THE OFFICIAL ENCYCLOPEDIA
OF THE NATIONAL HOCKEY LEAGUE®

TOTAL HOCKEY

DAN DIAMOND
EDITOR

RALPH DINGER   **JAMES DUPLACEY**   **ERIC ZWEIG**
MANAGING EDITORS

ERNIE FITZSIMMONS   **IGOR KUPERMAN**
CONSULTING STATISTICIAN   INTERNATIONAL EDITOR

GARY MEAGHER   **JOHN PASTERNAK**
SENIOR CONTRIBUTING EDITOR   DATA MANAGEMENT

**Andrews McMeel
Publishing**
Kansas City

Published by Total Sports
445 Park Avenue
New York, New York 10022

Distributed by:
Andrews McMeel Publishing
4520 Main Street
Kansas City, Missouri 64111

Distributed in Canada by:
Canadian Manda Group
1 Atlantic Avenue, #105
Toronto, Ontario M6K 3E7
Canada

For information about permission to reproduce
selections from this book, please write to:
Permissions
Total Sports
105 Abeel Street
Kingston, New York 12401

Total Sports™ is a trademark of Total Sports, Inc.
Total Hockey™ is a trademark of Total Sports, Inc.

Official Publication of the National Hockey League®

Library of Congress Catalog Card Number: 98-86782

ISBN 0-8362-7114-9

Printed in Canada

10 9 8 7 6 5 4 3

TOTAL HOCKEY

CONTENTS

III OTHER NORTH AMERICAN LEAGUES AND TEAMS

IV THE INTERNATIONAL GAME

V   OTHER FACETS OF THE GAME

VI   STATISTICAL AND BIOGRAPHICAL REGISTERS

OFFICE OF THE COMMISSIONER

Welcome to the first edition of Total Hockey, the biggest and best encyclopedia ever produced for our sport and one that I am sure you will spend many hours reading. Here, for the first time in one volume, is the definitive history of the game. From its beginnings in Windsor (Nova Scotia), Kingston (Ontario) and Montreal (Quebec), our game has grown to become the most international of sports, played and enjoyed by millions worldwide.

You now have the book that will tell you all that you want to know about hockey. Thanks to the skills and stamina of Total Sports and Dan Diamond and Associates, we are getting an unprecedented look at the history of the game.

We now have a complete record of every player who ever played in the National Hockey League. These records include every pertinent piece of information you could think of, from the player's hometown to his junior, minor pro and international records, as well as expanded NHL statistics and complete transaction histories.

If you want biographies of hundreds of key figures in the game's history -- players, coaches, managers, executives, inventors -- they are here. If you want the histories of each club ever to participate in the National Hockey League -- from the Montreal Wanderers to the Nashville Predators -- they are here.

Leafing through these pages will show you the greatness of NHL players. From Georges Vezina to Dominik Hasek, from Eddie Shore to Raymond Bourque, and from Howie Morenz to Wayne Gretzky, *Total Hockey* will give you all of the statistics and all of the stories.

You now have Adjusted Scoring statistics, a way to compare the stars of different eras -- Maurice Richard with Mark Messier, Jean Beliveau with Mario Lemieux, Bobby Orr with Chris Chelios, Gordie Howe with them all.

Total Hockey looks at all the pieces of the puzzle that create The Coolest Game on earth. Why is the puck flat and round and why is it called a puck? Why does the rink look as it does? What is life like in an NHL dressing room? What about the game off the ice? What are the best hockey movies and songs? If you want the answers, you have come to the right place.

For all of us who love hockey, *Total Hockey* takes us on a grand tour of our past and points us in the right direction for our future.

Read on and enjoy.

Gary B. Bettman

Gary B. Bettman
Commissioner

For everyone who cares for the game

Introduction

WELCOME TO *TOTAL HOCKEY*, the first official encyclopedia of the National Hockey League. The game of hockey is more than a century old and its most sought-after trophy, the Stanley Cup, is of similar vintage, but despite its years the sport retains its ability to change with the times, all the while surprising us with what goes on where it counts most: on the ice.

Nowhere was this more clearly demonstrated than at the Winter Olympics in February 1998. With skilled European players now a vital part of every NHL club, the league saw a bigger picture, structuring its season to allow the world's best players to play for their national Olympic teams in Nagano. Of the six "dream teams" that headed to Japan, four, it seemed, would contest the medals. In the end, Canada, Russia, Sweden and the United States fell by the wayside and it was a stunning performance by a purposeful Czech Republic team in support of goaltender Dominik Hasek that earned top place on the podium.

Total Hockey embodies these same attributes: it celebrates the history of the sport, pays close attention to how today's hockey works and, above all, respects the game and the accomplishments of the men (and women) who play it.

The book is divided into six sections:

- Section I deals with the origins of the game in Canada, the United States and Europe.
- Section II tells the story of the National Hockey League from its founding in 1917 to the 30-team circuit of the early 21st century.
- Section III reports on all other varieties of North American hockey including the junior, senior, collegiate and women's game.
- Section IV looks overseas, bringing together statistics and stories about international play.
- Section V covers hockey's many other facets including arenas, films, music, video games and history of the puck.
- Section VI presents complete registers for players, goaltenders and coaches that feature new stat categories that facilitate cross-era comparison of players. Biographical registers of top North American, international and women players are found here as well.

Several features within these sections break new ground:

"Movers and Shapers" *(page 82)* is a suite of stories that deal with people and forces that have determined the face of hockey.

"Inside the the NHL – Understanding the Business Side of Hockey" *(page 129)* is written by NHL vice president of public relations and media services Gary Meagher. It describes how the league works at the nuts-and-bolts level of trades, free-agency and standard player contracts. This information has never been gathered and presented before.

"The NHL Entry Draft" *(page 285)* by Chris Tredree and Paul Bontje analyzes each year's draft through text and tables that include NHL totals for each player selected.

"2002 and 2006 Olympic Teams" *(page 490)* utilizes an international array of journalists to evaluate the lessons of Nagano and presents preliminary rosters for the next two Winter Games for Canada, the Czech Republic, Finland, Russia, Sweden and the United States.

"Youth Hockey Around the World" *(page 571)* also uses the legwork of correspondents in major hockey countries to compare and contrast how young players are trained worldwide. Is it about having fun, winning games or developing pro players?

"The Evolution of Hockey Strategy" *(page 576)* goes beyond the chalkboard to examine the confluence of North American and European styles while providing a history of how the modern-era game is played. Stu Hackel worked closely with Harry Neale and Roger Neilson, two of the most knowledgeable analysts in hockey, to produce this illustrated story.

"Adjusted Scoring Statistics" *(page 626)* introduces a new method to compare players from different eras of hockey. These new stats, unique to *Total Hockey*, form the basis for an intriguing feature titled *Statistical Twins (page 627)* that marries cross-era combinations of players and produces surprising parallels.

Also worth noting are the "Introduction to the Player Registers" *(page 645)* and the explanatory page that proceeds *Total Hockey*'s Pre-Expansion Player, Modern Player and Goaltender registers. *(pages 646, 823 and 1601)* These pages contain valuable information on how to make best use of the numbers that make up the complete statistical record of every forward, defenseman or goaltender to see action in an NHL regular-season or playoff game.

More than 200 people did their best work to bring *Total Hockey* to life. They are profiled or acknowledged beginning on page 1875.

Has *Total Hockey* done it all? By no means. Already we are at work on new features for future editions that include career data panels for outstanding North American and European players who never appeared in the NHL, minor league coaching statistics and comprehensive won–lost–tied numbers for goaltenders in minor leagues and international competition.

Your comments, suggestion and corrections are extremely valuable to the *Total Hockey* editorial team. Contact information—and a list of 200 leagues touched on in the statistical registers—is found on page 1878.

Dan Diamond
July 1998

ORIGINS
OF THE
GAME

The 1906 Kenora Thistles. This squad won the
Stanley Cup in January 1907. Four of the men
in this photo are members of the Hockey
Hall of Fame: Si Griffis (front, left), Tom Phillips
(front, right), Tom Hooper (center) and
Bill McGimsie (back, right).

STANLEY CUP WINNERS
PRIOR TO THE FORMATION OF THE NHL
1893 TO 1917

SEASON	CHAMPIONS	MANAGER	COACH
1916-17	Seattle Metropolitans	Pete Muldoon	Pete Muldoon
1915-16	Montreal Canadiens	George Kennedy	George Kennedy
1914-15	Vancouver Millionaires	Frank Patrick	Frank Patrick
1913-14	Toronto Blueshirts	Jack Marshall	Scotty Davidson*
1912-13**	Quebec Bulldogs	Mike Quinn	Joe Malone*
1911-12	Quebec Bulldogs	Mike Quinn	Charles Nolan
1910-11	Ottawa Senators	Bruce Stuart*	
1909-10	Montreal Wanderers	Dickie Boon	Pud Glass*
1908-09	Ottawa Senators	Bruce Stuart*	
1907-08	Montreal Wanderers	Dickie Boon	Cecil Blachford
1906-07	Montreal Wanderers (Mar. 1907)	Dickie Boon	Cecil Blachford
1906-07	Kenora Thistles (Jan. 1907)	F.A. Hudson	Tommy Phillips*
1905-06	Montreal Wanderers	Cecil Blachford*	
1904-05	Ottawa Silver Seven	A.T. Smith	
1903-04	Ottawa Silver Seven	A.T. Smith	
1902-03	Ottawa Silver Seven	A.T. Smith	
1901-02	Montreal A.A.A.	Clare McKerrow	
1900-01	Winnipeg Victorias	Dan Bain	
1899-1900	Montreal Shamrocks	Harry Trihey*	
1898-99	Montreal Shamrocks	Harry Trihey*	
1897-98	Montreal Victorias	Frank Richardson	
1896-97	Montreal Victorias	Mike Grant*	
1895-96	Montreal Victorias (Dec. 1896)	Mike Grant*	
1895-96	Winnipeg Victorias (Feb. 1896)	Jack Armytage	
1894-95	Montreal Victorias	Mike Grant*	
1893-94	Montreal A.A.A.		
1892-93	Montreal A.A.A.		

* Indicates captain. Early teams were frequently run by their captain.
** Victoria defeated Quebec in challenge series. No official recognition.

CHAPTER 1

Ice Hockey in Nova Scotia

From Hurley to Hockey on Frozen Ponds

Garth Vaughan

CANADA'S OFFICIAL WINTER SPORT got its start in Windsor, Nova Scotia. Beginning around 1800, it developed gradually within the province. As it developed, so did all the required basic equipment. "Hockey" skates, wooden pucks, hand-made, one-piece hockey sticks, the rules of the game and the goal net all originated in Nova Scotia. The game first spread to New Brunswick in 1865, then to Montreal in 1875. Slowly and methodically, province by province, ice hockey spread until it arrived on the West Coast in 1890. Along the way it was taught to friends by players who had learned it from others. As it came to be played across the nation, the seventh player on the team was called the rover, also a Nova Scotia innovation. Unlike basketball, which was invented one day and played the next, ice hockey evolved slowly over decades, as the basic game became the game we know today.

All countries have games peculiar to their environment and climate. For the most part, ball games and stick-ball games known to America originated from a basic game called "camp" which developed following the Norman invasions of Britain in the 11th century. Townsfolk symbolically kicked out the invaders by kicking stones back and forth among themselves in fun. Played by individual neighbors at first, it was soon played by village teams. Community games thus developed which involved various objects being kicked, then hit with sticks on the ground, and finally in the air. Football, rugby, golf, field hockey, hurley, shinty, bandy, rounders and a host of variations evolved from this initial, simple game. In particular, the old English stick-ball game that combined hitting a ball in the air with the running of bases was known as rounders and later evolved into baseball in New York. Ice hockey, on the other hand, originated from stick-ball games played on the ground and then adapted to ice in Nova Scotia.

Windsor, Nova Scotia is situated on the shores of the Avon River which has the world's highest tides. The river banks were dyked by French Acadian settlers, creating prime farm land. Here the Acadians lived in harmony with the Mi'kmaq people who were indigenous to the area. The English arrived and built a military establishment in 1749. Called Fort Edward, it stood high above the town looking out over the Minas Basin. Strife led to the almost total decimation of the Mi'kmaq, and in 1755, to the expulsion of 4,000 Acadians to the eastern United States. Windsor had become an English stronghold.

Because the town was settled as early as 1684, it is natural that many things happened in Windsor before they happened elsewhere in Canada. Known as "the Little Town of Big Firsts," Windsor is the home of the first North American agricultural fair, the site of Canada's first college and the birthplace of the father of American humor, as well as the birthplace of ice hockey. Much of the initiative behind Windsor's contributions to the country came from the United Empire Loyalists. As the American

Revolutionary War ended, the name of King's College, New York, was changed to Columbia University, breaking the connection with England. Many United Empire Loyalists came to Nova Scotia and settled in and about Halifax and nearby Windsor. Reverend Charles Inglis, who had been a professor at King's College, was one such Loyalist who arrived in Halifax in 1783. He became the first Anglican bishop of the province and set about organizing a Canadian college so Anglican youth could be educated without having to go to Britain. Windsor was considered the playground of Halifax; Haligonians came to hunt and fish, watch horse racing and visit their elegant estates. In winter they enjoyed horse racing on the ice of lakes between the town and city. Inglis and others picked a 69-acre lot on one of Windsor's hills, with a view overlooking a magnificent pastoral scene, and proceeded to construct a school and college.

King's College School is the oldest independent school in Canada, established in Windsor in 1788. King's College, established a year later in Windsor, is Canada's first college. The students at King's came from London, New York, Boston, Rhode Island, Philadelphia, Bermuda, Ontario and New Brunswick, as well as Nova Scotia. Professors came from Oxford and Cambridge in England and other universities in Glasgow, Scotland, and Galway, Ireland. Windsor quickly became a center of culture and learning and was referred to by Halifax journalists as "the Athens of Nova Scotia." Professors brought with them the knowledge of their national field games and introduced the games to their students. English cricket and rounders, Scottish shinty and Irish hurley were favorite field games at the time. Boys at King's were the country's first group of young men affluent enough to afford time and equipment to engage in organized sport for entertainment.

America's most quoted author, Thomas Chandler Haliburton, was born in Windsor in 1796 and was educated at King's College School and King's College. With arts and law degrees, Haliburton became a judge and author of note. He wrote the first historical account of Nova Scotia in 1829 and created a fictional character named Sam Slick, a comic Yankee clockmaker noted for salesmanship and wise sayings. The first Canadian to acquire international acclaim as an author, Haliburton is commonly known as "the Father of American Humor." He also provides an important clue to the origin of ice hockey. In his writing in 1844, Haliburton reminisced about games students played at King's College School in his youth: ". . . you boys let out racin', yelpin', hollerin' and whoopin' like mad with pleasure, and the playground, with games at bass in the fields, or hurley on the long pond on the ice, or campin' out-a-night at Chester lakes to fish." This reference to ice hurley being played around 1800 is the earliest reference in English literature to a stick-ball game being played on ice.

The Chester lakes where the boys fished are 15 miles

away from the school, showing they were prepared to travel some distance on foot for sport. Games at bass (base) referred to rounders from which baseball later developed. Hurley is an Irish field game played year-round on the open fields of Ireland. In winter, Windsor's fields were deep with snow so the game was confined to three seasons. When ice formed on their skating ponds, King's College School students, obsessed with hurley, cleverly adapted it to the smooth, hard surface of the largest and longest of their favorite skating ponds and created a new winter sport, ice hurley.

As King's boys began playing hurley on ice, so began the evolution of Canada's great winter game, ice hockey. Nova Scotia's newspapers document the gradual and steady development of ice hurley into ice hockey within the province prior to its eventual spread across the nation. Ice hockey became Canada's game. In April, 1898, an article on ice hockey by Dr. A. H. Beaton, secretary of the Ontario Hockey Association, appeared in the Canadian Magazine. "Nearly twenty years ago," he wrote, "hockey, as a scientific sport, was introduced into Upper Canada from Nova Scotia, the latter being the indisputable home in Canada of this game."

From King's College, ice hurley spread to Fort Edward where soldiers also took up the new game. They traveled back and forth between Windsor, Halifax, and Dartmouth and the game gained impetus in the 1820s and 1830s as it was played on the magnificent Dartmouth lakes and frozen inlets of Halifax Harbour. Thomas H. Raddall, a noted Nova Scotia historic novelist, wrote of the soldiers in *Warden of the North* that "When [they] were transferred to military posts along the St. Lawrence and the Great Lakes, they took the game with them; and for some time afterwards continued to send to Dartmouth Indians for the necessary sticks." Many of the soldiers would have played cricket and the old English game of field hockey at home. Cricket was very popular among both the military stationed at Halifax and the students at King's College. They held exciting annual tournaments in which military teams traveled from Halifax to Windsor with their own band.

Both field hockey and cricket influenced ice hurley as it developed into ice hockey. Indeed, the game was sometimes called "wicket" and "cricket" as well as hurley and hockey. Mi'kmaq Natives in Nova Scotia communities, who had their own field and ice game called "Oochamkunutk," gradually joined with ice hurley players, melding their games. The Mi'kmaq referred to ice hurley as "Alchamadijik." The word hockey had been used in England as early as 1400 to describe a field game played by boys who carried produce in hock carts at harvest festivals. Since ice hockey developed in an English-dominated province, there is little reason to consider anything other than an English derivation of the name of the game. English officers by the name of Hockey (a common English family name) are known to have served in Nova Scotia in the mid-1800s. Oral history has it that one Colonel Hockey had his troops play the game in Windsor for winter exercise and that Hockey's game was later known simply as hockey. As for the derivation of the word "puck," it would appear to come directly from the game of hurley. When the ball used in hurley is struck with a hurley stick, it is said to be "pucked." Following a score, the goal tender is permitted a "puck out" from the goal mouth; when struck out of play to the side lines, the ball is returned by a "puck in." Beginners striking the ball about the field are said to be pucking

around. Is it any wonder that the elusive flat wooden disc used as ice hockey evolved was called a puck? Natives preferred black cherrywood for pucks, because the dark, leathery bark adhered tightly to the wood and also showed up plainly against snow and ice.

From its humble beginning among school boys and soldiers, the new game continued to develop and gained popularity among Nova Scotians for five decades before outsiders gave it notice. The *Boston Evening Gazette* printed a piece in December, 1859, entitled "Winter Sports in Nova Scotia," which told of the great skating ability of Nova Scotians and described hockey as it was then played. The editor added a note to the journalist's article saying he had sent to Nova Scotia for a set of sticks so that Bostonian skaters could give the game a try. In Nova Scotia at the time, the game still was being called ice hurley by some but ice hockey by others. This tradition continued for at least another two decades and eventually, coincident with other provinces taking up the game, the old name was dropped and ice hockey prevailed.

At the time of the Boston discovery, young James George Aylwin Creighton was a nine-year-old Halifax boy learning the game of ice hockey and developing skills as a figure skater. Following his education at Dalhousie University in Halifax, he became employed as an engineer in Montreal at the age of 22. There he taught new friends how to play ice hockey. Thus began the province-by-province introduction that was to take 15 years: from 1875 when hockey was first played publicly in Montreal until 1890 when it arrived at Winnipeg and Victoria. Henry Joseph, a noted Montreal athlete who played with Creighton in Montreal's first hockey game in 1875, later told the *Montreal Gazette* in a 1936 interview that Creighton was the leading spirit in the introduction of hockey into Montreal and added that he could not recall seeing hockey sticks in Montreal before that time, nor anybody playing hurley on skates. Finally, Joseph said that to Creighton should go the credit for the origin of ice hockey in Montreal.

While Creighton generally has received this credit, Montrealers have tended to downplay the history of hockey in Nova Scotia. Ninety years after Creighton's game was played first in Montreal, Nova Scotia provincial archivist Dr. C. Bruce Fergusson asked in June of 1965, "If Halifax Rules were used in the first game of 'true ice hockey,' which was played in Montreal in 1875, was it not reasonable to infer that those rules were evolved on ice, not solely on paper, in Halifax?"

Much of what is known of these early Halifax rules comes from Colonel B. A. Weston, a Dartmouth resident who served in the Fenian Raids and the North West Rebellion and who later became president of the Dartmouth Athletic Club. Weston played hockey in Halifax in the 1860s and, in 1937, he related "the main points of rules" followed at the time. He told of stones being first used to mark the goal, and of the wooden puck being required to remain on the ice. He also said that sticks were required to remain below the shoulder, and that teams were required to change ends when a goal was scored. Players had to remain on side, but forward passing *was* allowed. As ice hockey began in Montreal, it was played according to Halifax Hockey Club Rules, but the forward pass was not allowed. Not until the Dartmouth Chebuctos traveled to Quebec City in 1889 for a tournament was the excitement of the Nova Scotia forward pass tried in competition by the Montreal and Quebec players. It would be more than 30 years before

forward passing was adopted by the hockey establishment.

In Montreal, Creighton helped to move the game of hockey from frozen lakes and rivers to indoor ice rinks. This progression was much slower in his native Nova Scotia. Settlers from the old country had brought their skates with them to the area and skating outdoors became the most popular winter sporting activity in the province. Couples courted as they skated and many ended up skating through life together. Skaters did not like having ice hurley disrupt their sessions and fought to have the game banned! Parents objected to children's intense interest in the game, detracting from study time for school lessons. They also objected to having the children skip Sunday School to play the game. Ministers preached against ice hurley from their pulpits, calling it a desecration of the Sabbath. When Nova Scotia's first indoor rink ("rink" is a Scottish word meaning racecourse) appeared in 1862, it was for skating only; ice hurley or ice hockey was not allowed to be played on Nova Scotia rinks until 1883.

Despite this setback in the advancement of their new winter game, Nova Scotia had continued and would continue to be the source of many major contributions to the sport. In 1861, the Starr Manufacturing Company of Dartmouth began making high-class skates from quality steel for the world market. Skates used in the early 1800s had been hand-made locally, or imported from Britain, but had caused skaters all manner of trouble. Called stock skates or block skates because of the wooden stock or block used to hold the metal blades, they were held to boots with ropes or leather straps. Tight straps were necessary for security but tended to cut off circulation, thus aggravating already cold feet. Because the conventional block skates were so troublesome, Starr foreman John Forbes and his assistant Thomas Bateman invented self-fastening Acme Club Spring Skates, patented in 1863. These were held securely to soles and heels of boots with the mere flick of a lever. Applying skates at pond-side or in a cold rink was now a pleasure instead of a painful chore. Next, the Dartmouth company developed the Starr Hockey Skate, patented in 1866. This model had a rocker-shaped, wider blade with a rounded front and back for quick starts and stops as well as sudden turns that was ideal for ice hockey. Nova Scotians used these blades to play hockey for nine years before the game was played in Montreal. Photos of Montreal's early hockey teams show players using both Starr Acme Club and Starr Hockey Skates—the only self-fastening skates available at the time. Starr skates revolutionized skating and ice hockey. They were world-famous and the choice of skaters and hockey players well into the next century. Indeed, Boston Bruins manager Art Ross and the entire Boston Bruins hockey team endorsed Starr skates annually until as recently as 1927.

The Boston Bruins, and all hockey players of today, would have been known as "hockeyists" in the first century the game was played, and their sticks were known simply as "hockeys." Regardless of the difference in their title, contenders in early games wanted the best sticks available, then as now. Having made sticks for their own game, "Oochamkunutk," and being wood-carvers of necessity, the Mi'kmaq craftsmen were the natural choice to provide "hockeys" for Canada's hockeyists as they learned and developed the Nova Scotia game. From hornbeam trees, also commonly known as ironwood, harvested with roots attached, the Mi'kmaq carved powerfully strong and durable one-piece sticks, the blade coming from the root

and the handle from the trunk. After decades of providing such choice sticks, the supply of hornbeam became depleted and second-growth yellow birch was selected, proving to be a suitable alternative.

In 1875, J.G.A. Creighton had two dozen Mi'kmaq sticks sent up from his friends in Halifax for Montreal's first game. In 1886, as hockey began in Kingston, sticks were acquired for games from Nova Scotia as well. In 1943, Captain James T. Sutherland, the much-revered Kingston hockey hero, made a Kingston claim for ice hockey's origin which was accepted by the Canadian Amateur Hockey Association. Later, when it was pointed out to him that hockey sticks had been imported from Nova Scotia for Kingston's first games, he conceded that ice hockey must have been first played in Nova Scotia. Otherwise, he added, why send to Halifax for sticks?

Fifty years after Creighton had ordered his Mi'kmaq sticks for Montreal, the 1925 Eaton's Catalogue advertised that the Ontario Hockey Association continued to endorse "MicMac" brand sticks as their choice. They were sold across the nation and abroad for as little as 45 to 75 cents each, and cheaper by team lots of a dozen. MicMac "hockeys" were distributed from firms in Halifax, having been acquired from Native craftsmen in various parts of Nova Scotia. These sticks, like Starr skates, were popular across Canada into the 1930s, when both were squeezed from the market by competitors.

In addition to sticks and skates, much more of what would come to define modern hockey traces its roots to Nova Scotia. When ice hurley and ice hockey began, goals were first scored between rocks (as stated previously) which faced the sides of the ice surface to prevent scoring with long shots. In the 1880s, rocks were replaced with posts supported on wooden crosses, and moved so that they faced the ends of the ice surface as they do today. The goalkeeper, however, could be scored on from either the front or back as there was no net on the posts. Goal judges stood at the goal mouth and signaled goals with the ringing of a brass bell. Likewise, the referee used a hand bell to begin and end the play.

Ice hockey was well established across the nation by the turn of the 20th century and wooden covered rinks were built in many towns from coast to coast, often by volunteer labor, to bring ice hockey in out of the cold. On January 6, as the 1899 season got under way in Nova Scotia, the Halifax Wanderers and Crescents introduced the Nova Scotia Box Net, revolutionizing the job of the goal judge and goalkeeper. The Montreal Victorias and Shamrocks were next to use a goal net, the following season, in December 1899.

Prior to 1900, short shin pads without knee coverings were the only form of protection used by players. Mi'kmaq hockey players in Nova Scotia at the turn of the century used moose skin for shin and body protectors. Padded gloves first appeared in 1904. Knee, elbow, and shoulder pads did not appear until the 1930s and 1940s. Goalkeepers used the same stick as other players until the 1890s and were required to remain upright. Although a Dartmouth goaltender in 1889 wore shin guards to protect himself from being struck with sticks, it was not until the wrist shot was invented in Winnipeg in 1893, and the puck first was allowed officially off the ice, that larger (cricket) pads and a wider stick were required for the netminder. Both appear to have originated in Winnipeg. However, it was the black players of Nova Scotia, competing in the Coloured Hockey

League of the Maritimes, who first allowed goalkeepers to go down on the ice to stop pucks, in 1900. Major professional leagues like the Pacific Coast Hockey Association did not follow suit until 1912. The National Hockey League adopted the rule for its first season of 1917–18.

Not only is ice hockey both contagious and addictive, it is also as Canadian as the Maple Leaf and as Nova Scotian as the Bluenose. The spread of the game from place to place in Nova Scotia occurred as a result of players learning the game and teaching it to others. The pattern remained the same as the game spread to other provinces. Aylwin Creighton of Halifax, known to his friends as J.G.A.C., moved to Ottawa after his stay in Montreal, where he and others continued to play and teach the game in the early 1880s. Indeed, Creighton played with such notables as Edward and William Stanley, sons of Governor-General Lord Stanley, on an Ottawa team called the Rideau Rebels. Roddy McColl from New Glasgow, Nova Scotia, entered the Royal Military College in Kingston, Ontario in 1882 as cadet number 149 and is credited with teaching fellow cadets to play ice hockey, thus introducing the game to Kingston. RMC played its first games with the newly

formed Queen's University hockey team in 1886. Both teams were stacked with Nova Scotians and Quebecers. The principal of Queen's at the time was George Munro Grant of Pictou County, Nova Scotia, who had been called from his 14-year position as minister of Saint Matthew's Church in Halifax to become head of Queen's in 1877. Grant would have been well aware of wooden pucks, MicMac sticks, Starr hockey skates and the developing Nova Scotian winter game. Later, those who learned ice hockey in Nova Scotia, Ontario and Quebec and moved west to Manitoba, Saskatchewan and British Columbia taught new friends, while Ontario college teams carried the game to American colleges. Thus the organized Irish field game of hurley, adopted by students of King's College School and then adapted to ice in Windsor, Nova Scotia, developed into Canada's national winter sport, hockey, and became the world's fastest and most exciting winter game. Amazing!

On August 19, 1996, Cooperstown, New York, the Home of Baseball, was twinned with Windsor, Nova Scotia, the Birthplace of Hockey.

CHAPTER 2

Kingston, Ontario

A Special Place in Hockey History

Bill Fitsell

INGSTON, ONTARIO—the old garrison town and naval port and one-time capital of the United Canadas—has recorded a hockey heritage as rich as its multi-splendored social history. Originally named "Cataraqui"—a tribute to its native and French beginnings—and renamed King's Town after British occupation, the city has been pivotal in the early development and expansion of the game throughout Canada and the United States.

The city's hockey history has been inextricably interwoven with the progress and celebration of Canada's national winter game. This unique characteristic stems from two of its major institutions, Queen's University at Kingston and the Royal Military College of Canada, which seized on the game pioneered in eastern Canada and helped to spread it through Ontario and across the North American continent.

Queen's men and gentlemen cadets played a key role in the formation of the Ontario Hockey Association that became the forerunner of hockey administrations. Queen's was the first university in Canada to build its own covered rink on campus and introduced artificial ice in the mid-1920s, at a time when only large cities could afford such a facility. Despite McGill University's connection with the development of hockey in the 1870s, the first institution to challenge for the Stanley Cup was Queen's in 1895, and its tricolored squads made a total of three bids in the era of amateur Cup competition.

Kingstonians played a critical administrative role in the development of the game's rules and regulations. Queen's players were among the first to welcome touring ice polo players from the United States and to introduce the Canadian game to such cities as Pittsburgh, Washington and Baltimore in the 1890s. Kingston teams were also in demand for exhibition games from Detroit and Cleveland to Boston and New York. Kingston players—from Hall of Famers Marty Walsh and Bill Cook to Wayne Cashman and Doug Gilmour—have spread the city's name and enhanced its reputation throughout the National Hockey League and the world.

Appropriately for a community located at the confluence of Lake Ontario and the St. Lawrence River, Kingston's present Ontario Hockey League franchise, the Frontenacs—a name first used by a Kingston team in 1897—proudly displays a K-wheel crest similar to the main logo of the NHL Boston Bruins—the Hub City of Boston, Massachusetts. Kingston is "the hub of hockey" if not its home.

Situated halfway between Canada's two major hockey cities, Montreal and Toronto, linked by waterways to Canada's capital of Ottawa and to American ports, "the Limestone City" has been at the center of the century-old debate on the origins of the game since day one. The controversy started in 1903 when that fractious phrase "the birthplace of hockey" first appeared in a Kingston newspaper.

This claim was refuted by a Kingstonian, A.B. Cunningham, who played in the 1888 game between Queen's and RMC teams. Speaking at a 1903 banquet saluting one of Kingston's Ontario Hockey Association championship teams, the young lawyer credited the game's organized intro-

duction to Montreal a decade earlier. But the Kingston nativity myth grew and flourishes to this day.

The keystone of hockey's arch, locally and nationally, is not the highly visible and voluble Kingston-booster and broadcaster Donald Stewart Cherry (incidentally the only Kingstonian selected for Canada's 100 most influential citizens), but a venerable gentleman and hockey pioneer he reveres to this day, James Thomas Sutherland, the only Kingston-born citizen featured in the Canadian Encyclopedia of 1985. Creator of the 1903 birthplace report, Jim Sutherland was hockey's "legendmaker." He was a boy when the first organized game was played indoors in Montreal in 1875 and a teenager when the first report was published of a seven-aside game played on Kingston's harbor ice in 1886. But his memoirs erroneously claim he played in that historic game with a bandstand located at center ice.

A pioneer player and coach of champions, Jim Sutherland was a benchmark in the days before there was a bench—all seven players being on the ice. With booming voice, he pioneered the use of a megaphone to spur on his players and introduced preseason physical training to his amateur teams. A leading administrator in Ontario and Canadian hockey organizations during the 1910s and 1920s, he proposed four 15-minute periods for junior players and recommended rubberized goal posts to help eliminate injuries. Although a consummate amateur hockey advocate, he urged the reinstatement of professionals into amateur hockey and proposed a trophy in memory of players killed in the World War I—which became the OHA Memorial Cup for the Canadian junior championship.

Off the ice, the affable gentleman was a traveling shoe salesman and a hockey raconteur par excellence. He earned and retained the army rank of captain during World War I and with military determination kept the "hockey birthplace" pot boiling wherever he went. Immediately after the war, during which Capt. Sutherland served in Canada and England, the question "Where did the game start?" resurfaced. Prompting the debate was the publication of the first illustrated book on the game in 1924. Entitled *Canadian Hockey Year Book*, compiled by Joe King of Toronto, later of Kingston, it featured an article by Capt. Sutherland which stated: "I think it is generally admitted and has been substantially proven on many occasions that the actual birthplace of organized hockey is the City of Kingston in 1888." He offered little or no evidence in support of his argument, a feature which has bedeviled most arguments on hockey's birthplace.

The debate became international when one of Capt. Sutherland's local articles promoting Kingston as the "home of hockey" was republished in a 1927 New York Ranger program. His zeal and boundless enthusiasm kept Kingston in the forefront of the hot stove league discussion by authoring a 1929 article: "Who put hockey on the map?" and crediting noted Toronto and Montreal newspaper editors and columnists, who became his unswerving friends and supporters.

American sportswriter Frank G. Menke, who attempted to

unravel the mystery of hockey's origin, entered the discussion that year by contending the Canadian game derived from the Indian game of lacrosse. His first *All Sports Record Book*, while light on details of early hockey history, did introduce the claims of Montreal and Nova Scotia into the debate. Montreal, headed by McGill University officials, entered the verbal fray in 1930. Assistant physical education director F.M. Wagner, in a later letter to Capt. Sutherland wrote: "You will note that there is no claim here that the game was invented by anyone at McGill but we did find detailed descriptions of the game as played at McGill several years before hockey was originated in the opinion of many people at that time."

Dr. A.S. Lamb, director of physical education, recruited assistants Van Wagner and E.M. Orlick "in an effort to ferret out the secret of the beginning of ice hockey." Their findings not only documented the first games, with names of players, referees and goal judges, positions and early rules, but defined the introduction of pucks and flat-bladed sticks distinctive from the ball and short stick of shinny and field hockey.

Sutherland, now anointed by the press as "the father of organized hockey," fired back: "Kingston really is the home of hockey. A rink was formed on the ice in the harbor in front of Tete du Pont Barracks (now Fort Frontenac)." He conceded that "exhibition games" were played in Montreal but stuck to his contention that Kingston played the first organized games. Again he offered no strong evidence, relying on descriptions from a 19th century diary.

Throughout the Depression the controversy simmered. Men who played in the Montreal games of the late 1870s and early 1880s spoke up. Halifax newspapers joined the battle. Kingston sportswriters came through with a profound statement but stuck with the local legendmaker: "It is doubtful if the question of hockey origin will ever be settled to the satisfaction of everyone, but pending definite proof, we intend to string along with James T. [Sutherland]."

Kingston's claim continued to gain support from friends east and west of the city. Toronto newspaperman and OHA czar W.A. "Billy" Hewitt wrote in a 1937 Maple Leaf Gardens' program: "Kingston has generally been regarded in Canada as the birthplace of hockey and Capt. James Sutherland as the 'father of the game,' because of his long and sustained interest in the sport and the marvelous enthusiasm he has exhibited through the years." William J. Walshe, former Toronto sports columnist, after joining the *Kingston Whig-Standard*, cited Sutherland's ambition "to definitely establish Kingston as the home of organized hockey."

"Old-time hockey, like baseball," chimed in *Montreal Star* columnist Baz O'Meara, "suffers from the lack of authoritative history. There is too much obscurity about its beginnings, too little known of its early history, its great games, great personalities of the past. There are too few writers who have long experience in the sport. Too few old-time officials now active in the game, who can give it historical authority."

Ironically, baseball was instrumental in initiating a formal debate on hockey's origin. Capt. Sutherland, who had been watching with special interest the opening of the National Baseball Hall of Fame in Cooperstown, New York in 1939, seized the opportunity for hockey. In 1941, in the midst of the Second World War, he proposed to the Canadian Amateur Hockey Association, an organization he served for 40 years, that a study be made on the origin of hockey. The project soon became a movement to form a hockey hall of fame.

"If such a memorial is to be put on something of an enduring foundation it should be built and maintained in Montreal," wrote O'Meara. Kingston's daily responded: "Historic Kingston would be an ideal location for the shrine

of the puck sport. There is a good chance the Kingston bid will be successful. A hall of fame would be lost in a large metropolis like Montreal."

Sutherland and Hewitt, plus George Slater, President of the Quebec Senior Hockey League, were named to the study committee and the race was on. Authored by Capt. Sutherland, with cursory glances from the other two members, the CAHA's report, The Origin of Hockey in Canada was blatantly pro-Kingston and provoked a storm of protest, mainly from Montreal.

"This document is a conglomeration of contradictions and unsubstantiated statements," wrote E.M. Orlick in the *McGill News*. "It contains many dogmatic assertions and conclusions, but little, or nothing in the way of authentic first-source facts. It is not a report of an investigation on the origin of ice hockey, it is a poorly camouflaged presentation of the Kingston claims."

The Kingston claims proved to be successful, as on September 10–11, 1943 the NHL and the CAHA selected Kingston "as the most central site to erect a hall of fame as a memorial dedicated to perpetuate the memories of men who have done so much to develop national and internationally Canada's great winter sport—hockey."

In the 1940s, Capt. Sutherland basically ignored the Montreal claims, which were well documented with next-day newspaper reports and reminiscences of players from the early games. In his private papers, still folded in the original envelope, is the detailed presentation of McGill, with names dates and scores supporting the Montreal claim.

Kingston columnist Walshe said Kingston's selection was based mostly on account of its location for visitors. "The idea of the Hall of Fame is to perpetuate the memory of great stars and leaders of the game, not to honor any special place as the scene of the first game. Museums are established not where relics are found, but in places where they may be seen, studied or respected by the greatest numbers." Capt. Sutherland summed it up simply: "The City of Kingston was chosen as the site regardless as to where the first puck was shot."

Even following Kingston's selection as the hall of fame site, McGill Professor E.M. Orlick condemned Kingston's presentation as a "hoax" and maintained that the Ontario city had not "the slightest shred of an historical claim ... to the origin of ice hockey." Unfortunately, this argument doesn't quite stand up to later research and discoveries.

The Kingston claim was based mainly on the 1846–47 diary entry of the father of local historian Edwin Horsey, who wrote: "Most of the boys were quite at home on skates. They could cut the figure eight but 'shinny' was their delight." In the CAHA report written by Sutherland, someone with knowledge of Kingston as a garrison town had inserted "soldier" before boys and "great" before delight.

In 1843, a British army officer Arthur H. Freeling, stationed in Kingston wrote in his diary: "Began to skate this year, improved quickly and had great fun at hockey on the ice." To an amateur historian, this quotation seems to be a solid indication that skaters played a stick-ball game on ice in Kingston—32 years before the first organized game in Montreal. But in the view of Norman Anick, a historian for Canada's National Historic Sites and Monuments Board, this diary notation is ambiguous. "It does not specifically state that hockey on the ice was played by skaters, only that Freeling learned to skate and played hockey on the ice, with or without skates we are not informed."

Similar evidence of earlier stick-ball activity is recorded in the *Kingston Chronicle and Gazette* of the Scottish game of shinny being played on Kingston harbor ice for the second

consecutive year on New Year's Day, 1840: "At the appointed hour about 300 persons, including spectators, assembled on the ice in front of the town…The ball was flung up in the air between the two adverse chieftains as the signal to commence hostilities. A most vigorous contest was begun and maintained nearly three hours with unabated energy." Again no mention of skates is made.

At Montreal in 1842, shinty players were prevented by law from playing their recreational game on city streets, but the Halifax-Dartmouth area, with a myriad of lakes and bays, had long recorded people playing a similar game under a number of different names. In 1831 townsfolk and the military were reported in the Halifax press as playing "the spirit-stirring game of wicket" on the North West Arm.

By 1842 the game played on the Dartmouth lakes was called "ricket" and in 1859 the *Boston Evening Gazette* proclaimed the Nova Scotia game—"with skates on feet and hurleys or hockey (sticks) in hand"—as the most exciting game played on ice. "Whenever the ball is put through the ricket (a goal marked by two paving stones) a shout 'Game, ho!' resounds from shore to shore and dies away in a hundred echoes through the hills."

This freewheeling game, which was played in the Halifax area by 10, 15 or 20 players aside, was still called "ricket" by Haligonians as late as 1875, the year that Montrealers moved 'hockey' indoors, restricted the number of players (to nine), assigned a referee to enforce a no-forward passing rule and goal judges to determine the scores.

One of the captains of the two nine-man teams that played that historic game in Montreal's Victoria Skating Rink on March 3, 1875 and subsequent games, was Halifax-native James George Aylwin Creighton. Maritimers put great credit in the claim that he introduced "the Halifax rules" to Montreal, but newspaper reports indicate that the first games of the 1870s were played under "The Hockey Association" code as written for field hockey in 1875. In fact, Captain Creighton was cited for playing offside (ahead of the puck carrier), a style permitted in Halifax but not in Montreal.

The Montreal–Halifax games clashed in 1889, when the Dartmouth Chebuctos played four games in Montreal and Quebec City. The hosts predominated in all games whether played under the restricted passing game of Montreal or the wide-open, shinny-like Halifax regulations. Thereafter, Nova Scotia teams adopted the Montreal rules and the Halifax rules were forgotten.

As Halifax-born author J. Macdonald Oxley wrote in an 1891 magazine report on rink hockey: "As first played in Canada hockey went by various names, some of which were apparently merely local—hurley, shinny, rickets, and so forth—there was not much pretense to rules, each player taking part as best he knew how. No effort toward systematizing the game appears to have been made until the year 1875."

The centennial of organized hockey in 1975 was not celebrated in any way in the true birthplace of the organized sport—Montreal. McGill University did not display any interest in commemorating that first indoor game, but in recent years Montreal hockey historians have seized on their historic connections and taken the debate to that brash upstart—Windsor, N.S.—where the first recorded reference to "hockey" was in 1888 when King's College school team played a game against the Ramblers on Dartmouth Lakes.

Today only one city—Kingston—celebrates the game's roots in a formal and continuous way. The original local game was first commemorated at the opening of Kingston's first artificial ice rink in 1924 and Capt. Sutherland was involved in 1948 when the early military shinny game was re-enacted on Kingston harbor and captured in the first promotional hockey film ever shot.

The International Hockey Museum, once the sport's original hall of fame, has marked the first Kingston harbor game since the 1960s. Queen's and RMC, plus 2nd Regiment, Royal Canadian Horse Artillery, representing the garrison soldiers who first played a form of the game, compete for the Historic Hockey Trophy. Seven-man teams wearing toques and turtlenecks, use short field hockey sticks to propel a square puck between uprights frozen in the ice in front of historic Kingston City Hall. And according to the rules first developed and printed in Montreal, the centers faced the sides of the rink as in lacrosse, forward passing was prohibited and goaltenders were barred from lying, kneeling or sitting in making a stop.

And since 1986, Queen's and RMC varsity teams meet in the Carr-Harris Cup game, representing the longest rivalry between two hockey teams in the world—112 years by 1998—and counting. And just for good measure, Kingston is home every second year to the longest-running international hockey series. The Black Knights of the United States Military Academy of West Point, New York and the Paladins (formerly Redmen) of RMC meet amidst pomp, pageantry and bodychecks in a game that tops the intensity and personal importance of Stanley Cup games or the Army-Navy football game. It's war on ice!

The record of the spirited games played by the two military institutions is inscribed annually on illuminated boards in RMC's hallowed halls and also in the International Hockey Museum. The latter, a mythical institution until the International Hockey Hall of Fame was built in 1961 (the year the NHL opened its own shrine in Toronto) reflects the heritage of the game in Kingston and Canada.

One of the first communities to organize and promote boys' hockey, Kingston was the appropriate choice for the first Canadian midget championship tournament involving teams from 10 provinces and two territories in Canada's centennial year, 1967. And women's hockey, played here in 1894, has produced notable stars from Marguerite Carr-Harris and Katherine "Cookie" Cartwright to Jayna Hefford of the 1998 Canadian Olympic team.

Kingston has named its youth center arenas after local hockey champions—Jock Harty, Wally Elmer and the Cook Brothers, Bill and Bun of Ranger fame. And the late Gus Marker, a journeyman hockey player but a millionaire developer, named three streets after his favorite hockey people, Lionel Conacher, Howie Morenz and Capt. Sutherland.

The Kingston heritage runs deep. In an ornate case that once displayed jewelry is displayed the tricolor striped sweater of legendary captain Guy Curtis, who captained Queen's in two Stanley Cup series (in 1895 and 1899) and retired after a record 10-year career in university hockey. At Queen's Athletic Centre is the octagonal sided puck—looking much like a lump of coal—that was used in the first Kingston match in 1886. Alongside is the field hockey-type stick from the 1888 Queen's–RMC game. And front and center is an open 1893 magazine with a Montreal writer's comment that was ignored by Capt. Sutherland but eventually killed his birthplace dream: "Hockey skated up into Ontario from the Province of Quebec. It was quite old before it left home. … Its earliest stopping of importance seems to have been at Kingston (in the winter of) 1885–1886."

Kingston may not have been the place where hockey, as we know it, was born, but more than any other city in the world, it has done more to commemorate and celebrate hockey's early development.

CHAPTER 3

Out of the Mists of Memory

Montreal's Hockey History, 1875–1910

Michel Vigneault

HOW, WHEN AND WHERE—perhaps we will not ask why—did people start playing an ice game with sticks and a ball? When was that ball changed to a puck and what was that puck? How did the rest of the game evolve?

There are a number of theories and mysteries and at least three contenders for the title of hockey's first home, but one certain fact will concern us: a recognizable form of the game was played in Montreal in 1875 by university students and members of English, Scottish and Irish sporting clubs. French-speaking Quebecers had not yet taken up the new game.

Leaving aside the disputed evidence of distant and relative precedents in Europe or Greenland, the earliest account of an ice game dates back to a Dorchester team meeting the Uptown Club in Montreal on the last Saturday in February, 1837. The two teams met in a hurling game transferred from lawns to the surface that winter had wrought. Other records of games like Scottish shinny as played by military personnel in Halifax in 1851, in Ottawa in 1852 and in Kingston in 1855 all involved 100 or more soldiers playing around with a ball on a frozen river or lake. No rules were in force and there was no referee. It is not even certain how many players (if any) used skates. To illustrate just how shrouded and vexed is the mystery of hockey's definitive start, a committee formed by the Canadian Amateur Hockey Association in 1941 found that the first game of hockey was played in Kingston in 1855. The Kingston Hockey Hall of Fame, however, does not recognize that game but rather one played in the city in March, 1885 using Montreal rules, ignoring the well-documented Montreal game of 1875.

To begin at the beginning, perhaps the first question is: just what do we mean when we call a game hockey? For the duration, let us say it is a game played on ice, wearing skates, using sticks and a ball or puck, with a set of written rules (which shinny and hurling did not yet have), a referee and a goaltender (which neither game had either). With these basic elements, hockey can be—and has to be—played the same way anywhere in the world, as it is now. So where does it all start?

The *Montreal Gazette* on March 3, 1875 reported: "A game of Hockey will be played at the Victoria Skating Rink this evening between two nines chosen from among the members. Good fun may be expected, as some of the players are reputed to be exceedingly expert at the game. Some fears have been expressed on the part of intended spectators that accidents were likely to occur through the ball flying about in too lively a manner, to the imminent danger of lookers on, but we understand that the game will be played with a flat circular piece of wood, thus preventing all danger of its leaving the surface of the ice."

From the evidence of this small notice, we might infer that by then a group had been playing the game for some time. But it was at this precise point that they truly began to make modifications that would come to define a new sport.

As the game was to be played inside in front of spectators for the first time, a block of wood would replace a lacrosse ball to prevent possible damage—in the absence of boards, perhaps as much to windows as to people. Also, the game introduced goals like lacrosse (two sticks in the ice, eight feet apart and six feet tall). With no nets, the referee and the umpires (goal judges) had to decide if a goal had been scored. One new idea departs from the old British games of shinny, hurling or bandy (an early English form of field hockey). This was the ruling of no forward passing, which was adopted from rugby, a game most on these teams also played. Finally, a player was charged with protecting the goal, as in lacrosse. At this juncture, there were nine players on the ice on each team.

The *Montreal Gazette* reported on March 4 that "At the Rink last night a very large audience gathered to witness a novel contest on the ice. … Hockey is played usually with a ball, but last night, in order that no accident should happen, a flat block of wood was used, so that it should slide along the ice without rising, and thus going among the spectators to their discomfort. The game is like lacrosse in one sense—the block having to go through flags placed about 8 feet apart in the same manner as the rubber ball—but in the main the old country game of shinty gives the best idea of hockey. The players last night were eighteen in number—nine on each side—and were as follows: Mssrs Torrance (captain), Meagher, Potter, Goff, Barnston, Gardner, Griffin, Jarvis and Whiting. Creighton (captain), Campbell, Campbell, Esdail, Joseph, Henshaw, Chapman, Powell and Clouston. The match was an interesting and well-contested affair, the efforts of the players exciting much merriment as they wheeled and dodged each other, and notwithstanding the brilliant play of Captain Torrance's team, Captain Creighton's men carried the day, winning two games to the single of the Torrance nine. The game was concluded about half-past nine, and the spectators then adjourned well satisfied with the evening's entertainment."

Among these early players, we must make special note to remember the name of James George Aylwin Creighton. Born in Halifax, Nova Scotia, he came to Montreal in 1872 to work on the railroad after studying engineering at Dalhousie University. Five years later, he took up law at McGill and also worked as a writer for the *Gazette*. Later still, we find him in Ottawa, where he was working as a civil servant in 1882. All these progressions are central to the history of hockey. According to another of the players listed above, Henry Joseph, Creighton brought the basic structure of the game with him from Halifax, but transformed it in Montreal when he introduced the novelties already noted, and, as we will see shortly, probably wrote the first published rules. In Ottawa, he formed a team of public servants (the Rideau Rebels) which included two of

Lord Stanley's sons in its lineup.

Although there is considerable argument as to whether he transferred the game played in Halifax to Montreal, or if the games played in the two cities were quite different, there is general agreement that Creighton can lay claim to paternity in the birth of modern hockey. But if we are starting to think that the case is quite clear, we still must consider the situation of three McGill students who say they wrote the first rules of hockey.

In 1908, Richard F. Smith told the *Montreal Star* that he and two friends had come up with the rules of hockey in September, 1878. But as he also mentioned the victory of the Montreal Amateur Athletic Association at the Montreal Carnival of 1884 when it in fact occurred in 1885, perhaps the mists of his memory should not be fully relied upon. Further, in testimony separate from Smith and each other, W. L. Murray and W. R. Robertson both dated the rules of hockey to November, 1879. Robertson's brief (a letter in the Hockey Hall of Fame) is undated. Murray was sharing his recollections in 1936, when he was about 80 years old, and added that he played shinny on the St. Lawrence River in his youth. Perhaps we should exercise caution with his memory as well, since he refers to French Canadians playing shinny when in fact they did not take up hockey until after the 1890s. As for the rules, Murray said they tried them, starting with reducing a team from 15 down to seven and replacing the ball with a puck, all in one day. These modifications not only took time to evolve but were responses to particular—often in fact quite peculiar—circumstances, as we have seen and shall see again later.

The rules shown below were published in the *Gazette* on February 27, 1877, along with a summary of a game in which Creighton and his friends had played. (None of the three rival rules claimants had taken part.):

1. *The game shall be commenced and renewed by a Bully in the centre of the ground. Goals shall be changed after each game.*
2. *When a player hits the ball, any one of the same side who at such a moment of hitting is nearer to the opponents' goal line is out of play, and may not touch the ball himself, or in any way whatever prevent any other player from doing so, until the ball has been played. A player must always be on his own side of the ball.*
3. *The ball may be stopped, but not carried or knocked on by any part of the body. No player shall raise his stick above his shoulder. Charging from behind, tripping, collaring, kicking or shinning shall not be allowed.*
4. *When the ball is hit behind the goal line by the attacking side, it shall be brought out straight 15 yards, and started again by a Bully; but, if it is hit behind by any of the side whose goal line it is, a player of the opposite side shall [hit] it out from within one yard of the nearest corner; no player of the attacking side at that same time shall be within 20 yards of the goal line, and the defenders, with the exception of the goal-keeper, must be behind their goal line.*
5. *When the ball goes off at the side, a player of the opposite side to that which hit it out shall roll it out from the point on the boundary line at which it went off at right angles with the boundary line, and it shall not be in play until it has touched the ice, and the player rolling it in shall not play it until it has been played by another player, every player being then behind the ball.*
6. *On the infringement of any of the above rules, the ball shall be brought back and a Bully shall take place.*
7. *All disputes shall be settled by the umpires, or in the event of their disagreement, by the Referee.*

As Creighton was then a *Gazette* writer, it could be a safe assumption that he authored these rules. This may be a moot point though, as it seems the rules were forgotten quickly or at least not widely known. In the first book ever written on hockey (*Hockey: Canada's Royal Winter Game*, 1899) author Arthur Farrell, a Montreal Shamrocks player who was a member of Stanley Cup championship teams of 1899 and 1900, states that no rules were known prior to 1880. However, new rules added in 1886 and 1887 were all based on the version reprinted above.

With the game as we know it beginning to evolve, the next major phase of development came at the Montreal Winter Carnival, which was in essence the first hockey tournament. An initiative of English snowshoe clubs to promote Montreal throughout North America, the carnival lasted from 1883 to 1889. Hockey played a role in its first three years and became more popular in the process. In effect, the game had graduated to tournaments and a league of its own.

Only three teams were in competition at the first Winter Carnival in 1883, two from Montreal (the Victorias and McGill) and one from Quebec City. They played on a "rink" scraped on the St. Lawrence River. Another critical change to the game came about at this tournament because Quebec came with only seven players, and the Montreal teams had to drop two from their nine-man rosters. McGill won the round robin and was presented with a trophy which is now in the hands of the McCord Museum in Montreal, where one still can read the names of the winning players and the referee.

The next year, 1884, Quebec City declined to return after a Montreal team failed to show for a game in Quebec. Nevertheless, there were five teams that year, four from Montreal (the Wanderers, McGill, the Victorias and the Crystals) and one from Ottawa. The Ottawa club was not the Rideau Rebels—who would not be formed until 1888— but they did win the tournament, defeating McGill 3–0 in the finals. Seven-man teams were used at the carnival this year at the request of its organizers and became de facto the rule. There were problems maintaining a playable rink when heavy rains fell but all the games that could be played took place on an outdoor surface at McGill, with one exhibition game at the Victoria Rink.

Finally, in 1885, six teams were in competition, the defending champs from Ottawa and five clubs from Montreal (the Victorias, McGill, the Crystals, the Montreal Football Club and the Montreal Hockey Club, which was a part of the Montreal Amateur Athletic Association and indeed better known as the Montreal AAA, or the MAAA). It took nine periods for the Montreal Hockey Club to win its semifinal game against McGill, then another overtime to take the finals from Ottawa. This time the carnival tournament was played indoors, at the Crystal Rink.

It was with this set of games over three years at the Montreal Winter Carnival that hockey began to come into its own. The fact that McGill students came from outside Montreal and took their new skills and fervor back home was also a contributing factor to the game's growth in other regions of Canada (mainly Quebec and Ontario), Kingston being one notable instance, where the first league of sorts— a local affair involving four teams—was formed in 1885.

With hockey becoming more popular, teams from three cities tried a new kind of tournament for 1886 which would last the whole winter instead of just the week of the carnival in late January or early February. Six teams entered, in two divisions. The Montreal division included the MAAA,

the Victorias, McGill and the Crystals. Ottawa and Quebec formed the other division. In the Montreal division, the competition would be a round robin, while the other played a home-and-home series. The two winners would meet in a Dominion championship. In this first "season," the title game was played at the Crystal Rink between the Crystals and Quebec. In what may be seen to foreshadow the ongoing laments about violent play, the visitors forfeited the title when they quit the game. In the face of the home team's aggression, some Quebec players were unable to finish. The moment the team left the ice, the referee awarded the championship trophy to the Crystals.

This first season now behind them, the four Montreal teams and Ottawa took the next major step in 1887 when they formed a league, to be called the Amateur Hockey Association of Canada. (Quebec joined the following year.) All the teams would play more, and on a regular basis, but at this stage all the games were championship games in a challenge series. The champion defended its title at every game, while the league champion was the one who won the last game of the season. The anomalies of this structure saw the MAAA win the league championship in 1891 after winning only one game—the last one—while Ottawa had won all the games in the season except for that one. For 1892, a regular schedule was put forward and the team winning the most games was declared that season's champion.

This first inter-region league in Canada had been followed by other examples like the Ontario Hockey Association in 1890–91, but there was still one central factor to come into play before hockey became widely—and wildly—popular.

Frederick Arthur, Lord Stanley of Preston, Earl of Derby and Governor-General of Canada until he returned to England in 1892 was a sportsman and hockey fan whose sons were players with the Rideau Rebels. He also had a daughter who was one of the game's first women players. Lord Stanley attended many Ottawa hockey games during his tenure in Canada and in 1893 donated a trophy that was to be called the Dominion Hockey Challenge Cup. It instead became known by his own family name and has become virtually synonymous with hockey itself. First awarded to the MAAA as the 1893 AHAC champions, it thereafter became a challenge cup, meaning that any league champion could compete for it, on terms that were later laid down by Lord Stanley and his trustees in Ottawa, Sheriff John Sweetland and Philip Dansken Ross, the latter of whom was Montreal-born and played hockey there.

The Stanley Cup regulations of 1903 outline the rules that Stanley imposed in a document known as the "Deed of Gift" which states that: the then Governor-General, the Earl of Derby, before his departure from Canada in 1893 donated a challenge cup to be held from year to year by the championship Hockey Club of the Dominion. He appointed Sheriff Sweetland and Mr. P .D. Ross, of Ottawa, to act as trustees of the Cup, and requested them to suggest conditions to govern the competition. Meanwhile, his excellency directed that in 1893 the cup should be presented to the M.A.A.A. Hockey team of Montreal, champions of the A.H.A. of Canada, to be held by them until the close of the ensuing year. His excellency laid down the following preliminary conditions:

1. *The winners to give bond for the return of the cup in good order when required by the trustees for the purpose of being handed to any other team who may in turn win.*
2. *Each winning team to have at their own charge engraved on a silver ring fitted on the cup for the purpose the name*

of the team and they year won. (In the first instance the M.A.A.A. will find the cup already engraved for them.)
3. *The cup shall remain a challenge cup, and will not become property of any team, even if won more than once.*
4. *In case of any doubt as to the name of any club to claim the position of champions, the cup shall be held or awarded by the trustees as they may think right, their decision being absolute.*
5. *Should either trustee resign or otherwise drop out, the remaining trustee shall nominate a substitute.*

Lord Stanley, in view of the fact of several hockey associations existing in Canada, also asked the trustees to arrange means of making the cup open to all, and thus representative of the hockey championship as completely as possible, rather than of any one association.

The Trustees' Regulations, which have been used since 1893, are:

1. *So far as the Amateur Hockey Association of Canada is concerned, the cup goes with the championship each year, without the necessity of any special or extra contest. Similarly in any other association.*
2. *Challenges from outside the Amateur Hockey Association of Canada are recognized by the trustees only from champion clubs of senior provincial associations, and in the order received.*
3. *When a challenge is accepted, the trustees desire the two competing clubs to arrange by mutual agreement all terms of the contest themselves such as a choice of date, of rink, division of the gate money, selection of officials, etc., etc. The trustees do not wish to interfere in any way, shape or form if it can be avoided.*
4. *Where competing clubs fail to agree, the trustees have observed, and will continue to observe as far as practicable, the following principles.*
   a. *Cup to be awarded by the result of one match, or best two out of three, as seems fairest as regards other fixtures. The trustees would be willing, however, if desired, to allow the contest to be decided by a majority of the goals scored in two matches only (instead of best two matches in three).*
   b. *Contests to take place on ice in the home city, the date or dates and choice of rink to be made or approved by the trustees.*
   c. *The net gate money given by the rink to be equally divided between the competing teams.*
   d. *If the clubs fail to agree on a referee, the trustees to appoint one from outside the competing cities, the two clubs to share the expenses equally.*
   e. *If the clubs fail to agree on other officials, the trustees to authorize the referee to appoint them, the expense, if any, to be shared equally by the competing clubs.*
   f. *No second challenge recognized in one season from the same hockey association.*

With this set of rules and its object in place, hockey began to spread quickly across Canada into the United States and eventually to Europe and elsewhere. Up to 1914, when the Stanley Cup became exclusive to two leagues (the National Hockey Association and the Pacific Coast Hockey Association), many teams challenged for the trophy while league followed on league, often changing names more than anything else. During this time period the AHAC gave way to the Canadian Amateur Hockey League (1899–1905), the Eastern Canadian Amateur Hockey Association (1906–09), the Eastern Canada Hockey Association (1909), and the Canadian Hockey Association (1910). But in 20 years of Stanley Cup competition only

two teams outside the AHAC and its many successors had been successful in winning the Cup: the Winnipeg Victorias (1896, 1901) and the Kenora Thistles (1907).

We have yet to address the question of French-Canadian involvement in early Montreal-area hockey. Though French–English rivalry has become one of the central myths surrounding the game's origins, the truth of the matter is that French Canadians were not active participants before 1895, fully 20 years after we have established the start date of the Montreal game. The first French-Canadian teams weren't formed until some years after this date and their acceptance in local leagues wasn't immediate and required the support of the Irish.

Though there had been the occasional player like Charles Lamothe, captain of the Victorias in 1883, French Canadians generally started in hockey because of the setup of classical colleges in Montreal, where French and Irish Catholics studied together but in their own languages. Two colleges, Ste-Marie and Mont St-Louis, both bilingual, formed the core of an Irish hockey club, the Shamrocks. Though the Irish taught the French to play hockey in the college yard's rink, up to 1896 the Ste-Marie team was exclusively Irish, with players like Harry Trihey, Arthur Farrell and Jack Brennan (who would star later for the Shamrocks). Mont St-Louis had some French students on its team in 1895, including Louis Belcourt (who would join the Shamrocks in 1897, but was notably absent from the lineup when the team won the Stanley Cup in 1899 and 1900). In 1896, the college teams from Ste-Marie and Mont St-Louis merged to form the independent Orioles, though members still played for their respective colleges, thus producing an odd but workable combination of competing at one level and playing together at another.

In 1898, the Irish built their own college (Loyola) and parted physical company with their French friends. The ties between the two would remain strong, however, and play a critical role in the French gaining entry to Montreal's game. Not only did the first French players in the senior league play for the Shamrocks (Belcourt and Ernest Pagnuelo in 1897, Theophile Viau and Louis Hurtubise in 1902), but perhaps even more indicative of the Irish support—and how crucial it was—is the fact that the Shamrocks always voted in favor of having a French-Canadian team join the senior hockey ranks while other teams did not accept the French until 1905.

At about the same time that French-Canadian students first started to play the game, a new sporting club introduced a hockey team meant to be solely for francophone players, though a number of the players were actually Irish. This is where the difficult history of acceptance for French hockey teams begins. In 1894, a group of French-Canadian businessmen formed the Association Athletique d'Amateurs Nationale, known simply as *le National*. In the 1894–95 season, *le National* had two hockey teams (with all players from Mont St-Louis College) that played exhibition games. One of the teams beat the Junior Victorias, but mostly these teams suffered defeats. In 1898, a snowshoe club called *le Montagnard* built an ice rink and launched three new hockey teams which were placed in one of three leagues, depending on the calibre of the players. Most of these players were students at Ste-Marie College, effectively dividing the available francophone players by both college (Ste-Marie and Mont St-Louis) and club (*le National* and *le Montagnard*).

On their way to a Stanley Cup victory in 1899, the Shamrocks played an exhibition game against *le Montagnard*. To make it more even, they traded one player, Stephen Kent, for one Montagnard player, Hector Dalbec, who replaced Jack Brennan at forward. It hardly is surprising that the Shamrocks still won this game. In another sense, however, both teams ended up as losers: the game had been organized largely to encourage the acceptance of the francophone team in the ranks of Montreal senior hockey, but it did not succeed.

In 1900, with Montreal's French-Canadian hockey-playing college students advancing to university, a new school team emerged. The Université Laval à Montréal played its Quebec City counterpart, where a former Ste-Marie College student instigated the challenge. Meanwhile, *le National* and *le Montagnard*s continued their long, painful march toward the higher levels of hockey. Both were finally accepted into the intermediates in 1901 after a game between *le Montagnard* and the intermediate MAAA the year before. The two French teams helped to form a division along with McGill and the Pointe St-Charles team. *Le Montagnard* won the division while *le National* finished last and resigned from the league. In the semifinals, *le Montagnard* finished the series even with the MAAA but lost in terms of total goals by just one goal. It had been a good year, but not good enough to advance to the seniors. After another season, *le Montagnard* also resigned from the intermediate league when they saw there would no chance for advancement. (The Ottawa Aberdeens had won in 1902 but were not accepted as champions by the current rules.)

In 1904, the two French-Canadian teams merged for one season. *le National* was accepted into a new league, the Federal Amateur Hockey League (formed mainly under the leadership of the Montreal Wanderers), and the merger agreement called for *le National* to organize a team while *le Montagnard* provided its rink, free of charge, for games and practices. When this version of *le National* finished second in the Federal league standings, the mainstream senior league (then the Canadian Amateur Hockey League) at long last took notice and asked the team to join, which had been the main goal. But, perhaps ironically, the agreement between the two French clubs was now over. As *le National* joined the CAHL, *le Montagnard* was asked to form a team for the Federal league. Worse for *le National*, it lost its two main players from the 1904 season when Didier Pitre and Jack Laviolette left Montreal to turn professional in the United States. Both would later return and become prototype superstars for Montreal, but for now *le National* lasted only three games into the CAHL season (they lacked fans and kept losing) and then played only exhibition games. Meanwhile, *le Montagnard* stayed in the FAHL for two years. When the two clubs met again, in an exhibition game in 1906, *le National* won easily, 6–0, in a contest that was distinguished mainly by bloodshed.

The 1906–07 season would be the best yet for French hockey. With *le National* virtually defunct, *le Montagnard* acquired most of the best francophone players and lost only two games during the season. Their championship, and the chance to play for the Stanley Cup against the Montreal Wanderers, came into question, however, when the agenda at two of the Federal league meetings were dominated by protests to take away two Montagnard wins. With only two games remaining in the season, the team withdrew from the league. For the next two seasons, no French teams played organized senior hockey, but the Laval team was finally accepted in the University League in 1908 after a few

games against McGill in 1906 and 1907.

As Canadian senior hockey was becoming professional, a number of francophone players began coming back from the United States. Jack Laviolette and Didier Pitre would join the Montreal Shamrocks for the 1907–08 season and also played together in a major event the following year: an exhibition game of the best francophone players against the current Stanley Cup holders, the Montreal Wanderers. The game was scheduled at the Jubilee Rink in east end Montreal for March 10, 1909. That morning the French lineup was still not known, but that evening the roster was made up of Laviolette and Pitre, Edouard "Newsy" Lalonde, Emile Coutu, Joseph Dostaler, Robitaille and Alphonse Jette. All were well-known in Montreal except for Robitaille, who played for Pittsburgh in the International (Pro) Hockey League. To the surprise of a good many present, the francophone players emerged on the ice in the jerseys of *le National*.

The Wanderers won the game 9–8 but the exhibition game helped *le National* in its bid to return to league play in 1909–10. The sport's top league had just become the Canadian Hockey Association, but the situation in this league was anything but straightforward. At the meeting that saw *le National* reinstated, the Wanderers themselves were thrown out because their new owner wanted to play all his games at the Jubilee Rink (which he also owned), while the other CHA teams insisted on staying in the west end at the Westmount Arena. A team from Renfrew wanted to join the CHA this year but was also denied. Hence the Wanderers and Renfrew got together in a room next to the CHA meeting at Montreal's Windsor Hotel and formed a new league, the National Hockey Association. It is here that French Canada's truly unique hockey history begins to take the shape we still recognize today.

Renfrew was represented by the wealthy and strong-willed J. Ambrose O'Brien, whose family also owned a league in northern Ontario. O'Brien would deliver Cobalt and Haileybury as well as Renfrew to the NHA, but to bring out some crowds to the Jubilee Rink, the Wanderers proposed a new French team, to be called *les Canadiens*, and suggested Laviolette organize it. He would have the use of O'Brien's plentiful funds to build his new team, and as O'Brien and the Wanderers went to battle with CHA club owners over contracts, thus did the competition begin between *le National* and *les Canadiens* for the best French players. By December of 1909, both teams were claiming that they had signed many of the same ones. In fact, though, only one player had signed with both teams—and he had done so all in one day.

When Jack Laviolette telegraphed his good friend and erstwhile teammate Didier Pitre at his home in Sault Ste. Marie, he told him to join him in Ottawa to sign with the team he was putting together. Hearing of this, some *le National* administrators took a train to North Bay, Ontario, where they met Pitre first. Arriving in Ottawa later, Pitre said that he had signed already but Laviolette told him to sign his *Canadiens* contract anyway. *Les Canadiens* were to play their first game at home on January 5, 1910. Le National got an injunction against Pitre stating he was not to play or face prison. By the time the dispute went to court in February of that year, *le National* was no longer a team. The war between the NHA and the CHA had ended with an amalgamation on January 15, 1910.

Before the NHA–CHA coalition, there had been two professional hockey leagues with 10 teams in total—five of them in Montreal. After the merger, there was only the seven-team National Hockey Association. Three of its teams—the Wanderers, Shamrocks and Canadiens—were in Montreal. *Le National* was offered the Canadiens franchise if they would satisfy three conditions: play their home games at the Jubilee Rink; pay the salaries of all players on the Canadiens; and pay all debts incurred by the Canadiens. The Nationals were unwilling to take on the extra expense these conditions entailed and closed up shop, leaving the Canadiens as the only French-Canadian professional hockey team. The expanded Canadiens roster now included players from *le National*, but the squad had little success on the ice, winning only two of 12 games. The team might have fared better had Newsy Lalonde, the league's top scorer, not been loaned to Renfrew in an unsuccessful attempt to help that club win the championship. Because Ambrose O'Brien owned the Canadiens, Renfrew and two other NHA clubs, such personnel moves were not unheard of.

Since assuming ownership of the Canadiens, O'Brien had maintained that he wanted the club turned over to a French entrepreneur as soon as it was practical. However, in the summer of 1910, *le Club Athlétique Canadien* took O'Brien to court over the use of the name. In an out-of-court settlement, the club acquired the team and would own it until 1921 when the team was sold following the death of club manager George Kennedy. (Kennedy was born Georges Kendall, and while that name often appears in association with the hockey team, he went by Kennedy in English-speaking circles.)

The Montreal Canadiens won their first Stanley Cup in 1916, and while this was the initial victory for the French-Canadian team, it was not the first triumph for French-Canadian players. When the Winnipeg Victorias defeated the Montreal Shamrocks in 1901, Antoine "Tony" Gingras, born in St. Boniface, Manitoba, had become the first French Canadian to play for a Stanley Cup champion. Henri Menard had been the second when he was in goal for the Montreal Wanderers in 1906.

While hockey itself evolved from its start in Montreal and the city had a major role in all aspects of the game up to and after the formation of the NHL in 1917, the history of hockey in the city has become, for all intents and purposes, the history of the Montreal Canadiens as we known them today—the most successful club in the life of the sport and long past any need for the luck of the Irish.

CHAPTER 4

The Origins of American Hockey

Kevin Allen

ODDLY ENOUGH, one of the most important events in American hockey history occurred on a tennis court. The game's origin in the United States can be traced to a desert-hot summer day in 1894 when American and Canadian college athletes were competing at a tennis tournament in Niagara Falls. As they exited the court, conversation turned to winter activities and it was quickly discovered they were playing different versions of the same game. Canadians were developing hockey as we know it while the Americans were playing "ice polo." The objectives and strategy were the same, but ice polo was played with a ball and the stick resembled the one used today in field hockey. The rivals started comparing; boasting and challenges followed; before long, they were debating which sport gave greater excitement. To settle the question, a series of games was set up, to be played in Montreal, Ottawa, Toronto and Kingston, Ontario, in the winter of 1895.

In each city, one game of hockey and one of ice polo was scheduled.

To the Americans' surprise and dismay, the Canadians not only dominated all four of the hockey games but also managed to tie two of the ice polo matches. "It was pretty generally agreed among us as a result of that trip that the Canadian game was better than ours," U.S. participant Alexander Meikeljohn wrote about the series years later. Instantly enamored with this other game's speed, the Americans purchased all the sticks and hockey skates they could carry and took them back home. Within a few years, colleges and club teams along the Eastern seaboard had forsaken ice polo in favor of the faster and more thrilling sport. Meanwhile, Minnesotans were borrowing hockey from their Manitoba neighbors, players from Michigan's Upper Peninsula were starting to play against Canadian teams and hockey had quickly developed three significant and enthusiastic pockets of interest in the U.S. It also took root around Pittsburgh with the debut of the Western Pennsylvania and Interscholastic leagues until a fire at Schenley Park Casino Arena eventually stalled the game's growth there.

With the mining industry pumping huge amounts of money into Northern Michigan, a dentist named J.L. Gibson (a player on a team expelled from the Ontario Hockey Association in 1897–98 for paying some of its players) found enough investors to form America's (and the world's) first professional hockey league in 1904. The International [Professional] Hockey League included the Calumet-Larium Miners, the American Soo Indians, Pittsburgh, Houghton and Sault Ste. Marie (Ontario). The legendary Cyclone Taylor, for one, was enticed into the IPHL by hefty wages (it's believed he got a salary of more than $3,000), but it only survived until 1907.

The game needed a catalyst to gain wider acceptance and like so many other things American, needed a star to pin their dreams on. At the turn of the decade, they found one in Hobey Baker who was clearly the most important individual player in U.S. hockey's growth in the early years. Baker was a dashing and handsome center who was to college hockey from 1910 to 1914 what Wayne Gretzky was to the NHL in the 1980s.

Born to a wealthy family in Philadelphia, Baker was a schoolboy sensation in both hockey and football at St. Paul's School in Concord, New Hampshire. By the time the 5'9", 160-pound athlete arrived at Princeton, he was already a celebrity and his legend grew daily. By the end of his first (dual) sports seasons, observers were extolling his greatness the way basketball fans do today vis-à-vis Michael Jordan.

Baker had a blend of talent, courage and passion that had not yet been seen on a campus. He was a fearless halfback who brought crowds to their feet whenever he came near the ball; he dominated every game when he switched to play hockey. A dazzling skater, his raw speed seemed to mesmerize fans. When the puck found his stick, a buzz wound through a crowd anticipating a charge up the ice. He was once credited with 30 shots on goal in a game against Yale. As a sophomore, he had 92 points and led Princeton to an unbeaten season. Describing one of his goals, the *New York Times* wrote, "He carried the puck to every part of the ice surface without being stopped." But then the *Times* seemed particularly smitten by the Baker Phenomenon and it chronicled all his accomplishments with colorful prose. *Times* writers made it clear that they liked every layer of Baker, from the flashy way he moved on the ice to the noble manner with which he conducted himself when the game was over. In their eyes, the blonde bombshell was easily a prototype of the all-American boy.

Wherever Baker was scheduled to play, fans would line up to see him. To them, seeing Baker play hockey was like watching a magic show. They saw him perform acts of athleticism that simply could not be explained, like the time he seemed to run along the top of the boards to escape a defender. He controlled the puck as if it was attached to his stick by an invisible length of rope, as if he was running the-pea-and-the-shell game and the puck was the pea; now you see it, now you don't.

When Baker graduated, he declined turning pro. He was hardly tempted to give up his east coast lifestyle to play for the Portland Rosebuds, the new American team in the Pacific Coast Hockey Association. The Montreal Wanderers offered him $3,500, but money was no lure to Baker and he joined the St. Nick's amateur team in New York. By then, hockey had become a high-society sport and well-heeled businessmen came out in force to watch Baker dominate games.

St. Nick's defeated some prominent Canadian teams his first season, including the Montreal Stars during the Ross Cup series. But Baker longed for adventure—and of course there was a war—and by 1916 he was training as a fighter pilot. He was among the first American members of the Lafayette Escadrille Squadron shipped to France in 1917.

He painted his single-seat Spad in the orange and black Princeton colors and went into combat in April 1918.

Colleagues would later testify that he was a natural at dogfighting (as with so much in his life). He seemed to know how to make just the right aerial moves at precisely the moment he needed to, like he had on the ice rink. He brought down his first German aircraft in May 1918, the first of three in his combat career. "There was no finer man, nor a better pilot," recalls U.S. Major Charles Biddle, a long-time friend and flying companion. "He was very skillful and particularly fearless. He would have had an even greater record if he had been at the front more than he was."

Baker seemed to thrive on combat, presumably because it gave him the kind of adrenaline rush he got when he carried the football or stickhandled through the defense. He seemed more saddened than pleased when the War finally ended. Like a lot of other war veterans, Baker didn't seem sure what to do with his life.

A month after the war, Baker drove to the airfield and told his men he wanted to take one "last flight." This was in scary defiance of the combat pilot's deep superstition to never make an unneeded last flight, but given the fearless way he performed on the rink and gridiron, Baker perhaps never entertained the idea that he was indeed mortal. While he had known losses, he had never been beaten before December 18, 1918. Nothing and no one had compromised the conviction that he was invincible.

According to the *New York Times*, Baker went up in a recently repaired plane. As he coaxed it to an altitude of almost 2,000 feet, the engine sputtered to silence. He could have chosen to keep the plane level and crash-land a few miles from the airport (many pilots, including Baker himself, had walked away from crash-landings in the durable Spad), but he didn't want to suffer the embarrassment of losing a plane and immediately opted to turn back. Maybe he had time to think all of this through; maybe he acted as instinctively as he always had with a puck on his stick. In any event, as he turned the stalled plane, its nose was forced down. He struggled to pull it back up but he ran out of sky before he could complete the maneuver. He died on the way to the field hospital. He was 26.

So it was that the honor of being the first American in the NHL went to Jerry Geran of Holyoke, Massachusetts, who played against Baker in college, when he signed with the Montreal Wanderers in 1917–18 and played four games with no goals. Billed as "the second Hobey Baker," he didn't have that kind of ability. That year the Wanderers also signed Massachusetts native Raymie Skilton, a munitions expert posted in Montreal by the U.S. government who just wanted to play hockey and was signed by the cash-strapped team for one dollar.

In the early years of the next decade, the American player the NHL wanted most was Francis "Moose" Goheen. While Baker was dominating hockey in the east, Goheen was creating his own legend in Minnesota. He played on the USA's silver medal-winning 1920 Olympic team and then turned down contract offers from the Boston Bruins and Toronto Maple Leafs because he didn't want to surrender an excellent job with the Northern States Power Company. Playing in the NHL for less than his usual salary didn't seem to make sense to Goheen, who also picked up a bit extra playing for the St. Paul team in the American Hockey Association. And he wasn't alone. Many talented Minnesotans stayed at home in the AHA, a high-level league for the times. Some hockey historians argue con-

vincingly that Goheen's skills were on a par with Baker's and that what kept him from being as famous was a war record and a number of major articles in the *New York Times*.

"I've watched all the hockey players for 60 years and none could do as many things as Goheen," long-time Minnesota hockey aficionado Bob Fitzsimmons stated in a 1978 article in the *St. Paul Pioneer Press*. "He was a man born with skates on his feet. For him, the ice was like ground to the rest of us. He was truly the only hockey player I ever saw who combined speed, power, brute force, finesse and brains. God made Moose and threw away the mold."

Goheen often seemed like a racehorse in a field of hobbled nags. When he reached full speed, no opponent could catch him. Those who ventured too close often paid for their daring with damage caused by his stick. With his powerful stride, he was never more than seconds away from a score. He could be as tough as he was talented and he competed each night as if he was on a holy crusade. "Nothing in sports could ever beat the sight of Moose Goheen taking the puck, circling behind his own net and taking it down the rink, leaping over sticks along the way," said long-time Minneapolis announcer and sportswriter Halsey Hall in an interview with hockey historian Don Clark.

The first full-fledged, American-born NHL star was probably Taffy Abel, a barn-sized defenseman from Sault Ste. Marie, Michigan, 6'2" and 245 pounds when he arrived in the league with the New York Rangers in 1926. Considering that the majority of players in that era were about 5'9" and 165, it's not hard to imagine how physically imposing Abel was to opponents. He was also quick-tempered, which added to the fear factor they likely experienced. As a young player for the Soo Indians, he had recorded a one-punch knockout against a team manager who had reacted to a heartbreaking loss by saying, "There's always next game." Abel emphatically did not like to lose. "Off the ice, he was easygoing," recalls second cousin Bill Thorn. "On the ice, you didn't want to meet him."

Abel's game wasn't just about knocking opponents into the third row (although he was indeed a ferocious bodychecker). He could also skate well for a large man and it was said at the time that he churned like an open-throttle locomotive after he got going. Abel first caught the attention of NHL teams when general managers heard he had scored 15 goals in five games to help the Americans win the silver medal at the 1924 Olympics and he would deliver on that early promise. In his first season with the Rangers, he netted eight goals to place among the NHL's top-scoring defenseman.

Although Abel played three seasons for the Rangers and helped them win the 1928 Stanley Cup, general manager Lester Patrick always believed he should trim his girth (at various points in his career, Abel weighed as much as 260). When he refused to shed pounds, the Rangers sold him to the Chicago Black Hawks for $15,000—a whopping sum for a hockey transaction at that time.

In his seventh NHL season, Abel helped the Black Hawks win the Stanley Cup and then retired because owner Major Frederic McLaughlin wouldn't give him a raise he'd been promised.

As Abel was wrapping up his career, the NHL was just starting to view Eveleth, Minnesota as a spawning ground for hockey talent. Hockey was as much a staple in Eveleth as bread and potatoes and no city has meant more to hock-

ey in the United States. A mining community of 5,000 residents located 100 miles from the Canadian border and 60 miles from Duluth, Eveleth is to American hockey what Washington, D.C., is to politics and Nashville to country music. Its ability to produce elite-level players in the first half of the 20th century is one of the most astounding stories in hockey history.

In the 1930s, when there were only eight teams in the NHL, the Eveleth area managed to send two goaltenders to the league, Hall of Famer Frank Brimsek and Mike Karakas, who won NHL rookie of the year honors in 1935–36. Eveleth was also home to John Mariucci, one of the toughest NHL players in the 1930s, plus Joe Papike and Aldo Palazzari (who played briefly in the league, his NHL career prematurely ended when he lost an eye playing a pre-season game for the Rangers in 1944–45. His Eveleth-born son, Doug, made the NHL with the St. Louis Blues in 1974). Eveleth's influence also extended to college hockey and it has been documented that during the Depression, 147 Eveleth players were playing on various teams around the country.

Like Michigan's Upper Peninsula, Eveleth's ascendance as a hockey Mecca was fueled by its mining riches. The first recorded game in the community was played on January 23, 1903 when a team from Eveleth lost 5–2 to a team from Two Harbors, Minnesota. The city constructed its first indoor skating rink that same year. By 1914, it had four outdoor rinks. In the 1920s, hockey was such a major activity the mayor pushed for the construction of the 3,000-capacity Hippodrome rink, which opened on January 1, 1922.

In 1920–21, the Eveleth Reds began competing in the United States Amateur Hockey Association. Eveleth's division included teams from Houghton, Sault Ste. Marie [Ontario], the American Soo and Calumet, Michigan. In the national final, Eveleth lost to Cleveland 14–12 in a four-game total-goals series, but that was just the beginning. Eveleth fans got to see some of the best amateur hockey in the country before high operating costs and raids by pro teams forced the town to take a lower profile in 1926. During the early 1920s, the Eveleth team featured several prominent players—including Perk Galbraith, Vic Desjardins and Ching Johnson—who would play in the NHL. And Johnson, who had moved to Eveleth from his native Manitoba, would eventually be elected to the Hockey Hall of Fame.

But of all of the players born, raised and trained in the Eveleth program, Frank Brimsek and Mike Karakas achieved the most success. America usually celebrates Jim Craig's performance at the 1980 Olympics as the defining moment in American goaltending history, yet Karakas and Brimsek both won Stanley Cup championships long before he was born. Karakas helped the Black Hawks win the Stanley Cup in 1938 despite sneaking into the playoffs with a dismal record of 14–25–9. The 1937–38 Chicago team featured seven other U.S.-born players (Alex Levinsky, Carl Voss, Roger Jenkins, Doc Romnes, Louis Trudel, Virgil Johnson and Cully Dahlstrom) because owner Major McLaughlin was determined to prove Americans could compete in the NHL.

Karakas went on to earn 28 shutouts and a 2.92 goals-against average in eight NHL seasons. Brimsek led Boston to a Stanley Cup victory in his rookie season (1938–39) and retired from the NHL in 1950 with 40 shutouts and a 2.70 goals-against average over 10 seasons. Rocket Richard has called Brimsek the toughest goaltender he ever faced, but, "They were both very quiet guys," says Karakas's brother, Tommy. "Neither one of them was a Dennis Rodman type. They kept to themselves."

Yet a third Eveleth-area netminder reached the NHL in 1940–41 when Sam LoPresti became Chicago's goalie after Karakas was dealt to Montreal. Brimsek and Karakas were smallish goaltenders; LoPresti was a 215-pounder who looked like a fullback. He turned in one of the most remarkable goaltending performances in NHL history during his rookie season with a league-record 80 saves in a 3–2 loss to the Boston Bruins. LoPresti gave up the winning goal with 2:31 remaining as a shot caromed off his glove and fell into the net. (Years later, his son, Pete, played in the NHL and Lopresti was visiting in the Minnesota North Stars dressing room. When he noticed the size of the webbing in Pete's glove, he remarked, "If I'd had a glove that big, I wouldn't have missed that third goal.") It wasn't easy for the American pioneers to crack into NHL lineups that were usually exclusive Canadian clubs. Chicago's Doc Romnes (Lady Byng Trophy, 1936) and Cully Dahlstrom (Calder Trophy, 1936) were about the only other prominent Americans in the NHL in the 1930s. During his years with the Black Hawks, Mariucci felt that he had to fight regularly to prove he deserved to be in the league. He would later champion the cause of American players as coach at the University of Minnesota. When Palazzari joined the Rangers, Canadian teammates told him to "go home and play baseball." Palazzari said Canadians made him feel like "a germ that had just entered the body and the white corpuscles were ganging up on me."

It may be true that hockey tradition can't match—nor ever catch up to—the reverence that is regularly granted to baseball history in America. But it's just as true that hockey had its toehold in the American sporting landscape long before most people realize. In the first four decades of the 20th century, it was as popular in selected areas of the U.S. as anywhere in Canada. At least people in Eveleth and Houghton loved it with the same crazy passion as Canadian fans in Moose Jaw, Flin Flon and North Bay.

CHAPTER 5
The Origins of European Hockey

Denis Gibbons

WHILE CANADIAN HISTORIANS debate where the first ice hockey game in North America was played, the same kind of arguments are going on in Europe about the birthplace of hockey there.

Some say that in Great Britain ice hockey dates back to the 1850s when members of the Royal Family played a game on the frozen lake at Windsor Castle.

It is also said that Arthur Stanley, son of Lord Stanley of Preston for whom the Stanley Cup is named, returned to England in 1895 after his father served as Governor-General of Canada and cajoled the Royal Family into playing the game again, this time on a frozen pond at Buckingham Palace on a cold winter day. British historians do agree that the first demonstration match of ice hockey took place in Great Britain in 1895 and the first artificial hockey rink in Europe was constructed in London in 1903.

By comparison, it wasn't until the 1880s that soccer became established as an organized game in Great Britain, and not until the 1890s that it began to be played in continental Europe through the Victorian businessmen who traded across the continent. Soccer was also introduced to Europe by teachers of English who worked in colleges in Switzerland and France.

The Irish also lay claim to ice hockey, saying it evolved from hurling or hurley, although it's hard to figure out why it took Ireland until 1998 to join the International Ice Hockey Federation. There is even a 17th-century Dutch painting by Romein de Hooghe, showing characters zipping across ice on animal bones for skates, whacking at a flat rock with sticks formed from branches.

In all likelihood, ice hockey was being played in some form in several different European nations at the same time in the 19th century.

The Russians, it is known, had skates and sticks and a small object they tried to manipulate into a makeshift goal at either end of the ice. They used a ball instead of a puck and the ice surface was almost as big as a soccer field. But it was hockey.

Early Russian hockey was a game for aristocrats. An accident almost buried the sport forever. During a game the Arabian rubber ball was fired into a nobleman's eye causing serious damage. Hockey was then outlawed in Russia and the sport was not heard from again until the 1890s.

The first recorded hockey game between Russians and foreigners took place on the frozen Neva River in St. Petersburg in 1899. A local team called Sport played to a tie against a group of resident Englishmen. Among the players in this informal international match were world champion figure skater Alexei Lebedev and Russian speed-skating champion Alexander Pashin.

The Russians in those days stayed with the ball, a much bigger ice surface and more players. Their game was called Russian hockey and it evolved into what is more widely known as bandy, or in Russian—*hokkei s myachom* (hockey with a ball). Bandy, which is still played today, although

sometimes indoors and only at the top level by five nations—Russia, Finland, Sweden, Norway and the United States—provided a sound foundation for the Soviet ice hockey school, especially because it required so much skating and passing.

The first demonstration of Canadian hockey staged in Moscow took place in March of 1932, a few days after the Olympic hockey tournament at Lake Placid. The German team, which had won a bronze medal at the Olympics, was not very strong. The Germans lost 3–0 to the Central Army Sports Club, then 6–0 and 8–0 to the Moscow Selects. There were few spectators in the stands.

It was after a game of bandy at the Dynamo Stadium in February of 1946 that students from the Institute of Physical Education in Moscow demonstrated the game of Canadian hockey. It gained official status in December of the same year when the first USSR ice hockey championships got under way with 12 teams taking part.

Following the 1948 Olympic Games in St. Moritz, Switzerland in which Czechoslovakia narrowly missed winning a gold medal, the LTC club of Prague traveled to Moscow for three exhibition games with the Moscow Selects; its players were shocked to leave the Soviet Union with only a win and a tie. Czechoslovak players had long chats with the Soviets, shared their secrets with them, held training sessions with them and helped them master the skills of the game.

When the Soviets participated in the World Championship for the first time in 1954, there was only one artificial ice rink in the country. It was small and used primarily by figure skaters. Yet Vladimir Zabrodsky, the great Czechoslovak player, said that at the 1954 world tourney, in winning the gold medal, the Russians could not be held back unless they had the blades of their skates blunted.

In their development years the Soviets had first played with no hockey gloves and their knee pads and elbow pads were made from cotton wads. They wore soccer shin pads, wore no helmets and skated on the long blades of speed skates because that is all they had to use.

The Central Army Club had a sports camp in the Lenin Hills and because there were a lot of tall trees the ice would last a lot longer in the spring.

Anatoly Tarasov, the godfather of Soviet hockey, said workers would prepare the ice during the night, clean it and flood it so that at the coldest time of the night—3 or 4 a.m.—the players could start training. They would have to stop when the sun came up.

Eventually Tarasov received permission to use the artificial ice in the figure skating practice rink, which measured only 12 meters long by 10 meters wide. Hockey players were allowed to use it from two a.m. to six a.m., but there was room for only five players on the ice at a time and the team had to be broken up into small groups.

Josef Rossler-Orovsky, an all-round athlete, brought hockey sticks and a ball from Paris to Prague in 1890 and

translated the rules of a game played in France into Czech. Interestingly, the system used to award points according to those rules, by awarding one point for each goal and half-a-point for a corner shot, bears some resemblance to the existing goal-plus-assist scoring tables.

This was Czech national hockey, which soon became a good basis for the introduction of a new game of ice hockey. The spread of the new game was largely due to the efforts of Josef Gruss, a professor at Karlov University, who made the first translation of Canadian rules into Czech.

Gruss later was the chairman of the Czechoslovakian National Olympic Committee from 1929–1948 and became a member of the board of directors of the International Olympic Committee in 1946.

The first experiments in introducing Canadian hockey in Finland did not take place until the end of the 19th century when Professor Leonard Borgstrom arranged for early morning training sessions on the frozen north section of Helsinki Harbor. Interest in the new sport, however, waned and it did not appear again until 1927 in an effort backed by the management of the Finnish Speed Skating Union.

The ice skaters had for some time been unhappy about bandy, a game which required large ice rinks and thus stole the ice from the speed skaters. Ice hockey was included in the program of the Speed Skating Union, then one year later on the program of the Finnish Football Union.

The first match between teams from Finland and neighboring Sweden took place on January 29, 1928 when the Swedish champion, IK Gota, of Stockholm traveled to Helsinki and easily defeated the Helsinki Selects 8–1. In a rematch on February 26, the Swedish team won by an even larger margin of 10–1.

Finland had been part of Sweden for many years. Sweden's king conquered Finland in the year 1155 and it wasn't until 1809 that the two countries became separate nations again.

Today the rivalry between the two countries is so great that tickets for the Sweden–Finland game at the 1996 World Cup sold out in only 20 minutes.

Count Clarence von Rosen founded Stockholm's first ice hockey club in 1896.

The first international match in Sweden was played on January 31, 1921 when a team from Uppsala defeated a team from Berlin 4–1 in front of 2,022 spectators.

The first official hockey game in Germany was played on the frozen Lake Halensee in Berlin on February 4, 1897. Still the German Ice Hockey Union was not formed until 1963. Initially hockey was popular only in Bavaria where

the Alps provided the suitable climate. But by 1963 it was being played in industrial cities like Cologne, Dusseldorf and Krefeld.

Switzerland's first official hockey game took place in 1902 and, with a thriving economy today, the Swiss League offers the highest players' salaries in Europe.

Hockey in Hungary developed out of bandy. The first public game was played in Budapest in 1907. Seven years later the team of the Budapest Skating Union won international competitions in St. Moritz and Prague and was considered the best bandy team in Europe. An Englishman, John Dunlop, finally brought the game of Canadian ice hockey to Hungary in 1925 and the first matches were held between BKE and teams from Vienna.

In 1926 an artificial ice rink was built in Budapest and in the 1930s the Hungarian national team became one of the best in Europe, managing a 1–1 tie with Canada at the 1938 World Championship in Prague.

It was Stanko Bloudek, a champion discus thrower, who brought ice hockey to the Slovenian region of the former Yugoslavia. Bloudek undertook construction of the first ice rink in Ljubljana, brought the first ice hockey equipment there from Vienna and founded the first ice hockey club, Ilirija in 1928.

The quality of hockey in Poland before the Second World War improved with the help of many Polish-Canadians who had returned to their homeland.

Austria began to use transplanted Canadians heavily at the 1979 World B Pool Championships in Romania. Germany, Italy and France have also used Canadian-trained players who were able obtain passports from those respective European countries.

Over the years the Europeans have also learned a lot from North American professionals. The first tour of Europe by NHL clubs took place in 1938 when the Montreal Canadiens and Detroit Red Wings traveled by steamship to play a series of postseason exhibition games. Then at the conclusion of the 1958–59 season, the Boston Bruins and New York Rangers toured Europe, playing 23 exhibition games in Switzerland, England, France, Belgium, West Germany and Austria.

Since then NHL clubs like the New York Rangers, Washington Capitals and Winnipeg Jets (now the Phoenix Coyotes) have held training camps in Europe, and in the 1980s the Montreal Canadiens, Calgary Flames, Minnesota North Stars and the Capitals also played preseason exhibition games in the Soviet Union.

CHAPTER 6

Hockey on the Lake

The First International Tournament

Paul Kitchen

HE WAS NOT A HOCKEY PLAYER nor did he have any connection whatsoever with the sport, but when George Longley boarded the Montreal-bound train in Chicago in late February, 1885 he triggered a chain of events that would result in hockey history being made in Burlington, Vermont one year later.

Longley was a Pullman car conductor on the regular Grand Trunk Railway run between the two cities. He was looking forward to finally reaching home, a boarding house in downtown Montreal, especially since he was not feeling at all well. He was suffering feverishness, depression, chills and a cough. By the time the train arrived at Bonaventure Station on February 28, Longley was in no condition to proceed to his lodgings. Doctors succeeded in having him admitted to the crowded Hotel Dieu hospital, although at first they were not certain of the nature of his illness. It turned out to be smallpox, a highly contagious and often fatal disease transmitted through contamination of the air surrounding the victim and by way of infected objects and surfaces such as clothing, furniture and paper.

The failure of the hospital to promptly diagnose the complaint and to isolate the patient resulted in a rapid spread of the disease. Longley himself recovered and returned to his railway duties, but thousands of others were not so fortunate. The first death occurred on April 1. In the following months smallpox reached epidemic proportions and, by the end of its reign of terror, had claimed the lives of more than 3,000 Montrealers—some 2,500 being children under the age of 10 and mostly from working-class French-Canadian homes. Authorities estimated that 12,000 inhabitants of the city's population of 167,500 contracted the illness.

The commercial and social life of the city was disrupted. Business interests at first wanted newspapers to downplay the seriousness of the epidemic, but later joined forces to combat it by pressing officials to bring in compulsory vaccination and to quarantine those infected. Popular events where large numbers of people gathered were canceled, not the least of which was the Montreal Carnival slated for the winter of 1886.

The annual carnival, inaugurated in 1883, was a huge celebration of the joys of winter sport. Thousands of visitors from all parts of Canada, the United States and even Europe flowed into the city. They filled every hotel room and boarding house. Eagerly, they flocked to the dense program of skating competitions, curling matches, and tobogganing and sleighing demonstrations. In the evenings, there were fancy dress balls and dinners under the patronage of such luminaries as the Governor-General of Canada. Newspaper reporters from Ottawa, Toronto, Winnipeg, Boston, New York, Buffalo, Chicago, St. Louis and points between sent dispatches back home. Among the attractions was a curious new sport called hockey. Most spectators did not know what to make of it. They were dazzled by the game's speed and the dexterity of the players, but they were also a little taken aback by its rough edge.

By 1885, hockey, in an organized fashion, had been played for 10 years in Montreal, the birthplace of the formalized version as we know it. Even so, most of the city's inhabitants, not to mention visitors, were unfamiliar with the sport and newspapers struggled to find the right words to describe it. They likened it to rugby, lacrosse and the Irish game of hurley. The carnival, however, gave the game broad domestic and international exposure, a fact not lost on hockey leaders. Most of the participating clubs, such as McGill University, Victorias and Crystals, were locally based. The Quebec Hockey Club entered the first competition in 1883 and the Ottawa Hockey Club played in 1884 and 1885. The newly-formed Montreal Hockey Club joined the scene in 1885. There had never been an American entrant.

The Montreal Club, under the umbrella of the Montreal Amateur Athletic Association, were the 1885 victors. The rapid advancement of the team from inception to championship status was astonishing. Only in November of 1884 had the MAAA board of directors granted permission to one of their members to call a meeting for the purpose of starting a hockey club. Four days later the club was formed and the executive chosen. Two months hence the delighted team presented the carnival trophy to an appreciative board. The secretary-treasurer was immediately instructed to procure a trophy case, and the players anxiously looked forward to defending their title the following season.

But with the smallpox epidemic now causing the cancelation of the 1886 carnival, no one within hockey circles at first knew what to do about maintaining the momentum the carnival tournament afforded the game. As winter approached, there was talk in Ottawa of that city mounting a similar extravaganza since, as the *Ottawa Free Press* observed, "the smitten metropolis will be compelled this winter to forego its grand annual event." Soon though, the Ottawa mayor called off those plans, indicating it would be a "dangerous experiment" in light of Montreal's misfortune.

In Montreal, the carnival committee floated the idea of a "week of sports" as a substitute, presumably to keep it a primarily local affair since the stricken city would hardly be an attractive destination for outsiders.

Meanwhile, in the small city of Burlington, Vermont, nestled on the eastern shore of Lake Champlain, local sportsmen were making plans of their own. Members of the Burlington Coasting Club, according to that city's *Free Press*, had decided to organize a "week of winter sports, to which all the world should be welcome." Coasting, later known as bobsledding, was to be a central attraction but other sporting events would be arranged.

Officials were at pains to point out that when they conceived the idea, they were unaware of the cancelation of Montreal's carnival and, in any event, had in no way intended their own week to compete with that of the "City of the

North." It was only after the Montreal decision, organizers said, that it occurred to them it would be a good idea to borrow the project for a season and have a full-fledged Burlington Winter Carnival. Officials went north to seek advice on the running of such an event, and the *Burlington Free Press* was able to report that Montreal was being most cooperative "and has not only consented to our borrowing the name and spirit of her carnival, but has generously offered to assist us in every possible way."

There would be coasting, ice trotting, ice boating, skating races, snowshoe races, tobogganing, concerts, and a grand procession through the main streets. There would be hockey matches at the ice rink. Members of the Montreal Snowshoe Club would be coming down in force, and with them would be two crack Montreal hockey teams, the MAAA and the Crystals. The two teams were already great rivals that year, since they were competing in the Montreal city championship series that had finally been arranged. Everything was set for the week of February 15 to 19. The Ottawa Hockey Club, which had planned to compete, was practicing hard and for the occasion had ordered new sticks from the Caughnawaga reserve. The Ottawas had scheduled a warm-up match en route in Ogdensburg, New York. Mother Nature's intervention, bringing a blast of unseasonably mild weather, did not ruin plans but necessitated some adjustments. The organizing committee rescheduled the carnival for the following week and the Ottawa team bowed out of the hockey tournament.

The carnival week of February 22 to 26 was indeed all that Burlington could have envisioned. The air was crisp and cold. Retailers advertised suitable attire, including Canadian overshoes and moccasins available at Fisher & Boynton's Boot and Shoe House, and Canadian tuques and sashes at A.N. Percy & Co. The *Free Press* put out a special souvenir carnival issue which was distributed to such out-of-state cities as Boston, New York, Troy and Chicago. Somewhat wistfully, the *Montreal Gazette* told its readers that Burlington was "reaping a rare harvest of pleasure and profit through the success attending the gay gathering there."

The hockey tournament was the wrap-up sporting event scheduled for the late morning and afternoon of the 26th. Said the *Free Press*: "Hockey on the ice is one of the prettiest of carnival sports, with the colored costumes of the players, their rapid movements and the feats of skill accomplished." The paper did its best to picture the object of the players' attention. "The ball instead of being round is round one way and flat the other," wrote the reporter before finally nailing down the puck's description with the deft phrasing "like a boy's cartwheel sawed out of a board."

Competing with the MAAA and the Crystals in the three-team round robin was the local Van Ness House club. The Van Ness House was a prominent Burlington hotel and one of the centers of carnival socializing. Its members had never played a hockey game before and had only a few practice sessions. Nevertheless, in the spirit of athletic competition for which America is renowned, they ventured forth. At stake were gold medals for the members of the winning team and silver for the runners-up.

The rink was Lake Champlain, specifically the Central Vermont railroad slip. It was protected on three sides by docks which gave spectators an excellent vantage point. By 1886, organized hockey in Montreal had long been an indoor game, being played at the magnificent Victoria Skating Rink and the Crystal Rink. In a sense, the Canadian teams were returning to their outdoor roots. And the lake suited their American counterparts just fine. A terrific gale off the lake greeted the MAAA and the Crystals as they ventured onto the ice for what would be the first game of hockey ever played in the vicinity. Curiously, the referee and umpires were local residents, but since the rules of the game at that time were few and simple, no previous experience in interpreting and enforcing them seemed necessary.

Just one week earlier the same two teams, with almost exactly the same lineups, had met in the Montreal championship series. On that occasion the Crystals prevailed 3–1, thus setting the stage for a grudge match which, though it would have no bearing on the Montreal series, would give the MAAA a chance to restore their pride. And this they did when, after two scoreless 20-minute games, R. Smith "sent the ball through" to give the MAAA the sudden-death win. Friends of the victors greeted the result with deafening cheers.

At this point, true hockey history was about to be made, for the MAAA seven were now to face the Van Ness club in the first hockey tournament contest involving teams from two countries. The wind blew harder than ever through the frigid slip and gusting snow made visibility poor from the spectators' docks. Though the local team battled valiantly, again the MAAA came through, this time with a 3–0 victory in two games of 15 minutes duration. They took the gold medal honors. All that was left to be decided was the silver.

Probably because of the merciless weather and a general desire to conclude matters, the Crystals and Van Ness agreed to two 10-minute games to decide second spot. Forward J. McGoldrick of the Crystals scored in the first and that was sufficient, giving his team the victory. Observed the *Free Press*: "Hockey at once leaped into popularity on the part of those Burlingtonians who witnessed the game."

The MAAA and Crystals returned to Montreal where unfinished business awaited them the following week. In the match to decide the championship of Montreal, the Crystals defeated their arch rivals by a score of 4–2. They went on to win the championship of Canada in a less-than-conclusive manner when their Quebec City opponents refused to conclude the match due to disputes about player eligibility and rough play.

Meanwhile, the site of the first international tournament, the Vermont Central slip on Lake Champlain, was taken over by hordes of boys practicing their newly-discovered game.

Burlington Hockey Tournament Lineups

Van Ness House	MAAA	Crystals
L.C. Johnson	T.L. Paton	A. Cameron
C.H. Whitcomb	G. Lowe	J. Findlay
M.A. Kilvert	D. McIntyre	E. McCaffrey
W.H. Waters	F. Barlow	J. McGoldrick
E.S. Griffing	F. Crispo	W. Hutchison
H. Crane	W. Hodgson	J. Virtue
W. Laduke, Capt.	R. Smith	R. Laing, Capt.
	F. Larmonth, Capt.	

CHAPTER 7

Our Electrifying Game

Hockey in the Era of Gaslight

Brian McFarlane

FOR MOST OF THIS CENTURY (and elsewhere in this volume), fans and historians have debated the birthplace of hockey. There is solid pictorial evidence that people have been batting a ball around a field with a stick for hundreds, if not thousands, of years. Aside from Greek games, for example, paintings and tapestries of Dutch skaters knocking a spherical object around frozen canals date as far back as the 1600s. While such games can hardly be thought of as hockey even when they were transferred to ice, they were without doubt its forbears.

While a primitive form of hockey, "or ice-hurtling," as it was described in the *Montreal Gazette* in 1837, was played in many parts of Eastern Canada in the early 1800s, there were no organized games or leagues to play in until late in the century. Garth Vaughan, a *Total Hockey* contributor and member of the Windsor, Nova Scotia, Hockey Heritage Society, points out that hockey was played there almost 100 years before it existed in many other parts of Canada.

But it was in the era of gaslight, on March 3, 1875, that the first game of recognizable hockey with a set of rules governing the conduct of the players on the ice was played at Montreal's Victoria Rink. The ice surface measured 200 by 85 feet, which would become the standard size for rinks in North America.

Spectators at that first indoor match were warned to be on their guard at all times, as the puck, a circular piece of wood cut from a tree branch, was apt to fly off the ice. There were no boards surrounding the rink, but there was a low platform for people to stand on. Within a few years of this initial match, the piece of wood was replaced by a vulcanized rubber puck, invented in 1879.

The game received a huge boost at the Montreal Winter Carnival from 1883 to 1886 and it wasn't long before several teams in Montreal and Ottawa were organized to accommodate the rapidly growing number of hockey enthusiasts.

The first hockey league was established in Kingston, Ontario when four teams—Queen's University, Royal Military College, the Athletics and Kingston—agreed to play one another. In the championship game between Queen's and the Athletics, the flow of play was frequently interrupted. At that point in the game's evolution, the skate blade was not riveted but clamped onto a boot or a shoe. One of the goalie's skates was not clamped tightly and every shot that hit the blade knocked it off and the referee had to call time until it was replaced. Queen's won this first league title game by a 3–0 score. In the winter of 1886–87 the Amateur Hockey Association of Canada was formed. This body hoped to embrace and govern hockey in Quebec, Ontario and the Maritimes, but it wasn't long before the association was severely criticized for an apparent bias toward teams from Quebec. Member teams were the Montreal Amateur Athletic Association, the Montreal Vics, McGill, the Crystals (also from Montreal) and Ottawa. A

Quebec City team joined for the league's second season.

Toronto did not adopt hockey in a structured form until a league was organized and its first game took place in Toronto late in the 1888 season. The first game saw the Granites meet the Caledonians. By then, hockey itself was respectable, but still never on Sundays. Not long before this league was formed, Toronto boys were arrested for playing hockey on the harbor ice on the Sabbath. One outdoor ice surface used for games was said to be 500 feet long; it too was policed in "Toronto the Good." The Lord's Day Act was strictly upheld: no sports of any kind on a Sunday. By 1890, the Ontario Hockey Association had been formed to act as a regulatory body designed to supervise teams and leagues throughout the province. Within a year of its formation, the OHA included teams representing colleges and universities, politicians and bankers.

A decade later, in 1898–99, dissension rocked the Amateur Hockey Association of Canada, resulting in the birth of a new league. When the Ottawa Capitals (whose bid to join the league had been turned down the year before) were admitted into the AHA, three teams withdrew: the Victorias, Quebec and the Ottawa Hockey Club. The Montreal Hockey Club also withdrew and these four teams established the Canadian Amateur Hockey League. A fifth team, the Shamrocks, joined shortly after. With teams in Montreal (the Vics, the Shamrocks and the Montreal Hockey Club), Ottawa, and Quebec, the new league dominated hockey in Eastern Canada, producing the Stanley Cup-winning team six times in seven seasons even though by 1900 there were numerous hockey leagues, large and small, throughout Eastern Canada.

One of the clubs playing under the banner of the Ontario association was a popular team from Rideau Hall in Ottawa, the Rebels. On the team's OHA roster were two boys named Stanley, Arthur and Algernon, sons of the Governor-General, who had learned the game quickly. Their sister, Lady Isobel Stanley, was also a player, and may have been the first woman "hockeyist" to have her photograph taken with a stick and a puck, on the pond next to Government House in Ottawa. For several years there had been a carefully maintained rink there that was the focal point of lavish skating parties hosted by the Governor-General.

A reporter for an Ottawa newspaper witnessed a game one night between the ladies of the Ottawa Alphas and the Rideaus. The following day, he wrote: "That the Alpha ladies and the Rideaus can play hockey was well demonstrated at the Rideau rink last night. Both teams played grandly and surprised hundreds of the sterner sex who went to the match expecting to see many ludicrous scenes and have many good laughs. Indeed, before they were there very long, the mens' sympathies and admiration went out to the players and they became wildly enthusiastic."

While eastern teams still dominated hockey at its highest levels, leagues were also being formed all over the west.

The Manitoba and Northwestern [Ontario] Hockey League was active by 1892. By then, there were at least 30 teams in Winnipeg alone, with all the games played outdoors. Other associations were also established in the areas that would become Saskatchewan, Alberta, the Northwest Territories and the Yukon.

Players who wanted a test of their skills against other players and teams, near and far, in good weather and bad, had plenty to choose from if they found means to travel. In 1896, a Winnipeg team went to play in a tournament that was part of the St. Paul Winter Carnival in St. Paul, Minnesota. Other teams came from Chicago, Duluth and Fort Snelling. Seven German loving cups, with music boxes concealed in the bottom, were obtained by the tournament organizers to be awarded to the championship team. In their first game against St. Paul, the Winnipeg team had an easy time of it, winning 18–2. In the championship match, the Winnipeg boys scored a goal every few seconds, so often that officials lost track and stopped counting after 20 went into the net. "The southern boys made a plucky attempt to play the game but their efforts were crude," one of the victorious players told a reporter for the *Winnipeg Free Press*. "As for the German loving cups, they were not exactly up to their advertised value and mine was missing the music box which would have made it a much more attractive prize."

In December 1903, the Federal Amateur Hockey League was established as a result of the CAHL's refusal to admit new members. Four teams from three cities were charter members of the FAHL: Montreal Wanderers, Montreal Nationals, Ottawa Capitals and Cornwall. It was during this season that someone suggested painting a line between the goal posts to aid the goal umpires, who stood in back of the net. The Wanderers became the first champions of the new league and might have won the Stanley Cup had team owner James Strachan not ruined their chance. The trustees mandated a two-game playoff between the Wanderers and Ottawa, the CAHL champions. In Montreal, both teams played brilliantly and wound up 5–5; the outcome would have to be decided in overtime. Strachan decided the referee was incompetent, however, and vowed, "We'll not take the ice unless Kearns is replaced." The trustees huddled and moments later ordered the teams to restart the series—with two games to be played in Ottawa. Strachan insisted that the tied game be played over again—in Montreal. Ottawa vetoed that proposal and the series was abandoned. Ottawa went on to defeat Brandon 6–3 and 9–3 to retain the Stanley Cup.

According to hockey historian Mike Terran, the American Amateur Hockey League became the first organized league in the United States in 1889. Artificial ice was common in a handful of American cities at that time. The Brooklyn Skating Club won the league championship in 1899, with all games played on the St. Nicholas Rink in New York. By 1905, the Brooklyn club was in need of fresh talent (they had allowed 93 goals in eight games) so several top amateurs—but no professionals—were recruited from Canada. Brooklyn dropped out in 1906, but other teams carried on and the league lasted until 1917. A Philadelphia team appeared in the league standings for one season (1901) and a Boston club was represented for a few (1915 to 1917).

Hobey Baker of St. Nick's was the most renowned individual player in this league. A former Princeton star, he was the equal of any of the best Canadians, many of whom came with their teams to New York to play exhibition games at the end of each season. Killed in a plane crash in France at the end of World War I, Baker was inducted into the Hockey Hall of Fame in 1945. Indeed, Baker is in both the U.S. and Canadian Halls of Fame making him and "Moose" Goheen the only two non-professional American players ever to be so doubly honored. But if Baker had lived, he might well have starred in the U.S. version of the National Hockey League. Mike Terran comments on the existence of a short-lived NHL involving amateur teams from New York (Wanderers), Boston (Arenas and Charlestown Navy Yard) and Pittsburgh (Athletic Association). The circuit operated for only one year circa 1922, with Pittsburgh defeating Montreal Hochelaga for the title and a now all but forgotten honor called the Fellowes International Challenge Cup.

American hockey clubs had already shown a willingness to import some of the world's best players—and pay them for their services. Certain regions and teams in the States were beginning to offer financial inducements to the best Canadian (read amateur—maybe) players. A standard offer to a star player was $30 a week and maybe a job. One of the first teams to line up for players was Pittsburgh, where artificial ice was a big attraction. The manager of a Kingston team returned from a junket to Pittsburgh in 1902 and gave the following report to the *Toronto Globe*: "Pittsburgh is hockey crazy. Over 10,000 turned out for our three games there. The general admission being 35 cents and 75 cents for a box seat. The receipts were about $4,000 but all we got for our share was about $350, which, after expenses, will leave about enough to buy some postage stamps.

"But the Pittsburgh rink is a dream. Around the ice surface, which is about 275 feet by 125 feet wide, the seats are arranged in tiers above the boxes, which are fitted up luxuriously. The place is lighted by thousands of incandescent lamps. The band is always in attendance and there is every convenience for patrons, who, for skating sessions, can get their blades sharpened or acquire a pair without going outside the building. What a marvellous place it is."

By 1903, a dentist named J.L. Gibson was living in Houghton, Michigan, after leaving the Ontario town that was known as Berlin until World War I. In that previous home, which we now know as Kitchener, he had been a player on a team the Ontario Hockey Association expelled in 1898 after the members were rewarded with 10 dollar gold coins after an important victory. In Michigan, Gibson made history by creating the first fully professional team, Portage Lakes, hiring the best Canadian amateurs he could find and turning them pro. His imports whipped teams in other towns in the upper peninsula and environs so soundly that they in turn started to scour the Canadian wilderness for cash-strapped players to compete with Doc Gibson. In 1904, Gibson and his colleagues established the International (Pro) Hockey League. Portage Lakes continued to be the dominant team in the circuit.

While hockey's governing bodies decreed that no player could participate in Stanley Cup matches if he was not a bona fide amateur, debates raged for several years about the status of players and the issues involved. Who was an amateur and who was a mercenary pro? Could amateurs play with pros and remain amateurs? Could pros be reinstated as amateurs? The Amateur Athletic Union of Canada was called on to adjudicate many of these disputes.

For instance, by 1908 it was well established that the teams of the Ottawa Valley Hockey League (including Pembroke, Renfrew, Cornwall and Smiths Falls) all bid for the best players. And money talked. Cyclone Taylor, who

was then the Ty Cobb of hockey, was known to move from team to team, as was Art Ross—and always because they were well paid to do so.

It wouldn't be possible to operate any professional hockey league today without hundreds of players, most of them pretty well paid and a few of them extremely wealthy. But in 1911, when the Patrick brothers organized the Pacific Coast Hockey Association with franchises in Vancouver, Victoria and New Westminster, British Columbia only 23 players were required to fill the rosters of all three of the clubs. Every player was expected to be on the ice for the full 60 minutes of every match in the 15-game schedule. Some players earned extra money as referees in the league. The Patrick brothers had gained their experience in league management in the heart of the Rocky Mountains, in Nelson, British Columbia. In 1907–08 they worked for their father's lumber company and played for Nelson in the already established Kootenay Hockey League. Not only were they the best players in the league, but they raised money to replace the ramshackle 500-seat rink with one that housed 800 fans, and what's more had a roof. Lester took a leave of absence in December of 1908 to join Edmonton, one of several ringers, in an unsuccessful bid to win the Stanley Cup against the Montreal Wanderers. Edmonton paid him $100 for expenses, but he mailed back a cheque for $32, the money he had left in his pocket when he got back to Nelson. A year later, several eastern teams bid for his services and he opted to sign with Renfrew of the newly formed National Hockey Association. The team met his demand for $3,000 and also agreed to sign brother Frank for $2,000. After their Renfrew experience, the now seasoned hockey men came west again, to Vancouver and Victoria, where their vision included new arenas with artificial ice and a professional league that had some of the world's greatest players. And, like so many of the game's pioneers, they made their dream happen until it too was history in the world's fastest sport.

Meanwhile, in a virtually parallel universe perhaps inspired by the skills displayed by Lady Isobel Stanley a generation before, women's hockey teams flourished across Canada in this era, with the first known league for women operating in Quebec as early as 1900. Another inspiration and role model may have been Lady Minto, wife of the Earl of Minto, Canada's Governor-General from 1898 to 1904. Lady Minto once broke her leg while skating (was she perhaps playing hockey?) and was described by figure skating champion George Meagher thus: "I have seen all the best skaters in the world and I consider Her Excellency, the Countess of Minto, to be the peer of them all." At the turn of the century, American women were playing hockey on artificial ice in Philadelphia. Some teams played and practiced behind closed doors, with no men allowed. College teams with names like the Morning Glories and Love-Me-Littles played against one another. Soon leagues developed. Other teams bore such interesting monikers as the Icebergs, Snowflakes and Mad Old Hens. In 1927, a Queen's University player became the first goalie to wear a mask— a fencing mask. Michel Vigneault, who writes about early hockey in his native Montreal in this book (see page 10), has also written about the first professional hockey league for women. A small number of Quebec teams played in Montreal during the 1916 and 1917 seasons.

By this time, leagues from all over the country were sending challengers after the now-famous Stanley Cup that the Stanley children, and one of Lord Stanley's aides, Lord Kilcoursie, had encouraged the Governor-General to give hockey in 1893. It turned out to be a wonderful and lasting gift. In 1945, the gift of a small silver bowl would earn him a place of honor in the Hockey Hall of Fame in spite of the fact he himself never played, coached, managed or even saw a Stanley Cup game, having been recalled to England before the matches named after the $50 trophy commenced. But let's put the dry history aside and go back to that earliest era and see what we can by its gaslight. To gain a better perspective on how hockey was played and received then, let's start by reviewing in detail a Stanley Cup series of that time, when challenges for the Cup generated incredible excitement and interest for fans in the towns that competed. What follows are edited newspaper accounts of a series played in Montreal in 1896 between the Winnipeg Victorias and the Montreal Victorias (the Queen's legendary status is evidenced by the hundreds of hockey teams, among other things, named in her honor). Most accounts are from the *Winnipeg Free Press*.

Saturday, Feb 1, 1896: A week from next Monday, the Victoria hockey team leaves for Montreal to play the Victorias for the Stanley Cup, which carries with it the championship of Canada. That the Winnipeggers will win it is earnestly hoped for by every resident of the Canadian northwest. We have shown that Winnipeg is the curling center of the world, and if the Stanley Cup is brought to the bull's-eye of the Dominion, we will have proven our right to be called the hockey center of the world.

Tuesday, February 11: The sendoff yesterday from the Winnipeg station partook of the vociferous. Several hundred admiring friends of the Vics gathered at the depot and as the train pulled out three cheers and a tiger were given with an enthusiasm which was new to the CPR station. On the evening of Friday next, the greatest struggle in the history of hockey will take place. The championship of the world is at stake, an honor worthy of the best efforts of Winnipeg. Out from the west go seven of the prairie capital's most stalwart sons to do battle with the representatives of the 300,000 people who inhabit Canada's greatest city. If our champions fail, it will be before most worthy opponents. There must be over half a hundred regularly organized hockey clubs in Winnipeg, a truly marvellous state of affairs for a city of its pretensions.

Saturday, February 15: [Headline:] The Stalwart Sons of the Prairie Capital Show Easterners How to Play Hockey. Montrealers are Shutout on Their Own ice. Tremendous Local Interest in the Results.

This headline no doubt tells it all except for the score. And the score, 2–0, doesn't seem to account for much in the story written about the game:

There's joy in the ranks of the Winnipeg touring hockey contingent tonight. The magnificent Stanley Cup, emblematic of the championship of the Dominion, is theirs. They presented it to the Queen City of the west as a valentine, won as it was on February 14. Well and worthy was the victory, long and determined the battle, and for the first time in the history of the champions of the effete east, Montreal had to submit to a complete whitewash. The "Blizzards" from the land of the set-

ting sun which trouped into Montreal on Monday evening created no little stir in the breasts of Montrealers and in sporting circles. Their advent has been the topic of conversation for the past few days.

Alas for the frailty of human hopes, Montreal tonight is clothed in sackcloth and ashes and the sports have gone to sleepless beds with empty pocketbooks. The Peg contingents, on the other hand, have enough money to start a private bank. No less than 2,000 cold "plunkers" were passed over the Windsor Hotel counters tonight and went into the jeans of the Winnipeg supporters.

The game was played in the large Victoria Rink before a crowd of several thousand people...

McDougall got the face and the disc traveled toward the Winnipeg goal. Higginbotham lifted it gently in the other direction. Bain collared it and the Pegs swooped down on the Montreal goal. For five minutes it never got past the center line. Then the Montreal men quickened and there was some lively scurrying around the Winnipeg goal posts. Flett, with his wonderful lifts, made the spectators open their mouths in amazement. [Editor's note: A high backhand shot to get the puck out of danger was known as a "lift."] A particularly fine lift was taken advantage of when Howard got the puck in the corner, passed in front of the posts, and Armytage placed it fairly between the posts. Time: 10 minutes.

The Winnipeg yell went up from a dozen different portions of the rink where little knots of westerners had secured places of advantage...

[Later] Campbell managed to entice the disc past the Montreal goalkeeper and there was jubilation again in the ranks of the Winnipeg contingent. They surmised rightly that the victory was already theirs.

No more goals were taken by either side...

After the match, the Winnipegs were entertained to a pleasant supper by the officers of the vanquished club. The best of feeling prevailed.

Back in Winnipeg, a reporter for the *Free Press* wrote:

It is seldom that there have been evenings of rejoicing to equal last night. Everyone was interested in the success of the hockey team in the east, and by eight o'clock hundreds of persons had gathered in the hotels to listen to the returns as received on the CPR wires from Montreal.

The *Free Press* also printed an eyewitness account of the match. Joseph Carter, of the CPR ticket office, called the championship game one of the major events of the century.

Flett played the star game and Merritt's work in goal has never been excelled in Montreal. Bain being laid off [penalized] weakened the team. The referee was strictly impartial. He would never argue a case. His word was law. In the east, if a man plays offside he is warned by the referee. If he continues this practice, he is laid off for five minutes.

The Winnipeg club's share of the gate was $160, a small percent, but the lads didn't care if they never got a cent.

Friday, February 21: Mr. George H. Merritt, the man who won the Stanley Cup, returned to Winnipeg yes-

terday on the CPR train. The redoubtable "Whitey" is not yet recovered from his hard work in the big match a week ago today and many bruises on his body bear testimony to the hard shots he stopped so well. Merritt was met at the depot by a large number of enthusiastic friends who scrambled all over one another in their eagerness to shake his hand. Merritt made his way to the Winnipeg Hotel, there to refight the great battle before an audience of ready listeners. Mr. Merritt told a *Free Press* reporter that the rest of the players were enjoying themselves in Toronto and that they would reach the city Monday afternoon. He says they received the best of treatment wherever they went. Their entertainment in Montreal was pleasant, but the Victorias of that city plainly showed their great disappointment in losing the Cup which has adorned their club room for so many years. The caretaker of the rink was so worked up over the defeat that he shed enough tears to fill the big trophy.

The *Free Press* writer described the Cup itself:

The Stanley Cup is in the form of a punch bowl. It is of sterling silver and has about a two-gallon capacity. It will be brought up to the team next Monday along with the sticks and pucks used in the great game. It will be put on exhibition.

Tuesday, February 25: "A Heartily Welcomed Winnipeg Hockey Team Returns From Montreal"

A right royal welcome was extended to the Winnipeg hockey team yesterday on their return from Montreal, where they gained glory for themselves and fame for the province which was never prouder than yesterday to call them her sons. It was a welcome in keeping with the high honors the Vics have won.

Long before the train from the east was due, a steady stream of citizens of all sorts and sizes assembled at the CPR depot. When the inevitable "Here she comes!" started it ran through a crowd of several thousand people who swarmed the platform. When the iron horse made its appearance, a Union Jack was fluttering in front of its headlight and the cowcatcher was adorned with hockey sticks and brooms, symbolic of a clean sweep in Montreal. The engineer showed the pride he took in his work by wearing Winnipeg colors.

All eyes then turned to the rear sleeper from which the champions emerged, to be taken in charge by their enthusiastic friends. Captain Armytage led the procession and behind him came Mssrs Flett, Higginbotham, Bain, Campbell and Howard.

Mr. Merritt, the crack goalkeeper, had met the visitors down the line and landed with them.

High gray hats adorned with the club colors gave the champions a truly dignified appearance. To the tune of "See the Conquering Heroes Come," played by the Dragoon band which kindly lent its services to make the welcome a worthy one, the conquering heroes were escorted to the rear of the depot where Mr. Jordan had cabs at their disposal. The players and officers filled five cabs which, headed by the band, moved up Main Street. A great many other rigs followed and hundreds more moved along on foot.

The Stanley Cup trophy, coveted by every hockey team in the Dominion, occupied a prominent place in

the leading cab and was the center of the admiring eyes of those who lined the streets.

At the Manitoba Hotel, another immense crowd had gathered before the procession arrived, and when Mayor Jameson arose to speak, he was greeted by the shouts of several thousand proud citizens. The Mayor gave an eloquent address in which he extended from the city a warm welcome to the proud world champions. There were loud calls for Mr. Armytage, who upon rising was greeted by great cheers. The worthy captain took but a few minutes to thank his large audience for their enthusiastic welcome and stated that he hoped the Stanley Cup would long remain a prominent feature in the city of Winnipeg. At the conclusion of the speech-making, all adjourned to the hotel's smoking room, where the capacious trophy was filled to the brim with champagne.

That's what winning the Stanley Cup meant in the gaslight era, when the trophy was still just a baby, only three years old.

Incidentally, the Winnipeg Vics didn't hold the Cup long. In December of that same year, the Montreal Vics sought revenge. The big rink in Winnipeg was sold out far in advance, but the home team had lost a big star two months before this return match. At the peak of his career, 28-year-old Fred Higginbotham, star athlete and accomplished musician, was playing with some children and riding a pony when he ran into a clothesline. His spinal cord fractured, he died a few hours later in the arms of Joe Hall, his best friend who would later gain fame as a notorious "bad man" of hockey. Montreal recaptured the trophy, beating Winnipeg 6–5 at home.

When Winnipeg later returned to Montreal for a Stanley Cup series in 1903, the Bell Telephone Company provided a much-needed service. Bell put 10 extra girls on duty in its central station and they could have used more. Over 30,000 calls were answered and no less than 50 were incoming at one time. Every one asked the same question: "What's the score?"

In the earliest era of hockey, games were often played in public parks where bandstands were common. On a break-away, a player might have to decide rather quickly whether to veer left or right in a dash around the bandstand. It was a circuitous route to the goal, and players who kept their heads down were in constant peril of crashing right into the immovable structure. And it was far from uncommon for fans to get involved in the action. In a turn-of-the century match in Sudbury, a number of them landed right in the middle of play, but not by design. Over 30 spectators came down on the ice when the gallery's railing collapsed. Some landed on people directly beneath them and a number were seriously injured.

Flareups of temper were hardly unheard of. During a game in Ottawa in 1899, Ottawa star Chauncey Kirby had his stick grabbed as he skated along the boards. Kirby stopped and whacked the lad holding the stick on the jaw, a reaction that was "quite proper," according to an Ottawa reporter at the contest. When another Ottawa star, Weldy Young, lost his temper over critical remarks tossed his way, he "so far forgot himself as to jump into the crowd and assault a fresh young supporter of the opposing team. However, the latter had quite a number of friends with him and Young was roughly handled before he was thrown back on the ice." Fans too were quite often rowdy and had to be chastised. In 1899, the *Ottawa Citizen* stated: "It is hard to believe there are so many hoodlums in Ottawa. The manner in which Harvey Pulford was roasted by the crowd was a disgrace to decent sports." The paper quoted Bob Shillington, a famous coach: "Never in my life have I seen one player get such dirt as the Ottawa man was given by the crowd of hoodlums. They have but one equal and that is the Hamilton newsboy. There are two creatures that hiss—a snake and a goose. The former is venomous and the latter has no brains."

Referees and goal judges, then as now, had their critics. The *Toronto Telegram* weighed in in 1898: "There is little wonder at Waterloo objecting to Mr. King refereeing their game the other night. He is a tinhorn sport of the first water and should not be allowed in decent hockey circles."

The *Ottawa Citizen* decreed that a certain (unnamed) referee is "unfitted to the game and should stick to bowling. The next step before death is refereeing." One well-known referee had his own complaints. Fred Waghorne told newsmen in 1903: "I will not officiate in Stouffville ever again. No more little rinks for me. In future I will decline to referee in rinks where the ice surface is no larger than a billiard table."

Oddities were almost the rule in some of the earliest games. In a Stanley Cup match played between Rat Portage (Kenora) and Ottawa on March 12, 1903, the *Citizen* reported: "The ice was in wretched condition. In several places the water was two to three inches deep. On one occasion the puck slipped under the surface and disappeared. There was a delay while a player fished for it without success. In a second match, the visitors played two men in goal all during the game." In a model of understatement, the *Citizen* concluded: "Consequently, it made scoring a difficult problem for the Ottawas."

But complaints about ice conditions were common in those early days. Deep pools of water spoiled a game between Kingston and Belleville one warm day in March, 1894. The Kingston paper reported three or four inches of water on the open ice, but Belleville wouldn't pay Kingston's expenses if the team didn't play. What's more, the paper reported, "Belleville scored one of their two goals in a most peculiar way. While one player splashed water in the face of the Kingston goalie, another put the puck through for a goal."

The first outright professional league in Canada was in business for the 1908 season. Toronto, Guelph, Brantford and Berlin (Kitchener) were charter members of the Ontario Professional Hockey League. Since the teams traveled by trolley cars linking the cities, the league came to be known as the Trolley League. Leading scorer Newsy Lalonde had 29 goals in nine games. Berlin employed the fewest players (seven); the others clubs used 10 to 12. No doubt it is indicative of how rapidly progress took place that from such rough beginnings, in less than a decade the National Hockey League would come into being, setting the foundation for the highest level of the today's game.

CHAPTER 8

How Early Hockey was Reported

Peter Wilton

OTTAWA IN 1888 was certainly not at the cultural hub of the western world. Chosen mainly for its location—well away from the border with the United States—Ottawa was closer to a pioneer logging town than the capital of a nation. For Frederick Arthur Stanley, son of a British prime minister and accustomed to the inherited privilege of an aristocratic, upper class family, a posting as Governor-General to the colony of Canada must have seemed like traveling to the end of the civilized world.

As Governor-General, Lord Stanley only entered the political fray reluctantly, but he openly embraced the Canadian culture. Like much of the British upper class, Stanley was a sportsman and he enjoyed the new sports he encountered in Canada. Several of his seven sons played hockey with the Rideau Rebels, who skated on a rink behind Rideau Hall, the official residence of the Governor-General. In 1890, Arthur Stanley and the Rebels helped form the Ontario Hockey Association.

At the conclusion of the 1891–92 hockey season (and nearing the end of his term in Canada), Lord Stanley instructed Lord Kilcoursie to read a prepared statement for him at a hockey banquet in Ottawa. In this speech, Lord Stanley noted how much he and others had enjoyed hockey during the long Canadian winter months. In recognition of the game, he would purchase a silver cup for championship competition. The Stanley Cup was born.

Public interest in hockey can be gauged by the amount of coverage local newspapers were willing to give the Stanley Cup. On March 19, 1892, The Ottawa Citizen did not even mention the hockey banquet that had taken place in the city the night before, nor did the newspaper mention the speech delivered by Lord Kilcoursie or the donation of the Dominion Hockey Challenge Cup (as the Stanley Cup was formally known). When the first official Stanley Cup playoff game was held on March 22, 1894, the Citizen buried its three-paragraph article on the fifth page even though the game had involved a local team. The description of the on-ice action between the Ottawa Generals and the Montreal Amateur Athletic Association is brief, with the majority of the article concerning itself with the aftermath of the Montreal victory from Ottawa's perspective: "In the Ottawa dressing room Captain Young whose plucky play had won the admiration of friend and foe alike was stretched out on the floor in a faint. He was brought around after some little difficulty to listen to 'Lo Pean' [a Quebec folk song] which the enthusiastic Montreals were singing outside."

Early Stanley Cup coverage was less than what local newspapers gave to sports such as lacrosse or curling, and it seems the competition only warranted coverage if a local team was competing. During its first 10 years, three Montreal teams—the Amateur Athletic Association, the Shamrocks and the Victorias—controlled the Cup. Ottawa, the city in which the idea of the Cup was born and the capital of the country in which the game was created, continued to pay scant attention. On February 15, 1896, the Winnipeg Victorias captured the Stanley Cup from the Montreal Victorias. The Ottawa Citizen covered the game as follows: "Wild Woolly Westerners Win Montreal – February 14: The Winnipeg hockey team defeated the Victoria hockey team of Montreal by two goals to none."

This was the extent of the coverage in Ottawa, but while the Montreal–Winnipeg series may not have seemed newsworthy to the editors of the Citizen, it did capture the public imagination. After the rivalry between the two Victoria hockey clubs began, and the two teams traveled halfway across the country by rail to challenge each other, the amount of ink given to the Stanley Cup increased significantly.

For the first 45 years of the Stanley Cup's existence, the local newspaper was the only source of information on the outside world for the average citizen. However, by the turn of the 20th century, there already was emerging a glimmer of what the future would hold in the form of the telegraph. As interest in hockey grew, important games would be transmitted via railway telegraph to newspaper offices across the country by a Morse code operator who was set up within the arena. Crowds would gather in public places like hotel lobbies, railway stations and in front of newspaper offices to learn the results of the game as they came across the wire. This instant access to the game also allowed the newspapers to put out a supplement as soon as the results of the game were known. The majority of hockey fans would learn of their team from the newspapers, which gave a kind of saturated coverage similar in style to that of a modern play-by-play broadcast. The sports writers provided news such as who carried the puck on a particular rush or who was giving all their effort and who appeared to be sleeping through the game. Like radio and television today, these details gave added color for the readers and helped to create a following for the team. This style of total game coverage began to appear in Ottawa newspapers at the same time the famed Silver Seven began to dominate the game.

On March 11, 1903, the sports page of the Ottawa Citizen was filled with details of the Stanley Cup game of the night before, when Ottawa, led by one-eyed scoring sensation Frank McGee, defeated the Montreal Victorias 8–0 to take possession of the Stanley Cup. Almost a century later, the accounts of the game still give a sense of the excitement generated by this legendary team:

McGee shot on a good opening but was wide. Bowie made a fast rush but Moore stopped him. McGee nearly scored from a face[-off] in front of [the] Vics net. From another face, McGee slipped the rubber back to Suddie Gilmour and he drove it into the net like a bullet. Ottawa 2 Vics 0. ... Moore relieved a dangerous attack and McGee made a pretty rush but Lockerby cleverly blocked the shot. David Gilmour gave one of the prettiest exhibitions of stick handling going through the entire Vics team and scoring on a fast shot. Ottawa 3 Vics 0.

This type of coverage, using colorful and poetic descriptions of the game, carried on to describe each of Ottawa's eight goals. The newspaper gives not only a real feel for the game but also an example of the community pride in the local boys for being able to challenge the mighty Montreal team for the Stanley Cup.

The Silver Seven did not have a great deal of time to enjoy their victory because the Stanley Cup trustees had agreed that the winners would face the Rat Portage Thistles in a Stanley Cup challenge a mere two days after the conclusion of the Ottawa–Montreal series. The enthusiasm for coverage in the *Citizen* did not diminish despite the quick challenge. The same style of detailed and intense writing continued over the two-game total-goals series with the Thistles, as the Silver Seven skated to 6–2 and 4–2 victories. The reporting of the games between Ottawa and Rat Portage (later known as Kenora) also shows a growing sophistication amongst the readership:

> *As skaters and checkers the Thistles were in the Stanley Cup class, but the same may not be said of themselves regarding stick-handling and combination work [in passing the puck]. The Thistles rushes were mainly individual and they did not support each other at all well, frequently McGimsie or Griffis would go up ice at whirlwind speed, but when either passed, there was no one to take the pass and an opportunity was lost.*

The Thistles were the first of nine Stanley Cup challengers successfully turned back by the Ottawa Silver Seven between defeating the Montreal Vics in 1903 and finally losing to the Montreal Wanderers in March of 1906. Interest in and coverage of the team grew with their success.

In February of 1904, the Toronto Marlboros took on the Silver Seven in the first Stanley Cup challenge to come from that city. In Toronto, it was arranged that a steam whistle would be blown when the results of the game were known. Three whistles would indicate victory, while two would signal defeat. There was great anticipation as fans waited for the signal. Unfortunately for Toronto, the steam whistle sounded only twice as Ottawa remained champion.

Perhaps the Stanley Cup series from the Silver Seven era

which was best suited for the media of the day was the challenge which was accepted from Dawson City. Although the Dawson City team may have been the champions of the Klondike, it was apparent from the time the challenge was accepted that they were a team of virtual unknowns and, in all likelihood, not of the same caliber as the Silver Seven. The series would be a made-to-measure challenge for the newspapers to generate publicity.

The excitement created by the men of the gold rush less than 10 years after the mad dash to the Klondike captivated readers of Canada's newspapers. The incredible 4,000-mile journey by dog sled, foot, ferry and train made the Dawson City players celebrities before they even reached Ottawa. It was obvious from the opening face-off on January 13, 1905 that the two-game series was going to be terribly one-sided, but even a seven-goal Ottawa victory did not stop the crowds from showing up again three nights later: "With a score of 9 to 2 against them Dawson last night made their second appearance in Ottawa and that all confidence in the team's ability had not been lost by the public was evidenced by the fact that Dey's arena was again crowded."

The game, however, proved to be the biggest blowout in the history of the Stanley Cup as Frank McGee scored 14 goals to lead the Silver Seven to a 23–2 victory:

> *Thus by the unheard of and overwhelming majority of 28 goals [a two-game total of 32–4] has Ottawa proved to the world that the brand of hockey played in the Yukon and that which Ottawans are accustomed to witness are as widely divergent as the poles.*

But the results of the game were not all that mattered. The Dawson City team may have lost badly, but they had won the hearts of the hockey public. After the Stanley Cup series, the Klondikers went on to tour eastern Canada and posted a record of 13–9–1. Their appearances always generated lots of excitement in the local press. It is hard to judge if the newspapers fueled this excitement or merely reported it. Perhaps it was a combination of both. Whatever the case, it was in these earliest days of the Stanley Cup that the bond between the sport of hockey and the news media was formed.

CHAPTER 9

Pioneer Executive W.A. Hewitt

Hockey's Rapid Growth in the Early 1900s Challenged the Game's Organizers

Peter Wilton

THE PUBLIC VOICE OF HOCKEY transmitted across Canada—the voice that young boys heard in their imagination as they played their games on frozen ponds or back alleyways—was the voice of Foster Hewitt. Foster Hewitt developed the terms that defined the sport. He generated the excitement that captured the imagination of youngsters across the country and transported them from their family living rooms to Maple Leaf Gardens. But long before Foster's famed gondola in Maple Leaf Gardens, Hewitt's father had been the powerful private voice of hockey. Although the sound of W.A. Hewitt's voice has long been silenced, the effects of his decisions helped to define and structure the modern game of hockey.

William Abraham Hewitt was born into a working-class family in Cobourg, Ontario on May 15, 1875. The family moved to Toronto when he was four years old. There, three major pursuits kept young William and his three brothers occupied: school, work and sports. School and work were necessities. Sports was a passion. The place to view sports in Toronto a century ago was on Ward's Island. Hewitt and his friends would swim across the harbor to watch professional baseball, cricket and lacrosse, which all drew great crowds and excitement to the island. But the swim could be dangerous. It once nearly cost Hewitt his life when he got caught in a log jam and could not surface for air because the logs were so tightly packed. Hewitt's love for baseball took on a new meaning one hot summer's day on Ward's Island while watching the Toronto team practice. He was asked to play catch with one of the players, who was impressed by the boy's curve ball; a new style of pitch which the team's pitcher had yet to master. Hewitt was asked to practice pitch for the team. Many of the players had trouble hitting his curve.

In the winter, the Toronto harbor would freeze over and be transformed into a playground for the rich in their ice boats (a type of sailboat built on steel runners which could reach incredible speeds). For the less well-to-do, the frozen harbor was perfect for pleasure skating. While pleasure skating on Toronto harbor, Hewitt saw his first game of hockey. Fascinated by this new sport which seemed to combine the best elements of lacrosse, field hockey and soccer, Hewitt took up the game.

With the untimely death of his father, Hewitt's childhood and school days came to an abrupt end. He left Jarvis Collegiate at the age of 15 and secured a job as a reporter with the *Toronto News*. His first assignment was the police beat, but he soon was transferred to cover sports. At about the time that young Hewitt was being trained as a cub reporter, a group of 13 well-connected men met at the Queen's Hotel in Toronto to form a new amateur hockey association. Their plan was to make the competitions between their respective towns more structured and to play for defined championships. At this first meeting in November of 1890, the rules of the sport were agreed upon

and written down. The Governor-General of Canada, Lord Stanley of Preston, agreed to be a patron of the new organization, known as the Ontario Hockey Association (OHA). His decision hardly was surprising since one of the teams represented (the Rideau Rebels) played in his back garden. Two of Stanley's sons not only played for Ottawa's Rebel Hockey Club at this time, they were founding members of the OHA. In 1892, Lord Stanley donated a cup to be emblematic of amateur hockey supremacy in Canada. The Dominion Hockey Challenge Cup quickly became known as the Stanley Cup. Later, it would become the symbol of professional hockey greatness.

Hockey's popularity grew quickly in the years after the OHA was formed, and the changing attitudes toward the game could be seen in Toronto. Prior to the OHA, hockey was played by very few people. The arenas of the city had been geared towards pleasure skating. Often the ice surface was circular with a band shell in the middle which the skaters could circle around, arm in arm to the music. Hockey players might be hard pressed to guess which side of the band shell their opponent would skate around during a game provided they could get any ice time at all. The owners of the arenas viewed hockey players as an annoyance and saw pleasure skaters as the group that paid their bills. After the press, amongst whom was now W.A. Hewitt, began reporting on the game, interest grew. Fans began following the progress of local teams and, with the introduction of championship trophies, hockey was gaining ground rapidly as Canada's official winter sport.

As interest in hockey grew, so too did gambling. Individuals bet heavily on the outcome of games and this opened up an opportunity for con artists. One of the many flim-flams that arose was a scam to circumvent the OHA's strict residency rules, which stated that a player had to live in the area and register to play for a team prior to October 1 of the year before they were going to play. Towns without a great talent base would bring in a ringer from outside, give him a false birth certificate, put him on the roster, and hope that nobody in the towns that they were playing against would recognize him. Suddenly, a mediocre team was a powerhouse and the visiting team's supporters would clean up financially and divide the winnings.

Meanwhile, Hewitt's talent as a writer and his knowledge of sports were rewarded by the *News* when, at age 20, he was promoted to sports editor. Shortly afterwards (in 1897), the OHA passed tough regulations to combat the scams that were tarnishing hockey's image. The OHA ruled that any player who received money for games would be suspended, as would the entire team and its coaching staff. Any player who ever had played for money would be suspended and any trophies or awards granted to his team would be disallowed. The onus of this new bylaw was upon the individual accused of being a professional to prove that he was innocent. The introduction of these regulations coincided with

the appointment of a new member of the OHA board, the tough anti-professional proponent John Ross Robertson. Robertson was just one member among an executive of 11, but as owner of the *Evening Telegram* and a Member of Parliament in Canada's House of Commons, he was not only the richest OHA executive but also its best-connected and its strongest personality. Inevitably, he was able to dominate the OHA executive's agenda, and what Robertson wanted was amateur hockey untainted by money.

One of the first cases to enact the anti-professional stance of the OHA involved two teams from southwestern Ontario. The team from Berlin (which would become Kitchener during World War I) had won the Ontario intermediate championship in 1897 and moved up to the senior ranks in 1898. Its first senior game came against local rival Waterloo on January 6, 1898. The arena was filled with fans from both cities and the excitement was palpable. The rules of the day called for seven men per side with no substitutions, two 30-minute halves, and no forward passing. The game was hard-fought, with players from both sides playing through injuries. Berlin raced out to a 6–0 lead, but one top player took a slash to the cheek while another had his ankle cut badly by the puck. Both were dripping blood, but refused to leave the ice. Weakened, the Berlin team allowed Waterloo four goals in the second half but managed to hold on for a 6–4 victory. The mayor of Berlin was ecstatic with the victory. He visited the dressing room after the game and gave each player a souvenir 10-dollar coin as a memento.

The next morning's newspaper accounts of the Berlin–Waterloo game mentioned the mayor's generosity. The OHA executive was outraged. The gift was clearly a blatant violation of their newly passed anti-professional stand. The Berlin hockey club was requested to meet with the executive and explain the situation. At the hearing, the Berlin players argued that the coins were not going to be spent, but that a watchmaker was going to attach them to the back of their pocket watches. Unfortunately, very few of the players could produce their coins (most had spent them already) and the entire team was banned from the hockey.

Denied a winter of fun watching the Berlin-Waterloo rivalry, most fans of the area threw their support behind Waterloo. A 9–5 playoff loss to the Kingston Frontenacs appeared to end any championship dreams, but the game was ordered replayed because a member of the Kingston team had been playing for pay in New York. Waterloo won the rematch 7–3, then beat Listowel 10–4 for the OHA senior championship. However, professional charges were now brought against three Waterloo players and their title was taken away. There would be lasting feelings of bitterness towards the OHA from the fans of southwestern Ontario.

It was during the height of the reign of the anti-professional zealots on the OHA executive that W.A. Hewitt was asked to join in 1903. It was an appointment Hewitt accepted, and he was acclaimed to the position of secretary. At the age of 28, he was at the threshold of 58 years as a key decision-maker in one of the most influential hockey organizations in the world.

Hewitt had the ability to align himself with the right people and he quickly realized that the holder of the most influence within the OHA was John Ross Robertson, who was serving as president. The OHA executive no longer met at the Queen's Hotel, but in Robertson's *Telegram* office. At first, Robertson was dubious of Hewitt, who was, after all, the sports editor of a rival newspaper.

(Since January of 1900, it has been the *Toronto Star*.) His fears soon proved to be unfounded and the two became strong allies against the onslaught of professionalism.

An early example of the power wielded by W.A.H. (as he would become known) can be seen in his treatment of a teenage hockey player from Listowel during the winter of 1904–05. Long before he was known to the world as "Cyclone," Frederick Wellington Taylor was just a skinny 16-year-old kid who had an amazing talent for hockey. He was a fast skater and talented stickhandler who could score plenty of goals and had become something of a celebrity in his small town. When Hewitt learned of the Listowel whiz kid, he wanted him to play for the Toronto Marlboros. (Although there never has been a concrete link made between Hewitt and the Marlboros, accusations were made throughout his time with the OHA that he favored the big city's top team.) Taylor considered Hewitt's offer, but decided it would mean too big a change for him to move to Toronto and be away from his family and friends. Hewitt responded by telling Taylor that if he would not play hockey in Toronto, he would not play anywhere. Hewitt proved true to his word. Taylor tried without success to play for other OHA teams, but each application was returned with the request denied.

Taylor missed a full season of play because of his dispute with Hewitt and went through some very tough times, including the loss of his job at the piano stringing factory in Listowel. It was not until he was invited to play in Portage la Prairie, Manitoba in 1905–06 that Taylor was able to return to the game. (Hewitt's reach did not extend beyond Ontario's provincial boundaries.) Ironically, Taylor would leave Portage la Prairie during the year to join a fully professional team in Houghton, Michigan. Both the International (Pro) Hockey League and the Portage Lakes team he joined were operated by Dr. John Liddell "Jack" Gibson who had been a member of the Berlin team that was banned by the OHA in 1898.

Together Hewitt, Robertson and fellow board member Dwight Turner became known as "the Three White Czars" of the OHA. When a dispute arose about professionalism, residency or eligibility of a player, it was referred to the three czars, whose decision was final. Despite the fact that championships often were being determined in the office of Robertson as opposed to the ice rinks of Ontario, guidelines governing eligibility were tightened so that professionals were not even allowed to coach a team or be associated with them in any way for fear they might taint the purity of the OHA. This fixation took on the proportions of a witch hunt, with players living in fear that they were going to be accused of professionalism and be hauled before the three czars to prove their innocence.

By 1910, with the OHA still determined to be rid of the professionals, the National Hockey Association (forerunner of the NHL) started up as a purely professional league. Not only did the NHA gobble up many of the OHA's top intermediate and senior players, it eventually would stake its claim to the Stanley Cup. (In fact, with professional teams already competing for the Stanley Cup, Sir H. Montagu Allan of Montreal had donated a fine silver cup in 1908 for the sole competition of amateur teams in leagues like the OHA all across Canada.)

Others who gave the OHA grief during this time were the local mercantile leagues and, in particular, the banks. Each of the major banks had a hockey team and they were always looking for talented players. Bank games brought out large

crowds and it was a great promotion for a bank to win a game or, better yet, a championship. The banks would send scouts to watch for talented youngsters. When they came across prospects, they would offer them a job in the bank and promote them to the Toronto office, where they would play for the bank hockey team. The OHA resented the talent pool being skimmed this way but could do little to retaliate, since the banks were not a part of the OHA.

Though the OHA remained staunchly amateur, the league was still instrumental in some of the changes that helped shaped the modern game. Innovations of the era such as the blue line, goal creases, and six-man teams with substitutions found some of their earliest support in the Ontario Hockey Association.

In December of 1918, John Ross Robertson died. Although his influence had been waning in his later years, Robertson had been installed as a life member of the OHA and he continued to make his presence felt. It wasn't until after his death that the OHA finally began to ease its regulations surrounding professionals, allowing ex-pros to coach OHA teams and even to play for them. Professional athletes from other sports also were permitted to play hockey in the OHA. It was a lawyer by the name of George S. Dudley who had pushed hardest for these changes. Hewitt, sensing which way the wind was blowing, aligned himself with Dudley.

By this time, Hewitt was not only busy in his role as sports editor and OHA secretary, but he had become the registrar and treasurer of the Canadian Amateur Hockey Association in 1915. He had managed the Toronto Argonauts rugby football team in 1907 and 1908 and had convened the meeting in 1907 which organized the Big Four (a forerunner of the Canadian Football League). Still, he had time for more active involvement in hockey. In 1920, he accompanied the Allan Cup champion Winnipeg Falcons to Antwerp, Belgium for the first Olympic hockey tournament. Appalled by the general lack of knowledge about the game of hockey he found in Europe, Hewitt convinced the International Ice Hockey Federation to adopt the Canadian rules for the competition. The IIHF was so impressed by Hewitt they gave him the honor of refereeing the first Olympic game—an 8–0 win by Sweden over Belgium on April 23, 1920. The Falcons defeated Czechoslovakia 15–0, the United States 2–0 and Sweden 12–1 to earn a gold medal for Canada.

Following the 1920 Olympics, the International Ice Hockey Federation ruled that the tournament results would not be listed as official (though in 1983, the 1920 Games were recognized retroactively as the first World Championship.) Hewitt felt the IIHF decision took away from the Falcons' victory. However, in 1924, Hewitt served as general manager for the Toronto Granites team that won the gold medal at the first official Winter Olympics. So strong was the Canadian entry this year that legend has it goaltender Jack Cameron would leave his net during games to sign autographs for the young ladies in attendance. When questioned years later, Cameron denied the allegations though he did admit to leaving the net to talk to a young Norwegian figure skater named Sonja Henie. Four years later, Hewitt returned to the Olympics with the University of Toronto Varsity Grads and acted as general manager for another gold medal winner.

W.A. Hewitt remained involved with the Canadian Amateur Hockey Association until 1954 and stayed on with the OHA until 1961. He passed away on September 8, 1966. Hewitt had served as the manager of attractions at Maple Leaf Gardens when it opened in 1931 and was the public relations director of the Ontario Racing Commission when it opened in 1951. He also had been the long-time presiding steward on Canadian racing tracks. Hewitt not only witnessed much of Canadian sports history during his lifetime, he played an active role in the stewardship of hockey from an oddity seen only on Canada's frozen harbors to a sport televised and played all over the world

CHAPTER 10

The National Hockey Association

The Swashbuckling Roots of the NHL's Immediate Predecessor

Eric Zweig

WITH SKYROCKETING SALARIES fueling fears that Canadian markets are no longer large enough to compete with American cities, it almost seems impossible to believe that the league that became the NHL actually was formed by three small Ontario towns—which had a combined population that would not fill today's new arenas—plus two Montreal teams that played out of a 3,250-seat rink.

The NHL was formed in November of 1917 after a series of meetings which reorganized the National Hockey Association into the National Hockey League. The forerunner of the NHL had been created eight years before, though its roots can be traced back to 1907. At that time, the Stanley Cup was still a challenge trophy available to top teams all across Canada. In fact, the defending Stanley Cup champions hailed from the tiny town of Kenora, Ontario. Still, a Toronto newspaper chose to mock the Stanley Cup dreams of another small Ontario community:

"And now Renfrew talks of challenging for the Stanley Cup," the *Toronto Telegram* informed its readers on March 13, 1907, "and all because they have won a fence corner league [the Ottawa Valley Hockey League] and defeated a broken and discouraged band of Ottawas [Renfrew had defeated the former Silver Seven squad 9–5 in an exhibition game five days after Ottawa had been officially eliminated from Stanley Cup contention]. ... If Renfrew had any real stars on her team, some of the big teams would have gobbled them up long ago."

Not content to mock the hockey players, the *Telegram* also took a shot at the townsfolk one day later: "Renfrew have challenged for the Stanley Cup. Now don't laugh. If you've never lived in a country town you don't know how seriously those people take themselves. Anybody who went into Renfrew and gave voice to an opinion that there was a greater team on earth than Renfrew would be lucky if he escaped with his life."

But by the hockey season of 1909–10, there was no greater team on earth than Renfrew—or at least no greater collection of high-priced superstars.

Renfrew was denied a challenge for the Stanley Cup in 1907, but the town's hockey officials pressed on. By 1908–09, the decision was made to enter the professional ranks. To finance the team, Renfrew looked to its most prominent citizens. The tiny town in the Ottawa Valley had a population of just 4,000, yet two men who called Renfrew home were among the richest in Canada—lumber baron Alexander Barnet and railroad builder/mining magnate Michael John O'Brien. M.J. O'Brien and his son Ambrose already were supporting a hockey team in the Northern Ontario silver-mining town of Cobalt and could hardly turn down their hometown. However, Renfrew soon would learn that even victory in the new professional Federal League was not enough to impress the Stanley Cup trustees.

Both Cobalt and Renfrew issued Stanley Cup challenges in 1909. In late November of that year, Ambrose O'Brien traveled to Montreal where the Stanley Cup trustees were to reveal who would have a chance to play off against the defending champion Ottawa Senators. On November 24, 1909 they announced that Galt, Winnipeg and Edmonton had won the right to challenge (though only Galt and Edmonton did). Cobalt and Renfrew were ignored. But there was still one more chance for Renfrew. O'Brien was also in Montreal for the meetings of the Eastern Canada Hockey Association. If he could get his hometown team into the game's top professional league alongside the champion Senators, a challenge no longer would be necessary, as a league title probably would guarantee the Stanley Cup. O'Brien would state his case to the ECHA owners. He knew he had the support of Jimmy Gardner, who represented Montreal Wanderers owner P.J. Doran.

P.J. Doran had bought the Wanderers a year before and planned to move his team out of their 7,000-seat arena and into his 3,250-seat Jubilee rink. As the smaller capacity would mean a decrease in the gate receipts to be shared by visiting clubs, Doran's fellow owners were not impressed. With Ottawa leading the way, they voted the ECHA out of existence on November 25, 1909 and created a new league called the Canadian Hockey Association. The teams making up the CHA would be the Ottawa Senators, Quebec Bulldogs, Montreal Shamrocks, Montreal Nationals and All-Montreal. The Wanderers had been frozen out. Renfrew's application was denied as well.

Shortly after learning their fate, Jimmy Gardner met with Ambrose O'Brien and proposed that they form their own league. One week later, on December 2, 1909, the Wanderers, Renfrew, Cobalt and Haileybury formed the National Hockey Association. A fifth team was added two days later. Gardiner had convinced O'Brien to finance an all-French-Canadian team in Montreal to rival the Nationals of the CHA. The new NHA entry would be known as *les Canadiens* and share the tiny Jubilee Arena with the Wanderers.

The NHA would commence play with Cobalt at the Canadiens on January 5, 1910, six days after the scheduled start of the CHA. In the meantime, the two leagues went to war over the best players. The O'Briens controlled four of the five clubs in the NHA, and while their money helped attract stars like Newsy Lalonde and Didier Pitre to the Canadiens, Ambrose concentrated his efforts on bringing the Stanley Cup to Renfrew. Marty Walsh reportedly was offered $4,000 to leave Ottawa for Renfrew. When the 1909 scoring champion of the ECHA (with 38 goals in 12 games) refused to jump, O'Brien instead signed runner-up Herb Jordan of Quebec (who had scored 29 goals). Fred Whitcroft of the Edmonton Eskimos later jumped to Renfrew for $2,000. Frank Patrick also signed for $2,000. His more experienced brother, Lester Patrick, signed for $3,000. The largest contract to that point in hockey history

prompted Toronto newspapers to snicker, "Let us see: What salary does the average school teacher in Renfrew get?" But an even bigger deal was in the works.

Cyclone Taylor had been wooed by the O'Briens for their Cobalt team two years earlier when he returned to Canada from the International (Pro) Hockey League. He had signed with Ottawa instead and while Walsh was the Senators top scorer, Taylor was their biggest star (the Bobby Orr to Walsh's Phil Esposito). For weeks after the NHA was formed, Ottawa newspapers were filled with headlines documenting the attempts to lure Taylor to Renfrew. On December 28, 1909 he signed a contract said to be worth $5,250 for a 12-game season. The deal was considered the richest in North American team sports. (Ty Cobb was paid $6,500 that year, but had to play a 154-game baseball schedule.) Because Renfrew was famed for the quality of its dairy products, the hockey team was officially known as the Creamery Kings, but the huge contracts signed by its players had everyone calling them the Millionaires.

Taylor's signing had given the NHA instant credibility at the expense of the CHA. This, plus the fact that there were now five teams playing out of Montreal, saw the CHA draw poor crowds to its early games. A meeting between representatives of the rival organizations was called for January 15, 1910 amid talks the two leagues would amalgamate. Instead, the NHA offered to take in only the Senators and Shamrocks. The two teams jumped at the opportunity, abandoning the CHA which folded amid much bitterness from the teams that had been left out. The seven-team NHA was now hockey's major league and its schedule was revised to include the new clubs. With the defending champion Senators in the fold, an NHA championship would mean a Stanley Cup victory as well and it was freely predicted that Renfrew was the team to beat.

Despite their many stars, the Millionaires were slow to blend as a team. They did not hit their stride until acquiring Newsy Lalonde from the Canadiens midway through the season. Even then, a long road trip through northern Ontario left the team in poor shape for a key late-season game with the Wanderers. The Montreal team beat Renfrew 5–0 on February 25, then defeated the Senators 3–1 on March 5 to clinch the first NHA title and the Stanley Cup with a record of 11–1. The Wanderers also were presented with the O'Brien Trophy, which had been donated by M.J. O'Brien. Renfrew had to settle for humiliating Ottawa 17–2 in the second-last game of the season. Newsy Lalonde clinched the first NHA scoring title with nine goals in a 15–4 win over Cobalt in the season finale.

The 1909–10 season had been costly for hockey owners. M.J. O'Brien withdrew his financial support of Cobalt and Haileybury, whose franchises were replaced by the Quebec Bulldogs and the new Montreal Canadiens. George Kennedy, also known as "Kendall," was granted the new Montreal team after he threatened to sue because the name Canadiens was registered and incorporated to his *Club Athlétique Canadien*. (Kennedy was born Georges Kendall. In English-speaking circles he went by the name "Kennedy," but is identified as "G.W. Kendall, Treasurer" in the Montreal Canadiens team portrait of 1915–16.)

With Kennedy now in charge, the O'Briens no longer would be required to operate the original Canadiens either, though Ambrose would continue to operate the Millionaires. The Montreal Shamrocks would not be back for the 1910–11 season, leaving the NHA with just five teams. In a further effort to recoup their financial losses,

NHA owners chose to institute a salary cap of $5,000 per team. Another new wrinkle for the NHA's second season would be the replacement of two 30-minute halves with three 20-minute periods.

On November 23, 1910, rumors began to spread that a players' union would be formed to fight the salary cap. Bruce Stuart and Art Ross were at the forefront of the movement and began negotiating with their fellow players to establish a league of their own. Teams were to be placed in Montreal, Ottawa and nearby Brockville, but when the Montreal Arena refused to deal with any club but the Wanderers and attempts to secure ice time elsewhere fell through, players reluctantly began re-signing with their teams. Though most teams offered bonuses to get around the $5,000 cap or ignored it completely, salaries dropped considerably this season and the financial cuts cost Renfrew the services of Frank and Lester Patrick (who could not afford to leave the family business in British Columbia for such reduced rates). Ottawa proved the class of the NHA's scaled-down second season, winning the league title with a 13–3 record and replacing the Wanderers as Stanley Cup champions. After the season, the Senators crushed teams from Galt and Port Arthur by scores of 7–4 and 13–4 respectively in a pair of Stanley Cup challenges.

Further financial losses during the 1910–11 season convinced Ambrose O'Brien that Renfrew's population of 4,000 was simply too small to support pro hockey at the highest level. The man who had almost single-handedly created the NHA sold both his Renfrew franchise and the rights to the original Canadiens to Toronto interests. However, construction delays to the new Arena Gardens on Mutual Street meant neither the Toronto Blueshirts nor the Toronto Tecumsehs (who would later be known as the Ontarios, then Shamrocks) would actually begin play until 1912–13. The O'Brien Trophy became the official emblem of the NHA championship in 1911–12, and the league made the decision to abandon the rover in favor of six-man hockey (a goalie, two defenseman, a center and two wingers). Led by future NHL star Joe Malone, Quebec finished first in the NHA to win the O'Brien Trophy and unseat Ottawa as Stanley Cup Champions.

The biggest change in hockey for the 1911–12 season was Frank and Lester Patrick's creation of the Pacific Coast Hockey Association. Several NHA players helped fill out the rosters of the new PCHA teams in Vancouver, Victoria and New Westminster, including former Renfrew teammates Bert Lindsay, Bobby Rowe and Newsy Lalonde, and the NHA and PCHA would battle both for players and (soon) the Stanley Cup for the rest of the NHA's existence. Like the NHA, the PCHA would play three 20-minute periods, and though the Patricks chose to keep the position of rover, their new league would do much to modernize the rules of hockey. The PCHA tabulated assists as an official statistic (which the NHA copied in 1913–14), allowed goaltenders to sprawl on the ice to make saves (NHA goalies had to remain standing) and painted blue lines on the ice to divide the rink into zones (the NHA's ice had no markings). It also allowed forward passing in the neutral zone, while NHA players continued to advance the puck in the same way a rugby team advances the ball.

After winning the Stanley Cup in 1911–12, every member of the Quebec Bulldogs was offered a contract by teams in the PCHA for 1912–13. Goldie Prodgers, Eddie Oatman and Jack McDonald all went west (as did Cyclone Taylor this season), but with Joe Malone scoring 43 goals in 20

games and newcomer Tommy Smith adding 39 more, the Bulldogs still breezed to the NHA championship with a record of 16–4. Malone added nine goals in a 14–3 victory over the Sydney (Nova Scotia) Millionaires in game one of a Stanley Cup challenge series and then sat out the second game as Quebec cruised to a 6–2 victory. Two weeks later (March 24, 1913), the Bulldogs were in Victoria to take on the PCHA champion Aristocrats in a three-game exhibition series. Fortunately for Quebec the Stanley Cup was not on the line as Victoria won two of the three games. One year later, the challenge era in Stanley Cup history ended when the NHA and PCHA reach an agreement on an annual five-game Stanley Cup series to be played in the east and west in alternate years. The different rules from each league would be alternated game by game. Victoria was again the PCHA champions in 1913–14, but lost the Stanley Cup to the Toronto Blueshirts in three straight games.

Toronto's first Stanley Cup champions were led by Jack Marshall and Allan Davidson. Davidson soon would leave the team and sacrifice his life during World War I, but his 23 goals in 20 games in 1913–14 led the Blueshirts to a 13–7 record and a first-place tie with the Montreal Canadiens. Davidson then added two more goals as the Blueshirts claimed the NHA title with a 6–2 victory over Montreal in a two-game total-goals playoff. The 1914–15 NHA season also ended in a tie, with the Ottawa Senators and Montreal Wanderers both finishing 14–6. Ottawa emerged victorious in a playoff and traveled to the West Coast where they were defeated 6–2, 8–3 and 12–3 in a three-game sweep by the Vancouver Millionaires.

The NHA began feeling the effects of World War I during the 1914–15 season, as teams began losing players to military service and attendance dropped. As a result, salaries were slashed. The Montreal Wanderers advised their players they would be paid no more than $600 for the season (though that later was raised to $800 for the top stars). As in 1910–11, the players began to talk of forming their own league. Art Ross was again at the forefront of the movement and on November 30, 1914, he was banned from organized hockey for negotiating to sign players for the new league. But to ban Ross, the NHA also would have to ban the players he had negotiated with, which would have destroyed the rosters of the Wanderers and the Montreal Canadiens. Therefore, Ross was reinstated on December 18, but was suspended until January 7, 1915. On January 9, he signed with the Ottawa Senators.

The NHA was hit by troubles of a different sort in 1915–16. Toronto Shamrocks owner Eddie Livingstone bought the Toronto Blueshirts, which angered fellow owners who did not like the idea of Livingstone controlling both Toronto teams. He was ordered to sell the Shamrocks by November 20, 1915. However, virtually the entire Blueshirts rosters was signed away by a new PCHA team in Seattle. Livingstone then rebuilt his new team around the players under contract to his old club and simply folded the Shamrocks. The NHA was down to five clubs once again. The best of these five proved to be the Montreal Canadiens. With Newsy Lalonde leading the league with 28 goals in 24 games and Georges Vezina battling Clint Benedict as the top goaltender, the Canadiens posted a 16–7–1 record. They then defeated the PCHA's Portland Rosebuds for the first Stanley Cup victory in franchise history. The Canadiens were NHA champions again the following year but lost the Stanley Cup to the Seattle Metropolitans. However, there was much more to the story of 1916–17 than the first

Stanley Cup victory by an American-based team.

The season of 1916–17 would be the last for the NHA and the league's end would prove no less tumultuous than its beginning. Emmett Quinn, who had been president of the NHA since the merger with the CHA in 1910, resigned on October 28, 1916. (Frank Patrick had said there could be no peace between the two leagues while Quinn ran the NHA.) He was replaced by Major Frank Robinson of Montreal. One month earlier (September 30), the NHA had admitted a military team when the 228th Battalion was granted a franchise in Toronto. (Many hockey players had enlisted during the summer of 1916 and some of the best — including George and Howard McNamara, Goldie Prodgers, and Art Duncan — had joined the 228th.) With so many players in the army, the Ottawa Senators wanted to suspend operations for the season, but the idea was rejected and the team instead was placed under new management.

A decision was made to employ a split schedule for the 1916–17 NHA season, with the winner of the first half to meet the second-half winner to determine the league champion. The Canadiens and Ottawa finished the opening 10-game segment on January 27, 1917 with identical 7–3 records, but Montreal was awarded first place based on a better goal differential. The second half saw an equally tight battle between Ottawa and Quebec with the Bulldogs taking an 8–1 record into the season finale against the 7–2 Senators on March 3. Ottawa needed to win the game by seven goals to claim the second-half title and crushed Quebec 16–1. Frank Nighbor scored five times for Ottawa, while Quebec's Joe Malone was held scoreless, which meant the two players tied for the league scoring title with 41 goals apiece. Despite Ottawa's strong finish, the Senators lost the NHA playoff to the Canadiens.

As interesting as the season had been on the ice, greater drama occurred behind the scenes. One day before the first half had concluded, there were indications that the 228th Battalion was about to be sent overseas. Captain L.W. Reade assured the NHA that the team would be able to complete the second half, but on February 10, 1917, the regiment was shipped to Europe. A special meeting of the NHA was held the next day to determine how to salvage the season. Eddie Livingstone insisted that the league should organize a five-club, round-robin schedule, but the unpopular owner could not convince his fellow NHA directors. A decision was made instead to drop Livingstone's Blueshirts and the schedule was completed with just four teams. Toronto's players were divided among the rest of the remaining teams. Any compensation Livingstone received never was made public, though he was promised that his players would be returned at the end of the season. The players did indeed come back, but not to Livingstone's club. In an effort to be rid of him once and for all, the NHA's other owners reorganized as the National Hockey League in November of 1917. The NHL's Toronto franchise was granted to the owners of the Mutual Street Arena.

Not surprisingly, Eddie Livingstone did not go down without a fight. He did his best to interfere with the operation of the NHL and its Toronto team throughout the 1917–18 season, and his threats of lawsuits against the former NHA owners lasted into the 1918–19 campaign. Claiming that he had a majority of former NHA stockholders on his side, Livingstone forced a final meeting of the association on December 11, 1919, but he could not revive the old league. The NHA was dead, yet its eight-year existence had changed the course of hockey history.

CHAPTER 11

The Pacific Coast Hockey Association

Thomas D. Picard

DREAMS ... AMBITION ... POWER ... all played a part in the building of the Pacific Coast Hockey Association. Lester and Frank Patrick realized their dreams when father Joseph Patrick, a millionaire lumberman, retired after having successfully moved his business from Quebec to British Columbia. Using their father's financial support, the Patrick brothers announced the formation of the PCHA at the Hotel Vancouver on December 7, 1911. At that meeting Frank Patrick drafted a constitution that was similar to the eastern-based National Hockey Association. The playing rules, including the use of seven-man hockey, were adopted by the founders of the PCHA. W.P. Irving, a well-known executive of the Ontario Hockey Association, was appointed as the first president. Three franchises, Vancouver, Victoria and New Westminster, were granted for the initial PCHA season. The Vancouver Millionaires chose the uniform colors of maroon and white. Victoria Aristocrats chose red, white and blue and the New Westminster Royals were clad in orange and black attire.

Lester Patrick probably will go down in the annals of hockey history as one of the most innovative and shrewd individuals to be associated with the game. Aptly nicknamed "the Silver Fox," Lester Patrick contributed deeply to the improvement and evolution of professional hockey on every level. He was a player, playing every position from defense to rover to goalie. When the challenge presented itself, he would take on the extra duties of coaching, managing and operating the Victoria franchise. His ultimate ambition was to manage his own team and his own league. That dream became a reality with the formation of the Pacific Coast Hockey Association.

Frank Patrick was less famous than his brother. However, Frank probably would be considered the main architect and brains behind the formation of the PCHA and the direction that the league would take when confronting the National Hockey Association. Frank proposed some 20 rules that became part of the National Hockey League rule book. The multi-talented Patrick was not only the president of the PCHA for many years, he also was a star defenseman, coach, manager and owner of the Vancouver franchise. In 1926, he also was instrumental in engineering the biggest hockey deal to that time when he sold the entire Western Hockey League to eastern interests in New York, Detroit and Chicago for the first big expansion of the NHL to the United States.

The showcase for the Pacific Coast Hockey Association was to be a beautiful new ice arena located in Vancouver. The Georgia Street site, built for a princely sum of $175,000, was the largest ice arena in Canada at that time with a seating capacity of 10,000. The artificial ice surface measured 200' x 85' and was the first in Canada. Only New York's Madison Square Garden surpassed the Vancouver arena in size. Small by comparison, the Victoria ice arena would seat a capacity crowd of 4,000. New Westminster agreed to play all of its home games in Vancouver in 1911–12 as the Royal City Arena wouldn't be ready until the following season. To compete with the Eastern Canadian teams, the Patricks realized that, to gain major-league recognition, large and expensive ice arenas were a fact of life.

The Patrick brothers' major concern was finding high-caliber players to fill out the rosters for the three West Coast teams. Having played a number of years in eastern pro leagues, Frank and Lester acknowledged that the best place to plan their player raids would be the talent-rich National Hockey Association. Having played previously in Renfrew, Lester Patrick lured ex-teammates Bobby Rowe and Bert Lindsay, as well as Renfrew's Don Smith, to the West Coast. Patrick supplemented his Renfrew connection with Tom Dunderdale from the Quebec Bulldogs, Skinner Poulin from the Canadiens and Walter Smaill from the Montreal Wanderers. In fact, the complete starting lineup for the Aristocrats comprised ex-NHA veterans. Frank Patrick's septet was headed by ex-Canadiens and Renfrew star Newsy Lalonde. New Westminster's playing coach Jimmy Gardner, formerly with the Wanderers, enticed Ernie Johnson away from the Montreal team. Ken Mallen joined the Royals from Quebec and minding the nets was Ontario Professional Hockey League veteran Hugh Lehman.

The initial Pacific Coast Hockey Association season opened on January 2, 1912 in Victoria. At the 4,000-seat Victoria arena, 2,500 fans turned out to watch the Aristocrats take on the New Westminster Royals. Ran McDonald of the Royals had the honor of netting the first goal in PCHA history. McDonald, with four goals, paced the Royals to an 8–3 victory. The dubious distinction of first league penalty went to Don Smith of Victoria. Many of the league players had volunteered their services as on-ice officials. Vancouver's Tom Phillips acted as the referee. Frank Patrick showed his offensive prowess when he scored a record (for defensemen) six goals against New Westminster on March 5 as the Millionaires walloped the Royals 10–6. Frank would end the season as the highest scoring defenseman with 24 goals. The Millionaires' Newsy Lalonde, in his first and only PCHA season, was not only the scoring champ with 27 goals but was also the PCHA badman with 60 penalty minutes.

The New Westminster team proved to be the class of the initial PCHA season. Big stars for the Royals were playing coach Jimmy Gardner, Harry Hyland, Ran McDonald and Ken Mallen. Paced by Hyland's 26 goals, the Royals clinched the league championship on March 19 with a 7–5 victory over the Millionaires. The two teams were in a dead heat for first place until the Royals won their final two games and the Vancouver team closed off the season with a two-game losing streak. The Royals finished with a 9–6 record, Vancouver with seven wins and eight losses. Victoria came in last. By virtue of their first-place finish, the New Westminster Royals were declared PCHA champions. The league did not yet have any playoffs. This format

would remain in effect until the 1917–18 season.

The Pacific Coast Hockey Association began season number two by replacing W.P. Irving as president. Taking over the head duties was C.E. Doherty of New Westminster. Seeking to improve the quality of play, the PCHA decided to step up its efforts in raiding the National Hockey Association. The NHA's Quebec franchise was particularly hard-hit with the loss of three players. Jack McDonald moved to Vancouver with Goldie Prodgers going to Victoria and Eddie Oatman heading for New Westminster. To give the league a better balance in talent, Ernie "Moose" Johnson moved to New Westminster and Frank "Cyclone" Taylor made his PCHA debut with the Millionaires. Taylor, playing the rover position in seven-man hockey, would prove to be the greatest individual player in PCHA history as witnessed by his 160 goals in 135 games.

Other new players to make an impact in the PCHA's second year would be Bob Genge at Victoria and Charlie Tobin with the Royals. The only major losses for the league in 1912 came when Harry Hyland returned to the NHA Montreal Wanderers and Newsy Lalonde returned to the Canadiens. New Westminster still had problems with the construction of its arena. It was decided to play the Royals' home games at the Vancouver arena, the same as the previous year. However, for a change, the Royals decided to take some of their home games on the road. The last-place Royals, along with the Millionaires, played their last two games in Calgary and Regina on March 17 and 18. It proved be a huge success for the lowly Royals as they whipped the Vancouver septet by scores of 11–7 and 10–6. Giving the PCHA fans some added entertainment, a series of speed skating races were held at the Vancouver arena on January 14. In the preliminaries, Si Griffis showed his speed by edging Ernie Johnson, and Ken Mallen, surprisingly enough, got the better of Cyclone Taylor. Mallen won the trophy by outdistancing Si Griffis. On February 15, the PCHA tried the six-man game. The loss of the rover position did not win approval by the fans in attendance. (This experiment was set aside until the PCHA adopted an interlocking schedule with the Western Canada Hockey League in 1922–23.) Victoria won the league crown by defeating New Westminster 1–0 on March 7 to finish with a record of 10 wins and five losses. Victoria's Tom Dunderdale was scoring champ with 29 points, 24 of them goals.

The Quebec Bulldogs, NHA and Stanley Cup champs, decided to accept the challenge from the PCHA for an exhibition series and the Cup champs traveled to the West Coast. Because of the differences in the east–west rules, it was decided to play games one and three with seven-man hockey. Game two would enforce the six-man rules. Appropriately enough, Victoria won games one and three by scores of 7–5 and 6–1. Quebec won the middle affair 6–3. Leading scorers for the series were Lester Patrick of Victoria and Quebec's Tommy Smith with four goals each. (The Stanley Cup was not at stake during this series.)

Frank Patrick made his debut as PCHA president to start the 1913–14 season. He would retain that position until the demise of the league in 1923–24. This season brought about the invention of the blue line. As the PCHA rink dimensions were 200' x 85', Frank Patrick decided to divide the ice surface into three playing zones. The two blue lines were to be 67 feet apart, giving the rink approximately three equal playing areas. Also, for the first time, the forward pass would be allowed in the neutral zone. New eastern imports to appear on the scene this year were: Frank Nighbor from

Toronto and Albert "Dubbie" Kerr who had sat out the previous season in Ottawa. Former Canadien Didier "Cannonball" Pitre also made his PCHA debut in Vancouver. Unfortunately, "the Pembroke Peach," Frank Nighbor, broke his hand and was out of the Millionaires' lineup until January 27. Victoria would have to do without the services of Lester Patrick until January 23. Patrick broke his arm in the preseason. By coincidence, Victoria was in last place with a 4–5 record when Lester returned to action. With their coach and defenseman back, the Aristocrats took off in the standings with a six-game winning streak to finish the season in first place. However, the first sign of financial problems lurked around the corner. It was estimated that the New Westminster franchise had lost between $4,000 and $9,000 during the year. It was decided at the end of the season to transfer the troubled franchise. Although outscored by Tom Dunderdale 23–18, Cyclone Taylor managed to capture his first PCHA scoring title by virtue of having more assists, 14–3. Taylor finished with 32 points. Dubbie Kerr finished a close second with 31 points.

Victoria traveled east to play the NHA's Toronto Blueshirts to determine hockey's champion for the year. The PCHA representatives forgot one minor detail, however. They had overlooked the formality of submitting a formal challenge for the Stanley Cup and were not officially recognized as qualified challengers by the Stanley Cup trustees. Any potential dispute as to Victoria's right to claim the Cup was eliminated in a three-game sweep by the Blueshirts. The Patricks must have had a keen eye for talent, as Toronto stars Jack Walker, Cully Wilson and Frank Foyston eventually would make their way to the West Coast.

President Patrick brought in some more innovations for the 1914–15 season. The league adopted the National Hockey Association's idea of having the players' numbers on the backs of the uniforms. It was thought that it would be easier for the fans to identify the individual players. Also, to prevent some of the rough hockey of the past two years, bodychecking was prohibited within 10 feet of the boards. The New Westminster franchise was transferred to Portland and renamed the Rosebuds. For the first time, an American-based team would be eligible to compete for the Stanley Cup. Pete Muldoon took over as coach of the Portland team. The first trade of the PCHA saw Hugh Lehman and Ken Mallen transfer to Vancouver with Fred Harris moving to Portland. It was a tough year for Victoria's Tom Dunderdale. First, Dunderdale refused to play until he was offered a better contract. Threatened with suspension, the future Hall of Famer returned. Then, on December 11, 1914, Dunderdale suffered the embarrassment of scoring against his own goaltender, Bert Lindsay. Later in the game, he made amends by putting the puck behind Vancouver goalie Hugh Lehman. The Aristocrats lost 5–3. On the subject of embarrassing moments, on February 12, 1915 at Victoria, Frank Patrick returned to the Vancouver lineup. Forgetting to take off his skate guards, he took to the ice and proceeded to land face first, much to the delight of the partisan Victoria crowd. Future Hall of Famer Mickey MacKay made his debut in a Vancouver uniform, having played the previous season at Grand Forks, British Columbia in the Boundary League. Mickey would lead the PCHA in goal-scoring with 33. However, teammate Cyclone Taylor, with 23 goals and 22 assists for 45 points, would edge out MacKay for the scoring title by one point. Vancouver ended the season with a six-game winning streak to clinch the PCHA title with a 13–4 record.

Unfortunately, during the last game, Vancouver captain Si Griffis broke his leg and would miss the upcoming Stanley Cup series. Undaunted by the loss of their captain, the Millionaires awaited the arrival of the Ottawa Senators. Alternating the east-west rules, Vancouver won the three-game series 3–0 by scores of 6–2, 8–3 and 12–3. The powerful Vancouver attack was led by the trio of Cyclone Taylor, Frank Nighbor and Mickey MacKay. Cyclone led the series scorers with seven markers. For the very first time the Pacific Coast Hockey Association could lay claim to the coveted Stanley Cup!

The 1915–16 season marked a decided step up in the raiding activities of the PCHA. Expanding to four teams, President Patrick saw the need for extra quality players from the NHA. The newly formed Seattle Metropolitans secured the services of Toronto stars Jack Walker, Frank Foyston, Cully Wilson, Ed Carpenter and Harry "Hap" Holmes. The NHA retaliated by declaring that all PCHA players were free agents. Skinner Poulin, Frank Nighbor, Bert Lindsay and Walter Smaill all headed back to the NHA. Pete Muldoon took over as coach at Seattle. Edward Savage moved into Portland. The red, white and green-clad Metropolitans, with captain Frank Foyston as their leader, were the second U.S.-based team with a chance to win the Stanley Cup but it was Portland that outdistanced the other three teams to finish with a 13–5 record. Cyclone Taylor won another scoring title with 22 goals and 13 assists. Seattle's Bernie Morris paced the league with 23 goals. Portland's main strength was its superior defensive strategy. Ernie Johnson and Del Irvine led the defensive charge and Tommy Murray, a veteran goalie from Manitoba senior hockey circles, was the top netminder. The Portland Rosebuds would become the first team based in the United States to hold the distinction of actually playing for the Stanley Cup. President Patrick gave the Rosebuds permission to play the NHA in the championship series, however, because of his extreme dislike for NHA president Emmitt Quinn, Frank vowed that he would not be involved in any negotiations. According to the rules, Patrick issued an informal challenge to the Stanley trustees on behalf of Portland. The Rosebuds traveled to Montreal for the best-of-five series against *les Canadiens*. Once again using alternating east–west rules, the Habs squeaked out a 3–2 decision, winning the final game 2–1 on a goal by Goldie Prodgers.

The season of 1916–17 marked another franchise shift for the PCHA. Drawing small crowds, as most last-place teams do, the Aristocrats moved to Spokane, Washington to become the Canaries. Suddenly the PCHA shifted its power base to the United States, with Vancouver as the only Canadian franchise. Refusing to stand pat, the defending league champion Rosebuds added Manitoba senior hockey veterans Dick Irvin, Clem Loughlin and Stan Marples to their lineup.

Despite the loss of their superstar, Cyclone Taylor (out with an appendix operation until January 27), the Millionaires managed to hang on to second place in the standings. Playing only 12 games, Taylor managed to tally 14 goals and 15 assists. However, he was deprived of another scoring championship. Bernie Morris of the Metropolitans set a league record with 54 points, including 37 goals. The Millionaires' Gordon Roberts led all goal scorers with a league record 43. Seattle defeated Vancouver 7–4 on December 30 and first place was theirs to keep for the remainder of the year. They finished with 16 wins and eight losses. The move to Spokane proved to be another

failure. Attendance was very poor for the ex-Victoria franchise. The final game between the Canaries and Vancouver was canceled and the Spokane franchise folded. The Stanley Cup opened in Seattle with the Montreal Canadiens traveling west. The Stanley Cup was no longer a challenge trophy nor was it held by the champion team of the Dominion of Canada.

Confusion started the Cup series as the Canadiens were forced to drop Reg Noble from their lineup. It was concluded that Noble played with too many teams during the season to be eligible, including playing for Ottawa during the playoffs. Alternating east-west rules didn't seem to bother the Metropolitans. Led by Bernie Morris, Seattle trashed the Canadiens three games to one after dropping the first game. Seattle won the final match 9–1 as Morris pumped in six goals. His 14 goals in the four-game series was the most scored since the glory days of Frank McGee and the Ottawa Silver Seven.

To begin the 1917–18 season, President Patrick suspended the Spokane franchise, thus reducing the PCHA membership to three. However, for the first time, it was decided that the first- and second-place teams during the regular schedule would play a two game total goals playoff series for the PCHA championship. In a rule change, it was decided that there would be no substitutions for penalized players until three minutes had elapsed. More differences of opinion came up once again between the PCHA and NHA. NHA officials came to the conclusion that Gordon Roberts had been loaned to the Millionaires from the Wanderers the previous season. Needless to say, Frank Patrick didn't take this allegation too seriously. Roberts stayed on the West Coast, shifting his talents to Seattle. The league was very concerned about the lack of able-bodied hockey players due to World War I. They were hoping that the military would allow the players to use the hockey season as 'basic training' for military service. League stars such as Dick Irvin, Sibby Nichols and Art Duncan had enlisted already in the Canadian military. Stalwarts such as Ken Mallen and Frank Patrick retired (though Patrick would maintain all his management roles), leaving a huge gap in the PCHA team rosters. However, the league managed, via the suspension of the Spokane franchise, to put together three competitive teams. Seattle finished in first place with an 11–7 record. Close behind at 9–9 was Vancouver.

Once again, Cyclone Taylor was the main scoring threat. The Vancouver rover topped the league in scoring with 32 goals and 11 assists. Because of its first-place finish, Seattle decided to play the first game of the playoffs in Vancouver and the Millionaires held on for a 2–2 tie. Two nights later, in Seattle, Barney Stanley scored the winner for Vancouver in a 1–0 shutout. For the first time, the PCHA championship was not claimed by the team finishing first in the regular-season standings. The Millionaires traveled east to take on the new National Hockey League champions from Toronto in a best-of-five series. Toronto prevailed, winning the fifth game 2–1 on a goal by Corbett Denneny.

To begin the 1918–19 season, Frank Patrick was elected for his sixth consecutive term as president of the PCHA. The Portland Rosebuds franchise was suspended. Poor attendance, once again, was the determining factor. (The Portland team would resurface in 1925–26 when the Regina Capitals moved to the Oregon city.) Victoria, out of action for the past three years, rejoined the league this season. They adopted their previous name, the Aristocrats, with Lester Patrick returning as coach. On the player movement

scene, Art Duncan returned to the Vancouver lineup from overseas with the Military Cross. Also, Harry "Hap" Holmes left the Stanley Cup champs in Toronto for an extended stay with the Metropolitans. Manitoba native and PCHA tough guy Cully Wilson made his presence felt. Cully seemed to take a particular dislike to the Millionaires uniforms. On January 27, Wilson suffered a broken nose in a bout of fisticuffs with Vancouver's Lloyd Cook. Undaunted, he returned one game later. However, Wilson's future in the PCHA was clouded on February 26, 1919 when he nailed Millionaires star Mickey MacKay with a vicious cross-check that resulted in a compound fracture to Mickey's jaw. Wilson was assessed a $50 fine and a match penalty. MacKay was gone for the rest of the year and was also absent from the PCHA for all of the 1919–20 season. Despite the loss of their star player, Vancouver defeated Victoria in the last two games of the season to take first place by one point over Seattle. Cyclone Taylor captured his last PCHA scoring title with 23 goals and 11 assists. First-place Vancouver decided to play the first game of the finals at Seattle. Si Griffis came out of retirement to replace Mickey MacKay. Lloyd Cook moved up to rover and Griffis replaced Cook on defense.

The decision to open the playoffs in Seattle proved to be a mistake by Vancouver. Led by Frank Foyston's three goals, the Mets trashed the Millionaires by a 6–1 score. Two nights later Vancouver prevailed 4–1 but the first-game pounding proved to be too much as Seattle won the final series seven goals to five. The Montreal Canadiens traveled west to meet the PCHA champs. Alternating east-west rules were still in effect. Under western rules, Seattle whipped the Habs 7–0 with Foyston scoring a hat trick. Back to eastern rules, four goals by Newsy Lalonde powered Montreal to a 4–2 win. Foyston, with four goals, led the Metropolitans to a 7–2 victory in game three. Game four ended 0–0 after 20 minutes of overtime. The Canadiens tied the series at 2–2 (with one tie) when Odie Cleghorn popped the winner at 15:57 of overtime in game five. Then, a very serious problem broke out. The Spanish influenza epidemic, which had swept through North America, began to take its toll on the players. Joe Hall was hospitalized on March 30 with a high fever. He would die in a Seattle hospital on April 5, 1919. Four Canadiens players were bedridden with the flu along with manager George Kennedy. Kennedy offered to finish the series with Victoria players replacing the sick Montrealers. That request was refused by Seattle. The series was terminated and a Stanley Cup champion was not declared for the 1918–19 season.

In a carryover from the 1918–19 season, Cully Wilson was banished from the PCHA for his rough tactics, mainly because of the severe injury that he caused Mickey MacKay. MacKay was reinstated as an amateur for the 1919–20 campaign. Toronto lost three of its star players when Jack Adams and Alf Skinner jumped to Vancouver and Harry Meeking went to Victoria. The league was matched very evenly with only two games separating first from last place. Seattle finished the 1919–20 season in first place with a 12–10 record. One game back was Vancouver, and in the cellar was Victoria at 10–12. Seattle clinched the league title by defeating the Millionaires 12–10 before 7,000 fans. The scoring race went right down to the wire as well with Tom Dunderdale of Victoria edging out Seattle's Frank Foyston 33–29. Both players tied with 26 goals.

Seattle chose to open the playoffs at home. However, Vancouver pulled the upset, winning 3–1. Back in Vancouver, before over 9,000 fans, Frank Foyston put on a scoring clinic. His hat trick powered the Metropolitans to a 6–0 victory and the Mets took the finals seven goals to three. Seattle headed east to play the Ottawa Senators for the Cup. Frank Foyston was a one-man gang for the Mets in a losing cause. Ottawa took the first two games 3–2 and 3–0 with Frank scoring two goals in game one. Seattle rebounded to take games three and four with Foyston popping two goals in each game. Game five proved to be a disaster for the western club. Playing eastern rules, Ottawa blasted the Metropolitans 6–1. Jack Darragh was the star of the game with a hat trick for the Senators.

First order of business for the 1920–21 PCHA season was for President Patrick to refuse the reinstatement of Cully Wilson. However, after a one-year absence, Mickey MacKay returned to the Vancouver lineup. Realizing that the flow of eastern hockey talent heading west was drying up, Frank Patrick made his next excursion into new territory. By this time the Big Four League, located in Alberta and Saskatchewan, was vastly improving its caliber of play. Patrick had signed an agreement with the NHL, claiming all players west of the Lakehead (Thunder Bay, Ontario), if professional, would be property of the PCHA. In effect, this gave the NHL some needed protection from the endless raiding of talent by the PCHA. Patrick claimed that at least 10 players in the Big Four League were pros. He put up $1,000 to back his claim and challenged the Big Four to dispute it. Always on the lookout for talent, Patrick probably thought that he could make a serious bid for such prairie-based hockey stars as Dick Irvin, Herb Gardiner, George Hay and Harry Oliver. Lacking funds, the prairie league wouldn't take up Patrick on his claim. The Big Four League drifted into a netherworld of hockey, having neither amateur or professional status. One year later it would resurface as the professional Western Canada Hockey League.

In search for new talent for his Victoria team, Lester Patrick signed a hockey superstar named Frank Fredrickson. A veteran of senior hockey in Manitoba, Fredrickson was the star center for the 1920 Allan Cup and Olympic champion Winnipeg Falcons. Frank didn't make his move to the West Coast until three games into the season. After his debut, the Victoria franchise would never be the weak sister of the PCHA again. Despite missing those first three encounters, Fredrickson went on to become the 1920–21 PCHA scoring champ with 20 goals and 11 assists. Seattle's Frank Foyston was the top sniper with 26 goals. Not to be outdone by Tom Dunderdale from bygone days, Vancouver's Jack Adams gained some notoriety by scoring a goal into his own net for Victoria. A special night was held on March 4 at Victoria to commemorate to playing career of Ernie "Moose" Johnson. Various presentations were made and Lester Patrick's son, Murray, lovingly presented a cup on behalf of all the children of Victoria. (Murray "Muzz" Patrick would go on to a successful career in the NHL as both a player and executive.) The game was tied 4–4 tie after 60 minutes of overtime and was called a tie after an agreement between coaches Patrick and Muldoon.

As it turned out, that 4–4 tie prevented Seattle from catching Vancouver for first place in the final standings, Vancouver edging the Metropolitans 26 points to 25. The Millionaires were led by the powerful scoring foursome of Fred Harris, Jack Adams, Alf Skinner and Mickey MacKay. In the playoffs, it was no contest as Vancouver drubbed Seattle 7–0 and 6–2. Fred Harris sealed Seattle's fate in the first game by scoring four goals. The Stanley Cup was set

to go in Vancouver with the Ottawa Senators as the NHL reps. This series would prove to be a huge box-office success as more than 51,000 tickets were sold for the five games. The Millionaires pleased their sellout crowd with a resounding 3–1 victory in game one. Ottawa rebounded in game two. Vancouver squandered a two-goal lead as Harry "Punch" Broadbent scored the winner for a 4–3 victory. The two teams split games three and four by identical 3–2 scores. Everything would be settled in game five. More than 2,000 fans were turned away as the Millionaires and Senators prepared for battle. And a battle it was! In a rough game, Ottawa played shorthanded most of the time. The game was marred by many fights, and many $25 fines were assessed. It also marked the final game for Fred "Cyclone" Taylor (though he would later make a brief comeback). In the end, Ottawa prevailed as the Senators squeaked out a 2–1 victory. Jack Darragh was the game star as he netted both Ottawa goals.

Times were changing for the PCHA as the 1921–22 season approached. The professional Western Canada Hockey League was formed, causing another drain of hockey talent on the West Coast. A rule was approved awarding a penalty shot when a player with the puck was tripped deliberately while approaching the opposing goal. Also, to save playing time, overtime was limited to 20 minutes. The regular season began two weeks earlier than usual on December 5, 1921. The 1921–22 season would be the final one for future Hall of Famer Ernie "Moose" Johnson. Manitoba natives Clem and Wilf Loughlin were the defense pair for the Aristocrats. Moose moved over to the rover position and scored the final goal of his illustrious career against Seattle on January 13, 1922. Johnson hung up the blades for good five days later. Lester Patrick, once again, proved his versatility. Playing defense and coaching Victoria, Lester also played 10 minutes in the net on January 9 against the Millionaires. Aristocrats goalie Norm Fowler had been penalized for fighting with Mickey MacKay. Lester's play was perfect. He even went so far as to stop a penalty shot by Jack Adams! On January 19 Lester returned to the net for three minutes when Fowler got into an altercation with Vancouver's Alf Skinner. Again, another perfect outing. Referred to by newspaper reports as "the Praying Colonel," Lester had a slow and methodical way of dropping to his knees when making a save. Seattle finished first with a 12–11–1 record this year, one point ahead of Vancouver at 12 wins and 12 losses. "Jolly" Jack Adams was the scoring champ with 26 goals and four assists. The Seattle trio of Bernie Morris, Frank Foyston and Jim Riley powered their attack by scoring 46 of the team's 65 goals.

The competitiveness of the league was apparent in the championship series. Vancouver shut out the Metropolitans twice by the score of 1–0. Hugh Lehman racked up both goose eggs. Beginning in 1922, the PCHA champs were no longer the automatic reps for Western Canada in the Stanley Cup. Arrangements had been made for the PCHA champion to play the WCHL winner in a playoff series with the winner advancing to the Stanley Cup finals against the National Hockey League champs. The Millionaires thus advanced to the western playoff against the WCHL's Regina Capitals. Alternating sets of rules didn't seem to effect either team. Under Coast rules (seven-man) at Vancouver, Regina won 2–1 with Dick Irvin netting the winner. Reverting back to six-man hockey in Regina, Art Duncan scored three times as the Millionaires upset the Caps 4–0 to take the total-goal series. There was some

postgame mayhem as Regina's Amby Moran attacked referee Skinner Poulin in the dressing room, costing Amby a cool $100. The Millionaires traveled east to take on Toronto. Up to his old tricks, Frank Patrick added Victoria's Eddie Oatman to the lineup and proceeded to put brother Lester behind the Millionaires' bench. The first four games of the series were split as the western reps won while playing eastern rules and vice versa. The fifth and final game under eastern rules had the Toronto team walking away to a 5–1 victory. Babe Dye was the Toronto star in the series, scoring nine goals, including four in the finale. Jack Adams paced the Vancouver attack with six goals.

The 1922–23 season brought about the end of the rover position and the death of seven-man hockey on the West Coast. For some unknown reason, the PCHA was the last league, pro or amateur, to be using a system that dated back into the 1800s. This change was made because the PCHA had agreed to an interlocking schedule with the WCHL and the National Hockey League was tiring of the flip-flop rules in the Stanley Cup finals. Also, there were a number of rule changes made to conform with the other two pro leagues. It was made illegal for a team to use more than three men on defense. When not backchecking, all other players had to be advancing towards the opposing goal or have the puck in play. Any standing had to be done between the center area and the opposing blue line. Kicking the puck was permitted anywhere on the ice. However, no goal could be scored by such an action. Also, an offender would draw a two-minute minor penalty and the puck would be faced off at center ice.

The Vancouver franchise changed its name to the Maroons, reflecting the colors of their uniforms. The earliest opening of the PCHA regular season happened this year when Seattle defeated the Maroons on November 13 by an 8–2 score. But even before the season began, another dispute occurred between the PCHA and the WCHL regarding the playing rights to Dick Irvin. Despite playing for Regina the previous year, Patrick still claimed that Irvin belonged to the PCHA because of his playing days at Portland in 1917. The dispute was settled when the WCHL bought Irvin's contract and assigned him to Regina. Meanwhile, an agreement was ratified between the PCHA, WCHL and the NHL, bringing a truce between the three parties. Some of the highlights from the 1922–23 season included the final pro game for Cyclone Taylor on December 8 against Victoria. Also, Saskatoon's visit to Vancouver on January 29, 1923 saw player-coach Newsy Lalonde presented with a gold watch to commemorate his outstanding first season with the original Millionaires in 1911–12.

The PCHA demonstrated its superiority over the WCHL by winning the interlocking games 15–9. Paced by the high-scoring foursome of Frank Boucher, Alf Skinner, Mickey MacKay and Lloyd Cook, the Maroons landed in first place in the PCHA with a 17–12–1 record. Frank Fredrickson scored 39 goals for the Aristocrats and won the scoring title with an all-time high 55 points. Lester Patrick employed his Manitoba connections to secure, besides Fredrickson, the services of ex-Winnipeg Falcon Olympian Slim Halderson, Charles Dieldahl and the Loughlin brothers. The PCHA playoffs began March 7 at Victoria. The Maroons pounced on Victoria for a 3–0 victory to open the two-game total-goals series. Paced by Ernie Parkes' two goals, Hugh Lehman recorded the shutout. Back in Vancouver for game two, Victoria managed a narrow 3–2 win—not enough for the Aristocrats. The Maroons prevailed on aggregate by five goals to three.

The first Stanley Cup semifinals were set to go in Vancouver on March 16, 1923. A crowd of 9,000 fans jammed the Vancouver arena as the Ottawa Senators squeezed by the Maroons 1–0 in game one. Vancouver roared back to take game two 4–1 on the strength of two goals each from Frank Boucher and Art Duncan. Ottawa proceeded to wrap up the series by scores of 3–2 and 5–1. Punch Broadbent was the star for the Senators, pumping home two goals in each game. The Senators then faced the Edmonton Eskimos for the Stanley Cup and took the trophy back to Eastern Canada with two straight wins. An unusual feature of the series was the rivalry of two sets of brothers on the opposing teams, probably a Stanley Cup first. Vancouver's Frank Boucher and Corbett Denneny faced off against family members George Boucher and Cy Denneny of the Senators.

The 1923–24 season would prove to be the last year of existence for the PCHA. One of the rule changes no longer allowed goaltenders to play the puck behind their own net. Also, goalie pads were restricted to a maximum of 12 inches in width. To begin the year, Victoria changed its name from the Aristocrats to the Cougars. The interlocking schedule with the rival WCHL was in place once again.

Times were changing for the PCHA. The WCHL whipped the PCHA in the interlocking schedule as the prairie teams won 29 of the 48 contests. For the first time ever, all PCHA teams ended the regular season with losing records. The Metropolitans won a close race with a 14–16–0 record, one point ahead of Vancouver in the final standings. The Maroons' Art Duncan edged out Frank Fredrickson for the scoring race, finishing with 21 goals and nine assists. Once again, the first-place Seattle team was powered by the front-line trio of Jack Walker, Frank Foyston and Fred "Smokey" Harris. In the playoffs Seattle elected to play the first game at Vancouver. The Maroons and Mets battled to a 2–2 tie. In game two, at Seattle, Frank Boucher scored at 14 minutes of overtime to give Vancouver a 2–1 win and the PCHA title by four goals to three. The year's first series for the Stanley Cup involved the PCHA champs playing the Calgary Tigers of the WCHL. The winner of this series would receive a bye into the Stanley Cup finals. Game one of the series, in Vancouver, was the final victory of the season for the Maroons. Vancouver prevailed 3–1. Game two was played in Calgary, where old rival Cully Wilson extracted some revenge. Wilson whipped in three goals as the Tigers rebounded for a 6–3 triumph. The two teams then headed east to Winnipeg for game three. Calgary made it two straight with a 3–1 victory. The Maroons and Tigers then proceeded to Montreal for the final phase of the Stanley Cup playoffs. By virtue of their win, the Tigers awaited the winner of the Vancouver–Montreal series.

By the narrowest of margins, the Canadiens took two in a row from the Maroons. Billy Boucher scored the winner in game one, won 3–2 by the Habs. Game two was an all-Boucher affair. The Canadiens' Billy Boucher scored two goals for Montreal and brother Frank netted the lone Vancouver marker. Thus marked the final game of the Pacific Coast Hockey Association. Advancing to the finals, the Canadiens knocked off the Tigers two straight by 6–1 and 3–0 scores. Of note, game two was played under western rules with penalty shots, delayed penalties and kicking the puck allowed. Special circles were painted on the ice for the provision of penalty shots. The eastern fans were amused.

The 1924–25 season spelled the end of the Pacific Coast Hockey Association. The league was disbanded with the reduction of team membership to two, the Vancouver Maroons and Victoria Cougars. The Seattle Metropolitans, the first U.S.-based team to win the Stanley Cup, were but a faded memory. The two remaining PCHA teams applied, and received, franchises for the Western Canada Hockey League. The six teams agreed to a 28-game regular-season schedule and a three-team playoff format. Various ex-Seattle players were sent to WCHL teams. Victoria gained the most talent by adding Frank Foyston, Jack Walker, Gord Fraser and Hap Holmes. Edmonton added Archie Briden and Roy Rickey. Vancouver acquired the services of Fred Harris, and Bernie Morris moved to Calgary. Victoria was the better of the old PCHA teams, finishing the season in third place with a 16–12–0 record. The Maroons faded into fifth place, ending the year at 12 wins and 16 losses. Only the lowly Regina Capitals, at 8–20–0, were worse than the Maroons. Ex-PCHA stars still were making an impact in the individual scoring race. Vancouver's Mickey MacKay led the league with 27 goals and Frank Fredrickson finished third with 22 goals and eight assists. Bill Cook, Saskatoon's big right winger, edged out MacKay by one point with 21 goals and 13 assists to claim the scoring title. The semifinals began March 6 in Victoria. The hometown Cougars upset the second place Saskatoon Crescents 3–1. Back to Saskatoon, the Cougars hung on for a 3–3 tie, winning the series six goals to four. With Jack Walker leading the way, the Cougars pulled another upset by tying the first-place Calgary Tigers 1–1 and then winning 2–0 to clinch the WCHL championship three goals to one. Walker had scored goals in all four playoff games. The Stanley Cup finals were set to go on March 21 with the Montreal Canadiens traveling to the West Coast. Game one was played in Victoria and game two was moved to Vancouver, where over 11,000 fans were in attendance. The Cougars swept the first two games, 5–2 and 3–1. Once again, Jack Walker led the Cougar attack with two goals in each game. The Canadiens rebounded in game three, at Victoria, on the strength of a Howie Morenz hat trick for a 4–2 victory. However, the Western Canadian reps were not to denied in game four. Behind Frank Fredrickson's two-goal performance, the Cougars whipped the Habs 6–1, claiming the Stanley Cup—the last Stanley Cup victory by a non-NHL team and the only Cup win by a WCHL team.

The prevalent money problems of the old PCHA reappeared in the WCHL in 1925–26. It was becoming increasingly obvious that the western teams lacked the financial resources to compete with the National Hockey League. Besides that, there were rumors that the NHL was seriously considering a big move into some large United States markets. Western players were demanding salaries equal to their NHL counterparts. Frank Patrick once again disputed this claim of higher eastern salaries, knowing that the western league could not match any large salary demands and survive another season. Due to poor fan support and a last-place finish, the Regina Capitals moved their team to Portland, Oregon, minus Eddie Shore and Art Gagne. The league dropped the word Canada and became the Western Hockey League. The league opened the season on November 23 with the newly formed Portland Rosebuds edging Vancouver 3–2. Strong finishes propelled Edmonton and Victoria into first and third place respectively. Edmonton, at 19–11–0, finished one point ahead of Newsy Lalonde's Saskatoon team. By midseason, poor attendance was hurting the financial foundation of the WHL. Rumor

had it that the league would fold. Calgary dropped from last year's first-place finish to fifth and the Vancouver Maroons finished dead last at 10–18–2. Not even Portland, with future Hall of Famers Dick Irvin and George Hay, could make the playoffs. Victoria slipped into the final playoff spot with a 15–11–4 record. Once again, Saskatoon's Bill Cook was the top scorer with 44 points. Cook and Dick Irvin tied for the goal-scoring lead with 31. Victoria's strong suit proved to be its defensive play, led by future Hockey Hall of Fame goaltender Hap Holmes. Frank Fredrickson was the only Cougar to score more than 10 goals, leading the team with 16. Once again, in the playoffs, the Cougars played the role of underdog. In game one, ending in a 3–3 tie at Saskatoon, both coaches returned to action. Lester Patrick was on defense for the Cougars and Newsy Lalonde at center for the Crescents. At Victoria, the Cougars' Gord Fraser clinched the series, scoring the lone marker in a 1–0 Cougar win in game two. With no ice available in Edmonton, the final series switched to the West Coast with the Eskimos using Vancouver as home ice. In game one the Cougars upset the first-place Eskimos 3–1. With Jack Walker and Frank Foyston starring, the Cougars managed a 2–2 tie on Vancouver ice. By repeating the 1924–25 playoff results, the third-place Victoria Cougars remained WHL champs.

The Victoria team traveled to Montreal for the Stanley Cup finals, though this year's NHL champion was not the Canadiens but the Maroons. They blanked Victoria in the first two games by identical 3–0 scores. The Cougars escaped elimination in game three with a narrow 3–2 win. The last Stanley Cup game played by a non-NHL team was set for April 6, 1926. Nels Stewart, playing defense for the Maroons, took care of business that night. "Old Poison" netted both goals for the 2–0 victory, giving the Montreal team a 3–1 series win.

Facing reality, Frank Patrick realized that the western teams no longer could compete with the National Hockey League on a financial basis. With this in mind, Patrick proceeded to engineer the biggest transaction in hockey history. He sold virtually the entire Western Hockey League to the NHL. The eastern based league had decided to expand for the 1926–27 season and needed players to fill out the rosters in Detroit, Chicago and New York. The Black Hawks bought the entire Portland franchise. Added to the Hawks' lineup were such stars as Dick Irvin, George Hay and Charlie McVeigh along with Mickey MacKay and Hugh Lehman from Vancouver. Not to be outdone, Detroit named its team the Cougars and bought the Stanley Cup finalist Victoria club. Such stars as Frank Fredrickson, Frank Foyston, Jack Walker and Hap Holmes made their way to the Motor City. The New York Rangers picked up players from various WHL teams. Brothers Bill and Fred "Bun" Cook were reunited from Saskatoon and Frank Boucher came from Vancouver. The established teams also secured the talents of some high-quality stars from Western Canada. The Bruins added Edmonton's Eddie Shore and Duke Keats along with Calgary's Harry Oliver. Future Hall of Fame members Herb Gardiner and George Hainsworth headed east to the Canadiens. Calgary's tough defenseman and future NHL president Red Dutton moved into the Montreal Maroons lineup. Not to be outdone by the Rangers, the New York Americans added Saskatoon teammates Leo Reise and Laurie Scott. The Toronto St. Patricks added Corbett Denneny, also from Saskatoon. On the management side, WHL coaches made their mark in 1926–27. Art Duncan was Detroit's playing coach and Saskatoon's Newsy Lalonde was head man for the Americans. Pete Muldoon went to Chicago with the rest of the Portland team. Last, but not least, one of the main architects of western hockey, Lester Patrick, headed the New York Rangers franchise. The other mastermind of the PCHA, Frank Patrick, would make his entrance into the NHL in 1934–35 as the coach of Boston. Four of the 10 National Hockey League coaches in the 1926–27 season had coaching and managerial experience in the Pacific Coast and/or Western leagues.

Sadly, because of the economics of hockey, the greatest era in the history of the game in Western Canada had to come to an end. Fortunately, the league laid a foundation that was instrumental in the development of the modern game. Without the Patricks' ambitions, foresight and, most importantly, their dreams, hockey would not have evolved into its present-day form. More than eight decades later, the Patricks would be proud of the people who have followed in their footsteps.

Pacific Coast Hockey Association Champions

1912	New Westminster Royals
1913	Victoria Aristocrats
1914	Victoria Aristocrats
1915	Vancouver Millionaires
1916	Portland Rosebuds
1917	Seattle Metropolitans
1918	Vancouver Millionaires
1919	Seattle Metropolitans
1920	Seattle Metropolitans
1921	Vancouver Millionaires
1922	Vancouver Millionaires
1923	Vancouver Maroons
1924	Vancouver Maroons

Western Canada Hockey League Champions

1922	Regina Capitals
1923	Edmonton Eskimos
1924	Calgary Tigers
1925	Victoria Cougars

Western Hockey League Champions

1926	Victoria Cougars

CHAPTER 12
Hockey in World War I

Peter Wilton

On December 4, 1914, the cannons and machine guns stationed on the rich farmlands of rural France and Belgium continued to reap their bloody harvest. The echoes of the Great War could be heard in far-off villages, towns and isolated farms on both sides of the Front Line as the death toll continued to mount. The war would not be over by Christmas as the politicians had promised.

Thousands of miles away, in the Temple Building in Toronto, the board of directors for the Ontario Hockey Association was holding its annual meeting. Not surprisingly, the war in Europe dominated the agenda. Many on the board had close relatives fighting in the conflict, and with each passing day the teams of the OHA were losing more and more players to military service. As the minutes of that meeting show, the world of sports could not remain oblivious to the reality of war: "Much of the discussion at the meeting centered around the question of enlisted men and their residential eligibility. It was finally decided that enlisted men, no matter where located, could play with their home team, their regimental team, or with any team in the town in which their company or battalion was located. Any player who is under suspension from the OHA for any cause whatever, and who enlists for overseas service, shall automatically be reinstated and eligible for membership in the Association. This of course does not apply to professionals …"

One year later, the war raged on and another Christmas came and went with no end in sight. On December 30, 1915, James T. Sutherland, president of the Canadian Amateur Hockey Association and captain of the 146th Overseas Battalion, issued the following message:

In this, my first official note as president of the Canadian Amateur Hockey Association, I take the greatest pleasure in sending out to all officers and players in the many provincial associations connected with our governing body the heartfelt wish that the coming year of 1916 will bring to one and all the greatest amount of happiness and prosperity possible.

I feel, however, that I have a greater responsibility and duty to perform at this time and that is to point out to the great army of hockey players and officials scattered throughout our beloved Canada, from coast to coast, how great and urgent the need is for men to come forward and rally to the defense of our common cause, and strike a blow for liberty and justice that will re-echo around the world.

Canada's athletes have responded nobly to the call in the past, and will, I am sure, continue to do so. In a few short weeks, our hockey season will be over, and if there are any who have not made up their minds regarding their future course of action, let me say that, in my opinion, there should be only one conclusion, and that should be to exchange the stick and puck for a 'Ross rifle and a bayonet,' and take your place in the great army that is being forced to sweep the 'oppressors of humanity' from the face of the earth…

It takes nerve and gameness to play the game of hockey. The same qualities are necessary in the greater game that is now being played in France and on the other fighting fronts.

The thousands of hockey players throughout the Dominion of Canada have all the necessary qualifications. Therefore, I strongly urge all such to 'rally around the flag.' With every man doing his bit, Canada will raise an army of brains and brawn from our hockey enthusiasts the likes of which the world has never seen.

The bell has rung. Let every man 'play the greatest game of his life.' Over to center!

By the 1915–16 OHA season, schedules had been juggled to accommodate the surge in soldier teams (which had reached 17 in total), as military training schedules and the mobilization of army units might force these clubs to withdraw from the league with little notice. The majority of other senior and junior teams also had a large percentage of their players in the army. Many of the coaches and referees had enlisted as well. Out west, the Winnipeg 61st Battalion team (featuring future Hockey Hall of Famer "Bullet Joe" Simpson) won the Allan Cup in 1916 before being sent overseas. Another Winnipeg team, the Falcons (with future Hall of Famer Frank Fredrickson), saw every player who was of age enlist for military service. In 1916–17, the former Winnipeg Falcons played for the 223rd Battalion in Manitoba's Patriotic League. They trained with the army in Portage la Prairie and made their way into Winnipeg for games. In May of 1917, the 223rd Battalion was shipped overseas.

In the army, it did not matter that a soldier had been a hockey hero. Like thousands of others, the players were sent to the front-line trenches where they took part in the battles which so scarred Flanders. By the time of the armistice in 1918, many Winnipeg hockey heroes lay dead in the fields, buried in the newly dug military cemeteries of France. Amongst the dead were three former Falcons players: Olie Turnbull, Buster Thorsteinson and George Cumbers.

Far from receiving a hero's welcome, when the surviving members of the Falcons made it back to Winnipeg in 1919, they had to engage in a public battle with the board of hockey governors to be reinstated as a senior team. After a fight (via the newspapers), and a public outcry

against the treatment of the war veterans, the Falcons were permitted to play in a newly formed league with a team from Brandon and a team from Selkirk. The prewar rivalry between the Falcons and the Selkirk Fishermen heated up once again, much to the delight of their fans, who for decades afterward would pine for the return of the old Selkirk-Falcons series.

The Winnipeg Falcons not only proved themselves still capable by winning their new league title, they also defeated the champions of the established Winnipeg league that had made their return so difficult. They then went on to win the Allan Cup as Canada's senior amateur champions. As winners of the Allan Cup, the Falcons became the first Canadian hockey team to play in the Olympic Games in 1920, whereupon they won the gold medal. Unlike the welcome they had received on their return from the war, this time, as Olympic champions, they were treated as royalty with a parade in their honor, dinner with the mayor and a watch from the city. The Falcons had truly returned.

The city of Winnipeg certainly had no monopoly on hockey players who enlisted for military duty and/or played on Battalion teams before serving overseas. Among the heroes of the game who accepted the call to arms from all across the country was one of hockey's earliest legends: "One-Eyed" Frank McGee. Though he was already 32 years old, McGee signed up for military service on November 9, 1914. The former Ottawa sharp-shooter, known for his scoring prowess 10 years earlier when the Silver Seven dominated the Stanley Cup, performed one more amazing feat by passing his physical with perfect eyesight despite the fact he was said to be blind in one eye. This Ottawa native, the nephew of assassinated politician Darcy McGee, and a hero to many a hockey fan, was not spared the horrors of trench warfare. His speed and accuracy and the love of his fans were not enough to protect McGee from the bullets of France. He lost his life on September 16, 1916, while fighting in the Battle of the Somme.

Back in Canada, the Southam newspaper chain rapidly was gaining control of the country's print media, and Gordon Southam, the son of the founder, wanted to contribute to the war effort. He had two criteria—he wanted to form an artillery unit and he wanted the members of his unit to share his love of sport. His plan was that after the mandatory summer of military training in the Niagara region, his artillery unit would be stationed at the Canadian National Exhibition grounds in Toronto awaiting orders to ship out. While there, the unit would place a team in the Ontario Hockey Association.

With the backing of the family fortune, Gordon Southam formed the 40th Battery, known as the Sportsmen's Battery. One of the early individuals Southam approached to join his Battery was Conn Smythe, captain of the University of Toronto hockey team that had won the Ontario junior championship in 1914–15. Smythe already had joined the army and was a member of the 2nd Ottawa Battery but successfully transferred to Southam's 40th. It was up to Lieutenant Smythe to organize the Battery's hockey team and to get them accepted into the OHA. Despite its outward show of welcoming the soldier teams, Smythe found the OHA board of governors to be quite intense as they negotiated which teams the 40th Battery would compete against and determined their take of the gate receipts. The 40th Battery would compete in a

Toronto division with the Riversides (who boasted future Hall of Famer Reg Noble in their lineup), the Argos and the Toronto Rowing and Athletic Association. All games would be played at the Mutual Street Arena. The other hockey managers knew that crowds (and, therefore, the gate receipts) were traditionally smaller early in the season and would grow as the year progressed. Smythe did not yet know this and agreed that the 40th Battery would play as the home team during the first half of the season and the visitors during the second. This meant they would be receiving the larger portion of the gate during the time when crowds would be down.

"The old hockey men, I was told later, laughed at how they'd put one over on the kid," Smythe would write in his autobiography, "but the joke was on them. ... They'd misjudged the Patriotic sentiment in Toronto, plus our good players were starting to make us crowd favorites." In addition, the 40th Battery would be called overseas before the season concluded. "As a minor piece of retribution, this meant that the guys who had conned me in the scheduling weren't going to get the home-team break in gate money from us at all."

The 40th Battery began play in January, losing 8–3 to Reg Noble's Riversides in their first game. The *Toronto Telegram* informed its readers that one of the weaknesses of the army team was Conn Smythe's inability to backcheck effectively. This was the last game Smythe would play. Realizing his weakness, he put out the better players and concentrated on coaching. Among those better players was Jack Pethick, who played rover for the 40th Battery team and was the hero of many games. On January 17, 1916, the *Telegram* reported that "Pethick is going to be a hard man to handle. This soldier team, in fact, will take some [physical] beating from now on."

On January 26, 1916, Major Southam received orders that his battery soon would be heading overseas to France. Though the orders were secret, Southam let Smythe know and the two took up a local gambler's offer to bet heavily on the game. Southam and Smythe bet the team's entire gate receipts earned during their time in the OHA, a total of almost $2,800. Smythe let his team known that all of their money was riding on the game with the Argos, and the 40th Battery came out with a vengeance, racking up an 8–3 victory. "The 40th Battery came into their own last night," the *Telegram* said. "Just short of the winning touch in their last two meetings with the Argos, they came with a rush last night. The soldiers smothered the Argo attack from the start and added the final punch which had been lacking in their own offensive rushes." The 40th Battery had won a purse of more than $5,000 and with gate receipts of just over $1,000 had almost $7,000 in all. The money was used to improve their life over in France. Every man of the 40th Battery received a full Christmas dinner every Christmas that they were overseas.

The only unfortunate aspect of the team's lucrative victory was a brawl that broke out in the stands between supporters of the Battery and fans of the Argos. When the fisticuffs were over, one of the 40th Battery men was badly hurt. Worried that he would not be able to travel because of his injuries, the wounded man asked his teammates to cover for him. He boarded the ship with the rest of the soldiers but succumbed to his injuries (likely massive internal bleeding) during the trip and was buried at sea.

Like the many hockey soldiers who had proceeded and would follow them, no special treatment was given to these stars of the game in Europe. The 40th Battery took part in the Somme offensive and was part of the group that captured Vimy Ridge. A number of the hockey players, including rover Jack Pethick, who had been singled out for his skill, were killed in action. Gordon Southam was killed by an artillery shell. Smythe was disgusted by the commander that took over from his fallen leader and switched to the Royal Flying Corps. His flight instructor was Canadian flying ace Billy Barker.

Barker was an incredibly daring pilot, whose career in the sky was cut short when he was badly shot up during a dogfight over the fields of "No Man's Land." Smythe, who remained loyal to his former trainer and sensitive to the contribution which Barker had made to the war effort, later made him the first president of the Toronto Maple Leafs. "[It] didn't work out exactly as I had planned," Smythe would later write. "I thought that maybe a speech now and then from [Barker] in the dressing room would be good. Most of the players had missed the war, but certainly knew its most-decorated heroes. Many of the other directors had been in the war as well, but Barker was by far the most famous. However, he had trouble with alcohol. Trying to stay away from it he carried a case of ginger ale with him wherever he went, and when the impulse came he'd grab a ginger ale. But one night when I'd line him up to visit the dressing room before an important game, he had to go to Hamilton. On the way he reached down for a ginger ale. There wasn't any. He went into a hotel instead and got plastered, then headed back to Toronto hellbent for Maple Leaf Gardens. On the way up Jarvis Street his car skidded and turned upside down. He showed up on time in the dressing room, clothes torn and covered with blood, and didn't give a bad speech, at all, on the importance of morale. I don't know how much it actually helped morale, but it probably did make a few guys think about the dangers of drinking and driving."

In terms of hockey, World War I affected much more than just Canadian amateurs. In Europe, the International Ice Hockey Federation ceased operations from 1914 to 1920. In the United States, like Canada, the amateur game continued, though many American stars traded in their sticks for guns. Hobey Baker, American hockey's greatest star, was an airman in the famed Lafayette Esquadrille. The former Princeton star and a member of the famed St. Nicholas team in New York City had been in Europe at the time of the assassination of Austrian Archduke Ferdinand that triggered the start of World War I. Friends had a difficult time talking Baker out of enlisting in the British army. He returned to New York, but by 1916 was training to become a pilot. After the United States entered the war in 1917, Baker was among the first American flyers shipped to France, though it was not until April of 1918 that he saw his first combat—in a single-seater Spad painted in the Princeton colors of orange and black. He shot down three German planes by war's end and was decorated with the Croix de Guerre for heroism. Baker survived The Great War, but one month after the armistice of November 11, 1918, America's greatest hockey star was killed in a crash after taking to the skies for one last flight.

Like the amateur game, professional hockey in Canada was greatly affected during World War I. Vancouver was one of the first cities to feel it. As early as July of 1914 (a few days after the assassination of the Archduke), there were reports that German cruisers were prowling the waters of the Pacific just a few miles off the British Columbia coast. Guns were mounted at the entrance to Burrard Inlet and the entire Vancouver harbor was patrolled by the militia. Cyclone Taylor, star of the Vancouver Millionaires of the Pacific Coast Hockey Association and the number three man in the British Columbia Department of Immigration (where he worked when he wasn't playing hockey or lacrosse), had to pass through armed guards to get to his office on the Vancouver waterfront. Two weeks after Britain, and therefore Canada, declared war on Germany on August 5, 1914, Taylor volunteered for military service.

"I had no illusions about war, and I was not the soldier type," Taylor would tell biographer Eric Whitehead. He'd also been married just a few months before. "I wasn't anxious to serve overseas, but if they wanted me and needed me, I was willing and ready to go." A few days after he enlisted, immigration officers were declared exempt from military service (their work was categorized as vital to the national interest.) Private Frederick Wellington "Cyclone" Taylor of the Seaforth Highlanders was given an honorable discharge.

In the spring of 1915, Taylor's good friend Frank Patrick was reported to have enlisted for military service. The president of the Pacific Coast Hockey Association (as well as owner, coach and player of the Vancouver Millionaires) had offered to form a Sportsmen's Battalion similar to the ones being raised in the east. Two weeks later, writes Whitehead in his Patrick biography, a letter arrived from Ottawa stating that since Vancouver and Victoria were key ports and shipyard and naval-base communities, entertainment like hockey was considered vital to home-front morale. Both Frank and Lester Patrick were requested to stay put. However, by 1917, the Canadian government had commandeered the Victoria Arena for military purposes and Lester's hockey club was forced to move to Spokane, Washington. Pro hockey would not return to Victoria until after the war (1918–19).

In the east, the pro hockey cities of Toronto, Ottawa, Montreal and Quebec were less fearful of invasion than Vancouver and Victoria, but their teams would be no less affected by the war. Among the first National Hockey Association (forerunner of the NHL) players to enlist for military service was Allan "Scotty" Davidson. A scoring star with the 1914 Stanley Cup champion Toronto Blueshirts, Davidson signed up shortly after the outbreak of war and was killed in Belgium on June 6, 1915. By the 1916–17 season, dozens of NHA and past hockey players had enlisted. Attendance was suffering, as many of the game's former fans were also overseas or saw the game as too frivolous a pastime during the war. The Ottawa Senators asked to withdraw from the league for one season, but the team was operated under new management instead. Montreal Wanderers owner Sam Lichtenhein patriotically announced that only married men and munitions workers would be signed by his team (though the roster was not very different from the year before). The biggest change in the NHA for the 1916–17 season was the inclusion of an army team.

The 228th Battalion, or Northern Fusiliers, had recruit-

ed a great number of sportsmen from Toronto and Northern Ontario and was granted an NHA franchise on September 30, 1916. Among the khaki-clad hockey players was future Hall of Famer Howard McNamara, his brother George, Goldie Prodgers and Art Duncan of the PCHA. The team posted a 6–4 record in the first half of the NHA schedule but was sent overseas in February of 1917 and could not complete the season. To better balance the remainder of the schedule, the other NHA owners voted to drop Eddie Livingstone's Toronto team as well. Livingstone had long been a thorn in the side of the NHA and had angered both players and owners by battling the 228th Battalion over the rights to Duke Keats and refusing to allow Cy Denneny to join Ottawa, where he lived and worked when not playing hockey. In November of 1917, NHA owners reorganized as the National Hockey League in order to rid themselves of Livingstone. Though the Quebec Bulldogs and Montreal Wanderers were included in the new league, wartime financial losses spelled the end of both franchises (though he Bulldogs would be revived for a final season in 1919–20).

The First World War finally was over by the time the NHL began its second season of 1918–19. Fans looked forward to seeing their favorite players back on the ice, and though the armistice had been signed on November 11, 1918, few would be demobilized in time to start the season on December 21, 1918. Still, the war was over and hockey once again assumed an importance it had not enjoyed since 1914. That point was made clear when the Duke of Devonshire attended the Ottawa Senators home opener. It was the first time the Governor-General had appeared at a hockey game since the outbreak of war.

Much had changed in hockey during World War I and much would continue to change in the ensuing years. Many heroes of the game had given their lives, or at the very least the prime years of their career, to military service. The professional game would not recover fully until well into the 1920s. One man who was ready to be a part of this change was Conn Smythe. He had entered the war the son of a poor dreamer and emerged an officer who would go on to play a key role in forging the modern game of hockey. Twenty years later, he would follow the example of Gordon Southam and form a Sportsmen's Battalion when the world went to war a second time.

CHAPTER 13

The Stanley Cup Mystique

Milt Dunnell

WHEN LYNN AND MUZZ PATRICK discovered the Stanley Cup in a cardboard box down in the basement of their home in Victoria, British Columbia, they did what any grade-school-age students would be likely to do—especially if their father happened to be Lester Patrick, already a legend in hockey.

They got themselves a nail and attempted to add their names to those of the already anointed. Not being blessed with the powers of Nostradamus, they couldn't even guess their names would be engraved there eventually as members of the New York Rangers.

More than 70 years later, three Russian-born players, their names freshly cut into the Cup, were holding it aloft to the thunderous cheers of 62,000 fans attending a soccer match in Moscow. Among those paying homage to the Stanley Cup was Boris Yeltsin, head honcho of all the Russians.

The caper of Lester Patrick's kids didn't even make the local prints, of course, but the pilgrimage to Moscow of Igor Larionov, Vyacheslav Kozlov and Viacheslav Fetisov was big news, even in areas that still hadn't entered the debate on the neutral zone trap.

Thoughtful citizens were prompted to comment on the mystique of this trophy which the three members of the Detroit Red Wings had lugged back to Moscow. Wasn't that the same bowl that a group of Ottawa celebrants once dropkicked into the Rideau Canal, after they had closed one bar too many? Nobody seemed to accuse them of being iconoclastic. In fact, people laughed about it when the tale was rehashed at smokers and banquets.

Yes, it is the same old basin, the one that Lord Stanley of Preston left for hockey-crazed colonials when he completed his gig as the sixth Governor-General of Canada. But absolutely nobody, drunk or sober, is kicking the Stanley Cup around any more. Those days definitely are over. And you can take this to the bank: the Stanley Cup probably is the most popular sports trophy in the world at the moment.

Certainly, it is the most recognizable. And it got that way strictly on merit—no costly promotional campaign of flashing lights and crashing cymbals.

It comes closer to being The People's Cup than any other trophy in sport. They stand in line for hours to get a look at it, to study the names of hockey idols past and present. The secret of its popularity is its availability. It goes where there are people. It's friendly.

During what qualifies as the most successful barnstorming tour in the history of professional sport, the Stanley Cup traveled more than 40,000 miles in 50 days, commencing with the 1998 NHL All-Star Game in Vancouver. In stops at 29 cities, it helped charities to raise more than $2 million. And it didn't find a town that wouldn't just love to have it back.

You might even guess the trustees now responsible for its custody studied the treatment of some other sports cups and decided that mistakes had been made. They might even have known the saga of the America's Cup, the Stanley Cup of yachting. It long enjoyed the title of being the most prestigious prize in sport. But how many would recognize it?

Yes, there are some startling parallels between the America's Cup, and the Stanley. Both have backgrounds in Britain. An English yacht club commissioned the design of the America's Cup as the prize for an 1851 race around the Isle of Wight. After an American yacht won it, the trophy, a bottomless silver ewer that cost $500, narrowly escaped being thrown out as trash from the home of a wealthy sailor.

When the overbearing and unpopular New York Yacht Club came into sole possession of the cup in 1857, the pompous directors knew exactly what to do with it. They secured it to a table in their palatial quarters with a 40-inch bolt. That's where it stayed for 132 years, while the yacht club, frequently revising the rules to their own needs, ran up what was accepted as the longest winning streak in sports history.

And good for the New York Yacht Club. But how many of the unsalty millions in the streets got to see the sport's most publicized award? And good for the trustees of the Stanley Cup, who realize they have something special and want the whole world to help them enjoy it.

Another historic trophy that spent too much time in seclusion, especially during its early years, is the Davis Cup. Dedicated to the purpose of stimulating friendly international interest in tennis, the big silver dish failed in its purpose mainly because of early domination by the Australians. By 1910, both the U.S. and Britain were pleading for a greater display of the cup, in order to revive flagging interest. Where, exactly, was the Cup? It was on a sideboard at the home of Norman Brookes, one of the great Aussie players.

Yes, the National Hockey League has been criticized for taking over an award that the donor, Lord Stanley, directed should be for the championship of amateur hockey. At the time, there was no professional hockey and his lordship had no reason to expect there ever would be. His intention was to promote the popularity of hockey, which he and his family had learned to enjoy. It would be difficult to argue that the NHL has not done that. It has used the Stanley Cup to create enthusiasm for the sport in areas that previously were considered barren territory.

And there's more to come. Igor Larionov might have been more of a prophet than he intended to be when he spoke during that night at the stadium in Moscow. He said: "We (the Red Wings) have millions of fans who rooted for us all the way. It would be unfair not to bring this Cup and show it to them."

Those millions of fans—and millions more like them in Sweden and Finland and the former Czechoslovakia—are not going to be content to watch the tube indefinitely, especially after what happened at Nagano. They will want a piece of the action. Who's to say that European teams won't be competing for the Stanley Cup in the future?

Can't happen, you say? Less then 25 years ago, a deuce would get you 10 that a European player never would win one of the major awards in the National Hockey League. You would have been laughed out of the pub for suggesting a scenario such as the Jaromir Jagr story. Four score years before that, the thought of an American team winning the Stanley

would have been seen to be equally far-fetched. However, probably buried in the archives, there may be one of the most important decisions ever made concerning the trophy. The Pacific Coast Hockey Association had granted franchises to Portland and Seattle. Was either one of these U.S.-based clubs eligible to play for Lord Stanley's award?

Quietly, it appears now, William Foran, a trustee of the Cup, announced the decision. The Stanley Cup, he said, was emblematic of world championship in hockey and no longer was a challenge trophy, open to bids from organizations or individuals with stars in their eyes.

If Foran had decided otherwise, the Stanley Cup might have disappeared down the same faint trail left by the Allan Cup, once the coveted chalice of senior hockey in Canada. For many years, it has suffered anonymity. Seattle, of course, did win the Stanley Cup in 1917, becoming the first team based in the U.S. to do so.

Those first winners deserve to be remembered. Unlike later winners, their names were never inscribed on the Stanley Cup. So here they are, the 1917 Cup champion Seattle Metropolitans: Harry Holmes, Roy Rickey, Ed Carpenter, Jack Walker, Bernie Morris, Cully Wilson, Frank Foyston, Jim Riley and Bobby Rowe. That guy, Morris, scored six goals in one game! In today's NHL, who wouldn't like to be his agent?

Unfortunately, it is true that some of the most colorful chapters in any sport took place during the era in which dreamers could challenge and play for the Stanley Cup. That can't happen now. But reason had to set in somewhere.

There is nothing in the background of any other North American sport that compares to the 1905 bid for Stanley's hardware. It was pure Hollywood stuff outlandish, ridiculous, senseless, laughable—but still admirable.

The gold diggers of the Yukon had a dream. It turned out to be a nightmare but give them credit for trying to prove something they believed—or maybe just suspected. They had a hockey team that could beat the great Ottawa Silver Seven.

Taking off from Dawson City, allegedly by dog team on December 9, 1904, they covered an estimated 4,000 miles by boat, train, even by foot, before they arrived at Ottawa on January 12, 1905. Part of the expenses came out of their own pockets. There was no per diem to take care of shoeshines.

The Silver Seven proved to be impatient hosts. Their attitude was: You're here. Let's get this over with. The gold digger crew scored four goals in the two-game series. Ottawa scored 32. Ottawa star Frank McGee couldn't seem to get warmed up in the opening game and the Yukoners boasted they had his number. McGee scored 14 goals in the second game. Another dream shattered.

There were even nasty rumors that the Silver Seven doctored the ice to ensure that little Rat Portage (Kenora) did not upset the giants to make another absurd shot at the Cup come true. Rat Portage had pulled out all the stops for its bid, hiring some of the best players of the day and equipping them with the new tube skates that were fitted with thin blades.

In the opening game, the Ottawa Silver Seven got an alarming surprise. Those new blades really did work as speedy Rat Portage trounced their hosts by a score of 9–3.

In the second game, however, the thin blades seemed to become a handicap. They sank into the soft ice. One explanation of the ice was that the rink had been flooded shortly before the face-off. There also was some mention of salt. Things like that did happen. And play became so rough that Mike Grant, the referee, donned a hard hat. So much for the question of who wore the first helmet in hockey.

Ottawa won the second and third games. The Portagers went home, poorer but smarter. They had expected to profit handsomely from the proceeds but that didn't work out either. Total receipts were $7,791 before expenses were deducted. That was an Ottawa count, of course.

So spare the sighs of regret for the old days. The truth is that competition for the Stanley Cup, before the NHL took over and got it organized, was pretty much a turkey shoot.

Dawson City may be out of Stanley Cup orbit today but Detroit is in. Los Angeles and Miami are in. Moscow may not be too far away. Take your pick when it comes to return on the entertainment dollar.

And that is not to say the NHL system has been flawless. There seldom has been a dumber ruling in a major sport than Frank Calder, the first president of the NHL made in 1925 when he fined and suspended the entire Hamilton club for demanding $200 per head for taking part in the playoffs.

But the magic of the Cup was powerful even then. The Hamilton franchise was sold at once to New York interests. Maybe the purchase money did come from rum-running, as was alleged, but the New York Americans, as they became known, demonstrated that hockey belonged in New York. Madison Square Garden jumped into the action and the NHL got one of its strongest franchises, the New York Rangers.

Chicago and Detroit followed within a matter of months in a flurry of expansion. But even the booming NHL had trouble weathering the Depression and World War II.

Jobs were scarce and times were hard in the early 1930s but people still responded to events such as Mud Bruneteau's goal of March 25, 1936 in Montreal—at 2:25 in the morning! It gave the Detroit Red Wings a 1–0 win after 176 minutes and 30 seconds in the longest game of Stanley Cup history. That broke the record of 104:46 of overtime set at Toronto on April 3, 1933, when Ken Doraty of the Maple Leafs scored the goal that beat Boston 1–0. These were events that helped people forget their troubles, at least briefly.

A student of the occult sciences may even be tempted to conclude the good old Stanley Cup enjoys powers to make chicken salad out of chicken feathers. A reference point would be the 1942 playoff season.

By this time, the league had dwindled to six teams. Money was plentiful but butter and automobile tires were rationed. Hockey players were in a different kind of uniform and the question was whether hockey would be able to hang on until peace was restored. There was no doubt about the public's attitude. You had to know somebody in order to get a ticket.

But the game needed a shot in the arm. Enter Hap Day as freshman coach of the Toronto Maple Leafs. Hap really was far from happy. His team was down three games to zip in a best-of-seven set with the Detroit Red Wings, managed and coached by one of the shrewdest men in hockey, Jack Adams.

It's hockey history now but it was front page news then how Day shook up his lineup and avoided elimination by winning the fourth game of the series, right in Detroit. The ceremonial champagne had to accompany the Red Wings back to Toronto.

But the Leafs won again. This time, it was a 9–3 blowout and the Red Wings realized they were in trouble. And they never did get into that champagne. Day, a teetotaler, fell off the wagon after the Leafs won the series four games to three. He dipped a finger into the bubbly and licked it.

The series became increasingly tense, of course, and a lively sidebar was provided when Adams got onto the ice during the fourth game at Detroit. League president Calder, who was on hand, somehow got the idea that Jolly Jack was about to

tackle the referee, Mel Harwood. Adams said that conversation was all he had in mind. Adams was suspended.

Day went on to win the Cup in three successive seasons—the first time it had been done since the NHL took over Cup custody in 1926. It all added up to a publicity boom and applications for franchises from cities such as Cleveland, Los Angeles and San Francisco. All were rejected while the six-team league sailed serenely into an era of prosperity.

Even more momentous events were on the horizon to maintain the wave of popularity that the Leaf-Red Wings series had touched off. Can any coach in today's game picture himself looking along his bench and seeing Jacques Plante, Doug Harvey, Tom Johnson, Jean Beliveau, Boom Boom Geoffrion, Dickie Moore, Rocket Richard, Bert Olmstead, Henri Richard and Butch Bouchard—all them Hall of Famers?

A better question might be whether any general manager today could picture meeting such a payroll at current prices. Toe Blake had them all when he took his place behind the Montreal Canadiens bench for the first time in 1956. Rocket Richard, alone, was pro sport's best box-office property.

Toe was able to get his players to produce. Beliveau scored five goals in Toe's first playoff series. It was against the New York Rangers. In the finals, against Detroit, he potted seven more. Olmstead contributed eight assists in the two sets.

As just about every hockey fan knows, Blake won the prized jug in his first five tries behind the bench. It never had been done before and it almost certainly never will be again. Free agency, player agents and huge salaries have combined to make Toe's kind of team merely dream material.

Toe had to beat five other teams on his way to the Cup. Future coaches may have to defeat as many as 40 or even 50. The Europeans will be coming and the Asians are looking. One thing that can be said with assurance is that no city will monopolize the Cup as Montreal did through the glory years of Blake and Scotty Bowman.

That was a 15-Cup jog—of which eight were won by Toe's teams and five, including four in a row, by Scotty's. Never had two better rosters ever been billeted in the same town over a comparatively short period of time than those two dynasty teams. And, if it were possible to match them up in a series today, where would you put your pesos?

Would you go with the Pocket Rocket, the real Rocket, the Boomer (Geoffrion) and Le Gros Bill (Beliveau) or would it be with Bowman's crop of Hall of Famers?

Blake may have had a bit of an edge on offense, but Bowman wasn't exactly desperate in that area either. With sharpshooters such as Guy Lafleur, Steve Shutt, Jacques Lemaire and Yvan Cournoyer, in full flight, no goalie ever liked to see the Bowman bunch coming.

Defensively, it had to be said that Bowman was not suffering either. In front of goalie Ken Dryden, he sent out Serge Savard, Larry Robinson, Guy Lapointe and Brian Engblom who were among the game's greatest rearguards. Only one member of that group (Engblom) has escaped Hall of Fame attention. Robinson shares a record with Gordie Howe for most years in the Stanley Cup playoffs—20.

At the end of the century, there will be a flurry of polls to declare the greatest feats of Cup achievement. Even people who never saw any of the top teams play will be invited to participate. Just tap out a 1–900 number and vote.

In any serious poll, the Bowman and the Blake teams will get serious consideration. Any coach will say that winning an important trophy is tough enough. Defending it, they'll say, is even tougher. No other team ever did a better chore of

defending than the Blake and Bowman clubs.

Al Arbour's powerful Islanders of the early 1980s will get some votes and they will be well-earned. The Isles were not deep in marquee players but they are showing up in the Hall of Fame. Denis Potvin, Bryan Trottier, Mike Bossy and goalie Bill Smith already have made it.

In Mike Bossy, they had one of the most consistent goal-getters in Stanley Cup history. In three successive seasons, he scored 17 playoff goals, a feat not even Wayne Gretzky has duplicated. Twice during the Isles' triumphs, Mike's teammate Bryan Trottier was the leading scorer in the playoffs.

Partly because their achievements are so recent, but mainly because they have to be regarded as one of the finest teams ever assembled, the Edmonton Oilers of the Gretzky era will score heavily in the aforementioned end-of-century polls.

It's inevitable that they will be compared to the Canadiens of Blake and Bowman stewardship. Were they even better than those powerhouses? And where would they rate alongside those Detroit clubs of the early and mid-1950s?

Maybe it's all but forgotten now but the Red Wings of 1952 were hell on wheels when guys such as Gordie Howe, Ted Lindsay and Sid Abel were in full bloom. They swept the Canadiens and the Maple Leafs in eight straight games with goalie Terry Sawchuk logging four shutouts in Detroit. You know that record is for all time because there now are at least 16 teams in the playoffs.

The Edmonton Oilers, of course, don't have those four- and five-year winning strings to match the Bowman and Blake credentials. But five Stanley Cup possessions in seven years will get anyone's attention, especially since there are so many more teams to beat since expansion.

Even a casual glance at the Oilers' roster will impress any pollster. Wayne Gretzky, already acclaimed in one recent survey as the best player of the last 50 years, leads off. Then consider these names: Mark Messier, Jari Kurri, Glenn Anderson, Randy Gregg, Kevin Lowe, Paul Coffey, Grant Fuhr, Esa Tikkanen, Marty McSorley, Dave Hunter, Mike Krushelnyski. The beat goes on. If they are not the best team to come along, they at least are going to create some arguments in the bistros, where such decisions are challenged.

And they have left their skatetracks in the playoff computers. Since Gretzky holds most of the offensive records in the regular season, it's only right that many of the Stanley Cup laurels are his, too. His 122 playoff goals should stand for a long time unless Mark Messier and Jari Kurri enjoy huge late careers with teams that come up big in the playoffs. Gretzky's 260 assists look safe enough, too. His career points—382—can go to the bank. His closest pursuer, Messier, is almost 100 points behind him.

Polls may be nothing but window dressing, the critics are going to argue. They've got it all wrong when they say it about Stanley Cup polls. This is the People's Cup. And what the people say does matter.

For more than 100 years the Stanley Cup trophy has been the game's talisman, a focal point shared by players and fans. The shimmering silver bowl, collar and barrels have been displayed everywhere from Miami to Moscow where they have been admired and photographed by hundreds of thousands. The Cup's escapades—usually in the possession of a member of a winning team—are an action-adventure story all on their own. It's been the star of the show at small-town rinks and on late-night talk shows, all the while conveying the pride and joy of having reached hockey's pinnacle.

II

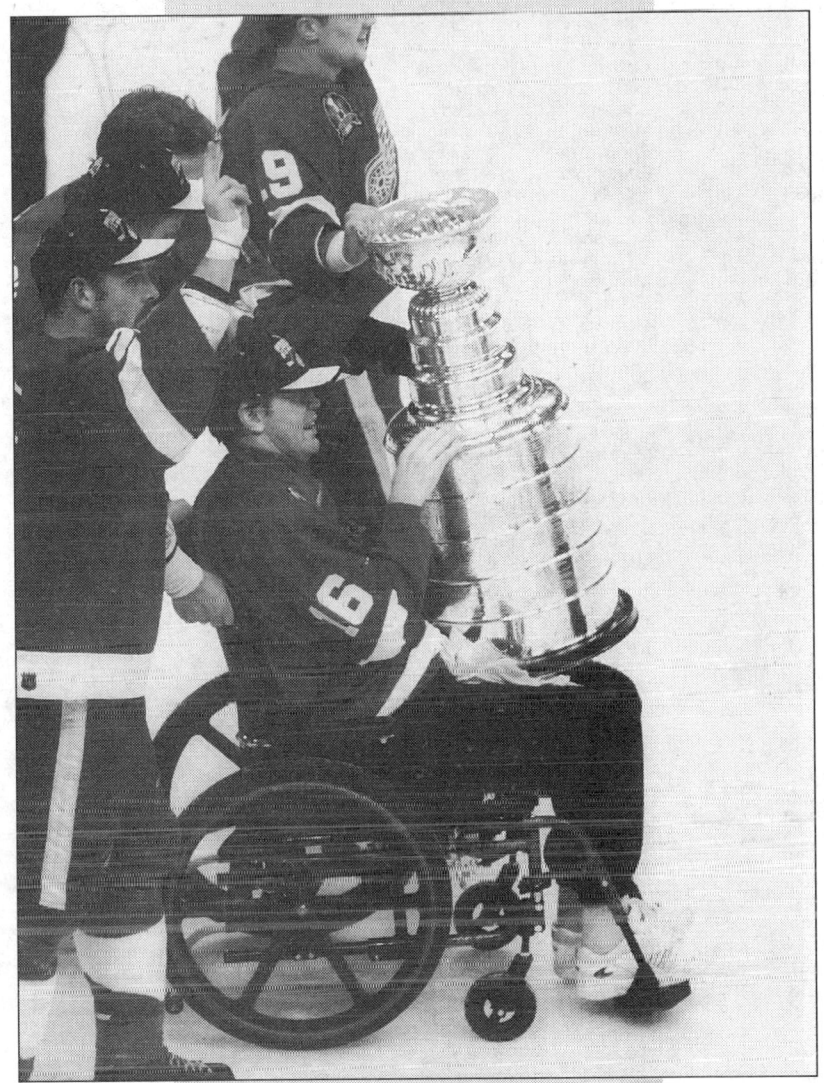

THE
NATIONAL
HOCKEY
LEAGUE

Vladimir Konstantinov and teammates,
Stanley Cup champions, 1998.

STANLEY CUP WINNERS
SINCE THE FORMATION OF THE NHL IN 1917

YEAR	W–L IN FINALS	WINNER	COACH	FINALIST	COACH
1998	4–0	Detroit	Scotty Bowman	Washington	Ron Wilson
1997	4–0	Detroit	Scotty Bowman	Philadelphia	Terry Murray
1996	4–0	Colorado	Marc Crawford	Florida	Doug MacLean
1995	4–0	New Jersey	Jacques Lemaire	Detroit	Scotty Bowman
1994	4–3	NY Rangers	Mike Keenan	Vancouver	Pat Quinn
1993	4–1	Montreal	Jacques Demers	Los Angeles	Barry Melrose
1992	4–0	Pittsburgh	Scotty Bowman	Chicago	Mike Keenan
1991	4–2	Pittsburgh	Bob Johnson	Minnesota	Bob Gainey
1990	4–1	Edmonton	John Muckler	Boston	Mike Milbury
1989	4–2	Calgary	Terry Crisp	Montreal	Pat Burns
1988	4–0	Edmonton	Glen Sather	Boston	Terry O'Reilly
1987	4–3	Edmonton	Glen Sather	Philadelphia	Mike Keenan
1986	4–1	Montreal	Jean Perron	Calgary	Bob Johnson
1985	4–1	Edmonton	Glen Sather	Philadelphia	Mike Keenan
1984	4–1	Edmonton	Glen Sather	NY Islanders	Al Arbour
1983	4–0	NY Islanders	Al Arbour	Edmonton	Glen Sather
1982	4–0	NY Islanders	Al Arbour	Vancouver	Roger Neilson
1981	4–1	NY Islanders	Al Arbour	Minnesota	Glen Sonmor
1980	4–2	NY Islanders	Al Arbour	Philadelphia	Pat Quinn
1979	4–1	Montreal	Scotty Bowman	NY Rangers	Fred Shero
1978	4–2	Montreal	Scotty Bowman	Boston	Don Cherry
1977	4–0	Montreal	Scotty Bowman	Boston	Don Cherry
1976	4–0	Montreal	Scotty Bowman	Philadelphia	Fred Shero
1975	4–2	Philadelphia	Fred Shero	Buffalo	Floyd Smith
1974	4–2	Philadelphia	Fred Shero	Boston	Bep Guidolin
1973	4–2	Montreal	Scotty Bowman	Chicago	Billy Reay
1972	4–2	Boston	Tom Johnson	NY Rangers	Emile Francis
1971	4–3	Montreal	Al MacNeil	Chicago	Billy Reay
1970	4–0	Boston	Harry Sinden	St. Louis	Scotty Bowman
1969	4–0	Montreal	Claude Ruel	St. Louis	Scotty Bowman
1968	4–0	Montreal	Toe Blake	St. Louis	Scotty Bowman
1967	4–2	Toronto	Punch Imlach	Montreal	Toe Blake
1966	4–2	Montreal	Toe Blake	Detroit	Sid Abel
1965	4–3	Montreal	Toe Blake	Chicago	Billy Reay
1964	4–3	Toronto	Punch Imlach	Detroit	Sid Abel
1963	4–1	Toronto	Punch Imlach	Detroit	Sid Abel
1962	4–2	Toronto	Punch Imlach	Chicago	Rudy Pilous
1961	4–2	Chicago	Rudy Pilous	Detroit	Sid Abel
1960	4–3	Montreal	Toe Blake	Toronto	Punch Imlach
1959	4–1	Montreal	Toe Blake	Toronto	Punch Imlach
1958	4–2	Montreal	Toe Blake	Boston	Milt Schmidt
1957	4–1	Montreal	Toe Blake	Boston	Milt Schmidt
1956	4–1	Montreal	Toe Blake	Detroit	Jimmy Skinner
1955	4–3	Detroit	Jimmy Skinner	Montreal	Dick Irvin
1954	4–3	Detroit	Tommy Ivan	Montreal	Dick Irvin
1953	4–1	Montreal	Dick Irvin	Boston	Lynn Patrick
1952	4–0	Detroit	Tommy Ivan	Montreal	Dick Irvin
1951	4–1	Toronto	Joe Primeau	Montreal	Dick Irvin
1950	4–3	Detroit	Tommy Ivan	NY Rangers	Lynn Patrick
1949	4–0	Toronto	Hap Day	Detroit	Tommy Ivan
1948	4–0	Toronto	Hap Day	Detroit	Tommy Ivan
1947	4–2	Toronto	Hap Day	Montreal	Dick Irvin
1946	4–1	Montreal	Dick Irvin	Boston	Dit Clapper
1945	4–3	Toronto	Hap Day	Detroit	Jack Adams
1944	4–0	Montreal	Dick Irvin	Chicago	Paul Thompson
1943	4–0	Detroit	Jack Adams	Boston	Art Ross
1942	4–3	Toronto	Hap Day	Detroit	Jack Adams
1941	4–0	Boston	Cooney Weiland	Detroit	Ebbie Goodfellow
1940	4–2	NY Rangers	Frank Boucher	Toronto	Dick Irvin
1939	4–1	Boston	Art Ross	Toronto	Dick Irvin
1938	3–1	Chicago	Bill Stewart	Toronto	Dick Irvin
1937	3–2	Detroit	Jack Adams	NY Rangers	Lester Patrick
1936	3–1	Detroit	Jack Adams	Toronto	Dick Irvin
1935	3–0	Mtl. Maroons	Tommy Gorman	Toronto	Dick Irvin
1934	3–1	Chicago	Tommy Gorman	Detroit	Herbie Lewis
1933	3–1	NY Rangers	Lester Patrick	Toronto	Dick Irvin
1932	3–0	Toronto	Dick Irvin	NY Rangers	Lester Patrick
1931	3–2	Montreal	Cecil Hart	Chicago	Dick Irvin
1930	2–0	Montreal	Cecil Hart	Boston	Art Ross
1929	2–0	Boston	Cy Denneny	NY Rangers	Lester Patrick
1928	3–2	NY Rangers	Lester Patrick	Mtl. Maroons	Eddie Gerard
1927	2–0–2	Ottawa	Dave Gill	Boston	Art Ross
		The National Hockey League assumed control of Stanley Cup competition after 1926			
1926	3–1	Mtl. Maroons	Eddie Gerard	Victoria	Lester Patrick
1925	3–1	Victoria	Lester Patrick	Montreal	Leo Dandurand
1924	2–0	Montreal	Leo Dandurand	Cgy. Tigers	
	2–0			Van. Maroons	
1923	2–0	Ottawa	Pete Green	Edm. Eskimos	
	3–1			Van. Maroons	
1922	3–2	Tor. St. Pats	Eddie Powers	Van. Millionaires	Frank Patrick
1921	3–2	Ottawa	Pete Green	Van. Millionaires	Frank Patrick
1920	3–2	Ottawa	Pete Green	Seattle	
1919	2–2–1	No decision – series between Montreal and Seattle cancelled due to influenza epidemic			
1918	3–2	Tor. Arenas	Dick Carroll	Van. Millionaires	Frank Patrick

CHAPTER 14

A Short History of the National Hockey League

THE FOUNDING OF A NEW LEAGUE

Brian McFarlane

NORTH AMERICA'S MOST EXCITING ERA of sports took place in the years after World War I.

Indeed, this colorful period came to be known as the Golden Age of Sport. Jack Dempsey in boxing, Babe Ruth in baseball, Bill Tilden in tennis and Bobby Jones in golf dominated the sports pages and became household names that are still not forgotten. In hockey, King Clancy, Eddie Shore, Aurel Joliat, Bill and Bun Cook and Howie Morenz became idols of the ice and stars of the National Hockey League.

But there wouldn't have been a National Hockey League had it not been for a number of quarrels and disputes between owners of teams in the National Hockey Association, the circuit that came just before the NHL. Such disagreements were particularly vitriolic during the 1916–17 season, in the unique situations of wartime.

In 1916, the NHA was comprised of six teams: Montreal Canadiens, Montreal Wanderers, Ottawa Senators, Quebec Bulldogs, the Torontos (often referred to as the Blueshirts or the Arenas) and a team of enlisted men, soldiers on skates representing the 228th Battalion, stationed in Toronto. Because of the war and a shortage of skilled players, Ottawa sought to withdraw from the league but was persuaded to stay on under new management. Sam Lichtenhein, manager of the Wanderers, came up with the patriotic idea that the Montreal club would sign only married men and munitions workers. But perhaps the biggest source of dispute was the team wearing khaki.

When the 228th Battalion recruited Gordon "Duke" Keats, one of his best players, Eddie Livingstone, owner of the Toronto team, protested so vehemently the Battalion commander allowed Keats to play for Toronto in his off-duty hours. But then most of the players in the league became angry when Livingstone refused to release Ottawa native Cy Denneny to his hometown, where he'd taken a job. Livingstone wanted the exorbitant sum of $1,800 and refused offers to trade for Denneny's release. Because of Livingstone's stance, a number of players talked about forming a union, or at least an association, though nothing came of it then. Eventually, Livingstone accepted $750 and goaltender Sammy Hebert for Denneny. Still, things could get worse: In less than a year, Livingstone was involved in a bitter battle with his fellow owners, threatened to start a new league, initiated lawsuits and injunctions and even claimed that Denneny's rights still belonged to him.

The boys in the 228th were a major attraction. Their khaki uniforms may have come across as what we'd call these days a fashion statement, but there was more to them than patriotic sentiment on ice. In their opening game, they scored no less than 10 goals to beat Ottawa 10–7. In a return

match in Ottawa, Howard McNamara (arguably the Battalion's most temperamental player) took two major penalties—including one for attacking the referee with his fists. He may have been somewhat surprised to receive a few solid punches in return from the no-nonsense Cooper Smeaton. But that was only a start. On February 3, 1917 in Quebec, the soldiers arrived late from Toronto, missed their pregame meal and were perchance in a foul mood. They took the Quebec players on at the outset and were pelted with bottles, programs and other debris from the stands. Police had to escort the visiting team to their dressing room, but an angry mob was waiting for them after the game and they did not reach the train station unscathed.

The 228th Battalion's stay in pro hockey, however eventful, was brief. Knowing that their future in hockey was unpredictable, the Battalion had taken out a $3,000 bond with the Ocean Accident and Guarantee Company against the possibility of their being called overseas prior to the end of the schedule. By January 27, 1917 the 228th had completed the first half of the NHA's split season with a 6–4 record (the Canadiens won the first half with a 7–3 mark), but on February 10 the club withdrew from the NHA because the Battalion was ordered to ship out. The following day, the league owners met and a shouting match resulted when Eddie Livingstone insisted on a revamping of the schedule. Before the meeting ended, Livingstone's team in Toronto had been dropped from the league and his players divided among the clubs that were left. Livingstone stormed out of the meeting an irate owner and former franchise holder.

The second half of the NHA's split season saw Ottawa emerge victorious and meet Montreal in a two-game total-goals playoff. After the Canadiens won the first game 5–2, huge crowds, with mounted police maintaining order, waited outside the arena in Ottawa, hoping for a chance to buy tickets for the second. Local recruiting officers worked up and down the line, trying to persuade able-bodied youth to sign up for military service. Not a single one chose to forgo watching hockey for a more serious life in the army and Ottawa won, but by only 4–2.

On the strength of its one-goal advantage, Montreal qualified to go west to meet Seattle, current champions of the Pacific Coast Hockey Association, for the Stanley Cup. On the coast, Seattle's Bernie Morris was sensational, scoring 14 goals against the Canadiens in the four-game series, which was won by Seattle three games to one. Game two was especially intense. A Seattle sportswriter wrote: "Harry Mummery threw himself into Jack Walker with such force that the frail forward of the Seattle team had to be stretched out and carried off the ice. Mummery and Rickey swung their sticks on one another's heads so hard that the raps could be heard up in the gods. Then Rickey and Couture staged a bout that would have furnished a lively reel for the movies." And to cap the climax of the most exciting scenes

ever enacted in the Seattle Arena, Newsy Lalonde swatted referee George Irvine across the face, whereupon judge of play Mickey Ion pitched into Lalonde and chased him off the ice, adding a fine of $25.

Thus ended the last season of play in the NHA, but if the eastern league owners thought they were in for a peaceful off-season, they were badly mistaken. Eddie Livingstone was still fuming, and he certainly wasn't just going away.

Even before the Stanley Cup was decided in 1917, Livingstone was demanding the expulsion of the Wanderers from the NHA, charging the team with attempting to lure two of his Toronto players to Montreal. Then he demanded $20,000 as his share of the Toronto Arena's profits for the 1916–17 season. When Arena officials offered him $6,000, he scoffed at the sum. He even railed against the team for providing the players with jackets.

Factions were forming and this small, local war escalating. Charlie Querrie, a highly respected sportsman and manager of the Toronto Arena, was approached by his friend Percy Quinn, a Toronto man who had purchased the Quebec franchise in the NHA. Quinn wanted to know if he could rent the Arena if he were to move. "Not on your life," Querrie answered. "If the Quebec team moves here, it will not get ice as long as you have any dealings at all with Mr. Livingstone."

Well heated, the climate of controversy between the Quinn–Livingstone side and the rest of the owners simmered all summer and boiled up again in the fall when Quinn and Livingstone announced the formation of a rival league, the Canadian Hockey Association. Quinn boasted that he had the exclusive rights to the ice in Ottawa and expected one or two clubs from that city to join his league. "That is absolutely false," declared E.P. Dey, owner of the Ottawa rink. "Mr.Quinn held an option on the ice here but his option expired some time ago. He sent us $25 and his cheque has been returned to him." The CHA also claimed to have an option on Montreal's Jubilee Rink, an arena affiliated with the Canadiens, then owned by George Kennedy. Kennedy wasn't worried, even when Livingstone's people made a night-time entry, turned on the hose and began making ice for the coming season. "If I can't get ice in Montreal, the Canadiens will play all their home games in Ottawa," he said. "The Ottawa rink seats twice as many fans as the Jubilee and I'll make twice as much money." But then Kennedy held strong opinions about Livingstone's plans for a rival league. "The new league is a joke, a scream. Just imagine anyone so foolish as to try to operate two teams in Ottawa. And to make jumps between Hamilton and Quebec. The latter is dead and the rink in Hamilton is not big enough. The NHA will be in operation again. Don't worry about that."

In Toronto, Eddie Livingstone talked of negotiating for the use of the Riverdale rink for his CHA team. The *Toronto Telegram* scoffed: "The Riverdale rink is a box. The attempt to rent it is like a drowning man grasping for something to hold him up. It is too narrow and brilliant play will be prevented by this condition." And when Livingstone repeated that he had control of Toronto's top players, team captain Ken Randall had a comeback. "Livingstone didn't pay me in 1916 and 1917. How can a contract still hold me?" Meanwhile, Percy Quinn applied for an injunction to prevent the Ottawa club from playing in the NHA, claiming once more that he had a prior arrangement to lease the ice in Ottawa.

While Livingstone's threat of a rival league appeared to be little more than empty rhetoric, talk of change was certainly in the air. There was much speculation after a meeting in Montreal on November 3 that the other NHA owners were planning to organize a new league, but six days later president Frank Robinson and secretary Frank Calder denied there were any changes planned. However, rumors of a new league again surfaced after another NHA meeting on November 10.

On November 17, it was announced that Quebec had dropped out of the NHA but that the league would continue to operate with the Wanderers, Canadiens, Ottawa, and Toronto. Five days later NHA owners met again in Montreal, but no official report of their discussions was released. The November 22 meeting was adjourned until November 24 but was not actually held until November 26 at Montreal's Windsor Hotel. On that day it was formally announced that there would be a new hockey league—the National Hockey League. Frank Calder would serve as president and franchises had been granted to the Montreal Canadiens, Montreal Wanderers and Ottawa Senators. Quebec had been present at the meetings, but would not yet operate an NHL team. A Toronto club was also admitted into the NHL. It would be owned by the Toronto Arena and operated by Charles Querrie.

Eddie Livingstone had been left out of the picture by his former fellow owners, but any fears that he might actually form a league of his own were all but put to rest when George Kennedy produced a signed lease for the use of the Jubilee Rink. The new hockey season was already fast approaching, and while there was still some litigation pending, the club owners felt optimistic about the future of the new league. "We ought to pass Eddie Livingstone a vote of thanks for solidifying our league," laughed George Kennedy when the meetings were over.

But Livingstone and Quinn weren't quite finished. They tried to obtain an injunction against the NHL to prevent the opening games of the new season from taking place. They notified the Ottawa Senators that the team had no rights to Hap Holmes, Alf Skinner, Jack Adams, Ken Randall, Gordon Meeking or Cy Denneny (for whom, as noted above, Livingstone received cash and a goaltender a few months earlier). Livingstone further claimed rights to several NHL players and warned them not to set foot on NHL ice. Quinn continued to insist he had a lease on the Ottawa ice and any team that played on it was doing so illegally.

In the middle of all of this strife, amid rumors of lawsuits, injunctions, threats and intimidation tactics, one veteran player showed a keen sense of humour. Having read in the papers that Percy Quinn had forbidden him from playing in the season opener, "Bad" Joe Hall wired Quinn and asked innocently: "I have read the papers. Am I permitted to play? I have no contract."

Not recognizing the sarcasm, Quinn wired back, "I regret you cannot play under any circumstances." Hall chuckled and went out and played. The next day he received another wire from Quinn. "You have been fined $200 for playing." Hall's reply was reported to be unprintable. Even in telegraphic form, the contents were said to be "hot enough to start a small fire without a match."

The first two games in NHL history were played on December 19, 1917. Toronto was beaten 10–9 by the visiting Montreal Wanderers with only 700 fans attending, even though soldiers in uniform were welcomed as guests of the management. The Montreal Canadiens captured their opener over the Ottawa Senators by 7–4, paced by

Joe Malone, who scored five of the seven goals. Picked up by Montreal when the Quebec club folded, Malone went on to record 44 goals in just 20 games that season.

The Wanderers' opening-game triumph over Toronto was their greatest NHL victory ever, if only because they did not have another. They took an 11–2 pounding from the Canadiens in their second game and then lost a pair to Ottawa by 6–3 and 9–2. Before their next start, a mysterious fire started up in the dressing room and spread quickly. It was out of control within minutes and the Westmount Arena was soon nothing but ashes. Fortunately, the Canadiens could move their home games to the Jubilee Rink, but the now aptly named Wanderers, left homeless, dropped out of hockey. The new NHL was reduced to a three-team circuit.

The Toronto Arenas (the name would not become official until the following year) won the first NHL championship and hosted the Vancouver Millionaires in the 1918 Stanley Cup playoffs, a best-of-five affair. In the final game, a goal by Corbett Denneny proved to be the winner in a 2–1 Toronto victory. Eddie Livingstone and Percy Quinn were left on the sidelines, maybe wondering what might have been. Stubborn, ambitious, confrontational characters, they could have easily played major roles when the new league was formed and become NHL pioneers had they not chosen to argue, scrap, threaten and litigate until other owners had just had enough. Today, their names are all but forgotten in the often told stories of NHL history.

SETTING THE FOUNDATION
1917–18 TO 1925–26

Bob Duff

RAPID GROWTH IN LEAGUE SIZE. Major expansion into the United States and grave Canadian fears that the Americans were "stealing our game." Contract holdouts. Soaring salaries. A players' strike that disrupts the Stanley Cup playoffs. Anti-defense rules designed to increase scoring. The first decade of the National Hockey League really wasn't all that different from the modern era.

Professional hockey was in dire straits as the governors of the National Hockey Association were set to gather in November 1917. The Great War raged in Europe and many of the game's top stars had traded in their skates and sticks for boots and rifles. "Pro Hockey on Last Legs" screamed the headline in the *Toronto Globe* on November 6, 1917 as the dearth of available hockey talent seemed ready to bring about the demise of the NHA, a league that had been in existence since 1909.

"The public want first-class hockey and unless we can furnish it for them, we will reserve the ice for skating purposes only," said E.D. Sheppard, president of the Montreal Arena Company, suggesting that pro hockey might not be part of the winter scenery that year.

With so many good young men heading off to war, the ranks of the NHA had dwindled to the old and infirm and the professional game had lost much of its fan support. "Futile attempts have been made to get amateur stars to become professionals to replace the worn-out oldtimers who have been playing on the NHA teams for year," noted the *Globe*. "Fast, young amateur stars have stolen the patronage from the pros."

On November 10, the governors of the NHA held a brief meeting in Montreal and afterwards announced that the league would suspend operations for the upcoming season, citing it as "unfeasible" with the scarcity of pro players. What people didn't know was that shortly after the NHA meeting adjourned, the owners of the Ottawa and Quebec franchises and the two Montreal clubs—the Canadiens and the Wanderers—gathered to hold a second meeting, welcoming a group representing the Toronto Arena Company.

Soon, the real reason for the suspension of the NHA would become public knowledge. it had less to do with a player shortage and more to do with getting rid of bombastic Toronto owner Eddie Livingstone. An earlier report in a Toronto newspaper had suggested there was "renewed determination on the part of the Ottawa, Montreal and Quebec clubs not to tolerate the Toronto club any longer."

A story in the November 12, 1917 edition of the *Toronto Globe* suggested that there was "something doing in pro hockey," amidst rumors of a new league being founded with Frank Calder, who had been secretary of the NHA, serving as president. "In a day or so, possibly later, developments may be looked for," hinted Quebec manager Mike Quinn.

It actually took two weeks until the new organization, the National Hockey League, was officially announced on November 26. As expected, Calder was named president. The loop consisted of five teams—Quebec, Ottawa, the two Montreal clubs and a new Toronto franchise. "A syndicate of Toronto sportsmen purchased the team," Calder stated, adding that "the new owners were thoroughly acceptable" to the other clubs of the league.

Team owners weren't as polite about the move as their league's new president. "He was always arguing about everything," Ottawa's Tommy Gorman said of Livingstone. "Without him, we can get down to the business of making money."

Not that the infant league didn't have other concerns. Immediately, the Quebec franchise took a leave of absence, reducing the NHL to a four-team outfit. The NHL's first season opened on December 19 and it was apparent that the name change wasn't fooling anyone as far as the quality of the product was concerned. Only 700 watched at Montreal's Westmount Arena as the Wanderers outscored Toronto 10–9.

It would be the only victory of their brief NHL history. The Westmount Arena burnt to the ground January 2, 1918. Both Montreal teams lost everything. The Canadiens scrounged up some new gear and moved into the tiny, 3,250-seat Jubilee Arena, but the Wanderers, citing operating losses of $30,000, elected to fold their franchise.

While teams were going down, NHL goaltenders couldn't —but that didn't stop them. League rules prohibited goalies from leaving their feet to make a save, but, as Ottawa's Clint Benedict pointed out "you could make it look like an accident" and get away with it. "The Praying Goaltender," as Benedict was known because he spent so much time on his knees, led to the league's first rule change. On January 9, 1918 Calder announced that goaltenders would be allowed to leave their feet to make a stop.

Announcing the rule change, Calder said of NHL netminders: "As far as I'm concerned, they can stand on their head if they choose to," coining a phrase still used by hockey people today.

Modern-day hockey fans wouldn't have recognized the NHL game in its infancy. Forward passing was not allowed, making stickhandling and skating required elements for

success. There were no zones on the ice, players were not allowed to kick the puck and immediate substitution was allowed in the event of a penalty, no matter how severe. Minor penalties were three minutes in length and goaltenders would serve their own penalties, meaning a forward or defenceman would have to take over in net for the duration of the sentence.

The winner of the NHL would meet the champions of the Pacific Coast Hockey Association, a loop run on the West Coast by the Patrick brothers, Frank and Lester, for the Stanley Cup. A third major league, the Western Canada Hockey League, formed on the Canadian prairies in 1921, also joined the competition for Lord Stanley's mug.

Rules varied from league to league. The Pacific league still played seven-player hockey, employing a rover, a position the NHA had dropped in 1911. Rules would be enforced on an alternating basis in Stanley Cup play, with the league having home-ice advantage playing the extra game under its rules.

Many PCHA rules were eventually adopted by the NHL, such as forward passing, dividing the rink into zones, playing short-handed while penalized and allowing players to kick the puck. The PCHA brought in the penalty shot in 1921, something the NHL did not do until the mid-1930s. The first time NHL fans got a look at the so-called free shot was in game two of the 1922 Stanley Cup finals when Toronto's Babe Dye fired his penalty shot over the net.

The PCHA was also considered more of a finesse and skating league than the NHL, which was known for its vicious brand of hockey. Seattle's Cully Wilson, banned from the PCHA in 1919 after a violent stick attack on Vancouver's Mickey Mackay, immediately signed with Hamilton of the NHL and proceeded to lead the league in penalty minutes in 1919–20.

Survival of the fittest was the name of the game in the early NHL and even the league's best players—stars like Newsy Lalonde, Punch Broadbent, Nels Stewart and Reg Noble—were as adept at applying the hickory as they were at using their sticks to direct the puck towards the goal.

Early NHL hockey wasn't the glamour game it is today. Harry Cameron, the highest-paid player on Toronto's 1918 Stanley Cup winner, earned $900. Joe Malone, who scored an amazing 44 goals in 20 games in 1917–18 (a league mark which would stand until 1944–45) became a part-time player in the 1918–19 season, playing just nine games for the Canadiens. "I had hooked on to a good job in Quebec City which promised a secure future, something hockey in those days couldn't," said Malone, who played only in Montreal's home games that season.

Paul Jacobs, a promising amateur defenseman signed by Toronto in 1918, quit the team after one game when he received a job offer in Montreal. Out west, PCHA stars Frank Foyston and Frank Fredrickson both left hockey briefly to enter private business—Foyston was a butcher and Fredrickson ran a music shop.

Low salaries meant convincing top amateurs to turn pro was nearly impossible, since the majority of them were well-educated and knew the real world offered the better future prospects than the ice rink. Besides, the best amateurs, or "Simon Pures," as they were called, were being paid quite handsomely—under the table, naturally—to remain with their teams.

The Canadiens and Senators were the dominant franchises in the league's first decade. Between them, they were the NHL representatives in six of the first nine Stanley Cup series. The Habs had won the Stanley Cup in 1916 and reached the finals in 1917, prior to the formation of the NHL. In 1919 they played in the ill-fated series in which no decision was reached.

The Spanish influenza epidemic worked its way through North America and it had already touched the NHL before Montreal headed west to play Seattle, the Pacific Coast champions.

The virus claimed the life of Ottawa defenseman Hamby Shore prior to the start of the season. By early 1919, the majority of the roster of Victoria's PCHA franchise was laid up with flu.

As the 1919 final wore on, five Montreal players became stricken with the illness. After five games, with the series deadlocked at 2–2–1 (including a 100-minute scoreless draw in game four), the Canadiens were so ill they couldn't ice a team. The Stanley Cup trustees offered the title to Seattle by default, but they refused to accept and the series was halted without a winner being declared. Canadiens defenseman Joe Hall never recovered from his illness and died April 5 in a Seattle hospital. Canadiens owner George Kennedy also never fully regained his health and died in the autumn of 1920.

Montreal had vanquished Ottawa in the league finals en route to Seattle, but the Senators were about to go to the top of the class. Goalie Benedict, defenseman Eddie Gerard, center Frank Nighbor and left winger Cy Denneny were already in place when the NHL was formed.

Rugged defenseman Sprague Cleghorn, considered the toughest NHLer of the era, was signed prior to the 1918–19 campaign. Completing the lineup of six starters was right winger Punch Broadbent, who returned to NHL play early in 1919 after serving in combat in World War I, where he was decorated for bravery.

Commencing with the 1919–20 season, Ottawa would take home the Stanley Cup three times in four seasons. So deep in talent were the Senators that during the 1921–22 season, rookie King Clancy and Frank Boucher, both future Hall of Famers, rarely got off the bench. The Senators swept both halves of the NHL's split season in 1919–20 and whipped Seattle in the Stanley Cup finals. When Ottawa opened up with five straight wins to start the 1920–21 campaign, the rest of the NHL screamed foul.

At issue was the Senators' defensive system. Simply explained, the Senators, once they secured a lead, would keep a forward and two defensemen in their own zone of the rink at all times. On the surface, other NHL clubs insisted this style of hockey would be the ruination of the game, but they also realized the effectiveness of Ottawa's system and began employing it. As scoring dwindled, the NHL decided to act and in 1924 adopted the anti-defense rule, which made it illegal for more than two defending players, other than the goaltender, to be in the defensive zone when the puck was not. "I think the fans want to see more scoring," Calder said in introducing the new regulation.

While some teams were thriving, the NHL was still seeking over-all stability. The Toronto Arenas folded in February 1919 and a new ownership group renamed the team the St. Patricks in 1919–20. Toronto entrepreneur Percy Quinn acquired an option on the dormant Quebec franchise in 1917–18, but when the league told him he couldn't move the club to Toronto, he tried to form his own league, the Canadian Hockey Association. He worked closely with Eddie Livingstone, but the new circuit never got off the ground.

Quebec finally rejoined the NHL in 1919. Its lone high-light came January 31, 1920 when Joe Malone potted seven goals against Toronto, an NHL record still on the books today. Malone had an eighth goal disallowed. After the season, the Quebec franchise was sold to Hamilton interests.

Calder felt it was necessary for the other clubs to ensure Hamilton could ice a competitive club. Toronto had loaned Dye to the Tigers prior to the season, but when he sniped two goals in Hamilton's 5–0 opening-night win over the Canadiens, they quickly recalled him. Citing a need to bring more balance into the league, on December 30, 1920, the NHL announced that both Broadbent and Cleghorn had been taken from the Senators and awarded to Hamilton. Senators' management felt they were being unfairly singled out and the issue became further muddled when both Broadbent and Cleghorn refused to report. By the end of the season, both players were back in Canada's capital city, helping Ottawa win Cup again.

Meanwhile, the Canadiens were floundering. Manager Leo Dandurand, who was part of a group that purchased the club for $11,000 from Kennedy's estate, sought reasons for the decline and early in the 1920–21 season, banned his players from driving their motor cars, feeling that it was causing their arm and leg muscles to cramp. The actual concern was dental in nature—Montreal's lineup was long in the tooth. While veteran Georges Vezina was still spectacular in goal, the forward unit of Lalonde, Didier Pitre and Louis Berlinquette had seen its best days.

The fans began to turn on Lalonde, who lost his job as the starting center to Odie Cleghorn in 1921 and quit the team in disgust. Lalonde returned to finish the 1921–22 campaign, but after the season Dandurand traded him to Saskatoon of the WCHL for $35,000 and the rights to an amateur named Aurel Joliat.

Sprague Cleghorn had been acquired and teamed with Billy Coutu to give the Habs the toughest defense pair in the NHL. Two other speedy amateurs, Howie Morenz and Billy Boucher, joined Joliat up front and the rebuilt Canadiens were Stanley Cup champions in 1924 and finalists in 1925—the season Victoria became the last team from outside the NHL to win the Stanley Cup. On-ice success was buoyed by the opening of two new facilities that served as home to the Montreal Canadiens—the Mount Royal Arena in January, 1920 and the $1 million Forum in November, 1924. The Forum was actually built to house a new Montreal franchise, the Maroons, who entered the NHL in 1924.

Maroons owner James Strachan paid $15,000 for his franchise—$11,000 of which was paid to the Canadiens for infringing on their territorial rights. Dandurand saw a natural intra-city rivalry quickly developing and he was right. The Maroons helped heat things up by icing a roster of English-speaking players from Ontario—the perfect foil to the Canadiens French-Canadian base. Strachan quickly assembled an outstanding team, purchasing veterans Benedict, Broadbent and Noble, while signing talented amateurs Stewart, Dunc Munro and Babe Siebert. It didn't hurt the rivalry when the Maroons won the Cup in 1925–26, their second season in the league.

The Hamilton Tigers, after four straight seasons out of the playoffs, finished first in 1924–25, but all was not joyous in Canada's Steel City. The NHL schedule had expanded from 24 to 30 games and while many teams had increased their salary structure, Hamilton was not one of them. Led by captain Shorty Green and goalie Jake

Forbes—who sat out the entire 1921–22 season in a contract dispute with Toronto—the club staged a walkout prior to the NHL final against the Canadiens, refusing to play unless each player was paid a $200 bonus. When the striking players refused to budge, Calder suspended the entire team, awarding the title to the Habs.

The NHL readied for its ninth season in the fall of 1925. Through it all, there had been one constant—Canadiens goaltender Georges Vezina. The ironman of the league, Vezina had never missed a game. He was the only original NHLer who could make this boast. In fact, he'd never missed a game in 16 years with the Habs. "His history in hockey is the history of the pro end of the sport since its inception," Dandurand said of Vezina.

At the Canadiens training camp, Vezina was bedridden with a severe cold. Despite a temperature of 102, he took to the ice for Montreal's season opener. He was unable to continue after the first period and gave way to backup Alphonse Lacroix. A few days later it was revealed that Vezina was suffering from tuberculosis. He had lost 35 pounds in six weeks.

The Canadiens had a game the day that Vezina found out about his illness and he didn't want to upset them, so he asked that no one be told until he had returned to his home in Chicoutimi, Quebec. When Vezina arrived at the Forum that morning, trainer Eddie Dufour assumed he was there to play goal and laid out Vezina's gear in his stall. Vezina sat quietly with his equipment, tears rolling down his cheeks. Then he took the jersey he had worn in the 1924 Stanley Cup finals and left, never to return. Vezina died March 26, 1925. A testament to his talent was evidenced by the fact that the Canadiens, who had reached the Stanley Cup finals the two previous seasons, finished last in the NHL in 1925–26.

"He was as loveable as he was athletic and I cannot say any more than that," Dandurand stated, paying tribute to his long-time goalic.

Perhaps it was fitting that Lacroix, the goaltender for the 1924 U.S. Olympic team, replaced Vezina, since many Canadians were convinced that their game was being taken over by Americans. NHL growth also extended south of the 49th parallel for the first time in 1924, when the Boston Bruins joined the league. The New York Americans, playing out of the 18,000-seat Madison Square Garden, and the Pittsburgh Pirates came aboard in 1925.

The Americans purchased the roster of the striking Tigers for $75,000 and Hamilton lost its NHL team. Each of the players had to pay a $200 fine and write a letter of apology to Calder before they could resume their careers.

The Pirates, with Odie Cleghorn as player-manager, made the playoffs in their first season. Cleghorn helped revolutionize the way the game was played by alternating three set forward lines.

Boston, which had struggled to draw fans in its first season, saw such a turnaround in 1925–26 that it announced plans to expand the size of its arena. New rinks were being built in Chicago, Newark and Jersey City. Ottawa president Frank Ahearn rejected a $100,000 bid for his franchise from the Jersey City group. Detroit, Chicago, Buffalo and a second New York group were also pursuing NHL franchises. Hockey was so popular at Madison Square Garden that Tex Rickard, a man who gained a worldwide reputation as a fight promoter, found the new game to be a gold mine.

"I can make bigger money with less worry and fewer risks out of hockey than I have been getting out of boxing,"

Rickard said, pointing to the large throngs attending Americans games, which often filled the rink.

There were rumors that a separate U.S. pro league was being organized, which would have two teams in New York, as well as franchises in Boston, Pittsburgh, Chicago, Detroit, Buffalo, Los Angeles, San Francisco, Seattle and Portland, Oregon. Eddie Livingstone, spurned by the NHL in 1917, was also trying to put together a rival pro league based in the U.S. "Hockey will sweep the United States from coast to coast within five years," predicted the *Toronto Globe* in a 1925 editorial.

Tom Duggan, managing director of the Americans franchise, scoffed at suggestions that America was usurping the Canadian game. "Stories in Canadian papers about the alleged Americanization of hockey are absurd," Duggan said. "The Canadian clubs are essential drawing cards and the New York club has no intention of ever cutting away from them."

The NHL was now attracting the top amateurs and playing in major centers. Salaries had grown with the league. Pittsburgh signed defenceman Lionel Conacher to a three-year deal at $7,500 a year. Other top earners included Dunc Munro ($7,000), Joe Simpson ($6,000) and Billy Burch ($6,500) of the Amerks and Toronto's Hap Day ($6,000). The NHL installed $35,000 salary caps on each club. Dandurand, who had purchased the Canadiens for $11,000 in 1921, insured the franchise for $150,000 in 1925.

Out west, things were headed in the other direction. The PCHA and WCHL had merged in 1924 and the owners of small-market teams situated on the Canadian prairies could see the handwriting on the wall. "It is a regrettable situation so far as the smaller Canadian centers are concerned," Calgary Tigers owner Lloyd Turner said. "In the larger American cities, they are prepared to pay higher prices. It is a situation that I felt would arise as soon as the United States cities took up hockey."

Big changes had already been undertaken and more were just around the corner. The NHL had opened on Broadway and it was a hit.

THE ESTABLISHMENT YEARS
1926–27 TO 1941–42

By Eric Zweig

THE STANLEY CUP became the exclusive property of the NHL for the 1926–27 season. Nothing better symbolized the importance of this era to the future of the NHL. Not only did the years between 1926–27 and 1941–42 see the game populated by some of the most colorful personalities in hockey history, it also introduced new rules and new franchises that would begin to define the modern NHL.

The 1920s have been called The Golden Age of Sports and with good reason. The Great War was over and gone with it was much of the rigid class structure that had existed before. A new generation of North Americans was in the mood to celebrate and the Roaring Twenties would be a time of great excess, with the pursuit of leisure taking on an importance it had not been allowed in the past. Music was jazzier, movies began to talk, and the popularity of sports exploded. Babe Ruth hit home runs farther and more often than anyone had ever seen. Red Grange tore up the gridiron at the University of Illinois, then gave the fledgling

National Football League an air of respectability when he signed with the Chicago Bears. Jack Dempsey was boxing's heavyweight champion until losing to Gene Tunney. Golf had Bobby Jones. Tennis had Bill Tilden and Helen Wills Moody. Even swimming had superstars in Johnny Weissmuller and Gertrude Ederle (who became the first woman to swim the English Channel in 1926). It was during this period of unprecedented sports popularity that the NHL grew from a tiny all-Canadian circuit into a major North American league.

When the NHL began play in 1917–18, it only had teams in Toronto, Ottawa, and Montreal and shared the Stanley Cup (and professional hockey supremacy) with the Pacific Coast Hockey Association. By 1921–22, the NHL was also in Hamilton and the Stanley Cup had become a three-league affair with the creation of the Western Canada Hockey League. The NHL had the advantage of the larger population base in the east, but the PCHA and WCHL compensated by banding together to play an interlocking schedule in 1922–23. The two leagues merged into one six-team circuit in 1924–25. The NHL also expanded to six teams that year, adding a second team in Montreal and making its first foray into the United States with the admission of the Boston Bruins.

The NHL had hoped to add teams in Boston and New York for the 1924–25 season, but Tex Rickard, who owned Madison Square Garden, had not yet been convinced to include an ice-making facility in his new building. Rickard apparently changed his mind after an invitation to Montreal to watch the Canadiens play during the 1924–25 season. He is said to have been so impressed by Howie Morenz that he finally agreed to install ice at the Garden provided that Morenz would be on hand for the first game there. Bootlegger "Big Bill" Dwyer purchased New York City's first NHL team for the 1925–26 season and the Americans played out of Rickard's 18,000-seat venue. Morenz led Montreal into Madison Square Garden on December 15, 1925 and scored a goal in the Canadiens' 3–1 win over the Americans in a game played before the Who's Who of New York society.

Hockey was a hit in the Big Apple and the New York Americans drew more fans in their first season than any four teams of the Western Canada Hockey League combined. The Pittsburgh Pirates had also been a success in 1925–26, reaching the playoffs in their first season. In just their second season, the Boston Bruins had demonstrated they were an emerging power and the Montreal Maroons were Stanley Cup champions while playing to sellout crowds in the 10,000-seat Montreal Forum. (The Canadiens did not become full-time Forum tenants until 1926–27.)

Having survived the instability of its early years, the NHL was now a financial success and potential owners were lining up to obtain teams in Chicago and Detroit for 1926–27. Tex Rickard also wanted his own New York franchise for Madison Square Garden. The sudden prosperity of the NHL was not lost on the owners of the Western Hockey League. With the NHL adding three more franchises, brothers Frank and Lester Patrick decided it was time to close up shop in the west. As Frank Patrick would later recall: "With our top salary range of about $4,000 we were already squeezing our population draw to its limits. [NHL players were now making close to $10,000] and there was no way we could keep good hockey players in the West beyond maybe one more season." Rather than cut their losses and operate as long as possible by selling off stars to the NHL,

"which would reduce our league to minor status," Patrick convinced five of the six WHL owners to entrust their players to him. "My plan," he recalled, "was to merge the five rosters into three strong teams and then sell the teams intact for $100,000 each."

Patrick's sale did not go entirely as planned, but he was more or less able to sell the roster of the Portland Rosebuds to the new owner of the Chicago Black Hawks and stock Detroit's new NHL team with players from the Victoria Cougars. (Detroit would be known as the Cougars for its first four seasons, before becoming the Falcons, and then the Red Wings in 1932–33.) The new team in New York was not willing to buy in bulk. Conn Smythe had already been hired to assemble the team (dubbed Tex's Rangers by the press as a play on words for Rickard and the famed Texas lawmen). The Rangers did purchase such WHL stars as Frank Boucher and Bill and Bun Cook and would later land Lester Patrick to replace Conn Smythe as coach and general manager. (Smythe would soon resurface in the NHL after buying the Toronto St. Pats and changing the name to Maple Leafs.) The Boston Bruins purchased $50,000 worth of WHL talent, including Eddie Shore, while other deals for individual WHL players created rights-of-ownership disputes, which eventually forced the NHL to sort out distribution. That done, the NHL emerged as hockey's only major professional league and the exclusive holder of the Stanley Cup.

The newly expanded 10-team NHL split into two five-team divisions. The Boston Bruins, Pittsburgh Pirates, New York Rangers, Chicago Black Hawks and Detroit Cougars played in the American Division, while the Montreal Canadiens, Montreal Maroons, Ottawa Senators, Toronto St. Pats/Maple Leafs and New York Americans played in the Canadian Division. Both Detroit and Chicago were expected to have new arenas ready as part of their inclusion in the NHL, but experienced delays. The Red Wings actually played their first season across the border in Windsor, Ontario before moving into the Olympia in 1927–28. The 1927–28 season also saw the Bruins move into the Boston Garden. As for the Black Hawks, Chicago Stadium would not be ready until December of 1929.

With the best available players now in one league, competition in the NHL was better than ever. Every man who finished among the top 10 in scoring in 1926–27 would later be elected to the Hockey Hall of Fame though the close competition ensured that over-all scoring was lower than ever with an average of only 3.80 goals-per-game. In an effort to increase offense, forward passing, which had been permitted since 1918–19, but only in the neutral zone between the two blue lines, was expanded to include the defensive zone. Still, goal-scoring fell to 3.67 goals-per-game in 1927–28. In 1928–29, scoring reached an all-time low with just 2.80 goals-per-game. This was the year in which George Hainsworth registered 22 shutouts in 44 games while posting a 0.92 goals-against average. Eight of the NHL's top 10 goaltenders had at least 10 shutouts that year and all 10 had averages below 2.00. Netminders like Boston's Tiny Thompson, Chicago's Chuck Gardiner, and Roy Worters of the New York Americans would continue to be among the best in the league for years.

In an effort to increase offense, the NHL finally authorized forward passing in all three zones in 1929–30. The only restriction was that the puck could not be passed across the blue line. However, there was nothing to prevent a player from parking himself in front of the opposing goal and waiting for a teammate to bring the puck across the blue line before feeding it to him. Players like Nels Stewart and Cooney Weiland employed this tactic to pile up goals, but the NHL soon realized the error of its ways. With scoring up a whopping four goals-per-game (to 6.91) through the first quarter of the season, the passing rules were amended to state that no player would be permitted to cross the blue line ahead of the puck. It was the birth of the modern offside rule and restored a more competitive balance between offense and defense in the NHL.

Forward passing is the greatest legacy to the rules of the game introduced during this time period, but over the next 10 seasons the NHL developed many other rules and innovations that are still part of the game. Though there is no record of a team ever trying to use two goaltenders at once, a rule was instituted for 1931–32 stating that teams could only have one goaltender on the ice at one time. In 1933–34, the NHL ruled that a visible time clock was required in every arena. Penalty shots were instituted in 1934–35. Rules governing icing the puck were put in place in 1937–38. Flooding the ice between periods became mandatory in 1940–41 and the system of one referee and two linesman to officiate games was instituted in 1941–42.

In addition to creating more offense, forward passing changed hockey from a game of individual rushes to one that focused on combination play. As a result, the 1930s became a time of great lines. Boston's Dynamite Line of Cooney Weiland, Dit Clapper and Dutch Gainor helped the Bruins follow up their first Stanley Cup victory in 1928–29 with a record of 38–5–1 in 1929–30 for an .875 winning percentage that remains the best in NHL history. Weiland led the NHL with 43 goals and 73 points in 44 games in 1929–30, but the Hart Trophy went to the Maroons' Nels Stewart. Stewart was triggerman for the powerful S-Line with Babe Seibert and Hooley Smith. The Toronto Maple Leafs unveiled the Kid Line of Busher Jackson, Joe Primeau, and Charlie Conacher in 1929–30. In 1931–32, they finished first, second, and fourth in the NHL scoring race and led the Maple Leafs to the Stanley Cup. Later, the Bruins featured the Kraut Line of Milt Schmidt, Bobby Bauer and Woody Dumart and won the Stanley Cup in 1939 and 1941.

The first of the NHL's great lines was the New York Rangers' trio of Bill Cook, Frank Boucher, and Bun Cook. Teamed up for the Rangers' first season, the elegant Boucher became the game's best passer and winner of the Lady Byng Trophy seven times in eight years between 1927–28 and 1934–35. Bill Cook was rivaled only by Charlie Conacher as the NHL's most dangerous scorer. Together with Bun Cook, they devised passing patterns that revolutionized offensive play and helped the Rangers win the Stanley Cup in 1928 and 1933. Boucher coached the team to a third Stanley Cup triumph in 1940. But even in an era that emphasized teamwork, two individuals stand out from the others: Eddie Shore and Howie Morenz.

Known as "the Stratford Streak," Morenz brought a combination of speed and skill to the NHL that was unsurpassed. He led the league in scoring in 1927–28 and in 1930–31, adding the Hart Trophy in both of those years and winning it again in 1931–32. Morenz also led the Canadiens to back-to-back Stanley Cup victories in 1930 and 1931 (after having won it previously in 1924). Above all, Morenz was the player fans of his era wanted to see. His appearance in the NHL's new American cities virtually guaranteed a sellout and he became known as "the Babe

Ruth of Hockey" for his box-office appeal. The funeral following his unexpected death on March 8, 1937 attracted more than 10,000 people to the Montreal Forum, while thousands more lined the route of the funeral cortege.

Like Morenz, Eddie Shore put fans in the stands. In a rough-and-tumble era, he took a backseat to no one, with a combination of skill and bravado that was matched by an explosive temper. When he took off on a rush, he would literally knock down opponents who got in his way. Shore was left scarred and toothless from his many on-ice battles, and nearly saw his career terminated after his hit from behind fractured Ace Bailey's skull in December of 1933, but he was no mere goon. Shore was named an All-Star eight years in a row (including seven selections to the NHL First All-Star Team) between 1930–31 and 1938–39 and is still the only defenseman to win the Hart Trophy four times. He was a key contributor to Boston's first Stanley Cup victory in 1929 and was still going strong when the Bruins won again 10 years later.

While Morenz, Shore, and others kept fans entertained with their on-ice exploits, the time period of 1926–27 to 1941–42 was also graced with larger-than-life personalities behind the scenes. Black Hawks owner Major Frederic McLaughlin fired coaches like a 1930s George Steinbrenner and watched his Chicago team win the Stanley Cup in 1934 and 1938. Jack Adams was hired to head up Detroit's hockey operations in 1927–28 and built the club into back-to-back Stanley Cup champions in 1936 and 1937. (He later built the Red Wings' great dynasty of 1949 to 1955.) However, it was Art Ross of the Bruins and Lester Patrick of the Rangers who were probably more responsible than anyone else for the success of NHL hockey in the United States.

Lifelong friends who had grown up together in Montreal and been star players themselves, Ross and Patrick did more than just build championship teams in Boston and New York—they made the Canadian game a part of the American sporting scene. Patrick was particularly adept at handling the influential New York press. "the Silver Fox," as he became known, would speak to the writers one-on-one or summon them in groups for seminars in which he would skillfully explain the intricacies of the game. By successfully courting the press, Patrick and his players were soon Manhattan celebrities while famous fans such as Babe Ruth and Lou Gehrig, mayor Jimmy Walker, movie stars Humphrey Bogart and George Raft, bandleader Cab Calloway, and a parade of Broadway's best and most recognizable faces made Madison Square Garden the place to be and be seen throughout the era.

In Canada, hockey did not require the hype it needed to survive in the United States and yet strong leadership certainly didn't hurt. When Conn Smythe put together a group to purchase the Toronto St. Pats on February 14, 1927 the Stanley Cup champions of 1922 were clearly a team in decline. The newly renamed Maple Leafs finished last in the Canadian Division in 1926–27 and would miss the playoffs again in 1927–28.

Though many on the team's board of directors disagreed, Smythe believed putting the team's games on the radio would help attract fans and Foster Hewitt's broadcasts did exactly that. Soon, all 8,000 seats at the Mutual Street Arena were being filled. In Montreal, Maroons and Canadiens games began to be broadcast as well, while in Toronto, Smythe dreamed of a bigger and better home for his hockey team. Maple Leafs Gardens was built in five months during the height of the Great Depression and opened on November 12, 1931. Though the Maple Leafs would lose 2–1 to Chicago that night, they would finish the 1931–32 season as Stanley Cup champions. By January of 1933, Hewitt's broadcasts from Maple Leaf Gardens were being carried on 20 radio stations across Canada. The nation's population was less than 10 million at the time. Audiences were estimated at almost one million per game.

While the Maple Leafs flourished despite the Depression, the same could not be said for all of the NHL's 10 teams. In 1927, the Senators won their fourth Stanley Cup title in six years, but U.S. expansion had left Ottawa with the league's smallest market, just 150,000 people. Unable to compete financially, the team began trading and selling stars, including King Clancy to the Toronto Maple Leafs for a record $35,000 on October 11, 1930.

Meanwhile, Pittsburgh's steel industry had been hit hard by the stock market crash in 1929 and the Pirates were also forced to peddle their star players. In 1930–31, the team relocated to become the Philadelphia Quakers. Both Ottawa and the Pittsburgh–Philadelphia franchise suspended operations prior to the 1931–32 season. The Senators returned to the NHL in 1932–33, but further poor performances both on the ice and at the box office doomed the club. The Senators moved south and became the St. Louis Eagles in 1934–35, but folded at year-end.

The 1934–35 season saw the Montreal Maroons win the Stanley Cup, but as in Ottawa, success did not mean financial stability. Both the Canadiens and the Maroons were struggling to attract fans during the Great Depression and with the prospects of war in Europe on the horizon, the Maroons' management withdrew its team from the league following a dismal 1937–38 season. With three teams gone, the NHL ended its divisional format and operated as one seven-team league in 1938–39. However, there was still one more problem franchise.

The New York Americans had preceded the Rangers into the NHL by one season, but as mere tenants at Madison Square Garden they never had the same economic advantages of the Rangers. Neither did they enjoy similar on-ice success, nor the same starry fan base. Years of financial instability and bailouts by the league turned the Americans into a virtual farm club, providing young talent to other NHL clubs and a rest home for veterans past their prime. The franchise hit bottom in 1940–41 with a last-place record of 8–29–11. Hoping to forge a new identity, the club became the Brooklyn Americans in 1941–42. After missing the playoffs again, operations were suspended for the duration of World War II. The franchise was never reactivated.

From the heady optimism of the Roaring Twenties, through the bleak years of the Great Depression, to the uncertainty of World War II, the NHL had gone through more changes in 16 seasons than it would again until 1967 and the years beyond. But the 'Original Six' teams that survived this era would carry the NHL into a new period of unprecedented stability and pave the way for the expansion that would follow.

THE ORIGINAL SIX
1942–43 TO 1966–67

Douglas Hunter

THE ERA OF THE NHL'S "ORIGINAL SIX," which ran from 1942–43 until 1966–67, has been called the golden age of professional hockey. The six teams—the Boston Bruins, Chicago Black Hawks, Detroit Red Wings, Toronto Maple Leafs, New York Rangers and Montreal Canadiens—that battled among themselves for Stanley Cup supremacy for 25 years were "original" in the sense that they preceded the expansion teams of 1967–68. But the Original Six was original in more ways than that. It's easy to view the league in those days before expansion, glowing pucks, multi-million-dollar player contracts and ever-increasing dominance by European and American players as a static, almost prosaic enterprise. But although the league's membership was static, the game would change considerably during this quarter century. With successive waves of new talent entering the NHL during and after the Second World War, playing a faster-breaking game made possible by the introduction of the center red line and the two-line offside in 1943–44, the Original Six was original in many ways. These were the years that ushered in firewagon hockey, the slapshot and the functional goaltender's mask. The NHL was defining itself, creating a modern game and modern heroes.

The league was an exclusive enterprise in those days. Only about 100 players had steady jobs, and it was hardest of all to break in as a goaltender—until 1965–66 teams carried only one. And with the advent of the 70-game schedule in 1949–50, teams faced each other 14 times during the regular season. This familiarity between teams—impossible to imagine today, when a team might face a non-conference rival only once in a season—for the most part bred contempt. Grudges were honed and vengeance regularly sought. Many players enjoyed long careers 15 or even 20 seasons—so feuds would be carried on over several seasons. Partly in response to gambling scandals that had dogged many sports, hockey included, Clarence Campbell introduced a rule after being named league president in 1946 banning fraternization between players on rival teams. The idea was to eliminate opportunities for game-fixing and to ensure public confidence that NHL rivalries were legitimate. It's doubtful such a rule would have been necessary. Although NHLers respected each other, and some inevitably were friends through playing for the same team in the past, the law of supply and demand did more than any league edict could to promote antagonism.

Observers who denounce today's game and harken back to a more stylish, gentlemanly era of play forget (or perhaps never noticed) just how vicious the NHL could be in those postwar years. Stick-swinging incidents and bench-clearing brawls were routine. On-ice officials were punched out. On September 28, 1946, the newly arrived Campbell defined hockey as "a game of speed and fierce bodily contact. If these go out, hockey will vanish." However, the game would become so violent at all levels that many fans feared for its survival.

The game was also the center of a number of controversies. Educators were alarmed by the influence the game had on the (lack of) dedication young athletes gave their studies. After the war, the NHL and its affiliated minor pro loops—which were growing in number and size—had a voracious appetite for new talent. Even the British professional ice hockey league was sending scouts into the Canadian hinterlands to find players. With so few jobs available in the NHL, it was felt, with no small amount of justification, that boys were being lured by dreams of professional glory into dead-end playing careers that would leave them with nothing to fall back on. Some officials in the Canadian amateur system also resented the way professional hockey had come to completely dominate their game, sponsoring clubs, paying de facto salaries to junior and senior players, and securing rights to players as young as 16.

The Canadian Amateur Hockey Association was in a sometimes-uneasy alliance with the National Hockey League, becoming its main source of talent in exchange for annual block payments. Before the Second World War, Americans could be found in the league in reasonable numbers. Two of the greatest goaltenders—Frank Brimsek in Boston, Mike Karakas in Chicago—were Minnesotans, and the Black Hawks had eight Americans in the lineup when they won the 1937–38 Stanley Cup. By the 1960s, the only American-born player with an NHL starting job was Tommy Williams of the Bruins. (The most notable American player of the era, Red Berenson, was born in Regina, Saskatchewan, although he was raised in the United States and played hockey at the University of Michigan before joining the Montreal Canadiens.) Americans would return to the game in large numbers beginning in the 1970s, but for many years the league was over 95 percent Canadian.

Many of those players hailed far from the major urban centers—from the Prairie provinces, or the mining towns of Quebec and Northern Ontario. They were scouted and signed as teens and fed into the development system at the junior level. Once their signature was on a C-form—a promise of professional services that allowed a professional club to call them up within one year—they were literally the property of a team for life. Players' rights remained with their teams even after retirement: an ex-player couldn't accept a coaching job with another club unless the arrangement was approved by the last team he played for. An NHL players association had been contemplated in 1946–47 but was abandoned when the league created a pension plan for its players. Another effort to organize, in 1957–58, was crushed by the owners. It would be 1967 before the players organized, and the resulting NHL Players' Association wasn't formally certified as a union until 1976. So, a player's career was subject completely to the whims of the team owners, and he could be promoted, demoted, traded, buried in the minor leagues, and paid whatever salary the owner deemed appropriate—all without recourse. Players lived in constant fear of losing their jobs, whether through injury, fading skills or by running afoul of management.

With a very few notable exceptions—such as Jean Beliveau, whom the Canadiens were desperate to sign and who ended an extended courtship by signing a five-year, $105,000 contract in 1953—NHLers for the most part earned only modest wages. In 1957, as part of the move to head off the players association, the minimum salary was set at $7,500. A journeyman player in the early 1960s made $10,000 to $15,000—about the same as a high-school principal or a police chief. And it was sometimes possible to make more money as a star in a minor league than as a marginal player in the NHL. At the close of World War II, for-

mer Chicago Black Hawk Bob Carse, who had nearly died as a German prisoner of war, weighed an offer from the American Hockey League's Cleveland Barons against a job selling insurance in Edmonton, Alberta. The Barons lured him back to the game with a two-year, $11,000 contract. At the time Carse was earning more in Cleveland than Gordie Howe was making in his first years as a Detroit Red Wing.

Still, while the structure could not compare to today's multi-million-dollar standards, it paid a far sight better than the vast majority of jobs, perhaps explaining why so many were prepared to abandon their education and a safer white-collar career for a chance to earn their living playing a vicious game. In the late 1940s, the best-paid laborers in Ontario were miners, who could make about $40 a week. For a teenager from one of those mining towns who was being offered $200 a week to play for an NHL club's amateur development team in the U.S., the math was elementary: five times as much money as his father made in a year, for only six months of work. And even during those six months, he would be "working" no more than a few hours a day.

Compared to hacking away at a vein of nickel or gold deep below the earth's surface, professional hockey seemed like a paid holiday. Of course, the odds against making this "easy" money were extremely long. Even a top-flight junior team could expect to send only a handful of players each season on to the NHL. For instance, the Montreal Royals won Canadian junior hockey's national championship (the Memorial Cup) in 1949. Only one member of that team, Dickie Moore, went on to an NHL career.

Despite the bountiful supply of talent available and the minimal demand for players, competition in the Original Six was frequently lopsided. The New York Rangers, winners of the 1940 Stanley Cup, lost their momentum in wartime and did not recover fully until after the 1967 expansion. They missed the playoffs 18 times in 24 years between 1942 and 1966. Their next Stanley Cup win didn't come until 1993–94. The Chicago Black Hawks turned in nine last-place finishes between 1946–47 and 1956–57. The Bruins, like the Rangers, were hobbled by wartime. A top team in the 1930s, and winners of the Cup in 1939 and 1941, the Bruins' limited player development resources prevented them from being consistent. But Boston management made the most of what they had and they built a sometimes-competitive club that played in (and lost) the Stanley Cup finals in 1943, 1946, 1953, 1957 and 1958.

The Toronto Maple Leafs were the dominant playoff team of the 1940s, winning the Stanley Cup four times in five seasons between 1946–47 and 1950–51. Coached by former captain Hap Day, these Leafs played a rugged two-way game and enjoyed superb goaltending in the clutch from Walter "Turk" Broda. But the team lost its way for most of the 1950s, bottoming out with a last-place finish in 1957–58. His hockey senses dulling, general manager Conn Smythe—who had fronted the purchase of the Toronto St. Patricks in 1927 and turned them into the Maple Leafs—made a series of debilitating trades, sacrificing scoring power just as the league's best teams were mounting powerful offenses.

The Detroit Red Wings and the Montreal Canadiens were the class of the league through the 1950s. The Red Wings, under coach/general manager Jack Adams, had come to the fore during the war years, appearing in the finals six times during the decade and winning the Cup in 1943. Adams relinquished the coaching duties to Tommy Ivan in 1947,

and together they created one of the most dynamic teams in NHL history. Their goaltender, Terry Sawchuk, who arrived to stay in 1950–51, may have been the greatest the game has ever seen. The defense featured the likes of Red Kelly, Marcel Pronovost and Bob Goldham, while their offensive stars comprised the famed and feared Production Line of Ted Lindsay, Gordie Howe and Sid Abel. The Red Wings defeated the upstart Rangers in double-overtime of the seventh game to win the 1949–50 Cup. Detroit won seven straight regular season titles from 1948–49 to 1954–55, appeared in seven finals between 1948 and 1956, and won the Stanley Cup four times.

At the outset of the Original Six era, Detroit's main rival was Toronto. The Leafs and Red Wings had tangled in seven-game finals in 1942 and 1945, both of which the Leafs won. But as the 1950s dawned, the league's main rivalry involved Detroit and Montreal. The Canadiens appeared in 10 consecutive finals from 1950–51 to 1959–60, and in the first half of the decade their blood feud with the Red Wings was unparalleled. The Red Wings defeated the Canadiens in 1952 in a four-game sweep as Detroit moved through the two playoff rounds without a single loss. After pausing in 1952–53 to give the Bruins a run at Montreal (in a series the Canadiens won in five), the Wings hooked up with the Habs in the next three finals. Detroit won the first two engagements, both of which went the full seven games. When Montreal won the third encounter in five in 1955–56, Detroit's reign was over, while the Canadiens had won the first of five consecutive Stanley Cup titles—a league record—winning 40 of 49 playoff games along the way.

The Canadiens team that came to dominate in the 1950s was a product of remarkable talent spotting. Few of their players had been acquired through trades; the team had signed the vast majority of its players as young amateurs and brought them along in the development system built by Frank Selke, Sr., who had joined the Habs as general manager in 1946 after a lengthy term in the Maple Leafs front office. Selke's system was not limited to francophone Quebec; it stretched across the country and featured such junior teams as Manitoba's St. Boniface Canadiens and Saskatchewan's Regina Pats. Selke's talent pipeline fed a steady stream of new recruits into the Canadiens lineup, which was coached by Dick Irvin from 1940 until 1955.

Irvin's main star was Maurice "Rocket" Richard, who first played for Montreal in 1942–43. His ferocious temper regularly got him into trouble with officials, and it was his outburst during a game in Boston on March 13, 1955, that became more famous than any goal he scored. In the midst of a brawl with Bruins defenseman Hal Laycoe, in which he broke a stick over Laycoe's back, Richard landed two punches in the face of a linesman. Clarence Campbell suspended him for the rest of the season and the playoffs. When Campbell appeared at the Montreal Forum to watch the Canadiens—sans Richard—play the Red Wings on March 17, the fans rioted and went on a destructive tear through Montreal.

After the Canadiens lost the 1955 finals to Detroit, Selke replaced Irvin with Toe Blake. The former Canadiens captain had had his career ended by a bad ankle fracture in January 1948; until then, he had been part of the great Punch Line with Richard and Elmer Lach. Selke figured Blake could do a better job of reining in the Rocket's volcanic temperament. The result was the streak of five consecutive Cup wins, and eight in the 13 seasons Blake ran the

Canadiens bench.

Montreal had so many wonderful players in the 1950s that it seems remiss not to list them all. But among the standouts were goaltender Jacques Plante, who won six Vezina Trophy titles with the Canadiens and introduced the modern fiberglass mask to the game in November 1959; center Jean Beliveau, a superstar for the ages who assumed the captaincy when Maurice Richard retired after the 1959–60 Cup win; the Rocket's younger brother, Henri "the Pocket Rocket," who came to the team in 1955, succeeded Beliveau as captain, and retired in 1975 with 11 Cup wins, more than another other player in NHL history; scoring stars Dickie Moore and Bernie "Boom Boom" Geoffrion, who brought the first fully developed slap shot to the NHL in 1950–51; and defenseman Doug Harvey, a seven-time Norris Trophy winner.

In 1958–59, Montreal encountered a relatively new Stanley Cup opponent, the Toronto Maple Leafs, who hadn't been in a final since defeating the Habs in 1951. George "Punch" Imlach had just taken over as coach and general manager, and the Leafs squeaked into the final playoff spot by a single point over the Rangers, then took seven games to upset the Bruins and make the finals. Though they lost to the Canadiens in five games, Toronto was back again to face Montreal in the 1959–60 finals. This time the Canadiens swept the Leafs, but a changing of the guard was taking place within the NHL: Montreal would be shut out of the next four finals, while Toronto and Chicago were ascendant.

In the early 1950s, player transactions were initiated by the league's other teams to keep the Hawks viable. Suddenly, in the late 1950s, Chicago emerged as a contender. The Black Hawks had benefited from the union-busting tactics of owners in Detroit and Toronto, who in 1957–58 shipped their principal players' association organizers to Chicago—where there was little chance of earning playoff bonus money—as punishment. Collecting Tod Sloan and Jim Thomson from the Maple Leafs, and Ted Lindsay and Glenn Hall from the Wings, Chicago had a foundation on which to build a champion. Its junior operations contributed stars like Bobby Hull and Stan Mikita, and a team that had missed the playoffs for the 11th time in 12 seasons in 1957–58 recovered so rapidly that it won the Stanley Cup in 1961.

Thus began the NHL's most competitive era. Every season from 1962–63 to 1966–67, the four playoff qualifiers had winning records, a circumstance not seen since 1953–54. In 1962–63, the most closely contested season in league history, only five points separated first-place Toronto from fourth-place Detroit. In these years, the playoffs were a toss-up between four evenly matched teams: Montreal, Detroit, Chicago and Toronto. Unfortunately, some of the success of these teams was built on the misery of the Bruins and the Rangers, both of whom had faded badly in the late 1950s.

The Maple Leafs prevailed in the playoff battles of the early 1960s, winning three straight Cup championships from 1962 to 1964 before giving way to a resurgent Canadiens team that emerged victorious four times over the next five seasons, a streak interrupted only by an aging Toronto team's last golden hurrah in 1967.

The Maple Leaf teams of the 1960s were the first truly engineered dynasty. Manager Punch Imlach retained established team veterans like Tim Horton, Ron Stewart and George Armstrong, and added such new talents from the farm system as Carl Brewer, Bob Baun, Dick Duff, Bob Nevin, Bob Pulford, Billy Harris and Ron Ellis. Then he stirred in veterans from other teams—Bert Olmstead from Montreal; Allan Stanley from Boston; Red Kelly, Al Arbour, Terry Sawchuk, Larry Hillman and Marcel Pronovost from Detroit; Ed Litzenberger from Chicago; and Andy Bathgate and Don McKenney from New York. It was a concoction that bore no resemblance to the carefully scouted and nurtured lineups of Detroit and Montreal in the 1950s, but it brought results.

The Black Hawks, despite a lineup chock full of all-stars, could not convert their regular season accomplishments into playoff success. They won in 1960–61—before the team's top players had fully developed into mature NHL stars—but would only return to the finals once, in 1965, losing to Montreal in seven games. Meanwhile, the Red Wings, a relentless checking outfit in the 1960s, reached the finals three times in four years and lost on every occasion.

The last Stanley Cup of the Original Six era was contested by the Leafs and the Canadiens. Chicago had run away with the regular season, winning their first league title, and claimed five of the six berths on the First All-Star Team. But Imlach's aging Leafs ground them down in six before doing the same to Montreal in the finals.

The league doubled in size for the 1967–68 season, and many good players who had been languishing in the minors surfaced for air. In 1969, the league's old recruitment and development system went by the wayside as the expanded league held its first universal Amateur Draft. Three years later, the NHL had a full-blown rival in the World Hockey Association, and the NHL's Canadian stars battled to maintain their country's global bragging rights in the sport as they tangled with the Soviet Union in an eight-game exhibition. A scant five years after its passing, the Original Six seemed like something out of ancient history.

To this day the players who had excelled during the NHL's second quarter century from 1942 to 1967 are remembered with a particular reverence and affection.

PUSHING THE BOUNDARIES
1967–68 TO 1978–79

Jeff Z. Klein and Karl-Eric Reif

A DECADE HAS BEEN REDISCOVERED. Someone opened a hockey time capsule full of 1970s memorabilia, and suddenly an era that until recently had been remembered only as a cultureless wasteland of bad clothes and bad hair is being recalled with nostalgic affection.

What artifacts were buried in that box? Let's take a quick look—ah! An equipment bag from the Kansas City Scouts ... a stained Flyers sweater ... Inge Hammarstrom's passport ... a season ticket order-form from the Miami Screaming Eagles ... a Canadiens Stanley Cup banner ... a pair of white skates and Henry Boucha's headband!

These artifacts come from an era that was curious, tumultuous, in some ways disastrous and sometimes a hugely entertaining time for hockey. It's all there: expansion, the Broad Street Bullies, the arrival of European players, the WHA, the elegance and excellence of Montreal's 1970s Cup dynasty, and yes, strange uniforms, long hair and side-burns.

In a larger sense, the 1970s really includes the first three seasons of the expansion era, starting in 1967–68. For a quarter century the NHL had been an insular six-team loop,

during which time Detroit owner Jim Norris also had an interest either in the Chicago, Boston, and New York franchises or their arenas. Stability reigned: from 1949 through 1966, Montreal never missed the playoffs, Detroit missed only twice, and Toronto just three times, while neither Chicago, Boston nor New York ever won a regular-season title in that span and combined to finish higher than third only six times.

By the mid-1960s, the prospect of substantial profits and the threat of a new major hockey league combined to convince the NHL's club owners to take a great leap forward, doubling in size by adding six new teams. A lot of politicking and networking determined which cities would be awarded new franchises; thus were created the St. Louis Blues, Pittsburgh Penguins, Minnesota North Stars, Los Angeles Kings, Oakland Seals and Philadelphia Flyers. The league split into two divisions, the established teams in the East and the expansion teams lumped together in the West, ensuring playoff participation and playoff dollars for the expansion sides.

A surprising amount of talent was available in that first expansion; plenty of NHL-worthy players who'd languished in the minors simply because they'd never gotten a real shot in the tiny six-team league, journeymen who blossomed in a bigger role on an expansion team, and an especially rich harvest of youngsters who could now step into the NHL right out of junior hockey. Expansion also extended the careers of many players to unprecedented lengths; with more NHL roster spots than established NHL talent, players just kept on playing through their thirties and sometimes past 40. It was strange to be an adult fan and see guys out on the ice older than your dad, but it provided a sense of history, a lovingly prolonged view of the torch being passed from one era to the next, and it made the expansion era unique.

The "Original Six" era closed and the expansion age opened with appropriate symmetry. Toronto closed the six-team chapter with a Stanley Cup victory in Canada's centennial year, and Montreal won the first Cup in hockey's new age. The Canadiens were rapidly aging in places— Jean Beliveau and Henri Richard were key centermen, and the venerable Gump Worsley split time in goal—and youthful in others, but blended well enough to win the Cup the first two years of the expansion era. Brilliant g.m. Sam Pollock moved veterans in and out with dazzling acumen to keep the team fresh and strong. The younger athletes— Jacques Lemaire, Yvan Cournoyer, Peter Mahovlich, goalie Ken Dryden—moved to the forefront as the Habs took the Cup again in 1971 and 1973. But the best was yet to come, as Montreal would stake out a Cup dynasty and establish themselves as the team of the 1970s.

There was room for only one team to dominate as the Canadiens did. And as the decade played out and each expansion side improved, the other clubs from the six-team era found the going tougher.

Boston, NHL doormats since the 1940s, turned the franchise's fortunes around with just two moves as expansion dawned: signing junior sensation Bobby Orr, and stealing Phil Esposito from Chicago in a still-infamous six-player trade. Both proceeded to rewrite the record book: Espo with some of the greatest goals-scoring seasons in history, Orr revolutionizing the way defense was played en route to becoming the best defenseman—some would simply say the best—ever to play the game. Together they galvanized the team that earned a reputation as "the Big Bad Bruins,"

a sneering, black-garbed, provoked-at-a-glance hit squad of a hockey team that seemed to run up seven or eight goals every night and beat the tar out of the opposition while they were at it. Boston won the Cup in 1970 and 1972, yet left the feeling there should have been more despite a remarkable string of consecutive postseason participation, including appearances in the 1974, 1977 and 1978 finals.

New York had last won it all in 1940 and since then had been even weaker than Boston. But like the Bruins the Rangers began building when expansion arrived, and by the early 1970s had assembled a swift, clean, skillful side able to contend for the Cup. Those Ranger teams reeked of style and featured the slick forward line of Jean Ratelle, Rod Gilbert and Vic Hadfield, centers like Walt Tkaczuk and Bobby Rousseau, young defenseman Brad Park (the poor man's Orr) and the great goaltending of Eddie Giacomin and Gilles Villemeure. This talent base enabled the team to reach the finals in 1972. But the Rangers always lacked some physical element, some critical mass for combustion. They faded in the mid-1970s, were rebuilt with the acquisition of Phil Esposito and WHA superstars Ulf Nilsson and Anders Hedberg, and returned to the finals in 1979. But this edition of the team—the 'Ooh-la-la' Rangers of the Ron Duguay-Don Murdoch-Ron Greschner years—had the bad timing to face the Montreal dynasty, and New York fans would have to wait until 1994.

Although they were snookered in the Esposito deal, Chicago still had superstars like Bobby Hull and Stan Mikita leading a team that had been strong through the 1960s. They wound up last among the old guard in the East in 1968–69 despite finishing over .500, but rebounded to win the division in 1969–70, and got a further boost when the NHL added two more expansion teams in 1970 and moved the Black Hawks in with the *arrivistes* of the West. With Bill White, Pat Stapleton, and Keith Magnuson leading a superb blue line corps and Tony Esposito in the nets, Chicago won the division in a cakewalk for the next three years, and twice went through to the finals. Both times, however, they fell to Montreal, first in a seven-game thriller in 1971, and then in a crazy-quilt comedy-of-errors finals of 1973. Then the prospect of healthy pay raises drove Hull and other key players into the beckoning arms of the World Hockey Association. Mikita and Esposito were still plugging away as the decade drew to a close, but weren't part of a contender in the latter half of the 1970s.

In Toronto, Maple Leaf owner Harold Ballard spent the decade embarrassing English-speaking Canada's favorite team with front-office chaos and boorish comments. In spite of him, the Leafs made the transition from the Dave Keon-Norm Ullman-George Armstrong era to the Darryl Sittler-Lanny McDonald-Borje Salming years without too many low spots, and often provided plenty of entertainment in the playoffs. The "Pyramid Power" series against Philadelphia and the 1978 seventh-game overtime series against the Islanders were particularly memorable as was Keon's joining the league-wide fashion trend, switching from his traditional crewcut to a pompadour with long sideburns. Although "the Buds" reached the semifinals only once in all that time, still harder times lay ahead for the franchise and its loyal fans in the 1980s.

Ironically, none of the Original Six fell further in the age of expansion than did Detroit. Led by veterans Gordie Howe and Alex Delvecchio, the Red Wings were still a respectable side as expansion dawned. But the club's front office soon made a habit of alienating their best players.

Howe retired, then joined the WHA, and young phenom Marcel Dionne escaped to Los Angeles. Mickey Redmond was lost to a career-ending injury. These developments left a journeyman cast, forcing goalie Jim Rutherford to face more rubber than probably any netminder of the 1970s. Detroit qualified for postseason play only twice from 1967 to 1983, and wouldn't contend until the late 1980s.

So for hockey's old guard in expansion's first decade-plus, Montreal thrived spectacularly, Boston found some glory and just missed more, and New York and Chicago fell just short in their brush with greatness. Even Toronto had its little moments and only Detroit withered away. The new teams were frequently more exciting than their established brethren, and often more colorful.

Second Six

The addition of six new franchises—California/Oakland, Los Angeles, Minnesota, Philadelphia, Pittsburgh and St. Louis—doubled the league's membership.

St. Louis, the city where the original Ottawa Senators went to die in the 1934–35, was the best of the expansion clubs in the late 1960s. General manager Lynn Patrick assembled a team of past-their-prime but extremely savvy veterans, starting with Hall of Famer Glenn Hall in goal. The Blues just missed the first West Division title, took it in 1969 and 1970, and went to the Stanley Cup finals in each of those first three expansion years, where they were on each occasion easily dispatched in four straight games by the NHL's old guard. Castoffs like centermen Red Berenson and Garry Unger became stars in St. Louis, three Plager brothers patrolled their blue line, Ernie Wakely, Eddie Staniowski and Jacques Caron shone briefly in goal, and stylish workers like Frank St. Marseille and Gary Sabourin defined the team's identity. St. Louis remained competitive though the first half of the decade, then decayed in the late 1970s, but the emergence of youngsters like Bernie Federko spelled hope for the 1980s in St. Louis.

Pittsburgh was another expansion city with plenty of hockey in its history. It had been home to an NHL club in an earlier era. The city also had been a charter member of the old International (Pro) Hockey League in 1904, was home to the NHL's Pirates in the 1920s and, with the Hornets, hosted a successful AHL franchise. The newly established NHL Penguins struggled until the mid-1970s. Players seemed to toil there forever, clad in those powder blue sweaters with the industrial-league look. Logging time in the Civic Arena were Ken Schinkel, Bryan Hextall Jr., Jean Pronovost, Syl Apps Jr., Lowell MacDonald, Ron Schock, Nick Harbaruk, Greg Polis, Val Fonteyne and fine goalies such as Les Binkley and Denis Herron who were bombarded with rubber nightly. The Penguins' first successful season, an 89-point effort in 1974–75, was the first of three consecutive campaigns over .500 as Greg Malone and Rick Kehoe improved the club. Still, the Pens finished more than two games over .500 just twice and won only three playoff series in their first dozen seasons. As the 1980s dawned, Mario Lemieux's arrival was still five years in the future.

The North Stars, set down in the high school and college hockey hotbed of Minnesota, were an entertaining side with plenty of color, and busy in the expansion playoff mix early on. The North Stars were loaded with veterans like Dean Prentice, Doug Mohns, Ted Harris, Ted Hampson, Bob Nevin, and Charlie Burns and his turban-shaped helmet, not to mention the venerable Gump Worsley, who along with Cesare Maniago gave the early Stars solid goaltending. J.P. Parise and Bill Goldsworthy were notable forwards, but Minnesota failed to build a contender and the Stars faded badly by the mid-1970s. They won only two playoff series until they absorbed the floundering Cleveland Barons in 1978; that influx of talent allowed them to shine briefly in the early 1980s.

Los Angeles had a history in the minors since the 1940s, but really got an expansion nod as a media center with a huge population. Expatriate Canadian Jack Kent Cooke, the team's eccentric owner, thought he had a built-in fan base for hockey with word that 300,000 ex-Canadians lived in metropolitan Los Angeles. "I found out why they moved," he said later. "They hated hockey." Unless you had a real passion for purple-and-gold—or at least Vic Venasky—the Kings had little to offer until the mid-1970s, when little Rogie Vachon from Montreal took over in goal, and Butch Goring and Juha Widing emerged as solid pivots. The Kings then acquired future Hall of Famer Marcel Dionne from Detroit and though the Kings won little in the 1970s, as the 1980s neared, they were an exciting team to watch.

Then there were the Seals, a team that seemed to have been born under an unfortunate star. No matter what they did, it turned sour or, just as often, hilarious. Disdaining the Amateur Draft, the Seals traded away their picks for journeymen. That strategy got them a second-place finish in their second season, but soon proved calamitous. A few worthy old-timers quickly came and went, but for the most part a parade of characters now fondly remembered only as answers to trivia questions filled the Seals bench, while their traded draft choices became superstars for other teams. The California Seals became the Oakland Seals and then the California Golden Seals when flamboyant baseball owner Charlie O. Finley bought the team and changed their yellow-and-aqua uniforms to green-and-gold with unforgettable white skates. But by any name and in any colors, the Seals finished last year after year, and there was nothing anyone from Joey Johnston and Carol Vadnais to Ivan Boldirev and Gilles Meloche to Len Frig and Morris Mott could do about it. The team moved to Cleveland in 1976, became the Barons, and spent two more years in the cellar before finally closing up shop and merging its roster with that of the struggling Minnesota North Stars.

The Philadelphia Flyers, though, were a book unto themselves—the most successful of the first wave of expansion while at the same time the most infamous. A decent side in their first few NHL campaigns, the Flyers opted to get much tougher. The Flyers took up where the Big Bad Bruins of the early 1970s had left off. Because of Philadelphia's success on the ice, some teams adopted elements of the Flyers' aggressive style.

Alongside their tough guys and plumbers, the Flyers had an elegant forward in Rick MacLeish as well as an effective first line in Bill Barber, Bobby Clarke and Reggie Leach. They were backstopped by the affable and spectacular Bernie Parent, the best goaltender of the 1970s. The Flyers were wildly successful, winning four straight division titles and back-to-back Stanley Cup titles in 1974 and 1975.

The NHL added two more new teams in 1970. Former Maple Leaf major-domo Punch Imlach quickly built an exciting, contending side in Buffalo, with acrobatic little Roger Crozier in net and one of the most spectacular young forward lines of the era, the French Connection of Gilbert Perreault, Rick Martin and Rene Robert, up front. Along with superb checking forwards like Craig Ramsay and Don

Luce and fine defensemen like Jim Schoenfeld and Bill Hajt, the Sabres reached the finals in just their fifth year of existence. While Buffalo remained among the league's best and most entertaining regular-season teams through the 1970s, the team had little playoff success.

Vancouver, on the other hand, was often as bland as its blue-and-green uniforms. Nifty little forwards like Andre Boudrias and Don Lever helped the Canucks win a division title in 1975, but Vancouver missed the playoffs in six of its first eight seasons and did not win a single playoff series in the 1970s. Goalie Dunc Wilson, though, may have set an NHL record for the largest muttonchops.

Crossing the Frozen Pond

Hockey in North America had certainly gotten bigger, but not necessarily better. In Europe and the Soviet Union, however, the game had both legitimacy and a style all its own. The Soviets earned the gold medal in every World Championship and Olympic tournament from 1963 to 1971. That Soviet hegemony stuck in Canada's collective craw, but the common wisdom over here was that the Soviets beat us in the Olympics because they were amateurs in name only, that our professionals would skate them dizzy if they ever met up. Hockey Canada arranged an eight-game Summit Series in 1972 between Canada's top NHL players and the Soviet Nationals to settle the issue, igniting a flag-waving, chest-thumping nationalistic fervor on these shores. Every hockey pundit in North America felt the NHLers would win in a cakewalk.

It began with embarrassing ease, as the NHL stars sprinted out to a 2–0 lead in game one in Montreal. Then everything went awry. The cream of the NHL staggered off goggle-eyed at game's end after the Soviets put on a skills exhibition and breezed to a 7–3 victory. Team Canada managed a win and a tie in the four games on Canadian ice, and the whole tournament was made a microcosm of the Cold War: their way of life against ours. In the end, the NHL players hacked their way to three heart-stopping victories in Moscow to close the series as narrow winners.

The Summit Series was a defining moment not only for North American hockey but for the Canadian identity; more than 25 years later this tournament is still constantly revisited, victory and defeat rolled into one, revered and reviewed, dissected and debated game by game and shot by shot. Paul Henderson's winning goal and the celebrations it touched off obscured the real point: the cloistered, self-absorbed North American version of the game had stagnated, and the game outside North America, so different, was now every bit as good.

Top Soviet club teams made the first of several midseason tours in 1975–76. Central Red Army and Montreal played to a memorable 3–3 tie on New Year's Eve, 1975. Four European national teams joined Canadian and American NHL stars in an inaugural Canada Cup tournament in September of 1976 with Canada defeating Czechoslovakia in the final.

EuroSoviet hockey was a revelation with its swirling, cycling, criss-crossing patterns of attack and emphasis on skating and passing, the very antithesis of the straight up-and-down-the-lanes North American style in which hitting, shooting and jamming the net were supreme. The Soviets couldn't leave their country to play here, but word circulated that there were many good players in Sweden, and the Leafs lured Inge Hammarstrom and Borje Salming to the Maple Leafs. Hammarstrom was adequate as an NHLer, but

Salming proved to be a gem who was smooth, skillful, smart and tough as any NHL defenseman.

The rival World Hockey Association began play in 1972–73, and from its inception, welcomed players from Europe. The WHA, organized by American Basketball Association entrepreneurs Gary Davidson and Dennis Murphy, set up shop with teams in a dozen towns. Six were cities bypassed by the NHL—Edmonton, Winnipeg, Quebec, Ottawa, Cleveland and Houston—and six went head-to-head with NHL teams in the bigger media centers or more hockey-crazed regions—New York, Los Angeles, Chicago, Philadelphia, Minnesota and New England. Some of the NHL's biggest stars jumped to WHA teams. Bobby Hull gave the new league credibility as did Frank Mahovlich, Paul Henderson, J.C. Tremblay, Dave Keon, Jacques Plante, Gordie Howe and others. While the WHA's on-ice product was not, at first, NHL quality, it soon wasn't far off, complete with its own garish uniforms and, on occasion, white skates.

Along with a horde of minor-leaguers, numerous NHLers flocked to the rebel circuit, lifting its quality, lowering the NHL's, and hiking the average player salary in both leagues. Some second-line NHLers like Andre Lacroix and Marc Tardif became superstars in the new league, but established NHL stars who jumped did not outshine them. Parity was further indicated by young WHA talents who later joined the NHL and remained stars there including Anders Hedberg, Ulf Nilsson, Mike Messier, Mike Gartner, Mark Howe and, of course, Wayne Gretzky.

The Winnipeg Jets won WHA championships with an electrifying, largely European roster and NHL scouts began to scour Scandinavia and Czechoslovakia for talent. By the second half of the 1970s, North American teams eagerly, if at first ineptly, began to copy the EuroSoviet offensive style. North American defense, on the other hand, diluted by expansion and the clutch-and-grab tactics in vogue in the early part of the decade, took longer to adapt.

The WHA operated on a financial tightrope for seven seasons before it went out of business in 1979. The only four teams that remained in constant operation through all seven WHA seasons—Edmonton, Quebec, Winnipeg, and New England (Hartford)—joined the NHL, albeit stripped of all but four players each.

The NHL's major reaction to the WHA was a desperate scramble to mint more NHL franchises. In a preemptive strike to head off the rebel loop's planting teams in cities in which neither league yet had a foothold, the NHL put the Flames in Atlanta and the Islanders in New York's Long Island suburbs in 1972, and then begat the Washington Capitals and Kansas City Scouts in 1974.

With as many 32 teams in the NHL and WHA combined and slim pickings available in expansion drafts, these new clubs weren't competitive. In addition, poor crowds forced several NHL franchises to relocate: Oakland moved to Cleveland, Kansas City decamped for Colorado, and Minnesota stayed afloat only because Cleveland failed. The novelty would soon wear off in Atlanta, as well, and Colorado would relocate to New Jersey.

One team rose above the thuggery that threatened to drag the game down in the 1970s. The Montreal Canadiens returned as conquering heroes in 1976, paragons of the best hockey had to offer. Many of the players who were part of great Montreal teams in the early 1970s were still in place, but in addition to this talent base, Guy Lafleur had blos-

somed into the game's most electrifying scorer, Steve Shutt proved a capable sniper on the opposite wing, checking forward Bob Gainey turned into a force of nature at playoff time, and Serge Savard, Larry Robinson, and Guy Lapointe—the Big Three on defense—were numbered among the best rearguards in the game.

In 1975–76, Montreal breezed through the regular season and early playoff rounds to face the defending Cup champion Flyers in the finals. In this showdown of hockey philosophies, the Canadiens swept Philadelphia aside in four straight games.

Montreal rarely took a night off for the rest of the decade. In the 1976–77 season, the Canadiens won a record 60 games and repeated in the finals with a four-game sweep of Boston. Another regular-season cakewalk followed in 1977–78, capped with another Cup victory over the Bruins. And the Canadiens topped their 115-point regular season in 1978–79 with a fourth consecutive Cup win, dashing the Rangers four games to one. The decade of the Seals and Scouts, of Peter Puck, of Fighting Saints and Golden Blades, of Hound Dog, the Hammer and the Moose, of Hockey Sock Rock, of white skates and giant sideburns ended with hockey artistry ascendant. The Islanders and Oilers—dynasties that followed the Canadiens—both used aspects of the Canadiens' system as models for their own.

99 AND 66
1979–80 TO 1991–92

Gary Mason

IT WOULD BE ONE OF HOCKEY'S MOST EXCITING ERAS. While the upstart World Hockey Association would draw its last breath, the National Hockey League would flourish on the ice in the 1980s and early 1990s, evolving into an international super-league employing great players from around the world. This period also would produce the games' last two dynasty teams—the New York Islanders and Edmonton Oilers—and would provide the setting for two of the game's greatest players to perform their magic—Wayne Gretzky and Mario Lemieux.

Off-ice, the era would be defined by the relationship between three men: chairman of the NHL's Board of Governors and owner of the Chicago Blackhawks Bill Wirtz, league president John Ziegler and Players' Association executive director Alan Eagleson. Through the WHA years as salaries soared, labor and management needed to work together creatively to ensure franchise stability and preserve players' jobs in the NHL. The triumvirate of Wirtz, Ziegler and Eagleson allowed this to happen but, by 1990 many players would become increasingly uncomfortable with this relationship. By October of 1992 Eagleson and Ziegler would be replaced and Wirtz's tenure as chairman of the Board of Governors ended.

The WHA had started in 1972. For seven years it challenged the NHL in cities across North America, signing some of the game's biggest names, most notably Bobby Hull, while allowing future stars like Gretzky and Mark Messier to make their professional debuts as teenagers. But the league's shaky financial foundation eventually collapsed and, in 1979, the NHL expanded into four WHA markets—Edmonton, Quebec, Hartford and Winnipeg. Before Edmonton joined the NHL, and was still operating in the WHA, the team purchased Gretzky, who first had

played with the Indianapolis Racers. Before Edmonton joined the NHL, it had to be assured it wouldn't lose the rights to Gretzky.

Meantime, another former expansion franchise, the New York Islanders, had quietly built an outstanding hockey team under the guidance of general manager Bill Torrey, coach Al Arbour and a gifted scouting staff.

The team revolved around its captain, All-Star defenseman Denis Potvin, forwards Bryan Trottier and Mike Bossy and goaltender Billy Smith. Like any great hockey team, the Islanders also had a talented supporting cast that included players like Clark Gillies, Bob Nystrom and Butch Goring. The Islanders were never flashy, they played a tough, disciplined game and made few mistakes. Their coach, Al Arbour, was a man of few expressions who rarely got flustered in the heat of battle. Arbour's composure under fire rubbed off on his team. Before retiring, Arbour would compile one of the most impressive coaching records in hockey.

The team's undisputed leader was also one of the finest defensemen in the game. Denis Potvin would go on to have a distinguished NHL career, breaking Bobby Orr's all-time scoring records for defensemen and becoming the first blueliner in the league to top 300 goals.

In 1979-80, their eighth NHL season, the Islanders became the second expansion team to win the Stanley Cup. Two players, Smith and Nystrom, had been with the team since its inception in 1972. The team would go on to win the Cup the next three years as well, becoming only the second NHL franchise in history to win four championships in a row. The Islanders would beat the Edmonton Oilers in four games to win their fourth Cup. The Oilers, however, would learn from their defeat.

Edmonton general manager Glen Sather, coach of the Oilers at the time, remembers walking by the Islander dressing room after the final game.

"They all had ice packs on," Sather recalled. "None of our guys were beat up like that. We just didn't know how hard we had to go to win. To be a Stanley Cup champion." They would learn.

Sather was building a different team from the conservative style of the Islanders. Sather had gone to Europe when he was coaching the Oilers in the WHA. He went to Finland and Sweden and he watched how midget hockey teams there practiced. He liked what he saw.

"They were teaching kids the fundamentals of the game," Sather recalled. "But they were also teaching them about switching lanes and creating open ice. " He saw defensemen jumping up into the play. It was a style that demanded creativeness and Sather knew he had one of the most creative players in the game—a slender kid from Brantford, Ontario, named Wayne Gretzky.

"I knew he was probably the most creative player who had skated in the NHL. He had tremendous peripheral vision," said Sather.

To emulate what he had seen in Europe, Sather needed players who could skate. And that's who he went after. Soon, the Oilers would have the likes of Jari Kurri, Glenn Anderson, Paul Coffey joining Gretzky and Mark Messier, a tough-as-nails forward with blazing speed. The team also found a great goaltender in Grant Fuhr. And they would need him. The Oilers had a high-octane offense. Defense was something they didn't pay as much attention to. The Oilers' European-style of play, which highlighted European players like Kurri, Esa Tikkanen, Jaroslav Pouzar, Reijo

Ruotsalainen and others, opened up the eyes of other NHL teams to the talent pool that existed overseas.

While great players like Toronto's Borje Salming had earlier proved that Europeans could not only play but thrive in the NHL, it would be the success of the Oilers and, earlier, the WHA's Winnipeg Jets that would up the stock of European players.

"The European players were highly skilled," said Sather. "And just as tough as we were." On May 19, 1984, in only their fifth NHL season, the Oilers captured the Stanley Cup for the first time. Edmonton defeated the defending champion Islanders 5–2 in game five to clinch the series. The torch had been passed from one dynasty to another. And the Oilers would dominate the rest of the decade.

"Our skill level was probably the biggest thing that made us so tough," Mark Messier remembered of those Oiler teams. "We forced all the teams to find better skilled players to be able to compete. Consequently, the ability and skill level of the entire league rose." Messier says the foundation of the Oilers was a special group of players that could play the game on anyone's terms.

"I think that was the biggest facet of that team," Messier said. "If you wanted to play it in the alley we could play it there. If you wanted to play it in the streets, we could play a fast, wide-open game. If you wanted tight-checking, we could beat you there. We could beat you at any game." Harry Neale, former NHL coach and general manager, had the unenviable task of facing the Oilers in the league's Smythe Division. He was coach of the Vancouver Canucks.

"They forced other teams, certainly in our division, into coping with their style," said Neale. "You weren't going to beat them if you were a slow-footed, checking team." Neale said the Oilers were especially deadly when teams were four on four. With Gretzky and Kurri on the ice and Paul Coffey on defense, Neale said, they could make the other team's four players look like minor-leaguers. Neale said when the league, in 1985, changed the rule concerning coincidental minors so teams would remain five aside and would no longer play with only four players, he referred to it as the Edmonton Oiler rule.

"I always said they changed the rule because the Oilers were scoring so many goals in four-on-four situations," Neale observed.

The key to the Oilers, however, was the incomparable talents of its captain, Wayne Gretzky.

"Gretzky terrified you," said Neale.

Gretzky's coach agreed.

"Wayne was really the main piece of the whole puzzle," said Sather. "He was such a great player he made the players around him better and they all developed from his confidence and the way he could play the game." Sather said it all started from practice. "Wayne never had a bad practice in 11 years." Gretzky would make his mark in the NHL right from the start. On a February night in 1980, he would tie the NHL record for most assists in one game with seven. His legend would grow from there. Gretzky, of course, would shatter and own endless NHL records.

As prolific a scorer as he was, Gretzky's greatest asset was his ability to set up others. He did things with the puck defenders never saw before. He would park himself behind an opponent's net and the moment a defender made a move, Gretzky seemed to find a teammate who was open. His position behind the net would become known as "Gretzky's office." He was a rare player who could take over a game himself. He was often double-shifted by his coach and

would play half the game. He was never the fastest player but he never had to be, so shifty were his moves.

The Oilers would win a second Cup in 1985, beating the Philadelphia Flyers in five games. Gretzky would win the Conn Smythe Trophy as the most valuable playoff performer. The Oilers looked like they might own the Cup forever. But they would falter the following year, enabling the Montreal Canadiens to win their 23rd Stanley Cup title behind the brilliant goaltending of a 20-year-old from Quebec named Patrick Roy. It would be the stunning debut of one of the game's great pressure goaltenders.

But the Oilers would reclaim hockey's greatest prize the next two seasons, beating the Flyers again in 1987 and the Boston Bruins the following year.

However, cracks were beginning to show in the great Oiler dynasty. The team's enormous success had driven up the value of its star players. Oiler owner Peter Pocklington was beginning to feel squeezed financially as the costs of doing business in the league began to soar. In November of 1987, the Oilers traded Paul Coffey to the Pittsburgh Penguins in a seven-player deal. It would set the stage for the most shocking trade in NHL history the following year.

On August 9, 1988, a sobbing Wayne Gretzky announced he was being traded to the Los Angeles Kings. Two other Oilers, Mike Krushelnyski and Marty McSorley would join him. In return, the Oilers got Jimmy Carson and Martin Gelinas plus L.A.'s first round picks in 1989, 1991 and 1993. Plus $15 million.

The move shocked a nation. Gretzky was a national hero in Canada and the thought of losing such a treasure seemed like heresy. Pocklington was vilified in his own city. Fans wanted to blame anybody, including Gretzky's new wife, actress Janet Jones, for luring him to the bright lights of Hollywood.

The trade would have profound ramifications on the NHL. First, Gretzky would become a glamorous spokesman for the game in the United States where someone of his stature was needed to sell the game. Almost overnight, Gretzky made hockey cool in sunny California. Some of Hollywood's biggest stars came to see him play.

There is little question that Gretzky's move precipitated the eventual expansion of the NHL game into several U.S. markets. In California, where Gretzky landed, franchises would later spring up in San Jose and Anaheim.

Beyond the impact Gretzky would have in the U.S., the trade would forever change the landscape of team-player relations. If Wayne Gretzky could be traded, then anyone could be traded.

"Once Wayne Gretzky got traded it changed everything," said Harry Neale. "Before you traded to make your team better. Now, teams were trading for economic reasons. And that's what the trade really highlighted; how the economics of hockey were changing." Once in L.A., Gretzky was told by the Kings' flamboyant owner Bruce McNall to write his own cheque. Gretzky would get close to $2 million a year, plus bonuses. It would set a new standard by which other players would want to be paid.

The Oilers would feel Gretzky's absence immediately. While still a strong team, The Great One's departure would be too much to handle the following season. The Calgary Flames would capture the Cup in 1989 and one of hockey's most enduring personalities, Lanny McDonald, would sip from the silver chalice for the first time in a long and distinguished career.

The Oilers, however, would bounce back and grab glory

one more time. It would be their most unlikely Cup victory and perhaps, in many ways, the most gratifying. In 1990, Mark Messier, now wearing the captain's "C" would lead his team to the Cup, beating the Boston Bruins in five games. It would be the final curtain call for one of the game's greatest dynasties. The economics of hockey would eventually force the Oilers to lose Messier, Anderson, Kurri and Fuhr. Only the team photos outside the Edmonton dressing would remain to remind future players of the past greatness that once occupied the room.

The Oilers, despite finishing below .500 in their first two seasons in the NHL, would accumulate the best overall record during the years 1979–80 to 1988–89. The Oilers racked up 996 points and a .623 winning percentage, just fractionally ahead of the Philadelphia Flyers.

While Gretzky would get most of the spotlight in the 1980s, he would eventually share center-stage with an emerging superstar in Pittsburgh.

Mario Lemieux became Pittsburgh's first pick, the top choice overall, in the 1984 Entry Draft. The lanky and stylish centre from the Laval Voisins of the Quebec Major Junior Hockey League had been touted by everyone as a sure-fire franchise player. He didn't disappoint.

In his first season, Lemieux reached the 100-point plateau. In 1987-88, he would stop Gretzky's string of eight consecutive MVP awards by winning the Hart Trophy. Pittsburgh's number 66 would also top Gretzky in the race for the Art Ross Trophy, finishing with 168 points, 19 more than number 99.

Lemieux and Gretzky weren't always on opposite sides of the ice. In 1987, the two joined forces for their country in the Canada Cup tournament. As expected Canada and the Soviet Union met in the final. The teams had split the first two games of the three-game series by identical scores of 6–5. In game three, the score was tied 5–5 in the dying minutes of regulation time when Gretzky broke down the left side of the ice with Lemieux trailing. Number 99 would wait until the last possible instant, drawing the Russian defenders toward him, before dropping a pass to Lemieux who snapped a shot to the top corner of the net, allowing Canada to win by the now-familiar score of 6–5. It may have been the second-greatest moment in the history of Canada and Russia's hockey rivalry, falling only in the shadow of Paul Henderson's goal in 1972.

Many felt Lemieux's game winner ignited him, pushed him to reach greater heights in hockey. If there was one frustration with Lemieux, it was that he didn't seem to possess the same passion for the game as Gretzky. But his skills were undeniably magnificent, enabling him to lead the Penguins to back-to-back Stanley Cup triumphs in 1991 and 1992.

Several tournaments and exhibition series with teams from the Soviet Union and other European hockey powers took place in the 1980s utilizing a variety of formats. The second edition of the six-nation Canada Cup was played in 1981, with the Soviets defeating Canada 8–1 in the championship game. Additional Canada Cup tournaments were played in 1984, 1987 (described above) and 1991 with Team Canada winning all three. Significantly, by 1991 Canada's final series opponent was not the Soviet Union but the United States.

Soviet teams and NHL clubs would stage a number of meetings throughout the 1980s. Central Red Army and Dynamo Moscow came over to play NHL teams in the 1979–80 season. The NHL teams won four of the nine games. In 1982–83, a Soviet all-star team played six NHL clubs, losing only to Edmonton and Calgary. The Central Red Army and Dynamo Moscow returned in 1985–86 and won eight out of 10 meetings with NHL teams.

Rendez-Vous 87 was played at Le Colisee in Quebec City, pitting the NHL All-Stars against the Soviet Nationals. The NHLers took the first game 4–3 but the Soviets won the second 5–3 with Valeri Kamensky starring for the Soviets. Additional Super Series were staged in 1988–89 and 1989–90 and 1990–91. Fifty-six games were played in all, with NHL teams winning 21 and Soviet clubs 29. Six games were tied.

NHL clubs also paid preseason visits to the Soviet Union. The Calgary Flames and Washington Capitals each played four Soviet opponents in September of 1989. The Minnesota North Stars and Montreal Canadiens played a similar schedule of games one year later.

The NHL would undergo a noticeable change in the demographic makeup of its players in the 1980s. The percentage of Canadian-born players, 82.1 percent in 1979–80, slipped to 75.5 percent by decade's end. The difference was made up in almost equal numbers by U.S.-born and European players. The decade also saw a dramatic increase in U.S. college and U.S. high school players selected in the annual NHL Entry Draft. Interest in U.S. hockey increased, particularly, after that country's upset gold medal at the 1980 Winter Olympics in Lake Placid. Several players on the team would have distinguished NHL careers. More importantly, the high-profile victory had a huge impact on the number of American children playing the game.

Soviet journeyman Sergei Priakhin became the first product of the Soviet hockey system permitted to join an NHL club when he signed a contract with the Calgary Flames in 1988–89. Beginning in 1989–90, top Soviet players like Sergei Makarov, Alexander Mogilny and Viacheslav Fetisov appeared in the NHL with many others to follow.

Several rule changes were introduced throughout the 1980s. By decade's end the league responded to growing concern about players being checked into the boards in an unsafe manner. The league ruled that any player who received a major penalty for boarding that resulted in an injury to the head or face of an opponent, also received an automatic game misconduct. Any player who incurred a total of two game misconduct penalties for boarding would be suspended for one game.

In 1982, rosters were expanded to 18 skaters plus two goaltenders from 17 skaters and two goaltenders. In 1983, a five-minute sudden-death overtime period was instituted.

Overall and average attendance at National Hockey League games rose to record levels throughout the 1980s. In 1979–80, the average league attendance was 12,747. By the end of the decade, average attendance had climbed to 14,908.

The 1980s would be a period of consolidation for the NHL—Atlanta's move to Calgary was the only franchise shift of the decade—but by the beginning of the 1990s, the league was poised for change. An additional team was added in 1991–92 when San Jose entered the league. Ottawa and Tampa Bay joined as expansion franchises in 1992–93 with Florida and Anaheim making the NHL into a 26-team circuit the following season.

Off the ice, criticism of NHL president John Ziegler's management style mounted. During the 1988 playoffs New Jersey Devils coach Jim Schoenfeld was suspended for clashing with referee Don Koharski after a game. When the

Devils obtained a temporary restraining order to overturn Schoenfeld's suspension, the referee and linesmen scheduled to work the next game refused to take the ice. The league found substitute officials and, after a lengthy delay the game was played that same Sunday evening.

The substitute referee had his own striped shirt but the new linesmen were forced to work the first period in oversized yellow practice jerseys. The officials did a good job, but after this "mini-crisis" media coverage came to revolve around the fact that Ziegler was not available to help resolve the issue. When added to an existing perception that he was aloof, this unfortunate incident—known as "Yellow Sunday"—strengthened growing opposition to Ziegler's regime among some members of the league's Board of Governors.

Fundamental changes also were under way at the NHL Players' Association which, since its inception, had been dominated by the personality and actions of its executive director Alan Eagleson. By the end of the 1980s many players had come to believe that Eagleson was too close to NHL club owners and accordingly was not acting in the players' best interests.

His involvements as an individual player agent and as the organizer of the Canada Cup international tournament placed him in what many felt were unacceptable conflicts of interest. These fears would later be realized when Eagleson was convicted on fraud charges in Boston and Toronto courtrooms in January of 1998.

In September 1990, a Michigan lawyer and player agent by the name of Bob Goodenow was brought aboard the NHLPA and after a two-year transition period, took over as Executive Director on January 1, 1992. His mandate was to revamp the operation.

"There was an association in name but not in operation," Goodenow said recently.

It wouldn't take long for NHL owners to realize they were now dealing with a new NHL Players' Association that was run along completely different lines than the one Eagleson had been operating.

In April of 1992, just four months after assuming control, Goodenow led the first league-wide players' strike in NHL history. As what would have been the final days of the regular season ticked by, the strike threatened the Stanley Cup playoffs.

The labor dispute lasted 10 days before a settlement was reached. The players acquired some improved free agency provisions and greater control over licensing of their likenesses. The players had served notice they were to be taken seriously by the owners.

"That was a major moment," said Goodenow. "The players were committed to getting the respect of the owners which they didn't feel they had before. I don't think the owners took the players seriously and it wasn't until the strike that they understood the players were serious." Goodenow would lead the players in other battles. It was clear that the NHL was much different than it was in 1979–80.

John Ziegler was replaced as league president by Gil Stein in 1992. A new office of the commissioner would soon be created with Gary Bettman elected to lead the NHL into a new era.

THE WORLD'S BEST
1992–93 TO 1998–99

Cammy Clark

TAMPA BAY LIGHTNING GENERAL MANAGER Phil Esposito sat in a Russian Orthodox Church in St. Petersburg, Florida, unable to understand most of the ceremony. But he got the gist of it. His middle daughter Carrie was marrying one of his right wingers, Russian Alexander Selivanov, who would soon be nicknamed "Son-in-law-ov."

"If this had happened 20 years ago, I would have disowned her," Esposito said in his matter-of-fact manner that has yet to mellow.

But good thing for Son-in-law-ov that it wasn't 1972 anymore, when Esposito said he would "have killed a Russian to win" the famous Summit Series. With the end of the Cold War, Russia no longer was "the Evil Empire" to North Americans. Selivanov didn't have to defect to leave his native land. He simply bought a plane ticket and within two years he was taking home an annual salary of $800,000, about double the highest salary Esposito ever received en route to the Hall of Fame with credentials that included 717 career goals, two Hart Trophy wins and two Stanley Cup championships.

Esposito, the father, was happy his daughter wouldn't be asking for money anymore. Esposito, the general manager, cringed at the salary he was paying Selivanov, who to that point hadn't won anything more than Carrie's heart.

Welcome to the new era of the NHL, when Russians became regulars, salaries skyrocketed, fabled arenas made way for state-of-the-art stadiums with luxury boxes, pucks were changed to blue dots on TV, two Canadian teams relocated, "zero tolerance" became a catch phrase, NHL players went to the Winter Olympics en masse, Brett Hull learned to backcheck and Wayne Gretzky no longer was the only hockey player people recognized south of the Mason-Dixon Line.

The new era unofficially began in 1992, when the league realized it was time to get into the 20th century before the 21st century arrived. A leadership overhaul took place to make way for people who believed that hockey's status quo needed changing.

The NHL Players' Association was the first to change. Gone was longtime executive director Alan Eagleson, who had been looking out for himself more than the players he represented and ultimately would be convicted of fraud and lose his place in the Hockey Hall of Fame. His place was taken by strong-willed Bob Goodenow. When the players went on strike for the first time in NHL history in the spring of 1992, they were armed with a leader whose tricks did not include rolling over and playing dead.

The strike ended in time for the playoffs to be saved, but not in time to save longtime president John Ziegler from losing his job. He was replaced on an interim basis by Gil Stein, the NHL's vice president and general counsel. Stein believed that the league could be a much bigger force on the North American sports scene with greater marketing efforts. He also pushed for the NHL to go to the Winter Olympics. But Stein, who would later get embroiled in a controversy over his election to the Hockey Hall of Fame, lobbied hardest for himself. He desperately wanted to become the first commissioner of the NHL but was seen to

be part of the old regime. It was time for new blood and, after considering several candidates, the NHL's Board of Governors elected NBA senior vice president Gary Bettman to superintend the league through what would prove to be a major growth spurt.

"In hindsight, he's exactly what we needed," longtime Boston Bruins executive Harry Sinden told the *Boston Globe* in 1996. "We couldn't have had a better person at the right time, in the right place. We got someone with energy, with knowledge, a guy who is current, upscale, vibrant— and someone who wasn't locked into our stupid traditions."

The days of croquet matches in period costumes after Board of Governors meetings in Florida were over. "When Gary came in, he was all business," former Tampa Bay Lightning governor David LeFevre said. "He was organized and right from the beginning everyone knew he was running the show."

Bettman, who had been a top executive at the NBA during its tremendous growth period of the 1980s, did not take the job until he had assurances from the league he would have power to make decisions on his own. The Board of Governors gave him the authority. Cumbersome league committees were eliminated as most of the business of the NHL was conducted out of league offices.

The NHL was "sort of sleepy in marketing themselves," said Tony Ponturo, vice president of corporate media and sports marketing for Anheuser-Busch. "We got excited about the new attitude of Bettman and his people. They offered all the ingredients in the pot, with the potential for big growth for a reasonable price. Plus we had a unique situation. Bud Ice was a natural fit with the Ice name."

Brett Hull, in his pre-backchecking days, described the NHL's previous efforts to sell the game by evoking the name of the game's top player: "Until now, the league's idea of marketing was Wayne, Wayne and more Wayne."

Increased exposure for the NHL was part of the rationale behind the granting of expansion franchises that took place before Bettman took over in 1993. Two new franchises— the Tampa Bay Lightning and Ottawa Senators—began play in the fall of 1992. Tampa represented a new market for the NHL. Ottawa marked the return of the league to a city where it had last fielded a team in 1933–34. Two other expansion franchises had been awarded one day before Bettman was elected: the Disney-owned Mighty Ducks of Anaheim and the Blockbuster-owned Florida Panthers.

The addition of four new franchises in important markets helped the NHL land its first U.S. network television contract in 20 years, with Fox-TV. The NHL also had heavy commitments on cable with ESPN and ESPN2. More games on more television outlets greatly increased viewers' options, though ratings numbers themselves often have shown little growth. At the same time, the NHL's presence on Hockey Night in Canada increased.

It didn't take long for Bettman to win over many who were skeptical of his approach to the business of the NHL.

"Bettman has advanced the league 10 years in the year and a half he's been here," Edmonton Oilers owner Peter Pocklington said in 1994. "He's brought energy, vision, leadership and a sense of how to make the business work."

The Bettman regime also has had its share of detractors. Many Canadians aren't happy that two Canadian-based teams—Quebec and Winnipeg—have moved to the United States. The 1998 proposal that more tax dollars or tax breaks should go to Canadian teams to help them remain competitive received mixed reviews in Canada as well.

Bettman took his share of criticism during the NHL's lockout of its players that resulted in the 1994–95 regular season being reduced to 48 games. The lockout came at an unfortunate time for the NHL. The New York Rangers, playing in the number one media market, had won their first Stanley Cup since 1940 after a thrilling seven-game Stanley Cup final series win over the Vancouver Canucks. But any audience-building momentum created by the Rangers compelling victory was halted in its tracks when the NHL shut its doors on October 1, 1994. Play was suspended for 103 days while the players and owners haggled over a luxury tax, salary caps and unrestricted free agency for a new collective bargaining agreement.

Christmas 1994 came and went with NHL players scattered throughout Europe. With the season on the verge of being canceled in January, Harry Sinden stated that the NHL's most recent proposal was, "our final, final, final, final final offer."

After 11th hour marathon negotiating sessions, a deal was struck as the players and owners approved a new CBA. One of the owners who opposed the deal was Marcel Aubut of the Quebec Nordiques whose franchise, in essence, had been handed a death sentence.

"I recognize that the majority of the industry can live with the agreement that was negotiated, but it is difficult to accept for a small market such as Quebec," he said.

"It would have been bad if we had lost a season," Bettman said. "I'm not happy we lost half a season. But we had to make a deal that was sensible." As it was, when play resumed on January 20, 1995, 468 games were lopped from the original 1994–95 regular-season schedule.

Expansion was the key to the overall growth of the NHL in the 1990s. Phil Esposito was part of the first new expansion wave in the early 1990s. Armed with nothing more than his smooth-talking charm and a plan that begged the question "Where's the beef?", he convinced the Board of Governors to grant an expansion franchise for the virgin hockey territory of Tampa Bay by promising what he knew the Board wanted to hear.

"Everybody thought I was nuts," Esposito said, but he set out to make believers of those who thought hockey would have as much chance in Florida as a female playing goal in the NHL. (Esposito tried this, too. Goaltender Manon Rheaume garnered plenty of publicity for the Lightning when she played one period in an exhibition game, but her real impact was in raising the profile of women's hockey.)

The Tampa Bay Hockey Group staged a preseason game in St. Petersburg between the Pittsburgh Penguins and Los Angeles Kings in the ThunderDome, a stadium built for a non-existent baseball team. An NHL record 25,581 people showed up. Two fights broke out in the stands. "I thought I was in New York," Esposito said.

"It would be good exposure for the league to play in Florida," said Wayne Gretzky, who played in that game for the Kings.

Hockey would show it could survive in Florida. The Lightning drew record crowds of 20,000-plus during their days in the ThunderDome. The Florida Panthers, who joined the league in 1993–94, are the team that brought you flying plastic rats and a storybook run to the Stanley Cup finals in only their third season.

But it became inevitable that some franchises in the smallest markets would be forced to relocate. With growth set against a backdrop of skyrocketing salaries, economics

forced the sale of the Quebec Nordiques to the Ascent Entertainment Group. Renamed and refinanced, the old Nordiques won the Stanley Cup in their first season as the Colorado Avalanche in Denver.

Winnipeg, despite a grassroots "Save the Jets" campaign, lost its team. New owners Richard Burke and Steven Gluckstern relocated the franchise to Arizona where it became the Phoenix Coyotes.

The Nordiques and Jets are both former WHA teams as are the Hartford Whalers who, in 1997–98, relocated to another exotic hockey market, North Carolina. Renamed the Carolina Hurricanes they began play in Greensboro as a new arena was being readied in Raleigh.

The Edmonton Oilers franchise is the only one of the four ex-WHA teams that joined the NHL in 1979–80 that has not been relocated, only after a prolonged campaign to save the team produced a community group of 35 investors to take over the club.

The NHL, which had only 21 teams as recently as 1991, will have 30 by the year 2000. The Nashville Predators begin play in 1998–99. Atlanta, home to the Flames before their move to Calgary in 1980, has acquired an expansion team called the Thrashers for the 1999–2000 season. Minneapolis-St. Paul, which lost its team in 1993 when the North Stars moved to Dallas, will also get a new team known as the Minnesota Wild and will begin play in 2000–01 alongside another new franchise, the Columbus (Ohio) Blue Jackets.

Many fear that the available pool of hockey talent will be significantly diluted by the addition of 125 or so more NHL jobs. But former Mighty Ducks of Anaheim coach Pierre Page disagrees. "We can expand because of the Europeans," he said. "We've gone from a redneck league to an international one."

The league has had a sprinkling of Swedes, Czechs and Finns for years, but the real influx didn't begin until the early 1990s, when players from Eastern Europe could come without having to defect.

Dave King was coach of the Calgary Flames when he said, "No one would argue that our game hasn't been improved by the Europeans. A person seeing his first game will invariably pick out a European player if you asked him to choose the best player in the game. That's because their skills are refined at such an early age."

The NHL's top three point scorers in 1997-98 were a Czech (Jaromir Jagr), a Swede (Peter Forsberg) and a Russian (Pavel Bure). The top two goal scorers were a Finn (Teemu Selanne) and a Slovak (Peter Bondra). In 1997–98, nearly a quarter of the NHL players (22.5 percent) came from outside North America, representing 16 countries. In the second round of the 1998 playoffs, 28% of the players still in contention for the Stanley Cup were Europeans.

In the Mighty Ducks locker room alone, six languages are spoken: English, French, Russian, Finnish, Sweden and Czech. "No other job you'd see that unless you were a U.N. ambassador," Ducks goalie Guy Hebert said.

The NHL has gone so international that the 48th All-Star Game in 1998 featured a new format: "North America" versus "The World."

"Somehow I think the World Team has more interest in the outcome, like they have something to prove," Pittsburgh coach Kevin Constantine said. "It has not always been easy for Europeans to come over here. I think it's a lot easier now. It's a lot more accepted now than it was 10 years ago. I think North American players felt the Europeans were probably taking their jobs. These Europeans had to suffer their fair share of ridicule."

The Europeans no longer have to worry about feeling inferior, especially after the 1998 Winter Olympics. In the first "Dream Team" Olympic tournament, the two favored teams, Canada and the United States, went home without a medal as the Czechs beat the Russians in the gold medal game and the Finns took the bronze.

Many branded the venture as a disaster, especially after disgruntled American players damaged their dorm rooms in the Olympic village, but Teemu Selanne said, "It was something unbelievable. I still think it was worth it. We've got to grow this game. The Olympics were good for hockey."

Selanne also was part of an historic series in Tokyo, Japan that opened the 1997–98 regular season. The Ducks and Vancouver Canucks split two games at Yoyogi Arena with the results counting in the standings. While the ice wasn't quite up to par, the venture was a big success as the 10,000-seat arena sold out in three hours with most tickets priced at $225.

During recent times, the league has also suffered its share of embarrassments. Bruce McNall, chairman of the NHL's Board of Governors and owner of the Los Angeles Kings was convicted of fraud and went to in jail. A little-known entrepreneur named John Spano came close to buying the New York Islanders before it was revealed that he had forged documents and wasn't creditworthy. There was Alan Eagleson's conviction for fraud in the U.S. and Canada. There was a mess in Tampa Bay, with absentee Japanese ownership eventually selling to Florida businessman Art Williams.

But through it all, Pierre Page said the NHL is still in it's "gold mine" phase in which the biggest winners appear to be the players. Their salaries have escalated, with no end in sight. Before Paul Kariya signed a two-year $14 million deal with the Mighty Ducks in December, 1997, teammate Guy Hebert said, "Paul is one of about five people who can write on a napkin how much he wants and get it. The rest of us would be shown the door."

Well, not exactly.

While almost every one of the other 650 or so NHL regulars certainly wouldn't be given the keys to the vault, the 1990s have been a lucrative time to be a player. All NHL players from pure scorers to enforcers, all-star goalies and third-line checking centers have benefited. The NHL has created numerous millionaires.

The average NHL salary was about $230,000 in 1992 and now it's well over $1 million and climbing. In 1996–97, there were 186 players making a million or more. The major reason for the escalation is "salary disclosure," according to Players' Association executive director Bob Goodenow. "It certainly wouldn't have happened under Al Eagleson. Some things had to change, no question. … At the end of the day, the objective of everyone who plays is to get paid in a way that reflects their value to the overall enterprise."

Brian Burke, former NHL senior vice president and director of hockey operations, said, "It's okay if salaries increase and the industry is healthy. Right now, hockey is riding a wave of popularity. But our revenues don't match up with football, baseball and basketball. I don't think salaries can continue to escalate."

The NHL also has shown growth through the substantial number of new arenas that have been constructed. Phil Esposito no longer can see hockey in two of the three are-

nas he once called home. Gone are Chicago Stadium and Boston Garden, rats and all.

The Montreal Forum, once known as the mecca of hockey, is no longer the home of the game's most successful franchise. But the feel of its legendary locker room was duplicated in the new building. No word if the ghost of Howie Morenz moved, too.

The Buffalo Memorial Auditorium, St. Louis Arena, Pacific Coliseum, Capital Centre and Spectrum no longer host the NHL. The Great Western Forum and Maple Leaf Gardens, the last of the "Original Six" buildings, are soon to be history, too.

During one of his last trips to Chicago Stadium, the Blackhawks' Hall of Fame goalie, Tony Esposito, took a piece of the cracked concrete as a souvenir. Gordie Howe kept a brick from Detroit's old Olympia and countless

hockey fans own pieces of the Montreal Forum, Boston Garden and other facilities where NHL clubs used to play.

The NHL doesn't expect to overtake the NBA, NFL or Major League Baseball anytime soon. But it is the most aggressive in going after new fans.

During the Bettman era, the NHL embarked on grassroots marketing efforts to reach boys and girls, aged six to 16 through street hockey and in-line hockey programs.

"We just want to be as good as we can be," Bettman said. "We're the league where the kids take the parents and not the parents taking he kids. And we have a lot of room for growth. When does a seven-year-old start getting control of the remote? Or buying his own tickets? We are now the sport of choice for seven-year-olds. Some day those kids are going to grow up and take their kids to games."

NHL FINAL STANDINGS AND TOP TEN SCORERS
1917–18 TO 1997-98

– Stanley Cup winner

1917-18

Team	GP	W	L	T	GF	GA	PTS
Montreal	22	13	9	0	115	84	26
*Toronto	22	13	9	0	108	109	26
Ottawa	22	9	13	0	102	114	18
**Mtl. Wanderers	6	1	5	0	17	35	2

** Montreal Arena burned down and Wanderers forced to withdraw. Canadiens and Toronto each counted a win for defaulted games.

Leading Scorers

Player	Club	GP	G	A	PTS
Malone, Joe	Montreal	20	44	4	48
Denneny, Cy	Ottawa	20	36	10	46
Noble, Reg	Toronto	20	30	10	40
Lalonde, Newsy	Montreal	14	23	7	30
Denneny, Corbett	Toronto	21	20	9	29
Cameron, Harry	Toronto	21	17	10	27
Pitre, Didier	Montreal	20	17	6	23
Gerard, Eddie	Ottawa	20	13	7	20
Darragh, Jack	Ottawa	18	14	5	19
Nighbor, Frank	Ottawa	10	11	8	19
Meeking, Harry	Toronto	21	10	9	19

1918-19

Team	GP	W	L	T	GF	GA	PTS
Ottawa	18	12	6	0	71	53	24
Montreal	18	10	8	0	88	78	20
Toronto	18	5	13	0	64	92	10

Leading Scorers

Player	Club	GP	G	A	PTS	PIM
Lalonde, Newsy	Montreal	17	23	10	33	42
Cleghorn, Odie	Montreal	18	21	6	27	33
Nighbor, Frank	Ottawa	18	18	9	27	27
Denneny, Cy	Ottawa	18	18	6	24	55
Pitre, Didier	Montreal	17	14	4	18	15
Skinner, Alf	Toronto	16	12	5	17	26
Cleghorn, Sprague	Ottawa	18	7	9	16	27
Cameron, Harry	Tor., Ott.	14	11	4	15	35
Darragh, Jack	Ottawa	14	11	4	15	30
Randall, Ken	Toronto	15	9	6	15	26

1919-20

Team	GP	W	L	T	GF	GA	PTS
*Ottawa	24	19	5	0	121	64	38
Montreal	24	13	11	0	129	113	26
Toronto	24	12	12	0	119	106	24
Quebec	24	4	20	0	91	177	8

Leading Scorers

Player	Club	GP	G	A	PTS	PIM
Malone, Joe	Quebec	24	39	10	49	12
Lalonde, Newsy	Montreal	23	37	9	46	34
Nighbor, Frank	Ottawa	23	26	15	41	18
Denneny, Corbett	Toronto	24	24	12	36	20
Darragh, Jack	Ottawa	23	22	14	36	22
Noble, Reg	Toronto	24	24	9	33	51
Arbour, Amos	Montreal	22	21	5	26	13
Wilson, Cully	Toronto	23	20	6	26	86
Pitre, Didier	Montreal	22	14	12	26	6
Broadbent, Punch	Ottawa	21	19	6	25	40

1920-21

Team	GP	W	L	T	GF	GA	PTS
Toronto	24	15	9	0	105	100	30
*Ottawa	24	14	10	0	97	75	28
Montreal	24	13	11	0	112	99	26
Hamilton	24	6	18	0	92	132	12

Leading Scorers

Player	Club	GP	G	A	PTS	PIM
Lalonde, Newsy	Montreal	24	32	11	43	36
Dye, Babe	Ham., Tor.	24	35	5	40	32
Denneny, Cy	Ottawa	24	34	5	39	10
Malone, Joe	Hamilton	20	28	9	37	6
Nighbor, Frank	Ottawa	24	19	10	29	10
Noble, Reg	Toronto	24	19	8	27	54
Cameron, Harry	Toronto	24	18	9	27	35
Prodgers, Goldie	Hamilton	24	18	9	27	8
Denneny, Corbett	Toronto	20	19	7	26	29
Darragh, Jack	Ottawa	24	11	15	26	20

1921-22

Team	GP	W	L	T	GF	GA	PTS
Ottawa	24	14	8	2	106	84	30
*Toronto	24	13	10	1	98	97	27
Montreal	24	12	11	1	88	94	25
Hamilton	24	7	17	0	88	105	14

Leading Scorers

Player	Club	GP	G	A	PTS	PIM
Broadbent, Punch	Ottawa	24	32	14	46	24
Denneny, Cy	Ottawa	22	27	12	39	18
Dye, Babe	Toronto	24	30	7	37	18
Malone, Joe	Hamilton	24	25	7	32	4
Cameron, Harry	Toronto	24	19	8	27	18
Denneny, Corbett	Toronto	24	19	7	26	28
Noble, Reg	Toronto	24	17	8	25	10
Cleghorn, Odie	Montreal	23	21	3	24	26
Cleghorn, Sprague	Montreal	24	17	7	24	63
Reise, Leo	Hamilton	24	9	14	23	8

1922-23

Team	GP	W	L	T	GF	GA	PTS
*Ottawa	24	14	9	1	77	54	29
Montreal	24	13	9	2	73	61	28
Toronto	24	13	10	1	82	88	27
Hamilton	24	6	18	0	81	110	12

Leading Scorers

Player	Club	GP	G	A	PTS	PIM
Dye, Babe	Toronto	22	26	11	37	19
Denneny, Cy	Ottawa	24	21	10	31	20
Adams, Jack	Toronto	23	19	9	28	42
Boucher, Billy	Montreal	24	23	4	27	52
Cleghorn, Odie	Montreal	24	19	7	26	14
Roach, Mickey	Hamilton	23	17	8	25	8
Boucher, George	Ottawa	23	15	9	24	44
Joliat, Aurel	Montreal	24	13	9	22	31
Noble, Reg	Toronto	24	12	10	22	41
Wilson, Cully	Hamilton	23	16	3	19	40

1923-24

Team	GP	W	L	T	GF	GA	PTS
Ottawa	24	16	8	0	74	54	32
*Montreal	24	13	11	0	59	48	26
Toronto	24	10	14	0	59	85	20
Hamilton	24	9	15	0	63	68	18

Leading Scorers

Player	Club	GP	G	A	PTS	PIM
Denneny, Cy	Ottawa	21	22	1	23	10
Boucher, Billy	Montreal	23	16	6	22	33
Joliat, Aurel	Montreal	24	15	5	20	19
Dye, Babe	Toronto	19	17	2	19	23
Boucher, George	Ottawa	21	14	5	19	28
Burch, Billy	Hamilton	24	16	2	18	4
Clancy, King	Ottawa	24	9	8	17	18
Adams, Jack	Toronto	22	13	3	16	49
Morenz, Howie	Montreal	24	13	3	16	20
Noble, Reg	Toronto	23	12	3	15	23

1924-25

Team	GP	W	L	T	GF	GA	PTS
Hamilton	30	19	10	1	90	60	39
Toronto	30	19	11	0	90	84	38
Montreal	30	17	11	2	93	56	36
Ottawa	30	17	12	1	83	66	35
Mtl. Maroons	30	9	19	2	45	65	20
Boston	30	6	24	0	49	119	12

Leading Scorers

Player	Club	GP	G	A	PTS	PIM
Dye, Babe	Toronto	29	38	6	44	41
Denneny, Cy	Ottawa	28	27	15	42	16
Joliat, Aurel	Montreal	24	29	11	40	85
Morenz, Howie	Montreal	30	27	7	34	31
Boucher, Billy	Montreal	30	18	13	31	92
Adams, Jack	Toronto	27	21	8	29	66
Burch, Billy	Hamilton	27	20	4	24	10
Green, Red	Hamilton	30	19	4	23	63
Herberts, Jimmy	Boston	30	17	5	22	50
Day, Hap	Toronto	26	10	12	22	27

1925-26

Team	GP	W	L	T	GF	GA	PTS
Ottawa	36	24	8	4	77	42	52
*Mtl. Maroons	36	20	11	5	91	73	45
Pittsburgh	36	19	16	1	82	70	39
Boston	36	17	15	4	92	85	38
NY Americans	36	12	20	4	68	89	28
Toronto	36	12	21	3	92	114	27
Montreal	36	11	24	1	79	108	23

Leading Scorers

Player	Club	GP	G	A	PTS	PIM
Stewart, Nels	Mtl. Maroons	36	34	8	42	119
Denneny, Cy	Ottawa	36	24	12	36	18
Cooper, Carson	Boston	36	28	3	31	10
Herberts, Jimmy	Boston	36	26	5	31	47
Morenz, Howie	Montreal	31	23	3	26	39
Adams, Jack	Toronto	36	21	5	26	52
Joliat, Aurel	Montreal	35	17	9	26	52
Burch, Billy	NY Americans	36	22	3	25	33
Smith, Hooley	Ottawa	28	16	9	25	53
Nighbor, Frank	Ottawa	35	12	13	25	40

1926-27

CANADIAN DIVISION

Team	GP	W	L	T	GF	GA	PTS
*Ottawa	44	30	10	4	86	69	64
Montreal	44	28	14	2	99	67	58
Mtl. Maroons	44	20	20	4	71	68	44
NY Americans	44	17	25	2	82	91	36
Toronto	44	15	24	5	79	94	35

AMERICAN DIVISION

Team	GP	W	L	T	GF	GA	PTS
New York	44	25	13	6	95	72	56
Boston	44	21	20	3	97	89	45
Chicago	44	19	22	3	115	116	41
Pittsburgh	44	15	26	3	79	108	33
Detroit	44	12	28	4	76	105	28

Leading Scorers

Player	Club	GP	G	A	PTS	PIM
Cook, Bill	New York	44	33	4	37	58
Irvin, Dick	Chicago	43	18	18	36	34
Morenz, Howie	Montreal	44	25	7	32	49
Fredrickson, Frank	Det., Bos.	41	18	13	31	46
Dye, Babe	Chicago	41	25	5	30	14
Bailey, Ace	Toronto	42	15	13	28	82
Boucher, Frank	New York	44	13	15	28	17
Burch, Billy	NY Americans	43	19	8	27	40
Oliver, Harry	Boston	42	18	6	24	17
Keats, Gordon	Bos., Det.	42	16	8	24	52

1927-28

CANADIAN DIVISION

Team	GP	W	L	T	GF	GA	PTS
Montreal	44	26	11	7	116	48	59
Mtl. Maroons	44	24	14	6	96	77	54
Ottawa	44	20	14	10	78	57	50
Toronto	44	18	18	8	89	88	44
NY Americans	44	11	27	6	63	128	28

AMERICAN DIVISION

Team	GP	W	L	T	GF	GA	PTS
Boston	44	20	13	11	77	70	51
*New York	44	19	16	9	94	79	47
Pittsburgh	44	19	17	8	67	76	46
Detroit	44	19	19	6	88	79	44
Chicago	44	7	34	3	68	134	17

Leading Scorers

Player	Club	GP	G	A	PTS	PIM
Morenz, Howie	Montreal	43	33	18	51	66
Joliat, Aurel	Montreal	44	28	11	39	105
Boucher, Frank	New York	44	23	12	35	15
Hay, George	Detroit	42	22	13	35	20
Stewart, Nels	Mtl. Maroons	41	27	7	34	104
Gagne, Art	Montreal	44	20	10	30	75
Cook, Fred	New York	44	14	14	28	45
Carson, Bill	Toronto	32	20	6	26	36
Finnigan, Frank	Ottawa	38	20	5	25	34
Cook, Bill	New York	43	18	6	24	42
Keats, Gordon	Det., Chi.	38	14	10	24	60

1928-29

CANADIAN DIVISION

Team	GP	W	L	T	GF	GA	PTS
Montreal	44	22	7	15	71	43	59
NY Americans	44	19	13	12	53	53	50
Toronto	44	21	18	5	85	69	47
Ottawa	44	14	17	13	54	67	41
Mtl. Maroons	44	15	20	9	67	65	39

AMERICAN DIVISION

Team	GP	W	L	T	GF	GA	PTS
*Boston	44	26	13	5	89	52	57
New York	44	21	13	10	72	65	52
Detroit	44	19	16	9	72	63	47
Pittsburgh	44	9	27	8	46	80	26
Chicago	44	7	29	8	33	85	22

Leading Scorers

Player	Club	GP	G	A	PTS	PIM
Bailey, Ace	Toronto	44	22	10	32	78
Stewart, Nels	Mtl. Maroons	44	21	8	29	74
Cooper, Carson	Detroit	43	18	9	27	14
Morenz, Howie	Montreal	42	17	10	27	47
Blair, Andy	Toronto	44	12	15	27	41
Boucher, Frank	New York	44	10	16	26	8
Oliver, Harry	Boston	43	17	6	23	24
Cook, Bill	New York	43	15	8	23	41
Ward, Jimmy	Mtl. Maroons	43	14	8	22	46

Seven players tied with 19 points

1929-30

CANADIAN DIVISION

Team	GP	W	L	T	GF	GA	PTS
Mtl. Maroons	44	23	16	5	141	114	51
*Montreal	44	21	14	9	142	114	51
Ottawa	44	21	15	8	138	118	50
Toronto	44	17	21	6	116	124	40
NY Americans	44	14	25	5	113	161	33

AMERICAN DIVISION

Team	GP	W	L	T	GF	GA	PTS
Boston	44	38	5	1	179	98	77
Chicago	44	21	18	5	117	111	47
New York	44	17	17	10	136	143	44
Detroit	44	14	24	6	117	133	34
Pittsburgh	44	5	36	3	102	185	13

Leading Scorers

Player	Club	GP	G	A	PTS	PIM
Weiland, Cooney	Boston	44	43	30	73	27
Boucher, Frank	New York	42	26	36	62	16
Clapper, Dit	Boston	44	41	20	61	48
Cook, Bill	New York	44	29	30	59	56
Kilrea, Hec	Ottawa	44	36	22	58	72
Stewart, Nels	Mtl. Maroons	44	39	16	55	81
Morenz, Howie	Montreal	44	40	10	50	72
Himes, Norm	NY Americans	44	28	22	50	15
Lamb, Joe	Ottawa	44	29	20	49	119
Gainor, Norm	Boston	42	18	31	49	39

1930-31

CANADIAN DIVISION

Team	GP	W	L	T	GF	GA	PTS
*Montreal	44	26	10	8	129	89	60
Toronto	44	22	13	9	118	99	53
Mtl. Maroons	44	20	18	6	105	106	46
NY Americans	44	18	16	10	76	74	46
Ottawa	44	10	30	4	91	142	24

AMERICAN DIVISION

Team	GP	W	L	T	GF	GA	PTS
Boston	44	28	10	6	143	90	62
Chicago	44	24	17	3	108	78	51
New York	44	19	16	9	106	87	47
Detroit	44	16	21	7	102	105	39
Philadelphia	44	4	36	4	76	184	12

Leading Scorers

Player	Club	GP	G	A	PTS	PIM
Morenz, Howie	Montreal	39	28	23	51	49
Goodfellow, Ebbie	Detroit	44	25	23	48	32
Conacher, Charlie	Toronto	37	31	12	43	78
Cook, Bill	New York	43	30	12	42	39
Bailey, Ace	Toronto	40	23	19	42	46
Primeau, Joe	Toronto	38	9	32	41	18
Stewart, Nels	Mtl. Maroons	42	25	14	39	75
Boucher, Frank	New York	44	12	27	39	20
Weiland, Cooney	Boston	44	25	13	38	14
Cook, Fred	New York	44	18	17	35	72
Joliat, Aurel	Montreal	43	13	22	35	73

1931-32

CANADIAN DIVISION

Team	GP	W	L	T	GF	GA	PTS
Montreal	48	25	16	7	128	111	57
*Toronto	48	23	18	7	155	127	53
Mtl. Maroons	48	19	22	7	142	139	45
NY Americans	48	16	24	8	95	142	40

AMERICAN DIVISION

Team	GP	W	L	T	GF	GA	PTS
New York	48	23	17	8	134	112	54
Chicago	48	18	19	11	86	101	47
Detroit	48	18	20	10	95	108	46
Boston	48	15	21	12	122	117	42

Leading Scorers

Player	Club	GP	G	A	PTS	PIM
Jackson, Harvey	Toronto	48	28	25	53	63
Primeau, Joe	Toronto	46	13	37	50	25
Morenz, Howie	Montreal	48	24	25	49	46
Conacher, Charlie	Toronto	44	34	14	48	66
Cook, Bill	New York	48	34	14	48	33
Trottier, Dave	Mtl. Maroons	48	26	18	44	94
Smith, Reg	Mtl. Maroons	43	11	33	44	49
Siebert, Albert	Mtl. Maroons	48	21	18	39	64
Clapper, Dit	Boston	48	17	22	39	21
Joliat, Aurel	Montreal	48	15	24	39	46

1932-33

CANADIAN DIVISION

Team	GP	W	L	T	GF	GA	PTS
Toronto	48	24	18	6	119	111	54
Mtl. Maroons	48	22	20	6	135	119	50
Montreal	48	18	25	5	92	115	41
NY Americans	48	15	22	11	91	118	41
Ottawa	48	11	27	10	88	131	32

AMERICAN DIVISION

Team	GP	W	L	T	GF	GA	PTS
Boston	48	25	15	8	124	88	58
Detroit	48	25	15	8	111	93	58
*New York	48	23	17	8	135	107	54
Chicago	48	16	20	12	88	101	44

Leading Scorers

Player	Club	GP	G	A	PTS	PIM
Cook, Bill	New York	48	28	22	50	51
Jackson, Harvey	Toronto	48	27	17	44	43
Northcott, Baldy	Mtl. Maroons	48	22	21	43	30
Smith, Reg	Mtl. Maroons	48	20	21	41	66
Haynes, Paul	Mtl. Maroons	48	16	25	41	18
Joliat, Aurel	Montreal	48	18	21	39	53
Barry, Marty	Boston	48	24	13	37	40
Cook, Fred	New York	48	22	15	37	35
Stewart, Nels	Boston	47	18	18	36	62
Morenz, Howie	Montreal	46	14	21	35	32
Gagnon, Johnny	Montreal	48	12	23	35	64
Shore, Eddie	Boston	48	8	27	35	102
Boucher, Frank	New York	47	7	28	35	4

1933-34

CANADIAN DIVISION

Team	GP	W	L	T	GF	GA	PTS
Toronto	48	26	13	9	174	119	61
Montreal	48	22	20	6	99	101	50
Mtl. Maroons	48	19	18	11	117	122	49
NY Americans	48	15	23	10	104	132	40
Ottawa	48	13	29	6	115	143	32

AMERICAN DIVISION

Team	GP	W	L	T	GF	GA	PTS
Detroit	48	24	14	10	113	98	58
*Chicago	48	20	17	11	88	83	51
New York	48	21	19	8	120	113	50
Boston	48	18	25	5	111	130	41

Leading Scorers

Player	Club	GP	G	A	PTS	PIM
Conacher, Charlie	Toronto	42	32	20	52	38
Primeau, Joe	Toronto	45	14	32	46	8
Boucher, Frank	New York	48	14	30	44	4
Barry, Marty	Boston	48	27	12	39	12
Dillon, Cecil	New York	48	13	26	39	10
Stewart, Nels	Boston	48	21	17	38	68
Jackson, Harvey	Toronto	38	20	18	38	38
Joliat, Aurel	Montreal	48	22	15	37	27
Smith, Reg	Mtl. Maroons	47	18	19	37	58
Thompson, Paul	Chicago	48	20	16	36	17

1934-35

CANADIAN DIVISION

Team	GP	W	L	T	GF	GA	PTS
Toronto	48	30	14	4	157	111	64
*Mtl. Maroons	48	24	19	5	123	92	53
Montreal	48	19	23	6	110	145	44
NY Americans	48	12	27	9	100	142	33
St. Louis	48	11	31	6	86	144	28

AMERICAN DIVISION

Team	GP	W	L	T	GF	GA	PTS
Boston	48	26	16	6	129	112	58
Chicago	48	26	17	5	118	88	57
New York	48	22	20	6	137	139	50
Detroit	48	19	22	7	127	114	45

Leading Scorers

Player	Club	GP	G	A	PTS	PIM
Conacher, Charlie	Toronto	47	36	21	57	24
Howe, Syd	St.L., Det.	50	22	25	47	34
Aurie, Larry	Detroit	48	17	29	46	24
Boucher, Frank	New York	48	13	32	45	2
Jackson, Harvey	Toronto	42	22	22	44	27
Lewis, Herb	Detroit	47	16	27	43	26
Chapman, Art	NY Americans	47	9	34	43	4
Barry, Marty	Boston	48	20	20	40	33
Schriner, Sweeney	NY Americans	48	18	22	40	6
Stewart, Nels	Boston	47	21	18	39	45
Thompson, Paul	Chicago	48	16	23	39	20

1935-36

CANADIAN DIVISION

Team	GP	W	L	T	GF	GA	PTS
Mtl. Maroons	48	22	16	10	114	106	54
Toronto	48	23	19	6	126	106	52
NY Americans	48	16	25	7	109	122	39
Montreal	48	11	26	11	82	123	33

AMERICAN DIVISION

Team	GP	W	L	T	GF	GA	PTS
*Detroit	48	24	16	8	124	103	56
Boston	48	22	20	6	92	83	50
Chicago	48	21	19	8	93	92	50
New York	48	19	17	12	91	96	50

Leading Scorers

Player	Club	GP	G	A	PTS	PIM
Schriner, Sweeney	NY Americans	48	19	26	45	8
Barry, Marty	Detroit	48	21	19	40	16
Thompson, Paul	Chicago	45	17	23	40	19
Thoms, Bill	Toronto	48	23	15	38	29
Conacher, Charlie	Toronto	44	23	15	38	74
Smith, Reg	Mtl. Maroons	47	19	19	38	75
Romnes, Doc	Chicago	48	13	25	38	6
Chapman, Art	NY Americans	47	10	28	38	14
Lewis, Herb	Detroit	45	14	23	37	25
Northcott, Baldy	Mtl. Maroons	48	15	21	36	41

1936-37

CANADIAN DIVISION

Team	GP	W	L	T	GF	GA	PTS
Montreal	48	24	18	6	115	111	54
Mtl. Maroons	48	22	17	9	126	110	53
Toronto	48	22	21	5	119	115	49
NY Americans	48	15	29	4	122	161	34

AMERICAN DIVISION

Team	GP	W	L	T	GF	GA	PTS
*Detroit	48	25	14	9	128	102	59
Boston	48	23	18	7	120	110	53
New York	48	19	20	9	117	106	47
Chicago	48	14	27	7	99	131	35

Leading Scorers

Player	Club	GP	G	A	PTS	PIM
Schriner, Sweeney	NY Americans	48	21	25	46	17
Apps, Syl	Toronto	48	16	29	45	10
Barry, Marty	Detroit	48	17	27	44	6
Aurie, Larry	Detroit	45	23	20	43	20
Jackson, Harvey	Toronto	46	21	19	40	12
Gagnon, Johnny	Montreal	48	20	16	36	38
Gracie, Bob	Mtl. Maroons	47	11	25	36	18
Stewart, Nels	Bos., NYA	43	23	12	35	37
Thompson, Paul	Chicago	47	17	18	35	28
Cowley, Bill	Boston	46	13	22	35	4

1937-38

CANADIAN DIVISION

Team	GP	W	L	T	GF	GA	PTS
Toronto	48	24	15	9	151	127	57
NY Americans	48	19	18	11	110	111	49
Montreal	48	18	17	13	123	128	49
Mtl. Maroons	48	12	30	6	101	149	30

AMERICAN DIVISION

Team	GP	W	L	T	GF	GA	PTS
Boston	48	30	11	7	142	89	67
New York	48	27	15	6	149	96	60
*Chicago	48	14	25	9	97	139	37
Detroit	48	12	25	11	99	133	35

Leading Scorers

Player	Club	GP	G	A	PTS	PIM
Drillon, Gord	Toronto	48	26	26	52	4
Apps, Syl	Toronto	47	21	29	50	9
Thompson, Paul	Chicago	48	22	22	44	14
Mantha, Georges	Montreal	47	23	19	42	12
Dillon, Cecil	New York	48	21	18	39	6
Cowley, Bill	Boston	48	17	22	39	8
Schriner, Sweeney	NY Americans	49	21	17	38	22
Thoms, Bill	Toronto	48	14	24	38	14
Smith, Clint	New York	48	14	23	37	0
Stewart, Nels	NY Americans	48	19	17	36	29
Colville, Neil	New York	45	17	19	36	11

1938-39

Team	GP	W	L	T	GF	GA	PTS
*Boston	48	36	10	2	156	76	74
New York	48	26	16	6	149	105	58
Toronto	48	19	20	9	114	107	47
NY Americans	48	17	21	10	119	157	44
Detroit	48	18	24	6	107	128	42
Montreal	48	15	24	9	115	146	39
Chicago	48	12	28	8	91	132	32

Leading Scorers

Player	Club	GP	G	A	PTS	PIM
Blake, Hector	Montreal	48	24	23	47	10
Schriner, Sweeney	NY Americans	48	13	31	44	20
Cowley, Bill	Boston	34	8	34	42	2
Smith, Clint	New York	48	21	20	41	2
Barry, Marty	Detroit	48	13	28	41	4
Apps, Syl	Toronto	44	15	25	40	4
Anderson, Tom	NY Americans	48	13	27	40	14
Gottselig, Johnny	Chicago	48	16	23	39	15
Haynes, Paul	Montreal	47	5	33	38	27
Conacher, Roy	Boston	47	26	11	37	12
Carr, Lorne	NY Americans	46	19	18	37	16
Colville, Neil	New York	48	18	19	37	12
Watson, Phil	New York	48	15	22	37	42

1939-40

Team	GP	W	L	T	GF	GA	PTS
Boston	48	31	12	5	170	98	67
*New York	48	27	11	10	136	77	64
Toronto	48	25	17	6	134	110	56
Chicago	48	23	19	6	112	120	52
Detroit	48	16	26	6	90	126	38
NY Americans	48	15	29	4	106	140	34
Montreal	48	10	33	5	90	167	25

Leading Scorers

Player	Club	GP	G	A	PTS	PIM
Schmidt, Milt	Boston	48	22	30	52	37
Dumart, Woody	Boston	48	22	21	43	16
Bauer, Bob	Boston	48	17	26	43	2
Drillon, Gord	Toronto	43	21	19	40	13
Cowley, Bill	Boston	48	13	27	40	24
Hextall, Bryan	New York	48	24	15	39	52
Colville, Neil	New York	48	19	19	38	22
Howe, Syd	Detroit	46	14	23	37	17
Blake, Hector	Montreal	48	17	19	36	48
Armstrong, M.	NY Americans	48	16	20	36	12

1940-41

Team	GP	W	L	T	GF	GA	PTS
*Boston	48	27	8	13	168	102	67
Toronto	48	28	14	6	145	99	62
Detroit	48	21	16	11	112	102	53
New York	48	21	19	8	143	125	50
Chicago	48	16	25	7	112	139	39
Montreal	48	16	26	6	121	147	38
NY Americans	48	8	29	11	99	186	27

Leading Scorers

Player	Club	GP	G	A	PTS	PIM
Cowley, Bill	Boston	46	17	45	62	16
Hextall, Bryan	New York	48	26	18	44	16
Drillon, Gord	Toronto	42	23	21	44	2
Apps, Syl	Toronto	41	20	24	44	6
Patrick, Lynn	New York	48	20	24	44	12
Howe, Syd	Detroit	48	20	24	44	8
Colville, Neil	New York	48	14	28	42	28
Wiseman, Eddie	Boston	48	16	24	40	10
Bauer, Bobby	Boston	48	17	22	39	2
Schriner, Sweeney	Toronto	48	24	14	38	6
Conacher, Roy	Boston	40	24	14	38	7
Schmidt, Milt	Boston	44	13	25	38	23

1941-42

Team	GP	W	L	T	GF	GA	PTS
New York	48	29	17	2	177	143	60
*Toronto	48	27	18	3	158	136	57
Boston	48	25	17	6	160	118	56
Chicago	48	22	23	3	145	155	47
Detroit	48	19	25	4	140	147	42
Montreal	48	18	27	3	134	173	39
Brooklyn	48	16	29	3	133	175	35

Leading Scorers

Player	Club	GP	G	A	PTS	PIM
Hextall, Bryan	New York	48	24	32	56	30
Patrick, Lynn	New York	47	32	22	54	18
Grosso, Don	Detroit	48	23	30	53	13
Watson, Phil	New York	48	15	37	52	48
Abel, Sid	Detroit	48	18	31	49	45
Blake, Hector	Montreal	47	17	28	45	19
Thoms, Bill	Chicago	47	15	30	45	8
Drillon, Gord	Toronto	48	23	18	41	6
Apps, Syl	Toronto	38	18	23	41	0
Anderson, Tom	Brooklyn	48	12	29	41	54

1942-43

Team	GP	W	L	T	GF	GA	PTS
*Detroit	50	25	14	11	169	124	61
Boston	50	24	17	9	195	176	57
Toronto	50	22	19	9	198	159	53
Montreal	50	19	19	12	181	191	50
Chicago	50	17	18	15	179	180	49
New York	50	11	31	8	161	253	30

Leading Scorers

Player	Club	GP	G	A	PTS	PIM
Bentley, Doug	Chicago	50	33	40	73	18
Cowley, Bill	Boston	48	27	45	72	10
Bentley, Max	Chicago	47	26	44	70	2
Patrick, Lynn	New York	50	22	39	61	28
Carr, Lorne	Toronto	50	27	33	60	15
Taylor, Billy	Toronto	50	18	42	60	2
Hextall, Bryan	New York	50	27	32	59	28
Blake, Hector	Montreal	48	23	36	59	28
Lach, Elmer	Montreal	45	18	40	58	14
O'Connor, Herb	Montreal	50	15	43	58	2

1943-44

Team	GP	W	L	T	GF	GA	PTS
*Montreal	50	38	5	7	234	109	83
Detroit	50	26	18	6	214	177	58
Toronto	50	23	23	4	214	174	50
Chicago	50	22	23	5	178	187	49
Boston	50	19	26	5	223	268	43
New York	50	6	39	5	162	310	17

Leading Scorers

Player	Club	GP	G	A	PTS	PIM
Cain, Herb	Boston	48	36	46	82	4
Bentley, Doug	Chicago	50	38	39	77	22
Carr, Lorne	Toronto	50	36	38	74	9
Liscombe, Carl	Detroit	50	36	37	73	17
Lach, Elmer	Montreal	48	24	48	72	23
Smith, Clint	Chicago	50	23	49	72	4
Cowley, Bill	Boston	36	30	41	71	12
Mosienko, Bill	Chicago	50	32	38	70	10
Jackson, Art	Boston	49	28	41	69	8
Bodnar, Gus	Toronto	50	22	40	62	18

1944-45

Team	GP	W	L	T	GF	GA	PTS
Montreal	50	38	8	4	228	121	80
Detroit	50	31	14	5	218	161	67
*Toronto	50	24	22	4	183	161	52
Boston	50	16	30	4	179	219	36
Chicago	50	13	30	7	141	194	33
New York	50	11	29	10	154	247	32

Leading Scorers

Player	Club	GP	G	A	PTS	PIM
Lach, Elmer	Montreal	50	26	54	80	37
Richard, Maurice	Montreal	50	50	23	73	36
Blake, Hector	Montreal	49	29	38	67	15
Cowley, Bill	Boston	49	25	40	65	2
Kennedy, Ted	Toronto	49	29	25	54	14
Mosienko, Bill	Chicago	50	28	26	54	0
Carveth, Joe	Detroit	50	26	28	54	6
DeMarco, Albert	New York	50	24	30	54	10
Smith, Clint	Chicago	50	23	31	54	0
Howe, Syd	Detroit	46	17	36	53	6

1945-46

Team	GP	W	L	T	GF	GA	PTS
*Montreal	50	28	17	5	172	134	61
Boston	50	24	18	8	167	156	56
Chicago	50	23	20	7	200	178	53
Detroit	50	20	20	10	146	159	50
Toronto	50	19	24	7	174	185	45
New York	50	13	28	9	144	191	35

Leading Scorers

Player	Club	GP	G	A	PTS	PIM
Bentley, Max	Chicago	47	31	30	61	6
Stewart, Gaye	Toronto	50	37	15	52	8
Blake, Hector	Montreal	50	29	21	50	2
Smith, Clint	Chicago	50	26	24	50	2
Richard, Maurice	Montreal	50	27	21	48	50
Mosienko, Bill	Chicago	40	18	30	48	12
DeMarco, Albert	New York	50	20	27	47	20
Lach, Elmer	Montreal	50	13	34	47	34
Kaleta, Alex	Chicago	49	19	27	46	17
Taylor, Billy	Toronto	48	23	18	41	14
Horeck, Pete	Chicago	50	20	21	41	34

1946-47

Team	GP	W	L	T	GF	GA	PTS
Montreal	60	34	16	10	189	138	78
*Toronto	60	31	19	10	209	172	72
Boston	60	26	23	11	190	175	63
Detroit	60	22	27	11	190	193	55
New York	60	22	32	6	167	186	50
Chicago	60	19	37	4	193	274	42

Leading Scorers

Player	Club	GP	G	A	PTS	PIM
Bentley, Max	Chicago	60	29	43	72	12
Richard, Maurice	Montreal	60	45	26	71	69
Taylor, Billy	Detroit	60	17	46	63	35
Schmidt, Milt	Boston	59	27	35	62	40
Kennedy, Ted	Toronto	60	28	32	60	27
Bentley, Doug	Chicago	52	21	34	55	18
Bauer, Bob	Boston	58	30	24	54	4
Conacher, Roy	Detroit	60	30	24	54	6
Mosienko, Bill	Chicago	59	25	27	52	2
Dumart, Woody	Boston	60	24	28	52	12

1947-48

Team	GP	W	L	T	GF	GA	PTS
*Toronto	60	32	15	13	182	143	77
Detroit	60	30	18	12	187	148	72
Boston	60	23	24	13	167	168	59
New York	60	21	26	13	176	201	55
Montreal	60	20	29	11	147	169	51
Chicago	60	20	34	6	195	225	46

Leading Scorers

Player	Club	GP	G	A	PTS	PIM
Lach, Elmer	Montreal	60	30	31	61	72
O'Connor, Buddy	New York	60	24	36	60	8
Bentley, Doug	Chicago	60	20	37	57	16
Stewart, Gaye	Tor., Chi.	61	27	29	56	83
Bentley, Max	Chi., Tor.	59	26	28	54	14
Poile, Bud	Tor., Chi.	58	25	29	54	17
Richard, Maurice	Montreal	53	28	25	53	89
Apps, Syl	Toronto	55	26	27	53	12
Lindsay, Ted	Detroit	60	33	19	52	95
Conacher, Roy	Chicago	52	22	27	49	4

1948-49

Team	GP	W	L	T	GF	GA	PTS
Detroit	60	34	19	7	195	145	75
Boston	60	29	23	8	178	163	66
Montreal	60	28	23	9	152	126	65
*Toronto	60	22	25	13	147	161	57
Chicago	60	21	31	8	173	211	50
New York	60	18	31	11	133	172	47

Leading Scorers

Player	Club	GP	G	A	PTS	PIM
Conacher, Roy	Chicago	60	26	42	68	8
Bentley, Doug	Chicago	58	23	43	66	38
Abel, Sid	Detroit	60	28	26	54	49
Lindsay, Ted	Detroit	50	26	28	54	97
Conacher, Jim	Det., Chi.	59	26	23	49	43
Ronty, Paul	Boston	60	20	29	49	11
Watson, Harry	Toronto	60	26	19	45	0
Reay, Billy	Montreal	60	22	23	45	33
Bodnar, Gus	Chicago	59	19	26	45	14
Peirson, John	Boston	59	22	21	43	45

1949-50

Team	GP	W	L	T	GF	GA	PTS
*Detroit	70	37	19	14	229	164	88
Montreal	70	29	22	19	172	150	77
Toronto	70	31	27	12	176	173	74
New York	70	28	31	11	170	189	67
Boston	70	22	32	16	198	228	60
Chicago	70	22	38	10	203	244	54

Leading Scorers

Player	Club	GP	G	A	PTS	PIM
Lindsay, Ted	Detroit	69	23	55	78	141
Abel, Sid	Detroit	69	34	35	69	46
Howe, Gordie	Detroit	70	35	33	68	69
Richard, Maurice	Montreal	70	43	22	65	114
Ronty, Paul	Boston	70	23	36	59	8
Conacher, Roy	Chicago	70	25	31	56	16
Bentley, Doug	Chicago	64	20	33	53	28
Peirson, John	Boston	57	27	25	52	49
Prystai, Metro	Chicago	65	29	22	51	31
Guidolin, Bep	Chicago	70	17	34	51	42

1950-51

Team	GP	W	L	T	GF	GA	PTS
Detroit	70	44	13	13	236	139	101
*Toronto	70	41	16	13	212	138	95
Montreal	70	25	30	15	173	184	65
Boston	70	22	30	18	178	197	62
New York	70	20	29	21	169	201	61
Chicago	70	13	47	10	171	280	36

Leading Scorers

Player	Club	GP	G	A	PTS	PIM
Howe, Gordie	Detroit	70	43	43	86	74
Richard, Maurice	Montreal	65	42	24	66	97
Bentley, Max	Toronto	67	21	41	62	34
Abel, Sid	Detroit	69	23	38	61	30
Schmidt, Milt	Boston	62	22	39	61	33
Kennedy, Ted	Toronto	63	18	43	61	32
Lindsay, Ted	Detroit	67	24	35	59	110
Sloan, Tod	Toronto	70	31	25	56	105
Kelly, Red	Detroit	70	17	37	54	24
Smith, Sid	Toronto	70	30	21	51	10
Gardner, Cal	Toronto	66	23	28	51	42

1951-52

Team	GP	W	L	T	GF	GA	PTS
*Detroit	70	44	14	12	215	133	100
Montreal	70	34	26	10	195	164	78
Toronto	70	29	25	16	168	157	74
Boston	70	25	29	16	162	176	66
New York	70	23	34	13	192	219	59
Chicago	70	17	44	9	158	241	43

Leading Scorers

Player	Club	GP	G	A	PTS	PIM
Howe, Gordie	Detroit	70	47	39	86	78
Lindsay, Ted	Detroit	70	30	39	69	123
Lach, Elmer	Montreal	70	15	50	65	36
Raleigh, Don	New York	70	19	42	61	14
Smith, Sid	Toronto	70	27	30	57	6
Geoffrion, Bernie	Montreal	67	30	24	54	66
Mosienko, Bill	Chicago	70	31	22	53	10
Abel, Sid	Detroit	62	17	36	53	32
Kennedy, Ted	Toronto	70	19	33	52	33
Schmidt, Milt	Boston	69	21	29	50	57
Peirson, John	Boston	68	20	30	50	30

1952-53

Team	GP	W	L	T	GF	GA	PTS
Detroit	70	36	16	18	222	133	90
*Montreal	70	28	23	19	155	148	75
Boston	70	28	29	13	152	172	69
Chicago	70	27	28	15	169	175	69
Toronto	70	27	30	13	156	167	67
New York	70	17	37	16	152	211	50

Leading Scorers

Player	Club	GP	G	A	PTS	PIM
Howe, Gordie	Detroit	70	49	46	95	57
Lindsay, Ted	Detroit	70	32	39	71	111
Richard, Maurice	Montreal	70	28	33	61	112
Hergesheimer, W.	New York	70	30	29	59	10
Delvecchio, Alex	Detroit	70	16	43	59	28
Ronty, Paul	New York	70	16	38	54	20
Prystai, Metro	Detroit	70	16	34	50	12
Kelly, Red	Detroit	70	19	27	46	8
Olmstead, Bert	Montreal	69	17	28	45	83
Mackell, Fleming	Boston	65	27	17	44	63
McFadden, Jim	Chicago	70	23	21	44	29

1953-54

Team	GP	W	L	T	GF	GA	PTS
*Detroit	70	37	19	14	191	132	88
Montreal	70	35	24	11	195	141	81
Toronto	70	32	24	14	152	131	78
Boston	70	32	28	10	177	181	74
New York	70	29	31	10	161	182	68
Chicago	70	12	51	7	133	242	31

Leading Scorers

Player	Club	GP	G	A	PTS	PIM
Howe, Gordie	Detroit	70	33	48	81	109
Richard, Maurice	Montreal	70	37	30	67	112
Lindsay, Ted	Detroit	70	26	36	62	110
Geoffrion, Bernie	Montreal	54	29	25	54	87
Olmstead, Bert	Montreal	70	15	37	52	85
Kelly, Red	Detroit	62	16	33	49	18
Reibel, Earl	Detroit	69	15	33	48	18
Sandford, Ed	Boston	70	16	31	47	42
Mackell, Fleming	Boston	67	15	32	47	60
Mosdell, Ken	Montreal	67	22	24	46	64
Ronty, Paul	New York	70	13	33	46	18

1954-55

Team	GP	W	L	T	GF	GA	PTS
*Detroit	70	42	17	11	204	134	95
Montreal	70	41	18	11	228	157	93
Toronto	70	24	24	22	147	135	70
Boston	70	23	26	21	169	188	67
New York	70	17	35	18	150	210	52
Chicago	70	13	40	17	161	235	43

Leading Scorers

Player	Club	GP	G	A	PTS	PIM
Geoffrion, Bernie	Montreal	70	38	37	75	57
Richard, Maurice	Montreal	67	38	36	74	125
Beliveau, Jean	Montreal	70	37	36	73	58
Reibel, Earl	Detroit	70	25	41	66	15
Howe, Gordie	Detroit	64	29	33	62	68
Sullivan, George	Chicago	69	19	42	61	51
Olmstead, Bert	Montreal	70	10	48	58	103
Smith, Sid	Toronto	70	33	21	54	14
Mosdell, Ken	Montreal	70	22	32	54	82
Lewicki, Danny	New York	70	29	24	53	8

1955-56

Team	GP	W	L	T	GF	GA	PTS
*Montreal	70	45	15	10	222	131	100
Detroit	70	30	24	16	183	148	76
New York	70	32	28	10	204	203	74
Toronto	70	24	33	13	153	181	61
Boston	70	23	34	13	147	185	59
Chicago	70	19	39	12	155	216	50

Leading Scorers

Player	Club	GP	G	A	PTS	PIM
Beliveau, Jean	Montreal	70	47	41	88	143
Howe, Gordie	Detroit	70	38	41	79	100
Richard, Maurice	Montreal	70	38	33	71	89
Olmstead, Bert	Montreal	70	14	56	70	94
Sloan, Tod	Toronto	70	37	29	66	100
Bathgate, Andy	New York	70	19	47	66	59
Geoffrion, Bernie	Montreal	59	29	33	62	66
Reibel, Earl	Detroit	68	17	39	56	10
Delvecchio, Alex	Detroit	70	25	26	51	24
Creighton, Dave	New York	70	20	31	51	43
Gadsby, Bill	New York	70	9	42	51	84

1956-57

Team	GP	W	L	T	GF	GA	PTS
Detroit	70	38	20	12	198	157	88
*Montreal	70	35	23	12	210	155	82
Boston	70	34	24	12	195	174	80
New York	70	26	30	14	184	227	66
Toronto	70	21	34	15	174	192	57
Chicago	70	16	39	15	169	225	47

Leading Scorers

Player	Club	GP	G	A	PTS	PIM
Howe, Gordie	Detroit	70	44	45	89	72
Lindsay, Ted	Detroit	70	30	55	85	103
Beliveau, Jean	Montreal	69	33	51	84	105
Bathgate, Andy	New York	70	27	50	77	60
Litzenberger, Ed	Chicago	70	32	32	64	48
Richard, Maurice	Montreal	63	33	29	62	74
McKenney, Don	Boston	69	21	39	60	31
Moore, Dickie	Montreal	70	29	29	58	56
Richard, Henri	Montreal	63	18	36	54	71
Ullman, Norm	Detroit	64	16	36	52	47

1957-58

Team	GP	W	L	T	GF	GA	PTS
*Montreal	70	43	17	10	250	158	96
New York	70	32	25	13	195	188	77
Detroit	70	29	29	12	176	207	70
Boston	70	27	28	15	199	194	69
Chicago	70	24	39	7	163	202	55
Toronto	70	21	38	11	192	226	53

Leading Scorers

Player	Club	GP	G	A	PTS	PIM
Moore, Dickie	Montreal	70	36	48	84	65
Richard, Henri	Montreal	67	28	52	80	56
Bathgate, Andy	New York	65	30	48	78	42
Howe, Gordie	Detroit	64	33	44	77	40
Horvath, Bronco	Boston	67	30	36	66	71
Litzenberger, Ed	Chicago	70	32	30	62	63
Mackell, Fleming	Boston	70	20	40	60	72
Beliveau, Jean	Montreal	55	27	32	59	93
Delvecchio, Alex	Detroit	70	21	38	59	22
McKenney, Don	Boston	70	28	30	58	22

1958-59

Team	GP	W	L	T	GF	GA	PTS
*Montreal	70	39	18	13	258	158	91
Boston	70	32	29	9	205	215	73
Chicago	70	28	29	13	197	208	69
Toronto	70	27	32	11	189	201	65
New York	70	26	32	12	201	217	64
Detroit	70	25	37	8	167	218	58

Leading Scorers

Player	Club	GP	G	A	PTS	PIM
Moore, Dickie	Montreal	70	41	55	96	61
Beliveau, Jean	Montreal	64	45	46	91	67
Bathgate, Andy	New York	70	40	48	88	48
Howe, Gordie	Detroit	70	32	46	78	57
Litzenberger, Ed	Chicago	70	33	44	77	37
Geoffrion, Bernie	Montreal	59	22	44	66	30
Sullivan, George	New York	70	21	42	63	56
Hebenton, Andy	New York	70	33	29	62	8
McKenney, Don	Boston	70	32	30	62	20
Sloan, Tod	Chicago	59	27	35	62	79

1959-60

Team	GP	W	L	T	GF	GA	PTS
*Montreal	70	40	18	12	255	178	92
Toronto	70	35	26	9	199	195	79
Chicago	70	28	29	13	191	180	69
Detroit	70	26	29	15	186	197	67
Boston	70	28	34	8	220	241	64
New York	70	17	38	15	187	247	49

Leading Scorers

Player	Club	GP	G	A	PTS	PIM
Hull, Bobby	Chicago	70	39	42	81	68
Horvath, Bronco	Boston	68	39	41	80	60
Beliveau, Jean	Montreal	60	34	40	74	57
Bathgate, Andy	New York	70	26	48	74	28
Richard, Henri	Montreal	70	30	43	73	66
Howe, Gordie	Detroit	70	28	45	73	46
Geoffrion, Bernie	Montreal	59	30	41	71	36
McKenney, Don	Boston	70	20	49	69	28
Stasiuk, Vic	Boston	69	29	39	68	121
Prentice, Dean	New York	70	32	34	66	43

1960-61

Team	GP	W	L	T	GF	GA	PTS
Montreal	70	41	19	10	254	188	92
Toronto	70	39	19	12	234	176	90
*Chicago	70	29	24	17	198	180	75
Detroit	70	25	29	16	195	215	66
New York	70	22	38	10	204	248	54
Boston	70	15	42	13	176	254	43

Leading Scorers

Player	Club	GP	G	A	PTS	PIM
Geoffrion, Bernie	Montreal	64	50	45	95	29
Beliveau, Jean	Montreal	69	32	58	90	57
Mahovlich, Frank	Toronto	70	48	36	84	131
Bathgate, Andy	New York	70	29	48	77	22
Howe, Gordie	Detroit	64	23	49	72	30
Ullman, Norm	Detroit	70	28	42	70	34
Kelly, Red	Toronto	64	20	50	70	12
Moore, Dickie	Montreal	57	35	34	69	62
Richard, Henri	Montreal	70	24	44	68	91
Delvecchio, Alex	Detroit	70	27	35	62	26

1961-62

Team	GP	W	L	T	GF	GA	PTS
Montreal	70	42	14	14	259	166	98
*Toronto	70	37	22	11	232	180	85
Chicago	70	31	26	13	217	186	75
New York	70	26	32	12	195	207	64
Detroit	70	23	33	14	184	219	60
Boston	70	15	47	8	177	306	38

Leading Scorers

Player	Club	GP	G	A	PTS	PIM
Hull, Bobby	Chicago	70	50	34	84	35
Bathgate, Andy	New York	70	28	56	84	44
Howe, Gordie	Detroit	70	33	44	77	54
Mikita, Stan	Chicago	70	25	52	77	97
Mahovlich, Frank	Toronto	70	33	38	71	87
Delvecchio, Alex	Detroit	70	26	43	69	18
Backstrom, Ralph	Montreal	66	27	38	65	29
Ullman, Norm	Detroit	70	26	38	64	54
Hay, Bill	Chicago	60	11	52	63	34
Provost, Claude	Montreal	70	33	29	62	22

1962-63

Team	GP	W	L	T	GF	GA	PTS
*Toronto	70	35	23	12	221	180	82
Chicago	70	32	21	17	194	178	81
Montreal	70	28	19	23	225	183	79
Detroit	70	32	25	13	200	194	77
New York	70	22	36	12	211	233	56
Boston	70	14	39	17	198	281	45

Leading Scorers

Player	Club	GP	G	A	PTS	PIM
Howe, Gordie	Detroit	70	38	48	86	100
Bathgate, Andy	New York	70	35	46	81	54
Mikita, Stan	Chicago	65	31	45	76	69
Mahovlich, Frank	Toronto	67	36	37	73	56
Richard, Henri	Montreal	67	23	50	73	57
Beliveau, Jean	Montreal	69	18	49	67	68
Bucyk, John	Boston	69	27	39	66	36
Delvecchio, Alex	Detroit	70	20	44	64	8
Hull, Bobby	Chicago	65	31	31	62	27
Oliver, Murray	Boston	65	22	40	62	38

1963-64

Team	GP	W	L	T	GF	GA	PTS
Montreal	70	36	21	13	209	167	85
Chicago	70	36	22	12	218	169	84
*Toronto	70	33	25	12	192	172	78
Detroit	70	30	29	11	191	204	71
New York	70	22	38	10	186	242	54
Boston	70	18	40	12	170	212	48

Leading Scorers

Player	Club	GP	G	A	PTS	PIM
Mikita, Stan	Chicago	70	39	50	89	146
Hull, Bobby	Chicago	70	43	44	87	50
Beliveau, Jean	Montreal	68	28	50	78	42
Bathgate, Andy	NYR, Tor.	71	19	58	77	34
Howe, Gordie	Detroit	69	26	47	73	70
Wharram, Ken	Chicago	70	39	32	71	18
Oliver, Murray	Boston	70	24	44	68	41
Goyette, Phil	New York	67	24	41	65	15
Gilbert, Rod	New York	70	24	40	64	62
Keon, Dave	Toronto	70	23	37	60	6

1964-65

Team	GP	W	L	T	GF	GA	PTS
Detroit	70	40	23	7	224	175	87
*Montreal	70	36	23	11	211	185	83
Chicago	70	34	28	8	224	176	76
Toronto	70	30	26	14	204	173	74
New York	70	20	38	12	179	246	52
Boston	70	21	43	6	166	253	48

Leading Scorers

Player	Club	GP	G	A	PTS	PIM
Mikita, Stan	Chicago	70	28	59	87	154
Ullman, Norm	Detroit	70	42	41	83	70
Howe, Gordie	Detroit	70	29	47	76	104
Hull, Bobby	Chicago	61	39	32	71	32
Delvecchio, Alex	Detroit	68	25	42	67	16
Provost, Claude	Montreal	70	27	37	64	28
Gilbert, Rod	New York	70	25	36	61	52
Pilote, Pierre	Chicago	68	14	45	59	162
Bucyk, John	Boston	68	26	29	55	24
Backstrom, Ralph	Montreal	70	25	30	55	41
Esposito, Phil	Chicago	70	23	32	55	44

1965-66

Team	GP	W	L	T	GF	GA	PTS
*Montreal	70	41	21	8	239	173	90
Chicago	70	37	25	8	240	187	82
Toronto	70	34	25	11	208	187	79
Detroit	70	31	27	12	221	194	74
Boston	70	21	43	6	174	275	48
New York	70	18	41	11	195	261	47

Leading Scorers

Player	Club	GP	G	A	PTS	PIM
Hull, Bobby	Chicago	65	54	43	97	70
Mikita, Stan	Chicago	68	30	48	78	58
Rousseau, Bobby	Montreal	70	30	48	78	20
Beliveau, Jean	Montreal	67	29	48	77	50
Howe, Gordie	Detroit	70	29	46	75	83
Ullman, Norm	Detroit	70	31	41	72	35
Delvecchio, Alex	Detroit	70	31	38	69	16
Nevin, Bob	New York	69	29	33	62	10
Richard, Henri	Montreal	62	22	39	61	47
Oliver, Murray	Boston	70	18	42	60	30

1966-67

Team	GP	W	L	T	GF	GA	PTS
Chicago	70	41	17	12	264	170	94
Montreal	70	32	25	13	202	188	77
*Toronto	70	32	27	11	204	211	75
New York	70	30	28	12	188	189	72
Detroit	70	27	39	4	212	241	58
Boston	70	17	43	10	182	253	44

Leading Scorers

Player	Club	GP	G	A	PTS	PIM
Mikita, Stan	Chicago	70	35	62	97	12
Hull, Bobby	Chicago	66	52	28	80	52
Ullman, Norm	Detroit	68	26	44	70	26
Wharram, Ken	Chicago	70	31	34	65	21
Howe, Gordie	Detroit	69	25	40	65	53
Rousseau, Bobby	Montreal	68	19	44	63	58
Esposito, Phil	Chicago	69	21	40	61	40
Goyette, Phil	New York	70	12	49	61	6
Mohns, Doug	Chicago	61	25	35	60	58
Richard, Henri	Montreal	65	21	34	55	28
Delvecchio, Alex	Detroit	70	17	38	55	10

1967-68

EAST DIVISION

Team	GP	W	L	T	GF	GA	PTS
*Montreal	74	42	22	10	236	167	94
New York	74	39	23	12	226	183	90
Boston	74	37	27	10	259	216	84
Chicago	74	32	26	16	212	222	80
Toronto	74	33	31	10	209	176	76
Detroit	74	27	35	12	245	257	66

WEST DIVISION

Team	GP	W	L	T	GF	GA	PTS
Philadelphia	74	31	32	11	173	179	73
Los Angeles	74	31	33	10	200	224	72
St. Louis	74	27	31	16	177	191	70
Minnesota	74	27	32	15	191	226	69
Pittsburgh	74	27	34	13	195	216	67
Oakland	74	15	42	17	153	219	47

Leading Scorers

Player	Club	GP	G	A	PTS	PIM
Mikita, Stan	Chicago	72	40	47	87	14
Esposito, Phil	Boston	74	35	49	84	21
Howe, Gordie	Detroit	74	39	43	82	53
Ratelle, Jean	New York	74	32	46	78	18
Gilbert, Rod	New York	73	29	48	77	12
Hull, Bobby	Chicago	71	44	31	75	39
Ullman, Norm	Det., Tor.	71	35	37	72	28
Delvecchio, Alex	Detroit	74	22	48	70	14
Bucyk, John	Boston	72	30	39	69	8
Wharram, Ken	Chicago	74	27	42	69	18

1968-69

EAST DIVISION

Team	GP	W	L	T	GF	GA	PTS
*Montreal	76	46	19	11	271	202	103
Boston	76	42	18	16	303	221	100
New York	76	41	26	9	231	196	91
Toronto	76	35	26	15	234	217	85
Detroit	76	33	31	12	239	221	78
Chicago	76	34	33	9	280	246	77

WEST DIVISION

Team	GP	W	L	T	GF	GA	PTS
St. Louis	76	37	25	14	204	157	88
Oakland	76	29	36	11	219	251	69
Philadelphia	76	20	35	21	174	225	61
Los Angeles	76	24	42	10	185	260	58
Pittsburgh	76	20	45	11	189	252	51
Minnesota	76	18	43	5	189	270	51

Leading Scorers

Player	Club	GP	G	A	PTS	PIM
Esposito, Phil	Boston	74	49	77	126	79
Hull, Bobby	Chicago	74	58	49	107	48
Howe, Gordie	Detroit	76	44	59	103	58
Mikita, Stan	Chicago	74	30	67	97	52
Hodge, Ken	Boston	75	45	45	90	75
Cournoyer, Yvan	Montreal	76	43	44	87	31
Delvecchio, Alex	Detroit	72	25	58	83	8
Berenson, Red	St. Louis	76	35	47	82	43
Beliveau, Jean	Montreal	69	33	49	82	55
Mahovlich, Frank	Detroit	76	49	29	78	38
Ratelle, Jean	New York	75	32	46	78	26

1969-70

EAST DIVISION

Team	GP	W	L	T	GF	GA	PTS
Chicago	76	45	22	9	250	170	99
*Boston	76	40	17	19	277	216	99
Detroit	76	40	21	15	246	199	95
New York	76	38	22	16	246	189	92
Montreal	76	38	22	16	244	201	92
Toronto	76	29	34	13	222	242	71

WEST DIVISION

Team	GP	W	L	T	GF	GA	PTS
St. Louis	76	37	27	12	224	179	86
Pittsburgh	76	26	38	12	182	238	64
Minnesota	76	19	35	22	224	257	60
Oakland	76	22	40	14	169	243	58
Philadelphia	76	17	35	24	197	225	58
Los Angeles	76	14	52	10	168	290	38

Leading Scorers

Player	Club	GP	G	A	PTS	PIM
Orr, Bobby	Boston	76	33	87	120	125
Esposito, Phil	Boston	76	43	56	99	50
Mikita, Stan	Chicago	76	39	47	86	50
Goyette, Phil	St. Louis	72	29	49	78	16
Tkaczuk, Walt	New York	76	27	50	77	38
Ratelle, Jean	New York	75	32	42	74	28
Berenson, Red	St. Louis	67	33	39	72	38
Parise, Jean-Paul	Minnesota	74	24	48	72	72
Howe, Gordie	Detroit	76	31	40	71	58
Mahovlich, Frank	Detroit	74	38	32	70	59
Balon, Dave	New York	76	33	37	70	100
McKenzie, John	Boston	72	29	41	70	114

1970-71

EAST DIVISION

Team	GP	W	L	T	GF	GA	PTS
Boston	78	57	14	7	399	207	121
New York	78	49	18	11	259	177	109
*Montreal	78	42	23	13	291	216	97
Toronto	78	37	33	8	248	211	82
Buffalo	78	24	39	15	217	291	63
Vancouver	78	24	46	8	229	296	56
Detroit	78	22	45	11	209	308	55

WEST DIVISION

Team	GP	W	L	T	GF	GA	PTS
Chicago	78	49	20	9	277	184	107
St. Louis	78	34	25	19	223	208	87
Philadelphia	78	28	33	17	207	225	73
Minnesota	78	28	34	16	191	223	72
Los Angeles	78	25	40	13	239	303	63
Pittsburgh	78	21	37	20	221	240	62
California	78	20	53	5	199	320	45

Leading Scorers

Player	Club	GP	G	A	PTS	PIM
Esposito, Phil	Boston	78	76	76	152	71
Orr, Bobby	Boston	78	37	102	139	91
Bucyk, John	Boston	78	51	65	116	8
Hodge, Ken	Boston	78	43	62	105	113
Hull, Bobby	Chicago	78	44	52	96	32
Ullman, Norm	Toronto	73	34	51	85	24
Cashman, Wayne	Boston	77	21	58	79	100
McKenzie, John	Boston	65	31	46	77	120
Keon, Dave	Toronto	76	38	38	76	4
Beliveau, Jean	Montreal	70	25	51	76	40
Stanfield, Fred	Boston	75	24	52	76	12

1971-72

EAST DIVISION

Team	GP	W	L	T	GF	GA	PTS
*Boston	78	54	13	11	330	204	119
New York	78	48	17	13	317	192	109
Montreal	78	46	16	16	307	205	108
Toronto	78	33	31	14	209	208	80
Detroit	78	33	35	10	261	262	76
Buffalo	78	16	43	19	203	289	51
Vancouver	78	20	50	8	203	297	48

WEST DIVISION

Team	GP	W	L	T	GF	GA	PTS
Chicago	78	46	17	15	256	166	107
Minnesota	78	37	29	12	212	191	86
St. Louis	78	28	39	11	208	247	67
Pittsburgh	78	26	38	14	220	258	66
Philadelphia	78	26	38	14	200	236	66
California	78	21	39	18	216	288	60
Los Angeles	78	20	49	9	206	305	49

Leading Scorers

Player	Club	GP	G	A	PTS	PIM
Esposito, Phil	Boston	76	66	67	133	76
Orr, Bobby	Boston	76	37	80	117	106
Ratelle, Jean	New York	63	46	63	109	4
Hadfield, Vic	New York	78	50	56	106	142
Gilbert, Rod	New York	73	43	54	97	64
Mahovlich, Frank	Montreal	76	43	53	96	36
Hull, Bobby	Chicago	78	50	43	93	24
Cournoyer, Yvan	Montreal	73	47	36	83	15
Bucyk, John	Boston	78	32	51	83	4
Clarke, Bobby	Philadelphia	78	35	46	81	87
Lemaire, Jacques	Montreal	77	32	49	81	26

1972-73

EAST DIVISION

Team	GP	W	L	T	GF	GA	PTS
*Montreal	78	52	10	16	329	184	120
Boston	78	51	22	5	330	235	107
NY Rangers	78	47	23	8	297	208	102
Buffalo	78	37	27	14	257	219	88
Detroit	78	37	29	12	265	243	86
Toronto	78	27	41	10	247	279	64
Vancouver	78	22	47	9	233	339	53
NY Islanders	78	12	60	6	170	347	30

WEST DIVISION

Team	GP	W	L	T	GF	GA	PTS
Chicago	78	42	27	9	284	225	93
Philadelphia	78	37	30	11	296	256	85
Minnesota	78	37	30	11	254	230	85
St. Louis	78	32	34	12	233	251	76
Pittsburgh	78	32	37	9	257	265	73
Los Angeles	78	31	36	11	232	245	73
Atlanta	78	25	38	15	191	239	65
California	78	16	46	16	213	323	48

Leading Scorers

Player	Club	GP	G	A	PTS	PIM
Esposito, Phil	Boston	78	55	75	130	87
Clarke, Bobby	Philadelphia	78	37	67	104	80
Orr, Bobby	Boston	63	29	72	101	99
MacLeish, Rick	Philadelphia	78	50	50	100	69
Lemaire, Jacques	Montreal	77	44	51	95	16
Ratelle, Jean	NY Rangers	78	41	53	94	12
Redmond, Mickey	Detroit	76	52	41	93	24
Bucyk, John	Boston	78	40	53	93	12
Mahovlich, Frank	Montreal	78	38	55	93	51
Pappin, Jim	Chicago	76	41	51	92	82

1973-74

EAST DIVISION

Team	GP	W	L	T	GF	GA	PTS
Boston	78	52	17	9	349	221	113
Montreal	78	45	24	9	293	240	99
NY Rangers	78	40	24	14	300	251	94
Toronto	78	35	27	16	274	230	86
Buffalo	78	32	34	12	242	250	76
Detroit	78	29	39	10	255	319	68
Vancouver	78	24	43	11	224	296	59
NY Islanders	78	19	41	18	182	247	56

WEST DIVISION

Team	GP	W	L	T	GF	GA	PTS
*Philadelphia	78	50	16	12	273	164	112
Chicago	78	41	14	23	272	164	105
Los Angeles	78	33	33	12	233	231	78
Atlanta	78	30	34	14	214	238	74
Pittsburgh	78	28	41	9	242	273	65
St. Louis	78	26	40	12	206	248	64
Minnesota	78	23	38	17	235	275	63
California	78	13	55	10	195	342	36

Leading Scorers

Player	Club	GP	G	A	PTS	PIM
Esposito, Phil	Boston	78	68	77	145	58
Orr, Bobby	Boston	74	32	90	122	82
Hodge, Ken	Boston	76	50	55	105	43
Cashman, Wayne	Boston	78	30	59	89	111
Clarke, Bobby	Philadelphia	77	35	52	87	113
Martin, Rick	Buffalo	78	52	34	86	38
Apps, Syl	Pittsburgh	75	24	61	85	37
Sittler, Darryl	Toronto	78	38	46	84	55
MacDonald, Lowell	Pittsburgh	78	43	39	82	14
Park, Brad	NY Rangers	78	25	57	82	148
Hextall, Dennis	Minnesota	78	20	62	82	138

1974-75

PRINCE OF WALES CONFERENCE

Norris Division

Team	GP	W	L	T	GF	GA	PTS
Montreal	80	47	14	19	374	225	113
Los Angeles	80	42	17	21	269	185	105
Pittsburgh	80	37	28	15	326	289	89
Detroit	80	23	45	12	259	335	58
Washington	80	8	67	5	181	446	21

Adams Division

Team	GP	W	L	T	GF	GA	PTS
Buffalo	80	49	16	15	354	240	113
Boston	80	40	26	14	345	245	94
Toronto	80	31	33	16	280	309	78
California	80	19	48	13	212	316	51

CLARENCE CAMPBELL CONFERENCE

Patrick Division

Team	GP	W	L	T	GF	GA	PTS
*Philadelphia	80	51	18	11	293	181	113
NY Rangers	80	37	29	14	319	276	88
NY Islanders	80	33	25	22	264	221	88
Atlanta	80	34	31	15	243	233	83

Smythe Division

Team	GP	W	L	T	GF	GA	PTS
Vancouver	80	38	32	10	271	254	86
St. Louis	80	35	31	14	269	267	84
Chicago	80	37	35	8	268	241	82
Minnesota	80	23	50	7	221	341	53
Kansas City	80	15	54	11	184	328	41

Leading Scorers

Player	Club	GP	G	A	PTS	PIM
Orr, Bobby	Boston	80	46	89	135	101
Esposito, Phil	Boston	79	61	66	127	62
Dionne, Marcel	Detroit	80	47	74	121	14
Lafleur, Guy	Montreal	70	53	66	119	37
Mahovlich, Pete	Montreal	80	35	82	117	64
Clarke, Bobby	Philadelphia	80	27	89	116	125
Robert, Rene	Buffalo	74	40	60	100	75
Gilbert, Rod	NY Rangers	76	36	61	97	22
Perreault, Gilbert	Buffalo	68	39	57	96	36
Martin, Rick	Buffalo	68	52	43	95	72

1975-76

PRINCE OF WALES CONFERENCE

Norris Division

Team	GP	W	L	T	GF	GA	PTS
*Montreal	80	58	11	11	337	174	127
Los Angeles	80	38	33	9	263	265	85
Pittsburgh	80	35	33	12	339	303	82
Detroit	80	26	44	10	226	300	62
Washington	80	11	59	10	224	394	32

Adams Division

Team	GP	W	L	T	GF	GA	PTS
Boston	80	48	15	17	313	237	113
Buffalo	80	46	21	13	339	240	105
Toronto	80	34	31	15	294	276	83
California	80	27	42	11	250	278	65

CLARENCE CAMPBELL CONFERENCE

Patrick Division

Team	GP	W	L	T	GF	GA	PTS
Philadelphia	80	51	13	16	348	209	118
NY Islanders	80	42	21	17	297	190	101
Atlanta	80	35	33	12	262	237	82
NY Rangers	80	29	42	9	262	333	67

Smythe Division

Team	GP	W	L	T	GF	GA	PTS
Chicago	80	32	30	18	254	261	82
Vancouver	80	33	32	15	271	272	81
St. Louis	80	29	37	14	249	290	72
Minnesota	80	20	53	7	195	303	47
Kansas City	80	12	56	12	190	351	36

Leading Scorers

Player	Club	GP	G	A	PTS	PIM
Lafleur, Guy	Montreal	80	56	69	125	36
Clarke, Bobby	Philadelphia	76	30	89	119	13
Perreault, Gilbert	Buffalo	80	44	69	113	36
Barber, Bill	Philadelphia	80	50	62	112	104
Larouche, Pierre	Pittsburgh	76	53	58	111	33
Ratelle, Jean	Bos., NYR	80	36	69	105	18
Mahovlich, Pete	Montreal	80	34	71	105	76
Pronovost, Jean	Pittsburgh	80	52	52	104	24
Sittler, Darryl	Toronto	79	41	59	100	90
Apps, Syl	Pittsburgh	80	32	67	99	24

1976-77

PRINCE OF WALES CONFERENCE

Norris Division

Team	GP	W	L	T	GF	GA	PTS
*Montreal	80	60	8	12	387	171	132
Los Angeles	80	34	31	15	271	241	83
Pittsburgh	80	34	33	13	240	252	81
Washington	80	24	42	14	221	307	62
Detroit	80	16	55	9	183	309	41

Adams Division

Team	GP	W	L	T	GF	GA	PTS
Boston	80	49	23	8	312	240	106
Buffalo	80	48	24	8	301	220	104
Toronto	80	33	32	15	301	285	81
Cleveland	80	25	42	13	240	292	63

CLARENCE CAMPBELL CONFERENCE

Patrick Division

Team	GP	W	L	T	GF	GA	PTS
Philadelphia	80	48	16	16	323	213	112
NY Islanders	80	47	21	12	288	193	106
Atlanta	80	34	34	12	264	265	80
NY Rangers	80	29	37	14	272	310	72

Smythe Division

Team	GP	W	L	T	GF	GA	PTS
St. Louis	80	32	39	9	239	276	73
Minnesota	80	23	39	18	240	310	64
Chicago	80	26	43	11	240	298	63
Vancouver	80	25	42	13	235	294	63
Colorado	80	20	46	14	226	307	54

Leading Scorers

Player	Club	GP	G	A	PTS	PIM
Lafleur, Guy	Montreal	80	56	80	136	20
Dionne, Marcel	Los Angeles	80	53	69	122	12
Shutt, Steve	Montreal	80	60	45	105	28
MacLeish, Rick	Philadelphia	79	49	48	97	42
Perreault, Gilbert	Buffalo	80	39	56	95	30
Young, Tim	Minnesota	80	29	66	95	58
Ratelle, Jean	Boston	78	33	61	94	22
McDonald, Lanny	Toronto	80	46	44	90	77
Sittler, Darryl	Toronto	73	38	52	90	89
Clarke, Bobby	Philadelphia	80	27	63	90	71

1977-78

PRINCE OF WALES CONFERENCE

NORRIS DIVISION

Team	GP	W	L	T	GF	GA	PTS
*Montreal	80	59	10	11	359	183	129
Detroit	80	32	34	14	252	266	78
Los Angeles	80	31	34	15	243	245	77
Pittsburgh	80	25	37	18	254	321	68
Washington	80	17	49	14	195	321	48

Adams Division

Team	GP	W	L	T	GF	GA	PTS
Boston	80	51	18	11	333	218	113
Buffalo	80	44	19	17	288	215	105
Toronto	80	41	29	10	271	237	92
Cleveland	80	22	45	13	230	325	57

CLARENCE CAMPBELL CONFERENCE

Patrick Division

Team	GP	W	L	T	GF	GA	PTS
NY Islanders	80	48	17	15	334	210	111
Philadelphia	80	45	20	15	296	200	105
Atlanta	80	34	27	19	274	252	87
NY Rangers	80	30	37	13	279	280	73

Smythe Division

Team	GP	W	L	T	GF	GA	PTS
Chicago	80	32	29	19	230	220	83
Colorado	80	19	40	21	257	305	59
Vancouver	80	20	43	17	239	320	57
St. Louis	80	20	47	13	195	304	53
Minnesota	80	18	53	9	218	325	45

Leading Scorers

Player	Club	GP	G	A	PTS	PIM
Lafleur, Guy	Montreal	79	60	72	132	26
Trottier, Bryan	NY Islanders	77	46	77	123	46
Sittler, Darryl	Toronto	80	45	72	117	100
Lemaire, Jacques	Montreal	76	36	61	97	14
Potvin, Denis	NY Islanders	80	30	64	94	81
Bossy, Mike	NY Islanders	73	53	38	91	6
O'Reilly, Terry	Boston	77	29	61	90	211
Perreault, Gilbert	Buffalo	79	41	48	89	20
Clarke, Bobby	Philadelphia	71	21	68	89	83
McDonald, Lanny	Toronto	74	47	40	87	54
Paiement, Wilf	Colorado	80	31	56	87	114

1978-79

PRINCE OF WALES CONFERENCE

Norris Division

Team	GP	W	L	T	GF	GA	PTS
*Montreal	80	52	17	11	337	204	115
Pittsburgh	80	36	31	13	281	279	85
Los Angeles	80	34	34	12	292	286	80
Washington	80	24	41	15	273	338	63
Detroit	80	23	41	16	252	295	62

Adams Division

Team	GP	W	L	T	GF	GA	PTS
Boston	80	43	23	14	316	270	100
Buffalo	80	36	28	16	280	263	88
Toronto	80	34	33	13	267	252	81
Minnesota	80	28	40	12	257	289	68

CLARENCE CAMPBELL CONFERENCE

Patrick Division

Team	GP	W	L	T	GF	GA	PTS
NY Islanders	80	51	15	14	358	214	116
Philadelphia	80	40	25	15	281	248	95
NY Rangers	80	40	29	11	316	292	91
Atlanta	80	41	31	8	327	280	90

Smythe Division

Team	GP	W	L	T	GF	GA	PTS
Chicago	80	29	36	15	244	277	73
Vancouver	80	25	42	13	217	291	63
St. Louis	80	18	50	12	249	348	48
Colorado	80	15	53	12	210	331	42

Leading Scorers

Player	Club	GP	G	A	PTS	PIM
Trottier, Bryan	NY Islanders	76	47	87	134	50
Dionne, Marcel	Los Angeles	80	59	71	130	30
Lafleur, Guy	Montreal	80	52	77	129	28
Bossy, Mike	NY Islanders	80	69	57	126	25
MacMillan, Bob	Atlanta	79	37	71	108	14
Chouinard, Guy	Atlanta	80	50	57	107	14
Potvin, Denis	NY Islanders	73	31	70	101	58
Federko, Bernie	St. Louis	74	31	64	95	14
Taylor, Dave	Los Angeles	78	43	48	91	124
Gillies, Clark	NY Islanders	75	35	56	91	68

1979-80

PRINCE OF WALES CONFERENCE

Norris Division

Team	GP	W	L	T	GF	GA	PTS
Montreal	80	47	20	13	328	240	107
Los Angeles	80	30	36	14	290	313	74
Pittsburgh	80	30	37	13	251	303	73
Hartford	80	27	34	19	303	312	73
Detroit	80	26	43	11	268	306	63
Adams Division							
Buffalo	80	47	17	16	318	201	110
Boston	80	46	21	13	310	234	105
Minnesota	80	36	28	16	311	253	88
Toronto	80	35	40	5	304	327	75
Quebec	80	25	44	11	248	313	61
CLARENCE CAMPBELL CONFERENCE							
Patrick Division							
Philadelphia	80	48	12	20	327	254	116
*NY Islanders	80	39	28	13	281	247	91
NY Rangers	80	38	32	10	308	284	86
Atlanta	80	35	32	13	282	269	83
Washington	80	27	40	13	261	293	67
Smythe Division							
Chicago	80	34	27	19	241	250	87
St. Louis	80	34	34	12	266	278	80
Vancouver	80	27	37	16	256	281	70
Edmonton	80	28	39	13	301	322	69
Winnipeg	80	20	49	11	214	314	51
Colorado	80	19	48	13	234	308	51

Leading Scorers

Player	Club	GP	G	A	PTS	PIM
Dionne, Marcel	Los Angeles	80	53	84	137	32
Gretzky, Wayne	Edmonton	79	51	86	137	21
Lafleur, Guy	Montreal	74	50	75	125	12
Perreault, Gilbert	Buffalo	80	40	66	106	57
Rogers, Mike	Hartford	80	44	61	105	10
Trottier, Bryan	NY Islanders	78	42	62	104	68
Simmer, Charlie	Los Angeles	64	56	45	101	65
Stoughton, Blaine	Hartford	80	56	44	100	16
Sittler, Darryl	Toronto	73	40	57	97	62
MacDonald, Blair	Edmonton	80	46	48	94	6
Federko, Bernie	St. Louis	79	38	56	94	24

1980-81

PRINCE OF WALES CONFERENCE

Norris Division

Team	GP	W	L	T	GF	GA	PTS
Montreal	80	45	22	13	332	232	103
Los Angeles	80	43	24	13	337	290	99
Pittsburgh	80	30	37	13	302	345	73
Hartford	80	21	41	18	292	372	60
Detroit	80	19	43	18	252	339	56
Adams Division							
Buffalo	80	39	20	21	327	250	99
Boston	80	37	30	13	316	272	87
Minnesota	80	35	28	17	291	263	87
Quebec	80	30	32	18	314	318	78
Toronto	80	28	37	15	322	367	71
CLARENCE CAMPBELL CONFERENCE							
Patrick Division							
*NY Islanders	80	48	18	14	355	260	110
Philadelphia	80	41	24	15	313	249	97
Calgary	80	39	27	14	329	298	92
NY Rangers	80	30	36	14	312	317	74
Washington	80	26	36	18	286	317	70
Smythe Division							
St. Louis	80	45	18	17	352	281	107
Chicago	80	31	33	16	304	315	78
Vancouver	80	28	32	20	289	301	76
Edmonton	80	29	35	16	328	327	74
Colorado	80	22	45	13	258	344	57
Winnipeg	80	9	57	14	246	400	32

Leading Scorers

Player	Club	GP	G	A	PTS	PIM
Gretzky, Wayne	Edmonton	80	55	109	164	28
Dionne, Marcel	Los Angeles	80	58	77	135	70
Nilsson, Kent	Calgary	80	49	82	131	26
Bossy, Mike	NY Islanders	79	68	51	119	32
Taylor, Dave	Los Angeles	72	47	65	112	130
Stastny, Peter	Quebec	77	39	70	109	37
Simmer, Charlie	Los Angeles	65	56	49	105	62
Rogers, Mike	Hartford	80	40	65	105	32
Federko, Bernie	St. Louis	78	31	73	104	47
Richard, Jacques	Quebec	78	52	51	103	39
Middleton, Rick	Boston	80	44	59	103	16
Trottier, Bryan	NY Islanders	73	31	72	103	74

1981-82

CLARENCE CAMPBELL CONFERENCE

Norris Division

Team	GP	W	L	T	GF	GA	PTS
Minnesota	80	37	23	20	346	288	94
Winnipeg	80	33	33	14	319	332	80
St. Louis	80	32	40	8	315	349	72
Chicago	80	30	38	12	332	363	72
Toronto	80	20	44	16	298	380	56
Detroit	80	21	47	12	270	351	54
Smythe Division							
Edmonton	80	48	17	15	417	295	111
Vancouver	80	30	33	17	290	286	77
Calgary	80	29	34	17	334	345	75
Los Angeles	80	24	41	15	314	369	63
Colorado	80	18	49	13	241	362	49
PRINCE OF WALES CONFERENCE							
Adams Division							
Montreal	80	46	17	17	360	223	109
Boston	80	43	27	10	323	285	96
Buffalo	80	39	26	15	307	273	93
Quebec	80	33	31	16	356	345	82
Hartford	80	21	41	18	264	351	60
Patrick Division							
*NY Islanders	80	54	16	10	385	250	118
NY Rangers	80	39	27	14	316	306	92
Philadelphia	80	38	31	11	325	313	87
Pittsburgh	80	31	36	13	310	337	75
Washington	80	26	41	13	319	338	65

Leading Scorers

Player	Club	GP	G	A	PTS	PIM
Gretzky, Wayne	Edmonton	80	92	120	212	26
Bossy, Mike	NY Islanders	80	64	83	147	22
Stastny, Peter	Quebec	80	46	93	139	91
Maruk, Dennis	Washington	80	60	76	136	128
Trottier, Bryan	NY Islanders	80	50	79	129	88
Savard, Denis	Chicago	80	32	87	119	82
Dionne, Marcel	Los Angeles	78	50	67	117	50
Smith, Bobby	Minnesota	80	43	71	114	82
Ciccarelli, Dino	Minnesota	76	55	51	106	138
Taylor, Dave	Los Angeles	78	39	67	106	130

1982-83

CLARENCE CAMPBELL CONFERENCE

Norris Division

Team	GP	W	L	T	GF	GA	PTS
Chicago	80	47	23	10	338	268	104
Minnesota	80	40	24	16	321	290	96
Toronto	80	28	40	12	293	330	68
St. Louis	80	25	40	15	285	316	65
Detroit	80	21	44	15	263	344	57
Smythe Division							
Edmonton	80	47	21	12	424	315	106
Calgary	80	32	34	14	321	317	78
Vancouver	80	30	35	15	303	309	75
Winnipeg	80	33	39	8	311	333	74
Los Angeles	80	27	41	12	308	365	66
PRINCE OF WALES CONFERENCE							
Adams Division							
Boston	80	50	20	10	327	228	110
Montreal	80	42	24	14	350	286	98
Buffalo	80	38	29	13	318	285	89
Quebec	80	34	34	12	343	336	80
Hartford	80	19	54	7	261	403	45
Patrick Division							
Philadelphia	80	49	23	8	326	240	106
*NY Islanders	80	42	26	12	302	226	96
Washington	80	39	25	16	306	283	94
NY Rangers	80	35	35	10	306	287	80
New Jersey	80	17	49	14	230	338	48
Pittsburgh	80	18	53	9	257	394	45

Leading Scorers

Player	Club	GP	G	A	PTS	PIM
Gretzky, Wayne	Edmonton	80	71	125	196	59
Stastny, Peter	Quebec	75	47	77	124	78
Savard, Denis	Chicago	78	35	86	121	99
Bossy, Mike	NY Islanders	79	60	58	118	20
Dionne, Marcel	Los Angeles	80	56	51	107	22
Pederson, Barry	Boston	77	46	61	107	47
Messier, Mark	Edmonton	77	48	58	106	72
Goulet, Michel	Quebec	80	57	48	105	51
Anderson, Glenn	Edmonton	72	48	56	104	70
Nilsson, Kent	Calgary	80	46	58	104	10
Kurri, Jari	Edmonton	80	45	59	104	22

1983-84

CLARENCE CAMPBELL CONFERENCE

Norris Division

Team	GP	W	L	T	GF	GA	PTS
Minnesota	80	39	31	10	345	344	88
St. Louis	80	32	41	7	293	316	71
Detroit	80	31	42	7	298	323	69
Chicago	80	30	42	8	277	311	68
Toronto	80	26	45	9	303	387	61
Smythe Division							
*Edmonton	80	57	18	5	446	314	119
Calgary	80	34	32	14	311	314	82
Vancouver	80	32	39	9	306	328	73
Winnipeg	80	31	38	11	340	374	73
Los Angeles	80	23	44	13	309	376	59
PRINCE OF WALES CONFERENCE							
Adams Division							
Boston	80	49	25	6	336	261	104
Buffalo	80	48	25	7	315	257	103
Quebec	80	42	28	10	360	278	94
Montreal	80	35	40	5	286	295	75
Hartford	80	28	42	10	288	320	66
Patrick Division							
NY Islanders	80	50	26	4	357	269	104
Washington	80	48	27	5	308	226	101
Philadelphia	80	44	26	10	350	290	98
NY Rangers	80	42	29	9	314	304	93
New Jersey	80	17	56	7	231	350	41
Pittsburgh	80	16	58	6	254	390	38

Leading Scorers

Player	Club	GP	G	A	PTS	PIM
Gretzky, Wayne	Edmonton	74	87	118	205	39
Coffey, Paul	Edmonton	80	40	86	126	104
Goulet, Michel	Quebec	75	56	65	121	76
Stastny, Peter	Quebec	80	46	73	119	73
Bossy, Mike	NY Islanders	67	51	67	118	8
Pederson, Barry	Boston	80	39	77	116	64
Kurri, Jari	Edmonton	64	52	61	113	14
Trottier, Bryan	NY Islanders	68	40	71	111	59
Federko, Bernie	St. Louis	79	41	66	107	43
Middleton, Rick	Boston	80	47	58	105	14

1984-85

CLARENCE CAMPBELL CONFERENCE

Norris Division

Team	GP	W	L	T	GF	GA	PTS
St. Louis	80	37	31	12	299	288	86
Chicago	80	38	35	7	309	299	83
Detroit	80	27	41	12	313	357	66
Minnesota	80	25	43	12	268	321	62
Toronto	80	20	52	8	253	358	48
Smythe Division							
*Edmonton	80	49	20	11	401	298	109
Winnipeg	80	43	27	10	358	332	96
Calgary	80	41	27	12	363	302	94
Los Angeles	80	34	32	14	339	326	82
Vancouver	80	25	46	9	284	401	59
PRINCE OF WALES CONFERENCE							
Adams Division							
Montreal	80	41	27	12	309	262	94
Quebec	80	41	30	9	323	275	91
Buffalo	80	38	28	14	290	237	90
Boston	80	36	34	10	303	287	82
Hartford	80	30	41	9	268	318	69
Patrick Division							
Philadelphia	80	53	20	7	348	241	113
Washington	80	46	25	9	322	240	101
NY Islanders	80	40	34	6	345	312	86
NY Rangers	80	26	44	10	295	345	62
New Jersey	80	22	48	10	264	346	54
Pittsburgh	80	24	51	5	276	385	53

Leading Scorers

Player	Club	GP	G	A	PTS	PIM
Gretzky, Wayne	Edmonton	80	73	135	208	52
Kurri, Jari	Edmonton	73	71	64	135	30
Hawerchuk, Dale	Winnipeg	80	53	77	130	74
Dionne, Marcel	Los Angeles	80	46	80	126	46
Coffey, Paul	Edmonton	80	37	84	121	97
Bossy, Mike	NY Islanders	76	58	59	117	38
Ogrodnick, John	Detroit	79	55	50	105	30
Savard, Denis	Chicago	79	38	67	105	56
Federko, Bernie	St. Louis	76	30	73	103	27
Gartner, Mike	Washington	80	50	52	102	71

1985-86

CLARENCE CAMPBELL CONFERENCE

Norris Division

Team	GP	W	L	T	GF	GA	PTS
Chicago	80	39	33	8	351	349	86
Minnesota	80	38	33	9	327	305	85
St. Louis	80	37	34	9	302	291	83
Toronto	80	25	48	7	311	386	57
Detroit	80	17	57	6	266	415	40
Smythe Division							
Edmonton	80	56	17	7	426	310	119
Calgary	80	40	31	9	354	315	89
Winnipeg	80	26	47	7	295	372	59
Vancouver	80	23	44	13	282	333	59
Los Angeles	80	23	49	8	284	389	54
PRINCE OF WALES CONFERENCE							
Adams Division							
Quebec	80	43	31	6	330	289	92
*Montreal	80	40	33	7	330	280	87
Boston	80	37	31	12	311	288	86
Hartford	80	40	36	4	332	302	84
Buffalo	80	37	37	6	296	291	80
Patrick Division							
Philadelphia	80	53	23	4	335	241	110
Washington	80	50	23	7	315	272	107
NY Islanders	80	39	29	12	327	284	90
NY Rangers	80	36	38	6	280	276	78
Pittsburgh	80	34	38	8	313	305	76
New Jersey	80	28	49	3	300	374	59

Leading Scorers

Player	Club	GP	G	A	PTS	PIM
Gretzky, Wayne	Edmonton	80	52	163	215	52
Lemieux, Mario	Pittsburgh	79	48	93	141	43
Coffey, Paul	Edmonton	79	48	90	138	120
Kurri, Jari	Edmonton	78	68	63	131	22
Bossy, Mike	NY Islanders	80	61	62	123	14
Stastny, Peter	Quebec	76	41	81	122	60
Savard, Denis	Chicago	80	47	69	116	111
Naslund, Mats	Montreal	80	43	67	110	16
Hawerchuk, Dale	Winnipeg	80	46	59	105	44
Broten, Neal	Minnesota	80	29	76	105	47

1986-87

CLARENCE CAMPBELL CONFERENCE

Norris Division

Team	GP	W	L	T	GF	GA	PTS
St. Louis	80	32	33	15	281	293	79
Detroit	80	34	36	10	260	274	78
Chicago	80	29	37	14	290	310	72
Toronto	80	32	42	6	286	319	70
Minnesota	80	30	40	10	290	314	70
Smythe Division							
*Edmonton	80	50	24	6	372	284	106
Calgary	80	46	31	3	318	289	95
Winnipeg	80	40	32	8	279	271	88
Los Angeles	80	31	41	8	318	341	70
Vancouver	80	29	43	8	282	314	66
PRINCE OF WALES CONFERENCE							
Adams Division							
Hartford	80	43	30	7	287	270	93
Montreal	80	41	29	10	277	241	92
Boston	80	39	34	7	301	276	85
Quebec	80	31	39	10	267	276	72
Buffalo	80	28	44	8	280	308	64
Patrick Division							
Philadelphia	80	46	26	8	310	245	100
Washington	80	38	32	10	285	278	86
NY Islanders	80	35	33	12	279	281	82
NY Rangers	80	34	38	8	307	323	76
Pittsburgh	80	30	38	12	297	290	72
New Jersey	80	29	45	6	293	368	64

Leading Scorers

Player	Club	GP	G	A	PTS	PIM
Gretzky, Wayne	Edmonton	79	62	121	183	28
Kurri, Jari	Edmonton	79	54	54	108	41
Lemieux, Mario	Pittsburgh	63	54	53	107	57
Messier, Mark	Edmonton	77	37	70	107	73
Gilmour, Doug	St. Louis	80	42	63	105	58
Ciccarelli, Dino	Minnesota	80	52	51	103	92
Hawerchuk, Dale	Winnipeg	80	47	53	100	54
Goulet, Michel	Quebec	75	49	47	96	61
Kerr, Tim	Philadelphia	75	58	37	95	57
Bourque, Ray	Boston	78	23	72	95	36

1987-88

CLARENCE CAMPBELL CONFERENCE

Norris Division

Team	GP	W	L	T	GF	GA	PTS
Detroit	80	41	28	11	322	269	93
St. Louis	80	34	38	8	278	294	76
Chicago	80	30	41	9	284	328	69
Toronto	80	21	49	10	273	345	52
Minnesota	80	19	48	13	242	349	51
Smythe Division							
Calgary	80	48	23	9	397	305	105
*Edmonton	80	44	25	11	363	288	99
Winnipeg	80	33	36	11	292	310	77
Los Angeles	80	30	42	8	318	359	68
Vancouver	80	25	46	9	272	320	59
PRINCE OF WALES CONFERENCE							
Adams Division							
Montreal	80	45	22	13	298	238	103
Boston	80	44	30	6	300	251	94
Buffalo	80	37	32	11	283	305	85
Hartford	80	35	38	7	249	267	77
Quebec	80	32	43	5	271	306	69
Patrick Division							
NY Islanders	80	39	31	10	308	267	88
Washington	80	38	33	9	281	249	85
Philadelphia	80	38	33	9	292	292	85
New Jersey	80	38	36	6	295	296	82
NY Rangers	80	36	34	10	300	283	82
Pittsburgh	80	36	35	9	319	316	81

Leading Scorers

Player	Club	GP	G	A	PTS	PIM
Lemieux, Mario	Pittsburgh	76	70	98	168	92
Gretzky, Wayne	Edmonton	64	40	109	149	24
Savard, Denis	Chicago	80	44	87	131	95
Hawerchuk, Dale	Winnipeg	80	44	77	121	59
Robitaille, Luc	Los Angeles	80	53	58	111	82
Stastny, Peter	Quebec	76	46	65	111	69
Messier, Mark	Edmonton	77	37	74	111	103
Carson, Jimmy	Los Angeles	80	55	52	107	45
Loob, Hakan	Calgary	80	50	56	106	47
Goulet, Michel	Quebec	80	48	58	106	56

1988-89

CLARENCE CAMPBELL CONFERENCE

Norris Division

Team	GP	W	L	T	GF	GA	PTS
Detroit	80	34	34	12	313	316	80
St. Louis	80	33	35	12	275	285	78
Minnesota	80	27	37	16	258	278	70
Chicago	80	27	41	12	297	335	66
Toronto	80	28	46	6	259	342	62
Smythe Division							
*Calgary	80	54	17	9	354	226	117
Los Angeles	80	42	31	7	376	335	91
Edmonton	80	38	34	8	325	306	84
Vancouver	80	33	39	8	251	253	74
Winnipeg	80	26	42	12	300	355	64
PRINCE OF WALES CONFERENCE							
Adams Division							
Montreal	80	53	18	9	315	218	115
Boston	80	37	29	14	289	256	88
Buffalo	80	38	35	7	291	299	83
Hartford	80	37	38	5	299	290	79
Quebec	80	27	46	7	269	342	61
Patrick Division							
Washington	80	41	29	10	305	259	92
Pittsburgh	80	40	33	7	347	349	87
NY Rangers	80	37	35	8	310	307	82
Philadelphia	80	36	36	8	307	285	80
New Jersey	80	27	41	12	281	325	66
NY Islanders	80	28	47	5	265	325	61

Leading Scorers

Player	Club	GP	G	A	PTS	PIM
Lemieux, Mario	Pittsburgh	76	85	114	199	100
Gretzky, Wayne	Los Angeles	78	54	114	168	26
Yzerman, Steve	Detroit	80	65	90	155	61
Nicholls, Bernie	Los Angeles	79	70	80	150	96
Brown, Rob	Pittsburgh	68	49	66	115	118
Coffey, Paul	Pittsburgh	75	30	83	113	193
Mullen, Joe	Calgary	79	51	59	110	16
Kurri, Jari	Edmonton	76	44	58	102	69
Carson, Jimmy	Edmonton	80	49	51	100	36
Robitaille, Luc	Los Angeles	78	46	52	98	65

1989-90

CLARENCE CAMPBELL CONFERENCE

Norris Division

Team	GP	W	L	T	GF	GA	PTS
Chicago	80	41	33	6	316	294	88
St. Louis	80	37	34	9	295	279	83
Toronto	80	38	38	4	337	358	80
Minnesota	80	36	40	4	284	291	76
Detroit	80	28	38	14	288	323	70
Smythe Division							
Calgary	80	42	23	15	348	265	99
*Edmonton	80	38	28	14	315	283	90
Winnipeg	80	37	32	11	298	290	85
Los Angeles	80	34	39	7	338	337	75
Vancouver	80	25	41	14	245	306	64
PRINCE OF WALES CONFERENCE							
Adams Division							
Boston	80	46	25	9	289	232	101
Buffalo	80	45	27	8	286	248	98
Montreal	80	41	28	11	288	234	93
Hartford	80	38	33	9	275	268	85
Quebec	80	12	61	7	240	407	31
Patrick Division							
NY Rangers	80	36	31	13	279	267	85
New Jersey	80	37	34	9	295	288	83
Washington	80	36	38	6	284	275	78
NY Islanders	80	31	38	11	281	288	73
Pittsburgh	80	32	40	8	318	359	72
Philadelphia	80	30	39	11	290	297	71

Leading Scorers

Player	Club	GP	G	A	PTS	PIM
Gretzky, Wayne	Los Angeles	73	40	102	142	42
Messier, Mark	Edmonton	79	45	84	129	79
Yzerman, Steve	Detroit	79	62	65	127	79
Lemieux, Mario	Pittsburgh	59	45	78	123	78
Hull, Brett	St. Louis	80	72	41	113	24
Nicholls, Bernie	L.A., NYR	79	39	73	112	86
Turgeon, Pierre	Buffalo	80	40	66	106	29
LaFontaine, Pat	NY Islanders	74	54	51	105	38
Coffey, Paul	Pittsburgh	80	29	74	103	95
Sakic, Joe	Quebec	80	39	63	102	27
Oates, Adam	St. Louis	80	23	79	102	30

1990-91

CLARENCE CAMPBELL CONFERENCE

Norris Division

Team	GP	W	L	T	GF	GA	PTS
Chicago	80	49	23	8	284	211	106
St. Louis	80	47	22	11	310	250	105
Detroit	80	34	38	8	273	298	76
Minnesota	80	27	39	14	256	266	68
Toronto	80	23	46	11	241	318	57
Smythe Division							
Los Angeles	80	46	24	10	340	254	102
Calgary	80	46	26	8	344	263	100
Edmonton	80	37	37	6	272	272	80
Vancouver	80	28	43	9	243	315	65
Winnipeg	80	26	43	11	260	288	63
PRINCE OF WALES CONFERENCE							
Adams Division							
Boston	80	44	24	12	299	264	100
Montreal	80	39	30	11	273	249	89
Buffalo	80	31	30	19	292	278	81
Hartford	80	31	38	11	238	276	73
Quebec	80	16	50	14	236	354	46
Patrick Division							
*Pittsburgh	80	41	33	6	342	305	88
NY Rangers	80	36	31	13	297	265	85
Washington	80	37	36	7	258	258	81
New Jersey	80	32	33	15	272	264	79
Philadelphia	80	33	37	10	252	267	76
NY Islanders	80	25	45	10	223	290	60

Leading Scorers

Player	Club	GP	G	A	PTS	PIM
Gretzky, Wayne	Los Angeles	78	41	122	163	16
Hull, Brett	St. Louis	78	86	45	131	22
Oates, Adam	St. Louis	61	25	90	115	29
Recchi, Mark	Pittsburgh	78	40	73	113	48
Cullen, John	Pit., Hfd.	78	39	71	110	101
Sakic, Joe	Quebec	80	48	61	109	24
Yzerman, Steve	Detroit	80	51	57	108	34
Fleury, Theo	Calgary	79	51	53	104	136
MacInnis, Al	Calgary	78	28	75	103	90
Larmer, Steve	Chicago	80	44	57	101	79

1991-92

CLARENCE CAMPBELL CONFERENCE

Norris Division

Team	GP	W	L	T	GF	GA	PTS
Detroit	80	43	25	12	320	256	98
Chicago	80	36	29	15	257	236	87
St. Louis	80	36	33	11	279	266	83
Minnesota	80	32	42	6	246	278	70
Toronto	80	30	43	7	234	294	67

Smythe Division

Team	GP	W	L	T	GF	GA	PTS
Vancouver	80	42	26	12	285	250	96
Los Angeles	80	35	31	14	287	296	84
Edmonton	80	36	34	10	295	297	82
Winnipeg	80	33	32	15	251	244	81
Calgary	80	31	37	12	296	305	74
San Jose	80	17	58	5	219	359	39

PRINCE OF WALES CONFERENCE

Adams Division

Team	GP	W	L	T	GF	GA	PTS
Montreal	80	41	28	11	267	207	93
Boston	80	36	32	12	270	275	84
Buffalo	80	31	37	12	289	299	74
Hartford	80	26	41	13	247	283	65
Quebec	80	20	48	12	255	318	52

Patrick Division

Team	GP	W	L	T	GF	GA	PTS
NY Rangers	80	50	25	5	321	246	105
Washington	80	45	27	8	330	275	98
*Pittsburgh	80	39	32	9	343	308	87
New Jersey	80	38	31	11	289	259	87
NY Islanders	80	34	35	11	291	299	79
Philadelphia	80	32	37	11	252	273	75

Leading Scorers

Player	Club	GP	G	A	PTS	PIM
Lemieux, Mario	Pittsburgh	64	44	87	131	94
Stevens, Kevin	Pittsburgh	80	54	69	123	254
Gretzky, Wayne	Los Angeles	74	31	90	121	34
Hull, Brett	St. Louis	73	70	39	109	48
Robitaille, Luc	Los Angeles	80	44	63	107	95
Messier, Mark	NY Rangers	79	35	72	107	76
Roenick, Jeremy	Chicago	80	53	50	103	23
Yzerman, Steve	Detroit	79	45	58	103	64
Leetch, Brian	NY Rangers	80	22	80	102	26
Oates, Adam	St. L., Bos.	80	20	79	99	22

1992-93

CLARENCE CAMPBELL CONFERENCE

Norris Division

Team	GP	W	L	T	GF	GA	PTS
Chicago	84	47	25	12	279	230	106
Detroit	84	47	28	9	369	280	103
Toronto	84	44	29	11	288	241	99
St. Louis	84	37	36	11	282	278	85
Minnesota	84	36	38	10	272	293	82
Tampa Bay	84	23	54	7	245	332	53

Smythe Division

Team	GP	W	L	T	GF	GA	PTS
Vancouver	84	46	29	9	346	278	101
Calgary	84	43	30	11	322	282	97
Los Angeles	84	39	35	10	338	340	88
Winnipeg	84	40	37	7	322	320	87
Edmonton	84	26	50	8	242	337	60
San Jose	84	11	71	2	218	414	24

PRINCE OF WALES CONFERENCE

Adams Division

Team	GP	W	L	T	GF	GA	PTS
Boston	84	51	26	7	332	268	109
Quebec	84	47	27	10	351	300	104
*Montreal	84	48	30	6	326	280	102
Buffalo	84	38	36	10	335	297	86
Hartford	84	26	52	6	284	369	58
Ottawa	84	10	70	4	202	395	24

Patrick Division

Team	GP	W	L	T	GF	GA	PTS
Pittsburgh	84	56	21	7	367	268	119
Washington	84	43	34	7	325	286	93
NY Islanders	84	40	37	7	335	297	87
New Jersey	84	40	37	7	308	299	87
Philadelphia	84	36	37	11	319	319	83
NY Rangers	84	34	39	11	304	308	79

Leading Scorers

Player	Club	GP	G	A	PTS	PIM
Lemieux, Mario	Pittsburgh	60	69	91	160	38
LaFontaine, Pat	Buffalo	84	53	95	148	63
Oates, Adam	Boston	84	45	97	142	32
Yzerman, Steve	Detroit	84	58	79	137	44
Selanne, Teemu	Winnipeg	84	76	56	132	45
Turgeon, Pierre	NY Islanders	83	58	74	132	26
Mogilny, Alex.	Buffalo	77	76	51	127	40
Gilmour, Doug	Toronto	83	32	95	127	100
Robitaille, Luc	Los Angeles	84	63	62	125	100
Recchi, Mark	Philadelphia	84	53	70	123	95

1993-94

EASTERN CONFERENCE

Northeast Division

Team	GP	W	L	T	GF	GA	PTS
Pittsburgh	84	44	27	13	299	285	101
Boston	84	42	29	13	289	252	97
Montreal	84	41	29	14	283	248	96
Buffalo	84	43	32	9	282	218	95
Quebec	84	34	42	8	277	292	76
Hartford	84	27	48	9	227	288	63
Ottawa	84	14	61	9	201	397	37

Atlantic Division

Team	GP	W	L	T	GF	GA	PTS
*NY Rangers	84	52	24	8	299	231	112
New Jersey	84	47	25	12	306	220	106
Washington	84	39	35	10	277	263	88
NY Islanders	84	36	36	12	282	264	84
Florida	84	33	34	17	233	233	83
Philadelphia	84	35	39	10	294	314	80
Tampa Bay	84	30	43	11	224	251	71

WESTERN CONFERENCE

Central Division

Team	GP	W	L	T	GF	GA	PTS
Detroit	84	46	30	8	356	275	100
Toronto	84	43	29	12	280	243	98
Dallas	84	42	29	13	286	265	97
St. Louis	84	40	33	11	270	283	91
Chicago	84	39	36	9	254	240	87
Winnipeg	84	24	51	9	245	344	57

Pacific Division

Team	GP	W	L	T	GF	GA	PTS
Calgary	84	42	29	13	302	256	97
Vancouver	84	41	40	3	279	276	85
San Jose	84	33	35	16	252	265	82
Anaheim	84	33	46	5	229	251	71
Los Angeles	84	27	45	12	294	322	66
Edmonton	84	25	45	14	261	305	64

Leading Scorers

Player	Club	GP	G	A	PTS	PIM
Gretzky, Wayne	Los Angeles	81	38	92	130	20
Fedorov, Sergei	Detroit	82	56	64	120	34
Oates, Adam	Boston	77	32	80	112	45
Gilmour, Doug	Toronto	83	27	84	111	105
Bure, Pavel	Vancouver	76	60	47	107	86
Roenick, Jeremy	Chicago	84	46	61	107	125
Recchi, Mark	Philadelphia	84	40	67	107	46
Shanahan, B.	St. Louis	81	52	50	102	211
Andreychuk, Dave	Toronto	83	53	46	99	98
Jagr, Jaromir	Pittsburgh	80	32	67	99	61

1994-95

EASTERN CONFERENCE

Northeast Division

Team	GP	W	L	T	GF	GA	PTS
Quebec	48	30	13	5	185	134	65
Pittsburgh	48	29	16	3	181	158	61
Boston	48	27	18	3	150	127	57
Buffalo	48	22	19	7	130	119	51
Hartford	48	19	24	5	127	141	43
Montreal	48	18	23	7	125	148	43
Ottawa	48	9	34	5	117	174	23

Atlantic Division

Team	GP	W	L	T	GF	GA	PTS
Philadelphia	48	28	16	4	150	132	60
*New Jersey	48	22	18	8	136	121	52
Washington	48	22	18	8	136	120	52
NY Rangers	48	22	23	3	139	134	47
Florida	48	20	22	6	115	127	46
Tampa Bay	48	17	28	3	120	144	37
NY Islanders	48	15	28	5	126	158	35

WESTERN CONFERENCE

Central Division

Team	GP	W	L	T	GF	GA	PTS
Detroit	48	33	11	4	180	117	70
St. Louis	48	28	15	5	178	135	61
Chicago	48	24	19	5	156	115	53
Toronto	48	21	19	8	135	146	50
Dallas	48	17	23	8	136	135	42
Winnipeg	48	16	25	7	157	177	39

Pacific Division

Team	GP	W	L	T	GF	GA	PTS
Calgary	48	24	17	7	163	135	55
Vancouver	48	18	18	12	153	148	48
San Jose	48	19	25	4	129	161	42
Los Angeles	48	16	23	9	142	174	41
Edmonton	48	17	27	4	136	183	38
Anaheim	48	16	27	5	125	164	37

Leading Scorers

Player	Club	GP	G	A	PTS	PIM
Jagr, Jaromir	Pittsburgh	48	32	38	70	37
Lindros, Eric	Philadelphia	46	29	41	70	60
Zhamnov, Alexei	Winnipeg	48	30	35	65	20
Sakic, Joe	Quebec	47	19	43	62	30
Francis, Ron	Pittsburgh	44	11	48	59	18
Fleury, Theoren	Calgary	47	29	29	58	112
Coffey, Paul	Detroit	45	14	44	58	72
Renberg, Mikael	Philadelphia	47	26	31	57	20
LeClair, John	Mtl., Phi.	46	26	28	54	30
Messier, Mark	NY Rangers	46	14	39	53	40
Oates, Adam	Boston	48	12	41	53	8

Top 10 All-Time Career Goals-Against Average

1.91	Alex Connell
1.91	George Hainsworth
2.02	Chuck Gardiner
2.04	Lorne Chabot
2.08	Tiny Thompson
2.16	Martin Brodeur
2.17	Dave Kerr
2.24	Ken Dryden
2.27	Roy Worters
2.31	Clint Benedict

Top 10 All-Time Career Shutouts

103	Terry Sawchuk
94	George Hainsworth
84	Glenn Hall
82	Jacques Plante
81	Tiny Thompson
81	Alex Connell
76	Tony Esposito
73	Lorne Chabot
71	Harry Lumley
66	Roy Worters

Top 10 All-Time Single Season Goals-Against Average

0.92	Geo. Hainsworth	1928-29	Montreal
1.06	Geo. Hainsworth	1927-28	Montreal
1.13	Alex Connell	1925-26	Ottawa
1.15	Tiny Thompson	1928-29	Boston
1.15	Roy Worters	1928-29	NY Americans
1.24	Alex Connell	1927-28	Ottawa
1.37	Dolly Dolson	1928-29	Detroit
1.41	John Ross Roach	1928-29	NY Rangers
1.42	Clint Benedict	1926-27	Mtl. Maroons
1.43	Alex Connell	1928-29	Ottawa

Top 10 All-Time Single Season Shutouts

22	Geo. Hainsworth	1928-29	Montreal
15	Hal Winkler	1927-28	Boston
15	Tony Esposito	1969-70	Chicago
15	Alex Connell	1927-28	Ottawa
15	Alex Connell	1925-26	Ottawa
14	Geo. Hainsworth	1926-27	Montreal
13	Roy Worters	1928-29	NY Americans
13	John Ross Roach	1928-29	NY Rangers
13	Harry Lumley	1953-54	Toronto
13	Geo. Hainsworth	1927-28	Montreal
13	Alex Connell	1926-27	Ottawa
13	Clint Benedict	1926-27	Mtl. Maroons
13	Dominik Hasek	1997-98	Buffalo

1995-96

EASTERN CONFERENCE

Northeast Division

Team	GP	W	L	T	GF	GA	PTS
Pittsburgh	82	49	29	4	362	284	102
Boston	82	40	31	11	282	269	91
Montreal	82	40	32	10	265	248	90
Hartford	82	34	39	9	237	259	77
Buffalo	82	33	42	7	247	262	73
Ottawa	82	18	59	5	191	291	41

Atlantic Division

Team	GP	W	L	T	GF	GA	PTS
Philadelphia	82	45	24	13	282	208	103
NY Rangers	82	41	27	14	272	237	96
Florida	82	41	31	10	254	234	92
Washington	82	39	32	11	234	204	89
Tampa Bay	82	38	32	12	238	248	88
New Jersey	82	37	33	12	215	202	86
NY Islanders	82	22	50	10	229	315	54

WESTERN CONFERENCE

Central Division

Team	GP	W	L	T	GF	GA	PTS
Detroit	82	62	13	7	325	181	131
Chicago	82	40	28	14	273	220	94
Toronto	82	34	36	12	247	252	80
St. Louis	82	32	34	16	219	248	80
Winnipeg	82	36	40	6	275	291	78
Dallas	82	26	42	14	227	280	66

Pacific Division

Team	GP	W	L	T	GF	GA	PTS
*Colorado	82	47	25	10	326	240	104
Calgary	82	34	37	11	241	240	79
Vancouver	82	32	35	15	278	278	79
Anaheim	82	35	39	8	234	247	78
Edmonton	82	30	44	8	240	304	68
Los Angeles	82	24	40	18	256	302	66
San Jose	82	20	55	7	252	357	47

Leading Scorers

Player	Club	GP	G	A	PTS	PIM
Lemieux, Mario	Pittsburgh	70	69	92	161	54
Jagr, Jaromir	Pittsburgh	82	62	87	149	96
Sakic, Joe	Colorado	82	51	69	120	44
Francis, Ron	Pittsburgh	77	27	92	119	56
Forsberg, Peter	Colorado	82	30	86	116	47
Lindros, Eric	Philadelphia	73	47	68	115	163
Kariya, Paul	Anaheim	82	50	58	108	20
Selanne, Teemu	Wpg., Ana.	79	40	68	108	22
Mogilny, Alex.	Vancouver	79	55	52	107	16
Fedorov, Sergei	Detroit	78	39	68	107	48

1996-97

EASTERN CONFERENCE

Northeast Division

Team	GP	W	L	T	GF	GA	PTS
Buffalo	82	40	30	12	237	208	92
Pittsburgh	82	38	36	8	285	280	84
Ottawa	82	31	36	15	226	234	77
Montreal	82	31	36	15	249	276	77
Hartford	82	32	39	11	226	256	75
Boston	82	26	47	9	234	300	61

Atlantic Division

Team	GP	W	L	T	GF	GA	PTS
New Jersey	82	45	23	14	231	182	104
Philadelphia	82	45	24	13	274	217	103
Florida	82	35	28	19	221	201	89
NY Rangers	82	38	34	10	258	231	86
Washington	82	33	40	9	214	231	75
Tampa Bay	82	32	40	10	217	247	74
NY Islanders	82	29	41	12	240	250	70

WESTERN CONFERENCE

Central Division

Team	GP	W	L	T	GF	GA	PTS
Dallas	82	48	26	8	252	198	104
*Detroit	82	38	26	18	253	197	94
Phoenix	82	38	37	7	240	243	83
St. Louis	82	36	35	11	236	239	83
Chicago	82	34	35	13	223	210	81
Toronto	82	30	44	8	230	273	68

Pacific Division

Team	GP	W	L	T	GF	GA	PTS
Colorado	82	49	24	9	277	205	107
Anaheim	82	36	33	13	245	233	85
Edmonton	82	36	37	9	252	247	81
Vancouver	82	35	40	7	257	273	77
Calgary	82	32	41	9	214	239	73
Los Angeles	82	28	43	11	214	268	67
San Jose	82	27	47	8	211	278	62

Leading Scorers

Player	Club	GP	G	A	PTS	PIM
Lemieux, Mario	Pittsburgh	76	50	72	122	65
Selanne, Teemu	Anaheim	78	51	58	109	34
Kariya, Paul	Anaheim	69	44	55	99	6
LeClair, John	Philadelphia	82	50	47	97	58
Gretzky, Wayne	NY Rangers	82	25	72	97	28
Jagr, Jaromir	Pittsburgh	63	47	48	95	40
Sundin, Mats	Toronto	82	41	53	94	59
Palffy, Zigmund	NY Islanders	80	48	42	90	43
Francis, Ron	Pittsburgh	81	27	63	90	20
Shanahan, B.	Hfd., Det.	81	47	41	88	131

1997-98

EASTERN CONFERENCE

Northeast Division

Team	GP	W	L	T	GF	GA	PTS
Pittsburgh	82	40	24	18	228	188	98
Boston	82	39	30	13	221	194	91
Buffalo	82	36	29	17	211	187	89
Montreal	82	37	32	13	235	208	87
Ottawa	82	34	33	15	193	200	83
Carolina	82	33	41	8	200	219	74

Atlantic Division

Team	GP	W	L	T	GF	GA	PTS
New Jersey	82	48	23	11	225	166	107
Philadelphia	82	42	29	11	242	193	95
Washington	82	40	30	12	219	202	92
NY Islanders	82	30	41	11	212	225	71
NY Rangers	82	25	39	18	197	231	68
Florida	82	24	43	15	203	256	63
Tampa Bay	82	17	55	10	151	269	44

WESTERN CONFERENCE

Central Division

Team	GP	W	L	T	GF	GA	PTS
Dallas	82	49	22	11	242	167	109
*Detroit	82	44	23	15	250	196	103
St. Louis	82	45	29	8	256	204	98
Phoenix	82	35	35	12	224	227	82
Chicago	82	30	39	13	192	199	73
Toronto	82	30	43	9	194	237	69

Pacific Division

Team	GP	W	L	T	GF	GA	PTS
Colorado	82	39	26	17	231	205	95
Los Angeles	82	38	33	11	227	225	87
Edmonton	82	35	37	10	215	224	80
San Jose	82	34	38	10	210	216	78
Calgary	82	26	41	15	217	252	67
Anaheim	82	26	43	13	205	261	65
Vancouver	82	25	43	14	224	273	64

Leading Scorers

Player	Club	GP	G	A	PTS	PIM
Jagr, Jaromir	Pittsburgh	77	35	67	102	64
Forsberg, Peter	Colorado	72	25	66	91	94
Bure, Pavel	Vancouver	82	51	39	90	48
Gretzky, Wayne	NY Rangers	82	23	67	90	28
LeClair, John	Philadelphia	82	51	36	87	32
Palffy, Zigmund	NY Islanders	82	45	42	87	34
Francis, Ron	Pittsburgh	81	25	62	87	20
Selanne, Teemu	Anaheim	73	52	34	86	30
Allison, Jason	Boston	81	33	50	83	60
Stumpel, Jozef	Los Angeles	77	21	58	79	53

Top 10 All-Time Career Goals Scored

885	Wayne Gretzky
801	Gordie Howe
731	Marcel Dionne
717	Phil Esposito
708	Mike Gartner
613	Mario Lemieux
610	Bobby Hull
602	Dino Ciccarelli
601	Jari Kurri
597	Mark Messier

Top 10 All-Time Career Assists

1910	Wayne Gretzky
1090	Paul Coffey
1049	Gordie Howe
1040	Marcel Dionne
1036	Ray Bourque
1015	Mark Messier
1006	Ron Francis
926	Stan Mikita
901	Bryan Trottier
891	Dale Hawerchuk

Top 10 All-Time Career Points Scored

2795	Wayne Gretzky
1850	Gordie Howe
1771	Marcel Dionne
1612	Mark Messier
1590	Phil Esposito
1494	Mario Lemieux
1473	Paul Coffey
1467	Stan Mikita
1434	Ron Francis
1425	Bryan Trottier

Top 10 All-Time Single Season Goals Scored

92	Wayne Gretzky	1981-82	Edmonton
87	Wayne Gretzky	1983-84	Edmonton
86	Brett Hull	1990-91	St. Louis
85	Mario Lemieux	1988-89	Pittsburgh
76	Teemu Selanne	1992-93	Winnipeg
76	Alex. Mogilny	1992-93	Buffalo
76	Phil Esposito	1970-71	Boston
73	Wayne Gretzky	1984-85	Edmonton
72	Brett Hull	1989-90	St. Louis
71	Wayne Gretzky	1982-83	Edmonton

Top 10 All-Time Single Season Assists

163	Wayne Gretzky	1985-86	Edmonton
135	Wayne Gretzky	1984-85	Edmonton
125	Wayne Gretzky	1982-83	Edmonton
122	Wayne Gretzky	1990-91	Los Angeles
121	Wayne Gretzky	1986-87	Edmonton
120	Wayne Gretzky	1981-82	Edmonton
118	Wayne Gretzky	1983-84	Edmonton
114	Wayne Gretzky	1988-89	Los Angeles
114	Mario Lemieux	1988-89	Pittsburgh
109	Wayne Gretzky	1987-88	Edmonton

Top 10 All-Time Single Season Points Scored

215	Wayne Gretzky	1985-86	Edmonton
212	Wayne Gretzky	1981-82	Edmonton
208	Wayne Gretzky	1984-85	Edmonton
205	Wayne Gretzky	1983-84	Edmonton
199	Mario Lemieux	1988-89	Pittsburgh
196	Wayne Gretzky	1982-83	Edmonton
183	Wayne Gretzky	1986-87	Edmonton
168	Wayne Gretzky	1988-89	Los Angeles
168	Mario Lemieux	1987-88	Pittsburgh
164	Wayne Gretzky	1980-81	Edmonton

CHAPTER 15

Movers and Shapers

People and Forces that have had an Impact on NHL Hockey

JACK ADAMS
RED WING ARCHITECT
Milt Dunnell

IT WASN'T EASY TO KNOW JACK ADAMS, although thousands of people on both sides of the Canada–U.S. border thought they did. But which Jack Adams?

The citation that accompanied the first presentation of the Lester Patrick Trophy helped to identify one Jack Adams. It stated the award was for long and meritorious service to hockey in the United States. Which was a gross understatement, of course. It could have stated that Jack Adams was responsible for making the city of Detroit almost as famous for its hockey team as it was for putting wheels under humans.

You're talking about the gregarious Jack Adams, now, the one who spent countless days beating the drums for his favorite sport as the ultimate in competitive entertainment or as a career for sons and nephews. Few professed to know or understand the Jack Adams of the rinks. There was no hint of the "Jolly Jack," as he liked to be called at rinkside. Once he glimpsed the red line, "Jolly Jack" was like a chameleon which changed color. He became the terror of referees; he berated opposing coaches and managers; he demanded justice, at league level, for his Red Wings, whom he saw as victims of malfeasance. He was fined. He was suspended. He was vilified by the media in other league cities. Some professed to want his expulsion, without ever getting around to claiming he was bad for hockey.

It sure would have been difficult to prove Adams had been bad for hockey in Detroit. Going into a town where the game was a little-known, back-burner operation, with a club that was broke, Adams won the NHL championship a dozen times as manager; seven times he won the Stanley Cup. In three of those seven seasons, he also was the coach.

Frank Calder, the first president of the NHL, recommended Adams to Detroit in 1927, hoping to get the faltering club back on its skates. Adams mistook the assignment as a permanent job and spent 35 years with the team. During most of that time, he never had a contract. When the original Jim Norris, a Canadian-born multi-millionaire, took over the bankrupt team in the early 1930s, he was asked whether Adams would remain as coach. He replied that Adams was entitled to probation for a year or so.

Norris was almost as fierce a competitor as Adams was. In the early years of ownership, he played a hands-on role in the team's operation, making his opinions known on player deals, sharing in the assessment of talent at training camp and even making road trips. In later years, his doctors told him he should no longer attend the games. His blood pressure couldn't stand it. He still demanded a phone call from his manager or coach the moment a game was over. Adams used to say that phone call was salt in the wound when the Red Wings lost.

"Pops," as they called Norris when he wasn't listening, never did learn to get philosophical about losing. He owned the Chicago Stadium, where the Black Hawks played, as well as the Olympia in Detroit. He also was a major shareholder in Madison Square Garden, home of the New York Rangers. This duplication of ownership gave hockey critics live ammunition. They cited the Norris interests and influence, sometimes sneering at the NHL as "the Norris House League." No one ever suggested, though, that Norris had a friendly thought for any club except the Red Wings.

Nor was Jack Adams ever accused of having lingering loyalty to the Toronto Maple Leafs or the old Ottawa Senators, although he had won the Stanley Cup in both cities as a player. The Toronto club was not yet known as the Maple Leafs, but Adams, at $900 per year, was said to be its highest-paid player. Once he took the Detroit job, Toronto almost immediately became his most detested enemy.

Although he was born in Canada (Fort William, Ontario) Adams never could understand why people who lived right across the river from Detroit in Windsor, Ontario would cheer for the Leafs whenever they met the Red Wings at the Olympia. To him, it was like disloyalty in a neighbor. Adams had become a naturalized American citizen himself. His reasoning was logical: "This city has been good to me." He entered vigorously into community affairs—even ran for city council. He lost. The voters might have decided the Jack Adams brand of democracy belonged in the Olympia.

Like most of the managers and coaches in the early years of professional hockey, Adams was a product of the frozen ponds that dotted Canada from December to early April. A kid learned quickly to skate and stickhandle if he wanted a share of the puck because play was a disorganized free-for-all. Adams did learn quickly. Before he was 17, he was playing for a senior team in northern Michigan. He turned pro officially with Toronto in 1918 and soon was lured to the Pacific Coast Hockey Association by the Patrick brothers, Frank and Lester, who had decided to raid the eastern leagues for talent.

Adams proved to be a good choice. He led the league with 26 goals in 1921–22. After three seasons with Vancouver, he returned to Toronto, where he remained until 1925–26. Then, the scent of another Stanley Cup took him to Ottawa. It was good thinking. The Senators were loaded: King Clancy, Frank Nighbor, Hooley Smith, Cy Denneny and other quality players. They won the Stanley Cup in 1927. Although no one could have suspected it then, this was an historic occasion. It marked the last time the Cup has been won by a team from Ottawa, where its donor, Lord Stanley, had the original inspiration for the trophy.

Although he had moved around freely enough as a player, Adams, in later years as manager and coach, had no trouble defending the rigid control which the NHL exercised over the movement of its players. The reserve clause in their contracts dictated that once a player signed, he was the

property of that club until his contract was sold or traded. Even young, unsigned players whose names appeared on the various teams' reserve lists were unapproachable.

Adams, like his contemporaries, argued the system was fair. They offered careers which were unavailable anywhere else and they were entitled to protect their talent. Amazingly there were few challenges to the arrangement. Playing in the NHL was a dream that wasn't to be threatened by talk about free agency.

One of Adams' big coups, of course, was the signing of Gordie Howe, especially since Howe, one of the greatest prizes in the history of the game, had slipped through the fingers of Lester Patrick. Although deservedly proud of his coup, Adams found excuses for Patrick. He preferred to point out that Howe was only 14 when he showed up at the New York Rangers tryout camp in Winnipeg. The Rangers scouts had provided Patrick with a rich crop of hopefuls more experienced than Howe was. In short, Patrick was a victim of his own riches. He had no time for 14-year-olds.

Adams claimed he might have missed Howe, too, if he hadn't broken up his own candidates into small groups, separating them from the regulars. That way, he got a better look at individuals. As soon as he saw Howe, he claimed, he knew he had something special. He had that right. Howe played 1,767 games in the NHL, scored 801 goals, then took a couple of years off before coming back for a second career in the World Hockey Association.

As Adams used to point out, though, the road to success in the NHL was pitted with traffic bumps, and few hockey personalities suffered greater embarrassment than he did in the 1941–42 Stanley Cup final. After winning the first three games from the seemingly outclassed Toronto Maple Leafs, the Red Wings went into a tailspin and lost the remaining four. This never had happened before (or since) in the Stanley Cup finals. Adams himself had contributed to his team's undoing when, frustrated with the officiating, he went on the ice, with seconds remaining in the fourth game, in an attempt to attack referee Mel Harwood. League president Frank Calder ignored the Detroit manager's contention that he merely wanted to question the official. Adams was fined and suspended.

Naturally, he took a severe beating in the press, especially outside Detroit. Some of the reviews were so vitriolic that Adams consulted a lawyer and threatened libel suits against some of his critics. None of them ever had to appear in court, but a few considered it advisable to skip assignments in Detroit until tempers cooled. When Adams was presented with a Lincoln car by his admirers in Detroit, 10 years later, congratulations came from many of the typewriter jockeys who had been most caustic.

They didn't make the mistake of concluding Adams had mellowed, however. And, within a year, they had evidence that the fires of competition still burned within his ample belly. The headlines read that Adams had put himself in jeopardy of a $1,000 fine for barging into the referee's room between periods of a game in Detroit. The opposition was the Montreal Canadiens, who were high on Adams' hate list, right behind Toronto. Again, Adams insisted a mistake had been made. He had been invited into the room, he said, to discuss something that had come up during the period. Unfortunately, referee Red Storey couldn't recall issuing the invitation.

As had happened to his boss, Jim Norris Sr., Adams eventually got the bad news: he shouldn't even watch games in which the Red Wings were involved. He compromised by leaving the games and walking the streets after the second period. Construction of the Yonge Street subway was under way in Toronto at the time, and Adams used to joke that he supervised the project. It didn't help his blood pressure much, though, because he was constantly asking the workers if they had heard any score from Maple Leaf Gardens.

Adams suffered the inevitable fate of managers and coaches in 1962. He got fired. He was 66 by that time and maybe it was time to go. But, after 44 years in the NHL, counting his years as a player, even his most relentless critics agreed he deserved better.

DEPRESSION HOCKEY
Stan Fischler

THE ERA SPANNING January 1, 1920, through October 29, 1929, is often referred to as the Roaring Twenties. Prohibition in the United States was accompanied by bootleg booze, shorter skirts were deployed in new dances, jazz was discovered by a wider, mixed audience; a general joie de vivre seemed a natural antidote to the hangover left behind after World War I ended. At first the National Hockey League responded slowly to the explosion in sports (along with everything else) that accompanied the 1920s. It wasn't until the 1924–25 season that the league expanded to include its first American team, the Boston Bruins. A year later, the deluge of new teams began with the New York Americans and Pittsburgh Pirates, soon to be followed by entries from Chicago, Detroit and a second from Manhattan, the Rangers.

When league owners convened for their annual meeting in September 1929, they could not have predicted the economic disaster that was so near at that point. They prepared for a 1929–30 campaign that would feature new rules that accentuated the offense as the Boston Bruins prepared to defend the Stanley Cup. Then came October 29, 1929, and all bets were off, everywhere. WALL STREET LAYS AN EGG, shouted a headline in *Variety*, the show business weekly, as just one example. Between 1929 and 1931, stock losses alone were estimated at $50 billion. The Great Depression quickly overcame North American life and would have a profound effect on the NHL too. The massive unemployment that was part and parcel of the Great Depression meant that hockey fans, like almost everyone else, had less to spend on entertainment—that is, if they had any money at all, or a source of it, i.e. a job.

At first the league weathered the economic storm with no significant negative effects, but as the Depression lengthened, attendance dropped and clubs folded. In 1930, the Pittsburgh franchise was moved to Philadelphia—with little success. The Quakers suffered through an abysmal 1930–31 season with four wins, four ties and 36 losses before they asked permission to cease operations at the September 26, 1931, club owners' meeting. Ottawa did likewise even though the Senators had enjoyed a more successful season. And considering the city's rich hockey heritage, the loss of Ottawa sent shockwaves throughout the hockey world. The franchise requested permission to lease its players until it could resume operations and Ottawa rejoined the league after a one-year absence, but the NHL board of governors later gave the Senators permission to move the franchise to St. Louis and the St. Louis Eagles were born in 1934.

No less affected by the Depression, the Eagles also suffered mightily at the gate and on the ice. At the time, the

team had one outstanding line: Syd Howe (no relation to Gordie) on left wing, Frank Finnigan on right wing and Bill Cowley at center. Howe was among the league's top scorers, Finnigan was a cagey and reliable veteran and Cowley displayed all the potential of a budding star. But the struggling franchise needed financial support and its first move was to deal Howe to Detroit for cash and Finnigan to Toronto for more cash. Eventually, Syd Howe and Bill Cowley ended up in the Hockey Hall of Fame. The St. Louis Eagles did not.

Playing their final game of the season in St. Louis on March 12, 1935, the Eagles closed at home with a flourish by defeating the Red Wings 3–2. The last game of that miserable year was on the road at Maple Leaf Gardens, where St. Louis lost 5 3. The standings at season's end showed the Eagles with 11 wins, six ties and 31 defeats—the year's worst in the league.

Obviously, the St. Louis franchise was in desperate trouble. On September 28, 1935, the club asked the NHL board of governors for permission to suspend operations for one year. The board refused and instead proposed that the league buy the rights to players under option to St. Louis, with the understanding that the money would be paid to the club if the league managed to sell the franchise. At a second meeting on October 15, 1935, the league agreed to buy the franchise and its players. The board of governors then assigned a cash value to each of the Eagles players and held a draft in which the league's lowest-placed teams had first crack at the available talent.

Such setbacks notwithstanding, the NHL was able to plod through the harsh years of the 1930s and survive with no less than two franchises in New York (the Americans and Rangers) and Montreal (the Canadiens and Maroons). Still, at a time when the continent's hit tunes were "Brother, Can You Spare a Dime" and "I Got a Right to Sing the Blues," novel methods were used to lure fans to hockey rinks. In Atlantic City, they were invited to bring a bag of food to Convention Hall in lieu of cash to see an exhibition game between the Rangers and the Atlantic City Sea Gulls. The result was the largest crowd ever to witness a hockey game to that point—22,157. Meanwhile, Detroit registered one of the smallest crowds—2,000. It was a barometer of things to come for the rest of the decade.

At Madison Square Garden, the Rangers–Americans rivalry thrived although management reluctantly agreed to a one-third reduction in prices to adjust to the lower cost of living and reduced salaries. And Garden officials, headed by Tom Lockhart, found yet another way to draw fans. Lockhart had organized the Eastern Amateur Hockey League, including a team in New York (the Rovers) which featured graduates from the Canadian juniors who were willing to play on the senior level as a stepping stone to the NHL. A Rangers farm team, the Rovers played on Sunday afternoons at the Garden for half the price of an NHL ticket and became so popular that crowds averaging 11,000 were not unusual during the Depression.

Meanwhile, as if to outface the Depression, Conn Smythe orchestrated construction of a new ice palace in Toronto. Defying doubters—and probably logic—Maple Leaf Gardens opened on schedule on November 12, 1931. On March 6, 1933, all banks in the United States were ordered closed by President Franklin Delano Roosevelt, whereupon Congress passed New Deal social and economic measures to ease the country through its economic woes. Only the repeal of Prohibition on December 5, 1933, offered some solace to the embattled nation—although not to Americans owner William "Big Bill" Dwyer, who had made his fortune as a bootlegger.

Fortunately, the quality of NHL hockey remained high. Marquee players such as Howie Morenz, Eddie Shore, King Clancy and Frank Boucher excited the crowds. Some of them resisted the league's plea for fiscal prudence, however, the most notable being crack defenseman Eddie Shore. At one point, he announced to the Boston media that he'd quit before taking a salary cut, as suggested by Bruins management. He eventually signed a contract for $7,500, the maximum allowed by the NHL in 1933. By 1935, it had become apparent that the Depression was not letting up. Without Dwyer's bankroll, the Americans hit the financial skids but remained competitive. In desperation, the league set a collective salary limit for clubs at $62,500, while no individual player would be permitted a contract in excess of $7,000. The American Congress passed the Social Security Act that same year.

Hockey fans still had a good deal to cheer about, particularly in Detroit, where a dynasty was in the making under the orchestration of Jack Adams. In 1936, the Motor City sextet won its first of two consecutive Stanley Cup titles, and en route engaged in one of the most memorable games in NHL annals.

On March 26, 1936, the Red Wings and Montreal Maroons played the longest NHL game ever. The playoff match lasted into a ninth period, by which time the veterans on both teams were fatigued beyond recovery. It became essential to employ the players with the most stamina left; naturally, those were the inexperienced young skaters like Moderre "Mud" Bruneteau, a fresh-faced Red Wing rookie—the youngest man in the longest game.

At the 16-minute mark of the sixth overtime period, Bruneteau went to work. He surrounded the puck in the Detroit zone and passed to Hec Kilrea. The two teammates proceeded to challenge the Montreal defense, Kilrea faking a return pass, then sliding it across the blue line.

Bruneteau cut behind the defense, retrieved the puck in front of goalie Lorne Chabot and banged it in for the winning goal. "Thank God Chabot fell down as I drove it in the net," said Bruneteau. "It was the funniest thing. The puck just stuck there in the twine and it didn't fall to the ice." After 116 minutes and 30 seconds of overtime, the Red Wings had at last defeated the Maroons—thanks to Mud Bruneteau. The marathon game—still the longest in NHL history—was one of a number of memorable events sprinkled throughout the Depression. While the economic crisis continued unabated through the late 1930s, big-league hockey was making big news. Some of it was sad, as in the case of its once greatest star, Howie Morenz, and some of it was glad, as in the emergence of fresh talent and sparkling new forwards line that—unlike today's game—often stayed together for a full season or more.

The years 1936, 1937 and 1938 were filled with such incidents. During the 1936–37 season, Morenz had regained his stardom with the Canadiens and appeared on target for a banner season when he suffered a badly broken leg and was hospitalized, where he died unexpectedly on March 8, 1937. Prior to an all-star game to benefit his family, some of Howie's equipment was auctioned off and the star's jersey was presented to his son, Howie Jr. Played at the Montreal Forum on November 2, 1937, the game featured a team of NHL stars against a squad that combined Canadiens and Maroons stars. The All-Stars won 6–5.

Meanwhile, Detroit's attempt to win an unprecedented third consecutive Stanley Cup championship was failing, leaving the race open to virtually every club. Particularly impressive were the Bruins, who had fashioned a forward line out of three youngsters from Kitchener, Ontario. (Prior to World War I the town was named Berlin.) Bobby Bauer, Milt Schmidt and Woody Dumart were dubbed the Kraut Line, or occasionally the Kitchener Kids. Boston was bragging about another trio—Charlie Sands, Bill Cowley and Ray Getliffe—that was as threatening as the Krauts. Not to be outdone, the Rangers formed a young line of their own featuring the brother act of Neil and Mac Colville along with Alex Shibicky to compete against the Americans' triumvirate of Sweeney Schriner, Art Chapman and Lorne Carr, who delivered headlines in the New York papers.

Yes, even the star-spangled Americans had a chance. Despite the fiscal crisis brought on by the Depression, the Americans—who had been taken over by the NHL itself—upstaged the wealthier and more secure Rangers. Amerks leader Red Dutton, who had become manager and coach, signed veteran defensemen Hap Day and Ching Johnson, who had been released by the Leafs and Rangers respectively, and added Earl Robertson in goal. Completely out of character, the Americans turned into contenders and actually finished in second place in the Canadian Division. Schriner led the team in goals (21) and scoring (38 points). "What made me so proud," said Dutton, "was that I signed Sweeney to his first pro contract. I brought him in along with Art Chapman and Lorne Carr, and together they made one of the greatest lines in hockey." In one of the finest intracity series in any sport, any time, the Americans took on the roundly loathed Rangers in the opening round of the 1937–38 playoffs. Dutton's Americans won the first game 2–1 on Johnny Sorrell's double-overtime goal; the Rangers rebounded, winning the second match 4–3; and the stage was set for the climactic finale on March 27, 1938, at Madison Square Garden. The largest crowd of the season, 16,340 fans, jammed the arena and saw a pulsating contest. Paced by Shibicky and Bryan Hextall, the Rangers jumped to a 2–0 lead. But Carr and Nels Stewart tied it and sent the game into overtime. Neither team could break the tie for two sudden-death periods. Finally, Carr scored the winner for Dutton at 0:40 of the third overtime.

"That," said Red, "was the greatest thrill I ever got in hockey. The Rangers had a high-priced team and beating them was like winning the Stanley Cup for us." The Americans were knocked out of the playoffs two games to one in the next round by Chicago and they never achieved such lofty heights again—but at least they survived. North of the border, the fiscally challenged Montreal Maroons became the next victim of the Depression, only three years after winning the Stanley Cup in 1935. Minus the Maroons, the NHL opened the 1938–39 season with only seven teams, five in the United States and two in Canada.

If any solace could be obtained from the Depression's effect on big-league hockey it was offered by ownership, who could legitimately claim that NHL quality and intensity were at a peak.

Maple Leafs front office aide (and later Canadiens managing director) Frank Selke Sr. noted that the Depression created an owners' market: "There were bread lines and men on street corners selling apples and widespread unemployment for years, starting in 1930. For a young Canadian to have a job playing hockey and to get paid pretty well for it was quite an asset. It was the kind of employment every player wanted to keep and that's one reason why they competed so hard in those years."

The onset of World War II brought about the end of the Great Depression as one trauma replaced another. Unfortunately, one last NHL victim was claimed—the lowly Americans. With his players enlisting in the armed services and his club crippled by huge debts, Dutton was forced to fold the franchise just when he was starting to pull out from under the debris of the Bill Dwyer days. "We had begun to pay off a lot of Bill's debts," said Dutton, "and it looked as though we were going to come out all right. A couple more years and we would have run the Rangers right out of the rink." By the time the Americans folded in the spring of 1942, the United States had entered World War II and the Great Depression was over.

From its inception until its conclusion at the start of the 1940s, North America's economic disaster had a profound effect on major-league hockey. It cost the NHL franchises in Pittsburgh, Philadelphia, Ottawa, St. Louis, Montreal and New York and the league was reduced to six teams, two in Canada and four in the United States. Even in postwar prosperity, the NHL would bear the Depression's scars through the mid-1960s, when it finally and robustly expanded from six to a dozen teams, as if to make up for the time wasted over three decades.

CONN SMYTHE: AN OWNER'S WILL
Milt Dunnell

THE SPORTS LITERATI will refrain kindly from ever using the term "new Maple Leaf Gardens," even lightly or in jest, when referring to the updated digs of Toronto's hockey heroes, when they finally unfurl their faded banners in the new Air Canada Centre in February of 1999.

Maple Leaf Gardens couldn't happen again. Nor could Constantine Falkland Smythe, alias "the Little Pistol," who had the dream which less far-sighted folk mistook for a nightmare.

Both Smythe and the hockey shrine which he created were contradictions and paradoxes. Consider: in the depth of the worst economic depression this century has witnessed and suffered, when there wasn't enough loose investment money lying around to finance the lean-to on a woodshed, Maple Leaf Gardens sprang out of the ground—in an area where it really wasn't welcome—in about the same amount of time it would take the committee on environmental acceptability today to set the date for its first meeting.

Consider too: Once Smythe had the building humming and the hockey team winning, he chased the unhappy brokers of the bullring right out into Church Street. The bullring, for those who came in after the first period, was a crowded area, back of the blue seats, where some of the town's most enterprising bookmakers offered odds on just about anything from first or last goal to the next unlucky fan who would get nicked by a flying puck. Male or female? Even money.

That someone would get nailed by a deflected shot was the best bet of the day. Protective glass above the boards was still the fantasy of some silly salesman. One thing on which the bookies were reluctant to offer odds was whether the next victim of a deflected shot would be dressed in a tai-

lor-made suit or a Holt Renfrew frock. It was odds-on that anyone within the orbit of a flying puck was fashionably clad.That was by decree of Constantine Falkland himself. Any seat subscriber who was guilty of favoring friends who showed up in the choice seats wearing a plain old leather jacket or a lettered sweatshirt would receive a curt reminder of the Gardens' dress code.

Smythe was right, of course, in banishing the bullring gang. But some of the very oddsmakers who got tossed out into the cold night have regarded themselves as victims of justice gone berserk. Wasn't it one of North America's most respected gamblers, Tex Rickard, who provided Smythe with at least part of the stake which he used to buy the old St. Pats franchise in the first place?

Smythe loved to tell the story himself. Colonel John Hammond, the director of Madison Square Garden, who had hired Smythe to put the New York Rangers together for their NHL debut in 1926, fired him before the season even started. The real reason was that he discovered he could get Lester Patrick, a much better-known name in hockey. His excuse was that Smythe had been at a football game at Toronto's Varsity Stadium when Babe Dye, a veteran player, became available for $17,500. Smythe had missed him. Chicago Black Hawks got him.

"I got Bun and Bill Cook and Frank Boucher for $17,500," Smythe argued. "For another $4,000, I got you Ching Johnson and Taffy Abel, two excellent defense players. I didn't want Dye." But Hammond had made up his mind. He also had decided that, since Smythe wouldn't even be going to New York, he wasn't entitled to his full salary of $10,000. The price would be $7,500.

Smythe got to meet Rickard, the president of Madison Square Garden, when he went to New York to see the team, which he had assembled, play the Montreal Maroons in their opening home game. Rickard asked him whether he thought the new team could make the game close. Smythe told him the Rangers would win—which they did. Rickard, the one-time owner of a famous casino in Goldfield, Nevada where Joe Gans and Battling Nelson fought, was impressed. He asked Smythe whether he would be interested in rejoining the Rangers as a consultant. Smythe retorted that he wouldn't even consider working for the Rangers after the experience with Hammond. Upon hearing the full story, Rickard, who had a reputation as a straight shooter, ordered Hammond to give Smythe a cheque for $2,500. In later years, Smythe would recall how he bet the money on the University of Toronto to beat McGill in a football game and then put the bundle on the New York Rangers to beat the St. Pats the first time they played in Toronto.

Now Smythe had enough money in his pocket that he need not feel embarrassed about approaching some of the town's wheelers and dealers to get them interested in buying the Toronto St. Patrick's franchise. The price was right. By today's standards, it was a steal—$165,000. The truth was, though, that the St. Pats were a pretty poor outfit. Not even the name was worth anything to the new owners. They changed it almost at once to Maple Leafs.

By 1930, with construction of his new building under way, Smythe knew that his team had to sign some name players to help sell tickets. One man he had in mind was King Clancy of the Ottawa Senators. But Clancy was going to cost a bundle—or what was considered a bundle at the time. Smythe's directors were willing to go only to $25,000. Not enough.

Once again, Smythe's willingness to gamble came into the picture. His two-year-old filly, Rare Jewel, was entered in a stakes race at Woodbine. Even his own trainer, Bill Campbell, told him she had no chance. The jockey, Dude Foden, had detected a hint of speed and durability in her, however. The racing public made her 100 to one and counting. Some of Smythe's rivals ridiculed him when he bet on her. He bet more. Foden gave the filly a rousing ride and she held off the favorite, Froth Blower, to win and pay $214 on a two-dollar win ticket. Smythe told his friends, Ed Bickle and Larkin Maloney, who were with him: "Now, I can buy King Clancy."

Smythe even insisted his presence at a horse park played an important part in the actual sale. An acquaintance, whom he met at the track, told him the directors of Montreal Maroons had scheduled a meeting to decide whether they should authorize their general manager, Jimmy Strachan, to offer the Ottawa club an unprecedented $35,000 for Clancy's contract.

"Before they held their meeting, I had closed the deal," Smythe liked to recall. "The price was $35,000 and two players whom we valued at $15,000. Anyone who doubts what the terms were (many skeptics did) is welcome to see the details, which I have right here in my desk."

Possibly as a promotional teaser which would inspire the fans, while also tossing a harpoon into the Maroons, the Leafs ran an advertisement in the local press inquiring whether they would favor Clancy's purchase. They knew what the answer would be. Obviously, Clancy was a Leaf before the ads appeared. Using the newspapers to irritate an opponent was a tactic which Smythe used on more than one occasion.

Smythe had a long-running feud with Art Ross, general manager and coach of the Boston Bruins. On one road trip, when the Leafs were billed to play in Boston Garden, Smythe had an advertisement placed in one of the Boston gazettes that read, in part: "If you're tired of what you've been looking at (the Bruins) come out tonight and see a decent team, the Toronto Maple Leafs, play hockey."

Ross, naturally, was furious. Smythe's defense, of course, was that he was inviting people to attend a game in the Bruins' building. Ross demanded that the league fine Smythe $1,000 for demeaning a rival team's product. When several other league executives sided with Ross, they were ridiculed by Smythe for lacking a sense of humor. The next time, he went to Boston Garden, he promised, he would be the perfect gentleman. And he kept his word, appearing in top hat and full dress suit near the Leaf bench before the face-off.

Such antics are left to club mascots today but the pioneers of pro hockey had no money at their disposal to pay for mascots. There were times when they scrambled for money to pay the meager salaries. They knew where they were going because they knew where they had been. And give them credit for making hockey their main concern—not a hobby. They were wrong a lot of the time, but they must have been right most of the time.

A look at the league today would permit that conclusion.

FROM STEEL RAILS TO JET TRAILS

Don O'Hanley

DISCUSS TRAVEL with a National Hockey League player and he'll probably state that it is the most difficult part of his job. It was not always thus. Let's return to the expansion year of 1926 when the National Hockey League added three clubs to the existing seven and divided the 10 members into the Canadian and American Divisions. Travel arrangements were made with the railroads and, on rare occasions, aboard coastal or Great Lakes steamships.

A 44-game schedule was in effect, with the season commencing in mid-November and ending in late March. The playoffs followed in April. The Boston Bruins, Chicago Black Hawks, Detroit Cougars, New York Rangers and Pittsburgh Pirates competed in the American Division. The Canadian grouping included the two Montreal clubs: Canadiens and Maroons, New York Americans, Ottawa Senators and the Toronto St. Patricks, who finished the season as the Maple Leafs when the franchise was sold in February 1927.

Teams played six games with each division member and four with each of the other group. The normal interval between games was three to five days and only once, at the end of the season, were two games scheduled on consecutive nights. It was a time of well-rested teams that played hard-nosed defensive hockey. Salaries were almost as low as the scores, but complaints are few when men get paid for what they enjoy doing. Most clubs carried only two forward lines, four defensemen, a spare skater and one goaltender. Traveling around the league was easy and carefree. To the average hockey player, it was a time for relaxation, strategy planning, card playing or horseplay.

There is a tendency today to downgrade railroad travel because the service was allowed to deteriorate in the 1960s. When the NHL was young in years, there was intense competition for passenger business and it was good advertising to carry a professional baseball or hockey club. Teams patronized the better trains of the day and a half-dozen railroads provided special Pullman service for them. A caste system of sorts existed among the players. Veterans got the lower berths on overnight trips with rookies and writers forced to occupy the uppers. The coach and general manager enjoyed the extra privacy of the drawing room in the standard 12-section and one-drawing-room heavyweight Pullman Company car. Placement of the vehicle was either at the front or rear of the train to prevent other passengers from passing through. An undisturbed night's rest was thus assured.

Let's use New York as a starting point for a road trip by the Rangers or Americans or a visiting club on its way home or onto the next game on "foreign" ice. New York Central's famous 'Water Level Route' took the club to Chicago and Detroit aboard the Lake Shore Limited, Wolverine, or Detroiter. If necessary, alternate routing could be obtained from the Pennsylvania Railroad on the Mercantile Express and Detroit Arrow. Normally, the Pennsylvania was used only for Pittsburgh trips. The Delaware & Hudson's Montreal Limited carried the teams to and from Montreal and connected with the Canadian National and Canadian Pacific for Ottawa and Toronto. The New York New Haven and Hartford's Knickerbocker Limited, consisting of reserved Pullman chair cars and a diner, was the deluxe Shore Line train to Boston. The New Haven boasted luxurious 'limiteds', world-famous Long Island Sound steamship service and a number of subsidiary transit companies. In Canada, the Canadian Pacific provided the last word in transportation from coast to coast and joined the Dominion with the British Empire with a veritable fleet of steamships. The Canadian National, operated by the government, served great cities and small towns with distinctive green, gold and black passenger equipment. Its system timetable contained 168 pages of service over some 290 separate routes. It was the largest railroad in North America.

In addition to providing a high standard of transportation, the railroads were proud of their dining cars which, like the old hotel restaurants, were a profitable sideline. Service and quality were maintained at a high standard and food was always freshly prepared in contrast to the precooked frozen variety offered on most airplanes. Many dining cars had a specialty such as Canadian Pacific's Rocky Mountain Trout, New Haven's Boston scrod, or New York Central's charcoal-broiled steaks. The Pennsylvania, self-proclaimed 'Standard Railroad of the World', was not known for outstanding cuisine, but it was adequate. The players had few complaints while dining on nicely served food at 60 or 70 miles per hour.

Just as there are convenient jet departures from not-so-convenient airports, the railroads offered frequent service to cities around the league with a choice of routes. A club might go from New York to Montreal via the New York Central connecting with either the Delaware & Hudson or Rutland Railroads; via the New Haven in connection with Canadian National or Boston & Maine/Canadian Pacific. All offered a choice of daytime or overnight trains.

Weather was seldom a problem and delays due to high winds, turbulence, or overcrowded landing strips were unknown. One didn't have to resort to tranquilizers or 80-proof cough syrup to calm the jitters before boarding a night express and players didn't retire due to the pressure of traveling.

A few franchises were moved around during the 1930s but travel habits remained pretty much the same. Pittsburgh transferred to Philadelphia and lasted one season. Ottawa moved to St. Louis but the change was a wasted effort and the club disbanded at the close of the 1934–35 season. The Montreal Maroons became a depression victim in 1938 causing the NHL to revert to a single grouping of seven clubs. The New York Americans, wards of the league, hung on until 1942 when most of their players entered the armed forces or were needed for essential war work. The faithful trains served the remaining six teams until the late 1950s.

The first team to take to the air was the Detroit Red Wings during the latter half of the 1938–39 season. They flew from Newark, New Jersey to Chicago on United Air Lines. A few weeks later Red Dutton's New York Americans came home from Chicago to Newark aboard a DC–3 "Mainliner." Remarkably, there was no major airport in the New York City metropolitan area in 1939.

Most clubs, however, preferred the dependable trains that they had used for so many years. The speed, safety and reliability of jet aircraft eventually led to almost total abandonment of rail passenger service and all professional sports teams changed their travel habits. The Montreal Canadiens were one of the last clubs to extensively travel by train. In many cases, it was the railroads themselves that forced them to take to the air. Reductions in service and inconve-

nient arrival and departure times hastened the change.

The National Hockey League has come a long way since the 1950s. When rail travel was the universal norm, the league was limited to cities that fell within a 1,000-square-mile radius. Universal air travel permitted unlimited geographic expansion. Distant cities such as Calgary, Edmonton, Los Angeles, Vancouver, Denver and San Jose were no longer perennial or potential minor-leaguers due to limitations of geography and travel time. Economic necessity dictated longer schedules and greater playoff participation. None of this would have been possible if travel speeds had not increased from 60 to many hundreds of miles per hour.

Those big green heavyweight Pullman Company cars, like the 44-game schedule, are things of the past. Life was a bit less complicated and perhaps more fun, but hockey remains as interesting as ever and considerably faster in keeping with the jet age. The teams have gone from the rails to the airways in quest of the Stanley Cup. Happy landing!

HOCKEY IN WORLD WAR II

Douglas Hunter

PROFESSIONAL HOCKEY, in no way immune to the impact of World War II on North American society, went through one of its greatest spasms of change during the six war years between 1939 and 1945. Some effects were directly related to the war, while others were coincidental. Still others were aftershocks from the Great Depression. The National Hockey League would emerge from the conflict stronger than at the outset, with a stabilized roster of teams and a game transformed by the introduction of the center red line. Along the way the league's competitive balance was turned virtually upside down and the careers of many of its stars would be interrupted. Those stars would also be the focus of controversy for the nature of their contributions to the war effort. While the league lost out on the talents of potential stars from the amateur, Canadian junior and minor-league ranks who paid the ultimate price during the conflict, it is difficult to name one NHL regular among the scores who entered the Canadian and American armed forces who died in military service.

The main challenge to the league's owners during the war years was to keep fans coming to the arenas. Rationing of vital materiel such as gasoline and rubber impaired fans' ability to drive their cars to games. (Late in the war, the U.S. government shut down horse racing to conserve these very items, which thoroughbred enthusiasts were consuming getting to and from the tracks.) Hockey teams in cities without extensive streetcar networks or subways were especially hard hit. The American Hockey League went from 10 teams at the war's outset to just six in 1943–44. Availability of players, however, was the primary concern: even if fans did bother to show up, what kind of hockey would they see?

While this was a problem faced by all professional sports, the fact that hockey straddled the Canada–U.S. border added some unique logistical and public-relations wrinkles. For one thing, while the vast majority of players were Canadian, all but two of the top 16 pro teams were based in the United States. Four issues regarding Canada's involvement in the war effort complicated the availability of NHL players: established NHLers and prospects alike showed a penchant for volunteering for military service; the Canadian government assigned a low labor priority to pro-

fessional hockey; the military draft; and wartime restrictions on cross-border employment and travel.

Unlike other Allied nations, Canada did not make overseas service compulsory for eligible males. Rather, a draft solely for home defense was introduced in 1940. This policy was made in large part because of overwhelming opposition in French Quebec to compulsory overseas service. Many prominent Quebec politicians sympathized with France's Vichy puppet regime, and Montreal mayor Camillien Houde was thrown in military prison for four years for inciting his citizens to refuse to register for the draft. But Quebec was not alone in its opposition. In the Prairie provinces, there was still resentment over the 1917 Canadian draft; it was widely felt that the government at the time had reneged on a promise that young men required for the harvest would not be conscripted.

Initially, home defense duties required little hardship. Those called up were required only to complete 30 days of basic training. In the fall of 1940, before the 1940–41 NHL season began, players were signing up in droves for home-defense militias and completing their 30 days training so that they could get on with playing hockey and not have to risk having their number called in midseason.

One of this scheme's most outspoken critics was Conn Smythe, the Toronto Maple Leafs' managing director and a veteran of the Great War. He made a super-human effort to get himself onto the firing line, and succeeded, shipping out as a major in the Royal Canadian Artillery with his own anti-aircraft battery.

Eventually the Canadian government took a viewpoint Smythe had held all along, concluding that the 30-day training program was inadequate and gradually increasing home-defense duties to three months, then six, then making service indefinite, with a tour of duty interruptible only by the end of hostilities. Members of Canada's "active" overseas force began to disparage the home-defense conscripts, labeling them "duty dodgers" and "Zombies"—painting them as "the living dead" of the war effort, neither pure civilians nor actively engaged in combat.

Perhaps more than any other group of civilians, professional hockey players' pride dictated that they not be tarred with the Zombie brush. When in January 1942 the first NHLers received their home-defense draft notices, the players felt they had no choice but to join the volunteer army overseas. Still, those who controlled professional hockey were not prepared to sit idly by and watch their investments die in combat. However unfair it may appear, other, less hazardous, duties were found for many (if not most) NHLers who were compelled to enlist. A common job for NHL draftees was as a physical-education instructor at a training base, and they were also often pressed into service on armed forces hockey teams with the intent of boosting civilian and enlisted morale. The most famous team was the Royal Canadian Air Force Flyers, a senior team stacked with enlisted NHLers, including the entire Kraut Line from the Boston Bruins—Woody Dumart, Bobby Bauer and Milt Schmidt. The Flyers won the 1942 Allan Cup, the Canadian senior hockey championship. Not to be outdone, New York Rangers coach Frank Boucher was instrumental in forming the Ottawa Commandos, an all-star army team created expressly for volunteers from professional hockey.

After the Commandos won the 1943 Allan Cup, teams from Canadian military camps, chock full of NHLers, accounted for most (and in some cases all) of the slots in provincial senior leagues. Bases were actively recruiting

major-league talents to serve as coaches and players, and there were justifiable fears that what was supposed to be a recreational pursuit for men undergoing basic training was becoming a shadow league for the NHL, keeping its players out of active combat while serving as a cash cow for the owners of arenas that hosted the games. Conn Smythe's Maple Leaf Gardens, for example, held the right to host all senior games held in Toronto, including those of the Toronto Army Daggers.

Shortly before midnight on October 18, 1943, the system was damaged beyond repair by a scandal involving Turk Broda, the star goaltender of the Toronto Maple Leafs. Broda was hauled off a Montreal-bound train by the Royal Canadian Mounted Police, claiming he was about to breach his draft notice. The *Montreal Gazette* got wind of the story, and claimed that Broda was on the train so he could enlist in a Montreal unit and play for the local army hockey team, but that the Mounties were spiriting him back home to make sure he played for the Toronto Army Daggers. A look at Broda's military records, made public 20 years after his death in 1992, shows that Broda was in no danger of breaching any draft notice—as a married father of three, he wasn't even draft-eligible. His records reveal that he had enlisted in the Royal Canadian Artillery in Toronto on October 15, three days before the incident on the train. Broda had apparently gone AWOL when taken into custody, and it does seem very likely that he was on his way to Montreal to accept a better offer than the one he had in Toronto to play military hockey.

As a result of the unfavorable publicity surrounding the Broda incident, the Toronto Daggers were ordered out of senior league play; by January 1944, military orders effectively brought an end to star-packed Canadian armed forces teams. NHLers did continue to play on military teams, however, and public resentment grew when it was revealed that some players had been on camp teams for two or more years while regular enlistees were being hurried through basic training in less than the prescribed eight months and being killed, wounded or captured overseas. Broda, for one, ended up going overseas and spending the war as a sporting ringer, playing softball and hockey on Canadian military teams.

The NHL, meanwhile, soldiered on with makeshift lineups of players who were beyond the reach of the Canadian draft. (The American draft also touched the league; most notably, the Bruins lost star goaltender Frank Brimsek, a Minnesota native, to U.S. Coast Guard duty.) Virtually the entire starting lineup of the New York Rangers, Stanley Cup champions of 1939–40, had disappeared into military service by midwar. Teams employed players who were too young, too old, or too married to be drafted. In a typical move, the Maple Leafs introduced 17-year-old Ted Kennedy to their lineup in 1943–44. Other players took advantage of medical deferrals to appear in NHL uniforms. Canadian military standards of fitness were very high—in retrospect, too high—and players with bum knees, shoulders and the like were turned aside as potential conscripts. It became an irony of wartime, particularly in the fall of 1944 when Canada was facing an acute shortage of infantry, that men deemed unfit for duty were making a living as professional hockey players. It was not a situation unique to hockey: during the winter of 1944–45, when American troops were suffering heavy losses in Europe and the Pacific, it was discovered that about 40 percent of the players in professional baseball in 1944 had been excused from military service on medical grounds.

Tommy Gorman, general manager of the Montreal Canadiens, cleverly exploited another draft loophole extended to men holding jobs in vital war industries. By ensuring Canadiens players secured jobs in industries such as shipbuilding and munitions manufacturing, Gorman was able to ice a mature and powerful lineup that proved to be the foundation on which 30 years' worth of great Canadiens teams were built. But the vital industry proviso was a double-edged sword: because professional hockey had been assigned a low labor priority by the Canadian government, potential players were not allowed to quit jobs of higher priority to accept starting positions with talent-starved clubs.

The resurgence of the Canadiens franchise was one of the major byproducts of the wartime NHL. Near death in 1940, the team was revived by Gorman's ingenuity, as well as the arrival of Dick Irvin, who'd spent the previous decade behind the bench in Toronto, and the introduction of a new generation of stars, among them Maurice Richard, Elmer Lach, Butch Bouchard and goaltender Bill Durnan. The Canadiens won the Stanley Cup in 1944 and utterly dominated the 1944–45 regular season, losing only eight of 50 games and securing five of the six First All-Star Team positions as linemates Richard and Lach respectively set new league records for goals (50) and assists (54). Though upset in the semifinals by a determined Leaf team, Montreal was on a roll that would produce the dominant teams of the 1950s, 1960s and 1970s.

As the Habs feasted, other teams starved. Already a league charity case when hostilities began, the New York Americans expired after the 1941–42 season, during which they were renamed the Brooklyn Americans. That left the league at six franchises, a configuration history would come to know as the "Original Six." Of the teams that survived the war, the Boston Bruins and New York Rangers, the league's top two teams from 1937–38 until 1939–40, suffered most, as their lineups were gutted by military call-ups. A return to peacetime saw the Rangers, the Cup champions of 1940, as perennial also-rans until after the 1967 expansion. It would be 1994 before they won another Stanley Cup title. The Bruins, Cup winners in 1939 and 1941, did manage to reach three Cup finals during the 1950s, but they were more down than up until a renaissance in the late 1960s. Joining Toronto and Montreal in the league's upper echelon after the war were the Detroit Red Wings. Last-place finishers in 1937–38, the Wings reached the Cup finals four times in the 1940s, winning in 1943. They would dominate the late 1940s and early 1950s with seven consecutive first-place finishes and four more Stanley Cup wins. The Chicago Black Hawks found success as elusive after the war as before it, unable to repeat their longshot Cup win of 1938. After reaching the finals against Montreal in 1943–44, the Blackhawks weren't seen again in Cup play until they won in 1961.

The game was substantially different after the war. In 1943–44, the NHL had changed the pace and flavor of its game entirely by introducing the center ice red line. Previously, a player could not make a forward pass across his own blue line and aggressive forechecking could bottle up a weaker team in its own end. The new rules allowed a player in his own defensive zone to make a breakout pass as far as the red line (but no farther, as a two-line pass resulted in an offside call) and created the high-speed, head-manning game we now take for granted. Many veterans whose careers had been interrupted by military service

found the faster-paced game too much for their advancing age and declining skills, and the way was paved for a number of fresh recruits such as Gordie Howe, Ted Lindsay and Ted Kennedy.

There is no question that wartime diluted the quality of the game. As Conn Smythe wrote from overseas to his chief scout, Squib Walker, in April 1944, "You have to admit that one NHLer is worth two wartime NHLers." Ted Kennedy reflects that while the game was not as well played as what followed, it was played with the same intensity. It was real hockey, and fans packed the arenas to see it.

The league was not untouched by the tragedy of war. Conn Smythe, having gotten overseas with his anti-aircraft battery, was seriously wounded in a Luftwaffe raid in July 1944 and returned home that September. Interim league president Red Dutton lost two sons in combat. And while casualties in the ranks of NHL regulars are difficult to spot, there were many bright prospects whose losses can only make one wonder what might have been. Detroit lost Joe Turner, a star goaltender in the AHL, who as a Canadian chose to join the U.S. Marines and was killed in action in northern Europe in January 1945. Leaf prospect Red Tilson, who had starred with the Oshawa Generals, was killed in action with a Canadian infantry regiment in October 1944. Red Hamill, a Leaf prospect who had been traded to the Rangers (playing 24 games with New York in 1942–43), was lost when his corvette patrol boat was torpedoed by a U-boat off Newfoundland in November 1944.

While these losses hurt the NHL, the league was not entitled to present these tragedies as evidence of win-the-war selflessness. As a business enterprise, the NHL made every effort to prosper in wartime, and it succeeded. While Maple Leaf Gardens hosted Victory Bond drives and bought bonds of its own, it never donated any profits from its operations to war charities, and its directors could have done so comfortably as earnings soared from $192,274 in 1939 to $315,763 in 1945. For all the privations and private losses, World War II was a fine time to own an NHL franchise.

HOCKEY DYNASTIES
AND NEAR-DYNASTIC TEAMS
Shirley Fischler

IN THE CHRONOLOGY of any major-league sports franchise, winning the trophy or award emblematic of the best in that sport three times consecutively would certainly constitute a dynasty. This definition, if you will, of what a dynasty is in major-league sports—three consecutive best-in-sport wins—applies equally to ice hockey and particularly to the National Hockey League.

By the above definition there have been few true dynasties in the National Hockey League. The reasons for this are myriad, having to do with the fact that a franchise is constantly evolving and changing: from behind the bench to every aspect of the team's composition. Unlike royal dynasties, where historically a single family tree can dominate the life of a culture or society for centuries, sports dynasties are short-lived and usually have a slightly changed player-composition from year to year even if the team does win the Stanley Cup three years in a row.

In fact, with all of the pressures to change and evolve along with the shortness of the average player's career, it's a bit of a miracle that there have been any dynasties in NHL

hockey at all. And with the large number of teams in the National Hockey League today, the chances of one team winning the Stanley Cup three years in a row are much less than prior to 1967–68, when the league began the modern era of expansion by doubling in size from the "Original Six" to 12 teams.

Which teams, then, have spawned the "dynasties?"

In fact, the team which spawned the first ice hockey dynasty of the 20th century pre-dated the formation of the National Hockey League and was situated in Ottawa, the national capital of Canada. The team was the Silver Seven, which won the Stanley Cup from 1902–03 through 1904–05. (Ottawa also defeated two Stanley Cup challengers during the 1905–06 season before losing the trophy to the Montreal Wanderers.)

Hockey played at the turn of the century was a far cry from the streamlined game of today: the slapshot, curved stick, goalie mask and helmet didn't exist; in fact, none of the players wore much in the way of equipment, protective or otherwise. Perhaps the most significant difference of all was the fact that hockey as played by the Ottawa Silver Seven was a seven-man game, with a sixth skater called the "rover."

The main intent of the game was the same, however: put the puck in the net, and as proof positive that the Ottawa Silver Seven merits the term "dynasty," there are six members of the team who are fixtures in the Hockey Hall of Fame.

The captain of the Ottawa Silver Seven in its Cup-winning days was defenseman Harvey Pulford who was one of the best body checkers of his era, but was also known as a clean and gentlemanly player. He was such a well-rounded athlete that he also participated in championship teams in football, lacrosse, boxing, rowing and squash. Pulford's career extended into his fifties.

Another Hall of Famer from the Silver Seven was a pint-sized chap by the name of Harry Westwick—nicknamed "Rat" for his small stature and pesky style of play. Harry joined Ottawa in 1895 and had his best season when the Silver Seven captured their third consecutive Cup in 1905, as he notched 24 goals in 13 games, playing the rover position. Westwick retired as a player in 1907 and became a National Hockey Association (forerunner of the National Hockey League) referee. He died in 1957.

Billy Gilmour and Frank McGee were also members of the Ottawa Silver Seven who ended up in the Hall of Fame, but by far the most famous and skilled of the two was McGee. To this day, the exploits of Frank McGee are still regarded as some of the most remarkable in Stanley Cup history. Blind in one eye, the dynamic McGee scored an amazing 14 goals in the final game of the championship series versus Dawson City in January, 1905. Eight of those goals were scored in succession in less than nine minutes, and four of them were notched in 140 seconds. His sixth, seventh and eighth goals were netted in a span of 90 seconds, a record which still stands as the fastest hat trick in Stanley Cup play. The legendary McGee was killed in action during World War I.

Pulford, Westwick, Gilmour and McGee were members of the Silver Seven throughout the team's entire dynasty (and all but Gilmour were also with the team for the 1905–06 season), while two other future Hall of Famers won the Stanley Cup twice with the Ottawa team. Forward Alf Smith, a native of Ottawa who started his career with other teams in his hometown and also played in Pittsburgh,

returned to Ottawa for the 1903–04 season and was a member of two Stanley Cup champions. Goaltender Bouse Hutton not only won the Stanley Cup in 1903 and 1904, but also played for teams that won the Canadian lacrosse and football titles in 1904. Another future Hall of Fame goaltender, Percy LeSueur, joined the Silver Seven during their unsuccessful Stanley Cup series with the Wanderers. After the Ottawa franchise became known as the Senators (no relation to the modern-day franchise), Lesueur helped the team win the Stanley Cup in 1909 and 1911.

The team which has not only won the Stanley Cup most often (23 times) since the establishment of the National Hockey League in 1917, but has had the longest dynasty (five consecutive Cup wins) and more dynastic eras (two) than any other NHL franchise, is the Montreal Canadiens. The Habs, as they're often called, also have the distinction of winning more than three consecutive championships in both of their dynastic eras (five from 1956 to 1960, four from 1976 to 1979), as well as winning the Cup two consecutive times on three different occasions (1930–31, 1965–66 and 1968–69).

In terms of hockey dynasties, there is no question that the 1956 to 1960 Montreal Canadiens were to the National Hockey League what the Murderers' Row New York Yankees of the 1920s were to baseball: quite, simply the greatest team of all time.

In goaltender Jacques Plante the Habs had one of the best, most creative netminders who ever guarded a crease. (Plante invented what would become today's goalie mask and also popularized the idea of the goaltender leaving his crease to handle the puck.) With blueliner Doug Harvey the Canadiens had one of the best defensemen ever to grace the ice and with the likes of the immortal Maurice (The Rocket) Richard, Henri (Pocket Rocket) Richard, Jean Beliveau and Boom Boom Geoffrion, arguably the most awesome array of shooters ever fielded on one team. And that was just for starters. Left winger Dickie Moore and defenseman Tom Johnson from that squad also are in the Hockey Hall of Fame, along with coach Hector (Toe) Blake. The Canadiens didn't have a flaw nor a weakness. Period.

"Their third line was better than most first lines on other teams," said former Ranger Aldo Guidolin. Guidolin was, of course, referring to players like Claude Provost, an efficient defensive forward, and skilled centers like youngsters Ralph Backstrom, Phil Goyette and Donnie Marshall. This Canadiens team was so superlative that the league ultimately instituted rule changes to cope with a power-play that simply overwhelmed other teams. At the time a player was to remain in the penalty box for the full two minutes of a minor penalty regardless of whether the team with the man advantage scored or not. So strong was the Habs' power-play that they frequently scored two or three goals during a two-minute penalty. (Jean Beliveau himself scored three goals in 44 seconds during a two-man advantage in a game played on November 5, 1955.) For the 1956–57 season the rule was changed, allowing a player serving a minor penalty to return to the ice when a goal was scored by the opposing team.

"They simply wanted to limit our power," recalled Rocket Richard, "but that still didn't stop us."

The Canadiens of this dynasty might well have won the Cup twice more (1955 and 1961) for a total of seven in a row, except for the fact that the Rocket was suspended for the entire playoffs of 1955 and had retired after the fifth straight victory in 1960. Obviously the absence of Richard hurt the team spiritually as well as in goals scored.

The Canadiens' dynasty of 1976 to 1979 had many of the ingredients of the Habs of 1956 to 1960, but in less ostentatious form. For example, goalie Ken Dryden (now president and general manager of the Toronto Maple Leafs) was excellent at his craft, but less showy and flamboyant than Jacques Plante. Guy Lafleur was a dazzling performer on the attack, but without the driving explosiveness of Maurice Richard. Larry Robinson was a tower of strength on the blue line, but did not match a young Doug Harvey at the peak of his game.

Then-Habs coach Scotty Bowman (who has since gone on to coach the Pittsburgh Penguins and the Detroit Red Wings to Stanley Cup victories) frequently lauded Dryden for his club's high attainment and other experts in the game backed him up. "Anytime you were fortunate enough to catch Montreal playing badly, Dryden stopped you anyway," said Bruins longtime general manager Harry Sinden. "In order to have a dynasty you have to have strong goaltending."

Dryden backstopped a mobile defense that featured (in addition to Robinson) Serge Savard, Guy Lapointe and in the last Cup year, Rod Langway. Lafleur, Steve Shutt and Jacques Lemaire were among the more gifted scorers, but the Habs also featured a number of grinding checkers, not the least of whom was Bob Gainey, whose bodycheck on Rangers defenseman Dave Maloney in 1979 helped his team win its fourth consecutive Stanley Cup title.

"We had lots of good players on that team," said Savard, "but Lafleur was the most important, because he had the ability to dominate a game."

The NHL franchise which falls second to the Canadiens in the number of Stanley Cup victories (13) has also had two "dynasties." The Toronto Maple Leafs (called the Torontos and the Arenas until 1919–20, when they became the St.Patricks—which they were until being renamed the Maple Leafs during the 1926–27 season) won the Stanley Cup three consecutive times from 1947 to 1949 and again from 1962 to 1964. The Maple Leafs are the only NHL club other than the Canadiens to have had more than one dynastic era.

Not only were the Toronto Maple Leafs, circa 1946 to 1951, one of the most arresting teams of all time, but they were a notable bunch for yet another reason. The club, managed by the irrepressible Conn Smythe and coached by scholarly Clarence (Hap) Day—later by Joe Primeau for the 1951 Cup win— became the NHL's first legitimate dynasty and, concomitantly, hockey's first post-World War II power.

Curiously, the Leafs had no business being a major force in the league, if their previous season was a barometer. They had missed the playoffs in 1945–46 with a fifth-place club and opened training camp in September of 1946 with an amalgam of unknown rookies and veterans, some of whom had just packed away their Canadian army uniforms. With few exceptions, the Leafs veterans were in mint condition and formed a solid nucleus around which Day could arrange his gifted rookies. Some of those rookies then proceeded to ripen faster than anyone had believed possible, particularly the defensive tandem of Gus Mortson and Jimmy Thomson, otherwise dubbed "the Gold Dust Twins."

Prime among the gifted youngsters was a center named Ted (Teeder) Kennedy, whose labored skating belied his creativity with the puck. While Kennedy was not the team captain—that honor belonged to the distinguished veteran centerman Syl Apps—Teeder often played the part in a

most natural way, giving Day not one, but two extraordinary centers who could rally the team in crisis. Likewise, the defense was anchored by a crowd-pleasing, puck-rushing blueliner named Wally Stanowski, who was more than willing to help the Gold Dust Twins, along with Garth Boesch and Bashin' Bill Barilko.

General manager Conn Smythe's ace-in-the-hole was superior goaltending. Walter (Turk) Broda had been a pre-War ace and delivered a Stanley Cup in 1942, when the Leafs had rallied from a three-game deficit in the finals to top the Detroit Red Wings. With their first of three Cup wins in 1947, Broda out-goaled the favored Montreal Canadiens, who had the formidable Bill Durnan in their net, enabling the Leafs to pull one of the greatest upsets in Stanley Cup history.

A year later, in 1948, the Leafs won again, and this time it was due in large part to the incredible trade which had been wrought by Conn Smythe. After acquiring super-center Max Bentley early in the 1947–48 season, Toronto had the best-balanced attack in the game and organized the first significant power-play in NHL annals, with Bentley patrolling the right point.

Syl Apps chose to retire from the game abruptly after the 1948 Cup finals and Smythe and the team suffered trade convulsions as the general manager attempted to compensate for the loss of the team's skilled captain. They did fill the opening better than had been expected and went on to win their third consecutive Cup in 1949 with Cal Gardner replacing Apps. The Toronto Maple Leafs had become the NHL's first real "dynasty". In fact, the Leaf hockey club, with Gardner at center, would go on to win another Cup in 1951, missing out as a five-Cup dynasty by losing in the Cup semifinals in 1950.

It would be another 13 years after the victory in 1949 before another Maple Leafs dynasty would emerge in the early 1960s, this one engineered and coached by the caustic and commanding Punch Imlach.

Imlach was an abrasive genius who originally signed on as assistant general manager, but in no time at all was promoted to general manager, while also assuming the coaching duties. His process of converting a dismal loser into a playoff club involved a number of clever signings, as well as the development of youngsters in the farm system.

Two of Punch's first moves proved to be brilliantly insightful. First, he signed Johnny Bower, an aging goaltender whom most thought was well past his best hockey years and looked too old to endure the NHL grind. Next, he made a deal for stay-at-home defenseman Allan Stanley, who had been booed out of Madison Square Garden while he was a New York Ranger and then played almost unnoticed for the Chicago Black Hawks and Boston Bruins.

Under Imlach's tutelage Bower flowered, suddenly acquiring a patina of youthful energy and a sharpness that exceeded his performance for the Rangers in 1953–54. Bower was so good for so long with Toronto that he eventually was inducted into the Hockey Hall of Fame.

In the meantime, Stanley was paired with that fireplug of a backliner Tim Horton, and suddenly developed into a bodychecking marvel and, most surprising of all, a leader in the locker room. Stanley, like Bower, would play so effectively as a Maple Leaf that he too would end up in the Hockey Hall of Fame.

Imlach was also blessed with another pair of blueliners who came from the Leafs' junior club, the Toronto Marlboros. Carl Brewer and Bob Baun became to the Leafs

of the 1960s what Gus Mortson and Jim Thomson had been to Hap Day's club of the late 1940s.

Then there was Leonard "Red" Kelly, who had been a superlative defenseman with the Detroit Red Wings until he fell out of favor with the Motor City boss Jack Adams and Imlach made a deal for the flame-haired player. Punch's next move was nothing short of astounding, as he converted Kelly into a center, a position at which Red became an instant star.

Soon there was a teamful of names that would become etched on the Stanley Cup: a big power forward named Frank Mahovlich had Kelly as his center, with one of the most underrated players of the 1960s, Bob Nevin, patrolling the right wing. Another line featured a quick little center named Dave Keon, whom many compared to the immortal Canadien, Howie Morenz, with Dick Duff and the team's captain, George "Chief" Armstrong, on the right side. Yet another trio was comprised of young Bob Pulford flanking veteran Bert Olmstead and wild man Eddie Shack.

It was the spring of 1962 that the Maple Leafs, with Imlach behind the bench wearing his ubiquitous fedora, stopped the Chicago Black Hawks in their bid for a second straight Stanley Cup title. The final game was a classic, with Chicago's Golden Jet, Bobby Hull, breaking a scoreless tie with one of his patented booming goals that had the crowd at noisy Chicago Stadium in frenzy. It was the third period and it looked certain that the home club would simply steamroll over the visiting Leafs. But Hull's goal had elicited such a clutter of debris on the ice that the lengthy time it took to clean up gave the Toronto club an opportunity to regroup. In no time at all, the Leafs tied the score and then put the winner past Glenn Hall for Imlach's first Stanley Cup win.

Employing the same core, Imlach produced another Cup champion a year later, first by routing Montreal four games to one and then repeating the feat against Detroit. The spring of 1964 saw almost the same scenario unfold—except that it took a full seven games to dispatch Montreal in the semis and another seven to erase Detroit for the Cup.

Imlach hoped to carry through to four straight championships, but his high-handed disciplinary measures had finally produced so many angry and disgruntled players that the team ceased to be as effective. Finally, in the 1965 semifinal round, the Canadiens ousted Toronto four games to two. The streak was over.

There is only one other team other than Montreal, in the annals of the NHL, which has won the Stanley Cup four consecutive times: the New York Islanders in the years 1980 through 1983. They are, to this day, the only team to have won 19 straight playoff series (concluding in 1984), and several names from those great Islanders teams have been entered in the rolls of the Hockey Hall of Fame.

But the beginnings of this modern expansion team could not have been less promising. In fact, at the end of their first season, 1972–73, the team had accumulated only 12 wins—a record low, and lost 60—a record high. Still, this wasn't a total calamity since it now meant that the Isles would be able to pick first in the Amateur Draft. General manager Bill Torrey, architect of this soon-to-become-legendary team, and his scouts had their eyes on a young defenseman named Denis Potvin, from the Ottawa 67's, who had broken many of Bobby Orr's old junior hockey scoring records.

The signing of Potvin and Torrey's decision to offer the coaching job to Al Arbour (they had begun with Phil Goyette, who was fired, and finished the first year with Earl

Ingarfield, who then stepped down at season's end) would prove to be two events that set the team on a course which would become the trail to the Stanley Cup.

By 1975 the team which had begun in the basement of the NHL had coalesced into a team which made the Stanley Cup playoffs. Then they met their arch-rival, the New York Rangers, in the best-of-five first round and stunned the hockey world by upsetting the Rangers in three games. They didn't stop there.

Until 1975 the only time an NHL team had ever lost three games straight in a best-of-seven series and then went on to win four consecutive games was the 1942 Toronto Maple Leafs. There was a huge difference between that Leafs team and the 1975 Isles, however; the Leafs had been well-stocked with all-stars and headliners, while the Isles of 1975 were a mish-mash of unsung veterans and untried striplings. Or, so it had appeared until now.

The astounding young Islanders had upset the New York Rangers. Now they proceeded to dig another hole for themselves, losing three straight to the Pittsburgh Penguins and then, incredibly, bouncing right back to win four in a row. Most remarkable of all, they came within a game of a second four-straight-after-losing-three versus the Philadelphia Flyers, which means they also came within a game of ending up in the Stanley Cup finals—just three years after being one of the worst teams in the league's history!

By 1978 the Islanders had become a real contender. They were graced with budding a superstar in Potvin, a hard-working and a talented young center named Bryan Trottier and a darting scoring whiz called Michael Bossy. They had the flying Swede, Bobby Nystrom, the seasoned defensive skills of Ed Westfall and arguably the finest goaltending combo in the league with Glenn "Chico" Resch and Billy Smith. But they just couldn't win the Cup. Until, in the spring of 1980, when Torrey traded right winger Billy Harris and defenseman Dave Lewis to Los Angeles for speedy center Butch Goring. Then the Islanders went on a tear that carried into the 1980 playoffs. Previously the Islanders had been accused of being too tight in crunch situations, but they responded with series wins over Los Angeles, Boston and Buffalo, before meeting the Flyers in the finals.

For the first time the Cup was within their grasp, and the Islanders came through with a four-games-to-two win over Philadelphia. In 1981 the Islanders marched past the Maple Leafs, Edmonton Oilers and the Rangers, before disposing of the Minnesota North Stars in a five-game final. They got a major scare in 1982 when Pittsburgh led by two goals in the decisive fifth game of their opening playoff series, but displayed their patented comeback qualities and took the game in overtime on a goal by John Tonelli. The Isles then edged the Rangers in six games and wiped out Quebec in four, as they did Vancouver in the finals. But their most impressive playoff run took place a year later, in 1983. They topped Washington (four games), the Rangers (six games) and the Bruins (six games) before taking on the powerful young Edmonton Oilers, led by the likes of Wayne Gretzky, Mark Messier and Paul Coffey. The combination of Billy Smith's feisty goaltending and timely scoring was too much for Edmonton. The Islanders swept the series in four straight and drank champagne from Lord Stanley's Cup for the fourth straight year.

As a postscript, the Islanders' "Drive for Five" in 1984 was even more heroic in many ways than any of their Stanley Cup victories. The team had finished the season atop the entire league and then fought their way through three brutally difficult playoff rounds, only to meet the Edmonton Oilers—still incredibly talented, but much, much wiser this year—again in the finals. By this time the Islanders were riddled with injury and tired, tired, tired. After 19 straight playoff series victories dating back to 1980, they succumbed to Edmonton in five games and what was possibly the second-greatest hockey dynasty in NHL history was on its way to oblivion.

There have been no other teams in the NHL which have won three or more consecutive Stanley Cup titles, but there are two others which merit mention because they won the Cup several times in matter of a few years. The Detroit Red Wings of the years 1950 to 1955 is one such team. In those six seasons the Wings garnered four Cup victories, missing out in 1951 and 1953. Furthermore, the team was laced with the great and the near-great, with immortals and Hall of Famers.

By the spring of 1950, Detroit general manager Jack Adams had assembled the trio which came to be called the Production Line, consisting of Gordie Howe, Ted Lindsay and the courtly veteran center, Sid Abel. Detroit's defense sported powerful Black Jack Stewart, Leo Reise Jr., and the aforementioned Red Kelly. In the nets was young albeit veteran Harry Lumley. Detroit went on to win the Stanley Cup in April of 1950, despite the fact that the Rangers pushed them to seven games in the finals and then into double overtime before a Detroit third-stringer named Pete Babando scored the winner.

At this point Detroit was on the threshold of a dynasty and looked ready to win for years to come, particularly with the acquisition of the talented young goaler, Terry Sawchuk. However, the Red Wings were embarrassed by Montreal in the six-game preliminary round in 1951, and the chance for consecutive Cup victories was destroyed.

Detroit recovered in 1952, winning the playoffs in eight straight games. Sawchuk produced four shutouts and in only one game did he give up more than one goal. However, in 1953, a much weaker Bruins team was able to get super defensive play from an elderly Woody Dumart, with clutch scoring from Jack McIntyre, and Boston eliminated Gordie Howe et al. in six games. Still, the Red Wings were simply too good to be kept down for long, as they demonstrated by winning the Cup two years straight, in 1954 and 1955. Furthermore, they finished first in the regular season every year during this six-season stretch (seven straight years in all), proving that the famed Production Line Red Wings of 1950 to 1955 belong in the ranks of the game's dynasties.

The same could be said of the Edmonton Oilers from the years 1984 through 1990. During those seven years the Oilers won the Stanley Cup five times, achieving two in a row twice and missing out only in 1986 and 1989.

This team had all of the necessary attributes of a dynasty: a coach and g.m., Glen Sather, who constructed a club of long-lasting greatness; superlative goaltending, in Grant Fuhr and Andy Moog; some of the best scoring in the history of the NHL, with Wayne Gretzky, Mark Messier, Jari Kurri and Glenn Anderson; and an often underrated defense led by the offense-minded Paul Coffey and the more stay-at-home Kevin Lowe. But the team's basic run-and-gun strategy of leaving their goaltender to make constant brilliant saves sometimes caught up with them, as the Calgary Flames did in 1986 after Edmonton had won the Cup in 1984 and 1985.

The Oilers rebounded nicely in 1987, however, beating

the Philadelphia Flyers in an exciting seven-game final.

Cracks and discontent had begun to accumulate on this oh-so-brilliant team, however, and when Paul Coffey balked at his contract terms and walked out on the team at the start of the 1987–88 season, he was traded to Pittsburgh and the dynasty had begun to be deconstructed. Still, the team recovered. Jeff Beukeboom stepped in to replace Coffey and the Oilers ended up winning their fourth Cup championship in five years.

Then what was arguably the most astounding trade in the history of the game occurred: owner Peter Pocklington and g.m./president Glen Sather traded "the Great One," Wayne Gretzky, to Bruce McNall's Los Angeles Kings. Surely the Edmonton Oilers would no longer be a presence felt in the higher echelons of the NHL.

Wrong. Even without The Great One, the Edmonton Oilers would win one more Cup. Two years after Wayne's World had shifted to La-La Land, Edmonton—with a nucleus which still contained Messier, Lowe and Craig MacTavish—gained the Cup in 1990. Then, as with all sports dynasties, management began the dismantling process in earnest.

Finally, there are several teams which won the Stanley Cup in two consecutive years, or two within three years, which deserve honorable mention among the NHL's dynasties. The Boston Bruins, who won the Stanley Cup in 1970 and 1972, for instance, were as heavily laced with talent as the Oilers or the Production Line Detroit team. Coached by Harry Sinden, the inner core of stars included Phil Esposito, Ken Hodge and Johnny Bucyk and the first offense-minded, high scoring defenseman of the modern era, Bobby Orr.

Like a Boston blueliner who preceded him by many years—Hall of Famer Eddie Shore—Orr could lead the team's rush, direct the power-play from the point, score at will and even play defense in his own end. Esposito took goal-scoring to new heights and bigger numbers, while teammates John Bucyk and Ken Hodge both became 50-goal scorers in their own right. Then there was the playboy defensive specialist and face-off artiste Derek Sanderson, as well as John (Pie) McKenzie and defenseman Ted Green. In the nets was Gerry Cheevers and his backup, Eddie Johnston.

When Boston won the Cup in 1970, many predicted that this would be the first of several consecutive championships. But the team came up short in discipline and drive in 1971, making an early and shocking exit from the playoffs after a record-setting regular season. The team exerted more self-discipline in 1972 and won their second Cup in three years. Again there was talk of a dynasty.

But in 1972 the World Hockey Association was born and by the start of 1972–73 training camp, Boston had lost Cheevers, Green and Sanderson to the WHA. Worse yet, Bobby Orr was beginning to show the effects of years of skating on two of the worst knees in sports. The Boston Bruins never became a true hockey dynasty, but they were oh, so tantalizingly close.

There was another, earlier Boston Bruins team which pulled off almost exactly the same feat, winning the Cup in 1939 and 1941. The great defenseman Eddie Shore—the core around which the Bruins first Stanley Cup champion had been built in 1929, was still with the club when it won the Cup in 1939. Not the overpowering force he had been a decade earlier, Shore was nonetheless still a muscular marvel in his declining years.

As with all the teams which have achieved dynastic or near-dynastic status, the Boston Bruins of 1939 to 1941 excelled in all areas. There was no smarter coach than Art Ross; no finer forward unit than the Kraut Line of Woody Dumart, Bobby Bauer and center Milt Schmidt and no tighter defense than Dit Clapper, Flash Hollett, Jack Portland and the ever-mighty Shore. Even their second-liners would have been starters on other teams: centerman Bill Cowley was arguably the most underrated playmaker of his era, if not all time; "Sudden Death" Mel Hill proved to be a clutch playoff performer and the team was admirably filled out with the likes of Roy Conacher, Herb Cain and Red Hamill.

Perhaps the most surprising aspect of the Bruins in this era was that failed to win the Cup three years in a row. They defeated the Maple Leafs to win Lord Stanley's mug in 1939, but yielded to a New York team destined to win in 1940, losing to the Rangers in six games even though they led by two games at one point. The spring of 1941 was witness to a splendid seven-game semifinal in which the Bruins defeated Toronto four games to three, then disposed of the Red Wings in four straight. But then hockey ran smack into World War II and soon the Kraut Line was enrolled in the Royal Canadian Air Force. The dynasty that almost was would never be.

The Philadelphia Flyers became the first modern expansion team to win the Stanley Cup in 1974, and then pulled off a repeat in 1975. Another of those talent-laden squads which appeared destined to go on into dynastic history, the club could not pull off a Triple Crown. Coached by Freddy Shero, the team boasted Bobby Clarke at center along with Bernie Parent in goal. Accompanied by sniper Reggie Leach and journeymen Gary Dornhoefer, Ross Lonsberry, Bob Kelly and Orest Kindrachuk, the Flyers took hitting and grinding to new heights.

The media loved to dwell on the somewhat bemused demeanor of Shero, thereby missing the fact that he was a master at what pundits would soon call "European" or "Soviet"-style hockey. Shero was one of the first to use an assistant coach and to modify the five-man attack—as opposed to the standard three-forward system—to include the defensemen in the scoring unit.

The Flyers reached the finals again in 1976, but a key element was missing: Bernie Parent had battled injuries for much of the year and was no longer at the top of his game. He was replaced by the less-skilled Wayne Stephenson and the Flyers lost the final in four straight games to Montreal, and have never won the Cup again.

The first team to win the Stanley Cup consecutively in the decade preceding the millennium was another modern expansion club: The Pittsburgh Penguins. Armed with one of the greatest players of any era—Mario Lemieux—the Penguins probably overcame more tragedy and near-tragedy than any other NHL team in order to win two championships.

By the 1990–91 season the building blocks of a dynasty had been assembled under the roof of the Igloo in downtown Pittsburgh: Off the ice general manager Craig Patrick had hired Scott Bowman (who had coached the Canadiens to five Cup victories) as director of player development and recruitment and had lured Bob Johnson away from USA Hockey (where he had gone after coaching the Calgary Flames for several seasons) to coach the Penguins. On the ice, Patrick had acquired the talented young goaltender Tom Barrasso from Buffalo. The offensively gifted defenseman Paul Coffey had come to the team in 1987 and was assisted

by more stay-at-home types such as Larry Murphy, Jim Paek, Randy Hillier and Jim Johnson—nothing spectacular, but steady. On the offense, besides the incomparable Lemieux, there was a blur of lesser-known faces: Bob Errey; journeyman-turned-scorer Joey Mullen; Kevin Stevens and a young Czech skater named Jaromir Jagr.

Near that season's trading deadline Patrick swung a major deal which would complete his team. On March 4, 1991, Patrick traded John Cullen, Zarley Zalapski and Jeff Parker to Hartford for the longtime "soul" of the Whalers, center Ron Francis, along with hulking (and mean) defenseman Ulf Samuelsson and Grant Jennings, also a blueliner.

By May 25, 1991, after an 8–0 win over the Minnesota North Stars, the Penguins became Stanley Cup champions for the first time in their 24-year history. On August 29 of that year coach Bob Johnson was diagnosed with brain tumors and operated upon that same night. Johnson was never able to return to Pittsburgh. By October 1 Scott Bowman has been named interim coach. Johnson passed away at his home in Colorado Springs on November 26, 1991. Despite the team's loss and despite the fact that their superstar Lemieux was slowly giving way to chronic back problems, and despite a brief players' strike, the Pens again marched to the playoffs, where they first took the Rangers in six games to win the Patrick Division (named after Craig's grandfather, Lester), then trounced the Bruins in four straight to take the Wales Conference title. Finally, on June 1, 1992, they swept the Chicago Blackhawks for their second consecutive Stanley Cup championship. Mario Lemieux won the Conn Smythe Trophy as the playoff MVP for the second year in a row.

Yet another team which seemed destined to achieve the Triple Crown of hockey championships, and thus gain dynastic status, the Pens seemed to be a virtual shoo-in for a third Cup in 1993. Then, on January 12, 1993, the Penguins announced that Lemieux has been diagnosed with a form of cancer called lymphoma, or Hodgkin's Disease. Lemieux underwent radiation therapy for a month and then, incredibly, returned to the Penguins lineup on March 2 and recorded two points that night.

Lemieux went on to astounding feats after being treated for a life-threatening disease—tallying at least one point in 18 of 20 games after returning and totaling 56 points in the remainder of the season. Mario scored 18 goals in the month of March alone, setting a club record for goals in one month. He even had four hat tricks, including back-to-back four-goal games on March 18 and March 20.

By the end of March, Pittsburgh had clinched first place in the Patrick Division for the second year in a row. A few days later the team had won its first Presidents' Trophy for the best record in the league overall. On April 9, 1993 the team set an NHL record when they defeat the New York Rangers 10–4 to register their 16th consecutive victory. The winning streak was extending to 17 with a 4–2 win over New York one night later. But in the playoffs on May 14, David Volek scored at 5:16 of overtime to give the New York Islanders a 4–3 win in the deciding game of the Patrick Division finals.

Despite his team's stunning early exit from the playoffs, Lemieux was awarded the Hart Memorial, the Art Ross and the Masterton trophies. Could the Penguins have won a third consecutive Cup if Lemieux hadn't missed 23 games?

And then there are the Detroit Red Wings of the late 1990s. Reminiscent of an earlier era, Detroit has once again won the Stanley Cup in back-to-back seasons (1997 and 1998), and appears poised to end the century in much the same way it was opened by that most venerable of dynasties, the Ottawa Silver Seven.

FRANK SELKE: THE GAME'S GREATEST GENERAL MANAGER

Frank Orr

ALTHOUGH FRANK SELKE WAS SMALL (5'7") in stature, he was a giant among NHL executives, the most successful front office man the league ever has known.

In his 34 years from 1930 to 1964 with the Toronto Maple Leafs as business manager and the Montreal Canadiens as managing director, Selke masterminded teams that won the Stanley Cup 13 times and were finalists in another 11 seasons.

Add the four Cup triumphs that the Leafs and Canadiens each won with basic rosters assembled by Selke after he left those jobs and his record is even more remarkable.

Selke's influence on the two oldest Canadian NHL franchises went far beyond the on-ice product. He was a key figure in the construction of Maple Leaf Gardens in Toronto in 1931 plus the upgrading and eventual rebuilding of the Montreal Forum when he moved to the Canadiens in 1946.

A native of Kitchener, Ontario, Selke was involved in amateur hockey there before he moved to Toronto in his "real" job as a business manager for the electricians' union. He coached two hockey teams in the 1920s, the semi-pro Toronto Ravinas and the Toronto Marlborough juniors, crossing paths as an opponent with another busy hockey coach and manager Conn Smythe. When Smythe bought the Toronto St. Patrick's, the city's NHL entry, in 1927, and changed the team name to the Maple Leafs, Selke slowly evolved into his assistant.

"I did a little bit of everything around the team from scouting for talent to selling ads and editing the program for games," Selke said.

Smythe's big ambition was to construct a new hockey building in Toronto because the old Mutual Street Arena wasn't large enough to support a top NHL club. But financing such a project at the start of The Great Depression was difficult.

Smythe's dream brought together three of hockey's most influential men—Smythe, Selke and play-by-play radio broadcaster Foster Hewitt. In the 1929–30 season, Smythe told Selke to produce a special program to sell the idea of a new home for the Leafs and include preliminary drawings of the structure.

On a Saturday night broadcast, Hewitt pitched his audience on the new booklet, to be mailed to anyone who sent in a dime. The Leafs planned to sell 32,000 programs over the entire season but 91,000 letters, each containing a dime and many with suggestions for the new rink, arrived after Hewitt's pitch.

"That huge response told us two things—how important a new building could be and the power of Hewitt's broadcasts," Selke recalled.

However, fund-raising to start construction was stalled when those involved met in a bank manager's office on King Street in Toronto in 1929. All revenue sources had been tapped and the funds needed to pay contracts with the

unions were still short several hundred thousand dollars.

The story goes that Selke bolted from the meeting and ran a mile to the Labor Council office on Church Street where the Allied Building Trades Council was in session. He asked them to back a plan under which workers would accept 20 percent of their salary in stock in the new building. The council did but, in reality, Selke had to sell the stock scheme to the business agents for 24 unions.

"It was hard times, construction work was scarce and I convinced them that 80 percent of a salary was better than none," Selke said.

The contractors followed the labor lead and bought stock packages, which, in turn, inspired the banks to increase their investment. Maple Leaf Gardens was built from scratch in an astonishing five months, opening on November 12, 1931.

The Selke–Smythe relationship never was a smooth one but together they built the Gardens and Maple Leafs into national institutions in Canada.

When Smythe wondered how to improve his team, Selke told him to move out the old players on the club and move in the excellent crop of youngsters Selke had assembled on the Marlboro juniors. Smythe guffawed but in the next couple of seasons added those youngsters—the Kid Line of Joe Primeau, Charlie Conacher and Busher Jackson, bashing defensemen Red Horner and forwards Alex Levinsky and Bob Gracie.The Leafs won only a single Stanley Cup title (1932) in that era but filled the Gardens. Selke and Smythe had many disagreements, especially on the type of players for the team.

"He (Smythe) said that players had to be big in stature to be winners and I didn't agree with him, although some size and toughness were necessary," Selke said. "We could have had two very talented but not large players from the west, Elmer Lach and Doug Bentley, plus the Kraut Line (Milt Schmidt, Woody Dumart and Bobby Bauer) from my hometown of Kitchener. Smythe said they were all too small but they all became important stars in the NHL."

When military call-ups for World War II service ravaged the rosters of NHL teams, Selke was able to use his knowledge of available talent to keep the Leafs at the top of the war-time league. They were Cup winners in 1942 and 1945. A major in the Canadian Army, Smythe went to war but even when based in England, he sent messages on how Selke, who was called business manager of the team, and coach Hap Day were to run the Leafs.

In 1942, Selke traded defenseman Frank Eddolls to the Montreal Canadiens for young center Ted "Teeder" Kennedy. Even though Kennedy went on to enjoy a fine NHL career and was among Smythe's favorite Maple Leafs, Smythe never forgave Selke for pulling the trigger on the deal without consulting him.

"It was great trade for the Leafs but Smythe could never admit that I or anyone else was a better judge of talent than him," Selke said.

Smythe returned from the war into a boardroom battle for control of the Leafs franchise. Selke sided with Ed Bickle and Bill MacBrien, club directors who were trying to gain control. When Smythe, backed by mining magnate Percy Gardner, won the ownership fight, Selke was finished with the Leafs. But the Leafs were not done. The large crop of splendid young players Selke had assembled won the Cup four times in the next five years.

Selke was immediately hired by the Canadiens, who had won the Stanley Cup title in 1946, to replace Tommy Gorman as managing director. The team had an aging but competitive roster and their arena, the old Montreal Forum, also was in shabby condition.

"When I walked into the Forum on a warm August day in 1946 to discuss my contract with the team, all I could smell in the building was dirty washrooms," Selke said. "I would not agree to any deal until the owners had committed $100,000 to cleaning up the arena."

The Canadiens spent much more on the building and gave Selke a large budget to build a model organization for the postwar NHL. The Canadiens poured money into the Quebec junior leagues plus minor hockey systems in such strong hockey cities as Winnipeg and Regina, giving the Montreal club the pick of top talent from many parts of Canada.

While the Leafs Selke had built and Smythe strengthened dominated the NHL with Cup wins in 1947, 1948, 1949 and 1951, and the Detroit Red Wings, with the young Gordie Howe, were a powerhouse, Selke carefully built the foundation of a strong farm system that was to sustain the Canadiens at the top through two decades.

"We looked for players with more than just talent," Selke said. "They had to be committed to the high standards of excellence in all parts of their lives that we made the trademark of the Canadiens' organization."

Goalie Jacques Plante, defensemen Doug Harvey, Tom Johnson, Bob Turner and Dollard St. Laurent, forwards Jean Beliveau, Maurice and Henry Richard, Bernie Geoffrion, Bert Olmstead, Dickie Moore, Marcel Bonin, Don Marshall, Claude Provost and Phil Goyette under the masterful coaching of Toe Blake gave the Canadiens of the 1950s a depth of talent perhaps unequaled in NHL history.

The team won the Stanley Cup in a record five consecutive seasons from 1956 to 1960, a string that easily could have been eight in a row because the Canadiens lost seven-game finals to the Red Wings in 1954 and 1955 after winning in 1953.

Selke did not want to retire from the job in 1964 when he reached the age of 70 but the ownership insisted. When he departed for his horse and cattle farm near Montreal, Selke again left behind an excellent stock of players—the Canadiens won four Cup championships in five seasons from 1965 to 1969—and an excellent replacement as managing director, Sam Pollock, whom Selke had groomed for the job.

THE ART AND CRAFT OF COACHING

Dick Irvin

THE HISTORY BOOKS OF HOCKEY do not tell us the identity of the game's first coach. The name of the first man to stand in front of his team, go over game strategies and deliver a pep talk, has been lost to the ages.

In the earliest days of competition for the Stanley Cup, teams almost always had a playing coach or playing manager. On only two occasions in the Stanley Cup's first 25 years (1902 and 1912), was the winning coach a non-playing member of the team.

In 1902 the Cup was won by the Montreal Amateur Athletic Association. The team picture includes 18 men: 10 players and eight civilians. In the latter group one "C. McKenna" is identified as "coach." The photo of the 1912 champion Quebec Bulldogs is much more crowded, with 24 people, but only nine are players. Included in the large group of civilian hangers-on is coach C. Nolan.

The last playing coaches of Stanley Cup-winning teams were Frank Patrick, with the Vancouver Millionaires in 1915, and Newsy Lalonde with the Montreal Canadiens the following year. We must remember that through those early years there weren't many players in uniform for coaches to coach. The sturdy warriors of the time were "ironmen," most of them playing the full 60 minutes. Then, as rosters increased, there was more need for a coach. Lalonde's 1916 Canadiens had 12 men in uniform, the most for a Cup-winning team until then.

Through the years many teams in amateur and minor pro hockey have employed playing coaches and there were a few in the NHL until the late 1960s. Legendary defenseman Doug Harvey was the playing coach of the New York Rangers in the 1961–62 season. Harvey led the Rangers to their first playoff position in four years and won the Norris Trophy as the NHL's outstanding defenseman. The last playing coach in the NHL was Charlie Burns, who held that position during 44 games with the Minnesota North Stars in the 1969–70 season. Today the NHL does not allow playing coaches.

As full-time bench coaches became the rule rather than the exception they had to deal with a problem that coaches still face today: discipline within the ranks of their team, on and off the ice. In 1917, shortly after the National Hockey League came into being, Charlie Querrie was appointed as the coach in Toronto. Querrie posted a set of rules on his team's dressing room wall which showed that, even then, coaches meant business. Querrie's rules read, in part:

- First and foremost, do not forget that I am running this club.
- You are expected to give your best services to the club. Your physical condition depends a lot on how you behave off the ice.
- You are being paid to play hockey and be a good fellow. If you do not want to be on the square and play hockey, turn in your uniform and go do some other work.

The basic ideas behind Charlie Querrie's 'rules' are not that much different than ideas held by coaches today, although back then it was easier for a coach to tell his players to "go do some other work." But there is much that is different today for the men who work behind the bench, especially when it comes to job security and length of service with one team. It was quite different for many coaches and managers in the early days of the NHL's modern era.

Jack Adams was hired by Detroit in 1927–28, the second year of the franchise. He was general manager of the team for the next 36 years, as well as coach through the first 21. Adams ran the Detroit organization just one way: his way. One of his favorite tricks was to walk around the dressing room before a game talking to his third- and fourth-line players with train tickets to Omaha, Nebraska prominently sticking out of his jacket pocket. Omaha was where the Red Wings had their farm team and the message was clear: play well tonight or you'll be on the train to Omaha. Adams was a fiery type who had more than his share of run-ins with opposing managers, coaches and referees. His attempts to get at the referee in the 1942 Stanley Cup finals resulted in a fine and suspension.

Art Ross was general manager of the Boston Bruins from the time they joined the NHL in 1924 until 1945. He also coached at various times, for a total of 16 years. In those days familiarity bred contempt and Ross was involved in ongoing and bitter disputes with some of his long-time rivals. Ross suffered a broken nose and lost a few teeth as the result of a fist fight with Red Dutton, the coach and general manager of the New York Americans. Another of Ross's rivals was Conn Smythe, the president and general manager of the Toronto Maple Leafs. When he heard the result of the Ross–Dutton fiasco, Smythe said: "It couldn't have happened to a more deserving recipient." Smythe himself exchanged punches with Bill Stewart, coach of the Chicago Black Hawks, prior to the first game of the 1938 Stanley Cup finals between their teams.

Lester Patrick was coach and general manager of the New York Rangers when they began play in 1926, and held both jobs for the next 13 years. Lester and his brother Frank were among the game's first great innovators. At one time the rule book included 20 items that had originated with one of the brothers, including the blue line. The Patricks' earned the title "the Royal Family of Hockey." Lester's sons, Lynn and Muzz, both played for and later coached the Rangers. Lynn's son Craig also played in the NHL and was general manager of the Pittsburgh Penguins when that team won the Stanley Cup in 1991 and 1992.

Beginning in 1940 the Montreal Canadiens had just two coaches, Dick Irvin and Hector "Toe" Blake, for the next 28 years. Irvin had the job for 15 years, Blake for 13. During their combined tenures the Canadiens finished first in the regular season 11 times, won the Stanley Cup 11 times, and missed the playoffs only once.

While coaches were more secure back then, there were exceptions—principally in Chicago where the original owner of the Black Hawks, Major Frederic McLaughlin, was a coach's nightmare. In the first 13 years he owned the team McLaughlin hired and fired 13 coaches. Two of them, Tommy Gorman and Bill Stewart, were let go shortly after they had coached the Major's team to Stanley Cup championships.

Many of today's coaches can relate to McLaughlin's victims. More than ever before, the coaching profession has become a precarious one. Management's motto seems to be: "If at first you don't succeed, you're gone," an attitude that is frustrating to the men behind the bench. Bob Murdoch, head coach in both Chicago and Winnipeg in the late 1980s, once said: "The insecurity, and at times the lack of respect for coaches, are discouraging." Others stress that the constantly escalating financial aspect of the game has owners demanding that their teams win "now."

During the 1997–98 season five of the seven teams in the NHL's Atlantic Division changed coaches. One of those changes saw Roger Neilson become coach of the Philadelphia Flyers, his seventh NHL head coaching job. A few months earlier Mike Keenan had taken over as coach of the Vancouver Canucks, his fifth team. Hockey's all-time winningest coach, Scotty Bowman, was with the Detroit Red Wings, his fifth stop behind an NHL bench. Resiliency in the marketplace is definitely an asset for anyone trying to earn a living as a coach in the NHL.

The path followed by coaches to the NHL has changed over the years. From the 1920s through until the late 1960s dominant, long-time winning coaches included Lester Patrick, Art Ross, Jack Adams, Hap Day, Dick Irvin, and Toe Blake. All have been elected to the Hockey Hall of Fame, but as players not coaches. Toe Blake retired in 1968 after coaching the Montreal Canadiens to the Stanley Cup for the eighth time. In the next 30 years only two Hall of Fame players coached Stanley Cup-winning teams: Tom Johnson with Boston in 1972 and Jacques Lemaire with New Jersey in 1995. During that same 30-year period only three other Cup-winning coaches—Glen Sather, Al Arbour, and Terry Crisp—had what could be termed lengthy NHL playing careers.

The era of the "career coach" has arrived. From 1990 to 1998 six different men were Stanley Cup-winning coaches. Only two, Jacques Lemaire and Marc Crawford, had played in the NHL. Lemaire played 998 games for the Montreal Canadiens, Crawford 196 for the Vancouver Canucks. The others, Scotty Bowman (who won three times), John Muckler, Bob Johnson, Jacques Demers and Mike Keenan never played in the NHL. In fact Bowman, Johnson, Demers, and Keenan never played professional hockey. By contrast, in the 30 years prior to 1990 only five Stanley Cup-winning coaches had not played hockey at the professional level.

Throughout the NHL's first six decades coaches were mainly a one-man show. They were the only person listed as "coach" on their team's payroll, and their duties sometimes extended beyond simply running their team in practices and games. They were often responsible for travel and hotel arrangements and organizing game-day meals for their players while on the road. And they were the only one standing behind the bench during the games. But with the advent of an ever-expanding map of professional hockey, much of that has changed.

In the early 1980s teams began hiring assistant coaches, often recently retired players. At first, having one assistant coach work behind the bench during games was a novelty. But their numbers increased as the NHL grew. Today teams may have as many as four or five assistant coaches who have specific assignments and who were hired after coaching careers at the college, junior, or minor pro level. Whereas coaches in the past handled all player changes during games, some teams now have an assistant who changes defense pairings and another who changes forward lines. Another assistant might be getting a different view of the game from a location high in the arena and communicating with those behind the bench via telephone. Most of the coaches in bygone years admitted they knew little about goaltending, unless they had been one in their playing days. Among today's assistants are goaltending coaches who work both with the goaltenders on the NHL team and with young prospects playing in junior or minor pro leagues.

Another modern aspect to coaching hockey is the use of videotape to study the opposition. Most teams employ someone who has the job of taping games involving other teams, then editing the tapes to show systems and tendencies opposing teams demonstrate on offense, defense, power-plays and penalty killing. In earlier days the only time a coach saw the opposition was when his team played them, although in the smaller NHL the teams played each other much more often than today. As well as talking to their players between periods, coaches now can show them video highlights, and lowlights, of the period just completed. Instant analysis is available in the dressing room as well as on television sets on the home front.

The changing face of the NHL appears to have brought an end to teams that could be termed 'dynasties' because of their domination of the rest of the league, especially during the playoffs. Beginning in 1956, either Toe Blake of the Canadiens or George "Punch" Imlach of the Maple Leafs was the Stanley Cup-winning coach 12 times in 13 years. The most recent examples of dynasties came in the period from 1976 to 1988, when three men—Scotty Bowman of the Montreal Canadiens, Al Arbour of the New York Islanders and Glen Sather of the Edmonton Oilers—all coached four Stanley Cup-winning teams during that time, accounting for 12 of 13 championships. In the next 10 years, eight different men coached Cup winners, with Bowman the only one to do it more than once.

One reason the NHL may have seen the last of its dynasties can be found in the movement of players from team to team, which to a large degree has been dictated by free agency and high salaries. Veteran coaches have found that sometimes it isn't easy to get their message across in a dressing room full of millionaires. Salaries of coaches have always lagged far behind salaries of players although in recent years things have been looking up for the men behind the bench.

The first coach to earn as much as $20,000 for one season was Dick Irvin Sr., who signed on for that amount with the Chicago Black Hawks in 1955. In 1963 Toe Blake confided to some of his players in Montreal that he was making $16,000 a year. At that time Blake had coached the Canadiens for nine seasons and had won the Stanley Cup five times.

During the 1997–98 season *The Hockey News* published the salaries of the 26 head coaches in the NHL. In U.S. dollars they ranged from a low of $236,000 for Jacques Martin of the Ottawa Senators to a high of $970,000 for Scotty Bowman of the Detroit Red Wings. Sixteen of the NHL's 26 coaches were earning $400,000 or more. The average salary for the league's players was about $1 million while for coaches it was a more modest $466,258. The salary gap still exists but it seems that, finally, the men who walk the coaching tightrope in the NHL are being better appreciated for what they do.

NHL TROPHIES AND AWARDS

Frank Orr

ALTHOUGH EVERY LEAGUE in professional team sports has a list of individual awards to hand out at the conclusion of each season, none has a lineup of trophies even close to the National Hockey League, both in number and esthetics.

Each June at a black-tie charity gala event televised nationally in Canada and the U.S., the winners of seven awards are announced and collect their silverware. Four other laurels announced earlier or based on statistical performance arc acknowledged.

Throw in several team trophies, a list headed of course by the Stanley Cup, and a very large table is required to hold the hardware.

The NHL First and Second All-Star teams are also announced to expand the list of acceptance speeches and the financial payout by the league. The individual awards and all-star selections are accompanied by fiscal rewards of $284,000, part of the NHL's $10,359,000 in prize loot comprising season, All-Star Game and playoff team booty and the individual prizes.

The NHL awards based on statistics include:

• The Art Ross Trophy, named in honor of the long-time manager and coach (1924 to 1954) of the Boston Bruins, goes "to the player who leads the league in scoring points at the end of the regular season," was first awarded in 1947.

• The William Jennings Trophy is awarded "to the goalkeeper(s) having played a minimum of 25 games for the team with the fewest goals scored against it." Jennings was president of the New York Rangers and when the award was donated in 1981–82, it replaced the Vezina Trophy as the award to the goalics on the best defensive team. The Vezina now is awarded to the top goalie as selected by the 26 general managers.

• The Bud Ice Plus–Minus Award was first awarded in the 1996–97 season "to the player, having played a minimum of 60 games who leads the league in plus–minus statistics at the end of the regular schedule." Plus–minus is the difference between goals for and against the team when the player is on the ice in equal manpower situations. (An award was first given to the NHL's plus–minus leader in 1982–83.)

The winners of the majority of NHL awards are selected by a poll of the Professional Hockey Writers' Association in all NHL cities.

• The Hart Trophy goes "to the player adjudged to be the most valuable to his team." The original trophy was donated in 1923 by Dr. David A. Hart, father of Cecil Hart, manager and coach of the Montreal Canadiens. The first Hart Trophy was retired to the Hockey Hall of Fame in 1960 and replaced by a new trophy.

• The Calder Trophy is "to the player selected as the most proficient in his first year of competition in the NHL." The trophy commemorates Frank Calder, NHL president from 1917 until his death in 1943.

• The Norris Trophy is awarded "to the defense player who demonstrates throughout the season the greatest all-round ability in the position." James Norris was the owner-president of the Detroit Red Wings.

• The Lady Byng Trophy goes "to the player adjudged to have exhibited the best type of sportsmanship and gentlemanly conduct combined with a high standard of playing ability." The trophy was donated originally in 1925 by Lady Byng, the wife of Canada's Governor-General.

• The Frank J. Selke Trophy goes "to the forward who best excels in the defensive aspects of the game." Selke was an executive for four decades with the Toronto Maple Leafs and Montreal Canadiens.

• The Conn Smythe Trophy is awarded "to the most valuable player in the playoffs." Smythe was owner and general manager of the Toronto Maple Leafs from 1927 to 1961 and builder of Maple Leaf Gardens.

• The Jack Adams Award goes "to the NHL coach adjudged to have contributed the most to his team's success." Voted by the NHL Broadcasters' Association, the award honors Adams, longtime general manager/coach of the Detroit Red Wings.

• The Vezina Trophy is presented to "the goalkeeper adjudged to be the best at his position," as voted by the general managers, was named for Georges Vezina, goalie of the Montreal Canadiens in the NHL's early days.

• The Bill Masterton Trophy is given to the NHL player who best exemplifies the qualities of perseverance, sportsmanship and dedication to hockey. It commemorates the late Bill Masterton of the Minnesota North Stars who died of head injuries suffered in a 1968 game.

• The King Clancy Trophy honors the man who spent 65 years in the NHL as a player, referee, coach and executive and is awarded "to the player who best exemplifies leadership qualities on and off the ice and has made a noteworthy humanitarian contribution in his community."

Two special NHL honors are the Lester Pearson Award and the Lester Patrick Trophy.

The Pearson Award honors the late Prime Minister of Canada and Nobel Peace prize winner Lester B. Pearson and goes to "the NHL's outstanding player as selected by members of the NHL Players' Association."

Named for one of the finest players of the game's early era and, later, one of the NHL's greatest coaches and executives, the Patrick award is "for outstanding service to hockey in the United States."

In addition to trophy winners, the hockey writers' group selects the 12 players on the two All-Star teams.

The winners of the awards and All-Star berths do more than supply lists of the game's greatest names. In many ways, those honored define much of hockey's history, the frames around its notable pictures.

During the 1997–98 season, *The Hockey News* celebrated its 50th anniversary. As a special event to celebrate the occasion, the publication had a panel of 50 voters, writers, broadcasters, hockey executives both active and retired, select the top 50 players in NHL history.

The tabulation of the results produced a "photo finish," a close vote in which Wayne Gretzky, the NHL's biggest star for the past 20 years; Bobby Orr, the brilliant defenseman of the late 1960s and early 1970s; and Gordie Howe, "Mr. Hockey," who had a 26-season NHL career plus additional time in the World Hockey Association, were picked as the top three players.

In his 19 seasons through the end of the 1997–98 schedule, Gretzky had collected 40 major awards and All-Star selections. With 33 honors in his 26 NHL seasons, Howe was second in numbers but third in the "greatest-ever" poll. Orr, who gathered the third-most awards, 25, but did it in only 12 seasons, was second in the top-50 poll.

The Hart Trophy is awarded to the player most valuable to his team, not the best player or the top star or the player of the year. Often this person represents all of the above, but on a few occasions this distinction between a pure MVP and the player most valuable to his team has produced Hart results open to second guessing.

For instance, the Hart was awarded to goalie Dominik Hasek of the Buffalo Sabres for the 1996–97 and 1997–98 seasons on the basis of his being the player who contributed the most to his club. As he also won the Lester Pearson Award and the Vezina in the same years, and second-guessers were silenced.

"At the end of most successful seasons, a team can look back over the games and say that goaltending was the big reason why we got a win here and a tie there, a dozen games where the points belong to the goalie," said John Muckler, the general manager of the Sabres in 1996–97.

"But it's tough to imagine a game in 1996–97 where we earned a win or a tie when Hasek's goaltending was not the dominant factor of our success. That season, the Hart award for him was perfect because no player in the league was as valuable to his team. If the award was to the player of the year, there were a half dozen guys who had extraordinary seasons of the caliber to win. But none was as important to their team as Hasek was to the Sabres."

Hasek is only the fifth goalie in 75 years to whom the Hart has been awarded and the first since Jacques Plante of the Montreal Canadiens in 1962. He is the only goalie to claim the honor twice.

An interesting twist on goalies and the Hart is that while the job is regarded as the most important position in the game, a goalie been named the most valuable player only eight percent of the time (six times in 75 seasons).

Obviously, the value of goalies increases in the Stanley Cup playoffs, where the Conn Smythe Trophy goes to the MVP in the postseason tournament. In the 34 years the Smythe has been awarded, 11 goalies accounting for 32 percent of the winners, have taken that hardware.

Of course, Gretzky, who owns a major portion of the NHL's offensive record book, has been awarded the Hart Trophy a record nine times, eight of them consecutively when he was with the Edmonton Oilers and once as a member of the Los Angeles Kings.

The mighty Howe was MVP six times and the defensemen who defined the two greatest eras of success by the Boston Bruins—Eddie Shore with four and Orr with three—follow. In fact only five other defensemen have won the Hart in 74 years.

To expand the theory that the best player in the league is not always the most valuable to his team, nine Hart Trophy winners were not named to the First All-Star Team at their position. Seven did earn Second-Team nominations while two MVPs (goalie Al Rollins of the Chicago Black Hawks in 1953–54 and center Teeder Kennedy of the Maple Leafs in 1954–55) were not on either star squad.

Rollins was one of only four Hart winners to have played on a team that did not qualify for the playoffs. The others were, Tom Anderson of the New York Americans in 1941–42, Andy Bathgate of the New York Rangers in 1958–59 and Mario Lemieux of the Pittsburgh Penguins in 1987–88.

In the 75 seasons that the MVP has been selected, 13 of the Hart winners for the regular schedule played on the Stanley Cup winner; five (Orr twice, Gretzky, Lemieux and Guy Lafleur of the Montreal Canadiens) were most valu-

able in both the schedule and the playoffs in the 34 years the Smythe has existed. As well, 32 scoring leaders and Art Ross Trophy winners have also won the Hart.

Gretzky also collected the Lady Byng Trophy as the most gentlemanly and effective player four times, one of the selections with an interesting number. A meager penalty total usually is a big part of the winner's repertoire but when number 99 was named Byng winner in 1991–92, he had 34 minutes in penalties. That's the second-highest total by any Byng recipient, topped only by the 40 minutes 1926–27 winner Billy Burch had gathered while a New York American.

Frank Boucher, the wonderful little center of the Rangers in the early days of the NHL, later coach and general manager of that team, collected the Byng a record seven times. Boucher recorded only 119 penalty minutes in 557 career games.

Although an assortment of defensemen over the years have played effective, aggressive hockey while seldom violating the rules, the backliners have received little support over the years in Byng voting. In only four seasons have defensemen won the award, Red Kelly of the Red Wings three times and the Wings' Bill Quackenbush in the 1948–49 season when he played the 60-game schedule without a penalty minute.

Another NHL trophy with many unusual twists in its history is the Jack Adams Award, since 1974 honoring the coach of the year.

No strong definition exists on what constitutes a superior coaching effort. Is it the lifting of a team a considerable way up the standings? Is it inspiring a good team to deliver excellent performances on a consistent basis? Is it convincing a weak team to play its best, delivering a sound, smart effort most nights?

The list of Adams winners includes coaches from all categories, although those who engineered dramatic improvements received the nod most times.

Coaches often joke that they do not want to win the Adams because it seems to carry a jinx: Win the Adams and be unemployed quickly!

In the 25 years the award has been presented, one coach, Ted Nolan of the Sabres in 1996–97, was fired days after he collected the trophy. Five winners were sacked during or at the end of the season after their win and seven more were gone from the job within two years of their Adams acceptance speech.

Having been involved in the most Stanley Cup wins (13), seven with the Maple Leafs and six as managing director of the Canadiens, Selke knew the type of player who rated highly on his list of assets.

"The backbone of any team is forwards who are at their best when the other team has the puck and can control the opposition's top shooters," Selke said when the NHL created the award bearing his name in 1977 for the best defensive forward.

"Of course, you need offensive stars, top defensemen and strong goaltending. But check the roster of any winning team and you will find a group of very good defensive forwards."

At the time the award was first presented, the Canadiens had a modest-scoring winger who was among the most valuable players in a roster of stars that was to win the Cup in four consecutive seasons. Bob Gainey was a splendid penalty-killer and the production of the NHL's strongest right wingers sagged against the Canadiens because of Gainey superior checking skills.

A high compliment for Gainey came from Viktor Tikhonov, the long-time coach of the Soviet Union national team and Central Red Army.

"Bob Gainey is the best technical hockey player in the world," Tikhonov said.

Gainey won the Selke Trophy in its first four seasons and an assortment of defensive specialists collected it in subsequent years. In recent seasons, however, the type of players winning the Selke has changed.

Because of NHL expansion and the dilution of talent, plus the budget constraints on some teams due to salary increases, many clubs cannot afford high-quality specialist players. Thus, the top stars must not only score goals, they must fill a large role in preventing scores. Many big shooters work on penalty-killing units and in situations when strong defense is required. Such big attack guns as Sergei Fedorov, Ron Francis and Doug Gilmour have won Selke awards in the 1990s and certainly not unjustly. Their heavy workload includes both even-strength and power-play duties plus penalty-killing time. Their skill makes them excellent in any role.

Suggestions have been made that the NHL needs two awards for defensemen, one for defensive backliners, another for "offensemen." While the Norris Trophy mandate dictates that all-round ability at the position must be considered, the chances of a defensive specialist collecting the award are very slim.

To be rated a top defenseman these days a player must have strong offensive skills and the point total to match. Blame some of that on Bobby Orr.

The NHL had excellent rushing defensemen throughout history from King Clancy to Babe Pratt to Doug Harvey, Red Kelly and Pierre Pilote. But Orr arrived and in his fourth season (1969–70) he won the NHL scoring title, a feat that up to that time was seen to be as strong a possibility as a pitcher leading the major leagues in home runs.

Orr's eight consecutive Norris wins started the trend of high-scoring defensemen. In the past 20 years, only one rearguard who could be classified as a defensive defenseman, Rod Langway of the Washington Capitals in 1982–83 (32 points) and 1983–84 (33), has won the Norris.

In the 14 seasons since Langway's 1984 Norris win, those collecting the best defenseman award (Ray Bourque, five; Paul Coffey and Chris Chelios, three each; Brian Leetch, two; and Rob Blake, one) have averaged more than 80 points in their Norris-winning seasons.

Since NHL All-Star Teams first were named in 1930–31, the selections have provoked as much discussion—yes, arguments—as any honors. Of course, the list of all-stars provides a guide rather than a definitive rating on the best at each position.

Perhaps the longest-running argument in NHL history was the debate on the greatest right winger, both in their era and total NHL history, Howe or Maurice Richard of the Canadiens.

During the 10-season stretch from 1948–49 to 1957–58 when the two players were in their peak form—from the time Howe arrived as a frontline player to the time age caught up with the Rocket—the outcome of the right wing All-Star vote was anticipated eagerly. In that time, Howe earned six first team and three second team selections while Richard had four and five.

But did that signify that Howe was the better player in that era? Although the playoff statistics do not figure in All-Star selections, which are based on performance during the schedule, the numbers for the postseasons in those 10 years add fuel to the "greatest RW" fire.

Each ace missed a playoff, Howe with an injury, Richard due to a suspension. But in the nine active springs, Richard played 87 games, scored 50 goals and had 25 assists for 75 points. Five of those goals were overtime winners as the Canadiens won the Stanley Cup four times in that stretch.

The Red Wings won the Cup four times, too, in those 10 seasons and in his nine playoffs, Howe had 36 goals and 46 assists for 72 points in 74 games.

Career longevity—Howe played 26 NHL seasons to 18 for Richard—allowed Howe to lead all NHL All-Stars with 21 selections, 12 to the first team and nine to the second, while Richard had 14, eight and six.

Second in All-Star nominations, and the leader among active players, is defenseman Raymond Bourque of the Boston Bruins. When he was not named to either 1996–97 All-Star Team, Bourque's streak was snapped at 17 (12 first, five second) selections.

While no NHL team has swept the six spots on the NHL First All-Star Team in one season, two clubs earned five of the nominations and placed a player on the second team.

In the 1944–45 season, the Canadiens had five first teamers: goalie Bill Durnan, defenseman Butch Bouchard and the Punch Line of Elmer Lach, Toe Blake and Rocket Richard. Defenseman Flash Hollett of the Red Wings spoiled the sweep, although defenceman Glen Harmon of the Canadiens was on the second team.

The Black Hawks placed five men on the first team in 1965–66: goalie Hall, defenseman Pilote, forwards Bobby Hull, Stan Mikita and Ken Wharram. Hawk defenseman Elmer Vasko was on the second team, losing the first-team selection to Tim Horton of the Maple Leafs.

The NHL All-Star Team from those with the most selections to the official first and second teams is not a bad little squad: Terry Sawchuk in goal, Raymond Bourque and Doug Harvey on defence and Wayne Gretzky at centre between Bobby Hull and Gordie Howe.

NATIONAL HOCKEY LEAGUE INDIVIDUAL TROPHY AND AWARD WINNERS

ART ROSS TROPHY
Scoring leader

1998	Jaromir Jagr, Pit.
1997	Mario Lemieux, Pit.
1996	Mario Lemieux, Pit.
1995	Jaromir Jagr, Pit.
1994	Wayne Gretzky, L.A.
1993	Mario Lemieux, Pit.
1992	Mario Lemieux, Pit.
1991	Wayne Gretzky, L.A.
1990	Wayne Gretzky, L.A.
1989	Mario Lemieux, Pit.
1988	Mario Lemieux, Pit.
1987	Wayne Gretzky, Edm.
1986	Wayne Gretzky, Edm.
1985	Wayne Gretzky, Edm.
1984	Wayne Gretzky, Edm.
1983	Wayne Gretzky, Edm.
1982	Wayne Gretzky, Edm.
1981	Wayne Gretzky, Edm.
1980	Marcel Dionne, L.A.
1979	Bryan Trottier, NYI
1978	Guy Lafleur, Mtl.
1977	Guy Lafleur, Mtl.
1976	Guy Lafleur, Mtl.
1975	Bobby Orr, Bos.
1974	Phil Esposito, Bos.
1973	Phil Esposito, Bos.
1972	Phil Esposito, Bos.
1971	Phil Esposito, Bos.
1970	Bobby Orr, Bos.
1969	Phil Esposito, Bos.
1968	Stan Mikita, Chi.
1967	Stan Mikita, Chi.
1966	Bobby Hull, Chi.
1965	Stan Mikita, Chi.
1964	Stan Mikita, Chi.
1963	Gordie Howe, Det.
1962	Bobby Hull, Chi.
1961	Bernie Geoffrion, Mtl.
1960	Bobby Hull, Chi.
1959	Dickie Moore, Mtl.
1958	Dickie Moore, Mtl.
1957	Gordie Howe, Det.
1956	Jean Beliveau, Mtl.
1955	Bernie Geoffrion, Mtl.
1954	Gordie Howe, Det.
1953	Gordie Howe, Det.
1952	Gordie Howe, Det.
1951	Gordie Howe, Det.
1950	Ted Lindsay, Det.
1949	Roy Conacher, Chi.
1948*	Elmer Lach, Mtl.
1947	Max Bentley, Chi.
1946	Max Bentley, Chi.
1945	Elmer Lach, Mtl.
1944	Herb Cain, Bos.
1943	Doug Bentley, Chi.
1942	Bryan Hextall, NYR
1941	Bill Cowley, Bos.
1940	Milt Schmidt, Bos.
1939	Toe Blake, Mtl.
1938	Gordie Drillon, Tor.
1937	Dave Schriner, NYA
1936	Dave Schriner, NYA
1935	Charlie Conacher, Tor.
1934	Charlie Conacher, Tor.
1933	Bill Cook, NYR
1932	Harvey Jackson, Tor.
1931	Howie Morenz, Mtl.
1930	Cooney Weiland, Bos.
1929	Ace Bailey, Tor.
1928	Howie Morenz, Mtl.
1927	Bill Cook, NYR
1926	Nels Stewart, Mtl.M.
1925	Babe Dye, Tor.
1924	Cy Denneny, Ott.
1923	Babe Dye, Tor.
1922	Punch Broadbent, Ott.
1921	Newsy Lalonde, Mtl.
1920	Joe Malone, Que.
1919	Newsy Lalonde, Mtl.
1918	Joe Malone, Mtl.

* Trophy first awarded in 1948. Scoring leader listed from 1918 to 1947.

HART TROPHY
Most valuable player

1998	Dominik Hasek, Buf.
1997	Dominik Hasek, Buf.
1996	Mario Lemieux, Pit.
1995	Eric Lindros, Phi.
1994	Sergei Fedorov, Det.
1993	Mario Lemieux, Pit.
1992	Mark Messier, NYR
1991	Brett Hull, St.L.
1990	Mark Messier, Edm.
1989	Wayne Gretzky, L.A.
1988	Mario Lemieux, Pit.
1987	Wayne Gretzky, Edm.
1986	Wayne Gretzky, Edm.
1985	Wayne Gretzky, Edm.
1984	Wayne Gretzky, Edm.
1983	Wayne Gretzky, Edm.
1982	Wayne Gretzky, Edm.
1981	Wayne Gretzky, Edm.
1980	Wayne Gretzky, Edm.
1979	Bryan Trottier, NYI
1978	Guy Lafleur, Mtl.
1977	Guy Lafleur, Mtl.
1976	Bobby Clarke, Phi.
1975	Bobby Clarke, Phi.
1974	Phil Esposito, Bos.
1973	Bobby Clarke, Phi.
1972	Bobby Orr, Bos.
1971	Bobby Orr, Bos.
1970	Bobby Orr, Bos.
1969	Phil Esposito, Bos.
1968	Stan Mikita, Chi.
1967	Stan Mikita, Chi.
1966	Bobby Hull, Chi.
1965	Bobby Hull, Chi.
1964	Jean Beliveau, Mtl.
1963	Gordie Howe, Det.
1962	Jacques Plante, Mtl.
1961	Bernie Geoffrion, Mtl.
1960	Gordie Howe, Det.
1959	Andy Bathgate, NYR
1958	Gordie Howe, Det.
1957	Gordie Howe, Det.
1956	Jean Beliveau, Mtl.
1955	Ted Kennedy, Tor.
1954	Al Rollins, Chi.
1953	Gordie Howe, Det.
1952	Gordie Howe, Det.
1951	Milt Schmidt, Bos.
1950	Chuck Rayner, NYR
1949	Sid Abel, Det.
1948	Buddy O'Connor, NYR
1947	Maurice Richard, Mtl.
1946	Max Bentley, Chi.
1945	Elmer Lach, Mtl.
1944	Babe Pratt, Tor.
1943	Bill Cowley, Bos.
1942	Tom Anderson, Bro.
1941	Bill Cowley, Bos.
1940	Ebbie Goodfellow, Det.
1939	Toe Blake, Mtl.
1938	Eddie Shore, Bos.
1937	Babe Siebert, Mtl.
1936	Eddie Shore, Bos.
1935	Eddie Shore, Bos.
1934	Aurel Joliat, Mtl.
1933	Eddie Shore, Bos.
1932	Howie Morenz, Mtl.
1931	Howie Morenz, Mtl.
1930	Nels Stewart, Mtl.M.
1929	Roy Worters, NYA
1928	Howie Morenz, Mtl.
1927	Herb Gardiner, Mtl.
1926	Nels Stewart, Mtl.M.
1925	Billy Burch, Ham.
1924	Frank Nighbor, Ott.

LADY BYNG TROPHY
Gentlemanly conduct

1998	Ron Francis, Pit.
1997	Paul Kariya, Ana.
1996	Paul Kariya, Ana.
1995	Ron Francis, Pit.
1994	Wayne Gretzky, L.A.
1993	Pierre Turgeon, NYI
1992	Wayne Gretzky, L.A.
1991	Wayne Gretzky, L.A.
1990	Brett Hull, St.L.
1989	Joe Mullen, Cgy.
1988	Mats Naslund, Mtl.
1987	Joe Mullen, Cgy.
1986	Mike Bossy, NYI
1985	Jari Kurri, Edm.
1984	Mike Bossy, NYI
1983	Mike Bossy, NYI
1982	Rick Middleton, Bos.
1981	Rick Kehoe, Pit.
1980	Wayne Gretzky, Edm.
1979	Bob MacMillan, Atl.
1978	Butch Goring, L.A.
1977	Marcel Dionne, L.A.
1976	Jean Ratelle, NYR-Bos.
1975	Marcel Dionne, Det.
1974	John Bucyk, Bos.
1973	Gilbert Perreault, Buf.
1972	Jean Ratelle, NYR
1971	John Bucyk, Bos.
1970	Phil Goyette, St.L.
1969	Alex Delvecchio, Det.
1968	Stan Mikita, Chi.
1967	Stan Mikita, Chi.
1966	Alex Delvecchio, Det.
1965	Bobby Hull, Chi.
1964	Ken Wharram, Chi.
1963	Dave Keon, Tor.
1962	Dave Keon, Tor.
1961	Red Kelly, Tor.
1960	Don McKenney, Bos.
1959	Alex Delvecchio, Det.
1958	Camille Henry, NYR
1957	Andy Hebenton, NYR
1956	Earl Reibel, Det.
1955	Sid Smith, Tor.
1954	Red Kelly, Det.
1953	Red Kelly, Det.
1952	Sid Smith, Tor.
1951	Red Kelly, Det.
1950	Edgar Laprade, NYR
1949	Bill Quackenbush, Det.
1948	Buddy O'Connor, NYR
1947	Bobby Bauer, Bos.
1946	Toe Blake, Mtl.
1945	Bill Mosienko, Chi.
1944	Clint Smith, Chi.
1943	Max Bentley, Chi.
1942	Syl Apps, Tor.
1941	Bobby Bauer, Bos.
1940	Bobby Bauer, Bos.
1939	Clint Smith, NYR
1938	Gordie Drillon, Tor.
1937	Marty Barry, Det.
1936	Doc Romnes, Chi.
1935	Frank Boucher, NYR
1934	Frank Boucher, NYR
1933	Frank Boucher, NYR
1932	Joe Primeau, Tor.
1931	Frank Boucher, NYR
1930	Frank Boucher, NYR
1929	Frank Boucher, NYR
1928	Frank Boucher, NYR
1927	Billy Burch, NYA
1926	Frank Nighbor, Ott.
1925	Frank Nighbor, Ott.

VEZINA TROPHY
Best goaltender

1998	Dominik Hasek, Buf.
1997	Dominik Hasek, Buf.
1996	Jim Carey, Wsh.
1995	Dominik Hasek, Buf.
1994	Dominik Hasek, Buf.
1993	Ed Belfour, Chi.
1992	Patrick Roy, Mtl.
1991	Ed Belfour, Chi.
1990	Patrick Roy, Mtl.
1989	Patrick Roy, Mtl.
1988	Grant Fuhr, Edm.
1987	Ron Hextall, Phi.
1986	John Vanbiesbrouck, NYR
1985	Pelle Lindbergh, Phi.
1984	Tom Barrasso, Buf.
1983	Pete Peeters, Bos.
1982	Billy Smith, NYI
1981	Richard Sevigny, Mtl.
	Denis Herron, Mtl.
	Michel Larocque, Mtl.
1980	Bob Sauve, Buf.
	Don Edwards, Buf.
1979	Ken Dryden, Mtl.
	Michel Larocque, Mtl.
1978	Ken Dryden, Mtl.
	Michel Larocque
1977	Ken Dryden, Mtl.
	Michel Larocque, Mtl.
1976	Ken Dryden, Mtl.
1975	Bernie Parent, Phi.
1974	Bernie Parent, Phi. (tie)
	Tony Esposito, Chi. (tie)
1973	Ken Dryden, Mtl.
1972	Tony Esposito, Chi.
	Gary Smith, Chi.
1971	Ed Giacomin, NYR
	Gilles Villemure, NYR
1970	Tony Esposito, Chi.
1969	Jacques Plante, St.L.
	Glenn Hall, St.L.
1968	Gump Worsley, Mtl.
	Rogatien Vachon, Mtl.
1967	Glenn Hall, Chi.
	Denis Dejordy, Chi.
1966	Gump Worsley, Mtl.
	Charlie Hodge, Mtl.
1965	Terry Sawchuk, Tor.
	Johnny Bower, Tor.
1964	Charlie Hodge, Mtl.
1963	Glenn Hall, Chi.
1962	Jacques Plante, Mtl.
1961	Johnny Bower, Tor.
1960	Jacques Plante, Mtl.
1959	Jacques Plante, Mtl.
1958	Jacques Plante, Mtl.
1957	Jacques Plante, Mtl.
1956	Jacques Plante, Mtl.
1955	Terry Sawchuk, Det.
1954	Harry Lumley, Tor.
1953	Terry Sawchuk, Det.
1952	Terry Sawchuk, Det.
1951	Al Rollins, Tor.
1950	Bill Durnan, Mtl.
1949	Bill Durnan, Mtl.
1948	Turk Broda, Tor.
1947	Bill Durnan, Mtl.
1946	Bill Durnan, Mtl.
1945	Bill Durnan, Mtl.
1944	Bill Durnan, Mtl.
1943	Johnny Mowers, Det.
1942	Frank Brimsek, Bos.
1941	Turk Broda, Tor.
1940	Dave Kerr, NYR
1939	Frank Brimsek, Bos.
1938	Tiny Thompson, Bos.
1937	Normie Smith, Det.
1936	Tiny Thompson, Bos.
1935	Lorne Chabot, Chi.
1934	Charlie Gardiner, Chi.

1933	Tiny Thompson, Bos.
1932	Charlie Gardiner, Chi.
1931	Roy Worters, NYA
1930	Tiny Thompson, Bos.
1929	George Hainsworth, Mtl.
1928	George Hainsworth, Mtl.
1927	George Hainsworth, Mtl.

CALDER MEMORIAL TROPHY
Best Rookie

1998	Sergei Samsonov, Bos.
1997	Bryan Berard, NYI
1996	Daniel Alfredsson, Ott.
1995	Peter Forsberg, Que.
1994	Martin Brodeur, N.J.
1993	Teemu Selanne, Wpg.
1992	Pavel Bure, Van.
1991	Ed Belfour, Chi.
1990	Sergei Makarov, Cgy.
1989	Brian Leetch, NYR
1988	Joe Nieuwendyk, Cgy.
1987	Luc Robitaille, L.A.
1986	Gary Suter, Cgy.
1985	Mario Lemieux, Pit.
1984	Tom Barrasso, Buf.
1983	Steve Larmer, Chi.
1982	Dale Hawerchuk, Wpg.
1981	Peter Stastny, Que.
1980	Ray Bourque, Bos.
1979	Bobby Smith, Min.
1978	Mike Bossy, NYI
1977	Willi Plett, Atl.
1976	Bryan Trottier, NYI
1975	Eric Vail, Atl.
1974	Denis Potvin, NYI
1973	Steve Vickers, NYR
1972	Ken Dryden, Mtl.
1971	Gilbert Perreault, Buf.
1970	Tony Esposito, Chi.
1969	Danny Grant, Min.
1968	Derek Sanderson, Bos.
1967	Bobby Orr, Bos.
1966	Brit Selby, Tor.
1965	Roger Crozier, Det.
1964	Jacques Laperriere, Mtl.
1963	Kent Douglas, Tor.
1962	Bobby Rousseau, Mtl.
1961	Dave Keon, Tor.
1960	Bill Hay, Chi.
1959	Ralph Backstrom, Mtl.
1958	Frank Mahovlich, Tor.
1957	Larry Regan, Bos.
1956	Glenn Hall, Det.
1955	Ed Litzenberger, Chi.
1954	Camille Henry, NYR
1953	Lorne Worsley, NYR
1952	Bernie Geoffrion, Mtl.
1951	Terry Sawchuk, Det.
1950	Jack Gelineau, Bos.
1949	Pentti Lund, NYR
1948	Jim McFadden, Det.
1947	Howie Meeker, Tor.
1946	Edgar Laprade, NYR
1945	Frank McCool, Tor.
1944	Gus Bodnar, Tor.
1943	Gaye Stewart, Tor.
1942	Grant Warwick, NYR
1941	Johnny Quilty, Mtl.
1940	Kilby MacDonald, NYR
1939	Frank Brimsek, Bos.
1938	Cully Dahlstrom, Chi.
1937	Syl Apps, Tor.
1936	Mike Karakas, Chi.
1935	Dave Schriner, NYA
1934	Russ Blinko, Mtl.M.
1933	Carl Voss, Det.

JAMES NORRIS TROPHY
Best defenseman

1998	Rob Blake, L.A.
1997	Brian Leetch, NYR
1996	Chris Chelios, Chi.
1995	Paul Coffey, Det.
1994	Ray Bourque, Bos.
1993	Chris Chelios, Chi.
1992	Brian Leetch, NYR
1991	Ray Bourque, Bos.
1990	Ray Bourque, Bos.
1989	Chris Chelios, Mtl
1988	Ray Bourque, Bos.
1987	Ray Bourque, Bos.
1986	Paul Coffey, Edm.
1985	Paul Coffey, Edm.
1984	Rod Langway, Wsh.
1983	Rod Langway, Wsh.
1982	Doug Wilson, Chi.
1981	Randy Carlyle, Pit.
1980	Larry Robinson, Mtl.
1979	Denis Potvin, NYI
1978	Denis Potvin, NYI
1977	Larry Robinson, Mtl.
1976	Denis Potvin, NYI
1975	Bobby Orr, Bos.
1974	Bobby Orr, Bos.
1973	Bobby Orr, Bos.
1972	Bobby Orr, Bos.
1971	Bobby Orr, Bos.
1970	Bobby Orr, Bos.
1969	Bobby Orr, Bos.
1968	Bobby Orr, Bos.
1967	Harry Howell, NYR
1966	Jacques Laperriere, Mtl.
1965	Pierre Pilote, Chi.
1964	Pierre Pilote, Chi.
1963	Pierre Pilote, Chi.
1962	Doug Harvey, NYR
1961	Doug Harvey, Mtl.
1960	Doug Harvey, Mtl.
1959	Tom Johnson, Mtl.
1958	Doug Harvey, Mtl.
1957	Doug Harvey, Mtl.
1956	Doug Harvey, Mtl.
1955	Doug Harvey, Mtl.
1954	Red Kelly, Det.

CONN SMYTHE TROPHY
Playoff MVP

1998	Steve Yzerman, Det.
1997	Mike Vernon, Det.
1996	Joe Sakic, Col.
1995	Claude Lemieux, N.J.
1994	Brian Leetch, NYR
1993	Patrick Roy, Mtl.
1992	Mario Lemieux, Pit.
1991	Mario Lemieux, Pit.
1990	Bill Ranford, Edm.
1989	Al MacInnis, Cgy.
1988	Wayne Gretzky, Edm.
1987	Ron Hextall, Phi.
1986	Patrick Roy, Mtl.
1985	Wayne Gretzky, Edm.
1984	Mark Messier, Edm.
1983	Billy Smith, NYI
1982	Mike Bossy, NYI
1981	Butch Goring, NYI
1980	Bryan Trottier, NYI
1979	Bob Gainey, Mtl.
1978	Larry Robinson, Mtl.
1977	Guy Lafleur, Mtl.
1976	Reggie Leach, Phi.
1975	Bernie Parent, Phi.
1974	Bernie Parent, Phi.
1973	Yvan Cournoyer, Mtl.
1972	Bobby Orr, Bos.
1971	Ken Dryden, Mtl.
1970	Bobby Orr, Bos.
1969	Serge Savard, Mtl.
1968	Glenn Hall, St.L.
1967	Dave Keon, Tor.
1966	Roger Crozier, Det.
1965	Jean Beliveau, Mtl

FRANK J. SELKE TROPHY
Best defensive forward

1998	Jere Lehtinen, Dal.
1997	Michael Peca, Buf.
1996	Sergei Fedorov, Det.
1995	Ron Francis, Pit.
1994	Sergei Fedorov, Det.
1993	Doug Gilmour, Tor.
1992	Guy Carbonneau, Mtl.
1991	Dirk Graham, Chi.
1990	Rick Meagher, St.L.
1989	Guy Carbonneau, Mtl.
1988	Guy Carbonneau, Mtl.
1987	Dave Poulin, Phi.
1986	Troy Murray, Chi.
1985	Craig Ramsay, Buf.
1984	Doug Jarvis, Wsh.
1983	Bobby Clarke, Phi.
1982	Steve Kasper, Bos.
1981	Bob Gainey, Mtl.
1980	Bob Gainey, Mtl.
1979	Bob Gainey, Mtl.
1978	Bob Gainey, Mtl.

BILL MASTERTON TROPHY
Perseverance and dedication to hockey

1998	Jamie McLennan, St.L.
1997	Tony Granato, S.J.
1996	Gary Roberts, Cgy.
1995	Pat LaFontaine, Buf.
1994	Cam Neely, Bos.
1993	Mario Lemieux, Pit.
1992	Mark Fitzpatrick, NYI
1991	Dave Taylor, L.A.
1990	Gord Kluzak, Bos.
1989	Tim Kerr, Phi.
1988	Bob Bourne, L.A.
1987	Doug Jarvis, Hfd.
1986	Charlie Simmer, Bos.
1985	Anders Hedberg, NYR
1984	Brad Park, Det.
1983	Lanny McDonald, Cgy.
1982	Glenn Resch, Col.
1981	Blake Dunlop, St.L.
1980	Al MacAdam, Min.
1979	Serge Savard, Mtl.
1978	Butch Goring, L.A.
1977	Ed Westfall, NYI
1976	Rod Gilbert, NYR
1975	Don Luce, Buf.
1974	Henri Richard, Mtl.
1973	Lowell MacDonald, Pit.
1972	Bobby Clarke, Phi.
1971	Jean Ratelle, NYR
1970	Pit Martin, Chi.
1969	Ted Hampson, Oak.
1968	Claude Provost, Mtl.

KING CLANCY MEMORIAL TROPHY
Leadership on and off the ice

1998	Kelly Chase, St.L.
1997	Trevor Linden, Van.
1996	Kris King, Wpg.
1995	Joe Nieuwendyk, Cgy.
1994	Adam Graves, NYR
1993	Dave Poulin, Bos.
1992	Ray Bourque, Bos.
1991	Dave Taylor, L.A.
1990	Kevin Lowe, Edm.
1989	Bryan Trottier, NYI
1988	Lanny McDonald, Cgy.

JACK ADAMS AWARD
Coach of the year

1998	Pat Burns, Bos.
1997	Ted Nolan, Buf.
1996	Scotty Bowman, Det.
1995	Marc Crawford, Que.
1994	Jacques Lemaire, N.J.
1993	Pat Burns, Tor.
1992	Pat Quinn, Van.
1991	Brian Sutter, St.L.
1990	Bob Murdoch, Wpg.
1989	Pat Burns, Mtl.
1988	Jacques Demers, Det.
1987	Jacques Demers, Det.
1986	Glen Sather, Edm.
1985	Mike Keenan, Phi.
1984	Bryan Murray, Wsh.
1983	Orval Tessier, Chi.
1982	Tom Watt, Wpg.
1981	Red Berenson, St.L.
1980	Pat Quinn, Phi.
1979	Al Arbour, NYI
1978	Bobby Kromm, Det.
1977	Scotty Bowman, Mtl.
1976	Don Cherry, Bos.
1975	Bob Pulford, L.A.
1974	Fred Shero, Phi.

WILLIAM M. JENNINGS TROPHY
Goaltender(s) on team allowing fewest goals

1998	Martin Brodeur, N.J.
1997	Martin Brodeur, N.J.
	Mike Dunham
1996	Chris Osgood, Det.
	Mike Vernon
1995	Ed Belfour, Chi.
1994	Dominik Hasek, Buf.
	Grant Fuhr
1993	Ed Belfour, Chi.
1992	Patrick Roy, Mtl.
1991	Ed Belfour, Chi.
1990	Andy Moog, Bos.
	Rejean Lemelin
1989	Patrick Roy, Mtl.
	Brian Hayward
1988	Patrick Roy, Mtl.
	Brian Hayward
1987	Patrick Roy, Mtl.
	Brian Hayward
1986	Bob Froese, Phi.
	Darren Jensen
1985	Tom Barrasso, Buf.
	Bob Sauve
1984	Al Jensen, Wsh.
	Pat Riggin
1983	Roland Melanson, NYI
	Billy Smith
1982	Rick Wamsley, Mtl.
	Denis Herron

LESTER B. PEARSON AWARD
Outstanding player selected by NHLPA

1998	Dominik Hasek, Buf.
1997	Dominik Hasek, Buf.
1996	Mario Lemieux, Pit.
1995	Eric Lindros, Phi.
1994	Sergei Fedorov, Det.
1993	Mario Lemieux, Pit.
1992	Mark Messier, NYR
1991	Brett Hull, St.L.
1990	Mark Messier, Edm.
1989	Steve Yzerman, Det.
1988	Mario Lemieux, Pit.
1987	Wayne Gretzky, Edm.
1986	Mario Lemieux, Pit.
1985	Wayne Gretzky, Edm.
1984	Wayne Gretzky, Edm.
1983	Wayne Gretzky, Edm.
1982	Wayne Gretzky, Edm.
1981	Mike Liut, St.L.
1980	Marcel Dionne, L.A.

PEARSON AWARD continued

1978	Guy Lafleur, Mtl.	1990
1979	Marcel Dionne, L.A.	1989
1978	Guy Lafleur, Mtl.	
1977	Guy Lafleur, Mtl.	
1976	Guy Lafleur, Mtl.	
1975	Bobby Orr, Bos.	1988
1974	Phil Esposito, Bos.	
1973	Bobby Clarke, Phi.	
1972	Jean Ratelle, NYR	1987

LESTER PATRICK TROPHY
Contributions to American hockey

1998	Peter Karmanos
	Neal Broten
	John Mayasich
	Max McNab
1997	Seymour H. Knox III
	Bill Cleary
	Pat LaFontaine
1996	George Gund
	Ken Morrow
	Milt Schmidt
1995	Joe Mullen
	Brian Mullen
	Bob Fleming
1994	Wayne Gretzky
	Robert Ridder
1993	*Frank Boucher
	*Mervyn (Red) Dutton
	Bruce McNall
	Gil Stein
1992	Al Arbour
	Art Berglund
	Lou Lamoriello
1991	Rod Gilbert

	Mike Ilitch
1990	Len Ceglarski
1989	Dan Kelly
	Lou Nanne
	*Lynn Patrick
	Bud Poile
1988	Keith Allen
	Fred Cusick
	Bob Johnson
	*Hobey Baker
1987	Frank Mathers
1986	John MacInnes
	Jack Riley
1985	Jack Butterfield
	Arthur M. Wirtz
1984	John A. Ziegler Jr.
	*Arthur Howie Ross
1983	Bill Torrey
1982	Emile P. Francis
1981	Charles M. Schulz
1980	Bobby Clarke
	Edward M. Snider
	Frederick A. Shero
	1980 U.S. Olympic Hockey Team
1979	Bobby Orr
1978	Phil Esposito
	Tom Fitzgerald
	William T. Tutt
	William W. Wirtz
1977	John P. Bucyk
	Murray A. Armstrong
	John Mariucci
1976	Stanley Mikita
	George A. Leader
	Bruce A. Norris
1975	Donald M. Clark
	William L. Chadwick

	Thomas N. Ivan
1974	Alex Delvecchio
	Murray Murdoch
	*Weston W. Adams, Sr.
	*Charles L. Crovat
1973	Walter L. Bush, Jr.
1972	Clarence S. Campbell
	John A. "Snooks" Kelly
	Ralph "Cooney" Weiland
	*James D. Norris
1971	William M. Jennings
	*John B. Sollenberger
	*Terrance G. Sawchuk
1970	Edward W. Shore
	*James C. V. Hendy
1969	Robert M. Hull
	*Edward J. Jeremiah
1968	Thomas F. Lockhart
	*Walter A. Brown
	*Gen. John R. Kilpatrick
1967	Gordon Howe
	*Charles F. Adams
	*James Norris, Sr.
1966	J.J. "Jack" Adams

* awarded posthumously

MASTERCARD CUTTING EDGE PLAY OF THE YEAR
Best play (as chosen by NHL fans)

1998	Shjon Podein, Phi.
1997	Valeri Kamensky, Col.
1996	Chris Osgood, Det.

BUD ICE PLUS–MINUS AWARD
Best plus–minus statistics

1998	Chris Pronger, St.L.
1997	John LeClair, Phi.

NORELCO FACE-OFF AWARD
Best face-off winning percentage

1998	Eric Lindros, Phi. (player)
1998	Dallas Stars (team award)

Team Award
PRESIDENTS' TROPHY
First place in the regular season

1998	Dallas Stars
1997	Colorado Avalanche
1996	Detroit Red Wings
1995	Detroit Red Wings
1994	New York Rangers
1993	Pittsburgh Penguins
1992	New York Rangers
1991	Chicago Blackhawks
1990	Boston Bruins
1989	Calgary Flames
1988	Calgary Flames
1987	Edmonton Oilers
1986	Edmonton Oilers

NHL All-Star Teams

Voting for the NHL All-Star Team is conducted among the representatives of the Professional Hockey Writers' Association at the end of the regular season. Following is a list of the First and Second All-Star Teams since their inception in 1930-31.

First Team	Position	Second Team	First Team	Position	Second Team	First Team	Position	Second Team
1997-98			**1992-93**			**1987-88**		
Hasek, Dominik, Buf.	G	Brodeur, Martin, N.J.	Belfour, Ed, Chi.	G	Barrasso, Tom, Pit.	Fuhr, Grant, Edm.	G	Roy, Patrick, Mtl.
Blake, Rob, L.A.	D	Pronger, Chris, St.L.	Chelios, Chris, Chi.	D	Murphy, Larry, Pit.	Bourque, Ray, Bos.	D	Suter, Gary, Cgy.
Lidstrom, Niklas, Det.	D	Niedermayer, Scott, N.J.	Bourque, Ray, Bos.	D	Iafrate, Al, Wsh.	Stevens, Scott, Wsh.	D	McCrimmon, Brad, Cgy.
Forsberg, Peter, Col.	C	Gretzky, Wayne, NYR	Lemieux, Mario, Pit.	C	LaFontaine, Pat, Buf.	Lemieux, Mario, Pit.	C	Gretzky, Wayne, Edm.
Jagr, Jaromir, Pit.	RW	Selanne, Teemu, Ana.	Selanne, Teemu, Wpg.	RW	Mogilny, Alexander, Buf.	Loob, Hakan, Cgy.	RW	Neely, Cam, Bos.
LeClair, John, Phi.	LW	Tkachuk, Keith, Phx.	Robitaille, Luc, L.A.	LW	Stevens, Kevin, Pit.	Robitaille, Luc, L.A.	LW	Goulet, Michel, Que.
1996-97			**1991-92**			**1986-87**		
Hasek, Dominik, Buf.	G	Brodeur, Martin, N.J.	Roy, Patrick, Mtl.	G	McLean, Kirk, Van.	Hextall, Ron, Phi.	G	Liut, Mike, Hfd.
Leetch, Brian, NYR	D	Chelios, Chris, Chi.	Leetch, Brian, NYR	D	Housley, Phil, Wpg.	Bourque, Ray, Bos.	D	Murphy, Larry, Wsh.
Ozolinsh, Sandis, Col.	D	Stevens, Scott, N.J.	Bourque, Ray, Bos.	D	Stevens, Scott, N.J.	Howe, Mark, Phi.	D	MacInnis, Al, Cgy.
Lemieux, Mario, Pit.	C	Gretzky, Wayne, NYR	Messier, Mark, NYR	C	Lemieux, Mario, Pit.	Gretzky, Wayne, Edm.	C	Lemieux, Mario, Pit.
Selanne, Teemu, Ana.	RW	Jagr, Jaromir, Pit.	Hull, Brett, St. L.	RW	Recchi, Mark, Pit., Phi.	Kurri, Jari, Edm.	RW	Kerr, Tim, Phi.
Kariya, Paul, Ana.	LW	LeClair, John, Phi.	Stevens, Kevin, Pit.	LW	Robitaille, Luc, L.A.	Goulet, Michel, Que.	LW	Robitaille, Luc, L.A.
1995-96			**1990-91**			**1985-86**		
Carey, Jim, Wsh.	G	Osgood, Chris, Det.	Belfour, Ed, Chi.	G	Roy, Patrick, Mtl.	Vanbiesbrouck, J., NYR	G	Froese, Bob, Phi.
Chelios, Chris, Chi.	D	Konstantinov, V., Det.	Bourque, Ray, Bos.	D	Chelios, Chris, Chi.	Coffey, Paul, Edm.	D	Robinson, Larry, Mtl.
Bourque, Ray, Bos.	D	Leetch, Brian, NYR	MacInnis, Al, Cgy.	D	Leetch, Brian, NYR	Howe, Mark, Phi.	D	Bourque, Ray, Bos.
Lemieux, Mario, Pit.	C	Lindros, Eric, Phi.	Gretzky, Wayne, L.A.	C	Oates, Adam, St. L.	Gretzky, Wayne, Edm.	C	Lemieux, Mario, Pit.
Jagr, Jaromir, Pit.	RW	Mogilny, Alexander, Van.	Hull, Brett, St. L.	RW	Neely, Cam, Bos.	Bossy, Mike, NYI	RW	Kurri, Jari, Edm.
Kariya, Paul, Ana.	LW	LeClair, John, Phi.	Robitaille, Luc, L.A.	LW	Stevens, Kevin, Pit.	Goulet, Michel, Que.	LW	Naslund, Mats, Mtl.
1994-95			**1989-90**			**1984-85**		
Hasek, Dominik, Buf.	G	Belfour, Ed, Chi.	Roy, Patrick, Mtl.	G	Puppa, Daren, Buf.	Lindbergh, Pelle, Phi.	G	Barrasso, Tom, Buf.
Coffey, Paul, Det.	D	Bourque, Ray, Bos.	Bourque, Ray, Bos.	D	Coffey, Paul, Pit.	Coffey, Paul, Edm.	D	Langway, Rod, Wsh.
Chelios, Chris, Chi.	D	Murphy, Larry, Pit.	MacInnis, Al, Cgy.	D	Wilson, Doug, Chi.	Bourque, Ray, Bos.	D	Wilson, Doug, Chi.
Lindros, Eric, Phi.	C	Zhamnov, Alexei, Wpg.	Messier, Mark, Edm.	C	Gretzky, Wayne, L.A.	Gretzky, Wayne, Edm.	C	Hawerchuk, Dale, Wpg.
Jagr, Jaromir, Pit.	RW	Fleury, Theoren, Cgy.	Hull, Brett, St. L.	RW	Neely, Cam, Bos.	Kurri, Jari, Edm.	RW	Bossy, Mike, NYI
LeClair, John, Mtl., Phi.	LW	Tkachuk, Keith, Wpg.	Robitaille, Luc, L.A.	LW	Bellows, Brian, Min.	Ogrodnick, John, Det.	LW	Tonelli, John, NYI
1993-94			**1988-89**			**1983-84**		
Hasek, Dominik, Buf.	G	Vanbiesbrouck, John, Fla.	Roy, Patrick, Mtl.	G	Vernon, Mike, Cgy.	Barrasso, Tom, Buf.	G	Riggin, Pat, Wsh.
Bourque, Ray, Bos.	D	MacInnis, Al, Cgy.	Chelios, Chris, Mtl.	D	MacInnis, Al, Cgy.	Langway, Rod, Wsh.	D	Coffey, Paul, Edm.
Stevens, Scott, N.J.	D	Leetch, Brian, NYR	Coffey, Paul, Pit.	D	Bourque, Ray, Bos.	Bourque, Ray, Bos.	D	Potvin, Denis, NYI
Fedorov, Sergei, Det.	C	Gretzky, Wayne, L.A.	Lemieux, Mario, Pit.	C	Gretzky, Wayne, L.A.	Gretzky, Wayne, Edm.	C	Trottier, Bryan, NYI
Bure, Pavel, Van.	RW	Neely, Cam, Bos.	Mullen, Joe, Cgy.	RW	Kurri, Jari, Edm.	Bossy, Mike, NYI	RW	Kurri, Jari, Edm.
Shanahan, Brendan, St. L.	LW	Graves, Adam, NYR	Robitaille, Luc, L.A.	LW	Gallant, Gerard, Det.	Goulet, Michel, Que.	LW	Messier, Mark, Edm.

First Team	Position	Second Team
1982-83		
Peeters, Pete, Bos.	G	Melanson, Roland, NYI
Howe, Mark, Phi.	D	Bourque, Ray, Bos.
Langway, Rod, Wsh.	D	Coffey, Paul, Edm.
Gretzky, Wayne, Edm.	C	Savard, Denis, Chi.
Bossy, Mike, NYI	RW	McDonald, Lanny, Cgy.
Messier, Mark, Edm.	LW	Goulet, Michel, Que.
1981-82		
Smith, Bill, NYI	G	Fuhr, Grant, Edm.
Wilson, Doug, Chi.	D	Coffey, Paul, Edm.
Bourque, Ray, Bos.	D	Engblom, Brian, Mtl.
Gretzky, Wayne, Edm.	C	Trottier, Bryan, NYI
Bossy, Mike, NYI	RW	Middleton, Rick, Bos.
Messier, Mark, Edm.	LW	Tonelli, John, NYI
1980-81		
Liut, Mike, St.L.	G	Lessard, Mario, L.A.
Potvin, Denis, NYI	D	Robinson, Larry, Mtl.
Carlyle, Randy, Pit.	D	Bourque, Ray, Bos.
Gretzky, Wayne, Edm.	C	Dionne, Marcel, L.A.
Bossy, Mike, NYI	RW	Taylor, Dave, L.A.
Simmer, Charlie, L.A.	LW	Barber, Bill, Phi.
1979-80		
Esposito, Tony, Chi.	G	Edwards, Don, Buf.
Robinson, Larry, Mtl.	D	Salming, Borje, Tor.
Bourque, Ray, Bos.	D	Schoenfeld, Jim, Buf.
Dionne, Marcel, L.A.	C	Gretzky, Wayne, Edm.
Lafleur, Guy, Mtl.	RW	Gare, Danny, Buf.
Simmer, Charlie, L.A.	LW	Shutt, Steve, Mtl.
1978-79		
Dryden, Ken, Mtl.	G	Resch, Glenn, NYI
Potvin, Denis, NYI	D	Salming, Borje, Tor.
Robinson, Larry, Mtl.	D	Savard, Serge, Mtl.
Trottier, Bryan, NYI	C	Dionne, Marcel, L.A.
Lafleur, Guy, Mtl.	RW	Bossy, Mike, NYI
Gillies, Clark, NYI	LW	Barber, Bill, Phi.
1977-78		
Dryden, Ken, Mtl.	G	Edwards, Don, Buf.
Potvin, Denis, NYI	D	Robinson, Larry, Mtl.
Park, Brad, Bos.	D	Salming, Borje, Tor.
Trottier, Bryan, NYI	C	Sittler, Darryl, Tor.
Lafleur, Guy, Mtl.	RW	Bossy, Mike, NYI
Gillies, Clark, NYI	LW	Shutt, Steve, Mtl.
1976-77		
Dryden, Ken, Mtl.	G	Vachon, Rogatien, L.A.
Robinson, Larry, Mtl.	D	Potvin, Denis, NYI
Salming, Borje, Tor.	D	Lapointe, Guy, Mtl.
Dionne, Marcel, L.A.	C	Perreault, Gilbert, Buf.
Lafleur, Guy, Mtl.	RW	McDonald, Lanny, Tor.
Shutt, Steve, Mtl.	LW	Martin, Richard, Buf.
1975-76		
Dryden, Ken, Mtl.	G	Resch, Glenn, NYI
Potvin, Denis, NYI	D	Salming, Borje, Tor.
Park, Brad, Bos.	D	Lapointe, Guy, Mtl.
Clarke, Bobby, Phi.	C	Perreault, Gilbert, Buf.
Lafleur, Guy, Mtl.	RW	Leach, Reggie, Phi.
Barber, Bill, Phi.	LW	Martin, Richard, Buf.
1974-75		
Parent, Bernie, Phi.	G	Vachon, Rogie, L.A.
Orr, Bobby, Bos.	D	Lapointe, Guy, Mtl.
Potvin, Denis, NYI	D	Salming, Borje, Tor.
Clarke, Bobby, Phi.	C	Esposito, Phil, Bos.
Lafleur, Guy, Mtl.	RW	Robert, Rene, Buf.
Martin, Richard, Buf.	LW	Vickers, Steve, NYR
1973-74		
Parent, Bernie, Phi.	G	Esposito, Tony, Chi.
Orr, Bobby, Bos.	D	White, Bill, Chi.
Park, Brad, NYR	D	Ashbee, Barry, Phi.
Esposito, Phil, Bos.	C	Clarke, Bobby, Phi.
Hodge, Ken, Bos.	RW	Redmond, Mickey, Det.
Martin, Richard, Buf.	LW	Cashman, Wayne, Bos.
1972-73		
Dryden, Ken, Mtl.	G	Esposito, Tony, Chi.
Orr, Bobby, Bos.	D	Park, Brad, NYR
Lapointe, Guy, Mtl.	D	White, Bill, Chi.
Esposito, Phil, Bos.	C	Clarke, Bobby, Phi.
Redmond, Mickey, Det.	RW	Cournoyer, Yvan, Mtl.
Mahovlich, Frank, Mtl.	LW	Hull, Dennis, Chi.

First Team	Position	Second Team
1971-72		
Esposito, Tony, Chi.	G	Dryden, Ken, Mtl.
Orr, Bobby, Bos.	D	White, Bill, Chi.
Park, Brad, NYR	D	Stapleton, Pat, Chi.
Esposito, Phil, Bos.	C	Ratelle, Jean, NYR
Gilbert, Rod, NYR	RW	Cournoyer, Yvan, Mtl.
Hull, Bobby, Chi.	LW	Hadfield, Vic, NYR
1970-71		
Giacomin, Ed, NYR	G	Plante, Jacques, Tor.
Orr, Bobby, Bos.	D	Park, Brad, NYR
Tremblay, J.C., Mtl.	D	Stapleton, Pat, Chi.
Esposito, Phil, Bos.	C	Keon, Dave, Tor.
Hodge, Ken, Bos.	RW	Cournoyer, Yvan, Mtl.
Bucyk, John, Bos.	LW	Hull, Bobby, Chi.
1969-70		
Esposito, Tony, Chi.	G	Giacomin, Ed, NYR
Orr, Bobby, Bos.	D	Brewer, Carl, Det.
Park, Brad, NYR	D	Laperriere, Jacques, Mtl.
Esposito, Phil, Bos.	C	Mikita, Stan, Chi.
Howe, Gordie, Det.	RW	McKenzie, John, Bos.
Hull, Bobby, Chi.	LW	Mahovlich, Frank, Det.
1968-69		
Hall, Glenn, St.L.	G	Giacomin, Ed, NYR
Orr, Bobby, Bos.	D	Green, Ted, Bos.
Horton, Tim, Tor.	D	Harris, Ted, Mtl.
Esposito, Phil, Bos.	C	Beliveau, Jean, Mtl.
Howe, Gordie, Det.	RW	Cournoyer, Yvan, Mtl.
Hull, Bobby, Chi.	LW	Mahovlich, Frank, Det.
1967-68		
Worsley, Lorne, Mtl.	G	Giacomin, Ed, NYR
Orr, Bobby, Bos.	D	Tremblay, J.C., Mtl.
Horton, Tim, Tor.	D	Neilson, Jim, NYR
Mikita, Stan, Chi.	C	Esposito, Phil, Bos.
Howe, Gordie, Det.	RW	Gilbert, Rod, NYR
Hull, Bobby, Chi.	LW	Bucyk, John, Bos.
1966-67		
Giacomin, Ed, NYR	G	Hall, Glenn, Chi.
Pilote, Pierre, Chi.	D	Horton, Tim, Tor.
Howell, Harry, NYR	D	Orr, Bobby, Bos.
Mikita, Stan, Chi.	C	Ullman, Norm, Det.
Wharram, Ken, Chi.	RW	Howe, Gordie, Det.
Hull, Bobby, Chi.	LW	Marshall, Don, NYR
1965-66		
Hall, Glenn, Chi.	G	Worsley, Lorne, Mtl.
Laperriere, Jacques, Mtl.	D	Stanley, Allan, Tor.
Pilote, Pierre, Chi.	D	Stapleton, Pat, Chi.
Mikita, Stan, Chi.	C	Beliveau, Jean, Mtl.
Howe, Gordie, Det.	RW	Rousseau, Bobby, Mtl.
Hull, Bobby, Chi.	LW	Mahovlich, Frank, Tor.
1964-65		
Crozier, Roger, Det.	G	Hodge, Charlie, Mtl.
Pilote, Pierre, Chi.	D	Gadsby, Bill, Det.
Laperriere, Jacques, Mtl.	D	Brewer, Carl, Tor.
Ullman, Norm, Det.	C	Mikita, Stan, Chi.
Provost, Claude, Mtl.	RW	Howe, Gordie, Det.
Hull, Bobby, Chi.	LW	Mahovlich, Frank, Tor.
1963-64		
Hall, Glenn, Chi.	G	Hodge, Charlie, Mtl.
Pilote, Pierre, Chi.	D	Vasko, Elmer, Chi.
Horton, Tim, Tor.	D	Laperriere, Jacques, Mtl.
Mikita, Stan, Chi.	C	Beliveau, Jean, Mtl.
Wharram, Ken, Chi	RW	Howe, Gordie, Det.
Hull, Bobby, Chi.	LW	Mahovlich, Frank, Tor.
1962-63		
Hall, Glenn, Chi.	G	Sawchuk, Terry, Det.
Pilote, Pierre, Chi.	D	Horton, Tim, Tor.
Brewer, Carl, Tor.	D	Vasko, Elmer, Chi.
Mikita, Stan, Chi.	C	Richard, Henri, Mtl.
Howe, Gordie, Det.	RW	Bathgate, Andy, NYR
Mahovlich, Frank, Tor.	LW	Hull, Bobby, Chi.
1961-62		
Plante, Jacques, Mtl.	G	Hall, Glenn, Chi.
Harvey, Doug, NYR	D	Brewer, Carl, Tor.
Talbot, Jean-Guy, Mtl.	D	Pilote, Pierre, Chi.
Mikita, Stan, Chi.	C	Keon, Dave, Tor.
Bathgate, Andy, NYR	RW	Howe, Gordie, Det.
Hull, Bobby, Chi.	LW	Mahovlich, Frank, Tor.

First Team	Position	Second Team
1960-61		
Bower, Johnny, Tor.	G	Hall, Glenn, Chi.
Harvey, Doug, Mtl.	D	Stanley, Allan, Tor.
Pronovost, Marcel, Det.	D	Pilote, Pierre, Chi.
Beliveau, Jean, Mtl.	C	Richard, Henri, Mtl.
Geoffrion, Bernie, Mtl.	RW	Howe, Gordie, Det.
Mahovlich, Frank, Tor.	LW	Moore, Dickie, Mtl.
1959-60		
Hall, Glenn, Chi.	G	Plante, Jacques, Mtl.
Harvey, Doug, Mtl.	D	Stanley, Allan, Tor.
Pronovost, Marcel, Det.	D	Pilote, Pierre, Chi.
Beliveau, Jean, Mtl.	C	Horvath, Bronco, Bos.
Howe, Gordie, Det.	RW	Geoffrion, Bernie, Mtl.
Hull, Bobby, Chi.	LW	Prentice, Dean, NYR
1958-59		
Plante, Jacques, Mtl.	G	Sawchuk, Terry, Det.
Johnson, Tom, Mtl.	D	Pronovost, Marcel, Det.
Gadsby, Bill, NYR	D	Harvey, Doug, Mtl.
Beliveau, Jean, Mtl.	C	Richard, Henri, Mtl.
Bathgate, Andy, NYR	RW	Howe, Gordie, Det.
Moore, Dickie, Mtl.	LW	Delvecchio, Alex, Det.
1957-58		
Hall, Glenn, Chi.	G	Plante, Jacques, Mtl.
Harvey, Doug, Mtl.	D	Flaman, Fern, Bos.
Gadsby, Bill, NYR	D	Pronovost, Marcel, Det.
Richard, Henri, Mtl.	C	Beliveau, Jean, Mtl.
Howe, Gordie, Det.	RW	Bathgate, Andy, NYR
Moore, Dickie, Mtl.	LW	Henry, Camille, NYR
1956-57		
Hall, Glenn, Det.	G	Plante, Jacques, Mtl.
Harvey, Doug, Mtl.	D	Flaman, Fern, Bos.
Kelly, Red, Det.	D	Gadsby, Bill, NYR
Beliveau, Jean, Mtl.	C	Litzenberger, Ed, Chi.
Howe, Gordie, Det.	RW	Richard, Maurice, Mtl.
Lindsay, Ted, Det.	LW	Chevrefils, Real, Bos.
1955-56		
Plante, Jacques, Mtl.	G	Hall, Glenn, Det.
Harvey, Doug, Mtl.	D	Kelly, Red, Det.
Gadsby, Bill, NYR	D	Johnson, Tom, Mtl.
Beliveau, Jean, Mtl.	C	Sloan, Tod, Tor.
Richard, Maurice, Mtl.	RW	Howe, Gordie, Det.
Lindsay, Ted, Det.	LW	Olmstead, Bert, Mtl.
1954-55		
Lumley, Harry, Tor.	G	Sawchuk, Terry, Det.
Harvey, Doug, Mtl.	D	Goldham, Bob, Det.
Kelly, Red, Det.	D	Flaman, Fern, Bos.
Beliveau, Jean, Mtl.	C	Mosdell, Ken, Mtl.
Richard, Maurice, Mtl.	RW	Geoffrion, Bernie, Mtl.
Smith, Sid, Tor.	LW	Lewicki, Danny, NYR
1953-54		
Lumley, Harry, Tor.	G	Sawchuk, Terry, Det.
Kelly, Red, Det.	D	Gadsby, Bill, Chi.
Harvey, Doug, Mtl.	D	Horton, Tim, Tor.
Mosdell, Ken, Mtl.	C	Kennedy, Ted, Tor.
Howe, Gordie, Det.	RW	Richard, Maurice, Mtl.
Lindsay, Ted, Det.	LW	Sandford, Ed, Bos.
1952-53		
Sawchuk, Terry, Det.	G	McNeil, Gerry, Mtl.
Kelly, Red, Det.	D	Quackenbush, Bill, Bos.
Harvey, Doug, Mtl.	D	Gadsby, Bill, Chi.
Mackell, Fleming, Bos.	C	Delvecchio, Alex, Det.
Howe, Gordie, Det.	RW	Richard, Maurice, Mtl.
Lindsay, Ted, Det.	LW	Olmstead, Bert, Mtl.
1951-52		
Sawchuk, Terry, Det.	G	Henry, Jim, Bos.
Kelly, Red, Det.	D	Buller, Hy, NYR
Harvey, Doug, Mtl.	D	Thomson, Jim, Tor.
Lach, Elmer, Mtl.	C	Schmidt, Milt, Bos.
Howe, Gordie, Det.	RW	Richard, Maurice, Mtl.
Lindsay, Ted, Det.	LW	Smith, Sid, Tor.
1950-51		
Sawchuk, Terry, Det.	G	Rayner, Chuck, NYR
Kelly, Red, Det.	D	Thomson, Jim, Tor.
Quackenbush, Bill, Bos.	D	Reise, Leo, Det.
Schmidt, Milt, Bos.	C (tied)	Abel, Sid, Det.
		Kennedy, Ted, Tor.
Howe, Gordie, Det.	RW	Richard, Maurice, Mtl.
Lindsay, Ted, Det.	LW	Smith, Sid, Tor.

1949-50

First team	Position	Second Team
Durnan, Bill, Mtl.	G	Rayner, Chuck, NYR
Mortson, Gus, Tor.	D	Reise, Leo, Det.
Reardon, Kenny, Mtl.	D	Kelly, Red, Det.
Abel, Sid, Det.	C	Kennedy, Ted, Tor.
Richard, Maurice, Mtl.	RW	Howe, Gordie, Det.
Lindsay, Ted, Det.	LW	Leswick, Tony, NYR

1948-49

First team	Position	Second Team
Durnan, Bill, Mtl.	G	Rayner, Chuck, NYR
Quackenbush, Bill, Det.	D	Harmon, Glen, Mtl.
Stewart, Jack, Det.	D	Reardon, Kenny, Mtl.
Abel, Sid, Det.	C	Bentley, Doug, Chi.
Richard, Maurice, Mtl.	RW	Howe, Gordie, Det.
Conacher, Roy, Chi.	LW	Lindsay, Ted, Det.

1947-48

First team	Position	Second Team
Broda, Turk, Tor.	G	Brimsek, Frank, Bos.
Quackenbush, Bill, Det.	D	Reardon, Kenny, Mtl.
Stewart, Jack, Det.	D	Colville, Neil, NYR
Lach, Elmer, Mtl.	C	O'Connor, Buddy, NYR
Richard, Maurice, Mtl.	RW	Poile, Bud, Chi.
Lindsay, Ted, Det.	LW	Stewart, Gaye, Chi.

1946-47

First team	Position	Second Team
Durnan, Bill, Mtl.	G	Brimsek, Frank, Bos.
Reardon, Kenny, Mtl.	D	Stewart, Jack, Det.
Bouchard, Emile, Mtl.	D	Quackenbush, Bill, Det.
Schmidt, Milt, Bos.	C	Bentley, Max, Chi.
Richard, Maurice, Mtl.	RW	Bauer, Bobby, Bos.
Bentley, Doug, Chi.	LW	Dumart, Woody, Bos.

1945-46

First team	Position	Second Team
Durnan, Bill, Mtl.	G	Brimsek, Frank, Bos.
Crawford, Jack, Bos.	D	Reardon, Kenny, Mtl.
Bouchard, Emile, Mtl.	D	Stewart, Jack, Det.
Bentley, Max, Chi.	C	Lach, Elmer, Mtl.
Richard, Maurice, Mtl.	RW	Mosienko, Bill, Chi.
Stewart, Gaye, Tor.	LW	Blake, Toe, Mtl.
Irvin, Dick, Mtl.	Coach	Gottselig, John, Chi.

1944-45

First team	Position	Second Team
Durnan, Bill, Mtl.	G	Karakas, Mike, Chi.
Bouchard, Emile, Mtl.	D	Harmon, Glen, Mtl.
Hollett, Bill, Det.	D	Pratt, Babe, Tor.
Lach, Elmer, Mtl.	C	Cowley, Bill, Bos.
Richard, Maurice, Mtl.	RW	Mosienko, Bill, Chi.
Blake, Toe, Mtl.	LW	Howe, Syd, Det.
Irvin, Dick, Mtl.	Coach	Adams, Jack, Det.

1943-44

First team	Position	Second Team
Durnan, Bill, Mtl.	G	Bibeault, Paul, Tor.
Seibert, Earl, Chi.	D	Bouchard, Emile, Mtl.
Pratt, Babe, Tor.	D	Clapper, Dit, Bos.
Cowley, Bill, Bos.	C	Lach, Elmer, Mtl.
Carr, Lorne, Tor.	RW	Richard, Maurice, Mtl.
Bentley, Doug, Chi.	LW	Cain, Herb, Bos.
Irvin, Dick, Mtl.	Coach	Day, "Hap, Tor.

1942-43

First team	Position	Second Team
Mowers, Johnny, Det.	G	Brimsek, Frank, Bos.
Seibert, Earl, Chi.	D	Crawford, Jack, Bos.
Stewart, Jack, Det.	D	Hollett, Bill, Bos.
Cowley, Bill, Bos.	C	Apps, Syl, Tor.
Carr, Lorne, Tor.	RW	Hextall, Bryan, NYR
Bentley, Doug, Chi.	LW	Patrick, Lynn, NYR
Adams, Jack, Det.	Coach	Ross, Art, Bos.

1941-42

First team	Position	Second Team
Brimsek, Frank, Bos.	G	Broda, Turk, Tor.
Seibert, Earl, Chi.	D	Egan, Pat, Bro.
Anderson, Tom, Bro.	D	McDonald, Bucko, Tor.
Apps, Syl, Tor.	C	Watson, Phil, NYR
Hextall, Bryan, NYR	RW	Drillon, Gord, Tor.
Patrick, Lynn, NYR	LW	Abel, Sid, Det.
Boucher, Frank, NYR	Coach	Thompson, Paul, Chi.

1940-41

First team	Position	Second Team
Broda, Turk, Tor.	G	Brimsek, Frank, Bos.
Clapper, Dit, Bos.	D	Seibert, Earl, Chi.
Stanowski, Wally, Tor.	D	Heller, Ott, NYR
Cowley, Bill, Bos.	C	Apps, Syl, Tor.
Hextall, Bryan, NYR	RW	Bauer, Bobby, Bos.
Schriner, Dave, Tor.	LW	Dumart, Woody, Bos.
Weiland, Cooney, Bos.	Coach	Irvin, Dick, Mtl.

1939-40

First team	Position	Second Team
Kerr, Dave, NYR	G	Brimsek, Frank, Bos.
Clapper, Dit, Bos.	D	Coulter, Art, NYR
Goodfellow, Ebbie, Det.	D	Seibert, Earl, Chi.
Schmidt, Milt, Bos.	C	Colville, Neil, NYR
Hextall, Bryan, NYR	RW	Bauer, Bobby, Bos.
Blake, Toe, Mtl.	LW	Dumart, Woody, Bos.
Thompson, Paul, Chi.	Coach	Boucher, Frank, NYR

1938-39

First team	Position	Second Team
Brimsek, Frank, Bos.	G	Robertson, Earl, NYA
Shore, Eddie, Bos.	D	Seibert, Earl, Chi.
Clapper, Dit, Bos.	D	Coulter, Art, NYR
Apps, Syl, Tor.	C	Colville, Neil, NYR
Drillon, Gord, Tor.	RW	Bauer, Bobby, Bos.
Blake, Toe, Mtl.	LW	Gottselig, Johnny, Chi.
Ross, Art, Bos.	Coach	Dutton, Red, NYA

1937-38

First team	Position	Second Team
Thompson, Tiny, Bos.	G	Kerr, Dave, NYR
Shore, Eddie, Bos.	D	Coulter, Art, NYR
Siebert, Babe, Mtl.	D	Seibert, Earl, Chi.
Cowley, Bill, Bos.	C	Apps, Syl, Tor.
Dillon, Cecil, NYR	RW	Dillon, Cecil, NYR
Drillon, Gord, Tor.	(tied)	Drillon, Gord, Tor.
Thompson, Paul, Chi.	LW	Blake, Toe, Mtl.
Patrick, Lester, NYR	Coach	Ross, Art, Bos.

1936-37

First team	Position	Second Team
Smith, Norm, Det.	G	Cude, Wilf, Mtl.
Siebert, Babe, Mtl.	D	Seibert, Earl, Chi.
Goodfellow, Ebbie, Det.	D	Conacher, Lionel, Mtl. M.
Barry, Marty, Det.	C	Chapman, Art, NYA
Aurie, Larry, Det.	RW	Dillon, Cecil, NYR
Jackson, Harvey, Tor.	LW	Schriner, Dave, NYA
Adams, Jack, Det.	Coach	Hart, Cecil, Mtl.

1935-36

First team	Position	Second Team
Thompson, Tiny, Bos.	G	Cude, Wilf, Mtl.
Shore, Eddie, Bos.	D	Seibert, Earl, Chi.
Siebert, Babe, Bos.	D	Goodfellow, Ebbie, Det.
Smith, Hooley, Mtl. M.	C	Thoms, Bill, Tor.
Conacher, Charlie, Tor.	RW	Dillon, Cecil, NYR
Schriner, Dave, NYA	LW	Thompson, Paul, Chi.
Patrick, Lester, NYR	Coach	Gorman, T.P., Mtl. M.

1934-35

First team	Position	Second Team
Chabot, Lorne, Chi.	G	Thompson, Tiny, Bos.
Shore, Eddie, Bos.	D	Wentworth, Cy, Mtl. M.
Seibert, Earl, NYR	D	Coulter, Art, Chi.
Boucher, Frank, NYR	C	Weiland, Cooney, Det.
Conacher, Charlie, Tor.	RW	Clapper, Dit, Bos.
Jackson, Harvey, Tor.	LW	Joliat, Aurel, Mtl.
Patrick, Lester, NYR	Coach	Irvin, Dick, Tor.

1933-34

First team	Position	Second Team
Gardiner, Charlie, Chi.	G	Worters, Roy, NYA
Clancy, King, Tor.	D	Shore, Eddie, Bos.
Conacher, Lionel, Chi.	D	Johnson, Ching, NYR
Boucher, Frank, NYR	C	Primeau, Joe, Tor.
Conacher, Charlie, Tor.	RW	Cook, Bill, NYR
Jackson, Harvey, Tor.	LW	Joliat, Aurel, Mtl.
Patrick, Lester, NYR	Coach	Irvin, Dick, Tor.

1932-33

First team	Position	Second Team
Roach, John Ross, Det.	G	Gardiner, Charlie, Chi.
Shore, Eddie, Bos.	D	Clancy, King, Tor.
Johnson, Ching, NYR	D	Conacher, Lionel, Mtl. M.
Boucher, Frank, NYR	C	Morenz, Howie, Mtl.
Cook, Bill, NYR	RW	Conacher, Charlie, Tor.
Northcott, Baldy, Mtl M.	LW	Jackson, Harvey, Tor.
Patrick, Lester, NYR	Coach	Irvin, Dick, Tor.

1931-32

First team	Position	Second Team
Gardiner, Charlie, Chi.	G	Worters, Roy, NYA
Shore, Eddie, Bos.	D	Mantha, Sylvio, Mtl.
Johnson, Ching, NYR	D	Clancy, King, Tor.
Morenz, Howie, Mtl.	C	Smith, Hooley, Mtl. M.
Cook, Bill, NYR	RW	Conacher, Charlie, Tor.
Jackson, Harvey, Tor.	LW	Joliat, Aurel, Mtl.
Patrick, Lester, NYR	Coach	Irvin, Dick, Tor.

1930-31

First team	Position	Second Team
Gardiner, Charlie, Chi.	G	Thompson, Tiny, Bos.
Shore, Eddie, Bos.	D	Mantha, Sylvio, Mtl.
Clancy, King, Tor.	D	Johnson, Ching, NYR
Morenz, Howie, Mtl.	C	Boucher, Frank, NYR
Cook, Bill, NYR	RW	Clapper, Dit, Bos.
Joliat, Aurel, Mtl.	LW	Cook, Bun, NYR
Patrick, Lester, NYR	Coach	Irvin, Dick, Chi.

TERRY SAWCHUK:
A GREAT
– AND GREATLY TROUBLED –
GOALTENDER

Brian Kendall

MOST HOCKEY HISTORIANS agree that the game has never seen a finer goaltender than Terrance Gordon Sawchuk, better remembered by teammates as "Uke" or Ukie," nicknames recalling his Ukrainian heritage. During Sawchuk's first five NHL seasons, his goals-against average never climbed above 1.99, an astonishing achievement. There were four Stanley Cup championships along the way—three with the powerhouse Detroit Red Wings of Gordie Howe and Ted Lindsay and Red Kelly, and a final, heartbreakingly heroic stand with the Toronto Maple Leafs during Canada's Centennial spring of 1967. He won the Calder Trophy in 1950–51 as the league's top rookie and won the Vezina Trophy on four occasions. He was elected to seven postseason all-star teams and in 1964 he surpassed George Hainsworth to become the all-time shutout leader.

Like so many of the greats, Sawchuk brought something new to the game. He was the first to adopt the crouch, bending so deeply that his chin almost touched his padded knees. He found that he was quicker from this position, especially when he had to kick out a leg to stop a shot, and from down low he was able to catch sight of the puck through the legs of opponents attempting to screen him. The famous "Sawchuk Crouch" was copied by a generation of young goalies.

An acrobat on ice, Sawchuk's every incredibly rapid movement was an explosion of action and a release of pent-up tension. Before he finally donned the Frankenstein face mask in 1962, it almost hurt to watch his face during a game. Every save appeared to cost him so much.

But all this is only part of the Sawchuk legend. "He was the greatest goalie I ever saw, and the most troubled athlete I ever knew," recalled Joe Falls, sports editor of the *Detroit Free Press* at the time of Sawchuk's tragic death in 1970. "The first time I met Terry Sawchuk he was raging with anger and shouting obscenities and throwing his skates at a reporter. This was in 1953. In all the years to follow, he never really changed."

Born in the working-class Winnipeg suburb of East Kildonan on December 28, 1929, Sawchuk became a netminder at the age of 10 when he inherited the goalie pads of his older brother Mike, who died suddenly of a heart attack at age 17. The passing of the brother he adored was but the first in a procession of family tragedies, injuries and accidents that would plague Sawchuk for the rest of his life.

By the time he was fifteen, Sawchuk starred for the Junior A Winnipeg Rangers. Signed after that initial campaign by Detroit Red Wing scout Bob Kinnear, the Wings shipped Sawchuk east the next season to the Ontario town of Galt, where they sponsored a squad in the Ontario Junior Hockey League, considered the top junior loop in Canada. The next fall Sawchuk, by now 17, proved the sensation of the Wings' training camp. "I've never seen a young goalie with more ability," raved Detroit coach Tommy Ivan. After just four more games of seasoning in the junior ranks, Detroit turned Sawchuk professional with Omaha of the United States Hockey League. There Sawchuk quickly made his mark, capturing the rookie of the year award for

1947–48. He repeated as top rookie the following year in the American Hockey League, after earning promotion to Indianapolis, the Wings' top farm club. The next season his superlative goaltending led Indianapolis to the AHL's championship, the Calder Cup.

Detroit general manager Jack Adams, whose squad had just won the 1950 Stanley Cup, felt so confident of Sawchuk's abilities that during the following summer he traded Harry Lumley, the Wings' incumbent netminder and himself a future Hall of Famer, to Chicago to make room for Sawchuk.

Thus began a five-year reign of excellence that saw Sawchuk capture the Calder Trophy (no one had ever before swept the freshman honors in hockey's top three professional leagues), win the Vezina Trophy three times, and help Detroit to three Stanley Cup championships.

As early as his sophomore season, Sawchuk was widely acclaimed as the greatest goaltender in the history of the game. "There simply isn't any question about it," insisted New York Rangers general manager Frank Boucher in January of 1952. "Oh, I know what some of the old-timers are going to say. That Sawchuk is just a kid and has to stand the test of time... But I'm sure that they'll be saying the same thing about Sawchuk years from now."

At the age of 22, Sawchuk had not only arrived as one of the game's marquee players, but he had been stamped as something unique, a goalie unlike any who had come before. Sawchuk's playoff performance that spring, when the Red Wings captured the Stanley Cup in the minimum eight games, remains unmatched by any goaltender in the modern era. He surrendered just five goals during the two playoff series against Toronto and Montreal for a minuscule goals-against average of 0.62. His four playoff shutouts equaled the record shared by Davey Kerr of the New York Rangers and Toronto's Frank McCool. But Kerr had needed nine games to get his four in 1937, and McCool thirteen in 1945.

The next season Sawchuk easily captured the Vezina Trophy, and he won it again in 1955 when Detroit took the second of two straight Stanley Cup titles. By now his credits included First Team All-Star selections in 1951, 1952 and 1953, and spots on the second squad in 1954 and 1955.

But despite the accolades, trouble loomed ahead for Sawchuk. Teammates noticed a souring of his personality as injuries and other troubles took their toll. Even for a goaltender, his litany of health problems seemed almost surreal. By the mid-1950s he had already suffered through several operations to remove bone chips from his right elbow, which he had injured playing football as a child. An eye injury while he was with Omaha almost ended his career before it really got started. His appendix had ruptured one off-season and another summer a lung collapsed in an automobile accident. In the years to come, Sawchuk would be troubled by neuritis, a painful inflammation of the nerves in his legs that doctors at first felt might eventually put him in a wheelchair; two herniated discs in his back further aggravated this condition. His upper back became severely swayed, caused by a condition called lordosis, the result of back muscles that had been shortened by years of crouching in goal. Sawchuk also suffered from insomnia, caused by the constant throbbing pain in his back and legs, and persistent migraine headaches.

"When it came time to waken him I often had to help him out of bed and, later, into the car for the trip to the rink,"

Sawchuk's wife, Pat, told an interviewer. "Then he'd take a painkiller pill, timing it so he would unstiffen by the time the buzzer sounded to skate out onto the ice."

Increasingly fond of drink, Sawchuk often showed up for practices in a foul mood, hung over from the night before. At the best of times, reporters approached him warily, hoping to be lucky enough to catch the goalie on one of his good days.

"His style was to listen placidly to a question, then look the reporter in the eye and snarl, 'get lost,' or words to that effect," Jim Proudfoot of the *Toronto Star* remembered. "A simple question, sensible in his case, such as 'how do you feel' would elicit this response: 'With my hands, dummy.' To a query about some on-ice incident—'you saw the game, didn't you?'"

Teammate Marcel Pronovost, who roomed with the goaltender for years on the road, often recalled how, when they first awoke in the morning, he would say good morning to Sawchuk in both French and English. "If he answered," recalled Pronovost, "I knew we would talk at least a little that day. But if he didn't reply, which was most days, we didn't speak the entire day."

Almost immediately after Detroit's Stanley Cup victory in 1955, Jack Adams stunned the hockey world by trading almost half of his championship squad in blockbuster deals with Chicago and Boston. Sawchuk, despite his recent Vezina win, was dispatched to the Bruins.

Adams explained that he made the trades to make room on the roster for such talented youngsters as Norm Ullman and Bronco Horvath. Slated to take Sawchuk's place in the Detroit goal was minor-league sensation Glenn Hall, another future Hall of Fame netminder.

Sawchuk never did adjust to life as a Boston Bruin. "Terry didn't like anything about Boston," remembered his friend Johnny Wilson, a teammate in Detroit. "He didn't like the city or even the arena. Terry was developed in a winning organization. And then suddenly he was with a team struggling to make the playoffs. I don't think he appreciated that."

Though Sawchuk played well, Boston finished out of the playoffs in fifth place in 1955–56. The next season both he and the team started strongly. By Christmas Sawchuk led the Vezina race and was playing so well that people were already talking him up as a potential candidate for the Hart Trophy as league MVP.

Then once again he was struck down by the injury whammy that had long been the bane of his existence. Sawchuk contracted infectious mononucleosis, a disease of the blood stream that affects the glands and causes loss of strength and a general feeling of lassitude. He entered hospital to begin a convalescence that was expected to last as long as two months.

But Sawchuk surprised everyone by returning to the Boston cage in less than three weeks. Doctors consulted by the press unanimously agreed that this was not nearly enough recuperation time from mono for an NHL goalie, who every game carried 35 pounds of soaking wet equipment and endured an unnaturally heightened level of physical and emotional stress. The suspicion quickly grew that the Bruins, desperate to secure a playoff spot, callously decided to roll the dice on Sawchuk's health and rush him back into the lineup.

Depression is often a side effect of mono, especially among sufferers who, like Sawchuk, don't get the rest and relaxation they need to start to feel better again. Night after night he lay in bed staring at the ceiling and smoking cigarettes. Disgusted by his indifferent play and confused by his emotional turmoil, Sawchuk announced to the Bruins that he was quitting the game.

Talk of retirement was nothing new for the high-strung netminder. Throughout his career—when he was sick or injured or depressed about a slump—Sawchuk would often threaten to quit. The difference was that this time he really meant it.

Sawchuk's walkout quickly became the biggest story in the game of hockey since the Richard Riot in Montreal two seasons before; front-page news in most league cities the next morning. Ironically, on the day that he announced his retirement, NHL headquarters in Montreal also announced the All-Star squads for the first half of the season. On the strength of his brilliant work before he became sick, Sawchuk out-polled all other goalies in the voting to earn a place on the first team.

At first the Bruins took a hard line against their errant goaltender, placing him on "permanent suspension." Then, realizing the magnitude of their loss, they softened their stance, asking him to reconsider. Finally, after acquiring the services of promising netminder Don Simmons from the AHL's Springfield Indians, they returned to their original hard line. "The game is bigger than Sawchuk," Boston general manager Lynn Patrick pronounced angrily.

And so the stage was set for Sawchuk's return to the Red Wings, who as it happened were in the market for a goaltender. Though Glenn Hall had been voted the league's top rookie, and was elected to the Second All-Star Team as a freshman and to the first team as a sophomore, the volatile Jack Adams had found him wanting. Adams placed most of the blame on Hall for the team's early exit from the playoffs that spring.

After time to recuperate and think it over back at his home in suburban Detroit, Sawchuk concluded that he would indeed like to continue his playing career, especially if a deal could be worked out transferring him back to the Red Wings. In truth, though he played for four other organizations during his career, Sawchuk was never really happy—or at least as happy as his irascible nature permitted—unless he was wearing Detroit's famous winged wheel.

That June of 1957 a deal was struck transferring Sawchuk back to Detroit in return for 22-year-old left winger Johnny Bucyk and an undisclosed sum of cash. Though unappreciated by Adams, Bucyk quickly blossomed into stardom with Boston, going on to score 545 goals for the Bruins over the next 21 seasons.

Sadly for Sawchuk, the Detroit squad he rejoined was but a pale shadow of the champions he had left behind in 1955. A string of disastrous trades had decimated one of the greatest teams in hockey history. After finishing in third place, Detroit was humiliated by Rocket Richard and the Montreal Canadiens in a semifinal sweep. The next year, 1958–59, the Red Wings hit rock bottom, finishing last in the standings for the first time in the club's history.

Sawchuk continued to play well, but by now he no longer necessarily ranked as the best goalie in the game. Many would have picked Montreal's Jacques Plante, Chicago's Glenn Hall, or possibly Toronto's Johnny Bower ahead of him. Still, Sawchuk was a standout on some good, though not great, Detroit teams in the early 1960s. Led by the ageless Gordie Howe, Alex Delvecchio and Norm Ullman up front, and anchored by a defense corps that included Marcel

Pronovost and Bill Gadsby, the Wings reached the Stanley Cup finals in 1961, 1963 and 1964.

By the start of the 1963–64 campaign Sawchuk was closing in on one of the most coveted records in hockey: George Hainsworth's mark of 94 career shutouts. His history-making 95th whitewash came in Montreal on January 18, 1964, after he foiled a third-period breakaway by John Ferguson to preserve a 2–0 score.

Coming off a season in which he had set the shutout record and been named team MVP, the by now 34-year-old fully expected to finish out his career with the Red Wings. But that spring Sawchuk was bitterly disappointed when Detroit set him free and Toronto claimed him in the third round of the annual intra-league waiver draft. His replacement in the Detroit goal would be young Roger Crozier, who had shared the job with Sawchuk for part of the previous season.

Punch Imlach's Maple Leafs had won the Stanley Cup the past three years, twice beating Detroit in the finals. Having Sawchuk and Johnny Bower, two future Hall of Famers, on the same squad seemed almost an embarrassment of riches. Bower recalled "going to Imlach and telling him that he'd just bought himself a Stanley Cup."

The two veterans, who had faced each other way back in the Calder Cup final of 1950, proceeded to form hockey's most formidable and famous goaltending platoon. They shared the Vezina that first season, 1964–65, and continued to provide Toronto with stellar protection for two more years. The Stanley Cup victory prophesied by Johnny Bower came to pass during Canada's Centennial spring of 1967, when the Maple Leafs beat Montreal in a thrilling six-game final.

Though bruised and ravaged by injuries, Sawchuk was at his most phenomenal in that series, just as he had been against the powerful Black Hawks of Bobby Hull and Stan Mikita in the semifinals. Many observers felt that even he, hockey's greatest netminder, had outdone himself. "I've never seen such goaling," said an awed Bobby Hull.

"It would be nice to go out a winner, the first star in a Cup-winning game," Sawchuk said afterwards, talking as he had so often before about quitting hockey. He was still contemplating retirement the following June when the Leafs chose to protect Johnny Bower rather than him in the original expansion draft, which saw the league grow from six to twelve teams. Made the draft's top pick by the Los Angeles Kings, Sawchuk found the offer of a $40,000 annual salary too rich to refuse and signed on for a minimum of two more years.

No one, including Sawchuk, knew it then, but he was pretty much through. The Stanley Cup victory with Toronto proved to be a glorious last hurrah. He struggled through one campaign with Los Angeles and then was sent packing to Detroit, where he was third goalie behind Roger Crozier

and Roy Edwards in 1968–69.

Yet still he kept on playing. After his wife divorced him, he needed the money for support payments for seven children. The final stop of an unparalleled career came with the New York Rangers the next season, when as the backup to Ed Giacomin, he made eight appearances, which included his 103rd and final shutout, a 6–0 decision over the Pittsburgh Penguins.

In all his life, Sawchuk had never felt so low as he did that season. His drinking, which had become progressively heavier with the passing years, got worse following the divorce. He became more irritable and even less tolerant of reporters, fans and anyone else outside a small, select circle of friends.

Then came the shocking end that shook the hockey world and made headlines across North America. Sawchuk, who shared a rented house on Long Island with his Ranger teammate Ron Stewart, got into a drunken argument with his friend over how much responsibility each had to clean up the place before handing the keys back to the owner, and about money Stewart felt was owed him for household expenses. During a brawl on their front yard, the goalie hit his stomach heavily on either Stewart's knee or a barbeque grill, nobody was certain which.

The tumble caused extensive damage to Sawchuk's liver and gall bladder. During the next month, he underwent surgery for the removal of his gall bladder and then to remove blood from his lacerated liver. The scarred and battered body Sawchuk had pushed so hard through 20 NHL seasons grew weaker by the day. Finally, on May 31, 1970, just hours after a final operation, he slipped away.

In the days that followed speculation abounded about the role Ron Stewart had played in the goalie's death. There was talk that Stewart would face a charge of involuntary manslaughter. But a Long Island grand jury deliberated less than half an hour before ruling that Sawchuk's death was "completely accidental."

Terry Sawchuk's legend has grown larger with every year since his tragic passing. In 1971, he was posthumously awarded the Lester Patrick Memorial Trophy—for "outstanding service to hockey in the United States." Also that year, voters waived the usual three-year waiting period and elected Sawchuk to the Hockey Hall of Fame. Then, on March 6, 1994 came the honour that would have pleased him the most. His beloved Red Wings officially retired Sawchuk's Number 1 and a commemorative banner was hoisted to the rafters of Joe Louis Arena. It hangs with the other retired numbers of Gordie Howe (9), Ted Lindsay (7), Sid Abel (12) and Alex Delvecchio (10).

"The Uke was the best goalie I ever saw," Gordie Howe marveled that glorious evening, "He was everything that a goalie should be."

FIGHTING AND HOCKEY IT'S PART OF THE GAME!?

Dan Diamond

THE HISTORIC ROYAL YORK HOTEL in Toronto was the scene; a speech to a business audience on the future of NHL hockey in Canada was the subject; the day was April 15, 1998, on the eve of the Stanley Cup playoffs. The guest speaker: NHL commissioner Gary Bettman.

While the speech to the Canadian Club was a prelude to a presentation less than two weeks later by the six Canadian-based NHL clubs to the Parliamentary Sub-Committee on Sport on a matter that has sparked considerable debate in recent years—namely the future viability of NHL teams in Montreal, Ottawa, Toronto, Calgary, Edmonton and Vancouver—the audience of more than 400 people was most interested in what transpired towards the very end of Bettman's presentation.

Following his speech, Bettman took a few questions from the audience on a variety of subjects. The final question touched a cord that has been the subject of numerous debates and discussions throughout the course of the NHL's 80-plus years.

The inquisitor wanted to know what the league intended to do about fighting in hockey.

Without hesitation, Bettman proceeded to stun the audience by asking for a show of hands as to who in the audience wanted to keep fighting in the NHL and who wished to have it eliminated. The result of the informal poll? Approximately half of the gathering in the room were for fighting and the other half wished to see it eliminated.

The room was polarized: Canadian television network executives voted both for and against its abolishment; executives from some of the country's biggest corporations also were split on fighting's value; members of the fifth estate—some for and some against; and most importantly, some of the most knowledgeable hockey fans in the world were also divided as to what place, if any, fighting should hold in their beloved game.

The Royal York Hotel has been the sight of dozens of NHL owners' meetings since the first time they gathered at the historic building in the heart of Canada's biggest city in 1929. It is safe to say though, that none of the business they have transacted down through the years generated more public interest than Bettman's straw poll conducted on the spur of the moment that April afternoon.

That people were divided on the issue of fighting in hockey should come as little surprise. A question posed to thousands of hockey fans in a league-commissioned market survey throughout Canada and the U.S. during the same month as Bettman's speech asked the question—Is there too much fighting in NHL hockey? The results: 13 percent of the respondents said there is too little fighting; 39 percent said that there is too much fighting and 48 said that there was neither too little or too much fighting in the game.

Such is the dilemma that has faced the leaders of the game for more than 80 years. What would the effect of eliminating fighting in today's game have on the league? Would some of those fans who buy tickets to the games be inclined not to do so? Would the game become even more popular among hard core fans as well as attract untold num-

bers of new fans without fighting?

To illustrate the effect of a fluctuation in the attendance of a sport that derives more than 60 percent of its revenue from ticket sales, a five percent fluctuation in attendance either way would mean untold millions in either revenue or losses. The upside would no doubt be terrific for all concerned, but how many franchises could live with the opposite result?

It is a question that has been asked since the beginning of hockey's time. But also one that is unanswerable. There are persuasive arguments both for and against fighting—and for that reason it remains a part of the game.

To be sure, the people entrusted with looking out for the best interests of the game have not stood still on the issue of rules to curb fighting. In the 1970s, for example, the more "tough guys" a team had the better off it was. For some teams, they couldn't have enough tough guys. Clearly, this has changed in the 1990s. There are some teams today that don't have a player whose principal role is to be a fighter on the roster. The pure fighter is fading out of the NHL as teams think they are better off with a good fourth-line checker than using an enforcer.

One of the two strictest pieces of legislation in this regard was adopted in 1987 when the league took steps to eliminate bench-clearing brawls, an element of the game in which fans seemed to be united in their distaste. (The others substantive change was the "third man in rule.")

To hockey fans, the 1970s are probably best remembered as much for two teams—"the Big Bad Bruins" and "the Broad Street Bullies"—as for a Montreal Canadiens club which put together a streak of four straight Stanley Cup championships from 1976 to 1979. The Boston Bruins and Philadelphia Flyers each won two Stanley Cup titles immediately prior the Canadiens' run and helped to popularize the art of intimidation through fisticuffs

The Bruins and, subsequently, the Flyers of the 1970s were two of the all-time best at intimidating their opposition. Teams hated to play them because they knew that they would be punished. Just as in today's NHL where 26 clubs attempt to copy the style of the two-time defending Stanley Cup champion Detroit Red Wings (as teams also tried to copy the style of the New Jersey Devils earlier this decade), so too did teams begin to employ in the 1970s the lumbering hockey player who could meet the challenge of a Bruin or a Flyer.

While the league averaged only one fight for every two games played (versus today's game which sees one fight for every 1.5 games played), the issue of fighting received much attention due to the frequency with which bench clearing brawls would occur. It was not uncommon for all players to leave their benches during the course of a game in the 1970s and take part in a brawl that could last up to 20 minutes.

In late 1975, the public attention to fighting and brawling reached a fever pitch when then Ontario Attorney General Roy McMurtry got into the act by threatening to charge NHL players with assault for their actions on the ice. He did just that on five occasions in the span of two years.

McMurtry defended his position at the time: "A hockey player can't get away with something on the ice if the tactics which he employs would cause him to face arrest out on a city street."

The league's reaction to the Attorney General's attempt to make use of the courts to police the NHL was summed up by then president Clarence Campbell in May, 1976:

"The hockey of today is patsy compared to what it was in the days of the six team NHL. The increased coverage via television and the expansion throughout the U.S. has placed it more in the spotlight. I still believe that it is up to the NHL to police its own game."

While Campbell would not admit to the role that McMurtry would play in ridding the game of some of the brawling, it seemed more than a little ironic that less than 12 months after McMurtry laid charges against several Philadelphia Flyers following a multi-player brawl during a playoff game in April 1976 in Toronto, the league adopted its "third man in" rule which called for the removal of a player from a game who became involved in a fight already in progress between two other players.

The adoption of this rule was seemingly the league's first admission that the game had been debased by the deliberately intimidating tactics of some players through the first half of the 1970s.

Bench-clearing brawls continued to escalate in numbers in the early 1980s before the league adopted a series of rule changes, culminating in 1987–88 with a piece of legislation that has effectively eliminated bench-clearing brawls from the game. That rule sees a 10-game suspension to the first player to leave the bench to start or join a fight. The second player to leave the bench, from either team is slapped with a five game suspension. While the league has had to suspend more than a dozen players since for 10 games, it is also true that the league has not had a bench-clearing brawl since 1987.

Bench clearings were also a significant part of the league's early era. In his description of an October 1950 game between the Canadiens and the Bruins, the *Boston Globe*'s Herb Ralby wrote: "Hockey fans must have thought they came to the Garden on the wrong night. 'Sugar' Ray Robinson was introduced between the first and second periods. He heads the fight card at the Garden tonight against Joe Rindone. But the 10,894 fans who came to see the season's local hockey opener last night at the Depot rink could justifiably have expected him to climb into the rink after watching the wild third period brawl.

"A dozen players, seven Bruins and five Canadiens staged the biggest donnybrook on Garden ice since Christmas night 1930, when the entire squads of the Bruins and the defunct Philadelphia team paired off in slugging bees all over the ice. It was the wildest brawl in the NHL, according to Canadiens coach Dick Irvin, since 1936 when 32 Toronto and Detroit players battled on Detroit ice in a Stanley Cup final."

One of hockey's greatest myths is that each club needs at least one roster spot to protect the star player on their team and give him the maximum amount of room on the ice in which to operate effectively without feeling intimidated. Marty McSorley has made a career of providing one of the game's greatest players, Wayne Gretzky, with the room to showcase his skills, first with the Oilers and then with the Kings. "Without fighting, you would increase those guys who don't look at themselves as being finesse players," he told the *Los Angeles Daily News*. "They try to intimidate your goal scorers through harassment. Your tough guys don't bother your goal scorers. ... The tough guys monitor the goal scorers and the tough guys get rid of the gnats; get rid of the annoying guys who slow the game down."

The most concerted effort to eliminate fighting in the NHL took place in the period from June to August, 1992. The matter was supposed to be on the agenda of the league's Board of Governors annual meeting in June, but the resignation of NHL president John Ziegler at that meeting led to the matter being tabled until August.

In the interim period, a great public debate raged among owners, general managers and coaches as each side—the abolitionists and the proponents of fighting—lobbied for public support. At issue, should the league adopt a rule that would remove a player from a game should he become involved in a fight. Two position papers were prepared by groups comprised of owners and general managers—one supporting fighting; the other, opposing it. The very public debate proved to be one of the most divisive chapters in NHL history as arguments from both sides found their way into the media.

The report of the anti-fighting group stated, "We have huge revenue growth potential with television in the United States. But until fighting is *prohibited*, cashing in on this opportunity will never happen."

The pro-fighting group, not surprisingly, drew an entirely different conclusion:

"There is a common misconception that the NHL cannot attract a national TV contract as a result of fisticuffs. Yet Molson, who is a franchise holder, a TV producer and a rightsholder wants fisticuffs in the game."

On the issue of the league's growth potential outside North America, both sides were also diametrically opposed. The anti-fighters: "European hockey absolutely does not allow fighting. Asian audiences will not accept systematic violence in team sports. Do we think that we will ever really expand into these markets as long as we allow fighting?"

The supporters of fighting thought so. "While the NHL has adopted many things from the European game that are good, Europeans have adopted the physical part of the NHL game. There are bigger, stronger Europeans joining the NHL every year."

The essence of the debate was crystallized in the following opposing stances: The pro-fighting side wrote: The North American psychology in sports favors the man who stands up for himself. He is applauded if he confronts a wrong. The issue comes down to what kind of a confrontation is desirable. Hockey players carry weapons [sticks]. Is the player who is frustrated by illegal tactics to respond with an accepted, safe and natural release of emotions through fisticuffs or is he to resort to stickwork?"

The abolitionists stated: "Hockey players are quality young men who have a tarnished image because of the public's perception that hockey is a sport with an accepted code of violence. We need to market our hockey players as gifted athletes—not bullies."

Finally, the debate dealt with the economics of fighting. Those who supported fighting wrote: "The NHL plays to 92 percent of capacity. This indicates that season-ticket holders, the casual fans, and sports fans in general like the game as it is. This is a business. With player salaries and costs increasing exponentially some member clubs are riding a tenuous line between fiscal failure and success. This is not the time to experiment. Elimination of fisticuffs may be a disaster ... and once removed will be impossible to reinstate without a media backlash."

The anti-fighting group responded by asking several crucial questions: "How many more potential fans stay away because of the fighting? Another key question we would ask is, 'Do we actually think fans would stop coming to the hockey games because we abolish fighting?' We feel we open the sport up to many more new fans and families by

eliminating the single most negative factor in our game today—the fighting."

It is an endless cycle of counter-balancing argument.

The trend in the NHL through the 1980s and 1990s has been to increase penalties for dangerous play like checking from behind and careless stickwork. These eliminate some of fighting's familiar flashpoints. But as we go forward—in the absence of any one resonant event that turns fans, broadcasters and advertisers against fisticuffs—gloves, on occasion, are likely to continue to drop in the NHL.

EXPANSION: THE NHL DOUBLES...
THEN TRIPLES
Shirley Fischler

BEFORE THE 1942–43 SEASON, the Brooklyn Americans, as the record book tells it, "retired from League" and the National Hockey League settled into the six-team circuit that was to be its format for the next quarter of a century. Over that span, especially in the 1960s, the word "tight" was often used to describe the governing body of the world's most exclusive ice club. Writer Jack Olsen, in an article, "Private Game: No Admittance" (*Sports Illustrated*, April 12, 1965) pictured the NHL as "A tight little island of close-fisted, inbred standpatters with a stranglehold on a grand professional game." His view was not particularly singular. Until February 8, 1966, when league president Clarence Campbell formally announced the addition of six new teams, the idea of expansion was generally as welcome among NHL leaders as a forward in the goal crease.

The earliest wave of expansion might be said to have started in 1924, when the Boston Bruins became the first team from the United States to join the league. In the same year, the Maroons presented Montreal another club to vie with the Canadiens. The following year, the Hamilton Tigers franchise, which had replaced the Quebec Bulldogs in 1920, was sold to New York, becoming the Americans, and the Pittsburgh Pirates were also admitted.

By the beginning of the 1926–27 season, the NHL ranks had swelled to an all-time high of 10 teams. In addition to the Bruins, Maroons, Canadiens, Americans and Pirates, there were the Toronto Maple Leafs and Ottawa Senators, as well as three new entries: the New York Rangers, Chicago Black Hawks and Detroit Cougars (later the Falcons, then the Red Wings). The league was divided into two five-team divisions, Canadian and American, with the New York Americans lined up with the four north-of-the-border clubs. From that time until 1967, any new NHL clubs resulted not from expansion but migration.

The Pittsburgh franchise became the Philadelphia Quakers in 1930; in 1931 Philadelphia folded. Ottawa, which had suspended operation in 1931–32, returned in 1932–33, became the St. Louis Eagles in 1934 and molted into oblivion in 1935. Three seasons later the Maroons disbanded, beating the Americans to extinction by four years.

After World War II, hockey, like all professional sports, began to reclaim its stars and solid regulars. The one-sided games of the wartime years subsided into more normal scores as the retreads and teenagers returned to the minors. Not only was the caliber of play up, but so were the attendance figures. In the postwar boom there was much ready money and sports shared amply in the entertainment dollar. The last-place Black Hawks of 1946–47 drew a crowd of 20,000 to Chicago Stadium as far along in the season as late February, and the Rangers, who had suffered much humiliation in the war years, again had a respectable team to attract consistently good crowds.

In May 1952 Jim Hendy, general manager of the Cleveland Barons, thought that his club was on the verge of leaving the American Hockey League to become the National Hockey League's seventh member. It had taken six months of beaverish activity to reach this point. A Cleveland sports columnist wrote: "Our city has been awarded a franchise in the NHL. This is the most pleasurable news of the year." He was a trifle premature.

Despite all indications that the Barons were "in," two months later they were turned down. "What do they want?" wailed Hendy, and the league responded with the following stipulations: $425,000 to cover the franchise, league reserve fund and working capital, and 60 percent of the stock to be owned by Cleveland residents. Hendy fulfilled these requests. His backers were solid and he seemed to have the support of member teams. He built up a farm system along major-league lines. President Clarence Campbell came out in favor of the Barons acceptance as a boon to hockey interest in the United States.

With seemingly only the formalities to be dispensed, the NHL suddenly shot a "no" from a curved stick. Included in the money raised to fulfill Cleveland's requirements were substantial advances against TV and radio earnings and concessions extending over two seasons. In the eyes of the NHL governors, this was not "working capital." Application denied.

A variety of reasons had made the NHL ultra-cautious. From the past there were the specters of all those failed franchises of the 1930s. In the present were new financial problems. Although there was no Depression, the postwar boom was over and people were not going out to see losers. Unfortunately there were two of those in the NHL at that moment. Between 1949–50 and 1956–57 the Black Hawks finished last seven out of eight times. From 1950–51 through 1954–55 the Rangers were fifth four times and in the cellar once. In that period there was nothing so enervating as a mid-week struggle between the league's two lowliest teams. At one such contest, a 1–1 tie that neither team seemed eager, nor particularly capable, of breaking, the Rangers management decided not to open the balcony at the old Madison Square Garden in deference to the size of the crowd. One literally could hear a puck drop. It was little wonder that the league sought new lands carefully, very carefully. Instead, the NHL strengthened from within.

The Black Hawks, with deliberate help from the stronger clubs, moved to fifth in 1957–58 and made the playoffs a year later. They were not out of the playoffs again 1969. Once their farm system began to produce the likes of Bobby Hull and Stan Mikita, they became self-sufficient. The Rangers, after a pocket renaissance from 1955–56 through 1957–58, fell back to the role of perennial also-ran until 1966–67, with the exception of 1961–62. They were joined by Boston, which did not participate in one playoff game from the spring of 1960 to the spring of 1968. However, there was an important difference between the doormats of the 1950s and the weak teams of the 1960s: the hometown rooters were still filling the arenas to see the latter play.

More specifically, they were coming to watch hockey. Television, described by Clarence Campbell in 1951, as "the greatest menace of the entertainment world," had helped magnify the appeal of the ice sport in already estab-

lished areas and spread its magnetic aura to unlikely corners, even to places where it had been only a dirty word. In Nashville, "hockey," prior to the arrival of the Eastern League's Dixie Flyers, was no more than a local joke. It took local residents a while before they could view the sign "Hockey Tonight" outside the arena without having a fit of thigh-slapping hysterics.

What began as local televising of certain home games, or parts of games, by each team in the early 1950s, eventually reached the network stage. In 1956–57 the Columbia Broadcasting System inaugurated a Saturday afternoon series from Boston, Chicago, Detroit and New York. Meanwhile, the Canadian Broadcasting Company's "Hockey Night in Canada" added TV to its weekly Saturday night radio broadcasts. None of these telecasts hurt attendance, but, in fact, boosted it in certain areas. The Rangers finished dead last again in 1965–66, but their practice of televising their Saturday night road contests made so many new fans for hockey that a pasteboard to one of their games at Madison Square Garden had become one of New York's hot tickets despite several losing seasons.

In the 1960s, hockey not only spread to the American south, but towns like Ft. Wayne, Indiana, in the International Hockey League were attracting bigger crowds to their games than "major-league" cities in other winter professional sports such as basketball. Before the 1961–62 season, San Francisco and Los Angeles joined the Western Hockey League. The success of these franchises in large population centers already represented by major-league teams in baseball and football became a constant spur to NHL expansion as the 1960s unfolded. The American Football League set up shop alongside the National Football League in 1960. Faced with the possibility of a third baseball league, the American League added two teams for the 1961 season, while the National League took in two new franchises for 1962. That spring, columnist Jim Murray of the *Los Angeles Times* wrote: "The National Hockey League makes a mockery of its title by restricting its franchises to six teams, waging a kind of private little tournament of 70 games just to eliminate two teams.

"Other big money sports are expanding," he continued, "but hockey likes it there in the back of the cave. Any businessman will tell you that in a dynamic economy you either grow or perish. Baseball had to be dragged, kicking and screaming, out of its rut. Football groped its way on the end of a short rope. Hockey just can't sit there in the dark forever, braiding buggy whips."

At the same time, Harold Ballard, one of the owners of the Toronto Maple Leafs, said: "If the right kind of people come to us with $5,000,000 and the right kind of plans, we'll listen. We'd be crazy not to." Although mitigated by some of the requirements, this was one of the rare positive statements on expansion to come from the NHL hierarchy at that time. Clarence Campbell's position for the league was couched in more conservative terms. "The league is not actively promoting or encouraging expansion of the numbers of its members at this time," he stated dryly. "But it is prepared to consider each individual application on its own merits."

By 1964, rumblings from the West Coast were edging toward the seismic. Coley Hall, a manipulator in Vancouver, but then the owner of the San Francisco Seals, said, "The time has come for the NHL to realize that Los Angeles and San Francisco can't wait; our hockey fans are just as major-league-conscious as fans of baseball and football and feel

they should be up there. An angry feeling is developing."

One of the more testy, anonymous quotes from the Pacific territory to reach print at that time was, "If the NHL won't expand to us, why don't we go outlaw, raid them groggy and find out if their control over hundreds of young players through B and C forms will stand up in law?"

The next flurry of expansion and excitement also came in 1964 from the Pacific Northwest. At the Western Hockey League's annual meeting in Seattle, Stafford Smythe, former president of the Toronto Maple Leafs, revealed that his club was willing to erect an $8,000,000 coliseum seating 20,000 in downtown Vancouver in time for the opening of the 1966–67 season. Smythe envisioned Vancouver as a member of a new six-team division. His accomplice, Harold Ballard, saw the new entry as part of the old circuit along with Los Angeles, San Francisco and St. Louis. Ballard made it clear that the Leafs' interest in Vancouver would be confined to building and operating the arena, with the franchise to be independently owned. What eventually became the main stumbling block was the contingency that the city donate the property for the arena site.

At first the City Council appeared to have agreed to this offer but almost immediately the motion was described as "a noncommittal resolution." Mayor William Rathie of Vancouver advocated a green light on the proposal. Although he won an election, the land grant was voted down by the taxpayers of Vancouver.

When the original proposition had come from the Maple Leafs, Clarence Campbell called it "kite-flying" and further threw around his presidential weight by stating: "I know that, as of this minute, they are not speaking for anybody official in the National Hockey League." However, he did say of Smythe and Ballard: "I agree with them that expansion is inevitable. With a show as good as ours, economics may someday either induce or force expansion."

The arguments against expansion were many. Travel expense was one. A major-league baseball team stays three or four days in one city when on the road; a hockey team plays one-night stands. Lack of talent was another. When baseball moved to Los Angeles and San Francisco it gave those cities established teams, but when it expanded it presented new teams that were hardly competitive. Campbell cited the "formation of a clown club" without directly naming the New York Mets. "We don't want any clown teams in the National Hockey League," he concluded. It was common thinking—and this prevailed until proved wrong during the actual playing of the 1967–68 season—that there were simply not enough good players available to make up two more NHL teams, let alone a new six-team division.

At the conclusion of the 1963–64 season it was reported that the NHL had played to 94.5 percent of its total seating capacity; this in a year when the fifth-place Rangers finished 17 points from the last playoff spot, and the Bruins trailed the New Yorkers by another six points. ("I'm for expansion," wrote one waggish columnist, "on the condition that it first include New York and Boston.") The standpatters could say, "What can we gain by expanding and adding to our expenses?" and the answer would have been, "Nothing," if not for one factor—television.

Aware of the lucrative deals garnered by baseball and football, the most forward-thinking of the NHL governors realized that in order to snare the TV dollar, major-league hockey would have to extend its nets over the length of the United States. On March 11, 1965, at a special meeting of club owners in New York's Plaza Hotel, the NHL

announced that it was expanding with the formation of a second six-team division, and would begin evaluating applications from responsible groups. The official acceptance in February 1966 found Los Angeles, San Francisco, St. Louis, Pittsburgh, Philadelphia and Minneapolis-St.Paul as the representatives of the new division. St. Louis was a surprise since it had not filed a formal application. Buffalo and Baltimore had been rejected. So had Vancouver and this rankled many Canadians. After all, here were six additions to the NHL and not one city was located in the country that was the cradle of hockey.

It is generally conceded that the younger governors like the Canadiens' David Molson and the Rangers' William Jennings were the prime movers in the expansion. For the daring jump to be successful, it was realized that the arrangement for stocking the new teams had to be equitable. When the Board of Governors thought they had a fair plan devised, the general managers balked. President Campbell explained the delay with: "I never met a generous general manager."

The approved plan called for each existing team to protect one goalie and 11 other players. When they lost a player, they could protect one more. This would go on until each new team had a roster of 20 players. The old teams would lose their number 12, 14, 16, 17 and 18 men to the expansion clubs. When the established teams' general managers heard this they moaned. The new members seemed satisfied. Only Campbell was reported to be not completely pleased. However he felt that an extended back up plan that called for all teams to be able to protect two goalies and only 14 others for the 1968 and 1969 intraleague drafts would help in the equalization. "The new teams won't have trouble picking out which 14 to protect," he said, "but the older teams … they're going to have problems.

"I visualize definite improvement in the new teams by 1968–69 because of the back up plan," Campbell added. "By 1970, they should have a glorious field day and I hope they do."

On June 6, 1967, the Expansion Draft was held in Montreal and the new teams received an opportunity to see what they were going to get for their initiation fee of $2,000,000. When the cigar smoke had cleared, there were those observers who felt the neophytes had been taken when they wound up paying what amounted to $100,000 each for bodies that ordinarily, under the regular draft price, cost only $30,000. Of course, for their $2,000,000 the new teams not only received 20 players but also an area in which to skate—provided one had the rink.

Even the players, pleased by the doubled job opportunities, had differing opinions. Forward Billy Hicke, drafted by the Oakland Seals, said of the new owners: "They didn't get a fair shake. The league was charitable with goaltenders, but that was all. Of the 20 players each team drafted, only six or seven are of NHL caliber."

Later, toward the tail end of the season, Philadelphia Flyers defenseman Ed Van Impe waxed positive about the new division. "Expansion was a good thing for hockey. These teams are good teams. There were a lot of good hockey players who never had a chance until this year. It's hard to imagine until this year there were only 120 spots open for major-league hockey players. Now it's 240. Expansion hasn't hurt. These guys are proving they belonged."

One thing expansion did was create more holdouts. Players who knew that they were vital to the new teams—especially the all-important goalies—drove hard bargains.

The older players realized that this was their last chance to cash in.

At the conclusion of the season, even the league's most ardent critics had to concede that the NHL version of expansion had been the most successful of any professional sport. The new teams, with the exception of Oakland, were all contenders for the four playoff spots. While Philadelphia finished first with 73 points, Pittsburgh was fifth, two points out of fourth, with 67 points. The six new clubs won 40, tied 18 and lost 86 in competition with the established division, a figure even a clairvoyant would have rejected in October.

The West Division playoffs were so closely played that all three series went the full seven games and one-third of those games were decided in sudden death overtime. When the St. Louis Blues bowed to the mighty Montreal Canadiens in four one-goal victories—two of them in overtime—the creators of expansion could sit back and admire an artistic triumph.

How did the new teams reach this level so quickly? Top caliber goaltending, certainly; lots of extra effort, for sure; complacency on the part of the old teams, partially. Prevailing over all was the feeling that the major-league benchwarmers, the locked-in minor-leaguers, and the fringe faction were all better than they had been rated. And, of course, the theory of different combinations was given a thorough testing—Player A may not play well with B and C, but put him with D (digger in the corners) and S (speedy up and down his wing) and you will see a different hockey player. The individual stars are always important but hockey is a team game, and an inventive coach can make a whole out of a lot of seemingly disparate parts.

For all the huzzahs over expansion's initial bloom, there were some who warned that there might be a sliding back when the junior players that the East Division clubs were able to protect would come to maturity and jet the old teams a few strides ahead again. Others warned of the consequences of trading away future choices in the universal draft of 20-year-olds. (Minnesota, for one, was heavily indebted to Montreal in this area.) The open draft of junior players began in 1967, but the size of established teams' sponsored lists did not begin to really shrink until after 1968 as the phasing out process neared its conclusion. Before the 1968 draft only 33 untouchables were left while 4,500 players were available. The figure was greater in 1969. Anyone turning 20 was eligible and the days of signing a fledgling at 14 were over. Scouting had become more important than ever.

So successful did the league fathers deem the first expansion that another followed in the fall of 1970. Vancouver and Buffalo made their respective debuts in the NHL following a realignment of divisions. Chicago was moved to the West Division while the two new entries joined the East section.

Meanwhile, other North American cities clamored for admittance to the NHL. In an interview during the 1970–71 season, William Jennings, the New York Rangers governor, said that he expected Atlanta and Long Island (New York) to become potential applicants by 1974. However, when the World Hockey Association revealed plans for opening in 1972, the NHL responded by admitting franchises in Long Island (the New York Islanders) and in Georgia, where the Atlanta Flames were born, for the 1972–73 season. For the first time in 30 years, the New York City metropolitan area had two NHL teams … in name at least. There were the

established Rangers who had not won the Stanley Cup in 32 years, and the brand new Islanders, who began the 1972–73 season looking as though they might never win a game.

The Islanders' problems began at the top and ran all the way to the bottom. Owner Roy Boe, who also owned the New York Nets basketball team, knew enough about hockey to hire Bill Torrey as general manager, but while Torrey would quickly build a great dynasty, there would be growing pains first. He ignored the newborn WHA and paid for it dearly when half his team jumped leagues, among them veteran forwards Norm Ferguson, Ted Hampson and Garry Peters. Torrey hired former Canadien/Ranger/Sabre Phil Goyette as his coach. Goyette was best known for skating with that Montreal-induced finesse and wearing pointed shoes off-ice. In other words, Phil was a nice guy but he had zero coaching experience. It didn't work.

In Atlanta, Bill Putnam, instrumental in forming a strong Philadelphia Flyers organization, was brought in as president of the Flames. He chose an excellent ex-scout named Cliff Fletcher to be his general manager. While the Islanders watched a huge chunk of their players march over to the WHA, Fletcher lost no one to the new league. Putnam named the explosive and erratic-tempered Bernie "Boom Boom" Geoffrion coach, and at first look, this seemed unwise, since Geoffrion's only other coaching assignment led to a bleeding ulcer. Instead, Geoffrion got his charges off to a winning start, and by midseason the Flames astoundingly found themselves in the midst of a West Division playoff race.

Atlanta's goaltending that first season was truly superior, with Quebecers Dan Bouchard and Phil Myre splitting the duties. First-round draft choice Jacques Richard was a disappointment, as the club's scoring leader turned out to be Bob Leiter. The defense corps was anchored by journeymen Noel Price and Pat Quinn and the youthful Randy Manery. Center Curt Bennett arrived at midseason to bolster the front line.

Although the World Hockey Association survived in spite of itself, the NHL continued to expand and in 1974 welcomed both the Washington Capitals and Kansas City Scouts. The choice of Washington as the sight of a new franchise was not as bizarre as some thought at the time. Washington had previously been a member of the old Eastern Amateur Hockey League. The Washington Eagles became the Washington Lions near the end of World War II, and reached their acme in the American Hockey League before dissolving in the 1950s. Next door to Washington, in Baltimore, there was also a long involvement with shinny. At the outset of World War II, with players rapidly disappearing into the services, the Curtis Bay Cutters were formed from a Coast Guard outfit in Baltimore. After the war Baltimore iced the Blades, and later, in 1962, entered the AHL with the Clippers. Throughout its hockey history, the Capital Area teams were feeders for the NHL and many a potential star labored below the Mason-Dixon line before making the bigs.

When Abe Pollin and his consortium of backers won the NHL Washington franchise, they decided to build a new arena, the Capital Centre, complete with huge instant-replay screens above center ice. Pollin, owner of the NBA's Washington Bullets basketball team, elected Milt Schmidt to put together his hockey team.

Schmidt, a Hall of Famer and center on the famous Bruins Kraut Line of the late 1930s and 1940s, had retired from playing in 1954 to coach the Bruins, becoming their general manager in 1967. He brought in Lefty McFadden as his assistant general manager, Jimmy Anderson as coach, and Red Sullivan as head scout. McFadden, a former writer, had organized the Dayton (Ohio) Gems of the International Hockey League; Anderson had played in the minors and coached in Springfield, Oklahoma City and Dayton; Sullivan had been a top NHL player and an indifferent coach with the Rangers and Pittsburgh. There was more talent behind the bench than there would be on it.

From the expansion and intraleague drafts Washington garnered the likes of second-rate forwards Denis Dupere, Dave Kryskow, Gord Brooks, Jack Egers, Pete Laframboise, Steve Atkinson, Mike Bloom and Lew Morrison. On defense they collected Bill Mikkelson, Gord Smith, and Yvon Labre. They drafted Ron Low and Michel Belhumeur for goal and purchased the aged, toupeed Doug Mohns from the Atlanta Flames to be father to the inexperienced defense and Bill Lesuk from the Los Angeles Kings to bolster the offense. Tommy Williams bolted the WHA's New England Whalers for the Capitals. Out of this potpourri of mediocrity, only Denis Dupere could be called something other than questionable, and in three seasons with Toronto he had never tallied more than 13 goals in one season.

Prior to this expansion round the NHL had a rule that no new club could trade away its Amateur Draft choice numbers for two years. Established teams such as Montreal had bolstered their clubs tremendously by robbing weak new clubs of their first round amateur numbers, depriving the expansion clubs of their opportunity for talented new blood. The Capitals had also learned from teams like the Islanders that it paid to sign draft choices fast, before they were enticed out of the league by the WHA. Schmidt signed defenseman Greg Joly of the Regina Pats and MVP in the Memorial Cup playoffs. He also signed the number two pick, winger Mike Marson of Sudbury, a chunky African-Canadian who showed up in training camp more than 20 pounds overweight. (In June 1975, however, the Caps traded away their first-round draft choice to the Stanley Cup-winning Philadelphia Flyers for veteran Bill Clement, apparently with NHL sanction.)

The Capitals were less than an artistic success in their early years but gradually developed a following and, in time, became a solid NHL franchise through the 1990s and a Stanley Cup finalist in 1998. The same could not be said for the other 1974 expansion club, the Kansas City Scouts.

The baby Scouts played out of Kansas City's new Kemper Arena. Missourians nurtured hopes that the state's second NHL club would fare as well as the Blues who, by this time, had become an institution of sorts in St. Louis. Relatively speaking, the Scouts did well—compared with the Capitals. While Washington finished with an abysmal 8–67–5 record for only 21 points, Kansas City was 15–54–1 for 41 points over the 80-game schedule.

The Capitals improved in 1975–76, but the Scouts remained stagnant and drew poorly enough to persuade the NHL that a franchise move was in order. After two dismal seasons in Kansas City, the franchise was transferred to Denver where it was rechristened the Colorado Rockies and gave fans at McNichols Arena little cause for jubilation. (This, incidentally, was not the only switch of the 1976–77 season; the California Golden Seals, formerly the Oakland Seals, were moved to the Richfield Coliseum where they became the Cleveland Barons.)

Eventually the expansion Scouts who had become the

Rockies would relocate once more, becoming the New Jersey Devils in 1982–83. After years of frustration in three different cities, the Devils would become Stanley Cup champions in 1995. Ironically, just one season after the Devils' victory, the Stanley Cup came to Colorado when Denver's second NHL franchise, the Avalanche (newly arrived from Quebec City) became NHL champions. Quebec had entered the league from the WHA, with Winnipeg, Hartford and Edmonton, in 1979 in the NHL's last expansion before the many franchise additions of the 1990s.

WRITING AND BROADCASTING

Dick Irvin

TODAY'S EXTENSIVE ELECTRONIC-AGE media coverage of hockey is a far cry from the days of the scribes who chronicled the game's early eras. The sport has been covered in the press from almost the first time someone on skates took a stick in his hand and chased a small object around a sheet of ice.

Historians trace hockey's roots back to a game called "ice hurley," which was introduced in Nova Scotia by Irish immigrants in the early 1800s. It was a field game in Ireland, and became a game played on ice when the early participants in the sport found themselves confronted by the long, cold winters in Canada.

In 1829 a reporter for the *Colonial Patriot* in Pictou, Nova Scotia, made reference to the game of hurley, calling it "break-shins," which led to pickup games being called "shinny." News of the game began to spread, albeit with different names such as 'wicket' and 'ricket.' The first time the game was written about in the United States may have been in the *Boston Evening Gazette*, November 5, 1859, when a reporter who had visited Nova Scotia referred to the game of "ricket" as a favorite on-ice winter pastime in the area. The name 'hockey' gradually evolved and seemed standard by the year 1863 when a newspaper reported: "…ten months after her marriage, the Princess of Wales rose abruptly from watching her husband play ice hockey and rushed home and delivered a son."

When the first organized indoor hockey game was played between students from McGill University at Montreal's Victoria Rink on March 3, 1875, local and out-of-town newspapers had reporters on the scene. There was a fight in the game, with the reporter from the *Daily British Whig* of Kingston, Ontario writing how "…lady spectators fled in confusion…" when the battle was taking place.

Among the earliest transmissions of the story of a hockey game occurred on December 30, 1896 when the Montreal Victorias played the Winnipeg Victorias for the Stanley Cup. The game was played in Winnipeg and ongoing reports were transmitted by telegraph back to Montreal. The play-by-play was then posted on bulletin boards set up at the Victoria Rink and in the ballroom of the Windsor Hotel. The telegraph transmission of important hockey games continued for many years. Fans of a team playing out of town would gather on the street in front of the local telegraph office, or newspaper, to await the news. In many cases it was relayed to them by someone who would come out of the telegraph office and bellow the latest information through a megaphone. When the Winnipeg Monarchs defeated the Melville Millionaires for the Allan Cup and the senior hockey championship of Canada in 1915, the final game was played in Melville. A report in a Winnipeg news-

paper the next day told of the scene in that city while the game was going on: "Winnipeg went wild with joy when the news was flashed over the wires. Thousands took advantage of the bulletin service to follow the progress of the game which was being played hundreds of miles away. The cheering kept up for hours after the happy news was flashed that the Monarchs had won."

Newspaper reporters had the field all to themselves in those days and became proficient in describing the game, play-by-play style, for their readers. Here's an example from that 1915 Winnipeg–Melville Allan Cup championship game: "Referee Caldwell faced the puck off at 8:35. Mullins secured and passed back to Harry Mackenzie, who gave to Billy and a rush was started for the Monarch goal. Bowman tested Murray with a low shot…" And on it went, a printed play-by-play of the entire game.

The intrepid scribes of that era have to be admired for their skill at reporting the game in that fashion and for their colorful descriptions of what they were watching. They worked, of course, without benefit of television replays, which are a boon today not only for analysts in the broadcast booth but for the print reporters at the game who can look up from their computers to check the slow motion replay. Coverage in the *Regina Leader* of a 1922 game in the Western Canada Hockey League included this description of the hectic finish: "As the minutes went by the Calgary team attacked like famished tigers but they could not break through the local defense. The Regina team shot the puck to the other end to gain time but, try as they might, Calgary could not break through the cordon of athletes which stood in front of the Regina net."

Other descriptive phrases in that 1922 game report included: "Regina attacked with vehemence," and "Laird stopped a hot one." It was mentioned that a dispute over a penalty was "settled amicably." Readers were informed that a Regina rush, "foozled at the Calgary defense."

The first man to broadcast a hockey game on the radio was Pete Parker, who called a Western Canada Hockey League game in Regina between the Regina Capitals and the Edmonton Eskimos on March 14, 1923. Eight days later a newspaper reporter for the *Toronto Star*, Foster Hewitt, was on the air in Toronto broadcasting an Ontario Hockey Association game between Toronto Parkdale and Kitchener for a radio station owned by his employer.

A few years later Hewitt was broadcasting NHL games of the Toronto St. Pats from the Mutual Street Arena. By November 12, 1931 the Toronto team had been renamed the Maple Leafs and Hewitt broadcast the first game played at a brand new Maple Leaf Gardens. That same night a Montreal Canadiens game was heard on the radio for the first time via a French language broadcast from the Montreal Forum as the Canadiens played the New York Rangers. Home games of the Montreal Maroons were also broadcast starting that season, in English. All of this was the forerunner to Hockey Night in Canada.

The first radio network started up January 1, 1933 when a network of 20 stations began carrying Saturday night games from both Toronto and Montreal (in English). At season's end that number had risen to 33 with an estimated audience of more than one million people. Surveys showed that 72 percent of all radios in Canada were tuned to a hockey broadcast on a Saturday night.

Hewitt and the others who were handling play-by-play were on their own. Color commentators had yet to arrive. Hewitt faced his first major test doing a game that began at

8:30 on the night of April 3, 1933 and ended at 1:45 in the morning, April 4. It was a playoff game between Toronto and the Boston Bruins which lasted 164 minutes and 47 seconds before Toronto's Ken Doraty scored the sudden-death winning goal on Boston goaltender Tiny Thompson in the fifth minute of the sixth overtime period. Hewitt called the entire game by himself and admitted afterward he had broadcast the last hour "in a daze," hardly knowing what he was saying.

That Toronto–Boston game was the longest ever played until then but Hewitt lost that particular broadcasting record three years later. On the opening night of the 1936 playoffs the Montreal Maroons and the Detroit Red Wings struggled through 176 minutes and 30 seconds of playing time at the Forum before Detroit's Mud Bruneteau scored the winning goal on Maroons goaltender Lorne Chabot. (Chabot had been the winning goaltender for Toronto in the 1933 marathon against Boston.) Unlike Hewitt, Charlie Harwood had help in the broadcast booth that night. A writer for the *Montreal Herald*, Elmer Ferguson, was working beside him doing color commentary.

Prior to television, hockey on the radio continued to captivate listeners across Canada via the descriptions of Foster Hewitt in Toronto and Charlie Harwood, Doug Smith and Michel Normandin in Montreal. At the same time, American-based teams were starting to air games described by other hockey broadcasting pioneers, including Bob Elson and Lloyd Pettit in Chicago, Bert Lee in New York, Fred Cusick in Boston and Budd Lynch in Detroit.

Television arrived on the hockey scene in Canada in 1952. That spring a closed-circuit telecast of one game of the Memorial Cup series for the junior championship of Canada was arranged in Toronto, with Foster Hewitt calling the play. On October 9, 1952 the first regular season NHL telecast originated from the Montreal Forum as the Canadiens opened the season against the Chicago Black Hawks. Rene Lecavelier, a French-language broadcasting legend in Montreal, handled the play-by-play on Radio Canada. Later that season another legend, Danny Gallivan, would begin broadcasting English language telecasts from the Montreal Forum on CBC-TV.

The Toronto Maple Leafs made their television debut when they played the Boston Bruins at Maple Leaf Gardens on November 1, 1952. Foster Hewitt was the announcer with his son Bill Hewitt taking over on the radio. It wasn't long before the younger Hewitt assumed more of a role on the telecasts while his father continued to work the radio games.

Similar to what happened in radio, the American-based NHL teams began televising their games on a local basis. The CBS network introduced hockey nationally with a "Game of the Week" package that began during the 1959–60 season. The broadcasters were Fred Cusick of Boston and a Canadian, Brian McFarlane, who would go on to a long career as a broadcaster, writer and hockey historian in his native country. Over the years regular network TV coverage in the United States has been sporadic. While there has never been anything comparable to Hockey Night in Canada in the United States, TV coverage on a national basis is broadening. In 1994 Fox Broadcasting signed a five-year, $50 million contract to televise NHL games. Its package begins with the All-Star Game in January and runs through to the end of the Stanley Cup finals. Many NHL teams also have cable-TV coverage of their games, home and away. Sports networks such as ESPN in the United States and TSN and RDS in Canada carry an extensive package of NHL games on a national basis.

The advent of television has meant a change in the way newspaper reporters do their job. There now is not as much play-by-play coverage of the games in print and more in the way of analysis, interviews and off-ice stories. Like the broadcasters, today's newspaper reporters owe a debt of gratitude to those who went before them. American writers who made their mark over the years included Leo Monohan, Fran Rosa and Tom Fitzgerald of Boston, Jim Burchard, Hugh Delano and Al Laney of New York, Ted Damata of the *Chicago Tribune* and Lewis Walter of Detroit.

Writers who are voted into the media section of the Hockey Hall of Fame receive the Elmer Ferguson Award, named in honor of the long time Montreal sportswriter. Other Canadian writers who made significant contributions include: Milt Dunnell, Red Burnett, Jim Vipond and Jim Proudfoot of Toronto and Charles Mayer, Baz O'Meara, Andy O'Brien, Dink Carroll and Marcel Desjardins of Montreal. Montreal's Red Fisher and the prolific hockey writer and historian, Stan Fischler of New York are veteran journalists who are still covering the game. *The Hockey News*, a weekly publication started on a small scale in the NHL's Montreal office in the late 1940s, is now a widely read international hockey institution.

As hockey has expanded, so has the media coverage of the game. The traveling entourage of NHL teams now usually includes representatives from all major newspapers in the teams' cities, plus crews to broadcast the game on radio and television. The media crush in dressing rooms after games, especially during the Stanley Cup playoffs, is unlike anything experienced by players and coaches when the league was smaller and the thirst for stories not as avid. The 1998 All-Star Game in Vancouver was covered by 800 journalists from all over the world.

Hockey Night in Canada on CBC-TV, still a national institution, now televises as many as three games early each Saturday evening during the regular season, plus a later game originating from the West Coast to complete a double-header. In the playoffs the CBC might carry at least one game every night during the five or six weeks leading up to the finals.

Today's fans expect and receive instant coverage both on the air and in print. Modern-day telecasts with their multitude of camera angles and replays are a far cry from the early 1950s when two or three cameras covered the game in black and white. Dozens of games are available on TV every week via satellite. Reporters at games use state-of-the-art computers that are hooked up directly from the press box in the arena to their newspaper back home.

The internet is now in play with up-to-the-minute information on leagues, teams and players available to fans who can surf the net. In 1998 the NHL's own web site, (www.nhl.com) was experiencing more than one million hits a day. It has all come a long way since the early days of the game when fans gathered on street corners awaiting news of a big game clicked to them over the miles by telegraph operators. Those involved way back then had no way of knowing they were pioneering the kind of media coverage which blankets the hockey world today.

THE RISE AND FALL OF R. ALAN EAGLESON

Scott Morrison

THE STORY OF R. ALAN EAGLESON—lawyer, player agent, founder of the NHL Players' Association, father of international hockey, convicted felon—is laced with what are mostly sad ironies. He grew up in the west-end suburb of New Toronto, the son of a factory worker, determined to make something of his life. He did so, becoming, arguably, the most powerful man in hockey, but now, arguably, he is its most disgraced. Once billed as the great emancipator of National Hockey League players, in the end he was proven a traitor and a crook when, in January of 1998, he was sentenced to 18 months in the Mimico Correctional Institute, just a few miles from where he was raised. The reputation and influence he had worked so hard to foster now lay in tatters.

History undoubtedly will remember Eagleson for the last chapter in his hockey career, a plea bargain and the guilty pleas to three counts of mail fraud in a Boston courtroom, then a day later guilty pleas to three more counts of fraud in a Toronto courtroom. And if that is his legacy, then so be it. But history cannot overlook the profound influence Eagleson had on the business of hockey. Some of it was positive, some of it wasn't, but Eagleson was clearly a powerbroker in the sport and the business of hockey for a quarter of a century. Hindsight simply offers clarity to his workings.

It was in 1966 that a young Toronto lawyer named Alan Eagleson was hired by budding superstar Bobby Orr to represent him in contract negotiations with the Boston Bruins. It is another of the many ironies, of course, that severed relations with Orr many years later would ultimately lead to Eagleson's fall from grace.

It was through a friendship with then-Toronto Maple Leafs center Bob Pulford, a friendship cultivated through their mutual involvement in lacrosse, that Eagleson was first introduced to the NHL back in the early 1960s. Eagleson met many of the Leaf greats, including the likes of Bobby Baun, Terry Sawchuk, Carl Brewer and others, through his friendship with Pulford, and Eagleson helped them with their contract negotiations and investments.

But it was the involvement with Orr that got Eagleson started on his remarkable rise to fame and fortune. At the time, in the summer of 1966, the Bruins had offered Orr, an 18-year-old superstar defenseman in the making with the Oshawa Generals, a two-year contract worth about $20,000, including bonuses. When Eagleson was done, however, the two-year deal had swelled to roughly $70,000, a salary stratosphere few had ever visited and the biggest contract ever given to a rookie. After that, as they say, the Eagle was in flight.

That same year Eagleson was asked by players on the Springfield Indians of the American Hockey League to act on their behalf with owner Eddie Shore, a hockey legend who had evolved into a hockey tyrant. The players had decided they could no longer work for Shore unless their working conditions were dramatically changed for the better. When they weren't, the players called in Eagleson, who threatened court action and proceeded to negotiate a settlement with management.

It was during Eagleson's visit to Springfield, though, that he met for lunch with Bobby Orr, who was joined by several of his Bruins teammates. They, in turn, invited Eagleson to meet with the rest of the players and to consider forming a players' union. Eagleson, who had a small stable of clients, gathered player opinion from around the league and within a few months had 110 players sign their support. The other 10 or so verbally gave their blessing. "Al's done more for hockey in two years than anybody else has done in 20," said Chicago Black Hawks superstar Bobby Hull at the time.

In late May of 1967 the brash and energetic 34-year-old Eagleson informed NHL president Clarence Campbell that he would be attending the league's annual meeting in Montreal and would be asking the NHL to recognize the Players' Association. Ten years earlier, of course, a New York lawyer named Milton N. Mound had tried to start a players union, but he was rebuked in his attempt. Many of the players who supported him, including former Detroit Red Wings star Ted Lindsay and Toronto players Jimmy Thomson and Tod Sloan, suffered the consequences by being traded to the last-place Chicago Black Hawks.

But there was no stopping Eagleson, who had virtually all the players in the league onside, and two week's later, on June 7, 1967, he convinced the league's governors to accept the association within 15 minutes of presenting them with the idea. In an article of the day written by journalist Trent Frayne, Eagleson was described in 1967 as being "the most influential figure in Canadian sports since Conn Smythe paid off the mortgage on Maple Leaf Gardens." In subsequent months, Eagleson got the league to raise the minimum from salary from $7,500 to $10,000. A more comprehensive medical plan was introduced and the players' pension plan was improved.

There was no question that for years the players had been underpaid and unappreciated by the owners and they had no retirement protection. To a large extent, Eagleson changed much of that. He vowed in the years ahead to change the standard player contract, to introduce the option clause, to get the players a share of television money, to allow them to pursue and retain endorsement deals, to change the waiver rules and gain greater freedom of movement.

The players finally had someone fighting for and protecting their rights and, at the time at least, they were grateful. No matter how the story evolved, Eagleson's early involvement in hockey, of acting on behalf of Orr and forming the union, changed the game forever. Much of the prosperity the players enjoy today would not have been possible if not for what transpired 32 years earlier.

Outside the NHLPA, Eagleson was expanding the services he offered as a player agent, adding former Leaf trainer Bob Haggert to run promotions and an accountant named Marvin Goldblatt to handle investments. The first prominent agent in hockey, Eagleson's involvement soon led to every player having representation at contract time.

In just a few short years, Eagleson had become a force to be reckoned with in the hockey world. As a player agent and as the executive director of the NHLPA, the Eagleson empire continued to grow, too. Considered by many acquaintances to be a man driven to acquire power, Eagleson had found it and continued to look for more of it.

Outside the hockey world, Eagleson became a Progressive Conservative member of the Ontario legislature in 1963. Five years later, after he had lost his elected seat, he won the presidency of the Conservative party and held the post for eight years, until 1976. His foray into the world of politics didn't dilute Eagleson's involvement in

hockey, however. He had proven from the beginning he was able to juggle many jobs and wear many different hats.

With the promise of enhancing their pensions, Eagleson took his players onto the international stage, beginning in 1972 when he had a hand in creating the first international summit between the powerful Soviet Union and a team of NHL players from Canada. Just how much credit Eagleson deserved for the series happening is a point of debate, but he certainly played a role and the end result was spectacular and far-reaching.

Indeed, it was a series that changed the face of hockey forever. It was eight games, winner take all. The first four games in September, 1972, were to be played in Canada, first in Montreal, then Toronto, Winnipeg and Vancouver. After a 10-day hiatus, the series would switch to four more games in Moscow. In the opinion of most North Americans, the series was going to prove the supremacy of Canadian hockey once and for all. For too many years Canada had sent teams of amateurs to the World Championships and the Olympics like so many sheep to slaughter. This time they would teach the Soviets a lesson.

When it was over, though, the Canadians and Soviets taught each other a lesson, that there was something to be learned from the way both countries prepared and played. And in the years to come, as the Iron Curtain peeled open and then ultimately ceased to be, the NHL would become the future home for players from all over Europe. And it was that 1972 series, won in the dying seconds of that eighth and final game on a goal from Canadian hero Paul Henderson, that changed the game forever. And it was Eagleson who was quick to take control and credit and then to build on this international success.

Two years after the historic summit, the renegade World Hockey Association assembled a team of its Canadian stars to play the Soviets in a similar eight-game series set up without any involvement from Eagleson. But while the WHA team was losing to the Soviets, Eagleson was working behind the scenes on a bigger and better tournament. It was to be called the Canada Cup, a miniature version of the World Cup of soccer, and would be run by Eagleson and the Players' Association, supposedly to benefit the players rather than NHL club owners. Eagleson by this time was the only man in hockey with the clout to make it work.

Through his various offices, he was able to get the NHL's okay for its players to participate in the Canada Cup. He could also deliver the top players to the tournament in his dual roles as super-agent and NHLPA executive director. His growing influence on hockey's international stage ensured the participation of the Soviets, Czechoslovakians, Swedes, Finns and Americans in what would prove to be the finest international tournament the game had seen.

The first Canada Cup was played in the fall of 1976. Subsequent tournaments would take place in 1981, 1984, 1987 and 1991. The host country won four out of five events, with Canada's overtime semifinal victory over the Soviet Union in 1984 and the three-game final in 1987 ranking as tournament highlights. (The format was revived and expanded in 1996 under a new name: The World Cup of Hockey. This time the tournament was a joint venture of the NHL, the NHLPA and the IIHF. Eagleson, no longer director of the NHLPA, was not involved).

While there is no denying that the international tournaments had a positive and profound affect on hockey, Eagleson's detractors would say that the co-operation of the NHL required to stage them was obtained by softening the players' demands for free agency and reducing the owners' pension fund contributions. In 1976, for instance, the players agreed to a collective bargaining agreement that included compensation to be paid to teams losing players to free agency. This compensation was so onerous that it effectively curtailed free agent signings, but in return the players received improvements to their pensions and the owners' approval to participate in the Canada Cup. These pension improvements, however, were funded by proceeds from the Canada Cup. In essence, the Eagleson-led players' association agreed to play games in an Eagleson-run tournament to generate revenue that was used to reduce the pension fund contributions of the NHL's club owners.

There is no denying that Eagleson helped to change the game at many levels and often for the better. He continued to negotiate improvements in collective bargaining agreements with the NHL, but with the benefit of hindsight, appeared to do so at an apparent price to the players. Salaries inched up and pensions improved, though free agency was always an unattainable carrot, negotiated away to keep Eagleson's international hockey ventures alive. In pure on-ice hockey terms, however, these Eagleson-led initiatives on the international front were huge. The results are seen in the number of talented European players that are a part of every NHL roster today.

It was through his involvement in international hockey, of course, that Eagleson became a Canadian icon with the adjectival phrase 'hockey czar' permanently welded to his name. He was the guy the players had to rescue from the grip of Soviet policemen in the final game of the 1972 series, the guy who proceeded to give the Soviet political system a middle-finger salute as the players hustled him across the ice to the safety of their bench. He was Captain Canada.

Eagleson's prominence and power continued to grow through that decade and the next with the start of the Canada Cup tournaments. His stable of clients also grew into the hundreds. He was named a director of Hockey Canada and, despite the apparent conflict of interest, he represented the NHL in all international hockey negotiations. Eagleson was decorated with the prestigious Order of Canada and was inducted into the Canadian Sports Hall of Fame and, later, the Hockey Hall of Fame. He was the friend of all variety of powerbrokers, from prime ministers, to premiers, to Supreme Court justices, to the wealthiest owners in hockey. A man of vision, Eagleson was often regarded as being equal parts bully and genius, driven by power, ambition and, ultimately, greed. But there was always the underlying belief that, character flaws and rough edges aside, Eagleson was helping to grow the game of hockey and make its players richer.

An autocratic ruler, Eagleson usually surrounded himself with his premier clients, negotiated them good contracts and put them in key positions in the NHLPA. When other players would question his power or his conflicts of interest, Eagleson would either beat them down verbally, or would have those players who were well looked-after convince them that all was well. He realized having the superstars onside gave him strength in his dealings with NHLPA members and with NHL team owners.

Critics of Eagleson would suggest he was far too cozy with the owners and league president John Ziegler and that he pushed for the NHL's 1979 expansion to include four former World Hockey Association franchises, effectively

killing the rival league. This deprived the players of considerable leverage, as the loss of the WHA combined with no effective free agency eliminated any pressure for salaries to keep going up. Salary growth was stopped.

Indeed, throughout the 1970s, Eagleson always maintained stability and peace between the players and the owners, supposedly for the over-all betterment of the game, but some say there was too much tranquility, that the labor peace came at a cost for the players and that the lines between labor and management often blurred. Many years later a class-action lawsuit was filed by some former players in Philadelphia charging that Eagleson colluded with former NHL president John Ziegler, chairman of the NHL's board of governors Bill Wirtz and the NHL's member clubs of that era to keep salaries down.

It cannot be denied, however, that the business of hockey grew during the Eagleson years and that when the NHL seemed on uncertain footing, its players didn't topple the league with a strike or labor stoppage. In many ways, it seems, they worked together to keep the game growing. Years later, many wondered whether they worked together more for the benefit of Eagleson and the owners, than for Eagleson and the players.

The first real crack in the Eagleson empire, though, came in April of 1980, when Orr—his first and most important superstar client—parted company with him after Eagleson had steered Orr away from the Bruins to the Black Hawks. Orr, whose career ended prematurely because of a series of severe knee injuries, would later claim he left the game flat broke and that Eagleson had neglected to inform him of an extremely lucrative final offer from the Bruins.

It was later in the decade, though, that others outside the game started to take notice of Eagleson's running of the Players' Association and the many hats he wore. Philadelphia-based lawyer Ed Garvey, a former director of the National Football League union, was hired by some NHL players to look into the affairs of Eagleson and the association. He was joined by two player agents, Rich Winter and Ron Salcer.

They argued that while Eagleson had promised the players much, the NHLPA hadn't gained any significant benefits for the players when compared to other professional sports. They charged in a private 55-page report written by Garvey that Eagleson had too many conflicts of interest, that while he represented the players on one hand, he acted for the owners on the other, and all the while was entrusted with negotiating the collective bargaining agreement between the two.

Eagleson withstood that tempest and others, but two years later in December of 1991, just one month after the FBI had launched an investigation into his dealings, Eagleson stepped down as the head of the NHLPA. He finally left the association he had founded a month after that, replaced during the All-Star weekend in Pittsburgh by Bob Goodenow, a labor lawyer and player agent who was based in Detroit.

Eagleson detractors maintained he had far too friendly a relationship with the NHL and Ziegler and that the union had fallen behind other sports in terms of gains won for its membership. Eagleson was portrayed in some circles as an salty-tongued individual who was out to gain more for himself than for his constituents.

Make no mistake, though, the Players' Association and the business of hockey were in for more and rapid change.

The NHLPA grew into a huge business, expanding its marketing activities, and under Goodenow it was involved in two labor stoppages—a strike and a lockout. But under Goodenow, the average player's salary rose to roughly $1.2 million in 1998. Ten years earlier it was $150,000.

In March of 1994 a Boston grand jury indicted Eagleson and arrest warrants were issued. In November of 1995 the class-action suit in Philadelphia was launched by several former NHL players, many of whom were the same players who once asked Eagleson to start their association.

Finally, in January of 1998 criminal investigations on both sides of the border ended with a negotiated settlement: guilty pleas in two courts, in two countries, a $1 million fine and an 18-month jail sentence. He served five months before entering a work-release program in May 1998, but by that time he had been expelled from the Canadian Sports Hall of Fame and, faced with mounting public pressure, had resigned from the Hockey Hall of Fame. Once the most influential man in hockey, the founder of an association to protect NHL players had ultimately stolen from them. From powerbroker to prisoner.

SCOUTING

Frank Bonello

Frank Bonello is the director of the NHL's Central Scouting Service. Each year Central Scouting evaluates approximately 1,500 players eligible for the upcoming NHL Entry Draft, ranks them and then distributes these rankings to the league's member clubs. Each team in the NHL employs its own scouts and does its own evaluations. Central Scouting's rankings are used by NHL scouting departments as a backup in making their final draft-day decisions.

EVERYTHING the Central Scouting Service does is directed at assessing players' potential to win jobs in the NHL, so our scouts seek out prospects wherever they are found. This means going beyond the primary sources—major junior, top European leagues and NCAA Division I colleges—to include Tier II junior in Canada, junior leagues in Europe and high schools, small colleges and junior clubs in the U.S. The end result is four separate final rankings: two covering skaters and goaltenders playing in North America and two covering the same categories everywhere else. For the purpose of ranking draft prospects, the designations "North America" and "Europe" don't refer to a player's country of origin. Instead they refer to where each player plays in his draft year. Moscow-born Valeri Bure played junior hockey in Tacoma of the Western Hockey League so he was ranked as a North American skater.

Wherever possible, a prospect is seen a minimum of five times, with highly ranked prospects being seen many more times than that. It's dangerous to base a decision on just a handful of viewings, as a player can have a bad game or a great game just when you happen to be scouting him. Both give a distorted picture. A scout's nightmare is when a general manager comes out to see a prospect that the scout is keen on and, in that particular game, the player disappoints. Sometimes this is enough to sour a general manager on that player despite the fact that the scout's high opinion may be based on seeing him a dozen times or more.

A recent addition to the scouting calendar has been top-

prospect games. Junior leagues have arranged special all-star games restricted to those players who have not been drafted. These games, which are usually accompanied by a skills competition, allow scouts to view talented undrafted players in a best-on-best format. A good performance by a player in one of these special games or in a short tournament can enhance his draft rating. It gives the scouts a reason to put him ahead of players of approximately the same potential. Conversely, a sub-par outing has less chance of bringing him down because he has been scouted in so many other circumstances.

We also like to have several scouts evaluate each player to get a wider range of opinion. It's not unusual for our scouts to come up with vastly different player rankings. In 1996 Dainius Zubrus played Tier II junior in Ontario and was ranked 22nd in the CSB's end-of-season rankings, but individual scouts had him rated as high as seventh over all. When the CSB's final rankings and comments on each player are distributed to the NHL's member clubs, the range of scouts' rankings for each player is published along with his overall ranking. (Philadelphia thought enough of Zubrus to draft him near the high end of his CSB range, 15th overall, and he proved to be a capable NHLer right from the start, playing 68 games in the 1996–97 regular season and scoring five goals in the playoffs as the Flyers reached the Stanley Cup finals.)

For forwards and defensemen, we grade from a high of 10 down to zero on each of skating, hockey sense, competitiveness, checking, puck skills and hockey sense, with skating being the most important grade. For goaltenders, we grade on quickness, puck control, competitiveness, skating, agility and, obviously most important of all, ability to stop the puck.

A grade of nine or 10 indicates a "cinch" guy—a Lindros or a Forsberg—who is going to play right away. A seven or an eight is a guy who's definitely going to play, maybe in two seasons. A six or a five indicates that the player is a maybe, likely an American Hockey League player. Our scouts enter game reports into a computer, which sorts the players roughly by the numbers.

In evaluating a player, I like to look at four important characteristics—productivity, competitiveness, talent and consistency. Productivity in hockey can be compared to a salesperson who is well dressed, attractive and makes a great first impression. You think: "This is the guy for me," but if in the end you find out he just can't sell, what good is he? He doesn't produce and that's the bottom line. In hockey, if you don't produce, it doesn't matter what your height, weight and talent are. The only thing that matters is what you do with your talent.

Competitiveness is the most important character trait that a hockey player can possess. Scouts try to answer the same questions for every prospect: Does he compete and to what degree and level? Does he get to the puck? Does he look like he wants the puck? Does he give everything he's got? A player's talents are wasted if he is not competitive. Scouts assess a player's competitiveness by observing his desire to finish a check or make a play. There is nothing more aggravating to a coach than to see a player who has talent fail to compete. This type of player usually doesn't stay too long with one team.

Competitiveness is also closely linked to consistency. Scouts are looking for the player who gives 100 percent all of the time, because you have to assume that that's the

effort that the player's opponents are going to give. Players who give a consistent effort aren't immune from bad games, but their highs and lows don't give a coach fits the way a "streaky" player does. The true streak player makes great plays one game and then lies down the next. Scouts are extremely wary of this "flash" ability. Regardless of how flashy a player might be when he's on a streak, no scout wants to recommend a player tagged as giving a good effort only part of the time. It's one of the reasons we try to see prospects in five or more games.

Though I've just said that without productivity and competitiveness, talent alone won't carry a player, talent remains an extremely important part of any scouting assessment. It is crucial to determine how difficult or easy it is for a player to perform at a high level. Naturally talented players make plays with ease. Less talented players might make the same plays, but have to work so hard to do so. Good players who have to struggle to get the job done—especially at skating—tend to have shorter careers than players who do things with much less effort.

Innate hockey sense is something that a prospect either does or does not possess. It's the magic of the game and is almost impossible to teach. I'm not talking about following a forechecking strategy or not passing the puck through the slot. Those are systems instituted by coaches. Hockey sense is the ability to make the right decision instantly: to shoot or stickhandle on a breakaway or to always find the open man with a pass. You can't teach this, so it's a plus if a player has this ability.

But on top of numerical rankings, there's a subjective analysis that can't be reduced to a computer entry. A player might have high numbers, but if you see that he pulls up in the corners or doesn't have the courage to go in front of the net, what do the numbers by themselves mean? The most complete picture of a prospect's potential comes from a combination of his numerical rankings combined with an assessment of the intangibles that set a top player apart: mental toughness, courage and confidence.

In addition to appraising a prospect's talent and competitiveness, a scout must form an opinion on what makes a player tick because it is the player's inner resources that will be called upon if he's going to meet the challenge of playing the game at its highest level. We have all seen "can't miss" prospects fail to make it in the NHL. These players are ticketed for stardom because they have all the visible talents, but it is usually the intangible qualities that are lacking when a sure-fire prospect can't move up to the next level.

By the time he is being scouted, every player has his own mindset about hockey. Players with a great deal of talent can usually ride their skills upward through youth and junior or college hockey, even if their attitude toward the game and their role in it is suspect. In the NHL, where talent levels are at their highest, pure talent is rarely enough to carry a player to success. The player's mindset often is the deciding factor. The prospect who arrives at his first pro camp committed to doing whatever he has to do to make the club is much better off than the player who comes to camp to see what it's like. If there was a reliable way of assessing this attitude, scouting would be much simpler.

Years ago when I was scouting for the Leafs, Toronto, Pittsburgh, Philadelphia and St Louis shared a computerized ranking system. The computer guys said that the Dallas Cowboys selected their players entirely based on these

rankings. No receiver under 6'3" would ever be considered regardless of what the scouts thought of him and how high he could jump. But hockey just doesn't work that way. "Heart" is a vital quality for a hockey player and can make up for other shortcomings. It's at the center of our discussions when we have our final ranking meetings. A player who we think is soft gets marked down, regardless of how well he skates or shoots.

Scouting for a team rather than for the Central Scouting Service brings with it special pressures. The amount of money paid to top prospects means that scouts are under pressure to pick the right player, particularly with first-round selections. Central Scouting assists team scouting operations by taking on some administrative tasks. Central Scouting publishes an integrated schedule that includes the games in almost all scouted leagues. This helps team scouts plan their itinerary of games. Early in the season, scouts from our bureau also survey Tier II junior, small colleges and high schools so that an advisory can be issued to team scouting departments helping them to focus on those players with potential at these levels.

The job of a team scout is also complicated by the need to modify recommendations to suit a club's most pressing needs. There are two schools of thought on this: pick the goalie, defenseman or forward your club needs to shore up its greatest weakness or pick the best athlete available and, if need be, acquire the specific help you need through trades. The answer is probably an approach somewhere between the two. If there is a group of eligible players with close to the same ability, pick the one that best meets your needs, but if one player is clearly superior, pick him regardless of his position.

At the draft table, it's impossible to rank a good goaltender against a good forward. If you're picking fifth and the top goaltender in the draft is still there, you have to look at your own club's depth. There's always a reluctance to take a goaltender with a high pick, as though it's a waste of draft choice, but that's foolish. The goaltender is the most important position on a hockey team. He's the guy who can win you a game all by himself, so why hesitate to take him third or fourth over all if you need a goaltender? We've seen that over the years, as teams have gotten over this prejudice and have taken goalies higher and higher in the draft. With goaltenders, the guy who is excellent in junior will usually be able to do well in the NHL. Success in junior (or college) is a slightly more reliable indicator for goaltenders than it is for forwards or defensemen, though, curiously, a lot of goaltenders prove to be better as pros than they were before they were drafted. There's no science to what works and what doesn't. Mike Palmateer was a goaltender who hated to practice and couldn't stop a basketball during workouts, but in a game he got himself wound up into such a pitch that he played wonderfully. Dominik Hasek isn't an example of any goaltending fundamentals except concentration and stopping the puck.

The commodity that's in shortest supply is solid defensemen, guys who are really good defensively and solid offensively. It's the old-fashioned type of defenseman, the stay-at-home guy who is scarce in the draft. Most young players would rather play another way, looking to have more fun.

For the last few years, a six-foot defenseman has been regarded as small. With 6'4" wingers, how is a six-foot guy going to move him out from the front of the net? But we're seeing good mobile defenseman at 5'10" or 5'11" who are

draft eligible. I believe that with expansion we're going to see more of these guys make it to the NHL. The expectation of size will have to come down. Today, we still mark a guy down if he's "just" 6'0", but there just aren't enough of the really big guys to go around. We're going to have to adjust our thinking and look for qualities other than sheer size. You can never say never. There are all sorts of guys in the NHL who you'd never have thought would make it. Rob Zamuner wasn't an outstanding junior, but is now an emerging star. We have to do a careful analysis of the kinds of players that have gone on to successful NHL careers and use that information to help us make accurate assessments of future prospects.

In recent years, we have gained additional information about top prospects through physical and medical tests. We operated various testing sites in the past, but beginning in 1998, we brought 100 top prospects, including 12 to 15 Europeans, to Toronto for three days of evaluation. Team scouts and management attend these sessions and have a chance to interview the players.

There are varying views on the value of player interviews to the extent that some teams do interviews and some don't. These days every prospect has an agent and, assuming the agent does his job, he has primed the kid on the kinds of questions that will be asked and the kinds of answers that are expected. They're even taught how to give a good firm handshake. So what does the team really learn in the interview? I wonder what it would have been like if Gordie Howe had been interviewed by Jack Adams when he was 16 and 17. Howe would probably have been too shy to even look Adams in the eye, but that doesn't mean he wasn't ready to play pro hockey.

If a North American player is drafted at 18 and doesn't sign, he can re-enter the draft as a 20-year-old, although the few players who choose this route rarely improve their spot in the draft unless the player dramatically improves between the ages of 18 and 20. If the player is much the same, a general manager would rather pick an 18-year-old because of his greater upside potential. Of course, fairly or unfairly, there's always a bit of a stigma attached to a kid who doesn't sign when he was first drafted. General managers can't help but wonder if they'll be able to sign him when another has already tried and failed.

Players who aren't drafted can stay in hockey by trying out for a minor pro team as a free agent. The East Coast Hockey League is particularly attractive to the undrafted young player.

Another challenge for scouts is trying to evaluate players who are playing against lesser competition. Jeremy Roenick, Brian Leetch and Phil Housley were all drafted when they were playing U.S. high school or prep school hockey. Two years later they were taking a regular turn in the NHL. When you scout a player who's playing high school or Tier II junior, you have to ask yourself: "What does this guy do that he should be able to do anywhere whether its in high school or a church league or in the NHL?" If he's a good skater, he's a good skater. If he can shoot hard here, he can shoot hard in the NHL. If he has hockey sense, he has hockey sense wherever he plays. On the other hand, if a kid is playing defense in high school and is just bowling over much smaller players, he won't be able to do this against the bigger and faster players he'd meet in top level junior or college hockey or in the pros.

Scouting is exceedingly democratic: it doesn't matter where you come from, whether your family is rich or poor

or what language you speak. If you can play, you'll be graded accordingly. There's always a quick positive reaction from a scout when he realizes that he's evaluating a prospect from a hockey family, but in the end the player has to have his own talent to make it. Three Gretzky brothers (Brent, Keith and Wayne) have played professional hockey. Only one made an impression. Three Richard brothers played for the Montreal Canadiens (Claude, Henri and Maurice). Two are Hall of Famers and one is the answer to a trivia question.

Years ago, Sweeney Schriner's son came to Toronto for a tryout with the Maple Leafs. Sweeney, an 11-year NHL veteran, called Stafford Smythe of the Leafs and asked permission for his son to bring a buddy with him to keep him company on his first visit to the big city. Schriner's son never made it, but his buddy turned out to be Ron Stewart, who went on to play 21 NHL seasons.

WAYNE GRETZKY: GREATNESS ASCENDANT

Jack Falla

FOR TWO DECADES, the ethereal Wayne Gretzky has lifted hockey to new and dizzying heights while establishing himself as the greatest player of all time. He transcends hockey and is the most statistically dominant player in the history of North American team sports, an athlete who ranks with basketball's Michael Jordan and soccer's Pele as one of the greatest offensive forces in the history of any sport and a man whose name will be mentioned in the same breath as Muhammad Ali's as one of the greatest athletes of the 20th century. By January of 1998, Gretzky held 62 NHL scoring records and was a certainty to retire with all-time career marks for goals, assists and points. He had an unprecedented 15 seasons with more than 100 points, four with more than 200. "He's made the record book obsolete," said former Minnesota general manager Lou Nanne. "His only point of reference is himself."

In 1997 *The Hockey News* named a committee of 50 hockey experts—former NHL players, past and present writers, broadcasters, coaches and hockey executives—to select and rank the 50 greatest players in NHL history. The experts voted Gretzky number one, ahead of the once seemingly incomparable Bobby Orr and Gordie Howe, who was third. "How great is Gretzky?" said committee member and Edmonton Oilers president and g.m. Glen Sather, who coached Gretzky for 10 seasons. "There aren't enough adjectives. Just look at his records and longevity."

Gretzky has rocketed past milestones so fast the numbers begin to blur into meaninglessness—so many of the records he breaks are his own anyway—but a few marks retain their ability to amaze. On October 26, 1997, in a game against Anaheim at New York's Madison Square Garden, Gretzky pushed back one of hockey's last statistical frontiers when he recorded his 1,851st assist, thus giving him more assists than the NHL's career number two scorer Gordie Howe had goals and assists combined. To put it more compellingly, if Gretzky never scored a goal he would still be the NHL's all-time scoring leader. Those are the kind of numbers that have defined Gretzky, who does not merely advance by small increments the boundaries of what was once thought humanly possible, but instead vaporizes old records, replacing them with new standards seemingly out of mortal reach.

"I think 163 assists in a season will be hard to beat. That and 215 points in a season," said Gretzky of the records he set with Edmonton in 1985–86. "And the 51-game scoring streak will stand for awhile," he said, the reference being to a 1983–84 consecutive game scoring streak that had sports writers across North America comparing Gretzky's accomplishment with Joe DiMaggio's 56-game hitting streak in baseball. But Gretzky had been putting up those kind of numbers long before he came to pro hockey.

378 Goals at Age 10

Gretzky began skating at age two on the Nith River near his grandparents' farm just outside of Brantford, Ontario. By age four, he had graduated to a backyard rink built by his father Walter behind the family's modest three-bedroom home on Varardi Street in Brantford. By age 10, he was scoring 378 goals—still an age group record—and 120 assists in Brantford's atom league. By the time he was 12 and playing in the prestigious International Pee Wee Hockey Tournament in Quebec City's Le Colisee, Gretzky was already so famous that he was besieged routinely by autograph seekers in every rink he played in. Gretzky played Tier II junior at age 14 and major junior at 15. He tried to get his team, the Sault Ste. Marie Greyhounds, to assign him jersey number 9 "because Gordie Howe was my favorite player and that was his number," but 9 belonged to a veteran player so Gretzky was given number 19 and, a few weeks later, number 99.

At 17 he turned pro with the World Hockey Association's Indianapolis Racers who quickly traded him to the Edmonton Oilers, where he was allowed to keep uniform number 99. He won WHA rookie of the year honors with a startling 46 goals and 110 points. Gretzky came into the NHL in 1979 when WHA franchises in Edmonton, Hartford, Quebec and Winnipeg joined the older league and the rest of the cash-strapped WHA disbanded. Many among the NHL cognoscenti thought Gretzky would fade when he started getting banged around in the more physical NHL. They thought wrong. "You can't hit Gretzky with a handful of confetti," said Nanne.

No one ever had seen a player like Gretzky. Though he was barely 6'0" and 155 pounds, could bench press a mere 140 pounds, had little better than average skating speed and possessed a shot that, while accurate, didn't remind anyone of Bobby Hull's, Gretzky's raptorial quickness to the puck, instinct for the creation and exploitation of space and darting elusiveness made him virtually uncheckable. "Gretzky sees a picture out there that no one else sees. It's difficult to describe because I've never seen the game he's looking at," said Boston Bruins president and g.m. Harry Sinden, who had coached Bobby Orr.

In an NHL debut even more impressive than Orr's or Howe's, Gretzky scored 51 goals in 1979–80, 55 in his second season and won the Hart Trophy for the first two of what would be a record eight consecutive selections as the league's MVP. "He's the greatest player I've ever seen," said former NHL goaltending great Glenn Hall, who had played against Orr and Howe and had been a teammate of Hull's. But of all Gretzky's records, the most jaw-droppingly incomprehensible may have been his utter obliteration of Maurice Richard's and Mike Bossy's 50 goals in 50 games, which had stood as a kind mythical statistical barrier since Richard first did it in 1944–45. On December 30, 1981, in a game against Philadelphia, Gretzky scored five goals to reach 50 in an unimaginable 39 games. After the

game and in defiance of NHL protocol, agog Flyers captain Bobby Clarke went into the Edmonton dressing room to tell Gretzky, "I know everything that's been written about you. I think none of it is adequate."

But Gretzky was only warming up. He fashioned a monster season in 1981–82 when he scored an NHL single-season record 92 goals along with 120 assists for 212 points on an Oilers team that gushed with talent. Edmonton had Paul Coffey, the greatest offensive defenseman since Orr, center Mark Messier, who was fast becoming the game's most fearsome power forward, and right winger Jari Kurri, the perfect complement for Gretzky, a quick-shooting, heady player who often veered from his off wing into the high slot to take and convert Gretzky's passes. But the greatest collection of scoring talent ever assembled in the NHL was eliminated in the Stanley Cup divisional semifinals by Los Angeles in 1982 and thoroughly embarrassed in a sweep by the four-time Stanley Cup-winning New York Islanders in the Cup finals of 1983. Hockey's greatest trophy would elude its greatest player until May 19, 1984, when the Oilers broomed the Islanders in four straight in a series that represented not only a changing of the guard but a changing of the game and ultimate validation for Gretzky.

The Sleek Inherit the Ice

In 1984 *Sports Illustrated* raved that "the sleek shall inherit the ice" as Gretzky and the Oilers showed that their hybrid Euro-swirl offense built on speed and backed by an admixture of North American grit could win and win big over orthodox North American bump-and-grind defense. "I hope we're an influence on the game," said Gretzky, shouting to a reporter out of the rollicking chaos and champagne mist of the Oilers championship locker room. "We proved that an offensive team can win the Cup and that can't do anything but help hockey." Winning the first of what would be four titles in five seasons gave Gretzky what he henceforth referred to as "my single biggest thrill in hockey."

Cheers for Tears

On August 9, 1988, 25 days after his marriage to American actress Janet Jones (the media called it "Canada's Royal Wedding") and less than three months after he'd led Edmonton to a fourth Stanley Cup title, Gretzky sat crying at an Edmonton press conference called to announce the trade of Gretzky, Marty McSorley and Mike Krushelnyski to the Los Angeles Kings for Jimmy Carson, Martin Gelinas, three first-round draft picks and—the biggest reason for the biggest trade in hockey history—15 million U.S. dollars to the Oilers cash-deprived owner Peter Pocklington. Gretzky later explained his dissolution to tears by recalling, "The roots that I was cutting off (in Edmonton) were deep. I started thinking of real basic things like scoring and congratulating each other. ... Everything with us was a celebration. We were constantly celebrating something: scoring, winning, championships, records. And ... I just started to cry."

But neither trade nor tears marked the end of the "Gretzky Era." Gretzky won three more league scoring titles, one more MVP award (1989) and led the Kings to the 1993 Stanley Cup finals (where they lost to Montreal), all the while giving the NHL an important boost in the consciousness of U.S. sports fans. What the trade also did was break up one of the greatest teams in NHL history. In the ensuing eight seasons with Los Angeles, 18 games with St. Louis—who acquired him from the Kings for a late season

and ultimately unsuccessful stretch run—and since his arrival with the New York Rangers as a free agent in 1996, Gretzky has not won the Cup. And in a sad touch of irony, on the same day Gretzky was traded to the Kings, a backhoe began digging up the yard behind his parents' house, scooping out the turf that once supported the backyard rink in preparation for the installation of an in-ground swimming pool, a gift from Wayne to his parents. It was that rink that had served as both launching pad and classroom for the game's greatest player.

Lord of the Rink

"Don't go where the puck was, go where the puck is going to be," was the mantra most commonly repeated by Gretzky's father Walter, an amateur hockey player whose understanding of the game far surpassed his modest physical skills. Wayne's eerie prescience about where the puck is going was acquired not only from his father's coaching, but also by young Wayne's curious habit of watching Hockey Night in Canada telecasts while tracing the path of the puck on a piece of cardboard on which he'd diagrammed the outline of a rink.

Wayne manifested an uncommon love for the game and Walter gave that love uncommon time and attention. Walter didn't push Wayne into hockey—"he didn't have to push me; I loved it," said Wayne—but he did everything to support his son's obsession. Family home movies show Wayne, at about age five, stickhandling through a slalom course of rubber cones set up by his father, a telephone repairman with Bell Canada. Walter also installed floodlights over the backyard rink so Wayne could play at night and often would stay out skating with his son long after the neighborhood kids had gone home. "My father and Glen Sather were the biggest influences on my hockey career," said Gretzky. "It's as if my father raised me until age 17, then said to (Sather) 'You take him from here.'" It was Sather who would do the pushing. "If I got 80 goals, Slats would tell me I could've had 85. He was never satisfied. But he always had faith in me (and) he made me a better player," recalled Gretzky. "It would be a crime to have the God-given talent Wayne has and not make the most of it because you didn't push hard enough," Sather explained, a player of modest talents who played with six teams in a nine-year NHL career.

But it is Walter who engendered the critically distinguishing elements of Wayne's game. The father stressed the advantages of making plays from behind an opponent's goal line where, as Wayne said, "You've got the whole play in front of you and the defensemen and goalie turned around." Gretzky has set up so many goals from behind the net that the area is often called "Wayne's office." It was also Walter who showed his son the advantages of curling away from the goal toward the boards, spreading and confusing the defense and creating space for passes to a trailer or a breaking winger. Indeed, if Gretzky has a "branch office" it is the 10 feet inside an opponent's blue line, the staging area for so many of his passes. And it was Walter who gave Wayne the tip that may well account for his largely injury-free career. "Go into a corner at an angle," said Walter, "When you go to the boards be turning quickly so no one gets a clean shot at you."

In his more than 20 years as a pro, few have had a clean shot at Gretzky, partly because of his technique and natural elusiveness and partly because Gretzky usually has been teamed with burly bodyguards such as Marty McSorley and Dave Semenko who would discourage any liberties. It was

Edmonton's Semenko who used to react to gratuitous violence against Gretzky with the chilling invitation to the offending party, "You and me better go for a canoe ride." "But I'm also not a banger and a crasher," commented Gretzky. "Guys who bang and crash wear down."

Gretzky doesn't play with the driving power of a Howe or the Gallic passion of a Lafleur but with a shorebird's sprightliness, flitting in lines and arcs that often seem unrelated to the flow of play until suddenly, inexplicably, Gretzky and the puck are at the same place at the same time. And it is at that joyful confluence that Gretzky will do the unexpected. "When you think he's going to shoot, he'll pass; and when you think he's going to pass, he'll shoot," said goalie Andy Moog, Gretzky's teammate for seven years in Edmonton. "And Wayne's got the lowest panic point in hockey," said Sather, referring to Gretzky's ability to hold the puck long past the point where any other player would have shot, passed or, more likely, turned it over.

"Joy and Energy"

Beyond his genius and imagination the Gretzkian game is also one of light and joy. "I love it," he enthused, "I love every part of it. Skating, playing, joking around with the guys in the dressing room." In Walter Gretzky's book *Gretzky*, Wayne is quoted as saying of his years in Edmonton, "It's just as well that I lived in a penthouse. If I lived at street level, the winter would come and I'd see kids playing road hockey, and before you know it I'd be out there with them and there would go my game that night."

Gretzky's love for the game is obvious even to those who know nothing of hockey. The late pop artist Andy Warhol, who painted a portrait of Gretzky in 1981, was asked what he saw in his subject: "As an artist, what I see in Wayne is great joy and energy," he said. Warhol added, "I think it's great when a sports star can look like a movie star." "The big thing with me is that I play emotionally," says Gretzky. "I used to let the emotion run away with me. If I got fouled I'd blame the ref ... now my attitude is, if the ref calls it, fine. If not, I'm not going to change his mind."

And the Days Dwindle Down

Though he is clearly now in the December of his career, Gretzky, in March of 1998, said he would play at least one more season with the New York Rangers, whom he led in scoring in 1997–98. "Even after I retire as a player we hope to stay in New York," says Gretzky whose sons Ty and Trevor play youth hockey on the same Manhattan team— both are forwards—and whose daughter Paulina is studying at New York's American Ballet Theater School, an achievement Gretzky likens to being "on an all-star team."

"I'd like to stay in hockey but not as a coach," he says. "I couldn't teach anybody else to do what I do because so much of it is instinctive." He says his principal involvement in hockey likely will be as a part-owner of the Canada-based hockey equipment maker Hespeler in which Gretzky invested during 1997. "I'm not just letting them use my name. I've made a serious financial investment in this company and I want to see us succeed," he says. But for now the game is the thing. "If there's been one big change in me it's that now I enjoy the moment more, I savor it ... and I think more about something my father once told me: 'Enjoy every shift because each one brings you one shift closer to your last.' "

HOCKEY ON THE INTERNET

Tom Hoffarth

IT REALLY SHOULD COME AS NO SURPRISE that the incredible popularity of hockey on the Internet has grown proportionally with the intensified enthusiasm that fans have for the sport all over the world. Fact is, the demographic studies done by those who are paid to know such things continually underscore one thing: if you play on the World Wide Web, you buy hockey tickets. Fans of both fall under the same general category—males in the 18 to 34 range making a decent living and leading an active lifestyle. Not to typecast—women's participation on both the Web and in the game has been loud and clear as well. But what has happened, then, is a very content marriage of the Web and the sport. The two come to complement each other in ways no other sport has enjoyed. It has become more than just an intense pastime for those who can't get enough information from the traditional media of radio, newspapers and television. For many, it has become a lifestyle.

The Internet, of course, is a 24-hour-a-day service station pumping information, opinion and any other kind of eye candy imaginable. It is accessible anywhere on the planet by anyone with a computer, a modem and the time to zip along a keyboard typing in strange-looking addresses that make no sense to anyone in the "outside" world. Experts predict more than 150 million people on the planet will use the Internet by the year 2000, a jump over the estimated 112 million who used it in 1998. In the United States alone, more than a third of the 103.2 million projected households will have Internet access. By some estimates, the Internet already accounts for about 20 percent of the total news intake by people who also have access to other media.

This black hole that constantly is referred to as cyberspace so far has come to produce no boundaries, making the possibilities endless to those who grease the wheels of its progress. And as most full-time experts involved in the Internet agree, we are nowhere near realizing the full potential of this technology. Consider this point in time as the world before the invention of electricity. You haven't seen anything yet.

Estimates are that more than 300 million Web pages are out there to be read, with hundreds added each day. By the year 2000, that total could be expanded by yet another 1,000 percent. A search for the word "hockey" on one of any Internet search engines may come up with more than 200,000 Web pages on more than 2,000 sites, but even this method of tracking down hockey-specific information is not quite fully reliable yet.

Those are the numbers that can either intimidate or initiate those who are simply courageous enough to grab a Web browser and surf the title waves.

For starters, every team in the National Hockey League has staked a claim on the World Wide Web. Every player employed by the NHL has his own a Web page on the NHLPA's site. The NHL has one of the most expansive sites on the 'Net. So does the Hockey Hall of Fame. So does every minor hockey league, European hockey leagues, semi-professional leagues. Anything with a stick, a puck and a net is on the 'Net.

But so is, it seems, the cyber thumbprint of every fan of the game who has learned the HTML coding. They've got something they're pretty sure no one else can offer, and here's the forum to show off their wares. Essentially, the

hockey community has embraced the Internet to a point that one can hardly imagine what it was like not to have this kind of cyber-universe bringing everything together.

Today, as the Internet continues to evolve and people find new ways to incorporate it into their day-to-day activities, most of the websites dedicated to pro teams have become accepted as extensions of the marketing department of each team—a place where fans can camp out and be deluged. A standard NHL team website, for example, has news about the organization, current schedules and rosters, ticket information (and, most importantly, the capability to take an order), fan club chat rooms, souvenirs to buy, plus an historical background. It may also have contests, trivia games and other interactive elements to entice the enthusiast.

The sites with a bit more sophistication introduce video and audio clips to those with the proper downloaded software. Listening to home games on the computer through the radio broadcast ignites those who have felt out of touch with their teams because they may have moved to another city. Future options likely will include watching a game on the computer, which will be hooked up to the television, along with the ability to pick and choose camera angles. The team locker rooms also could be viewed live, so computer users could watch the coach map out plays between periods and then listen as he talks to the players. So much technological advancement already has occurred in such a brief time that speculating on hockey's future on the Internet could be as wild as the imagination cares to make it. A click of the mouse could make those dreams come true before you have a chance to explain what just happened. As those Web masters in charge of these projects like to say, this is all just another work in progress.

In general, information about hockey is part of the fare at several all-purpose sports sites like ESPN SportsZone (http://espn.sportszone.com/nhl/), CBS Sportsline (http://-sportsline.com/u/hockey/), CNNSI (http://www.cnnsi.com/-hockey/) or the Yahoo! search engine site (http://-hockey.yahoo.com/). But more in-depth and narrow-targeted information is just as simple to find.

Any search for NHL information should start with the NHL's Interactive Cyber Enterprise (ICE), which has been one of the leaders in showing the 'Net's current capabilities and hinting to what's coming up. No other pro sports league can boast what this site (http://www.nhl.com) has accomplished, thanks in part to a partnership with computer giant IBM, which keeps up the state-of-the-art software. NHL ICE was the first to combine Web pages with all the teams in the league into a one-stop linked site. Schedules, statistics, daily scores, recaps, a fan forum and an NHL store is just the beginning of the site. A feature called "Grab the Mike" allows fans to pick any player in the league and grill him with questions just like Don Cherry. For example, there have been discussions with Jeremy Roenick about the escalating player salaries, with Chris Chelios about his favorite hockey commercials, even with referee Paul Stewart about his thoughts on what it takes to officiate NHL games. Another weekly feature, "Where Are They Now," profiles the game's legacy. Players who were featured during the 1997–98 season included Ken Morrow, Marcel Dionne, Craig Simpson, Mike Eruzione, Tiger Williams, Eddie Mio, Mike Bossy and Stan Mikita. Because the NHL owns the video rights to its games, there's never a lack of video clips on the site. Miss the sports news last night? Create your own highlight package with a 28.8-or-faster modem. What many click onto as their favorite place on NHL.com, how-ever, is live game-calls. Every NHL game is available free via RealAudio or NetShow plugins, from either team's flagship station, French or English (when available). Here, computer users all over the world—especially in Europe—keep close contact with their countrymen. So it's no surprise NHL teams like Detroit and Pittsburgh are the most popular on the site.

"We want to be the website of record, so the idea is to give fans everything—not just scores and recaps, but things they can't get anywhere else," said Refet Kaplan, the senior producer of NHL.com. "As a result, we have fans from Sweden and Finland especially that don't get any NHL information on a day-to-day basis except from this site. If Peter Forsberg or Teemu Selanne are doing anything in the NHL, they want to know about it. And the site is constantly in the state of re-evaluation. What we can't do today, we might be able to in a few months. We're determined to keep up with technology and the fan's desire to get more and more information faster and faster."

It's been a hit, all right. NHL.com experienced its greatest volume of visitors on March 24, 1998 when it received 9.1 million hits (the term hit refers to how many times each page is used by a computer visitor). Why that particular day? It was the league trading deadline.

If the Internet is youth-based, the NHL hasn't overlooked its next wave of fans. In March, 1998, it launched NHL4KIDS.com, combining interactive and educational games with features, contests, giveaways and access to much more. "This website was developed as part of an ongoing effort to target younger fans for the NHL," said Dina Gilbertie, vice president of youth marketing for the league. "We wanted to give kids a place to go where they could learn more about the game of hockey, but offer it in a way that had educational value and fun attached to it."

While the league has made huge strides with its sites, the league's players have developed their own identity through the NHLPA's website (http://www.nhlpa.com). Player sites with more than 2,500 photos allow fans to zero in on a particular favorite. Even if you're not sure how to spell the player's name, a search feature allows you to type in either the first or last name and presents a list of all those matches. Everything officially licensed by the NHLPA also is available, including trading cards, electronic games, jerseys, collectibles and fantasy games. The NHLPA biographies are a virtual cyber-trading card that include a player profile, current year stats and career stats for regular season and playoffs.

Also included are current compensation figures. Wayne Gretzky, for example, is listed as a $6.5 million man for those who wondered about his salary in 1998. That kind of information isn't available on Gretzky's own official site (http://www.gretzky.com), one of the few maintained by an all-sports website production team (in this case, CBS SportsLine, which also has sites built for basketball's Michael Jordan and golf's Tiger Woods). Nor are the fans who maintain a site for goaltender Martin Brodeur (http://www.martinbrodeur.com) and go so far as to advertise it weekly in *The Hockey News* about to dampen anyone's image of their idols by throwing around salary figures.

Although websites come and go on a frequent basis, we feel confident some will be helpful to those who are interested in exploring many other aspects of the game. The dedication of the Web masters on these sites is a dramatic example of the passion they have for the game, and they only want to share with all who want to know.

For example, women's hockey information: (http://-www.whockey.com or http://www.cs.utoronto.ca/~andria-Womens_hockey_info.html). Welcome to Andria Hunter's obsession. Taking her Masters of Science Knowledge from the Department of Computer Services at the University of Toronto, Hunter's hockey knowledge can be taken to new heights. The Peterborough, Ontario native attended the University of New Hampshire on a hockey scholarship and played on Canada's gold medal women's hockey team at the Women's World Championships in 1992 and 1994. She also played a year in Switzerland for DHC Langenthal of the Swiss women's A league. She also played at the University of Toronto. She says when she first started accessing the World Wide Web in 1994 there was no women's hockey information to be found, so she took it upon herself to organize the site. She covers local, national and international women's hockey, has a mailing list for those interested in getting more involved, references to Usenet Newsgroups (alt.sports.icehockey.women and alt.sport.hockey.women) and girls youth hockey discussions. Other topics include women in sports discussion forums, information on how to organize a women's tournament, playing and coaching opportunities in the soon-to-be formed Women's Professional Hockey League and college and club coaching opportunities. Also, there are links to sites like the Female Hockey Goalie's page (http://www.lookup.com/Homepages/89887/f_g.html) as well as home pages of women's hockey teams from all over the world, women's hockey equipment companies, articles on the subject, books, magazines and the women's display in the Hockey Hall of Fame.

Hockey magazines and newspapers: (http://www.geocities.com/Colosseum/Track/7342/). A list of almost every American and Canadian newspaper, magazine and journal that regularly features hockey stories, official and selected unofficial team pages, statistics and various hockey miscellany, covering the NHL, AHL, IHL, ECHL, WPHL and UHL. Compiled by New York Rangers fan Carole Sussman.

Hockey Hall of Fame: (http://www.hhof.com) and the United States Hockey Hall: (http://www.ushockeyhall.com/). The palace in Toronto and the one in Eveleth, Minnesota founded in the early 1970s offer virtual tours of the facilities, membership and souvenir hunting.

Disabled Hockey: (http://www.sledhockey.com). In Sweden and Canada, it's known as sledge hockey; in America, it's sled hockey. Either way, it's a way for people with various lower extremity disabilities (amputations, spinal cord injuries, cerebral palsy, etc.) to play the game on ice, using their arms to propel themselves by digging picks on the ends of two short hockey sticks and pulling themselves forward. The right and left sticks are miniature copies of a typical hockey stick except for the metal picks that are like a figure skate toe pick. Players are seated on the sleds, which are affixed to two hockey skate blades under the seat. The sleds are about three inches off the ice and between two and four feet long. The pucks, pads and checking are all the same. This is the site for the U.S. National Sled Team, but it includes links to the Official Paralympics, Disabled Sports USA, the British Sledge Hockey Association and the Cruisers Sledge Hockey team in Ontario, Canada.

Vintage table hockey games: (http://www.interlog.com/~reynolds/game/game1/html). If you've never heard of the Munro National Six-Men Hockey Game, said to be the world's first commercially successful game of its type, website creator Peter Reynolds has been building replicas of the 1954 model game as a pastime and wants to let everyone know about them. He also attempts to present a history of table hockey since there are no books about the subject he can find and companies that made these games long ago are no longer in business.

Backyard rinks: (http://www.barint.on.ca/byrinks/-index.html). Damian Agostini, from Barrie, Ontario thought that many of today's parents were too busy and tired after working all day to find quality time to spend with their children, so he created a company that makes safe do-it-yourself backyard ice rinks.

The science of hockey: (http://www.exploratorium.edu/-hockey/). Why is ice slippery? How fast is your reaction time? How much energy is generated by a mid-ice collision? How do you slap a puck 100 miles per hour? The site's author, Jim Spadaccini, has all the answers in easy-to-understand examples.

Fantasy hockey: they're abundant and exuberant about their existence. One quick example: Eddie Shore's Old Tyme Hockey League (http://members.tripod.com/~othl/), a 20-team APBA computer hockey league "competing in the spirit of Eddie Shore and Reg Dunlop," with teams in six states and two provinces.

The movie *Slap Shot*: (http://www.hansonbros.com). This is the official site of the Hanson brothers, made famous in the 1977 hockey cult movie staring Paul Newman. Other non-official sites include information from the aforementioned Eddie Shore fantasy league (http://members.tripod.com/~othl/slapshot.htm) and from the Daniel Rose Slap Shot site (http://luna.cas.usf.-edu/~rose/).

The Wildest Misfits in Hockey History: (http://www.-interlog.com/~ig/). Get to know Tiger Williams, Eddie Shore, Harold Ballard, Bugsy Watson, Spinner Spencer, Guy Lafleur, John Kordic, Bob Probert, Darius Kasparaitis, Don Cherry, the Hanson Brothers, Howie Young, Ching Johnson and Eddie Shack. To name a few.

Hockey's future: (http://www.hockeysfuture.com). Sound mysterious? It's really an in-depth look at the minor leagues along with NHL draft prognosis and a fan's list of his own top 50 websites.

The Joy of Hockey: (http://www.joyofhockey.com). A fellow named David Joy maintains the site. It's unofficial. It doesn't claim to be anything more than just a celebration of the game. Does he need any other excuse?

Need more sites? Set your own Web browser to a search engine and type in the word "hockey." The exploration is limitless.

A list of websites is found on page 128.

HOCKEY WEBSITES

GENERAL HOCKEY INFORMATION

ESPN SportsZone   http://espn.sportszone.com/nhl/
CBS Sportsline   http://sportsline.com/u/hockey/
CNNSI   http://www.cnnsi.com/hockey/
Yahoo! search engine   http://hockey.yahoo.com/

LEAGUE SITES

The official NHL site   http://www.nhl.com
The official NHL site for kids   http://www.nhl4kids.com
The official NHL Players' Association site   http://www.nhlpa.com
The American Hockey League   http://www.canoe.ca/AHL/home.htm
The International Hockey League   http://www.theihl.com/
The East Coast Hockey League   http://www.echl.org/

STAR PLAYERS

The Wayne Gretzky site   http://www.gretzky.com
The Martin Brodeur site   http://www.martinbrodeur.com

WOMEN'S HOCKEY

Women's hockey information   http://www.whockey.com
Female hockey goalies page   http://www.lookup.com/Homepages/89887/f_g.html

HALLS OF FAME

Hockey Hall of Fame   http://www.hhof.com
United States Hockey Hall of Fame   http://www.ushockeyhall.com/

MISCELLANEOUS

Backyard rinks   http://www.barint.on.ca/byrinks/index.html
Disabled hockey   http://www.sledhockey.com
Europeans in the NHL   http://www.euroreport.com/
Fantasy hockey   http://members.tripod.com/~othl/
The future of hockey   http://www.hockeysfuture.com
Goalie nicknames   http://www.angelfire.com/id/goalienicknames
Hockey nut   http://www.hockeynut.com/
Ice power   http://www.icepower.com
The hockey page of info   http://www.geocities.com/College Park/Quad/2387
The joy of hockey   http://www.joyofhockey.com
The wildest misfits in hockey history   http://www.interlog.com/~ig/
North Americans playing in Europe   http://www.geocities.com/Colosseum/5282/
Great hockey photos   http://www.bbshockey.com/bbs.htm
The science of hockey   http://www.exploratorium.edu/hockey/
"Slap Shot" movie sites   http://www.hansonbros.com
     http://members.tripod.com/~othl/slapshot.htm
     http://luna.cas.usf.edu/~rose/
Snacks for hockey   http://livingbeyondreality.com/Home.html#anchor510718
Vintage table hockey games   http://www.interlog.com/~reynolds/game/game1/html

PUBLICATIONS

SLAM! Canadian Sun newspapers hockey   http://www.canoe.ca/Hockey/home.html
The Hockey News   http://www.thn.com
The Sporting News   http://www.sportingnews.com/nhl/
Hockey newspapers and magazines   http://www.geocities.com/Colosseum/Track/7342/

BROADCASTERS

Canadian Broadcasting Corporation hockey   http://www.hockey.cbc.ca/
Fox Sports   http://www.foxsports.com/hockey/
The Sports Network   http://tsn.ca/nhl/

LINKS

Comprehensive college hockey links   http://www.ptialaska.net/~carlsonj/uafhockey/ehockey.html
Comprehensive European hockey links   http://www.enol.com/~liebmann/hockey/europe.htm

CHAPTER 16

Inside the National Hockey League

Off-ice Action: Understanding the Business Side of Hockey

Gary Meagher

At a meeting of representatives of hockey clubs held at the Windsor Hotel, Montreal, the following present, G.W. Kendall, S.E. Lichtenhein, T.P. Gorman, M.J. Quinn and Frank Calder, it was explained by the last named that in view of the suspension of operations by the National Hockey Association of Canada Limited, he had called the meeting at the suggestion of the Quebec Hockey Club to ascertain if some steps could not be taken to perpetuate the game of hockey.

Frank Calder was elected to the Chair and a discussion ensued after which it was moved by T.P. Gorman, seconded by G.W. Kendall: 'That the Canadiens, Wanderers, Ottawa and Quebec Hockey Clubs unite to comprise the National Hockey League'. The motion was carried.

It was then moved by M.J. Quinn seconded by G.W. Kendall that: 'This League agrees to operate under the rules and conditions governing the game of hockey prescribed by the National Hockey Association of Canada Limited'. The motion was carried.

At this stage, Mr. W.E. Northey, representing the Toronto Arena Company asked to be admitted to the meeting and was admitted. Mr. Northey explained that he was empowered by the interests he represented to say that in the event of a league being formed to contain four clubs, the Toronto Arenas desired to enter a team in the competition.

Upon this assurance M.J. Quinn on behalf of the Quebec Hockey Club declared the latter willing to withdraw provided a suitable arrangement could be made regarding players then the property of the Quebec Hockey Club.

After discussion it was unanimously agreed that the Quebec players be taken over by the league at a cost of $700 of which amount 50% should be paid to the Quebec Hockey Club by the club winning the championship, 30% by the second club and 20% by the third club in the race.

The meeting then proceeded to the election of officers. The following directors were elected S.E. Lichtenhein (Wanderers), Martin Rosenthal (Ottawa), G.W. Kendall (Canadiens) and a director to be named by the Toronto club.

M.J. Quinn was elected Honorary President with power to vote on matters pertaining to the general welfare of the league.

Frank Calder was elected President and Secretary-Treasurer at a salary of $800 on the understanding that there could be no appeal from his decisions.

After a schedule of Wednesday and Saturday games was adopted the meeting was adjourned.

From the Minutes of the
First NHL Board of Governors Meeting
November, 1917

ON THE ICE, the National Hockey League officially had its beginnings on December 19, 1917 as the Montreal Canadiens defeated Ottawa 7–4 and the Montreal Wanderers downed Toronto 10–9. Those historic games, however, were preceded by more than a month of meetings and backroom dealings by a group of gentlemen that were entrusted with the formation of the National Hockey League (NHL) following the demise of the National Hockey Association (NHA).

These meetings began in early November as the National Hockey Association's directors—S.E. Lichtenhein of the Wanderers, G.W. Kendall of the Canadiens, T.P. Gorman of Ottawa and M.J. Quinn of Quebec along with NHA secretary-treasurer Frank Calder—attempted to keep the league afloat. The numerous franchise problems in the preceding season, however, eventually led the NHA executives to start anew.

At the historic Board of Governors meeting from November 24-26 at Montreal's Windsor Hotel, the National Hockey League was formed. The crude 25-page constitution of the National Hockey Association, the predecessor of the NHL, was adopted as the governing document of the new league. As president-elect Calder told a sparse gathering of media in the late afternoon hours of Monday, November 26, the purpose of the new league was "the fostering and furtherance of the game of hockey to be governed by bylaws and rules."

While there were more than 250 owners meetings over the next half century which dealt with all aspects of developing the game, the second most important piece of off-ice business enacted by the Board of Governors took place on June 7, 1967 when the National Hockey League officially recognized the NHL Players' Association as the exclusive bargaining agent "for all of the present and future hockey players employed by the clubs with respect to certain terms and conditions of employment."

Eight years later, on May 4, 1976, the first Collective Bargaining Agreement was printed and distributed.

More than 80 years after its founding, the National Hockey League is still governed by a Board of Governors comprised of owners and club management personnel who establish the policies of the league and who, along with NHL commissioner Gary Bettman, uphold the 306-page *Lex Scripta* containing the league's constitution, bylaws and resolutions. Those documents, along with the 150-page *Collective Bargaining Agreement* between the league and the NHL Players' Association comprise the basis for managing the game off the ice.

Following is an "A-Z" look at the inner workings of today's National Hockey League along with some historical perspective on numerous aspects of the game and business.

AGE OF PLAYER

Today, a player must turn 18 years of age by September 15 of the year in which he is eligible to be drafted by an NHL club. The requirement that a player be 18 years old prior to competing in the NHL was first introduced in 1950 when then NHL president Clarence Campbell negotiated an agreement with all North American professional leagues that moved the age limit for signing players or placing their names on negotiation lists from 16 to 18.

Armand "Bep" Guidolin was the youngest player ever to play in the NHL. Guidolin was only 16 years old when he made his NHL debut for Boston in November 1942. Guidolin would go on to play nine years for Boston, Detroit and Chicago.

Patrick Marleau of the San Jose Sharks was as young as a player can be when he was drafted second overall in 1997. Marleau was born on September 15, 1979, and was the exact minimum age for 1997 draft eligibility. He made his NHL debut less than three weeks after his 18th birthday on October 1, 1997.

ASSIST

Before the beginning of the 1931–32 season a formal definition of an assist was adopted for the first time by the NHL's Board of Governors. It read as follows: "A goal shall be credited in the scoring records of a player who shall have propelled the puck into the opponent's goal. When such a goal shall have been scored as a result of an act of a player of the same side, such player shall be credited in the scoring records with an 'assist'. An assist may not be credited, however, to a player unless the act of 'assistance' took place within the defending zone of the opposing team. If a goal was scored from a rebound from a goal-keeper or from any part of the goal, credit for an 'assist' shall be given to the player whose shot caused such rebound."

BENCHES

In 1978–79, to remove an unfair advantage that some teams had in their home rinks where their player bench was located on the same side of the ice as the penalty bench (thus allowing for a quick substitution for a player when his penalty expired), the NHL introduced a rule that required that the player benches for both teams be located on the same side of the ice. A waiver was provided to teams whose buildings were built prior to 1978 to maintain their benches in their current position. By 1988–89, however, all teams were required to have both the home and visiting benches on the same side of the ice with the penalty bench located on the opposite side. This meant significant renovations in some NHL buildings.

BOARD OF GOVERNORS

The NHL is governed by a Board of Governors which establishes the policies of the league and upholds the constitution and bylaws. Each NHL club appoints a governor as well as alternate governors who are vested with the full power and authority to represent their club and bind it by their vote. The Board of Governors has two scheduled meetings during the year (June and December) as well as special meetings as necessary.

There is also a Chairman of the Board, a position first created in 1953. The chairman is elected for a two-year term.

The Board of Governors was officially formed in November 1925.

CENTRAL REGISTRY

The NHL's Central Registry Department is responsible for maintaining all player information. It maintains the NHL clubs' reserve lists which contain the names and vital status information of all players a club has proprietary rights to, either contractual rights or exclusive negotiation rights. It records the status of each player with regard to contracts, waivers, free agency etc. It tracks a player from the first time he is drafted until the completion of his career as a player.

CENTRAL SCOUTING

NHL Central Scouting (CSS) was established prior to the start of the 1975–76 season as a service for the NHL member clubs. CSS supplies the NHL clubs with personal and hockey information and rankings on draft-eligible players throughout the world; schedules, team rosters and directories for amateur leagues; weekly reports on injuries and roster changes of draft-eligible players; and video on draft-eligible players.

CSS consists of nine full-time and six part-time scouts, a director of scouting, and an administrative staff. The scouts file reports from more than 3,000 games throughout North America and Europe during a hockey season as well as coordinate medical and fitness testing for more than 150 draft-eligible players.

Two player rankings are done each season—one in late January and the final ranking in May.

COMMISSIONER

The NHL commissioner, as selected by the Board of Governors, serves as the chief executive officer of the league and is charged with protecting the integrity of the game and preserving public confidence in the league. The commissioner has the responsibility for the general supervision and direction of all business and affairs of the league and has all such powers as may be necessary or appropriate to fulfill his responsibilities.

The office of commissioner was created in December 1992 with the appointment of Gary B. Bettman. Mr. Bettman assumed office on February 1, 1993. Five others have served as the league's chief executive officer under the title of president. The five men are: Frank Calder (1917 to 1943); Mervyn "Red" Dutton (1943 to 1946); Clarence Campbell (1946 to 1977); John Ziegler (1977 to 1992) and Gil Stein (1992–1993).

CONSTITUTION, NHL

The purposes and objects of the National Hockey League, as stated in its constitution are:

a) To perpetuate hockey as one of the national games of the United States and Canada.

b) The promotion of the common interests of the members of the league, each member being an owner of a professional hockey club located in the United States or Canada.

c) The promulgation of rules governing the conduct of play of hockey games between the member clubs in the league, the relationships between players and member clubs, between member clubs and the league and between the member clubs and other hockey clubs, to the end that the public may be assured of a high standard of skill and fair play, integrity and good sportsmanship.

d) The arbitration and settlement of disputes between the

member clubs and between member clubs and players.

e) The education of the public, through advertising, radio and other media, to the end that professional hockey, as played according to the standards of the league, may gain popular support and acceptance as a wholesome entertainment.

f) The development of youth in mind and body and the teaching of fair play and good sportsmanship through the media of hockey.

CANADIAN SUPPLEMENTARY CURRENCY ASSISTANCE PLAN

The Canadian Supplementary Currency Assistance Plan was adopted on January 5, 1996. The plan has two key features to assist eligible Canadian clubs in addressing the disparity between the United States and Canadian dollars.

Canadian clubs in the bottom half of NHL revenues are eligible for assistance. Eligible clubs must qualify annually for assistance by either having revenues that are at least 80 percent of the NHL average or by selling defined numbers of season tickets, arena suites and dasherboards. Eligible qualifying clubs may receive up to $5 million in United States funds. The precise amount of assistance that eligible qualifying clubs will receive will depend on the magnitude of the currency differential, club revenues and the available pool for distribution.

Eligible Canadian clubs may also receive a subsidy for Group II players to whom they have tendered a qualifying offer and who receive offer sheets from U.S. teams. By way of example, if a player is presently earning $1 million in Canadian funds and is offered $1.5 million in U.S. funds and the currency differential is 40%, the subsidy would be calculated as follows.

1. New contract (CDN$) = $1.95 million
2. Old contract (CDN$)   = $1 million
3. Difference   = $950,000
4. Currency factor   = 40%
5. Subsidy   = $380,000 (CDN)

COLLECTIVE BARGAINING AGREEMENTS

The current Collective Bargaining Agreement between the NHL and the NHL Players' Association runs through September 15, 2004.

The NHL clubs first recognized the National Hockey League Players' Association as the exclusive representative of all players employed by the clubs in June 1967, prior to the NHL's first expansion from six to 12 teams.

From 1967 until the execution of their first formal Collective Bargaining Agreement on May 4, 1976, the clubs and the NHLPA reached agreements on business matters through collective bargaining, which were reflected in minutes of owner-player meetings, in standard players' contracts and in an arbitration agreement relating to said contracts.

On May 4, 1976, the NHLPA and the clubs published their first comprehensive, printed Collective Bargaining Agreement (CBA).

Although the CBA's stated term would not expire until September 30, 1980, one of the points agreed to was that the clubs and the NHLPA would continue the process of collective bargaining throughout its duration, through an "owner-player" council which would meet twice a year.

Through the establishment of this process of continuing negotiations, the players and owners were able to amend the CBA in May 1977, September 1977, January 1978, February 1979, June 1979, August 1979 and November 1979.

On August 1, 1981 a second comprehensive CBA between the clubs and the NHLPA was printed.

The CBA's stated term would expire September 15, 1984 but an ongoing dialogue continued which resulted in numerous changes to the agreement in the interim.

On November 1, 1984 a third comprehensive CBA between the clubs and the NHLPA was printed, which clarified existing terms that had previously been agreed to and incorporated all amendments to the prior CBA then in effect. The next expiry date for the CBA was September 15, 1986.

On June 1, 1988 a fourth comprehensive CBA was printed with the stated term set to expire on September 15, 1991.

The 1991–92 NHL season began without a CBA in place. Negotiations between the NHL and NHLPA were unsuccessful in averting a strike by the players on April 1, 1992. This spurred negotiations and a retroactive two-year CBA was reached on April 10. It would expire before the start of the 1993–94 season. *(See Labor Disruptions on page 136.)*

The 1993-94 season was also played without a CBA in place. Negotiations of varying levels of intensity took place through September of 1994. The NHL's club owners locked out the players, postponing the start of the 1994-95 season for what would prove to be 103 days. Play resumed on January 20, 1995. Teams played a 48-game schedule. *(See Labor Disruptions on page 137.)*

The CBA that resulted from the lockout had a clause that would have allowed either side to reopen negotiations, but that reopener was waived by both parties in October 1995. On June 25, in connection with the addition of four new expansion franchises on June 25, 1997, the agreement was extended through September 15, 2004.

CONTRACT, STANDARD PLAYER'S

A standard player's contract is an agreement between the club and player for a specified term for a specified salary. Following is a summary of some of the clauses contained in the Standard Player's Contract.

• A player is paid in consecutive semi-monthly installments from the commencement of the regular season until the conclusion of the regular season.

• A player agrees to give his best services to the club that has signed him and to play hockey only for that club unless his contract is release, assigned, exchanged or loaned by his club.

• A player also agrees to provide his services and to play hockey in all regular-season, All-Star, international, exhibition and Stanley Cup playoff games.

• If a player, in the sole judgment of the club's physician, is disabled and unable to perform his duties as a hockey player by reason of an injury sustained during the course of his employment as a hockey player, including travel with his team or on business requested by the club, he shall be entitled to receive his remaining salary due in accordance with the terms of this contract for the remaining stated term of this contract (excluding option period).

• The player and the club recognize and agree that the player's participation in other sports may impair or destroy his ability and skill as a hockey player. Accordingly the player agrees that he will not during the period of his contract engage or participate in football, baseball, softball, hockey, lacrosse, boxing, wrestling or other athletic sport without the written consent of the club.

• The club recognizes that the player owns exclusive rights to his individual personality, including his likeness. The player recognizes that the club owns exclusive rights to his name, emblems and uniform which the player wears as a hockey player for the club.

DEVELOPMENT CLUB

Some NHL clubs maintain a player-development club in one of the professional minor leagues, while others either share minor-league clubs or have working agreements to provide a certain number of players to a specific minor-league club.

ENTRY DRAFT, COMPENSATORY DRAFT SELECTION

Compensatory draft selections were introduced for the first time in the 1995 Entry Draft as a means of compensating clubs that are either unable to sign first-round draft choices or lose a Group III free agent who re-signs with another club and the club that lost the Group III free agent fails to sign another Group III free agent of equal or greater value. The determination of the value of these players is based on salary, honors earned, and certain performance achievements. A club may not receive a Group III compensatory pick until at least the 11th pick in the second round of the next following Entry Draft.

In the event that a club loses its draft rights to an unsigned rookie drafted in the first round of the Entry Draft, who is again eligible for the Entry Draft or becomes an unrestricted free agent, a compensatory draft selection is automatically granted to the club. The compensatory draft selection is the same numerical choice in the second round in the Entry Draft immediately following the date the club loses the rights to the player. For example, if a club cannot sign the third overall choice in the first round, it will receive the third choice in the second round of the next Entry Draft as compensation.

ENTRY DRAFT, DRAWING

The NHL draft drawing is a weighted lottery system that has been used since 1995 to determine the order of selection in the first round only of the Entry Draft for the non-playoff clubs from the previous season as well as expansion clubs (when applicable).

The draft drawing was adopted by the NHL's Board of Governors on March 24, 1994 in order to protect the integrity of the Entry Draft and the regular season, while continuing to ensure that the teams with the poorest records get the best selections. The club winning the draft drawing may not move up more than four positions in the draft order, while no club can fall back more than one position as a result of the draft drawing.

Under the weighted lottery system, the non-playoff team with the fewest regular-season points has the greatest chance of winning the drawing. Fourteen balls, numbered one to 14, are placed in a lottery machine and four are randomly drawn. There are 1,001 possible combinations and each of the clubs involved is assigned a specified number of those combinations. For example, in the 1998 draft drawing, the club with the fewest regular-season points received 280 (28%) possible combinations. The next club along with the expansion Nashville club each had an 18.5% chance of winning the drawing; while clubs four through 11 followed with a 10.9%, 7.9%, 5.7%, 4.1%, 2.8%, 1.9%, 1.2% and 0.5%, respectively, chance of winning. The combinations are assigned to the clubs by a computer on a random basis.

In 1995, Los Angeles moved from seventh to third by winning the drawing; Ottawa and Boston both retained the number-one draft position by winning the drawing in 1996 and 1997, respectively. Because clubs may trade future draft picks, the result of the drawing may sometimes appear complicated: Tampa Bay received the right to select first overall in 1998 as a result of two trades earlier in the 1997–98 season. The numbers assigned to Florida were selected at the draft drawing, but the Panthers had traded their first-round pick to San Jose earlier in the 1997–98 season, while Tampa Bay later that season made a trade with San Jose which gave the Lightning the option to trade first-round picks with the Sharks.

ENTRY DRAFT, LENGTH

The annual Entry Draft consists of nine rounds plus up to one round of compensatory draft selections.

ENTRY DRAFT, ELIGIBILITY

All players age 19 or older are eligible for claim in the Entry Draft except:
• A player on the reserve list of a club, other than as a tryout;
• A player who has been claimed in two prior entry drafts;
• A player who previously played in the league and became a free agent pursuant to the Collective Bargaining Agreement;
• A player age 21 or older who played hockey for at least one season in North America when he was age 18, 19 or 20.

In addition, any player who will be age 18 on or before September 15 in the year in which such Entry Draft is held, or reaches his 19th birthday between September 16 and December 31 inclusive, next following the Entry Draft, can become eligible by providing written notice to the league on an opt-in form.

ENTRY DRAFT, ORDER OF SELECTION

The draft drawing determines the order of selection for the first round of the Entry Draft. For rounds two through nine, the order of selection is determined as follows: teams not advancing to the playoffs draft in reverse order based on regular-season points, followed by those teams advancing to the playoffs. It is possible for a team finishing with more points to draft earlier than a team with fewer points, if the first team missed the playoffs because of the ranking in its respective conference.

ENTRY DRAFT, UNSIGNED DRAFT CHOICES

A player selected in the draft is registered on the club's reserve list as an "unsigned draft choice" and the club maintains exclusive right of negotiation up to and including June 1 of the calendar year next following the date of his selection. If a "bona fide offer" is made, the period of exclusive right of negotiation is extended up to and including the second June 1. The offer may be conditioned upon acceptance by the player within 30 days.

An unsigned draft choice who enters into an agreement with any organization or person other than the NHL club or club or with a club in a league affiliated with the NHL, may be retained on the reserve list as a "defected player." The NHL club may retain such a player on its reserve list for as long as the agreement is in effect.

A player selected in the draft who is either a college student at the time or becomes a college student by the next

June 1 following his draft, may be retained on the reserve list of a club so long as he remains a college student and thereafter for a period of 180 days plus the period between the end of said 180 days and the next June 1. A college player may also elect to be tendered a player contract at any time by filing the proper notice.

ENTRY DRAFT PLAYERS, EUROPEANS

All European players must be drafted by an NHL club prior to competing in the NHL. This, however, was not always the case. Beginning in the early 1980s the league began to phase in the process of drafting European players. By the late 1980s, the present-day rule was in place.

Players under contract to teams in International Ice Hockey Federation member countries may be signed by an NHL club in the year in which they are drafted through and including August 15. Once the signing deadline has passed, players under contract to IIHF teams or having signed a contract during the season with an IIHF team may not be signed by a National Hockey League club until the conclusion of the IIHF team's season.

ENTRY LEVEL SYSTEM, ASSIGNING OF 18- AND 19-YEAR-OLDS

During the first two seasons following the drafting of an 18-year-old player, the club he signs a contract with must first offer him to the club from which he was claimed before it may assign him out of the NHL.

During the first season following the drafting of a 19-year-old player or a player who reaches age 19 between September 16 and December 31, inclusive, of the year of his draft, the club he signs a contract with must first offer him to the club from which he was claimed before it may assign him out of the NHL.

A player aged 18 or 19 who was selected in the first three rounds of the Entry Draft and who has not been signed by his NHL club may not be retained by the club and must be returned to his junior team no later than the day prior to the opening of the NHL regular season.

A player aged 18 or 19 who was selected in the fourth or subsequent rounds who has not been signed by his NHL club may not be retained by the club and must be returned to his junior team no later than the fourth day prior to the opening of the NHL regular season.

An NHL club may not retain the services of a junior player signed after the start of the season, except under emergency conditions or after his junior club is no longer in competition.

With respect to forwards, an 18- or 19-year-old junior player may be recalled when the NHL club is in what is known as a third emergency (fewer than 16 skaters available to play). For defensemen, a junior player may be recalled when the NHL club is in a second emergency (fewer than 17 skaters available to play). With goaltenders, a junior may be recalled at any time when the NHL club is in an emergency.

An 18- or 19-year-old player may be assigned to the minor-league affiliate of his club when his junior team is no longer competing provided he has been listed on the club's minor-league eligibility list.

A junior player who signs an NHL contract and is subsequently returned to his junior team is entitled to receive a salary of $8,500.

ENTRY LEVEL SYSTEM, COMPENSATION

The Collective Bargaining Agreement has, since 1995, included a salary cap on entry level players as follows:

Draft Year	Entry Level Cap
1995	$850,000
1996	875,000
1997	925,000
1998	975,000
1999	1,025,000
2000	1,075,000
2001	1,130,000
2002	1,185,000
2003	1,240,000
2004	1,295,000

Other provisions of the entry level compensation system include:

• Maximum annual compensation includes salary and all bonuses other than certain specified legitimate performance bonuses. Bonuses, other than performance bonuses, are limited to 50% of player's annual compensation.

• Amounts of permitted bonuses can be individually negotiated by players.

• An entry level player has no rights to salary arbitration.

• Mandatory two-way contracts with the maximum minor-league salary component at no more than 50% of the NHL minimum. NHL minimum is at $150,000 through the 2000–2001 season.

ENTRY LEVEL SYSTEM, PLAYERS

Players 18 through 21 years of age when signing their first NHL contract must sign a three-year contract. Players age 22 and 23 when signing their first NHL contract must sign a two-year contract. while those age 24 when signing their first NHL contract must sign a one-year contract. Players who are 25 or older when they sign their first contract are not subject to the entry level system.

In the event that a signed 18- or 19-year-old player does not play at least 10 NHL games (regular season and/or playoffs) in his first season under contract, the term of his player contract and his number of years in the entry level system will be extended for a period of one year. The exception to this is a 19-year-old player who turns 20 years of age between September 16 and December 31 in his first contract year.

In the event that a player signs his first contract at age 18 and has had his Player Contract extended pursuant to the above, and such player does not play at least 10 NHL games (regular season and/or playoffs) in the second season under that player's player contract, then the term of his player contract and his number of years in the entry level system shall be extended for one additional year.

EQUIPMENT/UNIFORMS

Helmets — In 1979 all players entering the NHL were required to wear a helmet approved by the NHL's Rules Committee. Those in the league prior to 1979 were not. Beginning in 1992-93, all players had the option to play without a helmet, though only a handful did so. Craig MacTavish was the last player to go bare-headed.

Beginning in 1997, regulations were amended to require that certified helmets be worn by all players who either already wear a certified helmet or are 25 or younger.

Skates — In 1960, the Boston Bruins and Montreal Canadiens began wearing an improved skate that featured an injury-reducing plastic guard fitted to the rear end of the

blade. At the NHL's annual meeting in 1961, use of the CCM Pro-Guard Heel was made mandatory for all forwards and defensemen commencing with the 1961–62 season.

Sweaters – In August, 1970, the NHL's Board of Governors passed a resolution allowing the home team to put names on the back of player sweaters. Visiting teams could do the same only with the consent of the home club. Beginning with the 1977–78 season, it became mandatory for all players to have names on the backs of their sweaters.

Beginning in 1930 it became mandatory for each player to wear a number, measuring at least 10 inches in height, on the back of his sweater.

Sticks – The league first placed a limit on the maximum curvature of a stick blade in 1966–67 (½"). The maximum curvature was increased in 1968–69 to 1½" and reduced to 1" in 1969–70. The current maximum curvature (½") was adopted in 1970–71.

The approval for the use of an aluminum shaft stick by NHL players was first given in the 1981–82 season.

Goaltenders' facemask – Journeyman goaltender Andy Brown (who played for Detroit and Pittsburgh in the early 1970s) played his last NHL game on March 31, 1973 against the St. Louis Blues. Brown's appearance marked the last time an NHL goalie appeared in a game without the protection of a facemask.

The league began measuring goaltender pads and blockers on December 15, 1996.

EXPANSION

During the 33-year period between 1967 and the year 2000, the NHL will have expanded its membership from just six teams (in 1966–67) to 30 teams (in 2000–2001). The league's most active periods of expansion occurred in 1967 when its grew from six to 12 teams and during the 1990s when it moved from a 21-club league to its upcoming membership total of 30 teams.

First Expansion—1967: California (Seals), Los Angeles (Kings), Minnesota (North Stars), Philadelphia (Flyers), Pittsburgh (Penguins) and St. Louis (Blues) were added to the league, each paying a membership cost of $2 million.

The 1967 expansion process formally began on March 11, 1965 when then NHL president Clarence Campbell stated that the league "proposes to expand its operations through the formation of a second six-team division." Just under 12 months later the process was completed, when on February 7 and 8, the Board of Governors considered 14 different expansion applications, including five groups from Los Angeles, two from Pittsburgh and one each from San Francisco, Philadelphia, St. Louis, Minneapolis-St. Paul, Baltimore, Buffalo and Vancouver. St Louis was not represented at the meeting as an ownership group had yet to emerge. Cleveland and Louisville, Kentucky had also expressed interest but were not represented.

The procedure for stocking the new teams saw each of the "Original Six" teams protect 11 skaters and one goaltender with the expansion teams each drafting 18 skaters and two goaltenders. A "claim and fill" procedure was used during the draft that allowed a team that had had a player claimed by an expansion club to add one more player to its protected list.

Second Expansion—1970: Buffalo (Sabres) and Vancouver (Canucks) increased the league's membership from 12 to 14 teams. Each paid a membership cost of $6 million.

The origins of the 1970 expansion can be traced to the

financial difficulties of the California Seals. In December 1967, only three months into their inaugural season, the NHL began to lend the California franchise money so that it would be able to complete its first season. The financial difficulties of the California franchise led to a request in February 1969 by a Vancouver group to buy and transfer the team to the Canadian west coast city. At the same meeting, a Buffalo group represented by Seymour and Northrup Knox and Robert Swados offered to purchase the franchise and continue to operate it in the Bay area in the event the Vancouver proposal was rejected. By June 1969 they would own a portion of the California club.

The league formally adopted its plan of second expansion in October 1969 with the objective to add two new teams for the 1970–71 season. The plan included a franchise for Vancouver "if an acceptable applicant applies prior to December 1, 1969". Informal applications had been received from Atlanta, Baltimore, Buffalo, Cleveland, Kansas City and Washington D.C. By December 1969, conditional franchises had been awarded to Buffalo and Vancouver.

To stock the two new teams, each of the 12 existing teams protected 15 skaters and two goaltenders, with Buffalo and Vancouver selecting 18 skaters and two goaltenders. The two clubs also received the first two draft positions in the 1970 Amateur Draft.

Third Expansion—1972: Atlanta (Flames) and New York (Islanders) increased the league from 14 to 16 teams. Each was added at a membership cost of $6 million. In addition, the Islanders had to make a $4 million indemnity payment to the New York Rangers for moving into their home territory.

The 1972 expansion was actually part of a three-phase plan adopted by the Board of Governors on November 8, 1971 to counteract the plans of the newly formed World Hockey Association. In phase one, the league identified Atlanta and Long Island as desirable locations for franchises.

Phase two of the plan called for the admission of two new members for the 1974–75 season. Cities identified by the league as being potential members included Cleveland, Kansas City, Miami, Seattle, Portland (Oregon) and the Washington/Baltimore area. Phase three called for the NHL to expand to at least 24 teams during the 1970s. The league identified the need for additional teams in the Western part of the U.S. and in Canada.

To stock the Atlanta and New York Islanders franchises, each of the existing 14 teams protected 15 skaters and two goaltenders with the new clubs selecting 19 skaters and two goaltenders. The Islanders and Atlanta selected first and second, respectively, in the 1972 Amateur Draft.

Fourth Expansion—1974: Kansas City (Scouts) and Washington (Capitals) each were added for a franchise fee of $6 million, increasing the league's membership from 16 to 18 teams.

The Board of Governors reviewed 11 applications from eight different groups: Kansas City (four applicant groups) and one each from Cincinnati, Cleveland, Dallas, Indianapolis, Phoenix, San Diego and Washington.

The same draft procedures for both the Expansion and Amateur drafts in 1972 were used, with the exception that the two new teams drafted 22 skaters and two goaltenders each.

Following its fourth expansion, the league went about attempting to realize its stated goal of 24 teams by 1979. Prospective ownership groups from Denver, Seattle and San Diego were interviewed with the former two even

being granted conditional franchises in June 1974. Both groups, however, failed to meet the conditions of their membership.

Fifth Expansion—1979: The NHL's fifth expansion saw membership grow to 21 teams with Edmonton (Oilers), Hartford (Whalers), Quebec (Nordiques) and Winnipeg (Jets) paying franchise fees of $6 million each.

The addition of the four clubs from the World Hockey Association came in June 1979 after more than a year of discussions in which other WHA teams (Houston and Cincinnati) also attempted to gain entry into the league.

To stock the four former WHA teams now joining the NHL, each of the existing 17 teams protected 15 skaters and two goaltenders. Each of the four expansion teams drafted 15 skaters and two goaltenders and were also permitted a maximum of four priority selections from their 1978–79 WHA playing rosters. In the Entry Draft (formerly known as the Amateur Draft), the four expansion teams selected in the 18th through 21st positions.

Sixth Expansion—1991, 1992, 1993: San Jose (Sharks) was added for the 1991–92 season, bringing NHL membership to 22 teams. Ottawa (Senators) and Tampa Bay (Lightning) were added for the 1992–93 season, bringing NHL membership to 24 teams. Anaheim (Mighty Ducks) and Florida (Panthers) were added for the 1993–94 season, bringing NHL membership to 26 teams. The membership cost of each of the franchises from the sixth expansion was $50 million. The process by which the above teams were added is described here:

1991: In December 1989, the NHL's Board of Governors agreed in principle to become a league of 28 teams by the end of the century. On May 9, 1990, the Board approved the awarding of a conditional expansion franchise to the then owners of the Minnesota North Stars, George and Gordon Gund. On the same day, the Board also approved the sale of the North Stars to a group consisting of Howard Baldwin and Morris Belzberg.

1992: The 1992 expansion process began in June 1990 when the league sent out expansion application forms to 50 interested parties throughout North America. By August, a total of 11 applications representing 10 cities were received. The cities were: Hamilton, Houston, Miami, Milwaukee, Ottawa, Phoenix, San Diego (two), St. Petersburg, Seattle and Tampa Bay. Houston, San Diego, Milwaukee, Seattle and Phoenix would all withdraw from the process prior to formal presentations to the Board on December 5, 1990.

1993: The league had already identified Anaheim and South Florida as attractive expansion locations when the Board formally announced the two newest additions on December 10, 1992.

Seventh Expansion—1998, 1999, 2000: The league begins the process of growing to a 30-team league in 1998 with the addition of Nashville (Predators). Atlanta (Thrashers) will become the 28th team in 1999–2000, and Columbus (Blue Jackets) and Minnesota (Wild) make their debut in the 2000–2001 season.

The league's seventh expansion process began on June 26, 1996 when its was announced that the NHL would begin accepting applications for expansion teams. By November 1, 1996, the league had received 11 applications—Atlanta, Columbus, Hamilton, Houston (three applications), Minneapolis-St. Paul, Nashville, Norfolk/Virginia Beach/Newport News (Hampton Roads), Oklahoma City and Raleigh-Durham.

On January 13–14, expansion applicants' presentations

were made to the league's Expansion Committee and on February 19, the NHL announced that the list of active expansion applicants had been reduced from 11 to six. The applicants that remained under consideration were: Atlanta, Columbus, Houston, Minneapolis-St. Paul, Nashville and Oklahoma City. On June 17, 1997 the Expansion Committee formally recommended the addition of Nashville, Atlanta, Columbus and Minneapolis-St. Paul and on June 25, 1997 the league's Board of Governors approved the four new teams at a membership cost of $80 million per franchise.

FREE AGENCY

If a club makes a qualifying offer of contract to a player who does not have sufficient professional experience to qualify for Group II free agency, it maintains exclusive negotiation rights to him and he is not eligible for free agency.

FREE AGENCY, GROUP II PLAYER

Any player who meets the qualifications set forth in the following chart and is not a Group I player or a Group IV player, and is not an unrestricted free agent, becomes a Group II restricted free agent upon the expiration of his contract.

FIRST CONTRACT ELIGIBLE FOR GROUP II FREE AGENCY

SIGNING AGE	
18-21	plus three years professional experience
22-23	plus two years professional experience
24+	plus one year professional experience

Clubs must make qualifying offers to Group II free agents to maintain its rights of right of first refusal and/or draft choice compensation. A club's qualifying offer must be 110% of the prior year's NHL salary to players making the NHL average salary or less. For players earning more than the NHL average salary, the qualifying offer must be 100% of the prior year's NHL salary. The player's old club shall have the right to match any offer and retain the services of the player or, if it elects not to match, to receive draft choice compensation. A qualifying offer for players aged 26 or older must be at least $474,440 for the old club to retain the right to match, the amount is indexed annually beginning with the 1997–98 league year based on increases in the NHL average salary.

FREE AGENCY, GROUP II COMPENSATION

The level of draft-pick compensation that a club receives for losing a Group II free agent is determined by the salary offer the player receives from his new club. The following chart depicts the compensation that the player's old club is entitled to.

SALARY OFFER	DRAFT CHOICE COMPENSATION
$474,440 or below	None
$474,441 to 652,355	One 3rd round choice
$652,355 to 770,965	One 2nd round choice
$770,966 to 948,880	One 1st round choice
$948,881 to 1,186,100	One 1st round and one 3rd round choice
$1,186,101 to 1,423,320	One 1st round and one 2nd round choice
$1,423,321 to 1,660,540	Two 1st round choices
$1,660,541 to 2,016,370	Two 1st round and one 2nd round choice
Over $2,016,370	Three 1st round choices
Each additional million	Additional 1st round choice up to maximum of five

Clubs owing one pick must have it available in the next draft. Clubs owing two picks in the same round must have them available within the next three entry drafts. Clubs

owing three draft picks in the same round must have them available in the next four drafts and so forth. Clubs owing two draft picks in different rounds must have them available in the next draft. Also, clubs must use their own picks and not picks acquired from other clubs.

FREE AGENCY, GROUP II OFFER AND FIRST REFUSAL PROCEDURE

Once a Group II player signs an offer sheet from a new club, his old club, if applicable, has seven days to match that offer and retain the services of the player.

FREE AGENCY, GROUP III PLAYER

Any player who is 31 years of age or older as of June 30 of the end of the 1997–98, 1998–99, 1999–2000, 2000-01, 2001-02, 2002-03 or 2003-04 season and has four accrued seasons shall, if his contract expires, become an unrestricted free agent. Such player shall be completely free to negotiate and sign a contract with any club without restriction.

FREE AGENCY, GROUP IV PLAYER

A Group IV player is defined as a player who has never signed an NHL contract and who becomes a free agent after having met the conditions for a defected player. The NHL club owning his rights must make him a qualifying offer and receives only the right to match any offer sheet signed by the player with another NHL club.

FREE AGENCY, GROUP V PLAYER

A Group V player is defined as a player who has completed 10 or more professional seasons (minor league or NHL, excluding junior) and who did not earn in the final year of his contract more than that year's average league salary. This player may elect, once in his career, to negotiate and sign a contract with any club without restriction.

FREE AGENCY, GROUP VI PLAYER

A Group VI player is defined as a player age 25 or older who has completed three or more professional seasons, whose contract has expired and, in the case of a skater, has played less than 80 NHL games (regular season and/or playoffs), or in the case of a goaltender, less than 28 NHL games. A Group VI player is an unrestricted free agent at the end of his contract.

FREE AGENT, LIST

On July 1 of each year a free agent list is issued setting forth the names of those players who are free agents as of that date.

INJURED RESERVE LIST

A club may place a player on the injured reserve list if such player is injured or disabled and unable to perform his duties as a hockey player by reason of an injury sustained during the course of his employment as a hockey player after having passed the club's initial physical examination in that season.

A player who has an injury that renders him physically unable to play for a minimum of seven days after the date of the injury can be placed on the club's injured reserve list. Once a player is placed on injured reserve, the club may replace said player on its NHL roster with another player. All determinations that a player has suffered an injury warranting injured reserve list status must be made by the club's medical staff and in accordance with the club's medical standards.

A player placed on injured reserve is ineligible to compete in NHL games for a period of not less than seven days from the date of injury. A player will be eligible for activation beginning the eighth day from the date of injury.

Players on injured reserve may attend club meetings and meals, travel with their club and participate in practice sessions.

LABOR DISRUPTIONS

During its more than 80-year history, the NHL has been virtually free of labor strife. There have been only two labor disputes that forced the postponement of regular-season games—a 10-day players' strike in April 1992 and a 103-day lockout during the 1994–95 campaign.

There has also been one strike by on-ice officials. On November 15, 1993, the 58 members of the NHL Officials' Association initiated a strike. The strike lasted 16 days. The league and the NHLOA agreed upon a four-year collective bargaining agreement on November 30, 1993. Referees and linesmen returned to duty on December 2.

Details of the 1992 strike and 1994 lockout follow:

1992 Players' Strike

The process which led to the players' strike in 1992 actually began on May 14, 1991 when the NHL owners announced their intention to extend the Collective Bargaining Agreement by one year. This declaration was pursuant to a clause in the CBA which stated that a notice of termination and proposed revisions be provided "not less than 120 days prior to the 15th day of September, 1991." The league claimed that the NHLPA's notice of termination and proposed revisions on May 14 was defective as it did not provide any proposals for a revised CBA. The league later requested that the matter be heard by an arbitrator, while the NHLPA balked at any negotiations as long as the threat of an arbitration loomed.

On August 20, 1991, the league withdrew its request for arbitration thereby meeting the NHLPA's request and a month-long period of negotiating began in earnest. While the season commenced as scheduled in October, bargaining sessions ground to a halt between September 25, 1991 and March 9, 1992.

Numerous bargaining sessions during the month of March 1992 yielded very little in the way of progress, however, and on March 20, with the playoffs imminent, the NHLPA announced a strike deadline of March 30 if no agreement were concluded by that time. Forty minutes before the players were to strike NHLPA executive director Bob Goodenow announced a postponement of the deadline until April 1. On April 1, 1992, at 3:00 p.m. ET, with no agreement in place, the NHL players announced that, by a vote of 560–4, they would commence the first league-wide players' strike in NHL history.

A few moments later, President Ziegler announced at a news conference in the Sutton Place Hotel in Toronto: "It is with deep regret that I advise that effective 3:01 p.m. (EST) April 1, 1992, I have declared the 1991–92 NHL season suspended on a day-to-day basis until further notice. This action is required by reason of the unprecedented and regretful decision of the National Hockey League Players' Association to go on strike. Our concerns are for and with the great fans of hockey who will suffer the most from the action taken today by the NHLPA."

Despite the doom and gloom, little time was wasted getting back to the bargaining table as several negotiating sessions took place between April 1–7. Ziegler delivered a final offer to the NHLPA on April 7, with the provision that the offer be accepted by 12 noon Friday, April 10. Failing acceptance, the clubs would be unable to conclude their season and there would be no Stanley Cup playoff games. Later that day (April 7), less than four hours after receiving the offer, the NHLPA rejected the league's offer. Nevertheless, the offer remained open for acceptance until 3:00 p.m. on April 9. A marathon 14-hour bargaining session in New York eventually concluded with a new two-year Agreement (1991–92 and 1992–93) shortly before midnight on April 10.

At a news conference beginning at 12:04 a.m. on April 11 at the Plaza Hotel in New York, President Ziegler stated: "I'm pleased to report that after a very long day, at times a very difficult day, a day that demonstrated the spirit that traditionally has been between owners and players, we came to a meeting of the minds with respect to the essential provisions and have reached an agreement in principle."

Goodenow stated, "I guess to me the turning point was on Wednesday (April 1), I'd say about 6:00 p.m. There were some owners who came to Toronto with John Ziegler, and I had a feeling then that there was an ambition, a dedication to get this thing taken care of."

The season resumed on Sunday, April 12 with 11 of the remaining 30 regular-season games played. A full slate of Stanley Cup playoff games then ensued.

1994 Lockout

On May 10, 1993 the NHL Board of Governors voted not to terminate the CBA which was set to expire on September 15, 1993. Instead they wished to allow the agreement to remain in effect for an additional year in order to afford ample opportunity to reach a new comprehensive agreement. Ten days later, on May 20, Goodenow advised Bettman that the NHLPA had decided to end the CBA that September. Bettman said at the time: "The clubs had decided that, notwithstanding their unhappiness with numerous aspects of the agreement, the most prudent course was to opt for a year of stability and careful planning, in the hopes of avoiding the possibility of contentious labor negotiations during the summer and fall. We know that there are a great many issues to be resolved and we look forward to working closely with the players on those matters. We are disappointed that the agreement had to be reopened at this time. We will negotiate diligently and in good faith to reach a new CBA as soon as possible."

The league played under an expired Collective Bargaining Agreement for the entire 1993–94 season.

Over the 18 month period from June 1993 through January 1995, representatives of the NHL and NHLPA would meet formally and informally more than 40 times, but an agreement would not be reached until the NHL had closed its doors for 103 days from October 11, 1994 until January 20, 1995.

There was a five-month hiatus in the talks from March until August 1994, and when the negotiations did resume on August 19, 1994 it was against the backdrop of a series of takebacks in a 19-point plan (valued at $20 million) which the league intended to implement on September 1 in the absence of a new CBA. The intended purpose of the threat of the takebacks was to get the negotiations back on track, but following a two-hour meeting with the union, Commissioner Bettman stated, "We did not make as much progress as I would have hoped. It was a very small step in terms of the substance."

While the threat of a lockout loomed, training camps did open as scheduled on September 4 because of the fact that negotiations were in full swing in an attempt to reach an Agreement. By September 30, however, with no agreement in sight, the league announced a two-week postponement of the opening of the regular season. If an agreement was reached by then, a full regular-season complement of games would begin on October 15. By October 11, the NHL's Board of Governors voted to postpone indefinitely the start of the season and less than two weeks later (October 24), announced the cancelation of four games. Ten more games were lopped off the schedule on November 2. NHL stars such as Toronto's Mats Sundin and Doug Gilmour, Pittsburgh's Jaromir Jagr and Quebec's Peter Forsberg made their way overseas to maintain their conditioning in European leagues.

A month of more talks still produced nothing and on December 12 the Board of Governors authorized Commissioner Bettman to cancel the season if a 50-game schedule could not be played. January 16 was identified as the last possible starting date in order to play 50 games.

Finally, after two days of marathon bargaining (January 9–10) between the two principle negotiators—NHL commissioner Gary Bettman and NHLPA executive director Bob Goodenow—the league's offer was accepted, subject to ratification, by the NHLPA. A new six-year CBA was in place through September 15, 2000. Training camps opened on January 13 and a 48-game 1995 regular season began on January 20.

LAST LINE CHANGE

The rule which provides the home team with the last change of players prior to the resumption of play was introduced for the 1990–91 season.

"LAST MINUTE OF PLAY"

The NHL first required that a public address announcement be made of the last minute of a period for the 1946–47 season.

MARKETING THE GAME

In the second half of the 1990s the National Hockey League has taken a new view of the marketing of the game. The key principle in this new approach is exposure. Sponsorship agreements, licensing programs, grassroots fan development initiatives, broadcasting, publishing ventures and the use of new technology have all combined to increase exposure for the sport of hockey, NHL players and the league.

When the NHL signs an agreement with a new corporate partner, or extends an agreement with a longtime partner, the goal is to have the partner support the game in a variety of ways. No longer do sponsors buy a place in the game without providing support for programs that will help the sport grow.

For example, Nike has gotten into the hockey business and now sells equipment and licensed merchandise. But Nike also supports grassroots initiatives to get young people playing hockey in a program called Nike/NHL Street.

This program puts sticks and pucks in the hands of almost 300,000 young people a year.

Working with other partners such as Wendy's, Labatt, Anheuser Busch, IBM, Coca-Cola and Dodge, the NHL has drawn unprecedented exposure in the 1990s.

The overall growth of the licensing business has been reflected in the growth of sales of NHL licensed merchandise. In the 1998 business year, sales of NHL licensed products increased by more than 30 percent, outpacing the industry trend.

In 1993, the NHL identified fan development as a key area in trying to increase interest in the sport of hockey. Since then the NHL Fan Development Department has instituted a series of off-ice programs to attract new fans. The most intensive work has been done with a program known as NHL Breakout, a touring two-day street and in-line hockey tournament and interactive fan festival. In 1998, NHL Breakout will visit 22 cities and attract more than 300,000 participants and spectators.

The broadcast of NHL games on the Canadian Broadcasting Corporation's "Hockey Night in Canada" is the longest running regularly scheduled television program in North America. For the 1998-99 season, the NHL's Canadian cable partner changes to CTV Sports Net. In the United States, Fox Sports is the network broadcaster of NHL games and ESPN holds the cable rights.

On the Internet, nhl.com has become one of the most popular sports sites on the Worldwide Web. The result of a unique alliance with IBM, known as NHL ICE (NHL Interactive Cyber Enterprises), nhl.com gives hockey fans around the world real-time access to statistics, summaries, news, features and video of NHL games and the sport of hockey.

NATIONAL ANTHEMS

Although several teams had played their country's national anthem prior to games several years earlier, the NHL first required that the national anthem of the home club be played prior to a game for the 1946–47 season. For the 1987–88 season, the league expanded the regulation to its present-day form which requires, when a U.S. and Canadian club are competing, both national anthems be played.

OFFICIATING

The NHL's Officiating Department is responsible for the recruiting, assigning, training and evaluating of NHL referees and linesmen for preseason, regular season and Stanley Cup playoff games. In addition, the league assigns assigns referees for all games in the American Hockey League and for some games in the West Coast Hockey League, Western Professional Hockey League and the three Canadian major junior leagues. In 1997–98, NHL-assigned officials worked more than 2,100 games.

The 1997–98 staff consisted of 17 NHL referees, 33 NHL linesmen, 11 minor-league referees, 15 trainee referees, two linesmen trainees and nine supervisors.

The development system for officials mirrors that of a player with many of the NHL officials recruited while working junior and collegiate hockey before working their way up through the minor professional system.

During the NHL's inaugural season of 1917–18, local referees (one per game) were employed in each of the three NHL cities at a fee of $12.50 per game. The policy of using local referees for NHL games was discontinued in 1926 when the league appointed a full-time staff of six referees.

OVERTIME

Beginning in the 1983–84 season, the league instituted a five-minute "sudden death" overtime period for regular-season games.

PER DIEM

A per diem of $5 for players (players also paid their own hotel room and were allotted $2.50) was first introduced in the league during the 1930–31 season. A uniform per diem was introduced for players for the first time during the 1968–69 season ($15 per day with the proviso that on game days when clubs provided players with a steak dinner, only $7.50 was paid). Previously, clubs could decide what their team's per diem would be.

Today, a player's per diem is $70.

PLAYERS, EUROPEANS

Jaroslav Drobny, a member of the Czechoslovakian national team that won the International Ice Hockey Federation World Championships in 1947, was the first European player to appear on an NHL club's reserve list. Drobny was placed on Boston's negotiating list in 1949 but would never play in the NHL.

On March 29, 1989 Sergei Priakin, a right winger with the Soviet national team, became the first Soviet player to be permitted by the USSR Ice Hockey Federation to play in the NHL. Priakin signed a contract with the Calgary Flames.

PLAYOFF ELIGIBILITY

The idea of a playoff eligibility list was first introduced for the 1946 Stanley Cup playoffs when clubs were required to submit a list of 25 players (excluding goaltenders) who would be eligible to play in that year's playoffs to the league office by March 1. The only additions to the list after the deadline would be players returning from active military service overseas.

Today, only players on the reserve list of an NHL club at the trading deadline may participate in the Stanley Cup playoffs.

PROTECTIVE GLASS

Protective glass surrounding the boards first appeared in the NHL at Toronto's Maple Leaf Gardens in 1948. The use of protective glass in all NHL buildings became mandatory in the 1950s.

RESERVE LIST

During World War II, NHL team rosters were severely depleted as players fulfilled their military obligations. For that reason, the league had loose restrictions on roster limitations. Beginning on May 15, 1947, however, the league required that a club's reserve list not exceed 40 players.

Today, a member club may have on its reserve list, at any one time, not more than 90 players, which shall include the following:

- Not more than 50 players signed to standard player's contracts and not less than 24 players and three goalkeepers under contract. Age 18 and age 19 players who were returned to Canadian Major Junior Hockey clubs, and who have not played 11 games in the National

Hockey League in one season, are exempt from inclusion in the 50 player limit.

• Unsigned draft selections.

RINK-BOARD ADVERTISING

Clubs were first granted the right to advertise on rink boards beginning with the 1978–79 season. Such advertising first appeared in 1980 and by the 1989–90 season, all NHL clubs were using rink-board advertising.

Advertising on the ice surface first appeared in the early 1990s

ROSTER, 24-MAN

There may be a maximum of 24 players on each club's playing roster at any one time from the commencement of the NHL regular season through the trade deadline. Prior to the start of the season, each club must submit to the NHL its "opening day playing roster" which shall be comprised of not more than 24 players. Each club must have a roster of at least 20 players, composed of 18 skaters and two goaltenders. Players on injured reserve do not count in the 24-man limit.

ROSTER, PLAYING

The current playing roster of 18 skaters and two goaltenders was established for the 1982–83 season. The size of the playing roster has varied considerably in league history. In 1925–26, the playing roster was set at a 12-man maximum; it was increased to 15 players in 1929–30 and varied from 12 to 16 skaters plus goalies until 1971–72. Between 1971–72 and 1981–82, the playing roster was set at 17 skaters and two goalies.

SALARY, ARBITRATION

Salary arbitration is a process pursuant to which a club and a player may resolve a salary dispute by presenting their respective cases to an independent arbitrator in which they seek to establish the value of the player's contract. After each side has presented its case, the arbitrator makes a determination as to the appropriate salary for the player to be paid.

A player is eligible to elect salary arbitration if the player meets the qualifications set forth in the following chart:

First Contract Eligible for Salary Arbitration After ...

Signing Age	
18-20	Five years professional experience
21	Four years professional experience
22-23	Three years professional experience
24	Two years professional experience
25+	One year professional experience

SALARY, CAP

The only salary cap currently in place is for entry level players (see Entry Level System, Compensation).

In the league's formative years there was a salary cap, beginning in 1925–26 when the salary limit for a 12-player team was set at $35,000. That team cap grew to $70,000 (14-man roster plus goalies) in 1932–33 with the further provision that no player's salary could exceed $7,500. The cap was eliminated by the late 1930s after the Great Depression had ended.

SALARY, MINIMUM

A minimum player's salary of $7,000 was first introduced for the 1958–59 season.

For each of the 1998–99, 1999–00 and 2000–01 seasons, the minimum NHL salary is $150,000; 2001–02 $165,000; 2002–03 $175,000; 2003–04 $180,000; 2004–05 $185,000.

SALARY, MINOR LEAGUE

The minimum minor-league salary for a player is $25,000 (American Hockey League) and $27,500 (International Hockey League) for an entry level player; the maximum compensation $75,000 (50% of the NHL minimum salary for 1998–99 through 2000–01). The maximum compensation payable to a player who is playing major junior hockey is $8,500.

SUPPLEMENTARY DISCIPLINE

In accordance with NHL rules (Rule 33a of the Rule Book), an NHL club general manager has 24 hours following the completion of a game to request a review of an on-ice incident. A review may also be initiated by the NHL based on the game reports of the officials or supervisor of officials. A match penalty is automatically reviewed by the NHL.

After an initial screening of the videotape, the incident is either deemed not to warrant further action or to be "under review." Before a player can be disciplined he is entitled to a hearing, which may be conducted either in person or by telephone conference call.

All player suspension are without pay, meaning that a club must remit the player's salary for the period in which he is suspended to the league. Player fine money goes to the NHL's Emergency Assistance Fund to benefit former players. The NHL calculates the amount of money the player must forfeit due to the suspension. This is calculated on the following basis:

a) For first offenders (first incident requiring supplementary discipline in the form of a game suspension), player to forfeit one day's salary for each regular-season game lost (one divided by the total number of days in the season measured from the date of the NHL's first regular-season game to the last, irrespective of the player's club's schedule.

b) For repeat offenders (second or subsequent incidents requiring game suspension), player to forfeit one game's salary for each regular-season game lost (one divided by the number of regular season games for each regular season game suspended).

A player may also be fined up to $1,000, the maximum permitted under the Collective Bargaining Agreement.

SCOREBOARD

The use of scoreboards in all NHL arenas to show scores from out of town games became mandatory beginning in February 1955.

STANLEY CUP, ENGRAVING OF NAMES

The Stanley Cup is the oldest trophy competed for by professional athletes in North America and is the only trophy that provides for each player from the winning team to have his name engraved on it. Prior to the 1976–77 season, only those players who competed in the Stanley Cup playoffs were eligible to have their names engraved on the Stanley Cup. In January 1977, however, the NHL changed the criteria to allow players competing in 40 regular-season

games or one final-series game to have their names on the Cup. Since 1994, the league has allowed exceptions to this rule in the case of players who, by reason of injury, do not appear in the sufficient number of games.

TELEVISION

Prior to 1968, all broadcast revenues were divided according to international borders. With the exception of local market revenues that were reserved for the home team, all U.S. broadcast rights revenue was evenly distributed among the U.S.-based member clubs, while all Canadian broadcast rights revenues were evenly divided among the Canadian-based clubs. In 1968, the first version of the Trans-Border TV Rights Agreement was devised which saw the Canadian broadcast rightsholder (Molson) pay the U.S. broadcaster (CBS) for the right to air playoff games between two U.S.-based clubs within Canada. Molson, who owned the rights to cover games that involved two Canadian-based member clubs, did not have the right to cover any playoff games that involved two US-based clubs. The TBA was formed to allow Molson to cover the playoffs, in the event that no Canadian-based teams advance to the Stanley Cup finals. The sum that would be paid to the U.S. broadcaster was evenly split among all U.S. member clubs.

The TBA was altered a few more times, beginning in the early 1980s when Carling O'Keefe acquired the rights to cover home games between Canadian clubs and U.S. teams in Canada, while Molson continued to broadcast all home games between the Canadian teams. Since all broadcast rights were controlled by the clubs and not the NHL, it was possible to sell non-exclusive rights to a variety of broadcasters. However, this was changed in 1986 when it was announced that the league would sell the exclusive rights to broadcast coverage. The home team would reserve the right to provide its own exclusive coverage of home games within its local market, but the league's rightsholder would provide coverage to the rest of the nation. The division of such revenue would follow the previous guidelines of international boundaries.

The agreement was once again altered in accordance with the rise of U.S. cable. The NHL negotiated agreements with the emerging cable companies in the U.S. and revised the TBA so that all broadcast revenue from the sale of exclusive rights to both Canadian and U.S. networks and cable companies would be pooled and equally divided among all member clubs. This process of pooling and equal distribution of national television revenue remains in effect in today's NHL.

THIRD JERSEY

Third jerseys of five NHL teams—Anaheim, Boston, Los Angeles, Pittsburgh and Vancouver—were introduced for the first time on January 27, 1996.

TIE-BREAKING PROCEDURE, REGULAR-SEASON STANDINGS

At the conclusion of the regular season, the standing of the teams in each conference shall be determined in accordance with the following priorities in the order listed:
  a) The higher number of points earned by the club.
  b) The greater number of games won by the club.
  c) The higher number of points earned in games against each other among two or more clubs having equal standing under priorities (a) and (b).

NOTE: For the purpose of determining standings under priority (c) for two teams that have not played an equal number of games with each other, points earned in the first game played in the city that has the extra game shall not be included. However, when more than two teams are tied, the percentage of available points earned in games among each other shall be used to determine the standing.
  d) The greater differential between goals scored for and against by clubs having equal standing under priority (c).

A tie-breaking formula was first introduced in 1928–29 (most wins followed by better goal differential). In 1940, the criteria was changed to most wins; followed by fewest losses; most goals for; and fewest goals against. In 1970–71, the NHL adopted head-to-head results as the second criteria ahead of goals for and against. The current criteria were adopted beginning in 1984–85.

In 1969–70, the tie-breaking formula led to a bizarre regular-season finish. The New York Rangers, after leading the NHL standings for much of the 1969–70 season, found themselves in a must-win situation on the last day of the regular season in order to have a chance to qualify for the final postseason position in the East Division. They trailed the Montreal Canadiens by two points heading into the final day and also had to overcome a five-goal Montreal advantage that the Canadiens owned in the goals-for criteria. The Canadiens had scored 242 goals as compared to 237 goals for the Rangers heading into the final day of action, Sunday, April 5.

Playing an afternoon game at Madison Square Garden against Detroit, the Rangers gave themselves a chance, scoring nine goals in a 9–5 win, while outshooting the Red Wings 65–22. They pushed their points total to 92 and number of wins to 38 to tie the Canadiens for the last playoff spot and their goals-for total to 246, four better than Montreal.

Montreal still had one game to play—an evening encounter versus the Black Hawks at Chicago Stadium—where any of the following scenarios would get them into the playoffs ahead of the Rangers: a win, a tie or five goals scored.

A wild evening ensued. The Canadiens, trailing 3–2 entering the third period, fell behind 5–2 with less than 10 minutes to go in the game. Canadiens coach Claude Ruel, sensing his team would not get the tie or win, pulled goaltender Rogatien Vachon for an extra attacker at the 11:40 mark of the third period in the hope of scoring the necessary five goals. Five goals were scored ... but all by the Blackhawks into an empty Montreal net.

The Canadiens lost the game 10–2, and by failing to score five goals, were eliminated from participating in the Stanley Cup playoffs for the first time in 22 years. During the off-season, the NHL adopted head-to-head results as the second criteria (after wins) for breaking a tie between two clubs in the standings.

TIE-BREAKING PROCEDURE, ART ROSS TROPHY/INDIVIDUAL AWARDS

In 1979–80, Edmonton's Wayne Gretzky and Marcel Dionne of Los Angeles tied for the league lead in scoring with 137 points. Dionne was awarded the Art Ross Trophy based on his having scored 53 goals to Gretzky's 51 goals. The same situation had presented itself 18 years earlier when Bobby Hull and Andy Bathgate shared the scoring lead with 84 points. Hull was awarded the Art Ross Trophy based on his having scored 50 goals to Bathgate's 28.

Additional tie-break criteria were established for the 1987–88 season in the event that the tied players had scored equal number of goals. The player who had taken part in the fewest games would then be awarded the trophy, with the next tiebreaker (if necessary) being the earliest date of each player's first goal.

For the remainder of the league's individual awards, the number of first-place votes is the determining factor in breaking a tie followed by most second-place votes and so forth.

TIMING DEVICES

Game Clocks: Visible time clocks were first required in NHL rinks in 1933–34.

Goal Lights: In November 1938, the league passed a resolution requiring that all rinks be equipped with a "timing-lighting device" behind the goal, showing a green light at the expiry of each period. The new equipment made it impossible for the red goal light to be illuminated once the green light was on. Toronto was the first NHL club to have such a light installed in its rink—in March 1936.

Dressing Room: The league first required clocks in the dressing rooms to alert players of the amount of time remaining before the start of a game or period for the 1986–87 season.

TRANSFER OF PLAYERS

Trading Deadline: A club may loan players on its reserve list to clubs of any league affiliated with the NHL at any time up to 3:00 p.m. Eastern Time of the 26th day immediately preceding the final day of the regular season.

During the period following noon of the 26th day immediately preceding the final day of the regular season no player may be recalled from loan to a member club of any league affiliated with the league, except that:

a) an NHL club may exercise four recalls from a member club or clubs of a league affiliated with the NHL.

b) players may be recalled on an emergency basis.

c) Players may be recalled upon completion of the regular season and playoffs of the club to which they were loaned.

Emergency Recall: A player on loan to a club of any league affiliated with the NHL may be recalled under emergency conditions at any time. Emergency conditions are established when the playing strength of the NHL club, by reason of injury, illness or by league suspension, is reduced below the level of two goaltenders, six defensemen and 12 forwards. A player may be recalled for the duration of the emergency only.

IIHF/NHL: Any player under contract to an International Ice Hockey Federation team may be signed by an NHL club through July 15 of the year in which he will begin play in the NHL (e.g. July 15, 1998 is the signing deadline for a player for the 1998–99 season). For players drafted in the most recent Entry Draft, however, the deadline is August 15. The cost the NHL club must pay to the IIHF for any player signed between July 15 and August 15 is $100,000.

Any player who is under contract to an IIHF team; signs an NHL contract; has not yet reached his 20th birthday; is unable to earn a roster position on his NHL club by the first day of the NHL season and was not selected in the first round of the NHL Entry Draft may not be assigned by his NHL club to a minor-league affiliate but instead must be returned to his IIHF club for the balance of the IIHF season.

Players not under contract to an IIHF team or who were selected in the first round of the NHL Entry Draft or have reached their 20th birthday may be assigned by an NHL team to a minor-league club without restriction. All other player not signed by their NHL club must be returned to their IIHF club.

TRYOUT

An NHL club may enter into a tryout agreement with any amateur player whose eligibility for junior hockey is exhausted (ie. has attained or will have attained his 20th birthday by December 31 next following). Such tryout may not last for more than eight regular-season games.

VIDEO REPLAY

Video replay was first instituted in the NHL in the 1991–92 season with the following situations subject to review: puck crossing the goal line; puck in the net prior to the goal frame being dislodged; puck in the net prior to, or after expiration of time at the end of the period; puck directed into the net by a hand or foot; puck deflected into the net off an official; puck struck with a high stick (this criteria was actually added after the start of the 1991–92 season on December 6). Prior to the 1994–95 season, an additional criteria was added to establish the correct time on the game clock, while the man in the crease criteria was added in 1996–97.

Experimentation into using video replay for NHL games was first done in November 1985 in a U.S. collegiate game at Michigan State. Further experiments were conducted by the NHL on February 13-14, 1986 in the International Hockey League.

WAIVERS

Waivers were first introduced in the league in 1922. The new clause in the bylaws read: "No club in this league shall have the right to sell outright, option or otherwise exchange any of its players to any other league without first offering the services of such player or players to all NHL clubs at a price not to exceed $1,500." Today, waivers operate under that basic principle adopted in the league's early days.

WAIVER DRAFT (INTRA-LEAGUE DRAFT), REGULAR-SEASON WAIVERS

Parity in the six-team NHL had become of great concern to the NHL owners in the 1950–51 season when the last-place Chicago Black Hawks finished 65 points behind the league-leading Montreal Canadiens. A number of discussions ensued as to the feasibility of adopting a draft system to assist the weaker clubs with a player (or players) from the stronger clubs. In June 1952, the Intra-League Draft (the forerunner of the Waiver Draft) was adopted. It provided that each club would have the right to protect 25 professional players on its reserve list. In turn, the three lowest clubs in the league standings from the previous season were entitled to draft from the top three clubs two professional players. The top three clubs were then able to draft one professional player (not included on any protected list) from any other club with the draft price for any player established at $7,500.

Each year the NHL holds a Waiver Draft prior to the start of the regular season. The Waiver Draft is organized to allow each club an equal opportunity to acquire unprotected talent from the league's other member clubs. In September of each year, NHL clubs must submit a protect-

ed list consisting of 18 skaters and two goaltenders. The order of selection is based on the inverse order of standing from the previous regular season, beginning with only non-playoff teams selecting in the first round. Each subsequent round offers each member club an opportunity for selection. The draft is concluded when a round is completed without any clubs making a selection. In the first round, a team is not permitted to claim a player from a club in its own division. When a player is claimed he must immediately be placed on the claiming team's protected list, replacing a previously protected player who is now made available for claim by other clubs. A team losing a player is granted the option of receiving a cash payment from the claiming club or the player who is taken off the claiming team's protected list. No team shall lose more than three players, however, each club reserves the right to offer as many players as it so chooses. In addition, this three-man limit will increase according to the number of additional players the team claims in the draft.

Not every player is eligible for claim in the Waiver Draft. Exemptions are based on the players' age and experience in the league. For example, a player 18 years of age will not be eligible for the Waiver Draft for five years or until he has played in 160 NHL games.

Today, the number of years a player is exempt from the Waiver Draft is outlined below. The exemption ends once the player has played in the number of NHL regular-season and playoff games set forth in the applicable column below.

	GOALTENDERS				SKATERS		
AGE	YEARS FROM NHL SIGNING		NHL GAMES PLAYED	AGE	YEARS FROM NHL SIGNING		NHL GAMES PLAYED*
18	6	or	80	18	5	or	160
19	5	or	80	19	4	or	160
20	4	or	80	20	3	or	160
21	4	or	60	21	3	or	80
22	4	or	60	22	3	or	70
23	3	or	60	23	3	or	60
24	2	or	60	24	2	or	60
25+	1	or		25+	1	or	

For purposes of regular-season waivers and the Waiver Draft, the five-year exemption for an 18-year-old skater and four-year exemption for a 19-year-old skater are both reduced to three years commencing the first season that the 18- or 19-year-old plays in 11 games or more. The next two seasons, regardless of whether the skater plays any games in either season, shall count as the second and third years toward satisfying the exemption.

For purposes of regular-season waivers and the Waiver Draft, the six-year exemption for an 18-year-old goaltender and five-year exemption for a 19-year-old goaltender are both reduced to four years commencing the first season that the 18- or 19-year-old plays in 11 NHL games or more. The next three seasons, regardless of whether the goalie plays any games in any season, shall count as the next three years toward satisfying the exemption.

The first season in which a player who is age 20 or older plays in one or more "professional games" shall constitute the first year for calculating the number of years he is exempt from waivers.

A player 25 years or older who plays in one or more professional games in any season shall be exempt from regular-season waivers for the remainder of that season.

The rights granted to assign a player who is otherwise required to clear waivers to a minor-league club expire for any player, who, after clearing the Waiver Draft or regular-season waivers:

• is not sent to a minor-league club, or is recalled from a minor-league club (except on emergency recall) and;

• remains on an NHL roster for 30 days (cumulative) or plays 10 NHL games (cumulative).

ZAMBONI

A marked improvement in the playing conditions of the ice surface resulted in the early 1950s with the widespread adoption of the Zamboni ice-finishing machine that replaced the old practice of flooding the rink between periods. Instead of merely coating the ice with water, the Zamboni scraped away a layer of the old surface first, resulting in a quicker and smoother freeze.

With more clubs providing fans with between-periods entertainment on the ice, the league adopted a rule in early 1990s that requires teams to use two Zambonis to resurface the ice.

CHAPTER 17

Complete NHL Time Line

Information in 11 Categories about Each NHL Season since 1917–18

Bob Borgen and Bob Duff

EVERY HOCKEY FAN, from the senior who remembers paying 35 cents to watch the New York Americans at the old Garden to the 12-year-old excited by the coming of the Nashville Predators to her hometown, is connected to the history of the National Hockey League.

Even for the game's newest devotees, matters of history crowd in from all sides: Why do the Montreal Canadiens have a "CH" on their jerseys? Who were Hart, Norris, Vezina, Calder, Selke, Smythe and Stanley? Who put the "hat" in hat trick?

Older fans, remembering carefree times and the hockey heroes who captured their imaginations through radio broadcasts, newspapers or live attendance, tend to put a golden glow on games from 25-or-more years ago. This tendency dates back to hockey's early days. Some fans felt that the decision by the National Hockey Association to end seven-man hockey in 1911 irrevocably spoiled the game. A generation later, the addition of the center red line in 1943 was decried. By the 1980s, the six-team NHL of 1942 to 1967 was discussed in reverent tones. Today, it seems that the rough-and-tumble hockey of the 1970s has inched its way onto fans' sentimental hit parades.

From *Total Hockey*'s perspective, every era is special both in its own right and for the foundation it provides for everything that follows.

Each of the NHL's first 81 seasons contained singular achievements, significant trades, milestones and things worth knowing. A selection of those that stand out follows.

1910s	1917–18	1918–19	1919–20
Firsts	**Feb 18, 1918** • Montreal Canadiens goalie Georges Vezina recorded the first shutout in NHL history, blanking Toronto 9–0. It came in the third month of play, in the league's inaugural season.	**Dec 28, 1918** • Montreal Canadiens' Georges Vezina became the first NHL goalie to earn an assist. Teammate Newsy Lalonde picked up the puck after a Vezina save, skated the length of the ice and scored. It came in a 6–3 win over Toronto.	**Mar 10, 1920** • Quebec Bulldogs center Joe Malone became the first player in NHL history to score six goals in a game twice during his career. This time he led the Bulldogs to a 10–4 win over Ottawa.
Records	**Mar 2, 1918** • Joe Malone finished the first NHL season with a record 44 goals in 22 games, when Toronto beat Montreal 5–3. Malone's record stood until 1944–45 when Maurice Richard scored 50 goals.	**Feb 12, 1919** • Ottawa's Clint Benedict got his second shutout of the season, an NHL record, when the Senators won 7–0 over the visiting Montreal Canadiens.	**Jan 31, 1920** • Quebec's Joe Malone set an NHL record with seven goals in a 10–6 Bulldogs win over the visiting Toronto St. Patricks.
Did You Know?	**Dec 15, 1917** • The NHL's first exhibition game was played four days before the start of the regular season when the Canadiens and Montreal Wanderers played a benefit game for victims of the Halifax Explosion which had occurred 10 days earlier.	**Feb 20, 1919** • Ottawa goalie Clint Benedict led the Senators to a 9–3 win over Toronto, to finish the season with a 2.94 GAA, the lowest in the NHL's two-year history. One year earlier, Benedict had a 5.18 GAA, one of the worst in the league.	**Mar 6, 1920** • Toronto loaned goalie Howard Lockhart to Quebec for one game, and then beat the Bulldogs 11–2. Mickey Roach scored five goals to lead the scoring.
Milestones	**Dec 19, 1917** • Montreal Wanderers defenseman Dave Ritchie scored the first goal in NHL history (one minute into the NHL's first game) then added another goal in the third period, in a 10–9 opening night win over the visiting Toronto Arenas, before a crowd of 700 fans.	**Feb 18, 1919** • Ottawa's Cy Denneny scored his 62nd career goal (in a 4–3 win over the Toronto Arenas) to become the NHL's all-time leading goal scorer. Denneny passed Joe Malone.	**Jan 7, 1920** • Quebec Bulldogs' Joe Malone scored twice to become the NHL's all-time leading goal scorer, with 50. His two goals led the Bulldogs to a 4–3 win over the Toronto Arenas. He passed Cy Denneny, to reclaim his title.
Rookies	**Feb 19, 1918** • Toronto signed Jack Adams who went scoreless in eight games, but played six more years in the NHL, before becoming a coach and g.m. with Detroit.	**Feb 12, 1919** • Ottawa's Punch Broadbent scored the first goal of his NHL career in a 7–0 win over the visiting Montreal Canadiens.	**Dec 27, 1919** • Playing in his second game, Toronto's Babe Dye scored his first career NHL goal, in a 7–4 win over Quebec.
Transactions	**Jan 5, 1918** • Toronto claimed Hap Holmes from the Montreal Wanderers, after the team folded. Holmes was a Montreal property playing in the PCHA.	**Dec 14, 1918** • Toronto Arenas acquired Rusty Crawford from Ottawa, in exchange for a player to be named later (Harry Cameron).	**Jan 14, 1920** • Montreal Canadiens acquired Harry Cameron from Toronto, in exchange for Goldie Prodgers.
Teams	**Nov 26, 1917** • The NHL was founded. Teams included the Canadiens, Montreal Wanderers, Ottawa Senators, Toronto Arenas, and Quebec Bulldogs. Quebec didn't play in 1917–18.	**Feb 20, 1919** • Senators beat the Toronto Arenas 9–3 in Ottawa, to go 7–1–0 and win the NHL's second-half championship.	**Mar 3, 1920** • Montreal Canadiens set an NHL record for most goals in a game, in a 16–3 win over the Bulldogs in Quebec City.
Front Office	**Nov 26, 1917** • Frank Calder was elected as the NHL's first president.	**Dec 9, 1918** • Montreal Canadiens named Jack Laviolette as their new coach, assisting player-coach Newsy Lalonde in the running of the team.	**Dec 2, 1919** • Ottawa Senators fired coach Alf Smith, and named Pete Green as his replacement.
Playoffs	**Mar 20, 1918** • Toronto became the first NHL team to compete in the Stanley Cup finals, when they beat Vancouver of the PCHA 5–3 in Toronto. Reg Noble scored two goals and an assist in the first period to lead the way.	**Apr 1, 1919** • The final game for the 1919 Stanley Cup was canceled because of the worldwide epidemic of influenza. No winner was declared in the series between the Montreal Canadiens and Seattle Metropolitans.	**Mar 24, 1920** • Ottawa's Clint Benedict recorded the first of his NHL-record 15 career playoff shutouts in a 3–0 Senators win over the Seattle Metropolitans in game two of the Stanley Cup championship in Ottawa.
Business	**Jan 9, 1918** • The NHL announced a new rule permitting goaltenders to leave their feet while making a save. Previously a penalty was called if goaltenders sat or lay on the ice to stop the puck.	**Oct 20, 1918** • The NHL Board of Governors decreased the league's regular season schedule from 22 to 18 games.	**Nov 23, 1919** • The NHL's Quebec franchise announced it would "return" for the league's third season, after being dormant during the first two years of the NHL. Although first announced as the "Athletics," the club was finally called the "Bulldogs."
Births & Deaths	**Jan 22, 1918** • Elmer Lach born in Nokomis, Saskatchewan. **Feb 22, 1918** • Sid Abel born in Melville, Saskatchewan.	**Aug 21, 1918** • Billy Reay born in Winnipeg, Manitoba. **Apr 6, 1919** • Terry Reardon born in Winnipeg, Manitoba.	**Oct 10, 1919** • Edgar Laprade born in Mine Center, Ont. **Mar 1, 1920** • Max Bentley born in Delisle, Saskatchewan.

1920s

	1920–21	1921–22	1922–23	1923–24	1924–25
Firsts	**Mar 7, 1921** • Cy Denneny had six goals when Ottawa beat the Hamilton Tigers 12–5. Cy became part of the first brother combo to have six-goal games in the NHL. Brother Corbett also had six goals against Hamilton six weeks earlier.	**Feb 11, 1922** • After 20 minutes of overtime Toronto St. Patricks and Ottawa Senators settled for a 4–4 tie at Ottawa, in the first game in NHL history that ended in a tie.	**Jan 31, 1923** • Montreal Canadiens beat the Hamilton Tigers 5–4 in the first penalty-free game in NHL history.	**Feb 9, 1924** • The NHL's first individual award was created. The Hart Trophy would be given to the player judged the most valuable to his team during the season. Frank Nighbor was the first winner.	**Dec 17, 1924** • Goalies Jake Forbes of the Hamilton Tigers and Alex Connell of the Ottawa Senators played in the first 0–0 tie in NHL history.
Records	**Mar 7, 1921** • Toronto beat the visiting Montreal Canadiens 6–4, as Babe Dye of the St. Pats finished the season with 35 goals for a Toronto record. He would up the mark to 38 in 1924–25, a total that would remain a high for Toronto until 1960–61.	**Jan 14, 1922** • An NHL record was set when teammates (and brothers) Sprague and Odie Cleghorn each scored four goals in the Canadiens' 10–6 win over the Hamilton Tigers, in Montreal.	**Jan 6, 1923** • Senators center Frank Nighbor played in what was reported to be his sixth full game (without any time on the bench!) in a 2–1 win over the Toronto St. Patricks, in Ottawa. Nighbor scored six goals during the six-game span.	**Dec 26, 1923** • A record crowd of 8,300 fans (the most ever to see a hockey game in Ottawa) turned out to see the Senators beat the Canadiens 3–2.	**Mar 7, 1925** • Ottawa's rookie goalie Alex Connell set an NHL record with his seventh shutout of the season, in a 3–0 Senators win over the Toronto St. Pats.
Did You Know?	**Mar 7, 1921** • A 6–4 loss to Toronto in the final game of the year saw Montreal's Newsy Lalonde finish the season with 32 goals and 11 assists. Although he was third in goals, Lalonde won the scoring title due to his league-leading assists.	**Mar 2, 1922** • Toronto St. Pats beat the Vancouver Millionaires 6–0, in the final professional hockey game played with seven men on each side. Cy Denneny, the Leafs' "rover," scored a goal in the win.	**Mar 22, 1923** • Foster Hewitt (hockey's first regular radio announcer) used a telephone to broadcast his first hockey game. The game between intermediate teams from Kitchener and Toronto Parkdale took place at Toronto's Mutual Street Arena.	**Feb 20, 1924** • Canadiens fans waited two hours in the Mount Royal Arena, but the Ottawa Senators never showed up! The team was stranded on a snow-bound train 50 miles out of Ottawa. The game was played the next night (a 3–0 Habs win).	**Dec 1, 1924** • The Bruins beat the Montreal Maroons 2–1 at the Boston Arena in the first NHL game ever played in the United States.
Milestones	**Mar 5, 1921** • Ottawa's Clint Benedict became the first goaltender in NHL history to record 10 career shutouts, in a 1–0 Senators win over the Canadiens in Montreal.	**Feb 15, 1922** • Ottawa's Harry "Punch" Broadbent scored a goal in his 16th straight game, a standard that has not been matched, as the Senators tied the Canadiens 6–6 in Montreal.	**Feb 17, 1923** • Ottawa's Cy Denneny scored his 143rd career goal (in a 2–0 win over Montreal) to pass Joe Malone as the all-time NHL goal-scoring leader. It was the second time Denneny had become the NHL's goal leader. This time he held the record for 11 years.	**Mar 11, 1924** • The Montreal Canadiens won a two-game total-goals series 5–2 over Ottawa to claim the NHL championship.	**Jan 20, 1925** • Goaltender Clint Benedict became the first NHL goaltender to record 20 career shutouts as the Montreal Maroons beat the Bruins 2–0 at Boston.
Rookies	**Jan 5, 1921** • Toronto signed defenseman Billy "Red" Stuart.	**Dec 17, 1921** • Francis "King" Clancy played in the first game of his NHL career, as the Ottawa Senators beat Hamilton 3–2.	**Dec 16, 1922** • Montreal's Aurel Joliat scored twice in his NHL debut; a 7–2 Canadiens' loss at Toronto.	**Dec 26, 1923** • Montreal's Howie Morenz scored his first career NHL goal, in a 3–2 Canadiens loss to the Ottawa Senators.	**Jan 21, 1925** • Rookie Hap Day scored the first goal of his NHL career in the Toronto St. Patricks' 4–2 win over the Canadiens at Montreal.
Transactions	**Jan 26, 1921** • Toronto St. Patricks acquired Sprague Cleghorn from the Ottawa Senators.	**Nov 26, 1921** • Montreal Canadiens obtained Sprague Cleghorn from the Hamilton Tigers, in exchange for Amos Arbour and Harry Mummery.	**Sep 18, 1922** • Montreal Canadiens traded veteran Newsy Lalonde to the Saskatoon Sheiks of the WCHL, in exchange for the rights to then-amateur Aurel Joliat.	**Dec 14, 1923** • Toronto traded Ken Randall and cash to the Hamilton Tigers, in exchange for Bert Corbeau, Amos Arbour and George Carey.	**Jan 10, 1925** • Boston Bruins purchased Lionel Hitchman from Ottawa.
Teams	**Dec 22, 1920** • The first NHL game was played in Hamilton, Ontario, as goalie Howard Lockhart recorded the only shutout of his career in a 5–0 Tigers win over the Canadiens.	**Mar 8, 1922** • Despite a season-ending 7–2 loss to the Hamilton Tigers, the Ottawa Senators finished first in the NHL and led the league in most goals scored (106) and fewest goals allowed (84).	**Feb 28, 1923** • Ottawa beat Hamilton 6–3 to clinch first place for the fourth time in the NHL's first six seasons. The Senators went on to win the Stanley Cup for the third time in four years.	**Dec 29, 1923** • Shorty Green scored at 12:22 of overtime to give the Hamilton Tigers their first win at Ottawa, 3–2. The Tigers had been 0–13 against the Senators in Ottawa.	**Oct 11, 1924** • Boston Bruins and Montreal Maroons are granted franchises for $15,000. $11,000 of the Maroons' fees went to the Canadiens for infringement of their territory.
Front Office	**Nov 2, 1920** • Percy Thompson was named the general manager of the Hamilton Tigers, after the team relocated from Quebec City.	**Nov 1, 1921** • Toronto named Reg Noble as player/coach, and George O'Donoghue as manager of the St. Patricks. Eddie Powers would run the team from behind the bench.	**Mar 6, 1923** • Art Ross resigned as coach of the Hamilton Tigers. Percy Thompson assumed the team's managerial duties.	**Jan 16, 1924** • Hamilton Tigers (with a record of 6–8) named Percy Lesueur as their new coach, replacing Ken Randall, who remained with the team as a player.	**Oct 11, 1924** • Art Ross was named first manager of the Bruins, on the day that Boston was granted its NHL franchise.
Playoffs	**Apr 4, 1921** • Ottawa Senators defeated Vancouver Millionaires 2–1 in the decisive fifth game of their Stanley Cup series. Jack Darragh scored both goals for the Senators, who became the first NHL team to win back-to-back Stanley Cup titles.	**Mar 11, 1922** • Defenseman Art Duncan scored a hat trick as Vancouver won 4–0 at Regina in a Stanley Cup game. Duncan was the last defenseman to score a playoff hat trick until 1971, when Boston's Bobby Orr matched the record.	**Mar 31, 1923** • Ottawa's 18-year-old King Clancy played all six positions (including goalie for two minutes when Clint Benedict got a penalty) as the Senators beat Edmonton 1–0 in game two of the finals to become the 1922–23 Stanley Cup champions.	**Mar 25, 1924** • Montreal beat Calgary 3–0 in game two of the finals (played in Ottawa) to become the 1923–24 Stanley Cup champions. Georges Vezina got the shutout as the Canadiens won their first Cup title since the formation of the NHL in 1917–18.	**Mar 30, 1925** • Victoria Cougars of the WCHL beat the Montreal Canadiens 6–1 to become the last non-NHL team to win the Stanley Cup.
Business	**Nov 2, 1920** • Quebec Bulldogs franchise was transferred to Hamilton, Ontario, where they became known as the "Tigers."	**Nov 26, 1921** • NHL Board of Governors abandoned the "split schedule" and decided that the first- and second-place teams (at the end of the full schedule) would play for the league championship.	**Nov 14, 1922** • Art Ross was named coach of the Hamilton Tigers.	**Sep 30, 1923** • Montreal Canadiens signed Howie Morenz as a free agent.	**Nov 3, 1924** • The NHL increased the regular-season schedule from 24 to 30 games per team. This will later be the key reason behind the NHL's first players' strike, as the first-place Hamilton Tigers refuse to compete in the playoffs unless each player receives an additional $200.
Births & Deaths	**Aug 11, 1920** • Chuck Rayner born in Sutherland, Saskatchewan. **Apr 1, 1921** • Ken Reardon born in Winnipeg, Manitoba.	**Aug 4, 1921** • Maurice Richard born in Montreal, Quebec. **Mar 2, 1922** • Bill Quackenbush born in Toronto, Ontario	**Mar 17, 1923** • Tony Leswick born in Humboldt, Saskatchewan. **May 6, 1923** • Harry Watson born in Saskatoon, Sask.	**June 28, 1923** • Gaye Stewart born in Fort William, Ontario **Feb 10, 1924** • Bud Poile born in Fort William, Ontario.	**Nov 8, 1924** • Johnny Bower born in Prince Albert, Sask. **Dec 19, 1924** • Doug Harvey born in Montreal, Quebec.

1920s	1925–26	1926–27	1927–28	1928–29	1929–30
Firsts	**Jan 30, 1926** • Ottawa's Alex Connell became the first goaltender in NHL history to record 10 shutouts in one season, reaching the milestone in the Senators' 1–0 win over the New York Americans.	**Nov 16, 1926** • Hal Winkler became the first goaltender in NHL history to record a shutout in his first career game as the New York Rangers beat the visiting Montreal Maroons 1–0. Still, the Rangers would sell Winkler to Boston on Jan 17, 1927.	**Jan 14, 1928** • Hap Day scored his first career hat trick (and the first by any player in a Maple Leafs uniform) in a 6–1 win over the visiting New York Rangers.	**Mar 2, 1929** • Goaltender George Hainsworth became the first (and only) NHL goaltender to record 20 shutouts in one season when the Montreal Canadiens beat the Boston Bruins 3–0. Hainsworth ended the season with 22 shutouts.	**Feb 25, 1930** • Goaltender Alex Connell became the first goalie in NHL history to record 60 career shutouts, and Frank Finnigan scored two overtime goals, as Ottawa won 2–0 over the visiting Toronto Maple Leafs.
Records	**Dec 26, 1925** • New York Americans and Pittsburgh Pirates set an NHL record with 141 shots in a 3–1 victory by the Americans. New York held the shot edge, 73–68. Roy Worters made 70 saves for Pittsburgh, while Jake Forbes had 67 for New York.	**Mar 22, 1927** • Montreal's George Hainsworth set a record for first-year goaltenders with his 14th shutout of the season when the Canadiens beat the Bruins 1–0 in Boston.	**Feb 18, 1928** • Alex Connell of the Senators recorded his sixth consecutive shutout (still an NHL record) in a 1–0 win over the Montreal Canadiens in Ottawa.	**Feb 28, 1929** • Chicago Black Hawks set a record by being shut out for the eighth straight game when they settled for a 0–0 tie with the visiting New York Rangers.	**Mar 18, 1930** • Boston's Cooney Weiland had a hat trick in a 9–2 win over the Rangers in the final game of the season to give him an NHL-record 73 points (in 44 games).
Did You Know?	**Nov 28, 1925** • While playing in his 328th straight game for the Montreal Canadiens, goaltender Georges Vezina collapsed during the game against the Pittsburgh Pirates. Suffering from tuberculosis, Vezina died four months later.	**Mar 26, 1927** • Despite losing 4–3 to the visiting Boston Bruins on the final night of the season, the New York Rangers won the NHL's new American Division championship (with a record of 25–13–6) in their first season in the league.	**Apr 7, 1928** • 44-year-old coach Lester Patrick replaced injured netminder Lorne Chabot in goal and Frank Boucher scored at 7:05 of overtime to give the Rangers a 2–1 win over the Montreal Maroons in game two of the Stanley Cup finals.	**Jan 3, 1929** • Boston's legendary defenseman Eddie Shore drove through a blizzard to get from Boston to Montreal. Shore arrived late for the game but scored the only goal as the Bruins beat the Maroons 1–0.	**Feb 27, 1930** • New York Americans loaned their goaltender Roy Worters to the Montreal Canadiens for one night. Worters gave up two goals in a 6–2 win over the visiting Toronto Maple Leafs.
Milestones	**Jan 16, 1926** • Clint Benedict became the first goaltender to record 25 career NHL shutouts, when he led the Montreal Maroons to a 1–0 win over the Montreal Canadiens.	**Mar 3, 1927** • Ottawa Senators became the first NHL team to win 25 games in one season with a 2–1 victory at Pittsburgh. The Senators broke their own previous record of 24 wins, set in 1925–26.	**Mar 22, 1928** • Ottawa goalie Alex Connell became the first goaltender in history to record 50 career NHL shutouts as the Senators beat the visiting New York Americans 5–0.	**Feb 9, 1929** • Maroons' Clint Benedict became the NHL's all-time leader in shutouts when the 55th of his career moved him one ahead of Alex Connell. The milestone came as Montreal won 1–0 over the visiting Boston Bruins.	**Feb 20, 1930** • Montreal Maroons goalie Clint Benedict became the first goalie to wear a mask in an NHL game in a 3–3 tie against the New York Americans. Benedict wore the mask temporarily, during an injury.
Rookies	**Nov 10, 1925** • Pittsburgh Pirates (the NHL's newest team) announced the signing of Lionel Conacher, one of the top all-around athletes in Canada.	**Nov 16, 1926** • Rookie Eddie Shore made his NHL debut as the Boston Bruins opened their third NHL season with a 4–1 win over the Canadiens.	**Nov 15, 1927** • Boston's Dit Clapper scored his first NHL goal in the Bruins' season-opener, a 1–1 tie against the Chicago Black Hawks.	**Feb 28, 1929** • Boston goaltender Tiny Thompson recorded the 12th shutout of his rookie season as the Bruins beat the Senators 4–0 in Ottawa.	**Feb 6, 1930** • Toronto rookie Charlie Conacher scored his first career hat trick as the Maple Leafs tied 3–3 with the Montreal Maroons.
Transactions	**Jan 12, 1926** • Pittsburgh picked up Frank Lowery on waivers from the Maroons. Three days later, the Canadiens acquired Joe Matte on waivers from the Boston Bruins.	**Dec 16, 1926** • New York Americans acquired Lionel Conacher from Pittsburgh in exchange for Charlie Langlois and $2,000.	**Dec 15, 1927** • Montreal Canadiens acquired Charlie Langlois from Pittsburgh in exchange for Marty Burke.	**Oct 17, 1928** • Toronto acquired goaltender Lorne Chabot and Alex Gray from the New York Rangers in exchange for Butch Keeling and John Ross Roach.	**Dec 6, 1929** • Toronto signed Harvey "Busher" Jackson, who would become famous as a member of the Maple Leafs' Kid Line. Jackson made his NHL debut the next night.
Teams	**Sep 26, 1925** • The New York Americans purchased the roster of the suspended Hamilton Tigers for $75,000 when the Hamilton franchise was dropped from the NHL.	**May 15, 1926** • New York Rangers were officially granted a franchise. In addition, the NHL announced that Chicago and Detroit would join in November, giving the league 10 teams.	**Apr 14, 1928** • New York Rangers beat the Montreal Maroons 2–1 in game five of the finals to win their first Stanley Cup championship in just their second NHL season.	**Mar 29, 1929** • The Bruins beat the Rangers 2–1 in game two of their best-of-three series to win their first Stanley Cup title. The championship came in Boston's fifth NHL season.	**Feb 18, 1930** • Boston Bruins set an NHL record for most wins in a season, with their 31st of the year (and their 18th straight at home), in a 3–2 victory over the Montreal Maroons.
Front Office	**Oct 18, 1925** • Pittsburgh Pirates (the NHL's newest team) signed veteran Odie Cleghorn to coach and manage the club. He would also see some action as a player.	**Dec 14, 1926** • Ottawa's David Gill improved his record to 9–0–1 (the best start ever by a rookie coach) when the Senators beat the Americans 2–0. The undefeated streak ended two days later.	**May 17, 1927** • Jack Adams was named coach and general manager of the Detroit Cougars. He would control the Detroit team (later called the Red Wings) for the next 35 years.	**Oct 25, 1928** • Boston Bruins purchased veteran Cy Denneny from the Ottawa Senators and named him a player/coach for the 1928–29 season.	**Oct 22, 1929** • Montreal Maroons signed former NHL referee Dr. Jerry Laflamme as a bench coach. He would assist Dunc Munro, who functioned as the Maroons' player/coach.
Playoffs	**Apr 6, 1926** • Goalie Clint Benedict led the Montreal Maroons to their first Stanley Cup title, shutting out the Victoria Cougars 2–0 at the Montreal Forum to win the best of five series three games to one.	**Apr 2, 1927** • Lorne Chabot of the New York Rangers became the first rookie goalie in NHL history to get a shutout in his first playoff game when he and Boston's Hal Winkler traded shutouts in a scoreless tie in game one of the Stanley Cup semifinals.	**Apr 10, 1928** • Montreal Maroons goalie Clint Benedict recorded his 15th and final career playoff shutout (an NHL record) with a 2–0 win over the visiting New York Rangers in game three of their Stanley Cup championship series.	**Mar 28, 1929** • Boston Bruins and the New York Rangers clashed in the first NHL Stanley Cup final between two U.S.-based teams. Boston won 2–0 and 2–1 to capture their first championship title. Tiny Thompson provided stellar goaltending.	**Apr 3, 1930** • The Canadiens beat Boston 4–3 at the Forum to win the 1929–30 Stanley Cup championship in two straight games. For the defending Cup champ Bruins, who had the best regular season record (38–5–1), it marked their first back-to-back losses of the year.
Business	**Nov 26, 1925** • NHL announced a new "anti-defense" rule, which would prohibit teams from having more than two players in their own zone when the puck was not present. The league also increased the number of regular-season games from 30 to 36 for the upcoming season.	**May 4, 1926** • The NHL Board of Governors purchased the contracts of all the players in the Western Hockey League for $258,000. Most of the former Portland players were sold to the expansion Chicago Black Hawks. Players from the Victoria Cougars were sold to the new NHL team in Detroit.	**Sep 24, 1927** • The NHL passed new rules to allow forward passing in the defensive and neutral zones. In addition, sudden-death overtime in regular-season games was reduced from 20 minutes to 10 minutes.	**Sep 22, 1928** • The NHL passed new rules changing overtime in the regular season from 10 minutes of sudden-death to a full 10-minute extra period if games were tied at the end of regulation.	**Dec 16, 1929** • The "offside" rule had its origin at a Board of Governors meeting in Chicago. The new rule stated: "No attacking player shall be allowed to precede the play when entering the opposing defensive zone." The rule came into effect 5 days later.
Births & Deaths	**Jul 29, 1925** • Ted Lindsay born in Renfrew, Ontario. **Dec 12, 1925** • Ted Kennedy born in Humberstone, Ontario.	**Sept 4, 1926** • Bert Olmstead born in Scepter, Saskatchewan. **Nov 11, 1926** • Harry Lumley born in Owen Sound, Ontario.	**Jul 9, 1927** • Red Kelly born in Simcoe, Ontario. **Mar 31, 1928** • Gordie Howe born in Floral, Saskatchewan.	**Jan 17, 1929** • Jacques Plante born in Mont Carmel, Quebec. **May 14, 1929** • Gump Worsley born in Montreal, Quebec.	**Dec 28, 1929** • Terry Sawchuk born in Winnipeg, Manitoba. **Jan 12, 1930** • Tim Horton born in Cochrane, Ontario.

1930s	1930–31	1931–32	1932–33	1933–34	1934–35
Firsts	**Feb 14, 1931** • In an historic first, three assists were awarded on one NHL goal. Toronto's Charlie Conacher scored, with assists given to King Clancy, Joe Primeau and Busher Jackson. The goal gave the Maple Leafs a 1–1 tie with Detroit.	**Feb 11, 1932** • George Owen of Boston became the first U.S.-born player to score an NHL hat trick, but the host Bruins lost 7–4 to the Montreal Maroons.	**Mar 18, 1933** • Montreal's George Hainsworth became the first goaltender in NHL history to record 75 career shutouts as the Canadiens tied 0–0 with the visiting Boston Bruins.	**Feb 14, 1934** • The NHL held its first All-Star Game as a benefit for injured star Ace Bailey. Toronto defeated a team of All-Stars from the league's other seven teams 7–3 at Maple Leaf Gardens.	**Nov 10, 1934** • Canadiens' Armand Mondou was stopped by Toronto's George Hainsworth on the NHL's first penalty shot. Three days later Ralph "Scotty" Bowman of the St. Louis Eagles scored the first penalty shot goal in NHL history.
Records	**Jan 3, 1931** • Nels Stewart of the Montreal Maroons scored twice in a span of four seconds in the third period to set an NHL record (tied in 1995–96) for fastest two goals by one player. Stewart led his team to a 5–3 victory over the Boston Bruins.	**Dec 10, 1931** • Goaltender George Hainsworth set a record for all-time shutouts with the 64th of his career (to pass Alex Connell) as Montreal won 3–0 over the Americans at New York.	**Dec 4, 1932** • New York Americans' Ron Martin scored eight seconds after the opening face-off to set an NHL record for the fastest goal from the start of a game. New York won 4–2 over the visiting Montreal Canadiens.	**Mar 11, 1934** • NHL records were set when the Montreal Maroons scored four goals in the (mandatory) 10-minute overtime period to beat the Rangers 7–3 in New York. Russ Blinco led the scoring with two overtime goals.	**Nov 20, 1934** • Toronto's Harvey "Busher" Jackson set a record by scoring three goals in one period. He finished with four goals in the final period to lead the Leafs to 5–2 win over the St. Louis Eagles.
Did You Know?	**Nov 18, 1930** • Montreal's Howie Morenz took the first major penalty of his eight-year NHL career in a 5–2 Canadiens loss at Boston Garden.	**Mar 15, 1932** • With Toronto goalie Lorne Chabot in the penalty box for tripping, Boston scored goals against Leafs regulars Red Horner, Alex Levinsky and King Clancy. Chabot returned after the penalty expired, but the Bruins won 6–2.	**Mar 14, 1933** • Chicago forfeited the only game in team history when Black Hawk players refused to return to the ice after their coach Tom Gorman was ejected. Boston was awarded a 1–0 victory. (The Bruins led 3–2 at the time of the incident.)	**Jan 16, 1934** • Ken Doraty scored the only hat trick in NHL overtime history as Toronto defeated the Senators 7–4 at Ottawa. Overtime was a full 10-minute period at that time, not sudden death.	**Mar 16, 1935** • Charlie Conacher scored his 12th career hat trick as the Maple Leafs won 5–3 over the Montreal Canadiens. Conacher also took over in goal for injured netminder George Hainsworth and held Montreal scoreless for three minutes.
Milestones	**Feb 17, 1931** • Howie Morenz scored his milestone 200th career goal in the Canadiens' 2–0 win over the visiting Montreal Maroons.	**Feb 14, 1932** • Detroit goaltender Alex Connell recorded his 150th NHL career victory as the Red Wings won 3–1 over the visiting Black Hawks.	**Mar 12, 1933** • Detroit's John Ross Roach became the first goaltender in NHL history to record 200 career victories when the Red Wings won 3–1 over the visiting Montreal Canadiens.	**Dec 28, 1933** • Montreal's Howie Morenz scored twice to become the first 250-goal scorer in NHL history. The milestone came in a 4–3 loss to the visiting Boston Bruins.	**Jan 10, 1935** • The official scorer in New York made history by awarding four assists on a goal by Toronto's Joe Primeau. The milestone came in a 5–5 tie between the Maple Leafs and Americans.
Rookies	**Mar 21, 1931** • Goaltender Dave Kerr recorded the only shutout of his rookie season in the Montreal Maroons' 3–0 win over the rival Montreal Canadiens.	**Mar 22, 1932** • Rangers rookie Ott Heller, playing in his 21st career game on the final night of the season, scored his first two NHL goals as New York lost 5–4 to the Detroit Falcons.	**Dec 13, 1932** • Detroit rookie Gus Marker scored his first career goal in a 7–4 loss to the visiting Montreal Maroons.	**Dec 23, 1933** • Toronto's rookie defenseman William "Flash" Hollett scored his first career goal (and added an assist) in an 8–2 Maple Leafs win over the visiting Montreal Maroons.	**Jan 5, 1935** • St. Louis rookie Bill Cowley scored the first goal of his NHL career (the game winner in the third period) in a 2–1 Eagles win over the Maroons at Montreal.
Transactions	**Oct 10, 1930** • Toronto Maple Leafs announced the acquisition of King Clancy from Ottawa in exchange for Art Smith, Eric Pettinger and the record sum of $35,000 cash.	**Sep 26, 1931** • Detroit obtained Alex Connell, Hec Kilrea, Danny Cox and Alex Smith in the NHL Dispersal Draft, following the league's suspension of Ottawa and Philadelphia.	**Oct 5, 1932** • Detroit purchased goaltender John Ross Roach from the New York Rangers for $11,000. Roach went on to lead the NHL with 25 wins in 1932–33.	**Nov 26, 1933** • Detroit acquired Cooney Weiland from Ottawa in exchange for Carl Voss. Weiland went on to score 11 goals and 19 assists in 39 games with Detroit in 1933–34.	**Feb 22, 1935** • Montreal Maroons signed future Hall of Famer Hector "Toe" Blake. He would see little action before joining the Montreal Canadiens the following season.
Teams	**Nov 11, 1930** • The city of Philadelphia hosted its first NHL game as the Quakers were shut out 3–0 by the Rangers. The Quakers played just one season and were a dismal 4–36–4.	**Sep 26, 1931** • The NHL Board of Governors announced the suspension ("for one year, at least") of the Ottawa Senators and Philadelphia Quakers.	**Oct 5, 1932** • The new name Red Wings (along with new uniforms) was introduced to Detroit hockey fans. The team had previously been called the Cougars and then Falcons.	**Mar 15, 1934** • New York Americans beat the Senators 3–2 in what would be the final NHL game played in Ottawa until the league returned to Canada's capital in 1992–93.	**Sep 22, 1934** • The Ottawa Senators moved to St. Louis, where the team became known as the Eagles.
Front Office	**Oct 18, 1930** • NHL referee-in-chief Cooper Smeaton resigned from his post to become the new coach of the Philadelphia Quakers. The team had relocated from Pittsburgh to Philadelphia.	**Nov 27, 1931** • Toronto Maple Leafs fired coach Art Duncan and named Dick Irvin as his replacement. Irvin led the Leafs to the Stanley Cup and coached the team for the next eight years.	**Jan 14, 1933** • The Black Hawks named Tom Gorman their new coach. As the tenth coach in its seven-year history, Gorman would lead Chicago to its first Stanley Cup title in 1934.	**Apr 20, 1934** • Tommy Gorman resigned as coach of the Black Hawks, 10 days after leading the team to the Stanley Cup. Three weeks later, he was hired by the Montreal Maroons.	**May 14, 1934** • Tommy Gorman was named coach of the Montreal Maroons. He had coached Chicago to the Stanley Cup the previous season.
Playoffs	**Mar 26, 1931** • Boston's Art Ross became the first NHL coach to pull his goalie for an extra attacker as the Bruins lost 1–0 to the Canadiens in game two of the Stanley Cup semifinals. Sylvio Mantha scored the only goal and George Hainsworth got the shutout.	**Apr 5, 1932** • Toronto's Busher Jackson became the first player to score three goals in one period of a playoff game when he got a hat trick in the second period of a 6–4 Maple Leafs win over the Rangers in game one of the Stanley Cup finals at New York's Madison Square Garden.	**Apr 3, 1933** • Ken Doraty scored after 104:46 of overtime as Toronto defeated Boston 1–0 in game five of the Stanley Cup semifinals. The game was the longest in history at the time and remains the second-longest ever played in the NHL.	**Mar 22, 1934** • Herbie Lewis scored at 1:33 of OT (the first power-play overtime goal in NHL playoff history) to give the Red Wings a 2–1 win in Toronto in game one of their Stanley Cup semifinal series.	**Apr 9, 1935** • Montreal Maroons beat Toronto 4–1 in game three of the finals to become the 1935 Stanley Cup champions.
Business	**Sep 27, 1930** • At the annual NHL Governors' meeting, a new rule was passed: "The puck must be propelled into the attacking zone before any player of the attacking side can enter that zone."	**Sep 26, 1931** • The NHL Board of Governors increased the league's regular-season schedule from 44 to 48 games.	**May 10, 1932** • The NHL Board of Governors decided that no team's payroll would exceed $70,000 in 1932–33.	**Sep 30, 1933** • At the Board of Governors' NHL meeting it was decided that two referees would henceforth be used for each game instead of one referee and one linesman. This system lasted five years before it went back to one referee and one linesman.	**Sep 22, 1934** • The NHL approved a new rule to allow the awarding of penalty shots (to be taken from within a 10-foot circle 38 feet out from the goaltender) when an attacking player is fouled when in "a good scoring position."
Births & Deaths	**Jul 6, 1930** • George Armstrong born in Borlands Bay, Ont. **Feb 14, 1931** • Bernie Geoffrion born in Montreal, Quebec.	**Aug 31, 1931** • Jean Beliveau born in Trois Rivieres, Quebec. **Oct 3, 1931** • Glenn Hall born in Humboldt, Saskatchewan.	**Aug 28, 1932** • Andy Bathgate born in Winnipeg, Manitoba. **Dec 28, 1932** • Harry Howell born in Hamilton, Ontario.	**Oct 31, 1933** • Phil Goyette born in Lachine, Quebec. **Dec. 13, 1933** • Doug Mohns born in Capreol, Ontario.	**Nov 10, 1934** • Bill Sutherland born in Regina, Saskatchewan. **May 12, 1935** • John Bucyk born in Edmonton, Alberta.

1930s	1935–36	1936–37	1937–38	1938–39	1939–40
Firsts	**Jan 14, 1936** • Boston's Cecil "Tiny" Thompson became the first goaltender in NHL history to receive credit for an assist. It came in a 4–1 Bruins win over Toronto in Boston Garden.	**Nov 7, 1936** • New York Americans beat Toronto 3–2 in the first coast-to-coast radio broadcast of a hockey game in Canada.	**Dec 21, 1937** • Chicago's Paul Thompson became the first player in NHL history to score a goal against his brother when he scored on Bruins goalie Cecil "Tiny" Thompson at 19:51 of the third period in a 2–1 Black Hawks loss at Boston Garden.	**Mar 7, 1939** • Boston Bruins won the Prince of Wales trophy by clinching the NHL regular-season championship with a 3–0 win over the Red Wings in Boston. This was the first time the Prince of Wales trophy was awarded for this reason.	**Mar 17, 1940** • For the first time in history, one line (Boston's Milt Schmidt, Woody Dumart & Bobby Bauer) finished 1–2–3 in NHL scoring. A 7–2 win over Montreal in the final game that night gave the Bruins the NHL regular-season championship.
Records	**Mar 22, 1936** • New York Rangers won 3–1 at Boston on the final night of the season to finish with a record of 19–17–12, marking the first time in NHL history that every team in a division finished with records of over .500. The next time this would occur was in 1968–69.	**Jan 30, 1937** • Nels Stewart of the New York Americans set an NHL career scoring record with his 270th goal in a 4–0 win over the Canadiens. At the time, Howie Morenz was credited with 269 goals, though that would later be revised to 270. Stewart would score 324 goals	**Mar 13, 1938** • Detroit rookie Carl Liscombe scored the fastest three goals in NHL history in a 5–1 win over Chicago at the Olympia. His record time was 1:52. The record was broken 14 years later by Chicago's Bill Mosienko.	**Dec 20, 1938** • Boston's Frankie Brimsek set a record for rookie goalies with his sixth shutout in his eighth career game, a 3–0 win over the New York Americans.	**Jan 28, 1940** • Chicago's Les Cunningham had two goals and three assists in a span of 10:04 of the third period (in an 8–1 win over Montreal) to set an NHL record for most points by a player in one period.
Did You Know?	**Feb 2, 1936** • Boston defeated the New York Americans 2–1 at Boston Garden with all three goals scored in the final three minutes of the mandatory 10-minute overtime period.	**Nov 14, 1936** • Francis "King" Clancy scored on a penalty shot as the Maple Leafs beat Chicago 6–2. It was the final goal of Clancy's NHL playing career. The future Hall of Famer retired one week later.	**Apr 21, 1938** • Toe Blake scored the winning goal in overtime as Montreal beat Detroit 5–4 before a crowd of 8,000 in Earl's court, England in the first of a nine-game tour between the two teams. Games were played in England and France.	**Nov 15, 1938** • Boston extended its overtime undefeated streak to 37 games (10–0–27) with a 1–1 tie against Toronto. The 37-game streak, which began in December 1934, is the longest in NHL history.	**May 13, 1939** • At the annual NHL meetings, Boston's Art Ross submitted for consideration a new type of hockey stick with a metal handle and replaceable wooden blade. This came nearly 50 years before the modern-era aluminum stick.
Milestones	**Dec 17, 1935** • Canadiens and Rangers skated to a 1–1 tie in the 500th NHL game for five of the Ranger originals. The Cook brothers (Bill and Bun), along with Frank Boucher, Ching Johnson and Murray Murdoch were all presented with suitcases to honor the occasion.	**Mar 9, 1937** • New York Rangers' Frank Boucher became the first player in NHL history to amass 250 career assists. The milestone came in a 7–5 win over the New York Americans.	**Mar 17, 1938** • Nels Stewart of the New York Americans became the first player in NHL history to score 300 career goals. The milestone came in a 5–3 loss to the rival Rangers.	**Nov 20, 1938** • Boston's Tiny Thompson became the first NHL goaltender to record 250 career victories. The milestone came in a Bruins' 4–1 win over the visiting Detroit Red Wings.	**Feb 1, 1940** • Detroit goalie Tiny Thompson became the third NHL goaltender to record 80 career shutouts as the Red Wings beat the Rangers 2–0.
Rookies	**Feb 22, 1936** • Canadiens rookie Toe Blake scored his first career NHL goal as Montreal won 1–0 over the visiting New York Americans.	**Nov 5, 1936** • Rookies Turk Broda and Syl Apps made their NHL debuts when the Maple Leafs lost to the Red Wings 3–1 in Toronto on the opening night of the 1936–37 NHL season.	**Nov 4, 1973** • Earl Robertson became the fifth goaltender in NHL history to record a shutout in his first career regular-season game as the New York Americans won 3–0 at Chicago.	**Dec 1, 1938** • Boston rookie Frankie Brimsek played his first NHL game. He lost 2–0 to the Canadiens in Montreal, but went on to record six shutouts in his next seven games.	**Nov 19, 1939** • Toronto rookie Don Metz scored his first career NHL goal in a 7–1 Maple Leafs win over the Red Wings at Detroit.
Transactions	**Feb 13, 1936** • Montreal Canadiens purchased forward Hector "Toe" Blake from the Montreal Maroons.	**May 6, 1936** • Toronto Maple Leafs purchased amateur goaltender Walter "Turk" Broda from the Detroit Red Wings' organization for the sum of $8,000.	**Feb 13, 1938** • Detroit obtained Hap Emms from the New York Americans, in exchange for John Sorrell.	**Nov 28, 1938** • Detroit purchased veteran goaltender Tiny Thompson from the Boston Bruins for $15,000 and a player to be named later. Boston then called up rookie Frankie Brimsek	**Jan 25, 1940** • Boston Bruins defenseman Eddie Shore was traded to the New York Americans.
Teams	**Sep 28, 1935** • The St. Louis Eagles requested permission to suspend operations. The NHL refused and bought out the franchise one month later. A Dispersal Draft was held for the players.	**Mar 11, 1937** • The Red Wings clinched their second straight American Division title by beating the Rangers 4–2. Larry Aurie broke his leg during the game and missed the playoffs.	**Feb 22, 1938** • Boston won an NHL record seventh straight game as Tiny Thompson made 24 saves for a 2–0 win over Toronto at Boston Garden.	**Jun 22, 1938** • Montreal Maroons withdrew from the National Hockey League. The franchise folded two months later.	**Jan 14, 1940** • New York Rangers lost to Chicago 2–1 to end their team-record 10-game winning streak. The Rangers came back to win five straight for a total of 15 wins in 16 starts.
Front Office	**Sep 16, 1935** • Montreal Canadiens named Sylvio Mantha as their new coach replacing owner Leo Dandurand.	**July 30, 1936** • Cecil Hart was named coach and manager of the Montreal Canadiens.	**May 18, 1937** • Chicago Black Hawks named referee Bill Stewart their new coach, replacing Clem Loughlin. Stewart would lead the Black Hawks to the Stanley Cup in 1938.	**Jan 3, 1939** • Chicago Black Hawks fired coach Bill Stewart. Paul Thompson was named as his replacement. Stewart had led the Black Hawks to the Stanley Cup the previous spring.	**Aug 25, 1939** • Albert "Babe" Siebert, who had been named new coach of the Montreal Canadiens earlier in the summer, died in a drowning accident in Zurich, Ontario.
Playoffs	**Mar 24–25, 1936** • Mud Bruneteau scored as Detroit beat the Montreal Maroons 1–0 at 116:30 of overtime—five hours and 51 minutes after the opening face-off—in the longest game in NHL history. Goalie Norm Smith made 92 saves for the Red Wings.	**Mar 25, 1937** • Lionel Conacher of the Montreal Maroons took the NHL's first penalty shot in the playoffs. He was stopped by the Bruins' Tiny Thompson who went on to shut out the Maroons 4–0 in game two of the Stanley Cup quarterfinals in Boston.	**Apr 12, 1938** • Chicago beat Toronto 4–1 in game four of the finals to win the 1937–38 Stanley Cup championship. Eight American-born players skated for Chicago as the Black Hawks won the second Stanley Cup title in franchise history.	**Apr 16, 1939** • Boston Bruins defeated the Toronto Maple Leafs 3–1 to win the 1938–39 Stanley Cup championship in five games in the first best-of-seven Stanley Cup final. Previously, the championship series had been a best-of-five affair.	**Mar 19, 1940** • Syd Howe scored 25 seconds into overtime to give the Red Wings a 1–0 win over the New York Americans in game one of the Stanley Cup quarterfinals. At the time it was the fastest overtime goal in NHL playoff history.
Business	**Oct 15, 1935** • Boston Bruins obtained Bill Cowley from the NHL, which had taken over the financially troubled St. Louis Eagles franchise. Cowley went on to become the NHL's leading scorer in the 1930s and early 1940s.	**May 7, 1936** • At the NHL meetings in Detroit it was announced that the Montreal Canadiens had been granted first claim on all French Canadian amateur hockey players in all of Canada for a period of three years.	**Sep 24, 1937** • The NHL Board of Governors introduced legislation to discourage "icing" during the league's semi-annual meeting. The new rules would now cause a face-off in the defending zone if a team shot the puck all the way down the ice without scoring a goal.	**Sep 24, 1938** • The NHL announced its decision to operate as one seven-team division with each team playing 48 games.	**Feb 25, 1940** • New York Rangers faced the Canadiens in the first hockey game televised in the U.S. The game aired on station W2XBS in New York, with one camera in a fixed position, to 300 TV receivers in New York. The Rangers won 6–2 for their 14th straight home win.
Births & Deaths	**Dec 26, 1935** • Norm Ullman born in Provost, Alberta. **Feb 29, 1936** • Henri Richard born in Montreal, Quebec.	**Sep 7, 1936** • Orland Kurtenbach born in Cudworth, Sask. **Feb 11, 1937** • Eddie Shack born in Sudbury, Ontario.	**Jan 10, 1938** • Frank Mahovlich born in Timmins, Ontario. **Mar 18, 1938** • Bob Nevin born in South Porcupine, Ontario.	**Sep 5, 1938** • John Ferguson born in Vancouver, B.C. **Jan 3, 1939** • Bobby Hull born in Point Anne, Ontario.	**Mar 22, 1940** • Dave Keon born in Noranda, Quebec. **May 20, 1940** • Stan Mikita born in Skolce, Czech.

1940s

	1940–41	1941–42	1942–43	1943–44	1944–45
Firsts	**Mar 15, 1941** • Montreal Canadiens defeated the New York Americans 6–0 as Montreal coach Dick Irvin alternated goaltenders Bert Gardiner and Paul Bibeault in seven-minute intervals for the first "shared shutout" in NHL history.	**Mar 15, 1942** • Lynn Patrick scored twice as the New York Rangers clinched their first NHL regular-season championship by defeating Chicago 5–1.	**Jan 3, 1943** • Chicago's Reg Bentley scored a goal, with assists from brothers Max and Doug, in a 3–3 Black Hawks tie at New York. It was the first goal in NHL history with three points all from the same family!	**Jan 8, 1944** • Toronto's Babe Pratt became the first defenseman in NHL history to get six assists in a game. They came as the Leafs beat Boston 12–3 at Maple Leaf Garden.	**Mar 18, 1945** • In the final game of the 1944–45 season at Boston, Maurice "Rocket" Richard became the first player in NHL history to score 50 goals in a season as Montreal beat the Bruins 4–2. Richard scored his 50 goals in just 50 games.
Records	**Mar 4, 1941** • The Bruins set an NHL record with 83 shots against Chicago goalie Sam LoPresti in a 3–2 Boston win over the Black Hawks.	**Nov 5, 1942** • Detroit's Carl Liscombe set an NHL record with seven points (three goals and four assists) in one game as the Red Wings defeated the New York Rangers 12–5 at the Olympia.	**Jan 14, 1943** • Montreal's Alex Smart set a record for most goals by a rookie in his first NHL game. Smart had a hat trick (along with an assist) in a 5–1 win over Chicago. Smart went on to play just eight games in his NHL career.	**Jan 23, 1944** • Red Wings scored 15 consecutive goals, an NHL record, to beat the Rangers 15–0 in Detroit.	**Dec 28, 1944** • Montreal's Maurice Richard set a new scoring standard when he scored five goals and added three assists for a record eight-point night as the Canadiens beat Detroit 9–1.
Did You Know?	**Dec 1, 1940** • Four sets of brothers played in one NHL game: Rangers' Lynn & Muzz Patrick and Neil & Mac Colville against Chicago's brother acts of Max & Doug Bentley and Bob & Bill Carse. The Black Hawks won 4–1 at Chicago Stadium.	**Jan 6, 1942** • During a 3–2 Bruins win over Chicago in Boston Garden, an announcement was made to fans in attendance to "please return any pucks deflected into the stands, due to a wartime shortage of rubber".	**Nov 12, 1942** • 16-year-old Armand "Bep" Guidolin became the youngest player in NHL history when he appeared in his first game with the Boston Bruins, a 3–1 loss at Toronto.	**Feb 20, 1944** • Mike Karakas of the Black Hawks and the Maple Leafs' Paul Bibeault dueled to the only scoreless, penalty-free game in NHL history. The 0–0 tie, officiated by referee Bill Chadwick, took only 1:55 to play.	**Jan 18, 1945** • 7,687 fans waited in their seats at the Detroit Olympia as weather made the New York Rangers three hours late for their game. The Red Wings beat the Rangers 7–3 in a game that began at 11:15 p.m. and ended at 12:56 a.m.
Milestones	**Jan 18, 1941** • Boston's Dit Clapper scored his 200th career NHL goal in a 1–0 win over the Maple Leafs at Toronto.	**Nov 27, 1941** • Boston Bruins scored four goals in the overtime period, winning 6–2 over the New York Americans. Overtime was a mandatory 10-minute period before it was discontinued due to wartime travel restrictions in November 1942.	**Nov 10, 1942** • New York Rangers scored twice in overtime to beat the Black Hawks 5–3 in the final regular-season overtime game in 41 years.	**Nov 11, 1943** • Clint Smith scored the first empty-net goal in NHL history (after Bruins coach Art Ross pulled goalie Bert Gardiner with his team trailing 5–4). Smith made history at 19:12 of the final period and gave Chicago a 6–4 win at Boston Garden.	**Mar 8, 1945** • Detroit's Syd Howe became the NHL's all-time leading scorer with 516 career points (passing Nels Stewart). He set the record with an assist in a 7–3 win over New York.
Rookies	**Dec 1, 1940** • Chicago rookie Max Bentley scored the first goal of his NHL career in a 4–1 Black Hawks win over the visiting New York Rangers.	**Feb 7, 1942** • Toronto's rookie defenseman Bob Goldham scored the first goal of his NHL career, and added an assist, in a 6–4 Maple Leafs win over the visiting New York Rangers.	**Nov 8, 1942** • Rookie Maurice Richard scored his first NHL goal in a 10–4 Canadiens win over the Rangers in Montreal.	**Oct 30, 1943** • Toronto's Gus Bodnar set an NHL record for the fastest goal by a rookie by scoring just 15 seconds into his first NHL game. He later scored again in a 5–2 win over New York.	**Nov 2, 1944** • Detroit rookie Ted Lindsay scored his first NHL goal in a 10–3 Red Wings victory over the New York Rangers.
Transactions	**Nov 19, 1940** • Montreal Canadiens purchased veteran Jack Portland from the Chicago Black Hawks for $12,500.	**Dec 18, 1941** • Chicago Black Hawks purchased Red Hamill from Boston. Hamill went on to score 18 goals and nine assists in 34 games during the 1941–42 season.	**Mar 9, 1943** • Boston Bruins purchased Ab DeMarco from Toronto. DeMarco went on to score four goals and one assist in three games with the Bruins in 1942–43.	**Jan 5, 1944** • Detroit Red Wings obtained Bill "Flash" Hollett from the Boston Bruins in exchange for Pat Egan.	**Jan 2, 1945** • Chicago Black Hawks traded Earl Seibert to the Detroit Red Wings in exchange for Don Grosso, Cully Simon and Byron McDonald.
Teams	**Feb 23, 1941** • The Bruins set an NHL record by extending their unbeaten streak to 23 games (15–0–8) with a 3–1 win over the New York Americans at Boston Garden.	**Sep 12, 1941** • The Americans changed their home city designation from New York to Brooklyn.	**Sep 28, 1942** • The NHL shrunk to six teams as president Frank Calder announced that Madison Square Garden had declined to renew the lease of the Brooklyn Americans.	**Dec 11, 1943** • Following a 9–6 loss to Boston, the New York Rangers dropped to an 0–14–1 record, the worst start by any team in NHL history.	**Jan 21, 1945** • Boston set an NHL record for fastest four goals by one team, scoring four times in a 1:20 span during the second period of a 14–3 win over the Rangers.
Front Office	**Nov 3, 1940** • Dick Irvin coached his first game with the Montreal Canadiens, a 1–1 tie with the Bruins at the Forum.	**Nov 6, 1941** • Paul Thompson became the first coach in Black Hawks history to begin a fourth year behind the bench as Chicago won its season opener 1–0 over the Americans.	**Feb 5, 1943** • Mervyn "Red" Dutton was named the new NHL president, replacing Frank Calder, who had passed away the day before.	**Mar 18, 1944** • Jack Adams became the first coach in NHL history to record 350 career victories when the Red Wings beat the visiting Chicago Black Hawks 6–3.	**Nov 15, 1944** • Chicago Black Hawks fired coach Paul Thompson (in his seventh season with the team) and named Johnny Gottselig as his replacement.
Playoffs	**Mar 25, 1941** • Toronto's Nick Metz became the first NHL player to get three assists in one period of a playoff game. The assists came in the second period of the Toronto's 7–2 win over Boston in game three of the Stanley Cup semifinals at Maple Leaf Gardens.	**Apr 18, 1942** • Toronto completed the greatest comeback in playoff history with their fourth straight win, a 3–1 victory over Detroit, in game seven of the Stanley Cup finals. Leafs goalie Turk Broda allowed the Red Wings just seven goals in the final four games.	**Mar 25, 1943** • Harvey "Busher" Jackson scored the first overtime shorthanded goal in playoff history as the Bruins beat Montreal 3–2 in game three of the Stanley Cup semifinals. Jackson's winning goal came at 3:20 of overtime.	**Mar 23, 1944** • Montreal's Maurice Richard scored all five goals, and Toe Blake collected five assists, to lead the Canadiens to a 5–1 victory over Toronto in game two of the Stanley Cup semifinals.	**Apr 6, 1945** • Toronto's Frank McCool and Detroit's Harry Lumley became the first rookie goalies to meet in the Stanley Cup finals. The Leafs beat the Wings 1–0 to open the best-of-seven series. It was the first of three straight shutouts for McCool, as the Leafs would win the series four games to three.
Business	**Sep 12, 1940** • The NHL Board of Governors eliminated the requirement that only jersey numbers 1 to 19 be allowed to designate player in NHL games.	**Sep 12, 1941** • The NHL altered rules to establish minor and major penalty shots. Under the new rules, a minor shot would allow a player a shot at goal from a line 28 feet away.	**Nov 21, 1942** • The NHL Board of Governors announced that overtime would be discontinued in regular-season games because of conflicts with train schedules. Overtime was finally reinstated in the 1983–84 season after a 41-year absence.	**Sep 11, 1943** • The idea of a Hockey Hall of Fame was officially approved by the NHL.	**Oct 18, 1944** • Detroit Red Wings signed amateur Ted Lindsay to his first pro contract.
Births & Deaths	**Oct 3, 1940** • Jean Ratelle born in Lac St. Jean, Quebec. **Dec 7, 1940** • Gerry Cheevers born in St. Catharines, Ontario.	**Nov 22, 1941** • Jacques Laperriere born in Rouyn, Quebec. **Feb 20, 1942** • Phil Esposito born in Sault Ste. Marie, Ontario.	**Jan 28, 1943** • Paul Henderson born in Kincardine, Ontario. **Apr 23, 1943** • Tony Esposito born in Sault Ste. Marie, Ontario.	**Sep 2, 1943** • Glen Sather born in High River, Alberta. **Nov 22, 1943** • Yvan Cournoyer born in Drummondville, PQ.	**Nov 19, 1944** • Dennis Hull born in Pointe Anne, Ontario. **Apr 3, 1945** • Bernie Parent born in Montreal, Quebec.

1940s	1945–46	1946–47	1947–48	1948–49	1949–50
Firsts	**Jan 30, 1946** • NHL president Red Dutton made Babe Pratt the first player in league history to be suspended from the NHL for "conduct prejudicial to the welfare of hockey." Pratt had bet on hockey games, but never against his own team.	**Jan 8, 1947** • Toronto's Howie Meeker scored five goals to set an NHL record for goals in a game by a rookie as the Maple Leafs beat Chicago 10–4.	**Nov 13, 1947** • For the first time in league history, the NHL initiated the policy of having players raise their sticks to signify the scoring of a goal. Montreal's Billy Reay became the first to do so as the Canadiens beat Chicago 5–2 at the Forum.	**Nov 3, 1948** • Detroit's Gordie Howe made the first of his NHL record 21 All-Star appearances, helping the All-Stars to a 3–1 win over the Stanley Cup-champion Toronto Maple Leafs in a game played at Chicago Stadium.	**Feb 11, 1950** • Detroit's Gordie Howe scored his first career NHL hat trick, and added two assists, in a 9–4 Red Wings win at Boston.
Records	**Oct 24, 1945** • The NHL made the earliest season schedule start in league history (going back to 1917), and Chicago's Red Hamill scored two unassisted goals in the final seven minutes to give the Black Hawks a 5–4 win at Boston Garden.	**Mar 16, 1947** • Detroit's Billy Taylor set an NHL record with seven assists in a 10–6 win over the Black Hawks in Chicago.	**Nov 16, 1947** • Don Raleigh set an NHL record with three assists in a span of 1:21 during a 4–2 Rangers win over Montreal in New York.	**Nov 25, 1948** • Goaltender Turk Broda recorded a shutout, and Bill Ezinicki scored a goal and added an assist, as the Maple Leafs won 2–0 at Montreal. Ten major penalties were assessed in the game, a new NHL record.	**Mar 26, 1950** • Detroit's Ted Lindsay set an NHL record for most assists in a season when he picked up his 55th of the year in a 5–4 Red Wings loss to the visiting Black Hawks. Lindsay broke the record of Elmer Lach, who had 54 assists in 1944–45.
Did You Know?	**Jan 26, 1946** • Alex Kaleta scored four goals as the Black Hawks had a player score a hat trick for the third straight game. On this night, however, they lost 6–5 to the Maple Leafs in Toronto.	**Feb 12, 1947** • Boston's Dit Clapper officially retired (after a 20-year NHL career) in a ceremony at Boston Garden. He was granted immediate induction into the Hockey Hall of Fame and his uniform #5 was retired by the Bruins.	**Jan 21, 1948** • Don Gallinger scored twice to lead the Bruins to a 2–1 win over Toronto in Boston. The Bruins used two photographers to film their game for coaching purposes.	**Nov 10, 1948** • Due to unseasonable heat causing thick fog and soft ice inside the Boston Garden, referee Bill Chadwick halted a game with the Red Wings after nine minutes. Boston beat Detroit 4–1 when the game was replayed the next night.	**Dec 25, 1949** • New York Rangers extended their Christmas night undefeated streak to 21 years with a 3–1 home victory over the Maple Leafs. The win gave the Rangers a 16–1–1 lifetime record on Christmas, with their only loss coming in 1928.
Milestones	**Mar 10, 1946** • Playing near the end of his 11th (and final) NHL season, Maple Leafs veteran Sweeney Schriner scored his milestone 200th career goal in a 7–3 loss at Boston.	**Feb 12, 1947** • Boston's Bill Cowley picked up a goal and an assist in a 10–1 victory over the Rangers to become the NHL's all-time scoring leader. He passed Detroit's Syd Howe, who had retired with 528 points.	**Mar 21, 1948** • Toronto's Syl Apps scored a hat trick in the final regular-season game of his career to give him 201 NHL goals. The milestone came in the Maple Leafs' 5–2 win over the Red Wings in Detroit.	**Feb 3, 1949** • Toronto goalie Turk Broda became the second goaltender in NHL history (after Tiny Thompson) to record 250 career victories as the Maple Leafs won 4–1 over the Canadiens in Montreal.	**Mar 21, 1950** • Chicago's Frank Brimsek became the third NHL goaltender to record 250 career victories as the Black Hawks won 6–3 over the Rangers at New York. The first two 250-game winners were Tiny Thompson and Turk Broda.
Rookies	**Oct 27, 1945** • Rookie Billy Reay scored twice in the first game of his NHL career to lead the Canadiens to an 8–4 win over the Black Hawks in Montreal.	**Oct 16, 1946** • 18-year-old Gordie Howe scored his first NHL goal in his first career game as Detroit tied Toronto 3–3. Howe wore uniform #17 and also had two fights.	**Oct 16, 1947** • Montreal's rookie defenseman Doug Harvey played in his first career NHL game, a 2–1 Canadiens loss to the New York Rangers.	**Dec 15, 1948** • Rangers rookie defenseman Allan Stanley scored his first career goal as New York won 3–1 over the visiting Toronto Maple Leafs.	**Jan 15, 1950** • Red Wings rookie goalie Terry Sawchuk recorded his first career shutout as Detroit beat the Rangers 1–0.
Transactions	**Nov 1, 1945** • Gordie Howe (at age 16) signed his first professional hockey contract, with the Omaha Knights of the United States Hockey League. Omaha was a Red Wings farm club.	**May 30, 1946** • Toronto Maple Leafs signed amateur star Howie Meeker from the Stratford Seniors.	**Nov 3, 1947** • Chicago traded Max Bentley (the NHL's leading scorer the previous two seasons) to Toronto for Gus Bodnar, Bud Poile, Gaye Stewart, Bob Goldham and Ernie Dickens.	**Dec 9, 1948** • New York Rangers purchased defenseman Allan Stanley from Providence of the AHL for a reported $70,000.	**Aug 16, 1949** • Boston traded Pete Babando, along with Clare Martin, Lloyd Durham and Jim Peters, to Detroit for Bill Quackenbush and Pete Horeck.
Teams	**Jun 14, 1945** • The NHL Board of Governors turned down an application for a franchise in Philadelphia that would have begun play in 1946–47.	**Aug 1, 1946** • Montreal Canadiens named Frank Selke as their new managing director. Selke went on to run the Canadiens' for the next 18 years.	**Oct 13, 1947** • The Stanley Cup-champion Toronto Maple Leafs lost 4–3 to a group of NHL All-Stars in the first All-Star Game. Proceeds went to the players' pension fund.	**Dec 25, 1948** • Chuck Rayner got the shutout as the Rangers ran their Christmas record to 15–1–1 with a 2–0 win at Montreal. New York's only Christmas loss during this time was back in 1928.	**Jan 5, 1950** • The Montreal Canadiens celebrated their 40th anniversary by beating the Bruins 5–3. The Canadiens' first game was Jan 5, 1910 when they beat Cobalt 7–6 in the NHA.
Front Office	**Feb 21, 1946** • A previously rumored dramatic announcement was made when Lester Patrick resigned as g.m. of the New York Rangers. He was succeeded by coach Frank Boucher.	**Sep 4, 1946** • Clarence Campbell became president of the National Hockey League, replacing Red Dutton, who had presided over the NHL since the death of Frank Calder in 1943.	**Dec 27, 1947** • Chicago Black Hawks fired coach Johnny Gottselig and replaced him with Charlie Conacher.	**Dec 21, 1948** • Lynn Patrick was named as the new head coach of the New York Rangers, replacing Frank Boucher. Patrick became the third coach in Rangers history.	**Feb 5, 1950** • Montreal's Dick Irvin became the first coach in NHL history to win 500 games when the Canadiens beat the Bruins 5–3 at the Forum in Montreal.
Playoffs	**Mar 30, 1946** • Maurice Richard scored (at 9:08 of OT) the first of his NHL-record three overtime goals in the finals to give Montreal a 4–3 win over Boston in game one of the Stanley Cup finals.	**Apr 19, 1947** • Toronto's Ted Kennedy scored the winning goal (and added an assist) to beat the Canadiens 2–1 in game six of the finals. The victory gave Toronto the 1946–47 Stanley Cup championship, their third Stanley Cup title in six seasons.	**Apr 4, 1948** • Rookie defenseman Red Kelly scored a goal and added two assists in the first period (including an assist on Gordie Howe's first NHL playoff goal) as Detroit beat the Rangers 4–2 in the sixth and deciding game of their Stanley Cup semifinal series.	**Apr 16, 1949** • Toronto Maple Leafs became the first NHL team to win three straight Stanley Cup titles with a 5–1 victory over Detroit in game four of the Stanley Cup finals. The win was the Leafs' ninth straight in the finals.	**Apr 23, 1950** • In the first game seven of the Stanley Cup finals to go into overtime, Pete Babando scored at 28:31 of OT to give Detroit a 4–3 win over the Rangers—and the 1949–50 Stanley Cup championship.
Business	**Sept 7, 1945** • NHL president Red Dutton announced that, for the first time in the history of hockey, the rules adopted by the NHL would now be standard in all organized hockey, both professional and amateur.	**Sep 4, 1946** • The NHL increased the regular-season schedule from 50 to 60 games per team.	**Mar 9, 1948** • NHL president Clarence Campbell expelled New York's Billy Taylor and suspended Boston's Don Gallinger because of their gambling associations. They were alleged to have bet on hockey games, though none were "fixed." Taylor was reinstated in 1970.	**Jun 2, 1948** • At the NHL's annual meeting in Montreal, it was announced that the Art Ross Trophy would now be awarded annually to the scoring leader, rather than the outstanding player. Montreal's Elmer Lach was the first winner (with 61 points in 1947–48).	**Jun 1, 1949** • The NHL announced an increase of its regular-season schedule from 60 to 70 games. The schedule remained at 70 games until 1967–68.
Births & Deaths	**Sept 7, 1945** • Jacques Lemaire born in LaSalle, Quebec. **Jan 22, 1946** • Serge Savard born in Montreal, Quebec.	**Oct 10, 1946** • Peter Mahovlich born in Timmins, Ontario. **Apr 27, 1947** • Keith Magnuson born in Saskatoon, Sask.	**Aug 8, 1947** • Ken Dryden born in Hamilton, Ontario. **Mar 20, 1948** • Bobby Orr born in Parry Sound, Ontario.	**Jul 6, 1948** • Brad Park born in Toronto, Ontario. **Feb 17, 1949** • Jim Rutherford born in Beeton, Ontario.	**Aug 13, 1949** • Bobby Clarke born in Flin Flon, Manitoba. **Oct 14, 1949** • Dave Schultz born in Waldheim, Sask.

1950s	1950–51	1951–52	1952–53	1953–54	1954–55
Firsts	**Oct 8, 1950** • The first televised NHL All-Star Game was played in Detroit's Olympia Stadium. The Red Wings beat the All Stars 7–1 with Ted Lindsay getting the first All-Star hat trick, as well as assisting on Gordie Howe's first All-Star goal.	**Feb 10, 1952** • Detroit Red Wings rookie Johnny Wilson played the first of 580 straight games (an NHL record for many years) as the Red Wings defeated the Bruins 2–0 in Boston.	**Mar 22, 1953** • Gordie Howe became the first NHL player to win the Art Ross Trophy three times when he finished the season with a record 95 points.	**Oct 10, 1953** • Maurice Richard became the first player in NHL history to score 350 goals as the Canadiens won 4–1 over Detroit at the Forum.	**May 10, 1954** • Detroit's Red Kelly was named the first winner of the Norris Trophy as the NHL's top defenseman.
Records	**Mar 17, 1951** • Gordie Howe scored three goals and added an assist (as the Red Wings won 8–2 over Chicago) to break Herb Cain's scoring record of 82 points for a season set in 1943–44. Howe finished the year with 86 points	**Mar 23, 1952** • Chicago's Bill Mosienko set an NHL record for the fastest three goals by one player (21 seconds) as the Black Hawks beat the Rangers 7–6 at Madison Square Garden in New York on the final night of the 1951–52 season.	**Mar 5, 1953** • Gordie Howe scored two goals and added three assists to lead the Red Wings to a 7–1 win over the Rangers at the Olympia. With the five points Howe broke his own NHL record for most points for a single season (86).	**Oct 8, 1953** • Detroit's Earl Reibel set up four goals to set an NHL record for most assists by a player in his first NHL game as the Red Wings beat the Rangers 4–1 at the Olympia	**Feb 26, 1955** • Doug Harvey picked up his 41st assist of the season to set a new NHL record for assists in one season by a defenseman as the Canadiens won 4–1 over the Bruins at the Forum. Harvey broke the mark of 40 set by Toronto's Babe Pratt in 1943–44.
Did You Know?	**Mar 25, 1951** • Rookie Terry Sawchuk earned his 11th shutout of the season (to lead all NHL goaltenders) as Detroit beat Montreal 5–0.	**Nov 24, 1951** • Injuries forced Chicago trainer Moe Roberts to take over in goal and he helped in a 6–2 win over Detroit. At almost 46, Roberts was the oldest player to appear in an NHL game. His last NHL appearance had been in 1933–34.	**Oct 9, 1952** • Montreal's legendary announcer Danny Gallivan called his first NHL game on radio as the Canadiens lost to Chicago 3–2 in their season opener at the Forum.	**Jan 30, 1954** • For just the second time in NHL history (and the first time in 20 years), two brothers opposed each other as coaches when Muzz Patrick's Rangers beat Lynn Patrick's Bruins 8–3 in New York. Lester and Frank Patrick had been the first.	**Mar 10, 1955** • Toronto played at Montreal, but the biggest name in the game was Zamboni as the ice-cleaning machine made its NHL debut.
Milestones	**Dec 20, 1950** • Toronto's Turk Broda became the first goaltender in NHL history to record 300 career victories. The milestone came in the Maple Leafs' 6–1 win over the Montreal Canadiens.	**Feb 23, 1952** • Montreal's Elmer Lach became the NHL's all-time scoring leader when he got a goal and three assists in a 7–0 win over Chicago. Lach surpassed Bill Cowley (who had retired six years earlier with 548 career points).	**Nov 8, 1952** • Maurice Richard scored his 325th career goal to break the all-time record for NHL goals held by Nels Stewart. The milestone came in a 6–4 win over the Black Hawks in Montreal and exactly 10 years after Richard's first NHL goal.	**Dec 12, 1953** • Maurice Richard became the NHL's all-time scoring leader when his goal and two assists in a 7–2 win over the Rangers gave him 611 career NHL points, one more than injured teammate Elmer Lach, who had held the record since February 1952.	**Dec 18, 1954** • Maurice Richard became the first player in NHL history to score 400 career goals when the Canadiens defeated the Black Hawks 4–2 at Chicago.
Rookies	**Dec 16, 1950** • Jean Beliveau and Bernie Geoffrion both made their NHL debuts for Montreal in a 1–1 tie against the Rangers. Geoffrion scored his first NHL goal in the game.	**Nov 7, 1951** • Detroit rookie Alex Delvecchio scored the first two goals of his NHL career, and added an assist, in the Red Wings' 4–4 tie against the Rangers in New York.	**Jan 8, 1953** • Subbing for injured Terry Sawchuk, rookie Glenn Hall recorded the first shutout of his NHL career to lead the Red Wings to a 4–0 win over Boston at the Olympia.	**Feb 20, 1954** • Montreal's rookie goalie Jacques Plante recorded the first shutout of his NHL career, beating the Detroit Red Wings 2–0 at the Forum.	**Dec 9, 1954** • Montreal Canadiens rookie goalie Charlie Hodge picked up his first career shutout in a 2–0 win over the Maple Leafs at the Forum.
Transactions	**Dec 19, 1950** • Montreal Canadiens obtained Bert Olmstead from the Red Wings. Olmstead had been traded to Detroit just one week earlier, from Chicago.	**Jun 19, 1951** • New York Rangers traded Tony Leswick to Detroit in exchange for Gaye Stewart.	**Sep 11, 1952** • Chicago obtained Cal Gardner, along with Al Rollins, Ray Hannigan and Gus Mortson, from Toronto in exchange for Harry Lumley.	**Oct 3, 1953** • Jean Beliveau signed his first contract with the Montreal Canadiens.	**Nov 23, 1954** • Chicago traded Pete Conacher and Bill Gadsby to the Rangers in exchange for Allan Stanley and Nick Mickoski.
Teams	**Mar 15, 1951** • Detroit Red Wings set a new NHL record for most wins in a season with their 39th—a 4–0 victory over the visiting Bruins. Three teams had shared the record of 38 wins.	**Mar 12, 1952** • New York Rangers set a team record for the fastest four goals, scoring them in a span of 2:10 in the third period of a 10–2 win over the visiting Black Hawks.	**Mar 8, 1953** • Detroit Red Wings became the first NHL team to win five straight regular-season titles with a 3–1 win over the Toronto Maple Leafs.	**Oct 8, 1953** • Montreal began an NHL-record nine-year opening-night winning streak with a 3–0 win over the Black Hawks at the Forum.	**Oct 7, 1954** • Detroit Red Wings beat the visiting Toronto Maple Leafs 2–1 to set an NHL record by extending their season-opening undefeated streak to 15 games (14–0–1).
Front Office	**Mar 7, 1951** • 18-year-old Scotty Bowman suffered a severe head injury while playing in a junior hockey game. The injury ended his playing career, so Bowman turned to coaching.	**Dec 6, 1951** • Bill Cook was named the new coach of the New York Rangers, replacing Neil Colville.	**Mar 24, 1953** • King Clancy was named the new coach of the Toronto Maple Leafs following the resignation of Joe Primeau.	**Oct 22, 1953** • Montreal's Dick Irvin became the first coach in NHL history to win 600 career games when the Canadiens beat the Black Hawks 3–2 at Chicago	**Jul 7, 1954** • Tommy Ivan was named general manager of the Chicago Black Hawks, replacing Bill Tobin.
Playoffs	**Apr 21, 1951** • Toronto's Bill Barilko scored the Stanley Cup-winning goal at 2:53 of overtime to defeat Montreal 3–2 in game five of the finals. It was the only Stanley Cup series in NHL history in which every game ended in overtime. Barilko died in a plane crash on a fishing trip that summer.	**Mar 27, 1952** • Toronto's Turk Broda became the first goaltender in NHL history to play in 100 career playoff games when he faced the Red Wings in a 1–0 loss in game two of the Stanley Cup semifinals in Detroit.	**Mar 24, 1953** • Detroit's Terry Sawchuk tied an NHL record with his third straight playoff shutout, a 7–0 Red Wings win over Boston in game one of the Stanley Cup semifinals at the Olympia.	**Mar 25, 1954** • Montreal's Dickie Moore scored two goals and added four assists for an NHL-record six points in a playoff game as the Canadiens beat Boston 8–1 in game two of the Stanley Cup semifinals. Moore's record lasted for 29 years.	**Apr 12, 1955** • Dick Irvin became the first coach in NHL history to win 100 career playoff games when the Montreal Canadiens beat Detroit 6–3 in game six of the Stanley Cup finals.
Business	**May 30, 1950** • At the NHL meetings in Montreal, the league announced a rule change to allow for a "delayed whistle" when teams iced the puck at full strength. Henceforth, fast skaters on the offensive team could chase down the puck before the defending team touched it.	**Jun 6, 1951** • At the NHL meetings in Montreal, new league rules increased the goaltenders' crease from three-by-seven feet to four-by-eight feet. The league also imposed a penalty shot when any non-goalie picked up the puck in the crease.	**Dec 6, 1952** • Detroit's Alex Delvecchio had two assists and Terry Sawchuk shut out Chicago 2–0 in Indianapolis in the first regular-season game played outside an NHL city since 1928. Both teams' stadiums were unavailable that night.	**Jan 5, 1954** • Montreal g.m. Frank Selke complained about the use of "motion pictures" in making hockey rulings, but announced that he would not appeal an eight-game suspension of Bernie Geoffrion, who had been involved in a stick incident versus the Rangers on Dec. 20.	**Mar 13, 1955** • Montreal's Maurice "Rocket" Richard was ejected after punching a linesman in a fight during a 4–2 Canadiens loss to Boston. Three days later NHL president Clarence Campbell suspended Richard for the remainder of the season and playoffs. The decision sparked a riot in Montreal.
Births & Deaths	**Sep 18, 1950** • Darryl Sittler born in Kitchener, Ontario. **Apr 17, 1951** • Borje Salming born in Kiruna, Sweden.	**Aug 3, 1951** • Marcel Dionne born in Drummondville, Quebec. **Sep 20, 1951** • Guy Lafleur born in Thurso, Quebec.	**Jul 1, 1952** • Steve Shutt born in Toronto, Ontario. **Jul 11, 1952** • Bill Barber born in Callander, Ontario.	**Oct 29, 1953** • Denis Potvin born in Ottawa, Ontario. **Dec 13, 1953** • Bob Gainey born in Peterborough, Ontario.	**Mar 24, 1955** • Doug Jarvis born in Brantford, Ontario. **May 28, 1955** • Mark Howe born in Detroit, Michigan.

1950s	1955–56	1956–57	1957–58	1958–59	1959–60
Firsts	**Jan 23, 1956** • Montreal's Jean Beliveau became the first hockey player to make the cover of *Sports Illustrated* magazine.	**Jan 5, 1957** • CBS Television became the first U.S. network to televise an NHL game as the host New York Rangers beat Chicago 4–1 in an afternoon game at Madison Square Garden.	**Oct 19, 1957** • Montreal's Maurice Richard became the first player in NHL history to score 500 career goals. The milestone came in his 863rd career game, a 3–1 win over the Chicago Black Hawks.	**Mar 22, 1959** • Jean Beliveau became the first center in NHL history to score more than 90 points in a season. His 91st of the year broke his own record and led the Canadiens to a 4–2 win in New York.	**May 6, 1960** • Gordie Howe became the first player in NHL history to win the Hart Trophy as most valuable player five times in his career.
Records	**Feb 22, 1956** • Toronto defeated the Rangers 4–2 as Lou Fontinato set a new NHL penalty-minute record. Fontinato's 169 minutes broke the record of 167 set by Red Horner in the 1935–36 season.	**Mar 24, 1957** • Gordie Howe set a record by winning the Art Ross Trophy (as the NHL's leading scorer) for the fifth time. Howe earned two assists in the final game of the 1956–57 season (a 4–1 Red Wings win over Toronto) to finish with 44 goals and 45 assists for 89 total points.	**Nov 9, 1957** • Montreal's Claude Provost scored just four seconds into the second period to set an NHL record (later tied by Denis Savard) for fastest goal from start of a period. The Canadiens beat Boston 4–2.	**Mar 22, 1959** • Montreal's Dickie Moore set an NHL record for most points in a season when he scored a goal and an assist for his 96th point of the year in a 4–2 Canadiens win at New York. Moore broke Gordie Howe's record of 95 points set in 1952–53.	**Feb 13, 1960** • Bronco Horvath of Boston scored twice and had an assist to extend his NHL-record point-scoring streak to 22 straight games. The Bruins won the game 7–6 over Montreal.
Did You Know?	**Nov 5, 1955** • Montreal's Jean Beliveau scored all four goals, including three in 44 seconds during one power-play, in a 4–2 win over Boston. After the season, the NHL changed the rules to end a minor power-play after a goal was scored.	**Feb 11, 1957** • The NHL Players' Association was formed, with Detroit's Ted Lindsay elected as the first president. NHL owners soon crushed the fledgling organization and another decade would pass before NHL players formed a successful union.	**Jan 18, 1958** • Boston's rookie left winger Willie O'Ree skated onto the ice at the Montreal Forum to become the first black player in the NHL. He made his debut in the Bruins' 3–0 win over the Canadiens.	**Mar 3, 1959** • "Gordie Howe Night" was held in Detroit. Before the game, Howe skated out to receive a new car … and found his parents sitting in the back seat! Albert and Catherine Howe had come from Saskatchewan to see their first NHL game.	**Nov 1, 1959** • A new era in hockey dawned as Montreal goalie Jacques Plante returned to the ice wearing a mask after being hit in the face from a shot by Andy Bathgate. Plante led the Canadiens to a 3–1 victory over the Rangers in New York.
Milestones	**Mar 18, 1956** • Dick Irvin won his 690th (and final) career game as a coach when the Chicago Black Hawks won 3–2 in Boston on the final night of the season. Irvin remained the NHL's all-time win leader until Scotty Bowman broke the record 28 years later.	**Nov 18, 1956** • Detroit's Ted Lindsay scored three goals to become the fourth player in NHL history to top the 300-goal mark. Lindsay reached the milestone in an 8–3 victory over Montreal. The NHL's other 300-goal scorers at that time were Maurice Richard, Gordie Howe and Nels Stewart.	**Nov 28, 1957** • Gordie Howe picked up an assist during Detroit's 3–3 tie against Toronto to become the NHL's all time assist leader with 409. Howe broke the record set by Montreal's Elmer Lach.	**Dec 17, 1958** • Ted Lindsay scored two goals and added an assist to lead the Black Hawks to a 5–2 win over the Bruins at Chicago Stadium. With the two goals, Lindsay became the highest scoring left winger in NHL history, passing Aurel Joliat who retired with 270.	**Jan 16, 1960** • Gordie Howe scored a goal and an assist in his 888th career game to become the NHL's all-time leading scorer with 947 points. He passed Montreal's Maurice Richard as the Red Wings beat Chicago 3–1 in Detroit.
Rookies	**Oct 7, 1955** • Rangers rookie Andy Hebenton played the first of 630 consecutive games (an NHL record at the time) in New York's 7–4 win over Chicago.	**Mar 24, 1957** • Toronto rookie Frank Mahovlich scored the first goal of his NHL career. It came in the Maple Leafs' 4–1 loss at Detroit.	**Oct 22, 1957** • Chicago rookie Bobby Hull scored his first career NHL goal in a 2–1 win over the visiting Boston Bruins.	**Oct 23, 1958** • Montreal rookie Ralph Backstrom scored the first two goals of his NHL career, and added an assist, as the Canadiens won 9–1 over the Black Hawks at the Forum.	**Oct 7, 1959** • Chicago rookie Stan Mikita scored his first career goal in the Black Hawks' 5–2 opening-night win over the Rangers in Chicago.
Transactions	**Oct 13, 1955** • The Canadiens announced that Henri Richard had signed to a two-year contract with the team. He would go on to play for 11 Stanley Cup champions in Montreal.	**May 21, 1956** • Chicago purchased veteran goalie Harry Lumley and Eric Nesterenko from the Toronto Maple Leafs for $40,000.	**Jun 10, 1957** • The Red Wings reacquired goalie Terry Sawchuk from Boston in exchange for Johnny Bucyk. On Jul 23, 1957, Detroit traded Ted Lindsay and Glenn Hall to Chicago.	**Jun 3, 1958** • Toronto drafted goalie Johnny Bower from the New York Rangers. Bower went on to play 12 years with the Maple Leafs.	**Feb 10, 1960** • Detroit Red Wing traded Red Kelly to the Toronto Maple Leafs in exchange for Marc Reaume. Six days earlier, Kelly had refused a trade to the New York Rangers.
Teams	**Mar 18, 1956** • Montreal set an NHL record for most wins in a season, earning their 45th with a 3–1 victory over the Rangers in New York. Detroit had won 44 games in 1950–51.	**Mar 24, 1957** • Detroit Red Wings clinched their eighth first-place finish in nine seasons (an NHL record for dominance) when they beat the Maple Leafs 4–1 in their final game of the season.	**Sep 24, 1957** • Le Club de Hockey Canadien and the Canadian Arena Company were sold to Senator Hartland Molson and his brother, Thomas H.P. Molson.	**Mar 22, 1959** • Detroit Red Wings lost 6–4 to the visiting Toronto Maple Leafs to finish last overall in the NHL. Detroit had not finished last since its first NHL season of 1926–27.	**Mar 31, 1960** • Montreal ended the regular season with a 3–1 loss to the Rangers, but with eight future Hall of Famers in the lineup the Canadiens still finished first overall in the NHL.
Front Office	**Jun 8, 1955** • Hector "Toe" Blake was named coach of the Montreal Canadiens. He replaced Dick Irvin, who had coached the team for 15 years.	**Apr 11, 1956** • Toronto Maple Leafs named Howie Meeker as their new coach. Meeker replaced King Clancy, who was promoted to assistant g.m.	**Jan 2, 1958** • Detroit Red Wings named Sid Abel as their new coach, replacing Jimmy Skinner. Abel went on to coach the Red Wings for the next 10 years.	**Nov 21, 1958** • Toronto Maple Leafs named George "Punch" Imlach their new general manager. Eight days later, Imlach replaced Billy Reay as the Leafs' head coach.	**Nov 12, 1959** • Phil Watson ended his coaching career with the Rangers after hospitalization for an ulcer. He was replaced by Alf Pike.
Playoffs	**Apr 10, 1956** • Jean Beliveau had a goal and two assists as Montreal beat Detroit 3–1 in game five of the finals to become the 1955–56 Stanley Cup champions. It was the start of a record five straight Stanley Cup championships for the Canadiens.	**Apr 6, 1957** • Maurice Richard scored four goals to tie Newsy Lalonde and Ted Lindsay's playoff record for most goals in a Stanley Cup finals game as Montreal beat Boston 5–1.	**Apr 17, 1958** • Maurice Richard scored at 5:45 of OT for his sixth career playoff overtime goal as Montreal beat Boston 3–2 in game five of the Stanley Cup finals. Richard's six overtime goals remain an NHL record.	**Apr 18, 1959** • Montreal Canadiens won their fourth consecutive Stanley Cup championship with a 5–3 win over Toronto in game five of the finals. Rookie Ralph Backstrom led the scoring with a goal and three assists.	**Apr 14, 1960** • Jacques Plante recorded his 10th career playoff shutout as the Montreal Canadiens became the first (and only) team to win five consecutive Stanley Cup championships with a 4–0 win over Toronto.
Business	**Dec 29, 1955** • In a game between Montreal and Toronto, NHL officials wore new vertically striped black and white sweaters for the first time. The Canadiens won the game 5–2.	**Jun 6, 1956** • The NHL Board of Governors passed a rule allowing a player serving a minor penalty to return to the ice after a goal was scored by the opposition. Previously teams kept their power-play for the entire two minutes.	**Jun 5, 1957** • At the NHL meetings in Montreal, the league approved a plan for CBS to televise 21 games in the four U.S.-based NHL cities. The schedule was increased from the 10 games televised the previous year on an experimental basis.	**Jun 4, 1958** • The NHL meetings in Montreal produced the first signed agreement between the league's club owners and the players' association.	**Jun 10, 1959** • Boston Bruins selected Detroit's Charlie Burns and New York Rangers goalie Bruce Gamble at the Intra-League Draft held during the annual NHL meetings in Montreal.
Births & Deaths	**Dec 4, 1955** • Dave Taylor born in Levack, Ontario. **May 12, 1956** • Bernie Federko born in Foam Lake, Sask.	**Jul 17, 1956** • Bryan Trottier born in Val Marie, Saskatchewan. **Jan 22, 1957** • Mike Bossy born in Montreal, Quebec.	**Oct 2, 1957** • Gordie Roberts born in Detroit, Michigan. **Feb 12, 1958** • Bobby Smith born in North Sydney, Nova Scotia.	**Aug 15, 1958** • Craig MacTavish born in London, Ontario. **Apr 15, 1959** • Kevin Lowe born in Lachute, Quebec.	**Oct 29, 1959** • Mike Gartner born in Ottawa, Ontario. **May 18, 1960** • Jari Kurri born in Helsinki, Finland.

1960s	1960–61	1961–62	1962–63	1963–64	1964–65
Firsts	Oct 1, 1960 • Andy Hebenton scored the first shorthanded, game-winning goal in All-Star history as the Stars beat the Stanley Cup-champion Montreal Canadiens 2–1.	Nov 26, 1961 • Gordie Howe became the first player in NHL history to play in 1,000 career regular-season games when the Red Wings lost 4–1 at Chicago.	Nov 4, 1962 • Detroit's Bill Gadsby became the first defenseman in NHL history to score 500 career points. He reached the milestone in a 3–1 Red Wings win over Chicago.	Dec 4, 1963 • Boston's Andy Hebenton became the first player to appear in 581 consecutive NHL games (breaking the old mark of 580 set by John Wilson) as the Bruins tied Chicago 2–2.	Feb 4, 1965 • Terry Sawchuk became the first goaltender in NHL history to record 400 career victories as the Maple Leafs won 5–2 at Montreal.
Records	Nov 24, 1960 • Montreal's Dickie Moore scored his 20th goal of the season in his 21st game (a 3–1 loss at Detroit) to equal an NHL record for fastest 20 goals in a season (which had been set by former linemate Maurice Richard in 1944–45).	Oct 19, 1960 • Chicago rookie Reggie Fleming set an NHL record (later broken) with 37 penalty minutes in a 2–0 loss against the Rangers at New York. Fleming picked up one minor, three majors, a misconduct, and one game misconduct penalty.	Feb 20, 1963 • Tommy Williams of the Bruins set a record for U.S.-born players with his 21st goal of the season. It came in Boston's 3–3 tie against the New York Rangers.	Feb 8, 1964 • Detroit's Terry Sawchuk played in his 804th career game to break the NHL record for career games by a goalie (set by Harry Lumley). The Red Wings won the game 3–2 at Boston.	Mar 20, 1965 • Chicago's Pierre Pilote picked up two assists in a 3–2 loss at Montreal to give him 58 points for the year, a new NHL record for points by a defenseman. Pilote broke the record of 57 points set by Babe Pratt 21 years earlier.
Did You Know?	Oct 16, 1960 • Boston forward Jerry Toppazzini became the last non-goalie to take over in the nets for an injured netminder when he replaced Don Simmons in a 5–2 Bruins loss to the Chicago Black Hawks.	Jan 17, 1962 • Chicago Black Hawks goaltender Glenn Hall played in his 500th game (including the playoffs) and received a station wagon and other gifts from team management. The Black Hawks lost 7–3 to Montreal.	Jan 27, 1963 • Montreal won 3–1 in Chicago in a game where Canadiens goalie Jacques Plante took time out to measure the height of the Chicago goalposts. He discovered that they measured only 3'10" instead of the regulation 4'.	Mar 22, 1964 • Chicago won 4–3 at Boston as the Bruins' Ed Johnston became the final goaltender in NHL history to play every minute of every game for an entire season. Johnston finished the season 18–40–12 with a 3.01 goals-against average.	Feb 1, 1965 • Rangers right winger Rod Gilbert (who had been having severe back problems) underwent a spinal fusion operation. He missed the remainder of the 1964–65 season, but came back and played the next 11 seasons in the NHL.
Milestones	Nov 27, 1960 • Detroit's Gordie Howe became the first player in NHL history to score 1,000 career points as the Red Wings won 2–0 over Toronto. Howe's 1,000th point came in his 938th NHL game.	Mar 25, 1962 • Bobby Hull of the Black Hawks scored his milestone 50th goal of the season to tie the NHL record shared by Maurice Richard and Bernie Geoffrion. Chicago lost 4–1 to the Rangers at New York. Geoffrion had become the NHL's second 50-goal scorer just the season before.	Nov 10, 1962 • 31-year-old Chicago goalie Glenn Hall was forced to sit out a game due to a back injury, ending a streak of 503 consecutive games played over seven years. Denis DeJordy took Hall's place as the Black Hawks won 3–1 at Montreal.	Nov 10, 1963 • Detroit's Gordie Howe became the NHL's all-time leading goal scorer. He got #545 to move past Maurice Richard when the Red Wings beat Montreal 3–0.	Jan 9, 1965 • Bobby Hull scored twice in a 7–4 win over the Red Wings to become the Black Hawks' all-time leading goal scorer. Hull's two goals gave him 259 in his NHL career, one more than Bill Mosienko.
Rookies	Mar 4, 1961 • New York Rangers rookie Jean Ratelle scored the first goal of his NHL career, and added an assist, in a 5–4 loss to the Maple Leafs at Toronto.	Mar 18, 1962 • Red Berenson made his NHL debut with the Montreal Canadiens when they lost 6–2 at Boston.	Dec 15, 1962 • Boston goalie Eddie Johnston made his NHL debut (replacing Bob Perreault) in an 8–2 loss at Toronto. He proceeded to play in the next 160 consecutive games for Boston.	Jan 25, 1964 • Chicago rookie Phil Esposito scored his first career NHL goal in a 5–3 loss to the Red Wings.	Jan 27, 1965 • Ulf Sterner became the first Swedish-born player to appear in the NHL as New York beat Boston 5–2. Sterner's NHL career lasted only four games—all with the Rangers.
Transactions	Jan 24, 1961 • Detroit traded Murray Oliver, Gary Aldcorn and Tom McCarthy to Boston in exchange for Leo Labine and Vic Stasiuk.	Jun 14, 1961 • New York Rangers drafted young left winger Vic Hadfield from Chicago.	Jun 6, 1962 • Chicago obtained John McKenzie and Len Lunde from Detroit in exchange for Doug Barkley.	Jun 4, 1963 • New York Rangers traded Dave Balon, Leon Rochefort, Len Ronson and Gump Worsley to Montreal in exchange for Phil Goyette, Don Marshall and Jacques Plante.	Dec 22, 1964 • New York Rangers traded Dick Duff to Montreal in exchange for Bill Hicke.
Teams	Mar 19, 1961 • Montreal Canadiens beat the Red Wings 2–0 at Detroit on the final night of the season to finish first overall in the NHL standings for the fourth consecutive year.	Nov 23, 1961 • Stafford Smythe, Harold Ballard and John Bassett acquired control of Toronto's Maple Leaf Gardens.	Oct 6, 1962 • The defending Stanley Cup-champion Maple Leafs scored four first-period goals and held on for a 4–1 win over the All Stars at the 16th NHL All-Star Game in Toronto.	Nov 8, 1963 • Maple Leaf Gardens became the first NHL arena to install separate penalty-box doors for each team after Toronto's Bob Pulford fought Montreal's Terry Harper in the penalty box.	Dec 16, 1964 • Detroit Red Wings won the 1,000th game in franchise history, a 7–3 victory over the Rangers in New York.
Front Office	Jan 7, 1961 • Montreal's Frank Selke became the fourth general manager in NHL history to record 500 victories when the Canadiens beat the Rangers 6–3 in Montreal.	Jun 6, 1961 • Phil Watson was named the new coach of the Boston Bruins, replacing Milt Schmidt.	Apr 26, 1962 • Jack Adams announced his retirement after serving 35 years as the Detroit Red Wings general manager. Coach Sid Abel added the g.m. job to his portfolio.	Jun 4, 1963 • Billy Reay was named the new coach of the Chicago Black Hawks, replacing Rudy Pilous (who had been fired May 21). Reay went on to coach the Black Hawks for 13 years.	May 15, 1964 • Sam Pollock replaced Frank Selke as managing director of the Montreal Canadiens.
Playoffs	Apr 8, 1961 • Gordie Howe set a playoff record for most career assists during a 3–1 Red Wings win over Chicago in game two of the Stanley Cup finals. Howe's two assists in the game gave him 61 postseason set-ups, two more than Doug Harvey's previous record.	Apr 19, 1962 • Chicago's Stan Mikita picked up two assists to set two new playoff records: his 21 points broke Gordie Howe's record of 20 set in 1955 and his 15 assists also set a new record. Chicago lost 8–4 at Toronto in game five of the Stanley Cup finals.	Apr 9, 1963 • Toronto's Dick Duff set a Stanley Cup playoff record for fastest two goals from the start of a game. He scored twice against Terry Sawchuk in the first 1:08 as Toronto beat Detroit 4–2 in game one of the Stanley Cup finals.	Apr 5, 1964 • Detroit's Gordie Howe became the highest career point scorer in Stanley Cup playoff history when his goal (in a 3–2 loss at Chicago) gave him 127 career playoff points (in 122 games). Howe broke the mark held by Montreal's Maurice Richard.	Apr 11, 1965 • Detroit's Norm Ullman set a Stanley Cup playoff record for the fastest two goals—five seconds. Ullman scored at 17:35 and 17:40 of the second period as the Red Wings beat Chicago 4–2 in game five of the semifinals.
Business	Jun 7, 1960 • At the NHL meetings in Montreal, the Board of Governors announced that "Los Angeles and San Francisco will be considered first when expansion of the league is possible." The L.A. Kings and Oakland Seals entered the NHL seven years later.	Aug 26, 1961 • The original Hockey Hall of Fame building had its official opening in Toronto.	Jun 6, 1962 • Boston Bruins drafted goaltender Eddie Johnston from the Montreal Canadiens minor-league system, during the NHL meetings in Montreal.	Jun 5, 1963 • The NHL held its first Amateur Draft at the Queen Elizabeth Hotel in Montreal. Twenty-one players were selected. Montreal chose first and selected Garry Monahan.	Jun 10, 1964 • Toronto selected Dickie Moore from Montreal and goaltender Terry Sawchuk from Detroit in the annual NHL Intra-League Draft.
Births & Deaths	Jan 18, 1961 • Mark Messier born in Edmonton, Alberta. Jan 26, 1961 • Wayne Gretzky born in Brantford, Ontario.	Jun 1, 1961 • Paul Coffey born in Weston, Ontario. Jan 25, 1962 • Chris Chelios born in Chicago, Illinois.	Mar 1, 1963 • Ron Francis born in Sault Ste. Marie, Ontario. Apr 4, 1963 • Dale Hawerchuk born in Toronto, Ontario.	Jun 25, 1963 • Doug Gilmour born in Kingston, Ontario. Apr 1, 1964 • Scott Stevens born in Kitchener, Ontario.	Aug 9, 1964 • Brett Hull born in Belleville, Ontario. Jan 29, 1965 • Dominik Hasek born in Pardubice, Czech.

1960s	1965–66	1966–67	1967–68	1968–69	1969–70
Firsts	**Mar 12, 1966** • Chicago's Bobby Hull became the first player in NHL history to score more than 50 goals in one season. He got his 51st in a 4–2 win by the Black Hawks over the Rangers.	**Mar 18, 1967** • Bobby Hull became the first NHL player to have back-to-back 50-goal seasons when he scored his 50th of the year in a 9–5 loss at Toronto.	**Dec 7, 1967** • Montreal's John Ferguson became the first player in NHL history to be assessed a triple minor penalty in a 2–2 Canadiens tie against Detroit.	**Mar 2, 1969** • Boston's Phil Esposito scored twice to become the first player in NHL history to score 100 points in a season. His two goals came in a Bruins' 4–0 shutout win over Pittsburgh. Bobby Hull and Gordie Howe would also top 100 this year.	**Apr 5, 1970** • Boston's Bobby Orr had an assist in the final game of the season (a 3–1 win over Toronto) to become the first NHL defenseman to win the Art Ross Trophy. Orr finished with 33 goals and 87 assists for 120 points in 76 games.
Records	**Apr 3, 1966** • In the final game of the 1965–66 season, Chicago's Bobby Hull picked up an assist (during a 4–2 loss at Boston) to give him 97 points, the most ever by a player in one season. Hull broke Dickie Moore's NHL record of 96 points set in 1958–59.	**Oct 19, 1966** • Detroit's Gordie Howe set a longevity record when he played in the first game of his 21st consecutive season in the NHL (a 6–2 loss in Boston). Howe broke the mark of 20 seasons held by Dit Clapper and Bill Gadsby.	**Dec 7, 1967** • John Bucyk scored twice to set a record for career points by a Boston Bruin. His 576th point put him ahead of Milt Schmidt. The record came in a 3–1 win over New York at Boston Garden.	**Mar 20, 1969** • Bobby Orr scored his 21st goal of the season, a new record for defensemen, in a 5–5 Bruins tie against Chicago. Orr broke the mark set by Detroit's Flash Hollett in 1944–45.	**Mar 29, 1970** • Goalie Tony Esposito recorded his 15th shutout of the season, an NHL record for rookie goaltenders and the most ever in the modern era. Espo's 15th shutout came as the Black Hawks beat Toronto 4–0 at Chicago Stadium.
Did You Know?	**Feb 5, 1966** • Detroit's Bill Gadsby became the first NHL player to appear in 300 or more games with three different teams. Gadsby had previously played for Chicago and the New York Rangers.	**Jan 18, 1967** • For the first time in NHL history, the All-Star Game was held at midseason. The Stanley Cup-champion Canadiens beat the All-Stars 3–0 at the Forum. John Ferguson scored twice for Montreal.	**Jan 15, 1968** • Minnesota's Bill Masterton died two days after suffering a brain injury in a game against Oakland. It was the only death as a result of a game injury in the history of the National Hockey League.	**Feb 16, 1969** • St. Louis goalie Glenn Hall recorded his eighth shutout of the season to lead the Blues to a 6–0 win over Minnesota. Combined with Jacques Plante's five shutouts, the 13 by the Blues duo tied a modern NHL record.	**Mar 1, 1970** • Minnesota's Charlie Burns became the final player/coach in NHL history when he played in an 8–0 North Stars victory over the Toronto Maple Leafs. Burns was the North Stars' playing coach for the final month of the season.
Milestones	**Feb 3, 1966** • Detroit's Gordie Howe scored his 20th goal of the season (for the 17th consecutive time) when the Red Wings beat the Bruins 4–2 in Boston.	**Mar 4, 1967** • Terry Sawchuk became the first NHL goaltender to record 100 career shutouts when Toronto beat Chicago 3–0 at Maple Leaf Gardens.	**Feb 24, 1968** • Garry Unger began a record 914 consecutive game playing streak (lasting nearly 11 years) when Toronto beat Boston 1–0.	**Mar 20, 1969** • Chicago's Bobby Hull set an NHL record when he scored his 55th goal of the season in a 5–5 tie at Boston. Hull broke his own record of 54 (set in 1965–66) and finished the year with 58 goals.	**Mar 15, 1970** • The Bruins' Bobby Orr scored two goals and added two assists to become the first defenseman in NHL history to get 100 points in a season. The milestone came in Boston's 5–5 tie against Detroit.
Rookies	**Nov 3, 1965** • Rookie goaltender Bernie Parent made his NHL debut with the Boston Bruins in a 2–2 tie against Chicago.	**Oct 23, 1966** • Bruins rookie defenseman Bobby Orr fired a 50-foot shot past Montreal's Gump Worsley for his first NHL goal during a 3–2 Boston loss to the Canadiens.	**Oct 18, 1967** • Montreal rookie Jacques Lemaire scored the first goal of his NHL career in the Canadiens' 2–2 tie with the Rangers at New York.	**Dec 5, 1968** • Montreal's rookie goaltender Tony Esposito made his first NHL start and gave up two goals to brother Phil in a 2–2 tie between the Canadiens and Bruins in Boston Garden.	**Oct 30, 1969** • Rookie Bobby Clarke scored his first career NHL goal in Philadelphia's 3–3 tie against the Rangers at New York.
Transactions	**Jan 10, 1966** • Boston Bruins obtained John McKenzie from the New York Rangers in exchange for Reggie Fleming.	**Sep 3, 1966** • Bobby Orr signed his first NHL contract with the Boston Bruins. A two-year deal paying him $70,000 plus a signing bonus gave Orr the top salary in the game.	**May 15, 1967** • Phil Esposito, Ken Hodge and Fred Stanfield were traded from Chicago to Boston in exchange for Gilles Marotte, Pit Martin and goalie Jack Norris.	**May 21, 1968** • Pittsburgh Penguins purchased Jean Pronovost from Boston. Pronovost went on to play the next 10 years with the Penguins, collecting 316 goals and 287 assists.	**Jun 6, 1969** • Montreal Canadiens acquired Peter Mahovlich from Detroit in exchange for Garry Monahan.
Teams	**Jun 25, 1965** • The National Hockey League announced its intention to expand into new cities "of major league status." Two years later, the league doubled from six to 12 teams.	**Mar 12, 1967** • Chicago clinched the first regular-season league championship in team history with a 5–0 win over Toronto.	**Jun 5, 1967** • The Pittsburgh Penguins, Minnesota North Stars, Philadelphia Flyers, Los Angeles Kings, Oakland Seals and St. Louis Blues officially received their NHL franchises.	**Mar 29, 1969** • Montreal set an NHL record for most wins in a season with their 46th coming in a 5–3 victory over the visiting Bruins. Montreal had won 45 games back in 1955–56.	**May 22, 1970** • The Buffalo Sabres and Vancouver Canucks were officially granted NHL franchises for the 1970–71 season.
Front Office	**Dec 5, 1965** • New York Rangers general manager Emile Francis fired coach Red Sullivan and moved behind the Rangers bench for the first time in his career.	**Oct 19, 1966** • Harry Sinden coached his first NHL game, a 6–2 Boston Bruins win over the Red Wings.	**Nov 20, 1967** • Scotty Bowman was named the new head coach of the St. Louis Blues, replacing Lynn Patrick, who resigned. It was Bowman's first head coaching job in the NHL.	**Jun 4, 1968** • Bernie "Boom Boom" Geoffrion was named the new head coach of the New York Rangers, replacing Emile Francis (who remained as g.m.)	**Dec 29, 1969** • Charlie Burns replaced Wren Blair as the Minnesota North Stars coach. Two months later, he suited up again and became the final player/coach in NHL history.
Playoffs	**May 5, 1966** • Henri Richard scored the game winner at 2:20 of overtime as Montreal beat Detroit 3–2 in game six of the finals to win the 1966 Stanley Cup. Detroit goalie Roger Crozier won the Conn Smythe Trophy as playoff MVP despite the Red Wings' loss.	**May 2, 1967** • Toronto beat Montreal 3–1 in game six of the finals to become the 1967 Stanley Cup champions in the last Stanley Cup series between the two "Original Six" teams.	**Apr 9, 1968** • Minnesota's Wayne Connelly became the first player in NHL history to score on a penalty shot in the playoffs (after two others had missed). Connelly beat Terry Sawchuk during a 7–5 North Stars win over Los Angeles.	**Apr 2, 1969** • Toronto's Forbes Kennedy set a Stanley Cup playoff record for most penalties in one game with eight at Boston. Kennedy received four minors, two majors, a 10-minute misconduct, and a game misconduct as the Bruins beat the Maple Leafs 10–0.	**Apr 12, 1970** • Pittsburgh Penguins became the first team in NHL history to win its first four playoff games when Mike Briere scored at 8:28 of overtime for a 3–2 win over the Seals in game four of the quarterfinals at Oakland.
Business	**Jun 9, 1965** • Boston Bruins drafted 25-year-old goalie Gerry Cheevers from Toronto during the NHL Intra-League Draft.	**Feb 9, 1966** • Hockey's expansion era began as the governors of the NHL announced that six conditional franchises had been granted for the 1967–68 season: Los Angeles, San Francisco, Philadelphia, Pittsburgh, Minneapolis and St. Louis.	**Jun 8, 1967** • Los Angeles traded Ken Block to Toronto for veteran Red Kelly who retired as a player and became the Kings' first head coach.	**Jun 12, 1968** • The St. Louis Blues obtained veteran goaltender Jacques Plante from the New York Rangers in the NHL Intra-League Draft.	**Jun 11, 1969** • In the annual NHL summer draft, the Chicago Black Hawks claimed rookie goalie Tony Esposito from the Montreal Canadiens for $25,000.
Births & Deaths	**Oct 5, 1965** • Mario Lemieux born in Montreal, Quebec. **Oct 5, 1965** • Patrick Roy born in Quebec City, Quebec.	**Sep 22, 1966** • Mike Richter born in Philadelphia, PA. **Apr 29, 1967** • Curtis Joseph born in Keswick, Ontario.	**Sep 26, 1967** • Craig Janney born in Hartford, Connecticut. **Mar 3, 1968** • Brian Leetch born in Corpus Christi, Texas.	**Jun 29, 1968** • Theoren Fleury born in Oxbow, Saskatchewan. **Jan 23, 1969** • Brendan Shanahan born in Mimico, Ontario.	**Nov 1, 1969** • Tie Domi born in Windsor, Ontario. **Dec 13, 1969** • Sergei Fedorov born in Moscow, USSR.

1970s	1970–71	1971–72	1972–73	1973–74	1974–75
Firsts	**Feb 6, 1971** • Phil Esposito scored a goal and two assists to become the first player in NHL history to score 100 points in a season twice in his career. Esposito's milestone came in Boston's 4–3 win over the Buffalo Sabres.	**May 5, 1972** • Bobby Orr became the first player in NHL history to win the Hart Trophy (as the NHL's MVP) three straight seasons. He also became the first NHL player to win the Norris Trophy five years in a row.	**Mar 29, 1973** • Bobby Clarke of the Flyers became the first player from a post-'67 expansion team to score 100 points in a season. His 100th point was a goal that led the Flyers to a 4–2 win over the Atlanta Flames.	**Nov 15, 1973** • Bobby Orr scored three power-play goals and added four assists to become the first NHL defenseman to record seven points in one game as Boston beat the New York Rangers 10–2.	**Feb 8, 1975** • Phil Esposito had four goals and an assist to become the first player in NHL history to get 100 points or more six times. The milestone came as the Bruins beat the Red Wings 8–5 at Detroit.
Records	**Mar 18, 1971** • Gil Perreault scored his 35th goal of the season in Buffalo's 5–3 win over St. Louis to set a new NHL rookie record. Perreault broke the record of 34 held by Oakland's Norm Ferguson, Minnesota's Danny Grant and the Montreal Maroons' Nels Stewart.	**Mar 22, 1972** • Detroit's Marcel Dionne scored two goals and two assists to reach 75 points, a new NHL record for rookies, as the Red Wings won 6–3 at Los Angeles. Dionne broke the previous mark of 72 points set by Buffalo's Gil Perreault the year before.	**Dec 21, 1972** • Boston's Bobby Orr had an assist to set a new NHL record for career points (541) by a defenseman. It came in Orr's 423rd career NHL game, an 8–1 win over Detroit. Doug Harvey held the previous record, with 540 points in 1,113 games.	**Dec 9, 1973** • Buffalo's Rick Martin scored his 100th NHL goal in just his 174th career game (an NHL record at that time). It came in the Sabres' 5–2 win over the Maple Leafs at the Aud in Buffalo.	**Mar 28, 1975** • The Capitals recorded the only road victory in the team's first season when Nelson Pyatt's two third-period goals gave them a 5–3 win at Oakland. The win ended their NHL-record 37-game road losing streak. They finished the year 1–39–0 on the road.
Did You Know?	**Mar 20, 1971** • NHL history was made as two brothers faced each other in goal for the first time. Ken Dryden's Canadiens beat Dave Dryden's Sabres 5–2 at the Montreal Forum.	**Feb 8, 1972** • Despite suffering from discomfort in the first period, Flyers goalie Bruce Gamble led the team to a 3–1 win at Vancouver. After the game it was determined that Gamble had suffered a heart attack.	**Feb 6, 1973** • Playing his first NHL game at the age of 38, Connie Madigan became the oldest rookie in NHL history when he suited up for the St. Louis Blues in a 5–1 win over Vancouver.	**Feb 28, 1974** • Boston's 36-year-old rookie goalie Ross Brooks tied an NHL record with his 14th consecutive victory, an 8–1 win over Detroit at Boston Garden.	**Oct 23, 1974** • Washington's Michel Belhumeur faced two penalty shots and made two saves (against the Black Hawks' Jim Pappin and Stan Mikita). Despite his heroics, the Caps lost 3–2 at Chicago.
Milestones	**Oct 29, 1970** • Gordie Howe became the first player in NHL history to record 1,000 career assists when he picked up two (along with a goal) in a 5–3 Red Wings victory over Boston at the Olympia in Detroit.	**Feb 19, 1972** • Phil Esposito became the first player in NHL history to score 100 points in a season three times in his career. The milestone came when he picked up an assist in the Bruins' 6–4 win over the North Stars at Minnesota.	**May 18, 1973** • Boston's Bobby Orr was named the winner of the Norris Trophy. It was the first time in NHL history that a player had won an individual award six consecutive seasons.	**Apr 7, 1974** • Pittsburgh's Andy Brown became the last NHL goaltender to play without a mask when he played his final league game for the Penguins, a 6–3 loss to the Flame, at the Omni in Atlanta.	**Dec 29, 1974** • Brad Park picked up an assist to become the highest-scoring defenseman in Rangers history, breaking Harry Howell's record of 345 points as New York won 2–1 over the Kansas City Scouts at Madison Square Garden.
Rookies	**Mar 14, 1971** • Ken Dryden made his NHL debut when the Montreal Canadiens beat the Penguins 5–1 at Pittsburgh.	**Feb 10, 1972** • Montreal's Guy Lafleur had three goals in a 7–1 win over Chicago to become the first NHL rookie (in the modern era) to score three hat tricks in a season.	**Feb 3, 1973** • Montreal's rookie defenseman Larry Robinson scored his first career goal in a 7–1 Canadiens win over the Kings at Los Angeles.	**Oct 10, 1973** • Montreal rookie Bob Gainey played in his first NHL game when the Canadiens beat the North Stars 5–2 in Minnesota.	**Feb 8, 1975** • North Stars goalie Pete LoPresti recorded his first career shutout in a 5–0 win over the Flyers. He and Sam LoPresti became the first father and son both to record NHL shutouts.
Transactions	**Jun 10, 1970** • The Canadiens acquired Oakland's first choice in the 1971 draft in a multi-player deal. Exactly one year later, Montreal used the pick to select Guy Lafleur.	**Nov 4, 1971** • L.A. Kings traded Dale Hoganson, Dennis DeJordy, Noel Price and Doug Robinson to Montreal in exchange for goalie Rogie Vachon.	**Mar 2, 1973** • St. Louis Blues obtained defenseman Ab DeMarco from the New York Rangers, in exchange for Mike Murphy.	**May 12, 1973** • Toronto Maple Leafs signed Swedish defenseman Borje Salming and forward Inge Hammarstrom as free agents.	**May 24, 1974** • Philadelphia Flyers acquired Reggie Leach from the California Seals in exchange for Larry Wright, Al MacAdam and a first-round draft pick in 1974 (Ron Chipperfield).
Teams	**Mar 6, 1971** • Boston set a new NHL record for most wins in a season with their 47th in a 6–3 victory at Pittsburgh. The Bruins broke the record of 46 wins set by Montreal in 1968–69.	**Nov 9, 1971** • The NHL announced it had granted a franchise to Atlanta to start play in 1972–73. On Dec 31, 1971, a new franchise was awarded to the New York Islanders.	**Mar 1, 1973** • Philadelphia became the most penalized team in one season in NHL history when Bob Kelly's hooking penalty broke Vancouver's mark of 1,371 minutes set in 1970–71.	**Nov 10, 1973** • St. Louis beat Montreal 5–0 to become the first post-'67 expansion team to register 200 franchise victories.	**Jun 11, 1974** • The Kansas City Scouts and Washington Capitals officially received their NHL franchises.
Front Office	**Jan 8, 1971** • Detroit Red Wings fired general manager Sid Abel and named coach Ned Harkness as their new g.m.	**Jun 2, 1971** • The Philadelphia Flyers named Fred Shero as their new head coach, replacing Vic Stasiuk.	**Oct 5, 1972** • After his success in the just-concluded Canada-Russia series, Harry Sinden returned to the Boston Bruins as general manager. He had left in 1970 to work in private business.	**Jun 10, 1973** • Al Arbour signed a three-year contract with the Islanders as their new head coach, replacing Earl Ingarfield.	**Jun 13, 1974** • Don Cherry was named the new coach of the Boston Bruins, replacing Bep Guidolin.
Playoffs	**Apr 11, 1971** • Boston's Bobby Orr became the first defenseman in NHL history to score a hat trick in the Stanley Cup playoffs. It came in a 5–2 Bruins win at Montreal in game four of the quarterfinals. However, Ken Dryden's Canadiens went on to upset Boston in seven games and later won the Stanley Cup.	**May 4, 1972** • Bobby Orr scored his 17th career playoff goal to break the all-time postseason record for defensemen. Orr broke the mark set by Detroit's Red Kelly in a 5–2 Boston loss to the Rangers in game thee of the finals. Orr and the Bruins went on to win the Stanley Cup in six games.	**May 3, 1973** • Henri Richard set an NHL Stanley Cup record for career playoff games as he appeared in his 165th career playoff game; a 7–4 loss to Chicago in game three of the Stanley Cup finals. Richard broke the record of 164 games set by Red Kelly.	**May 19, 1974** • The Philadelphia Flyers became the first post-'67 expansion team to win the Stanley Cup, beating the Bruins 1–0 in game six of the finals.	**Apr 26, 1975** • New York Islanders beat Pittsburgh 1–0 in game seven of the Stanley Cup quarterfinals to become the second team in NHL history to win a best-of-seven series after losing the first three games. Toronto had accomplished the feat back in the 1942 finals.
Business	**Jun 11, 1970** • In the NHL Amateur Draft held in Montreal, the Buffalo Sabres used the first overall pick to select Gilbert Perreault.	**Jun 10, 1971** • In the NHL Amateur Draft held in Montreal, the Montreal Canadiens used the first pick overall to select Guy Lafleur.	**Jun 8, 1972** • In the NHL Amateur Draft held in Montreal, the expansion New York Islanders used the first overall pick to select Billy Harris.	**May 15, 1973** • In the NHL Amateur Draft held in Montreal, the New York Islanders used the first pick overall to select Denis Potvin.	**Jun 13, 1975** • The Pittsburgh Penguins declared bankruptcy. The team was sold by the NHL for $3,800,000.
Births & Deaths	**Jul 3, 1970** • Teemu Selanne born in Helsinki, Finland. **Mar 31, 1971** • Pavel Bure born in Moscow, USSR.	**Feb 15, 1972** • Jaromir Jagr born in Kladno, Czech. **May 6, 1972** • Martin Brodeur born in Montreal, Quebec	**Jan 13, 1973** • Nikolai Khabibulin born in Sverdlovsk, USSR. **Feb 28, 1973** • Eric Lindros born in London, Ontario.	**Jul 20, 1973** • Peter Forsberg born in Ornskoldsvik, Sweden. **Apr 12, 1974** • Roman Hamrlik born in Gottwaldov, Czech.	**Oct 16, 1974** • Paul Kariya born in Vancouver, B.C. **Feb 7, 1975** • Alexandre Daigle born in Montreal, Quebec.

1970s	1975–76	1976–77	1977–78	1978–79	1979–80
Firsts	**Mar 30, 1976** • Boston's Jean Ratelle became the first player in NHL history to score 100 points for two teams with a goal and two assists in a 4–4 tie with Buffalo. He had previously scored 109 points for the Rangers in 1971–72.	**Apr 3, 1977** • Montreal Canadiens became the first team in NHL history to win 60 games in a season when they beat the Capitals 2–1 at Washington to finish with a record of 60–8–12.	**Apr 1, 1978** • Mike Bossy of the New York Islanders became the first NHL rookie to score 50 goals when he scored twice in the Islanders' 3–2 win over the Washington Capitals.	**Mar 18, 1979** • Philadelphia beat the St. Louis Blues 5–3 in the first game in Flyers history where no Philadelphia player had any penalties!	**Feb 24, 1980** • Edmonton's Wayne Gretzky became the first player in NHL history to score 100 points in a season prior to his 20th birthday. His 100th career point came as an assist in just his 61st career game, a 4–2 Oilers loss to the Bruins.
Records	**Feb 7, 1976** • Darryl Sittler set an NHL record with 10 points in one game on six goals and four assists in an 11–4 Toronto win over Boston at Maple Leaf Garden. It was the last game goalie Dave Reece ever played in the NHL.	**Feb 2, 1977** • Toronto's Ian Turnbull set an NHL scoring record for defensemen with five goals in a 9–1 win over Detroit. Turnbull became the first NHL player to score five goals on just five shots.	**Dec 11, 1977** • Philadelphia's Tom Bladon set an NHL record for most points in a game by a defenseman. His eight points (four goals and four assists) led the Flyers to an 11–1 win over the Cleveland Barons.	**Dec 23, 1978** • Bryan Trottier set an NHL record with six points (three goals and three assists) in the second period as the Islanders beat the Rangers 9–4.	**Jan 6, 1980** • Philadelphia scored twice in the final period for a 4–2 win at Buffalo. The victory ran their NHL-record unbeaten streak to 35 games (25–0–10). The streak ended one night later with a loss to Minnesota.
Did You Know?	**Oct 8, 1975** • Doug Jarvis played the first of his NHL-record 964 consecutive games (over a span of 12 years). Jarvis started with Montreal, continued the streak with the Capitals, and ended it with Hartford in October 1987.	**Feb 14, 1977** • Philadelphia's Al Hill scored on his first two shots and added three assists to tie the NHL record for most points in a player's first career game. The Flyers beat St. Louis 6–4.	**Oct 12, 1977** • Guy Lapointe had a goal and two assists to lead the Canadiens to a 7–3 win over the North Stars at the Forum. The victory tied an NHL record as the Canadiens extended their opening night undefeated streak to 15 games (11–0–4).	**Mar 11, 1979** • Randy Holt of the Los Angeles Kings picked up an NHL-record nine penalties and 67 penalty minutes in one game. The outburst came in the first period of a 6–3 Kings loss at Philadelphia.	**Mar 9, 1980** • NHL history was made when Hartford's Gordie Howe skated on a line with his two sons (Mark and Marty). The trio skated one shift together mid-way through the game during a 1–1 Whalers tie with the Bruins at Boston.
Milestones	**Mar 13, 1976** • Chicago's Billy Reay became the winningest coach with one team in NHL history when he registered his 501st coaching victory as the Black Hawks won 4–1 at Minnesota. Toe Blake had previously collected exactly 500 wins with Montreal.	**Apr 3, 1977** • Guy Lafleur extended his NHL-record point-scoring streak to 28 games as Montreal won 2–1 at Washington. Lafleur scored 19 goals and had 42 assists for a total of 61 points during the 28-game streak.	**Mar 24, 1978** • Phil Esposito scored three goals and added an assist as the Rangers beat Washington 11–4. It was Esposito's 29th career hat trick, a new NHL record. the old mark of 28 career hat tricks was held by Bobby Hull.	**Feb 19, 1979** • Mike Bossy's 47th goal of the year helped the Islanders to an 8–3 win at Los Angeles. It was Bossy's 100th NHL goal in just his 129th game, the fastest 100 goals in NHL history.	**Nov 28, 1979** • Billy Smith became the first goalie in NHL history to get credit for a goal. He was the last Islander to touch the puck before Rob Ramage of Colorado put it into his own net. The Islanders lost the game 7–4 to the Rockies in Denver.
Rookies	**Mar 4, 1976** • Bryan Trottier of the Islanders set two NHL rookie records in a 3–3 tie with Vancouver; his 53rd assist broke Jude Drouin's mark of 52 and his 79th point passed Marcel Dionne.	**Feb 26, 1977** • St. Louis rookie Brian Sutter scored the first goal of his NHL career in a 5–1 loss to the visiting Philadelphia Flyers.	**Feb 24, 1978** • Colorado Rockies rookie Barry Beck scored his 18th goal to set an NHL rookie goal-scoring record for defensemen (breaking the record of 17 set by Denis Potvin in 1973–74).	**Oct 1, 1978** • Minnesota rookie Bobby Smith scored the first goal of his NHL career, and added an assist, in the North Stars' 7–2 win over the visiting Vancouver Canucks.	**Feb 2, 1980** • Philadelphia's rookie goaltender Pete Peeters earned his first NHL shutout to lead the Flyers to a 4–0 win at Pittsburgh. The win improved his season record to 20–0–5.
Transactions	**Nov 7, 1975** • Phil Esposito and Carol Vadnais were traded from Boston to the Rangers in exchange for Brad Park, Jean Ratelle and Joe Zanussi.	**May 26, 1976** • New York Rangers traded center Rick Middleton to the Boston Bruins for Ken Hodge.	**Nov 29, 1977** • Pittsburgh Penguins traded Pierre Larouche to Montreal in exchange for Pete Mahovlich and Peter Lee.	**Oct 9, 1978** • Los Angeles Kings obtained goaltender Ron Grahame from Boston for the Kings' 1979 first-round draft choice. The Bruins later used the pick to select Ray Bourque.	**Dec 29, 1979** • Toronto Maple Leafs traded Lanny McDonald and Joel Quenneville to the Colorado Rockies for Pat Hickey and Wilf Paiement.
Teams	**Apr 4, 1976** • Montreal set a new NHL record for most wins in a season with their 58th in a 4–3 victory at Washington. The Canadiens broke Boston's record of 57 wins in 1970–71.	**Oct 5, 1976** • The first regular-season NHL game was played in Denver when the Colorado Rockies (newly transferred from Kansas City) beat Toronto 4–2 at the McNichols Sports Arena.	**Apr 8, 1978** • Boston rookie Bob Miller scored his 20th goal of the season to give the Bruins 11 20-goal scorers on the team, a new NHL record.	**Jun 13, 1978** • The NHL Board of Governors unanimously agreed to a merger of the Cleveland Barons and the Minnesota North Stars.	**Jun 22, 1979** • Former WHA teams the Edmonton Oilers, Hartford Whalers, Quebec Nordiques and Winnipeg Jets joined the NHL, as it expanded to 21 teams.
Front Office	**Jan 7, 1976** • John Ferguson was named the new coach and general manager of the New York Rangers, replacing Emile Francis.	**Mar 3, 1977** • Edmonton Oilers (of the WHA) named their ex-player Glen Sather as the team's new head coach.	**Jul 6, 1977** • The Chicago Black Hawks named Bob Pulford as their new coach and general manager.	**Sep 4, 1978** • Sam Pollack resigned as general manager of the Canadiens after 14 years with the team. He was replaced by Irving Grundman.	**Nov 14, 1979** • Washington Capitals named Gary Green as their new head coach, replacing Dan Belisle. At age 26, Green became the youngest coach in NHL history.
Playoffs	**Apr 17, 1976** • Philadelphia's Reggie Leach set an NHL record by scoring a goal in his ninth consecutive playoff game, a 4–3 Flyers loss to Toronto in game four of the Stanley Cup quarterfinals.	**Apr 15, 1977** • Clark Gillies set a Stanley Cup playoff record with his fourth consecutive game-winning goal as the Islanders won 4–3 at Buffalo in game three of the quarterfinals	**May 16, 1978** • The Montreal Canadiens and Ken Dryden set team and goalie playoff records with their 10th straight win in the Stanley Cup finals (dating back to 1976). Guy Lafleur scored at 13.09 of OT in a 3–2 win over the visiting Bruins in game two of the 1978 finals.	**Apr 24, 1979** • The Rangers and Flyers set an NHL record for most goals in one period with nine in the third period of game five of the quarterfinals. New York won the period 6–3 and the game 8–3.	**Apr 8, 1980** • Hartford's Gordie Howe set an NHL record for most years in the playoffs (20) when the Whalers played in a 6–1 loss at Montreal. It was Howe's first NHL playoff appearance since the 1969–70 season. He broke the mark of 19 years in the playoffs set by Red Kelly.
Business	**Jun 23, 1975** • Los Angeles Kings signed free-agent Marcel Dionne from Detroit, along with Bart Crashley. The Red Wings obtained Dan Maloney and Terry Harper as compensation.	**Jul 14, 1976** • The NHL officially approved the transfer of the California Seals franchise to Cleveland. It was the NHL's first franchise move since 1934 when the Ottawa Senators became the St. Louis Eagles. The Kansas City Scouts also moved this year, becoming the Colorado Rockies.	**Jun 14, 1977** • In the NHL Amateur Draft held in Montreal, the Detroit Red Wings used the first pick overall to acquire Dale McCourt. Mike Bossy was chosen 15th by the Islanders.	**Jun 15, 1978** • In the NHL Amateur Draft held in Montreal, the Minnesota North Stars used the first pick overall to acquire Bobby Smith.	**Sep 28, 1979** • Minnesota North Stars signed free agent Dino Ciccarelli from the London Knights of the OHA. Ciccarelli had fractured his leg in junior hockey and went undrafted by all 21 NHL teams.
Births & Deaths	**Jul 24, 1975** • Jamie Langenbrunner born in Duluth, MN. **May 18, 1976** • Oleg Tverdovsky born in Donetsk, USSR.	**Aug 5, 1976** • Jeff Friesen born in Meadow Lake, Saskatchewan. **Mar 5, 1977** • Bryan Berard born in Woonsocket, RI.	**Jul 1, 1977** • Jarome Iginla born in Edmonton, Alberta. **Jan 21, 1978** • Andrei Zyuzin born in Ufa, USSR.	**Jun 16, 1978** • Dainius Zubrus born in Elektrenai, USSR. **Oct 27, 1978** • Sergei Samsonov born in Moscow, USSR.	**Jul 2, 1979** • Joe Thornton born in London, Ontario. **Sep 15, 1979** • Patrick Marleau born in Swift Current, Sask.

1980s	1980–81	1981–82	1982–83	1983–84	1984–85
Firsts	Oct 9, 1980 • Hartford's Mark Howe became the first defenseman in NHL history to score two shorthanded goals in a game. They came in the second period of an 8–6 Whalers loss to the Blues in St. Louis.	Mar 4, 1982 • Mike Bossy's hat trick in a 10–1 win over Toronto made him the first player in NHL history to score 50 goals in each of his first five seasons.	Feb 22, 1983 • Marcel Dionne of Los Angeles became the first player in NHL history to score 40 goals or more in nine seasons when he scored in the Kings' 5–3 win over Boston.	Mar 31, 1984 • Mike Bossy became the first player in NHL history to have seven straight 50-goal seasons when he scored his 50th and 51st of the year to lead the Islanders to a 3–1 win at Washington.	Nov 13, 1984 • Bernie Nicholls of Los Angeles became the first player in NHL history to score a goal in all four periods of a game. He scored once in each period, plus the overtime winner, when the Kings beat the Nordiques 5–4 in Quebec City.
Records	Mar 29, 1981 • Edmonton's Wayne Gretzky broke Phil Esposito's NHL record for most points in a season (152) with three assists in a 4–2 Oilers win at Detroit.	Feb 24, 1982 • Wayne Gretzky scored his 77th goal of the season to break the NHL record of 76 held by Phil Esposito. Gretzky finished with a hat trick in a 6–3 win at Buffalo and went on to score 92 goals for the season.	Jan 11, 1983 • Edmonton's Pat Hughes set an NHL record for fastest two shorthanded goals (25 seconds) in the second period of a 7–5 win at St. Louis. Hughes became the first player to break a Wayne Gretzky record.	Mar 6, 1984 • Winnipeg's Dale Hawerchuk set an NHL record with five assists in one period (the second) as the Jets won 7–3 in Los Angeles.	Dec 19, 1984 • Buffalo's Scotty Bowman became the winningest coach in NHL history with career victory #691 in the Sabres' 6–3 win at Chicago. Bowman surpassed Dick Irvin, who had won 690 games with the Maple Leafs, Canadiens and Black Hawks from 1930 to 1956.
Did You Know?	Mar 22, 1981 • Jim Rutherford became the first goalie in NHL history to play for three teams in one season when he led the Kings to a 7–5 win at Winnipeg. Rutherford started the year with Detroit before being traded to Toronto, then L.A. on Mar. 10.	Feb 11, 1982 • NHL history was made when referee Kerry Fraser awarded penalty shots to two Vancouver players in the same period! Thomas Gradin and Ivan Hlinka both scored on Gilles Gilbert in the third period of a 4–4 Canucks tie at Detroit.	Nov 28, 1982 • Rookie Ron Sutter made NHL history when he played in his first game with Philadelphia. It was the first time in league history that five brothers all played in the NHL. The Flyers tied the Canucks 5–5 in Vancouver.	Dec 18, 1983 • Wayne Gretzky had two goals and two assists for his 100th point of the season as the Oilers beat Winnipeg 7–5. Gretzky's 100th point came in the Oilers' 34th game of the season, the fastest 100 points in NHL history.	Oct 25, 1984 • Guy Lafleur scored his 518th and final goal as a member of the Montreal Canadiens in a 3–2 win over Buffalo. Lafleur's next NHL goal would come four years later with the New York Rangers.
Milestones	Nov 2, 1980 • The Flyers recorded the milestone 500th win in team history (a 4–2 victory over Boston in Philadelphia) at a time when no other expansion team had reached the 400-victory plateau.	Mar 25, 1982 • Wayne Gretzky scored two goals and had two assists to become the first player in NHL history to score 200 points in one season. The milestone came in a 7–2 Oilers win at Calgary. Gretzky finished the year with 212 points on 92 goals and 120 assists	Nov 13, 1982 • Chicago's Tony Esposito became the fourth goaltender in NHL history to record 400 career victories as the Black Hawks beat the Red Wings 3–2 in Detroit. The three previous 400-game winners were Terry Sawchuk, Jacques Plante and Glenn Hall.	Jan 27, 1984 • Wayne Gretzky extended his NHL-record consecutive point-scoring streak to 51 games in Edmonton's 3–3 tie with New Jersey. The streak began October 5, 1983. In total, Gretzky had 61 goals and 92 assists in the 51 games.	Dec 19, 1984 • While playing in just his 424th career game, Edmonton's Wayne Gretzky had two goals and four assists to become the fastest player in NHL history to reach 1,000 career points (breaking Guy Lafleur's record of 720 games). The Oilers won 7–3 over the visiting Los Angeles Kings.
Rookies	Oct 18, 1980 • Edmonton rookie Jari Kurri scored his first goal in a 5–5 tie with the Islanders. On Jan 2, 1981, Edmonton's rookie goaltender Andy Moog recorded his first victory (7–5 over Boston).	Oct 21, 1981 • Edmonton's Grant Fuhr got his first NHL victory, 5–2 over Hartford. On Nov 18, 1981, Whalers rookie Ron Francis got his first goal and first assist in an 8–5 win over Toronto.	Oct 6, 1982 • Rookie Steve Larmer scored the first goal of his NHL career, and added two assists, to lead the Black Hawks to a 3–3 tie against Toronto in Chicago.	Oct 5, 1983 • Detroit's Steve Yzerman scored his first goal in a 6–6 tie at Winnipeg. On Jan 18, 1984, Buffalo's Tom Barrasso got his first NHL shutout in a 4–0 win over L.A.	Oct 11, 1984 • Pittsburgh's Mario Lemieux scored his first goal on his first shift in a 4–3 loss at Boston. On Feb 23, 1985, Montreal's Patrick Roy debuted with a 6–4 win over Winnipeg.
Transactions	Aug 26, 1980 • Quebec Nordiques signed Peter and Anton Stastny after they defected from Czechoslovakia during a hockey tournament in Austria.	Nov 25, 1981 • Calgary Flames traded Bob MacMillan and Don Lever to the Colorado Rockies in exchange for Lanny McDonald.	Sep 9, 1982 • Montreal traded Rod Langway, Doug Jarvis, Craig Laughlin and Brian Engblom to Washington in exchange for Ryan Walter and Rick Green.	Oct 18, 1983 • Los Angeles traded defenseman Larry Murphy to the Washington Capitals for defenseman Brian Engblom and right winger Ken Houston.	Oct 1, 1984 • Los Angeles Kings signed free-agent defenseman Steve Duchesne to a contract.
Teams	Mar 19, 1981 • The Buffalo Sabres set an NHL record with nine goals in the second period of a 14–4 win over Toronto at Buffalo. The Sabres scored eight goals in a 4:52 span.	Feb 20, 1982 • New York Islanders set an NHL record with their 15th consecutive victory, 3–2 over the Colorado Rockies.	May 27, 1982 • Colorado Rockies were sold and moved to New Jersey, where they became known as the Devils.	Dec 15, 1983 • Philadelphia Flyers set an NHL record with three shorthanded goals in one period when they beat the Capitals 9–4 at Washington.	Nov 9, 1984 • Edmonton won 8–5 at Washington to set an NHL record for the longest undefeated streak from the start of the season (12–0–3).
Front Office	Nov 22, 1980 • Craig Patrick was named general manager and coach of the New York Rangers, replacing Fred Shero.	Nov 5, 1981 • Washington fired general manager. Max McNab and coach Garry Green. Roger Crozier became the new g.m. and interim coach. Bryan Murray was hired as coach six days later.	Jun 1, 1982 • Calgary Flames fired head coach Al MacNeil and hired Bob Johnson. Johnson joined the Flames after a 15-year stint as head coach at the University of Wisconsin.	May 27, 1983 • Ed Johnston was named the new general manager of the Pittsburgh Penguins, replacing Baz Bastien.	May 15, 1984 • Bobby Clarke retired as an NHL player and was named the new general manager of the Philadelphia Flyers. Nine days later, Clarke hired Mike Keenan as coach.
Playoffs	May 17, 1981 • Butch Goring became the first player in NHL history to score a playoff hat trick with two teams when he led the Islanders to a 7–5 win over Minnesota in game three of the 1981 Stanley Cup finals. Goring also had a three-goal game for Los Angeles. in 1977.	Apr 8, 1982 • Mikko Leinonen of the New York Rangers set a Stanley Cup playoff record for most assists in one game with six during a 7–3 win over Philadelphia in game two of the Patrick Division semifinals.	Apr 22, 1983 • The Islanders beat the Rangers 5–2 in game six of the Patrick Division finals at Madison Square Garden to win their 14th consecutive playoff series, an NHL record. (They ran the streak to 19 straight series wins before losing to Edmonton in the 1984 Stanley Cup finals).	Apr 8, 1984 • Calgary's Paul Reinhart became the first NHL defenseman to score two career playoff hat tricks as the Flames beat Vancouver 5–1 in game four of the Smythe Division semifinals.	May 7, 1985 • Edmonton beat Chicago 7–3 for the Oilers' 12th straight victory (then a playoff record) in game two of the Campbell Conference finals. The teams combined for three goals in 21 seconds in the third period, an NHL record.
Business	Jun 24, 1980 • The Atlanta Flames franchise moved to Calgary, Alberta.	Jun 10, 1981 • In the NHL Entry Draft held in Montreal, the Winnipeg Jets used the first pick overall to acquire Dale Hawerchuk.	Jun 9, 1982 • In the NHL Entry Draft held in Montreal, the Boston Bruins used the first pick overall to acquire Gord Kluzak.	Jun 8, 1983 • In the NHL Entry Draft held in Montreal, the Minnesota North Stars used the first pick overall to acquire Brian Lawton.	Jun 9, 1984 • In the NHL Entry Draft held in Montreal, the Pittsburgh Penguins used the first pick overall to select Mario Lemieux.
Births & Deaths	Tiny Thompson passed away on Feb 9, 1981 in Calgary, Alberta. Ken Doraty passed away on May 4, 1981 in Moose Jaw, Saskatchewan.	Lorne Duguid passed away on May 21, 1981 in Toronto, Ontario. Herb Cain passed away on Feb 15, 1982 in Newmarket, Ontario.	Mud Bruneteau passed away on Apr 15, 1982 in Houston, Texas Danny Cox passed away on Aug 8, 1982 in Thunder Bay, Ontario.	Roy Conacher passed away in Victoria, B.C. in December 1984. Eddie Bush passed away on May 31, 1984 in Collingwood Ontario.	Eddie Shore passed away on Mar 16, 1985. Cooney Weiland passed away on July 3, 1985.

1980s	1985–86	1986–87	1987–88	1988–89	1989–90
Firsts	**Mar 26, 1986** • Minnesota North Stars center Neal Broten became the first U.S.-born player to score 100 points in a season. He reached the century mark with two assists in a 6–1 North Stars victory at Toronto.	**Apr 4, 1987** • Denis Potvin of the Islanders scored twice (in a 6–6 tie with Buffalo) to become the first defenseman in NHL history to score 1,000 career points.	**Jan 4, 1988** • Toronto defenseman Borje Salming became the first European-trained player to appear in 1,000 career NHL games. The milestone came in the Maple Leafs' 7–7 tie against the Vancouver Canucks.	**Jun 6, 1989** • Wayne Gretzky became the first player in NHL history to win the same award nine times when he was named the recipient of the Hart Trophy after his first season with the Los Angeles Kings.	**Mar 20, 1989** • Pittsburgh's Paul Coffey became the first defenseman in NHL history to score 100 points in a season for two teams when he got his 100th point of the year in the Penguins' 7–2 loss at Minnesota.
Records	**Mar 8, 1986** • Philadelphia's Tim Kerr set an NHL record with his 29th power-play goal of the season in a 7–3 Flyers loss at New Jersey.	**Nov 11, 1986** • Minnesota's Dino Ciccarelli scored twice in his 15th game of the season (a 2–2 tie against Washington) to set a modern NHL record for the fastest 20 goals from the start of the season.	**Dec 19, 1987** • Boston's Ken Linseman and the Blues' Doug Gilmour scored goals two seconds apart in the third period to set an NHL record for fastest two goals. St. Louis won the game 7–5. Gilmour's goal came off a center-ice face-off into an empty net.	**Mar 30, 1989** • Mario Lemieux set an NHL record with his 13th shorthanded goal of the season (breaking the mark of 12 set by Wayne Gretzky in 1983–84), but Pittsburgh lost 9–5 to the visiting Hartford Whalers.	**Mar 17, 1990** • Wayne Gretzky had a goal and two assists to lead the Kings to a 5–4 win at Boston. The totals gave Gretzky 40-or-more goals for 11 straight seasons (an NHL record) and 100 or more assists for 10 straight seasons (also a record).
Did You Know?	**Dec 19, 1985** • Montreal Canadiens defenseman Larry Robinson scored the only hat trick of his 20-year NHL career in a 5–4 Canadiens loss to the Quebec Nordiques.	**Nov 1, 1986** • One month into Minnesota's 20th NHL season, Craig Hartsburg became the first defenseman in North Stars history to score a hat trick. It came in a 6–5 home loss to Chicago.	**Mar 15, 1988** • After starting the year with Pittsburgh, Edmonton's Craig Simpson became the first player in NHL history to score 50 goals while playing for two teams in one season. Simpson reached 50 in a 6–4 Oilers win over Buffalo.	**Dec 31, 1988** • Mario Lemieux scored five goals (including one on the power-play, one short-handed, one at even strength, one on a penalty shot, and one into an empty net). He also had three assists in an 8–6 Penguins win over New Jersey.	**Mar 31, 1990** • John Tanner made his NHL debut in goal for the Nordiques (in a 3–2 loss to Hartford), making Quebec the first team in NHL history to use seven goalies in one season.
Milestones	**Apr 2, 1986** • Paul Coffey of the Edmonton Oilers scored his 47th and 48th goals of the season in an 8–4 win against Vancouver to break Bobby Orr's NHL record for most goals by a defenseman. Orr had scored 46 goals in 1974–75.	**Apr 5, 1987** • Hartford's Doug Jarvis completed his 12th NHL season by playing in his 962nd straight game. Jarvis went on to play the first two games of the 1987–88 season before retiring with an NHL-record 964 straight games.	**Dec 8, 1987** • Ron Hextall became the second goalie in NHL history to get credit for scoring a goal, and the first to actually shoot and score, as the Flyers beat the Bruins 5–2 at the Spectrum. Hextall's goal went into an empty net at 18:48 of the third period.	**Apr 1, 1989** • Goalie Patrick Roy completed an unbeaten season at home as the Canadiens tied the Flyers 2–2 in Montreal. Roy finished the season 25–0–4 at the Forum.	**Oct 15, 1989** • Playing in Edmonton, Wayne Gretzky picked up a first-period assist for point #1,850 to tie Gordie Howe, then scored in the last minute of the game to become the NHL's all-time leading point scorer. He scored again in overtime to lead the Kings to a 5–4 win over the Oilers.
Rookies	**Apr 4, 1986** • Defenseman Gary Suter set an NHL record for most assists by a rookie with six in the Flames' 9–3 win over the Oilers in Calgary.	**Oct 9, 1986** • Luc Robitaille scored a goal in his first NHL game, but the Kings lost 4–3 to St. Louis. On Oct 26, 1986, Boston's Bill Ranford got his first shutout in a 6–0 win at Calgary.	**Nov 15, 1987** • Rookie Brett Hull scored his first career NHL hat trick with three straight goals in the final period to give the Flames an 8–4 win over the Canucks in Calgary.	**Mar 29, 1989** • Brian Leetch of the Rangers scored his 23rd goal in a 4–3 loss at Detroit. The goal broke Barry Beck's 1977–78 record of 22 goals by a rookie defenseman.	**Oct 5, 1989** • Alexander Mogilny scored his first NHL goal on his first shot of his first shift 20 seconds into his first game, leading the Sabres to an opening night 4–3 win over Quebec in Buffalo.
Transactions	**Jun 28, 1985** • Detroit Red Wings signed undrafted free agent Adam Oates after he had played three years of U.S. college hockey at Rensselaer Polytechnic Institute (RPI).	**Jun 6, 1986** • Boston Bruins obtained Cam Neely and Vancouver's first-round choice in the 1987 Entry Draft (Glen Wesley) from Vancouver in exchange for Barry Pederson.	**Mar 7, 1988** • St. Louis Blues obtained right winger Brett Hull from Calgary in exchange for defenseman Rob Ramage and goaltender Rick Wamsley.	**Aug 9, 1988** • Wayne Gretzky, Mike Krushelnyski and Marty McSorley were traded to the Kings from Edmonton for Jimmy Carson, Martin Gelinas, three first-round draft picks and cash.	**Jun 15, 1989** • Detroit traded Adam Oates and Paul MacLean to St. Louis for Bernie Federko and Tony McKegney. One day later, the Blues signed Curtis Joseph from the U of Wisconsin.
Teams	**Dec 11, 1985** • Edmonton beat the Black Hawks 12–9 in Chicago in the highest-scoring game in modern NHL history. The teams also set a record with 12 goals in the second period.	**Oct 18, 1986** • The Canadiens earned their 5,000th NHL point in a 5–3 win over Winnipeg. The win brought Montreal's 70-year NHL totals to 2,174–1,290–653 in 4,117 games.	**Dec 22, 1987** • New York Rangers played their 4,000th NHL game and their 2,000th career home game, a 6–4 loss to the Flyers. The loss gave them a record of 1,645–1,705–650.	**Dec 9, 1988** • NHL president John Ziegler announced plans to expand the league from 21 to 28 teams within the next decade.	**Nov 7, 1989** • Boston became just the second team in NHL history to win 2,000 games with a 5–4 overtime win over the Kings. Montreal was the only other NHL team with 2,000 wins.
Front Office	**Jun 11, 1985** • Jim Schoenfeld was named the Buffalo Sabres' new head coach, replacing Scotty Bowman. At age 32, Schoenfeld became the youngest coach in Sabres history.	**Jul 14, 1986** • Phil Esposito was named vice president and general manager of the New York Rangers, replacing Craig Patrick. In November, Espo would also become the team's head coach.	**Sep 10, 1987** • Lou Lamoriello took over as general manager of the New Jersey Devils, replacing Max McNab.	**Jun 20, 1988** • St. Louis Blues named 31-year-old Brian Sutter, who had played 12 years for the team, as their new head coach. Sutter replaced Jacques Martin.	**Jul 17, 1989** • New York Rangers hired Neil Smith as their new general manager, replacing Phil Esposito who had been fired two months earlier. Smith later hired Roger Neilson as coach.
Playoffs	**Apr 12, 1986** • Mike Bossy of the Islanders scored his 83rd career playoff goal to break Maurice Richard's long-held NHL record of 82. Bossy's 83rd came in a 3–1 Islanders loss to Washington in game three of the Patrick Division semifinals.	**Apr 9, 1987** • Edmonton's Wayne Gretzky had six assists, including his 177th career playoff point, to pass Jean Beliveau and put him into first place on the all-time playoff scoring list. The Oilers beat the Kings 13–3 in Edmonton.	**Apr 22, 1988** • New Jersey's Patrick Sundstrom set an NHL playoff record with eight points (three goals and five assists) to give the Devils a 10–4 win over Washington in game three of the Patrick Division finals.	**Apr 25, 1989** • Mario Lemieux tied five NHL playoff records with five goals and three assists in the Penguins' 10–7 win over Philadelphia in Game Five of the Patrick Division finals. Lemieux scored four goals in the first period, including three in a span of seven minutes.	**Apr 4, 1990** • Edmonton's Mark Messier set a new Stanley Cup record with his 11th career playoff shorthanded goal as the Oilers lost 7–5 to the Jets in game one of the Smythe Division semifinals. Messier broke the record of 10 that he had shared with Wayne Gretzky.
Business	**Jun 15, 1985** • In the NHL Entry Draft held in Toronto, the Maple Leafs used the first pick overall to select Wendel Clark.	**Jun 21, 1986** • In the NHL Entry Draft held in Montreal, the Detroit Red Wings used the first pick overall to acquire Joe Murphy.	**Jun 13, 1987** • In the NHL Entry Draft held in Detroit, the Sabres used the first pick overall to select Pierre Turgeon. At 17 years and 10 months, he became the youngest first overall pick in NHL history.	**Jun 11, 1988** • In the NHL Entry Draft held in Montreal, the Minnesota North Stars used the first pick overall to select Mike Modano.	**Jun 17, 1989** • At the NHL Draft held in Bloomington, Minnesota, the Quebec Nordiques used the first overall selection to pick Mats Sundin. Sundin became the first European player selected first overall.
Births & Deaths	Jacques Plante passed away on Feb 27, 1986 in Geneva, Switz. Bill Cook passed away on Apr 6, 1986 in Kingston, Ontario.	King Clancy passed away on Nov 8, 1986 in Toronto, Ontario. Red Dutton passed away on Mar 15, 1987.	Neil Colville passed away on Dec 26, 1987 in Richmond, B.C. Don Cook passed away on Mar 19, 1988 in Kingston, Ontario.	Joe Primeau passed away on May 14, 1989. Ab DeMarco passed away on May 25, 1989 in North Bay, Ontario.	Doug Harvey passed away on Dec 26, 1989. Hap Day passed away on Feb 17, 1990

1990s	1990–91	1991–92	1992–93	1993–94	1994–95
Firsts	**Jun 5, 1991** • Brett Hull became part of the first father-and-son team to win the Hart Trophy, as the St. Louis star won the NHL's MVP award in Toronto.	**Mar 7, 1992** • Pittsburgh's Kevin Stevens became the first player in NHL history to get 100 points and 200 penalty minutes in the same season when he picked up his 100th point of the year with an assist in a 5–3 loss in Los Angeles.	**Mar 28, 1993** • Alexei Zhamnov scored in a 3–3 tie against the Kings to make the Winnipeg Jets the first team in NHL history with four 20-goal rookies. Zhamnov joined Teemu Selanne, Evgeny Davydov and Keith Tkachuk as 20-goal rookies.	**Mar 26, 1994** • Toronto's Mike Gartner scored twice (in a 6–3 win over the Nordiques) to become the first player in NHL history to get 30 goals or more in 15 straight seasons.	**May 3, 1995** • Jaromir Jagr became the first European player to lead the NHL in scoring. Jagr and the Flyers' Eric Lindros tied with 70 points apiece in the shortened 48-game season, but Jagr led in goals (32–29) to win the Art Ross Trophy.
Records	**Mar 31, 1991** • Boston's Chris Nilan set an NHL record with 10 penalties in one game—six minors, two majors, a misconduct, and a game misconduct—in a 7–3 Bruins win over Hartford at Boston Garden.	**Dec 21, 1991** • Alexander Mogilny tied an NHL record with a goal scored just five seconds into the game, a 4–1 Sabres win over Toronto.	**Apr 15, 1993** • Winnipeg's Teemu Selanne finished his first season with NHL rookie scoring records of 76 goals and 132 points. Selanne and the Jets wrapped up the season with a 3–0 win over the Oilers.	**Mar 23, 1994** • Wayne Gretzky scored career goal #802 to pass Gordie Howe and set a new NHL record as the league's all-time leading goal scorer. The historic goal came in a game the Kings lost 6–3 to Vancouver at the Forum.	**Apr 28, 1995** • San Jose goaltender Arturs Irbe set an NHL record for most games played by a European-born goalie. He set the mark in his 158th career game, a 4–0 win over the visiting Los Angeles Kings.
Did You Know?	**Mar 9, 1991** • Calgary's Theoren Fleury scored three shorthanded goals and added an assist to lead the Flames to an 8–4 win at St. Louis.	**Mar 11, 1992** • Dave McLlwain tied an NHL record when he played his first game with Toronto (a 3–0 win at Minnesota). McLlwain became just the second player (Dennis O'Brien) to appear with four different NHL teams in one season.	**Mar 21, 1993** • Mario Lemieux and Kevin Stevens each scored a goal to become the first teammates to reach 50 goals in the same game. The Penguins won 6–4 over the Oilers in a neutral-site game played in Cleveland.	**Oct 20, 1993** • Wayne Gretzky had a goal and two assists in the first NHL game featuring two Gretzky brothers! Wayne played against his 21-year-old brother Brent (appearing in his second career game) as the Kings won 4–3 at Tampa Bay.	**Mar 8, 1995** • Montreal's Mark Recchi became the first player in NHL history to take penalty shots for two different NHL teams in one season. He was stopped by Buffalo's Dominik Hasek one month after missing with the Flyers against Ottawa.
Milestones	**Dec 27, 1990** • The Oilers recorded their 500th all-time NHL victory by defeating the Calgary Flames 4–1 in Edmonton. The win gave the Oilers a lifetime record of 500–295–120 for a winning percentage of .612, the best of any NHL team.	**Oct 17, 1991** • Paul Coffey had two assists to become the highest-scoring defenseman in NHL history with 1,053 career points (one more than former Islanders defenseman Denis Potvin). The milestone came as the Penguins beat the Islanders 8–5 at the Civic Arena.	**Dec 9, 1992** • Boston's Gordie Roberts became the first American-born player to play in 1,000 NHL games when the Bruins lost 5–2 in Buffalo.	**Dec 8, 1993** • Jari Kurri of the Kings became the highest scoring European-trained player in NHL history when he collected his 1,222nd career point in a 6–5 Los Angeles loss to the Florida Panthers. Kurri surpassed Peter Stastny, who had retired with 1,221 points.	**Feb 7, 1995** • Pittsburgh's Joe Mullen had two goals and added two assists (in a 7–3 win over the Florida Panthers) to become the first American-born player to score 1,000 points in the NHL.
Rookies	**Oct 7, 1990** • Pittsburgh's Jaromir Jagr scored his first goal in his second NHL game, a 7–4 win over the Devils. Dominik Hasek got his first victory in Chicago's 5–3 win at Buffalo.	**Nov 12, 1991** • Pavel Bure got his first two NHL goals as Vancouver beat L.A. 9–2. On Mar 26, 1992, New Jersey's Martin Brodeur made his NHL debut with a 4–2 win over Boston.	**Nov 15, 1992** • Philadelphia rookie Eric Lindros scored three goals for his first career NHL hat trick. He also added an assist to lead the Flyers to a 7–2 win over Ottawa at the Spectrum.	**Feb 24, 1994** • Rookie goaltender Chris Osgood recorded his first career NHL shutout as the Red Wings won 3–0 over the Hartford Whalers in Detroit.	**Jan 21, 1995** • Anaheim rookie Paul Kariya scored his first career NHL goal as the Mighty Ducks beat the Jets 4–3 at Winnipeg.
Transactions	**Jun 29, 1990** • Chicago traded Montreal native Denis Savard to the Canadiens in exchange for Chicago native Chris Chelios.	**Oct 4, 1991** • Edmonton Oilers traded Mark Messier to the New York Rangers for Bernie Nicholls, Steven Rice, and Louie DeBrusk.	**Aug 7, 1992** • Chicago Blackhawks traded goalie Dominik Hasek to Buffalo for Sabres goalie Stephane Beauregard and a fourth-round draft choice (Eric Daze) in 1993.	**Jun 25, 1993** • Dallas Stars obtained goalie Andy Moog from Boston in exchange for goaltender Jon Casey.	**Feb 9, 1995** • Philadelphia obtained John LeClair, Eric Desjardins and Gilbert Dionne from Montreal for Mark Recchi and Philadelphia's third-round pick in the 1995 Entry Draft.
Teams	**Dec 6, 1990** • The NHL announced the addition of two new teams for the 1992-93 season: Ottawa and Tampa Bay.	**Dec 16, 1991** • The Tampa Bay Lightning and Ottawa Senators were officially granted membership in the NHL. The teams would play their first NHL games 10 months later.	**Dec 10, 1992** • The NHL announced that conditional expansion franchises had been awarded to Anaheim and Miami. The teams were targeted to begin play in 1993–94.	**Oct 23, 1993** • Toronto set an NHL record for most wins from start of season with their ninth straight victory, a 2–0 win at Tampa Bay. The Leafs would push the streak to 10 in a row.	**Jan 31, 1995** • Quebec became the second team in NHL history to have a rookie coach win his first five games when Marc Crawford led the team to a 5–2 win over the Flyers.
Front Office	**Jun 19, 1990** • Bob Gainey was named the new head coach of the Minnesota North Stars. Gainey replaced Pierre Page.	**Jul 1, 1991** • The Maple Leafs announced the hiring of Cliff Fletcher as their new president and general manager. Fletcher replaced Floyd Smith as g.m. in Toronto	**Dec 11, 1992** • National Hockey League Governors named Gary Bettman as the first NHL commissioner in league history, effective Feb. 1, 1993.	**Apr 17, 1993** • The Rangers named Mike Keenan their new head coach, replacing interim coach Ron Smith (who had taken over for Roger Neilson).	**Jun 14, 1994** • Bobby Clarke was named as general manager and president of the Philadelphia Flyers. Clarke rejoined the team after serving one year as the g.m. of the Florida Panthers.
Playoffs	**Apr 10, 1991** • Wayne Gretzky scored his 93rd career playoff goal—the most in NHL history—to lead the Kings to a 6–1 win at Vancouver in game four of the Smythe Division semi-finals. Gretzky passed Jari Kurri, who had scored 92 career playoff goals.	**Apr 23, 1992** • Scotty Bowman became the NHL's all-time leader in playoff wins when he led the Penguins to a 6–4 victory over Washington in game three of the Patrick Division semifinals. Bowman passed Al Arbour, who had 114 career playoff wins with the Islanders.	**May 20, 1993** • Montreal set an NHL record with their seventh straight overtime playoff victory when Guy Carbonneau scored at 12:34 of OT for a 2–1 win over the Islanders in game three of the Wales Conference final in New York.	**Apr 20, 1994** • Chris Osgood became the fifth rookie goalie in NHL history to record a shutout in his first career playoff game. He led the Red Wings to a 4–0 win over the Sharks in game two of the Western Conference quarterfinals, in Detroit.	**May 27, 1995** • Paul Coffey passed Denis Potvin to become the highest-scoring defenseman in NHL playoff history. Coffey's goal and assist in the Red Wings' 6–2 win at San Jose gave him 166 career points and gave the Red Wings a four-game sweep of the Sharks.
Business	**May 9, 1990** • The NHL approved the sale of the Minnesota North Stars by George and Gordon Gund in exchange for their being granted the rights to a Bay Area team that would begin play in October 1991. Thus, the San Jose Sharks were born.	**Jun 22, 1991** • Eric Lindros was selected first overall by the Quebec Nordiques at the 1991 NHL Entry Draft in Buffalo, New York. A year later, Quebec traded Lindros to both the New York Rangers and Philadelphia. An arbitrator eventually upheld the deal with the Flyers.	**Mar 10, 1993** • Minnesota announced that the North Stars would move to Dallas after the 1992–93 season.	**Jun 26, 1993** • At the NHL Draft in Quebec City, the Ottawa Senators used the first pick overall to select Alexandre Daigle. The Senators had "earned" the top selection with a record of 10–70–4 in their first season of 1992–93.	**Jun 28, 1994** • At the NHL Draft in Hartford, the Florida Panthers used the first overall pick to select Ed Jovanovski.
Births & Deaths	Earl Seibert passed away in May of 1990. Sweeney Schriner passed away on July 4, 1990.	Bill Allum passed away on Mar 14, 1992 in Winnipeg Manitoba. Ace Bailey passed away on Apr 7, 1992 in Toronto, Ontario.	John Kordic passed away on Aug 8, 1992 in Quebec City, Quebec. Terry Reardon passed away on Feb 14, 1993 in Baltimore, Maryland.	Bill Cowley passed away on Dec 31, 1993. Bill Mosienko passed away on Jul 9, 1994 in Winnipeg, Manitoba	Bill Nyrop passed away on Dec 31, 1995. Eddie Mazur passed away on Jul 3, 1995 in St. Boniface, Manitoba.

1990s	1995–96	1996–97	1997–98
Firsts	**Mar 20, 1996** • Grant Fuhr became the first goaltender in NHL history to start 71 games in one season when he played for the St. Louis Blues in their 2–1 loss to the Stars in Dallas. The last goaltender to start 70 games in one season had been Eddie Johnson of the Boston Bruins in 1963–64. Fuhr went on to play 79 games, breaking his own record (75) for games by a goalie in one season.	**Mar 14, 1997** • Pittsburgh's Joey Mullen scored his 500th NHL goal and added an assist in the Penguins' 6–3 loss in Colorado. Mullen became the first American–born player to score 500 career goals. Mullen would retire after the season with 502 goals and 561 assists for 1,063 points. One day after Mullen scored his 500th career goal, New Jersey's Dave Andreychuk also reached the milestone.	**Oct 9, 1997** • New York Rangers became the first team in NHL history to tie their first four games of the season when they battled to a 1–1 draw against the Flames in Calgary. The Rangers never overcame a sluggish start to the season and missed the playoffs despite having the NHL's highest payroll in 1997–98.
Records	**Mar 3, 1996** • Tampa Bay's Terry Crisp became the first coach in NHL history to win 100 games with an expansion team when the Lightning won 2–0 over the visiting Chicago Blackhawks. The 1995–96 season would be Tampa's best, as the Lightning went 38–32–12 and reached the playoffs for the first time in franchise history. Crisp was the longest–tenured coach in the NHL when he was fired by Tampa Bay during the 1997–97 campaign.	**Jan 21, 1997** • Veteran defenseman Michel Petit set a record by playing for his ninth different NHL team when he suited up for his first game with the Flyers in a 3–3 tie against the visiting Dallas Stars. Petit joined his tenth team in 1997–98, playing 32 games with the Phoenix Coyotes. Petit has also been with Vancouver, the Rangers, Quebec, Toronto, Calgary, Los Angeles, Tampa Bay and Edmonton in his career.	**Apr 15, 1998** • Tie Domi set a Toronto Maple Leafs team record for most penalty minutes in one season when his 17 PIM in a 3–2 win over the visiting Chicago Blackhawks broke the record of 351 minutes set by Tiger Williams in 1977–78. Domi finished the season with 365 PIM, second in the NHL behind Vancouver's Donald Brashear who had 372 minutes in penalties.
Did You Know?	**Mar 22, 1996** • Sharks rookie Jan Caloun scored to give him his first four NHL goals on just four shots. Later in the game he finally missed on a shot for a shooting percentage of .800 at the start of his NHL career. San Jose beat Calgary 3–2. Caloun finished the season with eight goals and three assists in just 11 games.	**Apr 29, 1997** • Craig MacTavish, the last remaining player to appear in the NHL without a helmet, announced his retirement after 17 seasons. MacTavish had begun his career with Boston and concluded it with St. Louis. In between, he played on three Stanley Cup champions with the Edmonton Oilers and was with a fourth with the Rangers in 1994.	**Oct 26, 1997** • Steve Yzerman of Detroit broke former Red Wing Alex Delvecchio's NHL record of being the longest–serving captain in league history (11 years, 12 games) as Detroit beat the Canucks 5–1 at Vancouver.
Milestones	**Dec 13, 1995** • Detroit's Paul Coffey became the first NHL defenseman to get 1,000 career assists as the Red Wings won 3–1 over the visiting Chicago Blackhawks. Only Gordie Howe, Wayne Gretzky and Marcel Dionne had preceded Coffey to the milestone. To date, Raymond Bourque is the only other defenseman to top 1,000 career assists.	**Mar 6, 1997** • Mike Gartner scored twice to give him 30 goals for the season—for an NHL–record 17th time in his career. Gartner's Phoenix Coyotes won 5–0 in Tampa Bay. On Dec 14, 1997 Gartner became the fifth player in NHL history to score 700 goals, joining Wayne Gretzky, Gordie Howe, Phil Esposito and Marcel Dionne in the elite club.	**Mar 7, 1998** • Wayne Gretzky of the New York Rangers scored his 1,000th NHL goal (878 in the regular season and 122 in the playoffs) in a 6–3 Rangers loss to the Devils in New Jersey. He finished the year with 1,007 goals (885 and 122). With WHA totals included, Gretzky has 1,063 total goals through 1997–98. Gordie Howe's total for NHL and WHA regular season and playoffs is 1,071.
Rookies	**Dec 2, 1995** • Florida's Ed Jovanovski, the first pick in the 1994 NHL Draft, scored his first career goal as the Panthers won 5–3 at Hartford. On Dec15, 1995 Jets rookie Deron Quint scored two goals four seconds apart in a 9–5 win versus Edmonton, tying Nels Stewart's NHL record for the fastest two goals.	**Jan 21, 1997** • Patrick Lalime made 49 saves in Pittsburgh's 4–2 win over Calgary, improving his record to 14–0–2 and extending his NHL record for longest unbeaten streak to start a career. Lalime's streak was snapped two nights later in a 4–3 loss to Colorado. He ended the season at 21–12–2.	**Apr 9, 1998** • Boston's Sergei Samsonov became the only rookie to score 20 goals in 1997–98, then added his 21st as the Bruins beat the visiting New York Islanders 4–1. Samsonov went on to win the Calder Trophy as rookie of the year.
Transactions	**Dec 6, 1995** • Colorado obtained goaltender Patrick Roy and Mike Keane from Montreal. The two would help the Avalanche win the Stanley Cup . On Feb 7, 1996, the Mighty Ducks of Anaheim obtained Teemu Selanne in a multi–player deal with the Jets	**Jul 21, 1996** • The Rangers announced the signing of free agent Wayne Gretzky. On Oct 9, 1996, Detroit got Brendan Shanahan from Hartford for Keith Primeau and Paul Coffey. Coffey was later traded to Philadelphia in a deal involving Kevin Haller and draft choices on Dec 15, 1996.	**Jul 28, 1997** • Vancouver Canucks announced the signing of free agent Mark Messier. On Mar 24, 1998 a record was set when 38 players were involved in 19 trades before the deadline
Teams	**Apr 12, 1996** • The Red Wings set an NHL record with their 61st win of the year, a 5–3 victory over the Blackhawks. Detroit broke the record of 60 wins set by Montreal in 1976–77. The Red Wings went on to post a record of 62–13–7 and finished just one point behind the Canadiens record of 132 points in one season.	**Mar 25, 1997** • Hartford Whalers announced that they would move to play 5,000 games following the 1996–97 season. In 1997–98 they became the Carolina Hurricanes.	**Dec 1, 1997** • The Canadiens became the first team in history to play 5,000 NHL games. A 1–0 loss to the Penguins left Montreal with a record of 2,825–1,803–772 since 1917.
Front Office	**Dec 12, 1995** • New York Islanders named coach Mike Milbury as their new general manager. He replaced Don Maloney, who had been fired 10 days earlier. Milbury retained the dual role as coach and g.m. until midway through the 1996–97 season when he hired Rick Bowness to take over behind the bench.	**Feb 8, 1997** • Detroit's Scotty Bowman recorded the 1,000th NHL coaching victory of his career as the Red Wings won 6–5 in overtime at Pittsburgh.	**May 30, 1997** • Toronto Maple Leafs named Ken Dryden as the team's new president. Dryden replaced Cliff Fletcher, who had been fired six days earlier. On Aug 20, 1997 Dryden added the role of general manager to his portfolio.
Playoffs	**Apr 21, 1996** • Alexander Selivanov scored at 2:13 of overtime as the Lightning won 5–4 over the Flyers in game three of the Eastern Conference quarterfinals before a record crowd of 25,945 in Tampa Bay. The Lightning became the first NHL team to win its first two playoff games in overtime. Philadelphia would recover, however, and defeat Tampa Bay in six games	**Apr 24, 1997** • Patrick Roy set an NHL record with his 89th career playoff win, passing former New York Islander Billy Smith. Colorado beat the visiting Blackhawks 7–0 in game five of the Western Conference quarterfinals. Smith had been 88–36 in 132 playoff games and backstopped the Islanders to four consecutive Stanley Cup championships from 1980 to 1983. Through 1997–98, Roy is a three-time Stanley Cup champion and sports a playoff record of 99–59 in 160 games.	**Jun 11, 1998** • Detroit becomes the first team since the Montreal Canadiens in 1956 to rally from two goals down in the third period of a Stanley Cup game as they come back to beat Washington 5–4 in overtime in game two. Five nights later, the Red Wings wrapped up their second straight sweep of the Stanley Cup finals, defeating the Washington Capitals 4–1 in game four. Steve Yzerman won the Conn Smythe Trophy as playoff MVP.
Business	**May 25, 1995** • The NHL announced the sale of the Quebec Nordiques to COMSAT, who would move the team to Colorado. On Jan 19, 1996, the NHL Board of Governors approved the sale of the Winnipeg Jets, officially clearing the way for the team to move to Phoenix for the 1996–97 season.	**Jun 22, 1996** • In the NHL Entry Draft in St. Louis, the Ottawa Senators used the first overall pick to select Chris Phillips. A contract dispute almost cost the Senators a chance to sign Phillips, who made his NHL debut in 1997–98. With the 21st pick in the 1996 draft, San Jose chose Marco Sturm, making him the first German player ever chosen in the first round of the NHL draft. He also made his NHL debut in 1997–98.	**Jun 25, 1997** • The NHL officially approved expansion to 30 teams by the year 2000 with the announcement of new clubs in Atlanta, Columbus, Minnesota and Nashville. The Nashville Predators enter the league in 1998–99, with the Atlanta Thrashers coming on board in 1999–2000. The Minnesota Wild and Columbus Blue Jackets begin play in 2000–2001.
Births & Deaths	Roger Crozier passed away on Jan 11, 1996 in Landenberg, Pennsylvania. Jack "Tex" Evans passed away on Nov 10, 1996 in Manchester, Connecticut.	Al Rollins passed away on Jul 27, 1996 in Calgary, Alberta. Alex Motter passed away on Oct 18, 1996 in Livonia, Michigan.	Hal Laycoe passed away on Apr 28, 1998 in Vancouver, B.C. George Parsons passed away on Oakville, Ontario in June of 1998.

CHAPTER 18

NHL Franchise Histories

Profiles of Current and Former NHL Clubs

THE MIGHTY DUCKS OF ANAHEIM

Stan Fischler

LONG AFTER the Los Angeles Kings staked a claim in Southern California as a major player on the West Coast sports scene, there remained doubts that Jack Kent Cooke's club ever would seriously challenge professional basketball as a prime attraction. And even after Wayne Gretzky set up quarters in Inglewood, nobody—but nobody—ever imagined that a second National Hockey League club could be established in Tinseltown.

But that was prior to 1992 when a $103 million arena began taking shape in the city of Anaheim. Once a small town better known as the butt of Jack Benny jokes during the heyday of radio comedy, Anaheim had grown into prominence as the home of Disneyland as well as one of the major satellite communities of Greater Los Angeles. With that in mind, the city fathers erected a major-league facility that rivaled that of any city on the continent. It lacked only one critical element; a major-league team as a tenant.

For a time it appeared that Anaheim's rink would turn into a white elephant bigger than Dumbo but Michael Eisner would change all that. Head of the Disney Corporation, Eisner drove past the arena one day before it had been completed. Originally, he had thought it was an office building conveniently located down the street from his son's hockey rink but he learned from a city official that it would be a Madison Square Garden West.

"Who's playing there?" asked Eisner.

"Nobody yet," said the Anaheim official.

"Does somebody have a hockey franchise?" Eisner wanted to know.

"No," was the reply.

Eisner later conferred with Bruce McNall, then owner of the Kings, and learned that the NHL might, in fact, look kindly on a second major-league hockey team in Southern California. Eisner watched the film *Field of Dreams* and received further inspiration. "There was an arena and no team," the Disney chief said, "and I added two and two together. It came out to about 11 and I went and got the franchise."

Eisner's capsulization overlooked several other pertinent elements, but the key factor was that Anaheim badly wanted to be known as a metropolis in Orange County and the arena would help enhance that image. Once the building was in place, a team would be sought. Since the building was there and Eisner—whose passion for hockey was deeply-rooted—envisioned several positive possibilities for integrating it into his film business, all the pieces began to fall into place.

One of the first pieces was Disney's film *The Mighty Ducks*, which preceded the arena and became an instant hit. Grossing more than $50 million in North America, the movie whetted Eisner's appetite for an NHL franchise. This coincided with the transfer of NHL power from the conser-

vative regime of president John Ziegler to interim leader Gil Stein and to Gary Bettman, who was named the league's first commissioner late in 1992.

Under Bettman, the NHL was encouraging strong corporate ownership and, at the governors meetings in December 1992 both Disney (Anaheim) and Wayne Huizenga (South Florida) were awarded expansion franchises. The expansion fee for Florida was $50 million. In the case of Anaheim $25 million went to the NHL and the rest to McNall because of territorial indemnification. A second team in Southern California could conceivably cut deeply into the existing Kings fan base.

The moves to both Anaheim and South Florida were viewed with concern by league conservatives despite the obvious success of the Gund brothers' franchise in San Jose and what appeared to be good prospects for the Tampa Bay entry, which had played its first seasons at makeshift rinks. "There's great growth in hockey," Eisner enthused. "In the way hockey is shot (on television), we can be creative in creating stars. We do it in the movie business."

That very 'movie business' intruded heavily into hockey thinking from the very beginning in Anaheim. Instead of giving the new club a normal moniker such as Panthers—as in Florida—or Capitals—as in Washington—the new club was named after a film. To the dismay of traditionalists, Eisner's team became the Mighty Ducks of Anaheim.

Tony Tavares, who had much experience in the arena business and had worked briefly with McNall, became point man for the management team and he, in turn, hired Jack Ferreira as general manager and Pierre Gauthier to assist Ferreira.

A onetime goaltender for Boston University, Ferreira had considerable scouting and front-office experience with the New England Whalers, Calgary Flames and New York Rangers. The Montreal-born Gauthier won his spurs as scouting director for the Quebec Nordiques. Together they attended the NHL Expansion Draft at Quebec City in June 1993 and picked Guy Hebert as their number one goaltender after Florida had selected John Vanbiesbrouck.

For defensive experience, the Ducks opted for Devils veteran Alexei Kasatonov and Randy Ladouceur of Hartford. They also added Sean Hill, Bobby Dollas and Bill Houlder for the blue line corps. Up front, they plucked Steven King (Rangers), Tim Sweeney (Bruins), Stu Grimson (Chicago) and Troy Loney (Pittsburgh) among others.

The expansion draft was immediately followed by the Entry Draft at which Anaheim landed Paul Kariya from the University of Maine, even though he would be unavailable to the Mighty Ducks in their maiden season. The first freshman to win the Hobey Baker Award (best collegiate player in the USA), Kariya had played for the NCAA titlists and was projected as a superstar despite his smallish physique.

For head coach, Ferreira and Tavares settled on Ron Wilson, an assistant with the Vancouver Canucks who earlier had been an offensive-minded defenseman at Providence College—under Lou Lamoriello—and later in

the pros. Wilson's assistant would be former Bruin Al Sims, who had coached the International Hockey League's Fort Wayne Komets to a championship. Together, they constructed a team that played its first exhibition game at Anaheim on September 18, 1993 against the Pittsburgh Penguins. A crowd of 16,673 proved a good barometer of sellouts to come: more than 12,000 season tickets had been sold along with more than 40 luxury boxes.

On the ice the Mighty Ducks were just what had been expected of an expansion team, mediocre but promising. A win over the eventual Stanley Cup champion Rangers provided encouragement before a mid-autumn slump brought them back down to earth. Wilson, whose father Larry and uncle, Johnny, had been NHL regulars, earned the Mighty Ducks respect. He was sensitive to his player's needs and calm under fire. "I have yet to see him publically criticize a player," lauded Tavares. "Ron keeps his feelings well-camouflaged."

There was no concealing the affection of Anaheim fans. They began filling Arrowhead Pond early in the season and remained loyal throughout. On December 2, 1993 the Ducks visited Inglewood for the first time in a regular season game and a cross-county rivalry was born amid a flurry of fights and a 3–2 victory for the home team. Although the Kings would win again in the rematch at Anaheim, it had become evident that Wilson had devised a workable system to produce a competitive—if not thoroughly exciting—team during the first half of the season. As late as March 6, 1994 the Mighty Ducks still had a shot at a playoff berth and sat three points ahead of the Kings.

Not surprisingly, they faded in the stretch as the Sharks came on strong to finish high enough for postseason play. With five games remaining on the slate, the Mighty Ducks had been officially eliminated from the race but there was one consolation; they did finish ahead of Los Angeles. "That gave us a great feeling," Wilson admitted.

The Mighty Ducks concluded 1993–94 with 71 points (33–46–5), setting a first-year record with Florida for most wins in a season. They had 19 road wins, most ever by a first-year club in the NHL including a four-win road trip through Western Canada. Most importantly, the club captured the attention of Southern California hockey fans while the rival Kings were in a tailspin.

There was no diminishing of popularity in 1994–95, although the NHL lockout permitted only a 48-game season that didn't begin until January 1995. In the shortened schedule the Mighty Ducks were a microcosm of the 1993–94 team. They were competitive, staying in the playoff hunt through the homestretch, but were eliminated from contention with only two games remaining. Their 37 points (16–27–5) placed Anaheim in sixth place in the Pacific Division, although a strong finish (8–9–1) provided optimism for the future.

So did Kariya who, as a rookie, led the team in scoring with 39 points (18 goals, 21 assists) in 47 games. Rookie defenseman Oleg Tverdovsky blossomed into an offensive threat, while Guy Hebert's goaltending was reliable and Mikhail Shtalenkov was an effective backup. A testimony to fan loyalty were the 24 consecutive home sellouts at Arrowhead Pond.

The Mighty Ducks had become respected among league officials. Disney marketing—not to mention a sequel to the original Mighty Ducks movie—was copied by other teams. Despite the Ducks low standing, they managed to attract large crowds wherever they played, partly because of the

Disney connection and the attraction of the jerseys.

But by far the most significant landmark in the team's evolution was a trade completed on February 7, 1996. Ferreira dealt potential stars Tverdovsky and Chad Kilger—Anaheim's first-round, fourth overall pick in the 1995 Entry Draft—to Winnipeg for Finnish whiz Teemu Selanne and the rights to Marc Chouinard.

Teamed with Kariya, Selanne averaged more than a point a game in the stretch and was a prime reason why the Ducks nearly qualified for a Western Conference playoff spot. They finished tied for eighth in the conference with Winnipeg but lost the tie-breaker because the Jets had more wins. Nevertheless, Anaheim's 35 wins and 78 points were club records for one season and Selanne virtually guaranteed that the upswing would continue into 1996–97.

By now Wilson had established himself as a first-rate coach and the playoff berth obtained in the spring of 1997 underlined the point. Judiciously employing Selanne and Kariya—Steve Rucchin usually was third man on the first line—Wilson energized Anaheim to a 7–3–4 record for 18 points in March 1997 when his team needed it most. It was a franchise record for most points earned in one month. They followed that with an undefeated April (3–0–2) before qualifying for the playoff round.

With an overall mark of 36–33–13, the Mighty Ducks celebrated their first winning season and a new club record for points in a season. Kariya and Selanne combined for 208 points, second only to Jaromir Jagr–Mario Lemieux of Pittsburgh and ahead of Wayne Gretzky–Mark Messier of the Rangers by 27 points. Kariya finished first in game-winning goals (10) while Selanne was runner-up in league scoring with 109 points.

Appropriately, the Ducks collided with Phoenix—formerly the Winnipeg Jets—in the opening playoff round which exceeded dramatic expectations. After taking a two games to none lead, Anaheim lost the next three in a row before rebounding for a 3–2 overtime win in game six. Kariya, on a pass from Selanne, scored at 7:29 of sudden death to send the series to a seventh game. This time Hebert stopped all 31 shots he faced in earning his first playoff shutout.

Advancing to the second round, Anaheim faced the eventual Stanley Cup-winning Detroit Red Wings. Three out of the four games went into overtime but each time the Motor City sextet won. Game two extended through three sudden-death periods while the finale, game four, went into two overtimes before Brendan Shanahan delivered the coup de grace to the Mighty Ducks.

However, the highly successful run had a bitter aftermath. A dispute between Wilson and upper management resulted in a front office upheaval and the hiring of Pierre Page as Wilson's replacement. (The latter moved on to become head coach of the Washington Capitals.) No less upsetting was a contract collision between Kariya and the high command that left the superstar home in Vancouver while Selanne was compelled to carry the scoring load.

The disruptions left the Mighty Ducks in disarray although Selanne nobly performed extraordinary feats of skill to at least keep his club competitive. Eventually, Kariya returned with a new, enlarged pact but his comeback would be aborted by a serious concussion following a post-scoring hit delivered by Gary Suter of the Chicago Blackhawks.

Kariya never fully recovered from the blow during the season. The concussion, which produced disturbing side

effects, kept the Ducks ace sidelined through the early spring rush to the playoffs. Selanne, playing better than ever, kept the club alive but his contributions simply could not counter-balance the many debits which had accrued. One year after their dazzling playoff run the Mighty Ducks fell short of a playoff berth. The disappointing season cost Page his coaching position after just one year on the job.

How the Ducks succeed in future years will hinge mightily on how quickly Paul Kariya will be able to regain the standard of excellence he had set in previous years. The fiscal future is more certain, as fans continued to fill Arrowhead Pond in 1997–98 and attendance remained strong. If nothing else, fan support proved that Michael Eisner made the right move when he linked the Disney Corporation with the NHL.

Mighty Ducks of Anaheim Year-by-Year Record

Season	GP	W	L	T	GF	GA	Pts	Finish		Playoff Results
1993–94	84	33	46	5	229	251	71	4th	Pacific Div.	Out of Playoffs
1994–95	48	16	27	5	125	164	37	6th	Pacific Div.	Out of Playoffs
1995–96	82	35	39	8	234	247	78	4th	Pacific Div.	Out of Playoffs
1996–97	82	36	33	13	245	233	85	2nd	Pacific Div.	Lost Conf. Semifinal
1997–98	82	26	43	13	205	261	65	6th	Pacific Div.	Out of Playoffs

ATLANTA THRASHERS

ON JUNE 25, 1997, the National Hockey League awarded new expansion teams to Nashville, Columbus, Minnesota and Atlanta. The awarding of the Atlanta franchise saw NHL hockey return to Georgia, which had first entered the league in 1972–73. The lack of a major television contract and a crumbling real estate empire saw the Atlanta Flames sold to Calgary in 1980. Fan support was never seen as a problem in Atlanta, and TV and ownership won't be this time under Ted Turner and the Turner Broadcasting System, Inc.

The NHL will be a 28-team league (on its way to 30) when Atlanta comes on board for the 1999–2000 season, with teams split into three divisions in each of the Eastern and Western conferences. Atlanta will play in the Southeast Division of the Eastern Conference with the Carolina Hurricanes, Florida Panthers, Tampa Bay Lightning and Washington Capitals. The team will be known as the Thrashers.

The Thrashers name was taken from the state bird of Georgia—the Brown Thrasher—and the logo communicates the characteristics of fierce determination and speed. Team colors will be Capitol copper, Georgia bronze, Peachtree gold, Atlanta midnight blue and Thrasher ice blue. Don Waddell was hired as the club's general manager on June 23, 1998. An assistant g.m. in Detroit during the 1997–98 season, Waddell had previously served as the vice president general manager of the International Hockey League's Orlando Solar Bears from 1995 to 1997. His playing career includes three seasons in the Los Angeles Kings' farm system. Waddell was a member of the United States national team in 1983. An injury kept him from appearing with the 1980 "Miracle on Ice" United States Olympic hockey team.

BOSTON BRUINS

Stan Fischler

IN MANY WAYS IT WAS APPROPRIATE that the Boston Bruins became the first—and longest-running—American team in the National Hockey League. When the NHL was formed in 1917, the Boston Athletic Association was the defending American Amateur Hockey League champion. The city nicknamed Beantown had already become a hockey hub.

One of the ice game's champions was Charles Adams, who had sponsored an amateur club but became disenchanted after discovering that several rivals were spreading rather large gratuities among their players.

Ripe for a professional franchise, Adams was lobbied by a group that included Tom Duggan, Frank Sullivan and Russ Layton who insisted that a firsthand view of an NHL game would persuade the millionaire to invest his money in professional hockey. Adams agreed to attend the 1924 Stanley Cup finals between Calgary and a Montreal Canadiens club loaded with such legends as Georges Vezina, Howie Morenz, Aurel Joliat and Sprague Cleghorn.

"That did it," said Adams' son, Weston, who later would become club president. "When he returned home, he told us this was the greatest hockey he had ever seen. He wouldn't be happy until he had a franchise. ... Eddie Shore made hockey in Boston, but Montreal got us started." Adams wasted little time organizing his new enterprise. During his Canadian excursion he had met a crusty, dour Scot by the name of Art Ross who had once enjoyed a successful career as a player. He liked the man and promptly named him coach, general manager and scout of the new team. Eddie Shore, meanwhile, was playing defense in the old Western Canada Hockey League, where he already had earned the nickname "the Edmonton Express." But he was still a few years away from Boston; Ross had heard of Shore, but was dubious about his talents. He decided to ignore him, at least for the time being, and signed a number of qualified players, including goalie Alex Connell and Clarence "Hap" Day, who was later to be a star defenseman with Toronto and one of the NHL's most successful coaches. Other first-year Bruins were Carson Cooper, Hooley Smith, Ed Gorman, and Bert McCaffrey.

When the 1924–25 season ended, the Bruins' only claim to fame was that they were America's first NHL team. They barely held up the bottom of the six-team league; with a feeble record of six wins, 24 losses, the Boston group lagged far behind the Maroons, Ottawa, the Canadiens, Toronto and Hamilton.

"We had three teams that year," said Adams, "one coming, one going, and one playing." The best Bruins in their maiden NHL season were Jimmy Herberts and Carson Cooper, who had been outstanding amateurs in Ontario.

Despite their misfortune, the Bruins made a singular impact on Bostonians who began filling Boston Arena. Adams responded after two years by spending $50,000 on a massive infusion of talent. He landed Duke Keats, Perk Galbraith, Harry Oliver, Harry Meeking as well as the inimitable Eddie Shore from the folding Western Hockey League. With Shore as its centerpiece, the Bruins began muscling their way to a more prominent place in the NHL amid posh new surroundings on Causeway Street across from the elevated line.

Responding to the hockey mania, and with the backing of

Madison Square Garden money, promoters built a new arena, Boston Garden, over North Station and alongside the equally spiffy Manger Hotel. Originally named "Boston Madison Square Garden," the rink opened on November 20, 1928 for a game between the Bruins and Canadiens. Columnist Stanley Woodward recreated the scene on the pages of the *Boston Herald.* "It was a riot, a mob scene, re-enaction of the assault on the Bastille," wrote Woodward. "It is estimated that 17,500 persons, 3,000 in excess of the supposed capacity of the Garden, saw the game." One might have expected the crowd to behave itself once it obtained entrance to the rink. After all, this was the pre-micre of the "G-aa-den." But good manners were forgotten in that frenetic atmosphere. When referee George Mallinson ruled a Bruins foray offside, the fans bombarded the ice with garbage; or at least they tried to reach the rink with their missiles.

The game itself carved the mold for future developments decades later. Boston played host to the Montreal Canadiens and, despite harassment from the crowd and some lusty bodychecks by Shore and Co., the visitors won the game 1–0. Tall, dark and handsome Sylvio Mantha sent the 17,500 rooters home depressed when he outwitted Bruin captain Lionel Hitchman and scored with only two seconds remaining in the second period.

Within three seasons of the Bruins birth, Boston had a Stanley Cup contender. Although Art Ross's team lost to Ottawa in the 1927 finals, more than 29,000 applications were received by the Bruins for tickets. Two years later, they reached the finals again, this time against the Rangers. On March 29, 1929 the visiting Bostonians defeated New York 2–1 at Madison Square Garden to bring the Stanley Cup to the Hub for the first time.

Having acquired Cecil "Tiny" Thompson—formerly of the Minneapolis Millers—Ross boasted some of the best goaltending the league had ever seen. Thompson twice blanked the Canadiens in a three-game semifinal series and then held New York to only one goal in two games in the finals. He finished with a 0.60 goals-against average through the five playoff games and would eventually win the Vezina Trophy four times before being dealt to the Detroit Red Wings.

Nevertheless, Shore was the draw at Boston Garden. Occasionally, he would make grand entrances on to the ice. Once—with the Garden band playing "Hail To The Chief" as background music—Shore skated to his position in a matador's cloak, followed by a valet who removed Eddie's outer garment, allowing him to play. On another night the visiting New York Americans got even. They brought their own carpet, rolled it to center ice where Rabbit McVeigh emerged blowing kisses to the audience. The humiliated Shore vowed never to do the matador routine again.

The defenseman—equally renowned for his end-to-end rushes symbolized the macho hockey man of the early NHL days. After an injury left his ear hanging tenuously from the side of his head, Shore insisted on sewing it back on while an incredulous doctor held the mirror for him.

Another time a multi-car accident in downtown Boston delayed Shore sufficiently for him to miss the team train that rolled out of South Station for Montreal. Rather than miss the game, Shore commandeered a millionaire friend's limousine and directed the chauffeur north toward Canada. However, a blizzard severely limited visibility and convinced the chauffeur to give up the trek before the car had left the Boston suburbs. Shore took command and drove

through the night over the White Mountains of New Hampshire despite a number of mishaps along the way. The next night he played 58 out of 60 minutes—two minutes were spent in the penalty box—and scored the only goal in Boston's 1–0 victory.

Despite these heroics, Shore's career was marred by an ugly episode that nearly resulted in the death of Toronto Maple Leafs stickhandling expert Ace Bailey. The game, played on the night of December 12, 1933 at Boston Garden, was a typically robust Toronto–Boston encounter, aggravated by the intense rivalry between Ross and his Canadian counterpart Conn Smythe. The incident, which to this day remains the ugliest—and most controversial—in league history, began when King Clancy and Red Horner of Toronto simultaneously checked Shore into the boards near the Maple Leafs net.

When Shore recovered, he inexplicably concluded that Bailey had done the damage. Instead of pursuing Clancy, Shore moved on a collision course with Bailey whose back was to the Bruin.

"I looked back," Clancy recalled, "saw Shore scrambling to his feet and then hit Bailey across the back of the legs. Eddie thought he was retaliating against me. I know he never meant it to be that bad." It was worse. Horner went after Shore and pulverized him with a vicious sequence of punches. Bailey, who in Clancy's words "looked just awful," nearly died in the hospital. After two delicate brain operations, Ace's recuperation was miraculous but he never played hockey again. Shore was suspended for 16 games which Clancy called "fitting."

Shore's marquee personality tended to overshadow other Bruins who were outstanding in their own right. Aubrey "Dit" Clapper was an outstanding forward who would conclude his 20-year Boston career as a defenseman of equal ability. Few NHL players have been able to sustain two decades at a top level. Lionel Hitchman was every bit as good as Shore on the blue line but less belligerent. Frank Fredrickson, Harry Oliver, Norman "Dutch" Gainor and Ralph "Cooney" Weiland were among the other starry Bruins in their early years.

Ever the insightful thinker, Ross was the first NHL coach to pull his goaltender in a Stanley Cup playoff game. Unheard of at the time, the tactic was employed on March 26, 1931. Ross pulled Tiny Thompson for a sixth attacker in the last minute but the Montreal Canadiens were able to hold their 1–0 lead.

The Bruins Dynamite Line of Weiland, Clapper and Gainor comprised one of the better trios ever to don the brown and white. They helped Boston finish first five times in the American Division in the nine seasons between 1929–30 and 1937–38. By 1934 Ross had decided he wanted to concentrate on managing and hired Frank Patrick as coach. The salary of $10,500 was considered high for the time but worthwhile after Patrick moved the newly acquired Babe Seibert, renowned as a winger, to defense where he would work excellently with Shore. The Shore-Seibert combination would become one of the most feared blue line corps of the 1930s.

Patrick lasted two seasons behind the bench, doing well in the regular season but losing the first playoff round in successive years. Ross removed Patrick at the start of the 1936–37 season and returned to the bench himself. His sense of timing was excellent. The Bruins had signed a hard-nosed center from Kitchener, Ontario named Milt Schmidt and soon would add the kid's two pals, Bobby

Bauer and Woodrow Wilson "Woody" Dumart, who would form the outstanding Kraut Line.

When the NHL's two divisions amalgamated in 1938–39, Boston became the scourge of big-league hockey. Frank "Mister Zero" Brimsek replaced Tiny Thompson—traded to Detroit—in goal and blossomed into the best American-born goalie of all-time. En route to the 1939 Stanley Cup, the Bruins had heroes emerging from the ice cracks. One was Mel "Sudden Death" Hill, a chunky 175-pound athlete from Glenboro, Manitoba who specialized for a brief 12 days in beating the Rangers in overtime.

Boston won the best-of-seven semifinal four games to three; Hill secured three of the wins with overtime goals. Boston won the first three games, Rangers won the next three and, after the regulation 60 minutes of the seventh, they were tied 1–1. Hill won it with a goal after 48 minutes in overtime. Coach Lester Patrick of the losing Rangers had reason to be rueful. "I turned Hill down because he was too small. … I didn't think he could stand the strain of a full season and the tough playoffs." Hill didn't provide any heroics in the Cup final against Toronto, but none was needed. The Bruins dispatched the Leafs in five games and the team was hailed by many critics as the greatest of all time. "Every player was a major-leaguer," said Ross. "It was the best team I ever saw in my life."

Even after Shore left Boston to play for the New York Americans in 1940, the Bostonians continued to rule. In 1940–41, paced by the Krauts and Brimsek, the Bruins were coached by Cooney Weiland, who had moved behind the bench to replace Ross in 1939. The Beantown immortal directed his club to a seven-game semifinal playoff win over Toronto and then whipped Detroit four straight. The Krauts were magnificent, but no one was better than a deft center named Bill Cowley who had won the scoring championship and reached new levels of stickhandling agility.

Cowley would play consecutively through the 1946–47 season but the club's core soon would be demolished by World War II enlistments. Brimsek enlisted in the Coast Guard at Curtis Bay, Maryland while Schmidt, Dumart and Bauer signed up as a unit in the Royal Canadian Air Force. The Bruins would never be the same. At war's end, the four veterans returned to Boston, each having lost an edge during their service stint. Brimsek eventually was traded to Chicago and Bauer hung up his skates after the 1946–47 season—he returned for a one-game cameo appearance in 1951–52—leaving Schmidt and Dumart to carry the load. The former was superb for several years while the latter played a workmanlike checking role, which climaxed in the 1953 playoffs when Woody shadowed Gordie Howe efficiently enough to gain Boston a stunning upset over the defending Stanley Cup champion Red Wings.

After retiring, Schmidt became Bruins coach in 1954–55 with modest success. In an era dominated by the Canadiens and Red Wings, Boston invariably gained a playoff berth but never could annex another Stanley Cup. Stars such as defenseman Fern Flaman and the Uke Line (Bronco Horvath, Vic Stasiuk and Johnny Bucyk) ranked among the league's best but try as they might the high command was unable to round it out with top-notch goaltending. It wasn't until 1966–67 that Harry Sinden, an intense 37-year-old coach who never played a game in the NHL, was given control of the club. When Schmidt became general manager, he produced one of the most one-sided trades ever. From the Chicago Black Hawks, the Bruins obtained Phil Esposito, Fred Stanfield and Ken Hodge for three undistinguished skaters, Jack Norris, Pit Martin and Gilles Marotte.

Beginning in 1968, the Bruins began their ascent, abetted by the maturing wunderkind Bobby Orr, who was in the process of revolutionizing the game. Listed as a defenseman, the blond Orr employed extraordinary speed, puck control and shooting ability. Rather than stick to defensive play, Orr would lead attack after attack, combining like perfectly meshed gears with the finishing genius, Esposito.

The Era of Orr

In 1960, the Boston Bruins scouting staff discovered a 5'2", 110-pound 12-year old phenom in an all-Ontario bantam tournament. Defenseman Bobby Orr, a peewee playing with the bantam Parry Sound team, had impressed the Bruins.

Two years later, the Bruins successfully signed Orr to a standard junior amateur contract which brought him to the Oshawa Generals—a Bruins-sponsored junior farm club—as a 14-year old. He was nominated to the league's Second All-Star Team in his rookie season. Constantly improving, Orr remained in Oshawa until the age of 18 when he was signed to his first NHL contract, for a reported $60,000 plus bonuses over two years, at that time becoming the highest paid 18-year old in the history of the NHL.

Beginning with a Calder Trophy win in 1966–67, Orr spent 11 seasons with the Bruins helping them to two Stanley Cup titles, including their first in 29 years. He won the Norris Trophy in eight consecutive years, the Hart three times, the Conn Smythe twice and became the only defenseman to ever capture the Art Ross Trophy as the league's scoring champion, winning the award in 1970 and 1975. In addition, Orr was named to the NHL's First All-Star Team eight times and was nominated to the Second All-Star Team in his rookie season.

Knee injuries beginning in 1967–68 forced Orr to miss many games and shortened his career. During his second NHL season, he was on the receiving end of a hip check from Marcel Pronovost that tore the medial meniscus in his left knee. He underwent five knee operations between 1968 and 1975 before signing as a free agent with the Chicago Blackhawks. Orr played 20 games with Chicago before undergoing surgery for a sixth and final time before retiring prior to the 1978–79 regular season. He was immediately inducted into the Hockey Hall of Fame in 1979.

Orr and Esposito helped end the Bruins' Stanley Cup drought with a four-straight sweep of St. Louis in the 1970 finals. The feat was minimized by some because Boston's opponent, the Blues, was an expansion team loaded with retreads and assorted castaways. Yet the image that remains firmly set in the minds of Bostonians is that of an exuberant Orr flying through the air past St. Louis defenseman Noel Picard after the Beantown hero had fired the Cup-winning sudden-death goal past goalie Glenn Hall.

The triumph was partially marred by Sinden's unexpected resignation over a salary dispute. He was replaced by Tom Johnson, the Hall of Fame defenseman who had been Bruins assistant general manager. Although Johnson coached the Bruins to a first-place finish in the East Division, there were concerns about the team's country-club laissez-faire attitude. Favored to repeat as Cup champs, Esposito-Orr & Co. encountered a Montreal team

that seemed ripe for plucking in the opening playoff round. *Les Canadiens* started inexperienced rookie goalie Ken Dryden and, as expected, lost the opener to Boston. But Dryden grew progressively stronger as the series unfolded while the Bruins became more and more frustrated by the tall Cornell grad. The series ran a full seven games ending with a remarkable Montreal victory.

Few teams ever have been more determined to atone for a humiliation than the 1971–72 Bruins, one of the most powerful teams ever assembled. They finished the season with the best record—Esposito was leading scorer and Orr the most valuable player—and then marched all the way to the finals where they collided with a mighty Rangers team thirsting for New York's first Cup in 32 years. At times the Rangers appeared on the verge of a breakthrough but, with the series three games to two in Boston's favor, the Bruins came to Madison Square Garden and let Orr do the skating and shooting. He ended a scoreless tie with a dazzling pirouette and then fired what would be the winning goal in what ultimately was a 3–0 decision for the Bruins.

"We won every big game we had to win all season," said winning goalie Ed Johnston. "That's the sign of a good club and that's why we won the Cup." They won because Orr had flowered into the ultimate two-way player. "We played them pretty even," said Rangers captain Vic Hadfield, "but they had Bobby Orr and we didn't." At season's end, the Bruins—superficially, at least—had the makings of a dynasty. Johnston and Gerry Cheevers provided splendid goaltending while the Orr-centered defense was balanced and robust. Esposito, Hodge, Derek Sanderson and Ed Westfall each provided diverse ingredients necessary for champions while Johnson appeared adequate as coach.

But few could have forecast the upheaval that was ahead. The simultaneous arrival of the World Hockey Association and NHL expansion would rob the Bruins of pivotal players. Cheevers, Sanderson and captain Ted Green emigrated to the new WHA while Westfall was claimed by the expansion New York Islanders in 1972. The results were devastating for Boston. Johnson was fired in midseason and replaced by former Bruin Armand "Bep" Guidolin. The Canadiens swept past them in the regular season race, although Esposito won the scoring championship and Orr won the Norris Trophy as the best defenseman. But the playoffs were a disaster. Crippled by a knee injury Esposito left the Bruins without a top sniper and the Rangers knocked Boston out of the first round in five games.

The shock was almost as bad as it had been two years earlier and once again the Bruins vowed to regroup. True to their word, they finished an impressive (52–17–9) first with the usual prizes. Esposito took both the Hart and Art Ross trophies while Orr again earned the Norris and Johnny Bucyk won the Lady Byng. Most of the hockey world expected the Bruins to annex the Stanley Cup when they took on the expansion Philadelphia Flyers in the finals. But once again a hot goaltender—this time Bernie Parent—did them in and Boston exited in six games. The would-be dynasty was no more despite Orr's heroics. Bobby won the Norris yet again in 1975 but when the finals arrived it was Philadelphia versus Buffalo with Boston long gone.

Slowly yet relentlessly the Bruins lost their luster and eventually lost Phil Esposito and Bobby Orr as well. Esposito was traded to the Rangers with Carol Vadnais for Brad Park, Jean Ratelle and Joe Zanussi on November 7, 1975. On June 24, 1976, Orr, the defenseman who symbolized Bruins hockey as much as Eddie Shore had in an ear-lier era, signed as a free agent with the Chicago Black Hawks.

Devastating as the losses may have been, the Bruins were revitalized in a curious way. New owners—Sports Systems Corp. led by brothers Jeremy, Max and Lawrence Jacobs of Eggerts, New York—assumed control of the club on August 28, 1975. A career minor-league defenseman, Don "Grapes" Cherry, was hired as coach and infused an already rugged Boston squad with even more fire. They finished first in the Adams Division in 1976–77 and went all the way to the Stanley Cup finals before being dispatched by the Canadiens in four straight. Cherry brought them to the last round of the playoffs against Montreal again the following spring and even managed to win the first two games played at Boston Garden—tying the series at two apiece—before losing in six games.

By now Cherry's exuberance had made him the coaching toast of the league. Everyone seemed to love Grapes except g.m. Harry Sinden. A simmering feud was kept from exploding because Cherry delivered another first-place finish and a four-game playoff sweep of Pittsburgh in the quarterfinals. He peaked in the semifinals, bringing Boston back from a three-games-to-two deficit against Montreal. Game seven was a classic, with the Bruins leading until late in the third period when a too-many-men-on-the-ice penalty was called against them. Guy Lafleur scored for the Habs and Montreal won the game and the series in overtime.

Cherry was fired and the Bruins lost much of their luster. A year later they were eliminated from playoff contention by the Islanders, in 1981 by Minnesota and in 1982 by Quebec. They did have the 1982 Lady Byng winner in Rick Middleton, a top scorer in Barry Pederson and solid goaltending from Pete Peeters, but the Islanders proved too formidable in the playoffs and "Wait 'til Next Year" became the theme on Causeway Street. There would be no next year despite several valiant attempts. Sinden's adroit managing kept the Bruins in contention and they gained a playoff berth every season until 1996–97 when their record was ended. They were able to remain a top club because of Orr's successor as defense hero, Raymond Bourque.

Less flamboyant than Orr or Shore, Bourque nevertheless was exceptionally skilled as a skater, shooter and stickhandler and, unlike Orr, was miraculously durable. He helped Boston to the Stanley Cup finals in 1988—a four games to none loss to Edmonton—and again in 1990 when they took one game from a strong Oilers squad. Even though Bourque was a perpetual Norris Trophy candidate, his supporting cast was never sufficient to win the silver mug again.

The deteriorating state of Boston Garden was never more apparent than on the night of May 24, 1988 when an electrical failure plunged the building into darkness and forced postponement of the fourth game of the Stanley Cup finals. Construction would begin less than five years later on a modern replacement, the FleetCenter. The new facility opened prior to the 1995–96 season and played host to the NHL All-Star Game in January of 1996.

Following a non-playoff year in 1996–97, Sinden fired coach Steve Kasper and replaced him with the veteran Pat Burns. The new coach was presented with two first-round draft picks—Joe Thornton and Sergei Samsonov—as well as surprisingly good goaltending from ex-second-stringer Byron Dafoe.

While most critics believed that the Bostonians were too shallow to even reach a playoff berth in 1997–98, they surprised almost everyone by quickly moving over the .500 mark and remaining there throughout the season. Thornton

was a disappointment, but Samsonov—the Calder Trophy winner—led all rookies in scoring with 22 goals and 47 points while Jason Allison emerged as top-10 talent with 83 points. Mostly, though, it was the improved defense credited to Pat Burns' coaching system that saw the Bruins climb to fifth in the Eastern Conference. Bad breaks, as much as anything, saw Boston fall to the Washington Capitals in six games in the opening round of the 1998 playoffs.

Boston Bruins Year-by-Year Record

Season	GP	W	L	T	GF	GA	Pts	Finish		Playoff Results
1924–25	30	6	24	0	49	119	12	6th		Out of Playoffs
1925–26	36	17	15	4	92	85	38	4th		Out of Playoffs
1926–27	44	21	20	3	97	89	45	2nd	Amn. Div.	Lost Final
1927–28	44	20	13	11	77	70	51	1st	Amn. Div.	Lost Semifinal
1928–29	44	26	13	5	89	52	57	1st	Amn. Div.	Won Stanley Cup
1929–30	44	38	5	1	179	98	77	1st	Amn. Div.	Lost Final
1930–31	44	28	10	6	143	90	62	1st	Amn. Div.	Lost Semifinal
1931–32	48	15	21	12	122	117	42	4th	Amn. Div.	Out of Playoffs
1932–33	48	25	15	8	124	88	58	1st	Amn. Div.	Lost Semifinal
1933–34	48	18	25	5	111	130	41	4th	Amn. Div.	Out of Playoffs
1934–35	48	26	16	6	129	112	58	1st	Amn. Div.	Lost Semifinal
1935–36	48	22	20	6	92	83	50	2nd	Amn. Div.	Lost Quarterfinal
1936–37	48	23	18	7	120	110	53	2nd	Amn. Div.	Lost Quarterfinal
1937–38	48	30	11	7	142	89	67	1st	Amn. Div.	Lost Semifinal
1938–39	48	36	10	2	156	76	74	1st		Won Stanley Cup
1939–40	48	31	12	5	170	98	67	1st		Lost Semifinal
1940–41	48	27	8	13	168	102	67	1st		Won Stanley Cup
1941–42	48	25	17	6	160	118	56	3rd		Lost Semifinal
1942–43	50	24	17	9	195	176	57	2nd		Lost Final
1943–44	50	19	26	5	223	268	43	5th		Out of Playoffs
1944–45	50	16	30	4	179	219	36	4th		Lost Semifinal
1945–46	50	24	18	8	167	156	56	2nd		Lost Final
1946–47	60	26	23	11	190	175	63	3rd		Lost Semifinal
1947–48	60	23	24	13	167	168	59	3rd		Lost Semifinal
1948–49	60	29	23	8	178	163	66	2nd		Lost Semifinal
1949–50	70	22	32	16	198	228	60	5th		Out of Playoffs
1950–51	70	22	30	18	178	197	62	4th		Lost Semifinal
1951–52	70	25	29	16	162	176	66	4th		Lost Semifinal
1952–53	70	28	29	13	152	172	69	3rd		Lost Final
1953–54	70	32	28	10	177	181	74	4th		Lost Semifinal
1954–55	70	23	26	21	169	188	67	4th		Lost Semifinal
1955–56	70	23	34	13	147	185	59	5th		Out of Playoffs
1956–57	70	34	24	12	195	174	80	3rd		Lost Final
1957–58	70	27	28	15	199	194	69	4th		Lost Final
1958–59	70	32	29	9	205	215	73	2nd		Lost Semifinal
1959–60	70	28	34	8	220	241	64	5th		Out of Playoffs
1960–61	70	15	42	13	176	254	43	6th		Out of Playoffs
1961–62	70	15	47	8	177	306	38	6th		Out of Playoffs
1962–63	70	14	39	17	198	281	45	6th		Out of Playoffs
1963–64	70	18	40	12	170	212	48	6th		Out of Playoffs
1964–65	70	21	43	6	166	253	48	6th		Out of Playoffs
1965–66	70	21	43	6	174	275	48	5th		Out of Playoffs
1966–67	70	17	43	10	182	253	44	6th		Out of Playoffs
1967–68	74	37	27	10	259	216	84	3rd	East Div.	Lost Quarterfinal
1968–69	76	42	18	16	303	221	100	2nd	East Div.	Lost Semifinal
1969–70	76	40	17	19	277	216	99	2nd	East Div.	Won Stanley Cup
1970–71	78	57	14	7	399	207	121	1st	East Div.	Lost Quarterfinal
1971–72	78	54	13	11	330	204	119	1st	East Div.	Won Stanley Cup
1972–73	78	51	22	5	330	235	107	2nd	East Div.	Lost Quarterfinal
1973–74	78	52	17	9	349	221	113	1st	East Div.	Lost Final
1974–75	80	40	26	14	345	245	94	2nd	Adams Div.	Lost Prelim. Round
1975–76	80	48	15	17	313	237	113	1st	Adams Div.	Lost Semifinal
1976–77	80	49	23	8	312	240	106	1st	Adams Div.	Lost Final
1977–78	80	51	18	11	333	218	113	1st	Adams Div.	Lost Final
1978–79	80	43	23	14	316	270	100	1st	Adams Div.	Lost Semifinal
1979–80	80	46	21	13	310	234	105	2nd	Adams Div.	Lost Quarterfinal
1980–81	80	37	30	13	316	272	87	2nd	Adams Div.	Lost Prelim. Round
1981–82	80	43	27	10	323	285	96	2nd	Adams Div.	Lost Div. Final
1982–83	80	50	20	10	327	228	110	1st	Adams Div.	Lost Conf. Final
1983–84	80	49	25	6	336	261	104	1st	Adams Div.	Lost Div. Semifinal
1984–85	80	36	34	10	303	287	82	4th	Adams Div.	Lost Div. Semifinal
1985–86	80	37	31	12	311	288	86	3rd	Adams Div.	Lost Div. Semifinal
1986–87	80	39	34	7	301	276	85	3rd	Adams Div.	Lost Div. Semifinal
1987–88	80	44	30	6	300	251	94	2nd	Adams Div.	Lost Final
1988–89	80	37	29	14	289	256	88	2nd	Adams Div.	Lost Div. Final
1989–90	80	46	25	9	289	232	101	1st	Adams Div.	Lost Final
1990–91	80	44	24	12	299	264	100	1st	Adams Div.	Lost Conf. Final
1991–92	80	36	32	12	270	275	84	2nd	Adams Div.	Lost Conf. Final
1992–93	84	51	26	7	332	268	109	1st	Adams Div.	Lost Div. Semifinal
1993–94	84	42	29	13	289	252	97	2nd	Northeast Div.	Lost Conf. Semifinal
1994–95	48	27	18	3	150	127	57	3rd	Northeast Div.	Lost Conf. Quarterfinal
1995–96	82	40	31	11	282	269	91	2nd	Northeast Div.	Lost Conf. Quarterfinal
1996–97	82	26	47	9	234	300	61	6th	Northeast Div.	Out of Playoffs
1997–98	82	39	30	13	221	194	91	2nd	Northeast Div.	Lost Conf. Quarterfinal

BUFFALO SABRES

Brian McFarlane

THE BUFFALO SABRES National Hockey League franchise would not have been possible were it not for the vision, determination and dedication of two community-minded brothers—Seymour and Northrup Knox. The Sabres—and hockey in general—lost one of its finest sportsmen when Seymour Knox III passed away on May 22, 1996. Two-and-a-half years earlier, in November 1993, his induction into the Hockey Hall of Fame in the builders category was applauded throughout the hockey world. As a member of the NHL Board of Governors, and the guiding force behind the Sabres since their inception, his teams provided hockey fans in Western New York and Southern Ontario with many thrills, as well as the NHL's fifth-most-successful record in terms of winning percentage.

The story of the Buffalo Sabres begins in the mid-1960s. Seymour Knox III and Northrup "Norty" Knox spearheaded a drive for a Buffalo franchise when the NHL announced a doubling of the number of teams for the 1967–68 season. Despite a splendid written and oral presentation to the NHL governors at that time, one that included a well-prepared brochure listing Buffalo's virtues as locale for major-league sports, the city was not included in the list of new franchises awarded to Pittsburgh, Philadelphia, Los Angeles, Minnesota, Oakland and St. Louis.

Discouraged but unwilling to give up, the Knoxes joined the fraternity of NHL owners by buying shares in the Oakland Seals, an expansion franchise that had been praised for having selected the most talented players available in the NHL Expansion Draft. Despite this promise, the Seals flopped on the ice and at the box office.

When the NHL decided to add two more clubs for the 1970–71 season—at triple the 1967 cost—the Knoxes were still interested on behalf of Buffalo. On December 2, 1969 for a fee of $6 million apiece, Buffalo and Vancouver were named as the newest members of the NHL. At the time, the $6 million tab was considered to be an extraordinary price to pay for membership. (Today, almost 30 years later, it wouldn't pay Dominik Hasek's salary for one season.)

On January 16, 1969 a press conference was held in the Niagara Street offices of the yet-to-be-named club to announce the signing of George "Punch" Imlach as general manager and coach of the new franchise. Imlach had been fired by the Toronto Maple Leafs earlier in the year after leading the Leafs into the playoffs for 10 of his 11 years and coaching them to four Stanley Cup titles. "Running the Buffalo club will be the toughest job in pro hockey," Imlach said. "But the tougher it is the better I like it."

Imlach could never resist a dig at his former employers in Toronto. He chose uniforms similar to those worn by the old Cup-winning Maple Leaf teams he had managed in the 1960s, but instead of blue and white, he wanted blue and gold because, "We're classier than the Leafs."

A "Name the Team" contest in the spring of 1969 brought forth 13,000 suggestions, some of them over the top. Fortunately, the club rejected candidates like Mugwumps and Flying Zeppelins, settling on Sabres because the name reflected the steely determination to succeed at a lighting quick pace. Next came the annual June draft in Montreal and the dispersal of the best amateur talent. The two most-coveted players were Gilbert Perreault from the Montreal Jr. Canadiens and Dale Tallon of the Toronto Marlboros.

A "spin of the wheel" gave Buffalo first choice of the graduating juniors and Imlach didn't hesitate. He chose Perreault while Vancouver selected Tallon. Imlach had once coached Jean Beliveau in Quebec City and he figured Perreault might turn out to be almost as good. (Perreault's number 11 commemorated the result of that fateful spin of the wheel. Vancouver would get first pick if an even number came up; but when the pointer clicked to a stop on 11, Perreault was slated for Buffalo's blue and gold.)

The Buffalo Sabres entered the NHL at the beginning of the 1970s—a fascinating era in hockey history. A new league (the World Hockey Association) would soon spring up and competition for players would become fierce. Plans were under way for the first great international hockey clash in 1972 between Team Canada and the Soviets. There would be further expansion of the NHL. Philadelphia would adopt "the Broad Street Bullies" and, in 1974, become the first expansion team to win the Stanley Cup.

In the Sabres' first season, the Boston Bruins, with Phil Esposito and Bobby Orr leading the way, set 37 team records and topped the NHL standings with 57 wins and 121 points. The Bruins were stunned in the spring of 1971 when Montreal's rookie goaltender Ken Dryden stymied them in the first round of the playoffs. The Sabres turned in a respectable 24 wins and 63 points, good enough for fifth place in the East Division. They finished ahead of Vancouver (56 points) and Detroit (55). Gilbert Perreault proved he needed no further seasoning in the minors. He set a goal-scoring record for rookies with 38 goals and recorded enough points (72) to earn the Calder Trophy as the NHL's best rookie.

Left winger Rick Martin was the Sabres' top pick in the 1971 draft. In a normal year, with 44 goals and 74 points, Martin would have been a shoo-in as rookie of the year. But Ken Dryden's great goaltending for Montreal, in the eyes of the voters, was even more impressive. Martin and Perreault played brilliantly together while the search went on to find a right winger to fit their style. The 1971 amateur draft also produced Craig Ramsay and Bill Hajt. That year, general manager and coach Punch Imlach suffered heart problems and was persuaded to hand over the coaching duties to his longtime friend Joe Crozier.

In 1972 the Sabres traded Eddie Shack to Pittsburgh for unheralded Rene Robert. The deal gave Gilbert Perreault the right winger he'd been looking for and the French Connection Line was born. Defenseman Jim Schoenfeld was the team's number one draft choice in 1972. Larry Carriere and Peter McNab were other shrewd draft choices in 1972. In 1973 under Crozier, the Sabres earned their first playoff berth by defeating the St. Louis Blues 3–1 in the final game of the regular season and they went on to give Montreal a fright in the first round of the playoffs. After losing three straight games, the Sabres rebounded with a pair of victories. However, they lost their momentum in game six and bowed out of the postseason excitement.

Floyd Smith replaced Joe Crozier as the Sabres' coach in 1974 and guided the club to a 49–16–15 regular season record and 113 points, still the best numbers in the history of the franchise. Danny Gare joined the club that season and scored 31 goals. His first came 18 seconds after the opening whistle in his first NHL game, three seconds shy of the fastest goal by a rookie (Gus Bodnar in 1943). The following year Gare would jump to 50 goals.

The Sabres remained hot in the 1975 playoffs, ousting the Chicago Black Hawks in five games, then eliminating pow-

erful Montreal—a club that had enjoyed a 22-game undefeated streak during the season—in six. Defeating the Canadiens earned Buffalo a ticket to the Stanley Cup finals against the Philadelphia Flyers, the defending champions.

The final series matched the French Connection against the Flyers' potent combination of Clarke, Barber and Leach and the incredible goaltending of Bernie Parent. The Flyers captured the first two games but the Sabres rebounded for a pair of wins on home ice. The Sabres, who had never won at the Philadelphia Spectrum, lost game five by a 5–1 score.

Back in Buffalo's aging War Memorial Auditorium and facing elimination in game six, Roger Crozier replaced Gerry Desjardins in the Sabres goal. The contest was marred by thick fog which hovered over the ice throughout the match. The fog, which was caused by warm humid air coming in contact with the ice sheet, was so dense that the opposing goaltenders could not see each other and play was frequently interrupted so players could skate around with unfurled towels in an attempt to disperse the mist.

The Flyers' Parent came up with a 2–0 shutout, leaving Buffalo fans to wonder if the outcome would have been different if it had been played under ideal conditions. "We were a good young team then," forward Craig Ramsay would say later. "We thought we'd be back every year, taking a run at the Stanley Cup."

But it was not to be. A team that boasted five 30-plus goal scorers and a powerful defense remained one of the NHL's elite, but could never again generate enough playoff wins to reach the Stanley Cup finals. In 1976 the Sabres lost in the second round to the New York Islanders four games to two. The following spring the Islanders ousted them again in a second round sweep. In 1978 the Flyers pushed them aside in the second round and, in 1979 the Sabres, getting older now, were eliminated by Pittsburgh in the preliminary round. The decade ended with the Islanders—beginning a string of four Stanley Cups—ousting Buffalo in six games in the semifinals.

A highlight of the 1970s was the annual NHL All-Star Game, held in Buffalo in 1978. Rick Martin and Gilbert Perreault led the Wales Conference to an exciting 3–2 overtime victory. Martin scored the tying goal with 1:39 left in the third period and Perreault scored the winning goal after 3:55 of overtime.

Despite its string of playoff disappointments, Buffalo remained near the top of the NHL regular-season standings from the mid 1970s on. From 1974–75 through 1977–78 the team had never failed to top the 100-point plateau.

Imlach was fired after the 1978 playoffs and coach Marcel Pronovost also lost his job after the Sabres got off to a slow start in 1978–79. Imlach's dismissal was a direct result of a player revolt against his old-fashioned methods and philosophies. John Anderson was named interim manager until the Sabres were able to land renowned hockey man Scotty Bowman in 1979. Bowman had just coached the Montreal Canadiens to four consecutive Stanley Cup titles and wanted to add general manager's duties to his portfolio.

Bowman spent the next few seasons making widespread changes. He added players Mike Ramsey, Lindy Ruff, Hannu Virta, Phil Housley, Mike Foligno, Dave Andreychuk and goalies Tom Barrasso and Darren Puppa.

Bowman's maneuvers and coaching acumen bore results. In 1979–80 the Sabres had 110 points and, from 1980–81 through 1984–85, finished with 99, 93, 89, 103 and 90 points respectively.

In 1985 the Sabres drafted Keith Gretzky but he failed to make the team. On March 9, 1986 Gilbert Perreault, by now Buffalo's favorite athlete, scored his 500th career goal. He became the 12th NHLer to achieve that lofty plateau.

The club missed the playoffs with 80 points in 1985–86 and sputtered in 1986–87, resulting in Scotty Bowman dismissal. He was replaced by g.m. Gerry Meehan and coach Ted Sator.

In 1987, after 17 years, 512 goals and 1,326 points, Gilbert Perreault announced his retirement. Despite an offer from the club, he passed up a front office job. "I'm a hockey man, not a sweet talker," he said. He returned home to Quebec and would become a successful junior team owner and coach.

Gerry Meehan snared number one draft choice Pierre Turgeon in the 1987 Entry Draft, hoping that he'd landed a player of Perreault's stature. Turgeon rewarded Meehan with 88 and 106 points in his second and third seasons, but never quite replaced Perreault in the hearts of Sabres fans. Eventually (in October 1991), he would be traded to the Islanders, the key player in a deal that would bring Pat LaFontaine to Buffalo.

Ted Sator, a new coach added to the staff in 1986, was at the helm for the 1987–88 season and the team improved by 21 points. Sator would guide the team to two third-place finishes in the Adams Division and two first-round playoff eliminations.

Late in the 1988–89 season, goalie Clint Malarchuk suffered a frightening injury during a game with St. Louis. A skate blade slashed the goalie's neck and severed his jugular vein. The scene was so gruesome that several spectators fainted and television producers refused to show replays of the incident. Speedy medical attention saved Malarchuk's life and he made a complete recovery.

Rick Dudley became the Sabres' 12th coach in the team's 19-year history in 1989. The club made an impressive leap forward in 1989–90, finishing third overall with 45 wins and 98 points. During the season the club sought the help of a psychologist for talented Soviet defector Alexander Mogilny who revealed he had a fear of flying.

There was more playoff disappointment in 1990 when the Sabres, who'd finished with more wins, more points and more goals than Montreal, fell to the Canadiens in six games in the first round.

In the fall of 1990 Gilbert Perreault was inducted into the Hockey Hall of Fame and with much fanfare, the club retired his number 11 jersey.

Prior to the 1991–92 season, former Edmonton Oilers coach John Muckler was hired as director of hockey operations. Islanders star Pat LaFontaine, involved in a contract dispute with his team, was acquired by Buffalo, along with Randy Hillier, Randy Wood and a draft choice in return for Pierre Turgeon, Benoit Hogue, Uwe Krupp and Dave McLlwain. The Sabres managed 31 wins for the second straight season and were ousted by Boston in the first round of the playoffs.

John Muckler took over as coach of the Sabres for 1992–93 and winger Dave Andreychuk registered a hockey oddity during the season. After scoring 29 goals with the Sabres, he was traded to Toronto in exchange for goaltender Grant Fuhr. As a Maple Leaf, Andreychuk scored another 25, making him only the second NHL player to score 50 goals or more while splitting one season with two different teams. (Craig Simpson had scored a total of 56 goals split between Pittsburgh and Edmonton in 1987–88.)

In the playoffs, the Sabres surprised the Boston Bruins with a four-game sweep. It was the first time since 1983 that the Sabres had advanced to the second round. In round two, Alexander Mogilny suffered a broken leg against the Montreal Canadiens in game three. The Habs swept past Buffalo, then defeated the Islanders and the Los Angeles Kings to capture the Stanley Cup.

Dominik Hasek, who had been named the top player in Czechoslovakia in 1987, 1989 and 1990, had joined the Sabres prior to the 1992–93 season. After 20 games in that first campaign, he became Buffalo's number one goaltender in 1993–94. "The Dominator" responded by recording a 1.95 goal-against average, the lowest mark seen in the NHL since Bernie Parent's 1.85 in 1973–74. Hasek's .930 save percentage was the highest recorded since the NHL began to keep this statistic in the early 1980s. He was rewarded with the Vezina Trophy and a First All-Star Team selection.

Hasek's unorthodox and acrobatic goaltending made him a sensation in Buffalo and throughout the NHL. In the 1994 playoffs, he made 70 saves in game six of a first-round playoff matchup against New Jersey. The game was decided in the fourth overtime period, Buffalo winning on Dave Hannan's goal. It was the longest game in Sabres' history and ranked as the sixth-longest ever played in the NHL up to that time. The Devils went on to win the series in the seventh game by a 2–1 score.

In November 1994, Buffalo broadcaster Ted Darling was inducted into the media section of the Hockey Hall of Fame in Toronto.

In 1994–95, the Sabres slipped to 22 wins and 51 points in their division but still made the playoffs, only to be swept aside by Philadelphia in five games. Pat LaFontaine returned to the Buffalo lineup prior to the playoffs following a 16-month absence due to a torn anterior cruciate ligament. Dominik Hasek continued to frustrate the NHL's best scorers in 1994–95, winning a second consecutive Vezina Trophy while Pat LaFontaine was awarded the Bill Masterton trophy for sportsmanship and dedication to hockey.

On July 8, 1995 the Sabres traded Alexander Mogilny along with a draft choice to Vancouver in return for Michael Peca, Mike Wilson and the Canucks' first-round draft choice (Jay McKee) in the 1995 Entry Draft. Coach Ted Nolan left the St. Louis Blues to join the Buffalo Sabres. The Sabres would go on to finish fifth in the Northeast Division in 1995–96.

On May 22, 1996 Seymour Knox III passed away at age 70. Among his many legacies to the city was the new Marine Midland Arena, which would open that fall. Knox was posthumously awarded the Lester Patrick Trophy for outstanding service to hockey in the United States.

The opening of Marine Midland Arena, plus new team colors, logo and uniforms, coincided with on-ice improvement in 1996–97. With Ted Nolan in his second season as coach, the Sabres leaped to the top of the Northeast Division standings and finished with 92 points, eight more than second place Pittsburgh.

Dominik Hasek sustained a knee injury in the opening round of the playoffs against Ottawa. The Sabres called on backup goalie Steve Shields who responded with three wins, including a shutout in game six and an overtime thriller in game seven. But in the second round, Philadelphia's hot shooter John LeClair scored three winning goals against the Sabres and the Flyers captured the series four games to one.

The Sabres were in the spotlight at the annual postseason awards banquet in Toronto. Dominik Hasek won the Hart Trophy, the first time a goalie had been so honored since 1962 when Jacques Plante was named the league's most valuable player. Hasek also took home the Vezina Trophy for the third time in four years. Michael Peca, a 23-year-old center in just his second full season, joined Craig Ramsay as the only Sabres to win the Selke Trophy as the NHL's best defensive forward.

Despite a measure of on-ice success, antagonism had developed between Hasek and coach Nolan and between Nolan and g.m. John Muckler. Both Nolan and Muckler were replaced following the 1996–97 season. With Darcy Regier in the front office and ex-Sabre Lindy Ruff behind the bench, Buffalo started the 1997–98 season poorly but when Hasek moved his game into high gear in December (and played superbly for the Czech Republic at the Nagano Olympics), the Sabres became one of the league's best teams in the second half of the schedule.

Though only eight teams would score fewer goals than Buffalo, Hasek's brilliance was enough to get the Sabres into the playoffs with plenty of room to spare. His 2.09 goals-against average was fourth-lowest in the league, but it was his 13 shutouts (the highest total since Tony Esposito posted 15 in 1969–70) that grabbed most of the attention. He again earned both the Hart and Vezina trophies.

In the playoffs, Hasek's play, and the Sabres overall team speed, saw Buffalo upset the Philadelphia Flyers in the first round. The Sabres then swept the Montreal Canadiens before bowing out against the Washington Capitals in a six-game Eastern Conference final.

The team that had begun 1997–98 surrounded by question marks ended the season with anticipation of greater success to come.

Buffalo Sabres Year-by-Year Record

Season	GP	W	L	T	GF	GA	Pts	Finish		Playoff Results
1970–71	78	24	39	15	217	291	63	5th	Fast Div.	Out of Playoffs
1971–72	78	16	43	19	203	289	51	6th	East Div.	Out of Playoffs
1972–73	78	37	27	14	257	219	88	4th	East Div.	Lost Quarterfinal
1973–74	78	32	34	12	242	250	76	5th	East Div.	Out of Playoffs
1974–75	80	49	16	15	354	240	113	1st	Adams Div.	Lost Final
1975–76	80	46	21	13	339	240	105	2nd	Adams Div.	Lost Quarterfinal
1976–77	80	48	24	8	301	220	104	2nd	Adams Div.	Lost Quarterfinal
1977–78	80	44	19	17	288	215	105	2nd	Adams Div.	Lost Quarterfinal
1978–79	80	36	28	16	280	263	88	2nd	Adams Div.	Lost Prelim. Round
1979–80	80	47	17	16	318	201	110	1st	Adams Div.	Lost Semifinal
1980–81	80	39	20	21	327	250	99	1st	Adams Div.	Lost Quarterfinal
1981–82	80	39	26	15	307	273	93	3rd	Adams Div.	Lost Div. Semifinal
1982–83	80	38	29	13	318	285	89	3rd	Adams Div.	Lost Div. Final
1983–84	80	48	25	7	315	257	103	2nd	Adams Div.	Lost Div. Semifinal
1984–85	80	38	28	14	290	237	90	3rd	Adams Div.	Lost Div. Semifinal
1985–86	80	37	37	6	296	291	80	5th	Adams Div.	Out of Playoffs
1986–87	80	28	44	8	280	308	64	5th	Adams Div.	Out of Playoffs
1987–88	80	37	32	11	283	305	85	3rd	Adams Div.	Lost Div. Semifinal
1988–89	80	38	35	7	291	299	83	3rd	Adams Div.	Lost Div. Semifinal
1989–90	80	45	27	8	286	248	98	2nd	Adams Div.	Lost Div. Semifinal
1990–91	80	31	30	19	292	278	81	3rd	Adams Div.	Lost Div. Semifinal
1991–92	80	31	37	12	289	299	74	3rd	Adams Div.	Lost Div. Semifinal
1992–93	84	38	36	10	335	297	86	4th	Adams Div.	Lost Div. Final
1993–94	84	43	32	9	282	218	95	4th	Northeast Div.	Lost Conf. Quarterfinal
1994–95	48	22	19	7	130	119	51	4th	Northeast Div.	Lost Conf. Quarterfinal
1995–96	82	33	42	7	247	262	73	5th	Northeast Div.	Out of Playoffs
1996–97	82	40	30	12	237	208	92	1st	Northeast Div.	Lost Conf. Semifinal
1997–98	82	36	29	17	211	187	89	3rd	Northeast Div.	Lost Conf. Final

CALGARY/ATLANTA FLAMES

Mike Board

IT TOOK NO TIME for Calgary, a hockey town in the shadow of the Rocky Mountains to the west and the bald prairie to the east, to warm up to the National Hockey League. When the Atlanta Flames became the Calgary Flames in 1980, hockey immediately became the main sport, and the hottest ticket in town. The flaming "A" was replaced by a flaming "C" and there was hardly a heartbeat missed.

Playing to raucous crowds in the 7,000-seat Stampede Corral rink that first year, it looked as though the city had inherited a pretty good team to cheer for, too. "Nobody could beat us in the Corral," recalls then general manager Cliff Fletcher, the silver-haired wheeler-dealer who was with the organization for 20 years. "It was a very successful first season."

The NHL officially arrived on October 9, 1980 when the newborn Calgary Flames tied the Quebec Nordiques 5–5. With a 25–5–10 record in the Corral and a 39–27–14 record, the Flames finished third in the Patrick Division and seventh over all in the league. They then defeated Chicago and Philadelphia before losing to Minnesota in the Stanley Cup semifinals, four games to two.

With a new 20,000-seat rink being built across the street from the Corral, the future looked very bright indeed. Kent Nilsson, the enigmatic but supremely talented Swede, had a franchise record 82 assists and 131 points that first season in Calgary and just missed the 50-goal plateau, scoring 49. Pat Riggin had 21 wins in net. Jim Peplinski was a rookie, just beginning his famous glove in the face rubs en route to becoming one of the captains on Calgary's championship team of the future. Willi Plett hacked his way to 239 penalty minutes but nonetheless also scored 38 goals. Guy Chouinard had 83 points.

Ah, life in the land of snow and ice rather than the flowers and sunshine of Atlanta. The Atlanta franchise began playing in the league in 1972–73 and it appeared that Omni Sports group, a consortium of businessmen from the area, headed by Tom Cousins, was on solid ground. But that same year the wildcat World Hockey Association began operation and players were jumping from the NHL to the WHA for the big money being offered by the new league. That, in turn, threw a big wrench into the financing of the Atlanta team. "All the financial projections went out the window," recalls Fletcher.

Still, the team persevered for eight seasons, missing the playoffs only during its first and third years of operation. These early Flames were competitive, too. Teams that probably should have done better in the postseason but instead lost every first-round playoff matchup they entered. "They were always competitive but never won a playoff series. They always found a way to lose," says Fletcher.

As time went on the businessmen that Cousins had recruited faded from the picture, unwilling to put more money into the operation of a hockey franchise. When he sold the team to Nelson Skalbania, a Vancouver-based businessman, Cousins' stake in the team had increased from 20 percent to 89 percent. But Cousins sold the team for $16 million U.S., a record amount for an NHL team at the time. "It turned his whole experience into a profitable one," says Fletcher.

Skalbania had, in fact, jumped into the bidding late, gone high on his bid and basically undermined what three

Calgary businessmen had been negotiating. Doc and B.J. Seaman were the two instigators in placing an NHL team in Calgary. Harley Hotchkiss, another local businessman with ties to the oil patch that makes Calgary go around, was brought into the picture very early.

"There were two factors that got us involved. One was a great love of the game. All of us had played and Doc, had it not been for World War II, might have made it. I played, not very well mind you, at Michigan State in those early years," recalls Hotchkiss.

"All of us cared about the game. The second thing was that we cared about our community. We also knew that Calgary was competing for the Olympics and that meant that they would need a facility. They knew it would be easier if there was a longer-term tenant, a major tenant for the building."

Behind the scenes the Calgary group headed by the Seamans was well along in brokering the deal to purchase the Atlanta franchise when Canadian financier Skalbania entered the fray. In the end Skalbania would play a major bartering role in the Calgary franchise but one that drove the cost of the team much higher than what it was probably worth. "We had a price that was more favorable. Nelson, being Nelson, heard about it. We were a little constrained in our negotiations with the government and the building and our commitment to put money back into hockey development," explains Hotchkiss. "Nelson heard about it and negotiated a deal with Molson for the television rights for $6 million for 10 years and that gave him the money to make the down payment and he just blew us away. He made a higher bid and used the Molson deal to make it. For a week there, we thought we were all through."

Skalbania, based in Vancouver, immediately found it difficult to negotiate with the parties that the Seamans had been dealing with and called upon Norm Green, a Calgary businessman he had previously dealt with. In May of 1980 Green brought the two parties together and a deal was struck: Calgary interests would own 50 percent of the team and Skalbania the other 50 percent.

The Calgary owners were the Seamans, Hotchkiss, Green, Ralph Scurfield, then-owner of a Banff ski area called Sunshine Village who died in an avalanche in 1985 and Norm Kwong, a former running back with the Edmonton Eskimos who had a one percent share. By August of 1981, the local ownership had bought out Skalbania in two separate transactions.

"That was an expensive exercise for us. One was that we paid more than we should have and two we paid someone a premium to get him out," recalls Hotchkiss of the Skalbania era. "And Nelson left us with some loose ends, in just the way he dealt, that were expensive to clean up for several years after the fact. We ended up doing what we wanted to do. It took us a year and half and cost us a fair amount of money to get there."

When all was settled, the two Seamans, Hotchkiss, Scurfield and Green equally shared 90 percent of the team while Kwong increased his share to 10 percent. Skalbania had paid $16 million U.S. But by the time the dust had settled, the Calgary owners had spent between $20 and $30 million to complete the deal. With the raging success of the first season, however, there were few complaints.

The Flames moved from the Patrick Division to the Smythe Division for their second season in Calgary, one that began with much optimism but ended in disappointment. It was the year that the famous moustache, Lanny

McDonald, joined the team in a trade with the Colorado Rockies. McDonald would finish his playing career in Calgary, scoring a club record 66 goals in 1982–83 and serving as co-captain of the Stanley Cup champion team in 1988–89.

McDonald retired that summer and has since had his jersey raised to the roof of the current rink, the Canadian Airlines Saddledome, the only Flame jersey to be retired. McDonald still works in the Flames offices in the marketing department and there was a time when many figured he could have run for mayor and been elected in a landslide. But not even his presence could help the Flames in their second season as they finished with a 29–34–17 record and then bowed out in the first round of the playoffs to Vancouver, who went on to the Stanley Cup finals.

That would be a trend for Calgary, losing to teams that reached the Stanley Cup finals after beating the Flames in the first round of the playoffs. Usually it was Edmonton. But Vancouver in 1994 and Los Angeles in 1993 also handed Calgary first-round playoff defeats and proceeded all the way to the Stanley Cup finals.

After that second-year disappointment, the Flames changed direction on the ice. "That's when we realized we really did have a long way to go to build a winner," says Fletcher. "We only had to look 180 miles north to Edmonton to see an emerging dynasty." The 1982–83 season became a rebuilding year. The ultra-positive "Badger Bob" Johnson replaced Al MacNeil as coach. With Johnson's college background, the Flames began recruiting college free agents such as Neil Sheehy, Joel Otto and Colin Patterson, later drafting future captain and 50-goal scorer Joe Nieuwendyk out of Cornell.

Riding Nilsson's 104-point season and McDonald's 66 goals, the Flames reached the playoffs with a 32–34–14 record, defeated Vancouver in the first round and then lost to nemesis Edmonton in the division final. The Oilers would win the Stanley Cup the next two seasons as Fletcher and his staff hustled, traded and pieced together a team that could score, skate and hit with the Oilers. In toughness and grit he added Doug Risebrough. In the skill department he added a young Dan Quinn, Al MacInnis and Hakan Loob. Calgary-born Mike Vernon was added to the goaltending mix and the beginnings of the championship team were born. "We asked ourselves at the end of every day 'Did we get a little better today?'" remembers Fletcher.

In the fall of 1983 the Flames moved into what was then called the Olympic Saddledome, a unique-looking building that fit into the western flavor of the city as the roof is shaped like the saddle of a horse. That year the Flames took Edmonton to seven games in the Smythe Division finals, the closest the team had come to beating the Oilers, who again won the Stanley Cup that season.

It was there, perhaps, that one of the greatest hockey rivalries of the modern era developed. Those games were wars. As Wayne Gretzky and Paul Coffey and Hakan Loob, Kent Nilsson and Lanny McDonald battled on the skill side of the game, the likes of Doug Risebrough, Neil Sheehy, Tim Hunter and Jim Peplinski fought against Ken Linesman, Dave Semenko and Don Jackson in the trenches. They were games that meant everything to both teams. "It was tremendous. Anytime you played the Oilers you could feel the electricity in the building, playoffs or regular season," says Fletcher.

In 1984-85 the team achieved a high in points with 94 but bowed out disappointingly in the first round to Winnipeg.

The next season was the turning point. "That's when we caught the Oilers and went to the finals," says Fletcher, who dealt for scorer Joe Mullen, the first American-born player to score 500 goals. Gary Suter, a late-round draft pick, won the Calder Trophy, scoring 68 points from the blue line. Late in the season Fletcher acquire the gritty John Tonelli. Mike Vernon won 12 playoff games.

The key for the organization was that they had found a way to beat Edmonton, winning game seven in Edmonton on a goal that rookie Oiler defenseman Steve Smith put in his own net. Ironically Smith would return to Calgary as a coach in 1997 after his playing career, recalling that: "I probably could have been elected mayor of Calgary at that time."

"It was the most exhilarating experience in my hockey career," says Fletcher of that win in Edmonton and the short, 30-minute flight home. "We got to the airport and there were 25,000 people there. It was quite a scene. We felt a sense of accomplishment. In the minds of the southern Albertans, it was probably better than winning the Stanley Cup."

Which Calgary didn't do in 1986 as Montreal, led by Larry Robinson and a young Chris Chelios and Patrick Roy, eliminated the Flames in a five-game final.

In 1986 one of the team's original owners, Ralph Scurfield, died in an avalanche. His wife Sonia, took over his share of the Flames. For 10 years no other ownership changes took place but since that time, a number have occurred as increasing costs have put pressure on small market teams like the Flames.

In 1991 Green bought the Minnesota North Stars and the remaining Calgary owners bought up his shares. In 1994 the ownership again underwent a restructuring. "It was clear that the business was changing in a very dramatic way. The risks were higher and the costs were higher," says Hotchkiss. Simultaneously, Kwong and Scurfield were bought out and a new larger group of owners and partners were put in place.

"We looked for partners who had the same background as we did. Essentially community people who cared about the game and who were not in hockey ownership as something to make their livelihood at. We wanted to make economic sense, we have always said that and still do. We don't look on it as a kind of return on investment like we would seek in other investments," says Hotchkiss.

By 1995 the owners, the city and the federal government had combined to spend $40 million in renovations to the Saddledome as a way of increasing revenue for the team. As well, the owners took control of the building on a long-term lease, no longer having to deal with the intermediary Calgary Stampede which had operated the building since its inception in 1983. By 1998 there were nine owners in the Flames operation. Hotchkiss, the Seamans, local private merchant banker Murray Edwards and Tim Horton Donuts owner Ronald Joyce own about 23 percent each. The remainder is divided evenly between businessmen from Calgary: Allan Markin, Alvin Libin, Grant Bartlett and J.R. McCaig.

On the ice, the Edmonton Oilers would win the Stanley Cup in 1987 and 1988, although the Flames won the Presidents' Trophy in 1987–88 with a 48-23-9 regular season record, the same year that Joe Nieuwendyk won the Calder Trophy. Edmonton, however, disposed of Calgary in four games in the Smythe Division finals. From 1986 to 1991 the Flames had one of the best records in the NHL, and twice captured the Presidents' Trophy. Their playoff puzzle came together with a Stanley Cup win in 1989.

Coach Bob Johnson left Calgary in 1987 to join the Amateur Hockey Association of the United States in Colorado Springs. ("Badger Bob" would later return to the NHL and coach Pittsburgh to a Stanley Cup title before passing away after a battle with cancer.) Terry Crisp took over as coach while Fletcher continued to assemble a winning roster.

Doug Gilmour was brought on in a trade with St, Louis in 1988–89. Theo Fleury, the team's franchise player as the 1990s came to an end, was a rookie fourth-liner.

Gilmour, Mullen, Loob, Nieuwendyk, Suter and MacInnis formed perhaps the best power play the Flames have ever assembled. It had all the ingredients, including the rocket from the blue line that was MacInnis's shot. Oddly, the year they won the Cup they did not have to go through Edmonton, instead squeaking by Vancouver, thumping Los Angeles, grinding it out against Chicago and finally, defeating Montreal at the Forum, in game six to claim the Cup. It was the first time that the Canadiens had lost a Stanley Cup final series on home ice.

Lanny McDonald scored the final goal of his Hall of Fame career in game six at 4:24 of the second period, giving Calgary a 2–1 lead. Doug Gilmour scored the game winner at 11:02 on the power play before adding an empty-netter for the 4–2 Calgary win. They had reached the pinnacle. And since they have not come close. Crisp, the coach that took them to the Holy Grail of hockey, was fired a year later in a player mutiny that came after the 1990 playoffs, when Calgary was upset in the first round by Los Angeles.

Crisp was replaced on the bench by Doug Risebrough in 1990–91, a season that would be the last for Fletcher in the Flames organization. Fittingly, the team lost to Edmonton in the first round of the playoffs. The team Fletcher had chased all those years had chased him, too. "They had great players," says Fletcher of the Oilers. "They became the benchmark for the league. The key to matching up against Edmonton was that you had to be able to skate. It's still there. Even when they were missing the playoffs (mid-1990s) they could skate. No matter where they end up in the standings they are always a skating team."

Fletcher's leaving caused quite the stir in Calgary. After all, he was the only architect the team had known. "It had been 19 years. I just thought it was time for a change to get the juices going to 100 percent again," says Fletcher, who moved to Toronto as president and general manager. Risebrough, who had been under Fletcher's wing in the front office, took on the dual role of g.m. and coach. In one of the game's truly worst trades, Fletcher then picked the pocket of his pupil in January of 1992.

Fletcher acquired Doug Gilmour, who had walked out on the Flames in a contract dispute, Jamie Macoun, Ric Nattress, Kent Manderville and Rick Wamsley for Gary Leeman, Alexander Godynyuk, Jeff Reese, Michel Petit and Craig Berube. It was the largest trade in NHL history at the time and one that turned out to highly favor Toronto. Two seasons later, not one of the players Calgary had acquired was with the team and only Craig Berube, who was dealt to Washington, was taking a regular shift in the league. The Flames missed the playoffs entirely that season, although Gary Roberts scored 53 goals and vowed to name his next child after setup man Sergei Makarov.

The Flames had broken new ground in bringing Russian players to the NHL when they signed Sergei Priakin to a contract in 1990. "What we were trying to do was set up

things for down the road but eventually they eased the restrictions," recalls Fletcher. "Sergei Makarov was a moody player. He had been referred to as the Gretzky of Russian hockey and he certainly had his ideas on the game and he wasn't going to change them at 32 years old."

Having missed the playoffs for the time since moving to Calgary, the Flames gave Dave King, the former Canadian national team coach, his first NHL coaching job. In his three seasons behind the bench he directed the Flames to very credible regular-season records—all in the top 10 over all. But the team failed miserably in the playoffs, losing in the first round three consecutive seasons. It was also during these seasons that salaries began to rise, the league went through the lockout and running a small market team became a very different proposition.

One by one the Flames watched superstars depart: Mike Vernon to Detroit, Al MacInnis to St. Louis, Joe Nieuwendyk to Dallas, Gary Suter to Chicago, Gary Roberts, after two neck surgeries, to Carolina. Pierre Page replaced King behind the bench in 1995–96. After a terrible start to the season, Risebrough was fired as general manager and replaced by Al Coates. The Flames scraped into the playoffs but were swept by Chicago. Rebuilding was the order of the day.

The Flames missed the playoffs in Page's second year, finishing 21st over all in the league. Albertan and taskmaster Brian Sutter was named coach for 1997–98 as the rebuilding and the on-ice struggles continued. Calgary actually finished six points worse (with 67) under Sutter than they had under Page, and though they remained within hailing distance of eighth place in the Western Conference for much of the season the Flames were never really playoff contenders.

"What has made it difficult is the events of the last four or five years as far as costs, particularly salaries," says Hotchkiss. "That is a tough one. On one hand we want to be sensible in running our business. We have the capacity, if you look at our ownership, to compete in some of that. But does it make sense for the game long term? We don't think it does. I fully respect agents and players bargaining hard to get what they can get. But somehow there has to be some stability and some common sense or all of us involved are at some risk."

Hotchkiss, who was elected chairman of the Board of Governors of the NHL in 1995, isn't sure where the game or the franchise are headed with the escalation in salaries. The other factor that hurts Calgary is the Canadian dollar. Most of the Flames' expenses are in American funds yet the income for the club is mostly in Canadian dollars and, when the gap between the two currencies widens as it has done in the late 1990s, the Flames and the NHL's other Canadian teams are left at a disadvantage.

"The salaries slowed some (in 1997) but have taken off again and that really troubles me. We are looked upon as cheap. We're really not. We are willing to spend to have a competitive team. If that causes us to incur significant losses, we don't think that scenario can continue, not only for us, but for a whole lot of franchises. It just won't work. People get tired of it. Fans get tired of it. There has to be some balance between economic reality and costs."

In the lockout year, the team lost $12 million. Since that time it has been able to operate at a break-even point with expansion money and the currency equalization program that gives the Flames about $3 million a year. "We are struggling to stay on an even keel," said Hotchkiss.

The names of the future on the ice are Cale Hulse, Jarome Iginla, Todd Simpson, Daniel Tkachuk and Denis Gauthier. Cliff Fletcher believes Calgary will have a team long enough for the fans to see these young players take a run at a championship. "I think the city has the wherewithal to sustain a competitive team and keep it there forever," says Fletcher.

Calgary Flames Year-by-Year Record

Season	GP	W	L	T	GF	GA	Pts	Finish		Playoff Results
1972–73*	78	25	38	15	191	239	65	7th	West Div.	Out of Playoffs
1973–74*	78	30	34	14	214	238	74	4th	West Div.	Lost Quarterfinal
1974–75*	80	34	31	15	243	233	83	4th	Patrick Div.	Out of Playoffs
1975–76*	80	35	33	12	262	237	82	3rd	Patrick Div.	Lost Prelim. Round
1976–77*	80	34	34	12	264	265	80	3rd	Patrick Div.	Lost Prelim. Round
1977–78*	80	34	27	19	274	252	87	3rd	Patrick Div.	Lost Prelim. Round
1978–79*	80	41	31	8	327	280	90	4th	Patrick Div.	Lost Prelim. Round
1979–80*	80	35	32	13	282	269	83	4th	Patrick Div.	Lost Prelim. Round
1980–81	80	39	27	14	329	298	92	3rd	Patrick Div.	Lost Semifinal
1981–82	80	29	34	17	334	345	75	3rd	Smythe Div.	Lost Div. Semifinal
1982–83	80	32	34	14	321	317	78	2nd	Smythe Div.	Lost Div. Final
1983–84	80	34	32	14	311	314	82	2nd	Smythe Div.	Lost Div. Final
1984–85	80	41	27	12	363	302	94	3rd	Smythe Div.	Lost Div. Semifinal
1985–86	80	40	31	9	354	315	89	2nd	Smythe Div.	Lost Final
1986–87	80	46	31	3	318	289	95	2nd	Smythe Div.	Lost Div. Semifinal
1987–88	80	48	23	9	397	305	105	1st	Smythe Div.	Lost Div. Final
1988–89	80	54	17	9	354	226	117	1st	Smythe Div.	Won Stanley Cup
1989–90	80	42	23	15	348	265	99	1st	Smythe Div.	Lost Div. Semifinal
1990–91	80	46	26	8	344	263	100	2nd	Smythe Div.	Lost Div. Semifinal
1991–92	80	31	37	12	296	305	74	5th	Smythe Div.	Out of Playoffs
1992–93	84	43	30	11	322	282	97	2nd	Smythe Div.	Lost Div. Semifinal
1993–94	84	42	29	13	302	256	97	1st	Pacific Div.	Lost Conf. Quarterfinal
1994–95	48	24	17	7	163	135	55	1st	Pacific Div.	Lost Conf. Quarterfinal
1995–96	82	34	37	11	241	240	79	2nd	Pacific Div.	Lost Conf. Quarterfinal
1996–97	82	32	41	9	214	239	73	5th	Pacific Div.	Out of Playoffs
1997–98	82	26	41	15	217	252	67	5th	Pacific Div.	Out of Playoffs

* Atlanta Flames

THE CALIFORNIA/OAKLAND SEALS AND CLEVELAND BARONS

Stan Fischler

WHEN THE NATIONAL HOCKEY LEAGUE decided to expand west of the Mississippi River, the state of California was a natural target of growth. Both Los Angeles and San Francisco had a history of success at the minor-league level and each city had been mentioned as a potential big-league hockey site. But until the mid-1960s, NHL leaders had preferred the six-team cocoon ranging from Chicago on the west and Boston on the east and, despite being pressured to grow, both the governors and president Clarence Campbell continually rejected the suggestions.

When the NHL enjoyed unprecedented prosperity in the mid-1960s, the pressure to plant teams in both Northern and Southern California became irresistible. The Los Angeles entry went to Jack Kent Cooke while the Bay Area leader was a 28-year-old friend of New York Rangers president William Jennings. Barend (Barry) Van Gerbig was a jet-setter who owned pieces of Standard Oil of New Jersey as well as Union Carbide and looked like a blond beachboy just in from the surf. Van Gerbig had played goal for the varsity team at Princeton and graduated to marry the daughter of film icon Douglas Fairbanks, Jr. His godfather was legendary crooner Bing Crosby.

The seemingly well-heeled Van Gerbig and his partners purchased the San Francisco Seals of the Western League, a team which had played its home games out of the creaky Cow Palace in Daly City. In 1966-67, their final WHL season, their games were moved to a relatively palatial facility across the Bay. While Van Gerbig's intentions may have

been good, his geography was not. San Francisco, the revered city by the Golden Gate, would have been an ideal site for an NHL club, but it lacked a suitable arena. By contrast the Bay Area's second—and noticeably lesser—city, Oakland, boasted a brand-new facility with major-league dimensions. The Oakland-Alameda County Coliseum was chosen by Van Gerbig as home for his Oakland Seals because there was no other suitable facility around.

The choice of Oakland as the Seals base proved to be a mistake. Taciturn former NHL left winger Bert Olmstead was hired as general manager and coach. At the Montreal draft meeting in June 1967, Olmstead selected what looked like a winning lineup. His goalie, Charlie Hodge, had considerable NHL experience with the Canadiens while Bob Baun and Kent Douglas had skated for Maple Leafs Cup-winners. Gerry Ehman had been a proven goal scorer and Bill Hicke once had been touted as the natural heir to Maurice "Rocket" Richard with Montreal. The Seals also had drafted the young sons of former aces King Clancy, Babe Pratt and Bryan Hextall.

Before being replaced, Olmstead's record was a dismal 11–37–16. Meanwhile, the Seals were hellbent toward the cellar and a missed playoff in their first season. Even worse, the fan reaction alternated between cool and frigid. Attendance was terrible and early in the season Van Gerbig threatened to move the team if more fans didn't show up. By the time the Board of Governors convened for their March meeting in New York, there had been feelers to the Seals from Labatt Breweries of Canada Ltd., and two wealthy Canadians, Max Bell of Calgary and Frank McMahon of Vancouver. Labatt offered a loan of $680,000 (the amount that the league specified the Seals had to come up with by May 15) in order to move the franchise to Vancouver. Other interested bidders were Mel Swig, former owner of the old San Francisco Seals of the Western League; Ralph Wilson, owner of the Buffalo Bills football team; and Charles Finley, owner of the Oakland A's baseball club.

At the meeting a move to Vancouver was vetoed by an 8–4 vote. The league still could become healthy, and it was in no mood to depart from a large population area so vital to any television plans. (The CBS TV contract specifically stipulated the inclusion of the Bay area.) In August the Seals were purchased by the owners of the Harlem Globetrotters, Potter Palmer and George Gillett of Chicago, and John O'Neil Jr. of Miami. They were aided by the loan from Labatt. The three also had financial interests in the Atlanta Braves, the Miami Dolphins and the Atlanta Chiefs soccer team. Palmer and O'Neil had been partners, along with Van Gerbig, in the original Seals franchise. It was announced that Van Gerbig's future association with the team would be in an advisory capacity only. President Frank Selke Jr. became the general manager and a new man was hired to replace Bert Olmstead. He was Fred Glover.

Before the 1968–69 season, Glover was not the only new face in the Seals dressing room. Only seven of the 20 players originally drafted by the club remained. It was hoped that Bryan Watson and Carol Vadnais, drafted from the Canadiens, and Gary Jarrett and Doug Roberts, acquired from Detroit for Bobby Baun, would help Glover move the Seals upward. In front of the nets, Glover inherited, in addition to the diminutive Charlie Hodge, the 6'3" Gary Smith who, while promising, had shown an alarming tendency to stickhandle the puck across the blue line in his first season. Symbolic of the Seals NHL debut was one of his rushes. He

had outskated two of his teammates.

Few NHL goalies ever were bombarded the way Smith was during the 1969–70 and 1970–71 seasons. Prior to the latter campaign, Charles Finley, owner of the Oakland Athletics, bought the NHL club and changed its name to the California Golden Seals. He added colored skates, new jerseys and several other gimmicks but the Seals finished with the worst record of either division. One disaster led to another until February, 1974, when the team was purchased by the NHL. League president Clarence Campbell named Munson Campbell, a man with over 30 years experience in the inner workings of professional hockey, the president. Campbell had been named vice president of the California Seals under Finley in 1971 but left a year later to return to private business.

In his new role, Campbell attempted to find new ownership for the foundering Seals and eventually came up with hotelier Mel Swig. The hope was that a proposed new arena would be built in San Francisco for the Seals, but when it became apparent that the plans would never become reality, the club was moved to Cleveland during the 1976–77 campaign. Swig's ownership soon gave way to the Gund family, led by George Gund in June 1977. "There's a great hockey tradition in Cleveland," said Gund upon taking control of the franchise. "We would like to revive that and improve upon it. Our goal is to gain more and more friends and fans from all over northeastern Ohio."

But Gund could not solve yet another geography problem like the one that bedeviled the Seals in San Francisco. The new Cleveland Barons played their home games at the Coliseum in Richfield, Ohio. While it listed the largest seating capacity in the NHL at the time (18,544), the Coliseum was located in farmland far from downtown Cleveland and suffered sparse crowds in the Oakland tradition. The Barons record hardly encouraged sellouts. Under coach Jack "Tex" Evans, Cleveland finished the 1977–78 season with a 22–45–13 record and last place in the Adams Division. So poor was the club's financial condition that it merged with the Minnesota North Stars in time for the 1978–79 season. George Gund III was chairman of the board while his brother Gordon was named vice chairman. Lou Nanne was general manager and fellow NHL retiree Harry Howell ran the bench.

All things considered, the legacy of the Oakland-California Golden Seals/Cleveland Barons was less than encouraging. Both Oakland and Cleveland ceased to be NHL cities while the reconstituted North Stars—aided by the infusion of talent from the Barons—hardly were awesome. In 1978–79, despite the addition of Cleveland's players, the North Stars finished the campaign with a dismal 28–40–12 record that was not even good enough for a playoff berth.

California/Oakland/Cleveland Year-by-Year Record

Season	GP	W	L	T	GF	GA	Pts	Finish		Playoff Results
1967–68	74	15	42	17	153	219	47	6th	West Div.	Out of Playoffs
1968–69	76	29	36	11	219	251	69	2nd	West Div.	Lost Quarterfinal
1969–70	76	22	40	14	169	243	58	4th	West Div.	Lost Quarterfinal
1970–71	78	20	53	5	199	320	45	7th	West Div.	Out of Playoffs
1971–72	78	21	39	18	216	288	60	6th	West Div.	Out of Playoffs
1972–73	78	16	46	16	213	323	48	8th	West Div.	Out of Playoffs
1973–74	78	13	55	10	195	342	36	8th	West Div.	Out of Playoffs
1974–75	80	19	48	13	212	316	51	4th	Adams Div.	Out of Playoffs
1975–76	80	27	42	11	250	278	65	4th	Adams Div.	Out of Playoffs
1976–77	80	25	42	13	240	292	63	4th	Adams Div.	Out of Playoffs
1977–78	80	22	45	13	230	325	57	4th	Adams Div.	Out of Playoffs

CAROLINA HURRICANES AND HARTFORD WHALERS

Stan Fischler

IF EVER A NATIONAL HOCKEY LEAGUE franchise has described a roller coaster ride, the Carolina Hurricanes—whose roots can be found in the defunct World Hockey Association—is it. The Hurricanes started their existence as the New England Whalers in a league that many believed would never get started in the first place. But it did, and that was the beginning of a most unusual saga that moved from Boston to Springfield to Hartford and, most recently, Greensboro and Raleigh.

In the beginning, the seeds of the Whalers were planted in October 1971 by a pair of young sportsmen, Howard Baldwin and John Coburn Jr., who originally had planned to build a small hockey arena near Cape Cod. Out of this blueprint emerged one of the most powerful teams in the World Hockey Association. Having obtained backers for the proposed WHA team, Baldwin and Coburn flew to the league meetings in Miami and obtained a green light from the new league's bosses, Gary Davidson and Dennis Murphy. With the franchise in hand, Baldwin, a former business manager of the Jersey Devils of the old Eastern Hockey League, hired Jack Kelley, the Boston University coach, to manage and coach the Whalers. Kelley immediately hired Ron Ryan as assistant coach and director of player personnel.

Former Montreal Canadiens center Larry Pleau of Lynn, Massachusetts, was the first Whaler signed by Kelley, followed by NHL regulars Brad Selwood, Rick Ley and Jim Dorey, all former Toronto Maple Leafs, and Tim Sheehy of Boston College. On July 27, 1972, the Whalers signed former Boston Bruins defenseman Ted Green as captain and then signed other NHL aces such as Tom Webster, Al Smith and Tom Williams. On October 12, 1972, the Whalers played their first home game at Boston Garden before a crowd of 14,442, defeating the Philadelphia Blazers 4–3. A well-balanced unit, the Whalers went on to finish first and win the Avco World Cup.

However, the Whalers encountered financial problems because of competition from the NHL Boston Bruins, who featured Bobby Orr and Phil Esposito. Attendance remained less than satisfactory in the second season of operation, 1973–74, at Boston Garden. Kelley had assigned Ron Ryan the head coaching position and once again the Whalers moved to the top of the East Division. Because of the weak crowds, Baldwin began entertaining offers from other cities which coveted the franchise. He finally selected Hartford, which was building a new arena in the Connecticut city's civic center. A group of Hartford's leading businesses invested $1.5 million in the Whalers with a limited partnership, including a group of Boston investors. The companies included, among others, Aetna Life and Casualty, Connecticut Bank and Trust Company, United Aircraft, the *Hartford Courant* and the Greater Hartford Chamber of Commerce.

Instead of waiting until the end of the 1973–74 season, the Whalers moved their "home" games to the Eastern States Coliseum in Springfield, Massachusetts, because their new home in Hartford had yet to be completed. Playing their final games in Springfield late in the 1973–74 season had a negative effect on the Whalers. Although they finished first in their division, the Whalers were eliminated from the playoffs in a first-round, seven-game upset by the Chicago Cougars.

The Whalers continued to excel during the 1974–75 campaign, which was launched in Springfield and continued in Hartford late in the season upon completion of the 10,400-seat Civic Center arena. Once again they finished first in their division, but not without problems. En route to a match in Toronto on March 30, coach Ryan collapsed and was rushed to a hospital. He was replaced behind the bench by Kelley. On the plus side, the Whalers became an instant hit in Hartford, frequently selling out in the new building. It appeared that the Whalers, at last, had found a comfortable home although they were eliminated by Minnesota in the opening round of the 1975 playoffs in six games.

During their WHA existence, the Whalers boasted several luminaries, not the least of whom were Gordie Howe, Dave Keon, Bobby Hull and Mark Howe. Baldwin would eventually become president of the WHA and was the prime architect in hammering out the merger with the NHL. Baldwin gave up his WHA leadership role but, as a result, the Whalers, Edmonton Oilers, Winnipeg Jets and Quebec Nordiques became NHL members. The venerable Gordie Howe returned to the NHL at the age of 51 in 1979 as a member of Hartford. Howe finished his 32nd NHL season with 15 goals, including his 800th career regular-season tally. That same year, the Whalers traded for another Hall of Famer, Bobby Hull, and the two played on the same line for nine games.

The 1980–81 season saw Howe and his number nine retire and former director of hockey operations and first-ever Whaler draft choice Larry Pleau take over as coach, replacing the fired Don Blackburn. Also that summer, Pleau drafted an 18-year-old center fourth overall who would change Hartford hockey forever. Less than six months after being drafted, Ron Francis was leading the Ontario Hockey League in scoring until November 30, 1981, when he was brought up by the big club. He made an immediate impact. He would finish the year third in team scoring with 68 points in 56 games and helped to turn the 21st-ranked power-play into the best in the league for a three-month stretch. Despite missing the playoffs for the second straight year, the Whalers seemed destined for greatness.

But the 1982–83 campaign saw Larry Pleau return as bench boss replacing another fired coach, Larry Kish, and the Whalers did not qualify for postseason play, finishing with only 19 wins.

The 1983 offseason saw a total overhaul to the Hartford front office. Now coaching was Jack Evans and hired as general manager was Emile "the Cat" Francis. In two years, this tandem would eventually lead the hapless Whalers to unseen heights in the NHL. They surrounded perpetual all-star and crowd favorite Ron Francis with defenseman Joel Quenneville and winger Torrie Robertson and drafted Sylvain Turgeon over future stars such as Pat LaFontaine, Tom Barrasso, Steve Yzerman and Cam Neely, all of whom were available in that same draft year. Again, though, Hartford fans got an early summer.

After missing the playoffs yet again in the 1984–85 season, the Whalers traded for goalie (and Ron Francis' first cousin) Mike Liut. Liut helped the Whale to their first winning finish in seven years, and put them in the playoffs face-to-face with the Adams Division-leading Quebec Nordiques. Then, the unthinkable happened. The Whalers ousted Quebec in a three-game sweep to win their first NHL playoff round! Primed and ready for round two, the

Montreal Canadiens came calling. Miraculously, the Whalers upset the favored Habs in a game one overtime win. Montreal took games two and three but the Whalers roared back and won game four, again in extra time, thanks to rookie Kevin Dineen. The Habs took game five and a classic was on.

For it was in game six where Dineen, again, scored the most famous goal in Whaler history. The only tally of the game slipped past Montreal goalie Patrick Roy, and all of a sudden the Whalers were one game away from the unheard-of plateau of the Prince of Wales Conference finals. But whatever lofty hopes the Whaler faithful had were dashed when pesky Montreal rookie Claude Lemieux scored the series winner in overtime two nights later. Despite the crushing loss, Emile Francis was named *The Hockey News* and *The Sporting News* NHL executive of the year.

The next season, 1986–87, saw the Whalers capture their first and only Adams Division championship with 93 points. The celebration, however, was short-lived as the Nordiques upset the Whalers four games to two in the first round. Hartford returned to the postseason the following year but was again ousted in the first round, this time to rival Montreal. Following 1988–89, and another first-round loss to the Canadiens, Emile Francis was made team president and former goaltender Ed Johnston was named g.m. Pleau, who had returned to the bench for a third time the previous season, was fired and replaced by former Whaler Rick Ley. The next two seasons saw little excitement as the Whalers still could not win a playoff round, losing to the Boston Bruins in 1990.

Just as their unexpected triumph had happened in 1986, an unexpected blow came in March of 1991. Ron Francis, owner of most Hartford Whalers offensive records and arguably the most popular player ever to grace the Hartford Civic Center, was traded to Pittsburgh with Ulf Samuelsson and Grant Jennings for John Cullen, Zarley Zalapski and Jeff Parker. Francis would go on to win the Stanley Cup that year and the year after, and the Whalers never seemed to recover.

The 1991–92 season saw Dineen traded to Philadelphia and the Whalers knocked out again in the first round of the playoffs in a seven-game, double-overtime loss to the Canadiens. The next three years saw three separate coaches: Jimmy Roberts, Paul Holmgren and Pierre McGuire. Emile Francis retired after a 47-year hockey career. Brian Burke replaced Johnston as g.m. but soon resigned to become senior vice president and director of hockey operations for the NHL. He was replaced by Holmgren. On the day the 1994 NHL Entry Draft was held in Hartford, the team was sold to Compuware owner Peter Karmanos, Thomas Thewes and former NHL goaltender Jim Rutherford for $47.5 million. Rutherford became g.m. and president and Holmgren was named head coach.

The last huge trade made by the Whalers was the dealing of first-round draft choice Chris Pronger to St. Louis for All-Star power forward Brendan Shanahan in 1995. Shanahan would spend only one year (1995–96) in Whaler blue and green, as his desire to play on a Cup-contending team forced the Whale to trade him to Detroit for center Keith Primeau and future Hall of Fame defenseman Paul Coffey. Coffey, too, wasn't interested in rebuilding a franchise and made a trade demand, eventually getting sent to Philadelphia. In an ironic twist, Shanahan's Red Wings defeated Coffey's Flyers in the 1996–97 Stanley Cup finals.

But the end was near for the Hartford Whalers. On March 26, 1997, after another lackluster season in which the Whalers finished 32–39–11, good for no better than 10th place in the East, Peter Karmanos confirmed suspicions as he announced that the franchise would be playing somewhere else come the 1997–98 season. While some die-hard fans had done their best to prevent the move, launching the "Save the Whale" campaign in an effort to sell more tickets and convince Karmanos and Co. to stay, it was announced that the Whalers would relocate to Raleigh, North Carolina. A new arena was planned for the Hurricanes to play in by the turn of the century. Meanwhile, the team would be playing at Greensboro Coliseum, which overnight became one of the largest NHL's largest arenas. Kevin Dineen scored the last Whaler goal in history as Hartford defeated the Tampa Bay Lightning 2–1 in an emotional game on April 13, 1997. The Whalers finished out of the playoffs, but Karmanos predicted that the move to Carolina would be good for another 10 to 15 points.

It wasn't to be. The Carolina Hurricanes first season was, to put it mildly, a stormy one. In Greensboro, deep in the heart of college basketball and NASCAR country, the Hurricanes did not attract as much attention as they had wished. While the home opener drew 18,661 fans, attendance dropped after that. A few days after the opener, an announced crowd of 6,083 turned out to watch the 'Canes play the L.A. Kings. One fan was spotted sitting among a sea of empty seats holding aloft a sign that read "Great Sections Still Available!"

There were problems within the team as well. Geoff Sanderson, the leading scorer of the 1996–97 team with 67 points, was unhappy. He was traded away. Goalie Sean Burke, who had won four consecutive awards as the team MVP, did not play up to his usual standards. Plagued by this, as well as some off-ice problems, the successful goaltender also was traded. And finally, the team owners tried to lure All-Star Sergei Fedorov away from the Detroit Red Wings with a $38 million offer sheet designed to sink the Wings chances of matching. But match they did, leaving Carolina without the superstar center.

But there were some silver linings among the grey storm clouds that hung over the transferred franchise. Captain and leader Keith Primeau was an important part of Canada's entry at the 1998 Nagano Olympics and led the Hurricanes in scoring. Goalie Trevor Kidd, who had been acquired over the summer from Calgary, responded to the challenge of becoming a legit starting goaltender by posting career and franchise records with a 2.17 goals-against average and a .922 save percentage. Power forward Gary Roberts, who had played only 43 games since the end of the 1994 season because of injuries, joined the team after one year of retirement and went on to be the third leading scorer with 20 goals and 29 assists in only 61 games. And forward Sami Kapanen had a breakthrough year, amassing 63 points for a share of first place in team scoring, turning a few heads in the league in the process.

The 'Canes made a late season charge toward the playoffs, but an injury to Kidd braked the sprint as did wounds to other key players including Jeff O'Neill and Roberts. The Hurricanes ended their inaugural season in ninth place in the Eastern Conference, missing the playoffs.

Carolina Hurricanes Year-by-Year Record

Season	GP	W	L	T	GF	GA	Pts	Finish		Playoff Results
1979–80*	80	27	34	19	303	312	73	4th	Norris Div.	Lost Prelim. Round
1980–81*	80	21	41	18	292	372	60	4th	Norris Div.	Out of Playoffs
1981–82*	80	21	41	18	264	351	60	5th	Adams Div.	Out of Playoffs
1982–83*	80	19	54	7	261	403	45	5th	Adams Div.	Out of Playoffs
1983–84*	80	28	42	10	288	320	66	5th	Adams Div.	Out of Playoffs
1984–85*	80	30	41	9	268	318	69	5th	Adams Div.	Out of Playoffs
1985–86*	80	40	36	4	332	302	84	4th	Adams Div.	Lost Div. Final
1986–87*	80	43	30	7	287	270	93	1st	Adams Div.	Lost Div. Semifinal
1987–88*	80	35	38	7	249	267	77	4th	Adams Div.	Lost Div. Semifinal
1988–89*	80	37	38	5	299	290	79	4th	Adams Div.	Lost Div. Semifinal
1989–90*	80	38	33	9	275	268	85	4th	Adams Div.	Lost Div. Semifinal
1990–91*	80	31	38	11	238	276	73	4th	Adams Div.	Lost Div. Semifinal
1991–92*	80	26	41	13	247	283	65	4th	Adams Div.	Lost Div. Semifinal
1992–93	84	26	52	6	284	369	58	5th	Adams Div.	Out of Playoffs
1993–94*	84	27	48	9	227	288	63	6th	Northeast Div.	Out of Playoffs
1994–95*	48	19	24	5	127	141	43	5th	Northeast Div.	Out of Playoffs
1995–96*	82	34	39	9	237	259	77	4th	Northeast Div.	Out of Playoffs
1996–97*	82	32	39	11	226	256	75	5th	Northeast Div.	Out of Playoffs
1997–98	82	33	41	8	200	219	74	6th	Northeast Div.	Out of Playoffs

* Hartford Whalers

CHICAGO BLACKHAWKS

Stan Fischler

IF A HOLLYWOOD FILM WERE TO BE MADE about one of the "Original Six" National Hockey League teams, the Chicago Blackhawks would be the ideal subject. Their history, dating back to 1926, has touches of a Marx Brothers comedy, The Three Stooges, romance and a melodrama that Paramount scriptwriters would have trouble duplicating.

The Blackhawks' saga began during the mid-1920s with a telephone call to Major Frederic McLaughlin, a millionaire coffee baron and prominent American polo player. The Patrick brothers, Frank and Lester, who were disbanding the Western Hockey League, were on the other end of the wire. The WHL no longer could compete with the higher-salaried NHL and the Patrick were holding a fire sale.

They convinced McLaughlin that there was money to be made out of hockey and that Chicago could have a ready-made team by purchasing the Portland (Oregon) Rosebuds for $200,000. Fortified with about one hundred of his aristocratic Windy City friends, including H.R. Hardwick, the Major formed a consortium, bought the franchise, moved the Rosebuds to Illinois and changed their name.

As a commander of the 333rd Machine Gun Battalion of the U.S. Army's World War I Expeditionary Force, the Major belonged to the 85th Blackhawk Division and felt a many-faceted affection for the name. He also was aware that a Chief Blackhawk headed an Indian tribe that roamed the plains of the Midwest. After McLaughlin named the team, his wife Irene Castle—a world-renowned ballroom dancer who had teamed with her husband Vernon before he had died—designed the unique black, red and white striped uniforms with the head of Chief Blackhawk on the logo.

McLaughlin and friends moved the Rosebuds—now known as the Black Hawks—to Illinois and then found a home for them at the 6,000-seat Chicago Coliseum, which was more conspicuous for its odor than its design. More often than not the arena was home to cattle shows and smelled the part. Nevertheless with the aid of an ice plant, the Black Hawks were ready for play in the 1926–27 season and had the players to take aim at the Stanley Cup. (Until 1985–86, the name "Black Hawks" was usually—but not always—written as two words.)

Thanks to the Patricks, McLaughlin not only acquired a coach in Pete Muldoon but a package of players some of whom were the crème de la crème of western hockey. These included coach-in-waiting Dick Irvin, Rabbit McVeigh, Mickey Mackay, George Hay, Percy Traub and Bob Trapp. For added scoring power, Cecil "Babe" Dye was obtained from the Toronto St. Pats, although the brand new New York Rangers also were after his services. Dye had been the eighth-leading scorer the previous year. Goalie Jakie Forbes of the New York Americans called Dye the NHL's hardest shooter. "He was a terrible skater," said Forbes, "but he was foxy and he had tremendous wrists." Dye, who tied for second in goal-scoring with 25 red lights, helped the Black Hawks finish third in the NHL's American Division behind the Rangers and Boston whereupon McLaughlin—displaying an impatience that would be his hallmark—promptly fired Muldoon.

Whether the story is apocryphal or not remains debatable to this day. But legend has it that McLaughlin summoned Muldoon to his office at season's end and claimed that his club was good enough to finish first. According to the tale, Muldoon was amazed at McLaughlin's criticism, but not to the point of shutting up. "You're crazy!" he fumed. McLaughlin was outraged by such heresy. "You're fired!" he roared. Muldoon flared back in a black Irish snit. "Fire me, Major and you'll be sorry. The Hawks will never finish first! I'll put a curse on this team that will hoodoo it."

True hoodoo or not, the Chicagoans did seem cursed. During the 1927–28 training camp Dye broke his leg in a scrimmage prank and virtually ended his playing career. Without Dye to bolster their attack, the Hawks finished fifth in the American Division and wound up out of the playoffs. If they had anything worth cheering about, it was a young goaltender imported from the Winnipeg Maroons. His name was Charlie Gardiner, and he was slowly developing into one of the finds of the decade. Whenever he stepped between the goal pipes, he usually wore a broad smile. At first this seemed the height of presumptuousness, since his goalkeeping was hardly flawless. But he worked diligently at his trade. "He would come far out of the nets and sprawl on the ice in an effort to stop a score," reported Canadian writer Ron McAllister. "And even when his own team folded, he fought on and tried to defend his goal."

During the 1928–29 season, the Black Hawks began to take on a happier face. They were about to move their home base from the old Chicago Coliseum to a mammoth new structure that was being erected on West Madison Street. The Chicago Stadium would hold more than 18,000 people, making it the largest rink in the NHL. However, before the stadium opened, the Hawks were pushed out of the Coliseum and were without a home rink. Circumstances finally forced them to choose a bandbox arena in Fort Erie, Ontario for their home games. By 1929, Gardiner had improved so much that he finished second to the immortal George Hainsworth of the Montreal Canadiens in the race for the Vezina Trophy. In 1932, he would finally win the coveted prize and be named to the all-star team. In the 1929–30 season, the Black Hawks finished second to Boston, albeit a distant second, but they were eliminated by the Canadiens in the Stanley Cup semifinal. A year later they were runners-up to the Bruins again. However, this time they eliminated Toronto in the first round, New York in the second round, and advanced to the Cup finals before losing to the Canadiens.

After coaching the team in 1930–31, Irvin was released early in 1931-32 and promptly accepted a similar job with the Maple Leafs. It was too much to expect Major

McLaughlin to follow Irvin with an equally competent coach. Instead, the major chose a chap named Godfrey Matheson who had absolutely no big-league hockey coaching experience. Despite the Major's machinations, the Black Hawks sold Chicagoans on big-league hockey and the NHL was so popular that grain millionaire James Norris, himself a Canadian with ties to the Montreal Athletic Association, applied for a second Windy City franchise to share Chicago with the Black Hawks.

The Major wanted no part of that and stopped the Norris bid. But Norris went to war and organized a competitive team, the Chicago Shamrocks, and entered them in the American Association. Norris further embarrassed McLaughlin by hiring Tom Shaughnessy—recently fired by the Major—as Shamrocks coach.

Playing at the new Chicago Stadium, the Shamrocks drew healthy crowds in an unhealthy league. At season's end, Norris even issued a challenge for the Stanley Cup but was rejected by the NHL. When the American Association folded, McLaughlin moved his Black Hawks into the Stadium and they continued their futile pursuit of the Stanley Cup.

Despite a succession of mostly incompetent coaches, Charlie Gardiner's superlative goaltending kept the Hawks competitive. In 1933–34, Chicago finished second to Detroit while Gardiner allowed only 83 goals in 48 games and posted 10 shutouts. In 14 other games he permitted just one goal.

But astute Gardiner-watchers perceived that there was something unusual about the goalie's deportment, and they couldn't quite figure out what it was. Gardiner has lost his jovial manner and appeared melancholy. "He suddenly grew more serious," noted one observer. "Instead of relaxing, he kept on shouting to his teammates, more than ever before. He became intolerant of mistakes." There were many explanations, but it soon became apparent that Gardiner had been gravely ill all season. Two months after his heroic goaltending had led Chicago to its first Stanley Cup title, Gardiner collapsed and died of a brain hemorrhage in his hometown of Winnipeg. He was 29 years old.

Without Gardiner, the Black Hawks were no longer a Stanley Cup contender. But McLaughlin had an arresting idea for bringing glory back to his hockey club. An ardent chauvinist, he resented Canada's grip on hockey and believed that a team of all American-born players could well represent Chicago in the NHL.

He started with Mike Karakas (Aurora, Minnesota), Alex Levinsky (Syracuse, New York), Doc Romnes (White Bear, Minnesota) and Lou Trudel (Salem, Massachusetts. Although Canadian-born managers throughout the league mocked the Major, he urged his high command to add Americans whenever possible. By the 1937–38 season even the coach, Bill Stewart, was American. The Massachusetts-born major-league baseball umpire would frequently argue with the Major but Stewart usually prevailed.

When Stewart obtained Carl Voss from the Montreal Maroons, McLaughlin was absolutely convinced that his coach had goofed. After watching Voss in one game, the major insisted that he be cut from the squad as an obvious loser. This time Stewart was adamant. Voss would stay. And he did. Voss not only stayed, but he later played a part in Chicago's most stirring hockey triumph since the birth of the Black Hawks.

Meanwhile, the Americanized Black Hawks managed to plod along through the schedule at a slightly quicker pace than the Red Wings. The result was that Chicago finished third in the American Division, just two points ahead of its Detroit pursuers, but a good 30 points behind division-leading Boston. Their chances for winning the Stanley Cup were considered no better than 100–1. To begin with, the Hawks were the only one of the six qualifying teams to have less than a .500 record (14–25–9), and their first-round opponents were the Montreal Canadiens, who had a considerably more respectable 18–17–13 mark. Further complicating matters for Chicago was the fact that two of the three games would be played in the Montreal Forum.

Predictably, the Canadiens won the first match 6–4. But when the series shifted to Chicago, goalie Karakas shut out the Montrealers 4–0. Suddenly the Black Hawks were coming on strong. The final game was tied 2–2 after regulation time. It was decided in Chicago's favor when Lou Trudel's shot bounced off Paul Thompson and into Montreal's cage, although some observers insist that the puck was shot home by Mush March.

Now the Black Hawks were to face an equally aroused New York American sextet that had just routed its archrivals in Manhattan, the Rangers, in three games. Once again, the Hawks would have the benefit of only one home game in the best-of-three series. The Americans opened with a 3–1 victory at Madison Square Garden. But when the series shifted to Chicago, Karakas took over again and the teams battled to the end of regulation time without a score. The game was settled in sudden-death overtime on a goal by Cully Dahlstrom. In game three, Chicago clinched the series with a third-period goal by Doc Romnes. The final score was 3–2, and the Black Hawks advanced into the Stanley Cup finals against the Toronto Maple Leafs.

By now the betting odds had dropped considerably in Chicago's favor. But they soared again when it was learned that Karakas had suffered a broken big toe in the final game with the Americans. Karakas didn't realize the extent of the damage until he attempted to lace on his skates for the game with Toronto. He just couldn't make it, and the Hawks suddenly became desperate for a goaltender.

The Leafs were not in the least sympathetic to the Black Hawks and rejected requests for goaltending assistance. So the Chicago braintrust finally unearthed Alfie Moore, a minor-league goalie who purportedly was quaffing liquid refreshment in a Toronto pub when he was drafted to climb into the barrel for the Chicagoans. Moore answered the call and went into the Chicago nets on April 5, 1938 defeating Toronto 4–1 in the opening game of the series at Maple Leaf Gardens. From there Chicago went on to defeat Toronto in what was one of the singular upsets in Cup history. The Cup-winning goal was scored by Voss, thereby rewarding Stewart's faith in him.

Stewart was the coaching hero of Chicago until the following season. He was in fact ably coaching the team in 1938–39, but McLaughlin disagreed and fired the umpire after 21 games. From that point on—for more than two decades—the Windy City's hockey fortunes dipped. There would not be another championship at Chicago Stadium for almost a quarter of a century. There were, however, some fun years, particularly at the outset of World War II when a pair of fleet youngsters—Max and Doug Bentley—from Delisle, Saskatchewan and a speedy 19-year-old winger named Bill Mosienko teamed to form the Pony Line, one of the best little offensive trios the league has known.

In 1945–46 Max led the league in scoring while Doug and Mosie continued to dazzle. But the Hawks were going

nowhere and early in the 1947–48 season they shocked the Bentley family and Windy City fans by trading Max to the Toronto Maple Leafs in what then was one of the biggest deal in hockey history. The Leafs dispatched Gaye Stewart, Gus Bodnar, and Bud Poile—an entire forward line—as well as defensemen Bob Goldham and Ernie Dickens, to Chicago in return for Bentley and unobtrusive forward named Cy Thomas. The deal was correctly called one of the most extraordinary ever made, particularly because it separated the previously inseparable Bentley brothers. Conn Smythe, the Toronto boss, immediately claimed that the trade would become the basis for a hockey dynasty—and he was right. With centers such as Syl Apps, Ted Kennedy, and Bentley, he had the best offense in the league. The Leafs finished first that season and romped to the Cup.

In contrast, the Hawks, even augmented with the ex-Leafs, continued to struggle. They always seemed to come up with adequate scorers, but defense never seemed to be part of their vocabulary. The team acquired new ownership on September 11, 1952 when James Norris Sr., James D. Norris Jr. and Arthur Wirtz obtained control of the team. The Norrises already owned the Detroit Red Wings and had an interest in Madison Square Garden. By 1954 brothers Arthur and Michael Wirtz held controlling interest. Bill Wirtz also joined his father and uncle in reinvigorating the Black Hawks organization.

The Red Wings and Black Hawks became frequent trading partners and in 1952–53 a collection of ex-Detroiters including Jim McFadden, Jim Peters, George Gee, Gerry Couture and Lidio "Lee" Fogolin lifted Chicago to a fourth-place finish. With ex-Red Wing Sid Abel coaching while also doing considerable work at center, the Black Hawks marched into the Stanley Cup playoffs against the vaunted Canadiens. The Black Hawks' most important asset, both during the season and in the playoffs, was the goaltending of angular Al Rollins, perhaps the most underrated goalie the NHL has known. A former Maple Leaf, Rollins personally kicked and split his way through a remarkable season behind a none-too-encouraging defense.

In the playoffs it appeared at first that he'd capitulate before Montreal's big guns. The Canadiens won the first two games played in the Forum. But Chicago won two straight on their home grounds and then took the lead, three games to two by whipping the Canadiens 4–2 in Montreal. All that was required for Chicago to reach the Stanley Cup finals was a win at their friendly stadium on Madison Street. Try as they might, the Hawks couldn't swing it. They lost 3–0 at home and then were eliminated by losing 4–1 in Montreal.

It had been a gallant effort, and Chicago fans would have only the memory of it to sustain them during five more non-playoff years. The decline of the Hawks nearly caused owner Jim Norris to forsake his favorite game for more lucrative ventures. But Norris (whose father, James, had made a fortune in the grain business and founded the Red Wings' empire) was fond of hockey and was finally persuaded to invest a few million dollars in the rejuvenation of the Black Hawks franchise. He imported Tommy Ivan from the Detroit system and ordered him to develop a farm system from which Chicago could obtain a constant flow of young players. In the meantime, a few members of the league sympathized enough with the Chicago plight to promise help in some form or other. The talent-rich Canadiens finally cooperated by dealing the Hawks Ed Litzenberger, a muscular young forward of great promise.

By the 1955–56 season, the first trickles of new talent began flowing into Chicago Stadium. Such youngsters as Ken Wharram and Pierre Pilote, future NHL trophy winners, pulled on Black Hawk jerseys and hardly seemed out of place against their more accomplished opponents. Soon the St. Catharines farm club began funneling such young talents as Bobby Hull and Hank Ciesla, and veterans were traded for hopefully better prospects. Chicago finished fifth in 1957–58, and the signs were clear that better days were ahead. The next season they leaped into third place and gave Montreal a six-game run in the playoffs.

With Rudy Pilous at the helm, guiding the likes of Litzenberger, Hull, Pilote and Stan Mikita, Chicago remained a solid third-place team without making any playoff progress until 1961, when they again ran head-long into the Canadiens. Led by Glenn Hall's exceptional goaltending, Chicago captured the series 4–2 and then defeated Detroit in six games. It had taken 23 long and often miserable years for the Hawks to win the Stanley Cup.

After the final playoff game, instead of exploding into one of the loudest victory celebrations the sports world had ever heard, the Chicago dressing room was so quiet that it was possible to hear a puck drop. Only an occasional whoop seared the air while the tall Stanley Cup was installed on a massage table in the middle of the cramped room. Reg Fleming, the utility player whose goal for the shorthanded Hawks seemed to knock the sting out of the Wings, had an explanation. "I guess it's been so long for most of these guys," said Fleming, "they just don't know how to celebrate." Lantern-jawed defenseman Jack Evans had never played in a Stanley Cup final before. "I'm 35 now," said Evans, "I was beginning to think I'd never get my hands on that Cup. Now that I've got it, I just don't know what to say." Slumped in a quiet corner, almost hidden by a rack of overcoats, was the hero, Hall. He not only wasn't shouting, his voice was almost inaudible. "I'm a tired hockey player," said the sad-eyed goalie who, including playoffs, had played in 82 straight games that season. "Too tired to scream, but awfully enthused about the whole thing." A man with a gnarled face approached Hall. "Congratulations," he said. "I'm Mike Karakas." Hall smiled, not realizing that Karakas was the Black Hawks goaltender in 1938, when Chicago had last won the Cup.

The 1961 Black Hawks may have been the quietest and driest Cup winners hockey has known, for nobody was drenched with beer and nobody popped a champagne cork. "There's no champagne," said the jubilant Norris. "I didn't order any. I was afraid of jinxing the boys." With a Stanley Cup under their belts, the Hawks appeared ready for another assault on "the Muldoon jinx." Certainly, with stars like Hull, Hall, Mikita, and Pilote, they were the equal of any club in the league. But when the chips were down, they didn't produce. They looked like sure champs in 1962–63, but they bowed out in the stretch, and as a result coach Pilous was fired.

His successor, Billy Reay, who had once been fired by the Leafs, was imported from Buffalo in the American Hockey League. But the next season the Black Hawks missed again and landed in second place, just a solitary point behind the champion Canadiens. They were then humiliated by the fourth-place Red Wings, who ousted them from the semifinals in seven games. The only consolation for Reay was that Norris didn't fire him.

In the 1964–65 season, Chicago slipped to third place, and Reay still held his job. What saved him was a stirring

first-round playoff win over Detroit in seven games and a good showing in the seven game final against Montreal, ultimately won by the Canadiens. The 1965–66 season provided some glittering moments for Chicago fans. Bobby Hull scored his 300th NHL goal, and also became the first player to break the 50-goal barrier when he collected his 51st against Cesare Maniago on March 12. He broke the point record and won the Art Ross Trophy as well. Still, Chicago couldn't do better than second. The Hawks were victimized by Detroit again in the first Stanley Cup round. Another failure was added to the long Chicago skein.

Following the NHL's expansion from six to 12 teams in 1967, one of the most damaging events in franchise history occurred when Black Hawks general manager Tommy Ivan dealt Phil Esposito, Ken Hodge and Fred Stanfield to Boston for Gilles Marotte, Pit Martin and a minor-league goalie named Jack Norris. The three ex-Hawks, all young forwards, were responsible for a Boston surge. The rangy Esposito set an NHL record for points in a single season with 126 for the Bruins in 1968–69.

Despite the Bruins rise, the Black Hawks weren't dead for long. They finished first in the East Division in 1969–70 and then were transferred to the West Division in 1970–71 and finished on top once more. They wiped out Philadelphia in four straight games of the opening round of the 1971 playoffs; took the Rangers in an exhausting seven-game semifinals set; and succumbed to the Canadiens in the seventh game of the final series. Another telling blow occurred in 1972 when a contract dispute between the Wirtz family and Bobby Hull resulted in the Windy City hero bolting to the newly organized World Hockey Association. Despite NHL assertions that the WHA would quickly fold—causing Hull to return to the Black Hawks—it remained in business through the 1970s and Chicago lost its most colorful drawing card.

The Black Hawks survived and in some cases thrived without The Golden Jet. Thanks to productive performers such as Stan Mikita, Jim Pappin and Ivan Boldirev, the Black Hawks remained competitive, if not champions, during the WHA years.

But it wasn't until the 1991–92 season under Mike Keenan's coaching that they reached the Stanley Cup finals again. Despite the heroics of Ed "the Eagle" Belfour, Jeremy Roenick, Steve Larmer and Chicago-native Chris Chelios, they were eliminated by Pittsburgh in four straight games and have yet to reach similar heights again.

After 65 years in the historic Chicago Stadium, the Hawks moved across Madison Street for the 1994–95 season and into their new home, the United Center. The Chicago hosted the Edmonton Oilers in the new building's inaugural NHL game. Blackhawks forward Joe Murphy scored the first goal in United Center history as the home team defeated the Oilers 5–1 in the historic game.

By 1997–98, only Chelios remained of the Blackhawks' all-star nucleus from the early 1990s. Bob Pulford had departed as general manager after 20 years at the helm, turning over the position to Bob Murray. After a disastrous start to the season, the Blackhawks appeared to have their new house in order, but a weak finish saw the club miss postseason play for the first time since 1968–69. Third-year coach Craig Hartsburg lost his job, and the rebuilding process began anew with the hiring of former Blackhawk captain Dirk Graham to coach the team.

Chicago Blackhawks Year-by-Year Record

Season	GP	W	L	T	GF	GA	Pts	Finish		Playoff Results
1926–27	44	19	22	3	115	116	41	3rd	Amn. Div.	Lost Quarterfinal
1927–28	44	7	34	3	68	134	17	5th	Amn. Div.	Out of Playoffs
1928–29	44	7	29	8	33	85	22	5th	Amn. Div.	Out of Playoffs
1929–30	44	21	18	5	117	111	47	2nd	Amn. Div.	Lost Quarterfinal
1930–31	44	24	17	3	108	78	51	2nd	Amn. Div.	Lost Final
1931–32	48	18	19	11	86	101	47	2nd	Amn. Div.	Lost Quarterfinal
1932–33	48	16	20	12	88	101	44	4th	Amn. Div.	Out of Playoffs
1933–34	48	20	17	11	88	83	51	2nd	Amn. Div.	Won Stanley Cup
1934–35	48	26	17	5	118	88	57	2nd	Amn. Div.	Lost Quarterfinal
1935–36	48	21	19	8	93	92	50	3rd	Amn. Div.	Lost Quarterfinal
1936–37	48	14	27	7	99	131	35	4th	Amn. Div.	Out of Playoffs
1937–38	48	14	25	9	97	139	37	3rd	Amn. Div.	Won Stanley Cup
1938–39	48	12	28	8	91	132	32	7th		Out of Playoffs
1939–40	48	23	19	6	112	120	52	4th		Lost Quarterfinal
1940–41	48	16	25	7	112	139	39	5th		Lost Semifinal
1941–42	48	22	23	3	145	155	47	4th		Lost Quarterfinal
1942–43	50	17	18	15	179	180	49	5th		Out of Playoffs
1943–44	50	22	23	5	178	187	49	4th		Lost Final
1944–45	50	13	30	7	141	194	33	5th		Out of Playoffs
1945–46	50	23	20	7	200	178	53	3rd		Lost Semifinal
1946–47	60	19	37	4	193	274	42	6th		Out of Playoffs
1947–48	60	20	34	6	195	225	46	6th		Out of Playoffs
1948–49	60	21	31	8	173	211	50	5th		Out of Playoffs
1949–50	70	22	38	10	203	244	54	6th		Out of Playoffs
1950–51	70	13	47	10	171	280	36	6th		Out of Playoffs
1951–52	70	17	44	9	158	241	43	6th		Out of Playoffs
1952–53	70	27	28	15	169	175	69	4th		Lost Semifinal
1953–54	70	12	51	7	133	242	31	6th		Out of Playoffs
1954–55	70	13	40	17	161	235	43	6th		Out of Playoffs
1955–56	70	19	39	12	155	216	50	6th		Out of Playoffs
1956–57	70	16	39	15	169	225	47	6th		Out of Playoffs
1957–58	70	24	39	7	163	202	55	5th		Out of Playoffs
1958–59	70	28	29	13	197	208	69	3rd		Lost Semifinal
1959–60	70	28	29	13	191	180	69	3rd		Lost Semifinal
1960–61	70	29	24	17	198	180	75	3rd		Won Stanley Cup
1961–62	70	31	26	13	217	186	75	3rd		Lost Final
1962–63	70	32	21	17	194	178	81	2nd		Lost Semifinal
1963–64	70	36	22	12	218	169	84	2nd		Lost Semifinal
1964–65	70	34	28	8	224	176	76	3rd		Lost Final
1965–66	70	37	25	8	240	187	82	2nd		Lost Semifinal
1966–67	70	41	17	12	264	170	94	1st		Lost Semifinal
1967–68	74	32	26	16	212	222	80	4th	East Div.	Lost Semifinal
1968–69	76	34	33	9	280	246	77	6th	East Div.	Out of Playoffs
1969–70	76	45	22	9	250	170	99	1st	East Div.	Lost Semifinal
1970–71	78	49	20	9	277	184	107	1st	West Div.	Lost Final
1971–72	78	46	17	15	256	166	107	1st	West Div.	Lost Semifinal
1972–73	78	42	27	9	284	225	93	1st	West Div.	Lost Final
1973–74	78	41	14	23	272	164	105	2nd	West Div.	Lost Semifinal
1974–75	80	37	35	8	268	241	82	3rd	Smythe Div.	Lost Quarterfinal
1975–76	80	32	30	18	254	261	82	1st	Smythe Div.	Lost Quarterfinal
1976–77	80	26	43	11	240	298	63	3rd	Smythe Div.	Lost Prelim. Round
1977–78	80	32	29	19	230	220	83	1st	Smythe Div.	Lost Quarterfinal
1978–79	80	29	36	15	244	277	73	1st	Smythe Div.	Lost Quarterfinal
1979–80	80	34	27	19	241	250	87	1st	Smythe Div.	Lost Quarterfinal
1980–81	80	31	33	16	304	315	78	2nd	Smythe Div.	Lost Prelim. Round
1981–82	80	30	38	12	332	363	72	4th	Norris Div.	Lost Conf. Final
1982–83	80	47	23	10	338	268	104	1st	Norris Div.	Lost Conf. Final
1983–84	80	30	42	8	277	311	68	4th	Norris Div.	Lost Div. Semifinal
1984–85	80	38	35	7	309	299	83	2nd	Norris Div.	Lost Conf. Final
1985–86	80	39	33	8	351	349	86	1st	Norris Div.	Lost Div. Semifinal
1986–87	80	29	37	14	290	310	72	3rd	Norris Div.	Lost Div. Semifinal
1987–88	80	30	41	9	284	328	69	3rd	Norris Div.	Lost Div. Semifinal
1988–89	80	27	41	12	297	335	66	4th	Norris Div.	Lost Conf. Final
1989–90	80	41	33	6	316	294	88	1st	Norris Div.	Lost Conf. Final
1990–91	80	49	23	8	284	211	106	1st	Norris Div.	Lost Div. Semifinal
1991–92	80	36	29	15	257	236	87	2nd	Norris Div.	Lost Final
1992–93	84	47	25	12	279	230	106	1st	Norris Div.	Lost Div. Semifinal
1993–94	84	39	36	9	254	240	87	5th	Central Div.	Lost Conf. Quarterfinal
1994–95	48	24	19	5	156	115	53	3rd	Central Div.	Lost Conf. Final
1995–96	82	40	28	14	273	220	94	2nd	Central Div.	Lost Conf. Semifinal
1996–97	82	34	35	13	223	210	81	5th	Central Div.	Lost Conf. Quarterfinal
1997–98	82	30	39	13	192	199	73	5th	Central Div.	Out of Playoffs

COLORADO AVALANCHE AND QUEBEC NORDIQUES

Chrys Goyens

FOR THE TEAM'S ENTIRE EXISTENCE, the Quebec Nordiques struggled valiantly in the gigantic shadow cast by a building 150 miles southwest of the Quebec provincial capital. The building was the fabled Montreal Forum, home of the storied Montreal Canadiens, and the upstart team in the Habs' backyard would strive for equal billing for 23 years, seven of them spent in the World Hockey Association and 16 in the National Hockey League. No matter how arduous the task, the Nordiques would enjoy their share of success in "the Battle of Quebec." Ironically, when the franchise would relocate to Colorado, 2,000 miles to the southwest, the influence of the Montreal Canadiens would be felt in a much more positive way.

In 1971, Guy Lafleur was the latest in a long line of homegrown superstars who had excelled in junior hockey in Quebec City and then graduated to the Montreal Canadiens. This grated in the provincial capital. Lafleur was in the second month of his rookie season with Montreal when news came of a new professional league on November 1, 1971. The World Hockey Association would begin play the following October with 12 franchises. The following February, a group of six Quebec businessmen purchased the rights of the San Francisco franchise and moved it to Quebec where they would play as the Nordiques, a term that roughly translates to "North-men."

The Montreal influence was all pervasive, even as the infant franchise took its first toddling steps. Veteran Montreal defenseman Jean-Claude Tremblay was the first player signed by the new team, on July 20, 1972, and Maurice "Rocket" Richard joined him as the team's first coach. The new team even managed a $1 million offer for Jean Beliveau to come out of retirement, but the former Citadelle and Aces star opted to remain in the Montreal head office. The Nordiques played their first WHA game on October 11, 1972, a 3–0 loss to Gerry Cheevers and the Cleveland Crusaders. Three days later, after the team's second game, Richard admitted that he wasn't suited to coaching and resigned. Shortly thereafter, Hall of Fame netminder Jacques Plante joined the team as general manager.

Other former Canadiens, including the young duo of Marc Tardif and Rejean Houle (the team's top two draft picks in 1969), defenseman Dale Hoganson and a mix of veteran NHL and minor pro stars made Quebec a competitive team in its first seasons. Le Colisee was one of the best-attended WHA arenas. While other franchises in Canada and the United States foundered, the Nordiques built a loyal following in the province and were ready to challenge for the league's championship, the Avco Cup, by their third season. Young stars in the Quebec Junior League now had an alternative to the Canadiens and the NHL when draft time came. The Nordiques scored a coup in 1974 when they signed 18-year-old Remparts star Real "Buddy" Cloutier. A group of other young stars, including Rob Ramage, Craig Hartsburg, Michel Goulet, Gaston Gingras, Rick Vaive and Mark Napier would sign later with WHA teams, eventually forcing the NHL to lower its draft age to 18 from 20.

The Nordiques challenged for the Avco Cup in 1975 but were swept in the finals by the Houston Aeros, who boasted the unique trio of Gordie Howe and his two sons Mark and Marty. Two years later a local brewery invested $2 mil-

lion in the team and rookie coach Marc Boileau led the Nordiques to their first championship, as the team edged out the Winnipeg Jets and Bobby Hull in seven games. That victory was savored in Quebec City but paled against the exploits of the Montreal Canadiens. With Guy Lafleur in the midst of a six-year run of 50-goal seasons, the Canadiens captured the second of four straight titles and were recognized as the power in hockey. Even with a championship trophy on the mantelpiece, the Nordiques felt the chill in the shadows of the Forum.

Although some fans cried out for a championship series between the Stanley Cup and Avco Cup winners, few executives in pro hockey paid much mind. Though they didn't know it, the fans were a lot closer to a reunification championship than they dared hope, as talks of a merger between the leagues had begun in 1974 and were being taken seriously by both leagues now. With the WHA providing a windfall in players' salaries, and the new league siphoning off junior-aged talents like Wayne Gretzky, Mark Messier, the Howe brothers, Cam Connor and Rod Langway, as well as opening the doors wide to skilled Europeans like Ulf and Kent Nilsson and Anders Hedberg of Sweden, the NHL sought to institute damage control.

Merger talks were continuing at a desultory pace during the 1978–79 season when the Indianapolis Racers folded in midseason and set the events in motion which would see the NHL expand to include four former WHA teams the following September. The Edmonton Oilers, one of the strongest franchises in the WHA, were looking to a bright future when they picked up an 18-year-old center from the defunct Racers and signed him to a 21-year contract, worth somewhere between $4 million and $5 million. The contract linked Wayne Gretzky with the team through the end of the 1998–99 season, though "the Great One" would have the right to renegotiate after 10 years. Soon thereafter, the 17 NHL teams voted 14–3 in favor of an expansion to include the remaining WHA teams. Although six teams remained, only four—Quebec, Winnipeg, New England and Edmonton—would join the new league. The Cincinnati Stingers and the Birmingham Bulls would be dissolved. Significant talent was involved and dispersed throughout the newly expanded NHL via the Entry Draft, including the Cincinnati duo of Mark Messier and Mike Gartner, and "Baby Bulls" Goulet, Napier, Langway, Hartsburg, Ramage, Gingras and Vaive.

The Nordiques, like their WHA brethren, were given a rude welcome to the NHL. Coach Jacques Demers had several veterans available to him in the team's first year, among them Marc Tardif, Réal Cloutier, Robbie Ftorek, Dale Hoganson, Gerry Hart and Serge Bernier, and the team was astute in its inaugural pass at the drafting table, picking up Michel Goulet as well as junior stalwarts Dale Hunter and Lee Norwood.

A more significant draft was that of Czech star Anton Stastny, although it seemed the big winger might never make it across the Atlantic because the powerhouses of Eastern Europe jealously protected their talent. Still, at season's end, none of the new teams had a winning record, with the Hartford Whalers finishing fourth in the Norris Division, the Nordiques fifth and last in the Adams and Edmonton and Winnipeg finishing fourth and fifth respectively in the Smythe Division. Both Edmonton and Hartford were swept 3–0 in their best-of-five division semifinals, although the Whalers cost the Canadiens a second shot at five straight championships when wing Pat Boutette

downed Guy Lafleur with a season-ending knee injury.

While Winnipeg plummeted in 1980, Hartford, Edmonton and Quebec all moved up and gave indications of future greatness. Quebec's success was the result of several factors, the hiring of a feisty coach from Quebec's junior league, Michel Bergeron, some judicious draft choices and a special scouting expedition to Europe by team president Marcel Aubut and chief scout Gilles Léger. With the suspense and secrecy of a spy thriller, the Nordiques braintrust spirited away 1979 draft choice Anton Stastny and netted a bigger prize, older brother Peter, from Czechoslovakia in the summer of 1980.

With the emergence of Jacques Richard (52 goals) and Goulet (32 goals), the arrival of Hunter (19 goals), young defensemen Mario Marois and Normand Rochefort and newly acquired goalie Daniel Bouchard, the Nordiques surged immediately. But, the biggest influence by far was the Stastny brothers: both scored 39 goals and Peter added 70 assists to finish his Calder Trophy-winning season with 109 points, good for sixth place in the scoring race. Anton's 85 points would have won the rookie award for him any other year but that one.

And while the Canadiens were being swept by Edmonton in their best-of-five preliminary round, Quebec forced Philadelphia to five games before succumbing. Most significant was the fact that the Nordiques were seen as a rising force, while Montreal apparently was floundering, both on the ice and in the front office. "The Battle of Quebec" emerged as a premier NHL match-up in 1981–82 for several reasons. First and foremost, the Canadiens and Nordiques found themselves in the same division, the Adams, which meant a full slate of games at the Forum and Le Colisee each winter. Each game was no-holds-barred, and the same could be said for their first postseason meeting in April 1982. The Canadiens had rebounded to claim first in the Adams with 118 points, 43 better than the fourth-place Nordiques, but all observers agreed that regular-season statistics would have little bearing on the playoffs.

The Canadiens handily defeated Quebec 5–1 in the series opener, but the Nords rebounded 3–2 in the second game at the Forum and returned to Quebec with home-ice advantage to bounce the Canadiens 2–1. With Montreal on the ropes, it was Quebec's turn to falter and Montreal silenced a boisterous Colisee crowd with a 6–2 walkover. Game five was the stuff of legend, with the Nordiques taking a 2–0 lead into the third period, even though they had been outplayed significantly by the home team. Mario Tremblay, a fiery wing who became famous for his confrontations with Nordiques coach Bergeron, pulled the Habs within one at 10:49, and then Robert Picard drew Montreal even 80 seconds later.

The teams were tied 2–2 after regulation play, although the Canadiens had swarmed the Quebec net. Early in overtime, Montreal attacked the Quebec zone and a shot was blocked by Goulet, bouncing into the neutral zone where Dale Hunter and linemate Cloutier sped away on a two-on-one rush. Defenseman Rod Langway broke up a pass deep in his zone and the puck skittered behind the Montreal net. Hunter picked it up, sped around the net and shot it towards Rick Wamsley in the Canadiens goal. Everything went into slow motion at that point. Wamsley was down and appeared to have the puck under a pad, while Langway and Brian Engblom kept away Quebec attackers. Suddenly, a deathly silence enveloped the Forum. Hunter was raising his stick in jubilation, the referee was skating casually toward the

goal and pointing at the puck inside the cage, and the Nordiques bench was emptying a blue-and-white tidal wave over Hunter and Cloutier. The inferiority complex was over … the ghosts of Joe Malone, Jean Beliveau and Guy Lafleur (who played in the game) were exorcised. From that point on, 11:06 p.m. on April 13, 1982, the teams would meet as equals. The Nordiques would go on to defeat Boston 4–3 in the Adams Division finals before being swept by the Islanders in the Wales Conference finals. Those accomplishments would fade into obscurity, but the special feeling of that winning goal against the Canadiens is still felt in the provincial capital, almost 20 years later.

The Canadiens and Nordiques would face off in 113 regular-season games between 1979 and 1995. The Canadiens won 62 of the encounters, losing 39 and playing to 12 ties. The teams would meet five times in the playoffs. The Canadiens eliminated Quebec on three occasions (twice going on to win the Stanley Cup), while the Nordiques got the best of the Canadiens on the two other occasions but never went on to win the NHL's top prize. Nords–Habs playoffs were fraught with drama, including the game six brawl that marred the Good Friday series finale (Montreal won 5–3) in 1984, Peter Stastny's overtime goal in game seven of the 1985 division finals and Montreal's seven-game victory in 1987. The series that may have hurt the Quebec franchise the most came in 1993. After missing the playoffs for five straight seasons, which enabled the Nordiques to stockpile an impressive inventory of draft choices, Quebec fought the Bruins and Canadiens tooth-and-nail in the Adams Division, finishing second with 104 points, five behind Boston and two ahead of Montreal.

Those five years had been torture for the Nordiques faithful, and they sought vindication when the Adams Division semifinals began. The only relief of sorts during the five-year power outage had been the return of Guy Lafleur to Quebec. "The Flower" had retired from Montreal during the 1984–85 season, despondent at his apparent waning talent. After sitting out three seasons, during which he was inducted into the Hockey Hall of Fame, Lafleur came back for a single season with the Rangers and coach Michel Bergeron, and then the two were reunited in Quebec the following season. Lafleur would play two seasons for Quebec, scoring 24 goals and 38 assists in 98 games before putting a proper close to his playing career.

Lining up for the Nordiques against Montreal in 1993 were the harvests of so many rich draft years: Joe Sakic (1987, #15), Valery Kamensky (1987, #129), Mats Sundin (1989, #1), Adam Foote (1989, #22) and Owen Nolan (1990, #1). Not in the lineup, however, was the biggest draft prize, Eric Lindros. Lindros had told the hockey world that he would not play in Quebec and he had publicly accused team president Marcel Aubut of purposely losing games to guarantee the team's high draft position. The Nordiques drafted Lindros anyway, and both sides became involved in a year-long soap opera, with Lindros steadfastly refusing to sign, playing in the Canada Cup for Team Canada before returning to junior hockey. The Nordiques just as adamantly would not trade the superstar-in-waiting. The matter finally came to a head at the 1992 Entry Draft when Aubut entertained offers from all comers and eventually decided on a five-player package plus cash, offered by the New York Rangers.

At this point, Philadelphia vice president Jay Snider loudly complained that his team's offer had been verbally accepted by the Nordiques, and he would take his con-

tention to the league. Independent arbitrator Larry Bertuzzi, a Toronto-based lawyer, was appointed and he eventually ruled in favor of Philadelphia, and while that decision may have been embarrassing to the Nordiques president, the decision would definitely help the team. Coming to Quebec were forwards Peter Forsberg, Chris Simon and Mike Ricci, defensemen Kerry Huffman and Steve Duchesne, goalie Ron Hextall, draft choices in 1993 (Jocelyn Thibault) and 1994 (traded) and $15 million cash.

All but Huffman and Thibault were in the Quebec lineup against Montreal in 1993, as were other solid players such as Czech Martin Rucinsky and Russian Andrei Kovalenko, and the Nordiques immediately jumped into a 2–0 series lead with 3–2 (overtime) and 4–1 wins. The teams were stark contrasts. Quebec's lineup was chock-full of flashy European and North American talent, while Montreal's workmanlike team was led by "almost" superstars Kirk Muller, Brian Bellows and Vincent Damphousse, good young defensemen Mathieu Schneider, Patrick Brisebois and Eric Desjardins, and the world's best goalie, Quebec City native Patrick Roy.

Montreal got back into the series with a 2–1 overtime win on a Denis Savard goal and then evened things with a 3–2 victory at the Forum. The game which eventually took Quebec out of the series took place at Le Colisee, a 5–4 win by Montreal on Kirk Muller's overtime goal through Ron Hextall's legs as the Nordiques puckstopper desperately tried to cut across his net. Little could any of the Nordiques faithful suspect that Montreal's second overtime triumph would be a small step in what would turn out to be a 10-game overtime win streak that would bring the Canadiens their 24th Stanley Cup title. Two nights later, the aroused Habs thumped the dispirited Nords 6–2 at the Forum and the season was over. It was the last playoff meeting between the teams.

While the Nordiques players were struggling on the ice in the 1993–94 season, dropping to fifth place in the Adams and out of the playoffs, a similar uphill battle was being waged off the ice by their president. Marcel Aubut, who represented a consortium of owners of the team, had taken his case to his community, his city government and the provincial government.

The Nordiques were victims of the 1990s disease in sports, an outdated facility and too few revenue streams, and the only cure would be a state-of-the-art new building, with control of concessions and parking and tax breaks. The war of words was waged for two years, and the spirits and hopes of Quebec fans were raised in 1994–95 when the team under new coach Marc Crawford soared to the top of the Adams Division in a lockout-shortened season. Mats Sundin had been moved to Toronto for veteran wing Wendel Clark and defenseman Sylvain Lefebvre, and the young goaltending tandem of Jocelyn Thibault and Stephane Fiset showed poise beyond their years.

And then the bad news came all at once. The Nordiques were swept aside in six games by the Rangers, and three levels of government said no. Quebec's last game was a 4–2 loss at Madison Square Garden on May 16.

Nine days later, the Nordiques ownership group signed an agreement in principle with COMSAT Entertainment Group to sell the team. Ironically, it was on Canada Day, July 1, 1995 that the Nordiques announced that they were moving to Colorado. The "Battle of Quebec" was stilled forever. Despite the move, the long-reaching shadow of the Forum and the Montreal Canadiens would touch the hockey team once again, albeit in a positive manner.

The team's new home, Denver, "the Mile High City," had a tenuous connection with professional hockey since 1950 when the Falcons of the United States League, coached by Rangers legend Bill Cook, played out of the Denver University Arena, folding after a single season. A half-hearted effort occurred eight years later when the Denver Mavericks of the International Hockey League managed to get in a half-season at the Denver Coliseum before their transfer to Minneapolis. The Toronto Maple Leafs then installed the Denver Invaders of the Western Hockey League for the 1963–64 season before moving the farm team to British Columbia. The Central Hockey League Denver Spurs followed in 1968 and remained in town until 1976, playing one season in the World Hockey Association.

In 1974, Kansas City and Washington received NHL franchises. The Scouts lasted two seasons in Kansas City before moving to Colorado and the new McNichols Arena as the Colorado Rockies. A succession of coaches including John Wilson and the colorful Don Cherry led the team, and talented young stars like Rob Ramage, Barry Beck, Wilf Paiement and Lanny McDonald plied their trade with the Rockies until the franchise was moved to New Jersey after the 1981–82 season. Denver attempted half-hearted efforts at pro hockey after that (the Colorado Flames of the CHL in 1982–83, the Colorado Rangers from 1986 to 1989) and a successful team eluded the city until the Grizzlies appeared in 1993. A strong entry in the "I", the Grizzlies captured the International Hockey League championship in their inaugural season and averaged 12,000 fans per game at McNichols. When the Avalanche came to town two years later, the Grizzlies franchise moved to Salt Lake City.

It is rare that a team in a new city is competitive, and unlike the case of the Scouts/Rockies, this time Denver was getting a serious Stanley Cup contender. The team became a threat during the season, thanks to the influence of the Montreal Canadiens. The first move was made October 3, 1995, when former Habs winger Claude Lemieux was acquired from New Jersey in a three-way deal involving Steve Thomas of Toronto and Wendel Clark. Lemieux had debuted with the Canadiens late in the 1985–86 season and scored 10 goals during the playoffs, including the overtime marker that eliminated Hartford in game seven of the division finals. Four months before joining Colorado, he led New Jersey to their first Stanley Cup with 13 goals and won the Conn Smythe Trophy as playoff MVP. Three weeks later, the Avalanche traded power forward Owen Nolan to San Jose to acquire the defensive quarterback they needed in Sandis Ozolinsh, but the team's biggest move still was two months away and came in the form of a Christmas present from Montreal.

On December 2, the surging Detroit Red Wings invaded the Forum and handed the Canadiens a stinging 11–1 loss. The home team never would be the same. Rookie coach Mario Tremblay left veteran Patrick Roy in the net for two periods, during which he allowed nine goals, and Roy blew up at the bench when he was finally pulled from the game. In front of a national television audience, Roy passed in front of his coach and walked up to team president Ron Corey, sitting at ice level just behind the bench. "This is my last game in Montreal," he told the executive, and then tossed a "do you understand?" look Tremblay's way as he passed by the coach again. For three days, speculation was rampant that Roy was moving to Colorado. First, Colorado g.m. Pierre Lacroix was his former agent, and second, the Avalanche were one of the few talent-rich teams that could

Colorado Avalanche Year-by-Year Record

Season	GP	W	L	T	GF	GA	Pts	Finish		Playoff Results
1979–80*	80	25	44	11	248	313	61	5th	Adams Div.	Out of Playoffs
1980–81*	80	30	32	18	314	318	78	4th	Adams Div.	Lost Prelim. Round
1981–82*	80	33	31	16	356	345	82	4th	Adams Div.	Lost Conf. Final
1982–83*	80	34	34	12	343	336	80	4th	Adams Div.	Lost Div. Semifinal
1983–84*	80	42	28	10	360	278	94	3rd	Adams Div.	Lost Div. Final
1984–85*	80	41	30	9	323	275	91	2nd	Adams Div.	Lost Conf. Final
1985–86*	80	43	31	6	330	289	92	1st	Adams Div.	Lost Div. Semifinal
1986–87*	80	31	39	10	267	276	72	4th	Adams Div.	Lost Div. Final
1987–88*	80	32	43	5	271	306	69	5th	Adams Div.	Out of Playoffs
1988–89*	80	27	46	7	269	342	61	5th	Adams Div.	Out of Playoffs
1989–90*	80	12	61	7	240	407	31	5th	Adams Div.	Out of Playoffs
1990–91*	80	16	50	14	236	354	46	5th	Adams Div.	Out of Playoffs
1991–92*	80	20	48	12	255	318	52	5th	Adams Div.	Out of Playoffs
1992–93*	84	47	27	10	351	300	104	2nd	Adams Div.	Lost Div. Semifinal
1993–94*	84	34	42	8	277	292	76	5th	Northeast Div.	Out of Playoffs
1994–95*	48	30	13	5	185	134	65	1st	Northeast Div.	Lost Conf. Quarterfinal
1995–96	82	47	25	10	326	240	104	1st	Pacific Div.	Won Stanley Cup
1996–97	82	49	24	9	277	205	107	1st	Pacific Div.	Lost Conf. Final
1997–98	82	39	26	17	231	205	95	1st	Pacific Div.	Lost Conf. Quarterfinal

* Quebec Nordiques

put together an attractive package for Montreal. On December 6, the deal was announced: Roy and Montreal captain Mike Keane were on the way to "the Mile High City" for goalie Jocelyn Thibault and forwards Andrei Kovalenko and Martin Rucinsky. Avalanche defenseman Uwe Krupp was driving around Denver when he heard the news and said to himself, "We've got a great chance to win the whole thing now."

On June 10, 1996, less than a year after acquiring an NHL franchise, Colorado won the Stanley Cup on a goal by Krupp in the third overtime period after a masterful post-season by Roy. While the Colorado sweep over the Florida Panthers in the finals was the stuff of champions, the real victory came in the conference finals when the Avalanche bested favored Detroit, a team that had won an NHL record 62 games during the regular season. More importantly, the Red Wings were the team that had embarrassed Roy in Montreal and scored a 7–0 win over the Avalanche when he had changed teams. The Colorado team that started the conference final in Detroit was a team on a mission. Mike Keane won the first game with an overtime goal and then his fellow trade-mate Roy shut down the Wings 3–0 in game two. The teams split the games in Denver, then Detroit won their first home game, 5–2 in game five, and appeared ready to take control. But total team effort before a delirious home crowd gave the Avalanche a 4–1 win and a pass to the finals.

After Uwe Krupp's goal sealed the championship 10 days later, television stations sent their cameras into the streets of Quebec City to see if the locals were celebrating "their" first Stanley Cup, even though it now resided 2,000 miles to the west. The provincial capital was quiet, although action picked up that summer when local boy Patrick Roy stopped in to show off the Cup to family and friends. Quebec finally had its Stanley Cup, if only for a few hours.

The Avalanche have remained at the top of their conference with Detroit since 1996, although the team has not returned to the Stanley Cup finals. The nucleus of talent remains...Sakic, Forsberg, Roy, Ozolinsh, Kamensky,

Lemieux and Deadmarsh, but players such as Keane and Fiset have since moved on. After a bitter defeat to Edmonton in the first round of the 1998 playoffs, (a series Colorado led 3–1), Marc Crawford declined an offer of a contract extension and left the team. He was replaced by Bob Hartley, coach of the Avalanche's minor-league team at Hershey in the American Hockey League. During the season there had been a lot of talk about dissension and lack of focus in the dressing room.

Colorado is still a force to be reckoned with in the NHL's Western Conference, but how good a team it will continue to be is being questioned. A bit reminiscent of the Quebec days in the late 1980s, the Avalanche went into the 1998 Entry Draft with six of the first 52 picks. Moreover, the Ascent Entertainment Group (formerly COMSAT), will open the brand-new Pepsi Center in downtown Denver in 1999. It will seat 18,100 for hockey and feature 95 luxury suites and 1,850 executive club seats. It appears that this is one Denver hockey team that will be around for a while.

COLUMBUS BLUE JACKETS

COLUMBUS, OHIO OFFICIALLY BECAME a National Hockey League city on June 25, 1997 when the National Hockey League announced plans to place new franchises in Nashville, Atlanta, Minnesota and Columbus. Columbus and Minnesota will be the last of the four new expansion teams to take to the ice, entering the league for the 2000–2001 season.

By then, the NHL will be a 30-team circuit with three divisions of five teams making up both the Eastern and Western conferences. Columbus will play in the Central Division of the Western Conference with the Chicago Blackhawks, Detroit Red Wings, Nashville Predators and St. Louis Blues.

Principal owner of the NHL's Columbus franchise is John H. McConnell, who announced the selection of the team name Blue Jackets on November 11, 1997. "We wanted a name that reflected the spirit and pride that exists in Columbus," McConnell said. "The Blue Jacket [an insect] is aggressive, industrious, multi-tasked, resourceful and fast—many of the qualities exemplified by our community." The name was selected after a name-the-team contest which drew over 14,000 entries and thousands of different suggestions.

The primary Blue Jackets logo depicts a determined bug with plenty of attitude. "Stinger," complete with wings, antennae and clenched teeth, is outfitted with a blue coat featuring stars on the collar and a cap that are reminiscent of the American Civil War. The outfit is a tribute to the state of Ohio's rich historical heritage.

The Blue Jackets have started the process of putting some sting in their on-ice activities as well, hiring former Florida Panthers head coach Doug MacLean as the franchise's first general manager.

DALLAS STARS AND MINNESOTA NORTH STARS

Stan Fischler

WITH MORE THAN 15,000 LAKES that freeze over in the long, cold winters, hockey just seems to come naturally to Minnesota. With the exception of the Canadian provinces, no similar region produces as many hockey players, nor is the game played as much per square mile, as in Minnesota. So when the NHL decided to expand to 12 teams in 1967, it was arguably a foregone conclusion that somehow it would be included.

To bid for a franchise in 1967 (and to compete in the NHL), Minnesota had to produce a suitable arena. This requirement was fulfilled in less than a year when the splendid Metropolitan Sports Center in Bloomington was completed just prior to the start of the 1967–68 season. And with such eminent sportsmen as Gordon Ritz, Walter Bush, W. John Driscoll, Robert McNulty, Robert Ridder and Harry McNeely, Jr. on the North Stars' board to back the new entry, success was virtually guaranteed. Wren Blair, a veteran hockey organizer and the man who discovered superstar Bobby Orr, was named coach and general manager and the building of the North Stars was under way. The first game of the season was held at Bloomington on October 21, 1967, and the score was Minnesota North Stars 3, California Seals 1.

The young franchise was was dealt a stunning blow with the death of 29-year-old Bill Masterton in the early morning hours of January 15, 1968, two days after he sustained a brain injury in a game against Oakland. "Because he had the habit of giving everything he had for every second he was on the ice, Bill was the type of player who didn't have to score a lot of goals to help a club," said Wren Blair. Soon after the 1967–68 season, the NHL inaugurated a memorial award, the Bill Masterton Trophy, to be given to the player who most fit the description "unsung hero." Claude Provost of the Montreal Canadiens was the first winner.

The North Stars finished fourth in the West Division and reached the NHL playoffs in their rookie season. They eliminated the Los Angeles Kings in a rugged seven-game first-round series, fighting back from 2–0 and 3–2 deficits. Milan Marcetta won the sixth game with an overtime goal and then the Stars routed the Kings in Los Angeles 9–4. In the semifinals, Minnesota went up against the St. Louis Blues and carried the foe to seven games before losing 2–1 in double overtime.

In their second season, the North Stars finished in sixth place and out of the playoffs, but a complete house-cleaning by Blair turned things around and Minnesota moved up to third in 1969–70. Still, there was something missing, a stabilizing factor behind the bench to relieve Blair and provide the North Stars with the coaching guidance necessary for bigger wins. Blair finally found his man in Jack Gordon in 1970 and also infused the playing roster with significant names: defenseman Ted Harris, a hardrock ex-Canadien who became the team captain, veterans Doug Mohns and Lorne "Gump" Worsley and youngsters Jude Drouin and Barry Gibbs. Despite a fourth-place finish in 1970–71, the North Stars played mightily in the Stanley Cup competition, defeating the heavily favored St. Louis Blues in the first round.

Every young franchise requires a significant series to make it respectable. For the North Stars, it happened in April 1971 in a series with the fabled Montreal Canadiens. Conspicuous underdogs, the North Stars lost the series in six games, but not before giving the Montrealers considerable consternation. The Montrealers were impressed: "None of us realized that the North Stars were that good," said Peter Mahovlich of the Canadiens.

The Minnesotans obtained another measure of glory in the 1971–72 season, challenging Chicago for first place in the West before settling for a strong second-place position. Their eventual defeat by the Blues in the seventh game of the opening Cup round has gone down as a Stanley Cup classic and it enhanced the North Stars' appeal both at home and on the road.

Computations revealed that the North Stars' average attendance was 11,800 fans in their first NHL season, in a rink with a seating capacity of 15,095. By the third season the average had jumped to 14,351, and in the 1971–72 season it was next to impossible to find an empty seat in the building at any time. One reason for the club's popularity was its cast of characters.

It is doubtful that any NHL team ever boasted two such competent yet contrasting goaltenders as the Mutt and Jeff combination of Gump Worsley and Cesare Maniago. Worsley was short and round and tended his goal without the benefit of a protective face mask; tall and lean, Maniago wore a white mask with huge openings around the eyes that was suggestive of a World War I gas mask. Another marquee player was big, blond right winger Bill Goldsworthy. During 78 games in the 1971–72 season, he scored 31 goals and 31 assists for a team-leading 62 points, and did so with a flair and a shuffle that endeared him to rooters at the Metropolitan Sports Center. Adding to Goldsworthy's appeal was a post-scoring routine. Every one of his goals at home was accompanied by a shuffling little jig on the ice.

As the years went by, Minnesotans eventually found themselves with a winning team or two. After missing all but five games of the 1971–72 campaign, center Dennis Hextall played his first full season with Minnesota in 1972–73 and tallied 30 goals and 52 assists to lead the team in scoring. All-stars Barry Gibbs and J.P. Parise also contributed to a third-place finish in the West Division, but the Stars were defeated in the opening round of the playoffs by Philadelphia.

The next five seasons were disappointing, as the North Stars were transformed from the team that had so bravely spooked Montreal to an also-ran. Despite another fine season from Hextall and 20 goals from Goldsworthy in 1973–74, the Stars finished with a dreadful 23–38–17 record—dead last in the division and out of the playoffs. And the NHL's realignment in 1974–75 made no difference; they still finished out of the playoffs in the new Smythe Division. The 1975–76 season was not without its bright spots. Bill Hogaboam and Tim Young had breakout seasons, tying for the team lead in scoring with 51 points, and Goldsworthy popped in 24 goals. Still the team maintained its cellar-dweller status with a 20–53–7 record.

The 1976–77 season offered some hope that the North Stars might get over losing, as Young once again led the team in scoring with 95 points. Roland Eriksson (Minnesota's first Swedish import) added some always needed scoring punch to an improving team that managed to finish second in the Smythe despite a mediocre 23–39–18 record, and the second-place finish also meant that the Stars were back in the playoffs for the first time in four seasons. But whatever high hopes fans could have for

another gallant run reminiscent of the early 1970s was extinguished by the powerful Buffalo Sabres after just two games of the first round. The Sabres swept the best-of-three series 4–2 and 7–1.

Furthermore, the promise of 1976–77 was short-lived and the Stars' fall back to the bottom of the NHL pack was swift and disconcerting. They managed 18 wins and nine ties—and a whopping 53 losses. Eriksson and Young were once more the minority bright spots as they finished 1–2 respectively in team scoring; rookie defenseman Per-Olov Brasar also provided some spark.

Things looked bleak for the financially struggling North Stars until an unprecedented merger with another cash-strapped franchise breathed some life into their roster.

Since their inception in 1967, the Minnesota franchise had been owned by a group of investors led by team president Gordon Ritz. With the team fighting for its fiscal life, Ritz and company looked to cut their losses and sell to new investors, who, it so happened, were already owners of another struggling NHL franchise. Brothers George and Gordon Gund had also been suffering heavy monetary losses since they purchased the former Oakland Seals and moved them to Cleveland in 1976.

The Gunds knew it would be economic suicide to manage two losing hockey clubs at once. The solution? The two franchises merged and the Gunds assumed ownership of the Minnesota club while Cleveland folded. More significantly, all the players who had a contract with Cleveland were transferred to Minnesota and the 1978–79 North Stars hit the ice with eight former Cleveland Barons. Right winger Al MacAdam (who finished second in team scoring that season) and goaltender Gilles Meloche (who would start in Minnesota) proved to be the best of a bunch.

The most promising newcomer of 1978-79 was a talented young center by the name of Bobby Smith, who burst on the scene in Minnesota with 30 goals and 44 assists for 74 points in his first NHL season. Smith's production earned him the team lead in scoring and the Calder Trophy as the NHL's rookie of the year.

These new players left the North Stars much improved and by 1981 they were demonstrating their proficiency by advancing to the Stanley Cup finals against the defending champion New York Islanders.

The North Stars had the misfortune to meet an ascendant Islanders team in the final. Badly outgunned, they played gamely and averted a sweep with a 4–2 win in game four at home. The Islanders would clinch their second consecutive Cup title in with a 5–1 win in game five.

After a 94-point finish to lead the Norris Division in 1981–82, the Stars entered the playoffs with reason to believe that it might be the year they would finally sip from Lord Stanley's Cup. Bobby Smith's dependable scoring was abetted by two young phenoms that the team was developing, center Neal Broten (a Minnesota native) and right winger Dino Ciccarelli. Minnesota finished in first place and drew the Chicago Black Hawks in an opening-round playoff matchup. The Stars were shocked at home in the first two games of the series but responded. They blew out the Hawks in game three at Chicago. Still, they had gotten in over their heads by falling behind 2–0 in the series and were eliminated by a score of 5–2 in game four.

Again led by Broten, Smith and Ciccarelli, the Stars had another successful season in 1982–83, finishing a strong second in the Norris Division and setting a franchise record with 40 wins. They disposed of Toronto in four games in the first playoff round and again faced the Chicago Black Hawks. The result was another disappointment; the Stars won only game three.

Bobby Smith was traded to Montreal just 10 games into the 1983–84 season, but still the Stars regained the Norris Division title. Helping to fill the void created by Smith's absence were winger Brian Bellows, who contributed 44 goals, and defenseman Brad Maxwell, who notched 54 assists and accumulated 225 penalty minutes. In the first round of the playoffs, the Stars faced and defeated their nemesis from Chicago in a tough five-game series. The second-round series against the St. Louis Blues also went the distance, with Minnesota prevailing at 6:00 of overtime in game seven on a goal by Steve Payne. But the powerhouse Edmonton Oilers steamrollered the Stars with a fast four-game sweep in the Campbell Conference finals.

The North Stars' loss seemed to affect them next year. Despite finishing 18 games under .500, they earned a playoff berth, albeit against the first-place Blues. Most were anticipating a quick series. And indeed it was—but it was Minnesota that blindsided St. Louis with a sweep in the best-of-five first round. Keith Acton, who had been acquired from Montreal in the Bobby Smith trade, scored two game-winners in the series. The Stars were brought back down to earth in round two by—who else?—the Chicago Black Hawks.

The 1985–86 season was something of a bounce-back year. Broten bumped his numbers over 100 points for the first time in his career, Ciccarelli was back with 44 goals, a career year from left winger Scott Bjugstad yielded another 43 tallies, and Bellows popped in 31 more. The Stars finished in second and met St. Louis in the first round. The Blues, however, avenged the previous year's shocking defeat by turning the tables on the Stars and beating them three games to two. It would be the last playoff hockey the Stars would see action in for a while. Injuries cut short Broten's next two seasons, and despite the continued efforts of Ciccarelli and Bellows, the team finished out of the playoffs in 1986–87 and 1987–88.

Thanks to a pair of key trades, the North Stars found themselves back in the pack for the playoffs of 1989, two of the most significant components of their return having been forwards Dave Gagner and Mike Gartner, both new additions to the team. Gagner, who had been acquired from the New York Rangers in 1987, came out of nowhere to lead the Stars in scoring in 1988–89 with 78 points. Gartner, on the other hand, was already an established star in Washington when Minnesota traded for him in March of 1989. The price? Minnesota gave up fan-favorite Dino Ciccarelli to the Capitals, hoping that Gartner would be able to boost the Stars to an elusive Cup win. Also coming into prominence with the North Stars that year was goaltender Jon Casey, who took over as a full-time starter. Led by this new corps of would-be heroes—and, of course, Broten and Bellows—the Stars locked up third place in the Norris Division. They were again matched up against St. Louis in round one, and yet again the Blues were victorious, downing the North Stars in five games. Making matters worse, the Gartner gamble didn't pay off; he went scoreless in the series and the Stars traded him to the Rangers for Ulf Dahlen next season.

In 1990, Minnesota fans got their first glimpse of the man who would ultimately become their team's biggest star. Speedy center Mike Modano scored 29 goals and 46 assists for 75 points in his rookie campaign, earning him kudos as

the rookie of the year as chosen by *The Hockey News*.

Meanwhile, Bellows banged home an impressive 55 goals that season and Broten's playmaking was as good as ever. But once again an old nemesis was there to ground the Stars: Chicago ousted them in the first round of a hard-fought seven-game series.

But 1990 was tumultuous in other ways for the Stars. Owners George and Gordon Gund threatened to move the team elsewhere (San Jose) if they didn't find a buyer who would pay $50 million. At the 11th hour Howard Baldwin and Norm Green pulled together the resources and purchased the team. The Gunds were granted an NHL expansion franchise for San Jose and reached an agreement that saw them retain a portion of the players on the Minnesota reserve list. The new San Jose team—later called the Sharks—would select players from the Minnesota system at a dispersal draft after the 1990-91 season.

The old regime, headed by general manager Jack Ferreira and coach Pierre Page, was replaced by a new one featuring former Flyers captain Bob Clarke as g.m. and ex-Montreal hero Bob Gainey as coach.

The 1990–91 season began ominously enough for the North Stars, as they managed only one win in their first nine contests and endured a decidedly non-stellar opening three months before finally catching fire towards the end of January and carrying it through to mid-March.

Brian Propp, who had starred throughout the 1980s with Philadelphia, contributed 73 points and Bellows, Broten, Modano and Gagner all scored over 60. Bobby Smith, reacquired from Montreal prior to the season, also contributed. A late-season slump almost dropped them out of fourth place, but they managed to hang on and get to the playoffs.

What followed can only be described as a miracle run. Minnesota—a fourth-place team that had finished 12 games under .500—defeated their traditional playoff foes in the next three rounds. First it was a 4–2 series win over Norris Division champs Chicago, then a 4–2 win over St. Louis in round two. Goalie Jon Casey was nothing short of phenomenal in the opening rounds, outplaying rookie of the year counterpart Ed Belfour in round one and shutting down the deadly one-two punch of 86-goal scorer Brett Hull and super-playmaker Adam Oates in round two.

The Stars then went up against a completely revamped Edmonton Oilers in the Campbell Conference finals. Minnesota hadn't won in Edmonton in more than 11 years, but needed only five games to win the Campbell Conference championship.

The Stanley Cup finals pitted two surprise American teams: the Mario Lemieux-led Pittsburgh Penguins, playoff participants only once in the previous eight years, and Minnesota, a team that had finished the regular season with the sixth-worst record in the 21-team NHL. The teams split the first two games before Minnesota took the third 3–1. Jon Casey held the Penguins in check while Lemieux sat out the match with recurring back spasms but when he returned to the lineup in time for game four and the Penguins' offense kicked into high gear. Behind Super Mario, the Pens took control of the series with a pair of victories, 5–3 and 6–4. And with a three-games-to-two advantage, the Penguins went for the jugular in game six. Veteran Joey Mullen, whose career had been given up for dead earlier in the year, proved his worth by scoring two clutch goals in the early going. Lemieux stole the show with four points, and Pittsburgh embarrassed the shell-shocked Stars 8–0 to annex their first of two consecutive Stanley Cup championships.

The trip to the finals proved to be Minnesota's own final flirtation with a Stanley Cup title. Players who had peaked in that special spring of 1991 started losing their glow. Owner Norman Green's stewardship of the club had become ensnared with financial and legal problems and the North Stars followed up their gallant run by finishing in fourth place in the Norris Division in 1991–92 before losing to Detroit in seven games in the first playoff round. As if to add to the troubles, the Met Center itself, once a jewel among ice rinks, suddenly became an also-ran among arenas when the Target Center opened in downtown Minneapolis, and arrangements to move the North Stars from Bloomington's suburbs to the inner city failed while the team lost any hope of another championship run.

The dispersal draft to stock the new San Jose franchise was held on May 30, 1991. As per prior agreement the Sharks claimed four players from the Stars' NHL roster and 10 from their farm system. Going to San Jose from Minnesota were fan favorites like enforcer Shane Churla and goaltender Brian Hayward. Because they had staked the Sharks to a good portion of their new roster, the North Stars were allowed to select players from other NHL clubs in the 1991 Expansion Draft . They used this opportunity to grab veterans such as Kelly Kisio (who was actually later traded to San Jose when the Stars reclaimed Churla) and Charlie Huddy.

In 1992, changes were also taking place in the front office. Bob Clarke had moved on to run one of the NHL's new expansion teams, the Florida Panthers. That left Gainey to take on the role of general manager while retaining his slot as head coach. And despite Gainey's competence and Hall of Fame status, the Stars finished out of the playoffs in 1992–93.

Minnesota lost its NHL franchise in 1993. The North Stars were transferred to Dallas and became the first Texas-based team in the league. The word "North" was erased from the name. Thus truncated, the Dallas Stars' home games would be played at the 16,924-seat Reunion Arena, which had been home to the NBA Mavericks. Before the season began the Stars made one more drastic change, sending goalie Jon Casey to Boston for Andy Moog to complete an earlier deal.

In 1993–94—the Stars' first Texas season—the Stars acquired a new following en route to a 42–29–13 record and and third place in the Central Division. Behind the play of backup goalie Darcy Wakaluk, the Stars swept St. Louis in the first round of the playoffs, but neither Wakaluk nor Moog could fend off the Vancouver Canucks and the Stars fell in the second round four games to one.

In the lockout-shortened 1994–95 season, Dallas showed signs of weakness, finishing with a 17–23–8 record, fifth in the Central Division and barely making the postseason, where a five-game loss to Detroit predicated more major shakeups.

Norman Green sold the club to media mogul Tom Hicks in December 1995, but despite the infusion of cash and new blood, the Stars gave a harsh welcome to their new bosses when they finished with a 26–42–14 mark and didn't qualify for the 1995–96 postseason. On January 8, 1996, Gainey formally stepped down as coach to concentrate on his g.m. duties and brought Ken Hitchcock in to replace him. Hitchcock was coaching the Stars' International Hockey League affiliate in Kalamazoo when he got the call.

The addition of Hitchcock and dependable veterans like Guy Carbonneau and Joe Nieuwendyk couldn't help the Stars in what was ultimately a lost season—but they did lay the groundwork for a dramatic franchise turnaround. Dallas

finished 1996–97 with a handsome 48–26–8 mark and 104 points and won the Central Division crown with a 38-point jump from the previous season. Now an early round favorite, the Stars were upset in seven games by a red-hot Curtis Joseph in net for the Edmonton Oilers.

Taking much of the blame for the crushing upset was Moog, who was not re-signed by the Stars. For a new goaltender, Gainey looked no further than Ed "the Eagle" Belfour, who had been traded by Chicago to San Jose and had no intentions of re-signing with the struggling Sharks. Gainey also signed free-agent defenseman Shawn Chambers, late of the 1995 New Jersey Cup-winning team. Later in the season, Dallas also obtained forwards Mike Keane and Brian Skrudland from the Rangers. Both had prior experience as captains with the Canadiens and Panthers respectively, and both had played on Stanley Cup champions, Keane with Colorado and Skrudland with Montreal.

In a neck-and-neck race with the Devils and Red Wings for the best overall points record in 1997-98, the Stars won the Presidents' Trophy with 109 points (49–22–11) before taking a more determined run at the Stanley Cup. The road to the top wasn't easy, though. The Stars battled injuries during the entire season and at one time or another were missing such potent offensive forces as Nieuwendyk, Selke Trophy winner Jere Lehtinen and superstar Mike Modano. Leading the way in spite of those potentially disastrous absences were defensemen Sergei Zubov and Derian Hatcher who also gave the Stars a potent power-play.

With Belfour playing some of the best hockey of his life, Dallas eliminated San Jose in six games in the first round before exacting revenge on the Oilers in a five-game second-round test that featured The Eagle winning all but one of the duels with Curtis Joseph. But more injuries, particularly to Nieuwendyk (who was hurt in the first game against San Jose) caught up with the Stars in the Western Conference final. The Red Wings defeated Dallas in six games and went on to capture their second straight Stanley Cup championship.

Dallas Stars Year-by-Year Record

Season	GP	W	L	T	GF	GA	Pts	Finish	Playoff Results
1967–68*	74	27	32	15	191	226	69	4th West Div.	Lost Semifinal
1968–69*	76	18	43	15	189	270	51	6th West Div.	Out of Playoffs
1969–70*	76	19	35	22	224	257	60	3rd West Div.	Lost Quarterfinal
1970–71*	78	28	34	16	191	223	72	4th West Div.	Lost Semifinal
1971–72*	78	37	29	12	212	191	86	2nd West Div.	Lost Quarterfinal
1972–73*	78	37	30	11	254	230	85	3rd West Div.	Lost Quarterfinal
1973–74*	78	23	38	17	235	275	63	7th West Div.	Out of Playoffs
1974–75*	80	23	50	7	221	341	53	4th Smythe Div.	Out of Playoffs
1975–76*	80	20	53	7	195	303	47	4th Smythe Div.	Out of Playoffs
1976–77*	80	23	39	18	240	310	64	2nd Smythe Div.	Lost Prelim. Round
1977–78*	80	18	53	9	218	325	45	5th Smythe Div.	Out of Playoffs
1978–79*	80	28	40	12	257	289	68	4th Adams Div.	Out Of Playoffs
1979–80*	80	36	28	16	311	253	88	3rd Adams Div.	Lost Semifinal
1980–81*	80	35	28	17	291	263	87	3rd Adams Div.	Lost Final
1981–82*	80	37	23	20	346	288	94	1st Norris Div.	Lost Div. Semifinal
1982–83*	80	40	24	16	321	290	96	2nd Norris Div.	Lost Div. Final
1983–84*	80	39	31	10	345	344	88	1st Norris Div.	Lost Conf. Final
1984–85*	80	25	43	12	268	321	62	4th Norris Div.	Lost Div. Final
1985–86*	80	38	33	9	327	305	85	2nd Norris Div.	Lost Div. Semifinal
1986–87*	80	30	40	10	296	314	70	5th Norris Div.	Out of Playoffs
1987–88*	80	19	48	13	242	349	51	5th Norris Div.	Out of Playoffs
1988–89*	80	27	37	16	258	278	70	3rd Norris Div.	Lost Div. Semifinal
1989–90*	80	36	40	4	284	291	76	4th Norris Div.	Lost Div. Semifinal
1990–91*	80	27	39	14	256	266	68	4th Norris Div.	Lost Final
1991–92*	80	32	42	6	246	278	70	4th Norris Div.	Lost Div. Semifinal
1992–93*	84	36	38	10	272	293	82	5th Norris Div.	Out of Playoffs
1993–94	84	42	29	13	286	265	97	3rd Central Div.	Lost Conf. Semifinal
1994–95	48	17	23	8	136	135	42	5th Central Div.	Lost Conf. Quarterfinal
1995–96	82	26	42	14	227	280	66	6th Central Div.	Out of Playoffs
1996–97	82	48	26	8	252	198	104	1st Central Div.	Lost Conf. Quarterfinal
1997–98	82	49	22	11	242	167	109	1st Central Div.	Lost Conf. Final

*Minnesota North Stars

DETROIT RED WINGS

Bob Duff

THE MOTOR CITY'S PASSION for the game is etched at center ice of Joe Louis Arena. Detroit is Hockeytown. Has been for more than three-quarters of a century. Perhaps its proximity to the border explains Detroit's love for Canada's game. Whatever the reason, tickets to Red Wings games are harder to locate than imported cars with Michigan plates.

As the most successful American-based franchise in National Hockey League history, only the Montreal Canadiens and Toronto Maple Leafs have won more Stanley Cup titles than the nine captured by the Red Wings. The Detroit franchise has been part of the NHL since 1926. American expansion by the NHL brought the Boston Bruins into the fold in 1924, with the Pittsburgh Pirates and the New York Americans joining the following year.

The success of these moves led to more U.S. cities clamoring for NHL hockey and the league had no fewer than 11 bids for NHL franchises from American-based groups at its 1926 spring meetings, including five from Detroit. As early as March of 1926 one of the groups made a bold attempt to acquire the rights to Edmonton's franchise in the Western Hockey League and move it to Detroit. "Detroit will have professional hockey, of that there is no doubt," said James Connors, a representative of the Detroit Hockey Club.

On May 15, a group that included former pro netminder Percy LeSueur was awarded the franchise and Charles King was named club president. Players were secured when the roster of the WHL's Victoria Cougars was purchased for $100,000. Art Duncan, who led the Pacific Coast Hockey Association in scoring with Vancouver in 1923–24, was signed and named player-manager.

On paper, it looked like Detroit had bought itself instant status as a contender. Victoria had won the Stanley Cup in 1925 and was the losing finalist in 1926. Among the players acquired were goaltender Happy Holmes, who had backstopped four teams to Stanley Cup victories, and Frank Fredrickson, Jack Walker and Frank Foyston, superstars of the western circuits.

But the Stanley Cup is won on the ice and the Detroit club, which kept the Cougars nickname, soon found the nucleus of its roster was past its prime and no longer had what it took to contend. Detroit played all of its home games in Windsor, making it the first professional franchise to have a foreign country as home base. A disappointing first campaign concluded with a 12–28–4 record and a last-place finish in the NHL's five-team American Division. Financially, the team was more than $80,000 in the hole after just one season.

There would be plenty of changes before the puck would drop again. The most significant came May 16, 1927 when the Cougars announced that Jack Adams had been signed as manager. A star player who had just helped Ottawa win the Stanley Cup, Adams was chosen after the owners failed to lure Lester Patrick, who had coached the Cougars in the WHL, away from the New York Rangers.

The Olympia, Detroit's new rink, which was supposed to open February 1, 1927, finally debuted on November 22, 1927. Johnny Sheppard scored for the Cougars, who lost 2–1 to the Stanley Cup champion Senators.

Tight-fisted, indecisive ownership would be the trademark of Detroit's early years. Detroit made the playoffs just twice in its first seven seasons, losing in the first round on

both occasions. The club tried changing players, changing sweaters and changing names, going from the Cougars to the Falcons in 1930, but where the Cougars hadn't roared, the Falcons couldn't soar.

Distraught during one of his team's many slumps, Adams concluded that it was because the Cougars had loaned back-up goalie Porky Levine to Seattle of the Pacific Coast League, thus leaving his club with only one goalie to shoot at during practice. Team officials would not allow him to sign another netminder, so Adams had a wooden effigy of Porky constructed and outfitted in goalie equipment, including skates. The Detroit players pushed their pine Porky into place in front of the net during practice and sometimes took it out for pregame warmups.

Carving goaltenders out of plywood was a fact of life for Adams until the summer of 1932, when grain millionaire James Norris purchased the Detroit franchise. Norris had been a member of the Montreal Amateur Athletic Association, a sporting club with cycling roots. The MAAA's teams were known by their club emblem and these Winged Wheelers were the first winners of the Stanley Cup in 1893. Norris decided that a version of their logo was perfect for a team playing in the Motor City and on October 5, 1932 the club was renamed the Red Wings.

The winged wheel was also suitable, because this was a franchise that was about to turn things around and take off. Adams had used his eye for talent to methodically assemble the basis of a decent club. He added defenseman Doug Young and forwards Herbie Lewis, John Sorrell and Larry Aurie from the minor leagues and acquired the rights to amateur Ebbie Goodfellow from the New York Americans.

Detroit reached the Stanley Cup semifinals the first season with Norris as owner and in 1933–34—bolstered by the midseason acquisition of goalie Wilf Cude on loan from the Montreal Canadiens—Detroit qualified for the Stanley Cup finals for the first time. Although the Red Wings lost the final to the Chicago, Black Hawks, excitement was finally gripping the hockey fans of Detroit. But just when everything seemed rosy, a large hole was cut in the lineup when Cude was recalled by the Habs.

Minus its goalie, Detroit fell out of the playoff picture again in 1934–35, but Adams was still looking ahead. He dispatched $50,000 and defenseman Teddy Graham to the St. Louis Eagles for forward Syd Howe and defenseman Ralph (Scotty) Bowman. Adams also acquired Normie Smith from the Eagles to fill the void in net. He converted Goodfellow, who had been the club's scoring leader, from forward to defense.

The final piece of the puzzle fell into place when Adams met with Boston coach Frank Patrick during the 1935 Cup finals in Montreal. "If I had Cooney Weiland, my club would be here," Patrick said of the Detroit winger. "If I had Marty Barry," responded Adams, referring to Boston's number one center, "we'd win the Cup." On August 12, 1935 the deal was consummated—Barry and Art Giroux to Detroit for Weiland and Walt Buswell.

Adams proved a prophet. With Barry playing between Lewis and Aurie on the club's top forward unit, the Wings soared to the top of the NHL standings in 1935–36. Under the playoff format of the day, the first-place finishers from the league's two divisions would meet in the first round of the playoffs, with the winner advancing to the final. That meant Detroit would open at Montreal against the defending champion Maroons on March 24.

The game was scoreless after 60 minutes and through five overtime periods neither goaltender—Smith or Montreal's Lorne Chabot—had faltered. At the 4:47 mark of the sixth overtime period, the game became the longest ever in NHL history, surpassing the 164:46 mark set by Boston and Toronto in 1933.

Late in the sixth overtime, winger Moderre (Mud) Bruneteau, recalled from the minors just two weeks earlier, came over the boards with Howe and Hec Kilrea. After Smith thwarted a Montreal rush, Kilrea broke down ice, Bruneteau at his side. He fed Bruneteau, who deked the sliding Chabot and ended hockey's longest game after 176:30.

Smith stopped 89 shots in the game, which ended at 2:25 a.m. on March 25. He also shut out the Maroons in game two and his shutout sequence of 248:32 remains a Stanley Cup record. After sweeping the Maroons, the Red Wings Detroit bounced the Toronto Maple Leafs in the final to win their first Stanley Cup title.

Detroit became the first American-based franchise to win back-to-back Stanley Cup championships when the Wings downed the New York Rangers in 1937, even though minor-league goalie Earl Robertson, filling in for an injured Smith, played the final series. Buoyed by Robertson's performance, Adams sold minor-league goalie Turk Broda to Toronto shortly after the playoffs. It was a move he would live to regret.

The 1937–38 season would play a large role in mapping out Adams' future plans. Sticking with the same nucleus, he watched as his two-time Cup champs slipped out of the playoffs. Afterwards, Adams developed a theory that championship-caliber squads had a shelf life of approximately five years—a theory he would continue to put into practice.

The war years saw Detroit play in three straight finals. The Wings lost in 1941, won in 1943 and gained infamy in 1942. Taking a 3–0 lead in the best-of-seven series, Detroit lost game four and its coach when Adams was suspended by the NHL after assaulting referee Mel Harwood. Amazingly, Toronto—behind the goaltending of Broda—won four straight, the only time a team has rallied from a 3–0 deficit to win a best-of-seven Stanley Cup final.

Goaltender John Mowers, defenseman Black Jack Stewart and center Syd Howe were Detroit stars of this era. In a club-record 15–0 win over the Rangers on January 23, 1944 Howe posted a hat trick to surpass Lewis (148) as Detroit's career goal-scoring leader. Eleven days later, also against the Rangers, Howe set another club mark, scoring six times in a lopsided 12–2 win. "I wonder what the boys in the shop will say now," pondered the soft-spoken Howe, who, like many U.S.-based NHLers during World War II, worked a day job at a war plant.

By now, the face of the NHL had changed—shrinking from 10 teams to a six-team loop. Sponsorship of amateur teams by NHL clubs was now being employed to develop future talent. The league allotted each club the rights to all players playing within a 50-mile radius of that NHL city. That was good news for Toronto and Montreal and even Detroit, which could grab players from Southwestern Ontario. It didn't do much good at all for Boston or New York, which might explain why the Maple Leafs, Canadiens and Red Wings were the only teams to win the Stanley Cup from 1942 to 1960.

Detroit reached the finals in 1945 and nearly turned the tables on Toronto. The Leafs won the first three games, Detroit the next three, but Toronto rallied to take the deciding contest. Even though his club had played in four

Stanley Cup finals in five seasons, Adams stuck to his five-year plan. Harry Lumley replaced Mowers in goal. A rugged winger named Ted Lindsay and a slick center named Sid Abel moved into the lineup.

If the NHL's modern era is designated by the advent of the red line in 1943, the golden era of the Detroit franchise is earmarked by the arrival of Gordie Howe in 1946. Labeled "the best prospect I've seen in 20 years," by Adams, Howe had a goal in his first NHL game against Toronto and two games later displayed his legendary mean streak for the first time, running Chicago goalie Paul Bibeault when he wandered from his net to play the puck.

Detroit finished first in 1948–49, starting a streak of seven consecutive first-place finishes—an NHL record. The Wings reached the finals in both 1947–48 and 1948–49, but both times were vanquished by their nemesis Broda and the Maple Leafs.

By this time, Howe was considered the NHL's most complete player and Detroit's Production Line of Lindsay, Abel and Howe finished 1–2–3 in NHL scoring in 1949–50. This time, Detroit got the better of Broda and the Leafs in the playoffs, even though they had to do so without Howe. Howe suffered a severe head injury—but not a fractured skull, as is often reported—in Detroit's first playoff game in Toronto when he tried to hit Toronto's Teeder Kennedy, but miscalculated and put himself head-first into the boards.

"I enjoyed my last three Stanley Cups," reflected Howe, a six-time Hart Trophy winner, who captured the first of four consecutive NHL scoring crowns in 1950–51. "I don't remember much about the first one." His other three wins would come in the next four seasons. Terry Sawchuk replaced Lumley in goal, and Red Kelly, veteran Bob Goldham and Marcel Pronovost, pilfered out of Quebec from right under the Canadiens' noses, anchored the defense. Classy forward Alex Delvecchio, who would play 24 seasons in Detroit, was also added to the mix.

Detroit beat the New York Rangers in the 1950 final and had wins over Montreal in the Cup final series of 1952, 1954 and 1955. In 1952, the Red Wings became the first team to sweep through the playoffs without a loss, going 8–0. Sawchuk, considered by many to be the greatest goaltender in the game, posted four shutouts.

Wins in 1950 and 1954 had come in more dramatic fashion—game seven overtime goals. Pete Babando (1950) and Tony Leswick (1954) were the scorers. Detroit also vanquished the Canadiens in a seven-game final in 1955, prompting *The Hockey News* to predict that Detroit was plotting "to imprison the Stanley Cup for all time." Ever the wheeler dealer, Adams went to work on another rebuilding project shortly after the 1955 Cup win. He made a nine-player deal with Chicago and an eight-player trade with Boston which sent Sawchuk to the Bruins.

This time, the moves backfired. "He definitely took the heart and character out of that team with those trades and he didn't get much in return," said Hall of Fame defenseman Pronovost. Adams took issue with Lindsay's attempts to organize a player's union in 1957 and shipped him and goalie Glenn Hall to Chicago. He dealt talented young forward John Bucyk to Boston to get Sawchuk back. By 1958–59, the once-mighty Wings were a last-place club. Adams was gone in 1962, retiring to take over as president of the Central Hockey League.

The Red Wings reached the finals again in 1961, 1963,

1964 and 1966, but each time came out a loser, blowing the 1966 series after winning the first two games in Montreal. From 1967 to 1986, Detroit would reach the playoffs just four times. "They just got rid of so much great talent," said Howe, who retired in 1971 as the NHL's all-time scoring leader, having worn the winged wheel for a quarter-century. He was selected to 21 NHL all-star teams in 26 seasons.

"They made bad trades, the people didn't come up through the system and they made more bad trades trying to fill the holes."

Another Detroit revival was launched in 1982, when Mike and Marian Ilitch purchased the club from the Norris family, installing Jim Devellano as general manager. Devellano picked center Steve Yzerman in the first round of the 1983 NHL draft and he remains the pillar of the franchise today.

Under coach Jacques Demers, workmanlike Detroit clubs reached the Stanley Cup semifinals in 1987 and 1988, reviving fan interest. But the best was yet to come. In the 1989 draft, the Wings raided Europe for defensemen Nicklas Lidstrom and Vladimir Konstantinov and forward Sergei Fedorov. All were playing key roles in Detroit by the early 1990s.

Scotty Bowman, the NHL's winningest coach, was hired in 1993. A year later, the club acquired veteran goalie Mike Vernon from Calgary and reached the Stanley Cup finals for the first time since the 1966 fiasco.

Although swept by New Jersey, the Wings rebounded to set an NHL record with 62 wins (62–13–7) in 1995–96. Bowman picked up legends Igor Larionov and Slava Fetisov to play with Fedorov, Konstantinov and Slava Kozlov as part of an all-Russian unit. Rugged winger Brendan Shanahan and skilled defender Larry Murphy came aboard and in 1997, and in a sweep of Philadelphia, returned the Stanley Cup to the Motor City for the first time in 42 years.

The euphoria was short lived. Konstantinov and team masseur Sergei Manatsakanov suffered life-threatening head injuries in an automobile accident just a week after the final game. Vernon, who won the Conn Smythe Trophy as the most valuable player in the playoffs, was dealt to San Jose, following in the tradition of Jack Adams who had dealt away Harry Lumley (1950) and Sawchuk (1955) shortly after they'd won Cup titles.

In 1997–98, the Red Wings finished behind the Dallas Stars and the New Jersey Devils with the third-best record overall. In the playoffs, Chris Osgood provided steady goaltending (and rebounding heroically from the occasional weak goal), the Red Wings won 16 games to match Konstantinov's jersey number 16, concluding the postseason on June 16th with a sweep of the Washington Capitals for their second straight Stanley Cup title. After he accepted the NHL's top prize, (and his first career NHL individual honor, the Conn Smythe Trophy as playoff MVP), captain Steve Yzerman placed the Stanley Cup in the lap of Sergei Konstantinov who had been brought onto the ice in his wheelchair.

As the NHL's most successful team in the 1990s, Detroit should continue to contend. Solid ownership and management and a raucous fan base ensure that this will continue. "Winning has always been a priority around here," Yzerman said.

Hockeytown wouldn't have it any other way.

Detroit Red Wings Year-by-Year Record

Season	GP	W	L	T	GF	GA	Pts	Finish		Playoff Results
1926–27***	44	12	28	4	76	105	28	5th	Amn. Div.	Out of Playoffs
1927–28	44	19	19	6	88	79	44	4th	Amn. Div.	Out of Playoffs
1928–29	44	19	16	9	72	63	47	3rd	Amn. Div.	Lost Quarterfinal
1929–30	44	14	24	6	117	133	34	4th	Amn. Div.	Out of Playoffs
1930–31**	44	16	21	7	102	105	39	4th	Amn. Div.	Out of Playoffs
1931–32	48	18	20	10	95	108	46	3rd	Amn. Div.	Lost Quarterfinal
1932–33*	48	25	15	8	111	93	58	2nd	Amn. Div.	Lost Semifinal
1933–34	48	24	14	10	113	98	58	1st	Amn. Div.	Lost Final
1934–35	48	19	22	7	127	114	45	4th	Amn. Div.	Out of Playoffs
1935–36	48	24	16	8	124	103	56	1st	Amn. Div.	Won Stanley Cup
1936–37	48	25	14	9	128	102	59	1st	Amn. Div.	Won Stanley Cup
1937–38	48	12	25	11	99	133	35	4th	Amn. Div.	Out of Playoffs
1938–39	48	18	24	6	107	128	42	5th		Lost Semifinal
1939–40	48	16	26	6	90	126	38	5th		Lost Semifinal
1940–41	48	21	16	11	112	102	53	3rd		Lost Final
1941–42	48	19	25	4	140	147	42	5th		Lost Final
1942–43	50	25	14	11	169	124	61	1st		Won Stanley Cup
1943–44	50	26	18	6	214	177	58	2nd		Lost Semifinal
1944–45	50	31	14	5	218	161	67	2nd		Lost Final
1945–46	50	20	20	10	146	159	50	4th		Lost Semifinal
1946–47	60	22	27	11	190	193	55	4th		Lost Semifinal
1947–48	60	30	18	12	187	148	72	2nd		Lost Final
1948–49	60	34	19	7	195	145	75	1st		Lost Final
1949–50	70	37	19	14	229	164	88	1st		Won Stanley Cup
1950–51	70	44	13	13	236	139	101	1st		Lost Semifinal
1951–52	70	44	14	12	215	133	100	1st		Won Stanley Cup
1952–53	70	36	16	18	222	133	90	1st		Lost Semifinal
1953–54	70	37	19	14	191	132	88	1st		Won Stanley Cup
1954–55	70	42	17	11	204	134	95	1st		Won Stanley Cup
1955–56	70	30	24	16	183	148	76	2nd		Lost Final
1956–57	70	38	20	12	198	157	88	1st		Lost Semifinal
1957–58	70	29	29	12	176	207	70	3rd		Lost Semifinal
1958–59	70	25	37	8	167	218	58	6th		Out of Playoffs
1959–60	70	26	29	15	186	197	67	4th		Lost Semifinal
1960–61	70	25	29	16	195	215	66	4th		Lost Final
1961–62	70	23	33	14	184	219	60	5th		Out of Playoffs
1962–63	70	32	25	13	200	194	77	4th		Lost Final
1963–64	70	30	29	11	191	204	71	4th		Lost Final
1964–65	70	40	23	7	224	175	87	1st		Lost Semifinal
1965–66	70	31	27	12	221	194	74	4th		Lost Final
1966–67	70	27	39	4	212	241	58	5th		Out of Playoffs
1967–68	74	27	35	12	245	257	66	6th	East Div.	Out of Playoffs
1968–69	76	33	31	12	239	221	78	5th	East Div.	Out of Playoffs
1969–70	76	40	21	15	246	199	95	3rd	East Div.	Lost Quarterfinal
1970–71	78	22	45	11	209	308	55	7th	East Div.	Out of Playoffs
1971–72	78	33	35	10	261	262	76	5th	East Div.	Out of Playoffs
1972–73	78	37	29	12	265	243	86	5th	East Div.	Out of Playoffs
1973–74	78	29	39	10	255	319	68	6th	East Div.	Out of Playoffs
1974–75	80	23	45	12	259	335	58	4th	Norris Div.	Out of Playoffs
1975–76	80	26	44	10	226	300	62	4th	Norris Div.	Out of Playoffs
1976–77	80	16	55	9	183	309	41	5th	Norris Div.	Out of Playoffs
1977–78	80	32	34	14	252	266	78	2nd	Norris Div.	Lost Quarterfinal
1978–79	80	23	41	16	252	295	62	5th	Norris Div.	Out of Playoffs
1979–80	80	26	43	11	268	306	63	5th	Norris Div.	Out of Playoffs
1980–81	80	19	43	18	252	339	56	5th	Norris Div.	Out of Playoffs
1981–82	80	21	47	12	270	351	54	6th	Norris Div.	Out of Playoffs
1982–83	80	21	44	15	263	344	57	5th	Norris Div.	Out of Playoffs
1983–84	80	31	42	7	298	323	69	3rd	Norris Div.	Lost Div. Semifinal
1984–85	80	27	41	12	313	357	66	3rd	Norris Div.	Lost Div. Semifinal
1985–86	80	17	57	6	266	415	40	5th	Norris Div.	Out of Playoffs
1986–87	80	34	36	10	260	274	78	2nd	Norris Div.	Lost Conf. Final
1987–88	80	41	28	11	322	269	93	1st	Norris Div.	Lost Conf. Final
1988–89	80	34	34	12	313	316	80	1st	Norris Div.	Lost Div. Semifinal
1989–90	80	28	38	14	288	323	70	5th	Norris Div.	Out of Playoffs
1990–91	80	34	38	8	273	298	76	3rd	Norris Div.	Lost Div. Semifinal
1991–92	80	43	25	12	320	256	98	1st	Norris Div.	Lost Div. Final
1992–93	84	47	28	9	369	280	103	2nd	Norris Div.	Lost Div. Semifinal
1993–94	84	46	30	8	356	275	100	1st	Central Div.	Lost Conf. Quarterfinal
1994–95	48	33	11	4	180	117	70	1st	Central Div.	Lost Final
1995–96	82	62	13	7	325	181	131	1st	Central Div.	Lost Conf. Final
1996–97	82	38	26	18	253	197	94	2nd	Central Div.	Won Stanley Cup
1997–98	82	44	23	15	250	196	103	2nd	Central Div.	Won Stanley Cup

* Team name changed to Red Wings. ** Team name changed to Falcons. *** Team named Cougars.

EDMONTON OILERS

Brian McFarlane

AN NHL TEAM WITH A GLORIOUS PAST found itself facing an uncertain future in the spring of 1998. The Edmonton Oilers were up for sale. Local sportsmen were scrambling around, talking to bank managers, financial wizards and potential investors, attempting to raise millions of dollars in time to meet a Friday, March 13 deadline. Their goal was to save the team and keep it in Edmonton. (Les Alexander, owner of the Houston Rockets of the NBA, had offered to purchase the team, but there were fears he would move the club to Texas.)

A bizarre twist to the story occurred early in March when a New York businessman, citing a mysterious Swiss backer, claimed he would raise $100 million to keep the Oilers in Edmonton. His impressive financial credentials soon proved to be false. On Friday March 13, 1998, a local ownership group of 17 investors did rescue the franchise by announcing the decision to purchase. The sale was approved by the NHL on April 27. It was just another chapter in the colorful history of the Edmonton Oilers which dates back to the early 1970s.

In 1971, two entrepreneurs from California, Gary Davidson and Dennis Murphy, both of whom had been involved in the formation of the American Basketball Association, decided to incorporate a new professional hockey league and call it the World Hockey Association. They boldly announced they would compete for consumer dollars with the NHL.

Despite predictions by NHL moguls that "a rival league will never get off the ground or on the ice," the WHA opened for business during the 1972–73 season as a 12-team circuit with an Eastern and Western Division. The Alberta Oilers, with Bill Hunter as spokesman, Ray Kinasewich as coach, and Jim Harrison as the new league's early scoring leader, were in the Western Division. The Oilers were named for the province because initially the franchise was to split its games between Calgary and Edmonton. This idea was abandoned before the WHA opened for business.

In mid-February 1973, Bill Hunter took over as coach of the Oilers, replacing Kinasewich. The Oilers finished tied for fourth place with Minnesota and an extra game was needed to decide a playoff berth. Minnesota beat the Oilers 4–2.

In 1973–74, the team name was changed to Edmonton Oilers. For the second straight year the club finished with a record of 38–37–3 but this year the Oilers moved up a notch to third place. Jim Harrison played so well that Winnipeg owner Ben Hatskin compared him to his own superstar—Bobby Hull. Minnesota eliminated Edmonton in five games in the playoffs.

In 1974–75, Jacques Plante joined the Oilers but suffered a broken hand early in the season. Bill Hunter claimed the new arena to house his Oilers was "the finest hockey building in Canada." Prior to the 1975–76 season, center Norm Ullman, on the eve of his 40th birthday, signed with the Oilers and soon scored his 500th career goal. By midseason, coach Clare Drake's job was in jeopardy and in February Drake was replaced by general manager Bill Hunter. The Oilers finished in fourth place in the WHA's Canadian Division and were ousted by Winnipeg in the playoffs.

In 1976–77, the Oilers again finished in fourth place and failed to advance to the Avco Cup finals which were between Winnipeg and Quebec. The Nordiques would win the series in six games.

Prior to the 1977–78 season, six WHA cities—Edmonton, Quebec, Hartford, Winnipeg, Houston and Cincinnati—were told they would be welcomed into the NHL fold—for $2.9 million apiece. But at a subsequent

meeting, Leaf owner Harold Ballard persuaded some of the NHL governors to kill any merger plans. The war between the two leagues continued. The Oilers could not decide whether to continue operating or fold. Two weeks before the season opener two schedules were in place, one including the Oilers and one without. New owner Peter Pocklington was said to be trying to buy the NHL's Colorado Rockies. Meanwhile, the Oilers decided to play another season in the WHA and finished in fifth place in the revamped eight-team league. The Oilers were eliminated in the playoffs by New England, whose most famous player, Gordie Howe, became a grandfather during the series.

In 1978 the Edmonton Oilers dropped a bombshell on the world of hockey by announcing the acquisition of teenage sensation Wayne Gretzky from the Indianapolis Racers. The announced price for Gretzky, Eddie Mio and Peter Driscoll was $850,000. Racer fans were furious, and later, when the team folded, season ticket holders demand their money back. Gretzky, meanwhile, moved to Edmonton and signed a 21-year personal services contract with Peter Pocklington, the longest player agreement in hockey history, and one said to be worth between $4 and $5 million. The pact was signed at center ice before 12,000 fans on January 26, 1979, Gretzky's 18th birthday.

The NHL, by a vote of 14–3, agreed to accept four WHA clubs into its fold for the 1979–80 season. Edmonton was one of them. Cost of entry was $6 million. During the final WHA season of 1978–79 the Oilers led all clubs with 48 wins and 98 points. Gretzky was third in league scoring with 46 goals and 110 points. The Oilers were upset by the Winnipeg Jets in the final series for the Avco Cup and fans wondered if Wayne Gretzky would find life in the NHL more difficult than in the defunct WHA.

Edmonton and Winnipeg were placed in the Smythe Division of the NHL in 1979–80. The Oilers used one of their two Expansion Draft priority selections to retain Wayne Gretzky. In the annual NHL Entry Draft, Glen Sather selected teenager Mark Messier who had jumped from Tier II junior hockey to the Cincinnati Stingers of the WHA the previous season. On February 15, 1980 Wayne Gretzky tied Billy Taylor's NHL mark of seven assists in a game. Gretzky set a scoring record for first-year players with 137 points but was declared ineligible for the Calder Trophy or any first-year records because of his WHA service. Gretzky's 137 points tied the Kings' Marcel Dionne atop the NHL scoring list but Dionne won the Art Ross Trophy, by virtue of having scored 53 goals to Gretzky's 51. The Oilers finished the season in fourth place in their division but were swept aside by Philadelphia in the first round of the playoffs.

Bryan Watson was behind the Oiler bench for the 1980–81 season but was fired after just 18 games and Glen Sather replaced him. In the annual Canadian Press poll, Wayne Gretzky was selected as Canada's male athlete of the year. Gretzky finished the 1980–81 season with a league-record 164 points and the highest points-per-game average in NHL history—2.05. He surpassed Bill Cowley's mark of 1.97 set in 36 games in 1943–44. Gretzky established five other scoring records and reached the 300-career-point mark faster than any other player. In a major playoff upset, the 14th place Oilers stunned the third place Montreal Canadiens, eliminating the Habs in three straight games. "I guess we've come of age," chuckled rookie defenseman Paul Coffey. The Oilers then carried the New

York Islanders to six games before bowing out in the quarterfinals. Gretzky won both the Art Ross and Hart Trophies.

During the 1981–82 season, Wayne Gretzky signed a new contract calling for $20 million over the next 15 years which made him the NHL's highest paid player. Gretzky tied Phil Esposito's record of 76 goals in a single season and did it in 15 fewer games. His year-end accomplishments include a record number of goals (92), assists (120) and points (212), and a margin of 65 more points than runner-up Mike Bossy, while Edmonton cruised to top spot in the Smythe Division. Oiler fans were then shocked when the lowly Los Angeles Kings eliminated the Oilers in the first round of the playoffs. The teams set a playoff record for goals in the opener, won by the Kings 10–8. Once again, Gretzky had won the Ross and Hart trophies, while his unanimous choice for the Hart was a hockey first.

Gretzky captured most of the headlines again in 1982–83, winning the scoring crown for the third straight season. The Oilers finished third overall with 106 points but they amassed a record number of goals—424—and Gretzky, Messier and Glenn Anderson all topped 100 points. The Oilers reached the Stanley Cup finals only to be ousted in four games by the Islanders.

On November 19, 1983, Wayne Gretzky called the New Jersey Devils "a Mickey Mouse operation" and issued an apology two days later. Overshadowed in 1983–84 by Gretzky's remarkable season of 87 goals, 118 assists and 205 points was Paul Coffey's production—40 goals, 86 assists and 126 points. The Oilers smashed their own record for goals in a season with 446. In the spring of 1984, the Oilers once again advanced to the Stanley Cup finals. This time they overpowered the Islanders, winning the Stanley Cup in five games. Peter Pocklington said: "No question. I can see we're going to keep the Cup in Edmonton."

Midway through the 1984–85 season, Wayne Gretzky attained 1,000 career points—the fastest of any player in NHL history. He achieved the plateau in a mere 423 games. In the playoffs, the speed and depth of the Oilers was too much for the Kings, the Jets and then the Black Hawks. On May 30, 1985 at Northlands Coliseum, the Oilers bounced the Philadelphia Flyers 8–3 in game five of the final series and captured their second Stanley Cup. Gretzky compiled a record 47 playoff points in 18 games, a feat not yet surpassed.

The 1985–86 season saw Gretzky collect an amazing 215 points, breaking his own record. His total of 163 assists was—by itself—more points than any other player had ever scored in a season. Paul Coffey, with 48 goals, broke Bobby Orr's record for most goals by a defenseman. Jari Kurri became the first European player to win the goal-scoring title with 68. The Oilers finished on top of the standings with 119 points but lost to Calgary in the playoffs when rookie defenseman Steve Smith's clearing attempt resulted in an accidental goal against the Oilers in game seven.

In 1986–87, Wayne Gretzky scored an early-season hat trick, the 38th of his career and a new NHL record. On November 22, he reached the 500-goal plateau in just 575 games, easily beating Mike Bossy's mark of 500 goals in 689 games. The Oilers finished on top of the overall standings with 106 points and advanced to the Stanley Cup finals against the Philadelphia Flyers. The Oilers won the series in seven games and celebrated their third Stanley Cup victory.

Prior to the 1987–88 season Paul Coffey announced: "It will be impossible for me to wear the Oiler jersey ever again." He was irate over remarks made by Peter

Pocklington that allegedly questioned the two-time Norris Trophy winner's courage. Coffey was traded to Pittsburgh in return for Craig Simpson and defenseman Chris Joseph. Gretzky scored a goal to tie Mike Bossy for fifth place in career goals (573) but on the play he injured a knee and missed 13 games.

Later, Gretzky passed Gordie Howe to become the National Hockey League's all-time assists leader. The Oilers slipped to second place behind Calgary in the Smythe Division but they managed to eliminate the Flames in four games in the division final. The Oilers moved on to oust the Detroit Red Wings in the conference final. In the Cup finals they easily defeated Boston in four games to win their fourth Cup title in five years. Gretzky won the Conn Smythe Trophy after compiling 43 playoff points.

But Mario Lemieux captured the Hart Trophy, ending Gretzky's eight-year reign as hockey's top player. Hockey's most publicized wedding took place in Edmonton on July 16, 1988 when Wayne Gretzky married Hollywood actress and dancer Janet Jones.

On August 9, 1988 news of the greatest trade in history rocked the hockey world as Wayne Gretzky was dealt to the Los Angeles Kings, along with Marty McSorley, Mike Krushelnyski and minor-leaguer John Miner in return for Jimmy Carson, Martin Gelinas, three first-round draft picks and the rights to minor-league defenseman Craig Redmond. The Oilers also received $15 million cash. In a survey of Canadian hockey fans, 48 percent of respondents named Gretzky as the top player of the past 50 years. The Oilers slid to third place in the Smythe Division behind Los Angeles and first-place Calgary. In the first round of the playoffs, the Oilers blew a 3–1 lead in games and lost to Gretzky and the Kings.

The 1989–90 season got under way with John Muckler behind the Oiler bench. On October 15, 1989 Wayne Gretzky returned to Edmonton as a visiting player with the Kings and scored the tying goal against Bill Ranford late in the game. The goal marked his 1,851st regular-season point and broke Gordie Howe's record of 1,850. That same week, Jimmy Carson (a 100-point scorer for the Oilers in 1988–89) announced his retirement from hockey because he "can't get mentally up for the games." Glen Sather suspended him, then traded him, along with Kevin McLelland to Detroit in return for Joe Murphy, Adam Graves, Petr Klima and defenseman Jeff Sharples. On February 28, a brawl between the Kings and the Oilers at the Great Western Forum resulted in a record 85 penalties and 356 minutes. The Oilers established a league record with 44 penalties.

In the playoffs, the Oilers fell behind the Jets 3–1 in games in the opening round, then roared back with three straight wins. They then eliminated the Kings in four games in the Division finals before ousting Chicago in six for the Campbell Conference title. In the finals, just 21 months after Peter Pocklington had traded Gretzky, the Oilers held the Stanley Cup for the fifth time in seven years. They defeated Boston in five games in the Cup finals and goalie Bill Ranford captured the Conn Smythe Trophy. At the victory celebration, Mark Messier said: "This one's for you, Gretz." Mark Messier was named winner of the Hart Trophy for 1989–90.

Prior to the 1990–91 season, Jari Kurri returned to Europe to play hockey. Goalie Grant Fuhr received a one-year suspension after admitting to past substance abuse. Later, Fuhr's suspension was reduced to 60 games. The Oilers won just two of their first 15 games and almost slid into the basement. Come the playoffs, the Oilers, with Fuhr in goal, ousted Calgary in seven games and the Kings in six. Mark Messier was severely hobbled by injuries in the Conference finals and the Oilers lost to the Minnesota North Stars in six games.

In 1991–92, Ted Green replaced John Muckler as coach. The Oilers traded Grant Fuhr, Glenn Anderson and Craig Berube to Toronto and in return obtained Vincent Damphousse, Luke Richardson and Peter Ing. Three weeks later, Mark Messier left the club, signing with the New York Rangers. In the playoffs, the Oilers upset the Los Angeles Kings in six games and then claimed the Division title with a come-from-behind victory over the Vancouver Canucks. But Chicago proved to be too powerful for Edmonton in the Conference finals and swept the series, giving the Blackhawks 11 consecutive playoff wins.

When the Oilers struggled through the 1992–93 season, Glen Sather traded leading scorer Bernie Nicholls to New Jersey in return for Todd Elik and Zdeno Ciger. For the first time since they entered the NHL the Oilers missed the playoffs, finishing 27 points behind fourth-place Winnipeg. Owner Peter Pocklington announced he'd move the Oilers to Hamilton if he didn't get a better lease arrangement. He later filed a letter with the league requesting permission to move the Oilers.

In 1993–94 the Oilers slipped to the bottom of the renamed Pacific Division with a 25–45–14 record. Rookie coach George Burnett took over in 1994–95 but was fired after 35 games following a dressing room confrontation with Shayne Corson. Glen Sather replaced Burnett with Ron Low. The Oilers finished just one point ahead of the expansion Mighty Ducks of Anaheim during the lockout-shortened 48-game season.

In 1995–96, the Oilers missed the playoffs for the fourth year in a row with a fifth-place finish in the Pacific Division and a record of 30–44–8. The good news was the purchase of a luxury box in the Coliseum by Curtis Joseph to be used by sick and disabled children. In September, 1996 NHL commissioner Gary Bettman announced that Oilers season ticket sales must rise from 6,800 to 13,000 for the team to qualify for the NHL's Canadian Assistance Plan. Oiler fans bought the tickets.

In 1996–97, the Oilers crept close to .500 hockey with a 36–37–9 record and a third-place finish in the Pacific Division behind Colorado and Anaheim. In the playoffs, Curtis Joseph starred as the Oilers ousted the Dallas Stars (second overall) in seven games. But the Oilers couldn't match the speed and scoring of the Avalanche in round two and fell 4–1 in games. Coach Ron Low was rewarded with a contract extension.

Led by Doug Weight, the Oilers qualified for the 1998 playoffs and proceeded to engineer another upset, defeating the Colorado Avalanche in seven games after trailing three games to one. Goaltender Curtis Joseph and strong team defense held the Avalanche to just one goal over the final three games of the series. Facing the Stars in the second round, Edmonton could not continue the Cinderella story and was dropped by Dallas in five games.

Edmonton Oilers Year-by-Year Record

Season	GP	W	L	T	GF	GA	Pts	Finish	Playoff Results
1979–80	80	28	39	13	301	322	69	4th Smythe Div.	Lost Prelim. Round
1980–81	80	29	35	16	328	327	74	4th Smythe Div.	Lost Quarterfinal
1981–82	80	48	17	15	417	295	111	1st Smythe Div.	Lost Div. Semifinal
1982–83	80	47	21	12	424	315	106	1st Smythe Div.	Lost Final
1983–84	80	57	18	5	446	314	119	1st Smythe Div.	Won Stanley Cup
1984–85	80	49	20	11	401	298	109	1st Smythe Div.	Won Stanley Cup
1985–86	80	56	17	7	426	310	119	1st Smythe Div.	Lost Div. Final
1986–87	80	50	24	6	372	284	106	1st Smythe Div.	Won Stanley Cup
1987–88	80	44	25	11	363	288	99	2nd Smythe Div.	Won Stanley Cup
1988–89	80	38	34	8	325	306	84	3rd Smythe Div.	Lost Div. Semifinal
1989–90	80	38	28	14	315	283	90	2nd Smythe Div.	Won Stanley Cup
1990–91	80	37	37	6	272	272	80	3rd Smythe Div.	Lost Conf. Final
1991–92	80	36	34	10	295	297	82	3rd Smythe Div.	Lost Conf. Final
1992–93	84	26	50	8	242	337	60	5th Smythe Div.	Out of Playoffs
1993–94	84	25	45	14	261	305	64	6th Pacific Div.	Out of Playoffs
1994–95	48	17	27	4	136	183	38	5th Pacific Div.	Out of Playoffs
1995–96	82	30	44	8	240	304	68	5th Pacific Div.	Out of Playoffs
1996–97	82	36	37	9	252	247	81	3rd Pacific Div.	Lost Conf. Semifinal
1997–98	82	35	37	10	215	224	80	3rd Pacific Div.	Lost Conf. Semifinal

FLORIDA PANTHERS

Stan Fischler

THE IDEA OF PLANTING professional ice hockey in the Sunshine State was not as far-fetched as it seemed when H. Wayne Huizenga originally launched his NHL project in November 1992. An Eastern Hockey League team once played in Jacksonville, and the World Hockey Association actually granted a franchise to the Miami Screaming Eagles when that league was launched in 1972. The Screaming Eagles had a pretty big problem—they had signed only one player, goalie Bernie Parent, and no others—and never got off the ground. So it wasn't until the NHL targeted Tampa Bay, along with Ottawa, as an expansion franchise that one could take Florida seriously as a big-league venue.

Huizenga, who spent his early years in Chicago, was part-owner of the Miami Dolphins and had also purchased the expansion Florida Marlins baseball team. As chairman of Blockbuster Entertainment, he had already established himself as a major player in merchandising, but he had no interest in hockey. A chance meeting with then NHL board chairman and Los Angeles Kings head Bruce McNall altered this view when McNall and NHL interim president Gil Stein informed Huizenga that Disney would soon be admitted to the league as owners of an Anaheim franchise and another nationally known company like Blockbuster would be welcome at the same time. Although Huizenga may have had doubts about including a major-league hockey team in his portfolio, he took the gamble and on December 10, 1992, NHL owners okayed both the Miami and Anaheim applications. The two new franchises would begin operations for the 1993–94 season, which meant there was precious little time to organize a general staff and no time to build a new rink for the team-to-be.

The second challenge was met when the Miami Arena, home to the NBA Heat, was made available to Huizenga as a temporary home until a state-of-the-art facility could be constructed. As for the high command, the key selection would be the team's general manager and the race narrowed to Washington Capitals general manager David Poile and Philadelphia Flyers senior vice president Bob Clarke, who was holding a largely ceremonial position on Broad Street. Clarke was hired on March 1, 1993, and then signed a chief scout, Dennis Patterson, and an Eastern scout, Ron Harris. Needing a president to oversee the operation, Huizenga opted for Bill Torrey, architect of the New York Islanders Stanley Cup dynasty of the early 1980s. As a nickname,

Huizenga settled on "Panthers," in part because the Florida panther had been designated the official state animal—even though there were less than 100 existing in the wild when the hockey club chose *felis concolo coryi* as its logo.

In contrast, coaches were not in the least an endangered species. Clarke had plenty to choose from before he selected bushy-haired Roger Neilson, who had directed the New York Rangers to their most productive record in a half-century in 1991–92 when they finished with 105 points. Neilson was later fired by the Rangers. "I needed a job, to be sure," said Neilson, "and when Bobby Clarke came along, I welcomed the offer; not only to work with him but also to help design a brand-new franchise."

When it came to stocking the team, Neilson was fortunate. The NHL created more favorable rules—better than those accorded Ottawa and Tampa Bay—for Miami and Anaheim, and the Panthers hit the ground running. With Torrey and Clarke masterminding the selections, Neilson already had a team image in mind. It would resemble other clubs he had handled going back to his junior years in Peterborough, Ontario. If at all possible, the Panthers would be a lunch-pail team which operated at its best in the corners and other areas which required toughness. Assistant coaches Craig Ramsey, Lindy Ruff and Tom Webster seconded the notion.

One by one, the Panthers' draft choices fit and filled out the mold. Brian Skrudland would become team captain and was renowned for his work ethic, as were players such as Bill Lindsay, Tom Fitzgerald, Mike Hough and Dave Lowry. Others such as Gord Murphy and Scott Mellanby were proven big leaguers who seemed good enough to have been retained by their previous teams.

Goaltending can make or break a club, and in that Neilson got a big break. Onetime Rangers hero John Vanbiesbrouck was made available and was promptly snapped up by the Panthers. The new club thus not only secured a seasoned and competent netminder but also one with character, determination and, most of all, pride. "Respect was uppermost on my mind when I came to Miami," said Vanbiesbrouck. "The new group of us were united in wanting to prove to the rest of the league—and one another—that we could play at a competitive level with the rest even though we were a new, expansion team."

Bill Torrey recalled how promising a young goalie named Mark Fitzpatrick had been on Long Island before he contracted a mysterious ailment. He convinced Clarke to select him. Now Florida boasted a pair of puckstoppers with considerable competence and big-league experience. Then, just for good measure, Torrey added longtime Long Island pal and Cup-winning goalie Bill Smith as a consultant to Vanbiesbrouck and Fitzpatrick.

Surrounding the veterans with first-rate young players was the next objective, which meant adroit scouting among the Canadian junior ranks. Clarke's prize selection was Rob Niedermayer, a big, highly touted forward and kid brother of New Jersey Devils ace defenseman Scott Niedermayer. Plucked fifth overall in the Entry Draft, Rob Niedermayer was believed to be ready to make the difficult jump to the NHL directly from amateur hockey.

The brand-new Panthers opened training camp on September 10, 1993, and kicked off their first season on October 6 against the Blackhawks at Chicago Stadium. Despite suggestions that the new club could not help but be overwhelmed by one of the "Original Six," the final score was 4–4. If anything, it was a portent of things to come; mostly that the Panthers would indeed have a bite.

Scott Mellanby, who scored the team's first goal (from Niedermayer and Evgeny Davydov), would emerge as one of the Panthers' premier scorers. Skrudland, who scored the fourth and final goal of the game for Florida, would become the quintessential captain. A loss to St. Louis in game two was followed by a match at Tampa Bay's ThunderDome viewed by an NHL record 27,227. Vanbiesbrouck registered a 2–0 shutout and Florida had posted its first NHL victory. The 1–1–1 record after three games would prove meaningful over the long haul because it demonstrated that the new club was competitive but perhaps not dominant.

More important than wins and losses, South Florida sports fans had instantly taken to the team. They jammed Miami Arena for the opening-night loss to Pittsburgh and continued to pack the downtown rink thereafter, encouraging Huizenga to think he had made the right move. It was now only a matter of time before a larger building would be erected for the club.

Likewise, week by week Clarke blueprinted changes to improve the on-ice product. Late in the autumn he dealt Randy Gilhen and a fourth-round draft selection to the Jets for forward Stu Barnes, who had been a disappointment in Winnipeg after being selected first (fourth overall) in the 1989 draft. In no time at all, Barnes blossomed into a top offensive threat, coinciding with the Panthers turning into league threats in their own modest way.

A good example was provided when 14,706 people showed up for a game with the Rangers on December 22, 1993, and set an attendance record for Miami Arena. Energized by Vanbiesbrouck's 33 saves, the Panthers emerged with a 3–2 win that sent ripples throughout the league. By now it was clear that Torrey, Clarke and Neilson had crafted a team that could challenge for a berth in the playoffs. Even when they lost, they stayed close. Suddenly, established clubs began viewing them with alarm.

Past the halfway mark and into the home stretch, the Panthers continued their push. At one point they were five games over .500 and appeared capable of knocking the Islanders out for the final playoff spot. But then the dreaded slump occurred and the Panthers plummeted. In the final week of the schedule, Florida lost to Quebec and on the following night the Islanders defeated Tampa Bay to squeeze into the playoffs. Ironically, New York visited Miami Arena for the last game of the regular season. Although the game was meaningless in the standings, a capacity crowd toasted the local heroes. Vanbiesbrouck responded by defeating the Islanders and stopping Zigmund Palffy on a penalty shot.

The first-year results were impressive. The Panthers won 33 games and finished with 83 points. Their .494 won-lost percentage was the best for a first-year team in modern pro sports history. What's more, the club's people skills created a love affair between South Floridians and the Panthers that would grow even stronger in seasons to come. However, the front office suffered a blow when Clarke returned to Philadelphia to run the Flyers organization. His replacement would be Bryan Murray, who had established a good reputation in both coaching (for Washington) and managing (for Detroit).

With first pick in the 1994 Entry Draft, the Panthers selected Ed Jovanovski, a rugged defenseman with the Windsor Spitfires. Murray also obtained productive veterans such as Ray Sheppard, but in a lockout-shortened 1994–95 season, the Panthers didn't begin play until January 21, 1995, when they opened at Nassau Coliseum. The 2–1 loss would set a tone for the rest of the season.

Once again it was a case of close-but-no-cigar as Neilson brought his club to the brink in the final days of the schedule but had to settle for another non-playoff year. Granted, the Panthers missed by only one point, but that fact rankled management and the scapegoat was Neilson. Doug MacLean was appointed coach on July 24, 1995. When they fired him, management claimed that Neilson's defense-first orientation had slowed the club's progress. Murray was convinced that Jovanovski, who had remained in junior hockey for an extra year, would vegetate under Neilson but flourish with MacLean, and indeed Jovanovski quickly ripened into one of the NHL's prize rookies. And while most of the Panthers revered Neilson, they adapted to MacLean, who was considerably more emotional. And louder.

Under Neilson, the Panthers were lacking something to set them apart from teams like the Senators, Mighty Ducks or Lightning. This would change in the second game of the season at Miami Arena. A few minutes before game time, a rat darted into the Panthers locker-room, heading straight for Scott Mellanby. The Florida forward took his stick and used the rat as a puck, slapping it so hard it catapulted across the room and off the wall—dead. An hour later, he paced the Panthers to a 4–3 win over Calgary, scoring two goals. Following the victory, several reporters approached Mellanby, who was being kidded by Vanbiesbrouck. The three-goal hat trick was replaced at Miami Arena by the two-goal "rat trick."

When the dailies reported the rodent assault a day later, a number of fans picked up on it. When Mellanby registered another hot night, his goals were greeted with a shower of plastic and rubber toy rats. "The shower of rats started slowly," Mellanby recalled, "and then it picked up momentum. Pretty soon they were throwing rats no matter who scored, and all of a sudden we had an identity."

Toy rats became ubiquitous not only at Miami Arena but in other parts of South Florida as well during the 1995–96 season. Ironic as it was, the Panthers acquired a rat as their mascot not by design but by public acclamation. And because the club was enjoying its best season yet, the population of ersatz rats increased as the wins multiplied and enthusiasm grew.

In a matter of weeks, Robert Svehla, Bill Lindsay, Stu Barnes, Radek Dvorak and Gord Murphy had become household names in the Sunshine State, and under MacLean's direction the Panthers had become a better team than they had been in their previous two seasons. After 50 games, the club boasted a 31–14–5 mark and ranked among the NHL elite. Although a slump followed, the Panthers managed to stumble to the finish line with enough points to earn a playoff berth.

They were not expected to advance beyond the opening playoff since their first-round foe was the Boston Bruins, then the league's hottest team. But a three-goal outburst in the first period of the Panthers' initial playoff game set a tone for the series. They stunned Boston with a four-games-to-one upset and followed that up with a daunting challenge in the Philadelphia Flyers.

Still the pattern continued. In the first game, the Panthers scored twice (Barnes and Lowry) and let Vanbiesbrouck handle the rest. The result was a 2–0 decision that sent tremors up and down the Spectrum. The series would not prove as easy as the opener with Boston, but Florida prevailed again, this time in six games. Game six was a persuasive 4–1 rout. Among the highlights was the neutraliz-

ing of Philadelphia behemoth Eric Lindros by Jovanovski in an arresting exchange of bodychecks.

Having disposed of the Broad Street Bullies, the Panthers engaged Mario Lemieux and the Pittsburgh Penguins in round three, the Eastern Conference finals. Their confidence at an all-time high, MacLean and Co. continued on a roll, winning 5–1 at the Igloo. The Penguins rebounded in game two and eventually moved to a three-games-to-two advantage. But Florida rallied to win game six 4–3 on a Niedermayer goal with 6:02 left in regulation time, setting the stage for game seven in Pittsburgh.

Again the main man for the Panthers was Vanbiesbrouck. He thwarted the best Lemieux had to offer in a throbbing match that was tied 1–1 early in the third period. Instead of faltering, the Panthers counterattacked and permanently took the lead within five minutes on an unlikely long shot by Tom Fitzgerald that somehow befuddled Penguins goalie Tom Barrasso. A third goal by Johan Garpenlov clinched the improbable 3–1 decision. In only its third year, the expansion club was headed for the Stanley Cup finals.

Facing the Panthers for the Cup were the transplanted Quebec Nordiques, now playing out of Denver as the Colorado Avalanche. The series lasted only four games, although Florida hung tough in games three and four—3–2 and 1–0 losses, respectively—before bowing out as the NHL's Cinderella team of the 1990s.

The fact that Florida went down in a sweep was deceptive. In game four, which went into three sudden-death overtime periods, the Panthers hurled 63 shots at Avalanche goalie Patrick Roy. Deadlocked at 0–0, the game lasted beyond 1 a.m. on a damp Miami morning before Uwe Krupp, the hulking Colorado defenseman, blasted a slapshot past Vanbiesbrouck at 4:31 of the sixth period of play.

Disheartened though they were, South Floridians had become dedicated to their club. Approval had already been given for construction of a new arena in the city of Sunrise, which would be home to the Panthers by the start of the 1998–99 season. In the meantime, the team continued filling Miami Arena through 1996–97 with a zestful brand of hockey that was good enough for a second straight playoff berth. Some players who had been fringe performers in the past, defenseman Paul Laus for one, ripened under MacLean's tutelage and became first-rate players, while others, like Jovanovski, regressed. Injuries were more prevalent and slowed progress after a fast start. Still, the heroic nucleus of Vanbiesbrouck, Fitzgerald, Murphy, Mellanby and Lowry provided enough grit to keep Florida competitive.

There was, however, an important hitch which would have long-term ramifications. Bryan Murray had concluded that his club needed more size up front and had his eye on Chris Wells, a 6'6", 223-pound left wing/center who had played 54 NHL games for Pittsburgh in 1995–96 with modest results. On November 19, 1996, Murray obtained Wells for Stu Barnes and Jason Woolley.

At 5'11" and 174 pounds, Barnes had been one of the NHL's smaller centers, but he had been productive and popular in Miami. Defenseman Woolley was less effective but still a worthwhile contributor to the Panthers chemistry. Together, they left a major gap in the dressing room as well as on the ice. In contrast, Wells scored only two goals in 47 games and was conspicuous by his inconspicuousness.

The Panthers finished with a playoff-worthy 89 points, only three less than than the previous season, when they had won the conference championship. Their 19 ties led the NHL and their optimism still prevailed as they entered the playoffs against Wayne Gretzky, Mark Messier and the rest of the New York Rangers.

For a brief moment it appeared that the 1996 playoff success would be repeated.

Vanbiesbrouck thwarted New York 3–0 in the opener at Miami Arena, but the Rangers rebounded by the same score in game two and then annexed both games at Madison Square Garden.

MacLean had observed that if his club could somehow win game five, it could reverse the process and win the series. But the best Florida could do was push the match into overtime before Esa Tikkanen beat Vanbiesbrouck and sent the Panthers packing earlier than they had expected.

Overall, two playoffs in two years was a major positive for the young franchise, which appeared on the rise—until its high command changed in the off-season. When Lindy Ruff resigned as assistant coach to become head coach of the Buffalo Sabres in 1997–98, the Panthers lost a valuable resource behind the bench who was never adequately replaced. Once the season began, the evidence suggested problems. Jovanovski's play continued to decline, Vanbiesbrouck could not hold the club together on his own, and a perilous slump produced a major shakeup in the front office.

Murray fired MacLean and assumed the coach's role while remaining the manager. (After the season he would hire his brother Terry who had previously been an NHL head coach in Washington and Philadelphia.) By late March 1998, the Panthers had lost 13 consecutive games. "The underdog team that charmed South Florida and reached the Stanley Cup Finals only two years ago is no more," commented *Miami Herald* columnist Greg Cote.

Florida was eliminated from playoff contention long before the season's end, leaving a bitter taste with fans. But if there was a sweet use of the adversity, it was the prospect that starting in October 1998, the still young franchise would play its home games at a spanking new rink in suburban Sunrise and perhaps go from there to renewed, greater glory.

Florida Panthers Year-by-Year Record

Season	GP	W	L	T	GF	GA	Pts	Finish		Playoff Results
1993–94	84	33	34	17	233	233	83	5th	Atlantic Div.	Out of Playoffs
1994–95	48	20	22	6	115	127	46	5th	Atlantic Div.	Out of Playoffs
1995–96	82	41	31	10	254	234	92	3rd	Atlantic Div.	Lost Final
1996–97	82	35	28	19	221	201	89	3rd	Atlantic Div.	Lost Conf. Quarterfinal
1997–98	82	24	43	15	203	256	63	6th	Atlantic Div.	Out of Playoffs

HAMILTON TIGERS

Eric Zweig

AFTER FOUR STRAIGHT LAST-PLACE SEASONS, the Hamilton Tigers finished atop the NHL standings in 1924–25. However, a postseason strike by the Tigers players cost Hamilton a chance at the Stanley Cup that year and ultimately cost the city its NHL franchise. The league has never returned to Canada's Steel City, but Hamilton's loss ultimately proved to be hockey's gain as the Tigers became the New York Americans and helped sell the sport in the United States at a time when the NHL was hoping to establish itself south of the border.

Hamilton's first attempt to attract an NHL franchise came during the league's inaugural season of 1917–18 when arena owners in the city offered to take in the Montreal Wanderers after fire destroyed the Montreal Arena on January 2, 1918. Wanderers' owner Sam Lichtenhein chose to withdraw his franchise instead and Hamilton would have to wait three more years before attracting another unwanted franchise. Amid rumors that a new league with teams in Toronto, Hamilton, and Cleveland was being organized by E.J. Livingstone (the former Toronto owner who had been frozen out when the NHL was created), the owners of the Abso-Pure Ice Company paid $5,000 for the NHL franchise in Quebec City and moved it to Hamilton.

Abso-Pure had recently built a new 3,800-seat artificial ice rink in Hamilton and was looking for a hockey team to fill it. Unfortunately, the Quebec club they purchased had recorded just four wins against 20 losses during the 1919–20 season. Former Quebec players Eddie Carpenter, George Carey, Tom McCarthy and goalie Howie Lockhart were signed by the Hamilton Tigers, but the NHL recognized that more than a new name was needed to attract fans in the new city so the Montreal Canadiens sent Billy Couture for Harry Mummery, while the Toronto St. Pats supplied the Tigers with Joe Matte, Goldie Prodgers, and Babe Dye (though they quickly recalled Dye and sent Mickey Roach to Hamilton instead).

Mickey Roach and Goldie Prodgers would be productive players for the Tigers for several years, but the team's only true star during the 1920–21 season was Joe Malone. The legendary Quebec star signed with the Tigers four games into the season and went on to rank fourth in the NHL with 30 goals and 34 points in 1920–21. Still, Hamilton finished last in both halves of the league's split schedule, going 3–7–0 and 3–11–0. Malone was fourth in the league again with 25 goals and 32 points in 1921–22, but the Tigers showed little improvement and finished dead last with a record of 7–17–0 in a season that saw the league's split schedule abandoned.

Percy Thompson had been hired by the Abso-Pure Ice Company in 1920 to coach and manage its hockey team, but gave up his coaching position after the 1921–22 season to concentrate on building the Hamilton team. Thompson made several astute moves heading into the 1922–23 season, although it would still take some time before his wheeling and dealing paid off. Thompson signed former Toronto St. Pats goalie Vernon "Jake" Forbes to replace "Holes" Lockhart and also inked Toronto Aura Lee amateur star Billy Burch to his first pro contract. His most controversial move was trading Joe Malone to the Montreal Canadiens for Bert Corbeau and Edmond Bouchard. This deal worked out to the Tigers' advantage as Malone scored

just one goal in 20 games in Montreal while Bouchard led the NHL with 12 assists. Mickey Roach, Cully Wilson, Goldie Prodgers and Bert Corbeau picked up the goal-scoring slack in Hamilton and, although the Tigers' total of 81 goals was actually their lowest in three seasons, it marked the first time they did not finish last in the league in scoring. Unfortunately coach Art Ross saw the team post a 6–18–0 record for yet another last-place finish. The Tigers "improved" to 9–15–0 in 1923–24 but still finished last under new coach Percy LeSueur. However, two newcomers to the Hamilton lineup that year would help make the difference in 1924–25.

Brothers Redvers and Wilfred Green (known as Red and Shorty) had been amateur stars in their hometown of Sudbury, Ontario. Shorty had been courted by NHL teams since 1920 and Thompson's acquisition of the Green brothers was seen as a major coup for Hamilton. The Greens were reported to have signed two-year deals worth $6,000 at a time when top NHL stars were only being paid about $1,500 per year. Red and Shorty were placed on a line with center Billy Burch in Hamilton and the three proved to be a perfect fit as Burch went on to score 16 goals in 1923–24, which tied him for third in the NHL. When Thompson signed ex-Sudbury stars Alex McKinnon and Charlie Langlois for the Tigers' defense in 1924–25, Hamilton was poised for a breakthrough.

In an era when a team's starting players still played almost the entire game, having the four long-time Sudbury teammates in Hamilton made a big difference to the Tigers' teamwork. As early as the first game of the new season (a 5–3 win over the Ottawa Senators on November 29, 1924), local sportswriter Paddy Jones predicted that "Hamilton puck-chasers will not be the official doormats, as they were in former seasons." Under coach Jimmy Gardiner, Percy Thompson's Tigers raced out to a 10–4–1 record by the season's mid-point, then held off the hard-charging Toronto St. Pats to finish in first place by one point with a record of 19–10–1. Shorty Green finished the season with 18 goals, while brother Red scored 19. Billy Burch topped the team with 20 goals (sixth-best in the league) and earned the Hart Trophy as the most valuable player as Hamilton went from worst to first. Jake Forbes established a career best with a 1.96 goals-against average, which trailed only George Vezina's 1.81.

When the NHL's 1924–25 regular season ended on March 9, 1925, the 10 Tigers players promptly informed Percy Thompson they would not take part in the playoffs unless each man received an additional $200. The dispute became public two days later as the St. Pats and the Montreal Canadiens began the semifinal series that was supposed to determine Hamilton's playoff opponent. Team captain Shorty Green informed the press that "professional hockey is a money-making affair. The promoters are in the game for what they can make out of it and the players wouldn't be in the game if they didn't look at matters in the same light. Why then should we be asked to play two games merely for the sake of sweetening the league's finances?"

The Hamilton players certainly had legitimate reasons to feel they were entitled to additional money from their bosses. First, the NHL had undergone significant changes prior to the 1924–25 campaign. Expanding for the first time, the NHL hoped to gain a foothold in the U.S. market. Montreal entrepreneur Thomas Duggan had been working since 1922 to establish teams in New York and Boston, but by the fall of 1924 Tex Rickard had not yet been convinced to include

ice-making facilities in his new Madison Square Garden (which was also experiencing construction delays). There would be no team in New York yet, but on October 12, 1924 it was reported that James Strachan and Donat Raymond would pay the NHL $15,000 to establish a second team (soon to be known as the Maroons) in Montreal. Charles Adams paid the league another $15,000 and formed the Boston Bruins. Both new teams were formally admitted to the league on November 1, 1924.

Second, NHL owners had decided to increase the length of the season from 24 to 30 games in 1924–25 and also to expand the playoffs. In the past, the top two teams in the four-team league had met in a two-game total-goals playoff to determine which NHL club would face the champions of the Pacific Coast Hockey Association and/or the Western Canada Hockey League for the Stanley Cup. This year, the NHL decided that the second- and third-place teams in the six-team league would meet in a semifinal series with the winner to play the first-place team to determine the league's Stanley Cup representative. In addition, the NHL announced that the profits from all four playoff games would be divided evenly among the six team owners with no money guaranteed to go to the players.

Third, the Hamilton owners had already turned a record profit due to the Tigers' first winning season, while the players had worked harder than ever under contracts signed for a 24-game schedule. The players had all reported to training camp earlier than ever, played six more games than in the past, and were now expected to play at least two more unpaid playoff games. Other teams had given raises to their players or had provided generous Christmas bonuses. Hamilton had not.

Not surprisingly, NHL president Frank Calder did not share the players' point of view. He stated that NHL contracts required players to make their services available from December 1 to March 31, regardless of the length of the season. (It is interesting to note, however, that the 1924–25 NHL season had actually begun on November 29). Calder told the Hamilton players they were in violation of their contracts and would be fined or suspended if they refused to play. The players stated they would quit the sport rather than be taken advantage of. Shorty Green met with Calder on March 13, 1925 during the final game of the Toronto–Montreal playoff series, but no compromise could be reached. The Tigers would not play if they did not each receive $200 and so Hamilton was disqualified from the NHL finals. The players were suspended and fined $200. A plan to have the fourth-place Ottawa Senators meet the victorious Canadiens had proved unpopular, so Montreal was simply declared league champions. However, the Canadiens proved no match for the Victoria Cougars of the Western Canada Hockey League, who became the last non-NHL team ever to win the Stanley Cup.

On April 17, 1925 the NHL announced it would place a team in New York for the 1925–26 season (a team would later be added in Pittsburgh as well). "Big Bill" Dwyer, New York's most-celebrated Prohibition bootlegger, would own the team and Tommy Gorman would operate it out of Tex Rickard's now-completed 18,000-seat Madison Square Garden. In order to assure a solid showing in the most important American market, Dwyer bought the Hamilton franchise and players from Percy Thompson and Abso-Pure for $75,000. The Hamilton owners were only too happy to sell, having become convinced the league had outgrown their 3,800-seat arena and knowing that their players had

stated publicly that they would never play for them again.

Now known as the New York Americans, the former Hamilton players all received raises, with Shorty Green's salary reportedly bumped from $3,000 to $5,000. Billy Burch signed a three-year deal said to be worth between $18,000 and $25,000. As a native of Yonkers, New York and the most recent winner of the Hart Trophy, Burch would be the Americans' biggest drawing card and was promoted as "the Babe Ruth of Hockey." However, before the former Hamilton players could suit up in New York there was the matter of their fines and suspensions. Frank Calder required every player to offer an apology and request readmission to the league in writing. After a series of letters in which most players began by maintaining that they had been right to strike, Calder finally received the apologies he wanted. As for the fines, it remains unclear as to whether they were paid by the players, Tommy Gorman, or at all.

The first-place Hamilton Tigers dropped to fifth as the New York Americans in 1925–26, but the team proved to be a financial success. Tex Rickard was inspired to acquire his own franchise for 1926–27, which became the New York Rangers. Further American expansion placed new teams in Chicago and Detroit. The success in New York also helped convince brothers Frank and Lester Patrick to disband the Western Hockey League, leaving the new 10-team NHL as the dominant organization in hockey.

Hamilton Tigers Year-by-Year Record

Season	GP	W	L	T	GF	GA	Pts	Finish	Playoff Results
1920–21	24	6	18	0	92	132	12	4th	Out of Playoffs
1921–22	24	7	17	0	88	105	14	4th	Out of Playoffs
1922–23	24	6	18	0	81	110	12	4th	Out of Playoffs
1923–24	24	9	15	0	63	68	18	4th	Out of Playoffs
1924–25	30	19	10	1	90	60	39	1st	Suspended

LOS ANGELES KINGS

Stan Fischler

LONG BEFORE CANADIAN-BORN ENTREPRENEUR Jack Kent Cooke determined that the City of Angels deserved major-league hockey, Los Angeles had been eyed as a potential NHL market. The optimism was based on minor-league hockey successes in Southern California both before and after World War II as well as the natural growth of the state.

At one time, the thriving Pacific Coast Hockey League (later the Western Hockey League) embraced teams in Los Angeles as well as nearby Hollywood. During the immediate postwar years, the PCHL's Hollywood Wolves were linked with the NHL's Toronto Maple Leafs. The Wolves' most significant contribution as a farm team was defenseman Bill Barilko, who would in time score the 1951 Stanley Cup-winning goal for Toronto against the Montreal Canadiens.

Despite the rapid growth of Southern California in the 1940s and 1950s, the NHL ignored the area for several reasons, not the least of which was the absence of a major-league arena in which to hold games. But by the early 1960s, Cooke recognized the potential for major-league hockey in the Los Angeles area and paid $2 million for an expansion franchise for the 1967–68 season when the NHL doubled in size from six to 12 teams. Asked where he proposed to play home games, Cooke replied, "I'm going to build the most beautiful arena in the world, and it will be ready sometime in the opening season." True to his word,

Cooke supervised construction of his "Fabulous Forum" in suburban Inglewood, and when the $20 million project was completed, reviews were more than positive. "It must be seen to be believed," commented Eric Hutton in Canada's *Maclean's* magazine, "and maybe not even then. It is the gaudiest sports palace this side of the heyday of the Colosseum of Ancient Rome, of which the Forum is, in fact, a modernized copy."

For his first coach, Cooke hired Leonard "Red" Kelly, the former Detroit Red Wings and Toronto Maple Leafs star. He also purchased the Springfield Indians of the American Hockey League in order to develop minor-leaguers for his organization. From the Expansion Draft of 1967, the newly named Los Angeles Kings came away with Terry Sawchuk, who at one time was regarded as the premier goaltender in the world. Now in his twilight years, Sawchuk was, at best, a question mark. There was no question about Cooke's direction. In addition to Kelly he surrounded himself with top personnel including Larry Regan, a former Leafs center, as general manager. Los Angeles finished its first season in the expansion West Division only one point out of first place, and Cooke was voted executive of the year by *The Hockey News*.

The Kings were fourth in the West during their sophomore year but managed to make it to the semifinals before folding. By this time the best-laid plans of Cooke had become damaged by fate and mismanagement. The Kings next missed the playoffs for four years straight as Cooke proved more a problem than a blessing. Because of his brash style, he angered key members of the NHL Board of Governors, none of whom would do him any favors in the draft, or anywhere else. In 1969, Kelly quit the club to coach in Pittsburgh, and in 1971–72 Regan was replaced by Fred Glover, who had been fired recently by the California Seals.

The result was the Kings' worst finish ever, a mere 49 points, 11 less than the sickly Seals. There were major changes the next year. Veteran center Bob Pulford retired to go behind the bench while the defense was boosted by ex-Canadien Terry Harper and former Black Hawk Gilles Marotte. Los Angeles returned to playoff competition in 1973–74, but lacked a marquee superstar to tantalize the demanding California fans. A dispute a couple of thousand miles away turned out to be the solution to the Kings' quest for a big-name player.

Marcel Dionne had been the captain and foremost scorer on the Detroit Red Wings. In 1974–75 he had his finest season as a Red Wing, amassing 47 goals and 74 assists for 121 points, placing him behind only Phil Esposito and Bobby Orr in the NHL scoring race.

Despite his productive campaign, Dionne still felt underappreciated in Detroit so once the season ended, Marcel's agent Alan Eagleson informed the Red Wings that Dionne would be taking his services elsewhere. And so the big question: who would sign Marcel for 1975–76?

Six teams were in the early running—the Kings, the Canadiens, the Blues, the Sabres, the Maple Leafs and the Edmonton Oilers (of the World Hockey Association). Dionne's demands were high, as were the Red Wings', who were entitled to compensation from the team that signed him. Ultimately, the Kings, whose owner Jack Kent Cooke had just acquired Kareem Abdul-Jabbar for his basketball Lakers, offered the most money.

The Kings won the bidding war, and surrendered veteran defenseman Terry Harper and rugged forward Dan Maloney to Detroit. Cooke signed Marcel to a five-year, $1.5 million pact. Although Dionne and Cooke were pleased, Kings' coach Bob Pulford unhappily muttered that the deal was not in the best interests of his club.

Under Pulford's disciplined defensive style, the Kings previously had enjoyed an extremely successful season. Los Angeles had the fourth best won-lost record in the league, and only the Stanley Cup champion Philadelphia Flyers allowed fewer goals. Terry Harper had been the captain of the squad and the leader on defense. Maloney, a muscular winger, could score some goals and tend to checking. In Dionne, the Kings were adding a free-wheeling player whose style appeared conspicuously out of place in the Kings system. Coach Bob Pulford worried that Dionne's style of play might disrupt his previously sound club, both on and off the ice.

Pulford explained the situation: "I told Marcel that he couldn't float around center ice here the way he had in Detroit. He should retreat into the defensive end and work with the defenseman to get the puck out. That type of discipline was new to him, and I knew it would take time for him to learn our system."

But Pulford added hopefully: "Dionne may have been the best power forward in the NHL at that time. There was no doubt he was a valuable addition to our club."

"The Little Beaver" was up to the new challenge in California. "Everything I did there in L.A. was important," he said. "The little things meant more—holding your man, just standing in front of him—things that the average person just doesn't notice. They never mattered in Detroit.

"There was so much more enthusiasm there and a much bigger challenge. I felt like I wanted to play every game.

"I wouldn't be doing just one job—scoring. I'd play more conservatively. Don't misunderstand me, I wouldn't change my style too much. I just wouldn't get caught up ice."

To make sure Dionne had the legs and wind to not get caught up ice, Pulford immediately assigned him to the "fat squad," thinking that his ever-present paunch was a bit bigger than usual. ("I've always had a big stomach for a little guy. I like to eat. I was a big hamburger man.") Pulford put Dionne through rigorous stop-and-go skating drills following practice each day

After a brief period of adjustment with his new team, Marcel settled down and scored 40 goals and 54 assists for 94 points. However, the Kings no longer were the stingy defensive team they had been the year before. They gave up more goals, and instead of battling Montreal for first place in the NHL's Norris Division, the club found itself far back of the leader.

Perhaps the toughest night of the entire 1975–76 season for Dionne occurred on his return to Detroit. The Dionne-less Red Wings had been having trouble selling tickets, but 14,500 fans turned out to "greet" the man who, as a Red Wing, had scored more points than any other player in the first four years of his career. (This mark would soon be eclipsed, first by Mike Bossy and then by Wayne Gretzky.) Dionne's "greeting" was a disheartening distillation of boos and taunts. Frustrated by the jeers and by the persistent checking of the Red Wings' pesky Denis Polonich, the usually mild-mannered Dionne took a swipe at Polonich with his stick. At another point, he took a stiff check that knocked him down and sprained his arm. But he remained in the game.

"Marcel showed a lot of guts," observed teammate Mike Corrigan. "He withstood a lot of abuse. He pushed himself on and showed us he wanted to win."

It was a tough adjustment for Dionne to adapt to the Kings' style, but he made the necessary changes and was ready for the 1976–77 season, playing both at center and right wing.

Dionne became a new man, scoring goals and setting up teammates unselfishly, while diligently attending to the less glamorous job on defense. He was the only player to stay close to the Canadiens' Guy Lafleur in the scoring race. Marcel finished the 1976–77 season with 53 goals and 69 assists, and, for a pleasant change, earned rave reviews for his positive attitude.

"He was the complete opposite of everything the Detroit people said he was," said former Kings general manager Jake Milford. "In our games in Los Angeles he never wanted to be picked a star of the game and I don't even think he ever worried about the scoring race. He had become that much of a team player."

Scotty Bowman, who was the Montreal Canadiens coach at the time, was equally enthusiastic about Dionne. "If anything, he was too unselfish," said Bowman. "It's not as if he was just a shooter. He could make plays and sometimes I thought he even preferred to make plays."

Milford believed that the move to right wing helped Marcel improve his defensive game. "He checked better on the wing," Milford explained, "because it was easier for him to pick up his winger. Marcel was also able to shoot more from the wing."

Unfortunately, Dionne's improvement failed to help the Kings cope with the powerful Canadiens in the 1977 Norris Division race. In the playoffs, the Kings again failed to get past the quarterfinal round, although they hung tough against the feisty Boston Bruins after losing the first three games, finally bowing out in six.

Dionne won the Lady Byng Trophy and was named to the First All-Star Team in 1976–77. He was a Second Team All-Star in 1978–79 and went on to his best season on 1979–80, leading the NHL in scoring with 53 goals and 84 assists for a career-high 137 points. He also was named a First Team All-Star and won the Lester Pearson Award as the NHL player of the year as selected by his fellow players.

A prime reason for Dionne's point surplus was the quality of his linemates. Until the 1979–80 season, left winger Charlie Simmer bounced between the minors and the NHL, making no significant impact. But in 1979–80 Simmer became Dionne's regular linemate and tallied a league-leading 56 goals in only 64 games.

Filling out the Triple Crown Line was big right winger Dave Taylor who had been drafted by the Kings in June 1975. Taylor was the 14th King chosen in the 15th round, 210th overall. Taylor's grit and artistry produced 37 goals and 53 assists over 61 games in 1979–80 and set the stage for his great leap forward. In 72 games a season later he produced 47 goals and 65 assists for 112 points.

Taylor, who would become general manager of the Kings after the 1996–97 season, emerged as one of the NHL's most appealing athletes. When he was in his early years in California, Dave battled and eventually licked a stuttering problem. Beloved by his teammates, he was recognized by the NHL in 1991 when he became the only player to win the King Clancy Trophy for outstanding community service and the Masterton Trophy for dedication to hockey in the same season. He also reached 1,000-point milestone in 1990-91.

In addition to the members of the Triple Crown Line, another King with extraordinary appeal was goalie Rogatien (Rogie) Vachon. He came to Los Angeles in 1971–72 after winning Stanley Cup championships with Montreal in 1968, 1969 and 1971. Almost minuscule between the pipes, Vachon emerged as a heroic figure to the audience at Inglewood and would become one of California's most popular athletes. "When you're my size," said Vachon, "you've got to be a stand-up kind of person. I take my bruises but I won't back down. Never."

Unquestionably, Vachon ranks as the most competent goaltender in Kings history and was especially effective in the 1976 playoffs. The Kings eliminated Atlanta two games to none and then faced a powerful Boston Bruins team. Despite a 4–0 drubbing in the opening match at Boston Garden, Los Angeles rebounded with a 3–2 overtime win on the road and extended the favorites to a seventh game before succumbing.

He remained with Los Angeles through the 1977–78 season, during which time the Kings earned regular berths in playoffs but never developed significant headway. Vachon was traded to Detroit for the 1978–79 campaign without being adequately replaced. In 1979–80, the Kings employed a goaltending triumvirate of Mario Lessard, Ron Grahame and Doug Keans and finished second before being wiped out in the first round by the eventual Stanley Cup champion New York Islanders. The highlight of the year was Dionne winning the NHL scoring title. He also led the league in shots on goal with 348.

Dionne notwithstanding, the Kings remained a club mired in mediocrity during the early 1980s. They missed the playoffs in 1982–83 and 1983–84 as well as 1985–86. But better days and nights were on the horizon when Bruce McNall became co-owner of the Kings during the 1986–87 season and was named club president in September 1987. With gifted youngsters such as Luc Robitaille and Steve Duchesne, the Kings were positioned for a leap forward if they could obtain a major scorer and leader. That would happen on August 9, 1988 when Wayne Gretzky was acquired by Los Angeles along with Marty McSorley and Mike Krushelnyski for Jimmy Carson, Martin Gelinas, three first-round draft picks over the next five years and $15 million.

The Gretzky era in Los Angeles produced unprecedented attention for the NHL as well as a few successful years for the Kings. The Great One still possessed enormous scoring skills and in 1992–93 actually orchestrated a march to the Stanley Cup finals, a first in Los Angeles hockey history. After defeating Montreal in game one, the Kings led the Canadiens late in game two when McSorley was penalized for carrying an illegal stick. The Habs capitalized on the power-play, sending the game into overtime. Montreal scored the winner and went on to capture the Cup. That launched the downfall of Gretzky in California and the Kings as a contender. They missed the playoffs in the next four seasons, during which Gretzky moved on to St. Louis and eventually New York, while McNall was imprisoned for fraud.

Although it wasn't readily apparent at the time, another turning point in the Kings history took place on July 25, 1989. On that date the team signed Hall of Fame defenseman Larry Robinson as a free agent. He anchored the Kings defense in 1989–90 and spent three seasons on the blue line for Los Angeles. He was the second-highest scoring defenseman on the Kings in 1989–90 with 39 points (seven goals and 32 assists) and helped the team to a first-place finish in the Smythe Division in 1990–91.

During these three years Robinson not only made an indelible imprint because of his playing ability but also because of his character. After his retirement, he was named assistant coach of the New Jersey Devils beginning in 1993–94. Working with coach Jacques Lemaire, Robinson helped turn the Devils into a contender and, in 1995, into a Stanley Cup champion. It was evident that he was head coaching material and on July 26, 1995 the Kings gave him the opportunity to prove himself.

Assuming command of a foundering ship, Robinson patiently put it on an even keel and by 1997–98 had turned the Kings into a playoff contender once more. Under his guidance, Los Angeles finished with a plus-.500 record for the first time since 1992–93 and earned a playoff berth.

Nothing underlined the value of Robinson's coaching ability more than the improvement he brought about in defenseman Rob Blake who had been named team captain prior to the 1996–97 campaign.

If Robinson was symbolic of one aspect of the franchises rebound, Blake was part of another. A fourth round pick in the 1988 Entry Draft, Blake joined the Kings at the end of the 1989–90 season and had one goal and three assists for four points in eight playoff games. In his first full-season as a King, Blake was named to the NHL's All-Rookie Team as he led all rookie defenseman in scoring with 12 goals and 34 assists for 46 points. He has paced Kings defenseman in scoring on three separate occasions (1992–93, 1993–94 and 1997–98).

Blake played in his first NHL All-Star Game at Madison Square Garden in 1994 and he picked up an assist in the game. He posted career highs in goals (20), assists (48) and points (68) in 1993–94. Blake would play only 30 games over the next two seasons with a host of injuries from a nagging groin to a torn ligament in his left knee kept him out of action. His spirited comeback was slow but in the end it was well worth the wait.

The addition of Robinson, Blake's childhood idol, pushed Rob to the next level as he as named the winner of the Norris Trophy after the 1997–98 season. Blake had finally arrived.

"It's just awesome for Rob to win it," said Robinson after Blake beat out Niklas Lidstrom of Detroit and Chris Pronger of St. Louis for the award. "I think it lifts a huge, huge load off his shoulders. … He had been so close [to winning before] but then he was was always hurt, so he never won it. Now he has and he's worked hard to get there. It's a great building block for him and for us as a team."

"It was really tough [dealing with the pressure of] being tagged as a potential winner so early in my career … but [that] helps make it so exciting, to finally win it and to be considered at that level. It's somewhere I want to get back to each year now."

Blake and Robinson were not the only elements in the renaissance. New g.m. Dave Taylor worked closely with Robinson, bringing in younger talent. Three 1997 deals had a major impact on the franchise, starting with a March 18, 1997, trade that brought Glen Murray to Los Angeles for Ed Olczyk. Taylor and Robinson looked to rebuild around character and youth. Subsequent trades were made for Jozef Stumpel, Sandy Moger and Luc Robitaille (on his second tour of duty with the Kings). Each played a role in the Kings' resurgence in 1997–98.

Murray, who had been Boston's first-round choice in the 1991 Entry Draft, had his best season to date. The hulking winger scored 29 goals and 31 assists for 60 points and tied for the team lead in game-winning goals with seven.

Stumpel and Moger came over in a deal that worked for both sides. The Kings got a front-line center they needed as well as a tough winger while the Bruins got a starting goaltender in Byron Dafoe and a productive winger in Dimitri Khristich.

Stumpel led the Kings in scoring during the 1997–98 season with 21 goals and 58 assists for 79 points while managing a plus–minus of +17 to lead the team during the regular season.

Robitaille had a successful return to Los Angeles as he brought in his leadership and scoring touch. He was a force early in the season but an injury hampered the rest of his return. He still produced as evidenced by his 16 goals and 24 assists for 40 points in 57 games during the 1997–98 season.

An even earlier trade paid benefits this past season as Mattias Norstrom became a dependable everyday defenseman. He was third on the team with a plus–minus of +14, proving that he is ready to be a blueliner in L.A. for years to come.

Aside from trades, some of the Kings home grown talent started to show their worth as well. Vladimir Tsyplakov, the Kings third round daft pick in the 1995 Entry Draft had his best season yet. He set career-highs in goals (18), assists (34) and points (52). Tsyplakov was second on the team with a plus–minus rating of +15.

Off the ice another epoch of redevelopment began in October 1995 when Philip Anschutz and Edward Roski Jr. assumed ownership of the team. Apart from putting a winning product on the ice, the new ownership began thinking long-range—well into the 21st century. The cornerstone of their planning would be a new, state-of-the-art arena, not in the suburbs but rather located in downtown Los Angeles. Plans for the new arena were unveiled late in the 1997–98 season, thus ushering in a truly new era of major-league hockey.

Meanwhile, Taylor continued to reconstruct the team. In the 1998 Entry Draft he selected 6'6" defenseman Mathieu Biron from Shawinigan of the Quebec Major Junior Hockey League. Biron was ranked seventh by the Central Scouting Service among skaters but dropped into the Kings' lap when he was available with the 21st overall.

"We ranked him as one of the top 12 and we feel fortunate to get him," Taylor said. "We began a rebuilding process when Wayne Gretzky left. We finally have some youth, size and strength in our organization."

Los Angeles Kings Year-by-Year Record

Season	GP	W	L	T	GF	GA	Pts	Finish		Playoff Results
1967–68	74	31	33	10	200	224	72	2nd	West Div.	Lost Quarterfinal
1968–69	76	24	42	10	185	260	58	4th	West Div.	Lost Semifinal
1969–70	76	14	52	10	168	290	38	6th	West Div.	Out of Playoffs
1970–71	78	25	40	13	239	303	63	5th	West Div.	Out of Playoffs
1971–72	78	20	49	9	206	305	49	7th	West Div.	Out of Playoffs
1972–73	78	31	36	11	232	245	73	6th	West Div.	Out of Playoffs
1973–74	78	33	33	12	233	231	78	3rd	West Div.	Lost Quarterfinal
1974–75	80	42	17	21	269	185	105	2nd	Norris Div.	Lost Prelim. Round
1975–76	80	38	33	9	263	265	85	2nd	Norris Div.	Lost Quarterfinal
1976–77	80	34	31	15	271	241	83	2nd	Norris Div.	Lost Quarterfinal
1977–78	80	31	34	15	243	245	77	3rd	Norris Div.	Lost Prelim. Round
1978–79	80	34	34	12	292	286	80	3rd	Norris Div.	Lost Prelim. Round
1979–80	80	30	36	14	290	313	74	2nd	Norris Div.	Lost Prelim. Round
1980–81	80	43	24	13	337	290	99	2nd	Norris Div.	Lost Prelim. Round
1981–82	80	24	41	15	314	369	63	4th	Smythe Div.	Lost Div. Final
1982–83	80	27	41	12	308	365	66	5th	Smythe Div.	Out of Playoffs
1983–84	80	23	44	13	309	376	59	5th	Smythe Div.	Out of Playoffs
1984–85	80	34	32	14	339	326	82	4th	Smythe Div.	Lost Div. Semifinal
1985–86	80	23	49	8	284	389	54	5th	Smythe Div.	Out of Playoffs
1986–87	80	31	41	8	318	341	70	4th	Smythe Div.	Lost Div. Semifinal

Season	GP	W	L	T	GF	GA	Pts	Finish	Playoff Results
1987–88	80	30	42	8	318	359	68	4th Smythe Div.	Lost Div. Semifinal
1988–89	80	42	31	7	376	335	91	2nd Smythe Div.	Lost Div. Final
1989–90	80	34	39	7	338	337	75	4th Smythe Div.	Lost Div. Final
1990–91	80	46	24	10	340	254	102	1st Smythe Div.	Lost Div. Final
1991 92	80	35	31	14	287	296	84	2nd Smythe Div.	Lost Div. Semifinal
1992–93	84	39	35	10	338	340	88	3rd Smythe Div.	Lost Final
1993–94	84	27	45	12	294	322	66	5th Pacific Div.	Out of Playoffs
1994–95	48	16	23	9	142	174	41	4th Pacific Div.	Out of Playoffs
1995–96	82	24	40	18	256	302	66	6th Pacific Div.	Out of Playoffs
1996–97	82	28	43	11	214	268	67	6th Pacific Div.	Out of Playoffs
1997–98	82	38	33	11	227	225	87	2nd Pacific Div.	Lost Conf. Quarterfinal

MINNESOTA WILD

THE NHL WILL BE RETURNING to the hotbed of American high school and university hockey when the Minnesota Wild enter the league for the 2000–2001 season. The league announced its return to the Minneapolis–St. Paul area on June 25, 1997, when the National Hockey League welcomed Nashville, Atlanta, Columbus and Minnesota as new expansion teams. The NHL will be a 30-team circuit by the time Minnesota and Columbus come on board, with three divisions of five teams in each of the Eastern and Western conferences. Minnesota will join the Northwest Division of the Western Conference with the Calgary Flames, Colorado Avalanche, Edmonton Oilers and Vancouver Canucks.

The team name Wild for the Minnesota franchise was announced on January 22, 1998 following a name-the-team contest that ran for six months. "The selection of our team name is obviously an important step in developing our team's identity," said Jac K. Sperling, chief executive officer of the club. "We think it best represents what Minnesota hockey fans hold most dear — our rugged natural wilderness, the premier brand of hockey that's native to Minnesota and the great enthusiasm of all our hockey fans. The team logo depicts the word "wild" designed in an organic, naturalist form that includes the team's official colors of Iron Range red, forest green, harvest gold and Minnesota wheat.

When the Wild enter the NHL for the 2000–2001 season, they will be playing out of a brand new 18,600-seat arena in St. Paul.

MONTREAL CANADIENS

Chrys Goyens

FEW TEAMS IN HISTORY have done so much and meant so much to their sport and their followers than the Montreal Canadiens of the National Hockey League.

Modern marketing blitzes aside, few logos or team crests have approached the global recognition of the classic "CH" crest worn on the chest of Hall of Fame players for generations. The world recognizes two scarlet tunics from Canada, and the one worn by the fabled Royal Canadian Mounted Police is a distant runner-up for the international sports fan. "The Flying Frenchmen" did not always fly and weren't always Frenchmen, but their image and elan have endured for nine decades.

The Montreal Canadiens Hockey Club was born on December 4, 1909 — designed to add a French face to hockey in Montreal, until then the preserve of the mercantile English with their clubs like the Shamrocks, Wanderers and Victorias. Ironically, the first owner, J. Ambrose O'Brien, was neither a Montrealer nor a French Canadian. The scion of a wealthy mine-owning family, he sought to establish a French-Canadian club in the National Hockey Association where he already had an interest in a team in his hometown of Renfrew, Ontario. It was agreed that when French-speaking owners from Montreal could be found, ownership would be transferred as soon as possible. Jack Laviolette was hired to form and manage the team and the first lineup included the likes of veteran stars Edouard "Newsy" Lalonde, Didier Pitre, Art Bernier and George "Skinner" Poulin.

Early in its history, the club acquired the nickname "les habitants" or "the Habs," a French term first used to describe rugged farmer–settlers in New France, the 17th century predecessor of what is now Quebec. The French usage of the word "Canadien" at the time the team was formed had a similar meaning, and referred to the hard-working local people of Montreal.

The Canadiens played their first National Hockey Association game on natural ice at the Jubilee Arena on January 5, 1910, defeating the Cobalt Silver Kings 7–6. They were the real *bleu-blanc-rouge* (blue, white and red, the colors of the French flag from the staff radiating outward), wearing a blue sweater featuring a simple "C" of white, short, white pants and long, red wool socks. O'Brien's right to call his team *les Canadiens* was challenged by Georges Kendall, owner of a sporting association known as *le Club Athlétique Canadien*. The resulting out-of-court settlement saw ownership of the hockey team transferred to Kendall's athletic club. (Kendall used the name "George Kennedy" in his dealings with the predominately English-speaking commercial society that controlled business affairs in Montreal at this time.) Within three years, the team petitioned the league and was given the right to hire English-speaking players — homegrown French players were in short supply.

The Canadiens, wearing their now recognizable red-white-and-blue uniforms, but with the "CA" crest, won the franchise's first Stanley Cup on March 30, 1916, defeating the Portland Rosebuds of the Pacific Coast Hockey Association in a five-game series. Non-French speakers Skene Ronan and Goldie Prodgers scored the goals in that game and were supported by a stellar cast that included the legendary Georges Vezina in goal, Newsy Lalonde, Didier Pitre, Amos Arbour, Howard McNamara, Jack Laviolette, Louis Berlinquette, Jack Fournier and Bert Corbeau. Scant days after the Cup celebration, McNamara, Prodgers and Arbour enlisted in the army. Upon joining the fledgling National Hockey League as a founding member in November 1917, the team officially changed its name to club de hockey Canadien and added the now-famous letters "CH" for hockey Canadien to its familiar uniform.

Two years later, the Canadiens were poised for a second Stanley Cup when tragedy struck. After winning the National Hockey League title in a five game series with Ottawa, Montreal journeyed west to challenge the Seattle Metropolitans of the PCHA and their stars Frank Foyston, Muzz Murray, Jack Walker, Cully Wilson and Hap Holmes. After five games, the spirited series was deadlocked at two wins and a tie for each team, when fate intervened in the form of the Spanish Influenza pandemic that would kill an estimated 25 million from 1918 to 1920. The arrival of the disease on the West Coast coincided with the Canadiens visit and, with the final game scheduled for April 1, the Canadiens were unable to ice a team, with Newsy Lalonde, Billy Coutu, Louis Berlinquette, Jack McDonald, Joe Hall

and manager Kendall-Kennedy all down with the flu. The game was canceled and, for the only time in Stanley Cup history, no Cup holder was declared. Four days later, "Bad" Joe Hall, the veteran Canadiens defenseman, died in a Seattle hospital. Within a year, Kendall-Kennedy was dead of complications related to influenza.

While O'Brien put the first team on the ice, and Kendall-Kennedy nursed it through its first decade, the Canadiens did not acquire much of their mythic aura until a Franco-American from Bourbonnais, Illinois, came along to take control of the franchise. He was Leo Dandurand, a dandy who made and lost several fortunes in the sports world, especially in horse racing, where he was an owner of famous thoroughbreds as well as head of the Montreal Jockey Club for years.

With the fledgling NHL attempting to break out of its eastern Canadian niche and into the northeastern United States, it was imperative that salesmen who knew both markets take control of the sport. Dandurand was the right man in the right spot, a promoter extraordinaire who traveled in the same circles as New York's legendary Tex Rickard and Chicago's Major Frederic McLaughlin. If hockey was to make a go in markets like New York, Boston and Chicago, the visiting teams would have to capture the imagination of the American fans who were new to the game. "The Flying Frenchmen"—a term first used to describe some of the earliest Canadiens teams—were up to the task.

William Howard Morenz, a German-Canadian born in Mitchell, Ontario, who was spirited away to Montreal by Dandurand under the noses of the Toronto St. Pats, would become professional hockey's superstar in the Roaring Twenties. His support staff would include two diminutive skating buzzsaws, Aurel Joliat, a Swiss Protestant from Ottawa, Johnny "Black Cat" Gagnon, a product of Quebec's interior, as well as Georges Vezina, Billy Boucher, the Mantha brothers Sylvio and Georges, and the hardrock Cleghorn brothers, Odie and Sprague.

Morenz was discovered playing in railway league finals in Montreal, representing a team from Stratford, Ont. He was signed for $850. As training camp approached, he tried to get out of the deal, afraid that he wasn't good enough for the NHL and that he would lose his amateur standing because there was no minor professional league at the time. Dandurand stuck to his guns and a tearful Morenz was forced to join the Canadiens. The following March, Morenz led all playoff scorers with seven goals in six games and led the Canadiens to the Stanley Cup, the first of three championships he would win with the team.

Morenz, Joliat, Gagnon and the rest sold hockey on both sides of the border in the 1920s, helping several new franchises take root in Boston, New York (Americans and Rangers), Detroit (Cougars, later Falcons, and later still, Red Wings) and Chicago. As well, Dandurand's skill as a promoter and Morenz's on-ice heroics led to the creation of another franchise in Montreal, the Maroons, who would represent English Montreal against the darlings of French Montreal, *les Canadiens*.

A modern ice palace with the latest in artificial ice technology would accompany the Maroons arrival in the NHL. Called the Forum, it was constructed in 159 days in 1924 and was ready for action in late November when the new National Hockey League season got under way. Ironically, it would be inaugurated by the Canadiens, whose own Mount Royal Arena and its newly-installed artificial ice plant were plagued by electrical problems. On November 29, 1924, the Canadiens took part in the first ice hockey game ever played at the Forum, thumping the Toronto St. Pats 7–1. It took Billy Boucher only 56 seconds to score the first goal in what would become hockey's most venerated shrine. He added two more for a natural hat trick before the second period was two minutes old, and linemates Morenz and Joliat scored a pair each. The honor of the first score by a visitor went to Toronto center Jack Adams, who would return to the Forum many years later as the architect of the Detroit Red Wings dynasty of the 1930s, 1940s and 1950s.

For its first two seasons, the Forum was exclusively home to the Maroons. The Canadiens joined them starting with the 1926–27 season and would play there for another 70 years. The Maroons-Canadiens rivalry would galvanize Montreal hockey fans for more than a decade as "the Flying Frenchmen" would battle with the big, tough Maroons of the S-Line (Nels Stewart, Babe Siebert and Hooley Smith).

The new team, simply called Montreal in its inaugural season of 1924–25 because of a dispute over the use of its nickname "Maroons," was an expansion team playing against the defending Stanley Cup champions, but it still managed to tie the pair of games in "its" building that year, losing the three played at the Mount Royal Arena. However, the new building was a cash cow, filled to the rafters with 9,000 hockey fans each night, and it allowed the Maroons to make some judicious talent purchases in the summer of 1925.

Nels Stewart, Babe Siebert and Bill Phillips all joined the team that summer and drove the sophomore Maroons to a second-place finish in the NHL's Canadian Division behind Ottawa, while the Canadiens tumbled to seventh place with 11 wins and a tie in 36 games. Moreover, the lumbering giant, Stewart, outscored Morenz 34 goals to 23 to win the league scoring title. The Maroons easily dispatched the Pittsburgh Pirates 6–4 in a two-game total-goals series, and then did the same against the Senators, 2–1, in two bitterly-fought defensive games. Then came the Victoria Cougars, who had defeated the Canadiens the previous spring for the Stanley Cup. The Maroons scored 10 goals in their four-game Cup victory over the Cougars: eight of them—five by Stewart, two by Siebert and one by Phillips—tallied by the three players purchased the previous summer.

The Forum had its first Stanley Cup and Montreal its second in three years. However, the banner bore a stylized maroon M, and not the CH of the Canadiens. The Maroons would struggle valiantly for 13 seasons in the NHL, win another Cup in 1935, and on the way play in two "Games for the Ages" in their building: losing to Lester Patrick's New York Rangers in 1928 when the 44-year-old coach and general manager suited up to play goal for "the Blueshirts;" and, losing 1–0 to Detroit on March 24–25, 1936 on the famous Mud Bruneteau goal at 16:30 of the sixth period of overtime in the semifinals—the longest game in the history of the league.

With the Great Depression well entrenched by the late 1930s, Montreal no longer could support two teams and the Maroons were sold. The Maroons era had made Montreal the hockey hotbed of the league. Morenz and "the Flying Frenchmen" now returned to prominence, winning consecutive Stanley Cup championships in 1930 and 1931. With the win in 1924, and the two titles by the Maroons, Montreal would be the summer home to the Cup for five of 11 seasons. That kind of success could not prepare Montreal fans for what would become known as the *grand noirceur* or "great darkness" of the period between the

Maroons Cup in 1935 and the next success by a Montreal team in 1944. And nothing could prepare the hockey world for the unspeakable tragedy which would befall Howie Morenz in 1937.

Morenz had been hockey's major pinup during the 1920s, as his rocketing speed and fiery rink-long dashes thrilled fans in all NHL cities. Eventually, the rushes became fewer as age gained on "the Stratford Streak"—a.k.a. "the Mitchell Meteor," and in 1933 he was traded to Chicago. Morenz played a desultory season-and-a-half with the Black Hawks, and finished off the 1935–36 season with the New York Rangers before rejoining the Canadiens in the summer of 1936.

On January 28, 1937, in a rush that evoked Morenz at the peak of his powers, he burst into the Chicago zone at full speed. It would be the last rush by hockey's great hero of the day. Chicago defenseman Earl Seibert caught the Canadiens center with a hip check and Morenz lost his balance and fell toward the boards. Somehow, a skate jammed in a crack in the boards and Seibert arrived simultaneously. The sound of the leg breaking could be heard throughout the Forum.

Hospitalized, Howie Morenz kept up a brave appearance, but told teammate Aurel Joliat that he never would skate again. Still in hospital nearly two months later, weak and depressed, Morenz died suddenly on March 8, 1937, of a coronary embolism. Three days later, more than 10,000 people sat in silence in a jam-packed Forum during Morenz's funeral service. The city of Montreal was in mourning for Morenz for months. On the ice, the mourning period was extended some seven more years, until the arrival of the next Montreal superhero.

Montreal's previous superstar had come out of the machine shops of the Canadian Pacific Railway. The next one was the son of a machinist in the Montreal shops of the same CPR. Born Joseph Henri Maurice Richard, he would be known to the hockey world as "the Rocket" and would carry professional hockey and the NHL through the World War II era and into the modern age. As was the case with Morenz, Richard seemed to show some reluctance to burst onto the scene, suffering season-ending ankle and wrist injuries in the previous two campaigns before finally settling in the NHL during the 1943–44 season. Significantly, that ankle injury would keep him out of military service.

A bone of contention in English Canada during the 1940s was French Quebec's reluctance to embrace the war which involved the entire British Commonwealth. Anti-conscription riots broke out in Montreal and other Quebec centers, and local draft boards were seen from outside the province as notoriously lax. And although the Canadiens had their share of players in the country's uniform, the team was to all intents and purposes left intact. Veterans Hector "Toe" Blake and Elmer Lach teamed up with a "Rocket" right winger in 1943–44, and the Canadiens took off, winning an astonishing 38 games, tying seven and losing only five in a 50-game schedule. Richard's production included scoring all of his team's goals in a 5–1 playoff win over the Maple Leafs and in a 3–1 victory 10 days later over the Black Hawks. In nine playoff games, Richard scored 12 goals and the Canadiens had their first Stanley Cup since 1931, Montreal's first since 1935.

A year later, Richard soared into the Ruthian stratosphere with a feat that galvanized the sports world like no other since Babe Ruth had belted 60 homers in baseball's 1927 season. With the war winding down in Europe, Richard's exploits began taking over the front pages as the fiery competitor maintained a goal-a-game clip into January and then February. War-depleted lineups or not, opposing teams tried everything to stop Montreal's scoring machine and the superstar spent a significant amount of playing time in the penalty box for defending himself against all comers. Late in February, his two goals against Detroit gave Montreal a 5–2 win and Richard 43 in 38 games, tying Cooney Weiland for the second-highest season total in league history. A week later, a score against Toronto tied the legendary Joe Malone at 44, and he passed Malone in a Forum encounter against the Leafs several days later. With eight games remaining in the season, could Richard possibly tally five more for a magical 50?

By game 49, Richard had 49 goals and an emotional crowd was crammed into every nook and cranny of the Forum on the last Saturday of the season. Late in the game, a Chicago defenseman tripped Richard and the Rocket was awarded a penalty shot … and missed. It was not to be, at home, anyway. The following night, Richard scored his 50th goal of the season in Boston.

The arrival of Richard heralded a new era for the Canadiens, and although the team would win another Stanley Cup in 1946, the team's leap into the upper echelons of the league was the result of another new recruit. On August 1, 1946, the victim of a Toronto purge by Conn Smythe began work at the Forum as the Canadiens manager. The diminutive new leader was Frank Selke, and he would build the farm system that would allow the team to rival the Leafs and Red Wings during the late 1940s and then surpass all comers in the golden 1950s. Junior and senior leagues in Quebec and junior and senior teams in Manitoba, Alberta and Saskatchewan, as well as minor professional teams scattered throughout North America, ensured the Canadiens a rich bounty each season. It got to the point that Frank Selke's farm system paid for itself on the sales of players by the Canadiens to other NHL teams.

Richard had joined a team that included veterans Blake and Lach, as well as Ken Reardon, Butch Bouchard, goalie Bill Durnan and defenseman Doug Harvey, arguably the greatest rearguard of his era. However, the Montreal team that would emerge in the mid-1950s was based on Selke star harvests and future Hall of Famers Bernard "Boom Boom" Geoffrion, Jean Beliveau, Richard's younger brother Henri, Dickie Moore, Bert Olmstead, Jean-Guy Talbot, Phil Goyette, Don Marshall, Ralph Backstrom and the greatest character of them all, goaltender Jacques Plante.

Elements of the old and the new came together to win the Stanley Cup in 1953, but it would not be until the spring of 1956 that the team would take off in postseason play, setting a raft of records in the process. Local fans argue that the Canadiens might have won eight Cup titles in a row if not for a bit of luck and a decision by NHL president Clarence Campbell that ignited Montreal in 1955. In 1954, the Canadiens and Red Wings played to overtime in the seventh game of the finals, with Detroit's Tony Leswick sealing the issue. In 1955, although the team would go down in a seventh game at Detroit, the Cup actually had been lost weeks before, in Boston and Montreal. Late that season, the Canadiens and Wings were battling neck and neck for first place and the Canadiens were in Boston when Bruins defenseman Hal Laycoe, a former Hab and tennis partner of Richard's, clipped the Rocket with his stick during a rush. Richard could not be restrained; twice he attacked Laycoe and struck him with his stick while team-

mates and officials tried to calm him. And, with linesman Cliff Thompson pinning his arms, Richard managed to break free, striking the official twice and attacking Laycoe once again. He was ejected immediately with a match penalty and was ordered to a meeting at league headquarters in Montreal two days later.

A year earlier, Richard emerged unscathed from a similar incident with an official in Toronto and g.m. Conn Smythe of the Leafs and Detroit's Jack Adams took great pains to remind president Campbell of the results of his previous clemency. When Richard and manager Selke emerged from the meeting with president Campbell, Montreal went into shock, and then, rage. Richard, leading the league in scoring points for the first time in his career, had been suspended for the rest of the regular season (three games) and the playoffs. The city was divided along linguistic lines, with the French media and French-speaking mayor Jean Drapeau accusing Campbell of anti-French bias, and the English media adopting a law-and-order stance. Drapeau warned that his police might not be able to protect the NHL president if he attended a game the following evening on St. Patrick's Day.

A restive crowd thronged the Forum on March 17 for a first-place showdown with the visiting Wings, with another 10,000 or so fans milling about in an ugly mood outside the building. Late in the first period, with Detroit leading the dispirited Canadiens 4–1, Campbell sat down at his seat and was attacked by a fan in short order. Police intervened and a tear gas canister was set off, driving fans out of the building as the first period came to an end. The Red Wings were sitting quietly in their dressing room during the first intermission when a fire marshal declared that the game was over, and police took the players to their team bus. The Detroit bus was hardly out of sight of the Forum when Montreal erupted into a riot that trashed the downtown core and had the city seething for more than 24 hours. It took a special radio appeal by the Rocket to call an end to what would become known as "the Richard Riot." Detroit went on to capture first place and home-ice advantage in the playoffs, and Boom Boom Geoffrion won the scoring title, only to be vilified by his own fans for surpassing their beloved Rocket.

Montreal would not win the Cup that year, but it would be the last loss during Maurice Richard's career. On April 12, 1960, Richard scored on a backhand against Toronto's Johnny Bower as Montreal went on to a fifth straight Stanley Cup title. It was his 82nd playoff goal, 34th in the finals and the last of his career. Eventually all of his scoring records, 544 regular season goals, 988 points, would be surpassed. But no player would match the Rocket's impact during his era.

It was a testament to Frank Selke's skill as a hockey manager and administrator that his team took the powerful Red Wings to seven games in 1954 and 1955 minus several important players. Selke has built a juggernaut by then, and team leadership was moving from Maurice Richard and Butch Bouchard to Doug Harvey, Jean Beliveau, Henri Richard and Dickie Moore. The most distinctive of all was the 6'3" Beliveau, an elegant center with soft hands who had the strength to fight off opposing defensemen while scoring spectacular goals. The Canadiens had the luxury of two All-Star lines. The Richard brothers and Moore terrorized opposition defenses, only to be replaced by the trio of Beliveau, Geoffrion and Olmstead. With Hall of Famers like Harvey, Tom Johnson and Jean-Guy Talbot on the blue

line and five-time Vezina Trophy winner Plante in nets, the Canadiens were challenged rarely as they won the Stanley Cup five times in a row.

With Beliveau, Moore, Geoffrion, Henri Richard, Talbot and Plante emerging from the Quebec leagues, Montreal established a dynasty of individuals who would amass 154 Stanley Cup titles between them from 1956 to 1979. And they might have won more than that if they had been able to extract Beliveau from junior and senior teams in Quebec City where he starred for four years, making as much money as Rocket Richard and Gordie Howe playing "amateur" hockey. His arrival with the Canadiens for the 1953–54 season put the team over the top.

So powerful was the team's offense that the league was forced to change the rule governing minor penalties. Previous to the change, minors were served in their entirety even if a goal was scored on the shorthanded team. The Canadiens offense was so potent that the team sometimes scored two or three goals per opposition minor, putting games out of reach in the first period. The amended rule allowed the penalized player to return to the ice if a goal was scored against his team. Rule change notwithstanding, Geoffrion won the scoring title in 1954–55, Beliveau the following year and Moore in 1957–58 and 1958–59. At the other end of the ice, the Canadiens allowed the fewest goals against for five years running.

The most significant fact to emerge from Montreal's five-Cup run was that the Canadiens never were extended to seven games in any of the 10 playoff series and only played six games twice. There were five victories in five games and three sweeps, including eight straight wins in 1960. The Canadiens finally relinquished the Cup to Chicago in 1961, and after Punch Imlach's Leafs captured three straight championships, the Habs were back in contention in 1965, challenging a powerhouse Chicago team. Although many veterans of the five-straight team remained, direction of the team had moved from Frank Selke to Sam Pollock, and the rotund managing director would guide the team into the modern era of national TV on both sides of the border and a major NHL expansion.

Montreal won the Cup in 1965 and 1966 with a team built primarily through its farm system, and then came back with victories in 1968, 1969, 1971 and 1973 with teams built by trades and draft choices acquired by Pollock shortly before and during the early expansion era. The key to the entire process was the Montreal training camp for the 1965–66 season. While the team normally would invite 40 or so of its top pros to the team camp, Pollock brought in some 120 pros from throughout the system that year and had his scouts and talent spotters classify all of them. By the time the league would welcome six new teams with the Expansion Draft in 1967, Pollock had dismantled Selke's vast farm system and shipped more that 70 players throughout the league, accumulating draft selections as he went. Teams like St. Louis, Minnesota and Oakland immediately were competitive thanks to Canadiens farmhands, and Montreal's future throughout the coming decade was assured.

Stars like Guy Lafleur, Larry Robinson and Steve Shutt were accumulated in this fashion, guaranteeing a competitive team for years to come. Occasionally, "Trader Sam" got lucky as well. On such case was the acquisition of a lanky goalie from the Boston system, Ken Dryden. His trade to Montreal would haunt the Bruins for years to come. The acquisition of Lafleur provides a classic example of

Pollock's foresight. The Canadiens owned Oakland's first pick for the 1971 draft, and with the Seals in last place in the Western Division, it appeared that the selection would be first overall. Late in the season, however, the Los Angeles Kings began to falter and threatened to sink below the Seals in the standings. Pollock immediately dispatched veteran center Ralph Backstrom to the Kings and his leadership got the Kings over the hump.

On June 9, 1971, Jean Beliveau announced his retirement at the Queen Elizabeth Hotel in Montreal, site of the NHL meetings. A day later, the Canadiens drafted his replacement, Guy Lafleur, in the same room. And, for good measure, the team also picked up future Hall of Fame defenseman Larry Robinson an hour later.

In the mid-1960s, the Canadiens were a veteran team that included Beliveau, Henri Richard, Talbot, Ralph Backstrom and Claude Provost, bolstered by a large and strong defense corps that included newcomers Jacques Laperriere, Terry Harper and Ted Harris. They were strengthened up front by the additions of tough wingers Claude Larose and John Ferguson and the sheer explosiveness of Yvan "Roadrunner" Cournoyer. Gone were Plante, Geoffrion, Moore, Harvey and Johnson, but the team had enough talent to compete, with veteran goalies Lorne "Gump" Worsley and Charlie Hodge holding the fort.

Pollock tinkered with his team yearly. The team that won in 1965 and 1966 saw players like Provost, Harris, Hodge, Larose and Dick Duff moved to make room for newcomers like Rogatien Vachon, Tony Esposito, Serge Savard, Guy Lapointe, Jacques Lemaire, Pete Mahovlich and Mickey Redmond. The reconstructed Canadiens then turned around and burned the rising Bruins and Black Hawks in the 1968 and 1969 playoffs. By 1971, Hall of Fame goalies Worsley and Esposito had departed, as had scorers Redmond and Danny Grant. These departures made room for Ken Dryden and Frank Mahovlich respectively.

And by 1973, Beliveau, Ferguson, Vachon and Harper had departed, replaced by Marc Tardif, Rejean Houle, Guy Lafleur, Larry Robinson and Steve Shutt. In the period between the 1964–65 and 1972–73 seasons, Pollock managed to remake his entire team and win the Stanley Cup six times. Only five players, Henri Richard, Yvan Cournoyer, Jacques Laperriere, Jim Roberts and Claude Larose played for both the 1965 and 1973 Cup winners, although the latter two had been traded away and reacquired in the interim. Yet Canadiens players accumulated individual postseason statistics that are staggering in today's context: Henri Richard won 11 championships while Jean Beliveau and Yvan Cournoyer each won 10. Claude Provost was a part of nine Cup teams; Jacques Lemaire, eight; Jean-Guy Talbot, seven, and a raft of others won six or five championships.

Ice generalship was not a factor. When the popular and demanding Toe Blake asked to be replaced behind the Canadiens bench in 1968 after eight titles in 13 years, Pollock's team was strong enough to win the 1969 championship with rookie coach Claude Ruel calling the shots. Two years later, another rookie coach, Al MacNeil, replaced Ruel midway through the season and led the team to a championship, only to be replaced by Scotty Bowman the following September. Bowman would win five titles with Montreal in the 1970s before shuffling off to Buffalo.

The significance of the franchise's Stanley Cup wins in the late 1960s and early 1970s cannot be downplayed. While a workmanlike Montreal team was winning, it was preventing powerhouse teams from Chicago, Boston and New York from doing the same. The Black Hawks of Bobby and Dennis Hull, Stan Mikita, Phil Esposito, Chico Maki, Pierre Pilote, Ken Wharram and Glenn Hall was arguably the most potent NHL team in the mid-1960s, but only managed a 1961 Cup. Along came the Rangers of the Goal-A-Game (G-A-G) line of Jean Ratelle, Rod Gilbert and Vic Hadfield, with Brad Park and Jim Neilson on defense and Ed Giacomin in goal, and they were shut out in postseason play. Finally, Montreal outfought "the Big Bad Bruins" of the Orr-Esposito era, winning four titles to Boston's two at a time when many hockey observers expected the Bruins to sweep away everything in their path.

A classic example came in the April 1971, quarterfinals which pit the first-place Beantowners against the fourth-place Canadiens. After winning a 3–1 defensive struggle at the Garden, the Bruins were in cruise control, leading 5–1 late in the second period, when Henri Richard stole the puck from Bobby Orr and scored. Two minutes into the third period and the score was 5–4 on goals by Beliveau and Ferguson. Then, in rapid succession came goals by Beliveau, Lemaire and Frank Mahovlich and the Canadiens escaped a stunned Boston Garden with a 7–5 win en route to a series victory in seven games. Instrumental in that success was a goalie named Dryden, who then stymied the North Stars and Black Hawks after playing only seven regular-season games that spring.

The onset of the World Hockey Association would cripple the Bruins, Rangers and Black Hawks, and although the Canadiens lost some players (Houle, Tardif, J.C. Tremblay and Frank Mahovlich) to the new league, the team was in better shape than most NHL entries. Lafleur struggled in his first three seasons, alternating between right wing and center on different lines, finally emerging as the league's superstar in 1974–75. A cross between the elegance of Beliveau and the fire of the Rocket, he electrified NHL audiences nightly with his rink-long dashes, his blond hair streaming behind him. Pollock put together a stellar supporting cast that included Cournoyer, Shutt, Lemaire, Peter Mahovlich, Doug Risebrough, Yvon Lambert, Mario Tremblay and the incomparable Bob Gainey on the forward lines, and "the Big Three" of Larry Robinson, Guy Lapointe and Serge Savard anchoring an airtight defense backstopped by Dryden.

That team ended the "three-peat" aspirations of the Philadelphia Flyers in May 1976, outdueling "the Broad Street Bullies" in the corners with bangers like Pierre Bouchard, Lambert and Rick Chartraw, and outfinessing them with the likes of Lafleur, Shutt and Mahovlich. Four straight championships resulted, as the Habs fended off strong teams in Boston, Buffalo and New York (Islanders) until injury and age caught up with them in 1980. The last Canadiens dynasty came to an end on April 27, 1980, in a 3–2 Forum loss to the youthful Minnesota North Stars. Gone a year earlier to retirement were young Jacques Lemaire, 33, and Ken Dryden, 31. Gone also was Scotty Bowman, miffed because Sam Pollock would not name him as his own replacement when he opted to remain with the Bronfman family which sold the team to the Molson Breweries empire in 1978. Pollock selected Irving Grundman, his assistant in the previous decade, but not a hockey man, and although Grundman managed a Cup in 1979, his leadership was under perpetual challenge in the strident Montreal media.

Grundman's major mistake was attempting to replace Bowman with the colorful Bernie Geoffrion, who had

coached the Rangers and later the expansion Atlanta Flames, stepping down both times for health reasons. Boomer lasted 30 games in Montreal and was replaced, as Toe Blake had been, by Claude Ruel. The team still was competitive, but the early 1980s belonged to the Islanders and the Edmonton Oilers. A nucleus of talent that included Robinson, Savard and Gainey, and quality additions like Ryan Walter, Bobby Smith, Rick Green, Chris Chelios and Mats Naslund kept the team near the top of the league standings. Montreal could not afford to dwell on the successes of the Oilers and Islanders, however, because the challenge to their hegemony came from their own backyard. In 1979, the NHL expanded to include the four remaining teams in the World Hockey Association, and suddenly the province of Quebec was no longer the exclusive preserve of the Canadiens, with the Nordiques challenging them from the provincial capital.

When Quebec managed to eliminate Montreal in their first playoff confrontation, a best-of-five series in 1982, the second floor at the Forum went into shock. The Nordiques noisily claimed to be the league's "French" team, relegating the Canadiens to "English" status in their own backyard, even though the talent of the team revolved about two Slovaks, brothers Peter and Anton Stastny, and a feisty Ontario farm boy named Dale Hunter. That was remedied with the hiring of Ronald Corey as team president, and his decision to replace Grundman with former star Serge Savard.

In the spring of 1984, the Canadiens gained a measure of revenge by ousting the Nordiques in the bitterly fought six-game Adams Division finals, which included a huge Good Friday brawl in the final contest. Montreal went on to lose to the Islanders in six games in the conference finals, but the Canadiens had given notice that they were back in the chase. In June 1984, Savard and the Canadiens had a dream draft, selecting Czech defector Petr Svoboda and Shayne Corson in the first round and adding Stephane Richer and goaltender Patrick Roy in the second. They once again lost to the Nordiques in the playoffs, on Peter Stastny's overtime goal in game seven, but were poised to challenge the league in 1986, when Svoboda, Richer and, most importantly, Roy, joined the team as regulars.

Patrick Roy was a cross between Jacques Plante and Ken Dryden, impressive credentials indeed in Montreal. And like Plante and Dryden before him, he took the team to a Stanley Cup triumph in his rookie season. When Montreal had fallen to Quebec in 1985, the scapegoat was goaltender Steve Penney, a journeyman who had enjoyed two decent seasons in Montreal but was unable to provide the championship backstopping the team needed. That changed in 1986, as Roy was unbeatable in the playoffs, helping the Canadiens to sweep the Bruins 3–0 in their best-of-five division semifinals, and then out-battling Hartford's Mike Liut in the division finals that went down to overtime in game seven before rookie Claude Lemieux ended it. The Canadiens disposed of the Rangers in five games, including a spectacular overtime win in game three (again a goal by Lemieux) that saw Roy hold off the aroused Rangers single-handedly, including 13 stops (44 overall) in extra time. The final was a formality, Montreal defeating Calgary in five close games, and Roy posed happily in the team's dressing room at the Saddledome with his arms around the Conn Smythe Trophy (playoff MVP) and the Stanley Cup.

Seven years later, Roy once again was aroused in post-season and led a much changed team—only Roy and Guy Carbonneau remained from the 1986 champions—to the

franchise's 24th Stanley Cup and 23rd in the team's NHL history. The 1986 and 1993 victories gave Montreal a unique and enviable record in professional sports in North America, making them the only long-established team to win a league championship in each decade in which it has played. The 24 championships lead baseball's New York Yankees by one and basketball's Boston Celtics by seven.

In March 1996, the fabulous Forum featured its last Canadiens home game, a 4–1 win over the Dallas Stars, and the team moved across town to the spanking new Molson Centre. The team that made the move, however, had few connections with the Stanley Cup, including the championship won less than three years before. In the fashion of professional sport in the 1990s and the new world of free agency and liberal player movement, only four Canadiens remained from the team that had won Cup #24.

Gone to Philadelphia were John LeClair and the memories of his two overtime goals in "The Fabulous Forum" in Inglewood that eviscerated Wayne Gretzky and the Kings. Joining "Marmaduke" in the Philly shuffle was Eric Desjardins, whose three goals, including one in overtime, in the pivotal second game of the Kings series, set Montreal on the road to championship.

Gone were longtime NHL stars Kirk Muller, Brian Bellows, Denis Savard, Guy Carbonneau, and Mathieu Schneider. Gone, too, were journeymen who played huge roles in the 1993 conquest, Lyle Odelein, Jean-Jacques Daigneault, Gilbert Dionne, Paul Di Pietro, Mike Keane, Andre Racicot and Kevin Haller. Veterans Rob Ramage and Gary Leeman were out of the NHL, having departed on a Cup-winning note. And farthest gone was King Patrick, in a spectacular and very public tantrum against rookie coach Mario Tremblay seen nationwide on Hockey Night in Canada during an 11–1 Forum shellacking at the hands of Detroit. Roy's snubbing of his coach and embarrassing of team president Ronald Corey forced the reluctant Canadiens to trade him to Colorado, where he won the Stanley Cup six months later.

Thrust to center-stage was the next generation of Canadiens: Mark Recchi from Philadelphia, Andrei Kovalenko, Martin Rucinsky and Jocelyn Thibault from the Avalanche, as well as Pierre Turgeon and Vladimir Malakhov from the Islanders (for Muller and Schneider).

The 1993 champions were an all-North American aggregation, not a whiff of Europe to them. That would change immediately. Not only would Kovalenko, Rucinsky and Malakhov arrive by trades, the Canadiens would find European-trained talent on both sides of the Atlantic, drafting diminutive Valeri Bure, brother of Vancouver's Pavel, from the Western Hockey League in 1991, and a feisty Finnish centre, Saku Koivu, from Turku's TPS team in 1993.

Also spotted in transatlantic travels by team scouts were Swedish rearguard Peter Popovic, Finnish defenseman Marko Kiprusoff (who decided after one season that the NHL was not for him), Czechs Thomas Vokoun, a goalie, and Miroslav Guren, a defenseman, Austrian-born centers Martin Hohenberger and Gregor Baumgartner, Swedish wingers Niklas Anger and Peter Strom and Finnish forwards Timo Vertala and Arto Kuki.

And when Bure was eventually traded to Calgary in 1998, a Swede, Jonas Hoglund, came in the return package. Significantly, the Canadiens began trading heavily under new managing director Rejean Houle. Rejoining the team were former Habs Stephane Richer (from New Jersey for Odelein) and Shayne Corson (from St. Louis in a package

that included Pierre Turgeon), defensemen Stephane Quintal and Zarley Zalapski, and forward Scott Thornton, while defensive center Marc Bureau was signed as a free agent.

A fast, skillful team, Montreal can play firewagon hockey on those nights when the neutral zone trap is forsaken by the opposition. They proved this in a six-game upset of the Pittsburgh Penguins in the first round of the 1998 playoffs. The Canadiens still take pride in the old "Flying Frenchmen" label, and as was the case with Morenz, Joliat et al in the 1920s, they are half right. Most importantly, they are recognized around the league as a scrappy team that always comes to play.

With CHarisma and CHaracter.

Montreal Canadiens Year-by-Year Record

Season	GP	W	L	T	GF	GA	Pts	Finish		Playoff Results
1917–18	22	13	9	0	115	84	26	1st and 3rd*		Lost NHL Final
1918–19	18	10	8	0	88	78	20	1st and 2nd*		NHL Champion **
1919–20	24	13	11	0	129	113	26	2nd and 3rd*		Out of Playoffs
1920–21	24	13	11	0	112	99	26	3rd and 2nd*		Out of Playoffs
1921–22	24	12	11	1	88	94	25	3rd		Out of Playoffs
1922–23	24	13	9	2	73	61	28	2nd		Lost NHL Final
1923–24	24	13	11	0	59	48	26	2nd		Won Stanley Cup
1924–25	30	17	11	2	93	56	36	3rd		Lost Final
1925–26	36	11	24	1	79	108	23	7th		Out of Playoffs
1926–27	44	28	14	2	99	67	58	2nd	Cdn. Div.	Lost Semifinal
1927–28	44	26	11	7	116	48	59	1st	Cdn. Div.	Lost Semifinal
1928–29	44	22	7	15	71	43	59	1st	Cdn. Div.	Lost Semifinal
1929–30	44	21	14	9	142	114	51	2nd	Cdn. Div.	Won Stanley Cup
1930–31	44	26	10	8	129	89	60	1st	Cdn. Div.	Won Stanley Cup
1931–32	48	25	16	7	128	111	57	1st	Cdn. Div.	Lost Semifinal
1932–33	48	18	25	5	92	115	41	3rd	Cdn. Div.	Lost Quarterfinal
1933–34	48	22	20	6	99	101	50	2nd	Cdn. Div.	Lost Quarterfinal
1934–35	48	19	23	6	110	145	44	3rd	Cdn. Div.	Lost Quarterfinal
1935–36	48	11	26	11	82	123	33	4th	Cdn. Div.	Out of Playoffs
1936–37	48	24	18	6	115	111	54	1st	Cdn. Div.	Lost Semifinal
1937–38	48	18	17	13	123	128	49	3rd	Cdn. Div.	Lost Quarterfinal
1938–39	48	15	24	9	115	146	39	6th		Lost Quarterfinal
1939–40	48	10	33	5	90	167	25	7th		Out of Playoffs
1940–41	48	16	26	6	121	147	38	6th		Lost Quarterfinal
1941–42	48	18	27	3	134	173	39	6th		Lost Quarterfinal
1942–43	50	19	19	12	181	191	50	4th		Lost Semifinal
1943–44	50	38	5	7	234	109	83	1st		Won Stanley Cup
1944–45	50	38	8	4	228	121	80	1st		Lost Semifinal
1945–46	50	28	17	5	172	134	61	1st		Won Stanley Cup
1946–47	60	34	16	10	189	138	78	1st		Lost Final
1947–48	60	20	29	11	147	169	51	5th		Out of Playoffs
1948–49	60	28	23	9	152	126	65	3rd		Lost Semifinal
1949–50	70	29	22	19	172	150	77	2nd		Lost Semifinal
1950–51	70	25	30	15	173	184	65	3rd		Lost Final
1951–52	70	34	26	10	195	164	78	2nd		Lost Final
1952–53	70	28	23	19	155	148	75	2nd		Won Stanley Cup
1953–54	70	35	24	11	195	141	81	2nd		Lost Final
1954–55	70	41	18	11	228	157	93	2nd		Lost Final
1955–56	70	45	15	10	222	131	100	1st		Won Stanley Cup
1956–57	70	35	23	12	210	155	82	2nd		Won Stanley Cup
1957–58	70	43	17	10	250	158	96	1st		Won Stanley Cup
1958–59	70	39	18	13	258	158	91	1st		Won Stanley Cup
1959–60	70	40	18	12	255	178	92	1st		Won Stanley Cup
1960–61	70	41	19	10	254	188	92	1st		Lost Semifinal
1961–62	70	42	14	14	259	166	98	1st		Lost Semifinal
1962–63	70	28	19	23	225	183	79	3rd		Lost Semifinal
1963–64	70	36	21	13	209	167	85	1st		Lost Semifinal
1964–65	70	36	23	11	211	185	83	2nd		Won Stanley Cup
1965–66	70	41	21	8	239	173	90	1st		Won Stanley Cup
1966–67	70	32	25	13	202	188	77	2nd		Lost Final
1967–68	74	42	22	10	236	167	94	1st	East Div.	Won Stanley Cup
1968–69	76	46	19	11	271	202	103	1st	East Div.	Won Stanley Cup
1969–70	76	38	22	16	244	201	92	5th	East Div.	Out of Playoffs
1970–71	78	42	23	13	291	216	97	3rd	East Div.	Won Stanley Cup
1971–72	78	46	16	16	307	205	108	3rd	East Div.	Lost Quarterfinal
1972–73	78	52	10	16	329	184	120	1st	East Div.	Won Stanley Cup
1973–74	78	45	24	9	293	240	99	2nd	East Div.	Lost Quarterfinal
1974–75	80	47	14	19	374	225	113	1st	Norris Div.	Lost Semifinal
1975–76	80	58	11	11	337	174	127	1st	Norris Div.	Won Stanley Cup
1976–77	80	60	8	12	387	171	132	1st	Norris Div.	Won Stanley Cup
1977–78	80	59	10	11	359	183	129	1st	Norris Div.	Won Stanley Cup
1978–79	80	52	17	11	337	204	115	1st	Norris Div.	Won Stanley Cup
1979–80	80	47	20	13	328	240	107	1st	Norris Div.	Lost Quarterfinal
1980–81	80	45	22	13	332	232	103	1st	Norris Div.	Lost Prelim. Round
1981–82	80	46	17	17	360	223	109	1st	Adams Div.	Lost Div. Semifinal
1982–83	80	42	24	14	350	286	98	2nd	Adams Div.	Lost Div. Semifinal
1983–84	80	35	40	5	286	295	75	4th	Adams Div.	Lost Conf. Final

Montreal Canadiens Year-by-Year Record *continued*

Season	GP	W	L	T	GF	GA	Pts	Finish		Playoff Results
1984–85	80	41	27	12	309	262	94	1st	Adams Div.	Lost Div. Final
1985–86	80	40	33	7	330	280	87	2nd	Adams Div.	Won Stanley Cup
1986–87	80	41	29	10	277	241	92	2nd	Adams Div.	Lost Conf. Final
1987–88	80	45	22	13	298	238	103	1st	Adams Div.	Lost Div. Final
1988–89	80	53	18	9	315	218	115	1st	Adams Div.	Lost Final
1989–90	80	41	28	11	288	234	93	3rd	Adams Div.	Lost Div. Final
1990–91	80	39	30	11	273	249	89	2nd	Adams Div.	Lost Div. Final
1991–92	80	41	28	11	267	207	93	1st	Adams Div.	Lost Div. Final
1992–93	84	48	30	6	326	280	102	3rd	Adams Div.	Won Stanley Cup
1993–94	84	41	29	14	283	248	96	3rd	Northeast Div.	Lost Conf. Quarterfinal
1994–95	48	18	23	7	125	148	43	6th	Northeast Div.	Out of Playoffs
1995–96	82	40	32	10	265	248	90	3rd	Northeast Div.	Lost Conf. Quarterfinal
1996–97	82	31	36	15	249	276	77	4th	Northeast Div.	Lost Conf. Quarterfinal
1997–98	82	37	32	13	235	208	87	4th	Northeast Div.	Lost Conf. Semifinal

* Season played in two halves with no combined standing at end.
From 1917–18 through 1925–26 NHL champions played against western champions for Stanley Cup.
** Stanley Cup series with Seattle of the PCHA suspended due to influenza epidemic.

THE MONTREAL MAROONS
Eric Zweig

THE MONTREAL MAROONS played for 14 seasons in the NHL, from 1924–25 to 1937–38, during which they were consistently among the league's best teams and won the Stanley Cup twice. The team boasted some of the top stars of the era, including Nels Stewart, the NHL's first 300-goal scorer, future Hockey Hall of Famers Hooley Smith and Babe Siebert and goaltending legends Clint Benedict and Alex Connell, and they played the longest game in NHL history on March 24–25, 1936 when they lost to the Detroit Red Wings 1–0 after 116 minutes and 30 seconds of overtime. But the Maroons' greatest legacy to their city and the NHL was the Montreal Forum.

Hockey may not have been born in Montreal, but it certainly grew up there. It was there that it first moved indoors from frozen lakes, rivers and ponds when James Creighton captained a team of McGill University students and Montreal football players against a club representing the Victoria skating rink, where the game was played on March 3, 1875. How much it resembled what would become modern hockey is still hotly debated, but what we can state for certain is that from that date on Montreal became hockey's center. From the time the Amateur Hockey Association of Canada (the first national league) was formed in 1886–87 until well into the first decade of the 20th century, it was not uncommon to find as many as three Montreal teams represented in the top leagues of the day.

The Montreal Victorias, Montreal Amateur Athletic Association and Montreal Shamrocks dominated the game during this era, winning Stanley Cup titles in nine of the first 10 years the trophy was presented. While the Cup was still strictly for amateur players from 1893 to 1902, the Montreal Wanderers would help usher in the professional era and win the Cup in 1906, 1907, 1908 and finally in 1909–10, the season in which the Canadiens started.

Like their predecessors, the Wanderers were English Montreal's favorite franchise while the Canadiens were created to tap into the francophone market. Both teams played out of the Montreal (or Westmount) Arena during most of their days in the old National Hockey Association, and both were still playing at the Arena when the NHL was formed in November of 1917.

After fire destroyed the Montreal Arena on January 2, 1918, the Canadiens took up residence in the old Jubilee Rink (with capacity of only 3,250) while the Wanderers withdrew from the league. For the first time in its hockey history, Montreal was left without a team that represented

its anglophone population and an adequate facility to show-case the game.

Built in 1920 to house the Canadiens, the Mount Royal Arena relied on natural ice, which spelled havoc for sched-uling in the event of mild weather. By March 1922 English Montreal was mobilizing both to build a new rink and to return to the NHL. Ironically, a French Canadian, Donat Raymond, would make it all happen when he and William Northey (long involved with the game at the amateur level and the former manager of the Montreal Arena) appealed to Canadian Pacific Railway Chairman Edward W. Beatty, whose influence and financial support led to the creation of the Canadian Arena Company Limited in January 1924. Construction began in late spring and by fall the Montreal Forum stood at the corner of St. Catherine and Atwater.

With the rink taken care of, Raymond and Northey then turned to James Strachan to assemble a team. Strachan, a member of a prominent Montreal bakery family, had creat-ed the Wanderers back in 1903 and operated the team for several seasons. On October 12, 1924 it was reported that Strachan and Raymond would be granted an NHL franchise for $15,000. On November 1, 1924 the NHL formally admitted the new Montreal team, along with its first American entry, the Boston Bruins. Yet another French Canadian had been instrumental behind the scenes in arranging for Montreal's new NHL franchise. Leo Dandurand, owner of the Canadiens, facilitated the admit-tance of a second, English Montreal team as part of a gen-tlemen's agreement that would allow him to move the Canadiens into the Forum when his lease expired at the Mount Royal Arena in 1926. In fact, because the natural ice surface at the Arena was not ready in time for the 1924–25 season opener, the Canadiens actually played the very first game at the Forum, on November 29, 1924.

The new Montreal team was known only as the Montreal Professional Hockey Club during its first season. The own-ers had hoped to use the Wanderers name, but the rights apparently belonged to former Wanderers player and man-ager Dickie Boon, whose request for compensation would not be forthcoming. In its first season, the Montreal roster was comprised mostly of veteran castoffs (though Clint Benedict, Punch Broadbent and Reg Noble would prove they still had some life left). Rookies up from the amateur ranks included Dunc Munro, a prize acquisition from the Toronto Granites who had won an Olympic gold medal in February of 1924. The team was just 9–19–2 in its first sea-son of 1924–25 and was spared last place only by the 6–24–0 record of their expansion cousins in Boston. But with sellout crowds flocking to the Forum, success would come quickly. In its second season, the team became known by the color of its uniforms and had acquired three new players to wear them. Nels Stewart, Babe Siebert and Bill Phillips would transform the Montreal Maroons franchise.

Born in Montreal but raised in Toronto, Nels Stewart had developed into a goal-scoring star while playing amateur hockey in Cleveland during the early 1920s. Stewart was a slow, plodding skater, but he had size and strength and would become known as "Old Poison" for the deadly accu-racy of his shot. It found the net a league-leading 34 times in 36 games during the 1925–26 season, earning Stewart not only a scoring title but also the Hart Trophy as the NHL's most valuable player for lifting the Maroons from second-last the year before to second from the top in its sec-ond season.

Having thus reached the playoffs in only their second year, the Maroons faced the Pittsburgh Pirates in a two-game total-goals series. Stewart was shut out in that series, but three goals by Bill Phillips gave the Maroons a 6–4 vic-tory. The first-place Ottawa Senators were favored to defeat the Maroons for the NHL championship, but ex-Senators Clint Benedict and Punch Broadbent had something to say about that. Broadbent scored the lone Montreal goal in a 1–1 tie in the first game, while Benedict recorded a shutout in game two. Babe Siebert's goal gave the team a 2–1 series victory that entitled the Maroons to play for the Stanley Cup against the Western Hockey League champion Victoria Cougars. Nels Stewart, who had yet to score in the playoffs, fired six goals in four games against Victoria, including both goals in the 2–0 victory that gave the Maroons the series three games to one.

The 1926–27 season saw the NHL expand to 10 teams and split into Canadian and American divisions. The Maroons, now defending Stanley Cup champions, slumped to third place in the Canadian Division, while the rival Montreal Canadiens finished second. Under the new NHL playoff format, the two tenants of the Montreal Forum would meet in the postseason for the first time. Crowds of more than 11,000 fans jammed the arena—whose capacity was said to be only 10,000—for each of the two-game quar-terfinal series. Howie Morenz won it for the Canadiens 2–1 with an overtime goal in game two. The Maroons would get revenge in the semifinals the following year, however, when Russell Oatman's overtime goal gave them a 3–2 total-score victory over the Canadiens and put them into the Stanley Cup final against the New York Rangers. Every game of the best-of-five final that year would be played at the Forum because the circus was performing at Madison Square Garden, yet the Rangers would beat the Maroons three games to two. Incidentally, this was the series in which Rangers coach Lester Patrick made an emergency appearance in goal after Lorne Chabot was hit above the eye by a Nels Stewart backhand shot in game two.

The Maroons fell to last place in the Canadian Division in 1928–29, but rebounded to remain a power in the league well into the 1930s. Nels Stewart was again the most valu-able player in 1929–30, and the S-Line of Stewart, Babe Siebert and Hooley Smith remained among the league's most dangerous until both Stewart and Siebert were traded in 1932–33. By then, Baldy Northcott, Dave Trottier and Jimmy Ward had emerged as new stars, and with Russ Blinco named rookie of the year in 1933–34, the Maroons were more than able to compensate for the loss of the two future Hall of Famers. In 1935, the Montreal team became Stanley Cup champions for the second time.

Former Maroon Lionel Conacher had returned to Montreal in 1934–35 after having won the Stanley Cup in Chicago the year before. Another key acquisition that sea-son was Alex Connell, who was acquired by Tommy Gorman, hired as coach and general manager of the Maroons in 1934–35 after coaching the Black Hawks to the Stanley Cup in 1934. Connell gave the Montreal team its first star goaltender since Clint Benedict left in the 1929–30 season. (Ironically, it was Connell's arrival in Ottawa 10 years earlier that had convinced the Senators to let Benedict go to Montreal.) Connell helped the Maroons post the sec-ond-best defensive record in the NHL during the 1934–35 season, then sparkled en route to the Stanley Cup with a pair of shutouts and just eight goals against in seven play-off games.

With the line of Hooley Smith, Baldy Northcott and

Jimmy Ward leading the way, the Maroons followed up their Stanley Cup victory with a Canadian Division title in 1935–36, but even with so much success, fan support was beginning to wane. In fact, attendance had been in decline in Montreal and around the league since the onset of the Depression, but now the Maroons really began to feel the economic pinch. Hooley Smith was an all-star in 1935–36, but salary concerns saw him peddled to the Boston Bruins prior to the 1936–37 campaign. The Maroons opened the season poorly without him and attendance suffered all the more. A strong finish nearly saw the Maroons catch the Canadiens for top spot in their division, but attendance never recovered. The retirement of Lionel Conacher and Alex Connell further weakened the team in 1937–38, but Tommy Gorman hoped that hiring King Clancy as coach would fill the Maroons with a fighting spirit. It didn't. Following a three-game losing streak that saw the team fall into last place with a record of 6–11–1, Clancy resigned as coach on December 31, 1937, and Gorman went back behind the bench. At the time it was said that Clancy hadn't enforced enough discipline; others put the blame for the team's poor play on the low wages Gorman was paying.

The Maroons continued to slump under Gorman and attendance worsened amid talk the city might be better served by just one professional hockey team. A 6–3 loss to the Canadiens on March 17, 1938 saw the Maroons finish the season with the league's worst record of 12–30–6 and miss the playoffs for the first time in nine years. It would be the last game the Maroons ever played. With the threat of war in Europe making the economic future even more uncertain, the team requested permission to suspend operations for one year, which the NHL granted on August 25, 1938. After the year off, the Montreal Maroons advised the NHL on May 13, 1939 that they would no longer operate a franchise. Within a year, the Canadian Arena Company would acquire the complete stock and assets of the Montreal Canadiens. The Canadiens were also drawing poorly at this time, but Donat Raymond would assure that at least one Montreal club would survive. The man who had built the Forum and created the Maroons continued to absorb financial losses while Tommy Gorman and coach Dick Irvin rebuilt the Canadiens. By 1944, the team had won its first Stanley Cup in 13 years and would go on to become the most successful franchise in hockey history.

Montreal Maroons Year-by-Year Record

Season	GP	W	L	T	GF	GA	Pts	Finish		Playoff Results
1924–25	30	9	19	2	45	65	20	5th		Out of Playoffs
1925–26	36	20	11	5	91	73	45	2nd		Won Stanley Cup
1926–27	44	20	20	4	71	68	44	3rd	Cdn. Div.	Lost Quarterfinal
1927–28	44	24	14	6	96	77	54	2nd	Cdn. Div.	Lost Final
1928–29	44	15	20	9	67	65	39	5th	Cdn. Div.	Out of Playoffs
1929–30	44	23	16	5	141	114	51	1st	Cdn. Div.	Lost Semifinal
1930–31	44	20	18	6	105	106	46	3rd	Cdn. Div.	Lost Quarterfinal
1931–32	48	19	22	7	142	139	45	3rd	Cdn. Div.	Lost Semifinal
1932–33	48	22	20	6	135	119	50	2nd	Cdn. Div.	Lost Quarterfinal
1933–34	48	19	18	11	117	122	49	3rd	Cdn. Div.	Lost Semifinal
1934–35	48	24	19	5	123	92	53	2nd	Cdn. Div.	Won Stanley Cup
1935–36	48	22	16	10	114	106	54	1st	Cdn. Div.	Lost Semifinal
1936–37	48	22	17	9	126	110	53	2nd	Cdn. Div.	Lost Semifinal
1937–38	48	12	30	6	101	149	30	4th	Cdn. Div.	Out of Playoffs

MONTREAL WANDERERS

Eric Zweig

THE MONTREAL WANDERERS officially came into existence on December 5, 1903 and departed the hockey scene on January 4, 1918, two days after their home arena was destroyed by fire. Yet, while they lasted less than 15 seasons and have now been gone for more than 80 years, the Montreal Wanderers remain one of the legendary names in hockey history. In the team's brief lifetime, 16 future Hockey Hall of Famers played for the Wanderers and the team was Stanley Cup champions in 1906, 1907, 1908 and 1910. But, even more than success, controversy defined the Montreal Wanderers throughout their brief existence.

The Wanderers were organized by James Strachan (who would later help form the Montreal Maroons). Strachan was granted a team in the Federal Amateur Hockey League, along with the Ottawa Capitals, Cornwall and the Montreal Nationals, when the new league was formed on December 5, 1903. FAHL President William Foran of the Capitals explained that the new league was created because the Canadian Amateur Hockey League had excluded the entry of new teams from their organization. Perhaps the exclusion of the Wanderers was due to the fact that Strachan had raided the roster of the CAHL's Montreal Amateur Athletic Association hockey club to stock his new team. Of the nine players who played at least two games for the Wanderers during the six-game 1903–04 FAHL season, six (Jack Marshall, Jimmy Gardner, Cecil Blachford, Dickie Boon, Billy Bellingham and goalie Billy Nicholson) had been with the rival Montreal organization the previous season. All except Blachford had also been members of the AAA's Stanley Cup-winning team of 1902. That team had been dubbed "the Little Men of Iron" for the tenacious way they hung on to defeat the Winnipeg Victorias and in later years the nickname was frequently applied to the Wanderers.

The powerful aggregation of former champions had little trouble with the competition in the FAHL as the Wanderers romped to the championship with a perfect 6–0 record. A two-game total goals Stanley Cup challenge match was then arranged between the Wanderers and the Ottawa Silver Seven. Ottawa, too, had seen its share of controversy that year. The defending Stanley Cup champions had resigned from the CAHL in midseason and there had been some discussion as to whether or not they still had the right to retain the Stanley Cup. The trustees sided with the Silver Seven, but the Stanley Cup series between the season's two most troublesome teams provided yet more problems.

The series opened in Montreal on March 2, 1904 and an extremely physical game ended in a 5–5 tie after 60 minutes (then played in two 30-minute halves). Unhappy with the refereeing, the Wanderers refused to play overtime and the game remained a tie. The Stanley Cup trustees ordered a new two-game set with both games to be played in Ottawa, but the Wanderers refused to take part unless the tied game was replayed in Montreal. After plenty of harsh words from James Strachan, the series was abandoned and the Silver Seven went on to defeat a team from Brandon, Manitoba, in a new Stanley Cup challenge.

Prior to the 1904–05 season, the Wanderers again applied for entry in the Canadian Amateur Hockey League (which added two teams that year) but were refused. The Silver Seven joined them in the Federal League this year, although there were rumors both teams would abandon the FAHL for

a place in the CAHL. The rumors heated up again prior to the 1905–06 season but the Wanderers would be in the center of a much more surprising development.

Although both the Wanderers and Silver Seven had announced in late November their intentions to remain in the Federal League, the two teams became involved in the formation of a new league on December 11, 1906. The Eastern Canada Amateur Hockey Association would consist of the Wanderers and Ottawa from the FAHL, and the Montreal Victorias, Quebec Bulldogs, Montreal AAA and Montreal Shamrocks of the CAHL. With a few additions, the constitution of the CAHL was adopted for the new ECAHA. The Arena Trophy was to be emblematic of the league champion. (The Stanley Cup was still a challenge trophy in those days, open to any league in Canada.)

Bolstered by the additions of future Hall of Famers Lester Patrick, Moose Johnson and Ernie Russell, the Wanderers proved the equal of the defending Stanley Cup champions from Ottawa and the two teams finished the first ECAHA season with identical 9–1 records. To break the tie, a two-game total-goals playoff was scheduled. The winner would not only claim the new Arena Trophy but also the Stanley Cup. The first game was played in Montreal on March 14, 1906 and resulted in a shocking 9–1 victory for the Wanderers. Game two was played in Ottawa three nights later, and the Wanderers chose not to protest when the Silver Seven unveiled former Smiths Falls star Percy LeSueur in goal. The change appeared not to matter, as the Wanderers scored an early goal to take a 10–1 lead overall but then the defending champions began to chip away at the lead. Frank McGee scored twice and Harry Smith once before half time, and with Smith scoring four more goals in the second half the Silver Seven stormed back to tie the series at 10–10. With Ottawa fans poised to see their heroes end a fourth consecutive season as Stanley Cup champions, Lester Patrick scored two late goals and the Wanderers ended the Silver Sevens' championship reign with a 12–10 victory.

Not content to rest on their laurels as champions, James Strachan and the Wanderers began to stir up new trouble at the annual meeting of the Eastern Canada Amateur Hockey Association on November 11, 1906. Strachan was instrumental in pushing to allow professional players into the league along with amateurs. The rule was passed (against the objections of the Montreal AAA and Montreal Victorias) on condition that the status of each team's players had to be published in the newspapers. The Wanderers signed new goaltender Riley Hern and defenseman Hod Stuart to professional contracts, as well as existing players Pud Glass, Moose Johnson and Jack Marshall, while Lester Patrick, Cecil Blachford, Ernie Russell and Rod Kennedy retained their amateur status. The Wanderers made further waves at the ECAHA meetings when they announced they would withdraw from the league unless they were permitted to meet a team from New Glasgow, Nova Scotia in a preseason Stanley Cup challenge. Permission was granted and the Wanderers scored easy 10–3 and 7–2 victories on December 27 and 29, 1906. The Wanderers began the ECAHA season on January 2, 1907 and posted three straight victories before taking time off to accept another Stanley Cup challenge.

The Kenora Thistles had challenged the Ottawa Silver Seven in 1903 and 1905 when the town was still known as Rat Portage. The team had been a power in northwestern Ontario and Manitoba for several years by 1907 and had a

roster that boasted future Hall of Famers in Tommy Phillips, Tom Hooper, Billy McGimsie and Si Griffis. Art Ross was also added to the lineup for the challenge against the Wanderers, yet it was still considered an upset when the Thistles scored a 4–2 victory in the first game on January 17. Tommy Phillips scored all four goals and added three more in an 8–6 win four nights later as the Thistles lifted the Stanley Cup.

Spurred on by the desire to win back the trophy, the Wanderers blazed through the remainder of the ECAHA season. With Ernie Russell leading the way (he would score 42 goals in nine league games), the Wanderers recorded wins of 11–3, 5–2, 16–3, 13–5, 18–5, 10–6, and 16–5, to finish the season 10–0 and head west to Winnipeg for a Stanley Cup rematch with Kenora. This time, the Thistles had bolstered their attack with Ottawa stars Alf Smith and Rat Westwick, but the Wanderers scored a 7–2 victory in the first game on March 23, 1907. Though Kenora won the second game 6–5, the Wanderers took the total-goal series 12–8 and were Stanley Cup champions once again. Another ECAHA title in 1907–08 gave them their third straight Arena Trophy (which currently resides in the Hockey Hall of Fame in Toronto) and successful defenses against teams from Ottawa, Toronto, Winnipeg and Edmonton kept the Stanley Cup in Montreal through one more year. Lester Patrick went west to British Columbia to work in the family lumber business and Hod Stuart had drowned during the summer of 1907, but the addition of Art Ross and Hod's brother Bruce Stuart to the Wanderers lineup helped offset the loss.

The 1908–09 season saw the Eastern Canada Amateur Hockey Association become the Eastern Canada Hockey Association after the withdrawal of the strictly amateur Montreal Victorias and Montreal AAA. Ottawa (now known as the Senators) beat the Wanderers in the final game of the season to win the ECHA title and the Stanley Cup, but the Wanderers would return to the top in 1910 — though not without more controversy.

The Wanderers, by this time, had been sold to P.J. Doran, who owned the Jubilee Arena in Montreal. Although his arena had about half the capacity of the Wanderers previous home, Doran proposed to move his team into his rink for the 1909–10 season. This idea was not well received by other teams, whose share of the gate receipts would now be significantly less. As a result, Doran's fellow owners voted the ECHA out of existence on November 25, 1909 and created the new Canadian Hockey Association. This league would not include the Wanderers, nor the team from Renfrew, Ontario that the Wanderers supported for inclusion in the ECHA.

Having both been snubbed, the Wanderers joined with Renfrew to form a rival hockey league — the National Hockey Association. Backed by Renfrew millionaire M.J. O'Brien and run by his son Ambrose, the NHA went to war with the CHA, driving up salaries as they bought talented stars like Cyclone Taylor and Lester Patrick for their Renfrew club and creating a new all-French team in Montreal known as *les Canadiens*. (The Wanderers, like virtually all other Montreal teams, had relied on English/Irish Montreal for both players and their fans.) By mid-January, it was apparent the NHA was winning the war and the Montreal Shamrocks and Ottawa Senators abandoned the CHA for the new league. With Ottawa now in tow, the NHA held the Stanley Cup and it was predicted that the championship battle would be between Renfrew and the

Senators. However, the Wanderers upset the experts. The addition of Harry Hyland to the now-familiar roster of Hern, Marshall, Johnson, Glass, Blachford, Gardner and Russell helped the Wanderers post an 11–1 record that gave them both the NHA title and the Stanley Cup.

Ownership of the Wanderers again changed hands for the 1910–11 season and the team moved back to the larger Montreal Arena. However, the glory days of the franchise were over. With the exception of the 1914–15 season (when they lost the league title to the Ottawa Senators in a two-game playoff), the Wanderers were little more than also-rans during the final seven seasons of the NHA. Sam Lichtenhein's ownership during this period was marked by financial struggles. The war over players with the rival Pacific Coast Hockey Association drove up salaries, while the War in Europe depleted rosters and lessened hockey's box office appeal.

When the teams of the NHA reorganized to form the NHL in November of 1917, the Wanderers were included but Lichtenhein's team was clearly in trouble. As late as December 12, 1917 it appeared that the Wanderers might not be able to produce a team due to injuries and military commitments. However, when the NHL season opened seven days later, the Wanderers' cast of aging veterans and unproven youngsters defeated Toronto 10–9—though only 700 fans saw the game. Two nights later, the rival Canadiens crushed the Wanderers 11–2 and Lichtenhein threatened to withdraw from the NHL unless he could get more players. A 6–3 loss to Ottawa was followed by a 9–2 loss to the Senators on December 29. It would be the last game the Wanderers ever played.

On January 2, 1918 fire destroyed the Montreal Arena. The blaze was attributed to an unknown cause in the Wanderers' dressing room. The Montreal Canadiens announced they would play out the season in the Wanderers' old home, the Jubilee Arena. The arena in Hamilton, Ontario offered to take in the Wanderers, but when the other NHL teams refused to provide the addition players he wanted, Lichtenhein withdrew his club on January 4, 1918. A colorful and controversial era in hockey history was over.

Montreal Wanderers Year-by-Year Record

Season	GP	W	L	T	GF	GA	Pts	Finish	Playoff Results
1917–18	6	1	5	0	17	35	2	Withdrew	

NASHVILLE PREDATORS

THE NHL BECOMES A 27-TEAM LEAGUE (on its way to 30) with the debut of the Nashville Predators in 1998–99. Nashville is the first of four new teams (Atlanta, Minnesota and Columbus) to hit the ice after all were welcomed into the league as expansion clubs on June 25, 1997. The Predators play out of the Central Division of the Western Conference along with the Chicago Blackhawks, Detroit Red Wings, and St. Louis Blues. (The Columbus Blue Jackets will be added to the division for the 2000–2001 season.) Their home rink is the new Nashville Arena.

The Predators name was announced for Nashville's first major-league sports franchise on November 13, 1997 by club chairman and majority owner Craig Leipold and president Jack Diller. "This is another major step in creating a permanent identity for Nashville's franchise," Leipold said. "Given the intense nature of hockey, combined with the

game's speed and skill, Predators is a natural fit, and it is the name Nashville fans chose for their team." Said Diller: "We wanted our hockey club to be a reflection of the community … [and] Predators was the name of choice. … The image of a predator is one who succeeds and wins, something we hope our team will do often when we begin play." For a logo, the team chose a dramatic profile of a saber-toothed tiger, which was native in prehistoric times to the region that is now Nashville. Team colors are dark blue, silver, orange and gold. On March 28, 1998, the Predators topped the 12,000-mark in seasons tickets (a condition of expansion set out by the NHL) through the strength of a community-wide effort involving business leaders and individual hockey fans.

The first major order of business for team president Jack Diller had been to hire David Poile as executive vice president of hockey operations and general manager on July 9, 1997. Poile had served as general manager of the Washington Capitals since 1982 and had helped build the team into a perennial contender. He had begun his career in hockey administration with the expansion Atlanta Flames in 1972 and worked himself up to the position of assistant general manager in both Atlanta and Calgary. His father, Bud Poile, had played seven years in the NHL and was the general manager of expansion teams in both Philadelphia and Vancouver. A little less than a month after his own hiring in Nashville, Poile signed Barry Trotz as the team's first head coach. Trotz had spent the past four seasons as the head coach of the Portland Pirates, Washington's farm club in the American Hockey League.

Roster-building commenced on June 26, 1998 at the Expansion Draft in Buffalo (see below). A day later, a trade with the San Jose Sharks landed Nashville the second pick in the NHL Entry Draft and the Predators choice highly regarded junior prospect David Legwand. A rookie in the Ontario Hockey League in 1997–98, Legwand had 54 goals and 51 assists in just 59 games for the Plymouth Whalers and became the first rookie (and second American-born player) to be named the OHL's most valuable player.

NASHVILLE EXPANSION DRAFT SELECTIONS

PLAYER	POSITION	PREVIOUS CLUB
Chris Armstrong	D	Florida Panthers
Blair Atcheynum	RW	St. Louis Blues
Joel Bouchard	D	Calgary Flames
Bob Boughner	D	Buffalo Sabres
Paul Brousseau	RW	Tampa Bay Lightning
Doug Brown	RW	Detroit Red Wings
Andrew Brunette	LW	Washington Capitals
Frederic Chabot	G	Los Angeles Kings
Patrick Cote	LW	Dallas Stars
J.J. Daigneault	D	New York Islanders
Jeff Daniels	LW	Carolina Hurricanes
Craig Darby	LW	Philadelphia Flyers
Mike Dunham	G	New Jersey Devils
Doug Friedman	C	Edmonton Oilers
Tony Hrkac	C	Pittsburgh Penguins
Al Iafrate	D	San Jose Sharks
Greg Johnson	C	Chicago Blackhawks
Uwe Krupp	D	Colorado Avalanche
Denny Lambert	LW	Ottawa Senators
Mike Richter	G	New York Rangers
Mikhail Shtalenkov	G	Mighty Ducks of Anaheim
John Slaney	D	Phoenix Coyotes
Mike Sullivan	C	Boston Bruins
Tomas Vokoun	G	Montreal Canadiens
Scott Walker	C	Vancouver Canucks
Rob Zettler	D	Toronto Maple Leafs

NEW JERSEY DEVILS, COLORADO ROCKIES AND KANSAS CITY SCOUTS

Stan Fischler

IN ITS RELATIVELY SHORT life in the National Hockey League, the New Jersey Devils franchise has embodied the personalities of its two leaders, John McMullen and Lou Lamoriello. The Devils have been disciplined, well-organized, fiscally responsible, brash and forthright. They have gone in the space of a decade from the league's laughing stock—Wayne Gretzky once called the Devils a "Mickey Mouse operation"—to a Stanley Cup champion and consistent challenger for the Presidents' Trophy as the NHL's regular-season champion.

Actually, the Devils began their existence not in New Jersey but Missouri as the Kansas City Scouts. During the league's expansion decade, the 1970s, teams had been admitted from Long Island and Atlanta in 1972 followed by Washington and Kansas City two years later. Playing out of the brand-new Kemper Arena, the Scouts had little to offer in their rookie season. Facing competition from the two-year-old World Hockey Association, the Scouts scrambled for talent and had little apart from the solid goaltending of Denis Herron, the power shooting from Simon Nolet and the hope that high-priced rookie Wilf Paiement would make his three-year $500,000 contract look worthwhile.

Former Detroit Red Wings hero Sid Abel was named general manager, and he did the best with what he had but, admittedly, it was not much. "Neither the Capitals nor ourselves were exactly overloaded with stars," said Abel. By comparison with the Capitals, the Scouts did relatively well. Kansas City finished with 41 points, 20 more than Washington, but that was the extent of the jubilation. A year later Kansas City slipped to 36 points while attendance slipped to a point of no return. With the NHL's approval, the franchise was moved to Denver where it was rechristened the Colorado Rockies and continued to lose hockey games.

Under coach Johnny Wilson, the Rockies finished last in the Smythe Division (20–46–14) and offered little to attract the Rocky Mountain fans other than Paiement, who began fulfilling his early notices. There was little difference between the franchise in Kansas City and Denver other than the fact that Rockies lasted six years rather than two and for a brief, colorful period Don Cherry took over as coach. Cherry had become a major personality by the time the 1979–80 season was half over, although his team once again was at or near the bottom of the Smythe Division.

"My goalies were Hardy Astrom, Bill McKenzie and Bill Oleschuk," said Cherry. "I never thought of myself as a connoisseur of goaltenders, but one look at the guys we had between the pipes convinced me that our goalie problems weren't big, they were colossal. When I came home one day after practice, I said to my wife, 'Either our team has the best shooters in the NHL or the worst goaltenders.' Unfortunately for me it was the latter."

Cherry was succeeded by Billy MacMillan in 1980–81, by which time it had become obvious that Denver was not buying into the Rockies. New Jersey trucking executive Arthur Imperatore, who had purchased the team, threatened to move the franchise to a new arena in his home state's Meadowlands within view of the Manhattan skyline. But the Rangers, Islanders and Flyers—each of whom had veto power—nixed the idea, whereupon Imperatore sold the club to Buffalo cable television magnate Peter Gilbert and former Colorado lieutenant governor Mark Hogan.

MacMillan failed to nudge the Rockies into a playoff berth but somehow was promoted to general manager while former NHL defenseman Bert Marshall took over behind the bench. After 24 games (3–17–4), he was fired and replaced by Marshall Johnston, whose effectiveness was not much better than his predecessors. By this time, Gilbert wanted out and found a buyer in Dr. John J. McMullen. Renowned in sporting circles, Dr. McMullen first ventured into baseball as a limited partner of the New York Yankees and later would own the Houston Astros. A New Jersey native, Dr. McMullen graduated from Montclair High Schools and received a B.S. Degree in Electrical Engineering from the U.S. Naval Academy in 1940. He served in the navy during World War II and resigned with the rank of commander in 1954. During naval service, he earned a Master of Science degree in Naval Architecture and Marine Engineering from M.I.T. and a Doctor of Mechanical Engineering degree from Swiss Federal Institute in Zurich.

Throughout his life, McMullen remained an avid sports fan and became convinced that the state of New Jersey could support an NHL team at The Meadowlands. On May 27, 1982 it became official. McMullen, along with John C. Whitehead, now the chairman of AEA Investors, Inc., and former New Jersey governor Brendan T. Byrne, purchased the Rockies and received NHL approval to shift the franchise to The Meadowlands. It was not, however, a simple transaction. McMullen had to indemnify the Flyers, Rangers and Islanders handsomely for "invading" their territory. But McMullen, who had an excellent track record owning the Houston Astros, was neither daunted by the indemnity nor the losing team which he had inherited. "Our fans in New Jersey will be tolerant for a few years," he said. "In time we should be able to improve ourselves." McMullen named longtime hockey executive Max McNab vice president in charge of hockey operations and Billy MacMillan as general manager and coach. The team was renamed the Devils and opened its first training camp in the Garden State on September 11, 1982 in Totowa.

As the players streamed into camp from all parts of Canada and the United States, the Devils roster began taking shape. Among the NHLers, there was Joel Quenneville, Bob Lorimer, Joe Cirella, Aaron Broten and Steve Tambellini, along with former Islanders goaltender Chico Resch. A veteran of several shellings as a member of the Colorado Rockies, Resch wasted no time telling reporters how previous management had hurt the franchise. "They made some bad moves in the past," said Resch. "Many of the mistakes were because of pressure from the former ownership. There were a lot of panic moves made in an attempt to produce an instant winner. Now we're moving in a positive direction. The only way to accomplish anything in this game is by drafting blue-chip players and being patient with them."

On September 17, 1982, the Devils beat the Washington Capitals 3–1. It was their first game—and first win—since they escaped the hopeless situation in Colorado and came east. New Jersey fans would be treated to the home exhibition debut of the team on September 21, 1982. Facing them would be the New York Rangers, a team that soon became a keen rival. Dr. McMullen accelerated the rivalry possibilities by twitting the denizens of Madison Square Garden in

a pregame comment that was well-covered by the media. "I believe we're going to be a lot more aggressive than the Rangers," said Dr. McMullen. "They're complacent because they're sold out." Seizing on the observation, the *New York Post* headlined the story RANGERS ANGRY OVER McMULLEN REMARK.

Perhaps they were, but McMullen couldn't have cared less. He wanted his team to put on a good showing against the 56-year-old franchise from across the Hudson River and he was amply rewarded, although the Devils did not win despite two goals from Merlin Malinowski. The 9,193 fans were well entertained, yet MacMillan was disappointed. "We still have a long way to go," he opined.

It is doubtful that McMullen realized precisely how long it would take for his Devils to become a playoff contender. They finished their first season with a record of 17 wins, 49 losses and 14 ties, placing them fifth in the six-team Patrick Division. And while they missed postseason play, the Devils did leave an imprint on the Metropolitan Area hockey scene. "We're making some progress," said Aaron Broten. "Last year we didn't know if the team would be in Denver or wherever. Now we know we're going to be in New Jersey next year."

But 1983–84 was no kinder to New Jersey's franchise. If one episode could encapsulate the club's futility, it would be a game at Northlands Coliseum in Edmonton on November 19, 1983. Ron Low started in goal for New Jersey. He was well-known to Edmonton fans and players, having played for the Oilers over four seasons before being traded to the Devils in 1983. While not a spectacular netminder, Low was a favorite with just about everyone, even those in opposing uniforms. "We had pretty strong ties," said Edmonton defenseman Kevin Lowe, "because Ronnie had been a part of our team when we were just beginning to jell. He was one guy you always could talk to no matter what uniform he was wearing."

Much as they liked Low, the Oilers were merciless in their treatment of him that evening. They pumped eight goals past him through two periods of play and were so overwhelming that MacMillan felt obligated to pull his starter and replace Ron with Resch for the third period. The Devils kept the score respectable until the final 10 minutes, when Edmonton players acted like piranhas to a wounded deer. They swarmed around Resch and riddled him with five goals. The final tally was 13–4, representing the largest score ever run up against the franchise. And the swarming was not over.

Reporters descended on the Oilers dressing room for comments, especially from Wayne Gretzky, who had eight points on three goals and five assists. By this point in time, The Great One had become THE premier personality in hockey, and his words carried extra weight when he delivered a peroration. On this night, he had plenty to say.

Prodded with leading questions from the newsmen, Gretzky was lured into a denunciation that he would have avoided, if he had the luxury of replay. But he answered spontaneously when queried about the bombardment of his buddy Low. "It got to a point where it wasn't even funny," said Gretzky. "How long has it been for them? Three years? Five? Seven? Probably closer to nine. Well, it's time they got their act together. They're ruining the whole league. They had better stop running a Mickey Mouse operation and put somebody on ice. It's not a question of not working. It's a question of talent. I feel sorry for Ronnie and New Jersey. The 37 shots we took were all good shots. They

struggled in Kansas City, they were awful in Colorado and now look what's happening."

There was a lull before the backdraft blew out the media doors. The 13–4 game took place on Saturday night in Edmonton, after most of the New Jersey-New York newspapers had their last editions put to bed. Little other than the scoring results appeared in most Sunday papers, but by Monday the headlines were blaring all over the country. GRETZKY TAKES A SLAP AT DEVILS ORGANIZATION barked the headline in *USA Today*. *The New York Post* was more direct. GRETZKY: DEVILS ARE A MICKEY MOUSE TEAM. The Mickey Mouse theme began snowballing. To his surprise, Gretzky began feeling the heat and experiencing considerable remorse the more he considered his intemperate putdown. What surprised him was the groundswell of public opinion against his tirade. "You'd have thought I'd criticized Miss Newark or something," said Gretzky. "The fans went crazy against me. In retrospect, I probably shouldn't have said it, but I was feeling so bad about the way we'd killed them and I liked some of their guys, Ronnie Low and Chico Resch. I made a mistake of trying to divert the blame from those guys, but maybe it wasn't my place to lay blame or divert it."

The fallout from the Gretzky fiasco led to MacMillan being dismissed as general manager and head coach. Max McNab was named general manager and Tom McVie, who had been coaching the Maine Mariners, was promoted to head coach. The results were insignificant. The Devils finished fifth again (17–56–7) and now had the stigma of Gretzky's insult tarnishing their image. Only an upgrade of the on-ice product would make a difference, but that was not to be; at least not in the immediate future. If there was hope, it was provided by draft choices such as Kirk Muller and John MacLean, who infused energy into the machine if not sufficient wins. In 1985–86, the club dropped to sixth place (28–49–3) but MacLean's 21 goals earmarked him for future stardom. In addition, rugged, young defenseman Ken Daneyko had established himself as the most robust hitter on the Devils and one of the early fan favorites.

Management had placed Doug Carpenter in charge of coaching and while the redhead provided a sense of discipline and purpose in the young club, the coveted playoff berth was still beyond reach. Try as he might, Carpenter was unsuccessful, although he did lift the club to an all-time high of 29 wins and 64 points despite the sixth-place finish. The club's turning point began on April 24, 1987, when president Bob Butera resigned and McMullen named Lou Lamoriello as his successor. For two decades Lamoriello had been the guiding force behind Providence College's hockey success and coached the Friars for 15 years beginning with the 1968–69 season. He had ascended to the post of athletic director at Providence in 1982 and became commissioner of Hockey East in 1983.

"In Lou Lamoriello," said Dr. McMullen, "the Devils have a hockey man who has earned a great respect for his accomplishments at and away from the rink, and for both his hockey and his business acumen. I look forward to working with Lou as we take the Devils through the next steps of our development—the playoff and the Stanley Cup." Lamoriello, a 1963 graduate of Providence, guided the Friars to an impressive winning percentage (248–179–13) and ten postseason tournaments in his 15 years behind the bench, including a 1983 NCAA Final Four appearance in his final season. A year after becoming athletic director, he was one of five founders of the Hockey

East Association. He was selected by his peers to serve as commissioner of the seven-team league which, under his direction, has become one of the most prestigious hockey conferences in the country.

"Since the establishment of the NHL franchise in New Jersey," said Lamoriello, "the Devils have always impressed me with strong ownership and unlimited potential. After meeting and getting to know Dr. McMullen, I am convinced of this, as well as Dr. McMullen's commitment to winning in a first-class manner." When McNab was moved up to a vice presidency, Lamoriello became general manager as well and began a serious evaluation of talent. Following a 9–3 loss to the Rangers at Madison Square Garden on December 16, 1987, Lamoriello decided to replace Carpenter. The search for a new coach took more than a month but on January 26, 1988, Jim Schoenfeld was introduced as the new bench boss.

Schoenfeld was one of two key additions who would transform the Devils from perennial losers to a playoff team. The other was goaltender Sean Burke, who had been drafted by New Jersey in 1985 and had come to the team following the 1988 Winter Olympic Games at Calgary. In his first game as a Devil at Boston Garden, Burke defeated the Bruins 7–6 in overtime, on a goal by Andy Brickley. Although nobody knew it for sure at the time, this was the start of something big. Slowly, relentlessly, the Devils began a long climb toward a playoff berth that culminated with a decisive game at Chicago Stadium on April 3, 1988. Trailing the Rangers throughout the homestretch, the Devils could oust their rivals by defeating the Blackhawks. The game went into sudden-death overtime before John MacLean beat goalie Darren Pang at 2:21 to give New Jersey its victory and first taste of postseason play.

The Devils then upset the first-place Islanders in the opening round and followed that with a seven-game series win—again MacLean scored the decisive goal—over favored Washington. Facing Boston in the third round, the Devils unexpectedly became involved in a brouhaha at the end of game three at Byrne Arena. Coach Jim Schoenfeld engaged in a verbal bout with referee Don Koharski that continued in a hallway leading from the ice to the dressing rooms. When NHL vice president Brian O'Neill—NHL president John Ziegler was reportedly out-of-town—suspended Schoenfeld, the Devils charged that no hearing was held and the right of appeal should be honored.

Taking their case to Bergen County Superior Court Judge James F. Madden, the Devils won a temporary restraining order that lifted Schoenfeld's suspension. The decision was rendered minutes before game time on Mother's Day, May 8, the night on which game four was to be played. Upon hearing of the judge's decision, the referee and linesmen refused to take the ice. The NHL responded by hiring three off-ice officials—Paul McInnis, Vin Godleski and Jim Sullivan—to officiate the game. Skates were found for all three. Only one had a striped shirt. The other two donned yellow practice jerseys and took the ice one hour and six minutes after the scheduled start of the game. (Two more striped shirts were found for the start of period two.) The Devils won 3–1 and the replacement officials won praise for their efforts.

New Jersey took Boston to seven games before succumbing 6–2 in the finale at Boston Garden. "Our club has proven that we no longer will be two easy points for every opponent," said Lamoriello. Instead of providing an impetus for bigger things, the big run to the playoffs proved illu-

sory. In 1988–89, they missed the postseason again but rebounded the following season with a second-place finish after John Cunniff had replaced Schoenfeld as coach. A first-round exit dimmed the luster and Cunniff exited in the middle of the 1990–91 season in favor of Tom McVie. The Devils continued to play competitively, reaching the playoffs but never advancing past the first round, even after Herb Brooks succeeded McVie for the 1992–93 campaign.

A new era dawned on June 28, 1993 when Jacques Lemaire, a member of eight Stanley Cup-winning Montreal Canadiens teams, was named New Jersey's seventh head coach, while former teammate Larry Robinson came aboard as Lemaire's assistant. The results were remarkable. In his first season, Lemaire guided the Devils to their best-ever record, 47–25–12, good for second place in the division. They then defeated Boston and Buffalo in the first two playoff rounds before extending the Rangers to double-overtime of the seventh game.

A year later, in a lockout-shortened season, the Devils finished second again and entered the playoffs as distinct underdogs to the Boston Bruins. Paced by Claude Lemieux and Stephane Richer, New Jersey opened with a 5–0 win on the road and proceeded to demolish the Bruins in five games. Facing Pittsburgh, the Devils fell behind by a game, losing 3–2 at the Civic Center, but rebounded for a 4–2 victory at Pittsburgh and closed out the series with three more wins.

Next on the agenda was Philadelphia, with the Devils again opening on the road. It hardly mattered. They beat the Flyers in two straight at the Spectrum and won the series in six. Lemieux, Richer and goalie Martin Brodeur continued to excel as New Jersey reached the finals against the Red Wings at Joe Louis Arena. Lemieux tallied the winner (2–1) in game one, setting the stage for a surprisingly easy rout. After winning 4–2 in game two, the Devils wrapped up the series with consecutive 5–2 victories before capacity crowds of 19,004 at the Meadowlands. NHL commissioner Gary Bettman presented the Cup to captain Scott Stevens and then congratulated John McMullen.

But the days of celebration were clouded in uncertainty. In a dispute with the New Jersey Sports and Exposition Authority—the landlord of Byrne Arena—McMullen threatened to move his club to Nashville where a brand-new rink was being completed and financial enticements were difficult to refuse. After a summer of intense negotiations with the involvement of Bettman, a compromise was hammered out which included a new lease that extended through the start of the 21st century.

In their defense of the Stanley Cup, the Devils proved a disappointment, although their record in 1995–96 was 37–33–12, good for 86 points. Yet they were eliminated from playoff contention on the final weekend of the season, losing to Ottawa at home and thus enabling the Tampa Bay Lightning to earn its first playoff berth. However, Lemaire was able to galvanize his team the following year, lifting New Jersey to first place both in the division and the conference. Martin Brodeur had established himself as one of the league's foremost goaltenders while Scott Stevens was a rock on the blue line. Lacking a gunner, the Devils nevertheless spread the goals among four well-balanced lines led by the likes of Bobby Holik, Dave Andreychuk and Randy McKay.

The Devils seemed on course for another long playoff run in the spring of 1997 until Andreychuk—the club's best two-way forward—badly broke his ankle in the club's final

game of the season at Philadelphia. Although New Jersey defeated Montreal in a five-game opening playoff round, Lemaire's team seemed somewhat off-kilter. This was confirmed in the second round when the Rangers—after losing the first match—won four straight to eliminate the Devils.

Lamoriello made some lineup alterations for 1997–98, dipping into his Albany River Rats farm club for reinforcements. Youngsters such as Brad Bombardir, Patrik Elias and Sheldon Souray were added to the lineup and paid off handsomely. New Jersey finished with a club record 107 points (48–23–11), falling just short of winning the Presidents' Trophy. First in their division and first in their conference, the Devils were rated among the Stanley Cup favorites. However, late-season injuries to Doug Gilmour and Randy McKay disrupted the momentum, and instead of approaching the playoffs with a rush, the Devils limped into the first round and were stunned by an Ottawa Senators team that eliminated them in six games.

Despite the defeat, New Jersey had established itself as a formidable organization. Attendance reached an all-time high during the 1997–98 season with an average of more than 17,000 per game, and the Albany farm club continued to excel in the American Hockey League. Meanwhile, McMullen revealed plans to build an arena of his own on the Hudson River shores in the city of Hoboken. Although full approval had yet to be granted, McMullen projected that the new building that would straddle the historic Delaware, Lackawanna and Western Railroad terminal could be completed as early as the year 2004.

If nothing else, the blueprints demonstrated that the Devils had come a long way since the dim, dismal days of the franchise in Kansas City and Denver.

New Jersey Devils Year-by-Year Record

Season	GP	W	L	T	GF	GA	Pts	Finish		Playoff Results
1974–75*	80	15	54	11	184	328	41	5th	Smythe Div.	Out of Playoffs
1975–76*	80	12	56	12	190	351	36	5th	Smythe Div.	Out of Playoffs
1976–77**	80	20	46	14	226	307	54	5th	Smythe Div.	Out of Playoffs
1977–78**	80	19	40	21	257	305	59	2nd	Smythe Div.	Lost Prelim. Round
1978–79**	80	15	53	12	210	331	42	4th	Smythe Div.	Out of Playoffs
1979–80**	80	19	48	13	234	308	51	6th	Smythe Div.	Out of Playoffs
1980–81**	80	22	45	13	258	344	57	5th	Smythe Div.	Out of Playoffs
1981–82**	80	18	49	13	241	362	49	5th	Smythe Div.	Out of Playoffs
1982–83	80	00	17	49	14	230	338	48	5th	Patrick Div.	Out of Playoffs
1983–84	80	17	56	7	231	350	41	5th	Patrick Div.	Out of Playoffs
1984–85	80	22	48	10	264	346	54	5th	Patrick Div.	Out of Playoffs
1985–86	80	28	49	3	300	374	59	6th	Patrick Div.	Out of Playoffs
1986–87	80	29	45	6	293	368	64	6th	Patrick Div.	Out of Playoffs
1987–88	80	38	36	6	295	296	82	4th	Patrick Div.	Lost Conf. Final
1988–89	80	27	41	12	281	325	66	5th	Patrick Div.	Out of Playoffs
1989–90	80	37	34	9	295	288	83	2nd	Patrick Div.	Lost Div. Semifinal
1990–91	80	32	33	15	272	264	79	4th	Patrick Div.	Lost Div. Semifinal
1991–92	80	38	31	11	289	259	87	4th	Patrick Div.	Lost Div. Semifinal
1992–93	84	40	37	7	308	299	87	4th	Patrick Div.	Lost Div. Semifinal
1993–94	84	47	25	12	306	220	106	2nd	Atlantic Div.	Lost Conf. Final
1994–95	48	22	18	8	136	121	52	2nd	Atlantic Div.	Won Stanley Cup
1995–96	82	37	33	12	215	202	86	6th	Atlantic Div.	Out of Playoffs
1996–97	82	45	23	14	231	182	104	1st	Atlantic Div.	Lost Conf. Semifinal
1997–98	82	48	23	11	225	166	107	1st	Atlantic Div.	Lost Conf. Quarterfinal

* Kansas City Scouts. ** Colorado Rockies.

NEW YORK AMERICANS AND BROOKLYN AMERICANS

Stan Fischler

IF THE NEW YORK AMERICANS could have had a baseball counterpart it would have been the St. Louis Browns, who played second-fiddle to the Cardinals in the Mound City. Likewise, the Amerks—as New York headline writers liked to call them—were bottom banana to the Rangers with whom they shared Madison Square Garden on Eighth Avenue and 50th Street. The Browns never won a World Series and in their 16-year life the Americans never won a Stanley Cup, nor even made it to the finals.

Yet in their own bizarre way, the star-spangled skaters oozed excitement both on the ice and off. And they are truly historic, having been the first National Hockey League team to represent New York City. They entered the NHL for the 1925–26 season, one year before the Rangers were granted a franchise, and became a barometer for future NHL expansion.

At a time when journalist Damon Runyon was glorifying the guys and dolls of Broadway, the Americans boasted a list of characters that could have filled Runyon's columns. And by far the best was William V. Dwyer, founder of the Amerks who also happened to be one of America's most notorious bootleggers during the halcyon Prohibition years of the Roaring Twenties.

Such Runyonesque characters as gangsters Owney Madden, Dutch Schultz and Legs Diamond shared Dwyer's compound in the Forrest Hotel, just around the corner from Times Square and only a half-block from Madison Square Garden. Runyon knew them well since he, too, rented rooms in the Forrest.

Not especially versed in hockey knowledge, Dwyer happened upon the Americans in a typically curious way. Having already expanded to Boston, the NHL targeted Manhattan as its next site but lacked a buyer. William MacBeth, a Canadian who wrote for the *New York Herald-Tribune* newspaper, knew about the NHL's interest and believed that hockey would become a cash cow on Broadway. Friendly with Dwyer, MacBeth persuaded the liquor boss to buy the waiting New York franchise, knowing full well that George "Tex" Rickard, impresario of the new Madison Square Garden, had been toying with the idea of purchasing a franchise for his soon-to-open new arena.

Since Rickard was lukewarm to hockey, Dwyer—with MacBeth's incessant prodding—finally made his move. The bootlegger was lucky in more ways than one. For starters, the Hamilton Tigers players had pulled a protest walkout during the 1925 playoffs and were suspended by NHL president Frank Calder. The players' strike, combined with Hamilton's relatively small drawing power, made the Ontario franchise ripe for movement. On April 17, 1925 the Hamilton players were officially "suspended" and fined $200 apiece. At that same league meeting it was announced that the franchise would be transferred from Ontario to New York and would be rechristened the Americans.

For $75,000 Dwyer obtained a team that had finished first in the NHL during the 1924–25 campaign and was primed to be competitive. Led by Red Green, the Americans—nee Tigers—included top talents Billy Burch, Red's brother Shorty Green, Leo Reise Sr., Alex McKinnon and a speedster who immediately caught the fans' fancy, "Bullet" Joe Simpson.

With appropriate pomp and circumstance, the Americans played their first NHL game at the Garden on December 15, 1925 against the Montreal Canadiens. Although they lost, 3–1, the Amerks impressed everyone including the legion of bluebloods who graced the side arena. But Dwyer, who had directed the trafficking of more than $42 million worth of beer and whiskey over a period of 14 months, had more pressing concerns.

He had been nailed by the feds after attempting a rum-running scheme that involved bogus destroyer escorts and a repatriated German World War I submarine. (Dwyer would be dispatched to Atlanta Penitentiary for two years on a bootlegging charge in June 1927.) While this was a blow to the Americans' owner, it hardly sidetracked the team.

With MacBeth handling their publicity and Tommy Gorman managing them, the Americans became an instant hit on Broadway, partly because of their ability and partly because of their star quality. Unfortunately, the press agent overplayed his hand in touting Burch and Simpson. Bullet Joe was labeled "the Blue Streak from Saskatoon" and Burch "the Babe Ruth of Hockey" at a time when Ruth was knocking baseballs out of Yankee Stadium. New Yorkers, unschooled in hockey fundamentals, seized upon the nicknames and immediately made these two their favorites, demanding a goal from them each time Billy or Joe would touch the puck.

Conscious of their newly created audience, Burch and Simpson responded by stressing their individual exploits. "Every time one of them passed to another player," wrote Frank Graham Sr., who covered sports for the *New York Sun*, "the spectators howled in rage and disappointment. Seeking to please the customers, Billy and Joe did as little passing as possible. This resulted in spectacular but futile one-man raids on the enemies' nets and a rapid disintegration of the team play necessary to ensure victories, as the other players then all tried to get into the act as individuals."

So popular were the Americans that Garden ownership decided to obtain a big-league team as well; this despite the fact that Dwyer had an unwritten "guarantee" from the Garden that his club would have sole rights to the New York area. Under scrutiny from law enforcement authorities, the bootlegger was in no position to threaten Garden president Colonel John Hammond who—with Rickard's blessing—had laid the groundwork for the Rangers' debut just a year after the Americans had become the Big Apple's hockey darlings.

Apart from the Rangers competition, what infuriated Dwyer was the rent-free status of the new franchise compared with his Amerks, whose rent bill grew steeper by the season. These indignities sparked a rivalry that quickly flamed into one of the best in a city that featured the Brooklyn Dodgers versus the New York Giants and, if a World Series meeting took place, either of these clubs against the New York Yankees.

Fortified with Roy "Shrimp" Worters peerless goaltending, the Americans remained a competitive team during the late 1920s—despite Worters' short stint with the Montreal Maroons—but not as good as the Rangers. When the Broadway Blueshirts won their first Stanley Cup in their second season (1927–28) they instantly became the patricians of New York hockey while the Amerks took on the image of also-rans.

The only good news for Dwyer was his parole at the start of the 1928–29 season. His Amerks finished second in the Canadian Division (19–13–12) that year but were knocked out of the playoffs by the Rangers. A trend had been set that would prove irreversible. By 1933 the Americans were still Cup-less while the Rangers had not only won their second championship but clearly had become the elite NHL team in Gotham.

Although Dwyer remained a member of the league Board of Governors until 1937, his fiscal infusions into his hockey club had ended. Big Bill went broke after the government won a $3,715,907 action against him, causing the league to take over the team in 1936–37. That plus the end of Prohibition finished Dwyer but not the Amerks.

Mervyn "Red" Dutton, who had become playing coach, was the scion of a wealthy western Canadian contracting family. With the Great Depression playing havoc with finances, Dutton would occasionally shell out money to Dwyer or write a personal check for the team.

"Once I had to lend Bill $20,000 when he was down in Miami Beach," Dutton recalled. "He blew it all in a crap game. We had a lot of headaches then because we were always short of money and had that tough contract with the Garden. Many's the day I'd look up at the sky and pray it wouldn't rain so we'd have a good crowd and could pay the salaries. Of course, the league would stand behind us, but I wanted the club to be able to pay the bills on its own."

Despite the Depression and other hardships, Dutton managed to keep the Americans afloat both on and off the ice. Deft trades enabled him to ice a competitive team and in at least one instance a Stanley Cup threat. That happened during the 1937–38 season when his club finished second in the Canadian Division and Red's protege, Dave "Sweeney" Schriner, placed seventh in scoring. "What made me so proud," said Red, "was that I signed Schriner to his first pro contract. I brought him in along with Art Chapman and Lorne Carr and together they made one of the greatest lines in hockey."

The Amerks faced the Rangers in the best-of-three play-offs round. This time Dutton's sextet won the opener 2–1 on Johnny Sorrell's overtime goal. The Rangers rebounded, winning the second match 4–3 and setting the stage for the climactic finale on March 27, 1938 at the Garden.

The largest crowd of the season, 16,340 fans, jammed the arena and saw a riveting contest. Paced by Alex Shibicky and Bryan Hextall, the Rangers jumped into a 2–0 lead but Lorne Carr and Nels Stewart tied the game for the Amerks, sending it into overtime. Neither team could break the tie for three sudden-death periods before Carr finally scored the winner for Dutton and Company.

"That," Dutton states, "was the greatest thrill I ever got in hockey. The Rangers had a high-priced team then and beating them was like winning the Stanley Cup to us."

Unfortunately, the Americans were knocked out of the playoffs by Chicago, two games to one, in the next round and were never to achieve such lofty heights again, although their fans continued to root them on, just as Brooklyn's "Faithful" supported the Dodgers. "We had fans mostly from Brooklyn," said Dutton, "while the Rangers had the hotsy-totsy ones from New York."

A year later the Americans made the playoffs only to be eliminated in the first round, two games to none, by Toronto. They slipped out of playoff contention in 1939–40 and finished dead last in 1940–41. World War II had broken out and many Canadian-born players quit hockey to join the armed forces. By 1940–41 Dutton had lost 14 of 16 players to the Canadian army and other branches of the services.

Dutton's last ploy to save the franchise—the infusion of new blood—was blunted by the war. When the 1941–42

season started, he changed the club's name to the Brooklyn Americans; this was a token gesture to stimulate a Brooklyn–New York rivalry, although all Americans' home games were still played at the Garden. The Amerks finished last again but, surprisingly, had come up with several young players such as goalie Chuck Rayner and defenseman Pat Egan who showed considerable promise.

However, the war effort soon took Rayner and several other Americans and at start of the 1942–43 season Dutton was forced to fold the club just when he was starting to pull out from under the debris of the Dwyer days. "We had begun to pay off a lot of Bill's debts," said Dutton, "and it looked as though we were going to come out of it all right. A couple more years and we would have run the Rangers right out of the rink." Instead, the Americans vanished and a glorious hockey era came to a sad close.

New York Americans Year-by-Year Record

Season	GP	W	L	T	GF	GA	Pts	Finish		Playoff Results
1941–42	48	16	29	3	133	175	35	7th		Out of Playoffs
1940–41	48	8	29	11	99	186	27	7th		Out of Playoffs
1939–40	48	15	29	4	106	140	34	6th		Lost Quarterfinal
1938–39	48	17	21	10	119	157	44	4th		Lost Quarterfinal
1937–38	48	19	18	11	110	111	49	2nd	Cdn. Div.	Lost Semifinal
1936–37	48	15	29	4	122	161	34	4th	Cdn. Div.	Out of Playoffs
1935–36	48	16	25	7	109	122	39	3rd	Cdn. Div.	Lost Semifinal
1934–35	48	12	27	9	100	142	33	4th	Cdn. Div.	Out of Playoffs
1933–34	48	15	23	10	104	132	40	4th	Cdn. Div.	Out of Playoffs
1932–33	48	15	22	11	91	118	41	4th	Cdn. Div.	Out of Playoffs
1931–32	48	16	24	8	95	142	40	4th	Cdn. Div.	Out of Playoffs
1930–31	44	18	16	10	76	74	46	4th	Cdn. Div.	Out of Playoffs
1929–30	44	14	25	5	113	161	33	5th	Cdn. Div.	Out of Playoffs
1928–29	44	19	13	12	53	53	50	2nd	Cdn. Div.	Lost Quarterfinal
1927–28	44	11	27	6	63	128	28	5th	Cdn. Div.	Out of Playoffs
1926–27	44	17	25	2	82	91	36	4th	Cdn. Div.	Out of Playoffs
1925–26	36	12	20	4	68	89	28	4th	Cdn. Div.	Out of Playoffs

NEW YORK ISLANDERS

Stan Fischler

HOCKEY'S HERITAGE in Nassau and Suffolk counties, which comprise Long Island, predates the National Hockey League's arrival in Uniondale by many decades. Various forms of the ice game were played by the Island's bluebloods, some of whom combined to skate for the Sands Point (Long Island) Tigers, a popular club in the Metropolitan League. Hall of Fame NHL referee Bill Chadwick broke in with the neighboring Jamaica Hawks before graduating to the Eastern League.

However, the professional game was not evident on the Island until well after World War II primarily because no suitable facility was available. It wasn't until New York Rangers business manager Tom Lockhart realized the potential of the burgeoning metropolitan suburbs that a major hockey foothold was established in Suffolk County. Lockhart built the Long Island Arena in a hitherto unknown village called Commack and transferred the Rangers' Eastern League farm club, the Rovers to the new building. Future Hall of Fame goalie Ed Giacomin was a member of the original team.

The team eventually was sold to electrical contractor Al Baron and had its name changed to the Long Island Ducks. In that form the club enjoyed considerable popularity and helped inspire construction of a major-league facility in nearby Uniondale.

When Nassau Veterans Memorial Coliseum was designed in 1970, the NHL decided to place an expansion franchise on Long Island as well as another in Atlanta.

Businessman Roy Boe, who already owned the New York Nets of the infant American Basketball Association, badly wanted to add big-league hockey to his portfolio.

The NHL was asking $6 million per franchise so Boe persuaded 19 other investors besides himself to purchase the franchise and pay off a $4 million territorial fee to the Rangers, who were a mere 25 miles away. He also hired William Arthur (Bill) Torrey, who had previously been chief executive of the Oakland Seals, as his general manager. Torrey's task was daunting because the World Hockey Association was set to debut in October 1972 precisely when his club was to premiere, as well as the Atlanta Flames.

"The difference between Atlanta and Long Island back then was that in Atlanta they were going to have to sell hockey," Torrey remembered. "They didn't know much about it down there. On Long Island, they already knew all about hockey. I thought that would give us the edge." Torrey's opening season nucleus included coach Phil Goyette, a former Montreal Canadiens and Rangers ace; top draft pick Billy Harris, a fleet right wing with a powerful shot; versatile checking forward Ed Westfall, who had played for two Stanley Cup-winning Bruins teams; and rugged defenseman Gerry Hart.

Other members of the first-year club included Gerry Desjardins, the former Black Hawks goalie who had a permanently bent arm following an injury; flame-haired Terry Crisp, who had been an effective utility player with the St. Louis Blues; veteran goalie Denis Dejordy and left winger Germain Gagnon, who had been purchased from Montreal; right wing Craig Cameron, late of the Minnesota North Stars; defenceman Ken Murray, formerly the property of the Buffalo Sabres; and center Tom Miller, a product of Denver University, who also had come out of the Buffalo system.

Torrey's most colorful selection would be a 24-year-old out of the U.S. hockey system—goaltender Glenn "Chico" Resch, who had played for the University of Minnesota-Duluth before turning pro with the Muskegon Mohawks of the International Hockey League. "Resch could be the sleeper at training camp," said Torrey. "I've only seen him play a few games, but in the games I saw, he was the outstanding player." Although Resch would take additional time to hone his skills, Torrey's shrewd evaluation would be remembered years later.

The Islanders opening season would be memorable for its mediocrity—with the exception of Nassau Coliseum, which NHL president Clarence Campbell deemed "a magnificent place to watch hockey." It opened on October 7, 1972 when a crowd of 12,221 turned out to see the Islanders lose 3–2 to the Flames. Westfall scored the first goal in Islanders history and would prove to be a formidable captain during the team's formative years.

On October 12, 1972 the Isles won their first NHL game, beating the Kings 3–2 at Inglewood. The winning goal was delivered by Germaine Gagnon while Billy Harris notched the other two. But after 25 games, the Islanders only had three wins, two ties and 20 losses. Although the club admittedly was weak, it had hoped to be more competitive, as far as the high command was concerned. After considerable review, Torrey decided in midseason to replace Goyette with Earl Ingarfield.

Ingarfield replaced Goyette as coach on January 29, 1973 but the results were hardly encouraging. No less than 32 players would wear the blue and orange that first season,

and none of them would score 30 goals or more than 50 points. As expected, Billy Harris, the Long Island hunk, led the team with 28 goals; no one else had more than 19. At one point, the team lost 12 straight games, never won more than three in a row, and in one particularly futile stretch compiled a 1–20–1 record on the road.

The team's overall won-lost record showed that the Islanders had captured only 12 games, a record low, and lost 60, a record high. They finished 72 points behind the Rangers, who nevertheless had helped the Islanders forge the kind of white-hot rivalry Boe had envisioned—even though the Rangers won all six regular-season meetings by outscoring the upstarts from Long Island 25–5. Among the rookies the most encouraging were pugnacious Garry Howatt and hard-working Bob Nystrom, who were elevated to the big club in March 1973. Islanders fans immediately took a liking to both players and thoroughly enjoyed watching the 5'9" Howatt push around some of the league's bigger customers.

The Islanders' last-place finish guaranteed them the first pick in the Amateur Draft, which was one of the best in history, led by Ottawa 67's defenseman Denis Potvin. Torrey resisted several offers from Canadiens general manager Sam Pollock for the rights to Potvin and made Denis his top choice. "I didn't want to be traded to Montreal," Potvin recalled, "because I was afraid I'd be under tremendous pressure to be an instant superstar. And I knew that there was a long list of players who had cracked under the strain of having to live up to those demanding Montreal rooters."

If anything. Potvin needed a coach who would stress the defensive fundamentals that might have eluded him in the junior ranks. When Ingarfield asked to be relieved of the coaching job, Torrey offered the position to the bespectacled Al Arbour, long considered the "defenseman's defenseman" when he skated for the Detroit Red Wings, Chicago Black Hawks, Toronto Maple Leafs and St. Louis Blues. As a player, Arbour had been a member of four Stanley Cup-winning teams, but he nearly didn't come to Long Island.

Arbour, who had coached the Blues on and off from 1970 to 1973, hesitated at first because of his sour opinion of the Big Apple. "My wife Claire and I were under the impression that Long Island was just like New York City—overcrowded and dirty," Arbour said. "We changed our mind after taking a tour of the Island." When he and his wife discovered the more bucolic atmosphere of Long Island, Arbour accepted the position.

The addition of Arbour to his general staff was one of Torrey's most meaningful moves. Arbour quickly brought discipline and toughness to the sophomore—and sometimes sophomoric—Islanders. Under Goyette the team had regularly broken training rules, but Arbour changed all that. An 11 p.m. curfew on the eve of games was instituted and rigorously enforced, and Al began fining players who were late, whether it was for the bus, the plane or practice. Then he doubled the fines for second offenders. The strict new regime began on the first day of training camp, when Al insisted that each and every player jog from the motel to the practice rink.

Even with Arbour, Potvin and Westfall the Islanders struggled in 1973–74, finishing last (19–41–18) in the Eastern Division with the second-worst record in the entire league. They did gain respect in goal. Billy Smith had emerged as a combative netminder with a knack of making the hardest saves at the most critical moments. He finished the season with a 3.07 goals-against average and a guaran-

tee of many more years in the NHL. Smith and Resch would become a tandem through the club's first Stanley Cup season.

It wasn't until the autumn of 1974 that the Isles began turning the competitive corner. Torrey had selected Clark Gillies, a big left winger, as his first draft pick and later added Gillies' pal, Bob Bourne, a swift left winger with a short fuse. At midseason Torrey completed a landmark trade with Minnesota, obtaining left wing J.P. Parise and center Jude Drouin for Ernie Hicke, Doug Rombough and Craig Cameron, none of whom would be factors in future NHL years.

Working with Westfall, Parise and Drouin provided New York with a dependable scoring and checking line. In a neck-and-neck battle with Atlanta for a final playoff berth, the Islanders prevailed in the homestretch, finishing with 33 wins compared to 19 the previous season.

The 1975 playoff experience figured to be remarkably short. Facing the Islanders in the first round was a powerful Rangers squad sprinkled with future Hall of Famers such as Rod Gilbert, Brad Park and Ed Giacomin. The best-of-three series was expected to be completed with a two-straight Rangers rout because of experience and talent.

Instead, the Islanders won with a stirring sudden-death victory on Parise's goal—on a pass from Drouin—with only 11 seconds elapsed in the overtime. Torrey's young club had gained instant recognition and respectability. The *Philadelphia Bulletin* commented: "The Islanders proved that wet-behind-the-ears is a better condition than egg-on-the-face. Furthermore, the Islanders had advanced to the second round against a Pittsburgh Penguins franchise that also was rated a prohibitive favorite. For three games, the Isles appeared lost, but facing elimination they won three in a row. Not only did they tie the series but a folk hero was born after goalie Chico Resch smothered a shot by Ron Schock which had rebounded to him after it had hit the goal post. Resch pulled himself to his feet and kissed the red piping, an act that forever endeared him to the fans.

In another melodramatic moment, Westfall ended the series by breaking a 0–0 tie late in the third period of the seventh game with a backhander past goalie Gary Inness. Thus the Isles found their place in history alongside the 1942 Toronto Maple Leafs as the only NHL clubs to have surmounted a three-game deficit in the playoffs and win four straight.

Defying all odds, the Islanders took on the defending champion Philadelphia Flyers, lost three straight and then rebounded for another remarkable comeback. With the series tied at three and the deciding game in Philadelphia, the Flyers produced the ultimate good luck charm, a venerable vocalist named Kate Smith, otherwise known as "the Songbird of the South."

Miss Smith had sung "God Bless America" before many Flyers games—often with a recording substituted for the real thing—giving the home club a record of 40–3–1 on those occasions. Islanders captain Ed Westfall attempted to break the jinx by presenting Kate with a bouquet of yellow roses but it didn't work. Philadelphia triumphed 4–1. The Isles miracle run had a long-term benefit for the team. Beating the Rangers gave them bragging rights in the New York Metropolitan area and the two separate comeback performances captured the imagination of NHL fans while boosting the young club's confidence. Meanwhile, Torrey continued building the foundation of what eventually would be a dynasty.

To his promising attacking corps he added a rugged center named Bryan Trottier for the 1975–76 season and a year later Michael Bossy was picked first (15th overall) in the 1977 draft. Gillies, Trottier and Bossy would in time become Trio Grande not to mention the best line ever to skate in Nassau. Gifted though they were, the Islanders were missing a key element in team chemistry and balance. This was evident when underdog Toronto eliminated them in a vicious, seven-game 1978 playoff that was followed a year later by a humiliating six-game series loss to the Rangers after the Isles had become the first expansion team to lead the NHL with a 51–15–14 mark and dominated the rest of the league. "We have a monkey on our back," said Islanders forward Bob Bourne.

To remove the monkey, Torrey made key changes. He added World Hockey Association defenseman Dave Langevin and gold medal Olympian Ken Morrow after the U.S. won at Lake Placid in 1980. But his most important move was obtaining center Butch Goring from Los Angeles for defenseman Dave Lewis and right wing Billy Harris.

"With Butchie at center," said Denis Potvin, "there was a sense of hope we didn't have before." Sure enough, the revitalized Islanders reached the Stanley Cup finals against the Flyers. Leading three games to two, the Isles hosted the sixth game on a warm spring afternoon. The game was tied 4–4 when the biggest goal in franchise history was scored. It began at center ice where Lorne Henning pounced on the unattended rubber. His wings had already begun to skate on a kind of looping diagonal; John Tonelli from left to right and Nystrom from right to left. The criss-cross momentarily froze the Philadelphia defense of Andre Dupont and Bob Dailey. Henning instantly slipped the puck to Tonelli, who strode past a clinging Dupont.

"Bob and I were blitzing," said Tonelli. Dailey, almost riveted to the ice, watched in horror as Nystrom eluded him and skated hell-bent down the left side toward goalie Pete Peeters. Because he was on his "off" wing, Nystrom carried his curved stick in the "wrong" position; that is, with the curve going in the opposite direction, to the left. "I had a warp on my stick that didn't allow me to backhand at the best of times," said Nystrom. "I don't think I had ever scored on my backhand."

Tonelli had an option. He could shoot from the right side or he could pass to Nystrom. The shot would have been an easier choice because it eliminated the possibility of the cross-ice feed being intercepted by the back-pedaling Flyers. "I decided to give him the puck," said Tonelli. Taking the gamble, Tonelli flipped the puck as Nystrom moved to within striking distance of Peeters. The pass was exquisitely timed and Nystrom knew it as the puck arrived on his stick. "I just knew that I had to get it up," he said. "I whacked at it." Peeters slid across the goalmouth in a desperate attempt to get his pads on the puck. But Nystrom already had jabbed at the rubber, changing its trajectory so that it deflected off his stick and into the net before the befuddled goalie could cover the crease. The time was 7:11.

Nystrom's deflection was the start of something big. The Islanders won additional Stanley Cup titles in 1981, 1982 and 1983. The victims, successively, were Minnesota, Vancouver and Edmonton, the latter two exiting in four straight games while the North Stars lasted five.

To enhance the dynasty, Torrey continually juggled his roster. Additions such as defensemen Gord Lane and Mike McEwen played pivotal roles in the Cup years as did forwards Wayne Merrick and Anders Kallur. But the steady work of tempestuous goalie Billy Smith provided the last line of defense so necessary to a champion. For grit there were the Sutter brothers, Duane and Brent, as well as one of the NHL's all-time underrated defensemen, Stefan Persson, not to mention fellow Swede Tomas Jonsson.

In their "Drive for Five," the Islanders came close. They etched their names in the history book by completing a total of 19 consecutive playoff series victories when they won the first three rounds of the 1984 playoffs. By the time they reached the finals against a young, healthy Edmonton team, Al Arbour's skaters were wounded beyond repair. They split the first two games on Long Island before flying to Edmonton and three straight games at Northlands Coliseum. By the end of the fifth game the league had a new champion and Torrey returned to the drawing board to reshape his squad.

Two key additions—forwards Pat LaFontaine and Patrick Flatley—fortified the attack, while Kelly Hrudey was designated as the number-two goalie behind Bill Smith. But the shocker was Arbour's decision to retire after 13 seasons behind the Islanders bench. He was replaced by Terry Simpson, who was pacing the matting on April 18–19, 1987 when the Islanders participated in their longest game. Played at Capital Centre in Landover, Maryland, the seventh game of the Washington–Islanders series lasted until 8:47 of the fourth overtime period when LaFontaine jumped over the boards as the puck moved around the Capitals end of the rink. Defenseman Gord Dineen gambled behind the net and the puck skipped to LaFontaine at the blue line. "I just turned around and gave it my best shot," said LaFontaine. It beat goalie Bob Mason just seconds before 2 a.m.

The Islanders remained competitive through the late 1980s under the ownership of John Pickett. In 1987–88 they won the Patrick Division title and faced New Jersey in the opening playoff round. The Devils had gained a playoff berth on the final night of the season and seemed to be easy pickings, but New Jersey physically manhandled the Isles and wiped them out in six games. "I'm bitterly disappointed," said Torrey. "We played six mediocre games." Not only were the Isles eliminated but they lost their best defenseman, Denis Potvin, to retirement, and a severe depression settled over the club in 1988–89 when they finished with a record of 28–47–5, their worst season since the second year of the franchise. Bill Smith retired, leaving youthful Mark Fitzpatrick and Jeff Hackett to battle for the goaltending job.

Torrey persuaded Arbour to come out of retirement but there was little improvement until late in the 1989–90 season when the Isles were able to clinch a playoff berth on the final night of the season—March 31, 1990—beating Philadelphia while Buffalo toppled Pittsburgh in sudden-death overtime on Uwe Krupp's slapshot.

It was the next-to-last high point of what would become a terribly disappointing decade. Only in 1992–93 was there a renaissance as a gutsy team including Ray Ferraro, Steve Thomas, Benoit Hogue and Tom Fitzgerald kept them competitive while Pierre Turgeon—obtained from Buffalo in a deal for Pat LaFontaine—led the scoring and ebullient Glenn Healy surfaced as the new netminding favorite. Turgeon capped a homestretch drive by scoring an overtime goal against the Rangers at Madison Square Garden on April 2, 1993 for a 3–2 Islanders win. It was Turgeon's 50th goal of the season. A few days later the Rangers were eliminated, guaranteeing the Islanders a playoff berth and

matchup with Washington in the first round.

New York won the series in six games, but the bad news was a blindside cheap shot delivered by Dale Hunter of the Capitals against Turgeon after he had scored the Islanders fifth goal that left the star with a shoulder separation and concussion. Undaunted, the Isles next took favored Pittsburgh to a seventh game and won it at the Igloo when Czech-born David Volek steered a Ferraro pass behind Tom Barrasso at 5:16 of the first overtime to complete the unexpected upset. "Somehow," said Hogue, "we were going to find a way to win." The dream ended in the next round as the eventual Stanley Cup-winning Montreal Canadiens ousted the Islanders in five games. "You don't always get an opportunity to be this close," lamented Healy, who had become something of a folk hero on Long Island.

Healy's words were prophetic. A number of personnel moves—including the loss of the popular goalie—changed the team's chemistry, although it did manage another playoff berth in 1994. With Healy moved to the Rangers, Ron Hextall became the resident goaltender. On some nights he was peerless and others powerless. But in a tense stretch drive, he enabled his new club to gain a playoff berth with a 2–0 win over the Lightning at Tampa Bay during the last week of the regular season.

Facing the Rangers in the first round, the Islanders—especially Hextall—disintegrated, losing four straight and setting the stage for a dismal playoff drought through the remainder of the 1990s. Adding insult to injury was Pickett's decision to sell the team to so-called tycoon John Spano. Before the sale could be consummated, Spano was indicted on several fraud counts and eventually sentenced to prison.

Pickett regained control of the team and in 1997 sold the Islanders to New York Sports Ventures, a group headed by Steven Gluckstern, Howard Milstein, Edward Milstein and David Seldin. The new owners took command during the 1997–98 season, another disappointing year during which general manager Mike Milbury fired coach Rick Bowness and finished the year behind the bench as well.

New York Islanders Year-by-Year Record

Season	GP	W	L	T	GF	GA	Pts	Finish		Playoff Results
1972–73	78	12	60	6	170	347	30	8th	East Div.	Out of Playoffs
1973–74	78	19	41	18	182	247	56	8th	East Div.	Out of Playoffs
1974–75	80	33	25	22	264	221	88	3rd	Patrick Div.	Lost Semifinal
1975–76	80	42	21	17	297	190	101	2nd	Patrick Div.	Lost Semifinal
1976–77	80	47	21	12	288	193	106	2nd	Patrick Div.	Lost Semifinal
1977–78	80	48	17	15	334	210	111	1st	Patrick Div.	Lost Quarterfinal
1978–79	80	51	15	14	358	214	116	1st	Patrick Div.	Lost Semifinal
1979–80	80	39	28	13	281	247	91	2nd	Patrick Div.	Won Stanley Cup
1980–81	80	48	18	14	355	260	110	1st	Patrick Div.	Won Stanley Cup
1981–82	80	54	16	10	385	250	118	1st	Patrick Div.	Won Stanley Cup
1982–83	80	42	26	12	302	226	96	2nd	Patrick Div.	Won Stanley Cup
1983–84	80	50	26	4	357	269	104	1st	Patrick Div.	Lost Final
1984–85	80	40	34	6	345	312	86	3rd	Patrick Div.	Lost Div. Final
1985–86	80	39	29	12	327	284	90	3rd	Patrick Div.	Lost Div. Semifinal
1986–87	80	35	33	12	279	281	82	3rd	Patrick Div.	Lost Div. Final
1987–88	80	39	31	10	308	267	88	1st	Patrick Div.	Lost Div. Semifinal
1988–89	80	28	47	5	265	325	61	6th	Patrick Div.	Out of Playoffs
1989–90	80	31	38	11	281	288	73	4th	Patrick Div.	Lost Div. Semifinal
1990–91	80	25	45	10	223	290	60	6th	Patrick Div.	Out of Playoffs
1991–92	80	34	35	11	291	299	79	5th	Patrick Div.	Out of Playoffs
1992–93	84	40	37	7	335	297	87	3rd	Patrick Div.	Lost Conf. Final
1993–94	84	36	36	12	282	264	84	4th	Atlantic Div.	Lost Conf. Quarterfinal
1994–95	48	15	28	5	126	158	35	7th	Atlantic Div.	Out of Playoffs
1995–96	82	22	50	10	229	315	54	7th	Atlantic Div.	Out of Playoffs
1996–97	82	29	41	12	240	250	70	7th	Atlantic Div.	Out of Playoffs
1997–98	82	30	41	11	212	225	71	4th	Atlantic Div.	Out of Playoffs

NEW YORK RANGERS

Stan Fischler

THE RANGERS WERE BORN out of a New York City hockey boom that was rooted in a popular series of exhibition games played at the old St. Nicholas Arena on Manhattan's Upper West Side shortly after the turn of the century. But it wasn't until the ice game's popularity was confirmed on a big-league level in 1925–26 by the New York Americans that the Broadway Blueshirts finally were awarded an NHL franchise.

None of this would have been possible had a Kansas City-born, Texas-bred entrepreneur named George Lewis Rickard not made a fortune promoting fights in New York. By 1924 when the New York Life Insurance Company decided to raze old Madison Square Garden and build a 40-story office building, Rickard had become Manhattan's most renowned sportsman. He rounded up a syndicate of businessmen—his self-proclaimed "600 millionaires"—and organized the Madison Square Garden Corporation. By December 15, 1925 the new Garden was up and flourishing, with its lone NHL tenant, the New York Americans, playing the Montreal Canadiens.

Once Rickard realized that hockey was a hit on Broadway, he concluded that the Garden should organize its own team—the Americans were merely renting the arena—and along with MSG president Colonel John S. Hammond laid the groundwork for a second New York franchise. Rickard and Hammond designated Conn Smythe, a bright, young Torontonian who already had a reputation for successfully managing hockey teams, to organize the Rangers. Since the strong-willed Hammond paid close attention to the hockey club, the Colonel and Smythe developed a strong but stormy relationship.

Smythe adroitly signed a nucleus of superb players, including the amateur defense pair of Ivan "Ching" Johnson and Clarence "Taffy" Abel, names soon to become bywords among New York sports fans. By far Smythe's best moves were the acquisitions of center Frank Boucher, left winger Fred "Bun" Cook and right winger Bill Cook. The brothers Cook and Boucher—all Hall of Famers—would comprise one of the finest forward lines ever to grace the NHL.

Smythe also chose wisely in goal with Lorne Chabot and when the Rangers gathered for their first training camp at Toronto's little Ravina rink in the fall of 1926, their roster appeared competitive if not downright formidable. Unfortunately for Smythe, Hammond disagreed. "Conn," said Hammond, "we can't start the season with a bunch of rank amateurs like this." Believing that he knew better, the equally obstinate Smythe shot back: "The hell we can't!" He turned his back on his boss and marched directly to the workout. Shortly after the scrimmage had concluded, Hammond summoned Smythe to his office and fired him.

The Colonel had been well-prepared for this moment, having already summoned former Pacific Coast Hockey Association co-organizer and former player Lester Patrick to Toronto. The moment Smythe departed, Patrick became coach of the Rangers for the-then astronomical fee of $18,000 a year. It marked the beginning of a long and lovely relationship.

Patrick not only oozed the kind of class that Rickard revered, he also knew as much about hockey as Smythe and proved it by taking over the Rangers without missing a beat. One day he called a team meeting and announced:

"Gentlemen, when we start playing in the National Hockey League you're going to win some games and you're going to lose some. I just want to stress this: If you lose more than you win, you won't be around." Beginning with an opening night 1–0 victory over the powerful Montreal Maroons on November 17, 1926, the Rangers obliged Patrick by winning more than losing. They also proved Smythe correct in his assessment of the team.

Paced by the Cook-Boucher line as well as stout defense and solid goaltending, the Rangers became immediate contenders while coach Patrick emerged as a major personality in the Big Apple along with Babe Ruth and Lou Gehrig. "Lester didn't adjust to New York," said Americans manager Tommy Gorman, "New York adjusted to him." In only their second NHL season the Rangers reached the Stanley Cup finals against the Maroons. They had achieved a rare balance from goal through defense to the forward lines but they had one obstacle that was unconquerable; they couldn't defeat Ringling Brothers and Barnum and Bailey.

"It was tremendously difficult for a Ranger team in those days," said Boucher. "We couldn't play the finals on our home ice in New York because the arena was booked with the circus. We had to play every game at the Montreal Forum." The appearance of the elephants at playoff time would haunt the Blueshirts for nearly four decades, but playing all games on the Maroons' home ice hardly was daunting for the Rangers. More challenging was the search for a goaltender after Chabot was injured during the second game. In an era when NHL clubs carried only one goalie, it was commonplace for teams to "borrow" a neutral netminder. Patrick asked permission to use either Alex Connell of Ottawa Senators or a minor-leaguer, Hughie McCormick, both of whom were in the stands. When Maroons manager Eddie Gerard refused, Patrick went to his dressing room, huddled with Bun Cook and Boucher and then turned to trainer Harry Westerby and asserted, "Harry, I'm in goal." Already down one game to none, the Rangers desperately needed this win and Patrick heroically stopped all but one shot as the teams completed regulation time tied, 1–1. According to *Montreal Star* columnist Baz O'Meara, Patrick performed "prodigious feats of netminding." The climax to the remarkable evening came when Boucher scored the game winner in overtime.

Eventually, Patrick was replaced in goal by an obscure goalie named Joe Miller on loan from the Americans. Tied at two games apiece, the Rangers and Maroons met in game five to decide the championship. As coach Patrick had earlier, Miller held Montreal to one goal while Boucher managed both scores for New York. The final score was 2–1. In their second NHL season the Rangers had won their first Stanley Cup. Upon returning to Manhattan, the Blueshirts was suitably hailed as conquering heroes. They were greeted on the steps of City Hall by a beaming Mayor Jimmy "Beau James" Walker, himself a regular at Madison Square Garden games, and a crowd of proud New Yorkers. The Rangers had arrived.

Under Patrick's orchestration, their standard of excellence was maintained through the early 1930s, although they didn't win another Stanley Cup until 1933. The core of the original Cup-winners was intact except for Chabot and Abel, who had been traded, when they faced Toronto in the 1933 finals. Ironically, Smythe, who was running the Maple Leafs, watched in frustration as the very players he had signed for New York dominated his Toronto skaters. Bill Cook led the Rangers to a 1–0 victory in the fourth and final

game, although he was now 35 years old and apparently past his prime.

Two Stanley Cup titles in only seven seasons was a laudable achievement for Patrick and his Rangers who were feted in a glittering victory party at the Astor Hotel in the center of Times Square. The celebration was significant in another way because it served as an introductory platform for the Rangers new president, General John Reed Kilpatrick. A World War I hero, Kilpatrick was the ideal boss for Patrick and the two set out to rejuvenate what was an aging hockey team. The feat was accomplished by means of an elaborate farm system that would eventually comprise The Three Rs — New Haven Ramblers, New York Rovers and Lake Placid Roamers.

However, the original revivifying sources came from Patrick's American League farm club in Philadelphia not to mention Lester's own family. His sons, Lynn — the eldest and most productive as a scorer — and Murray had been outstanding athletes in hockey, track, bicycling, baseball, rugby, football and basketball. Murray — later known as Muzz — was so adept in the ring that he became an amateur boxing champion. As the Cooks and Boucher were phased out of the lineup, the likes of Bryan Hextall, Phil Watson, Dutch Hiller, the Colville Brothers (Neil and Mac) Alex Shibicky and goalie Davey Kerr moved in, along with Lynn up front and Muzz on defense. By the time World War II had exploded in the fall of 1939, Patrick's Rangers were as powerful as his club of a dozen years earlier. Only this time Boucher was behind the bench coaching instead of occupying his familiar spot on the ice at center.

The 1939–40 Rangers were an extraordinary group of players. At one point in the season they had recorded 24 victories or ties in 25 games. They developed the strategy of offensive penalty-killing and popularized pulling the goalie for a sixth attacker in the final minute of play. With exquisite irony, they advanced to the Stanley Cup finals against Smythe's Maple Leafs once more and defeated them in six games. Forced out of their Madison Square Garden home by the circus, the Rangers played the last two games at Maple Leaf Gardens, winning both in overtime. Lester accepted the Stanley Cup from NHL president Frank Calder and then posed for an historic picture; a father and two sons on a Cup-winner at the same time.

Since their inception, the Rangers now had won the Stanley Cup three times and, with a young roster, it appeared that more championships were in the offing. But World War II would change that. Within months the Blueshirts roster was decimated by armed forces enlistments and by 1942 both Muzz and Lynn were in uniform. It was the beginning of a long and dismal run for the Rangers with relief coming well after the war's end. By that time Lester had retired and Boucher took over both managing and coaching. New York's only bright season was 1949–50 when some adroit trades elevated the Rangers to playoff contention. They reached the finals — naturally playing all home games on the road — against Detroit and forced the Red Wings to double overtime in the seventh game before losing on a Pete Babando goal.

The Frank Boucher era ended with his dismissal at the end of the 1954–55 season, just after he had successfully reorganized the farm system, centered on the Guelph Biltmore Madhatters of the Ontario Hockey Association. Future Hall of Famers such as Harry Howell and Andy Bathgate graduated to the Blueshirts along with goalie Lorne "Gump" Worsley who had been developed on the

Rangers Eastern League farm club, the Rovers.

With Muzz Patrick managing and Phil Watson coaching, the club enjoyed a few bright moments in the late 1950s before fading again under Watson's tyrannical rule. By 1964 Patrick was gone, replaced by onetime—though only briefly—Ranger goalie Emile "the Cat" Francis. A native of North Battleford, Saskatchewan, Francis restored the franchise to a modicum of dignity and championship potential.

Francis' goaltending discovery Ed Giacomin anchored an impressive lineup that included the G-A-G (Goal-A-Game) Line centered by Jean Ratelle and flanked by Rod Gilbert on the right and Vic Hadfield. Although not as popular as Patrick, Francis became a Big Apple favorite who enjoyed innovation as much as his predecessor. The Cat even lured onetime NHL scoring champion Bernie "Boom Boom" Geoffrion out of retirement in a move that paid immediate dividends, a second playoff berth in two years in 1967–68. But try as he might, Francis could not craft a Cup-winner, although the 1971–72 team reached the finals before losing to Bobby Orr and the Boston Bruins in six games. Unable to replenish his aging lineup with young stars, Francis lost favor with management and soon was replaced by former Ranger-basher John Ferguson.

This was a trying time for Rangers fans. An expansion franchise in adjoining Nassau County had become a winner faster than anyone had expected. In the 1974–75 season—only the third in franchise history—the New York Islanders not only reached the playoffs but unceremoniously ousted the vaunted Rangers in the opening round. Revenge, of sorts, was obtained four seasons later when the Blueshirts, now guided by former Philadelphia Flyers coach Fred Shero, upset the Islanders in a six-game series and reached the Stanley Cup finals against the defending champion Montreal Canadiens. A New York victory in the opener at the Forum was followed by a two-goal Rangers lead in game two, but the Habs soon counterattacked and won four straight games and another Cup title.

One by one New York coaches and managers came and went, but that coveted fourth Stanley Cup appeared more distant than ever. Craig Patrick—Lynn's son and grandson of Lester—provided hope in the early 1980s along with Lake Placid Olympic hero Herb Brooks. With the latter behind the bench, the Blueshirts introduced a revolutionary game plan that blended European with North American hockey styles. During the 1983–84 playoffs, Brooks' Rangers extended the four-time Cup champion Islanders to a full five games before losing in sudden-death overtime. Again, the team crested and then plummeted while management desperately searched for a Cup-winning formula. Meanwhile, expansion teams were passing them by as Philadelphia had won two championships, Edmonton crafted a late 1980s Stanley Cup dynasty and Calgary won a title before the decade was over. The likes of Phil Esposito in the front office and Michel Bergeron behind the bench did little to bring the club closer to a championship.

The gloom over Broadway was lifted at the start of the 1990s when Craig Patrick draftee Brian Leetch established himself as a premier defenseman on the Rangers blue line. "He's reminiscent of the great Doug Harvey," said Esposito. "There were few better puckhandling defensemen than Harvey." Leetch won the Norris Trophy in 1992, not coincidentally in the same season that Mark Messier was lured away from Edmonton in a colossal deal that saw Rangers' young general manager Neil Smith dispatch minor-league prospects Louie DeBrusk and Steven Rice to the Oilers along with the popular center Bernie Nicholls and an unnamed but substantial amount of cash.

For the first time in 50 years the Rangers had the best NHL record in 1991–92 (50–25–5), thanks in large part to Messier's leadership, his 107 points and an all-round performance that earned him the Hart Trophy. Still, it wasn't enough. Pittsburgh won the Cup for the second straight year. Messier's presence notwithstanding, the Rangers fell to the bottom of the division in 1992–93 and missed the playoffs as injuries and personnel strife disrupted the organization. Messier was openly critical of coach Roger Neilson, who was fired and replaced by Mike Keenan.

The turnabout was dramatic. Under Keenan's iron-fisted rule, the Rangers rebounded to the top, finishing with the league's best regular-season record (52–24–8) and a relentless march through the playoffs. They stumbled in a third-round encounter with the New Jersey Devils, falling behind three games to two. But Messier scored a hat trick in game six and third-liner Stephane Matteau put them in the finals with an overtime goal in the seventh match.

New York required seven games before disposing of Vancouver in the 1994 finals. Leetch, who won the Conn Smythe Trophy and tallied 34 points, detonated the seventh game win with a goal in the first period. Goalie Mike Richter withstood a late-game Canucks assault to preserve the victory and give The Big Apple its first Stanley Cup since 1940. A sign carried by one fan in the stands read "NOW I CAN DIE IN PEACE." There was, however, no peace in the Rangers front office. Keenan and Smith had been feuding all season and, instead of bringing the high command together, the Cup triumph pulled them farther apart. By mid-summer 1994 Keenan had left New York to become general manager and coach of the St. Louis Blues. Smith replaced him with assistant coach Colin Campbell.

In a lockout-shortened 1994–95 season the Rangers betrayed their age by playoff time. Messier proved no match for the younger, stronger Eric Lindros and his teammates saw their one-year reign collapse almost as quickly as it had begun. Smith moved quickly, obtaining Wayne Gretzky—The Great One had moved from Edmonton to Los Angeles and St. Louis—and suddenly Broadway was abuzz with hockey frenzy. The former Oilers cronies, Gretzky and Messier, infused the Rangers with new life. Along with Adam Graves, Alexei Kovalev, Ulf Samuelsson, Richter and Leetch, the Rangers had elite written all over them, although their regular-season record was less than awesome. But once the playoffs began, the old pros delivered. Gretzky personally took over the opening round series against Florida and delivered a five-game victory. Second-round opponent New Jersey looked impressive shutting out the Rangers in game one but Richter turned impregnable and again the New Yorkers annexed a series in five.

An opening game win in round three against Philadelphia suggested that the finals—and even a Cup—were reachable. But injuries and age combined to enervate the Blueshirts. Lindros & Co. rolled over them in the next four games, ending hopes for a Gretzky-Messier return to the finals. As captain, Messier had been an unqualified leader on Broadway, but the general staff had more and more come to the conclusion that he was overstepping his power base. A dismal performance in the Philadelphia series led general manager Smith to conclude that Messier's value would diminish in the seasons ahead. The Rangers did make the captain an offer to return but it was not deemed

suitable for Messier. Instead he chose a more lucrative Canucks contract and signed with Vancouver.

The decision caused shockwaves up and down Seventh Avenue. Garden officials were assailed for failing to retain the captain but Smith and others countered that a reasonable offer was made and rejected by the Messier camp. Instead, the Rangers obtained Pat LaFontaine from Buffalo, sending the Sabres a second-round draft pick. Smith also obtained free agent veterans Brian Skrudland and Mike Keane, losing second-string goalie Glenn Healy to the Maple Leafs. Prior to the opening game, fellow general managers told Smith that he had a potential Stanley Cup-winner if LaFontaine had fully recovered from the concussions which had sidelined him in Buffalo.

In no time at all LaFontaine surged to the lead among Rangers scorers and little-regarded acquisitions such as Tim Sweeney became surprisingly productive. Kovalev, who had suffered a serious knee injury in 1996–97, returned in mint condition; and there was Richter, who had starred in Uncle Sam's World Cup victory prior to training camp.

Yet it wasn't enough. The Rangers hiccuped their way through the first half of the season. At the all-star break they were still under the .500 mark. In the end, they missed the playoffs despite strong play by Wayne Gretzky over the last two months of the season.

New York Rangers Year-by-Year Record

Season	GP	W	L	T	GF	GA	Pts	Finish		Playoff Results
1926–27	44	25	13	6	95	72	56	1st	Amn. Div.	Lost Quarterfinal
1927–28	44	19	16	9	94	79	47	2nd	Amn. Div.	Won Stanley Cup
1928–29	44	21	13	10	72	65	52	2nd	Amn. Div.	Lost Final
1929–30	44	17	17	10	136	143	44	3rd	Amn. Div.	Lost Semifinal
1930–31	44	19	16	9	106	87	47	3rd	Amn. Div.	Lost Semifinal
1931–32	48	23	17	8	134	112	54	1st	Amn. Div.	Lost Final
1932–33	48	23	17	8	135	107	54	3rd	Amn. Div.	Won Stanley Cup
1933–34	48	21	19	8	120	113	50	3rd	Amn. Div.	Lost Quarterfinal
1934–35	48	22	20	6	137	139	50	3rd	Amn. Div.	Lost Semifinal
1935–36	48	19	17	12	91	96	50	4th	Amn. Div.	Out of Playoffs
1936–37	48	19	20	9	117	106	47	3rd	Amn. Div.	Lost Final
1937–38	48	27	15	6	149	96	60	2nd	Amn. Div.	Lost Quarterfinal
1938–39	48	26	16	6	149	105	58	2nd		Lost Semifinal
1939–40	48	27	11	10	136	77	64	2nd		Won Stanley Cup
1940–41	48	21	19	8	143	125	50	4th		Lost Quarterfinal
1941–42	48	29	17	2	177	143	60	1st		Lost Semifinal
1942–43	50	11	31	8	161	253	30	6th		Out of Playoffs
1943–44	50	6	39	5	102	310	17	6th		Out of Playoffs
1944–45	50	11	29	10	154	247	32	6th		Out of Playoffs
1945–46	50	13	28	9	144	191	35	6th		Out of Playoffs
1946–47	60	22	32	6	167	186	50	5th		Out of Playoffs
1947–48	60	21	26	13	176	201	55	4th		Lost Semifinal
1948–49	60	18	31	11	133	172	47	6th		Out of Playoffs
1949–50	70	28	31	11	170	189	67	4th		Lost Final
1950–51	70	20	29	21	169	201	61	5th		Out of Playoffs
1951–52	70	23	34	13	192	219	59	5th		Out of Playoffs
1952–53	70	17	37	16	152	211	50	6th		Out of Playoffs
1953–54	70	29	31	10	161	182	68	5th		Out of Playoffs
1954–55	70	17	35	18	150	210	52	5th		Out of Playoffs
1955–56	70	32	28	10	204	203	74	3rd		Lost Semifinal
1956–57	70	26	30	14	184	227	66	4th		Lost Semifinal
1957–58	70	32	25	13	195	188	77	2nd		Lost Semifinal
1958–59	70	26	32	12	201	217	64	5th		Out of Playoffs
1959–60	70	17	38	15	187	247	49	6th		Out of Playoffs
1960–61	70	22	38	10	204	248	54	5th		Out of Playoffs
1961–62	70	26	32	12	195	207	64	4th		Lost Semifinal
1962–63	70	22	36	12	211	233	56	5th		Out of Playoffs
1963–64	70	22	38	10	186	242	54	5th		Out of Playoffs
1964–65	70	20	38	12	179	246	52	5th		Out of Playoffs
1965–66	70	18	41	11	195	261	47	6th		Out of Playoffs
1966–67	70	30	28	12	188	189	72	4th		Lost Semifinal
1967–68	74	39	23	12	226	183	90	2nd	East Div.	Lost Quarterfinal
1968–69	76	41	26	9	231	196	91	3rd	East Div.	Lost Quarterfinal
1969–70	76	38	22	16	246	189	92	4th	East Div.	Lost Quarterfinal
1970–71	78	49	18	11	259	177	109	2nd	East Div.	Lost Semifinal
1971–72	78	48	17	13	317	192	109	2nd	East Div.	Lost Final
1972–73	78	47	23	8	297	208	102	3rd	East Div.	Lost Semifinal
1973–74	78	40	24	14	300	251	94	3rd	East Div.	Lost Semifinal
1974–75	80	37	29	14	319	276	88	2nd	Patrick Div.	Lost Prelim. Round

New York Rangers Year-by-Year Record continued

Season	GP	W	L	T	GF	GA	Pts	Finish		Playoff Results
1975–76	80	29	42	9	262	333	67	4th	Patrick Div.	Out of Playoffs
1976–77	80	29	37	14	272	310	72	4th	Patrick Div.	Out of Playoffs
1977–78	80	30	37	13	279	280	73	4th	Patrick Div.	Lost Prelim. Round
1978–79	80	40	29	11	316	292	91	3rd	Patrick Div.	Lost Final
1979–80	80	38	32	10	308	284	86	3rd	Patrick Div.	Lost Quarterfinal
1980–81	80	30	36	14	312	317	74	4th	Patrick Div.	Lost Semifinal
1981–82	80	39	27	14	316	306	92	2nd	Patrick Div.	Lost Div. Final
1982–83	80	35	35	10	306	287	80	4th	Patrick Div.	Lost Div. Final
1983–84	80	42	29	9	314	304	93	4th	Patrick Div.	Lost Div. Semifinal
1984–85	80	26	44	10	295	345	62	4th	Patrick Div.	Lost Div. Semifinal
1985–86	80	36	38	6	280	276	78	4th	Patrick Div.	Lost Conf. Final
1986–87	80	34	38	8	307	323	76	4th	Patrick Div.	Lost Div. Semifinal
1987–88	80	36	34	10	300	283	82	5th	Patrick Div.	Out of Playoffs
1988–89	80	37	35	8	310	307	82	3rd	Patrick Div.	Lost Div. Semifinal
1989–90	80	36	31	13	279	267	85	1st	Patrick Div.	Lost Div. Final
1990–91	80	36	31	13	297	265	85	2nd	Patrick Div.	Lost Div. Semifinal
1991–92	80	50	25	5	321	246	105	1st	Patrick Div.	Lost Div. Final
1992–93	84	34	39	11	304	308	79	6th	Patrick Div.	Out of Playoffs
1993–94	84	52	24	8	299	231	112	1st	Atlantic Div.	Won Stanley Cup
1994–95	48	22	23	3	139	134	47	4th	Atlantic Div.	Lost Conf. Semifinal
1995–96	82	41	27	14	272	237	96	2nd	Atlantic Div.	Lost Conf. Semifinal
1996–97	82	38	34	10	258	231	86	4th	Atlantic Div.	Lost Conf. Final
1997–98	82	25	39	18	197	231	68	5th	Atlantic Div.	Out of Playoffs

OTTAWA SENATORS
1917–18 TO 1933–34
Brian McFarlane

OTTAWA HAS ONE OF THE RICHEST TRADITIONS of any hockey city in North America. Teams from Canada's capital have brought honor and distinction to the city almost from the beginning of hockey's emergence as Canada's great winter game. At the Montreal Winter Carnival of 1884, an Ottawa team competed against four Montreal squads and beat McGill University in the finals. This was Ottawa's first appearance at the Montreal event which was in its second year as hockey's initial championship event.

Over a dozen famous teams have represented Ottawa since those early days; the Ottawas, Victorias, Capitals, Silver Seven, Montagnards, Primroses, Canadiens, Rebels, Rideaus, Cliffsides, Flyers, Commandos and, of course, the famous Senators.

From 1893 to 1934, when Ottawa teams were eligible to compete for the Stanley Cup, the Ottawa Silver Seven and Senator teams combined for nine championship seasons. This Stanley Cup record was unprecedented at the time and remains tied with Detroit for third behind the 24 victories of the Montreal Canadiens and the 13 of the Toronto Maple Leafs/St. Pats/Arenas. (A case can also be made that the 1914 Stanley Cup victory of the Toronto Blueshirts gives the franchise 14 championships.) In addition to the city's Stanley Cup wins, four Ottawa teams have captured the Allan Cup, symbolic of senior hockey supremacy, since it was donated in 1908.

Ottawa was a charter member of the National Hockey League when it was formed during a series of meetings in November of 1917 at the Windsor Hotel in Montreal. The Senators did not capture their first Stanley Cup as NHL champions until 1920 when they hosted the Seattle Metropolitans, the first team from a U.S. city to win the Cup (back in 1917) and the 1920 Pacific Coast Hockey Association champions. Weather played a big part in the outcome. Before a sellout crowd of 7,500, Ottawa captured the first game on soft ice by a 3–2 score. In game two, the ice now covered by water, Ottawa won again 3–0. After Seattle captured game three 3–1 on ice conditions that were intolerable, the final two games were shifted to the new

artificial ice surface in Toronto. Seattle outskated Ottawa in game four, winning 5–2 but the Senators fought back to defeat the visitors 6–1 in the deciding game. Ottawa left for home, clutching its the Stanley Cup.

In 1921, Ottawa posted an 8–2–0 record to win the first half of the NHL's split-season schedule. After slumping to third place in the second half. the Senators caught fire in the playoffs and earned the right to meet the Vancouver Millionaires in Vancouver in the Cup finals. Before 10,000 fans, the largest crowed ever to see a playoff game to that time, the hometown squad scored a 3–1 victory but the Senators bounced back for a 4–3 victory in game two then scored a 3–2 win in game three. Vancouver then fought back with a 3–2 victory of its own and the stage was set for the final contest. Thousands of fans were turned away from the Denman Arena where the Senators and the Millionaires clashed, the Senators winning 2–1 and skating off with Ottawa's seventh Cup triumph.

In 1923, the Senators again met Vancouver for the Stanley Cup (though the West Coast team was now known as the Maroons), but not before Ottawa emerged from the NHL playoffs battered and bruised. On March 7 in Montreal, the Senators and the Canadiens clashed in a memorable playoff game. Montreal tough guys Sprague Cleghorn and Billy Coutu ran wild, using fists and sticks to knock several Ottawa players all but senseless. Both the Montreal badmen were ejected from the game. Further punishment was meted out by Montreal manager Leo Dandurand who suspended his own players from further participation in the series. Ottawa won the series and headed west to meet the Maroons.

Ottawa's Punch Broadbent scored the only goal in the Senators' opening-game victory. Vancouver won game two 4–1 but lost game three by a 3–2 score. The Senators captured the final game in this best-of-five series by 5–1. But the Senators' season wasn't over. The Edmonton Eskimos of the Western Canada Hockey League had traveled to Vancouver and were anxious to face the Senators in a follow-up series for the Cup—a best of three affair. Ottawa defeated the Albertans 2–1 in the first game and 1–0 in the second encounter.

It was in game two that Ottawa star Frank "King" Clancy played every position on the ice including goal. In that era, goaltenders served their own penalties and when Senator netminder Clint Benedict was banished to the box for two minutes, he casually handed his goal stick to Clancy, who guarded the net until Benedict returned. On their departure for Ottawa, the Senators were described by Vancouver's Frank Patrick as "the greatest team I have ever seen."

Artificial ice came to Ottawa on November 30, 1923 when the new Auditorium opened for hockey business featuring an exhibition game between the Edmonton Eskimos and the Senators.

By the 1926–27 season, the rival professional leagues of the west had collapsed and the Stanley Cup became exclusively an NHL trophy. The final Stanley Cup championship won by an Ottawa team emerged from a 1927 playoff series between the Senators and the Boston Bruins. It was during this series that a Boston player received a lifetime suspension from the game. In the opener played in Boston, the Bruins and the Senators fought to a scoreless draw, despite 20 minutes of overtime. Two days later, the Senators beat the Bruins 3–1. The third game, back in Ottawa, ended in a 1–1 score. The fourth and final game was a mild affair until late in the game when a series of savage fights broke out. Boston's Billy Coutu (late of the Canadiens) assaulted one of the game officials in the corridor following the game, won by Ottawa by a 3–1 score, and received a lifetime suspension from hockey. Coutu was reinstated a few years later when it was too late for him to cause any more trouble at the NHL level.

Despite the Senators' success on the ice, NHL expansion into the United States had left Ottawa as by far the smallest market in the NHL and the team was facing serious financial problems. The first official notice of the difficulties the team was facing came at the NHL meetings in September of 1927 when Ottawa management requested that the team receive a larger percentage of the box office receipts from road games. (As perennial champions, the Senators were always a large draw on the road.) Next, the Senators sold Hooley Smith to the Montreal Maroons. Ed Gorman was sold to Toronto and Jack Adams was permitted to retire. The Senators slipped to third in the standings of the NHL's Canadian Division and the defending Stanley Cup champions were eliminated by the Montreal Maroons in the first round of the playoffs.

The Senators continued to ship out expensive talent in 1928–29 when they sent Cy Denneny to the Bruins and Punch Broadbent to the New York Americans. Ottawa fell to fourth in the standings and missed the playoffs. Prior to the 1929–30 season, the Senators again requested an increased share of the road receipts. In January, they shipped an aging Frank Nighbor to the Toronto Maple Leafs. With King Clancy and Alex Connell as the only stars left in Ottawa, the Senators managed to slip into the playoffs that year, but were handled easily by the New York Rangers in the opening round.

Prior to the 1930–31 season, one of hockey's biggest deals took place in the off-season. Toronto owner Conn Smythe won a bundle on a horse named Rare Jewel at the race track one day. He took his winnings and used them as a down payment to purchase Ottawa's star defenseman King Clancy. Ottawa fans mourned the loss of Clancy, one of the game's most colorful personalities. The $35,000 cash received for Clancy wasn't enough to solve the Senators' financial woes and as the team continued to slip in the standings reports began circulating that the team might be sold. Before the start of the 1931–32 season, Ottawa requested a year's leave of absence from the NHL. Ottawa players were distributed around the league and fans in the capital lamented the fact that, for the first time since 1893, no Ottawa team was eligible to compete for the Stanley Cup. The Senators returned to the NHL fold under new management for the 1933–34 season but finished with the poorest record (13–29–6) of the league's nine teams and arrangements were made to transfer the once-proud franchise to St. Louis.

The final NHL game of that era was played in Ottawa at the Auditorium on March 15, 1934. The New York Americans defeated the Senators 3–2. When Americans' goalie Roy Worters received a deep gash over the eye in this match, Ottawa loaned the visitors its backup goaltender Alex Connell, who had been benched and humiliated by his manager earlier in the season. Connell played brilliantly for the visitors and was the number one star of the contest. Over 6,500 fans applauded Connell, then left the arena with solemn faces, knowing it was the end of a memorable era in Canadian hockey.

Ottawa Senators Year-by-Year Record, 1917–1934

Season	GP	W	L	T	GF	GA	Pts	Finish		Playoff Results
1917–18	22	9	13	0	102	114	18	3rd		Out of Playoffs
1918–19	18	12	6	0	71	53	24	1st		Lost NHL Final
1919–20	24	19	5	0	121	64	38	1st		Won Stanley Cup
1920–21	24	14	10	0	97	75	28	2nd		Won Stanley Cup
1921–22	24	14	8	2	106	84	30	1st		Lost NHL Final
1922–23	24	14	9	1	77	54	29	1st		Won Stanley Cup
1923–24	24	16	8	0	74	54	32	1st		Lost NHL Final
1924–25	30	17	12	1	83	66	35	4th		Out of Playoffs
1925–26	36	24	8	4	77	42	52	1st		Lost NHL Final
1926–27	44	30	10	4	86	69	64	1st	Cdn. Div.	Won Stanley Cup
1927–28	44	20	14	10	78	57	50	3rd	Cdn. Div.	Lost Quarterfinal
1928–29	44	14	17	13	54	67	41	4th	Cdn. Div.	Out of Playoffs
1929–30	44	21	15	8	138	118	50	3rd	Cdn. Div.	Lost Quarterfinal
1930–31	44	10	30	4	91	142	24	5th	Cdn. Div.	Out of Playoffs
1931–32			Did Not Play							
1932–33	48	11	27	10	88	131	32	5th	Cdn. Div.	Out of Playoffs
1933–34	48	13	29	6	115	143	32	5th	Cdn. Div.	Out of Playoffs

OTTAWA SENATORS
1992–93 TO DATE

Bruce Garrioch

THE DREAM, SO THE LEGEND NOW GOES, started in a dressing room in the winter of 1989. As the boys from Terrace Investments peeled off their equipment on a Saturday morning at a suburban arena in Ottawa, Bruce Firestone, Randy Sexton and Cyril Leeder came up with the idea to bring a National Hockey League team back to life. Firestone, a visionary with big dreams but little money to back them up, suggested to Sexton and Leeder a land holding the small real estate firm had in Kanata—a suburb in the west end of the city—would be a perfect place for an NHL team complete with a 22,500-seat arena, shopping centre and hotel.

It seemed easy enough. The National Hockey League was looking for two expansion franchises and the city fit the bill to house a team. There would be hurdles along the way but nobody would doubt the success hockey could have in Ottawa. It was, after all, small-town Canada. The country where the game was born. How could the NHL go against an area of a million people where the team would be embraced?

The history of hockey in Ottawa is long and rich. The Stanley Cup was born in the city. The Ottawa Silver Seven team was one of the most powerful clubs of the early 1900s. Before the original Senators moved to St. Louis in 1933–34, the city had nine Stanley Cup victories. In the eyes of Firestone, the capital needed a hockey team and he was the man to bring it back. Instead of viewing the announcement of his bid for a team with excitement, there was resounding laughter. The media thought the release they received that sunny June afternoon in 1989 from Terrace Investments was a joke. Nobody was really serious about bringing the greatest game in the world back to Ottawa ... or were they?

"It's not that the area isn't big enough to support a professional hockey team," said former Ottawa mayor Jim Durrell, who later joined the Senators as team president because Firestone was so inspired in a speech he gave to the NHL's board of governors. "It's just that we're not going to get it." After calling a local press conference at which original Senators great Frank Finnigan was on hand to remind people of the old Senators' past accomplishments in their city, fans started to take them seriously. More than 18,000 fans anted up a non-refundable $50 deposit on season tick-

ets because they believed—like Firestone—the area could support pro hockey.

For a year, Firestone, Sexton and Leeder lobbied NHL owners, governors and general managers in an attempt to get them to believe in the city. They fought political types constantly, trying to get the land rezoned where they would build the Ottawa Palladium so that it could be used for commercial development. The battle was going to be a lot more difficult than they thought. It was obvious the city wanted hockey back, but nobody wanted to say for sure these were the men who could make it possible. Firestone was ripped in the media. People wondered if he actually had the backing to get the job done. Privately, he and his partners vowed to battle the odds, and they used Tom Petty's "Don't Back Down" as their theme song when the chances of making the dream a reality seemed dark.

Armed with an impressive hardcover book outlining their bid, the Senators made their way to the Board of Governors meeting at The Breakers in Palm Beach, Florida, complete with the Ottawa Fire Fighters Marching Band, determined to take their best shot. As the meeting progressed, the Ottawa group received little indication that their bid had been well received, but on December 6, 1990 with the announcement imminent, Firestone was summoned to a room where the governors were gathered prior to a press conference. He was handed a piece of paper that contained just two words —"Tampa" and "Ottawa"—and with that simple gesture, Firestone burst into tears. Ottawa had scored.

There was joy at the announcement and season tickets were snapped up by fans immediately as they went on sale. Still, raising the $50 million (U.S.) franchise fee and getting the funding for the $150 million Palladium—which had been downsized to 18,500—would prove to be difficult. It almost cost them the franchise. That's when Rod Bryden entered the picture. A local businessman and friend of Firestone's, Bryden was brought on board to find investors in the team. Getting the funding for the franchise fee was hardly easy. They pushed the envelope as far as they could and had to spend the late hours of one night in a downtown office to make sure the money was in place for a $22.5 million payment.

Once the expansion fee was paid and the franchise's future secured, the team began to build its hockey department. Sexton was the man in charge. Mel Bridgman, a member of the Philadelphia Flyers "Broad Street Bullies" with an impressive education from the Wharton School of Business, was assigned the tough job of building the team with the help of former Montreal Canadiens great John Ferguson. Only days before the Expansion Draft, highly touted coach Rick Bowness was fired by the Boston Bruins and immediately hired as the Senators first coach. The step from Beantown to Bytown was going to be a challenge; however, he brought with him a respectable coaching record and a willingness to show patience in building a team from the ground up.

The first mistake by Bridgman, and one of the most embarrassing for the franchise, came at the Expansion Draft in a downtown hotel in Montreal. The final list was misplaced by Ferguson and the Senators attempted to draft two players who were ineligible. Twice they were told to make a new selection and it left the organization looking bad from the start. "Ottawa apologizes," said Bridgman. The selections they did decide to keep were mostly journeymen NHLers or players who had good years in the minor leagues

but no longer were considered prospects. Ken Hammond and Brad Shaw were among those who formed the defense. Laurie Boschman, the club's first captain, led a weak list of forwards. It would be up to Peter Sidorkiewicz to handle the goaltending duties.

Only days later at the Entry Draft table in Montreal, fans could have cut the silence with a knife after the club made relative unknown Alexei Yashin from the Moscow Dynamo its number one pick and the second overall selection. Fans had heard nothing about him. The top-rated player in the draft, Roman Hamrlik, went to Tampa Bay. A trainload of people from Ottawa clapped politely. Ferguson talked about Yashin's start potential. Nobody knew it would become a reality.

The players gathered in September in Hull, Ottawa's twin city. More than 80 bodies were looking for a shot in the NHL. Oddly enough, it was Larry Skinner, a former NHLer and an employee of an Ottawa newspaper hired to try out for the team, who was one of the best performers in the club's rookie camp. It was time to face reality: the fans had better be prepared for a difficult season. "It was special to hear that first player's skate hit the ice. It's something I've thought about a lot," said Sexton that day. "It's a simple thing but it's a sound I'm going to remember for the rest of my life. We've finally arrived."

Opening night against the Montreal Canadiens on October 8, 1992, was incredible. The fans packed the cozy 10,500-seat Civic Centre—the club's home until the arena still troubled by financial problems was completed—and with a national television audience watching on Hockey Night in Canada, the Senators did the unthinkable by beating the Habs 5–3. It was a special night. Really, though, it would be the last bit of joy for the season. They would not win a road game for 39 games. Boschman, the man assigned the captaincy, showed he could not do it anymore. Instead, the player who carried the torch was defenseman Brad Marsh and he was a healthy scratch in the first game. The American Hockey League players—Neil Brady, Lonnie Loach and Mark Lamb—who wanted a chance in the "Big Show" couldn't make the jump. Yashin decided to stay in Russia an extra year. The team finished with a 10–70–4 record for 24 points which made them one of the worst expansion teams of all time.

Asked to breakfast by Bryden—who had been installed as chief operating officer—the morning after getting a vote of confidence on local television, Bridgman was fired unceremoniously. What was the meeting like? "Well, I didn't eat my breakfast," said Bridgman. He had suspected all along he would be the fall guy and his worst nightmare came true. Sexton was installed as g.m.—the job he always had coveted—and a new era began. The only thing people in Ottawa were smiling about was the fact the club sealed up the number-one pick at the 1993 NHL Entry Draft. The Senators made no secret of the fact they would use the selection for highly touted Victoriaville Tigres superstar Alexandre Daigle. He was every marketer's dream. He was young, French and had superstar quality. He would be just the tonic the franchise needed to build the Palladium and they mistakenly handed him an unprecedented five-year, $12.5 million contract to get the job done.

But in Firestone's final act as owner of the team, he left in a sea of disarray and disgust. During an off-the-record session with reporters at a team party in Quebec City following the draft, he suggested the team purposely lost games so the Senators could guarantee themselves Daigle.

Only days after Firestone's ownership was bought out conveniently by Bryden, the NHL launched a full investigation. The result was a $100,000 (U.S.) fine to the organization, but the club was found not guilty.

The next season started with promise and hope. Yashin reported to camp and looked brilliant. Daigle had his flashy speed. Craig Billington was the new goaltender of record. It couldn't get worse than the season before. The team looked like it was going places. Even financing for the Palladium was falling into place and there was a belief in the region the rink was going to get built. The Senators actually were surrounded by excitement.

Yashin finished with 77 points—including 35 goals—and was voted to play in the NHL All-Star Game while Daigle had 20 goals and 31 assists. Unfortunately, the record didn't get much better on the ice. The team finished with 37 points. The questions started about Sexton's leadership because Yashin and agent Mark Gandler claimed the organization had made a verbal promise to renegotiate Yashin's contract. It was the start of yet another nightmare.

A war of words stretched through the summer. Yashin didn't report to training camp and 1995 number one selection Bryan Berard walked out of camp because Sexton didn't make him a contract offer. The NHL lockout stole the headlines while Yashin worked out with the Ottawa 67's junior team. A deal was struck to bring Yashin back into the fold just hours before the team left to play its first game of the shortened 48-game schedule in January when the lockout was settled. Again, all seemed well in the world.

Another disappointing season passed under Sexton and Bowness and still Bryden refused to make a move. He claimed to have confidence in the direction the team was going. Then, another battle with Yashin broke out and confidence in management reached an all-time low. Ferguson walked out on the team because he didn't agree with the club's position to trade Yashin. "Just get the guy signed and get him into camp. You don't trade talent like that. You give him what he's worth and move on. Don't fight with your best player," said Ferguson, who was warned he would be fired before quitting.

On opening night of the 1995–96 season, Yashin was on the front page of the local newspaper with his sticks packed up and headed for Russia. He practiced for a week with Moscow Dynamo and suited up for a couple of games before the International Ice Hockey Federation suspended him. An attempt to have his contract declared null and void by an NHL arbitrator was turned down. Twenty games into the year, Bowness was fired and Dave Allison—a career minor-leaguer with no NHL coaching experience—was Sexton's hand-picked successor. The move didn't work. Only weeks later, Sexton was shown the door by Bryden with Anaheim Mighty Ducks assistant g.m. Pierre Gauthier hired to take over the hockey operation. He moved swiftly by bringing Yashin back into the fold—signing him to a five-year, $13 million U.S. contract. Excitement was building, the team was ready to move into the Palladium in January 1996, and there was a sense of direction to the franchise. But Gauthier wasn't finished.

Allison, who had only two victories since taking over from Bowness, was fired on January 24 and replaced by Colorado Avalanche assistant Jacques Martin. The move came only hours after Gauthier pulled off an important three-way trade with the Toronto Maple Leafs and New York Islanders which brought the club young defenseman Wade Redden and goaltender Damian Rhodes. It was a

move which signalled there was a new era in Ottawa. "It's going to be a process," said Martin, the day he was hired. "We want a team that's going to compete, work hard and give us a chance to win. The most important thing is for this team is to work hard. You want to be a team you know your opponent is going to respect. They've got some good young talent here and we build on it for the future."

In 38 games behind the bench, Martin had a respectable 10–24–4 record. It doesn't sound impressive but judging by what had gone on with the organization, it looked pretty good to fans. The move to get Rhodes injected life into the team. Swede Daniel Alfredsson was selected the NHL's rookie of the year. By the time the season ended, fans had confidence and Bryden had backed away from the scene. Former L.A. Kings president Roy Mlakar, who carried a strong background in marketing, was installed to take over.

The summer of 1996 was a flurry of activity. By the time training camp ended, Gauthier and Martin had made ten changes to the roster. The only consistency in the lineup was Yashin, Alfredsson, Daigle, Redden and Rhodes, along with 1994 number one selection Radek Bonk and veteran captain Randy Cunneyworth. Virtually every other part had changed but the Senators were expected to compete for a playoff spot.

Competing and actually getting there were two different stories. Goaltender Ron Tugnutt, signed to be a backup to Rhodes in the off-season, emerged as the hero down the stretch when the former went down with a season-ending ankle injury in late February. The Senators needed help getting into the playoffs but did themselves a favor by going 9–3–1 down the stretch to seal up seventh place in the Eastern Conference on the final night of the season.

Defenseman Steve Duchesne took a pass from Yashin with just over a minute remaining to fire the shot heard around Ottawa that broke a 0–0 tie and vaulted the Senators into the playoffs. It was a magical evening. Outside the arena, horns beeped and fans started lining up for playoff tickets which sold in a span of 40 minutes. "It was great," said Duchesne, dispatched to St. Louis in the off-season. "That was the most fun I've had in my career. It was something you'll never forget."

Backed by Tugnutt, the "Cinderella" Senators faced the Sabres in the first round. It appeared Ottawa was going to knock off Buffalo after taking a 3–2 lead in the series after five games. The series had everything. Sabres goalie Dominik Hasek had left with a mysterious groin injury which called his character into question. Backup goalie Steve Shields had no playoff experience. Buffalo tough guy Matthew Barnaby was flapping at the mouth and Senators fans were primed for victory.

A 3–0 loss to Buffalo in the sixth game at home set the stage for a dramatic game seven at the Marine Midland Arena. With the game tied 2–2, it was Derek Plante who saved the day for the Sabres by throwing a puck at the net in overtime which slipped through Tugnutt's glove to seal the victory. For a moment, the Senators sat slumped around their playoff hero, not sure what to do. The dream of getting to the postseason had ended in disappointment and defeat. At home, a city mourned the loss of its heroes.

After the initial disappointment passed, the Senators viewed their run to the playoffs as a good sign for the future. Changes were kept to a minimum in the summer. Tugnutt was signed to a new three-year deal. Defenseman Chris Phillips, the club's top draft pick in 1996 from the Western Hockey League's Prince Albert Raiders, was added to the roster at the start of the 1997–98 season. Alfredsson joined the club six games into the season after signing a new five-year, $10 million U.S. deal. The average attendance in the building leaped by more than 2,000 additional tickets sold per game.

Not everything stayed the same. Daigle left. Gauthier finally gave up on him in January 1998, shipping him to the Philadelphia Flyers in exchange for Pat Falloon and prospect Vaclav Prospal. Carrying the weight of the contract he signed with the club just hours before the draft, Daigle couldn't have success in Ottawa. There was simply too much pressure on him. He needed a change to jump-start his career.

After finishing the regular schedule with a franchise-record 83 points, Ottawa faced the powerful New Jersey Devils in the opening round of the 1998 playoffs. Although some insiders thought the speedy Senators were capable of beating the older, slower Devils, no one was prepared for what happened. New Jersey simply could not cope with Ottawa's skating skills, and the Senators dominated en route to a six-game upset. Though a five-game loss to the Washington Capitals followed, 1997–98 had been a very successful season.

Shortly after the 1998 NHL Entry Draft, Pierre Gauthier announced his resignation, stating that his young family came first. Rick Dudley, who previously was g.m. of the successful Detroit Vipers franchise in the International Hockey League, was hired as the Senators' fourth general manager.

A five-year first phase of growth has ended, and the Senators have reached respectability. There were firings along the way. Firestone and Sexton are distant memories. Only Leeder—who never was involved in the hockey operation—remains from the original founders of the club. Ottawa fans don't like to look back at the past.

They look at what the future is going to bring to this franchise. It's difficult for Canadian teams to compete in the new NHL. That's why the Senators are trying to build around their young players. Yashin, Alfredsson, Redden and Phillips are the cornerstone of the franchise. They are the foundations for the future and the players this team is going to rely on in its quest to bring a 10th Stanley Cup championship to Ottawa.

It seemed like a longshot the day it was discussed in that dressing room following a Saturday morning pickup game, but the men who realized the dream think about it every time they hear the Hockey Night in Canada theme.

Ottawa Senators Year-by-Year Record, 1992–1998

Season	GP	W	L	T	GF	GA	Pts	Finish		Playoff Results
1992–93	84	10	70	4	202	395	24	6th	Adams Div.	Out of Playoffs
1993–94	84	14	61	9	201	397	37	7th	Northeast Div.	Out of Playoffs
1994–95	48	9	34	5	117	174	23	7th	Northeast Div.	Out of Playoffs
1995–96	82	18	59	5	191	291	41	6th	Northeast Div.	Out of Playoffs
1996–97	82	31	36	15	226	234	77	3rd	Northeast Div.	Lost Conf. Quarterfinal
1997–98	82	34	33	15	193	200	83	5th	Northeast Div.	Lost Conf. Semifinal

PHILADELPHIA FLYERS

Stan Fischler

WHEN A GROUP OF INVESTORS from the City of Brotherly Love declared that they wanted to purchase an NHL franchise to begin play in the 1967–68 season, they were cautioned that big-league hockey simply wouldn't sell in Philadelphia.

The one previous flirtation between the NHL and Philadelphia during the Great Depression was a dismal failure. Benny Leonard, once boxing's lightweight champion of the world, owned the league's old Pittsburgh franchise and moved it to Broad Street. He renamed his club the Quakers and promised to build a brand new arena along the lines of Madison Square Garden that would replace Philadelphia's antiquated rink. Unfortunately, the Quakers couldn't even fill their tiny old Arena. And for good reason; Leonard's inept club had won only five games in Pittsburgh during the 1929–30 campaign, losing 36 and tying three. They were even worse in Philadelphia, going 4–36–4. They did not win a single game from November 29, 1930 to January 10, 1931 and set a league record, losing 15 consecutive matches.

Not long after that Leonard lost his team to bankruptcy and, on September 26, 1931, NHL president Frank Calder made it official that the franchise was suspended. Fortunately, pro hockey was not suspended indefinitely in Philadelphia. Various forms of the minor-league variety were featured at the Arena including the Ramblers, an American Hockey League farm team of the New York Rangers which groomed several stars for the Broadway Blueshirts.

From time to time attempts were made to reintroduce NHL hockey to Pennsylvania but the absence of a large, modern arena proved a major obstacle. It wasn't until the NHL contemplated its major expansion in the mid-1960s that Philadelphia entered the ice picture once more.

This time a new facility was on the horizon as well as substantial financial backing. For $2 million a new franchise was granted to a group headed by Bill Putnam and Jerry Wolman. They named their prospective team the Flyers and immediately purchased an AHL team, the Quebec Aces, before the Flyers ever took the ice. This gave them depth and experience that would prove a large factor in their early success.

When the historic 1967–68 season began, the NHL ballooned from six to a dozen teams. In addition to Philadelphia, the expansion clubs included Oakland, Los Angeles, Minnesota, Pittsburgh and St. Louis. Fiscal problems forced Wolman out of the picture before the maiden season was over. His 60 percent share was sold to Ed Snider. Putnam controlled 25 percent and Joe Scott, a Philadelphia sportsman, had the remaining 15.

Pivotal to the early success of the Flyers was their choice of front office personnel. Putnam chose Norman "Bud" Poile as general manager and he, in turn, picked Keith Allen to be coach. Both Poile and Allen had successful records in the Western Hockey League as coaches and general managers; Poile at Edmonton and San Francisco; Allen at Seattle. Poile, who scored 107 goals with five NHL teams during his career, was an all-star with the Black Hawks in 1948. Allen, who played only 28 games for the Red Wings, was an outstanding minor-league defenseman, and is another in a long line who have proven that you don't have to be

an NHL star to be a fine coach. Both men, in their mid-40s, had been around long enough to know the talent on the farms. In the 1967 Expansion Draft they picked up two 22-year-old goalies from the Bruins, Doug Favell and Bernie Parent, who were good enough to combine for the lead in the Vezina Trophy race in the season's first half and finish third overall with a combined average of 2.42. Each man registered four shutouts.

From Chicago, they snared defenseman Ed Van Impe, runner-up to Bobby Orr for the Calder Trophy the previous season, defenseman John Miszuk, center Lou Angotti and wingman Pat Hannigan. Boston also yielded defenseman Joe Watson and forwards Gary Dornhoefer and Forbes Kennedy. From Montreal came Jean Gauthier, Leon Rochefort and Garry Peters; from Toronto, Brit Selby. Forwards such as Don Blackburn, Bill Sutherland and Ed Hoekstra, who had never before received a chance to play in the NHL (Blackburn had been with Boston for six games in 1962–63), were allowed to display their talents in the big time thanks to expansion.

From Quebec there were the familiar NHL names like Claude LaForge, John Hanna and Jean-Guy Gendron. Before the season ended, some of the fine young prospects, acquired with the Quebec purchase, had made themselves known. There were Simon Nolet and Andre Lacroix. The latter, leading scorer in the AHL who lost out to Nolet when called up to the Flyers, scored six goals and eight assists in 18 games, and added two goals and three assists in the playoffs. Lacroix was not yet 23 years old at the time.

Experts believed that the Flyers would be competitive within the West Division but not of championship caliber. The favorites were the Oakland Seals whose lineup was sprinkled with first-rate NHL skaters and veteran goalie Charlie Hodge.

"We've got to be in the top three in the expansion division," said Poile, following an exhibition record of three wins, three losses, and two ties. "I think we're going to jell and be a factor in the race." The Flyers opened the season on October 11, 1967 at Oakland, losing 5–1 to the Seals. On October 14 they lost 4–2 to the Los Angeles Kings. Their first victory came in the third game, at St. Louis, when Hoekstra scored the winning goal in a 2–1 triumph.

Meanwhile, Philadelphians eagerly awaited the world premiere of the Flyers at the Spectrum. The date was October 19, 1967. The opponents were the Pittsburgh Penguins. It was a game that almost didn't begin because the Flyers didn't have tickets to get into the rink. An hour before game time Bill Sutherland and four of his teammates approached the players' entrance on the lower level and were abruptly stopped by a large man attired in a splendid blue uniform.

"Ticket please," the usher requested.

The players stared at one another like so many Jack Bennys awaiting the punch line. There was one, of course, but it wasn't funny. "I'm sorry," said the man, "but I can't let anybody in without a ticket." Sutherland explained that he was a member of the Flyers and that the usher simply was carrying his devotion to orders a bit too far. But the large man was unmoved even after Flyers president Bill Putnam and Myrna Snider, wife of the team's principal stockholder, tried to intercede. Acknowledging a dead end when he saw one, Sutherland finally led his mates to another corner of the Spectrum where they found an unguarded door and then, like burglars, stole through the cavernous passageways down to their new dressing room. "That

usher," said John Brogan of the *Bulletin*, "threatened Philadelphia's first major-league hockey game in 37 years."

Ironically, Putnam was concerned that not enough people would pass through the Spectrum turnstiles. The rink's capacity was 14,558 seats; hopefully at least three-quarters of them would be filled at face-off time. Putnam himself predicted a crowd of 12,000. The official count was 7,812 and Putnam agreed he had been misled. "They told me this was a gate town," he explained. "I don't know what happened but we sure didn't do much business at the gate tonight." Slowly, the Flyers began attracting a following and it was evident that Poile and Allen had built not only a respectable team but one that appeared quite capable of winning the West Division championship and the Clarence Campbell Bowl.

A key reason for their success was the effectiveness of 39-year-old defenseman Larry "the Rock" Zeidel, who had two brief stints with Detroit and one full season with Chicago in the early 1950s but had toiled for 16 seasons in the minors. Zeidel had helped spearhead the Flyers to first place when an extraordinary event took place; the roof of the Spectrum was blown off during a freak late winter storm. The disaster forced the Flyers out of their home and for 31 days they were compelled to play "home" games at a neutral site, Le Colisee, in Quebec City, not to mention the usual catalog of road matches in foreign rinks.

All things considered, the Flyers adapted well, particularly to their new home in north of the border. After they had beaten Minnesota at Le Colisee, defenseman Joe Watson, who had scored the winning goal said: "If we have to play away from Philly, this is the best place to play. The guys who played here in Quebec in past years give it that little extra because they know the fans who supported them in the past are out there cheering them on."

At a "home game" played in New York, where the fans love an underdog, they had booed the Flyers and cheered the Seals. "We won't go back there," grumbled general manager Bud Poile, "unless it's for the Stanley Cup finals." In Toronto, on the other hand, the fans supported them in a Maple Leaf Gardens home match against the hated Bruins, but the magnanimous Maple Leaf management charged the Flyers 50 percent of the gate as their rink rental.

Meanwhile the hole in the Spectrum's top became the most famous flaw in Philadelphia since the Liberty Bell. In the new Madison Square Garden a fan was complaining about the small number of seats from which one could actually see the entire rink. A second fan offered that although the Spectrum contained 2,500 fewer seats than the Garden, one could see well from anywhere in the building. "Yeah," chimed in a third party, "you could fly over in a heeliocopter and see da game troo da roof." The Spectrum became a joke—but not to the Flyers—and in Philadelphia it had become a political puck. It took 19 days for the city government to reach a decision to begin repairs on the building. Finally, with two games remaining in the regular schedule, it was announced that the Spectrum would reopen in time for the Stanley Cup playoffs.

During the troubled time there was talk that the Flyers would be leaving for another location permanently, even though in their first season they had scored a solid hit with the fans. It was estimated that the Flyer organization lost approximately $400,000 when they were unable to play their last seven home games at the Spectrum. "We felt sure we'd play before sellout crowds," cried Poile.

The team that had edged Los Angeles 73 points to 72 for

the Clarence Campbell Bowl came home from the final regular-season game at Pittsburgh with a four-game losing streak. (The last loss, by a 5–1 margin, was due, in part, to a champagne party that began at 1:30 a.m. in the morning of the game, actuated by the news from Oakland that the Seals had tied the Kings, thereby making it impossible for them to catch the Flyers.) Though elated, they were a road-weary band.

That stretch run debilitated the Flyers at playoff time. They were eliminated in a tense, seven-game opening round by the St. Louis Blues and were forced to regroup for the 1968–69 season. More importantly, their gallant run had captured the hearts of Philadelphia fans and it soon became apparent that the franchise which skeptics earlier had denigrated was on its way to becoming a fiscal success.

Artistically, it was another story. Like other expansion teams, the Flyers tried to blend the old with the new but had difficulty finding a superstar to lead the team. It wasn't until after the heartbreaking loss of a playoff berth on the final night of the 1971–72 season that the Flyers reached their first major turning point.

Previously, the Philadelphia lineup had been sprinkled with smaller players who tended to be pushed around by more muscular opponents. This was evident in two playoff series with St. Louis, not to mention the success off the Big, Bad Bruins who won the Stanley Cup in 1970 and 1972. Owner Ed Snider chose a more belligerent philosophy which was endorsed by new coach Fred "the Fog" Shero and the young captain Bobby Clarke. What emerged was the club that became renowned as the Broad Street Bullies. Its evolution was slow, steady and painful—but mostly to the opposition. Once Keith Allen took over as general manager, the Flyers lineup became pockmarked with pugilists, the most notorious of all being Dave "the Hammer" Schultz, who came to epitomize the new hit-first-ask-questions-later credo at the Spectrum.

Allen wisely surrounded the tough core with burgeoning aces such as Bill Barber and Rick MacLeish, not to mention wise veterans like Ed Van Impe and Barry Ashbee. Most of all he boasted a catalyst in captain Clarke and a superior goaltender in Bernie Parent.

The total package was an intimidating team with enough talent, chemistry and coaching to emerge as the first expansion franchise with Stanley Cup potential. During the 1974 playoffs that potential was realized as the Flyers upset the New York Rangers and ultimately the Bruins to win the title. While critics carped over their occasionally brutish behavior, the Flyers countered that enforcers such as Schultz were also capable players and The Hammer actually became a 20-goal scorer.

What's more, the Flyers proved they were not flukes, winning a second straight Stanley Cup title in 1975 and following that with a third trip to the finals in the spring of 1976. In what was billed as the Good versus Bad playoff, the Flyers took on a skilled Montreal club but without the services of Parent. Swept in four games, Philadelphia had nevertheless emerged as a league power and demonstrated that expansion could work.

By this time Broad Street had become a hockey mecca and it remained that way through the decade and into the 1980s. The Flyers reached the finals again in 1980 only to be ousted in six games by an even younger expansion club, the New York Islanders. Throughout the glory epoch, Clarke shone as the most visible—and adored—Flyer. His tenacity and fierce determination put an imprimatur on the

club that would remain until his retirement in 1984. he was immediately appointed the club's vice president and general manager.

Despite losing Clarke from the lineup, the Flyers made a trip to the finals in 1985, thanks to the galvanic Mike Keenan. Though they lost to Edmonton in five games, a new era of success dawned at the Spectrum. A minuscule Swedish goalie named Pelle Lindbergh had become a new idol and would remain so until his death in an auto accident on a dark road near the club's practice rink in Voorhees, New Jersey on November 10, 1985. With unexpected ease, the Flyers replaced Lindbergh with Ron Hextall.

Under Keenan's stern stewardship, the Flyers reached the finals again in 1987 only to be ousted again by Wayne Gretzky, Mark Messier and the mighty Edmonton Oilers in seven games. Hextall's gallant play in the losing effort earned him the Conn Smythe Trophy. The Keenan era abruptly ended in 1988 and he was followed behind the bench by former Flyer Paul Holmgren.

Surprisingly, Clarke's hold on management unravelled in 1990 when he left Broad Street to become general manager of the Minnesota North Stars. His successor, Russ Farwell (1990 to 1994), underachieved during what was one of the more dismal epochs on Broad Street. The Flyers would miss the playoffs for five straight years.

The one source of optimism was the acquisition of wunderkind Eric Lindros in 1992, an oversized center who previously had refused to report to the Quebec Nordiques when first drafted in 1991. A year later, 1992's draft day was replete with intrigue and last-minute machinations, Philadelphia and the Rangers both thought they had struck a deal with Quebec owner Marcel Aubut to obtain the prospect and it would take the ruling of an independent arbitrator to decide in favor of the Flyers. To obtain Lindros Philadelphia relinquished Hextall, Kerry Huffman, Chris Simon, Peter Forsberg, Steve Duchesne, Mike Ricci, first round draft choices in the 1993 and 1994 Entry Drafts and $15 million to the Nordiques.

The hulking Lindros proved an instant attraction and cornerstone of the franchise as it embarked on construction of a new arena—completed prior to the 1996–97 season—that would adjoin the aging Spectrum. Lindros proved to be a superstar talent, but through his first three NHL seasons, missed 46 games due to injury as the Flyers missed two playoff berths. Meanwhile, coaches were changed almost as frequently as new seasons. Holmgren was replaced in 1991 by Bill Dineen who was replaced in 1993 by Terry Simpson.

The breakthrough finally occurred in the 1994–95 season when the Flyers hired Terry Murray as coach and traded right winger Mark Recchi to Montreal for defenseman Eric Desjardins and right winger John LeClair, an underachiever with the Habs who was dealt out of frustration by general manager Serge Savard. LeClair would become the first Philadelphian to enjoy three consecutive 50-goal seasons since Tim Kerr's four-peat in the 1980s.

After five non-playoff years, the additions of LeClair and Desjardins, plus the return of Hextall via trade with the Islanders, and general manager Bobby Clarke from the Florida Panthers, turned the Flyers into division champions in the lockout-shortened 1994–95 season. In the playoffs, they skated past Buffalo and the Rangers only to be shut

down in six games by the eventual Stanley Cup champions, the New Jersey Devils. Lindros was awarded the Hart Trophy as league MVP.

Another first-place finish followed in 1995–96 but so did another playoff collapse, this time at the hands of the upstart Florida Panthers. Goaltending was being tagged as the main culprit. The tandem of Hextall and Wrentham, Massachusetts native Garth Snow did little to wow Philly fans or make them legitimate contenders in the eyes of many. That didn't stop the Flyers, though, from finishing second in the Atlantic Division in 1996–97. The acquisition of defender Paul Coffey, a second straight 50-goal effort from LeClair and seemingly improved goaltending carried the team to the Stanley Cup finals where they were smothered by the Detroit Red Wings in four straight games.

A summer of discontent followed. Murray was replaced with Wayne Cashman prior to the 1997–98 season. The Flyers signed free-agent center Chris Gratton from the Tampa Bay Lightning for a multi-million-dollar, multi-year contract that made the 23-year-old the second-highest paid player in the league. But by December of that year, the Flyers were running a distant second to the Devils and changes were in order. Philadelphia acquired underachieving Ottawa Senators winger Alexandre Daigle for budding forward Vaclav Prospal and center Pat Falloon. Next was the demotion of Cashman to assistant coach and the hiring of Roger Neilson as head coach in February 1998. At the 1998 trading deadline, 1996–97 All-Rookie Team defenseman Janne Niinimaa was sent to Edmonton for defenseman Dan McGillis. A Flyers team built on toughness was hurt when the NHL began to crack down on obstruction fouls late in the 1997–98 season, and in the playoffs, Philadelphia's lumbering giants proved no match for the small but speedy Sabres. Dominik Hasek and his Buffalo teammates knocked the Flyers out of the postseason tournament in just five games.

Philadelphia Flyers Year-by-Year Record

Season	GP	W	L	T	GF	GA	Pts	Finish		Playoff Results
1967–68	74	31	32	11	173	179	73	1st	West Div.	Lost Quarterfinal
1968–69	76	20	35	21	174	225	61	3rd	West Div.	Lost Quarterfinal
1969–70	76	17	35	24	197	225	58	5th	West Div.	Out of Playoffs
1970–71	78	28	33	17	207	225	73	3rd	West Div.	Lost Quarterfinal
1971–72	78	26	38	14	200	236	66	5th	West Div.	Out of Playoffs
1972–73	78	37	30	11	296	256	85	2nd	West Div.	Lost Semifinal
1973–74	78	50	16	12	273	164	112	1st	West Div.	Won Stanley Cup
1974–75	80	51	18	11	293	181	113	1st	Patrick Div.	Won Stanley Cup
1975–76	80	51	13	16	348	209	118	1st	Patrick Div.	Lost Final
1976–77	80	48	16	16	323	213	112	1st	Patrick Div.	Lost Semifinal
1977–78	80	45	20	15	296	200	105	2nd	Patrick Div.	Lost Semifinal
1978–79	80	40	25	15	281	248	95	2nd	Patrick Div.	Lost Quarterfinal
1979–80	80	48	12	20	327	254	116	1st	Patrick Div.	Lost Final
1980–81	80	41	24	15	313	249	97	2nd	Patrick Div.	Lost Quarterfinal
1981–82	80	38	31	11	325	313	87	3rd.	Patrick Div.	Lost Div. Semifinal
1982–83	80	49	23	8	326	240	106	1st	Patrick Div.	Lost Div. Semifinal
1983–84	80	44	26	10	350	290	98	3rd	Patrick Div.	Lost Div. Semifinal
1984–85	80	53	20	7	348	241	113	1st	Patrick Div.	Lost Final
1985–86	80	53	23	4	335	241	110	1st	Patrick Div.	Lost Div. Semifinal
1986–87	80	46	26	8	310	245	100	1st	Patrick Div.	Lost Final
1987–88	80	38	33	9	292	292	85	3rd	Patrick Div.	Lost Div. Semifinal
1988–89	80	36	36	8	307	285	80	4th	Patrick Div.	Lost Conf. Final
1989–90	80	30	39	11	290	297	71	6th	Patrick Div.	Out of Playoffs
1990–91	80	33	37	10	252	267	76	5th	Patrick Div.	Out of Playoffs
1991–92	80	32	37	11	252	273	75	6th	Patrick Div.	Out of Playoffs
1992–93	84	36	37	11	319	319	83	5th	Patrick Div.	Out of Playoffs
1993–94	84	35	39	10	294	314	80	6th	Atlantic Div.	Out of Playoffs
1994–95	48	28	16	4	150	132	60	1st	Atlantic Div.	Lost Conf. Final
1995–96	82	45	24	13	282	208	103	1st	Atlantic Div.	Lost Conf. Semifinal
1996–97	82	45	24	13	274	217	103	2nd	Atlantic Div.	Lost Final
1997–98	82	42	29	11	242	193	95	2nd	Atlantic Div.	Lost Conf. Quarterfinal

PHILADELPHIA QUAKERS

Eric Zweig

THE NHL FIRST CAME TO PHILADELPHIA long before expansion in 1967, arriving in the City of Brotherly Love in 1930 when the Pittsburgh Pirates moved across state. The team was dubbed the Philadelphia Quakers, after the religious community of the Pennsylvania countryside.

Pittsburgh had become the third American city in the NHL (after Boston and New York) when the Pirates were officially granted a franchise in 1925–26. Though the city had a long hockey tradition, and the team made the playoffs twice in its first three seasons, the Pirates were not a financial success. After the stock market crash in October of 1929 weakened the city's steel industry and the Pirates struggled through a 5–36–3 season, owner Benny Leonard decided to relocate. The transfer of Pittsburgh's home games to Philadelphia was accepted by the NHL's Board of Governors on October 18, 1930.

Twelve players who had worn the yellow and black of the Pittsburgh Pirates in 1929–30 suited up in the orange and black of the Philadelphia Quakers in 1930–31. Hugh Darragh, Hib Milks, Tex White and Herb Drury had been with the franchise since its NHL debut in 1925–26, though only Milks would suffer through the entire season in Philadelphia. Future Hockey Hall of Fame referee Cooper Smeaton had resigned as the NHL's referee-in-chief to coach the Quakers. The roster was bolstered by future star Syd Howe and new goalie Wilf Cude (who would later become a two-time All-Star), but Smeaton would be refereeing again by 1931–32.

The first NHL game in Philadelphia took place on November 11, 1930 with the New York Rangers defeating the Quakers 3–0. It would take until their third game before the Quakers scored their first goal. Philadelphia was 1–4–1 after beating the Toronto Maple for its first victory on November 25, but the Quakers' next win would not come until January 10, 1931 when they beat the Montreal Maroons 4–3 in overtime. A 2–1 loss to the Montreal Canadiens three nights later saw Philadelphia hit the midway point of the season at 2–20–1. The second half of the season brought a pair of wins over the Detroit Falcons (2–0 on February 17 and 7–5 on March 12) as the Quakers finished the season with a record of 4–36–4.

Philadelphia's 76 goals in 1930–31 tied the New York Americans for the lowest in the league but while the Americans only allowed an NHL-best 74 goals against, Philadelphia surrendered 184, which was 42 more than the next worst team (the Ottawa Senators) and almost double the league average of 97 goals allowed by the NHL's other nine teams. Philadelphia's four victories tied a league record for futility established by the Quebec Bulldogs during a 24-game season in 1919–20, and the Quakers' winning percentage of .136 would remain the worst in NHL history until the Washington Capitals went 8–67–5 for a .131 winning percentage in 1974–75.

At the NHL Board of Governors meeting on September 26, 1931 it was announced that both the Ottawa Senators and the Pittsburgh-Philadelphia franchise would suspend operations for 1931–32. The Pennsylvania club continued to receive permission to suspend operations for two more years while still being represented on the NHL Board of Governors. An application to suspend operations yet again was accepted on September 22, 1934, but this time with the proviso that the club would no longer have a representative on the board. Finally, at the NHL meeting on May 7, 1936 the franchise was formally canceled. The NHL did not return to Pittsburgh or Philadelphia until the Penguins and Flyers began play in 1967.

Philadelphia Quakers Year-by-Year Record

Season	GP	W	L	T	GF	GA	Pts	Finish		Playoff Results
1930–31	44	4	36	4	76	184	12	5th.	Amn. Div.	Out of Playoffs

PHOENIX COYOTES AND WINNIPEG JETS

Tim Campbell

THE SYMBOLISM OF THE TRANSFER of the Winnipeg Jets to Phoenix in 1996 is unmistakable. The franchise, three times a champion of the renegade World Hockey Association—the rebels that put Winnipeg back on the hockey map and changed the face of the pro game—had been in a competitive desert for many years since. Never with a shortage of headliners before or since the move, the team reborn as the Phoenix Coyotes in its new, larger, richer home still has found the NHL's ultimate prize, the Stanley Cup, as elusive as ever.

In 19 NHL years through 1997–98, the franchise posted a winning record only six times, won only two playoff series and never has won so much as a game in the second round of the Stanley Cup tournament. Elite stars such as Dale Hawerchuk and Teemu Selanne—both Calder Trophy winners—and Keith Tkachuk and Jeremy Roenick have been caught in the drought, their personal victories and records only small consolations in the frustrating quest that now continues in the sizzling American Southwest. An earlier group of worshiped players, the likes of "the Golden Jet" Bobby Hull and linemates Ulf Nilsson and Anders Hedberg, set high standards the franchise always has been held to but never matched once it joined the NHL in 1979–80.

The Winnipeg Jets franchise actually was born in the mid-1960s with little fanfare or commotion. Spearheaded by entrepreneur Ben Hatskin, the junior Jets were admitted to the Western Canada Junior Hockey League in 1967. The team was named simply because Hatskin was a friend and admirer of Sonny Werblin, owner of the NFL's New York Jets. The new hockey team met with only limited success but Hatskin was hooked on both the game and ownership. So when Gary Davidson and Dennis Murphy came up with the brainstorm of piecing together a pro league to rival the NHL, Hatskin joined the 12-team WHA in 1971, the WHA's first games were played in 1972–73.

It wasn't regarded with much interest or credibility by hockey's establishment, but it took only a couple of high-profile signings to change all of that. For good, talented goalie Bernie Parent led the defections to the WHA and Hatskin was not far behind with his coup de grace. His target was "the Golden Jet," Hull, the ultimate scoring machine, said he found most of Hatskin's early overtures merely a nuisance. In that mindset, Hull jokingly told the Winnipeg organization that he needed a million dollars to jump leagues. The jest turned out to be the best news his bank account ever received.

Hull found out that Hatskin and his new partners weren't kidding around. Some intense negotiations and deal-bro-

kering with other WHA franchises to contribute half of the $2.75 million contract led to Hull's decision to switch leagues. He inked the deal June 27, 1972 in St. Paul, Minnesota, then jetted off to Winnipeg for a symbolic signing at the city's epicenter, the corner of Portage Avenue and Main Street. The NHL was aghast. One of its marquee players, even if he was 32, had abandoned the unquestioned tradition and script for all players. Worse for the grand old league, it touched off a flurry of defections that numbered 60 by the time the first WHA schedule had begun.

The defections were followed as quickly with lawsuits from NHL clubs, who held that the reserve clause bound players to teams, even if their contracts had expired. Still, the Jets had taken on another Chicago winger, Christian Bordeleau, and several players from other NHL organizations including Cal Swenson (Toronto), Garth Rizzuto (Vancouver), Steve Cuddie (Buffalo), Bobby Ash (Rangers), Larry Hornung (St. Louis) and veteran players Bob Woytowich, Wally Boyer, Ab McDonald and Billy Sutherland.

The legal actions continued into August of 1972 (costing Hull a spot on Team Canada's 1972 roster), but the Jets did not sit still. Not only did they name Hull as the team's first coach, but they hired Nick Mickoski as his assistant and named Ab McDonald their first captain. Hull did not suit up for the franchise's first pro game in Madison Square Garden on October 12, 1972, against the New York Raiders, a 6–4 win. In fact, he missed 15 games until an American judge tossed out the NHL suits as "harassment."

Despite the forced hiatus, the Golden Jet fired 51 goals and 103 points that inaugural season to help put the WHA in business and Winnipeg in the headlines. Playing on the Luxury Line, with Bordeleau and Normie Beaudin, Hull and the Jets went all the way to the Avco Cup finals before losing to New England. After a mediocre second year, Hatskin dispatched confidante and scout Billy Robinson to Sweden to bolster the club's lineup—a philosophy much ahead of its time but one eventually adopted by teams everywhere. The mission brought Nilsson, Hedberg, defenseman Lars-Erik Sjoberg and others to Winnipeg and became the catalyst for a new and high-tempo brand of offensive hockey that made the Jets immensely successful in the remaining WHA years.

The slick, swift style the Swedes played with Hull (who scored 77 goals that season) on the "Production line," and the addition of rock-solid competitors like Sjoberg and Finnish stars Veli-Pekka Ketola and Heikki Riihiranta had the Jets on their way, though they had to endure one more frustrating year.

In the fall of 1975, three more Swedes joined the team— Willy Lindstrom, Mats Lindh and Dan Labraaten—and the Jets had become a truly international collection. They won the WHA title in that season, made the finals in 1977 and won the final two Avco Cup titles in 1978 and 1979. And in those days, it was the Jets that held the upper hand against their rivals from Edmonton. Those speedy, skill-oriented strategies were not lost on future Oilers coach and g.m. Glen Sather, who later used that same blueprint for the powerhouse Stanley Cup winners in the 1980s.

While the Jets were dominating the WHA in the late 1970s, the league eventually ran up against some insurmountable problems, most of them financial. Folding and moving franchises was simply no way to do business. However, as one of the league's strongest entities, the Jets eventually became one of four clubs that were accepted into

the NHL's expansion of 1979. About a year earlier, a green, local lawyer named Barry Shenkarow and Winnipeg businessman Michael Gobuty had become part of the ownership team. The deal was cut to have the Jets, Edmonton, Hartford and Quebec join the NHL, but admittance came with some harsh conditions attached. The successful hockey team Winnipeggers had come to love was more or less disbanded. Hull was in his final days as a player. Hedberg and Nilsson had been lured to the New York Rangers, and Jets general manager John Ferguson was caught between a rock and a hard place, allowed to retain only two skaters and two goaltenders before the Expansion Draft.

Ferguson selected Jimmy Mann, a fierce fighter but not much else, as the Jets' first player in the NHL Entry Draft, 19th overall. The team fared a little better in later rounds, choosing Dave Christian, Tim Watters and a player who turned out to be one of the classiest and most admirable performers in the franchise's history, Thomas Steen. Under coach Tom McVie and Billy Sutherland, now his assistant, the Jets opened their first NHL season in Pittsburgh, October 10, 1979, with a 4–2 loss. Their first NHL goal came from Morris Lukowich, who went on to lead the club with 35 goals and 74 points in that first rag-tag season. It produced 20 wins, something of a miracle in itself, and the Jets managed to tie Colorado in last place with 51 points.

That was the good news. The bad news was that the Jets weren't much different than most expansion teams, finding the road even tougher to travel in the second season. The team went 30 games without victory in one stretch, went through three coaches (McVie, Sutherland and the man who later would be g.m., Mike Smith) and ended up a distant last in the NHL with only nine wins (9–57–14) and 32 points. Of course, what goes down usually comes up, and the Jets rebound in the 1981–82 season was one of the most dramatic on record. The club posted a .500 mark that year, 33–33–14, finishing second in the Norris Division to Minnesota.

There were reasons for this turnaround. The worst record at least gives a team the top draft pick and the Jets used theirs in 1981 to choose a franchise player named Dale Hawerchuk, the darling junior with the all-world talent from the Cornwall Royals. Like the organization's first franchise player, Bobby Hull, Hawerchuk was signed in a ceremony at Winnipeg's most famous intersection. Known as "Ducky" because of his squat skating style, Hawerchuk broke into the NHL with a flourish. His scoring exploits from junior translated instantly into the pro game, amounting to 45 goals and 103 points and giving him a lock on top rookie honors. The Jets had hired career college coach Tom Watt from the University of Toronto and the combination was enough to bring them immediate respectability. While Hawerchuk won the Calder, Watt was rewarded with the Jack Adams Award as NHL coach of the year.

An ominous tendency for early playoff exits began in that spring of 1982 when the Jets lost to St. Louis in the first round of the playoffs. In the following two years, it happened against the powerful Edmonton Oilers in straight games each time. That type of stagnation and eventual strained relations between Hawerchuk and the coach cost Watt his job. A minor breakthrough occurred in the spring of 1985, when a very balanced Jets team dropped the Calgary Flames in the first round and at least lived to fight the Oilers in the second. Again an Edmonton sweep took the many of the positives out of a season where six different Jets had 30 goals—Hawerchuk (53, plus 77 assists and

an All-Star berth), Paul MacLean (41), Laurie Boschman (32), Brian Mullen (32), Doug Smail (31) and Steen (30). An experienced defense led by Randy Carlyle and Dave Ellett had been so promising.

That season, under coach Barry Long, the Jets hit a high-water mark of 43 wins and 96 points, and it was the last time the franchise finished as high as second in its division. So many people still utter "what if," referring to Hawerchuk's broken ribs suffered in the first-round victory over Calgary. The Jets fell back to 59 points the very next season, and the yo-yo trend of good season followed by bad was well under way. Long was replaced by Dan Maloney, who as per the script, brought the team back up to 88 points in 1986–87.

That was another exciting spring in Winnipeg, Hawerchuk's fifth with more than 100 points. The Jets won a stirring first-round playoff matchup against the Calgary Flames in six games—the last time the team made it past the first round—but it was the same old story against the Oilers. The second-round series lasted the minimum four games, taking the Jets postseason record against Edmonton to 0–14. From 88 points, the Jets slipped back again the following season to 77 and the 1988 playoffs brought a familiar opponent, the Oilers. This time, the underdogs managed a shorthand winning goal from hometown product Randy Gilhen and actually won a game, but a five-game triumph for Edmonton left the overall tally at 1–18. That, as much as anything, cost the always-boisterous Ferguson his job in October of 1988.

Long-time scout and assistant g.m. Mike Smith was brought in as general manager first on an interim basis and then as a permanent appointment, but by the time he started rearranging the team's role players and depth, the season was lost. Maloney was a casualty, and the Jets finished a 64-point, out-of-playoffs year under Rick Bowness. Bob Murdoch took over as the new coach in 1989–90 and predictably, the team perked up once again. It rebounded to 85 points with a very workmanlike approach but there seemed to be no way around that old nemesis, the Oilers.

This time, however, the playoff matchup was a classic. It wasn't even supposed to be a fair fight, but the drama and excitement in the spring of 1990 went to new levels in Winnipeg Arena. Winnipeg jumped out to a 3–1 lead in the series, including Dave Ellett's double-overtime marker that for many Jets fans remains one of the club's greatest NHL moments. But Jari Kurri, Mark Messier and Grant Fuhr still proved too much for Winnipeg in seven games and the Oilers marched on to the Stanley Cup.

As the cigar-chomping Ferguson was known for his volatile temper, Smith's style also became the subject for much scrutiny. The introspective and highly educated general manager made frequent trades (71 during his five-year tenure) and stocked the Jets reserve list with European players, mainly Russian. Smith also became known as a frugal manager and formidable negotiator, a trait which may have been good for the team's bottom line but alienated several important players.

Hawerchuk eventually became disgruntled at the forever-sideways moves of the franchise and his trade request was granted by Smith after the seven-game loss to the Oilers in 1990. The catch was Buffalo's highly talented defenseman Phil Housley, who himself became a contractual headache and was traded to St. Louis in September of 1993. The same fate befell goalie Bob Essensa, who had broken in as a virtual unknown in 1989. Essensa was a Vezina finalist in 1991–92, but negotiations never solved anything and led to a landmark salary arbitration case that the goaltender eventually won—the first $1 million arbitration award in NHL history. Essensa, however, was traded in March, 1994, a disastrous 57-point season during which Smith was fired.

After the Hawerchuk trade, the Jets had sagged to 63 points under Murdoch in 1990-91 and the coach was replaced. Smith this time looked much closer to home for his next coach and found Oak River, Manitoba native John Paddock. Paddock had spent most of his playing time in the minors and had assembled an impressive resume behind the bench of several successful American Hockey League clubs. Paddock took over in the fall of 1991 and moved the team to two straight playoff berths, with improved point totals (81, 87) each year, a first for the franchise. But the Vancouver Canucks had taken the place of the Oilers as impenetrable playoff obstacles and defeated the Jets in consecutive years, 1992 and 1993.

Smith was responsible for drafting or bringing much of the new wave of talent to the franchise—including Selanne, Teppo Numminen, Alexei Zhamnov, Tkachuk and goalie Nikolai Khabibulin—something history should not forget. But Shenkarow, the team's president, could go no further with Smith and dismissed him in January of 1994.

Paddock the coach became Paddock the coach and general manager. His instant priority was not to change the talent as much as the chemistry of his floundering team and that brought about the acquisition of some grit, in the persons of Dallas Drake and Dave Manson, before the end of the season.

Paddock had benefited from the introduction of Selanne, a 1988 draft pick, to the NHL in the fall of 1992. Such an injection of speed and skill, not to mention charisma, vaulted "the Finnish Flash" to instant stardom. Teemu-mania not only had a hold of Winnipeg but nearly every place in the NHL. Selanne, 22 when he played his first NHL game, smashed records for goals by freshmen with 76 (tying Alexander Mogilny for the overall league lead) and points with 132. And the fact that "the Flash" picked up his own torrid pace in the season's second half made him the unanimous selection (all 50 first-place votes) as the Calder Trophy winner over the likes of Eric Lindros and Felix Potvin.

The lockout-shortened season of 1994–95 proved to be the beginning of the end for the franchise in Winnipeg. Burdened with the city's decaying arena (built in the 1950s and renovated several times) and escalating NHL salaries, Shenkarow and his private ownership group (holding 64 percent) were caught in a financial squeeze. Provincial and city governments held a 36 percent stake and had a grip on the team's purse strings after agreeing to fund any operating losses in 1991. That's when, in a vacuum of civic leadership, the bureaucracies decided to study the matter further instead of proceeding with the construction of a new, downtown arena for about $65 million Cdn.

The covering of losses was the panacea to Shenkarow to be patient. It also turned out to be a short-sighted guarantee in the wake of rising salaries, and eventually became a political lightning rod that was the underlying poison for whatever hope there might have been to save the franchise in Winnipeg. Shenkarow obviously had gotten a sweetheart deal and was blamed for most of the mess, but it was political leaders who signed on the bottom line.

Two distinct groups emerged to try to rescue the situation in 1994 and 1995. But the tenuous labor peace that was

achieved after a three-month lockout didn't bode well for Winnipeg, because no firm grip on rising salaries was gained by NHL owners. Manitoba Entertainment Complex (MEC) was the first group to try to arrange the purchase of the team and construction of a new, revenue-enhancing arena. Shenkarow, in his 1991 agreement with governments, had agreed to sell the franchise to approved buyers for $32 million Canadian by 1996. MEC, however, after first blaming NHL commissioner Gary Bettman, couldn't finalize an agreement with Shenkarow on the sale of the team or with different government bodies on the arena financing, and flew the white flag in early May.

After missing the playoffs, an emotional in-arena funeral to retire the team logo and Steen's number 25 was held only days before a second group called Spirit of Manitoba surfaced. Spirit's effort was buoyed by community efforts that included a downtown riverside rally attended by 35,000 people as well as by other fund-raising endeavors that came to be called "Operation Grassroots." Winnipeg's city council and Manitoba's provincial government each endorsed contributions to construction of a new facility, but Shenkarow's August deadline to consummate a deal with the group could not be met.

Mostly, the deal was just too complicated, had too many strings attached, involved too many personal and political agendas and the Shenkarow group's $32 million takeout price for its privately held shares was a simple transaction. Bettman's summation of the mess was painfully accurate—that it was a simple case that nobody in the Manitoba capital wanted to step up and own the team. Winnipeg fans and taxpayers had run the emotional gamut from death to life, back to the inevitable and impending departure. While the recriminations resounded—some blamed Shenkarow for not wanting to relinquish control, politicians for submarining the process and local business leaders for being selfish—Winnipeg was left with a lame-duck team for the 1995–96 season because all the political and financial wrangling went past the league deadline for transferring locations.

And so they played, to poor crowds that eventually averaged 11,316 (74 percent of capacity) in what really wasn't much of a "Season To Remember," as the franchise had dubbed it. The club's 36–40–6 record was overshadowed by Tkachuk's huge new five-year contract, the terms of which were dictated by an offer sheet tendered by the Chicago Blackhawks, and by the unpopular trade of citywide favorite Teemu Selanne who went to Anaheim for Oleg Tverdovsky and Chad Kilger.

On the ice, the club struggled to the bitter end to squeeze into the playoffs. Tkachuk's 50th goal in the second-to-last game of the season sparked a final burst of enthusiasm for the team, though the Jets had drawn the powerful, first-seeded Detroit Red Wings in the first round of the Western Conference playoffs. Winnipeg, with its white-clad, frenzied fans, got in its licks to take the Wings to six games, but Norm MacIver's goal in the 3–1, game six loss on April 28, 1996 closed the book on Winnipeg in the NHL.

Exactly 1,400 regular and postseason NHL games had been played by the Jets, who were turned into Phoenix Coyotes after a $68-million (U.S.) franchise purchase by Richard Burke and Steven Gluckstern moved the club to Arizona. Coach Terry Simpson, who most agreed had performed well in keeping together a lame-duck team, lost his job in the transition, as ties to Winnipeg were cut by the new owners. Along with players and equipment, Burke and

Gluckstern had bought an unimpressive performance history. Paddock, who had stepped aside as coach in the spring of 1995, was also a casualty just two months into the team's new season in Phoenix. Vice president Bobby Smith, hired by Burke, took over the job of running the team.

With rookie Don Hay running the first show in the desert, the Coyotes played inconsistently again, but eventually finished at 38–37–7, in spite of a losing record in their new home rink, America West Arena. The team survived a lengthy holdout by Roenick, who was traded for Zhamnov during the off-season, and matched up against the Mighty Ducks of Anaheim in the first playoff round.

Phoenix imported the white-out from Winnipeg for the postseason, but all it brought them was the same old grief. The Coyotes were knocked out by the Ducks in a seventh game, in spite of six goals in seven games by Tkachuk, who had become the first American-born player to lead the NHL in goals during the regular-season with 52. The defeat surprisingly prompted Smith to dismiss Hay, and Jim Schoenfeld was brought in to coach year number two in Phoenix.

Tkachuk was restored to the captaincy a year after his messy contract situation in "the Season To Remember," but the Coyotes also enlisted the services of free-agent Rick Tocchet in the summer of 1997 to assist in leadership areas. The club qualified for the playoffs with a .500 record in 1997–98, but was eliminated in the first round of the Western Conference playoffs by the eventual Stanley Cup champions from Detroit.

Phoenix Coyotes Year-by-Year Record

Season	GP	W	L	T	GF	GA	Pts	Finish		Playoff Results
1979–80*	80	20	49	11	214	314	51	5th	Smythe Div.	Out of Playoffs
1980–81*	80	9	57	14	246	400	32	6th	Smythe Div.	Out of Playoffs
1981–82*	80	33	33	14	319	332	80	2nd	Norris Div.	Lost Div. Semifinal
1982–83*	80	33	39	8	311	333	74	4th	Smythe Div.	Lost Div. Semifinal
1983–84*	80	31	38	11	340	374	73	4th	Smythe Div.	Lost Div. Semifinal
1984–85*	80	43	27	10	358	332	96	2nd	Smythe Div.	Lost Div. Final
1985–86*	80	26	47	7	295	372	59	3rd	Smythe Div.	Lost Div. Semifinal
1986–87*	80	40	32	8	279	271	88	3rd	Smythe Div.	Lost Div. Final
1987–88*	80	33	36	11	292	310	77	3rd	Smythe Div.	Lost Div. Semifinal
1988–89*	80	26	42	12	300	355	64	5th	Smythe Div.	Out of Playoffs
1989–90*	80	37	32	11	298	290	85	3rd	Smythe Div.	Lost Div. Semifinal
1990–91*	80	26	43	11	260	288	63	5th	Smythe Div.	Out of Playoffs
1991–92*	80	33	32	15	251	244	81	4th	Smythe Div.	Lost Div. Semifinal
1992–93*	84	40	37	7	322	320	87	4th	Smythe Div.	Lost Div. Semifinal
1993–94	84	24	51	9	245	344	57	6th	Central Div.	Out of Playoffs
1994–95	48	16	25	7	157	177	39	6th	Central Div.	Out of Playoffs
1995–96*	82	36	40	6	275	291	78	5th	Central Div.	Lost Conf. Quarterfinal
1996–97	82	38	37	7	240	243	83	3rd	Central Div.	Lost Conf. Quarterfinal
1997–98	82	35	35	12	224	227	82	4th	Central Div.	Lost Conf. Quarterfinal

* Winnipeg Jets

PITTSBURGH PENGUINS

Stan Fischler

THE TEAM GRACED with the likes of Mario Lemieux, Jaromir Jagr and Ron Francis and honored with two consecutive Stanley Cup championships became one of the National Hockey League's marquee franchises in the last decade of the 20th century. The elegant Lemieux had joined Gretzky as major-league hockey's foremost performers. Francis, always revered by NHL insiders, gained recognition as one of the league's premier two-way centers, and if it were possible the Czech born Jagr created moves that not even the magnificent Lemieux could duplicate.

Add to that the quintessential galvanic coach in Bob Johnson, followed by all-time winner Scott Bowman and the sum total was Stanley Cup championships in 1991 and

1992. This was made possible despite an aging arena in a relatively small market during a time when superstar salaries were sky rocketing to new highs. The overall architect who made this uniquely successful club possible was former World Hockey Association president Howard Baldwin, who had blossomed into the prototypically successful contemporary club owner.

Baldwin adroitly allowed general manager Craig Patrick to formulate a winning franchise around Lemieux after unsuccessful seasons in the mid-1980s. The Baldwin-Patrick duo transformed the team from laughingstock to model franchise for the rest of the industry. However, this was not the case when Pittsburgh entered the NHL during the great expansion of 1967–68. Before a puck was dropped many observers felt that the new Pittsburgh entry in the National Hockey League had lost a face-off. The winning name in the contest to give the team an identifying symbol was Penguins. Coach Red Sullivan's immediate reaction was: "I can see it now. The day after we play a bad game the sportswriters will say: 'They skated like a bunch of nuns.'" Although there were nights during the season when the Penguins exhibited some bad habits, no one advised them to get to a nunnery because the management dressed them in pale blue rather than black an white.

The team symbol, a penguin skating along, stick in hand, flowing scarf from neck, was nowhere to be seen on the uniform. Only the word "Pittsburgh" adorned the front of each jersey; in 1969, the Penguins symbol, sans scarf, was added in a new uniform design. One particularly plausible answer as to why "Penguins" was chosen is that the Civic Arena, completed in 1961 at the cost of $22 million, is called "the Igloo" because of its roof's shape. Whatever the reason, the name of the team only added to the disgruntlement of Pittsburgh's hockey fans, already angry over the loss of the Hornets, their longtime American Hockey League member that had won both the regular season AHL title and the Calder Cup in 1967. Although they were now to see the Howes, Hulls and Beliveaus, the ice fans in the Steel City no longer had a team they identified with and had to be won over.

From the mid-1930s, when John H. Harris bought a franchise in the AHL, the name Hornets had been symbolic of Pittsburgh hockey and a training ground, first for Detroit but later, and more famously, for Toronto Maple Leafs farmhands. When the old Duquesne Gardens on Craig Street was torn down in the 1950s, there was an absence of hockey in Pittsburgh for five years until the Civic Arena opened and the Hornets returned for the 1961–62 season.

The NHL's previous stay in Pittsburgh lasted from the fall of 1925 through the 1929–30 season. The Pirates, who took their name from the National League baseball team, did quite well in their first year, finishing third. In the playoffs, they lost to the Montreal Maroons. In 1926–27 they became part of the American Division and ended up fourth, out of the playoffs, but bounced back the next year to finish third. This was to be Pittsburgh's last quest for the Stanley Cup. In 1928–29 the Pirates won nine and tied eight in 44 games, and the next season they won only five and tied three. This led, in 1930–31, to a move Philadelphia as the Quakers and an even lower estate. The NHL did not return to Pennsylvania until 1967.

In their first year in the NHL, the Penguins, unlike the Pirates, did not make the playoffs. They came close enough, however, to make one think that if they had not sustained a series of injuries to key men, they would have sneaked in. The race was that tight.

In the Expansion Draft of 1967, general manager Jack Riley and coach Red Sullivan sought players with experience and wound up with the oldest club—average age 32. Riley, a popular hockey man who had run the Rochester team of the AHL, and then became president of that league before joining the Penguins, explained: "We have a modern building but we do not have a brand new arena as do four of the clubs. A new building excites the fans for a year or two. … We won the Calder Cup last year. Our fans don't want a building program, they're used to winners. We felt we had to put quality on the ice immediately. I'm aware of some of the potential problems, but we tried to select players with pride—good competitors who will go all out. The older players have been winning in hockey in recent years, so that's the way we went."

Three of the important draftees were Earl Ingarfield, Ken Schinkel and Andy Bathgate. All were over 30 and had something else in common. They had played for the New York Rangers where the Penguin coach, Sullivan, had played and coached. In fact, the Pittsburgh roster began to resemble an old Rangers list with defenseman Al MacNeil and forwards Val Fonteyne and Mel Pearson.

Players like Noel Price, Billy Dea and Al Stratton had also worn Ranger livery at one time in their careers. When third-round draft choice Larry Jeffrey was traded to New York for forward Paul Andrea, defenseman Dunc McCallum and handyman George Konik, a Ranger look was really in evidence. To these ex-Rangers, Riley and Sullivan added wingers Ab McDonald, Bob Dillabough and Keith McCreary from Detroit, Boston and Montreal and defenseman Leo Boivin from Detroit.

Before the 1966 season, Pittsburgh had purchased three defensemen—Ted Lanyon, Dick Mattiussi and Bill Speer— and goaltender Les Binkley from the Cleveland Barons. At the time, the Pens had no farm team of their own so the four were spread around the minors and convened with the rest of the squad at Brantford, Ontario for training camp. A hot battle for the two goaltending jobs developed among Binkley, rookie Joe Daley, veteran Hank Bassen and amateur Marv Edwards. Bassen, who as a Hornet had led his team to the Calder Cup the previous year, was garnered in a trade with Detroit just before the season opened. He figured to do a job and be colorfully popular at the same time. What he hadn't anticipated was just how good Binkley was.

In Boston, Binkley made 33 saves and shut out the Bruins 1–0. It was one of six shutouts, tying him for second place in that department with Lorne Worsley and Cesare Maniago behind Ed Giacomin's eight. In 54 games he compiled a solid 2.87 average. However, in the futile pursuit of a playoff berth, Binkley broke his finger in a 6–6 tie in Oakland. The Penguins blew a big lead and lost a vital point along with their ace goalie. It was to their credit that they kept battling right to the end of the campaign. Binkley, having recovered, returned in time to lead them to victory in three of their last four winning games. When it was all over, they had as many wins as the North Stars but two less points.

Despite missing the playoffs, there were signs of encouragement in the Penguin nest. Pittsburgh fandom, resentful and skeptical at first, had been won over, and late in the season the club's majority interest was sold to a group of Michigan investors, headed by Donald H. Parsons, board chairman of the Bank of the Commonwealth of Detroit, who announced that the Penguins would remain in

Pittsburgh. The only expansion was of a player development club in Amarillo, Texas of the Central Professional Hockey League that was abandoned a year later.

The Michigan group retained as president Jack E. McGregor, a youthful Pennsylvania state senator with the fresh, eager look of a Junior A hockey player. It had been McGregor along with Pittsburgh lawyer Pete Block who assembled the men, including representatives from the Heinz and Mellon families, to bring NHL hockey to Pittsburgh. These original investors required help after losing about $700,000 in a disastrous soccer promotion with the now-defunct Phantoms of that city. McGregor admitted that the soccer fiasco had been a factor in making the stock available but he also cited "unforeseen expenses" as a for instance, the proposed settlements with the American and Western Hockey Leagues, the figures being "far, far greater than anticipated." Before selling to the Detroit financiers, Pittsburgh played off bids from the Atlanta Braves baseball team and the Avon cosmetics company. Early in the 1967–68 season rumors flew to the effect that the Braves were buying in and moving the team to Atlanta the next season. This did not help public relations. When McGregor announced that the deal was off, he said that he was, "sorry in a sense because of my total respect for key management officials in the Braves organization and happy in a sense because it helps squash the rumor that the Braves were going to steal the franchise and take it out of town.

"It is absolutely untrue," he added, without a trace of a smile, "that the Braves backed out of this because they didn't like the name "Penguins." Rumors of a franchise move notwithstanding, the Pens kept plugging away and actually gained their first playoff berth in April 1970 under the direction of Red Kelly. Pittsburgh moved smartly into the semifinals before being eliminated by St. Louis. Delighted with the play of rookie forward Michel Briere, the Penguins looked forward to next year but tragedy struck shortly after the 1969–70 season. Briere was seriously injured in an automobile accident in Northern Quebec and never recovered. After a long convalescence, the young player died during the 1971 playoffs. Without Briere, the Penguins had been unable to gain a playoff berth in 1971.

That year did see the team sold again, this time to a Pittsburgh-based group lead by Thayer R. "Tad" Potter, who installed himself as general partner and CEO. Other changes included Kelly stepping down as general manager and Jack Riley replacing him, and the acquisition of the flamboyant Eddie Shack in exchange for future Buffalo Sabres star Rene Robert. All these moves didn't help the on-ice product, though, as Pittsburgh was swept in the first round of the playoffs by Chicago. The Penguins continued their hot and cold ways for the next three seasons. Despite setting a still enduring NHL record for the fastest five goals scored by one team (two minutes, seven seconds) and Greg Polis winning the 1972–73 All-Star Game MVP award, they missed the playoffs that season and the next.

But there was a turnaround in the 1974–75 campaign. Behind Jean Pronovost, Syl Apps (that year's All-Star MVP) and rookie Pierre Larouche, Pittsburgh climbed to a 37–28–15 record, third best in the new Norris Division. After sweeping the Blues in the preliminary round, the Penguins went into the quarterfinals against the New York Islanders and quickly established a three-games-to-none lead going into game four.

It was then that Pittsburgh suffered one of the most ignominious setbacks in playoff history. They lost the next three

games in a row, setting the stage for a winner-take-all seventh game at home. The game remained scoreless through the middle of the third period when the Islanders forced the puck deep into the Pittsburgh end. Isles defenseman Bert Marshall passed to right winger Ed Westfall who fired the puck into the top inside corner of the net, beating goalie Garry Inness. The final score was 1–0, leaving Pittsburgh in a state of shock.

The following seasons didn't help ease the pain of the Islander upset and the Penguins suffered back-to-back preliminary round losses to Toronto in the 1976 and 1977 playoffs and a no-show in 1978. Although the 1978–79 Penguins finished second in their division, they too didn't fare well, surrendering to the Boston Bruins in straight games in the quarterfinals.

The Penguins unveiled a new uniform in 1979, doffing the old blue and white and adopting the black and gold color scheme of the baseball Pirates and football Steelers. This didn't sit well with Boston, which had been wearing almost identical hues. The Bruins protested, but to no avail as the Penguins cited a precedent set by the Pittsburgh Hockey Club of the 1920s, similar wearers of black and gold uniforms. Three straight first-round playoff losses in 1980, 1981 and 1982 followed in what would prove to be the franchise's only playoff appearances until 1989.

Mediocrity characterized the franchise but also had its virtues. Because of a last-place finish in 1983–84, the Penguins were able to select Mario Lemieux first in the 1984 Entry draft. Considered the finest young player to arrive in the NHL since Wayne Gretzky, the oversized Lemieux arrived at training camp in 1984 and immediately dazzled onlookers with his comprehensive talent. Lemieux won the Calder Trophy as rookie of the year in 1985 and followed that with a nomination to the Second All-Star Team in 1986 and 1987. A season later he won the Hart Trophy as most valuable player as well as the Art Ross (leading scorer) while being named to the First All-Star squad. Despite these accomplishments, the Penguins missed the playoffs every season through 1987–88. However, in 1988–89 Pittsburgh finished second in the Patrick Division and gained a playoff berth while establishing themselves as a Stanley Cup contender.

When Craig Patrick was named general manager on December 5, 1989 a new era in Pittsburgh hockey leadership was launched. Patrick's most significant move was a multi-player trade he completed on March 4, 1990. To the Hartford Whalers went John Cullen, Zarley Zalapski and Jeff Parker and coming to the Igloo were Ulf Samuelsson, Grant Jennings and, the symbol of Hartford hockey, Ron Francis. At the time, Francis was the Whalers' captain and is still the club's franchise leader in points, goals, assists, seasons and games played.

An equally crucial move by Patrick took place at the 1990 Entry Draft where he held the fifth selection overall. While Owen Nolan, Petr Nedved, Keith Primeau and Mike Ricci were picked in that order, the Penguins g.m. opted for a tall, gangly Czech named Jaromir Jagr, who would emerge as the second coming of Lemieux. On June 12, 1990 Patrick hired collegiate legend "Badger Bob" Johnson as head coach. With Johnson at the helm, the Penguins won their first division title in 1990–91 and proceeded to defeat Minnesota in six games to win the Stanley Cup. Lemieux was voted the Conn Smythe Trophy as the playoffs most valuable player and had surpassed Gretzky as the NHL's most dominant performer.

A significant ownership change took place in 1991 when the DeBartolo family sold the franchise to a partnership that included Howard Baldwin, Morris Belzberg and Thomas Ruta. Baldwin, who had been president of the World Hockey Association and head of the Hartford Whalers, became the hands-on leader of the hockey club as it was entering its golden era. Lemieux's dominance continued through 1991–92 as Mario swept the Hart and Ross trophies with a combination of stickhandling and shooting artistry that also made him a First Team All-Star. He also was the NHL's plus–minus leader. Not surprisingly, Pittsburgh gained its second consecutive Stanley Cup championship with a four-game sweep of Chicago. However, tragedy marred the season for the Penguins. On August 29, 1991 Johnson was diagnosed with brain tumors and was replaced behind the bench on October 1, 1991 by Scott Bowman, who had been the club's director of player development and Johnson's *consigliore* during the first Cup triumph.

Johnson died at the age of 60 on November 26, 1991 in Colorado Springs. Nevertheless, with Bowman guiding the team, Pittsburgh expected a third Stanley Cup in 1993 because of the club's talented nucleus of superb players. The Penguins underlined the point by finishing first in the Patrick Division and winning the Presidents' Trophy for most points in the league. But tragedy struck again. Mario Lemieux, who had previously battled debilitating back injuries, was diagnosed with Hodgkin's disease, a mild form of cancer. Radiation treatments lasted from February 1 to March 2. Amazingly, Lemieux returned to the lineup immediately and won another scoring title.

All signs pointed to a third-straight championship as Pittsburgh eliminated New Jersey's Devils in a five-game opening round. Whether the Penguins were too cocky entering the second-round series against the Islanders remains a moot question. When New York won the first match 3–2, the Penguins were back on their heels en route to one of the league's most extraordinary upsets.

With their reputations on the line, the Penguins came back to dominate the next two games, winning 3–0 and 3–1. But thanks to Tom Fitzgerald's two shorthanded goals, the Isles took game four 6–5. Now it was personal. Game five featured Lemieux, Larry Murphy and Rick Tocchet scoring goals in the first two minutes and the Islanders couldn't recover. The Penguins were now one game away from their third-straight conference final when the Islanders won game six 7–5.

Game seven proved to be a classic on every level. Rallying to tie the game 3–3 in the final minutes of the third period, the Penguins appeared ready to win in the game overtime until David Volek stunned the capacity crowd with a slapshot goal, beating Tom Barrasso at 5:16 of the first overtime period.

Although the Penguins finished first in 1993–94, they were without Lemieux for all but 22 games because of illness. They were eliminated by Washington in the first round and began retooling for the future. This was made even more imperative after Lemieux announced in August 1994 that he would take a one-year leave of absence from the game. Jagr inherited the leadership role and won the Art Ross Trophy in the lockout-shortened 1994–95 season.

After a second-place finish in the Northeast Division, Pittsburgh defeated Washington in the opening playoff round but was eliminated in five games by New Jersey in round two.

Lemieux startled the hockey world with his return from medical leave in October 1995. He scored his 500th career goal on October 28, 1995 and finished the season with an Art Ross-winning 69 goals and 92 assists for 161 points. Jagr was runner-up with 149 points. The Penguins never would win another Stanley Cup with Lemieux in the line-up, although they did play more memorable games. During the 1996 playoffs, they played a marathon four-overtime game against the Capitals, defeating Washington on Petr Nedved's goal after 79:15 of extended play.

Uncertainty characterized the Penguins' play during 1996–97, culminating with the firing of coach Ed Johnston on March 3, 1997. He was replaced on an interim basis by g.m. Patrick. Lemieux retired at the conclusion of the 1996–97 season after Pittsburgh was eliminated in a five-game opening-round series with Philadelphia.

In May of 1997, Roger Marino joined Howard Baldwin as co-owner and co-managing director of the franchise. During the off-season, Craig Patrick named the defense-oriented Kevin Constantine as head coach. Although Constantine occasionally clashed with Jagr over his disciplinary tactics and heavy defensive orientation, the Penguins surprised the critics with a strong performance, finishing first in the Northeast Division with 98 points. Jagr won the Art Ross Trophy while Tom Barrasso turned in a strong comeback effort in goal. The year would end in disappointment, however, as the Montreal Canadiens eliminated the Penguins in six games in the opening round of the 1998 playoffs.

Pittsburgh Penguins Year-by-Year Record

Season	GP	W	L	T	GF	GA	Pts	Finish		Playoff Results
1967–68	74	27	34	13	195	216	67	5th	West Div.	Out of Playoffs
1968–69	76	20	45	11	189	252	51	5th	West Div.	Out of Playoffs
1969–70	76	26	38	12	182	238	64	2nd	West Div.	Lost Semifinal
1970–71	78	21	37	20	221	240	62	6th	West Div.	Out of Playoffs
1971–72	78	20	30	14	220	258	54	4th	West Div.	Lost Quarterfinal
1972–73	78	32	37	9	257	265	73	5th	West Div.	Out of Playoffs
1973–74	78	28	41	9	242	273	65	5th	West Div.	Out of Playoffs
1974–75	80	37	28	15	326	289	89	3rd	Norris Div.	Lost Quarterfinal
1975–76	80	35	33	12	339	303	82	3rd	Norris Div.	Lost Prelim. Round
1976–77	80	34	33	13	240	252	81	3rd	Norris Div.	Lost Prelim. Round
1977–78	80	25	37	18	254	321	68	4th	Norris Div.	Out of Playoffs
1978–79	80	36	31	13	281	279	85	2nd	Norris Div.	Lost Quarterfinal
1979–80	80	30	37	13	251	303	73	3rd	Norris Div.	Lost Prelim. Round
1980–81	80	30	37	13	302	345	73	3rd	Norris Div.	Lost Prelim. Round
1981–82	80	31	36	13	310	337	75	4th	Patrick Div.	Lost Div. Semifinal
1982–83	80	18	53	9	257	394	45	6th	Patrick Div.	Out of Playoffs
1983–84	80	16	58	6	254	390	38	6th	Patrick Div.	Out of Playoffs
1984–85	80	24	51	5	276	385	53	6th	Patrick Div.	Out of Playoffs
1985–86	80	34	38	8	313	305	76	5th	Patrick Div.	Out of Playoffs
1986–87	80	30	38	12	297	290	72	5th	Patrick Div.	Out of Playoffs
1987–88	80	36	35	9	319	316	81	6th	Patrick Div.	Out of Playoffs
1988–89	80	40	33	7	347	349	87	2nd	Patrick Div.	Lost Div. Final
1989–90	80	32	40	8	318	359	72	5th	Patrick Div.	Out of Playoffs
1990–91	80	41	33	6	342	305	88	1st	Patrick Div.	Won Stanley Cup
1991–92	80	39	32	9	343	308	87	3rd	Patrick Div.	Won Stanley Cup
1992–93	84	56	21	7	367	268	119	1st	Patrick Div.	Lost Div. Final
1993–94	84	44	27	13	299	285	101	1st	Northeast Div.	Lost Conf. Quarterfinal
1994–95	48	29	16	3	181	158	61	2nd	Northeast Div.	Lost Conf. Semifinal
1995–96	82	49	29	4	362	284	102	1st	Northeast Div.	Lost Conf. Final
1996–97	82	38	36	8	285	280	84	2nd	Northeast Div.	Lost Conf. Quarterfinal
1997–98	82	40	24	18	228	188	98	1st	Northeast Div.	Lost Conf. Quarterfinal

PITTSBURGH PIRATES

Eric Zweig

WHEN THE NATIONAL HOCKEY LEAGUE first expanded into the United States in 1924, it placed a team in Boston. On September 22, 1925 the NHL's second U.S. franchise was formally announced, as the Hamilton Tigers became the New York Americans. The NHL's third franchise in the United States was granted on November 7, 1925. The team in Pittsburgh would be owned by fight promoter and ex-boxer Benny Leonard. It would begin its first NHL season three weeks later.

Hockey already had a long history in Pittsburgh at the time the city was awarded an NHL franchise. The Steel City had a team in hockey's first fully professional league (the International (Pro) Hockey League, which operated from 1904 to 1907) and later competed in the United States Amateur Hockey Association. In fact, the Pittsburgh Yellow Jackets had been USAHA national champions in 1924 and 1925 and it was the players of this team that stocked Pittsburgh's 1925–26 NHL roster.

Future Hockey Hall of Famer and Canadian male athlete of the half century Lionel Conacher had been the leader of the Yellow Jackets since his arrival in Pittsburgh to play football at Duquesne University in the fall of 1923. He recruited friends like goalie Roy Worters, Hugh Darragh, and Harold "Baldy" Cotton from top amateur clubs in Toronto and Ottawa to join him in Pittsburgh, and when the NHL arrived in town they all accepted the offer to turn pro, as did Yellow Jackets teammates Hib Milks, Duke McCurry, Tex White and Herb Drury. As professionals, they would now be known as the Pittsburgh Pirates—the same as the city's baseball team.

Former NHL and National Hockey Association tough guy and scoring star Odie Cleghorn was hired to coach the Pirates (and would occasionally see some ice time as well—including a game in goal on December 18, 1925 when Worters had pneumonia and Pittsburgh beat the Americans 3–2). Little was expected from Cleghorn's roster of amateurs, but his innovative coaching tactics saw the Pirates finish in third place in the seven-team NHL with a record of 19–16–1.

Because his team did not have the star talent others did, Cleghorn employed three set forward lines at a time when most teams simply played their best players for as long as possible. He also became the first NHL coach to change his players on the fly.

The Pirates were the only team in the NHL not to have a player rank among the league's top–10 scorers in 1925–26, but with a solid team approach and Roy Worters' 1.90 goals-against-average and seven shutouts (both second in the league behind Ottawa's Alex Connell who led the league with a 1.12 average and 15 shutouts) Pittsburgh grabbed the last spot in the playoffs with one more point than the Boston Bruins. The Montreal Maroons then defeated the Pirates 6–4 in a two-game total-goals series and went on to win the Stanley Cup.

The 1926–27 season saw the NHL add the New York Rangers, Chicago Black Hawks, and Detroit Cougars (later the Falcons, then the Red Wings), who joined Pittsburgh and Boston in the newly created American Division. The league was also bolstered by an influx of talent after the Western Hockey League ceased operations. Most of the western players stocked the rosters of the NHL's newest teams, though future stars like Eddie Shore (Bruins) and George Hainsworth (Montreal Canadiens) found their way onto existing clubs. The Pirates only acquisition was Ty Arbour from the Vancouver Maroons.

Pittsburgh headed into its second season with virtually the same roster as the year before, but Lionel Conacher was soon traded to the New York Americans for Charlie Langlois. "the Big Train" would be sorely missed as the Pirates' defensive record ballooned to the second-worst in the NHL behind only the expansion Black Hawks. Pittsburgh finished the year fourth in the American Division with a 15–26–3 record and missed the playoffs. A few minor roster adjustments and Roy Worters' return to form saw the Pirates reach the playoffs again in 1927–28 after going 19–17–8. As in 1926, Pittsburgh was beaten in the first round by the team that would go on to win the Stanley Cup—this time the New York Rangers.

Despite their success on the ice, the Pirates were not receiving much fan support in Pittsburgh. Like the Ottawa Senators, they began peddling talent to help their finances. Roy Worters was sent to the New York Americans for Joe Miller, and Baldy Cotton was sold to the Toronto Maple Leafs. Mickey MacKay was added to the roster and later traded to the Boston Bruins for Frank Fredrickson, but both former Pacific Coast Hockey Association stars were now past their prime. The Pirates plummeted to 9–27–8 in 1928–29 and were spared last place overall in the NHL only by the Chicago Black Hawks' dreadful 7–29–8 season.

Odie Cleghorn resigned after the 1928–29 campaign and became an NHL referee. Frank Fredrickson took over as playing coach in Pittsburgh (though a serious knee injury would limit his playing to just nine games) but he could do nothing to change the team's fortunes. The Pirates suffered through a 5–36–3 season and the combination of a last-place team plus the stock market crash (which had seriously depressed the steel industry) doomed professional hockey in Pittsburgh.

The Pirates were transferred to Philadelphia for the 1930–31 season, but the results were only worse. The Philadelphia Quakers went 4–36–4 and at the NHL Board of Governors meeting on September 26, 1931, it was announced that both the Ottawa Senators and the Pittsburgh-Philadelphia franchise would suspend operations for 1931–32. The Senators would live on for a few more years, but the Pittsburgh club would not. The Pirates owners were again given permission to suspend operations at each of the next five preseason NHL governors meetings. Finally, at the NHL meetings on May 7, 1936 the Pittsburgh franchise was formally canceled. The NHL did not return to Pittsburgh or Philadelphia for more than 30 years until the Penguins and Flyers began play in 1967.

Pittsburgh Pirates Year-by-Year Record

Season	GP	W	L	T	GF	GA	Pts	Finish		Playoff Results
1925–26	36	19	16	1	82	70	39	3rd		Out of Playoffs
1926–27	44	15	26	3	79	108	33	4th.	Amn. Div.	Out of Playoffs
1927–28	44	19	17	8	67	76	46	3rd.	Amn. Div.	Out of Playoffs
1928–29	44	9	27	8	46	80	26	4th.	Amn. Div.	Out of Playoffs
1929–30	44	5	36	3	102	185	13	5th.	Amn. Div.	Out of Playoffs

QUEBEC BULLDOGS

Eric Zweig

THE BULLDOGS NICKNAME for Quebec City's hockey team dates back to at least 1909, and though it was used infrequently by the newspapers of the day, a bulldog was prominently displayed in the 1913 team picture. The team itself traces its roots all the way back to 1886 and the formation of the Amateur Hockey Association of Canada (the first national hockey league). A Quebec team also played at the Montreal Winter Carnival in 1883. Quebec continued to be represented in a variety of top Canadian hockey leagues until 1909–10 when the Bulldogs were left out of hockey that year after the Ottawa Senators and Montreal Shamrocks abandoned the Canadian Hockey Association for the rival National Hockey Association. A realignment of the NHA in 1910–11 brought Quebec back into the fold. By 1912 the Bulldogs were Stanley Cup champions. Quebec retained the Stanley Cup by repeating as NHA champs in 1913 and by pounding a team from Sydney, Nova Scotia 14–3 and 6–2 in a two-game Stanley Cup challenge. The Bulldogs' Cup reign came to an end in 1914 when the Toronto Blueshirts unseated them as NHA champions.

Quebec's roster from the Stanley Cup years boasted future Hall of Famers Joe Malone, Paddy Moran, Joe Hall, Tommy Smith, and Russell Crawford, as well as other stars of the day like Eddie Oatman, Jack Marks, Jack McDonald, and Harry Mummery. All were of English, Irish, or Scottish descent, as not a single French Canadian appeared on the Bulldogs roster in either season. In fact, though the they represented the capital city of the province of Quebec, there are no more than a handful of French Canadians who played for the team. Even the Bulldogs nickname had been chosen to express the ideals of courage represented by 19th century Britain.

Joe Malone was the greatest star in the history of the Quebec franchise. He joined the club as a 19-year-old in 1909 and his goal-scoring feats became legendary during seven seasons in the NHA. His greatest year came in the first season of the NHL when he scored 44 goals in 20 games. Those goals, however, were not scored in the uniform of the Quebec Bulldogs, but as a member of the Montreal Canadiens. The Bulldogs were charter members when the NHL was formed in November of 1917, but the financially troubled franchise did not operate a team that year and its players were dispersed throughout the NHL.

Quebec finally iced a team during the NHL's third season of 1919–20 and although many of the Bulldogs' star players returned only Malone proved still capable. He led the NHL with 39 goals (including a record seven in one game on January 31, 1920) and 48 points, but Quebec finished with a dismal 4–20–0 record.

Prior to the 1920–21 season, the Quebec franchise was transferred to Hamilton where it became known as the Tigers. After five seasons in the Ontario city, the team moved again and became the New York Americans. Quebec City did not return to the NHL until 1979 when the Nordiques were absorbed from the World Hockey Association. That team, too, wound up in the United States when the it became the Colorado Avalanche in 1995.

ST. LOUIS BLUES

Jeff Gordon

THE ST. LOUIS BLUES could erect a glittering Hall of Fame to enshrine all the hockey greats the franchise has employed. Start at the top with "the Great One," Wayne Gretzky, and move down the list of star forwards: Dale Hawerchuk, Peter Stastny, Dickie Moore, Bernie Federko, Brett Hull, Doug Gilmour, Glenn Anderson, Joey Mullen, Adam Oates, Brendan Shanahan, Pierre Turgeon, Garry Unger, Guy Carbonneau and Brian Sutter.

The Blues have employed some of the great defensemen, too, with Al MacInnis, Scott Stevens, Phil Housley, Doug Harvey, Guy Lapointe, Don Awrey, Rob Ramage and Bob and Barclay Plager. Goaltending hasn't been a problem, either. The franchise started with all-time greats Glenn Hall and Jacques Plante and also welcomed the likes of Mike Liut, Curtis Joseph and Grant Fuhr. Their coaching register is as impressive, with Stanley Cup winners Al Arbour, Scotty Bowman, Jacques Demers and Mike Keenan. Legendary architects Lynn Patrick and Emile Francis once ran the Blues, and championship team builders Cliff Fletcher and Jimmy Devellano had stints on the St. Louis hockey staff. Calling Blues action over the years was Dan Kelly, one of hockey's all-time broadcasting greats.

The Blues enjoyed some team success, too, reaching the Cup finals in the first three seasons out of the expansion bracket. From 1979 to 1998, the club reached the playoffs 19 times in a row … yet the team had no Stanley Cup titles to show for its first 30 years of hockey. The franchise also has been scarred by tragedies greater than playoff disappointment. Young defenseman Bobby Gassoff was killed in a motorcycle crash after attending a team function. Dan Kelly lost his battle with cancer while still in his prime and Barclay Plager succumbed to brain tumors while serving as an assistant coach. Banners commemorating them hang in the rafters of Kiel Center. The Blues have been like family to St. Louis. "The people here are great people," Brian Sutter says. "They always expected hard work, whether it was from goal scorers or checkers. Barclay Plager, Rob Ramage, they really respected those people."

Hockey began auspiciously in St. Louis in 1967–68. The Blues were the best of the NHL's six expansion teams, playing a disciplined defensive game that allowed them to outperform the other fledgling franchises. That commitment to winning in the early years helped establish a loyal and vocal fan base. "What got everybody excited, from the players standpoint, and what got the fans excited, was when the team took off," recalls Red Berenson, "You could feel the momentum building. It went right through the playoffs and stayed right through the first four or five years." While the franchise has just celebrated its 30th anniversary, it's that first playoff run that remains the most exciting in Blues' history. Midway through their inaugural campaign, Scotty Bowman convinced future Hall of Fame forward Dickie Moore to test his wonky knees and give the club a veteran voice in the dressing room. Moore, who hadn't laced up the blades since retiring at the end of the 1964–65 season, quickly established himself as the team leader. Moore insisted that the team meet after every road game and go out together to sit down and talk about the game they had just played. "It was like that in Montreal," Bob Plager remembers, "If they went somewhere, they all went together. It was like that for years in St. Louis after that." Moore also

Quebec Bulldogs Year-by-Year Record

Season	GP	W	L	T	GF	GA	Pts	Finish	Playoff Results
1919–20	24	4	20	0	91	177	8	4th	Out of Playoffs

quickly turned up the heat in the dressing room. After one disgruntled player tossed his jersey to the floor in frustration, Moore reprimanded the offender. "That's your sweater," Moore told his startled teammate, "That's your life. That emblem, that Blue Note, must never hit the floor again." It was a speech that Moore had heard Jean Beliveau deliver many times in the hallowed Montreal Canadiens locker room. With Moore and, later, Doug Harvey providing the emotional lift, the Blues survived two gruelling seven game marathons against Los Angeles and Minnesota before reaching the Stanley Cup finals. Waiting there to welcome them were the well-rested Montreal Canadiens, still steaming from their loss to the underdog Toronto Maple Leafs twelve months earlier. The Habs weren't about to let this pooch loose. The Blues fought hard, losing in four one-goal games, but it was clear the gap in talent was too wide for the Blues to overcome. "There was nothing more unfair than expansion," Glenn Hall recalls. "The existing teams kept all the players. The expansion teams were left with the guys they thought were over the hill. The league was very lucky St. Louis represented the expansion teams very well or the league might have gone belly up."

The franchise flourished for the game's ultimate players' owner, Sidney J. Salomon Jr. His family had bought the team for $2 million and the St. Louis Arena from Chicago Black Hawks owners Arthur and Bill Wirtz for $4 million. The "Original Six" teams were run by strict and penurious men, but Salomon provided cars for his players and treated them to Florida vacations. The Blues acquired a bunch of all-stars in the twilight of their careers and they loved St. Louis. "It was unique compared to what was going on in the league," Hall says. "You were just like cattle, bought and sold and auctioned off. The only way we could return the favor to the Salomons was to go out and give a good effort every night."

Hall and Plante were stellar in goal and the Plagers, Barclay and Bob, led a gritty defense that also featured Arbour and Harvey. Red Berenson, Ab McDonald and Gary Sabourin led the offense. Berenson's six-goal game in Philadelphia during the 1968–69 season remains one of the great milestones for the franchise. "The Salomons brought in a lot of charismatic players who developed a relationship with the fans," says former Blues vice president Susie Mathieu, who spent the better part of two decades serving the franchise in a variety of roles. "That cemented the future. They set a foundation between the players and the fans and the team and the fans that helped us survive all the ups and downs the franchise has seen."

Bowman added the general manager's portfolio to his resume in 1968 and he continued to mold his oldtimers into a lovable team that filled the old St. Louis Arena. The Blues were hot, so hot that the National Basketball Association's St. Louis Hawks played second fiddle for a season before fleeing to Atlanta in 1968. Alas, the good times would not last. The Blues continued to be the best of the bunch in the West Division, reaching the Stanley Cup finals again in both 1969 and 1970. Once there, however, they were unable to win a game against their "Original Six" opponents, dropping four-game decisions to Montreal and Boston. Then, in 1971, Sidney Salomon III took a larger role in running his father's franchise and the result was constant upheaval from 1971, when Bowman left, until 1977.

The coaches came and went, with Arbour, Sid Abel, Bill McCreary, Jean-Guy Talbot, Lou Angotti, Garry Young, Leo Boivin and Emile Francis spending time on the bench.

The general managers came and went, with Abel, Charles Catto, Gerry Ehman and Denis Ball holding the job from 1972 to 1976. Only Garry Unger's flashy scoring kept fans interested until the Salomons' final day. "We never did anything that would knowingly hurt our hockey club," Salomon III would say. The challenge of the World Hockey Association, escalating costs and declining revenues pushed the franchise to the brink of financial ruin. Out of the gloom came Emile "the Cat" Francis, who took over as general manager, caretaker, security guard and saviour. If the Cat was going to save the Blues, he would need all of his nine lives to do it.

After a financially devastating 1976–77 season that saw the Blues pare down their staff to only three employees, Francis was able to convince Ralston Purina chairman R. Hal Dean to invest in the team. On July 27, 1977, barely concealing a smile as smug as the cat that ate the canary, Francis announced that the St. Louis Blues had been reborn. On paper, at least. In 1978–79, the Blues slipped off the bottom rung of the NHL ladder, winning just 18 games under coach Barclay Plager. Yet, once again, Francis was able to rebuild the crumbling foundation. Ralston Purina repainted the old bandbox known as the Arena and rechristened it the Checkerdome. In the 1976 Amateur Draft, Francis had selected Bernie Federko, Brian Sutter and Mike Liut who would go on to become the cornerstones of the team in the 1980s. Runners-and-gunners like Wayne Babych (picked third overall in 1978) and Perry Turnbull (taken second in 1979) were added to the nucleus and by 1980–81, the Blues had a 107-point juggernaut for Red Berenson, who took over as coach during the previous season.

"It was a very exciting time for me," Francis says. "There we were, on the brink of extinction, then to come all the way back the way we did and get the support we needed … that was like a dream come true." Francis couldn't sustain that success, though. Almost as quickly, it all came tumbling down. The Blues finished eight games under .500 in 1981–82 and continued their free-fall the following season, collecting only 65 points, the fourth-lowest total in club history. Berenson got canned, Dean retired and Ralston Purina soon lost interest in hockey. Citing losses of $1.8 million per year, the company put the team up for sale. When the league blocked the sale of the Blues to Saskatoon interests in 1983, the company padlocked the Checkerdome and left the franchise on the NHL's doorstep. The Blues, with their ownership unresolved, did not participate in the 1983 NHL Entry Draft.

Enter entrepreneur Harry Ornest, who bought the franchise off the scrap heap. He, new general manager Ron Caron and coach Jacques Demers quickly made the Blues profitable and competitive. "There was no doubt St. Louis was a good hockey town, but it needed a total turnaround to salvage the franchise," Caron says. "I call the Ornest years the years of survival." Federko, Sutter and Doug Gilmour, a gritty two-way center whose desire and determination more than made up for his lack of size, led the charge back up the NHL ladder. Caron traded furiously, shuffling stars (like Liut and Mullen) and draft picks for lots of affordable, competent veterans. Many of these veterans may have lacked flash, but their lunch-bucket work ethic helped transform the team into the type of blue-collar hockey club that the city had rallied behind so vigorously in the early years. "Sutter, Federko and Ramage—these players did a lot for this franchise," Plager remembers, "A lot of veterans would have just gone through the motions."

This regime peaked in the 1986 playoffs with the "Monday Night Miracle" game. After being stretched to the limit to eliminate Minnesota and Toronto, the Blues had their backs against the wall once again in their semifinal series against the Calgary Flames. Needing a home-ice victory to force a seventh and deciding game, the Blues trailed 5–2 with less than 12 minutes remaining in the game and their season. Once again, it was a member of the Lunch-Bucket Brigade that provided the dramatics. In the fifth and deciding match of the Minnesota series, Ed Beers' first playoff goal as a member of the Blues was the deciding tally in a 6–3 win. In game seven of the St. Louis–Toronto grudge match, the final playoff goal of Mark LaVallee's career was the winning goal that eliminated the Leafs. The unlikely hero on this madcap Monday night was Greg Paslawski, a hard-plugging foot soldier who was originally signed as an undrafted—and unwanted—free agent by the Montreal Canadiens. "Paws" notched a pair of late third-period goals to even the affair after Brian Sutter had lit the comeback torch with a nifty goal at the 8:08 mark of the final stanza. Twenty minutes later, Doug Wickenheiser—who had received his fair share of hard knocks when the Montreal Canadiens selected him ahead of hometown hero Denis Savard in the 1980 Entry Draft—slipped a rebound past Mike Vernon to give the Blues a comeback win for the ages. Paslawski notched 10 playoff goals in the greatest spring of his career, more than he would score in the rest of his postseason career combined. The 6–5 victory forced a decisive seventh game of the Western Conference finals, but the Flames extinguished the Blues' Stanley Cup aspirations with a 2–1 win back in the Saddledome. Doug Gilmour and Bernie Federko tied for the playoff lead in points, becoming the first—and only—players to lead the postseason scoring parade without making it to the finals.

"I have a lot of souvenirs from hockey," Demers says. "First is my Stanley Cup ring in Montreal. I got two coaches of the year in Detroit and four times in nine years I made it to the final four. But I will never forget 6–5 in overtime in game six against Calgary. To come back and win and hear that major standing ovation the fans gave us, I will never forget that."

Demers left for Detroit after that season and Ornest, like the other owners before him, also decided to move on. He sold the team to a local ownership group led by Michael Shanahan during the 1986–87 season. However, with Ron Caron still aboard, the club remained in capable hands. Within two years, Caron had landed Brett Hull, Adam Oates and Curtis Joseph in addition to face-off wizard Peter Zezel and defenseman Jeff Brown, who tallied 21 goals from his office on the blue line in 1988–89. Later, through astute trades and eye-opening free agent acquisitions, Caron brought such high-profile names such as Scott Stevens, Brendan Shanahan, Phil Housley, Al MacInnis and Steve Duchesne into the St. Louis fold. Still, the coup-de-grace was the steal of Brett Hull from the Calgary Flames, paying them back in full for the disappointing playoff loss in 1986. Deemed uncoachable, lazy and uninterested in improving his game, Hull was an enigma to many of the scouts and coaches that took him under their wing. In St. Louis, however, the offensive system was molded around Hull, his deadly accurate shot and his uncanny ability to find open ice, and once there, deliver the goods. With Adam Oates supplying picture-perfect passes, Hull became the NHL's top sniper. The Golden Brett reached the 70-goal plateau in three consecutive seasons, including his Hart Trophy-winning campaign of 1990–91 when he slipped 86 pucks past enemy goaltenders, the most by any player in NHL history not called Gretzky. Hull's exploits helped to broaden local interest in the team. The Blues filled the arena, made the playoffs every year and began multiplying both their revenue and payroll in a giddy bid for greatness. Shanahan, Caron and team president Jack Quinn (another holdout from the Ornest regime) became notorious raiders, issuing a slew of offer sheets, trading for other team's holdouts and generally ticking off their colleagues.

In 1990–91, the Blues had a breakout 105-point season behind Hull but, as in most seasons, the club couldn't get past the second round of the playoffs. Though this front office never got to the final four with coaches Jacques Martin, Brian Sutter, Bob Plager and Bob Berry, it did turn the Blues into a mainstream sports success. The team's success inspired the top St. Louis corporations to come together, buy the team from Shanahan and build the new Kiel Center, which opened in downtown St. Louis in 1994.

Shanahan was reduced to a figurehead, then run out of the organization. His last stab at glory was to hire Mike Keenan as general manager and coach. Keenan brought a lot of baggage with him, but he also carried a reputation as a winner. He tested the patience of the Blues' fans early, unloading Petr Nedved, Craig Janney and Brendan Shanahan within a year of his stepping into the front office. Many of the dedicated St. Louis fans never forgave Keenan for casting off Brendan Shanahan. The quick-witted power forward was a local favorite and one of the most outgoing of the all the pro athletes in the city, who generously gave his time and effort to charities and special events. There was another tempest brewing, as well. Relations between Keenan and Brett Hull were acrimonious at best, and when Iron Mike stripped Hull of his captaincy, the battle of wills was on. In an effort to stem the tide of unrest, Keenan made a bold move, acquiring potential free agent Wayne Gretzky for the final playoff push in the 1995–96 season. Any hopes for a lengthy playoff run were dashed early when Grant Fuhr suffered a season-ending knee injury in the first game of the postseason against the Toronto Maple Leafs. Although backup Jon Casey performed admirably, the Blues lacked the consistent offensive attack required to reach the highest level. The Great One came close to resurrecting the club's Stanley Cup hopes with 16 points in 13 games, but in the end the Blues' lack of fire power caught up to them. The Blues did manage to stretch Detroit to double overtime in the seventh game in the Western Conference semifinals, but a Steve Yzerman goal gave the Wings a 1–0 victory and ended Keenan's quest for the Cup. As expected, the Great One headed for the Great White Way and the New York Rangers via free agency, leaving the St. Louis ship in stormy waters. The war of words between Keenan and Hull escalated and the product on the ice suffered. Finally, on December 19, 1996, the Keenan era ended, with both he and Jack Quinn being ushered out of town. Ron Caron came out of quasi-retirement to serve as interim general manager, helping new team president Mark Sauer hire coach Joel Quenneville and general manager Larry Pleau. Together, they tried to get the franchise back to the basics of drafting talent, grooming players and building up for another run at the elusive Stanley Cup.

As the franchise has done countless times in the past, the Blues made a remarkable recovery in 1997–98. Even Brett Hull bought into Quenneville's defense-first philosophy, proving himself to be a better-than-adequate penalty killer

and checker. Still, the Blues had enough all-around fire-power to lead the NHL with 256 goals and finished with 98 points for the league's fourth-best record. The Blues overwhelmed the Los Angeles Kings with a four-game sweep to open the playoffs and were given an excellent chance of knocking off defending champion Detroit in round two. It was not to be however, as the Red Wings eliminated St. Louis for the third year in a row en route to their second straight Stanley Cup title.

The Brett Hull era also came to close in St. Louis after a decade of highlight reel goals and mile-wide smiles when the Golden Brett signed as a free agent with Dallas. Still, there remains plenty of room for optimism. The Blues resigned veteran rearguard Al MacInnis, ensuring that the league's most powerful shooter will finish his career in St. Louis. The emergence of Chris Pronger as a potential superstar continued in 1997–98, as the young rearguard was named team captain and led the league with a plus–minus rating of plus 47, a remarkable achievement for a 23-year-old blueliner. With the masterful MacInnis at his side, Pronger should be one of the NHL's top rearguards for years to come. As the Blues celebrated their past, the future appeared bright.

St. Louis Blues Year-by-Year Record

Season	GP	W	L	T	GF	GA	Pts	Finish		Playoff Results
1967–68	74	27	31	16	177	191	70	3rd	West Div.	Lost Final
1968–69	76	37	25	14	204	157	88	1st	West Div.	Lost Final
1969–70	76	37	27	12	224	179	86	1st	West Div.	Lost Final
1970–71	78	34	25	19	223	208	87	2nd	West Div.	Lost Quarterfinal
1971–72	78	28	39	11	208	247	67	3rd	West Div.	Lost Semifinal
1972–73	78	32	34	12	233	251	76	4th	West Div.	Lost Quarterfinal
1973–74	78	26	40	12	206	248	64	6th	West Div.	Out of Playoffs
1974–75	80	35	31	14	269	267	84	2nd	Smythe Div.	Lost Prelim. Round
1975–76	80	29	37	14	249	290	72	3rd	Smythe Div.	Lost Prelim. Round
1976–77	80	32	39	9	239	276	73	1st	Smythe Div.	Lost Quarterfinal
1977–78	80	20	47	13	195	304	53	4th	Smythe Div.	Out of Playoffs
1978–79	80	18	50	12	249	348	48	3rd	Smythe Div.	Out of Playoffs
1979–80	80	34	34	12	266	278	80	2nd	Smythe Div.	Lost Prelim. Round
1980–81	80	45	18	17	352	281	107	1st	Smythe Div.	Lost Quarterfinal
1981–82	80	32	40	8	315	349	72	3rd	Norris Div.	Lost Div. Final
1982–83	80	25	40	15	285	316	65	4th	Norris Div.	Lost Div. Semifinal
1983–84	80	32	41	7	293	316	71	2nd	Norris Div.	Lost Div. Final
1984–85	80	37	31	12	299	288	86	1st	Norris Div.	Lost Div. Semifinal
1985–86	80	37	34	9	302	291	83	3rd	Norris Div.	Lost Conf. Final
1986–87	80	32	33	15	281	293	79	1st	Norris Div.	Lost Div. Semifinal
1987–88	80	34	38	8	278	294	76	2nd	Norris Div.	Lost Div. Final
1988–89	80	33	35	12	275	285	78	2nd	Norris Div.	Lost Div. Final
1989–90	80	37	34	9	295	279	83	2nd	Norris Div.	Lost Div. Final
1990–91	80	47	22	11	310	250	105	2nd	Norris Div.	Lost Div. Final
1991–92	80	36	33	11	279	266	83	3rd	Norris Div.	Lost Div. Semifinal
1992–93	84	37	36	11	282	278	85	4th	Norris Div.	Lost Div. Final
1993–94	84	40	33	11	270	283	91	4th	Central Div.	Lost Conf. Quarterfinal
1994–95	48	28	15	5	178	135	61	2nd	Central Div.	Lost Conf. Quarterfinal
1995–96	82	32	34	16	219	248	80	4th	Central Div.	Lost Conf. Semifinal
1996–97	82	36	35	11	236	239	83	4th	Central Div.	Lost Conf. Quarterfinal
1997–98	82	45	29	8	256	204	98	3rd	Central Div.	Lost Conf. Semifinal

ST. LOUIS EAGLES

Eric Zweig

THE OTTAWA SENATORS WON THE STANLEY CUP four times in the 1920s, but were victims of the Great Depression.

Senators owner Tommy Ahearne absorbed losses for years, but at the NHL Board of Governors meeting on September 22, 1934, the directors of the Ottawa club sought permission to move their team to St. Louis. Permission was granted, even though a franchise application from St. Louis had been rejected at an NHL meeting two years earlier due to excessive travel expenses. Redmond Quinn would continue to guide operations from Ottawa while Clare Brunton would run the team in Missouri.

The Ottawa Senators were now the St. Louis Eagles, but there were problems from the start. St. Louis was already home to an American Hockey Association team called the Flyers. Owners of this club contended that there was an agreement between the AHA and the NHL that prevented the latter from placing a team west of the Mississippi and threatened to file a $200,000 damage suit. However, no suit was filed and the Eagles were able to play out the season.

The Eagles began the 1934–35 season with much the same roster the Senators had employed in 1933–34, but the arrival in St. Louis of an NHL team that had gone 13–29–6 the previous season did not excite fans there any more than it had in Ottawa. Attendance began at 12,600 on opening night (November 8, 1934) but quickly declined. By early December, the Eagles were already beginning to trade away players and when the team fell to 2–11–0 after a loss on December 9 coach Eddie Gerard was fired in favor of George Boucher. By February, Clare Brunton and Redmond Quinn were denying rumors that home games would be switched back to Ottawa or that the club had any plans to leave St. Louis. However, Syd Howe (the Eagles' top player and the second-leading scorer in the NHL that season) was then sold to the Detroit Red Wings along with Scotty Bowman. Frank Finnigan was sold to the Toronto Maple Leafs.

When the season ended on March 19, 1935 the Eagles were in last place with a record of 11–31–6. The annual NHL meeting on May 11 left the status of the Ottawa/St. Louis franchise unsettled, but at a league meeting on September 28 Redmond Quinn asked if the team could suspend operations for a year as it had done in Ottawa in 1931–32. On October 15 the NHL governors decided to terminated the team instead. The NHL bought out the franchise and took over ownership of the players, who were then drafted throughout the league. The prize pick in the draft wound up going to the Boston Bruins, who selected sixth. Bill Cowley had attracted little attention as a rookie in St. Louis but would go on to become one of the league's top stars in Boston during the 1940s. The NHL finally returned to St. Louis in 1967. It was not back in Ottawa until 1992.

St. Louis Eagles Year-by-Year Record

Season	GP	W	L	T	GF	GA	Pts	Finish		Playoff Results
1934–35	48	11	31	6	86	144	28	5th	Cdn. Div.	Out of Playoffs

SAN JOSE SHARKS

Ross McKeon

ON MAY 9, 1990 the National Hockey League granted approval for George and Gordon Gund to sell the Minnesota North Stars in return for the rights to an expansion franchise in the San Francisco Bay Area that would begin to play in the 1991–92 season. Despite past failures, the league was attracted to the region because it had grown to boast eight million residents and presented the fourth-largest media market in the United States.

Pro hockey was no stranger to the area, but success and longevity never had gone hand-in-hand. In 1928, the sport dawned in the Bay Area with the creation of the California Hockey League. Imported players from Canada formed a basis for San Francisco and Oakland-based teams. The league dissolved by 1930 due to poor economic conditions. In 1948, the three-year-old Pacific Coast Hockey League turned pro, and famed NHL defenseman Eddie Shore bought the league-member Oakland Oaks. By 1950, however, Shore abandoned the financially strapped team and the PCHL faltered.

By 1961, the San Francisco Seals, formerly a pro team from Edmonton, joined the Western Hockey League and won the first of consecutive titles in 1963. In 1966, the team moved to the Oakland Coliseum Arena for their final season in the WHL. Attendance dwindled during the transitional campaign prior to the unveiling of the NHL's first expansion venture into the Bay Area. In 1967, the Oakland Seals were added as one of six new franchises as the NHL doubled from its "Original Six" to 12 teams. Struggling at the gate and in the standings, the Seals went through numerous owners before ending a nine-year run in the Bay Area by moving to Cleveland for the start of the 1976–77 NHL season.

On September 6, 1990, it was announced the newest Bay Area franchise would be known as the Sharks. The team colors of Pacific teal, gray, black and white would not be unveiled until February 12, 1991. To determine the team's nickname, a contest had been held in which 5,700 entries accounting for more than 2,300 different nicknames were entered by the public. Entries were submitted from 47 of the 50 American states, every Canadian province and overseas from as far away as Italy. The most popular names, besides the eventual winner, included Blades, Breakers, Breeze, Condors, Fog, Gold, Golden Gators, Golden Skaters, Grizzlies, Icebreakers, Knights, Redwoods, Sea Lions and Waves.

A week after announcing the nickname, the team's majority owner George Gund and San Jose mayor Tom McEnery announced that the South Bay city would be the permanent home for the NHL franchise. The Sharks would play two years at the Cow Palace in Daly City, located just outside the San Francisco city limits, before moving to a new arena in downtown San Jose for the 1993–94 campaign. On April 12, 1991 the Sharks chose George Kingston to be the team's initial head coach. The 52-year-old Canadian from Biggar, Saskatchewan had little previous NHL experience among his 30 years in hockey. Kingston had spent 20 years as head coach at the University of Calgary. In the NHL, he worked as a part-time assistant with the Calgary Flames from 1980 to 1982 and as an assistant coach in 1988–89 with the Minnesota North Stars.

Nine days after paying the league the balance of a $50-million entrance fee, the Sharks obtained their first 34 players in dispersal and expansion drafts held on May 30, 1991. San Jose inherited 24 players off Minnesota's reserve list, mostly young players from the North Stars affiliate, Kalamazoo of the International Hockey League, or those playing in the college or junior ranks. Among those players included Arturs Irbe, Brian Hayward, Neil Wilkinson, Rob Zettler, Doug Zmolek, Link Gaetz and Jarmo Myllys. The Sharks selected an additional 10 players from the other NHL teams' unprotected lists in the Expansion Draft. Jeff Hackett and Jayson More were among those chosen.

On June 22, 1991 the Sharks participated in their first NHL Entry Draft and selected right winger Pat Falloon from the Western Hockey League's Spokane Chiefs with the second overall pick. The Sharks also picked Ray Whitney and Sandis Ozolinsh. Just as the team was preparing to begin its first training camp, general manager Jack Ferreira engineered a trade with Chicago to bring popular defenseman Doug Wilson to the Sharks in exchange for a minor-league player and a draft pick. The 14-year Blackhawk became San Jose's first captain.

The Sharks first game on October 4, 1991 ended in a 4–3 loss at Vancouver. The visitors rallied for three goals in the final period to tie the score before Trevor Linden provided the game winner with just 19 seconds remaining in regulation. Journeyman forward Craig Coxe scored the first goal in club history at 4:09 of the third period. In the second game at the Cow Palace, the Sharks posted their first win on October 8 against the Calgary Flames. Kelly Kisio broke a tie by scoring a power-play goal with 3:15 left in regulation to support winning goalie Brian Hayward in San Jose's 4–3 triumph.

There were a number of other firsts. Calgary was the victim again on November 30 as the Sharks earned their initial road victory with a 2–1 triumph over the host Flames. Wilson became the first San Jose representative in an All-Star Game, as he suited up for the Campbell Conference on January 18, 1992 in Philadelphia. And goalie Jeff Hackett was selected as the team's most valuable player for the season as voted upon by Bay Area media. San Jose faced a lot of adversity in its first season. The Sharks experienced an early-season 13-game losing streak, three four-game skids and two stretches of seven consecutive losses—including one to close out the year. In addition, they surrendered a league-high 359 goals.

"I'm very proud of every guy who donned a Sharks uniform," Neil Wilkinson said after his third NHL season was complete. "Against the odds, we went out every night to win. We never backed down from anybody. We lost a lot of one-goal games and a lot of games where we were behind and had to struggle back. I think we can learn from it." The Sharks were involved in 25 one-goal games, fourth-most in the NHL. They led the league with 17 one-goal losses and dropped 13 of 14 two-goal decisions. San Jose finished last in the six-team Smythe Division with a 17–58–5 record in a season that included a 10-day work stoppage. The 19-year-old Falloon led the Sharks in goals (25) and points (59), but it would be the best season he'd produce in a San Jose sweater. The team's tough guy, Link Gaetz, who had a near cult following already, ranked among the league leaders with 326 penalty minutes. Trouble seemed to follow Gaetz, who after a number of run-ins with the law was involved in a near-fatal car crash in which he was left with a bruised brain stem. After 48 games in 1991–92, Gaetz never would play in the NHL again.

It didn't take long once the season ended for change to occur. Jack Ferreira, a highly-respected manager around the league, was fired on June 26, 1992. He lost a power struggle with Chuck Grillo, director of player personnel, who convinced initial team president Art Savage a change was needed. Besides remaining in his capacity, Grillo was elevated to vice president and given one-third of the general manager's responsibilities he'd share with Kingston and former assistant g.m. Dean Lombardi. It was a move that would prove problematic, eventually bringing about the nickname of "three-headed monster" to describe San Jose's new leadership.

San Jose had a relatively quiet off-season following the front-office shakeup, too quiet as it would soon find out. Participating in their second draft, the Sharks drafted, among others, Mike Rathje, Andrei Nazarov and Marcus Ragnarsson. The team did not otherwise acquire any other talent it could put into the lineup. The Sharks second season would be their last one in the intimate and sometimes odorous confines of the Cow Palace, the team's temporary home while a new building was under construction 50 miles south in San Jose. An opening-night 4–3 win against visiting Winnipeg in overtime provided a false illusion of how 1992–93 would unfold. The Sharks proceeded to lose their next nine games in a harbinger of things to come. Mired in last place, and hopelessly out of playoff contention at 6–31–2 on January 3, the Sharks still had more than half a season to go. The next night they would embark on an NHL record-tying 17-game losing streak. From January 4 to February 12, San Jose would lose five games by one goal and score one or fewer goals eight times. Along the way, the Sharks suffered a franchise-worst loss with a 13–1 shellacking in Calgary. Flames right winger Theoren Fleury set a modern-day league record by posting a plus–minus rating of +9. The ineptitude finally ended with a 3–2 victory over Winnipeg on February 14, 1993.

One of the season's few bright spots, Latvian goaltender Arturs Irbe, was in the net that night. The goalie who would develop into a fan favorite in years to come won only seven of 33 decisions in his first full season in the NHL. He provided one of the season's few highlights by stopping 39 Los Angeles shots during a 6–0 victory on November 17, 1992 for the first Sharks shutout in history. Rookie right winger Rob Gaudreau made a splash by recording the team's first hat trick in just his second NHL game. It came during a 7–5 loss to visiting Hartford on December 3, 1992. Gaudreau would repeat the three-goal feat four games later during an 8–7 overtime loss to visiting Quebec. Gaudreau was rewarded as the league's rookie of the month for December, a time in which he scored 14 goals and 19 points and set a club-mark 12-game point scoring streak (December 3–29).

The one-goal win on Valentine's Day over the Jets stopped the bleeding only momentarily as the Sharks would win just four more times in their last 26 outings. San Jose endured a 13-game losing streak from March 9 to April 4. Losing 16 of its final 17 games, San Jose ended a miserable second season with an 11–71–2 record to set a league record for most losses in a single NHL campaign. Four days into the off-season, Kingston was fired. The Sharks were about to open their first season in San Jose Arena, a state-of-the-art building that featured 64 luxury boxes and seating for 17,190 at a cost of $162.5 million. They would do it with Kevin Constantine behind the bench. The 35-year-old entered the season as the league's youngest coach. One year removed from winning the Turner Cup with San Jose's

minor-league affiliate, Kansas City of the International Hockey League, Constantine was familiar with San Jose's personnel and direction since he'd been part of the franchise from its inception.

The Sharks would make their initial season in San Jose a memorable one. Despite getting off to an 0–8–1 start, the players rallied behind Constantine's defense-first approach to make the playoffs for the first time, and they established an NHL record for the greatest single-season turnaround— 58 points better than 1992–93's total of 24. The reunion of Russian hockey greats Sergei Makarov and Igor Larionov to form two-thirds of a potent first line, the maturation of young defenseman Sandis Ozolinsh and the workmanlike goaltending of Arturs Irbe sparked the team to a 33–35–16 record and an eighth-place finish in the Western Conference standings. But the Sharks were not done there. In the first round of the playoffs they drew top-seed Detroit, a team they had beaten only once in 11 previous meetings. San Jose set the tone for an upset by skating off with game one in Detroit, 5–4. The heavily-favored Wings won the next two games and held a 3–1 edge early in game four when San Jose turned the series around. The Sharks scored three unanswered goals for a series-tying 4–3 triumph. Three days later San Jose took a 3–2 edge with a 6–4 victory. The scene switched back to Joe Louis Arena, where the hosts dominated San Jose 7–1 and appeared headed for the kill in game seven. But midway through the third period of a 2–2 game, Detroit goaltender Chris Osgood wandered too far out of his crease, then threw a puck up the left boards that Jamie Baker intercepted and deposited back into an empty net with 6:35 remaining for the series clincher.

Next it was on to Toronto, and the Sharks won game one again by one goal, 3–2. "Cinderella" San Jose eventually took a 3–2 game lead and headed back to Toronto with a chance to reach hockey's final four. It nearly came in game six, and when that didn't happen it never came at all. Johan Garpenlov hit the crossbar with the game tied 2–2. Then, in overtime, the slick-skating, ever-opportunistic Ozolinsh led a rush into the Toronto zone that had game winner written all over it. However, inexplicably, the 21-year-old native of Latvia literally passed up on a high percentage shot from the slot, instead dishing too far ahead toward a surprised Larionov. The play turned back up ice and before the Sharks could utter the words "conference finals," Mike Gartner had bagged the game winner for the Maple Leafs at 8:53. Game seven was Toronto's from start to finish. It ended 4–2 and so did San Jose's most exciting season.

Constantine was recognized by finishing second in voting for the Jack Adams Award. Irbe, who set a league record for most minutes played in a season (4,412) had accompanied his country-mate Ozolinsh to the All-Star Game in New York. A seemingly reborn Makarov, who listed his age as 35 though he was thought to be older, set a team mark with 30 goals. And the Sharks formed a strong bond with their hometown fans that would last for quite some time. The lovefest in the Bay Area that was now Sharks hockey had to wait until late January of 1995 to resume because league labor strife forced the postponement of play from October, 1995, until the turn of the calendar year. San Jose picked up right where it left off, shooting 5–1–1 out of the gate to raise already high expectations. Qualifying for a second straight postseason would become a challenge, however, as the team slumped by losing 10 of its next 16 before having a home game on March 10 against Detroit postponed because of heavy rain and flooding around San

Jose Arena. Knowing a loss in the season finale would preclude an invitation to the playoffs, the Sharks tied Vancouver 3–3 to sneak into seventh place with an otherwise disappointing 19–25–4 record.

Like its first-round opponent a season ago, the Sharks drew a foe that was ripe for an upset. Calgary had lost six straight first-round matchups since its Stanley Cup triumph in 1989, and that was all the Flames read about prior to meeting the Sharks. San Jose won the first two games in Calgary, shockingly lost the middle three, then returned home to win 5–3 before clinching in Calgary with a 5–4 win. Backup goalie Wade Flaherty, who had bailed out a faltering Irbe in the series, got the call for game seven on the strength of a 30-save effort. Flaherty was brilliant in the finale. He stopped a franchise playoff-record 56 shots. Ray Whitney redirected a Makarov feed past his former junior teammate—goalie Trevor Kidd—with 1:54 gone in the second overtime. The win allowed the Sharks to move on with a 5–4 triumph despite having been outshot 60–30 by the stunned Flames.

Revenge-seeking Detroit was waiting in round two, and the Red Wings would leave no room for error this time. They completely dominated San Jose, outscoring the Sharks 24–6, while outshooting them on the average of 37–15 per game during the four-game win. The postseason disappointment was softened by the outstanding showing of rookie Jeff Friesen, who stepped right into the lineup after being selected 11th overall the previous June to finish as the team's regular-season goal-scoring leader (15) and as San Jose's third scorer overall (25 points). He was the first Shark to be named to an NHL All-Rookie Team.

All the success and giddiness that surrounded the seemingly up-and-coming franchise would come crashing down, however. One by one, the heroes fell. His confidence already shaken by the loss of his status as the team's number one goalie, Irbe experienced an off-season mishap when he was attacked by his dog. He required delicate surgery to repair injuries to his hands and left wrist. He and Flaherty would get off to awful starts in 1995–96. An out-of-shape Makarov never made it out of training camp. A frustrated Larionov had a run-in with Constantine and demanded a trade. He was gone by October 24. Ozolinsh was dealt two days later to Colorado in return for a much-needed scorer, Owen Nolan. Constantine didn't last much longer. Despite having signed a new three-year deal the first week of the season, he was fired two months later on December 2 after the team managed to win only three of its first 25 games (3–18–4). It turned out Constantine wasn't the problem. Interim coach Jim Wiley could do little with a group that quit and malingered throughout the sorry campaign. The Sharks, retooling over the final months of the season, finished ahead of only Ottawa in the overall standings at 20–55–7. The team's first draft choice, Pat Falloon, was traded. San Jose gave up on Irbe when it acquired Chris Terreri. Player personnel director Chuck Grillo was fired and Dean Lombardi was named general manager. Surprisingly, the Sharks sold out all 41 home games. In midseason, one ray of light appeared when George Gund was named a recipient of the Lester Patrick Trophy, awarded for outstanding service and contributions to hockey in the United States.

Rebuilding would prove tedious. Grillo's risky drafts hadn't panned out. Lombardi started over from scratch. He had to weed the organization of veterans who had gotten used to losing, evaluate youth to determine who had viable NHL potential and acquire players who would compete on a nightly basis. Lombardi turned the roster over before the 1996–97 season, securing no less than eight seasoned veterans with a winning track record including Todd Gill, Al Iafrate, Kelly Hrudey, Marty McSorley, Tony Granato, Bernie Nicholls, Tim Hunter and Todd Ewen. Once the new campaign began, Lombardi continued adding by signing Ron Sutter, Greg Hawgood and former Sharks captain Bob Errey for a second go-around. And, in his boldest move, Lombardi acquired veteran goalie Ed Belfour from Chicago. Belfour would be an unrestricted free agent at season's end, but Lombardi was convinced once the two-time Vezina winner saw first-hand San Jose's renewed commitment to winning he'd be sure to stay.

The one mistake Lombardi made in all of his moves, however, was the hiring of ex-Anaheim assistant Al Sims as the team's fourth head coach. Sims never earned the respect of his players and the result was a very long season. The underachieving Sharks finished 25th overall again, posting a 27–47–8 record. They produced a league-low 211 goals and fell 19 points short of a playoff spot.

The lone bright spot was Tony Granato's selection as the NHL's Masterton Award winner. Granato made a successful comeback from brain surgery and was honored for perseverance and dedication to the game. Iafrate saw his first action after two injury-riddled campaigns in Boston. His impact was felt as the Sharks went 17–17–4 with "the Freighter" in the lineup, but he was out more than he was in.

Sims was fired on May 9. Exactly one month later, former Blackhawks coach Darryl Sutter was lured out of retirement and hired to lead San Jose into the 1997–98 season. Belfour bolted for Dallas on the second day free agents were allowed to sign. Lombardi acquired 1997 Conn Smythe Trophy winner Mike Vernon from Detroit.

The two-time champion would handle the job of number-one goaltender as the Sharks also welcomed newcomers Murray Craven, Stephane Matteau, Shawn Burr, Bill Houlder and rookies Patrick Marleau, Marco Sturm and Andrei Zyuzin for renewed hope and enthusiasm in 1997–98.

Though a dispute with Sutter caused captain Todd Gill to remove the 'C' from his sweater, and later led to his being traded to St. Louis, the season proved to be a success. The Sharks won a franchise-high 34 games and returned to the playoffs after a two-year absence. Unfortunately, San Jose hooked up with the regular season's strongest team when they faced the Dallas Stars to open the postseason. Although they won twice on home ice, the Sharks were eliminated in six games.

San Jose Sharks Year-by-Year Record

Season	GP	W	L	T	GF	GA	Pts	Finish		Playoff Results
1991–92	80	17	58	5	219	359	39	6th	Smythe Div.	Out of Playoffs
1992–93	84	11	71	2	218	414	24	6th	Smythe Div.	Out of Playoffs
1993–94	84	33	35	16	252	265	82	3rd	Pacific Div.	Lost Conf. Semifinal
1994–95	48	19	25	4	129	161	42	3rd	Pacific Div.	Lost Conf. Semifinal
1995–96	82	20	55	7	252	357	47	7th	Pacific Div.	Out of Playoffs
1996–97	82	27	47	8	211	278	62	7th	Pacific Div.	Out of Playoffs
1997–98	82	34	38	10	210	216	78	4th	Pacific Div.	Lost Conf. Quarterfinal

TAMPA BAY LIGHTNING

Stan Fischler

LIGHTNING CAN BRIGHTEN A NIGHT SKY and it can cause serious physical and mental damage. Tampa Bay's National Hockey League franchise has done both since it was conceived in 1990, played its first game in 1992 and fitfully struggled through the decade of the 1990s.

Prior to the late 1980s, there had been considerable skepticism about the possibilities of major-league hockey in steamy Florida. An attempt by the World Hockey Association to establish a foothold in Miami during the early 1970s ended in failure before a game was ever played. But in December 1989 the NHL announced a grand plan to expand to 28 teams by the year 2000 and, in March of the next year Hall of Famer Phil Esposito came to the conclusion that the Tampa–St. Petersburg area was prime for NHL expansion.

Teaming with Florida attorney Henry Lee Paul, son of longtime baseball executive Gabe Paul, and Mel Lowell, a former Madison Square Garden official, Esposito laid the groundwork for acceptance. His first move was to promote an exhibition game at the massive Florida Suncoast Dome between the Los Angeles Kings and Pittsburgh Penguins on September 19, 1990. With appropriate fuss and fanfare, the game drew a crowd of 25,581—the largest to see an NHL game. Pittsburgh won the match 5–3 and Tampa Coliseum, Inc. agreed to finance construction of a multi-purpose arena next to Tampa Stadium.

Still cautious, the NHL dispatched an expeditionary force to Tampa Bay on November 1, 1990 to gauge interest and decide whether the league should formally invade Florida. NHL vice president Gil Stein opined: "This area is ready for an NHL expansion franchise." Less than five weeks later Tampa Bay and Ottawa were awarded conditional franchises to play in 1992–93.

That was the good news. The bad news was that, almost from the very beginning, the original ownership group led by Esposito needed cash for the 1990 expansion fee. It had been expected that the Pritzger family, owner of the Hyatt Corporation among other holdings, would put up the $50 million expansion fee but Pritzger decided to stay out of the hockey business, leaving Esposito and Paul to find another substantial backer.

It was then that Esposito did what no other NHL executive had done; he jetted to the Orient in search of funding. He started with a $2 million infusion and eventually boosted it with support from such Japanese firms as Kokusai Green, Nippon Green and Tokyo Tower. Esposito liked to humorously recall that some of the negotiations took place between drinks. "The more we drank," said Esposito, "the more it (the deal) made sense. I said 'hockey' but they thought I had said 'sake'."

Lowell: "Our meetings with Kokusai took place in hotel bars in the Ginza at odd hours." Significantly, Takashi Okubo, the key man at Kokusai Green, never attended any of the meetings. Even then, at least one NHL owner had his doubts about the manner in which the Lightning's application was being processed. "It was a terrible expansion process," said New Jersey Devils owner John McMullen. "I voiced my concerns but I was only one voice." The fiscal clouds became darker in June 1991 when the team missed a $22.5 million franchise installment payment. That moved Kokusai Green into action and it felt obliged to take a majority stake in the franchise.

In September 1991 the Lightning received league approval for a restructured partnership with Lightning Partners—owned by Kokusai Green—assuming the role of general partner. Esposito's group had now been formally replaced by the Japanese majority owners.

In December 1991 the NHL granted permanent membership status to both the Lightning and Ottawa Senators. On the operating front Phil Esposito emerged as the general manager, with brother Tony heading the scouting division. As for a playing venue, the club opted for the Florida State Fairgrounds Expo Hall as a temporary home until a permanent arena was built in Tampa.

Despite the innumerable obstacles—both financial and political—the Lightning managed to take the ice for the first time on September 12, 1992 at the Lakeland Civic Center in Lakeland, Florida. If that wasn't news enough, Esposito stunned the hockey world by signing a female goaltender, Manon Rheaume to a tryout form. The attractive French Canadian made history on September 23, 1992 by becoming the first woman to play one of the four major professional sports when she started against St. Louis in a preseason game. Rheaume made seven saves during 20 minutes of action and later was awarded a contract with Atlanta, Tampa Bay's International Hockey League affiliate.

On opening night a sellout crowd of 10,425 jammed Expo Hall cheering the Lightning to a 7–3 victory over Chicago. Chris Kontos, a reject of several NHL teams, scored four goals for Tampa Bay. As expected, the Lightning played like an expansion team, although there were conspicuous highlights. One of the earliest took place on November 7, 1992 when defenseman Doug Crossman set a team record for most points in a game with six against the New York Islanders. Crossman's third goal of the game provided the win in sudden-death for the Lightning's first overtime victory in team history.

Of all the discards picked up by Esposito the most impressive was Brian Bradley who finished the season with a team-leading 42 goals and 44 assists for 86 points. Bradley also became the first All-Star in team history, skating for the Campbell Conference in the 44th NHL All-Star Game in Montreal. In the end Tampa Bay finished sixth in the Norris Division (23–54–7) and to nobody's surprise missed the playoffs.

For their second season, the Lightning moved out of the drafty, barn-like Expo Hall to St. Petersburg's Florida Suncoast Dome, which was designed as a baseball stadium but was reconfigured to handle hockey. It would have 28,000 seats for NHL games and would later be renamed the Thunderdome.

Underlying all the excitement were negative fiscal currents. Starting in 1992, the club was so cash-strapped that Lightning officials were constantly concerned about failure to make payroll and the potential collapse of the team. "There never was enough cash," said Mel Lowell. "There never was enough oxygen to breathe."

Nevertheless, Phil Esposito continued to fortify his lineup. In July 1993 he signed free agent Gerard Gallant, who had enjoyed eight successful seasons in Detroit and was a four-time 30-goal scorer. With his first selection (third overall), Esposito selected Chris Gratton, a big forward, in the Entry Draft and he also acquired five-time 30-goal scorer Petr Klima from Edmonton for future considerations.

Some of the choices were good while others failed miserably. Klima led the Lightning in scoring with 28 goals in 1993–94, but Gallant would prove to be a major disap-

pointment. Conversely, Daren Puppa, who was obtained from the Florida Panthers in phase two of the 1993 Expansion Draft, proved to be the formidable goaltender the club required to remain competitive.

During the 1993–94 season, Puppa played in 63 games and won 23 out of the 30 victories produced by the Lightning. His 2.71 goals-against-average was remarkable considering the modest defense in front of him, and the Lightning's climb to fifth place was directly attributable to Puppa's netminding. Any doubts that Tampa Bay was hockey country were dispelled on October 9, 1993 when the club set an NHL single-game attendance mark with 27,227 fans witnessing the Lightning home opener against Florida. The move across the bay to St. Petersburg did nothing to deter interest and the team's record of 30–43–11 was a further boost despite a second straight year without making the playoffs.

The team drew 805,901, over 41 games for an average of 19,656, but many of the seats were low-priced or giveaways and the financial woes continued. During the autumn of 1994 the Internal Revenue Service and the State of Florida were prepared to file liens on the Lightning for $750,000 in past due taxes. Other debts were also piling up and to handle them Kokusai Green borrowed against many of the team's revenue streams.

In 1995 Kokusai Green demanded that all limited partners produce an additional $885,000 for each $1 million limited partnership or lose their entire investment. Upon learning of that, Mel Lowell sued the team, withdrawing the action only when the NHL persuaded Kokusai to withdraw the demand and repay most of the original investment to partners who wanted out. When his contract was not renewed by the team, Lowell left his job as executive vice president of the team.

These events coincided with yet another non-playoff season. Finishing sixth during the lockout-shortened campaign, the club won 17 games, lost 28 and tied three for sixth place. Its two leading scorers, Bradley and Klima, netted just 13 goals apiece. Bradley was the team leader with 40 points. If any solace was to be obtained, it could only come from Puppa's heroic goaltending. He actually brought his goals-against-average down to 2.68 and won all but four of his team's victories.

The turnabout for the Lightning's fortunes took place in October 1995 when Paul Ysebaert was named the first captain in team history and young defenseman Roman Hamrlik surfaced as one of the best offensive point men in the NHL. Between Puppa's goaltending, Hamrlik's versatility on defense and attack and Terry Crisp's spirited coaching, the Lightning made its first serious bid for a playoff berth.

On March 5, 1996 Hamrlik's two goals and Puppa's shutout gave Tampa Bay a 2–0 win for the franchise's 100th victory. It came against Chicago which, coincidentally, had been the opponent when the Lightning won their first game in 1992. And when the chips were down in the homestretch, the Lightning would not falter. On March 13, Tampa Bay tied Philadelphia 1–1, setting a club record with a seven-game unbeaten streak (5–0–2).

Through early April, the Lightning and defending champion New Jersey Devils engaged in a neck-and-neck race for the final playoff berth. On April 13, 1996, a day off for Crisp's skaters, the Devils lost at home to Ottawa thereby clinching a postseason spot for Tampa Bay. A powerful Philadelphia club faced the Lightning and won 7–3 at The Spectrum in the opener, but an overtime goal by Brian

Bellows provided the underdogs with a 2–1 win in game two. Then came the stunner: returning to the confines of their home rink, the Lightning defeated Philadelphia 5–4 on Alexander Selivanov's goal in overtime.

It proved to be the Lightning's last gasp. The Flyers next ran off 4–1, 4–1 and 6–1 victories to capture the series. However, fan support was stronger than ever and on April 23, 1996 the Lightning set an all-time NHL attendance record of 28,183 for game four of the playoff series. Even more encouraging was news that the club's new home, the Tampa-based Ice Palace, was ready for occupancy at the start of the 1996–97 season. Located within a puck's shot of the bay, the Ice Palace won admirers with its tasteful exterior and magnificent interior appointments.

Opening night at the new building was October 20, 1996 when the home team defeated the New York Rangers 5–3 in front of 20,543 fans. Original Lightning team member Brian Bradley scored the first goal in the Ice Palace at 11:46 of the first period while second-string goaltender Corey Schwab—standing in for the injured Puppa—recorded a three-period total of 32 saves.

It was an auspicious debut for a season of disappointment. A troublesome back kayoed Puppa, causing coach Crisp to alternate Schwab and Rick Tabaracci in goal. Strong offensive efforts by Dino Ciccarelli and John Cullen enabled the Lightning to stay in the playoff hunt. On March 4, 1997 Ciccarelli scored the 1,000th goal in Lightning history in the first period of a 6–3 win over the Islanders at Nassau Coliseum.

Tampa Bay had a shot at another playoff berth right up to the final weekend of the season, but it was not to be. At season's end the Lightning finished with 32 wins—only six less than the previous year—but 40 losses and 10 ties meant they fell short of an opportunity to participate in the postseason. If any solace was derived from the demise it came on April 10, 1997 when the Lightning set an Ice Palace attendance record of 20,667 in the final home game of the season, a 4–3 win over Pittsburgh.

By this time the Japanese-based ownership had begun a determined effort to sell the team. The organization's debt had passed the $50 million mark and would reach $100 million by 1998. The Las Vegas-based Maloof family spent eight months trying to hammer out a deal but never was able to personally contact the mysterious Japanese owner Takashi Okubo. "Not only did I never speak to Okubo in our eight months [of trying to make a deal], I began to wonder if he ever existed," said Tony Guanci, a consultant for the Maloofs.

Instead of buying the Lightning, the Maloofs purchased the NBA Sacramento Kings. One problem was that Kokusai Green originally had set a price of $230 million for the team and its 40-year sweetheart lease with the Ice Palace but the price dropped to $167 million as other suitors became harder and harder to find.

Okubo, who had poured $90 million into the team but had never attended a game, became more and more the subject of scrutiny as the 1997–98 season unfolded. It would be a traumatic year for the Lightning.

For starters, John Cullen, who had been diagnosed with cancer, learned in September 1997 that radiation and chemotherapy treatments had not been successful and that he would have to undergo a bone-marrow transplant. Doctors reported that his chances of recovery—once reported to be better than 90 percent—were now no better than 75 percent.

A month later forward Troy Mallette discovered that a natural narrowing of the spinal chord would compel him to miss the entire season and could be career threatening. In November, Ciccarelli was sidelined because of immense pain caused by floating debris in his elbow. Surgery forced him out of the lineup for a month, whereupon Brian Bradley suffered a severe concussion.

At virtually the same time promising forward Vladimir Vujtek was felled by pericarditis, a rare virus that infected his heart. He, too, was lost for the season. As if to put a capper on the catastrophes, assistant equipment manager Jim Pickard was diagnosed with pancreatitis and was lost for all but the final two weeks of the campaign.

To Tampa fans, the most egregious loss was that of Chris Gratton, the 6'4", 218-pound center who received a five-year, $16.5 million free agent offer sheet from the Philadelphia Flyers in the summer of 1997.

Unable to match the bid, Phil Esposito later explained to an arbitrator that he couldn't decipher the Philadelphia's proposal because some of the numbers on the fax were smudged. Arbitrator John Sands didn't buy that argument, but the Lightning escaped a total disaster when Philadelphia agreed to trade Mikael Renberg and Karl Dykhuis to Tampa Bay for the four first-round draft picks that the Flyers would have lost to the Lightning in the original offer sheet plan. But by December 1997 Renberg had broken his wrist and was lost for a month.

Meanwhile, Phil Esposito had fired Terry Crisp, placed Rick Paterson in the head coaching slot and then replaced him with Jacques Demers. No matter who was behind the bench, the Lightning required Puppa's top goaltending to survive, but in a game against Boston in December 1997, the goalie left complaining of back spasms. He was lost for the rest of the year.

As expected, the club concluded the 1997–98 season with the worst record of its six-year existence. With only 17 wins in 82 games, the Lightning lost 55 matches, one more than in their maiden season. Leading scorer Paul Ysebaert totaled only 40 points and top goal scorers Renberg and Selivanov, had a mere 16 apiece.

At season's end NHL commissioner Gary Bettman revealed that the league was diligently working to consummate a sale of the team that would eliminate "99.9 percent" of the team's problems. "There are difficulties in having distant ownership," said Bettman, "particularly if that ownership is not familiar with the sports business. At this point I'll define 'local interest' as North America. I'll take somebody within a six-hour flight!"

In May 1998 it appeared that the Lightning's luck was beginning to take a turn for the better. John Cullen learned that his cancer was in remission. "I got a clean bill of health," said Cullen, who had non-Hodgkin's lymphoma. "It was hard but I stayed positive the whole way. I knew I could beat this thing."

No less heartening was news that a front office shakeup was under way and that potential new buyers were on the horizon. Steve Oto resigned as Lightning chief executive officer and president, replaced by Chuck Hasegawa. Art Williams, a wealthy retired insurance executive from Palm Beach, purchased the club.

The club's on-ice future received a considerable boost at the 1998 NHL Entry Draft when, using the first overall draft selection, the Lightning picked highly-regarded center Vincent Lecavalier from the Rimouski Oceanic of the Quebec Major Junior Hockey League.

Tampa Bay Lightning Year-by-Year Record

Season	GP	W	L	T	GF	GA	Pts	Finish		Playoff Results
1992–93	84	23	54	7	245	332	53	6th	Norris Div.	Out of Playoffs
1993–94	84	30	43	11	224	251	71	7th	Atlantic Div.	Out of Playoffs
1994–95	48	17	28	3	120	144	37	6th	Atlantic Div.	Out of Playoffs
1995–96	82	38	32	12	138	248	88	6th	Atlantic Div.	Lost Conf. Quarterfinal
1996–97	82	32	40	10	217	247	74	6th	Atlantic Div.	Out of Playoffs
1997–98	82	17	55	10	151	269	83	7th	Atlantic Div.	Out of Playoffs

TORONTO MAPLE LEAFS

Brian McFarlane

WHEN TORONTO MADE ITS NHL DEBUT against the Montreal Wanderers on December 19, 1917 the team scored nine goals—and lost the game. The Wanderers, so devoid of talent that they had talked of dropping out of hockey one week earlier, edged Toronto 10–9 in that historic match, witnessed by a mere 700 souls. To help fill the seats, soldiers in uniform were admitted as guests of the management.

Both teams were troubled clubs playing in a wobbly league which was not yet a month old. The NHL, formed in a series of meetings between November 22 and November 26, 1917 originally comprised teams from Quebec, Ottawa and two clubs from Montreal—the Canadiens and the Wanderers. Toronto was included in the mix with the stipulation that former owner Eddie Livingstone not be involved in any way. Livingstone was not a popular chap—at least not with his hockey brethren. The Toronto team was admitted to the NHL under the ownership of the city's Mutual Street Arena, hence the name the Toronto Arenas. (This name has been traditionally attached to Toronto's NHL team of 1917–18, but it appears that the name was not actually used until the following season.)

How could anyone have known on that opening night that the Wanderers' first victory would be their last in the NHL? A few days later, after three losses in which they gave up 26 goals, their arena burned to the ground and they were forced to withdraw from the league. How could anyone have known that Toronto's first game would begin a hockey tradition that would last to the end of the century and encompass more than 5,000 games?

Despite the fact those original Toronto players quarreled with management and were hit by fines for breaking training, the team won the second half of the NHL's split schedule, defeated Montreal in a playoff series and captured the Stanley Cup with by winning a best-of-five series with the Vancouver Millionaires of the Pacific Coast Hockey Association. And they did it on a surface of artificial ice—the only such surface in the NHL. While it was Toronto's first Cup win under the NHL banner, a 1914 team playing in the National Hockey Association is credited with bringing Lord Stanley's basin to the Queen City for the first time. Some interesting new rules governed hockey in 1914. A goaltender who deliberately fell to the ice to block a shot was subject to a $2 fine, a player who deliberately hurt an opposing player was punished with a match penalty—and a $15 fine. And the league executives decided it was time to give credit to players who assisted on goals.

The 1914 Toronto team—known as the Blueshirts—hosted the Victoria Aristocrats of the PCHA that season, even though Victoria had neglected to submit a formal challenge for the Stanley Cup. The Blueshirts won by scores of 5–2, 6–5 (in overtime) and 2–1. Goaltender Harry Holmes and defenseman Harry Cameron also played on the 1918 cham-

pionship team. Why not? They were well paid for their efforts. By 1918 Holmes was earning $700 per season, Cameron $900. The total payroll for the 10 players on the Toronto roster was $6,150.

Despite winning the Stanley Cup in the NHL's first season, the Toronto Arenas struggled in 1918–19 and, in fact, withdrew from the league on February 20, 1919. The team was back for the 1919–20 season after having been reorganized as the Toronto St. Patricks. In 1922, the St. Pats squad surprised the hockey world by defeating the Ottawa Senators in the NHL playoffs and then toppling Vancouver in five games in the finals for the Stanley Cup. Toronto's Babe Dye led all playoff scorers with 11 goals in seven games. It was in the 1922 Stanley Cup series that Vancouver's Art Duncan tripped Dye and Dye was awarded the first penalty shot in Stanley Cup history. His shot from 36 feet out sailed high over the goalie's head. Dye had been the NHL's top goal scorer in 1920–21 (35 goals) and would top the league again with 26 in 1922–23. Dye's 38 goals in 1924–25 were a career high and his 44 points that season also led the NHL.

Meanwhile, in March of 1923, a teenaged newspaper reporter named Foster Hewitt began broadcasting hockey games from Mutual Street Arena on the *Toronto Star*'s new radio station, CFCA. It wouldn't be long before Hewitt's voice would become the most familiar one in all of Canada.

By 1926–27 the NHL had franchises in New York (the Americans), Boston and Pittsburgh. Other teams clamored for admission—the New York Rangers, the Chicago Black Hawks and the Detroit Cougars (later the Falcons and the Red Wings). Young Conn Smythe was hired to assemble the original Rangers but was fired before the first game was played in New York. Lester Patrick, older and more experienced, was signed to replace him. New York's loss soon became Toronto's gain.

Following his dismissal in New York, Smythe vowed he would someday organize another team, one capable of beating the Rangers. He managed to raise $160,000, enough to purchase the last-place St. Pats in February of 1927. He promptly renamed the team the Toronto Maple Leafs. He also switched the uniform colors from green and white to blue and white. Smythe soon needed additional money, some to purchase King Clancy from Ottawa and a lot more to finance the building of a new arena, the largest in Canada.

As Foster Hewitt's broadcasts attracted more and more fans, Smythe soon realized he could not accommodate them all at the Mutual Street Arena and he began formulating plans for a new ice palace—Maple Leaf Gardens. When financing the project became a major undertaking Smythe—and his energetic assistant Frank Selke—turned to the trade unions and bartered Gardens' stock in return for labor. In what has been called "a miracle of engineering," the new ice palace was erected in six months and at a bargain price—$1.5 million. Some called it "Smythe's folly" and predicted he'd "never fill the place."

With Hap Day and King Clancy on defense and the Kid Line of Charlie Conacher, Joe Primeau and Busher Jackson up front, the Leafs became a powerful force in the NHL. Through the decades that followed, the Gardens was always full to overflowing and those fortunate stalwarts Smythe selected to don his steel blades, to pull on his coveted jerseys of blue and white became hockey exemplars, idolized by millions, more popular than Tom Mix or Hopalong Cassidy of movie fame. In 1931–32, their first year on

Gardens' ice, the Leafs swept to the Stanley Cup, ousting the Rangers in the finals in three straight games. Early in the season, Smythe had replaced coach Art Duncan with Dick Irvin, who had been fired by Chicago. Irvin brought the Leafs from last place to first place within a month.

On December 12, 1933 Ace Bailey, one of Smythe's star performers and one of the few Leaf players ever to win a scoring title (1928–29), almost lost his life in a game played at the Boston Garden. Knocked to the ice by Bruins tough guy Eddie Shore, Bailey suffered a fractured skull and hovered close to death for several hours following emergency brain surgery. He recovered but never played again. Two months later, a benefit game was played for Bailey at Maple Leaf Gardens. Great sportsman that he was, Bailey walked to center ice and shook hands with the irascible Shore.

On April 3, 1933 the Leafs and the Bruins began a playoff game at Maple Leaf Gardens that would develop into the longest game ever played in the building. The game went into the sixth overtime before little Ken Doraty, a Leaf forward, scored the lone goal of the contest. Doraty is remembered for little else. (In 1936, a longer playoff game, another six-overtime marathon, would be played in Montreal between the Maroons and the Red Wings.)

In 1940, Dick Irvin resigned as Leaf coach and accepted a similar position with the Montreal Canadiens. Hap Day was Irvin's successor and figured prominently in one of hockey's most dramatic comebacks. In 1942, after Detroit took a 3–0 lead in games over Toronto in the Stanley Cup finals, Day made some player changes and the Leafs roared back with three straight wins to tie the series. They won the Cup with a 3–1 victory in a thrilling seventh game. It's the only time a club has come back from such a deficit in the Stanley Cup finals.

Goaltender Frank McCool was a Toronto hero in the Stanley Cup finals of 1945. The Red Wings had defeated the Leafs in eight of 10 games played during the regular season, but when they met in the finals, McCool was brilliant, setting a playoff record with three shutouts. The Leafs won the Cup in seven games. One of the stars of that team was defenseman Babe Pratt, who had won the Hart Trophy in 1944. Pratt would be expelled from hockey in 1945–46 for wagering on games and, although he was reinstated on February 14, 1946 following a 16-day absence from the game, his days in Toronto were numbered. Pratt was traded to the Boston Bruins after the season and finished his playing days in the minors.

The Leafs regained the Stanley Cup in the spring of 1947. Ted Kennedy's winning goal in a 2–1 victory over Montreal in game six of the finals brought the Cup back to Maple Leaf Gardens. Early the following season, Conn Smythe traded several players to Chicago in order to land Max Bentley, a superstar of the era. Smythe's gamble paid off when the Leafs swept to a second straight Cup win, ousting Detroit four straight in the finals. In the spring of 1949, coach Hap Day established a remarkable record by leading his team to five Stanley Cup titles in eight years. Once again, Detroit finished as runners-up.

The 1950–51 season is remembered for Bill Barilko's Stanley Cup-winning goal. When Toronto met Montreal in the 1951 finals, each game in the series required overtime. Game five was the most dramatic. Montreal had the game almost won when the Leafs yanked their goalie and Tod Sloan scored at 19:28 of the third to tie the score. At 2:53 of the overtime, Bill Barilko galloped in from the blue line and drilled the series-winning goal past Gerry McNeil. Barilko

died tragically in a plane crash a few weeks later.

On February 1, 1955 Conn Smythe, 60, stepped down as general manager of the Leafs and handed the position to Hap Day. Leaf fans, however, had little to cheer about during this era. The club finished in last place for the first time in history in 1956–57. In August 1958, Toronto signed 33-year-old minor-league goaltender Johnny Bower and rookie Carl Brewer. Allan Stanley was acquired from Boston and assistant general manager Punch Imlach took over as general manager in November. One of his first moves was to fire Billy Reay and add the coaching job to his own portfolio. He installed rookie Dave Keon at center and grabbed Eddie Shack from the Rangers in a deal. Imlach's "Cinderella Leafs" climbed from last place into the playoffs that season but lost in the finals to a powerful Montreal club. In February 1960, Imlach snared Red Kelly from Detroit and switched him from defense to center. Once again the Leafs reached the finals and once again they lost to Montreal, who captured their fifth straight Stanley Cup championship.

In November 1961, Conn Smythe officially stepped aside and sold his 50,000 shares in the Maple Leafs franchise— 60 percent of the voting rights—to his son Stafford, Harold Ballard and *Toronto Telegram* owner John Bassett for $2 million dollars. The Leafs won the Stanley Cup in 1962, dethroning the Chicago Black Hawks, and they retained the trophy by ousting Detroit in the 1963 finals. The following season, Punch Imlach dealt Dick Duff, Bob Nevin, Arnie Brown, Rod Seiling and Bill Collins to the Rangers in return for Andy Bathgate and Don McKenney. Bathgate and McKenney proved to be a big help as the Leafs won their third consecutive Cup title in 1964. In the final series against Detroit, hardrock defenseman Bobby Baun scored the winning goal in game six in overtime while playing on a cracked anklebone. Toronto captured the Cup once more in the 1960s. With NHL expansion looming, Imlach's veterans—the oldest club ever to reach the finals—ousted Montreal in six games in 1967 behind the superb goaltending of Terry Sawchuk and Johnny Bower. "Bower," Imlach once said, "is the most remarkable athlete in the world."

When his team slumped in 1967–68, Imlach sent Frank Mahovlich (a player he couldn't get along with), Pete Stemkowski and Garry Unger, along with the rights to retired Carl Brewer (another Leaf who drove Imlach to distraction), to Detroit for Norm Ullman, Paul Henderson and Floyd Smith. But the Leafs were no longer championship material. After they were eliminated in the 1968 playoffs by Boston, Imlach was fired by Stafford Smythe. Jim Gregory took over as general manager and John McLellan was assigned the coaching job.

In the summer of 1969, Harold Ballard and Stafford Smythe faced charges of tax evasion. John Bassett, unwilling to be associated with partners who faced jail terms, sold his shares to Ballard and Smythe for close to $6 million. Smythe died before he could be sentenced. Upon the death of his partner, Ballard bought Smythe's shares, with help from his friend Don Giffin, who arranged for a loan of $7.4 million. Ballard, now in full control of the franchise and the Gardens, had his jail sentenced postponed until after the Canada–Soviet series of 1972. Then he was whisked off to jail to serve three concurrent three-year terms. He served only a year and returned to put his personal ruinous stamp on hockey at Maple Leaf Gardens for most of the next two decades.

Upon his return to Toronto, Ballard scoffed at reports the newly formed World Hockey Association would give him any trouble. As a result his organization lost no less than 14 players to the rival loop, including such young stars as Jim Dorey, Rick Ley, Jim Harrison and the brilliant young goaltender Bernie Parent. Though they were no longer the powerhouse club of the 1960s, Ballard's Leafs played decent hockey throughout most of the 1970s. One of game's great moments took place on February 7, 1976 when Leaf captain Darryl Sittler scored a record 10 points (six goals and four assists) in a game against Boston. Sittler capped an outstanding year by scoring five goals in a playoff game against Philadelphia and later scoring the winning goal in overtime for Team Canada against Czechoslovakia in the final of the inaugural Canada Cup series in September of 1976. In 1977–78, the Leafs, with new coach Roger Neilson replacing Red Kelly behind the bench, stunned the New York Islanders in the playoff quarterfinals, winning in overtime in game seven on a Lanny McDonald goal.

Late in the 1978–79 season, Harold Ballard fired coach Roger Neilson after a March 1 loss to Montreal, then found he had nobody to replace him. He rehired Neilson prior to the next game, then fired him a second time a few weeks later. He also fired Jim Gregory and dumped chief scout Bob Davidson. The Leafs were about to head into a steep decline. Ballard talked of hiring Scotty Bowman to run his team. Then it was Don Cherry. But he refused to pay Bowman what other clubs would and he waited too long to make Cherry an offer. Bowman went to Buffalo, taking Neilson with him. Cherry wound up in Colorado. Ballard decided to bring back Punch Imlach and promised him full control. It would prove to be a huge mistake.

Imlach's dictatorial ways paid big dividends for the Maple Leafs of the 1960s, but his tactics didn't work with the Leafs of the 1980s. When players raised his ire he got rid of them. He feuded with Darryl Sittler and fumed because Sittler had a no-trade clause in his contract. Maliciously, he traded Sittler's best friend Lanny McDonald, along with Joel Quenneville to Colorado for Pat Hickey and Wilf Paiement. He sent Pat Boutette to Hartford, Dave Hutchison to Chicago, Tiger Williams to Vancouver. The players disliked him to the extent that they tacked his photo to a dart board in a pub close to the Gardens. He brought back retired players in Larry Carriere and Carl Brewer and installed old pals as coaches, first Floyd Smith and then Joe Crozier. When Imlach suffered two heart attacks and required bypass surgery during the 1980–81 season, Ballard didn't fire him. He simply said his manager wouldn't be back because of ill health. When Imlach did return, his parking spot was gone.

When Imlach was pushed aside, Ballard took over. He appointed Gerry McNamara as general manager. It was another unpopular move, but McNamara remained on the job through the 1987–88 season. Thirty-year-old Gord Stellick (who had begun working for the Leafs while still in high school) and loyal Floyd Smith followed McNamara in the general manager's chair, while Leaf coaches in the 1980s included Joe Crozier, Mike Nykoluk, Dan Maloney, John Brophy, Doug Carpenter and George Armstrong.

It was the most dismal decade in Leaf history. It is perhaps symbolic that team founder Conn Smythe had passed away at age 85 on November 18, 1980. Smythe had led his Leafs to seven Stanley Cup championships during his tenure as manager and had seen them win 11 in his lifetime.

Darryl Sittler had resigned as Leaf captain under Imlach but was persuaded by Ballard to resume that role when Punch's future became uncertain because of his heart prob-

lems. But Sittler was grossly underpaid compared to other stars in the league. When he requested a raise, Ballard told him to think about joining another team. During the 1981–82 season, Sittler agreed to join the Philadelphia Flyers, at a handsome increase in pay. He had set club records for goals (389), assists (527) and points (916) during his career in Toronto.

Though the club missed the playoffs four times in eight years during the mid-1980s, Leaf fans at least could witness some impressive individual efforts. Rick Vaive became the first Leaf player to score 50 or more goals in a season with 54 in 1981–82, and topped 50 again each of the next two years. Later in the decade Gary Leeman totaled 51 goals.

In November 1986, King Clancy died after a gall bladder operation. The death of his great friend left Harold Ballard devastated despite the consoling words of Yolanda, the lady in his life. In the later years of his own life, the saga of Harold and Yolanda would play out like a soap opera in the Toronto media. In April 1990, Ballard passed away at age 86, leaving a once-great hockey franchise in tatters.

Donald Giffin, Steve Stavro and Donald Crump stepped in as executors of the Ballard estate to sort out the mess both on and off the ice, which included a debt of $60 million. Floyd Smith was retained as general manager and Doug Carpenter as the coach. He soon gave way to Tom Watt. Smith made a major trade blunder when he acquired Tom Kurvers, a mediocre defenseman, from New Jersey in return for the Leafs' top draft choice the following year. If Quebec hadn't nosedived that year to sink lower than the Leafs, and Smith had retained his pick, Toronto would have been in a position to draft Eric Lindros.

On June 4, 1991 Cliff Fletcher was hired as president, chief operating officer and general manager of the Leafs. Fletcher was signed to a five-year, $4 million contract. He immediately reshaped the front office, named popular Wendel Clark as captain and masterminded a number of shrewd deals to improve the questionable product on the ice. On January 2, 1992 he hit the jackpot by sweet-talking his Calgary counterpart, Doug Risebrough, into giving up Doug Gilmour, Jamie Macoun, Ric Nattress, Kent Manderville and Rick Wamsley in return for Gary Leeman, Michel Petit, Alexander Godynyuk, Craig Berube and Jeff Reese. Gilmour, always a prolific scorer, was the plum in the pudding. He swiftly became a superstar in Toronto.

Fletcher's next major move was to sign Pat Burns as coach, replacing Tom Watt. Burns had resigned from the Montreal Canadiens in May 1992. Within hours he was the Maple Leaf mentor. In his first season Burns guided his Leafs to third place in their division and to 99 points in the standings. Gilmour and Burns orchestrated a stunning seven-game upset of Detroit in the first round of the 1993 playoffs and a seven-game victory over St. Louis in round two. Another seven game matchup ended with the Los Angeles Kings terminating the most exciting hockey season in Toronto in recent memory. Hockey—top quality hockey—was back at Maple Leaf Gardens.

In the playoffs of 1994, the Leafs eliminated Chicago in six and San Jose in seven. But a five-game playoff loss to Vancouver ended their season. Undaunted, Fletcher kept making moves. At the annual draft sessions in Hartford, Fletcher traded Wendel Clark, Sylvain Lefebvre and Landon Wilson to Quebec for Mats Sundin, Garth Butcher and Todd Warriner.

Ordered by owner Steve Stavro to trim the payroll, on June 22, 1996 Fletcher traded Mike Gartner to Phoenix

(Gartner claimed he had a verbal no-trade agreement with the g.m.) and Dave Gagner to Calgary. One of the few highlights of the 1996–97 season was a goaltender bout between mild-mannered Felix Potvin and mercurial Ron Hextall. When Hextall rumbled down the ice seeking battle, Potvin gave him a solid licking. A major late-season deal saw Doug Gilmour traded to New Jersey, along with Dave Ellett, in return for Steve Sullivan, Jason Smith and Alyn McCauley, a junior star. At the trade deadline, Fletcher sent Larry Murphy to Detroit and Kirk Muller to the Panthers.

Despite the many moves in an attempt to salvage the season, Toronto finished in last place in the Central Division and missed the playoffs. The next move would involve Fletcher himself. He was dismissed as CEO, president and g.m. on May 24, 1997. Meanwhile, as things were coming apart on the ice, the Toronto team was enduring allegations that would soon see two former Gardens' workers charged with indecent assault and gross indecency for alleged assaults on teenaged boys during the 1970s and 1980s.

In a surprise move six days after Fletcher's departure, Hall of Fame goaltender Ken Dryden, 49, accepted the job as president of the Toronto Maple Leafs. Though he had no managerial experience, Dryden promised a better team on the ice and better hot dogs at the concession stands. "I'm here because it feels right to be here," Dryden said. On August 20, 1997 Dryden named himself to the position of general manager and named Anders Hedberg, Mike Smith, and Bill Watters to his management team. Mike Murphy was retained as coach but was presented with perhaps an even less talented roster than the team that had missed the playoffs in Fletcher's final season. With only Mats Sundin proving capable offensively, the Leafs struggled to score goals throughout the 1997–98 season and missed the playoffs for the second year in a row. Club president and general manager Ken Dryden fired Mike Murphy on June 23, 1998 and replaced him with Pat Quinn three days later.

Toronto Maple Leafs Year-by-Year Record

Season	GP	W	L	T	GF	GA	Pts	Finish		Playoff Results
1917	18	22	13	9	108	109	26	2nd and 1st***		Won Stanley Cup
1918–19	18	5	13	0	64	92	10	3rd and 3rd***		Out of Playoffs
1919–20**	24	12	12	0	119	106	24	3rd and 2nd***		Out of Playoffs
1920–21	24	15	9	0	105	100	30	2nd and 1st***		Lost NHL Final
1921–22	24	13	10	1	98	97	27	2nd		Won Stanley Cup
1922–23	24	13	10	1	82	88	27	3rd		Out of Playoffs
1923–24	24	10	14	0	59	85	20	3rd		Out of Playoffs
1924–25	30	19	11	0	90	84	38	2nd		Lost NHL Semifinal
1925–26	36	12	21	3	92	114	27	6th		Out of Playoffs
1926–27*	44	15	24	5	79	94	35	5th	Cdn. Div.	Out of Playoffs
1927–28	44	18	18	8	89	88	44	4th	Cdn. Div.	Out of Playoffs
1928–29	44	21	18	5	85	69	47	3rd	Cdn. Div.	Lost Semifinal
1929–30	44	17	21	6	116	124	40	4th	Cdn. Div.	Out of Playoffs
1930–31	44	22	13	9	118	99	53	2nd	Cdn. Div.	Lost Quarterfinal
1931–32	48	23	18	7	155	127	53	2nd	Cdn. Div.	Won Stanley Cup
1932–33	48	24	18	6	119	111	54	1st	Cdn. Div.	Lost Final
1933–34	48	26	13	9	174	119	61	1st	Cdn. Div.	Lost Semifinal
1934–35	48	30	14	4	157	111	64	1st	Cdn. Div.	Lost Final
1935–36	48	23	19	6	126	106	52	2nd	Cdn. Div.	Lost Final
1936–37	48	22	21	5	119	115	49	3rd	Cdn. Div	Lost Quarterfinal
1937–38	48	24	15	9	151	127	57	1st	Cdn. Div.	Lost Final
1938–39	48	19	20	9	114	107	47	3rd		Lost Final
1939–40	48	25	17	6	134	110	56	3rd		Lost Final
1940–41	48	28	14	6	145	99	62	2nd		Lost Semifinal
1941–42	48	27	18	3	158	136	57	2nd		Won Stanley Cup
1942–43	50	22	19	9	198	159	53	3rd		Lost Semifinal
1943–44	50	23	23	4	214	174	50	3rd		Lost Semifinal
1944–45	50	24	22	4	183	161	52	3rd		Won Stanley Cup
1945–46	50	19	24	7	174	185	45	5th		Out of Playoffs
1946–47	60	31	19	10	209	172	72	2nd		Won Stanley Cup
1947–48	60	32	15	13	182	143	77	1st		Won Stanley Cup
1948–49	60	22	25	13	147	161	57	4th		Won Stanley Cup
1949–50	70	31	27	12	176	173	74	3rd		Lost Semifinal
1950–51	70	41	16	13	212	138	95	2nd		Won Stanley Cup
1951–52	70	29	25	16	168	157	74	3rd		Lost Semifinal
1952	53	70	27	30	13	156	167	67	5th	Out of Playoffs

Toronto Maple Leafs Year-by-Year Record continued

Season	GP	W	L	T	GF	GA	Pts	Finish		Playoff Results
1953–54	70	32	24	14	152	131	78	3rd		Lost Semifinal
1954–55	70	24	24	22	147	135	70	3rd		Lost Semifinal
1955–56	70	24	33	13	153	181	61	4th		Lost Semifinal
1956–57	70	21	34	15	174	192	57	5th		Out of Playoffs
1957–58	70	21	38	11	192	226	53	6th		Out of Playoffs
1958–59	70	27	32	11	189	201	65	4th		Lost Final
1959–60	70	35	26	9	199	195	79	2nd		Lost Final
1960–61	70	39	19	12	234	176	90	2nd		Lost Semifinal
1961–62	70	37	22	11	232	180	85	2nd		Won Stanley Cup
1962–63	70	35	23	12	221	180	82	1st		Won Stanley Cup
1963–64	70	33	25	12	192	172	78	3rd		Won Stanley Cup
1964–65	70	30	26	14	204	173	74	4th		Lost Semifinal
1965–66	70	34	25	11	208	187	79	3rd		Lost Semifinal
1966–67	70	32	27	11	204	211	75	3rd		Won Stanley Cup
1967–68	74	33	31	10	209	176	76	5th	East Div.	Out of Playoffs
1968–69	76	35	26	15	234	217	85	4th	East Div.	Lost Quarterfinal
1969–70	76	29	34	13	222	242	71	6th	East Div.	Out of Playoffs
1970–71	78	37	33	8	248	211	82	4th	East Div.	Lost Quarterfinal
1971–72	78	33	31	14	209	208	80	4th	East Div.	Lost Quarterfinal
1972–73	78	27	41	10	247	279	64	6th	East Div.	Out of Playoffs
1973–74	78	35	27	16	274	230	86	4th	East Div.	Lost Quarterfinal
1974–75	80	31	33	16	280	309	78	3rd	Adams Div.	Lost Quarterfinal
1975–76	80	34	31	15	294	276	83	3rd	Adams Div.	Lost Quarterfinal
1976–77	80	33	32	15	301	285	81	3rd	Adams Div.	Lost Quarterfinal
1977–78	80	41	29	10	271	237	92	3rd	Adams Div.	Lost Semifinal
1978–79	80	34	33	13	267	252	81	3rd	Adams Div.	Lost Quarterfinal
1979–80	80	35	40	5	304	327	75	4th	Adams Div.	Lost Prelim. Round
1980–81	80	28	37	15	322	367	71	5th	Adams Div.	Lost Prelim. Round
1981–82	80	20	44	16	298	380	56	5th	Norris Div.	Out of Playoffs
1982–83	80	28	40	12	293	330	68	3rd	Norris Div.	Lost Div. Semifinal
1983–84	80	26	45	9	303	387	61	5th	Norris Div.	Out of Playoffs
1984–85	80	20	52	8	253	358	48	5th	Norris Div.	Out of Playoffs
1985–86	80	25	48	7	311	386	57	4th	Norris Div.	Lost Div. Final
1986–87	80	32	42	6	286	319	70	4th	Norris Div.	Lost Div. Final
1987–88	80	21	49	10	273	345	52	4th	Norris Div.	Lost Div. Semifinal
1988–89	80	28	46	6	259	342	62	5th	Norris Div.	Out of Playoffs
1989–90	80	38	38	4	337	358	80	3rd	Norris Div.	Lost Div. Semifinal
1990–91	80	23	46	11	241	318	57	5th	Norris Div.	Out of Playoffs
1991–92	80	30	43	7	234	294	67	5th	Norris Div.	Out of Playoffs
1992–93	84	44	29	11	288	241	99	3rd	Norris Div.	Lost Conf. Final
1993–94	84	43	29	12	280	243	98	2nd	Central Div.	Lost Conf. Final
1994–95	48	21	19	8	135	146	50	4th	Central Div.	Lost Conf. Quarterfinal
1995–96	82	34	36	12	247	252	80	3rd	Central Div.	Lost Conf. Quarterfinal
1996–97	82	30	44	8	230	273	68	6th	Central Div.	Out of Playoffs
1997–98	82	30	43	9	194	237	69	6th	Central Div.	Out of Playoffs

  * Name changed from St. Patricks to Maple Leafs.
  ** Name changed from Arenas to St. Patricks.
  *** Season played in two halves with no combined standing at end.

VANCOUVER CANUCKS

Brian McFarlane

THE VANCOUVER CANUCKS played their first National Hockey League game on October 9, 1970. Even though the Canucks lost the match to the Los Angeles Kings by a score of 3 to 1, Vancouver fans went home happy. They were delighted to finally see NHL hockey played in British Columbia.

While professional hockey was not new to Vancouver, only fans who'd been around in the 1920s could tell younger fans about the big-league excitement of it. Only they could remember the thrill of watching heroes like Fred "Cyclone" Taylor, Mickey MacKay and goaltender Hugh Lehman as they brought the Stanley Cup to Vancouver. Only they could produce fading newspaper clippings and point with pride to a photo of the 1915 champions posing in their uniforms with the big V on front, their skates digging into the mud and slush outside the arena. In the background an arena worker looks on, unaware that his image is being captured for eternity, a blue collar type in close proximity to the hockey superstars of the day.

The Vancouver Millionaires had played some glorious hockey in the old Pacific Coast Hockey Association, a creation of brothers Frank and Lester Patrick, before it disbanded in the mid-1920s. The Western Canada Hockey League soon followed, changed its name to the Western Hockey League, and before long, with the Patricks acting as negotiators, all the league's top players were sold en masse, swallowed up by the wealthy NHL club owners in the east.

The Millionaires had won Vancouver's one and only Stanley Cup before the NHL was born, in that wartime season of 1915. That year Vancouver, with Frank Patrick as manager, coach and player, had rolled to the Pacific Coast league title with 13 wins and four defeats in the 18-game schedule. Vancouver's Mickey MacKay was the league's individual scoring leader with 34 goals in 17 games. Cyclone Taylor scored 23 goals in 16 games and Frank Nighbor, imported from the Ottawa Valley where he was known as "the Pembroke Peach," finished third in league scoring with 22 goals in 17 games.

Vancouver faced Ottawa, the NHA champions, for the Stanley Cup in the first Cup series ever played west of Winnipeg. The best-of-five series was played at the Denman Street Arena and 7,000 fans turned out for the first game, won by the Millionaires by a 6–2 score. Cyclone Taylor led the way with a pair of goals. Taylor scored three times in the second game, an 8–3 rout for the mighty Millionaires. Ottawa successfully tied up Taylor in game three but that allowed another brilliant scorer to break loose—Barney Stanley. Stanley scored four goals in a 12–3 trouncing of the visitors. Mickey MacKay and Frank Nighbor almost matched Stanley's output, each scoring three goals. The Stanley Cup traveled to the coast for the first time and hockey experts predicted the talented Millionaires would hold onto it for a few more years.

But the Millionaires' reign was short-lived. The following year, Portland, with 13 wins, shot to the top of the PCHA standings, while Vancouver, with only nine wins, slipped into a second place tie with Seattle. During the 1917–18 season, Cyclone Taylor, who had gained fame several years earlier for scoring a goal for Renfrew while skating backwards, duplicated his feat in a game against Seattle. He scored the winner in overtime with his back to the Seattle netminder. Vancouver journeyed east to meet Toronto for the Stanley Cup that season and tied the best of five series with a decisive 8–1 victory in game four. But the visitors wilted in game five and lost by a 2–1 count. It was a disappointing finish for the Millionaires who anticipated winning a second Stanley Cup title.

In the spring of 1921, Vancouver hosted Ottawa in a memorable Stanley Cup series, one that lasted five games and drew over 50,000 fans. Alf Skinner and Jack Adams were Vancouver's top scorers that season while Mickey MacKay was still an idol with the fans. It was Adams who created a bit of history when he scored against his own goalie during a regular season game—and the official scorer credited him with a goal. It had never happened before and it hasn't happened since. Ottawa won the fifth and deciding game of the 1921 series by a 2–1 score, with Ottawa's two roughhouse players, Eddie Gerard and Sprague Cleghorn, picking up 10 penalties between them. Cleghorn's appearance was a bit of a mystery for he had played most of the season, including the eastern playoffs, with Toronto.

In the spring of 1922, the Millionaires again traveled to Toronto where they met the Toronto St. Pats for the Stanley Cup. Jack Adams scored six goals in five games but his output wasn't enough as the St. Pats won the series and the Stanley Cup three games to two. A year later, Vancouver

lost to Ottawa in a four-game Stanley Cup series played in Vancouver. In 1924, two western teams, Vancouver and Calgary, journeyed east to Montreal to play the Canadiens for the Stanley Cup. Vancouver had emerged as PCHA champions while Calgary captured the Western Canada Hockey League title. The Canadiens toppled Vancouver 3–2 and 2–1 in a two-game series and went on to beat Calgary by 6–1 and 3–0 to capture the Cup.

The 1923–24 season marked the final year for the PCHA. Vancouver joined the WCHL for the 1924–25 season and finished in fifth place, out of the playoffs. For the 1925–26 season, the WCHL became the Western Hockey League, dropping Canada from its name after the addition of U.S.-based franchise in Portland, Oregon. Vancouver's performance in the new circuit was dismal—a last-place finish.

During the season, NHL president Frank Calder scoffed at reports that players in the his league were making huge salaries and one Toronto reporter supported him, stating that a top NHL wage would be around $3,000. Cyclone Taylor had made as much and more while playing for Renfrew 15 years earlier. Still, after Montreal won the Stanley Cup in 1926, Frank Patrick was convinced that western clubs couldn't compete financially with teams in the east. Therefore, he arranged for the sale of all the pros from the WHL to NHL clubs. (Saskatoon was the one organization that made its own deal without Patrick's help.)

Vancouver fans sighed, knowing they'd probably have to settle for minor-league hockey for the next little while. And they did—for a long while—until 1970.

In 1965, when the NHL announced plans to expand into six new hockey markets, Vancouver representatives were front and center seeking a franchise to represent western Canada. Fred Hume, former mayor of the city and owner of the minor-league Vancouver Canucks, announced that he would apply for a franchise. Mayor William Rathie announced that the city, with financial help from the province, would build a $12 million arena and support Hume's bid. But Rathie had his knuckles rapped when Premier Bennett said the province would come up with only a third, not half of the finances needed, and only if the federal government would also throw in a third. In Ottawa, Northern Affairs minister Arthur Laing said: "Forget it, boys. We're not throwing in anything."

Initially, Cyrus McLean, chairman of the board of B.C. Telephone, and the legendary broadcaster Foster Hewitt were named as the prospective owners of the Vancouver entry in the NHL. McLean had purchased the minor-league Canucks from Fred Hume, who was then in failing health. But the McLean–Hewitt presentation to the league governors at a 1966 meeting in New York was sloppily prepared. It fell short, was in fact scoffed at, and they were not granted a franchise. One reason for the failed bid may have stemmed from Toronto Maple Leafs owner Stafford Smythe's distaste for Vancouver after the city failed to approve a Smythe plan to build an arena on city-owned land a few months earlier. When Smythe's proposal to build a 20,000-seat arena on a $2.5 million parcel of prime land—for a token sum of $1—was turned down by a referendum, Smythe left the city in a huff, describing it as "a bush league town." He vowed to keep it from getting an NHL franchise "in my lifetime." Another reason for denial may be attributed to Chicago Black Hawks' influential owner, James D. Norris. It was said Norris would have preferred to see some of his personal friends involved in the Vancouver bid—men like Frank McMahon, Max Bell and Red Dutton, all pow-

erful figures in sports and business in western Canada.

Meanwhile, Captain Harry Terry, president of the Pacific National Exhibition, had decided that, come hell or high water, a new rink should adorn the Vancouver Exhibition grounds. And Terry had an ace up his sleeve. He knew that the federal government would come through with low-interest loans and grants for such an edifice because of new legislation promising funding of winter and summer fairs, etc. Fred Hume liked Terry's enthusiasm—and the site that Terry proposed. Hume offered to build a $6.5 million, 22,000 seat arena at the PNE. By then, Terry had extracted promises from three levels of government to provide financing and politely turned down Hume's offer. It was agreed that the federal and provincial governments would put up $2 million each, the city would be liable for another $1 million. Through private funding the city would also commit to another $1 million.

A contest provided a name—Pacific Coliseum—and construction got under way. The arena was dedicated on January 8, 1968 with the Ice Capades as entertainment. A month later, the first hockey game was played between the Montreal Oldtimers and the Western All-Stars. It attracted 16,511 fans, at the time the largest crowd to see a game in Canada. Obviously, Vancouver had a thirst for hockey. Now it hungered for an NHL team.

By the time of the follow-up NHL expansion, which began with the 1970–71 season, the Vancouver ownership picture had changed. Foster Hewitt was no longer involved and Cyrus McLean was thrust into a secondary role among the new majority owners, the Medicor Group of Minneapolis, with Tom Scallen as president. The new ownership group had bought the minor-league Western Hockey League Vancouver Canucks team and successfully negotiated with the NHL for an expansion franchise. At a cost of $6 million apiece, both the new Vancouver Canucks hockey team and the other successful applicant, the Buffalo Sabres, would be entitled to pick 20 players in an expansion draft. In an effort to maintain the league's competitive balance, both Buffalo and Vancouver were placed in the East Division despite the geographical contradiction. In October, the start of the 1970–71 season, the newly formed Canucks would begin to play in the eyeball-popping Pacific Coliseum. A new era for hockey in Vancouver had begun.

The first general manager of the Canucks was Norman "Bud" Poile, the former g.m. of the Philadelphia Flyers, a team that had entered the league in 1967 in the original doubling of the NHL. There was grumbling in some quarters when Poile was selected over Joe Crozier who had run the minor-league Canucks with much success. Poile in turn selected Hal Laycoe, formerly of the Los Angeles Kings, to coach the Canucks in their inaugural season.

In the Expansion Draft, the 12 established teams were allowed to protect 15 skaters and two goaltenders. Each time an existing team lost a player they were allowed to protect another. Thus, the two new expansion teams would be able to acquire two third-ranked goalies each and start with the chance of selecting at least the 16th and 18th best position players of each existing team in the draft. Considering that six of the existing teams were former expansion teams themselves with only three years in the league, the pickings were indeed slim.

Under those draft rules, the Canucks were relatively pleased with their new talent. Their first choice was Gary Doak, a former Boston Bruin who was thought of as a young defenseman with promise. Also chosen was Orland

Kurtenbach, a tough player and future team leader, as well as Rosaire Paiement and Ray Cullen, two forwards with proven scoring ability. Wayne Maki, who scored only seven goals in 66 games with Chicago and St. Louis, contributed a career-high 25 goals (and 63 points) in that first season—a pleasant surprise. From their minor-league team, which had captured two straight Western Hockey League playoff titles, the Canucks plucked goaltender George Gardner, as well as veterans Marc Reaume and Len Lunde.

Following that June 1970 expansion draft, general manager Poile, in what could be described as gallows humor, suggested to his coach Laycoe: "There you are Hal, there's $6 million worth of talent, don't foul it up." The 18 position players the Canucks drafted had scored a very unimpressive total of 37 goals in the 1969–70 NHL season. But the immediate future of the Canucks—and the Sabres—depended largely on the amateur draft of junior players. After a "spin of the wheel" at the June 9 draft meetings in Montreal, the Canucks picked second (after losing Gilbert Perreault to Punch Imlach's Buffalo Sabres). Poile selected talented defenseman Dale Tallon as the Canucks' first choice and another defender, Jim Hargreaves, with his second. From that nucleus, the Canucks filled out their initial roster. Many Canuck fans still refer to June 9, 1970 as Black Tuesday because of the loss of Perreault.

There was much enthusiasm for the fledgling franchise both on and off the ice. In preseason games the Canucks displayed an aggressive style of play and sold 12,000 season tickets prior to the opener. They counted on playing their home games to better than 90% of seating capacity at the 15,553-seat Pacific Coliseum. The Canucks were happy to announce that all tickets for the home opener were sold and the fans were anticipating a first-night victory to successfully kick-start the new franchise.

For that historic Friday night opener against the Kings, there were so many dignitaries present at rinkside that someone observed, "there was hardly an unstuffed shirt to be found." Although the Canucks lost to the Kings by 3–2 there were some notable 'firsts.' The first prolonged ovation was for 87-year-old Cyclone Taylor, who had helped Vancouver capture its only Stanley Cup in 1915. The other major ovation was for the first Canucks goal, scored by unheralded defenseman Barry Wilkins at 2:14 of the third period against the Kings' Denis Dejordy. Another notable 'first' was the first misconduct in Canucks' history, handed out to defenseman Pat Quinn who years later would coach and manage the Canucks and take them to within one game of winning the Stanley Cup.

In another unusual event, it was discovered there were unsold seats for the opener. But this was no fault of the Vancouver fans. It seems the Vancouver ticket manager had relied on a computer system which had falsely indicated that all the available tickets were sold when, in fact, over a thousand were still available. The Canucks, anxious to have a first-rate operation, commenced a search for a new ticket manager. With the opening night loss behind them, the Canucks waited until Sunday, October 11 to achieve their first win by a score of 5–3 over Toronto. It was also the first sellout at the Pacific Coliseum.

Early in November, the Canucks recorded their first road victory, a 4–1 win over Buffalo. Canuck goalie Dunc Wilson stopped the team's first penalty shot when he foiled Sabre Paul Andrea. By mid-December, the Canucks had rolled to a 10–3–2 record and had established a club record with six straight home victories. But they were still a long way from contending for the Stanley Cup. The Canucks finished their first season out of the playoffs but achieved 56 points in a 78-game schedule. The Canucks finished below their expansion cousins the Buffalo Sabres by seven points but did manage to finish one point ahead of Detroit, an "Original Six" team, in the East Division standings.

The Canucks struggled through the next three seasons, finishing with 48, 53 and 59 points. Then, with a happy-go-lucky goaltender named Gary Smith in the net, obtained from Chicago with Jerry Korab in return for Dale Tallon, they soared to first place in the Smythe Division with 86 points in their fifth season of 1974–75. Hockey writer Tony Gallagher touted Smith for the Hart Trophy that season but voters in the east weren't listening. In the playoffs, the Canucks lost to a powerful Montreal club in the fifth game of the quarterfinals in overtime.

Tony Gallagher recalls a few ice follies in those early days of the franchise, which included two Medicor representatives, Tom Scallen, the head of Northwest Sports Enterprises, and Lyman Walters of Minneapolis, another principal in the corporation owning the team, getting themselves indicted on embezzlement charges. This was after they paid $2.85 million for the Western Hockey League Canucks and six weeks after being granted a berth in the NHL. The theft of club funds was calculated at $3 million. Northwest was a subsidiary of Medicor of Minnesota, a company once recommended as a ideal hockey partner to the Canucks by NHL president Clarence Campbell. Walters, incidentally, had angered hockey fans everywhere by suggesting the name Canucks was a poor one and might have to be changed. On the day the theft story broke, Bud Poile announced to the press: "Gentlemen, I have some bad news and some good news The good news is that our owners have been charged with swiping $3 million. The bad news is we have to play the Boston Bruins tonight."

Problems between coaches and players drew attention from time to time. When Vic Stasiuk replaced Hal Laycoe as coach in 1972, he called a practice at 7:30 one morning. Tiny Bobby Lalonde refused to a finish a drill to Stasiuk's liking and there was a near-revolt by the players. Bill McCreary soon replaced Stasiuk, then Phil Maloney replaced McCreary and there was harmony for a time. Maloney took on the additional role of general manager in 1974, fired himself as coach and brought in Orland Kurtenbach to run the bench. Jake Milford took over as general manager in 1977 and was succeeded by Harry Neale in 1982. Jack Gordon managed the club from 1985 to 1987 when Pat Quinn came aboard. Throughout the early years, the scouting was poor and, as a result, the drafting of players was questionable.

When the Medicor people stepped away from hockey and the club was put up for sale, the Griffiths family moved forward to rescue the organization. Frank Griffiths' wife Emily is often credited with making the final decision to purchase the club. Griffiths had been highly successful in the broadcast business and he genuinely wanted to put something back into the community. The new ownership provided a degree of stability and things began to look up on the ice. Harry Neale was hired as coach in 1978 and by 1982 the Canucks found themselves sailing into the Stanley Cup finals. Neale, suspended for 10 games after challenging some fans in Quebec, wasn't around for the fun. His assistant, Roger Neilson, took the spotlight behind the bench, and captured headlines after he waved a white towel at referee Bob Myers in mock surrender during a playoff game in

Chicago. Tiger Williams and the other Canucks followed suit, hoisting towels on their hockey sticks. The club was fined $10,000 for ridiculing the game officials. When the team returned home for the next game, almost every Vancouver fan waved a white towel enthusiastically. The Canucks disposed of the Black Hawks and advanced to the finals against the Islanders, only to lose in four straight games. One day after their defeat, 100,000 Vancouverites honored their underdog heroes with a civic parade. Thomas Gradin, Stan Smyl, and Ivan Boldirev were the team's top scorers, but the star of the surprising playoff run had been goaltender Richard Brodeur.

The success of 1982 did not carry over into subsequent seasons as the team struggled annually to reach the playoffs and failed to advance beyond the first round when it did. Highlights in these years included Patrick Sundstrom's seven-point night on February 29, 1984 when he set a new club record with six assists in one game and joined Billy Taylor and Bobby Orr as just the third player in history to have six assists in a road game. That season also saw Tony Tanti set a club record with 45 goals. On February 28, 1986 Richard Brodeur became the first Canuck netminder to register 100 career wins in a 3–1 victory over Philadelphia.

On January 9, 1987 the Canucks announced that Pat Quinn had accepted the position as general manager and president in Vancouver. Quinn was under contract as coach of the Los Angeles Kings at the time, and league president John Ziegler issued a fine of $310,000 (later reduced to $10,000 by the B.C. Supreme Court) for tampering. Quinn was not permitted to assume his dual roles until May 1, and soon after hired Bob McCammon as his coach and Brian Burke as director of hockey operations. After collecting just 59 points during the 80-game 1987–88 season, the Canucks held the second selection overall in the 1988 Entry Draft and Quinn used the pick to obtain Trevor Linden.

Linden entered the NHL as the league's youngest player in 1988–89 after having helped the Medicine Hat Tigers win back-to-back Memorial Cup championships. He set a Canucks rookie record with 30 goals and was named Vancouver's most valuable player while finishing as the runner up behind Brian Leetch in voting for the Calder Trophy as rookie of the year. Kirk McLean established himself as one of the top goalies in the NHL, posting a record of 20–17–3 with a 3.08 goals-against average to finish third in voting for the Vezina Trophy. The Canucks won 33 games and set a club record with just 253 goals allowed. In the playoffs, Vancouver was beaten in the first round but they were the only team to take the eventual Stanley Cup champion Calgary Flames to the seven-game limit, losing 4–3 in overtime in the final game.

On July 1, 1989 the Canucks signed former Soviet star Igor Larionov. The move came just a few days after Vancouver had selected Pavel Bure in the fourth round of the 1989 Entry Draft. Bure's draft eligibility was questioned, but was resolved in the Canucks' favor several months later. He joined the Canucks for the 1991–92 season, scoring 34 goals to break new team captain Trevor Linden's club rookie record. "the Russian Rocket" also became the first Canucks player to win a major postseason award when he was named the winner of the Calder Trophy. Pat Quinn, who had added coaching duties to his portfolio in January of 1991, joined Bure on the winners' podium as he captured the Jack Adams Award as coach of the year. Quinn had guided the Canucks to first place in the Smythe Division for the first time since 1974–75. with a record of 42-26-12.

It was another first place finish in 1992–93, as two club records set the preceding season were shattered when the Canucks registered 47 wins and 101 points. Pavel Bure became the first Canuck to be voted to play in the All-Star Game and finished the season with 60 goals and 110 points—both club records. On April 2, 1993 team owner Frank Griffiths was inducted into the Hockey Hall of Fame. A year later he passed away after a lengthy illness. Griffiths had purchased the financially troubled team in 1974.

On April 13, 1994 Pavel Bure reached 60 goals for the second straight season. Later in the month, Bure scored at 2:20 of the second overtime period to give Vancouver a 4–3 win over Calgary. It was the club's third straight overtime win in a come-from-behind seven-game playoff victory. In May, after eliminating the Dallas Stars, goalie Kirk McLean blanked the Leafs in back-to-back playoff games en route to a five-game victory in the Campbell Conference finals. The Canucks advanced to the Stanley Cup finals and played in June for the first time in their history.

Greg Adams' goal at 19:26 of overtime gave the Canucks a 3–2 win over the Rangers in game one of the finals before New York reeled off three straight wins. Heading back to Madison Square Garden for game five, the Canucks stayed alive with a 6–3 victory, then forced a seventh game with a 4–1 win at home. Back in New York, the Rangers sweated out a 3–2 victory for their first Cup triumph in 54 years. Pavel Bure's 16 goals led all playoff performers, while Trevor Linden's 12 tied Mark Messier for second best.

In March 1995, Seattle businessman John E. McCaw purchased a majority interest in the Canucks and also gained control of the new $163 million General Motors Place arena and the NBA's Vancouver Grizzlies. The Canucks eliminated St. Louis in the first playoff round but new coach Rick Ley's team was swept aside by Chicago in four games in the second round.

On July 8, 1995 the Canucks reunited former junior hockey teammates Alexander Mogilny and Pavel Bure when they acquired Mogilny from Buffalo. Later, Trevor Linden was signed to a new multi-year contract. On October 9, 1995 the Canucks played their first regular-season game at General Motors Place and lost 5–3 to Detroit. Mike Ridley scored the first regular-season goal in the new ice palace. The 1995–96 season saw Mogilny join Bure as the only 50-goal scorers in franchise history as he collected 55 goals and had 107 points. On March 23, 1996 the Canucks passed an attendance record with 28 sellouts at GM Place and an average attendance of 17,795 fans. On March 28, 1996 Pat Quinn took over the coaching reigns again following the dismissal of Rick Ley. After finishing 25 points behind first-place Colorado in the Pacific Division, the Canucks were eliminated by the Avalanche in six games in the first playoff round.

After the season, Quinn hired former Canadian national team coach Tom Renney to coach the Canucks. The team had difficulty adjusting to Renney's weak-side lock system in 1996–97. Some complained about his leadership, and the Canucks finished out of the playoffs. In June 1997, the club introduced new team colors and a logo of a killer whale breaking through ice shaped in the letter C. Mark Messier was signed as an expensive free agent (three years at more than $20 million) and Trevor Linden chose to relinquish the captaincy to the newly acquired team leader. The 1997–98 season, however, proved to be a disaster. Pat Quinn was fired after a poor start and Renney was released a short time later. Mike Keenan was brought in to coach and by the end

of January, was given the authority to make personnel changes. Keenan had feuded with Linden since his arrival and traded the popular player to the New York Islanders in February. Though Keenan's shakeups improved the team marginally, Vancouver still missed the playoffs for the second year in a row. In June of 1998, Brian Burke returned to the Canucks as the club's new general manager.

Throughout their history, the Canucks have enjoyed moderate, if not spectacular success, reaching the Stanley Cup finals in 1982 and in 1994. Hope still runs high in Vancouver for more playoff success with stars such as Mattias Ohlund, Mark Messier, Pavel Bure, and Alexander Mogilny. Canuck fans await Vancouver's first Stanley Cup victory since Cyclone Taylor and the Millionaires last won the coveted trophy back in 1915.

Vancouver Canucks Year-by-Year Record

Season	GP	W	L	T	GF	GA	Pts	Finish		Playoff Results
1970–71	78	24	46	8	229	296	56	6th	East Div.	Out of Playoffs
1971–72	78	20	50	8	203	297	48	7th	East Div.	Out of Playoffs
1972–73	78	22	47	9	233	339	53	7th	East Div.	Out of Playoffs
1973–74	78	24	43	11	224	296	59	7th	East Div.	Out of Playoffs
1974–75	80	38	32	10	271	254	86	1st	Smythe Div.	Lost Quarterfinal
1975–76	80	33	32	15	271	272	81	2nd	Smythe Div.	Lost Prelim. Round
1976–77	80	25	42	13	235	294	63	4th	Smythe Div.	Out of Playoffs
1977–78	80	20	43	17	239	320	57	3rd	Smythe Div.	Out of Playoffs
1978–79	80	25	42	13	217	291	63	2nd	Smythe Div.	Lost Prelim. Round
1979–80	80	27	37	16	256	281	70	3rd	Smythe Div.	Lost Prelim. Round
1980–81	80	28	32	20	289	301	76	3rd	Smythe Div.	Lost Prelim. Round
1981–82	80	30	33	17	290	286	77	2nd	Smythe Div.	Lost Final
1982–83	80	30	35	15	303	309	75	3rd	Smythe Div.	Lost Div. Semifinal
1983–84	80	32	39	9	306	328	73	3rd	Smythe Div.	Lost Div. Semifinal
1984–85	80	25	46	9	284	401	59	5th	Smythe Div.	Out of Playoffs
1985–86	80	23	44	13	282	333	59	4th	Smythe Div.	Lost Div. Semifinal
1986–87	80	29	43	8	282	314	66	5th	Smythe Div.	Out of Playoffs
1987–88	80	25	46	9	272	320	59	5th	Smythe Div.	Out of Playoffs
1988–89	80	33	39	8	251	253	74	4th	Smythe Div.	Lost Div. Semifinal
1989–90	80	25	41	14	245	306	64	5th	Smythe Div.	Out of Playoffs
1990–91	80	28	43	9	243	315	65	4th	Smythe Div.	Lost Div. Semifinal
1991–92	80	42	26	12	285	250	96	1st	Smythe Div.	Lost Div. Final
1992–93	84	46	29	9	346	278	101	1st	Smythe Div.	Lost Div. Final
1993–94	84	41	40	3	279	276	85	2nd	Pacific Div.	Lost Final
1994–95	48	18	18	12	153	148	48	2nd	Pacific Div.	Lost Conf. Semifinal
1995–96	82	32	35	15	278	278	79	3rd	Pacific Div.	Lost Conf. Quarterfinal
1996–97	82	35	40	7	257	273	77	4th	Pacific Div.	Out of Playoffs
1997–98	82	25	43	14	224	273	64	7th	Pacific Div.	Out of Playoffs

WASHINGTON CAPITALS

Stan Fischler

THE DISTRICT OF COLUMBIA is renowned for its monuments. Many have housed and continue to honor great moments in politics, justice and history and the statesmen who made and attended them. Among them it has one to hockey, a distinctive edifice with a curved roof adorned with a series of spikes that set it apart. It is here that professional hockey was born in Washington, as conceived by an ice-making mogul from the Netherlands.

His main line of business was refrigeration, but Mike Uline also took a keen interest in sports, particularly the game played on ice—preferably his. Convinced that pro hockey had a future in the shadow of the White House, Uline constructed a state-of-the-art arena just before America's entry into World War II.

With all due immodesty, he named the rink Uline's Arena, christened his team the Washington Ulines and proceeded to enter his club in the American Hockey League as soon as he'd hired popular New York Rangers defenseman Ivan "Ching" Johnson as player-coach. When the armed forces of both Canada and the United States claimed most

of the able-bodied hockey players, Uline disbanded his AHL team for the duration. He later entered a team, the Washington Lions—whose sweaters displayed a distinctive "U" on the crest—in the Eastern Amateur League and they drew well enough for him to reenter the AHL.

For years thereafter, Washington remained a minor-league hockey outpost and training ground for the likes of Hall of Famer Ed Giacomin (who became a star with the New York Rangers), but major-league hockey never seemed possible in D.C. if only because Uline Arena lacked NHL seating capacity. Washington's entry into the big league would require a man with another vision.

When Abe Pollin announced in 1972 that he planned to bring an NHL team to America's national capital, the Washington sportsman—who had headed his own construction firm—was advised by a Las Vegas bookmaker that the odds were 600–1 against him. Undaunted, Pollin personally delivered his application to the NHL office in Montreal on the final day of acceptance and made his presentation at the Board of Governors meetings in May 1972. Aware that he was an underdog among 10 competitors for two expansion franchise openings, Pollin spent five days in a Montreal hotel, lobbying hockey's power brokers on Washington's behalf. His presentation was impressive enough to get him the franchise, on the condition that a suitable arena would be available by 1974–75.

Pollin already owned the NBA Baltimore Bullets and envisioned a new arena that would house both his major-league teams somewhere in the Capital District, but bickering and bureaucratic delays over who—or which city—would build the arena frustrated his plans. Finally he decided he would construct the rink with his own funds, on a site he would personally choose, and bypassed both Washington and Baltimore for a tract of former farmland in Landover, Maryland. There he opened blueprints for an $18-million arena to be known as the Capital Centre, complete with the British (and Canadian) spelling of "center."

The minimum target date for completion was thought to be two years. Instead, the arena was completed in 15 months from ground-breaking to opening. It seated 17,962 for hockey and boasted that every spectator was guaranteed a seat no further than 200 feet from center ice.

Furthermore, at a time when other NHL arenas were not even considering premium seating, Pollin arranged for 40 luxury sky suites to be clustered along the upper levels, with private elevators serving the area. Each suite included a reception area, powder room, wet bar, wall-to-wall carpeting, closed circuit and commercial television and a panoramic view of the arena's floor.

What the fans would see was not especially appetizing. Former American Hockey League star Jimmy Anderson was behind the bench and Hall of Famer Milt Schmidt was managing, but the Capitals were competing against the three-year-old World Hockey Association and the NHL expansion Kansas City Scouts for talent. The result was a patchwork conspicuously lacking in talent on both the attack and defense. Washington's leading scorer, Tommy Williams (22 goals, 36 assists), was a Boston Bruins discard, and the supporting cast, with the notable exception of heroic goalie Ron Low, had even fewer credentials. The team's major hope was an African-Canadian named Mike Marson who had been the top scorer with the Sudbury Wolves in the Ontario Hockey Association before the Caps picked him in the 1974 Entry Draft. Marson was only the second black to reach the NHL, the first having been Willie

O'Ree, who played for Boston in 1960–61 after a two-game trial in 1957–58. Marson finished as the Caps' third-leading scorer with 16 goals and 28 points. Precisely how Washingtonians would respond to hockey was underscored on opening night (October 9, 1974) when a crowd of 17,500 turned out to see the New York Rangers defeat the Caps 6–3. Sellouts were not the norm, but there were enough substantial gates to persuade Pollin he had made a good move—and this despite several records for futility set by the 1974–75 edition of his team. These include:

CATEGORY	CAPS' RECORD	DATE	VS.	OLD NHL RECORD	
Most losses in a season	67	3/20/75	MIN	1972–73 NYI	60
Most consecutive losses	17	3/23/75	ATL	1930–31 PHI Q	15
Most consecutive road losses	37	2/1/75	VAN	1973–74 CAL	24
Fewest points in a season (min. 70 game schedule)	21	3/23/75	ATL	1972–73 NYI	30
Most home defeats	33	3/20/75	MIN	1972–73 NYI	25
Most goals against	446	3/2/75	VAN	1972–73 NYI	347
Most power play GA	94	3/18/75	PHI	1970–71 VAN	81
Most shorthanded GA	18	3/20/75	MIN	1973–74 CAL	14
Fewest road victories	1			Held by many teams	2
Fewest victories in a season (min. 70 game schedule)	8			1953–54 CHI	12
				1972–73 NYI	12
Most road losses	39			1973–74 CAL	37

It would have been difficult for Pollin's puckchasers to do worse in their second season, but the improvement proved to be minuscule. The Capitals launched the season with Schmidt both managing and coaching. After 36 games, his record was three wins, five ties and 28 losses. Worse, there were enough complaints about his stewardship to inspire Pollin to make a wholesale change in the high command. Central Hockey League president Max McNab was imported as general manager, and McNab in turn hired Tom McVie to handle the skating rabble from behind the bench.

"I coached a dozen games before we won," McVie recalls, "but I'd always been gung ho for the next workout. 'Gentlemen,' I would say, 'I have these things planned for today. We'll do some two-on-ones, some three-on-ones...' And I saw the looks on them, like, 'This guy is crazy.' I went on and on with it and they just leaned on their sticks and listened. Finally I asked if anybody had anything to say.

"One of my defensemen, Bob Paradise, said, 'Why are we doing this when we know we're going to bleeping lose anyway?' I looked at him and said, 'Well, then, why don't we all go to Abe Pollin's office and tell him we are disbanding the team!'" Pollin didn't disband the team after the second year. (By way of comparison, the Scouts left Kansas City for Denver.) In 1975–76, the Capitals won 11, tied 10 and lost 59. An otherwise obscure forward named Nelson Pyatt led the team's scorers with 49 points. McVie, who won eight, tied five and lost 31, was retained to coach the following year.

McNab's regime was marked by a significant improvement. In 1976–77, the team's record leaped to a more reasonable 24–42–14 thanks to key acquisitions such as Guy Charron (who led the team in scoring with 82 points), Bryan Watson and Gerry Meehan. Unfortunately for McVie, the upward trend didn't continue. In 1977–78, the Caps' record dropped to 17–49–14.

"It was the low point in my career," McVie allowed. "It was my first NHL job and I gave my soul. I put the team ahead of my family and health. I took a day off once with my wife, and when I came back, Danny Belisle was in my coach's chair. They said, 'You're gone!' That taught me a lesson. Ever since then, I take my chair with me and never go on vacations."

With Belisle coaching in their fifth year of existence (1978–79), the Capitals registered their best record yet with 63 points (24–41–15)—but still missed the playoffs. Fleet little Dennis Maruk became an overnight sensation as he led the team in scoring with 90 points (31 goals, 59 assists); hard-shooting Tom Rowe also had 31 goals; Gary Inness played capably in goal.

Belisle's tenure was short-lived, however. The victim of a poor start (4–10–2) in 1979–80, he was yanked after 16 games in favor of a youthful Gary Green, 26 years old, who had coached the Peterborough, Ontario, Junior A team and Hershey of the AHL. Green was the youngest coach in NHL history. "I don't consider talent overall as the most important factor in winning," he said.

"What wins is belief in yourself, intensity, desire and discipline." He made good on his words and produced the best yet Capitals coaching record (23–30–11), but it was a case of too little, too late and a playoffs berth eluded the franchise for the sixth consecutive year in spite of starry efforts by Maruk, Mike Gartner and Ryan Walter that offered hope for the future.

Even with his new—albeit brief—major-league experience, Green could not shake the Capitals' playoffs jinx in 1980–81 either. The club finished with a 26–36–18 record, but his youth and enthusiasm notwithstanding, Green simply couldn't find the necessary mix. He lasted 13 games into the 1981–82 season, winning but a single game and losing a dozen before he got the hook. Assistant G.M. Roger Crozier handled one game (a tie) until Bryan Murray could be named the head coach. And Murray almost did the unthinkable—coaching a Washington team to a .500 mark—with a 25–28–13 record.

Washington was certainly capable of generating positive headlines. In June 1981, McNab, choosing third overall in the Entry Draft, selected New England hero Bob Carpenter as his first pick—the first American ever drafted in the NHL's first round. In a cover story, *Sports Illustrated* had dubbed him "the Can't Miss Kid," and Carpenter delivered: 32 goals and 35 assists for 67 points as a rookie in the 1981–82 season.

Still, the ongoing playoff drought finally compelled Pollin to make another change in his general staff. On August 30, 1982, McNab was dropped as general manager in favor of 33-year-old David Poile, who became the youngest G.M. in NHL history. David's father, Norman "Bud" Poile, had been an NHL star and later a top hockey executive, and David had done his front office basic training with Atlanta and Calgary before moving to Landover. But nothing in his past suggested he would make the blockbuster move that made Washington at long last a contender.

On September 10, 1982, shortly after training camp started, Poile sent defenseman Rick Green and forward Ryan Walter to Montreal for defensemen Rod Langway and Brian Engblom as well as forwards Doug Jarvis and Craig Laughlin. And few deals for any team at any time have ever produced a more dramatic impact. The former Canadiens infused the Capitals with a winning spirit that was translated into the club's first season above .500.

Washington finished third in the Patrick Division with a record of 39–25–16 before losing (three games to one) to the Stanley Cup champion New York Islanders in the playoffs. Langway won the Norris Trophy as the NHL's best defenseman and Scott Stevens made an instant impact as a rookie defenseman with nine goals and 16 assists for 25 points (and 195 penalty minutes) in 77 games. With Langway leading the way on the ice and in the dressing room, Washington improved to second place (48–27–5) in

1983–84. The captain again won the Norris Trophy, Doug Jarvis the Selke Trophy as the NHL's best defensive forward, the goaltending tandem of Al Jensen and Pat Riggin the Jennings Trophy for having the fewest goals against, and to top off Washington's biggest year yet for awards, Murray took the Jack Adams Award as coach of the year. Still, the defending champion Islanders once more eliminated them from the Stanley Cup run, four games to one.

Murray's effervescent coaching continued to keep the Capitals near the top of the Patrick Division. In 1984–85, they finished third overall with 101 points and featured two 50-goal scorers in Bobby Carpenter (53) and Mike Gartner (50). "It was a positive development," says Poile. "But the problem was that too much of our scoring was concentrated in those two people. We needed secondary threats to make things more complicated for defenses around the league." Poile's point was emphasized when the Islanders eliminated Washington three games to two in the divisional semifinals. If nothing else, it highlighted the Capitals postseason dilemma: The team was strong, but something was missing when the playoffs chips were down.

After winning 50 regular-season games for the first time in franchise history, Murray appeared to have a Cup-worthy team in the spring of 1986. Carpenter, Gartner, Dave Christian and Bengt Gustafsson paced the attack while Al Jensen provided grade-A goaltending. Heavy favorites to defeat New York in the playoffs, the Capitals were upset four games to two and by now had taken on the distinct image of playoffs chokers, a state of affairs that moved Poile to action.

Once again he executed an arresting deal. On New Year's Day 1987, he delivered Carpenter and a second-round draft choice to the Rangers for Kelly Miller, Mike Ridley and Bob Crawford. Carpenter was a bust on Broadway, lasting less than three months before being dealt again—this time to Los Angeles—while Ridley and Miller excelled in a dual capacity as scoring threats and penalty killers. Remarkably, defenseman Larry Murphy led Washington in points (81); Gartner's 41 goals were tops in that department.

Still nothing changed vis-a-vis playoffs. After a 38–32–10 season, the Caps encountered their traditional nemesis, the Islanders, in the divisional semifinals. The series wound down to an excruciatingly close seventh game at Capital Center. When the fans finally departed, it was six hours after the opening face-off and they had witnessed the most memorable game of the 1980s—a quadruple-overtime thriller in which the Isles ultimately prevailed 3–2.

Consider the final statistics after the six-plus periods that April 18th: 132 shots on goal, 75 by Washington. And it wasn't just the outrageous totals; it was the number of quality chances that Kelly Hrudey for the Isles and Bob Mason for the Caps turned away. The netminders matched each other save for save. A spectacular glove save that Hrudey wrapped around a Bobby Gould slapper was answered by point-blank stops that Mason made on Bob Bassen and Duane Sutter.

Mason lost his helmet in a goalmouth flurry in the second overtime—and still managed to thwart two close-in shots.

"Each guy had their own method of trying to relax during the intermissions," recalls Isles right winger Pat Flatley. "It was popular to lie on your back on the floor with your feet up on the locker stalls. Pat LaFontaine kept yelling, 'Who's gonna be the hero?'"

"Right before that shift, I remember [Isles equipment manager] Jimmy Pickard drenching me with a water bottle

to cool me off," adds LaFontaine. "I looked into the stands—some people looked stressed out, a few others were sleeping. I saw the time-of-day clock—it said 1:56 a.m. Right then, the organist started playing the Twilight Zone theme. I thought to myself, 'Is this really happening?'"

It was at 1:56 a.m. on Easter Sunday that LaFontaine ground out a blue line slapshot that put the Caps out of their misery. Washington had suffered another premature season's end, and the Islanders lost the next round to the Flyers, but the 1987 playoffs are still mainly remembered for the Easter Epic.

The pattern of playoff futility continued through the Bryan Murray regime in spite of heartening regular-season efforts. In 1987–88, a record of 38–33–9 took second place in the Patrick Division. The playoffs result? Lost in the second round to New Jersey, four games to three. In 1988–89, a 41–29–10 record finished first place in the Patrick Division. The playoffs result? A first round loss to the Flyers.

The 1989–90 campaign brought a breakthrough. After posting 18–24–4 in the first half of the season, Poile decided to take action and replaced head coach Bryan Murray with his brother, Terry. This time there was an improvement: Washington reached the third round of the playoffs before losing to Boston in four straight games.

Meanwhile the face of the Capitals was changing. In 1990–91, rookie Peter Bondra showed flashes of brilliance behind usual point producers Mike Ridley and Michal Pivonka. The blue line was solidified with rock-solid Kevin Hatcher and smooth-skating Calle Johansson. In 1994, the Caps acquired playmaker Joe Juneau from Boston for defenseman Al Iafrate. Rounding out the new look was goalie Jim Carey, who posted a stunning 18–6 record in his rookie year and 35–24–9 with nine shutouts the year after, good enough to capture the 1996 Vezina Trophy. The final step in the process of change saw the Capital Centre renamed the U.S. Air Arena.

Despite the many alterations, the Caps' legendary lack of luck in the playoffs continued. In 1994–95, Washington was ousted by the Pittsburgh Penguins, as usual in the first round; they experienced a case of déjà vu in 1995–96 when the Penguins were back and another four-overtime nail-biter ensued—and once again the Caps were on the short end of the scoreboard when Peter Nedved beat goalie Olaf Kolzig with a screened slapshot.

Every year that Washington failed to reach the Stanley Cup finals brought Poile under more fire from the hometown media. Still, he retained Pollin's confidence until the end of the 1996–97 season. This time, for the first time in 15 years, the Caps didn't even get to the playoffs to fail.

Poile executed a late-season deal that at first seemed to save his job when he sent the suddenly struggling Carey and young forwards Anson Carter and Jason Allison to Boston for top playmaker Adam Oates, former Philadelphia captain Rick Tocchet and one-time Conn Smythe Trophy-winning goalie Bill Ranford. But it wasn't enough, and finally Pollin decided. He replaced Poile with former left winger George McPhee on June 9, 1997. (As many suspected, Poile wasn't out of work long. By the end of the summer, he had been hired as g.m. of the Nashville Predators expansion team that begins play in the 1998–99 season.) Also released was head coach Jim Schoenfeld, who had replaced Terry Murray in 1993–94.

The first major coup of the McPhee era was hiring Ron Wilson as head coach. Wilson had coached the Anaheim Mighty Ducks to their first playoffs berth and series win in

1996, then guided Team USA to a victory at the World Cup of Hockey. A dispute with Anaheim high command paved the way for Wilson's arrival on Capital Hill, where he discovered a major change in the Capitals' ambience. After playing in Landover for 24 years, the team moved into a spanking new arena in downtown Washington, near the city's Chinatown. Commercially named MCI Center, the rink signaled a gamble that Pollin could lure the suburban fans from Maryland and Virginia into the inner city that had been off-limits to many of them in the past, but the change of venue was temporarily disappointing in terms of attendance. Crowds were smaller than anticipated until the Capitals turned on the heat in the homestretch of 1997–98 and reached the playoffs.

Under Wilson, the Caps responded to a coach who had succeeded with Anaheim. They suffered through a season pockmarked by injuries but still finished third in the Atlantic Division with a 40–30–12 record and eliminated Boston in the first round of the playoffs. At least part of the success came from Wilson's unorthodox coaching: using popsicle sticks to illustrate plays and having water pistol fights to stimulate his skaters in practice. "Ron is very good at keeping a team loose with snide remarks," says future Vancouver Canucks general manager Brian Burke, who played alongside Wilson at Providence College. "He's very sarcastic."

Wilson guided Washington into the second playoff round against Ottawa and the battle between the two national capitals went to the American city in five games. Olaf Kolzig had enjoyed an excellent season in 1997–98. His 33 wins, five shutouts and 2.20 goals-against average had all ranked among the best in the game, but in the postseason, "Ollie the Goalie" truly came into his own. He outplayed Dominik Hasek as Washington beat Buffalo to win the Eastern Conference championship and advance to the Stanley Cup finals for the first time. But the ultimate mission would not be accomplished. Though Wilson scoffed at speculation that the Detroit Red Wings would complete the Stanley Cup's fourth consecutive sweep, the defending champions did just that and retained their title with four straight wins.

Washington Capitals Year-by-Year Record

Season	GP	W	L	T	GF	GA	Pts	Finish		Playoff Results
1974–75	80	8	67	5	181	446	21	5th	Norris Div.	Out of Playoffs
1975–76	80	11	59	10	224	394	32	5th	Norris Div.	Out of Playoffs
1976–77	80	24	42	14	221	307	62	4th	Norris Div.	Out of Playoffs
1977–78	80	17	49	14	195	321	48	5th	Norris Div.	Out of Playoffs
1978–79	80	24	41	15	273	338	63	4th	Norris Div.	Out of Playoffs
1979–80	80	27	40	13	261	293	67	5th	Patrick Div.	Out of Playoffs
1980–81	80	26	36	18	286	317	70	5th	Patrick Div.	Out of Playoffs
1981–82	80	26	41	13	319	338	65	5th	Patrick Div.	Out of Playoffs
1982–83	80	39	25	16	306	283	94	3rd	Patrick Div.	Lost Div. Semifinal
1983–84	80	48	27	5	308	226	101	2nd	Patrick Div.	Lost Div. Semifinal
1984–85	80	46	25	9	322	240	101	2nd	Patrick Div.	Lost Div. Final
1985–86	80	50	23	7	315	272	107	2nd	Patrick Div.	Lost Div. Semifinal
1986–87	80	38	32	10	285	278	86	2nd	Patrick Div.	Lost Div. Final
1987–88	80	38	33	9	281	249	85	2nd	Patrick Div.	Lost Div. Semifinal
1988–89	80	41	29	10	305	259	92	1st	Patrick Div.	Lost Conf. Final
1989–90	80	36	38	6	284	275	78	3rd	Patrick Div.	Lost Div. Final
1990–91	80	37	36	7	258	258	81	3rd	Patrick Div.	Lost Div. Semifinal
1991–92	80	45	27	8	330	275	98	2nd	Patrick Div.	Lost Div. Semifinal
1992–93	84	43	34	7	325	286	93	2nd	Patrick Div.	Lost Conf. Semifinal
1993–94	84	39	35	10	277	263	88	3rd	Atlantic Div.	Lost Conf. Quarterfinal
1994–95	48	22	18	8	136	120	52	3rd	Atlantic Div.	Lost Conf. Quarterfinal
1995–96	82	39	32	11	234	204	89	4th	Atlantic Div.	Out of Playoffs
1996–97	82	33	40	9	214	231	75	5th	Atlantic Div.	Lost Final
1997–98	82	40	30	12	219	202	92	3rd	Atlantic Div.	

CHAPTER 19

Year-by-Year

Regular-season and Playoff Summaries

Eric Zweig

IN A SERIES OF MEETINGS held between November 22 and November 26, 1917, team owners from the National Hockey Association met to form a new league, the National Hockey League. Former NHA secretary Frank Calder was chosen as the new circuit's first president. Notably absent from the meetings was Toronto owner Eddie Livingstone, who was not popular among his fellow owners; instead, the NHL's Toronto franchise was given to the directors of the Arena Gardens.

In addition to Toronto, the NHL's charter members were the Montreal Canadiens, Montreal Wanderers, Ottawa Senators and Quebec Bulldogs. The Bulldogs, however, elected not to operate their team until the 1919–20 season and the Wanderers withdrew from the league after just six games when their home arena burned down.

1917–18

The star of the NHL's first season was Joe Malone of the Canadiens, who had 44 goals in just 20 games.

Clubs played a split schedule. The Canadiens won the first half, but were defeated in a playoff for the NHL championship by the leaders of the second half, the Torontos—or the Arenas as they are more commonly known.

In the rival Pacific Coast Hockey Association, Gordie Roberts and Bernie Morris led the Seattle Metropolitans to a first–place finish, but league scoring champion Cyclone Taylor and the Vancouver Millionaires knocked them out in the playoffs, earning the right to travel east to play Toronto for the Stanley Cup.

The Stanley Cup series went the full five-game limit, with Toronto emerging victorious. Incidentally, the PCHA still played seven-man hockey (using a rover) and also allowed limited forward passing, which was not added in the NHL until the following season. To accommodate for the differences, the teams alternated between eastern and western rules during the series. Each team won the games played under its rules.

1918–19

The NHL fielded only three teams in the 1918–19 season and a 20-game split schedule was drawn up, with the winners of the two halves to meet for the league title. The Montreal Canadiens, led by Newsy Lalonde (who would claim the league scoring title with 21 goals and 9 assists), were the class of the NHL's first half, posting a 7–3 record. In the second half, the Ottawa Senators had won seven of eight games when the season was cut short when the Toronto Arenas ran into financial difficulties and had to withdraw from the league.

Left with only two teams, the NHL decided to stage a best-of-seven series between Ottawa and Montreal to determine a league champion. The Canadiens proved to be surprisingly easy winners of this showdown, taking the first three games and winning the series in five.

The NHL championship entitled Montreal to play the Seattle Metropolitans of the Pacific Coast Hockey Association for the Stanley Cup. Reversing the results of the previous season, Seattle had finished second in the PCHA before knocking off the first-place Vancouver Millionaires in the playoffs. The Victoria Aristocrats once again missed the playoffs.

The Stanley Cup finals were played in Seattle, with the Mets taking the opener 7–0 under western rules that included the use of the rover. As had happened the year before, alternate games were played under eastern and western rules. The series proved hard-fought and evenly matched, as each team had recorded two wins and a tie through five games. The deciding game was scheduled for April 1, but the onset of a worldwide Spanish influenza epidemic intervened. Several Canadiens players were too sick to continue and the series was abandoned. Canadiens star "Bad Joe" Hall lost his life to the illness four days later. It was the only year that no Stanley Cup champion would be declared.

1919–20

The 1919–20 season saw the NHL regrouping after a rocky 1918–19 campaign. On the eve of the regular season the Toronto club found new owners, was renamed the St. Patricks and rejoined the NHL. Meanwhile the Quebec Bulldogs, one of the NHL's founding members, finally exercised its franchise and iced a team. A number of players who'd taken jobs elsewhere returned to Quebec City, most notably Joe Malone. Though Quebec would post a dismal 4–20 record, Malone was the league's top scorer with 39 goals and nine assists for 48 points. On January 31, 1920, Malone also set an NHL record which still stands when he scored seven goals in a single game in the Bulldogs' 10–6 victory over Toronto.

The NHL again played a split season, but this year the Ottawa Senators negated the need for a playoff by winning both halves. Led by stars Frank Nighbor, Cy Denneny, Jack Darragh, Punch Broadbent and goalie Clint Benedict, the Senators were 9–3 in the first half and 10–2 in the second.

The competition was much tighter in the Pacific Coast Hockey Association, where just two wins separated the three teams. The Seattle Metropolitans clinched first place on the second-last night of the season and finished 12–10. The Vancouver Millionaires went 11–11, while the Victoria Aristocrats again missed the playoffs with a 10–12 record. Vancouver beat the Mets 3–1 in game one in Seattle, but lost 6–0 at home as the Metropolitans advanced to the Stanley Cup finals with a 7–3 victory in the two-game total-goals series.

The Stanley Cup final was slated for Ottawa, but warm weather forced the final two games of the series to be moved to the artificial ice of the Toronto Arena. Despite the

disruption, the Senators prevailed with a 6–1 victory in the fifth and deciding game of the best-of-five affair.

1920–21

The first franchise shift in NHL history took place as the Quebec Bulldogs moved to Hamilton and became the Tigers. The change of venue did little to improve the team's fortunes: Though other NHL teams contributed players to bolster Hamilton's roster, the Tigers finished last in both halves of the split season, going 3–7 and 3–11.

The defending Stanley Cup champion Ottawa Senators were the best team in the NHL's first half, posting an 8–2 record, but they slumped to third place in the second half. Former Senator Sprague Cleghorn helped Toronto post a 10–4 record to win the second half, edging out the 9–5 Canadiens. Toronto's Babe Dye led the league with 35 goals, one better than Ottawa's Cy Denneny. Montreal's Newsy Lalonde had 33 goals, but his eight assists gave him 41 points to lead the league. Despite poor support, Hamilton's Joe Malone was fourth in both goals and points, with 30 goals and four assists. It was defense, though, that made the difference in the playoffs, as Ottawa twice blanked Toronto, 5–0 and 2–0, for an easy win in the total-goals series. Clint Benedict was brilliant in net, while Eddie Gerard and George Boucher were solid on defense.

Ottawa traveled west to face the Vancouver Millionaires of the Pacific Coast Hockey Association for the Stanley Cup. For the second straight year, the PCHA had gone down to the wire. The Millionaires were 13–11–0 to Seattle's 12–11–1. The Victoria Aristocrats were in their usual third-place spot at 10–13–1, but the debut this season of Frank Fredrickson offered hope for future improvement. Vancouver crushed the Metropolitans 7–0 and 6–2 in the playoffs.

The first game of the Stanley Cup series drew a record crowd of 10,000 fans, as Vancouver beat Ottawa 3–1. The Senators, though, were able to retain the trophy with a victory in five games that were witnessed by an estimated 51,000 fans.

1921–22

Professional hockey prospered as the 1920s roared. In November of 1921 the Montreal Canadiens were sold to Leo Dandurand, Joseph Cattarinich and Louis Letourneau for a reported $11,000. Bigger news came out of the Prairies with the rise of a third professional league to rival the NHL and Pacific Coast Hockey Association. The Western Canada Hockey League boasted teams in Calgary, Edmonton, Regina and Saskatoon.

The NHL abandoned the split-season format for 1921–22, adopting the PCHA's playoff scheme under which the first- and second-place teams met for the league championship. The defending Stanley Cup champion Ottawa Senators, who added King Clancy and Frank Boucher to a star-studded lineup, were again the league's best with a 14–8–2 record. Ottawa's Punch Broadbent led the NHL in scoring with 32 goals and 14 assists and established an NHL record that still stands today, scoring in 16 consecutive games. Still, the second-place Toronto St. Pats pulled off an upset in the two-game total-goals playoff.

In the west, the PCHA had another tight finish, with Seattle going 12–11–1, Vancouver finishing 12–12–0 and Victoria 11–12–1. The Millionaires then defeated the first-place Metropolitans with a pair of 1–0 shutouts by Hugh Lehman. Edmonton was the first-place club in the WCHL's inaugural season, but the Regina Capitals, having first

knocked off the Calgary Tigers in a playoff to determine second place, defeated the Eskimos to claim the first league championship.

Regina and Vancouver met in a two-game total-goals series to determine the west's challenger for the Stanley Cup. After a 2–1 win, Regina was shut out 4–0 and it was the Millionaires who earned the right to go to Toronto to play for the Stanley Cup. The final went a full five games before the St. Patricks emerged victorious. Babe Dye of Toronto was the series star with nine goals.

1922–23

A controversial deal marked the preseason in 1922–23. Veteran star Newsy Lalonde of the Montreal Canadiens was sold to the Western Canada league's Saskatoon Crescents without being offered on waivers to other NHL clubs. The dispute was resolved when NHL president Frank Calder ruled Lalonde would be considered traded for a top Saskatoon prospect named Aurel Joliat. Joliat became an instant star in Montreal and helped the Canadiens edge out the Toronto St. Pats for second place and a playoff spot behind the Ottawa Senators.

Ottawa won the playoff opener 2–0 despite the dirty play of Montreal defensemen Sprague Cleghorn and Bill Couture. The pair were suspended from game two by Canadiens owner Leo Dandurand. Still, Montreal hung on in the second game, taking a 2–0 lead, but Cy Denneny scored for Ottawa and gave the Senators a 3–2 victory in the total-goals series.

Out west, the Pacific Coast Hockey Association finally made the switch to six-man hockey, abandoning the rover position. The move allowed the PCHA and the WCHL to play an interlocking schedule, though the two leagues would maintain separate standings and playoffs. Vancouver finished first in the PCHA, but the real story was in Victoria where Frank Fredrickson's scoring exploits led the Aristocrats to the playoffs for the first time in 10 years. Still, it was Vancouver, now known as the Maroons, who won the league title in the playoffs. Newsy Lalonde won the WCHL scoring title, though his Saskatoon club finished last. Edmonton's 19–10–1 record had the Eskimos comfortably in first place, though they needed overtime to beat Regina 4–3 in the two-game total-goals playoff.

The NHL champion Senators first defeated Vancouver three games to one in a best-of-five affair, then swept the WCHL champion Eskimos 2–0 in a best-of-three series to claim their third Stanley Cup title in four years.

1923–24

The defending Stanley Cup champion Ottawa Senators were under new ownership for the 1923–24 season, and moved into the new 11,000-seat Ottawa Auditorium. Longtime star and captain Eddie Gerard was forced to retire due to illness, but the Senators were still the class of the NHL, cruising to a first-place finish with a 16–8–0 record. Ottawa's Frank Nighbor was the first winner of the Hart Trophy—donated by Dr. David Hart, father of Montreal Canadiens coach and manager Cecil Hart—to recognize the league's most valuable player.

The Canadiens introduced a talented newcomer named Howie Morenz this season, and finished comfortably ahead of Toronto and Hamilton (who finished last for the fourth straight year) to make the playoffs. Montreal then surprised Ottawa with victories of 1–0 and 4–2 to claim the NHL championship.

On the other side of the continent, the Pacific Coast Hockey Association and Western Canada Hockey League once again played an interlocking schedule, with Seattle proving to be the PCHA's best. As in the NHL, there was a playoff upset as second-place Vancouver eliminated Seattle. In the WCHL, future NHL star Bill Cook led the loop in scoring, but his Saskatoon team finished out of the playoffs behind Calgary and Regina. Calgary was the only first-place team to survive the postseason.

Canadiens owner Leo Dandurand wanted the two western champions to face each other in a playoff to send only one team east, but Frank Patrick of the PCHA insisted the NHL champs play both Vancouver and Calgary. Montreal gave in and swept both teams in two straight games. Howie Morenz scored seven goals in the Canadiens' six playoff games as Montreal won its first Stanley Cup since the club was part of the old NHA in 1916.

1924–25

There were changes throughout professional hockey in 1924–25. The NHL expanded to six teams, adding its first American club, the Boston Bruins, and a second Montreal team (later known as the Maroons) that would play its home games at the new Montreal Forum. In the west, the Seattle Metropolitans folded, marking the end of the Pacific Coast Hockey Association. Vancouver and Victoria joined Calgary, Edmonton, Regina and Saskatoon in a revamped Western Canada Hockey League.

With expansion, the NHL extended its season from 24 to 30 games and changed the playoff structure. The first-place team would now receive a bye into the finals and meet the winner of a series between the second- and third-place teams. The Hamilton Tigers, who'd placed last in each of the previous four seasons, went 19–10–1 this year to finish one point ahead of the Toronto St. Pats for first place. But the Tigers' players were upset that the season had been lengthened by 25 percent without a comparable increase in their salaries and they refused to take part in the playoffs unless they received an extra $200 each. President Frank Calder suspended the players and announced that the winner of a playoff between the Canadiens and St. Patricks would receive the new Prince of Wales Trophy as the NHL's regular-season champion. Montreal won and earned the right to play for the Stanley Cup.

In the west, Victoria had added Seattle stars Jack Walker, Frank Foyston and Hap Holmes to a roster that already boasted future Hall of Famer Frank Fredrickson, and though they only finished third, the Cougars (as they were now known) beat Saskatoon and Calgary in the playoffs to earn a chance at hockey's top prize. Victoria then beat Montreal to become the last non-NHL team to win the Stanley Cup.

1925–26

On September 22, 1925, the NHL held its first meeting in the United States, when a special session was convened in New York to discuss the admission of a new expansion team for that city. The Hamilton Tigers were being dropped and the New York Americans would take Hamilton's place place and employ its players. Another new team, the Pittsburgh Pirates, also joined the league for 1925–26, bringing membership to seven teams. The Pirates were stocked with players from the American amateur champion Pittsburgh Yellow Jackets and included such stars as Lionel Conacher and Roy Worters.

Coached by Odie Cleghorn, Pittsburgh finished in third place and made the playoffs in its first season. The Pirates were just ahead of the much-improved Boston Bruins, but the Montreal Maroons showed even greater improvement. Young stars like Babe Siebert and Nels Stewart (who won the NHL scoring title and the Hart Trophy) helped lift the Maroons into second place, beat Pittsburgh in the playoffs, then knock off the first-place Ottawa Senators for the NHL championship.

In the Western Canada Hockey League, poor fan support in Regina saw the franchise transferred to Portland, Oregon. Consequently, the word "Canada" was dropped from the league's name. The defending Stanley Cup champion Victoria Cougars limped through the first half of the season, but came alive late to finish third. Victoria then knocked off Saskatoon and Edmonton to claim the Western Hockey League championship.

Victoria came east to Montreal in what proved to be the last Stanley Cup final involving a team from a league other than the NHL. The Maroons won the best-of-five series in four games, claiming the first of what would be many Stanley Cup championships won on Forum ice.

1926–27

With American expansion proving successful, the NHL prepared to add three more U.S. teams for the 1926–27 season. Much of that growth was at the expense of the Western Hockey League which, lacking the larger, richer markets of the east, closed its doors. The NHL's new Chicago franchise, the Black Hawks, bought the entire roster of the WHL's Portland Rosebuds. Similarly, the Victoria Cougars were sold to eastern interests and joined the NHL as the Detroit Cougars.

The Bruins rescued defenseman Eddie Shore from the Edmonton Eskimos, while the newly formed New York Rangers used such WHL stars as Frank Boucher and brothers Bill and Bun Cook to hit the ground running in the NHL. Conn Smythe was originally hired to build, coach and manage the Rangers, but a clash with management saw him ousted in favor of WHL impresario Lester Patrick. Smythe bought the Toronto St. Patricks later in the 1926–27 season and renamed them the Maple Leafs.

With league membership now at 10 teams, the NHL was split into Canadian and American Divisions. Boston, Pittsburgh, Chicago, Detroit and the Rangers comprised the American Division, while Ottawa, Toronto, the Montreal Maroons and Canadiens and, oddly enough, the New York Americans made up the Canadian Division. The top three teams from each division would make the playoffs, with the first-place teams earning a bye into their division finals.

The Rangers were first in the American Division, but Boston beat Chicago before upsetting New York to become the first U.S.-based NHL team to reach the Stanley Cup finals. Ottawa won the Canadian Division, then beat the Bruins to claim their fourth Cup title of the decade.

1927–28

The NHL was now hockey's undisputed major professional league and business was booming. As a sign of the league's growing confidence, it did away with salary cap restrictions and increased the transfer fee for players on waivers from $2,500 to $5,000. There was, however, one cause for concern. The powerhouse Ottawa Senators, playing in what was now the league's smallest market, were losing money despite their Stanley Cup success and were

forced to sell Hooley Smith to the Montreal Maroons.

Stars from the NHL's early days were now retired or reaching the ends of their careers and a new generation of superstars was taking their place. The New York Rangers had Frank Boucher and Bill and Bun Cook. Boston boasted Eddie Shore, Dit Clapper and Cooney Weiland. The Maroons would soon team Hooley Smith with Nels Stewart and Babe Siebert to form the powerful "S" Line, but the Montreal Canadiens had the greatest star of all in Howie Morenz.

Morenz led the NHL in scoring in 1927–28 with 33 goals and 18 assists in the 44-game regular season and won the Hart Trophy as the Canadiens finished first in the Canadian Division. The Habs were upset, however, by the rival Maroons in the playoffs.

In the American Division, Boston finished first, but the second-place Rangers beat the Pittsburgh Pirates and eliminated the Bruins to advance to the Stanley Cup final. Because a circus was booked into Madison Square Garden, all five games of the series were played at the Montreal Forum. The second game provided a legendary moment when 44-year-old Ranger coach Lester Patrick took over in goal after an injury to Lorne Chabot. Patrick's Rangers won the game 2–1 in overtime and went on to become only the second American team (after the 1917 Seattle Metropolitans) to win the Stanley Cup with a victory in the full five games.

1928–29

In 1919–20, the league's four clubs had averaged nearly five goals each per game, but during the ensuing decade an emphasis on defense meant only the top-scoring teams approached three per game. But 1928–29 was the year the NHL reached its offensive nadir—the 10 teams scored fewer than 1.5 goals per game, with last-place Chicago netting just 33 in 44 games. Ace Bailey of the Toronto Maple Leafs led the league with just 22 goals and 10 assists, and Nels Stewart of the Maroons, with 21, was the only other man in the league to score more than 20.

Meanwhile, all but two of the league's first-string goalies recorded at least 10 shutouts. The Montreal Canadiens' George Hainsworth led the way, setting a record that still stands with 22 shutouts, and posting a remarkable 0.92 goals-against average on his way to his third consecutive Vezina Trophy.

The playoff format was altered this year. The top three teams from both the Canadian and American divisions still made the playoffs, but each second- and third-place finisher would meet its counterpart from the other division in a two-game total-goals series. The winners would compete in a best-of three-series for a berth in the Stanley Cup finals. Meanwhile, the two first-place teams played a best-of-five series for the other spot in the finals.

The Canadiens and Bruins finished atop their respective divisions and engaged in a close-checking semifinal. Boston recorded 1–0 victories in each of the first two games, as Tiny Thompson turned away every shot he faced and Cooney Weiland scored both Bruin goals. They completed the sweep with a 3–2 victory in game three. The Rangers knocked off the Americans and then the Toronto Maple Leafs to provide Boston's opposition in the first all-American Stanley Cup final. The best-of-three set went to the Bruins in two straight as Boston celebrated its first Stanley Cup victory.

1929–30

After the previous season's offensive drought, the NHL made significant rule changes to increase scoring in 1929–30. The most important new rule allowed forward passing in the offensive zone—previously it had only been allowed in a team's neutral and defensive zones. But the changes quickly proved too effective, as forwards began to station themselves in front of the opposition goal and wait for passes. So, on December 21, 1929, the NHL legislated that no attacking player would be allowed to proceed the puck across the blue line. The modern offside rule was born.

Bruins coach Art Ross had schooled his players well in the new rules and Boston was by far the best team in the NHL, posting a 38–5–1 record for an .875 winning percentage that still remains a league record. Cooney Weiland's league-leading 43 goals nearly doubled Ace Bailey's high of 22 the year before and his 73 points were by far a new league record. Linemate Dit Clapper had 41 goals, while Dutch Gainor, the third member of the Dynamite Line, recorded 31 assists, second-best in the league. Boston's Tiny Thompson won the Vezina Trophy, though his 2.19 goals-against average was nearly double what it had been the year before. Veteran goaltender Clint Benedict chose to retire late in the season after a crude leather facemask failed to adequately protect his broken nose.

The Bruins cruised into the Stanley Cup final after sweeping the Montreal Maroons to open the playoffs. The Canadiens provided the opposition after beating the Black Hawks and Rangers. Boston was heavily favored, but Montreal swept the best-of-three series, handing the Bruins back-to-back losses for the first time all season. Partly as a result of the surprising sweep, the Stanley Cup final would be increased to a best-of-five affair in the future.

1930–31

The Great Depression began to take its toll on the NHL by the 1930–31 season. Even in the best of times, the Ottawa Senators had been finding the economic going rough. Now, the situation was even worse. Several Senators were sold off prior to the start of the season, most notably King Clancy, who was purchased by the Toronto Maple Leafs for $35,000 and two players. Toronto immediately improved to second place in the Canadian Division, while Ottawa slumped to last place with a 10–30–4 mark.

The Pittsburgh Pirates had also been been in trouble for several years, and, after a 5–36–3 season in 1929–30, the franchise was moved to Philadelphia. Renamed the Quakers, the relocated team proved even worse this year as they limped through a 4–36–4 campaign.

At the other end of the spectrum, the Boston Bruins were the NHL's best for the second year in a row, finishing atop the American Division with a 28–10–6 record. League-leading scorer Howie Morenz powered the Montreal Canadiens to top spot in the Canadian Division and earned his second Hart Trophy as most valuable player.

In a rematch of the previous season's Stanley Cup final, the Canadiens beat Boston in five games to open the playoffs. The Chicago Black Hawks made their first appearance in the finals after knocking off the Toronto Maple Leafs and the New York Rangers.

The series opened before huge crowds at the Chicago Stadium, where the teams split two games before conclud-

ing the series at the Montreal Forum. The Black Hawks won game three before the Canadiens rallied to defend their Cup title by winning the fourth and fifth games.

1931–32

The NHL's fortunes between the two world wars matched those of the countries it played in. The league had grown from four to 10 teams in the space of just four seasons in the Roaring Twenties, but this season would see it suffering from the impact of the Great Depression. One of the casualties was the Philadelphia Quakers, who closed shop after only one year following five seasons in Pittsburgh as the Pirates. More shocking was the decision of the Ottawa Senators to withdraw from play. Ottawa was a founding member of the NHL, had won its first Stanley Cup in 1903 (long before the NHL even existed) and had won the Cup four times in the 1920s.

Meanwhile, Conn Smythe's Toronto Maple Leafs seemed to be the picture of optimism. Against long odds, Conn Smythe had built his hockey palace, Maple Leaf Gardens, which opened on November 12, 1931, with a disappointing 2–1 loss to Chicago. The Leafs rebounded to win a club-record 23 games (23–18–7) in the newly expanded 48-game season and their Kid Line of Joe Primeau, Busher Jackson and Charlie Conacher emerged as full-fledged superstars. Jackson led the league with 53 points on 28 goals and 25 assists and Primeau's 37 assists topped the loop, while Conacher's 34 goals tied him with Bill Cook for top spot in the NHL.

Toronto finished second behind the Montreal Canadiens in the Canadian Division, but advanced to the Stanley Cup finals with playoff victories over the Chicago Black Hawks and Montreal Maroons. Meanwhile, the Canadiens were eliminated by the American Division–winning New York Rangers. The Rangers had a week off before meeting Toronto in the Stanley Cup final, but the rest was of no benefit. Toronto took the opener 6–4 in New York, won game two 6–2 in Boston after the circus forced the series out of Madison Square Garden, then completed the sweep with a 6–4 victory at home. It was Toronto's first Stanley Cup victory since the St. Patricks won it 10 years before.

1932–33

After a one-year absence, the Ottawa Senators returned to the NHL for the 1932–33 season, but finished last in the league with an 11–27–10 mark. In Toronto, the defending Stanley Cup champions climbed to top spot in the Canadian Division, and starting this year Foster Hewitt's broadcasts from Maple Leaf Gardens could be heard nationally, over a network of 20 radio stations. The Montreal Maroons placed second to Toronto, while their rink-mates, the Canadiens, edged the New York Americans for the final playoff spot.

In the American Division, the Rangers, Boston and Detroit (now under new ownership and renamed the Red Wings) battled for top spot, with only Chicago out of the running. The Black Hawks fired two coaches before settling on Tommy Gorman. A dispute over rent at the Chicago Stadium saw the team spend the first month of the season at the old Chicago Coliseum. Eddie Shore won the Hart Trophy for the first of four times in his career as the Bruins finished on top of the division. Detroit finished second despite an identical 25–15–8 record. The Rangers finished third but came on strong in the postseason, knocking off the Canadiens and Red Wings to advance to the Stanley Cup final.

In the battle of first-place finishers, Toronto beat Boston in five games. The series finale on April 3 was the longest game to date in NHL history, as Ken Doraty scored at 4:46 of the sixth overtime period to give the Maple Leafs a 1–0 victory. The game ended at 1:50 a.m. on the 4th, but the Leafs were in New York later that night to open the Stanley Cup final. The Rangers breezed to a 5–1 victory and won the series in four games, avenging their sweep at the hands of the Leafs the previous spring.

1933–34

As the Great Depression worsened, so did its effect on the NHL. Although the Detroit Red Wings were now safely under the ownership of multi-millionaire James Norris and his son James D. Norris of Olympia Incorporated, the Ottawa Senators were on shaky financial ground after 1932–33, and so were the New York Americans. NHL president Frank Calder quickly put down rumors that the teams might merge. Meanwhile in Montreal, it was beginning to look as if there was room for only one team, as the Montreal Maroons were having trouble drawing fans to the Forum, the rink they shared with the Canadiens.

Despite league-wide economic hardship, Boston's Eddie Shore refused to accept a pay cut after winning the Hart Trophy and sat out the first three games of the season before agreeing to a $7,500 contract. Shore would be in the hockey headlines again a month later after one of the darkest incidents in NHL history.

On December 12, 1933, the Toronto Maple Leafs were in Boston to play the Bruins. The game got chippy and Shore was tripped by King Clancy after a rink-long rush. Shore retaliated angrily by checking the first Leaf he could see, Ace Bailey, from behind. Bailey's skull was fractured as he fell over backward and his head hit the ice. It was 10 days before doctors were even sure the wounded Maple Leafs would live. As it was, Bailey's hockey career was over. Shore was suspended for 16 games—one-third of the 48-game schedule. On February 14, 1934, an NHL All-Star Game was played to benefit Bailey and his family.

The Chicago Black Hawks, led by the exploits of goaltender Charlie Gardiner, won their first Stanley Cup. Gardiner played in the Bailey benefit game and also earned his second Vezina Trophy this year. Shortly after Chicago's Stanley Cup victory, Gardiner died of a brain tumor. He was 30 years old.

1934–35

The Ottawa Senators finally succumbed to financial woes prior to the 1934–35 season, as the once-proud franchise abandoned the Canadian capital to become the St. Louis Eagles. The change of venue did not improve the club's fortunes, however, and, after finishing last with an 11–31–6 record, the club folded for good. Meanwhile, driven by hard economic times, the NHL lowered its salary cap to $62,500 per team and a maximum of $7,000 per player. The move didn't help the New York Americans' players, who complained that they weren't being paid.

Because of the salary cap, the Montreal Canadiens were forced to trade aging superstar Howie Morenz to the Chicago Black Hawks. Goalie Lorne Chabot was included in the deal to replace the late Charlie Gardiner. Chabot would enjoy a career year and won the Vezina Trophy. The Canadiens received Lionel Conacher and two other players, then they dealt Conacher to the Montreal Maroons, where he was reunited with coach Tommy Gorman, who, despite

winning the Stanley Cup in 1934, had been fired by the Black Hawks.

On the ice, Charlie Conacher led the league in scoring and his Toronto Maple Leafs easily outdistanced the Maroons for top spot in the Canadian Division. The Boston Bruins, who had fallen to last place the previous year, regained their usual perch atop the American Division standings and Eddie Shore took home the Hart Trophy for a second time. The Lady Byng Trophy, for sportsmanship, was won by Frank Boucher of the New York Rangers. It was the seventh time in eight years Boucher had won the award, and in recognition of that fact he was given permanent possession of the original trophy.

In the playoffs, Toronto knocked off Boston to advance to the Stanley Cup final, while the Maroons defeated the Black Hawks and Rangers before upsetting the Leafs for the league championship.

1935–36

Despite their Stanley Cup win, the Montreal Maroons continued to struggle at the box office. So did the Canadiens, who were sold by Leo Dandurand and Joseph Cattarinich to the Canadian Arena Company prior to the 1935–36 season.

A dispersal draft was held to distribute the players belonging to the defunct St. Louis Eagles and the Boston Bruins got a diamond in the rough in Bill Cowley, who would blossom into a superstar. Boston also traded Marty Barry to the Detroit Red Wings, where he teamed with Larry Aurie and Herbie Lewis to form one of the league's top lines.

The Wings emerged as the best in the league this season, winning the American Division with a 24–16–8 record. The Maroons won the Canadian Division with the nearly identical mark of 22–16–10. The teams were so evenly matched in the first game of their playoff series that it took until 16:30 of the sixth overtime period for Mud Bruneteau to beat Lorne Chabot for the game's only goal.

Not only had Detroit's Normie Smith recorded a shutout in the longest game in NHL history, he went on to blank the Maroons for 60 minutes more in game two—another 1–0 victory—then allowed only one goal in a 2–1 win that swept the series. Smith's goals-against average for the series was a minuscule 0.20.

The New York Americans made the playoffs for the first time since 1929 and beat the Chicago Black Hawks in their first series before falling to the Toronto Maple Leafs. It was the Leafs' fourth trip to the finals in five years, but they would come away empty-handed for the third year in a row as the Red Wings earned their first NHL championship.

1936–37

The Toronto Maple Leafs unveiled several new players for the 1936–37 season. Center Syl Apps would earn honors as rookie of the year, as his playmaking skills blended perfectly with first-year sniper Gordie Drillon. Goalie Turk Broda also made his debut this season. In Montreal, it was an old name that made headlines, as Howie Morenz returned to the Canadiens after stints with the Black Hawks and Rangers. Morenz took his place at center between his old linemates Aurel Joliat and Johnny Gagnon. The three were now past their prime, but the Canadiens were showing much improvement over the previous year's last-place finish, thanks largely to youngster Toe Blake, who shouldered most of the offensive load.

Meanwhile, reaching the playoffs the previous season had done little to help the New York Americans' bottom line; the NHL was forced to take over operation of the club before the start of the season.

On January 28, 1937, Morenz caught the tip of his skate in the boards at the Montreal Forum, badly breaking his leg above the ankle. On March 8, the hockey world was stunned to learn that Morenz had died in hospital. A heart attack was given as the cause of death. Thousands of fans filed past Morenz's body, which lay in state at the Forum, and thousands more lined the route of the funeral procession that took him to the cemetery.

Despite the loss of their great superstar, the Canadiens won the Canadian Division, but were knocked out of the playoffs by the Red Wings. Detroit then became the first American franchise to win back-to-back Stanley Cup titles when they defeated the New York Rangers.

1937–38

The NHL had lost its first great superstar the year before and so the 1937–38 season began with a memorial All-Star Game in honor of Howie Morenz. A team made up of Montreal Canadiens and Maroons took on the best from the NHL's other six teams. The event raised $20,000 for the Morenz family.

Nels Stewart, who'd overtaken Morenz as the NHL's all-time career goal-scoring leader the year before, notched his 300th goal in 1937–38, while Boston's Eddie Shore returned from a serious back injury the previous year to win his fourth and final Hart Trophy.

Shore's Bruins were the best in the NHL in the regular season, winning the American Division over a strong New York Ranger squad. The Chicago Black Hawks snuck into the playoffs with a weak 14–25–9 third-place finish. The Toronto Maple Leafs won the Canadian Division behind the stellar play of scoring leader Gordie Drillon and runner-up Syl Apps. Boston's stronger defense had them favored to beat Toronto in the playoffs, but Turk Broda's stellar goaltending sparked an upset as the Leafs advanced to the Stanley Cup final for the fifth time in seven years.

Despite a poor regular season (and spared a last-place finish only by Detroit's shocking collapse from first to worst), the Black Hawks came alive in the playoffs. Chicago upset the Canadiens and Americans, though their win over New York cost them the services of netminder Mike Karakas, who suffered a broken toe. Ex-NHLer Alfie Moore took over in goal and stunned the Leafs with a 3–1 victory in game one. Moore was then declared ineligible and Chicago lost game two 5–1 with farmhand Paul Goodman between the pipes. Karakas subsequently returned, wearing a specially-fitted skate, and the Black Hawks won the next two games to take the Stanley Cup. Two facts distinguished the Chicago win: they were the first club with a losing record to win the Cup, and they did it with a roster that was 50 percent comprised of American-born players.

1938–39

The Montreal Maroons' last-place finish in 1937–38 proved the final nail in their coffin. They suspended operations prior to the 1938–39 season, leaving the NHL with just seven teams. As a result, the league reverted to a single division for the first time since 1926–27. Six of the seven teams would qualify for the postseason: the first- and second-place clubs would play a seven-game semifinal, while the third- and fourth-place teams would meet in a best-of-

three quarterfinal, as did the fifth- and sixth-place finishers. The quarterfinal winners would then compete in a three-game semifinal series. The Stanley Cup final would be a best-of-seven series.

The Detroit Red Wings replaced goaltender Normie Smith at the start of the season. Manager Jack Adams purchased Tiny Thompson from the Boston Bruins. Thompson had won the Vezina Trophy for the fourth time the year before—then a league record—but Bruins manager Art Ross knew he had a worthy replacement in Frank Brimsek. "Mr. Zero," as he became known, led the league with 10 shutouts, won the Vezina Trophy with a 1.56 goals-against average, and was named to the First All-Star Team as the Bruins cruised to a first-place finish.

Though the 36–10–2 Bruins had 10 more victories and 16 more points than the second-place Rangers, it took Boston the full seven games to eliminate New York in the semifinals. Mel Hill earned the nickname "Sudden Death" by scoring three overtime goals in the series. The third-place Leafs beat the Americans and Red Wings to reach the finals, then lost to the Bruins in five games as the Stanley Cup returned to Boston for the first time in 10 years.

1939–40

War broke out in Europe before the NHL started the 1939–40 season, but the league was determined to continue operations with as little disruption as possible. Economic conditions were beginning to improve with the end of the Great Depression, but the New York Americans were still strapped for cash. As a result, they peddled their best player, Sweeney Schriner, to the Toronto Maple Leafs for cash and four players, including the aging Busher Jackson. Jackson would team with ex-Kid Line mate Charlie Conacher on an Americans roster that had become something of a haven for fading stars. Former Bruin great Eddie Shore would play out his career alongside the two ex-Leafs, but the Americans would tumble to sixth place, ahead of only the Montreal Canadiens, who were in the cellar for the first time since 1925–26.

The loss of Shore did not hinder the Bruins in 1939–40, as Kraut Line stars Milt Schmidt, Woody Dumart and Bobby Bauer finished 1–2–3 in the league scoring race. Teammate Bill Cowley came in fifth. The defending Stanley Cup champions posted the best record in the NHL for the third consecutive season, but were upset by the second-place New York Rangers in six games in their semifinal. New York's opposition in the finals was third-place Toronto, who had advanced with wins over the Chicago Black Hawks and Detroit Red Wings.

The Stanley Cup series opened in New York, with the Rangers winning the first two games. As happened so many times to the Rangers over the years, the circus at Madison Square Garden forced the rest of the series to be played in Toronto. The Leafs won games three and four, but a pair of overtime victories gave the Rangers their third Stanley Cup title in 13 seasons. It would be 54 years before the Rangers won the Stanley Cup again.

1940–41

Determined to rebuild after their last-place finish in 1939-40, the Canadiens hired a new coach—Dick Irvin, who had enjoyed great success with the Toronto Maple Leafs in the 1930s. Though he would help the Canadiens qualify for the playoffs this season, the return to glory in

Montreal was still several seasons in the offing.

At the other end of the spectrum, the Boston Bruins—despite failing to repeat as Stanley Cup champions in 1940—kept their team intact for 1940–41. General manager Art Ross's patience was rewarded with a fourth consecutive first-place finish and the team's second Stanley Cup title in three years. Bill Cowley led the NHL in scoring with 62 points, 18 more than the five players who finished tied for second. Bruins teammates Eddie Wiseman, Bobby Bauer, Roy Conacher and Milt Schmidt all joined Cowley in the top 10, while Frank Brimsek led the league with six shutouts. The Bruins set an NHL record with a 23-game undefeated streak and they set another record on March 4, 1941, when they fired 83 shots against the Black Hawks. Chicago goalie Sam LoPresti made 80 saves in a 3–2 loss.

In the playoffs, Boston defeated the second-place Maple Leafs in a thrilling seven-game semifinal. Third-place Detroit supplied the opposition for the Stanley Cup after the Red Wing eliminated the New York Rangers and Chicago. Boston then beat Detroit in the first four-game sweep in Stanley Cup history. The victory would prove to be Boston's last until 1970.

1941–42

After the 1940–41 season, the NHL turned over ownership of the New York Americans to club manager Red Dutton. He tried to spark a local rivalry by changing the team's name to the Brooklyn Americans. Dutton even moved to the borough, and encouraged his players to do the same. Although the club practiced in Brooklyn, games would continue to be played at Madison Square Garden. Still, the cash-strapped team was forced to sell off its few remaining stars, and the 1941–42 season would prove to be the Amerks' swan song.

The rival New York Rangers enjoyed much more success than their crosstown cousins. The team had slumped after their 1940 Stanley Cup victory, but rebounded to first place in 1941–42. Bryan Hextall led the way, winning the NHL scoring title. His 54 points were two more than runner-up and linemate Lynn Patrick, and four more than his other linemate, Phil Watson, who finished fourth in the scoring race. The Rangers held off the Toronto Maple Leafs in a tight race for top spot. The Boston Bruins finished a close third despite losing their entire Kraut Line to military service midway through the season.

In the playoffs, Toronto upset the Rangers in the semifinals, but dropped the first three games of the finals to the Detroit Red Wings. Then coach Hap Day shook up his roster, benching Gordie Drillon and Bucko McDonald in favor of Don Metz and Hank Goldup, and the team roared back to win the next four games and the Stanley Cup. Though this was their seventh trip to the finals since 1932, it was the Maple Leafs' first Stanley Cup title since then.

1942–43

With the departure of the Brooklyn Americans, the National Hockey League, after growing to as many as 10 teams, was reduced in 1942–43 to what would become known as the "Original Six." There were concerns that even the six surviving teams would be sidelined if the increased Canadian and American participation in World War II forced the cancelation of hockey, but such fears were put to rest by NHL President Frank Calder. On September 28, 1942, he announced that government officials in both the

United States and Canada had decided the game should continue "in the interest of public morale."

Still, with at least 80 players serving in the armed forces, the NHL's clubs faced severe manpower shortages. The Boston Bruins had lost their entire Kraut Line of Milt Schmidt, Woody Dumart and Bobby Bauer, while seven Toronto Maple Leaf players were in the army. The New York Rangers were hit particularly hard, losing brothers Neil and Mac Colville, Alex Shibicky, Jim Henry and Art Coulter to wartime service.

On November 21, three weeks after the start of the 1942–43 season, the league announced regular-season overtime was being discontinued due to wartime travel restrictions. It was the last major decision president Frank Calder would ever make, as he died of heart failure on February 4, 1943. Former New York Americans player and manager Mervyn "Red" Dutton succeeded him as the NHL's second president.

Offense increased during the 1942–43 season, and the Chicago Black Hawks' Doug Bentley led the NHL with 73 points (tying Cooney Weiland's single-season record set back in 1929–30). Though the Detroit Red Wings failed to produce a top–10 scorer, they finished first in the regular-season standings and captured the Stanley Cup, avenging the previous year's defeat when they had lost to Toronto after leading the series three games to none.

1943–44

The National Hockey League Board of Governors made a decision at the league meetings in September 1943 that has since been interpreted as the beginning of hockey's modern era: They voted to add a red line at center ice. Players could now pass the puck from their own zone into the neutral zone, as far as the red line. The idea was to reduce the number of offside calls, thus opening up the defensively-oriented style of play that dominated. It was hoped that a game that offered more offense would keep customers clicking through the turnstiles out while NHL owners suffered through both player and cash shortages during the World War II.

Military obligations continued to take talent from NHL rosters during the 1943–44 campaign. The Stanley Cup champion Detroit Red Wings lost nine starters to military service, while the New York Rangers, already badly depleted, lost five more players, including top scorer Lynn Patrick. The Rangers suffered through a horrendous 6–39–5 season in 1943–44, allowing a then-record 310 goals in just 50 games. Goaltender Ken "Tubby" McAuley's 6.20 goals-against average is still the highest single-season mark in league history among goalies appearing in at least 30 games.

The Rangers' woefully inept defense played a part in a league-wide offensive explosion. Four teams scored 200 or more goals, and three players, led by Herb Cain's 82 points for the Boston Bruins, eclipsed the old single-season scoring record of 73 points. On February 3, 1944, Detroit's Syd Howe scored six goals in a single game. The Montreal Canadiens led the league with a record 234 goals and also posted the NHL's best defensive record as they cruised home as regular-season champions, 25 points ahead of their closes competitor, the Detroit Red Wings.

The Habs' Rocket Richard scored 12 goals in nine post-season games—including five in one game against the Toronto Maple Leafs—to lead the Canadiens to their first Stanley Cup title in 14 years.

1944–45

With the war in Europe winding down, players who had performed military service slowly began trickling back to NHL rosters in 1944–45, though most teams were still thinly stocked. Picking up the slack were several talented newcomers who made their NHL debuts this season, including Ted Lindsay and Harry Lumley with the Detroit Red Wings, Toronto's Frank McCool and Bill Moe with the New York Rangers. The undisputed star of the 1944–45 season, though, was Rocket Richard.

Scoring at a season-long pace of a goal per game, the Canadiens' right wing enjoyed a record-setting night on December 28, 1944, scoring five goals and adding three assists in a 9–1 Montreal victory over the Detroit Red Wings. Later in the season, Richard surpassed Joe Malone's single-season scoring record of 44 goals (set during the NHL's 22-game inaugural season of 1917–18) when he scored his 45th on February 25, 1945. By season's end, Richard had scored 50 goals in 50 games.

The Rocket was not the only record-setting player during the 1944–45 campaign. His linemate Elmer Lach set a new standard with 54 assists en route to winning the league scoring title with 80 points. Syd Howe's 515th career point during that season put him ahead of Nels Stewart as the NHL's all-time leader, while his Detroit Red Wing teammate Flash Hollett became the first defenseman to score 20 goals in a season.

Montreal's Bill Durnan won his second consecutive Vezina Trophy, as the Canadiens once again finished first. In the playoffs, however, the Canadiens were the targets of a semifinal upset by the Toronto Maple Leafs. Leaf goalie Frank McCool, 1945's rookie of the year, opened the finals with three consecutive shutouts as the Leafs held on to beat Detroit in seven games and win the Stanley Cup.

1945–46

With the World War II ended, more than 40 players returned from military service to their respective NHL rosters for the start of training camp in 1945. The Boston Bruins welcomed back Milt Schmidt, Woody Dumart, Bobby Bauer and goaltender Frank Brimsek. Art Ross, deciding to concentrate on his role as general manager, turned over the coaching honors to Dit Clapper, who would also continue to play for Boston. The revitalized Bruins battled the Montreal Canadiens for much of the 1945–46 season before settling for second place.

The New York Rangers welcomed back stars Lynn and Muzz Patrick, Neil Colville and goalie Chuck Rayner. Their lineup also boasted rookie of the year Edgar Laprade, but hard times continued as the club finished last in every major statistical category for the third year in a row and wound up in last place again. The going was also tough in Toronto, where the Maple Leafs opened the season without goaltender Frank McCool. Even Turk Broda's return from the military in January 1946 could not salvage a season that saw Toronto become just the second NHL team to miss the playoffs the year after winning the Stanley Cup.

The Montreal Canadiens endured a scoring slump by the Punch Line of Rocket Richard, Elmer Lach and Toe Blake, as well as an injury to goalie Bill Durnan, yet they once again finished first in the regular season. Their top trio regained its scoring touch in the playoffs, finishing 1–2–3 in postseason scoring as the Canadiens won the Stanley Cup for the second time in three seasons, beating Boston in the final.

1946–47

Postwar reconstruction of the NHL began in earnest prior to the 1946–47 season. Clarence Campbell was named the NHL's third president, succeeding Red Dutton, rosters were replenished with returning veterans and the regular season was extended from 50 to 60 games.

In Toronto, Frank Selke, who had guided the Maple Leafs during Conn Smythe's military service, lost a power struggle with the team's board of directors and left to run the Montreal Canadiens. Fully in charge of his team again, Smythe cleared out a number of aging stars to make room for youngsters like Bill Barilko, Sid Smith, Calder Trophy–winner Howie Meeker and Garth Boesch, and hockey's newest dynasty was formed.

Max Bentley, playing on the Chicago Black Hawks' Pony Line with brother Doug and Bill Mosienko, led the NHL with 72 points, and Punch Line star Rocket Richard regained his scoring touch to pot 45 goals. Milt Schmidt and Woody Dumart of Boston's Kraut Line also returned to the NHL's top 10 scorers in 1946–47. On March 16, 1947, Billy Taylor of the Detroit Red Wings collected a record seven assists in a single game, while the Leafs' Howie Meeker set a rookie record on January 8 with five goals in one contest.

The Leafs finished the regular season in second place behind Montreal and knocked off the Red Wings in five games in the semifinals. Toronto dropped the opening game of the finals 6–0 to the Canadiens before winning the Stanley Cup in six games.

1947–48

The 1947–48 NHL season began with the All-Star Game, an idea which had been proposed the previous season. A collection of NHL greats defeated the defending Stanley Cup champion Toronto Maple Leafs 4–3. Unfortunately, this spirited game was marred by an injury to Chicago Black Hawks' star Bill Mosienko, who suffered a fractured ankle. A similar injury also ended the career of Toe Blake, thus breaking up the Montreal Canadiens' much-feared Punch Line. It was also the end of an era in Boston, where Bobby Bauer's retirement broke up the Kraut Line. Meanwhile Detroit saw the rise of a new offensive force when Red Wings coach Tommy Ivan teamed second-year forward Gordie Howe on a line with Ted Lindsay and Sid Abel, creating the Production Line.

In Toronto, Conn Smythe was not satisfied with the defending Stanley Cup champions' depth. He wanted a third center to complement Syl Apps and Teeder Kennedy, a need made all the more pressing by Apps's talk of retirement. The Leafs opened the season undefeated in six games, but after a loss to the Rangers on November 2, Smythe orchestrated the biggest trade in NHL history, sending Bud Poile, Bob Goldham, Ernie Dickens, Gaye Stewart and Gus Bodnar to the Chicago Black Hawks for perennial All-Star and slick puck-handler Max Bentley, along with rookie Cy Thomas.

With Bentley bolstering their attack, the Leafs soared to a 32–15–13 record and a first-place finish. In the playoffs, Toronto downed the Bruins in five games before sweeping the Detroit Red Wings for their second consecutive Stanley Cup championship.

On a dark note, two of the league's finest playmakers, Billy Taylor of the Rangers and Boston's Don Gallinger, were handed lifetime suspensions for gambling.

1948–49

The 1948–49 season opened on a sour note for the New York Rangers. The team was enjoying a productive training camp when Bill Moe, Edgar Laprade, Buddy O'Connor, Frank Eddolls and Tony Leswick were all injured in a car accident. Three of the five sustained only minor injuries, but O'Connor and Eddolls would be lost for at least two months. The Rangers opened the season 6–11–6, costing Frank Boucher his coaching job. Lynn Patrick took over behind the bench, but the Rangers still wound up missing the playoffs by 10 points.

Joining New York on the sidelines come postseason were the Chicago Black Hawks, who finished fifth in the six-team league despite the fact that teammates Roy Conacher and Doug Bentley were a comfortable 1–2 atop the NHL scoring leaders. For much of the season, it appeared the two-time Cup champion Maple Leafs would miss the playoffs. Hurt by the retirements of Nick Metz and Syl Apps, and besieged by injuries all season, only a late-season collapse by the Rangers and Hawks got the Leafs into the playoffs. The brilliant goaltending of Bill Durnan, who had 10 shutouts on the season—including a modern-day record four in a row at one stretch—carried the Montreal Canadiens to a third-place finish. The Detroit Red Wings easily topped the Boston Bruins to wind up first in the regular-season standings.

In the playoffs, the Leafs came to life. Healthy for the first time all season, Toronto downed Boston in five games, then swept Detroit for the second straight year to win their third consecutive Stanley Cup title. They were the first fourth-place regular-season finisher to win the trophy.

1949–50

The Detroit Red Wings won eight of their first 10 games to start the 1949–50 season and they never looked back. Despite a surprising trade that saw them swap star defenseman Bill Quackenbush to the Boston Bruins for four players, and an injury to goalie Harry Lumley, the Red Wings were the best in hockey. The Quackenbush trade allowed Red Kelly to take a more prominent role on the club's defense, while the Lumley injury let Detroit preview goaltender Terry Sawchuk. Offensively, the Production Line of Ted Lindsay, Sid Abel and Gordie Howe finished 1–2–3 in league scoring.

In Montreal, goalie Bill Durnan won the Vezina Trophy for the sixth time in seven seasons, and Rocket Richard returned to form with 43 goals, but the Canadiens finished a distant second to Detroit in the standings. The Toronto Maple Leafs were third, while the disappointing Bruins dropped to fifth and missed the playoffs. Despite a lineup that featured five 20-goal scorers, the Chicago Black Hawks finished last and had problems drawing fans.

The surprise of the 1949–50 season was the Broadway revival of the New York Rangers. A well-balanced attack and the stellar goaltending of Chuck Rayner, who earned the Hart Trophy as most valuable player, led the Rangers to a fourth-place finish and just their second postseason appearance since 1943.

In the playoffs, the Red Wings knocked off Toronto despite a severe head injury to Gordie Howe. The Rangers defeated Montreal in the semifinals, but were forced to play the entire final series against Detroit on the road because the circus was booked into Madison Square Garden. Still, the Rangers pushed the Red Wings to seven games before

Pete Babando (acquired in the Quackenbush trade) scored in the second overtime to give Detroit the Stanley Cup.

1950–51

The Detroit Red Wings were defending Stanley Cup champions and clear favorites to repeat, but there were changes in the Motor City for 1950–51. In the biggest trade in NHL history, Detroit sent Harry Lumley, Jack Stewart, Al Dewsbury, Don Morrison and Pete Babando to the Chicago Black Hawks for Jim Henry, Bob Goldham, Gaye Stewart and Metro Prystai. Lumley had been the NHL's winningest goalie the previous two seasons, but was deemed expendable with the emergence of Terry Sawchuk.

During the off-season, the NHL decided to maintain the 70-game schedule introduced the year before, and Detroit took advantage of the extra 10 games to rewrite the record book, winning 44 games and posting 101 points—the first 100-point season in NHL history. Sawchuk was in net for each of the victories, setting an individual record, and he won the Calder Trophy as rookie of the year. Gordie Howe bounced back from a head injury suffered in last year's playoffs to win the Art Ross Trophy with an all-time NHL high of 86 points. Despite their great success, however, the Red Wings were eliminated in six games in the semifinals by the third-place Montreal Canadiens.

Under new coach Joe Primeau, the Toronto Maple Leafs had battled Detroit all season long and established a club record with 95 points. The Maple Leafs knocked off the fourth-place Boston Bruins in five games, then beat Montreal in five for their fifth Stanley Cup victory in seven years. Each of the five games in the finals went to overtime, with Bill Barilko scoring the series-winner. Three months later, Barilko disappeared on a fishing trip to northern Ontario. The wreckage of the plane that contained his body would not be discovered until 1962. By strange coincidence, the Leafs would not win the Cup again until that same year.

1951–52

For the second year in a row, the Detroit Red Wings made changes to a talented roster and came out ahead. Six players were sold to the Chicago Black Hawks, with Jack Adams convinced that rookie Alex Delvecchio and newcomer Tony Leswick would help pick up the slack. Adams was right, as the Red Wings cruised to their second straight 44-win season and easily finished atop the NHL standings with 100 points. Gordie Howe earned both the Hart and Art Ross trophies, while Terry Sawchuk won the Vezina Trophy with a 1.90 goals-against average and 12 shutouts.

The Montreal Canadiens finished in second place in 1951–52. The team was without Rocket Richard due to injuries for much of the season, but Bernie "Boom Boom" Geoffrion bolstered the offense with 30 goals and was named rookie of the year. Dickie Moore joined the team in December and recorded 33 points in 33 games. The Toronto Maple Leafs, struggling to score goals throughout the season, finished four points behind Montreal for third place. The Boston Bruins claimed the last playoff spot, while the New York Rangers and Chicago Black Hawks finished fifth and sixth respectively. On the last night of the regular season, Chicago's Bill Mosienko put his name in the record book by scoring three goals in 21 seconds during a 7–6 win over the Rangers.

The Red Wings proved to be even better in the playoffs than during the regular season, sweeping Toronto in the semifinals and then sweeping Montreal in the finals to capture the Stanley Cup in just eight games, the minimum number required. Terry Sawchuk did not allow a single goal on home ice during both rounds of the playoffs, posting a 0.62 goals-against average and recording four shutouts in postseason play.

1952–53

Big changes in Chicago this season saw the Black Hawks make the playoffs for the first time since 1946. On September 11, 1952, the three owners of the Chicago Stadium—James Norris, Sr., James D. Norris, and Arthur Wirtz—acquired control of the hockey team. They lured Sid Abel away from the Detroit Red Wings to become a playing coach, and they dealt goalie Harry Lumley to the Toronto Maple Leafs for Al Rollins, Ray Hannigan, Gus Mortson and Cal Gardner.

Despite the loss of Abel, the Red Wings remained the NHL's best team. Alex Delvecchio joined Gordie Howe and Ted Lindsay on the team's top line, which remained as productive as ever. Gordie Howe netted 49 goals during the 1952–53 season and won the Art Ross Trophy with a league-record 95 points. Detroit finished the regular season in first place for the fifth straight season, while the Montreal Canadiens again finished second. Rocket Richard's scored his 325th career goal during the season, surpassing Nels Stewart as the NHL's all-time leader.

There was concern in Toronto that the Maple Leafs were getting old as the team struggled to score goals for the second year in a row. The fears proved well-founded as the Leafs missed the playoffs, finishing two points back of Chicago and the Boston Bruins, who were tied with 69 points. The Rangers dropped to the basement, but the debuts of Gump Worsley, Andy Bathgate, Dean Prentice and Harry Howell provided reason for optimism at Madison Square Garden.

Chicago's return to the postseason lasted seven games before Montreal, with Jacques Plante starring in goal, eliminated them. The Bruins then stunned the Red Wings in a six-game semifinal, but fell to the Canadiens in five in the Stanley Cup final.

1953–54

A familiar cast of characters led the Detroit Red Wings to their sixth first-place finish in a row. Gordie Howe won the Art Ross Trophy for the fourth consecutive year as the NHL's leading scorer. Terry Sawchuk registered 12 shutouts and a 1.92 goals-against average and Red Kelly became the first winner of the James Norris Memorial Trophy as the NHL's best defenseman.

After a prolonged courtship, the Montreal Canadiens finally signed Jean Beliveau this season, but injuries would limit him to just 44 games. Injuries also sidelined Dickie Moore, while a pair of suspensions forced the Habs to do without Boom Boom Geoffrion for 16 games. Rocket Richard led the league with 37 goals, and his 67 points were second only to Gordie Howe as Montreal still managed to finish the regular season in second place.

King Clancy took over the coaching reins in Toronto and, emphasizing defense, led the Maple Leafs back into the playoffs with a third-place finish. Goalie Harry Lumley had 13 shutouts and a 1.86 goals-against average to win the Vezina Trophy. The Boston Bruins grabbed fourth place, while the New York Rangers and Chicago Black Hawks missed the playoffs. The Black Hawks were a woeful

12–51–7 and yet goalie Al Rollins still managed to compile a decent 3.23 goals-against average and was rewarded with the Hart Trophy as the player most valuable to his team.

In the playoffs, the Red Wings, still stinging from last year's postseason disappointment, were not be denied. They downed Toronto in five games, while Montreal swept Boston. The finals came down to a seventh game, with Detroit's Tony Leswick scoring the Stanley Cup winner on a bad bounce in overtime for a 2–1 victory.

1954–55

Conn Smythe stepped aside as general manager of the Toronto Maple Leafs prior to the 1954–55 season, turning over the job to Hap Day. Boston's general manager Art Ross also retired after running the Bruins since their inception in 1924. In Chicago, Sid Abel resigned as Black Hawks coach amid fears the franchise might fold and Tommy Ivan gave up coaching the Detroit Red Wings to become Chicago's general manager. Elmer Lach retired in Montreal and Jacques Plante took over from Gerry McNeil in the Canadiens' goal, but there would be a much bigger story involving the Habs this season.

Though he was the NHL's greatest goal scorer, Rocket Richard had never won the Art Ross Trophy. He appeared destined to capture his first scoring title in 1954–55, until his legendary temper got the better of him. On March 13, 1955, Richard punched linesman Cliff Thompson after a stick-swinging incident with Boston's Hal Laycoe. NHL president Clarence Campbell suspended Richard for the season's final three games and all of the playoffs. When Campbell showed up at the Montreal Forum on the night of March 17, a riot broke out. Only a radio plea by Richard the following day was able to restore peace to the city.

At the time of his suspension, the Rocket led Boom Boom Geoffrion by two points in the NHL scoring race and the Canadiens were two points up on Detroit for top spot in the standings. With Richard out, Geoffrion passed him for the scoring title and Detroit claimed first place for the seventh consecutive season. In the playoffs, the Red Wings swept Toronto, while Montreal beat Boston in five. In the finals, the Red Wings again got the better of the Canadiens, winning the Stanley Cup in seven games.

1955–56

After two straight losses to the Detroit Red Wings in the Stanley Cup finals, the Montreal Canadiens made several key changes for the 1955–56 season, in the process assembling the greatest dynasty in NHL history. With Doug Harvey now the key to the Canadiens' defense, veteran Butch Bouchard was phased out, opening a spot for newcomer Bob Turner. Henri Richard, the Rocket's brother, and Claude Provost were also added to the lineup. The key change, however, was the decision to replace coach Dick Irvin with Toe Blake. Irvin returned to Chicago, where he'd begun his NHL playing and coaching careers, to try and resurrect the Black Hawks.

There were more changes in Detroit in 1955–56, but unlike past moves, this season's trade hurt the team. With Glenn Hall emerging as a top-notch goaltender, Jack Adams dealt Terry Sawchuk and three other players to the Boston Bruins, but of the five players Detroit received in return only Warren Godfrey lasted the entire season.

With Jean Beliveau's 47 goals and 88 points leading the league, and Jacques Plante winning the Vezina Trophy in goal, the Canadiens cruised to an NHL record 45 victories

and the first 100-point season in franchise history. Detroit was a distant second with 76 points, while the New York Rangers established franchise highs with 32 wins and 74 points. The Toronto Maple Leafs slipped into the final playoff spot, with two more points than Boston's 59.

In the playoffs, Montreal disposed of New York in five games while Detroit dispatched Toronto just as easily. This year, the Red Wings proved no match for the Canadiens as Montreal won the Stanley Cup in five games. No other team would win it for the rest of the decade.

1956–57

After losing both their regular-season and Stanley Cup crowns to the Montreal Canadiens, it was expected that the Detroit Red Wings would make big changes for the 1956–57 season, but Jack Adams made only minor adjustments. His team responded with a first-place finish. Injuries to Montreal stars Boom Boom Geoffrion, Rocket Richard, Henri Richard and Jacques Plante helped Detroit's cause, but so too did the play of Gordie Howe. Howe edged teammate Ted Lindsay by four points to win the Art Ross Trophy for the fifth time and also took home the Hart as most valuable player.

The Boston Bruins proved a pleasant surprise this season, though injuries and illness forced them to replace goalie Terry Sawchuk with rookie Don Simmons for much of the year. A solid offense, led by Real Chevrefils' 31 goals, saw Boston finish just two points behind Montreal for third place in the standings. The New York Rangers grabbed the final playoff spot, while the Toronto Maple Leafs fell to fifth place under rookie coach Howie Meeker. Tommy Ivan replaced an ailing Dick Irvin as coach in Chicago, but the Black Hawks finished in the league basement for the fourth year in a row.

In the semifinals, Boston threw a tight-checking blanket over Detroit's top line of Lindsay, Howe and Alex Delvecchio enabling them to upset the first-place Red Wings in five games. Montreal needed just five games to knock off New York, with Rocket Richard scoring the series winner in overtime. Two nights later, Richard opened the Stanley Cup finals with a four-goal effort in a 5–1 Canadiens win. Montreal cruised to its second consecutive Stanley Cup title in five games.

1957–58

In February 1957, a group of NHL players tried to form a union. The attempt was not welcomed by NHL owners, who crushed the fledgling association during the 1957–58 season. Ted Lindsay had been the leader of the players' fight for rights and Jack Adams punished his great star with a trade to the lowly Chicago Black Hawks. Lindsay and goalie Glenn Hall were both dealt to Chicago, who also introduced a rookie named Bobby Hull this season and finally began to show signs of improvement after years of horrible hockey, though they would miss the playoffs again this season.

The Boston Bruins also proved beneficiaries of Jack Adams' wheeling and dealing, acquiring John Bucyk in a deal that returned Terry Sawchuk to Detroit. Another key Bruin addition was Bronco Horvath, who came over from the Montreal Canadiens. The star-studded Canadiens, who kept their team basically intact, set an NHL record with 250 goals and cruised to first place in the standings. Dickie Moore led the league in goals and points, while Henri Richard topped the loop in assists. Jacques Plante won the

Vezina Trophy, while Rocket Richard became the first player in league history to score 500 goals. The New York Rangers finished a surprising second to Montreal. The Toronto Maple Leafs, who fired general manager Howie Meeker before the club had even played a game, slipped to last place for the first time since 1919 when the team had been known as the Arenas.

Montreal swept Detroit in the semifinals while Boston upset New York to set up a rematch of the previous year's final. This time, the Bruins proved a stubborn foe, but the powerful Canadiens prevailed in six games to capture their third consecutive Stanley Cup.

1958–59

The Montreal Canadiens were the class of the NHL again in 1958–59, finishing well atop the regular-season standings and becoming the first team in league history to win four consecutive Stanley Cup titles. Jacques Plante won the Vezina Trophy for the fourth straight season, while Tom Johnson won the Norris Trophy as top defenseman, ending teammate Doug Harvey's four-year reign. Dickie Moore won his second consecutive Art Ross Trophy and set a new NHL scoring record with 96 points.

The Boston Bruins climbed to second place, while the Chicago Black Hawks, backed by the solid goaltending of Glenn Hall, reached the playoffs for just the second time in 13 years. The Hawks featured an excellent defense, and a young Bobby Hull complemented a veteran forward unit that included Ted Lindsay and Tod Sloan. The Canadiens' fierce rival for much of the decade, the Detroit Red Wings, fell to last place.

The New York Rangers appeared to have the fourth and final playoff spot sewn up before one of the great collapses in hockey history. Punch Imlach, who'd been named general manager of the Toronto Maple Leafs early in the 1958–59 season, had promptly named himself head coach. But the Leafs, who had missed the playoffs two years in a row, were slow to respond. In fact, with just five games left in the season, Toronto was still seven points behind the Rangers. But the Leafs won those last five games, while New York dropped six of seven, and the Leafs clinched a playoff spot on the last night of the season.

Toronto's roll continued into the playoffs, as they defeated Boston in the semifinals in seven games. The Canadiens, however, needed just five games to cool off the Leafs and claim an NHL record-setting fourth consecutive Stanley Cup championship.

1959–60

Bobby Hull emerged as an NHL superstar in 1959–60. Teamed on a line with Bill Hay and Murray Balfour, the Chicago Black Hawks' "Golden Jet" was involved in a season-long battle for the NHL scoring title with Bronco Horvath of the Boston Bruins. Hull emerged victorious, ending the year with 39 goals and 42 assists to Horvath's 39 and 41. A promising newcomer was added to the Chicago roster, as Stan Mikita centered a line with Ted Lindsay and Kenny Wharram. Glenn Hall, as always, was solid in goal as the Black Hawks emerged from an early-season slump to finish in third place and reach the playoffs in consecutive seasons for the first time since the early 1940s.

The Toronto Maple Leafs, who had rallied into the playoffs the previous season under Punch Imlach, enjoyed a solid second-place finish in 1959–60, as once again the Montreal Canadiens came out on top. The Detroit Red Wings rebounded from last season's trip to the cellar, climbing into fourth place. The Boston Bruins and New York Rangers missed the playoffs.

In their semifinal series, the Canadiens assigned Claude Provost to shadow Bobby Hull and he limited the NHL's scoring leader to just one goal in a four-game sweep as Montreal reached the Stanley Cup final for the tenth year in a row. The other semifinal featured Toronto and Detroit, with the Leafs winning in six. The Canadiens were heavy favorites in the finals and had little trouble with the Leafs, winning in four to duplicate Detroit's 1952 feat of sweeping the playoffs, and setting a new standard with five consecutive Stanley Cup wins. Rocket Richard scored what would prove to be the final goal of his legendary career in the third game of the Leafs series.

1960–61

Throughout the summer, Montreal newspapers were filled with rumors about Rocket Richard's imminent retirement. Although Richard was with the Canadiens when they opened training camp, he announced on September 15, 1960—only hours after scoring four goals in an intrasquad scrimmage—that his brilliant career was over. He had scored a record 544 goals in the regular season and added 82 more in the playoffs. Even more importantly, he had been the heart and soul of hockey in Montreal.

As Richard made his exit, two players took aim at one of his most legendary accomplishments. Though the NHL season had lengthened from 50 games to 70, no one had so far managed to duplicate Richard's 50-goal season of 1944–45. This year, Frank Mahovlich of the Toronto Maple Leafs was scoring at a record rate, but he slumped down the stretch just as Montreal's Boom Boom Geoffrion got red hot. Season's end found Mahovlich with 48 goals, but Geoffrion reached the magic 50 and added 45 assists to win the Art Ross Trophy. Punch Imlach had much improved his Toronto club, putting ex-defenseman Red Kelly at center on a line with Mahovlich and rookie Bob Nevin. Another first-year Leaf, center Dave Keon, was also impressive, scoring 20 goals and winning the Calder Trophy.

The four playoff qualifiers finished in the same order as last year: Montreal, Toronto, Chicago, Detroit. The Chicago Black Hawks surprised Montreal in the semifinals, winning in six games and dashing the Canadiens' hopes of a sixth consecutive Cup win. The fourth-place Red Wings upset Toronto, setting up the first all–U.S. final since 1950, but they could not contain the Black Hawks, who won in six games to capture their first Stanley Cup title since 1938.

1961–62

Though their five-year reign as Stanley Cup champions had ended the previous spring, the Montreal Canadiens resisted the urge to overhaul their aging roster for 1961–62. One major change, though, saw the Canadiens allow superstar defenseman Doug Harvey to move to the New York Rangers, where he became a playing coach. The Canadiens received tough guy Lou Fontinato in return. The Rangers responded by climbing to fourth place and back into the postseason, though the play of Andy Bathgate was probably more responsible than Harvey's coaching.

All season long, Bathgate and Bobby Hull of the defending Stanley Cup champion Chicago Black Hawks battled for the scoring title. The duel between the slick playmaker and powerful goal scorer went right down to the final game, when Hull became just the third player in history to score

50 goals by beating the Rangers' Gump Worsley. Bathgate collected his 56th assist against the Black Hawks that night, and the two players ended tied with 88 points. Hull was awarded the Art Ross Trophy because he had more goals.

For the third year in a row, the top two teams in the regular season were the Canadiens and the Toronto Maple Leafs. The Detroit Red Wings missed the playoffs, while the Boston Bruins were a dismal 15–47–8 and finished last for the second year running. The Canadiens took the first two games from Chicago in their semifinal series, but then lost four in a row as the Black Hawks returned to the finals. The Leafs beat New York in six games. An injury to Johnny Bower forced the Leafs to switch to Don Simmons in goal after four games with Chicago, and he led Toronto to victory in six. It was Toronto's first Stanley Cup triumph since their overtime thriller in 1951.

1962–63

Having won the Cup the previous spring, Punch Imlach and the Toronto Maple Leafs entered the 1962–63 season with the team virtually intact, though top scorer Frank Mahovlich was nearly sold to the Chicago Black Hawks for $1 million. Only five points separated the first- and fourth-place teams in the tightest season-long competition in league history, with the Leafs finishing on top for the first time since 1947–48. The Black Hawks' 81 points were just one behind Toronto, though a remarkable streak ended in Chicago when a sore back forced Glenn Hall out of goal after playing 502 consecutive complete games. Injuries also hampered the Montreal Canadiens, who slipped to third for their worst performance since 1950–51. The Detroit Red Wings finished fourth in a rebuilding year that saw Jack Adams step down after 35 years as general manager.

Sid Abel added the general manager's portfolio to his Detroit coaching duties, and it was his former Production Line-mate Gordie Howe who led the resurgence. Mr. Hockey earned the Art Ross Trophy as the NHL's leading scorer with 86 points, while also garnering the Hart Trophy as MVP. It was the sixth and final time he'd receive either honor. Andy Bathgate was runner-up for the Art Ross for the second year in a row, though his New York Rangers slipped to fifth place. The Boston Bruins occupied the basement for the third straight year.

Toronto and Montreal met in the semifinals, with Johnny Bower collecting two shutouts and allowing the Canadiens just six goals in a five-game Leafs victory. The Black Hawks took the first two games from Detroit in their series before the Red Wings rallied to win in six. The finals featured tight defensive play, in which the Leafs prevailed in five evenly matched games to win their second consecutive Stanley Cup title.

1963–64

After three early playoff exits, the Montreal Canadiens swung a major trade with the New York Rangers prior to the 1963–64 season. The Habs sent Jacques Plante, Phil Goyette and Don Marshall to New York for Dave Balon, Len Ronson, Leon Rochefort and Gump Worsley, though it would be Charlie Hodge rather than Worsley who would see most of the action in the Canadiens' goal. Tom Johnson went to the Boston Bruins, and Dickie Moore retired and was replaced by John Ferguson. Montreal responded to the changes with a first-place finish, one point ahead of the Chicago Black Hawks.

Billy Reay was the new coach in Chicago, where team-mates Bobby Hull and Stan Mikita dueled for the scoring title. Hull led the league with 43 goals, but Mikita's 89 points on 39 goals and 50 assists were two better than the Golden Jet. Two major career records were broken by Detroit Red Wings players during the 1963–64 season— Gordie Howe surpassed Rocket Richard's mark of 544 goals, while Terry Sawchuk passed George Hainsworth with his 95th career shutout. The Red Wings slumped in the early going under the pressure of Howe's record chase, but rallied to a fourth-place finish.

The defending Stanley Cup champion Toronto Maple Leafs also found the going rough until a huge late-season trade saw them acquire Andy Bathgate and Don McKenney from the New York Rangers for five players. The Leafs ended the season in third place while New York missed the playoffs for the second year in a row. The Boston Bruins finished last for the fourth straight season.

For the first time since the best-of-seven format was introduced in 1939, all three playoff series went the distance, with the Maple Leafs knocking off Montreal and Detroit for their third consecutive Stanley Cup triumph.

1964–65

After 18 seasons, during which he had built the greatest dynasty in hockey history, Frank Selke retired as managing director of the Montreal Canadiens prior to the 1964–65 season. He was succeeded by Sam Pollock. Several youngsters were also added to the roster to replace aging and departing veterans, but it was the play of long-time greats Jean Beliveau and Henri Richard that had the Canadiens off to a flying start. Injuries, though, saw Montreal slump to a second-place finish in the regular season.

The top team in the NHL this season was the Detroit Red Wings, who had not finished first since 1956–57. The team was sparked by the comeback of Ted Lindsay after a four-year retirement, but it was the play of young goalie Roger Crozier, as well as the offensive power of Gordie Howe, Alex Delvecchio and Norm Ullman that fueled the Red Wings' resurgence. Ullman led the NHL with 42 goals, and his 83 points trailed only Stan Mikita's 87. Mikita and the Chicago Black Hawks fought Montreal and Detroit in a three-way battle for first place, but had to settle for third. A string of injuries saw the three-time defending Stanley Cup champion Toronto Maple Leafs fall into fourth place, while, for the fifth time in six years, the New York Rangers and Boston Bruins both failed to make the playoffs.

The Leafs' reign as Stanley Cup champions came to an early end when the Canadiens beat them in a six-game semifinal. Chicago knocked off Detroit in seven games, reversing the results of a season ago. The Canadiens then knocked off Chicago in a tough seven-game series to win the Stanley Cup. Jean Beliveau was named the inaugural winner of the Conn Smythe Trophy as playoff MVP.

1965–66

Bobby Hull became hockey's all-time single-season scoring leader in 1965–66, collecting 54 goals and 97 points, both league records. Goal number 51 came on March 12, 1966, before a packed house at Chicago Stadium. Hull won the Art Ross Trophy for the third time, as well as earning his second consecutive Hart Trophy selection as league MVP. The Golden Jet's brilliant play had the Chicago Black Hawks in a season-long battle for top spot with the Montreal Canadiens, though they would have to settle for second place this year.

The Detroit Red Wings, who had finished first the previous season but been eliminated in the first playoff round, made some lineup adjustments, including an eight-player swap with the Toronto Maple Leafs in which the principals were rugged defenseman Marcel Pronovost—headed for Toronto—and center Andy Bathgate—going to the Wings. Detroit was further buoyed by Gordie Howe's 600th goal, but a career-ending injury to defenseman Doug Barkley saw them slump to fourth place. The aging Maple Leafs came in third. The Boston Bruins finally climbed out of last place, finishing one point ahead of the New York Rangers. Promising youngsters like Ted Green, Don Awrey and Gerry Cheevers gave reason for optimism in Boston once the league expanded for the 1967–68 season—a decision that the league announced on February 9, 1966.

For the third year in a row, Detroit met the Black Hawks in the semifinals. Chicago was heavily favored, but the Red Wings won in six games. Montreal knocked off Toronto in six, and claimed their second straight Stanley Cup title with another six-game victory over Detroit. Red Wings goalie Roger Crozier won the Conn Smythe Trophy as playoff MVP for his outstanding play in a losing effort.

1966–67

The NHL's final season as a six-team loop saw the Chicago Black Hawks finish in first place for the first time in franchise history, which dated back to 1926. Bobby Hull's 52 goals led the league as Chicago established a new team goal-scoring record with 264, but Stan Mikita was the big story as he won the Art Ross Trophy with 97 points and the Hart Trophy as MVP. The reformed tough guy also won the Lady Byng Trophy, becoming in the process the first NHL player to capture three major awards in one season.

The two-time defending Stanley Cup champion Montreal Canadiens finished second to Chicago in the regular season, though their 77 points left them 17 out of top spot. A veteran band of Toronto Maple Leafs, augmented by youngsters like Jim Pappin and Pete Stemkowski, finished third, while the New York Rangers returned to the postseason after missing the playoffs in seven of eight previous seasons. The Detroit Red Wings fell into fifth place, while the Boston Bruins slipped back into the basement. The debut of Bobby Orr and the appointment of Harry Sinden as coach suggested their days as also-rans were coming to an end.

New York's return to the playoffs was short-lived, as Montreal swept them out of the semifinals. Toronto and goalie Terry Sawchuk stunned Chicago in six games to set up an all-Canadian final in Canada's centennial year. The Canadiens were expected to add a Stanley Cup win to Montreal's Expo 67 festivities (a place had been reserved for the trophy in the Quebec pavilion at the world's fair) but instead, an aging gang of Toronto players, including Sawchuk, George Armstrong, Johnny Bower, Allan Stanley and Red Kelly, closed out hockey's six-team era with what would prove to be coach Punch Imlach's fourth and last Stanley Cup victory.

1967–68

The NHL doubled its membership for 1967–68, adding the Philadelphia Flyers, Los Angeles Kings, St. Louis Blues, Minnesota North Stars, Pittsburgh Penguins and Oakland Seals. The expanded 12-team league was split into two divisions, with the "Original Six" teams in the East Division and the new clubs in the West. The regular season was expanded to 74 games, with each team playing 50 against divisional rivals and 24 against the other division. The top four teams in each division would make the playoffs, with the quarterfinals and semifinals determining the champion of each division, who would then play for the Stanley Cup. This playoff format guaranteed an established team would meet an expansion team in the final round.

An elaborate expansion draft, plus much preseason wheeling and dealing, meant the NHL's newest clubs all had some veteran talent, though two of the more interesting trades involved only the old-line teams. The Boston Bruins acquired Phil Esposito, Ken Hodge and Fred Stanfield from Chicago for Gilles Marotte, Pit Martin and Jack Norris, while the Maple Leafs sent Frank Mahovlich, Pete Stemkowski, Garry Unger and the rights to Carl Brewer to the Red Wings for Norm Ullman, Paul Henderson and Floyd Smith. Both Toronto and Detroit failed to make the playoffs, but Boston's big deal helped the Bruins return to the postseason for the first time since 1959. Bobby Orr helped too, winning the Norris Trophy as best defenseman in only his second season.

Except for Oakland, the expansion teams were evenly matched, with just six points separating the top five teams. Philadelphia took first place, but St. Louis proved the best in the playoffs. The Blues were no match for the East champion Canadiens, though, as Montreal swept St. Louis to win the Stanley Cup.

1968–69

The 1968–69 season saw the Boston Bruins' emergence as an NHL powerhouse. Bobby Orr was by far the league's best defenseman and Phil Esposito proved to be its best offensive star. Esposito became the first player to top 100 points when he finished the season with 49 goals and 77 assists. New York's Goal-A-Game Line of Jean Ratelle, Vic Hadfield and Rod Gilbert was also leading the Rangers back to respectability.

In Chicago, the Black Hawks signed Bobby Hull to a three-year deal worth $100,000 per season and he responded with a record 58 goals. Hull and Detroit's ageless Gordie Howe also topped 100 points this season, though their teams failed to make the playoffs in the East. Montreal was the top club in the regular season with 103 points (three more than Boston) and once again advanced to the Stanley Cup finals with a pair of playoff series victories.

For the second year in a row, St. Louis proved to be the best in the West, topping all the new teams with 88 points. The Blues had enticed Jacques Plante out of retirement to join Glenn Hall in a stellar goaltending tandem. The veterans combined for 13 shutouts and shared the Vezina Trophy by backstopping the league's stingiest defense. The Blues also had some offensive talent, as Red Berenson tied an NHL record with six goals in a single game. He finished the year with 35 goals and 47 assists and was the only West Division player to crack the top 10 in league scoring.

For the second year in a row, future Canadiens coach Scotty Bowman led the St. Louis Blues against Montreal in the Stanley Cup final and, for the second year in a row, the Canadiens swept the series in four close games.

1969–70

There was a fierce battle for playoff spots in the East Division in 1969–70, with the two-time defending Stanley Cup champion Montreal Canadiens missing the postseason despite a 92-point season that topped any team in the West. The Toronto Maple Leafs were last in the East with 71

points, making it the first time in NHL history that no Canadian teams qualified for the playoffs.

Bobby Hull joined Gordie Howe and Rocket Richard in the 500-goal club, but the highlight of the season for the first-place Black Hawks was the remarkable goaltending of Tony Esposito. The rookie netminder posted a modern-era record 15 shutouts and won both the Vezina and Calder trophies. Bobby Orr enjoyed a sizzling record-breaking season in Boston, becoming the first defenseman to lead the NHL in scoring. In addition to winning the Art Ross Trophy as scoring leader, Orr also won his third straight Norris Trophy as the league's best blueliner.

Once again, the St. Louis Blues were the top team in the West Division, finishing well ahead of the Pittsburgh Penguins. The Blues advanced to their third consecutive Stanley Cup final by eliminating the Minnesota North Stars, then Pittsburgh in the playoffs. This year, Boston would be their opponent in the finals. The Bruins needed six games to defeat the New York Rangers, then surprised Chicago with a four-game sweep.

Long-suffering Bruins star Johnny Bucyk celebrated his first appearance in the Stanley Cup final since 1958 with a hat trick in game one. Following two more Bruins victories, Bobby Orr completed the series sweep with an overtime goal in game four and became the subject of one of hockey's most famous photographs when he went flying through the air after being upended by the Blues' Noel Picard. The Stanley Cup was back in Boston for the first time since 1941.

1970–71

Two cities that narrowly missed joining the NHL in 1967 were added to the league in 1970–71. Despite the geographic contradiction, the Buffalo Sabres and Vancouver Canucks were both placed in the East Division. To improve the competitive balance between the two divisions, the Chicago Black Hawks moved into the West, and the season, extended to 78 games, featured a balanced schedule. The playoff format was also altered so that teams would cross divisional lines after the opening round.

The Boston Bruins, as their Stanley Cup predecessors had done in 1929, followed up their championship with a record-breaking season. The 1970–71 edition of the Bruins set NHL all-time single-season records with 57 victories, 121 points and 399 goals. Phil Esposito set new records with 76 goals and 152 points, while Bobby Orr established a new mark with 102 assists. Esposito, Orr, Johnny Bucyk and Ken Hodge finished 1–2–3–4 in the NHL scoring race as all four topped 100 points, while Espo and Bucyk became the first teammates to top 50 goals in a single season. Unfortunately these Bruins were also like that 1929–30 team in that they couldn't get past the Montreal Canadiens.

Though he had played just six games late in the regular season, Montreal made Ken Dryden their number-one goalie for their quarterfinal series against Boston. Dryden completely stymied the powerful Bruins as Montreal pulled off a stunning seven-game upset. The Canadiens then defeated the Minnesota North Stars to advance to the finals. Chicago provided the opposition, but the Stanley Cup returned to Montreal in a tight seven-game series. Henri Richard scored the Cup-winning goal after feuding with coach Al MacNeil earlier in the series. Dryden earned the Conn Smythe Trophy as playoff MVP.

The NHL lost two of its greats when Jean Beliveau and Gordie Howe announced their retirements—although Howe, it would turn out, was not done just yet.

1971–72

The Montreal Canadiens made two moves before the 1971–72 season that ensured the success of the franchise for years to come. Scotty Bowman was hired as coach and, after a series of trades to ensure they landed the number-one pick, Guy Lafleur was selected in the draft. "The Flower" slowly blossomed into the league's top star, while Rick Martin, selected fifth overall by Buffalo, provided the Sabres with more immediate benefits. Martin set a rookie record with 44 goals, but the Calder Trophy went to Ken Dryden, who had not played enough regular-season games in 1970–71 to lose his rookie status.

For the second straight year, the Boston Bruins and New York Rangers proved to be the top teams in the regular season. Boston's Phil Esposito and Bobby Orr finished 1–2 in the NHL scoring race, while New York's Goal-A-Game Line of Jean Ratelle, Vic Hadfield and Rod Gilbert finished 3–4–5. Bobby Clarke of the Philadelphia Flyers was establishing himself as a star and was the only player from an expansion team to crack the top 10.

With the previous year's playoff upset still in mind, the Bruins downed the Toronto Maple Leafs in five games, then swept the St. Louis Blues in four to advance to the Stanley Cup final. The Rangers, who had edged Montreal by just one point in the regular-season standings, knocked off the Canadiens in six, then swept the West Division–leading Chicago Black Hawks to reach the finals for the first time since 1950.

The Boston–New York Stanley Cup matchup was the first since 1960 to feature the NHL's top two regular-season teams, and the first-place Bruins emerged victorious in six games. Bobby Orr became the first two-time winner of the Conn Smythe Trophy, earning playoff MVP honors as he had in 1970.

1972–73

The hockey universe changed forever in 1972. The NHL had a major professional rival for the first time since the 1926 demise of the old Western Hockey League with the establishment of the World Hockey Association. The new 12-team league featured the Alberta Oilers, Winnipeg Jets, Chicago Cougars, Houston Aeros, Los Angeles Sharks and Minnesota Fighting Saints in the Western Division, while the Eastern Division was comprised of the Cleveland Crusaders, New England Whalers, Quebec Nordiques, Ottawa Nationals, Philadelphia Blazers and New York Raiders.

The WHA raided NHL rosters of talent, securing such players as Bernie Parent, Gerry Cheevers and J.C. Tremblay, though the real coup was Winnipeg's signing of Bobby Hull to a 10-year deal worth $2.75 million. The league was also a place for NHL journeymen such as Andre Lacroix and Danny Lawson to shine. Lawson scored a league-leading 61 goals, while Lacroix topped the loop with 124 points. The Whalers beat Hull's Jets in the Avco Cup final to claim the first WHA championship.

Before either league opened its 1972–73 schedule, hockey fans around the world focused their attention on an eight-game series pitting an all-NHL Team Canada against the Soviet Union's national team. The Soviets were perennial amateur champions, but Canadian fans were confident their top professionals would put the Russians in their place. The Canadians quickly found that the Soviets were a superb team and struggled valiantly to raise their play to meet the challenge. Only Paul Henderson's goal with 34

seconds to play in game eight secured a narrow victory for Team Canada. The Soviets' superior training techniques and strong skating and passing skills would influence the future of hockey in North America.

The NHL responded to the WHA's challenge by adding the New York Islanders and Atlanta Flames this year, but the season's best performances came from traditional favorites. The Boston Bruins' Phil Esposito won his third consecutive scoring title, while the Montreal Canadiens finished first overall in the regular season and later beat the Chicago Black Hawks in six games in the finals to win the Stanley Cup. A one-game challenge issued by the WHA champion Whalers went unheeded by the NHL.

1973–74

During the 1972–73 season, Bobby Clarke had finished second to Phil Esposito in NHL scoring with 104 points, making him the first player from an expansion team to top the 100-point plateau. His Philadelphia Flyers had finished 37–30–11 for their first winning season, and the Flyers' captain was the first member of a non–Original Six team to win the Hart Trophy as most valuable player. During the 1973–74 campaign, the Flyers would emerge as the new NHL powerhouse.

Known as "the Broad Street Bullies" for their intimidating play, the Flyers featured offensive talent in Clarke, Reggie Leach and Rick MacLeish, a strong defense boasting Tom Bladon and Andre "Moose" Dupont and prototypical tough guys like Dave Schultz and Don Saleski, all extremely well-coached by Fred Shero. Bernie Parent, back with the Flyers after a season with the WHA's Philadelphia Blazers, provided excellent goaltending, sharing the Vezina Trophy with Tony Esposito of the Chicago Black Hawks. The Flyers recorded a 50–16–12 mark to lead the West Division with 112 points, just one point behind the Boston Bruins for top spot overall. Boston's Phil Esposito, Bobby Orr, Ken Hodge and Wayne Cashman finished 1–2–3–4 on the NHL scoring list.

In the postseason, the Bruins and Philadelphia continued to be the league's best teams as they marched through the playoffs toward a showdown for the Stanley Cup. Boston won game one of the final 3–2 on a late goal by Bobby Orr, but the Flyers became the first expansion team to win a Stanley Cup final series game with a 3–2 victory of their own in game two. By game six, with Kate Smith belting out *God Bless America*, Philadelphia was the NHL's first expansion champion after a 1–0 triumph. Rick MacLeish had the game's only goal, while Bernie Parent's shutout sealed his selection as Conn Smythe Trophy winner.

The World Hockey Association was back with a 12-team lineup for the 1973–74 season, although franchise shifts had landed teams in Toronto (the Toros, formerly the Ottawa Nationals) and Vancouver (the former Philadelphia Blazers). The rival league dropped another bombshell when Gordie Howe ended a two-year retirement to join sons Mark and Marty with the Houston Aeros. The 45-year-old wonder scored 31 goals and added 69 assists and helped Houston win the Avco Cup. Former NHLer Mike Walton led WHA scoring with 57 goals and 117 points.

1974–75

It was another expansion year for the NHL, which added the Kansas City Scouts and Washington Capitals and the 18-team league was reorganized into four divisions named after some of the game's builders. The Norris and Adams divisions made up the Prince of Wales Conference, while the Clarence Campbell Conference housed the Patrick and Smythe divisions. The Philadelphia Flyers, Buffalo Sabres and Montreal Canadiens led the Patrick, Adams and Norris divisions respectively, each finishing with 113 points, while the Vancouver Canucks were the surprise winners of the Smythe Division with 86 points in the newly expanded 80-game season. Under a new playoff format, the top three teams in each division qualified, with the four first-place teams receiving a bye into the quarterfinals while the others battled through a preliminary round.

The 1975 Stanley Cup finals marked the first battle between two expansion teams. The Flyers, buoyed by Bobby Clarke's second Hart Trophy performance in as many years and Bernie Parent's Vezina win, led the league with 51 wins and eliminated the Toronto Maple Leafs and New York Islanders to reach the finals for the second year in a row. The Islanders had battled back from a 3–0 deficit to beat Pittsburgh in the quarterfinals, and nearly duplicated the feat against Philadelphia. Meanwhile the Sabres knocked off the Black Hawks and the Canadiens to play for the Stanley Cup in only their fifth season. The Flyers successfully defended their Cup title in a six-game final series remembered for the fog that rose from the ice at Buffalo's Memorial Auditorium and frequently interrupted play.

The regular season also saw the emergence of new individual talents. Veterans Bobby Orr and Phil Esposito finished 1–2 atop the NHL scoring list, but right behind them were Marcel Dionne and Guy Lafleur, who were finally showing the promise that had made them the top two selections in the 1971 Amateur Draft.

The WHA also expanded this year, adding the Phoenix Roadrunners and Indianapolis Racers, although several of the 12 "established" franchises moved before (and even during) the season. The innovative league created a Canadian Division of Vancouver, Edmonton, Winnipeg, Toronto and Quebec. Bobby Hull set a pro hockey record with 77 goals for Winnipeg, while Andre Lacroix of San Diego had a record 106 assists, but Gordie Howe's Houston Aeros emerged on top, winning their second Avco Cup title.

1975–76

The Montreal Canadiens returned to the NHL's summit in 1975–76, collecting a league-record 58 wins and 127 points. Guy Lafleur won the first of three consecutive Art Ross trophies, leading the league with 56 goals and 125 points, while Ken Dryden earned the Vezina Trophy with a 2.03 goals-against average. The Norris Trophy this year went to Denis Potvin of the New York Islanders, ending Bobby Orr's streak of eight consecutive Norris Trophy wins. Orr was forced to undergo two knee operations and played just 10 games during the 1975–76 season.

Orr's was not the only significant absence from the Boston Bruins' lineup. In November, Harry Sinden stunned the hockey world by dealing Phil Esposito and Carol Vadnais to the New York Rangers for Jean Ratelle, Brad Park and Joe Zanussi. The blockbuster helped revitalize an aging roster, allowing Boston to claim top spot in the Adams Division and to remain one of the NHL's top club for years to come. In another surprising move, Marcel Dionne left the Detroit Red Wings as a free agent. He was signed by the Los Angeles Kings, who sent Dan Maloney, Terry Harper and a draft choice to Detroit as compensation.

The two-time defending Stanley Cup champion Philadelphia Flyers enjoyed another outstanding season,

leading the Patrick Division with 118 points. Philadelphia beat the Toronto Maple Leafs in a quarterfinal series that saw both Reggie Leach and Toronto's Darryl Sittler tie the playoff record of five goals in a game, then the Flyers defeated Boston to reach the finals. Montreal advanced with wins over the Chicago Black Hawks and the Islanders, capping their season with a Stanley Cup sweep.

The WHA once again opened the season with 14 teams playing in the Canadian, Eastern, and Western divisions, though the Cincinnati Stingers and Denver Spurs replaced teams in Chicago and Baltimore, and the Vancouver Blazers became the Calgary Cowboys.

The Spurs and the Minnesota Fighting Saints both folded before the season's end. Quebec enjoyed the year's best individual performances, as Marc Tardif led the league with 71 goals and 148 points and tied teammate J.C. Tremblay with 77 assists, while goalie Richard Brodeur had 44 wins. But the Winnipeg Jets, led by Bobby Hull, Ulf Nilsson and Anders Hedberg, won the Avco Cup, denying Houston a third straight title by registering a four-game sweep in the championship series.

1976–77

Two of the NHL's weakest clubs found new homes for the 1976–77 season—the first franchise shifts since the Ottawa Senators moved to St. Louis in 1934–35. The Kansas City Scouts headed for Denver, where they would now be known as the Colorado Rockies, while the California Golden Seals left Oakland for the Rust Belt, setting up shop as the Cleveland Barons. Wilf Paiement scored 41 goals for the Rockies, who improved by 18 points over their last year in Kansas City, but both Colorado and Cleveland finished last in their respective divisions. Only the woeful 41-point effort by the Detroit Red Wings kept the two transplanted clubs out of the NHL cellar.

At the other end of the standings, the Montreal Canadiens surpassed their brilliant record of the previous season with a mark of 60–8–12 for 132 points. The Canadiens lost just once on home ice, going 33–1–6 at the Forum. Guy Lafleur won his second straight scoring title with 136 points and also won the Hart Trophy as MVP. Steve Shutt led the NHL with 60 goals, Larry Robinson won the Norris Trophy as best defenseman, and Ken Dryden and Michel "Bunny" Larocque shared the Vezina Trophy. The Philadelphia Flyers also had another great year, leading the Patrick Division with 112 points. The New York Islanders were second with 106, a point total that was good enough for Boston to win the Adams Division title. The Bruins and New York Rangers made another trade—though not as sensational as the previous year's Esposito deal—acquiring Rick Middleton for Ken Hodge. Still, the deal would pay dividends for Boston.

St. Louis, with just 73 points in 80 games, finished first in the Smythe Division but was swept out of the playoffs by the Canadiens, who then beat the Islanders to return to the Stanley Cup final. Boston provided the opposition after eliminating the Los Angeles Kings and Philadelphia. The Canadiens won the first three games, with Boston playing their best hockey of the series in game four before Jacques Lemaire scored in overtime to complete the sweep.

The WHA opened the 1976–77 season with 12 teams, the same number as at the end of 1975–76, but there were two more franchise shifts. The Toronto Toros moved to Alabama, becoming the Birmingham Bulls, while the Cleveland Crusaders moved to Minnesota as the second incarnation of the Fighting Saints. The new Saints proved no more viable than the old, folding before season's end.

Anders Hedberg of Winnipeg led the league with 70 goals, while teammate Ulf Nilsson was tops with 85 assists. The scoring title went to Quebec's Real Cloutier with 66 goals and 75 assists for 141 points. The Nordiques beat the Jets for the Avco Cup in a seven-game championship series.

1977–78

The off-season was eventful for the World Hockey Association, as six teams applied for entry into the NHL. The vote among NHL owners was close, but not close enough, and with Phoenix, Calgary and San Diego ceasing operations, the WHA entered its sixth season with just eight teams. The Houston Aeros, a perennial power, were weakened by the departure of Marty, Mark and Gordie Howe to the New England Whalers, and would also fold in the spring of 1978. Bolstered by the arrival of Gordie and sons, the Whalers beat the Winnipeg Jets for the Avco Cup. Meanwhile, Marc Tardif of the Quebec Nordiques was the league's top scorer with 65 goals and 89 assists.

In the NHL, the Montreal Canadiens dominated play for the third consecutive season. The Canadiens were 59–10–11 on the year and their 129 points led the Norris Division by 51 points over a much-improved Detroit Red Wings team. Guy Lafleur won the Art Ross Trophy for the third year in succession and won the Hart Trophy for the second straight year. Ken Dryden and Bunny Larocque again shared the Vezina Trophy. Bob Gainey won the newly created Selke Trophy as the NHL's best defensive forward. It was an honor he would win again in each of the next three seasons.

The New York Islanders won their first Patrick Division title this year with 111 points. Bryan Trottier's 123 points were second behind Lafleur's 132 in the NHL scoring race, while teammate Mike Bossy set a rookie record with 53 goals. Denis Potvin finished fifth in scoring with 30 goals and 64 assists and earned his second Norris Trophy win as the league's best defenseman. But despite their great regular season, the Islanders' year ended in disappointment when Lanny McDonald's seventh-game overtime goal gave the Toronto Maple Leafs a quarterfinal series upset. Toronto had enjoyed a 92-point year under rookie coach Roger Neilson, but couldn't get past Montreal in the semifinals as the Canadiens swept Toronto en route to the finals.

For the second year in a row, Don Cherry's Bruins faced Montreal in the final. Boston had won the Adams Division with 113 points and had needed just nine games to eliminate the Chicago Black Hawks and Philadelphia Flyers. Boston provided much tougher competition this year, but the Canadiens still made it three straight Stanley Cup titles with a six-game victory. Larry Robinson and Guy Lafleur tied for the postseason scoring lead, with the big defenseman taking home the Conn Smythe Trophy as playoff MVP.

1978–79

After another summer of fruitless merger talks with the NHL, the World Hockey Association prepared for its seventh season with seven teams lumped into a single division. Early in the year, the Indianapolis Racers went out of business. The team made one significant deal before folding, selling the contract of 17-year-old Wayne Gretzky to the Edmonton Oilers. Gretzky scored 46 goals and added 64 assists as a rookie and led Edmonton to a first-place finish. His 110 points ranked third in WHA scoring. The Quebec

Nordiques' Real Cloutier led the league again with 75 goals and 54 assists.

In the playoffs, the Winnipeg Jets beat the Oilers for the last-ever Avco Cup championship in league history. On March 29, 1979, the NHL announced it would take in four WHA teams the following season: Edmonton, Winnipeg, Quebec, and the New England Whalers. The two remaining clubs, the Cincinnati Stingers and Birmingham Bulls, were paid to go out of business.

The WHA's instability had many of its top players rushing to sign with NHL clubs prior to the 1978–79 season. The New York Rangers doled out big bucks for Swedish stars Ulf Nilsson and Anders Hedberg, who got two-year contracts worth $1 million. The Rangers also hired former Philadelphia Flyer coach Fred Shero to fill the dual role of coach and general manager. New York's 91 points this season were 18 better than the previous year, but good for only third place in the Patrick Division. First place in the Patrick belonged to New York Islanders, whose 116 points edged out the Montreal Canadiens at 115 for top spot in the overall standings. Bryan Trottier earned both the Art Ross and Hart trophies, but once again a great Islanders season would end in playoff disappointment. Phil Esposito had led the Rangers to victories over the Los Angeles Kings and Philadelphia, but it was goalie John Davidson who made the difference when the team knocked off the Islanders in a six-game semifinal.

The Rangers' opponent for the Stanley Cup was Montreal, who had reached the final for the fourth consecutive year after a thrilling seven-game semifinal with the Bruins. The deciding game turned on a late Boston bench minor for having too many men on the ice. On the ensuing power-play, Montreal tied the score and went on to win in overtime. The Rangers took full advantage of the Canadiens' fatigue in a 4–1 series-opening victory, but Montreal stormed back to take the next four games for their fourth consecutive Stanley Cup championship. Bob Gainey earned the Conn Smythe Trophy as playoff MVP.

1979–80

A year after the struggling Cleveland Barons merged with the Minnesota North Stars, reducing the NHL to 17 teams, the league was growing again as it absorbed the four survivors of the World Hockey Association: the Edmonton Oilers, Winnipeg Jets, Quebec Nordiques and Hartford (formerly New England) Whalers.

The National Hockey League benefited from an influx of talent created by the WHA's demise. Most notable was the return of legends Bobby Hull, Dave Keon and 51-year-old Gordie Howe, who would score 15 goals for Hartford. At the other end of their careers were young players like Mike Gartner, Rick Vaive, Michel Goulet and Mark Messier, who'd played in the WHA as underage pros. But it was the youngest of the WHA's refugees who would prove to be the greatest NHLer of all.

Beginning his pro career at the age of 17, Wayne Gretzky had finished third in WHA scoring in 1978–79. He had been a point-scoring machine all his young life, but few expected his WHA performance to translate into NHL success. Getting better as the year progressed, Gretzky proved the doubters wrong, enjoying a late-season surge that saw him tie Marcel Dionne for the league league with 137 points. The Art Ross Trophy, however, went to the Los Angeles Kings superstar because his 53 goals were two more than Gretzky's 51. "The Great One", as Gretzky would become

known, was also denied the Calder Trophy because the his season he spent in the WHA meant he wasn't considered an NHL rookie, but his brilliance was recognized with both the Hart and Lady Byng trophies. Gretzky's great play also managed to sneak Edmonton into the 16th and final playoff spot, though the Oilers were knocked off in three straight games by Philadelphia. The Flyers set a professional sports record during the season with a 35-game unbeaten streak en route to a first-place finish in the overall standings.

The four-time defending Stanley Cup champion Montreal Canadiens underwent a major overhaul before the 1979–80 season. Goalie Ken Dryden announced his retirement and Scotty Bowman resigned as coach to run the Buffalo Sabres. Bowman was replaced by Canadiens legend Boom Boom Geoffrion, who in turn gave way to Claude Ruel during the season. Montreal managed to finish atop the Norris Division with 107 points, but a quarterfinal defeat at the hands of the Minnesota North Stars ended the team's quest for a record-tying fifth straight Stanley Cup. The Cup wound up instead with the New York Islanders when Bob Nystrom's overtime goal upset favored Philadelphia in a six-game final.

1980–81

The defending Stanley Cup champion New York Islanders proved to be the best again during the 1980–81 season. The Islanders' 110 points topped both the Patrick Division and the overall NHL standings, just three points ahead of the Smythe Division's surprising St. Louis Blues. The Canadiens were the NHL's third-best team with 103 points, but Montreal was stunned in the first round of the playoffs when the Edmonton Oilers eliminated them in three straight games. The victory was a clear sign that the balance of power in the NHL had shifted from the older, established teams. Edmonton's playoff success continued as they lasted six games in the second round before bowing out against the Islanders.

The Oilers featured a host of talented young players—Glenn Anderson, Jari Kurri, Paul Coffey, Kevin Lowe and Mark Messier—but the undisputed leader was Wayne Gretzky, who began to rewrite the NHL record book this year. He broke Bobby's Orr's single-season assist record by seven with 109, and his 55 goals gave him 164 points, easily breaking Phil Esposito's record of 152. It was the first of seven consecutive Art Ross Trophy wins for Gretzky, and the second of eight straight Hart Trophy selections. The Oilers had a provincial rival this season, as the Atlanta Flames moved north to Calgary.

Two of Edmonton's fellow WHA refugees did not fare as well in 1980–81. The Hartford Whalers, now without the retired Gordie Howe, fell out of the playoffs, while the Jets suffered through one of the worst season's in hockey history. Winnipeg's 9–57–14 mark was the worst in the NHL since the Washington Capitals went 8–67–5 in 1974–75. The Jets suffered through 30 games without a victory at one point, establishing a new NHL record for futility.

Meanwhile the Quebec Nordiques unveiled brothers Anton and Peter Stastny this season, with 25-year-old Peter setting a rookie scoring record with 109 points. A third Stastny brother, Marian, would join Quebec in 1981–82. Another new name appeared among the NHL scoring leaders this season, as Calgary's Kent Nilsson placed third with 131 points. The NHL goal-scoring crown went to Mike Bossy of the Islanders, who netted 68 goals and equaled Rocket Richard's legendary feat of 50 goals in 50 games.

After eliminating the Oilers in the quarterfinals, Bossy and the Islanders swept the Rangers to return to the Stanley Cup final. Their opponents were the upstart Minnesota North Stars, but the Islanders proved too powerful, needing only five games to win their second consecutive Cup. Bossy, Bryan Trottier and Denis Potvin were the offensive stars, but the determined hustle of Butch Goring was rewarded with the Conn Smythe Trophy.

1981–82

In just their third season in the NHL, the Edmonton Oilers arrived as a powerhouse in 1981–82, winning the Smythe Division with 111 points and finishing second overall to the two-time defending Stanley Cup champion New York Islanders. Wayne Gretzky was the story of the regular season, collecting goals and assists in bunches from the very beginning of the schedule. A year after Mike Bossy had duplicated Rocket Richard's mark of 50 goals in 50 games, Gretzky obliterated this record. His five-goal performance on December 30, 1981, gave him 50 in just 39 games. On February 24, 1982, Gretzky broke Phil Esposito's single-season record with his 77th goal and pushed his total to 92 by season's end. The Great One also broke his own record with 120 assists, giving him an astounding total of 212 points. The Oilers set a new NHL record with 417 goals this year, though none of their other improving young stars managed to join Gretzky in the league's top 10. Edmonton unveiled goalie Grant Fuhr this season and his netminding would soon prove the perfect complement to the team's high-powered offense.

The NHL realigned geographically this year and changed its playoff format to emphasize divisional play. Teams played for division, then conference titles, to determine the two Stanley Cup finalists. The Oilers finished 48 points ahead of fourth-place Los Angeles, but were eliminated by the Kings in the first round of the Smythe Division playoffs. The third game of the best-of-five series saw the Kings rebound from a 5–0 deficit to win in overtime in a game that became known as "the Miracle on Manchester" after the site of the Los Angeles Forum.

There were plenty of other playoff upsets in the Campbell Conference this year, with the Vancouver Canucks (third in the Smythe) and Chicago Black Hawks (fourth in the Norris) advancing to the conference final. In the Prince of Wales Conference, the fourth-place Nordiques eliminated the first-place Montreal Canadiens in "the Battle of Quebec," then beat the Boston Bruins for the Adams Division title. Only in the Patrick Division did things go according to expectations, as the Islanders emerged victorious. The New York club then swept Quebec to return to the Stanley Cup finals against Vancouver.

Game one found the Canucks leading 5–4 with only seven minutes to play before Mike Bossy tied it up and then won it in overtime. Richard Brodeur provided Vancouver with excellent goaltending, which kept the games close, but the Islanders claimed their third straight Stanley Cup title with a series sweep. The Conn Smythe Trophy for playoff MVP went to Bossy, whose 17 postseason goals led all scorers.

1982–83

The Boston Bruins returned to the top of the NHL standings for the first time since 1973–74 with 110 points. Barry Pederson's 46 goals and 61 assists placed him among the NHL's top 10 in scoring and Rick Middleton's 49 goals led

the team, but defense was the key to the Bruins' success. Ray Bourque was named to the Second All-Star Team—the fourth All-Star selection of his four-year career—while Pete Peeters earned the Vezina Trophy with 40 wins and a 2.36 goals-against average. His eight shutouts this season would prove to be the best single-season total of the 1980s. A sad note in Boston this season was the brain hemorrhage suffered by second-year winger Normand Leveille. He survived the illness, but his hockey career was over.

The three-time defending Stanley Cup champion New York Islanders started the season slowly, but came on strong. Still, they wound up in second place in the Patrick Division behind the Philadelphia Flyers. (The Patrick Division included a new team this year, as the Colorado Rockies had become the New Jersey Devils.) In the playoffs, Philadelphia lost to the New York Rangers in the first round, while the Islanders beat the Washington Capitals and then the Rangers to set up a Wales Conference showdown with Boston. The Bruins had defeated the Quebec Nordiques and Buffalo Sabres, but after a six-game conference final, the Islanders were headed back to the Stanley Cup finals for the fourth year in a row.

In the Campbell Conference, the Chicago Black Hawks enjoyed an excellent season. Denis Savard finished third in the league with 121 points, Al Secord scored 54 goals, and rookie of the year Steve Larmer notched 43. Chicago topped the Norris Division with 104 points and beat the St. Louis Blues and Minnesota North Stars in the playoffs before falling to the Edmonton Oilers in the conference final.

After the playoff disappointment of the previous season, the Edmonton Oilers rebounded. Although Wayne Gretzky "slumped" to 71 goals, his 125 assists were a new league high and his 196 points were 72 more than runner-up Peter Stastny—the widest gap ever between first and second place in the scoring derby. Gretzky's teammates Mark Messier, Glenn Anderson, and Jari Kurri each collected at least 40 goals and 100 points and joined him among the top 10 scorers this season as the Oilers broke their own league record with 424 goals.

The Stanley Cup final between the Oilers and Islanders was much anticipated, but the high-flying newcomers did not yet have the experience necessary to better the defending champions. The Islanders kept Gretzky off the scoresheet and held the Oilers to just six goals as they won their fourth consecutive Stanley Cup title in a four-game sweep.

1983–84

Overtime returned to the NHL regular season for the first time since 1942 when wartime travel restrictions had curtailed the practice. In the event of a tie after 60 minutes, teams would play a five-minute sudden-death session. If no one scored, the game would remain a tie.

Following their Stanley Cup loss to the New York Islanders the previous year, the Edmonton Oilers posted a 119-point season in 1983–84 and, for the third year in a row, set an all-time record with 446 goals. Not surprisingly, it was Wayne Gretzky who led the way as he tallied 87 goals and 118 assists for 205 points. Paul Coffey emerged as the best offensive defenseman since Bobby Orr, collecting 40 goals and 86 assists to finish second to Gretzky in the league scoring race. Jari Kurri had 52 goals and 61 assists to finish seventh in scoring, while Glenn Anderson had 54 goals as the Oilers become the first team to boast three 50-goal scorers in one season.

The New York Islanders showed every indication in the regular season that they were a legitimate threat to equal the Montreal Canadiens' record of five consecutive Stanley Cup championships. The Islanders posted 104 points to lead the Patrick Division after a tight race with the much-improved Washington Capitals, who set a franchise high with 101 points. The Boston Bruins, also with 104 points, won the Adams Division by a single point over the Buffalo Sabres. Buffalo was sparked by 18-year-old goalie Tom Barrasso, who won both the Calder and Vezina trophies. The Montreal Canadiens tumbled to fourth place in the division with their first sub-.500 season since 1948–49.

In a move reminiscent of their 1971 decision to go with Ken Dryden, the Habs elected to open the playoffs with rookie Steve Penney in goal, even though he had played only four games during the season. Penney responded by leading Montreal to upsets of Boston and the Quebec Nordiques. His hot hand even carried the Canadiens to two wins to open the Prince of Wales Conference championship before the Islanders recovered to win four in a row and advance to play for the Stanley Cup once again.

Playoff victories over the Winnipeg Jets, Calgary Flames and Minnesota North Stars meant Edmonton would face the Islanders in the finals for the second year in a row. The teams split the first two games before the Oilers' offense clicked into high gear. Edmonton won three in a row, outscoring the Isles 19–6, to take the series in five and deny the Islanders a fifth straight Stanley Cup title. Wayne Gretzky led all playoff performers with 35 points, but the Conn Smythe Trophy for playoff MVP went to rugged teammate Mark Messier.

1984–85

Chosen first overall in the 1984 Entry Draft, Pittsburgh center Mario Lemieux recorded 43 goals and 57 assists en route to winning the Calder Trophy as rookie of the year. Within a few seasons, Lemieux would be credited with saving the Penguins franchise and would rival Wayne Gretzky as the greatest player in the game. This year, however, the Penguins recorded just 53 points and finished ahead of only the Toronto Maple Leafs in the NHL's overall standings.

Meanwhile, Gretzky and his Edmonton Oilers continued to dominate the league. Gretzky set yet another single-season record with 135 assists, and he added 73 goals for a total 208 points. Linemate Jari Kurri's 71 goals and 135 points trailed only Gretzky in the league scoring race. Edmonton's Smythe Division rivals, the Winnipeg Jets and Calgary Flames, were also among the league's best this season and the league's top five scorers were all from the Smythe Division: Gretzky, Kurri, Winnipeg's Dale Hawerchuk, Marcel Dionne of Los Angeles and Oiler defenseman Paul Coffey.

The top team overall, however, was the Philadelphia Flyers. Former captain Bobby Clarke was now the general manager and new coach Mike Keenan got 53 wins and 113 points out of his troops. Tim Kerr led the team with 54 goals, but it was a stingy defense, led by Mark Howe and the Vezina Trophy–winning goaltending of Pelle Lindbergh, that was key to Philadelphia's success. The Flyers outdistanced the Washington Capitals for top spot in the Patrick Division, while the New York Islanders slipped to third place. The Islanders upset Washington in the playoffs, but suffered their earliest postseason ouster since 1979 when they lost to Philadelphia in the second round. The Montreal Canadiens survived the midseason retirement of

Guy Lafleur to lead the Adams Division, but lost to Quebec in the playoffs. The Nordiques then fell to the Flyers in the Wales Conference final.

Bernie Federko's 103 points led the St. Louis Blues to first place in the Norris Division, but it was the Chicago Black Hawks who survived the playoffs before falling to Edmonton in a six-game Campbell Conference final that saw the powerful Oilers score a record 44 goals. Philadelphia beat Edmonton 4–1 in game one of the finals, before the Oilers won three tight games to take a commanding lead in the series. The Oilers wrapped it up with an offensive explosion that resulted in an 8–3 victory in game five and their second straight Stanley Cup title. Jari Kurri tied former Flyer Reggie Leach's record with 19 goals in the postseason, while Wayne Gretzky had 17 goals and 30 assists for a playoff-record 47 points, earning him the Conn Smythe Trophy.

1985–86

Just as the explosive Montreal Canadiens power-play of the late 1950s had caused the NHL to change its rules (allowing a penalized player to return to the ice before the two minutes expired if a goal was scored), the Edmonton Oilers' abundance of firepower caused the league to allow player substitutions on coincidental minor penalties, virtually eliminating the four-on-four situations that favored teams with superior skill.

The rule change did little to put the brakes on the Oilers, as the two-time defending Stanley Cup champions wrapped up their fifth consecutive Smythe Division title. The Oilers also returned to the top spot in the overall standings with 119 points and became the inaugural winners of the Presidents' Trophy for finishing in first place. Wayne Gretzky broke his own single-season record with 215 points, mainly by shattering his assist record with an astounding total of 163. Gretzky's assist total alone would have been enough to win the scoring title, as Mario Lemieux of the Pittsburgh Penguins finished second with 141 points. Paul Coffey also enjoyed a record-breaking year, surpassing Bobby Orr's standard of 46 goals by a defenseman with 48. Coffey added 90 assists to finish third in the scoring race. Jari Kurri's 68 goals and 63 assists saw him finish fourth.

As in Wayne Gretzky's 212-point campaign of 1981–82, regular-season records didn't translate into playoff prosperity as the rival Calgary Flames eliminated the Oilers in a seven-game Smythe Division final. The series-winning goal came when Edmonton defenseman Steve Smith bounced a clearing pass off goalie Grant Fuhr into his own net. Calgary then defeated the Norris Division champion St. Louis Blues in seven games to reach the Stanley Cup finals.

Upsets also abounded in the Prince of Wales Conference, where the Montreal Canadiens prevailed, setting up the first all-Canadian final since 1967. Mats Naslund's 110 points made him the first Hab to crack the top 10 in scoring since Guy Lafleur in 1980. Rookie Brian Skrudland scored the fastest overtime goal in history after just nine seconds for a 3–2 win over Calgary in game two of the Stanley Cup finals, and newcomer Claude Lemieux had 10 goals in the playoffs. But the most important rookie of all was Patrick Roy. He posted a 1.92 goals-against average in the playoffs and backstopped Montreal to a five-game Stanley Cup victory. Roy was the first rookie since Harry Lumley in 1945 to register a shutout in the finals when he blanked the Flames for a 1–0 victory in game four and was a deserving recipient of the Conn Smythe Trophy as playoff MVP.

1986–87

Numerous coaching changes took place before and during the 1986–87 season. The New York Islanders named Terry Simpson their new head coach and promoted four-time Stanley Cup winner Al Arbour to vice president. The New York Rangers named Phil Esposito their new general manager, and he made 19 trades during the course of the year. He also fired coach Ted Sator after just 19 games and took over the chores himself when an inner-ear infection sidelined Sator's replacement, Tom Webster. Sator was hired by the Buffalo Sabres, replacing Craig Ramsay, who had replaced Scotty Bowman. In Boston, the Bruins fired Butch Goring and hired Terry O'Reilly.

Four of the five Norris Division teams made coaching changes. Jacques Demers left St. Louis for the Detroit Red Wings and the Blues replaced him with Jacques Martin. In Minnesota, the North Stars sacked Glen Sonmor in favor of Lorne Henning and the Toronto Maple Leafs turned to John Brophy after firing Dan Maloney. Bob Pulford stayed on as Chicago's coach, but the team did change the spelling of its nickname from Black Hawks to Blackhawks after discovering that the moniker had been spelled as one word in the club's original NHL charter.

In an attempt to limit upsets, the first round of the playoffs was extended to a best-of-seven series. The New York Islanders and Washington Capitals took the new format to its limit—and then some. Pat LaFontaine's goal in the fourth overtime period of game seven provided the Islanders with the victory.

Fueled by their playoff defeat in 1986, the Edmonton Oilers again led the regular season, though their 106 points were the fewest by a first-place team since 1969–70. Wayne Gretzky won the Art Ross Trophy for the seventh consecutive season with 62 goals and 121 assists. He was awarded the Hart Trophy as MVP for an eighth consecutive season as well. After playoff victories over the Los Angeles Kings, Winnipeg Jets and Detroit Red Wings, Edmonton faced Philadelphia, the NHL's only other 100-point team, for the Stanley Cup.

The Oilers jumped out to a three-games-to-one lead in the finals, but the Flyers rallied to tie the series. It was Edmonton's turn to come back in game seven as they turned an early 1–0 deficit into a 3–1 victory and their third Cup championship. Wayne Gretzky hoisted the Stanley Cup and then passed it to Steve Smith, whose errant clearing pass the year before had knocked Edmonton out of the playoffs. Flyer goalie Ron Hextall played well enough in defeat to win the Conn Smythe Trophy as, for the second year in a row, a rookie goalie was named playoff MVP. Hextall also won the Vezina Trophy as the NHL's top goaltender.

1987–88

During the late summer of 1987, the fourth Canada Cup tournament took place and it marked the rise of Mario Lemieux as a true superstar. Playing on a line with Wayne Gretzky, Lemieux's work ethic and mental approach finally caught up with his immense physical skills. He was the tournament's top goal scorer and netted the dramatic series-winning goal against the Soviets on a feed from Gretzky late in the final game. By the end of the regular season, Lemieux had unseated Gretzky as NHL scoring champion and ended his eight-year hold on the Hart Trophy.

Lemieux's brilliant play and the acquisition of Paul Coffey from the Edmonton Oilers saw Pittsburgh post its best record in 10 years, but the Penguins' 81 points were still not enough to make the playoffs in the tight Patrick Division where only seven points separated the six teams. The New York Islanders finished first, followed by the Washington Capitals and Philadelphia Flyers. In a game against Boston on December 8, 1987, Flyers goalie Ron Hextall became the first NHL netminder to shoot the puck the length of the ice for a goal into an empty net.

Fourth place in the Patrick Division went to the New Jersey Devils, who made the playoffs for the first time in 10 years and just the second time in franchise history. Led by the goaltending of Canadian national team star Sean Burke, the surprising Devils reached the Wales Conference final before they fell to the Bruins. Boston had finished second behind the Montreal Canadiens—who boasted the league's best defensive record as well as 50-goal scorer Stephane Richer—in the Adams Division, but the Bruins prevailed in the division final, beating Montreal for the first time in 18 playoff series dating back to 1945.

The Presidents' Trophy for first place overall went to Calgary with 105 points, but their Alberta rivals, the defending Stanley Cup champion Edmonton Oilers, made easy work of the Flames in the Smythe Division final, sweeping the series in four games.

The Oilers went on to beat the Detroit Red Wings, the Norris Division champions, to play Boston for the Stanley Cup. Edmonton swept the Bruins to win their fourth Stanley Cup championship in five years, although the series actually went five games—late in the second period of game four, with the score tied 3–3, a power failure at Boston Garden forced the game's suspension. Wayne Gretzky won the Conn Smythe Trophy after setting a new record with 13 points in the finals. The Oilers celebrated their Stanley Cup triumph with an impromptu group photo at center ice. Little did anyone know that the picture documented the end of an era.

1988–89

The hockey world was shocked on August 9, 1988, when the Edmonton Oilers and Los Angeles Kings announced a trade virtually without parallel in sports history. Wayne Gretzky, Mike Krushelnyski and Marty McSorley were L.A.-bound, while the Oilers would receive Jimmy Carson, Martin Gelinas, the Kings' first-round draft choices in 1989, 1991 and 1993 plus a reported $15 million in cash. Fans in Edmonton, and across Canada, bemoaned the loss of the Great One, while the citizens of southern California would be turned on to hockey as never before.

Showing a flair for the dramatic worthy of his Hollywood surroundings, Gretzky scored a goal on his very first shot of the 1988–89 season. He led the Kings to a 91-point season, good for second place in the Smythe Division and the team's best showing since 1981. His 114 assists tied Mario Lemieux for top spot in the NHL, and though Lemieux's 85 goals to Gretzky's 54 meant Mario retained the Art Ross Trophy, Gretzky was awarded the Hart Trophy as MVP for a ninth time. Gretzky also brought out the greatest in his Los Angeles teammates—Bernie Nicholls, with 70 goals and 80 assists, and Luc Robitaille, with 46 goals and 52 assists, were also among the top 10 in scoring.

L.A. faced Edmonton in the first round of the playoffs and defeated Gretzky's former teammates in seven games. The Kings were swept aside in the Smythe Division final, however, by the Calgary Flames, the NHL's best team during the regular season with 117 points. Joe Mullen set career highs with 51 goals and 110 points, while Joe

Nieuwendyk followed up his 51-goal rookie performance with another 51 goals this season. In the Norris Division, Flames castoff Brett Hull emerged as a star, scoring 41 goals for the St. Louis Blues, while in Detroit, Steve Yzerman led the Red Wings with 65 goals and 90 assists. Still, it was the Chicago Blackhawks who emerged from the Norris Division before falling to the Flames in five games.

Led by Mario Lemieux, Pittsburgh was back in the playoffs after six years. The Penguins took on the New York Rangers—who boasted rookie stars Brian Leetch and Tony Granato, and who had convinced Guy Lafleur to come out of retirement—and eliminated the Blueshirts in the first round. The Philadelphia Flyers knocked Pittsburgh out, then went on to lose to the Montreal Canadiens—led by rookie coach Pat Burns to the league's second-best record with 115 points—in the Prince of Wales Conference final.

Calgary opened the Cup finals at home with a 3–2 victory and, after splitting the next four games, took a one-game series lead back to Montreal for game six. The Canadiens had never allowed an opponent to beat them for the Stanley Cup on Forum ice, but the Flames defied history with a 4–2 victory. Lanny McDonald, who had recorded his 500th goal and 1,000th point during the season—scored a key goal in the final game and retired a Stanley Cup champion.

1989–90

The NHL enjoyed unprecedented box-office success in 1989–90, as attendance was up for the 11th year in a row. But the story this season was growing parity and tight divisional races. Under rookie coach Mike Milbury, the Boston Bruins won the Presidents' Trophy with 101 points, marking the first season since 1970–71 that only one team broke the 100-point barrier. Cam Neely led the offense with 55 goals, while Ray Bourque earned his third Norris Trophy in four years as the NHL's best defenseman. Goalies Reggie Lemelin and Andy Moog allowed the fewest goals in the league and shared the Jennings Trophy. The Bruins survived a seven-game scare from the Hartford Whalers in the first round of playoffs before beating the Montreal Canadiens and Washington Capitals to reach the Stanley Cup finals for the second time in three years. At the other end of the standings, the return of Guy Lafleur to the city where he'd starred as a Junior couldn't save the Quebec Nordiques, whose 61 losses and 31 points were the worst the league had seen since 1975.

An injury to Mario Lemieux kept him out of 21 games this season and saw the Pittsburgh Penguins miss the playoffs. His absence made it possible for Wayne Gretzky to reclaim the Art Ross Trophy. Although his 142 points represented his lowest total since his first NHL season, the Great One continued his assault on the record book. On October 15, 1989, Gretzky became the NHL's all-time scoring leader when he surpassed Gordie Howe's career total of 1,850 points—fittingly enough, in a game at Edmonton's Northlands Coliseum. His former Oilers teammate Mark Messier established a career high with 129 points on 45 goals and 84 assists, earning him the Hart Trophy as most valuable player. St. Louis Blue Brett Hull led the NHL, and set a new record for right wingers, with 72 goals.

Fourth-place Los Angeles upset the defending Stanley Cup champion Calgary Flames in the Smythe Division semis before falling to Messier and the Oilers in four straight. Edmonton advanced to play for the Stanley Cup after a six-game Campbell Conference final victory over the Chicago Blackhawks, who had won the Norris Division in their first

year under ex–Philadelphia Flyers coach Mike Keenan.

Game one of the Stanley Cup final needed 55 minutes of overtime before Petr Klima gave Edmonton a 3–2 victory. A 7–2 win followed in game two, and the Oilers rolled to victory in five games. Messier, Glenn Anderson, Jari Kurri and Kevin Lowe all earned their fifth Stanley Cup rings, and the play of youngsters Adam Graves, Joe Murphy and Martin Gelinas had also figured prominently. The Conn Smythe Trophy for playoff MVP went to goalie Bill Ranford, who was in net for all 16 of Edmonton's postseason victories.

1990–91

The 1990–91 season featured a great race for the Presidents' Trophy, with five teams, representing three of the league's four divisions, in the hunt for first place overall. The Boston Bruins again proved the best in the Adams Division with 100 points. Ray Bourque won the Norris Trophy for the fourth time and Cam Neely scored 51 goals. The Calgary Flames also had 100 points this season, but top spot in the Smythe Division went to the Los Angeles Kings, first-place finishers for the first time in franchise history with 102 points. The Kings were led by Wayne Gretzky who earned his ninth scoring title with 41 goals and 122 assists. Gretzky also took home the Lady Byng Trophy.

But the battle for first place overall came down to Norris Division rivals St. Louis and Chicago. The Blues had Hart Trophy winner Brett Hull's 86 goals on their side, but the Blackhawks edged them out with 106 points to the Blues' 105. Defense was the key in Chicago, where goalie Ed Belfour won the Vezina Trophy as well as the Calder as rookie of the year. In the playoffs, both Norris Division titans were eliminated by the surprising Minnesota North Stars, who racked up a third playoff upset when they knocked off the Edmonton Oilers in the Campbell Conference finals. The defending Stanley Cup champions, who'd slipped to a third-place .500 record, had upset Calgary and Los Angeles before falling to Minnesota.

In the Patrick Division, the Pittsburgh Penguins opened the season without Mario Lemieux (who missed 54 games because of back surgery), but developed a balanced attack led by Mark Recchi, Kevin Stevens and Paul Coffey. Lemieux's late-season return, and a trade that brought Ron Francis and Ulf Samuelsson from Hartford, propelled the Penguins to their first-ever division title with 88 points. Pittsburgh defeated the New Jersey Devils and Washington Capitals to reach the Wales Conference final for the first time. After dropping the first two games to Boston, the Penguins won four in a row and advanced to play Minnesota for the Stanley Cup.

The matchup of Pittsburgh and Minnesota marked the first time since 1934, when the Detroit Red Wings faced Chicago, that neither finalist had ever won the Stanley Cup. The North Stars won games one and three of the series, but Pittsburgh held a 3–2 lead after five games. The Penguins' offensive power finally proved too great in game six, and Pittsburgh claimed its first Stanley Cup title with an 8–0 victory. Mario Lemieux led all postseason performers with 44 points to win the Conn Smythe Trophy as playoff MVP.

1991–92

The 1991–92 season was the league's 75th, and the "Original Six" franchises—Boston, Chicago, Detroit, Montreal, New York Rangers and Toronto—commemorated the occasion by wearing vintage uniforms for selected

games. The Rangers were the season's top team with 105 points on a club-record 50 victories, leading the league for the first time since 1941–42. Mark Messier, traded to New York by the Edmonton Oilers just before the start of the season, won the Hart Trophy, becoming only the second player after former teammate Wayne Gretzky to be named the league's most valuable player with two different teams.

Gretzky and Mario Lemieux both lost time to injuries this season, but Lemieux regained the NHL scoring title with 44 goals and 87 assists. Pittsburgh Penguins teammate Kevin Stevens was second in scoring with 123 points, while Gretzky was third with 31 goals and 90 assists. For the third season in a row, Brett Hull of the St. Louis Blues led the league in goals, this time with 70.

A 10-day players' strike late in year jeopardized the conclusion of the season and pushed back the start of the playoffs to April 18, the latest date in history. The delayed first round proved to be one of the most exciting in history, as six of the eight series went to the full seven games. Boston, Detroit, the Pittsburgh Penguins and Vancouver Canucks all rebounded from 3–1 deficits to win their series. For the first time since 1980, all four division leaders (Montreal, the Rangers, Detroit and Vancouver) advanced to the second round, though each team lost in their respective division finals. Chicago got past Edmonton to advance to the Stanley Cup final from the Campbell Conference, while Pittsburgh beat Boston for the Wales Conference championship.

The Penguins' season had been eventful: new owners had taken over and popular coach Bob Johnson had died in November 1991. The team was not to be denied under interim coach Scotty Bowman, even though the Blackhawks had set a playoff record with 11 consecutive wins en route to the Stanley Cup finals, and took an early 3–0 lead in game one before Pittsburgh rallied for a last-minute 5–4 win. The Penguins went on to sweep the series, with their four straight victories giving them 11 consecutive playoff wins. The Conn Smythe Trophy for playoff MVP went to Mario Lemieux, who joined Bernie Parent of the Philadelphia Flyers as the only players to win the award two years in a row.

The league awarded its first new franchise since 1979, adding the San Jose Sharks, as NHL hockey returned to the San Francisco Bay area for the first time since 1976. The Sharks' teal and black jersey with its shark-biting-stick logo quickly became a top seller, ushering in a new era of marketing and merchandising consciousness around the NHL.

1992–93

Major changes took place during the summer of 1992. League president John Ziegler resigned and was replaced for a short time by Gil Stein. A new position of commissioner was created in December 1992 with the election of Gary Bettman. Meanwhile, NHL membership reached 24 teams with the addition of the Tampa Bay Lightning and Ottawa Senators. The Senators' home opener marked the first NHL game played in the Canadian capital since 1934, but there were even more amazing resurrections during the Stanley Cup's 100th-anniversary season.

The Toronto Maple Leafs repaid their long-suffering fans with a return to the upper echelon under former Montreal Canadiens coach Pat Burns. Longtime Atlanta-Calgary Flames executive Cliff Fletcher had taken over as president and general manager the year before and acquired Doug Gilmour and Grant Fuhr in a pair of blockbuster trades. With Felix Potvin now ready to emerge as the number-one goalie, Fletcher traded Fuhr to the Buffalo Sabres during

the 1992–93 season for sniper Dave Andreychuk. With Andreychuk converting his passes, Gilmour enjoyed career highs with 95 assists and 127 points, and with the Leafs adhering to Burns's defensive philosophy, Toronto set club records with 44 wins and 99 points during the expanded 84-game season. In the playoffs, the Leafs knocked off the Detroit Red Wings in a thrilling seven-game Norris Division semifinal, then beat the St. Louis Blues to win the division final.

Wayne Gretzky also enjoyed a brilliant comeback. The Great One missed the first 39 games of the season due to a career-threatening back injury, but he returned to action on January 6, 1993 and collected 65 points in 45 games. Gretzky was in top form by the playoffs, leading the Los Angeles Kings to victories over the Calgary Flames and Vancouver Canucks before eliminating to the Leafs in seven games to reach the Stanley Cup final for the first time in franchise history.

One day before Gretzky's return to the Kings, the Pittsburgh Penguins announced that Mario Lemieux had Hodgkin's disease, a form of cancer. Lemieux missed 24 games while receiving treatment, then returned to claim the NHL scoring title and spark Pittsburgh to a record 17-game winning streak that led the Penguins to first place overall. Lemieux was bothered by back spasms in the playoffs and the New York Islanders stunned the Penguins in the Patrick Division final before falling to the Montreal Canadiens in the Wales Conference championship.

The 100th anniversary of the Stanley Cup matched the game's greatest franchise against arguably its greatest player and it was the Montreal Canadiens who came out ahead of Wayne Gretzky and the Los Angeles Kings in five games. Montreal won its 24th Stanley Cup title on Patrick Roy's brilliant playoff goaltending and an amazing 10 consecutive overtime victories, including three against Los Angeles.

1993–94

The 1993–94 season was the NHL's third consecutive expansion year as the Miami-based Florida Panthers and the Mighty Ducks of Anaheim joined the fold. The league moved into another southern city as the Minnesota North Stars relocated to Texas, becoming the Dallas Stars. The division and conference names were also changed to geographic designations: the Adams, Patrick, Norris and Smythe divisions became the Northeast, Atlantic, Central and Pacific. The Prince of Wales and Clarence Campbell conferences were now known respectively as the Eastern and Western.

Previous expansions had all produced an explosion of offense, but defense came to the forefront in the new 26-team NHL. In 1992–93 only two goaltenders had posted goals-against averages below 3.00; in 1993–94, 19 goalies broke that barrier, led by Vezina Trophy winner Dominik Hasek of the Buffalo Sabres, whose 1.95 average made him the first netminder below 2.00 since Bernie Parent of the Philadelphia Flyers in 1973–74.

Pittsburgh Penguins superstar Mario Lemieux did not figure in the scoring race this season, as injuries and illness limited him to just 22 games. Pat LaFontaine of the Buffalo Sabres, runner-up to Lemieux in 1992–93, missed 68 games with a knee injury. Teemu Selanne of the Winnipeg Jets, who scored 76 goals as a rookie the year before, played just 51 games, while budding superstar Eric Lindros of the Philadelphia Flyers missed 19 games with injuries.

Despite the drop in offense, Wayne Gretzky still managed to become the greatest goal scorer in NHL history. On March 23, 1994, the Los Angeles Kings superstar took passes from teammates Marty McSorley and Luc Robitaille and beat Kirk McLean of the Vancouver Canucks for his 802nd career goal, breaking Gordie Howe's record of 801. Gretzky finished the year with 38 goals and 92 assists, earning his 10th scoring title. The Hart Trophy went to Sergei Fedorov of the Detroit Red Wings, who was runner-up to Gretzky for the Art Ross and also earned the Selke Trophy as the NHL's best defensive forward.

The New York Rangers proved to be the best in the NHL this year, setting franchise records with 52 wins and 112 points under coach Mike Keenan. They beat the New York Islanders and Washington Capitals before defeating the New Jersey Devils in a thrilling seven-game Eastern Conference final. The Vancouver Canucks provided the opposition for the Stanley Cup. Vancouver won game one, but the Rangers took the next three in a row. The Canucks rallied for two wins to force a seventh game, but the Rangers finally snapped their 54-year Stanley Cup jinx with a 3–2 victory.

1994–95

A 103-day lockout resulted in the NHL's shortest regular season in 53 years. The 1994–95 season did not begin until January 20, 1995, but the abbreviated 48-game schedule was packed with plenty of excitement.

The Pittsburgh Penguins were without Mario Lemieux for the entire year, as he took the season off to recuperate from the lingering effects of back injuries and his battle with cancer, but the team remained in fine form, opening the season with a 12–0–1 mark. The Quebec Nordiques, not to be outdone, streaked out of the gate at 12–1–0 and the two teams battled for top spot in the Northeast Division until the final night of the season. Quebec, who had swapped Mats Sundin to Toronto in a deal for Wendel Clark and Sylvain Lefebvre, emerged victorious with 65 points to Pittsburgh's 61.

The Penguins' Jaromir Jagr broke through as a superstar, leading the NHL with 70 points on 32 goals and 38 assists. Eric Lindros earned the Hart Trophy for leading the Philadelphia Flyers to top spot in the Atlantic Division. Lindros equaled Jagr's 70 points, but missed out on the Art Ross Trophy because he had only scored 29 goals.

The defending Stanley Cup champion New York Rangers battled all season just to earn a berth in the playoffs. They snuck in as the eighth and final qualifier in the Eastern Conference. Montreal wasn't so lucky. Despite acquiring Mark Recchi for John LeClair in a blockbuster deal with Philadelphia, and swapping captain Kirk Muller to the New York Islanders for Pierre Turgeon, the Canadiens missed the playoffs for the first time in 25 years. The Rangers managed to upset the Quebec Nordiques in the first round before losing to Philadelphia. Pittsburgh reached the second round before falling to the New Jersey Devils, who then beat the Flyers to advance to the Stanley Cup final for the first time in franchise history.

In the Western Conference, the Detroit Red Wings cruised to top spot in the Central Division with a record of 33–11–4. With their 70 points, Detroit finished first overall in the NHL standings for the first time since 1964–65. The Red Wings then beat the Dallas Stars before avenging the previous year's first-round loss to the San Jose Sharks with a four-game sweep. After a five-game victory over the Chicago Blackhawks for the Western Conference title, Detroit was back in the Stanley Cup final for the first time in 29 years.

Under coach Jacques Lemaire, the Devils had successfully employed a defensive scheme known as the "neutral-zone trap" throughout the Eastern Conference playoffs, but their detractors doubted they could shut down the powerful Red Wings. The Devils proved the pundits wrong, completely closing down Detroit's attack in a surprising four-game sweep of the Stanley Cup finals.

1995–96

After their first-place finish the year before, most expected the Detroit Red Wings to come out flying in 1995–96 and they didn't disappoint. Coach Scotty Bowman's squad exceeded even his great Montreal Canadiens teams of the late 1970s with an NHL-record 62 victories, though Detroit's 62–13–7 mark produced one less point than the record 132 collected by Bowman's 60–8–12 Canadiens of 1976–77. Meanwhile, 1994–95's top Eastern Conference team, the Quebec Nordiques, moved to Denver, becoming the Colorado Avalanche and playing in the Pacific Division. The Avalanche would beat the Wings in a six-game Western Conference final.

After sitting out the 1994–95 season, Mario Lemieux came back to score 69 goals in 70 games and win his fifth scoring title with 161 points. Lemieux won the Hart Trophy as most valuable player for the fifth time. Things did not go as well for Wayne Gretzky this season. The Great One and his Los Angeles Kings were both slumping when he was dealt to the St. Louis Blues in February. Another significant trade this season saw Patrick Roy swapped to Colorado after a dispute with Canadiens coach Mario Tremblay.

Several young players took their place among the NHL's elite. Jaromir Jagr followed up his Art Ross performance of the previous season with 149 points, while Joe Sakic of the Avalanche finished third in league scoring with 120 points. Teammate Peter Forsberg (rookie of the year in 1994–95) collected 116 points, while Eric Lindros of the Philadelphia Flyers had 115. Paul Kariya fulfilled the promise expected of him with 50 goals and 58 assists for the Mighty Ducks of Anaheim and was teamed with a linemate who complemented his talents when Teemu Selanne was acquired from the Winnipeg Jets.

In the Eastern Conference, the Florida Panthers made the playoffs in just their third season and rode the hot goaltending of John Vanbiesbrouck past the Boston Bruins, Philadelphia Flyers and Pittsburgh Penguins to the Stanley Cup finals which opened in Denver with the Avalanche scoring 3–1 and 8–1 victories. The Panthers played better when the series moved to Miami, but Colorado completed the sweep with 3–2 and 1–0 wins. Uwe Krupp scored the Stanley Cup-winning goal at 4:31 of the third overtime period. Joe Sakic won the Conn Smythe Trophy, while Claude Lemieux (previously a winner in Montreal and New Jersey) became only the fourth player in history to celebrate Stanley Cup titles with three different teams.

1996–97

There were many changes throughout the 1996–97 season, beginning with the United States dethroning Canada as the top hockey nation at the inaugural World Cup of Hockey. Major trades this season involved Jeremy Roenick, Brendan Shanahan, Paul Coffey, Adam Oates, Bill Ranford, Ed Belfour and Doug Gilmour. Wayne Gretzky took his act

to Broadway, signing as a free agent with the New York Rangers and Mario Lemieux staged a farewell tour, retiring at season's end at the age of 31. Lemieux went out in style, winning the Art Ross Trophy for a sixth time with 122 points. Wayne Gretzky tied Lemieux for the league lead with 72 assists and added 25 goals to lead the Rangers in scoring with 97 points. Lemieux and Teemu Selanne were the only players to top 100 points in a season dominated by defense. The southward migration of NHL franchises also continued this year as the Winnipeg Jets moved to Phoenix, setting up shop as the Coyotes.

Goaltenders all around the league posted outstanding numbers, but Martin Brodeur of the New Jersey Devils was the most impressive. His 1.88 goals-against average was the lowest in the NHL since Tony Esposito's 1.77 in 1971–72 and his 10 shutouts made him the first to reach double digits since Ken Dryden in 1976–77. Brodeur and backup Mike Dunham shared the Jennings Trophy, but the Vezina Trophy went to Dominik Hasek. The Buffalo star also became the first goaltender since Jacques Plante in 1962 to win the Hart Trophy after leading the Sabres to a surprising first-place finish in the Northeast Division.

The Sabres needed overtime in the seventh game to subdue an improved Ottawa Senators team in the first round of the playoffs. The Philadelphia Flyers—en route to the Stanley Cup finals—then eliminated the Sabres and New York to advance.

In the Western Conference, the defending Stanley Cup champion Colorado Avalanche topped the NHL standings with 107 points. The Detroit Red Wings followed up their record-breaking season with an "ordinary" 94-point campaign and they had trouble getting past the St. Louis Blues to open the playoffs. A four-game sweep of the Mighty Ducks of Anaheim followed before the Red Wings avenged the previous spring's loss to the Avalanche with a six-game victory for the Western Conference championship. Goalie Mike Vernon won the Conn Smythe Trophy as playoff MVP. The Stanley Cup returned to Detroit for the first time since 1955 as the Red Wings defeated the Philadelphia Flyers in four consecutive games.

1997–98

The 1997-98 season saw the Red Wings win their second consecutive Stanley Cup title with a four-game sweep of the Washington Capitals. It was Detroit's second consecutive championship. The Red Wings had been the third-best team during the regular season, posting 103 points to trail both the Dallas Stars and New Jersey Devils. Detroit's success had been a true team effort; their team total of 250 goals was the second-highest in the NHL (behind the St. Louis Blues' 256) despite the fact that no Detroit player ranked among the NHL's top 20 scorers.

Jaromir Jagr was the league's leading scorer with 102 points. His total was the lowest to top the NHL in a full season since Stan Mikita's 87 points in 1967–68 and marked the first time since Bobby Orr in 1969–70 that only one NHL player had more than 100 points. Jagr's strong play helped the Pittsburgh Penguins to a surprising first-place finish in the Northeast Division in the first season following the retirement of Mario Lemieux. Jagr also helped the Czech Republic win a gold medal in hockey at the Winter Olympics in Nagano, Japan.

The participation of NHL players at the Winter Olympics resulted in the most evenly matched hockey competition in Winter Games history. North American fans were disappointed by the early elimination of the United States and by Canada's fourth-place finish. The Russians, led by Pavel Bure, appeared headed for the gold until they ran into Dominik Hasek in the championship game. Hasek blanked Russia 1–0 to clinch the Czech Republic's first Olympic gold medal.

Hasek enjoyed another brilliant season in 1997–98. He shook off a slow start to lead the NHL with 13 shutouts, and his 33 wins and 2.09 goals-against average also ranked among the leaders. With his second consecutive Hart Trophy win, he became the first goalie to earn multiple MVP awards. Hasek's play led Buffalo to the Eastern Conference finals, where the Sabres lost to Washington in six games. Upsets had marked the Eastern playoffs, particularly in the first round where the Sabres knocked off the Philadelphia Flyers, the Montreal Canadiens surprised Pittsburgh, and the Ottawa Senators stunned the Devils.

The playoffs went more according to form in the Western Conference, as Detroit defeated Phoenix and St. Louis to meet a Dallas team that had knocked off the San Jose Sharks and Edmonton Oilers. The Western Conference final matchup of the defending Cup champion (Detroit) against the league's best club in the regular season (Dallas) was compelling, but the Red Wings, led by captain Steve Yzerman, eliminated the Stars in six games.

CHAPTER 20

The NHL Entry Draft

History and Analysis of the NHL's Principal Player Source

Text by Chris Tredree • Tables by Paul Bontje

The NHL's Entry Draft and its predecessor, the Amateur Draft, have been the gateway to the league for star players from all over the world. In the chapter that follows, each year's draft is described and accompanied by a table that lists every drafted player along with his NHL career totals if applicable. Drafted players or goaltenders with no statistics in these tables never played—or have yet to play—in the NHL.

IN AN EFFORT TO ELIMINATE the sponsorship of amateur teams and players by its member clubs, the National Hockey League began seeking to develop a drafting system that would provide each team with an equal opportunity to acquire amateur players.

During the 1962–63 regular season, NHL president Clarence Campbell first introduced his plans to organize the drafting of amateur talent. "I'm trying to work out a system whereby all amateur players who will attain their 17th birthdays before August of each year will be available for drafting by NHL teams in the reverse order of the standing," Campbell commented. "We're ultimately hopeful it will produce a uniform opportunity for each team to acquire a star player." The end result was the establishment of the NHL's Amateur Draft.

It was decided that eligibility for the Amateur Draft would be based on age, with a determination that all amateur players who would reach 17 years old between the period of August 1, 1963 to July 31, 1964 would be eligible for drafting. Any amateur player whose name appeared on NHL sponsorship lists prior to May 1, 1963 would be exempt from the draft.

Each NHL team would be granted four selections to be conducted according to a specific predetermined order. Teams were given the opportunity to choose their draft seeding in the reverse order of standing of the 1961–62 regular season. The Boston Bruins, who finished in last place in 1961–62, were granted the first choice of seeding and selected the third drafting position. The set order of selection saw the Montreal Canadiens get the first pick, followed by the Detroit Red Wings, Boston, the New York Rangers, the Chicago Black Hawks and the Toronto Maple Leafs. This order would rotate for each successive Amateur Draft, meaning Detroit would have the first overall pick for the next draft, with Boston moving up to second and so on, with Montreal dropping down to the last pick. This system would allow each team to have the first pick in turn over a six-year period. Although each team would have four picks, a team was not obligated to exercise them all.

At the conclusion of each draft, the NHL teams would have to pay $2,000 as compensation to the amateur teams of each of their selected players. Any player drafted would be kept on the drafting club's reserve list until his 18th birthday, at which time negotiations toward a professional contract could commence.

Due to the unique situation of the Montreal Canadiens, it was agreed to protect the French-Canadian flavor of the team. Therefore, the Canadiens were granted the option to select up to two players of French-Canadian heritage before any other team could exercise its first selections in the Amateur Draft. These cultural picks would be in lieu of their first and second selections in the draft order. The Canadiens were not obligated to exercise this option.

1963

On June 5, 1963 the National Hockey League conducted its first Amateur Draft in Montreal's Queen Elizabeth Hotel. The Canadiens waived their right to exercise the cultural option and went directly to the first choice, making Garry Monahan of the St. Michael's Juveniles in Toronto the first player to be selected in the NHL Amateur Draft. At 16 years and seven months, Monahan remains the youngest player to be selected first overall. Although Monahan only appeared in 14 games with the Canadiens, he spent 12 seasons in the NHL before continuing his career with a professional league in Japan. "The draft was new at that time and nobody really knew anything about it," observed Monahan in retrospect. "You have to remember that most junior players were already signed by one of the six NHL teams that were playing at the time."

Since most of the top junior players were on sponsored lists and ineligible for drafting, it was widely believed that no star players would be obtained through the Amateur Draft—especially in its first year of operation. However, to the surprise of many, such a player did emerge. Pete Mahovlich, younger brother of NHL superstar Frank, was drafted second overall by Detroit. Mahovlich went on to enjoy 16 seasons in the NHL, appearing with the Red Wings, Canadiens and the Pittsburgh Penguins.

He collected 773 career points (288 goals and 485 assists) and played on four Stanley Cup champions with the Canadiens (1971, 1973, 1976 and 1977) before retiring in 1980–81.

The 1963 Amateur Draft saw 21 players selected by the six NHL teams. Chicago and Detroit were the only teams who opted not to use all of their selections. After the draft, the NHL revised the age of draft eligibility to include players reaching their 17th birthdays between August 1, 1964 and July 1, 1965 for the next year.

1963

PICK	TEAM	NAME	DRAFTED FROM	NHL PLAYERS: POS / NHL GOALTENDERS: POS	GP GP	G W	A GA	PTS SO	PIM AVG
1	MTL	Garry Monahan	St. Michael's Juveniles	LW	748	116	169	285	484
2	DET	Pete Mahovlich	St. Michael's Juveniles	C	884	288	485	773	916
3	BOS	Orest Romashyna	New Hamburg Jr. C						
4	NYR	Al Osborne	Weston Jr. B	RW					
5	CHI	Art Hampson	Trenton Midgets						
6	TOR	Walt McKechnie	London Jr. B	C	955	214	392	606	469
7	MTL	Rodney Presswood	Georgetown Midgets						
8	DET	Bill Cosburn	Bick's Pickles						
9	BOS	Terrance Lane	Georgetown Midgets						
10	NYR	Terry Jones	Weston Midgets						
11	CHI	Wayne Davidson	Georgetown Midgets						
12	TOR	Neil Clairmont	Parry Sound Midgets	LW					

1963 continued PICK TEAM NAME	DRAFTED FROM	NHL PLAYERS: POS NHL GOALTENDERS: POS	GP GP	G W	A GA	PTS SO	PIM AVG
13 MTL Roy Pugh	Aurora Jr. C	C					
14 BOS Roger Bamburak	Isaac Brock	RW					
15 NYR Mike Cummings	Georgetown Midgets						
16 CHI Bill Carson	Brampton Midgets						
17 TOR Jim McKenny	Neil McNeil Jr. A	D	604	82	247	329	294
18 MTL Glen Shirton	Port Colborne Midgets	D					
19 BOS Jim Blair	Georgetown Midgets						
20 NYR Campbell Alleson	Portage la Prairie Jr.						
21 TOR Gerry Meehan	Neil McNeil Jr. A	C	670	180	243	423	111

1964

Under the same rulings that applied to its predecessor, the second Amateur Draft was conducted on June 11, 1964. Due to the lack of unprotected 17-year-olds perceived to have the potential to emerge as NHL stars, the issue of raising the draft age surfaced and would continue until the effects of sponsorship disappeared.

The 1964 Amateur Draft saw 24 players selected as all of the NHL teams exercised their four picks. The Canadiens once again passed on their cultural option, allowing the Detroit Red wings to choose Quebec-born Claude Gauthier as the first overall selection. The 1964 draft would mark the first time the top four selections never appeared in an NHL game. The drafts in 1965 and 1967 stand as the only other examples of such poor drafting.

As in 1963, the 1964 draft featured the effects of family relations as Syl Apps Jr., son of former Maple Leaf star and Hockey Hall of Famer Syl Apps, was selected 21st by the New York Rangers. Despite his late selection, Apps went on to play 10 seasons in the NHL, tallying 183 goals and 423 assists for 606 career points in 727 games.

A little-known aspect of the 1964 Amateur Draft is the fact that the Boston Bruins selected unprotected goaltender Ken Dryden from the Etobicoke Junior B team. Although Boston drafted him, Dryden never appeared in a Bruins jersey, opting to attend Cornell University instead. During his time there, he was obtained by the Montreal Canadiens. Dryden was first introduced to the NHL during the 1971 playoffs, where he backstopped the Canadiens to the Stanley Cup.

"He goes to college, studies law, writes exams and works for Ralph Nader in the summer," wrote *The Hockey News* during the 1971–72 campaign. "He's in the thick of contention for rookie of the year honors, yet he already holds the Conn Smythe Trophy as the best man in the playoffs. This guy is very nearly in a class by himself."

His immediate success in the NHL is one of many distinguishing characteristics of Ken Dryden. As the brother of Dave Dryden, the two formed the first goaltending brother act in the NHL. He was also recognized as the league's biggest goaltender at 6'4" and 210 pounds. In addition to his Conn Smythe and Calder Trophy wins, he is a five-time winner of the Vezina Trophy as the NHL's best goaltender (1973, 1976, 1977, 1978, 1979) and was the runner-up to Bobby Orr for the Hart Trophy as the NHL's MVP in 1971–72. Dryden was inducted into the Hockey Hall of Fame in 1983 and is now the president and general manager of the Toronto Maple Leafs.

1964

PICK TEAM NAME	DRAFTED FROM	NHL PLAYERS: POS NHL GOALTENDERS: POS	GP GP	G W	A GA	PTS SO	PIM AVG
1 DET Claude Gauthier	Rosemount Midgets						
2 BOS Alec Campbell	Strathroy Midgets	RW					
3 NYR Robert Graham	Toronto Marlboro Midgets	D					
4 CHI Richard Bayes	Dixie Midgets	C					
5 TOR Thomas Martin	Toronto Marlboro Midgets	RW	3	1	0	1	0
6 MTL Claude Chagnon	Rosemount Midgets						

1964 continued PICK TEAM NAME	DRAFTED FROM	NHL PLAYERS: POS NHL GOALTENDERS: POS	GP GP	G W	A GA	PTS SO	PIM AVG
7 DET Brian Watts	Toronto Marlboro Midgets	LW	4	0	0	0	0
8 BOS Jim Booth	Sault Ste. Marie Midgets	LW					
9 NYR Tim Ecclestone	Etobicoke Jr. B	LW	692	126	233	359	344
10 CHI Jan Popiel	Georgetown Midgets	LW					
11 TOR Dave Cotey	Aurora Jr. C						
12 MTL Guy Allen	Stamford Jr. B	D					
13 DET Ralph Buchanan	Montreal East Intermediates	D					
14 BOS Ken Dryden	Etobicoke Jr. B	G	397	258	870	46	2.24
15 NYR Gordon Lowe	Toronto Marlboro Midgets	D					
16 CHI Carl Hadfield	Dixie Jr. B	RW					
17 TOR Mike Pelyk	Toronto Marlboro Midgets	D	441	26	88	114	566
18 MTL Paul Reid	Kingston Midgets						
19 DET Rene Leclerc	Hamilton Jr. B	RW	87	10	11	21	105
20 BOS Blair Allister	Ingersoll Jr. B						
21 NYR Syl Apps Jr.	Kingston Midgets	C	727	183	423	606	311
22 CHI Moe L'Abbe	Rosemount Midgets	RW	5	0	1	1	0
23 TOR Jim Dorey	Stamford Jr. B	D	232	25	74	99	553
24 MTL Michel Jacques	Megantic Jr. B	LW					

1965

In 1965, the NHL officially altered the age of eligibility for all players entering the Amateur Draft.

In order to be drafted, a player now had to be 18 years of age. Any player whose name appeared on the NHL's sponsorship lists as of April 1, 1965 would be exempt from the draft. To accommodate the raised age of eligibility, the age for contract negotiations was also revised to keep players on the drafting team's reserve list until their 19th birthday, at which point a pro contract could be offered.

An interesting agreement was executed for the 1965 Amateur Draft between the NHL and the other pro leagues (the American Hockey League, the Western Hockey League and the Central Professional Hockey League).

The partnership allowed these leagues to participate in the draft when all of the NHL clubs had completed their picks. At that point, the AHL and WHL would be granted three picks each while the CPHL could take two selections. Despite their newly found rights, only one player was selected by a non-NHL club. The AHL's Pittsburgh Hornets selected Gary Beattie of the Gananoque Junior C team as the last pick.

The effects of sponsorship were made apparent, as the 1965 Amateur Draft is considered to be the weakest draft in NHL history. Due to the lack of talent among unsponsored 18-year-olds, only 11 players were selected by NHL teams, the fewest number of players to be selected in the history of the Amateur Draft. The top four players never appeared in an NHL game.

The New York Rangers selected Andre Veilleux of the Montreal Rangers Junior B club as the first pick overall. The Rangers were originally seeded as the second pick, however the Boston Bruins opted not to exercise their number-one seeding due to the thin talent pool. The lack of available talent also prompted the Toronto Maple Leafs not to participate in the draft at all.

1965

PICK TEAM NAME	DRAFTED FROM	NHL PLAYERS: POS NHL GOALTENDERS: POS	GP GP	G W	A GA	PTS SO	PIM AVG
1 NYR Andre Veilleux	Montreal Jr. B	RW					
2 CHI Andrew Culligan	St. Michael's Jr. B						
3 DET George Forgie	Flin Flon Jrs.	D					
4 BOS Joe Bailey	St. Thomas Jr. B						
5 MTL Pierre Bouchard	St. Vincent de Paul Jr. B	D	595	24	82	106	433
6 NYR George Surmay	Kelvin Juveniles	G					
7 CHI Brian McKenney	Smiths Falls Jr.						
8 DET Bob Birdsell	Stettler	RW					
9 BOS Bill Ramsay	Winnipeg Jrs.						
10 NYR Michel Parizeau	Montreal Jr. B	C	58	3	14	17	18
11 PIT-AHL Gary Beattie	Gananoque Jr. C						

1966

For the first time since its inception, the Amateur Draft changed its location. The 1966 Amateur Draft was conducted in Montreal's Mount Royal Hotel on April 25, 1966. This is the earliest date that the draft has been conducted. In contrast to the previous year, the 1966 Amateur Draft displayed a much more promising crop of unprotected young prospects. Each of the member clubs used all of their four picks, resulting in 24 players being selected. Having passed the previous year, Boston took the first pick and selected Barry Gibbs of the Estevan Bruins. Gibbs became the first defenseman to be selected first overall. He went on to enjoy a 13-year career in the NHL, recording 282 points (58 goals, 224 assists) with five different clubs before retiring in 1979–80.

Although the draft was now in its fourth year of operation, the system of sponsorship would continue to affect the talent pool of draft-eligible prospects for another two years. As a result, the odds of discovering a future superstar from the Amateur Draft were still considered slim. However, the 1966 Amateur Draft unearthed just such a player when the New York Rangers drafted defenseman Brad Park second overall. As an unprotected prospect, Park played his junior hockey with the Toronto Marlboros before breaking into the NHL in the 1968–69 season as a 20-year-old. Although most of the attention was fixed on products of sponsored lists, the media took notice of Park's long-term potential: "Whether he wins the Calder Trophy as the NHL's best rookie or not, Park is the best first-year man in the league. He will be a star when some of those who may get more votes will not be in the league."

This observation was remarkably true, as Park was denied the Calder and went on to spend 17 seasons in the NHL, posting a career record of 213 goals and 683 assists for 896 points in 1,113 games. He is recognized as one of the best all-around defensemen to play the game. Park was named as a runner-up for the Norris Trophy as the league's top defenseman six times (1970, 1971, 1972, 1974, 1976, 1978), although in an era dominated first by Bobby Orr and then Denis Potvin he never won the award. In 1984, he captured the Masterton Trophy recognizing his perseverance and dedication to the sport of hockey. Park became the second alumnus of the Amateur Draft to be inducted into the Hockey Hall of Fame in 1988. A second Masterton Trophy winner came out of the 1966 draft when center Don Luce, selected 14th overall by the Rangers, captured the award with the Buffalo Sabres in 1975.

1966

PICK	TEAM	NAME	DRAFTED FROM	NHL PLAYERS: POS / NHL GOALTENDERS: POS	GP / GP	G / W	A / GA	PTS / SO	PIM / AVG
1	BOS	Barry Gibbs	Estevan	D	797	58	224	282	945
2	NYR	Brad Park	Toronto	D	1113	213	683	896	1429
3	CHI	Terry Caffery	Toronto	C	14	0	0	0	0
4	TOR	John Wright	West Clair Jr. B	C	127	16	36	52	67
5	MTL	Phil Myre	Shawinigan	G	439	149	1482	14	3.53
6	DET	Steve Atkinson	Niagara Falls	RW	302	60	51	111	104
7	BOS	Rick Smith	Hamilton	D	687	52	167	219	560
8	NYR	Joey Johnston	Peterborough	LW	331	85	106	191	320
9	CHI	Ron Dussiaume	Oshawa	LW					
10	TOR	Cam Crosby	Toronto						
11	MTL	Maurice St. Jacques	London	C					
12	DET	Jim Whittaker	Oshawa	D					
13	BOS	Garnet Bailey	Edmonton	LW	568	107	171	278	633
14	NYR	Don Luce	Kitchener	C	894	225	329	554	364
15	CHI	Larry Gibbons	Markham Jr. B	D					
16	TOR	Rick Ley	Niagara Falls	D	310	12	72	84	528
17	MTL	Jude Drouin	Verdun	C	666	151	305	456	346
18	DET	Lee Carpenter	Hamilton Jr. B	D					
19	BOS	Tom Webster	Niagara Falls	RW	102	33	42	75	61
20	NYR	Jack Egers	Kitchener Jr. B	RW	284	64	69	133	154
21	CHI	Brian Morenz	Oshawa	LW					
22	TOR	Dale MacLeish	Peterborough	C					
23	MTL	Bob Pate	Montreal	D					
24	DET	Grant Cole	St. Michael's Jr. B	G					

1967

The National Hockey League underwent extensive change prior to the 1967–68 season as expansion doubled its size from six to 12 teams. The six new teams were incorporated into the 1967 Amateur Draft, which then saw a necessary revision to its method of determining the order of selection.

In order to prevent the already existing clubs from acquiring the absolute top junior prospects, it was agreed that the expansion teams (playing in the West Division) would be granted the first six drafting positions. The order of the expansion teams would be determined by allotment, while the "Original Six" teams (now in the East Division) would continue on their previous rotating basis. The final order of selection for the 1967 draft was the Los Angeles Kings, the Pittsburgh Penguins, the Oakland Seals, the Minnesota North Stars and the Philadelphia Flyers, at which point the original order of selection for the East Division would begin with the Rangers. The expansion St. Louis Blues made no selections that year.

The age of eligibility was changed in 1967, with only all amateur players who were 20 years of age or older now considered eligible for drafting. The effects of the age change were similar to those witnessed in the 1965 Amateur Draft when the age of eligibility was raised to 18. A definite lack of talent within the drafting pool of eligible amateur players prompted the NHL to allow the expansion clubs to select overage juniors whose names appeared on NHL-sponsored lists. However, for every sponsored player a team selected, it had make a payment of $5,000 to that player's amateur team as compensation, making the choice an expensive investment.

On June 7, 1967 only 18 players were selected in the draft and for the third time none of the top four picks would appear in an NHL game. The Los Angeles Kings made history as the first expansion club to participate in the Amateur Draft when they selected Rick Pagnutti of the Garson Native Sons.

Pagnutti was the Kings' only selection in the 1967 draft as they opted not to exercise their other draft picks. No team used all four of their designated selections.

Perhaps due to the thin talent pool in the common amateur ranks, National Hockey League teams sought talent in other amateur leagues such as the U.S. collegiate system. The Detroit Red Wings broke into a new realm when they drafted Michigan Tech's Alan Karlander 17th overall. The move proved to be a success, as Karlander went on to play four seasons with the Red Wings, tallying 36 goals and 56 assists for 92 points in 212 games. Karlander was only one of two players selected in the 1967 draft to play in the NHL, the other being the Flyers' first pick (fifth overall) Serge Bernier, who collected 197 points (78 goals, 119 assists) in 302 games and also starred in the World Hockey Association.

There were four sponsored players taken in the Special Internal Draft of sponsored juniors. Philadelphia took two players, drafting Toronto's John Marshall and Ken Schutz. Pittsburgh selected New York's Frank Francis, while Minnesota drafted Andre Aubrey from the Rangers' protected list.

At the conclusion of the draft, this special clause was terminated.

1967

PICK	TEAM	NAME	DRAFTED FROM	NHL PLAYERS: POS	GP	G	A	PTS	PIM
				NHL GOALTENDERS: POS	GP	W	GA	SO	AVG
1	L.A.	Rick Pagnutti	Garson	D					
2	PIT	Steve Rexe	Belleville Srs.	G					
3	OAK	Ken Hicks	Brandon						
4	MIN	Wayne Cheesman	Whitby Jr. B	D					
5	PHI	Serge Bernier	Sorel	RW	302	78	119	197	234
6	NYR	Robert Dickson	Chatham Jr. B	LW					
7	CHI	Bob Tombari	Sault Ste. Marie	LW					
8	MTL	Elgin McCann	Weyburn Jr. A	RW					
9	DET	Ron Barkwell	Flin Flon						
10	BOS	Meehan Bonnar	St. Thomas Jr. B	RW					
11	PIT	Bob Smith	Sault Ste. Marie	C					
12	OAK	Garry Wood	Fort Frances	D					
13	MIN	Larry Mick	Pembroke Jr. A						
14	PHI	Al Sarault	Pembroke Jr. A	D					
15	NYR	Brian Tosh	Smiths Falls Jr.	D					
16	TOR	Bob Kelly	Port Arthur Jr.	LW	425	87	109	196	687
17	DET	Al Karlander	Michigan Tech	C	212	36	56	92	70
18	OAK	Kevin Smith	Halifax Jr.	D					

1968

Prior to the 1967 draft, the NHL worked ahead of schedule establishing procedures that would be applied to the Amateur Draft in 1968 and 1969. Of primary focus was the order of selection. It was finally decided that it would be based on the reverse order of the standing for the previous year and that this guideline would apply to all member clubs, thereby abandoning the long-standing rotation that was first established in 1963. However, the order of selection would be a mix between the two divisions.

The last-place team in the West Division would be granted the first pick, followed by the last-place club in the East Division. The West Division team that placed second-last would go third, followed by the fifth-place team in the East Division. At this point the remaining four West Division teams would be granted the next four selections, while the remaining East Division teams would take the last four spots. These last eight spots would remain according to the reverse order of standing in each division.

While this new system of determining draft order was devised to aid the expansion teams, a new mode of transaction began to be practiced by NHL clubs. The new teams began to trade away their draft picks for packages of veteran talent, while the established teams sought to improve their drafting position. Therefore, it was not uncommon to see the first round dominated by one team.

Another issue facing the NHL was Montreal's cultural option. The Canadiens had yet to exercise this option since it had originally been granted, and it was decided that the team should be required to exercise at least one of its priority choices in every Amateur Draft. The choices would remain in lieu of their respective first and second choices in the drafting order.

Prior to the 1968 Amateur Draft, the Canadiens had acquired the first selections of both the Oakland Seals and the Detroit Red Wings through trades. As Oakland was the last-place team in the West Division, and Detroit the last-place team in the East, Montreal would be granted the first two selections of the draft.

In addition, by using their cultural option, Montreal had the first three picks in 1968, marking the only time in history that one team owned the top three drafting positions. With their priority selection, the Canadiens drafted goaltender Michel Plasse of the Drummondville juniors. Plasse remains the only goaltender to be selected before any other player in an Amateur Draft. Montreal's following two choices were Robert Belisle of the Montreal North Beavers

and Jim Pritchard of the Winnipeg Jets. Plasse was the only Montreal selection to have a career in the NHL, lasting 12 years before retiring in 1981–82.

Gary Edwards, the only other goaltender taken in the 1968 Amateur Draft, also enjoyed a long career spanning 13 seasons. In 1975, Edwards and Rogie Vachon were the runners-up to Bernie Parent for the Vezina Trophy awarded to the league's top goaltender.

1968

PICK	TEAM	NAME	DRAFTED FROM	NHL PLAYERS: POS	GP	G	A	PTS	PIM
				NHL GOALTENDERS: POS	GP	W	GA	SO	AVG
1	MTL	Michel Plasse	Drummondville	G	299	92	1058	2	3.79
2	MTL	Roger Belisle	Montreal North Beavers						
3	MTL	Jim Pritchard	Winnipeg	D					
4	PIT	Garry Swain	Niagara Falls	C	9	1	1	2	0
5	MIN	Jim Benzelock	Winnipeg	RW					
6	ST.L.	Gary Edwards	Toronto	G	286	88	973	11	3.65
7	L.A.	Jim McInally	Hamilton	D					
8	PHI	Lew Morrison	Flin Flon	RW	564	39	52	91	107
9	CHI	John Marks	North Dakota	LW	657	112	163	275	330
10	TOR	Brad Selwood	Niagara Falls	D	163	7	40	47	153
11	DET	Steve Andrascik	Flin Flon	RW					
12	BOS	Danny Schock	Estevan	LW	20	1	2	3	0
13	OAK	Doug Smith	Winnipeg	C					
14	PIT	Ron Snell	Regina	RW	7	3	2	5	6
15	MIN	Marc Rioux	Verdun	C					
16	ST.L.	Curt Bennett	Brown	LW	580	152	182	334	347
17	DET	Herb Boxer	Michigan Tech	RW					
18	BOS	Fraser Rice	Halifax Jr.	C					
19	NYR	Bruce Buchanan	Weyburn Jr. A	D					
20	OAK	Jim Trewin	Flin Flon	D					
21	PIT	Dave Simpson	Port Arthur Jr.	D					
22	MIN	Glen Lindsay	Saskatoon	G					
23	MTL	Don Grierson	North Bay Jr. A	RW					
24	BOS	Brian St. John	U. of Toronto	C					

1969

By June 12, 1969 the National Hockey League had finally reached its goal in terms of the Amateur Draft, as for the first time the effects of sponsorship would not play a role in the available junior prospects. The 1969 draft would provide every team with an equal opportunity to acquire the absolutely best talent the junior ranks had to offer. The only restriction on the draft was the age of eligibility, which remained at 20 years of age. The NHL maintained that no eligible player would be exempt from the draft with the exception of Europeans who would need to be released from their respective associations.

The order of selection was based on the reverse order of the overall standing within the league. Therefore the divisional standing had no bearing on draft position. It was ruled that draft selection would continue until every member club declared that their participation was complete.

The Montreal Canadiens made another extreme impact on the draft this year when they exercised both priority selections before any other team could select. Their cultural option gave the Canadiens a distinct advantage in the 1969 draft, since the two players who were considered to be the top available prospects were of French-Canadian descent. Montreal took full advantage of the clause and selected teammates Rejean Houle and Marc Tardif of the Montreal Junior Canadiens as the first and second picks.

After the draft, it was ruled that the Canadiens could not exercise the priority selections unless all of the NHL general managers unanimously agreed to reinstate the option on a yearly basis. The Canadiens have not exercised the option since, and today the clause is considered non-existent.

Unlike most drafted players, Houle joined the Canadiens immediately, though he played only nine NHL games in 1969–70. He was a regular on the team when Montreal won

the Stanley Cup in 1971 and 1973. After three seasons with the Quebec Nordiques in the WHA, Houle returned to Montreal and helped the Canadiens capture the Stanley Cup again in 1977, 1978 and 1979. In all, he spent 11 years in the NHL, recording 408 points (161 goals, 247 assists) in 635 games. He retired in 1982–83 and is currently the Canadiens general manager. Marc Tardif also made the club in 1969–70 and went on to play eight seasons in the NHL, posting a career record of 194 goals and 207 assists for 401 points in 517 games. He is also one of the top scorers in the history of the WHA.

Although Montreal had clearly dominated the 1969 Amateur Draft, it was the Philadelphia Flyers who walked away with the year's prize catch. Center Bobby Clarke had won consecutive scoring titles in the Western Canada Junior League with the Flin Flon Bombers and was considered to be one of the top three talents in Canada. However, Clarke was a diabetic and was thus considered to be a high-risk draft choice. The Flyers decided to take the risk and drafted Clarke 17th overall. He went on to become the heart and soul of the franchise, winning the Hart Trophy in 1973, 1975 and 1976 as the league's MVP.

Clarke spent nine seasons as the Flyers' captain, leading them to consecutive Stanley Cup championships in 1974 and 1975 as the Flyers became the first expansion club to win the title. In only his fourth season, and prior to winning his first Hart Trophy, Clarke was already being recognized and praised by his teammates. "Bobby is every bit as valuable to us as Gordie Howe is to the Red Wings," Flyers winger Simon Nolet stated. "He's every bit as valuable to us as Bobby Orr or Phil Esposito are to the Bruins. Every team must have a leader, a guy who can carry the club when things aren't going so well. Well, that's something that fits Bobby perfectly. He really means a lot to us."

In 1987, Clarke was inducted into the Hockey Hall of Fame and his number 16 jersey has been retired by the club. With a career record of 358 goals and 852 assists for 1,210 points in 1,144 games, Clarke ranks as the Flyers all-time leader in most offensive categories. Currently, Clarke is president and general manager of the Flyers. He remains a perfect example of one club's gamble for success.

The Kings should be credited for finding the most underrated player in the 1969 Amateur Draft when they made Butch Goring their final choice, 51st overall. Goring joined the Kings immediately after the draft and made an impact on the NHL in his first year, scoring 13 goals and collecting 23 assists for 36 points in only 59 games. He went on to capture the Lady Byng Trophy as the most gentlemanly player in 1978. His dedication and perseverance for the game also earned him the Masterton Trophy in the same year. On March 10, 1980 Goring joined the New York Islanders and became an integral part of one of the most heralded hockey dynasties as the Islanders went on to win four consecutive Stanley Cup championships. Goring captured the Conn Smythe Trophy as the playoffs MVP in 1981. He spent 16 seasons in the NHL, performing for the Kings, the Islanders and the Boston Bruins before retiring in 1984–85 with 375 career goals and 513 assists for 888 points.

The 1969 draft also boasted an international flavor as it featured the first European-born player to be selected in the Amateur Draft. The St. Louis Blues opted to take Tommi Salmelainen, a native of Sweden, 66th overall. Although he never appeared in an NHL game, the move represented an expanded view of the hockey pool by the NHL as teams began to search the world for the best available talent.

1969

PICK	TEAM	NAME	DRAFTED FROM	NHL PLAYERS: POS / NHL GOALTENDERS: POS	GP	G / W	A / GA	PTS / SO	PIM / AVG
FIRST ROUND									
1	MTL	Rejean Houle	Montreal	L/RW	635	161	247	408	395
2	MTL	Marc Tardif	Montreal	LW	517	194	207	401	443
3	BOS	Don Tannahill	Niagara Falls	LW	111	30	33	63	25
4	BOS	Frank Spring	Edmonton	RW	61	14	20	34	12
5	MIN	Dick Redmond	St. Catharines	D	771	133	312	445	504
6	PHI	Bob Currier	Cornwall	C					
7	OAK	Tony Featherstone	Peterborough	RW	130	17	21	38	65
8	NYR	Andre Dupont	Montreal	D	800	59	185	244	1986
9	TOR	Ernie Moser	Estevan	RW					
10	DET	Jim Rutherford	Hamilton	G	457	151	1576	14	3.65
11	BOS	Ivan Boldirev	Oshawa	C	1052	361	505	866	507
12	NYR	Pierre Jarry	Ottawa	LW	344	88	117	205	142
13	CHI	J.P. Bordeleau	Montreal	RW	519	97	126	223	143
14	MIN	Dennis O'Brien	St. Catharines	D	592	31	91	122	1017
SECOND ROUND									
15	PIT	Rick Kessell	Oshawa	C	135	4	24	28	6
16	L.A.	Dale Hoganson	Estevan	D	343	13	77	90	186
17	PHI	Bobby Clarke	Flin Flon	C	1144	358	852	1210	1453
18	OAK	Ron Stackhouse	Peterborough	D	889	87	372	459	824
19	ST.L.	Mike Lowe	Loyola College	C					
20	TOR	Doug Brindley	Niagara Falls	LW/C	3	0	0	0	0
21	DET	Ron Garwasiuk	Regina	LW					
22	BOS	Art Quoquochi	Montreal	RW					
23	NYR	Bert Wilson	London	LW	478	37	44	81	646
24	CHI	Larry Romanchych	Flin Flon	RW	298	68	97	165	102
25	MIN	Gilles Gilbert	London	G	416	192	1290	18	3.27
26	PIT	Michel Briere	Shawinigan	C	76	12	32	44	20
27	L.A.	Gregg Boddy	Edmonton	D	273	23	44	67	263
28	PHI	Willie Brossart	Estevan	LW	129	1	14	15	88
OTHER ROUNDS									
29	OAK	Don O'Donoghue	St. Catharines	RW	125	18	17	35	35
30	ST.L.	Bernard Gagnon	Michigan	C					
31	TOR	Larry McIntyre	Moose Jaw	D	41	0	3	3	26
32	MTL	Bobby Sheehan	St. Catharines	C	310	48	63	111	50
33	DET	Wayne Hawrysh	Flin Flon	RW					
34	BOS	Nels Jacobson	Winnipeg	LW					
35	NYR	Kevin Morrison	St Jerome	D	41	4	11	15	23
36	CHI	Milt Black	Winnipeg	RW					
37	MIN	Fred O'Donnell	Oshawa	RW	115	15	11	26	98
38	PIT	Yvon Labre	Toronto	D	371	14	87	101	788
39	L.A.	Bruce Landon	Peterborough	G					
40	PHI	Michel Belhumeur	Drummondville	G	65	9	254	0	4.61
41	OAK	Pierre Farmer	Shawinigan	D					
42	ST.L.	Victor Teal	St. Catharines	RW	1	0	0	0	0
43	TOR	Frank Hughes	Edmonton	LW	5	0	0	0	0
44	MTL	Murray Anderson	Flin Flon	D	40	0	1	1	68
45	DET	Wayne Chernecki	Winnipeg	C					
46	BOS	Ron Fairbrother	Saskatoon	LW					
47	NYR	Bruce Hollemond	Moose Jaw	LW					
48	CHI	Daryl Maggs	Calgary	D	135	14	19	33	54
49	MIN	Pierre Jutras	Shawinigan	LW					
50	PIT	Ed Patenaude	Calgary	RW					
51	L.A.	Butch Goring	Dauphin Jr. A	C	1107	375	513	888	102
52	PHI	Dave Schultz	Sorel	LW	535	79	121	200	2294
53	OAK	Warren Harrison	Sorel	C					
54	ST.L.	Brian Glenwright	Kitchener	LW					
55	TOR	Brian Spencer	Swift Current	LW	553	80	143	223	634
56	MTL	Garry Doyle	Ottawa	G					
57	DET	Wally Olds	Minnesota-Duluth	D					
58	BOS	Jeremy Wright	Calgary	C					
59	NYR	Gordon Smith	Cornwall	D					
60	CHI	Mike Baumgartner	North Dakota	D	17	0	0	0	0
61	MIN	Bob Walton	Niagara Falls	C					
62	PIT	Paul Hoganson	Toronto	G	2	0	7	0	7.37
63	MTL	Guy Delparte	London	LW	48	1	8	9	18
64	PHI	Don Saleski	Regina	RW	543	128	125	253	629
65	OAK	Neil Nicholson	London	D	39	3	1	4	23
66	ST.L.	Tommi Salmelainen	HIFK Helsinki, FIN	LW					
67	TOR	Bob Neufeld	Dauphin Jr. A	LW					
68	MTL	Lynn Powis	U. of Denver	C	130	19	33	52	25
69	BOS	Jim Jones	Peterborough	D	2	0	0	0	0
70	ST.L.	Dale Yutsyk	Colorado College	LW					
71	CHI	Dave Hudson	North Dakota	C	409	59	124	183	89
72	MIN	Rick Thompson	Niagara Falls	D					
73	ST.L.	Bob Collyard	Colorado College	C	10	1	3	4	4
74	MTL	Ian Wilkie	Edmonton	G					
75	MTL	Dale Power	Peterborough	C					
76	OAK	Pete Vipond	Oshawa	LW	3	0	0	0	0
77	ST.L.	Dave Pulkkinen	Oshawa	LW/D	2	0	0	0	0
78	MIN	Cal Russell	Hamilton	RW					
79	MTL	Frank Hamill	Toronto	RW					
80	ST.L.	Pat Lange	Sudbury	C					
81	PHI	Claude Chartre	Drummondville	C					
82	ST.L.	John Converse	Estevan						
83	MTL	Gilles Drolet	Quebec						
84	MTL	Darrel Knibbs	Lethbridge	C					

1970

The 1970 Amateur Draft featured the participation of the NHL's second phase of expansion as the newly awarded Buffalo Sabres and Vancouver Canucks franchises were granted the first and second picks respectively. Due to the problem of expansion teams having the tendency to trade their draft picks for packages of players from the NHL's strongest teams, the league issued a clause in the draft that forbid expansion clubs from trading their first picks and once that player was signed they were obligated to remain with the club for at least three seasons. Such trades by other NHL teams were very evident in the 1970 draft. The Stanley Cup champion Boston Bruins had acquired the first picks of Los Angeles and Philadelphia, while the Montreal Canadiens (who won the Stanley Cup in 1969) had also traded to acquire higher drafting positions by obtaining Oakland's and Minnesota's first picks.

In 1970 the Buffalo Sabres used the first overall pick to select Gilbert Perreault. (With the second pick of the 1970 draft, the Canucks selected highly touted defenseman Dale Tallon, who would spend only three seasons with Vancouver.) Perreault became an instant star in the NHL, posting 72 points (38 goals, 34 assists) in 78 games in his rookie season to capture the Calder Trophy as the rookie of the year in 1970–71.

In 1973, Perreault added another award to his resume as he accepted the Lady Byng Trophy as the league's most gentlemanly player. Two years later, he led the Sabres to the Stanley Cup finals where they were defeated by the powerful Philadelphia Flyers. The Sabres have not returned to the finals since. Perreault remained the exclusive property of the Sabres as he spent his entire 17-year career in a Buffalo uniform. He is a member of the 500-goal club, scoring 512 times and also ranks among the all-time leaders with 814 assists. Perreault centered Rene Robert and Richard Martin on Buffalo's French Connection, one of the most productive forward lines in NHL history. He remains the Sabres' highest-scoring player and has been honored with the retirement of his number 11 jersey, which currently hangs from the rafters of the Marine Midland Arena. In 1990 Perreault was inducted to the Hockey Hall of Fame.

Although the first round of the 1970 draft displayed both Boston and Montreal's genius for acquiring high draft picks, it also showed the potential for weakness among even the league's best organizations. Boston selected two of the most dangerous snipers of all-time in Reggie Leach and Rick MacLeish. However, MacLeish was traded to the Flyers prior to the commencement of the regular season and never wore the Boston jersey. Leach spent two seasons with the Bruins but failed to develop fast enough for Boston management and was also traded. He eventually joined MacLeish in Philadelphia and the two were instrumental in the Flyers' success in the 1970s. On April 1, 1976 Leach became only the second player in NHL history to record 60 goals in one season, joining Boston's Phil Esposito. Leach also proved to be one of the best playoff performers when he set a league record with 19 goals in 16 games in the 1976 postseason, including nine goals in one series (five games), which also stands as a league record. With 381 career goals, Leach still ranks among the game's all-time leaders. MacLeish tallied 339 goals.

Montreal's scouting weakness was illustrated by the Canadiens' selection of goaltender Ray Martiniuk as their first pick (fifth overall) in 1970. Martiniuk failed to gradu-

ate into the NHL, while two first-rate goaltenders were hiding in the crowd, including a future Hall of Famer. Goaltender Billy Smith became known as one of the most fierce competitors on the ice, an uncharacteristic role for a goaltender. His physical style of play resonates throughout the goaltending ranks of today, making him one of the most influential players at that position. An unorthodox milestone that Smith holds came during the 1979–80 season when he became the first goaltender credited with a goal for his team.

Originally drafted by Los Angeles, he backstopped the Kings' minor-league Springfield Kings of the American Hockey League to an unexpected championship title in 1971. He is best known for his outstanding performance with the New York Islanders to whom he was sent in the 1972 Expansion Draft. Smith captured the Vezina Trophy as the league's top goaltender in 1982 and the William M. Jennings Trophy, which he shared with Rollie Melanson as the top goaltending tandem, in 1983. He was a premier performer for the Islanders as they captured four consecutive Stanley Cup championships. Smith won the Conn Smythe as the playoff MVP in 1983. Ten years later, he was elected to the Hall of Fame.

In addition to Perreault and Smith, another future Hall of Famer was chosen in the 1970 Amateur Draft. Toronto selected Darryl Sittler eighth overall and he went on to become the leading scorer in Maple Leafs history. In a 15-year career with Toronto, Detroit and Philadelphia, he totaled 484 goals and 637 assists. Both Sittler and Reggie Leach are tied (along with Newsy Lalonde, Maurice Richard and Mario Lemieux) for the league record for most goals scored in one playoff game with five. Sittler also holds the NHL record for most points in one game which he set against Boston on February 7, 1976 after he tallied six goals and four assists for a 10-point performance.

1970

PICK	TEAM	NAME	DRAFTED FROM	NHL PLAYERS: POS / NHL GOALTENDERS: POS	GP / GP	G / W	A / GA	PTS / SO	PIM / AVG
FIRST ROUND									
1	BUF	Gilbert Perreault	Montreal	C	1191	512	814	1326	500
2	VAN	Dale Tallon	Toronto	D	642	98	238	336	568
3	BOS	Reggie Leach	Flin Flon	RW	934	381	285	666	387
4	BOS	Rick MacLeish	Peterborough	C	846	349	410	759	434
5	MTL	Ray Martyniuk	Flin Flon	G					
6	MTL	Chuck Lefley	Canadian National	LW	407	128	164	292	137
7	PIT	Greg Polis	Estevan	LW	615	174	169	343	391
8	TOR	Darryl Sittler	London	C	1096	484	637	1121	948
9	BOS	Ron Plumb	Peterborough	D	26	3	4	7	14
10	CAL	Chris Oddleifson	Winnipeg	C	524	95	191	286	464
11	NYR	Norm Gratton	Montreal	LW	201	39	44	83	64
12	DET	Serge Lajeunesse	Montreal	D/RW	103	1	4	5	103
13	BOS	Robert Stewart	Oshawa	D	575	27	101	128	809
14	CHI	Dan Maloney	London	LW	737	192	259	451	1489
SECOND ROUND									
15	BUF	Butch Deadmarsh	Brandon	LW	137	12	5	17	155
16	VAN	Jim Hargreaves	Winnipeg	D	66	1	7	8	105
17	MIN	Fred Harvey	Hamilton	RW	407	90	118	208	131
18	PHI	Bill Clement	Ottawa	C	719	148	208	356	383
19	CAL	Pete Laframboise	Ottawa	LW/C	227	33	55	88	70
20	MIN	Fred Barrett	Toronto	D	745	25	123	148	671
21	PIT	John A. Stewart	Flin Flon	LW	258	58	60	118	158
22	L.A.	Errol Thompson	Charlottetown Sr.	LW	599	208	185	393	184
23	ST.L.	Murray Keogan	Minnesota-Duluth	C					
24	L.A.	Al McDonough	St. Catharines	RW	237	73	88	161	73
25	NYR	Mike Murphy	Toronto	RW	831	238	318	556	514
26	DET	Bobby Guindon	Montreal	LW	6	0	1	1	0
27	BOS	Dan Bouchard	London	G	655	286	2061	27	3.26
28	CHI	Michel Archambault	Drummondville	LW	3	0	0	0	0
OTHER ROUNDS									
29	BUF	Steve Cuddie	Toronto	D					
30	VAN	Ed Dyck	Calgary	G	49	8	178	1	4.35
31	MTL	Steve Carlyle	Red Deer Jr. A	D					
32	PHI	Bob Kelly	Oshawa	LW	837	154	208	362	1454
33	CAL	Randy Rota	Calgary	C/LW	212	38	39	77	60
34	MIN	Dennis Patterson	Peterborough	D	138	6	22	28	67

PICK	TEAM	NAME	DRAFTED FROM	NHL PLAYERS: POS / NHL GOALTENDERS: POS	GP / GP	G / W	A / GA	PTS / SO	PIM / AVG
35	PIT	Larry Bignell	Edmonton	D	20	0	3	3	2
36	TOR	Gerry O'Flaherty	Kitchener	LW	438	99	95	194	168
37	ST.L.	Ron Climie	Hamilton	LW					
38	L.A.	Terry Holbrook	London	RW	43	3	6	9	4
39	NYR	Wendell Bennett	Weyburn Jr. A	D					
40	DET	Yvon Lambert	Drummondville	LW	683	206	273	479	340
41	BOS	Ray Brownlee	U. of Brandon	C					
42	CHI	Len Frig	Calgary	D	311	13	51	64	479
43	BUF	Randy Wyrozub	Edmonton	C	100	8	10	18	10
44	VAN	Brent Taylor	Estevan	RW					
45	MTL	Cal Hammond	Flin Flon	G					
46	PHI	Jacques Lapierre	Shawinigan	D					
47	CAL	Ted McAneeley	Edmonton	D	158	8	35	43	141
48	MIN	Dave Cressman	Kitchener	LW	85	6	8	14	37
49	PIT	Connie Forey	Ottawa	LW	4	0	0	0	2
50	TOR	Bob Gryp	Boston U.	LW	74	11	13	24	33
51	ST.L.	Gord Brooks	London	RW	70	7	18	25	37
52	MTL	John French	Toronto	LW					
53	NYR	Andre St. Pierre	Drummondville	D					
54	DET	Tom Johnston	Toronto	RW					
55	BOS	Gordon Davies	Toronto	LW					
56	CHI	Walt Ledingham	Minnesota-Duluth	LW	15	0	2	2	4
57	BUF	Mike Morton	Shawinigan	RW					
58	VAN	Bill McFadden	Swift Current	F					
59	L.A.	Billy Smith	Cornwall	G	680	305	2031	22	3.17
60	PHI	Doug Kerslake	Edmonton	RW					
61	OAK	Ray Gibbs	Charlottetown Sr.	G					
62	MIN	Henry Lehvonen	Kitchener	D					
63	PIT	Stephen Cardwell	Oshawa	LW					
64	TOR	Luc Simard	Trois-Rivieres	RW					
65	ST.L.	Mike Stevens	Minnesota-Duluth	D					
66	MTL	Rick Wilson	North Dakota	D	239	6	26	32	165
67	NYR	Gary Coalter	Hamilton	RW	34	2	4	6	2
68	DET	Tom Mellor	Boston College	D	26	2	4	6	25
69	BOS	Robert Roselle	Sorel	LW					
70	CHI	Gilles Meloche	Verdun	G	788	270	2756	20	3.64
71	BUF	Mike Keeler	Niagara Falls	D					
72	VAN	Dave Gilmour	London	LW					
73	L.A.	Gerry Bradbury	London	C					
74	PHI	Dennis Giannini	London	LW					
75	OAK	Doug Moyes	Sorel	RW					
76	MIN	Murray McNeill	Calgary	LW					
77	PIT	Bob Fitchner	Brandon	C	78	12	20	32	59
78	TOR	Calvin Booth	Weyburn Jr. A	LW					
79	ST.L.	Claude Moreau	Montreal	D					
80	MTL	Robert Brown	Boston U.	D					
81	NYR	Duane Wylie	St. Catharines	C	14	3	3	6	2
82	DET	Bernie MacNeil	Espanola Jr.	LW	4	0	0	0	0
83	BOS	Murray Wing	North Dakota	D	1	0	1	1	0
84	BUF	Tim Regan	Boston U.	G					
85	ST.L.	Jack Taggart	U. of Denver	D					
86	L.A.	Brian Carlin	Calgary	LW	5	1	0	1	0
87	PHI	Hank Nowak	Oshawa	LW	180	26	29	55	161
88	OAK	Terry Murray	Ottawa	D	302	4	76	80	199
89	MIN	Gary Geldart	London	D	4	0	0	0	5
90	PIT	Jim Pearson	St. Catharines	RW					
91	TOR	Paul Larose	Quebec	RW					
92	CAL	Terry Marshall	Brandon	D					
93	MTL	Bob Fowler	Estevan	RW					
94	NYR	Wayne Bell	Estevan	G					
95	DET	Ed Hays	U. of Denver	C					
96	BOS	Glen Siddall	Kitchener	LW					
97	BUF	Doug Rombough	St. Catharines	C	150	24	27	51	80
98	L.A.	Brian Chinnick	Peterborough	C					
99	PHI	Garry Cunningham	St. Catharines	D					
100	OAK	Al Henry	North Dakota	D					
101	MIN	Mickey Donaldson	Peterborough	LW					
102	PIT	Cam Newton	Kitchener	G	16	4	51	0	3.76
103	TOR	Ron Low	Dauphin Jr. A	G	382	102	1163	4	4.28
104	ST.L.	Dave Iataryn	Niagara Falls	G	2	1	10	0	7.50
105	MTL	Rick Jordan	Boston U.	D					
106	NYR	Pierre Brind'Amour	Montreal	LW					
107	BUF	Luc Nadeau	Drummondville	C					
108	ST.L.	Bob Winograd	Colorado College	D					
109	PHI	Jean Daigle	Sorel	LW					
110	PIT	Ron Lemieux	Dauphin Jr. A	RW					
111	ST.L.	Mike Lampman	U. of Denver	LW	96	17	20	37	34
112	ST.L.	Jeff Rotsch	Wisconsin	D					
113	ST.L.	Al Calver	Kitchener	D					
114	ST.L.	Gerry MacDonald	St. Francis Xavier	D					
115	ST.L.	Gerald Haines	Kenora						

1971

The 1971 Amateur Draft focused once again on weaker teams trading away their draft picks. NHL president Clarence Campbell proposed taking action against teams who dealt their picks and to place further restrictions on team's actions during the Amateur Draft. Over the past two drafts, the Montreal Canadiens and other "Original Six" franchises had stocked up on first-round picks, thereby monopolizing the NHL Amateur Draft and defeating the purpose of promoting parity between the league's "haves" and "have-nots."

"If we're ever going to get parity in the NHL, some embargo must be placed on the trading of amateur draft choices," said Clarence Campbell. "The clubs should at least wait to see what they've got in these amateurs before giving them away."

The issue was raised due to the Canadiens' acquisition of California's first-round pick which, based on the reverse order of standing, happened to be the first overall selection. To the Canadiens' delight, the 1971 junior crop featured two of the greatest players ever available in an NHL Amateur Draft. They had been engaged in dramatic battles for the junior scoring races and even faced off in the Memorial Cup. It was reported that in the Memorial Cup of 1971, "the personal confrontation between Quebec's great star Guy Lafleur and St. Catharines' scoring ace Marcel Dionne, both generally rated as the top two picks in the forthcoming NHL summer amateur draft, was the feature highlight of the series." Lafleur ended up leading his Quebec team to the championship title, defeating Dionne to begin the long-standing rivalry between the two talents.

Lafleur, dubbed "Mr. Everything," was drafted first overall by the Canadiens with Dionne going second to the Red Wings. A third French-Canadian, Jocelyn Guevremont, went third overall, marking the first time that three French-Canadian players went 1–2–3 to three different teams in an Amateur Draft. Vancouver picked up Guevremont as its first choice.

Lafleur went on to capture five Stanley Cup championships with the Canadiens and a collection of individual awards that includes the Art Ross Trophy (three times) as the scoring champion, back-to-back Hart Trophy MVP awards, a Conn Smythe as the best player in the postseason, and the Lester B. Pearson Award on three occasions. His career point total ranks among the best in NHL history as he collected 560 goals and 793 assists. Lafleur's number 10 is one of seven jerseys that currently hang from the rafters of the Molson Centre.

Although Dionne never won a Stanley Cup title or even made it to the finals, he did capture the Art Ross Trophy as top scorer, the Lady Byng Trophy as most gentlemanly player and two consecutive Lester B. Pearson Awards as Players' Association MVP. Dionne's career record of 731 goals and 1,040 assists smashed Lafleur's career point totals. To date, his 1,771 points trail only Wayne Gretzky and Gordie Howe in NHL history. Dionne's number 16 sweater has been retired by the Los Angeles Kings. Both Dionne (1992) and Lafleur (1988) are members of the Hockey Hall of Fame, making the 1971 draft the only one in which the first two picks have been enshrined in the Hall.

Another French-Canadian prospect from 1971 that made an incredible mark on the NHL was Rick Martin who was selected fifth overall by the Buffalo Sabres. It seemed that the Sabres had struck gold immediately, as their first pick in

their second season smashed their current star Gil bert Perreault's league record for rookie goals. Martin notched 44 goals in his first season and finished as the runner-up to Ken Dryden as the rookie of the year in 1972. Martin's career peaked once the Sabres placed him with Perreault and Rene Robert to form the talented French Connection. The trio's jerseys have all been honored by the club, including the retirement of Martin's number 7. During his 11-year career, he posted a 384 goals and 317 assists for 701 points in 685 games.

Montreal captured another superstar in the 1971 draft when it selected Larry Robinson 20th overall on a pick acquired from Los Angeles. Robinson, a 6'2", 190-pound defenseman, made an immediate impression in the NHL. He captured the Norris Trophy twice as the top blueliner (1977, 1980) and won the Conn Smythe as the playoff MVP in 1978.

He helped the Canadiens to six Cup championships, the last in 1986. In his 20 NHL seasons, Robinson collected 208 goals and 750 assists for 958 points in 1,384 games. Robinson was also inducted into the Hall of Fame in 1995.

Other future NHL award winners selected in the 1971 draft included Steve Vickers, selected 10th overall by the Rangers and winner of the Calder Trophy in 1973; Craig Ramsay, 19th overall and winner of the Frank J. Selke Trophy in 1985; and 22nd pick Rick Kehoe, who captured the Lady Byng in 1981.

1971

PICK	TEAM	NAME	DRAFTED FROM	NHL PLAYERS: POS NHL GOALTENDERS: POS	GP GP	G W	A GA	PTS SO	PIM AVG
FIRST ROUND									
1	MTL	Guy Lafleur	Quebec	RW	1126	560	793	1353	399
2	DET	Marcel Dionne	St. Catharines	C	1348	731	1040	1771	600
3	VAN	Jocelyn Guevremont	Montreal	D	571	84	223	307	319
4	ST.L.	Gene Carr	Flin Flon	C	465	79	136	215	365
5	BUF	Rick Martin	Montreal	LW	685	384	317	701	477
6	BOS	Ron Jones	Edmonton	D	54	1	4	5	31
7	MTL	Chuck Arnason	Flin Flon	RW	401	109	90	199	122
8	PHI	Larry Wright	Regina	C	106	4	8	12	19
9	PHI	Pierre Plante	Drummondville	RW	599	125	172	297	599
10	NYR	Steve Vickers	Toronto	LW	698	246	340	586	330
11	MTL	Murray Wilson	Ottawa	LW	386	94	95	189	162
12	CHI	Dan Spring	Edmonton	C					
13	NYR	Steve Durbano	Toronto	D	220	13	60	73	1127
14	BOS	Terry O'Reilly	Oshawa	RW	891	204	402	606	2095
SECOND ROUND									
15	CAL	Ken Baird	Flin Flon	D	10	0	2	2	15
16	DET	Henry Boucha	U.S. Nationals	C	247	53	49	102	157
17	VAN	Bobby Lalonde	Montreal	C	641	124	210	334	298
18	PIT	Brian McKenzie	St. Catharines	LW	6	1	1	2	4
19	BUF	Craig Ramsay	Peterborough	LW	1070	252	420	672	201
20	MTL	Larry Robinson	Kitchener	D	1384	208	750	958	793
21	MIN	Rod Norrish	Regina	LW	21	3	3	6	2
22	TOR	Rick Kehoe	Hamilton	RW	906	371	396	767	120
23	TOR	Dave Fortier	St. Catharines	D	205	8	21	29	335
24	MTL	Michel Deguise	Sorel	G					
25	MTL	Terry French	Ottawa	C					
26	CHI	Dave Kryskow	Edmonton	LW	231	33	56	89	174
27	NYR	Tom Williams	Hamilton	LW	397	115	138	253	73
28	BOS	Curt Ridley	Portage la Prairie Jr.	G	104	27	355	1	3.87
OTHER ROUNDS									
29	CAL	Rich LeDuc	Trois-Rivieres	C	130	28	38	66	69
30	DET	Ralph Hopiavuouri	Toronto	D					
31	MTL	Jim Cahoon	North Dakota	C					
32	PIT	Joe Noris	Toronto	C/D	55	2	5	7	22
33	BUF	Bill Hajt	Saskatoon	D	854	42	202	244	433
34	L.A.	Vic Venasky	U. of Denver	C	430	61	101	162	66
35	MIN	Ron Wilson	Flin Flon	D					
36	PHI	Glen Irwin	Estevan	D					
37	TOR	Gavin Kirk	Toronto	C					
38	ST.L.	John Garrett	Peterborough	G	207	68	837	1	4.27
39	VAN	Richard Lemieux	Montreal	C	274	39	82	121	132
40	CHI	Bob Peppler	St. Catharines	LW					
41	NYR	Terry West	London	C					
42	BOS	Dave Bonter	Estevan	C					
43	CAL	Hartland Monahan	Montreal	RW	334	61	80	141	163
44	DET	George Hulme	St. Catharines	G					
45	MTL	Ed Sidebottom	Estevan	D					

PICK	TEAM	NAME	DRAFTED FROM	NHL PLAYERS: POS NHL GOALTENDERS: POS	GP GP	G W	A GA	PTS SO	PIM AVG
46	PIT	Gerald Methe	Oshawa	D					
47	BUF	Bob Richer	Trois-Rivieres	C	3	0	0	0	0
48	L.A.	Neil Komadoski	Winnipeg	D	502	16	76	92	632
49	MIN	Mike Legge	Winnipeg	LW					
50	PHI	Ted Scharf	Kitchener	RW					
51	TOR	Rick Cunningham	Peterborough	D					
52	ST.L.	Derek Harker	Edmonton	D					
53	MTL	Greg Hubick	Minnesota-Duluth	D	77	6	9	15	10
54	CHI	Clyde Simon	St. Catharines	RW					
55	NYR	Jerry Butler	Hamilton	RW	641	99	120	219	515
56	BOS	Dave Hynes	Harvard	LW	22	4	0	4	2
57	CAL	Ray Belanger	Shawinigan	G					
58	DET	Earl Anderson	North Dakota	RW	109	19	19	38	22
59	VAN	Mike McNiven	Halifax Jr.	D					
60	PIT	Dave Murphy	North Dakota	G					
61	BUF	Steve Warr	Clarkson	D					
62	L.A.	Gary Crosby	Michigan Tech	C					
63	MIN	Brian McBratney	St. Catharines	D					
64	PHI	Don McCulloch	Niagara Falls	D					
65	TOR	Bob Sykes	Sudbury	LW	2	0	0	0	0
66	ST.L.	Wayne Gibbs	Calgary	D					
67	MTL	Mike Busniuk	U. of Denver	D	143	3	23	26	297
68	CHI	Dean Blais	U. of Minnesota	LW					
69	NYR	Fraser Robertson	Lethbridge	D					
70	BOS	Bert Scott	Edmonton	C					
71	CAL	Gerry Egers	Sudbury	D					
72	DET	Charlie Shaw	Toronto	D					
73	VAN	Tim Steeves	Prince Edward Islanders Jr.	D					
74	PIT	Ian Williams	U. of Notre Dame	RW					
75	BUF	Pierre Duguay	Quebec	C					
76	L.A.	Camille Lapierre	Montreal	C					
77	MIN	Al Globensky	Montreal	D					
78	PHI	Yvon Bilodeau	Estevan	D					
79	TOR	Mike Ruest	Cornwall	D					
80	ST.L.	Bernie Doan	Calgary	D					
81	MTL	Ross Butler	Winnipeg	LW					
82	CHI	Jim Johnston	Wisconsin	C					
83	NYR	Wayne Wood	Montreal	G					
84	BOS	Bob McMahon	St. Catharines	D					
85	CAL	Al Simmons	Winnipeg	D	11	0	1	1	21
86	DET	Jim Nahrgang	Michigan Tech	D	57	5	12	17	34
87	VAN	Bill Green	U. of Notre Dame	D					
88	PIT	Doug Elliott	Harvard	D					
89	L.A.	Peter Harasym	Clarkson	LW					
90	L.A.	Norm Dube	Sherbrooke	LW	57	8	10	18	54
91	MIN	Bruce Abbey	Peterborough	D					
92	PHI	Bob Gerrard	Regina	RW					
93	MTL	Dale Smedsmo	Bemidji State College	LW	4	0	0	0	0
94	ST.L.	Dave Smith	Regina	D					
95	MTL	Peter Sullivan	Oshawa	C	126	28	54	82	40
96	NYR	Douglas Keeler	Ottawa	C					
97	NYR	Jean Denis Royal	St-Jerome	D					
98	TOR	Steve Johnson	Verdun	D					
99	CAL	Angus Beck	Charlottetown Jr.	C					
100	DET	Bob Boyd	Michigan State	D					
101	VAN	Norm Cherry	Wisconsin	RW					
102	VAN	Bob Murphy	Cornwall	LW					
103	L.A.	Lorne Stamler	Michigan Tech	LW	116	14	11	25	16
104	CAL	Red Lyons	Halifax Jr.	LW					
105	MIN	Russ Frieson	Hamilton	C					
106	PHI	Jerome Mrazek	Minnesota-Duluth	G	1	0	1	0	10.00
107	TOR	Bob Burns	Cdn. Armed Forces	D					
108	ST.L.	Jim Collins	Flin Flon	LW					
109	NYR	Gene Sobchuk	Regina	LW/C	1	0	0	0	0
110	NYR	Jim Ivison	Brandon	D					
111	NYR	Andre Peloffy	Rosemount Jr. A	C	9	0	0	0	0
112	NYR	Elston Evoy	Sault Ste. Marie	C					
113	MIN	Mike Antonovich	Minnesota-Duluth	C	87	10	15	25	37
114	NYR	Gerald Lecompte	Sherbrooke	D					
115	NYR	Wayne Forsey	Swift Current	LW					
116	NYR	Bill Forrest	Hamilton	D					
117	MIN	Richard Coutu	Rosemount Jr. A	G					

1972

It was a record-setting year at the drafting tables in 1972 as the selection process became the longest since the inception of the Amateur Draft in 1963. After 3 hours and 52 minutes, 152 players were selected by the NHL teams, the most taken in one draft to that point.

The 1972–73 season featured the NHL's third round of expansion and two new clubs, the New York Islanders and Atlanta Flames, participated in the Amateur Draft. Once again, the first picks of the expansion clubs were to remain

with the team for at least three seasons. The Islanders were granted the first overall pick and made Billy Harris, the captain of the powerful Toronto Marlboros junior team, the club's first amateur selection. Harris went on to compile 558 points (231 goals, 327 assists) over a successful 12-year career.

Once again, the Montreal Canadiens controlled the 1972 NHL Amateur Draft, as they had acquired four first-round selections. The Canadiens obtained the first picks of Los Angeles, California and Minnesota, locking up the fourth, sixth, and eighth positions on top of their original 14th selection.

In order, Montreal g.m. Sam Pollock selected future Hall of Famer Steve Shutt of the Toronto Marlboros; Ottawa 67's goaltender Michel "Bunny" Larocque; Shutt's junior linemate Dave Gardner; and John Van Boxmeer of St. Catharines. At the conclusion of the draft, Pollock stated, "I was able to get every one of the four players I wanted with those four first-round picks." However, only Shutt developed into a star player. In his 13 seasons with the Canadiens, he accumulated a career record of 424 goals to rank among the NHL's all-time top scorers. Shutt was an integral piece in the Canadiens dynasty as he helped them to five Stanley Cup titles. Recognized as one of the most dangerous goal scorers of his era, Shutt spent his best years on a line with Guy Lafleur and Pete Mahovlich, scoring 60 goals in 1976–77. He was inducted into the Hall of Fame in 1993. Although, Larocque was a three-time recipient of the Vezina Trophy as a member of the league's best goaltending tandem, his career was shadowed by the remarkable performance of teammate Ken Dryden.

Following on their selection of Billy Smith, the Islanders drafted the first major building block towards their Stanley Cup dynasty when they selected Bob Nystrom 33rd overall in 1972. Nystrom, born in Sweden but raised in Kamloops, British Columbia, was left out of the prospect watch and was one of the most underrated players in the 1972 crop of graduating juniors. However, the Islanders recognized something other than talent when they scouted Nystrom. He stood out as one of the most dedicated and competitive players available, and displayed those qualities throughout his 14-year career, all of which was spent with the Islanders. "The most important things for a kid are pride in himself and desire," said Nystrom. "I was often told that I'd have a hard time making the pros, but if a guy wants to make the team badly enough, he will."

Although he only accumulated 513 points in 900 games, Nystrom was forever enshrined in the hearts of fans at the Nassau Coliseum in 1980 when he scored the game-winning goal in overtime of the sixth game of the finals to clinch the club's first Stanley Cup. Nystrom's number 24 jersey was retired by the Islanders on April 1, 1995.

The Flyers, selecting seventh in the order, drafted Bill Barber as their first choice in 1972. Immediately entering the NHL for the 1972–73 season, Barber was named as the runner-up behind Steve Vickers for the Calder Trophy as the league's top rookie after scoring 30 goals. As one of the most talented young players in the league, Barber received very little fanfare, prompting Flyers g.m. Keith Allen to comment: "What does he have to do to get recognized? He's got to be the most underrated player in hockey." Barber developed into one of the most effective special-team players in the NHL and helped the Flyers capture two consecutive Stanley Cup championships. With Bobby Clarke and Reg Leach the line set an NHL record on April

3, 1976 when they pushed their combined season totals to 141 goals. With 420 goals, Barber ranks as top goal scorer in Flyers history. His number 7 was retired by the club on October 11, 1990 just after his induction to the Hockey Hall of Fame.

Peter McNab, son of former NHLer Max McNab, was selected by the Sabres as the 85th pick in 1972. As a late draft choice, McNab emerged as the draft's biggest surprise success. Raised in San Diego, California, McNab played his youth hockey there. He played in the California Junior League before going to play collegiate hockey the University of Denver. After a top-scoring performance in the AHL with the Cincinnati Swords, McNab moved to the NHL where he compiled 363 goals and 813 points in 14 seasons to become (at the time) the top-scoring player ever to emerge from the U.S. collegiate ranks. At 6'4" and 210 pounds, he used his size to his advantage. "He's so big that guys realize it's kind of senseless trying to belt him," said coach Floyd Smith. "Besides, he's very nimble. Somebody makes a move to hit him with a check and he just steps around them and is on his way."

1972

PICK	TEAM	NAME	DRAFTED FROM	NHL PLAYERS: POS NHL GOALTENDERS: POS	GP GP	G W	A GA	PTS SO	PIM AVG
FIRST ROUND									
1	NYI	Bill Harris	Toronto	RW	897	231	327	558	394
2	ATL	Jacques Richard	Quebec	LW	556	160	187	347	307
3	VAN	Don Lever	Niagara Falls	LW	1020	313	367	680	593
4	MTL	Steve Shutt	Toronto	LW	930	424	393	817	410
5	BUF	Jim Schoenfeld	Niagara Falls	D	719	51	204	255	1132
6	MTL	Michel Larocque	Ottawa	G	312	160	978	17	3.33
7	PHI	Bill Barber	Kitchener	LW	903	420	463	883	623
8	MTL	Dave Gardner	Toronto	C	350	75	115	190	41
9	ST.L.	Wayne Merrick	Ottawa	C	774	191	265	456	303
10	NYR	Albert Blanchard	Kitchener	LW					
11	TOR	George Ferguson	Toronto	C	797	160	238	398	431
12	MIN	Jerry Byers	Kitchener	LW	43	3	4	7	15
13	CHI	Phil Russell	Edmonton	D	1016	99	325	424	2038
14	MTL	John Van Boxmeer	Guelph	D	588	84	274	358	465
15	NYR	Bob MacMillan	St. Catharines	RW	753	228	349	577	260
16	BOS	Mike Bloom	St. Catharines	LW	201	30	47	77	215
SECOND ROUND									
17	NYI	Lorne Henning	New Westminster	C	544	73	111	184	102
18	ATL	Dwight Bialowas	Regina	D	164	11	46	57	46
19	VAN	Bryan McSheffrey	Ottawa	RW	90	13	7	20	44
20	L.A.	Don Kozak	Edmonton	RW	437	96	86	182	480
21	NYR	Lawrence Sacharuk	Saskatoon	D	151	29	33	62	42
22	CAL	Tom Cassidy	Kitchener	C	26	3	4	7	15
23	PHI	Tom Bladon	Edmonton	D	610	73	197	270	392
24	PIT	Jack Lynch	Oshawa	D	382	24	106	130	336
25	BUF	Larry Carriere	Loyola College	D	367	16	74	90	462
26	DET	Pierre Guite	St. Catharines	LW					
27	TOR	Randy Osburn	London	LW	27	0	2	2	0
28	CAL	Stan Weir	Medicine Hat	C	642	139	207	346	183
29	CHI	Brian Ogilvie	Edmonton	C	90	15	21	36	29
30	PIT	Bernie Lukowich	New Westminster	RW	79	13	15	28	34
31	NYR	Rene Villemure	Shawinigan	LW					
32	BOS	Wayne Elder	London	D					
33	NYI	Bob Nystrom	Calgary	RW	900	235	278	513	1248
34	ATL	Jean Lemieux	Sherbrooke	D	204	23	63	86	39
35	VAN	Paul Raymer	Peterborough	LW					
36	L.A.	Dave Hutchison	London	D	584	19	97	116	1550
37	PHI	Jim McMasters	Calgary	D					
38	CAL	Paul Shakes	St. Catharines	D	21	0	4	4	12
39	PHI	Jimmy Watson	Calgary	D	613	38	148	186	492
40	PIT	Denis Herron	Trois-Rivieres	G	462	146	1579	10	3.70
41	ST.L.	Jean Hamel	Drummondville	D	699	26	95	121	766
42	DET	Bob Krieger	U. of Denver	C					
43	TOR	Denis Deslauriers	Shawinigan	D					
44	MIN	Terry Ryan	Hamilton	C					
45	CHI	Mike Veisor	Peterborough	G	139	41	532	5	4.09
46	MTL	Ed Gilbert	Hamilton	C	166	21	31	52	22
47	NYR	Gerry Teeple	Cornwall	C					
48	BOS	Michel Boudreau	Laval	C					
49	NYI	Ron Smith	Cornwall	D	11	1	1	2	14
50	ATL	Don Martineau	New Westminster	RW	90	6	10	16	63
51	VAN	Ron Homenuke	Calgary	RW	1	0	0	0	0
52	L.A.	John Dobie	Regina	D					
53	BUF	Richard Campeau	Sorel	D					
54	CAL	Claude St. Sauveur	Sherbrooke	C	79	24	24	48	23

1972 *continued*

PICK	TEAM	NAME	DRAFTED FROM	NHL PLAYERS: POS / NHL GOALTENDERS: POS	GP	G / W	A / GA	PTS / SO	PIM / AVG
55	PHI	Al MacAdam	University of PEI	RW	864	240	351	591	509
56	PIT	Ron Lalonde	Peterborough	C	397	45	78	123	106
57	ST.L.	Murray Myers	Saskatoon	D					
58	DET	Danny Gruen	Thunder Bay Jr. A	LW	49	9	13	22	19
59	TOR	Brian Bowles	Cornwall	D					
60	MIN	Tom Thomson	Toronto	D					
61	CHI	Tom Peluso	U. of Denver	LW					
62	MTL	Dave Ellenbass	Cornell	G					
63	NYR	Doug Horbul	Calgary	LW	4	1	0	1	2
64	BOS	Les Jackson	New Westminster	LW					
65	NYI	Richard Grenier	Verdun	C	10	1	1	2	2
66	MTL	Bill Nyrop	U. of Notre Dame	D	207	12	51	63	101
67	VAN	Larry Bolonchuk	Winnipeg	D	74	3	9	12	97
68	L.A.	Bernie Germaine	Regina	G	1	0	0	0	
69	BUF	Gilles Gratton	Oshawa	G	47	13	154	0	4.02
70	CAL	Tim Jacobs	St. Catharines	G	46	0	10	10	35
71	PHI	Daryl Fedorak	Victoria	G	2	0	0	0	
72	PIT	Brian Walker	Calgary	C					
73	ST.L.	Dave Johnson	Cornwall	LW					
74	DET	Dennis Johnson	North Dakota	LW					
75	TOR	Michel Plante	Drummondville	LW					
76	MIN	Chris Ahrens	Kitchener	D	52	0	3	3	84
77	CHI	Rejean Giroux	Quebec	RW					
78	ATL	Jean-Paul Martin	Shawinigan	C					
79	NYR	Martin Gateman	Hamilton	D					
80	BOS	Brian Coates	Brandon	LW					
81	NYI	Derek Black	Calgary	LW					
82	ATL	Frank Blum	Sarnia Jr. B	G					
83	VAN	Dave McLelland	Brandon	G	2	1	10	0	5.00
84	L.A.	Mike Usitalo	Michigan Tech	LW					
85	BUF	Peter McNab	U. of Denver	C	954	363	450	813	179
86	CAL	Jacques Lefebvre	Shawinigan	G					
87	PHI	Dave Hastings	Charlottetown Jr.	G					
88	PIT	Jeff Ablett	Medicine Hat	LW					
89	ST.L.	Tom Simpson	Oshawa	RW					
90	DET	Bill Miller	Medicine Hat	D					
91	TOR	Dave Shardlow	Flin Flon	LW					
92	MIN	Steve West	Oshawa	C					
93	CHI	Rob Palmer	U. of Denver	C	16	0	3	3	2
94	MTL	D'Arcy Ryan	Yale	LW					
95	NYR	Ken Ireland	New Westminster	C					
96	BOS	Peter Gaw	Ottawa	RW					
97	NYI	Richard Brodeur	Cornwall	G	385	131	1410	6	3.85
98	ATL	Scott Smith	Regina	LW					
99	VAN	Dan Gloor	Peterborough	C	2	0	0	0	0
100	L.A.	Glen Toner	Regina	LW					
101	NYI	Don McLaughlin	Brandon	LW					
102	CAL	Mike Amodeo	Oshawa	D	19	0	0	0	2
103	PHI	Serge Beaudoin	Trois-Rivieres	D	3	0	0	0	0
104	PIT	D'Arcy Keating	U. of Notre Dame	RW					
105	ST.L.	Brian Coughlin	Verdun	D					
106	DET	Glenn Seperich	Kitchener	G					
107	TOR	Monte Miron	Clarkson	D					
108	MIN	Chris Meloff	Kitchener	D					
109	CHI	Terry Smith	Edmonton	C					
110	MTL	Yves Archambault	Sorel	G					
111	NYR	Jeff Hunt	Winnipeg	LW					
112	BOS	Gordie Clark	New Hampshire	RW	8	0	1	1	0
113	NYI	Derek Kuntz	Medicine Hat	LW					
114	ATL	Dave Murphy	Hamilton	C					
115	VAN	Dennis McCord	London	D	3	0	0	0	6
116	MIN	Scott MacPhail	Montreal	RW					
117	NYI	Rene Lavasseur	Shawinigan	D					
118	CAL	Brent Meeke	Niagara Falls	D	75	9	22	31	8
119	PHI	Pat Russell	Vancouver	RW					
120	PIT	Yves Bergeron	Shawinigan	RW	3	0	0	0	0
121	ST.L.	Gary Winchester	Wisconsin	C					
122	DET	Mike Ford	Brandon	D					
123	TOR	Peter Williams	University of PEI	D					
124	MIN	Bob Lundeen	Wisconsin	D					
125	CHI	Billy Reay, Jr.	Wisconsin	RW					
126	MTL	Graham Parsons	Red Deer Jr. A	G					
127	NYR	Yvon Blais	Cornwall	LW					
128	BOS	Roy Carmichael	New Westminster	D					
129	NYI	Yvan Rolando	Drummondville	RW					
130	ATL	Pierre Roy	Quebec	D					
131	VAN	Steve Stone	Niagara Falls	RW	2	0	0	0	0
132	ATL	Jean Lamarre	Quebec	RW					
133	NYI	Bill Ennos	Vancouver	RW					
134	CAL	Denis Meloche	Drummondville	C					
135	PHI	Ray Boutin	Sorel	G					
136	PIT	Jay Babcock	London	D					
137	NYR	Pierre Archambault	St-Jerome	D					
138	DET	George Kuzmicz	Cornell	D					
139	TOR	Pat Boutette	Minnesota-Duluth	C/RW	756	171	282	453	1354
140	MIN	Glen Mikkelson	Brandon	RW					
141	CHI	Gary Donaldson	Victoria	RW	1	0	0	0	0
142	MTL	Edward Bumbacco	U. of Notre Dame	LW					
143	TOR	Gary Schofield	Clarkson	D					
144	NYI	Garry Howatt	Flin Flon	LW	720	112	156	268	1836
145	MIN	Steve Lyon	Peterborough	D	3	0	0	0	2
146	NYI	Rene Lambert	St-Jerome	RW					
147	MIN	Juri Kudrosov	Kitchener	C					
148	MIN	Marcel Comeau	Edmonton	C					
149	PIT	Don Atchison	Saskatoon	G					
150	DET	Dave Arundel	Wisconsin	D					
151	MTL	Fred Riggall	Dartmouth	RW					
152	MTL	Ron Leblanc	U. of Moncton	RW					

1973

The 1973 NHL Amateur Draft was hailed as one of the deepest since its inception and featured a star-studded first round. The Islanders once again had the first overall selection, which they used to secure junior defenseman Denis Potvin. Potvin had been touted as the sure first pick after he broke many of Bobby Orr's junior scoring records. As a blueliner with an obvious abundance of offensive talent, Potvin's greatest asset was his ability to excel at the physical aspects of the game. "Denis will put the hitting back in defense," commented Potvin's junior coach Leo Boivin. "There's very little hitting today and what there is doesn't amount to much. But this kid loves to hit. I've never seen anybody, I say anybody, lay them out like Denis does. And they're all good, clean checks. He can score, set up plays and his passes seldom miss. Oh, they'll try and rough him up when he hits the pros but they'll have a time of it. He's still growing."

At 6'0" and 205 pounds, Potvin entered the NHL and emerged as the Islanders' leading scorer with 17 goals and 54 points, setting new league records for goals and points for rookie defensemen.

Potvin owned the voting as the rookie of the year and became the first NHL award winner for the Islanders with the Calder Trophy in 1973. It marked the first time that the top two players selected in the previous year's Amateur Draft finished one-two in Calder voting. Second draft selection Tom Lysiak of the Atlanta Flames was runner-up. Prior to the draft, the Islanders signed Potvin's older brother Jean. It was rumored that the move was to ensure that Denis would sign with the Islanders during a time of fierce competition for players between the NHL and the WHA.

Potvin became the cornerstone of the Islanders' dynasty as their captain and one of the most prominent players of all time. He is a three-time Norris Trophy winner as the NHL's best defenseman (1976, 1978 and 1979) and was the runner-up for the Hart Trophy as the league MVP behind Bobby Clarke in 1976. Potvin became the first Islander to have his jersey retired and was inducted into the Hall of Fame in 1991.

The St. Louis Blues made history as they drafted goaltender John Davidson as the fifth selection in 1973, marking the earliest that a goaltender would be drafted. (Although Michel Plasse was selected first in the 1968 draft, he qualified under the cultural option of the Montreal Canadiens). Davidson was highly touted and had been compared to the size and style of goaltending great Ken Dryden. He spent two seasons with the Blues, putting up impressive numbers in his freshman year with a 3.03 goals-against average. In his third year he was traded to the New York Rangers. "We thought highly of Davidson when he was a junior and we believe he's a tremendous goalie," said Rangers g.m. Emile Francis. "We didn't have a young goalie on our team until Davidson came along. We think

he'll help quite a bit." Davidson spent 10 seasons in the NHL and helped the Rangers reach the Stanley Cup finals in 1979 before retiring to enter broadcasting.

Lanny McDonald was a star junior sniper selected fourth overall by the Maple Leafs in 1973. After weak performances in his first two seasons in the NHL, it was thought that McDonald was a poor first-round selection. Once he was paired with Leaf star Darryl Sittler, he went on to record outstanding numbers with the club. "What Lanny needed was time. It's tough to break into this league from junior, especially under his circumstances," said Toronto coach Red Kelly about the highly-touted winger.

McDonald ended his career with the Calgary Flames, spending four seasons as the team's captain. He led the Flames to a Stanley Cup championship in 1989. McDonald captured the Masterton Trophy for his perseverance and dedication to hockey and became the first recipient of the King Clancy Trophy for leadership and community work. His 500 goals rank him among the highest goal scorers in NHL history and his 506 assists gave him 1,006 career points. McDonald's number 9 remains the only jersey retired by the Flames.

"What has happened to me in hockey over the past 16 years really is a dream come true," said McDonald. "Seeing my number raised to the rafters of the Saddledome will be another great moment, something I will never forget." In 1990, Lanny was inducted into the Hockey Hall of Fame.

The surprise pick of the 1973 Amateur Draft was forward Bob Gainey, taken eighth overall by the Montreal Canadiens. Finishing 67th in the junior scoring race, it was assumed that Gainey would be selected later in the draft, but he illustrated his strongest asset as a reliable defensive forward and immediately joined Montreal's strong lineup. Gainey captured the Frank J. Selke Trophy four consecutive years and is considered to be one of the best two-way players to grace the NHL. "He has given the checking role respectability," said NHL coach Roger Neilson, Gainey's junior coach. "You think of him among the five or six most valuable players in the league." In 1979, Gainey was awarded the Conn Smythe Trophy as the playoff MVP when Montreal capped its fourth year as Cup champions. As captain, he led the Canadiens back to to the Stanley Cup in 1986. Gainey's selection and subsequent career demonstrated the skill of the Canadiens' scouting department, as he was inducted into the Hall of Fame in 1990 along with Lanny McDonald. The 1973 draft marked the last time that the Canadiens drafted a future Hall of Famer in the first round of the Amateur Draft. Gainey is currently the general manager of the Dallas Stars.

The third pick (48th overall) by the St. Louis Blues in 1973 was Bob Gassoff, who was killed in a motorcycle accident during the summer of 1977. After his death, *The Hockey News* reported: "With the death of Bob Gassoff the National Hockey League has lost one of its most aggressive and colorful performers." The Blues have honored Gassoff by retiring his number 3 to the rafters of the Kiel Center.

1973

PICK	TEAM	NAME	DRAFTED FROM	NHL PLAYERS: POS / NHL GOALTENDERS: POS	GP / GP	G / W	A / GA	PTS / SO	PIM / AVG
FIRST ROUND									
1	NYI	Denis Potvin	Ottawa	D	1060	310	742	1052	1354
2	ATL	Tom Lysiak	Medicine Hat	C	919	292	551	843	567
3	VAN	Dennis Ververgaert	London	RW	583	176	216	392	247
4	TOR	Lanny McDonald	Medicine Hat	RW	1111	500	506	1006	899
5	ST.L.	John Davidson	Calgary	G	301	123	1004	7	3.52
6	BOS	Andre Savard	Quebec	C	790	211	271	482	411
7	PIT	Blaine Stoughton	Flin Flon	RW	526	258	191	449	204
8	MTL	Bob Gainey	Peterborough	LW	1160	239	262	501	585
9	VAN	Bob Dailey	Toronto	D	561	94	231	325	814
10	TOR	Bob Neely	Peterborough	LW	283	39	59	98	266
11	DET	Terry Richardson	New Westminster	G	20	3	85	0	5.63
12	BUF	Morris Titanic	Sudbury	LW	19	0	0	0	
13	CHI	Darcy Rota	Edmonton	LW	794	256	239	495	973
14	NYR	Rick Middleton	Oshawa	RW	1005	448	540	988	157
15	TOR	Ian Turnbull	Ottawa	D	628	123	317	440	736
16	ATL	Vic Mercredi	New Westminster	C	2	0	0	0	0
SECOND ROUND									
17	MTL	Glenn Goldup	Toronto	RW	291	52	67	119	303
18	MIN	Blake Dunlop	Ottawa	C	550	130	274	404	172
19	VAN	Paulin Bordeleau	Toronto	RW	183	33	56	89	47
20	PHI	Larry Goodenough	London	D	242	22	77	99	179
21	ATL	Eric Vail	Sudbury	LW	591	216	260	476	281
22	MTL	Peter Marrin	Toronto	C					
23	PIT	Wayne Bianchin	Flin Flon	LW	276	68	41	109	137
24	ST.L.	George Pesut	Saskatoon	D	92	3	22	25	130
25	MIN	John Rogers	Edmonton	RW	14	2	4	6	0
26	PHI	Brent Leavins	Swift Current	LW					
27	PIT	Colin Campbell	Peterborough	D	636	25	103	128	1292
28	BUF	Jean Landry	Quebec	D					
29	CHI	Reg Thomas	London	LW	39	9	7	16	6
30	NYR	Pat Hickey	Hamilton	LW	646	192	212	404	351
31	BOS	Jimmy Jones	Peterborough	RW	148	13	18	31	68
32	MTL	Ron Andruff	Flin Flon	C	153	19	36	55	54
OTHER ROUNDS									
33	NYI	Dave Lewis	Saskatoon	D	1008	36	187	223	953
34	CAL	Jeff Jacques	St. Catharines	RW					
35	VAN	Paul Sheard	Ottawa	RW					
36	BOS	Doug Gibson	Peterborough	C	63	9	19	28	0
37	MTL	Ed Humphreys	Saskatoon	G					
38	L.A.	Russ Walker	Saskatoon	RW	17	1	0	1	41
39	DET	Nelson Pyatt	Oshawa	C	296	71	63	134	69
40	PHI	Robert Stumpf	New Westminster	RW/D	10	1	1	2	20
41	MIN	Rick Chinnick	Peterborough	RW	4	0	2	2	0
42	PHI	Mike Clarke	Calgary	C					
43	DET	Robbie Neale	Brandon	LW					
44	BUF	Andre Deschamps	Quebec	LW					
45	CHI	Randy Holt	Sudbury	D	395	4	37	41	1438
46	NYR	John Campbell	Sault Ste. Marie	C					
47	BOS	Al Sims	Cornwall	D	475	49	116	165	286
48	ST.L.	Bob Gassoff	Medicine Hat	D	245	11	47	58	866
49	NYI	Andre St. Laurent	Montreal	C	644	129	187	316	749
50	CAL	Ron Serafini	St. Catharines	D	2	0	0	0	2
51	VAN	Keith Mackie	Edmonton	D					
52	TOR	Francois Rochon	Sherbrooke	LW					
53	ATL	Dean Talafous	Wisconsin	RW	497	104	154	258	163
54	L.A.	Jim McCrimmon	Medicine Hat	D	2	0	0	0	0
55	PIT	Dennis Owchar	Toronto	D	288	30	85	115	200
56	MTL	Al Hangelben	North Dakota	D	185	21	48	69	396
57	MIN	Tom Colley	Sudbury	C	1	0	0	0	2
58	PHI	Dale Cook	Victoria	LW					
59	DET	Mike Korney	Winnipeg	RW	77	9	10	19	59
60	BUF	Yvon Dupuis	Quebec	RW					
61	CHI	Dave Elliott	Winnipeg	LW					
62	NYR	Brian Molvik	Calgary	D					
63	BOS	Steve Langdon	London	LW	7	0	1	1	2
64	MTL	Richard Latulippe	Quebec	C					
65	NYI	Ron Kennedy	New Westminster	RW					
66	CAL	Jim Moxey	Hamilton	RW	127	22	27	49	59
67	VAN	Paul O'Neil	Boston U.	C/RW	6	0	0	0	0
68	TOR	Gord Titcomb	St. Catharines	LW					
69	ATL	John Flesch	Lake Superior State	LW	124	18	23	41	117
70	L.A.	Dennis Abgrall	Saskatoon	RW	13	0	2	2	4
71	PIT	Guido Tenesi	Oshawa	D					
72	ST.L.	Bill Laing	Saskatoon	LW					
73	MIN	Lowell Ostlund	Saskatoon	D					
74	PHI	Michel Latreille	Montreal	D					
75	DET	Blair Stewart	Winnipeg	C	229	34	44	78	326
76	BUF	Bob Smulders	Peterborough	RW					
77	CHI	Dan Hinton	Sault Ste. Marie	LW	14	0	0	0	16
78	NYR	Pierre Laganiere	Sherbrooke	RW					
79	BOS	Peter Crosbie	London	G					
80	MTL	Gerry Gibbons	St. Mary's U.	D					
81	NYI	Keith Smith	Brown	LW					
82	CAL	William Trognitz	Thunder Bay Jr. A	LW					
83	VAN	Jim Cowell	Ottawa	C					
84	TOR	Doug Marit	Regina	D					
85	ATL	Ken Houston	Chatham Jr. B	RW	570	161	167	328	624
86	L.A.	Blair MacDonald	Cornwall	RW	219	91	100	191	65
87	PIT	Don Seiling	Oshawa	LW					
88	ST.L.	Randy Smith	Edmonton	C	3	0	0	0	0
89	MIN	David Lee	Ottawa	LW					
90	PHI	Doug Ferguson	Hamilton	D					
91	DET	Glenn Cickello	Hamilton	D					
92	BUF	Neil Korzack	Peterborough	LW					

1973 *continued*

PICK	TEAM	NAME	DRAFTED FROM	NHL PLAYERS: POS / NHL GOALTENDERS: POS	GP	G / W	A / GA	PTS / SO	PIM / AVG
93	CHI	Gary Doerksen	Winnipeg	C					
94	NYR	Dwayne Pentland	Brandon	D					
95	BOS	J-P Bourgouyne	Shawinigan	D					
96	MTL	Dennis Patry	Drummondville	RW					
97	NYI	Don Cutts	RPI	G	6	1	16	0	3.57
98	CAL	Paul Tantardini	Downsview Jr.	LW					
99	VAN	Clay Hebenton	Portland	G					
100	TOR	Dan Follett	Downsview Jr.	G					
101	ATL	Tom Machowski	Wisconsin	D					
102	L.A.	Roly Kimble	Hamilton	G					
103	PIT	Terry Ewasiuk	Victoria	LW					
104	ST.L.	John Wensink	Cornwall	LW	403	70	68	138	840
105	MIN	Lou Nistico	London	C	3	0	0	0	0
106	PHI	Tom Young	Sudbury	D					
107	DET	Brian Middleton	U. of Alberta	D					
108	BUF	Bob Young	U. of Denver	D					
109	CHI	Wayne Dye	New Westminster	LW					
110	NYI	Dennis Andersen	New Westminster	D					
111	BOS	Walter Johnson	Oshawa	RW					
112	MTL	Michel Belisle	Montreal	C					
113	NYI	Mike Kennedy	Kitchener	RW					
114	CAL	Bruce Greig	Vancouver	LW	9	0	1	1	46
115	VAN	John Senkpiel	Vancouver	LW					
116	TOR	Les Burgess	Kitchener	LW					
117	ATL	Bob Law	North Dakota	RW					
118	DET	Dennis Polonich	Flin Flon	C/RW	390	59	82	141	1242
119	PIT	Fred Comrie	Edmonton	C					
120	ST.L.	John Tetreault	Drummondville	LW					
121	MIN	George Beveridge	Kitchener	D					
122	PHI	Norm Barnes	Michigan State	D	156	6	38	44	178
123	DET	George Lyle	Michigan Tech	LW	99	24	38	62	51
124	BUF	Tim O'Connell	Vermont	RW					
125	CHI	Jim Koleff	Hamilton	C					
126	NYI	Denis Desgagnes	Sorel	C					
127	BOS	Virgil Gates	Swift Current	D					
128	MTL	Mario Desjardins	Sherbrooke	LW					
129	NYI	Bob Lorimer	Michigan Tech	D	529	22	90	112	431
130	CAL	Larry Patey	Braintree H.S.	C	717	153	163	316	631
131	VAN	Peter Folco	Quebec	D	2	0	0	0	0
132	TOR	Dave Pay	Wisconsin	LW					
133	ATL	Bob Bilodeau	New Westminster	D					
134	PIT	Gord Lane	New Westminster	D	539	19	94	113	1228
135	DET	Dennis O'Brien	Laurentian	D					
136	MIN	Jim Johnston	Peterborough	C					
137	PHI	Dan O'Donohue	Sault Ste. Marie	D					
138	DET	Tom Newman	Kitchener	D					
139	DET	Ray Bibeau	Montreal	D					
140	CHI	Jack Johnson	Wisconsin	LW					
141	CHI	Steve Alley	Wisconsin	LW	15	3	3	6	11
142	BOS	Jim Pettie	St. Catharines	G	21	9	71	1	3.68
143	MTL	Bob Wright	Pembroke Jr. A						
144	TOR	Lee Palmer	Clarkson	D					
145	CAL	Doug Mahood	Sault Ste. Marie	RW					
146	VAN	Terry McDougall	Swift Current	C					
147	TOR	Bob Peace	Cornell	F					
148	ATL	Glen Surbey	Loyola College	D					
149	ATL	Guy Ross	Sherbrooke	D					
150	PIT	Randy Aimoe	Medicine Hat	D					
151	DET	Kevin Neville	Toronto	G					
152	MIN	Sam Clegg	Medicine Hat	G					
153	PHI	Brian Dick	Winnipeg	RW					
154	DET	Ken Gibb	North Dakota	D					
155	DET	Mitch Brandt	U. of Denver						
156	CHI	Rick Clubbe	North Dakota	RW					
157	BOS	Yvan Bouillon	Cornwall	C					
158	MTL	Alain Labrecque	Trois-Rivieres	C					
159	TOR	Norm McLeod	Ottawa M&W Rangers	LW					
160	CAL	Angelo Moretto	Michigan	C	5	1	2	3	2
161	MIN	Russ Wiechnik	Calgary	C					
162	ATL	Greg Fox	Michigan	D	494	14	92	106	637
163	MIN	Max Hansen	Sudbury	LW					
164	PIT	Don McLeod	Saskatoon	G	18	3	74	0	5.05
165	CHI	Gene Strate	Edmonton	D					
166	MTL	Gord Halliday	U. of Pennsylvania						
167	MTL	Cap Raeder	New Hampshire	G					
168	MTL	Louis Chiasson	Trois-Rivieres	C					

1974

With the rival World Hockey Association signing underage talent before these players were eligible for the NHL draft, the 1974 Amateur Draft featured the re-emergence of the age-of-eligibility issue. It was agreed that teams could select one 18-year-old prospect in the Amateur Draft, with the underage selection limited to the first two rounds. In addition, the NHL decided it would be in its best interest to conduct the draft in secrecy via conference call from the NHL headquarters in Montreal in order to restrict the WHA from immediately bartering with players before the NHL clubs could make any contract offers.

Two new expansion clubs, Washington and Kansas City, were granted the first two picks respectively. The Capitals selected defenseman Greg Joly. Capitals g.m. Milt Schmidt said, "His clutch play in pressure games convinced our scouts and me that he is the kind of player we want. He seemed to play his best hockey in the playoffs and the Memorial Cup. He is the kind of rushing defenseman everybody has been looking for since Bobby Orr started having such success with Boston." Joly spent only two years with the Capitals before being traded to Detroit. After sustaining a major wrist injury, Joly's career eventually came to an end after nine years in the NHL. Despite being touted as a Bobby Orr-style offensive blueliner, he only compiled a career record of 21 goals and 76 assists for 97 points in 365 games. The Scouts used the second pick to take Wilf Paiement. He went on to become one of the NHL's most traveled veterans, playing for seven teams in his 14-year career. Paiement posted 356 goals and 458 assists for 814 points before retiring in 1987–88.

The Islanders once again came out of the Amateur Draft with the talent necessary for them to further construct their dynasty. Drafting 6'3", 215-pound winger Clark Gillies, the Islanders had acquired one of the most gifted physical forces ever available in the draft. The Islanders director of player personnel Earl Ingarfield commented on his attraction to Gillies' junior performance: "What impressed me most about Clark was how well he skates and handles the puck for such a big man. I also remember the way he fought that first season and earned the respect of every player in the league."

In 14 years, Gillies compiled 319 goals and 378 assists as well as 1,023 penalty minutes. He was a primary figure in the Islanders' four-year hold on the Stanley Cup. On December 7, 1996 he became the fourth Islander to have his jersey retired.

While Gillies became a key team leader, the best choice by the Islanders in 1974 was the selection of Bryan Trottier 22nd overall. An underrated junior talent, Trottier entered the NHL without much publicity or expectation in 1975–76 and went on to set rookie records for assists (63) and points (95) and finished among the top 12 scorers in the league. He was awarded the Calder Trophy as the rookie of the year, becoming the second Islander to do so. Trottier became an instant star as he stabilized the Islanders' weak offensive corps. "It's his poise that really stands out," said teammate Billy Harris. "He's always calm, regardless of the situation. And he's got tremendous hockey sense. He is, if there's such a thing, a natural-born center." Trottier became known as one of the most dominating centers in the NHL. He was a superb face-off man and was also recognized as perhaps the best all-around talent in the league.

Trottier went on to collect an NHL scoring championship and the Hart Trophy in 1978–79, the Conn Smythe Trophy in 1980 and the King Clancy Award in 1989. On February 13, 1990 Trottier became only the 15th player in the history of the NHL to record 500 goals. He retired with 524 goals and 901 assists for 1,425 points and was inducted into the Hockey Hall of Fame in 1997.

Three other promising talents emerged from the draft's lower selections in 1974 as Guy Chouinard, selected 28th,

Danny Gare, 29th overall and Charlie Simmer, taken 39th, all became top NHL talents. Gare had 354 goals in his career, while Simmer scored 342 times and the two tied for the league lead with 56 goals in 1979–80. Simmer is best known as the left winger with Marcel Dionne and Dave Taylor on the Los Angeles Kings' Triple Crown line. The often-injured sniper also won the Masterton Trophy in 1986. Chouinard went on to record 575 points (205 goals, 370 assists) in 578 games during his 10-year career. His son Eric was chosen by the Montreal Canadiens in the first round of the 1998 Entry Draft.

The emphasis of the physical aspect of the game was evident in the 1974 draft with the first-round selection of Clark Gillies and the second-round selection of Dave "Tiger" Williams (31st overall). Williams played a boisterous physical game, and would be a frequent visitor to NHL penalty boxes, racking up 3,966 penalty minutes in 712 games. This total remains the all-time league record.

The influence of the WHA was felt in 1974 when talented underage defenseman Mark Howe, son of Gordie Howe, signed with the Houston Aeros of the WHA despite being drafted 25th overall by the Boston Bruins. The loss of Howe is a prime example of the conflict between the two major pro leagues in their race to acquire amateur talent.

The 1974 Amateur Draft also demonstrated the NHL's changing international flavor. Although they had been participating in the league for quite sometime, the selection of Europeans was still uncommon. Six Europeans were drafted, but the surprise came when an Asian player was chosen. The Buffalo Sabres drafted Taro Tsujimoto, a native of Japan, as the 183rd player selected. A member of the Tokyo Katanas in the Japanese system, Tsujimoto became the first Asian-born player taken in the NHL Amateur Draft. He never appeared in an NHL game.

1974

PICK	TEAM	NAME	DRAFTED FROM	NHL PLAYERS: POS / NHL GOALTENDERS: POS	GP / GP	G / W	A / GA	PTS / SO	PIM / AVG
FIRST ROUND									
1	WSH	Greg Joly	Regina	D	365	21	76	97	250
2	K.C.	Wilf Paiement	St. Catharines	RW	946	356	458	814	1757
3	CAL	Rick Hampton	St. Catharines	LW/D	337	59	113	172	147
4	NYI	Clark Gillies	Regina	LW	958	319	378	697	1023
5	MTL	Cam Connor	Flin Flon	RW	89	9	22	31	256
6	MIN	Doug Hicks	Flin Flon	D	561	37	131	168	442
7	MTL	Doug Risebrough	Kitchener	C	740	185	286	471	1542
8	PIT	Pierre Larouche	Sorel	C	812	395	427	822	237
9	DET	Bill Lochead	Oshawa	LW	330	69	62	131	180
10	MTL	Rick Chartraw	Kitchener	D/RW	420	28	64	92	399
11	BUF	Lee Fogolin	Oshawa	D	924	44	195	239	1318
12	MTL	Mario Tremblay	Montreal	RW	852	258	326	584	1043
13	TOR	Jack Valiquette	Sault Ste. Marie	C	350	84	134	218	79
14	NYR	Dave Maloney	Kitchener	D	657	71	246	317	1154
15	MTL	Gordon McTavish	Sudbury	C	11	1	3	4	2
16	CHI	Grant Mulvey	Calgary	RW	586	149	135	284	816
17	CAL	Ron Chipperfield	Brandon	C	83	22	24	46	34
18	BOS	Don Larway	Swift Current	RW					
SECOND ROUND									
19	WSH	Mike Marson	Sudbury	LW	196	24	24	48	233
20	K.C.	Glen Burdon	Regina	C	11	0	2	2	0
21	CAL	Bruce Affleck	U. of Denver	D	280	14	66	80	86
22	NYI	Bryan Trottier	Swift Current	C	1279	524	901	1425	912
23	VAN	Ron Sedlbauer	Kitchener	LW	430	143	86	229	210
24	MIN	Richard Nantais	Quebec	LW	63	5	4	9	79
25	BOS	Mark Howe	Toronto	D	929	197	545	742	455
26	ST.L.	Bob Hess	New Westminster	D	329	27	95	122	178
27	PIT	Jacques Cossette	Sorel	RW	64	8	6	14	29
28	ATL	Guy Chouinard	Quebec	C	578	205	370	575	120
29	BUF	Danny Gare	Calgary	RW	827	354	331	685	1285
30	MTL	Gary MacGregor	Cornwall	C					
31	TOR	Dave Williams	Swift Current	LW	962	241	272	513	3966
32	NYR	Ron Greschner	New Westminster	D	982	179	431	610	1226
33	MTL	Gilles Lupien	Montreal	D	226	5	25	30	416
34	CHI	Alain Daigle	Trois-Rivieres	RW	389	56	50	106	122
35	PHI	Don McLean	Sudbury	D	9	0	0	0	6
36	BOS	Peter Sturgeon	Kitchener	LW	6	0	1	1	2

PICK	TEAM	NAME	DRAFTED FROM	NHL PLAYERS: POS / NHL GOALTENDERS: POS	GP / GP	G / W	A / GA	PTS / SO	PIM / AVG
OTHER ROUNDS									
37	WSH	John Paddock	Brandon	RW	87	8	14	22	86
38	K.C.	Bob Bourne	Saskatoon	C	964	258	324	582	605
39	CAL	Charlie Simmer	Sault Ste. Marie	LW	712	342	369	711	544
40	NYI	Brad Anderson	Victoria	C					
41	VAN	John Hughes	Toronto	D	70	2	14	16	211
42	MIN	Pete LoPresti	U. of Denver	G	175	43	668	5	4.07
43	ST.L.	Gordon Buynak	Kingston	D	4	0	0	0	2
44	DET	Dan Mandryk	Calgary	C					
45	DET	Bill Evo	Peterborough	RW					
46	ATL	Dick Spannbauer	Minnesota-Duluth	D					
47	BUF	Michel Deziel	Sorel	LW					
48	L.A.	Gary Sargent	Fargo-Moorhead	D	402	61	161	222	273
49	TOR	Per A. Alexandersson	Leksand, SWE	C					
50	NYR	Jerry Holland	Calgary	LW	37	8	4	12	6
51	MTL	Marty Howe	Toronto	D	197	2	29	31	99
52	CHI	Bob Murray	Cornwall	D	1008	132	382	514	873
53	PHI	Bob Sirois	Montreal	RW	286	92	120	212	42
54	BOS	Tom Edur	Toronto	D	158	17	70	87	67
55	WSH	Paul Nicholson	London	LW	62	4	8	12	18
56	K.C.	Roger Lemelin	London	D	36	1	2	3	27
57	CAL	Tom Price	Ottawa	D	29	0	2	2	12
58	ATL	Pat Ribble	Oshawa	D	349	19	60	79	365
59	VAN	Harold Snepsts	Edmonton	D	1033	38	195	233	2009
60	MIN	Kim MacDougall	Regina	D	1	0	0	0	0
61	MTL	Barry Legge	Winnipeg	D	107	1	11	12	144
62	PIT	Mario Faubert	St. Louis U.	D	231	21	90	111	292
63	DET	Michel Bergeron	Sorel	RW	229	80	58	138	165
64	ATL	Cam Botting	Niagara Falls	RW	2	0	1	1	0
65	BUF	Paul McIntosh	Peterborough	D	48	0	2	2	66
66	L.A.	Brad Winton	Toronto	C					
67	TOR	Pete Driscoll	Kingston	LW	60	3	8	11	97
68	NYR	Boyd Anderson	Medicine Hat	LW					
69	MTL	Mike McKegney	Kitchener	RW					
70	CHI	Terry Ruskowski	Swift Current	C	630	113	313	426	1354
71	PHI	Randy Andreachuk	Kamloops	C					
72	BOS	Bill Reed	Sault Ste. Marie	D					
73	WSH	Jack Patterson	Kamloops	C					
74	K.C.	Mark Lomenda	Victoria	RW					
75	CAL	Jim Warden	Michigan Tech	G					
76	NYI	Carlo Torresan	Sorel	D					
77	VAN	Mike Rogers	Calgary	C	484	202	317	519	184
78	MIN	Ron Ashton	Saskatoon	D					
79	ST.L.	Mike Zuke	Michigan Tech	C	455	86	196	282	220
80	PIT	Bruce Aberhart	London	G					
81	DET	John Taft	Wisconsin	D	15	0	2	2	4
82	ATL	Jerry Badiuk	Kitchener	D					
83	BUF	Garry Lariviere	St. Catharines	D	219	6	57	63	167
84	L.A.	J. Paul Evans	Kitchener	C	103	14	25	39	34
85	TOR	Mike Palmateer	Toronto	G	356	149	1183	17	3.53
86	NYR	Dennis Olmstead	Wisconsin	C					
87	ST.L.	Donald Wheldon	London	D	2	0	0	0	0
88	CHI	Dave Logan	Laval	D	218	5	29	34	470
89	PHI	Dennis Sobchuk	Regina	C	35	5	6	11	2
90	BOS	Jim Bateman	Quebec	LW					
91	WSH	Brian Kinsella	Oshawa	C	10	0	1	1	0
92	K.C.	John Shewchuk	St. Paul Jr. A	C					
93	CAL	Tom Sundberg	St. Paul Jr. A	C/LW					
94	NYI	Sid Prysunka	New Westminster	R/LW					
95	VAN	Andy Spruce	London	LW	172	31	42	73	111
96	MIN	John Sheridan	Minnesota-Duluth	C					
97	ST.L.	Mike Thompson	Victoria	D					
98	PIT	William Schneider	Minnesota-Duluth	LW					
99	DET	Don Dufek	Michigan	LW					
100	ATL	Bill Moen	U. of Minnesota	G					
101	BUF	Dave Given	Brown	D					
102	L.A.	Marty Mathews	Flin Flon	LW					
103	TOR	Bill Hassard	Wexford Jr.	C					
104	NYR	Eddie Johnstone	Medicine Hat	RW	426	122	136	258	375
105	MTL	John C. Stewart	Bowling Green	C	2	0	0	0	0
106	CHI	Bob Volpe	Sudbury	G					
107	PHI	Willie Friesen	Swift Current	LW					
108	BOS	Bill Best	Sudbury	LW					
109	WSH	Garth Malarchuk	Calgary	G					
110	K.C.	Mike J. Boland	Sault Ste. Marie	D	23	1	2	3	29
111	CAL	Tom Anderson	St. Paul Jr. A	D					
112	NYI	Dave Langevin	Minnesota-Duluth	D	513	12	107	119	530
113	VAN	Jim Clarke	Toronto	D					
114	MIN	Dave Heitz	Fargo-Moorhead	G					
115	ST.L.	Terry Casey	St. Catharines	RW					
116	PIT	Robbie Laird	Regina	C	1	0	0	0	0
117	DET	Jack Carlson	Marquette Sr.	LW	236	30	15	45	417
118	ATL	Peter Brown	Boston U.	D					
119	BUF	Bernard Noreau	Laval	RW					
120	L.A.	Harvey Stewart	Flin Flon	G					
121	TOR	Kevin Devine	Toronto	LW	2	0	1	1	8
122	NYR	John Memryk	Winnipeg	G					

1974 *continued*

PICK	TEAM	NAME	DRAFTED FROM	NHL PLAYERS: POS / NHL GOALTENDERS: POS	GP	G	A	PTS	PIM
123	MTL	Joe Micheletti	Minnesota-Duluth	D	158	11	60	71	114
124	CHI	Eddie Mio	Colorado College	G	192	64	705	4	4.06
125	PHI	Reggie Lemelin	Sherbrooke	G	507	236	1613	12	3.46
126	BOS	Ray Maluta	Flin Flon	D	25	2	3	5	6
127	WSH	John Nazar	Cornwall	LW					
128	CAL	Jim McCabe	Welland Jr. B	C					
129	NYI	David Inkpen	Edmonton	D					
130	VAN	Robbie Watt	Flin Flon	LW					
131	MIN	Roland Eriksson	Tunabro, SWE	C	193	48	95	143	26
132	ST.L.	Rod Tordoff	Swift Current	D					
133	PIT	Larry Finck	St. Catharines	D					
134	DET	Greg Steele	Calgary	D					
135	ATL	Tom Lindskog	Michigan	D					
136	BUF	Charles Constantin	Quebec	C					
137	L.A.	John Held	London	D					
138	TOR	Kevin Kemp	Ottawa	D	3	0	0	0	4
139	NYR	Greg Holst	Kingston	C	11	0	0	0	0
140	MTL	Jamie Hislop	New Hampshire	RW	345	75	103	178	86
141	CHI	Mike St. Cyr	Kitchener	D					
142	PHI	Steve Short	Minnesota Jr. Stars	LW	6	0	0	0	2
143	BOS	Darryl Drader	North Dakota	D					
144	WSH	Kelvin Erickson	Calgary	G					
145	K.C.	Brian Kurliak	North Bay	LW					
146	NYI	Jim Foubister	Victoria	G					
147	VAN	Marc Gaudreault	Lake Superior State	D					
148	MIN	Dave Staffen	Ottawa	C					
149	ST.L.	Paul-Andre Touzin	Shawinigan	G					
150	PIT	James Chicoyne	Brandon	D					
151	DET	Glenn McLeod	Sudbury	D					
152	ATL	Larry Hopkins	Oshawa	LW	60	13	16	29	26
153	BUF	Rick Jodzio	Hamilton	LW	70	2	8	10	71
154	L.A.	Mario Lessard	Sherbrooke	G	240	92	843	9	3.74
155	TOR	Dave Syvret	St. Catharines	D					
156	NYR	Claude Arvisais	Shawinigan	C					
157	MTL	Gord Stewart	Kamloops	C					
158	CHI	Stephen Colp	Michigan State	C					
159	PHI	Peter McKenzie	St. Francis Xavier	D					
160	BOS	Peter Roberts	St. Cloud Jr.	C					
161	WSH	Tony White	Kitchener	LW	164	37	28	65	104
162	K.C.	Denis Carufel	Sorel	D					
163	NYI	Bob Ferguson	Cornwall	C					
164	MIN	Brian Anderson	New Westminster	D					
165	ST.L.	Jack Ahern	Brown	D					
166	PIT	Rick Uhrich	Regina	RW					
167	ATL	Louis Loranger	Shawinigan	C					
168	BUF	Derek Smith	Ottawa	C/LW	335	78	116	194	60
169	L.A.	Derrick Emerson	Montreal	RW					
170	TOR	Andy Stoesz	Selkirk Jr.	G					
171	NYR	Ken Dodd	New Westminster	LW					
172	MTL	Charlie Luksa	Kitchener	D	8	0	1	1	4
173	CHI	Rick Fraser	Oshawa	D					
174	PHI	Marcel Labrosse	Shawinigan	C					
175	BOS	Peter Waselovich	North Dakota	G					
176	WSH	Ron Pronchuk	Brandon	D					
177	K.C.	Soren Johansson	Djurgarden, SWE	C					
178	NYI	Murray Fleck	Estevan	D					
179	MIN	Duane Bray	Flin Flon	D					
180	ST.L.	Mitch Babin	North Bay	C	8	0	0	0	0
181	PIT	Serge Gamelin	Sorel	RW					
182	ATL	Randy Montgomery	Welland Jr. B	LW					
183	BUF		invalid claim						
184	L.A.	Jacques Locas	Quebec	C					
185	TOR	Martin Feschuk	Saskatoon	D					
186	NYR	Ralph Krentz	Brandon	LW					
187	MTL	Cliff Cox	New Hampshire	C					
188	CHI	Jean Bernier	Shawinigan	D					
189	PHI	Scott Jessee	Michigan Tech	RW					
190	WSH	Dave McKee	Oshawa	RW					
191	K.C.	Mats Ulander	Boden, SWE	D					
192	NYI	David Rooke	Cornwall	D					
193	MIN	Don Hay	New Westminster	RW					
194	ST.L.	Doug Allan	New Westminster	G					
195	PIT	Richard Perron	Quebec	D					
196	BUF	Bob Geoffrion	Cornwall	LW					
197	L.A.	Lindsay Thomson	U. of Denver	C					
198	NYR	Larry Jacques	Ottawa	RW					
199	MTL	Dave Lumley	New Hampshire	RW	437	98	160	258	680
200	CHI	Dwane Byers	Sherbrooke	RW					
201	PHI	Richard Guay	Chicoutimi	G					
202	WSH	Scott Mabley	Sault Ste. Marie	D					
203	K.C.	Edward Pizunski	Peterborough	D					
204	NYI	Neil Smith	Brockville Jr. A	D					
205	MIN	Brian Holderness	Saskatoon	G					
206	PIT	Richard Hindmarch	U. of Calgary	RW					
207	L.A.	Craig Brickley	U. of Pennsylvania	C					
208	NYR	Tom Gastle	Peterborough	LW					

			DRAFTED	NHL PLAYERS: POS	GP	G	A	PTS	PIM

PICK	TEAM	NAME	FROM	NHL GOALTENDERS: POS	GP	W	GA	SO	AVG
209	MTL	Mike Hobin	Hamilton	C					
210	CHI	Glen Ing	Victoria	RW					
211	PHI	Brad Morrow	Minnesota-Duluth	D					
212	WSH	Bernard Plante	Trois-Rivieres	LW					
213	K.C.	Willie Wing	Hamilton	RW					
214	NYI	Stefan Persson	Brynas Gavle, SWE	D	622	52	317	369	574
215	MIN	Frank Taylor	Brandon	D					
216	PIT	Bill Davis	Colgate	D					
217	L.A.	Brad K*uglin	U. of Pennsylvania	LW					
218	NYR	Eric Brubacher	Kingston	C					
219	PHI	Craig Arvidson	Minnesota-Duluth	LW					
220	WSH	Jacques Chiasson	Drummondville	RW					
221	NYI	Dave Otness	Wisconsin	C					
222	MIN	Jeff Hymanson	St. Cloud Jr.	C					
223	PIT	James Mathers	Northeastern	D					
224	NYR	Russell Hall	Winnipeg	RW					
225	WSH	Bill Bell	Regina	LW					
226	NYI	Jim Murray	Michigan Tech	D					
227	NYR	Bill Kriski	Winnipeg	G					
228	WSH	Robert Blanchet	Kitchener	G					
229	NYI	Mike Dibble	Wisconsin	G					
230	NYR	Kevin Treacy	Cornwall	RW					
231	WSH	Johnny Bower	Downsview Jr.	G	552	250	1347	37	2.52
232	NYI	Brian Bye	Kitchener	LW					
233	NYR	Ken Gassoff	Medicine Hat	C					
234	WSH	Yves Plouffe	Sorel	D					
235	NYI	Martti Jarkko	Tappara Tampere, FIN	D					
236	NYR	Cliff Bast	Medicine Hat	D					
237	WSH	Terry Bozack	Pembroke Jr. A	D					
238	NYI	Ron Phillips	St. Catharines	D					
239	NYR	Jim Mayer	Michigan Tech	RW	4	0	0	0	0
240	WSH	Gord Cole	Brandon	LW					
241	NYR	Warren Miller	Minnesota-Duluth	RW	262	40	50	90	137
242	WSH	Mike Cosentino	Hamilton	C					
243	NYR	Kevin Walker	Cornell	D					
244	WSH	John Duncan	Cornwall	D					
245	NYR	Jim Warner	Minnesota Jr.	RW	32	0	3	3	10
246	WSH	Barry Kerfoot	Smiths Falls Jr.	RW					
247	WSH	Ron Poole	Kamloops	C					

1975

Due to the NHL's decision to allow the best 18-year-olds to be drafted the previous year, the 1975 draft lacked star potential. "The cream was all skimmed off last year," said Montreal coach Scotty Bowman. "This is a pretty ordinary crop." The draft was once again conducted in secrecy from the NHL's Montreal office via conference call. Only 20-year-old prospects would be eligible for drafting. The 1975 Amateur Draft was unique since it was the first draft to provide a ranking of the top eligible talent through the newly developed Central Scouting Bureau. Central Scouting compiled a ranking of the top junior talents and provided the list to the teams to be used as a guideline for drafting.

Since it was obvious that superstars were simply not available in the 1975 crop of graduating juniors, the intangible that would determine a player's value was attitude. It was not uncommon for teams to conduct personal interviews with prospects prior to the draft to evaluate the player. The ultimate winner in both the talent and attitude departments was Mel Bridgman of the Victoria Cougars.

Bridgman's coach, Pat Ginnell, previously coached the Flin Flon Bombers. He commented: "There's nothing bad I could say about Mel. He's the best I've had since [Bobby] Clarke. I don't want to say his playmaking is as good as Clarke's, but Mel has a lot of potential." On June 3, 1975 the Philadelphia Flyers, who had acquired last-place Washington's first choice in the draft, selected the Western Canada Hockey League scoring champion.

"Our scouts were unanimous," said Flyers g.m. Keith Allen. "When I asked them which player they would choose if they could pick one, they all chose Bridgman. The computer system also ranked Mel number one. It is the opinion of the scouts that Mel will step right in with the Flyers next year and we couldn't be happier." Bridgman joined the Flyers lineup the following year and went on to

enjoy 14 seasons in the NHL scoring 252 goals and adding 449 assists.

The 1975 draft showed the strength of the underdog, as most of the players who made an impact on the NHL were late selections. For example, the Atlanta Flames selected Willi Plett as the 80th player overall. He emerged as the league's top rookie for 1976–77, capturing the Calder Trophy and going on to collect 437 points (222 goals, 215 assists) over a 13-year career. The biggest surprise of the draft, and perhaps the most underrated player to be taken during the 1970s, was a 5'9", 145-pound sophomore at Clarkson College named Dave Taylor. Taylor was selected 210th overall by the Los Angeles Kings. "I was a little squirt when I went to Clarkson," said Taylor. "Luckily I grew both in height and weight. I guess that's why I wasn't selected until the 15th round." In 1976–77 he returned to Clarkson where he tied the U.S. college scoring record for one season with 108 points in 34 games before being promoted to the Kings lineup. A late bloomer, Taylor eventually grew to be 6'0" and 185 pounds to begin his NHL career. As the missing piece to complete the Kings' powerful Triple Crown line with Marcel Dionne and Charlie Simmer, Taylor went on to enjoy 17 seasons with the Kings, tallying 431 goals and 638 assists for 1,069 points to rank among the all-time NHL leaders in each category. He was awarded the King Clancy and Bill Masterton trophies in 1991 and served as the Kings' captain for four seasons. In 1987–88, Taylor became the highest-scoring player from the U.S. collegiate system, surpassing Peter McNab's 813 NHL points.

The only other significant career to emerge from the first round of the 1975 draft was goaltender Bob Sauve. As the 17th overall pick by the Sabres, Sauve developed into one of Buffalo's premier goaltenders. Four years into his career in 1979–80, Sauve was named a co-winner of the Vezina Trophy as the best goaltender in the NHL, which he shared with the 89th selection of the 1975 draft and Buffalo teammate Don Edwards. Sauve also shared the Jennings Trophy in 1984–85 with Tom Barrasso. He posted a career record of 182 wins, 154 losses and 54 ties and a lifetime goals-against average of 3.48.

Although Edwards was a late pick for the Sabres, he went on to set Buffalo team records in games played (307), minutes played (17,969) and wins (156).

The international invasion continued into the 1975 Amateur Draft, as the Flyers selected Viktor Khatulev as the 160th overall pick. He is recognized as the first Soviet player to be selected in the NHL draft. He never appeared in an NHL game.

1975

PICK	TEAM	NAME	DRAFTED FROM	NHL PLAYERS: POS / NHL GOALTENDERS: POS	GP / GP	G / W	A / GA	PTS / SO	PIM / AVG
FIRST ROUND									
1	PHI	Mel Bridgman	Victoria	C	977	252	449	701	1625
2	K.C.	Barry Dean	Medicine Hat	LW	165	25	56	81	146
3	CAL	Ralph Klassen	Saskatoon	C	497	52	93	145	120
4	MIN	Bryan Maxwell	Medicine Hat	D	331	18	77	95	745
5	DET	Rick Lapointe	Victoria	D	664	44	176	220	831
6	TOR	Don Ashby	Calgary	C	188	40	56	96	40
7	CHI	Greg Vaydik	Medicine Hat	C	5	0	0	0	0
8	ATL	Richard Mulhern	Sherbrooke	D	303	27	93	120	217
9	MTL	Robin Sadler	Edmonton	D					
10	VAN	Rick Blight	Brandon	RW	326	96	125	221	170
11	NYI	Pat Price	Saskatoon	D	726	43	218	261	1456
12	NYR	Wayne Dillon	Toronto	C	229	43	66	109	60
13	PIT	Gord Laxton	New Westminster	G	17	4	74	0	5.55
14	BOS	Doug Halward	Peterborough	D	653	69	224	293	774
15	MTL	Pierre Mondou	Montreal	C	548	194	262	456	179
16	L.A.	Tim Young	Ottawa	C	628	195	341	536	438
17	BUF	Bob Sauve	Laval	G	420	182	1377	8	3.48

PICK	TEAM	NAME	DRAFTED FROM	NHL PLAYERS: POS / NHL GOALTENDERS: POS	GP / GP	G / W	A / GA	PTS / SO	PIM / AVG
18	WSH	Alex Forsyth	Kingston	C	1	0	0	0	0
SECOND ROUND									
19	WSH	Peter Scamurra	Peterborough	D	132	8	25	33	59
20	K.C.	Don Cairns	Victoria	LW	9	0	1	1	2
21	CAL	Dennis Maruk	London	C	888	356	522	878	761
22	MTL	Brian Engblom	Wisconsin	D	659	29	177	206	599
23	DET	Jerry Rollins	Winnipeg	D					
24	TOR	Doug Jarvis	Peterborough	C	964	139	264	403	263
25	CHI	Daniel Arndt	Saskatoon	LW					
26	ATL	Rick Bowness	Montreal	RW	173	18	37	55	191
27	ST.L.	Ed Staniowski	Regina	G	219	67	818	2	4.06
28	VAN	Brad Gassoff	Kamloops	LW	122	19	17	36	163
29	NYI	Dave Salvian	St. Catharines	RW					
30	NYR	Doug Soetaert	Edmonton	G	284	110	1030	6	3.97
31	PIT	Russ Anderson	Minnesota-Duluth	D	519	22	99	121	1086
32	BOS	Barry Smith	New Westminster	C	114	7	7	14	10
33	L.A.	Terry Bucyk	Lethbridge	RW					
34	MTL	Kevin Greenbank	Winnipeg	RW					
35	BUF	Ken Breitenbach	St. Catharines	D	68	1	13	14	49
36	ST.L.	Jamie Masters	Ottawa	D	33	1	13	14	2
OTHER ROUNDS									
37	DET	Al Cameron	New Westminster	D	282	11	44	55	356
38	K.C.	Neil Lyseng	Kamloops	RW					
39	CAL	John Tweedle	Lake Superior State	RW					
40	MIN	Paul Harrison	Oshawa	G	109	28	408	2	4.22
41	MIN	Alex Pirus	U. of Notre Dame	RW	159	30	28	58	94
42	TOR	Bruce Boudreau	Toronto	C	141	28	42	70	46
43	CHI	Mike O'Connell	Kingston	D	860	105	334	439	605
44	BUF	Terry Martin	London	LW	479	104	101	205	202
45	DET	Blair Davidson	Flin Flon	D					
46	VAN	Normand Lapointe	Trois-Rivieres	G					
47	NYI	Joe Fortunato	Kitchener	LW					
48	NYR	Greg Hickey	Hamilton	LW	1	0	0	0	0
49	PIT	Paul Baxter	Winnipeg	D	472	48	121	169	1564
50	DET	Clarke Hamilton	U. of Notre Dame	LW					
51	MTL	Paul Woods	Sault Ste. Marie	LW	501	72	124	196	276
52	MTL	Pat Hughes	Michigan	RW	573	130	128	258	646
53	BUF	Gary McAdam	St. Catharines	LW	534	96	132	228	243
54	PHI	Bob Ritchie	Sorel	LW	29	8	4	12	10
55	WSH	Blair MacKasey	Montreal	D	1	0	0	0	2
56	K.C.	Ron Delorme	Lethbridge	C	524	83	83	166	667
57	CAL	Greg Smith	Colorado College	D	829	56	232	288	1110
58	MIN	Steve Jensen	Michigan Tech	LW	438	113	107	220	318
59	DET	Mike Wirachowsky	Regina	D					
60	BOS	Rick Adduono	St. Catharines	C	4	0	0	0	2
61	CHI	Pierre Giroux	Hull	C	6	1	0	1	17
62	ATL	Dale Ross	Ottawa	LW					
63	ST.L.	Rick Bourbonnais	Ottawa	RW	71	9	15	24	20
64	VAN	Glen Richardson	Hamilton	LW	24	3	6	9	19
65	NYI	Andre Lepage	Montreal	G					
66	NYR	Bill Cheropita	St. Catharines	G					
67	PIT	Stuart Younger	Michigan State	LW					
68	BOS	Denis Daigle	Montreal	LW					
69	L.A.	Andre Leduc	Sherbrooke	D					
70	MTL	Dave Gorman	St. Catharines	RW	3	0	0	0	0
71	BUF	Greg Neeld	Calgary	D					
72	PHI	Rick St. Croix	Oshawa	G	129	49	450	2	3.71
73	WSH	Craig Crawford	Toronto	LW					
74	K.C.	Terry McDonald	Kamloops	D	8	0	1	1	6
75	CAL	Doug Young	Michigan Tech	D					
76	MIN	David Norris	Hamilton	LW					
77	DET	Mike Wong	Montreal	C	22	1	1	2	12
78	TOR	Ted Long	Hamilton	D					
79	CHI	Bob Hoffmeyer	Saskatoon	D	198	14	52	66	325
80	ATL	Willi Plett	St. Catharines	RW	834	222	215	437	2572
81	ST.L.	Jim Gustafson	Victoria	C					
82	VAN	Doug Murray	Brandon	LW					
83	NYI	Denis McLean	Calgary	LW					
84	NYR	Larry Huras	Kitchener	D	2	0	0	0	0
85	PIT	Kim Clackson	Victoria	D	106	0	8	8	370
86	BOS	Stan Jonathan	Peterborough	LW	411	91	110	201	751
87	L.A.	Dave Miglia	Trois-Rivieres	D					
88	MTL	Jim Turkiewicz	Peterborough	D					
89	BUF	Don Edwards	Kitchener	G	459	208	1449	16	3.32
90	PHI	Gary Morrison	Michigan	RW	43	1	15	16	70
91	WSH	Roger Swanson	Flin Flon	G					
92	K.C.	Eric Sanderson	Victoria	LW					
93	CAL	Larry Hendrick	Calgary	G					
94	MIN	Greg Clause	Hamilton	RW					
95	DET	Mike Harazny	Regina	D					
96	TOR	Kevin Campbell	St. Lawrence U.	D					
97	CHI	Tom Ulseth	Wisconsin	RW					
98	ATL	Paul Heaver	Oshawa	D					
99	ST.L.	Jack Brownschidle	U. of Notre Dame	D	494	39	162	201	151
100	VAN	Bob Watson	Flin Flon	RW					
101	NYI	Mike Sleep	New Westminster	RW					
102	NYR	Randy Koch	Vermont	LW					

1975 *continued*

PICK	TEAM	NAME	DRAFTED FROM	NHL PLAYERS: POS / NHL GOALTENDERS: POS	GP	G / W	A / GA	PTS / SO	PIM / AVG
103	PIT	Peter Morrison	Victoria	LW					
104	BOS	Matti Hagman	HIFK Helsinki, FIN	C	237	56	89	145	36
105	L.A.	Bob Russell	Sudbury	C					
106	MTL	Michel Lachance	Montreal	D	21	0	4	4	22
107	BUF	Jim Minor	Regina	LW					
108	PHI	Paul Holmgren	U. of Minnesota	RW	527	144	179	323	1684
109	WSH	Clark Jantzie	U. of Alberta	LW					
110	K.C.	Bill Oleschuk	Saskatoon	G	55	7	188	1	3.98
111	CAL	Rick Shinske	New Westminster	C	63	5	16	21	10
112	MIN	Francois Robert	Sherbrooke	D					
113	DET	Jean-Luc Phaneuf	Montreal	C					
114	TOR	Mario Rouillard	Trois-Rivieres	RW					
115	CHI	Ted Bulley	Hull	LW	414	101	113	214	704
116	ATL	Dale McMullin	Brandon	LW					
117	ST.L.	Doug Lindskog	Michigan	LW					
118	VAN	Brian Shmyr	New Westminster	C					
119	NYI	Ritchie Hansen	Sudbury	C	20	2	8	10	4
120	NYR	Claude Larose	Sherbrooke	LW	25	4	7	11	2
121	PIT	Mike Will	Edmonton	C					
122	BOS	Gary Carr	Toronto	G					
123	L.A.	Dave Faulkner	Regina	C					
124	MTL	Tim Burke	New Hampshire	D					
125	BUF	Grant Rowe	Ottawa	D					
126	PHI	Dana Decker	Michigan Tech	LW					
127	WSH	Mike Fryia	Peterborough	LW					
128	K.C.	Joe Baker	Minnesota-Duluth	D					
129	CAL	Doug Schoenfeld	Cambridge Sr.	D					
130	MIN	Dean Magee	Colorado College	LW	7	0	0	0	4
131	DET	Steve Carlson	Johnstown NAHL	C	52	9	12	21	23
132	TOR	Ron Wilson	Providence	D	177	26	67	93	68
133	CHI	Paul Jensen	Michigan Tech	D					
134	ATL	Rick Piche	Brandon	D					
135	ST.L.	Dick Lamby	Salem State	D	22	0	5	5	22
136	VAN	Allan Fleck	New Westminster	LW					
137	NYI	Bob Sunderland	Boston U.	D					
138	NYR	Bill Hamilton	St. Catharines	RW					
139	PIT	Tapio Levo	Assat Pori, FIN	D	107	16	53	69	36
140	BOS	Bo Berglund	Djurgarden, SWE	LW					
141	L.A.	Bill Reber	Vermont	RW					
142	MTL	Craig Norwich	Wisconsin	D	104	17	58	75	60
143	BUF	Alex Tidey	Lethbridge	RW	9	0	0	0	8
144	WSH	Jim Ofrim	U. of Alberta	C					
145	K.C.	Scott Williams	Flin Flon	LW					
146	CAL	Jim Weaver	Kingston	G					
147	MIN	Terry Angel	Oshawa	RW					
148	DET	Gary Vaughn	Medicine Hat	RW					
149	TOR	Paul F. Evans	Peterborough	C/LW	11	1	1	2	21
150	ATL	Nick Sanza	Sherbrooke	G					
151	ST.L.	Dave McNabb	Wisconsin	G					
152	VAN	Bob McNeice	New Westminster	D					
153	NYI	Don Blair	Ottawa	RW					
154	NYR	Bud Stefanski	Oshawa	C	1	0	0	0	0
155	PIT	Bryan Shutt	Bowling Green	LW					
156	BOS	Joe Rando	New Hampshire	D					
157	L.A.	Sean Sullivan	Hamilton	D					
158	MTL	Paul Clarke	U. of Notre Dame	D					
159	BUF	Andy Whitby	Oshawa	RW					
160	PHI	Viktor Khatulev	Dynamo Riga, USSR	C					
161	WSH	Malcolm Zinger	Kamloops	RW					
162	ST.L.	Greg Agar	Merritt Jr. A	RW					
163	MIN	Michel Blais	Kingston	D					
164	DET	Jean Thibodeau	Shawinigan	C					
165	TOR	Jean Latendresse	Shawinigan	D					
166	TOR	Paul Crowley	Sudbury	RW					
167	ATL	Brian O'Connell	St. Louis U.	G					
168	NYI	Joey Girardin	Winnipeg	D					
169	NYR	Daniel Beaulieu	Quebec	LW					
170	PIT	Frank Salive	Peterborough	G					
171	BOS	Kevin Nugent	U. of Notre Dame	G					
172	L.A.	Brian Petrovek	Harvard	G					
173	MTL	Bob Ferriter	Boston College	C					
174	BUF	Len Moyer	U. of Notre Dame	G					
175	PHI	Duffy Smith	Bowling Green	D					
176	DET	David Hanson	Colorado College	D	33	1	1	2	65
177	MIN	Earl Sargent	Fargo-Moorhead	RW					
178	DET	Robin Larson	Minnesota-Duluth	D					
179	TOR	Dan D'Alvise	Royal York Jr.	C					
180	TOR	Jack Laine	Bowling Green	RW					
181	ATL	Joe Augustine	Austin Prep	D					
182	VAN	Sid Veysey	Sherbrooke	C	1	0	0	0	0
183	NYI	Geoff Green	Sudbury	RW					
184	NYR	John McMorrow	Providence	D					
185	PIT	John Glynne	Vermont	D					
186	L.A.	Tom Goddard	North Dakota	RW					
187	MTL	David Bell	Harvard	C					
188	TOR	Ken Holland	Medicine Hat	G	4	0	17	0	4.95
189	TOR	Bob Barnes	Hamilton	D					
190	MIN	Gilles Cloutier	Shawinigan	G					
191	TOR	Gary Burns	New Hampshire	LW/C	11	2	2	4	18
192	ATL	Torbjorn Nilsson	Skelleftea, SWE	RW					
193	TOR	Jim Montgomery	Hull	C					
194	NYI	Kari Makkonen	Assat Pori, FIN	RW	9	2	2	4	0
195	NYR	Tom McNamara	Vermont	G					
196	PIT	Lex Hudson	U. of Denver	D	2	0	0	0	0
197	L.A.	Mario Viens	Cornwall	G					
198	MTL	Carl Jackson	U. of Pennsylvania	C					
199	TOR	Rick Martin	London	RW					
200	NYR	Steve Roberts	Providence	D					
201	NYR	Paul Dionne	Princeton	D					
202	PIT	Dan Tsubouchi	St. Louis U.	RW					
203	L.A.	Chuck Carpenter	Yale	C					
204	MTL	Michel Brisebois	Sherbrooke	C					
205	NYR	Cecil Luckern	New Hampshire	LW					
206	PIT	Bronislav Stankovsky	Fargo-Moorhead	LW					
207	L.A.	Bob Fish	Fargo-Moorhead	LW					
208	MTL	Roger Bourque	U. of Notre Dame	D					
209	NYR	John Corriveau	New Hampshire	RW					
210	L.A.	Dave Taylor	Clarkson	RW	1111	431	638	1069	1589
211	MTL	Jim Lundquist	Brown	D					
212	NYR	Tom Funke	Fargo-Moorhead	LW					
213	L.A.	Robert Shaw	Clarkson	D					
214	MTL	Don Madson	Fargo-Moorhead	C					
215	MTL	Bob Bain	New Hampshire	D					
216	ATL	Gary Gill	Sault Ste. Marie	LW					
217	PIT	Kelly Secord	New Westminster	RW					

1976

As the direct competition with the WHA continued to grow, the new trend surrounding the NHL's Amateur Draft was the race to sign the top draft choices in order to prevent losing them to counter-offers from WHA clubs. However, NHL general managers made clear that only the top 18 players would end up being signed following the 1976 draft, as all the contract attention would be focused on them. Those players selected in the second round and lower would have to attend NHL training camps in an attempt to prove themselves worthy of an opportunity to appear on an NHL roster.

This approach was taken due to the dramatic fluctuation in the cost of signing players to pro contracts.

"That's the outlook facing some 200 or more Canadian major junior hockey league players who were born in 1956 and another 40-odd American college players who are in their graduating year," stated *The Hockey News*. "They are the prime targets of the NHL clubs, who this year will put results of the newly innovative Central Scouting Bureau, directed by Jack Button and his nine-man scouting staff, to work for them in evaluating what players they want to draft. Button's season-long fact-finding mission will provide guidelines for the NHL team on the available players, but won't tell them who to pick."

Once again the NHL had felt the effects of the underage acquisitions from two years ago when they were forced to select from a less talented crop of graduating juniors. Only 135 players were drafted and only nine of the top 18 picks were signed to NHL contracts. As in the previous year, a player's value was measured according to his attitude and the role that he would be able to fill. The Washington Capitals drafted Rick Green, the OHA's defenseman of the year, with the first pick overall.

After the Amateur Draft, Capitals general manager Max McNab commented: "When you look at the kids who could have been available this year you realize a lot of good ones weren't there. Still we feel there are a lot of solid players who'll help the teams. I know we're satisfied we got Green because we've got to start cutting down our goals against and we believe he's the type of defenseman who can help. We had offers to trade our first choice away but we think

we've got to start building our own loyalties." In the style of the classic blueliner, Green spent 15 years in the NHL as a player who excelled in all of the defensive aspects of the game scoring only 43 goals in 845 games. Green was traded to the Montreal Canadiens in 1982–83, where he helped them reach the Stanley Cup finals twice. He was part of a Cup winner in 1986.

The California Seals made draft history whey they selected Sweden's Bjorn Johansson fifth overall. He was the player from outside North America to be taken in the first round of the Amateur Draft. "We're really pleased with this year's draft," said Seals g.m. Bill McCreary. "In Johansson, we have an aggressive player, a very good skater with a fine shot. He is an excellent puck carrier and has an added dimension that's not always found: toughness." The 6'0", 185-pound Swede appeared in only 15 NHL games, recording two points with the Cleveland Barons. The Seals also selected Jouni Rinne, a native of Finland, as their sixth pick in 1976, 95th overall.

Of the eight non-North American born players selected in the draft, one emerged as a star. Atlanta drafted Swede Kent Nilsson with its fifth choice, 64th overall. He went on to collect 686 points (264 goals, 422 assists) over a nine-year career and has been credited as one of the pioneers for European success in the NHL. Nilsson was a member of the Stanley Cup champion Edmonton Oilers in 1987.

St. Louis came out of the 1976 draft in a similar situation as the Islanders in 1974 as they were able to acquire two of the franchise's most influential talents. With the seventh pick overall, the Blues selected Bernie Federko. He had come into the draft just after setting a new WCHL scoring record with 187 points (72 goals and 115 assists), a record previously held by Bobby Clarke (173 points). Federko developed into one of the team's star players, setting Blues' records for most points (1,073), assists (721), and games played (927).

Although Federko was highly touted going into the draft, the Blues struck gold when they selected lower-ranked Brian Sutter as the 20th pick overall. Sutter brought an aggressive approach to the game combined with offensive prowess. He spent 12 seasons with the Blues compiling 303 goals, 333 assists and 1,786 penalty minutes in 779 games. He was the first of six Sutter brothers to play in the NHL and spent nine seasons as the Blues captain before retiring in 1987–88 to a career as a head coach. He captured the Jack Adams Award as the coach of the year in 1991 after leading the Blues to a second place overall finish. He is currently the head coach of the Calgary Flames. Both Federko's and Sutter's jerseys have been honored by the Blues and hang from the rafters of the Kiel Center.

There were two incidents at the 1976 draft that made apparent the conflict that existed between the NHL and the WHA. The Cincinnati Stingers had pursued Toronto's first pick, Randy Carlyle, and claimed to have signed him to a contract. The Leafs gambled on a tip that the document signed by Carlyle was not legally binding, and drafted him 30th overall. The result was in the favor of the Leafs as Carlyle had only signed a letter of intent from the Stingers. He quickly signed with the Leafs and, although he never lived up to expectations in Toronto, Carlyle went on to become one of the league's marquee blueliners and was the recipient of the Norris Trophy as the best defenseman in 1981. He appeared in 1,055 games over a 17-year career, becoming only the 73rd player in NHL history to reach the 1,000-game plateau. The other clash between the NHL and

WHA in 1976 involved Mike Liut. The goaltender was selected 56th overall by St. Louis but opted to sign with the WHA Stingers and did not enter the NHL until the WHA disbanded in 1979–80.

1976

PICK	TEAM	NAME	DRAFTED FROM	NHL PLAYERS: POS / NHL GOALTENDERS: POS	GP / GP	G / W	A / GA	PTS / SO	PIM / AVG
FIRST ROUND									
1	WSH	Rick Green	London	D	845	43	220	263	588
2	PIT	Blair Chapman	Saskatoon	RW	402	106	125	231	158
3	MIN	Glen Sharpley	Hull	C	389	117	161	278	199
4	DET	Fred Williams	Saskatoon	C	44	2	5	7	10
5	CAL	Bjorn Johansson	Orebro, SWE	D	15	1	1	2	10
6	NYR	Don Murdoch	Medicine Hat	RW	320	121	117	238	155
7	ST.L.	Bernie Federko	Saskatoon	C	1000	369	761	1130	487
8	ATL	Dave Shand	Peterborough	D	421	19	84	103	544
9	CHI	Real Cloutier	Quebec	RW	317	146	198	344	119
10	ATL	Harold Phillipoff	New Westminster	LW	141	26	57	83	267
11	K.C.	Paul Gardner	Oshawa	C	447	201	201	402	207
12	MTL	Peter Lee	Ottawa	RW	431	114	131	245	257
13	MTL	Rod Schutt	Sudbury	LW	286	77	92	169	177
14	NYI	Alex McKendry	Sudbury	L/HW	46	3	6	9	21
15	WSH	Greg Carroll	Medicine Hat	C	131	20	34	54	44
16	BOS	Clayton Pachal	New Westminster	C/LW	35	2	3	5	95
17	PHI	Mark Suzor	Kingston	D	64	4	16	20	60
18	MTL	Bruce Baker	Ottawa	RW					
SECOND ROUND									
19	PIT	Greg Malone	Oshawa	C	704	191	310	501	661
20	ST.L.	Brian Sutter	Lethbridge	LW	779	303	333	636	1786
21	L.A.	Steve Clippingdale	New Westminster	IW	19	1	2	3	9
22	DET	Reed Larson	Minnesota-Duluth	D	904	222	463	685	1391
23	CAL	Vern Stenlund	London	C	4	0	0	0	0
24	NYR	Dave Farrish	Sudbury	D	430	17	110	127	440
25	ST.L.	John Smrke	Toronto	LW	103	11	17	28	33
26	VAN	Bob Manno	St. Catharines	D	371	41	131	172	274
27	CHI	Jeff McDill	Victoria	RW	1	0	0	0	0
28	ATL	Bobby Simpson	Sherbrooke	LW	175	35	29	64	98
29	PIT	Peter Marsh	Sherbrooke	RW	278	48	71	119	224
30	TOR	Randy Carlyle	Sudbury	D	1055	148	499	647	1400
31	MIN	Jim Roberts	Ottawa	IW	106	17	23	40	33
32	NYI	Mike Kaszycki	Sault Ste. Marie	C	226	42	80	122	108
33	BUF	Joe Kowal	Hamilton	LW	22	0	5	5	13
34	BOS	Lorry Gloeckner	Victoria	D	13	0	2	2	6
35	PHI	Drew Callander	Regina	C/RW	39	6	2	8	7
36	MTL	Barry Melrose	Kamloops	D	300	10	23	33	728
OTHER ROUNDS									
37	WSH	Tom Rowe	London	RW	357	85	100	185	615
38	K.C.	Mike Kitchen	Toronto	D	474	12	62	74	370
39	MIN	Don Jackson	U. of Notre Dame	D	311	16	52	68	640
40	DET	Fred Berry	New Westminster	C	3	0	0	0	0
41	CAL	Mike Fidler	Boston U.	IW	271	84	97	181	124
42	NYR	Mike McEwen	Toronto	D	716	108	296	404	460
43	ST.L.	Jim Kirkpatrick	Toronto	D					
44	VAN	Rob Flockhart	Kamloops	LW	55	2	5	7	14
45	CHI	Thomas Gradin	MoDo Ornskoldsvik, SWE	C	677	209	384	593	298
46	ATL	Rick Hodgson	Calgary	D	6	0	0	0	6
47	PIT	Morris Lukowich	Medicine Hat	LW	582	199	219	418	584
48	TOR	Alain Belanger	Sherbrooke	RW	9	0	1	1	6
49	L.A.	Don Moores	Kamloops	C					
50	NYI	Garth MacGuigan	Montreal	C	5	0	1	1	2
51	MIN	Ron Zanussi	London	RW	299	52	83	135	373
52	TOR	Gary McFayden	Hull	RW					
53	PHI	Craig Hamner	St. Paul Jr. A	D					
54	MTL	Bill Baker	Minnesota-Duluth	D	143	7	25	32	175
55	WSH	Al Glendinning	Calgary	D					
56	ST.L.	Mike Liut	Bowling Green	G	663	294	2219	25	3.49
57	MIN	Mike Federko	Hamilton	D					
58	DET	Kevin Schamehorn	New Westminster	RW	10	0	0	0	17
59	CAL	Warren Young	Michigan Tech	C	236	72	77	149	472
60	NYR	Claude Periard	Trois-Rivieres	LW					
61	ST.L.	Paul Skidmore	Boston College	G	2	1	6	0	3.00
62	VAN	Elmer Ray	Calgary	LW					
63	CHI	David Debol	Michigan	C	92	26	26	52	4
64	ATL	Kent Nilsson	Djurgarden, SWE	C	553	264	422	686	116
65	PIT	Greg Redquest	Oshawa	G	1	0	3	0	13.85
66	TOR	Tim Williams	Victoria	D					
67	L.A.	Bob Mears	Kingston	G					
68	NYI	Ken Morrow	Bowling Green	D	550	17	88	105	309
69	BUF	Henry Maze	Edmonton	LW					
70	BOS	Bob Miller	Ottawa	C	404	75	119	194	220
71	PHI	Dave Hynek	Kingston	LW					
72	MTL	Ed Clarey	Cornwall	RW					
73	WSH	Doug Patey	Sault Ste. Marie	RW	45	4	2	6	8
74	K.C.	Rick McIntyre	Oshawa	LW					
75	MIN	Phil Vorchota	Minnesota-Duluth	C					
76	DET	Dwight Schofield	London	D	211	8	22	30	631

1976 *continued*

PICK	TEAM	NAME	DRAFTED FROM	POS	GP	G	A	PTS	PIM
77	CAL	Darcy Regier	Lethbridge	D	26	0	2	2	35
78	NYR	Doug Gaines	St. Catharines	C					
79	CAL	Cal Sandbeck	U. of Denver	D					
80	VAN	Rick Durston	Victoria	LW					
81	CHI	Terry McDonald	Edmonton	C					
82	ATL	Mark Earp	Kamloops	G					
83	PIT	Brendan Lowe	Sherbrooke	D					
84	TOR	Greg Hotham	Kingston	D	230	15	74	89	139
85	L.A.	Robert Ross Palmer	Michigan	D	320	9	101	110	115
86	NYI	Mike Hordy	Sault Ste. Marie	D	11	0	0	0	7
87	BUF	Ron Roscoe	Hamilton	D					
88	BOS	Peter Vandemark	Oshawa	LW					
89	PHI	Robin Lang	Cornell	D					
90	MTL	Maurice Barrette	Quebec	D					
91	WSH	Jim Bedard	Sudbury	G	73	17	278	1	3.94
92	K.C.	Larry Skinner	Ottawa	C	47	10	12	22	8
93	MIN	Dave Delich	Colorado College	C					
94	DET	Tony Horvath	Sault Ste. Marie	G					
95	CAL	Jouni Rinne	Lukko Rauma, FIN	RW					
96	NYR	Barry Scully	Kingston	RW					
97	ST.L.	Nels Goddard	Michigan Tech	D					
98	VAN	Rob Tudor	Regina	RW/C	28	4	4	8	19
99	CHI	John Peterson	U. of Notre Dame	G					
100	WSH	Don Wilson	St. Catharines	D					
101	PIT	Vic Sirko	Oshawa	D					
102	TOR	Dan Djakalovic	Kitchener	C					
103	L.A.	Larry McRae	Windsor	G					
104	NYI	Yvon Vautour	Laval	RW	204	26	33	59	401
105	BUF	Don Lemieux	Trois-Rivieres	D					
106	BOS	Ted Olson	Calgary	LW					
107	PHI	Paul Klasinski	St. Paul Jr. A	LW					
108	MTL	Pierre Brassard	Cornwall	LW					
109	WSH	Dale Rideout	Flin Flon	G					
110	MIN	Jeff Barr	Michigan State	D					
111	DET	Fern LeBlanc	Sherbrooke	C	34	5	6	11	0
112	NYR	Remi Levesque	Quebec	C					
113	ST.L.	Mike Eaves	Wisconsin	C	324	83	143	226	80
114	VAN	Brad Rhiness	Kingston	C					
115	CHI	John Rothstein	Minnesota-Duluth	RW					
116	TOR	Chuck Skjodt	Windsor	C					
117	PHI	Ray Kurpis	Austin Prep	RW					
118	MTL	Rick Gosselin	Flin Flon	C					
119	WSH	Allan Dumba	Regina	RW					
120	DET	Claude Legris	Sorel	G	4	0	4	0	2.64
121	ST.L.	Jacques Soguel	Davos, SUI	C					
122	VAN	Stu Ostlund	Michigan Tech	C					
123	MTL	John Gregory	Wisconsin	D					
124	ST.L.	David Dornself	Providence	D					
125	MTL	Bruce Horsch	Michigan Tech	G					
126	ST.L.	Brad Wilson	Providence	C					
127	MTL	John Tavella	Sault Ste. Marie	LW					
128	ST.L.	Don Hoene	Michigan	RW					
129	MTL	Mark Davidson	Flin Flon	RW					
130	ST.L.	Goran Lindblom	Skelleftea, SWE	D					
131	MTL	Bill Wells	Cornwall	LW					
132	ST.L.	Jim Bales	U. of Denver	G					
133	MTL	Ron Wilson	St. Catharines	C	832	110	216	326	415
134	ST.L.	Anders Hakansson	AIK Solna, SWE	LW	330	52	46	98	141
135	ST.L.	Juhani Wallenius	Lukko Rauma, FIN	C					

1977

On June 14, 1977 the NHL conducted its third Amateur Draft via confidential conference call, selecting 185 players in what was looked at as one of the strongest crops of juniors in the past few years. The NHL had instituted a new clause in the draft making it possible for a drafted player to re-enter the draft the following year if he had not signed a pro contract 48 hours prior to the successive draft. This allowed for a larger and deeper draft pool. With continuing competition from the WHA, the NHL clubs signed 13 first-round selections including Detroit's first overall pick Dale McCourt.

McCourt became one of the few rookies to step into the NHL and lead his team in scoring. Tallying 72 points (33 goals, 39 assists), he was identified as a future superstar and was sought by the Los Angeles Kings who wanted McCourt as compensation for losing star goaltender Rogie Vachon to Detroit through free agency following the 1977–78 season. After a highly publicized year-long lawsuit, McCourt

fought the decision and won. However, the case placed an enormous amount of pressure on the young player and McCourt was never able to live up to the superstar billing. He retired after seven seasons with 194 goals and 284 assists for 478 points in 532 games.

The 1977 draft boasted a lot of NHL families, as defenseman Doug Wilson would join his older brother Murray of the Canadiens in the NHL. Other relatives included goaltender Moe Robinson, brother of Montreal superstar Larry. Moe never appeared in an NHL game. Ric Seiling was a brother of Rod, a member of the St. Louis Blues. Even McCourt was the nephew of former Toronto star George Armstrong. The 1977 draft also featured one of the largest crops of junior goaltending talent available. Goaltenders Pete Peeters (135th overall), Greg Millen (102nd overall), Glenn Hanlon (40th overall), Murray Bannerman (58th overall) and Richard Sevigny (124th overall) all went on to enjoy successful careers in the NHL. Peeters and Sevigny each captured the Vezina Trophy as the NHL's top goaltender, Sevigny earning it in 1981 while Peeters received the award in 1983.

The Colorado Rockies (formerly the Kansas City Scouts) had the second pick in 1977 and selected 6'3", 215-pound defenseman Barry Beck. Beck had an immediate impact as he stepped into the NHL to set new league records for goals (22) and points (60) by a rookie defensemen. He also earned a spot on the Campbell Conference team for the 1977–78 All-Star Game. "He's been our quarterback all year," said Rockies head coach Pat Kelly. "From the very first day of training camp, he looked like he'd been in this league four or five years. He just doesn't fluster." Beck was named as the runner-up for the Calder Trophy as rookie of the year. He went on to collect 355 points in his 10-year career.

Two other marquee defensemen were selected in the 1977 draft. The Chicago Black Hawks took Doug Wilson as the sixth selection overall while the Montreal Canadiens opted for Rod Langway as the 36th pick. Wilson went on to enjoy a 16-year career with 237 goals and 590 assists for 827 points to rank among the top-scoring defensemen in history. Wilson was regarded as having the league's hardest slapshot and was recognized as the best defenseman when he captured the Norris Trophy in 1982.

Langway, known more for his defensive abilities than his offensive skills, also enjoyed an excellent career in the NHL. He became one of the most prominent defenseman in the NHL, winning the Norris Trophy as a member of the Washington Capitals in 1983 and 1984. He had previously been a member of the 1979 Stanley Cup champion Montreal Canadiens. Langway is the Capitals' longest serving captain, a role he assumed for 11 seasons The team retired his jersey early in the 1997–98 season.

The New York Islanders once again emerged as the real winners in the draft, selecting two more gems as late picks. They obtained one of the NHL's greatest goal scorers of all time when they opted for junior sniper Mike Bossy as the 15th selection. Bossy had just finished setting the junior record for career goals with 309 markers over five seasons. However, he was regarded as a player who neglected the defensive aspects of the game and teams were looking for more all-around talent. But the Islanders needed an offensive specialist, which is exactly what they found in Bossy. Immediately stepping into the league, Bossy became the first rookie in league history to score 50 goals (finishing with 53) and came within four points of Bryan Trottier's

rookie record when he added 38 assists for 91 points.

The following season Bossy set an NHL mark by scoring his 100th goal in the 129th regular-season game of his NHL career, eclipsing Maurice Richard's record of 134 games. Prior to being drafted, Islanders scout Ed Chadwick commented, "Bossy's a natural scorer. He's a hell of a skater, plays his position well and never has his back to the play." Bossy proved his scoring touch as he recorded 573 goals in his career to rank among the game's all-time leaders. He scored his 1,000th point in his 656th game, third-fastest to this milestone. He compiled a career record of 573 goals and 553 assists for 1,126 points in 752 games before being forced into retirement by a severe neck injury that resulted from being hit from behind. Bossy was immediately inducted into the Hall of Fame as the three-year grace period was waived. He had been awarded the Calder Trophy as the league's best rookie in 1978, and was a three-time recipient of the Lady Byng Trophy recognizing gentlemanly play. He received the Conn Smythe Trophy as MVP of the 1982 playoffs. As a primary member of the Islander dynasty that captured four consecutive Stanley Cup championships, Bossy's jersey, number 22, has been retired by the club.

The other important role player the Islanders acquired in the 1977 draft was forward John Tonelli, whom they obtained with the 33rd selection overall. Tonelli compiled a career record of 325 goals and 511 assists for 836 points in 1,028 games to rank him among the NHL's top 100 in each category. Tonelli was also a key player for the Islanders during their reign as four-time Stanley Cup champions.

1977

FIRST ROUND

PICK	TEAM	NAME	DRAFTED FROM	POS	GP	G	A	PTS	PIM
1	DET	Dale McCourt	St. Catharines	C	532	194	284	478	124
2	COL	Barry Beck	New Westminster	D	615	104	251	355	1016
3	WSH	Robert Picard	Montreal	D	899	104	319	423	1025
4	VAN	Jere Gillis	Sherbrooke	LW	386	78	95	173	230
5	CLE	Mike Crombeen	Kingston	RW	475	55	68	123	218
6	CHI	Doug Wilson	Ottawa	D	1024	237	590	827	830
7	MIN	Brad Maxwell	New Westminster	D	612	98	270	368	1292
8	NYR	Lucien DeBlois	Sorel	C	993	249	276	525	814
9	ST.L.	Scott Campbell	London	D	80	4	21	25	243
10	MTL	Mark Napier	Toronto	RW	767	235	306	541	157
11	TOR	John Anderson	Toronto	RW	814	282	349	631	263
12	TOR	Trevor Johansen	Toronto	D	286	11	46	57	282
13	NYR	Ron Duguay	Sudbury	C/RW	864	274	346	620	582
14	BUF	Ric Seiling	St. Catharines	RW/C	738	179	208	387	573
15	NYI	Mike Bossy	Laval	RW	752	573	553	1126	210
16	BOS	Dwight Foster	Kitchener	RW	541	111	163	274	420
17	PHI	Kevin McCarthy	Winnipeg	D	537	67	191	258	527
18	MTL	Norm Dupont	Montreal	LW	256	55	85	140	52

SECOND ROUND

PICK	TEAM	NAME	DRAFTED FROM	POS	GP	G	A	PTS	PIM
19	CHI	Jean Savard	Quebec	C	43	7	12	19	29
20	ATL	Miles Zaharko	New Westminster	D	129	5	32	37	84
21	WSH	Mark Lofthouse	New Westminster	RW/C	181	42	38	80	73
22	VAN	Jeff Bandura	Portland	D	2	0	1	1	0
23	CLE	Dan Chicoine	Sherbrooke	RW	31	1	2	3	12
24	TOR	Bob Gladney	Oshawa	D	14	1	5	6	4
25	MIN	Dave Semenko	Brandon	LW	575	65	88	153	1175
26	NYR	Mike Keating	St. Catharines	LW	1	0	0	0	0
27	ST.L.	Neil Labatte	Toronto	D	26	0	2	2	19
28	ATL	Don Laurence	Kitchener	C	79	15	22	37	14
29	TOR	Rocky Saganiuk	Lethbridge	RW/C	259	57	65	122	201
30	PIT	Jim Hamilton	London	RW	95	14	18	32	28
31	ATL	Brian Hill	Medicine Hat	RW	19	1	1	2	4
32	BUF	Ronald Areshenkoff	Medicine Hat	C	4	0	0	0	0
33	NYI	John Tonelli	Toronto	LW	1028	325	511	836	911
34	BOS	Dave Parro	Saskatoon	G	77	21	274	2	4.09
35	PHI	Tom Gorence	U. of Minnesota	RW	303	58	53	111	89
36	MTL	Rod Langway	New Hampshire	D	994	51	278	329	849

OTHER ROUNDS

PICK	TEAM	NAME	DRAFTED FROM	POS	GP	G	A	PTS	PIM
37	DET	Rick Vasko	Peterborough	D	31	3	7	10	29
38	COL	Doug Berry	U. of Denver	C	121	10	33	43	25
39	WSH	Eddy Godin	Quebec	RW	27	3	6	9	12
40	VAN	Glen Hanlon	Brandon	G	477	167	1561	13	3.60
41	CLE	Reg Kerr	Kamloops	LW	263	66	94	160	169
42	CLE	Guy Lash	Winnipeg	RW					
43	MTL	Alain Cote	Chicoutimi	LW	696	103	190	293	383
44	NYR	Steve Baker	Union College	G	57	20	190	3	3.70

PICK	TEAM	NAME	DRAFTED FROM	NHL PLAYERS: POS / NHL GOALTENDERS: POS	GP	G / W	A / GA	PTS / SO	PIM / AVG
45	ST.L.	Tom Roulston	Winnipeg	C/RW	195	47	49	96	74
46	MTL	Pierre Lagace	Quebec	LW					
47	COL	Randy Pierce	Sudbury	RW	277	62	76	138	223
48	PIT	Kim Davis	Flin Flon	C	36	5	7	12	51
49	MTL	Moe Robinson	Kingston	D	1	0	0	0	0
50	NYI	Hector Marini	Sudbury	RW	154	27	46	73	246
51	NYI	Bruce Andres	New Westminster	LW					
52	BOS	Mike Forbes	St. Catharines	D	50	1	11	12	41
53	PHI	Dave Hoyda	Portland	LW	132	6	17	23	299
54	MTL	Gordie Roberts	Victoria	D	1097	61	359	420	1582
55	DET	John Hilworth	Medicine Hat	D	57	1	1	2	89
56	VAN	Dave Morrow	Calgary	C/D					
57	WSH	Nelson Burton	Quebec	LW	8	1	0	1	21
58	VAN	Murray Bannerman	Victoria	G	289	116	1051	8	3.83
59	CLE	John Baby	Sudbury	D	26	2	8	10	26
60	CHI	Randy Ireland	Portland	G		Re-entered Draft in 1978			
61	MIN	Kevin McCloskey	Calgary	D					
62	NYR	Mario Marois	Quebec	D	955	76	357	433	1746
63	ST.L.	Tony Currie	Portland	RW	290	92	119	211	83
64	MTL	Robbie Holland	Montreal	G	44	11	171	1	4.08
65	TOR	Dan Eastman	London	C		Re-entered Draft in 1978			
66	PIT	Mark Johnson	Wisconsin	C	669	203	305	508	260
67	PHI	Yves Guillemette	Shawinigan	G					
68	BUF	Bill Stewart	Niagara Falls	D	261	7	64	71	424
69	NYI	Steve Stoyanovich	RPI	C	23	3	5	8	11
70	BOS	Brian McGregor	Saskatoon	RW					
71	PHI	Rene Hamelin	Shawinigan	LW					
72	ATL	Jim Craig	Boston U.	G	30	11	100	0	3.78
73	DET	Jim Korn	Providence	D	597	66	122	188	1801
74	COL	Mike Dwyer	Niagara Falls	LW	31	2	6	8	25
75	WSH	Denis Turcotte	Quebec	C					
76	VAN	Steve Hazlett	St. Catharines	LW	1	0	0	0	0
77	CLE	Owen Lloyd	Medicine Hat	D					
78	CHI	Gary Platt	Sorel	D					
79	MIN	Robert Parent	Kingston	D					
80	NYR	Benoit Gosselin	Trois-Rivieres	LW	7	0	0	0	33
81	ST.L.	Bruce Hamilton	Saskatoon	LW					
82	ATL	Kurt Christoferson	Colorado College	D					
83	TOR	John Wilson	Windsor	LW					
84	L.A.	Julian Baretta	Wisconsin	G					
85	L.A.	Warren Holmes	Ottawa	C	45	8	18	26	7
86	BUF	Richard Sirois	Laval	G		Re-entered Draft in 1978			
87	NYI	Markus Mattsson	Ilves Tampere, FIN	G	92	21	343	6	4.11
88	BOS	Douglas Butler	St. Louis U.	D					
89	PHI	Dan Clark	Kamloops	D		Re-entered Draft in 1978			
90	MTL	Gaetan Rochette	Shawinigan	LW					
91	DET	Jim Baxter	Union College	G					
92	COL	Dan Lempe	Minnesota-Duluth	C					
93	WSH	Perry Schnarr	U. of Denver	RW					
94	VAN	Brian Drumm	Peterborough	LW					
95	CLE	Jeff Allan	Hull	D	4	0	0	0	2
96	CHI	Jack O'Callahan	Boston U.	D	389	27	104	131	541
97	MIN	Jamie Gallimore	Kamloops	RW	2	0	0	0	0
98	NYR	John Bethel	Boston U.	LW	17	0	2	2	4
99	ST.L.	Gary McMonagle	Peterborough	C					
100	ATL	Bernard Harbec	Laval	C					
101	TOR	Roy Sommer	Calgary	LW/C	3	1	0	1	7
102	PIT	Greg Millen	Peterborough	G	604	215	2281	17	3.87
103	L.A.	Randy Rudnyk	New Westminster	RW					
104	BUF	Wayne Ramsey	Brandon	D	2	0	0	0	
105	NYI	Steve Letzgus	Michigan Tech	D					
106	BOS	Keith Johnson	Saskatoon	D					
107	PHI	Alain Chaput	Sorel	C					
108	MTL	Bill Himmelwright	North Dakota	D					
109	DET	Randy Wilson	Providence	LW					
110	COL	Rick Doyle	London	LW					
111	WSH	Rollie Boutin	Lethbridge	G	22	7	75	0	3.96
112	VAN	Ray Creasey	New Westminster	C					
113	CLE	Mark Toffolo	Chicoutimi	D		Re-entered Draft in 1978			
114	CHI	Floyd Lahache	Sherbrooke	RW					
115	MIN	Jean-Pierre Sanvido	Trois-Rivieres	G					
116	NYR	Bob Sullivan	Chicoutimi	LW	62	18	19	37	18
117	ST.L.	Matti Forss	Lukko Rauma, FIN	C					
118	ATL	Bobby Gould	New Hampshire	RW	697	145	159	304	572
119	TOR	Lynn Jorgensen	Toronto	LW					
120	L.A.	Robert Suter	Wisconsin	D					
121	NYI	Harald Luckner	Farjestad Karlstad, SWE	C		Re-entered Draft in 1978			
122	BOS	Ralph Cox	New Hampshire	RW					
123	PHI	Richard Dalpe	Trois-Rivieres	C					
124	MTL	Richard Sevigny	Sherbrooke	G	176	80	507	5	3.21
125	DET	Raymond Roy	Sherbrooke	C					
126	COL	Joe Contini	St. Catharines	C	68	17	21	38	34
127	WSH	Brent Tremblay	Trois-Rivieres	D	10	1	0	1	6
128	CLE	Grant Fakin	Lethbridge	LW					
129	CHI	Jeff Geiger	Ottawa	D					
130	MIN	Greg Tebbutt	Victoria	D	26	0	3	3	35

1977 *continued*

PICK	TEAM	NAME	DRAFTED FROM	NHL PLAYERS: POS / NHL GOALTENDERS: POS	GP	G / W	A / GA	PTS / SO	PIM / AVG
131	NYR	Lance Nethery	Cornell	C	41	11	14	25	14
132	ST.L.	Raimo Hirvonen	HIFK Helsinki, FIN	C					
133	ATL	Jim Bennett	Brown	LW					
134	TOR	Kevin Howe	Sault Ste. Marie	C/D					
135	PHI	Pete Peeters	Medicine Hat	G	489	246	1424	21	3.08
136	PHI	Clint Eccles	Kamloops	LW					
137	MTL	Keith Hendrickson	U. of Minnesota	D					
138	BOS	Mario Claude	Sherbrooke	D					
139	PHI	Mike Greeder	St. Paul Jr. A	D					
140	MTL	Mike Reilly	Colorado College	RW					
141	DET	Kip Churchill	Union College	C					
142	COL	Jack Hughes	Harvard	D	46	2	5	7	104
143	WSH	Don Michelletti	U. of Minnesota	LW					
144	CHI	Stephen Ough	Laval	D					
145	MIN	Keith Hanson	Austin Prep	D	25	0	2	2	77
146	NYR	Alex Jeans	U. of Toronto	RW					
147	ST.L.	Bjorn Olsson	Farjestad Karlstad, SWE	D					
148	ATL	Tim Harrer	U. of Minnesota	RW	3	0	0	0	2
149	TOR	Ray Robertson	St. Lawrence U.	D					
150	PHI	Tom Bauer	Providence	LW					
151	PHI	Mike Bauman	Hull	LW					
152	MTL	Barry Borrett	Cornwall	G					
153	PHI	Bruce Crowder	New Hampshire	RW	243	47	51	98	156
154	MTL	Sid Tanchak	Clarkson	C					
155	DET	Lance Gatoni	U. of Toronto	D					
156	WSH	Archie Henderson	Victoria	RW	23	3	1	4	92
157	NYR	Peter Raps	Western Michigan	LW					
158	PHI	Rob Nicholson	St. Paul Jr. A	D					
159	PHI	Dave Isherwood	Winnipeg	C					
160	MTL	Mark Holden	Brown	G	8	2	25	0	4.03
161	PHI	Steve Jones	Ohio State	G					
162	MTL	Craig Laughlin	Clarkson	RW	549	136	205	341	364
163	DET	Rob Plumb	Kingston	LW	14	3	2	5	2
164	NYR	Mike Brown	Western Michigan	RW					
165	PHI	Jim Trainor	Harvard	D					
166	PHI	Dan Poulin	Kitchener	D	3	1	1	2	2
167	MTL	Daniel Poulin	Chicoutimi	D					
168	PHI	Rod McNair	Ohio State	D					
169	MTL	Tom McDonell	Ottawa	C					
170	DET	Alain Belanger	Trois-Rivieres	RW					
171	NYR	Mark Miller	Michigan	LW					
172	PHI	Mike Laycock	Brown	G					
173	MTL	Gary Garelli	Toronto	C/RW					
174	MTL	Carey Walker	New Westminster	G					
175	DET	Dean Willers	Union College	C					
176	MTL	Mark Wells	Bowling Green	C					
177	MTL	Stan Palmer	U. of Minnesota	D					
178	DET	Roland Cloutier	Trois-Rivieres	C	34	8	9	17	2
179	MTL	Jean Belisle	Chicoutimi	G					
180	MTL	Bob Daly	Ottawa	G					
181	DET	Edward Hill	Vermont	RW					
182	MTL	Bob Boileau	Boston U.	RW					
183	MTL	John Costello	Lowell Tech College	C					
184	DET	Val James	Quebec	LW	11	0	0	0	30
185	DET	Grant Morin	Calgary	RW					

1978

The Amateur Draft in 1977 and 1978 indicated a change in attitude by the NHL's member clubs toward the trading of top draft picks, as the majority of teams recognized the value in young prospects and chose to hold on to their top choices. The 1978 draft was felt to offer a better-than-average crop of junior graduates, with most of the talent on offense. In an effort to strengthen the draft pool, the NHL announced an agreement with the Canadian Major Junior Hockey League that would see the NHL provide strong financial support to the Canadian junior leagues to further develop premium junior talent.

"We advised the major junior hockey representatives that so long as they continue to maintain and improve their development programs and continue to provide skilled hockey players, they can count on our financial and moral support," said NHL president John Ziegler. "Provided there are no significant changes in the quantity, quality and skill level of the players coming out of junior hockey, the amounts to be paid to minor hockey for each player can be increased each year so that by 1980 the National Hockey League may be paying a maximum of $30,000 per player."

On June 15, 1978 the Amateur Draft returned to the Queen Elizabeth Hotel in Montreal, abandoning the secretive conference call format. The last-place Minnesota North Stars had the first pick and selected junior sensation Bobby Smith. Smith had just set an Ontario junior record for most points in one season and stepped immediately into the NHL to lead all rookies in scoring with 30 goals and 44 assists and was the only first-year player to lead his team in scoring. "Bobby Smith arrived here under tremendous pressure, accepted it and lived up to his advance notices," said Minnesota general manager Lou Nanne. "He's a mature young man and showed it by his ability to handle that pressure. Bobby has the attitude of a winner, an attitude we feel will make the players around him winners." Smith captured the Calder Trophy as the NHL's best rookie in 1979 and, as a member of the Montreal Canadiens, he later captured the Stanley Cup in 1986.

Washington used the second pick to select Ryan Walter, an all-round player scouts compared to Flyers star Bobby Clarke. He was touted as an excellent checker and special-teams expert. His shot made him a dangerous point man and his playmaking skills allowed him to excel as a center on the power play. He was also said to be the best face-off man in the Western Junior Hockey League. But perhaps his strongest asset was his leadership qualities. "The thing that stands out about Ryan Walter," said Washington g.m. Max McNab "is his attitude. He plays a physical, unselfish game, and he has national league anticipation. It's the intangibles that make him so valuable." Prior to his first training camp, Walter had to undergo surgery to repair torn cartilage in his knee. Seven weeks into the season, Walter made his NHL debut notching a goal and an assist. He tallied 56 points (28 goals, 28 assists) in 69 games to finish as the runner-up to Bobby Smith in the Calder Trophy race. It marked only the second time that the winner and runner-up for the Calder were the first and second picks in the previous Amateur Draft (the first time being 1974). Walter went on to score 264 goals while setting up 382 others for 646 career points in 1,003 NHL games. He was also a member of the 1986 Stanley Cup-winning Montreal Canadiens.

Two of the most underrated yet consistent players in the NHL were selected in the 1978 Amateur Draft. The Bruins chose Craig MacTavish, the Eastern Collegiate Athletic Conference's rookie of the year for 1978, as the 153rd pick. MacTavish immediately established himself as an aggressive player and one of the league's best checkers. He would later help the Edmonton Oilers win three Stanley Cup championships and aided the New York Rangers to the Cup in 1994. Although he was respected for his hard work, he will forever be remembered as the last player to play without a helmet, retiring bareheaded in 1997–98. MacTavish had compiled 480 points (213 goals and 267 assists) over a 14-year career.

Seeking leadership, the Vancouver Canucks opted for the extremely consistent Stan Smyl. Smyl had been touted as a proven winner, leading his team to the Memorial Cup in four consecutive years, winning it the final two times. He was marked as a strong leader, a super checker and an average goal scorer by the scouts; however, Smyl remained in the mix until the 40th pick. He eventually led the Canucks to the Stanley Cup finals in 1982, and his career totals of 262 goals, 411 assists and 673 points in 896 games remain club records. On November 3, 1991 Smyl's number 12 jersey was retired by the Canucks.

Family was once again present in the Amateur Draft, as

Darryl Sutter, the second of the biggest brother act to enter the NHL, was drafted by the Chicago Black Hawks 179th overall. Sutter, who played a similar aggressive style as his brother Brian, went on to play eight seasons with the Hawks before retiring to enter a career in coaching. He is currently the head coach of the San Jose Sharks.

Czechoslovakian-born Anton Stastny introduced the NHL to another significant brother act. Anton was selected 198th overall by the Philadelphia Flyers and later played nine years in the NHL after breaking in with the Quebec Nordiques. His two brothers, Marian and Peter, soon joined him as they were signed as free agents by Quebec. Peter is recognized as one of the NHL's most prolific scorers and is the second-leading European scorer in NHL history behind Jari Kurri. Another brother act entered the NHL when the Canadiens chose Dave Hunter as the 17th pick overall. Dave later entered the NHL with the Edmonton Oilers in the 1980 season and would captured three Stanley Cup championships. His brothers Mark and Dale also joined him in the NHL via the draft. Finally, Mike Meeker, son of Toronto great Howie Meeker, was selected 25th overall by the Pittsburgh Penguins in 1978. Meeker appeared in only four NHL games and failed to register a point.

Another Soviet talent was taken this year as the Montreal Canadiens selected Viacheslav Fetisov with the 201st pick. Fetisov was not granted a release from the Soviet Union and was barred from coming to North America to play until political changes during the late 1980s cleared the way for him to enter the NHL. He was the oldest player in the league in 1998.

1978

PICK	TEAM	NAME	DRAFTED FROM	NHL PLAYERS: POS	GP	G	A	PTS	PIM
				NHL GOALTENDERS: POS	GP	W	GA	SO	AVG
FIRST ROUND									
1	MIN	Bobby Smith	Ottawa	C	1077	357	679	1036	917
2	WSH	Ryan Walter	Seattle	C/LW	1003	264	382	646	946
3	ST.L.	Wayne Babych	Portland	RW	519	192	246	438	498
4	VAN	Bill Derlago	Brandon	C	555	189	227	416	247
5	COL	Mike Gillis	Kingston	LW	246	33	43	76	186
6	PHI	Behn Wilson	Kingston	D	601	98	260	358	1480
7	PHI	Ken Linseman	Kingston	C	860	256	551	807	1727
8	MTL	Danny Geoffrion	Cornwall	RW	111	20	32	52	99
9	DET	Willie Huber	Hamilton	D	655	104	217	321	950
10	CHI	Tim Higgins	Ottawa	RW	706	154	198	352	719
11	ATL	Brad Marsh	London	D	1086	23	175	198	1241
12	DET	Brent Peterson	Portland	C	620	72	141	213	484
13	BUF	Larry Playfair	Portland	D	688	26	94	120	1812
14	PHI	Danny Lucas	Sault Ste. Marie	RW	6	1	0	1	0
15	NYI	Steve Tambellini	Lethbridge	C	553	160	150	310	105
16	BOS	Al Secord	Hamilton	LW	766	273	222	495	2093
17	MTL	Dave Hunter	Sudbury	LW	746	133	190	323	918
18	WSH	Tim Coulis	Hamilton	LW	47	4	5	9	138
SECOND ROUND									
19	MIN	Steve Payne	Ottawa	LW	613	228	238	466	435
20	WSH	Paul Mulvey	Portland	LW	225	30	51	81	613
21	TOR	Joel Quenneville	Windsor	D	803	54	136	190	705
22	VAN	Curt Fraser	Victoria	LW	704	193	240	433	1306
23	MIN	Paul MacKinnon	Peterborough	D	147	5	23	28	91
24	MIN	Steve Christoff	Minnesota-Duluth	C	248	77	64	141	108
25	PIT	Mike Meeker	Peterborough	RW	4	0	0	0	5
26	NYR	Don Maloney	Kitchener	LW	765	214	350	564	815
27	COL	Merlin Malinowski	Medicine Hat	C	282	54	111	165	121
28	DET	Glenn Hicks	Flin Flon	LW	108	6	12	18	127
29	CHI	Doug Lecuyer	Portland	LW	126	11	31	42	178
30	MTL	Dale Yakiwchuk	Portland	C					
31	DET	Al Jensen	Hamilton	G	179	95	557	8	3.35
32	BUF	Tony McKegney	Kingston	LW	912	320	319	639	517
33	PHI	Mike Simurda	Kingston	RW					
34	NYI	Randy Johnston	Peterborough	D	4	0	0	0	4
35	BOS	Graeme Nicolson	Cornwall	D	52	2	7	9	60
36	MTL	Ron Carter	Sherbrooke	RW	2	0	0	0	
OTHER ROUNDS									
37	PHI	Gord Salt	Michigan Tech	RW					
38	WSH	Glen Currie	Laval	C	326	39	79	118	100
39	ST.L.	Steve Harrison	Toronto	D					
40	VAN	Stan Smyl	New Westminster	RW	896	262	411	673	1556

PICK	TEAM	NAME	DRAFTED FROM	NHL PLAYERS: POS	GP	G	A	PTS	PIM
				NHL GOALTENDERS: POS	GP	W	GA	SO	AVG
41	COL	Paul Messier	U. of Denver	C	9	0	0	0	4
42	MTL	Richard David	Trois-Rivières	LW	31	4	4	8	10
43	NYR	Ray Markham	Flin Flon	C	14	1	1	2	21
44	NYR	Dean Turner	Michigan	D	35	1	0	1	59
45	WSH	Jay Johnston	Hamilton	D	8	0	0	0	13
46	CHI	Rick Paterson	Cornwall	C	430	50	43	93	136
47	ATL	Tim Bernhardt	Cornwall	G	67	17	267	0	4.27
48	TOR	Mark Kirton	Peterborough	C	266	57	56	113	121
49	BUF	Rob McClanahan	Minnesota-Duluth	C	224	38	63	101	126
50	PHI	Glen Cochrane	Victoria	D	411	17	72	89	1556
51	NYI	Dwayne Lowdermilk	Seattle	D	2	0	1	1	2
52	BOS	Brad Knelson	Lethbridge	D					
53	DET	Doug Derkson	New Westminster	C					
54	MIN	Curt Giles	Minnesota-Duluth	D	895	43	199	242	733
55	WSH	Bengt-Ake Gustafsson	Farjestad Karlstad, SWE	RW	629	196	359	555	196
56	VAN	Harald Luckner	Farjestad Karlstad, SWE	C					
57	VAN	Brad Smith	Sudbury	RW	222	28	34	62	591
58	COL	Dave Watson	Sault Ste. Marie	LW	18	0	1	1	10
59	NYR	Dave Silk	Boston U.	RW	249	54	59	113	271
60	NYR	Andre Dore	Quebec	D	257	14	81	95	261
61	PIT	Shane Pearsall	Ottawa	LW					
62	DET	Bjorne Skaare	Ottawa	C	1	0	0	0	0
63	CHI	Brian Young	New Westminster	D	8	0	2	2	6
64	ATL	Jim MacRae	London	LW					
65	TOR	Bob Parent	Kitchener	G	3	0	15	0	5.62
66	BUF	Mike Gazdic	Sudbury	D					
67	PHI	Russ Wilderman	Seattle	C					
68	BOS	George Buat	Seattle	RW					
69	MTL	Kevin Reeves	Montreal	C					
70	MIN	Roy Kerling	Cornell	LW					
71	WSH	Lou Franceschetti	Niagara Falls	RW	459	59	81	140	747
72	ST.L.	Kevin Willison	Billings	D					
73	COL	Tim Thomlison	Billings	G					
74	COL	Rod Guimont	Lethbridge	RW					
75	PIT	Rob Garner	Toronto	C	1	0	0	0	0
76	NYR	Mike McDougal	Port Huron IHL	RW	61	8	10	18	43
77	L.A.	Paul Mancini	Sault Ste. Marie	LW					
78	DET	Ted Nolan	Sault Ste. Marie	C	78	6	16	22	105
79	CHI	Mark Murphy	Toronto	LW					
80	ATL	Gord Wappel	Regina	D	20	1	1	2	10
81	TOR	Jordy Douglas	Flin Flon	LW	268	76	62	138	160
82	BUF	Randy Ireland	Portland	G	2	0	3		06.000
83	PHI	Brad Tamblyn	U. of Toronto	D					
84	NYI	Greg Hay	Michigan Tech	LW					
85	MTL	Darryl MacLeod	Boston U.	LW					
86	MTL	Mike Boyd	Sault Ste. Marie	D					
87	MIN	Bob Bergloff	Minnesota-Duluth	D	2	0	0		5
88	WSH	Vince Magnan	U. of Denver	LW					
89	ST.L.	Jim Nill	Medicine Hat	RW	524	58	87	145	854
90	VAN	Gerry Minor	Regina	C	140	11	21	32	173
91	COL	John Hynes	Harvard	G					
92	TOR	Mel Hewitt	Calgary	D/LW					
93	NYR	Tom Laidlaw	Northern Michigan	D	705	25	139	164	717
94	L.A.	Doug Keans	Ottawa	G	210	96	666	4	3.51
95	DET	Sylvain Locas	Sherbrooke	C					
96	CHI	Dave Feamster	Colorado College	D	169	13	24	37	154
97	ATL	Greg Meredith	U. of Notre Dame	RW	38	6	4	10	8
98	TOR	Normand Lefebvre	Trois-Rivières	RW					
99	BUF	Cam MacGregor	Cornwall	LW					
100	PHI	Mark Taylor	North Dakota	C	209	42	68	110	73
101	NYI	Kelly Davis	Flin Flon	LW/D					
102	BOS	Jeff Brubaker	Peterborough	LW	178	16	9	25	512
103	MTL	Keith Acton	Peterborough	C	1023	226	358	584	1172
104	MIN	Kim Spencer	Victoria	D					
105	WSH	Mats Hallin	Sodertalje, SWE	LW	152	17	14	31	193
106	ST.L.	Steve Stockman	Cornwall	C					
107	VAN	Dave Ross	Portland	R/LW					
108	COL	Andy Clark	Lake Superior State	D					
109	ST.L.	Paul MacLean	Hull	RW	719	324	349	673	968
110	NYR	Dan Clark	Milwaukee (IHL)	D	4	0	1	1	6
111	L.A.	Don Waddell	Northern Michigan	D	1	0	0	0	0
112	DET	Wes George	Saskatoon	LW					
113	CHI	Dave Mancuso	Windsor	D					
114	ATL	Dave Hindmarch	U. of Alberta	RW	99	21	17	38	25
115	TOR	John Scammel	Lethbridge	D					
116	BUF	Dan Eastman	Saginaw (IHL)	C					
117	PHI	Mike Ewanouski	Boston College	RW					
118	NYI	Richard Pepin	Laval	RW					
119	BOS	Murray Skinner	Lake Superior State	G					
120	MIL	Jim Lawson	Brown	RW					
121	MIN	Mike Cotter	Bowling Green	D					
122	WSH	Rick Sirois	Milwaukee (IHL)	G					
123	ST.L.	Denis Houle	Hamilton	RW					
124	VAN	Steve O'Neill	Providence	LW					
125	COL	John Olver	Michigan	RW/C					
126	PHI	Jerry Price	Portland	G					
127	NYR	Greg Kostenko	Ohio State	D					

1978 *continued*

PICK	TEAM	NAME	DRAFTED FROM	NHL PLAYERS: POS / NHL GOALTENDERS: POS	GP	G / W	A / GA	PTS / SO	PIM / AVG
128	L.A.	Rob Mierkalns	Hamilton	C					
129	DET	John Barrett	Windsor	D	488	20	77	97	604
130	CHI	Sandy Ross	Colgate	D					
131	ATL	Dave Morrison	Calgary	RW					
132	TOR	Kevin Reinhart	Kitchener	D					
133	BUF	Eric Strobel	Minnesota-Duluth	C					
134	PHI	Darre Switzer	Medicine Hat	D					
135	NYI	Dave Cameron	University of PEI	C	168	25	28	53	238
136	BOS	Richard Hehir	Boston College	C					
137	MTL	Larry Landon	RPI	RW	9	0	0	0	2
138	MIN	Brent Gogol	Billings	D					
139	WSH	Denis Pomerleau	Trois-Rivieres	RW					
140	ST.L.	Tony Meagher	Boston U.	RW					
141	VAN	Charlie Antetomaso	Boston College	D					
142	COL	Kevin Krook	Regina	D	3	0	0	0	2
143	ST.L.	Rick Simpson	Medicine Hat	C/RW					
144	NYR	Brian McDavid	Kitchener	D					
145	L.A.	Ric Scully	Brown	LW					
146	DET	Jim Malazdrewicz	St. Boniface Jr. A	LW					
147	CHI	Mark Locken	Niagara Falls	G					
148	ATL	Doug Todd	Michigan	RW					
149	TOR	Mike Waghorne	New Hampshire	D					
150	BUF	Eugene O'Sullivan	Calgary	C					
151	PHI	Greg Francis	St. Lawrence U.	D					
152	NYI	Paul Joswiak	Minnesota-Duluth	G					
153	BOS	Craig MacTavish	University of Lowell	C	1093	213	267	480	891
154	MTL	Kevin Constantine	RPI	G					
155	MIN	Mark Seide	Bloomington Jr.	LW/D					
156	WSH	Barry Heard	London	G					
157	ST.L.	Jim Lockhurst	Kingston	G					
158	VAN	Richard Martens	New Westminster	G					
159	COL	Jeff Jensen	Lake Superior State	LW					
160	ST.L.	Bob Froese	Niagara Falls	G	242	128	694	13	3.10
161	NYR	Mark Rodrigues	Yale	G					
162	L.A.	Brad Thiessen	Toronto	C					
163	DET	Geoff Shaw	Hamilton	RW					
164	CHI	Glenn Van	Colorado College	D					
165	ATL	Mark Green	Sherbrooke	C					
166	TOR	Laurie Cuvelier	St. Francis Xavier	D					
167	PHI	Rick Berard	St. Mary's U.	LW/D					
168	PHI	Don Lucia	U. of Notre Dame	D					
169	NYI	Scott Cameron	U. of Notre Dame	D					
170	ST.L.	Dan Lerg	Michigan	C					
171	MTL	John Swan	McGill University	C					
172	WSH	Mark Toffolo	Port Huron IHL	D					
173	ST.L.	Risto Siltanen	Ilves Tampere, FIN	D	562	90	265	355	266
174	COL	Bo Ericson	AIK Solna, SWE	D					
175	ST.L.	Dan Hermansson	Karlskoga, SWE	LW					
176	NYR	Steve Weeks	Northern Michigan	G	290	111	989	5	3.74
177	L.A.	Jim Armstrong	Clarkson	LW/C					
178	DET	Carl Van Harrewyn	New Westminster	D/RW					
179	CHI	Darryl Sutter	Lethbridge	LW	406	161	118	279	288
180	ATL	Robert Sullivan	New Haven/Toledo (IHL)	C/LW					
181	ST.L.	Jean-Francois Boutin	Verdun	LW					
182	PHI	Mark Berge	North Dakota	D					
183	PHI	Ken Moore	Clarkson	G					
184	NYI	Christer Lowdahl	Oreboro, SWE	C/LW					
185	ST.L.	John Sullivan	Providence	RW					
186	MTL	Daniel Metivier	Hull	RW					
187	WSH	Paul Hogan	Regina	LW					
188	ST.L.	Serge Menard	Montreal	RW					
189	WSH	Steve Barger	Boston College	RW					
190	COL	Jari Viitala	Ilves Tampere, FIN	C/LW					
191	ST.L.	Don Boyd	RPI	D/C					
192	NYR	Pierre Daigneault	St. Laurent College	LW					
193	L.A.	Claude Larochelle	Hull	C					
194	DET	Ladislav Svozil	TJ Vitkovice, TCH	LW					
195	PHI	Jim Olson	St. Paul Jr. A	C					
196	ATL	Bernhard Englbrecht	Landshut, FRG	G					
197	ST.L.	Paul Stasiuk	Providence	LW					
198	PHI	Anton Stastny	Slovan Bratislava, TCH	LW	*Re-entered Draft in 1979*				
199	NYI	Gunnar Persson	Brynas Gavle, SWE	D					
200	ST.L.	Gerd Truntschka	Landshut, FRG	C/LW					
201	MTL	Viacheslav Fetisov	CSKA Moscow, USSR	D	*Re-entered Draft in 1983*				
202	WSH	Rod Pacholsuk	Michigan	D					
203	ST.L.	Viktor Shkurdyuk	SKA Leningrad, USSR	RW					
204	COL	Ulf Zetterstrom	Kiruna, SWE	LW					
205	ST.L.	Carl Bloomberg	St. Louis U.	G					
206	NYR	Chris McLaughlin	Dartmouth	D					
207	ST.L.	Terry Kitching	St. Louis U.	LW					
208	DET	Tom Bailey	Kingston	RW					
209	ST.L.	Brian O'Connor	Boston U.	D					
210	ST.L.	Brian Crombeen	Kingston	D					
211	ST.L.	Mike Pidgeon	Oshawa	C					
212	MTL	Jeff Mars	Michigan	RW					
213	WSH	Wes Jarvis	Windsor	C	237	31	55	86	98
214	ST.L.	John Cochrane	Harvard	RW					

PICK	TEAM	NAME	DRAFTED FROM	NHL PLAYERS: POS / NHL GOALTENDERS: POS	GP	G / W	A / GA	PTS / SO	PIM / AVG
215	WSH	Ray Irwin	Oshawa	D					
216	ST.L.	Joe Casey	Boston College	D					
217	NYR	Todd Johnson	Boston U.	C					
218	ST.L.	Jim Farrell	Princeton	C					
219	DET	Larry Lozinski	Flin Flon	G	30	6	105	0	4.32
220	ST.L.	Frank Johnson	Providence	D					
221	ST.L.	Blair Wheeler	Yale	D					
222	MTL	Greg Tignanelli	Northern Michigan	LW					
223	NYR	Dan McCarthy	Sudbury	C	5	4	0	4	4
224	DET	Randy Betty	New Westminster	LW					
225	MTL	George Goulakos	St. Lawrence U.	LW					
226	DET	Brian Crawley	St. Lawrence U.	D					
227	MTL	Ken Moodie	Colgate	RW					
228	DET	Doug Feasby	Toronto	C					
229	MTL	Serge Leblanc	Vermont	D					
230	MTL	Bob Magnuson	Merrimack	C					
231	MTL	Chris Nilan	Northeastern	RW	688	110	115	225	3043
232	MTL	Rick Wilson	St. Lawrence U.	G					
233	MTL	Louis Sleigher	Chicoutimi	RW	194	46	53	99	146
234	MTL	Doug Robb	Billings	RW					

1979

A new era for the NHL began in 1979. The amalgamation of the WHA with the NHL eliminated its direct competition as four WHA teams joined the NHL. The convergence called for a complete restructuring of the draft beginning with the name officially being changed to Entry Draft rather than the Amateur Draft. Since much of the WHA's talent would be eligible for drafting, it would be inaccurate to refer to them as amateurs since they had professional experience. In addition, it was decided that the NHL would include the drafting of underage talent for the first time since 1974. However, an ongoing debate regarding eligibility restrictions forced the draft to be delayed. Finally, it was agreed that the age of eligibility would be 20 years old, but that NHL teams would be able to draft 19-year-olds if they so chose. All 19-year-olds who were involved with the WHA would be included in the drafting pot.

However, if a team selected a 19-year-old, that player would have to remain on the roster or be immediately offered back to the junior club he was with prior to his involvement in the WHA. If the junior club refused to repossess the player then the team could send him to the minors. The 1979 draft format would see the existing 17 NHL clubs choose according to the reverse order of standing while the new WHA clubs would fill the last four drafting seeds. Each team was to pick for six rounds for a maximum total of 126 players selected.

On August 9, 1979 the first NHL Entry Draft was conducted behind closed doors at Montreal's Queen Elizabeth Hotel. The drafting pool had never been bigger or deeper and it boasted the best talent yet available in an NHL draft. "Usually, a club must commit itself to taking the best athlete available," said Washington general manager Max McNab. "This year, with the inclusion of the underage players, it looks like one of the best drafts in history. A bottom club, drafting by position, isn't going to get hurt, because so many of this crop look like solid NHL players." It was believed that the WHA underage players would be the focus for the first picks, with a particular emphasis on defensemen. The last-place Colorado Rockies lived up to the expectations as they selected defenseman Rob Ramage, a First Team All-Star with the WHA's Birmingham Bulls. At 20 years and five months, Ramage remains the oldest player ever selected first.

Ramage spent 15 years in the NHL, capturing the Stanley Cup with the 1989 Calgary Flames and the 1993 Montreal Canadiens. Playing with eight teams throughout his career, he was one of the most traveled veterans in the NHL, post-

ing 564 points in 1,044 games. "It was a good decision to turn pro a year early," said Ramage of his WHA experience. "I had the chance for an immediate step on the way to the NHL, to play in a good league where I improved much more quickly than I would have in junior."

Clearly the best defensive talent acquired in the draft was 19-year-old Raymond Bourque, selected eighth overall by the Boston Bruins on a draft pick they had acquired from the Los Angeles Kings. Bourque immediately joined the Bruins for the 1979–80 season and set a new NHL record for most points by a rookie defenseman with 65 (17 goals, 48 assists) in 80 games. He captured the Calder Trophy as rookie of the year and was named to the first of 17 consecutive all-star teams. Today, Bourque is a five-time Norris Trophy winner as the NHL's best defenseman and is recognized as one of the greatest players in NHL history. "Oh, he's going to be a phenomenal hockey player," said Bruin veteran Brad Park during Bourque's first season. "There's no doubt in my mind that he's going to make one heck of a mark on the game. He's the finest rookie defenseman I've ever seen come into the league."

Two of the best offensive players to appear in the NHL were also selected in the 1979 draft, as Mike Gartner and Michel Goulet were chosen fourth and 20th respectively. Both were underage products of the WHA. Goulet went on to record 548 goals and 1,152 points. Gartner has long been known as one of the most explosive skaters in the NHL and is also the only player to record 30 or more goals in 15 consecutive NHL seasons. He is one of only five players to score more than 700 career goals. Remarkably, neither Gartner nor Goulet ever received a major NHL award nor have they played on a Stanley Cup winner.

The historical focus of the 1979 Entry Draft falls upon the actions of the Edmonton Oilers, as they quickly built one of the most powerful dynasties in hockey history. Allowed to reclaim Wayne Gretzky and an underage junior prior to the draft, the Oilers then managed to obtain three of the most talented and underrated players available in the draft. With their first pick, the Oilers opted for defenseman Kevin Lowe as the 21st choice. "He's smart and he'll learn what you teach him," said Lowe's junior coach Rene Drolet. "Everybody has respect for Kevin. He's a complete player." Lowe has enjoyed 19 seasons as one of the most effective defensive blueliners in the NHL.

The second pick of the Oilers is deemed to be the biggest steal from any Entry Draft as the Oilers selected Mark Messier 48th overall. Messier has gone on to become the fifth-highest point scorer in NHL history, after beginning his pro career at age 18 when he joined the WHA in 1978–79. When the Oilers drafted him Glen Sather commented: "This is a boy who jumped all the way from Tier II to the pros in one season and didn't look terribly out of place. I think he'll make a hell of a choice for us." Messier joined the Oilers as the second-youngest player in the NHL behind teammate Wayne Gretzky.

As an aggressive physical force combined with tremendous offensive talent, Messier set the mold for the NHL power forward. "Name me one other team that's got a third-rounder playing regularly," said Sather. "He's better than some number-one picks." Messier has gone on to collect the Conn Smythe Trophy and on two occasions each, the Hart Trophy as MVP and the Lester B. Pearson Award as NHL Players' Association MVP. He also has been named to five NHL All-Star teams.

The third selection of the Oilers in 1979 was used to obtain forward Glenn Anderson, picked 69th overall. Anderson was a virtual unknown who had spent the 1978–79 season at the University of Denver where he finished as the team's leading scorer. "I remember when I became really sold on him," recalled Oilers assistant coach Bryan Watson. "It was at the Olympics in Lake Placid (in 1980). Canada was playing Poland and I think they might have lost without Anderson. He set up good scoring chances four times on one shift." Anderson became known for his reckless style of offensive play just as he has become known as one of the most naturally gifted snipers in NHL history. With a career record of 498 goals and 601 assists, Anderson's 1,099 points rank him among the NHL's all-time leaders.

Lowe, Messier and Anderson all played integral roles in the Edmonton dynasty, helping the Oilers capture five Stanley Cup championships. The three veterans were reunited with the New York Rangers in 1994, as they led the club to its first Stanley Cup championship in 54 years.

As the league expanded in 1979, so did the NHL's brother acts as Duane Sutter was selected 17th overall by the New York Islanders. It marked the third consecutive year that a Sutter brother entered the NHL via the Entry Draft. The Hunter family also became more prevalent within the league as Dale joined the Quebec Nordiques as the 41st choice in the draft. Known for his incredibly aggressive play, Hunter holds the second-highest penalty-minute total in league history behind Tiger Williams.

The 1979 Entry Draft also marked the first significant ground-breaking by a U.S.-born player. Neal Broten, a 5'8", 165-pound product of the University of Minnesota, was the 42nd player taken in the draft, selected by the Minnesota North Stars. Broten entered the NHL in 1980–81 after capturing the NCAA title. He had been named the first recipient of the Hobey Baker Award as the top collegiate player in the United States.

A year earlier, Broten had won an Olympic gold medal with the "Miracle on Ice" U.S. Olympic team. He went on to become the first U.S.-born talent to collect 100 points in a season with 105 in 1985–86 on 29 goals and 76 assists and was the NHL's all-time leading American born scorer until being surpassed by Joe Mullen. "With every point he scores, he becomes more and more of an inspiration for American kids," North Stars assistant g.m. John Mariucci said of Broten. "We talk about the Russians, Finns, Swedes and Americans, but face it, nobody can touch the Canadians for the number of good players. But it doesn't hurt to shoot for them and Neal is leading the way."

An historical footnote to the 1979 draft was the choice of previously drafted Anton Stastny, making him the first player to be selected a second time as a result of re-entering the draft. Stastny was the 83rd player chosen and the fourth pick of the Quebec Nordiques.

1979

PICK	TEAM	NAME	DRAFTED FROM	NHL PLAYERS: POS NHL GOALTENDERS: POS	GP GP	G W	A GA	PTS SO	PIM AVG
FIRST ROUND									
1	COL	Rob Ramage	London	D	1044	139	425	564	2226
2	ST.L.	Perry Turnbull	Portland	C	608	188	163	351	1245
3	DET	Mike Foligno	Sudbury	RW	1018	355	372	727	2049
4	WSH	Mike Gartner	Niagara Falls	RW	1432	708	627	1335	1159
5	VAN	Rick Vaive	Sherbrooke	RW	876	441	347	788	1445
6	MIN	Craig Hartsburg	Sault Ste. Marie	D	570	98	315	413	818
7	CHI	Keith Brown	Portland	D	876	68	274	342	916
8	BOS	Ray Bourque	Verdun	D	1372	375	1036	1411	1033
9	TOR	Laurie Boschman	Brandon	C	1009	229	348	577	2265
10	MIN	Tom McCarthy	Oshawa	LW	460	178	221	399	330
11	BUF	Mike Ramsey	Minnesota-Duluth	D	1070	79	266	345	1012

1979 *continued*

PICK	TEAM	NAME	DRAFTED FROM	POS	GP	G	A	PTS	PIM
12	ATL	Paul Reinhart	Kitchener	D	648	133	426	559	277
13	NYR	Doug Sulliman	Kitchener	RW	631	160	168	328	175
14	PHI	Brian Propp	Brandon	LW	1016	425	579	1004	830
15	BOS	Brad McCrimmon	Brandon	D	1222	81	322	403	1416
16	L.A.	Jay Wells	Kingston	D	1098	47	216	263	2359
17	NYI	Duane Sutter	Lethbridge	RW	731	139	203	342	1333
18	HFD	Ray Allison	Brandon	RW	238	64	93	157	223
19	WPG	Jimmy Mann	Sherbrooke	RW	293	10	20	30	895
20	QUE	Michel Goulet	Quebec	LW	1089	548	604	1152	825
21	EDM	Kevin Lowe	Quebec	D	1254	84	347	431	1498

SECOND ROUND

PICK	TEAM	NAME	DRAFTED FROM	POS	GP	G	A	PTS	PIM
22	PHI	Blake Wesley	Portland	D	298	18	46	64	486
23	ATL	Mike Perovich	Brandon	D					
24	WSH	Errol Rausse	Seattle	LW	31	7	3	10	0
25	NYI	Tomas Jonsson	MoDo Ornskoldsvik, SWE	D	552	85	259	344	482
26	VAN	Brent Ashton	Saskatoon	LW	998	284	345	629	635
27	MTL	Gaston Gingras	Hamilton	D	476	61	174	235	161
28	CHI	Tim Trimper	Peterborough	LW	190	30	36	66	153
29	L.A.	Dean Hopkins	London	RW	223	23	51	74	306
30	L.A.	Mark Hardy	Montreal	D	915	62	306	368	1293
31	PIT	Paul Marshall	Brantford	LW	95	15	18	33	17
32	BUF	Lindy Ruff	Lethbridge	D/LW	691	105	195	300	1264

Goaltender rows (POS GP W GA SO AVG):

PICK	TEAM	NAME	DRAFTED FROM	POS	GP	W	GA	SO	AVG
33	ATL	Pat Riggin	London	G	350	153	1135	11	3.43
34	NYR	Ed Hospodar	Ottawa	D	450	17	51	68	1314
35	PHI	Pelle Lindbergh	AIK Solna, SWE	G	157	87	503	7	3.30
36	BOS	Doug Morrison	Lethbridge	RW	23	7	3	10	15
37	MTL	Mats Naslund	Brynas Gavle, SWE	LW	651	251	383	634	111
38	NYI	Billy Carroll	London	C	322	30	54	84	113
39	HFD	Stu G. Smith	Peterborough	D	77	2	10	12	95
40	WPG	Dave Christian	North Dakota	RW	1009	340	433	773	284
41	QUE	Dale Hunter	Sudbury	C	1345	321	688	1009	3446
42	MIN	Neal Broten	Minnesota-Duluth	C	1099	289	634	923	569

OTHER ROUNDS

PICK	TEAM	NAME	DRAFTED FROM	POS	GP	G	A	PTS	PIM
43	MTL	Craig Levie	Edmonton	D	183	22	53	75	177
44	MTL	Guy Carbonneau	Chicoutimi	C	1175	246	385	631	753
45	DET	Jody Gage	Kitchener	RW	68	14	15	29	26
46	DET	Boris Fistric	New Westminster	D					
47	VAN	Ken Ellacott	Peterborough	G	12	2	41	0	4.43
48	EDM	Mark Messier	St. Albert Jr. A	C	1354	597	1015	1612	1654
49	CHI	Bill Gardner	Peterborough	C	380	73	115	188	68
50	L.A.	John Paul Kelly	New Westminster	LW	400	54	70	124	366
51	TOR	Norm Aubin	Verdun	C	69	18	13	31	30
52	PIT	Bennett Wolf	Kitchener	D	30	0	1	1	133
53	BUF	Mark Robinson	Victoria	D					
54	ATL	Tim Hunter	Seattle	RW	815	62	76	138	3146
55	BUF	Jacques Cloutier	Trois-Rivieres	G	255	82	778	3	3.64
56	PHI	Lindsay Carson	Billings	C	373	66	80	146	524
57	BOS	Keith Crowder	Peterborough	RW	662	223	271	494	1344
58	MTL	Rick Wamsley	Brantford	G	407	204	1287	12	3.34
59	NYI	Rollie Melanson	Windsor	G	291	129	995	6	3.63
60	HFD	Don Nachbaur	Billings	C	223	23	46	69	465
61	WPG	Bill Whelton	North Dakota	D	2	0	0	0	0
62	QUE	Lee Norwood	Oshawa	D	503	58	153	211	1099
63	MIN	Kevin Maxwell	North Dakota	C	66	6	15	21	61
64	COL	Steve Peters	Oshawa	C	2	0	1	1	0
65	ST.L.	Bob Crawford	Cornwall	RW	246	71	71	142	72
66	DET	John Ogrodnick	New Westminster	LW	928	402	425	827	260
67	WSH	Harvie Pocza	Billings	LW	3	0	0	0	2
68	VAN	Art Rutland	Sault Ste. Marie	C					
69	EDM	Glenn Anderson	U. of Denver	RW	1129	498	601	1099	1120
70	CHI	Lou Begin	Sherbrooke	LW					
71	L.A.	John Gibson	Niagara Falls	D	48	0	2	2	120
72	TOR	Vince Tremblay	Quebec	G	58	12	223	1	4.80
73	PIT	Brian Cross	Brantford	D					
74	BUF	Gilles Hamel	Laval	LW	519	127	147	274	276
75	ATL	Jim Peplinski	Toronto	RW	711	161	263	424	1467
76	NYR	Pat Conacher	Saskatoon	LW	521	63	76	139	235
77	PHI	Don Gillen	Brandon	RW	35	2	4	6	22
78	BOS	Larry Melnyk	New Westminster	D	432	11	63	74	686
79	MTL	Dave Orleski	New Westminster	LW	2	0	0	0	0
80	NYI	Tim Lockridge	Brandon	D					
81	HFD	Ray Neufeld	Edmonton	RW	595	157	200	357	816
82	WPG	Pat Daley	Montreal	RW	12	1	0	1	13
83	QUE	Anton Stastny	Slovan Bratislava, TCH	LW	650	252	384	636	150
84	EDM	Maxwell Kostovich	Portland	LW					
85	COL	Gary Dillon	Toronto	C	13	1	1	2	29
86	ST.L.	Mark Reeds	Peterborough	RW	365	45	114	159	135
87	DET	Joe Paterson	London	LW	291	19	37	56	829
88	WSH	Tim Tookey	Portland	C	106	22	36	58	71
89	VAN	Dirk Graham	Regina	L/RW	772	219	270	489	917
90	MIN	Jim Dobson	Portland	RW	12	0	0	0	6
91	CHI	Lowell Loveday	Kingston	D					
92	L.A.	Jim Brown	U. of Notre Dame	D	3	0	1	1	5
93	TOR	Frank Nigro	London	C	68	8	18	26	39
94	PIT	Nick Ricci	Niagara Falls	G	19	7	79	0	4.36
95	BUF	Alan Haworth	Sherbrooke	C	524	189	211	400	425
96	ATL	Brad Kempthorne	Brandon	C/RW					
97	NYR	Dan Makuch	Clarkson	RW					
98	PHI	Thomas Eriksson	Djurgarden, SWE	D	208	22	76	98	107
99	BOS	Marco Baron	Montreal	G	86	34	292	1	3.63
100	MTL	Yvan Joly	Ottawa	RW	2	0	0	0	0
101	NYI	Glenn Duncan	Toronto	LW					
102	HFD	Mark Renaud	Niagara Falls	D	152	6	50	56	86
103	WPG	Thomas Steen	Leksand, SWE	C	950	264	553	817	753
104	QUE	Pierre Lacroix	Trois-Rivieres	D	274	24	108	132	197
105	EDM	Mike Toal	Portland	C	3	0	0	0	0
106	COL	Bob Attwell	Peterborough	RW	22	1	5	6	0
107	ST.L.	Gilles Leduc	Verdun	LW					
108	DET	Carmine Cirella	Peterborough	LW					
109	WSH	Greg Theberge	Peterborough	D	153	15	63	78	73
110	VAN	Shane Swan	Sudbury	D					
111	MIN	Brian Gualazzi	Sault Ste. Marie	D					
112	CHI	Doug Crossman	Ottawa	D	914	105	359	464	534
113	L.A.	Jay MacFarlane	Wisconsin	D					
114	TOR	Bill McCreary Jr.	Colgate	RW	12	1	0	1	4
115	PIT	Marc Chorney	North Dakota	D	210	8	27	35	209
116	BUF	Rick Knickle	Brandon	G	14	7	44	0	3.74
117	ATL	Glenn Johnson	U. of Denver	C					
118	NYR	Stan Adams	Niagara Falls	C					
119	PHI	Gord Williams	Lethbridge	RW	2	0	0	0	2
120	BOS	Mike Krushelnyski	Montreal	LW/C	897	241	328	569	699
121	MTL	Greg Moffett	New Hampshire	LW					
122	NYI	John Gibb	Bowling Green	D					
123	HFD	Dave McDonald	Brandon	LW					
124	WPG	Tim Watters	Michigan Tech	D	741	26	151	177	1289
125	QUE	Scott McGeown	Toronto	D					
126	EDM	Blair Barnes	Windsor	RW	1	0	0	0	0

1980

In 1980, the Entry Draft was transformed into a public event. For the first time since its inception, the Montreal Forum hosted the Entry Draft and the event was attended by more than 2,500 hockey fans. As was decided prior in 1979, all junior players aged 18 would be eligible for drafting by NHL clubs in 1980. Although the drafting of underage juniors was viewed as controversial, player agent Art Kaminsky wanted to know: "Why should a player who has the ability to play pro at 18 be held back two years? Both Bobby Orr and Bobby Hull were in the NHL at age 18, so why all the fuss?"

Junior organizations believed that underage drafting was ruining their leagues, while NHL clubs believed that it provided an advantage to the strong teams since they could afford to select underage talent and provide them with the necessary time to mature without any risk of losing them to a rival club. It was thought that restrictions should be placed on the teams who draft underage junior talent as was previously practiced in 1974. Therefore, all underage draftees would be exempt from being farmed to minor-league affiliates. If an underage player did not make the NHL roster he must be returned to his junior club.

Montreal had acquired the first pick from the Colorado Rockies in a 1976 trade and used it to select Doug Wickenheiser. Though he was the top prospect from the Western Hockey League, the Canadiens were criticized for this choice since it was expected that Montreal native Denis Savard would be the preferred pick. To make matters worse, Wickenheiser's career failed to reap the rewards that was expected, while Savard (selected third overall by Chicago) developed into one of the NHL's premiere performers. He collected 75 points (28 goals, 47 assists) in his rookie campaign with the Black Hawks, setting club records for rookie points and assists. In his sophomore year, Savard joined Bobby Hull as the second player in Black Hawks history to record over 100 points in one season, posting 32 goals and 87 assists for 119 points. Savard went on to record 473 goals and 865 assists for 1,338 points to rank among the top scorers in NHL history. After his first

season, his potential was critiqued by *The Hockey News*: "He brings to the rink the French flair for excitement. His moves are Mikita-like. But just as Hull could, this 20-year-old center can suddenly lift people from their seats." Referred to as a "hockey magic act," Savard was recognized as one of hockey's most agile skaters and slickest playmakers. He was eventually traded to the Canadiens in 1990, but although he was a member of a Stanley Cup champion in Montreal in 1993 he was no longer the dynamic playmaker he had been in Chicago.

The Los Angeles Kings and the Black Hawks walked away from the 1980 Entry Draft looking similar to the Edmonton Oilers in 1979, as they both were able to claim two of the best players in the draft as fourth-round selections. Highly underrated forwards Bernie Nicholls, the 73rd player selected, and Steve Larmer, picked 120th overall, developed into two of the most potent offensive forces in the NHL. Both Nicholls and Larmer returned to their respective junior clubs for the 1980–81 season and both graduated to the AHL the following year. After recording 55 goals in 77 games in the minors, Nicholls was promoted to the Kings lineup where he went on to become one of the club's premier scorers. His 70 goals and 150 points in 1988–89 rank among the greatest single-season totals in league history and his career totals rank among the NHL's all-time leaders. Larmer became a regular with the Black Hawks in 1982–83 and complemented Savard at right wing. With a 90-point performance (43 goals, 47 assists) in his first year, he captured the Calder Trophy as rookie of the year. Larmer collected 441 goals and 571 assists during his career, but will best be known as one of the NHL's ironmen, appearing in 884 consecutive games.

The Edmonton Oilers managed to further build their dynasty in 1980 by acquiring defenseman Paul Coffey and Finnish sniper Jari Kurri with the eighth and 69th picks. Coffey has become the highest-scoring defensemen in the history of the NHL and one of the top scorers of all-time. He has collected over 100 points in five different seasons and captured the Norris Trophy as the league's best defenseman three times. Kurri established himself as the top-scoring non-North American-born player in NHL history. Although Europeans had been participating in the NHL for quite some time, there were relatively few Finnish players, which put Kurri in a position to pioneer the future of Finnish prominence in the NHL.

"When a Swede comes to North America he has something to shoot for. He can look at Borje Salming or Ulf Nilsson or Anders Hedberg and feel he was in the same company as them in Sweden," said player agent Don Baizley. "But for a Finn, there's been nobody who has really made it. Jari has the potential to break through the barrier." With a Lady Byng Trophy, five Stanley Cup championships, twice a runner-up for the Art Ross Trophy and more points than any other European player, Kurri has paved the way for many international stars.

The 1980 Entry Draft continued to follow the trend of family ties as Brent Sutter was drafted 17th overall to join three of his brothers in the NHL. Two other brothers, Kurt and Scot Kleinendorst, were selected as the third and fourth picks of the New York Rangers. Scot was the only brother to play in the NHL. The other trend that was further explored in 1980 was the drafting of U.S. talent, as New York City native Brian Mullen was taken from the University of Wisconsin. Mullen was chosen 128th overall by the Winnipeg Jets. Compiling 622 points (260 goals and

362) in 11 seasons, he became recognized as another significant U.S.-born hockey talent in the NHL.

1980

PICK	TEAM	NAME	DRAFTED FROM	NHL PLAYERS: POS NHL GOALTENDERS: POS	GP GP	G W	A GA	PTS SO	PIM AVG
FIRST ROUND									
1	MTL	Doug Wickenheiser	Regina	C	556	111	165	276	286
2	WPG	Dave Babych	Portland	D	1154	140	575	715	948
3	CHI	Denis Savard	Montreal	C	1196	473	865	1338	1336
4	L.A.	Larry Murphy	Peterborough	D	1397	265	838	1103	985
5	WSH	Darren Veitch	Regina	D	511	48	209	257	296
6	EDM	Paul Coffey	Kitchener	D					
7	VAN	Rick Lanz	Oshawa	D	569	65	221	286	448
8	HFD	Fred Arthur	Cornwall	D	80	1	8	9	49
9	PIT	Mike Bullard	Brantford	C	727	329	345	674	703
10	L.A.	Jim Fox	Ottawa	RW	578	186	293	479	143
11	DET	Mike Blaisdell	Regina	RW	343	70	84	154	166
12	ST.L.	Rik Wilson	Kingston	D	251	25	65	90	220
13	CGY	Denis Cyr	Montreal	RW	193	41	43	84	36
14	NYR	Jim Malone	Toronto	C					
15	CHI	Jerome Dupont	Toronto	D	214	7	29	36	468
16	MIN	Brad Palmer	Victoria	LW	168	32	38	70	58
17	NYI	Brent Sutter	Red Deer Jr. A	C	1111	363	466	829	1054
18	BOS	Barry Pederson	Victoria	C	701	238	416	654	472
19	COL	Paul Gagne	Windsor	LW	390	110	101	211	127
20	BUF	Steve Patrick	Brandon	RW	250	40	68	108	242
21	PHI	Mike Stothers	Kingston	D	30	0	2	2	65
SECOND ROUND									
22	COL	Joe Ward	Seattle	C	4	0	0	0	2
23	WPG	Moe Mantha	Toronto	D	656	81	289	370	501
24	QUE	Normand Rochefort	Quebec	D	598	39	119	158	570
25	TOR	Craig Muni	Kingston	D	819	28	119	148	775
26	TOR	Bob McGill	Victoria	D	705	17	55	72	1766
27	MTL	Ric Nattress	Brantford	D	536	29	135	164	377
28	CHI	Steve Ludzik	Niagara Falls	C	424	46	93	139	333
29	HFD	Michel Galarneau	Hull	C	78	7	10	17	34
30	CHI	Ken Solheim	Medicine Hat	LW	135	19	20	39	34
31	CGY	Tony Curtale	Brantford	D	2	0	0	0	0
32	CGY	Kevin LaVallee	Brantford	LW	366	110	125	235	85
33	L.A.	Greg Terrion	Brantford	LW	561	93	150	243	339
34	L.A.	Dave Morrison	Peterborough	RW	39	3	3	6	4
35	NYR	Mike Allison	Sudbury	LW	499	102	166	268	630
36	CHI	Len Dawes	Victoria	D					
37	MIN	Don Beaupre	Sudbury	G	667	268	2151	17	3.45
38	NYI	Kelly Hrudey	Medicine Hat	G	677	271	2174	17	3.43
39	CGY	Steve Konroyd	Oshawa	D	895	41	195	236	863
40	MTL	John Chabot	Hull	C	508	84	228	312	85
41	BUF	Mike Moller	Lethbridge	RW	134	15	28	43	41
42	PHI	Jay Fraser	Ottawa	LW					
OTHER ROUNDS									
43	TOR	Fred Boimistruck	Cornwall	D	83	4	14	18	45
44	WPG	Murray Eaves	Michigan	C	57	4	13	17	9
45	MTL	John Newberry	Nanaimo	C	22	0	4	4	6
46	DET	Mark Osborne	Niagara Falls	LW	919	212	319	531	1152
47	WSH	Don Miele	Providence	RW					
48	EDM	Shawn Babcock	Windsor	RW					
49	VAN	Andy Schliebener	Peterborough	D	84	2	11	13	74
50	HFD	Mickey Volcan	North Dakota	D	162	8	33	41	146
51	PIT	Randy Boyd	Ottawa	D	257	20	67	87	328
52	L.A.	Steve Bozek	Northern Michigan	LW	641	164	167	331	309
53	MIN	Randy Velischek	Providence	D	509	21	76	97	401
54	ST.L.	Jim Pavese	Kitchener	D	328	13	44	57	689
55	WSH	Torrie Robertson	Victoria	LW	442	49	99	148	1751
56	BUF	Sean McKenna	Sherbrooke	RW	414	82	80	162	181
57	CHI	Troy Murray	St. Albert Jr. A	C	915	230	354	584	875
58	CHI	Marcel Frere	Billings	LW					
59	NYI	Dave Simpson	London	C					
60	BOS	Tom Fergus	Peterborough	C	726	235	346	581	499
61	MTL	Craig Ludwig	North Dakota	D	1176	36	178	214	1350
62	BUF	Jay North	Bloomington-Jefferson H.S.	C					
63	PHI	Paul Mercier	Sudbury	D					
64	COL	Rick LaFerriere	Peterborough	G	1	0	1	0	3.00
65	WPG	Guy Fournier	Shawinigan	C					
66	QUE	Jay Miller	New Hampshire	LW	446	40	44	84	1723
67	CHI	Carey Wilson	Dartmouth	C	552	169	258	427	314
68	NYI	Monty Trottier	Billings	C					
69	EDM	Jari Kurri	Jokerit Helsinki, FIN	RW	1251	601	797	1398	545
70	VAN	Marc Crawford	Cornwall	LW	176	19	31	50	229
71	HFD	Kevin McClelland	Niagara Falls	RW	588	68	112	180	1672
72	PIT	Tony Feltrin	Victoria	D	48	3	3	6	65
73	L.A.	Bernie Nicholls	Kingston	C	1117	475	732	1207	1288
74	TOR	Stewart Gavin	Toronto	LW	768	130	155	285	584
75	ST.L.	Bob Brooke	Yale	C	447	69	97	166	520
76	CGY	Marc Roy	Trois-Rivieres	RW					
77	NYR	Kurt Kleinendorst	Providence	C					
78	CHI	Brian Shaw	Portland	RW					

1980 continued

PICK	TEAM	NAME	DRAFTED FROM	NHL PLAYERS: POS / NHL GOALTENDERS: POS	GP	G / W	A / GA	PTS / SO	PIM / AVG
79	MIN	Mark Huglen	Roseau H.S.	D					
80	NYI	Greg Gilbert	Toronto	LW	837	150	228	378	576
81	BOS	Steve Kasper	Verdun	C	821	177	291	468	554
82	MTL	Jeff Teal	U. of Minnesota	RW	6	0	1	1	0
83	BUF	Jim Wiemer	Peterborough	D	325	29	72	101	378
84	PHI	Taras Zytynsky	Montreal	D					
85	COL	Ed Cooper	Portland	LW	49	8	7	15	46
86	WPG	Glen Ostir	Portland	D					
87	QUE	Basil McRae	London	LW	576	53	83	136	2457
88	DET	Mike Corrigan	Cornwall	LW	594	152	195	347	698
89	WSH	Timo Blomqvist	Jokerit Helsinki, FIN	D	243	4	53	57	293
90	EDM	Walt Poddubny	Kingston	LW	468	184	238	422	454
91	VAN	Darrell May	Portland	G	6	1	31	0	5.11
92	HFD	Darren Jensen	North Dakota	G	30	15	95	2	3.81
93	PIT	Doug Shedden	Sault Ste. Marie	C	416	139	186	325	176
94	L.A.	Alan Graves	Seattle	LW					
95	TOR	Hugh Larkin	Sault Ste. Marie	RW					
96	ST.L.	Alain Lemieux	Chicoutimi	C	119	28	44	72	38
97	CGY	Randy Turnbull	Portland	D	1	0	0	0	2
98	NYR	Scot Kleinendorst	Providence	D	281	12	46	58	452
99	CHI	Kevin Ginnell	Medicine Hat	C					
100	MIN	David H. Jensen	Minnesota-Duluth	D	18	0	2	2	11
101	NYI	Ken Leiter	Michigan State	D	143	14	36	50	62
102	BOS	Randy Hillier	Sudbury	D	543	16	110	126	906
103	MTL	Remi Gagne	Chicoutimi	RW					
104	BUF	Dirk Rueter	Sault Ste. Marie	D					
105	PHI	Dan Held	Seattle	C					
106	COL	Aaron Broten	Minnesota-Duluth	LW/C	748	186	329	515	441
107	WPG	Ron Loustel	Saskatoon	G	1	0	10	0	10.00
108	QUE	Mark Kumpel	University of Lowell	RW	288	38	46	84	113
109	DET	Wayne Crawford	Toronto	C					
110	WSH	Todd Bidner	Toronto	LW	12	2	1	3	7
111	EDM	Mike Winther	Brandon	C					
112	VAN	Ken Berry	Canadian Olympic	LW	55	8	10	18	30
113	HFD	Mario Cerri	Ottawa	C					
114	PIT	Pat Graham	Niagara Falls	LW	103	11	17	28	136
115	L.A.	Darren Eliot	Cornell	G	89	25	377	1	4.59
116	TOR	Ron Dennis	Princeton	G					
117	ST.L.	Perry Anderson	Brantford	LW	400	50	59	109	1051
118	CGY	John Multan	Portland	RW					
119	NYR	Reijo Ruotsalainen	Karpat Oulu, FIN	D	446	107	237	344	180
120	CHI	Steve Larmer	Niagara Falls	RW	1006	441	571	1012	532
121	MIN	Dan Zavarise	Cornwall	D					
122	NYI	Dan Revell	Oshawa	RW					
123	BOS	Steve Lyons	Matignon H.S.	LW					
124	MTL	Mike McPhee	RPI	LW	744	200	199	399	661
125	BUF	Daniel Naud	Verdun	D					
126	PHI	Brian Tutt	Calgary	D	7	1	0	1	2
127	COL	Dan Fascinato	Ottawa	D					
128	WPG	Brian Mullen	U.S. Jr. National Team	RW	832	260	362	622	414
129	QUE	Gaston Therrien	Quebec	D	22	0	8	8	12
130	DET	Mike Braun	Niagara Falls	D					
131	WSH	Frank Perkins	Sudbury	RW					
132	EDM	Andy Moog	Billings	G	713	372	2097	28	3.13
133	VAN	Doug Lidster	Colorado College	D	880	75	268	343	669
134	HFD	Mike Martin	Sudbury	D					
135	WPG	Mike Lauen	Michigan Tech	RW	4	0	1	1	0
136	L.A.	Mike O'Connor	Michigan Tech	D					
137	TOR	Russ Adam	Kitchener	C	8	1	2	3	11
138	ST.L.	Roger Hagglund	Bjorkloven Umea, SWE	D	3	0	0	0	0
139	CGY	Dave Newsom	Brantford	LW					
140	NYR	Bob Scurfield	Western Michigan	C					
141	CHI	Sean Simpson	Ottawa	C					
142	MIN	Bill Stewart	U. of Denver	RW					
143	NYI	Mark Hamway	Michigan State	RW	53	5	13	18	9
144	BOS	Tony McMurchy	New Westminster	C					
145	MTL	Bill Norton	Clarkson	LW					
146	BUF	Jari Paavola	TPS Turku, FIN	G					
147	PHI	Ross Fitzpatrick	Western Michigan	C	20	5	2	7	0
148	COL	Andre Hidi	Peterborough	LW	7	2	1	3	9
149	WPG	Sandy Beadle	Northeastern	LW	6	1	0	1	2
150	QUE	Michel Bolduc	Chicoutimi	D	10	0	0	0	6
151	DET	John Beukeboom	Peterborough	D					
152	WSH	Bruce Raboin	Providence	D					
153	EDM	Rob Polman Tuin	Michigan Tech	G					
154	VAN	John O'Connor	Vermont	D					
155	HFD	Brent Denat	Michigan Tech	LW					
156	PIT	Bob Geale	Portland	C	1	0	0	0	2
157	L.A.	Bill O'Dwyer	Boston College	C	120	9	13	22	113
158	TOR	Fred Perlini	Toronto	C	8	2	3	5	0
159	ST.L.	Pat Rabbit	Billings	LW					
160	CGY	Claude Drouin	Quebec	C					
161	NYR	Bart Wilson	Toronto	D					
162	CHI	Jim Ralph	Ottawa	G					
163	MIN	Jeff Walters	Peterborough	RW					
164	NYI	Morrison Gare	Penticton Jr. A	RW					
165	BOS	Mike Moffat	Kingston	G	19	7	70	0	4.29
166	MTL	Steve Penney	Shawinigan	G	91	35	313	1	3.62
167	BUF	Randy Cunneyworth	Ottawa	LW	852	187	223	410	1280
168	PHI	Mark Botell	Brantford	D	32	4	10	14	31
169	COL	Shawn MacKenzie	Windsor	G	4	0	15	0	6.92
170	WPG	Edward Christian	Warroad H.S.	LW					
171	QUE	Chris Tanguay	Trois-Rivieres	RW	2	0	0	0	0
172	DET	Dave Miles	Brantford	RW					
173	WSH	Peter Andersson	Timra, SWE	D	172	10	41	51	81
174	EDM	Lars-Gunnar Petterson	Lulea, SWE	D					
175	VAN	Patrik Sundstrom	Bjorkloven Umea, SWE	C	679	219	369	588	349
176	HFD	Paul Fricker	Michigan	G					
177	PIT	Brian Lundberg	Michigan	D	1	0	0	0	2
178	L.A.	Daryl Evans	Niagara Falls	LW	113	22	30	52	25
179	TOR	Darwin McCutcheon	Toronto	D	1	0	0	0	2
180	ST.L.	Peter Lindgren	Hammarby Stockholm, SWE	D					
181	CGY	Hakan Loob	Farjestad Karlstad, SWE	RW	450	193	236	429	189
182	NYR	Chris Wray	Boston College	RW					
183	CHI	Don Dietrich	Brandon	D	28	0	7	7	10
184	MIN	Bob Lakso	Aurora H.S.	LW	3	0	0	0	4
185	NYI	Peter Steblyk	Medicine Hat	D					
186	BOS	Michael Thelven	Djurgarden, SWE	D	207	20	80	100	217
187	MTL	John Schmidt	U. of Notre Dame	D					
188	BUF	Dave Beckon	Peterborough	C					
189	PHI	Peter Dineen	Kingston	D	13	0	2	2	13
190	COL	Bob Jansch	Victoria	RW					
191	WPG	Dave Chartier	Brandon	C	Re-entered Draft in 1982				
192	QUE	William Robinson	Acton-Boxboro H.S.	D					
193	DET	Brian Rorabeck	Niagara Falls	D					
194	WSH	Tony Camazzola	Brandon	D	3	0	0	0	4
195	PHI	Bob O'Brien	Dixie Jr. B	RW					
196	VAN	Grant Martin	Kitchener	LW	44	0	4	4	55
197	HFD	Lorne Bokshowan	Saskatoon	C					
198	PIT	Steve McKenzie	St. Albert Jr. A	D					
199	L.A.	Kim Collins	Bowling Green	LW					
200	TOR	Paul Higgins	Henry Carr H.S.	RW	25	0	0	0	152
201	ST.L.	John Smyth	Calgary	D					
202	CGY	Steven Fletcher	Hull	LW/D	3	0	0	0	5
203	NYR	Anders Backstrom	Brynas Gavle, SWE	D					
204	CHI	Dan Frawley	Sudbury	RW	273	37	40	77	674
205	MIN	Dave Richter	Michigan	D	365	9	40	49	1030
206	NYI	Glenn Johannesen	Red Deer Jr. A	LW	2	0	0	0	0
207	BOS	Jens Ohling	Djurgarden, SWE	LW					
208	MTL	Scott Robinson	U. of Denver	G					
209	BUF	John Bader	Irondale H.S.	LW					
210	PHI	Andy Brickley	Bowling Green	LW/C	385	82	140	222	81

1981

The drafting of underage talent received tremendous attention prior to the 1981 Entry Draft. The NHL teams' eagerness to immediately incorporate underage draft choices in their rosters left junior ranks relatively thin in talent and slowed the development of other players. The NHL's involvement further disrupted the junior leagues with the constant return and recall of drafted players. "Where I have some difficulty and where we have to meet on some common ground in our negotiations on the recall and use of junior players by the NHL teams is that point in time when the player is sent back to his junior team," said Ontario Hockey League commissioner and Canadian Hockey League executive director David Branch during talks with the NHL.

"If a date can be set where those final returns to junior can be made, as well as a final decision by the NHL teams on what players they want to keep, call up, whatever, would be a big step." The result of these talks led the NHL to enact a rule saying that all junior players were to be returned by the beginning of the junior season and once a player was returned to his junior club, he could not be recalled until his junior club's season and playoffs had concluded.

In an attempt to reach a larger talent pool the NHL began negotiations with international federations from Finland and Czechoslovakia to seek an agreement that would allow international players to play in the NHL. Although NHL teams were able to draft non-North American-born players, they could not play in the NHL without being released from

their respective hockey federations or, according to IIHF rules, until 18 months after being drafted.

For the first time since 1978, the junior crop boasted a consensus number-one draft pick in 1981. Scoring phenom Dale Hawerchuk was selected first overall by the Winnipeg Jets. The Cornwall star had just received MVP honors from the Quebec Junior Hockey League and was recognized as the most outstanding player in the Canadian Major Junior Hockey League. As the leading scorer in the Quebec league, Hawerchuk also led his team to the Memorial Cup and received the MVP award for the tournament. "I've been waiting for Dale for two years," said Jets g.m. John Ferguson. "When I saw him as a 16-year-old in Brandon, I was sold on him then." As the NHL's rookie of the year for 1982, Hawerchuk set a record for a drafted rookie with 103 points (45 goals, 58 assists). He went on to post a career record of 518 goals and 891 assists for 1,409 points, which ranked him as the 10th-highest scorer in NHL history at the time of his retirement. Hawerchuk became one of the youngest players to captain an NHL team, earning the position at 21 years of age in the fourth year of his career. The Jets used their second pick in 1981 to select Scott Arniel, Hawerchuk's junior linemate .

Following the Jets selection of Hawerchuk, the Washington Capitals pulled off an 11th-hour trade, swapping their first- and second-round picks to the Colorado Rockies for their first- and third-round picks in order to move up two positions in the drafting order. With their newly acquired first pick, the Capitals drafted Bobby Carpenter third overall. As a product of the St. John's Prep School in Danvers, Massachusetts, Carpenter became the first U.S. high school prospect ever selected in the first round of the Entry Draft. As a 17-year-old, Carpenter had already received an extreme amount of public attention in the U.S., even appearing on the cover of *Sports Illustrated*. He immediately jumped from high school to the NHL and set club records for goals (32), points (67) and shots on goal for a rookie in 1981–82. In the 1984–85 season, Carpenter tallied 53 goals and 42 assists to become the first American to post a 50-goal season. Ten years later, Carpenter captured the Stanley Cup with the New Jersey Devils in 1995.

Although the Capitals had stolen Hartford's most desired prospect when they traded up to take Carpenter, the Whalers managed to land one of the NHL's best when they selected forward Ron Francis fourth. Francis had been a quiet prospect who was overshadowed by the excellence of Hawerchuk and Carpenter; however, as one of the highest scorers in the history of hockey and a two-time Stanley Cup champion, Francis has become known as one of the NHL's finest ambassadors.

Francis did not make an immediate jump to the NHL as he returned to his junior club for an additional year of seasoning. "I think going back to junior was good for me," said Francis in his rookie season with the Whalers. "Had I stayed in Hartford and started slowly, who knows what would have happened to my confidence. As it was, I went back to junior, got off to a great start, and was ready for when the call came."

NHL teams selected 25 goaltenders in 1981, the most ever taken in an Entry Draft. The most prominent of those goaltenders was Grant Fuhr. Selected by Edmonton eighth overall, Fuhr became the first goaltender to be taken in the first round since 1975 and the first black goaltender ever selected. He had led the Victoria Cougars to the WHL title in the previous year and would soon become an integral

piece of the Edmonton dynasty, backstopping them to five Stanley Cup championships. He was awarded the Vezina Trophy as the league's best goaltender in 1988. Another marquee goaltender selected in the 1981 draft was Mike Vernon, selected by Calgary 56th overall. Vernon went on to capture a Stanley Cup championship with the Flames in 1989 and the Detroit Red Wings in 1997 when he was named Conn Smythe Trophy winner as the MVP for the postseason.

The 15th player selected in the 1981 draft emerged as the best blueliner available, as the Flames laid claim to Al MacInnis. Known for his extremely powerful shot and offensive ability, MacInnis became an instant star with the Flames, eventually capturing the Conn Smythe when Calgary won the Stanley Cup in 1989 and finishing as the runner-up behind Ray Bourque for the Norris Trophy in 1990 and 1991 as one of the league's best defensemen.

1981

PICK	TEAM	NAME	DRAFTED FROM	NHL PLAYERS: POS / NHL GOALTENDERS: POS	GP / GP	G / W	A / GA	PTS / SO	PIM / AVG
FIRST ROUND									
1	WPG	Dale Hawerchuk	Cornwall	C	1188	518	891	1409	730
2	L.A.	Doug Smith	Ottawa	C	535	115	138	253	624
3	WSH	Bob Carpenter	St. John's Prep	C	1122	318	400	718	883
4	HFD	Ron Francis	Sault Ste. Marie	C	1247	428	1006	1434	833
5	COL	Joe Cirella	Oshawa	D	828	64	211	275	1446
6	TOR	Jim Benning	Portland	D	605	52	191	243	461
7	MTL	Mark Hunter	Brantford	RW	628	213	171	384	1426
8	EDM	Grant Fuhr	Victoria	G	806	382	2590	23	3.41
9	NYR	James Patrick	Prince Albert	D	935	126	439	565	655
10	VAN	Garth Butcher	Regina	D	897	48	158	206	2302
11	QUE	Randy Moller	Lethbridge	D	815	45	180	225	1692
12	CHI	Tony Tanti	Oshawa	RW	697	287	273	560	661
13	MIN	Ron Meighan	Niagara Falls	D	48	3	7	10	18
14	BOS	Normand Leveille	Chicoutimi	LW	75	17	25	42	49
15	CGY	Al MacInnis	Kitchener	D	1060	270	733	1003	1226
16	PHI	Steve Smith	Sault Ste. Marie	D	18	0	1	1	15
17	BUF	Jiri Dudacek	Poldi SONP Kladno, TCH	RW					
18	MTL	Gilbert Delorme	Chicoutimi	D	541	31	92	123	520
19	MTL	Jan Ingman	Farjestad Karlstad, SWE	LW					
20	ST.L.	Marty Ruff	Lethbridge	D					
21	NYI	Paul Boutilier	Sherbrooke	D	288	27	83	110	358
SECOND ROUND									
22	WPG	Scott Arniel	Cornwall	LW	730	149	189	338	599
23	DET	Claude Loiselle	Windsor	C	616	92	117	209	1149
24	TOR	Gary Yaremchuk	Portland	C	34	1	4	5	28
25	CHI	Kevin Griffin	Portland	LW					
26	COL	Rich Chernomaz	Victoria	RW	51	9	7	16	18
27	MIN	Dave Donnelly	St. Albert Jr. A	C	137	15	24	39	150
28	PIT	Steve Gatzos	Sault Ste. Marie	RW	89	15	20	35	83
29	EDM	Todd Strueby	Regina	LW	5	0	1	1	2
30	NYR	Jan Erixon	Skelleftea, SWE	LW	556	57	159	216	167
31	MIN	Mike Sands	Sudbury	G	6	0	26	0	5.17
32	MTL	Lars Eriksson	Brynas Gavle, SWE	G					
33	MIN	Tom Hirsch	Patrick Henry H.S.	D	31	1	7	8	30
34	MIN	Dave Preuss	St. Thomas Academy	RW					
35	BOS	Luc Dufour	Chicoutimi	LW	167	23	21	44	199
36	ST.L.	Hakan Nordin	Farjestad Karlstad, SWE	D					
37	PHI	Rich Costello	Natick H.S.	C	12	2	2	4	2
38	BUF	Hannu Virta	TPS Turku, FIN	D	245	25	101	126	66
39	L.A.	Dean Kennedy	Brandon	D	692	24	103	127	1095
40	MTL	Chris Chelios	Moose Jaw	D	1001	156	606	762	2189
41	MIN	Jali Wahlsten	TPS Turku, FIN	C					
42	NYI	Gord Dineen	Sault Ste. Marie	D	528	16	90	106	693
OTHER ROUNDS									
43	WPG	Jyrki Seppa	Ilves Tampere, FIN	D	13	0	2	2	6
44	DET	Corrado Micalef	Sherbrooke	G	113	26	409	2	4.24
45	WSH	Eric Calder	Cornwall	D	2	0	0	0	0
46	MTL	Dieter Hegen	ESV Kaufbeuren, FRG	C					
47	PHI	Barry Tabobondung	Oshawa	LW					
48	COL	Uli Hiemer	Fussen, FRG	D	143	19	54	73	176
49	PIT	Tom Thornbury	Niagara Falls	D	14	1	8	9	16
50	NYR	Peter Sundstrom	Bjorkloven Umea, SWE	LW	338	61	83	144	120
51	NYR	Mark Morrison	Victoria	C	10	1	1	2	0
52	VAN	Jean-Marc Lanthier	Sorel	RW	105	16	16	32	29
53	QUE	Jean-Marc Gaulin	Sorel	RW	26	4	3	7	8
54	CHI	Darrel Anholt	Calgary	D	1	0	0	0	0
55	TOR	Ernie Godden	Windsor	C	5	1	1	2	6
56	CGY	Mike Vernon	Calgary	G	624	331	1825	18	3.06
57	NYI	Ron Handy	Sault Ste. Marie	LW	14	0	3	3	0
58	PHI	Ken Strong	Peterborough	LW	15	2	4	6	0
59	BUF	Jim Aldred	Kingston	LW					

1981 *continued*

PICK	TEAM	NAME	DRAFTED FROM	POS	GP	G	A	PTS	PIM
60	BUF	Colin Chisholm	Calgary	D	1	0	0	0	0
61	HFD	Paul MacDermid	Windsor	RW	690	116	142	258	1303
62	ST.L.	Gord Donnelly	Sherbrooke	D	554	28	41	69	2069
63	NYI	Neal Coulter	Toronto	RW	26	5	5	10	11
64	WPG	Kirk McCaskill	Vermont	C					
65	PHI	Dave Michayluk	Regina	LW	14	2	6	8	8
66	COL	Gus Greco	Windsor	C					
67	HFD	Mike Hoffman	Brantford	LW	9	1	3	4	2
68	WSH	Tony Kellin	Grand Rapids H.S.	D					
69	MIN	Terry Tait	Sault Ste. Marie	C					
70	PIT	Norm Schmidt	Oshawa	D	125	23	33	56	73
71	EDM	Paul Houck	Kelowna	RW	16	1	2	3	2
72	NYR	John Vanbiesbrouck	Sault Ste. Marie	G	717	306	2124	29	3.12
73	VAN	Wendell Young	Kitchener	G	187	59	618	2	3.94
74	QUE	Clint Malarchuk	Portland	G	338	141	1100	12	3.47
75	CHI	Perry Pelensky	Portland	RW	4	0	0	0	5
76	MIN	Jim Malwitz	Grand Rapids H.S.	C					
77	BOS	Scott McLellan	Niagara Falls	RW	2	0	0	0	0
78	CGY	Peter Madach	HV-71 Jonkoping, SWE	C					
79	PHI	Ken Latta	Sault Ste. Marie	RW					
80	BUF	Jeff Eatough	Cornwall	RW	1	0	0	0	0
81	L.A.	Marty Dallman	RPI	C	6	0	1	1	0
82	MTL	Kjell Dahlin	Timra, SWE	RW	166	57	59	116	10
83	BUF	Anders Wikberg	Timra, SWE	LW					
84	NYI	Todd Lumbard	Brandon	G					
85	WPG	Marc Behrend	Wisconsin	G	39	12	160	1	4.82
86	DET	Larry Trader	London	D	91	5	13	18	74
87	COL	Doug Speck	Peterborough	D					
88	MTL	Steve Rooney	Canton H.S.	LW	154	15	13	28	496
89	WSH	Mike Siltala	Kingston	RW	7	1	0	1	2
90	TOR	Normand Lefrancois	Trois-Rivieres	LW					
91	WSH	Peter Sidorkiewicz	Oshawa	G	246	79	832	8	3.60
92	EDM	Phil Drouillard	Niagara Falls	LW					
93	HFD	Bill Maguire	Niagara Falls	D					
94	NYI	Jacques Sylvestre	Sorel	C					
95	QUE	Edward Lee	Princeton	RW	2	0	0	0	5
96	CHI	Doug Chessell	London	G					
97	MIN	Kelly Hubbard	Portland	D					
98	BOS	Joe Mantione	Cornwall	G					
99	CGY	Mario Simioni	Toronto	RW					
100	PHI	Justin Hanley	Kingston	C					
101	BUF	Mauri Eivola	TPS Turku, FIN	C					
102	TOR	Barry Bringley	Calgary	C					
103	HFD	Dan Bourbonnais	Calgary	LW	59	3	25	28	11
104	ST.L.	Mike Hickey	Sudbury	C					
105	VAN	Moe Lemay	Ottawa	LW	317	72	94	166	442
106	WPG	Bob O'Connor	Boston College	G					
107	DET	Gerard Gallant	Sherbrooke	LW	615	211	269	480	1674
108	COL	Bruce Driver	Wisconsin	D	922	96	390	486	670
109	PIT	Paul Edwards	Oshawa	D					
110	WSH	Jim McGeough	Billings	C	57	7	10	17	32
111	EDM	Steve Smith	London	D	702	71	283	354	2000
112	PIT	Rod Buskas	Medicine Hat	D	556	19	63	82	1294
113	EDM	Marc Habscheid	Saskatoon	RW/C	345	72	91	163	171
114	NYR	Eric Magnuson	RPI	C					
115	VAN	Stu Kulak	Victoria	RW	90	8	4	12	130
116	QUE	Mike Eagles	Kitchener	C/LW	776	68	120	188	863
117	CHI	Bill Schafhauser	Northern Michigan	D					
118	MIN	Paul Guay	Mount St. Charles H.S.	RW	117	11	23	34	92
119	BOS	Bruce Milton	Boston U.	D					
120	CGY	Todd Hooey	Windsor	RW					
121	PHI	Andre Villeneuve	Chicoutimi	D					
122	BUF	Ali Butorac	Ottawa	D/LW					
123	L.A.	Brad Thompson	London	D					
124	MTL	Tom Anastos	Paddock Pool H.S.	RW					
125	ST.L.	Peter Aslin	AIK Solna, SWE	G					
126	NYI	Chuck Brimmer	Kingston	C					
127	WPG	Peter Nilsson	Hammarby Stockholm, SWE	C					
128	DET	Greg Stefan	Oshawa	G	299	115	1068	5	3.92
129	COL	Jeff Larmer	Kitchener	LW	158	37	51	88	57
130	HFD	John Mokosak	Victoria	D	41	0	2	2	96
131	WSH	Risto Jalo	Ilves Tampere, FIN	C	3	0	3	3	0
132	TOR	Andrew Wright	Peterborough	D					
133	PIT	Geoff Wilson	Winnipeg	RW					
134	L.A.	Craig Hurley	Saskatoon	D					
135	NYR	Mike Guentzel	Greenway/Coleraine H.S.	D					
136	VAN	Bruce Holloway	Regina	D	2	0	0	0	0
137	PHI	Vladimir Svitek	HC Kosice, TCH	RW					
138	CHI	Marc Centrone	Lethbridge	C/RW					
139	MIN	Jim Archibald	Moose Jaw	RW	16	1	2	3	45
140	BOS	Mats Thelin	AIK Solna, SWE	D	163	8	19	27	107
141	CGY	Rick Heppner	Mount View H.S.	D					
142	PHI	Gil Hudon	Prince Albert	G					
143	BUF	Heikki Leime	TPS Turku, FIN	D					
144	L.A.	Peter Sawkins	St. Paul Academy	D					
145	MTL	Tom Kurvers	Minnesota-Duluth	D	659	93	328	421	350
146	ST.L.	Erik Holmberg	Sodertalje, SWE	C					

PICK	TEAM	NAME	DRAFTED FROM	POS	GP	G	A	PTS	PIM
147	NYI	Teppo Virta	TPS Turku, FIN	RW					
148	WPG	Dan McFall	Buffalo Jr. Sabres	D	9	0	1	1	0
149	DET	Rick Zombo	Austin Prep	D	652	24	130	154	728
150	COL	Tony Arima	Jokerit Helsinki, FIN	LW					
151	HFD	Denis Dore	Chicoutimi	RW					
152	WSH	Gaetan Duchesne	Quebec	LW	1028	179	254	433	617
153	TOR	Richard Turmel	Shawinigan	D					
154	PIT	Mitch Lamoureux	Oshawa	C	73	11	9	20	59
155	EDM	Mike Sturgeon	Kelowna	D					
156	NYR	Ari Lahtenmaki	HIFK Helsinki, FIN	RW					
157	VAN	Petri Skriko	SaiPa Lappeenranta, FIN	LW	541	183	222	405	246
158	QUE	Andre Cote	Quebec	RW					
159	CHI	Johan Mellstrom	Falun, SWE	LW					
160	MIN	Kari Kanervo	TPS Turku, FIN	C					
161	BOS	Armel Parisee	Chicoutimi	D					
162	CGY	Dale DeGray	Oshawa	D	153	18	47	65	195
163	PHI	Steve Taylor	Providence	LW					
164	BUF	Gaetano Orlando	Providence	C	98	18	26	44	51
165	L.A.	Dan Brennan	North Dakota	LW	8	0	1	1	9
166	MTL	Paul Gess	Jefferson H.S.	RW					
167	ST.L.	Alain Vigneault	Trois-Rivieres	D	42	2	5	7	82
168	NYI	Bill Dowd	Ottawa	D					
169	WPG	Greg Dick	St. Mary's H.S.	G					
170	DET	Don Leblanc	Moncton Jr.	LW					
171	COL	Tim Army	Providence	C					
172	HFD	Jeff Poeschl	Northern Michigan	G					
173	WSH	George White	New Hampshire	LW					
174	TOR	Greg Barber	Victoria	D					
175	PIT	Dean Defazio	Brantford	LW	22	0	2	2	28
176	EDM	Miloslav Horava	Poldi SOMP Kladno, TCH	D	80	5	17	22	38
177	NYR	Paul Reifenberger	Anoka H.S.	C					
178	VAN	Frank Caprice	London	G	102	31	391	1	4.20
179	QUE	Marc Brisebois	Sorel	RW					
180	L.A.	John Benns	Billings	LW					
181	MIN	Scott Bjugstad	Minnesota-Duluth	RW	317	76	68	144	144
182	BOS	Don Sylvestri	Clarkson	G	3	0	6	0	3.53
183	CGY	George Boudreau	Matignon H.S.	D					
184	PHI	Len Hachborn	Brantford	C	102	20	39	59	29
185	BUF	Venci Sebek	Niagara Falls	D					
186	L.A.	Allan Tuer	Regina	D	57	1	1	2	208
187	MTL	Scott Ferguson	Edina West H.S.	D	0				
188	ST.L.	Dan Wood	Kingston	RW					
189	NYI	Scott MacLellan	Burlington Jr. B	RW					
190	WPG	Vladimir Kadlec	TJ Vitkovice, TCH	D					
191	DET	Robert Nordmark	Lulea, SWE	D					
192	COL	John Johannson	Wisconsin	C	5	0	0	0	0
193	HFD	Larry Power	Kitchener	C					
194	WSH	Chris Valentine	Sorel	C	105	43	52	95	127
195	TOR	Marc Magnan	Lethbridge	LW	4	0	1	1	5
196	PIT	Dave Hannan	Brantford	C	841	114	191	305	942
197	EDM	Gord Sherven	Weyburn Jr. A	C	97	13	22	35	33
198	NYR	Mario Proulx	Providence	G					
199	VAN	Rejean Vignola	Shawinigan	C					
200	QUE	Kari Takko	Assat Pori, FIN	G	Re-entered Draft in 1984				
201	CHI	Sylvain Roy	Hull	D					
202	MIN	Steve Kudebeh	Breck H.S.	G					
203	BOS	Richard Bourque	Sherbrooke	LW					
204	CGY	Bruce Eakin	Saskatoon	C	13	2	2	4	4
205	PHI	Steve Tsujiura	Medicine Hat	C					
206	BUF	Warren Harper	Prince Albert	RW					
207	L.A.	Jeff Baikie	Cornell	LW					
208	MTL	Danny Burrows	Belleville	G					
209	ST.L.	Richard Zemlak	Spokane	RW	132	2	12	14	587
210	NYI	Dave Randerson	Stratford Jr. B	RW					
211	WPG	Dave Kirwin	Irondale H.S.	D					

1982

Prior to the 1982 Entry Draft the NHL made amends to the rule of prospects re-entering the draft pool. It was decided that players who had been selected in two previous entry drafts would be exempt from eligibility for a third. Any player who fell under this ruling would have to depend on free agency in order to continue pursuing a professional career.

Brian Bellows of the Kitchener Rangers was expected to be selected first overall in 1982 and many teams rallied and scrambled in an attempt to obtain a higher drafting position to better their chances at acquiring top prospects. The selection of Bellows atop the draft was deemed to be such a sure thing that the media had dubbed the 1982 proceedings "The Brian Bellows Derby." "There's no question that the differ-

ence between Bellows and the next three or four players has closed considerably in the last six months," said an NHL scout. "But he's still the best. He showed it this week (at the Memorial Cup) and I'll be very surprised if the Bruins don't take him." Boston, however, proved that it is never safe to assume anything as they used the first overall pick, which they had acquired from the Colorado Rockies, to obtain defenseman Gord Kluzak. At 6'4" and 200 pounds, Kluzak was extremely impressive on the blue line, but he had missed most of his final junior year due to a knee injury, an injury that proved to be disastrous for the Bruins and Kluzak throughout his career. He was forced to miss his entire third year in 1984–85 due to knee problems. He made an attempt to return to play the following season only to be reinjured and forced to sit out the entire 1986–87 season. Kluzak returned to play one more time, appearing in only 77 games over the next three seasons. His constant dedication to continue his career earned him the Masterton Trophy in 1990 before he retired in 1991.

Bellows, on the other hand, was drafted second overall by the Minnesota North Stars, who had arranged to swap first-round picks with Detroit. Bellows immediately joined the North Stars and became the second-highest scoring rookie in the league with 65 points (35 goals, 30 assists). Bellows has placed himself among the top NHL scorers of all-time over his lengthy career and captured the Stanley Cup with the Montreal Canadiens in 1993.

The first round of the 1982 draft introduced two players who would become two of the best defensemen in the NHL. First, the Washington Capitals selected Scott Stevens fifth overall. Stevens was heralded as a master of his position, a defensive blueliner and one of the most punishing hitters ever made available in the Entry Draft. Today, Stevens is known for his leadership and extremely tough play and remains one of the most feared players in the NHL. Stevens was voted the runner-up to Ray Bourque for the Norris Trophy as the league's best defenseman in 1988. Immediately following the selection of Stevens, the Buffalo Sabres used the first of three first-round picks to draft South St. Paul High School's Phil Housley. Touted as an offensive defenseman who could play as a forward, Housley became one of the NHL's best rushing blueliners. After posting 19 goals and 47 assists for 66 points in his rookie season, Housley was named as the runner-up to Steve Larmer for the Calder Trophy in 1983, continuing the trend of emerging U.S.-born talent. Another offensive defenseman taken in the 1982 draft was Gary Leeman of the Regina Pats. Leeman, named the WHL's top defenseman in 1982–83, was selected by the Maple Leafs as the 24th pick. He went on to record 51 goals and 95 points for the Leafs in 1989–90 as a right winger.

Family was strongly represented in the first round of 1982 as five players had NHL family ties. The last of the Sutters were selected, twin brothers Ron and Rich joined Brian, Darryl, Duane and Brent in the NHL. With Ron going to Hartford fourth overall and Rich being picked 10th by Pittsburgh it marked the first time that twins would be taken in the first round of the Entry Draft. Other relations included Rocky Trottier, younger brother of Islanders superstar Bryan (eighth overall to New Jersey); Ken Yaremchuk, younger brother of Toronto prospect Gary (seventh overall to Chicago); and Jim Playfair, younger brother of Buffalo defenseman Larry (20th overall to Edmonton).

The Hartford Whalers could be considered most success-

ful drafting team in 1982 as they acquired Kevin Dineen 56th overall, Ulf Samuelsson 67th and Ray Ferraro 88th. Dineen and Ferraro have enjoyed successful and underrated careers, while. Samuelsson is known as one of the most feared defensemen in the NHL. He captured two consecutive Stanley Cup championships with the Pittsburgh Penguins. Swedish talent Tomas Sandstrom was introduced to the NHL when he was selected by the New York Rangers 36th overall. Sandstrom has gone on to become the fifth-highest-scoring European in NHL history.

There were two dark horses that emerged from the 1982 Entry Draft as prominent NHLers, as Pat Verbeek and Doug Gilmour were taken 43rd and 134th overall respectively. Despite leading the OHL in scoring with 177 points, Gilmour was overlooked by the NHL until the seventh round because of his small size. Gilmour reinvented himself as a defensive specialist early in his career before emerging as one of the league's top offensive talents as well. In 1993 Gilmour received the Frank J. Selke Trophy as the NHL's best defensive forward while finishing as the runner-up for the Hart Trophy behind Mario Lemieux. Verbeek has compiled impressive career totals that rank him among the NHL's all-time leaders in both goals and penalty minutes.

1982

PICK	TEAM	NAME	DRAFTED FROM	NHL PLAYERS: POS / NHL GOALTENDERS: POS	GP	G / W	A / GA	PTS / SO	PIM / AVG
FIRST ROUND									
1	BOS	Gord Kluzak	Nanaimo	D	299	25	98	123	543
2	MIN	Brian Bellows	Kitchener	LW	1112	468	518	986	692
3	TOR	Gary Nylund	Portland	D	608	32	139	171	1235
4	PHI	Ron Sutter	Lethbridge	C	935	196	314	510	1266
5	WSH	Scott Stevens	Kitchener	D	1200	166	606	772	2440
6	BUF	Phil Housley	South St. Paul H.S.	D	1131	291	730	1021	662
7	CHI	Ken Yaremchuk	Portland	C	235	36	56	92	106
8	N.J.	Rocky Trottier	Nanaimo	RW	38	6	4	10	2
9	BUF	Paul Cyr	Victoria	LW	470	101	140	241	623
10	PIT	Rich Sutter	Lethbridge	RW	874	149	166	315	1411
11	VAN	Michel Petit	Sherbrooke	D	827	90	238	328	1839
12	WPG	Jim Kyte	Cornwall	D	598	17	49	66	1342
13	QUE	David Shaw	Kitchener	D	769	41	153	194	906
14	HFD	Paul Lawless	Windsor	LW	239	40	77	126	64
15	NYR	Chris Kontos	Toronto	LW/C	230	54	69	123	103
16	BUF	Dave Andreychuk	Oshawa	LW	1158	517	595	1112	842
17	DET	Murray Craven	Medicine Hat	LW	1009	262	481	743	502
18	N.J.	Ken Daneyko	Seattle	D	910	32	110	142	2178
19	MTL	Alain Heroux	Chicoutimi	LW					
20	EDM	Jim Playfair	Portland	D	21	2	4	6	51
21	NYI	Pat Flatley	Wisconsin	RW	780	170	340	510	686
SECOND ROUND									
22	BOS	Brian Curran	Portland	D	381	7	33	40	1461
23	DET	Yves Courteau	Laval	RW	22	2	5	7	4
24	TOR	Gary Leeman	Regina	D	667	199	267	466	531
25	TOR	Peter Ihnacak	Sparta Praha, TCH	C	417	102	165	267	175
26	BUF	Mike Anderson	North St. Paul H.S.	C					
27	L.A.	Michael Heidt	Calgary	D	6	0	1	1	7
28	CHI	Rene Badeau	Quebec	D					
29	CGY	Dave Reierson	Prince Albert	D	2	0	0	0	2
30	BUF	Jens Johansson	Pitea, SWE	D					
31	MTL	Jocelyn Gauvreau	Granby	D	2	0	0	0	0
32	MTL	Kent Carlson	St. Lawrence U.	D	113	7	11	18	148
33	MTL	David Maley	Edina H.S.	LW	466	43	81	124	1043
34	QUE	Paul Gillis	Niagara Falls	C	624	88	154	242	1498
35	HFD	Mark Paterson	Ottawa	D	29	3	3	6	33
36	NYR	Tomas Sandstrom	Farjestad Karlstad, SWE	RW	925	379	445	824	1151
37	CGY	Rich Kromm	Portland	LW	372	70	103	173	138
38	PIT	Tim Hrynewich	Sudbury	LW	55	6	8	14	82
39	BOS	Lyndon Byers	Regina	RW	279	28	43	71	1081
40	MTL	Scott Sandelin	Hibbing H.S.	D	25	0	4	4	2
41	EDM	Steve Graves	Sault Ste. Marie	LW	35	5	4	9	10
42	NYI	Vern Smith	Lethbridge	D	1	0	0	0	0
OTHER ROUNDS									
43	N.J.	Pat Verbeek	Sudbury	R/LW	1147	461	470	931	2532
44	DET	Carmine Vani	Kingston	LW					
45	TOR	Ken Wregget	Lethbridge	G	519	201	1780	8	3.75
46	PHI	Miroslav Dvorak	Motor Ceske Budejovice, TCH	D	193	11	74	85	51
47	PHI	Bill Campbell	Montreal	D					
48	L.A.	Steve Seguin	Kingston	L/RW	5	0	0	0	9

1982 continued

PICK	TEAM	NAME	DRAFTED FROM	POS	GP	G	A	PTS	PIM
49	CHI	Tom McMurchy	Brandon	RW	55	8	4	12	65
50	ST.L.	Mike Posavad	Peterborough	D	8	0	0	0	0
51	CGY	Jim Laing	Clarkson	D					
52	PIT	Troy Loney	Lethbridge	LW	624	87	110	197	1091
53	VAN	Yves Lapointe	Shawinigan	LW					
54	N.J.	Dave Kasper	Sherbrooke	C					
55	QUE	Mario Gosselin	Shawinigan	G	241	91	801	6	3.74
56	HFD	Kevin Dineen	U. of Denver	RW	925	330	372	702	1875
57	NYR	Corey Millen	Cloquet H.S.	C	335	90	119	209	236
58	WSH	Milan Novy	Poldi SOMP Kladno, TCH	C	73	18	30	48	16
59	MIN	Wally Chapman	Edina H.S.	C					
60	BOS	David Reid	Peterborough	LW	750	147	177	324	188
61	MTL	Scott Harlow	S.S. Braves H.S.	LW	1	0	1	1	0
62	EDM	Brent Loney	Cornwall	LW					
63	NYI	Garry Lacey	Toronto	LW					
64	L.A.	Dave Gans	Oshawa	C	6	0	0	0	2
65	CGY	Dave Meszaros	Toronto	G					
66	DET	Craig Coxe	St. Albert Jr. A	LW	235	14	31	45	713
67	HFD	Ulf Samuelsson	Leksand, SWE	D	960	52	265	317	2296
68	BUF	Timo Jutila	Tappara Tampere, FIN	D	10	1	5	6	13
69	MTL	John Devoe	Edina H.S.	RW					
70	CHI	Bill Watson	Prince Albert	RW	115	23	36	59	12
71	VAN	Shawn Kilroy	Peterborough	G					
72	CGY	Mark Lamb	Nanaimo	C	403	46	100	146	291
73	TOR	Vladimir Ruzicka	CHZ Litvinov, TCH	C	233	82	85	167	129
74	WPG	Tom Martin	Kelowna Jr.	LW	92	12	11	23	249
75	WPG	Dave Ellett	Ottawa Jr. A	D	1023	151	401	552	948
76	QUE	Jiri Lala	Dukla Jihlava, TCH	RW					
77	PHI	Mikael Hjalm	MoDo Ornskoldsvik, SWE	R/LW					
78	NYR	Chris Jensen	Kelowna Jr.	RW	74	9	12	21	27
79	BUF	Jeff Hamilton	Providence	R/LW					
80	MIN	Bob Rouse	Nanaimo	D	965	37	169	206	1496
81	MIN	Dusan Pasek	Slovan Bratislava, TCH	C	48	4	10	14	30
82	L.A.	Dave Ross	Seattle	D					
83	EDM	Jaroslav Pouzar	Motor Ceske Budejovice, TCH	LW	186	34	48	82	135
84	NYI	Alan Kerr	Seattle	RW	391	72	94	166	826
85	N.J.	Scott Brydges	Mariner H.S.	D					
86	DET	Brad Shaw	Ottawa	D	361	22	137	159	200
87	TOR	Eduard Uvira	CHZ Litvinov, TCH	D					
88	HFD	Ray Ferraro	Penticton Jr. A	C	955	333	377	710	976
89	WSH	Dean Evason	Kamloops	C	803	139	233	372	1002
90	L.A.	Darcy Roy	Ottawa	LW					
91	CHI	Brad Beck	Penticton Jr. A	D					
92	ST.L.	Scott Machej	Calgary	C/LW					
93	CGY	Lou Kiriakou	Toronto	D					
94	PIT	Grant Sasser	Portland	C	3	0	0	0	0
95	L.A.	Ulf Isaksson	AIK Solna, SWE	LW	50	7	15	22	10
96	WPG	Tim Mishler	East Grand Forks H.S.	C					
97	QUE	Phil Stanger	Seattle	LW					
98	PHI	Todd Bergen	Prince Albert	C	14	11	5	16	4
99	TOR	Sylvain Charland	Shawinigan	LW					
100	BUF	Robert Logan	West Island Jr.	RW	42	10	5	15	0
101	MIN	Marty Wiitala	Superior H.S.	C					
102	BOS	Bob Nicholson	London	D					
103	MTL	Kevin Houle	Acton-Boxboro H.S.	LW					
104	EDM	Dwayne Boettger	Toronto	D					
105	NYI	Rene Breton	Granby	C					
106	N.J.	Mike Moher	Kitchener	RW	9	0	1	1	28
107	DET	Claude Vilgrain	Laval	RW	89	21	32	53	78
108	TOR	Ron Dreger	Saskatoon	LW					
109	HFD	Randy Gilhen	Winnipeg	C	457	55	60	115	314
110	WSH	Ed Kastelic	London	R/LW	220	11	10	21	719
111	BUF	Jeff Parker	Mariner H.S.	RW	141	16	19	35	163
112	CHI	Mark Hatcher	Niagara Falls	D					
113	ST.L.	Perry Ganchar	Saskatoon	RW	42	3	7	10	36
114	CGY	Jeff Vaive	Ottawa	C					
115	TOR	Craig Kales	Niagara Falls	RW					
116	VAN	Taylor Hall	Regina	LW	41	7	9	16	29
117	MTL	Ernie Vargas	Coon Rapids H.S.	C					
118	CGY	Mats Kihlstrom	Sodertalje, SWE	D					
119	PHI	Ron Hextall	Brandon	G	585	286	1671	23	2.99
120	NYR	Tony Granato	Northwood Prep	LW	630	232	226	458	1267
121	BUF	Jacob Gustavsson	Almtuna, SWE	G					
122	MIN	Todd Carlile	North St. Paul H.S.	D					
123	BOS	Bob Sweeney	Acton-Boxboro H.S.	C/RW	639	125	163	288	799
124	MTL	Michael Dark	Sarnia Jr. B	D	43	5	6	11	14
125	EDM	Raimo Summanen	Reipas Lahti, FIN	LW	151	36	40	76	35
126	NYI	Roger Kortko	Saskatoon	C	79	7	17	24	28
127	N.J.	Paul Fulcher	London	LW					
128	DET	Greg Hudas	Redford Jr.	D					
129	TOR	Dom Campedelli	Cohasset H.S.	D	2	0	0	0	0
130	HFD	Jim Johannson	Rochester Mayo H.S.	C					
131	QUE	Daniel Poudrier	Shawinigan	D	25	1	5	6	10
132	L.A.	Viktor Nechayev	SKA Leningrad, USSR	C	3	1	0	1	0
133	CHI	Jay Ness	Roseau H.S.	C					
134	ST.L.	Doug Gilmour	Cornwall	C	1125	381	795	1176	1028
135	CGY	Brad Ramsden	Peterborough	RW					
136	PIT	Brent Couture	Lethbridge	D					
137	VAN	Parie Proft	Calgary	D					
138	WPG	Derek Ray	Seattle Jr. B	LW					
139	TOR	Jeff Triano	Toronto	D					
140	PHI	David Brown	Saskatoon	RW	729	45	52	97	1789
141	NYR	Sergei Kapustin	Spartak Moscow, USSR	LW					
142	BUF	Allen Bishop	Niagara Falls	D					
143	MIN	Viktor Zhluktov	CSKA Moscow, USSR	LW					
144	BOS	John Meulenbroeks	Brantford	D					
145	MTL	Hannu Jarvenpaa	Karpat Oulu, FIN	RW		Re-entered Draft in 1986			
146	EDM	Brian Small	Ottawa	RW					
147	NYI	John Tiano	Winthrop H.S.	C					
148	N.J.	John Hutchings	Oshawa	D					
149	DET	Pat Lahey	Windsor	C					
150	MTL	Steve Smith	St. Lawrence U.	D					
151	HFD	Mickey Kramptoich	Hibbing H.S.	C					
152	WSH	Wally Schreiber	Regina	RW	41	8	10	18	12
153	L.A.	Peter Helander	Skelleftea, SWE	D	7	0	1	1	0
154	CHI	Jeff Smith	London	LW					
155	ST.L.	Chris Delaney	Boston College	LW					
156	CGY	Roy Myllari	Cornwall	D					
157	PIT	Peter Derksen	Portland	LW					
158	VAN	Newell Brown	Michigan State	C					
159	WPG	Guy Gosselin	John Marshall H.S.	D	5	0	0	0	6
160	NYR	Brian Glynn	Buffalo Jr.	C					
161	PHI	Alain Lavigne	Shawinigan	RW					
162	NYR	Jan Karlsson	Kiruna, SWE	D					
163	BUF	Claude Verret	Trois-Rivieres	C	14	2	5	7	2
164	MIN	Paul Miller	Crookstown H.S.	C	3	0	3	3	0
165	MTL	Tony Fiore	Montreal	C					
166	MTL	Tom Koliouspoulos	Fraser H.S.	RW					
167	EDM	Dean Clark	St. Albert Jr. A	D	1	0	0	0	0
168	NYI	Todd Okerlund	Burnsville H.S.	RW	4	0	0	0	2
169	N.J.	Alan Hepple	Ottawa	D	3	0	0	0	7
170	DET	Gary Cullen	Cornell	C					
171	TOR	Miroslav Ihnacak	VSZ Kosice, TCH	LW	56	8	9	17	39
172	HFD	Kevin Skilliter	Cornwall	D					
173	WSH	Jamie Reeves	Saskatoon Jr. A	G					
174	L.A.	Dave Chartier	Saskatoon	C	1	0	0	0	0
175	CHI	Phil Patterson	Ottawa	RW					
176	ST.L.	Matt Christensen	Aurora H.S.	C					
177	CGY	Ted Pearson	Wisconsin	LW					
178	PIT	Greg Gravel	Windsor	C					
179	VAN	Don McLaren	Ottawa	RW					
180	WPG	Tom Ward	Richfield H.S.	D					
181	QUE	Mike Hough	Kitchener	LW	696	100	156	256	673
182	PHI	Magnus Roupe	Farjestad Karlstad, SWE	LW	40	3	5	8	42
183	NYR	Kelly Miller	Michigan State	LW	995	179	277	456	483
184	BUF	Rob Norman	Cornwall	RW					
185	MIN	Pat Micheletti	Hibbing H.S.	C	12	2	0	2	8
186	BOS	Doug Kostynski	Kamloops	C	15	3	1	4	4
187	MTL	Brian Williams	Sioux City Jr. A	C					
188	EDM	Ian Wood	Penticton Jr. A	G					
189	NYI	Gord Paddock	Saskatoon Jr. A	D					
190	N.J.	Brent Shaw	Seattle	RW					
191	DET	Brent Meckling	Calgary Jr. A	D					
192	TOR	Leigh Verstraete	Calgary	RW	8	0	1	1	14
193	NYR	Simo Saarinen	HIFK Helsinki, FIN	D	8	0	0	0	0
194	WSH	Juha Nurmi	Tappara Tampere, FIN	C					
195	L.A.	John Franzosa	Brown	G					
196	CHI	James Camazzola	Penticton Jr. A	LW	3	0	0	0	0
197	ST.L.	John Shumski	RPI	C/RW					
198	CGY	Jim Uens	Oshawa	C/RW					
199	PIT	Stu Wenaas	Winnipeg	D					
200	VAN	Al Raymond	Niagara Falls	LW					
201	WPG	Mike Savage	Sudbury	LW					
202	QUE	Vincent Lukac	Dukla Jihlava, TCH	LW					
203	PHI	Tom Allen	Michigan Tech	G					
204	NYR	Bob Lowes	Prince Albert	G					
205	BUF	Mike Craig	Nanaimo	G					
206	MIN	Arnold Kadlec	CHZ Litvinov, TCH	D					
207	BOS	Tony Gilliard	Niagara Falls	LW					
208	MTL	Bob Emery	Matignon H.S.	D					
209	EDM	Grant Dion	Cowichan Valley Jr.	D					
210	NYI	Eric Faust	Henry Carr Jr. B	D					
211	N.J.	Scott Fusco	Harvard	LW					
212	DET	Mike Stern	Oshawa	LW					
213	TOR	Tim Loven	Red River H.S.	D					
214	HFD	Martin Linse	Djurgarden, SWE	C					
215	WSH	Wayne Prestage	Seattle	C					
216	L.A.	Ray Shero	St. Lawrence U.	LW					
217	CHI	Mike James	Ottawa	D					
218	ST.L.	Brian Ahern	West St. Paul H.S.	LW					
219	CGY	Rick Erdall	Minnesota-Duluth	C					
220	PIT	Chris McCauley	London	RW					
221	VAN	Steve Driscoll	Cornwall	LW					
222	WPG	Bob Shaw	Penticton Jr. A	RW					

PICK	TEAM	NAME	DRAFTED FROM	NHL PLAYERS: POS NHL GOALTENDERS: POS	GP GP	G W	A GA	PTS SO	PIM AVG
223	QUE	Andre Martin	Montreal	D					
224	PHI	Rick Gal	Lethbridge	LW					
225	NYR	Andy Otto	Northwood Prep	D					
226	BUF	Jim Plankers	Cloquet H.S.	D					
227	MIN	Scott Knutson	Warroad H.S.	C					
228	BOS	Tommy Lehmann	Stocksund, SWE	C	36	5	5	10	16
229	MTL	Darren Acheson	Fort Saskatchewan	C					
230	EDM	Chris Smith	Regina	G					
231	NYI	Pat Goff	Alexander Ramsey H.S.	D					
232	N.J.	Dan Dorion	Austin Prep	C	4	1	1	2	2
233	DET	Shaun Regan	Brantford	RW					
234	TOR	Jim Appleby	Winnipeg	G					
235	HFD	Randy Cameron	Winnipeg	D					
236	WSH	Jim Holden	Peterborough	G					
237	L.A.	Mats Ulander	AIK Stockholm, SWE	RW					
238	CHI	Bob Andrea	Dartmouth Jr.	D					
239	ST.L.	Peter Smith	U. of Maine	G					
240	CGY	Dale Thompson	Calgary Jr. A	RW					
241	PIT	Stan Bautch	Hibbing H.S.	G					
242	VAN	Shawn Green	Victoria	RW					
243	WPG	Jan Urban Ericson	AIK Solna, SWE	LW					
244	QUE	Jozef Lukac	VSŽ Kosice, TCH	C					
245	PHI	Mark Vichorek	Sioux City Jr. A	D					
246	NYR	Dwayne Robinson	New Hampshire	D					
247	WSH	Marco Callas	St. Louis Jr. B	C					
248	QUE	Jan Jasko	Slovan Bratislava, TCH	LW					
249	BOS	Bruno Campese	Northern Michigan	G					
250	MTL	Bill Brauer	Edina H.S.	D					
251	EDM	Jeff Crawford	Regina	LW					
252	NYI	Jim Koudys	Sudbury	D					

1983

The 1983 NHL Entry Draft paled in comparison to the 1982 event, as there were no standout superstars evident in the junior crop. "Not only does this year's draft lack depth in terms of numbers of good prospects available," said an NHL scout. "But it may also lack quality at the top. Not only is there no Bellows this year, there is also no Kluzak, Nylund or Housley." It was believed that not many of the 1983 draftees would be able to make an immediate jump to the NHL; however, like every draft, 1983 had its surprises.

The biggest surprise was the dominance of U.S.-born talent among the early selections as five Americans were drafted in the first round. Brian Lawton, a product of Mount St. Charles High School in Rhode Island, was selected first overall by the Minnesota North Stars, eclipsing the number one-ranked Pat LaFontaine. Lawton became the first U.S.-born player to be selected first and the highest drafted prospect from the U.S. high school system. LaFontaine, the first U.S.-born talent to be ranked as the top prospect by Central Scouting, was surprisingly passed over as the second pick and was taken third overall by the powerhouse New York Islanders. Goaltender Tom Barrasso was selected fifth overall by the Buffalo Sabres, joining John Davidson and Ray Martiniuk as the highest-drafted goaltenders in history. Alfie Turcotte and David Jensen completed the U.S. blitz as they were selected 17th and 20th respectively. "I guess we all owe something to Bobby Carpenter and Phil Housley," said Lawton. "They were both drafted high in the first round and both of them proved that a U.S. high school player could not only jump directly to the NHL, but star in the league."

"Whenever you're picked number one and don't do as well as expected, people start to jump on you. They put all the blame on you," said Lawton. Never quite able to adapt and develop in the NHL, he went on to record only 266 points for six different clubs in nine NHL seasons. LaFontaine, on the other hand, quickly became one of the NHL's most dangerous players. He is among the NHL's all-time leading scorers and is the third-highest-scoring U.S.-born player in NHL history. LaFontaine was named the

NHL's Performer of the Year in 1990 and earned the Masterton Trophy in 1995.

Tom Barrasso holds the distinction of being the first American high school goalie to be accorded first-round status. Barrasso jumped immediately into the NHL, posting an impressive 2.84 goals-against average in 42 games with the Sabres to capture the Calder Trophy as the league's top rookie, another milestone for a U.S.-born talent. Buffalo also acquired an additional goaltender in 1983 with the selection of Daren Puppa with their sixth pick, 74th overall. Puppa was named runner-up for the Vezina Trophy in 1990 and was nominated for the award again in 1996.

Although the 1983 draft was dubbed "The Year of the Yankee," Americans were not the only prominent invaders of the NHL, as 14% of the players chosen were classified as internationals. Finnish super-pest Esa Tikkanen led the Europeans by being selected 80th overall by the Edmonton Oilers. Czechoslovakian star Petr Klima and goaltending wizard Dominik Hasek were selected 86th and 199th overall respectively. However, it was the drafting of Soviet superstars that grabbed the most attention. After outstanding performances in major international competition such as the Olympics and the Canada Cup tournaments, the NHL pursued the top Soviet talents. Goaltender Vladislav Tretiak, touted as the world's greatest netminder, was taken 138th overall by the Canadiens. Tretiak never got the opportunity to play in the NHL but he was inducted into the Hockey Hall of Fame in 1989.

Defensemen Viacheslav Fetisov and Alexei Kasatonov were taken 150th and 225th by the New Jersey Devils. It was the second time that Fetisov had been selected in the Entry Draft, as the Canadiens had taken him 201st overall in 1978. The Calgary Flames took Soviet scorer Sergei Makarov 231st overall. Makarov would become the first Russian to win a major NHL award when he captured the Calder Trophy as rookie of the year in 1990. Eligibility for the award was revised after Makarov received the trophy, barring players 26 years of age or older from qualifying. Makarov was a crafty 32-year-old veteran of international hockey when he became an NHL rookie.

The role of the power forward was emphasized in the 1983 draft as Cam Neely, Rick Tocchet and Kevin Stevens were selected. Aggressive physical play combined with outstanding offensive talent made their patented style of play the popular and most effective player mold for the wave of the future.

The 1983 NHL Entry Draft was conducted under a shadow cast by the financial woes of the St. Louis Blues. After suffering severe monetary losses over the past few years, the Blues experienced a change in ownership, which resulted in the franchise's failure to participate in the Entry Draft.

1983

PICK	TEAM	NAME	DRAFTED FROM	NHL PLAYERS: POS NHL GOALTENDERS: POS	GP GP	G W	A GA	PTS SO	PIM AVG
FIRST ROUND									
1	MIN	Brian Lawton	Mount St. Charles H.S.	LW	483	112	154	266	401
2	HFD	Sylvain Turgeon	Hull	LW	669	269	226	495	691
3	NYI	Pat LaFontaine	Verdun	C	865	468	545	1013	552
4	DET	Steve Yzerman	Peterborough	C	1098	563	846	1409	740
5	BUF	Tom Barrasso	Acton-Boxboro H.S.	G	665	326	2110	30	3.32
6	N.J.	John MacLean	Oshawa	RW	985	360	373	733	1196
7	TOR	Russ Courtnall	Victoria	RW	972	291	434	725	538
8	WPG	Andrew McBain	North Bay	RW	608	129	172	301	633
9	VAN	Cam Neely	Portland	RW	726	395	299	694	1241
10	BUF	Normand Lacombe	New Hampshire	RW	319	53	62	115	196
11	BUF	Adam Creighton	Ottawa	C	708	187	216	403	1077
12	NYR	Dave Gagner	Brantford	C	877	312	379	691	955
13	CGY	Dan Quinn	Belleville	C	805	266	419	685	533
14	WPG	Bobby Dollas	Laval	D	505	36	80	116	361

1983 *continued*

PICK	TEAM	NAME	DRAFTED FROM	POS	GP	G	A	PTS	PIM
					GP	W	GA	SO	AVG
15	PIT	Bob Errey	Peterborough	LW	895	170	212	382	1005
16	NYI	Gerald Diduck	Lethbridge	D	848	56	151	207	1489
17	MTL	Alfie Turcotte	Portland	C	112	17	29	46	49
18	CHI	Bruce Cassidy	Ottawa	D	36	4	13	17	10
19	EDM	Jeff Beukeboom	Sault Ste. Marie	D	759	30	120	150	1830
20	HFD	David A. Jensen	Lawrence Academy	C	69	9	13	22	22
21	BOS	Nevin Markwart	Regina	LW	309	41	68	109	794

SECOND ROUND

PICK	TEAM	NAME	DRAFTED FROM	POS	GP	G	A	PTS	PIM
22	PIT	Todd Charlesworth	Oshawa	D	93	3	9	12	47
23	HFD	Ville Siren	Ilves Tampere, FIN	D	290	14	68	82	276
24	N.J.	Shawn Evans	Peterborough	D	9	1	0	1	2
25	DET	Lane Lambert	Saskatoon	RW	283	58	66	124	521
26	MTL	Claude Lemieux	Trois-Rivieres	RW	836	298	302	600	1392
27	MTL	Sergio Momesso	Shawinigan	LW	710	152	193	345	1557
28	TOR	Jeff Jackson	Brantford	LW	263	38	48	86	313
29	WPG	Brad Berry	St. Albert Jr. A	D	241	4	28	32	323
30	VAN	David Bruce	Kitchener	LW	234	48	39	87	338
31	BUF	John Tucker	Kitchener	C	656	177	259	436	285
32	QUE	Yves Heroux	Chicoutimi	RW	1	0	0	0	0
33	NYR	Randy Heath	Portland	LW	13	2	4	6	15
34	BUF	Richard Hajdu	Kamloops	LW	5	0	0	0	4
35	MTL	Todd Francis	Brantford	RW					
36	MIN	Malcolm Parks	St. Albert Jr. A	C					
37	NYI	Garnet McKechney	Kitchener	RW					
38	MIN	Frantisek Musil	Tesla Pardubice, TCH	D	745	34	101	135	1203
39	CHI	Wayne Presley	Kitchener	RW	684	155	147	302	953
40	EDM	Mike Golden	Reading H.S.	C					
41	PHI	Peter Zezel	Toronto	C	832	213	381	594	419
42	BOS	Greg Johnston	Toronto	RW	187	26	29	55	124

OTHER ROUNDS

PICK	TEAM	NAME	DRAFTED FROM	POS	GP	G	A	PTS	PIM
43	WPG	Peter Taglianetti	Providence	D	451	18	74	92	1106
44	PHI	Derrick Smith	Peterborough	LW	537	82	92	174	373
45	MTL	Daniel Letendre	Quebec	RW					
46	DET	Bob Probert	Brantford	LW	648	144	181	325	2701
47	L.A.	Bruce Shoebottom	Peterborough	D	35	1	4	5	53
48	ST.L.	no selection							
49	TOR	Allan Bester	Brantford	G	219	73	786	7	4.01
50	NYR	Vesa Salo	Lukko Rauma, FIN	D					
51	VAN	Scott Tottle	Peterborough	RW					
52	CGY	Brian Bradley	London	C	651	182	321	503	528
53	QUE	Bruce Bell	Windsor	D	209	12	64	76	113
54	NYR	Gord Walker	Portland	RW	31	3	4	7	23
55	QUE	Iiro Jarvi	HIFK Helsinki, FIN	RW	116	18	43	61	58
56	CGY	Perry Berezan	St. Albert Jr. A	C	378	61	75	136	279
57	MIN	Mitch Messier	Notre Dame Sask. Juvenile	C	20	0	2	2	11
58	NYI	Mike Neill	Sault Ste. Marie	D					
59	PIT	Mike Rowe	Toronto	D	11	0	0	0	11
60	CHI	Marc Bergevin	Chicoutimi	D	859	30	114	144	823
61	EDM	Mike Flanagan	Acton-Boxboro H.S.	D					
62	HFD	Leif Karlsson	Mora, SWE	D					
63	BOS	Greg Puhalski	Kitchener	LW					
64	PIT	Frank Pietrangelo	Minnesota-Duluth	G	141	46	490	1	4.12
65	HFD	Dave MacLean	Belleville	RW					
66	NYI	Mikko Makela	Ilves Tampere, FIN	LW	423	118	147	265	139
67	CGY	John Bekkers	Regina	C					
68	L.A.	Guy Benoit	Shawinigan	C					
69	ST.L.	no selection							
70	DET	David Korol	Winnipeg	D					
71	WPG	Bob Essensa	Henry Carr Jr. B	G	329	130	992	16	3.28
72	VAN	Tim Lorentz	Portland	LW					
73	CGY	Kevan Guy	Medicine Hat	D	156	5	20	25	138
74	HFD	Ron Chyzowski	St. Albert Jr. A	C					
75	NYR	Peter Andersson	Orebro, SWE	D	47	6	13	19	20
76	BUF	Daren Puppa	Kirkland Lake	G	411	173	1152	17	3.02
77	WSH	Tim Bergland	Lincoln H.S.	RW	182	17	26	43	75
78	MIN	Brian Durand	Cloquet H.S.	C					
79	CGY	Bill Claviter	Virginia H.S.	LW					
80	MTL	John Kordic	Portland	RW	244	17	18	35	997
81	CHI	Tarek Howard	Olds Jr. A	D					
82	EDM	Esa Tikkanen	HIFK Helsinki, FIN	LW	845	244	383	627	1039
83	PHI	Alan Bourbeau	Acton-Boxboro H.S.	C					
84	BOS	Alain Larochelle	Saskatoon	G					
85	TOR	Dan Hodgson	Prince Albert	C	114	29	45	74	64
86	NYI	Bob Caulfield	Detroit Lakes H.S.	RW					
87	N.J.	Chris Terreri	Providence	G	364	137	1037	8	3.10
88	DET	Petr Klima	Dukla Jihlava, TCH	R/LW	773	312	260	572	667
89	L.A.	Bob LaForest	North Bay	RW	5	1	0	1	2
90	ST.L.	no selection							
91	DET	Joe Kocur	Saskatoon	RW	781	78	77	155	2432
92	WPG	Harry Armstrong	Dubuque Jr. A	D					
93	VAN	Doug Quinn	Nanaimo	D					
94	CGY	Igor Liba	Dukla Jihlava, TCH	LW	37	7	18	25	36
95	QUE	Luc Guenette	Quebec	G					
96	NYR	Jim Andonoff	Belleville	RW					
97	BUF	Jayson Meyer	Regina	D					
98	WSH	Martin Bouliane	Granby	C					
99	MIN	Rich Geist	St. Paul Academy	C					
100	NYI	Ron Viglasi	Victoria	D					
101	MTL	Dan Wurst	Edina H.S.	D					
102	CHI	Kevin Robinson	Toronto	D					
103	L.A.	Garry Galley	Bowling Green	D	963	106	428	534	1077
104	PHI	Jerome Carrier	Verdun	D					
105	BOS	Allen Pederson	Medicine Hat	D	428	5	36	41	487
106	PIT	Patrick Emond	Hull	C					
107	HFD	Brian Johnson	Silver Bay H.S.	RW	3	0	0	0	5
108	N.J.	Gordon Mark	Kamloops	D	85	3	10	13	187
109	DET	Chris Pusey	Brantford	G	1	0	3	0	4.50
110	L.A.	Dave Lundmark	Virginia H.S.	D					
111	ST.L.	no selection							
112	L.A.	Kevin Stevens	Silver Lake H.S.	LW	668	292	346	638	1265
113	WPG	Joel Baillargeon	Hull	LW	20	0	2	2	31
114	VAN	Dave Lowry	London	LW	798	126	136	262	1018
115	CGY	Grant Blair	Harvard	G					
116	QUE	Brad Walcott	Kingston	D					
117	NYR	Bob Alexander	Rosemount H.S.	D					
118	BUF	Jim Hofford	Windsor	D	18	0	0	0	47
119	CHI	Jari Torkki	Lukko Rauma, FIN	LW	4	1	0	1	0
120	MIN	Tom McComb	Mount St. Charles H.S.	D					
121	NYI	Darin Illikainen	Hermantown H.S.	D					
122	MTL	Arto Javanainen	Assat Pori, FIN	RW	Re-entered Draft in 1984				
123	CHI	Mark Lavarre	Stratford Jr. B	RW	78	9	16	25	58
124	EDM	Don Barber	Kelowna	R/LW	115	25	32	57	64
125	PHI	Rick Tocchet	Sault Ste. Marie	RW	909	385	436	821	2626
126	BOS	Terry Taillefer	St. Albert Jr. A	G					
127	PIT	Paul Ames	Billerica H.S.	C					
128	HFD	Joe Reekie	North Bay	D	Re-entered Draft in 1985				
129	N.J.	Greg Evtushevski	Kamloops	RW					
130	DET	Bob Pierson	London	LW					
131	L.A.	Tim Burgess	Oshawa	D					
132	ST.L.	no selection							
133	TOR	Cam Plante	Brandon	D	2	0	0	0	0
134	WPG	Iain Duncan	North York Jr. B	LW	127	34	55	89	149
135	VAN	Terry Maki	Brantford	LW					
136	CGY	Jeff Hogg	Oshawa	G					
137	QUE	Craig Mack	East Grand Forks H.S.	D					
138	NYR	Steve Orth	St. Cloud Tech H.S.	C					
139	BUF	Christian Ruuttu	Assat Pori, FIN	C	621	134	298	432	714
140	WSH	Dwaine Hutton	Kelowna	C					
141	MIN	Sean Toomey	Cretin H.S.	LW	1	0	0	0	0
142	NYI	Jim Sprenger	Cloquet H.S.	D					
143	MTL	Vladislav Tretiak	CSKA Moscow, USSR	G					
144	CHI	Scott Birnie	Cornwall	RW					
145	EDM	Dale Derkatch	Regina	C					
146	PHI	Bobby Mormina	Longueuil	D					
147	BOS	Ian Armstrong	Peterborough	D					
148	HFD	Chris Duperron	Chicoutimi	D					
149	HFD	James Falle	Clarkson	G					
150	N.J.	Viacheslav Fetisov	CSKA Moscow, USSR	D	546	36	192	228	656
151	DET	Craig Butz	Kelowna	D					
152	L.A.	Ken Hammond	RPI	D	193	18	29	47	290
153	ST.L.	no selection							
154	TOR	Paul Bifano	Burnaby Jr.	LW					
155	WPG	Ron Pessetti	Western Michigan	D					
156	VAN	John Labatt	Minnetonka H.S.	C					
157	CGY	Chris MacDonald	Western Michigan	D					
158	QUE	Tommy Albelin	Djurgarden, SWE	D	614	35	163	198	359
159	NYR	Peter Marcov	Welland Jr. B	LW					
160	BUF	Don McSween	Regina Jr. A	D	47	3	10	13	55
161	WSH	Marty Abrams	Pembroke Jr. A	G					
162	MIN	Don Biggs	Oshawa	C	12	2	0	2	8
163	NYI	Dale Henry	Saskatoon	LW	132	13	26	39	263
164	MTL	Rob Bryden	Henry Carr Jr. B	LW					
165	CHI	Kent Paynter	Kitchener	D	37	1	3	4	69
166	EDM	Ralph Vos	Abbotsford Jr.	G	1	0	3	0	4.50
167	PHI	Pelle Eklund	AIK Solna, SWE	C	594	120	335	455	109
168	BOS	Francois Olivier	St-Jean	LW					
169	PIT	Marty Ketola	St. Cloquet H.S.	RW					
170	HFD	Bill Fordy	Guelph	LW					
171	N.J.	Jay Octeau	Mount St. Charles H.S.	D					
172	DET	Dave Sikorski	Cornwall	D					
173	L.A.	Bruce Fishback	Mariner H.S.	C					
174	ST.L.	no selection							
175	TOR	Cliff Albrecht	Princeton	D					
176	WPG	Todd Flichel	Gloucester	D	6	0	1	1	4
177	MTL	Allan Measures	Calgary	D					
178	CGY	Rob Kivell	Victoria	D					
179	QUE	Wayne Groulx	Sault Ste. Marie	C	1	0	0	0	0
180	NYR	Paul Jerrard	Notre Dame Jr. A	D	5	0	0	0	4
181	BUF	Tim Hoover	Sault Ste. Marie	D					
182	WSH	David Cowan	Washburn H.S.	LW					
183	MIN	Paul Pulis	Hibbing H.S.	RW					
184	NYI	Kevin Vescio	North Bay	D					
185	MTL	Grant MacKay	U. of Calgary	D					
186	CHI	Brian Noonan	Archbishop Williams H.S.	RW	622	116	159	275	518

PICK	TEAM	NAME	DRAFTED FROM	NHL PLAYERS: POS / NHL GOALTENDERS: POS	GP	G / W	A / GA	PTS / SO	PIM / AVG
187	EDM	Dave Roach	New Westminster	G					
188	PHI	Rob Nichols	Kitchener	LW					
189	BOS	Harri Laurila	Reipas Lahti, FIN	D					
190	PIT	Alec Haidy	Sault Ste. Marie	RW					
191	TOR	Greg Rolston	Michael Power H.S.	RW					
192	N.J.	Alexander Chernykh	Khimik Voskresensk, USSR	C					
193	DET	Stu Grimson	Regina	LW	Re-entered Draft in 1985				
194	L.A.	Thomas Ahlen	Skelleftea, SWE	D					
195	ST.L.		no selection						
196	TOR	Brian Ross	Kitchener	D					
197	WPG	Cory Wright	Dubuque Jr. A	RW					
198	VAN	Roger Grillo	U. of Maine	D					
199	CGY	Tom Pratt	Kimball Union Academy	D					
200	QUE	Scott Shaunessy	St. John's Prep	D/LW	7	0	0	0	23
201	HFD	Reine Karlsson	Sodertalje, SWE	LW					
202	BUF	Mark Ferner	Kamloops	D	91	3	10	13	51
203	WSH	Yves Beaudoin	Shawinigan	D	11	0	0	0	5
204	MIN	Milos Riha	TJ Gottwaldov, TCH	LW					
205	NYI	Dave Shellington	Cornwall	LW					
206	MTL	Thomas Rundqvist	Farjestad Karlstad, SWE	C	2	0	1	1	0
207	CHI	Dominik Hasek	Tesla Pardubice, TCH	G	350	165	782	33	2.34
208	EDM	Warren Yadlowski	Calgary	C					
209	PHI	William McCormick	Westminster Heights H.S.	C					
210	BOS	Paul Fitzsimmons	Northeastern	D					
211	PIT	Garth Hildebrand	Calgary	LW					
212	HFD	Allan Acton	Saskatoon	LW					
213	N.J.	Allan Stewart	Prince Albert	LW	64	6	4	10	243
214	DET	Jeff Frank	Regina	RW					
215	L.A.	Miroslav Blaha	Motor Ceske Budejovice, TCH	RW					
216	ST.L.		no selection						
217	TOR	Mike Tomlak	Cornwall	C/LW	141	15	22	37	103
218	WPG	Eric Cormier	St. Georges	LW					
219	VAN	Steve Kayser	Vermont	D					
220	CGY	Jaroslav Benak	Dukla Jihlava, TCH	LW					
221	MIN	Oldrich Valek	Dukla Jihlava, TCH	RW					
222	NYR	Bryan Walker	Portland	D					
223	BUF	Uwe Krupp	Koln, FRG	D	695	66	209	275	636
224	WSH	Alain Raymond	Trois-Rivieres	G	1	0	2	0	3.00
225	WSH	Anders Huss	Brynas Gavle, SWE	C					
226	NYI	John Bjorkman	Warroad H.S.	C					
227	MTL	Jeff Perpich	Hibbing H.S.	D					
228	CHI	Steve Pepin	St-Jean	C					
229	EDM	John Miner	Regina	D	14	2	3	5	16
230	PHI	Brian Jopling	Williston Academy	G					
231	BOS	Norm Foster	Penticton Jr. A	G	13	7	34	0	3.27
232	PIT	Dave Goertz	Regina	D	2	0	0	0	2
233	HFD	Darcy Kaminski	Lethbridge	D					
234	N.J.	Alexei Kasatonov	CSKA Moscow, USSR	D	383	38	122	160	320
235	DET	Charles Chiatto	Cranbrook H.S.	C					
236	L.A.	Chad Johnson	Roseau H.S.	C					
237	ST.L.		no selection						
238	TOR	Ron Choules	Trois-Rivieres	LW					
239	WPG	Jamie Husgen	Des Moines Jr. A	D					
240	VAN	Jay Mazur	Breck H.S.	C/RW	47	11	7	18	20
241	CGY	Sergei Makarov	CSKA Moscow, USSR	RW	424	134	250	384	317
242	QUE	Bo Berglund	Djurgarden, SWE	RW	130	28	39	67	40
243	NYR	Ulf Nilsson	Skelleftea, SWE	C	170	57	112	169	85
244	BUF	Marc Hamelin	Shawinigan	G					
245	BUF	Kermit Salfi	Northwood Prep	LW					
246	MIN	Paul Roff	Edina H.S.	RW					
247	NYI	Peter McGeough	Henricken H.S.	RW					
248	MTL	Jean-Guy Bergeron	Shawinigan	D					
249	QUE	Jindrich Kokrment	CHZ Litvinov, TCH	C					
250	EDM	Steve Woodburn	Verdun	D					
251	PHI	Harold Duvall	Belmont Hill H.S.	LW					
252	BOS	Greg Murphy	Trinity-Pawling H.S.	D					

1984

For the first time in NHL history the Entry Draft was publicly televised in 1984, expanding the event further into the public eye. The Canadian Broadcasting Company provided live coverage of the draft, broadcasting coast-to-coast in Canada in both French and English. International talent was again a focus at the 1984 Entry Draft as the NHL arranged for the European Sports Services, a Finnish-based scouting service, to provide a ranking of European prospects eligible for drafting.

The 1984 NHL Entry Draft proved to be the most exciting since 1973, when Denis Potvin went first. It produced the greatest player selected in an Entry Draft, when Mario Lemieux went first overall by the Pittsburgh Penguins.

After rewriting the junior record books, the 6'4", 200-pound scoring phenomenon was touted as a sure-fire franchise player coming into the NHL. "You look at the guys who have been great players out of this league but he's broken every record they have," said Penguins g.m. Eddie Johnston. "We need that big, dominant guy and this guy's presence is felt. He's got great skills. It's 99.9 percent [sure that] this guy can come in. He's the best player in the country." Although Lemieux refused to don the Penguin jersey or pose for pictures due to a dispute with club management, he suited up with the Penguins in 1984–85 and recorded his first 100-point season with 43 goals and 57 assists in his rookie year. He captured the Calder Trophy to start an impressive collection of NHL awards that eventually saw him win the Hart Trophy three times; the Art Ross Trophy six times, the Lester B. Pearson Award four times, the Masterton Trophy once and the Conn Smythe Trophy in 1991 and 1992 when he led the Penguins to back-to-back Stanley Cup wins. His 613 goals and 881 assists for 1,494 points in just 745 games rank him as one of the NHL's most elite talents in history. He was the second-fastest player to record 500 goals and 1,000 points, reaching the milestones in 605 and 513 games respectively, to trail only Wayne Gretzky. After retiring in 1996–97, Lemieux became the ninth player to be inducted into the Hockey Hall of Fame without waiting the three-year grace period.

Although all of the attention settled on Lemieux in 1984, there remained a substantial number of dark horses in the draft pool. Among them was Brett Hull, son of former NHL great Bobby. Hull was taken 117th overall by Calgary and emerged as one of the NHL's greatest snipers after a trade to the St. Louis Blues. He would set a record for goals by a right winger with 86 in 1990–91. He also captured the Hart Trophy as the league's MVP in 1991 and the Lady Byng Trophy as the most gentlemanly player in 1990. The Los Angeles Kings uncovered a diamond when they drafted Luc Robitaille 171st. Robitaille went on to capture rookie of the year honors in 1987 as he led all first-year players in scoring with 84 points on 45 goals and 39 assists. Robitaille went on to set NHL single-season records for most goals and points by a left winger, with 63 goals and 123 points in 1992–93.

The Calgary Flames drafted defenseman Gary Suter 180th overall. He captured the 1986 Calder Trophy to become the second U.S.-born talent to receive the award. The American factor was once again apparent in 1984 when three U.S.-born talents were selected in the first round of the Entry Draft. Chicago native Ed Olczyk was selected by his hometown Black Hawks third overall, while Michigan native Al Iafrate followed as the fourth selection when he was picked by the Maple Leafs. Big defenseman Kevin Hatcher completed the trio as the 17th overall selection by the Washington Capitals.

Although goaltending talent was considered to be relatively thin in the 1984 draft, the Montreal Canadiens grabbed Patrick Roy 51st overall. Roy became a superstar in the NHL when he backstopped the Montreal Canadiens to a Stanley Cup championship in his rookie year of 1985–86 and captured the Conn Smythe Trophy as the MVP of the postseason, following a similar path as former Canadiens netminder Ken Dryden. Roy has won the Vezina Trophy three times and the Conn Smythe Trophy twice in addition to his three Stanley Cup rings. He is known as one of the greatest goaltenders of all-time and stands as the goaltender with the most wins in postseason play.

1984

PICK	TEAM	NAME	DRAFTED FROM	POS	GP	G / W	A / GA	PTS / SO	PIM / AVG
FIRST ROUND									
1	PIT	Mario Lemieux	Laval	C	745	613	881	1494	737
2	N.J.	Kirk Muller	Guelph	LW	1032	334	542	876	1078
3	CHI	Ed Olczyk	Team USA	C	937	330	435	765	833
4	TOR	Al Iafrate	Belleville	D	799	152	311	463	1301
5	MTL	Petr Svoboda	CHZ Litvinov, TCH	D	880	50	297	347	1313
6	L.A.	Craig Redmond	U. of Denver	D	191	16	68	84	134
7	DET	Shawn Burr	Kitchener	LW/C	856	181	256	437	1040
8	MTL	Shayne Corson	Brantford	LW	809	221	328	549	1708
9	PIT	Doug Bodger	Kamloops	D	993	103	410	513	969
10	VAN	J-J Daigneault	Longueuil	D	775	50	182	232	593
11	HFD	Sylvain Cote	Quebec	D	877	99	240	339	441
12	CGY	Gary Roberts	Ottawa	LW	646	277	277	554	1839
13	MIN	David Quinn	Kent Prep	D					
14	NYR	Terry Carkner	Peterborough	D	796	40	179	219	1534
15	QUE	Trevor Stienburg	Guelph	RW	71	8	4	12	161
16	PIT	Roger Belanger	Kingston	C	44	3	5	8	32
17	WSH	Kevin Hatcher	North Bay	D	960	208	390	598	1292
18	BUF	Mikael Andersson	Vastra Frolunda, SWE	LW	659	91	159	250	126
19	BOS	Dave Pasin	Prince Albert	RW	76	18	19	37	50
20	NYI	Duncan MacPherson	Saskatoon	D					
21	EDM	Selmar Odelein	Regina	D	18	0	2	2	35
SECOND ROUND									
22	PHI	Greg Smyth	London	D	229	4	16	20	783
23	N.J.	Craig Billington	Belleville	G	264	88	874	7	3.80
24	L.A.	Brian Wilks	Kitchener	C	48	4	8	12	27
25	TOR	Todd Gill	Windsor	D	793	72	248	320	1064
26	ST.L.	Brian Benning	Portland	D	568	63	233	296	963
27	PHI	Scott Mellanby	Henry Carr Jr. B	RW	872	238	291	529	1734
28	DET	Doug Houda	Calgary	D	556	19	62	81	1090
29	MTL	Stephane Richer	Granby	RW	866	380	341	721	560
30	WPG	Peter Douris	New Hampshire	RW	321	54	67	121	80
31	VAN	Jeff Rohlicek	Portland	C	9	0	0	0	8
32	ST.L.	Tony Hrkac	Orillia Jr. A	C	382	75	148	223	84
33	CGY	Ken Sabourin	Sault Ste. Marie	D	74	2	8	10	201
34	WSH	Stephen Leach	Matignon H.S.	RW	615	127	147	274	911
35	NYR	Raimo Helminen	Ilves Tampere, FIN	C	117	13	46	59	16
36	QUE	Jeff Brown	Sudbury	D	747	154	430	584	498
37	PHI	Jeff Chychrun	Kingston	D	262	3	22	25	744
38	CGY	Paul Ranheim	Edina H.S.	LW	629	125	157	282	177
39	BUF	Doug Trapp	Regina	LW	2	0	0	0	0
40	BOS	Ray Podloski	Portland	C	8	0	1	1	22
41	NYI	Bruce Melanson	Oshawa	RW					
42	EDM	Daryl Reaugh	Kamloops	G	27	8	72	1	3.47
OTHER ROUNDS									
43	PHI	David McLay	Kelowna	LW					
44	N.J.	Neil Davey	Michigan State	D					
45	CHI	Trent Yawney	Saskatoon	D	573	27	102	129	751
46	MIN	Ken Hodge	St. John's Prep	C/RW	142	39	48	87	32
47	PHI	John Stevens	Oshawa	D	53	0	10	10	48
48	L.A.	John English	Sault Ste. Marie	D	3	1	3	4	4
49	DET	Milan Chalupa	Dukla Jihlava, TCH	D	14	0	5	5	6
50	ST.L.	Toby Ducolon	Bellows Academy	RW					
51	MTL	Patrick Roy	Granby	G	717	380	1875	41	2.69
52	VAN	David Saunders	St. Lawrence U.	LW	56	7	13	20	10
53	ST.L.	Robert Dirk	Regina	D	402	13	29	42	786
54	MTL	Graeme Bonar	Sault Ste. Marie	RW					
55	VAN	Landis Chaulk	Calgary	LW					
56	ST.L.	Alan Perry	Mount St. Charles H.S.	G					
57	QUE	Steven Finn	Laval	D	725	34	78	112	1724
58	VAN	Mike Stevens	Kitchener	LW	23	1	4	5	29
59	WSH	Michal Pivonka	Poldi SOMP Kladno, TCH	C	789	176	412	588	466
60	BUF	Ray Sheppard	Cornwall	RW	696	322	257	579	192
61	BOS	Jeff Cornelius	Toronto	D					
62	NYI	Jeff Norton	Cushing Academy	D	591	46	278	324	484
63	EDM	Todd Norman	Hill-Murray H.S.	C					
64	PIT	Mark Teevens	Peterborough	RW					
65	MTL	Lee Brodeur	Grafton H.S.	RW					
66	CHI	Tommy Eriksson	MoDo Ornskoldsvik, SWE	C					
67	TOR	Jeff Reese	London	G	172	52	521	5	3.65
68	WPG	Chris Mills	Bramalea Jr. B	D					
69	L.A.	Thomas Glavine	Billerica H.S.	C					
70	NYI	Doug Wieck	Rochester Mayo H.S.	LW					
71	ST.L.	Graham Herring	Longueuil	D					
72	WPG	Sean Clement	Brockville Jr. A	D					
73	VAN	Brian Bertuzzi	Kamloops	C					
74	N.J.	Paul Ysebaert	Petrolia Jr. B	C	522	149	186	335	215
75	CGY	Petr Rosol	Dukla Jihlava, TCH	LW					
76	MIN	Miroslav Maly	Bayreuth, FRG	D					
77	NYR	Paul Broten	Roseau H.S.	RW	322	46	55	101	264
78	QUE	Terry Perkins	Portland	RW					
79	PHI	Dave Hanson	Grand Forks H.S.	D	33	1	1	2	65
80	WSH	Kris King	Peterborough	LW	730	61	79	140	1862
81	BUF	Bob Halkidis	London	D	256	8	32	40	825
82	BOS	Bob Joyce	Notre Dame Jr. A	LW	158	34	49	83	90
83	NYI	Ari Haanpaa	Ilves Tampere, FIN	RW	60	6	11	17	37
84	EDM	Rich Novak	Richmond Jr.	RW					
85	PIT	Arto Javanainen	Assat Pori, FIN	RW	14	4	1	5	2
86	N.J.	Jon Morris	Chelmsford H.S.	C	103	16	33	49	47
87	L.A.	David Grannis	South St. Paul H.S.	RW					
88	TOR	Jack Capuano	Kent Prep	D	6	0	0	0	0
89	MIN	Jiri Poner	Landshut, FRG	RW					
90	CHI	Timo Lehkonen	Jokerit Helsinki, FIN	D					
91	DET	Mats Lundstrom	Skelleftea, SWE	LW					
92	ST.L.	Scott Paluch	Chicago Jr.	D					
93	WPG	Scott Schneider	Colorado College	C					
94	VAN	Brett MacDonald	North Bay	D	1	0	0	0	0
95	MTL	Gerald Johannson	Swift Current	D					
96	CGY	Joel Paunio	HIFK Helsinki, FIN	LW					
97	MIN	Kari Takko	Assat Pori, FIN	G	142	37	475	1	3.90
98	NYR	Clark Donatelli	Stratford Jr. B	LW	35	3	4	7	39
99	WPG	Brent Severyn	Seattle	LW	298	9	28	37	775
100	PHI	Brian Dobbin	London	RW	63	7	8	15	61
101	CHI	Darin Sceviour	Lethbridge	RW	1	0	0	0	0
102	BUF	Joel Rampton	Sault Ste. Marie	LW					
103	BOS	Mike Bishop	London	G					
104	NYI	Mike Murray	London	C	1	0	0	0	0
105	EDM	Richard Lambert	Henry Carr Jr. B	LW					
106	EDM	Emanuel Viveiros	Prince Albert	D	29	1	11	12	6
107	N.J.	Kirk McLean	Oshawa	G	537	221	1702	20	3.29
108	L.A.	Greg Strome	North Dakota	G					
109	TOR	Fabian Joseph	Victoria	C					
110	HFD	Mike Millar	Brantford	RW	78	18	18	36	12
111	CHI	Chris Clifford	Kingston	G	2	0	0	0	0.00
112	DET	Randy Hansch	Victoria	G					
113	ST.L.	Steve Tuttle	Richmond Jr.	RW	144	28	28	56	12
114	WPG	Gary Lorden	Bishop Hendricken H.S.	D					
115	VAN	Jeff Korchinski	Clarkson	D					
116	MTL	Jim Nesich	Verdun	RW/C					
117	CGY	Brett Hull	Penticton Jr. A	RW	801	554	433	987	298
118	MIN	Gary McColgan	Oshawa	LW					
119	NYR	Kjell Samuelsson	Leksand, SWE	D	767	47	134	181	1187
120	QUE	Darren Cota	Kelowna	RW					
121	PHI	John Dzikowski	Brandon	LW					
122	WSH	Vito Cramarossa	Toronto	RW					
123	BUF	James Gasseau	Drummondville	D					
124	BOS	Randy Oswald	Michigan Tech	D					
125	NYI	Jim Wilharm	Minnetonka H.S.	D					
126	EDM	Ivan Dornic	Dukla Trencin, TCH	LW					
127	PIT	Tom Ryan	Newton North H.S.	D					
128	N.J.	Ian Ferguson	Oshawa	D					
129	L.A.	Timothy Hanley	Deerfield Academy	C					
130	TOR	Joseph McInnis	Watertown H.S.	C					
131	HFD	Mike Vellucci	Belleville	D	2	0	0	0	11
132	CHI	Mike Stapleton	Cornwall	C	507	50	84	134	268
133	DET	Stefan Larsson	Vastra Frolunda, SWE	D					
134	ST.L.	Cliff Ronning	New Westminster	C	695	196	363	559	291
135	WPG	Luciano Borsato	Bramalea Jr. B	C	203	35	55	90	113
136	VAN	Blaine Chrest	Portland	C					
137	MTL	Scott Mactavish	Fredericton H.S.	D					
138	CGY	Kevan Melrose	Red Deer Jr. A	D					
139	MIN	Vladimir Kyhos	CHZ Litvinov, TCH	LW					
140	NYR	Thomas Hussey	St. Andrew's H.S.	LW					
141	QUE	Henrik Cedergren	Brynas Gavle, SWE	RW					
142	PHI	Tom Allen	Kitchener	D					
143	WSH	Timo Iljima	Karpat Oulu, FIN	C					
144	BUF	Darcy Wakaluk	Kelowna	G	191	67	524	9	3.22
145	BOS	Mark Thietke	Saskatoon	D					
146	NYI	Kelly Murphy	Notre Dame Jr. A	D					
147	EDM	Heikki Riihijarvi	Kiekko-Espoo, FIN	D					
148	ST.L.	Don Porter	Michigan Tech	LW					
149	N.J.	Vladimir Kames	Dukla Jihlava, TCH	C					
150	L.A.	Shannon Deegan	Vermont	G					
151	TOR	Derek Laxdal	Brandon	RW	67	12	7	19	90
152	DET	Lars Karlsson	Farjestad Karlstad, SWE	LW					
153	CHI	Glen Greenough	Sudbury	RW					
154	DET	Urban Nordin	MoDo Ornskoldsvik, SWE	C					
155	ST.L.	Jim Vesey	Columbus H.S.	C/RW	15	1	2	3	7
156	WPG	Brad Jones	Michigan	LW	148	25	31	56	122
157	VAN	Jim Agnew	Brandon	D	81	0	1	1	257
158	MTL	Brad McCaughey	Ann Arbor H.S.	RW					
159	CGY	Jiri Hrdina	Sparta Praha, TCH	C	250	45	85	130	92
160	MIN	Darin Macinnis	Kent Prep	G					
161	NYR	Brian Nelson	Willmar H.S.	C					
162	QUE	Jyrki Maki	Simley H.S.	D					
163	PHI	Luke Vitale	Henry Carr Jr. B	C					
164	WSH	Frank Joo	Regina	D					
165	BUF	Orvar Stambert	Djurgarden, SWE	D					
166	BOS	Don Sweeney	St. Paul's H.S.	D	670	41	157	198	466
167	NYI	Franco Desantis	Verdun	D					
168	EDM	Todd Ewen	New Westminster	RW	518	36	40	76	1911
169	PIT	John Del Col	Toronto	LW					

PICK	TEAM	NAME	DRAFTED FROM	POS	GP	G	A	PTS	PIM
170	N.J.	Mike Roth	Hill-Murray H.S.	D					
171	L.A.	Luc Robitaille	Hull	LW	889	478	524	1002	793
172	TOR	Dan Turner	Medicine Hat	LW					
173	HFD	John Deveraux	Scituate H.S.	C					
174	CHI	Ralph Difiore	Shawinigan	D					
175	DET	Bill Shibicky	Michigan State	C					
176	ST.L.	Daniel Jomphe	Granby	LW					
177	WPG	Gord Whitaker	Colorado College	RW					
178	VAN	Rex Grant	Kamloops	G					
179	MTL	Eric Demers	Shawinigan	LW					
180	CGY	Gary Suter	Wisconsin	D	918	181	563	744	1156
181	MIN	Duane Wahlin	Johnson H.S.	RW					
182	NYR	Ville Kentala	HIFK Helsinki, FIN	LW					
183	QUE	Guy Ouellette	Quebec	C					
184	PHI	Billy Powers	Matignon H.S.	C					
185	WSH	Jim Thomson	Toronto	RW	115	4	3	7	416
186	BOS	Kevin Heffernan	Weymouth H.S.	C					
187	NYI	Tom Warden	North Bay	C					
188	NYR	Heinz Ehlers	Leksand, SWE	C					
189	PIT	Steve Hurt	Hill-Murray H.S.	RW					
190	N.J.	Mike Peluso	Greenway H.S.	LW	458	38	52	90	1951
191	L.A.	Jeff Crossman	Western Michigan	C					
192	TOR	David Buckley	Trinity-Pawling H.S.	D					
193	HFD	Brent Regan	St. Albert Jr. A	RW					
194	CHI	Joakim Persson	S/G Hockey 83 Gavle, SWE	RW					
195	DET	Jay Rose	New Prep H.S.	D					
196	ST.L.	Tom Tilley	Orillia Jr. A	D	174	4	38	42	89
197	WPG	Rick Forest	Melville Jr. A	LW					
198	VAN	Ed Lowney	Boston U.	RW					
199	MTL	Ron Anncar	San Diego U.	D					
200	CGY	Petr Rucka	Sparta Praha, TCH	C					
201	MIN	Michael Orn	Stillwater H.S.	C					
202	NYR	Kevin Miller	Redford Jr.	C	574	146	176	322	414
203	QUE	Ken Quinney	Calgary	RW	59	7	13	20	23
204	PHI	Daryn Fersovich	St. Albert Jr. A	C					
205	WSH	Paul Cavallini	Henry Carr Jr. B	D	564	56	177	233	750
206	BUF	Brian McKinnon	Ottawa	C					
207	BOS	J. D. Urbanic	Windsor	LW					
208	NYI	David Volek	Slavia Praha, TCH	L/RW	396	95	154	249	201
209	EDM	Joel Curtis	Oshawa	LW					
210	PIT	Jim Steen	Moorehead H.S.	C					
211	N.J.	Jarkko Piiparinen	Klekkorelpas, FIN.	C					
212	L.A.	Paul Kenny	Cornwall	C					
213	TOR	Mikael Wurst	Ohio State	LW					
214	HFD	Jim Culhane	Western Michigan	D	6	0	1	1	4
215	CHI	Bill Brown	Simley H.S.	C					
216	DET	Tim Kaiser	Guelph	RW/D					
217	ST.L.	Mark Cupolo	Guelph	LW					
218	WPG	Mike Warus	Lake Superior State	RW					
219	VAN	Doug Clarke	Colorado College	D					
220	MTL	Dave Tanner	Notre Dame Jr. A	D					
221	CGY	Stefan Jonsson	Sodertalje, SWE	D					
222	MIN	Tom Terwilliger	Edina H.S.	D					
223	NYR	Tom Lorentz	Brady H.S.	C					
224	CHI	David Mackey	Victoria	LW	126	8	12	20	305
225	WSH	Mikhail Tatarinov	Sokol Kiev, USSR	D	161	21	48	69	184
226	BUF	Grant Delcourt	Kelowna	RW					
227	BOS	Bill Kopecky	Austin Prep	C					
228	NYI	Russ Becker	Virginia H.S.	D					
229	EDM	Simon Wheeldon	Victoria	C	15	0	2	2	10
230	PIT	Mark Ziliotto	Streetsville Jr. B	LW					
231	N.J.	Chris Kienne	Springfield Jr. B	D					
232	L.A.	Brian Martin	Belleville	C					
233	TOR	Peter Slanina	VSZ Kosice, TCH	D					
234	HFD	Peter Abric	North Bay	G					
235	CHI	Dan Williams	Chicago Jr.	D					
236	DET	Tom Nickolau	Guelph	C					
237	ST.L.	Mark Lanigan	U. of Waterloo	D					
238	WPG	Jim Edmonds	Cornell	G					
239	VAN	Ed Kister	London	D					
240	MTL	Troy Crosby	Verdun	G					
241	CGY	Rudolf Suchanek	Motor Ceske Budejovice, TCH	D					
242	MIN	Mike Nightengale	Simley H.S.	D					
243	NYR	Scott Brower	Lloydminster Jr.	G					
244	QUE	Peter Loob	Sodertalje, SWE	D	8	1	2	3	0
245	PHI	Juraj Bakos	VSZ Kosice, TCH	D					
246	WSH	Per Schedrin	Brynas Gavlo, SWE	D					
247	BUF	Sean Baker	Seattle	LW					
248	BOS	Jim Newhouse	Matignon H.S.	LW					
249	NYI	Allister Brown	New Hampshire	D					
250	EDM	Darren Gani	Belleville	D					

1985

Although the rankings compiled by the Central Scouting Bureau were confidential, it was decided that a report on all eligible players excluding their specific ratings would be published and provided to the media in 1985 to help support the growing interest generated by the Entry Draft. This report included biographies of top prospects.

Following such a successful crop in 1984, the 1985 draft was extremely thin in franchise-type players. "As far as number one overall, no individual jumps to the forefront as an automatic," said player agent Don Meehan. Once again, the top-ranked player was edged in the selections, as Wendel Clark was drafted first overall ahead of top-rated sniper Craig Simpson.

Clark, the WHL's top defenseman for 1984–85, was drafted by the Toronto Maple Leafs and joined the roster immediately to become one of the club's most dangerous forwards. "We have lots of good young defensemen," said Toronto head coach Dan Maloney. "Wendel has tremendous offensive power. The biggest part of his game is his skating and shooting. For that reason, we're leaning towards looking at him as a forward." Posting 34 goals and 45 points in his rookie season, Clark proved his offensive ability and was the runner-up behind defenseman Gary Suter for the Calder Trophy as the league's best rookie. Known for his tough play and powerful wrist shot, Clark became an instant favorite in Toronto.

The second round of the draft was dominated by goaltenders, as Sean Burke, Troy Gamble and Kay Whitmore were taken as the 24th, 25th and 26th picks. Northwood Prep School goaltender Mike Richter was also selected in the second round as the 28th choice and, along with a center selected in the same round, proved to be the top catches of the Draft. Cornell University's Joe Nieuwendyk was selected 27th overall by the Calgary Flames and went on in 1987–88 to join Mike Bossy as just the second rookie to score 50 goals. He had 51 goals and 41 assists and captured the Calder Trophy in 1988. After playing a huge role in the Calgary's Stanley Cup championship in 1989, Nieuwendyk has gone on to star in Dallas. He received the King Clancy Trophy in 1995 and remains one of the league's premier players.

An additional buzz surrounded the 1985 draft as the NHL was about to be introduced to another Gretzky. Keith Gretzky, younger brother of the greatest hockey talent in the world, was drafted 56th overall by the Buffalo Sabres. "There is no doubt there is going to be a lot of hoopla about having Keith on this team," said Buffalo head coach Jim Schoenfeld. "The first thing you have to do is mention the name and that draws attention." Despite the extremely favorable genetic pool, Keith Gretzky never graduated into the NHL.

The Vancouver Canucks once again enhanced the international flavor of the draft as Soviet superstar Igor Larionov was selected 214th overall. Larionov is currently one of the most valued veterans in the NHL today and helped the Detroit Red Wings to the Stanley Cup in 1997 and 1998. In addition, the Pittsburgh Penguins selected defenseman Jim Paek, who became the first South Korean-born player to be drafted into the NHL. Paek was a member of back-to-back Stanley Cup championships with the Penguins, becoming the first Asian-born player to have his name engraved on the Cup.

1985

Header legend: For NHL PLAYERS columns are POS, GP, G, A, PTS, PIM. For NHL GOALTENDERS columns are POS, GP, W, GA, SO, AVG.

FIRST ROUND

PICK	TEAM	NAME	DRAFTED FROM	POS	GP	G/W	A/GA	PTS/SO	PIM/AVG
1	TOR	Wendel Clark	Saskatoon	D	683	294	216	510	1619
2	PIT	Craig Simpson	Michigan State	LW	634	247	250	497	659
3	N.J.	Craig Wolanin	Kitchener	D	695	40	133	173	894
4	VAN	Jim Sandlak	Calgary	D	549	110	119	229	821
5	HFD	Dana Murzyn	London	RW	826	52	150	202	1550
6	NYI	Brad Dalgarno	Hamilton	RW	321	49	71	120	332
7	NYR	Ulf Dahlen	Ostersund, SWE	RW	686	231	249	480	194
8	DET	Brent Fedyk	Regina	LW	403	93	106	199	278
9	L.A.	Craig Duncanson	Sudbury	LW	38	5	4	9	61
10	L.A.	Dan Gratton	Oshawa	C	7	1	0	1	5
11	CHI	Dave Manson	Prince Albert	D	844	91	253	344	2449
12	MTL	Jose Charbonneau	Drummondville	RW	71	9	13	22	67
13	NYI	Derek King	Sault Ste. Marie	LW	727	235	316	551	389
14	BUF	Calle Johansson	Vastra Frolunda, SWE	D	783	92	323	415	417
15	QUE	David Latta	Kitchener	LW	36	4	8	12	4
16	MTL	Tom Chorske	Minneapolis SW H.S.	RW	537	114	114	228	215
17	CGY	Chris Biotti	Belmont Hill H.S.	D					
18	WPG	Ryan Stewart	Kamloops	C	3	1	0	1	0
19	WSH	Yvon Corriveau	Toronto	LW	280	48	40	88	310
20	EDM	Scott Metcalfe	Kingston	LW	19	1	2	3	18
21	PHI	Glen Seabrooke	Peterborough	C	19	1	6	7	4

SECOND ROUND

PICK	TEAM	NAME	DRAFTED FROM	POS	GP	G/W	A/GA	PTS/SO	PIM/AVG
22	TOR	Ken Spangler	Calgary	D					
23	PIT	Lee Giffin	Oshawa	RW	27	1	3	4	9
24	N.J.	Sean Burke	Toronto	G	470	178	1447	16	3.29
25	VAN	Troy Gamble	Medicine Hat	G	72	22	229	1	3.61
26	HFD	Kay Whitmore	Peterborough	G	149	59	487	4	3.51
27	CGY	Joe Nieuwendyk	Cornell	C	768	397	371	768	433
28	NYR	Mike Richter	Northwood Prep	G	424	203	1162	18	2.89
29	DET	Jeff Sharples	Kelowna	D	105	14	35	49	70
30	L.A.	Par Edlund	Bjorkloven Umea, SWE	RW					
31	BOS	Alain G. Cote	Quebec	D	119	2	18	20	124
32	N.J.	Eric Weinrich	North Yarmouth Academy	D	602	41	185	226	489
33	MTL	Todd Richards	Armstrong H.S.	D	8	0	4	4	4
34	NYI	Brad Lauer	Regina	LW	323	44	67	111	218
35	BUF	Benoit Hogue	St-Jean	C	670	197	279	476	750
36	QUE	Jason Lafreniere	Hamilton	C	146	34	53	87	22
37	ST.L.	Herb Raglan	Kingston	RW	343	33	56	89	775
38	CGY	Jeff Wenaas	Medicine Hat	C					
39	WPG	Roger Ohman	Leksand, SWE	D					
40	WSH	John Druce	Peterborough	RW	531	113	126	239	347
41	EDM	Todd Carnelley	Kamloops	D					
42	PHI	Bruce Rendall	Chatham Jr. B	LW					

OTHER ROUNDS

PICK	TEAM	NAME	DRAFTED FROM	POS	GP	G/W	A/GA	PTS/SO	PIM/AVG
43	TOR	Dave Thomlinson	Brandon	LW	42	1	3	4	50
44	ST.L.	Myles O'Connor	Stratford Jr. B	D	43	3	4	7	69
45	N.J.	Nelson Emerson	Notre Dame Jr. A	RW	524	151	236	387	398
46	VAN	Shane Doyle	Belleville	D					
47	MTL	Rocky Dundas	Spokane	RW	5	0	0	0	14
48	PHI	Darryl Gilmour	Moose Jaw	G					
49	NYR	Sam Lindstahl	Sodertalje, SWE	G					
50	DET	Steve Chiasson	Guelph	D	723	92	297	389	1091
51	MIN	Stephane Roy	Granby	C	12	1	0	1	0
52	BOS	Bill Ranford	New Westminster	G	595	230	1885	14	3.39
53	CHI	Andy Helmuth	Ottawa	G					
54	ST.L.	Ned Desmond	Hotchkiss H.S.	D					
55	NYI	Jeff Finley	Portland	D	335	7	42	49	251
56	BUF	Keith Gretzky	Windsor	C					
57	QUE	Max Middendorf	Sudbury	RW	13	2	4	6	6
58	PIT	Bruce Racine	Northeastern	G	11	0	12	0	3.13
59	CGY	Lane Macdonald	Harvard	LW					
60	WPG	Daniel Berthiaume	Chicoutimi	G	215	81	714	5	3.67
61	WSH	Rob Murray	Peterborough	C	94	3	13	16	107
62	EDM	Michael Ware	Hamilton	RW	5	0	1	1	15
63	PHI	Shane Whelan	Oshawa	C					
64	TOR	Greg Vey	Peterborough	C					
65	QUE	Peter Massey	New Hampton H.S.	LW					
66	N.J.	Gregg Polak	Lincoln H.S.	LW					
67	VAN	Randy Siska	Medicine Hat	C					
68	HFD	Gary Callaghan	Belleville	C					
69	MIN	Mike Berger	Lethbridge	D	30	3	1	4	67
70	NYR	Pat Janostin	Notre Dame Jr. A	D					
71	DET	Mark Gowans	Windsor	G					
72	L.A.	Perry Florio	Kent Prep	D					
73	BOS	Jaime Kelly	Scituate H.S.	RW					
74	CHI	Daniel Vincelette	Drummondville	LW	193	20	22	42	351
75	MTL	Martin Desjardins	Trois-Rivieres	C	8	0	2	2	2
76	NYI	Kevin Herom	Moose Jaw	LW					
77	BUF	Dave Moylan	Sudbury	D					
78	QUE	David Espe	White Bear Lake H.S.	D					
79	MTL	Brent Gilchrist	Kelowna	LW	617	125	152	277	307
80	CGY	Roger Johansson	Troja, SWE	D	161	9	34	43	163
81	WPG	Fredrik Olausson	Farjestad Karlstad, SWE	D	787	112	356	468	348
82	WSH	Bill Houlder	North Bay	D	454	41	130	171	220
83	WSH	Larry Shaw	Peterborough	D					
84	PHI	Paul Marshall	Northwood Prep	D					
85	TOR	Jeff Serowik	Lawrence Academy	D	2	0	0	0	0
86	PIT	Steve Gotaas	Prince Albert	C	49	6	9	15	53
87	CHI	Rick Herbert	Portland	D					
88	VAN	Robert Kron	Zetor Brno, TCH	LW	497	110	129	239	87
89	NYI	Tommy Hedlund	AIK Solna, SWE	D					
90	MIN	Dwight Mullins	Lethbridge	C					
91	NYR	Brad Stephan	Hastings H.S.	LW					
92	DET	Chris Luongo	St. Clair Shores H.S.	D	218	8	23	31	176
93	L.A.	Petr Prajsler	Tesla Pardubice, TCH	D	46	3	10	13	51
94	BOS	Steve Moore	London Jr. B	D					
95	CHI	Brad Belland	Sudbury	C					
96	MTL	Tom Sagissor	Hastings H.S.	C					
97	NYI	Jeff Sveen	Boston U.	C					
98	BUF	Ken Priestlay	Victoria	C	168	27	34	61	63
99	QUE	Bruce Major	Richmond Jr.	C	4	0	0	0	0
100	ST.L.	Dan Brooks	St. Thomas Academy	C					
101	CGY	Esa Keskinen	TPS Turku, FIN	C					
102	WPG	John Borrell	Burnsville H.S.	RW					
103	WSH	Claude Dumas	Granby	C					
104	EDM	Tomas Kapusta	TJ Gottwaldov, TCH	C					
105	PHI	Daril Holmes	Kingston	RW					
106	TOR	Jiri Latal	Sparta Praha, TCH	D	92	12	36	48	24
107	PIT	Kevin Clemens	Regina	LW					
108	N.J.	Bill McMillan	Peterborough	RW					
109	VAN	Martin Hrstka	Ingstav Brno, TCH	LW					
110	HFD	Shane Churla	Medicine Hat	RW	488	26	45	71	2301
111	MIN	Michael Mullowney	Deerfield Academy	D					
112	NYR	Brian McReynolds	Orillia Jr. A	C	30	1	5	6	8
113	DET	Randy McKay	Michigan Tech	RW	574	93	114	207	1314
114	PIT	Stuart Marston	Longueuil	D					
115	BOS	Gord Hynes	Medicine Hat	D	52	3	9	12	22
116	CHI	Jonas Heed	Sodertalje, SWE	D					
117	BOS	Donald Dufresne	Trois-Rivieres	D	268	6	36	42	258
118	NYI	Rod Dallman	Prince Albert	LW	6	1	0	1	26
119	BUF	Joe Reekie	Cornwall	D	641	21	107	128	1062
120	QUE	Andy Akervik	Claire H.S.	C					
121	ST.L.	Rich Burchill	Catholic Memorial H.S.	C					
122	CGY	Tim Sweeney	Weymouth North H.S.	LW	291	55	83	138	123
123	WPG	Danton Cole	Aurora Jr. A	C/RW	318	58	60	118	125
124	WSH	Doug Stromback	Kitchener	RW					
125	EDM	Brian Tessier	North Bay	G					
126	PHI	Ken Alexander	Kitchener	D					
127	TOR	Tim Bean	North Bay	LW					
128	PIT	Steve Titus	Cornwall	G					
129	N.J.	Kevin Schrader	Burnsville H.S.	D					
130	VAN	Brian McFarlane	Seattle	RW					
131	HFD	Chris Brant	Sault Ste. Marie	LW					
132	MIN	Michael Kelfer	St. John's Prep	C					
133	NYR	Neil Pilon	Kamloops	D					
134	DET	Thomas Bjur	AIK Solna, SWE	RW					
135	L.A.	Tim Flannigan	Michigan Tech	RW					
136	BOS	Per Martinelle	AIK Solna, SWE	RW					
137	CHI	Victor Posa	Wisconsin	LW/D	2	0	0	0	2
138	ST.L.	Pat Jablonski	Detroit Compuware Jr. A	G	128	28	413	1	3.74
139	NYI	Kurt Lackten	Moose Jaw	RW					
140	BUF	Petri Matikainen	Sapko Savonlinna, FIN	D					
141	QUE	Mike Oliverio	Sault Ste. Marie	C					
142	MTL	Ed Cristofoli	Penticton Jr. A	RW	9	0	1	1	4
143	CGY	Stu Grimson	Regina	LW	504	9	17	26	1528
144	WPG	Brent Mowery	Summerland Jr.	LW					
145	WSH	Jamie Nadjiwan	Sudbury	LW					
146	EDM	Shawn Tyers	Kitchener	RW					
147	PHI	Tony Horacek	Kelowna	LW	154	10	19	29	316
148	TOR	Andy Donahue	Belmont Hill H.S.	C					
149	PIT	Paul Stanton	Catholic Memorial H.S.	D	295	14	49	63	262
150	N.J.	Ed Krayer	St. Paul's H.S.	C					
151	VAN	Hakan Ahlund	Orebro, SWE	RW					
152	HFD	Brian Puhalsky	Notre Dame Jr. A	LW					
153	MIN	Ross Johnson	Mayo H.S.	C					
154	NYR	Larry Bernard	Seattle	LW					
155	DET	Mike Luckraft	Burnsville H.S.	D					
156	L.A.	John Hyduke	Hibbing H.S.	D					
157	BOS	Randy Burridge	Peterborough	LW	706	199	251	450	458
158	CHI	John Reid	Belleville	G					
159	ST.L.	Scott Brickey	Port Huron Jr.	RW					
160	NYI	Hank Lammens	St. Lawrence U.	D	27	1	2	3	22
161	BUF	Trent Kaese	Lethbridge	RW	1	0	0	0	0
162	QUE	Mario Brunetta	Quebec	G	40	12	128	0	3.90
163	MTL	Mike Claringbull	Medicine Hat	D					
164	CGY	Nate Smith	Lawrence Academy	D					
165	WPG	Tom Draper	Vermont	G	53	19	173	1	3.70
166	WSH	Mark Haarmann	Oshawa	D					
167	EDM	Tony Fairfield	St. Albert Jr. A	RW					
168	PHI	Mike Cusack	Dubuque Jr. A	RW					
169	TOR	Todd Whittemore	Kent Prep	C					

PICK	TEAM	NAME	DRAFTED FROM	NHL PLAYERS: POS / NHL GOALTENDERS: POS	GP	G / W	A / GA	PTS / SO	PIM / AVG
170	PIT	Jim Paek	Oshawa	D	217	5	29	34	155
171	N.J.	Jamie Huscroft	Seattle	D	308	5	31	36	964
172	VAN	Curtis Hunt	Prince Albert	D					
173	HFD	Greg Dornbach	Miami of Ohio	C					
174	MIN	Tim Helmer	Ottawa	C					
175	NYR	Stephane Brochu	Quebec	D	1	0	0	0	0
176	DET	Rob Schenna	St. John's Prep	D					
177	L.A.	Steve Horner	Henry Carr Jr. B	RW					
178	BOS	Gord Cruickshank	Providence	C					
179	CHI	Richard Laplante	Vermont	C					
180	ST.L.	Jeff Urban	Minnetonka H.S.	LW					
181	NYI	Rich Wiest	Lethbridge	C					
182	BUF	Jiri Sejba	Dukla Jihlava, TCH	LW	11	0	2	2	8
183	QUE	Brit Peer	Sault Ste. Marie	RW					
184	MTL	Roger Beedon	Sarnia Jr. B	G					
185	CGY	Darryl Olsen	St. Albert Jr. A	D	1	0	0	0	0
186	WPG	Nevin Kardum	Henry Carr Jr. B	C					
187	WSH	Steve Hollett	Sault Ste. Marie	C					
188	EDM	Kelly Buchberger	Moose Jaw	RW	743	78	154	232	1679
189	PHI	Gord Murphy	Oshawa	D	711	81	208	289	589
190	TOR	Bobby Reynolds	St. Clair Shores H.S.	LW	7	1	1	2	0
191	PIT	Steve Shaunessy	Reading H.S.	D					
192	N.J.	Terry Shold	International Falls H.S.	LW					
193	VAN	Carl Valimont	University of Lowell	D					
194	HFD	Paul Tory	Illinois-Chicago	C					
195	MIN	Gordon Ernst	Cranston East H.S.	C					
196	NYR	Steve Nemeth	Lethbridge	C	12	2	0	2	2
197	DET	Erik Hamalainen	Lukko Rauma, FIN	D					
198	MTL	Maurice Mansi	RPI	C					
199	BOS	Dave Buda	Streetsville Jr. B	LW					
200	CHI	Brad Hamilton	Aurora Jr. A	D					
201	ST.L.	Vince Guidotti	Noble and Greenough H.S.	D					
202	NYI	Real Arsenault	Prince Andrew H.S.	LW					
203	BUF	Boyd Sutton	Stratford Jr. B	C					
204	QUE	Tom Sasso	Babson College	C					
205	MTL	Chad Arthur	Stratford Jr. B	LW					
206	CGY	Peter Romberg	Iserlohn, FRG	D					
207	WPG	Dave Quigley	U. of Moncton	G					
208	WSH	Dallas Eakins	Peterborough	D	80	0	5	5	167
209	EDM	Mario Barbe	Chicoutimi	D					
210	BOS	Bob Beers	Buffalo Jr.	D	258	28	79	107	225
211	TOR	Tim Armstrong	Toronto	C	11	1	0	1	6
212	PIT	Doug Greschuk	St. Albert Jr. A	D					
213	N.J.	Jamie McKinley	Guelph	C					
214	VAN	Igor Larionov	CSKA Moscow, USSR	C	509	115	282	397	242
215	HFD	Jerry Pawlowski	Harvard	D					
216	MIN	Ladislav Lubina	Tesla Pardubice, TCH	RW					
217	NYR	Robert Burakovsky	Leksand, SWE	RW	23	2	3	5	6
218	DET	Bo Svanberg	Farjestad Karlstad, SWE	LW					
219	L.A.	Trent Ciprick	Brandon	RW					
220	BOS	John Byce	Madison Memorial H.S.	C	21	2	3	5	6
221	CHI	Ian Pound	Kitchener	D					
222	ST.L.	Ron Saatzer	Hopkins H.S.	C					
223	NYI	Mike Volpe	St. Mary's U.	G					
224	BUF	Guy Larose	Guelph	C	70	10	9	19	63
225	QUE	Gary Murphy	Arlington Catholic H.S.	D					
226	MTL	Mike Bishop	Sarnia Jr. B	G					
226	MTL	Mike Bishop	Sarnia Jr. B	D					
227	CGY	Alexander Kozhevnikov	Spartak Moscow, USSR	LW					
228	WPG	Chris Norton	Cornell	D					
229	WSH	Steve Hrynewich	Ottawa	LW					
230	EDM	Peter Headon	Notre Dame Jr. A	C					
231	PHI	Rod Williams	Kelowna	RW					
232	TOR	Mitch Murphy	St. Paul's H.S.	G					
233	PIT	Gregory Choules	Chicoutimi	LW					
234	N.J.	David Williams	Choate	D	173	11	53	64	157
235	VAN	Darren Taylor	Calgary	LW					
236	HFD	Bruce Hill	U. of Denver	LW					
237	MIN	Tommy Sjodin	Timra, SWE	D	106	8	40	48	52
238	NYR	Rudy Poeschek	Kamloops	RW/D	336	6	25	31	760
239	DET	Mikael Lindman	AIK Solna, SWE	LW					
240	L.A.	Marian Horwath	Slovan Bratislava, TCH	LW					
241	BOS	Marc West	Burlington Jr. B	C					
242	CHI	Rick Braccia	Avon Old Farms H.S.	LW					
243	ST.L.	Dave Jecha	Minnetonka H.S.	D					
244	NYI	Tony Grenier	Prince Albert	C					
245	BUF	Ken Baumgartner	Prince Albert	LW	627	12	38	50	2125
246	QUE	Jean Bois	Trois-Rivieres	LW					
247	MTL	John Ferguson Jr.	Winnipeg South Blues Jr.	LW					
248	CGY	Bill Gregoire	Victoria	D					
249	WPG	Anssi Melametsa	HIFK Helsinki, FIN	LW	27	0	3	3	2
250	WSH	Frank Dimuzio	Belleville	C					
251	EDM	John Haley	Hull H.S.	G					
252	PHI	Paul Maurice	Windsor	D					

1986

The 1986 NHL Entry Draft would be remembered for its many new firsts rather than its crop of graduating junior prospects. For the first time since the draft had started to be broadcast throughout Canada, it was not covered in 1986 (due to the World Cup of Soccer). For the first (and only time) since the modern draft was created in 1969 there was no trading, as each team had retained its original pick in the first round. In addition, there were no Europeans drafted in the first round (the crop of international prospects was labeled as the weakest in years), while talented goaltenders were relatively scarce in the 1986 draft pool. However, the primary story of the 1986 Entry Draft was that for the first time a product of a U.S. college team was selected first overall when Joe Murphy of Michigan State was taken by the Detroit Red Wings. As the top-ranked prospect entering the draft, many teams offered packages of players to Detroit in order to acquire the first pick, however Detroit g.m. Jimmy Devellano stated: "Numbers won't help the Detroit Red Wings. We need quality and Joe Murphy is a quality player." Murphy was recognized as the Central Collegiate Hockey Association rookie of the year and had played an integral role in helping his team capture the NCAA title. However, he played only five games with the Red Wings before being sent to the minors in 1986–87. In his first full season in 1987–88, Murphy recorded only 19 points (10 goals, nine assists) in 50 games. He has gone on to be an effective role player in his career, helping Edmonton win the Stanley Cup in 1990, though his play has hardly been characteristic of a first draft pick.

The 1986 Entry Draft became known as another "Year of the American" as seven U.S.-born talents were selected in the first round. Jimmy Carson, a sniper from the Quebec junior league, was selected second overall by the Los Angeles Kings. High school star Brian Leetch was taken ninth by the New York Rangers, while Boston collegians Scott Young and Craig Janney were selected 11th and 13th respectively. George Pelawa, a 6'3", 235-pound winger, and Tom Fitzgerald rounded out the American invasion as the 16th and 17th players selected. "What I think you're seeing are the full effects of NHL expansion and the Bobby Orr-era," said Jack Button, director of player personnel for the Capitals. "The kids we're drafting this year were born in 1968, which was the first full year for the 12-team NHL. These kids have grown up with the NHL all around them. It was also the time when Orr and the Bruins were getting ready to take a run at the Stanley Cup. I don't think you can underestimate the influence that had on American youth."

Carson jumped immediately into the NHL and posted impressive numbers with 37 goals and 42 assists in his rookie year. His 55 goals in 1987–88 set a single-season record for an American-born player, but Carson will always be remembered as the primary player that Edmonton received from the Kings in the blockbuster trade that brought Wayne Gretzky to Los Angeles. Craig Janney and Scott Young both went on to success in their rookie years and remain as key players on their NHL clubs today. Pelawa failed to break into the NHL, while Brian Leetch became the impact player of the 1986 Entry Draft. The recipient of the Calder Trophy as the rookie of the year for 1989, twice awarded the Norris Trophy as the NHL's best defenseman, and the Conn Smythe Trophy winner when the Rangers won the Stanley Cup in 1994, Leetch is recognized as one of the NHL's premiere blueliners.

For the second consecutive year, the Vancouver Canucks selected a Soviet superstar with a late draft pick, as Vladimir Krutov was selected 238th overall. Despite his international success, he would played only one NHL season, collecting just 34 points (11 goals, 23 assists) in 1989–90. Another late international pick was the selection of Tony Hand as the last player taken, 245th overall by the Edmonton Oilers, in the draft. Hand became the first NHL product from Scotland's hockey system.

1986

PICK	TEAM	DRAFTED NAME	NHL PLAYERS: FROM	POS	GP	G	A	PTS	PIM
FIRST ROUND									
1	DET	Joe Murphy	Michigan State	RW	634	195	252	447	623
2	L.A.	Jimmy Carson	Verdun	C	626	275	286	561	254
3	N.J.	Neil Brady	Medicine Hat	C	89	9	22	31	95
4	PIT	Zarley Zalapski	Canadian National	D	625	99	283	382	678
5	BUF	Shawn Anderson	Canadian National	D	255	11	51	62	117
6	TOR	Vincent Damphousse	Laval	C	928	328	552	880	828
7	VAN	Dan Woodley	Portland	RW	5	2	0	2	17
8	WPG	Pat Elynuik	Prince Albert	RW	506	154	188	342	459
9	NYR	Brian Leetch	Avon Old Farms H.S.	D	725	164	536	700	357
10	ST.L.	Jocelyn Lemieux	Laval	RW	598	80	84	164	740
11	HFD	Scott Young	Boston U.	RW	672	186	259	445	251
12	MIN	Warren Babe	Lethbridge	LW	21	2	5	7	23
13	BOS	Craig Janney	Boston College	C	704	183	541	724	156
14	CHI	Everett Sanipass	Verdun	LW	164	25	34	59	358
15	MTL	Mark Pederson	Medicine Hat	LW	169	35	50	85	77
16	CGY	George Pelawa	Bemidji H.S.	RW					
17	NYI	Tom Fitzgerald	Austin Prep	RW/C	569	81	112	193	403
18	QUE	Ken McRae	Sudbury	C	137	14	21	35	364
19	WSH	Jeff Greenlaw	Canadian National	LW	57	3	6	9	108
20	PHI	Kerry Huffman	Guelph	D	401	37	108	145	361
21	EDM	Kim Issel	Prince Albert	RW	4	0	0	0	0
SECOND ROUND									
22	DET	Adam Graves	Windsor	C	748	232	216	448	1003
23	PHI	Jukka Seppo	Sport Vaasa, FIN	LW					
24	N.J.	Todd Copeland	Belmont Hill H.S.	D					
25	PIT	Dave Capuano	Mount St. Charles H.S.	LW	104	17	38	55	56
26	BUF	Greg Brown	St. Mark's H.S.	D	94	4	14	18	86
27	MTL	Benoit Brunet	Hull	LW	333	61	104	165	161
28	PHI	Kent Hawley	Ottawa	C					
29	WPG	Teppo Numminen	Tappara Tampere, FIN	D	711	66	277	343	273
30	MIN	Neil Wilkinson	Selkirk Jr.	D	436	16	67	83	791
31	ST.L.	Mike Posma	Buffalo Jr.	D					
32	HFD	Marc LaForge	Kingston	LW	14	0	0	0	64
33	MIN	Dean Kolstad	Prince Albert	D	40	1	7	8	69
34	BOS	Pekka Tirkkonen	Sapko Savonlinna, FIN	C					
35	CHI	Mark Kurzawski	Windsor	D					
36	TOR	Darryl Shannon	Windsor	D	390	19	77	96	378
37	CGY	Brian Glynn	Saskatoon	D	431	25	79	104	410
38	NYI	Dennis Vaske	Armstrong H.S.	D	232	5	41	46	247
39	QUE	Jean-Marc Routhier	Hull	RW	8	0	0	0	9
40	WSH	Steve Seftel	Kingston	LW	4	0	0	0	2
41	QUE	Stephane Guerard	Shawinigan	D	34	0	0	0	40
42	EDM	Jamie Nichols	Portland	LW					
OTHER ROUNDS									
43	DET	Derek Mayer	U. of Denver	D	17	2	2	4	8
44	L.A.	\Denis Larocque	Guelph	D	8	0	1	1	18
45	N.J.	Janne Ojanen	Tappara Tampere, FIN	C	98	21	23	44	28
46	PIT	Brad Aitken	Sault Ste. Marie	LW	14	1	3	4	25
47	BUF	Bob Corkum	U. of Maine	C	448	73	75	148	208
48	TOR	Sean Boland	Toronto						
49	VAN	Don Gibson	Winkler Jr. A	D	14	0	3	3	20
50	WPG	Esa Palosaari	Karpat Oulu, FIN	RW					
51	NYR	Bret Walter	U. of Alberta	C					
52	ST.L.	Tony Hejna	Nichols H.S.	LW					
53	NYR	Shawn Clouston	U. of Alberta	RW					
54	MIN	Rick Bennett	Wilbraham Monson H.S.	LW	15	1	1	2	13
55	MIN	Rob Zettler	Sault Ste. Marie	D	477	4	55	59	788
56	BUF	Kevin Kerr	Windsor	RW					
57	MTL	Jyrki Lumme	Ilves Tampere, FIN	D	654	85	260	345	430
58	MIN	Brad Turner	Calgary	D	3	0	0	0	0
59	NYI	Bill Berg	Toronto	LW	502	53	65	118	460
60	WSH	Shawn Simpson	Sault Ste. Marie	G					
61	WSH	Jim Hrivnak	Merrimack	G	85	34	262	0	3.73
62	N.J.	Marc Laniel	Oshawa	D					
63	EDM	Ron Shudra	Kamloops	D	10	0	5	5	6
64	DET	Tim Cheveldae	Saskatoon	G	340	149	1116	10	3.49
65	L.A.	Sylvain Couturier	Laval	C	33	4	5	9	4
66	N.J.	Anders Carlsson	Sodertalje, SWE	C	104	7	26	33	34
67	PIT	Rob Brown	Kamloops	RW	435	167	224	391	573
68	BUF	David Baseggio	Yale	D					
69	TOR	Kent Hulst	Windsor	C					

PICK	TEAM	DRAFTED NAME	NHL PLAYERS: FROM	POS	GP	G	A	PTS	PIM
70	VAN	Ron Stern	Longueuil	RW	493	64	72	136	1768
71	WPG	Hannu Jarvenpaa	Karpat Oulu, FIN	RW	114	11	26	37	83
72	NYR	Mark Janssens	Regina	C	587	39	67	106	1251
73	ST.L.	Glen Featherstone	Windsor	D	384	19	61	80	939
74	HFD	Brian Chapman	Belleville	D	3	0	0	0	29
75	MIN	Kirk Tomlinson	Hamilton	C	1	0	0	0	0
76	BOS	Dean Hall	St. James Jr. A	C					
77	CHI	Frantisek Kucera	Sparta Praha, TCH	D	354	21	75	96	227
78	MTL	Brent Bobyck	Notre Dame Midgets	LW					
79	CGY	Tom Quinlan	Hill-Murray H.S.	RW					
80	NYI	Shawn Byram	Regina	LW	5	0	0	0	14
81	QUE	Ron Tugnutt	Peterborough	G	304	90	966	8	3.56
82	WSH	Erin Ginnel	Calgary	C					
83	PHI	Mark Bar	Peterborough	D					
84	EDM	Dan Currie	Sault Ste. Marie	LW	22	2	1	3	4
85	DET	Johan Garpenlov	Nacka, SWE	LW	472	104	174	278	203
86	L.A.	Dave Guden	Roxbury Latin	LW					
87	ST.L.	Michael Wolak	Kitchener	C					
88	PIT	Sandy Smith	Brainerd H.S.	C					
89	BUF	Larry Rooney	Thayer Academy	F					
90	TOR	Scott Taylor	Kitchener	D					
91	VAN	Eric Murano	Calgary	RW					
92	WPG	Craig Endean	Seattle	LW	2	0	1	1	0
93	NYR	Jeff Bloemberg	North Bay	D	43	3	6	9	25
94	MTL	Eric Aubertin	Granby	LW					
95	PHI	Bill Horn	Western Michigan						
96	MIN	Jari Gronstrand	Tappara Tampere, FIN	D	185	8	26	34	135
97	BOS	Matt Pesklewis	St. Albert Jr. A	LW					
98	CHI	Lonnie Loach	Guelph	LW	56	10	13	23	29
99	MTL	Mario Milani	Verdun	RW					
100	CGY	Scott Bloom	Burnsville H.S.	LW					
101	NYI	Dean Sexsmith	Brandon	C					
102	QUE	Gerald Bzdel	Regina	D					
103	WSH	John Purves	Hamilton	RW	7	1	0	1	0
104	NYI	Todd McLellan	Saskatoon	C	5	1	1	2	0
105	EDM	David Haas	London	LW	7	2	1	3	7
106	DET	Jay Stark	Portland	D					
107	L.A.	Robb Stauber	Duluth Denfield H.S.	G	62	21	209	1	3.81
108	N.J.	Troy Crowder	Hamilton	RW	150	9	7	16	433
109	PIT	Jeff Daniels	Oshawa	LW	156	8	13	21	36
110	BUF	Miguel Baldris	Shawinigan	D					
111	TOR	Stephane Giguere	St-Jean	LW					
112	VAN	Steve Herniman	Cornwall	D					
113	WPG	Robertson Bateman	St. Laurent College	RW					
114	NYR	Darren Turcotte	North Bay	C	586	191	210	401	281
115	ST.L.	Mike O' Toole	Markham Jr. B	R/LW					
116	HFD	Joe Quinn	Calgary	RW					
117	QUE	Scott White	Michigan Tech	D					
118	BOS	Garth Premak	New Westminster	D					
119	CHI	Mario Doyon	Drummondville	D	28	3	4	7	16
120	MTL	Steve Bisson	Sault Ste. Marie	D					
121	CGY	John Parker	White Bear Lake H.S.	C					
122	NYI	Tony Schmalzbauer	Hill-Murray H.S.	D					
123	QUE	Morgan Samuelsson	Boden, SWE	F					
124	WSH	Stefan Nilsson	Lulea, SWE	C					
125	PHI	Steve Scheifele	Stratford Jr. B	RW					
126	EDM	Jim Ennis	Boston U.	D	5	1	0	1	10
127	DET	Per Djoos	Mora, SWE	D	82	2	31	33	58
128	L.A.	Sean Krakiwsky	Calgary	RW					
129	N.J.	Kevin Todd	Prince Albert	C	383	70	133	203	225
130	PIT	Doug Hobson	Prince Albert	D					
131	BUF	Mike Hartman	North Bay	LW	397	43	35	78	1388
132	TOR	Danny Hie	Ottawa	C					
133	VAN	Jon Helgeson	Roseau H.S.	C					
134	QUE	Mark Vermette	Lake Superior State	RW	67	6	13	18	33
135	NYR	Robb Graham	Guelph	RW					
136	ST.L.	Andy May	Bramalea Jr. B	C					
137	HFD	Steve Torrel	Hibbing H.S.	C					
138	NYI	Will Anderson	Victoria						
139	BOS	Paul Beraldo	Sault Ste. Marie	RW	10	0	0	0	4
140	CHI	Mike Hudson	Sudbury	C/LW	416	49	87	136	414
141	MTL	Lyle Odelein	Moose Jaw	D	578	27	107	134	1648
142	CGY	Rick Lessard	Ottawa	D	15	0	4	4	18
143	NYI	Richard Pilon	Prince Albert AAA	D	448	6	48	54	1403
144	QUE	Jean F. Nault	Granby	C					
145	WSH	Peter Choma	Belleville	RW					
146	PHI	Sami Wahlsten	TPS Turku, FIN	F					
147	EDM	Ivan Matulik	Slovan Bratislava, TCH	LW					
148	DET	Dean Morton	Oshawa	D	1	1	0	1	2
149	L.A.	Rene Chapdelaine	Lake Superior State	D	32	0	2	2	32
150	N.J.	Ryan Pardoski	Calgary	LW					
151	PIT	Steve Rohlik	Hill-Murray H.S.						
152	BUF	Francois Guay	Laval	C	1	0	0	0	0
153	TOR	Stephen Brennan	New Prep H.S.	F					
154	VAN	Jeff Noble	Kitchener	C					
155	WPG	Frank Furlan	Sherwood Park Jr. A	G					
156	NYR	Barry Chyzowski	St. Albert Jr. A	C					

PICK	TEAM	NAME	DRAFTED FROM	NHL PLAYERS: POS / NHL GOALTENDERS: POS	GP	G / W	A / GA	PTS / SO	PIM / AVG
157	ST.L.	Randy Skarda	St. Thomas Academy	D	26	0	5	5	11
158	HFD	Ron Hoover	Western Michigan	C	18	4	0	4	31
159	MIN	Scott Mathias	U. of Denver	C					
160	BOS	Brian Ferreira	Falmouth H.S.	RW					
161	CHI	Marty Nanne	Minnesota-Duluth	RW					
162	MTL	Rick Hayward	Hull	D	4	0	0	0	5
163	CGY	Mark Olsen	Colorado College	D					
164	NYI	Peter Harris	Haverhill H.S.	G					
165	QUE	Keith Miller	Guelph	LW					
166	WSH	Lee Davidson	Penticton Jr. A	C					
167	PHI	Murray Baron	Vernon Jr. A	D	525	24	55	79	873
168	EDM	Nicolas Beaulieu	Drummondville	LW					
169	DET	Marc Potvin	Stratford Jr. B	RW	121	3	5	8	456
170	L.A.	Trevor Pochipinski	Penticton Jr. A	D					
171	N.J.	Scott McCormack	St. Paul's H.S.						
172	PIT	Dave McLlwain	North Bay	C/RW	501	100	107	207	292
173	BUF	Shawn Whitham	Providence	D					
174	TOR	Brian Bellefeuille	Canterbury H.S.	LW					
175	VAN	Matt Merton	Stratford Jr. B	G					
176	WPG	Mark Green	New Hampton H.S.	C					
177	NYR	Pat Scanlon	Cretin H.S.						
178	ST.L.	Martyn Ball	St. Michael's Jr. B	LW					
179	HFD	Robert Glasgow	Sherwood Park Jr. A	RW					
180	MIN	Lance Pitlick	Cooper H.S.	D	178	8	19	27	167
181	BOS	Jeff Flaherty	Weymouth H.S.	RW					
182	CHI	Geoff Benic	Windsor	LW					
183	MTL	Antonin Routa	Poldi SOMP Kladno, TCH	D					
184	CGY	Scott Sharples	Penticton Jr. A	G	1	0	4	0	3.69
185	NYI	Jeff Jablonski	London Jr. B	LW					
186	QUE	Pierre Millier	Chicoutimi	D					
187	WSH	Tero Toivola	Tappara Tampere, FIN	F					
188	PHI	Blaine Rude	Fergus Falls	RW					
189	EDM	Mike Greenlay	Calgary Midget AAA	G	2	0	4	0	12.00
190	DET	Scott King	Vernon Jr. A	G	2	0	3	0	2.95
191	L.A.	Paul Kelly	Guelph	D					
192	N.J.	Frederic Chabot	St. Foy Midget AAA	G	21	3	46	0	3.32
193	PIT	Kelly Cain	London	C					
194	BUF	Kenton Rein	Prince Albert	G					
195	TOR	Sean Davidson	Toronto	RW					
196	VAN	Marc Lyons	Kingston	D					
197	WPG	John Blue	Minnesota-Duluth	G	46	16	126	1	3.00
198	NYR	Joe Ranger	London	D					
199	ST.L.	Rod Thacker	Hamilton	D					
200	HFD	Sean Evoy	Cornwall	G					
201	MIN	Dan Keczmer	Detroit Little Caesar's	D	173	8	32	40	150
202	BOS	Greg Hawgood	Kamloops	D	377	53	142	195	392
203	CHI	Glen Lowes	Toronto						
204	MTL	Eric Bohemier	Hull	G					
205	CGY	Doug Pickell	Kamloops	LW					
206	NYI	Kerry Clark	Saskatoon	RW					
207	QUE	Chris Lappin	Canterbury H.S.	D					
208	WSH	Bobby Babcock	Sault Ste. Marie	D	2	0	0	0	2
209	PHI	Shaun Sabol	St. Paul Jr.	D	2	0	0	0	0
210	EDM	Matt Lanza	Winthrop H.S.	D					
211	DET	Tom Bissett	Michigan Tech	C	5	0	0	0	0
212	L.A.	Russ Mann	St. Lawrence U.	D					
213	N.J.	John Andersen	Oshawa	LW					
214	PIT	Stan Drulia	Belleville	RW	24	2	1	3	10
215	BUF	Tony Arndt	Portland	D					
216	TOR	Mark Holick	Saskatoon	RW					
217	VAN	Todd Hawkins	Belleville	L/RW	10	0	0	0	15
218	WPG	Matt Cote	Lake Superior State						
219	NYR	Russell Parent	South Winnipeg Jr.	D					
220	ST.L.	Terry MacLean	Longueuil	C					
221	HFD	Cal Brown	Penticton Jr. A	D					
222	MIN	Garth Joy	Hamilton	D					
223	BOS	Steffan Malmqvist	Leksand, SWE	F					
224	CHI	Chris Thayer	Kent Prep	C					
225	MTL	Charlie Moore	Belleville	LW					
226	CGY	Anders Lindstrom	Timra, SWE	C					
227	NYI	Dan Beaudette	St. Thomas Academy						
228	QUE	Martin Latreille	Laval	D					
229	WSH	John Schratz	Amherst Jr. B	D					
230	PHI	Brett Lawrence	Rochester Jr. B	RW					
231	EDM	Mojmir Bozik	HC Kosice, TCH	D					
232	DET	Peter Ekroth	Sodertalje, SWE	D					
233	L.A.	Brian Hayton	Guelph	LW					
234	ST.L.	Bill Butler	Northwood Prep	LW					
235	PIT	Rob Wilson	Sudbury	D					
236	N.J.	Doug Kirton	Orillia Jr. A	F					
237	TOR	Brian Hoard	Hamilton	D					
238	VAN	Vladimir Krutov	CSKA Moscow, USSR	LW	61	11	23	34	20
239	WPG	Arto Blomsten	Djurgarden, SWE	D	25	0	4	4	8
240	NYR	Soren True	Skobakken, DEN	F					
241	ST.L.	David O'Brien	Northeastern	RW					
242	HFD	Brian Verbeek	Kingston	C					
243	MIN	Kurt Stahura	Williston Academy	LW					

PICK	TEAM	NAME	DRAFTED FROM	NHL PLAYERS: POS / NHL GOALTENDERS: POS	GP	G / W	A / GA	PTS / SO	PIM / AVG
244	BOS	Joel Gardner	Sarnia Jr. B	C					
245	CHI	Sean Williams	Oshawa	C	2	0	0	0	4
246	MTL	Karel Svoboda	Skoda Plzen, TCH	R/LW					
247	CGY	Antonin Stavjana	TJ Gottwaldov, TCH	D					
248	NYI	Paul Thompson	Northern Manitoba AAA	D					
249	QUE	Sean Boudreault	Mount St. Charles H.S.	F					
250	WSH	Scott McCrory	Oshawa	C					
251	PHI	Daniel Stephano	Northwood Prep	G					
252	EDM	Tony Hand	Murrayfield Racers, GBR	C					

1987

The 1987 NHL Entry Draft boasted one of the best crops of junior talent since 1979, as the Canadian junior leagues filled the first round after the previous three drafts had been dominated by the American high school and college systems. The Buffalo Sabres were granted the first overall selection, their first since drafting superstar Gil Perreault in 1970, and used the top choice to select another stellar French-Canadian prospect. Pierre Turgeon had previously been selected into the Quebec Major Junior Hockey League first overall and had completed his junior career as the consensus number-one pick.

The brother of Sylvain Turgeon (who had been Hartford's first-round draft choice in 1983), Pierre joined the Sabres immediately in 1987–88 but recorded only 42 points (14 goals, 28 assists) in 76 games. However, he quickly improved by doubling the total the following year and recorded his first 100-point season with 40 goals and 66 assists in his third season of 1989–90. Turgeon's best season came following a trade to the New York Islanders when he had 58 goals and 74 assists for 132 points in 1992–93 and received the Lady Byng Trophy as the league's most gentlemanly player.

Following Turgeon, there remained a collection of future superstars in the 1987 talent pool. Brendan Shanahan, touted as a franchise player as the top Ontario Hockey League prospect, was selected by the New Jersey Devils with the second overall pick. Similar to Turgeon, Shanahan was immediately recruited by the Devils for the following season where he collected only 26 points (seven goals, 19 assists) in 65 games. However, Shanahan also consistently improved his numbers each year, eventually reaching a career high in 1993–94 with a 52 goals and 50 assists for the St. Louis Blues.

Shanahan has clearly established himself as one of today's most dangerous offensive threats, yet the 6'3", 218-pound power forward is also one of the NHL's most aggressive talents as he has never finished a season with fewer than 100 penalty minutes.

Another impressive talent taken in the first round of the 1987 draft was Bryan Fogarty. Selected ninth overall by Quebec after shattering junior scoring records for defenseman, Fogarty could not overcome off-ice problems. However, Quebec also landed Joe Sakic with the 15th pick in the first round. He required an extra year of seasoning in the WHL, where he finished the year as the league's MVP and earned player of the year honors as well as tying for the league's scoring championship before breaking into the NHL in 1988–89. He has gone on to become one of the top offensive stars in the game and led the Colorado Avalanche to a Stanley Cup title in 1996 in the franchise's first year after leaving Quebec.

One of the darkest horses to come out of the Entry Draft was selected in 1987. A 61-goal scorer with Moose Jaw of the WHL in 1986–87, Theoren Fleury stood just 5'6" and

weighed only 160 pounds and was thus considered a high-risk pick since the drafting trend seemed to place a strong emphasis on size. The Calgary Flames decided to take the risk and drafted him 166th overall as their ninth choice. Like Joe Sakic, Fleury would return to the WHL after being drafted, tying Sakic as the league's top scorer with 160 points in 1987–88. In 1989–90 he became a regular in Calgary and has gone on to become the Flames' all-time leading scorer. As the smallest player in the NHL, he remains one of the most effective and exciting players in the league.

The Montreal Canadiens emerged as the most successful team in the draft as they acquired high-scoring forwards Andrew Cassels (17th overall) and John LeClair (33rd), as well as top blueliners Eric Desjardins (38th overall) and Mathieu Schneider (44th).

1987
FIRST ROUND

PICK	TEAM	NAME	DRAFTED FROM	NHL PLAYERS: POS NHL GOALTENDERS: POS	GP GP	G W	A GA	PTS SO	PIM AVG
1	BUF	Pierre Turgeon	Granby	C	810	366	566	932	275
2	N.J.	Brendan Shanahan	London	LW	788	363	380	743	1626
3	BOS	Glen Wesley	Portland	D	803	99	305	404	635
4	L.A.	Wayne McBean	Medicine Hat	D	211	10	39	49	168
5	PIT	Chris Joseph	Seattle	D	418	36	99	135	523
6	MIN	Dave Archibald	Portland	C/LW	323	57	67	124	139
7	TOR	Luke Richardson	Peterborough	D	795	26	104	130	1325
8	CHI	Jimmy Waite	Chicoutimi	G	90	22	252	3	3.47
9	QUE	Bryan Fogarty	Kingston	D	156	22	52	74	119
10	NYR	Jayson More	New Westminster	D	388	18	52	70	684
11	DET	Yves Racine	Longueuil	D	508	37	194	231	439
12	ST.L.	Keith Osborne	North Bay	RW	16	1	3	4	16
13	NYI	Dean Chynoweth	Medicine Hat	D	241	4	18	22	667
14	BOS	Stephane Quintal	Granby	D	593	38	109	147	860
15	QUE	Joe Sakic	Swift Current	C	719	334	549	883	311
16	WPG	Bryan Marchment	Belleville	D	478	25	84	109	1430
17	MTL	Andrew Cassels	Ottawa	C	579	122	299	421	274
18	HFD	Jody Hull	Peterborough	RW	526	99	105	204	110
19	CGY	Bryan Deasley	Michigan	LW					
20	PHI	Darren Rumble	Kitchener	D	157	10	22	32	181
21	EDM	Peter Soberlak	Swift Current	LW					

SECOND ROUND

PICK	TEAM	NAME	DRAFTED FROM	POS	GP	G/W	A/GA	PTS/SO	PIM/AVG
22	BUF	Brad Miller	Regina	D	82	1	5	6	321
23	N.J.	Ricard Persson	Ostersund, SWE	D	67	6	9	15	53
24	VAN	Rob Murphy	Laval	C	125	9	12	21	152
25	CGY	Stephane Matteau	Hull	LW	524	100	118	218	534
26	PIT	Rick Tabaracci	Cornwall	G	260	88	704	13	3.03
27	L.A.	Mark Fitzpatrick	Medicine Hat	G	299	107	881	8	3.14
28	TOR	Daniel Marois	Chicoutimi	RW	350	117	93	210	419
29	CHI	Ryan McGill	Swift Current	D	151	4	15	19	391
30	PHI	Jeff Harding	St. Michael's Jr. B	RW	15	0	0	0	47
31	NYR	Daniel Lacroix	Granby	LW	183	11	7	18	366
32	DET	Gord Kruppke	Prince Albert	D	23	0	0	0	32
33	MTL	John LeClair	Bellows Academy	LW	507	226	222	448	265
34	NYI	Jeff Hackett	Oshawa	G	284	83	824	14	3.13
35	MIN	Scott McCrady	Medicine Hat	D					
36	WSH	Jeff Ballantyne	Ottawa	D					
37	WPG	Patrik Ericksson	Brynas Gavle, SWE	C					
38	MTL	Eric Desjardins	Granby	D	678	73	255	328	494
39	HFD	Adam Burt	North Bay	D	575	36	103	139	829
40	CGY	Kevin Grant	Kitchener	D					
41	DET	Bob Wilkie	Swift Current	D	18	2	5	7	10
42	EDM	Brad Werenka	Northern Michigan	D	133	8	30	38	100

OTHER ROUNDS

PICK	TEAM	NAME	DRAFTED FROM	POS	GP	G/W	A/GA	PTS/SO	PIM/AVG
43	L.A.	Ross Wilson	Peterborough	RW					
44	MTL	Mathieu Schneider	Cornwall	D	553	95	216	311	561
45	VAN	Steve Veilleux	Trois-Rivieres	D					
46	NYR	Simon Gagne	Laval	RW					
47	PIT	Jamie Leach	Hamilton	RW	81	11	9	20	12
48	MIN	Kevin Kaminski	Saskatoon	C	139	3	10	13	528
49	TOR	John McIntyre	Guelph	C	351	24	54	78	516
50	CHI	Cam Russell	Hull	D	354	8	19	27	778
51	QUE	Jim Sprott	London	D					
52	DET	Dennis Holland	Portland	C					
53	BUF	Andrew MacVicar	Peterborough	LW					
54	ST.L.	Kevin Miehm	Ottawa	C	22	1	4	5	8
55	NYI	Dean Ewen	Spokane	LW					
56	BOS	Todd Lalonde	Sudbury	LW					
57	WSH	Steve Maltais	Cornwall	LW	94	9	15	24	41
58	MTL	Francois Gravel	Shawinigan	G					
59	ST.L.	Robert Nordmark	Lulea, SWE	D	236	13	70	83	254
60	CHI	Mike Dagenais	Peterborough	D					

PICK	TEAM	NAME	DRAFTED FROM	NHL PLAYERS: POS NHL GOALTENDERS: POS	GP GP	G W	A GA	PTS SO	PIM AVG
61	CGY	Scott Mahoney	Oshawa	LW					
62	PHI	Martin Hostak	Sparta Praha, TCH	C	55	3	11	14	24
63	EDM	Geoff Smith	St. Albert Jr. A	D	458	18	73	91	280
64	EDM	Peter Eriksson	HV-71 Jonkoping, SWE	LW	20	3	3	6	24
65	N.J.	Brian Sullivan	Springfield Jr. B	RW	2	0	1	1	0
66	VAN	Doug Torrel	Hibbing H.S.	C					
67	BOS	Darwin McPherson	New Westminster	D					
68	PIT	Risto Kurkinen	JyP HT Jyvaskyla, FIN	LW					
69	NYR	Mike Sullivan	Boston U.	C	453	41	62	103	137
70	CGY	Tim Harris	Pickering Jr. B	RW					
71	TOR	Joe Sacco	Medford H.S.	LW	418	76	84	160	207
72	QUE	Kip Miller	Michigan State	C	90	14	25	39	31
73	MIN	John Weisbrod	Choate	C					
74	DET	Mark Reimer	Saskatoon	G					
75	ST.L.	Darren Smith	North Bay	LW					
76	NYI	George Maneluk	Brandon	G	4	1	15	0	6.43
77	WSH	Matt DelGuidice	St. Anselm College	G	11	2	28	0	3.87
78	WSH	Tyler Larter	Sault Ste. Marie	C	1	0	0	0	0
79	WPG	Don McLennan	U. of Denver	D					
80	MTL	Kris Miller	Greenway H.S.	D					
81	HFD	Terry Yake	Brandon	RW	270	58	85	143	144
82	ST.L.	Andy Rymsha	Western Michigan	D	6	0	0	0	23
83	PHI	Tomaz Eriksson	Djurgarden, SWE	LW					
84	BUF	John Bradley	New Hampton H.S.	G					
85	BUF	David Pergola	Belmont Hill H.S.	RW					
86	N.J.	Kevin Dean	Culver Military Academy	D	136	3	19	22	50
87	VAN	Sean Fabian	Hill-Murray H.S.	D					
88	MIN	Teppo Kivela	Jokerit Helsinki, FIN	C					
89	PIT	Jeff Waver	Hamilton	D					
90	L.A.	Mike Vukonich	Duluth Denfield H.S.	C					
91	TOR	Mike Eastwood	Pembroke Jr. A	C	322	39	58	97	145
92	CHI	Ulf Sandstrom	MoDo Ornskoldsvik, SWE	RW					
93	QUE	Rob Mendel	Wisconsin	D					
94	NYR	Eric O'Borsky	Yale	C					
95	DET	Radomir Brazda	Tesla Pardubice, TCH	D					
96	WPG	Ken Gernander	Greenway H.S.	C	10	2	3	5	4
97	NYI	Petr Vlk	Dukla Jihlava, TCH	LW					
98	BOS	Ted Donato	Catholic Memorial H.S.	LW	451	112	139	251	275
99	WSH	Pat Beauchesne	Moose Jaw	D					
100	WPG	Darrin Amundson	Duluth East H.S.	C					
101	MTL	Steve McCool	Hill H.S.	D					
102	HFD	Marc Rousseau	U. of Denver	D					
103	CGY	Tim Corkery	Ferris State	D					
104	PHI	Bill Gall	New Hampton H.S.	RW					
105	EDM	Shaun Van Allen	Saskatoon	C	357	40	96	136	226
106	BUF	Chris Marshall	Boston College H.S.	LW					
107	N.J.	Ben Hankinson	Edina H.S.	RW	43	3	3	6	45
108	VAN	Garry Valk	Sherwood Park Jr. A	LW	474	69	92	161	570
109	MIN	D'arcy Norton	Kamloops	LW					
110	PIT	Shawn McEachern	Matignon H.S.	LW	447	120	145	265	196
111	L.A.	Greg Batters	Victoria	RW					
112	TOR	Damian Rhodes	Richfield H.S.	G	183	63	455	8	2.61
113	CHI	Mike McCormick	Richmond Jr.	D					
114	QUE	Garth Snow	Mount St. Charles H.S.	G	109	47	268	3	2.74
115	NYR	Ludek Cajka	Dukla Jihlava, TCH	D					
116	DET	Sean Clifford	Ohio State	D					
117	ST.L.	Rob Robinson	Miami of Ohio	D	22	0	1	1	8
118	NYI	Rob DiMaio	Medicine Hat	C	427	58	77	135	458
119	BOS	Matt Glennon	Archbishop Williams H.S.	LW	3	0	0	0	2
120	WSH	Rich Defreitas	St. Mark's H.S.	D					
121	WPG	Joe Harwell	Hill-Murray H.S.	D					
122	MTL	Les Kuntar	Nichols H.S.	G	6	2	16	0	3.18
123	HFD	Jeff Cyr	Michigan Tech	D					
124	CGY	Joe Aloi	Hull	D					
125	PHI	Tony Link	Dimond H.S.	D					
126	EDM	Radek Toupal	Motor Ceske Budejovice, TCH	RW					
127	BUF	Paul Flanagan	New Hampton H.S.	D					
128	N.J.	Tom Neziol	Miami of Ohio	LW					
129	VAN	Todd Fanning	Ohio State	G					
130	MIN	Timo Kulonen	KalPa Kuopio, FIN	D					
131	PIT	Jim Bodden	Chatham Jr. B	C					
132	L.A.	Kyosti Karjalainen	Brynas Gavle, SWE	RW	28	1	8	9	12
133	DET	Trevor Jobe	Moose Jaw	LW					
134	CHI	Stephen Tepper	Westboro H.S.	RW	1	0	0	0	0
135	QUE	Tim Hanus	Minnetonka H.S.	LW					
136	NYR	Clint Thomas	Bartlet H.S.	D					
137	DET	Mike Bober	Laval	LW					
138	ST.L.	Todd Crabtree	Governor Dummer H.S.	LW					
139	NYI	Knut Walbye	Furuset Oslo, NOR	C					
140	BOS	Rob Cheevers	Boston College	G					
141	WSH	Devon Oleniuk	Kamloops	D					
142	WPG	Todd Hartje	Harvard	C					
143	MTL	Rob Kelley	Matignon H.S.	LW					
144	HFD	Greg Wolf	Buffalo Regal Midgets	D					
145	CGY	Peter Ciavaglia	Nichols H.S.	C	5	0	0	0	0
146	PHI	Mark Strapon	Hayward H.S.	D					
147	EDM	Tomas Srsen	Zetor Brno, TCH	RW	2	0	0	0	0

PICK	TEAM	NAME	DRAFTED FROM	NHL PLAYERS: POS / NHL GOALTENDERS: POS	GP / GP	G / W	A / GA	PTS / SO	PIM / AVG
148	BUF	Sean Dooley	Groton	D					
149	N.J.	Jim Dowd	Brick H.S.	C	144	17	37	54	35
150	VAN	Viktor Tyumenev	Spartak Moscow, USSR	C					
151	MIN	Don Schmidt	Kamloops	D					
152	PIT	Jiri Kucera	Dukla Jihlava, TCH	RW					
153	BUF	Tim Roberts	Deerfield Academy	C					
154	TOR	Chris Jensen	Northwood Prep	RW					
155	CHI	John Reilly	Phillips Andover H.S.	LW					
156	QUE	Jake Enebank	Northfield H.S.	LW					
157	NYR	Charles Wiegand	Essex Junction H.S.	C					
158	DET	Kevin Scott	Vernon Jr. A	C					
159	ST.L.	Guy Hebert	Hamilton College	G	300	115	819	16	2.91
160	NYI	Jeff Saterdalen	Jefferson H.S.	RW					
161	BOS	Chris Winnes	Northwood Prep	RW	33	1	6	7	6
162	WSH	Thomas Sjogren	Vastra Frolunda, SWE	RW					
163	WPG	Markku Kyllonen	Karpat Oulu, FIN	LW	9	0	2	2	2
164	MTL	Will Geist	St. Paul Academy	D					
165	HFD	John Moore	Yale	C					
166	CGY	Theoren Fleury	Moose Jaw	RW	731	334	427	761	1271
167	PHI	Darryl Ingham	U. of Manitoba	RW					
168	EDM	Age Ellingsen	Storhamer, NOR	D					
169	BUF	Grant Tkachuk	Saskatoon	LW					
170	N.J.	John Blessman	Toronto	D					
171	VAN	Greg Daly	New Hampton H.S.	D					
172	MIN	Jarmo Myllys	Lukko Rauma, FIN	G	39	4	161	0	5.23
173	PIT	Jack MacDougall	New Prep H.S.	RW					
174	L.A.	Jeff Gawlicki	Northern Michigan	LW					
175	TOR	Brian Blad	Belleville	D					
176	CHI	Lance Werness	Burnsville H.S.	RW					
177	QUE	Jaroslav Sevcik	Zetor Brno, TCH	LW	13	0	2	2	2
178	NYR	Eric Burrill	Tartan H.S.	RW					
179	DET	Mikko Haapakoski	Karpat Oulu, FIN	D					
180	ST.L.	Robert Dumas	Seattle	D					
181	NYI	Shawn Howard	Penticton Jr. A	D					
182	BOS	Paul Ohman	St. John's Prep	D					
183	QUE	Ladislav Tresl	Zetor Brno, TCH	C					
184	WPG	Jim Fernolz	White Bear Lake H.S.	RW					
185	MTL	Eric Tremblay	Drummondville	D					
186	HFD	Joe Day	St. Lawrence U.	C	72	1	10	11	87
187	CGY	Mark Osiecki	Madison Jr. A	D	93	3	11	14	43
188	PHI	Bruce McDonald	Loomis-Chaffee H.S.	RW					
189	EDM	Gavin Armstrong	RPI	G					
190	BUF	Ian Herbers	Swift Current	D	22	0	2	2	32
191	N.J.	Peter Fry	Victoria	G					
192	VAN	John Fletcher	Clarkson	G					
193	MIN	Larry Olimb	Warroad H.S.	D					
194	PIT	Daryn McBride	U. of Denver	C					
195	L.A.	John Preston	Boston U	C					
196	TOR	Ron Bernacci	Hamilton College	C					
197	CHI	Dale Marquette	Brandon	LW					
198	QUE	Darren Nauss	North Battleford Jr.	RW					
199	NYR	David Porter	Northern Michigan	LW					
200	DET	Darin Bannister	Illinois-Chicago	D					
201	ST.L.	David Marvin	Warroad H.S.	D					
202	NYI	John Herlihy	Babson College	RW					
203	BOS	Casey Jones	Cornell	C					
204	WSH	Chris Clarke	Pembroke Jr. A	D					
205	NYR	Brett Barnett	Wexford Jr. B	RW					
206	MTL	Barry McKinlay	Illinois-Chicago	D					
207	ST.L.	Andy Cesarski	Culver Military Academy	D					
208	CGY	William Sedergren	Springfield Jr. B	D					
209	PHI	Steve Morrow	Westminster H.S.	D					
210	EDM	Mike Tinkham	Newburyport H.S.	RW					
211	BUF	David Littman	Boston College	G	3	0	14	0	5.96
212	N.J.	Alain Charland	Drummondville	C					
213	VAN	Roger Hansson	Rogle Angelholm, SWE	LW					
214	MIN	Mark Felicio	Northwood Prep	G					
215	PIT	Mark Carlson	Philadelphia Jr.	RW					
216	L.A.	Rostislav Vlach	TJ Gottwaldov, TCH	RW					
217	TOR	Ken Alexander	Hamilton	LW					
218	CHI	Bill Lacouture	Natick H.S.	RW					
219	QUE	Mike Williams	Ferris State	G					
220	NYR	Lance Marciano	Choate	D					
221	DET	Craig Quinlan	Hill-Murray H.S.	D					
222	ST.L.	Dan Rolfe	Brockville Jr. A	D					
223	NYI	Michael Erickson	St. John's Hill H.S.	D					
224	BOS	Eric Lemarque	Northern Michigan	RW					
225	WSH	Milos Vanik	EHC Freiburg, FRG	C					
226	WPG	Roger Rougelot	Madison Jr. A	G					
227	MTL	Ed Ronan	Andover Academy	RW	182	13	23	36	101
228	HFD	Kevin Sullivan	Princeton	RW					
229	CGY	Peter Hasselblad	Orebro, SWE	D					
230	PHI	Darius Rusnak	Slovan Bratislava, TCH	C					
231	EDM	Jeff Pauletti	Minnesota-Duluth	D					
232	BUF	Allan MacIssac	Guelph	LW					
233	VAN	Neil Eisenhut	Langley Jr.	C	16	1	3	4	21
234	VAN	Matt Evo	Country Day H.S.	LW					
235	MIN	Dave Shields	U. of Denver	C					
236	PIT	Ake Lilljebjorn	Brynas Gavle, SWE	G					
237	L.A.	Mikael Lindholm	Brynas Gavle, SWE	C	18	2	2	4	2
238	TOR	Alex Weinrich	North Yarmouth Academy	C					
239	CHI	Mike Lappin	Northwood Prep	C					
240	WSH	Dan Brettschneider	Burnsville H.S.	RW					
241	EDM	Jesper Duus	Rodoure SK, DEN	D					
242	DET	Tomas Jansson	IK Talje, SWE	D					
243	ST.L.	Ray Savard	Regina	C					
244	NYI	Will Averhill	Belmont Hill H.S.	D					
245	BOS	Sean Gorman	Matignon H.S.	D					
246	WSH	Ryan Kummo	RPI	D					
247	WPG	Hans Goran Elo	Djurgarden, SWE	G					
248	MTL	Bryan Herring	Dubuque Jr. A	C					
249	HFD	Steve Laurin	Dartmouth	G					
250	CGY	Magnus Svensson	Leksand, SWE	D	46	4	14	18	31
251	PHI	Dale Roehl	Minnetonka H.S.	G					
252	EDM	Igor Vyazmikin	CSKA Moscow, USSR	R/LW	4	1	0	1	0

1988

The 1988 NHL Entry Draft was one of the most publicized events in the history of the draft. Teams and media were engulfed by the closest race between two junior players for the prestigious position as the top-ranked prospect. Both talents starred in the WHL throughout their junior career and both featured extremely different styles of play. One was a U.S.-born finesse player who oozed natural playmaking ability and picture-perfect goal-scoring, while the other was a power forward who excelled in physical play and hard work. "(Trevor) Linden's closer to the NHL than anybody in the draft. The guy plays every shift, no matter what rink he's in. He has a big, big heart. He knows how to win," said one NHL scout. "(Mike) Modano has the ability to be a tremendous star down the road. He's very talented and could be a franchise player." The final result was the selection of Livonia, Michigan native Mike Modano first overall by the Minnesota North Stars.

Modano became the second U.S.-born talent that the North Stars had selected first overall, but unlike the underachieving Brian Lawton in 1983, Modano quickly became one of the most exciting players in the NHL, being named the runner-up to Sergei Makarov for the Calder Trophy as the league's top rookie in 1990. He helped Minnesota to an appearance in the Stanley Cup finals in 1991 and remains as one of the league's premier players with the Dallas Stars. Linden immediately entered the NHL in the 1988–89 season where he also was the runner-up for the Calder honors behind Brian Leetch. As captain of the Canucks, Linden led them to the Stanley Cup finals in 1994. He was the heart and soul of the team until his trade to the New York Islanders in 1997–98.

In addition to the two top prospects, the 1988 draft featured star players from every developmental system. Chicago's first pick was Jeremy Roenick, who had dominated the U.S. high school circuit with Thayer Academy. Roenick has developed into one of the NHL's most charismatic snipers. Rod Brind'Amour was taken by the St. Louis Blues as the ninth overall pick. Brind'Amour had emerged from the Saskatchewan Junior Hockey League's Notre Dame College Hounds. He has established himself as a multi-talented player who has the ability to check strongly as well as playing a finesse game. Brind'Amour played an integral role with the Flyers as they reached the 1997 Stanley Cup finals.

The steal of the first round would prove to be the Winnipeg Jets' pick of Teemu Selanne from Finland with the 10th choice overall. Although he did not enter the NHL until five seasons after being drafted, Selanne demolished

the rookie record books after tallying 76 goals and 132 points in 1992–93.

It was the first time that a rookie had lead the NHL in goals (Alexander Mogilny also had 76 that year) and Selanne was a runaway winner of the Calder Trophy. He continues to star as one of the NHL's top snipers with the Mighty Ducks of Anaheim.

The 1988 draft could be referred to as the year of the dark horse, as noted talents such as Mark Recchi (67th overall), Tony Amonte (68th), Rob Blake (70th), Joe Juneau (81st) and Dmitri Khristich (120th overall) were all late selections who have developed into premiere NHL talents. Juneau posted 102 points on 32 goals and 70 assists in his rookie season and finished as the runner-up to Selanne in the Calder Trophy race.

The Russian invasion also continued in 1989 as Alexander Mogilny (89th overall), Valeri Kamensky (129th), Alexander Semak (207th), Alexei Gusarov (213th) and Sergei Priakin (252nd overall) dominated the final rounds of the draft. Priakin became the first Soviet player to be permitted to play in the NHL when he signed with the Calgary Flames on March 29, 1989.

1988

PICK	TEAM	NAME	DRAFTED FROM	NHL PLAYERS: POS / NHL GOALTENDERS: POS	GP / GP	G / W	A / GA	PTS / SO	PIM / AVG
FIRST ROUND									
1	MIN	Mike Modano	Prince Albert	C	633	277	377	654	456
2	VAN	Trevor Linden	Medicine Hat	C/RW	727	257	329	586	578
3	QUE	Curtis Leschyshyn	Saskatoon	D	661	40	130	170	508
4	PIT	Darrin Shannon	Windsor	LW	506	87	163	250	344
5	QUE	Daniel Dore	Drummondville	RW	17	2	3	5	59
6	TOR	Scott Pearson	Kingston	LW	290	56	41	97	615
7	L.A.	Martin Gelinas	Hull	LW	987	168	161	329	367
8	CHI	Jeremy Roenick	Thayer Academy	C	675	320	401	721	788
9	ST.L.	Rod Brind'Amour	Notre Dame Jr. A	C	696	249	380	629	651
10	WPG	Teemu Selanne	Jokerit Helsinki, FIN	RW	410	266	271	537	155
11	HFD	Chris Govedaris	Toronto	LW	45	4	6	10	24
12	N.J.	Corey Foster	Peterborough	D	45	5	6	11	24
13	BUF	Joel Savage	Victoria	RW	3	0	1	1	0
14	PHI	Claude Boivin	Drummondville	LW	132	12	19	31	364
15	WSH	Reggie Savage	Victoriaville	C	34	5	7	12	28
16	NYI	Kevin Cheveldayoff	Brandon	D					
17	DET	Kory Kocur	Saskatoon	RW					
18	BOS	Robert Cimetta	Toronto	L/RW	103	16	16	32	66
19	EDM	Francois Leroux	St-Jean	D	249	3	20	23	577
20	MTL	Eric Charron	Trois-Rivieres	D	97	2	6	8	76
21	CGY	Jason Muzzatti	Michigan State	G	62	13	167	1	3.32
SECOND ROUND									
22	NYR	Troy Mallette	Sault Ste. Marie	LW	456	51	68	119	1226
23	N.J.	Jeff Christian	London	LW	18	2	2	4	17
24	QUE	Stephane Fiset	Victoriaville	G	292	123	865	12	3.17
25	PIT	Mark Major	North Bay	LW	2	0	0	0	5
26	NYR	Murray Duval	Spokane	RW					
27	TOR	Tie Domi	Peterborough	RW	486	42	63	105	2260
28	L.A.	Paul Holden	London	D					
29	NYI	Wayne Doucet	Hamilton	LW					
30	ST.L.	Adrien Plavsic	New Hampshire	D	214	16	56	72	161
31	WPG	Russell Romaniuk	St. Boniface Jr. A	LW	102	13	14	27	63
32	HFD	Barry Richter	Culver Military Academy	D	54	5	14	19	32
33	VAN	Leif Rohlin	Vasteras, SWE	D	96	8	24	32	40
34	MTL	Martin St. Amour	Verdun	LW	1	0	0	0	2
35	PHI	Pat Murray	Michigan State	LW	25	3	1	4	15
36	WSH	Tim Taylor	London	C	218	35	33	68	164
37	NYI	Sean Lebrun	New Westminster	LW					
38	DET	Serge Anglehart	Drummondville	D					
39	EDM	Petro Koivunen	Kiekko-Espoo, FIN	C					
40	MIN	Link Gaetz	Spokane	D	65	6	8	14	412
41	WSH	Todd Bartley	Dauphin Jr. A	D					
42	CGY	Todd Harkins	Miami of Ohio	C	48	3	3	6	78
OTHER ROUNDS									
43	MIN	Shaun Kane	Springfield Jr. B	D					
44	VAN	Dane Jackson	Vernon Jr. A	RW	45	12	6	18	58
45	QUE	Petri Aaltonen	HIFK Helsinki, FIN	C					
46	MTL	Neil Carnes	Verdun	C					
47	DET	Guy Dupuis	Hull	D					
48	TOR	Peter Ing	Windsor	G	74	20	266	1	4.05
49	L.A.	John Van Kessel	North Bay	RW					
50	CHI	Trevor Dam	London	RW					
51	ST.L.	Rob Fournier	North Bay	G					

PICK	TEAM	NAME	DRAFTED FROM	NHL PLAYERS: POS / NHL GOALTENDERS: POS	GP / GP	G / W	A / GA	PTS / SO	PIM / AVG
52	WPG	Stephane Beauregard	St-Jean	G	90	19	268	2	3.65
53	EDM	Trevor Sim	Seattle	RW	3	0	1	1	2
54	N.J.	Zdeno Ciger	ZTS Martin, TCH	LW	296	82	121	203	75
55	BUF	Darcy Loewen	Spokane	LW	135	4	8	12	211
56	PHI	Craig Fisher	Oshawa Jr. B	C	12	0	0	0	2
57	WSH	Duane Derksen	Winkler Jr. A	G					
58	NYI	Danny Lorenz	Seattle	G	8	1	25	0	4.20
59	DET	Petr Hrbek	Sparta Praha, TCH	RW					
60	BOS	Stephen Heinze	Lawrence Academy	RW	367	97	77	174	209
61	EDM	Collin Bauer	Saskatoon	D					
62	PIT	Daniel Gauthier	Victoriaville	LW	5	0	0	0	0
63	PHI	Dominic Roussel	Trois-Rivieres	G	146	64	414	5	3.19
64	MIN	Jeffrey Stolp	Greenway H.S.	G					
65	N.J.	Matt Ruchty	Bowling Green	LW					
66	QUE	Darin Kimble	Prince Albert	RW	311	23	20	43	1082
67	PIT	Mark Recchi	Kamloops	RW	710	317	472	789	535
68	NYR	Tony Amonte	Thayer Academy	RW	533	203	232	435	374
69	TOR	Ted Crowley	Lawrence Academy	D	21	1	2	3	10
70	L.A.	Rob Blake	Bowling Green	D	469	91	197	288	742
71	CHI	Stefan Elvenas	Rogle Angelholm, SWE	RW					
72	ST.L.	Jaan Luik	Miami of Ohio	D					
73	WPG	Brian Hunt	Oshawa	C					
74	HFD	Dean Dyer	Lake Superior State	C					
75	N.J.	Scott Luik	Miami of Ohio	RW					
76	BUF	Keith Carney	Mount St. Charles H.S.	D	342	19	62	81	370
77	PHI	Scott Lagrand	Hotchkiss H.S.	G					
78	WSH	Bob Krauss	Lethbridge	D					
79	NYI	Andre Brassard	Trois-Rivieres	D					
80	DET	Sheldon Kennedy	Swift Current	RW	310	49	58	107	233
81	BOS	Joe Juneau	RPI	C	410	99	287	386	150
82	EDM	Cam Brauer	RPI	D					
83	MTL	Patrik Kjellberg	Falun, SWE	LW	7	0	0	0	2
84	CGY	Gary Socha	Tabor Academy	C					
85	CGY	Tomas Forslund	Leksand, SWE	RW	44	5	11	16	12
86	TOR	Leonard Esau	Humboldt Jr. A	D	27	0	10	10	24
87	QUE	Stephane Venne	Vermont	D					
88	PIT	Greg Andrusak	Minnesota-Duluth	D	12	0	4	4	8
89	BUF	Alexander Mogilny	CSKA Moscow, USSR	RW	587	315	354	669	273
90	CGY	Scott Matusovich	Canterbury H.S.	D					
91	L.A.	Jeff Robison	Mount St. Charles H.S.	D					
92	CHI	Joe Cleary	Stratford Jr. B	D					
93	MTL	Peter Popovic	Vasteras, SWE	D	303	7	48	55	173
94	WPG	Anthony Joseph	Oshawa	RW	2	1	0	1	0
95	HFD	Scott Morrow	Northwood Prep	LW	4	0	0	0	0
96	N.J.	Chris Nelson	Rochester Jr. A	D					
97	BUF	Rob Ray	Cornwall	RW	569	33	34	67	2268
98	PHI	Edward O'Brien	Cushing Academy	LW					
99	NYR	Martin Bergeron	Drummondville	C					
100	NYI	Paul Rutherford	Ohio State	C					
101	WPG	Benoit Lebeau	Merrimack	LW					
102	BOS	Daniel Murphy	Gunnery H.S.	D					
103	EDM	Don Martin	London	LW					
104	MTL	Jean-Claude Bergeron	Verdun	G	72	21	232	1	3.69
105	ST.L.	Dave Lacouture	Natick H.S.	RW					
106	BUF	David Di Vita	Lake Superior State	G					
107	VAN	Corrie D'Alessio	Cornell	G	1	0	0	0	0.00
108	QUE	Ed Ward	Michigan	RW	154	14	19	33	222
109	L.A.	Micah Aivazoff	Victoria	C	92	4	6	10	46
110	NYR	Dennis Vial	Hamilton	LW	242	4	15	19	794
111	NYI	Pavel Gross	Sparta Praha, TCH	RW					
112	L.A.	Robert Larsson	Skelleftea, SWE	D					
113	CHI	Justin Lafayette	Ferris State	LW					
114	ST.L.	Dan Fowler	U. of Maine	D					
115	WPG	Ronald Jones	Windsor	RW					
116	HFD	Corey Beaulieu	Seattle	D					
117	N.J.	Chad Johnson	Rochester Jr. A	C					
118	BUF	Mike McLaughlin	Choate	LW					
119	PHI	Gordie Franti	Calumet H.S.	C					
120	PHI	Dimitri Khristich	Sokol Kiev, USSR	LW/C	548	196	240	436	322
121	NYI	Jason Rathbone	Brookline H.S.	RW					
122	VAN	Phil Von Stefenelli	Boston U.	D	43	0	5	5	23
123	BOS	Derek Geary	Gloucester	RW					
124	EDM	Len Barrie	Victoria	C	64	5	13	18	93
125	MTL	Patrik Carnback	Vastra Frolunda, SWE	C	154	24	38	62	122
126	CGY	Jonas Bergqvist	Leksand, SWE	RW	22	2	5	7	10
127	WPG	Markus Akerblom	Bjorkloven Umea, SWE	C					
128	VAN	Dixon Ward	Red Deer Jr. A	RW	317	59	83	142	279
129	QUE	Valeri Kamensky	CSKA Moscow, USSR	LW	395	152	218	370	275
130	PIT	Troy Mick	Portland	LW					
131	NYR	Mike Rosati	Hamilton	G					
132	TOR	Matt Mallgrave	St. Paul's H.S.	C					
133	L.A.	Jeff Kruesel	John Marshall H.S.	G					
134	CHI	Craig Woodcroft	Colgate	LW					
135	ST.L.	Matt Hayes	New Hampton H.S.	D					
136	ST.L.	Jukka Marttila	Tappara Tampere, FIN	G					
137	HFD	Kerry Russell	Michigan State	RW					
138	N.J.	Chad Erickson	Warroad H.S.	G	2	1	9	0	4.50

PICK	TEAM	NAME	DRAFTED FROM	NHL PLAYERS: POS / NHL GOALTENDERS: POS	GP	G / W	A / GA	PTS / SO	PIM / AVG
139	BUF	Mike Griffith	Ottawa	RW					
140	PHI	Jamie Cooke	Bramalea Jr. B	RW					
141	WSH	Keith Jones	Niagara Falls Jr. B	RW	348	88	92	180	581
142	NYI	Yves Gaucher	Chicoutimi	LW					
143	DET	Kelly Hurd	Michigan Tech	RW					
144	WSH	Brad Schlegel	London	D	48	1	8	9	10
145	EDM	Mike Glover	Sault Ste. Marie	RW					
146	MTL	Tim Chase	Tabor Academy	C					
147	CGY	Stefan Nilsson	HV-71 Jonkoping, SWE	LW					
148	MIN	Ken MacArthur	U. of Denver	D					
149	VAN	Greg Geldar	St. Albert Jr. A	C					
150	QUE	Sakari Lindfors	HIFK Helsinki, FIN	G					
151	PIT	Jeff Blaeser	St. John's Prep	LW					
152	NYR	Eric Couvrette	St-Jean	LW					
153	TOR	Peter Elvenas	Rogle Angelholm, SWE	C					
154	L.A.	Timo Peltomaa	Ilves Tampere, FIN	RW					
155	CHI	Jon Pojar	Roseville H.S.	LW					
156	ST.L.	John McCoy	Edina H.S.	LW					
157	WPG	Mark Smith	Trinity-Pawling H.S.	C					
158	HFD	Jim Burke	U. of Maine	D					
159	N.J.	Bryan Lafort	Waltham H.S.	G					
160	BUF	Daniel Ruoho	Madison Memorial H.S.	D					
161	PHI	Johan Salle	Malmo, SWE	D					
162	WSH	Todd Hilditch	Penticton Jr. A	D					
163	NYI	Marty McInnis	Milton Academy	C	422	101	148	249	151
164	DET	Brian McCormack	St. Paul's H.S.	D					
165	BOS	Mark Krys	Boston U.	D					
166	EDM	Shjon Podein	Minnesota-Duluth	LW	355	59	59	118	249
167	MTL	Sean Hill	Duluth East H.S.	D	284	18	60	78	314
168	CGY	Troy Kennedy	Brandon	RW					
169	MIN	Travis Richards	Armstrong H.S.	D	3	0	0	0	2
170	VAN	Roger Akerstrom	Lulea, SWE	D					
171	QUE	Dan Wiebe	U. of Alberta	LW					
172	PIT	Rob Gaudreau	Bishop Hendricken H.S.	RW	231	51	54	105	69
173	NYI	Shorty Forrest	St. Cloud State	D					
174	TOR	Mike Delay	Canterbury H.S.	D					
175	L.A.	Jim Larkin	Mount St. Charles H.S.	LW					
176	CHI	Mathew Hentges	Edina H.S.	D					
177	ST.L.	Tony Twist	Saskatoon	LW	382	8	12	20	972
178	WPG	Mike Helber	Ann Arbor H.S.	C					
179	HFD	Mark Hirth	Michigan State	C					
180	N.J.	Sergei Sveltov	Dynamo Moscow, USSR	RW					
181	BUF	Wade Flaherty	Victoria	G	69	14	208	4	3.80
182	PHI	Brian Arthur	Etobicoke Jr. B	D					
183	WSH	Petr Pavlas	Dukla Trencin, TCH	D					
184	NYI	Jeff Blumer	U. of St. Thomas	RW					
185	DET	Jody Praznik	Colorado College	D					
186	BOS	Jon Rohloff	Grand Rapids H.S.	D	150	7	25	32	129
187	EDM	Tim Cole	Woburn H.S.	G					
188	MTL	Harijs Vitolinsh	Dynamo Riga, USSR	C	Re-entered Draft in 1993				
189	CGY	Brett Peterson	St. Paul Jr. A	D					
190	MIN	Ari Matilainen	Assat Pori, FIN	RW					
191	VAN	Paul Constantin	Burlington Jr. B	C					
192	WSH	Mark Sorensen	Michigan	D					
193	PIT	David Pancoe	Hamilton	LW					
194	NYR	Paul Cain	Cornwall	C					
195	TOR	David Sacco	Medford H.S.	RW	35	5	13	18	22
196	L.A.	Brad Hyatt	Windsor	D					
197	CHI	Daniel Maurice	Chicoutimi	C					
198	ST.L.	Bret Hedican	North St. Paul H.S.	D	375	16	93	109	341
199	WPG	Pavel Kostichkin	CSKA Moscow, USSR	C					
200	HFD	Wayde Bucsis	Prince Albert	RW					
201	N.J.	Bob Woods	Brandon	D					
202	NYR	Eric Fenton	North Yarmouth Academy	C					
203	PHI	Jeff Dandretta	Cushing Academy	RW					
204	WSH	Claudio Scremin	U. of Maine	D	17	0	1	1	29
205	NYI	Jeff Kampersal	St. John's Prep	D					
206	DET	Glen Goodall	Seattle	C					
207	N.J.	Alexander Semak	Dynamo Moscow, USSR	C	289	83	91	174	187
208	EDM	Vladimir Zubkov	CSKA Moscow, USSR	D					
209	MTL	Yuri Krivokhizha	Dynamo Minsk, USSR	D					
210	CGY	Guy Darveau	Victoriaville	D					
211	MIN	Grant Bischoff	Minnesota-Duluth	LW					
212	VAN	Chris Wolanin	Illinois-Chicago	D					
213	QUE	Alexei Gusarov	CSKA Moscow, USSR	D	468	33	108	141	261
214	PIT	Cory Laylin	St. Cloud Appollo H.S.	LW					
215	NYR	Peter Fiorentino	Sault Ste. Marie	D	1	0	0	0	0
216	TOR	Mike Gregorio	Cushing Academy	G					
217	L.A.	Doug Laprade	Lake Superior State	RW					
218	CHI	Dirk Tenzer	St. Paul's H.S.	D					
219	ST.L.	Heath Deboer	Spring Lake Park H.S.	D					
220	WPG	Kevin Heise	Lethbridge	LW					
221	HFD	Rob White	St. Lawrence U.	D					
222	N.J.	Charles Hughes	Catholic Memorial H.S.	G					
223	BUF	Thomas Nieman	Choate	RW					
224	PHI	Scott Billey	Madison Jr. A	RW					
225	WSH	Chris Venkus	Western Michigan	RW					
226	NYI	Phillip Neururer	Osseo H.S.	D					
227	DET	Darren Colbourne	Cornwall	RW					
228	BOS	Eric Reisman	Ohio State	D					
229	EDM	Darin MacDonald	Boston U.	LW					
230	MTL	Kevin Dahl	Bowling Green	D	181	7	22	29	149
231	CGY	Dave Tretowicz	Clarkson	D					
232	MIN	Trent Andisson	Cornwall	LW					
233	VAN	Stefan Nilsson	Troja, SWE	C					
233	VAN	Steffan Nilsson	Troja, SWE	LW					
234	QUE	Claude Lapointe	Laval	C	439	67	93	160	415
235	PIT	Darren Stolk	Lethbridge	D					
236	NYR	Keith Slifstien	Choate	RW					
237	TOR	Peter DeBoer	Windsor	RW					
238	L.A.	Joe Flanagan	Canterbury H.S.	C					
239	CHI	Andreas Lupzig	Landshut, FRG	C					
240	ST.L.	Michael Francis	Harvard	G					
241	WPG	Kyle Galloway	U. of Manitoba	D					
242	HFD	Dan Slatalla	Deerfield Academy	LW					
243	N.J.	Robert Wallwork	Miami of Ohio	C					
244	BUF	Michael Pohl	Rosenheim, FRG	C					
245	PHI	Drahomir Kadlec	Dukla Jihlava, TCH	D					
246	WSH	Ron Pascucci	Belmont Hill H.S.	D					
247	NYI	Joe Caprini	Babson College	G					
248	DET	Donald Stone	Michigan	C					
249	BOS	Doug Jones	Kitchener	D					
250	EDM	Tim Tisdale	Swift Current	C					
251	MTL	Dave Kunda	U. of Guelph	D					
252	CGY	Sergei Priakin	Krylja Sovetov, USSR	RW	46	3	8	11	2

1989

The 1989 Entry Draft saw the first non-North American prospect chosen first overall in an NHL draft. The Quebec Nordiques selected center Mats Sundin, a 6'4", 215-pound native of Bromma, Sweden with the number-one choice. After remaining in the Swedish Elite League for one more season before entering the NHL, Sundin has developed into one of the league's most dominating forwards both with the Nordiques and after his 1994 trade to Toronto.

The 1989 draft was a big year for international talent, producing stars from Sweden, Czechoslovakia and the Soviet Union. Swedish defenseman Nicklas Lidstrom was taken 53rd overall by the Detroit Red Wings. Joining the team in 1991-92, Lidstrom collected 60 points (11 goals, 49 assists) and was named to the NHL All-Rookie Team. The two-way blueliner has become one of the most prolific defensemen in the league, playing an integral role in the Red Wings' rise to the top of the NHL and their Stanley Cup titles in 1997 and 1998. Lidstrom has also received recognition as a finalist for the 1998 Norris Trophy.

Most European players were taken late in the draft despite their star potential. Due to the political state of their native countries they were considered to be a potential risk to NHL clubs. Bobby Holik became the second Czech to be taken in the first round of an NHL Entry Draft as the Hartford Whalers selected him 10th overall. (The first had been Petr Svoboda, drafted fifth overall in 1984.) Fellow Czech Robert Reichel was also taken as the 70th pick in 1989, going to the Calgary Flames. Reichel remained in the Czech League for an additional season, leading the league in points and goals before breaking into the NHL with the Flames in 1990–91.

The Soviet Union provided two of today's most exciting NHL players when Central Red Army linemates Sergei Fedorov and Pavel Bure were drafted 74th and 113th respectively in 1989. Bure was awarded rookie of the year honors for the Soviet National League in 1988–89 before coming into the NHL in 1991–92. Dubbed "the Russian Rocket" because of his explosive speed, Bure recorded 34 goals and 60 points in his rookie year to capture the Calder Trophy, making him the second Russian to be so honored. To date, Bure has posted three seasons with 50 goals or

more. He reached the 100-point plateau in his sophomore season, collecting 110 points (60 goals, 50 assists), and led the Vancouver Canucks to the Stanley Cup finals in 1994. Fedorov joined the Red Wings in 1990–91 where a 79-point performance earned him a spot on the NHL All-Rookie Team. He has continued to be an effective scorer, enjoying his best season in 1993–94 when he posted 120 points (56 goals, 64 assists) and was recognized as the NHL's most outstanding player with the Lester Pearson Trophy, and became the first non-North American player to receive the Hart Trophy as the league's MVP. Fedorov also received the Frank J. Selke Trophy as the league's top defensive forward, another first for a non-North American player. He won it again in 1996 and, in 1997 and 1998, contributed to Detroit's consecutive Stanley Cup titles.

The Washington Capitals chose the two most prominent goaltenders in the draft by selecting Olaf Kolzig in the first round, 19th overall, and Byron Dafoe as the 35th selection. Kolzig and Dafoe share remarkable similarities. Not only are they both internationally born, but they have played hockey together at every level throughout their entire lives and even shared the Hap Holmes Trophy in 1994 for allowing the fewest goals-against in the AHL. Kolzig was born in Johannesburg, South Africa but plays internationally for Germany, while Dafoe was born in Sussex, England.

One of the worst first-round operations in Entry Draft history occurred in 1989 as the Toronto Maple Leafs entered the process with three picks in the first round. The Leafs selected three teammates from the Belleville Bulls of the Ontario Hockey League. Their first pick was used to obtain center Scott Thornton third overall. Right winger Rob Pearson was their second choice as the 12th pick and defenseman Steve Bancroft closed the first round as the 21st selection. None of the three players ever developed in the NHL. Pearson spent the most time in Toronto posting 49 goals and 42 assists for 91 points in 192 games as a Leaf, and a career record of 56 goals and 54 assists in 269 games before being assigned to the minors. Thornton has a career record of just 40 goals and 52 assists in 382 games, with only four of those points achieved in a Leaf jersey. Bancroft has only appeared in one NHL game, playing for the Chicago Blackhawks. He has never recorded an NHL point.

The 1989 Entry Draft produced the fewest 18-year-old players to immediately enter the NHL, as second overall pick Dave Chyzowski appeared in 34 games with the New York Islanders before being assigned to their AHL affiliate. The Minnesota North stars selected the oldest player ever taken in the draft when they opted for 37-year-old Helmut Balderis as the 238th pick. Balderis was a native of the Soviet Union who would play just 26 games with the North Stars in 1989–90 and collect nine points (three goals and six assists) before retiring later that same year.

1989

PICK	TEAM	NAME	DRAFTED FROM	NHL PLAYERS: POS / NHL GOALTENDERS: POS	GP / GP	G / W	A / GA	PTS / SO	PIM / AVG
FIRST ROUND									
1	QUE	Mats Sundin	Nacka, SWE	C/RW	611	265	367	632	485
2	NYI	Dave Chyzowski	Kamloops	LW	126	15	16	31	144
3	TOR	Scott Thornton	Belleville	C	382	40	52	92	701
4	WPG	Stu Barnes	Tri-City	C	433	121	152	273	184
5	N.J.	Bill Guerin	Springfield Jr. B	RW	420	121	122	243	549
6	CHI	Adam Bennett	Sudbury	D	69	3	8	11	69
7	MIN	Doug Zmolek	John Marshall H.S.	D	362	9	32	41	743
8	VAN	Jason Herter	North Dakota	D	1	0	1	1	0
9	ST.L.	Jason Marshall	Vernon Jr. A	D	172	5	16	21	375
10	HFD	Bobby Holik	Dukla Jihlava, TCH	LW	560	150	187	337	535
11	DET	Mike Sillinger	Regina	C	371	68	114	182	147
12	TOR	Rob Pearson	Belleville	RW	269	56	54	110	645

PICK	TEAM	NAME	DRAFTED FROM	NHL PLAYERS: POS / NHL GOALTENDERS: POS	GP / GP	G / W	A / GA	PTS / SO	PIM / AVG
13	MTL	Lindsay Vallis	Seattle	D	1	0	0	0	0
14	BUF	Kevin Haller	Regina	D	462	36	81	117	666
15	EDM	Jason Soules	Niagara Falls	D					
16	PIT	Jamie Heward	Regina	D	25	1	4	5	6
17	BOS	Shayne Stevenson	Kitchener	RW	27	0	2	2	35
18	N.J.	Jason Miller	Medicine Hat	LW	6	0	0	0	0
19	WSH	Olaf Kolzig	Tri-City	G	135	47	320	7	2.59
20	NYR	Steven Rice	Kitchener	RW	329	64	61	125	275
21	TOR	Steve Bancroft	Belleville	D	1	0	0	0	0
SECOND ROUND									
22	QUE	Adam Foote	Sault Ste. Marie	D	435	18	74	92	678
23	NYI	Travis Green	Spokane	C	410	97	156	253	274
24	CGY	Kent Manderville	Notre Dame Jr. A	LW	294	21	29	50	189
25	WPG	Dan Ratushny	Cornell	D	1	0	1	1	2
26	N.J.	Jarrod Skalde	Oshawa	C	78	11	18	29	36
27	CHI	Michael Speer	Guelph	D					
28	MIN	Mike Craig	Oshawa	RW	420	71	97	168	548
29	VAN	Robert Woodward	Deerfield Academy	LW					
30	MTL	Patrice Brisebois	Laval	D	391	39	127	166	348
31	ST.L.	Rick Corriveau	London	D	Re-entered Draft in 1991				
32	DET	Bob Boughner	Sault Ste. Marie	D	177	2	11	13	494
33	PHI	Greg Johnson	Thunder Bay Jr. A	C	283	52	79	131	132
34	PHI	Patrik Juhlin	Vasteras, SWE	LW	56	7	6	13	23
35	WSH	Byron Dafoe	Portland	G	162	60	446	7	2.99
36	EDM	Richard Borgo	Kitchener	G					
37	PIT	Paul Laus	Niagara Falls	D	308	5	36	41	1089
38	BOS	Mike Parson	Guelph	G					
39	L.A.	Brent Thompson	Medicine Hat	D	121	1	10	11	352
40	NYR	Jason Prosofsky	Medicine Hat	RW					
41	MTL	Steve Larouche	Trois-Rivieres	C	26	9	9	18	10
42	CGY	Ted Drury	Fairfield Prep	C	272	33	44	77	247
OTHER ROUNDS									
43	QUE	Stephane Morin	Chicoutimi	C	90	16	39	55	52
44	NYI	Jason Zent	Nichols H.S.	LW	25	3	3	6	13
45	NYR	Rob Zamuner	Guelph	LW	426	77	107	184	301
46	WPG	Jason Cirone	Cornwall	C	3	0	0	0	2
47	N.J.	Scott Pellerin	U. of Maine	LW	186	28	43	71	140
48	CHI	Bob Kellogg	Springfield Jr. B	D					
49	NYR	Louie DeBrusk	London	LW	282	20	14	34	963
50	CGY	Veli-Pekka Kautonen	HIFK Helsinki, FIN	D					
51	MTL	Pierre Sevigny	Trois-Rivieres	LW	78	4	5	9	64
52	HFD	Blair Atcheynum	Moose Jaw	RW	65	11	16	27	10
53	DET	Nicklas Lidstrom	Vasteras, SWE	D	531	87	279	366	150
54	QUE	John Tanner	Peterborough	G	21	2	65	1	3.60
55	ST.L.	Denny Felsner	Michigan	LW	18	1	4	5	6
56	BUF	Scott Thomas	Nichols H.S.	RW	39	3	3	6	23
57	BOS	Wes Walz	Lethbridge	C	169	27	51	78	71
58	PIT	John Brill	Grand Rapids H.S.	D					
59	WSH	Jim Mathieson	Regina	D	2	0	0	0	4
60	MIN	Murray Garbutt	Medicine Hat	C					
61	WSH	Jason Woolley	Michigan State	D	254	26	97	123	129
62	WPG	Kris Draper	Canadian National	C	287	38	38	76	212
63	CGY	Corey Lyons	Lethbridge	RW					
64	WPG	Mark Brownschidle	Boston U.	D					
65	NYI	Brent Grieve	Oshawa	LW	97	20	16	36	87
66	TOR	Matt Martin	Avon Old Farms H.S.	D	76	0	5	5	71
67	NYR	Jim Cummins	Michigan State	RW	263	14	16	30	911
68	NYI	Niklas Andersson	Vastra Frolunda, SWE	LW	129	26	44	70	73
69	WPG	Allain Roy	Harvard	G					
70	CGY	Robert Reichel	CHZ Litvinov, TCH	C	519	183	255	438	252
71	VAN	Brett Hauer	Richfield H.S.	D	29	4	2	6	30
72	PHI	Reid Simpson	Prince Albert	LW	105	4	11	15	289
73	HFD	Jim McKenzie	Victoria	LW	489	29	25	54	1158
74	DET	Sergei Fedorov	CSKA Moscow, USSR	C	527	248	361	609	371
75	MIN	Jean-Francois Quintin	Shawinigan	LW	22	5	5	10	4
76	MTL	Eric Dubois	Laval	D					
77	BUF	Doug Macdonald	Wisconsin	LW	11	1	0	1	2
78	EDM	Josef Beranek	CHZ Litvinov, TCH	LW	324	77	88	165	275
79	PIT	Todd Nelson	Prince Albert	D	3	1	0	1	2
80	BOS	Jackson Penney	Victoria	C					
81	L.A.	Jim Maher	Illinois-Chicago	D					
82	WSH	Trent Klatt	Osseo H.S.	RW	385	75	114	189	174
83	MTL	Andre Racicot	Granby	G	68	26	196	2	3.50
84	CGY	Ryan O'Leary	Hermantown H.S.	C					
85	NYI	Kevin Kaiser	Minnesota-Duluth	LW					
86	NYI	Jace Reed	Grand Rapids H.S.	D					
87	MIN	Pat MacLeod	Kamloops	D	53	5	13	18	14
88	NYR	Aaron Miller	Niagara Jr. A	D	126	7	17	24	72
89	N.J.	Mike Heinke	Avon Old Farms H.S.	G					
90	NYI	Steve Young	Moose Jaw	RW					
91	MIN	Bryan Schoen	Minnetonka H.S.	G					
92	EDM	Peter White	Michigan State	C	62	10	12	22	2
93	ST.L.	Daniel Laperriere	St. Lawrence U.	D	48	2	5	7	27
94	HFD	James Black	Portland	C	186	33	29	62	60
95	DET	Shawn McCosh	Niagara Falls	C	9	1	0	1	6
96	TOR	Keith Carney	Mount St. Charles H.S.	D					
97	MIN	Rhys Hollyman	Miami of Ohio	D					

PICK	TEAM	NAME	DRAFTED FROM	POS	GP	G	A	PTS	PIM
98	BUF	Ken Sutton	Saskatoon	D	303	21	69	90	291
99	NYI	Kevin O'Sullivan	Catholic Memorial H.S.	D					
100	PIT	Tom Nevers	Edina H.S.	C					
101	BOS	Mark Montanari	Kitchener	C					
102	L.A.	Eric Ricard	Granby	D					
103	L.A.	Thomas Newman	Blaine H.S.	G					
104	MTL	Marc Deschamps	Cornell	D					
105	CGY	Toby Kearney	Belmont Hill H.S.	LW					
106	QUE	Dan Lambert	Swift Current	D	29	6	9	15	22
107	BUF	Bill Pye	Northern Michigan	G					
108	TOR	David Burke	Cornell	D					
109	WPG	Dan Bylsma	Bowling Green	LW	148	6	15	21	65
110	N.J.	David Emma	Boston College	C	28	5	6	11	2
111	CHI	Tommi Pullola	Sport Vaasa, FIN	C					
112	MIN	Scott Cashman	Kanata Jr.	G					
113	VAN	Pavel Bure	CSKA Moscow, USSR	RW	428	254	224	478	328
114	ST.L.	David Roberts	Avon Old Farms H.S.	LW	125	20	33	53	85
115	HFD	Jerome Bechard	Moose Jaw	LW					
116	DET	Dallas Drake	Northern Michigan	C	369	86	139	225	331
117	PHI	Niklas Eriksson	Leksand, SWE	C					
118	NYR	Joby Messier	Michigan State	D	25	0	4	4	24
119	BUF	Mike Barkley	U. of Maine	RW					
120	EDM	Anatoli Semenov	Dynamo Moscow, USSR	C/LW	362	68	126	194	122
121	PIT	Mike Markovich	U. of Denver	D					
122	BOS	Stephen Foster	Catholic Memorial H.S.	D					
123	L.A.	Daniel Rydmark	Farjestad Karlstad, SWE	C					
124	ST.L.	Derek Frenette	Ferris State	LW					
125	TOR	Michael Doers	Northwood Prep	RW					
126	PIT	Mike Needham	Kamloops	RW	86	9	5	14	16
127	QUE	Sergei Mylnikov	Traktor Chelyabinsk, USSR	G	10	1	47	0	4.96
128	NYI	Jon Larson	Roseau H.S.	D					
129	TOR	Keith Merkler	Portledge H.S.	LW					
130	WPG	Pekka Peltola	HPK Hameenlinna, FIN	RW					
131	WPG	Doug Evans	Michigan	LW	355	48	87	135	502
132	CHI	Tracy Edgeland	Prince Albert	LW					
133	NYI	Brett Harkins	Detroit Compuware Jr. A	LW	53	4	18	22	14
134	VAN	James Revenburg	Windsor	RW					
135	ST.L.	Jeff Batters	Alaska-Anchorage	D	16	0	0	0	28
136	HFD	Scott Daniels	Regina	LW	148	8	12	20	667
137	DET	Scott Zygulski	Culver Military Academy	D					
138	PHI	John Callahan Jr.	Belmont Hill H.S.	C					
139	NYR	Greg Leahy	Portland	C					
140	EDM	Davis Payne	Michigan Tech	LW	22	0	1	1	14
141	EDM	Sergei Yashin	Dynamo Moscow, USSR	LW					
142	PIT	Patrick Schafhauser	Hill-Murray H.S.	D					
143	BOS	Otto Hascak	Dukla Trencin, TCH	RW					
144	L.A.	Ted Kramer	Michigan	RW					
145	WSH	Dave Lorentz	Peterborough	LW					
146	MTL	Craig Ferguson	Yale	RW	24	1	1	2	6
147	CGY	Alex Nikolic	Cornell	LW					
148	QUE	Paul Krake	Alaska-Anchorage	G					
149	NYI	Phil Huber	Kamloops	LW					
150	TOR	Derek Langille	North Bay	D					
151	WPG	Jim Solly	Bowling Green	C					
152	N.J.	Sergei Starikov	CSKA Moscow, USSR	D	16	0	1	1	0
153	CHI	Milan Tichy	Skoda Plzen, TCH	D	23	0	5	5	40
154	MIN	Jonathon Pratt	Pingree Prep	G					
155	VAN	Rob Sangster	Kitchener	LW					
156	ST.L.	Kevin Plager	Parkway North H.S.	RW					
157	HFD	Raymond Saumier	Trois-Rivieres	RW					
158	DET	Andy Suhy	Western Michigan	D					
159	PHI	Sverre Sears	Belmont Hill H.S.	D					
160	NYR	Greg Spenrath	Tri-City	LW					
161	BUF	Derek Plante	Cloquet H.S.	C	354	87	134	221	114
162	EDM	Darcy Martini	Michigan Tech	D	2	0	0	0	0
163	PIT	Dave Shute	Victoria	C					
164	BOS	Rick Allain	Kitchener	D					
165	L.A.	Sean Whyte	Guelph	RW	21	0	2	2	12
166	WSH	Dean Holoien	Saskatoon	D					
167	MTL	Patrick Lebeau	St-Jean	LW	7	2	2	4	4
168	CGY	Kevin Wortman	American Int'l College	D	5	0	0	0	2
169	QUE	Viacheslav Bykov	CSKA Moscow, USSR	C					
170	NYI	Matthew Robbins	New Hampton H.S.	C					
171	TOR	Jeffrey St. Laurent	Berwick H.S.	RW					
172	WPG	Stephane Gauvin	Cornell	LW					
173	N.J.	Andre Faust	Princeton	C	47	10	7	17	14
174	CHI	Jason Greyerbiehl	Colgate	LW					
175	MIN	Kenneth Blum	St. Joseph H.S.	C					
176	VAN	Sandy Moger	Lake Superior State	C	194	38	36	74	186
177	ST.L.	John Roderick	Rindge and Latin Academy	D					
178	HFD	Michel Picard	Trois-Rivieres	LW	112	16	27	43	85
179	DET	Bob Jones	Sault Ste. Marie	LW	2	0	0	0	0
180	PHI	Glen Wisser	Philadelphia Jr.	RW					
181	NYR	Mark Bavis	Cushing Academy	C					
182	L.A.	Jim Giacin	Culver Military Academy	LW					
183	BUF	Donald Audette	Laval	RW	409	164	125	289	323
184	PIT	Andrew Wolf	Victoria	D					
185	BOS	James Lavish	Deerfield Academy	RW					
186	L.A.	Martin Maskarinec	Sparta Praha, TCH	D					
187	WSH	Victor Gervais	Seattle	C					
188	MTL	Roy Mitchell	Portland	D	3	0	0	0	0
189	CGY	Sergei Gomolyako	Traktor Chelyabinsk, USSR	C					
190	QUE	Andrei Khomutov	CSKA Moscow, USSR	RW					
191	NYI	Vladimir Malakhov	CSKA Moscow, USSR	D	380	56	176	232	377
192	TOR	Justin Tomberlin	Greenway H.S.	C					
193	WPG	Joe Larson	Minnetonka H.S.	C					
194	BUF	Mark Astley	Lake Superior State	D	75	4	19	23	92
195	CHI	Matt Saunders	Northeastern	LW					
196	MIN	Arturs Irbe	Dynamo Riga, USSR	G	259	88	774	13	3.26
197	VAN	Gus Morschauser	Kitchener	G					
198	ST.L.	John Valo	Detroit Compuware Jr. A	D					
199	HFD	Trevor Buchanan	Kamloops	LW					
200	DET	Greg Bignell	Belleville	D					
201	NYR	Al Kummu	Humboldt Jr. A	D					
202	NYR	Roman Oksiuta	Khimik Voskresensk, USSR	RW	153	46	41	87	100
203	BUF	John Nelson	Toronto	C					
204	DET	Rick Judson	Illinois-Chicago	LW					
205	PIT	Greg Hagen	Hill-Murray H.S.	RW					
206	BOS	Geoff Simpson	Estevan Jr. A	D					
207	L.A.	Jim Hiller	Melville Jr. A	RW	63	8	12	20	116
208	WSH	Jiri Vykoukal	DS Olomouc, TCH	D					
209	MTL	Ed Henrich	Nichols H.S.	D					
210	CGY	Dan Sawyer	Ramapo Jr.	D					
211	QUE	Byron Witkowski	Nipiwan Jr. A	LW					
212	NYI	Kelly Ens	Lethbridge	C					
213	TOR	Mike Jackson	Toronto	RW					
214	WPG	Bradley Podiak	Wayzata H.S.	LW					
215	N.J.	Jason Simon	Windsor	LW	5	0	0	0	34
216	CHI	Mike Kozak	Clarkson	RW					
217	MIN	Tom Pederson	Minnesota-Duluth	D	240	20	49	69	142
218	VAN	Hayden O'Rear	Lathrop H.S.	D					
219	ST.L.	Brian Lukowski	Niagara Jr. A	G					
220	HFD	John Battice	London	D					
221	DET	Vladimir Konstantinov	CSKA Moscow, USSR	D	446	47	128	175	838
222	PHI	Matt Brait	St. Michael's Jr. B	D					
223	NYR	Steve Locke	Niagara Falls	LW					
224	BUF	Todd Henderson	Thunder Bay Jr. A	G					
225	EDM	Roman Bozek	Motor Ceske Budejovice, TCH	RW					
226	PIT	Scott Farrell	Spokane	D					
227	BOS	David Franzosa	Boston College	LW					
228	L.A.	Steve Jaques	Tri-City	D					
229	WSH	Sidorov Andrei	Sokol Kiev, USSR	C					
230	MTL	Justin Duberman	North Dakota	RW	4	0	0	0	0
231	CGY	Alexander Yudin	Dynamo Moscow, USSR	D					
232	QUE	Noel Rahn	Edina H.S.	C					
233	NYI	Iain Fraser	Oshawa	C	94	23	23	46	31
234	TOR	Steve Chartrand	Drummondville	LW					
235	WPG	Evgeny Davydov	CSKA Moscow, USSR	LW	155	40	39	79	120
236	N.J.	Peter Larsson	Sodertalje, SWE	C					
237	CHI	Michael Doneghery	Catholic Memorial H.S.	G					
238	MIN	Helmut Balderis	Dynamo Riga, USSR	RW	26	3	6	9	2
239	VAN	Darcy Cahill	Cornwall	C					
240	WPG	Sergei Kharin	Krylja Sovetov, USSR	RW	7	2	3	5	2
241	EDM	Peter Kasowski	Swift Current	C					
242	DET	Joseph Frederick	Madison Jr. A	RW					
243	PHI	James Pollio	Vermont Academy	LW					
244	NYR	Ken MacDermid	Hull	LW					
245	BUF	Michael Bavis	Cushing Academy	RW					
246	DET	Jason Glickman	Hull	G					
247	PIT	Jason Smart	Saskatoon	C					
248	VAN	Jan Bergman	Sodertalje, SWE	D					
249	L.A.	Kevin Sneddon	Harvard	D					
250	WSH	Ken House	Miami of Ohio	C					
251	MTL	Steve Cadieux	Shawinigan	C					
252	CGY	Kenneth Kennholt	Djurgarden, SWE	D					

1990

In 1990, the NHL announced that the Central Scouting Bureau would be responsible for producing a ranking of all 18- and 19-year-old prospects eligible for the draft and who were expected to be selected within the first three rounds. The list would include all North American and non-North American talents. If a player under 20 years of age was not on the list he would not be eligible for the draft. However, non-North Americans who were 21 years old would not be listed but would still be eligible for drafting. There was a particular interest placed on European players, especially those who hailed from the Eastern Bloc countries.

Beginning in 1987, the drafting of Eastern Bloc talent had become popular for later rounds due to the risk of limited access to them. However, with the first-round selection of Bobby Holik by the Whalers, it was assumed that more teams would make strides towards Czechoslovakian and Soviet players in the first three rounds.

Attention focused on two Czech players as the draft approached. The first was center Petr Nedved. Nedved surprised the world by defecting from Czechoslovakia during a midget tournament in Calgary at the age of 16. He entered the WHL, playing for the Seattle Thunderbirds and burned up the junior leagues with his explosive skating and creative playmaking. "He's faster and more explosive than the other prospects," said a scout. "Speed kills and he's got it. He sees the ice so well. He invents new ways to score goals." Nedved was drafted second overall by the Vancouver Canucks after being recognized as the major junior rookie of the year. The other Czech player was scoring phenomenon Jaromir Jagr, a 6'2", 198-pound left winger who was considered by many to be the best eligible player in the world. "He's a top-notch international player," a scout exclaimed. "He's a very big guy who skates extremely well and plays well in traffic." Jagr, drafted fifth overall by the Penguins, stepped immediately into the NHL and seemed a perfect fit with Penguin franchise player Mario Lemieux. In Jagr's rookie year the Penguins captured the Stanley Cup for the first time. He contributed 13 points (three goals and 10 assists) in 24 playoff games to earn his first Cup ring. As a sophomore, Jagr recorded a 69-point regular season before notching 24 points in the playoffs to help the Penguins to their second consecutive Stanley Cup victory. Jagr has gone on to become one of the league's premier scorers, winning the Art Ross Trophy in 1994–95 and 1997–98, and is considered to be one of the best one-on-one players in the world today.

The 1990 draft saw six 18-year-olds immediately enter the NHL, as Nedved and Jagr were joined by first overall pick Owen Nolan, CHL player of the year Mike Ricci, OHL scoring champion Keith Primeau and defenseman Drake Berehowsky. Touted as a tough offensive talent, he became the second consecutive first overall selection for the Quebec Nordiques. To date Nolan has appeared in three NHL All-Star games, representing Quebec in 1992 and San Jose in 1996 and 1997. Although he was the top-ranked prospect by Central Scouting, Mike Ricci was selected fourth overall by the Philadelphia Flyers and is one of only three first rounders from 1990 to have his name inscribed on the Stanley Cup, after helping the Colorado Avalanche capture hockey's greatest prize in 1996.

Considered a late bloomer at the junior level, Keith Primeau was taken third overall by the Detroit Red Wings. At 6'4" and 217 pounds, Primeau stood out as the biggest prospect in the draft: "In two or three years, I think he may turn out to be the best of the group," said Primeau's junior coach George Burnett. The Red Wings traded him to Hartford prior to their 1996–97 Stanley Cup victory, but Primeau was a member of the Canadian Olympic team that competed in Nagano, Japan in 1998. Drake Berehowsky battled injuries much of the time as he spent six seasons traveling between the NHL and various minor-league teams after being selected 10th overall by the Maple Leafs. In 1997–98, he played 67 games with the Edmonton Oilers.

Top-ranked goaltender Trevor Kidd was touted as an impact player and was taken 11th overall by the Calgary Flames, but the winner in the goaltending lottery was the

New Jersey Devils. Selecting Martin Brodeur 19th overall and Mike Dunham as the 53rd pick, the Devils had acquired what would become the best goaltending tandem in the NHL. The two went on to capture the William Jennings Trophy in 1996–97. Brodeur has been the real star, capturing the Calder Trophy as the league's top rookie in 1994, leading the Devils to their first Stanley Cup victory in 1995 and being named as the runner-up to Dominik Hasek for the Vezina Trophy as the best goaltender in 1997 and 1998. In 1996, Brodeur set an NHL record for minutes played in one season as he appeared in net for 4,433 minutes of play. On April 17, 1997 Brodeur scored a goal against the Montreal Canadiens in a playoff game.

Top U.S. talents Derian Hatcher (brother of Washington Capitals blueliner Kevin Hatcher), high school star Keith Tkachuk and U.S. college star Doug Weight all emerged from the 1990 Entry Draft. All three have played an integral role in the rising success of hockey in the United States. In addition to being superstar players on their respective NHL clubs, they also helped Team USA defeat Canada in the inaugural World Cup of Hockey in 1996. Three Russian stars were also selected in 1990, as top forward Vyacheslav Kozlov, defenseman Sergei Zubov and Sergei Nemchinov were all drafted into the NHL. All three have appeared on Stanley Cup-winning teams; both Nemchinov and Zubov were members of the 1994 New York Rangers while Kozlov helped Detroit to the title in 1997 and 1998.

1990

PICK	TEAM	NAME	DRAFTED FROM	NHL PLAYERS: POS / NHL GOALTENDERS: POS	GP / GP	G / W	A / GA	PTS / SO	PIM / AVG
FIRST ROUND									
1	QUE	Owen Nolan	Cornwall	RW	487	191	198	389	976
2	VAN	Petr Nedved	Seattle	C	441	158	179	337	320
3	DET	Keith Primeau	Niagara Falls	C	519	149	195	344	1052
4	PHI	Mike Ricci	Peterborough	C	544	141	207	348	576
5	PIT	Jaromir Jagr	Poldi Kladno, TCH	RW	581	301	434	735	435
6	NYI	Scott Scissons	Saskatoon	C	2	0	0	0	0
7	L.A.	Darryl Sydor	Kamloops	D	475	41	166	207	392
8	MIN	Derian Hatcher	North Bay	D	448	46	116	162	940
9	WSH	John Slaney	Cornwall	D	188	19	51	70	75
10	TOR	Drake Berehowsky	Kingston	D	196	7	32	39	346
11	CGY	Trevor Kidd	Brandon	G	225	93	557	13	2.69
12	MTL	Turner Stevenson	Seattle	RW	252	27	36	63	462
13	NYR	Michael Stewart	Michigan State	D					
14	BUF	Brad May	Niagara Falls	LW	452	76	92	168	1364
15	HFD	Mark Greig	Lethbridge	RW	95	8	20	28	76
16	CHI	Karl Dykhuis	Hull	D	273	17	53	70	287
17	EDM	Scott Allison	Prince Albert	C					
18	VAN	Shawn Antoski	North Bay	LW	183	3	5	8	599
19	WPG	Keith Tkachuk	Malden Catholic H.S.	LW	458	236	205	441	1167
20	N.J.	Martin Brodeur	St-Hyacinthe	G	305	162	627	32	2.16
21	BOS	Bryan Smolinski	Michigan State	C	362	115	134	249	241
SECOND ROUND									
22	QUE	Ryan Hughes	Cornell	C	3	0	0	0	0
23	VAN	Jiri Slegr	CHZ Litvinov, TCH	D	280	20	90	110	424
24	N.J.	David Harlock	Michigan	D	14	0	0	0	4
25	PHI	Chris Simon	Ottawa	LW	216	40	55	95	758
26	NYR	Nicolas Perreault	Hawkesbury Jr. A	D					
27	NYI	Chris Taylor	London	C	22	0	4	4	4
28	L.A.	Brandy Semchuk	Canadian Olympic	RW	1	0	0	0	2
29	N.J.	Chris Gotziaman	Roseau H.S.	RW					
30	WSH	Rod Pasma	Cornwall	D					
31	TOR	Felix Potvin	Chicoutimi	G	364	157	1007	12	2.86
32	CGY	Vesa Viitakoski	SaiPa Lappeenranta, FIN	LW	23	2	4	6	8
33	ST.L.	Craig Johnson	Hill-Murray H.S.	LW/C	180	37	38	75	110
34	NYR	Doug Weight	Lake Superior State	C	504	128	320	448	448
35	WPG	Mike Muller	Wayzata H.S.	D					
36	HFD	Geoff Sanderson	Swift Current	LW	514	200	181	381	219
37	CHI	Ivan Droppa	Partizan Liptovsky Mik's, TCH	D	19	0	1	1	14
38	EDM	Alexandre Legault	Boston U.	RW					
39	MTL	Ryan Kuwabara	Ottawa	RW					
40	PHI	Mikael Renberg	Pitea, SWE	RW	326	125	154	279	200
41	CGY	Etienne Belzile	Cornell	D					
42	PHI	Terran Sandwith	Tri-City	D					
OTHER ROUNDS									
43	QUE	Brad Zavisha	Seattle	LW	2	0	0	0	0
44	PHI	Kimbi Daniels	Swift Current	C	27	1	2	3	4

PICK	TEAM	NAME	DRAFTED FROM	POS	GP	G / W	A / GA	PTS / SO	PIM / AVG
45	DET	Vyacheslav Kozlov	Khimik Voskresensk, USSR	C	384	135	148	283	273
46	PHI	Bill Armstrong	Oshawa	D					
47	PHI	Chris Therien	Northwood Prep	D	279	14	65	79	271
48	NYI	Dan Plante	Edina H.S.	RW	159	9	14	23	135
49	L.A.	Bill Bergman	Belleville	LW					
50	MIN	Laurie Billeck	Prince Albert	D					
51	WSH	Chris Longo	Peterborough	RW					
52	PHI	Al Kinisky	Seattle	LW					
53	N.J.	Michael Dunham	Canterbury H.S.	G	41	13	72	3	2.42
54	ST.L.	Patrice Tardif	Lennoxville Jr.	C	65	7	11	18	78
55	NYR	John Vary	North Bay	D					
56	N.J.	Brad Bombardir	Powell River Jr. A	D	43	1	5	6	8
57	HFD	Mike Lenarduzzi	Sault Ste. Marie	G	4	1	10	0	3.17
58	MTL	Charles Poulin	St-Hyacinthe	C					
59	EDM	Joe Crowley	Lawrence Academy	LW					
60	MTL	Robert Guillet	Longueuil	RW					
61	PIT	Joe Dziedzic	Edison H.S.	LW	128	14	14	28	131
62	CGY	Glen Mears	Rochester Jr. A	D					
63	BOS	Cam Stewart	Elmira Jr. B	LW	83	3	7	10	72
64	N.J.	Mike Bodnarchuk	Kingston	RW					
65	VAN	Darin Bader	Saskatoon	LW					
66	DET	Stewart Malgunas	Seattle	D	115	1	4	5	136
67	EDM	Joel Blain	Hull	LW					
68	PIT	Chris Tamer	Michigan	D	242	8	21	29	556
69	NYR	Jeff Nielsen	Grand Rapids H.S.	RW	34	4	5	9	18
70	MIN	Cal McGowan	Kamloops	C					
71	MIN	Frank Kovacs	Regina	LW					
72	WSH	Randy Pearce	Kitchener	LW					
73	TOR	Darby Hendrickson	Richfield H.S.	C	214	26	21	47	198
74	WPG	Roman Meluzin	Zetor Brno, TCH	RW					
75	WPG	Scott Levins	Tri-City	C/RW	124	13	20	33	316
76	NYR	Rick Willis	Pingree Prep	LW					
77	WPG	Alexei Zhamnov	Dynamo Moscow, USSR	C	379	144	234	378	322
78	HFD	Chris Bright	Moose Jaw	C					
79	CHI	Chris Tucker	Jefferson H.S.	C					
80	TOR	Greg Walters	Ottawa	C					
81	MTL	Gilbert Dionne	Kitchener	LW	223	61	79	140	108
82	BUF	Brian McCarthy	Pingree Prep	C					
83	CGY	Paul Kruse	Kamloops	LW	368	35	33	68	912
84	BOS	Jerome Buckley	Northwood Prep	RW					
85	NYR	Sergei Zubov	CSKA Moscow, USSR	D	380	64	258	322	123
86	VAN	Gino Odjick	Laval	LW	457	46	52	98	2158
87	DET	Tony Burns	Duluth Denfield H.S.	D					
88	PHI	Dan Kordic	Medicine Hat	LW	195	4	8	12	582
89	PIT	Brian Farrell	Avon Old Farms H.S.	C					
90	NYI	Chris Marinucci	Grand Rapids H.S.	C	13	1	4	5	2
91	L.A.	David Goverde	Sudbury	G	5	1	29	0	6.26
92	MIN	Enrico Ciccone	Trois-Rivieres	D	312	7	17	24	1328
93	WSH	Brian Sakic	Tri-City	C					
94	WSH	Mark Ouimet	Michigan	C					
95	N.J.	Dean Malkoc	Kamloops	D	114	1	2	3	292
96	ST.L.	Jason Ruff	Lethbridge	LW	14	3	3	6	10
97	BUF	Richard Smehlik	TJ Vitkovice, TCH	D	337	36	97	133	279
98	WPG	Craig Martin	Hull	RW	21	0	1	1	24
99	NYR	Lubos Rob	Motor Ceske Budejovice, TCH	C					
100	BUF	Todd Bojcun	Peterborough	G					
101	EDM	Greg Louder	Cushing Academy	G					
102	MTL	Paul Di Pietro	Sudbury	C	192	31	49	80	96
103	BUF	Brad Pascall	North Dakota	D					
104	N.J.	Petr Kuchyna	Dukla Jihlava, TCH	D					
105	BOS	Michael Bales	Ohio State	G	23	2	77	0	4.12
106	QUE	Jeff Parrott	Minnesota-Duluth	D					
107	PIT	Ian Moran	Belmont Hill H.S.	D	124	6	12	18	88
108	DET	Claude Barthe	Victoriaville	D					
109	PHI	Viacheslav Butsayev	CSKA Moscow, USSR	C	124	17	25	42	129
110	PIT	Denis Casey	Colorado College	G					
111	NYI	Joni Lehto	Ottawa	D					
112	L.A.	Erik Andersson	Danderyd, SWE	C	Re-entered Draft in 1997				
113	MIN	Roman Turek	VTJ Pisek, TCH	G	29	14	58	1	2.19
114	WSH	Andrei Kovalev	Dynamo Moscow, USSR	RW					
115	TOR	Alexander Godynyuk	Sokol Kiev, USSR	D	223	10	39	49	224
116	N.J.	Lubomir Kolnik	Dukla Trencin, TCH	RW					
117	ST.L.	Kurtis Miller	Rochester Jr. A	LW					
118	NYR	Jason Weinrich	Springfield Jr. B	D					
119	WPG	Daniel Jardemyr	Uppsala, SWE	D					
120	HFD	Cory Keenan	Kitchener	DC					
121	CHI	Brett Stickney	St. Paul's H.S.	C					
122	EDM	Keijo Sailynoja	Jokerit Helsinki, FIN	LW					
123	MTL	Craig Conroy	Northwood Prep	C	155	21	40	61	91
124	CHI	Derek Edgerly	Stoneham H.S.	C					
125	CGY	Chris Tschupp	Trinity-Pawling H.S.	C					
126	BOS	Mark Woolf	Spokane	RW					
127	QUE	Dwayne Norris	Michigan State	RW	20	2	4	6	8
128	VAN	Daryl Filipek	Ferris State	D					
129	DET	Jason York	Kitchener	D	261	12	63	75	233
130	PIT	Mike Valila	Tappara Tampere, FIN	C					
131	PIT	Ken Plaquin	Michigan Tech	D					
132	NYI	Michael Guilbert	Governor Dummer H.S.	D					
133	L.A.	Robert Lang	CHZ Litvinov, TCH	C	201	28	52	80	42
134	MIN	Jeff Levy	Rochester Jr. A	G					
135	WSH	Roman Kontsek	Dukla Trencin, TCH	RW					
136	TOR	Eric Lacroix	Governor Dummer H.S.	LW	283	59	56	115	276
137	N.J.	Chris McAlpine	Roseville H.S.	D	93	3	10	13	77
138	ST.L.	Wayne Conlan	Trinity-Pawling H.S.	C					
139	NYR	Brian Lonsinger	Choate	D					
140	WPG	John Lilley	Cushing Academy	RW	23	3	8	11	13
141	HFD	Jergus Baca	VSZ Kosice, TCH	D	10	0	2	2	14
142	BUF	Viktor Gordiouk	Krylja Sovetov, USSR	LW	26	3	8	11	0
143	EDM	Mike Power	Western Michigan	G					
144	MTL	Stephen Rohr	Culver Military Academy	RW					
145	PIT	Pat Neaton	Michigan	D	9	1	1	2	12
146	CGY	Dimitri Frolov	Dynamo Moscow, USSR	D					
147	BOS	Jim Mackey	Hotchkiss H.S.	D					
148	QUE	Andrei Kovalenko	CSKA Moscow, USSR	RW	394	123	140	263	292
149	VAN	Paul O'Hagan	Oshawa	D					
150	DET	Wes McCauley	Michigan State	D					
151	PHI	Patrik Englund	AIK Solna, SWE	LW					
152	PIT	Petteri Koskimaki	Boston U.	C					
153	NYI	Sylvain Fleury	Longueuil	LW					
154	L.A.	Dean Hulett	Lake Superior State	RW					
155	MIN	Doug Barrault	Lethbridge	RW	4	0	0	0	2
156	WSH	Peter Bondra	HC Kosice, TCH	RW	544	285	205	490	379
157	TOR	Dan Stiver	Michigan	RW					
158	QUE	Alexander Karpovtsev	Dynamo Moscow, USSR	D	278	21	75	96	211
159	WSH	Steve Martell	London	RW					
160	NYR	Todd Hedlund	Roseau H.S.	RW					
161	HFD	Henrik Andersson	Vasteras, SWE	D					
162	HFD	Martin D'Orsonnens	Clarkson	D					
163	CHI	Hugo Belanger	Clarkson	LW					
164	EDM	Roman Mejzlik	Dukla Jihlava, TCH	LW/C					
165	MTL	Brent Fleetwood	Portland	LW					
166	BUF	Milan Nedoma	Zetor Brno, TCH	D					
167	CGY	Shawn Murray	Hill-Murray H.S.	G					
168	BOS	John Gruden	Waterloo Jr. A	D	59	0	7	7	28
169	QUE	Pat Mazzoli	Humboldt Jr. A	G					
170	VAN	Mark Cipriano	Victoria	RW					
171	DET	Anthony Gruba	Hill-Murray H.S.	RW					
172	PHI	Toni Porkka	Lukko Rauma, FIN	D					
173	PIT	Ladislav Karabin	Slovan Bratislava, TCH	LW	9	0	0	0	2
174	NYI	John Joyce	Avon Old Farms H.S.	C					
175	L.A.	Denis Leblanc	St-Hyacinthe	C					
176	MIN	Joe Biondi	Minnesota-Duluth	C					
177	WSH	Ken Klee	Bowling Green	RW	220	18	14	32	262
178	TOR	Robert Horyna	Dukla Jihlava, TCH	D					
179	N.J.	Jaroslav Modry	Motor Ceske Budejovice, TCH	D	155	9	35	44	87
180	ST.L.	Parris Duffus	Melfort Jr. A	G	1	0	1	0	2.07
181	NYR	Andrew Silverman	Beverly H.S.	D					
182	WPG	Rauli Raitanen	Assat Pori, FIN	C					
183	HFD	Corey Osmak	Nipiwan Jr. A	C					
184	CHI	Owen Lessard	Owen Sound	LW					
185	EDM	Richard Zemlicka	Sparta Praha, TCH	RW					
186	MTL	Derek Maguire	Delbarton H.S.	D					
187	BUF	Jason Winch	Niagara Falls	LW					
188	CGY	Mike Murray	Cushing Academy	RW					
189	BOS	Darren Wetherill	Minot Jr. A	D					
190	QUE	Scott Davis	U. of Manitoba	D					
191	VAN	Troy Neumier	Prince Albert	D					
192	DET	Travis Tucker	Avon Old Farms H.S.	D					
193	PHI	Greg Hanson	Bloomington-Kennedy H.S.	D					
194	PIT	Timothy Fingerhut	Canterbury H.S.	LW					
195	NYI	Richard Enga	Culver Military Academy	C					
196	L.A.	Patrik Ross	HV-71 Jonkoping, SWE	RW					
197	MIN	Troy Binnie	Ottawa	RW					
198	WSH	Michael Boback	Providence	C					
199	TOR	Rob Chebator	Arlington Catholic H.S.	D					
200	N.J.	Corey Schwab	Seattle	G	57	13	126	3	2.89
201	ST.L.	Steve Widmeyer	U. of Maine	RW					
202	NYR	Jon Hillebrandt	Monona Grove H.S.	G					
203	WPG	Mika Alatalo	Koo Koo Kouvola, FIN	LW					
204	TOR	Espen Knutsen	Valerengen, NOR	C	19	3	0	3	6
205	CHI	Erik Peterson	Brockton H.S.	C					
206	EDM	Petr Korinek	Skoda Plzen, TCH	C					
207	MTL	Mark Kettelhut	Duluth East H.S.	D					
208	BUF	Sylvain Naud	Laval	RW					
209	CGY	Rob Sumner	Victoria	D					
210	BOS	Dean Capuano	Mount St. Charles H.S.	D					
211	QUE	Mika Stromberg	Jokerit Helsinki, FIN	D					
212	VAN	Tyler Ertel	North Bay	C					
213	DET	Brett Larson	Duluth Denfield H.S.	D					
214	PHI	Tommy Soderstrom	Djurgarden, SWE	G	156	45	496	10	3.63
215	PIT	Michael Thompson	Michigan State	RW					
216	NYI	Martin Lacroix	St. Lawrence U.	RW					
217	L.A.	K.J.(Kevin) White	Windsor	C					
218	MIN	Ole Eskild Dahlstrom	Furuset Oslo, NOR	C					

1990 *continued*

PICK	TEAM	NAME	DRAFTED FROM	NHL PLAYERS: POS / NHL GOALTENDERS: POS	GP / GP	G / W	A / GA	PTS / SO	PIM / AVG
219	WSH	Alan Brown	Colgate	D					
220	TOR	Scott Malone	Northfield H.S.	D					
221	N.J.	Valeri Zelepukin	Khimik Voskresensk, USSR	LW	408	87	143	230	406
222	ST.L.	Joe Hawley	Peterborough	RW					
223	NYR	Brett Lievers	Wayzata H.S.	C					
224	WPG	Sergei Selyanin	Khimik Voskresensk, USSR	D					
225	HFD	Tommie Eriksen	Prince Albert	D					
226	CHI	Steve Dubinsky	Clarkson	C	173	9	22	31	95
227	EDM	invalid claim							
228	MTL	John Uniac	Kitchener	D					
229	BUF	Kenneth Martin	Belmont Hill H.S.	LW					
230	CGY	invalid claim							
231	BOS	Andy Bezeau	Niagara Falls	LW					
232	QUE	Wade Klippenstein	Alaska-Fairbanks	LW					
233	VAN	Karri Kivi	Ilves Tampere, FIN	D					
234	DET	John Hendry	Lake Superior State	LW					
235	PHI	William Lund	Roseau H.S.	C					
236	PIT	Brian Bruininks	Colorado College	D					
237	NYI	Andy Shier	Detroit Compuware Jr. A	C					
238	L.A.	Troy Mohns	Colgate	D					
239	MIN	John McKersie	West H.S.	G					
240	WSH	Todd Hlushko	London	C	79	8	13	21	84
241	TOR	Nick Vachon	Governor Dummer H.S.	C	1	0	0	0	0
242	N.J.	Todd Reirden	Tabor Academy	D					
243	ST.L.	Joe Fleming	Xaverian H.S.	D					
244	NYR	Sergei Nemchinov	Krylja Sovetov, USSR	C	498	117	142	259	179
245	WPG	Keith Morris	Alaska-Anchorage	C					
246	HFD	Denis Chalifoux	Laval	C					
247	CHI	Dino Grossi	Northeastern	RW					
248	EDM	Sami Nuutinen	Kiekko-Espoo, FIN	D					
249	MTL	Sergei Martynyuk	Torpedo Yaroslavl, USSR	LW					
250	BUF	Brad Rubachuk	Lethbridge	C					
251	CGY	Leo Gudas	Sparta Praha, TCH	D					
252	BOS	Ted Miskolczi	Belleville	D					

1991

The 1991 Entry Draft in Buffalo's Memorial Auditorium saw the NHL's first wave of expansion in the 1990s with the participation of the San Jose Sharks. It was decided that the Sharks would select second in every round of the draft.

The 1991 draft was surrounded with excitement since it was the day that the NHL would acquire the most talked-about prospect since 1984. "In this draft, there is Lindros and then there's everyone else," said a scout. "He came into this season as the number-one guy and at no time was the ranking ever threatened. He is an outstanding prospect, the best since Mario Lemieux." At 6'4" and 228 pounds, 17-year-old Eric Lindros had attracted an enormous amount of attention in the hockey world.

He had been the first overall pick for the Sault Ste. Marie Greyhounds in the OHL draft and had forced the OHL to rewrite its rule book to let him play for a team closer to his home in Toronto. The Greyhounds received three players, two draft picks and approximately $80,000 to classify as the biggest trade in junior history as Lindros went to play for the Oshawa Generals. In his first year with the Generals, he helped them capture the Memorial Cup and was named to the tournament's all-star team.

Despite appearing in only 25 OHL games in 1990, Lindros shared player of the year honors with junior star Mike Ricci. In 1991, Lindros captured the junior scoring title, MVP award and player of the year awards as he entered the draft as the most publicized prospect in Entry Draft history.

"There'll be no suspense this time," said Nordiques director of player personnel Pierre Gauthier. "In the past, for a variety of reasons, it wasn't in our best interest to say in advance who would be our top pick. With Mats Sundin (1989) and Owen Nolan (1990), there was some element of surprise when we picked them. This year, Eric Lindros is the guy. There will be no surprises." However, after becoming the first overall selection, Lindros refused to don the

Nordiques' jersey and held out against signing with the club. After the draft, Lindros became the only player to participate in a Canada Cup tournament for Team Canada without any NHL experience.

On June 30, 1992 the Philadelphia Flyers acquired the rights to Lindros in the biggest trade in the history of the NHL as they sent six players, two first-round draft picks and cash to Quebec. Lindros has since become the foundation of the Flyers, capturing the Lester Pearson Trophy as the league's most outstanding player and earning MVP honors with the Hart Trophy in 1995. Lindros is arguably the most complete player ever to play the game as he combines excellent offensive skill and playmaking abilities with an extreme physical game and is considered by many to be the most dominating player in hockey today.

Aside from Lindros, the talent pool in 1991 was considered extremely thin. The Sharks picked Pat Falloon second overall and he gave an impressive performance as a rookie, but quickly diminished. Third overall selection Scott Niedermayer was the first defenseman taken in 1991. He came into the league touted as an offensive defenseman and quickly developed into one of the NHL's premiere blueliners. Niedermayer was a key player in the New Jersey Devils' Stanley Cup victory in 1995.

On the international level, the 1991 draft was one of the best with potential NHL stars expected to come from the Eastern Bloc countries and Sweden. Right wing Alexei Kovalev became the first Russian-born player to be taken in the first round as the New York Rangers chose him 15th overall. Slovakian sniper Zigmund Palffy was selected 26th overall, while star defensive talents Sandis Ozolinsh (30th), Dmitri Mironov (160th), Igor Kravchuk (71st), Alexei Zhitnik (81st) and Janne Laukkanen (156th) were also drafted. Prior to any of those choices, however, one of the NHL's best superstar talents was selected under the shadow of Eric Lindros.

Although he was ranked only 17th on the European list by Central Scouting, Swedish forward Peter Forsberg was the first European selected in the draft as the Flyers took him sixth overall. Forsberg was one of the players sent to Quebec in the Lindros trade and entered the league in 1994–95. Collecting 50 points (15 goals, 35 assists) in 47 games in a season shortened by a labor dispute, Forsberg captured the Calder Trophy as the NHL's top rookie. He went on to record a 116-point season in his sophomore year as the Nordiques became the Colorado Avalanche and won the Stanley Cup. His 91 points in 1997–98 saw him finish as the runner-up to Jaromir Jagr in the NHL's scoring race.

1991

PICK	TEAM	NAME	DRAFTED FROM	NHL PLAYERS: POS / NHL GOALTENDERS: POS	GP / GP	G / W	A / GA	PTS / SO	PIM / AVG
FIRST ROUND									
1	QUE	Eric Lindros	Oshawa	C	360	223	284	507	743
2	S.J.	Pat Falloon	Spokane	RW	430	117	134	251	107
3	N.J.	Scott Niedermayer	Kamloops	D	454	52	179	231	246
4	NYI	Scott Lachance	Boston U.	D	391	25	71	96	318
5	WPG	Aaron Ward	Michigan	D	107	8	11	19	105
6	PHI	Peter Forsberg	MoDo Ornskoldsvik, SWE	C	266	98	245	343	230
7	VAN	Alek Stojanov	Hamilton	RW	107	2	5	7	222
8	MIN	Richard Matvichuk	Saskatoon	D	296	16	46	62	283
9	HFD	Patrick Poulin	St-Hyacinthe	LW	391	74	96	170	242
10	DET	Martin Lapointe	Laval	RW	311	49	54	103	499
11	N.J.	Brian Rolston	Detroit Compuware Jr. A	C	255	54	63	117	61
12	EDM	Tyler Wright	Swift Current	C	168	8	7	15	252
13	BUF	Philippe Boucher	Granby	D	229	28	60	88	152
14	WSH	Pat Peake	Detroit	C	134	28	41	69	105
15	NYR	Alexei Kovalev	Dynamo Moscow, USSR	RW	388	116	152	268	447
16	PIT	Markus Naslund	MoDo Ornskoldsvik, SWE	RW	315	63	82	145	157
17	MTL	Brent Bilodeau	Seattle	D					
18	BOS	Glen Murray	Sudbury	RW	375	88	80	168	245

PICK	TEAM	NAME	DRAFTED FROM	POS	GP	G	A	PTS	PIM
19	CGY	Niklas Sundblad	AIK Solna, SWE	RW	2	0	0	0	0
20	EDM	Martin Rucinsky	CHZ Litvinov, TCH	LW	389	109	165	274	339
21	WSH	Trevor Halverson	North Bay	LW					
22	CHI	Dean McAmmond	Prince Albert	C	243	52	86	138	113

SECOND ROUND

PICK	TEAM	NAME	DRAFTED FROM	POS	GP	G	A	PTS	PIM
23	S.J.	Ray Whitney	Spokane	C	277	81	105	186	80
24	QUE	Rene Corbet	Drummondville	LW	194	32	37	69	235
25	WSH	Eric Lavigne	Hull	D	1	0	0	0	0
26	NYI	Zigmund Palffy	AC Nitra, TCH	LW	281	146	135	281	139
27	ST.L.	Steve Staios	Niagara Falls	D	152	6	18	24	229
28	MTL	Jim Campbell	Northwood Prep	C	160	47	42	89	159
29	VAN	Jassen Cullimore	Peterborough	D	141	5	11	16	130
30	S.J.	Sandis Ozolinsh	Dynamo Riga, USSR	D	385	92	193	285	301
31	HFD	Martin Hamrlik	TJ Zlin, TCH	D					
32	DET	Jamie Pushor	Lethbridge	D	144	6	15	21	227
33	N.J.	Donevan Hextall	Prince Albert	LW					
34	EDM	Andrew Verner	Peterborough	G					
35	BUF	Jason Dawe	Peterborough	LW	303	80	81	161	138
36	WSH	Jeff Nelson	Prince Albert	C	43	1	7	8	18
37	NYR	Darcy Werenka	Lethbridge	D					
38	PIT	Rusty Fitzgerald	Duluth East H.S.	C	25	2	2	4	12
39	CHI	Michael Pomichter	Springfield Jr. B	C					
40	BOS	Jozef Stumpel	AC Nitra, TCH	C	351	75	180	255	107
41	CGY	Francois Groleau	Shawinigan	D	8	0	1	1	6
42	L.A.	Guy Leveque	Cornwall	C	17	2	2	4	21
43	MTL	Craig Darby	Albany Academy	C	35	2	8	10	2
44	CHI	Jamie Matthews	Sudbury	C	Re-entered Draft in 1993				

OTHER ROUNDS

PICK	TEAM	NAME	DRAFTED FROM	POS	GP	G/W	A/GA	PTS/SO	PIM/AVG
45	S.J.	Dody Wood	Seattle	C	106	8	10	18	471
46	QUE	Rich Brennan	Tabor Academy	D	13	1	2	3	2
47	TOR	Yanic Perreault	Trois-Rivieres	C	237	69	66	135	88
48	NYI	Jamie McLennan	Lethbridge	G	86	33	227	2	2.86
49	WPG	Dmitri Filimonov	Dynamo Moscow, USSR	D	30	1	4	5	18
50	PHI	Yanick Dupre	Drummondville	LW	35	2	0	2	16
51	VAN	Sean Pronger	Bowling Green	C	113	13	23	36	58
52	CGY	Sandy McCarthy	Laval	RW	290	30	30	60	801
53	HFD	Todd Hall	Hamden H.S.	D					
54	DET	Chris Osgood	Medicine Hat	G	221	132	498	20	2.33
55	N.J.	Fredrik Lindqvist	Djurgarden, SWE	C					
56	EDM	George Breen	Cushing Academy	RW					
57	BUF	Jason Young	Sudbury	LW					
58	WSH	Steve Konowalchuk	Portland	C	373	77	106	183	332
59	HFD	Michael Nylander	Huddinge, SWE	C	276	54	126	180	112
60	PIT	Shane Peacock	Lethbridge	D					
61	MTL	Yves Sarault	St-Jean	LW	63	5	3	8	14
62	BOS	Marcel Cousineau	Beauport	G	15	3	31	1	3.19
63	CGY	Brian Caruso	Minnesota-Duluth	LW					
64	ST.L.	Kyle Reeves	Tri-City	RW					
65	ST.L.	Nathan LaFayette	Cornwall	C	154	15	18	33	68
66	CHI	Bobby House	Brandon	RW					
67	S.J.	Kerry Toporowski	Spokane	D					
68	QUE	Dave Karpa	Ferris State	D	323	12	56	68	963
69	TOR	Terry Chitaroni	Sudbury	C					
70	NYI	Milan Hnilicka	Poldi Kladno, TCH	G					
71	CHI	Igor Kravchuk	CSKA Moscow, USSR	D	419	49	141	190	158
72	BUF	Peter Ambroziak	Ottawa	LW	12	0	1	1	0
73	MTL	Vladimir Vujtek	Tri-City	LW	102	7	29	36	38
74	MIN	Mike Torchia	Kitchener	G	6	3	18	0	3.30
75	HFD	Jim Storm	Michigan Tech	LW	84	7	15	22	44
76	DET	Michael Knuble	Kalamazoo Jr. A	RW	62	8	6	14	16
77	N.J.	Bradley Willner	Richfield H.S.	D					
78	EDM	Mario Nobili	Longueuil	LW					
79	L.A.	Keith Redmond	Bowling Green	LW	12	1	0	1	20
80	WSH	Justin Morrison	Kingston	C					
81	L.A.	Alexei Zhitnik	Sokol Kiev, USSR	D	429	56	174	230	497
82	PIT	Joe Tamminen	Virginia H.S.	C					
83	MTL	Sylvain Lapointe	Clarkson	D					
84	BOS	Brad Tiley	Sault Ste. Marie	D	1	0	0	0	0
85	CGY	Steven Magnusson	Anoka H.S.	C					
86	PHI	Aris Brimanis	Bowling Green	D	21	0	3	3	12
87	ST.L.	Grayden Reid	Owen Sound	C					
88	CHI	Zac Boyer	Kamloops	RW	3	0	0	0	0
89	S.J.	Dan Ryder	Sudbury	G					
90	QUE	Patrick Labrecque	St-Jean	G	2	0	7	0	4.29
91	WPG	Sha Ylonen	Kiekko-Espoo, FIN	C	57	1	11	12	10
92	NYI	Steve Junker	Spokane	LW	5	0	0	0	0
93	EDM	Ryan Haggerty	Westminster H.S.	C					
94	PHI	Yanick Degrace	Trois-Rivieres	G					
95	VAN	Dan Kesa	Prince Albert	RW	22	2	4	6	18
96	NYR	Corey Machanic	Vermont	D					
97	MIN	Mike Kennedy	U. of British Columbia	C	144	16	36	52	110
98	DET	Dimitri Motkov	CSKA Moscow, USSR	D					
99	WPG	Yan Kaminsky	Dynamo Moscow, USSR	RW	26	3	2	5	4
100	MTL	Brad Layzell	RPI	D					
101	BUF	Steve Shields	Michigan	G	31	7	80	0	2.91
102	TOR	Alexei Kudashov	Krylja Sovetov, USSR	C	25	1	0	1	4
103	QUE	Bill Lindsay	Tri-City	LW	435	57	89	146	430
104	PIT	Robert Melanson	Hull	D					
105	MTL	Tony Prpic	Culver Military Academy	RW					
106	BOS	Mariusz Czerkawski	GKS Tychy, POL	RW	265	69	72	141	88
107	CGY	Jerome Butler	Roseau H.S.	G					
108	L.A.	Pauli Jaks	Ambri Piotta, SUI	G	1	0	2	0	3.00
109	ST.L.	Jeff Callinan	Minnetonka H.S.	G					
110	CHI	Maco Balkovec	Merritt Jr. A	D					
111	S.J.	Frank Nilsson	Vasteras, SWE	C					
112	CHI	Kevin St. Jacques	Lethbridge	LW					
113	TOR	Jeff Perry	Owen Sound	LW					
114	NYI	Robert Valicevic	Detroit Red Wings Jr. A	RW					
115	WPG	Jeff Sebastian	Seattle	D					
116	PHI	Clayton Norris	Medicine Hat	RW					
117	VAN	Yevgeny Namestnikov	Torpedo Niz. Novogord, USSR	D	41	0	9	9	22
118	MIN	Mark Lawrence	Detroit	RW	17	0	1	1	19
119	HFD	Mike Harding	Northern Michigan	RW					
120	NYI	Alexander Kuzminsky	Sokol Kiev, USSR	C					
121	N.J.	Curt Regnier	Prince Albert	RW					
122	PHI	Dimitri Yushkevich	Torpedo Yaroslavl, USSR	D	412	20	93	113	392
123	BUF	Sean O'Donnell	Sudbury	D	221	9	34	43	499
124	BUF	Brian Holzinger	Detroit Jr. A	C	212	46	63	109	127
125	NYR	Fredrik Jax	Leksand, SWE	RW					
126	PIT	Brian Clifford	Nichols H.S.	C					
127	MTL	Oleg Petrov	CSKA Moscow, USSR	RW	112	20	26	46	39
128	NYR	Barry Young	Sudbury	D					
129	CGY	Bobby Marshall	Miami of Ohio	D					
130	L.A.	Brett Seguin	Ottawa	C					
131	ST.L.	Bruce Gardiner	Colgate	C	122	18	21	39	99
132	CHI	Jacques Auger	Wisconsin	D					
133	S.J.	Jaroslav Otevrel	TJ Zlin, TCH	LW	16	3	4	7	2
134	QUE	Mikael Johansson	Djurgarden, SWE	C					
135	TOR	Martin Prochazka	Poldi Kladno, TCH	RW	29	2	4	6	8
136	NYI	Andreas Johansson	Falun, SWE	C	95	9	20	29	40
137	MIN	Geoff Finch	Brown	G					
138	PHI	Andrei Lomakin	Dynamo Moscow, USSR	RW	215	42	62	104	92
139	VAN	Brent Thurston	Spokane	LW					
140	CGY	Matt Hoffman	Oshawa	LW					
141	HFD	Brian Mueller	South Kent H.S.	D					
142	DET	Igor Malykhin	CSKA Moscow, USSR	D					
143	N.J.	David Craievich	Oshawa	D					
144	EDM	David Oliver	Michigan	RW	155	39	36	75	62
145	BUF	Chris Snell	Ottawa	D	34	2	7	9	24
146	WSH	Dave Morissette	Shawinigan	LW					
147	NYR	John Rushin	Kennedy H.S.	C					
148	PIT	Ed Patterson	Kamloops	RW	68	3	3	6	56
149	MTL	Brady Kramer	Haverford H.S.	C					
150	CGY	Gary Golczewski	Trinity-Pawling H.S.	LW					
151	CGY	Kelly Harper	Michigan State	C					
152	L.A.	Kelly Fairchild	Grand Rapids H.S.	C	23	0	3	3	4
153	ST.L.	Terry Hollinger	Lethbridge	D	7	0	0	0	2
154	CHI	Scott Kirton	Powell River Jr. A	RW					
155	S.J.	Dean Grillo	Warroad H.S.	RW					
156	QUE	Janne Laukkanen	Reipas Lahti, FIN	D	170	8	40	48	158
157	QUE	Aaron Asp	Ferris State	C					
158	NYI	Todd Sparks	Hull	LW					
159	WPG	Jeff Ricciardi	Ottawa	D					
160	TOR	Dmitri Mironov	Krylja Sovetov, USSR	D	401	46	168	214	454
161	VAN	Eric Johnson	Armstrong H.S.	RW					
162	BUF	Jiri Kuntos	Dukla Jihlava, TCH	D					
163	HFD	Steve Yule	Kamloops	D					
164	TOR	Robb McIntyre	Dubuque Jr. A	LW					
165	N.J.	Paul Wolanski	Niagara Falls	D					
166	EDM	Gary Kitching	Thunder Bay Jr. A	C					
167	TOR	Tomas Kucharcik	Dukla Jihlava, TCH	C					
168	WSH	Rick Corriveau	London	D					
169	NYR	Corey Hirsch	Kamloops	G	85	30	249	3	3.15
170	PIT	Peter McLaughlin	Belmont Hill H.S.	D					
171	MTL	Brian Savage	Miami of Ohio	LW	260	87	69	156	130
172	BOS	Jay Moser	Park H.S.	D					
173	CGY	David St. Pierre	Longueuil	C					
174	MIN	Michael Burkett	Michigan State	LW					
175	ST.L.	Chris Kenady	St. Paul Jr. A	RW	5	0	2	2	0
176	CHI	Roch Belley	Niagara Falls	G					
177	S.J.	Corwin Saurdiff	Waterloo Jr. A	G					
178	QUE	Adam Bartell	Niagara Jr. A	D					
179	TOR	Guy Lehoux	Drummondville	D					
180	NYI	John Johnson	Niagara Falls	C					
181	WPG	Sean Gauthier	Kingston	G					
182	PHI	James Bode	Armstrong H.S.	RW					
183	VAN	David Neilson	Prince Albert	LW					
184	HFD	Derek Herlofsky	St. Paul Jr. A	G					
185	HFD	Chris Belanger	Western Michigan	D					
186	DET	Jim Bermingham	Laval	C					
187	N.J.	Daniel Reimann	Anoka H.S.	D					
188	NYI	Brent Brekke	Western Michigan	D					
189	BUF	Tony Iob	Sault Ste. Marie	LW					
190	WSH	Trevor Duhaime	St-Jean	RW					

1991 *continued*

PICK	TEAM	NAME	DRAFTED FROM	NHL PLAYERS: POS / NHL GOALTENDERS: POS	GP	G / W	A / GA	PTS / SO	PIM / AVG
191	NYR	Vyachesl Uvayev	Spartak Moscow, USSR	D					
192	PIT	Jeff Lembke	Omaha Jr. A	G					
193	MTL	Scott Fraser	Dartmouth	C	44	14	11	25	10
194	BOS	Daniel Hodge	Merrimack	D					
195	CGY	David Struch	Saskatoon	C	4	0	0	0	4
196	L.A.	Craig Brown	Western Michigan	G					
197	ST.L.	Jed Fiebelkorn	Osseo H.S.	RW					
198	CHI	Scott MacDonald	Choate	D					
199	S.J.	Dale Craigwell	Oshawa	C	98	11	18	29	28
200	QUE	Paul Koch	Omaha Jr. A	D					
201	TOR	Gary Miller	North Bay	D					
202	NYI	Robert Canavan	Hingham H.S.	LW					
203	WPG	Igor Ulanov	Khimik Voskresensk, USSR	D	351	11	68	79	706
204	PHI	Josh Bartell	Rome Free Academy	D					
205	VAN	Brad Barton	Kitchener	D					
206	MIN	Tom Nemeth	Cornwall	LW					
207	HFD	Jason Currie	Clarkson	G					
208	DET	Jason Firth	Kitchener	C					
209	WSH	Rob Leask	Hamilton	D					
210	EDM	Vegar Barlie	Valerengen, NOR	RW					
211	BUF	Spencer Meany	St. Lawrence U.	RW					
212	WSH	Carl Leblanc	Granby	D					
213	NYR	Jamie Ram	Michigan Tech	G	1	0	0	0	0.00
214	PIT	Chris Tok	Greenway H.S.	D					
215	MTL	Greg MacEachern	Laval	D					
216	BOS	Steve Norton	Michigan State	D					
217	CGY	Sergei Zolotov	Krylja Sovetov, USSR	LW					
218	L.A.	Mattias Olsson	Farjestad Karlstad, SWE	D					
219	ST.L.	Chris MacKenzie	Colgate	LW					
220	CHI	Alexander Andrijevski	Dynamo Moscow, USSR	RW	1	0	0	0	0
221	S.J.	Aaron Kriss	Cranbrook H.S.	D					
222	QUE	Doug Friedman	Boston U.	LW	16	0	0	0	20
223	TOR	Johnathon Kelley	Arlington Catholic H.S.	C					
224	NYI	Marcus Thuresson	Leksand, SWE	C					
225	WPG	Jason Jennings	Western Michigan	RW					
226	PHI	Neil Little	RPI	G					
227	VAN	Jason Fitzsimmons	Moose Jaw	G					
228	MIN	Shayne Green	Kamloops	RW					
229	HFD	Mike Santonelli	Matignon H.S.	C					
230	DET	Bart Turner	Michigan State	LW					
231	N.J.	Kevin Riehl	Medicine Hat	C					
232	EDM	Yevgeny Belosheiken	CSKA Moscow, USSR	G					
233	BUF	Mikhail Volkov	Krylja Sovetov, USSR	RW					
234	WSH	Rob Puchniak	Lethbridge	D					
235	NYR	Vitali Chinakhov	Torpedo Yaroslavl, USSR	C					
236	PIT	Paul Dyck	Moose Jaw	D					
237	MTL	Paul Lepler	Rochester Jr. A	D					
238	BOS	Stephen Lombardi	Deerfield Academy	C					
239	CGY	Marko Jantunen	Reipas Lahti, FIN	C	3	0	0	0	0
240	L.A.	Andre Bouliane	Longueuil	G					
241	ST.L.	Kevin Rappana	Duluth East H.S.	D					
242	CHI	Mike Larkin	Rice Memorial H.S.	D					
243	S.J.	Mikhail Kravets	SKA Leningrad, USSR	RW	2	0	0	0	0
244	QUE	Eric Meloche	Drummondville	RW					
245	TOR	Chris O'Rourke	Alaska-Fairbanks	D					
246	NYI	Marty Schriner	North Dakota	C					
247	WPG	Sergei Sorokin	Dynamo Moscow, USSR	D					
248	PHI	John Porco	Belleville	C					
249	VAN	Xavier Majic	RPI	C					
250	MIN	Jukka Suomalainen	GrIFK Kauniainen, FIN	D					
251	HFD	Rob Peters	Ohio State	D					
252	DET	Andrew Miller	Wexford Jr. B	RW					
253	N.J.	Jason Hehr	Kelowna Jr. A	D					
254	EDM	Juha Riihijarvi	Karpat Oulu, FIN	RW					
255	BUF	Michael Smith	Lake Superior State	D					
256	WSH	Bill Kovacs	Sudbury	LW					
257	NYR	Brian Wiseman	Michigan	C	3	0	0	0	0
258	PIT	Pasi Huura	Ilves Tampere, FIN	D					
259	MTL	Dale Hooper	Springfield Jr. B	D					
260	BOS	Torsten Kienass	Dynamo Berlin, FRG	D					
261	CGY	Andrei Trefilov	Dynamo Moscow, USSR	G	49	12	138	2	3.34
262	L.A.	Michael Gaul	St. Lawrence U.	D					
263	ST.L.	Mike Veisor	Springfield Jr. B	G					
264	CHI	Scott Dean	Lake Forest H.S.	D					

1992

The NHL Entry Draft returned to the Montreal Forum for the eighth time in 1992 where it was characterized by a record number of non-North American talent being selected by NHL clubs. A total of 84 Europeans were taken, accounting for 31.4 percent of all players drafted. Eleven were taken in the first round, including the top two picks. It marked the first time that two non-North American players would occupy the first and second overall positions. Defenseman Roman Hamrlik, a native of the Czech Republic, was selected first overall by the expansion Tampa Bay Lightning. Despite being ranked third on the Central Scouting European lists, Hamrlik became only the second European to be taken first overall. (Mats Sundin was the first in 1989.) Russian-born Alexei Yashin, who was taken by the second expansion team, the Ottawa Senators, became the highest-drafted Russian in Entry Draft history when he went second. Russian defenseman Darius Kasparaitis was selected fifth overall by the New York Islanders.

Due to the inclusion of the two new expansion franchises, the NHL decided to determine the drafting order by means of a coin toss. The team that won the toss would be granted the first overall pick, while the other team would follow with the second pick. This order would rotate every round, therefore granting the two expansion teams the first two picks throughout the draft. To avoid the problems that were encountered during the expansion of the 1960s and 1970s, the expansion clubs were restricted from trading their first-round picks prior to the draft, and could not trade their first-round prospect before one full season.

For the second consecutive year there were no goaltenders taken in the first round, a trend that had been becoming popular since 1987. The first goaltender drafted was U.S. high school prodigy Jim Carey, 32nd overall. The ranking of goaltenders was surrounded with skepticism. "It's always difficult to get a true handle on U.S. high school goalies because the caliber of shooter isn't that high," said a scout. Void of grand expectations, Carey broke into the NHL in 1994–95 and was named to the NHL's All-Rookie Team after finishing as the runner-up to Peter Forsberg for the Calder Trophy. In his sophomore season, Carey led the league with nine shutouts and an outstanding 2.26 goals-against average to capture the Vezina Trophy as the NHL's best goaltender. Since these incredible feats, however, Carey has disappeared from NHL play and is currently in the minor leagues. An additional award winner came from the 1992 draft in center Michael Peca, selected 40th overall. Peca has emerged as one of the league's best defensive forwards and received the Frank J. Selke Trophy in 1997.

The 1992 Entry Draft was a big year for NHL family ties. First overall pick Roman Hamrlik joined his brother Martin who had been selected 31st overall in 1991 by the Hartford Whalers. Russian defenseman Boris Mironov (27th overall) joined his brother and fellow blueliner Dmitri, while Valeri Bure (33rd overall), brother of Pavel, was selected by the Montreal Canadiens. Twin brothers Peter and Chris Ferraro were taken by the New York Rangers, becoming the second set of twins (after Rich and Ron Sutter) to be taken via the Entry Draft. The NHL welcomed another Gretzky with the 49th pick as the Lightning drafted Brent Gretzky, youngest brother of Wayne. Brent has only appeared in 13 NHL games, collecting a goal and three assists, and is currently playing in the minors. Ryan Sittler, son of Hall of Famer Darryl Sittler, was selected seventh overall by the Philadelphia Flyers, but has never played an NHL game.

The NHL also saw the second Japanese-trained player enter the league in 1992 as the Montreal Canadiens opted to take Hiroyuki Miura with the 260th selection. The 6'3", 187-pound defenseman from Kushiro High School in Hokkaido, Japan has never appeared in an NHL game. Two

dark horse talents did emerge from the late rounds of the draft, as Russian goaltender Nikolai Khabibulin was taken 204th and forward Anson Carter was drafted 220th.

1992

PICK	TEAM	NAME	DRAFTED FROM	NHL PLAYERS: POS / NHL GOALTENDERS: POS	GP / GP	G / W	A / GA	PTS / SO	PIM / AVG
FIRST ROUND									
1	T.B.	Roman Hamrlik	ZPS Zlin, TCH	D	418	58	153	211	522
2	OTT	Alexei Yashin	Dynamo Moscow, CIS	C	340	134	175	309	138
3	S.J.	Mike Rathje	Medicine Hat	D	228	6	43	49	182
4	QUE	Todd Warriner	Windsor	LW	182	24	37	61	87
5	NYI	Darius Kasparaitis	Dynamo Moscow, CIS	D	370	12	64	76	650
6	CGY	Cory Stillman	Windsor	C	214	49	63	112	97
7	PHI	Ryan Sittler	Nichols H.S.	LW					
8	TOR	Brandon Convery	Sudbury	C	57	7	12	19	24
9	HFD	Robert Petrovicky	Dukla Trencin, TCH	C	126	17	24	41	94
10	S.J.	Andrei Nazarov	Dynamo Moscow, CIS	LW	183	24	29	53	548
11	BUF	David Cooper	Medicine Hat	D	28	3	7	10	24
12	CHI	Sergei Krivokrasov	CSKA Moscow, CIS	RW	225	42	41	83	146
13	EDM	Joe Hulbig	St. Sebastian's H.S.	LW	23	2	2	4	2
14	WSH	Sergei Gonchar	Traktor Chelyabinsk, CIS	D	238	35	64	99	184
15	PHI	Jason Bowen	Tri-City	LW	77	2	6	8	109
16	BOS	Dmitri Kvartalnov	San Diego IHL	LW	112	42	49	91	26
17	WPG	Sergei Bautin	Dynamo Moscow, CIS	D	132	5	25	30	176
18	N.J.	Jason Smith	Regina	D	266	6	26	32	283
19	PIT	Martin Straka	HC Skoda Plzen, TCH	C	370	77	135	212	150
20	MTL	David Wilkie	Kamloops	D	120	9	19	28	94
21	VAN	Libor Polasek	TJ Vitkovice, TCH	C					
22	DET	Curtis Bowen	Ottawa	LW					
23	TOR	Grant Marshall	Ottawa	RW	200	24	34	58	305
24	NYR	Peter Ferraro	Waterloo Jr. A	C	37	3	5	8	14
SECOND ROUND									
25	OTT	Chad Penney	North Bay	LW	3	0	0	0	2
26	T.B.	Drew Bannister	Sault Ste. Marie	D	139	4	23	27	137
27	WPG	Boris Mironov	CSKA Moscow, CIS	D	322	38	111	149	436
28	QUE	Paul Brousseau	Hull	RW	25	1	3	4	29
29	QUE	Tuomas Gronman	Tacoma	D	38	1	3	4	38
30	CGY	Chris O'Sullivan	Catholic Memorial H.S.	D	39	2	10	12	12
31	PHI	Denis Metlyuk	Lada Togliatti, CIS	C					
32	WSH	Jim Carey	Catholic Memorial H.S.	G	168	78	403	16	2.55
33	MTL	Valeri Bure	Spokane	RW	231	51	68	119	75
34	MIN	Jarkko Varvio	HPK Hameenlinna, FIN	RW	13	3	4	7	4
35	BUF	Jozef Cierny	ZTK Zvolen, TCH	LW	1	0	0	0	0
36	CHI	Jeff Shantz	Regina	C	305	35	80	115	151
37	EDM	Martin Reichel	Freiburg, GER	RW					
38	ST.L.	Igor Korolev	Dynamo Moscow, CIS	RW	384	60	113	173	162
39	L.A.	Justin Hocking	Spokane	D	1	0	0	0	0
40	VAN	Michael Peca	Ottawa	C	245	55	77	132	236
41	CHI	Sergei Klimovich	Dynamo Moscow, CIS	C	1	0	0	0	2
42	N.J.	Sergei Brylin	CSKA Moscow, CIS	C	123	14	18	32	54
43	PIT	Marc Hussey	Moose Jaw	D					
44	MTL	Keli Corpse	Kingston	C					
45	VAN	Mike Fountain	Oshawa	G	9	2	24	1	3.53
46	DET	Darren McCarty	Belleville	RW	300	63	91	154	710
47	HFD	Andrei Nikolishin	Dynamo Moscow, CIS	LW	200	37	76	113	90
48	NYR	Mattias Norstrom	AIK Solna, SWE	D	207	4	40	44	222
OTHER ROUNDS									
49	T.B.	Brent Gretzky	Belleville	C	13	1	3	4	2
50	OTT	Patrick Traverse	Shawinigan	D	5	0	0	0	2
51	S.J.	Alexander Cherbayev	Khimik Voskresensk, CIS	LW					
52	QUE	Emmanuel Fernandez	Laval	G	8	1	24	0	3.82
53	WSH	Stefan Ustorf	ESV Kaufbeuren, GER	C	54	7	10	17	16
54	CGY	Mathias Johansson	Farjestad Karlstad, SWE	C					
55	BOS	Sergei Zholtok	Riga Stars, CIS	C	160	24	31	55	37
56	NYI	Jarrett Deuling	Kamloops	LW	15	0	1	1	11
57	HFD	Jan Vopat	HC Chemo. Litvinov, TCH	D	65	6	14	20	36
58	MIN	Jeff Bes	Guelph	C					
59	BUF	Ondrej Steiner	HC Skoda Plzen, TCH	C					
60	WPG	Jeremy Stevenson	Cornwall	LW		Re-entered Draft in 1994			
61	EDM	Simon Roy	Shawinigan	D					
62	ST.L.	Vitali Karamnov	Dynamo Moscow, CIS	LW	92	12	20	32	65
63	L.A.	Sandy Allan	North Bay	G					
64	ST.L.	Vitali Prokhorov	Spartak Moscow, CIS	LW	83	19	11	30	35
65	EDM	Kirk Maltby	Owen Sound	RW	301	39	31	70	354
66	N.J.	Cale Hulse	Portland	D	153	6	28	34	280
67	PIT	Travis Thiessen	Moose Jaw	D					
68	MTL	Craig Rivet	Kingston	D	120	1	11	12	206
69	VAN	Jeff Connolly	St. Sebastian's H.S.	C					
70	DET	Sylvain Cloutier	Guelph	C					
71	WSH	Martin Gendron	St-Hyacinthe	RW	30	4	2	6	10
72	NYR	Eric Cairns	Detroit	D	79	0	4	4	239
73	OTT	Radek Hamr	Sparta Praha, TCH	D	11	0	0	0	0
74	T.B.	Aaron Gavey	Sault Ste. Marie	C	156	18	18	36	126
75	S.J.	Jan Caloun	HC Chemo. Litvinov, TCH	RW	13	8	3	11	0
76	QUE	Ian McIntyre	Beauport	D					
77	TOR	Nikolai Borschevsky	Spartak Moscow, CIS	RW	162	49	73	122	44
78	CGY	Robert Svehla	Dukla Trencin, TCH	D	247	31	116	147	293
79	IIFD	Kevin Smyth	Moose Jaw	LW	58	6	8	14	31
80	BUF	Dean Melanson	St-Hyacinthe	D	5	0	0	0	4
81	HFD	Jason McBain	Portland	D	9	0	0	0	0
82	MTL	Louis Bernard	Drummondville	D					
83	BUF	Matthew Barnaby	Beauport	RW	273	43	65	108	1105
84	WPG	Mark Visheau	London	D	1	0	0	0	0
85	NYR	Chris Ferraro	Waterloo Jr. A	RW	60	5	5	10	49
86	ST.L.	Lee Leslie	Prince Albert	LW					
87	L.A.	Kevin Brown	Belleville	RW	45	3	7	10	28
88	MIN	Jere Lehtinen	Kiekko-Espoo, FIN	RW	192	45	68	113	38
89	CHI	Andy MacIntyre	Saskatoon	LW					
90	N.J.	Vitali Tomilin	Krylja Sovetov, CIS	C					
91	PIT	Todd Klassen	Tri-City	D					
92	MTL	Marc Lamothe	Kingston	G					
93	VAN	Brent Tully	Peterborough	D					
94	N.J.	Scott McCabe	GPD Midgets	D					
95	TOR	Mark Raiter	Saskatoon	D					
96	EDM	Ralph Intranuovo	Sault Ste. Marie	C	22	2	4	6	4
97	T.B.	Brantt Myhres	Lethbridge	RW	85	5	1	6	386
98	OTT	Daniel Guerard	Victoriaville	RW	2	0	0	0	0
99	S.J.	Marcus Ragnarsson	Djurgarden, SWE	D	219	16	65	81	170
100	QUE	Charlie Wasley	St. Paul Jr. A	D					
101	TOR	Janne Gronvall	Lukko Rauma, FIN	D					
102	CGY	Sami Helenius	Jokerit Helsinki, FIN	D	3	0	1	1	0
103	PHI	Vladislav Buljin	Dizelist Penza, CIS	D					
104	NYI	Thomas Klimt	HC Skoda Plzen, TCH	C					
105	NYI	Ryan Durhie	Spokane	C					
106	TOR	Chris Deruiter	Kingston Jr. A	RW					
107	BUF	Markus Ketterer	Jokerit Helsinki, FIN	G					
108	BUF	Yuri Khmylev	Krylja Sovetov, CIS	LW	263	64	88	152	133
109	EDM	Joaquin Gage	Portland	G	18	2	52	0	3.82
110	VAN	Brian Loney	Ohio State	RW	12	2	3	5	6
111	L.A.	Jeff Shevalier	North Bay	LW	27	5	9	14	6
112	BOS	Scott Bailey	Spokane	G	19	6	55	0	3.42
113	CHI	Tim Hogan	Michigan	D					
114	N.J.	Ryan Black	Peterborough	LW					
115	PIT	Philippe DeRouville	Verdun	G	3	1	9	0	3.16
116	MTL	Don Chase	Springfield Jr. B	C					
117	VAN	Adrian Aucoin	Boston U.	D	155	13	33	46	118
118	DET	Mike Sullivan	Reading H.S.	D					
119	WSH	John Varrga	Tacoma	LW					
120	NYR	Dmitri Starostenko	CSKA Moscow, CIS	LW					
121	OTT	Al Sinclair	Michigan	C					
122	T.B.	Martin Tanguay	Verdun	C					
123	S.J.	Michal Sykora	Tacoma	D	208	9	41	50	159
124	QUE	Paxton Schulte	Spokane	LW	2	0	0	0	4
125	TOR	Mikael Hakansson	Nacka, SWE	C					
126	CGY	Ravil Yakubov	Dynamo Moscow, CIS	C					
127	PHI	Roman Zolotov	Dynamo Moscow, CIS	D					
128	NYI	Derek Armstrong	Sudbury	C	79	9	10	19	56
129	CGY	Joel Bouchard	Verdun	D	126	9	12	21	110
130	MIN	Michael Johnson	Ottawa	D					
131	BUF	Paul Rushforth	North Bay	D					
132	WPG	Alexander Alexeyev	Sokol Kiev, CIS	D					
133	BOS	Jiri Dopita	DS Olomuc, TCH	C					
134	ST.L.	Bob Lachance	Springfield Jr. B	RW					
135	L.A.	Rem Murray	Michigan State	LW	143	20	29	49	55
136	BOS	Grigori Panteleev	Riga Stars, CIS	LW	54	8	6	14	12
137	CHI	Gerry Skrypec	Ottawa	D					
138	N.J.	Daniel Trebil	Bloomington-Jefferson H.S.	D	50	3	4	7	25
139	PIT	Artem Kopot	Traktor Chelyabinsk, CIS	D					
140	MIL	Martin Sychra	Zetor Brno, TCH	C					
141	VAN	Jason Clark	St. Thomas Jr. B	C					
142	DET	Jason MacDonald	Owen Sound	RW					
143	HFD	Jarrett Reid	Sault Ste. Marie	C					
144	NYR	David Dal Grande	Ottawa Jr. A	D					
145	T.B.	Derek Wilkinson	Detroit	G	17	2	44	0	3.88
146	OTT	Jaroslav Miklenda	DS Olomuc, TCH	D					
147	S.J.	Eric Dellerose	Trois-Rivieres	LW					
148	QUE	Martin Lepage	Hull	D					
149	TOR	Patrik Augusta	Dukla Jihlava, TCH	RW	2	0	0	0	0
150	CGY	Pavel Rajnoha	ZPS Zlin, TCH	D					
151	PHI	Kirk Daubenspeck	Culver Military Academy	G					
152	NYI	Vladimir Grachev	Dynamo-2 Moscow, CIS	LW					
153	HFD	Ken Belanger	Ottawa	LW	65	3	3	6	239
154	MIN	Kyle Peterson	Thunder Bay Jr. A	C					
155	WPG	Artur Oktyabrev	CSKA Moscow, CIS	D					
156	WPG	Andrei Raisky	Torpedo Ust-Kamen'k, CIS	C					
157	EDM	Steve Gibson	Windsor	LW					
158	ST.L.	Ian Laperriere	Drummondville	C	248	33	55	88	473
159	NYI	Steve O'Rourke	Tri-City	RW					
160	ST.L.	Lance Burns	Lethbridge	C					
161	CHI	Mike Prokopec	Cornwall	RW	15	0	0	0	11
162	N.J.	Geordie Kinnear	Peterborough	D					
163	PIT	Jan Alinc	HC Chemo. Litvinov, TCH	C					
164	MTL	Christian Proulx	St-Jean	D	7	1	2	3	20

1992 continued

PICK	TEAM	NAME	DRAFTED FROM	NHL PLAYERS: POS / NHL GOALTENDERS: POS	GP	G / W	A / GA	PTS / SO	PIM / AVG
165	VAN	Scott Hollis	Oshawa	RW					
166	DET	Greg Scott	Niagara Falls	G					
167	WSH	Mark Matier	Sault Ste. Marie	D					
168	NYR	Matt Oates	Miami of Ohio	LW					
169	OTT	Jay Kenney	Canterbury H.S.	D					
170	T.B.	Dennis Maxwell	Niagara Falls	C					
171	S.J.	Ryan Smith	Brandon	D					
172	QUE	Mike Jickling	Spokane	C					
173	TOR	Ryan Vandenbussche	Cornwall	RW	31	2	1	3	73
174	CGY	Ryan Mulhern	Canterbury H.S.	C	3	0	0	0	0
175	PHI	Claude Jutras Jr.	Hull	RW					
176	NYI	Jason Widmer	Lethbridge	D	7	0	1	1	7
177	HFD	Konstantin Korotkov	Spartak Moscow, CIS	C					
178	MIN	Juha Lind	Jokerit Helsinki, FIN	C	39	2	3	5	6
179	BUF	Dean Tiltgen	Tri-City	C					
180	ST.L.	Igor Boldin	Spartak Moscow, CIS	C					
181	EDM	Kyuin Shim	Sherwood Park Jr. A	RW					
182	ST.L.	Nick Naumenko	Dubuque Jr. A	D					
183	DET	Justin Krall	Omaha Jr. A	D					
184	BOS	Kurt Seher	Seattle	D					
185	CHI	Layne Roland	Portland	RW					
186	N.J.	Stephane Yelle	Oshawa	C	231	29	46	75	116
187	PIT	Fran Bussey	Duluth East H.S.	C					
188	MTL	Michael Burman	North Bay	D					
189	DET	C. J. Denomme	Kitchener	G					
190	EDM	Colin Schmidt	Regina Midgets	C					
191	WSH	Mike Mathers	Kamloops	LW					
192	NYR	Mickey Elick	Wisconsin	D					
193	T.B.	Andrew Kemper	Seattle	D					
194	OTT	Claude Savoie Jr.	Victoriaville	RW					
195	S.J.	Chris Burns	Thunder Bay Jr. A	G					
196	QUE	Steve Passmore	Victoria	G					
197	TOR	Wayne Clarke	RPI	RW					
198	CGY	Brandon Carper	Bowling Green	D					
199	PHI	Jonas Hakansson	Malmo, SWE	LW					
200	NYI	Daniel Paradis	Chicoutimi	C					
201	HFD	Greg Zwakman	Edina H.S.	D					
202	MIN	Lars Edstrom	Lulea, SWE	LW					
203	BUF	Todd Simon	Niagara Falls	C	15	0	1	1	0
204	WPG	Nikolai Khabibulin	CSKA Moscow, CIS	G	221	94	605	13	2.93
205	EDM	Marko Tuomainen	Clarkson	RW	4	0	0	0	0
206	ST.L.	Todd Harris	Tri-City	D					
207	L.A.	Magnus Wernblom	MoDo Ornskoldsvik, SWE	RW					
208	BOS	Mattias Timander	MoDo Ornskoldsvik, SWE	D	64	2	9	11	20
209	CHI	David Hymovitz	Thayer Academy	LW					
210	N.J.	Jeff Toms	Sault Ste. Marie	LW	81	6	14	20	25
211	PIT	Brian Bonin	White Bear Lake H.S.	C					
212	MTL	Earl Cronan	St. Mark's H.S.	LW					
213	VAN	Sonny Mignacca	Medicine Hat	G					
214	DET	Jeff Walker	Peterborough	D					
215	WSH	Brian Stagg	Kingston	RW					
216	NYR	Daniel Brierley	Choate	D					
217	OTT	Jake Grimes	Belleville	C					
218	T.B.	Marc Tardif	Shawinigan	LW					
219	L.A.	Alexander Kholomeyev	Izorhets St. Petersburg, CIS	LW					
220	QUE	Anson Carter	Wexford Jr. A	C	116	27	34	61	40
221	TOR	Sergei Simonov	Kristall Saratov, CIS	D					
222	CGY	Jonas Hoglund	Farjestad Karlstad, SWE	LW	146	31	29	60	34
223	PHI	Chris Herperger	Swift Current	LW					
224	NYI	David Wainwright	Thayer Academy	D					
225	HFD	Steven Halko	Thornhill Jr. A	D	18	0	2	2	10
226	MIN	Jeff Rolmo	Blaine H.S.	C					
227	BUF	Rick Kowalsky	Sault Ste. Marie	RW					
228	WPG	Yevgeny Garanin	Khimik Voskresensk, CIS	C					
229	WPG	Teemu Numminen	Stoneham H.S.	C					
230	ST.L.	Yuri Gunko	Sokol Kiev, CIS	D					
231	L.A.	Ryan Pisiak	Prince Albert	RW					
232	BOS	Chris Crombie	London	LW					
233	CHI	Richard Raymond	Cornwall	D					
234	N.J.	Heath Weenk	Regina	D					
235	PIT	Brian Callahan	Belmont Hill H.S.	C					
236	MTL	Trent Cavicchi	Dartmouth Midgets	G					
237	VAN	Mark Wotton	Saskatoon	D	42	3	6	9	25
238	DET	Daniel McGillis	Hawkesbury Jr. A	D	153	17	36	53	161
239	WSH	Gregory Callahan	Belmont Hill H.S.	D					
240	NYR	Vladimir Vorobiev	Metallurg Cherepovets, CIS	LW	31	7	7	14	12
241	T.B.	Tom MacDonald	Sault Ste. Marie	D					
242	OTT	Tomas Jelinek	HPK Hameenlinna, FIN	RW	49	7	6	13	52
243	S.J.	Victor Ignatjev	Riga Stars, CIS	D					
244	QUE	Aaron Ellis	Culver Military Academy	G					
245	TOR	Nathan Dempsey	Regina	LW	14	1	1	2	2
246	CGY	Andrei Potaichuk	Krylja Sovetov, CIS	RW					
247	PHI	Patrice Paquin	Beauport	LW					
248	NYI	Andrei Vasiliev	CSKA Moscow, CIS	LW	15	2	5	7	6
249	HFD	Joacim Esbjors	Vastra Frolunda, SWE	D					
250	MIN	Jeffrey Moen	Roseville H.S.	D					
251	BUF	Chris Clancy	Cornwall	LW					
252	WPG	Andrei Karpovstev	Dynamo Moscow, CIS	RW					
253	EDM	Bryan Rasmussen	St. Louis Park H.S.	LW					
254	WPG	Ivan Vologzhaninov	Sokol Kiev, CIS	RW					
255	L.A.	Jukka Tiilikainen	Kiekko-Espoo, FIN	LW					
256	BOS	Denis Chervyakov	Riga Stars, CIS	D	2	0	0	0	2
257	BOS	Yevgeny Pavlov	SKA St. Petersburg, CIS	LW					
258	N.J.	Vladislav Yakovenko	Argus Moscow, CIS	LW					
259	ST.L.	Wade Salzman	Duluth East H.S.	G					
260	MTL	Hiroyuki Miura	Kushiro High School, JPN	D					
261	VAN	Aaron Boh	Spokane	D					
262	DET	Ryan Bach	Notre Dame Jr. A	G					
263	WSH	Billy Jo MacPherson	Oshawa	LW					
264	OTT	Petter Ronnqvist	Nacka, SWE	G					

1993

The 1993 Entry Draft was highly anticipated by NHL teams and the surrounding hockey media as it was believed that the graduating crop of prospects was the best to emerge in 13 years. *The Hockey News* reported: "The 1993 NHL Entry Draft contains more talent than any in years and could rival the famous draft of 1979 for the quantity and quality of players it sends to the NHL." Ten players immediately entered the NHL as 18-year-olds from the 1993 draft, including the top-ranked prospect Alexandre Daigle, a highly touted player who was known for his explosive speed and skating ability. "He would be in the top 20 percent of the league's skaters his first day," said Ottawa Senators scout Jim Nill. Daigle was selected first overall by the Senators and made history by signing a trend-setting multi-million-dollar contract before ever playing in an NHL game. His highly anticipated debut in the NHL resulted in a 51-point season which he repeated in 1996–97. Daigle never developed into the franchise-type player that was expected of him in Ottawa and he was traded to the Philadelphia Flyers during the 1997–98 season.

The first round featured another talent that was touted as a franchise player despite a fifth overall ranking by Central Scouting. Left winger Paul Kariya, a native of Vancouver, British Columbia who is of Japanese descent, prompted the media to report: "Paul Kariya enters the 1993 entry draft as one of the most highly touted pure playmakers since Wayne Gretzky descended from the heavens some 14 years ago."

In 1993, Kariya had become the first freshman to capture the Hobey Baker Award as the best player in the U.S. collegiate system. With 24 goals and 93 points in 39 games, Kariya led the University of Maine to the NCAA title. Drafted fourth overall by the Mighty Ducks of Anaheim, he entered the NHL in 1994–95 and recorded 39 points in 47 games to earn a spot on the NHL All-Rookie Team. He recorded his first 100-point season in his sophomore year and is considered to be one of the most talented players in the NHL today. He became just the eighth player to capture the Lady Byng Trophy as the league's most gentlemanly player two years in a row (1995–96 and 1996–97) and was also the runner-up to Dominik Hasek for the Hart Trophy as the NHL's MVP in 1997.

Two of the NHL's tallest defensemen were taken in the first round in 1993 as Chris Pronger (second) and Mike Wilson (20th) both came into the NHL standing 6'6". Pronger was voted to the 1994 NHL All-Rookie Team and has developed into one of the NHL's premier blueliners as he captained the St. Louis Blues at the age of 23 and competed with Team Canada in the 1998 Winter Olympics. Pronger was also recognized as a finalist for the 1998 Norris Trophy. Other emerging defensive talents selected in the 1993 draft were Sweden's Kenny Jonsson (12th) and

Finland's Janne Niinimaa (36th). Niinimaa and Jonsson were honored with selections to the NHL's All-Rookie Team in 1997 and 1995 respectively.

Chris Gratton was touted as the best power forward in the 1993 draft. "When this guy hits you," one NHL scout said, "you stay hit." the 6'4", 218-pound Gratton was selected third overall by the Tampa Bay Lightning and stepped directly into the NHL, but joined the Philadelphia Flyers as a free agent prior to the 1997–98 season. Center Jason Arnott was taken with the seventh pick in the first round by the Edmonton Oilers and immediately entered the league as an 18-year-old. It appeared that the Oilers had drafted a diamond when Arnott recorded 68 points (33 goals, 35 assists) in his first season. However he has struggled since.

Top international talent was once again brought into the league in 1993, as forwards Niklas Sundstrom and Saku Koivu were taken eighth and 21st respectively. At just 5'9" and 162 pounds, Koivu was rated sixth on Central Scouting's European listing but was considered to be somewhat of a risk due to his size. However, his talent was too rich to pass up. "He's one hell of a hockey player," said a scout. "In spite of his size, there isn't anything he can't do." Koivu has been a solid performer since coming into the NHL in 1995–96, but has been plagued by injuries.

Goaltending talent was rather unique in the 1993 drafting pool, as both the top-ranked goaltender and the second-lowest-rated netminder made the biggest news in the NHL. After becoming the first netminder to earn player of the year honors in the Quebec junior league, Jocelyn Thibault was selected 10th overall and became only the sixth goaltender to appear in the NHL as an 18-year-old. Patrick Lalime was taken 156th overall by the Pittsburgh Penguins and didn't break into the NHL until 1996–97. Lalime came into the league as a virtual no-name prospect who went on to surpass Ken Dryden's record for the longest undefeated streak by a rookie goaltender with 14 wins and two ties for 16 consecutive games.

There were a number of dark horse talents to emerge from the 1993 draft, as Eric Daze (90th) became a finalist for the Calder Trophy as rookie of the year for 1995–96 and has emerged as one of the most promising young power forwards in the league, while Czech natives Michal Grosek (145th) and Pavol Demitra (227th) both immediately broke into the NHL as 18-year-old talents and have emerged as key performers with their respective teams.

1993

PICK	TEAM	NAME	DRAFTED FROM	NHL PLAYERS: POS / NHL GOALTENDERS: POS	GP / GP	G / W	A / GA	PTS / SO	PIM / AVG
FIRST ROUND									
1	OTT	Alexandre Daigle	Victoriaville	C	338	83	115	198	125
2	HFD	Chris Pronger	Peterborough	D	362	37	103	140	600
3	T.B.	Chris Gratton	Kingston	C	376	89	142	231	677
4	ANA	Paul Kariya	U of Maine	LW	220	129	148	277	53
5	FLA	Rob Niedermayer	Medicine Hat	C	288	61	89	150	289
6	S.J.	Viktor Kozlov	Dynamo Moscow, CIS	LW	220	41	51	92	64
7	EDM	Jason Arnott	Oshawa	C	321	105	149	254	510
8	NYR	Niklas Sundstrom	MoDo Ornskoldsvik, SWE	LW	234	52	68	120	58
9	DAL	Todd Harvey	Detroit	C	239	38	61	99	449
10	QUE	Jocelyn Thibault	Sherbrooke	G	205	87	529	7	2.80
11	WSH	Brendan Witt	Seattle	D	156	6	12	18	285
12	TOR	Kenny Jonsson	Rogle Angelholm, SWE	D	267	23	77	100	130
13	N.J.	Denis Pederson	Prince Albert	C	160	30	34	64	159
14	QUE	Adam Deadmarsh	Portland	C	277	85	83	168	459
15	WPG	Mats Lindgren	Skelleftea, SWE	C	151	24	27	51	54
16	EDM	Nick Stajduhar	London	D	2	0	0	0	4
17	WSH	Jason Allison	London	C	186	43	81	124	102
18	CGY	Jesper Mattsson	Malmo, SWE	C					
19	TOR	Landon Wilson	Dubuque Jr. A	RW	84	10	17	27	85
20	VAN	Mike Wilson	Sudbury	D	201	10	21	31	140
21	MTL	Saku Koivu	TPS Turku, FIN	C	201	51	107	158	126
22	DET	Anders Eriksson	MoDo Ornskoldsvik, SWE	D	90	7	20	27	44

PICK	TEAM	NAME	DRAFTED FROM	NHL PLAYERS: POS / NHL GOALTENDERS: POS	GP / GP	G / W	A / GA	PTS / SO	PIM / AVG
23	NYI	Todd Bertuzzi	Guelph	C	214	41	54	95	272
24	CHI	Eric Lecompte	Hull	LW					
25	BOS	Kevyn Adams	Miami of Ohio	C	5	0	0	0	7
26	PIT	Stefan Bergkvist	Leksand, SWE	D	7	0	0	0	9
SECOND ROUND									
27	OTT	Radim Bicanek	Dukla Jihlava, TCH	D	28	0	1	1	8
28	S.J.	Shean Donovan	Ottawa	RW	228	30	24	54	157
29	T.B.	Tyler Moss	Kingston	G	6	2	20	0	3.27
30	ANA	Nikolai Tsulygin	Salavat Yulayev Ufa, CIS	D	22	0	1	1	8
31	WPG	Scott Langkow	Portland	G	4	0	10	0	4.20
32	PIT	Jay Pandolfo	Boston U.	LW	69	7	11	18	10
33	EDM	David Vyborny	Sparta Praha, TCH	C					
34	NYR	Lee Sorochan	Lethbridge	D					
35	DAL	Jamie Langenbrunner	Cloquet H.S.	C	171	38	57	95	120
36	PHI	Janne Niinimaa	Karpat Oulu, FIN	D	154	8	79	87	120
37	ST.L.	Maxim Bets	Spokane	LW	3	0	0	0	0
38	BUF	Denis Tsygurov	Lada Togliatti, CIS	D	51	1	5	6	45
39	N.J.	Brendan Morrison	Penticton Jr. A	C	11	5	4	9	0
40	NYI	Bryan McCabe	Spokane	D	246	19	56	75	530
41	FLA	Kevin Weekes	Owen Sound	G	11	0	32	0	3.96
42	L.A.	Shayne Toporowski	Prince Albert	RW	3	0	0	0	7
43	WPG	Alexei Budayev	Kristall Elektrostal, CIS	C					
44	CGY	Jamie Allison	Detroit	D	64	3	8	11	139
45	S.J.	Vlastimil Kroupa	HC Chemo. Litvinov, TCH	D	105	4	19	23	66
46	VAN	Rick Girard	Swift Current	C					
47	MTL	Rory Fitzpatrick	Sudbury	D	50	0	3	3	26
48	DET	Jon Coleman	Andover Academy	D					
49	QUE	Ashley Buckberger	Swift Current	RW					
50	CHI	Eric Manlow	Kitchener	C					
51	BOS	Matt Alvey	Springfield Jr. B	RW					
52	PIT	Domenic Pittis	Lethbridge	C	1	0	0	0	0
OTHER ROUNDS									
53	OTT	Patrick Charbonneau	Victoriaville	G					
54	CHI	Bogdan Savenko	Niagara Falls	RW					
55	T.B.	Allan Egeland	Tacoma	C	17	0	0	0	16
56	ANA	Valeri Karpov	Traktor Chelyabinsk, CIS	RW	76	14	15	29	32
57	FLA	Chris Armstrong	Moose Jaw	D					
58	S.J.	Ville Peltonen	HIFK Helsinki, FIN	LW	59	4	14	18	14
59	EDM	Kevin Paden	Detroit	C/LW					
60	EDM	Alexander Kerch	Pardaugava Riga, CIS	LW	5	0	0	0	2
61	NYR	Maxim Galanov	Lada Togliatti, CIS	D	6	0	1	1	2
62	PIT	Dave Roche	Peterborough	C	132	12	12	24	285
63	ST.L.	Jamie Rivers	Sudbury	D	77	4	9	13	44
64	BUF	Ethan Philpott	Andover Academy	RW					
65	N.J.	Krzysztof Oliwa	Welland Jr. B	LW	74	2	3	5	300
66	NYI	Vladimir Chebaturkin	Kristall Elektrostal, CIS	D	2	0	2	2	0
67	FLA	Mikael Tjallden	MoDo Ornskoldsvik, SWE	D					
68	L.A.	Jeff Mitchell	Detroit	C/RW	7	0	0	0	7
69	WSH	Patrick Boileau	Laval	D	1	0	0	0	0
70	CGY	Dan Tompkins	Omaha Jr. A	LW					
71	PHI	Vaclav Prospal	Motor Cooke Budejovice, TCH	C	74	11	29	40	25
72	HFD	Marek Malik	TJ Vitkovice, TCH	D	55	1	6	7	54
73	MTL	Sebastien Bordeleau	Hull	C	85	8	17	25	38
74	DET	Kevin Hilton	Michigan	C					
75	QUE	Bill Pierce	Lawrence Academy	C					
76	CHI	Ryan Huska	Kamloops	LW	1	0	0	0	0
77	PHI	Milos Holan	TJ Vitkovice, TCH	D	49	5	11	16	42
78	FLA	Steve Washburn	Ottawa	C	77	14	15	29	36
79	WPG	Ruslan Batyrshin	Dynamo-2 Moscow, CIS	D	2	0	0	0	6
80	S.J.	Alexander Osadchy	CSKA Moscow, CIS	D					
81	T.B.	Marian Kacir	Owen Sound	RW					
82	ANA	Joel Gagnon	Oshawa	G					
83	FLA	Bill McCauley	Detroit	C	Re-entered Draft in 1995				
84	HFD	Trevor Roenick	Boston Jr.	RW					
85	MTL	Adam Wiesel	Springfield Jr. B	D					
86	NYR	Sergei Olimpiyev	Dynamo Minsk, CIS	LW					
87	DAL	Chad Lang	Peterborough	G					
88	BOS	Charles Paquette	Sherbrooke	D					
89	ST.L.	Jamal Mayers	Western Michigan	C	6	0	1	1	2
90	CHI	Eric Daze	Beauport	LW	235	84	54	138	58
91	OTT	Cosmo Dupaul	Victoriaville	C					
92	NYI	Warren Luhning	Calgary Jr. A	RW	8	0	0	0	0
93	WPG	Ravil Gusmanov	Traktor Chelyabinsk, CIS	LW	4	0	0	0	0
94	L.A.	Bob Wren	Detroit	LW	3	0	0	0	0
95	CGY	Jason Smith	Princeton	D					
96	CGY	Marty Murray	Brandon	C	19	3	3	6	6
97	DET	John Jakopin	St. Michael's Jr. B	D	2	0	0	0	4
98	VAN	Dieter Kochan	Kelowna Jr. A	G					
99	MTL	Jean-Francois Houle	Northwood Prep	LW					
100	DET	Benoit Larose	Laval	D	Re-entered Draft in 1995				
101	QUE	Ryan Tocher	Niagara Falls	D					
102	CHI	Patrik Pysz	Augsburg, GER	C					
103	BOS	Shawn Bates	Medford H.S.	C	13	2	0	2	2
104	PIT	J. Andersson-Junkka	Kiruna, SWE	D					
105	L.A.	Frederick Beaubien	St-Hyacinthe	G					
106	S.J.	Andrei Buschan	Sokol Kiev, CIS	D					

1993 *continued*

PICK	TEAM	NAME	DRAFTED FROM	POS	GP	G/W	A/GA	PTS/SO	PIM/AVG
107	T.B.	Ryan Brown	Swift Current	D					
108	ANA	Mikhail Shtalenkov	Milwaukee IHL	G	122	34	320	3	3.14
109	FLA	Todd MacDonald	Tacoma	G					
110	N.J.	John Guirestante	London	RW					
111	EDM	Miroslav Satan	Dukla Trencin, TCH	C	217	65	54	119	82
112	NYR	Gary Roach	Sault Ste. Marie	D					
113	MTL	Jeff Lank	Prince Albert	D	Re-entered Draft in 1995				
114	PHI	Vladimir Krechin	Traktor Chelyabinsk, CIS	LW					
115	HFD	Nolan Pratt	Portland	D	32	0	4	4	50
116	BUF	Richard Safarik	AC Nitra, TCH	RW					
117	L.A.	Jason Saal	Detroit	G					
118	NYI	Tommy Salo	Vasteras, SWE	G	136	45	356	9	2.83
119	WPG	Larry Courville	Newmarket	LW	Re-entered Draft in 1995				
120	L.A.	Tomas Vlasak	Slavia Praha, TCH	C					
121	CGY	Darryl Lafrance	Oshawa	C					
122	CGY	John Emmons	Yale	C					
123	TOR	Zdenek Nedved	Sudbury	RW	31	4	6	10	14
124	VAN	Scott Walker	Owen Sound	C	197	10	34	44	466
125	MTL	Dion Darling	Spokane	D					
126	DET	Norm Maracle	Saskatoon	G	4	2	6	0	2.02
127	QUE	Anders Myrvold	Farjestad Karlstad, SWE	D	13	0	3	3	10
128	CHI	Jonni Vauhkonen	Reipas Lahti, FIN	RW					
129	BOS	Andrei Sapozhnikov	Traktor Chelyabinsk, CIS	D					
130	PIT	Chris Kelleher	St. Sebastian's H.S.	D					
131	OTT	Rick Bodkin	Sudbury	C					
132	S.J.	Petri Varis	Assat Pori, FIN	LW	1	0	0	0	0
133	T.B.	Kiley Hill	Sault Ste. Marie	LW					
134	ANA	Antti Aalto	TPS Turku, FIN	C	3	0	0	0	0
135	FLA	Alain Nasreddine	Drummondville	D					
136	DAL	Rick Mrozik	Cloquet H.S.	D					
137	QUE	Nicholas Checco	Bloomington-Jefferson H.S.	C					
138	NYR	Dave Trofimenkoff	Lethbridge	G					
139	DAL	Per Svartvadet	MoDo Ornskoldsvik, SWE	C					
140	PHI	Mike Crowley	Bloomington-Jefferson H.S.	D	8	2	2	4	8
141	ST.L.	Todd Kelman	Vernon Jr. A	D					
142	BUF	Kevin Pozzo	Moose Jaw	D					
143	N.J.	Steve Brule	St-Jean	C					
144	NYI	Peter LeBoutillier	Red Deer	RW	Re-entered Draft in 1995				
145	WPG	Michal Grosek	ZPS Zlin, TCH	LW	199	34	47	81	183
146	L.A.	Jere Karalahti	HIFK Helsinki, FIN	D					
147	WSH	Frank Banham	Saskatoon	RW	24	9	2	11	12
148	CGY	Andreas Karlsson	Leksand, SWE	C					
149	TOR	Paul Vincent	Cushing Academy	C					
150	VAN	Troy Creurer	Notre Dame Jr. A	D					
150	VAN	Troy Creurer	Notre Dame Jr. A	D					
151	MTL	Darcy Tucker	Kamloops	C	150	14	26	40	256
152	DET	Tim Spitzig	Kitchener	RW					
153	QUE	Christian Matte	Granby	RW	10	1	1	2	6
154	S.J.	Fredrik Oduya	Ottawa	D					
155	BOS	Milt Mastad	Seattle	D					
156	PIT	Patrick Lalime	Shawinigan	G	39	21	101	3	2.94
157	S.J.	Sergei Poleschuk	Krylja Sovetov-2, CIS	D					
158	S.J.	Anatoli Filetov	Torpedo Ust-Kamen'k, CIS	RW					
159	T.B.	Matthieu Raby	Victoriaville	D					
160	ANA	Matt Peterson	Osseo H.S.	D					
161	FLA	Trevor Doyle	Kingston	D					
162	NYR	Sergei Kondrashkin	Metallurg Cherepovets, CIS	RW					
163	EDM	Alexander Zhurik	Dynamo Minsk, CIS	D					
164	NYR	Todd Marchant	Clarkson	C	285	60	74	134	215
165	DAL	Jeremy Stasiuk	Spokane	RW					
166	PHI	Aaron Israel	Harvard	G					
167	ST.L.	Mike Buzak	Michigan State	G					
168	BUF	Sergei Petrenko	Dynamo Moscow, CIS	LW	14	0	4	4	0
169	N.J.	Nikolai Zavarukhin	Salavat Yulayev Ufa, CIS	C					
170	NYI	Darren Van Impe	Red Deer	D	160	8	33	41	148
171	WPG	Martin Woods	Victoriaville	D					
172	L.A.	Justin Martin	Essex Junction H.S.	RW					
173	WSH	Daniel Hendrickson	St. Paul Jr. A	RW					
174	WSH	Andrew Brunette	Owen Sound	LW	62	18	22	40	24
175	TOR	Jeff Andrews	North Bay	LW					
176	VAN	Yevgeni Bobariko	Torpedo Nizhny Novgorod, CISC						
177	MTL	David Ruhly	Culver Military Academy	LW					
178	DET	Yuri Yeresko	CSKA Moscow, CIS	D					
179	QUE	David Ling	Kingston	RW	3	0	0	0	0
180	CHI	Tom White	Westminster H.S.	C					
181	BOS	Ryan Golden	Reading H.S.	C					
182	PIT	Sean Selmser	Red Deer	LW					
183	OTT	Jason Disher	Kingston	D					
184	S.J.	Todd Holt	Swift Current	RW					
185	T.B.	Ryan Nauss	Peterborough	LW					
186	ANA	Tom Askey	Ohio State	G	7	0	12	0	2.64
187	FLA	Briane Thompson	Sault Ste. Marie	D					
188	HFD	Manny Legace	Niagara Falls	G					
189	EDM	Martin Bakula	Alaska-Anchorage	D					
190	NYR	Ed Campbell	Omaha Jr. A	D					
191	DAL	Rob Lurtsema	Burnsville H.S.	LW					
192	PHI	Paul Healey	Prince Albert	RW	6	0	0	0	12
193	ST.L.	Eric Boguniecki	Westminster H.S.	C					
194	BUF	Mike Barrie	Victoria	C					
195	N.J.	Thomas Cullen	Wexford Jr. A	D					
196	NYI	Rod Hinks	Sudbury	C					
197	WPG	Adrian Murray	Newmarket	D					
198	L.A.	John-Tra Dillabough	Wexford Jr. A	C					
199	WSH	Joel Poirer	Sudbury	LW					
200	CGY	Derek Sylvester	Niagara Falls	RW					
201	TOR	David Brumby	Tri-City	G					
202	VAN	Sean Tallaire	Lake Superior State	RW					
203	MTL	Alan Letang	Newmarket	D					
204	DET	Vitezslav Skuta	TJ Vitkovice, TCH	D					
205	QUE	Petr Franek	HC Chemo. Litvinov, TCH	G					
206	CHI	Sergei Petrov	Cloquet H.S.	LW					
207	BOS	Hal Gill	Nashoba H.S.	D	68	2	4	6	47
208	PIT	Larry McMorran	Seattle	C					
209	OTT	Toby Kvalevog	Bemidji State College	G					
210	S.J.	Jonas Forsberg	Djurgarden, SWE	G					
211	T.B.	Alexandre Laporte	Victoriaville	D					
212	ANA	Vitali Kozel	Khimik Novopolotsk, CIS	C					
213	FLA	Chad Cabana	Tri-City	LW					
214	HFD	Dmitri Gorenko	CSKA Moscow, CIS	LW					
215	EDM	Brad Norton	Cushing Academy	D					
216	NYR	Ken Shepard	Oshawa	G					
217	WPG	Vladimir Potapov	Kristall Elektrostal, CIS	RW					
218	PHI	Tripp Tracy	Harvard	G					
219	ST.L.	Michael Grier	St. Sebastian's H.S.	RW	145	24	23	47	118
220	BUF	Barrie Moore	Sudbury	LW	38	2	6	8	18
221	N.J.	Judd Lambert	Chilliwack Jr. A	G					
222	NYI	Daniel Johansson	Rogle Angelholm, SWE	D					
223	WPG	Ilja Stashenkov	Krylja Sovetov, CIS	D					
224	L.A.	Martin Strbak	ZPA Presov, TCH	D					
225	WSH	Jason Gladney	Kitchener	D					
226	PHI	E.J. Bradley	Tabor Academy	C					
227	OTT	Pavol Demitra	Dukla Trencin, TCH	LW	128	37	44	81	34
228	WPG	Harijs Vitolinsh	Chur, SUI	C	8	0	0	0	4
229	MTL	Alexandre Duchesne	Drummondville	LW					
230	DET	Ryan Shanahan	Sudbury	RW					
231	QUE	Vincent Auger	Hawkesbury Jr. A	C					
232	CHI	Mike Rusk	Guelph	D					
233	BOS	Joel Prpic	Waterloo Jr. B	C	1	0	0	0	2
234	PIT	Timothy Harberts	Wayzata H.S.	C					
235	OTT	Rick Schuwerk	Canterbury H.S.	D					
236	S.J.	Jeff Salajko	Ottawa	G					
237	T.B.	Brett Duncan	Seattle	D					
238	ANA	Anatoli Fedotov	Moncton AHL	D	4	0	2	2	0
239	FLA	John Demarco	Archbishop Williams H.S.	D					
240	HFD	Wes Swinson	Kitchener	D					
241	EDM	Oleg Maltsev	Traktor Chelyabinsk, CIS	LW					
242	NYR	Andrei Kudinov	Traktor Chelyabinsk, CIS	RW					
243	DAL	Jordan Willis	London	G	1	0	1	0	3.16
244	PHI	Jeff Staples	Brandon	D					
245	ST.L.	Libor Prochazka	Poldi Kladno, TCH	D					
246	BUF	Chris Davis	Calgary Jr. A	G					
247	N.J.	Jimmy Provencher	St-Jean	RW					
248	NYI	Stephane Larocque	Sherbrooke	RW					
249	DAL	Bill Lang	North Bay	C					
250	L.A.	Kimmo Timonen	KalPa Kuopio, FIN	D					
251	WSH	Mark Selinger	Rosenheim, FRG	G					
252	CGY	German Titov	TPS Turku, FIN	C	345	107	121	228	142
253	TOR	Kyle Ferguson	Michigan Tech	RW					
254	VAN	Bert Robertsson	Sodertalje, SWE	D	30	2	4	6	24
255	MTL	Brian Larochelle	Phillips-Exeter H.S.	G					
256	DET	James Kosecki	Berkshire H.S.	G					
257	QUE	Mark Pivetz	Saskatoon Jr. A	D					
258	CHI	Mike McGhan	Prince Albert	LW					
259	BOS	Joakim Persson	Hammarby Stockholm, SWE	G					
260	PIT	Leonid Toropchenko	Springfield AHL	D					
261	NYR	Pavel Komarov	Torpedo Niz. Novogord, CIS	D					
262	S.J.	Jamie Matthews	Sudbury	C					
263	T.B.	Mark Szoke	Lethbridge	LW					
264	ANA	David Penney	Worcester Academy	LW					
265	FLA	Eric Montreuil	Chicoutimi	C					
266	HFD	Igor Chibirev	Fort Wayne IHL	C	45	7	12	19	2
267	CHI	Ilja Byakin	Landshut, GER	D	57	8	25	33	44
268	NYR	Maxim Smelnitsky	Traktor Chelyabinsk, CIS	RW					
269	DAL	Cory Peterson	Bloomington-Jefferson H.S.	D					
270	PHI	Ken Hemenway	Alaska All-Stars	D					
271	ST.L.	Alexander Vasilevski	Victoria	RW	4	0	0	0	2
272	BUF	Scott Nichol	Portland	C	5	0	0	0	14
273	N.J.	Mike Legg	London Jr. B	RW					
274	NYI	Carl Charland	Hull	LW					
275	ST.L.	Christer Olsson	Brynas Gavle, SWE	D	56	4	12	16	24
276	L.A.	Patrick Howald	Lugano, SUI	LW					
277	WSH	Dany Bousquet	Penticton Jr. A	C					
278	CGY	Burke Murphy	St. Lawrence U.	LW					
279	TOR	Mikhail Lapin	Western Michigan	D					

PICK	TEAM	NAME	DRAFTED FROM	NHL PLAYERS: POS	GP	G	A	PTS	PIM
				NHL GOALTENDERS: POS	GP	W	GA	SO	AVG
279	MTL	Russell Guzior	Culver Military Academy	C					
280	VAN	Sergei Tkachenko	Hamilton AHL	G					
282	DET	Gordon Hunt	Detroit Compuware Jr. A	C					
283	QUE	John Hillman	St. Paul Jr. A	C					
284	CHI	Tom Noble	Catholic Memorial H.S.	G					
285	WPG	Russell Hewson	Swift Current	LW					
286	PIT	Hans Jonsson	MoDo Ornskoldsvik, SWE	D					

1994

The 1994 Entry Draft featured a first round that included a number of players of similar talents, making exact ranking difficult. There was a surprising last-minute flurry of trades involving draft picks. Top-ranked prospect Radek Bonk was passed over until the third selection, where he was chosen by Ottawa.

The Florida Panthers opted to take defenseman Ed Jovanovski as the first pick. Jovanovski's story was unique since he did not start playing hockey until he was 11 years old, the age that many future stars are first noticed by hockey scouts. After just six years in hockey he was taken first overall into the NHL.

"Just watching him and the progress he's made in a relatively short career, and his ability to handle each new level that he's played at, convinced us that whenever he's ready to play, he'll be able to step up," said Panthers president Bill Torrey. In his first season, Jovanovski was named to the All-Rookie Team in 1996 and was also recognized as a runner-up for the Calder Trophy behind winner Daniel Alfredsson and Eric Daze. Jovanovski established himself as one on the league's best hitters and played an integral role in the Panthers surprise entry to the Stanley Cup finals in 1996.

Another defenseman was taken second overall in 1993, as the Mighty Ducks of Anaheim took Russian-born Oleg Tverdovsky. As a second pick, Tverdovsky joined Alexei Yashin as the highest-drafted Russians in Entry Draft history and has developed into one of the NHL's most promising offensive blueliners.

The Edmonton Oilers were blessed with two top-10 picks as they selected Jason Bonsignore and Ryan Smyth with the fourth and sixth selections. Smyth made a big impression in his sophomore year with 39 goals and 22 assists for 61 points. Although he was plagued with injuries during his third season in 1997–98, Smyth remains an integral part of the Oilers' future.

The first-round trading blitz began with the Quebec Nordiques, who had the ninth and 10th picks before trading their ninth to the Islanders in return for New York's 12th overall selection. Quebec then dealt its 10th pick to Toronto who in turn dealt it to Washington for the Capitals' 16th pick. This incredible round of trades surrounded one particular prospect who was coveted by the four teams. The prospect was Brett Lindros, the less talented but more aggressive younger brother of NHL prodigy Eric Lindros who wound up going to the Islanders with the ninth pick. "Brett is exactly what this franchise needs," said Islanders g.m. Don Maloney. "We're not looking for him to be the beacon of this franchise. He's rough around the edges, but we will give him time to develop."

Lindros played only two seasons in the NHL before retiring prematurely due to concussions. Lindros was one of three relatives of hockey stars taken in the first round; the others were Keith's brother Wayne Primeau (17th overall), and Alexander Kharlamov (15th overall), who is the son of Soviet superstar Valeri Kharlamov who starred for the

Soviet Union in the historic Summit Series of 1972.

Another surprise in 1994 was the drafting of three goaltenders in the first round, the most to be selected so early. The Los Angeles Kings took Jamie Storr seventh overall and the Maple Leafs took Eric Fichaud with their 16th pick, while Dan Cloutier closed out the first round as the 26th pick by the New York Rangers.

The 1994 draft crop saw six 18-year-olds immediately enter the NHL, as Tverdovsky, Smyth, Primeau, Jason Wiemer (8th overall), Jeff Friesen (11th overall) and Richard Park (50th overall) all joined their respective clubs. Friesen was named to the NHL's All-Rookie Team in 1995 and has since become the all-time leading scorer for the San Jose Sharks. Park came into the NHL as a unique prospect who was a Korean-born talent trained in California.

Two dark horse talents came out of the 1994 Entry Draft as Russian native Sergei Berezin was drafted 256th by the Toronto Maple Leafs. Berezin went on to be named to the NHL's All-Rookie Team in 1997. The other more prominent dark horse was Swedish native Daniel Alfredsson. Alfredsson was passed over for three years before being drafted as a 21-year-old. Ranked as the second-highest overage Swedish talent by Central Scouting, Alfredsson was taken 133rd overall by the Ottawa Senators. He entered the NHL in 1995–96 and became the only rookie to lead his team in scoring with 26 goals and 35 assists for 61 points in 82 games. Alfredsson captured the Calder Trophy and was named to the All-Rookie Team.

1994

PICK	TEAM	NAME	DRAFTED FROM	NHL PLAYERS: POS	GP	G	A	PTS	PIM
				NHL GOALTENDERS: POS	GP	W	GA	SO	AVG
FIRST ROUND									
1	FLA	Ed Jovanovski	Windsor	D	212	26	41	67	467
2	ANA	Oleg Tverdovsky	Krylja Sovetov, CIS	D	246	27	89	116	97
3	OTT	Radek Bonk	Las Vegas IHL	C	236	31	49	80	94
4	EDM	Jason Bonsignore	Niagara Falls	C	56	3	10	13	26
5	HFD	Jeff O'Neill	Guelph	C	211	41	55	96	147
6	EDM	Ryan Smyth	Moose Jaw	LW	198	61	44	105	148
7	L.A.	Jamie Storr	Owen Sound	G	32	15	74	2	2.60
8	T.B.	Jason Wiemer	Portland	C	244	31	28	59	419
9	NYI	Brett Lindros	Kingston	RW	51	2	5	7	147
10	WSH	Nolan Baumgartner	Kamloops	D	5	0	1	1	0
11	S.J.	Jeff Friesen	Regina	C	288	89	107	196	171
12	QUE	Wade Belak	Saskatoon	D	10	1	1	2	00
13	VAN	Mattias Ohlund	Pitea, SWE	D	77	7	23	30	76
14	CHI	Ethan Moreau	Niagara Falls	LW	144	24	26	50	200
15	WSH	Alexander Kharlamov	CSKA Moscow, CIS	C					
16	TOR	Eric Fichaud	Chicoutimi	G	75	19	199	1	3.14
17	BUF	Wayne Primeau	Owen Sound	C	117	9	10	19	151
18	MTL	Brad Brown	North Bay	D	8	0	0	0	22
19	CGY	Chris Dingman	Brandon	LW	70	3	3	6	149
20	DAL	Jason Botterill	Michigan	LW	4	0	0	0	19
21	BOS	Evgeni Ryabchikov	Molot Perm, CIS	G					
22	QUE	Jeff Kealty	Catholic Memorial H.S.	D					
23	DET	Yan Golubovsky	Dynamo-2 Moscow, CIS	D	12	0	2	2	6
24	PIT	Chris Wells	Seattle	C	162	9	18	27	148
25	N.J.	Vadim Sharifjanov	Salavat Yulayev Ufa, CIS	RW	2	0	0	0	0
26	NYR	Dan Cloutier	Sault Ste. Marie	G	12	4	23	0	2.50
SECOND ROUND									
27	FLA	Rhett Warrener	Saskatoon	D	169	4	16	20	233
28	ANA	Johan Davidsson	HV-71 Jonkoping, SWE	C					
29	OTT	Stanislav Neckar	HC Ceske Budejovice, CZE	D	195	6	14	20	124
30	WPG	Deron Quint	Seattle	D	110	12	31	43	42
31	FLA	Jason Podollan	Spokane	RW	29	1	4	5	10
32	EDM	Mike Watt	Stratford Jr. B	LW	14	1	2	3	4
33	L.A.	Matt Johnson	Peterborough	LW	133	4	7	11	550
34	T.B.	Colin Cloutier	Brandon	C					
35	QUE	Josef Marha	Dukla Jihlava, CZE	C	31	9	11	20	4
36	FLA	Ryan Johnson	Thunder Bay Jr. A	C	10	0	2	2	0
37	S.J.	Angel Nikolov	HC Chemo. Litvinov, CZE	D					
38	NYI	Jason Holland	Kamloops	D	12	1	0	1	4
39	QUE	Robb Gordon	Powell River Jr. A	C					
40	CHI	Jean-Yves Leroux	Beauport	LW	67	6	8	14	60
41	WSH	Scott Cherrey	North Bay	LW					
42	VAN	Dave Scatchard	Portland	C	76	13	11	24	165
43	BUF	Curtis Brown	Moose Jaw	C	96	17	16	33	54
44	MTL	Jose Theodore	St-Jean	G	17	5	54	0	3.90

1994 *continued*

PICK	TEAM	NAME	DRAFTED FROM	POS	GP	G	A	PTS	PIM
45	CGY	Dmitri Ryabykin	Dynamo-2 Moscow, CIS	D					
46	DAL	Lee Jinman	North Bay	C					
47	BOS	Daniel Goneau	Laval	LW		Re-entered Draft in 1996			
48	TOR	Sean Haggerty	Detroit	LW	6	0	0	0	0
49	DET	Mathieu Dandenault	Sherbrooke	RW	167	13	28	41	77
50	PIT	Richard Park	Belleville	C	84	5	10	15	56
51	N.J.	Patrik Elias	HC Kladno, CZE	LW	92	20	22	42	30
52	NYR	Rudolf Vercik	Slovan Bratislava, SVK	LW					

OTHER ROUNDS

PICK	TEAM	NAME	DRAFTED FROM	POS	GP	G	A	PTS	PIM
53	EDM	Corey Neilson	North Bay	D					
54	MTL	Chris Murray	Kamloops	RW	168	13	11	24	409
55	T.B.	Vadim Yepanchindev	Spartak Moscow, CIS	C					
56	WPG	Dorian Anneck	Victoria	C					
57	PIT	Sven Butenschon	Brandon	D	8	0	0	0	6
58	WPG	Tavis Hansen	Tacoma	C	2	0	0	0	0
59	L.A.	Vitali Yachmenev	North Bay	RW	149	29	57	86	30
60	EDM	Brad Symes	Portland	D					
61	QUE	Sebastien Bety	Drummondville	D					
62	PHI	Artem Anisimov	Itil Kazan, CIS	D					
63	NYI	Jason Strudwick	Kamloops	D	29	0	2	2	72
64	TOR	Fredrik Modin	Sundsvall Timra, SWE	LW	150	22	23	45	56
65	VAN	Chad Allan	Saskatoon	D					
66	S.J.	Alexei Yegorov	SKA St. Petersburg, CIS	C	11	3	3	6	2
67	ANA	Craig Reichert	Red Deer	RW	3	0	0	0	0
68	ST.L.	Stephane Roy	Val d'Or	C					
69	BUF	Rumun Ndur	Guelph	D	3	0	0	0	4
70	MTL	Marko Kiprusoff	TPS Turku, FIN	D	24	0	4	4	8
71	N.J.	Sheldon Souray	Tri-City	D	60	3	7	10	85
72	QUE	Chris Drury	Fairfield Prep	C					
73	PIT	Greg Crozier	Lawrence Academy	LW					
74	MTL	Martin Belanger	Granby	D					
75	DET	Sean Gillam	Spokane	D					
76	PIT	Alexei Krivchenkov	CSKA Moscow, CIS	D					
77	CGY	Chris Clark	Springfield Jr. B	RW					
78	NYR	Adam Smith	Tacoma	D					
79	EDM	Adam Copeland	Burlington Jr. B	RW					
80	ANA	Byron Briske	Red Deer	D					
81	OTT	Bryan Masotta	Hotchkiss H.S.	G					
82	WPG	Steve Cheredaryk	Medicine Hat	D					
83	HFD	Hnat Domenichelli	Kamloops	C	54	12	10	22	15
84	FLA	David Nemirovsky	Ottawa	RW	89	16	21	37	42
85	CHI	Steve McLaren	North Bay	D					
86	T.B.	Dmitri Klevakin	Spartak Moscow, CIS	RW					
87	QUE	Milan Hejduk	HC Pardubice, CZE	RW					
88	PHI	Adam Magarrell	Brandon	D					
89	S.J.	Vaclav Varada	HC Vitkovice, CZE	RW	33	5	6	11	17
90	NYI	Brad Lukowich	Kamloops	D	4	0	1	1	2
91	CGY	Ryan Duthie	Spokane	C					
92	VAN	Mike Dubinsky	Brandon	RW					
93	WSH	Matt Herr	Hotchkiss H.S.	C					
94	ST.L.	Tyler Harlton	Vernon Jr. A	D					
95	EDM	Jussi Tarvainen	KalPa Kuopio, FIN	D					
96	MTL	Arto Kuki	Kiekko-Espoo, FIN	C					
97	CGY	Johan Finnstrom	Rogle Angelholm, SWE	D					
98	DAL	Jamie Wright	Guelph	LW	21	4	2	6	2
99	BOS	Eric Nickulas	Cushing Academy	C					
100	NYR	Alexander Korobolin	Traktor Chelyabinsk, CIS	D					
101	PHI	Sebastien Vallee	Victoriaville	LW					
102	PIT	Thomas O'Connor	Springfield Jr. B	D					
103	N.J.	Zdenek Skorepa	HC Chemo. Litvinov, CZE	RW					
104	NYR	Sylvain Blouin	Laval	LW	7	0	0	0	23
105	FLA	Dave Geris	Windsor	D					
106	ANA	Pavel Trnka	HC Skoda Plzen, CZE	D	48	3	4	7	40
107	CGY	Nils Ekman	Hammarby Stockholm, SWE	LW					
108	WPG	Craig Mills	Belleville	RW	24	0	5	5	34
109	HFD	Ryan Risidore	Guelph	D					
110	EDM	Jon Gaskins	Dubuque Jr. B	D					
111	L.A.	Chris Schmidt	Seattle	C					
112	NYI	Mark McArthur	Guelph	G					
113	QUE	Tony Tuzzolino	Michigan State	RW	1	0	0	0	2
114	DET	Frederic Deschenes	Granby	G					
115	S.J.	Brian Swanson	Omaha Jr. A	C					
116	NYI	Albert O'Connell	St. Sebastian's H.S.	LW					
117	VAN	Yanick Dube	Laval	C					
118	CHI	Marc Dupuis	Belleville	D					
119	WSH	Yanick Jean	Chicoutimi	D					
120	ST.L.	Edvin Frylen	Vasteras, SWE	D					
121	BUF	Sergei Klimentiev	Medicine Hat	D					
122	MTL	Jimmy Drolet	St-Hyacinthe	D					
123	CGY	Frank Appel	Dusseldorf, GER	D					
124	DAL	Marty Turco	Cambridge Jr. B	G					
125	BOS	Darren Wright	Prince Albert	D					
126	TOR	Mark Deyell	Saskatoon	C					
127	DET	Doug Battaglia	Brockville Jr. A	LW					
128	PIT	Clint Johnson	Duluth East H.S.	LW					
129	N.J.	Christian Gosselin	St-Hyacinthe	D					
130	NYR	Martin Ethier	Beauport	D					
131	OTT	Mike Gaffney	St. John's Prep	D					
132	ANA	Bates Battaglia	Caledon Jr. A	LW	33	2	4	6	10
133	OTT	Daniel Alfredsson	Vastra Frolunda, SWE	RW	213	67	110	177	76
134	N.J.	Ryan Smart	Meadville H.S.	C					
135	NYR	Yuri Litvinov	Krylja Sovetov, CIS	C					
136	EDM	Terry Marchant	Niagara Jr. A	LW					
137	T.B.	Daniel Juden	Governor Dummer H.S.	RW					
138	T.B.	Bryce Salvador	Lethbridge	D					
139	QUE	Nicholas Windsor	Cornwall	D					
140	PHI	Alexander Selivanov	Spartak Moscow, CIS	RW	261	72	64	136	253
141	S.J.	Alexander Korolyuk	Krylja Sovetov, CIS	C	19	2	3	5	6
142	NYI	Jason Stewart	Simley H.S.	RW					
143	WPG	Steve Vezina	Beauport	G					
144	CHI	Jim Enson	North Bay	C					
145	WSH	Dmitri Mekeshkin	Avangard Omsk, CIS	D					
146	WPG	Chris Kibermanis	Red Deer	D					
147	BUF	Cal Benazic	Medicine Hat	D					
148	MTL	Joel Irving	Regina Midgets	C					
149	CGY	Patrick Haltia	Grums, SWE	G					
150	DAL	Yevgeny Petrochinin	Spartak Moscow, CIS	D					
151	BOS	Andre Roy	Chicoutimi	LW	13	0	2	2	12
152	TOR	Karri White	Newmarket	D					
153	DET	Pavel Agarkov	Krylja Sovetov, CIS	RW					
154	PIT	Valentin Morozov	CSKA Moscow, CIS	C					
155	N.J.	Luciano Caravaggio	Michigan Tech	G					
156	NYR	David Brosseau	Shawinigan	C					
157	FLA	Matt O'Dette	Kitchener	D					
158	ANA	Mark Welsing	Wisconsin Jr. A	D					
159	OTT	Doug Sproule	Hotchkiss H.S.	LW					
160	EDM	Chris Sheptak	Olds Jr. A	LW					
161	PIT	Serge Aubin	Granby	C					
162	EDM	Dmitri Shulga	Tivali Minsk, CIS	RW					
163	L.A.	Luc Gagne	Sudbury	RW					
164	T.B.	Chris Maillet	Red Deer	D					
165	QUE	Calvin Elfring	Powell River Jr. A	D					
166	PHI	Colin Forbes	Sherwood Park Jr. A	LW	66	13	7	20	59
167	S.J.	Sergei Gorbachev	Dynamo Moscow, CIS	RW					
168	BUF	Steve Plouffe	Granby	G					
169	VAN	Yuri Kuznetsov	Avangard Omsk, CIS	C					
170	CHI	Tyler Prosofsky	Tacoma	C		Re-entered Draft in 1996			
171	WSH	Daniel Reja	London	C					
172	ST.L.	Roman Vopat	HC Chemo. Litvinov, CZE	C	79	6	11	17	163
173	BUF	Shane Hnidy	Prince Albert	D					
174	MTL	Jessie Rezansoff	Regina	RW					
175	CGY	Ladislav Kohn	Swift Current	RW	9	1	1	2	2
176	BUF	Steve Webb	Peterborough	RW	61	1	4	5	179
177	BOS	Jeremy Schaeffer	Medicine Hat	LW					
178	TOR	Tommi Rajamaki	Assat Pori, FIN	D					
179	EDM	Chris Wickenheiser	Red Deer	G					
180	PIT	Drew Palmer	Seattle	D					
181	N.J.	Jeff Williams	Guelph	C					
182	NYR	Alexei Lazarenko	CSKA-2 Moscow, CIS	LW					
183	FLA	Jason Boudrias	Laval	C					
184	ANA	Brad Englehart	Kimball Union Academy	C					
185	EDM	Rob Guinn	Newmarket	D					
186	WPG	Ramil Saifullin	Avangard Omsk, CIS	C					
187	HFD	Tom Buckley	St. Joseph H.S.	C					
188	EDM	Jason Reid	St. Andrew's H.S.	D					
189	L.A.	Andrew Dale	Sudbury	C					
190	T.B.	Alexei Baranov	Dynamo-2 Moscow, CIS	C					
191	QUE	Jay Bertsch	Spokane	RW		Re-entered Draft in 1996			
192	PHI	Derek Diener	Lethbridge	D					
193	S.J.	Eric Landry	Guelph	C	12	1	0	1	4
194	NYI	Mike Loach	Windsor	C					
195	VAN	Rob Trumbley	Moose Jaw	C					
196	CHI	Mike Josephson	Kamloops	LW					
197	WSH	Chris Patrick	Kent Prep	LW					
198	ST.L.	Steve Noble	Stratford Jr. B	C					
199	BUF	Bob Westerby	Kamloops	LW					
200	MTL	Peter Strom	Vastra Frolunda, SWE	LW					
201	CGY	Keith McCambridge	Swift Current	D					
202	PHI	Raymond Giroux	Powasson Jr.	D					
203	NYI	Peter Hogardh	Vastra Frolunda, SWE	C					
204	TOR	Rob Butler	Niagara Jr. A	LW					
205	DET	Jason Elliot	Kimberley Jr. A	G					
206	PIT	Boris Zelenko	CSKA Moscow, CIS	LW					
207	N.J.	Eric Bertrand	Granby	LW					
208	NYR	Craig Anderson	Park Center H.S.	D					
209	NYR	Vitali Yeremeyev	Torpedo Ust-Kamen'k, CIS	G					
210	OTT	Frederic Cassivi	St-Hyacinthe	G					
211	OTT	Danny Dupont	Laval	D					
212	WPG	Henrik Smangs	Leksand, SWE	D					
213	HFD	Ashlin Halfnight	Harvard	C					
214	EDM	Jeremy Jablonski	Victoria	G					
215	L.A.	Jan Nemecek	HC Ceske Budejovice, CZE	D					
216	T.B.	Yuri Smirnov	Spartak Moscow, CIS	C					
217	QUE	Tim Thomas	Vermont	G					

PICK	TEAM	NAME	DRAFTED FROM	NHL PLAYERS: POS / NHL GOALTENDERS: POS	GP	G / W	A / GA	PTS / SO	PIM / AVG
218	PHI	Johan Hedberg	Leksand, SWE	G					
219	S.J.	Yevgeni Nabokov	Torpedo Ust-Kamen'k, CIS	G					
220	NYI	Gord Walsh	Kingston	LW					
221	VAN	Bill Muckalt	Kelowna Jr. A	RW					
222	CHI	Lubomir Jandera	HC Chemo. Litvinov, CZE	D					
223	WSH	John Tuohy	Kent Prep	D					
224	ST.L.	Marc Stephan	Tri-City	C					
225	BUF	Craig Millar	Swift Current	D	12	4	0	4	10
226	MTL	Tomas Vokoun	HC Kladno, CZE	G	1	0	4	0	12.00
227	CGY	Jorgen Jonsson	Rogle Angelholm, SWE	LW					
228	DAL	Marty Flichel	Tacoma	RW					
229	BOS	John Grahame	Sioux City Jr. A	G					
230	HFD	Matt Ball	Detroit	RW					
231	DET	Jeff Mikesch	Michigan Tech	C					
232	PIT	Jason Godbout	Hill-Murray H.S.	D					
233	N.J.	Steve Sullivan	Sault Ste. Marie	C	133	28	47	75	85
234	NYR	Eric Boulton	Oshawa	LW					
235	FLA	Tero Lehtera	Kiekko-Espoo, FIN	LW					
236	ANA	Tommi Miettinen	KalPa Kuopio, FIN	C					
237	OTT	Stephen MacKinnon	Cushing Academy	LW					
238	WPG	Mike Mader	Loomis-Chaffee H.S.	D					
239	HFD	Brian Regan	Westminster H.S.	G					
240	S.J.	Tomas Pisa	HC Pardubice, CZE	RW					
241	L.A.	Sergei Shalomai	Spartak Moscow, CIS	LW					
242	T.B.	Shawn Gervais	Seattle	C					
243	QUE	Chris Pittmann	Kitchener	LW					
244	PHI	Andre Payette	Sault Ste. Marie	C					
245	S.J.	Aniket Dhadphale	Marquette Elec. AAA	C					
246	NYI	Kirk Dewaele	Lethbridge	D					
247	VAN	Tyson Nash	Kamloops	LW					
248	CHI	Lars Weibel	Lugano, SUI	G					
249	WSH	Richard Zednik	IS Banska Bystrica, SVK	LW	77	19	10	29	32
250	ST.L.	Kevin Harper	Wexford Jr. A	D					
251	BUF	Mark Polak	Medicine Hat	C					
252	MTL	Chris Aldous	Northwood Prep	D					
253	CGY	Mike Peluso	Omaha Jr. A	C					
254	DAL	Jimmy Roy	Thunder Bay Jr. A	C					
255	BOS	Neil Savary	Hull	G					
256	TOR	Sergei Berezin	Khimik Voskresensk, CIS	RW	141	41	31	72	12
257	DET	Tomas Holmstrom	Boden, SWE	LW	104	11	20	31	77
258	PIT	Mikhail Kazakevich	Torpedo Yaroslavl, CIS	LW					
259	N.J.	Scott Swanjord	Waterloo Jr. A	G					
260	NYR	Radoslav Kropac	Slovan Bratislava, SVK	RW					
261	FLA	Per Gustafsson	HV-71 Jonkoping, SWE	D	89	8	27	35	38
262	ANA	Jeremy Stevenson	Sault Ste. Marie	LW	53	3	6	9	127
263	CHI	Rob Mara	Belmont Hill H.S.	RW					
264	WPG	Jason Iscol	Prince Albert	LW					
265	HFD	Steve Nimigon	Niagara Falls	LW					
266	EDM	Ladislav Benysek	HC Olomouc Jr., CZE	D	2	0	0	0	0
267	NYR	Jamie Butt	Tacoma	LW					
268	T.B.	Brian White	Arlington Catholic H.S.	D					
269	N.J.	Mike Hanson	Minot H.S.	C					
270	PHI	Jan Lipiansky	Slovan Bratislava, SVK	LW					
271	S.J.	David Beauregard	St-Hyacinthe	LW					
272	NYI	Dick Tarnstrom	AIK Solna, SWE	D					
273	VAN	Robert Longpre	Medicine Hat	C					
274	OTT	Antti Tormanen	Jokerit Helsinki, FIN	RW	50	7	8	15	28
275	WSH	Sergei Tertyshny	Traktor Chelyabinsk, CIS	D					
276	ST.L.	Scott Fankhouser	Loomis-Chaffee H.S.	G					
277	BUF	Shayne Wright	Owen Sound	D					
278	MTL	Ross Parsons	Regina	D					
279	CGY	Pavel Torgayev	TPS Turku, FIN	LW	41	6	10	16	14
280	DAL	Chris Szysky	Swift Current	RW					
281	BOS	Andrei Yakhanov	Salavat Yulayev Ufa, CIS	D					
282	TOR	Doug Nolan	Catholic Memorial H.S.	LW					
283	DET	Toivo Suursoo	Krylja Sovetov, CIS	LW					
284	PIT	Brian Leitza	Sioux City Jr. A	G					
285	QUE	Steven Low	Sherbrooke	D					
286	NYR	Kim Johnsson	Malmo, SWE	D					

1995

"Opting in" became part of each year's Entry Draft procedure starting in 1995. The opting-in process required 18-year-olds and 19-year-olds born between September 16 and December 31 who hoped to be drafted to formally register with the league. The NHL's Central Registry department would confirm their eligibility and place their names on a list of available players. This process remains as a mandatory procedure for the Entry Draft.

The 1995 Entry Draft saw a defenseman taken first overall for the second consecutive year. Top-ranked prospect Bryan Berard, a native of Woonsocket, Rhode Island, was drafted by the Ottawa Senators and became just the third U.S.-born player to be selected first, joining Brian Lawton and Mike Modano. (Berard later joined Eric Lindros as the only first pick in the Entry Draft never to appear in uniform for the team that drafted him. He was a hold out from the Senators and was traded to the New York Islanders.) Prior to the draft, junior coach Paul Maurice stated: "There's always a lot of hype any time someone like this comes along. But with Bryan, it is warranted. He's the player everyone said he was going to be."

Berard captured top rookie honors in the Canadian Hockey League and was the CHL's top defenseman for two consecutive seasons. Upon entering the NHL, Berard made an immediate impact as one of the most promising and dangerous offensive blueliners. After recording eight goals and 40 assists in 1996–97, Berard captured the Calder Trophy and was named to the NHL All-Rookie Team.

The top three players selected in the 1995 draft were all defensemen as Wade Redden and Finnish native Aki-Petteri Berg were selected second and third respectively. Redden wound up going to Ottawa in the trade that sent Bryan Berard to the Islanders and he has developed into one of the league's most promising stay-at-home defensemen with the Senators, playing with the maturity and poise of an NHL veteran.

Berg, on the other hand, was touted as an offensive-minded defenseman who played a very physical game. To date, he has yet to demonstrate this consistently in the NHL.

Following the trend of 1994, there were three goaltenders selected in the first round of the 1995 draft. Jean-Sebastien Giguere was selected 13th overall followed by top-ranked goaltender Martin Biron who was selected 16th after receiving top rookie and top goaltending honors in the Quebec junior league. The Colorado Avalanche took Marc Denis 25th overall.

Ten 18-year-old talents immediately entered the NHL from the 1995 draft, as Chad Kilger (4th), Shane Doan (7th), Kyle McLaren (9th), Radek Dvorak (10th), Jarome Iginla (11th), Jay McKee (14th), Petr Sykora (18th), Jason Doig (34th), Aki-Petteri Berg and Martin Biron joined their respective NHL clubs. Biron became only the seventh goaltender to appear in the NHL as an 18-year-old.

McLaren and Dvorak played 74 and 62 games respectively as 18-year-olds. McLaren was selected to the NHL All-Rookie Team in 1996, where he was joined by Sykora. As the youngest talent on the Florida Panthers, Dvorak helped them to an appearance in the Stanley Cup finals in 1996. Iginla also emerged as a promising young talent in the NHL as he earned a selection to the NHL's All-Rookie Team in 1997.

Talents that emerged from later choices in the 1995 draft crop include 1997 CHL player of the year Alyn McCauley (79th) and overage Finnish talent Sami Kapanen (87th) who led the Carolina Hurricanes in scoring with a 26 goals and 37 assists for 63 points in 1997–98. Per Axelsson (177th), a native of Sweden, recorded 27 points (eight goals and 19 assists) in his rookie season with the Boston Bruins, while Cameron Mann (99th overall) has developed into one of the most promising prospects in the Bruins minor system.

1995

PICK	TEAM	NAME	DRAFTED FROM	NHL PLAYERS: POS / NHL GOALTENDERS: POS	GP / GP	G / W	A / GA	PTS / SO	PIM / AVG
FIRST ROUND									
1	OTT	Bryan Berard	Detroit	D	157	22	72	94	145
2	NYI	Wade Redden	Brandon	D	162	14	38	52	68
3	L.A.	Aki-Petteri Berg	Kiekko-67 Turku, FIN	D	164	2	21	23	114
4	ANA	Chad Kilger	Kingston	C	130	14	22	36	57
5	T.B.	Daymond Langkow	Tri-City	C	151	23	28	51	97
6	EDM	Steve Kelly	Prince Albert	C	51	3	3	6	29
7	WPG	Shane Doan	Kamloops	RW	170	16	24	40	185
8	MTL	Terry Ryan	Tri-City	LW	7	0	0	0	31
9	BOS	Kyle McLaren	Tacoma	D	198	15	41	56	183
10	FLA	Radek Dvorak	HC Ceske Budejovice, TCH	LW	219	43	59	102	83
11	DAL	Jarome Iginla	Kamloops	RW	152	34	48	82	66
12	S.J.	Teemo Riihijarvi	Kiekko-Espoo, FIN	RW					
13	HFD	J-S Giguere	Halifax	G	8	1	24	0	3.65
14	BUF	Jay McKee	Niagara Falls	D	100	2	23	25	79
15	TOR	Jeff Ware	Oshawa	D	15	0	0	0	6
16	BUF	Martin Biron	Beauport	G	3	0	10	0	5.04
17	WSH	Brad Church	Prince Albert	LW	2	0	0	0	0
18	N.J.	Petr Sykora	Detroit	C	140	35	46	81	58
19	CHI	Dmitri Nabokov	Krylja Sovetov, CIS	C	25	7	4	11	10
20	CGY	Denis Gauthier	Drummondville	D	10	0	0	0	16
21	BOS	Sean Brown	Belleville	D	23	0	1	1	47
22	PHI	Brian Boucher	Tri-City	G					
23	WSH	Miika Elomo	Kiekko-67 Turku, FIN	LW					
24	PIT	Alexei Morozov	Krylja Sovetov, CIS	RW	76	13	13	26	8
25	COL	Marc Denis	Chicoutimi	G	1	0	3	0	3.00
26	DET	Maxim Kuznetsov	Dynamo Moscow, CIS	D					
SECOND ROUND									
27	OTT	Marc Moro	Kingston	D	1	0	0	0	0
28	NYI	Jan Hlavac	Sparta Praha, CZE	LW					
29	ANA	Brian Wesenberg	Guelph	RW					
30	T.B.	Mike McBain	Red Deer	D	27	0	1	1	8
31	EDM	Georges Laraque	St-Jean	RW	11	0	0	0	59
32	WPG	Marc Chouinard	Beauport	C					
33	L.A.	Donald MacLean	Beauport	C	22	5	2	7	4
34	WPG	Jason Doig	Laval	D	19	1	2	3	40
35	HFD	Sergei Fedotov	Dynamo Moscow, CIS	D					
36	FLA	Aaron MacDonald	Swift Current	G					
37	DAL	Patrick Cote	Beauport	LW	8	0	0	0	47
38	S.J.	Peter Roed	White Bear Lake H.S.	C					
39	NYR	Christian Dube	Sherbrooke	C	27	1	1	2	4
40	VAN	Chris McAllister	Saskatoon	D	36	1	2	3	106
41	NYI	D.J. Smith	Windsor	D	8	0	1	1	7
42	BUF	Mark Dutiaume	Brandon	LW					
43	WSH	Dwayne Hay	Guelph	LW	2	0	0	0	2
44	N.J.	Nathan Perrott	Oshawa	RW					
45	CHI	Christian Laflamme	Beauport	D	76	0	12	12	61
46	CGY	Pavel Smirnov	Molot Perm, CIS	C/RW					
47	BOS	Paxton Schafer	Medicine Hat	G	3	0	6	0	4.68
48	PHI	Shane Kenny	Owen Sound	D					
49	ST.L.	Jochen Hecht	Mannheim, GER	C					
50	L.A.	Pavel Rosa	HC Chemo. Litvinov, CZE	RW					
51	COL	Nic Beaudoin	Detroit	LW					
52	DET	Philippe Audet	Granby	LW					
OTHER ROUNDS									
53	OTT	Brad Larsen	Swift Current	LW		Re-entered Draft in 1997			
54	TOR	Ryan Pepperall	Kitchener	RW					
55	ANA	Mike Leclerc	Brandon	LW	12	1	1	2	6
56	T.B.	Shane Willis	Prince Albert	RW		Re-entered Draft in 1997			
57	EDM	Lukas Zib	HC Ceske Budejovice, CZE	D					
58	DET	Darryl Laplante	Moose Jaw	C	2	0	0	0	0
59	L.A.	Vladimir Tsyplakov	Fort Wayne IHL	LW	163	39	62	101	34
60	MTL	Miloslav Guren	ZPS Zlin, CZE	D					
61	VAN	Larry Courville	Oshawa	LW	33	1	2	3	16
62	FLA	Mike O'Grady	Lethbridge	D					
63	DAL	Petr Buzek	Dukla Jihlava, CZE	D	2	0	0	0	2
64	S.J.	Marko Makinen	TPS Turku, FIN	RW					
65	NYR	Mike Martin	Windsor	D					
66	VAN	Peter Schaefer	Brandon	LW					
67	WPG	Brad Isbister	Portland	RW	66	9	8	17	102
68	BUF	Mathieu Sunderland	Drummondville	RW					
69	DAL	Sergei Gusev	CSK VVS Samara, CIS	D	9	0	0	0	2
70	N.J.	Sergei Vyshedkevich	Dynamo Moscow, CIS	D					
71	CHI	Kevin McKay	Moose Jaw	LW					
72	CGY	Rocky Thompson	Medicine Hat	D	12	0	0	0	61
73	BOS	Bill McCauley	Detroit	C					
74	MTL	Martin Hohenberger	Prince George	LW					
75	ST.L.	Scott Roche	North Bay	G					
76	PIT	Jean-Sebastien Aubin	Sherbrooke	G					
77	COL	John Tripp	Oshawa	RW		Re-entered Draft in 1997			
78	N.J.	David Gosselin	Sherbrooke	RW					
79	MTL	Alyn McCauley	Ottawa	C	60	6	10	16	6
80	FLA	Dave Duerden	Peterborough	LW					
81	COL	Tomi Kallio	Kiekko-67 Turku, FIN	LW					
82	CHI	Chris Van Dyk	Windsor	D					
83	EDM	Mike Minard	Chilliwack Jr. A	G					
84	WPG	Justin Kurtz	Brandon	D					
85	HFD	Ian MacNeil	Oshawa	C					
86	MTL	Jonathan Delisle	Hull	RW					
87	HFD	Sami Kapanen	HIFK Helsinki, FIN	LW	161	44	53	97	24
88	FLA	Daniel Tjarnqvist	Rogle Angelholm, SWE	D					
89	OTT	Kevin Bolibruck	Peterborough	D					
90	S.J.	Vesa Toskala	Ilves Tampere, FIN	G					
91	NYR	Marc Savard	Oshawa	C	28	1	5	6	4
92	VAN	Lloyd Shaw	Seattle	D					
93	WSH	Sebastien Charpentier	Laval	G					
94	BUF	Matt Davidson	Portland	RW					
95	WSH	Joel Theriault	Beauport	D					
96	N.J.	Henrik Rehnberg	Farjestad Karlstad, SWE	D					
97	CHI	Pavel Kriz	Tri-City	D					
98	CGY	Jan Labraaten	Farjestad Karlstad, SWE	LW					
99	BOS	Cameron Mann	Peterborough	RW	9	0	1	1	4
100	PHI	Radovan Somik	ZTS Martin, SVK	LW					
101	ST.L.	Michal Handzus	IS Banska Bystrica, SVK	C					
102	PIT	Oleg Belov	CSKA Moscow, CIS	C					
103	OTT	Kevin Boyd	London	LW					
104	DET	Anatoli Ustyugov	Torpedo Yaroslavl, CIS	LW					
105	WSH	Benoit Gratton	Laval	LW	6	0	1	1	6
106	NYI	Vladimir Orszagh	IS Banska Bystrica, SVK	RW	11	0	1	1	2
107	ANA	Igor Nikulin	Severstal Cherepovets, CIS	RW					
108	T.B.	Konst'in Golokhvastov	Dynamo Moscow, CIS	RW					
109	EDM	Jan Snopek	Oshawa	D					
110	NYR	Alexei Vasiliev	Torpedo-2 Yaroslavl, CIS	D					
111	BUF	Marian Menhart	HC Chemo. Litvinov, CZE	D					
112	MTL	Niklas Anger	Djurgarden, SWE	RW					
113	HFD	Hugh Hamilton	Spokane	D					
114	FLA	Francois Cloutier	Hull	LW					
115	DAL	Wade Strand	Regina	D					
116	S.J.	Miikka Kiprusoff	TPS Turku, FIN	G					
117	NYR	Dale Purinton	Tacoma	D					
118	L.A.	Jason Morgan	Kingston	C	14	1	0	1	4
119	BUF	Kevin Popp	Seattle	D					
120	VAN	Todd Norman	Guelph	LW					
121	WPG	Brian Elder	Brandon	G					
122	N.J.	Chris Mason	Prince George	G					
123	BUF	Daniel Bienvenue	Val d'Or	LW					
124	WSH	Joel Cort	Guelph	D					
125	DET	Chad Wilchynski	Regina	D					
126	DET	David Arsenault	Drummondville	G					
127	ST.L.	Jeff Ambrosio	Belleville	LW					
128	PIT	Jan Hrdina	Seattle	C					
129	COL	Brent Johnson	Owen Sound	G					
130	S.J.	Michal Bros	HC Olomouc, CZE	C					
131	OTT	David Hruska	Banik Sokolov, CZE	RW					
132	PHI	Dmitry Tertyshny	Traktor Chelyabinsk, CIS	D					
133	ANA	Peter LeBoutillier	Red Deer	RW	35	2	1	3	176
134	T.B.	Eduard Pershin	Dynamo Moscow, CIS	RW					
135	PHI	Jamie Sokolsky	Belleville	D					
136	WPG	Sylvain Daigle	Shawinigan	G					
137	L.A.	Igor Melyakov	Torpedo Yaroslavl, CIS	LW					
138	MTL	Boyd Olson	Tri-City	C					
139	TOR	Doug Bonner	Seattle	G					
140	S.J.	Timo Hakanen	Assat Pori, FIN	C					
141	DAL	Dominic Marleau	Victoriaville	D					
142	S.J.	Jaroslav Kudrna	Penticton Jr. A	LW					
143	NYR	Peter Slamiar	ZTK Zvolen, SVK	LW					
144	VAN	Brent Sopel	Swift Current	D					
145	TOR	Yannick Tremblay	Beauport	D	43	2	4	6	6
146	CHI	Marc Magliarditi	Des Moines Jr. A	G					
147	WSH	Frederick Jobin	Laval	D					
148	N.J.	Adam Young	Windsor	D					
149	CHI	Marty Wilford	Oshawa	D					
150	CGY	Clarke Wilm	Saskatoon	C					
151	BOS	Yevgeny Shaldybin	Torpedo Yaroslavl, CIS	D	3	1	0	1	0
152	PHI	Martin Spanhel	ZPS Zlin, CZE	LW					
153	ST.L.	Denis Hamel	Chicoutimi	LW					
154	PIT	Alexei Kolkunov	Krylja Sovetov, CIS	C					
155	COL	John Cirjak	Spokane	RW					
156	DET	Tyler Perry	Seattle	C					
157	L.A.	Benoit Larose	Sherbrooke	D					
158	NYI	Andrew Taylor	Detroit	LW					
159	ANA	Mike LaPlante	Calgary	D					
160	T.B.	Cory Murphy	Sault Ste. Marie	D					
161	EDM	Martin Cerven	Dukla Trencin, SVK	C					
162	WPG	Paul Traynor	Kitchener	D					
163	L.A.	Juha Vuorivirta	Tappara Tampere, FIN	C					
164	MTL	Stephane Robidas	Shawinigan	D					
165	HFD	Byron Ritchie	Lethbridge	C					
166	FLA	Peter Worrell	Hull	LW	19	0	0	0	153
167	S.J.	Brad Mehalko	Lethbridge	RW					
168	S.J.	Robert Jindrich	HC Interconex Plzen, CZE	D					
169	NYR	Jeff Heil	Wisconsin-River Falls	G					

PICK	TEAM	NAME	DRAFTED FROM	POS	GP	G	A	PTS	PIM
170	VAN	Stewart Bodtker	Colorado College	C					
171	TOR	Marek Melenovsky	Dukla Jihlava, CZE	C					
172	BUF	Brian Scott	Kitchener	LW					
173	DAL	Jeff Dewar	Moose Jaw	RW					
174	N.J.	Richard Rochefort	Sudbury	C					
175	CHI	Steve Tardif	Drummondville	C					
176	CGY	Ryan Gillis	North Bay	D					
177	BOS	Per-Johan Axelsson	Vastra Frolunda, SWE	LW	82	8	19	27	38
178	PHI	Martin Streit	HC Olomouc, CZE	LW					
179	ST.L.	J-L Grand Pierre	Val d'Or	D					
180	PIT	Derrick Pyke	Halifax	RW					
181	COL	Dan Smith	U. of British Columbia	D					
182	DET	Per Eklund	Djurgarden, SWE	LW					
183	OTT	Kaj Linna	Boston U.	D					
184	OTT	Ray Schultz	Tri-City	D	13	0	1	1	45
185	ANA	Igor Karpenko	Sokol Kiev, CIS	G					
186	T.B.	Joe Cardarelli	Spokane	LW					
187	EDM	Stephen Douglas	Niagara Falls	D					
188	WPG	Jaroslav Obsut	North Battleford	D					
189	WPG	Fredrik Loven	Djurgarden, SWE	C					
190	MTL	Greg Hart	Kamloops	RW					
191	HFD	Milan Kostolny	Detroit	RW					
192	FLA	Filip Kuba	HC Vitkovice, CZE	D					
193	DAL	Anatoli Koveshnikov	Sokol Kiev, CIS	RW					
194	S.J.	Ryan Kraft	Minnesota-Duluth	C					
195	NYR	Ilja Gorokhov	Torpedo Yaroslavl, CIS	D					
196	VAN	Tyler Willis	Swift Current	RW					
197	TOR	Mark Murphy	Stratford Jr. B	LW					
198	BUF	Mike Zanutto	Oshawa	C					
199	WSH	Vasili Turkovsky	CSKA Moscow, CIS	D					
200	N.J.	Frederic Henry	Granby	G					
201	CHI	Casey Hankinson	Minnesota-Duluth	LW					
202	DAL	Sergei Luchinkin	Dynamo Moscow, CIS	RW					
203	BOS	Sergei Zhukov	Torpedo Yaroslavl, CIS	D					
204	PHI	Ruslan Shafikov	Salavat Yulayev Ufa, CIS	C					
205	ST.L.	Derek Bekar	Powell River Jr. A	C					
206	PIT	Sergei Voronov	Dynamo Moscow, CIS	D					
207	COL	Tomi Hirvonen	Ilves Tampere, FIN	C					
208	DET	Andrei Samokhvalov	Torpedo Ust-Kamen'k, CIS	RW					
209	ST.L.	Libor Zabransky	HC Ceske Budejovice, TCH	D	40	1	6	7	50
210	NYI	David MacDonald	Sudbury	G					
211	NYI	Mike Broda	Moose Jaw	LW					
212	T.B.	Zac Bierk	Peterborough	G	13	1	30	0	4.16
213	EDM	Jiri Antonin	HC Pardubice, CZE	D					
214	WPG	Rob Deciantis	Kitchener	C					
215	L.A.	Brian Stewart	Sault Ste. Marie	D					
216	MTL	Eric Houde	Halifax	C	22	1	2	3	2
217	HFD	Mike Rucinski	Detroit	D	9	0	1	1	2
218	FLA	David Lemanowicz	Spokane	G					
219	DAL	Stephen Lowe	Sault Ste. Marie	C					
220	S.J.	Mikko Markkanen	TPS Turku, FIN	RW					
221	NYR	Bob Maudie	Kamloops	C					
222	VAN	Jason Cugnet	Kelowna Jr. A	G					
223	TOR	Daniil Markov	Spartak Moscow, CIS	D	25	2	5	7	28
224	BUF	Rob Skrlac	Kamloops	LW					
225	WSH	Scott Swanson	Omaha Jr. A	D					
226	N.J.	Colin O'Hara	Winnipeg Jr. A	D					
227	CHI	Mike Pittman	Guelph	C					
228	COL	Chris George	Sarnia	RW					
229	BOS	Jonathon Murphy	Peterborough	D					
230	PHI	Jeff Lank	Prince Albert	D					
231	OTT	Erik Kaminski	Cleveland Jr.	RW					
232	PIT	Frank Ivankovic	Oshawa	G					
233	CGY	Steve Shirreffs	Hotchkiss H.S.	D					
234	DET	David Engblom	Vallentuna, SWE	C					

1996

The 1996 Entry Draft saw a defenseman selected first overall for the third consecutive year as top-ranked prospect Chris Phillips was taken by the Ottawa Senators. After receiving rookie of the year honors in the WHL, Phillips' junior coach Chris Stewart stated: "The thing that struck me was I knew he'd be a good player and I knew I wouldn't have a problem with him. But I didn't realize that he would start off on the first power-play unit, he would start off on the first penalty-killing unit, and he would contribute in the magnitude that he did, especially in the first 20 games." Although drafted as a defenseman, Phillips has played a dual role with the Senators, being used as a forward as well. The San Jose Sharks took another defenseman as the second overall pick, selecting the Russian-born Andrei Zyuzin.

Unlike the previous two drafts, the crop was thin in goaltending talent as only one goaltender was taken in the first round. The Pittsburgh Penguins took top-ranked netminder Craig Hillier 23rd overall.

A dark horse talent was taken in the first round as the Mighty Ducks of Anaheim took overage defenseman Ruslan Salei. Salei, a native of Belarus, played with the Las Vegas Thunder of the IHL, following in the footsteps of Radek Bonk and Petr Sykora as first-round picks to come from the IHL. Salei immediately entered the league with the Ducks and has emerged as one of the club's premier defensemen. However, the Cinderella story of the 1996 draft was the selection and development of Lithuanian-born Danius Zubrus. Drafted from Ontario's provincial (Tier II) junior league, Zubrus was taken 15th overall by the Philadelphia Flyers and was the only 18-year-old talent to immediately break into the NHL. Not only did Zubrus make the Flyers' roster, he was promoted to the first line, forming the missing link on the team's Legion of Doom line with captain Eric Lindros and John LeClair. Though Zubrus recorded only 21 points (eight goals and 13 assists) in his rookie season, he was selected to the NHL's All-Rookie Team in 1997. Zubrus is one of very few players to appear in the Stanley Cup finals as an 18-year-old.

Like the few previous drafts, the 1996 crop will continue to produce new NHL talent. Some of the most noticeable players who have already emerged are Calgary's first two choices, defensemen Derek Morris (13th) and Steve Begin (40th). Morris enjoyed a solid rookie season in 1997–98 and received strong consideration for the Calder Trophy and the All-Rookie Team. In addition, German-born Marco Sturm also made an impact in his first season in the NHL recording 30 points for the Sharks in 1997–98.

The 1996 Entry Draft saw another dimension added to the NHL as the New York Islanders selected the tallest player to appear in the NHL. The 6'8" Czech-born defenseman Zdeno Chara was taken as the 56th player in the draft and graduated to the league in 1997–98.

1996

PICK	TEAM	NAME	DRAFTED FROM	POS	GP	G	A	PTS	PIM
FIRST ROUND									
1	OTT	Chris Phillips	Prince Albert	D	72	5	11	16	38
2	S.J.	Andrei Zyuzin	Salavat Yulayev Ufa, CIS	D	56	6	7	13	66
3	NYI	Jean-Pierre Dumont	Val d'Or	RW					
4	WSH	Alexander Volchkov	Barrie	C					
5	DAL	Richard Jackman	Sault Ste. Marie	D					
6	EDM	Boyd Devereaux	Kitchener	C	38	1	4	5	6
7	BUF	Erik Rasmussen	Minnesota-Duluth	C	21	2	3	5	14
8	BOS	Johnathan Aitken	Medicine Hat	D					
9	ANA	Ruslan Salei	Las Vegas IHL	D	96	5	11	16	107
10	N.J.	Lance Ward	Red Deer	D					
11	PHX	Dan Focht	Tri-City	D					
12	VAN	Josh Holden	Regina	C					
13	CGY	Derek Morris	Regina	D	82	9	20	29	88
14	ST.L.	Marty Reasoner	Boston College	C					
15	PHI	Dainius Zubrus	Pembroke Jr. A	RW	137	16	38	54	64
16	T.B.	Mario Larocque	Hull	D					
17	WSH	Jaroslav Svejkovsky	Tri-City	RW	36	11	4	15	14
18	MTL	Matt Higgins	Moose Jaw	C	1	0	0	0	0
19	EDM	Matthieu Descoteaux	Shawinigan	D					
20	FLA	Marcus Nilson	Djurgarden, SWE	LW					
21	S.J.	Marco Sturm	Landshut, GER	C	74	10	20	30	40
22	NYR	Jeff Brown	Sarnia	D					
23	PIT	Craig Hillier	Ottawa	G					
24	PHX	Daniel Briere	Drummondville	C	5	1	0	1	2
25	COL	Peter Ratchuk	Shattuck St. Mary's H.S.	D					
26	DET	Jesse Wallin	Red Deer	D					
SECOND ROUND									
27	BUF	Cory Sarich	Saskatoon	D					
28	PIT	Pavel Skrbek	HC Poldi Kladno, CZE	D					
29	NYI	Dan Lacouture	Junior Whalers	LW					
30	L.A.	Josh Green	Medicine Hat	LW					

1996 continued

PICK	TEAM	NAME	DRAFTED FROM	NHL PLAYERS: POS / NHL GOALTENDERS: POS	GP	G/W	A/GA	PTS/SO	PIM/AVG
31	CHI	Remi Royer	St-Hyacinthe	D					
32	EDM	Chris Hajt	Guelph	D					
33	BUF	Darren Van Oene	Brandon	LW					
34	HFD	Trevor Wasyluk	Medicine Hat	LW					
35	ANA	Matt Cullen	St. Cloud State	C	61	6	21	27	23
36	TOR	Marek Posmyk	Dukla Jihlava, CZE	D					
37	L.A.	Marian Cisar	Slovan Bratislava, SVK	RW					
38	N.J.	Wes Mason	Sarnia	LW					
39	CGY	Travis Brigley	Lethbridge	LW	2	0	0	0	2
40	CGY	Steve Begin	Val d'Or	C	5	0	0	0	23
41	N.J.	Joshua Dewolf	Twin Cities Jr.	D					
42	CHI	Jeff Paul	Niagara Falls	D					
43	WSH	Jan Bulis	Barrie	C	48	5	11	16	18
44	MTL	Mathieu Garon	Victoriaville	G					
45	BOS	Henry Kuster	Medicine Hat	RW					
46	CHI	Geoff Peters	Niagara Falls	C					
47	N.J.	Pierre Dagenais	Moncton	LW					
48	NYR	Daniel Goneau	Granby	LW	52	12	3	15	14
49	N.J.	Colin White	Hull	D					
50	TOR	Francis Larivee	Laval	G					
51	COL	Yuri Babenko	Krylja Sovetov, CIS	C					
52	DET	Aren Miller	Spokane	G					

OTHER ROUNDS

PICK	TEAM	NAME	DRAFTED FROM	POS	GP	G/W	A/GA	PTS/SO	PIM/AVG
53	BOS	Eric Naud	St-Hyacinthe	LW					
54	BUF	Francois Methot	St-Hyacinthe	C					
55	S.J.	Terry Friesen	Swift Current	G					
56	NYI	Zdeno Chara	Dukla Trencin, SVK	D	25	0	1	1	50
57	L.A.	Greg Phillips	Saskatoon	C					
58	WSH	Sergei Zimakov	Krylja Sovetov, CIS	D					
59	EDM	Tom Poti	Cushing Academy	D					
60	FLA	Chris Allen	Kingston	D	1	0	0	0	2
61	HFD	Andrei Petrunin	CSKA Moscow, CIS	RW					
62	PHX	Per-Anton Lundstrom	MoDo Ornskoldsvik, SWE	D					
63	N.J.	Scott Parker	Kelowna	RW	Re-entered Draft in 1998				
64	PHI	Chester Gallant	Niagara Falls	RW					
65	FLA	Oleg Kvasha	CSKA Moscow, CIS	LW					
66	TOR	Mike Lankshear	Guelph	D					
67	ST.L.	Gordie Dwyer	Beauport	LW					
68	TOR	Konstantin Kalmikov	Detroit	LW					
69	T.B.	Curtis Tipler	Regina	RW					
70	DAL	Jonathan Sim	Sarnia	C					
71	MTL	Arron Asham	Red Deer	RW					
72	PIT	Boyd Kane	Regina	LW					
73	CGY	Dmitri Vlasenkov	Torpedo Yaroslavl, CIS	LW					
74	WSH	Dave Weninger	Michigan Tech	G					
75	VAN	Zenith Komarniski	Tri-City	D					
76	NYR	Dmitri Subbotin	CSKA Moscow, CIS	LW					
77	PIT	Boris Protsenko	Calgary	RW					
78	WSH	Shawn McNeil	Kamloops	C					
79	COL	Mark Parrish	St. Cloud State	LW					
80	BOS	Jason Doyle	Sault Ste. Marie	RW					
81	OTT	Antti-Jussi Niemi	Jokerit Helsinki, FIN	D					
82	FLA	Joey Tetarenko	Portland	D					
83	NYI	Tyrone Garner	Oshawa	G					
84	L.A.	Mikael Simons	Mora, SWE	C					
85	WSH	Justin Davis	Kingston	RW					
86	TOR	Jason Sessa	Lake Superior State	RW					
87	BUF	Kurt Walsh	Owen Sound	RW					
88	HFD	Craig MacDonald	Harvard	C					
89	CGY	Toni Lydman	Reipas Lahti, FIN	D					
90	DAL	Mike Hurley	Tri-City	RW					
91	N.J.	Josef Boumedienne	Huddinge, SWE	D					
92	MTL	Kim Staal	Malmo, SWE	C					
93	VAN	Jonas Soling	Huddinge, SWE	RW					
94	CGY	Christian Lefebvre	Granby	D	Re-entered Draft in 1998				
95	ST.L.	Jonathan Zukiwsky	Red Deer	C					
96	L.A.	Eric Belanger	Beauport	C					
97	ST.L.	Andrei Petrakov	Avtomobilist Yekat'burg, CIS	RW					
98	COL	Ben Storey	Harvard	D					
99	MTL	Etienne Drapeau	Beauport	C					
100	BOS	Trent Whitfield	Spokane	C					
101	N.J.	Josh MacNevin	Vernon Jr. A	D					
102	S.J.	Matt Bradley	Kingston	RW					
103	TOR	Vladimir Antipov	Torpedo Yaroslavl, CIS	RW					
104	HFD	Steve Wasylko	Detroit	C					
105	PIT	Michal Rozsival	Dukla Jihlava, CZE	D					
106	BUF	Mike Martone	Peterborough	D					
107	COL	Randy Petruk	Kamloops	G					
108	DET	Johan Forsander	HV-71 Jonkoping, SWE	LW					
109	NYI	Andy Berenzweig	Michigan	D					
110	TOR	Peter Cava	Sault Ste. Marie	C					
111	TOR	Brandon Sugden	London	D					
112	DAL	Ryan Christie	Owen Sound	LW					
113	DAL	Yevgeny Tsybuk	Torpedo Yaroslavl, CIS	D					
114	EDM	Brian Urick	U. of Notre Dame	RW					
115	BUF	Alexei Tezikov	Lada Togliatti, CIS	D					
116	HFD	Mark McMahon	Kitchener	D					
117	ANA	Brendan Buckley	Boston College	D					
118	N.J.	Glenn Crawford	Windsor	C					
119	PHX	Richard Lintner	Dukla Trencin, SVK	D					
120	L.A.	Jesse Black	Niagara Falls	D					
121	VAN	Tyler Prosofsky	Kelowna	C					
122	CGY	Josef Straka	HC Chemo. Litvinov, CZE	C					
123	L.A.	Peter Hogan	Oshawa	D					
124	PHI	Per-Ragnar Bergqvist	Leksand, SWE	G					
125	T.B.	Jason Robinson	Niagara Falls	D					
126	WSH	Matthew Lahey	Peterborough	LW					
127	MTL	Daniel Archambault	Val d'Or	C					
128	NYI	Peter Sachl	HC Ceske Budejovice, CZE	C					
129	FLA	Andrew Long	Guelph	RW					
130	CHI	Andy Johnson	Peterborough	D					
131	NYR	Colin Pepperall	Niagara Falls	LW					
132	BOS	Elias Abrahamsson	Halifax	D					
133	PHI	Jesse Boulerice	Detroit	D					
134	COL	Luke Curtin	Kelowna	LW					
135	DET	Michal Podolka	Sault Ste. Marie	G					
136	OTT	Andreas Dackell	Brynas Gavle, SWE	RW	161	27	37	64	32
137	S.J.	Michel Larocque	Boston U.	G					
138	NYI	Todd Miller	Sarnia	C					
139	PHX	Robert Esche	Detroit	G					
140	TOR	Dmitri Yakushin	Pembroke Jr. A	D					
141	EDM	Bryan Randall	Medicine Hat	C					
142	BUF	Ryan Davis	Owen Sound	RW					
143	HFD	Aaron Baker	Tri-City	G					
144	DET	Magnus Nilsson	Vita Hasten, SWE	RW					
145	N.J.	Sean Ritchlin	Michigan	RW					
146	COL	Brian Willsie	Guelph	RW					
147	VAN	Nolan McDonald	Vermont	G					
148	TOR	Chris Bogas	Michigan State	D					
149	ANA	Blaine Russell	Prince Albert	G					
150	PIT	Peter Bergman	Kamloops	C					
151	TOR	Lucio DeMartinis	Shawinigan	LW					
152	T.B.	Nikolai Ignatov	CSKA Moscow, CIS	D					
153	WSH	Andrew Van Bruggen	Northern Michigan	RW					
154	MTL	Brett Clark	U. of Maine	D	41	1	0	1	20
155	BOS	Chris Lane	Spokane	D					
156	FLA	Gaetan Poirier	Merrimack	LW					
157	T.B.	Xavier Delisle	Granby	C					
158	NYR	Ola Sandberg	Djurgarden, SWE	D					
159	ST.L.	Stephen Wagner	Olds Jr. A	G					
160	COL	Kai Fischer	Dusseldorf, GER	G					
161	BUF	Darren Mortier	Sarnia	C					
162	DET	Alexandre Jacques	Shawinigan	C					
163	OTT	Francois Hardy	Val d'Or	D					
164	S.J.	Jake Deadmarsh	Kamloops	D					
165	NYI	Joe Prestifilippo	Hotchkiss H.S.	G					
166	DAL	Eoin McInerney	London	G					
167	COL	Dan Hinote	Army	RW					
168	EDM	David Bernier	St-Hyacinthe	C					
169	ST.L.	Daniel Corso	Victoriaville	C					
170	EDM	Brandon Lafrance	Ohio State	RW					
171	HFD	Greg Kuznik	Seattle	D					
172	ANA	Timo Ahmaoja	JyP HT Jyvaskyla, FIN	D					
173	N.J.	Daryl Andrews	Melfort Jr. A	D					
174	PHX	Trevor Letowski	Sarnia	C					
175	VAN	Clint Cabana	Medicine Hat	D					
176	COL	Samual Pahlsson	MoDo Ornskoldsvik, SWE	C					
177	ST.L.	Reed Low	Moose Jaw	RW					
178	TOR	Reggie Berg	Minnesota-Duluth	C					
179	T.B.	Pavel Kubina	HC Vitkovice, CZE	D	10	1	2	3	22
180	WSH	Michael Anderson	Minnesota-Duluth	RW					
181	MTL	Timo Vertala	JyP HT Jyvaskyla, FIN	RW					
182	BOS	Thomas Brown	Sarnia	D					
183	FLA	Alexandre Couture	Victoriaville	D					
184	CHI	Mike Vellinga	Guelph	D					
185	NYR	Jeff Dessner	Taft H.S.	D					
186	PIT	Eric Meloche	Cornwall	RW					
187	PHI	Roman Malov	Avangard Omsk, CIS	LW					
188	COL	Roman Pylner	HC Chemo. Litvinov, CZE	C					
189	DET	Colin Beardsmore	North Bay	C					
190	L.A.	Stephen Valiquette	Sudbury	G					
191	S.J.	Cory Cyrenne	Brandon	C					
192	NYI	Evgeny Korolev	Peterborough	D					
193	L.A.	Kai Nurminen	HV-71 Jonkoping, SWE	LW	67	16	11	27	22
194	DAL	Joel Kwiatkowski	Prince George	D					
195	EDM	Fernando Pisani	St. Albert Jr. A	C/LW					
196	ST.L.	Andrej Podkonicky	ZTK Zvolen, SVK	C					
197	HFD	Kevin Marsh	Calgary	LW					
198	ANA	Kevin Kellett	Prince Albert	D					
199	N.J.	Willie Mitchell	Melfort Jr. A	D					
200	PHX	Nicholas Lent	Omaha Jr. A	RW					
201	VAN	Jeff Scissons	Vernon Jr. A	C					
202	CGY	Ryan Wade	Kelowna	RW					
203	ST.L.	Tony Hutchins	Lawrence Academy	C					

PICK	TEAM	NAME	DRAFTED FROM	NHL PLAYERS: POS NHL GOALTENDERS: POS	GP GP	G W	A GA	PTS SO	PIM AVG
204	TOR	Tomas Kaberle	HC Poldi Kladno, CZE	D					
205	N.J.	Jay Bertsch	Spokane	RW					
206	WSH	Oleg Orekhovsky	Dynamo Moscow, CIS	D					
207	MTL	Mattia Baldi	Ambri Piotta, SUI	F					
208	BOS	Bob Prier	St. Lawrence U.	RW					
209	FLA	Denis Khloptonov	CSKA Moscow, CIS	G					
210	CHI	Chris Twerdun	Moose Jaw	D					
211	NYR	Ryan McKie	London	D					
212	OTT	Erich Goldmann	Mannheim, GER	D					
213	PHI	Jeff Milleker	Moose Jaw	D					
214	COL	Matthew Scorsune	Hotchkiss H.S.	D					
215	DET	Craig Stahl	Tri-City	RW					
216	OTT	Ivan Ciernik	HC Nitra, SVK	LW	2	0	0	0	0
217	S.J.	David Thibeault	Drummondville	LW					
218	NYI	Mike Muzechka	Calgary	D					
219	L.A.	Sebastien Simard	Drummondville	LW					
220	DAL	Nick Bootland	Guelph	LW					
221	EDM	John Hultberg	Kingston	G					
222	BUF	Scott Buhler	Medicine Hat	G					
223	HFD	Craig Adams	Harvard	RW					
224	ANA	Tobias Johansson	Malmo, SWE	LW					
225	N.J.	Pasi Petrilainen	Tappara Tampere, FIN	D					
226	PHX	Marc-Etienne Hubert	Laval	C					
227	VAN	Lubomir Vaic	HC Kosice, SVK	C	5	1	1	2	2
228	CGY	Ronald Petrovicky	Prince George	RW					
229	ST.L.	Konstantin Shafranov	Fort Wayne IHL	RW	5	2	1	3	0
230	TOR	Jared Hope	Spokane	C					
231	HFD	Askhat Rakhmatullin	Salavat Yulayev Ufa, CIS	LW					
232	WSH	Chad Cavanagh	London	C					
233	MTL	Michel Tremblay	Shawinigan	LW					
234	BOS	Anders Soderberg	MoDo Ornskoldsvik, SWE	RW					
235	FLA	Russell Smith	Hull	D					
236	CHI	Andrei Kozyrev	Severstal Cherepovets, CIS	D					
237	NYR	Ronnie Sundin	Vastra Frolunda, SWE	D	1	0	0	0	0
238	PIT	Timo Seikkula	Junkkarit Kalajoki, FIN	C					
239	OTT	Sami Salo	TPS Turku, FIN	D					
240	COL	Justin Clark	Michigan	RW					
241	DET	Evgeny Afanasiev	Detroit L.C. Midgets	LW					

1997

The 1997 Entry Draft was hailed as the best in years as forward Joe Thornton became the most publicized prospect since Eric Lindros in 1991. Thornton was touted as the consensus number one pick where he remained, selected by the Bruins first overall. Thornton is expected to develop into a franchise player; however, it was the Bruins' second choice that really made an impression in the NHL in 1997–98. Russian-born Sergei Samsonov was drafted eighth overall by the Bruins from the IHL's Detroit Vipers. Both Thornton and Samsonov entered the NHL as 18-year-olds, but Thornton went on to record only seven points (three goals and four assists), Samsonov posted 22 goals and 25 assists to lead all rookie scorers with 47 points and finish the season with the Boston's fourth-highest point total. He won the Calder Trophy as the NHL's top rookie.

In total there were seven 18-year-old talents who immediately entered the NHL from the 1997 draft crop, including offensive talents Patrick Marleau (second overall by the San Jose Sharks), Finnish born Olli Jokinen (third by the Los Angels Kings), Newfoundland native Daniel Cleary (10th by the Chicago Blackhawks) and Marian Hossa (12th by the Ottawa Senators). However, only Thornton, Marleau and Samsonov lasted the entire year with their respective big-league clubs.

Marleau was the youngest player to enter the draft, as he turned 17 on the date of eligibility, thus making him the youngest player in the NHL. Top goaltending talent Roberto Luongo became the highest-drafted goaltender in Entry Draft history when the New York Islanders selected him fourth overall. The Islanders had the opportunity to select two consecutive picks, and took blueliner Eric Brewer fifth. The Blackhawks were also had two first-round picks, taking Cleary and Alaskan-born Ty Jones.

1997

PICK	TEAM	NAME	DRAFTED FROM	NHL PLAYERS: POS NHL GOALTENDERS: POS	GP GP	G W	A GA	PTS SO	PIM AVG
FIRST ROUND									
1	BOS	Joe Thornton	Sault Ste. Marie	C	55	3	4	7	19
2	S.J.	Patrick Marleau	Seattle	C	74	13	19	32	14
3	L.A.	Olli Jokinen	HIFK Helsinki, FIN	C	8	0	0	0	6
4	NYI	Roberto Luongo	Val d'Or	G					
5	NYI	Eric Brewer	Prince George	D					
6	CGY	Daniel Tkaczuk	Barrie	C					
7	T.B.	Paul Mara	Sudbury	D					
8	BOS	Sergei Samsonov	Detroit	LW	81	22	25	47	8
9	WSH	Nicholas Boynton	Ottawa	D					
10	VAN	Brad Ference	Spokane	D					
11	MTL	Jason Ward	Erie	RW/C					
12	OTT	Marian Hossa	Dukla Trencin, SVK	LW	7	0	1	1	0
13	CHI	Daniel Cleary	Belleville	LW	6	0	0	0	0
14	EDM	Michel Riesen	Biel-Bienne, SUI	LW					
15	L.A.	Matt Zultek	Ottawa	LW					
16	CHI	Ty Jones	Spokane	RW					
17	PIT	Robert Dome	Las Vegas IHL	RW	30	5	2	7	12
18	ANA	Mikael Holmqvist	Djurgarden, SWE	C					
19	NYR	Stefan Cherneski	Brandon	RW					
20	FLA	Mike Brown	Red Deer	C					
21	BUF	Mika Noronen	Tappara Tampere, FIN	G					
22	CAR	Nikos Tselios	Belleville	D					
23	S.J.	Scott Hannan	Kelowna	D					
24	N.J.	J-F Damphousse	Moncton	G					
25	DAL	Brenden Morrow	Portland	LW					
26	COL	Kevin Grimes	Kingston	D					
SECOND ROUND									
27	BOS	Ben Clymer	Minnesota-Duluth	D					
28	CAR	Brad DeFauw	North Dakota	LW					
29	L.A.	Scott Barney	Peterborough	C					
30	PHI	Jean-Marc Pelletier	Cornell	G					
31	NYI	Jeff Zehr	Windsor	LW/C					
32	CGY	Evan Lindsay	Prince Albert	G					
33	T.B.	Kyle Kos	Red Deer	D					
34	VAN	Ryan Bonni	Saskatoon	D					
35	WSH	Jean-Francois Fortin	Sherbrooke	D					
36	VAN	Harold Druken	Detroit	C					
37	MTL	Gregor Baumgartner	Laval	LW					
38	N.J.	Stanislav Gron	Slovan Bratislava, SVK	C					
39	CHI	Jeremy Reich	Seattle	C					
40	ST.L.	Tyler Rennette	North Bay	C					
41	EDM	Patrick Dovigi	Erie	G					
42	CGY	John Tripp	Oshawa	RW					
43	PHX	Juha Gustafsson	Kiekko-Espoo, FIN	D					
44	PIT	Brian Gaffaney	North Iowa Jr. A	D					
45	ANA	Maxim Balmochnykh	Lada Togliatti, RUS	LW					
46	NYR	Wes Jarvis	Kitchener	D					
47	FLA	Kristian Huselius	Farjestad Karlstad, SWE	LW					
48	BUF	Henrik Tallinder	AIK Solna, SWE	D					
49	DET	Yuri Butsayev	Lada Togliatti, RUS	C					
50	PHI	Pat Kavanagh	Peterborough	RW					
51	CGY	Dmitri Kokorev	Dynamo-2 Moscow, RUS	D					
52	DAL	Roman Lyashenko	Torpedo Yaroslavl, RUS	C					
53	COL	Graham Belak	Edmonton	C					
OTHER ROUNDS									
54	BOS	Mattias Karlin	MoDo Ornskoldsvik, SWE	C/RW					
55	COL	Rick Berry	Seattle	D					
56	FLA	Vratislav Cech	Kitchener	D					
57	TOR	Jeff Farkas	Boston College	C					
58	OTT	Jani Hurme	TPS Turku, FIN	G					
59	NYI	Jarrett Smith	Prince George	C					
60	CGY	Derek Schutz	Spokane	C					
61	T.B.	Matt Elich	Windsor	RW					
62	PHI	Kris Mallette	Kelowna	D					
63	BOS	Lee Goren	North Dakota	RW					
64	VAN	Kyle Freadrich	Regina	LW					
65	MTL	Ilkka Mikkola	Karpat Oulu, FIN	D					
66	OTT	Josh Langfeld	Lincoln Jr.	RW					
67	CHI	Mike Souza	New Hampshire	LW					
68	EDM	Sergei Yerkovich	Las Vegas IHL	D					
69	BUF	Maxim Afinogenov	Dynamo Moscow, RUS	RW					
70	CGY	Erik Andersson	U. of Denver	C	12	2	1	3	8
71	PIT	Josef Melichar	HC Ceske Budejovice, CZE	D					
72	ANA	Jay LeGault	London	LW					
73	NYR	Burke Henry	Brandon	D					
74	FLA	Nick Smith	Barrie	C					
75	BUF	Jeff Martin	Windsor	C					
76	DET	Petr Sykora	HC Poji. IB Pardubice, CZE	C					
77	DAL	Steve Gainey	Kamloops	C					
78	COL	Ville Nieminen	Tappara Tampere, FIN	RW					
79	NYI	Robert Schnabel	Slavia Praha, CZE	D					
80	CAR	Francis Lessard	Val d'Or	D					
81	BOS	Karol Bartanus	Drummondville	RW					
82	S.J.	Adam Colagiacomo	Oshawa	RW					

1997 *continued*

PICK	TEAM	NAME	DRAFTED FROM	POS	GP	G	A	PTS	PIM
83	L.A.	Joseph Corvo	Western Michigan	D					
84	TOR	Adam Mair	Owen Sound	C					
85	NYI	Petr Mika	Slavia Praha, CZE	LW					
86	ST.L.	Didier Tremblay	Halifax	D					
87	COL	Brad Larsen	Swift Current	LW	1	0	0	0	0
88	CAR	Shane Willis	Lethbridge	RW					
89	WSH	Curtis Cruickshank	Kingston	G					
90	VAN	Chris Stanley	Belleville	C					
91	MTL	Daniel Tetrault	Brandon	D					
92	CGY	Chris St. Croix	Kamloops	D					
93	NYR	Tomi Kallarsson	HPK Hameenlinna, FIN	D					
94	EDM	Jonas Elofsson	Farjestad Karlstad, SWE	D					
95	FLA	Ivan Novoseltsev	Krylja Sovetov, RUS	RW					
96	PHX	Scott McCallum	Tri-City	D					
97	PIT	Alexandre Mathieu	Halifax	D					
98	ST.L.	Jan Horacek	Slavia Praha, CZE	D					
99	L.A.	Sean Blanchard	Ottawa	D					
100	CGY	Ryan Ready	Belleville	LW					
101	BUF	Luc Theoret	Lethbridge	D					
102	DET	Quintin Laing	Kelowna	LW					
103	PHI	Mikhail Chernov	Torpedo-2 Yaroslavl, RUS	D					
104	N.J.	Lucas Nehrling	Sarnia	D					
105	DAL	Marc Kristofferson	Mora, SWE	D					
106	ST.L.	Jame Pollock	Seattle	D					
107	S.J.	Adam Nittel	Erie	RW					
108	T.B.	Mark Thompson	Regina	D					
109	T.B.	Jan Sulc	HC Chemo. Litvinov, CZE	C					
110	CHI	Benjamin Simon	U. of Notre Dame	C					
111	TOR	Frantisek Mrazek	HC Ceske Budejovice, CZE	LW					
112	T.B.	Karel Betik	Kelowna	D					
113	CGY	Martin Moise	Beauport	LW					
114	VAN	David Darguzas	Edmonton	C					
115	NYI	Adam Edinger	Bowling Green	C					
116	WSH	Kevin Caulfield	Boston College	RW					
117	VAN	Matt Cockell	Saskatoon	G					
118	MTL	Konstantin Sidulov	Traktor Chelyabinsk, RUS	LW					
119	OTT	Magnus Arvedson	Farjestad Karlstad, SWE	C	61	11	15	26	36
120	CHI	Peter Gardiner	RPI	RW					
121	EDM	Jason Chimera	Medicine Hat	C					
122	MTL	Gennady Razin	Kamloops	D					
123	PHX	Curtis Suter	Spokane	D					
124	PIT	Harlan Pratt	Prince Albert	D					
125	ANA	Luc Vaillancourt	Beauport	G					
126	NYR	Jason McLean	Moose Jaw	G					
127	FLA	Pat Parthenais	Detroit	D					
128	BUF	Torrey DiRoberto	Seattle	C					
129	DET	John Wikstrom	Lulea, SWE	D					
130	CHI	Kyle Calder	Regina	C					
131	N.J.	Jiri Bicek	HC Kosice, SVK	LW					
132	DAL	Teemu Elomo	TPS Turku, FIN	LW					
133	COL	Aaron Miskovich	Green Bay Jr.	C					
134	NYR	Johan Lindbom	HV-71 Jonkoping, SWE	LW	38	1	3	4	28
135	BOS	Denis Timofeyev	CSKA-2 Moscow, RUS	D					
136	NYR	Michael York	Michigan State	C					
137	L.A.	Richard Seeley	Prince Albert	D					
138	TOR	Eric Gooldy	Detroit	LW					
139	NYI	Bobby Leavins	Brandon	LW					
140	CGY	Ilja Demidov	Dynamo-2 Moscow, RUS	D					
141	EDM	Peter Sarno	Windsor	C					
142	CAR	Kyle Dafoe	Owen Sound	D					
143	WSH	Henrik Petre	Djurgarden, SWE	D					
144	VAN	Matt Cooke	Windsor	LW					
145	MTL	Jonathan Desroches	Granby	D					
146	OTT	Jeff Sullivan	Halifax	D					
147	CHI	Heath Gordon	Green Bay Jr.	LW					
148	VAN	Larry Shapley	Welland Jr. B	LW					
149	ST.L.	Nicholas Bilotto	Beauport	D					
150	L.A.	Jeff Katcher	Brandon	D					
151	PHX	Robert Francz	Peterborough	LW					
152	PIT	Petr Havelka	Sparta Praha, CZE	LW					
153	T.B.	Andrei Skopintsev	TPS Turku, FIN	D					
154	NYR	Shawn Degagne	Kitchener	G					
155	FLA	Keith Delaney	Barrie	C					
156	BUF	Brian Campbell	Ottawa	D					
157	DET	B.J. Young	Red Deer	RW					
158	PHI	Jordon Flodell	Moose Jaw	D					
159	N.J.	Sascha Goc	Schwenningen, GER	D					
160	DAL	Alexei Timkin	Torpedo-2 Yaroslavl, RUS	RW					
161	COL	David Aebischer	Fribourg-Gotteron, SUI	G					
162	OTT	Joel Trottier	Ottawa	RW					
163	S.J.	Joel Dusabek	U. of Notre Dame	RW					
164	PHI	Todd Fedoruk	Kelowna	LW					
165	TOR	Hugo Marchand	Victoriaville	D					
166	NYI	Kris Knoblauch	Edmonton	LW					
167	CGY	Jeremy Rondeau	Swift Current	LW					
168	T.B.	Justin Jack	Kelowna	RW					
169	CAR	Andrew Merrick	Michigan	C					
170	T.B.	Eero Somervuori	Jokerit Helsinki, FIN	RW					
171	VAN	Rod Leroux	Seattle	D					
172	MTL	Ben Guite	U. of Maine	D					
173	OTT	Robin Bacul	Slavia Praha, CZE	RW					
174	CHI	Jerad Smith	Portland	D					
175	NYR	Johan Holmqvist	Brynas Gavle, SWE	G					
176	EDM	Kevin Olibruck	Peterborough	D					
177	ST.L.	Ladislav Nagy	Dragon Presov, CZE	C					
178	ANA	Tony Mohagen	Seattle	LW					
179	PIT	Mark Moore	Harvard	D					
180	BOS	Jim Baxter	Oshawa	D					
181	ANA	Mat Snesrund	North Iowa Jr. A	D					
182	NYR	Mike Mottau	Boston College	D					
183	FLA	Tyler Palmer	Lake Superior State	D					
184	BUF	Jeremy Adduono	Sudbury	RW					
185	T.B.	Samuel St. Pierre	Victoriaville	RW					
186	DET	Mike Laceby	Kingston	C					
187	EDM	Chad Hinz	Moose Jaw	C					
188	N.J.	Mathieu Benoit	Chicoutimi	RW					
189	DAL	Jeff McKercher	Barrie	D					
190	TOR	Shawn Thornton	Peterborough	RW					
191	BOS	Antti Laaksonen	U. of Denver	LW					
192	S.J.	Cam Severson	Prince Albert	LW					
193	L.A.	Jay Kopischke	North Iowa Jr. A	LW					
194	TOR	Russ Bartlett	Phillips-Exeter H.S.	C					
195	CAR	Niklas Nordgren	MoDo Ornskoldsvik, SWE	LW					
196	NYI	Jeremy Symington	Petrolia Jr. B	G					
197	MTL	Petr Kubos	Petra Vsetin, CZE	D					
198	T.B.	Shawn Skolney	Seattle	D					
199	CAR	Randy Fitzgerald	Detroit	LW					
200	WSH	Pierre-Luc Therrien	Drummondville	G					
201	VAN	Denis Martynyuk	CSKA-2 Moscow, RUS	LW					
202	MTL	Andrei Sidyakin	Salavat Yulayev Ufa, RUS	RW					
203	OTT	Nick Gillis	Cushing Academy	RW					
204	CHI	Sergei Shikhanov	Lada Togliatti, RUS	RW					
205	EDM	Chris Kerr	Sudbury	D					
206	ST.L.	Bobby Haglund	Des Moines Jr. A	LW					
207	PHX	Alexander Andreyev	Weyburn Jr. A	D					
208	PIT	Andrew Ference	Portland	D					
209	ANA	Rene Stussi	Thurgau, SUI	LW					
210	NYR	Andrew Proskurnicki	Sarnia	LW					
211	FLA	Doug Schueller	Twin Cities Jr.	D					
212	BUF	Kamil Pros	HC Chemo. Litvinov, CZE	C					
213	DET	Steve Wilejto	Prince Albert	C					
214	PHI	Marko Kauppinen	JyP HT Jyvaskyla, FIN	D					
215	N.J.	Scott Clemmensen	Des Moines Jr. A	G					
216	DAL	Alexei Komarov	Dynamo-2 Moscow, RUS	D					
217	COL	Doug Schmidt	Waterloo Jr. A	D					
218	BOS	Eric Van Acker	Chicoutimi	RW					
219	S.J.	Mark Smith	Lethbridge	C					
220	L.A.	Konrad Brand	Medicine Hat	D					
221	TOR	Jonathan Hedstrom	Skelleftea, SWE	RW					
222	NYI	Ryan Clark	Lincoln Jr.	D					
223	CGY	Dustin Paul	Moose Jaw	RW					
224	T.B.	Paul Comrie	U. of Denver	C					
225	CAR	Kent McDonell	Guelph	RW					
226	WSH	Matt Oikawa	St. Lawrence U.	RW					
227	VAN	Peter Brady	Powell River Jr. A	G					
228	MTL	Jarl-Espen Ygranes	Furuset Oslo, NOR	D					
229	OTT	Karel Rachunek	ZPS Zlin, CZE	D					
230	CHI	Chris Feil	Ohio State	D					
231	EDM	Alexander Fomichev	St. Albert Jr. A	G					
232	ST.L.	Dmitri Plekhanov	Neftekhimik Nizhk., RUS	D					
233	PHX	Wyatt Smith	Minnesota-Duluth	C					
234	PIT	Eric Lind	Avon Old Farms H.S.	D					
235	ANA	Tommi Degerman	Boston U.	LW					
236	NYR	Richard Miller	Providence	D					
237	FLA	Benoit Cote	Shawinigan	C					
238	BUF	Dylan Kemp	Lethbridge	D					
239	DET	Greg Willers	Kingston	D					
240	PHI	Par Styf	MoDo Ornskoldsvik, SWE	D					
241	N.J.	Jan Srdinko	Petra Vsetin, CZE	D					
242	DAL	Brett McLean	Kelowna	C					
243	COL	Kyle Kidney	Salisbury H.S.	LW					
244	ST.L.	Marek Ivan	Lethbridge	C					
245	COL	Stephen Lafleur	Belleville	D					
246	BOS	Jay Henderson	Edmonton	LW					

1998

The NHL Entry Draft returned to Buffalo for the second time in 1998. The top-rated prospects in each of the three Major Junior leagues were drafted 1–2–3.

The Tampa Bay Lightning owned the draft's first overall selection for the second time in franchise history, having selected defenseman Roman Hamrlik with the number-one pick in 1992. Six years later, the Lightning opted for offensive power as they selected top ranked prospect Vincent Lecavalier from the Rimouski Oceanic of the QMJHL. Lecavalier had been highly touted throughout his junior career and was an early favorite to go first overall.

Throughout the season, Lecavalier had shared the spotlight with David Legwand, the top U.S.-born prospect who was ranked number two. Legwand, who had scored 54 goals with the OHL's Plymouth Whalers in 1997–98, became the first draftee of the expansion Nashville Predators franchise when he was taken as the second pick.

Brad Stuart, a big defenseman from the Regina Pats of the WHL, was selected third overall by San Jose. Bryan Allen from the Oshawa Generals became the second defenseman selected when Vancouver used the 4th overall pick to select him.

The 1998 Entry Draft's first European player was taken 5th overall by Anaheim. The Mighty Ducks selected defenseman Vitali Vishnevsky from Torpedo-2 Yaroslavl in the Russian Hockey League.

1998

PICK	TEAM	NAME	DRAFTED FROM	NHL PLAYERS: POS / NHL GOALTENDERS: POS	GP	G / W	A / GA	PTS / SO	PIM / AVG
FIRST ROUND									
1	T.B.	Vincent Lecavalier	Rimouski	C					
2	NSH	David Legwand	Plymouth	C					
3	S.J.	Brad Stuart	Regina	D					
4	VAN	Bryan Allen	Oshawa	D					
5	ANA	Vitaly Vishnevsky	Torpedo-2 Yaroslavl, RUS	D					
6	CGY	Rico Fata	London	C					
7	NYR	Manny Malhotra	Guelph	C					
8	CHI	Mark Bell	Ottawa	LW					
9	NYI	Michael Rupp	Erie	LW					
10	TOR	Nikolai Antropov	Torpedo Ust-Kamen'k, KAZ	C					
11	CAR	Jeff Heerema	Sarnia	RW					
12	COL	Alex Tanguay	Halifax	C					
13	EDM	Michael Henrich	Barrie	RW					
14	PHX	Patrick DesRochers	Sarnia	G					
15	OTT	Mathieu Chouinard	Shawinigan	G					
16	MTL	Eric Chouinard	Quebec	C					
17	COL	Martin Skoula	Barrie	D					
18	BUF	Dimitri Kalinin	Traktor Chelyabinsk, RUS	D					
19	COL	Robyn Regehr	Kamloops	D					
20	COL	Scott Parker	Kelowna	D					
21	L.A.	Mathieu Biron	Shawinigan	D					
22	PHI	Simon Gagne	Quebec	C					
23	PIT	Milan Kraft	Keramika Plzen Jr., CZE	C					
24	ST.L.	Christian Backman	Vastra Frolunda Jr., SWE	D					
25	DET	Jiri Fischer	Hull	D					
26	N.J.	Mike Van Ryn	U. of Michigan	D					
27	N.J.	Scott Gomez	Tri City	C					
SECOND ROUND									
28	COL	Ramzi Abid	Chicoutimi	LW					
29	S.J.	Jonathon Cheechoo	Belleville	RW					
30	FLA	Kyle Rossiter	Spokane	D					
31	VAN	Artem Chubarov	Dynamo Moscow, RUS	C					
32	ANA	Stephen Peat	Red Deer	D					
33	CGY	Blair Betts	Prince George	C					
34	BUF	Andrew Peters	Oshawa	LW					
35	TOR	Petr Svoboda	Havlickuv Brod, CZE	D					
36	NYI	Chris Neilson	Calgary	C					
37	N.J.	Christian Berglund	Farjestad Karl. Jr., SWE	C					
38	COL	Philippe Sauve	Rimouski	G					
39	DAL	John Erskine	London	D					
40	NYR	Randy Copley	Cape Breton	RW					
41	ST.L.	Maxim Linnik	St. Thomas Jr. B	D					
42	PHI	Jason Beckett	Seattle	D					
43	PHX	Ossi Vaananen	Jokerit Helsinki Jr., FIN	D					
44	OTT	Mike Fisher	Sudbury	C					
45	MTL	Mike Ribeiro	Rouyn-Noranda	C					
46	L.A.	Justin Papineau	Belleville	C					
47	BUF	Norman Milley	Sudbury	RW					
48	BOS	Jonathon Girard	Laval	D					
49	WSH	Jomar Cruz	Brandon	G					
50	BUF	Jaroslav Kristek	ZPS Zlin, CZE	RW					
51	PHI	Ian Forbes	Guelph	D					
52	BOS	Bobby Allen	Boston College	D					
53	COL	Steve Moore	Harvard	C					
54	PIT	Alexander Zevakhin	CSKA Moscow, RUS	RW					
55	DET	Ryan Barnes	Sudbury	LW					
56	DET	Tomek Valtonen	Ilves Tampere Jr., FIN	LW					
57	DAL	Tyler Bouck	Prince George	RW					
OTHER ROUNDS									
58	OTT	Chris Bala	Harvard	LW					
59	WSH	Todd Hornung	Portland	C					
60	NSH	Denis Arkhipov	Ak Bars Kazan, RUS	LW					
61	FLA	Joe DiPenta	Boston U.	D					
62	CGY	Paul Manning	Colorado College	D					
63	FLA	Lance Ward	Red Deer	D					
64	T.B.	Brad Richards	Rimouski	LW					
65	S.J.	Eric LaPlante	Halifax	LW					
66	NYR	Jason Labarbera	Portland	G					
67	EDM	Alex Henry	London	D					
68	VAN	Jarkko Ruutu	HIFK Helsinki, FIN	LW					
69	TOR	Jamie Hodson	Brandon	G					
70	CAR	Kevin Holdridge	Plymouth	D					
71	CAR	Erik Cole	Clarkson	LW					
72	T.B.	Dimitry Afanasenkov	Torpedo-2 Yaroslavl, RUS	LW					
73	PHX	Pat O'Leary	Robbinsdale-Armstrong H.S.	C					
74	OTT	Julien Vauclair	Lugano, SWI	D					
75	MTL	Francois Beauchemin	Laval	D					
76	L.A.	Alexei Volkov	Krylja Sovetov-2, RUS	G					
77	BUF	Mike Pandolfo	St. Sebastian's H.S.	LW					
78	BOS	Peter Nordstrom	Farjestad Karl. Jr., SWE	LW					
79	COL	Yevgeny Lazarev	Kitchener Jr. B	LW					
80	PIT	David Cameron	Prince Albert	C					
81	VAN	Justin Morrison	Colorado College	RW					
82	N.J.	Brian Gionta	Boston College	RW					
83	ST.L.	Matt Walker	Portland	D					
84	DET	Jake McCracken	Sault Ste. Marie	G					
85	NSH	Geoff Koch	U. of Michigan	LW					
86	DAL	Gabriel Karlsson	HV 71 Jonkoping Jr., SWE	C					
87	TOR	Alexei Ponikarovsky	Dynamo-2 Moscow, RUS	LW					
88	NSH	Kent Sauer	North Iowa Jr. A	D					
89	FLA	Ryan Jardine	Sault Ste. Marie	LW					
90	VAN	Regan Darby	Tri-City	D					
91	CAR	Josef Vasicek	Slavia Praha Jr., CZE	C					
92	T.B.	Eric Beaudoin	Guelph	LW					
93	CAR	Tommy Westlund	Brynas Gavle, SWE	RW					
94	CHI	Matthias Trattnig	U. of Maine	C					
95	NYI	Andy Burnham	Windsor	RW					
96	N.J.	Mikko Jokela	HIFK Helsinki, FIN	D					
97	CAR	Chris Madden	Guelph	G					
98	S.J.	Rob Davison	North Bay	D					
99	EDM	Shawn Horcoff	Michigan State	C					
100	PHX	Ryan Vanbuskirk	Sarnia	D					
101	OTT	Petr Schastlivy	Torpedo Yaroslavl, RUS	LW					
102	CGY	Shaun Sutter	Lethbridge	C					
103	L.A.	Kip Brennan	Sudbury	D					
104	S.J.	Miroslav Zalesak	Plastika Nitra, SVK	RW					
105	N.J.	Pierre Dagenais	Rouyn-Noranda	LW					
106	WSH	Krys Barch	London	LW					
107	WSH	Chris Corrinet	Princeton	RW					
108	CGY	Dany Sabourin	Sherbrooke	G					
109	PHI	Jean Philippe Morin	Drummondville	D					
110	PIT	Scott Myers	Prince George	G					
111	DET	Brent Hobday	Moose Jaw	C					
112	ANA	Viktor Wallin	HV 71 Jonkoping Jr., SWE	LW					
113	EDM	Kristain Antila	Ilves Tampere, FIN	G					
114	NYR	Boyd Kane	Regina	LW					
115	PHX	Jay Leach	Providence College	D					
116	PHX	Josh Blackburn	Lincoln Jr. A	G					
117	FLA	Jaroslav Spacek	Farjestad Karlstad, SWE	D					
118	WSH	Mike Siklenka	Lloydminster	D					
119	N.J.	Anton But	Torpedo Yaroslavl 2, RUS	RW					
120	CGY	Brent Gauvreau	Oshawa	RW					
121	T.B.	Curtis Rich	Calgary	D					
122	PHI	Patrick Leahy	Miami of Ohio	RW					
123	NYI	Jiri Dopita	Petra Vsetin, CZE	C					
124	PHI	Francis Belanger	Rimouski	LW					
125	WSH	Erik Wendell	Maple Grove H.S.	C					
126	TOR	Morgan Warren	Moncton	RW					
127	S.J.	Brandon Coulter	Oshawa	LW					
128	EDM	Paul Elliott	Medicine Hat	D					
129	PHX	Robert Schnabel	Red Deer	D					
130	OTT	Gavin McLeod	Kelowna	D					
131	NYR	Tomas Kloucek	Slavia Praha Jr., CZE	D					

1998 continued

PICK	TEAM	NAME	DRAFTED FROM	POS
132	MTL	Andrei Bashkirov	Fort Wayne/Las Vegas	LW
133	L.A.	Joe Rullier	Rimouski	D
134	PIT	Robert Scuderi	Boston College	D
135	BOS	Andrew Raycroft	Sudbury	G
136	VAN	David Jonsson	Leksand, SWE	D
137	BUF	Aaron Goldade	Brandon	C
138	NSH	Martin Beauchesne	Sherbrooke	D
139	PHI	Garrett Prosofsky	Saskatoon	C
140	VAN	Rick Bertran	Kitchener	D
141	COL	Kristinn Timmons	Tri-City	LW
142	DET	Calle Steen	Hammarby SWE	LW
143	N.J.	Ryan Flinn	Laval	LW
144	EDM	Oleg Smirnov	Kristall Elektrostal, RUS	RW
145	S.J.	Mikael Samuelsson	Sodertalje, SWE	LW
146	T.B.	Sergei Kuznetsov	Torpedo Yaroslavl 2, RUS	C
147	NSH	Craig Brunel	Prince Albert	RW
148	FLA	Chris Ovington	Red Deer	D
149	VAN	Paul Cabana	Fort McMurray	RW
150	ANA	Trent Hunter	Prince George	RW
151	DET	Adam DeLeeuw	Barrie	LW
152	MTL	Gordie Dwyer	Quebec	LW
153	DAL	Pavel Patera	AIK Solna, SWE	LW
154	TOR	Allan Rourke	Kitchener	D
155	NYI	Kevin Clauson	Western Michigan	D
156	CHI	Kent Huskins	Clarkson	D
157	ST.L.	Brad Voth	Medicine Hat	D
158	CHI	Jari Viuhkola	Karpat Oulu, FIN	C
159	EDM	Trevor Ettinger	Cape Breton	D
160	PHX	Rickard Wallin	Farjestad Karl. Jr., SWE	C
161	OTT	Christopher Neil	North Bay	RW
162	MTL	Andrei Markov	Khimik Voskresensk, RUS	D
163	L.A.	Tomas Zizka	ZPS Zlin, CZE	D
164	BUF	Ales Kotalik	Ceske Budejovice Jr., CZE	RW
165	BOS	Ryan Milanovic	Kitchener	LW
166	CHI	Jonathan Pelletier	Drummondville	G
167	COL	Alexander Ryazantsev	Victoriaville	D
168	PHI	Antero Niittymaki	TPS Turku Jr., FIN	G
169	PIT	Jan Fadmy	Slavia Praha, CZE	C
170	ST.L.	Andrei Trochinsky	Torpedo Ust-Kamen'k, KAZ	C
171	DET	Pavel Datsyuk	Dynamo-E. Yeka'burg, RUS	C
172	N.J.	Jacques Lariviere	Moncton	LW
173	DAL	Niko Kapanen	HPK Hameenlinna, FIN	C
174	T.B.	Brett Allan	Swift Current	C
175	PHI	Cam Ondrik	Medicine Hat	G
176	FLA	B.J. Ketcheson	Peterborough	D
177	VAN	Vincent Malts	Hull	RW
178	ANA	Jesse Fibiger	U. of Minnesota-Duluth	D
179	WSH	Nathan Forster	Seattle	D
180	NYR	Stefan Lundqvist	Brynas Gavle, SWE	LW
181	TOR	Jonathan Gagnon	Cape Breton	C
182	NYI	Evgeny Korolev	London	D
183	CHI	Tyler Arnason	Fargo-Moorehead Jr. A	C
184	CAR	Donald Smith	Clarkson	C
185	S.J.	Robert Mulick	Sault Ste. Marie	D
186	EDM	Michael Morrison	Exeter H.S.	G
187	PHX	Erik Westrum	U. of Minnesota	C
188	OTT	Michael Periard	Shawinigan	D
189	MTL	Andrei Kruchinin	Lada Togliatti, RUS	D
190	L.A.	Tommi Hannus	TPS Turku Jr., FIN	C
191	BUF	Brad Moran	Calgary	C
192	CGY	Radek Duda	Sparta Praha, Cze	RW
193	WSH	Ratislav Stana	HC Kosice, SVK	G
194	T.B.	Oak Hewer	Sault Ste. Marie	C
195	PHI	Tomas Divisek	Slavia Praha, CZE	LW
196	PIT	Joel Scherban	London	C
197	ST.L.	Brad Twordik	Brandon	C
198	DET	Jeremy Goetzinger	Prince Albert	D
199	N.J.	Erik Jensen	Des Moines Jr. A	RW
200	DAL	Scott Perry	Boston University	C
201	MTL	Craig Murray	Penticton	C
202	NSH	Martin Bartek	Sherbrooke	LW
203	FLA	Ian Jacobs	Ottawa	RW
204	VAN	Graig Mischler	Northeastern	C
205	ANA	David Bernier	Quebec	RW
206	CGY	Jonas Frogren	Farjestad Karl. Jr., SWE	D
207	NYR	Johan Witehall	Leksand, SWE	LW
208	CAR	Jaroslav Svoboda	HC Olomouc, CZE	LW
209	NYI	Frederik Brindamour	Sherbrooke	G
210	CHI	Sean Griffin	Kingston	D
211	CAR	Mark Kosick	U. of Michigan	C
212	S.J.	Jim Fahey	Catholic Memorial H.S.	D
213	EDM	Christian Lefebvre	Baie-Comeau	D
214	PHX	Justin Hanson	Moose Jaw	RW
215	TOR	Dwight Wolfe	Halifax	D
216	MTL	Michael Ryder	Hull	C
217	L.A.	Jim Henkel	New England	C
218	BUF	David Moravec	HC Vitkovice, CZE	RW
219	VAN	Curtis Valentine	Bowling Green	LW
220	WSH	Michael Farrell	Providence College	D
221	T.B.	Daniel Hulak	Swift Current	D
222	PHI	Lubomir Pistek	Slovan Bratislava Jr., CZE	RW
223	OTT	Sergei Verenikin	Torpedo Yaroslavl, RUS	LW
224	PIT	Mika Lehto	Assat Pori Jr., FIN	G
225	ST.L.	Vevgeny Pastukh	Torpedo Yaroslavl, RUS	LW
226	DET	David Petrasek	HV 71 Jonkoping, SWE	D
227	N.J.	Marko Ahosilta	KalPa Kuopio Jr., FIN	C
228	TOR	Mihail Travnicek	Chemo. Litvinov Jr., CZE	RW
229	T.B.	Chris Lyness	Rouyn-Noranda	D
230	NSH	Karlis Skrastins	TPS Turku, FIN	D
231	FLA	Adrian Wischer	EHC Kloten, SWI	C
232	VAN	Jason Metcalfe	London	D
233	ANA	Pelle Prestberg	Farjestad Karlstad, SWE	LW
234	CGY	Kevin Mitchell	Guelph	D
235	NYR	Jan Mertzig	Lulea, SWE	D
236	TOR	Sergei Rostov	Dynamo-2 Moscow, RUS	D
237	NYI	Ben Blais	Walpole H.S.	D
238	CHI	Alexandre Couture	Sherbrooke	LW
239	CAR	Brent McDonald	Red Deer	C
240	CHI	Andrei Yershov	Khimik Voskresensk, RUS	D
241	EDM	Maxim Spiridonov	London	RW
242	NYI	Jason Doyle	Owen Sound	RW
243	PHI	Petr Hubacek	Kometa Brno, CZE	C
244	PIT	Toby Peterson	Colorado College	C
245	ANA	Andreas Andersson	HV 71 Jonkoping, SWE	G
246	OTT	Rastisla Pavlikovsky	Utah	C
247	MTL	Darcy Harris	Kitchener	RW
248	L.A.	Matthew Yeats	Olds	G
249	BUF	Edo Terglav	Baie-Comeau	RW
250	NYI	Radek Matejovsky	Slavia Praha, CZE	RW
251	WSH	Blake Evans	Tri-City	C
252	T.B.	Martin Cibak	HK 32 Liptovsky Mik's, SVK	C
253	PHI	Bruno St. Jacques	Baie-Comeau	D
254	PIT	Matt Hussey	Avon Old Farms H.S.	C
255	ST.L.	John Pohl	Red Wing H.S.	C
256	DET	Petja Pietilainen	Saskatoon	LW
257	N.J.	Ryan Held	Kitchener	C
258	PHI	Sergei Skrobat	Dynamo-2 Moscow, RUS	D

From its quiet beginnings as a draft of unsponsored 17-year-olds in 1963 (when just 17 players were selected) to today's big crowds, live television coverage and much anticipated draft rankings, the NHL Entry Draft has become a rite of passage for the world's best young hockey players and for their families. From draft day deals to surprising late-round picks, it remains one of the most dramatic days on each year's hockey calendar.

CHAPTER 21

The Changing Rink

How the Evolution of the Ice Sheet Parallels Hockey's History

James Duplacey

BEGINNING WITH A SINGLE FACE-OFF DOT, advancements in the game of hockey have occurred in concert with modifications to the lines, circles and colors painted just below the surface of the ice.

The blue line evolved as offside rules and forward pass-ing zones were defined. The center-ice red line was a "temporary" measure instituted in 1943–44 to reduce breakaway opportunities as club rosters were weakened when regular players enlisted in the armed services.

1917–18

The center-ice face-off dot and lines between the goal posts are the only marking on an otherwise blank sheet of ice.

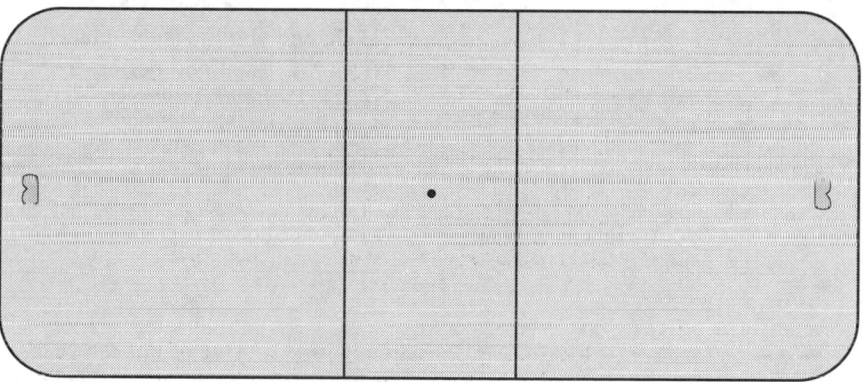

1918–19

Blue lines are added to the ice, 80 feet from the end boards. The surface was thus formally divided into three zones with forward passing permitted in the middle "neutral zone." Kicking the puck was also permitted in the neutral zone.

1926–27

Each blue line is moved 10 feet closer to the end boards, placing them 60 feet in front of each goal and expanding the neutral zone to 60 feet.

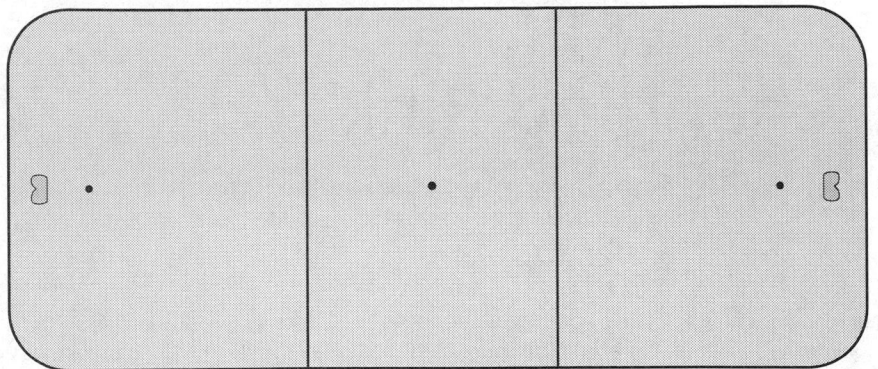

1929–30

Additional face-off dots are added to the ice surface exactly 10 feet in front of each goal. Every time a goaltender failed to clear the puck after making a save, a face-off would be held at the dot in front of his net. No player other than the goalie was permitted to stand between the face-off spot and the goal.

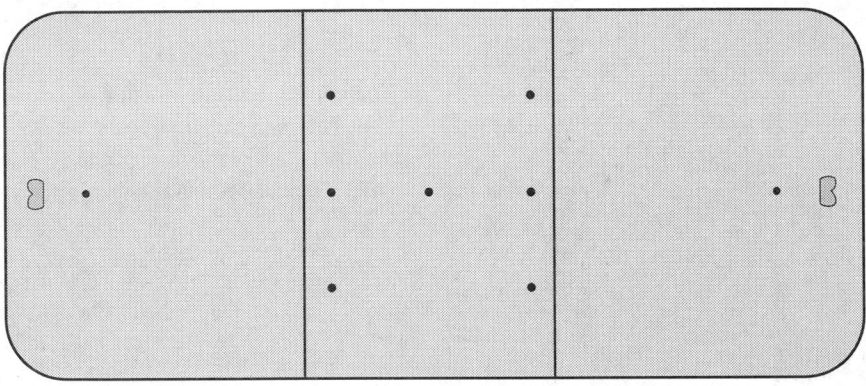

1931–32

Three additional face-off spots are added outside each blue line.

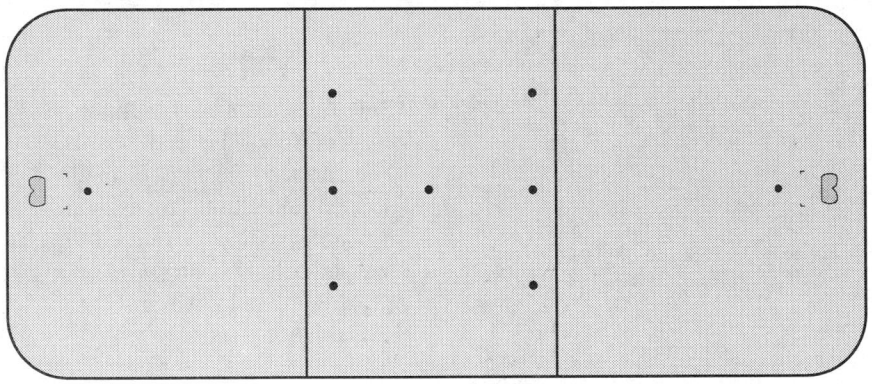

1933–34

L-shaped boundaries placed in front of each net define a goaltender's safe area (8' x 5').

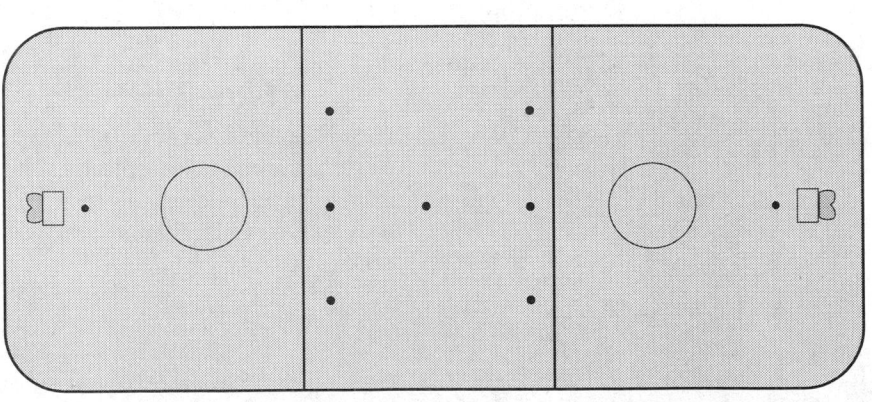

1934–35

A 20-foot diameter penalty shot circle is added in front of each goal. The center of the circle is 38 feet from the goal line. A player is awarded a penalty shot if he is tripped and prevented from shooting while having no other player to pass to. The shot must be taken from within the penalty shot circle. The goalie must not advance more than one foot from the front of his net. A full goal crease (8' x 5') is also painted on the ice.

1937–38

Two face-off spots are added in each defensive zone. The face-off spot directly in front of each goal is removed. A goal line running the entire width of the ice is added, as new rules governing icing the puck are introduced.

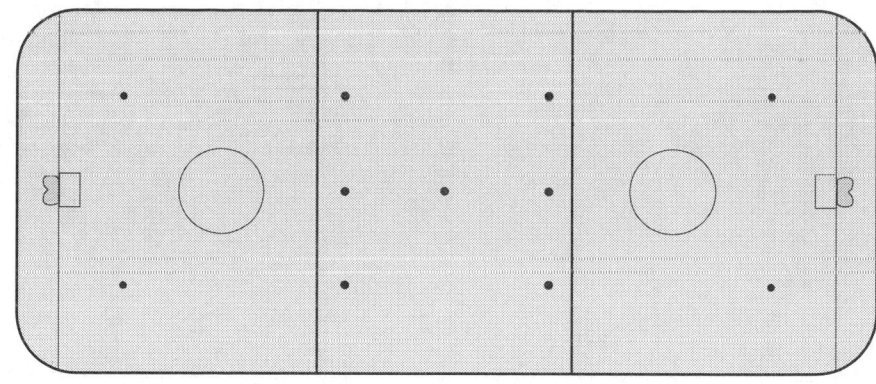

1938–39

The width of each blue line is increased to 12 inches.

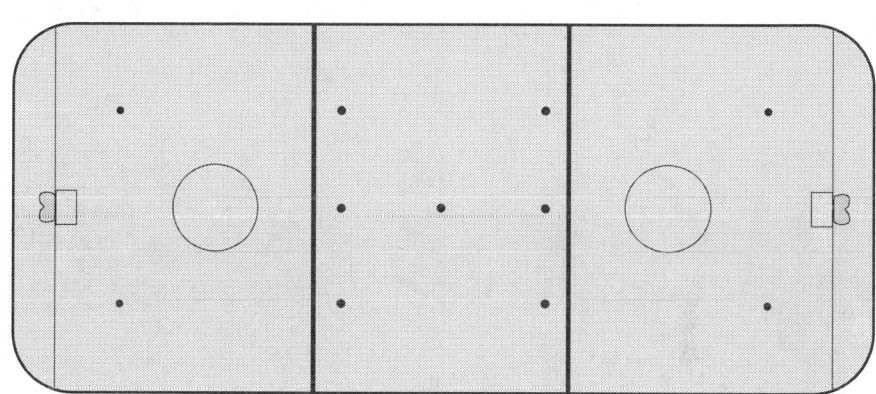

1939–40

The size of the goal crease is modified to 7' x 3'.

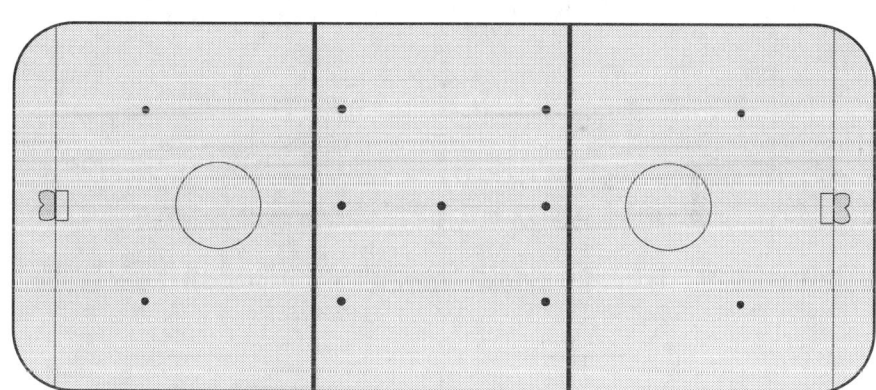

1941–42

Twenty-foot face-off circles are added at center ice and in each corner. The penalty shot circles are replaced with a short penalty shot line 28 feet in front of the goal. Penalty shots are classified as minor and major, with minor penalty shots to be taken from the line. For major penalty shots (assigned when a player is tripped on a breakaway) the player is permitted to skate in on the goaltender from the penalty shot line.

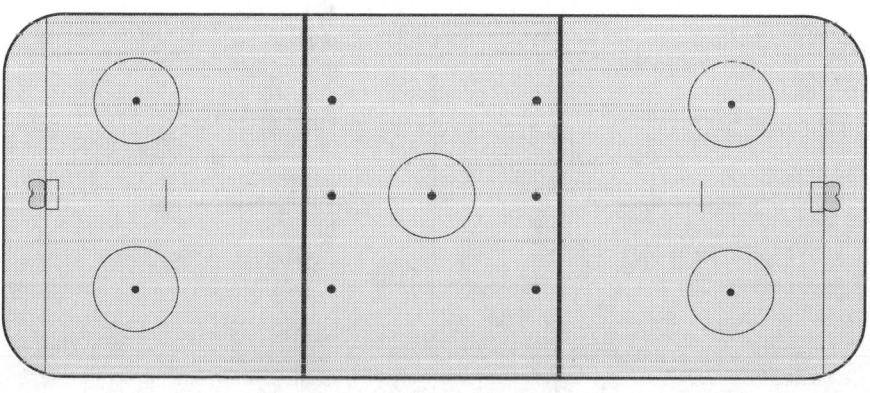

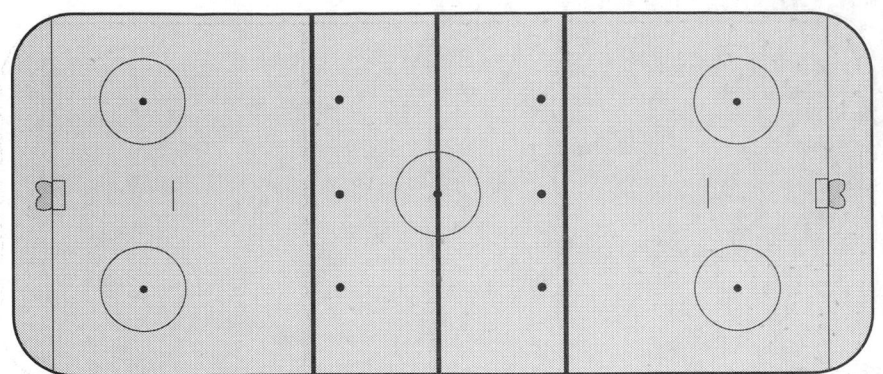

1943–44

A center-ice red line is added to the rink. The red line is introduced to speed up the game and reduce off-side calls. This innovation marks the beginning of the modern era in the NHL.

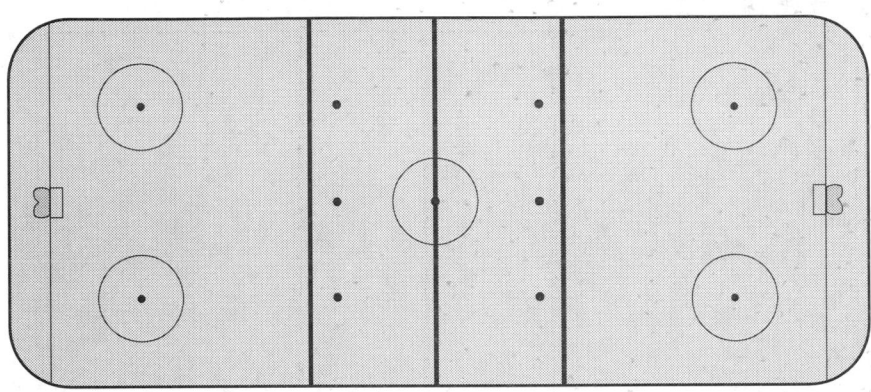

1945–46

The penalty shot line is deleted, with penalty shots to be taken from the center ice face-off dot. Minor penalty shots are eliminated.

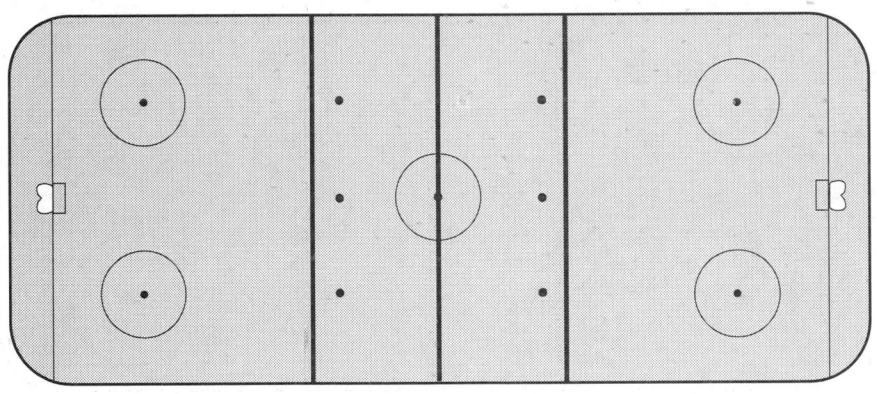

1947–48

The area defined by the goal line and the base of the net is painted white. This move is made to aid referees and goal judges in determining when a goal has been scored.

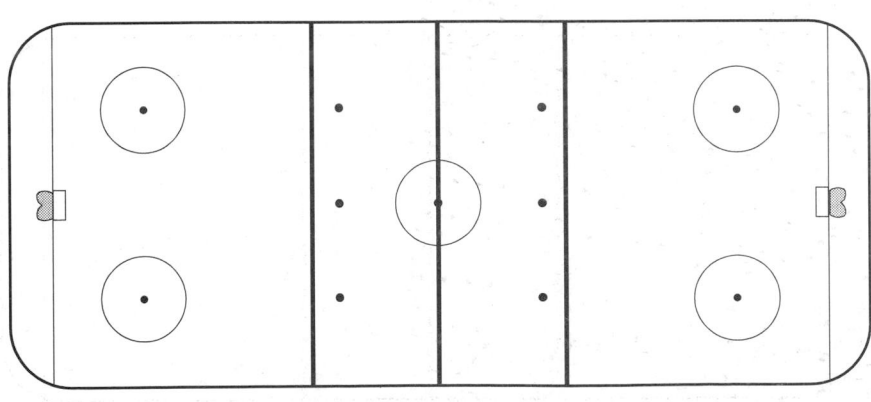

1949–50

The entire ice surface is painted white following the popularity of the white goal area among fans and officials. The new white ice surface makes the puck more visible to fans in the stands, as well as those watching on the new medium of television.

1951–52

The size of the goal crease is increased to 8' x 4'. Face-off circles are expanded to 30 feet in diameter and hash marks are added to the circles in the two defensive zones to keep players onside when lining up for face-offs. The two center face-off dots are eliminated in the neutral zone, and a referee's crease is added.

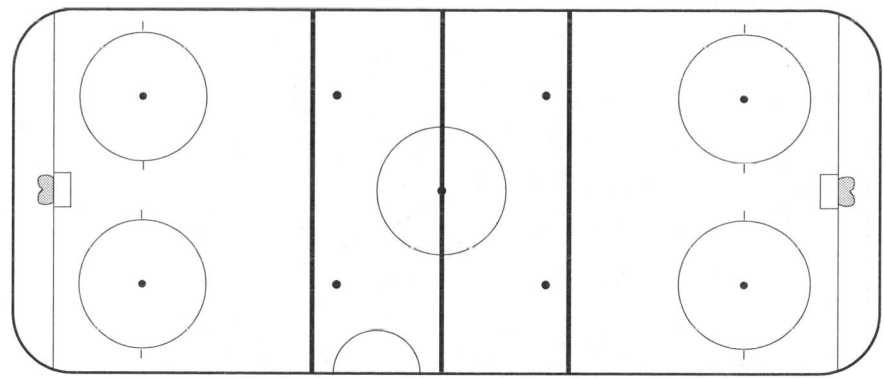

1961–62

"Crosshairs" are added to the face-off spots in the defensive zones. (These lines would undergo numerous design changes prior to the adoption of L-shaped marks in 1996–97.)

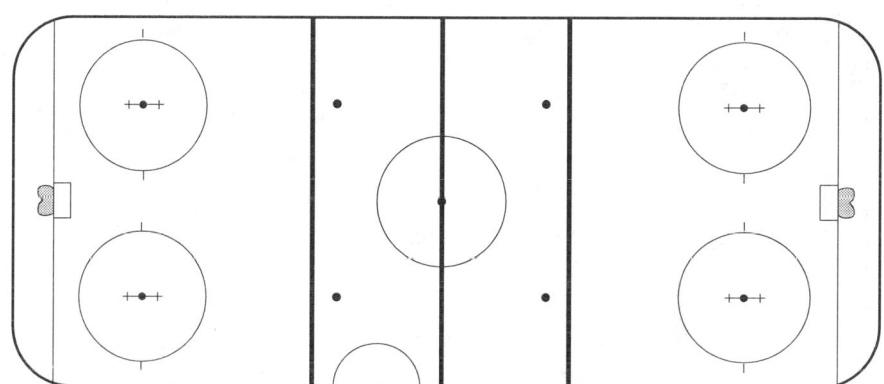

1964–65

Use of a checkered center red line is officially added to the NHL rule book. The checkered line had begun to be used in some rinks as early as 1957.

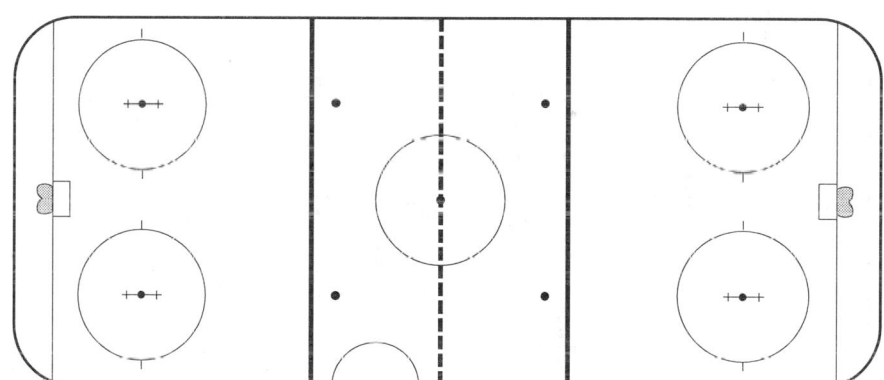

1982–83

Double hash marks and modified dots in the face off circles replace the previous markings in the defensive zone.

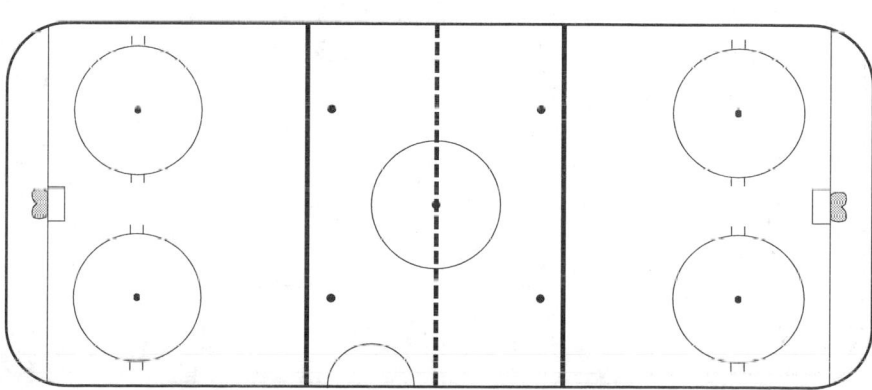

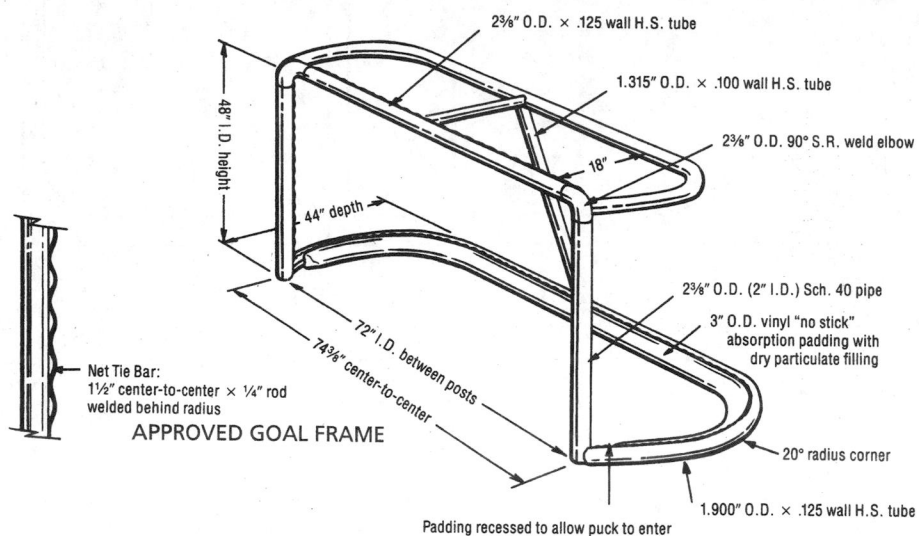

2⅜" O.D. × .125 wall H.S. tube

1.315" O.D. × .100 wall H.S. tube

2⅜" O.D. 90° S.R. weld elbow

48" I.D. height

18"

44" depth

2⅜" O.D. (2" I.D.) Sch. 40 pipe

3" O.D. vinyl "no stick" absorption padding with dry particulate filling

Net Tie Bar:
1½" center-to-center × ¼" rod welded behind radius

72" I.D. between posts

74⅜" center-to-center

APPROVED GOAL FRAME

20° radius corner

1.900" O.D. × .125 wall H.S. tube

Padding recessed to allow puck to enter

1984–85

After decades of using the Art Ross net, the goal frame is modified. The switch comes four years after Mark Howe was severely injured by the point in the middle of the base of the net. (The base of the old goal frame was shaped like the number "3".) The 1984–85 season also saw the iron pegs that had been used to hold goal nets in position replaced by the new magnetic Megg-Net (designed by Dennis Meggs and Terry Riley). In 1993–94, the Megg-Net would be replaced by the Marsh peg, a bendable plastic pin that holds the net in position more firmly and reduces the many stoppages in play that had come from the net being knocked off its moorings.

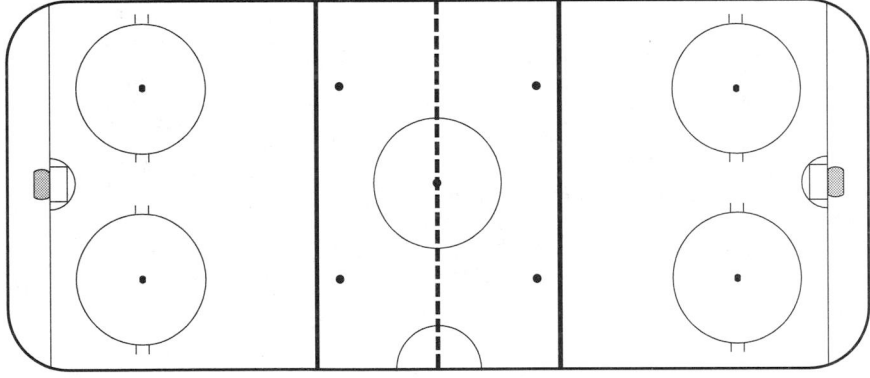

1986–87

A round goal crease is added, surrounding the traditional rectangular crease. The original goal crease remained 8'x 4' with lines two inches thick forming a box beginning one foot from each goal post. The additional semi-circle is six feet in radius from the center of the goal line and is also painted with a two-inch line.

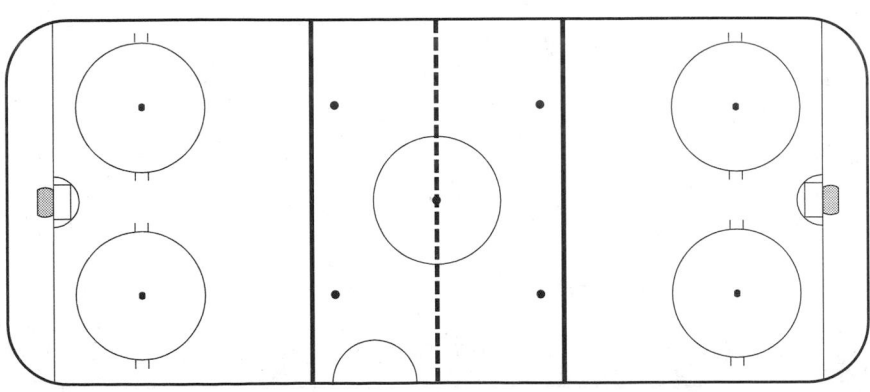

1990–91

In an effort to increase offense by giving players more room to operate behind the net, the goal lines, blue lines and defensive zone face-off circles and dots are all moved out one foot further from the back boards, increasing the distance behind the goal line from 10 feet to 11 feet. The neutral zone decreases from 60 feet to 58 feet.

1991–92

The rectangular goal crease is eliminated. L-shaped markings with both lines five inches long are placed just inside the edge of the semi-circle crease, marking the upper corners of the old goal crease. The entire goal crease, as well as the area enclosed by the goal line and the base of the net, is tinted blue.

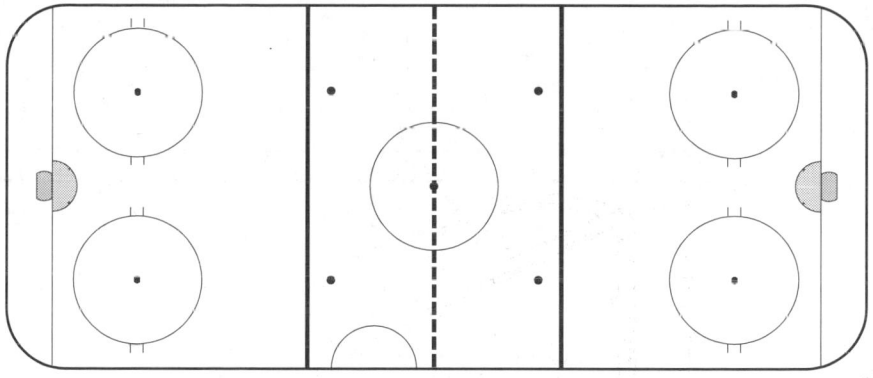

1995–96

The goal area (inside the net from behind the goal line to the base of the goal frame) is tinted white.

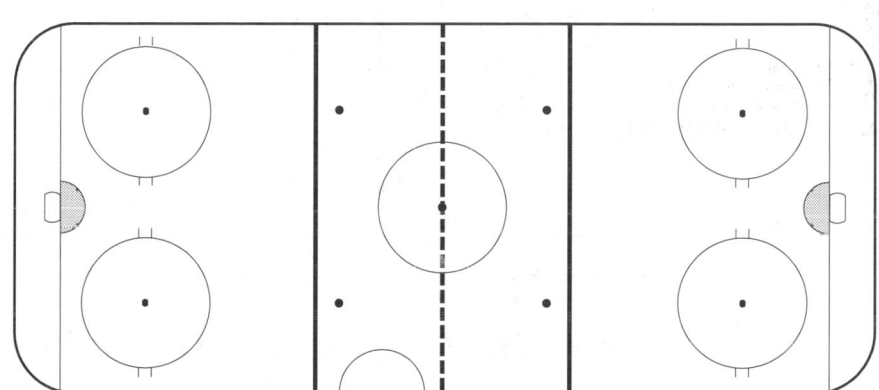

1996–97

L-shaped positioning marks are added to the two face-off spots in each defensive end.

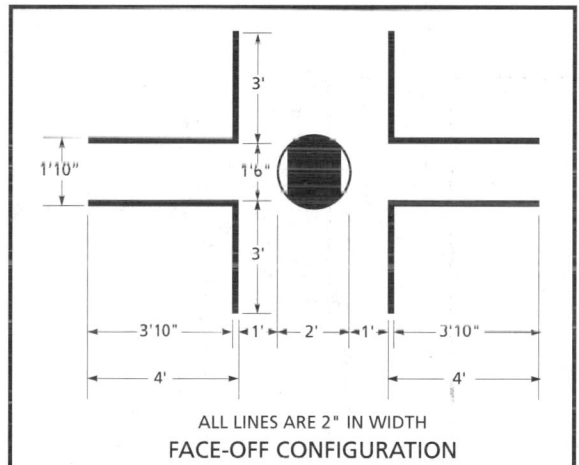

ALL LINES ARE 2" IN WIDTH
FACE-OFF CONFIGURATION

1998–99

The goal lines, blue lines and defensive zone face-off circles, L-marks and dots are all moved two feet closer to center, creating 13 feet of room from the end boards to the goal lines and shrinking the neutral zone from 58 feet to 54 feet. The new configuration is designed give players more room to operate behind the goal and discourage goaltenders from playing the puck. To cut down on in-the-crease violations, the size of the goal crease is altered so that it extends only one foot beyond each goal post and straight down from the L-shaped markings at the top of the crease. Only the top of the crease remains rounded.

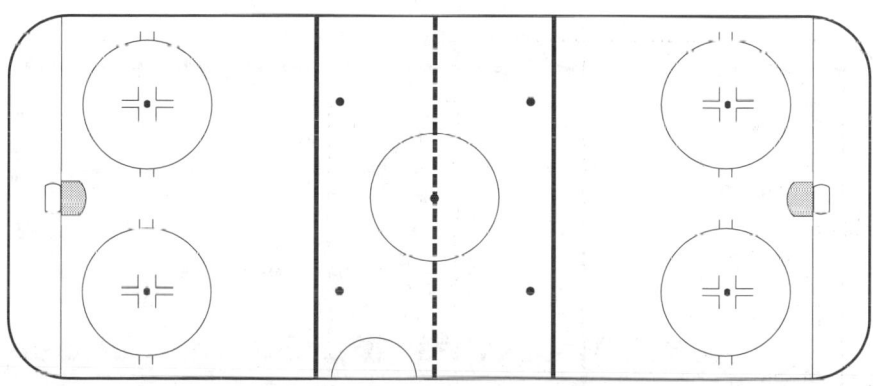

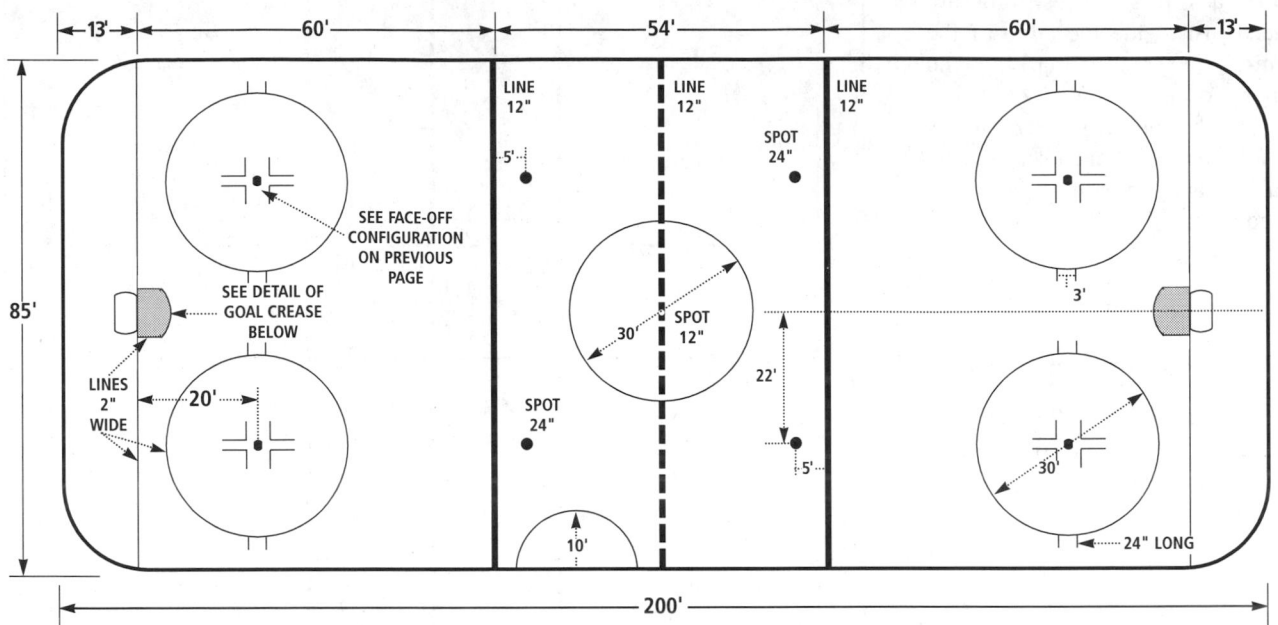

NHL Rink Markings and Dimensions, 1998–99

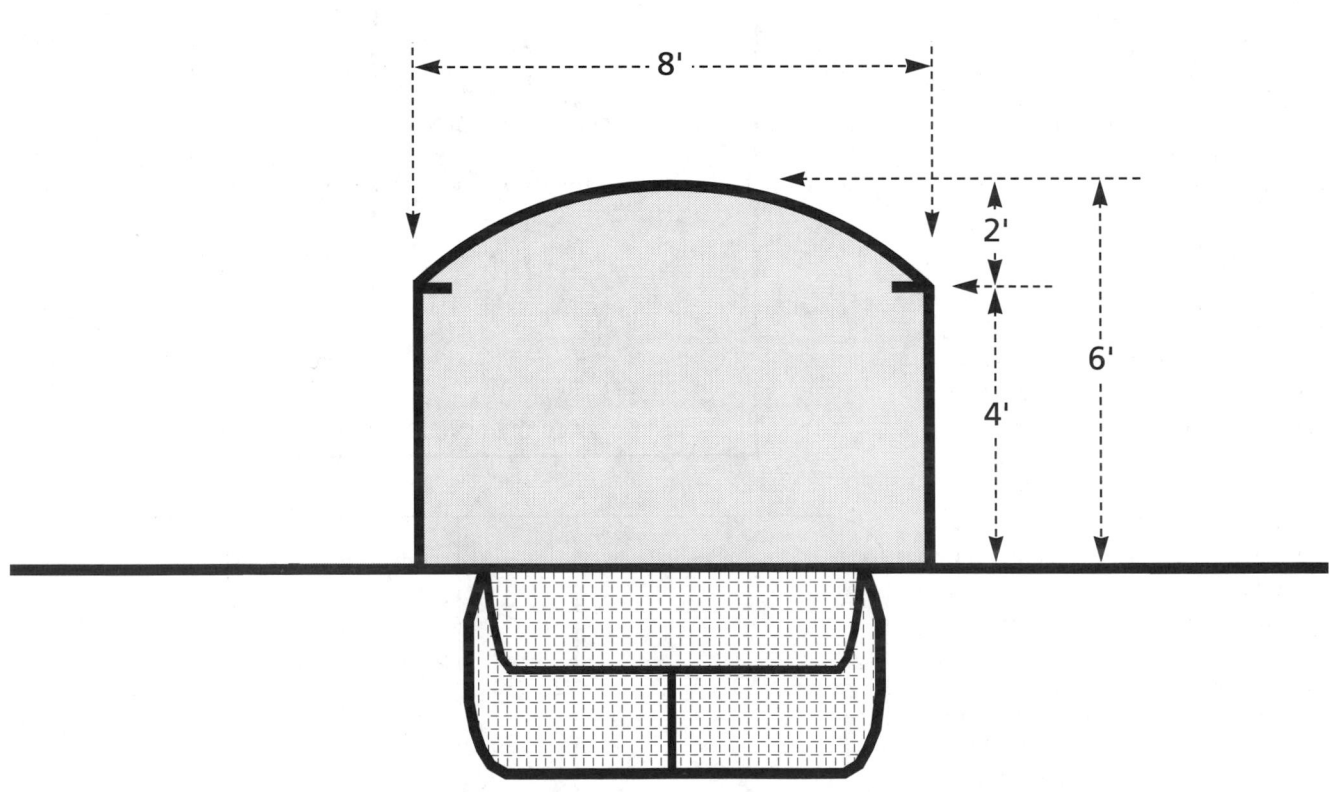

NHL Goal Crease Markings and Dimensions, 1998–99

CHAPTER 22
Names of the Game
Families, Forward Lines and Nicknames

THE FAMILY FACTOR IN HOCKEY

Glen R. Goodhand

FAMILY TREES have been just as integral to Canada's national game as ice and skates, sticks and pucks. The longest-standing championship emblem of any North American team sport takes us back to a family infatuated with the game. We speak, of course, of Sir Frederick Arthur, Lord Stanley of Preston, Canada's sixth Governor-General, and his seven sons. Lord Stanley quickly became a devout fan, thanks to his boys, who grew into enthusiastic puckchasers and formed a team of aristocratic types which they tagged the Rideau Rebels. In his book *Stanley Cup Fever*, Brian McFarlane comments, "(They) formed the first and last vice-regal hockey club in Canada, and although they did not last long, their influence is still felt today." Details are not plentiful, but it is known that the Rebels traveled to other cities to challenge teams in this fast-growing sport and even tackled the powerful Ottawa City Club for the Dominion championship (which they lost). As a result, their father donated that famous trophy which bears his name today. Initially it was intended for amateur shinny supremacy in Canada, but since 1908 has been up for grabs by professionals only.

As the number of leagues grew, so did the appearance of players with identical surnames. In 1897, there were the Davidsons with the Montreal Victorias and the Murphys with the Ottawa Capitals. In 1902, Rod and Magnus Flett represented the Winnipeg squad that challenged for the Cup. A year later Dave, Suddy and Billy Gilmour contributed to the Ottawa Silver Seven's crowning in the Canadian Amateur Hockey League which was the equivalent of the NHL today. During the same decade the Quebec septet boasted the Power brothers, Chubby, Rocket and Joe. Meanwhile, the Smith brothers of Ottawa were beginning to emerge as a hockey force. Alf, Harry and Tommy were the best of them, making it to the elite leagues. But all seven soon linked up with teams at some level of shinny. Both Alf and Harry had fiery tempers and gained the reputation as ruffians, while Tommy stuck more to the finesse aspect of the game. Hod and Bruce Stuart cannot be overlooked when hockey siblings are listed. Both were enshrined in the Hall of Fame after illustrious careers in the International and Eastern Canada loops. The former died prematurely as a result of a swimming accident, but Bruce continued into the early campaigns of the National Hockey Association.

In the Ontario Professional Hockey League, Canada's first openly monied fraternity, which spanned 1907–08 to 1910–11, the McNamaras, the Cochranes, the Seiberts and the Mercers made their presence known. The McNamaras especially deserve to be singled out. Until the Plagers (Barclay, Bob and Bill) who played for St. Louis in the 1960s, they formed one of the most threatening defenses ever to grace the ice lanes. However, unlike the bashing

Plagers, this trio invited respect simply because of their size. Waterloo was privileged to employ all three during the 1910–11 campaign. George and Howard honed their skills in the old Eastern Canada Amateur Hockey Association, while Harold lined up with Edmonton in 1908. George is the best known of the triad. Along with Howard he was a member of that unique contingent, the 228th Battalion, the only service team ever to be part of a major professional league. He was elected to the Hockey Hall of Fame in 1952. Following his career on the ice, he became the very wealthy owner of a successful construction company in the Toronto area. Generous to a fault, many down-on-their-luck army buddies or former hockey mates benefited from his philanthropy. It was said when he died some 50 men were receiving regular cash remittances at his request.

George's son, Paul McNamara, was pursued by the Boston Bruins when he played for St. Mike's junior team, but when a deal could not be made to have him come to the Maple Leafs, in deference to his father, he chose education and business instead. He was on the board of directors of Maple Leaf Gardens for many years.

One would be remiss not to mention the McGregor brothers from Almonte, Ontario. While brother Willard quietly spent time in the Lakehead displaying his shinny talents, Edwin (Mag) became known as "the Tourist" because of his "have stick and skates, will travel" philosophy. In 1910–11 alone, counting an exhibition tilt with the Tecumsehs lacrosse club, of which he was a valued member, he displayed the colors of no less than five hockey teams. He was in Port Arthur for the Christmas week, came home for a one-night stand with his hometown amateurs and alternated between Port Hope of the Lakeshore Pro circuit and Berlin of the OPHL throughout the campaign.

Because families tended to be much larger in those days, and because exhibitions of any kind were a big attraction, the early days of shinny were ripe for contests involving teams made up entirely of brothers. As early as 1899 Ottawa's local papers heralded this invitation: "The Robert McCracken family hockey team challenges any other family team to a match!" On that occasion it probably would have been better if the challenge had been issued. The Simms clan answered with a 12–0 rout. With a hint of sarcasm, the press reported the following day, "The McCrackens never were in the game!"

Probably because of the status of Henry Smith of Rideauville (Ottawa), the game which received the most ink was never played. When the eight McLarens of Perth published a similar challenge on February 5, 1904, theirs dared to dangle this opportunity to "ANY FAMILY TEAM IN THE WORLD." The offer was taken up by the Doyle brothers of Newmarket, the Clement brothers of Toronto and the Christmas brothers of parts unknown ... plus the aforementioned Smiths, who couldn't let the challenge go unanswered. In fact, they arranged some practice games with the Ottawa Beavers to prepare for the on-ice collision.

Unfortunately (or maybe fortunately for the Perth siblings), both the Smiths and the challengers had family members involved in crucial playoffs in the Canadian Amateur Hockey League, the Upper Ottawa Valley Hockey League and the Ontario Hockey Association, preventing them from taking time off for exhibition games. Kitchener could boast three such sibling squads: the Seiberts, the Schnarrs and the Kargos. The Seibert gang, of which Oliver, Eddie and Jimmy were the best known, took up this unique tradition in 1905, defeating the King family and the Schnarrs on a number of occasions. This novel practice continued on into the 1920s, with the latter clan of eight still active in this way. As late as 1922, they traveled extensively in the eastern USA playing exhibition games. As well, the Carroll brothers of Moncton made the headlines at the East Coast in 1923, by taking on the professional Victorias and whipping them three games straight.

From time to time, even in the 1950s, the press would point out unique situations involving families. In 1954, the Orono, Ontario junior squad, the Orphans, boasted eight brothers skating side by side, coached by none other than their proud papa. In 1959 the famed Bruins Kraut Line was reunited through the sons of Schmidt, Bauer and Dumart, in a four-minute showcase on national television from Boston. They were joined by Fern Flaman's son Terry, Craig and Glenn Patrick and (manager Lynn's boys) and Curt Bennett, imitating father Harvey, a one-time Bruin, along with Lance Reardon, Mitch Boivin and Bobby Pierson, sons of Terry, Leo and Johnny. They squared off against the Wellesley Pee-Wees.

The more hockey became a business, of course, the less time there was for such tomfoolery. However, this did not lessen the impact of the family factor on the game. While the Stanleys may be looked upon as hockey's "First Family," The Patricks, Lester and Frank, formed the roots of hockey's "Royal Family." They dominated as players from 1904 until the mid-1920s in several leagues, and jointly embarked on one of the most daring enterprises in all of shinny history, forming the Pacific Coast Association in 1912, competing boldly with the NHA in major-level hockey. Innovations, said to number at least 20, which they introduced to increase the pace of the sport—like the penalty shot, playoffs and forward passing—have had a profound impact which continues to this day. Both became successful in coaching and managerial roles in the NHL as well, Lester in New York and Frank in Boston. The former's sons, Lynn and Muzz, followed in their father's footsteps, both on and off the ice. Lynn's boys, Glenn and Craig, persevered to make the NHL as players, with Craig also becoming successful as a general manager with the Rangers and Pittsburgh.

Only one other clan can boast three generations represented on the ice in the NHL, namely the Hextalls. Bryan Sr. was a star in his own right in the 1930s and 1940s. His boys Bryan Jr. and Dennis battled their way up and down the league in a combined seven different arenas, collecting an aggregate 2,136 minutes in penalties. Bryan Jr.'s offspring, Ron, continues in this rugged family tradition, giving and taking no quarter, even though he does so from the goal crease. He is also the only netminder to have actually scored two goals in the NHL.

Ottawa has been called the cradle of hockey by some, and the cradles in the Boucher household certainly have produced some rare talent. Beginning with George (Buck) in 1917–18, and followed by Frank, Billy and Bobby, these four siblings ran up a combined total of 1,239 regular-season contests in the NHL. At one time the two older brothers skated together in Ottawa. They are both members of the Hall of Fame, not only for contributions on the ice, but for their skills behind the bench. The two younger boys were teammates in Montreal in the mid-1920s, although they failed to reach the heights marked by their older brothers. And while Frank was winning Lady Byng trophies, another pair, Odie and Sprague Cleghorn, were winding down their impressive careers which began with the Renfrew Millionaires in 1910-11. Odie mesmerized the opposition with his stickhandling wizardry while Sprague banged bodies and heads with reckless abandon, earning the reputation as one of the meanest defensemen ever to lace on skates. He claimed he only "gave back what was dished out to him," but he did so in the Biblical sense—four-fold. He was so rough his own manager once fined him for dirty play. Considered washed up when he broke both legs in 1918, he was purchased by Ottawa for the price of a train ticket. He starred for eight more years, then coached the Maroons. Odie graduated to playing coach with Pittsburgh in 1926 and actually was pressed into service as goalie for a game. He also officiated in the NHL. The two, always inseparable, died just five days apart in 1956.

As the Depression hit, the Conachers, Lionel, Charlie and Roy, blazed into the hockey scene. The eldest, Lionel, was Canada's athlete of the first half-century. Charlie became one of the greatest right wingers of all time, possessing a booming shot which could shatter rink end boards, and Roy, the baby of the trio, finished as a 200-goal scorer in the "Original Six" era. Competing with this Toronto family for top honors in "the Dirty Thirties" was a trio from Kingston by the name of Cook. Unlike the older Conacher brothers, Bill and Bun were sufficiently close in age to compete with several different centers, first in the old Western Hockey League and then in the NHL. Along with Frank Boucher, they formed one of the all-time great forward lines. All three have been inducted into the Hockey Hall of Fame. Like the Conachers, a younger brother came upon the scene later. However, Bud managed only 55 games in the big time. An amusing sidelight to the two families features Roy Conacher. Though selling concessions at Maple Leaf Gardens while big brother Charlie was part of the famed Kid Line, he maintained the Cook–Boucher combination was the best triumvirate in the world.

The Bentleys must be given the nod as the "family of the 1940s," with Max and Doug both eventually inducted into the Hall of Fame. Both won scoring championships and were voted to all-star teams several times. They were joined by brother Reg on December 3, 1942, to form the first all-brother forward line in the history of the NHL. It would be 40 years before the Stastnys would duplicate that feat. While Reg couldn't cut it at the NHL level, "the Dipsy Doodle Dandies From Delisle" consistently puzzled defenders with their water bug maneuvers, deking rearguards out of their britches.

The argument about whether Gordie Howe or Maurice Richard was the best NHL right winger in the 1950s has probably been laid to rest. But when it comes to sibling scoring, "the Rocket" received more help from little brother Henri than "Mr. Hockey" did from his sibling, Victor. The Habs' famous duet tallied 902 times; the Howes, with Vic scoring three markers, totaled 804. The next decade witnessed another battle royal for scoring honors, with the Mahovlich brothers, Frank and Peter, pitted against Bobby

and Dennis Hull. "The Big M" and "the Little M" had several inches on them in height, but the Pointe Anne boys lit 913 red lamps compared to 821 by the boys from Timmins. It will be interesting to see what Wayne Gretzky and brother Brent (with one goal) will manage to tally before their respective careers wrap up.

The mention of the Howes brings us to the rarest of all feats in major-league shinny: namely, a father playing together on the same team with his sons. The phenomenon has been reviewed scores of times. When the Houston Aeros of the World Hockey Association vied for the services of sons Mark and Marty, it was a family decision that they take a package deal which included 45-year-old Gordie, who had been out of active service for two years. Not only did "Mr. Elbows" fit in, but he scored 100 points to end up third in league scoring and was chosen an all-star at right wing. Mark was rookie of the year and made the second all-star team as a left winger. After three seasons with the Texas contingent they shifted to New England with the Whalers. From that vantage point they would enjoy the opening face-off as Hartford played its first game in the NHL in 1979. If there was a question about their success because of an "inferior league" it was soon put to rest after one go-round through the NHL. While only the Howes can claim major-league status of this kind, there have been two other situations similar at the minor pro level. In 1973, the Western Hockey League's Andy Hebenton, who was then 44, was joined by his son Clay. However, they played on different teams; Dad skated at right wing for Portland while his boy tended goal for Seattle. Then, in 1995, Mike and Jeff Antonovich toiled side by side for the Quad City Mallards against the Madison Monsters in the Colonial circuit (now the United Hockey League). Mike, the father, had been involved both in the WHA and NHL from 1972 through 1984, while Jeff was just a rookie.

With the six Sutter boys making their debuts in the world's premier circuit one after another over a five-year period, a new record was set for the number of players from one household to make it to the NHL. There have been several trios like the Carsons, the Kilreas, Leswicks, Hannigans, Cullens, Bennetts, Pronovosts, Rousseaus and Hillmans. The Bouchers, with four, had held the highest total previously. Doubtless this accomplishment never will be repeated or forgotten. And with their coaching skills so evident, their presence will be felt for many years to come. With the drafting of Rich and Ron in 1982, another element of distinction came to the fore, the number of twins who have made the big time. According to Lester Patrick, when Frank and Don Porteous caught on with the Washington Lions of the American Hockey League in 1947, it was the first instance of twins in the monied ranks. Had not Roy Conacher's twin, Bert, lost an eye through a fluke accident in the home, they would have held that distinction. He had great potential as a big leaguer. The Porteous boys, however, never made it to those dizzying heights of the NHL. Rich and Ron did. And not only were they the first to reach the NHL, but when Rich joined the Flyers in 1984, they were the first to skate side by side under the same banner. When manager Bob Clarke split them up by trading Rich to Vancouver in 1987, he received a generous piece of their father's mind for doing so. They were fortunate enough to become compadres again in 1991–92 with the Blues.

Patrik Sundstrom made the jump to the NHL in 1983 with Vancouver and twin Peter caught on with the Rangers a year later. But it wasn't until Peter's last campaign in North America that they became teammates with the New Jersey Devils. Though they tended to be shy, they fooled everyone one night in a game in Madison Square Garden by switching sweaters. But the record books can't be fooled, Patrik was simply a better player, a reality that has been typical not only with twins but with other brothers. Of the 207 sibling acts in NHL history, out of the 70 combinations which can rate a star status for at least one brother, 70 percent of them involve a player of inferior talent. Another such scenario almost transpired with the Wilson brothers. Carey Wilson, whose father Dr. Gerry Wilson played briefly with the Canadiens before choosing a medical career, caught on with Calgary. His brother Jeff was a good player, but not good enough. They skated together in the Swedish elite circuit but only Carey reached the NHL.

In the fall of 1984 the Winnipeg Jets circulated a posed picture of Paul and Perry Pooley in Jets livery. It was in conjunction with the announcement that this was the first instance of twins turning pro together with the same NHL team. Paul eventually skated in 14 contests for the Manitoba club, but Perry never got beyond the AHL. After two seasons they both went back to school. Since then, the Ferraro boys, Peter and Chris, have hurdled the line between minor and major-leaguers, first with the Rangers and then with Pittsburgh. At this point it would appear that they may be the closest ever to identical twins matching one another talent-wise as well as in appearance. At one point, it appeared as if there might be a new family phenomenon on the horizon—triplets. Craig, Glenn, and Brian Seabury insisted on sticking together and Division College of the NCAA took them as a package deal. However, very little has been heard of them since 1989–90.

While it is more common for brothers to play on opposing teams than to be teammates, it has been a rare thing for them to oppose one another in the role of coaches. When Lester and Frank Patrick formed the Pacific Coast Hockey Association they always skated in different directions. Most often, however, they were in team livery as well in executive positions. But on December 16, 1934, now in the NHL, they faced one another exclusively as bench bosses. Lester's Rangers defeated Frank's Bruins 2–1. Twenty years later it was Patrick versus Patrick again. On January 20, 1954, Lester's sons, Muzz and Lynn, lined up against one another. Again the Rangers, tutored by Muzz, whipped Lynn's Beantowners 8–3. On January 20, 1977, it was Johnny and Larry Wilson's turn. The *Windsor Star*, published just across the river from Detroit, where Johnny's Rockies would be hosted by Larry's Red Wings, quipped that their Mom, Carol, "couldn't lose no matter for whom she cheered!" But Larry did, to his older brother, 3–1. On October 6, 1990, Terry Murray brought his Caps into Detroit to take on Bryan's "Winged Wheelers." Again the home team didn't fare well in this unique contest, losing 6–4. Since then, it seems everywhere you look there is a Sutter; with Brian in Calgary, Darryl in San Jose and Brent assisting in Florida, household rivalry is inevitable.

Another aspect of the family factor is father-son combinations. To date, as near as can be determined, 70 dads have passed along their hockey genes to their offspring in sufficient quantity for them to make it to the top. There were also tandems in pre-NHL days, Harry "Rat" Westwick of Ottawa Silver Seven fame and his son Tommy, for instance, who played in the OPHL; Oliver Seibert, who played in the International (Pro) Hockey League in 1905, and his boy, Earl. Both are members of the Hockey Hall of Fame, mak

ing them first father and son playing combination so honored. Likewise Gordie Wilson, who had a cup of tea with the Bruins in the 1954–55, was the son of Hall of Famer Phat Wilson, who anchored Port Arthur's Allan Cup contingents in the 1920s.

One of the NHL's first illustrious duos would be Bert Lindsay, best known for his role with the Renfrew Millionaires and Victoria Aristocrats, but also a key member of the NHL Toronto Arenas in 1919, and Ted. The latter was called "Scarface" and "Terrible Ted" because he was one of the fiercest competitors, pound for pound, who ever graced the "Original Six" era. Even in nothing-at-stake oldtimers' games, he was so rambunctious, organizers stopped inviting him to participate.

Leo Reise Sr. and Leo Jr. are of that ancient vintage. Dad, who had only one eye, began his major-league career with the Hamilton Tigers, shifting with them to the Big Apple when they became the New York Americans. Junior broke in with Chicago in 1945–46 but skated mostly with Detroit. Leo Sr. dropped completely from the hockey scene when he retired, content to enjoy the peace and quiet of country living. Years later, he agreed to coach a Hamilton senior team. During the years he had been away from hockey the center red line had been added. Seeing it for the first time at the team's first practice, he announced, "The first thing we have to do is get rid of these darn curling marks!"

Other oldtimers whose offspring emulated their sire's choice of career were Ab DeMarco and Ab Jr., Babe Pratt and Tracy, Louis Holmes and Chuck, Jack Mackell and Fleming as well as Peanuts O'Flaherty and Gerry. At least two curiosities emanate from the father-son combinations. One is the matter of compared abilities.

It is fascinating to discover that few second generation skaters made as much of an impact in the NHL as did their fathers. Danny Geoffrion, for instance, couldn't carry his father's skates. Nor could Hank Goldup's boy, Glenn. Gordie Hampson, Ken Hodge Jr., Earl Ingarfield Jr., Daniel Laperriere and Jamie Leach, Reggie's son, fall into the same category. Rob Robinson and Guy Larose (the sons of Doug and Claude, respectively) could have their names added to such a list as well.

Some exceptions to that rule are Gene Carr, who carved deeper ruts in the ice than his pop, Red; Gary "Suitcase" Smith, who will be remembered longer than father Des; and Mike Walton, who required much more ink for stats sheets than his immediate ancestor, Robert. Had John Cullen not been afflicted with cancer, his superiority over Barry would have been even more distinct.

In some instances an accurate comparison is impossible. Emile "the Cat" Francis was a goalie, Bobby was a forward; likewise Adam and Andy Brown, Hank and Bob Bassen, Rogie and Nick Vachon as well as Harvey Bennett and his three boys. As for those who have proven themselves to be on par with their "old man," we might refer to Dave and Adam Creighton, Bobby Hull and Brett, Reg and Pete LoPresti, Rags and Herb Raglan as well as Larry and Ron Wilson. Statistics-wise, Syl Apps Jr. didn't appear to be far behind his illustrious dad, but, as for pure talent, he was short-circuited in that department.

The other area of interest relates to the suspicion of nepotism. One thing is certain; the Patrick family could never be accused of favoritism. Lester was frankly skeptical about Lynn's ability in the first place. He was also fearful of what fans might think if he, as general manager and coach of the Rangers, picked Lynn ahead of some other prospect. But the Cook brothers, as well as Frank Boucher, assured "the Silver Fox" that his boy was a major-leaguer. When Conn Smythe dropped into his office one day and offered $75,000 in cash for his prodigy, he felt reassured that the advice given him was sound. When Peter McNab's days were waning in Buffalo, father Max, then manager of Washington, considered making a pitch for his son's services. Both agreed that there would have been pressure placed upon each of them and the idea was dropped. Perhaps it was a wise decision. Pete went on to outscore the elder McNab by 353 goals to 16, and most of them came after he went to Boston, not to the District of Columbia.

But this question will not go away: would Brent Imlach ever have made it into a Maple Leafs uniform had not Punch been at the helm of Toronto? Would Terry Clancy have lasted 86 games in the same livery had King not been one of the coaching staff? Gerry Abel's only match in the big time was with his father's Red Wings in 1966–67. The Patricks were afraid of such suspicions, the McNabs avoided any possibility of it, but when it came to Bill and Kevin Dineen, it was thrust upon them. When the latter was traded to the Flyers in November of 1992, that move was followed by the hiring of his dad to be the Philly coach three weeks later. In a candid comment about the scenario, the younger Dineen said "he expected no special treatment from his father." He didn't get it. If he fouled up, his father was right on his case, as with any other player. It is also interesting to note that Bill Dineen played with Gordie Howe and coached Mark Howe.

Some random family anecdotes include: in 1920, when Ottawa netminder Clint Benedict picked a fight with Corb Denneny, his capital city teammate Cy Denneny took his brother's side and hauled "Benny" out of the fray. All three Plager brothers were goalies during their minor-league careers at one time or another. In 1964-65, Jimmy Peters Jr., called up for one game with the Red Wings, skated between Gordie Howe and Ted Lindsay, a position his father, Jim Sr., had held briefly in the 1950s.

The aforementioned seven Smith brothers of Ottawa fame had 1989 counterparts in the Stanfields. Although only Fred (the most famous), Jim and Jack made it to the NHL, four others were in organized shinny, with Joe and Vic having professional potential. Out of 22 sons of well-known NHL players, including Howie Morenz Jr., Lorne Chabot Jr., Brian Lindsay (Ted), Wayne Mosdell (Ken), Dennis Olmstead (Bert), Lee Fogolin (Lee) and Dave and Paul Gardner (Cal), only six made it to the big time. Brian Smith, while skating for L.A., created the first instance of a player scoring a goal against his brother. Gary was in net for Oakland. Foster and Bill Hewitt formed a combo which probably would be impossible to imitate, with a son following in his play-by-play footsteps, combining a total of 59 years as the "voices of the Toronto Maple Leafs."

Hockey was undoubtedly far from the mind of FBI director J. Edgar Hoover when he said, "The home is the citadel of American life! If the home is lost, all is lost!" The NHL, as well as leagues which preceded it, would not be lost if the family element was not included … but it would have left some huge gaps.

NHL FATHERS AND SONS
(Fathers listed first)

A
ABEL, Syd and Gerry
APPS, Syl and Syl Jr.
ATTWELL, Ron and Bob

B
BASSEN, Hank and Bob
BENNETT, Harvey and Harvey Jr.,
  Curt and Bill
BOILEAU, Rene and Marc
BORDELEAU, Paulin and Sebastien
BOUCHARD, Butch and Pierre
BROWN, Adam and Andy
BUBLA, Jiri and Jiri Slegr
BUCHANAN, Bucky and Ron

C
CARR, Red and Gene
CLANCY, King and Terry
CONACHER, Charlie and Pete
CONACHER, Lionel and Brian
CREIGHTON, Dave and Adam
CULLEN, Barry and John

D
DeMARCO, Ab and Ab Jr.
DINEEN, Bill and Kevin, Gord and Peter
DUBE, Norm and Christian

F
FERGUSON, Norm and Craig
FRANCIS, Emile and Bobby
FOGOLIN, Lidio and Lee

G
GARDNER, Cal and Dave and Paul
GEOFFRION, Bernie and Danny
GOLDUP, Hank and Glenn

H
HAMPSON, Ted and Gord
HAWORTH, Gord and Alan
HEXTALL, Bryan and Bryan Jr.
  and Dennis
HEXTALL, Bryan Jr. and Ron
HICKS, Wayne and Alex
HODGE, Ken and Ken Jr.
HOLMES, Lou and Chuck
HOWE, Gordie and Mark and Marty
HULL, Bobby and Brett

I
INGARFIELD, Earl and Earl Jr.

J
JOHANSEN, Bill (Johnson) and Trevor

L
LAFRENIERE, Roger and Jason
LAPERRIERE, Jacques and Daniel
LAROSE, Claude and Guy
LEACH, Reggie and Jamie
LINDSAY, Bert and Ted
LoPRESTI, Sam and Pete

M
MACKELL, Jack and Fleming
McCREARY, Bill and Bill E.
McMAHON, Mike and Mike W.
McNAB, Max and Peter
MORRISON, Jim and Dave

O
O'FLAHERTY, Peanuts and Gerry

P
PALAZZARI, Aldo and Doug
PATRICK, Lester and Muzz and Lynn
PATRICK, Lynn and Craig and Glenn
PETERS, Jim and Jimmy.
PRATT, Babe and Tracy

R
RAGLAN, Clare and Herb
REISE, Leo and Leo Jr.
RIGGIN, Dennis and Pat
ROBERTS, Doug and David
ROBINSON, Doug and Rob

S
SMITH, Des and Brian and Gary
SMITH, Stu E. and Brian
SMRKE, Stan and John
STAPLETON, Pat and Mike

V
VACHON, Rogie and Nick

W
WALTON, Bob and Mike
WARD, Don and Joe
WILSON, Larry and Ron
WILSON, Jerry and Carey
WILSON, Rik and Landon

NHL BROTHER COMBINATIONS

A
ALLEN, George and Viv
ALLISON, Mike and Dave
ANDERSSON, Mikael and Niklas
ARBOUR, John and Ty

B
BABYCH, Wayne and Dave
BARRETT, Fred and John
BATHGATE, Andy and Frank
BELL, Joe and Gordie
BENNETT, Curt, Harvey Jr. and Bill
BENNING, Jim and Brian
BENTLEY, Doug, Max and Reg
BERRY, Doug and Ken
BLAIR, Chuck and George
BORDELEAU, J.P., Paulin and Chris
BOUCHER, Frank, George,
  Bobby and Billy
BOURCIER, Conrad and Jean
BRODERICK, Ken and Len
BROTEN, Neal, Aaron and Paul
BROWN, Doug and Greg
BROWNSCHIDLE, Jeff and Jack
BRUNETEAU, Eddie and Mud
BRYDSON, Glenn and Gord
BUSNIUK, Ron and Mike

C
CAFFERY, Jack and Terry
CALLANDAR, Drew and John
CAMAZZOLA, James and Tony
CAPUANO, Jack and Dave
CARLSON, Jack and Steve
CARSE, Bob and Bill
CARSON, Bill, Gerry and Frank
CAVALLINI, Gino and Paul
CHERRY, Don and Dick
CLEGHORN, Sprague and Odie
COLVILLE, Mac and Neil
CONACHER, Lionel, Charlie and Roy
COOK, Bill, Bun and Bud
COULTER, Art and Tommy
COSTELLO, Les and Murray
COURTNALL, Geoff and Russ
CROWDER, Keith and Bruce
CRAWFORD, Bob, Marc and Lou
CULLEN, Brian, Barry and Ray

D
DAMORE, Nick and Hank
DARRAGH, Harold and Jack
DENNENY, Cy and Corb
DILLON, Wayne and Gary
DINEEN, Kevin, Gord and Peter
DIONNE, Marcel and Gilbert
DRYDEN, Ken and Dave

E
EAVES, Murray and Mike
ESPOSITO, Phil and Tony

NHL BROTHER COMBINATIONS
continued

F
FILLION, Bob and Marcel
FINNIGAN, Ed and Frank
FLOCKHART, Ron and Bob
FRASER, Archie and Harry

G
GARDNER, Paul and Dave
GASSOFF, Bob and Brad
GILLIS, Mike and Paul
GLOVER, Fred and Howie
GOULD, John and Larry
GRATTON, Gilles and Norm
GREEN, Red and Shorty
GREIG, Mark and Bruce
GRETZKY, Wayne and Brent

H
HAMEL, Jean and Gilles
HANNIGAN, Pat, Gordie and Ray
HANSON, Ossie and Emil
HARKINS, Todd and Brett
HARRIS, Fred and Henry
HATCHER, Kevin and Derian
HEXTALL, Bryan Jr. and Dennis
HERGESHEIMER, Wally and Phil
HICKEY, Pat and Greg
HICKE, Bill and Ernie
HICKS, Glenn and Doug
HILLMAN, Larry, Wayne and Floyd
HOEKSTRA, Ed and Cecil
HOLT, Gary and Randy
HOWE, Gordie and Vic
HOWE, Marty and Mark
HOWELL, Harry and Ron
HULL, Bobby and Dennis
HUNTER, Dave, Dale and Mark

I
IHNACAK, Peter and Miroslav

J
JACKSON, Busher and Art
JERWA, Joe and Frank
JOHNSON, Greg and Ryan
JOLIET, Aurel and Bobby
JONES, Bob and Jim

K
KANNEGIESSER, Gord and Sheldon
KILREA, Wally, Hec and Ken
KITCHEN, Mike and Bill
KORDIC, John and Dan
KULLMAN, Arnie and Eddie
KYLE, Bill and Gus

L
LaFOREST, Bob and Mark
LARMER, Steve and Jeff
LEBEAU, Stephan and Patrick
LEFLEY, Chuck and Bryan
LEMIEUX, Alain and Mario
LEMIEUX, Claude and Jocelyn
LEPINE, Pit and Hec

LESWICK, Tony, Peter and Jack
LINDEN, Trevor and Jamie
LINDROS, Eric and Brett
LOOB, Peter and Hakan
LOUGHLIN, Clem and Wilf
LOWREY, Gerry and Fred

M
MacMILLAN, Billy and Bob
MAHOVLICH, Frank and Pete
MAKI, Chico and Wayne
MALONEY, Don and Dave
MANERY, Randy and Kris
MANTHA, Sylvio and Georges
McATEE, Norm and Jud
McCRAE, Basil and Chris
McCREARY, Keith and Bill
MENARD, Howie and Hillary
MESSIER, Joby and Mitch
MESSIER, Mark and Paul
METZ, Don and Nick
MICHALUK, Art and John
MICHELETTI, Pat and Joe
MEISSNER, Dick and Barrie
MILLER, Bob and Paul
MILLER, Kelly, Kevin and Kip
MIRONOV, Dmitri and Boris
MOKOSAK, John and Carl
MOLLER, Mike and Randy
MORRISON, Mark and Doug
MORRISON, Rod and Don
MULLEN, Joe and Brian
MULVEY, Grant and Paul
MURDOCH, Don and Bob

N
NELSON, Jeff and Todd
NIEDERMAYER, Scott and Rob
NIELSON, Jeff and Kirk

O
ODELEIN, Lyle and Selmar
O'SHEA, Kevin and Danny

P
PAIEMENT, Rosaire and Wilf
PATEY, Larry and Doug
PATRICK, James and Steve
PATRICK, Muzz and Lynn
PATRICK, Craig and Glenn
PETTINGER, Gord and Eric
PICARD, Roger and Noel
PLAGER, Barclay, Bob and Bill
PLAYFAIR, Larry and Jim
PLUMB, Rob and Ron
POILE, Don and Bud
POTVIN, Denis and Jean
PRENTICE, Dean and Eric
PRIMEAU, Kevin and Wayne
PRONGER, Chris and Sean
PRONOVOST, Marcel, Jean and Claude

Q
QUACKENBUSH, Bill and Max

R
REARDON, Ken and Terry
REDMOND, Mickey and Dick
RICHARD, Maurice and Henri
RIVERS, Shawn and Jamie
ROBERGE, Mario and Serge
ROBINSON, Larry and Moe
ROCHE, Earl and Michel
ROBERTS, Doug and Gordie
ROBERTSON, Torrie and Gordie
ROUSSEAU, Bobby, Roland and Guy
ROY, Patrick and Stephane

S
SABOURIN, Bob and Gary
SACCO, David and Joe
SAUVE, J.F. and Bob
SCHMAUTZ, Bobby and Cliff
SCHMIDT, Joe and Jackie
SCHOCK, Ron and Danny
SEILING, Rod and Ric
SHANNON, Gerry and Charles
SHANNON, Darrin and Darryl
SHEPPARD, Johnny and Frank
SHILL, Jack and Bill
SHEEHY, Tim and Neil
SIMON, Cully and Thain
SMITH, Gary and Brian
SMITH, Kenny and Don A.
SMITH, Des and Roger
SMITH, Carl and Dalton
SMITH, Billy and Gord
SMYTH, Kevin and Ryan
SOBCHUCK, Gene and Dennis
STANFIELD, Fred, Jack and Jim
STANKIEWICZ, Edward and Myron
STASTNY, Peter, Marian and Anton
STEVENS, Scott and Mike
SUNDSTROM, Peter and Patrik
SULLIVAN, Frank and Peter
SUTTER, Brian, Brent, Duane,
    Darryl, Ron and Rich

T
TAYLOR, Tim and Chris
TEAL, Skip and Skeeter
THOMPSON, Tiny and Paul
TOPPAZZINI, Gerry and Zellio
TROTTIER, Bryan and Rocky
TURGEON, Pierre and Sylvain

V
VOPAT, Jan and Roman

W
WARWICK, Grant and Bill
WATSON, Joe and Jimmy
WEBSTER, Don and Chick
WESLEY, Blake and Glen
WILLIAMS, Gord and Fred
WILLIAMS, Tom and Warren
WILSON, Larry and Johnny
WILSON, Murray and Doug

Y
YAREMCHUK, Gary and Ken

FORWARD LINES

John Halligan

Special thanks to Ron Boileau, Steve Charendoff and
Glen R. Goodhand for their research on forward combinations.

WHERE, OH WHERE have all the great lines gone? For the most part, not literally but figuratively, they've gone to the great ice patch in the sky.

Like the drop pass, the rover and leather helmets, hockey lines nowadays are more frequently remembered than they are experienced. There are exceptions, of course, but fundamental changes to the game itself—technology, coaching strategies and frequent player movement—have all conspired against three teammates staying together as a single line for a significant period of time.

Hockey lines—and their nicknames—have been with us for three quarters of a century or so. Often, the names have changed, or been used interchangeably, by more than one or two different combinations. The names run the gamut, quite literally from A to Z, in an alphabet soup that is as diverse as the game of hockey itself.

Even in decline, hockey lines have proven to be a hardy sort. Over the decades, they have taken their monikers from every corner, be it age, size, ethnicity and often pure whimsy.

Herewith, hockey's greatest lines over the years:

In most instances, linemates names are listed from left to right with left wing first, followed by center and right wing. Seasons listed for lines are approximate as line combinations were formed, named, broken up and re-formed as club needs dictated.

A

"A" LINE
Bun Cook – Frank Boucher – Bill Cook
New York Rangers, 1926–1936
So named for the Eighth Avenue subway line—the A Train—that was constructed along Eighth Avenue beneath the old Madison Square Garden.

ATOMIC LINE
Church Russell – Cal Gardner – Rene Trudell
New York Rangers, 1940s
This trio was also known as the Rover Line and the Winnipeg Kid Line.

B

BACON LINE
Sweeney Schriner – Gus Bodnar – Lorne Carr
Toronto Maple Leafs, 1940s
They brought home the bacon.

BANANA LINE
John Tonelli – Wayne Merrick – Bob Nystrom
New York Islanders, 1970s–1980s
They wore yellow jerseys in practice.

BASH, DASH & STASH
Pat Boutette – Mike Rogers – Blaine Stoughton
Hartford Whalers, 1979 to 1981

BEE LINE
Alan Kuntz – Clint Smith – Grant Warwick
New York Rangers, 1941–42

BIG LINE
Gordie Drillon – Syl Apps – Nick Metz.
Toronto Maple Leafs, 1930s–1940s
Numerous other lines named the Big Line over the years.

BLACK ACES
Any team, any era. Particularly during the playoffs. Three, four or more players who do not regularly play in games, but practice together away from the regular team. Hockey's version of a taxi squad. Nickname dates to the Springfield Indians of legendary Eddie Shore in the 1940s.

BLANKET LINE
Woody Dumart – Milt Schmidt – Joe Klukay
Boston Bruins, 1950s
They covered the opposition.

BOILERMAKER LINE
Roy Conacher – Doug Bentley – Bill Mosienko
Chicago Black Hawks, 1948 to 1950
The Black Hawks trio of Bert Olmstead, Metro Prystai and Bep Guidolin was also know as the Boilermaker Line.

BRAT LINE
Tiger Williams – Jack Valiquette – Pat Boutette
Toronto Maple Leafs, 1970s
They all played an abrasive style.

BREAD LINE
Mac Colville – Neil Colville – Alex Shibicky
New York Rangers, 1930s–1940s
They were the team's bread and butter. The name was not related to the actual bread lines that formed during the Great Depression

BULLDOG LINE
Steve Vickers – Walt Tkaczuk – Bill Fairbairn
New York Rangers, 1970s
Tenacious checkers all. Dave Balon preceded Vickers at left wing in the late 1960s

BUZZ-SAW LINE
Bob Berry – Juha Widing – Mike Byers
Los Angeles Kings, 1970s

C

CENTURY LINE
Lowell MacDonald – Syl Apps – Jean Pronovost
Pittsburgh Penguins, 1970s
A veteran threesome that was also known as the MAP Line and the Bicentennial Line; Doug Bentley – Edgar Laprade – Max Bentley of the New York Rangers, 1953–54, were also known as the Century Line.

CHAOS LINE
Marc Crawford – Ron Delorme – Gary Lupul
Vancouver Canucks, 1980s

CLUB CHAOS
Rich Sutter – Steve Bozek – Stan Smyl
Vancouver Canucks, 1980s

THE CLYDESDALES
Curt Fraser – Eddie Olczyk – Troy Murray
Chicago Blackhawks, 1980s

CRASH LINE
Randy McKay – Bobby Holik – Mike Peluso
New Jersey Devils, 1990s

CRAZY EIGHTS
Brent Fedyk – Eric Lindros – Mark Recchi
Philadelphia Flyers, 1993 to 1995
Numbers 8, 18 and 88.

CRISIS LINE
Brian Lawton – Dennis Maruk – Brian Bellows
Minnesota North Stars, 1980s

CURRY LINE
Luc Robitaille – Tomas Sandstrom – Jari Kurri
Los Angeles Kings, 1990s
Hot like curry; also known as the International Line.

CYCLONE LINE
Bob Davidson – Art Jackson – Nick Metz
Toronto Maple Leafs, 1930s

D

DAD LINE
Gordie Drillon – Syl Apps – Bob Davidson
Toronto Maple Leafs, 1930s–1940s

DESTRUCTION LINE
Scott Daniels – Mark Janssens – Kelly Chase
Hartford Whalers, 1995–96

DIAPER LINE
David Jensen – Eddie Olczyk – Pat LaFontaine
United States Olympic team, 1984

DICE LINE
Richard Kromm – Carey Wilson – Colin Patterson
Calgary Flames, 1980s

DOGS OF WAR
Wayne Cashman – Phil Esposito – Ken Hodge
Boston Bruins, 1960s–1970s

DONUT LINE
A name used in jest. Any team, any era. Two talented wingers with a no-name center. A line with a "hole in the middle."

DYNAMITE LINE
Cooney Weiland – Dutch Gainor – Dit Clapper
Boston Bruins, 1920s–1930s

F

FLOCKY HOCKEY
Brian Propp – Ron Flockhart – Ray Allison
Philadelphia Flyers, 1980s

FLOWER POWER
Steve Shutt – Peter Mahovlich – Guy Lafleur
Montreal Canadiens, 1970s

FLYING FORTS
Gaye Stewart – Gus Bodnar – Bud Poile
Toronto Maple Leafs, Chicago Black Hawks, 1940s
They all hailed from Fort William, Ontario.

FOSSIL LINE
Peter McNab – Mel Bridgman – Rich Preston
New Jersey Devils, 1985–86
Age was creeping up on this trio.

FRENCH CONNECTION
Richard Martin – Gilbert Perreault – Rene Robert
Buffalo Sabres, 1970s

FTD LINE
Sylvain Turgeon – Ron Francis – Kevin Dineen
Hartford Whalers, 1980s
They always delivered.

G

G LINE
Clark Gillies – Butch Goring – Greg Gilbert
New York Islanders, 1980s

G-A-G Line
Vic Hadfield – Jean Ratelle – Rod Gilbert
New York Rangers, 1960s–1970s
The name stood for Goal-A-Game; later it was changed to the T-A-G Line for Two-A-Game. Ratelle, Gilbert and Steve Vickers were known as the G-A-G II Line

GABBY LINE
Ray Getliffe – Murph Chamberlain – Phil Watson
Montreal Canadiens, 1943–44
Dirk Irvin called them holler guys.

GEM LINE
Mark Osborne – Eddie Olczyk – Gary Leeman
Toronto Maple Leafs, 1980s
Their first initials supplied the name.

GMC LINE
Brett Callighen – Wayne Gretzky – Blair MacDonald
Edmonton Oilers, 1979–80.
Their last initials supplied the name.

GO GO LINE
Larry Lund – Andre Hinse – Frank Hughes
Houston Aeros (WHA), 1970s

GOL LINE
Danny Grant – Danny O'Shea – Claude Larose
Minnesota North Stars, 1968 to 1970

GREEN LINE
Jack Adams – Elmer Lach – Tony Demers
Montreal Canadiens, 1940–41
Named for their youth and inexperience, like the Kid Line

GRIND LINE
Basil McRae – Dave Gagner – Stew Gavin
Minnesota North Stars, 1987 to 1992

GRIND LINE
Kirk Maltby – Kris Draper – Joe Kocur
Detroit Red Wings, 1997–98

H

HELICOPTER LINE
A line with a great center and no-name wings. Used in jest, like the Donut Line.

HEM LINE
Frank Mahovlich – Billy Harris – Gerry Ehman
Toronto Maple Leafs, 1950s–1960s

HOUND LINE
Wendel Clark – Gary Leeman – Russ Courtnall
Toronto Maple Leafs, 1980s
All three played midget hockey for the Notre Dame Hounds in Wilcox, Saskatchewan.

HOT LINE
Ron Murphy – Phil Esposito – Ken Hodge
Boston Bruins, 1960s
Johnny Bucyk – Fred Stanfield – Johnny McKenzie
Boston Bruins, 1970s
Bobby Hull – Ulf Nilsson – Anders Hedberg
Winnipeg Jets (WHA), 1970s
And many others on various teams.

HUM LINE
Paul Henderson – Norm Ullman – Bruce MacGregor
Detroit Red Wings, 1960s

HUSKY LINE
Harry Watson – Billy Taylor – Cal Gardner
Toronto Maple Leafs, 1940s–1950s

K

KID LINE
Harvey "Busher" Jackson – Joe Primeau – Charlie Conacher
Toronto Maple Leafs, 1930s
Teamed up as inexperienced NHL youngsters, they became the most famous Toronto line of all time.

KID LINE 2
Ted Kennedy – Howie Meeker – Vic Lynn
Toronto Maple Leafs, 1940s
Brit Selby – Pete Stemkowski – Ron Ellis
Toronto Maple Leafs, 1960s
There have been many other Kid Lines on other teams.

KGB LINE
Anders Kallur – Butch Goring – Bob Bourne
New York Islanders, 1980s

KLM LINE
Vladimir Krutov – Igor Larionov – Sergei Makarov
USSR, 1980s

KRAUT LINE

Woody Dumart – Milt Schmidt – Bobby Bauer
Boston Bruins, 1930s–1940s

The most famous line in Boston Bruins history. During World War Two, they were renamed The Kitchener Kids as all three hailed from the Kitchener-Waterloo area of Ontario (an area heavily populated by people of German descent, which had contributed to the original Kraut Line moniker).

KSS LINE

Ted Kennedy – Sid Smith – Tod Sloan
Toronto Maple Leafs, 1940s–1950s

L

L LINE

Tony Leswick – Edgar Laprade – Pentti Lund
New York Rangers, 1940s

LCB LINE

Reggie Leach – Bob Clarke – Bill Barber
Philadelphia Flyers, 1970s–1980s

Also known as the Godfather Line.

LEG LINE

Paul Lawless – Dean Evason – Stewart Gavin
Hartford Whalers, 1985–86

THE LEGION OF DOOM

John LeClair – Eric Lindros – Mikael Renberg
Philadelphia Flyers, 1995 to 97

LIFE LINE

Brian Propp – Pelle Eklund – Rick Tocchet
Philadelphia Flyers, 1980s
Geoff Courtnall – Cliff Ronning – Trevor Linden
Vancouver Canucks, 1990s
Jim Morrison – Jim Thomson – George Armstrong
Toronto Maple Leafs, 1950s

Short-lived line as Morrison and Thomson were mainly defensemen.

LIGHTNING LINE

Norm Dussault – Billy Reay – Leo Gravelle
Montreal Canadiens, 1940s

LINIMENT LINE

Don Grosso – Sid Abel – Eddie Wares
Detroit Red Wings, 1940s

LONG ISLAND ELECTRIC COMPANY

Clark Gillies – Bryan Trottier – Billy Harris
New York Islanders, 1970s

First great Islanders line, they lit up arenas around the NHL

LUXURY LINE

Bobby Hull – Christian Bordeleau – Norm Beaudin
Winnipeg Jets (WHA), 1970s

M

MAD LINE

Nick Metz – Syl Apps – Gord Drillon
Toronto Maple Leafs, 1930s–1940s

MAFIA LINE

Don Maloney – Phil Esposito – Don Murdoch
New York Rangers, 1970s–1980s

The Godfather, Esposito, and two Dons.

MEATBALL LINE

Bert Olmstead – Metro Prystai – Bep Guidolin
Chicago Black Hawks, 1940s

MIKE LINE

Mike McPhee – Mike Modano – Mike Craig
Minnesota North Stars, 1992–93

MILLION DOLLAR LINE

Bobby Hull – Bill Hay – Murray Balfour
Chicago Black Hawks, 1960s

MPH LINE

Bobby Hull – Stan Mikita – Jim Pappin
Chicago Black Hawks, 1960s

MUSCLE LINE

Ken Smith – Paul Ronty – Johnny Peirson
Boston Bruins, 1947 to 1950

N

NICK 'EM, NOCK 'EM, NEUF 'EM

Nick Fotiu – Don Nachbaur – Ray Neufeld
Hartford Whalers, 1980–81

Also known as NICKY-NACKY-NEUKY.

O

OFF BROADWAY LINE

Tom Williams – Gene Carr – Mike Murphy
New York Rangers, 1973–74

OLD SMOOTHIES

Don Marshall – Phil Goyette – Bob Nevin
New York Rangers, 1964 to 1969

OPTION LINE

Kevin Stevens – John Cullen – Mark Recchi
Pittsburgh Penguins, 1988 to 1991

OVER THE HILL LINE

John Tonelli – Doug Risebrough – Lanny McDonald
Calgary Flames, 1986 to 1988

Also known as the Not Ready For Retirement Line.

P

PAPOOSE LINE

Pete Conacher – Murray Costello – Larry Wilson
Chicago Black Hawks, 1953–54

They were all just 20 years old.

PAPPY LINE

Ted Lindsay – Tod Sloan – Ed Litzenberger
Chicago Black Hawks, 1957 to 1960

PIPE LINE

Peter Klima – Bernie Nicholls – Joe Murphy
Edmonton Oilers, 1991–92

PLUMBER LINE

Greg Adams – Alan Haworth – Craig Laughlin
Washington Capitals, 1980s

PONY LINE

Doug Bentley – Max Bentley – Bill Mosienko
Chicago Black Hawks, 1940s

PONY EXPRESS

Andre Boudrias – Richard Lemieux – Bobby Lalonde
Vancouver Canucks, 1972 to 1974

POWERHOUSE LINE

Lynn Patrick – Phil Watson – Bryan Hextall
New York Rangers, 1930s–1940s

PPS LINE

Bob Pulford – Pete Stemkowski – Jim Pappin
Toronto Maple Leafs, 1960s

PRODUCTION LINE

Ted Lindsay – Sid Abel – Gordie Howe
Detroit Red Wings, 1940s–1950s

The most famous line in Detroit history and probably the most famous line in NHL history.
Named for their prolific offensive ability and the production of the assembly lines in the Motor City.

PRODUCTION LINE 2

Frank Mahovlich – Alex Delvecchio – Gordie Howe
Detroit Red Wings, 1960s

PUNCH LINE

Toe Blake – Elmer Lach – Maurice Richard
Montreal Canadiens, 1940s.

R

RAT PATROL
Brian Propp – Ken Linseman – Paul Holmgren
Philadelphia Flyers, 1978 to 1982

RAZZLE DAZZLE LINE
Pierre Morin – Buddy O'Connor – Jerry Heffernan
Montreal Canadiens, 1941–42

REPRODUCTION LINE
Gaye Stewart – Metro Prystai – George Gee
Chicago Black Hawks, 1948–49

ROARING TWENTIES LINE
Bob Kelly – Dennis Maruk – Jean Pronovost
Washington Capitals, 1980–81
     They all had numbers in the 20s.

ROCKS
Johnny Wilson – Duke Edmunson – Gerry James
Toronto Maple Leafs, 1959 to 60
     Also known as the Clothes Line.

RPM LINE
Terry Ruskowski – Rich Preston – Grant Mulvey
Chicago Black Hawks, 1979 to 1983

S

S LINE
Babe Siebert – Nels Stewart – Hooley Smith
Montreal Maroons, 1929 to 1932
     Also know as the 3-S-Line.

SAW LINE
Harry Watson – Tod Sloan – George Armstrong
Toronto Maple Leafs, 1947 to 1954

SCOOTER LINE
Doug Mohns – Stan Mikita – Ken Wharram
Chicago Black Hawks, 1964 to 1969

SH-BOOM LINE
Real Chevrifils – Fleming Mackell – Leo Labine
Boston Bruins, 1952 to 1959
     Also known as the Crew Cuts.

SHIFT DISTURBERS
Rick Tocchet – Ron Sutter – Rich Sutter
Philadelphia Flyers, 1984 to 1986

SHINK-SHACK-SHOCK
Eddie Shack – Ron Schock – Ken Schinkel
Pittsburgh Penguins, 1971 to 1973

SIZZLE LINE
Dickie Moore – Jean Beliveau – Bernie Geoffrion
Montreal Canadiens, 1951 to 1963
     Also known as the Dream Line.

S-O-S LINE
Harry Watson – Red Sullivan – Eddie Litzenberger
Chicago Black Hawks, 1955–56
     Strong On Scoring.

SPECIAL K LINE
Paul Kariya – Chad Kilger – Todd Krygier
Anaheim Mighty Ducks, 1995–96

SPEEDBALL LINE
Aurel Joliat – Howie Morenz – Johnny Gagnon
Montreal Canadiens, 1930 to 1934

SPROUT LINE
Bep Guidolin – Don Gallinger – John Schmidt
Boston Bruins, 1942–43
     So called due to their youth and the fact that they were
     playing with the Bruins when Schmidt, Dumart and Bauer
     of the Kraut Line were serving in the Canadian Air Force.
     Guidolin, Gallinger and Bill Shill were also known as the
     Sprout Line.

SST LINE
Petri Skriko – Patrik Sundstrom – Tony Tanti
Vancouver Canucks, 1984 to 1987

SWAT LINE
Tiger Williams – Patrik Sundstrom – Tony Tanti
Vancouver Canucks, 1980s

T

THREE ACES
Dick Duff – Tod Sloan – George Armstrong
Toronto Maple Leafs, 1955 to 1958

THREE FEATHERS
Joe Klukay – Max Bentley – Ray Timgren
Toronto Maple Leafs, 1948 to 1952

THREE GUN LINE
Roy Conacher – Bill Cowley – Eddie Wiseman
Boston Bruins, 1940 to 1942

THREE-M LINE
Bob Murdoch – Dennis Maruk – Al MacAdam
Cleveland Barons, 1976 to 1978

TRE KRONER LINE
Bengt Lundholm – Thomas Steen – Willy Lindstrom
Winnipeg Jets, 1980s
     Named for the emblem on the Swedish flag. Also
     known as the Swedish Connection.

TRICKY TRIO
Vic Lynn – Ted Kennedy – Howie Meeker
Toronto Maple Leafs, 1946 to 1950

TRIO GRANDE
Clark Gillies – Bryan Trottier – Mike Bossy
New York Islanders, 1970s–1980s
     Also known as the Long Island Electrical Company.

TRIPLE CROWN LINE
Charlie Simmer – Marcel Dionne – Dave Taylor
Los Angeles Kings, 1970s–1980s

TYPHOON LINE
Kenny Smith – Frank Mario– Bill Cupulo
Boston Bruins, 1944–45

U

UKE LINE
Johnny Bucyk – Bronco Horvath – Vic Stasiuk
Boston Bruins, 1957 to 1961
     All three players were of Ukrainian descent.

UNITED NATIONS LINE
Valery Kamensky – Peter Forsberg – Claude Lemieux
Colorado Avalanche, 1995 to 1997
     Also known as Barrage-A-Trois.

W

WILLY, BILLY & SILLY
Dave Semenko – Billy Carroll – Willy Lindstrom
Edmonton Oilers, 1984–85
Jay Miller – Billy O'Dwyer – Willi Plett
Boston Bruins, 1987–88

WING LINE
Paul Henderson – Norm Ullman – Floyd Smith
Toronto Maple Leafs, 1968 to 1970
     So named because all three were acquired in the same
     trade from the Detroit Red Wings.

WOOLWORTH LINE
Nick Metz – Art Jackson – Pep Kelly
Toronto Maple Leafs, 1934 to 1937
     Metz wore number 5, Kelly number 15 and Jackson
     number 20, popular prices of the day at Woolworth
     stores.

WRECKING LINE
Floyd Curry – Ken Mosdell – Calum MacKay
Montreal Canadiens, 1949 to 1955

WHERE HAVE ALL THE NICKNAMES GONE?

Glen R. Goodhand

CURRENT PROFESSIONAL HOCKEY is missing three specific elements that gave "the good old days" color of which its modern counterpart knows nothing:

- the excitement generated by stickhandling reminiscent of Max Bentley, Ted Kennedy and Bill Cowley, as opposed to the run-and-gun tactics of the 1970s, 1980s, and 1990s.
- Honest bodychecking in open ice instead of the "roller-derby" board bashing practiced today and disguised as "solid hitting."
- An atmosphere of comradeship that inspired, among other things, the constant reference to players by nicknames, rather than their given names that appeared on their birth certificates.

A quick review of an early day's "Who's Who" on big-league ice surfaces records the bynames of stars like Pud Glass, Riley Hern, Dubbie Kerr, Sibby Nichols, Mickey McKay, Babe Siebert, Wingy Johnson, and Ants Antas. These personalities graced the pages of local papers, and were on the lips of loyal fans during those "Golden Years" of hockey.

Oh, similar handles do infiltrate the contemporary scene; readers can find them in virtually every NHL team fact book. But these are mostly pet names, seldom getting farther than dressing rooms or game interactions. Mark Osborne has been "Ossie" during his stint with four different clubs; Paul Coffey was "Coff" in Edmonton, Pittsburgh and Philly; and Al Iafrate has borne the burden of being "Skiis" wherever he has laced on his oversized blades. But even the media makes little of these in-house agnomens.

The last pure nicknames in recent years, the kind that used to replace first names in stats columns, for instance, belonged to Michel (Bunny) Larocque, Eldon (Pokey) Reddick, Dave (Tiger) Williams, and particularly Butch Goring. Goring's proper name, Robert, may only have been known by his parents, his wife and team executives who signed his contract. As for Larocque, he revealed that he had buck teeth as a boy, hence the rabbit-like reference. In James Lawton's chronicle of the Saskatchewan-born Williams, chapter one was introduced with these words: "He has been known as 'Tiger' from his first day on the frozen river at Weyburn." Pokey Reddick, meanwhile, maintained the kind of pace around home, especially when chores were to be done, that prompted his father to address him in this fashion.

But genuine nicknames—the kind described above—are virtually unknown in pro circuits today. Like so much of the light-hearted, "good-time Charlie" atmosphere that was in vogue in hockey's fledgling years, they have been replaced with salary arbitration and player agents. Who can argue that something had to be done to offset the perpetual treatment of shinny's artisans by pawns of power-hungry dictators? Babe Pratt once quipped that he dropped his paycheck on the way to the bank one day, and "an ant with a hernia picked it up and ran off with it!" Perhaps it cannot be expected that, in these days of economic Russian Roulette, the carefree attitude concerning money exhibited by the stars of days gone by should be initiated. (King Clancy declared he would have played even if they hadn't paid

him.) But a little "lightening-up" today might just bring part of that "Gashouse Gang" spirit back into the game. And that would benefit both players and fans. It is probably no coincidence that personal epithets began to disappear about the same time that the Players' Association was in its embryo form. Surely this great game could have become a business (which is the way they refer to it now), without losing part of its heart and soul ... something called fun!

Over 300 agnomens of a significant nature appear in the player registers of the NHA and NHL, which date back to 1910. About one-third of these represent those which almost completely replaced a player's John Henry both publicly and privately. For instance Mush March was almost never addressed as Harold; Taffy Abel seldom heard anyone call for Clarence; Rip Riopelle's given name was Howard, but Danny Gallivan would no more echo that moniker than say: "The puck is in the net!" Even the most astute historian may be hard-pressed to recall that Hooley Smith was really Reginald and that Red Kelly was christened Leonard. The seemingly endless list of nicknames include both the sublime and the ridiculous, the baffling and the bizarre. Overall, nicknames fall into at least 18 different categories.

Nationality noms de plume

Five well-known skaters of Germanic background were called "Dutch": Herb Cain, Wilbert Hiller, Earl Reibel, Frank Nighbor, and Armond Delmonte. Alex Levinsky was "Mine Boy" because, when his father used to watch him play at Maple Leaf Gardens, he would proudly let it be known in proper Yiddish grammatical construction: "That's *mine boy* out there!"

Irwin Boyd, as one of the first American-born players in the NHL was addressed as "Yank." Pat Egan's real name was Martin. His father, however, was a very patriotic Irishman, and the Egan home was identified by a large shamrock. In derision his friends tagged young Martin as "Pat." But he must hold some kind of record for aliases. A number of players have borne two nicknames, but he managed to attract no less than six. Other than the one already mentioned, he was "Marty," "Joe," "the Great Egg," "Wild Tad from Tundrus" and "the Skating Boxcar."

It is no surprise that native North Americans should be affectionately called "Chief." Such was the case with Jim Nielson, Ron Delorme, and George Armstrong. The account of the latter officially being dubbed "Chief Shoot-The-Puck," adorned with headdress and all, by the Ojibwas of Morely Alberta, is quite well known. Fred Saskamoose, the first treaty Indian to play any appreciable number of games in the big time, similarly was honored by the Sandy Lake, Saskatchewan tribe as "Chief Running Deer." What may not be common knowledge is that Bobby Hull, widely known as "the Golden Jet," in a 1965 interview refers to being "Chief Great Star ... which is what Indians christened me several years ago!"

One other "Chief" was John Bucyk. But he was not of Indian extraction. He reveals that linemate Bronco Horvath started it all. Apparently Horvath was such a take-charge guy, he was accused of treating his wingers like an Indian chief shouting commands to his braves. But he argued that Bucyk was "the Chief" because of the way he went into the corners and tomahawked the puck off rival's sticks and out in front of the net to his waiting center.

There are several versions concerning how Ivan Johnson became "Ching." He himself related that, while he had ori-

ental features, it was his cooking skills that did the trick. His dad always flooded a rink in the backyard. His mother tired of the neighborhood kids ruining her linoleum, so Pop built a shack for skate changing. Soon the youthful Ivan was providing snacks for the hungry hockeyists, "mostly french fries," he recalls. As a result (in a less politically-correct era) he acquired the nickname "Chinaman." When he played for the Winnipeg Monarchs a sportswriter changed it to "Ching" and the short form stuck!

Although those from the Lone Star State would probably disagree, it is probably stretching it a bit to include Jack Evans in this category. The big defenseman hardly ever spoke, but when he did it was with such a slow drawl that it reminded his mates of someone from Texas; hence, "Tex" became his moniker.

As much as an afterthought as it is, Pavel Bure as "the Russian Rocket" cannot be overlooked.

Physical Attributes

It is no strain on the imagination to discern how Roy Worters was dubbed "Shrimp." He was 5'3" and weight 135 pounds. Wilf (Shorty) Green and Bill (Wee Willie) Mosienko contracted their descriptive monikers for much the same reason. Woodrow (Porky) Dumart and Kenneth (Tubby) McAuley radiated slightly different attributes in their renown. Don (Bones) Raleigh had the unique distinction of draping 150 pounds on a six-foot frame. His coach, Muzz Patrick, insisted that Bones dished out the most painful body checks because he was so bony that "he cuts 'em when he hits 'em!"

Jim Conacher, who is no relation to the famous family of the same name, was built along similar lines, and was tagged with "Pencil." When Grant Warwick played with the Regina Rangers for the Allan Cup in 1940–41, Scotty Cameron thought that his shortness of stature reminded him of a stockiness, a blunt look, which was best described by "Knobby." (Sort of "knee high to a door knob"). Henri Richard owned part of his byname to his older brother; but he was tagged "the Pocket Rocket" because of his stature as well.

Sid Abel was "Ole Boot Nose" for the most obvious reasons; John Sherratt Stewart was "Black Jack" because of his swarthy complexion; J.D. Henderson was "Long John" because of his height. Lawrence Northcott was called "Baldy" purely out of sarcasm, because of his magnificent head of thick, dark hair. But Calum (Baldy) McKay came out of the barber shop almost scalped one day during his junior career, and picked up that agnomen.

Clint Albright was called "Professor" when he skated for the Rangers, both because he looked like one and because of his pursuit of higher education. John Morrison was a talented track and field athlete in the off-season. He broke his legs on rough ground with such frequency that his ever present artificial supports gained him the name "Crutchy."

Sarcasm also netted Cecil (Tiny) Thompson his sobriquet. It was not because he was a runt, but due to the fact that the was the biggest kid on his "midget" team. He played at 5'10" and 170 pounds in the NHL at a time when goaltenders were generally much smaller. Paul Reinhart was dubbed "Rhino" since some teammates said he was "as big as a Rhinoceros." Chubby cheeks did both Harry Lumley and Alex Delvecchio in. The former was referred to as "Ole Apple Cheeks" and the latter, although his weight problems seemed to disappear as he grew older, fell heir to "Fatso," or just plain "Fats."

Animal Agnomens

A host of pucksters, for various reasons, had wildlife designations connected to their ID's. The 6'3" Elmer Vasko heard shout of "Moose" whenever he charged down the Chicago Stadium ice. Because Eddie Mazur looked like a "Spider," all arms and legs, Bernie Geoffrion skated up to him at practice one day and christened him with his nickname. John McCormick's extra long neck and protruding Adam's apple reminded many of a "Goose." A thick thatch of raven-colored hair earned Johnny Gagnon the title "Black Cat." The lightning speed and darting mannerisms of Charlie McVeigh earned him the title "Rabbit."

Although Mrs. Fred Cook insists that brother Bill called her husband Bun because of his big nose, the constant reference to him as "Bunny" in newspapers suggests that his quickness on skates is the more likely explanation. When he coached in the American Hockey League he lost his temper so often they added another backhanded tribute: "Hot Cross Bun." Gordon Kuhn played only a few games for the New York Americans in 1933, but his reputation of always being under his opponent's skin, harassing them or "dogging" them, earned him the name Doggie.

Harry Westwick shared that the Quebec Chronicle gave a rather unfriendly report on a game in which he played for Ottawa against Quebec in 1896: it called Harvey Pulford "the Bytown Slugger," Weldy Young a "thug," and Westwick a "miserable, insignificant rat!" After that he was Rat Westwick. It is common knowledge that Walter (Turk) Broda came by his handle because, as a chubby kid with freckles, when he got angry, his neck reddened like a tomato and he looked like a fowl with the mumps. One day a kid shouted, "look at the turkey!" It was shortened later to Turk, but it stuck. Camille Henry slithered in behind defending players for quick deflections, which earned him the title "the Eel."

Grace Sutter, the mother who holds the record for having the most sons from one family in the NHL, candidly reveals that Duane was first known as Dog around home because he was always whining. Family photos picture him crying on almost every occasion. When he and Brent went together to play Junior A in Red Deer, it naturally fell to the younger of the two to have "Pup" attached to his ID!

How Yogi Berra's favorite payer, Clifford Purpur, was dubbed "Fido" is enough to keep any researcher on the edge of his seat. Purpur himself reveals that a Minneapolis sportswriter named Fred Matthewson reported that Cliff was "busier than a springer (bird dog) in a field full of pheasants." The next day the name was made public, and it stuck. But even that cannot touch a 1965 *Hockey Pictorial* reference to an amateur prospect named Donald Duck, no less. San Francisco's Bud Poile spoke of him as a bright prospect, but that his name was "quite a burden to carry." The thing is it wasn't a nickname—it was for real!

While our fine feathered friends are technically not animals, they do belong to that same kingdom. Larry Robinson and Don Saleski shared a common moniker, "Big Bird."

Employment Epithets

Whether real or imagined, former or off-season jobs hounded several players, especially before 1950. Edouard Lalonde once worked in a print shop, and "Newsy," not his given name, ever appeared in the formal columns of league statistics. Alex Connell was a fireman in Ottawa, and his moniker was appendaged with that fact. Jimmy Herberts

worked on the Great Lakes tankers when he wasn't cruising down the ice lanes and was appropriately known as "Sailor." Claire Alexander was a milkman in Collingwood, and was thus tagged. Bill Juzda worked in the off-season as a fireman on the CNR, eventually earning his engineer's license. So they just called him "the Honest Brakeman."

While we can vouch for only one of them ever riding a horse, at least four NHLers, including Bill Cowley and Eric Pettinger, answered to "Cowboy." It was Bill Flett, who hailed from Alberta, who decidedly knew one end of such animals from the other. In his younger years he participated in rodeos!

John O'Flaherty gives his own account of how he got to be "Peanuts". "My brother sold programs at Maple Leaf Gardens; since I wanted to see the Leafs play I got a job selling concessions, like peanuts, popcorn and soft drinks. One day a sportswriter saw me, recognized me, and hung the nickname on me." In days gone by, athletes who could take care of themselves were often called "Bucko" (as in Wilfred McDonald) or "Butch." But in Clarence Keeling's case, his father was a butcher!

Dr. Bill Carson was a practicing dentist when he played for Toronto in the 1920s, as was Charles (Doc) Stewart, stalwart goalie in the Bruins' early years. In fact, the founder of the first professional hockey league in the world, the International (Pro) League of 1904 to 1907, Kitchener's Doc Gibson, also specialized in extracting molars. Dr. Rod Smylie, a member of the Stanley Cup champion Toronto St. Pats in 1922, went into family practice after his playing days were through. Randy Gregg was a qualified physician while he played out his career with the Edmonton Oilers.

But I'm satisfied that no contemporary of either Elwyn (Doc) Romnes, or Gerry (Doc) Couture ever allowed either to pull his teeth or remove his appendix. The former used to carry his limited amount of equipment around in a bag resembling one a doctor might use, and the latter spent two years studying medicine at the University of Saskatchewan. While he may never be a backbencher, Serge Savard's interest in politics prompted his friends to call him "the Senator."

Personality Prænoms

Wild Bill Ezinicki was just that, a human misguided missile knocking opponents down with abandon. The same can be said about Dave (The Hammer) Shultz, and "Terrible Ted" (alias Scarface) Lindsay! Theodore Green was a second generation "Terrible Ted." Ivan Irwin was crowned "Ivan the Terrible" after the infamous Middle Ages Grand Duke of Moscow. Albert Leduc used to get up such a head of steam when skating that it was uncertain if he could be stopped (or even stop himself); so he was dubbed "Battleship." Brian Conacher opines that his dad, Lionel, due to the way he ran in football, legs churning high and powerfully like a train barreling down the tracks, prompted him to become "the Big Train." Still along the line of engines, Doug Mohns shares that a fellow Barrie Flyer junior player decided he should be "Diesel." The former Bruin and Black Hawk testifies that there was a dual reason for this: "I came from a railroad town (Capreol, Ontario, where his dad was an engineer), and I guess I had a pretty good engine!" Leapin' Louie Fontinato's nickname was hung on him because every time a penalty was called against him he jumped off the ice like somebody had stabbed him with a pitchfork, and made more facial gestures than a professional wrestler.

Sarcasm was responsible for Alex Kaleta's second nickname. When he played in Chicago the Canmore, Alberta product went by "Sea Biscuit" after the famous racehorse. When he found himself before the rambunctious Madison Square Garden fans, however, his shortcomings soon came to the fore. Because he was somewhat timid when it came to going into the corners to battle for the puck, those paying customers decided he should be known from henceforth as "Killer." Ouch!

Imagine what a burden it was for Frank McCool, the wartime goalie for the Toronto Maple Leafs, to rely upon copious amounts of milk to keep his flaming stomach from getting the better of him. Then to be saddled with a nickname like "Ulcers." Enough is enough! Rookie Roland (Roly) McLenahan exhibited quite the opposite disposition: while skating for the Red Wings in the 1946 playoffs he failed to get excited about this tense situation. While the rest of the team chewed their fingernails he munched on peanuts, earning him the title of "Fearless Fosdick."

Thomas B. O'Neill, Q.C., was probably the only Maple Leaf Gardens usher to be promoted to right wing for the same organization. That was in 1943–44. One day Conn Smythe heard him playing the piano and decided that it was such poor playing that he added $100 to his contract so he could afford lessons. But he contracted his famous nickname not from the piano but because he had an abiding love of debate. While at St. Michael's College one day he persisted in his point of view until one of the priests cut him off with, "Why don't you sit down, Windy?" When Viv Allen was growing up he had difficulty expressing himself because he stuttered. When his voice should have been changing it took on a decidedly high-pitched quality. Naturally his schoolmates called him "Squeaky." Often it was shortened to "Squeak." When he and brother George graduated to junior hockey in North Battleford, Saskatchewan, his moniker was ripe to add some color to the local scene. However, because a well-known skater of a previous era bore the nickname "Squee," the public address announcer asked Viv if he could adapt his handle for nostalgia sake. Even his wife still calls him Squee and the quality of his voice yet betrays the reason he is so recognized. As an aside he shares that he was never very fond of his given name. When he asked his mother why she had laid it on him, her reply was that it was a biblical name. "I read the bible through twice and couldn't find it," he recalls. Upon reporting that to his mother, she teased: "Well, it was the only way I could get you to read it!"

Humility had no place when Bill Hollett embarked on his major-league career. Asked if he had a nickname, he replied without hesitating: "Just call me 'Flash'." Few knew him otherwise. Fifty years later, tongue-in-cheek, Glen Sather exhibited the same modesty. When questioned how he acquired the alias, "Slats," he explained that his coach, Eddie Johnston, was responsible. "He couldn't say Sather, I guess." This revelation came in the presence of a Soviet reporter, who had come to cover the 1984 Canada Cup competition. Enquiring what Slats meant, the Team Canada mentor deadpanned: "Superstar."

Monarchical Monograms

Most hockey fans recall that Frank (King) Clancy inherited his byname from his father, who was "King of the Heelers" (heeling was a rugby-football term in bygone days). Frank didn't like to be called that, but the media planted it on him, and he couldn't stop them. Borje Salming

was also called King. That resulted from a tantrum in practice one day, during which he hurled his stick into the stands. Jim McKenny yelled at him: "You big donkey! Who do you think you are? King of Sweden?"

Only one player of account was ever ranked one notch lower than a monarch, and that was Claude Earl (Prince Charlie) Rayner. For no apparent reason his playmates called him Charlie when he was a boy. The first reference to "Prince Charlie" appears to have been on February 4, 1940 when a reporter commented that a "snap shot by Bill Mosienko spoiled Prince Charlie's hallmark performance." The number of "Dukes" in shinny history is multiple, including George Harris, Laudus Dukowski, and Gary Edmunson. Another, Gordon (Duke) Keats, came by his sobriquet early in life. As a boy in North Bay, Ontario his pals named him after a battleship. Joe Klukay was afforded an extra dubbing when writer Annas Stukas decided he had an aristocratic air about him. He became "the Duke of Paducah" and could never shake it.

While this title doesn't reach those regal heights, to be a Count is no trifle. Don Grosso immediately stood out as a newcomer on Detroit ice. His thatch of thick shiny black hair reminded some of Count Dracula of Transylvania. So he became "Count." There is a popular photo of the Detroit forward, sitting beside Ab Demarco Sr., who shared this honored moniker.

Media Monikers

Hubert Jacques Martin is better knows as "Pit." His father began calling him that after a character in a French-Canadian comic strip while he was still growing up in Noranda, Quebec. The funny papers were responsible for Clint Smith's alternate name as well. Snuffy Smith became such a dominant personality in the Barney Google strip, that he eventually outshone the original headliner. The transfer to Clint was helped along when a teammate skated to the public address announcer to urge that it be heralded that Snuffy Smith scored. Lorne Worsley confesses that when he was 10 a classmate concluded he resembled Sidney Smith's Andy Gump; so "Gump" it was from then on. The Saskatchewan Sports Hall of Fame submits that Harold March became known as "Mush" because of a cartoon character in Dick Tracy called Mush Mouth.

Ronald Maki revealed to Randy Schultz, whose syndicated feature, "Where are they now?" appeared in *The Hockey News* in 1985, that he was "Chico" long before he ever laced on skates. This was due to the fact that his mother's favorite Marx brother was the eldest, Leonard or "Chico." Gordie Howe decided that Marcel Dionne reminded him of Red Ryder's Indian sidekick … and he was branded "L'il Beaver." Montreal's humble giant Jean Beliveau rose to stardom about the time a popular song, "Le Gros Bill," hit the charts. Soon it was applied to the smooth-skating center. Clare Raglan began his career when Rags Ragglan was starring in movie comedies. The same alias became his. Reginald Smith was known almost exclusively as Hooley. He owed his epithet to cartoon character, Happy Hooligan. Fun lovers just couldn't resist the temptation when Steve Kasper appeared on the scene and "the Friendly Ghost" appeared in quotation marks whenever he merited mention on the sports pages. Likewise, Red Berenson's rise to prominence coincided with Snoopy's comic-strip fantasies about the Red Baron, a World War I flying ace. Ron Ellis, a teammate of Alain Belanger, is certain that husky forward's sobriquet, "Bam Bam," came from "The Flintstones." Like

Barney Rubble's son he possessed unusual strength.

The cruelest cartoon nickname of all was reserved for a referee. George Gravel's surname invited the reversal of the name of Dick Tracy's Gravel Gertie; hence "Gertie" Gravel. As if whistle-tooters don't have it tough enough!

Skills Signatures

Most historians laud Howie Morenz, "the Mitchell Meteor" or "the Stratford Streak," for his blinding speed. However, there are testimonies from the past that claim that Hec Kilrea could keep pace with him; so the latter earned the title "Hurricane." The branding of Fred Taylor is legend. When Taylor starred in his first home game with the 1907–08 Ottawa Senators, Malcolm Price of the *Free Press* wrote: "They used to call him the Whirlwind of the International League, but he has become the Cyclone of the Eastern League." But there was another "Cyclone" in the big leagues. Marvin Wentworth, a scoring defenseman, was a standout with the old Montreal Maroons in the mid-1930s. He was so impressed that he became Taylor's namesake. The late Al Parsely wrote: "Of course 'Cyclone' was clipped to 'Cy', but Marvin was all but forgotten except on official documents!"

"Sudden Death" Mel Hill, with his famous run of overtime goals in the playoffs of 1939, could deposit the rubber disk when it really counted. Frankie (Mr. Zero) Brimsek could keep them out—six shutouts in seven games as a rookie, no less! "Tony O" Esposito took a page from his book, ringing up 15 whitewashes in his first full campaign between the pipes in 1969–70. Nels Stewart was "Ole Poison" to his opponents. Not only was he deadly around the net, as he parked his big frame in the right position to shovel goals home, but according to Ching Johnson, "Nels was poison alright. … You had to watch him all the time for your own safety." Don McKenny had many of the same qualities that Camille Henry had; so became knows as "Slip." H. Joseph Simpson, whom Newsy Lalonde once called "the greatest living hockey player," could have been branded "Bullet Joe" for two reasons. He was wounded twice on World War I battlefields and he could also skate like the wind. But it was the latter that earned him this flattering title.

Boom Boom Geoffrion's resounding "bang" of the puck against the arena boards earned him his alias when he was still in junior hockey. When a local scribe said he was going to refer to him as "Boom" from now on, the fun-loving forward replied, "Make it two booms!" But two equally famous skaters set precedents along this line two and three decades earlier respectively. Didier Pitre was called "Cannonball" because he constantly splintered the dashers wherever he played. Big Charlie Conacher wasn't known as "the Big Bomber" for nothing. His magnificent wrist shot drove more than one netminder back into the twine, and at least once the puck went right through the boards of "the house that Conn built."

No two pucksters were ever less alike than Max Bentley and Maurice Richard. Bentley was "the Dipsy Doodle Dandy," a handle he shared with his brother Doug, because that's the way he finessed his way through the opposition. Conversely, Richard was like a bull-in-a-china-shop! Countless opponents referred to the "red glare" of his eyes as he barged toward the goal area. That may be part of the reason he became "the Rocket." More than one hockey personality is credited with coining this handle; but it is most likely that it was the warning of fellow Hab Ray Getliffe

that he sounded during scrimmages: "Here comes the Rocket." Gordie Howe's "Mr. Hockey," and Glenn Hall's "Mr. Goalie" titles fall into the 'nuff said department

Appendage Appellations

Wayne Gretzky isn't the only ice jockey to be called "the Great." In the 1940s Eddie Dorohoy was recognized as "the Great Gabbo." Had he been able to score as well as he could talk, he would be in the Hall of Fame. He was also called "Pistol" because he shot his mouth off so much. The reputations of Yvan (The Roadrunner) Cournoyer, Eddie (The Edmonton Express) Shore, Frank (The Big M) Mahovlich, and Eddie (The Entertainer) Shack need no enhancing. Until he passed away just a couple of years ago, Frank Finnigan was the last remaining member of the original Ottawa Senators. He was known as "the Shawville Express" because he regularly rode the train down from his Quebec hometown to the Canadian capital for games. Reggie Leach became known as "the Rifle" following his record-setting goal-scoring feat in the 1976 playoffs.

The Fair Sex

Several years ago Johnny Cash sang about a "Boy Named Sue." Would you believe it, someone had the gall to shackle a 1913 member of the Toronto Blueshirts of the NHA, Archie McLean, with that very tag? At least eight other professional skaters over the years have born the brunt of the same treatment. Bill Taylor of the Ontario Professional Hockey League's Brantford team was "Lady;" apparently because the dapper dresser was a "ladies' man." In the 1930s Emile Drouin responded to "Polly," and in 1929 Francis Calligan of the Rangers got stuck with "Pats." There was also Arthur (Dolly) Swift, Nelson (Nellie) Podlosky and (Toots) Holloway.

A 1930s popular song is obviously to be thanked for James O'Neill to be burdened with "Peggy." But poor Eric Nesterenko! When Chicago fans concluded that he was just out for a skate, they scorned him with "Sonja," with reference to the championship figure skater Sonja Henie. Allan Stanley received the same ribbing in Madison Square Garden for his non-aggressive playing style.

Childhood Misnomers

Victor is not a particularly difficult word to get one's tongue around. But it was for Aubrey Clapper's little brother. It came out "Ditter" and was abbreviated to "Dit." The same applied in Hector Blake's household. "Toe" was a lot easier to pronounce, so Toe he was, forever and a day. Herbert O'Connor and Frank Boll shared an almost identical experience, the inability of siblings to say "brother." In O'Connor's case it came out "Buddy" and few knew him as anything else. With Boll, the adjective added was no problem; but "brother" was ... so "little buzzer" he became. Typically it was shortened to "Buzz." That, not his style of play, is responsible for this colorful moniker.

Billy Harris (the one who played with the Toronto Maple Leafs) was born in 1935. His grandmother had a son the same year. He and this "uncle" grew up playing together. Somehow he couldn't manage "Billy" and it came out "Hinky." It stuck with him the whole time he was in Toronto. Armand Guidolin came from an Italian home. When he was born, in her broken English, his mother clucked over her little "beppie." His brothers and sisters simply shortened it to "Bep."

Ted Kennedy's nickname rained down from the seats in Maple Leaf Gardens for years, as the voice of Jim Arnott cried, "C'mon Teeder." A childhood acquaintance had trouble with Theodore, and it came out "Teeder." It more or less slipped out, but the battle cry was heard many an evening afterwards.

All Grit and Guts

Over the years some names have just exuded the aura of being rough and tough. In fact, The Dictionary of American Slang defines those two characteristics are inherent in one called "Butch." Butches, regardless of their real names, stand out in a crowd. What NHLer ever radiated that more than Robert Goring? His generally dishevelled appearance and his gung-ho style of play betrays this characteristic.

Those who tried to tangle with Emile Bouchard, the one-time Canadiens captain, quickly realized why Butch was appropriate for him as well. It is said he was so bombastic during his first training camp that veteran Murph Chamberlain appealed to Dick Irwin: "If I were you I'd order this young elephant to calm down, or you will find yourself without any players to open the season." Gus, Bud, and Buck radiate the same character traits.

Inviting Innovations

Some player's names just dare some to annexing them. What else would you call Mark LaForest, but "Trees?" If your last name is Goodenough ... "Izzy" just comes naturally. Frank Beaton just had to be called "Seldom," and Mr. Smyl, Stanley "Steamer." With a handle like Campbell you couldn't escape being "Soupy," and what better way to address the late Bill Masterton than "Bat?" Although he weighed only 150 pounds, Larry Kwong answered to "King."

There were three NHLers who wore the ID of "Hap." Leighton Emms always looked like a thunder cloud, and seemed never to crack a smile. No matter what mood he was in, Clarence Day was "Happy." There is a little anecdote that followed Hap around. Seems on a tour of the Western provinces he stopped briefly in Saskatoon. Standing by the boards one night he spied Reg Bentley, now skating for the local senior contingent. Bentley noticed him and looked puzzled, as if he were trying to place him. The former Leaf, sensing this, explained "Happy Day." "Happy day to you, too," he responded; and skated off. Herb Hamel, who played briefly with Toronto, because of his disposition and his short fling with the Leafs, was playfully willed Mr. Day's nickname.

It took very little ingenuity to hang "Comet" on Len Haley. Merlin Malinowski's name fostered the title, "the Magician;" and Bernie Nicholl's post-goal-scoring celebration prompted the handle, "the Pumper Nicholl Kid." Fans, peers, and newspaper reporters must have fallen over one another trying to be first to refer to Tim Watters as "Muddy."

Food Fantasies

Goalie James Henry apparently couldn't keep his fingers out of neighbors' sugar bowls, and he reaped the infamy of being "Sugar Jim." Andy Hebenton had the same weakness when it came to potatoes. "Preferably mashed, piled alongside a steak, with gravy flooding them," he used to confess. "That's why we call him 'Spuds'," offered coach Phil Watson. Clarence (Taffy) Abel likewise had a sweet tooth, so his agnomen resulted from his addiction to Atlantic saltwater taffy.

"Have Skates, Will Travel"

In shinny's early days, when "professional" was a dirty word, talented players were much in demand all over the country. They would skip from place to place, wherever there was a fast buck to be made. In 1911 Edwin "Mag" McGregor sported the sweater of no less than five different teams, prompting hockeyists to refer to him as "the Tourist." Gary Smith strapped on the big pads for no less than 10 major-league teams, and invited the name "Suitcase."

Everyone is aware that Gordie Howe and Glenn Hall are justifiably known as "Mr. Hockey" and "Mr. Goalie." But hockey historian W.J. (Bill) Fitsell found a 1900 newspaper article that contains what is probably the greatest hockey nickname outside "Peter Puck" Pocklington. The article reveals that "Hockey" Dixon of Barrie was investigated by the Southern Ontario Hockey Association, because he played with Welland in Buffalo that season. Walter H. Dixon was listed as playing with the Toronto Granites in 1896 and Berlin in 1897. Apparently he was among the transients of the era who moved around wherever there was a "hockey" job.

Baseball By-lines

Dave Schriner, Cecil Dye and Walter Pratt can attribute their handles to baseball. The Russian-born Schriner grew up in Calgary, where he idolized a semi-pro slugger, Bill Sweeny. His attempts at emulating his hero led to the inevitable, the tag of "L'il Sweeny." As he grew, the L'il part disappeared. With Pratt it related to skill, not admiration. One day while filling in on his older brother's team in Winnipeg, he had a better-than-average day at the plate. "He's a regular Babe Ruth," cracked one of his mates and it stuck! Dye, on the other hand, was a professional ballplayer in the off season, and his mates couldn't resist teasing him with "Babe" too.

Awful Aliases

We cannot, with good conscience, consider this essay complete without noting a handful of nicknames, which cannot be considered anything other than bizarre. Bert Corbeau embarked on his NHL career the same year the loop was born. When he died, sports pages headlined his epitaph with, *Old Pig Iron Passes Away.*

For some reason not commonly known, New York Ranger Alf Pike was tagged "the Embalmer." How would you like to have your family read game reports described you as "Cement Head?" Jim Hargreaves had that stigma to bear. Earl Walsh, according to one report, was called "Flat" because he lived in one!

Odds and Sods

George Imlach is not the only puck chaser to be called "Punch," but no one earned it in more painful fashion. While playing for a Toronto Senior A hockey team in the 1940s, Imlach was bowled over in a road game at the Windsor Arena, and struck his head on the ice. When the trainer rushed to administer smelling salts, he soon had to duck Imlach's flying fists. Imlach thought someone had decked him and he was retaliating. "George! Come out of it," the medic urged. "Don't go punchy on me." A journalist reported that Imlach was "punch drunk" that night due to the concussion he received. In time, "Punchy" was reduced to just plain "Punch."

How Harvey Jackson became "Busher" has been reiterated many times over. When asked by trainer Tim Daley to help tote gear, the young left winger sasses: "Nothing doing. I'm a hockey player not an equipment man!" "Why you fresh young busher!" Daley retorted. What may not be realized is that he wasn't addressing him as a "bush leaguer," because that expression didn't become popular until 1949. It emanated from a series authored by Ring Lardner that appeared in the *Saturday Evening Post* between 1914 and 1918. One particular character was a young "busher," a greenhorn rookie ball player, who disregarded training rules, refused to take advice, yet beamed overconfidence in his abilities as a player.

Winston Juckes was always referred to as "Bing." His first coach in Hamiota, Manitoba was Chuck Lindsay. Whenever the fast-skating forward bulged the twine, his bench boss would shout "Bingo!" It was shortened to just plain Bing. Aloyisius Martin Sloan, also known as "Slinker," was delivered from his parental designation by the local druggist in his hometown of Vinton, Quebec. It seems Frank Douglas was a horse racing buff, and had admired the record of a famous jockey of the late 1800s. Sloan was small for his age, and Douglas christened him "Tod" after the renowned rider.

Players aren't the only hockey people who get saddled with weird handles. Spiff Evans, Toronto public relations director in the 1950s, played Little League in a sandlot circuit near his home. One afternoon his mom sent him to the playground decked out in a sailor suit. The third baseman, Jack Foy, looked startled and teased: "My! Don't you look spiffy?" So "Spiff" it was.

Irvine (Ace) Bailey's nickname has been credited to many things: some say that trainer Tim Daley hung the tag on him when he won the scoring championship in 1929. The same Daley is alleged to have so honored him because he brought him luck playing cards. But Bailey himself claimed that friends were always hitting him up for a dollar or two in the depression era. He most often helped them out. In response to "where was he able to come up with it all the time?" he would answer: "It came from my 'ace in the hole'."

The WHA's Mike Dubois was known as "Plywood." (*Bois* is French for wood.) The prefix was a matter of choice. Language was responsible for Hugh Bolton's rather odd appellation as well. Al Nickolson did a feature on the big rookie defenseman in the February 2, 1952 Maple Leaf Gardens program. While Bolton was still with the Marlie Seniors, teammate Scotty Mair dubbed him "Yug." Mair's contention was that it was Scottish for Hugh. Bolton was never sure if he should believe him or not.

Nicknames are not a modern innovation. According to Elsdon Smith they date back to ancient Egypt, where people were known to each other by Dog, Ape or Grasshopper, etc. The expression in English was originally "ekename," or "also name," but later became "nickname." Often these names were used in pleasantry or ridicule, but often were crudely accurate in their descriptiveness. What was good enough for Pharaoh should be good enough for modern hockey.

Bring back old-fashioned ekenames!

The game needs that kind of shot in the arm!

III

OTHER
NORTH
AMERICAN
LEAGUES
AND TEAMS

The Edmonton Oil Kings, 1960 Memorial Cup
finalists. From left: Bobby Marik, Eddie Joyal,
Cliff Pennington and Bruce MacGregor.

CHAPTER 23

The World Hockey Association

Assessing the Impact of the "Rival League"

Shirley Fischler

DEFYING ALL HOCKEY SHIBBOLETHS, a group of California entrepreneurs launched what they labeled a second major league of the ice sport in 1972. Organized by Santa Ana attorney Gary Davidson and promoter Dennis Murphy, the World Hockey Association took on the National Hockey League against long odds. Neither Davidson nor Murphy had any previous hockey experience and because of that fact alone the imminent demise of the WHA was predicted freely at the very start.

On February 12, 1972, the WHA held its first player draft at the Royal Coach Inn in Anaheim, California. Until then the WHA had no profound impact on the NHL. Elders of the established circuit refused to recognize the new threat and moved along with plans for further expansion of their own. But two weeks later, the first shock rippled through the established hockey world when Bernie Parent, one of the most gifted young NHL goaltenders, made public his intent to sign with a WHA team. At the time Parent was supposed to play in Florida with the proposed Miami Screaming Eagles, but the team never go off the ground. Instead he joined the Philadelphia Blazers.

Parent's decision was the catalyst for other NHL players to jump to the new circuit and, one by one, major signings were announced. WHA teams spirited away the likes of Derek Sanderson, Ted Green and J.C. Tremblay from their respective NHL teams. But the biggest coup was the signing of Bobby Hull to a 10-year $2.75 million contract. The WHA opened its first season on October 11, 1972, with Quebec at Cleveland and Edmonton at Ottawa. Edmonton's Ron Anderson scored the first-ever WHA regular season goal.

The league opened with 12 teams spread over two divisions: New England (Boston), Cleveland, Philadelphia, Ottawa, Quebec and New York were in the Eastern Division; Winnipeg, Houston, Los Angeles, Alberta (Edmonton), Minnesota (St. Paul) and Chicago were in the Western Division. In the first playoff finals New England (Whalers) defeated Winnipeg (Jets) four games to one to win the WHA's inaugural playoff championship.

Not only did the WHA survive its first year of operations, it also held its first All-Star Game—January 6, 1973 at Quebec City—and had one of its games shown on the CBS television network. Danny Lawson became the first WHA player to reach the 50-goal plateau on February 22, 1973 in Ottawa.

Some NHL officials took the WHA challenge seriously and in April, 1973, secret meetings were held between Gary Davidson and an NHL group led by William Jennings, president of the New York Rangers, in an effort to hammer out an agreement, but no pact was forthcoming. Davidson announced that the WHA would continue to operate independently. "We believe that the NHL's reserve clause is wrong," said Davidson. "It would be impossible for us to consider any formal association with the NHL so long as

they still have it." More importantly, the old guard among the NHL governors was adamantly opposed to any agreement with the WHA and maintained hopes of eliminating the maverick league.

In its second year, the WHA added to its trophy collection by making a deal with the Avco Financial Services organization which lent its name to the WHA's black, lucite and silver Stanley Cup-sized championship trophy. Hereafter, the winner of the WHA playoff would become the holder of the Avco World Trophy. In May 1974, the WHA Houston Aeros captured the Avco World Trophy in 14 games, sweeping Winnipeg in the quarterfinals, taking Minnesota in six, then sweeping Chicago in the finals.

Like the NHL, the WHA was struggling through tumultuous times and reorganization was the order of the day. In June 1974, the league divided into three divisions (Canadian, West, East) and a "wild card" team playoff format was adopted. Phoenix and Indianapolis were the new expansion teams. Another blow was dealt the NHL when the WHA's Toronto Toros persuaded superstar Frank Mahovlich to leave the established league.

In contrast to the NHL, the WHA owners instantly realized that there was a motherlode of rich talent to be mined in Europe. The Winnipeg Jets, in particular, stocked their roster with Swedes and Finns rather than Canadians, and, as a result, Ulf Nilsson and Anders Hedberg teamed with veteran Bobby Hull to comprise one of the most formidable attacking units of the 1970s. The WHA made another meaningful inroad on the international level when it persuaded Soviet hockey officials to sanction an eight-game series between a WHA all-star squad and a similar team from Russia. The tourney took place in the fall of 1974, with the Soviets easy winners.

Its setbacks notwithstanding, the WHA continued to grow because of one pivotal element: the spectacular growth of new arena construction throughout North America and the demand, in every city, for suitable tenants. Whereas the NHL was more demanding by far in setting forth conditions for entry, the WHA gladly would accept any franchise bidder, as long as an attractive arena was located in the city in question. Thus, Cincinnati, which was not likely to become an NHL entry any time soon, was welcomed into the WHA in 1975, upon completion of the handsome Riverfront Arena. Cleveland—the building actually was located in distant Richfield, Ohio—also had a new arena, as did Indianapolis and Edmonton.

From the outset, one of the most frequently debated questions among hockey fans was the quality of WHA play in relation to that of the NHL. Clearly, the new league lacked the depth of stars still in the older circuit, but it did offer some interesting talents: the Swedes, two talented Finnish players, two Czechs and, of course, Bobby Hull, Gordie Howe and his two youngsters, Mark and Marty. Scoring came easier in the WHA and when Bobby Hull equaled

Maurice Richard's venerable NHL record of 50 goals in 50 games on February 14, 1975, the achievement was greeted with less than overwhelming enthusiasm.

Some players who made the leap from the NHL to the WHA reconsidered and returned, among them Parent and Sanderson; but others, such as Hull, stuck with the new league. More than anyone, Hull proved to be the foremost gate attraction in the WHA and further helped the league's cause by his graciousness with fans and the media. On December 14, 1975, Hull received still more attention when he became the first WHA player to score 200 goals in league play.

Franchise rumblings were heard after the 1975-76 season, when the league realigned back into two divisions, eliminating the Canadian Division. The Toronto Toros could not compete with the NHL's venerated Toronto Maple Leafs and emigrated to Birmingham, Alabama to become the Bulls. Likewise, the Crusaders became a losing proposition in Cleveland and moved to St.Paul. Birmingham proved to be a pleasant addition to the league, but St.Paul couldn't make it past 42 games before folding. It was a portent of things to come. By the end of the 1977–78 season, the WHA had dwindled from 12 to eight teams, having lost St. Paul, Calgary, Phoenix and San Diego.

There was, however, new hope on the diplomatic front. Howard Baldwin, new WHA president, enjoyed a very positive relationship with two key National Hockey League leaders: Ed Snider, owner of the Philadelphia Flyers, and John Ziegler, new president of the NHL. The endless, unspoken WHA–NHL war was bleeding both leagues white and a spirit of reconciliation once again brought the leaders together. Only this time there was more understanding on both sides of the bargaining table and a realization that a peace pact of some kind was in order. The result was that four WHA teams—the Edmonton Oilers, the New England (renamed Hartford) Whalers, the Quebec Nordiques and the Winnipeg Jets—were admitted to an expanded NHL, effective following the 1978–79 season. The World Hockey Association, after seven seasons of tumultuous operation, ceased to exist.

In many ways the WHA had a profound impact on the North American professional hockey scene. The competition for talent sent player salaries skyrocketing to all-time highs. The WHA spread pro hockey to new areas, but sometimes these gains were offset by inefficient management practices that ultimately turned fans away from the game. As a result, cities that had been long acclaimed for their support of minor professional franchises—among them San Diego and Cleveland—found themselves temporarily transformed into hockey wastelands.

The progressive nature of the WHA leadership resulted in a heavy accent on European talent, a trend then followed by the NHL, and an increase in many of the game's skills. Further, the WHA recognized cities heretofore ignored as potential moneymakers or dismissed as lacking a big league market by the NHL. On the legal front, the WHA fought many battles and won a significant number of challenges. It was the WHA which experimented with teenage stars, ultimately leading the NHL to abolish its rules forbidding the signing of players under 20 years of age. It was the WHA which signed the electrifying Wayne Gretzky at a time when some in hockey circles were unsure of the lad, disparaging him as too thin, too weak, maybe even too

unskilled and not likely to become a major factor in the major-league game!

The WHA spawned interest, created a group of gifted hockey executives and offered an interesting form of sports entertainment throughout the 1970s. But more than anything else, the league demonstrated in the 1970s that there wasn't room in North America for more than one major professional league. That is why the World Hockey Association is now a footnote in the lore of the game.

The following are the teams and nicknames for the clubs that made up the WHA and what has happened to those four clubs which merged into the NHL.

WORLD HOCKEY ASSOCIATION FRANCHISE GUIDE

ALBERTA OILERS 1972–73
renamed the Edmonton Oilers prior to the 1973–74 season

BALTIMORE BLADES 1974–75 formerly Michigan Stags

BIRMINGHAM BULLS 1976–77 to 1978–79 formerly Toronto Toros

CALGARY COWBOYS 1975–76 to 1976–77 formerly Vancouver Blazers

CHICAGO COUGARS 1972–73 to 1974–75

CINCINNATI STINGERS 1975–76 to 1978–79

CLEVELAND CRUSADERS 1972–73 to 1975–76
moved to Minnesota in 1976 and renamed Minnesota Fighting Saints

DENVER SPURS 1975–76
moved to Ottawa during the 1975–76 season and renamed Ottawa Civics

EDMONTON OILERS 1973–74 to 1978–79
previously named Alberta Oilers; joined NHL in 1979; still in the NHL

HOUSTON AEROS 1972–73 to 1977–78

INDIANAPOLIS RACERS 1974–75 to 1978–79

JERSEY KNIGHTS 1973–74
formerly New York Golden Blades; moved to San Diego in 1974 and renamed San Diego Mariners

LOS ANGELES SHARKS 1972–73 to 1973–74
moved to Detroit in 1974 and renamed Michigan Stags

MICHIGAN STAGS 1974–75
formerly Los Angeles Sharks; moved to Baltimore during the 1974–75 season and renamed Baltimore Blades

MINNESOTA FIGHTING SAINTS 1972–73 to 1975–76; 1976–77
folded in February 1976; revived as relocated Cleveland franchise in July 1976

NEW ENGLAND WHALERS 1972–73 to 1978–79
joined NHL in 1979 and renamed Hartford Whalers; moved to North Carolina in 1997 and renamed Carolina Hurricanes

NEW YORK GOLDEN BLADES 1973–74
formerly New York Raiders; moved to New Jersey during the 1973–74 season and renamed the Jersey Knights

NEW YORK RAIDERS 1972–73
renamed New York Golden Blades in 1973

OTTAWA CIVICS 1975–76 formerly Denver Spurs

OTTAWA NATIONALS 1972–73
moved to Toronto in 1973 and renamed Toronto Toros

PHILADELPHIA BLAZERS 1972–73
moved to Vancouver in 1973 and renamed Vancouver Blazers

PHOENIX ROADRUNNERS 1974–75 to 1976–77

QUEBEC NORDIQUES 1972–73 to 1978–79
joined NHL in 1979; moved to Denver in 1995 and renamed Colorado Avalanche

SAN DIEGO MARINERS 1974–75 to 1976–77 formerly Jersey Knights

TORONTO TOROS 1973–74 to 1975–76
formerly Ottawa Nationals; moved to Birmingham in 1976 and renamed Birmingham Bulls

VANCOUVER BLAZERS 1973–74 to 1974–75
formerly Philadelphia Blazers; moved to Calgary in 1975 and renamed Calgary Cowboys

WINNIPEG JETS 1972–73 to 1978–79
joined NHL in 1979; moved to Phoenix in 1996 and renamed Phoenix Coyotes

CHAPTER 24

Minor Pro Hockey in the 1920s, 1930s and 1940s

Ernie Fitzsimmons

WITH MORE THAN 2,500 PEOPLE playing professional hockey per season in the late 1990s, it is hard to realize that less than 100 years ago there was no pro hockey at all. It was just over 70 years ago that minor pro hockey as we know it swung into action.

The first leagues to start openly paying players began in the United States in 1902–03, though Pittsburgh teams had paid future Hall of Famer Riley Hern to play goal in 1901–02. Over the next few years play-for-pay leagues would spring up across most of Canada and parts of the northern United States. The first fully professional league was the original International (Pro) Hockey league, organized in 1904–05 with franchises in Calumet, Houghton and Sault Ste. Marie, Michigan as well as Pittsburgh and Sault Ste. Marie, Ontario. Other early pro leagues were the Eastern Canada Hockey Association (Montreal-Ottawa-Quebec), the Ontario Professional Hockey League (Toronto and southwestern Ontario), the Eastern Ontario Professional Hockey League, the Temiskaming league (Cobalt-Haileybury) and the New Ontario league (Thunder Bay), plus leagues in Manitoba and Saskatchewan.

By the second decade of the 20th century many of these early pro leagues had dropped out of hockey, but the Patrick family formed a new major league called the Pacific Coast Hockey Association in 1911, later amalgamating with the Western Canada Hockey League to ice a credible rival to the NHL that would last until 1925–26. The Maritime league continued until 1914–15 but players had to be released to play in that league, although there was some talk of the Maritimes becoming the first development league. Those thoughts perished with the outbreak of World War I in 1914. The National Hockey Association (forerunner of the NHL) even talked of folding in 1916–17, but after the war ended there was an influx of players, and the first renewed sign that affiliate teams were needed was when Toronto loaned Ken Randall and Gord Meeking to the semi-pro Sydney Millionaires in 1918–19.

In 1920–21, the Maritime Independent League was formed because players who had performed in the Maritime Pro League couldn't get reinstated to play elsewhere. By 1923–24 there was talk of the new Maritime league becoming the first full minor pro league. A few players like Bill "Red" Stuart, Stan Jackson, Ted Stackhouse, Pat Nolan and Charlie Fraser got NHL trials while playing in the MIHL, and both George Carroll and Jack Ingram of Moncton went to the NHL after the league folded in 1924.

Because of the lack of minor pro leagues to train players for the NHL in the early 1920s the United States Amateur Hockey Association West became a fertile training ground for prospects. It was a thinly veiled senior league that brought in such star players as Herb Lewis, Cecil "Tiny" Thompson, Ivan "Ching" Johnson, Clarence "Taffy" Abel, Roy Worters, Percy Galbraith, Ralph "Cooney" Weiland

and Nels Stewart. Stewart was wanted by several NHL teams after leading the USAHA West in scoring in 1922–23, but he had such a lucrative deal with Cleveland that he chose to stay put. He would lead the league in scoring two more times before finally accepting an offer from the Montreal Maroons in 1925–26. Once in the NHL he enjoyed one of the greatest rookie seasons of all-time, topping the league in goals (34) and points (42) while leading the Maroons to the Stanley Cup. Stewart was voted as the NHL's most valuable player and awarded the Hart Trophy. Eight of the top 10 scorers in the USAHA West in 1924–25 went on to play in the NHL, with Stewart, Lionel Conacher and Herb Lewis all later inducted into the Hockey Hall of Fame. Virtually all of the players from the 1924–25 U.S. amateur champion Pittsburgh Yellow Jackets, who had played in the USAHA West, joined the NHL as the Pittsburgh Pirates in 1925–26.

When Frank and Lester Patrick folded their league after the 1925–26 campaign, the newly expanded NHL couldn't handle all of the pro players kicking around. The result was the formation of the very first minor pro leagues in 1926–27, when four new leagues were started. Two of these, the Canadian-American (Can-Am) league, and the Canadian Professional (Can-Pro) loop combined to form one league, the International-American Hockey League, in 1936–37. This league was the forerunner of the American Hockey League.

The Can-Am league was formed in Springfield, Massachusetts in 1926 with franchises awarded to New Haven, Quebec, Boston, Providence and Springfield under the watchful eye of president Gordon Clapp of Boston. Art Ross was running the Boston Bruins and he immediately placed his own team in the Can-Am league called the Boston Tigers. He kept his prospects there until 1935–36, and stars like Dit Clapper, Bobby Bauer and Woody Dumart got their start with the Tigers.

Lester Patrick showed similar vision as head of the expansion New York Rangers and ran the Indians club in Springfield. Patrick kept his best farmhands there until 1932–33. The plan worked, as Earl Seibert, Ott Heller, Cecil Dillon, Andy Aikenhead and others all became Rangers regulars. Patrick moved his farmhands to Philadelphia in 1933–34 and kept them there until well into the Second World War. The Montreal Canadiens started a long-lasting relationship with the Providence Reds, but the Reds owned most of their own players. New Haven and Quebec were independent franchises who got their players where they could. The Philadelphia Arrows were added to the Can-Am in 1927–28 and the league operated with five or six teams until the end of the 1935–36 campaign. Judge James Dooley of Providence took over as president in 1929.

The Can-Pro league was started in Windsor, Ontario with Charles King as president, and had teams in the Canadian

cities of Stratford, London, Hamilton, Niagara Falls and Windsor for the 1926–27 campaign. The Montreal Maroons established an on-going connection with the Windsor Bulldogs which lasted into the mid-1930s. In 1927–28 the Detroit NHL franchise placed a club known as the Detroit Olympics in the Can-Pro league and kept its farmhands with that club until 1935–36. The Maroons developed star goalies Davey Kerr and Norm Smith in Windsor, along with regular players like Baldy Northcott and Hap Emms, while Detroit produced Turk Broda, Carl Liscombe, Mud Bruneteau and Bill Brydge. Toronto didn't establish a regular minor-league connection during the earliest days. The Maple Leafs had players at London of the Can-Pro league in the late 1920s, but their first lasting relationship was with the Syracuse Stars from 1931–32 until 1938–39. Gordie Drillon, Reg Hamilton, Bob Davidson, Nick Metz, Pete Langelle, Flash Hollett, Bill Thoms and Wally Stanowski all made their pro debuts with the Stars.

The New York Americans were probably the only NHL team who spent significant money on their minor pro system and yet failed to produce a winner. The Amerks had their players in Niagara Falls in 1926–27 and in New Haven from 1928–29 until 1937–38. They also had players with more than one farm team through the early 1930s, but when players developed they persisted in trading them for aging big-name veterans.

Detroit had been the first U.S. city to join the Can-Pro league, but Buffalo came along in 1928–29, and when Cleveland, Pittsburgh and Syracuse were added in 1929–30 it was obvious that a name change was in order for the league, since only Windsor and London remained of the Canadian cities. The league was dubbed the International Hockey League for the 1929–30 season. Creating some confusion that year was the fact that a farm league to the IHL called the Canadian Professional League was organized with teams in Galt, Guelph, Kitchener and Brantford. In 1930–31 the league was called the Ontario Professional Hockey League with teams in Guelph, Kitchener, Niagara Falls, Stratford and Oshawa. After that season Ontario cities dropped out of minor pro hockey until the Eastern Professional league came along in 1959–60.

The Maritime Senior league had been hiring strong imports since the early 1930s, but folded in December of 1934 when branch-to-branch transfers were refused. Many of the Maritimes players congregated in Saint John for a series of semi-pro exhibition games and there was persistent talk that Saint John would join the Can-Am league in 1935–36. This never happened and it was 1971–72 before the Nova Scotia Voyageurs set up shop in Halifax as the next pro team in the Maritimes.

The first major change in the setup of the minor leagues came in 1936–37 when the Can-Am and IHL combined to form the IAHL (this season is considered to be the first year of the current AHL). Of the 13 teams from these two leagues eight banded together to form the new loop with the number cut to seven when the Buffalo Bisons folded after just 11 games. It was a shame to lose the strong London and Windsor franchises that had been in the International league for all 10 years, but the Depression was having a bad effect on all leagues. John D. Chick was in charge of the Western Division of the IAHL, while Maurice Podoloff of New Haven looked after the east. Podoloff remained as AHL president until 1951–52.

With no more Canadian franchises in the IAHL, the name was changed to the American Hockey League in 1941–42.

A high of 10 franchises was reached that season, but the Second World War soon whittled that number to six teams for the 1943–44 campaign. After the War the complement jumped back to 10 teams in 1946–47. Providence was the only franchise to have a minor pro team through 25 years of minor-league hockey up until 1950–51, with New Haven represented for 23 seasons, while St. Louis (21), Cleveland (21), Buffalo (20) and Springfield (19) were represented most of the time. The AHL (including the Canadian-American and the IHL), was the major provider of star players to the NHL prior to 1951. Graduates of these leagues read like a Who's Who of Hockey with the likes of Johnny Bower, Frank Brimsek, Chuck Rayner, Al Rollins, Tim Horton, Doug Harvey, Tom Johnson, Bob Goldham, Fern Flaman, Jim Thomson, Allan Stanley, Marty Barry, Tod Sloan, Sid Abel, George Armstrong, Toe Blake, Milt Schmidt and Syd Howe.

Perhaps one of the main reasons why the Detroit Red Wings became such a powerhouse in the late 1940s and early 1950s was because they were the first team to establish multiple farm teams. When they folded the Olympics after the 1935–36 campaign, the Red Wings moved their allegiance to the Pittsburgh Hornets (IAHL) franchise from 1936–37 until 1944–45. In 1939–40 they also provided players for the Indianapolis Caps IAHL team in a relationship that lasted into the early 1950s. For those same years they also stocked the Omaha Knights of the American Hockey Association/United States Hockey League—except for the war years of 1942 to 1945.

With so many players in their system it stood to reason that some should excel as the Red Wings produced three of the best goalies of all time in Harry Lumley, Terry Sawchuk and Glenn Hall at Indianapolis. Other good players like Earl Reibel, Johnny Wilson, Marcel Pronovost, Benny Woit, Marty Pavelich, Lee Fogolin, Bill Quackenbush, Al Dewsbury, Gerry Couture, Joe Carveth and Carl Liscombe spent significant time with the Caps.

While the AHL and its forerunners were the main suppliers of NHL talent through the 1940s, they were not the only leagues to showcase talented players. Back in 1926–27, the USAHA had declared itself as fully professional and was renamed the American Hockey Association. Franchises were awarded to Duluth, Minneapolis, Winnipeg, St. Paul, Chicago and Detroit (who folded after only six games).

The AHA operated without any affiliation with the NHL. Its long-range plan was to use as many U.S.-born players as possible and eventually challenge for the Stanley Cup. Because of these aims, there were as many American-born pro players in the 1920s and 1930s as there were at any time until the 1980s. Players like Doc Romnes, Vic Desjardins and Cully Dahlstrom would likely never have played in the NHL without first getting their chance in the AHA.

The first AHA president was A.H. Warren of St. Paul, Minnesota and the secretary-treasurer was William Grant of Duluth. In 1927–28 Grant started a new franchise in Kansas City and he is one of the few people in hockey who were at the same time president, general manager and coach of their team. In 1932–33 his Greyhounds won the AHA title. That season he had also served as AHA president. Grant relinquished all of his other duties to remain on as AHA president in 1933–34.

When former NHA franchise holder Eddie Livingstone got wind of the fact that Chicago would have a team in the NHL in 1926–27, he got the rights to Chicago's main hockey arena and started a team called the Chicago Cardinals in

the AHA. His antics caused lawsuits that were several years being settled. St. Louis and Tulsa joined the AHA in 1928–29 and remained through until the entire league withdrew for the war years after the 1941–42 season. St. Paul and Minneapolis had joined the so-called senior Central Hockey League in 1932–33, but by 1934–35 they were back with the AHA as that league and the CHL played an adjoining schedule. When Ottawa transferred its NHL franchise to St. Louis for the 1934–35 season the new Eagles went up against the established AHA St. Louis Flyers and the first-place minor pro team won the battle. The Eagles folded after just one season.

A year after playing their interlocking schedule, the AHA and the CHL merged for the 1935–36 campaign. In all, Kansas City was in for 15 of the 16 AHA seasons, while St. Louis and Tulsa were members for 14. St. Paul and Minneapolis played 11 years in the AHA and three with the CHL. Omaha got its first pro franchise in 1939–40, while Fort Worth and Dallas joined for the final season of 1941–42. During its existence the AHA proved to be a haven for former big leaguers like Red Stuart, Cully Wilson, Red Green, John Gottselig, Butch Keeling, Marty Barry, Harry Cameron and others who extended their playing careers. The AHA did develop their own players as planned, but teams could not resist the big money when NHL clubs came to purchase players. By October of 1932 the AHA had signed an agreement with the NHL resulting in each league respecting the other's contract. Players developed in the AHA who went on to solid NHL careers include: Bill Mosienko, Charlie Gardiner, Tiny Thompson (who had an amazing 0.35 playoff goals-against average with the Minneapolis Millers in 1927–28), Cooney Weiland, Mike Karakas, Vic Ripley, John Gottselig and Lolo Couture.

The fourth minor pro league to debut after the 1925–26 collapse of major-league hockey in the west was the Prairie Hockey League. The Prairie league was formed under president W.E. Sanborn with franchises in Calgary, Edmonton, Regina, Saskatoon and Moose Jaw for the 1926–27 season. The bigger cities of Calgary and Edmonton dropped out in 1927–28 and the league folded after that year. The Chicago Black Hawks were short of player reserves, so they bought the Saskatoon franchise to get at players like Earl Miller and Val Hoffinger.

The Patrick family couldn't keep their hands out of western hockey and when a stronger league called the Pacific Coast Hockey League was formed with teams in Seattle, Portland, Victoria and Vancouver for the 1928–29 campaign, the Vancouver franchise was run by Guy Patrick, a brother of Frank and Lester. (With a few breaks, this league operated until 1973–74.) There was no league in the west in 1931–32 and a new loop called the Western Canada Hockey League, with teams in Calgary, Edmonton and Vancouver, started in 1932–33. The league changed its name to the Northwest Hockey League in 1933–34 and added teams

from Portland and Seattle. By 1936–37 the Alberta teams were again gone and the name was changed back to the PCHL. There were teams in Vancouver, Oakland, Portland and Seattle, although Oakland moved to Spokane during the season and stayed there for a few more years. In 1939–40 Guy Patrick won his fourth title in seven years in Vancouver, then challenged the Chicago Black Hawks to an unofficial playoff after the season. The PCHL champs swamped the visitors 6–0 in game one and edged the Hawks 4–3 in the second tilt before Chicago regrouped to win 4–2, 7–6 and 7–3.

World War II had a major effect on pro hockey as the Brooklyn (New York) Americans dropped out of the NHL in 1942. The PCHL had folded in 1941, followed by the AHA in 1942. By 1943–44 there were only 12 pro teams in the NHL and AHL combined as most of the best pro players were scattered throughout senior or military leagues all across North America. With the end of World War II, a large hockey revival took place. The NHL did not deviate from its six teams until 1967–68, but by 1946–47 the AHL had jumped to 10 teams, while the new United States Hockey League iced eight more. The USHL was really a revival of the old AHA with teams in Kansas City, Omaha, St. Paul, Tulsa, Fort Worth, Dallas and Minneapolis. It lasted until the 1950–51 season. The PCHL had come back in 1945–46 as what was called a senior league, though a look at the rosters would indicate that they had some pretty high-priced help. During the postwar hockey boom the PCHL turned pro again in 1948–49 with teams in New Westminster, Tacoma, Vancouver, Portland and Seattle. Victoria came in for the 1949–50 campaign and the league flourished for many years using much the same formula as the IHL of the 1990s. Although the PCHL and its various other western leagues were run as independent operations up until 1950, they did manage to develop star players like Clint Smith, Bryan Hextall, Lorne Carr, Norm "Dutch" Gainer, Wally Hergesheimer and Andy Hebenton for the NHL. In addition to the many minor pro circuits, there were also numerous so-called amateur organizations like the Eastern Amateur Hockey League that provided players with a good income and at least six senior leagues in Canada, plus leagues in England and Scotland, were paying outsiders again by 1946–47.

There were far fewer independent minor-league hockey teams after the late 1940s revival. Detroit had players in Indianapolis, St. Louis and Omaha; Montreal had a hand in Buffalo, Dallas, Houston, San Diego and Victoria; the Rangers were in New Haven, Minneapolis, St. Paul and Tacoma; Toronto in Pittsburgh, Tulsa and Los Angeles; Chicago had players in Kansas City and Tulsa while Boston placed most of their players in Hershey. These multiple sponsorships continued until NHL expansion in 1967, when teams gradually started cutting back on the number of pro players in their system until most ended up supplying only one team by the late 1990s.

MINOR PRO FRANCHISES, 1926–27 TO 1950–51

Team	League	First and Last Seasons	NHL affiliation
Boston Tigers	Can-Am	1926–27 – 1935–36	Boston
Bronx Tigers	Can-Am	1931–32	Americans/Rangers
Buffalo Bisons	IHL	1928–29 – 1935–36	
	AHL	1940–41 – 1969–70	Canadiens/Rangers/Chicago
Buffalo Majors	AHA	1930–31 – 1931–32	
Calgary Tigers	Prairie	1926–27	
	WCHL	1932–33	
	NWHL	1933–34 – 1935–36	
Chicago Cardinals	AHA	1926–27	
Chicago Shamrocks	AHA	1930–31 – 1932–32	
Cincinnati Mohawks	AHL	1949–50 – 1951–52	Canadiens/Rangers
Cleveland Indians	IHL	1929–30 – 1933–34	
Cleveland Falcons	IHL	1934–35 – 1935–36	
Cleveland Barons	AHL	1936–37 – 1971–72	Rangers/Canadiens/Minnesota
Coral Gables Seminoles	Tropical	1938–39	
Dallas Texans	AHA	1941–42	
	USHL	1945–46 – 1948–49	Canadiens
Denver Falcons	USHL	1950–51	Rangers
Detroit Greyhounds	AHA	1926–27	
Detroit Olympics	Can-Pro/IHL	1927–28 – 1935–36	Detroit
Duluth Hornets	AHA	1926–27 – 1932–33	
Edmonton Eskimos	Prairie	1926–27	
	WCHL	1932–33	
	NWHL	1933–34 – 1935–36	
Eveleth Rangers	CHL	1934–35	
Fort Worth Rangers	AHA	1941–42	
	USHL	1945–46 – 1948–49	Rangers
Fresno Falcons	PCHL	1948–49 – 1949–50	
Galt Terriers	Can-Pro	1929–30	
	OPHL	1930–31	
Guelph Maple Leafs	OPHL	1930–31	
Hamilton Tigers	Can-Pro/IHL	1926–27 – 1929–30	
Havana Tropicals	Tropical	1938–39	
Hershey Bears	AHL	1938–39 – present day	"Original Six"/Pittsburgh/Philadelphia
Hollywood Millionaires	California	1927–28 – 1929–30	
		1932–33	
Hollywood Stars	California	1931–32	
Houston Huskies	USHL	1946–47 – 1948–49	Canadiens
Indianapolis Caps	AHL	1939–40 – 1951–52	Detroit
Kansas City Pla-Mors	AHA	1927–28 – 1931–32	
	USHL	1945–46 – 1948–49	Chicago
Kansas City Greyhounds	AHA	1932–33 – 1939–40	
Kansas City Americans	AHA	1940–41 – 1941–42	Chicago
Kansas City Royals	USHL	1950–51	Rangers
Kitchener Millionaires	Can-Pro	1927–28	
Kitchener Flying Dutchmen	Can-Pro	1928–29 – 1929–30	
Kitchener Silverwoods	OPHL	1930–31	
London Tecumsehs	Can-Pro	1926–27 – 1935–36	Toronto/Chicago
Los Angeles Palais-de-Glace	California	1925–26	
Los Angeles Richfield Oil	California	1925–26 – 1929–30	
Los Angeles Culver City	California	1925–26	
Los Angeles Globe Ice Cream	California	1926–27	
Los Angeles Wintergarden	California	1926–27	
Los Angeles Millionaires	California	1930–31	
Los Angeles Angels	California	1931–32	
Los Angeles Monarchs	PCHL	1948–49 – 1949–50	Toronto
Louisville Blades	USHL	1949–50	Canadiens
Miami Clippers	Tropical	1938–39	
Miami Beach Pirates	Tropical	1938–39	
Milwaukee Seagulls	USHL	1950–51	Chicago
Minneapolis Millers	AHA	1926–27 – 1930–31	
	CHL	1934–35	
	AHA	1936–37 – 1941–42	Rangers
	USHL	1945–46 – 1949–50	Rangers
Moose Jaw Maroons	Prairie	1926–27 – 1927–28	

Minor Pro Franchises, 1926–27 to 1950–51 *continued*

TEAM	LEAGUE	FIRST AND LAST SEASONS	NHL AFFILIATION
New Haven Eagles	Can-Am/AHL	1926–27 – 1942–43	NY Americans/Canadiens
	AHL	1945–46	
		1950–51	
New Haven Ramblers	AHL	1946–47 – 1949–50	Rangers
Newark Bulldogs	Can-Am	1928–29	
New Westminster Royals	PCHL	1948–49 – 1958–59	Toronto
Niagara Falls Cataracts	Can-Pro	1926–27 – 1929–30	
	OPHL	1930–31	
Oakland Sheiks	California	1928–29 – 1932–33	
Oakland Checkers	California	1930–31	
Oakland Clippers	PCHA	1936–37 – Moved to Spokane during season	
Oakland Oaks	PCHL	1948–49 – 1949–50	Springfield (AHL)
Oklahoma City Warriors	AHA	1933–34 – 1935–36	
Omaha Knights	AHA	1939–40 – 1941–42	Detroit
	USHL	1945–46 – 1950–51	Detroit
Oshawa Patricians	OPHL	1930–31	
Philadelphia Arrows	Can-Am	1927–28 – 1934–35	Americans/Rangers
Philadelphia Ramblers	IAHL	1935–36 – 1939–40	Rangers
Philadelphia Rockets	AHL	1940–41 – 1948–49	
Pittsburgh Yellow Jackets	IHL	1930–31 – 1931–32	
Pittsburgh Shamrocks	IHL	1935–36	
Pittsburgh Hornets	IAHL	1936–37 – 1955–56	Detroit/Toronto
Portland Buckaroos	PCHL	1928–29 – 1930–31	
	NWHL	1933–34 – 1935–36	
	PCHL	1936–37 – 1940–41	
Portland Penguins	PCHL	1948–49 – 1949–50	
Portland Eagles	PCHL	1950–51	
Providence Reds	Can-Am/AHL	1926–27 – 1976–77	"Original Six"
Quebec Castors	Can-Am	1926–27 – 1927–28	
	Can-Am	1932–33 – 1934–35	Maroons
Seattle Olympics	PCHL	1940–41	
Seattle Ironmen	PCHL	1948–49 – 1951–52	
Spokane Clippers	PCHL	1936–37 – 1938–39	
Spokane Bombers	PCHL	1940–41	
Springfield Indians	Can-Am	1926–27 – 1932–33	Rangers
	Can-Am/IAHL/AHL	1935–36 – 1941–42	Canadiens/Americans
	AHL	1946–47 – 1950–51	
Stratford Nationals	Can-Pro	1926–27 – 1927–28	
	OPHL	1930–31	Maroons
Syracuse Stars	IHL	1930–31 – 1939–40	Toronto
Tacoma Tigers	PCHL	1930–31	
Tacoma Rockets	PCHL	1948–49 – 1952–53	Rangers
Toronto Ravinas	Can-Pro	1927–28	
Toronto Millionaires	Can-Pro/IHL	1928–29 – 1929–30	
Tulsa Oilers	AHA	1928–29 – 1941–42	
	USHL	1945–46 – 1950–51	Toronto/Boston
Vancouver Lions	PCHL	1928–29 – 1930–31	
	NWHL	1933–34 – 1935–36	
	PCHL	1936–37 – 1940–41	
Vancouver Maroons	WCHL	1932–33 – Moved from Regina during season	
Vancouver Canucks	PCHL/WHL	1948–49 – 1969–70	Rangers
Victoria Cubs	PCHL	1928–29 – 1929–30	
Victoria Cougars	PCHL/WHL	1949–50 – 1960–61	Canadiens/Boston
Washington Lions	AHL	1941–42 – 1942–43	Canadiens
	AHL	1947–48 – 1948–49	
Wichita Blue Jays	AHA	1932–33	
Wichita Vikings	AHA	1933–34 – folded after three games	
Wichita Skyhawks	AHA	1935–36 – 1939–40	
Windsor Bulldogs	Can-Pro/IHL	1926–27 – 1935–36	Maroons/Detroit
Winnipeg Maroons	AHA	1926–27 – 1927–28	Chicago

CHAPTER 25

The Modern Minors

Minor Pro Hockey's Surprising Southern Boom

Eric Zweig

WHEN EIGHT TEAMS BANDED TOGETHEr in 1936–37 to form the American Hockey League, the professional hockey universe consisted of the eight NHL clubs and just 15 other minor pro teams competing in three leagues across North America. By 1997–98, beyond the 26 NHL franchises, there were seven minor leagues counting 102 clubs as members, and expectations of further growth at both levels.

Like the other minor leagues of the day, the American league's primary mandate was, and remains, to develop talent for the National Hockey League. But in today's minor leagues, salesmanship and show business are as highly valued as the ability to skate and shoot. This new emphasis is reflected in the team nicknames.

Where teams once were known rather prosaically as the Bisons, Eagles, Reds or Stars, with the Wichita Skyhawks of the American Hockey Association or the Pittsburgh Yellow Jackets of the Eastern league on the exotic edge, contemporary teams are more likely to be called the Mudbugs, RiverFrogs, Sabercats or Lizard Kings. The minors have spread far beyond their traditional locales in the northeastern and midwestern United States into the deep South and the sunbelt of the southwest. Even the failure of two minor leagues during the 1990s (the Sunshine Hockey League and the Southern Hockey League) hasn't stemmed minor professional hockey's spread across the North American continent.

As it has been for most of its existence, the American Hockey League is the top development league for the National Hockey League. Each franchise is required to be affiliated with an NHL team, and the league's 18 clubs were linked to 24 of the NHL's 26 teams in 1997–98, with seven clubs owned outright by their NHL parents. In 1998–99 the AHL will add the Lowell (Massachusetts) Loch Monsters, owned by the New York Islanders, and the 1999–2000 season will mark the debut of a team in Wilkes-Barre, Pennsylvania which will be the farm team for the Pittsburgh Penguins, who currently co-sponsor the Syracuse Crunch with the Vancouver Canucks.

The Philadelphia Flyers added an interesting wrinkle to the AHL in 1996 when they ended their association with the Hershey Bears and launched the Philadelphia Phantoms as a farm club, both for players and fans. With the Flyers having moved into the new CoreStates Center, the Phantoms took over their old arena, the Spectrum, and led the league in attendance with average crowds of 9,182 en route to the AHL championship.

Each AHL team is guaranteed a set number of players from their parent club(s), but they are also free to sign free agents and conduct their own professional tryouts. Players must be at least 18 years old by December 31 in order to be eligible to play in the AHL. As most of the league's players are on NHL contracts, there is no preset salary range. The American Hockey League plays NHL rules, except that a single point is awarded to a team that loses in overtime.

The International Hockey League was formed on December 5, 1945, and has operated continuously since the 1945–46 season. It's interesting to note that the names of both the American and International leagues have been something of a misnomer for more than 30 years: the AHL has had at least one Canadian-based team in every season since 1959–60, while the "I" was strictly American following the withdrawal of southwestern Ontario's Chatham Maroons and Windsor Bulldogs after the 1963–64 season. Not until 1996, when franchises were placed in the former NHL cities of Winnipeg and Quebec, did the IHL once again become international.

Between 1987–88 and 1995–96, the IHL expanded from nine teams to 19 and has grown beyond its original base in Michigan, where four of its clubs are still located, into large metropolitan areas such as Houston, Cleveland and Cincinnati. In 1994–95, the IHL made forays into existing NHL cities with the Chicago Wolves and Detroit Vipers. The addition of the Vipers represented a sort of homecoming for the league, which had begun its existence in Detroit and Windsor, Ontario, under the guidance of Red Wings general manager Jack Adams. The Vipers have become the IHL's flagship franchise, often attracting capacity crowds of 20,182 to their home arena, the Palace in suburban Auburn Hills, Michigan. Total IHL attendance now regularly tops five million fans per season. A testament to the league's viability is the fact that the latest expansion team, in New Orleans, paid an $8-million fee to join the circuit.

The IHL's early-1990s growth spurt seemed to have the league on a collision course with the NHL. In addition to the teams in Chicago and Detroit, teams were placed in Long Beach, California, and San Francisco, both near NHL cities. Relations between the IHL and its senior counterpart soured and many National league clubs canceled their IHL affiliations. Only four of 18 teams had an NHL affiliation in 1997–98. Under new chief operating officer Doug Moss (former president of the Buffalo Sabres) the league is working to improve its relationship with the NHL. A sign of renewed cooperation with the major league is the selection of the Milwaukee Admirals as the farm team for the NHL's expansion Nashville Predators. The IHL hopes to establish more working agreements. IHL teams, however will remain under independent ownership.

One major difference between the NHL and the "I" is the use of shootouts to break ties. The shootout was adopted in 1985–86, and is used to determine a winner if a game remains tied after a five-minute overtime period is played. Teams losing in a shootout receive one point. This rule has been adopted by every minor league below the "I".

Because it is not a developmental league, the IHL has no firm policy regarding the age of its players. It does employ

a salary cap which has been as high as $1.4 million per team but will drop to $1.1 million by the end of the current collective bargaining agreement in 2001–02. The average salary for IHL players is estimated at $50,000, with elite players making around $100,000. (The league's highest-paid player in 1997–98 was Hubie McDonough of the Orlando Solar Bears at $243,000.) The minimum wage increases from $25,000 to $27,500 in 1998–99. The IHL is committed to a policy that at least half its arena's seats (or at least 5,000) are to be sold for $10 or less.

If the "I" and the "A" represent the top rung of minor professional hockey in North America, next on the ladder would be the East Coast Hockey League. The ECHL grew out of the old Atlantic Coast league and was set up in 1988 to provide a place for players who were not drafted by NHL teams to develop their skills. Through the 1997–98 season, the "E" has sent some 80 players on to the NHL. It is hockey's largest minor league, fielding 25 teams in 1997–98 with hopes of expanding to as many as 32 by the turn of the century. Sixteen teams had secondary affiliations with NHL clubs in 1997–98. ECHL teams usually carry no more than four or five of an NHL team's prospects and it is not uncommon for players from several NHL clubs to play together on one ECHL team. The ECHL considers itself a development league and rules prohibit its teams from carrying more than four players on their 18-man rosters who have more than 200 games of professional experience. A salary cap of $8,000 per team per week is in force and players earn a minimum of $300 per week. The minimum age to play in the ECHL is 19 (though a player must also have used up his Junior eligibility). The average age is 23.

The East Coast Hockey League was comprised of just five teams when it began play in 1988–89 (the Johnstown Chiefs and Erie Panthers in Pennsylvania; the Knoxville Cherokees in Tennessee; the Carolina Thunderbirds and the Virginia Lancers). Its rapid growth in what are mainly non-traditional hockey markets, combined with the 1990s' emphasis on marketing, has given rise to some of the strangest team names and logos in all of hockey, including the Louisiana Ice Gators, the Baton Rouge Kingfish, the Louisville RiverFrogs, the Jacksonville Lizard Kings, the Pensacola Ice Pilots, the PeeDee Pride and the Mobile Mysticks.

Though expansion is generally limited by the travel expenses league owners are willing to incur, competition between leagues for players and cities has become much stronger in the low minors in recent years. The oldest of the four lower minor leagues is the United Hockey League, which was founded as the Colonial Hockey League in 1991. The original name was chosen to reflect what was planned as a New England–based circuit, but the league actually ended up placing teams on both sides of the border, primarily around the Great Lakes. This international setup led to a name change, to the United Hockey League, in 1997–98, and a new logo was created featuring both the Canadian and American flags.

The league has continued to grow, icing 10 teams in 1997–98, and stretching from the Thunder Bay (Ontario) Thunder Cats in the north to the Winston-Salem (North Carolina) Icehawks in the south. The league has moved into a number of markets the IHL and AHL have abandoned (Flint, Muskegon, Port Huron and Saginaw in Michigan and Binghamton and Utica in New York), and is trying to

grow to 16 teams by 1999–2000, with expansion confirmed into St. Charles, Missouri (near St. Louis); Rockford, Illinois; and Mansfield, Ohio.

Each of the 10 teams in the "U" in 1997–98 was independently owned, though seven had an affiliation with teams in either the National, International or American leagues. The Port Huron Border Cats lead the way, linked to the NHL's Florida Panthers, the Beast of New Haven (Florida's AHL farm club) and the IHL's Las Vegas Thunder. The Quad City Mallards also have multiple agreements, with both the Portland Pirates (the Washington Capitals' AHL team) and the San Antonio Dragons of the IHL. Generally, the higher minor leagues send players to the United league when they require more ice time or need to improve a specific skill. Recently, however, a growing number of players have started in the "U" and moved up, and the NHL has begun to scout the league more aggressively. The loop held its first All-Star Game in 1997–98.

Rinks in the United Hockey League seat an average of 4,000 fans, topped by Quad City's 9,200-seat arena in Moline, Illinois (called "the Mark" after Mark Twain). Attendance in 1997–98 averaged about 3,100 and has increased in every year of the league's operation.

Teams carry a maximum of 21 players and the salary cap of $8,800 per team per week is monitored weekly by the league office. Through 1997–98, teams were required to carry at least three rookies and were allowed no more than nine players with more than 200 games of professional experience. Beginning with the 1998–99 season, teams will have to carry an additional rookie, and "veterans" will be limited to seven per club. UHL teams generally travel by bus, though Thunder Bay, playing in the loop's most remote city, flies to some road games. The schedule is set up to keep travel expenses to a minimum, with fewer, but longer, excursions and by sending teams on the road during dates when their home arenas are otherwise occupied.

The "new" Central Hockey League began operations in 1992–93. It's the creation of Ray Miron, a former NHL general manager with the Colorado Rockies and a longtime coach and general manager of the Tulsa Oilers and Oklahoma City Blazers in the original CHL, which operated from 1963 until 1984. Many of the cities that competed in the old CHL, including Tulsa and Oklahoma City, are represented in the new league, but the loop sits further down the hockey development chain than it used to. Still, four former CHL players found their way onto NHL rosters between 1993 and 1998.

The new league is closely tied to the International Hockey League—both the Columbus Cottonmouths and the Wichita Thunder are directly affiliated with IHL teams, and five of the CHL's 10 teams in 1997–98 were owned by Horn Chen, who also owns the IHL's Indianapolis Ice. Despite this cozy arrangement, the "I" placed a team in San Antonio, Texas, displacing the Central league franchise in that city. Topeka (Kansas) joins the "C" in 1998–99, and North Little Rock (Arkansas) and Chattanooga (Tennessee) are seen as future expansion sites. The league currently operates in Arkansas, Tennessee, Texas, Georgia, North Carolina, Kansas and Oklahoma. Teams travel primarily by bus, though they make one or two air trips during the season.

Average attendance in the Central Hockey League has so far managed to remain above that of the other leagues of similar caliber, but the Western Professional Hockey League, based mainly in Texas, seems to have designs on

much of the same territory as the CHL and has already established a rival franchise to the CHL team in Fort Worth, Texas. The WPHL will pose a very real challenge to the Central league.

CHL teams have a salary limit of $6,600 per week to pay a 17-man roster. There is no maximum age restriction, but teams can carry no more than five players with 200 games of professional experience. Among the more unusual team nicknames in the CHL are the Huntsville Channel Cats and the Macon Whoopee.

Hockey's two newest minor leagues are the West Coast Hockey League and the Western Professional Hockey League. The WPHL began in 1996–97 with five teams in Texas and one in New Mexico, and doubled its size to 12 teams in 1997–98, moving into Louisiana with the Lake Charles Ice Pirates, the Monroe Moccasins and the Shreveport Mudbugs. The league will continue its explosive growth in 1998–99, with plans to add the Arkansas Glaciercats, the Tupelo (Mississippi) T-Rex and the Corpus Christi (Texas) Icerays. The league is also eyeing Abilene, Texas; Pueblo, Colorado; and Alexandria, Louisiana as expansion sites. The franchise fee, which was $100,000 in the league's first season, increased to $250,000 for 1997–98 and $400,000 in 1998–99. Despite the league's aggressive approach to franchise growth, the WPHL plans to remain a league that's regional in its scope, so that travel expenses can be kept low.

The WPHL covers territory that has largely been untapped by hockey in the past, a fact driven home during the league's first season, when some fans left games after two periods because they didn't know there was a third still to come. Still, the circuit has drawn more than 4,000 fans per game over its first two campaigns, a result that's been aided by the fact that many cities in the league enjoy rivalries based on geography or on competition in other sports such as college football.

In an effort to attract quality players, the WPHL has set a salary cap of $10,000 per team per week, easily the highest of the low minor pro leagues. With 20-man rosters, a player's average payday is $500 per week. By increasing its mandatory rookie quota to five players in 1998–99, the WPHL hopes to showcase younger talent poised to move up through the hockey ranks. Two of the league's teams are currently affiliated with the International Hockey League, and negotiations are ongoing to hook up every club with an IHL team. While it will probably be years before a WPHL player makes his way onto an NHL roster, the league has no lack of NHL connections. Former players Lee Norwood (the Central Texas Stampede) and Garry Unger (the New Mexico Scorpions) coach in the league, while Blaine Stoughton is general manager of the Austin Ice-Bats. Kevin Lowe of the Edmonton Oilers is a member of the league's board of governors. Current NHL players Joe Murphy and Bernie Nicholls co-own the New Mexico Scorpions, while Andy Moog is a part-owner of the Fort Worth Brahmas. Former Montreal Canadiens backup goaltender Andre Racicot began the 1997–98 season with the WPHL franchise in Monroe, Louisiana before leaving to play hockey in England.

Hockey attained an unprecedented level of popularity after the trade of Wayne Gretzky to the Los Angeles Kings in August 1988. Gretzky's presence in southern California helped the NHL expand into markets it had never before considered, and the major league's growth mirrored an increased interest in minor pro hockey throughout the United States. Even so, no professional hockey teams existed west of the Rocky Mountains below the IHL level until the creation of the West Coast Hockey League in 1995–96.

The WCHL opened for business with six teams in three states: the (Fairbanks) Alaska Gold Kings and their in-state rival the Anchorage Aces, the Reno Renegades in Nevada, and the Fresno Fighting Falcons, Bakersfield Fog and San Diego Gulls in California. After the league's second season the Fairbanks club withdrew, but it is slated to resume play in 1998–99 in Colorado Springs as the Colorado Gold Kings. In 1997–98 the league expanded into four new cities and three new states with the admission of the Tacoma (Washington) Sabercats, the (Boise) Idaho Steelheads, and the Phoenix Mustangs and Tucson Gila Monsters in Arizona. The Reno franchise changed its name to the Rage that season. During each of its first three seasons the league has also hosted a touring Russian squad.

While there are no other immediate expansion plans in the works, several California cities are building new arenas, providing potential new sites for franchises. The WCHL is also eyeing locations in Washington, Oregon and British Columbia.

The West Coast league's salary cap allows its member clubs a budget of only $7,125 per team per week for a roster of 19 players—an average salary of just $375 per week. Players are, however, permitted to double as coaches or work in the front office, which can mean more money for some players while stretching team budgets. Teams must carry at least three rookies, a quota the league plans to expand to six, but teams are encouraged to carry as many veterans as possible to maintain a high level of competition. The location of many teams in or near large cities and popular vacation spots makes the league more attractive to players and the WCHL is unique in the minors in that teams travel primarily by plane—air fares in the west are often cheaper than buses are in the east.

Former NHLers Walt Poddubny (Anchorage) and Ron Flockhart (Reno), as well as Wayne Gretzky's brother Keith (Bakersfield), all coach in the WCHL, and some NHL teams have begun to scout its players. The league is more closely associated, however, with the IHL. The Tacoma Sabercats are directly affiliated with the Las Vegas Thunder, while the San Diego Gulls are loosely aligned with the Long Beach Ice Dogs. In addition, Cleveland, Quebec and Utah all had players on assignment to WCHL teams in 1997–98, while approximately 50 WCHL players have been called up to various IHL teams during the league's first three seasons. The WCHL fan base has grown each year, with average attendance climbing from 2,963 in 1995–96, to 3,016 in 1996–97, and 3,663 in 1997–98. The San Diego Gulls have been the league's best draw, with attendance topping 5,000 fans per game, while the Tacoma Sabercats hosted a league-record crowd of more than 14,000 in March 1998.

CHAPTER 26

Early Professional, Early Senior, WHA and Modern Minor Professional League Standings

Ernie Fitzsimmons

1893

AMATEUR HOCKEY ASSOCIATION

	GP	W	L	T	GF	GA	Pts
*Montreal AAA	8	7	1	1	38	18	14
Ottawa HC	8	6	2	0	49	22	12
Montreal Crystals	8	3	5	0	25	34	6
Quebec HC	8	2	5	1	23	46	5
Montreal Victorias	8	1	6	1	20	35	3

1894

AMATEUR HOCKEY ASSOCIATION

	GP	W	L	T	GF	GA	Pts
*Montreal AAA	8	5	3	0	25	15	10
Ottawa HC	8	5	3	0	24	16	10
Montreal Victorias	8	5	3	0	36	20	10
Quebec HC	8	5	3	0	26	27	10
Montreal Crystals	0	8	0	0	10	43	0

1895

AMATEUR HOCKEY ASSOCIATION

	GP	W	L	T	GF	GA	Pts
*Montreal Victorias	8	6	2	0	35	20	12
Montreal AAA	8	4	4	0	33	22	8
Ottawa HC	8	4	4	0	25	24	8
Montreal Crystals	7	3	4	0	21	39	6
Quebec HC	7	2	5	0	18	27	4

1896

AMATEUR HOCKEY ASSOCIATION

	GP	W	L	T	GF	GA	Pts
*Montreal Victorias	8	7	1	0	41	24	14
Ottawa HC	8	6	2	0	22	16	12
Quebec HC	8	4	4	0	23	23	8
Montreal AAA	8	2	6	0	24	33	4
Montreal Shamrocks	8	1	7	0	16	30	2

1897

AMATEUR HOCKEY ASSOCIATION

	GP	W	L	T	GF	GA	Pts
*Montreal Victorias	8	7	1	0	48	26	14
Ottawa HC	8	5	3	0	25	18	10
Montreal AAA	8	5	3	0	31	26	10
Quebec HC	8	2	6	0	22	46	4
Montreal Shamrocks	8	1	7	0	27	37	2

1898

AMATEUR HOCKEY ASSOCIATION

	GP	W	L	T	GF	GA	Pts
*Montreal Victorias	8	8	0	0	53	33	16
Montreal AAA	8	4	3	0	34	21	10
Montreal Shamrocks	8	3	5	0	25	36	6
Quebec HC	8	2	6	0	29	35	4
Ottawa HC	8	2	6	0	28	44	4

1899

CANADIAN AMATEUR HOCKEY LEAGUE

	GP	W	L	T	GF	GA	Pts
*Montreal Shamrocks	8	7	1	0	40	21	14
Montreal Victorias	8	6	2	0	44	23	12
Ottawa HC	8	4	4	0	21	43	8
Montreal AAA	8	3	5	0	30	29	6
Quebec HC	8	0	8	0	12	31	0

Champions are indicated by an asterisk (*).

1900

CANADIAN AMATEUR HOCKEY LEAGUE

	GP	W	L	T	GF	GA	Pts
*Montreal Shamrocks	8	7	1	0	49	26	14
Montreal AAA	8	5	3	0	34	36	10
Ottawa HC	8	4	4	0	28	19	8
Montreal Victorias	8	2	6	0	44	55	4
Quebec HC	8	2	6	0	33	52	4

1901

CANADIAN AMATEUR HOCKEY LEAGUE

	GP	W	L	T	GF	GA	Pts
*Ottawa HC	8	7	0	1	33	20	15
Montreal Victorias	8	4	3	1	45	32	9
Montreal Shamrocks	8	4	4	0	30	25	8
Montreal AAA	8	3	5	0	28	37	6
Quebec HC	8	1	7	0	21	43	2

1902

CANADIAN AMATEUR HOCKEY LEAGUE

	GP	W	L	T	GF	GA	Pts
*Montreal AAA	8	6	2	0	39	15	12
Ottawa HC	8	5	3	0	35	15	10
Montreal Victorias	8	4	4	0	36	25	8
Quebec HC	8	4	4	0	26	34	8
Montreal Shamrocks	8	1	7	0	15	62	2

1903

CANADIAN AMATEUR HOCKEY LEAGUE

	GP	W	L	T	GF	GA	Pts
*Ottawa HC	8	6	2	0	47	26	8
Montreal Victorias	8	6	2	0	48	33	8
Montreal AAA	7	4	3	0	34	19	8
Quebec HC	8	3	4	0	30	46	6
Montreal Shamrocks	8	0	8	0	21	56	0

1904

CANADIAN AMATEUR HOCKEY LEAGUE

	GP	W	L	T	GF	GA	Pts
*Quebec HC	8	7	1	0	50	37	14
Montreal Victorias	8	5	3	0	75	48	10
Montreal AAA	8	3	5	0	34	49	6
Montreal Shamrocks	8	1	7	0	32	75	2
Ottawa HC	8	4	4	0	32	15	8

• *Ottawa resigned 02/08/04 Results not counted in final standings*

FEDERAL AMATEUR HOCKEY LEAGUE

	GP	W	L	T	GF	GA	Pts
*Montreal Wanderers	6	6	0	0	38	18	12
Montreal Nationals	6	3	3	0	27	27	6
Cornwall HC	6	2	4	0	20	27	0
Ottawa Capitals	6	1	5	0	28	41	2

1905

CANADIAN AMATEUR HOCKEY LEAGUE

	GP	W	L	T	GF	GA	Pts
*Montreal Victorias	10	9	1	0	64	32	18
Quebec HC	10	8	2	0	78	45	16
Montreal AAA	10	7	3	0	54	42	14
Montreal Shamrocks	10	3	7	0	41	62	6
Montreal Westmount	10	3	7	0	55	75	6
Montreal Nationals	10	0	10	0	6	42	0

FEDERAL AMATEUR HOCKEY LEAGUE

	GP	W	L	T	GF	GA	Pts
*Ottawa HC	8	7	1	0	60	19	14
Montreal Wanderers	8	6	2	0	44	27	12
Brockville HC	8	4	4	0	34	30	8
Cornwall HC	8	3	5	0	18	37	6
Ottawa Montagnards	8	0	8	0	19	62	0

INTERNATIONAL PRO HOCKEY LEAGUE

	GP	W	L	T	GF	GA	Pts
*Calumet-Larium Miners	24	18	5	1	131	75	37
Houghton-Portage Lakes	24	15	7	2	98	81	32
Michigan Soo Indians	24	10	13	1	81	79	21
Pittsburgh Pro HC	24	8	15	1	82	114	17
Canadian Soo	24	6	17	1	97	140	13

1906

EASTERN CANADA AMATEUR HOCKEY LEAGUE

	GP	W	L	T	GF	GA	Pts
*Ottawa Silver Seven	10	9	1	0	90	42	18
Montreal Wanderers	10	9	1	0	74	38	18
Montreal Victorias	10	6	4	0	76	73	12
Quebec HC	10	3	7	0	57	70	6
Montreal AAA	10	3	7	0	49	63	6
Montreal Shamrocks	10	0	10	0	30	90	0

FEDERAL AMATEUR HOCKEY LEAGUE

	GP	W	L	T	GF	GA	Pts
*Smiths Falls HC	7	7	0	0	35	13	14
Ottawa Victorias	8	4	4	0	48	42	8
Brockville HC	7	3	4	0	55	32	6
Cornwall HC	6	2	4	0	16	30	4
Ottawa Montagnards	4	0	4	0	2	39	0

INTERNATIONAL PRO HOCKEY LEAGUE

	GP	W	L	T	GF	GA	Pts
*Houghton-Portage Lakes	24	19	5	0	105	70	38
Michigan Soo Indians	24	18	6	0	126	57	36
Pittsburgh Pro HC	24	15	9	0	121	84	30
Calumet Miners	24	7	17	0	48	108	14
Canadian Soo	24	1	23	0	56	137	2

1907

EASTERN CANADA AMATEUR HOCKEY ASSOC.

	GP	W	L	T	GF	GA	Pts
*Montreal Wanderers	10	10	0	...	105	39	20
Ottawa Silver Seven	10	7	3	...	76	54	14
Montreal Victorias	10	6	4	...	101	70	12
Montreal AAA	10	3	7	...	58	83	6
Quebec HC	10	2	8	...	62	88	4
Montreal Shamrocks	10	2	8	...	52	120	4

INTERNATIONAL PRO HOCKEY LEAGUE

	GP	W	L	T	GF	GA	Pts
*Houghton-Portage Lakes	24	16	8	0	102	102	32
Canadian Soo	24	13	11	0	124	123	26
Pittsburgh Pro HC	25	12	12	1	94	82	25
Michigan Soo Indians	24	11	13	0	103	88	22
Calumet Wanderers	25	8	16	1	96	124	17

MANITOBA PROFESSIONAL HOCKEY LEAGUE

	GP	W	L	T	GF	GA	Pts
Brandon Wheat Kings	9	5	2	2	50	39	12
Portage-la-Prairie	9	5	3	1	35	33	11
*Kenora Thistles	6	4	2	0	38	19	8
Winnipeg Strathconas	10	1	8	1	38	70	3

1907-08

EASTERN CANADA AMATEUR HOCKEY ASSOC.

	GP	W	L	T	GF	GA	Pts
*Montreal Wanderers	10	8	2	...	63	52	16
Ottawa Silver Seven	10	7	3	...	86	51	14
Quebec HC	10	5	5	...	81	74	10
Montreal Shamrocks	10	5	5	...	53	49	10
Montreal Victorias	10	4	6	...	73	78	8
Montreal AAA	10	1	9	...	53	105	2

ONTARIO PROFESSIONAL HOCKEY LEAGUE

	GP	W	L	T	GF	GA	Pts
*Toronto Professionals	12	10	2	...	88	55	20
Berlin Dutchmen	12	7	5	...	57	49	14
Brantford Indians	12	5	7	...	65	79	10
Guelph Professionals	12	2	10	...	33	60	4

MANITOBA PROFESSIONAL HOCKEY LEAGUE

	GP	W	L	T	GF	GA	Pts
Winnipeg Maple Leafs	16	10	6	0	107	89	20
Portage la Prairie	15	8	7	0	76	73	16
Winnipeg Strathconas	15	5	10	0	92	113	10
Kenora Thistles §	...	...	...	...	...	...	...
Brandon Wheat Kings ¶	...	...	...	...	...	...	...

§ folded 01/01/08   ¶ folded 01/03/08

1908-09

EASTERN CANADA AMATEUR HOCKEY ASSOCIATION

	GP	W	L	T	GF	GA	Pts
* Ottawa Senators	12	10	2	...	117	63	20
Montreal Wanderers	12	9	3	...	82	61	18
Quebec Bulldogs	12	3	9	...	78	106	6
Montreal Shamrocks	12	2	10	...	56	103	4

ONTARIO PROFESSIONAL HOCKEY LEAGUE

	GP	W	L	T	GF	GA	Pts
* Brantford Indians	14	10	4	1	123	100	21
Galt Professionals	14	10	4	1	107	91	21
Berlin Dutchmen	15	9	6	0	96	72	18
Toronto Professionals	15	5	10	0	105	111	10
Guelph Professionals	6	1	5	0	28	56	2
St. Catharines Pros	6	0	6	0	29	58	0

MANITOBA PROFESSIONAL HOCKEY LEAGUE

First Half

	GP	W	L	T	GF	GA	Pts
Winnipeg Maple Leafs	4	4	0	0	37	21	8
Winnipeg Shamrocks	4	1	3	0	22	29	2
Winnipeg Winnipegs §	2	0	2	0	13	22	0

§ folded 01/09/09

Second Half

	GP	W	L	T	GF	GA	Pts
* Winnipeg Shamrocks	5	4	1	0	48	35	8
Winnipeg Maple Leafs	5	1	4	0	35	48	2

1909-10

CANADIAN HOCKEY ASSOCIATION

	GP	W	L	T	GF	GA	Pts
Ottawa Senators	2	2	0	0	29	9	4
All-Montreal HC	4	2	2	0	20	25	4
Quebec Bulldogs	3	2	1	0	20	22	4
Montreal Shamrocks	3	2	1	0	29	17	4
Montreal Nationals	4	0	4	0	25	26	0

• CHA folded on 01/15/10 • No champion determined

ONTARIO PROFESSIONAL HOCKEY LEAGUE

	GP	W	L	T	GF	GA	Pts
Berlin Dutchmen	17	11	6	...	103	74	22
* Waterloo Professionals	15	8	7	...	77	70	16
Brantford Indians	14	7	7	...	79	76	14
Galt Professionals	16	5	11	...	63	102	10

NATIONAL HOCKEY ASSOCIATION

	GP	W	L	T	GF	GA	Pts
* Montreal Wanderers	12	11	1	0	91	41	22
Ottawa Senators	12	9	3	0	89	66	18
Renfrew Creamery Kings	12	8	3	1	96	54	17
Cobalt Silver Kings	12	4	8	0	79	104	8
Haileybury HC	12	4	8	0	77	83	8
Montreal Shamrocks	12	3	8	1	52	95	7
Montreal Canadiens	12	2	10	0	59	100	4

1910-11

NATIONAL HOCKEY ASSOCIATION

	GP	W	L	T	GF	GA	Pts
* Ottawa Senators	16	13	3	...	122	69	26
Montreal Canadiens	16	8	8	...	66	62	16
Renfrew Creamery Kings	16	8	8	...	91	101	16
Montreal Wanderers	16	7	9	...	73	88	14
Quebec Bulldogs	16	4	12	...	65	97	8

ONTARIO PROFESSIONAL HOCKEY LEAGUE

	GP	W	L	T	GF	GA	Pts
* Galt Professionals	19	13	6	...	134	99	26
Waterloo Professionals	19	13	6	...	85	78	26
Berlin Dutchmen	18	10	8	...	93	87	20
Brantford Indians	18	1	17	...	59	107	2

INTERPROVINCIAL PROFESSIONAL HOCKEY LEAGUE

	GP	W	L	T	GF	GA	Pts
* Moncton Victorias	8	6	2	0	35	12	12
Halifax Crescents	8	5	3	0	45	41	10
New Glasgow Cubs	8	1	7	0	35	66	2

1911-12

NATIONAL HOCKEY ASSOCIATION

	GP	W	L	T	GF	GA	Pts
* Quebec Bulldogs	18	10	8	...	81	79	20
Ottawa Senators	18	9	9	...	99	93	18
Montreal Wanderers	18	9	9	...	95	96	18
Montreal Canadiens	18	8	10	...	59	66	16

PACIFIC COAST HOCKEY ASSOCIATION

	GP	W	L	T	GF	GA	Pts
* New Westm'ster Royals	15	9	6	...	78	77	18
Vancouver Millionaires	15	7	8	...	102	102	14
Victoria Aristocrats	16	7	9	...	81	81	14

MARITIME PROFESSIONAL HOCKEY LEAGUE

	GP	W	L	T	GF	GA	Pts
* Moncton Victorias	18	12	6	0	106	80	24
New Glasgow Cubs	18	10	8	0	108	80	20
Halifax Crescents	18	7	11	0	94	122	14
Halifax Socials	18	7	11	0	100	126	14

1912-13

NATIONAL HOCKEY ASSOCIATION

	GP	W	L	T	GF	GA	Pts
* Quebec Bulldogs	20	16	4	...	112	75	32
Montreal Wanderers	20	10	10	...	93	90	20
Ottawa Senators	20	9	11	...	87	81	18
Toronto Blueshirts	20	9	11	...	86	95	18
Montreal Canadiens	20	9	11	...	83	81	18
Toronto Tecumsehs	20	7	13	...	59	98	14

PACIFIC COAST HOCKEY ASSOCIATION

	GP	W	L	T	GF	GA	Pts
* Victoria Aristocrats	15	10	5	...	68	56	20
Vancouver Millionaires	16	7	9	...	84	89	14
New Westm'ster Royals	15	6	9	...	67	74	12

MARITIME PROFESSIONAL HOCKEY LEAGUE

	GP	W	L	T	GF	GA	Pts
* Sydney Millionaires	16	11	5	0	71	60	22
New Glasgow Cubs	16	10	6	0	89	58	20
Moncton Victorias	16	9	7	0	73	63	18
Halifax Socials	16	8	8	0	66	67	16
Halifax Crescents	16	2	14	0	44	95	4

1913-14

NATIONAL HOCKEY ASSOCIATION

	GP	W	L	T	GF	GA	Pts
Montreal Canadiens	20	13	7	...	85	65	26
* Toronto Blueshirts	20	13	7	...	93	65	26
Quebec Bulldogs	20	12	8	...	111	73	24
Ottawa Senators	20	11	9	...	65	71	22
Montreal Wanderers	20	7	13	...	102	125	14
Toronto Ontarios	20	4	16	...	61	118	8

PACIFIC COAST HOCKEY ASSOCIATION

	GP	W	L	T	GF	GA	Pts
* Victoria Aristocrats	15	10	5	...	80	67	20
New Westm'ster Royals	16	7	9	...	75	81	14
Vancouver Millionaires	15	6	9	...	76	83	12

MARITIME PROFESSIONAL HOCKEY LEAGUE

	GP	W	L	T	GF	GA	Pts
* Sydney Millionaires	24	16	8	0	131	113	32
N. Glasgow Blk Foxes	24	16	8	0	162	117	32
Halifax Crescents	24	12	12	0	108	107	26
Halifax Socials	24	4	20	0	97	161	10

1914-15

NATIONAL HOCKEY ASSOCIATION

	GP	W	L	T	GF	GA	Pts
* Ottawa Senators	20	14	6	...	74	65	28
Montreal Wanderers	20	14	6	...	127	82	28
Quebec Bulldogs	20	11	9	...	85	85	22
Toronto Blueshirts	20	8	12	...	66	84	16
Tor. Ontarios/Shamrocks	20	7	13	...	76	86	14
Montreal Canadiens	20	6	14	...	65	81	12

PACIFIC COAST HOCKEY ASSOCIATION

	GP	W	L	T	GF	GA	Pts
* Vancouver Millionaires	17	13	4	...	115	71	26
Portland Rosebuds	18	9	9	...	91	83	18
Victoria Aristocrats	17	4	13	...	64	116	8

EASTERN PROFESSIONAL HOCKEY LEAGUE

	GP	W	L	T	GF	GA	Pts
Glace Bay Miners	7	5	2	0	37	24	10
N. Glasgow Blk Foxes §	7	3	4	0	32	46	6
Sydney Millionaires	8	3	5	0	46	45	6

§ folded 01/31/15

• EPHL folded 02/07/15 • No champion determined

1915-16

NATIONAL HOCKEY ASSOCIATION

	GP	W	L	T	GF	GA	Pts
* Montreal Canadiens	24	16	7	1	104	76	33
Ottawa Senators	24	13	11	0	78	72	26
Quebec Bulldogs	24	10	12	2	91	98	22
Montreal Wanderers	24	10	14	0	90	116	20
Toronto Blueshirts	24	9	14	1	97	98	19

PACIFIC COAST HOCKEY ASSOCIATION

	GP	W	L	T	GF	GA	Pts
* Portland Rosebuds	18	13	5	...	71	50	26
Vancouver Millionaires	18	9	9	...	75	69	18
Seattle Metropolitans	18	9	9	...	68	67	18
Victoria Aristocrats	18	5	13	...	74	102	10

1916-17

NATIONAL HOCKEY ASSOCIATION

First Half

	GP	W	L	T	GF	GA	Pts
* Montreal Canadiens	10	7	3	...	58	38	14
Ottawa Senators	10	7	3	...	56	41	14
Toronto 228th §	10	6	4	...	70	57	12
Toronto Blueshirts ¶	10	5	5	...	50	45	10
Montreal Wanderers	10	3	7	...	56	72	6
Quebec Bulldogs	10	2	8	...	43	80	4

§ called overseas 02/11/17   ¶ folded 02/11/17

Second Half

	GP	W	L	T	GF	GA	Pts
Ottawa Senators	10	8	2	...	63	22	16
Quebec Bulldogs	10	8	2	...	54	46	16
Montreal Canadiens	10	3	7	...	31	42	6
Montreal Wanderers	10	2	8	...	38	65	4

PACIFIC COAST HOCKEY ASSOCIATION

	GP	W	L	T	GF	GA	Pts
* Seattle Metropolitans	24	16	8	...	125	80	32
Vancouver Millionaires	23	14	9	...	131	124	28
Portland Rosebuds	24	9	15	...	114	112	18
Spokane Canaries	23	8	15	...	89	143	16

1917-18

PACIFIC COAST HOCKEY ASSOCIATION

	GP	W	L	T	GF	GA	Pts
Seattle Metropolitans	18	11	7	...	67	65	22
* Vancouver Millionaires	18	9	9	...	70	60	18
Portland Rosebuds	18	7	11	...	63	75	14

1918-19

PACIFIC COAST HOCKEY ASSOCIATION

	GP	W	L	T	GF	GA	Pts
Vancouver Millionaires	20	12	8	...	72	55	24
* Seattle Metropolitans	20	11	9	...	66	46	22
Victoria Aristocrats	20	7	13	...	44	81	14

1919-20

PACIFIC COAST HOCKEY ASSOCIATION

	GP	W	L	T	GF	GA	Pts
* Seattle Metropolitans	22	12	10	...	59	55	24
Vancouver Millionaires	22	11	11	...	75	65	22
Victoria Aristocrats	22	10	12	...	57	71	20

1920-21

PACIFIC COAST HOCKEY ASSOCIATION

	GP	W	L	T	GF	GA	Pts
* Vancouver Millionaires	24	13	11	0	86	78	26
Seattle Metropolitans	24	12	11	1	77	68	25
Victoria Aristocrats	24	10	13	1	71	88	21

1921-22

PACIFIC COAST HOCKEY ASSOCIATION

	GP	W	L	T	GF	GA	Pts
Seattle Metropolitans	24	12	11	1	65	64	25
* Vancouver Millionaires	24	12	12	0	77	68	24
Victoria Aristocrats	24	11	12	1	61	71	23

WESTERN CANADA HOCKEY LEAGUE

	GP	W	L	T	GF	GA	Pts
Edmonton Eskimos	24	15	9	...	117	76	30
* Regina Capitals	24	14	10	...	94	78	28
Calgary Tigers	24	14	10	...	75	62	28
Sask-Moose Jaw	24	5	19	...	67	137	10

1922-23

PACIFIC COAST HOCKEY ASSOCIATION

	GP	W	L	T	GF	GA	Pts
* Vancouver Maroons	30	17	12	1	116	88	35
Victoria Cougars	30	16	14	0	94	85	32
Seattle Metropolitans	30	15	15	0	100	106	30

Western Canada Hockey League

	GP	W	L	T	GF	GA	Pts
Edmonton Eskimos	30	19	10	1	112	90	39
*Regina Capitals	30	16	14	0	93	97	32
Calgary Tigers	30	12	18	0	91	106	24
Saskatoon Crescents	30	8	20	2	91	125	18

1923-24

Pacific Coast Hockey Association

	GP	W	L	T	GF	GA	Pts
Seattle Metropolitans	30	14	16	0	84	99	28
*Vancouver Maroons	30	13	16	1	87	80	27
Victoria Cougars	30	11	18	1	78	103	23

Western Canada Hockey League

	GP	W	L	T	GF	GA	Pts
*Calgary Tigers	30	18	11	1	83	72	37
Regina Capitals	30	17	11	2	83	67	36
Saskatoon Crescents	30	15	12	3	91	73	33
Edmonton Eskimos	30	11	15	4	69	81	26

1924-25

Western Canada Hockey League

	GP	W	L	T	GF	GA	Pts
Calgary Tigers	28	17	11	0	96	80	34
Saskatoon Crescents	28	16	11	1	102	75	33
*Victoria Cougars	28	16	12	0	84	63	32
Edmonton Eskimos	28	14	13	1	97	109	29
Vancouver Maroons	28	12	16	0	91	102	24
Regina Capitals	28	8	20	0	82	123	16

1925-26

Western Hockey League

	GP	W	L	T	GF	GA	Pts
Edmonton Eskimos	30	19	11	0	94	77	38
Saskatoon Crescents	30	18	11	1	93	64	37
*Victoria Cougars	30	15	11	4	68	53	34
Portland Rosebuds	30	12	16	2	84	110	26
Calgary Tigers	30	10	17	3	71	80	23
Vancouver Maroons	30	10	18	2	64	90	22

1926-27

Canadian-American Hockey League

	GP	W	L	T	GF	GA	Pts
New Haven Eagles	32	18	14	0	73	66	36
*Springfield Indians	32	14	13	5	59	53	33
Quebec Castors	32	15	14	3	69	67	33
Boston Tigers	32	14	15	3	48	46	31
Providence Reds	32	12	17	3	50	67	27

American Hockey Association

	GP	W	L	T	GF	GA	Pts
*Duluth Hornets	38	20	10	8	90	46	48
Minneapolis Millers	38	17	11	10	60	51	44
Winnipeg Maroons	38	19	14	5	83	77	43
St. Paul Saints	37	17	15	5	46	67	39
Detroit Greyhounds §	10	0	10	0	5	22	0

§ folded

Canadian Professional Hockey League

	GP	W	L	T	GF	GA	Pts
Stratford Nationals	32	20	12	0	92	81	40
*London Panthers	32	16	15	1	89	78	33
Hamilton Tigers	32	16	15	1	81	78	33
Windsor Hornets	32	14	17	1	72	95	29
Niagara Falls Cataracts	32	12	19	1	78	81	25

1927-28

Canadian-American Hockey League

	GP	W	L	T	GF	GA	Pts
*Springfield Indians	40	24	13	3	90	71	51
Boston Tigers	40	21	14	5	80	71	47
Quebec Castors	40	18	14	8	70	68	44
New Haven Eagles	40	16	20	4	81	90	36
Providence Reds	40	13	19	8	88	83	34
Philadelphia Arrows	40	13	25	2	79	107	28

Canadian Professional Hockey League

	GP	W	L	T	GF	GA	Pts
*Stratford Nationals	42	25	12	5	...	...	55
Detroit Olympics	42	24	14	4	...	...	52
Toronto Ravinas	42	20	18	4	...	...	44
Kitchener Millionaires	42	19	17	6	...	...	44
Hamilton Tigers	42	19	17	6	...	...	44
Niagara Falls Cataracts	42	13	17	12	...	...	38
Windsor Hornets	42	13	24	5	...	...	31
London Panthers	42	14	26	2	...	...	30

American Hockey Association

	GP	W	L	T	GF	GA	Pts
Duluth Hornets	40	18	9	13	63	49	49
Kansas City Pla-Mors	40	18	14	8	61	53	44
*Minneapolis Millers	40	18	17	5	64	50	41
St. Paul Saints	40	14	17	9	76	87	37
Winnipeg Maroons	40	11	22	7	68	93	29

1928-29

Canadian-American Hockey League

	GP	W	L	T	GF	GA	Pts
*Boston Tigers	40	21	11	8	72	56	50
Providence Reds	40	18	12	10	64	58	46
New Haven Eagles	40	15	15	10	73	68	40
Springfield Indians	40	13	14	13	60	58	39
Newark Bulldogs	40	12	21	7	60	73	31
Philadelphia Arrows	40	12	21	7	60	73	31

American Hockey Association

	GP	W	L	T	GF	GA	Pts
*Tulsa Oilers	40	23	9	8	125	63	54
Minneapolis Millers	40	18	12	10	77	51	46
St. Paul Saints	40	20	17	3	88	98	43
Kansas City Pla-Mors	40	17	16	7	66	75	41
Duluth Hornets	40	15	21	4	66	70	34
St. Louis Flyers	40	10	28	2	73	138	22

Canadian Professional Hockey League

	GP	W	L	T	GF	GA	Pts
Detroit Olympics	42	27	10	5	131	67	59
*Windsor Bulldogs	42	25	12	5	114	76	55
Toronto Millionaires	42	19	16	7	94	88	45
Kitchener Flying Dutch.	42	19	19	4	105	118	42
Buffalo Bisons	42	17	18	7	89	72	41
London Panthers	42	16	22	4	86	113	36
Hamilton Tigers	42	14	24	4	83	115	32
Niagara Falls Cataracts	42	12	28	2	70	128	26

Pacific Coast Hockey League

	GP	W	L	T	GF	GA	Pts
*Vancouver Lions	36	25	8	3	87	54	54
Seattle Eskimos	36	17	17	2	75	76	36
Portland Buckaroos	36	14	17	5	64	72	33
Victoria Cubs	36	8	22	6	68	91	22

California Hockey League

	GP	W	L	T	GF	GA	Pts
*Oakland Sheiks	36	18	13	5	67	64	41
San Francisco	36	15	14	6	83	89	36
Los Angeles Richfields	36	15	17	4	56	60	34
Hollywood Millionaires	36	14	17	5	73	66	33

1929-30

Canadian-American Hockey League

	GP	W	L	T	GF	GA	Pts
*Providence Reds	40	24	11	5	120	98	53
Philadelphia Arrows	40	20	18	2	120	121	41
Boston Tigers	40	17	18	5	136	129	39
New Haven Eagles	40	14	20	6	94	101	34
Springfield Indians	40	15	23	2	96	120	32

International-American Hockey League

	GP	W	L	T	GF	GA	Pts
*Cleveland Indians	42	24	9	9	125	78	57
Buffalo Bisons	42	26	12	4	102	67	56
London Panthers	42	24	13	5	117	93	53
Detroit Olympics	42	21	12	9	120	74	51
Windsor Bulldogs	42	20	14	8	123	93	48
Hamilton Tigers	42	9	25	8	95	128	26
Toronto Millionaires	42	10	28	4	84	172	24
Niagara Falls Cataracts	42	7	28	7	72	133	21

American Hockey Association

	GP	W	L	T	GF	GA	Pts
*Kansas City Pla-Mors	48	21	13	14	75	65	58
Duluth Hornets	48	18	13	17	87	83	53
Tulsa Oilers	48	18	14	16	94	79	52
St. Paul Saints	48	18	16	14	93	90	50
Minneapolis Millers	48	15	21	12	82	83	42
St. Louis Flyers	48	12	25	11	98	129	35

Canadian Professional Hockey League

	GP	W	L	T	GF	GA	Pts
*Guelph Maple Leafs	30	17	10	3	112	83	37
Galt Terriers	30	15	12	3	89	104	33
Kitchener Fly. Dutchmen	30	13	16	1	76	74	27
Brantford Indians	30	10	17	3	68	83	23

Pacific Coast Hockey League

	GP	W	L	T	GF	GA	Pts
*Vancouver Lions	36	20	8	8	86	46	48
Portland Buckaroos	36	20	10	6	64	34	46
Seattle Eskimos	36	15	13	8	77	58	38
Victoria Cubs	36	5	29	2	43	132	12

California Hockey League

	GP	W	L	T	GF	GA	Pts
*Oakland Sheiks	42	24	12	6	121	72	54
San Francisco Tigers	42	15	16	11	98	109	41
Los Angeles Richfields	42	17	19	6	91	122	40
Hollywood Millionaires	42	13	22	7	100	107	33

1930-31

Canadian-American Hockey League

	GP	W	L	T	GF	GA	Pts
*Springfield Indians	40	29	9	2	167	99	60
Providence Reds	40	23	11	6	132	96	52
Boston Tigers	40	14	22	4	96	114	32
Philadelphia Arrows	40	12	22	6	84	108	30
New Haven Eagles	40	9	23	8	78	140	26

International-American Hockey League

	GP	W	L	T	GF	GA	Pts
Buffalo Bisons	48	30	13	5	115	76	65
*Windsor Bulldogs	48	30	13	5	141	114	57
Cleveland Indians	48	25	16	7	131	112	54
Pittsburgh Yelo Jackets	48	21	18	9	101	108	51
London Tecumsehs	48	21	21	6	89	83	48
Detroit Olympics	48	18	28	2	100	127	38
Syracuse Stars	48	9	34	5	114	171	23

American Hockey Association

	GP	W	L	T	GF	GA	Pts
*Tulsa Oilers	48	30	15	3	152	112	60
Kansas City Pla-Mors	48	28	16	4	99	63	56
Duluth Hornets	48	28	19	1	118	92	56
Buffalo Majors	46	25	17	4	116	90	50
Chicago Shamrocks	47	24	21	2	118	97	48
Minneapolis Millers	46	11	33	2	65	136	22
St. Louis Flyers	47	11	36	0	84	162	22

• No points awarded for ties.

Ontario Professional Hockey League

	GP	W	L	T	GF	GA	Pts
Guelph Maple Leafs	30	16	12	2	107	86	34
*Niagara Falls Cataracts	30	14	12	4	82	66	32
Stratford Nationals	30	14	14	2	98	93	30
Galt Terriers	30	13	15	2	84	103	28
Oshawa Patricias	30	12	14	4	94	86	28
Kitchener Silverwoods	30	13	15	2	70	101	28

Pacific Coast Hockey League

	GP	W	L	T	GF	GA	Pts
Seattle Eskimos	34	16	9	9	64	51	41
*Vancouver Lions	35	14	13	8	61	61	36
Portland Buckaroos	35	12	15	8	60	61	32
Tacoma Tigers §	10	2	7	1	12	24	5

§ folded 01/31

California Hockey League

	GP	W	L	T	GF	GA	Pts
*Oakland Sheiks	40	25	14	1	117	79	51
Oakland Checkers	41	20	17	4	109	117	44
Los Angeles Millionaires	39	16	17	6	93	91	38
San Francisco Tigers §	27	12	14	1	73	75	25
San Fran Blk Hawks ¶	31	9	20	2	69	99	20

§ folded 02/12/31 ¶ folded 02/23/31

1931-32

Canadian-American Hockey League

	GP	W	L	T	GF	GA	Pts
*Providence Reds	40	23	11	6	138	108	52
Boston Cubs	40	21	16	3	116	108	45
New Haven Eagles	40	19	15	6	113	75	44
Bronx Tigers	40	18	15	7	94	90	43
Philadelphia Arrows	40	13	22	5	85	114	31
Springfield Indians	40	10	25	5	85	136	25

International-American Hockey League

	GP	W	L	T	GF	GA	Pts
*Buffalo Bisons	48	25	14	9	106	80	59
London Tecumsehs	48	21	15	12	92	70	54
Windsor Bulldogs	48	21	16	11	123	104	52
Detroit Olympics	48	19	19	10	96	97	48
Pittsburgh Yelo Jackets	48	17	22	9	91	118	43
Syracuse Stars	48	16	23	9	111	118	41
Cleveland Indians	48	15	25	8	110	142	38

American Hockey Association

	GP	W	L	T	GF	GA	Pts
*Chicago Shamrocks	48	30	13	5	121	72	60
Kansas City Pla-Mors	48	28	18	2	95	62	56
Duluth Hornets	48	21	24	3	97	97	42
St. Louis Flyers	48	18	22	8	80	97	36
Tulsa Oilers	48	16	29	3	85	121	35
Buffalo Majors §	24	7	14	3	28	57	14

• No points awarded for ties § folded 01/30/32

California Hockey League

	GP	W	L	T	GF	GA	Pts
*Hollywood Stars	31	20	7	4	134	86	44
San Francisco Rangers	30	12	12	6	100	110	30
Oakland Sheiks	30	11	12	7	99	85	29
Los Angeles Angels	31	9	21	1	112	154	19

1932-33

Canadian-American Hockey League

	GP	W	L	T	GF	GA	Pts
Philadelphia Arrows	48	29	12	7	153	95	65
Providence Reds	48	26	16	6	129	117	58
*Boston Cubs	48	21	18	9	136	119	51
New Haven Eagles	48	16	27	5	100	137	37
Quebec Castors	48	11	30	7	106	156	29
Springfield Indians §	13	6	5	2	29	29	14

§ folded, results did not count

International-American Hockey League

	GP	W	L	T	GF	GA	Pts
London Tecumsehs	44	27	9	8	111	66	62
*Buffalo Bisons	44	26	12	6	128	70	58
Syracuse Stars	44	23	15	6	136	119	52
Windsor Bulldogs	44	16	22	6	87	120	38
Detroit Olympics	44	10	27	5	100	147	25
Cleveland Indians	44	10	27	5	75	115	25

American Hockey Association

First Half	GP	W	L	T	GF	GA	Pts
*K.C. Greyhounds	22	14	8	0	48	48	28
St. Louis Flyers	21	11	9	1	48	43	22
St. Paul Saints	21	8	12	1	46	51	16
Duluth Hornets	18	7	11	0	42	44	14
Second Half							
Tulsa Oilers	24	13	11	0	68	69	26
St. Louis Flyers	24	13	11	0	64	47	26
*K.C. Greyhounds	24	11	12	1	58	58	22
Wichita Blue Jays	24	10	13	1	70	86	20

• Duluth relocated to Wichita • St. Paul relocated to Tulsa • No points awarded for ties

Western Canada Hockey League

	GP	W	L	T	GF	GA	Pts
*Calgary Tigers	30	16	10	4	70	61	36
Regina/Vancouver	30	15	13	2	110	97	32
Edmonton Eskimos	30	11	14	5	81	86	27
Saskatoon Crescents	30	11	16	3	82	99	25

California Hockey League

	GP	W	L	T	GF	GA	Pts
*Oakland Sheiks	29	16	11	2	100	92	34
Hollywood Millionaires§	34	15	16	3	151	161	33
San Francisco Rangers	29	11	15	3	118	116	25

§ folded 01/28/33

Tri-State Hockey League

	GP	W	L	T	GF	GA	Pts
Atlantic City Seagulls	18	15	1	2	100	27	32
Baltimore Orioles	18	12	5	1	43	33	25
Hershey B'Ars	18	6	11	1	69	58	13
Philadelphia Comets	16	0	16	0	25	119	0

1933-34

Canadian-American Hockey League

	GP	W	L	T	GF	GA	Pts
*Providence Reds	41	19	13	9	91	92	47
Boston Tiger Cubs	41	18	16	7	112	104	42
Philadelphia Arrows	41	18	16	7	121	101	42
Quebec Castors §	44	19	16	9	96	88	41
New Haven Eagles	41	12	25	4	96	88	28

§ played five 1-point games

International-American Hockey League

	GP	W	L	T	GF	GA	Pts
Detroit Olympics	44	23	16	5	104	98	51
Buffalo Bisons	44	20	13	11	90	66	51
*London Tecumsehs	44	18	17	9	92	80	43
Syracuse Stars	44	19	21	4	114	120	42
Windsor Bulldogs	44	18	23	3	84	103	39
Cleveland Falcons	44	16	24	4	104	121	38

American Hockey Association

	GP	W	L	T	GF	GA	Pts
*K.C. Greyhounds	48	26	18	4	106	87	52
St. Louis Flyers	48	26	18	4	97	84	52
Tulsa Oilers	48	23	25	0	107	110	46
Oklahoma City Warriors	48	16	30	2	86	115	32
Wichita Vikings §	3	0	3	0	3	9	0

• No points awarded for ties § folded 12/04/33

North West Hockey League

	GP	W	L	T	GF	GA	Pts
*Calgary Tigers	34	17	11	6	117	76	40
Edmonton Eskimos	34	18	12	4	98	91	40
Vancouver Lions	34	17	16	1	95	111	35
Seattle Seahawks	34	15	17	2	80	95	32
Portland Buckaroos	34	10	21	3	80	116	23

Eastern Amateur Hockey League

	GP	W	L	T	GF	GA	Pts
*Baltimore Orioles	24	18	4	2	98	52	38
Atlantic City Seagulls	20	15	4	1	109	39	31
Hershey B'ars	26	14	11	1	77	63	29
Bronx Tigers	20	8	9	3	51	54	19
NY Hamilton Crescents	20	6	14	0	28	76	12
New York Athletic Club	15	4	9	2	32	[illegible]	10
St. Nicholas HC	17	0	14	3	28	74	3

1934-35

Canadian-American Hockey League

	GP	W	L	T	GF	GA	Pts
*Boston Bruin Cubs	48	29	13	6	185	125	64
Quebec Castors	48	23	19	6	141	123	52
Providence Reds	48	15	30	3	122	160	33
New Haven Eagles	48	16	23	9	125	145	41
Philadelphia Arrows	48	15	30	3	122	160	33

International-American Hockey League

	GP	W	L	T	GF	GA	Pts
*Detroit Olympics	44	21	15	8	116	88	42
London Tecumsehs	44	21	17	6	98	110	40
Syracuse Stars	44	20	20	4	128	118	40
Cleveland Falcons	44	20	23	1	115	132	40
Buffalo Bisons	44	20	18	6	113	110	28
Windsor Bulldogs	44	14	23	7	94	116	

American Hockey Association

	GP	W	L	T	GF	GA	Pts
*St. Louis Flyers	48	29	15	4	151	102	58
Tulsa Oilers	48	23	21	4	111	98	46
K.C. Greyhounds	48	23	25	0	82	102	46
Oklahoma City Warriors	48	15	28	5	88	133	30

North West Hockey League

	GP	W	L	T	GF	GA	Pts
Seattle Seahawks	32	20	9	3	98	69	43
Portland Buckaroos	32	15	10	7	83	72	37
*Vancouver Lions	32	15	11	6	105	81	36
Edmonton Eskimos	26	7	15	4	77	101	18
Calgary Tigers	26	3	15	8	60	104	14

Eastern Hockey League

	GP	W	L	T	GF	GA	Pts
*NY-Hamilton Crescents	21	15	5	1	67	35	31
Hershey B'ars	21	10	9	2	60	56	22
Atlantic City Seagulls	21	8	10	3	44	64	19
Baltimore Orioles	21	4	13	4	41	57	12

1935-36

Canadian-American Hockey League

	GP	W	L	T	GF	GA	Pts
*Philadelphia Ramblers	48	27	18	3	151	106	57
Providence Reds	47	21	20	6	105	127	48
Springfield Indians	48	21	22	5	131	129	47
Boston Bruins	47	20	23	4	128	127	44
New Haven Eagles	48	19	25	4	122	149	42

International-American Hockey League

Western Division	GP	W	L	T	GF	GA	Pts
*Detroit Olympics	47	26	18	3	127	101	55
Cleveland Falcons	48	25	19	4	149	146	54
Windsor Bulldogs	48	18	19	11	121	120	47
Pittsburgh Shamrocks	46	18	27	1	137	170	37
Eastern Division							
Syracuse Stars	48	26	19	3	167	130	55
Buffalo Bisons	48	22	20	6	109	101	50
London Tecumsehs	48	23	22	3	118	125	49
Rochester Cardinals	47	15	29	3	104	137	33

American Hockey Association

	GP	W	L	T	GF	GA	Pts
St. Paul Saints	48	32	13	3	153	99	64
*St. Louis Flyers	48	27	17	4	115	90	52
OK City Mpls. Warriors	40	21	22	5	92	[illegible]	42
Tulsa Oilers	48	21	27	0	99	140	42
K.C. Greyhounds	48	20	26	2	94	105	40
Wichita Skyhawks	48	16	32	0	81	114	32

• No points awarded for ties
• Oklahoma City relocated to Minneapolis 03/12/36

North West Hockey League

	GP	W	L	T	GF	GA	Pts
*Seattle Seahawks	39	19	14	6	100	86	44
Portland Buckaroos	40	18	14	8	88	67	44
Vancouver Lions	40	18	17	5	125	117	41
Edmonton Eskimos	39	14	18	7	97	105	35
Calgary Tigers	40	15	21	4	107	141	34

Eastern Amateur Hockey League

	GP	W	L	T	GF	GA	Pts
Hershey B'ars	40	27	11	2	119	78	56
Pittsburgh Yelo Jackets	40	22	16	2	108	74	46
Atlantic City Seagulls	40	21	18	1	101	111	43
New York Rovers	40	16	21	3	108	110	35
*Baltimore Orioles	40	9	29	2	78	141	20

1936-37

• IAHL and Can-Am amalgamate to form AHL

American Hockey League

Eastern Division	GP	W	L	T	GF	GA	Pts
Philadelphia Ramblers	48	26	14	8	149	106	60
Springfield Indians	48	22	17	9	117	125	53
Providence Reds	48	21	20	7	122	125	49
New Haven Eagles	48	14	28	6	107	142	34
Western Division							
*Syracuse Stars	48	27	16	5	173	129	59
Pittsburgh Hornets	48	21	22	5	73	124	47
Clevlnd Falcons-Barons	48	13	27	8	113	152	34
Buffalo Bisons §	11	3	8	0	23	30	6

§ folded 12/09/36

American Hockey Association

	GP	W	L	T	GF	GA	Pts
St. Louis Flyers	48	32	13	4	143	90	64
*Minneapolis Millers	48	23	21	4	102	105	46
K.C. Greyhounds	48	21	23	4	78	95	42
St. Paul Saints	48	21	24	3	90	102	42
Wichita Skyhawks	48	18	27	3	84	87	36
Tulsa Oilers	48	17	24	7	67	85	34

• No points awarded for ties

Pacific Coast Hockey League

	GP	W	L	T	GF	GA	Pts
*Portland Buckaroos	39	21	13	5	95	72	47
Vancouver Lions	36	16	12	8	111	86	40
Oakland-Spokane	39	14	18	7	85	96	35
Seattle Seahawks	38	13	21	4	78	115	30

Eastern Amateur Hockey League

	GP	W	L	T	GF	GA	Pts
Hershey Bars	48	25	15	8	133	105	58
*Atlantic City Sea Gulls	48	27	19	2	148	120	56
Pittsburgh Yelo Jackets	48	19	24	5	119	147	43
New York Rovers	48	18	23	7	130	144	43
Baltimore Orioles	48	16	24	8	121	135	40

1937-38

American Hockey League

Eastern Division	GP	W	L	T	GF	GA	Pts
*Providence Reds	48	25	16	7	114	86	57
Philadelphia Ramblers	48	26	18	4	134	108	56
New Haven Eagles	48	13	28	7	93	131	33
Springfield Indians	48	10	30	8	96	140	28
Western Division							
Cleveland Barons	48	25	12	11	126	114	61
Pittsburgh Hornets	48	22	18	8	100	104	52
Syracuse Stars	48	21	20	7	142	122	49

American Hockey Association

	GP	W	L	T	GF	GA	Pts
*St. Louis Flyers	48	29	14	5	143	102	58
Minneapolis Millers	48	24	15	9	140	100	48
Wichita Skyhawks	48	23	21	4	125	133	46
Tulsa Oilers	48	22	21	5	111	93	44
K.C. Greyhounds	48	21	22	5	120	120	42
St. Paul Saints	48	10	36	2	87	178	20

• No points awarded for ties

Pacific Coast Hockey League

	GP	W	L	T	GF	GA	Pts
*Seattle Seahawks	42	20	14	8	123	100	48
Vancouver Lions	42	19	18	5	87	91	43
Portland Buckaroos	42	16	18	8	88	84	40
Spokane Clippers	42	16	21	5	90	113	37

Eastern Amateur Hockey League

	GP	W	L	T	GF	GA	Pts
Hershey B'ars	58	32	15	11	197	136	75
*Atlantic City Seagulls	58	31	16	11	199	169	73
New York Rovers	58	29	23	6	193	179	64
Baltimore Orioles	58	21	29	8	177	195	50
Bronx Tigers	40	2	32	6	54	141	10

1938-39

American Hockey League

Eastern Division	GP	W	L	T	GF	GA	Pts
Philadelphia Ramblers	54	32	17	5	214	161	69
Providence Reds	54	21	22	11	136	153	53
Springfield Indians	54	16	29	9	121	179	41
New Haven Eagles	54	14	30	10	114	174	38
Western Division							
Hershey Bears	54	31	18	5	140	110	67
Syracuse Stars	54	26	19	9	152	117	61
*Cleveland Barons	54	23	22	9	145	138	55
Pittsburgh Hornets	54	22	28	4	176	166	48

American Hockey Association

	GP	W	L	T	GF	GA	Pts
*St. Louis Flyers	48	36	12	0	183	95	72
Minneapolis Millers	48	31	17	0	214	139	62
Tulsa Oilers	48	25	23	0	137	153	50
St. Paul Saints	48	24	24	0	149	142	48
K.C. Greyhounds	48	15	33	0	133	225	30
Wichita Skyhawks	48	12	35	0	113	175	26

PACIFIC COAST HOCKEY LEAGUE

	GP	W	L	T	GF	GA	Pts
*Portland Buckaroos	48	31	9	8	180	114	70
Seattle Seahawks	48	21	21	6	168	167	48
Vancouver Lions	48	15	24	9	139	195	39
Spokane Clippers	48	14	27	7	144	155	35

TROPICAL HOCKEY LEAGUE

	GP	W	L	T	GF	GA	Pts
*Coral Gables Seminoles	14	12	2	0	85	53	24
Miami Clippers	14	7	7	0	55	62	14
Miami Beach Pirates	15	6	9	0	61	71	12
Havana Tropicals	15	4	11	0	69	84	8

EASTERN AMATEUR HOCKEY LEAGUE

	GP	W	L	T	GF	GA	Pts
*New York Rovers	53	31	13	9	196	121	71
Baltimore Orioles	53	26	22	5	180	165	57
Atlantic City Seagulls	53	22	25	6	166	180	50
Hershey Cubs	53	19	29	5	156	187	43
Canada	20	4	13	3	....	....	11

• Games played against Canada in Wills Trophy Tournament counted in standings

1939-40

AMERICAN HOCKEY LEAGUE

Eastern Division	GP	W	L	T	GF	GA	Pts
*Providence Reds	54	27	19	8	161	157	62
New Haven Eagles	54	27	24	3	177	183	57
Springfield Indians	54	24	24	6	166	149	54
Philadelphia Ramblers	54	15	31	8	133	170	38
Western Division							
Indianapolis Capitals	56	26	20	10	174	144	62
Pittsburgh Hornets	56	27	24	5	154	156	59
Hershey Bears	56	25	22	9	152	133	59
Cleveland Barons	56	24	24	8	127	130	56
Syracuse Stars	56	20	27	9	147	169	49

AMERICAN HOCKEY ASSOCIATION

	GP	W	L	T	GF	GA	Pts
St. Louis Flyers	48	37	11	0	195	99	74
St. Paul Saints	47	29	18	0	159	121	58
Minneapolis Millers	48	26	22	0	170	140	52
*Omaha Knights	48	25	23	0	149	131	50
K.C. Greyhounds	48	20	28	0	129	175	40
Tulsa Oilers •	46	16	30	0	141	180	32
Wichita Skyhawks •	45	12	33	0	97	184	24

• played one 4-point game

PACIFIC COAST HOCKEY LEAGUE

	GP	W	L	T	GF	GA	Pts
*Vancouver Lions	40	22	16	2	132	126	46
Portland Buckaroos	40	17	18	5	96	99	39
Seattle Seahawks	40	16	21	3	120	125	35

EASTERN AMATEUR HOCKEY LEAGUE

	GP	W	L	T	GF	GA	Pts
*Baltimore Orioles	61	38	21	2	263	185	78
Washington Eagles	61	32	25	4	259	229	68
New York Rovers	61	31	26	4	274	247	66
Atlantic City Seagulls	61	25	31	5	207	242	55
Rivervale Skeeters	61	16	38	7	173	267	39

1940-41

AMERICAN HOCKEY LEAGUE

Eastern Division	GP	W	L	T	GF	GA	Pts
Providence Reds	56	31	21	4	196	171	66
New Haven Eagles	56	27	21	8	179	153	62
Springfield Indians	56	26	21	9	157	149	61
Philadelphia Rockets	56	25	25	6	166	167	56
Western Division							
*Cleveland Barons	56	26	21	9	177	162	61
Hershey Bears	56	24	23	9	193	189	57
Pittsburgh Hornets	56	21	29	6	156	170	48
Buffalo Bisons	56	19	27	10	148	176	48
Indianapolis Capitals	56	17	28	11	133	168	45

AMERICAN HOCKEY ASSOCIATION

	GP	W	L	T	GF	GA	Pts
*St. Louis Flyers	48	31	17	0	139	99	62
Kansas City Americans	48	25	23	0	150	152	50
Minneapolis Millers	48	25	23	0	136	106	50
St. Paul Saints	48	25	23	0	113	116	50
Omaha Knights	48	24	24	0	138	130	48
Tulsa Oilers	48	14	34	0	121	194	28

PACIFIC COAST HOCKEY LEAGUE

	GP	W	L	T	GF	GA	Pts
Spokane Bombers	48	25	18	5	146	127	55
*Vancouver Lions	48	22	21	5	163	167	47
Seattle Olympics	48	20	21	7	158	167	47
Portland Buckaroos	48	20	27	1	130	158	41

EASTERN AMATEUR HOCKEY LEAGUE

	GP	W	L	T	GF	GA	Pts
Washington Eagles	65	42	15	8	280	196	92
Baltimore Orioles	65	36	23	6	240	194	78
*Atlantic City Seagulls	65	32	28	5	253	256	69
Rivervale Skeeters	65	29	34	2	217	240	60
Boston Olympics	65	23	36	6	203	242	52
New York Rovers	65	19	45	1	218	283	39

1941-42

AMERICAN HOCKEY LEAGUE

Eastern Division	GP	W	L	T	GF	GA	Pts
Springfield Indians	56	31	20	5	213	167	67
New Haven Eagles	56	26	26	4	182	219	56
Washington Lions	56	20	30	6	160	172	46
Providence Reds	56	17	32	7	205	237	41
Philadelphia Rockets	56	11	41	4	157	254	26
Western Division							
*Indianapolis Capitals	56	34	15	7	204	144	75
Hershey Bears	56	33	17	6	207	169	72
Cleveland Barons	56	33	19	4	174	152	70
Buffalo Bisons	56	25	25	6	182	157	56
Pittsburgh Hornets	56	23	28	5	210	223	51

AMERICAN HOCKEY ASSOCIATION

Northern Division	GP	W	L	T	GF	GA	Pts
St. Louis Flyers	50	30	15	5	141	103	65
St. Paul Saints	50	28	17	5	141	99	61
*Omaha Knights	50	24	20	6	171	149	54
Minneapolis Millers	50	22	25	3	141	158	47
Southern Division							
Kansas City Americans	50	31	17	2	185	157	64
Fort Worth Rangers	50	25	23	2	190	176	52
Tulsa Oilers	50	13	34	3	120	188	29
Dallas Texans	50	12	34	4	131	190	28

EASTERN AMATEUR HOCKEY LEAGUE

	GP	W	L	T	GF	GA	Pts
*New York Rovers	60	34	20	6	272	197	74
Boston Olympics	60	34	20	6	263	218	74
Johnstown Bluebirds	60	34	20	6	248	215	74
Washington Eagles	60	28	27	5	261	253	61
Baltimore Orioles	60	26	30	4	252	262	56
Atlantic City Seagulls	60	20	39	1	239	316	41
Rivervale Skeeters	60	18	38	4	191	265	40

1942-43

AMERICAN HOCKEY LEAGUE

	GP	W	L	T	GF	GA	Pts
Hershey Bears	56	35	13	8	240	166	78
*Buffalo Bisons	56	28	21	7	189	143	63
Indianapolis Capitals	56	29	23	4	211	181	62
Pittsburgh Hornets	56	26	24	6	183	203	58
Providence Reds	56	27	27	2	211	216	56
Cleveland Barons	56	21	29	6	190	196	48
Washington Lions	56	14	34	8	184	272	36
New Haven Eagles §	32	9	18	5	85	116	23

§ folded 01/18/43

EASTERN AMATEUR HOCKEY LEAGUE

	GP	W	L	T	GF	GA	Pts
*U.S. Coast Guard	46	32	13	1	224	138	65
New York Rovers	46	24	20	2	197	158	50
Philadelphia Falcons	46	24	21	1	186	184	49
Boston Olympics	46	17	27	2	164	195	36

1943-44

AMERICAN HOCKEY LEAGUE

Eastern Division	GP	W	L	T	GF	GA	Pts
Hershey Bears	56	30	16	8	181	133	68
*Buffalo Bisons	54	25	16	13	201	168	63
Providence Reds	52	11	36	5	126	214	27
Western Division							
Cleveland Barons	54	33	14	7	224	176	73
Indianapolis Capitals	54	20	18	16	156	156	56
Pittsburgh Hornets	52	12	31	9	140	181	33

EASTERN AMATEUR HOCKEY LEAGUE

	GP	W	L	T	GF	GA	Pts
*Boston Olympics	45	39	4	2	250	93	80
New York Rovers	45	20	20	5	210	222	45
Philadelphia Falcons	45	17	23	5	185	207	39
New Haven Crescents	45	6	34	6	179	302	16

• U.S. Coast Guard folded 11/28/43. Played exhibitions only.

1944-45

AMERICAN HOCKEY LEAGUE

Eastern Division	GP	W	L	T	GF	GA	Pts
Buffalo Bisons	60	31	21	8	200	182	70
Hershey Bears	60	28	24	8	197	186	64
Providence Reds	60	23	31	6	241	249	52
Western Division							
*Cleveland Barons	60	34	16	10	256	199	78
Indianapolis Capitals	60	25	24	11	169	167	61
Pittsburgh Hornets	60	26	27	7	267	247	59
St. Louis Flyers	60	14	38	8	157	257	36

EASTERN AMATEUR HOCKEY LEAGUE

	GP	W	L	T	GF	GA	Pts
*Boston Olympics	48	32	13	3	295	178	67
Baltimore Orioles	48	28	19	1	228	177	57
Philadelphia Falcons	48	23	21	4	242	232	50
Washington Lions	48	15	28	5	212	310	35
New York Rovers	48	12	29	7	176	256	31

1945-46

AMERICAN HOCKEY LEAGUE

Eastern Division	GP	W	L	T	GF	GA	Pts
*Buffalo Bisons	62	38	16	8	270	196	84
Hershey Bears	62	26	26	10	213	221	62
Providence Reds	62	23	33	6	221	254	52
New Haven Eagles	62	14	38	10	199	263	38
Western Division							
Indianapolis Capitals	62	33	20	9	286	238	75
Pittsburgh Hornets	62	30	22	10	262	226	70
Cleveland Barons	62	28	26	8	269	254	64
St. Louis Flyers	62	21	32	9	198	266	51

UNITED STATES HOCKEY LEAGUE

	GP	W	L	T	GF	GA	Pts
*Kansas City Pla-Mors	56	35	17	4	271	185	74
Omaha Knights	56	31	22	3	210	190	65
St. Paul Saints	56	28	26	2	208	186	58
Tulsa Oilers	56	27	25	4	269	230	58
Fort Worth Rangers	56	24	31	1	186	238	49
Dallas Texans	56	21	32	3	218	259	45
Minneapolis Millers	56	20	33	3	192	262	43

PACIFIC COAST HOCKEY LEAGUE

North Division	GP	W	L	T	GF	GA	Pts
*Vancouver Canucks	58	37	21	0	308	247	74
Portland Eagles	58	29	29	0	257	261	58
Seattle Ironmen	58	29	29	0	251	214	58
New Westm'ster Royals	58	20	32	0	228	268	52
South Division							
Oakland Oaks	40	25	15	0	188	159	50
Hollywood Wolves	40	21	19	0	157	157	42
San Diego Skyhawks	40	21	19	0	145	139	42
Los Angeles Monarchs	40	17	23	0	189	208	34
San Fran. Shamrocks	40	11	29	0	159	229	22

QUEBEC SENIOR HOCKEY LEAGUE

	GP	W	L	T	GF	GA	Pts
*Montreal Royals	40	30	8	2	209	131	62
Ottawa Senators	40	24	14	2	212	157	50
Shawinigan Cataracts	40	18	20	2	158	193	38
Quebec Aces	40	17	20	3	149	169	37
Valleyfield Braves	40	15	22	3	163	184	33
Hull Volants	40	9	29	2	158	211	20

INTERNATIONAL HOCKEY LEAGUE

	GP	W	L	T	GF	GA	Pts
Det. Bright's Goodyears	15	9	3	3	90	70	21
Windsor Gotfredsons	15	8	4	3	90	72	19
*Detroit Auto Club	15	8	7	0	82	81	16
Windsor Spitfires	15	1	12	2	50	89	4

EASTERN AMATEUR HOCKEY LEAGUE

	GP	W	L	T	GF	GA	Pts
*Boston Olympics	52	32	12	8	258	162	72
Philadelphia Falcons	52	26	21	5	180	186	57
New York Rovers	52	25	20	7	240	181	57
Baltimore Clippers	52	19	25	8	164	205	46
Washington Lions	52	8	32	12	128	236	28

WESTERN CANADA SENIOR HOCKEY LEAGUE

	GP	W	L	T	GF	GA	Pts
*Calgary Stampeders	36	28	7	1	219	95	57
Edmonton Flyers	36	24	10	2	181	130	50
Saskatoon Elks	36	14	19	2	104	147	30
Regina Caps	36	2	32	1	95	227	5

1946-47

American Hockey League

Eastern Division	GP	W	L	T	GF	GA	Pts
*Hershey Bears	64	36	16	12	276	174	84
Springfield Indians	64	24	29	11	202	220	59
New Haven Ramblers	64	23	31	10	199	218	56
Providence Reds	64	21	33	10	226	281	52
Philadelphia Rockets	64	5	52	7	188	400	17
Western Division							
Cleveland Barons	64	38	18	8	272	215	84
Buffalo Bisons	64	36	17	11	257	173	83
Pittsburgh Hornets	64	35	19	10	260	188	80
Indianapolis Capitals	64	33	18	13	285	215	79
St. Louis Flyers	64	17	35	12	211	292	46

United States Hockey League

North Division	GP	W	L	T	GF	GA	Pts
Omaha Knights	60	29	16	15	225	181	73
*Kansas City Pla-Mors	60	29	20	11	264	197	69
Minneapolis Millers	60	28	22	10	214	197	66
St. Paul Saints	60	27	27	6	216	234	60
South Division							
Dallas Texans	60	27	18	15	232	218	69
Fort Worth Rangers	60	22	27	11	195	214	55
Tulsa Oilers	60	17	31	12	203	259	46
Houston Huskies	60	14	32	14	210	259	42

Pacific Coast Hockey League

North Division	GP	W	L	T	GF	GA	Pts
Portland Eagles	60	39	21	0	281	216	78
Seattle Ironmen	60	34	25	1	263	195	69
Vancouver Canucks	60	30	29	1	267	287	61
New Westm'ster Royals	60	29	29	2	257	270	60
Tacoma Rockets	60	16	42	2	223	324	34
South Division							
Hollywood Wolves	60	43	16	1	238	138	87
*Los Angeles Monarchs	60	36	24	0	308	260	72
San Diego Skyhawks	60	33	26	1	194	160	67
Fresno Falcons	60	26	33	1	236	252	53
Oakland Oaks	60	22	38	0	253	306	44
San Fran. Shamrocks	60	17	42	1	217	329	35

Quebec Senior Hockey League

	GP	W	L	T	GF	GA	Pts
Ottawa Senators	40	26	10	4	206	148	56
*Montreal Royals	40	25	13	2	173	124	52
Quebec Aces	40	19	15	6	159	158	44
Shawinigan Cataracts	40	14	23	3	135	175	31
Valleyfield Braves	40	8	31	1	142	210	17

International Hockey League

	GP	W	L	T	GF	GA	Pts
Windsor Staffords	28	17	8	3	167	138	37
*Windsor Spitfires	28	14	10	4	162	141	32
Det. Bright's Goodyears	28	13	9	6	154	128	32
Det. Metal Mouldings	28	9	13	6	89	122	24
Detroit Auto Club	28	7	20	1	113	156	15

Eastern Amateur Hockey League

	GP	W	L	T	GF	GA	Pts
New York Rovers	56	30	22	4	232	202	64
Washington Lions	56	24	24	8	235	252	56
*Boston Olympics	56	25	26	5	284	273	55
Baltimore Clippers	56	18	30	8	203	253	44

Western Canada Senior Hockey League

	GP	W	L	T	GF	GA	Pts
*Calgary Stampeders	40	27	9	4	187	105	57
Edmonton Flyers	40	24	10	2	174	139	46
Lethbridge Maple Leafs	40	20	17	3	177	159	43
Saskatoon Elks	40	15	23	2	151	210	32
Regina Caps	40	10	29	1	125	201	21

1947-48

American Hockey League

Eastern Division	GP	W	L	T	GF	GA	Pts
Providence Reds	68	41	23	4	342	277	86
New Haven Ramblers	68	31	30	7	254	242	69
Hershey Bears	68	25	30	13	240	273	63
Philadelphia Rockets	68	22	41	5	260	331	49
Springfield Indians	68	19	42	7	237	308	45
Washington Lions	68	17	45	6	241	369	40
Western Division							
*Cleveland Barons	68	43	13	12	332	197	98
Pittsburgh Hornets	68	38	18	12	238	170	88
Buffalo Bisons	68	41	23	4	277	238	86
Indianapolis Capitals	68	32	30	6	293	260	70
St. Louis Flyers	68	22	30	10	242	291	54

United States Hockey League

North Division	GP	W	L	T	GF	GA	Pts
Kansas City Pla-Mors	66	35	27	4	274	244	74
Minneapolis Millers	66	34	26	6	259	228	74
Omaha Knights	66	32	27	7	275	252	71
St. Paul Saints	66	30	30	6	236	245	66
South Division							
*Houston Huskies	66	36	27	3	317	267	75
Fort Worth Rangers	66	30	31	5	230	234	65
Tulsa Oilers	66	23	34	9	222	275	55
Dallas Texans	66	21	39	6	208	276	48

Pacific Coast Hockey League

North Division	GP	W	L	T	GF	GA	Pts
Seattle Ironmen	66	42	21	3	311	209	87
Tacoma Rockets	66	34	28	4	294	281	72
*Vancouver Canucks	66	34	29	3	284	264	71
New Westm'ster Royals	66	27	38	1	293	322	55
Portland Eagles	66	17	46	3	256	345	37
South Division							
Los Angeles Monarchs	66	36	26	4	306	270	76
San Francisco Shamrocks	66	35	29	2	243	227	72
San Diego Skyhawks	66	32	31	3	242	258	67
Fresno Falcons	66	30	32	4	229	236	64
Oakland Oaks	66	29	36	1	236	252	59

Quebec Senior Hockey League

	GP	W	L	T	GF	GA	Pts
*Ottawa Senators	48	35	11	2	271	139	72
Montreal Royals	48	34	14	0	241	159	68
Shawinigan Cataracts	48	26	17	5	206	189	57
Quebec Aces	48	23	20	5	175	185	51
Valleyfield Braves	48	16	31	1	207	251	33
New York Rovers §	48	14	32	1	150	220	29
Boston Olympics §	48	12	35	0	173	287	24

§ also played in EHL

International Hockey League

	GP	W	L	T	GF	GA	Pts
Windsor Spitfires	30	19	10	1	151	105	39
*Toledo Mercurys	30	15	10	5	113	98	35
Det. Metal Mouldings	30	15	12	3	135	139	33
Det. Bright's Goodyears	30	13	14	3	157	149	29
Detroit Auto Club	30	13	16	1	161	155	27
Windsor Staffords	30	8	21	1	117	188	17

Eastern Amateur Hockey League

	GP	W	L	T	GF	GA	Pts
*Baltimore Clippers	48	31	16	1	246	154	63
New York Rovers §	48	27	19	2	125	150	56
Atlantic City Seagulls	48	17	25	6	167	196	40
Boston Olympics §	48	14	29	5	139	177	33

§ also played in QSHL

- *All teams played a series of 4-point games*

Western Canada Senior Hockey League

	GP	W	L	T	GF	GA	Pts
Calgary Stampeders	48	28	19	1	225	191	57
Regina Caps	48	26	21	1	225	226	53
*Edmonton Flyers	48	24	22	2	231	184	50
Lethbridge Maple Leafs	48	20	24	4	175	209	44
Saskatoon Quakers	48	8	38	2	144	307	18

1948-49

American Hockey League

Eastern Division	GP	W	L	T	GF	GA	Pts
*Providence Reds	68	44	18	6	347	219	94
Hershey Bears	68	28	35	5	256	261	61
Springfield Indians	68	22	37	9	240	276	53
New Haven Ramblers	68	20	40	8	223	286	48
Philadelphia Rockets	68	15	48	5	230	407	35
Washington Lions	68	11	53	4	179	401	26
Western Division							
Cleveland Barons	68	41	18	9	294	192	91
Pittsburgh Hornets	68	39	17	12	288	209	90
Buffalo Bisons	68	41	21	6	286	251	88
Indianapolis Capitals	68	39	19	10	301	175	88
St. Louis Flyers	68	33	27	8	246	213	74

Eastern Amateur Hockey League

- *EHL did not operate in 1948-49*

United States Hockey League

North Division	GP	W	L	T	GF	GA	Pts
*St. Paul Saints	66	36	20	10	284	210	82
Kansas City Pla-Mors	66	30	23	13	261	206	73
Omaha Knights	66	28	25	13	226	220	69
Minneapolis Millers	66	27	24	15	223	211	69
South Division							
Tulsa Oilers	66	33	23	10	281	216	76
Dallas Texans	66	24	27	15	246	251	63
Fort Worth Rangers	66	24	35	7	217	298	55
Houston Huskies	66	17	42	7	200	326	41

Pacific Coast Hockey League

Northern Division	GP	W	L	T	GF	GA	Pts
New Westm'ster Royals	70	39	26	5	285	229	83
Tacoma Rockets	70	34	31	5	239	262	73
Vancouver Canucks	70	33	31	6	262	256	72
Portland Penguins	70	32	31	7	246	236	71
Seattle Ironmen	70	29	36	5	225	246	63
Southern Division							
Fresno Falcons	70	33	30	7	213	211	73
Oakland Oaks	70	33	33	4	241	222	70
*San Diego Skyhawks	70	32	35	3	249	275	67
Los Angeles Monarchs	70	28	33	9	246	271	65
San Fran. Shamrocks	70	29	36	5	273	271	63

Quebec Senior Hockey League

	GP	W	L	T	GF	GA	Pts
*Ottawa Senators	60	44	15	1	341	207	89
Sherbrk Red Raiders	60	41	16	3	263	176	85
Montreal Royals §	59	35	19	5	216	178	77
Valleyfield Braves	60	29	30	1	265	270	59
Quebec Aces	60	22	32	6	186	213	50
Shawinigan Cataracts	60	18	40	2	201	292	38
New York Rovers §	59	10	47	2	191	328	22

§ played one 4-point game

International Hockey League

North Division	GP	W	L	T	GF	GA	Pts
Toledo Mercurys	35	20	7	8	185	140	48
Detroit Jerry Lynch	31	16	6	9	163	125	44a
Detroit Auto Club	31	17	11	3	146	130	39b
*Windsor Het. Spitfires	31	15	11	5	152	144	39c
Det. Bright's Goodyears	31	8	16	7	135	154	28d
Windsor Ryancretes	31	0	25	6	89	177	6

- *All teams except Toledo played 4-point games*

South Division	GP	W	L	T	GF	GA	Pts
Louisville Blades	32	21	5	6	192	127	48
Toledo Mercurys	32	21	7	4	173	93	46
Milwaukee Clarks	32	16	15	1	148	139	33
Muncie Flyers	32	9	19	4	103	168	22
Akron Americans	32	4	25	3	111	200	11

Western Canada Senior Hockey League

	GP	W	L	T	GF	GA	Pts
*Regina Capitals	48	33	13	2	214	150	68
Edmonton Flyers	48	30	17	1	262	172	61
Calgary Stampeders	48	23	22	3	220	177	49
Lethbridge Maple Leafs	48	20	24	4	175	209	44
Saskatoon Quakers	48	8	38	2	144	307	18

1949-50

American Hockey League

Eastern Division	GP	W	L	T	GF	GA	Pts
Buffalo Bisons	70	32	29	9	226	208	73
Providence Reds	70	34	33	3	268	267	71
Springfield Indians	70	28	34	8	245	258	64
New Haven Ramblers	70	24	36	10	196	250	58
Hershey Bears	70	21	39	10	229	310	52
Western Division							
Cleveland Barons	70	45	15	10	357	230	100
*Indianapolis Capitals	70	35	24	11	267	231	81
St. Louis Flyers	70	34	28	8	258	250	76
Pittsburgh Hornets	70	29	26	15	215	185	73
Cincinnati Mohawks	70	19	37	14	185	257	52

United States Hockey League

	GP	W	L	T	GF	GA	Pts
Omaha Knights	70	41	22	7	313	240	89
*Minneapolis Millers	70	33	28	9	297	257	75
Kansas City Mohawks	70	30	28	12	293	267	72
St. Paul Saints	70	29	30	11	253	289	69
Tulsa Oilers	70	25	33	12	276	302	62
Louisville Blades	70	22	39	9	256	333	53

Pacific Coast Hockey League

Northern Division	GP	W	L	T	GF	GA	Pts
*New Westm'ster Royals	71	36	19	16	291	233	88
Tacoma Rockets	70	34	27	6	302	238	77
Vancouver Canucks	70	33	28	9	300	263	75
Seattle Ironmen	70	32	27	11	212	237	75
Portland Penguins	71	32	30	9	237	229	73
Victoria Cougars	70	22	42	6	218	307	50
Southern Division							
San Fran. Shamrocks	71	35	27	9	266	233	79
Los Angeles Monarchs	70	30	30	10	259	247	70
San Diego Skyhawks	70	27	33	10	211	236	64
Fresno Falcons	70	21	34	14	197	239	56
Oakland Oaks §	29	10	14	5	78	109	25

§ folded 12/16/49

Quebec Senior Hockey League

	GP	W	L	T	GF	GA	Pts
*Sherbrooke Saints	60	39	20	1	246	173	79
Quebec Aces	60	35	22	3	207	175	73
Ottawa Senators	60	31	25	4	251	240	66
Montreal Royals	60	27	24	9	206	188	63
Valleyfield Braves	60	25	26	9	216	200	59
Chicoutimi Sagueneens	60	22	35	3	172	236	47
Shawinigan Cataracts	60	15	42	3	184	270	33

International Hockey League

	GP	W	L	T	GF	GA	Pts
Sarnia Sailors	40	26	11	3	219	136	55
Detroit Auto Club	40	19	14	7	170	139	45
*Chatham Maroons	40	19	18	3	152	148	41
Detroit Hettche	40	15	21	4	157	191	34
Windsor Ryancretes	40	10	25	5	152	236	25

Eastern Amateur Hockey League

	GP	W	L	T	GF	GA	Pts
Toledo Buckeyes	51	26	13	12	188	142	64
*New York Rovers	47	25	17	7	195	133	57
Grand Rapids Rockets	61	26	21	14	230	225	66
Boston Olympics	43	16	20	7	146	169	39
Milwaukee Clarks	51	19	24	8	191	210	46
Atlantic City Seagulls	47	14	31	2	122	193	30
Cleveland Knights §	18	4	10	4	....	....	12
Baltimore Clippers §	12	5	7	0	....	....	10

§ folded 12/20/49

Western Canada Senior Hockey League

	GP	W	L	T	GF	GA	Pts
Edmonton Flyers	50	27	18	5	238	174	59
*Calgary Stampeders	50	22	23	5	176	163	49
Saskatoon Quakers	50	24	25	1	190	227	49
Regina Capitals	50	19	28	5	171	211	43

1950-51

American Hockey League

Eastern Division	GP	W	L	T	GF	GA	Pts
Buffalo Bisons	70	40	26	4	309	284	84
Hershey Bears	70	38	28	4	256	242	80
Springfield Indians	70	27	37	6	268	254	60
Providence Reds	70	24	41	5	247	303	53
New Haven Ramblers §	28	5	23	0	74	154	10
§ folded 12/10/51							
Western Division							
*Cleveland Barons	71	44	22	5	281	221	93
Indianapolis Capitals	70	38	29	3	287	255	79
Pittsburgh Hornets	71	31	33	7	212	177	69
St. Louis Flyers	70	32	34	4	233	252	68
Cincinnati Mohawks	70	28	34	8	203	228	64

United States Hockey League

	GP	W	L	T	GF	GA	Pts
*Omaha Knights	64	43	17	4	306	211	90
St. Paul Saints	64	33	26	5	213	186	71
Denver Falcons	64	31	31	2	233	232	64
Tulsa Oilers	64	30	31	3	248	237	63
Kansas City Royals	64	22	36	6	231	287	50
Milwaukee Seagulls	64	20	38	6	202	280	46

Pacific Coast Hockey League

	GP	W	L	T	GF	GA	Pts
*Victoria Cougars	70	35	20	15	250	216	85
New Westm'ster Royals	70	38	24	8	267	205	84
Tacoma Rockets	70	27	26	17	219	222	71
Portland Eagles	70	30	32	8	266	255	68
Seattle Ironmen	70	23	36	11	214	249	57
Vancouver Canucks	70	19	34	17	216	285	55

Quebec Senior Hockey League

	GP	W	L	T	GF	GA	Pts
*Valleyfield Braves	60	37	19	4	227	178	78
Quebec Aces	60	31	22	7	228	195	69
Ottawa Senators	60	29	23	8	214	189	66
Chicoutimi Sagueneens	60	28	29	3	200	203	59
Montreal Royals	60	27	28	5	220	216	59
Sherbrooke Saints	60	24	30	6	193	209	54
Shawinigan Cataracts	60	15	40	5	181	273	35

International Hockey League

	GP	W	L	T	GF	GA	Pts
Grand Rapids Rockets	56	39	11	6	274	165	84
Toledo Mercurys	56	35	15	6	290	174	76
*Chatham Maroons	52	25	23	4	211	215	59a
Sarnia Sailors	52	24	19	9	226	191	59b
Detroit Auto Club	52	10	32	10	136	238	31c
Detroit Hettche	52	6	39	7	112	226	19

• Chatham, Sarnia, Detroit Auto and Detroit Hettche played 4-point games

Eastern Amateur Hockey League

	GP	W	L	T	GF	GA	Pts
Johnstown Jets	54	26	25	3	195	194	55
Boston Olympics	54	25	24	5	187	191	55
*Atlantic City Seagulls	54	23	24	7	231	218	53
New York Rovers	54	22	23	9	168	178	53

Western Canada Senior Hockey League

	GP	W	L	T	GF	GA	Pts
Calgary Stampeders	60	38	21	1	282	202	77
Edmonton Flyers	60	34	25	1	242	198	69
*Saskatoon Quakers	59	31	27	1	246	234	63
Regina Caps	59	14	44	1	173	309	29

Maritime Major Hockey League

	GP	W	L	T	GF	GA	Pts
*Charlottetown Islanders	77	49	23	5	340	216	102
Halifax St. Mary's	78	42	33	3	328	294	87
Saint John Beavers	78	36	39	3	293	310	75
Moncton Hawks	77	20	52	5	251	392	45

1951-52

American Hockey League

Eastern Division	GP	W	L	T	GF	GA	Pts
Hershey Bears	68	35	28	5	256	215	75
Providence Reds	68	32	33	3	263	270	67
Buffalo Bisons	68	28	36	4	230	298	60
Syracuse Warriors	68	25	42	1	211	272	51
Western Division							
*Pittsburgh Hornets	68	46	19	3	267	179	95
Cleveland Barons	68	44	19	5	265	166	93
Cincinnati Mohawks	68	29	33	6	183	228	64
St. Louis Flyers	68	28	39	1	256	262	57
Indianapolis Capitals	68	22	40	6	232	273	50

Pacific Coast Hockey League

	GP	W	L	T	GF	GA	Pts
New Westm'ster Royals	70	40	19	11	286	200	91
*Saskatoon Quakers	70	35	21	14	273	225	84
Tacoma Rockets	70	34	25	11	293	244	79
Seattle Ironmen	70	30	31	9	252	280	69
Edmonton Flyers	70	30	32	8	244	246	68
Victoria Cougars	70	25	38	7	242	296	57
Calgary Stampeders	70	24	37	9	278	320	57
Vancouver Canucks	70	23	38	9	226	283	55

Quebec Senior Hockey League

	GP	W	L	T	GF	GA	Pts
*Quebec Aces	60	37	16	7	230	168	81
Montreal Royals	60	30	24	6	219	204	66
Chicoutimi Sagueneens	60	26	25	9	210	179	61
Ottawa Senators	60	26	28	6	177	195	58
Sherbrooke Saints	60	24	29	7	155	183	55
Valleyfield Braves	60	24	30	6	169	178	54
Shawinigan Cataracts	60	19	34	7	147	200	45

International Hockey League

	GP	W	L	T	GF	GA	Pts
Grand Rapids Rockets	48	29	13	6	213	156	64
*Toledo Mercurys	48	24	18	6	210	192	54
Troy Bruins	48	23	19	6	211	180	52
Chatham Maroons	48	22	23	3	206	218	47
Detroit Hettche	48	10	35	3	138	232	23

Eastern Amateur Hockey League

	GP	W	L	T	GF	GA	Pts
*Johnstown Jets	65	39	21	5	264	186	83
Boston Olympics	66	38	27	1	246	240	77
N. Haven Tomahawks	66	37	27	2	256	241	76
Springfield Indians	66	33	29	4	247	235	70
Atlantic City Seagulls	65	26	36	3	255	281	55
New York Rovers	61	25	34	2	233	231	52
Washington Lions §	36	9	24	3	124	155	21
Philadelphia Falcons ¶	25	8	17	0	68	124	16

§ folded 01/25/52 ¶ folded 12/17/52

Maritime Major Hockey League

	GP	W	L	T	GF	GA	Pts
*Saint John Beavers	90	53	24	13	360	231	119
Charlottetown Islanders	90	42	39	9	317	316	93
Halifax St.Mary's	90	41	41	8	333	339	90
Glace Bay Miners	90	37	43	10	320	342	84
Sydney Millionaires	90	35	43	12	285	326	82
Moncton Hawks	90	30	48	12	268	329	72

1952-53

American Hockey League

	GP	W	L	T	GF	GA	Pts
Cleveland Barons	64	42	20	2	248	164	86
*Pittsburgh Hornets	64	37	21	6	223	149	80
Syracuse Warriors	64	31	31	2	213	201	64
Hershey Bears	64	31	32	1	208	217	63
Providence Reds	64	27	36	1	215	254	55
St. Louis Flyers	64	26	37	1	212	258	53
Buffalo Bisons	64	22	39	3	160	236	47

Quebec Hockey League

	GP	W	L	T	GF	GA	Pts
*Chicoutimi Sagueneens	60	33	15	12	213	149	78
Montreal Royals	60	32	22	6	201	162	70
Valleyfield Braves	60	27	25	8	175	178	62
Ottawa Senators	60	27	26	7	171	191	61
Sherbrooke Saints	60	25	28	7	184	175	57
Quebec Aces	60	22	26	12	178	197	56
Shawinigan Cataracts	60	15	39	6	171	241	56

International Hockey League

	GP	W	L	T	GF	GA	Pts
*Cincinnati Mohawks	60	43	13	4	310	152	90
Troy Bruins	60	34	21	5	264	221	73
Toledo Mercurys	60	32	25	3	210	207	67
Grand Rapids Rockets	60	27	32	1	231	257	55
Fort Wayne Komets	60	20	38	2	182	244	42
Milwaukee Chiefs	60	15	42	3	234	350	33

Eastern Amateur Hockey League

	GP	W	L	T	GF	GA	Pts
Springfield Indians	60	39	19	2	296	234	80
*Johnstown Jets	60	28	29	3	226	244	59
New Haven Nutmegs	60	28	31	1	251	223	57
Washington Lions	60	26	31	3	201	215	55
Troy Uncle Sam Trojans	60	23	34	3	220	278	49

Western Hockey League

• PCHL and WCSHL amalgamate to form WHL

	GP	W	L	T	GF	GA	Pts
Saskatoon Quakers	70	35	26	9	268	240	79
Vancouver Canucks	70	32	28	10	227	216	74
Calgary Stampeders	70	31	27	12	254	252	74
*Edmonton Flyers	70	31	28	11	263	227	73
Seattle Bombers	70	30	32	8	232	225	68
New Westm'ster Royals	70	29	33	8	217	254	66
Tacoma Rockets	70	27	31	12	246	249	66
Victoria Cougars	70	26	36	8	244	278	60

Maritime Major Hockey League

	GP	W	L	T	GF	GA	Pts
*Halifax Atlantics	84	47	33	4	350	308	98
Charlottetown Islanders	84	45	35	4	307	261	94
Glace Bay Miners	84	40	40	4	278	280	84
Sydney Millionaires	84	28	52	4	228	314	60

1953-54

American Hockey League

	GP	W	L	T	GF	GA	Pts
Buffalo Bisons	70	39	24	7	283	217	85
Hershey Bears	70	37	29	4	274	243	78
*Cleveland Barons	70	38	32	0	269	227	76
Pittsburgh Hornets	70	34	31	5	250	222	73
Providence Reds	70	26	40	4	211	276	56
Syracuse Warriors	70	24	42	4	215	317	52

Quebec Hockey League

	GP	W	L	T	GF	GA	Pts
Chicoutimi Sagueneens	72	40	25	7	261	197	87
Montreal Royals	72	40	25	7	257	203	87
Ottawa Senators	72	34	32	6	223	212	74
*Quebec Aces	72	30	34	8	216	212	68
Sherbrooke Saints	72	30	36	6	223	244	66
Valleyfield Braves	72	31	38	3	207	252	65
Springfield Indians	72	25	40	7	222	289	57

International Hockey League

	GP	W	L	T	GF	GA	Pts
*Cincinnati Mohawks	64	47	15	2	325	153	96
Marion Barons	64	40	24	0	279	207	80
Johnstown Jets	64	35	26	3	254	221	73
Toledo Mercurys	64	33	26	5	221	157	71
Troy Bruins	64	31	32	1	241	258	63
Fort Wayne Komets	64	29	30	5	203	220	63
Grand Rapids Rockets	64	29	32	3	252	274	61
Louisville Shooting Stars	64	18	42	4	202	331	40
Milwaukee Chiefs	64	13	48	3	187	343	29

Western Hockey League

	GP	W	L	T	GF	GA	Pts
Vancouver Canucks	70	39	24	7	218	174	85
*Calgary Stampeders	70	38	25	7	266	206	83
Saskatoon Quakers	70	32	29	9	226	214	73
Edmonton Flyers	70	29	30	11	246	260	69
Victoria Cougars	70	27	32	11	203	223	65
New Westm'ster Royals	70	28	34	8	218	261	64
Seattle Bombers	70	22	41	7	209	248	51

Maritime Major Hockey League

	GP	W	L	T	GF	GA	Pts
*Halifax Atlantics	78	42	33	3	361	314	87
Sydney Millionaires	78	40	35	3	262	257	83
Glace Bay Miners	78	34	39	2	286	304	72
Charlottetown Islanders	78	33	42	0	290	324	66

Eastern Amateur Hockey League

• EHL did not operate in 1953-54

1954-55

American Hockey League

	GP	W	L	T	GF	GA	Pts
*Pittsburgh Hornets	64	31	25	8	187	180	70
Cleveland Barons	64	32	29	3	254	222	67
Springfield Indians	64	32	29	3	251	233	67
Buffalo Bisons	64	31	28	5	248	228	67
Hershey Bears	64	29	28	7	217	225	65
Providence Reds	64	21	37	6	194	263	48

Quebec Hockey League

	GP	W	L	T	GF	GA	Pts
*Shawinigan Cataracts	62	39	20	3	228	145	81
Quebec Aces	60	31	27	2	206	208	64
Montreal Royals	62	30	28	4	232	207	64
Chicoutimi Sagueneens	61	29	29	3	216	212	61
Valleyfield Braves	62	21	39	2	178	261	44
Ottawa Senators §	27	10	17	0	63	90	20

§ folded 12/21/54

International Hockey League

	GP	W	L	T	GF	GA	Pts
*Cincinnati Mohawks	60	40	19	1	268	164	81
Troy Bruins	60	31	27	2	190	180	64
Toledo Mercurys	60	31	29	0	183	196	62
Grand Rapids Rockets	60	28	31	1	199	215	57
Johnstown Jets	60	25	34	1	188	215	51
Fort Wayne Komets	60	22	37	1	181	235	45

Eastern Hockey League

	GP	W	L	T	GF	GA	Pts
Washington Lions	49	26	21	2	204	175	54
*New Haven Blades	46	23	21	2	201	199	48
Baltimore Clippers	47	22	23	2	208	180	46
Clinton Comets §	22	15	7	0	111	75	30
Worcester Warriors §	20	3	17	0	59	154	6

§ played partial schedule

Western Hockey League

	GP	W	L	T	GF	GA	Pts
*Edmonton Flyers	70	39	20	11	273	204	89
Victoria Cougars	70	33	29	8	237	199	74
Vancouver Canucks	70	31	30	9	207	202	71
Calgary Stampeders	70	29	29	12	262	258	70
New Westm'ster Royals	70	29	32	9	249	299	67
Saskatoon Quakers	70	19	40	11	207	273	49

1955-56

American Hockey League

	GP	W	L	T	GF	GA	Pts
*Providence Reds	64	45	17	2	263	193	92
Pittsburgh Hornets	64	43	17	4	271	186	90
Buffalo Bisons	64	29	30	5	239	250	63
Cleveland Barons	64	26	31	7	225	231	59
Hershey Bears	64	19	39	6	218	271	44
Springfield Indians	64	17	45	2	212	297	36

Quebec Hockey League

	GP	W	L	T	GF	GA	Pts
Shawinigan Cataracts	64	43	18	3	243	166	89
*Montreal Royals	64	34	23	7	192	162	75
Chicoutimi Sagueneens	64	32	28	4	212	188	68
Quebec Aces	64	23	37	4	190	230	50
Trois-Rivieres Lions	64	18	44	2	159	250	38

International Hockey League

	GP	W	L	T	GF	GA	Pts
*Cincinnati Mohawks	60	45	13	2	336	159	92
Troy Bruins	60	39	20	1	216	152	79
Fort Wayne Komets	60	29	29	2	272	219	60
Toledo-Marion Mercurys	60	25	30	5	178	229	55
Grand Rapids Rockets	60	24	33	3	198	237	51
Indianapolis Chiefs	60	11	48	1	126	330	23

Eastern Hockey League

	GP	W	L	T	GF	GA	Pts
*New Haven Blades	64	43	18	3	318	206	89
Clinton Comets	64	33	28	3	298	269	69
Washington Lions	64	33	28	3	258	267	69
Johnstown Jets	64	32	32	0	312	298	64
Baltimore Clippers	64	23	40	1	236	327	47
Philadelphia Ramblers	64	23	41	0	246	301	46

Western Hockey League

Prairie Division	GP	W	L	T	GF	GA	Pts
*Winnipeg Warriors	70	40	28	2	248	212	82
Calgary Stampeders	70	40	30	0	292	242	80
Edmonton Flyers	70	33	34	3	236	256	69
Saskatoon Quakers	70	27	35	8	208	249	62
Regina-Brandon Regals	70	23	39	8	199	243	54
Coast Division							
Vancouver Canucks	70	38	28	4	252	181	80
Victoria Cougars	70	35	30	5	206	196	75
New Westm'ster Royals	70	31	37	2	238	258	64
Seattle Americans	70	31	37	2	201	243	64

1956-57

American Hockey League

	GP	W	L	T	GF	GA	Pts
Providence Reds	64	34	22	8	236	168	76
*Cleveland Barons	64	35	26	3	249	210	73
Rochester Americans	64	34	25	5	224	199	73
Hershey Bears	64	32	28	4	223	237	68
Buffalo Bisons	64	25	37	2	209	270	52
Springfield Indians	64	19	41	4	217	274	42

Quebec Hockey League

	GP	W	L	T	GF	GA	Pts
*Quebec Aces	68	40	21	7	226	175	87
Chicoutimi Sagueneens	68	34	28	6	225	199	75
Trois-Rivieres Lions	68	29	32	7	168	197	65
Montreal Royals	68	28	34	6	191	211	62
Shawinigan Cataracts	68	24	35	9	202	213	57
Hull-Ottawa Jr. Canadiens	20	7	12	1	57	74	15

• Hull-Ottawa played 20-game exhibition schedule that counted in standings

International Hockey League

	GP	W	L	T	GF	GA	Pts
*Cincinnati Mohawks	60	50	9	1	245	113	101
Indianapolis Chiefs	60	26	29	5	168	177	57
Huntington Hornets	60	26	30	4	180	188	56
Toledo Mercurys	60	26	30	4	166	186	56
Fort Wayne Komets	60	25	29	6	170	177	56
Troy Bruins	60	15	41	4	135	223	34

Eastern Hockey League

	GP	W	L	T	GF	GA	Pts
*Charlotte Checkers	64	50	13	1	364	239	101
Philadelphia Ramblers	64	34	27	3	277	233	71
New Haven Blades	64	31	30	3	276	263	65
Johnstown Jets	64	31	33	0	320	290	62
Clinton Comets	64	23	39	2	254	325	48
Washington Lions	64	18	45	1	256	397	37

Western Hockey League

Prairie Division	GP	W	L	T	GF	GA	Pts
*Brandon Regals	70	44	22	4	250	186	92
Edmonton Flyers	70	39	27	4	239	212	82
Calgary Stampeders	70	29	37	4	220	230	62
Winnipeg Warriors	70	23	45	2	198	273	48
Coast Division							
Seattle Americans	70	36	28	6	263	225	78
New Westm'ster Royals	70	34	31	5	215	235	73
Victoria Cougars	70	29	34	7	208	204	65
Vancouver Canucks	70	27	37	6	203	231	60

1957-58

American Hockey League

	GP	W	L	T	GF	GA	Pts
*Hershey Bears	70	39	24	7	241	198	85
Cleveland Barons	70	39	28	3	232	163	81
Providence Reds	70	33	32	5	237	220	71
Springfield Indians	70	29	33	8	231	246	66
Rochester Americans	70	29	35	6	205	242	64
Buffalo Bisons	70	25	42	3	224	301	53

Quebec Hockey League

	GP	W	L	T	GF	GA	Pts
Chicoutimi Sagueneens	64	35	24	5	241	209	75
*Shawinigan Cataracts	64	31	28	5	243	235	67
Montreal Royals	64	29	30	5	227	219	63
Quebec Aces	64	29	31	4	224	233	62
Trois-Rivieres Lions	64	24	35	5	176	215	53

International Hockey League

	GP	W	L	T	GF	GA	Pts
Cincinnati Mohawks	64	43	16	5	303	176	91
Fort Wayne Komets	64	28	28	8	213	224	64
Louisville Rebels	64	30	31	3	239	263	63
*Indianapolis Chiefs	64	28	30	6	209	208	62
Toledo Mercurys	64	26	32	6	214	248	58
Troy Bruins	64	20	38	6	192	251	46

Eastern Hockey League

	GP	W	L	T	GF	GA	Pts
Charlotte Clippers	64	38	25	1	275	243	77
*Washington Presidents	64	36	24	4	221	195	76
New Haven Blades	64	33	26	5	204	180	71
Johnstown Jets	64	31	30	3	228	225	65
Philadelphia Ramblers	64	30	31	3	210	211	63
Clinton Comets	64	15	47	2	186	270	32

Western Hockey League

Coast Division	GP	W	L	T	GF	GA	Pts
*Vancouver Canucks	70	44	21	5	238	174	93
New Westm'ster Royals	70	39	28	3	254	223	81
Seattle Americans	70	32	32	6	234	231	70
Victoria Cougars	70	10	50	2	225	313	38
Prairie Division							
Winnipeg Warriors	70	39	26	5	263	211	83
Edmonton Flyers	70	38	28	4	264	225	80
Calgary Stampeders	70	30	35	5	222	223	65
Sask.-St. Paul Regals	70	25	45	0	214	324	50

1958-59

American Hockey League

	GP	W	L	T	GF	GA	Pts
Buffalo Bisons	70	38	28	4	233	201	80
Cleveland Indians	70	37	30	3	261	252	77
Rochester Americans	70	34	31	5	242	209	73
*Hershey Bears	70	32	32	6	200	202	70
Springfield Indians	70	30	38	2	253	282	62
Providence Reds	70	28	40	2	222	265	58

Quebec Hockey League

	GP	W	L	T	GF	GA	Pts
*Montreal Royals	62	34	22	6	206	162	74
Trois-Rivieres Lions	62	30	29	3	194	184	63
Chicoutimi Sagueneens	62	30	31	1	238	236	61
Quebec Aces	62	21	33	8	176	232	50

International Hockey League

	GP	W	L	T	GF	GA	Pts
*Louisville Rebels	60	35	24	1	280	197	71
Fort Wayne Komets	60	32	27	1	236	213	65
Troy Bruins	60	30	28	2	245	283	62
Indianapolis Chiefs	60	26	30	4	231	247	56
Toledo Mercurys	60	22	36	2	196	248	46

Eastern Hockey League

	GP	W	L	T	GF	GA	Pts
*Clinton Comets	64	41	21	2	291	180	84
Johnstown Jets	64	33	28	3	252	223	69
New Haven Blades	64	29	31	4	201	216	69
Philadelphia Ramblers	64	30	33	1	215	237	61
Washington Presidents	64	29	35	0	242	271	58
Charlotte Checkers	64	24	38	2	209	283	50

Western Hockey League

Coast Division	GP	W	L	T	GF	GA	Pts
*Seattle Totems	70	40	27	3	277	225	83
Vancouver Canucks	70	31	28	11	220	214	73
Victoria Cougars	70	30	35	5	219	254	65
Spokane Spokes	70	26	38	6	217	275	58
New Westm'ster Royals	70	23	45	2	237	301	48
Western Hockey League							
Calgary Stampeders	64	42	21	1	263	196	85
Edmonton Flyers	64	33	28	3	205	207	69
Winnipeg Warriors	64	31	31	2	256	228	64
Saskatoon Quakers	64	29	31	4	208	201	62

1959-60

American Hockey League

	GP	W	L	T	GF	GA	Pts
*Springfield Indians	72	43	23	6	280	219	92
Rochester Americans	72	40	27	5	285	211	85
Providence Reds	72	38	32	2	251	237	78
Cleveland Barons	72	34	30	8	267	229	76
Buffalo Bisons	72	33	35	4	251	271	70
Hershey Bears	72	28	37	7	226	238	63
Quebec Aces	72	19	51	2	178	333	40

Eastern Professional Hockey League

	GP	W	L	T	GF	GA	Pts
Sudbury Wolves	70	36	26	8	310	283	80
*Montreal Royals	70	30	26	14	215	198	74
Hull-Ottawa Canadiens	70	31	28	11	249	241	73
Trois-Rivieres Lions	70	30	31	9	226	235	69
Soo Thunderbirds	70	27	32	11	248	262	65
Kingston Frontenacs	70	28	39	3	297	326	59

International Hockey League

East Division	GP	W	L	T	GF	GA	Pts
Fort Wayne Komets	68	50	16	2	312	187	102
Louisville Rebels	68	37	30	1	303	276	75
Toledo-St. Louis	68	28	36	4	266	298	60
Indianapolis Chiefs	68	25	40	3	234	322	53
West Division							
*St. Paul Saints	68	41	21	6	261	188	88
Minneapolis Millers	68	39	27	2	297	233	80
Milwaukee Falcons	67	24	42	1	251	314	49
Omaha Knights	67	15	47	5	198	303	35

Eastern Hockey League

North Division	GP	W	L	T	GF	GA	Pts
Clinton Comets	64	35	27	2	244	202	72
New Haven Blades	64	32	29	3	217	189	67
Philadelphia Ramblers	64	31	30	3	226	219	65
New York Rovers	64	19	44	1	205	294	39
South Division							
*Johnstown Jets	64	45	18	1	255	176	91
Charlotte Clippers	64	31	29	4	243	244	66
Greensboro Generals	64	26	33	5	229	250	57
Washington Presidents	64	25	34	5	207	252	55

Western Hockey League

	GP	W	L	T	GF	GA	Pts
*Vancouver Canucks	70	44	20	6	230	177	94
Seattle Totems	70	38	28	4	270	219	80
Edmonton Flyers	70	37	29	4	246	240	78
Victoria Cougars	70	37	29	4	227	194	78
Calgary Stampeders	70	32	36	2	245	227	66
Winnipeg Warriors	70	25	42	3	224	262	53
Spokane Comets	70	19	48	3	201	326	41

1960-61

American Hockey League

	GP	W	L	T	GF	GA	Pts
*Springfield Indians	72	49	22	1	344	206	99
Hershey Bears	72	36	32	4	218	210	76
Cleveland Barons	72	36	35	1	231	234	73
Buffalo Bisons	72	35	34	3	259	261	73
Rochester Americans	72	32	36	4	261	244	68
Quebec Aces	72	30	39	3	217	267	63
Providence Reds	72	26	46	0	225	333	52

Eastern Professional Hockey League

	GP	W	L	T	GF	GA	Pts
*Hull-Ottawa Canadiens	70	41	20	9	268	187	91
Soo Thunderbirds	70	32	29	9	236	234	73
Kitchener-W Dutchmen	70	31	28	11	220	215	73
Kingston Frontenacs	70	29	33	8	259	269	66
Sudbury Wolves	70	28	33	9	236	257	65
Montreal Royals	70	19	37	14	167	224	52

International Hockey League

East Division	GP	W	L	T	GF	GA	Pts
Toledo Mercurys	70	36	33	1	274	260	73
Fort Wayne Komets	69	31	35	3	304	265	65
Muskegon Zephyrs	70	25	41	4	243	319	54
Indianapolis Chiefs	70	20	46	4	217	313	44
West Division							
Minneapolis Millers	72	50	20	2	323	229	102
*St. Paul Saints	72	46	22	4	309	233	96
Omaha Knights	70	35	32	3	254	235	73
Milwaukee Falcons §	17	1	15	1	45	115	3

§ folded 11/26/60

Eastern Hockey League

North Division	GP	W	L	T	GF	GA	Pts
New Haven Blades	64	38	25	1	278	221	77
Clinton Comets	64	30	32	2	267	228	62
Jersey Devils	64	24	39	1	215	254	49
New York Rovers	64	18	45	1	196	293	37
South Division							
Greensboro Generals	64	40	22	2	339	257	82
*Johnstown Jets	64	40	22	2	273	215	82
Philadelphia Ramblers	64	32	28	4	227	278	68
Charlotte Checkers	64	25	34	5	221	265	55

Western Hockey League

	GP	W	L	T	GF	GA	Pts
Calgary Stampeders	70	44	22	4	300	215	92
*Portland Buckaroos	70	38	23	9	242	192	85
Vancouver Canucks	70	38	29	3	208	191	79
Seattle Totems	70	37	28	5	262	222	79
Spokane Comets	70	33	34	3	247	258	69
Victoria Cougars	70	27	41	2	220	267	56
Edmonton Flyers	70	27	43	0	229	295	54
Winnipeg Warriors	70	21	45	4	191	259	46

1961-62

American Hockey League

Eastern Division	GP	W	L	T	GF	GA	Pts
*Springfield Indians	70	45	22	3	292	194	93
Hershey Bears	70	37	28	5	236	213	79
Providence Reds	70	36	32	2	261	267	74
Quebec Aces	70	30	36	4	208	207	64
Western Division							
Cleveland Barons	70	39	28	3	255	203	81
Buffalo Bisons	70	36	31	3	247	219	75
Rochester Americans	70	33	31	6	234	240	72
Pittsburgh Hornets	70	10	58	2	177	367	22

Eastern Professional Hockey League

	GP	W	L	T	GF	GA	Pts
*Hull-Ottawa Canadiens	70	38	21	11	233	172	87
Kingston Frontenacs	70	38	24	8	274	224	84
Kitchener Beavers	70	36	24	10	263	217	82
Sudbury Wolves	70	27	31	12	235	271	66
North Bay Trappers	70	23	37	10	186	229	56
Soo Greyhounds	70	17	42	11	207	285	45

International Hockey League

	GP	W	L	T	GF	GA	Pts
*Muskegon Zephyrs	68	43	23	2	334	242	88
St. Paul Saints	68	42	25	1	291	209	85
Minneapolis Millers	68	41	26	1	261	234	83
Omaha Knights	68	37	28	3	264	227	77
Fort Wayne Komets	68	33	31	4	265	245	70
Indianapolis Chiefs	68	19	49	0	220	348	38
Toledo Mercurys	68	17	50	1	222	352	35

Eastern Hockey League

North Division	GP	W	L	T	GF	GA	Pts
Clinton Comets	68	45	22	1	314	204	91
*Johnstown Jets	68	41	26	1	296	255	83
New Haven Blades	68	34	34	0	239	224	68
Long Island Ducks	68	26	41	1	234	266	53
Southern Division							
Greensboro Generals	68	36	30	2	284	258	74
Knoxville Knights	68	30	35	3	216	256	63
Philadelphia Ramblers	68	28	38	2	265	341	58
Charlotte Checkers	68	26	40	2	226	270	54

Western Hockey League

North Division	GP	W	L	T	GF	GA	Pts
*Edmonton Flyers	70	39	27	4	296	245	82
Calgary Stampeders	70	36	29	5	292	271	77
Seattle Totems	70	36	29	5	244	222	77
Vancouver Canucks	70	18	48	4	223	324	40
South Division							
Portland Buckaroos	70	42	23	5	265	203	89
Spokane Comets	70	37	28	5	272	242	79
San Francisco Seals	70	29	39	2	229	270	60
Los Angeles Blades	70	25	39	6	265	259	56

1962-63

American Hockey League

East Division	GP	W	L	T	GF	GA	Pts
Providence Reds	72	38	29	5	239	203	81
Hershey Bears	72	36	28	8	262	231	80
Baltimore Clippers	72	35	30	7	226	244	77
Quebec Aces	72	33	28	11	206	210	77
Springfield Indians	72	33	31	8	282	236	74
West Division							
*Buffalo Bisons	72	41	24	7	237	199	89
Cleveland Barons	72	31	34	7	270	253	69
Rochester Americans	72	24	39	9	241	270	57
Pittsburgh Hornets	72	20	48	4	200	317	44

Eastern Professional Hockey League

	GP	W	L	T	GF	GA	Pts
Kingston Frontenacs	72	42	19	11	300	229	95
*Hull-Ottawa Canadiens	72	40	25	7	279	224	87
Sudbury Wolves	72	27	32	13	294	305	67
St. Louis Braves	72	26	37	9	275	304	61

International Hockey League

	GP	W	L	T	GF	GA	Pts
*Fort Wayne Komets	70	35	30	5	283	255	75
Minneapolis Millers	70	36	32	2	296	301	74
Muskegon Zephyrs	70	34	31	5	328	326	73
Omaha Knights	70	30	35	5	252	248	65
Port Huron Flags	70	28	26	6	246	273	62
St. Paul Saints	70	23	44	3	241	328	49

Eastern Hockey League

Northern Division	GP	W	L	T	GF	GA	Pts
Clinton Comets	68	38	24	6	289	186	82
Long Island Ducks	68	36	28	4	287	261	76
Johnstown Jets	68	34	31	3	254	309	71
Philadelphia Ramblers	68	29	36	3	287	304	61
New Haven Blades	68	27	40	1	249	293	55
Southern Division							
*Greensboro Generals	68	40	26	2	305	263	82
Knoxville Knights	68	37	28	3	295	245	77
Charlotte Checkers	68	35	31	2	242	264	72
Nashville Dixie Flyers	68	16	48	4	181	264	36

Western Hockey League

North Division	GP	W	L	T	GF	GA	Pts
Vancouver Canucks	70	35	31	4	243	234	74
Seattle Totems	70	35	33	2	239	237	72
Edmonton Flyers	70	24	44	2	215	309	50
Calgary Stampeders	70	23	45	2	227	284	48
South Division							
Portland Buckaroos	70	43	21	6	279	184	92
*San Francisco Seals	70	44	25	1	288	219	89
Los Angeles Blades	70	35	32	3	235	226	73
Spokane Comets	70	30	38	2	219	252	62

1963-64

American Hockey League

East Division	GP	W	L	T	GF	GA	Pts
Quebec Aces	72	41	30	1	258	225	83
Hershey Bears	72	36	31	5	236	249	77
Providence Reds	72	32	35	5	248	239	69
Baltimore Clippers	72	32	37	3	200	220	67
Springfield Indians	72	23	44	5	238	292	51
West Division							
Pittsburgh Hornets	72	40	29	3	242	196	83
Rochester Americans	72	40	30	2	256	223	82
*Cleveland Barons	72	37	30	5	239	207	79
Buffalo Bisons	72	25	40	7	194	260	57

Western Hockey League

	GP	W	L	T	GF	GA	Pts
Denver Invaders	70	44	23	3	271	202	91
Portland Buckaroos	70	33	30	7	229	228	73
Los Angeles Blades	70	31	31	8	218	244	70
*San Francisco Seals	70	32	35	3	228	262	67
Seattle Totems	70	29	35	6	247	228	64
Vancouver Canucks	70	26	41	3	229	258	55

Central Professional Hockey League

	GP	W	L	T	GF	GA	Pts
*Omaha Knights	72	44	19	9	311	218	97
St. Paul Rangers	72	38	30	4	259	230	80
Minneapolis Bruins	72	36	29	7	294	270	79
St. Louis Braves	72	33	32	7	316	275	73
Cincinnati Wings	72	12	53	7	207	394	31

International Hockey League

	GP	W	L	T	GF	GA	Pts
*Toledo Blades	70	41	25	4	278	207	86
Fort Wayne Komets	70	41	28	1	322	264	83
Port Huron Flags	70	37	31	2	279	279	76
Windsor Bulldogs	70	32	35	3	226	280	67
Des Moines Oak Leafs	70	31	35	4	272	266	66
Muskegon Zephyrs	70	31	36	3	298	312	65
Chatham Maroons	70	21	44	5	211	278	47

Eastern Hockey League

Northern Division	GP	W	L	T	GF	GA	Pts
Johnstown Jets	72	41	26	5	297	245	87
*Clinton Comets	72	37	28	7	289	215	81
Long Island Ducks	72	32	34	6	245	263	70
New Haven Blades	72	27	42	3	252	296	57
Philadelphia Ramblers	72	21	44	7	261	374	49
Southern Division							
Greensboro Generals	72	41	29	2	294	257	84
Knoxville Knights	72	40	31	1	340	289	81
Nashville Dixie Flyers	72	37	31	4	231	242	78
Charlotte Checkers	72	30	41	1	276	304	61

1964-65

American Hockey League

East Division	GP	W	L	T	GF	GA	Pts
Quebec Aces	72	44	26	2	280	223	90
Hershey Bears	72	36	32	4	246	243	76
Baltimore Clippers	72	35	32	5	275	249	75
Springfield Indians	72	29	39	4	237	273	62
Providence Reds	72	20	50	2	193	312	42
West Division							
*Rochester Americans	72	48	21	3	310	199	99
Buffalo Bisons	72	40	26	6	261	218	86
Pittsburgh Hornets	72	29	36	7	228	256	65
Cleveland Barons	72	24	43	5	228	285	53

Western Hockey League

	GP	W	L	T	GF	GA	Pts
*Portland Buckaroos	70	42	23	5	267	216	89
Seattle Totems	70	36	30	4	204	198	76
Vancouver Canucks	70	32	32	6	262	243	70
Victoria Cougars	70	32	36	2	246	242	66
San Francisco Seals	70	31	37	2	255	283	64
Los Angeles Blades	70	26	41	3	217	269	55

Central Professional Hockey League

	GP	W	L	T	GF	GA	Pts
*St. Paul Rangers	70	41	23	6	281	223	88
Omaha Knights	70	37	25	8	246	238	82
Minneapolis Bruins	70	36	27	7	239	193	79
Tulsa Oilers	70	35	27	8	254	224	78
Memphis Wings	70	26	35	9	243	245	61
St. Louis Braves	70	13	51	6	189	329	32

International Hockey League

	GP	W	L	T	GF	GA	Pts
Port Huron Flags	70	43	22	5	336	258	91
*Fort Wayne Komets	70	40	25	5	344	240	85
Des Moines Oak Leafs	70	39	26	5	303	277	83
Toledo Blades	70	32	36	2	297	327	66
Dayton Gems	70	23	45	2	283	396	48
Muskegon Zephyrs	70	22	45	3	320	385	47

Eastern Hockey League

North Division	GP	W	L	T	GF	GA	Pts
*Long Island Ducks	72	50	20	2	336	182	102
Clinton Comets	72	42	29	1	279	233	85
Johnstown Jets	72	41	31	0	330	294	82
New Jersey Devils	72	34	34	4	297	312	72
New York Rovers	72	25	39	8	206	270	58
New Haven Blades	72	19	52	1	238	379	39
South Division							
Nashville Dixie Flyers	72	54	18	0	349	296	108
Greensboro Generals	72	37	33	2	333	301	76
Charlotte Checkers	72	35	35	2	262	286	72
Knoxville Knights	72	34	36	2	281	284	70
Jacksonville Rockets	72	13	57	2	211	385	28

1965-66

American Hockey League

East Division	GP	W	L	T	GF	GA	Pts
Quebec Aces	72	47	21	4	337	226	98
Hershey Bears	72	37	30	5	268	232	79
Springfield Indians	72	31	38	3	207	235	65
Baltimore Clippers	72	27	43	2	212	254	56
Providence Reds	72	20	49	3	184	310	43
West Division							
*Rochester Americans	72	46	21	5	288	221	97
Cleveland Barons	72	38	32	2	243	217	78
Pittsburgh Hornets	72	38	33	1	236	218	77
Buffalo Bisons	72	29	40	3	215	243	61

Western Hockey League

	GP	W	L	T	GF	GA	Pts
Portland Buckaroos	72	43	24	5	271	218	91
*Victoria Cougars	72	40	28	4	260	243	84
Vancouver Canucks	72	33	35	4	252	233	70
San Francisco Seals	72	32	36	4	243	248	68
Seattle Totems	72	32	37	3	231	256	67
Los Angeles Blades	72	22	48	2	236	329	46

Central Professional Hockey League

	GP	W	L	T	GF	GA	Pts
Minnesota Rangers	70	34	25	11	229	197	79
*Oklahoma City Blazers	70	31	26	13	188	203	75
Tulsa Oilers	70	29	29	12	218	198	70
St. Louis Braves	70	30	31	9	226	217	69
Houston Apollos	70	27	32	11	221	244	65
Memphis Wings	70	25	33	12	200	223	62

International Hockey League

	GP	W	L	T	GF	GA	Pts
Muskegon Mohawks	70	46	19	5	376	314	97
Fort Wayne Komets	70	38	26	6	312	289	82
*Port Huron Flags	70	34	32	4	308	274	72
Dayton Gems	70	33	35	2	347	322	68
Des Moines Oak Leafs	70	29	40	1	263	319	59
Toledo Blades	70	20	48	2	248	366	42

Eastern Hockey League

North Division	GP	W	L	T	GF	GA	Pts
Long Island Ducks	72	46	23	3	292	208	95
Clinton Comets	72	41	28	3	276	212	85
Johnstown Jets	72	39	31	2	303	267	80
New Haven Blades	72	27	43	2	283	353	56
New Jersey Devils	72	25	43	4	239	311	54
South Division							
*Nashville Dixie Flyers	72	42	23	7	277	179	91
Charlotte Checkers	72	42	30	0	300	251	84
Greensboro Generals	72	37	31	4	291	263	78
Knoxville Knights	72	34	36	2	278	261	70
Jacksonville Rockets	72	12	57	3	207	441	27

1966-67

American Hockey League

East Division	GP	W	L	T	GF	GA	Pts
Hershey Bears	72	38	24	10	273	216	86
Baltimore Clippers	72	35	27	10	252	247	80
Quebec Aces	72	35	30	7	275	249	77
Springfield Indians	72	32	31	9	267	261	73
Providence Reds	72	13	46	13	210	329	39
West Division							
*Pittsburgh Hornets	72	41	21	10	282	209	92
Rochester Americans	72	38	25	9	300	223	85
Cleveland Barons	72	36	27	9	284	230	81
Buffalo Bisons	72	14	51	7	207	386	35

Western Hockey League

	GP	W	L	T	GF	GA	Pts
Portland Buckaroos	72	41	24	7	255	209	89
*Seattle Totems	72	39	26	7	220	195	85
Vancouver Canucks	72	38	32	2	228	215	78
California Seals	72	32	30	10	228	242	74
Victoria Cougars	72	30	34	8	224	232	68
Los Angeles Blades	72	29	38	5	260	286	63
San Diego Gulls	72	22	47	3	222	266	47

Central Professional Hockey League

	GP	W	L	T	GF	GA	Pts
*Oklahoma City Blazers	70	38	23	9	233	196	85
Omaha Knights	70	36	24	10	262	203	82
Houston Apollos	70	32	28	10	255	229	74
Memphis Wings	70	30	32	8	230	259	68
St. Louis Braves	70	24	26	20	229	236	68
Tulsa Oilers	70	14	41	15	183	269	43

International Hockey League

	GP	W	L	T	GF	GA	Pts
Dayton Gems	72	44	25	3	315	282	91
Fort Wayne Komets	72	40	31	1	274	234	81
*Toledo Blades	72	39	31	2	284	247	80
Des Moines Oak Leafs	72	36	32	4	256	264	76
Port Huron Flags	72	34	33	5	314	300	73
Muskegon Mohawks	72	27	43	2	262	299	56
Columbus Checkers	72	23	48	1	294	373	47

Eastern Hockey League

North Division	GP	W	L	T	GF	GA	Pts
Clinton Comets	72	44	26	2	285	202	90
New Jersey Devils	72	39	30	3	292	210	81
Johnstown Jets	72	34	36	2	267	290	70
Long Island Ducks	72	29	39	4	198	233	62
New Haven Blades	72	27	44	1	241	346	55
South Division							
*Nashville Dixie Flyers	72	51	19	2	287	169	104
Charlotte Checkers	72	36	33	3	259	235	75
Greensboro Generals	72	35	37	0	265	279	70
Knoxville Knights	72	27	42	3	232	268	57
Florida Rockets	72	27	43	2	222	315	56

1967-68

American Hockey League

Eastern Division	GP	W	L	T	GF	GA	Pts
Hershey Bears	72	34	30	8	270	248	76
Springfield Kings	72	31	33	8	247	276	70
Providence Reds	72	30	33	9	235	272	69
Baltimore Clippers	72	28	34	10	2136	255	66
Western Division							
*Rochester Americans	72	38	25	9	273	233	85
Quebec Aces	72	33	28	11	277	240	77
Buffalo Bisons	72	32	28	12	239	224	76
Cleveland Barons	72	28	30	14	236	255	70

Western Hockey League

	GP	W	L	T	GF	GA	Pts
Portland Buckaroos	72	40	26	6	246	168	86
*Seattle Totems	72	35	30	7	207	199	77
San Diego Gulls	72	31	36	5	241	236	67
Phoenix Roadrunners	72	28	40	4	215	276	60
Vancouver Canucks	72	26	41	5	213	258	57

Central Professional Hockey League

Northern Division	GP	W	L	T	GF	GA	Pts
*Tulsa Oilers	70	37	22	11	278	241	85
Kansas City Blues	70	31	29	10	249	243	72
Memphis South Stars	70	24	34	12	206	244	60
Omaha Knights	70	14	46	10	167	272	38
Southern Division							
Oklahoma City Blazers	70	38	20	12	245	174	88
Fort Worth Wings	70	34	25	11	245	199	79
Dallas Black Hawks	70	30	29	11	230	251	71
Houston Apollos	70	28	31	11	220	216	67

International Hockey League

	GP	W	L	T	GF	GA	Pts
*Muskegon Mohawks	72	43	17	12	305	216	98
Dayton Gems	72	33	27	12	332	275	78
Columbus Checkers	72	32	30	10	312	300	74
Fort Wayne Komets	72	30	29	13	282	272	73
Toledo Blades	72	29	29	14	261	307	72
Port Huron Flags	72	25	36	11	269	243	61
Des Moines Oak Leafs	72	19	43	10	244	292	48

Eastern Hockey League

Northern Division	GP	W	L	T	GF	GA	Pts
*Clinton Comets	72	57	5	10	436	185	124
New Haven Blades	72	43	22	7	387	242	93
Johnstown Jets	72	38	25	9	386	273	85
Long Island Ducks	72	29	36	7	333	329	65
New Jersey Devils	72	17	51	4	251	458	38
Syracuse Blazers	72	12	57	3	277	583	27
Southern Division							
Greensboro Generals	72	46	20	6	364	248	98
Charlotte Checkers	72	42	21	9	333	243	93
Nashville Dixie Flyers	72	42	23	7	341	256	91
Florida Rockets	72	30	34	8	262	288	68
Knoxville Knights	72	23	43	6	250	294	52
Salem Rebels	72	11	53	8	211	432	30

1968-69

American Hockey League

Eastern Division	GP	W	L	T	GF	GA	Pts
*Hershey Bears	74	41	27	6	307	234	88
Baltimore Clippers	74	33	34	7	266	257	73
Providence Reds	74	32	36	6	242	284	70
Springfield Kings	74	27	30	11	257	174	65
Western Division							
Buffalo Bisons	74	41	18	15	282	192	97
Cleveland Barons	74	30	32	12	213	245	72
Quebec Aces	74	26	34	14	235	258	66
Rochester Americans	74	25	38	11	237	295	61

Western Hockey League

	GP	W	L	T	GF	GA	Pts
Portland Buckaroos	74	40	18	16	291	201	96
*Vancouver Canucks	74	36	24	14	259	223	86
San Diego Gulls	74	33	29	12	273	260	78
Seattle Totems	74	33	30	11	236	238	77
Phoenix Roadrunners	74	21	41	12	199	282	54
Denver Spurs	74	23	44	7	254	308	53

Central Professional Hockey League

Northern Division	GP	W	L	T	GF	GA	Pts
Tulsa Oilers	72	28	28	16	248	238	72
Kansas City Blues	72	26	28	18	236	242	70
Omaha Knights	72	29	32	11	249	252	69
Memphis South Stars	72	14	41	17	206	302	45
Southern Division							
Oklahoma City Blazers	72	40	19	14	295	225	93
*Dallas Black Hawks	72	37	25	10	264	218	84
Houston Apollos	72	34	26	12	224	204	80
Amarillo Wranglers	72	29	32	11	237	259	69
Fort Worth Wings	72	23	29	20	213	232	66

International Hockey League

	GP	W	L	T	GF	GA	Pts
*Dayton Gems	72	40	21	11	313	227	91
Toledo Blades	72	41	23	8	282	235	90
Muskegon Mohawks	72	34	29	9	332	287	77
Port Huron Flags	72	28	30	14	285	289	70
Fort Wayne Komets	72	24	33	15	235	262	63
Columbus Checkers	72	26	37	9	286	333	61
Des Moines Oak Leafs	72	21	41	10	226	326	52

Eastern Hockey League

Northern Division	GP	W	L	T	GF	GA	Pts
*Clinton Comets	72	44	18	10	284	181	98
Johnstown Jets	72	42	23	7	358	230	91
New Haven Blades	72	39	23	10	343	271	88
Long Island Ducks	72	27	37	8	256	318	62
New Jersey Devils	72	26	39	7	245	301	59
Syracuse Blazers	72	9	59	4	178	401	22
Southern Division							
Greensboro Generals	72	41	22	9	350	279	91
Nashville Dixie Flyers	72	41	25	6	336	253	88
Charlotte Checkers	72	37	29	6	274	281	80
Jacksonville Rockets	72	27	37	8	267	295	62
Salem Rebels	72	24	45	3	240	321	51

1969-70

American Hockey League

Eastern Division	GP	W	L	T	GF	GA	Pts
Montreal Voyageurs	72	43	15	14	327	195	100
Springfield Kings	72	38	29	5	287	287	81
Quebec Aces	72	27	39	6	221	272	60
Providence Reds	72	23	36	3	218	267	49
Western Division							
*Buffalo Bisons	72	40	17	15	280	193	95
Hershey Bears	72	28	28	16	247	249	72
Baltimore Clippers	72	25	30	17	230	252	67
Cleveland Barons	72	23	33	16	222	255	62
Rochester Americans	72	18	38	16	253	315	52

Western Hockey League

	GP	W	L	T	GF	GA	Pts
*Vancouver Canucks	72	47	17	8	334	219	102
Portland Buckaroos	72	42	23	7	322	241	91
San Diego Gulls	72	33	29	10	263	242	76
Seattle Totems	73	30	35	8	240	260	68
Phoenix Roadrunners	73	27	34	12	252	257	66
Denver Spurs	72	24	37	11	250	316	59
Salt Lake Gold. Eagles	72	15	43	14	240	366	44

• Seattle & Phoenix played extra game to decide fourth place

Central Hockey League

	GP	W	L	T	GF	GA	Pts
*Omaha Knights	72	36	26	10	247	212	82
Iowa Stars	72	35	26	11	252	232	81
Tulsa Oilers	72	35	27	10	230	202	80
Fort Worth Wings	72	31	25	16	217	206	78
Dallas Black Hawks	72	30	37	5	236	241	65
Oklahoma City Blazers	72	26	30	7	233	236	59
Kansas City Blues	72	24	37	11	228	233	59

International Hockey League

Northern Division	GP	W	L	T	GF	GA	Pts
Muskegon Mohawks	72	46	18	8	366	271	100
Port Huron Flags	72	37	28	7	272	270	81
Fort Wayne Komets	72	26	38	8	241	266	60
Flint Generals	72	21	39	12	218	270	54
Southern Division							
*Dayton Gems	72	38	30	4	296	271	80
Toledo Blades	72	32	33	7	241	265	71
Des Moines Oak Leafs	72	31	33	8	261	254	70
Columbus Checkers	72	24	36	12	289	307	60

Eastern Hockey League

Northern Division	GP	W	L	T	GF	GA	Pts
*Clinton Comets	74	50	16	8	394	222	108
New Haven Blades	74	39	20	15	377	244	93
Johnstown Jets	74	27	33	14	318	344	68
Syracuse Blazers	74	23	37	14	292	350	60
Long Island Ducks	74	24	44	6	261	364	54
New Jersey Devils	74	20	48	6	278	440	46
Southern Division							
Greensboro Generals	74	45	22	7	333	241	97
Salem Rebels	74	37	27	10	279	266	84
Charlotte Checkers	74	34	31	9	284	266	77
Jacksonville Rockets	74	27	37	10	282	355	64
Nashville Dixie Flyers	74	27	38	9	279	305	63

1970-71

American Hockey League

East Division	GP	W	L	T	GF	GA	Pts
Providence Reds	72	28	31	13	257	270	69
Montreal Voyageurs	72	27	31	14	215	239	68
*Springfield Kings	72	29	35	8	244	281	66
Quebec Aces	72	25	31	16	211	240	66
West Division							
Baltimore Clippers	72	40	23	9	263	224	89
Cleveland Barons	72	39	26	7	272	208	85
Hershey Bears	72	31	31	10	238	212	72
Rochester Americans	72	25	36	11	222	248	61

WESTERN HOCKEY LEAGUE

	GP	W	L	T	GF	GA	Pts
*Portland Buckaroos	72	48	17	7	306	210	103
Phoenix Roadrunners	72	36	27	9	271	234	81
San Diego Gulls	72	33	27	12	248	223	78
Denver Spurs	72	25	31	16	242	253	66
Seattle Totems	72	27	36	9	223	260	63
Salt Lake Gold. Eagles	72	18	49	5	217	327	41

CENTRAL HOCKEY LEAGUE

	GP	W	L	T	GF	GA	Pts
*Omaha Knights	72	45	16	11	312	216	101
Dallas Black Hawks	72	36	28	8	276	246	80
Fort Worth Wings	72	35	28	9	232	198	79
Oklahoma City Blazers	72	30	30	12	258	273	72
Kansas City Blues	72	30	31	11	214	223	71
Tulsa Oilers	72	27	37	8	252	275	62
Amarillo Wranglers	72	14	47	11	216	329	39

INTERNATIONAL HOCKEY LEAGUE

	GP	W	L	T	GF	GA	Pts
Muskegon Mohawks	72	42	24	6	300	212	91
Des Moines Oak Leafs	72	38	23	11	286	233	87
Dayton Gems	72	36	29	7	263	263	79
Flint Generals	72	33	32	7	247	224	73
Fort Wayne Komets	72	28	32	12	221	233	68
*Port Huron Flags	72	25	36	11	248	292	61
Toledo Hornets	72	17	44	11	211	319	45

EASTERN HOCKEY LEAGUE

Northern Division	GP	W	L	T	GF	GA	Pts
New Haven Blades	74	38	21	15	339	244	91
Syracuse Blazers	74	36	30	8	302	284	80
Johnstown Jets	74	30	29	15	273	297	75
Clinton Comets	74	31	32	11	257	233	73
Long Island Ducks	74	29	35	10	283	296	68
New Jersey Devils	74	22	39	13	282	353	57
Southern Division							
*Charlotte Checkers	74	55	12	7	383	153	117
Greensboro Generals	74	44	21	8	340	234	96
Salem Rebels	74	31	34	9	257	303	71
Nashville Dixie Flyers	74	26	42	5	270	342	57
Jacksonville Rockets	74	11	58	5	206	453	27

1971-72

AMERICAN HOCKEY LEAGUE

Eastern Division	GP	W	L	T	GF	GA	Pts
Boston Braves	76	41	21	14	260	191	96
*Nova Scotia Voyageurs	76	41	21	14	274	202	96
Springfield Kings	76	31	30	15	273	266	77
Providence Reds	76	28	37	11	250	274	67
Rochester Americans	76	28	38	10	242	311	66
Western Division							
Baltimore Clippers	76	34	31	11	240	249	79
Hershey Bears	76	33	30	13	266	253	79
Cincinnati Swords	76	30	28	18	252	258	78
Cleveland Barons	76	32	34	10	269	263	74
Richmond Robins	76	29	34	13	237	218	71
Tidewater Wings	76	22	45	9	197	275	53

WESTERN HOCKEY LEAGUE

	GP	W	L	T	GF	GA	Pts
*Denver Spurs	72	44	20	8	293	209	96
Phoenix Roadrunners	72	40	27	5	283	235	85
Portland Buckaroos	72	38	31	3	301	271	79
San Diego Gulls	72	32	31	9	241	243	73
Salt Lake Gold. Eagles	72	29	33	10	250	254	68
Seattle Totems	72	12	53	7	175	331	31

CENTRAL HOCKEY LEAGUE

	GP	W	L	T	GF	GA	Pts
*Dallas Black Hawks	72	43	22	7	317	232	93
Tulsa Oilers	72	34	30	8	256	243	76
Fort Worth Wings	72	30	30	12	238	246	72
Oklahoma City Blazers	72	29	34	9	235	273	67
Omaha Knights	72	29	35	8	241	260	66
Kansas City Blues	72	21	35	16	244	277	58

INTERNATIONAL HOCKEY LEAGUE

Northern Division	GP	W	L	T	GF	GA	Pts
Muskegon Mohawks	72	49	21	2	328	231	100
*Port Huron Wings	72	37	31	4	276	262	78
Flint Generals	72	31	36	5	253	259	67
Toledo Hornets	72	26	46	0	270	371	52
Southern Division							
Dayton Gems	72	49	23	0	319	243	98
Fort Wayne Komets	72	37	33	2	291	244	76
Des Moines Oak Leafs	72	35	34	3	296	278	73
Columbus Seals	72	15	55	2	220	365	32

EASTERN HOCKEY LEAGUE

Northern Division	GP	W	L	T	GF	GA	Pts
Syracuse Blazers	75	38	27	10	340	276	86
Johnstown Jets	75	33	28	14	290	269	80
Clinton Comets	75	30	32	13	272	278	73
New Haven Blades	75	30	35	10	307	333	70
Long Island Ducks	75	25	40	10	237	294	60
Jersey Devils							
Southern Division							
*Charlotte Checkers	73	47	18	8	330	180	102
Greensboro Generals	73	34	27	12	284	252	80
Roanoke Valley Rebels	73	30	33	10	241	266	70
St. Petersburg Suns	73	27	34	12	248	291	66
Jacksonville Rockets §	28	6	20	2	81	160	14

§ folded 12/13/72

1972-73

WORLD HOCKEY ASSOCIATION

Eastern Division	GP	W	L	T	GF	GA	Pts
*New England Whalers	78	46	30	2	318	263	94
Cleveland Crusaders	78	43	32	3	287	239	89
Philadelphia Blazers	78	38	40	0	288	305	76
Ottawa Nationals	78	35	39	4	279	301	74
Quebec Nordiques	78	33	40	5	276	313	71
New York Raiders	78	33	43	2	303	334	68
Western Division							
Winnipeg Jets	78	43	31	4	285	249	90
Houston Aeros	78	39	35	4	284	269	82
Los Angeles Sharks	78	37	35	6	259	250	80
Minn. Fighting Saints	78	38	37	3	250	269	79
Alberta Oilers	78	38	37	3	269	256	79
Chicago Cougars	78	26	50	2	245	295	54

AMERICAN HOCKEY LEAGUE

Eastern Division	GP	W	L	T	GF	GA	Pts
Nova Scotia Voyageurs	76	43	18	15	316	191	101
Boston Braves	76	34	29	13	248	256	81
Rochester Americans	76	33	31	12	239	276	78
Providence Reds	76	32	30	14	253	255	78
Springfield Kings	76	18	42	16	265	344	52
N. Haven Nighthawks	76	16	40	20	246	331	52
Western Division							
*Cincinnati Swords	76	54	17	5	351	206	113
Hershey Bears	76	42	23	11	326	231	95
Virginia Wings	76	38	22	16	258	221	92
Richmond Robins	76	30	36	10	272	280	70
Jacksonville Barons	76	23	44	9	251	329	55
Baltimore Clippers	76	17	48	11	210	315	45

WESTERN HOCKEY LEAGUE

	GP	W	L	T	GF	GA	Pts
*Phoenix Roadrunners	72	37	26	9	310	250	83
Salt Lake Gold. Eagles	72	32	25	15	288	259	79
San Diego Gulls	72	32	29	11	239	223	75
Denver Spurs	72	27	32	13	264	275	67
Seattle Totems	72	26	32	14	270	286	66
Portland Buckaroos	72	21	39	12	226	287	54

CENTRAL HOCKEY LEAGUE

	GP	W	L	T	GF	GA	Pts
Dallas Black Hawks	72	38	23	11	256	208	87
*Omaha Knights	72	35	27	10	262	263	80
Fort Worth Wings	72	31	35	6	254	267	68
Tulsa Oilers	72	26	37	9	259	308	61

INTERNATIONAL HOCKEY LEAGUE

North Division	GP	W	L	T	GF	GA	Pts
Flint Generals	74	44	29	1	347	281	89
Port Huron Wings	73	41	31	1	266	237	83
Toledo Hornets	74	36	33	5	257	261	77
Muskegon Mohawks	74	36	34	4	302	259	76
Saginaw Gears	74	30	41	3	305	304	63
South Division							
*Fort Wayne Komets	74	48	23	3	308	219	99
Dayton Gems	73	44	25	4	308	235	92
Des Moines Capitols	74	30	41	3	279	360	63
Columbus Seals	74	10	62	2	177	393	22

EASTERN HOCKEY LEAGUE

Central Division	GP	W	L	T	GF	GA	Pts
Cape Cod Cubs	76	36	29	11	338	314	83
Rhode Island Reds	76	32	35	9	320	307	73
Long Island Ducks	76	26	43	7	287	386	59
Jersey Devils	76	23	41	12	239	300	58
Northern Division							
*Syracuse Blazers	76	63	9	4	453	190	130
Johnstown Jets	76	36	28	12	283	255	84
Clinton Comets	76	18	51	7	256	415	43
New England Blades §	24	9	13	2	91	109	20
§ folded 12/06/73							
Southern Division							
Roanoke Valley Rebels	76	40	25	11	345	276	91
Greensboro Generals	76	40	28	8	391	315	88
Suncoast Suns	76	30	37	9	301	365	69
Charlotte Checkers	76	26	40	10	241	313	62

1973-74

WORLD HOCKEY ASSOCIATION

Eastern Division	GP	W	L	T	GF	GA	Pts
New England Whalers	78	43	31	4	291	260	90
Toronto Toros	78	41	33	4	304	272	86
Cleveland Crusaders	78	37	32	9	266	264	83
Chicago Cougars	78	38	35	5	271	273	81
Quebec Nordiques	78	38	36	4	306	280	80
NY Blades/NJ Knights	78	32	42	4	268	313	68
Western Division							
*Houston Aeros	78	48	25	5	318	219	101
Minn. Fighting Saints	78	44	32	2	332	275	90
Edmonton Oilers	78	38	37	3	268	269	79
Winnipeg Jets	78	34	39	5	264	296	73
Vancouver Blazers	78	27	50	1	278	345	55
Los Angeles Sharks	78	25	53	0	239	339	50

AMERICAN HOCKEY LEAGUE

Northern Division	GP	W	L	T	GF	GA	Pts
Rochester Americans	76	42	21	13	296	248	97
Providence Reds	76	38	26	12	330	244	88
Nova Scotia Voyageurs	76	37	27	12	263	223	86
N. Haven Nighthawks	76	35	31	10	291	275	80
Boston Braves	76	23	40	13	239	297	59
Springfield Kings	76	21	40	15	251	327	57
Southern Division							
Baltimore Clippers	76	42	24	10	310	232	94
*Hershey Bears	76	39	23	14	320	241	92
Cincinnati Swords	76	40	25	11	273	233	91
Richmond Robins	76	22	40	14	248	320	58
Jacksonville Barons	76	24	44	8	244	334	56
Virginia Wings	76	22	44	10	216	307	54

WESTERN HOCKEY LEAGUE

	GP	W	L	T	GF	GA	Pts
*Phoenix Roadrunners	78	43	32	3	300	273	89
Salt Lake Gold. Eagles	78	41	33	4	356	297	86
San Diego Gulls	78	40	33	5	278	281	85
Portland Buckaroos	78	39	33	6	292	258	84
Seattle Totems	78	32	42	4	288	319	68
Denver Spurs	78	28	50	0	249	335	56

CENTRAL HOCKEY LEAGUE

	GP	W	L	T	GF	GA	Pts
Oklahoma City Blazers	72	36	25	11	280	230	83
Omaha Knights	72	34	23	15	259	217	83
*Dallas Black Hawks	72	29	26	17	220	227	75
Fort Worth Wings	72	30	28	14	237	241	74
Tulsa Oilers	72	28	31	13	233	239	69
Albuquerque 6-Guns	72	16	40	18	188	263	48

INTERNATIONAL HOCKEY LEAGUE

North Division	GP	W	L	T	GF	GA	Pts
Muskegon Mohawks	76	44	62	6	272	234	94
Saginaw Gears	76	38	34	4	310	282	80
Toledo Hornets	76	33	42	1	260	302	67
Flint Generals	76	30	43	3	251	288	63
Port Huron Wings	76	29	44	3	229	268	61
South Division							
*Des Moines Capitols	76	45	25	6	316	247	96
Columbus Owls	76	40	34	2	288	270	82
Dayton Gems	76	38	35	3	272	247	79
Fort Wayne Komets	76	31	45	0	245	305	62

EASTERN HOCKEY LEAGUE

- *EHL folds to become NAHL and SHL*

NORTH AMERICAN HOCKEY LEAGUE

	GP	W	L	T	GF	GA	Pts
*Syracuse Blazers	74	54	16	4	358	218	112
Maine Nordiques	74	45	26	3	393	339	93
Long Island Cougars	74	35	36	3	310	274	73
Cape Cod Cubs	74	34	39	1	338	345	69
Johnstown Jets	74	32	38	4	267	302	68
Binghamton Dusters	74	28	41	5	275	356	61
Mohawk Valley Comets	74	20	52	2	238	367	42

SOUTHERN HOCKEY LEAGUE

	GP	W	L	T	GF	GA	Pts
*Roanoke Valley Rebels	72	53	19	0	366	244	106
Charlotte Checkers	71	44	27	1	309	227	89
Greensboro Generals	71	33	37	1	285	310	67
Winston-Salem P. Bears	72	26	44	2	283	363	54
Macon Whoopees §	61	22	38	2	244	290	46
Suncoast Suns ¶	31	9	22	0	123	176	18

§ folded 02/15/74 ¶ folded 12/19/73

1974-75

WORLD HOCKEY ASSOCIATION

Eastern Division	GP	W	L	T	GF	GA	Pts
New England Whalers	78	43	30	5	274	279	91
Cleveland Crusaders	78	35	40	3	236	258	73
Chicago Cougars	78	30	47	1	261	312	61
Indianapolis Racers	78	18	57	3	216	338	39
Western Division							
*Houston Aeros	78	53	25	0	369	247	106
San Diego Mariners	78	43	31	4	326	268	90
Minn. Fighting Saints	78	42	33	3	308	279	87
Phoenix Roadrunners	78	39	31	8	300	264	86
Michigan-Baltimore	78	21	53	4	205	341	46
Canadian Division							
Quebec Nordiques	78	46	32	0	331	299	92
Toronto Toros	78	43	33	2	349	304	88
Winnipeg Jets	78	38	35	5	322	293	81
Vancouver Blazers	78	37	39	2	256	270	76
Edmonton Oilers	78	36	38	4	279	279	76

AMERICAN HOCKEY LEAGUE

Northern Division	GP	W	L	T	GF	GA	Pts
Providence Reds	76	43	21	12	317	263	98
Rochester Americans	76	42	25	9	317	243	93
Nova Scotia Voyageurs	75	40	26	9	270	227	89
*Springfield Indians	75	33	30	12	299	256	78
N. Haven Nighthawks	76	30	35	11	282	302	71
Southern Division							
Virginia Wings	75	31	31	13	254	250	75
Richmond Robins	75	29	39	7	261	293	65
Hershey Bears	75	27	38	10	259	303	64
Syracuse Eagles	75	21	43	11	254	332	53
Baltimore Clippers §	46	14	22	10	136	180	38

§ folded 01/23/75

CENTRAL HOCKEY LEAGUE

North Division	GP	W	L	T	GF	GA	Pts
*Salt Lake Gold. Eagles	78	43	24	11	317	245	97
Denver Spurs	78	36	29	13	285	263	85
Omaha Knights	78	34	33	11	254	268	79
Seattle Totems	78	29	38	11	258	296	69
South Division							
Dallas Black Hawks	78	40	30	8	302	259	88
Oklahoma City Blazers	78	33	33	12	267	267	78
Tulsa Oilers	78	27	41	10	262	289	64
Fort Worth Texans	78	26	40	12	264	322	64

INTERNATIONAL HOCKEY LEAGUE

North Division	GP	W	L	T	GF	GA	Pts
Muskegon Mohawks	75	48	24	3	325	240	99
Flint Generals	75	44	26	5	287	220	93
Saginaw Gears	75	43	29	3	302	259	89
Port Huron Flags	76	35	38	3	255	270	73
Kalamazoo Wings	75	17	53	5	203	318	39
Lansing Lancers §	41	12	28	1	145	216	25
§ folded 01/16/75							
South Division							
Dayton Gems	75	46	26	3	297	256	95
Columbus Owls	76	40	32	4	307	275	84
*Toledo Goaldiggers	76	34	38	4	285	275	72
Des Moines Capitols	76	31	38	7	253	264	69
Fort Wayne Komets	76	26	44	6	247	313	58

NORTH AMERICAN HOCKEY LEAGUE

	GP	W	L	T	GF	GA	Pts
Syracuse Blazers	74	46	25	3	345	232	95
Philadelphia Firebirds	74	40	31	3	310	289	83
Binghamton Dusters	74	39	32	3	293	285	81
*Johnstown Jets	74	38	32	4	274	255	80
Cape Cod Codders	74	32	38	4	319	310	68
Mohawk Valley Comets	74	31	38	5	312	345	67
Long Island Cougars	74	29	46	5	271	280	63
Maine Nordiques	74	27	46	1	266	394	55

SOUTHERN HOCKEY LEAGUE

	GP	W	L	T	GF	GA	Pts
*Charlotte Checkers	72	50	21	1	370	256	101
Hampton Gulls	72	43	28	1	323	262	87
Winston-Salem P. Bears	72	32	40	0	300	345	64
Roanoke Valley Rebels	72	29	41	2	296	304	60
Greensboro Generals	72	23	47	2	262	384	48

1975-76

WORLD HOCKEY ASSOCIATION

Eastern Division	GP	W	L	T	GF	GA	Pts
Indianapolis Racers	80	35	39	6	245	247	76
Cleveland Crusaders	80	35	40	5	273	279	75
New England Whalers	80	33	40	7	255	290	73
Cincinnati Stingers	80	35	44	1	285	340	71
Western Division							
Houston Aeros	80	53	27	0	205	341	263
Phoenix Roadrunners	80	39	35	6	205	302	287
San Diego Mariners	80	36	38	6	205	303	290
Minn. Fighting Saints §	59	30	25	4	205	211	212
Denver-Ottawa ¶	41	14	26	1	205	134	172
§ folded 02/27/76 ¶ folded 01/17/76							
Canadian Division							
*Winnipeg Jets	81	52	27	2	345	254	106
Quebec Nordiques	81	50	27	4	371	316	104
Calgary Cowboys	80	41	35	4	307	282	86
Edmonton Oilers	81	27	49	5	268	345	59
Toronto Toros	81	24	52	5	335	398	53

AMERICAN HOCKEY LEAGUE

Northern Division	GP	W	L	T	GF	GA	Pts
*Nova Scotia Voyageurs	76	48	20	8	326	209	104
Rochester Americans	76	42	25	9	304	243	93
Providence Reds	76	34	34	8	294	300	76
Springfield Indians	76	33	39	4	267	321	70
Southern Division							
Hershey Bears	76	39	31	6	304	275	84
Richmond Robins	76	29	39	8	262	297	66
N. Haven Nighthawks	76	29	39	8	261	295	66
Baltimore Clippers	76	21	48	7	238	316	49

CENTRAL HOCKEY LEAGUE

	GP	W	L	T	GF	GA	Pts
*Tulsa Oilers	76	45	21	10	301	228	100
Dallas Black Hawks	76	41	24	11	282	211	93
Salt Lake Gold. Eagles	76	37	35	4	300	299	78
Oklahoma City Blazers	76	32	34	10	256	263	74
Fort Worth Texans	76	29	31	16	287	271	74
Tucson Mavericks	76	14	53	9	242	396	37

INTERNATIONAL HOCKEY LEAGUE

North Division	GP	W	L	T	GF	GA	Pts
Saginaw Gears	78	43	26	9	339	293	95
Port Huron Flags	78	36	31	11	304	291	83
Flint Generals	78	34	30	14	285	254	82
Muskegon Mohawks	78	34	31	13	260	238	81
Kalamazoo Wings	78	27	41	10	273	326	64
South Division							
*Dayton Gems	78	47	21	10	340	240	104
Fort Wayne Komets	78	28	36	14	289	309	70
Toledo Goaldiggers	78	27	37	14	269	293	68
Columbus Owls	78	24	47	7	251	366	55

NORTH AMERICAN HOCKEY LEAGUE

Eastern Division	GP	W	L	T	GF	GA	Pts
Beauce Jaros	74	54	18	2	462	306	110
Syracuse Blazers	74	38	33	3	284	278	79
Mohawk Valley Comets	74	30	40	4	306	354	64
Cape Cod Codders §	74	24	25	3	244	227	51
Maine Nordiques	74	18	55	1	295	450	37
§ folded 02/13/76							
Western Division							
Johnstown Jets	74	47	25	2	346	257	96
*Philadelphia Firebirds	74	45	29	0	373	319	90
Erie Blades	74	37	36	1	310	298	75
Buffalo Norsemen	74	30	44	0	323	375	60
Binghamton Dusters	74	27	45	2	258	337	56

SOUTHERN HOCKEY LEAGUE

	GP	W	L	T	GF	GA	Pts
*Charlotte Checkers	72	42	20	10	302	206	94
Hampton Gulls	72	33	23	16	262	234	82
Winston-Salem P. Bears	72	30	29	13	252	253	73
Roanoke Valley Rebels	72	29	28	15	239	238	73
Tidewater Sharks	72	24	34	14	230	260	62
Greensboro Generals	72	18	42	12	221	317	48

1976-77

WORLD HOCKEY ASSOCIATION

Eastern Division	GP	W	L	T	GF	GA	Pts
*Quebec Nordiques	81	47	31	3	353	295	97
Cincinnati Stingers	81	39	37	5	354	303	83
Indianapolis Racers	81	36	37	8	276	305	80
New England Whalers	81	35	40	6	275	290	76
Birmingham Bulls	81	31	46	4	289	309	66
Minn. Fighting Saints §	42	19	18	5	136	129	43
§ folded 01/17/76							
Western Division							
Houston Aeros	80	50	24	6	320	241	106
Winnipeg Jets	80	46	32	2	366	291	94
San Diego Mariners	81	40	37	4	284	283	84
Edmonton Oilers	81	34	43	4	243	304	72
Calgary Cowboys	81	31	43	7	252	296	69
Phoenix Roadrunners	80	28	48	4	281	383	60

AMERICAN HOCKEY LEAGUE

	GP	W	L	T	GF	GA	Pts
*Nova Scotia Voyageurs	80	52	22	6	308	225	110
N. Haven Nighthawks	80	43	31	6	333	287	92
Rochester Americans	80	42	33	5	320	273	89
Hershey Bears	80	36	38	6	282	293	78
Springfield Indians	80	28	51	1	302	390	57
Rhode Island Reds	80	25	51	4	282	359	54

CENTRAL HOCKEY LEAGUE

	GP	W	L	T	GF	GA	Pts
*Kansas City Blues	76	46	21	9	322	225	101
Dallas Black Hawks	76	35	25	16	281	231	86
Tulsa Oilers	76	37	29	10	314	289	84
Fort Worth Texans	76	35	32	9	272	261	79
Salt Lake Gold. Eagles	76	31	39	6	276	288	68
Oklahoma City Blazers	76	15	53	8	245	416	38

INTERNATIONAL HOCKEY LEAGUE

North Division	GP	W	L	T	GF	GA	Pts
*Saginaw Gears	78	40	27	11	338	292	91
Kalamazoo Wings	78	38	27	13	325	290	89
Flint Generals	78	35	33	10	342	306	80
Muskegon Mohawks	78	31	36	11	294	322	73
Port Huron Flags	78	27	43	8	268	328	62
South Division							
Toledo Goaldiggers	78	40	31	7	321	317	87
Dayton Gems	78	35	38	5	304	312	75
Fort Wayne Komets	78	32	36	10	301	311	74
Columbus Owls	78	28	35	15	294	309	71

NORTH AMERICAN HOCKEY LEAGUE

	GP	W	L	T	GF	GA	Pts
Syracuse Blazers	73	48	22	3	372	261	99
Maine Nordiques	74	40	29	5	311	284	85
Binghamton Dusters	74	41	31	2	363	324	84
Philadelphia Firebirds	74	38	33	3	319	294	79
Erie Blades	74	37	33	4	257	251	78
Mohawk Valley Comets	74	29	42	3	316	387	61
Johnstown Jets	73	22	49	2	253	334	46
Beauce Jaros §	30	6	22	2	109	165	14

§ folded 12/22/76

SOUTHERN HOCKEY LEAGUE

	GP	W	L	T	GF	GA	Pts
Hampton Gulls	50	32	16	2	198	152	66
Tidewater Sharks §	41	26	13	2	158	131	54
Charlotte Checkers	50	22	25	3	180	186	47
Baltimore Clippers	47	21	24	2	182	169	44
Richmond Wildcats §	38	21	16	1	160	144	43
Greensboro Generals §	40	15	24	1	140	173	31
Winston-Salem P. Twins	42	11	30	1	130	193	23

• SHL folded 01/31/77 • No champion was crowned
§ folded 01/07/77

1977-78

WORLD HOCKEY ASSOCIATION

	GP	W	L	T	GF	GA	Pts
*Winnipeg Jets	80	50	28	2	381	270	102
New England Whalers	80	44	31	5	335	269	93
Houston Aeros	80	42	34	4	296	302	88
Quebec Nordiques	80	40	37	3	349	347	83
Edmonton Oilers	80	38	39	3	309	307	79
Birmingham Bulls	80	36	41	3	287	314	75
Cincinnati Stingers	80	35	42	3	298	332	73
Indianapolis Racers	80	24	51	5	267	353	53
Soviet All Stars	8	3	4	1	27	36	7
Czechoslovakia	8	1	6	1	21	40	3

• Games vs. Soviet All-Stars and Czechoslovakia counted in standings

AMERICAN HOCKEY LEAGUE

Northern Division	GP	W	L	T	GF	GA	Pts
*Maine Mariners	80	43	28	9	305	256	95
Nova Scotia Voyageurs	81	37	28	16	304	250	90
Springfield Indians	81	39	33	9	348	350	87
Binghamton Whalers	81	27	46	8	287	377	62
Southern Division							
Rochester Americans	81	43	31	7	332	296	93
N. Haven Nighthawks	80	38	31	11	313	292	87
Philadelphia Firebirds	81	35	35	11	294	290	81
Hershey Bears	81	27	44	10	281	324	64
Hampton Gulls	46	15	28	3	142	171	33

§ folded 02/02/78

CENTRAL HOCKEY LEAGUE

	GP	W	L	T	GF	GA	Pts
*Fort Worth Texans	76	44	29	3	262	251	91
Salt Lake Gold. Eagles	76	42	31	3	283	238	87
Dallas Black Hawks	77	38	36	3	204	281	79
Tulsa Oilers	76	34	39	3	264	273	71
K.C. Red Wings	76	33	40	3	266	257	69
Phoenix Roadrunners §	27	4	20	3	75	134	11

§ folded 12/13/78

INTERNATIONAL HOCKEY LEAGUE

North Division	GP	W	L	T	GF	GA	Pts
Saginaw Gears	80	40	28	12	360	278	92
Kalamazoo Wings	80	35	31	14	315	288	84
Flint Generals	80	36	34	10	364	381	82
Port Huron Flags	80	33	32	15	322	331	81
Muskegon Mohawks	80	27	42	11	290	322	65
South Division							
Fort Wayne Komets	80	40	23	17	305	287	97
*Toledo Goaldiggers	80	34	28	18	331	316	86
Milwaukee Admirals	80	27	38	15	257	299	69
Dayton-G. Rapids Owls	80	27	43	10	290	332	64

PACIFIC HOCKEY LEAGUE

	GP	W	L	T	GF	GA	Pts
*San Fran. Shamrocks	42	24	17	1	185	156	49
Phoenix Roadrunners	42	24	17	1	195	168	49
San Diego Mariners	42	20	22	0	171	175	40
Long Beach	42	15	27	0	163	217	30

1978-79

World Hockey Association

	GP	W	L	T	GF	GA	Pts
Edmonton Oilers	80	48	30	2	340	266	98
Quebec Nordiques	80	41	34	5	288	271	87
*Winnipeg Jets	80	39	35	6	307	306	84
New England Whalers	80	37	34	9	298	287	83
Cincinnati Stingers	80	33	41	6	274	284	72
Birmingham Bulls	80	32	42	6	286	311	70
Indianapolis Racers §	25	5	18	2	78	130	12
Soviet All Stars	6	4	1	1	27	20	9
Czechoslovakia	6	1	4	1	14	33	3
Finland	1	0	1	0	4	8	0

• Soviet All Stars, Czechoslovakia and Finland games counted in the standings
§ folded 12/15/78

American Hockey League

Northern Division	GP	W	L	T	GF	GA	Pts
*Maine Mariners	80	45	22	13	350	252	103
New Brunswick Hawks	80	41	29	10	315	288	92
Nova Scotia Voyageurs	80	39	37	4	313	302	82
Springfield Indians	80	33	38	9	289	290	75
Southern Division							
N. Haven Nighthawks	80	46	25	9	346	271	101
Hershey Bears	79	35	36	8	311	324	78
Binghamton Whalers	79	32	42	5	300	320	69
Rochester Americans	80	26	42	12	289	349	64
Philadelphia Firebirds	80	23	49	8	230	347	54

Central Hockey League

	GP	W	L	T	GF	GA	Pts
Salt Lake Gold. Eagles	76	47	22	7	314	209	101
*Dallas Black Hawks	76	45	28	3	339	289	93
Kansas City Red Wings	76	37	36	3	301	306	77
Fort Worth Texans	76	33	39	4	260	277	70
Oklahoma City Stars	76	34	41	1	277	311	69
Tulsa Oilers	76	21	51	4	258	357	46

International Hockey League

North Division	GP	W	L	T	GF	GA	Pts
Port Huron Flags	80	44	29	7	393	292	95
*Kalamazoo Wings	80	40	28	12	368	327	92
Saginaw Gears	80	35	35	10	326	322	80
Flint Generals	80	35	40	5	356	349	75
Muskegon Mohawks	80	15	58	7	275	475	37
South Division							
Grand Rapids Owls	80	50	21	9	368	267	109
Fort Wayne Komets	80	45	9	6	386	327	96
Toledo Goaldiggers	80	35	32	13	320	302	83
Milwaukee Admirals	80	21	48	11	260	391	53

Pacific Hockey League

	GP	W	L	T	GF	GA	Pts
Phoenix Roadrunners	60	37	20	3	234	206	77
San Diego Hawks	58	34	22	2	270	192	70
Spokane Flyers	55	32	22	1	246	198	65
Tucson Rustlers	58	20	38	0	215	305	40
Los Angeles Blades §	22	7	14	1	84	190	1
San Fran. Shamrocks	23	4	18	1	68	167	9

• League folded after regular season • No champion was crowned
§ folded 01/03/79 ¶ folded 01/03/79

1979-80

American Hockey League

Northern Division	GP	W	L	T	GF	GA	Pts
New Brunswick Hawks	79	44	27	8	325	271	96
Nova Scotia Voyageurs	79	43	29	7	331	271	93
Maine Mariners	80	41	28	11	307	266	93
Adiron Red Wings	80	32	37	11	297	309	75
Springfield Indians	80	31	37	12	292	302	74
Southern Division							
N. Haven Nighthawks	80	46	25	9	350	305	101
*Hershey Bears	80	35	39	6	289	273	76
Syracuse Firebirds	80	31	42	7	303	364	69
Rochester Americans	80	28	42	10	260	327	66
Binghamton Whalers	80	24	49	7	268	334	55

Central Hockey League

	GP	W	L	T	GF	GA	Pts
*Salt Lake Gold. Eagles	80	49	24	7	342	259	105
Indianapolis Checkers	79	40	32	7	275	238	87
Fort Worth Texans	80	37	34	9	312	298	83
Birmingham Bulls	80	36	39	5	260	295	77
Tulsa Oilers	80	34	37	9	241	256	77
Houston Apollos	80	32	38	10	300	319	74
Oklahoma City Stars	80	33	44	3	261	268	69
Dallas Black Hawks	80	29	43	8	291	334	66
Cincinnati Stingers §	33	11	21	1	108	151	23

§ folded 12/17/80

International Hockey League

North Division	GP	W	L	T	GF	GA	Pts
*Kalamazoo Wings	80	45	26	9	366	274	99
Saginaw Gears	80	43	27	10	349	306	96
Port Huron Flags	80	38	26	16	352	300	92
Flint Generals	80	35	32	13	298	316	83
Muskegon Mohawks	80	29	43	8	317	330	66
South Division							
Fort Wayne Komets	80	40	27	13	343	311	93
Toledo Goaldiggers	80	28	34	18	293	345	74
Milwaukee Admirals	80	29	41	10	327	402	68
Grand Rapids Owls	80	27	41	12	327	340	66
Dayton Gems	80	28	45	7	307	355	63

Eastern Hockey League

	GP	W	L	T	GF	GA	Pts
*Erie Blades	70	46	21	3	349	241	95
Richmond Rifles	69	40	23	6	315	240	86
Baltimore Clippers	69	41	25	4	308	225	86
Utica Mohawks	70	30	34	6	274	287	66
Johnstown Red Wings	70	24	45	1	281	384	49
Hampton Aces	70	17	49	4	214	364	38

1980-81

American Hockey League

Northern Division	GP	W	L	T	GF	GA	Pts
Maine Mariners	80	45	28	7	319	292	97
New Brunswick Hawks	80	37	33	10	317	298	84
Nova Scotia Voyageurs	80	38	37	5	335	298	81
Springfield Indians	80	34	41	5	312	343	73
Southern Division							
Hershey Bears	80	47	24	9	357	299	103
*Adiron Red Wings	80	35	40	5	305	328	75
Binghamton Whalers	80	32	42	6	296	336	70
N. Haven Nighthawks	80	29	40	11	295	321	69
Rochester Americans	80	30	42	8	295	316	68

Central Hockey League

	GP	W	L	T	GF	GA	Pts
Dallas Black Hawks	79	56	16	7	356	233	119
*Salt Lake Gold. Eagles	80	46	29	5	368	295	97
Indianapolis Checkers	80	44	30	6	306	238	94
Oklahoma City Stars	79	39	28	2	312	328	80
Tulsa Oilers	79	33	42	4	285	312	70
Wichita Wind	80	32	45	3	307	346	67
Fort Worth Texans	80	24	53	3	201	309	51
Birmingham Bulls §	58	17	37	4	204	277	38
Houston Apollos ¶	33	12	13	8	97	98	32

§ folded 02/24/81 ¶ folded 01/08/81

International Hockey League

East Division	GP	W	L	T	GF	GA	Pts
*Saginaw Gears	82	45	29	8	392	289	98
Port Huron Flags	82	31	35	16	337	377	78
Flint Generals	82	32	42	8	324	363	72
Toledo Goaldiggers	82	26	47	9	303	392	61
West Division							
Kalamazoo Wings	82	52	20	10	369	244	114
Fort Wayne Komets	82	37	30	15	337	303	89
Milwaukee Admirals	82	32	35	15	354	371	79
Muskegon Mohawks	82	28	45	9	274	351	65

Eastern Hockey League

	GP	W	L	T	GF	GA	Pts
Erie Blades*	72	52	14	6	407	252	110
Richmond Rifles	72	38	29	5	331	295	81
Salem Raiders	72	32	31	9	272	289	73
Baltimore Clippers	72	29	36	7	278	286	65
Hampton Aces	72	17	49	6	282	385	40
Syracuse Hornets §	10	0	9	1	36	99	1

§ folded 11/13/81

1981-82

American Hockey League

Northern Division	GP	W	L	T	GF	GA	Pts
*New Brunswick Hawks	80	48	21	11	338	338	107
Maine Mariners	80	47	26	7	325	325	101
Nova Scotia Voyageurs	80	35	35	10	330	330	80
Springfield Indians	80	32	43	5	278	278	69
Fredericton Express	80	20	55	5	275	275	45
Southern Division							
Binghamton Whalers	80	46	28	6	329	266	98
Rochester Americans	80	40	31	9	325	286	89
N. Haven Nighthawks	80	39	33	8	292	276	86
Hershey Bears	80	36	38	6	316	347	78
Adiron Red Wings	80	34	37	9	299	285	77
Erie Blades	80	22	52	6	317	425	50

Central Hockey League

North Division	GP	W	L	T	GF	GA	Pts
Salt Lake Gold. Eagles	80	47	30	3	368	329	97
Cincinnati Tigers	80	46	30	4	375	340	96
*Indianapolis Checkers	80	42	33	5	319	259	89
Nashville South Stars	80	41	35	4	313	319	86
South Division							
Wichita Wind	80	44	33	3	343	289	91
Tulsa Oilers	80	43	36	1	355	324	87
Dallas Black Hawks	80	37	37	6	394	382	80
Oklahoma City Stars	80	25	54	1	300	397	51
Fort Worth Texans	80	20	57	3	273	401	43

International Hockey League

	GP	W	L	OTL	T	GF	GA	Pts
*Toledo Goaldiggers	82	53	25	1	4	407	320	111
Milwaukee Admirals	82	41	34	2	7	385	351	91
Kalamazoo Wings	82	41	36	2	5	355	333	89
Fort Wayne Komets	82	35	41	5	6	368	375	81
Saginaw Gears	82	36	38	0	8	401	402	80
Flint Generals	82	32	45	5	5	310	353	74
Muskegon Mohawks	82	30	49	1	3	319	411	64

• Teams receive one point for overtime tie and one point for overtime loss

Atlantic Coast Hockey League

	GP	W	L	T	GF	GA	Pts
Salem Raiders	47	32	15	0	246	161	64
*Mohawk Valley Stars	47	28	18	1	225	198	57
Baltimore Skipjacks	48	22	23	3	204	189	47
Winston-Salem T'birds	50	14	33	3	179	265	31
Cape Cod Buccaneers §	39	17	21	1	130	158	35
Schenectady Chiefs ¶	9	4	5	0	38	45	8
Fitchburg Trappers •	6	2	4	0	26	32	4

§ folded 02/01/82 ¶ folded 11/16/81 • folded 11/06/81

1982-83

American Hockey League

Northern Division	GP	W	L	T	GF	GA	Pts
Fredericton Express	80	45	27	8	348	284	98
Nova Scotia Voyageurs	80	41	34	5	378	333	87
Maine Mariners	80	39	33	8	342	309	86
Adiron Red Wings	80	36	39	5	329	343	77
Moncton Alpines	80	34	39	7	304	315	75
Sherbrooke Jets	80	22	54	4	288	390	48
Southern Division							
*Rochester Americans	80	46	25	9	389	325	101
Hershey Bears	80	40	35	5	313	308	85
N. Haven Nighthawks	80	38	34	8	337	329	84
Binghamton Whalers	80	36	36	8	320	333	80
Baltimore Skipjacks	80	35	36	9	362	366	79
St. Catharines Saints	80	33	41	6	335	368	72
Springfield Indians	80	31	43	6	282	324	68

Central Hockey League

	GP	W	L	T	GF	GA	Pts
*Indianapolis Checkers	80	50	28	2	335	242	102
Colorado Flames	80	41	36	3	322	322	85
Birmingham S. Stars	80	41	37	2	297	297	84
Salt Lake Gold. Eagles	80	41	38	1	318	312	83
Tulsa Oilers	80	29	48	3	286	346	61
Wichita Wind	80	29	48	3	286	346	61

International Hockey League

East Division	GP	W	L	OTL	T	GF	GA	Pts
*Toledo Goaldiggers	82	51	21	1	10	362	269	113
Fort Wayne Komets	82	45	26	2	11	377	344	103
Flint Generals	82	35	36	1	11	317	340	82
Saginaw Gears	82	29	44	4	9	332	376	71
West Division								
Milwaukee Admirals	82	43	30	3	9	407	312	98
Kalamazoo Wings	82	32	44	6	6	311	341	76
Muskegon Mohawks	82	29	41	1	12	335	354	71
Peoria Prancers	82	25	47	2	10	330	435	62

Atlantic Coast Hockey League

	GP	W	L	OTL	GF	GA	Pts
Carolina Thunderbirds	68	51	10	7	376	208	111
*Erie Golden Blades	64	39	21	4	345	276	83
Mohawk Valley Stars	65	30	33	2	311	306	54
Virginia Raiders	65	20	36	9	257	306	51
Hampton Roads Gulls §	42	16	24	2	170	213	35
Nashville South Stars	58	11	43	4	239	389	28

• Teams receive one point for overtime loss
§ folded 02/02/83

1983-84

American Hockey League

Northern Division	GP	W	L	T	GF	GA	Pts
Fredericton Express	80	45	30	5	340	262	95
Adiron Red Wings	80	37	29	14	344	330	88
*Maine Mariners	80	33	36	11	310	312	77
Nova Scotia Voyageurs	80	32	37	11	277	288	75
Moncton Alpines	80	32	40	8	251	278	72
Sherbrooke Jets	80	22	53	5	301	419	49
Southern Division							
Baltimore Skipjacks	80	46	24	10	384	304	102
Rochester Americans	80	46	32	2	363	300	94
St. Catharines Saints	80	43	31	6	364	346	92
Springfield Indians	80	39	35	6	344	340	84
N. Haven Nighthawks	80	36	40	4	365	371	76
Binghamton Whalers	80	33	43	4	359	388	70
Hershey Bears	80	28	42	10	320	384	66

International Hockey League

	GP	W	L	OTL	T	GF	GA	Pts
Fort Wayne Komets	82	52	23	1	7	371	273	112
Milwaukee Admirals	82	46	30	3	6	403	335	101
Flint Generals	82	41	32	2	9	375	319	93
*Toledo Goaldiggers	82	41	36	4	5	326	318	91
Kalamazoo Wings	82	37	38	2	7	333	316	83
Peoria Prancers	82	29	48	3	5	298	392	66
Muskegon Mohawks	82	19	58	3	5	282	435	46

Atlantic Coast Hockey League

	GP	W	L	OTL	GF	GA	Pts
Carolina Thunderbirds	72	43	24	5	381	300	92
Erie Golden Blades	72	42	26	4	371	310	91
Virginia Lancers	73	34	37	2	384	400	71
Mohawk Valley Stars	74	28	38	7	322	370	60
Pinebridge Bucks	72	25	47	0	329	422	52
Birmingham Bulls §	3	2	1	0	17	8	4

§ folded 10/26/84

1984-85

American Hockey League

Northern Division	GP	W	L	T	GF	GA	Pts
Maine Mariners	80	38	32	10	296	266	86
Fredericton Express	80	36	36	8	279	301	80
*Sherbrooke Canadiens	80	37	38	5	323	329	79
Nova Scotia Oilers	80	36	37	7	292	295	79
Adiron Red Wings	80	35	37	8	290	336	78
Moncton Gold. Flames	80	32	40	8	291	300	72
Southern Division							
Binghamton Whalers	80	52	20	8	388	265	112
Baltimore Skipjacks	80	45	27	8	326	252	98
Rochester Americans	80	40	27	13	333	301	93
Springfield Indians	80	36	40	4	322	326	76
N. Haven Nighthawks	80	31	41	8	315	341	70
Hershey Bears	80	26	43	11	315	339	63
St. Catharines Saints	80	24	50	6	272	391	54

International Hockey League

East Division	GP	W	L	OTL	T	GF	GA	Pts
Muskegon Mohawks	82	50	29	0	3	374	291	103
Flint Generals	82	43	35	3	4	349	340	93
Kalamazoo Wings	82	40	35	2	7	323	297	89
Toledo Goaldiggers	82	32	45	3	5	292	362	72
West Division								
*Peoria Rivermen	82	48	25	0	9	357	275	105
Fort Wayne Komets	82	37	34	5	11	339	327	90
Salt Lake Gold. Eagles	82	35	39	4	8	332	323	82
Indianapolis Checkers	82	31	47	3	4	264	318	69
Milwaukee Admirals	82	25	52	5	5	292	389	60

Atlantic Coast Hockey League

	GP	W	L	T	GF	GA	Pts
Carolina Thunderbirds	64	53	11	0	374	228	107
*Erie Golden Blades	64	41	23	0	362	261	83
Pinebridge Bucks	64	33	31	0	306	298	72
Virginia Lancers	64	19	45	0	248	434	42
Mohawk Valley Stars	64	14	50	0	290	417	33

1985-86

American Hockey League

Northern Division	GP	W	L	T	GF	GA	Pts
*Adiron Red Wings	80	41	31	8	330	298	90
Maine Mariners	80	40	31	9	274	285	89
Moncton Gold. Flames	80	34	34	12	294	307	80
Fredericton Express	80	35	37	8	319	311	78
Sherbrooke Canadiens	80	33	38	9	340	341	75
Nova Scotia Oilers	80	29	43	8	314	353	66
Southern Division							
Hershey Bears	80	48	29	3	346	292	99
Binghamton Whalers	80	41	34	5	316	290	87
St. Catharines Saints	80	38	37	5	304	308	81
N. Haven Nighthawks	80	36	37	7	340	343	79
Springfield Indians	80	36	39	5	301	309	77
Rochester Americans	80	34	39	7	320	337	75
Baltimore Skipjacks	80	28	44	8	271	304	64

International Hockey League

East Division	GP	W	L	OTL	T	GF	GA	Pts
*Musk. Lumberjacks	82	50	32	5	0	378	294	105
Kalamazoo Wings	82	47	35	6	0	345	314	100
Saginaw Generals	82	41	41	8	0	322	290	90
Toledo Goaldiggers	82	24	58	10	0	305	427	58
Flint Spirits	82	16	66	6	0	271	497	38
West Division								
Fort Wayne Komets	82	52	30	8	0	350	266	112
Milwaukee Admirals	82	48	33	5	1	371	310	102
Peoria Rivermen	82	46	36	5	0	339	300	97
Salt Lake Gold. Eagles	82	44	38	2	0	347	326	90
Indianapolis Checkers	82	41	40	5	1	302	306	88

Atlantic Coast Hockey League

	GP	W	L	T	GF	GA	Pts
Carolina Thunderbirds	62	49	13	0	395	220	104
*Erie Golden Blades	64	34	30	0	371	321	74
Virginia Lancers	61	27	34	0	293	338	61
Mohawk Valley Comets	62	23	39	0	259	332	49
New York Slapshots	59	21	38	0	260	367	43

1986-87

American Hockey League

Northern Division	GP	W	L	T	GF	GA	Pts
Sherbrooke Canadiens	80	50	28	2	328	257	102
Adiron Red Wings	80	44	31	5	329	296	93
Moncton Gold. Flames	80	43	31	6	338	315	92
Nova Scotia Oilers	80	38	39	3	318	315	79
Maine Mariners	80	35	40	5	272	298	75
Fredericton Express	80	32	43	5	292	357	69
Southern Division							
*Rochester Americans	80	47	26	7	315	263	101
Binghamton Whalers	80	47	26	7	309	259	101
N. Haven Nighthawks	80	44	25	11	331	315	99
Hershey Bears	80	43	36	1	329	309	87
Baltimore Skipjacks	80	35	37	8	277	295	78
Springfield Indians	80	34	40	6	296	344	74
Newmarket Saints	80	28	48	4	226	337	60

International Hockey League

East Division	GP	W	L	OTL	GF	GA	Pts
Musk Lumberjacks	82	47	30	5	366	286	99
Saginaw Generals	82	44	32	6	383	344	94
Flint Spirits	82	42	33	7	343	361	91
Kalamazoo Wings	82	36	38	8	331	353	80
West Division							
Fort Wayne Komets	82	48	26	8	343	284	104
*Salt Lake Gold. Eagles	82	39	31	12	360	357	90
Milwaukee Admirals	82	41	37	4	342	358	86
Indianapolis Checkers	82	37	38	7	360	387	81
Peoria Rivermen	82	31	42	9	264	362	71

Atlantic Coast Hockey League

	GP	W	L	T	GF	GA	Pts
*Virginia Lancers	56	36	19	0	280	218	75
Erie Golden Blades	55	28	22	0	250	246	58
Mohawk Valley Comets	54	23	31	0	260	292	49
Carolina Thunderbirds	54	23	31	0	252	278	48

Troy Slapshots folded 11/17/87

1987-88

American Hockey League

Northern Division	GP	W	L	OTL	T	GF	GA	Pts
Maine Mariners	80	44	29	4	7	308	284	99
Fredericton Express	80	42	30	3	8	370	318	95
Sherbrke Canadiens	80	42	34	1	4	316	243	89
Nova Scotia Oilers	80	35	36	2	9	323	343	81
N. Haven Nighthawks	80	33	40	3	7	288	307	76
Moncton Hawks	80	27	45	2	8	286	358	64
Springfield Indians	80	27	45	1	8	269	333	63
Southern Division								
*Hershey Bears	80	50	27	2	3	343	256	105
Rochester Americans	80	46	27	1	7	328	272	100
Adiron Red Wings	80	42	27	4	11	306	275	99
Binghamton Whalers	80	38	34	3	8	353	300	87
Utica Devils	80	34	35	2	11	318	307	81
Newmarket Saints	80	33	39	6	8	282	328	80
Baltimore Skipjacks	80	13	58	6	9	268	434	35

• Teams receive one point for an overtime loss

International Hockey League

East Division	GP	W	L	OTL	GF	GA	Pts
Musk Lumberjacks	82	58	14	10	415	269	126
Fort Wayne Komets	82	48	30	4	343	310	100
Saginaw Hawks	82	45	30	7	325	294	97
Flint Spirits	82	42	31	9	395	389	93
Kalamazoo Wings	82	37	33	12	328	360	86
West Division							
Colorado Rangers	82	44	35	3	344	354	91
*Salt Lake Gold. Eagles	82	40	34	8	308	303	88
Peoria Rivermen	82	34	41	7	301	338	75
Milwaukee Admirals	82	21	54	7	288	430	49

• Teams receive one point for an overtime loss

All-American Hockey League

	GP	W	L	OTL	GF	GA	Pts
Virginia Lancers	43	37	5	1	321	129	75
*Carolina Thunderbirds	49	34	15	0	355	182	68
Johnstown Chiefs §	26	13	13	0	157	115	26
Miami Valley Sabres	37	17	19	1	217	260	35
Danville Fighting Saints	35	15	20	0	240	317	30
Jackson All-Americans	40	14	21	5	227	318	33
Port Huron Clippers	38	9	28	1	212	347	19
Michigan Stars	14	2	12	0	68	130	4

• Miami, Danville, Jackson and Port Huron folded after regular season § played 2nd half of season only ¶ folded 11/30/87

1988-89

American Hockey League

Northern Division	GP	W	L	T	GF	GA	Pts
Sherbrooke Canadiens	80	47	24	9	348	261	103
Halifax Citadels	80	42	30	8	345	300	92
Moncton Hawks	80	37	34	9	320	313	83
N. Haven Nighthawks	80	35	35	10	325	309	80
Maine Mariners	80	32	40	8	262	317	72
Springfield Indians	80	32	44	4	287	341	68
Cape Breton Oilers	80	27	47	6	308	388	60
Southern Division							
*Adiron Red Wings	80	47	27	6	369	294	100
Hershey Bears	80	40	30	10	361	309	90
Utica Devils	80	37	34	9	309	295	83
Newmarket Saints	80	38	36	6	339	334	82
Rochester Americans	80	38	37	5	305	302	81
Baltimore Skipjacks	80	30	46	4	317	347	64
Binghamton Whalers	80	28	46	6	307	392	62

International Hockey League

East Division	GP	W	L	OTL	GF	GA	Pts
*Musk Lumberjacks	82	57	18	7	433	308	121
Saginaw Hawks	82	46	26	10	378	294	102
Fort Wayne Komets	82	46	30	6	293	274	98
Kalamazoo Wings	82	39	36	7	345	350	85
Flint Spirits	82	22	54	6	287	428	50
West Division							
Salt Lake Gold. Eagles	82	56	22	3	369	294	116
Milwaukee Admirals	82	54	23	5	399	323	113
Denver Rangers	82	33	42	7	323	394	73
Peoria Rivermen	82	31	42	9	339	383	71
Indianapolis Ice	82	26	54	2	312	430	54

East Coast Hockey League

	GP	W	L	OTL	GF	GA	Pts
Erie Panthers	60	37	20	3	327	256	77
Johnstown Chiefs	60	32	22	6	295	251	70
Knoxville Cherokees	60	32	27	1	266	286	65
*Carolina Thunderbirds	60	27	32	1	266	329	55
Virginia Lancers	60	22	30	8	266	298	52

1989-90

American Hockey League

Northern Division	GP	W	L	T	GF	GA	Pts
Sherbrooke Canadiens	80	45	23	12	301	247	102
Cape Breton Oilers	80	39	34	7	317	306	85
*Springfield Indians	80	38	38	4	317	310	80
Halifax Citadels	80	37	37	6	317	300	80
Maine Mariners	80	31	38	11	294	317	73
Moncton Hawks	80	33	42	5	266	303	71
N. Haven Nighthawks	80	32	41	7	283	316	71
Southern Division							
Rochester Americans	80	43	28	9	337	286	95
Adiron Red Wings	80	42	27	11	330	304	95
Baltimore Skipjacks	80	43	30	7	302	265	93
Utica Devils	80	44	32	4	354	315	92
Newmarket Saints	80	31	33	16	305	318	78
Hershey Bears	80	32	38	10	298	296	74
Binghamton Whalers	80	11	60	9	229	366	31

International Hockey League

East Division	GP	W	L	OTL	GF	GA	Pts
Musk Lumberjacks	82	55	21	6	389	304	116
Kalamazoo Wings	82	53	23	6	389	311	112
Flint Spirits	82	40	36	6	326	358	86
Fort Wayne Komets	82	37	34	11	316	345	85
West Division							
*Indianapolis Ice	82	53	21	8	315	237	114
Salt Lake Gold. Eagles	82	37	36	9	326	311	83
Milwaukee Admirals	82	36	39	7	316	370	79
Peoria Rivermen	82	31	38	13	317	378	75
Phoenix Roadrunners	82	27	44	11	314	394	65

East Coast Hockey League

	GP	W	L	OTL	GF	GA	Pts
Winston-Salem T'birds	60	38	16	6	312	257	82
Erie Panthers	60	38	16	6	357	251	82
Virginia Lancers	60	36	18	6	261	218	78
*Greensboro Monarchs	60	29	27	4	283	283	62
Hampton Rds Admirals	60	29	29	2	252	267	60
Nashville Knights	60	26	30	4	248	289	56
Johnstown Chiefs	60	23	31	6	233	291	52
Knoxville Cherokees	60	21	33	6	230	300	48

1990-91

AMERICAN HOCKEY LEAGUE

Northern Division	GP	W	L	T	GF	GA	Pts
*Springfield Indians	80	43	27	10	348	281	96
Cape Breton Oilers	80	41	31	8	306	301	90
Moncton Hawks	80	36	32	12	270	267	84
Fred'n Canadiens	80	36	35	9	295	292	81
Maine Mariners	80	34	34	12	269	284	80
Halifax Citadels	80	33	35	12	338	340	78
N. Haven Nighthawks	80	24	45	11	246	324	59
Southern Division							
Rochester Americans	80	45	26	9	326	253	99
Binghamton Rangers	80	44	30	6	318	274	94
Baltimore Skipjacks	80	39	34	7	325	289	85
Hershey Bears	80	33	35	12	313	324	78
Adiron Red Wings	80	33	37	10	320	346	76
Utica Devils	80	36	42	2	325	346	74
Capital Dist. Islanders	80	28	43	9	284	323	65
Newmarket Saints	80	26	45	9	278	317	61

INTERNATIONAL HOCKEY LEAGUE

East Division	GP	W	L	OTL	GF	GA	Pts
Kalamazoo Wings	82	52	29	1	354	302	105
Indianapolis Ice	82	48	29	5	342	264	101
Fort Wayne Komets	83	43	35	5	369	335	91
Musk Lumberjacks	83	38	40	5	305	352	81
Albany Choppers §	55	22	30	3	191	232	47
§ folded 02/15/91							
West Division							
*Peoria Rivermen	82	58	19	5	405	261	121
Salt Lake Gold. Eagles	83	50	28	5	353	296	105
Phoenix Roadrunners	83	38	36	9	326	343	85
Milwaukee Admirals	82	36	43	3	275	316	75
San Diego Gulls	83	30	45	8	273	362	68
Kansas City Blades	82	25	53	4	255	385	54

EAST COAST HOCKEY LEAGUE

East Division	GP	W	L	OTL	GF	GA	Pts
*Hampton Rds Admirals	64	38	20	6	300	248	82
Johnstown Chiefs	64	32	29	3	324	287	67
Erie Panthers	64	31	30	3	302	302	65
Richmond Renegades	64	29	29	6	300	307	64
Roanoke Valley Rebels	64	25	32	7	218	295	57
West Division							
Knoxville Cherokees	64	46	13	5	377	230	97
Cincinnati Cyclones	64	37	24	3	285	281	77
Greensboro Monarchs	64	34	27	3	275	268	71
Louisville IceHawks	64	31	29	4	251	309	66
Nashville Knights	64	29	31	4	307	317	62
Winston-Salem T'birds	64	20	41	3	228	323	43

1991-92

AMERICAN HOCKEY LEAGUE

Atlantic Division	GP	W	L	T	GF	GA	Pts
Fred'n Canadiens	80	43	27	10	314	254	96
St. John's Maple Leafs	80	39	29	12	325	285	90
Cape Breton Oilers	80	36	34	10	336	330	82
Moncton Hawks	80	32	38	10	285	299	74
Halifax Citadels	80	25	38	17	280	324	67
Northern Division							
Springfield Indians	80	43	29	8	308	277	94
*Adiron Red Wings	80	40	36	4	335	309	84
N. Haven Nighthawks	80	39	37	4	305	309	82
Capital District Islanders	80	32	37	11	261	289	75
Maine Mariners	80	23	47	10	296	352	56
Southern Division							
Binghamton Rangers	80	41	30	9	318	277	91
Rochester Americans	80	37	31	12	292	248	86
Hershey Bears	80	36	33	11	313	337	83
Utica Devils	80	34	40	6	268	313	74
Baltimore Skipjacks	80	28	42	10	287	320	66

INTERNATIONAL HOCKEY LEAGUE

East Division	GP	W	L	OTL	GF	GA	Pts
Fort Wayne Komets	82	52	22	8	340	287	112
Musk Lumberjacks	82	41	28	13	306	293	95
Milwaukee Admirals	82	38	36	8	306	309	84
Kalamazoo Wings	82	37	35	10	292	312	84
Indianapolis Ice	82	31	41	10	272	329	72
West Division							
*Kansas City Blades	82	56	22	4	302	248	116
Peoria Rivermen	82	48	25	9	333	300	105
San Diego Gulls	82	45	28	9	340	298	99
Salt Lake Gold. Eagles	82	33	40	9	252	304	75
Phoenix Roadrunners	82	29	46	7	275	338	65

EAST COAST HOCKEY LEAGUE

East Division	GP	W	L	OTL	GF	GA	Pts
Greensboro Monarchs	64	43	17	4	297	252	90
*Hampton Rds Admirals	64	42	20	2	298	220	86
Winston-Salem T'birds	64	36	24	4	270	245	76
Richmond Renegades	64	30	27	7	263	263	67
Raleigh IceCaps	64	25	33	6	228	284	56
Roanoke Valley Rebels	64	21	36	7	236	313	49
Knoxville Cherokees	64	20	36	8	265	355	48
West Division							
Toledo Storm	64	46	15	3	367	240	95
Cincinnati Cyclones	64	36	20	8	329	284	80
Johnstown Chiefs	64	36	23	5	294	248	77
Erie Panthers	64	33	27	4	284	309	70
Dayton Bombers	64	32	26	6	305	300	70
Louisville IceHawks	64	31	25	8	315	306	70
Columbus Chill	64	25	30	9	298	341	59
Nashville Knights	64	24	36	4	246	335	52

COLONIAL HOCKEY LEAGUE

	GP	W	L	OTL	T	GF	GA	Pts
Michigan Falcons	60	34	22	3	4	296	257	75
Brantford Smoke	60	34	22	0	4	327	265	72
*T. Bay Thunder Hawks	60	26	28	4	6	309	289	62
St. Thomas Wildcats	60	24	29	2	7	263	288	57
Flint Bulldogs	60	20	37	2	3	272	368	45

• Teams receive one point for overtime tie and one point for overtime loss

1992-93

AMERICAN HOCKEY LEAGUE

Atlantic Division	GP	W	L	T	GF	GA	Pts
St. John's Maple Leafs	80	41	26	13	351	308	95
Fred'n Canadiens	80	38	31	11	314	278	87
*Cape Breton Oilers	80	36	32	12	356	336	84
Moncton Hawks	80	31	33	16	292	306	78
Halifax Citadels	80	33	37	10	312	348	76
Northern Division							
Providence Bruins	80	46	32	2	384	348	94
Adiron Red Wings	80	36	35	9	331	308	81
Capital Dist. Islanders	80	34	34	12	280	285	80
Springfield Indians	80	25	41	14	282	336	64
N. Haven Nighthawks	80	22	47	11	262	343	55
Southern Division							
Binghamton Rangers	80	57	13	10	392	246	124
Rochester Americans	80	40	33	7	348	332	87
Utica Devils	80	33	36	11	325	354	77
Baltimore Skipjacks	80	28	40	12	318	353	68
Hershey Bears	80	27	41	12	316	339	66
Hamilton Canucks	80	29	45	6	284	327	64

INTERNATIONAL HOCKEY LEAGUE

Atlantic Division	GP	W	L	OTL	GF	GA	Pts
Atlanta Knights	82	52	23	7	333	291	111
Cleveland Lumberjacks	82	39	34	9	329	330	87
Cincinnati Cyclones	82	27	48	7	305	364	61
Central Division							
*Fort Wayne Komets	82	49	27	6	339	294	104
Indianapolis Ice	82	34	39	9	324	347	77
Kalamazoo Wings	82	29	42	11	291	367	69
Midwest Division							
Milwaukee Admirals	82	49	23	10	329	280	108
Kansas City Blades	82	46	26	10	318	288	102
Peoria Rivermen	82	41	33	8	297	307	90
Pacific Division							
San Diego Gulls	82	62	12	8	381	229	132
Salt Lake Gold. Eagles	82	38	39	5	269	305	81
Phoenix Roadrunners	82	26	50	6	248	361	58

EAST COAST HOCKEY LEAGUE

East Division	GP	W	L	OTL	GF	GA	Pts
Wheeling Thunderbirds	64	40	16	8	314	223	88
Hampton Rds Admirals	64	37	21	6	294	235	80
Raleigh IceCaps	64	37	22	5	289	262	79
Johnstown Chiefs	64	34	23	7	281	264	75
Richmond Renegades	64	34	28	2	292	292	70
Greensboro Monarchs	64	33	29	2	256	261	68
Roanoke Val. Rampage	64	14	49	1	227	387	29
West Division							
*Toledo Storm	64	36	17	11	316	238	83
Dayton Bombers	64	35	23	6	282	270	76
Nashville Knights	64	36	25	3	312	305	75
Erie Panthers	64	35	25	4	305	307	74
Louisville IceHawks	64	30	27	7	302	293	67
Birmingham Bulls	64	30	29	5	290	313	65
Columbus Chill	64	30	30	4	257	256	64
Knoxville Cherokees	64	19	39	6	212	323	44

CENTRAL HOCKEY LEAGUE

	GP	W	L	OTL	GF	GA	Pts
Oklahoma City Blazers	60	39	18	3	291	232	81
*Tulsa Oilers	60	35	22	3	270	230	73
Dallas Freeze	60	31	25	4	276	242	66
Memphis RiverKings	60	26	27	7	253	272	59
Fort Worth Fire	60	24	29	7	252	288	55
Wichita Thunder	60	25	33	2	242	320	52

• Teams receive one point for an overtime loss

COLONIAL HOCKEY LEAGUE

	GP	W	L	SOL	GF	GA	Pts
*Brantford Smoke	60	39	18	3	308	264	81
Detroit Falcons	60	36	20	4	239	239	76
T' Bay Thunder Hawks	60	32	24	4	271	271	68
Muskegon Fury	60	28	27	5	278	278	61
St. Thomas Wildcats	60	27	27	6	322	322	60
Flint Generals	60	27	29	4	296	296	58
Chatham Wheels	60	21	35	4	344	344	46

• Teams receive one point for a shootout loss

1993-94

AMERICAN HOCKEY LEAGUE

Atlantic Division	GP	W	L	T	GF	GA	Pts
St. John's Maple Leafs	80	45	23	12	360	287	102
Saint John Flames	80	37	33	10	304	305	84
Moncton Hawks	80	37	36	7	310	303	81
Cape Breton Oilers	80	32	35	13	316	339	77
Fred'n Canadiens	80	31	42	7	294	296	69
PEI Senators	80	23	49	8	269	356	54
Northern Division							
Adiron Red Wings	80	45	27	8	333	273	98
*Portland Pirates	80	43	27	10	328	269	96
Albany River Rats	80	38	34	8	312	315	84
Springfield Indians	80	29	38	13	309	327	71
Providence Bruins	80	28	39	13	283	319	69
Southern Division							
Hershey Bears	80	38	31	11	306	298	87
Hamilton Canucks	80	36	37	7	302	305	79
Cornwall Aces	80	33	36	11	294	295	77
Rochester Americans	80	31	34	15	277	300	77
Binghamton Rangers	80	33	38	9	312	322	75

INTERNATIONAL HOCKEY LEAGUE

Atlantic Division	GP	W	L	SOL	GF	GA	Pts
Kalamazoo Wings	81	48	26	7	337	297	103
Fort Wayne Komets	81	41	29	11	347	297	93
Cleveland Lumberjacks	81	31	36	14	278	344	76
Central Division							
Peoria Rivermen	81	51	24	6	327	294	108
Cincinnati Cyclones	81	49	23	9	336	282	107
Indianapolis Ice	81	28	46	7	257	329	63
Midwest Division							
*Atlanta Knights	81	45	22	14	321	282	104
Milwaukee Admirals	81	40	24	17	338	302	97
Kansas City Blades	81	40	31	10	326	327	90
Russian Penguins	13	2	9	2	35	64	6
Pacific Division							
Las Vegas Thunder	81	52	18	11	319	282	115
San Diego Gulls	81	42	28	11	311	302	95
Phoenix Roadrunners	81	40	36	5	313	309	85
Salt Lake Gold. Eagles	81	24	52	5	243	377	53

• Teams receive one point for a shootout loss
• Games vs. touring Russian Penguins counted in standings

EAST COAST HOCKEY LEAGUE

East Division	GP	W	L	OTL	GF	GA	Pts
Hampton Rds Admirals	68	41	19	8	298	246	90
Raleigh IceCaps	68	41	20	7	296	221	79
Greensboro Monarchs	68	41	21	6	319	262	88
Charlotte Checkers	68	39	25	4	281	271	82
Roanoke Express	68	37	28	3	300	290	77
S. Carolina Stingrays	68	33	26	9	294	291	75
Richmond Renegades	68	34	29	5	286	293	73
West Division							
Knoxville Cherokees	68	44	18	6	325	246	94
Birmingham Bulls	68	44	20	4	340	268	92
Nashville Knights	68	26	36	6	255	289	58
Huntsville Blast	68	20	39	9	241	315	49
Louisville IceHawks	68	16	44	8	236	356	40
Huntington Blizzard	68	14	49	5	191	413	33
North Division							
*Toledo Storm	68	44	20	4	338	289	92
Columbus Chill	68	41	20	7	344	285	89
Wheeling Thunderbirds	68	38	23	7	327	289	83
Johnstown Chiefs	68	37	27	4	323	308	78
Dayton Bombers	68	29	31	8	316	308	66
Erie Panthers	68	27	36	5	264	334	59

CENTRAL HOCKEY LEAGUE

	GP	W	L	OTL	GF	GA	Pts
*Wichita Thunder	64	40	18	6	309	275	86
Tulsa Oilers	64	36	24	4	347	281	76
Oklahoma City Blazers	64	35	23	6	260	246	76
Dallas Freeze	64	31	25	8	304	309	70
Memphis RiverKings	64	25	34	5	243	294	55
Fort Worth Fire	64	25	37	2	253	311	52

COLONIAL HOCKEY LEAGUE

East Division	GP	W	L	SOL	GF	GA	Pts
*Thunder Bay Senators	64	45	15	4	331	236	94
Brantford Smoke	64	28	26	10	308	348	66
St. Thomas Wildcats	64	22	34	8	284	343	52
Utica Bulldogs	64	21	39	4	226	330	46
West Division							
Chatham Wheels	64	39	18	7	336	281	85
Muskegon Fury	64	35	24	5	319	301	75
Detroit Falcons	64	34	25	5	296	275	73
Flint Generals	64	32	23	9	328	314	73

1994-95

AMERICAN HOCKEY LEAGUE

Atlantic Division	GP	W	L	T	GF	GA	Pts
PEI Senators	80	41	31	8	305	271	90
St. John's Maple Leafs	80	33	37	10	263	263	76
Fred'n Canadiens	80	35	40	5	274	288	75
Saint John Flames	80	27	40	13	250	286	67
Cape Breton Oilers	80	27	44	9	298	342	63
Northern Division							
*Albany River Rats	80	46	17	17	293	219	109
Portland Pirates	80	46	22	12	333	233	104
Providence Bruins	80	39	30	11	300	268	89
Adiron Red Wings	80	32	38	10	271	294	74
Springfield Falcons	80	31	37	12	269	289	74
Worcester Icecats	80	24	45	11	234	300	59
Southern Division							
Binghamton Rangers	80	43	30	7	302	261	93
Cornwall Aces	80	38	33	9	236	248	85
Hershey Bears	80	34	36	10	275	300	78
Rochester Americans	80	35	38	7	300	304	77
Syracuse Crunch	80	29	42	9	288	325	67

INTERNATIONAL HOCKEY LEAGUE

North Division	GP	W	L	SOL	GF	GA	Pts
Detroit Vipers	81	48	27	6	311	273	102
Kalamazoo Wings	81	43	24	14	288	249	100
Chicago Wolves	81	34	33	13	261	306	82
Cleveland Lumberjacks	81	34	37	10	306	339	78
Midwest Division							
Peoria Rivermen	81	51	19	11	311	245	113
Cincinnati Cyclones	81	49	22	10	305	272	108
Fort Wayne Komets	81	34	39	8	296	324	76
Indianapolis Ice	81	32	41	8	273	330	72
Central Division							
Milwaukee Admirals	81	44	27	10	317	298	98
Houston Aeros	81	38	35	8	272	283	84
Atlanta Knights	81	39	38	5	279	296	83
Minnesota Moose	81	34	35	12	271	336	80
Kansas City Blades	81	35	40	6	277	300	76
Southwest Division							
*Denver Grizzlies	81	57	18	6	339	235	120
Las Vegas Thunder	81	46	30	5	328	278	97
Phoenix Roadrunners	81	41	26	14	325	310	96
San Diego Gulls	81	37	36	8	268	301	82
Soviet Wings	16	1	14	2	37	89	4

• *Games vs. touring Soviet Wings counted in standings*

EAST COAST HOCKEY LEAGUE

East Division							
*Richmond Renegades	68	41	20	7	271	232	89
Roanoke Express	68	39	19	10	255	223	88
Charlotte Checkers	68	37	22	9	274	261	83
Hampton Rds Admirals	68	37	23	8	255	239	82
Greensboro Monarchs	68	31	28	9	277	293	71
Raleigh IceCaps	68	23	39	6	239	295	52
North Division							
Wheeling Thunderbirds	68	46	17	5	313	243	97
Dayton Bombers	68	42	17	9	307	224	93
Toledo Storm	68	41	22	5	287	230	87
Columbus Chill	68	31	32	5	282	315	67
Johnstown Chiefs	68	31	32	5	256	297	67
Erie Panthers	68	18	46	4	256	356	40
South Division							
S. Carolina Stingrays	68	42	19	7	255	215	91
Tallahassee T'Sharks	68	36	25	7	268	227	79
Nashville Knights	68	32	30	6	263	279	70
Knoxville Cherokees	68	30	30	8	241	267	68
Huntington Blizzard	68	28	37	3	224	275	59
Birmingham Bulls	68	26	38	4	273	325	56

CENTRAL HOCKEY LEAGUE

	GP	W	L	SOL	GF	GA	Pts
*Wichita Thunder	66	44	18	4	320	268	92
San Antonio Iguanas	66	37	22	7	336	281	81
Tulsa Oilers	66	36	24	6	307	281	78
Oklahoma City Blazers	66	34	23	9	274	267	77
Fort Worth Fire	66	32	26	8	314	288	72
Memphis Riverkings	66	24	35	7	259	327	55
Dallas Freeze	66	24	36	6	266	364	54

• *Teams receive one point for a shootout loss*

COLONIAL HOCKEY LEAGUE

East Division	GP	W	L	SOL	GF	GA	Pts
*Thunder Bay Senators	74	48	22	4	341	279	100
London Wildcats	74	34	38	2	341	380	70
Utica Blizzard	74	31	38	5	299	349	67
Brantford Smoke	74	26	36	12	299	357	64
West Division							
Detroit Falcons	74	45	27	2	329	273	92
Muskegon Fury	74	42	27	5	333	286	89
Saginaw Wheels	74	36	31	7	306	321	79
Flint Generals	74	34	34	6	350	353	74

1995-96

AMERICAN HOCKEY LEAGUE

Atlantic Division	GP	W	L	OTL	T	GF	GA	Pts
PEI Senators	80	38	36	3	6	303	313	85
Saint John Flames	80	35	34	4	11	272	264	85
St. John's Mpl Leafs	80	31	35	4	14	248	274	80
Fred'n Canadiens	80	34	35	0	11	307	308	79
Cape Breton Oilers	80	33	44	4	3	290	323	73
Northern Division								
Springfield Falcons	80	42	27	5	11	272	215	100
Worcester Icecats	80	36	32	4	12	242	244	88
Portland Pirates	80	32	38	4	10	282	283	78
Providence Bruins	80	30	40	4	10	249	280	74
Central Division								
Albany River Rats	80	54	19	0	7	322	218	115
Adiron Red Wings	80	38	34	2	8	271	247	86
*Rochester Americans	80	37	38	4	5	294	297	83
Cornwall Aces	80	34	39	5	7	249	251	80
Syracuse Crunch	80	31	44	7	5	257	307	74
Southern Division								
Binghamton Rangers	80	39	34	3	7	333	331	88
Hershey Bears	80	36	33	3	11	301	287	86
Baltimore Bandits	80	33	38	2	9	279	299	77
Carolina Monarchs	80	28	41	3	11	313	343	70

• *Teams receive one point for an overtime loss*

INTERNATIONAL HOCKEY LEAGUE

East Division	GP	W	L	SOL	GF	GA	Pts
Cincinnati Cyclones	82	51	22	9	318	247	111
Michigan K-Wings	82	40	24	18	290	272	98
Indianapolis Ice	82	43	33	6	304	295	92
Fort Wayne Komets	82	39	35	8	276	296	86
Central Division							
Orlando Solar Bears	82	52	24	6	352	307	110
Detroit Vipers	82	48	28	6	310	274	102
Cleveland Lumberjacks	82	43	27	12	334	330	98
Atlanta Knights	82	32	41	9	282	348	73
Houston Aeros	82	29	45	8	262	328	66
Midwest Division							
Milwaukee Admirals	82	40	32	10	290	307	90
Chicago Wolves	82	40	34	8	288	310	88
Peoria Rivermen	82	39	38	5	274	290	83
Kansas City Blades	82	39	38	5	288	326	83
Minnesota Moose	82	30	45	7	254	332	67
Southwest Division							
Las Vegas Thunder	82	57	17	8	380	249	122
*Utah Grizzlies	82	49	29	4	291	232	102
San Francisco Spiders	82	40	32	10	278	283	90
Phoenix Roadrunners	82	36	35	11	267	281	83
Los Angeles Ice Dogs	82	32	36	14	305	336	78

EAST COAST HOCKEY LEAGUE

East Division	GP	W	L	OTL	GF	GA	Pts
Richmond Renegades	70	46	11	13	314	225	105
*Charlotte Checkers	70	45	21	4	294	250	94
S. Carolina Stingrays	70	40	22	8	284	251	88
Roanoke Express	70	36	28	6	231	260	78
Hampton Rds Admirals	70	32	25	13	278	265	77
Raleigh IceCaps	70	23	34	13	215	266	59
North Division							
Toledo Storm	70	48	14	8	301	240	104
Wheeling Thunderbirds	70	42	23	5	289	261	89
Louisville RiverFrogs	70	39	24	7	288	237	85
Columbus Chill	70	37	28	5	285	268	79
Dayton Bombers	70	35	28	7	247	237	77
Erie Panthers	70	25	40	5	227	293	55
Johnstown Chiefs	70	21	38	11	249	322	53
Huntington Blizzard	70	21	39	10	232	309	52
South Division							
Louisiana Ice Gators	70	43	21	6	312	261	92
Nashville Knights	70	42	22	6	368	307	90
Tallahassee T'Sharks	70	42	22	6	283	260	90
Knoxville Cherokees	70	37	29	4	323	303	78
Jacksonville Lizard Kings	70	33	29	8	267	288	74
Birmingham Bulls	70	26	39	5	258	360	57
Mobile Mysticks	70	22	37	11	265	325	55

CENTRAL HOCKEY LEAGUE

	GP	W	L	SOL	GF	GA	Pts
*Oklahoma City Blazers	64	47	13	4	327	224	98
San Antonio Iguanas	64	39	17	8	313	240	86
Memphis Riverkings	64	34	24	6	308	271	74
Tulsa Oilers	64	26	33	5	244	302	57
Fort Worth Fire	64	24	34	6	244	289	54
Wichita Thunder	64	22	39	3	270	380	47

COLONIAL HOCKEY LEAGUE

East Division	GP	W	L	SOL	GF	GA	Pts
*Flint Generals	74	51	18	5	347	248	107
Brantford Smoke	74	45	24	5	336	283	95
Detroit Falcons	74	33	32	9	275	310	75
Saginaw Wheels	74	32	35	7	299	341	71
Utica Blizzard	74	29	39	6	285	339	64
West Division							
Muskegon Fury	74	40	27	7	273	248	87
Thunder Bay Senators	74	36	26	12	302	289	84
Madison Monsters	74	37	30	7	267	284	81
Quad City Mallards	74	30	39	5	269	311	65

WEST COAST HOCKEY LEAGUE

	GP	W	L	OTL	GF	GA	Pts
*San Diego Gulls	58	49	7	2	350	232	100
Fresno Falcons	58	30	21	7	270	232	67
Reno Renegades	58	26	24	8	271	283	60
Alaska Gold Kings	58	23	25	10	256	307	56
Anchorage Aces	58	24	29	5	271	299	53
Bakersfield Fog	58	24	29	5	271	323	53
CSKA Moscow	12	4	6	2	50	63	10

• *Games vs. touring CSKA Moscow team counted in standings*

SOUTHERN HOCKEY LEAGUE

	GP	W	L	OTL	GF	GA	Pts
Lakeland Prowlers	60	41	13	6	342	229	88
Daytona Breakers	60	33	20	7	297	251	73
Win.-Salem Mammoths	60	30	23	7	273	274	67
Huntsville Channel Cats	60	27	31	2	274	294	56
*West Palm Beach	60	26	32	2	251	319	54
Jacksonville Bullets	60	23	33	4	282	352	50

1996-97

AMERICAN HOCKEY LEAGUE

Canadian Division	GP	W	L	OTL	T	GF	GA	Pts
St. John's Mpl Leafs	80	36	28	6	10	265	264	88
Saint John Flames	80	28	36	3	13	237	269	72
Hamilton Bulldogs	80	28	39	4	9	220	276	69
Fred'n Canadiens	80	26	44	2	8	234	283	62
Empire State Division								
Rochester Americans	80	40	30	1	9	298	257	90
Albany River Rats	80	38	28	2	12	258	249	90
Adiron Red Wings	80	38	28	5	9	269	231	90
Syracuse Crunch	80	32	38	0	10	241	265	74
Binghamton Rangers	80	27	38	2	13	245	300	69
New England Division								
Worcester Icecats	80	43	23	5	9	256	234	100
*Springfield Falcons	80	41	25	2	12	268	229	96
Portland Pirates	80	37	26	7	10	279	264	91
Providence Bruins	80	35	40	2	3	262	289	75
Mid-Atlantic Division								
Phil. Phantoms	80	49	18	3	10	325	230	111
*Hershey Bears	80	43	22	5	10	273	220	101
KY Thoroughblades	80	36	35	0	9	278	284	81
Baltimore Bandits	80	30	37	3	10	251	285	73
Carolina Monarchs	80	28	43	5	4	273	303	65

INTERNATIONAL HOCKEY LEAGUE

Northeast Division							
Detroit Vipers	82	57	17	8	280	188	122
Orlando Solar Bears	82	53	24	5	305	232	111
Cincinnati Cyclones	82	43	29	10	254	248	96
Quebec Rafales	82	41	30	11	287	248	93
Grand Rapids Griffins	82	40	30	12	244	246	92
Central Division							
Indianapolis Ice	82	44	29	9	289	230	97
Cleveland Lumberjacks	82	40	32	10	286	280	90
Michigan K Wings	82	31	44	7	208	272	69
Fort Wayne Komets	82	28	47	7	223	318	63
Midwest Division							
San Antonio Dragons	82	45	30	7	276	278	97
Kansas City Blades	82	38	29	15	271	270	91
Chicago Wolves	82	40	36	6	276	290	86
Milwaukee Admirals	82	38	36	8	253	298	84
Manitoba Moose	82	32	40	10	262	300	74
Southwest Division							
Long Beach Ice Dogs	82	54	19	9	309	247	117
Houston Aeros	82	44	30	8	247	228	96
Utah Grizzlies	82	43	33	6	259	254	92
Las Vegas Thunder	82	41	34	7	287	299	89
Phoenix Roadrunners	82	27	42	13	239	309	67

EAST COAST HOCKEY LEAGUE

East Division	GP	W	L	SOL	GF	GA	Pts
*S. Carolina Stingrays	70	45	15	10	345	253	100
Hampton Rds Admirals	70	46	19	5	286	223	97
Richmond Renegades	70	41	25	4	252	235	86
Roanoke Express	70	38	26	6	262	250	82
Charlotte Checkers	70	35	28	7	27	267	77
Raleigh Icecaps	70	30	33	7	256	293	67
Knoxville Cherokees	70	24	43	3	260	343	51
North Division							
Columbus Chill	70	44	21	5	257	208	93
Peoria Rivermen	70	43	21	6	219	208	92
Daytona Bombers	70	36	26	8	258	208	80
Wheeling Thunderbirds	70	36	29	5	291	208	77
Toledo Storm	70	32	28	10	248	208	74
Huntington Blizzard	70	33	33	4	296	208	70
Louisville RiverFrogs	70	29	31	10	290	208	68
Johnstown Chiefs	70	24	39	7	354	208	55
South Division							
Tallahassee T'Sharks	70	39	23	8	263	236	86
Birmingham Bulls	70	36	25	9	291	296	81
Louisiana Ice Gators	70	38	28	4	292	244	80
Mobile Mysticks	70	34	25	11	257	263	79
Mississippi Sea Wolves	70	34	26	10	241	245	78
Pensacola Ice Pilots	70	36	31	3	275	275	75
Baton Rouge Kingfish	70	31	33	6	222	238	68
Jacksonville Lizard Kings	70	21	37	12	220	299	54

• *Teams receive one point for a shootout loss*

CENTRAL HOCKEY LEAGUE

Eastern Division	GP	W	L	SOL	GF	GA	Pts
Huntsville Channel Cats	66	39	24	3	311	297	81
Macon Whoopee	66	38	24	4	276	237	80
Memphis RiverKings	66	35	27	4	278	260	74
Columb. Cottonmouths	66	32	28	6	292	291	70
Nashville Nighthawks	66	12	52	2	219	359	26

Western Division	GP	W	L	SOL	GF	GA	Pts
Oklahoma City Blazers	66	48	12	6	307	200	102
*Fort Worth Fire	66	45	16	5	279	210	95
Tulsa Oilers	66	30	32	4	286	284	64
Wichita Thunder	66	25	31	10	279	324	60
San Antonio Iguanas	66	26	36	4	261	326	56

COLONIAL HOCKEY LEAGUE

East Division	GP	W	L	SOL	GF	GA	Pts
Flint Generals	74	55	18	1	371	232	111
Brantford Smoke	74	42	25	7	321	286	91
Port Huron Border Cats	74	38	31	5	280	288	81
Utica Blizzard	74	22	42	10	278	385	54
Saginaw Lumber Kings	74	21	48	5	263	399	47

West Division	GP	W	L	SOL	GF	GA	Pts
*Quad City Mallards	74	51	20	3	384	245	105
Madison Monsters	74	46	21	7	315	259	99
Thunder Bay Senators	74	43	23	8	333	266	94
Muskegon Fury	74	39	29	6	268	257	84
Dayton Ice Bandits	74	13	53	8	216	412	34

WEST COAST HOCKEY LEAGUE

	GP	W	L	SOL	GF	GA	Pts
*San Diego Gulls	64	50	12	2	400	210	102
Anchorage Aces	64	41	18	5	349	260	87
Fresno Falcons	64	38	20	6	313	254	82
Bakersfield Fog	64	33	26	5	345	325	71
Reno Renegades	64	16	43	5	252	418	37
Alaska Gold Kings	64	13	47	4	230	423	30
CSKA Moscow	12	7	4	1	56	55	15

• Games vs. CSKA Moscow touring team counted in standings

WESTERN PROFESSIONAL HOCKEY LEAGUE

	GP	W	L	SOL	GF	GA	Pts
New Mexico Scorpions	64	42	20	2	323	258	86
Austin Ice-Bats	64	35	22	7	271	249	77
*El Paso Buzzards	64	33	23	8	284	272	74
Central Tex. Stampede	64	35	27	2	243	229	72
Waco Wizards	64	30	30	4	220	249	64
Amarillo Rattlers	64	17	39	8	239	323	42

1997-98

AMERICAN HOCKEY LEAGUE

Atlantic Division	GP	W	L	OTL	T	GF	GA	Pts
Saint John Flames	80	43	24	0	13	231	201	99
Fred'n Canadiens	80	33	32	5	10	245	244	81
Portland Pirates	80	33	33	2	12	241	247	80
St. John's Mpl Leafs	80	25	32	5	18	233	254	73

New England Division	GP	W	L	OTL	T	GF	GA	Pts
Springfield Falcons	80	45	26	2	7	278	248	99
Hartford Wolf Pack	80	43	24	1	12	272	227	99
New Haven Beasts	80	38	33	2	7	256	239	85
Worcester Icecats	80	34	31	6	9	267	268	83
Providence Bruins	80	19	49	5	7	211	301	50

Empire Division	GP	W	L	OTL	T	GF	GA	Pts
Albany River Rats	80	43	20	6	11	290	223	103
Hamilton Bulldogs	80	36	22	5	17	264	242	94
Syracuse Crunch	80	35	32	2	11	272	285	83
Adiron Red Wings	80	31	37	3	9	245	275	74
Rochester Americans	80	30	38	0	12	238	260	72

Mid-Atlantic Division	GP	W	L	OTL	T	GF	GA	Pts
*Phil. Phantoms	80	47	21	2	10	314	249	106
Hershey Bears	80	36	31	6	7	238	235	85
KY Thoroughblades	80	29	39	3	9	241	278	70
Cinci Mighty Ducks	80	23	37	7	13	243	303	66

INTERNATIONAL HOCKEY LEAGUE

Northeast Division	GP	W	L	SOL	GF	GA	Pts
Detroit Vipers	82	47	20	15	267	232	109
Orlando Solar Bears	82	42	30	10	258	251	94
Grand Rapids Griffins	82	38	31	13	225	242	89
Quebec Rafales	82	27	48	7	211	292	61

Central Division	GP	W	L	SOL	GF	GA	Pts
Fort Wayne Komets	82	47	29	6	270	243	100
Cincinnati Cyclones	82	40	30	12	275	254	92
Indianapolis Ice	82	40	36	6	245	261	86
Cleveland Lumberjacks	82	35	37	10	228	262	80
Michigan K-Wings	82	36	39	7	223	261	79

Midwest Division	GP	W	L	SOL	GF	GA	Pts
*Chicago Wolves	82	55	24	3	301	258	113
Kansas City Blades	82	41	29	12	269	258	94
Milwaukee Admirals	82	43	34	5	267	262	91
Manitoba Moose	82	39	36	7	269	254	85

Southwest Division	GP	W	L	SOL	GF	GA	Pts
Long Beach Ice Dogs	82	53	20	9	282	210	115
Houston Aeros	82	50	22	10	268	214	110
Utah Grizzlies	82	47	27	8	276	234	102
Las Vegas Thunder	82	33	39	10	260	305	76
San Antonio Dragons	82	25	49	8	233	334	58

EAST COAST HOCKEY LEAGUE

Northeast Division	GP	W	L	SOL	GF	GA	Pts
Roanoke Express	70	42	21	7	235	208	91
Wheeling Nailers	70	37	24	9	255	255	83
Chesapk Icebreakers	70	34	28	8	252	239	76
*Hampton Rds Admirals	70	32	28	10	222	225	74
Richmond Renegades	70	30	33	7	218	277	67
Johnstown Chiefs	70	23	41	6	219	297	52

Northwest Division	GP	W	L	SOL	GF	GA	Pts
Peoria Rivermen	70	44	19	7	296	213	95
Toledo Storm	70	41	21	8	251	210	90
Daytona Bombers	70	36	26	8	255	256	80
Huntington Blizzard	70	34	29	7	230	259	75
Columbus Chill	70	33	30	7	221	220	73
Louisville RiverFrogs	70	32	31	7	228	257	71

Southeast Division	GP	W	L	SOL	GF	GA	Pts
S. Carolina Stingrays	70	41	23	6	246	218	88
Charlotte Checkers	70	35	24	11	251	237	81
Pee Dee Pride	70	34	25	11	214	215	79
Jacksnville Lizard Kings	70	35	29	6	243	239	76
Raleigh Icecaps	70	32	33	5	236	254	69
Tallahassee T'Sharks	70	24	44	2	210	320	50

Southwest Division	GP	W	L	SOL	GF	GA	Pts
Louisiana Icegators	70	43	17	10	298	232	96
Birmingham Bulls	70	39	23	8	293	257	86
Pensacola Ice Pilots	70	36	24	10	276	262	82
New Orleans Brass	70	36	24	10	278	263	82
Mobile Mysticks	70	35	27	8	236	233	78
Mississippi Sea Wolves	70	34	27	9	225	224	77
Baton Rouge Kingfish	70	33	27	10	220	238	76

CENTRAL HOCKEY LEAGUE

Eastern Division	GP	W	L	SOL	GF	GA	Pts
*Columb. Cottonmouths	70	51	13	6	341	219	108
Nashville Ice Flyers	70	41	19	10	274	246	92
Huntsville Channel Cats	70	40	22	8	333	281	88
Macon Whoopee	70	38	25	7	249	234	83
Fayetteville Force	70	25	42	3	247	348	53

Western Division	GP	W	L	SOL	GF	GA	Pts
Oklahoma City Blazers	70	48	19	3	319	237	99
Wichita Thunder	70	35	31	4	302	303	74
Tulsa Oilers	70	34	31	5	308	274	73
Memphis RiverKings	70	25	40	5	239	287	55
Fort Worth Fire	70	13	53	4	214	397	30

UNITED HOCKEY LEAGUE

East Division	GP	W	L	SOL	GF	GA	Pts
Flint Generals	74	46	22	6	371	278	98
Brantford Smoke	74	33	27	14	312	307	80
Port Huron Border Cats	74	31	33	10	256	303	72
Binghamton Icemen	74	25	40	9	237	339	59
Saginaw Lumber Kings	74	23	46	5	231	342	51

West Division	GP	W	L	SOL	GF	GA	Pts
*Quad City Mallards	74	55	18	1	360	257	111
Muskegon Fury	74	43	23	8	341	244	94
T. Bay Thunder Cats	74	42	26	6	337	304	90
Madison Monsters	74	39	24	11	271	265	89
Winst.-Salem Icehawks	74	33	38	3	228	305	69

WEST COAST HOCKEY LEAGUE

North Division	GP	W	L	SOL	GF	GA	Pts
Tacoma Sabercats	64	42	19	3	300	214	87
Anchorage Aces	64	36	20	8	308	261	80
Idaho Steelheads	64	27	30	7	253	275	61
Reno Rage	64	23	39	2	219	297	48

South Division	GP	W	L	SOL	GF	GA	Pts
*San Diego Gulls	64	53	10	1	347	198	107
Phoenix Mustangs	64	36	25	3	267	235	75
Fresno's Fight. Falcons	64	33	29	2	273	262	68
Bakersfield Fog	64	22	37	5	226	330	49
Tucson Gila Monsters	64	16	43	5	213	334	37

WESTERN PROFESSIONAL HOCKEY LEAGUE

Eastern Division	GP	W	L	SOL	GF	GA	Pts
Fort Worth Bulls	69	41	17	11	296	219	93
Shreveport Mudbugs	69	42	20	7	308	228	91
Central Tex. Stampede	69	40	23	6	258	251	86
Austin Ice-Bats	69	35	23	11	247	255	81
Lake Chas. Ice Pirates	69	35	28	6	273	280	76
Monroe Moccasins	69	35	32	2	225	223	72
Waco Wizards	69	18	48	3	203	319	39

Western Division	GP	W	L	SOL	GF	GA	Pts
*El Paso Buzzards	69	43	20	6	338	252	92
New Mexico Scorpions	69	42	20	7	324	236	91
San Angelo Outlaws	69	29	34	6	280	326	64
Amarillo Rattlers	69	25	32	12	228	300	62
Odessa Jackalopes	69	26	37	6	262	360	58

CHAPTER 27

Senior Hockey and the Allan Cup

Once the Highest Level of the Sport, Senior Hockey is Almost Extinct

Ed Sweeney

THERE HAS BEEN A DRAMATIC DECLINE in senior hockey in Canada these recent years and senior amateur hockey could be very near its demise. Only a handful of teams are left to compete for the Canadian senior hockey championship and the Allan Cup. This is quite a drastic change from the early days of hockey when the amateur game was the only game in town.

In 1885 the first hockey league in Canada was formed in Kingston, Ontario, paving the way for other cities like Montreal, Quebec, Ottawa, Toronto, Peterborough, London and Niagara Falls to form senior hockey league teams. The Amateur Hockey Association of Canada was formed in 1886–87 and in 1890 the Ontario Hockey Association was organized.

This was the era of seven-man hockey teams and 60-minute men as the clubs were only allowed to carry one spare and could only use him in case of injury. The championship team was decided by whoever finished in first place in the league standings at the end of the regular-season schedule. There was no competition from the West even though Winnipeg had formed a senior hockey league in 1891.

In March of 1892, Lord Stanley of Preston, the sixth Governor-General of Canada announced his intention to obtain a Dominion Hockey Challenge Cup. The first recipient of the trophy that was soon known as the Stanley Cup was the Montreal AAA club in 1893.

In 1896 the Winnipeg Victorias traveled to Montreal and blanked the hometown Victorias 2–0, bringing the Stanley Cup west for the first time. Team captain Jack Armytage scored the winning goal in the game while Winnipeg goaltender George "Whitey" Merritt wore white cricket pads. Dan Bain, a future Hockey Hall of Famer, appeared in the Winnipeg Victorias lineup and got his first taste of Stanley Cup play. The Montreal club challenged Winnipeg later that year and with Hockey Hall of Famers Mike Grant and Graham Drinkwater, recaptured the Stanley Cup for the easterners. At the turn of the century hockey was on the move as were some of the future Hockey Hall of Fame players. Lester Patrick appeared with Brandon during the 1904 season, Fred "Cyclone" Taylor played with Portage la Prairie in 1905–06, Art Ross and Joe Hall were in Kenora's 1907 lineup and Edouard "Newsy" Lalonde played one game with Portage in 1907–08.

Of the many great early championship teams, the Ottawa Silver Seven club was perhaps the best. They won the Stanley Cup in 1903, 1904 and 1905 and successfully defeated two challengers during the 1906 season before losing to the Montreal Wanderers.

There were six Hockey Hall of Famers in the Ottawa lineup: Frank McGee, Harvey Pulford, Harry Westwick, Alf Smith, Billy Gilmour and netminder Bouse Hutton. It was around this time that professional hockey came into the picture and in 1908–09 the word amateur was dropped from the Eastern Canada Amateur Hockey Association.

With top teams now willing to pay high salaries for talent, senior amateur clubs found they could not compete successfully with these professional outfits. As the Stanley Cup became the championship trophy of professional hockey senior amateur hockey in Canada was left without a championship cup. This problem was rectified in 1908 when Sir Montagu Allan of Montreal came forward and donated a new hockey trophy. The Allan Cup would be presented annually to the senior amateur hockey champions of Canada. There is a lot of history connected with the Allan Cup over the many years that have followed and longtime senior hockey fans like to spin stories of rinks jammed to the rafters from Glace Bay to Trail. Their anecdotes usually include folklore about the Trail Smoke Eaters, Edmonton Flyers, Toronto Dentals, Moncton Hawks, Whitby Dunlops, Saskatoon Quakers, Winnipeg Maroons and Thunder Bay Twins. They also feature names like Dick Irvin, "Bullet" Joe Simpson, Jerry LaFlamme, George Hainsworth, Frank Fredrickson, Reginald "Hooley" Smith, Grant Warwick, Bill Durnan and Harry Sinden.

In its heyday senior hockey in Canada rivalled, and in some places exceeded, the professional National Hockey League in terms of popularity. NHL teams would only ever represent a handful of Canadian cities (and just Toronto and Montreal from 1934 until 1970) while virtually every community of any size across the country could ice a senior amateur team. Players on these teams lived in the community year-round. Most of them had grown up there. To the fans, they were friends, neighbors and co-workers. Even when teams brought in "ringers" to bolster their roster, they would be given jobs in town and become a part of the community. The game had a much less mercenary feel than did early pro hockey and could foster genuine civic pride and fierce local rivalries. The Allan Cup was as big a deal on the hockey calendar as the Stanley Cup, and its East–West playoff format pushed the game's local rivalries across both regional and provincial boundaries and made senior amateur hockey a truly national spectacle.

The Ottawa Cliffsides were the first winners of the Allan Cup and in 1909 Queen's University of Kingston won the crown. Toronto St. Michael's College captured the Allan Cup in 1910 with team captain Jerry LaFlamme leading the charge. The Winnipeg Victorias were the first western club to win the Allan Cup in 1911 and became the first team to win back-to-back Canadian senior hockey championships when they repeated in 1912. In December of 1914 the Canadian Amateur Hockey Association was formed with branches in the provinces of Quebec, Ontario, Manitoba, Saskatchewan, Alberta and British Columbia.

Remembering St. Mike's

In terms of its hockey history, St. Michael's College in Toronto is generally associated with the junior game, winning the Memorial Cup four times while

sending more than 140 players to the NHL. But hockey history at St. Mike's predates the birth of the Memorial Cup in 1919 by more than a decade and it was the senior game that provided the school with its first national championship.

St. Michael's College was founded in 1852 but it was not until after the turn of the 20th century that the Catholic institution began to integrate into Protestant Ontario. Beginning with the school year of 1904–05, Father Henry Carr committed the College to adopting the high school curriculum prescribed by the Ontario department of education. Carr also believed that sports was a key to community involvement and formed the school's first hockey team in 1906. Competing with clubs from St. Andrew's College in Aurora and Upper Canada College in Toronto, St. Mike's won league titles in 1907 and 1908. Carr's hockey team challenged Stratford for the Ontario Hockey Association junior championship in 1908, but was defeated.

Despite the loss, Carr moved St. Michael's into the senior OHA in 1909 and promptly won the John Ross Robertson Cup as league champions. The following year, St. Michael's went through the season undefeated, not only retaining the Robertson trophy but going on to capture the Allan Cup. A new tradition of hockey excellence had been born.

The Winnipeg Monarchs were the 1915 Allan Cup winners with Hockey Hall of Famers Dick Irvin and Fred "Steamer" Maxwell playing key roles in the championship season. Irvin scored the Cup-winning goal in the final that year as the Winnipeg club defeated the Melville Millionaires 4–2. World War I was now raging in Europe and many of the hockey players joined the Canadian Armed Forces. Hockey was still being played during the war years from 1914 until 1918 and leagues still operated in Canada. The senior loops took on names like the Military and Patriotic leagues and in 1916 the Winnipeg 61st Battalion, led by Hockey Hall of Famer "Bullet" Joe Simpson, captured the Allan Cup. The Kitchener club defeated the Winnipeg Ypres, a military team, and won the 1918 Allan Cup title. Hockey Hall of Famer goaltender George Hainsworth was outstanding in the nets for Kitchener.

In 1920 the Winnipeg Falcons were the Allan Cup champions, beating Toronto Varsity in the final. After their Cup victory, the CAHA asked the Winnipeg club to represent Canada at the 1920 Olympics in Antwerp, Belgium. The Falcons defeated Czechoslovakia, the United States and Sweden in the tournament and captured the gold medal in the first demonstration of hockey at the Olympics. Frank Fredrickson, a future Hockey Hall of Famer, led the Falcons with 12 goals in three games.

The Toronto Granites, who were Allan Cup champions in 1922 and 1923 represented Canada in the first Winter Olympics held at Chamonix, France in 1924. Team Canada demolished all opposition in its road to the gold medal with victories over Czechoslovakia, Sweden, Switzerland, Great Britain and the United States. In the five games Canada scored a total of 110 goals while allowing only three. Harry Watson led the Canadians with 36 goals in the tournament while Bert McCaffery chipped in with 20 and Reginald "Hooley" Smith added another 18 markers. Both Watson and Smith were later elected to the Hockey Hall of Fame. Another team member was defenseman and captain Dunc Munro, who would also captain the Montreal Maroons

when they won the 1926 Stanley Cup title.

The Port Arthur Bearcats won back-to-back Allan Cup titles in 1925 and 1926, defeating the University of Toronto in the Canadian senior final both years. Port Arthur's Lorne Chabot was the best amateur goalkeeper in the country during these years and would later backstop the 1927–28 New York Rangers and the 1931–32 Toronto Maple Leafs to Stanley Cup victories.

The University of Toronto made its third straight Allan Cup final in 1927, this time against Fort William, and captured the championship with a 2–1 overtime triumph in the final game. All four games of the series were played in Vancouver and this was the first time that British Columbia had hosted the senior final. As Allan Cup winners, the University of Toronto represented Canada at the 1928 Winter Olympics in St. Moritz, Switzerland. Canada continued its dominance of international hockey as the Varsity Grads defeated Sweden 11–0, Great Britain 14–0 and Switzerland 13–0 to capture the gold medal. Hugh Plaxton and Dave Trottier led the Canadians with 12 goals apiece in the three-game set while goaltenders Joe Sullivan and Stuffy Mueller were both unbeatable in the net. It was a good year for scholastic hockey clubs in 1928, as the University of Manitoba won the Allan Cup championship over the Montreal Victorias in the final at Ottawa. Andy Blair was one of the westerners' key players and would later play a role in the Toronto Maple Leafs' 1932 Stanley Cup victory.

In 1931 the Winnipeg Hockey Club captured the Allan Cup and represented Canada at the 1932 Winter Olympics held at Lake Placid, New York. With only four countries represented that year, the officials decided on a double round-robin tournament for the first and only time in Olympic history. The Canadians were hard pressed to win the championship as they battled the United States to a 2–2 tie that could not be broken despite 30 minutes of overtime. Wally Munson led Canada in the scoring department with seven goals in the six-game series.

In 1933 the Moncton Hawks became the first Maritime team to win the Allan Cup as they recorded two shutout victories over the Saskatoon Quakers in the Canadian senior hockey final at Vancouver. Moncton goaltender Jimmy Foster was simply outstanding in both games, stopping everything the Quakers had to offer. Moncton repeated in the following campaign as Canadian senior hockey champions and Allan Cup holders. The Hawks defeated Fort William two games to one in the final played at Toronto's Maple Leaf Gardens. Jimmy Foster was again at his very best in the Moncton goal while teammate Dub James led the team in scoring with six points. One of the officials in the series was Clarence Campbell who would later become the president of the National Hockey League.

The Maritime provinces continued their hold on the Allan Cup in 1935 when the Halifax Wolverines won the Canadian senior hockey championship, defeating the Port Arthur Bearcats in the final in front of their hometown fans. The Wolverines were designated to represent Canada in the 1936 Winter Olympics at Garmisch-Partenkirchen, Germany. However, before the 1935–36 season began, several members of the Halifax team had jumped to other clubs and the CAHA replaced them with a hybrid team that included several members of the Port Arthur Bearcats. It was a disappointing 1936 Olympics for the Canadian club as they lost only one game in the tournament, but this 2–1 loss to Great Britain was enough to hand the gold medal to

the British team. Canada settled for second place. It was also a very controversial tournament as the Olympic officials had overturned the rules and format.

The Trail Smoke Eaters won the Allan Cup in 1938 with a three-games-to-one victory over the Cornwall Flyers in the championship finals. A key figure for Trail was Johnny McCreedy who would later be a member of two Stanley Cup-winning teams with the Toronto Maple Leafs. The Smoke Eaters represented Canada in the 1939 World Hockey Championships in Switzerland. They won all eight games of the tournament, scoring 42 goals against the opposition while allowing only one goal, and returned home as gold medal winners.

World War II began in Europe in the fall of 1939 and there was no sports competition internationally until 1947.

The Winnipeg Falcons

So high was the caliber of senior amateur hockey in Canada that until 1961, the Allan Cup champions and other top clubs could generally be counted on to bring home Olympic and World Championship gold. Canada's domination in international hockey began with the Winnipeg Falcons in 1920.

With World War I finally over, and the international sporting world hoping to return to normal after the cancelation of the 1916 Olympics in Berlin, it was decided to stage a spring sports festival in April of 1920 as a lead-in to the Antwerp Games. Canada would send its Allan Cup champion to the Olympic tournament, but there was one problem. The Allan Cup playoffs had not finished until March 29 and the Olympic hockey tournament was scheduled to start on April 20. The Falcons, who had traveled east to defeat the University of Toronto, would not have time to return to Winnipeg before leaving for Belgium. (Transatlantic travel meant boarding a steamship in 1920.) But for the Falcons, overcoming adversity was nothing new. Funds for new clothes and uniforms were hastily raised by the hockey community in Toronto, and the Winnipeg team left by train, first for Montreal, then St. John, New Brunswick, where they set sail for Europe on April 3.

The Falcons long voyage to Belgium had begun in the 1890s when Winnipeg's Icelandic community had began to form its own athletic clubs. The Icelandic Athletic Club and the Vikings played their first hockey game in 1896 and it drew so much interest from the Icelandic community in Winnipeg that it was decided to form a league. It consisted of just the two teams. By 1908, finances were running low and the rent was rising at local ice rinks, so what resulted was the merger of the Vikings and IACs into one team. The Winnipeg Falcons were born, taking their name from the national bird of Iceland. Unfortunately, the Falcons found no place to play. The teams of Winnipeg's British-Protestant majority wanted no part of the immigrant squad and it was not until 1912 that they could form a rival league in which to play. Only after the player shortages and patriotic fervor created by World War I were the Falcons finally permitted to play with the other top Winnipeg teams. Yet after the war, even though every Falcons man of military age had served overseas, the Icelandic team was again on the outs.

Forced to structure a rival league again in 1919–20, the Falcons not only won the championship of the Manitoba Senior Hockey League, they then defeated the champions of Winnipeg, beat Fort William for the championship of Western Canada and went on to win the Allan Cup. After winning Olympic gold, the Falcons returned to civic receptions in Toronto and Winnipeg, where the city's hockey fans had always appreciated the team even if the hockey establishment hadn't.

Senior hockey continued in Canada throughout World War II with an abundance of military teams, some of which would be stocked with NHL players who had been drafted for war service but had not yet been shipped overseas. Future NHL star Bill Durnan helped the Kirkland Lake Blue Devils capture the Allan Cup in 1940, while fellow goaltender "Sugar" Jim Henry and future NHLer Grant Warwick led the Regina Rangers to victory in 1941. In 1942 the Ottawa RCAF Flyers hockey club captured the Canadian senior championship by defeating the Port Arthur Bearcats three games to two in the finals. The Flyers were bolstered by the Boston Bruins' famed line of Milt Schmidt, Woody Dumart and Bobby Bauer who all played key roles in the victory. Edgar Laprade played well for Port Arthur in the series and in 1948 would win the Calder Trophy as rookie of the year with the New York Rangers.

The Ottawa Army Commandos won the 1943 Allan Cup title by defeating the Victoria Army Club three games to one in the final. Reg Reardon and Neil Colville were two future Hockey Hall of Fame members that sparked Ottawa's championship club, while "Sugar" Jim Henry played on his second Allan Cup winner in three years. In 1944 the Quebec Aces were the senior hockey champions of Canada and winners of the Allan Cup. They were led to victory by team captain Billy Reay who would go on and play on Stanley Cup championship clubs with the Montreal Canadiens in 1945–46 and 1952–53. Reay would also coach after his playing days for 17 seasons with the Toronto Maple Leafs and Chicago Black Hawks.

There was no Allan Cup competition in 1945 (it being the sixth year of the World War II) and the majority of hockey players of military age were in the Canadian Armed Forces. World War II ended in 1945 and hockey leagues resumed action on all fronts in Canada. The Calgary Stampeders ruled the senior hockey picture in 1946, winning the Allan Cup over the Hamilton Tigers by a four-games-to-one margin in the championship series. In the 1946–47 campaign the Montreal Royals dominated senior hockey in the east all season and then went on to defeat the defending Cup holders from Calgary in a tough seven-game final to win the Allan Cup. Six of the Royals players found themselves in the NHL with the Montreal Canadiens the following season: Gerry McNeil, Floyd Curry, Rip Riopelle, Tod Campeau, Jacques Locas and Doug Harvey. It would be 18 years before the Allan Cup would return to Quebec courtesy of the Sherbrooke Beavers in 1965.

In 1948 the Olympic Games resumed and were held at St. Moritz, Switzerland. The CAHA changed its format by sending a group of RCAF amateur players instead of the previous Allan Cup champions. In the tournament Team Canada (the RCAF Flyers) was led by forwards Wally Halder and George Mara. Canada and Czechoslovakia completed the tourney with identical records of 7–0–1 but the gold medal was awarded to the Canadians because of a better scoring differential.

The Ottawa Senators (called the "Barber Poles" because of their striped jerseys) were Allan Cup finalists in 1948,

losing the final to the Edmonton Flyers four games to one. Goaltender Al Rollins was a standout in the Flyers net and would go on to a fine NHL career. (He would win the Hart Trophy as NHL MVP with Chicago in 1953–54.) Ottawa came back the following campaign and this time made no mistake in the final, beating the Regina Capitals four games to one to win the Allan Cup. Even with former NHL greats "Sudden Death" Mel Hill and Dave "Sweeney" Schriner, Regina could not skate or generate any offense against their eastern opposition.

One of the greatest amateur goaltenders in this era of hockey was Ottawa's Bill "Legs" Fraser. He was certainly a crowd favorite and after every Ottawa victory "Legs" would throw his goalstick into the stands. Fraser never played in the NHL but did have numerous offers from the professional clubs. He turned them all down.

The Toronto Marlboros were the senior amateur hockey champions of Canada in 1950. In the Allan Cup final that year the Marlboros defeated the Calgary Stampeders four games to one. Members of the winning team included Frank "Flash" Hollett who was on Stanley Cup championship clubs with the Boston Bruins in 1938–39 and 1940–41. Another member of the team was George Armstrong who would later play his entire NHL career (and be on four Stanley Cup-winning teams) with Toronto Maple Leafs. He was inducted into the Hockey Hall of Fame in 1975. Another Maple Leafs Hall of Famer, Joe Primeau, coached the Marlies this year. Having won the Memorial Cup as a coach with St. Michael's in 1947, Primeau would score an unprecedented hat trick by coaching the Maple Leafs to the Stanley Cup in 1951.

Canada was represented by the Edmonton Mercurys at the 1952 Winter Olympics at Oslo, Norway. The Canadians were most impressive in this tournament, starting with seven straight victories which led up to the gold medal game against the United States. It was a hard-fought match that finished in a 3–3 draw, giving the Mercurys the Olympic championship. Canada has not won an Olympic gold medal since this victory by the senior amateurs from Edmonton.

In 1954 the Penticton Vees captured the Canadian senior hockey championship with an exciting four-games-to-three triumph over the Sudbury Wolves in the finals. After falling behind three games to one, Penticton stormed back to win the last three contests and the series. The newly crowned Allan Cup winners were led by the Warwick brothers, Grant (playing coach), Dick and Billy who all played key roles in the victory.

The Penticton Vees represented Canada in the 1955 World Championships at Krefeld, Germany. With the championship on the line, Penticton blanked the Soviet Union by a 5–0 score. The Vees were led to victory with a two-goal performance by Billy Warwick in the final game.

The European Challenge

On January 12, 1953, Canadian Amateur Hockey Association president W.B. George announced that Canada would not be sending a team to the 1953 World Championships.

"Every year we spend $10,000 to send a Canadian hockey team to Europe to play 40 exhibition games [and the IIHF World Championships]," George explained to the press. "All of these games are played to packed houses that only enrich European hockey coffers. In return we are subjected to constant, unnec-essary abuse over our Canadian style of play."

It was difficult to find a team willing to make the trip when Canada returned to the World Championships in 1954, but the CAHA finally found the East York Lyndhursts of suburban Toronto. Though not up to the caliber of previous Canadian entries, the Lyndhursts easily outscored their opponents 57–5 in winning their first six games. Facing the USSR in the final game, the Lyndhursts were crushed 7–2 and the Soviets became the world hockey champions at their very first tournament.

Canada's hockey honor would be restored the following year by the Penticton Vees. Named for three varieties of peaches—the Vedette, the Valiant and the Veteran—the Vees had been formed in the British Columbia Okanagan Valley orchard city in 1950 but did not play their first game until 1951–52. Led by Warwick brothers Dick, Billy and Grant (whose amateur status had been restored after his NHL career) the Vees were Allan Cup finalists in just their second season and Allan Cup champions in 1954. Penticton's IIHF World Championship victory in 1955 seemed almost a case of too much, too fast and instead of wanting more, fans lost interest. The team withdrew from hockey after losing $15,000 in 1955–56.

The last Canadian senior amateur team to win a world championship also hailed from British Columbia. Though their jersey depicted the stacks of the Cominco mine, the Trail Smoke Eaters had actually been named in 1929 after star center Carroll Kendall skated around the ice puffing on a pipe that an irate fan had thrown onto the ice. The "Smokies" became world champs for the first time 10 years later but it is their victory in 1961 that has become a part of Canadian hockey folklore. Every member of the team was a hometown boy except captain Cal Hockley, who was imported from nearby Fernie, B.C. in 1956. Trail is still represented by a Smoke Eaters team and Hockley is captain of the world championship alumni club, known affectionately around town as "the 61ers."

In the 1955 Allan Cup final, the Kitchener-Waterloo Dutchmen delighted their hometown fans with a four-games-to-one series triumph over the Fort William Beavers. Ken Laufman, who led the OHA in scoring during the regular season with 61 points in 50 games, was their leader in the playoffs. In goal for the Dutchmen was Denis Brodeur (father of the New Jersey Devils' Martin) who was the OHA's leading netminder during the regular campaign. The Kitchener-Waterloo coach was Bobby Bauer of Boston Bruin fame. The Kitchener-Waterloo Dutchmen represented Canada in the 1956 Winter Olympics at Cortina, Italy. In the final round of the tournament Canada suffered a 4–1 loss to United States and then a 2–0 setback at the hands of the Soviet Nationals. It was a very disappointing third-place finish for the Canadians at these Olympics and the bronze medal was not what they had expected.

The Whitby Dunlops captured the 1957 OHA and Eastern senior hockey championships and met the Western-winning Spokane Flyers in the finals played at Toronto's Maple Leaf Gardens. It marked the first time a United States team had qualified for the Allan Cup series. Whitby, however, made short work of the Americans by upending Spokane four games to none. The 1958 World Championships were held at Oslo, Norway and the defending Allan Cup champions from Whitby were the Canadian representatives for the

tournament. Bob Attersley tallied the winning goal in the final game as Canada defeated the Soviet Nationals 4–2 and captured the world title. Team captain for the Canadian squad was defenseman Harry Sinden who would later coach the 1969–70 Boston Bruins to a Stanley Cup victory. Harry was also the Team Canada coach in the historic 1972 Summit Series.

The Belleville McFarlands were Canadian senior hockey champions in 1958, but it was an uphill battle all the way as they came back from a three-games-to-one series deficit against the Kelowna Packers to win the final and the Allan Cup. Belleville won the seventh game of the final in Kelowna by an 8–5 score as Russ Kowalchuk sparked the winners with three goals while playing coach Ike Hildebrand and Minnie Menard chipped in with two tallies each. In 1959, Canada was represented by Belleville at the world hockey tournament in Prague, Czechoslovakia. Ike Hildebrand was still the McFarlands' playing coach and was assisted by Billy Reay who made the overseas trip as Belleville's business manager. The McFarlands won the tournament with a record of seven wins and one loss and fulfilled the real purpose of their mission by defeating the Soviet Nationals by a 3–1 count.

The Canadian senior hockey championship of 1959 was won by the Whitby Dunlops who captured their second Allan Cup in three years by defeating the Vernon Canadians four games to one. Key performers for the Dunlops were playing coach Sid Smith (a former Toronto Maple Leaf) and team captain Harry Sinden who was a tower of strength on defence. Another member of the winning squad was Pete Babando who scored the 1950 Stanley Cup winning goal in overtime for the Detroit Red Wings. The Dunlops declined the invitation to represent Canada at the 1960 Winter Olympics in Squaw Valley, California, thus paving the way for the Kitchener-Waterloo Dutchmen to appear in their second successive Olympics. The Canadians played a fine tournament and only a 2–1 loss to the United States prevented them from winning the championship. Fred Etcher of the Canadian team was the leading tournament scorer with 21 points in seven games for the silver medal winners. Bobby Rousseau and Cliff Pennington also played for Canada in the tournament. In 1962 Rousseau was the Calder Trophy winner with the Montreal Canadiens and Pennington was the runner-up for the top rookie award as a member of the Boston Bruins.

The Chatham Maroons won the Canadian senior hockey crown in 1960, defeating the Trail Smoke Eaters in the final four games to none with one game tied. Goaltender Cesare Maniago was outstanding for the Allan Cup champions throughout the playoffs. Maniago would later play 15 years in the NHL with five different teams. At the 1961 World Championships in Geneva, Switzerland, Canada was represented by the Smoke Eaters after Chatham turned down the invitation. The Canadians opened the tournament with a 1–1 draw against Czechoslovakia and thereafter, both teams won all their games before the final day which meant that the Smoke Eaters needed to defeat the Soviet national team by four goals in the final game. A late third-period goal by Norm Lenardon gave the Canadian team a 5–1 victory and the 1961 world hockey title.

In 1962, the Trail Smoke Eaters won the Canadian senior hockey championship by defeating the Montreal Olympics in the final. The following year, Trail once again represented Canada at the world hockey tourney in Stockholm, Sweden. This time the Smoke Eaters finished the tourna-

ment in fourth place behind national teams from the Soviet Union, Sweden and Czechoslovakia. After 1963, neither the Allan Cup winners nor other top senior clubs would represent Canada in international competition. Father David Bauer's national team would take over the hockey program and represent Canada in the Olympic and IIHF World Championships from 1964 until 1969. Afterwards, Canada would not play international events until NHL players were allowed to take part.

One of the most overpowering victories in Allan Cup history was recorded in 1967 by the Drummondville Eagles who captured the prized trophy with a four-games-to-none final series triumph over the Calgary Spurs. Drummondville netminder Claude Cyr turned in a sparkling series performance in registering shutouts in all four games which amounted to 240 minutes of flawless goaltending. The Galt Hornets captured the Allan Cup in 1969 with a four-games-to-none sweep of the Calgary Stampeders. In 1971 Galt won its second Canadian senior hockey crown in three years by again defeating the same Stampeders club four games to none in the final. Vance Millar led his Galt teammates in that championship game scoring two goals, including the Cup winner.

In 1970 the Spokane Jets defeated the Orillia Terriers four games to two in the senior final and became the first United States team in 62 years of Allan Cup competition to win the Canadian senior hockey trophy. The Jets won their second Allan Cup title in three years in 1972 when they upended the Barrie Flyers four games to two. Barrie won the Allan Cup for the first time in 1974, beating the Cranbrook Royals in the Canadian senior hockey final four games to two. The Thunder Bay Twins captured the Canadian senior hockey championship in 1975 by defeating the defending Cup holders from Barrie four games to two in the Allan Cup final. Tom Deacon was the main marksman for the Twins in that final game scoring three goals, including the winner in a 6–4 Thunder Bay victory. In 1976 the Spokane Flyers won the Allan Cup again with a four-games-to-none victory over the Barrie Flyers, who were making their fourth appearance in the championship series in the past five years.

The Brantford Alexanders captured the Canadian senior hockey championship in 1977 with a four-games-to-one series victory over the defending Allan Cup champions from Spokane. In the final game of the series, Fred Speck deflected Denny McLean's pass into the net for the winning goal. Jack Egers, who had played with the Washington Capitals during the previous season, scored nine goals in the finals and was named the most valuable player in the series. In 1980 the Spokane Flyers recaptured the Canadian senior hockey crown with a four-game Allan Cup sweep of the Cambridge Hornets. It was the fourth Allan Cup victory by a Spokane team since 1970.

Newfoundland's Near Victory

Despite the fact that Newfoundland did not join Canada until 1949, organized hockey on "The Rock" dates back to 1899, when the first league was formed. The province's senior league became powerful enough in the 1980s to challenge for the Allan Cup and in 1985 the Corner Brook Royals lost at home in the finals to Thunder Bay after leading three games to none.

In 1986, Corner Brook reached the eastern finals against Flamboro, Ontario—a team featuring ex-NHLers Rocky Saganiuk, Stan Jonathan and goalie

Ken Ellacott. The Royals won a high-scoring, wild affair in seven games to advance to the national Allan Cup finals in Nelson, British Columbia. Playing with the support of 30 loud Newfoundland fans who crossed canada to support their team, Steve MacKenzie was the game one star, as his hat trick paced the Royals to a 6–4 win. Then, Royals goalie Dave Matte made 40 saves in a 6–5 victory, following it up with 37 more in a 5–2 triumph, placing his team within one win of the title again. The well-balanced Royals easily took game four 7–0 to complete the road sweep against a physically intimidating Nelson squad. It was the island's sole national championship. Several years later, the Newfoundland league folded after pricing itself out of existence with expensive "import" players.

The Thunder Bay Twins were the Canadian senior hockey team of the 1980s, winning four Allan Cup titles during the decade. They captured the senior hockey championship in 1984, 1985, 1988 and 1989. Along with their first Cup win in 1975, it gave the Twins a total of five Allan Cup victories, which is the most won by any club in Canadian senior hockey history.

By the time Thunder Bay had come to dominate senior hockey, fewer and fewer Canadian communities were displaying the fan support and corporate financial backing necessary to ice a top-level amateur club. Declining interest would force a number of provincial associations to cancel their senior series due to a shortage of teams. The Ontario Hockey Association suspended its senior A series after the 1991–92 season, signaling the close of the oldest league in hockey. Still, the Allan Cup continues and in the 1990s the Warroad Lakers of Minnesota did what no Canadian senior hockey club had ever done before by winning the trophy three years in a row.

In the 1994 Allan Cup final, Warroad defeated the St. Boniface Mohawks 5–2 to claim their first Allan Cup title. The following year the Lakers won the championship with a 3–2 victory over the Stony Plain Eagles. They won their third straight Canadian senior amateur hockey crown in 1996 by once again beating the Stony Plain Eagles 6–1. The Powell River Regals denied the Lakers a fourth straight title when they beat Warroad 7–3 in the 1997 Allan Cup finals. This United States-based team was located just six miles below the Canadian border in Manitoba and was founded by Cal Marvin (who managed the three championship teams) some 50 years before. Marvin was honored in 1997 by the province of Manitoba, where the Lakers played most of their games, when he was inducted in to the Manitoba Hockey Hall of Fame.

There are a number of reasons for the decline of senior amateur hockey in recent years and many of them read like a litany of complaints about the modern world. Globalization of the economy and modern telecommunications mean people can—and do—know more about what is happening half a world away than in their own backyard. Community pride is not what it once was and a hockey fan in small-town Saskatchewan is more likely to relate to the Mighty Ducks of Anaheim than the Prince Albert Raiders. Businesses cannot hand out jobs just because a person can play hockey, nor would the public let them. In a fast-paced, modern world, senior hockey has become like a relic on an archaeological site—if you dig deep enough, you'll find a fascinating history.

Allan Cup Winners

1908	Ottawa Cliffsides	1939	Port Arthur	1971	Galt Hornets
1909	Kingston Queen's University	1940	Kirkland Lake Blue Devils	1969	Galt Hornets
1910	Toronto St. Michael's	1941	Regina Rangers	1970	Spokane Jets
1911	Winnipeg Victorias	1942	Ottawa RCAF	1972	Spokane Jets
1912	Winnipeg Victorias	1943	Ottawa Commandos	1973	Orillia Terriers
1913	Winnipeg Hockey Club	1944	Quebec Aces	1974	Barrie Flyers
1914	Regina Victorias	1945	no competition	1975	Thunder Bay Twins
1915	Winnipeg Monarchs	1946	Calgary Stampeders	1976	Spokane Flyers
1916	Winnipeg 61st Battalion	1947	Montreal Royals	1977	Brantford Alexanders
1917	Toronto Dentals	1948	Edmonton Flyers	1978	Kimberley Dynamiters
1918	Kitchener Hockey Club	1949	Ottawa Senators	1979	Petrolia Squires
1919	Hamilton Tigers	1950	Toronto Marlboros	1980	Spokane Flyers
1920	Winnipeg Falcons	1951	Owen Sound Mercurys	1981	Petrolia Squires
1921	University of Toronto	1952	Fort Francis Canadiens	1982	Cranbrook Royals
1922	Toronto Granites	1953	Kitchener-Waterloo Dutchmen	1983	Cambridge Hornets
1923	Toronto Granites	1954	Penticton V's	1984	Thunder Bay Twins
1924	Sault Ste. Marie Greyhounds	1955	Kitchener-Waterloo Dutchmen	1985	Thunder Bay Twins
1925	Port Arthur	1956	Vernon Canadiens	1986	Cornerbrook Royals
1926	Port Arthur	1957	Whitby Dunlops	1987	Brantford Motts
1927	Toronto Varsity Grads	1958	Belleville McFarlands	1988	Thunder Bay Twins
1928	University of Manitoba	1959	Whitby Dunlops	1989	Thunder Bay Twins
1929	Port Arthur	1960	Chatham Maroons	1990	Chomedy Laval Warriors
1930	Montreal AAA	1961	Galt Terriers	1991	Charlottetown Islanders
1931	Winnipeg Hockey Club	1962	Trail Smoke Eaters	1992	Saint John Vito's
1932	Toronto Nationals	1963	Windsor Bulldogs	1993	Whitehorse Huskies
1933	Moncton Hawks	1964	Winnipeg Maroons	1994	Warroad Lakers
1934	Moncton Hawks	1965	Sherbrooke Beavers	1995	Warroad Lakers
1935	Halifax Wolverines	1966	Drumheller Miners	1996	Warroad Lakers
1936	Kimberley Dynamiters	1967	Drummondville Eagles	1997	Powell River Regals
1937	Sudbury Tigers	1968	Victoriaville Tigers	1998	Truro Bearcats
1938	Trail Smoke Eaters				

CHAPTER 28

Junior Hockey and the Memorial Cup

The 80-year Quest for the Top Trophy in a Young Man's Game

Ed Sweeney

JUNIOR HOCKEY has been played for more than 100 years. It all began in 1890–91 when the Ontario Hockey Association was formed and a few short years later the Kingston Limestones were crowned the first OHA junior hockey champions. There were other forms of junior hockey played across Canada at the turn of the century but a formation of Provincial leagues was not a reality until the Canadian Amateur Hockey Association came into existence in 1914.

As we head toward the 21st century, the world of junior hockey has seen much growth from its early Canadian roots. The junior game has experienced boom times in Europe and is growing rapidly in the United States. On the world level, Canada has dominated competition at the World Junior Championships, winning 10 gold medals since the tournament was established in 1977, including five in a row from 1993 to 1997. Canada's long-time hockey rival the Soviet Union/C.I.S. claimed nine golds, the most recent of which came in 1992.

Globally, the World Junior Championships attract almost as many national teams to its B, C, and D tournaments as do the World Championships.

In Canada, the game has evolved from its old designations of Junior A and Junior B. The top level of modern junior hockey is known as major junior and consists of three leagues: the Ontario Hockey League, the Quebec Major Junior Hockey League and the Western Hockey League. Each spring the champion of each of these three leagues plus a host club compete for the Memorial Cup. Other contemporary junior leagues are classified as Junior A, B or C. Regional Junior A champions play for the Royal Bank Cup in an annual national championship tournament. In recent years, NHL teams have drafted an increasing number of players from Canadian Junior A and B, as well as from U.S. junior clubs, but the top breeding ground for NHL talent continues to be Major Junior hockey.

Most players on Major Junior rosters are 17, 18 or 19 years old. Each team is also allowed to carry three "over-age" 20-year-olds and, in rare cases, 15 and 16-year-olds have suited up.

The OHL, QMJHL and WHL combine to form the Canadian Hockey League which provides major junior hockey with a national (and international) presence as both the Ontario and Western leagues have teams in the United States as well as Canada. The 1998–99 season will see 53 major junior franchises in operation in eight Canadian provinces and four American states. Even the top club team prize in junior hockey, the Memorial Cup, went international in 1983 when it was won by the Portland Winter Hawks. The Spokane Chiefs became the second U.S.-based champion in 1991.

In its original form, the Memorial Cup had been emblematic of junior hockey supremacy in Canada only. It was back in March of 1919, shortly after World War I had ended, that the CAHA set forth to promote junior hockey in

Canada. The hockey body was aided by the Ontario Hockey Association who donated the OHA Memorial Cup Trophy for the Canadian championship of junior teams in national competition. The idea of such a trophy was proposed and promoted by Captain James T. Sutherland, a past president of the OHA and CAHA, and was in memory of the many Canadian hockey players who had made the supreme sacrifice for their country in World War I from 1914 to 1918. It was also in memory of two of the Kingston Frontenacs' finest players and Hockey Hall of Famers, Captain's Alan "Scotty" Davidson and George T. Richardson who were both killed in action during the Great War. Another Hockey Hall of Famer honored was John Ross Robertson, a former OHA president who, during his six-year tenure, had donated three trophies for annual competition, designating one each to be awarded the champions of senior, intermediate and junior divisions. He never lived to see the trophy which was originally called the John Ross Robertson OHA Memorial Cup, as he died on May 31, 1918.

The Saskatchewan Amateur Hockey Association donated a trophy to the CAHA in memory of Captain Edward Lyman "Hick" Abbott of Regina who had lost his life in the war. Abbott was a fine player of his day and was a member of the Regina Victorias, the 1914 Allan Cup champions. The trophy would be presented each year to the junior champions of Western Canada. In 1919 another trophy was introduced by the Manitoba Amateur Hockey Association in memory of Captain Ollie Turnbull who had also lost his life in World War I. This trophy would be presented annually to the Junior A champions of Manitoba. The Regina Patricias were the first to claim the Abbott Cup in 1919 when they defeated the Manitoba junior champions, the Young Men's Lutheran Club of Winnipeg, in the Western final.

The first OHA Memorial Cup final was played on March 19, 1919 at the Toronto Arena between the University of Toronto Schools and Regina Patricias. It was a two-game total-goals series with the eastern champions overpowering Regina by 14–3 and 15–5 scores for a 29–8 total-goal victory. Team captain Jack Aggett and Don Jeffreys led the Toronto club with nine goals apiece in the two games. Another member of Toronto's championship squad, defenseman Duncan (Dunc) Munro would later go on to establish an unprecedented feat by adding an Allan Cup championship (1922 and 1923 Toronto Granites), Olympic championship (1924 when the Granites represented Canada) and a Stanley Cup championship (1926 Montreal Maroons) to his Memorial Cup victory.

Lou Marsh, a legendary sports writer with the *Toronto Star* officiated both games in 1919 while Jack Hughes, a hockey star from Winnipeg, worked the opening match. Bill Finlay, a sports editor of the *Winnipeg Free Press* aided Marsh in game two.

As the 1920s roared in so did junior hockey all across

Canada. The sports' fans began filling arenas to watch the brand of high level hockey that good junior players provided. One reason given for this new-found popularity was the Memorial Cup competition and the East–West rivalry. In the first decade of the Canadian junior hockey championships the western clubs managed to win five Memorial Cup titles and trailed the east by only one game in the much followed championship series.

In the 1919–20 campaign, the Toronto Canoe Club powered its way through all opposition and won the Memorial Cup. The Canoe Club defeated the Selkirk Fishermen in a two-game total-goals final and then dispatched Fort William in a "sudden death" game with the likes of Roy Worters, Lionel Conacher and captain Billy Burch who were all key figures in the Toronto Canoe Club's road to the Canadian junior hockey championship. Burch would later join the NHL's Hamilton Tigers and in the 1924–25 campaign, led them to a first-place finish. He was the Hart Trophy recipient as league MVP that season. Goaltender Worters went on to a fine NHL career with the Pittsburgh Pirates and New York Americans and was the Hart Trophy winner in 1928–29. He won the Vezina Trophy in 1931 as the NHL's top goaltender. Defenceman Lionel Conacher (the Big Train) was a member of two Stanley Cup-winning teams during his 12-year NHL career and was twice runner-up for the Hart Trophy award. Conacher was voted Canada's athlete of the first half of the century by a Canadian Press poll in 1950. All three players were later elected to the Hockey Hall of Fame.

The Winnipeg Falcons beat the Stratford Midgets in the 1921 Cup final as the western team upset the eastern champions 11–9 in the two-game total-goals series at Toronto. One of the Stratford players was the legendary Howie Morenz who dazzled the fans with his speed and hockey ability. Morenz would sign an NHL contract with Montreal in 1924 and would play on three Stanley Cup winners with the Canadiens. He led the NHL in scoring twice and was the first three time recipient of the Hart Trophy. Howie was noted as the top hockey player of this first half century and was one of the first players to be elected to the Hockey Hall of Fame in 1945.

Many other junior hockey players from this decade went on to great NHL careers. Murray Murdoch of the 1923 University of Manitoba team is one of these. He led the western varsity club to the Memorial Cup that year, scoring nine goals against Kitchener in the two-game final. Murray was the first player to ink a contract with the new NHL expansion New York Rangers in 1926. He was a member of two Rangers Stanley Cup-winning teams and was the National Hockey League's first ironman, playing 508 consecutive games in 11 years with the New York Rangers.

Another Hockey Hall of Famer, Herbie Lewis, played his junior hockey with Calgary in 1923 and 1924 and was a member of Stanley Cup championship teams with Detroit in 1936 and 1937. Ralph "Cooney" Weiland played his junior hockey with the OHA's Owen Sound Greys and was a key member of their 1924 Canadian junior championship team. He turned pro with the Boston Bruins and in the 1929–30 season captured the NHL scoring crown with a record 73 points in 44 games. Another Owen Sound team member was Mel "Butch" Keeling who later played on the 1933 New York Rangers Stanley Cup-winning team.

Ken Doraty, another player of note, was with the Regina Pats, Memorial Cup champions of 1925. Ken's one claim to fame happened on April 3, 1933 while with the Toronto Maple Leafs in a playoff game gainst Boston. He tallied the winning marker after 104:46 of overtime. The game stands as the second-longest match played in NHL history.

The Memorial Cup Goes West

The Memorial Cup traveled west for the first time when the Winnipeg Falcons beat the Stratford Midgets in 1921. The win followed on the heels of the senior Winnipeg Falcons' Allan Cup and Olympic championships of 1920. Originally formed in 1912 as an amalgamation of the Vikings and the Icelandic Athletic Club, the Falcons players (who were Lutherans of Icelandic decent) faced much prejudice from the British-Protestant majority in Winnipeg as they strove to reach their hockey goals. The Falcons junior team was formed from the Young Mens Lutheran Club in Winnipeg, but its roster contained fewer players of Icelandic decent then did the senior Falcons.

The junior Falcons raced out to a 9–2 lead over Stratford in game one of the two-game total goal Memorial Cup series behind three goals from Wally Fridfinnson. The Midgets struck back with a 7–2 win in game two, including a hat trick from Howie Morenz, but Winnipeg still took the series 11–9 in aggregate. Falcons goalie Scotty Comfort was given immense credit for allowing only seven goals under Stratford's relentless attack in the second game. Falcons defenseman Harry Neil would later coach the Winnipeg Monarchs to Memorial Cup championships in 1935 and 1937, while teammate Art Somers would play seven years in the NHL with Chicago and New York and win the Stanley Cup with the Rangers in 1933.

A group of junior hockey players followed which included Paul Thompson who was a member of the 1926 Calgary club that won the Canadian junior title. Paul went on to a 13-year NHL career with New York Rangers (Stanley Cup winners in 1928) and Chicago Black Hawks (Cup winners in 1934 and 1938). Carl Voss was a Memorial Cup finalist with Kingston in 1926 and was the first NHL rookie of the year trophy winner in 1933 with the Detroit Red Wings. He also scored the Stanley Cup-winning goal in the 1938 final for the Black Hawks.

Harold "Mush" March played on the Canadian junior championship-winning Regina Monarchs in 1928. A veteran of 17 NHL seasons with Chicago Black Hawks, "Mush" will be remembered for his overtime goal in the 1934 final over Detroit which gave the Black Hawks their first Stanley Cup championship. One player from the Memorial Cup-losing team that year was the Ottawa Gunners' Syd Howe who also went on to play 17 NHL seasons. In a NHL game on February 3, 1944 against the New York Rangers, Detroit's Syd Howe tallied six goals as the Red Wings hammered the Rangers 12–2.

Toronto saw its third Memorial Cup champion crowned in 1929 when the Marlboros won the coveted trophy for the first time. The team was coached by Frank Selke and led by two future NHL stars, Charlie Conacher and Harvey "Busher" Jackson. Jackson captured the NHL scoring crown in 1932 with the Toronto Maple Leafs while teammate Conacher led all scorers in 1934 and 1935. They both played on their only Stanley Cup winner in 1932 with the Leafs where they formed Toronto's famous "Kid Line" with Joe Primeau. The trio were all later inducted into the Hockey Hall of Fame. Another member of the Marlies club

was Hall of Famer defenseman Reginald "Red" Horner who followed his two teammates to the Maple Leafs. Earl Seibert was a solid defenseman with the OHA's Kitchener Colts juniors and played on Stanley Cup winners with the New York Rangers in 1932–33 and the Chicago Black Hawks in 1937–38. He was elected to the Hockey Hall of Fame in 1963. Two future Hockey Hall of Fame goaltenders from Canadian junior hockey in the 1920s were Cecil "Tiny" Thompson, who played with Calgary, and Charlie Gardiner, who was with the Winnipeg Tigers.

In the 1930s, Canadian junior hockey continued to produce more and more players for the National Hockey League. The 1930 Memorial Cup final, for example, sent six players to the NHL. From the Cup-winning Regina Pats were Frank "Buzz" Boll, Gord Pettinger and Eddie Wiseman while the West Toronto Nationals sent up Bob Gracie, John "Red" Doran and Bill Thoms.

Another future Hall of Famer was Bill Cowley of the Ottawa Primroses, Memorial Cup finalists in 1931. Cowley led the Boston Bruins to a couple of Stanley Cup victories (1939 and 1941) and won the NHL scoring title in 1940–41. He was also awarded the Hart Trophy in 1940–41 and 1942–43.

Dave "Sweeney" Schriner is another Hockey Hall of Famer who played his junior hockey in Calgary. He broke into the NHL in 1934–35 with the New York Americans and captured the rookie of the year award. Schriner won the NHL scoring crown in 1935–36 and 1936–37 and was a member of Stanley Cup championship teams with the Toronto Maple Leafs in 1942 and 1945.

In 1931 and 1932 Clint Smith was with the Saskatoon juniors. He joined the NHL in 1937 with the New York Rangers and was on their 1940 Stanley Cup-winning team. He captured the Lady Byng Trophy in 1939 and 1944 and is a member of the Hockey Hall of Fame. Bill Durnan first achieved recognition with the junior Sudbury Wolves in 1931–32 and later became the NHL's top goaltender of the 1940s with Montreal Canadiens. He won the Vezina Trophy six out of seven seasons and was a six-time NHL First Team All-Star and a two-time Stanley Cup champion with the Montreal Canadiens (1944 and 1946). Bill was inducted into the Hockey Hall of Fame in 1963.

The Sudbury Wolves captured the Canadian junior title in 1932 with future NHL great Hector "Toe" Blake in their lineup. Blake would later play on three Stanley winners (the 1935 Montreal Maroons and 1944 and 1946 Montreal Canadiens) and was the NHL scoring champion and Hart Trophy recipient in 1938–39. He was also named the Lady Byng Trophy winner in 1946. He later coached the Montreal Canadiens to another eight Stanley Cup victories and is a member of the Hockey Hall of Fame.

Bryan Hextall was on the Memorial Cup-losing Winnipeg Monarchs when Blake's Sudbury team won in 1932. Hextall was a member of the 1940 New York Rangers Stanley Cup championship club and captured the NHL scoring crown in 1942. Hextall's two sons, Bryan Jr., and Dennis, later played in the NHL as does his grandson Ron. Bryan Sr. was elected into the Hockey Hall of Fame in 1969.

The George T. Richardson trophy was donated in memory of this fine hockey player form Kingston, Ontario who had lost his life in World War I. The trophy was presented to the Canadian Amateur Hockey Association by his brother, James A. Richardson of Winnipeg, in 1932. The silver cup trophy is presented annually to the junior hockey champions of Eastern Canada.

In 1934 the Toronto St. Michael's College club assembled one of the finest junior hockey teams in the country. They won the OHA title and the Canadian junior hockey crown that year. There were eight players from that Toronto championship squad who went on to play in the NHL, including Hockey Hall of Famer Bobby Bauer. The others were Reg Hamilton, Regis "Pep" Kelly, Art Jackson, Nick Metz, Don Willson, Clarence Drouillard and Harvey Teno. Bauer shifted to Kitchener the next season and was teamed with Milt Schmidt and Woodrow "Woody" Dumart and the Kraut Line was born.

In 1937–38 the trio moved up to the Boston Bruins, leading the NHL club to four straight first-place finishes and Stanley Cup triumphs in 1939 and 1941. Bobby was singled out for his clean play and sportsmanship in 1940, 1941 and 1947 when he was awarded the Lady Byng Trophy. In a 10-year NHL career he only accumulated 36 penalty minutes. Milt Schmidt would capture the NHL scoring crown in 1940 and the Hart Trophy in 1951. Schmidt, Bauer and Dumart are all members of the Hockey Hall of Fame.

Walter "Turk" Broda played junior hockey with Brandon in 1932–33 and led the club to the provincial championship. He began his NHL career with Toronto Maple Leafs and would backstop the Leafs to five Stanley Cup titles while winning the Vezina Trophy three times. His last Vezina win was shared with Al Rollins in 1951. Broda later coached the Toronto Marlboros to Memorial Cup victories in 1955 and 1956. He was elected to the Hockey Hall of Fame in 1967.

Sylvanus "Syl" Apps played junior hockey in Paris, Ontario and signed with the Toronto Maple Leafs in 1936. He captured the Calder Trophy as NHL rookie of the year and was the Lady Byng winner in 1942. Syl played on three Toronto Stanley Cup championship teams and in 1961 he was inducted into the Hockey Hall of Fame. Another Hall of Famer from that era of junior hockey was Walter "Babe" Pratt who played with the Kenora Thistles and was the Manitoba Junior Hockey League scoring champion in 1935. Pratt later played on the 1940 Stanley Cup champion New York Rangers and the 1945 Toronto Maple Leafs where he scored the Stanley Cup-winning goal. In a game on January 8, 1944, Pratt became the first defenseman to record six assists as Toronto blasted Boston 12–3. Babe had a great 1943–44 season and was awarded the Hart Trophy.

In 1936 the West Toronto Nationals emerged as Canadian junior hockey champions. One player in the Toronto lineup was Roy Conacher who would later play on Stanley Cup-winning teams with Boston in 1939 and 1941. Conacher's best NHL season was 1948–49 with Chicago when he captured the Art Ross Trophy as the league's leading scorer.

Herbert "Buddy" O'Connor played junior hockey with Montreal in 1935 and later played on two Stanley Cup winners with the Canadiens. He captured the Hart Trophy in 1948 with the New York Rangers and is a member of the Hockey Hall of Fame.

The Winnipeg Monarchs were the class of Canadian junior hockey in 1937, winning their second Memorial Cup in three years. The Monarchs produced one of the top-rated lines in all of junior hockey that season with team captain Alf Pike, Johnny McCreedy and Dick Kowcinak. Pike was later a member of the 1940 Stanley Cup champion New York Rangers and coached the NHL club after retiring as a player. Johnny McCreedy and Dick Kowcinak played on the Allan Cup champion Trail Smoke Eaters the following season and also in 1939 when the senior club won the IIHF World Championship. McCreedy turned pro with the

Toronto Maple Leafs and was a member of their 1942 and 1945 Stanley Cup winners. Another Monarchs team player was Pete Langelle, who also played with Toronto and scored the Leafs' 1942 Cup-winning goal.

John "Black Jack" Stewart was a solid defenseman with the Detroit Red Wings and Chicago Black Hawks during his 12-year NHL career. The future Hall of Famer played his junior hockey with the Portage Terriers in 1936 and 1937. He was named to five NHL All-Star teams and was a member of Stanley Cup championship clubs with the Detroit Red Wings in 1943 and 1950.

In 1938 the Oshawa Generals were rated by many as the top junior club in Canada and their star, Billy Taylor, the top player in the country. However the western champion St. Boniface Seals would prove all the experts wrong as they upset Oshawa in the Memorial Cup final before record crowds at Maple Leaf Gardens in Toronto. The Seals were led by defenseman Wally Stanowski and Billy Reay who both went on to fine NHL careers. Stanowski would play on four Toronto Maple Leaf Stanley Cup-winning teams (1942, 1945, 1947, and 1948) while Reay was on Montreal Canadiens Stanley Cup championship teams in 1946 and 1953. Bill Reay joined the coaching ranks after his playing days and piloted the Toronto Maple Leafs and Chicago Black Hawks over a 17-year career and recorded 541 victories.

Billy Taylor redeemed himself the following campaign, leading Oshawa to the Canadian junior hockey crown. The team captain won his second OHA junior hockey scoring title that year and tallied nine times in the four-game 1939 Cup final to spark Oshawa to victory. He played on the 1942 Stanley Cup-winning Toronto Maple Leafs and later with Detroit set a NHL record with seven assists as the Red Wings hammered Chicago 10–5 on March 16, 1947. Hall of Famer Ken Reardon was with the Edmonton club in the 1939 Memorial Cup final and made this comment on Taylor: "He scored five goals in game one of the final against us and was just a one-man show the entire series."

Full Houses Despite Hard Times

Despite the difficult times of the Great Depression, junior hockey continued to draw large crowds during the 1930s. By 1932, junior players who had been used to performing in front of a few hundred spectators were now performing in front of thousands in the brand new Maple Leaf Gardens in Toronto. Throughout the 1930s, all of the Memorial Cup finals took place either in Winnipeg, where games were played in Shea's Amphitheatre (adjacent to Shea's Brewery) or in Toronto, where the Mutual Street Arena hosted the games in 1931 before the Memorial Cup settled into Maple Leafs Gardens in 1933. With crowds approaching 10,000 fans, the Newmarket Redmen defeated the Regina Pats in three games. With the growing crowds came expansion to a best-of-five format in 1937. Foster Hewitt began broadcasting the games on radio.

The Memorial Cup continued to attract record crowds throughout the 1940s despite World War II. The series alternated between Toronto and Winnipeg for the first few years of the decade before moving to Maple Leaf Gardens exclusively in 1943. The Memorial Cup finals were expanded to a best-of-seven format that year and though the series only went six games, the Oshawa Generals and Winnipeg

Rangers attracted 73,867 fans for an average of 12,311 per game. Winnipeg took the series with a 4–3 win in game six that was witnessed by 14,485 fans. In 1947, the Memorial Cup went on the road again, with games hosted in Winnipeg, Regina, and Moose Jaw, Saskatchewan. The Montreal Royals became Quebec's first Memorial Cup winner playing in Winnipeg in 1949. In 1950 the tournament was held at the Montreal Forum for the first time.

World War II began in 1939 in Europe and Canada was at war again. The National Hockey League and Canadian junior hockey leagues still operated during the six-year ordeal that was to follow and only the senior hockey leagues were changed to military hockey leagues.

Saskatchewan produced many junior hockey players for the NHL over the years and, in the late 1930s and early 1940s, sent five future Hall of Famers to the big league. Sid Abel broke into the NHL in 1938–39 with Detroit Red Wings and in 1949 was named the Hart Trophy winner. Doug Bentley was next when he made the Chicago Black Hawk club in 1939–40 and was the NHL's scoring champion in 1943. Max Bentley followed his brother to Chicago in 1940–41 and would capture the scoring title in 1946 and 1947. He was also the Lady Byng winner in 1943 and Hart Trophy winner in 1946.

Elmer Lach entered the NHL with the Montreal Canadiens in 1940–41 and won the scoring crown in 1945 and 1946 and the Hart Trophy in 1945.

Charlie "Chuck" Rayner played his first junior hockey with the Saskatoon Wesleys at age 16 in 1936–37 and later with the Kenora Thistles of the Manitoba Junior Hockey League from 1937–38 to 1939–40. He began his NHL career with the New York Americans in 1940–41 and after the war joined the New York Rangers. In 1950 he became only the second goaltender to win the Hart Trophy.

Then came a Manitoban, Billy Mosienko who played just one year of junior hockey with the Winnipeg Monarchs in 1939–40 before turning pro with the Chicago Black Hawks. The future Hall of Famer captured the Lady Byng Trophy in 1945 and is still the NHL record holder of the three fastest goals in 21 seconds. "Wee Willie" set the record in a game played on March 23, 1952 at Madison Square Garden as his Chicago Black Hawks registered a 7–6 victory over the New York Rangers.

Maurice "Rocket" Richard played with Verdun of the Quebec Junior Hockey League in 1938–39 and 1939–40. Richard made his NHL debut in 1942–43 with the Montreal Canadiens and was a member of eight Stanley Cup winners in his brilliant career. The Rocket was the Hart Trophy recipient in 1947 and was elected into the Hockey Hall of Fame in 1961.

One of the top defenseman in NHL history was Doug Harvey who began his hockey career in the Quebec Junior Hockey League with Montreal in 1942–43. The Hall of Famer played on six Stanley Cup-winning teams with the Montreal Canadiens and won the Norris Trophy as top NHL defenseman seven times.

Albert "Red" Tilson played with the Oshawa juniors in 1942 and 1943 as the Generals were Memorial Cup finalists both years. Tilson lost his life the following year in battle during World War II. The Red Tilson Trophy, awarded to the Most Valuable Player in the Ontario junior league was established in his honor and the annual award has been presented since 1945.

Ted Lindsay played junior hockey with St. Michael's College in Toronto as well as with the Oshawa Generals and was part of their 1944 Canadian junior championship team. He turned pro with Detroit in 1944–45 and was a key member of four Red Wings Stanley Cup winners. Ted won the NHL scoring crown in 1950 and was inducted into the Hockey Hall of Fame in 1966.

Gordie Howe played his minor hockey in Saskatoon and in 1944–45 journeyed east and joined the OHA Galt junior Red Wings. Gordie broke into the NHL in 1946–47 with Detroit and led the Red Wings to four Stanley Cup championships, scoring the winning goal in the 1955 final. He was nicknamed "Mr. Hockey" and that was exactly what he was for 26 NHL seasons and 1,767 games. Howe was named to 21 All-Star teams and was a six-time NHL scoring champion and a recipient of the Hart Trophy another six times. Gordie is, and always will be, a great ambassador for the game of hockey. In 1972 he was elected to the Hockey Hall of Fame.

Terry Sawchuk played one year of junior hockey with the Winnipeg Rangers and in 1946–47 he tended goal for the Windsor Spitfires. Terry became the Detroit Red Wings' regular netminder in 1950–51 and won the Calder Trophy as rookie of the year. He would go on to play on four Stanley Cup winners with Detroit and Toronto and was a four-time Vezina Trophy recipient. Terry recorded a record 103 shutouts in his starry career and was elected to the Hockey Hall of Fame in 1971.

A standout defenseman by the name of Leonard "Red" Kelly was first noticed when he was a member of the 1947 Memorial Cup champion St. Michael's Majors. In his 20-year NHL career, Kelly won the Lady Byng Trophy four times, was the first winner of the Norris Trophy and played on eight Stanley Cup championship teams with the Detroit Red Wings and Toronto Maple Leafs. He was inducted into the Hockey Hall of Fame in 1969.

Goaltender Jacques Plante played his junior hockey in the Quebec league and began his NHL career in 1952–53 with the Montreal Canadiens. He backstopped Montreal to six Stanley Cup titles and would put his name on the Vezina Trophy a record seven times. In 1962 he became only the fourth goalie to win the Hart Trophy. Plante recorded a total of 82 shutouts in his career and was the first goaltender to wear a mask on a regular basis. He was elected to the Hockey Hall of Fame in 1978.

Dickie Moore played on two straight Memorial Cup-winning teams, the Montreal Royals in 1949 and the Montreal Junior Canadiens in 1950. These were the first two teams from Quebec to win Canada's national junior championship. Moore began his NHL career in 1951–52 with Montreal and helped the Canadiens to six Stanley Cup wins and twice led the NHL in scoring (1958 and 1959). Moore was inducted into the Hockey Hall of Fame in 1974.

There were also a dozen Canadian junior hockey players in the 1940s that were later elected into the Hockey Hall of Fame. Harry Watson, Fern Flaman, Bill Gadsby, Johnny Bower, Bert Olmstead, Tom Johnson, Bill Quackenbush, Alex Delvecchio, Marcel Pronovost, Glenn Hall, Tim Horton and George Armstrong.

Bernie "Boom Boom" Geoffrion played junior hockey with the Montreal Nationals in 1950–51 and moved up to the Montreal Canadiens the following season, winning the Calder Trophy. He was on six Stanley Cup championship teams with Montreal, won the Art Ross Trophy twice and the Hart Trophy once in 1961. Geoffrion was elected to the Hockey Hall of Fame in 1972.

Jean Beliveau played junior hockey with Victoriaville and Quebec before signing with the Montreal Canadiens in 1953. In 1956 Beliveau won the NHL scoring title and Hart Trophy and captured his second Hart Trophy in 1964. He led the Montreal Canadiens to a total of 10 Stanley Cup wins and was the first recipient of the Conn Smythe Trophy in 1965 as playoff MVP. Jean was inducted into the Hockey Hall of Fame in 1972.

Andy Bathgate played all his minor hockey in Winnipeg and then went east to the Guelph juniors and captained the Biltmores to the Memorial Cup in 1952. Bathgate made his NHL debut the following season with the New York Rangers and in 1959 he was the Hart Trophy recipient. Andy was later traded to Toronto and scored the Leafs' Stanley Cup-winning goal in 1964. He was elected to the Hockey Hall of Fame in 1978.

From 1951–52 to 1954–55 Henri Richard played in the Quebec Junior Hockey League with Montreal. The following season he joined the Montreal Canadiens and followed in the footsteps of his older brother, the illustrious Maurice Richard. Henri was a member of a record 11 Stanley Cup teams and twice scored the Cup-winning goal. He won the Masterton Trophy in 1974 and was elected into the Hockey Hall of Fame in 1979.

The Inkerman Rockets

A farming community of 100 people in the lower Ottawa Valley, the tiny town of Inkerman, Ontario boasted a junior hockey team that captivated fans from Kingston to Montreal for a brief period in the late 1940s and early 1950s. The brainchild of Lloyd Laporte, a school teacher from nearby Winchester who wanted to give local players an opportunity to play organized hockey, the Inkerman Rockets played in the Winchester and District Intermediate League. Aided by local farmers who contributed five dollars apiece, Laporte was able to obtain red and white jerseys on sale for his team and named them the Rockets to match the "R" logo that was already stitched on the sweaters. The Rockets would win five consecutive Ottawa and District championships and reached the 1951 Memorial Cup quarterfinals. Among the Rockets players that year was future hockey author and broadcaster Brian McFarlane, who had the unenviable task of covering Jean Beliveau in the big game. Beliveau's Quebec Citadelles proved too much for the small-town team, though they would fall to the eventual Memorial Cup champion Barrie Flyers in the eastern championship game.

Hockey Hall of Famer Bobby Hull played junior hockey in the OHA with the St. Catharines Teepees in 1955–56 and 1956–57 before joining the Chicago Black Hawks. He won the NHL scoring crown three times, the Hart Trophy twice and the Lady Byng Trophy once. Bobby was on one Stanley Cup winner in 1961 with Chicago and was elected to the Hall in 1983.

Like Hull, Stan Mikita played his junior hockey with St. Catharines and in 1959 he moved up to the Chicago Black Hawks. Stan would capture the NHL scoring title four times over a 20-year career and is still the only player to win the Art Ross, Hart and Lady Byng trophies in the same season. Mikita then duplicated his 1966–67 trophy haul by accomplishing the rare triple again the following year. He was a

member of the Chicago's 1961 Stanley Cup championship team and was inducted into the Hockey Hall of Fame in 1983. Other Hockey Hall of Famers to play Canadian junior hockey in the 1950s were Johnny Bucyk, Norm Ullman, Harry Howell, Rod Gilbert, Jean Ratelle, Bobby Pulford, Frank Mahovlich, Pierre Pilote and Dave Keon.

Phil Esposito played his junior hockey with St. Catharines in 1961–62 and broke into the NHL with Chicago in 1963–64. After being traded by Chicago to Boston in 1967, "Espo" won the Art Ross Trophy five times and was the first NHL player to record 100 points in a season (1968–69). He was also a two-time Hart Trophy recipient and was a member of two Boston Stanley Cup winning teams. Phil was inducted into the Hockey Hall of Fame in 1984.

One of the top defencemen of all-time, Bobby Orr played his junior hockey with Oshawa, leading the Generals to the 1966 Memorial Cup final. Bobby began his NHL career in 1966–67 with the Boston Bruins and was the Calder Trophy winner. He then went on to claim eight straight Norris Trophy wins as the NHL's top defenseman. He was the first rearguard to win the Art Ross Trophy (in 1970) and was the scoring champion again in 1975. Orr was the Hart Trophy winner three straight years and led the Boston Bruins to Stanley Cup victories in 1970 and 1972. He scored the Cup-winning goal and won the Conn Smythe Trophy as playoff MVP in both years. Bobby Orr was inducted into the Hockey Hall of Fame in 1979.

Bobby Clarke played all of his minor hockey including junior in Flin Flon, Manitoba. He led the Bombers to the Manitoba Junior Hockey League championship in 1967 and captured the league's scoring title with 183 points. Bobby played his best two junior years with Flin Flon in the WCHL and led that league in scoring both seasons while capturing the MVP honors in 1969. He broke into the NHL with Philadelphia in 1969–70 and captained the Flyers to Stanley Cup championships in 1974 and 1975. Clarke was named the Hart Trophy recipient three times (1973, 1975 and 1976). He was also the winner of the Masterton Trophy in 1972 for perseverance and dedication to hockey and was inducted into the Hockey Hall of Fame in 1987.

In 1969 the NHL held its first Amateur Draft and from the first 24 selections, 16 players from the Ontario Junior Hockey League were chosen. Another six came from the Western Hockey League while one came from the Quebec Junior League. The Canadian junior team of the 1960s was the Edmonton Oil Kings, winners of the Abbott Trophy as western champions seven straight years from 1960 to 1966. The Oil Kings also won two Memorial Cup championships. Other Hockey Hall of Famers that played Canadian junior hockey in the 1960s were, Bernie Parent, Serge Savard, Guy Lapointe, Brad Park, Darryl Sittler, Gilbert Perreault, Denis Potvin and Marcel Dionne.

At the 1970 CAHA annual meeting the delegates gave their approval for a split-level Junior A setup that would embrace only the OHA, WCHL and the QAHA, forerunners of today's three major junior leagues. The rest of the country would be relegated to a lower tier of competition. The Manitoba Amateur Hockey Association came forward in 1970 and donated the Manitoba Centennial Cup Trophy to the Canadian Amateur Hockey Association. This trophy would be presented annually to the Junior A Canadian Junior Hockey Champions. In 1996 the Centennial Cup trophy was retired and was replaced by the Royal Bank Cup.

After leading the Quebec Remparts to the 1971 Memorial Cup championship in his final year of junior hockey, Guy

Lafleur was drafted first overall by the Montreal Canadiens later that year. He went on to win three straight NHL scoring crowns and captured the Hart Trophy in 1977 and 1978. Guy was a member of five Stanley Cup championship teams with the Canadiens and was the 1976 Conn Smythe Trophy winner. Lafleur was elected to the Hockey Hall of Fame in 1988.

In 1972 the Memorial Cup playoff final was changed to a round-robin tournament with the champions of the Ontario Quebec and Western Hockey League's meeting in the final.

Toronto's Championship Teams

The city of Toronto has been home to 14 Memorial Cup championship teams, including the St. Michael's Majors (1934, 1945, 1947 and 1961), the West Toronto Redmen (1936), the Toronto Canoe Club (1920) and the University of Toronto Schools (1919). The most successful junior club in Canadian hockey history is the Toronto Marlboros who won the Memorial Cup a record seven times (1929, 1955, 1956, 1964, 1967, 1973 and 1975).

The Toronto Marlborough Hockey Club took its name from the Duke of Marlborough after team secretary Fred Waghorne wrote him in 1903 to obtain permission to use his name and crown for the athletic club. The club's first Ontario junior championship came in 1903 when the Marlboros beat the Kingston Frontenac-Beechgroves. As champions of the OHA, the Marlboros challenged Ottawa for the (still strictly amateur) Stanley Cup in 1904. After a respectable showing in a 6–3 loss in game one, the Marlies were crushed 11–2 by the Silver Seven in the series finale.

Almost 70 years later, the Toronto Marlboros enjoyed a record-setting season in 1972–73 with 47 wins and 103 points. The team boasted stars like Mark and Marty Howe, Paulin Bordeleau, Wayne Dillon and Mike Palmateer, and the sellout crowd of 16,485 they drew for the deciding game of the OHA final that year was the largest attendance ever for a junior game at Maple Leaf Gardens. The Marlies would win the Memorial Cup in 1973 and again in 1975, but were no longer attracting many fans in the 1980s. After the 1988–89 season, the Marlboros left Toronto and became the Hamilton Dukes. Major junior hockey would not be back in Toronto until 1997 when St. Michael's College returned to the ranks as a member of the Ontario Hockey League.

Bryan Trottier played junior hockey in Swift Current and Lethbridge. He was drafted by New York Islanders in 1972 and made his NHL debut in 1975–76 with the Isles, winning the Calder Trophy. He was the Art Ross and Hart Trophy winner in 1979. Trottier played on six Stanley Cup winners, four with the Islanders and two with the Pittsburgh Penguins. In 1980 he was selected the Conn Smythe Trophy winners as playoff MVP. He was inducted into the Hockey Hall of Fame in 1997.

There were also three of Trottier's New York Islanders teammates that shared the four consecutive Stanley Cup victories of 1980 to 1983 who were elected to the Hockey Hall of Fame. Defenceman Denis Potvin played five seasons with the Ottawa 67's juniors before joining the New York Islanders in 1973–74. He was named the Calder Trophy winner that campaign and captured the Norris Trophy in 1976, 1978 and 1979. Goaltender Billy Smith

was with the Cornwall Royals juniors and in 1970 was drafted by the L.A. Kings. He was claimed by the New York Islanders from Los Angeles in 1972 Expansion Draft. Smith's lone individual NHL award came in 1982 when he captured the Vezina Trophy. Mike Bossy played junior hockey for Laval and in four seasons scored a total of 308 goals with the Voisins. In his first NHL season with New York Islanders in 1977–78 he was awarded the Calder Trophy after scoring a rookie-record 53 goals. Mike was also the 1982 Conn Smythe Trophy winner and a three-time Lady Byng recipient.

Steve Shutt played junior with the Toronto Marlboros against Larry Robinson who was with the Kitchener Rangers in 1970–71. Both players were drafted by the Montreal Canadiens and played on the 1973 Stanley Cup winner in their first NHL season. Shutt would be a member of five Stanley Cup winners and Robinson six, all with the Montreal Canadiens. Shutt was elected to the Hockey Hall of Fame in 1993 and Robinson followed in 1995.

Lanny McDonald played with the Medicine Hat Tigers of the Western Hockey League in both 1971–72 and 1972–73 before joining the Maple Leafs in 1973–74. He won the Masterton Trophy in 1983 and played on a Stanley Cup winner at the end of his playing career with the Calgary Flames in 1989. McDonald was elected to the Hockey Hall of Fame in 1992.

Wayne Gretzky played his last year of junior hockey in 1977–76 with the Sault Ste. Marie Greyhounds. He turned pro the following season at age 17 with the Indianapolis Racers of the World Hockey Association and was traded to the Edmonton Oilers after playing only eight games. Wayne went on to a great NHL career and either holds or shares more than 60 NHL individual records. He has won the Art Ross Trophy 10 times, the Hart Trophy nine times and the Lady Byng Trophy on four occasions. Gretzky was a member of four Stanley Cup winning teams with Edmonton and in 1985 and 1988 was named the Conn Smythe Trophy recipient.

Mark Messier played junior hockey with the St. Albert Saints of the Alberta Junior Hockey League in 1977–78. He broke into the NHL in 1979–80 with Edmonton after one season in the World Hockey Association and was a member

of five Oilers Stanley Cup championship teams, winning the Conn Smythe Trophy in 1984. Mark also captained the New York Rangers to their 1994 Stanley Cup victory. Messier captured the Hart Trophy in 1990 with Edmonton and in 1992 with the Rangers.

Mario Lemieux was with Laval of the Quebec Hockey League and played three years of junior with the Voisins and was the Canadian junior hockey player of the year in 1984 when he set records for most goals (133) and points (282) in a season. Lemieux was the Pittsburgh Penguins' first choice, first overall in the 1984 NHL Draft and was the Calder Trophy winner in 1985. He went on to captain Pittsburgh's Stanley Cup championship teams in 1991 and 1992 and was the Conn Smythe Trophy winner both years. Mario won the Art Ross Trophy on six occasions and was a two-time Hart Trophy winner. Lemieux was elected to the Hockey Hall of Fame in 1997.

Another provincial Junior A player was Brett Hull who was with the Penticton Knights of the British Columbia Junior Hockey League in 1983–84. Brett followed his famous father Bobby's footsteps into the NHL and won the Lady Byng Trophy in 1990 and the Hart Trophy in 1991 while with the St. Louis Blues. Paul Kariya also played in Penticton before joining the University of Maine Black Bears and the Mighty Ducks of Anaheim. He represented Canada at the 1994 Winter Olympics and was the NHL's First Team All-Star left winger in 1995–96 and 1996–97.

Eric Lindros was a key player in the Oshawa Generals' 1990 Memorial Cup victory. The following OHL season with Oshawa, Lindros won the Eddie Powers Memorial Trophy (leading scorer) and the Albert "Red" Tilson Trophy as the league's MVP. He was drafted number one in 1991 by Quebec but would not sign with the Nordiques and was later traded to Philadelphia. In 1994–95, his third season with the Flyers, Lindros was voted the Hart Trophy winner.

The Memorial Cup has been in competition for 80 years and is still one of the most important events on the hockey calendar. Junior hockey for all these many years has been and continues to be a focal point for the communities in which it is played and the main contributor of players to professional hockey.

Memorial Cup Winners

1919	University of Toronto Schools	1939	Oshawa Generals	1959	Winnipeg Braves	1979	Peterborough Petes
1920	Toronto Canoe Club Paddlers	1940	Oshawa Generals	1960	St. Catharines Tee Pees	1980	Cornwall Royals
1921	Winnipeg Falcons	1941	Winnipeg Rangers	1961	Toronto St. Michael's Majors	1981	Cornwall Royals
1922	Fort William War Veterans	1942	Portage la Prairie Terriers	1962	Hamilton Red Wings	1982	Kitchener Rangers
1923	University of Manitoba Bisons	1943	Winnipeg Rangers	1963	Edmonton Oil Kings	1983	Portland Winter Hawks
1924	Owen Sound Greys	1944	Oshawa Generals	1964	Toronto Marlboros	1984	Ottawa 67's
1925	Regina Pats	1945	Toronto St. Michael's Majors	1965	Niagara Falls Flyers	1985	Prince Albert Raiders
1926	Calgary Canadians	1946	Winnipeg Monarchs	1966	Edmonton Oil Kings	1986	Guelph Platers
1927	Owen Sound Greys	1947	Toronto St. Michael's Majors	1967	Toronto Marlboros	1987	Medicine Hat Tigers
1928	Regina Monarchs	1948	Port Arthur West End Bruins	1968	Niagara Falls Flyers	1988	Medicine Hat Tigers
1929	Toronto Marlboros	1949	Montreal Royals	1969	Montreal Junior Canadiens	1989	Swift Current Broncos
1930	Regina Pats	1950	Montreal Junior Canadiens	1970	Montreal Junior Canadiens	1990	Oshawa Generals
1931	Elmwood Millionaires	1951	Barrie Flyers	1971	Quebec Remparts	1991	Spokane Chiefs
1932	Sudbury Cub Wolves	1952	Guelph Biltmore Mad Hatters	1972	Cornwall Royals	1992	Kamloops Blazers
1933	Newmarket Redmen	1953	Barrie Flyers	1973	Toronto Marlboros	1993	Sault Ste. Marie Greyhounds
1934	Toronto St. Michael's Majors	1954	St. Catharines Tee Pees	1974	Regina Pats	1994	Kamloops Blazers
1935	Winnipeg Monarchs	1955	Toronto Marlboros	1975	Toronto Marlboros	1995	Kamloops Blazers
1936	West Toronto Nationals	1956	Toronto Marlboros	1976	Hamilton Fincups	1996	Granby Predateurs
1937	Winnipeg Monarchs	1957	Flin Flon Bombers	1977	New Westminster Bruins	1997	Hull Olympiques
1938	St. Boniface Seals	1958	Ottawa-Hull Canadiens	1978	New Westminster Bruins	1998	Portland Winter Hawks

CHAPTER 29

NCAA Hockey

Kevin Allen

ONE OF THE CHARMING ASPECTS of U.S. college hockey is that it has resisted the urge to become fully grown up. In a sports world dominated by marketing, logos and corporate sponsorship, there's still an endearing rah-rah quality that won't go away. The college game doesn't depart from the pros just because there's no red line and players wear full-face shields. College hockey is as much about painted faces, outrageous student bodies, colorful mascots, bare-chested fans, vulgar chanting and lively bands as it is about goals and assists. About 43% of the players in U.S. college hockey are in fact Canadian, but the zaniness is uniquely American.

"College hockey isn't just about the guys going on to the pros from the big schools," says Hockey East commissioner Joe Bertagna. "It's a lot of little venues where it's the only game in town."

College hockey is a 10-hour bus ride to take on Lake Superior State College in a packed house in Sault Ste. Marie, Michigan. College hockey is North Dakota band members leaning over the plexiglass and almost nailing the other team's players with enthusiastic trombone slides. College hockey is Bowling Green holding a "Ron Mason look-alike contest" when the Falcons' former coach returned to his old home rink employed as the coach of Michigan State. College hockey is fans in every college arena screaming "Sieve, Sieve" every time an opposing goaltender lets in a goal.

These kinds of hijinks have been going on forever in college hockey, probably since the first documented game was played in Baltimore between Johns Hopkins and Yale on February 3, 1896. The *Baltimore Sun* carried a report of this game that said it drew "the largest crowd of the season," from which we might easily extrapolate that others were played before then.

Rivalries are steeped in tradition and history. The one between Harvard and Brown began in January 1898; no two schools have faced each other more often than Harvard and Yale, with 201 meetings dating back to just before the turn of the century as of 1998–99. Competition was keen even from the beginning. In 1897, the University of Maryland hired three high-priced attorneys to fight a court challenge to its McNaughton Cup championship when the losing team claimed a referee had allowed a goal that appeared to be "too high."

Early in the 20th century, college hockey was well received in the east and most of the top games were played to large, loud, boisterous crowds. By the 1930s, it enjoyed a high level of popularity, particularly in the Boston area, where a Harvard–Yale game could draw 14,000. Hockey also spread to the West Coast, where USC, UCLA and Loyola also had club teams. But college hockey as we recognize it today didn't really begin until World War II ended.

The Eddie Jeremiah-coached Dartmouth squad was modern college hockey's first juggernaut squad. In the early 1940s, no other team could match Dartmouth. They won 46 consecutive games at one stretch, showing virtually no hint of vulnerability until the University of Michigan defeated them for the championship at the first NCAA tournament in 1948. The next year, Dartmouth fell to Boston College in the NCAA finals. Given how strong its program was in that era, no one would have believed that Dartmouth wouldn't return to the Final Four again until 1979. The main architect of the early success, Jeremiah was a principled man who was always trying to tidy up the NCAA rules to make the competition as fair as it could be. "He is to college hockey what Ted Williams was to baseball," said another great coach, Snooks Kelley, in 1966. "Being on Jerry's team was like being with a Broadway musical and it was a long run," said former player Jim Malone when Jeremiah retired in 1967.

The introduction of the NCAA championship clearly changed the landscape of college hockey. With a Holy Grail to pursue, western teams began to recruit older Canadians (much to the chagrin of the coaches in the east who thought this gave Western schools an unfair advantage). Teams from the west won 18 of the first 20 titles, with coach Vic Heylinger's Michigan team winning six more (1951, 1952, 1953, 1955, 1956 and 1964) after the initial victory in 1948, while Denver won five (1958, 1960, 1961, 1968 and 1969). The rules were so lax that Wally Maxwell was allowed to play for Michigan in the 1957 NCAA tournament even though he had played two games for the NHL's Toronto Maple Leafs four years earlier. Colorado College had a 36-year-old player named Jack Smith. U.S. college hockey became the final destination for Canadians who had no further options in the pros or in Canada. "Tony Frasca was 30 when he was coaching at Colorado College and he had players who were older than he was," noted former Colorado College player Art Berglund. "Only the real talented Americans got a chance to play at some schools."

Not every coach in the west believed in using Canadian players. Minnesota's John Mariucci (one of the few Americans to play in the NHL in the 1930s) began to lobby for reforming the rules and increasing the use of American-born players. "John wasn't anti-Canadian," recalls one of his players, 1980 Olympic coach Herb Brooks. "He was pro-American."

Incensed one night when his players were manhandled by Denver's older Canadian players, Mariucci vowed he would never play Denver again and in 1958 he called in some of his friendship markers to convince officials at Minnesota, Michigan State, the University of Michigan and Michigan Tech to leave the Western Intercollegiate Hockey League. The top college teams in the West re-formed as the Western Collegiate Hockey Association in 1959. It would be quite a few years before Mariucci was comfortable playing Denver. When he was forced to do so at the NCAA tournament in 1961, he had Lou Nanne, a naturalized American player, carry a sign that read, "We fry Canadian bacon."

While Mariucci was lobbying for reform in the West, equally colorful characters were changing the game in the East. Cornell's Ned Harkness was a feisty coach who didn't

like losing and didn't think much of the west's dominance in the NCAA finals. Boston University's Jack Kelley was another fire-breathing coach with little patience (and less humor) for losing.

Everyone who knows Kelley seems to have a story about his competitiveness and intense rivalry with Boston College and its long-time coach, Snooks Kelley. One that has stood the test of time concerns a chair turned to kindling. In 1972, the college hockey community knew Jack Kelley was planning to quit at Boston University and each of his opponents decided to give him a gift. The Boston College officials made the mistake of presenting Kelley with a BC chair—before the BC–BU game. Legend has it that Jack Kelley broke the chair into pieces when his team lost in what coincidentally was Snooks Kelley's 500th career win. Jack Kelley himself says the tale has been exaggerated over time. "All I can tell you is that I've never seen that chair in our house or in his office," says his son, Mark, a scout with the Pittsburgh Penguins. Jack Parker was Jack Kelley's assistant. As he remembers the situation, "Oh, he threw it, and was kicking it. I'm not saying he broke it."

Under Harkness and Kelley, Cornell and Boston University were at last able to break the chains of the west's domination. In 1967, Cornell won the NCAA title and BU finished second, the first time a team from the east had won since Rensselaer Polytechnic in 1954. Cornell won again in 1970 while Boston University won back-to-back titles in 1971 and 1972. The name most associated with hockey at Cornell in that era is Hall of Famer Ken Dryden, who played goal for Cornell before signing with the Montreal Canadiens. Dryden, now president of the Maple Leafs, was one of the most advanced, technically sound goaltenders in NCAA history, but the most celebrated Cornell team of that era is the 1969–70 squad, the only Division I team in college hockey history to record a perfect season en route to an NCAA championship.

The Big Red was 29–0 that season; the closest they came to a loss was in the Eastern Collegiate Athletic Conference Game when John Hughes scored with 14 seconds left to leave Cornell 3–2 up against Clarkson. "Most people would be willing to bet that Ken Dryden was the goaltender on that team," says Joe Bertagna, a former Harvard goaltender and current Hockey East commissioner, "but he wasn't." The 6'4", 210-pound Dryden graduated the season before and Cornell's new goaltender, Brian Cropper, was 5'5" and barely weighed 125 pounds with a pocketful of change.

Most coaches figured that Cornell's years of dominance would be over when Dryden left, but they hadn't counted on the star player of the 1969–70 team. Dan Lodboa was a rocket-fueled speedster with a nifty scoring touch who was much chagrined when Harkness switched him from left wing to defense, but he ended up being the country's best puck-carrying defenseman. He scored 24 goals in the season and netted three third-period goals to help Cornell beat Clarkson 6–4 in the 1970 NCAA championship game. "He was my Bobby Orr," said Harkness years later. "Boa was the greatest hockey player I ever coached, the greatest college player I ever saw."

Over the past 28 years, only the 1992–93 Maine team has come close to matching Cornell's feat of the perfect season when the Black Bears went 42–1–2 and Paul Kariya won the Hobey Baker Award as college player of the year. "He dominated college hockey like Michael Jordan dominated basketball," says Maine coach Shawn Walsh. "He was electrifying." The goalies on that team were Garth Snow, now

with the Vancouver Canucks, and Mike Dunham, now with the new Nashville Predators. The Black Bears beat Lake Superior State for the national championship that year, and in 1994–95 they defeated Michigan in what is considered one of the greatest games in NCAA hockey history. It was also the longest game in NCAA history. Dan Shermerhorn scored 28 seconds into the third overtime to give the Black Bears a 4–3 win in the semifinals. With end-to-end action throughout the game, Maine goaltender Blair Allison and Michigan's Marty Turco combined for 99 saves. "It was an unbelievable game," Walsh says. "It was hard to call anyone a loser in that game." Indeed, Turco's disappointment would be eased by winning NCAA titles in 1996 and 1998.

The other game that makes anyone's list of top games in NCAA history is Bowling Green's 5–4 win over Minnesota-Duluth in the 1984 NCAA championship game. That contest lasted 97 minutes and 11 seconds before Gino Cavallini scored for Bowling Green's victory (Cavallini eventually played in the NHL with Calgary, St. Louis and Quebec.) "That game was like fighters cold-cocking each other. No one would go down," said writer Mike Prisuta, who covered the game.

But college hockey history is rich in great players, colorful coaches and legendary stories, none more telling than the tale of the snow-covered Beanpot Tournament of 1978.

The Beanpot Tournament (which began in December of 1952) brings together teams from Harvard, Boston University, Boston College and Northeastern for an annual tournament to crown the city championships. Next to a national championship, winning this may mean more to these players than anything else they accomplish in hockey. Students and fans also take it quite seriously, which explains what happened during the blizzard of 1978.

As the games were being played in the Boston Garden, the snow kept coming down. In the middle of the second game, the announcer on the public address suggested that those in attendance go home because the city was being hammered by the worst blizzard in its history. But a good many didn't want to go home and spent the night in the Garden, foraging for leftover popcorn and overcooked hot dogs. People were sacked out all over the building.

In 1962, University of Michigan player Red Berenson earned a rough ride by becoming the first player in that era to jump directly from college hockey to the pros. Berenson played for the Montreal Canadiens the night after he played for the Wolverines in an NCAA consolation game.

Berenson says his NHL peers looked at him as if he had sprouted three heads. "I was considered an intellectual geek." And indeed he returned to his roots as the Wolverines' head coach since 1984–85.

Since Berenson's debut, college players' foothold in the NHL has strengthened each year and they are now in abundant supply. Among the NHL's leading scorers in 1997–98 are an array of former college players including John LeClair (Vermont), Adam Oates (RPI), Rod Brind'Amour (Michigan State), Tony Amonte (Boston University), Brett Hull (Minnesota-Duluth), Doug Weight (Lake Superior State), Joe Nieuwendyk (Cornell), Keith Tkachuk (Boston University) and goals-against leader Ed Belfour (North Dakota).

Coaches have played a major role in developing the game. We have touched on the pivotal roles played by Eddie Jeremiah in the east and John Mariucci in the west, but college hockey never had a better promoter than Wisconsin coach Bob Johnson, who became known simply

as "Badger Bob." Johnson took his players to shopping malls in full gear and had them give talks on the use of equipment. And he promoted the game even more with what he could do on the ice, leading Wisconsin to NCAA titles in 1973, 1977 and 1981. "No man was ever more enthusiastic about hockey than Bob Johnson," says Art Berglund.

Still, the NHL resisted hiring college coaches (particularly after Harkness was given a try and proved a bust with the Detroit Red Wings in the 1970s) until former Minnesota and U.S. Olympic coach Herb Brooks was hired by the New York Rangers in 1981. In 1982, his long-time rival Johnson was named coach of the Calgary Flames.

The Minnesota Gophers program remains one of the most successful in college hockey. They have made a record 25 NCAA tournament appearances, including the last 13 in a row through 1997–98. And what makes the program unique is that it relies predominantly on Minnesota-bred players. Michigan (which won the first NCAA title in 1948) won its NCAA-record ninth in 1998. Boston University has 24 NCAA tournament appearances, many of them with Jack Parker behind the bench. He replaced Jack Kelley in 1973 and is expected to record his 600th win in the 1998–99 season. He's fourth on the all-time list but still more than 200 short of Michigan State's Ron Mason, who holds the college record of 808 heading into the 1998–99 season.

College hockey has tremendous respect for its history. The Boston University–Boston College rivalry is as fresh today as it was when Jack Kelley and Snooks Kelly were behind the two benches. Bragging rights are still extremely important in college hockey. "What makes a difference in college hockey is the fans and school spirit aspect," observed Mike Prisuta. "BU in the east and Michigan in the west are famous for their choreographed cheers for each situation in a game. And they all know what to do. It can be very intimidating."

Imagine what the players thought the night Goldy the Gopher recorded a huge takedown of Bucky the Badger in the pregame hoopla surrounding a Minnesota–Wisconsin game. North Dakota fans may have crossed the line at one game when they threw a dead gopher on the ice, just to let Minnesota know what their players would look like when North Dakota reduced them to road kill. College hockey arenas are one of the few venues where you can catch a 60-year-old, bespectacled history professor taking part in the organized public chanting of expletives perhaps best deleted when he doesn't like a high-sticking call. Through the years at Harvard, in the rare moments when the hockey squad's struggling, the famously well-heeled and supposedly intellectually superior student body has chanted, "That's all right, that's OK, you're going to work for us someday." Bertagna didn't enjoy that one much when he played. He preferred Harvard's reaction to the rumors Ned Harkness was enrolling Canadian players in Cornell's agriculture program. When players from Cornell arrived at the Harvard arena, they were greeted by signs that read, "Welcome Canada's future farmers," or "Hey, Cornell, if you're here, who's milking the cows?"

No one is sure what school's fans started playing a major role first. It is thought to have been more pronounced in the east before it became fashionable in the west. "Some people make the case that the wise guy cheers might have some sort of Ivy League band history. They have an irreverence," Bertagna says. But it's all in good fun, and most coaches wouldn't want the game to lose the edge that it gets from fans' antics. Even goaltenders, who usually take the brunt of fan zaniness, don't seem to mind. Everyone who loves the game has their fond memories: the Boston University band playing the Peter Gunn theme a good many years ago now, Wisconsin's repeated rendition of the Budweiser song, the closest the game has yet come to an overall theme song. Players know they have played a real away game when they leave Badgerland with their ears ringing to it. They all preserve the closeness of the fraternity—even if the sport hasn't grown like it could.

"What's interesting is our uniqueness is also what holds us back," Bertagna explains. "We have [big schools like] Michigan and Ohio State … but a big part of who we are is Saturday night in Potsdam, New York, or Saturday night in Sault Ste. Marie [Lake Superior] or Houghton [Michigan Tech]. Houston Field House in Troy, New York, [RPI] and Gutterson [Arena] in Burlington [Vermont]. These are great storied places that are a big part of our tradition. We have some unusually small schools where we are the only game in town."

As television expresses more interest, there is a concern that the small college teams will be squeezed out, especially if bigger schools embrace the sport. "Unfortunately, the world is changing, and we have a dilemma," Bertagna concludes. "How do we advance our game without it being done at the expense of our game?"

NCAA Champions

1948	Michigan Wolverines	1965	Michigan Tech Huskies	1982	North Dakota Fighting Sioux
1949	Boston College Eagles	1966	Michigan State Spartans	1983	Wisconsin Badgers
1950	Colorado College Tigers	1967	Cornell Big Red	1984	Bowling Green Falcons
1951	Michigan Wolverines	1968	Denver Pioneers	1985	RPI Engineers
1952	Michigan Wolverines	1969	Denver Pioneers	1986	Michigan State Spartans
1953	Michigan Wolverines	1970	Cornell Big Red	1987	North Dakota Fighting Sioux
1954	RPI Engineers	1971	Boston University Terriers	1988	Lake Superior Lakers
1955	Michigan Wolverines	1972	Boston University Terriers	1989	Harvard Crimson
1956	Michigan Wolverines	1973	Wisconsin Badgers	1990	Wisconsin Badgers
1957	Colorado College Tigers	1974	Minnesota Golden Gophers	1991	Northern Michigan U. Wildcats
1958	Denver Pioneers	1975	Michigan Tech Huskies	1992	Lake Superior Lakers
1959	North Dakota Fighting Sioux	1976	Minnesota Golden Gophers	1993	University of Maine Black Bears
1960	Denver Pioneers	1977	Wisconsin Badgers	1994	Lake Superior Lakers
1961	Denver Pioneers	1978	Boston University Terriers	1995	Boston University Terriers
1962	Michigan Tech Huskies	1979	Minnesota Golden Gophers	1996	Michigan Wolverines
1963	North Dakota Fighting Sioux	1980	North Dakota Fighting Sioux	1997	North Dakota Fighting Sioux
1964	Michigan Wolverines	1981	Wisconsin Badgers	1998	Michigan Wolverines

CHAPTER 30
Canadian College Hockey
Hockey's Best-kept Secret
Steve Knowles

ONCE CALLED CANADA'S BEST KEPT SECRET, collegiate hockey no longer takes a back seat in the country's hockey community. With 33 schools icing teams during the 1997–98 season, the Canadian Interuniversity Athletic Union continues a rich tradition of hockey excellence that dates back to 1877 when McGill University of Montreal formed the first organized hockey club. In 1886 Queen's University and the Royal Military College of Canada ushered in intercollegiate hockey when they played the first organized game in Kingston, Ontario. Since then Canadian university teams have competed for the Stanley Cup, Allan Cup and Memorial Cup. Canadian college players have skated in the NHL and on the international stage at the Olympics, World championships and World Student Games.

The Early Years

Although the precise origins of the game of hockey remain strongly debated by historians, what can be proven is that the game of ice hockey evolved in Canada, and that the first recorded game to be played indoors took place in Montreal at the Victoria Skating Rink on March 3, 1875. That historic contest had its first connection with Canadian universities as the two teams of nine players were composed of, and captained by, students from McGill University. Serving as captain of one of the teams was James George Aylwin Creighton, who drafted the first rules for ice hockey after he and other friends, including fellow McGill classmate Henry Joseph, tried to play lacrosse on skates at the Victoria Rink. Creighton's team was victorious in this first game by a 2–1 score.

In 1877 McGill became the first university in the world to ice an intercollegiate team. The *McGill University Gazette* of February 1, 1877, reported that McGill students officially formed an organized ice hockey club and played its first game against the Montreal Victorias. McGill's first officially organized game was a 2–1 victory over the Victorias on January 31, 1877. In its first season of hockey, McGill would finish with a 2–1 record in three games against the Victorias.

The roster of McGill's first ice hockey team consisted of Archibald Dunbar Taylor, who was elected the team president, Harry Abbott (team captain), R.J. Howard, Fred Torrence, Lorne Campbell (goalie), W. Redpath, Nelson, Coverhill and Dawson. This group of students were the first in a long line of student-athletes who have represented McGill in an intercollegiate hockey program that continues to this day.

In 1883 the Montreal Winter Carnival hosted the first ice hockey tournament. Three teams were featured in the competition as McGill was joined by the Montreal Victorias and a team from Quebec City. The tournament rules stipulated that the teams would consist of seven men and that two 30-minute halves would be played with a 10-minute intermis-

sion. McGill defeated the Victorias 1–0 and then tied Quebec 2–2 to win the world's first official hockey championship. McGill's victory saw the school receive a silver cup, then valued at $750. The original trophy, along with a replica of the game puck, is on display at McGill's McCord Museum of Canadian History. The championship McGill squad, whose names are engraved on the trophy, consisted of goalie A.P. Low, point J.M. Elder, cover point P.D. Green and forwards Richard W. Smith, W.L. Murray, J.A. Kinlock (captain) and P.L. Foster.

On December 8, 1886 the first official hockey league, the Amateur Hockey Association of Canada, was formed in Montreal. McGill was one of five charter members of the AHA's senior division which also included the Montreal Amateur Athletic Association, the Montreal Victorias, the Ottawa Hockey Club and the Montreal Crystals. The first game played in league history took place on January 7, 1887 as the Crystals earned a 3–1 victory over McGill.

While McGill was an integral part of the development of hockey and its rules in the Montreal area, graduates of the school also helped to organize and develop the game in other locations. One McGill grad, Edward Thornton Taylor, went to Kingston, Ontario and introduced the game to the cadets at the Royal Military College of Canada in 1877.

Kingston was a hotbed of hockey as early as 1855 when a form of the game was played on the frozen harbor by British soldiers stationed in the area. Along with the cadets at RMC, Kingston was also home to Queen's University and this proximity saw the schools become arch rivals. The rivalry began with football and in 1886 the RMC cadets challenged Queen's to a game of hockey—the first organized intercollegiate game in history.

A community skating rink just off shore from the Fort Frontenac barracks was the site of the game. The rink featured a large wooden bandstand right in the middle of the ice, which prevented the opposing goalies from seeing one another. Despite this obstacle, the game was played in a spirited manner. Lennox Irving, captain of the Queen's squad, became the first player to score a goal in intercollegiate play as he netted the winner in a 1–0 victory. A Queen's account says the winning goal was scored by Irving, "an excellent skater", who "swept up to the RMC goal, bounced the puck off the goalie's shoulder, struck the rebounding puck in midair, and knocked it into the goal for the game."

The next season RMC gained revenge with a 4–0 victory over Queen's and the collegiate game was on its way in Canada.

Ten seasons after playing the first intercollegiate game, Queen's recorded another first as the Golden Gaels became the first, and only, collegiate team to challenge for the Stanley Cup. In 1895 Queen's made its first of three challenges for Lord Stanley's Cup when they faced-off against the Montreal Amateur Athletic Association on March 9,

1895. Montreal AAA won the challenge defeating Queen's 5–1. Queen's would also challenge for the Cup in 1899 and 1906. In March 1899 the Golden Gaels lost 6–2 to the Montreal Shamrocks and in 1906 they dropped two games to the Ottawa Silver Seven by scores of 16–7 and 12–7 on February 27 and 28. For Queen's, it was their final attempt at winning the Stanley Cup and it marked the last time that a collegiate team would compete for hockey's most illustrious trophy. Although Queen's failed to win the Stanley Cup, it did capture the 1909 Allan Cup as Canada's senior amateur champions.

Marty Walsh was a member of the Queen's team during the Golden Gaels' Stanley Cup challenge in 1906 and although he did not win the prized trophy for his university, Walsh would later sip champagne from the Cup. In 1907–08 he scored 28 goals for the Ottawa Senators to tie for the Eastern Canada Amateur Hockey Association goal-scoring lead with Russell Bowie of the Montreal Victorias. Walsh and the Senators won the Stanley Cup in 1908–09 and he was a member of the Ottawa team that successfully defended the Cup against challengers from Galt and Edmonton early in the 1909–10 season. Walsh scored six goals in Ottawa's 12–3 win over Galt on January 5, 1910. It would be one of several high-scoring games for the talented Kingston native as Walsh scored six-or-more goals in four games during his career. He netted a career-high 10 goals against Port Arthur in a Stanley Cup challenge on March 16, 1911 as he fell four goals shy of the Cup record for goals in a game set by Frank McGee of the Ottawa Silver Seven in 1905.

Walsh's next Stanley Cup victory came in 1910–11 as the Queen's alumnus helped Ottawa win the championship of the National Hockey Association (forerunner of the NHL) and defeat Galt and Port Arthur in Stanley Cup challenges. In total, Walsh scored 25 goals in eight Stanley Cup playoff games and was a scoring leader in each of the Eastern Canada Hockey Association and the NHA. He was elected to the Hockey Hall of Fame in 1962.

During the final decade of the 19th century, McGill hockey enjoyed one of its most historic eras as four players who went on to become Honoured Members of the Hockey Hall of Fame skated for the Montreal school. Fred Scanlan, Arthur F. Farrell and Harry J. Trihey were members of McGill's hockey team from 1898 to 1900 and Charles Graham Drinkwater was a member from 1894 to 1898. This quartet of McGill stars, along with Jack Brannen, who also skated for McGill from 1898 to 1900, would combine to win 12 Stanley Cup championships. Three of the McGill skaters—Trihey, Scanlan and Farrell—formed one of the greatest forward lines in early hockey history and helped the Montreal Shamrocks win back-to-back Stanley Cup titles in 1899 and 1900. Trihey, the captain of both Shamrock championship teams, netted a hat trick and Farrell scored twice in Montreal's 6–2 win over Queen's in 1899. Trihey and Drinkwater were inducted into the Hockey Hall of Fame in 1950. They were joined by Farrell and Scanlon in 1965.

Three more future members of the Hockey Hall of Fame would join McGill in the 1900s as Lester Patrick and Billy Gilmour made their debut in a McGill uniform in 1900–01. They would be followed by Patrick's younger brother, Frank, in 1904. All three players would become McGill captains and would go on to win several Stanley Cup championships. Lester Patrick would win the Stanley Cup as a player with the Montreal Wanderers in 1906 and 1907 and

later win four more as a coach and general manager with the Victoria Cougars in 1925 and the New York Rangers in 1928, 1933 and 1940. The younger Patrick was a playing-manager with the Vancouver Millionaires when they won the Cup in 1915. Gilmour won three consecutive Stanley Cup titles as a member of the Ottawa Silver Seven in 1903, 1904 and 1905.

The Next Step

As the game of hockey became more popular and gained increased recognition throughout Canada, the intercollegiate version of the sport also continued to grow. Ever since the first game between Queen's and RMC in 1886, universities had been adopting the sport as part of their athletic programs with teams taking to the ice throughout the Maritimes, Ontario and Quebec. These teams played at a variety of levels of competition ranging from intramural to senior leagues, including the Stanley Cup challenges of Queen's University. There were some intercollegiate games played during this time, but there was no official league for college teams.

Included among the early intercollegiate games were three of major significance. Two decades after McGill met Harvard University in the first international collegiate football game, the schools met on the ice at Victoria Rink in Montreal on February 23, 1894. McGill would win the game 14–1 in what is believed to be the first collegiate hockey game to be played between teams from Canada and the United States. Another cross-border match-up took place in December of 1895 when Queen's made a trip to New York and defeated the Yale University Elis 3–0. What would prove to be another durable collegiate hockey rivalry began on February 2, 1895, when Queen's skated to a 6–5 victory over McGill in Kingston.

In 1901–02 an intercollegiate league was proposed after a meeting with several teams in Quebec and Ontario. The Canadian Intercollegiate Hockey Union became a reality on January 7, 1903 when McGill, Queen's and the University of Toronto Varsity Blues officially formed Canada's first collegiate hockey league. The first season saw the CIHU take a small step as only three games were played. McGill won the inaugural "Queen's Cup", which was presented by Queen's University in the first season. The Queen's Cup, which is currently awarded to the champion of the Ontario University Athletics conference, is the second oldest trophy competed for in Canadian intercollegiate history.

McGill and Queen's would both win two of the first four CIHU championships before Toronto captured the title in 1906–07. It was the first championship for the Varsity Blues since Toronto began its hockey team on January 15, 1891 and the beginning of one of the most successful programs in the country. During their storied history, the Varsity Blues have won the Queen's Cup a total of 41 times, including 10 consecutive seasons from 1919–20 to 1928–29 and eight more from 1965–66 to 1972–73.

As with McGill, Toronto's early years saw several of hockey's eventual elite involved with the Varsity Blues. Hall of Famer Conn Smythe was the captain of the 1915 Varsity Blues which won the Ontario junior championship. He coached Toronto from 1923 to 1926 and lead the Blues to the 1927 Allan Cup. This victory was the third Allan Cup title for the school as the varsity team had first won the trophy in 1921 after the Toronto Dentals had been victorious in 1917.

The 1927 victory earned Toronto the right to represent

Canada at the 1928 Olympic Games in St. Moritz, Switzerland. The Varsity Grads won the gold medal with a 3–0 record at the second Winter Olympic Games, outscoring the opposition 38–0.

Smythe is only one of several prominent coaches in Toronto's history. The list also includes former Canadian Prime Minister Lester Pearson (1926 to 1928), Maple Leaf Ace Bailey (1935 to 1940, 1945 to 1949), Judge Joseph Kane (1962 to 1965), Tom Watt (1966 to 1979, 1985) and Mike Keenan (1984).

The First World War halted intercollegiate play for four seasons from 1915–16 to 1918–19, but the CIHU returned to action in 1919–20. Over the next 21 seasons, from 1919–20 to 1939–40, the CIHU fluctuated in size from a low of two teams in the years following the 1929 stock market crash to four teams. During this span the original three members of the league were joined at various times by teams from the University of Montreal, the University of Western Ontario and Laval University.

In 1936–37 one of the most unique arrangements in intercollegiate sport occurred. That season saw the formation of the International Intercollegiate Hockey League which brought together teams from the CIHU and the U.S.-based Ivy League. McGill, Toronto, Queen's and Montreal were joined by Harvard, Yale, Princeton and Dartmouth to form an eight-team league which played a 10-game schedule. McGill won the first three IIHL titles from 1936–37 to 1938–39 as they compiled a record of 28–2.

In 1939–40 league membership fell to seven teams as Montreal withdrew from the circuit. Toronto went undefeated with an 8–0–0 record to capture the final championship in IIHL history before the league ceased operations due to World War II.

With the end of World War II, intercollegiate hockey resumed play across Canada. In Ontario and Quebec, the CIHU faded from the scene but was replaced by the four-team Senior Intercollegiate Hockey League which included McGill, Toronto, Queen's and Laval.

While intercollegiate hockey was evolving in Ontario and Quebec, the sport was also enjoying success on the campuses of universities in Atlantic and Western Canada. In the Maritimes, hockey had been played at universities since the late 19th century with competition between Dalhousie, St. Francis Xavier, Kings College and Acadia in Nova Scotia and the University of New Brunswick and Mount Allison University in New Brunswick. These schools formed the Maritimes Intercollegiate Athletic Association in 1910 and competed in a variety of sports including hockey, rugby, track, tennis and basketball.

Following the First World War, the MIAA expanded to a total membership of 10 schools and in 1968 the conference became the Atlantic Intercollegiate Athletic Association with the addition of Memorial University of Newfoundland. In April of 1974 the AIAA once again changed its name, becoming the Atlantic Universities Athletic Association.

St. Francis Xavier University, from Antigonish, Nova Scotia, was an early powerhouse in the MIAA as the X-Men captured 17 of 32 MIAA championships from 1928–29 to 1961–62, including 14 of 18 the titles contested from 1940–41 to 1958–59. The 1950s belonged to the X-Men as they won every title from 1950 to 1959, with the exception of 1952–53 when no conference champion was declared because of the collapse of the arena which was hosting the MIAA championship. Also prominent on the

East Coast was Mount Allison University, winners of six of nine MIAA championships from 1930–31 to 1938–39. The Mounties won three consecutive titles from 1931 to 1933, one in 1935 and two more in 1938 and 1939.

Western Canada was also home to much intercollegiate hockey with teams in each of the four western provinces. The University of Alberta Golden Bears began play during the 1908–09 season as a member of the Edmonton Collegiate League. In Manitoba, the University of Manitoba Bisons were members of the local Winnipeg hockey league, while in Saskatoon the University of Saskatchewan Huskies were formed in the early 1910s. At Vancouver the University of British Columbia has iced a hockey team since 1915–16.

The early years of all four western schools saw the hockey teams compete in local city leagues as well as provincial senior and intermediate leagues as there was no formal intercollegiate league. However, several of the teams played exhibition games against each other.

The first such game occurred on February 27, 1911 when Alberta visited Saskatoon and defeated Saskatchewan 16–0 as Roy Goodridge scored a Golden Bears team-record eight goals. This record still stands.

In the fall of 1919 intercollegiate athletics in the west took a monumental step forward as Alberta, Manitoba and Saskatchewan met at the Hotel MacDonald in Edmonton to form an athletic conference for the western universities. The Western Intercollegiate Athletic Union was the product of this meeting and in January of 1920 the first hockey game was played. Manitoba won the first WCIAU title as the Bisons won three of their four games to finish two points ahead of second-place Alberta.

In the early 1920s three western schools enjoyed particular success. In 1920-21 the UBC Thunderbirds won the Savage Cup as British Columbia Senior A champions and earned the right to move on to the Allan Cup playoffs. (The Thunderbirds were unable to skate for the Allan Cup as final exams conflicted with the playoff schedule.) The University of Manitoba won the 1923 Memorial Cup and captured the Manitoba Amateur Hockey Association junior championship in 1922, 1923 and 1925. Saskatchewan reached the Allan Cup finals in 1923 after having won the Saskatchewan and Western Canadian senior titles. Other Canadian universities to advance in the Memorial Cup playoffs included Quebec's Loyola College in 1920 and McGill in 1923.

In 1922, Dr. J. Halpenny of the University of Saskatchewan donated a trophy to the WCIAU to be awarded to the annual champion. The Halpenny Trophy was competed for on an annual basis until 1950, with the exception of several seasons during the 1930s and early 1940s, when competition was halted due to the Depression and World War II. In March of 1950 the Halpenny Trophy was retired in the permanent possession of Alberta after the Golden Bears won the trophy for the 17th consecutive season. The Halpenny Trophy was replaced by the W.G. Hardy Trophy in 1950–51.

The Hardy Trophy was named after Dr. W. George Hardy, a professor of Classics at the University of Alberta, who coached the Golden Bears from 1924 to 1928. Hardy was renowned for both his academic and athletic endeavors and served as president of the Alberta Amateur Hockey Association from 1931 to 1933, the Canadian Amateur Hockey Association from 1938 to 1939 and the International Ice Hockey Federation from 1948 to 1951.

The Canadian Interuniversity Athletic Union

In 1961 the Canadian Intercollegiate Athletic Union was formed as the governing body for intercollegiate sport in Canada. The CIAU, which would change its name to the present Canadian Interuniversity Athletic Union in 1978, began with five regional conferences—the Maritime Intercollegiate Athletic Association, Ottawa-St. Lawrence Intercollegiate Athletic Association, the Ontario-Quebec Athletic Association, Ontario Intercollegiate Athletic Association and the Western Canadian Intercollegiate Athletic Association.

Through the years the CIAU has grown and this growth has resulted in several different alignments in the various conferences across the country. In the Maritimes, the AUAA has grown from six teams to as many as 10, and currently has nine teams playing in two divisions. Intercollegiate hockey in Quebec saw the Ontario-Quebec Association thrive for a decade as the conference began ranged in size from four to nine teams. In 1970–71 the OQAA became the Quebec University Athletic Association and eight schools competed for the conference title. In the early 1980s a trend developed that saw several QUAA schools drop their hockey programs due to budget constraints and by 1986–87 the conference was down to only four teams. In 1987 the *Université du Québec à Chicoutimi* dropped its hockey program, leaving McGill, Concordia and *Québec à Trois-Rivières* as the only remaining Quebec universities with an active hockey program. The three surviving members of the QUAA then joined the Ontario Universities Athletic Association in time for the 1987–88 season, where they remain today.

In Ontario, collegiate hockey continued to flourish with as many as 16 teams competing for the conference title. The conference has seen several changes to its membership and make-up over the years, but currently has 16 teams competing in four four-team divisions.

College hockey in the western provinces saw the original WCIAU move from its three charter members—Alberta, Manitoba and Saskatchewan—to a two-team league for several years in the 1930s and 1940s. In 1956–57 the conference expanded to four teams with the addition of the Brandon College Caps. Brandon played two seasons in the WCIAU before withdrawing, but the Caps were replaced by the University of British Columbia Thunderbirds in 1961–62.

The WCIAU became the Western Canadian Intercollegiate Athletic Association in 1962–63 and the conference membership grew to eight teams by 1970–71 as the University of Calgary joined in 1964–65 and was followed by the University of Winnipeg in 1968–69, the University of Victoria in 1969–70 and the return of Brandon to the fold that same season. From 1969–70 to 1971–72, the WCIAU remained an eight-team conference, but in 1972–73 it separated into two new leagues. Alberta, Saskatchewan, Calgary, UBC and Victoria formed the Canada West University Athletic Association while Brandon, Manitoba and Winnipeg began the Great Plains Athletic Conference.

Victoria would drop its hockey program in 1973–74 after suffering through four seasons with an overall record of 3–75–0. The Vikings departure left the CWUAA with four teams for the next 11 seasons until 1984–85 when the University of Lethbridge Pronghorns joined the association. While the CWUAA remained stable, GPAC was growing as Lakehead University began play in 1972–73 and won the

conference's first title that season. GPAC upped its membership to five teams in 1976–77 with the addition of the University of Regina Cougars. Winnipeg and Lakehead shelved their hockey programs in the mid 1980s, leaving GPAC membership at three with only Brandon, Manitoba and Regina icing squads. In 1985–86 the CWUAA and remaining GPAC teams merged to form an eight-team conference under the banner of the CWUAA.

Currently, CIAU hockey has a total of 33 teams in three separate conferences competing for the University Cup national championship.

The University Cup

With the formation of the CIAU in 1961 as the governing body of intercollegiate athletics in Canada, the concept of national championships became a reality. The 1962–63 season saw the first CIAU championships held in hockey and basketball. The annual CIAU hockey champion has been awarded the University Cup since the first national championship was played. Queen's University and the Royal Military College of Canada—the two schools that participated in the first intercollegiate game in history—donated the University Cup to the CIAU in recognition of the contribution made to the game of hockey by outstanding university players.

During the course of its history, the format of the University Cup playoffs has varied. The first two tournaments in 1962–63 and 1963–64 were co-hosted by Queen's and the Royal Military College and featured four teams playing two semifinal games which led to a championship and consolation final. Since then the tournament has varied from four- to six-team fields featuring conference champions, host and wild card teams to progressive best-of-three regional series between conference champions. The championship tournament has been contested in sites across Canada from Edmonton and Calgary in the west to Moncton and Charlottetown in the east. For 10 seasons, from 1987–88 to 1996–97, the University of Toronto's Varsity Arena was host to the national tournament and from 1992–93 to 1996–97 Maple Leaf Gardens was the site of the CIAU championship game. In 1997–98 the tournament returned to the west as the University of Saskatchewan earned the right to host the final for three seasons (1997–98 to 1999–2000) at Saskatchewan Place in Saskatoon.

Through 1998 a total of 13 teams have won the University Cup since 1962–63. The McMaster University Marlins, in their only tournament appearance, won the inaugural championship with a 3–2 victory over the UBC Thunderbirds. Joining McMaster as CIAU champions are the Toronto Varsity Blues with a CIAU record 10 titles, the Alberta Golden Bears (8), the Moncton Aigles Bleus (4), the York Yeomen (3), the Acadia Axemen (2), the Trois-Rivieres Patriotes (2) and the Guelph Gryphons, Lethbridge Pronghorns, Manitoba Bisons, New Brunswick Varsity Reds, Saskatchewan Huskies and Waterloo Warriors who have each won the University Cup once. Of the 13 championship teams, two, Toronto and Alberta, have combined to win exactly half of the 36 University Cup titles.

Toronto, under the guidance of Tom Watt (CIAU coach of the year in 1971 and the National Hockey League's coach of the year with the Winnipeg Jets in 1981–82) won its first University Cup title in 1965–66. It was the first of Toronto's 10 titles and it began an unprecedented streak of success for the Varsity Blues as they would win seven University Cup competitions in a span of eight seasons from 1965–66 to

1972–73, including five straight from 1968–69 to 1972–73. The final four championships in Toronto's amazing streak came against the same opponent. From 1969–70 through 1972–73 the Varsity Blues would face the St. Mary's University Huskies of the AUAA for the national crown. St. Mary's, from Halifax, Nova Scotia, was coached by Bob Boucher, who would guide the Huskies to the AUAA championship eight times in nine seasons from 1968–69 to 1976–77. Toronto recorded one-goal victories in three of its four games with Huskies as the Varsity Blues won 3–2 in 1970 and 1973 and 5–4 in 1971. Back-to-back titles in 1975–76 and 1976–77 gave the Varsity Blues their eighth and ninth University Cup victories under Watt and Toronto won its 10th national championship in 1983–84 as Mike Keenan guided the team to a 9–1 victory over the Concordia Stingers.

The only team that can match the success of Toronto has been the Alberta Golden Bears. The Edmonton-based school has made a record 23 appearances at the University Cup tournament reaching the championship game on 12 occasions and winning the University Cup honors eight times, including once in each of the four decades of trophy competition. Alberta won its first title in 1963–64 and earned its second four years later with an exciting last-minute victory over Loyola College. Before a crowd of 12,000 at the Montreal Forum, Ron Cebryk netted the game-winning goal with only 17 seconds remaining to give the Golden Bears a 5–4 win over the hometown Warriors and the 1967–68 University Cup. For Alberta Golden Bears head coach Clare Drake the national title was his second of the season. Drake, who ended his 28 seasons behind the Alberta bench as the winningest coach in North American intercollegiate hockey with a record of 697–296–37, had earlier guided the Golden Bears football team to the 1967 Vanier Cup—the Canadian college football championship. It is the only time in CIAU history that one coach has won national championships in two sports during the same season.

For four seasons from 1976–77 to 1979–80, the Golden Bears were the dominant team in the CIAU as they appeared in four consecutive University Cup finals, winning three consecutively from 1977–78 to 1979–80. Alberta would win again in 1985–86 and capture their eighth title in 1991–92.

Toronto's crosstown rival, the York University Yeomen, have also had a successful record in University Cup play, winning three CIAU championships in seven appearances. The Yeomen first won in 1984–85 with a 3–2 victory over Alberta as Don McLaren accounted for all of York's scoring with a first-period hat trick. The Yeomen would return to national prominence with consecutive championships in 1987–88 and 1988–89. Dave Chambers guided the Yeomen to victory in 1985 and went on to become head coach of the NHL's Quebec Nordiques in 1989–90.

In 1980–81 the Moncton Aigles Bleus won their first of two consecutive University Cup titles with a 4–2 victory over Saskatchewan. With Jean Perron, the future coach of the 1986 Stanley Cup champion Montreal Canadiens, behind the bench Moncton would become one of the powerhouses of the CIAU. After winning in 1980–81, the Aigles Bleus would repeat in 1981–82 with another win over Saskatchewan. Louis Durocher's goal with 33 seconds remaining in regulation time capped a third-period comeback for Moncton which saw the Aigles Bleus score three goals to rally from a 2–0 deficit.

The 1980s saw the UQTR Patriotes emerge as one of Canada's premier teams. The team from Trois-Rivières, Quebec made eight University Cup appearances in 15 seasons and won the University Cup twice. Serving as host of the 1983–84 tournament, the Patriotes made their debut in the championship and finished fourth after dropping two games to eventual CIAU titlist Toronto. UQTR dominated the QUAA for the next several seasons and advanced to the 1985–86 title game where they lost 5–2 to Alberta. A year later, Clement Jodoin would take the Patriotes a step further as UQTR became the first team from the QUAA to win a national championship with a 6–3 win over Saskatchewan. UQTR's second title came in 1990–91 as they skated past the Golden Bears.

Moncton would capture its third and fourth University Cup titles in 1989–90 and 1994–95, but the Aigles Bleus are only the most successful of three teams from the AUAA which have won a total of seven University Cup championships. The Acadia Axemen claimed the nation's top trophy twice, winning in 1992–93 and 1995–96. Since 1991–92, when they made their first appearance in the University Cup tournament, the Axemen have made five appearances in the tourney and have reached the championship game a total of four times. The latest AUAA team to capture the national crown is the Varsity Reds of the University of New Brunswick. After making appearances in the 1963–64 and 1983–84 tournaments, the Varsity Reds reached the championship game in 1996–97, dropping a 4–3 decision to the Guelph Gryphons. After losing the 1997 final, New Brunswick set its sights on returning to the final in 1997–98. With a team of veterans committed to a common goal, the Varsity Reds were ranked number one in the nation for all but one week of the season. They reached the University Cup final once again where they defeated conference rival Acadia 6–3.

Several teams have enjoyed success at the conference level, but have not been able to capture the University Cup. As noted earlier, St. Mary's lost four consecutive national finals to Toronto in the early 1970s. The Huskies disappointment can be matched by the Concordia Stingers, Calgary Dinosaurs and St. Francis Xavier X-Men.

Concordia was the dominant team in the Quebec Universities Athletic Association from the mid-1970s to the mid-1980s. Leading the way was head coach Paul Arsenault who won 17 conference championships during his 22-season career. With Arsenault behind the bench, Concordia made nine appearances in the University Cup tournament and reached the championship twice, losing to Saskatchewan in 1983 and Toronto in 1984. Calgary and St. Francis Xavier have made nine and six visits, respectively, to the tournament without a title as both schools have yet to reach the championship final.

For the Saskatchewan Huskies and Guelph Gryphons, the disappointment of missed chances was washed away with a final victory. Dave King, longtime coach of the Canadian Olympic team and an NHL head coach with the Calgary Flames, returned to his alma mater in Saskatoon in 1979–80 and the former Huskies' forward built Saskatchewan into a force in the CWUAA. Under King, the current assistant coach of the Montreal Canadiens, the Huskies won three consecutive Canada West conference titles from 1980–81 to 1982–83 and advanced to the University Cup championship game in each season. The Huskies suffered disappointing losses to Moncton in the title game in their first two appearances before winning the 1982–83 national crown with a 6–2 victory over Concordia.

For Guelph, the road to the top was a long one as the Gryphons finally earned the University Cup in 1996–97 in their seventh appearance. Guelph made its first journey to the national tournament in 1975–76 as OUAA champions and advanced to the title game before losing 7–2 to Toronto. Guelph would not return to the final game for 18 seasons, but when they did the Gryphons would play in four championship games in a span of four seasons from 1993–94 to 1996–97. The Gryphons lost 5–2 to Lethbridge in 1994 and 5–1 against Moncton in 1995 before winning the Cup in 1997. Marlin Muylaert was the driving force behind Guelph's success in the 1990s. In his first season at Guelph, Muylaert and the Gryphons missed the post-season. It would be the only time that Guelph would fail to qualify for the playoffs under Muylaert (who is married to former 1984 Canadian Olympic swimming gold medalist Anne Ottenbreit). From 1989–90 to their championship season of 1996–97, the Gryphons would qualify for the playoffs eight times, win two OUAA Queen's Cup conference titles, qualify for the University Cup tournament three times and win the CIAU title once.

Recently, the CIAU and NCAA have established a cross-border challenge match between the two national governing bodies. Named the World University Hockey Challenge, all-star teams from the CIAU and NCAA have faced-off against each other at Joe Louis Arena in Detroit. In an exciting overtime victory, the CIAU took the inaugural game 6–5 in 1997. The NCAA won 3–1 in 1998.

The CIAU and the NHL

Although not known as a pipeline to the National Hockey League, the CIAU has sent its share of players, coaches and administrators to the professional ranks.

From hockey's beginning, players from Canadian universities have played a vital role in the development and expansion of the sport. In the early years, students from McGill, Queen's and Toronto helped to formulate hockey rules and develop the sport's equipment. Today, players from CIAU teams are skating for NHL teams as well as teams at other levels of professional hockey in North America and Europe.

Some of the great names in hockey history started their hockey careers at Canadian universities. Hall of Famers Lester and Frank Patrick played collegiate hockey at McGill before moving on to make their mark in the NHL as players and coaches. Conn Smythe was the captain of Toronto's Varsity Blues in 1915 and went on to build the Toronto Maple Leafs into one of the NHL's most storied teams. Another former Canadian university student to have a direct impact on the NHL was Clarence Campbell. Campbell was a Rhodes Scholar from the University of Alberta who began his hockey career as an administrator and referee in local hockey leagues in Edmonton prior to World War II. He succeeded Red Dutton as president of the NHL in 1946 and during his 31 years as NHL president, Campbell helped to establish the NHL Pension Society in 1946 and spearheaded the league's expansion from six to 12 teams in 1967–68. The longest serving president in NHL history, he was elected to the Hockey Hall of Fame in 1966.

Another former Canadian university student would become most influential in the growth of the Stanley Cup into hockey's most prized trophy. When Lord Stanley of Preston donated the trophy named after him to Canadian hockey in 1893, one of the trustees he appointed to insure the integrity of the Cup was Philip Dansken Ross of

Ottawa. The former McGill hockey and football star played an integral role in the decisions concerning the Stanley Cup and its evolvement into the oldest trophy in North American professional sport. Elected to the Hall of Fame in 1976, Ross had served as trustee of the Stanley Cup for 56 years until his death in 1949.

In addition to the administration of the Stanley Cup, players from the CIAU have been members of Cup winning teams. Only 54 players in the history of the Stanley Cup have won five or more championships since the trophy was first awarded in 1893. Among those five-time Stanley Cup champions is Randy Gregg. A defenceman with the University of Alberta, Gregg was a member of two CIAU national championship teams with the Golden Bears and was the 1979 recipient of the Senator Joseph A. Sullivan Trophy as the nation's most outstanding player. After graduating from Alberta with his degree in Medicine, Gregg was captain of the 1980 Canadian Olympic team and then played two seasons in Japan before joining the Edmonton Oilers where he was a member of five Stanley Cup championship teams playing alongside the likes of Wayne Gretzky, Mark Messier, Kevin Lowe, Jari Kurri, Grant Fuhr and Paul Coffey.

McGill is the home of 13 players to have won the Stanley Cup. Included among these champions are Hall of Famer Art Ross, the Patrick brothers, Percival Molson and Billy Gilmour. Among McGill's NHLers is goaltender Jack Gelineau, the winner of the Calder Memorial Trophy as the NHL's rookie of the year. Gelineau won the award in 1949–50 after recording three shutouts and a 3.28 goals-against average in 67 games.

Joining Gelineau on the NHL's honor roll is Al MacAdam. MacAdam played for the University of Prince Edward Island Panthers before embarking on an NHL career that would see him play 12 seasons with Philadelphia, Calgary, Cleveland, Minnesota and Vancouver. In 1979–80 he led the Minnesota North Stars in scoring and was the winner of the Bill Masterton Trophy which is awarded annually to the NHL player who best exemplifies perseverance, sportsmanship and dedication to hockey.

One of the first collegians from western Canada to make the NHL was Alberta defenceman Dave MacKay who played one season with the Chicago Black Hawks in 1940–41. After his rookie season in "the Windy City," MacKay cut short his NHL career, and, like many Canadians, joined the war effort, serving three years with the Canadian Army Engineers.

The 1997–98 season saw several CIAU graduates in the NHL. The Mighty Ducks of Anaheim had two former Canadian collegians on their roster as Steve Rucchin of the University of Western Ontario Mustangs centered two of the NHL's superstars—Teemu Selanne and Paul Kariya—and Brent Severyn of Alberta spent his sixth season in the league. Joining Rucchin and Severyn on NHL rosters were defenceman Cory Cross (Alberta) of the Tampa Bay Lightning, forwards Mike Kennedy (UBC) of Dallas and Stu Grimson (Manitoba) of Carolina. These players continue a line of CIAU student-athletes who have made their way to the NHL, following in the skate strides of players such as Bob Berry.

Berry played eight seasons in the NHL from 1968–69 to 1976–77 with the Montreal Canadiens and Los Angeles Kings after an outstanding career as an all-star forward with the Sir George Williams University Georgians of the

Ottawa–St. Lawrence Athletic Association in the mid-1960s. Following his playing career, Berry served as head coach of Los Angeles, Montreal, Pittsburgh and St. Louis and was the runner-up for the Jack Adams Award as the NHL's coach of the year with the Kings in 1980–81.

Other Canadian collegians to play in the NHL include former goaltenders Ken Lockett of Guelph, (Vancouver Canucks), Toronto's Gary Inness (Pittsburgh, Philadelphia, Washington), UBC's Ken Broderick (Minnesota, Boston), Ross McKay (Hartford) of Saskatchewan, Bernie Wolfe (Washington) of Sir George Williams and Jim Corsi (Edmonton) of Loyola and Concordia. Larry Carriere, a stalwart defenceman with Loyola College in Montreal, was drafted by the Buffalo Sabres 25th overall in the 1972 NHL Amateur Draft and played seven seasons with five NHL teams. He is now the assistant to the Sabres' general manager. Another blueliner of note was Bob Murdoch of the Waterloo Warriors. An OUAA all-star, Murdoch won the Stanley Cup with Montreal in 1971 and 1973 during a 12-year NHL career. He would go on to coach in the NHL with Chicago and Winnipeg.

The most prolific CIAU scorer to play in the NHL was Manitoba's Mike Ridley. The CIAU's outstanding player and freshman of the year in 1983–84, Ridley led the Bisons to two GPAC titles during his collegiate career before turning pro with the New York Rangers in the 1985–86 season. Scoring 22 goals and 65 points in his rookie season, Ridley was named to the NHL's All-Rookie Team that season. During a 12-year NHL career from 1985–86 to 1996–97, Ridley would score 292 goals and 466 assists for 758 points in 866 career games.

The CIAU can also be found behind the bench in the NHL, as there have been a host of former Canadian college coaches in the league, including two winners of the Jack Adams Award. In 1997–98 there were several former CIAU coaches plying their trade in the NHL. Among the bench bosses were Vancouver Canucks head coach Mike Keenan. Keenan, who guided the Toronto Varsity Blues to the 1984 CIAU title, has coached five NHL teams including one Stanley Cup champion and three Cup finalists. The Jack Adams Award winner in 1984–85 with Philadelphia, Keenan took the Flyers to the Stanley Cup finals in 1985 and 1987 and the Chicago Blackhawks in 1991–92 before winning the Stanley Cup with the New York Rangers in 1993–94. Keenan's career has also seen him guide Team Canada to Canada Cup championships in 1987 and 1991 and the Rochester Americans to the 1982–83 American Hockey League Calder Cup title.

The other CIAU coach to be named the NHL coach of the year is Tom Watt. Like Keenan, Watt was coach of the University of Toronto before turning pro and led the Varsity Blues to a CIAU record nine University Cup championships while compiling a career coaching record of 410–102–34 in 15 seasons. Watt won the Jack Adams Award in 1981–82 with the Winnipeg Jets. He would also coach Vancouver and Toronto during his career and was an assistant coach with Vancouver and Calgary, helping the Flames win the Stanley Cup in 1988–89.

Joining Keenan and Watt among the NHL coaching ranks was the Florida Panthers' Doug MacLean. The former UPEI player and New Brunswick Varsity Reds head coach guided the Panthers to the 1996 Stanley Cup finals and was a finalist for the Jack Adams Award that season. Relieved of his coaching duties midway through the 1997–98 season, MacLean has since been named the general manager of the NHL expansion Columbus Blue Jackets.

Also behind the bench for NHL teams in 1997–98 were Anaheim's Pierre Page (Dalhousie), Montreal assistant coaches Dave King (Saskatchewan) and Clement Jodoin (Trois-Rivières), New York Rangers assistant Bill Moores (Alberta), New York Islanders assistant Wayne Fleming (Manitoba) and Vancouver assistant Terry Bangen (McGill). Clare Drake (Alberta), Harry Neale (Toronto), Gary Green (Guelph), Jean Perron (Moncton), George Kingston (Calgary), Dave Chambers (Saskatchewan, Guelph and York), Ron Smith (York), Conn Smythe (Toronto), Art Ross (McGill), George Burnett (McGill), Doug Carpenter (MacDonald College), Kevin Primeau (Alberta) and Charles Thiffault (Sherbrooke) are others to become head or assistant coaches in the NHL after playing and/or coaching in the CIAU.

NHL front offices have also had their fair share of former CIAU coaches and players in important roles. John Blackwell, a former student trainer with Alberta served his eighth season as the Philadelphia Flyers' assistant general manager during 1997–98. Blackwell spent four seasons with Alberta in the late 1960s and early 1970s before joining the Edmonton Oilers in 1972–73 while they were a member of the World Hockey Association. He would spend 18 seasons with Edmonton in various roles in the front office and contribute to the Oilers' five Stanley Cup titles before moving on to the Flyers in 1990–91. Former Regina Cougars head coach Al Murray has served as the Los Angeles Kings director of amateur scouting since 1988–89. Jim Nill, a former forward with the Calgary Dinosaurs, has been the director of player development for the Detroit Red Wings for four seasons.

On the World Stage

As well as its contribution to the NHL, the CIAU has made a significant contribution to Canada's role on the world hockey stage.

In August of 1962, Father David Bauer unveiled a plan to establish a Canadian national hockey team which would represent the country at the Olympics and World Championships. The Canadian Amateur Hockey Association accepted the plan and Bauer put together a group of top CIAU and senior players, who would prepare for international competition in Vancouver at the University of British Columbia. Prior to the national program, Bauer, the brother of NHL star Bobby Bauer, had guided the Toronto St. Michael's junior team to the 1961 Memorial Cup title. Bauer's success would carry over to Canada's national program as he officially began his role as coach on August 21, 1963.

In its first major competition, the Canadian national team, which had four members of the 1962–63 CIAU finalist UBC Thunderbirds on the roster, placed fourth at the 1964 Winter Olympics in Innsbruck, Austria, with a 5–2–0 record. Canada's only losses were to the gold medal winning Russians and the Czechs, who won the bronze medal. Bauer, who was elected to the Hockey Hall of Fame in 1989, would continue with the national program through the 1968 Winter Olympics, winning a bronze medal at the World Championships in 1966 and 1967 and at the Grenoble Olympic Games. On the Canadian roster in 1968 were Ken Broderick, Barry MacKenzie and Terry O'Malley of UBC, Herb Pinder of Manitoba and Toronto's Steve Monteith.

Following the 1968 Olympic Games, Canada withdrew

from international play over the issue of professionalism and it would not be until 1980 that Canadians would once again skate at the Olympic Games.

Prominent behind Canada's return to the Olympic stage was Father Bauer. Serving as the managing director, Bauer brought together a team composed mainly of CIAU players and selected Clare Drake (Alberta), Tom Watt (Toronto) and Lorne Davis to serve as co-coaches. Between Drake and Watt, the two had combined to win 13 of 14 CIAU titles between 1966 and 1979.

Based in Calgary, the 1980 Canadian Olympic team included 15 CIAU players: Randy Gregg, who was selected captain, John Devaney, Don Spring, Kevin Primeau and Dave Hindmarch of Alberta; Warren Anderson, Joe Grant, Dan D'Alvise, Stelio Zupancich, Cary Farelli and Shane Pearsall of Toronto, UBC's Terry O'Malley and Ron Paterson, Paul MacLean of the Dalhousie Tigers and Jim Nill of Calgary. For O'Malley, it was his third Olympic appearance having previously represented Canada in 1964 and 1968. In its return to the Olympics, Canada would finish sixth at Lake Placid, New York.

Following the 1980 Olympics, Hockey Canada decided to continue Bauer's national program on a full-time basis with the team headquartered in Calgary. Dave King of the University of Saskatchewan was named the head coach of Team Canada and the 1980 CIAU coach of the year would guide the team at three Olympics. Under King, Canada finished fourth at both the 1984 Games at Sarajevo, Yugoslavia and at Calgary in 1988 before winning a silver medal at Albertville, France in 1992. He would also coach Canada at four World Championship tournaments and participate in a gold medal win for Canada at the World Junior Championships in 1982. He added a bronze in 1983.

During King's tenure with Team Canada, he had several CIAU players as members of the Olympic team. In 1984 Warren Anderson and Darren Lowe (Toronto), Robin Bartel (Saskatchewan), Vaughn Karpan (Manitoba) wore the maple leaf, while George Kingston (Calgary) and Jean Perron (Moncton) served as King's assistants. Moncton's Claude Vilgrain was a member of the 1988 team and was joined Karpan and Gregg.

For both Gregg and Karpan, it marked their second stint with the Olympic program. There were no CIAU players on Team Canada at the 1992 Olympics in Albertville, but the 1994 team in Lillehammer, Norway had Saskatchewan defenceman Ken Lovsin on the roster. UQTR head coach Dany Dube was an assistant to head coach Tom Renney and George Kingston served in management as the team's director of hockey operations.

Besides the players on the Canadian Olympic team, there have been several players from the CIAU representing other countries at the Olympics and world championships. Ron Fischer of Calgary (1988, 1992) and Rick Amann of UBC (1992, 1994) were both members of Germany's Olympic team, while Regina's Rick Nasheim skated for Austria in 1994 and 1998. A trio of Calgary Dinosaurs represented the CIAU at the 1998 games in Nagano, Japan. Defenceman Chad Biafore skated for Italy and Matt Kabayama and Steve Tsujiura were members of the host Japanese Olympic team.

Even prior to Father Bauer's national program at UBC in 1964, Canadian university athletes had often represented their country internationally. In 1928 the University of Toronto Grads won the Olympic gold medal at St. Moritz. One member of the team was Dr. Joseph A. Sullivan. Playing goal for Canada, Sullivan earned two shutouts to backstop the Grads to an undefeated record. Following the Games, Sullivan would go on to serve in Canada's senate and the trophy awarded to the CIAU's outstanding player is named in his honour.

The CIAU has also represented Canada at the World Student Games five times since 1968. That season the Toronto Varsity Blues won a bronze medal for Canada at Innsbruck and in 1972 a CIAU all-star team won silver at Lake Placid. In 1980 the Alberta Golden Bears won the gold medal in Jaca, Spain and later earned a bronze medal in 1987 in Strbske Pleso, Czechoslovakia. Canada's was last represented at the World Student Games in January, 1997 by an all-star squad from the CWUAA, which came home with a bronze medal.

Over the years CIAU student-athletes and coaches have also represented Canada at international tournaments such as the Canada Cup, Spengler Cup, Izvestia Cup, the World Championships and the World Junior Championships. In the process they have helped to carry on the rich tradition of Canadian intercollegiate hockey.

CIAU Champions

1963	McMaster Marlins
1964	Alberta Golden Bears
1965	Manitoba Bisons
1966	Toronto Varsity Blues
1967	Toronto Varsity Blues
1968	Alberta Golden Bears
1969	Toronto Varsity Blues
1970	Toronto Varsity Blues
1971	Toronto Varsity Blues
1972	Toronto Varsity Blues
1973	Toronto Varsity Blues
1974	Waterloo Warriors
1975	Alberta Golden Bears
1976	Toronto Varsity Blues
1977	Toronto Varsity Blues
1978	Alberta Golden Bears
1979	Alberta Golden Bears
1980	Alberta Golden Bears
1981	Moncton Aigles Bleus
1982	Moncton Aigles Bleus
1983	Saskatchewan Huskies
1984	Toronto Varsity Blues
1985	York Yeomen
1986	Alberta Golden Bears
1987	Trois-Rivieres Patriotes
1988	York Yeomen
1989	York Yeomen
1990	Moncton Aigles Bleus
1991	Trois-Rivieres Patriotes
1992	Alberta Golden Bears
1993	Acadia Axemen
1994	Lethbridge Pronghorns
1995	Moncton Aigles Bleus
1996	Acadia Axemen
1997	Guelph Gryphons
1998	New Brunswick Varsity Reds

CHAPTER 31

A Woman's Game

Nagano Saw It Come of Age, but Women's Hockey has Its Own Rich History

Shirley Fischler

IT WAS 1956 WHEN DEFENSEMAN ABBY HOFFMAN made headlines across Canada, largely because of a proposed swimming party. Abby Hoffman was a nine-year-old girl who had been selected to play in the Timmy Tyke minor hockey tournament, and the swimming party was proposed for the "boys" of the team after the tournament.

Hoffman had managed to disguise her sex throughout the season by dressing at home, which most of the kids did, and by wearing her hair in a boyish close crop. But the proposed swimming party, combined with the necessity of producing a birth certificate (which clearly would show her sex as female) in order to participate in the tourney, was Abby's downfall. However, determined to play in the league and the tournament, Abby and her family took hockey off the ice and into the courts. The Ontario Supreme Court ruled against Abby and she remained banished from the league. Undaunted, Abby went on to a distinguished track career, competing in four Olympics, the British Empire Games and the Pan-American Games.

In April 1982, in remembrance of Hoffman's struggle to play hockey, the Ontario Women's Hockey Association (OWHA) played their first annual Abby Hoffman Cup (a national women's tournament) in Brantford, Ontario. In truth, though, Abby Hoffman had not forged a new trail for women in hockey, nor was the Abby Hoffman Cup Tourney the first truly national women's ice hockey tournament. Women are known to have played hockey as far back as the nineteenth century.

In 1889, only a month after Lord Stanley (who later contributed the Stanley Cup) and his family had appeared at the annual Ottawa Winter Carnival and witnessed this popular, new game of ice hockey, the local press reported that Lord Stanley's daughter, Isobel, had played for a Government House team in a victory over the Rideau ladies' hockey team. In 1896, a young woman who was reputed to be one of the fastest skaters in the province of Saskatchewan, Annie McIntyre, helped organize a women's hockey team. In the province of Alberta, the *Medicine Hat Times* reported on March 11, 1897 about a game between two women's teams. And before the turn of the century, there were women's teams in Calgary, Banff, Medicine Hat, Red Deer, Vancouver, Kingston, Toronto, Ottawa, Montreal, Quebec City, Fredericton, Saint John and Moncton—although women were discouraged from playing the game in Prince Edward Island and Cape Breton. In 1900, three women's teams from Montreal and one each from Trois-Rivieres and Quebec City formed a league in Quebec.

From a copy of the OWHA's newsletter, a faded picture of the Ottawa Canadian Banknote team of 1905 shows six ladylike players dressed in ankle-length skirts, turtleneck sweaters and tasseled toques. Peeking out from under one long, flowing skirt, however, is a pair of genuine hockey skates, not figure skates. As one looks at this aged testimony to women's hockey, one must remember that at that time

men did not wear any significant protective gear when they played the game either. In fact, women's ice hockey was a popular, avidly played and surprisingly well-attended sport through the 1920s and 1930s in Canada and small, isolated sections of the United States.

Women's hockey leagues in Ontario attracted both media attention and spectator interest through the 1920s. There was even an East–West (national) championship annually in Canada. At that time, Canada was a nation of small towns connected by the national railroad system and the women hockey players would take off in railroad cars and live in them (on sidings) until the tourney was over. Of course, this meant that the East–West event always had to take place between towns that were connected by the railroads.

The games took place on outdoor ice and records indicate that over 3,000 people watched one East–West tourney in Fort William, Ontario. In the 1930s, the Preston (Ontario) Rivulettes were the winningest and best-known women's hockey team in all of Canada, with an astounding record of only two losses in more than 350 games. The Rivulettes were the Canadian women's hockey champions for an entire decade, from 1930 to 1940—something even the fabled Montreal Canadiens cannot claim.

The history of women's hockey, both in Canada and the United States, parallels the status of women overall. Women achieved great strides in civil rights and cultural freedom prior to World War II, culminating with a huge influx of women into the job market when the men went off to fight from 1939 through 1945. After the war, however, the men returned, women were forced back into the home, and a new era of conservatism toward women and their role in society began, which extended into the early 1960s.

The rise and fall and further rise of women's hockey echoes this history. Participation and interest in women's hockey peaked before World War II, then waned during the war years (reflecting what was happening at the highest levels of men's professional hockey). After World War II, women's hockey of the 1950s and early 1960s reflected the prevalent attitude toward women: they should be feminine, weak, frivolous and decorative. Women no longer used hockey skates, but darted about, giggling and flirting, on white figure skates, wearing no protective equipment whatsoever. Stories of the time dealt more with hair styles and fashion than with skating, shooting prowess or stickhandling, and one "cute" story—with voluptuous starlet Jayne Mansfield on the ice wielding a hockey stick and a vacuous smirk—personified the devaluation of women's participation in nearly all sports, and definitely in all sports which were traditionally a masculine domain.

This is why Abby Hoffman's effort to compete in a boys' hockey league all the way back in 1956 remains so astounding. At a time when other girls and women never were encouraged and often were discouraged to compete with men—at any level or in any any kind of endeavor—and to

act and appear as feminine as possible, Hoffman played as an equal with boys her age and succeeded.

Arnold Bruner, then of the *Toronto Daily Star*, described a typical women's hockey game of the period: "It was a gentlemanly—oops—ladylike game of hockey with the girls, some wearing no more protective equipment than flimsy blouses, doing everything they could to keep from bumping into each other."

By the mid-1960s, reflecting the activism of the times, women's hockey began to take on a more serious nature. In British Columbia, Jack Campbell and Doug Dionne wanted to get ice time for their daughters and other interested girls, and at the beginning of the 1963–64 season they received one hour of ice per week from the Killarney Community Centre Association. In Burnaby (a suburb of Vancouver), a women's softball team became a hockey team when they could get the ice time. By 1965–66, there was a five-team girls league and age divisions of junior, intermediate and senior were formed. Within a couple of years, there were 25 teams in the lower British Columbia mainland and 12 teams on Vancouver Island. Soon, teams from the interior of the province began to join what became the B.C. Girls' Ice Hockey Association. By the 1970s, girls' teams from British Columbia were traveling to the eastern provinces on tours. One team went to Finland for exhibitions, another traveled to Japan for a tourney.

British Columbia and Ontario were not the only hotbeds of women's hockey, however. In Saskatchewan, one story has it that NHL greats Max and Doug Bentley's earliest (and stiffest, it is told) competition came from their own sisters. Besides Max and Doug, the Bentleys sent four other brothers from their Saskatchewan home into professional hockey. But, according to Bill Bentley, the family's father, it was not the boys but the girls, seven sisters in all, who were the family's better hockey players when young.

"The girls had a hockey team when they were kids," explained Papa Bentley, "and they could beat the blisters off the boys nine times out of ten!"

Likewise, in traditional U.S. hockey areas such as Massachusetts women's hockey flourished. Leagues grew in the late 1960s and early 1970s, with women's rediscovery of "liberation."

Although women rushed to join girls and women's teams and leagues, there were isolated women who tried to join the men's teams, like Abby Hoffman before them. Karen Koch, 19, tried to play for a Senior A men's club in Michigan and already had played goal for a Northern Michigan University fraternity team. Karen even moved to Toronto in an effort to find a men's team that would let her play, but there was an Ontario Hockey Association rule prohibiting women's playing on men's teams. For a short time in 1970, Jane Yearwood, 10, played goal for a boys' team in an organized league in Edmonton, Alberta. Jane was remarkable in that she had been playing goal since the age of five and did so without a mask.

Gail Cummings, 11, tried out for the goalie slot on a Huntsville Minor Hockey Association all-star team, and in October 1976, she signed a Canadian Amateur Hockey Association player registration certificate. She played four games with the team before she was notified by coach Barry Webb that her certificate had been rejected. Like Hoffman, Gail and her family took the matter all the way up to the Ontario Supreme Court, where she was ultimately rejected.

More than a decade later, a high school senior in the unlikely town of Oyster Bay, Long Island, New York won a discrimination suit against the town, and Barbara Broidy officially was allowed to play with the boys in the town's high school ice hockey league. Unfortunately, the ruling came down just as Barbara was about to go off to college and her chance to play with the boys was almost completely gone.

Whatever the image, the fears and the difficulties, by 1982 there were more than 12,000 girls and women playing hockey in the Canadian province of Ontario alone. In the U.S., the women's division of USA Hockey (formerly AHAUS—the Amateur Hockey Association of the United States) had 116 teams registered, covering the spectrum from Squirt (12 years and up), through Senior A (women 20 and older), including 35 women's and girls' teams in Massachusetts alone.

Canadian college and universities operated women's teams in the 1980s and by the close of the decade, the quality of the women's game had advanced. Concordia University in Montreal was a power in the women's game, attracting top players from both Canada and the U.S.

In the U.S., the Eastern Collegiate Athletic Conference began sponsoring women's collegiate hockey in 1984. By the mid-1990s there were more than 65 colleges and universities in the East and Midwest that sponsored either women's varsity or club ice hockey teams. The main event in U.S. women's college hockey is the ECAC Women's Championship Tournament.

In the meantime, from 1990–91 through 1996–97, the number of girls and women registered with USA Hockey almost quadrupled, swelling from 5,573, to more than 23,000 in five age categories ranging from "nine and under" to "senior" (20 and over), with the "nine and under" group comprising almost 30 percent of the total.

In 1993 another breakthrough came when the NCAA officially recognized women's ice hockey as an emerging sport. This recognition has enabled collegiate women's ice hockey to graduate from a regional to a national sport. However, NCAA rules require that in order for a women's sport to hold an annual national championship tournament at least 40 colleges or universities must offer varsity ice hockey programs for women, and these varsity programs have to exist for at least two years.

"I believe that over the next six years there will be a huge number of schools adding the sport," said Cornell women's ice hockey coach Julie Andeberhan. In fact, it was predicted that the women's version of ice hockey would qualify under the NCAA rules for a national championship by the 2000–01 season.

In 1994 the state of Minnesota became the first to designate girls' ice hockey as a varsity sport at the high school level. As a result the number of Minnesota high schools with varsity girls' hockey teams jumped from 24 in 1994–95 to more than triple that number (85) in 1997–98.

Also in 1994, USA Hockey created the women's equivalent of the college hockey Hobey Baker Award: the USA Hockey Women's Hockey Player of the Year Award, which was won the first time by Erin Whitten, a goaltender from Glens Falls, New York, who also became the starting goaltender for Team USA.

On the international level women's ice hockey was growing, too, with the initial World Invitational Tournament taking place in 1987 in North York and Mississauga, Ontario. Simultaneously pressure was being applied to the International Ice Hockey Federation (IIHF) to create a

world championship for women and after IIHF president Dr. Gunther Sabetzki attended the European Women's Championship in 1989, he began to formulate plans for a Women's World Championship.

The plans were realized in 1990, when the first-ever IIHF Women's World Championship took place in Ottawa. The Canadian women's team nabbed the gold, the U.S. women took silver and Finland returned home with the bronze. Cornell's Julie Andeberhan was a member of that silver medal-winning 1990 U.S. women's team.

"It was like my dream come true," she recalled. "It was something that I always hoped for and now it was happening.

"A lot of my time playing sports had been spent just trying to pursue excellence and not really having a concrete idea of what I could do. Finally, here was a chance to play on the U.S. team with such great players and for the first time understand what it is to play on an international level."

A momentous leap forward for women's ice hockey happened in 1992 when the International Olympic Committee (IOC) chose to include it as a full-medal sport in the 2002 Winter Olympics which would take place in Salt Lake City, Utah. In the meantime, either the 1994 or 1998 Winter Olympic host could include women's ice hockey as a medal sport if they so chose. The Japanese Olympic Organizing Committee, hosts of the 1998 Winter Olympics in Nagano, opted to include women's hockey.

The second IIHF Women's World Championship also took place in 1992 and the venue moved to Tampere, Finland, although the results were identical to the first world tourney: Canada, gold; U.S., silver; Finland, bronze. The third world event would take place in Lake Placid, New York, in 1994, with results unchanged for the third consecutive time.

In April 1997 the fourth IIHF Women's World Championship took place in Kitchener, Ontario, serving as a qualifier for the 1998 Olympic Winter Games. Team USA was now coached by Ben Smith, formerly the men's ice hockey coach at Northeastern University. Guided by Smith, the U.S. women almost pulled off a major upset, yielding only to the Canadian women's team 4–3 in overtime (thereby giving the Canadian women a perfect 20–0 record in international competition).

Outside of the international and collegiate competitions, in 1992 a young Quebec goaltender created professional ice hockey history when she was given the chance to appear in a Tampa Bay Lightning exhibition game against the St. Louis Blues. Before a huge but skeptical crowd of 27,000 in the ThunderDome, Manon Rheaume played the game's first period in the Tampa net. When she exited the goal after one period, the score was 2–2.

Although Manon did not make the Lightning's regular squad for the 1992–93 season, she did play with Tampa's farm team in the International Hockey League. She was invited to the next Lightning preseason training camp and appeared in another exhibition game—this time versus the Boston Bruins. Rheaume subsequently played several more seasons in the minor leagues, backstopping for the Charlotte Checkers and Knoxville Cherokees of the East Coast Hockey League, the Las Vegas Thunder of the IHL and the Reno Renegades of the West Coast Hockey League—belying the accusations that her playing professional men's hockey was just a one-time publicity stunt. (Rheaume did not play minor pro men's hockey in 1997-98 in order to honor her commitment to the Canadian Women's Olympic team.)

While Rheaume and Erin Whitten remain the only women to play in the minors, the fact that they played on mixed-gender teams was not unique. Unfortunately, Canadian Hockey (formerly the Canadian Amateur Hockey Association) does not keep records of girls and young women playing on boys' youth hockey teams, so the true number of girls and young women playing ice hockey in Canada are not yet accurate (that number was officially listed at 23,922 in 1996.)

But USA Hockey—which is well aware of the fact that the number of girls' and women's teams and leagues in the U.S. has not kept pace at all with the rise in participation—says that a majority of the 20,319 registered girls and women playing hockey outside of the collegiate system in 1996 are doing so on mixed-gender teams.

"Growing up playing mostly with the boys in youth hockey programs," recalled Maria Dennis, a former Yale hockey player and member of the board of directors of USA Hockey, "people would come up to me and say, 'you skate so wonderfully,' and I would say, 'thank you.' Then they'd say, 'you skate like a guy,' to which I'd reply, 'I don't skate like a guy; I skate like a hockey player.'"

And when the women hockey players sallied forth on Olympic ice in Nagano, Japan—whether they began playing ice hockey disguised as boys, or played girls' hockey in Duluth, Springfield or Trois-Rivieres—they would be wearing equipment designed for women and they would play their own game, with their own rules.

CHAPTER 32
Significant Others
Little-known and "Forgotten" Teams

THE OXFORD CANADIANS

Peter Wilton

DURING THE EARLY 1920s, and again in the early 1930s, a team from Oxford, England, made up largely of Canadian Rhodes Scholars, dominated ice hockey in Europe. Through their skill on the ice, and their grace and charm off it, they were able not only to win games but to serve as ambassadors for their sport in the villages, cities, towns and resorts in which they played. Their efforts did much to popularize hockey in Europe.

In the fall of 1921, Lester Pearson, Roland Michener and R.H. (Dick) Bonnycastle met at Oxford University. Pearson would go on to become the 14th Prime Minister of Canada; Michener, the Governor-General of Canada and Bonnycastle the first mayor of Greater Winnipeg. The bond between these three men was forged not on debating clubs (although each of their futures would be defined by the elegance of their words), but on the ice with the Oxford Ice Hockey Club.

In the early 1920s, Oxford University was diminished greatly by the losses sustained in World War I. Certainly it tried to maintain its traditions, but the university had paid a high price for King and country. Of the 3,000 students and teachers who had enlisted "to do their bit," 2,700 had been killed. Amongst the dead were eight class leaders, the son of a British prime minister and a generation of future British leaders in politics, arts, science and commerce. After the war, another 25 million people worldwide died of influenza. Across the historic grounds of Oxford, plaques to the dead were appearing. Returning service personnel—witness to unimaginable horrors—were seized by a need to enjoy the moment.

Sports took on a new and greater meaning for this generation which had been a part of so much sorrow. The landscape and traditions had been altered forever.

From backgrounds shaped by disease and years of war, a team of young men were brought together by the common love of hockey. Under the direction of their captain, K.E. Taylor, Pearson, Michener and Bonnycastle, along with E.B. Pitblado, H. Fleming, F.L. Neylan, F.M. Bacon and C.B. Clark, would go on to become one of the greatest hockey teams ever assembled by Oxford. They would dominate European hockey over the next three years.

An example of the leadership displayed by Taylor is the effort he put into preparing his team for the 1921 edition of the annual game between Cambridge and Oxford known as the Varsity match. (The two collegiate rivals had been playing this contest since 1900, with the game held in Switzerland since 1902. The schools did not play from 1914 to 1919 because of the war.) Taylor arranged for Oxford to play a series of games against a Manchester hockey team prior to the 1921 Varsity match. The captain of Cambridge made no such arrangements for his team. Oxford defeated Cambridge 27–0 that year for the most lopsided victory in

Varsity history. So strong was the Oxford team that the fans who encircled the outdoor arena were betting heavily on the margin of victory. After just five minutes, one gentleman refused to sell a pool ticket that required Oxford to win by 40 goals, believing it might be a winner. In the end, it was the combination of Taylor, Pitblado and Bonnycastle that had emerged as the great stars of the game.

During their Christmas tour in 1921, Oxford competed against the Swiss national team and won by a margin of 9–0. They went on to post bigger victories over the home clubs in the ski resorts of Davos and St. Moritz. By the end of the tour, the Oxford hockey team had won the international tournament that was the forerunner of the Spengler Cup. Oxford's dominance over the course of its tour can be measured by its goals for and against: Oxford scored 87 times while allowing just two goals. In February of 1922, five members of this Oxford team were invited to join the British National Ice Hockey Team for an international tournament in St. Moritz. It was largely due to the play of E.B. Pitblado, H. Fleming, F.L. Neylan, F.M. Bacon and C.B. Clark that Britain won the tournament. The determination shown by the Oxford players is exemplified by Fleming, who was pushed to the ice during the first game and bit his tongue so badly it was nearly severed. Fleming had the injury stitched up and went on to play so impressively throughout the rest of the tournament that some believe England would not have won without him.

An interesting aspect of the early Oxford hockey tours is that the games were watched by the Europeans in much the same way they would view a stage performance or a concert. The ladies and gentlemen who attended these games were largely from the upper classes and would dress in proper evening clothes. In the Berlin Ice Palace, the indoor arena was surrounded by a dining room in which the hockey fans would be served their dinner and wine while the game was going on for their entertainment. The young Oxford players loved the glitter and glamour of the continental urban and ski resort scene. They did not receive any money for playing hockey but were given room and board in many of the finest hotels. Their leisure time was filled with sight-seeing and skiing. After the game, they were much sought-after guests and enjoyed the company of some of the most attractive women in Europe. Lester Pearson always treasured a menu which he had had signed by Gladys Cooper, a glamorous silent movie star of the era, who had danced with him at the Grand Hotel and Belvedere in Davos.

During the Christmas tour of 1922–23, captain Taylor once again led the Oxford hockey team to great success—though the Varsity match was a much more even game than the blowout of the year before. Cambridge captain H. G. Joseph had picked his team very carefully, ensuring that almost all the members had played hockey in either Canada or the United States and arranging for his team to have plenty of practice. Taking the lead from Taylor, Joseph also brought in some teams to compete against Cambridge. But

despite his best efforts, the score of the Varsity match was 7–1 in favor of Oxford. This marked the first year in which Oxford and Cambridge both sent a second team to Davos. The two teams were well-matched and put on a good game, which the Oxford Cosmopolitans won by a score of 5–2.

The Christmas break of 1922–23 proved once again that the Oxford Ice Hockey Club dominated European hockey. They played against the German national team in Berlin, and against local club teams in Paris and in Davos, as well as playing the British army team at St. Moritz. Oxford was victorious in every game. The German newspapers, impressed by Lester Pearson's skating style, nicknamed him "Herr Zig Zag."

The 1923–24 school year marked the end of this extraordinarily successful Oxford team, as the squad's key players graduated that spring. Its last season had been no less triumphant than the first two. Despite a 1924 tournament that was plagued by heavy snowfall and bad weather, the Oxford team came out victorious over Cambridge as well as the British Olympic team, although there are no scores available to show the extent of the Oxford victories.

In 1926, Clarence Campbell won a Rhodes Scholarship to Oxford. His main sporting interest was baseball (having played semi-pro ball in Canada prior to coming to England) and once at Oxford he formed the Oxford Baseball Club. Each Sunday, the baseball team traveled to London to play against the London team. Campbell also played for the Oxford Ice Hockey Club between 1927 and 1929. His style of play was rugged and he was certainly one of the better players on the Oxford team. In appreciation for his fine play and his efforts as team captain, Campbell was presented with a miniature of the Anspang Cup (for competition between Davos and the university teams) and the Patton Cup (for the English league championship) after winning the annual Varsity match in 1929. C.T. Wylde, the captain of Cambridge also was presented with a miniature of the Patton Cup. Campbell's connection to hockey certainly did not end at Oxford. He went on to become an NHL referee and then president of the National Hockey League in 1946.

Another Bonnycastle brother arrived at Oxford as a Rhodes Scholar in 1929. Larry Bonnycastle had played hockey in his home province of Manitoba and it was natural that he should follow his older brother's lead and join the Oxford Hockey Club. The team of his era would prove to be the equal of his brother's squad of the early 1920s, as Larry Bonnycastle had the golden scoring touch. Goaltender C.H. "Herbie" Little of the Oxford squad was one of the greatest goaltenders in Europe at the time. Some 65 years later, he recalled the team's winning formula: "Larry would put the puck in the net at one end, and I would keep it out at the other."

Bonnycastle's other teammates in his three years at Oxford included John D. Babbitt (a left-handed right winger who had great success with his backhand), G. Stanley, Orvald A. "Snooks" Gratius, A.S. "Si" Leach, Leland A. Watson (the only American on the team), Archie Humble, B.S. Keirstead, Ronald Martland (who was top of his class at Oxford, received a double law degree and later became a judge on the Supreme Court of Canada) and James E. Coyne. In 1933, Jim Coyne saved his Oxford teammates from financial destitution during their Christmas tour of Europe after a Czech border guard impounded all their money. As the team pondered their options, Coyne magically produced an American Express check he had hidden in the heel of his shoe. Such financial wizardry would

come in handy in later life as Coyne went on to become the governor of the Bank of Canada.

During the Christmas holiday European tour of 1930–31, Oxford won the Anspang Cup for the fourth time. The fourth win of the Anspang entitled the Oxford team to keep the trophy, but it was agreed by the players to offer it up for perpetual competition between varsity teams. On February 13, 1931, a combined varsity team made up of the top players from Oxford and Cambridge was put together with W.G. Speechly as captain. The combined club met a touring Toronto team known as the Canadas at Golders Green rink in London and defeated them by a score of 13–0.

Following their Anspang Cup victory, the Oxford team had continued its tour of Europe and met the German national team in Berlin. During the intermission of the hockey game, the fans were entertained not by the scraping of the ice but by the graceful figure skating of Sonja Henie. Hugh Morrison recalls that the Oxford team owed quite a debt of gratitude to Ms. Henie: "We were delayed in Hanover en route to Berlin. By the time we arrived, the crowd had been waiting for close to an hour for us to rush from the station to the Berlin Ice Arena. We got changed and took to the ice. The crowd had been kept entertained by Sonja Henie during this time. It was her skating that kept the fans from leaving."

As captain of the Oxford Ice Hockey Club, it was the honor of Larry Bonnycastle to present Ms. Henie with flowers. Bonnycastle's future wife, Mary Andrews, was watching from the stands as he made his way out with the flowers. She recalls that, after the game, Larry confided to her that his legs had been shaking badly—he had not realized how difficult it was to skate without the aid of a hockey stick.

With the success of the Oxford team and the obvious European interest in the sport, hockey began taking on an increased importance as a display of nation pride. With the success of a team reflecting more and more on its hometown or nation, European teams began to pursue better players for their rosters, and these players were overwhelmingly Canadian. The Oxford Ice Hockey Club already featured a mainly Canadian roster, but the team was given a further boost when the town built a new ice arena that was the same size as the Montreal Forum. The new rink was a tremendous advantage for the Oxford team, as arenas were rare in Britain at the time. Prior to the creation of the arena in Oxford, the team had to travel as far as Manchester to practice. With the new arena, the "dark blues" were able to practice as often as four times per week.

On February 6, 1932, the Varsity match between Oxford and Cambridge was played in the London suburb of Richmond. This marked the first time in 30 years that the two teams would meet in England instead of Switzerland. The results proved one-sided, as the combination of Bonnycastle and Babbitt, backed by Little in goal, was too strong for the rookie-laden Cambridge roster. Oxford won the game 7–0. The headlines of the *Oxford Mail* the following morning read: "Oxfords Great Win at Richmond and a Triumph for Bonnycastle … in which the speed of the Oxford forwards were opposed to the dour defensive tactics of the [Cambridge] light blues."

The strength of the 1931–32 Oxford team can be measured again by their successful European tour. The team would win yet another Anspang Cup as well as the Spengler Cup (as the top club team in Europe), in addition to winning the Patton Cup as the league champion in England. Among the highlights of the season was holding the Boston

Olympics to a tie. This team of top American amateurs would win the World Championship in 1933 and already had beaten the national teams of England and France when they met the Oxford Canadians as part of their 1932 European Tour. The Oxford team very nearly beat the American champions, missing on a scoring opportunity late in the game. Reported the press afterwards: "It is hard to find praise high enough for the University team ... Not only did the university hold its side, they often looked more dangerous than the visitors." In appreciation of the team's efforts and successes in Europe this season, the players were presented with gold medals by the mayor of Oxford. As captain of the team, and its top scorer, Larry Bonnycastle made an acceptance speech.

Unlike the rough and tumble games being played by the North American professional teams of the era, European teams, including Oxford and Cambridge, played a much cleaner game. The rules for infractions such as boarding were enforced strictly. Fighting was forbidden absolutely and would mean an automatic game misconduct. Hugh Morrison remembers playing a game in a small town in Europe in which the referee called an offside that was clearly not offside: "I started arguing the call with the ref. A man from the audience came down from his seat and told me that he was a graduate of Oxford and was ashamed of my behavior. He went on to say that students from Oxford simply did not behave in this manner and that arguing a call with a ref would not be tolerated by students wearing the colors of Oxford."

In the spring of 1932, Larry Bonnycastle graduated from Oxford University, and so came to a close one of the greatest hockey careers of that era. During the following year, the efforts of goalie C.H. Little resulted in the university somewhat reluctantly agreeing to award hockey club members the formal athletic honor known as a "Half Blue" for their sporting achievements. The decision had come too late for Bonnycastle, perhaps the greatest player to wear the Oxford hockey sweater. Despite Little's strongest lobbying, the university refused to award Bonnycastle the color retroactively. Nonetheless, many, including Hugh MacLennan, a distinguished Canadian author who was a Rhodes Scholar in the early 1930s, looked upon Larry Bonnycastle as the one individual who, more than anyone else, sold the game of hockey to the Europeans.

The departure of Bonnycastle greatly diminished the offensive strength of the Oxford Ice Hockey Club. Within a year, the interest in hockey in England lost its momentum along with Oxford's supremacy of the game. The hockey arena that Bonnycastle had helped to fill with chanting and singing fans stood largely empty. Without the European champions, interest in hockey fell. The arena was closed and converted into a cinema. It would be another 50 years before Oxford would boast an ice arena again.

C.H. Little hung up his goalie pads after the 1933 season despite an attempt to sign him by the Toronto Maple Leafs. Little wanted to retire a winner and never played competitive hockey again. His interest in hockey at Oxford remained, though the sport there was clearly in decline. Little hoped to sponsor a tournament and donated a silver cup to the college. Two years later, his cup was found abandoned in a coal bin. It was returned to Mr. Little, who was shocked to find the trophy and the sport of hockey treated so shabbily. The "cupper" which he donated is used now as a rose bowl in his Toronto apartment.

The days of glory of Oxford hockey ended with the graduation of Bonnycastle and the subsequent graduations of Little and John D. Babbitt. While interest in the game may have waned in England, it had taken root firmly in Europe. This is the true legacy of a team of amateur academics who, for a brief time, ruled supreme in the game they loved.

THE COAST GUARD CUTTERS

Stan Fischler

IT MAY COME AS A SURPRISE to many American hockey historians, but the most accomplished collection of players to represent Uncle Sam on ice belonged neither to the 1960 nor 1980 gold medal Olympians who won their championships at Squaw Valley and Lake Placid, respectively.

Comprised almost exclusively of collegians or recent university graduates, the Olympians were more glamorous—in the melodramatic, Horatio Alger, Hollywood style—than talented although their victories symbolized many hockey virtues.

By contrast, a virtually forgotten group of star-spangled skaters playing out of Baltimore, Maryland unquestionably remains the finest non-National Hockey League team ever to perform in league competition. The United States Coast Guard Cutters club, unfortunately, performed in a pre-television, pre-hype era and consequently their feats remained relatively unchronicled, although they won two consecutive championships and thoroughly dominated the competition in their two seasons of operation.

A product of World War II, the Cutters were created shortly after the Japanese attack on Pearl Harbor. A former Michigan-born player, C.R. MacLean was assigned to the Coast Guard's Curtis Bay Yard in Baltimore. A Lieutenant Commander, MacLean was the Yard's Personnel Officer and foremost hockey fan.

"If a hockey player had a choice of service in which to enlist," said Mike Nardello, a New York Rangers prospect, "Commander MacLean would encourage them to join the Coast Guard."

During the summer of 1942 MacLean began networking and soon he had enough players to organize a team. He contacted Tom Lockhart, president of the Amateur Hockey Association of the United States. Lockhart also was head of the Eastern Amateur Hockey League (EAHL), one of the top breeding grounds for NHL players.

"Prior to the war," Nardello recalled, "the Eastern League played in Baltimore. But like so many clubs it had to disband because so many players entered the armed forces."

Lockhart approved the Cutters as the EAHL's replacement club in Baltimore. They would play against the New York Rovers—a Rangers farm club playing out of Madison Square Garden—the Boston Olympics, the Bruins' EAHL counterpart, and the Philadelphia Falcons, an independent team whose home was the Arena.

What lifted the Coast Guard head and shoulders above any of their American rivals, before or since, was the quality of personnel, not to mention the depth at each position. Once MacLean's clarion call was sounded, stickhandlers from virtually every league responded, especially the NHL. And many were future Hall of Famers.

Art Coulter had just captained the Rangers to first place during the 1941–42 National Hockey League season—he also had led them to the 1940 Stanley Cup—and debated whether to enlist. He took the train to Baltimore and signed on with the Coast Guard.

So did Frank Brimsek, alias Mister Zero, who to this day

is regarded as the premier goaltender in Boston Bruins history. A native of Eveleth, Minnesota—appropriately home of the U.S. Hockey Hall of Fame—Brimsek was netminder for Boston's Stanley Cup wins in 1939 and 1941.

"The amazing thing was that Frankie had to fight for the number one job," said Bob Gilray, another member of the Cutters, "because we had two other top goalies."

Each a star in the powerful minor-league American Hockey Association, goalies Muzz Murray and Hub Nelson battled Brimsek for lead goalie. The result was that the netminding was divided by thirds but always nonpareil.

Johnny Mariucci, an All-American football hero at the University of Minnesota, and a starting defenseman for the Chicago Black Hawks, took the train from the Windy City to Baltimore. Mariucci teamed with AHA ace Manny Cotlow—a Jewish defenseman who would just as soon eat railroad spikes as T-bone steaks—to give the Cutters a frightening back line duo.

No less tough was Bob Dill, a Golden Gloves champ from St.Paul, who would graduate to the New York Rangers defense after his stint in the Coast Guard. (After Dill scored the winning goal against the Rovers one Sunday, the next day's New York Daily Mirror headlined it "Dill Pickles Clincher.")

From Detroit came Alex Motter, who had been a member of the Red Wings 1942 Stanley Cup finalists that had taken the Toronto Maple Leafs to seven games before losing. Motter, a forward, and Bud Cook, kid brother of legendary Rangers Bill and Bun Cook, were ingredients in the Coast Guard's high-octane attack.

The big-leaguers notwithstanding, primary energy for the Cutters machine was infused by players from hotbeds such as the Minnesota Iron Range and Northern Michigan. A prime example was the top line comprised of Gilray, Joe Kucler and Eddie Olson.

"I was playing in the Marquette (Michigan) area with Muzz Murray," said Gilray. "Our coach was the former NHL defenseman Taffy Abel. He got a letter from Commander MacLean asking Taffy if any of his players were interested in playing hockey for the Coast Guard.

"Muzz and I had been on a waiting list to join the Coast Guard. When Commander McLean found out we wanted to play hockey we were told to report to the Coast Guard's Chicago base the next day. A Captain Stewart asked me to raise my hand and proceeded to swear me in. His first words were 'Where are your skates?' When I told him I left them at home he said: 'You better mail for them immediately!' I was playing hockey within two days."

Mike Nardello was one of the rare New York-born Rangers prospects. A high school star, the fleet forward played in the Metropolitan Amateur Hockey League for the Manhattan Arrows when he was spotted by Rangers manager Lester Patrick. Eventually, Nardello became the only New Yorker to play for the Coast Guard varsity.

"I was going to high school at St. Frances Prep," recalls Nardello, "and playing for the Eastern League's New York Rovers at the same time. Eddie Olson of the Cutters encouraged me to join the Coast Guard when I graduated from high school and had to be drafted. I graduated from high school on January 28, 1943. On February 1, I was sworn into the Coast Guard. Before going to boot camp, I got a chance to play one game for the Cutters. It was against the Rovers. In the span of one week I played for and against the Rovers and the Coast Guard."

One by one, from all points between South Boston and San Francisco, the stickhandlers converged on the Curtis Bay Yard. Eddie Barry, who eventually would play for the Boston Bruins, packed his gear in Wellesley, Massachusetts and made his way to Baltimore. Mel Harwood, who had refereed the 1942 Stanley Cup finals, enlisted in what New York Daily News reporter Dick Young called "Hooligan's Navy" and immediately was named coach of the Cutters.

"Harwood was an excellent coach," said Cotlow. "He certainly had the respect of the players. He was good to us and the players paid him back. Harwood got the most out of us."

If Harwood had a problem it was finding enough ice time for his bell-bottomed skaters. They were required to fulfill their military obligations by day and only then were able to practice at Carlin's Iceland arena in Baltimore. Then there was the matter of numbers.

Harwood was so overloaded with talent he divided the Cutters into two teams—the Cutters and the Clippers—who competed against each other when they weren't involved in Eastern League action. They once played a brutal four-game series that Cotlow described as "the most physical games of my life." George Taylor, writing in the Baltimore News-Post, observed "the rubber tilt was more exciting than the Stanley Cup playoffs." When the Clippers and Cutters united against a common foe, they were virtually unbeatable, winning the U.S. National Senior Open championship of the Amateur Hockey Association in 1943 and 1944.

To gauge how powerful the Cutters were—apart from the fact that they overwhelmed Eastern League foes and won two national titles—one must consider their exhibition game slate as well. For diversion, the Cutters would play against strong Canadian service teams liberally sprinkled with pros and invariably beat them. In a contest against the Allan Cup champion Ottawa Commandos, led by ex-Rangers stars Neil Colville and Alex Shibicky, as well as Joe Cooper of the Black Hawks, the Cutters triumphed 5–2.

The only downer was a loss to the Stanley Cup champion Red Wings on January 6, 1943, before a capacity crowd in Baltimore. With Brimsek in goal, the Cutters hung tough until well into the third period—they trailed 4–3, but were ultimately shellacked 8–3.

"They didn't intimidate us," said Cotlow, "but they were a little smarter."

Despite the patriotic aura that engulfed North America, the Cutters were hardly popular outside Baltimore. They played a take-no-prisoners type of game and frequently roughed up the enemy as well as outscored them. Cotlow was the most rambunctious of the sextet.

"Manny," recalled Kucler, "was quite a character. If the crowd got on Manny for making a bad play, he would set them off by waving his arms or stick at them. You should have heard them boo then. Manny didn't care. He would just keep it up."

"Manny," added McLean, "was an unbelievable show-off. I remember him throwing his stick in the air. He became really adept at achieving a great deal of height after a while."

Cotlow: "I always felt that if the fans didn't cheer or boo you might as well not be playing."

The special ambience which surrounded the Cutters was embellished not only by their personalities but their uniforms and musicians as well. They wore unusual red, white and blue, star spangled jerseys with crossed anchors on the front. Unlike any other hockey club, they were accompanied by a nimble 30-piece marching band that played Semper Paratus—Always Ready, the Coast Guard marching song—at every game.

Nardello was on Madison Square Garden ice for a singularly significant event in the team's short history. Winner of the EAHL's James J. Walker Cup, among their many accomplishments, the Cutters actually were presented the trophy by New York's dashing Mayor Jimmy (Beau James) Walker in ceremonies near the conclusion of the 1943–44 season. It marked one of Walker's last public appearances.

Likewise, it signalled the end of the brief, though sparkling, Coast Guard reign. By mid-1944 the Allied war effort had reached a critical juncture and the need for reinforcements was grave. The idea that two dozen sailors could spend fall and winter playing hockey along the eastern seaboard did not sit well with some elements of the public.

"A lot of parents of servicemen couldn't understand why their sons were overseas fighting and we were still playing hockey," said Kulcer. "The Coast Guard was under a lot of pressure to break us up."

Olson: "They said that Joe was playing his last game for us and then would be shipping out. As soon as Joe left they began getting rid of the other guys and by then, we knew the honeymoon was over."

Those who saw the Cutters on a regular basis agree that they were genuine champions and bristling characters as well. Emile "the Cat" Francis, who played goal for the Philadelphia Falcons and faced the Cutters many times, ranked them among the best clubs of their kind.

"There was nothing quite like them before or since," said Francis, who later became an NHL goaltender as well as big-league coach and general manager.

At war's end, many of the Cutters—including Coulter—retired from pro hockey. However, Mariucci and Brimsek resumed their NHL careers and Nardello played minor-league hockey for the Clinton Comets.

Their feats, for the most part, were forgotten as they gradually left the ice realm. But Nardello, who became an NHL off-ice official at New Jersey Devils games in the mid-1980s and continued at the post through the late 1990s, insisted that the Cutters never received sufficient recognition for their excellence.

Whether they were the greatest American team or not is debatable but neither their uniqueness nor their championships can be questioned.

THE WARROAD LAKERS
1946–47 TO 1996–97
Roger A. Godin

THERE IS A BIT OF HOCKEY HISTORY not much known outside of Northern Minnesota and Western Canada, but one which needs to be told. It is the story of the most successful senior hockey team in the United States. It is also the story of one man's dedication to Canada's national game in small-town America and how that dedication could turn this same small town into a producer of top hockey talent for half a century.

Warroad is a community of some 1,700 people located in Northwestern Minnesota on the shores of the Lake of the Woods about 11 miles south of the Manitoba border. Its principal industrial firm is Marvin Windows, a major enterprise which markets products internationally. Agriculture, logging, fishing and the manufacture of hockey sticks are other commercial activities. The Marvin family has played a significant role in the community's life. Most notable are the brothers Bill, Tut (Randolph), Jack and Frank along

with sister Mary. Bill is the retired mastermind behind Marvin Windows, which employs 3,000 people. Tut, a company vice president, is retired as well; Jack is a vice president who handles the firm's lumber and hardware retail operations, while Frank, now deceased, was in charge of the company's Canadian operations. Mary left Warroad early for a career in Minneapolis-St. Paul. However, by far the best-known family member is Cal, who has owned and operated various motels and restaurants in the community. What he also has operated with a successful passion for 50 years is the Warroad Lakers.

Cal Marvin came back from World War II service with the Marine Corps after having participated in some of the most grueling South Pacific campaigns. He had played hockey before the war and he and others from the area were anxious to renew their part-time ice careers. Along with Dan McKinnon of nearby Williams, he approached the University of North Dakota in Grand Forks about heading a varsity program. The university accepted the idea and thus was born not only the Fighting Sioux but the Warroad Lakers. The young men of Warroad and its environs spent three to four years playing college hockey and drove home on Sundays to play for the Lakers. The team's name came from the nearby Lake of the Woods. The first Lakers team had 13 players and, besides Marvin and McKinnon, featured Clarence Schmidt, also from Williams, who had a brief wartime stint with the Boston Bruins, and Gordie Christian, who would play for the 1956 U.S. Olympic team. Rube Bjorkman, another early Laker, played for both the 1948 and 1952 U.S. Olympic squads. They played their home games on an outdoor rink behind the school and wore the colors of the Boston Bruins. There were no masks, mouthguards, helmets or Zambonis.

The Lakers played in the States-Dominion League for three years and continued to play on outside artificial ice until November, 1949, when Warroad Memorial Arena was opened. Cal Marvin had led the effort to build an indoor arena as a parallel activity to his involvement with the team. Fundraising efforts began on February 20, 1947, and the project was completed for a cost of only $30,000, as all labor was donated. The building was erected as a memorial to those who had died in the service of their country. It seated 1,800, but did not have the luxury of locker rooms at first. The players would change across the street in a local business and then walk to the arena. An artificial ice plant was added in the late 1960s.

By the 1950–51 season, the team was playing in the Northwest Hockey League with Crookston, Roseau, Hallock, Thief River Falls and Grand Forks. This would be the first of many league changes over the team's history. The first significant achievement for the Lakers occurred in 1955 when they won the United States intermediate championship against the Grand Falls Americans in that Montana city. The following year saw the club play the U.S. Olympic team for the first time, losing 6–2 in Eveleth, Minnesota. In 1958, the town was christened with the nickname "Hockeytown USA" by their mayor, Morris Taylor. Cal Marvin, who now was coaching the team exclusively, took a year's sabbatical to go behind the bench for the 1957–58 U.S. national team. The Marvin-coached Nationals finished fifth at the World Championships in Oslo and then became the first U.S. sports team to tour the Soviet Union after World War II. When Marvin returned to Warroad the next season, he coached the Lakers to a 7–1 victory over the Nationals in Warroad.

The late 1950s saw the Lakers' Sammy Graftstrom named as rookie of the year in the Ontario-Minnesota League. The team featured such former NHL players as goaltender Sugar Jim Henry (New York Rangers, Boston Bruins) and defenseman Ed Kryzanowski (Boston Bruins, Chicago Black Hawks). Somewhat before this time, Bob Johnson, who would coach Wisconsin to three NCAA titles and lead Pittsburgh to a Stanley Cup, played for the Lakers when he was coaching Warroad High School.

As the decade closed, the team abandoned the Boston Bruins black and gold colors and adopted red, white and blue. Running a senior hockey team always was challenging financially and the club resorted to community auctions, bingo games, turkey shoots, fishing contests and even a male style show to raise funds.

The Lakers continued to be successful in league play as they expanded their international activities. One of the most significant events in Lakers history occurred in January 1960, when they defeated the U.S. Olympic team 6–4. A few weeks later this same U.S. team won an upset gold medal at Squaw Valley, California. Brothers Bill and Roger Christian of the Lakers were in the U.S. lineup, following in the footsteps of their brother Gordie and Dan McKinnon who were on the 1956 team. In March 1962, both the Swedish and Norwegian teams visited Warroad on their way to the world tournament in Colorado Springs, Colorado. It was a return trip for the Swedes, who had stopped in "Hockeytown" in 1960.

The Christian brothers returned to the U.S. Olympic team in 1964 but got back in time to join the Lakers as they accomplished another significant milestone by capturing the Canadian intermediate title by defeating Kamloops, British Columbia, and taking the Edmonton Journal Trophy. They became the first American-based team to win a Canadian amateur hockey championship. The previous year, long-time Laker board member John Heneman began keeping statistics and while the early records are a bit lean, they do show that Bill Juzda, a member of the Stanley Cup-winning Toronto Maple Leafs in 1949 and 1951, was in the Lakers lineup in 1964–65 and for a limited number of games the following year.

"Hockey sticks by hockey players," the trademark phrase for Christian Brothers, Inc., got under way in 1964 as the two brothers launched their stick-making business. The Lakers reached the Western Canada finals of the Allan Cup in 1965 before losing to Nelson, British Columbia. While the Lakers achieved success in the Manitoba Senior Hockey League during the remainder of the decade, their Canadian intermediate victory and defeat of the 1960 U.S. Olympic team were the highlights of the 1960s.

Henry Boucha, an outstanding Warroad high school player, had a brief Lakers career in the early 1970s before he joined the 1972 U.S. Olympic team that won a silver medal in Sapporo, Japan. Boucha went on to play with the Detroit Red Wings and Minnesota North Stars before an eye injury brought a premature end to his career. Another Lakers milestone occurred in 1974 when the team won its second Canadian intermediate title by defeating the Embron (Ontario) Panthers, three games to none at nearby Roseau, Minnesota. This achievement earned them the Hardy Cup, a trophy not in existence at the time of their first intermediate victory in 1964. While Canadians might not have been happy with a U.S. victory, they would take considerable pride in the fact that 15 of the 21 Lakers were from north of the border. Blaine Comstock, a backup goaltender on the

Hardy Cup team, went on to play for the United States at the 1976 Winter Olympics. Earlier in 1974, Roger Christian was honored on a special day for his 18 years of service with the team. Success at the intermediate level continued in the late 1970s as the club was the Western Canadian intermediate champion in 1977, losing to Campbellton, New Brunswick, in the finals. In 1979, they reached the Western Canadian intermediate finals before losing to Quesnal, British Columbia.

As the 1980s opened, Lakers fans were pleased to see one of their own on the U.S. Olympic team once more. Dave Christian, son of Bill (who had retired after the 1979–80 season), was part of the "Miracle on Ice" as the United States won a surprising gold medal at Lake Placid. He subsequently played 16 years in the NHL with Winnipeg, Washington, Boston, St. Louis and Chicago. The Olympic team visited Warroad in both 1980 and 1984, while the Lakers tied the 1983 U.S. national team 6–6. The 1983–84 team toured Europe and compiled a 5–0 record against teams in Holland, France, Austria and West Germany. That same year a second indoor rink was built in the town and named the Olympic Arena. Under the chairmanship of Bill Christian, volunteers erected a metal building at a cost of $150,000. An ice plant was added later in the decade. The mid-to-late 1980s saw the beginnings of league membership problems that would plague the club until the end. In 1985, the Lakers became members of the Southeastern Manitoba Hockey League, but their membership was contingent on a yearly vote and eventually that vote went against them. While the league cited travel problems as the reason for the ouster there would appear to be some basis for the belief that their success was the root of the problem. The Lakers won the league title in 1985, 1987 and 1989. In addition to that they were Manitoba intermediate champions in 1989 and 1990.

As the 1990s began, the Lakers found a home in the Central Amateur Senior Hockey League, known popularly as the CASH League. The price for membership was that the Lakers would not be permitted any players from Manitoba. It did not really matter, as the locals were as successful in the CASH League as earlier teams had been in the Southeastern Manitoba Hockey League. The Lakers won the league title in 1992 and 1993 as well as advancing to the Allan Cup final four in both those seasons. In January, 1992, the Warroad club took its second trip to Europe and finished with a 3–1 record against the French, German and Austrian squads. The following month, Chris Imes became the ninth Laker to play for the United States in the Olympics when he suited up at Lillehammer, Norway.

On July 23, 1993, a new arena to replace the original Gardens was dedicated. Plans had begun back in 1989 for the new facility, as the old Gardens was a wood structure and it was feared it might be lost to fire or wind. As might be expected, Cal Marvin headed up the steering committee and his efforts were aided considerably by a $500,000 gift from brother Tut as well as another sizeable donation from brother Jack. The total cost of the new building was $4.5 million. The new Gardens played host to the Allan Cup finals in April, 1994 making Warroad the smallest city ever to host the event and only the second venue in the U.S. to do so. (Spokane, Washington had hosted the 1980 finals.) The Lakers had continued to play in the CASH League and, after advancing through various playoff levels, they carried a 33–5 record into the finals. The team featured 11 former NCAA Division I college players including Steve Johnson

(North Dakota), Chris Imes (Maine), Larry Olimb (Minnesota) and veteran Scott Knutson (Chicago Circle). The Lakers emerged victorious with a 5–2 win over the St. Boniface, Manitoba Mohawks. Warroad had won the Allan Cup on their own ice with an entirely homegrown roster.

The next year, after playing in the Southeastern Manitoba League, the Lakers returned to the Allan Cup finals at Stoney Plain, Alberta. They defeated the host Eagles 3–2 on Wyatt Smith's third-period goal and the goaltending of Todd Kreibach. Stoney Plain was once again the opponent in the 1996 finals at Unity, Saskatchewan. The Lakers played an independent schedule that season and were going for the "three-peat," a feat never before accomplished in Allan Cup competition. (Three Winnipeg victories from 1911 to 1913 were accomplished by two different teams.) The Eagles scored the first goal, but it would be the only one they would get as Warroad responded with two goals in each period for a 6–1 victory and a third straight title.

The continuing difficulty of finding a league to play in was taking its toll on founder/manager Cal Marvin. While the Lakers played in the Hanover–Tache League in 1996–97, Marvin announced before the season that it would be the Lakers' last. Once again, Warroad fought its way to the Allan Cup finals at Powell River, British Columbia, but four titles in a row was not to be as the Powell River Regals defeated the Lakers 7–3 in their very last game to return the coveted trophy to Canada. Prior to the finals and earlier playoffs, a 50-year reunion for all Lakers alumni was staged on March 15, 1997, as Minnesota Governor Arne Carlson proclaimed "Cal Marvin Day" in the state. It was one of many honors for Cal, who has been elected to the United States Hockey Hall of Fame, Manitoba Hockey Hall of Fame, University of North Dakota Athletic Hall of Fame and the Warroad High School Athletic Hall of Fame. The day featured a banquet, gift giving, speeches, reminiscences and a Lakers playoff victory.

Nephew Bob Marvin summed it all up when he said of his uncle: "We are grateful for all that you have given us. You've taught us how to really enjoy winter. You've taught us how to make things happen. You've taught us all about patience and perseverance. You've taught us how to win and once in a while how to lose. You've held our attention with your wit and wisdom."

Warroad Laker Achievements

1997	Allan Cup Finalists
1996	Allan Cup Champions
1995	Allan Cup Champions
1994	Allan Cup Champions
1993	CASH League and Manitoba-Sask. Champions
1992	CASH League and Manitoba-Sask. Champions
1991	CASH League Finalists
1990	Manitoba Intermediate AA Champions
1990	Southeastern Manitoba Hockey League Champions
1989	Manitoba Intermediate Champions
1987	Southeastern Manitoba Hockey League Champions
1985	Southeastern Manitoba Hockey League Champions
1980	Central Amateur Senior Hockey League Champions
1979	Western Canadian Intermediate Finalists
1976	Manitoba Eastern Hockey League Champions
1975	Manitoba Eastern Hockey League Champions
1974	Canadian Intermediate Champions
1973	Manitoba/Thunder Bay Intermediate Champions
1972	Central Canadian Hockey League Champions
1971	Western Canadian Intermediate Champions

Warroad Laker Achievements

1970	Manitoba Senior Hockey League Champions
1969	Manitoba Senior Hockey League Champions
1966	Manitoba Senior Hockey League Champions
1965	Western Canada Allan Cup Finalists
1964	Canadian Intermediate Champions
1963	Canadian Intermediate Finalists
1961	Ont./Minn. Hockey League Champions
1960	Ont./Minn. Hockey League and Cranford Cup Champions
1959	Ont./Minn. Hockey League and Cranford Cup Champions
1958	Cranford Cup Champions
1956	Northwest Hockey League Champions
1955	United States National Intermediate Champions

THE CANADIAN NATIONAL TEAM 1963 TO 1970

Morris Mott

THE CANADIAN NATIONAL HOCKEY TEAM was established in 1963 and ceased operations in 1970. It represented Canada at the Winter Olympic Games in 1964 and 1968, as well as at the World Hockey Championships in 1965, 1966, 1967 and 1969. It finished third in the 1968 Olympics and fourth in 1964. It finished third in the World Championship in 1966 and 1967, fourth in 1965 and 1969. These results were disappointing at the time. However, in the 1970s and 1980s, the national team's record began to be viewed more favorably, because by this time European teams performed very well against Canada's best professionals.

The man most responsible for creating the national team was Father David Bauer (1925–1988). Bauer had been a very good junior player at St. Michael's College in Toronto in the 1940s. (In 1944 he, Gus Mortson and Ted Lindsay were picked up from St. Mike's by the Oshawa Generals for the Memorial Cup finals against the Trail Smoke Eaters. Oshawa swept Trail in four games straight.) He considered playing pro hockey for a farm team of the Boston Bruins, and had he done so it is almost certain he soon would have joined his older brother, Bobby Bauer, who enjoyed a successful career on the Bruins famous "Kraut Line." But David decided against a pro career because he felt that as a pro athlete his intellectual and spiritual development would be stifled. He became a Roman Catholic priest, returned to St. Mike's and coached both hockey and football there.

The high point of Bauer's coaching career at St. Mike's occurred in 1961 when he led the Majors, as the College team was called, to the Memorial Cup championship. But by this time he and other influential people at St. Mike's had become disillusioned with Junior A hockey. The next year St. Mike's dropped out of the Ontario Hockey Association's Junior A series and Bauer was moved by his Basilian superiors to St. Mark's College, part of the University of British Columbia in Vancouver.

The main reason that Father Bauer, the St. Mike's officials and many other people across the Dominion had become disillusioned with junior hockey was that junior teams were tied so closely to, and controlled by, NHL teams. In those days NHL teams "sponsored" junior teams. Young men with hockey ability, from the age of 15 or 16, were encouraged to become the best player they could be and to leave school or at least to spend little time and ener-

gy on their studies. Too often these adolescents turned into journeymen minor professional or senior players. They discovered that they were not able to make a good living in hockey, but that they had neither the skills nor the training to begin a promising career outside the sport. They were, in a word, exploited by the people who controlled professional and junior teams.

At about the same time that Canadians became aware of the dark side of junior and pro hockey, they were coming to realize that Canada's best Senior A clubs were no longer good enough to win against the top European teams. Since the 1920s, the Canadian Amateur Hockey Association almost always had sent the Allan Cup winner to the next year's World or Olympic tournament. By the 1950s, these Senior A teams were having trouble, particularly against teams from the Soviet Union. The senior teams especially struggled at the Olympic Games, because in the Olympics, as opposed to the World Championships, "reinstated" amateurs (former pros) were not eligible. In fact, by 1961, the year that Bauer led St. Mike's to the Memorial Cup victory, Canadian senior teams had lost the last two Olympic Games and it did not seem probable that a senior team would do better at the next Olympics, scheduled for 1964.

In 1962, there came a further indication that senior teams could no longer be relied upon to represent Canada successfully. In that year the International Ice Hockey Federation's World Championship was held in Colorado Springs, Colorado. Neither the Soviet Union nor Czechoslovakia sent a team. They boycotted the tournament because at that time the USA did not recognize (Communist) East Germany and the Americans refused to allow East German athletes to attend. Canadians expected an easy victory for their team, but the Galt Terriers finished second to the team from Sweden.

Father Bauer attended that tournament. The games in Colorado Springs confirmed an opinion he had formed already: he could establish a team of junior or college players who could perform better than senior teams now could, especially in Olympic tournaments where the stricter standards of amateurism applied.

Bauer soon arranged a meeting with Art Potter of Edmonton and Gordon Juckes of Melville, Saskatchewan, the President and Secretary-Manager, respectively, of the Canadian Amateur Hockey Association. He told them of his desire to form a team of young players who would enroll at the University of British Columbia and represent Canada at the 1964 Olympic Games in Innsbruck, Austria. Potter and Juckes invited Bauer to present his ideas later that year to the delegates at the annual meeting of the CAHA. Bauer did so. The delegates accepted his proposal and agreed to provide some financial support. The national team was born.

The next year, in 1963, the Trail Smoke Eaters Senior A team, who had won the World Championship in 1961, finished fourth. This seemed to confirm the need for the new team for which Bauer already was recruiting. Some very good young players were coming to UBC, some of them graduates of Bauer's 1961 team at St. Mike's.

Why was the national team formed? Primarily for two purposes. The first was to provide the opportunity for young men to demonstrate, especially to pro and junior operators, that they could play high-caliber hockey while at the same time earning university degrees. The second was to give Canada better representation at World and Olympic tournaments than it had enjoyed recently or than it could expect to receive in the future from Senior A teams.

There were also two other purposes, understated perhaps, but certainly more important to Bauer than to others involved in creating the team. One was to provide a meaningful alternative to pro hockey for good players coming out of junior. Part of the reason a "second" national team was established in Ottawa in 1967 (it lasted until 1969), and part of the reason there was talk of eventually establishing a third and fourth team, was to make the "Nat" alternative available to more players. The final reason for founding the national team was to establish an institution that would contribute to national unity. Bauer often spoke of the Nats as an entity that could bring together the different ethnic, religious and regional communities in Canada. He was the chief recruiter for the team from start to finish, and the main requirement for every player he obtained was the capacity to help the team on the ice. But he also consciously sought players from all parts of the Dominion, especially those who were part of an ethnic or linguistic minority, who could help the Nats become the unifying symbol he envisioned.

At Innsbruck in 1964, the Nats nearly won the gold medal. In their final game they lost to the Soviets 3–2. Had they won that game, they would have taken the championship, but the loss left them in a three-way tie for second. As a result of a controversial, last-minute decision by the directors of the International Ice Hockey Federation, the tie was broken by considering goals for and against in all games. Canada finished fourth. (A little-known fact should be mentioned here. The International Ice Hockey Federation recognized the 1964 Olympic tournament as the World Championship tournament for that year. However, for World Championship purposes there was a different tie-breaking formula than the one used for Olympic purposes. So Canada finished third in the World Championship, but fourth in the Olympics.)

One of the members of that 1964 team was Brian Conacher. He was the son of Lionel Conacher, who was chosen Canada's greatest athlete of the first half of the 20th century, and after Brian left the Nats, he enjoyed a fine NHL career.

In 1970, he wrote a book entitled *Hockey In Canada: The Way It Is!* It still can be read profitably on a number of subjects, and one of those subjects is the national team. In 1964 he wrote that the Nats had two weaknesses. They lacked "scoring punch" and they needed a "strong rushing defenseman" who could make the key move to get the puck out of the defensive zone.

These weaknesses were evident right from 1964 through 1969. Most of the forwards were good skaters, good checkers and good passers, but none of them could really blast the puck and strike fear into the heart of a goaltender. The defensemen were terrific defensively, extremely tough to beat in one-on-one situations. But only one of them, Carl Brewer, the former Maple Leaf who played in 1967 in Vienna, was a creative passer out of his own end, and none of them had the kind of hard point shot point that was, by the late 1960s, becoming one of the prerequisites for elite-level NHL defensemen (Orr, Park, Laperriere, Stapleton).

In other words, the team was not as strong offensively as it needed to be. At the same time, it was very strong defensively. The players worked hard on their checking, and especially on mastering the checking systems that Father Bauer emphasized, systems that could bottle up any team but which did not facilitate the transition from defense to offense. Moreover, the team played disciplined hockey, which was a tribute to its coaches. Father Bauer was suc-

ceeded by Gord Simpson in 1965 and Jack McLeod from 1966 through 1969. (McLeod coached the team through most of the 1965–66 season. However, just before the World Championships, in an effort to add more offense, a decision was taken to have McLeod play. Father Bauer took over behind the bench.)

The team also received good goaltending, usually from Seth Martin, Ken Broderick or Wayne Stephenson. All three of them went on to have successful years as pros, and Martin was already a legend in Europe by 1964 because of his play with the Trail Smoke Eaters in 1961 and 1963. These strengths allowed the Nats to compile a surprisingly good record over the years against teams from minor professional leagues (15 wins, eight losses, five ties, according to Conacher) and even against NHL teams (four wins and six losses). They also allowed the Nats to stay close to the top European squads, but seldom to beat them.

After the Olympics of 1964, the team was moved from Vancouver to Winnipeg. The latter was close to Central Pro League teams who had indicated a willingness to play exhibition games. It also had a very fine arena, built in 1955, and no pro team as a tenant. Some of the Nats who had enrolled at UBC now transferred to the University of Manitoba. They joined members of the Winnipeg Maroons, the Senior A team that had won the Allan Cup in 1964. The amalgamation never worked. Some of the Maroons were not good enough to play top-level European teams. Some of the Nats from Vancouver concentrated too much on their university studies and not enough on hockey. The World Championships that year were held in Tampere, Finland. The Canadian team finished fourth, and deserved to.

In 1965–66, some good young players joined the team in Winnipeg. They soon became competitive with the Soviets, especially after several games against them on the December-January tour across the country that was becoming more or less an annual affair. In Ljubljana, Yugoslavia, at the World Championships, the team finished third. In those years only four teams could really expect to win a medal: the Swedes, Czechs, Soviets and Canadians. Canada finished ahead of Sweden but behind the other two contenders. The lack of scoring power was evident in the 3–0 loss to the first-place Soviets and the 2–1 loss to the second-place Czechs.

After the loss to the team from Czechoslovakia, an incident occurred that nearly destroyed the team. The refereeing in that game had been atrocious, even by the very low standards of European officiating at the time. In the dressing room immediately following the match, and then back at the team's hotel until early in the morning, the players and other members of the team, along with some members of the press and even a diplomat, debated whether or not to quit the tournament without playing the final game against the Soviets. Had the players decided not to play, the national team would have died right there, and probably the players would have been suspended by the CAHA. The incident has been summarized capably in a number of places, especially in the very good books on international hockey by Scott Young (*War On Ice*) and Jim Coleman (*Hockey Is Our Game!*). Only one new piece of information will be added here.

This is that the man who convinced some of the players they should stay was Dr. Jack Waugh of Winnipeg. Jack Waugh and Reid Taylor were the volunteer team doctors. They were like volunteer team doctors on dozens of top-level amateur teams in Canada in the days before medicare: sometimes they were paid for their services, sometimes they were not, and they were much, much more than pill-

pushers and stitchers. They were friends of the players, and no doctor was ever a better friend to his teammates than Jack Waugh was on the night he stood up in a crowded hotel room in Ljubljana and spoke quietly of the players' "moral obligation to the Canadian people."

In 1967, the Nats had their strongest team. Carl Brewer was on that squad. So was Jack Bownass, who had played tough hockey for about 15 years in various senior and pro leagues, including the NHL, and who played extremely well for the Nats. The team won the CAHA's Centennial Invitational Tournament held in Winnipeg early in January during Canada's 100th year. In the World Championships held in Vienna, however, the Nats finished third once more, and again they could have used more firepower. In seven games, they scored 28 goals, but only a total of two came in the three games against the Swedes, Czechs and Soviets.

In 1968, the team that prepared for the Olympics in Grenoble, France, was nearly as strong as the team of 1967. Brewer and Bownass were former pros and therefore were not eligible, but Brian Glennie (who later played for the Toronto Maple Leafs) was added to the defense. There were also good new forwards in Gerry Pinder, Herb Pinder Jr. and Steve Monteith. And then there were the players who had been around for two or three years or even longer (not all of them actually played in the Olympic tournament): Broderick and Stephenson in goal; Barry Mackenzie, Paul Conlin, Terry O'Malley, Gary Begg, Marshall Johnston on defense; Gary Dineen, Ray Cadieux, Fran Huck, Roger Bourbonnais, Morris Mott, Danny O'Shea, Ted Hargreaves, Bill MacMillan and Jean Cusson up front. In the early games they beat the Americans, the East Germans and the West Germans, as expected, but suffered a surprising loss to the Finns. Then they beat the Czechs 3–2 and the Swedes 3–0. The final game would be against the Soviets. A win would mean the gold medal. A loss or a tie, because of the way the tournament had evolved and especially because of the loss to Finland, would mean the bronze.

The Soviets won 5–0. The Nats actually played a solid game, but they hardly had a good scoring chance against a team which, except in goal (where Victor Konovalenko was not as strong as his successor, Vladislav Tretiak), was not noticeably weaker than the Soviet team that competed against the NHL's best in the Summit Series of 1972.

After the 1968 Olympics, many players from the national team moved on to professional hockey or to other careers. Those players who remained concentrated, perhaps too much, on their university classes. Some good young players joined either the Winnipeg or Ottawa team: among them were Bob Murdoch, Steve Carlyle, Jack Taggart, Jim Irving, Ken Stephanson, Ab DeMarco, Bill Heindl, Richie Bayes, Chuck Lefley, Terry Caffery, Steve King, Kevin O'Shea, and (at the World Championships in Stockholm) Ken Dryden. Many of these players became outstanding professionals, but in March of 1969 they were not ready to take on the best Europeans. In the Stockholm tournament that year, six teams played a new double round-robin format. Canada won each of its two games against Finland and the United States; Canada lost each of its two games against Czechoslovakia, Sweden and the Soviet Union. The Canadians scored 26 goals in their 10 games, whereas the Czechoslovakians scored 40, the Swedes 45 and the Soviets 59. In the six games they played against the medal-winning teams, Canada scored only nine times.

Already, by the time this Stockholm tournament was played in 1969, big changes in the organization and admin-

istration of the national team had occurred. In 1968, Pierre Trudeau replaced Lester Pearson as Prime Minister. Trudeau and his government were very conscious of the role that success in international sports could play in gaining international prestige and in fostering national unity. In 1968, Trudeau announced the creation of a Task Force on Sport. Among other things, the Task Force would suggest ways in which Canadian performances in international competition could be improved.

As far as hockey was concerned, the main recommendation of the Task Force was acted upon by the federal government even before the official report was released. Hockey Canada was established in February, 1969. It was composed of representatives of the federal government, the CAHA, Canada's NHL teams, the NHL Players' Association and eventually both the Canadian Interuniversity Athletic Union and, later, the World Hockey Association. It was given two responsibilities. One was to foster the development of hockey (especially the skill level of players and the competence of coaches). The other was to manage and operate the teams that represented Canada in international tournaments. In order to carry out the latter job, Hockey Canada would work with the CAHA, which held the Canadian vote in the International Ice Hockey Federation, but the CAHA would follow directions from Hockey Canada. Of course, since it was represented on the board of directors of Hockey Canada, the CAHA could help shape the instructions that Hockey Canada gave.

Hockey Canada had more money to support the national team than the CAHA had ever been able to devote to it. The players' allowances went up considerably. In fact, in some cases (depending on individual circumstances and especially the number of dependents a player had) the allowance more than doubled. However, there was more pressure on the players to win than ever before and less concern for academic progress.

Hockey Canada also had a mandate from the federal government to work towards more "open" tournaments: that is, to convince the International Ice Hockey Federation that Canada should be allowed to use professionals in international play, and to convince the IIHF also that the state-supported amateurs of the Communist countries were really professionals. In the summer of 1969, partly because the 1970 World Championships were to be held in Winnipeg and Montreal, a majority of delegates at the IIHF annual meeting agreed to allow Canada to use as many as nine minor-league pros for this one year. Then the whole amateur–professional issue would be studied with a view to finding long-term solutions.

However, early in January, 1970, the IIHF's executive council decided to reverse the decision to allow Canada to use professionals. Just why this happened is not exactly clear. It may be that some members of the IIHF were legitimately concerned that players who competed against the Canadian pros in 1970 would be declared ineligible for the Olympic Games in 1972 and later. It may be that the Soviets and others were concerned by the strong showings that the national team, bolstered by pros, made in tournaments in Leningrad and Moscow in September and December, respectively. Whatever the thinking of the various European nations was, the repercussion for Hockey Canada was that it would not be allowed to ice any professionals. Hockey Canada immediately canceled the tournament (it was rescheduled for Stockholm) and announced that for the time being Canada would not participate in international hockey.

There was no longer any need for the national team. A few commitments to play games in Canada were honored, but the national team essentially was defunct on January 4, 1970—the day Canada pulled out of international hockey. The players soon went into pro hockey, or finished their education with financial assistance from Hockey Canada, which helped all members of the team complete their degrees.

Did the national team fulfill the purposes for which it had been established? The answer has to be a qualified "yes." In some ways it contributed to national unity; certainly there are people in Newfoundland who say that when their own George Faulkner played so well on the national team that went to Ljubljana in 1966, they felt more Canadian than they ever had. And the team did provide an alternative to pro hockey for good junior players who were not sure-fire NHLers. Moreover, it seems clear that the team did represent Canada better than Senior A teams could have in the mid to late-1960s. Above all, it did provide a place through which good players could show that they could play a high level of hockey while succeeding in school. Several Nats became teachers, some became businessmen, a few moved into the front office of professional hockey teams, a couple became civil servants, at least half a dozen became lawyers and one became a medical doctor. The national team certainly proved that education and hockey could be combined.

In 1979, a new national team was formed by Hockey Canada. It still exists. But the new national team never has had the same purposes and roles as the old team of the 1960s because of the immense changes that took place in Canadian and international hockey in the 1970s and 1980s.

The members of the post–1979 Nats often have been university students. However, since the 1970s, young players have been able to combine hockey and education in many ways, and usually the national team was not the best way, as it had been in the 1960s. For one thing, the new Nats had to do far more traveling throughout the hockey season than the old Nats ever did, so the new Nats generally had to be part-time students, or students taking a year off school. Moreover, by the late 1970s and the 1980s, university hockey had improved immensely, and many universities provided scholarships or bursaries for hockey players. Finally, by the 1970s and 1980s, junior operators had a much more enlightened attitude toward education than they had shown in the 1950s and 1960s. Some junior teams even helped pay tuition for their players at a university or community college.

In a strict hockey sense, too, the new national team was different than the old. Except in the Olympics of 1980, in which the team failed to advance to the medal round but performed much better than its results indicated, the team no longer represents Canada in the most important international competitions. Since 1972, the Europeans had shown they could play against the best Canadian professionals. By 1977, the IIHF World Championships had become completely open to pros and between 1984 and 1988 the Olympic Games gradually became so. This meant that the modern national team became a squad used by Hockey Canada to represent Canada at significant but second-level tournaments (such as the Izvestia tournament in Russia) and, because of the high-quality coaches the Nationals have hired, a team used by pro clubs to develop players who need top-class skill development and playing time against talented opponents.

The national team of the 1960s had more complex and occasionally contradictory responsibilities. It's probable that Father Bauer asked the team to accomplish too much:

to obtain a higher education, to serve as a unifying force for Canadians, to offer an alternative to NHL farm systems and to compete with the best European national teams.

The young men who were on that team succeeded to some degree in fulfilling Bauer's expectations. For doing so, they received—and they deserve—respect that stops short of veneration.

THE BATHURST PAPERMAKERS, 1970–71 HARDY CUP CHAMPIONS

Jim Regan

ON THE NORTHERN TIP OF NEW BRUNSWICK, Canada's picture province, 70 miles from what *Sports Illustrated* once called some of the best salmon fishing in the world, sits the city of Bathurst. Bobby Orr, Ted Williams, Jack Nicklaus, Jimmy Carter and other luminaries who could afford the tab came for the salmon fishing, but there was something else that distinguished this town: hard-rock competitive hockey. Throughout its 65-year history, the Bathurst Papermakers played senior or intermediate hockey, filling their own and their opponents' rinks from the Quebec border to the small towns of Newfoundland.

Senior and intermediate hockey were the top two levels of the adult amateur game in Canada. Players past junior age were eligible for both levels. Generally it was budget and arena capacity that separated senior and intermediate leagues. Senior hockey's national champion was awarded the Allan Cup; the top intermediate team—an honor claimed by the Papermakers in 1971—won the Hardy Cup.

In the Maritimes many players with professional experience up to and including the NHL returned to play with senior or intermediate clubs and, with only 120 NHL jobs in the six-team era, many gifted players were content to stay home and use their hockey skills to help them secure a steady job in a plant or mill that sponsored a team. The result was excellent hockey hotly contested in Bathurst and other Maritime towns.

The Bathurst Papermakers were known by sports fans throughout Eastern Canada and were a source of great pride to their town and to all of northern New Brunswick. It all started with an eight-man roster in 1920. Typical of the time, protective gear was confined to knee and shin pads and reinforced gloves.

From this modest nucleus, the team, composed of employees from the local pulp and paper mill, went on to accumulate many laurels, starting with the Maritime Senior Championship. On March 9, 1929 the Papermakers defeated the Halifax Wolverines 1–0 before a crowd of 8,000. That same year, the wooden-roofed Bathurst Arena collapsed after a heavy snowfall. A steel structure was built in its place and the Papermakers soldiered on.

Bathurst borders the beautiful Bay of Chaleur. Its inhabitants are largely English and Acadian with a leavening of Irish, Scottish and Jewish. The population of the town is 11,000 with additional people living in fishing and logging hamlets like Tracadie, Shippagan, St. Isodore and Caraquet, all of which are within 60 miles of Bathurst.

While pulp and paper, fishing, and mining provided jobs in Bathurst and its small liberal arts college produced numerous civil servants and politicians including Canada's current Governor-General Romeo Leblanc, it was hockey that stitched the town together. Outdoor rinks—and there were many—hosted an array of local teams from peewee to juvenile. One such rink was 25 miles from Bathurst at a private boys school on the Jacquet River. On a cold winter Sunday afternoon in the late 1960s, the protocol of the day stipulated that the home team had the wind in the first and third periods while the visitors supplied logs for the wood-burning stove in the dressing rooms. Most of the priests that ran the school came from Quebec and had played hockey. They actively participated in refereeing, coaching, or yelling at poor passes and great plays alike. Their rink was truly an altar where the real teaching of religion took place.

If Father Boudreau's backhand got by you, it was certain that the stations of the cross in the cathedral in Bathurst or Holy Family Church in West Bathurst would be frequented more readily for spiritual rejuvenation. There were no chalk talks in the confessional or diagrams of passing plays distributed before Sunday sermon, but everybody knew that Father Thistle would cut short his 12 o'clock sermon so that one could either hurry to the rink or, if the Papermakers were playing at home, beat the rush to the Bathurst Arena for an afternoon tilt against an opponent from the very competitive North Shore Intermediate A Hockey League.

The Papermakers' top rival was the Campbellton Tigers, a fast-skating club based an hour to the west. Campbellton was a team of skaters and the sheet of ice in their rink was patterned after the Montreal Forum. Because the Bathurst Arena was modeled on snug Boston Garden, the corners in 'Tiger Town' were safer and the passing lanes wider and faster. Other teams in the loop were the Dalhousie Rangers, located next door to Campbellton, and the Chatham Ironmen and Newcastle Legionnaires. All five teams were located within a 200-mile radius.

These five clubs in the North Shore league shared the sports pages of New Brunswick's two leading dailies with a corresponding four-team Southern League comprised of Saint John, Moncton, Fredericton and a fourth club that played out of various communities over the years. The *Moncton Times* and the *Saint John Telegram* gave extensive coverage to intermediate hockey. The largest towns and biggest rinks in the province were located in the south, but players in the Southern League knew that the North Shore Hockey League played a great brand of hockey.

Power in New Brunswick, whether in party politics or hockey administration, was concentrated in the more affluent south. Calling the shots at the New Brunswick Amateur Hockey Association were two southerners, secretary-registrar Len Poore and Dr. William MacGillivary, Dean of the Faculty of Physical Education at the University of New Brunswick and later the chairman of the Canadian Amateur Hockey Association. The first northern New Brunswicker to make his mark on the NBAHA was James MacLaggan who had moved from Peterborough, Ontario to Bathurst in the 1950s. When he first got involved, MacLaggan was told that no northerner could become president of the NBAHA. Time would reveal a different story.

In the 1940s, Bathurst's best hockey was played at the high school level. Campbellton-born Jack Furlotte, who later coached the Papermakers, played a fiercely competitive brand of hockey as a member of the 1945, 1946 and 1947 high school teams that won provincial and Maritime championships. Clifford Kennah was Furlotte's math partner at school and proved to have a full understanding of the geometry of the corners and the calculus of play in the slot, from where he was able to score many exciting goals.

Playing for Bathurst High School meant early morning and late evening practices. After the local figure skating club and public skaters finished using the Bathurst Arena, the high school team took to the ice—if homework was completed. When the playoffs were completed in April, many students turned aside an occasional letter from an NCAA school or from Junior A teams in Quebec and Ontario to complete their studies and final exams. Some of these talented hockey players left to pursue hockey outside the Maritimes, but many stayed after their high school careers ended and found jobs in the paper mill, the town works department or the local hardware store, which enabled them to earn a living while playing lots of intermediate hockey.

For the best players, it was a reasonably comfortable life that was able to attract some big-name professionals from Quebec at the midpoint of their careers. Salaries reached $350 per week as part of a package that included a job, a place to live and a spot on the North Shore club's roster.

The Papermakers' coach in the 1950s was Ev Doucet, whose colorful language and ever-present pipe made him the local equivalent of Toronto's loquacious King Clancy. Doucet understood the delicate balance of local hockey politics and knew just when to add an import to the roster and when to stick with the locals. In 1954–55 a 40-goal Quebec import by the name of Moe Lamirande joined Doug and Keir Howat from the small town of Sussex, New Brunswick to form the nucleus of a team that attracted attention throughout the Maritimes. Lamirande and the Howats were joined by Dicker Macdonald from Sydney, Nova Scotia, who added fight in the corners and speed to the net, enabling him to score goals that brought the fans to their feet.

In 1958 a balcony collapsed at the east end of the rink. No one was hurt, so the imperturbable Bathurst fans accommodated the displaced balcony dwellers after only a short stoppage of play.

In the late 1950s, the Papermakers became the first New Brunswick team to win a Maritime Intermediate A hockey championship. The team at that time was led by Rolly Rossignol, a former Montreal Canadien. He joined local greats Fred McKay, Earl Cooper and Bob MacMinn to make the Papermakers a source of pride throughout the region.

The Chatham Ironmen challenged the Papermakers with an import-rich roster that included players such as "Wild" Bill Malone who caught the eye of several NHL scouts. The Ironmen built their roster by signing players from leagues throughout Quebec and Ontario, as well as from the International and American leagues. Despite this stacked lineup, the Ironmen still could not manage to beat Bathurst consistently. The Papermakers drew upon their winning tradition and from the mysterious black ointment concocted by trainer Ron Wheeler and equipment manager Lou Anderson. Wheeler was the town's recreation director and, when he wasn't trainer to the Papermakers, was trainer to a stable of horses, so his mystery ointment had been perfected down the backstretches of several regional race tracks.

Jack Furlotte, the coach of the Papermakers who was later inducted into the Sports Hall of Fame in Bathurst, agreed that this rubdown formulation was a great remedy for the aches and sprains that were part of Intermediate A hockey. But he cautioned that one had to be extremely careful not to get any of the potion on strategic parts of one's anatomy, because it burned like hell and wouldn't come off! Ask Art Malais, a member of the 1971 Hardy Cup champions, who once made this mistake and spent several hours in the shower attempting to deal with a dark stain on his manhood.

Malais scrubbed and scrubbed before he was told about the antidote: white vinegar would do the trick every time!

Malais's predicament aside, it was the 1971 edition of the Papermakers that brought Bathurst a measure of fame that spread beyond the Maritimes. At the beginning of the season, management felt that the team had the ability to go all the way. A decision was made by Bathurst's municipal council to underwrite the cost of hosting a national Hardy Cup final if the team made the playoffs and won its way into the tournament. James MacLaggan, Bathurst's man on the provincial hockey executive, lobbied for all he was worth against southern New Brunswickers' traditional bias against the north, arguing that the Papermakers' organization could bring off the huge task of hosting a national tournament.

Many of the men who had been part of the Papermakers from the 1920s to the 1960s had remained in Bathurst. They would make sure that Bathurst's organization would be first rate. All the Papermakers had to do was keep winning on the ice and that they did, beginning with a 35-game regular-season schedule and continuing into the best-of-seven league and provincial playoffs. Millworkers, miners and teachers by day and hockey heroes by night, Bathurst clinched the North Shore crown by eliminating the Campbellton Tigers in five games. Two Southern League teams, the Saint John Mooseheads and the Fredericton Capitals, were defeated by the Papermakers en route to the provincial intermediate title.

The Maritime playdowns proved anticlimactic. A team from Newfoundland journeyed to the Bathurst Arena and left humiliated, with one game ending in a 14–4 victory for the Papermakers. This one-sided win set the stage for an Eastern Canadian final. According to Canadian Amateur Hockey Association rules, teams reaching the semifinal round of a national championship were permitted to strengthen their rosters by adding up to three players from other clubs in their league. The Papermakers voted to stay with their local players. No last-minute additions would disrupt the chemistry of this championship-bound team.

Embrun, Ontario provided the Papermakers' opponents in the best-of-five Eastern Canadian intermediate final. Embrun was a talented hockey club staffed by many players with Allan Cup playoff experience that was put to good use in game one, an 8–1 Embrun win. Bathurst captain Joe Hachey, a former Montreal Junior Canadien, and coach Jack Furlotte convened a team meeting to discuss strategy. The conclusion was a simple one: go to the body in game two.

This take-no-prisoners approach yielded a 4–1 win for the Papermakers, to the delight of 4,500 spectators packed tightly into the Bathurst Arena. Reporters criticized the Papermakers for rough play in game two as official protests were made to the tournament executive, the NBAIIA and the CAHA. No protest was upheld, allowing the series to go on. Bathurst prevailed in the next two contests, winning close games by scores of 2–1 and 3–1.

The Papermakers had their wish: a berth in a Hardy Cup national intermediate championship series played in Bathurst. Their opponents in the best-of-five national final were the Western Canadian champions from Rosetown, Saskatchewan.

The national final was a best-of-five series. From the outset it appeared that the series was going to be a close one as the Rosetown Red Wings matched up well against the Papermakers. The usual controversy with selection of officials was quickly put to rest by Len Poore of the NBAHA. There would be no administrative delays: the championship

would be fairly decided on the ice, not in the boardroom of the local Legion hall.

The Friday evening opener was filled with tension. The pregame introductions drew equal amounts of cheering for the home team and booing for the westerners. The game went back and forth and was deadlocked after 60 minutes. Bathurst team captain Joe Hachey brought the house to a roar when he potted the winner. The Papermakers had struck first blood.

The second game of the series was played Saturday night. Hard-working Art Malais gave Bathurst the lead early in the first period when he blasted home Jim Craik's pass from behind the Rosetown cage at the 1:36 mark.

The game was a tough one: four major penalties were assessed along with two game misconducts for joining a fight already in progress. A few moments after this had been sorted out, Bob Degrace, a local restaurateur and former chairman of the Canadian Food and Restaurant Association, scrambled a few eggs with his right elbow, the result of which saw a Rosetown Red Wing counting stars. The ensuing penalty proved costly as Rosetown's Keith Robson squared the match just seven seconds into the power-play with a goal at 16:00 of the second.

The winning goal came off the stick of Bathurst's Lou Ouellette, an ex-Oshawa General who had played for a time with Bobby Orr. His first goal of the series at 10:48 of the final period proved to be the winner, giving Bathurst a 2–1 victory and a two-game lead in the series.

At the end of the game Rosetown launched a protest based on an incorrect icing call with 18 seconds remaining on the clock. The resulting face-off forced the Red Wings to remove their sixth attacker and put their goalie back in the net. The protest wasn't a calm one. Players pushed to get at the linesman who made the icing call, resulting in the ejection of Rosetown's Terry Simpson. Although he steadfastly denied making physical contact with the official, he was suspended for the remainder of the tournament.

The next day, a determined Bathurst squad set out to complete a three-game final series sweep. Enthusiastic supporters filled Bathurst Arena on Sunday hoping to see their hometown team win a national championship, something no other New Brunswick squad had done since the Moncton Hawks won the Allan Cup in 1932–33. Father Thistle had cut short his sermon for a good cause, as a congregation's worth of spiritual rejuvenation would occur that afternoon at the rink.

Bathurst took the lead early as team spokesperson Paul Ouellette (Lou's older brother) scored the important first goal just 55 seconds into the contest. Fellow teacher Aurelle Hachey put the Papermakers ahead 2–0 at 6:08 with an unassisted marker. Aurelle was a last-minute replacement called up from an intermediate B team. The Hacheys were a family of gifted all-round athletes. Brother Sam was the team's goaltender while Aurelle and a third brother, Paul, won New Brunswick's amateur golf championship on several occasions.

It took the Rosetown Red Wings nearly 18 minutes of play in the second period to finally beat Sam Hachey's spectacular goaltending. Gerry Follick tipped in Neil Torrance's drive from the blue line to cut the Papermakers' lead to a lone goal. Hachey's strong play in net kept the Papermakers in front until they broke the game wide open in the third period with three goals, a pair by Lou Ouellette and one by Jim Craik. When the final buzzer went the score was 5–2 and the celebration was on.

This final game victory was the culmination of an outstanding postseason. The Papermakers had won 15 of 16 playoff games and had swept three of their four playoff series en route to the Canadian Intermediate A Hockey championship. Captain Joe Hachey—no relation to Aurelle and Sam—hoisted the Hardy Cup on behalf of everyone in northern New Brunswick. This team of home-brewed players was a national champion.

The North Shore League flourished through the 1970s as the Campbellton Tigers won the Hardy Cup in each of the next three seasons. In recent years there has been little of this kind of sponsored amateur hockey in New Brunswick. The minor pro American Hockey League expanded into the Maritimes in the 1980s and, more recently, a Quebec Major Junior Hockey League team opened its doors in Moncton. With NHL hockey streaming in on cable and satellite television, intermediate hockey no longer has the power to pack the local arena and fuel young fans' dreams. But for those who remember what went on in the Bathurst Arena in the spring of 1971, the Papermakers offer a dictionary definition of the phrase: "That's hockey."

IV

THE
INTERNATIONAL
GAME

Future U.S. Hockey Hall of Famer John Mayasich checks Stanislav Petukhov of the Soviet Union at the 1960 Winter Olympics in Squaw Valley, California. The U.S. won the game 3–2 and would go on to win its first Olympic hockey gold medal.

CHAPTER 33

The International Ice Hockey Federation

Denis Gibbons

INTERNATIONAL ICE HOCKEY FANS who recognize Russia, Sweden, Finland and the Czech Republic as the four powerhouse nations of Europe might be surprised to learn that none of these countries was on board when the sport became organized on the continent 90 years ago. The Ligue Internationale de Hockey sur Glace, now known as the International Ice Hockey Federation, was founded in 1908 by the representatives of four national federations—Belgium, Great Britain, France and Switzerland.

The IIHF, which now has 53 member federations, not only from Europe but also North America, Asia and Africa, has adopted countries like Mexico, Greece, Andorra and Ireland in recent years. The growth of hockey throughout the world has not been explosive, but it has been steady. For more than a decade the LIGH/IIHF was a purely European institution. It was only in 1920 that Canada, the mother country of the sport, as well as the neighboring United States, joined the federation. Today the game is still in constant development, with the new sport of inline hockey contributing to even faster growth of the IIHF.

The IIHF now conducts World Championship tournaments annually for men's teams in four different pools, as well as four pools of World Junior Championships. It also holds a World Championship for women, the annual European (under-18) Junior Championship, the Continental Cup (formerly European Cup) competition for club champions and organizes the hockey tournament of the Olympic Games every four years. Still, political problems have thrown a monkey wrench into competitions from time to time. In 1957, both Canada and the United States did not participate in the World Championship in Moscow in protest of the Soviet invasion of Hungary the previous year. To show their disgust with the treatment of the team of the German Democratic Republic, which was not granted entry visas to the U.S., the Soviet Union and Czechoslovakia did not participate in the 1962 World tournament at Colorado Springs.

But the greatest setback for the IIHF was the absence of Canada from two Olympics and seven World tournaments between 1970 and 1976. A quarter of a century ago, teams competing in the World Championship and Olympics were not allowed to use professionals, even though officials in the West viewed the players of the Soviet Union and Czechoslovakia as pros because they really did nothing else but play hockey for 11 months of the year. Canada, complaining that all of its best players were playing as professionals in the NHL, had found competition with its amateur national team, strengthened only by reinstated pros, very difficult in the 1960s against the rapidly improving European countries. In World Championship and Olympic play, Canada was able to win only three bronze medals.

During the IIHF Congress at Lausanne, Switzerland in the summer of 1969, Canada proposed that the World Championship be thrown wide open with all countries allowed to use professionals. Although the proposal was easily defeated, some countries changed their votes when another proposal was made that Canada be allowed nine professionals, none of them to be active in the NHL. It was a tie vote until IIHF president Bunny Ahearne cast the deciding vote in favor of Canada using nine non-NHL pros at the 1970 World Championships, scheduled for Montreal and Winnipeg. Russia had voted against the motion fearing that allowing teams to use professionals would jeopardize their eligibility for the Olympics. The International Olympic Committee heard about the decision and wrote the IIHF warning that if professionals of any kind were used on national teams they would, as the Russians feared, be ineligible for the Olympics.

In a later meeting in Switzerland in January of 1970, Ahearne presented correspondence from Avery Brundage, president of the IOC, and informed Canada the IIHF could not go along with the move to allow Canada the use of nine minor pros. Aside from making Canada ineligible for Olympic play, some countries were afraid that they also would be out of the Olympics just because they played against Canada. Canada came back with a compromise that the 1970 tournament go ahead as scheduled, but only as an exhibition and that the World Championships be postponed for a year until the IIHF could get a clearer ruling on the use of pros from the IOC. But this was rejected. So, although $300,000 worth of tickets had been sold for the 1970 World tournament, Canada withdrew and the IIHF was forced to scramble to get Sweden to host it for the second year in a row.

In 1975, the IIHF finally approved the use of NHL pros in the World Championship. But because Canada did not return to competition until 1977, the United States was the first country to use NHLers at the 1976 World Championships in Poland. But it did little good as the Americans placed fourth and out of the medals. Toronto lawyer Alan Eagleson, who doubled as head of Hockey Canada and the NHLPA, negotiated his country's return to the World Championships in exchange for IIHF assurance that the top European nations would take part in a new venture, the Canada Cup, every four years. Canada made an inauspicious return to the World tournament at Vienna in 1977 with a team of NHLers whose teams had missed the playoffs, absorbing an 11–1 shellacking at the hands of the Soviet Union on opening day and, like the American team the year before, finishing only fourth. In fact, it wasn't until 1994 that Canada would win another World Championships (at Milan) and 1996 until the U.S. won any kind of a medal, a bronze at Vienna. In the meantime, Canada, using its best pros, won four of the five Canada Cup tournaments held in North America in the fall of 1976, 1981, 1984, 1987 and 1991. The 1996 World Cup of Hockey, a joint effort of the

NHL and NHLPA, was held under the auspices of the IIHF. The United States won $300,000 (Cdn.) in prize money by defeating Canada two games to one in a thrilling best-of-three final, which started in Philadelphia and wound up in Montreal.

The IIHF faced a complicated situation after the Berlin Wall fell in November of 1989, leading to a gradual change from Communism to democracy in the Eastern European countries. On January 1, 1992, the Soviet Union was transformed into the Commonwealth of Independent States (CIS) and later former Soviet republics became countries on their own each with membership in the international federation. Then in 1993 Czechoslovakia divided into two separate nations—the Czech Republic and Slovakia. In the case of the former Czechoslovakia, the IIHF ruled that since its national team had been made up mostly of Czech players, the Czech Republic would remain in the A Pool of the World Championships. Slovakia protested, but to no avail, and it was placed in the C Pool of the 1994 World Championships. (Former Soviet republics Latvia, Belarus, Kazakhstan and the Ukraine began play in the C Pool in 1993.) Slovakia, Belarus and Latvia quickly climbed the ladder to the A Pool and it is likely that Kazakhstan and the Ukraine will qualify for 1999's A event. The success of these additional competitors from behind the old Iron Curtain threatened to knock central European countries like Austria, Italy, France and Switzerland down to the B Pool. The IIHF, fearful it would lose much needed advertising revenue from these nations if their teams were relegated, decided to increase the number of entries for the 1998 World Championships in Switzerland from 12 to 16.

Starting with the 1998 World tournament, the national team of the host country automatically participates to ensure that the tournament is a financial success for the organizing committee. The best team from the Far East is included, helping to promote ice hockey in that growing market and creating further sponsorship opportunities for the IIHF. Regional qualification tournaments will be held to declare the other entries, serving to increase interest in those markets.

Maintaining spectator interest in the 1960s and 1970s when the Soviet Union was dominating World tournaments was also a headache for IIHF officials. Although the Soviet Union had not played in the World Championships until 1954, by 1979 it had won 16 out of a possible 25 gold medals and fans were getting bored watching lopsided games. The IIHF decided on a new format for the 1983 World Championships in West Germany. In future, rather than have only a single round robin, the top four teams would enter a medal round, with no points to carry over from the preliminary round. The Soviets, at the peak of their game, didn't even flinch as they breezed to another gold medal with a 9–0–1 record, but the pressure of entering what was virtually a brand-new tournament in the medal round finally caught up with them at Prague in 1985. After posting a perfect 7–0–0 record in the preliminaries, they lost to both Canada and Czechoslovakia in the medal round and had to settle for a bronze medal. They were perfect in the preliminaries again at the 1987 World Championships in Vienna, outscoring their seven opponents by a total of 52–8. But a 2–2 tie with Sweden and a scoreless draw with Canada cost them the gold medal. They finished second behind Sweden. If you look at the tournament as a whole, they became only the second team in history to go undefeated (8–0–2) and not win the gold medal.

Czechoslovakia also finished second with a record of 7–0–1 at the 1948 tournament in St. Moritz.

A further change in format took place for the 1992 World Championships in Prague. The entry list was increased to 12 teams, which competed in two groups of six with the top four teams in each group qualifying for the playoffs. Quarterfinals and semifinals were followed by sudden-death games for the bronze and gold medals. Sweden defeated Finland for the gold medal. The first IIHF-sanctioned World Junior Championships took place in the 1976–77 season in the towns of Zvolen and Banska Bystrica, Czechoslovakia, and in the last two decades the tournament has become a must on the itinerary of NHL scouts looking for talent under the age of 20. The Soviet Union defeated Canada, represented by the St. Catharines Fincups, 6–4 to win the first gold medal. Canada and the Soviet Union (CIS, Russia) have developed a keen rivalry, with Canada winning 10 of the championships and their arch-rivals nine. In the 1995–96 season, the tournament expanded from eight to 10 teams.

Interest in women's hockey also had been growing around the world, and during the meeting of the IOC executive board in June of 1993, the organizing committee of the Nagano Olympic Winter Games officially agreed to include a competition for women in the program. The first international hockey tournament for women was held in 1985 when Fran Rider, president of the Ontario Women's Hockey Association, invited teams from North America, Europe and Asia to Brampton for the Dominion Ladies Hockey Tournament. Two teams each from Canada and the U.S. were joined by West Germany and the Netherlands.

Finally, in 1989, the IIHF sanctioned a European Championship for women and plans were laid for the top five finishers to join Canada, the United States and one team from Asia in the first World Women's Championships in 1990. A crowd of 9,000 packed the Civic Centre in Ottawa to watch Canada defeat the United States 5–2 for the gold medal of the 1990 World tournament. Canada also won gold medals at the 1992 World tournament in Finland, 1994 at Lake Placid and 1997 in Kitchener, Ontario. But when women's hockey was introduced in the Olympics at Nagano in 1998, the United States won the first gold medal, upsetting the world champions from Canada 3–1.

In-line hockey has caught the fancy of sportsmen around the world and in 1995 the IIHF included the sport in its program. The first World Championships in this discipline was held in the summer of 1996 in St. Paul, Minnesota. Eleven countries took part, with the United States winning the title.

Meanwhile, with many European stars emigrating to North America to pursue lucrative careers in the NHL, and the threat that the NHL itself might expand into Europe, the IIHF once again was moved to act. The result was the formation of the European Hockey League for the 1996–97 season, with 20 top clubs from 14 different countries participating. Clubs competed in the EHL and their domestic leagues at the same time, with each club having to play only two EHL games per month from October to December. Games were played in 19 different cities in the best arenas available. The first champion was TPS Turku of Finland. TPS defeated Moscow Dynamo in the finals.

There remained one last hurdle for the IIHF to clear before the arrival of the new millennium. For years fans had been clamoring to have NHL pros take part not only in the World Championships but also the Olympics. The final agreement regarding participation of NHL players in the

1998 Olympics in Nagano was reached during the IIHF Semi-Annual Congress in Budapest in September of 1995. NHL owners agreed to shut down the league for 16 days and to work with the IIHF and NHL Players' Association on a three-stage tournament in which Canada, the United States, Russia, Sweden, Finland and the Czech Republic would be given byes into the final round. In June of that year, IIHF President Rene Fasel had been elected to the International Olympic Committee, the first ice hockey representative to be named to such a post. The first Olympic tournament involving NHL pros was full of upsets. Canada, the United States and Sweden were the favorites, but Canada was the only team of that trio to make the semifinals before losing to the Czech Republic in a shootout. The Czechs, behind the outstanding goaltending of Dominik Hasek, went on to shut out Russia 1–0 to win their first Olympic gold medal.

There were hitches in the Olympic experiment. Slovakia flew seven NHL players over to Japan, expecting to strengthen their team when they won their qualifying group and advanced to the final round. But the Slovaks were upset by Kazakhstan and, because the Slovaks left only two spots open on their preliminary round roster, five of the seven pros didn't even play a game. Midway through the tournament it was discovered that Swedish defenceman Ulf Samuelsson had obtained United States citizenship, which under Swedish law nullified his citizenship in his homeland, thus making him ineligible for Olympic play. Samuelsson was barred for the rest of the tournament, but Sweden was allowed to continue. Most embarrassingly, some players from the U.S. team reacted badly to their early elimination, damaging dorm rooms in the Olympic village. Though the cost of repairs was relatively small ($3,000), the media gave the story extensive coverage around the world, tarnishing the image of the U.S. Olympic Committee and the NHL.

Overall, though, the trial run was deemed a success. Besides the tournament in Salt Lake City in the year 2002, international hockey fans can look forward to the 1999 World Championships in Lillehammer, Norway, popular site of the 1994 Olympic Games, and the World tournament of 2000 in St. Petersburg, Russia, the first time since 1986 that it has been held in that country. The IIHF also has opened an International Hockey Hall of Fame in Zurich and started a program of building up its own archives through the collection of photographs, films, tapes from previous tournaments and statistical materials. In addition, the IIHF has worked with the Hockey Hall of Fame in Toronto on the development of a large world hockey display that opened in June of 1998. This supplements the collection of international memorabilia housed in the smaller International Hockey Hall of Fame at Kingston, Ontario, where the development of ice hockey in all member countries can be followed. In 1997, the IIHF also signed a contract with CWL Marketing AG which will extend until the year 2003 with an option to 2007. Since 1989, the company has managed to increase the hours of television programming for the World Championships.

Over the years the IIHF has benefitted from the efforts of a lot of outstanding players, brilliant coaches and hardworking executives. Thirty of them were inducted into the IIHF Hall of Fame in 1997. The inductees are: Walter Wasservogel of Austria; Father David Bauer, Gordon Juckes, Bob Lebel, Victor Lindquist, Seth Martin and Harry Sinden of Canada; Vaclav Bubnik, Jaroslav Drobny, Vladimir Kostka, Vaclav Nedomansky and Vladimir Zabrodsky of the former Czechoslovakia; Urpo Ylonen of Finland; Louis Magnus of France; Erich Kuhnhackl and Dr. Gunther Sabetzki of Germany; Bunny Ahearne of Great Britain; Vsevolod Bobrov, Anatoly Tarasov, Andrei Starovoitov, Alexander Ragulin and Vladislav Tretiak of the former Soviet Union; Richard Torriani of Switzerland; Arne Grunander, Anders Hedberg and Sven Tumba of Sweden; along with Walter Brown, Bill Cleary, Gerry Cosby and John Mayasich of the United States.

Five IIHF honorees plus former IIHF president William Thayer Tutt are also members of the Hockey Hall of Fame in Toronto. The honored members are: Paul Loicq, a former member of the Belgian national team who served as president of the IIHF for 20 years starting in 1927; Anatoly Tarasov, a great builder of Russian hockey who coached the Soviet Union to nine straight World Championships and three straight Olympic titles before retiring in 1972; John Francis "Bunny" Ahearne, who managed the British national team to an Olympic gold medal in 1936 and built the World Championship into a major television attraction after he was elected IIHF president in 1957; William Thayer Tutt of the United States, who offered his family-owned arena in Colorado Springs for the first NCAA hockey tournament and later served as president of the IIHF; Vladislav Tretiak, the great Soviet goaltender who won three Olympic gold medals and 10 World Championships during a brilliant 14-year career; Dr. Gunther Sabetzki of Germany, who served as president of the IIHF from 1975–94 and played a major

CHAPTER 34

From Andorra to Yugoslavia

The History of Hockey and Its Structure Today in Each IIHF Nation

Igor Kuperman

EACH IIHF MEMBER NATION is listed here in alphabetical order. Each country's name is followed by the formal name of its national hockey federation.

ANDORRA
Federacion Andorrana d'Esports de Gel
Ice Hockey Committee

HISTORY: Ice hockey did not begin in Andorra until the 1990s. The lack of ice and equipment has slowed the development of the game in the country, but a major step towards popularizing hockey was made in 1996–97 when the city of Canillo hosted the D Pool World Championships.

HOCKEY TODAY: Teams from Andorra currently play exhibition games only.

AUSTRALIA
Australian Ice Hockey Federation

HISTORY: The history of Australian ice hockey began in 1907 when a group of young skaters from Melbourne issued a challenge to the crew of the American battleship Baltimore. The game drew a capacity crowd to the Melbourne Glaciarium and attracted considerable attention in the press. Though the home team was defeated by the Americans, the game had found its feet in Australia. In 1908, games were played in the country's two artificial indoor ice rinks in Sydney and Melbourne. By 1909, there were four hockey clubs in the province of Victoria and two more in New South Wales. The first inter-provincial games in Australia were played that year, with Melbourne (Victoria) defeating Sydney (New South Wales) two games to one. This early chapter in Australian hockey history came to a close with the outbreak of the First World War in 1914. It was many years before the game was played again.

Hockey in Australia experienced a revival during the 1950s. The country joined the International Ice Hockey Federation in 1950, though the Australian Ice Hockey Federation was not founded until 1954. The popularity of the game declined during the late 1950s and early 1960s due to the shortage of rinks in the country, though Australia did compete in hockey at the 1960 Winter Olympics in Squaw Valley, California. This marked the Australian national team's international debut (their first game was a 12–1 loss to the United States on February 18, 1960). In later years, the arrival of Eastern Bloc immigrants to Australia helped to boost the number of hockey players in the country to around 3,500.

HOCKEY TODAY: Because of the huge distances between settlements in Australia, there is no national league competition. Australia's most prestigious hockey trophy is the Goodall Cup, which was presented by Melbourne player John Goodall in 1921. Since 1991–92, selected teams have been playing off for the Goodall Cup. In 1997–98, four teams representing different areas of the country played a round-robin tournament to decide the Goodall Cup champion.

The different provinces across Australia have teams playing in their own leagues. The Superleague, with teams from New South Wales and the Australian Capital Territory, is the country's most important league and attracts the largest audience. The best of this league's 14 arenas is the Macquarie (with a capacity of 3,500) which is located in a shopping mall in suburban Sydney. In addition to the Eastcoast Superleague, there are leagues in Queensland and Victoria. Each league has playoffs to determine a regional championship.

In recent years, the national emphasis has been on developing junior hockey with seasonal clinics and top overseas and local coaches hosting provincial clinics. Players under 21 compete for the Brown Trophy, while those under 16 play for the Tange Trophy. The President's Cup has been inaugurated by the Australian Ice Hockey Federation for boys and girls under age 13 as an introduction to the sport in a fun and less competitive atmosphere.

AUSTRIA
Osterreichischer Eishockeyverband

HISTORY: The first mention of hockey in Austria occurred on January 12, 1896, when the Vienna newspaper *Allgemeine Sport-Zeitung* printed an article called "Hockey Game," which was, in fact, about bandy (field hockey on ice). The article described the game as being played on a surface measuring 60 x 100 meters and involving seven players per team. It was mentioned that the game was already popular in Prague (which was, at the time, a part of the Austro-Hungarian Empire).

Bandy arrived in Austria in 1899 when the first game was played in Vienna. The sport spread quickly across the country and teams soon were organized in other cities. The first international bandy game involving Austria took place in 1901 when a team from Vienna was defeated 17–3 by Slavia Prague. Around the same time, three Austrian clubs organized an ice hockey committee, and though the new sport could not yet match the popularity of bandy, it had made huge strides by 1911 when almost all bandy players began to play hockey. The first artificial ice rink had opened in Vienna on November 10, 1909, and this did much to increase the popularity of hockey.

The Austrian Hockey Union was created on January 15, 1912 and Austria was admitted into the International Ice Hockey Federation on March 18, 1912. Austria played its first international game on February 2, 1912 at the European Championships and lost to Bohemia 5–0. Austria was represented at the European Championships in 1913, though at this time the only national championship that existed in Austria was for bandy. Still, the popularity of hockey grew quickly and regional hockey unions started to form. Canadian Blake Watson (who also helped to coach in Germany) did much to advance the game in Austria. In 1922, the country held its first national ice hockey championship.

The development of hockey slowed in Austria during the 1930s and 1940s, with the decline attributed to financial difficulties, a lack of coaches and a shrinking player base. However, by the end of the 1950s, Austrian clubs began recruiting coaches and players from abroad—particularly from Czechoslovakia and Canada, and later from the Soviet Union. The level of competition in Austria increased and in 1965 the Bundesliga was created.

HOCKEY TODAY: In 1997–98, the 11 best Austrian clubs began the season in the Alpenliga along with teams from Italy and Slovenia. After playing a quadruple round-robin schedule, the Austrian clubs are ranked according to their Alpenliga standings and the three top teams move on to the Austrian League-Division 1. The Austrian teams ranking fourth through sixth then participate in a double round-robin series with the winner becoming the fourth team to qualify for the Austrian League-Division 1 playoffs. Best-of-seven series are played in the semifinals and finals.

Austrian League Division 2 is divided into East (eight teams) and West (seven teams) with teams playing a double round-robin schedule within these groups. The top three teams from each group then play a double round robin among themselves, while the remaining teams play a separate double round robin in the East and West. The two teams that win the East and West series then join the top six teams in the playoffs. Quarterfinals, semifinals and finals are all a best-of-three. There is no promotion after the playoffs.

The next level of competition in Austria below Division 2 is in the regional leagues. There are also national championships for junior, midget and other age groups broken down into under 20, under 16, under 14, under 12 and under 10.

AZERBAIJAN
Azerbaidzhanskaya Federatsiya Hokkeya

HISTORY: The Ice Hockey Federation of the Republic of Azerbaijan was founded in 1991 as a part of the Soviet Ice Hockey Federation. After the breakup of the Soviet Union, Azerbaijan became an independent country in 1992. The federation joined the International Ice Hockey Federation on May 6, 1992.

HOCKEY TODAY: There is no national championship in Azerbaijan.

BELARUS
Federatsiya Hokkeya Belarusi

HISTORY: Hockey in the Soviet Republic of Belorussia (now the independent country Belarus) became very popular right after World War II when ice hockey made its first inroads in the Soviet Union. In 1946, Torpedo Minsk (later Dynamo Minsk and now Tivali Minsk) was formed and began to play in the top Soviet division. After the breakup of the Soviet Union, the team from Minsk played in the Inter-State Hockey League. Since 1996, Tivali Minsk and three other Belarus clubs (Polimir Novopolotsk, Yunost Minsk and Neman Grodno) have played in the East European Hockey League along with teams from the Ukraine, Latvia, Lithuania and a team from Poland.

The Ice Hockey Federation of the Belarus Republic became independent in 1992 after the breakup of the Soviet Union. Belarus became a member of the International Ice Hockey Federation on May 6, 1992, and staged its first independent national championship in 1992–93. Dynamo Minsk was the winner. Belarus played its first international game against the Ukraine in 1992. The Belarus national team made its debut at the World Championships in the C Pool in 1994 and has progressed rapidly since. In 1998, Belarus played at the Olympics and in the A Pool of the World Championships.

Oleg Mikulchik (Winnipeg and Anaheim), Vladimir Tsyplakov (Los Angeles) and Ruslan Salei (Anaheim) are Belarus natives who have reached the NHL. Andrei Kovalev is under contract in the Washington Capitals organization.

HOCKEY TODAY: In 1997–98, the top four clubs in Belarus played a quadruple round-robin tournament to declare the country's champion.

BELGIUM
Koninklijke Belgische Ijshockey Federatie

HISTORY: Bandy (field hockey on ice) was first played in Belgium in Brussels and Antwerp in 1899. Soon, bandy players began learning to play ice hockey and in 1908 the Royal Belgian Ice Hockey Federation was founded. Belgians were very active in the roots of ice hockey in Europe and on December 8, 1908 Belgium joined France, Bohemia, England and Switzerland as the fifth member of the *Ligue Internationale de Hockey sur Glace* (which became the IIHF in 1911).

Hockey quickly became a popular sport in Belgium and the first national championship was held in 1912. It was won by Brussels IHSC. Belgians also had great success on the European scene, beating France 6–2 in their first international game in 1906. At the first official European Championships in 1910, Belgium tied gold medal-winning Great Britain 1–1 and earned a bronze medal, doing so again in 1911 and 1914. Belgium won the European Championship in Munich in 1913 and earned a silver medal in 1927. The first Olympic hockey tournament (which would later be recognized by the IIHF as the first World Championships) was held in Antwerp in April of 1920 in conjunction with the upcoming Summer Olympic Games.

Paul Loicq, who was president of the IIHF for 25 years (1922 to 1947), is the most famous Belgian in the history of international hockey, but the country's most legendary hockey player is Jef Lekens of Antwerp. He played in nine World and/or European championships between 1929 and 1955 and was also an international referee during the 1950s. From 1961 through 1966, he coached the Belgian national team.

HOCKEY TODAY: In 1997–98, the top six Belgian clubs played a double round-robin schedule with the top four teams advancing to the playoffs. Semifinals and finals are played in a best-of-three format while third place is decided with a two-game total-goals series between the two losers of the semifinals. Belgium also has a second division with 10 teams, a reserve division and junior leagues for players under 18, 16 and 14 years old.

BRAZIL
Confederacao Brasileira de Desportos Terrestres

HISTORY: The first ice hockey games in Brazil were played in 1967 in the ice hall (which used to be a casino) of the hotel Quitandinha in Petropolis (40 miles from Rio de Janeiro). Games took place there for eight years until the hotel was closed. During that time, the CCEG Rio de Janeiro team was the best in Brazil.

Hockey resumed in Brazil in 1978 with teams playing on a rink used for performances of the ice show Holiday on Ice. The revival of hockey in Brazil is attributed to businessman Erwin Dietenhofer of Munich, Germany. His efforts made possible the creation of the Brazil Ice Sport Union and the organization Brazil Hockey as part of the sports union. Dietenhofer served as the first president of both Brazil Hockey and the Brazil Ice Sport Union.

Brazil joined the International Ice Hockey Federation in November of 1984. In 1985, the country had five senior teams and five junior clubs, 180 senior and 130 junior players and five arenas with artificial ice. However, only one rink with a regulation-sized ice surface existed (in Rio de Janeiro).

HOCKEY TODAY: Currently, there are four regulation-size hockey arenas in Brazil located in Rio de Janeiro, Sao Paulo, Brasilia and Riberao Preto. Generally, these arenas are located in the so-called "play centers" of large supermarkets. There are also temporary ice facilities located in Belo Horizonte, Recife and Petropolis. There is no national hockey championship in Brazil.

BULGARIA
Bulgarska Federatsiya po Hokej na Led

HISTORY: The history of hockey in Bulgaria began in 1929 when the Bulgarian Skating Club was created. A handful of players took part in a few intra-squad games and later played against each other on newly created teams: AS–23 and FC–13. Sources indicate the Bulgarian national team played its first international game against Yugoslavia on January 17, 1942 and won 4–2.

Hockey was revived in Bulgaria after World War II and in 1946 the Bulgarian Skating and Ice Hockey Federation (now the Bulgarian Ice Hockey Federation) was founded. In Sofia, the old Yunak sports arena was converted into a hockey rink and the country's first tournament was held in 1949. Four teams participated—Spartak, Slavia, Levski and Sredec—with Spartak emerging victorious. Also that year, Akademik won the first Sofia championship.

Hockey became popular in Bulgaria and in 1950 five new sports clubs were founded, each with their own hockey team. In 1952, the country's first national championship took place on the ice of a frozen lake near the Musala mountains. The first national junior tournament also was held that year. Bulgaria's first artificial ice rink opened in Sofia in 1960. After joining the International Ice Hockey Federation on July 25, 1963, Bulgaria began to play regularly at the World and European Championships.

HOCKEY TODAY: In 1997–98, the top five clubs in Bulgaria participated in a double round-robin schedule with the best four teams advancing to a best-of-five playoff round. The two playoff winners meet to determine the gold and silver medal, while the two losing teams play for the bronze medal. A national junior championship is held annually and a national midget competition began in 1971.

CANADA
Canadian Hockey

HISTORY: The game of hockey was born in Canada. Conflicting claims surround the origins of the game, but it is accepted generally that antecedents of hockey were played in various garrison towns and in Montreal, where the sport first flourished. A hockey game first was advertised in a Montreal newspaper in 1875. The game rapidly took root in Ottawa, Toronto and soon after, throughout the young country.

In 1893, Canada's Governor-General, Lord Stanley of Preston, donated a silver bowl to be awarded to the top senior amateur team in the country. This Dominion Hockey Challenge Cup soon came to be known by the name of its patron.

By the turn of the century, hockey was played in every part of Canada. Even before 1910, openly professional players were competing for the Stanley Cup. Accounts of the exploits of storied teams such as the Ottawa Silver Seven, Montreal Wanderers and Renfrew Millionaires filled the newspapers of the day. The National Hockey League was established in 1917 and by the end of its first decade, it stood alone as the game's number one professional circuit.

As the game in Canada became increasingly professionalized, the Allan Cup was donated in 1908 to honor Canada's senior amateur champions. In 1914, the Canadian Amateur Hockey Association was created and in 1920 the CAHA was accepted by the International Ice Hockey Federation as Canada's representative in international hockey. Canada competed at the 1920 Olympics in Antwerp, Belgium and was represented by the Allan Cup champion Winnipeg Falcons, who easily won the gold medal at the event later considered to be the first World Championships. The Toronto Granites won gold as well at the first Winter Olympics in 1924, outscoring their opponents 110–3. Hockey Hall of Fame member Harry Watson scored 36 goals at that tournament. Canada's gold medal streak came to an end in 1933 when the National Sea Fleas, managed by future Toronto Maple Leafs owner Harold Ballard, lost 2–1 to the United States at the World Championships in Prague.

By using top amateur club teams, Canada was able to remain the dominant nation in international hockey until 1954. That year, the Senior B East York Lyndhursts were defeated by the Soviet national team when the USSR made its debut at the World Championships. Senior clubs continued to carry Canada's colors into the early 1960s, with teams like the Penticton Vees and Whitby Dunlops still able to defeat the Soviets.

However, the Trail Smoke Eaters would prove to be the last Canadian senior amateur club to win the World Championship when they captured the title in 1961.

In the early 1960s, Father David Bauer, coach of the 1961 Memorial Cup-winning St. Michael's junior team in Toronto, presented a plan to develop a Canadian national hockey

team. The CAHA accepted Bauer's proposal and the "Nats" were launched at the University of British Columbia.

The Nats were a good club, but the Soviet hockey system was in full flower during the 1960s. The best finishes by Father Bauer's squad were third-place bronze medals at the 1966 and 1967 World Championships and at the 1968 Olympics.

Canada withdrew from international competition after 1969. Hockey Canada was created that year to improve Canada's performance in international play. Beginning with the famed eight-game series against the Soviet Union's superb national team in 1972, professional players started to participate in some international events. Canada dominated play throughout the history of the Canada Cup tournament from 1976 to 1991. This event always saw Team Canada employ its very best professional skaters and goaltenders.

Hockey Canada and its successor, Canadian Hockey, have developed and operated successful national junior and national/Olympic team programs. Canada has won 10 World Junior Championships since 1982 and Team Canada earned silver medals at the Olympics in 1992 and 1994.

A team stocked mainly with National Hockey league players brought Canada its first world championship title since 1961 at the IIHF 1994 World Championships, and Canada won the world title again in 1997. However, the loss to the United States at the World Cup of Hockey in 1996 and the disappointing performance of the 1998 Olympic team have stung Canadian fans' pride in their country's hockey prowess.

Canadian Hockey has supported the development of women's hockey in the country and has operated a national women's team that won four consecutive gold medals at the IIHF Women's World Championships. The Canadian team finished second behind the United States when women's hockey made its Olympic debut in 1998.

HOCKEY TODAY: Though Canadian teams are struggling to survive in the economics of sports in the 1990s, and there are only six teams from Canada currently playing in the NHL, the National Hockey League remains the top league in Canada as it has since its formation in 1917.

Canadian cities also are represented in the biggest minor professional leagues of North America. While many more players from the United States and Europe are playing professional hockey in North America, Canada still provides more players than any other country.

More Canadian prospects are beginning to play at American universities, but the top junior hockey players in Canada mainly continue to play in the three major junior leagues that make up the Canadian Hockey League—the Ontario Hockey League, the Quebec Major Junior Hockey League and the Western Hockey League. All three leagues are mainly Canadian-based, though both the OHL and the WHL have American franchises. An increasing number of European and American players are entering the ranks of Canadian junior hockey, though the overwhelming number of players are still grow up in Canada.

Below the top junior leagues, Canadian players can compete at several different levels in many different age groups. Canada's recent disappointments at the international level are causing Canadian Hockey to take a serious look at its youth programs, but it remains true that more young people are playing hockey in Canada than in any of the other major hockey nations.

CHINA
Ice Hockey Association of the People's Republic of China

HISTORY: The roots of Chinese ice hockey date back to 1915 when a few games took place in Sen Jan (Mugden). The next mention of hockey in China does not occur until January 26, 1935 when the country's first tournament took place as part of the First Winter Spartakaide Games.

The Ice Hockey Association of the People's Republic of China was founded in 1951. Two years later, the first national championship was held. In 1956, the National Winter Sports Federation was founded and in March of that year the Chinese national team made its international debut at the Universiade in Wroclaw, Poland. China joined the International Ice Hockey Federation on July 25, 1963, and played its first game in the C Pool of the World and European Championships in Miercurea Ciuc, Romania on March 3, 1972. China beat Bulgaria 4–3.

HOCKEY TODAY: In 1997–98, the best seven clubs in China played for the national title (including two teams each from Qiqihar, Harbin and Jiamusi). After playing a round-robin schedule, the top four teams advance to the national league championship where they play a quadruple round-robin format followed by one-game semifinals. The winners then play for the national title while the losers meet to decide third place. China also has a second division with six teams. Due to a lack of indoor rinks, many teams in China still play on natural ice in the country's mountain region.

CHINESE TAIPEI
Chinese Taipei Skating Association

HISTORY: The Chinese Taipei Skating Association was founded in 1980. Two years later, in 1982, the first national championship took place. In 1983, Chinese Taipei became a member of the International Ice Hockey Federation.

The debut of the Chinese Taipei national team took place in 1987 in Perth, Australia, when the team played at the D Pool World Championships. (Due to Asian political considerations, results with Chinese Taipei didn't count in the final standings.) The national team tied its first game 2–2 versus Hong Kong on March 13, 1987.

HOCKEY TODAY: A national championship is held almost every year. Polar Bears Taipei is the most successful team.

CROATIA
Hrvatski Savez Hokeja na Ledu

HISTORY: The roots of ice hockey in Croatia go back to 1906 when the first hockey team in Yugoslavia (HASK—the Croatian Academic Sports Club) was formed in the city of Zagreb. The first official hockey games also took place in Zagreb in 1916–17 when HASK played a two-game series against I.IISK (I. Croatian Sports Club). HASK won the first game 2–0 but lost the second 6–0. In 1930, the Yugoslav Ice Hockey Federation was founded in Zagreb. Not surprisingly, clubs from Zagreb were among the best in Yugoslavia for many years.

In 1991, the Croatian Ice Hockey Association was founded and the first Croatian national championship was won by HK Zagreb in 1992. The newly independent nation joined the International Ice Hockey Federation on May 6,

1992, and the Croatian national team made its debut in the C2 Pool of the IIHF World Championships in Barcelona, Spain in 1994.

HOCKEY TODAY: In 1997–98, there were about 400 hockey players in Croatia playing on two indoor and two outdoor rinks. Croatia's top four teams play a quadruple round-robin schedule with all four teams then advancing to the play-offs. Semifinals are a best-of-three, while the finals use a best-of-five format.

CZECH REPUBLIC
Cesky Svaz Ledniho Hokeje

HISTORY: The game of bandy (field hockey on ice) was introduced to Czechoslovakia by Josef Rossler-Orovsky in 1890 when the country was known as Bohemia. Orovsky brought sticks and a ball to Bohemia from Paris and translated rules that had been brought into the country from England. When the game of ice hockey first was demonstrated in Prague in 1905 by Canadian Ruck Anderson, the country's bandy background provided players with a solid basis for the new game. As a result, hockey's growth here occurred much sooner than in countries like Sweden and Finland, whose climates were better suited to the game.

The spread of hockey in the future Czechoslovakia was largely due to the efforts of Josef Gruss, a professor at Karlov University who made the first translation of Canadian rules into Czech. In the summer of 1908, Gruss began establishing the first hockey clubs in Prague (I. CLTK, Slavia, AC Sparta, ASK and others) which led to the formation in principle of a Czech Hockey Union (Cesky Svaz Hokejovi) on November 6, 1908. Because Gruss was well-connected with the founder of the *Ligue Internationale de Hockey sur Glace* (which became the International Ice Hockey Federation in 1911), Bohemia joined France as the second member of the LIHG on November 15, 1908. (When Bohemia became Czechoslovakia after World War I, it was readmitted to the IIHF under its new name on April 26, 1920.)

The constituent meeting of the Czech Hockey Union actually was not held until December 11, 1908. Speed skating champion Jaroslav Potucek was elected as the first chairman of the ice hockey union, which included 12 member clubs. An invitation was extended to the Czech players to attend the upcoming inaugural international hockey tournament in Chamonix and seven Prague players went to France with their bandy equipment. Although they lost all four games they played, the experience proved invaluable. In 1911, the Bohemian national team won the European Championship. Their victory in 1912 was annulled later due to a technicality, but Bohemia won again in 1914. After World War I, the Czechoslovakian national team continued to rank as one of the top squads in Europe, winning the European championships again in 1922, 1925, 1929 and 1933.

Czechoslovakian hockey progressed rapidly during the 1930s. The first artificial ice rink opened in Prague on January 17, 1931, with the University of Manitoba playing LTC Prague in the inaugural game en route to representing Canada at the World Championships in Poland. Also in 1931, Slovakia's Hockey Union merged with the Czech Hockey Union to form the Czechoslovakian Hockey Union. Prior to that, there had been separate national Czech championships (since 1910) and Slovak Championships (since 1930). National championships have been held regularly since 1936–37.

Czechoslovakian hockey continued to flourish after World War II despite two tragic events. The Czechs had won the World Championships with Canada absent in 1947, and tied the Canadian team at the 1948 Olympics before settling for the silver medal, but five national team members were killed in a plane crash in November of 1948. Still, Czechoslovakia was able to beat Canada to win the World Championship in 1949. The Czechs would be denied a chance to repeat in 1950 when the entire team was arrested prior to the tournament amid accusations the players planned to defect. The Soviet Union would emerge as a world power in 1954, but Czechoslovakia would continue to rank among the best teams in Europe. After the fall of Communism, the Czech Republic succeeded Czechoslovakia in the IIHF in 1993 and won the World Championship in 1996 and an Olympic gold medal in 1998.

HOCKEY TODAY: In 1997–98, the Czech Republic Extraleague comprised 14 teams playing a quadruple round-robin, 52-game regular season. The top eight teams advance to the playoffs, where series are a best-of-five. In a promotion/relegation round, the two bottom teams from the Extraleague play a set of best-of-seven series against the two top teams from the First League. The First League also has 14 teams playing a quadruple round-robin schedule. The Second League has two divisions with 16 teams in each. The top juniors in the Czech Republic play in the Junior Extraleague, which consists of two divisions with 10 teams in each.

DENMARK
Danmarks Ishockey Union

HISTORY: The first mention of hockey (bandy) in Denmark dates back to the beginning of the 20th century when the members of KSF Copenhagen (Copenhagen Skating Club, founded in 1869) tried the new game. The growth of hockey proceeded slowly in the country and did not begin in earnest until the creation of the Dansk (now Danmarks) Ishockey Union on November 27, 1949. Prior to that date, the only ice hockey association in Denmark had been a branch of the Danish Winter Sports Federation. Through that organization, Denmark had become a member of the International Ice Hockey Federation on April 27, 1946.

The first appearance of Danish hockey players on the world stage resulted in what remains the worst defeat in international hockey at its highest level. On February 12, 1949, Denmark was defeated 47–0 by Canada at the World and European Championships in Stockholm, Sweden. Nevertheless, Denmark kept sending its national teams to the World and European tournaments and the development of hockey in the country progressed. Danish clubs began to extend invitations to coaches from North America, and in 1954–55 the first national championship was held. Since 1960, all games have been played on indoor rinks. By the 1970s, Danish teams began employing talented coaches from other European nations, particularly Czechoslovakia.

HOCKEY TODAY: In 1997–98, the top 10 clubs in Denmark played in the Elitserien. After a quadruple round-robin schedule, the top six teams advance to the Superisligan, where they play each other three times (15 games for each team). The top two teams after this stage advance to the playoffs while the four other teams join the top four teams from Division 1

for a new eight-team, double round-robin series. The top two teams from this set also qualify for the playoffs. Semifinals and finals are five-game series, while the two losers in the semifinals play a best-of-three series to determine third place. Junior and midget clubs in Denmark have competed for national titles since 1962.

ESTONIA
Eesti Jaahoki Federatsiooni

HISTORY: Like so many European nations, hockey in Estonia developed out of the game of bandy which was being played in Tallinn prior to World War I. By the 1930s, there were many hockey clubs in Estonia, with most of the teams concentrated in Revel (now Tallinn) and the university town of Dorpat (now Tartu). The first national championship took place in 1934 and was won by Kalev Tallinn. Later, Kalev, the Tartu academic sport club, and Sport Tallinn dominated competition in Estonia.

The Estonian Ice Hockey Federation was founded in 1921 when Estonia was an independent country and was re-established in 1991 as a part of the Soviet Ice Hockey Federation. Estonia originally joined the International Ice Hockey Federation on February 17, 1937, but was excluded from the IIHF after World War II (on April 27, 1946). During this time, Estonia never sent its national team to the World and European Championships and restricted its play to exhibition games against other Baltic countries and Finland. Estonia was represented at the World Championships in Prague in 1938—by referee Raoul Saue. The Estonian national team played its first game on February 20, 1937, losing 2–1 to Finland in Helsinki. Estonia won the second game of the series 2–1, but dropped the final game 9–1. The country's last international game was a 3–0 victory over Lithuania in February of 1941. The most famous Estonian player in prewar Europe was a 6'7" giant known as Tipner, who later became well-known as a soccer goalkeeper. Another internationally known Estonian player was Juha Sevo, who played for the HC Augsburg team in Germany after World War II. After becoming part of the Soviet Union, the best Estonian club (Dynamo Tallinn) played in the top division of the Soviet league from 1946 to 1953. After 1955, Dynamo Tallinn played only for the Estonian Republic Championship.

The newly independent nation of Estonia again became a member of the IIHF on May 6, 1992 and played in the C2 Pool World Championships in 1994.

HOCKEY TODAY: The five best Estonian clubs played in the country's top league in 1997–98 with the winner of the national title determined after a 20-game season (each club plays the others five times). The top four teams qualify for the playoffs for the Estonian Cup. The semifinals consist of just one game while the final employs a two-game total-goals format.

FINLAND
Suomen Jaakiekkoliitto

HISTORY: The first attempt to introduce hockey to Finland was made by professor Leonard Borgstrom at the end of the 19th century. Training sessions were held in the early mornings in the North Harbour area (Pohjoisranta) in Helsinki and were reported by the press. "The new ice sport is called hockey," the Finnish sports newspaper *Suomen Urheilulehti* told its readers in 1899. "The players divided into two

groups of skaters on ice and hit the puck with sticks trying to get it into their opponent's goal, two poles over one meter high set one and a half meters from each other. The game is very entertaining and requires strong arms and legs, as well as nerves, determination, and speed."

Interest in the new sport waned, however, and the second coming of hockey to Finland did not occur until 1927 under the instigation of the Finnish Skating Union. Skaters long had been unhappy with bandy because the huge surface because this game required resulted in competition for ice time with speed skaters. The Finnish speed skating organization had seen "Canadian" hockey in Sweden and at the Olympic Games in Antwerp in 1920 and had come to the conclusion that this game could be played without interfering with their skating competitions. As a result, hockey was added to the program of the Finnish Skating Union. The skating union published the first set of rules for hockey in Finland based on the rules of the International Ice Hockey Federation. The first club game was played in Tampere on January 15, 1928. Finland was admitted to the IIHF through the efforts of the skating union on February 10, 1928.

A year after the Finnish Skating Union had become involved with hockey, the country's soccer union added hockey to its program in 1928 and published its own set of rules based on those of the Canadian Amateur Hockey Association. The soccer union initially restricted its participation to organizing tournaments. The first national championship was held in 1928 and won by Viipurin Reipas. The soccer union also entered the international scene by inviting the Swedish champions (IK Gota of Stockholm) to play in Helsinki on January 29, 1928. The game received widespread publicity and resulted in an 8–1 victory by the Swedish team.

Recognizing the need for cooperation, representatives from both the Finnish Skating Union and the Finnish Soccer Union formed the Finnish Ice Hockey Association on January 20, 1929. The new group organized an expanded national championship and found resources to pay visiting Swedish coaches. The lack of coaches in Finland limited the work of the new hockey association to the Helsinki-Tampere-Turku area during the 1930s, but this approach made it possible to keep the teams' traveling expenses at a minimum.

Interest in hockey grew rapidly in Finland and even the national team's 0–5–0 record at its World Championship debut in 1939 was accepted as a useful step in gaining experience and knowledge of the game. However, Finland soon was seen to be losing ground to the other European countries due to its inadequate training facilities. While the best players in Europe had been practicing on artificial ice rinks, Finnish players were still totally dependent on the weather. Though Finland's first artificial rink did not open until November 22, 1955, in Tampere, the country had by that time experienced a great hockey boom due to the development of a hockey equipment manufacturing industry that had made Finland one of Europe's leading equipment exporters. The result of that had seen an unprecedented interest in hockey among Finnish youth.

Finally, by the 1960s, the Finnish national team arrived as a real force at the international level. The Finns won their first medal (a silver) at the European Championship in 1962, but their greatest successes came at the junior level, winning a silver medal at the World Junior Championships in 1974 and gold in 1978. In 1988, the Finnish national team earned a silver

medal at the Olympics and in 1992 they finished in second place behind Sweden at the World Championship. In 1995, Finland beat Sweden to win its first World Championship. The Finns have added bronze medals at the Olympics in 1994 and 1998.

HOCKEY TODAY: The top league in Finland, the SM-Liiga, was founded in 1975. There were 12 teams playing a 48-game schedule in this league in 1997–98. The eight top teams advance to the playoffs, which are played in a best-of-five format (plus a one-game series to decide third place among the two losers in the semifinals).

Finland's Division 1 comprises 12 teams who play a quadruple round-robin regular season. Six teams advance to the playoffs with the three winners from these best-of-five series moving on to play with the worst team from SM-Liiga in the semifinals and finals.

Division 2 is made up of seven different groups containing between eight and 10 teams. Each group plays a double round robin with the best team in each group qualifying for a promotional pool. Winners from this pool are advanced to Division 1 for the next season. Finland also has regional divisions 3, 4, 5 and 6.

Junior hockey is very well-organized in Finland, with the country's top junior players (aged 18–21) playing in three leagues: SM-Liiga, Division 1 and Division 2. Players under 17 play in Junior B competitions with their own SM-Liiga and Division 1. Junior C players (under 16) also have their own SM-Liiga and Division 1.

FRANCE
Federation Francaise
des Sports de Glace
Comite National de Hockey sur Glace

HISTORY: France is one of a few European countries which has been playing hockey since the end of the 19th century. The game was introduced in France by Canadian George Meagher, who brought a rule book and coaching instructions to Paris in 1894. Meagher began running practices to teach the elements of hockey to the French, but the first official game did not take place until 1903 when a team from Paris beat a Lyon team 2–1. It was also in 1903 that Europe's first official hockey club, the Patineurs de Paris, was formed. They played their first international game against a team from London.

France held its first national hockey championship in 1904, making it the second country in Europe (behind Great Britain) to stage one. Patineurs de Paris were France's first champions. The French national team played its first game against Belgium in 1906. In 1907, an ice hockey association was founded as part of the French Federation of Ice Sports. One year later, France, England, Belgium and Switzerland founded the Ligue Internationale de Hockey sur Glace, forerunner of the International Ice Hockey Federation. On October 20, 1908, France became the first member of the new organization and Frenchman Louis Magnus became its first president. The first international tournament took place in 1908 in Chamonix, France, with teams from Paris, London, Lausanne, Brussels and Prague taking part. Paris finished second behind London. The French national team competed at the first World Championships, held in conjunction with the Antwerp Olympics in 1920, losing its first game 4–0 to Sweden on April 25. Still, France would rank among the top countries in Europe during the 1920s and 1930s, winning a silver medal at

the European Championship in 1923 and a gold medal the following year.

HOCKEY TODAY: In 1997–98, the 12 teams of the Ligue Nationale play an initial double round-robin schedule before dividing into two divisions. The top six teams play another double round robin series in the Division Elite, while the lower six teams play a double round robin in the Division Excellence. The top two teams from the Division Excellence then join the six teams from Division Elite for the playoffs. Quarterfinals, semifinals and finals are played in a best-of-five format. The losing teams in the semifinals play a best-of-five series to decide third place, while the quarterfinals losers play off to determine fifth through eighth place. The champions of France receive the Magnus Cup, though the best teams also compete for the French Cup.

French hockey also has a Nationale 1 League, with eight teams in the East and eight in the West playing a double round-robin schedule. Nationale 2 League has three six-team divisions: South, Northeast and Northwest. There is a Division 3 league.

Junior and midget teams in France began competing for the French national title in their age categories during the 1950s. Later, four other age groups began playing for national titles.

GERMANY
Deutscher Eishockey Bund E.V.

HISTORY: The beginning of ice sports in Germany goes back to 1888 when the German National Skating Union was founded in Berlin. Among its other duties, the union was in charge of bandy players in Germany. The first game of hockey in the country took place on Lake Halensee in Berlin on February 4, 1897. By 1901, the first hockey team had been created with players practicing at a rink on the grounds of the Berlin Zoo. Germany's first indoor arena opened in Berlin in 1909 and by 1910 hockey had become so popular that Berlin held its first city championship. Ten teams took part, with the tournament being won by the Berliner Schlittschuh Club. The Berliner SC had helped to christen Germany's first indoor arena the year before in an international tournament with teams from London and Paris. In 1912, Berliner SC would win Germany's first national championship.

On September 19, 1909, Germany had become the sixth nation in the world, after Belgium, Bohemia, England, Switzerland and France, to join the League Internationale de Hockey sur Glace (forerunner of the International Ice Hockey Federation). In 1910, the Germans won the silver medal at the first official European Championships. German hockey players quickly became among the best in Europe and never failed to win a medal at the European Championships through 1914. So popular was hockey in Germany at this time that the European tournament was held in Berlin in both 1911 and 1914 and in Munich in 1913. After World War I, Germany was excluded from the IIHF from 1920 until January 11, 1926. However, even during this period of time, German teams continued to play internationally at the Spengler Cup. Berliner SC won that tournament in 1924, and again in 1926 and 1928.

The success of Berliner SC on the international scene was not a surprise to the European hockey community. The team was coached by two Canadians—Dr. Blake Watson and Dr.

Roche—who also coached the German national team to great success. Stocked mainly by players from Berliner SC roster, the German national team finished third, earned a bronze medal in its return to the European Championships in 1927. Before the outbreak of World War II, the German national team would win two European Championships, while earning three silver medals and seven bronze medals. Germany also won a silver medal at the 1930 World Championship, a bronze medal at the 1932 Olympics and a bronze medal at the World Championships in 1934.

After World War II, Germany was excluded from the IIHF again but reinstated as the Federal Republic of Germany (West Germany) on March 10, 1951. During its absence from the world scene, the Germans created the Oberliga in 1947–48 as the top league in the country. Eleven years later, the Oberliga was replaced by the Bundesliga. Other steps toward strengthening ice hockey in Germany were made on June 16, 1963, when the Germany Hockey Union was founded. It consisted of 32 teams in eight provincial associations. Dr. Gunther Sabetzki of Dusseldorf was elected as one of the first two presidents of the union. He would serve as president of the IIHF from 1975 to 1994.

German hockey authorities always have attempted to boost the popularity of the game in their country by inviting foreign players. Traditionally, German club teams usually carried two or three foreign players per team, but those numbers have increased greatly since the creation of the Deutsche Eishockey League—Germany's first professional league—in 1994.

HOCKEY TODAY: In 1997–98, the Deutsche Eishockey League was made up of 16 teams. A double round-robin schedule is played with the top six teams advancing to a second stage, where each one will play the others four times with their points added to their first-stage totals. Meanwhile, the teams finishing seventh to 16th play a double round robin with the best two teams from that stage joining up with the six top teams for the playoffs. All playoff series are a best-of-five. The eight teams that have failed to qualify for the playoffs take part in their own play-down series, and the four winning teams remain in the DEL for the next year. A series is then played among the four losing teams, with the two winners also staying in the DEL. The two losing teams face the two best teams from 1.Liga in a best-of-three playoff with the winners of this series promoted to the DEL.

The lower divisions in Germany hockey are 1.Liga and 2.Liga, both with groups in the north and south. There are also seven regional leagues. The junior Bundesliga is also divided into North and South divisions. There are national competitions among junior and boys teams of different age groups.

GREAT BRITAIN
British Ice Hockey Association

HISTORY: The roots of British ice hockey go far back into history. In about 1600, skates equipped with metal blades were introduced to Britain from Holland and in 1642 the Edinburgh Skating Club (believed to be Britain's oldest skating organization) was formed. Skating became a very popular sport in Great Britain under the reign of Charles II and the *Art of Skating* by Robert Jones was published in 1772. Many sketches and paintings during the 18th and 19th centuries depict people skating on frozen lakes and rivers, often using sticks and a

ball or some other object. In 1876, the world's first artificial ice rinks were opened in London.

The first official ice hockey game played outside of Canada is said to have been Cambridge University versus Oxford University at St. Moritz, Switzerland in 1885. Oxford won 6–0. What was played in that match, however, was probably not ice hockey as the game is known today. A very important part in popularizing hockey in Britain belongs to the Stanley brothers. The Honorable Arthur Stanley, son of Lord Stanley of Preston (then Governor-General of Canada) formed the Rideau Rebels hockey club in Ottawa in 1888. Five year later, in 1893, he and his hockey-playing brothers helped to persuade their father to present the Stanley Cup. In the same year, A.C.A.Wade, one of Britain's first hockey writers, recalled playing the game at Gravenhurst in Bedfordshire.

After their return to England, the Stanley brothers continued their efforts to popularize ice hockey in Great Britain. During the hard winter of 1895, the lake of Buckingham Palace was frozen over and a palace team which included the Prince of Wales (later King Edward VII), the Duke of York (the future King George V), Lord Mildmay, Sir Francis Astley-Corbett, Sir William Bromley Davenport and Mr. Ronald Moncrieff played the Stanley team led by Arthur Stanley and four of his brothers. The Palace team was beaten easily by the experienced Stanley squad. However, it remains unclear as to whether or not the game played was truly ice hockey—both sides were using bandy sticks. The Stanley family continued its missionary work and in 1896–97 Arthur Stanley and five of his brothers played the Niagara Hall ice rink team and defeated them easily. Two Stanley brothers, A.F. and F.W., also played for an Old Wellingtonians team which lost to Niagara 2–0 on January 1, 1899.

Despite the importance of the Stanley family in the history of British ice hockey, the "Founding Father" of the sport in the United Kingdom is considered to be Major B.M. "Peter" Patton. It was he who approached Admiral Maxe, founder of the Princes' Skating Club in London, and asked for permission to form a hockey team at the rink. Permission was granted and the first game took place in February of 1897. Patton was 21 at the time and did not retire from the game until 1931, when he was 55. Over the years, the team he formed often represented England abroad. The Princes played and won an international bandy tournament in Davos, Switzerland in 1904 and also beat France in Lyon that same year. In 1908, the Princes gave England victory in the first indoor international ice hockey tournament when they defeated Germany and France in Berlin. The first official European Championship was held in Switzerland in 1910 and Peter Patton was on hand to captain England to victory. In 1913, he founded the British Ice Hockey Association (BIHA). He revived it in 1923 after it had been disbanded during the First World War.

The first English Ice Hockey League was formed in 1903–04 with five teams participating: the Princes club, the London Canadians, Cambridge University and two teams from Henglers Circus Ice Rink (also known as the National Ice Palace)—Argyll and the Amateur Skating Club. The London Canadians won the first championship.

In 1908, England joined France, Belgium and Switzerland in the founding of the *Ligue Internationale de Hockey sur Glace*, forerunner of the International Ice Hockey Federation. That same year, the first hockey games played in Scotland took place in Glasgow. The Scottish Ice Hockey Association was formed in 1929. Britain remained a European hockey power until World War II, culminating in Olympic, World and European championships at Garmisch-Partenkirchen, Germany in 1936.

HOCKEY TODAY: The British League folded at the end of the 1995–96 season and the leading 23 teams split into three leagues running independently of each other and the governing BIHA. League membership depended heavily upon how many overseas players a club was willing to sign as well as a club's geographical location. Beginning in 1997–98, the eight-team Superleague comprised most of the clubs who were formerly members of the Premier Division in the British League. The winner of the Superleague is considered to be the national champion. The eight teams play a 42-game schedule after which all of them advance to the playoffs. The teams finishing first, third, fifth and seventh are then placed in Group A, with the four other teams in Group B. After a double round robin within each group, the two best teams from each group advance to the semifinals. Both the semifinals and finals consist of a single game.

The eight teams playing in Britain's Premier League and the seven clubs in the Northern Premier League are mainly members of the old Division 1. In the Premier League, the eight teams play each other eight times (for a 56-game schedule per team) with the top six qualifying for the playoffs. Those teams then play a double round-robin series with the top two teams competing in a two-game total-goals finals. The winner then meets the Northern Premier League playoff champion in the Premier Leagues Championship finals.

The seven teams of the Northern Premier League play each other six times for a 36-game schedule. Afterwards, all seven teams are split into two groups for a double round-robin playoff round. The top two teams from each group then advance to play in a final four-team, double round robin with the top team emerging as the Northern Premier League champion and qualifying to play against the Premier League champion.

Superleague teams are permitted to employ overseas players without any restrictions. Premier League clubs have an agreement to allow three per team. The Northern Premier League has the toughest eligibility rules, allowing only three players who require an International Transfer Card (ITC) regardless of passport. In addition, the Northern Premier League imposes a salary cap of £75,000 compared to £250,000 in the Premier League. The Superleague has no salary cap. The Superleague and the Premier League have formed companies to operate and administer their organizations—Ice Hockey Superleague Ltd. and the Premier Ice Hockey League Ltd.

The 20-team English League (with 12 teams in the Southern Conference and eight in the Northern) is run by the English Ice Hockey Association for teams with smaller budgets. These teams rely mostly on players born and trained in Britain. The junior English Under-19 League has nine teams in its North Conference and seven teams in the South.

GREECE
Elliniki Omospondia Pagodromion

HISTORY: Ice hockey in Greece was introduced in Thessaloniki by Czechoslovakian emigrants in the early 1980s. Romanians and Canadians built ice rinks in Greece, but most of them were not of standard hockey size. A regulation-sized facility did exist at the sports stadium at Neo Faliro but it was used generally for basketball. Ice was only available for about two or three weeks in November.

Despite the difficulties, Greece joined the International Ice Hockey Federation in April of 1987. By then, Greece had four different hockey clubs. The Flying Ice Skaters in Athens had a senior and a junior team as well as a beginners club with 32 children between the age of six and 10. Albatros Athens had a senior team. The Chalkis Ice Hockey Club (based about 50 miles outside of Athens) had a senior and a junior team, as did Aris Thessaloniki. The first Greek national hockey championship took place in 1988–89 and was won by Aris Thessaloniki. There has been no national championship in Greece since 1992.

In 1989, Greece's ice hockey association became a section of the Hellenic Ice Sports Federation. Three years later, the Greek national team made its first international appearance at the C2 Pool of the World Championships. Greece was a winner in its national team debut, defeating Turkey 15–3 on March 21, 1992 in Johannesburg, South Africa.

HOCKEY TODAY: Greek teams have played in the C Pools of the IIHF World Championships and the World Junior Championships on several occasions during the 1990s.

HONG KONG
Hong Kong Ice Hockey Association

HISTORY: The Hong Kong Ice Hockey Association was founded on August 8, 1980. Hong Kong joined the International Ice Hockey Federation on March 31, 1983 and made its debut on the world stage at the D Pool World Championships in Perth, Australia in 1987. Hong Kong tied Taiwan 2–2 in its first international game on March 13, 1987 and went on to win the Fair Play Cup at the world tournament.

Although there was plenty of hockey activity in Hong Kong, local teams (usually stocked with Canadian and American players) did not compete for a national championship until 1995–96. The first title was won by a team sponsored by Planet Hollywood.

HOCKEY TODAY: In 1997–98, seven teams played in the Hong Kong league. A triple round-robin schedule sees each team play 18 games. After that, the two top teams meet in a one-game playoff for the national title.

HUNGARY
Magyar Jegkorong Szovetseg

HISTORY: The roots of hockey in Hungary begin with the sport of bandy (field hockey on ice). The country's first bandy team was formed in 1905 and the first public bandy game was held in Budapest two years later. In 1914, the BKE Budapest team, representing the Budapest Skating Union, won international bandy competitions in St. Moritz and Prague and was considered the best bandy team in Europe. The appeal of bandy was stopped, however, by the introduction of a new game—"Canadian" ice hockey. Hockey was introduced to Hungary by Englishman John Dunlop in 1925 and the first real hockey game in Hungary was staged on December 26 of that year between BKE and a team from Vienna. Vienna won the game 1–0.

The Hungarian Winter Sports Federation had

been founded in 1908 and ice hockey was given a division within the federation. (Today, hockey in Hungary is represented by the Hungarian Ice Hockey Federation). Hungary joined the International Ice Hockey Federation on January 24, 1927 and that same day the Hungarian national team played its first game, losing 6–0 to Austria.

Hungary had gotten its first artificial ice rink (an outdoor facility) in Budapest in 1926, but the Hungarians still had a lot to learn about hockey. At the European Championship in Vienna in 1927, Hungary's national team finished last. Two years later, Hungary hosted the tournament during the bitterly cold winter of 1929 and by the 1930s the Hungarians had become one of the top teams in Europe. In 1934, a touring Canadian team could only manage a scoreless tie against the Hungarian national team at an exhibition match in Budapest. In 1937, Hungary held its first national championship (won by the BKE Budapest hockey club) and at the IIHF World Championships in Prague in 1938, the Hungarians managed a 1–1 tie against the gold medal-winning Canadian team. The big hero of the Hungarian team was goaltender Istvan Hircsak, who was considered one of the best in Europe at the time.

World War II stopped the development of hockey in Hungary for nearly 10 years, but interest in the game rose again by the late 1940s. In later years, training methods were significantly improved by Czechoslovakian coach Vladimir Kominek, who led the Hungarian national team between 1959 and 1964.

HOCKEY TODAY: In 1997–98, the top five clubs in Hungary played each other seven times for a 28-game schedule. The national championship is determined after a best-of-three playoff between the top two teams in the league. The top four teams compete for the Hungarian Medicor Cup, playing one-game semifinals and finals. Some games in the league are played on outdoor rinks. Ten clubs play in Hungary's second division. Junior teams have been competing for a national title since 1954, midget teams since 1961.

ICELAND
Icelandic Skating Association

HISTORY: Hockey in Iceland began in 1937, when the first games were played. The first national championship was held in 1968–69 and won by Skautefelag Akureyri. However, after two years of national competition, the development of hockey in Iceland slowed down. The Icelandic national championship was revived in 1978–79 but it did not take place every year. Skautefelag Akureyri is still the country's best hockey team.

The Icelandic Skating Association, as a part of the of Ithrottasambaud Islands (Sports Union of Iceland), was created in 1987 and included an Ice Hockey Division. Iceland joined the International Ice Hockey Federation on May 6, 1992 and made its debut on the world stage in 1997 when the Icelandic national junior team (under-18) played at the D Pool of the European Junior Championships. In 1998, Iceland had a junior team (under 20) at the D Pool of the World Junior Championships.

HOCKEY TODAY: In 1997–98, Iceland had 360 registered players (including 130 senior players) and two outdoor hockey arenas. Three teams compete in the national league, playing a double round-robin schedule. The top two teams then meet in a best-of-five finals for the Icelandic national title.

INDIA
Winter Games Federation of India

HISTORY: The Winter Games Federation of India was founded in 1979 and became a member of the International Ice Hockey Federation in 1989. The first two clubs to play hockey in India were Bombay IHC and Madras IHC, though the majority of hockey in the country has been played by two other clubs: the Shimla Ice Skating Club in the Himalayan Mountains and the Ladakh Ice Skating Club in Leh near the Tibet border. The distance between these two hockey cities is about 1,000 miles and the teams travel by plane when playing one another. However, because Leh in located in a valley in the Himalayan Mountains, air travel often is difficult because of heavy clouds. The teams only travel when clear skies permit, so they often will continue to play games against one another until improved weather conditions allow a return flight.

HOCKEY TODAY: There are about 100 hockey players in India. Many more are interested in playing but the lack of facilities has slowed hockey's development. Currently, there are no national competitions.

IRELAND
Irish Ice Hockey Association

HISTORY: Ice hockey in Ireland did not gain popularity until the 1980s when the game's supporters began to form new teams. Much of the activity took place in Dublin. The first official game took place on April 21, 1982 between the Dublin Stags and the Liverpool Leopards of England. Dublin won 11–7.

HOCKEY TODAY: There is no national championship in Ireland yet and the country has not been active on the international scene.

ISRAEL
Ice Hockey Federation of Israel

HISTORY: The first ice skating rink in Israel opened in January of 1986. It is located in Kiryat Motzkin, a suburb of Haifa in northern Israel. Hockey practices began in April of 1986 with former Canadian players as instructors. Shortly after formal instruction began, "shinny" hockey started and attracted many players who formerly lived in Canada, the United States, the Soviet Union and other traditional hockey countries.

In May of 1988, a new and larger skating rink opened in the city of Bat Yam near Tel Aviv. That same year, the Israel Ice Hockey and Figure Skating Association was founded. One of the first hockey games played in Israel was an exhibition game in July of 1988 between teams representing the rinks in Kiryat Motzkin and Bat Yam. Bat Yam won the game 8–5 before 200 spectators. Marcus Silverberg scored a hat trick and was the hero of the game.

Israel's national team played its first game in 1989–90 against a team made up of Canadian UN peacekeepers posted in the Golan Heights. Although the Israeli team featured several immigrant Jewish players from North America and the USSR, it was a native Israeli (18-year-old Gal Assa of Bat Yam) who scored the country's first goal. The first Israeli championship was played in the summer of 1990 with HC Haifa defeating Jerusalem in the playoffs. Because most of the rinks in Israel were too small for a normal hockey game, teams played with only four skaters per side.

The Israel Ice Hockey and Figure Skating Association (now the Ice Hockey Federation of Israel) joined the International Ice Hockey Federation on May 2, 1991. Israel's national team made its debut at the World Championships in the C2 Pool in 1992, losing its first game versus Spain by a score of 23–4 in Johannesburg, South Africa on March 22. Israeli hockey has received a major boost in recent years with the opening of an almost Olympic-sized skating rink at the Canada Centre in Metulla in 1995.

HOCKEY TODAY: In 1997–98, the six best Israeli clubs played a double round-robin schedule for the first stage of the national championship. The top four teams then qualify for playoffs. All series consist of one game only.

ITALY
Federazione Italiana Sport del Ghiaccio

HISTORY: The first attempts to introduce ice hockey to Italy were made in Torino in 1911 when a skating club called Circolo Pattinatori Valentino organized Italy's first hockey team. After playing a series of scrimmage games, Circolo Pattinatori Valentino played its first official game later in the year against a team from Lyon, France. Soon, hockey was gaining popularity in Italy—particularly in the north where winter mountain resorts had lots of natural ice.

The first hockey teams started to appear in Italy during the early 1920s and the country's first indoor ice rink opened in Milan on December 28, 1923. The Hockey Club Milano (which had played roller hockey) soon was playing ice hockey in the new arena. Italy's first hockey association was created in 1924 and later was admitted into the International Ice Hockey Federation. In 1925, the Italian Federation of Winter Sports was founded. The hockey association became a part of the Federation in 1926.

Italy had staged its first national hockey championship in 1924–25 but it was not until 1935 that the first national league was formed. It was made up of seven teams. From the very beginning, Italian clubs have relied heavily on Canadians of Italian descent and the eligibility of these Canadians to play for the national team helped to make it strong. By the 1970s, Italian-Canadian players helped to boost hockey in the northern part of the country, producing such strong club teams as Val Gardena, Bolzano, Brunico and Merano.

HOCKEY TODAY: In 1997–98, the Serie A league (Italy's top league) comprised 11 teams. The teams play a double round-robin schedule in the first stage, with those who finish fifth to 11th playing another double round robin. The best two teams from this stage then join the top four clubs in the final round. After that double round-robin series (with three points for a win, one for a tie), the top four teams advance to the playoffs. Semifinals are a best-of-three affair while the finals are a best-of-five. In addition to the Serie A league, a few of Italy's top teams also compete in the Alpenliga.

The next level of hockey in Italy below Serie A is Serie B1 and B2. Serie B1 has 10 teams playing a quadruple round-robin with the top eight teams advancing to the playoffs. Best-of-three series are played in the quarterfinals, with the semifinals and finals both being best-of-five. Serie B2 is divided into two groups—Group A (eight teams) and Group B (nine teams). The Serie C league has four teams. Italian juniors (under 20) have been playing

for a national championship since 1962. In 1997–98, seven teams battled for Italy's national junior title. There are also national competitions for those under 18 (11 teams), under 16 (16 teams in two groups), under 14 (eight teams), under 12 and under 10-years-old.

JAPAN
Japan Ice Hockey Federation

HISTORY: Ice hockey was brought to Japan by the English at the beginning of the 20th century. The new game quickly became popular (particularly in the northern regions of the country) and in 1929 teams located in from Tokyo, Waseda and Tomakomai founded the Japan Ice Hockey Federation.

The Japan Ice Hockey Federation became a member of the International Ice Hockey Federation on January 26, 1930. That same year, the IIHF made a decision to hold its World Hockey Championships in conjunction with the European Championships if a team was present from either Canada, the United States or Japan. The Japanese national team played its first international game at the World Championships in Davos, Switzerland in 1930, losing to England 3–0. Japan's national team continued to participate in major tournaments. At the 1936 Winter Olympics in Garmisch-Partenkirchen, Germany, Japanese goaltender Teiji Honma surprised everyone by wearing a mask. After World War II, Japan was barred from the IIHF on April 27, 1946. The Japan Ice Hockey Federation was not reinstated until March 10, 1951.

Traditionally, Japanese teams had quite a few foreign players on their rosters, especially from Canada and Russia. In 1984, the Japan Ice Hockey Federation banned the use of foreign players (though foreigners could continue to coach). This ruling was overturned during the 1990s and foreign players have returned.

HOCKEY TODAY: In 1997–98, Japan's national league comprised six teams. Each team plays the others six times for a 30-game schedule, after which the top four clubs qualify for the playoffs. Semifinals and finals are played in a best-of-three format. Japan's national champion receives the National Cup. The country's second division is comprised of regional leagues.

KAZAKHSTAN
Federatsiya Hokkeya Kazakhstana

HISTORY: Hockey in Kazakhstan dates back to the 1950s when the first teams were created in what was then known as the Soviet Republic of Kazakhstan. Torpedo Ust-Kamenogorsk became Kazakhstan's best team and in 1987–88 it made its debut in the top Soviet league after playing in lower divisions for many years.

The Kazakhstan Ice Hockey Federation was created as part of the Soviet Ice Hockey Federation in 1991. It became a separate organization when Kazakhstan gained its independence in 1992, uniting the region's four teams— Torpedo Ust-Kamenogorsk, ShVSM Ust-Kamenogorsk, Bulat Temirtau and Avtomobilist Karaganda (later Bulat Karaganda). The Kazakhstan national team made its debut at the St. Petersburg Grand Prix tournament on April 14, 1992 and beat the Ukrainian national team 5–1. On May 6, 1992 Kazakhstan became a member of the International Ice Hockey Federation and in 1993 the national team made its World Championship debut in the C Pool. Torpedo Ust-Kamenogorsk became the first Kazakh champion in 1993, though all four

Kazakhstan teams continued to compete among the Russian teams after the breakup of the Soviet Union. Until 1996, Torpedo Ust-Kamenogorsk and Bulat Karaganda played in the Inter-State Hockey League.

The best hockey player developed in Kazakhstan to date is Boris Alexandrov, who played for the Moscow Central Red Army and the Soviet national team in the late 1970s. Alexandrov won an Olympic gold medal with the Soviet team in 1976. Kazakh native Yevgeny Poladjev played for Spartak and the Soviet national team in the late 1960s and early 1970s. Andrei Raisky of Kazakhstan was signed by the Winnipeg Jets in 1992 and played in the club's farm system. Konstantin Shafranov made his NHL debut with the St. Louis Blues in 1996–97. The Toronto Maple Leafs selected Nikolai Antropov 10th overall in the 1998 NHL Entry Draft.

HOCKEY TODAY: In 1997–98, five Kazakhstan teams battled for the national title. The champion was determined after a double round-robin schedule. The best team in Kazakhstan, Torpedo Ust-Kamenogorsk, also played in the second division of the Russian league.

LATVIA
Latvijas Hokeja Federacija

HISTORY: Like most other European countries, hockey in Latvia developed from the traditional game of bandy (field hockey on ice). Bandy championships were taking place in Riga prior to World War I and the city later became the center of hockey in Latvia. Three Riga-based teams—the German Club Union, the university sport club US (Universitates Sports) and the army sports club ASK—became some of the best-known teams in Europe by the 1930s. Latvia held its first championship in 1931–32, with nine teams taking part. The national championship of the Republic of Latvia (as a part of the Soviet Union) began in 1946 and was held every year until the breakup of the USSR.

The Latvian Ice Hockey Federation was founded on January 5, 1923 and became a member of the International Ice Hockey Federation on February 22, 1931. The Latvian national team played its first international game on February 27, 1932 and beat Lithuania 3–0. Its first international tournament was the 1932 European Championships in Berlin. Prior to World War II, Latvia took part in five World Championships, including the 1936 Olympic Games in Garmisch-Partenkirchen, Germany. The most successful Latvian player of this time period was Leonid Vedejs, who played in 34 out of 36 international games for Latvia between 1932 and 1940. Latvia's final international match was a 2–1 victory over Estonia in Riga on March 10, 1940. On April 27, 1946, Latvia was ejected from the IIHF after becoming a part of the Soviet Union.

Following its incorporation into the Soviet Union after World War II, the best Latvian teams began to play for the USSR championship and Latvian players often acted as coaches for other Soviet players. The most successful Latvian team was Dynamo Riga, which produced the legendary Soviet national team coach Viktor Tikhonov. (Tikhonov worked for Dynamo Riga from 1971 to 1977.) The three most outstanding Latvian players are Helmut Balderis, who starred for the Soviet national team from 1976 to 1983, and current NHLers Arturs Irbe and Sandis Ozolinsh.

After regaining its independence following

the breakup of the Soviet Union, Latvia again held a national championship in 1991–92. On May 6, 1992, Latvia rejoined the International Ice Hockey Federation.

HOCKEY TODAY: In 1997–98, eight clubs played in the top Latvian league. Teams play a double round robin in the league's first stage, with the top four teams then advancing to play in another double round robin to determine a champion. Teams that finish fifth through eighth after stage one also play a consolation double round-robin stage. Latvian teams also play in the East European Hockey League along with teams from the Ukraine, Belarus, Lithuania and Poland.

LITHUANIA
Lietuvos Ledo Ritulio Federacija

HISTORY: Hockey in Lithuania was developed from the traditional game of bandy, as it was in most other European countries. The first ice hockey activity in Lithuania took place in the 1920s. Teams were formed in the cities of Kaunas and Memel (now Klaipeda) and the first national championship was held in 1926. LFLS Kaunas won Lithuania's first title. The Lithuanian Ice Hockey Federation was founded on October 14, 1932 and Lithuania joined the International Ice Hockey Federation in 1932. It was expelled on April 26, 1946 after becoming a part of the Soviet Union following World War II. The newly independent Lithuania had its hockey federation reinstated in 1991 and rejoined the IIHF on May 6, 1992.

The Lithuanian national team played its first international game on February 27, 1932 when it was beaten 3–0 by Latvia. Lithuania made its debut at the World Championships in Prague in 1938 and beat Romania 1–0 for its only victory in its first game of the tournament. Lithuania played its last international game in Kaunus in 1941 and suffered a 3–0 loss to Estonia. After the country became a part of the Soviet Union, Spartak Kaunus (later Zalgiris Kaunas) played in either the first or second division of the Soviet league. After 1955, the team played only in the Lithuanian Republican Championship.

Lithuania finally returned to the world stage in 1995, playing in the C2 Pool of the IIHF World Championships. Two Lithuanians— Darius Kasparaitis and Dainius Zubrus—are currently playing in the NHL.

HOCKEY TODAY: In 1997–98, the best Lithuanian team (Energija Elektrenai) played in the East European Hockey League along with teams representing the Ukraine, Belarus, Latvia and Poland. Four other Lithuanian teams play in the country's top division. Each team plays the other three six times for an 18-game schedule. The teams that finish second and third play a two-game total-goals series to determine the league's third-best team. The first-place team plays a two-game total-goals series against Energija Elektrenai to determine the Lithuanian national champion.

LUXEMBOURG
Federation Luxembourgeoise de Hockey sur Glace

HISTORY: Luxembourg's Ice Hockey Federation is one of the oldest in Europe, having been formed in 1912. Luxembourg joined the International Ice Hockey Federation on March 23, 1912, but the popularity of hockey in the country grew slowly. Luxembourg did not hold

its first national championship until 1978. Only two hockey teams existed in the country at that time and Hiversport Luxembourg defeated Beaufort Echternach for the championship. In 1984, financial difficulties forced the two teams to merge into one new club called HC Luxembourg. For two years, HC Luxembourg played exhibition games against teams from West Germany, France, the Netherlands, Belgium, Switzerland and Canada and also participated in the European Champions Cup. All home games for HC Luxembourg took place at either the indoor arena of Luxembourg-Stadt or the outdoor rink in Echternach. In 1986–87, HC Luxembourg changed its name to Tornado and played in the Rheinland-Pfalz regional league in West Germany.

The Luxembourg national team made its debut on the international scene at the C2 Pool of the World Championships in 1992. The team lost its first game to the Republic of South Africa by a lopsided score of 23–0 on March 21, 1992 in Johannesburg. In 1998, Luxembourg iced a national junior team (under 18) in the D Pool of the European Junior Championships.

HOCKEY TODAY: In 1997–98, the national champion of Luxembourg was determined in a playoff for the Luxembourg Cup. Four teams from Luxembourg as well as teams from Germany, Belgium and France take part in the tournament. Ten teams in total are split into Division A and Division B and play a double round robin with each division. Based on the rankings from both divisions, the two top Luxembourg teams play one game for their country's national championship.

MEXICO
*Federacion Mexicana de Deportes
Invernales A.C.*

HISTORY: The earliest mention of ice hockey in Mexico dates back to 1964; however, the Mexican Federation of Winter Sports was not founded until 1984. Mexico joined the International Ice Hockey Federation in 1985. At the time, Mexico boasted two indoor rinks (one in Mexico City and one in Guadalajara) and six hockey teams. The first national championship was held in 1988–89 and was won by the Association del Estado de Mexico.

HOCKEY TODAY: Currently, there is no Mexican championship. Mexico competed internationally for the first time in 1997 when a national junior team (under 20) competed in the D Pool of the World Junior Championships.

NETHERLANDS
Nederlandse Ijshockey Bond

HISTORY: The history of ice hockey in the Netherlands can be traced back to the 16th century, as artists from that period have depicted people playing "hockey" on frozen ponds with sticks and a ball. These pictures are the oldest in Europe showing people playing with sticks and, as such, it is safe to say that bandy, as an early form of hockey, likely developed in the Netherlands. Despite this early start, hockey was not introduced in the Netherlands until the early 1930s. The country's first artificial ice rink was build in the Hague in 1937, though the first indoor arena did not appear until 1961 in Amsterdam.

The Dutch Ice Hockey Union was founded on September 6, 1934 and the Netherlands joined the International Ice Hockey Federation on

January 20, 1935. The best teams in the country began competing for a national championship in 1937, but no championship was held from 1950 to 1963 because of a lack of teams. The 1960s saw Dutch clubs begin to invite players and coaches from Canada and the United States, with personnel from other European countries added later. All Dutch hockey clubs are sponsored by different companies, with the names of those companies included in the name of the team.

The Dutch national team made its debut on the international scene with a 4–0 loss to Belgium in Amsterdam on January 5, 1935. Two weeks later, the Netherlands made its first appearance at the World and European Championships in Davos, Switzerland. The Netherlands lost their first game 6–0 to Hungary on January 19, but went on to win the Fair Play Cup at the 1935 tournament. After playing in the lower levels of international hockey following the introduction of the pool system, the Dutch team made its A Pool debut in 1981.

HOCKEY TODAY: In 1997–98, the top division in the Netherlands was the eight-team Eredivisie. After a double round-robin schedule, the top four teams play another double round-robin series to determine the standings for the play-offs. Semifinals and finals are played in a best-of-seven format. Meanwhile, the teams ranked fifth through eighth after the original double round robin play their own new double round robin and playoff games. After the national championship, the top two clubs play one game for the Netherlands Cup. The next levels of hockey in the country are Division 1 (six teams) and Division 2 (eight teams). National junior competitions began in 1968.

NEW ZEALAND
New Zealand Ice Hockey Federation

HISTORY: Ice hockey has been played in New Zealand for over 60 years. Many of the early games were played on the frozen ponds in the South Canterbury mountains and teams were made up of local farm workers who had regular access to the ice. The first organized hockey tournament in New Zealand was held at Opawa near Albury in 1937. Teams competed for the Erewhon Cup, which had been presented by Wyndham Barker to the Mt. Harper club before being turned over to the newly formed New Zealand Ice Skating Association in 1937. This new association was formed at a meeting following the inaugural tournament in Opawa and though it was established for the organization of hockey, it soon became more concerned with speed skating and figure skating. Despite this fact, hockey continued to be played in an organized fashion in New Zealand except during the war years of 1939 to 1945 and from 1978 to 1982 when poor winters caused a lack of ice. In the early days of hockey in New Zealand, teams from Mt. Harper, Windwhistle, Tekapo, Irishman Creek, Fairlie, Opawa, Mt. Hull and Canterbury were regular competitors.

In 1954, the New Zealand Ice Skating Association formed an Ice Hockey Committee to administer the game. Vic Hahn was appointed chairman and the Erewhon Cup series was divided into three sections (Otago, South Canterbury and Canterbury) to cut down on travel. It was decided later that all Erewhon Cup competitions would be played on outdoor rinks. In 1957, a new competition confined to South Canterbury provided additional interest in the game. The McKerrow Memorial Cup had been

donated in the memory of Graham McKerrow, a prominent New Zealand hockey player who drowned in Saltwater Creek at Timaru after going through the ice during hockey practice.

Another notable year in New Zealand hockey history is 1963, when a team from the Hakoah Club in Melbourne, Australia made the first international visit to New Zealand by a hockey team, for a series of games at Christchurch and Tekapo. The Australian visit also marked the first time a hockey game was televised in New Zealand when Hakoah played the Hawks of Christchurch and beat them 8–6.

New Zealand became a member of the International Ice Hockey Federation on May 2, 1977. On September 14, 1986 all 19 ice hockey associations and clubs of New Zealand met at Tekapo in order to form a new federation to help develop and coordinate the game throughout the country. Thus, the New Zealand Ice Hockey Federation was created. The inaugural national club championship games for the Norm Hawker Shield were held at the Big Apple rink in Christchurch over the weekend of June 19–21, 1987. Ten teams entered the competition with the Manuwai Warriors of Auckland winning the title. That same year, a national competition for Provincial Select teams was held and won by Canterbury. Also in 1987, the New Zealand national team made its debut in the D Pool of the World Championships. The first official game took place in Perth, Australia on March 13, 1987 and resulted in a 35–2 loss to South Korea.

HOCKEY TODAY: New Zealand has several ice hockey associations which hold their own regional championships: Canterbury, Southern Districts, Queen City, Auckland, Albury, Oturehua, Alexandra, Queenstown, Gore and Ranfurly.

NORWAY
Norges Ishockeyforbund

HISTORY: The roots of hockey in Norway go back to the late 1920s when the game first began to be played in the northern part of the country. Like many other European countries, the first ice hockey players in Norway had a great deal of previous experience playing bandy. The first hockey teams in Norway were created in 1932 in Trondheim, Sandviken and Tromso. The first Norwegian national championship was played in 1934–35 and was won by the Trygg SFK club of Oslo. The 1934–35 season also saw the formation of the Norwegian Ice Hockey Union on September 18, 1934, and the inclusion of Norway in the International Ice Hockey Federation on January 20, 1935.

The Norwegian national team began its official history on February 13, 1937 when Norway was defeated 13–2 by Switzerland in the opening game of the IIHF World and European Championships. However, Norway would make its mark on the international scene by winning a bronze medal at the European Championships in 1951 and 1962. Norway's performance in 1951 also saw them finish fourth in the World Championship tournament—the highest placing ever for the team.

HOCKEY TODAY: In 1997–98, the Eliteserien— the top division of Norwegian hockey—was made up of 10 teams. After a 44-game season, the top four teams advance to the playoffs where the semifinals and finals are played in a best-of-five format. The team that finishes last in the Eliteserien is relegated to Division 1 for the following year while the top team in Division 1 is

promoted to the Eliteserien. In addition, the team that finishes second-last in the Eliteserien plays a best-of-three series with the second-best team in Division 1 to determine the final team in the Eliteserien the following season.

Division 1 consists of eight teams who play a quadruple round-robin season. Division 2 also has eight teams playing a quadruple round-robin schedule. Division 3 is divided into groups based on geographic region.

Since the late 1950s, junior and midget teams in Norway have played for a national title in their age category. The top division in junior hockey features eight teams, while the top midget division has seven teams. Both leagues play a quadruple round-robin tournament.

NORTH KOREA
Ice Hockey Association of the
Democratic People's Republic of Korea

HISTORY: The game of ice hockey in the People's Democratic Republic of Korea (North Korea) became popular during the 1950s when Soviet and Chinese workers taught the game and its rules in the capital city of Pyongyang. The Ice Hockey Association of the Democratic People's Republic of Korea was founded in 1955. North Korea became a member of the IIHF on August 8, 1964.

North Korea's first national championship was held in 1956 and was won by Amnokang Pyongyang. However, the North Korean national team did not make its debut until 1974 when it competed in the C Pool of the World Championships. The team lost its first official game to Italy 11–2 on March 8, 1974, but rebounded for surprising victories over China and Australia.

HOCKEY TODAY: North Korea's only indoor arena is in Pyongyang. It has a seating capacity of 8,000. Eight teams play in the country's top division while a second division consisting of four teams also plays a league schedule.

POLAND
Polski Zwiazek Hokeja na Lodzie

HISTORY: Ice hockey has a long history in Poland. Two hockey teams (Polonia and AZS) were formed in Warsaw in 1922, playing their first game (a 3–0 win by AZS) on February 17. Students at the Warsaw Academic Sports Union (AZS) soon were promoting the game, but hockey in Poland did not really begin to advance until 1924 when Canadian immigrant Wilhelm Rybak began demonstrating the rules and techniques of the game.

Four clubs in Warsaw established the Polish Ice Hockey Union in January of 1925 and the Union joined the International Ice Hockey Federation on January 11, 1926. Six teams took part in the first Polish national championship in 1927. In 1931, an outdoor hockey arena was built in Katowice.

Poland first participated in international tournaments in 1926 and has been entering the World Championships ever since. Polish hockey flourished during the late 1920s and early 1930s with the national team bolstered by the use of Polish-Canadians who had returned to their native country.

Among these players was Polish national team captain Tadeusz Adamowski. Brothers Adam and Aleksander Kowalski also returned from Canada and were among the best players in Europe prior to World War II. Aleksander Kowalski lost his life in the war, as did goal-

tender Jozef Stogowski, who had participated in 11 World and European Championships for Poland. A hockey rink in his hometown of Kopernik bears his name in tribute.

Polish hockey was slow to recover after World War II, but the sport slowly began to take root again. The construction of the country's first indoor artificial ice rinks in the early 1950s helped to spur a rebirth of the game.

HOCKEY TODAY: In 1997–98, the top division of Polish hockey comprised 13 teams. The six best teams play in Group A and face each other eight times for a 40-game season. The seven clubs in Group B play a quadruple round-robin schedule. All six teams from Group A and the top two teams from Group B qualify for the playoffs. Quarterfinals are played in a best-of-three format, semifinals are best-of-five and the finals are a best-of-seven. The two semifinal losers meet in a best-of-five series to decide third place, while losers from the quarterfinals play a consolation round to determine fifth through eighth place. The four best Group B teams that miss the playoffs play their own series to decide ninth through 12th place. National junior and midget competitions have been held in Poland since 1955.

ROMANIA
Federatia Romana de Hochei pe Gheata

HISTORY: Ice hockey began in Romania in 1921 when the first games took place in Miercurea Cuic. The popularity of the game grew quickly and in 1924 the Romania Ice Hockey Association was founded. On January 24, 1924, Romania joined the International Ice Hockey Federation. Until 1927, Romania's hockey association was a part of the Romanian Winter Sports Committee. In 1927, the Romanian Winter Sports Committee became the Romanian Ice Sports Committee. Four years later, it became the Romanian Winter Sports Federation. Today, the Romanian Ice Hockey Federation is in charge of the sport.

Romania's first national hockey championship was held in 1925 and won by Brasovia Brasov. The popularity of the sport increased after the country's first artificial ice rink was built in 1931, though many games continued to be played on natural ice surfaces in the country's mountain areas. Major steps towards developing the game took place in the 1940s and 1950s, including the construction of new ice rinks in Bucharest, Galati and Miercurea Ciuc in 1958. Coaches from Czechoslovakia and the Soviet Union also helped to develop hockey in Romania.

Romania made its international debut at the World and European Championships in Poland in 1931, losing its first game to the United States 15–0 on February 2 in Krynica.

HOCKEY TODAY: In 1997–98, six teams played in Romania's top division. The country's national champion is determined during a quadruple round-robin (20-game) schedule. There is also a second division in the country. Junior and midget teams have been playing for a national championship since 1960.

RUSSIA
Federatsiya Hokkeya Rossii

HISTORY: "Canadian" hockey was first demonstrated in the former Soviet Union in Moscow in March of 1932, shortly after the Olympic hockey tournament in Lake Placid. A German trade

union team called Ficheti played a series of exhibition games against the Central Red Army Sports Club and the Moscow Selects. The games attracted a small number of spectators to an outdoor rink and resulted in a 3–0 win by the Red Army and 6–0 and 8–0 victories by the Selects. The Soviet teams were comprised of bandy players (field hockey on ice) and neither the players nor the spectators were impressed with the new game. (Among the players was Alexander Igumnov, future Soviet hockey coach who developed such world-class players as Vyacheslav Starshinov, Anatoli Firsov, the Mayorov brothers, Boris and Yevgeny, Alexander Yakushev, Vladimir Shadrin and others).

The *Fizkultura i Sport* magazine gave a detailed report on the first hockey games in Russia, explaining that the rules were not to its liking: "With the rules such as they are, hockey appears to be purely individualistic and primitive," the article stated, stressing that forward passing was not permitted, which forced players to carry the puck (rather than pass it) almost all the time. "The game is very poor in combinations [passing] and in this regard cannot be favorably compared to bandy. From the viewpoint of its technique, the game is also quite primitive. The question of whether there is any need to cultivate Canadian hockey in our country should be answered negatively."

Even before the *Fizkultura* article, the Soviet sports press had derided what was called "Western hockey," describing it as a bourgeois game and therefore unacceptable to proletarian athletes. In addition, the foreign game had a strong native rival in bandy—or Russian hockey—which had been widespread in the country since the 1890s. However, despite its overall unpopularity, hockey had its supporters. "An advantage of Canadian hockey," stated the Leningrad magazine *Spartak* in its November 1931 issue, "is in the size of the ice fields. It would be possible to set up a hockey ground on any skating rink." In 1933, an attempt was made to start hockey in Moscow. The regulations of the Moscow bandy championship stipulated that five clubs—Central Army Sports Club, Promkooperatsiya, Dukat, Serp i Molot and Dynamo—were each to be represented by a hockey team as well, with the results of those games to count towards the championship. However, a shortage of proper sticks meant the hockey plans never materialized.

The next serious attempt to introduce hockey to the Soviet Union was undertaken in 1935 following a letter by K. Kvashnin, captain of the Moscow Bandy Selects, to the newspaper *Krasnyi Sport*. Kvashnin proposed to start playing the new game "as soon as possible," but plans for the game were not implemented until the winter of 1938 when the Moscow Sports Committee made it mandatory for top league clubs playing bandy in the Moscow championship to have a team of "Canadians" as well. Efforts to manufacture equipment with no competent advisors proved unsuccessful and so this attempt to start hockey also failed.

Nevertheless, the development of Soviet hockey did not stop. In 1939, the game was introduced into the curriculum of the Physical Culture Institute in Moscow. Arrangements were made to stage demonstrations of games, seminars were planned for players to share their experiences and experts in the manufacturing of hockey equipment were invited to Moscow from the Soviet Baltic republics of Latvia, Estonia and Lithuania. (The three formerly independent republics would remain members of the

International Ice Hockey Federation until 1946.)

World War II interrupted the development of hockey in the Soviet Union, but training resumed as soon as the war was over. The opening games of the first official Soviet championship were played on December 22, 1946 and the first goal was scored by Arkady Chernyshev—future coach of the Soviet national team. A major turning point in Soviet hockey occurred in February of 1948 with the historic visit of the LTC Prague team of Czechoslovakia. Almost every player on the Prague team had been a member of the Czech national squad which had received a silver medal at the recently concluded Olympic Games in St. Moritz, Switzerland. The results of the three-game series (the Moscow Selects won 6–3, lost 5–3 and tied 2–2) surprised everyone, but even more surprising was the success of the Soviet national team when it entered the World Championships for the first time in 1954. The USSR defeated Canada 7–2 in the gold medal game and would remain a power in international hockey until the breakup of the Soviet Union in 1992. Since then, Russia has become the successor to the former USSR, though the Russians struggled on the international hockey stage before earning a silver medal at the Olympics in Nagano in 1998 with a team of players with NHL experience.

HOCKEY TODAY: In 1997–98, the Russian Hockey League consisted of three leagues: the Superleague, Top League and Regional League. The Superleague comprises two groups of 14 teams, divided into East and West Divisions. Each team plays a double round robin within its division. The top 10 teams in each group then advance to the championship round, where they play another double round robin against the teams of the other division. The regular-season champion and medal winners are determined after this round. The top 16 teams then advance to the Russian Cup playoffs. The first three rounds of the playoffs see teams playing best-of-three series, with the finals being a best-of-five.

Beneath the Superleague is the Top League, which is made up of 17 teams (nine in the East and eight in the West). Each team plays a quadruple round robin within its division. The top two teams from each division and eight teams from the Superleague (the four bottom teams from each division after the first stage) are then placed in a promotion pool. The 12 teams then play a double round robin, with the two winning teams to join the Superleague the following season. The Regional League consists of five regional divisions. Regional competitions also are held every year for youth teams aged 13 to 18 with the winners taking part in the All-Russian finals. These national finals help to determine the top youth and junior teams in the country and identify prospects for the upper leagues. All aspects of hockey development in Russia are managed by the Russian Hockey Federation.

SINGAPORE
Skating Federation of Singapore

HISTORY: After initial efforts by the Touras and Marine teams to establish hockey in Singapore in the 1970s, students at the University of Singapore have begun taking up the game in recent years.

HOCKEY TODAY: So far no league has been formed, with student teams playing only exhibition games.

SLOVAKIA
Slovensky Zvaz Ladoveho Hokeja

HISTORY: The roots of hockey in Slovakia date back to the end of the 19th century when skating associations first began to appear in Bratislava (1871), Presov (1872), Poprad (1881) and Banska Bystrica (1889). Bandy was being played in Slovakia by 1902, but the first organized game of hockey did not take place until January of 1921 in the Petrzalka area of Bratislava. CSSK Bratislava defeated SK Velke Mezirici 9–2. Three years later, in 1924, CSSK Bratislava played Slovakia's first international game, losing to Wiener EV of Austria 6–1.

Hockey in Slovakia received a major boost in popularity after the European Championships of 1925 were held in Stary Smokovec and won by the host Czechoslovakians. In 1929, the Tatra Cup was held in Czechoslovakia for the first time. (Today, it is the second-oldest hockey tournament in Europe after the Spengler Cup in Switzerland.) Just one year later, the Slovakia Hockey Union organized its first official competition—the Slovak national championship. In 1931, however, the Slovak Union joined with the Czech Union to form the Czechoslovakian Hockey Union. The Slovakian Union would remain in charge of teams in Slovakia, and by 1932 the union was organized into three divisions: West, Central and East. In 1940, the union was renamed the Championship of the Slovak Republic and a new league—the Slovakian Hockey League—was formed. Also in 1940, the first artificial ice rink was opened in the city of Bratislava. Prior to this, all hockey games had been played outdoors.

After World War II, the clubs from Slovakia started to play permanently in the Czechoslovakian League. Three Slovak teams became national champions: Slovan Bratislava (1979), VSZ Kosice (1986 and 1988) and Dukla Trencin (1992). These clubs produced international stars like Vladimir Dzurilla, Jozef Golonka, Vaclav Nedomansky, Peter, Marian and Anton Stastny, Vincent Lukac, Darius Rusnak, Igor Liba, Dusan Pasek, Robert Svehla, Peter Bondra, Zigmund Palffy and others.

Shortly after the separation of Czechoslovakia into two independent countries in 1993, Slovakia qualified for its first Olympics by winning a qualification tournament held in Sheffield, England. Peter Stastny (who had represented Czechoslovakia at the Lake Placid Olympics in 1980) carried his new nation's flag in Lillehammer, Norway in 1994. Slovakia finished in sixth place at the tournament. Later the same year, Slovakia made its debut at the World Championships in the C Pool. It took only two years (and two tournament victories) to earn a promotion to the A Pool in 1996.

HOCKEY TODAY: In 1997–98, the Slovak Extraleague was made up of 10 teams playing a quadruple round-robin series. At the completion of the regular schedule, the top six clubs play a double round robin after which the top four teams qualify for the playoffs, which are played in a best-of-five format. The fifth and sixth-place clubs play their own best-of-three series. The clubs that finish from seventh to tenth in the Extraleague play a double round-robin promotion/relegation pool with the top four clubs from the First League. The four top teams from this series are promoted to the Slovak Extraleague.

Slovakia's First League has existed since 1963 as a part of the Czechoslovakian League under the name of the Slovak National Hockey League. It comprises 12 clubs playing a quadru-

ple round-robin schedule. The Second League is divided into three divisions. The East Division consists of six teams; the West Division has five teams; and the Central Division has four. Two sets of junior leagues, divided by age, each consist of 16 teams.

SLOVENIA
Hokejska Zveza Slovenije

HISTORY: The history of hockey in Slovenia officially began on February 7, 1929, when the new hockey section of the Ilirija Sports Club in Ljubljana played against a team from Kamnik, a small town near the Slovenian capital. Ilirija won the game 15–1. The team in Kamnik only had been formed at the urging of Ilirija and it fell apart after the game.

Credit for introducing hockey to Slovenia is given to Stanko Bloudek, who brought the first hockey equipment to Ljubljana from Vienna in 1928 and founded the Ilirija hockey club with Viktor Vodisek. After the demise of Kamnik, the Ilirija team had to find opponents in Austria and would play games against KAC of Klagenfurt and VSV of Villach. During the 1930s, new hockey teams were formed in Croatia and Serbia but this still provided little competition for Ilirija. The team was considered so strong that it was proclaimed the national champion of Yugoslavia by the Skating and Ice Hockey Federation in both 1937 and 1938 without playing a single game. In 1939, Irilija was again the national champion after winning a tournament in Zagreb.

The development of hockey continued in Yugoslavia after World War II, with Slovenia figuring prominently. The Slovenian club Jesenice was the champion of Yugoslavia 15 years in a row from 1957 to 1971 and players from Slovenia made up the majority of the Yugoslav national team.

The Ice Hockey Federation of Slovenia was founded in 1991 and the newly independent nation of Slovenia joined the International Ice Hockey Federation on May 6, 1992. Slovenia had held its first national championship (won by Acroni Jesenice) that year and the Slovenian national team had played its first international game on March 20, 1992, losing to Austria 1–0 in Klagenfurt. The country's debut in the C Pool of the IIHF World Championships took place on home ice in Ljubljana and Bled in 1993.

HOCKEY TODAY: The Slovenian championship is decided through a complicated system, with the country's top division divided into three groups. In 1997–98, the top three Slovenian teams (Group A) began play in the 40-game Alpenliga with teams from France and Italy. Meanwhile, Group B (made up of five Slovenian and three Croatian teams) played a double round-robin schedule with the five Slovenian teams then playing a separate double round-robin tournament. Following this, the three teams from Group A play twice each against the five Slovenian teams from Group B. After this round, the three Group A teams and the best team from Group B advance to a final group, while the four remaining teams are relegated to the consolation group. Both new groups play a double round-robin schedule. After that, the top two teams from the final group play a best-of-seven series for the national championship. The two remaining teams from the final group play a best-of-three series to decide third place. Slovenian teams also play in the international Alpenliga.

SOUTH AFRICA
South African Ice Hockey Association

HISTORY: Ice hockey as an organized sport has been played in South Africa for more than 60 years. Its origins date back to the construction of an ice rink at Wembley Stadium which was built during for the British Empire Exhibition staged in Johannesburg during the mid-1930s. The sport reached the peak of its popularity in the late 1960s and early 1970s when a semi-professional league was run at the old Wembley rink. The high level of immigration into South Africa had brought many people who had been involved in or watched hockey in their home countries. The majority of players in South Africa's first semi-pro league formed ethnically-based teams of Canadians, Germans, Austrians and Swiss with some South African players included. By the 1970s, though, attendance for games dropped and the importation of overseas players became more expensive. There was also a scarcity of ice and little time for young players to learn to skate and practice.

In recent years, the construction of additional rinks in Johannesburg, as well as new facilities in Pretoria and Cresta, has seen an increase in the number of people learning to skate and becoming involved in hockey. Presently, there are nine ice rinks in South Africa, including three that are of international size. The hockey center of hockey in South Africa is the province of Transvaal. Almost 80 percent of the approximately 1,000 players in South Africa come from this area.

The South African Ice Hockey Association was founded in 1936 and became a member of the International Ice Hockey Federation on February 25, 1937. In 1938, South Africa's hockey players played their first international game when they took on a team from Toronto. The South African national team played its first official game in the C Pool of the World and European Championships in Lausanne, Switzerland, on March 3, 1961, losing 12–3 to Yugoslavia. National championships have been held in the country since 1992 when the Roodenpoort Flyers became South Africa's first national champions.

HOCKEY TODAY: In 1997–98, four clubs played 18 games each in South Africa's top division (the Transvaal League) to determine the country's national champion. Six teams play in the second division, including three B-teams of the top division clubs.

SOUTH KOREA
Korean Ice Hockey Association

HISTORY: Although the Korean Ice Hockey Association was founded in 1928 and the first national champion (Yonsei University) was crowned in 1930, the modern history of South Korea's national championship began in 1946. Since then, university teams mainly located in the capital city of Seoul have competed annually for the South Korean championship. Korea joined the International Ice Hockey Federation on July 25, 1963.

In recent years, attendance for hockey games in South Korea has averaged about 4,000 fans, particularly when Yonsei University and Korea University (the dominant teams of 1990s) are playing. The Korean army and some major corporations also have their own hockey teams.

HOCKEY TODAY: Currently, there are two indoor rinks of international standards in Seoul—Tae

Reung and Mok Dong. In 1997–98, the Korean league was made up of seven teams (five of which represent universities). They play a double round-robin schedule with three points awarded for a win. The first-place team then receives a bye into the finals, while the second and third-place teams play off in a best-of-three semifinals. The finals are played in a best-of-five format.

SPAIN
Federacion Espanola Deportes de Invierno

HISTORY: In the early days of Spanish ice hockey, the game was played on natural rinks in the Pyrenees Mountains and the capital city of Madrid. The game first made an impact in the country at the beginning of the 20th century with a series of exhibition games featuring Canadian and British players. Spain's first indoor rink with artificial ice was built in Madrid in the 1930s. Four clubs created a hockey association in the early 1920s as a division of the Spanish Field Hockey Federation. The Spanish Winter Sports Federation was founded in 1923. On March 10 of that year, Spain joined the International Ice Hockey Federation. The country participated at the 1924 European Championships in Madrid but lost 12–0 to Switzerland in its first international game on March 12, 1924. Spain also played at the 1926 European Championships.

For the next 25 years, ice hockey was rarely played in Spain, though roller hockey was very popular. The game was revived in the 1950s, but with only a few games played among the country's three hockey teams. During the 1970s, some of the country's top soccer clubs (such as FC Barcelona) began to sponsor hockey teams as well. In 1971, Spain's first modern indoor arena opened in San Sebastian and in 1972–73 the Real Sociedad team of San Sebastian won Spain's first official championship.

HOCKEY TODAY: The best six teams in Spain played a triple round-robin schedule in 1997–98, with the top four clubs advancing to the playoffs. After a best-of-three semifinals, the winners meet for the championship while the losers play off for third place. The top two teams in Spain also play one game for the prestigious King's Cup trophy. There is a national junior championship as well.

SWEDEN
Svenska Ishockeyforbundet

HISTORY: American Roul La Mat is credited with introducing the game of hockey to Sweden. La Mat was a movie distributor who arrived in Stockholm in 1919. Already familiar with "Canadian" hockey, La Mat became fascinated by the game of bandy, which had been played in Sweden since 1896. He was impressed with the talent of the local players and believed their excellent skating skills would make them successful in hockey as well. It was La Mat's idea to enter Sweden in the Olympic hockey tournament in 1920 (this tournament was recognized later as the first World Championship), though it is unclear how he managed to convince the Swedish Olympic Committee to send a hockey team to Antwerp, considering no one in the country really understood the game at this time. Still, the committee did agree, though it granted only third-class travel expenses.

Picking Sweden's first national hockey team was not easy. The country had only one experienced player at that time. He was Nils Molander, who had been living in Germany since 1908 and played hockey for the team operated by Berliner SC. Eventually, the decision was made to send Molander to the Olympics along with the 10 best bandy players from the cities of Stockholm, Uppsala and Gavle. They received jerseys from the Swedish national soccer team, while the rest of their equipment remained bandy-style. However, once they arrived in Antwerp, the Swedes received proper hockey sticks from the American team as a gesture of generosity towards their compatriot La Mat, who served as coach of the Swedish team. Despite their newcomer status, Sweden made an impressive showing at the Olympics, finishing fourth behind Canada, the U.S. and Czechoslovakia. The gold medal-winning Winnipeg Falcons were so impressed by the Swedish team, they decided to let them score a goal. (Sweden's goal in the 12–1 defeat was the only one Canada allowed in the tournament.)

Hockey found many supporters in Sweden after the Olympic tournament. As a reward for its team's strong showing, Sweden was named the host city of the European Championships in 1921 and won the event after only one other nation (Czechoslovakia) showed up. This success, however modest, gave a real boost to the development of hockey in Sweden and on November 17, 1922 seven teams from Stockholm founded the Swedish Ice Hockey Union. In 1923, the Swedish hockey union was admitted to the Royal Sports Union of Sweden. Isaac Westergren served as the first chairman of the hockey union, to be replaced two years later by Anton Johansson, who occupied the post for 24 years.

National championships have been held in Sweden since 1922, with the first title being won by IK Gota, whose team included several players from the 1920 national team. By 1925, the game had begun to spread across the country from its roots in Stockholm, and by 1927, interest in Swedish hockey brought the first visit of a Canadian team to the country with the arrival of the Victoria Hockey Club of Montreal. The first artificial ice rink in Sweden was built into an airplane hangar in 1931 and it remained the country's only indoor arena until 1938, hosting 1,032 games over that time.

The Swedish Ice Hockey Union was instrumental in establishing hockey as one of the most popular sports in the country. It also has been responsible for maintaining a unique list of the greatest players in the country's history. The "Stor Grabb" (Great Men) are determined according to a special system of points. Fittingly, the list is headed by Swedish hockey pioneer Nils Molander of the 1920 national team, who is accorded the title of Stor Grabb #1. Over the years, Sweden's national team has come to be known as Tre Kronor (Three Crowns) for the emblem on its uniform. To date, Sweden has won the World Championships in 1953, 1957, 1962, 1987, 1991, 1992 and 1998. They also won an Olympic gold medal in 1994.

HOCKEY TODAY: Sweden's Elite League (Elitserien) was created in 1975. In 1997–98, the Elitserien features 12 teams playing a schedule of 50 games each. The eight best teams qualify for the playoffs, which are played in best-of-five series. The two bottom clubs play off in a double round-robin, promotion/relegation series against the four best teams from Division 1. The top two teams from this double round-robin

series are promoted to the Elitserien.

Division 1 has four groups (North, South, East, West) consisting of eight to 10 teams. After a double round-robin regular season, the two best teams from each group advance to play in another round-robin series to determine which four teams will move up to the promotion/relegation series. Division 2 has eight groups (two each in the North, South, East and West) with 10 to 12 teams in each group.

Top junior players in Sweden played in the Junior Elitserien, which is broken up into age groups of under 20, under 18, under 16 and under 14.

SWITZERLAND
Schweizerischer Eishockeyverband

HISTORY: Bandy was being played in Switzerland by the late 19th century, but British tourists and students later convinced Swiss bandy players to switch to hockey due to the lack of large ice surfaces in the country. The first hockey games were played in Switzerland in 1902, and soon eight clubs in the French part of Switzerland created the country's first hockey league. After the incorporation of the Swiss Hockey Union on September 27, 1908, this league officially was designated as the Swiss League. However, union officials chose to make the Swiss League an open league with clubs from other countries invited to battle for the championship. These open championships took place for five years between 1909 and 1913. Since 1916, Switzerland has held tournaments for Swiss clubs only.

Swiss players began playing games abroad shortly after the sport was taken up, with the first game taking place on December 19, 1904 in Lyon, France. One of the Swiss players in the two-game series against the Hockey Club Lyon was Max Sillig—future president of the International Ice Hockey Federation. The games consisted of two 20-minute periods. Switzerland lost the first game 3–1 but rebounded to win game two by the same score. Through the initiative of Sillig and Louis Dufour, Switzerland joined France, Bohemia and England as the fourth member of the *Ligue Internationale de Hockey sur Glace* (forerunner of the IIHF) on November 23, 1908.

Switzerland took part in the first international hockey tournament along with teams from England, France, Belgium and Bohemia, in Chamonix, France in 1909. The Swiss national team played its first game on January 23, 1909 and lost 3–0 to Great Britain, who went on to win the tournament. Switzerland finished third. A year later, Switzerland hosted the first official European Championships with games played on the natural ice of a frozen lake in the Alps near Montreux. Games at this tournament consisted of two 30-minute halves.

Hockey now was becoming popular in all parts of Switzerland, with the Akademischer Sports Club of Zurich having become the first team from the German part of the country to join the Swiss Hockey Union in 1910. In 1926, the first indoor artificial ice rink was built in Davos. Three years earlier, Dr. Carl Spengler of Davos created what has become the longest-running event for European club teams when he originated the tournament for the Spengler Cup. Over the years, Swiss hockey players would become among the best in Europe as Switzerland won four European Championships, while adding six silver and seven bronze medals. Swiss teams also won one silver and eight bronze medals at

the World Championships, including bronze medals at the Olympics in 1928 and 1948.

HOCKEY TODAY: By 1977, the top teams in Switzerland were playing in the Nationalliga A. In 1997–98, Nationalliga A had 11 teams playing a quadruple round-robin schedule. The top eight teams advance to the playoffs, which are played in a best-of-seven format. Switzerland's other national league, Nationalliga B, contains 12 teams split into East and West Conferences. A double round-robin schedule is played to determine the top three teams in each conference who advance to play in another double round-robin series. Meanwhile, the lower three teams in each conference play their own double round robin and the two top teams from this group join the six best clubs in the league playoffs, which are played in a best-of-five format. The winner of the Nationalliga B playoffs is promoted to Nationalliga A.

Lower levels of Swiss hockey include the 1.Liga (with three groups containing 36 teams), the 2.Liga (with six groups containing 57 teams) and the 3.Liga (with 12 groups and 99 teams). Top juniors in Switzerland play in the Elite A League, which has eight teams. There is also an Elite B League with eight teams each in the East and West Division.

THAILAND
Thailand Ice Skating Association

HISTORY: The Thailand Ice Skating Association was founded in 1986. Three years later, in April of 1989, the association joined the International Ice Hockey Federation.

HOCKEY TODAY: There is no national championship in the country, but the game is very popular among students at the University of Bangkok. Thailand participated in the 1998 Asia-Oceania Junior Championship.

TURKEY
Turkiye Buz Sporlari Federasyonu

HISTORY: The Turkish Ice Sports Federation, formerly known as the Turkish Skating and Skiing Union, was created in 1991. It governs ice hockey in Turkey. In May of 1991, Turkey became a member of the International Ice Hockey Federation and in 1992 the Turkish national team made its debut in the C2 Pool of the World Championships. Turkey's first hockey club was Eagologlu Istanbul and a national championship was played for the first time in 1992–93. In 1995, Turkey's national junior team (under 18) made its debut at the C2 Pool of the European Junior Championships. By 1997, more than 300 hockey players were registered in Turkey, playing on three indoor arenas and one outdoor rink. In 1997–98, the Turkish national team played in the D Pool at the World Championships and a junior team competed in the D Pool of the World Junior Championships.

HOCKEY TODAY: In 1997–98, six Turkish clubs played a double round-robin schedule in the country's top league. The winner of this tournament becomes the national champion.

UKRAINE
Federatsiya Hokkeya Ukrainy

HISTORY: Hockey has a long history in the Ukraine, dating back to 1912 when two teams

from Kharkov (Gelferikh and Feniks) played a series of exhibition games. The real development of Ukrainian hockey, however, began in 1946 when the game started to catch on in the Soviet Union. Spartak Uzhgorod played games against Vodnik Arkhangelsk in the Dynamo soccer stadium in Kiev and the team was invited to participate in the first Soviet championship in 1946–47. Prior to World War II, Uzhgorod had been part of Czechoslovakia, a country with a long hockey heritage. Players from Uzhgorod had excellent equipment and could compete well against other Soviet clubs during the first championship.

The first championship of the Ukrainian Republic took place in 1949 and was won by Lokomotiv Kharkov. In 1963, Dynamo Kiev (later Sokol Kiev) was created. It would become the best team in the Ukraine and participate in the top division of the Soviet League. In 1985, Sokol Kiev won the bronze medal in the Soviet Championship. After the breakup of the Soviet Union, Sokol Kiev played in the Inter-State Hockey League. Since 1996, Sokol Kiev has played in the East European Hockey League along with Ldinka Kiev of the Ukraine and teams from Belarus, Latvia, Lithuania and a team from Poland. Sokol Kiev also won the first Ukrainian national championship in 1992.

Before the breakup of the Soviet Union, the Ukrainian Ice Hockey Federation was a part of the Soviet federation. It became an independent body in 1992 and joined the International Ice Hockey Federation on May 6 of that year. The Ukrainian national team had made its debut at the St. Petersburg Grand Prix on April 13, 1992, tying the Russian national B-team 3–3. The Ukraine made its first appearance at the World Championships in the C Pool in 1993.

While many Canadian-born players of Ukrainian descent have played in the NHL, the first Ukrainian-trained to reach the NHL was Alexander Godynyuk, who made his debut with the Toronto Maple Leafs in 1990–91. Dimitri Khristich (Washington, Los Angeles, Boston), Alexei Zhitnik (Los Angeles, Buffalo) and Oleg Tverdovsky (Anaheim, Phoenix) are among the others who have followed.

HOCKEY TODAY: In 1997–98, the seven best Ukrainian clubs played for the national title. They play a double round-robin schedule with the top four team advancing to the playoffs. All playoffs rounds—semifinal, the third-place game and final—consist of just a single game.

UNITED STATES
USA Hockey

HISTORY: Hockey's origins in the United States are almost as old as they are in Canada, though it was not until Canadian teams began to tour the northeastern United States in the late 19th century that the game really caught on. Canadians were paid to play in the U.S. as part of hockey's first professional league in the early 1900s. The United States did not meet teams from outside North America until 1920. That year, the Americans made their international debut at the Antwerp Olympics. Led by Hall of Fame member Moose Goheen, they took the silver medal, losing only to Canada.

Until the creation of the United States Amateur Hockey Association in 1920, amateur hockey had been controlled by the International Skating Union. In 1924, the Americans repeated as silver medalists at the Chamonix Olympics. In 1924–25, the Boston Bruins became the first

team based in the United States to play in the National Hockey League.

At the end of the 1925–26 season the USAHA disbanded and left amateur hockey in the United States without a governing body until 1930, when the Amateur Athletic Union took over. In the meantime, the U.S. missed the 1928 Olympics and 1930 World Championships.

The first entirely American team to represent the country internationally was the Boston Olympics, a squad composed of Massachusetts-born players. The team placed second behind Canada in the 1931 World Championships and won another silver medal at the 1932 Olympics in Lake Placid. The USA finally upset Canada in 1933 to win its first and only World Championship in a non-Olympic year.

The growth of the game in the 1930s was sporadic. Canadian imports were taking most college hockey scholarships and there was no clear policy to develop young American players. More emphasis was placed on developing home-grown players after the Amateur Hockey Association of the United States was formed in 1937. Still, squabbles between AHAUS and the Amateur Athletic Union hampered American hockey and were not resolved until after the 1948 Olympics. With AHAUS fully in control, Olympic silver medals were won in 1952 and 1956. Notable members of the U.S. national team included Jack Riley, John Mayasich and Bill Cleary.

The 1960 Winter Olympics, staged in Squaw Valley, California, were a spectacular success for American hockey. Led by goaltender Jack McCartan, the Americans defeated Canada and the Soviet Union en route to the gold medal. This triumph spurred interest in hockey and U.S. college programs began to see more American talent. High school hockey programs in Minnesota, Massachusetts and other states began to feed increasingly skilled players into the college hockey system.

The U.S. won a surprising silver medal at the 1972 Olympics with a team that included Mark Howe and Robbie Ftorek on its roster, but the late 1960s and 1970s were not a good time for American hockey. In 1969, the United States sent more men to the moon than it did to the National Hockey League. Internationally, using

a team built around a nucleus of college players, Team USA was relegated to the IIHF's B Pool in the early to mid-1970s. Coached by Canadian Bob Pulford, Team USA finished fifth among six teams at the inaugural Canada Cup tournament in 1976.

Another Olympic triumph—widely known as the "Miracle on Ice"—took place in 1980 in Lake Placid. Many of the players on this team went on to enjoy successful careers in the NHL and the upstart squad helped to spur renewed interest in hockey in the United States. With more Americans going on to NHL careers, the late NHL and NCAA coach "Badger" Bob Johnson revamped the national team program in 1987, making greater use of NHL players. By 1991, Team USA finished runner-up at the 1991 Canada Cup. A bronze medal at the 1996 World Championships was followed with a win over Canada at the World Cup of Hockey. While the Americans were a disappointment in men's hockey at the 1998 Olympics in Nagano, the women's team that had finished second behind Canada at four consecutive World Championships finally beat its arch- rival to win the gold medal.

HOCKEY TODAY: The overwhelming majority of National Hockey League franchises are based in the United States, with more to come as the NHL expands into the new century. While most players in the NHL are still Canadians, the number of Americans in the league has increased significantly in the years since the U.S. Olympic gold medal victory in 1980. Many of the NHL's top stars today are American-born.

More American players are finding their way onto the rosters of the top major junior teams in the Canadian Hockey League and American cities are represented in both the Ontario Hockey League and the Western Hockey League. Junior hockey programs are growing in the United States, though most American prospects continue to find their way to the NHL from university teams in the National Collegiate Athletic Association.

In terms of youth hockey, USA Hockey is the national governing body that oversees the development of the sport. USA Hockey is divided into 11 districts throughout the United States. Each

district has a registrar, referee-in-chief, coach-in-chief and an administrator who facilitates learn-to-play programs for youth players and their parents. Hockey registration has increased rapidly in recent years. USA Hockey is responsible for organizing and training American teams for international competitions.

YUGOSLAVIA
Savez Hokeja na Ledu Jugoslavije

HISTORY: The origins of ice hockey in Yugoslavia date back to the early 20th century. The first team—HASK (Croatian Academic Sports Club)—was founded in Zagreb in 1906. The first official hockey games in Yugoslavia were not played until 1916–17 when HASK and another Zagreb club (I.HSK) played each other in a two-game series. HASK won the first game 2–0, while I.HSK won the second 6–0. In 1921, the Yugoslav Winter Sports Union was created in Ljubljana. In 1930, the Yugoslav Ice Hockey Union was created out of the Winter Sports Union. The Yugoslavian national team played its first game on January 30, 1934 in Ljubljana and lost 1–0 to Romania.

Yugoslavia became a member of the International Ice Hockey Federation in February of 1939. Earlier that year, the country held its first national championship. Four teams competed in the tournament on January 6, 1939, with Ilirija Ljubljana emerging as champion. The first rinks with artificial ice were opened in Ljubljana and Jesenice in 1954.

Hockey has always enjoyed great popularity in the northern regions of the country, especially in the area that is now Slovenia. Since 1991, Slovenia and Croatia have had their own independent hockey associations.

HOCKEY TODAY: In 1997–98, the top five Yugoslavian teams played a triple round-robin schedule (12 games each) with the top four clubs qualifying for the playoffs. Semifinals and finals are played in a best-of-three format. National championships for boys and juniors are held in four different age groups. A championship playdown for junior teams was first played in 1962. The corresponding boys event has been staged since 1972.

CHAPTER 35

Miracles on Ice

International Hockey's Greatest Triumphs and Tragedies

THE 1936 BRITISH OLYMPIC TEAM

Phil Drackett

THE EXCITED VOICE of an unknown, young Canadian commentator crackling across the airwaves from an open-air ice rink high in the Bavarian Alps first brought hockey to the attention of the British public. The year was 1936, Germany was hosting the Winter Olympics and the august British Broadcasting Corporation had so far forgotten itself as to schedule some match commentaries for peak evening listening-time. It needed a commentator, and Bob Bowman, a humble sub-editor working for the BBC Empire Services, got the job. He was the only Canadian broadcaster they could find.

Great Britain was playing the highly fancied USA squad.

"The score is still nothing-nothing. We're in the second overtime period—eighty minutes of hockey and still no goal has been scored. Erhardt, the British captain, is taking the puck down the ice now. He's skating fast and he's at the American defense, but he's been sidetracked into a corner and can't get his shot away. Both teams are piling into the corner to get that puck and there's a great scramble going on. There's a left-hook to the body and a right-cross to the jaw. Fists and sticks are flying everywhere. No, ladies and gentlemen, this is not a rebroadcast of the Petersen Neusel fight. This is just a broadcast of an ice hockey match between Great Britain and the United States of America being played during the Winter Olympics at Garmisch-Partenkirchen."

Then, to the frustration and fury of thousands of listeners, the BBC pulled the plug. To be fair to the BBC, the commentary had over-run already by three-quarters of an hour, a piano recital had been scrapped and the main news bulletin was late. The uproar made headlines. The BBC had 600 telephone calls and a stack of telegrams and letters. Bowman became famous overnight and was signed by a national newspaper as a featured sports columnist. The great British public suddenly became aware of the existence of ice hockey and this launched a boom which was to survive the World War II and last into the 1960s. The Empire Pool at Wembley and Empress Hall at Earl's Court were open already and Harringay Arena would be in action for the 1936–37 season, giving London three new 10,000-seat ice rinks.

Hockey, in various forms, had been played in England for hundreds of years, but growth had been much slower than across the Atlantic, mainly due to the lack of natural ice. Although England had won the first official European Championship in 1910, it was not until after World War I that properly organized leagues came into being. By the time of the Garmisch Olympics, there were still only seven teams in the English League, despite the boost Wembley Stadium's opening in 1934 had given the game.

However, playing standards were improving and the British Ice Hockey Association had a new president, successful business executive Philip Vassar Hunter. He had learned to play hockey on the frozen fens of East Anglia, where, allegedly, the game originated centuries earlier. He recruited a new secretary for the association, a jovial Irish travel agent named J.F. "Bunny" Ahearne, who never had been on skates in his life. This unlikely couple determined that Great Britain would compete in the 1936 Olympics and would improve on their past record. In 1924, the British had finished third behind Canada and the United States and, in 1928, fourth to Canada, Switzerland and Sweden. Both British teams had been largely composed of Canadian Army officers and university graduates living in the U.K.

Hunter and Ahearne decided that the 1936 entry must have puckchasers who were both British-born and good, so it was decreed that each of the seven league teams must have a minimum of four British-born skaters, thus creating a pool of at least 28 players to choose from. The other requirement was a first-class coach. They chose Canada's finest. Percy Nicklin, a burly graduate of minor professional "knock 'em down and drag 'em out" hockey, twice had led the Moncton Hawks to the Allan Cup, emblematic of Canada's senior amateur championship. He was recruiting players from Canada for the Brighton Tigers and Richmond Hawks of the English League and was to coach Richmond himself, so a deal was worked out whereby he would coach the British squad as well.

Several British-born players were among those he brought across the Atlantic, and one of them was to prove a priceless asset. Jimmy Foster, a dour Glaswegian goalminder, nicknamed "the Parson" because he once harbored thoughts of entering the church, was reckoned by many to be the best goalie in the world, even better than those playing in the NHL. The pros were not paying big money and it was said that Foster got a more lucrative contract in England. Nicklin decided to build his team around Foster, adopt a defensive strategy and choose strong, tireless, two-way skaters who would cover closely and backcheck every time their own goal was threatened.

A series of trial matches was staged and, of course, as coach of Richmond, Nicklin had plenty of opportunities to study the available talent. Given a free hand, he came up with Jimmy Foster and Art Child in goal; captain Carl Erhardt, Bob Wyman, Jimmy Borland and Gordon Dailley, defense; and forwards Edgar Brenchley, Jimmy Chappell, Alex Archer, Gerry Davey, Archie Stinchcombe, Johnny Coward and Jack Kilpatrick. All but Dailley were born in Britain, though all but Erhardt and Wyman had been taught hockey in Canada.

Born in Glasgow on September 13, 1907, Foster did not make headlines until after breaking his leg in two places

and being warned that he might never play again. But play again he did and in four seasons with Moncton he smashed every record in the book. The first netminder to register two straight shutouts in the Allan Cup finals (2–0 and 3–0 against the Saskatoon Quakers in 1931–32), he played in all but one of Moncton's 220 games while he was on the roster, and once went 417 minutes without being scored on (a Canadian record). Years later, Dr. Bob Broderick of McGill University, who later captained Streatham in the English National League, recalled watching Foster in the later stages of his career, playing in the Quebec Senior League. "He would stop a high shot on the back of the stick hand and smother the puck with the other hand as it hit the glove. It demanded flawless timing and the way Jimmy did it, with a graceful upsweep of both arms, was pretty to watch. But then Jimmy had style."

Foster's backup, Art Child of the Wembley Lions, English-born in 1916, had similar shutout exploits in minor hockey. As a 13-year-old, he conceded only one goal in a 17-game schedule. The captain—and oldest man in the Olympic tournament—Carl Erhardt, was born on February 15, 1897, and celebrated his 39th birthday during the Games. He learned his hockey in Germany and Switzerland, where he went to school, and first played for Great Britain in 1931. He captained the team in the 1935 World Championships. A rusher and an awkward man to get around, Erhardt had the old Corinthian approach, which meant that although he was rarely, if ever, guilty of dirty play, he wasn't above flattening an attacker who presumed too much.

Four of the team had been born in London within a few miles of each other, although they didn't know one another prior to being taken to Canada by their parents. Wyman and Archer had been born in the West Ham neighborhood, Davey in Barking, and Brenchley was also a Londoner. Wyman, small for a defenseman, was still a rough handful and compensated for lack of inches with exceptional speed, having been a British half-mile and mile speed skating champion and record-holder. Davey, who was with Streatham, was one of the most experienced internationalists among the forwards, although one of the youngest. He was only 16 when his mother brought him back to England from Port Arthur, Ontario, and was drafted onto the national team almost right away. By the time of Garmisch, he had been chosen to play 100 times for his country.

Archer, a crafty winger with the Wembley Lions, learned his hockey around Winnipeg but was also a good soccer player, and he had to make a choice between the two sports. Brenchley, a right-hand shot who could play center or wing, was very similar in many respects.

Even more versatile were Dailley and Borland, both of whom were equally at home on the blue line or up front, thus increasing Nicklin's options. Dailley, born in Winnipeg on July 24, 1911, joined the Grosvenor House Canadians in 1931 and played for them when they won the English Championship in 1933–34 (when he was first chosen for the national team). In 1934 he was signed by Wembley. Under the Olympic rules then prevailing he was eligible for Britain because he had played for her in international matches prior to the Games. Manchester-born Borland (Brighton Tigers) was the same age as Dailley and played with him on the Grosvenor House title-winning team and with Great Britain.

The rest of the team, like Borland, were Northerners. Archie Stinchcombe (Streatham) and Jimmy Chappell (Earl's Court Rangers) both came from Yorkshire, but Stinchcombe was taken to Canada at six months, whereas Chappell was 10 years old when his parents emigrated. He was a late starter in hockey but soon caught up, playing with Ontario schools and the intermediate champions before signing with the famed Oshawa Generals.

Stinchcombe played with the OHA champion Windsor Mic Macs and he and brother Jack (three years older) were scheduled to play at the 1932 Olympics in Lake Placid, but in the end Great Britain, along with most other European nations, could not afford to send a team to the United States. It might have given Stinchcombe a remarkable record, for he was to captain Great Britain in the 1948 Olympics.

Coward, whose second home was Fort Frances, Ontario, was a Richmond player like Brenchley and Foster. He was a controversial choice for the Olympic team, having a poor record as a marksman, although he was a good, strong skater. "Nicklin wanted me as a defensive skater. I hardly ever went over the opposing team's blue line. But if anybody broke loose it was my job to stop them from scoring."

The lineup was completed with the youngest member, John Kilpatrick, of the Wembley Lions, who was just 18 when he played against Sweden in Great Britain's opening match. He was believed to be the youngest player in the tournament.

This was the group which, under the leadership of Nicklin, set off for Germany on what was regarded as a forlorn hope against the might of Canada, unbeaten in Olympic history, and the strongly-fancied Americans. The British were not even fancied to take the European title since Germany, the host nation, Switzerland, Czechoslovakia and Austria all had strong teams. However, Canada had problems. Normally represented by the previous season's Allan Cup Champions (in 1935, the Halifax Wolverines) the Canadian Amateur Hockey Association found that the Halifax coach and five star players had signed for clubs offering better pay.

So, the CAHA chose the losing Allan Cup finalists, Port Arthur Bearcats, to represent Canada. The Montreal Royals, who had lost to Halifax in the semifinals but given them a harder fight than Port Arthur, objected. Finally, a team was chosen comprising four Halifax men, two from Montreal and seven from Port Arthur. Four days before the team was due to sail for Europe it was announced that Montreal's Ralph St. Germain was being added to the team and that the four Halifax men were being dropped for asking for "broken-time" payments to maintain their families while they were away. All hell broke loose, but the Association would not give way, and named Pud Kitchen (Toronto Dukes), Hugh Farquharson, called "hockey's best amateur," and Ken Farmer (Montreal Victorias) plus goalminder Dinty Moore (Port Colborne Sailors) to replace the unfortunate quartet. Not content with his own troubles, CAHA President E. A. Gilroy ("not an easy man to deal with," commented Erhardt) objected to a number of players in the English League, including some of the Olympic team, because they allegedly did not have permission to leave the jurisdiction of his association. Jimmy Haggarty of the Wembley Lions was one of those on the list but his name mysteriously disappeared from it—after the CAHA had decided to add him to Canada's Olympic lineup! Eventually, Gilroy gave way—for the period of the Olympics only. Cynics observed that he didn't think Great Britain had a chance anyway.

Britain began against Sweden with Foster in goal, Erhardt and Borland on defense (in those days it was common for a defense pair to play right through the game), Brenchley centering Archer and Kilpatrick and Chappell between Davey and Dailley. With three minutes gone, Brenchley fired a long shot from behind the blue line and caught the Swedish netminder napping. From the face-off, Brenchley got the puck to Archer, the right winger laid one on Kilpatrick's stick and the youngster bulged the rigging, only to hear the referee call offside. The Swedes were on the offensive in the second period but Foster came up with a couple of brilliant saves. In the third, the Scandinavians collected a couple of quick penalties, Dailley took a pass from Borland to beat the Swedish goalie, Carlsson—but a Swedish defender got his stick to the puck and cleared it off the line. The Swedes came back but Nicklin kept switching his lines and Foster did the rest.

Japan was next, more experienced than many realized, having competed in the World Championships as far back as 1930. Nicklin, still seeking his best lineup, brought in Wyman to partner Erhardt on defense, moving Borland up to center in place of Chappell. Coward and Stinchcombe were brought in for their first games, replacing Davey and Kilpatrick. Brenchley picked up a loose puck around the net halfway through the first period, drew Honma out and put Britain ahead. Two minutes later, Archer's backhand went into the net off the goalie's arm. The Japanese goal continued his charmed life in the second period, and early in the third a penalty to Wyman brought the Japanese back into the game. Towards the end they tired and Jimmy Borland broke away to make it 3–0, taking Britain into the next round. Sweden later beat Japan 2–0 to also go forward.

In the tournament's Group A, Canada lived up to its reputation and blasted its way past Austria, Latvia and Poland, Austria beating the other two for its passport into the second round. Group C went much as expected with the Czechs and Hungary going through, France and Belgium going out. The shocks came in Group B, where two of the most fancied European teams, Germany and Switzerland, were pitted against the U.S. and rank outsiders Italy. The Americans almost blew it, losing 2–1 to the lowly Italians. They then beat Switzerland but scrambled home against Germany with the only goal of the game. Germany also went through.

There were no easy rides from there on in. Great Britain drew Canada, Germany and Hungary in the next round; the U.S. was grouped with Austria, Sweden and Czechoslovakia on the other side of the draw. Britain's first match was against Canada and Nicklin had to select his strongest roster. Foster in goal and Erhardt the captain were automatic choices. To partner Erhardt on defense, Nicklin chose Dailley, whose size and speed gave him the edge over Borland and Wyman. Four of the forwards—Chappell, Davey, Archer and Brenchley—picked themselves. It left two to choose from four—Coward, Stinchcombe, Kilpatrick and Borland. Coward, the best backchecker on the team, and Stinchcombe, improving with every game, got the nod.

On the eve of the big match, the blow fell. Davey, a goal scorer on a team otherwise noted for defense, took to his bed with the flu. Then, an hour before face-off, he appeared in the dressing room, heavy-eyed and pale-faced, and announced he was going to play. In a drama right out of the *Boys' Own Paper*, he put Great Britain ahead after only 40 seconds with one of the long shots which seemed to be a

British speciality. Ten thousand fans went wild. The British had their supporters, but many of the crowd were Germans suddenly awake to the possibility that if Britain could upset the Canadians, Germany might yet take the championship. The thrills came thick and fast. The crowds forgot the cold, although they stamped their feet hard enough, the noise ringing round the stadium. They applauded enthusiastically the great plays and miraculous saves of both sides.

Then at 13:40, Ralph St. Germain, Montreal Royals captain, tied the game. He came out of the corner to score from close in, the first goal Foster had conceded in the tournament. But the Glaswegian was at his brilliant best in the second period. Chappell outskated opponents to the corners and the Erhardt–Dailley duo was rock-like on the blue line. It went into the third with the teams deadlocked but the odds on Canada. The British were outgunned and outclassed but still Foster came up with save after save. There were just 90 seconds on the clock when Canada regrouped for another all-out attack on the phlegmatic, gum-chewing goaltender. As they hit the British blue line, Dailley lunged forward, intercepted the puck and found himself in the clear with only the lone figure of the Canadian custodian in the distance.

Brenchley, quick to realize the situation, skated furiously after his defenseman. Dailley let fly as soon as he got in range, the shot was padded away but Brenchley raced in to sink the rebound. Great Britain 2, Canada 1.

Following their victory over the Canadians, Britain then drew 1–1 with Germany after three overtime periods and beat Hungary 5–1 to reach the medal round with Canada, who had beaten Germany 6–2 and Hungary 15–0. In the other grouping, the U.S. topped the table by defeating Sweden, Czechoslovakia and Austria with the Czechs also advancing.

Under the tournament rules, teams did not play any opponent a second time, so Britain did not have to meet Canada again nor did the U.S. have to play the Czechs. The first match of the finals was for the European championship and saw Great Britain beat the Czechs 5–0 with a hat trick from Davey and singles from Chappell and, just to prove he could do it, Coward.

Canada beat the Czechs by an even bigger margin, 7–0, before the British and Americans met in the game Bob Bowman described so enthusiastically over the airwaves. Scoreless after three overtime periods, the result effectively ended Canada's hopes but left the U.S. with an outside chance. If the Americans could beat Canada in the final match without conceding a goal or win by 5–1 or more, they could take the title on goal average. It didn't happen. Tired after their marathon the previous night, and with skipper Johnny Garrison injured, they were defeated 1–0.

The final standings were:

  1) Great Britain
  2) Canada
  3) U.S.
  4) Czechoslovakia

Britain became the first team in hockey history to win the Olympic, World and European Championships. The entire team was elected to British hockey's hall of fame, the only team so honored, but for all of them nothing ever would equal the night a bunch of "no-hopers" defeated the might of Canada. Nicklin could well have said those words immortalized by another coach:

"Win this one and we will walk together forever."

THE LOST GENERATION:
THE CZECHOSLOVAKIAN NATIONAL TEAM OF 1950

Igor Kuperman

ON SATURDAY, MARCH 11, 1950, a group of athletes who couldn't hide their emotions gathered at the Prague airport. The Czechoslovakian national hockey team was ready and waiting for a flight to London, where the Wembley Empire Pool would host the World Championships. They were on their way to defend the world title they had won the previous year by defeating the mighty Canadians. The crew of an aging Dakota was also waiting impatiently, but the players still weren't on board. The departure time came, and went, and the players and flight crew still waited. Finally, after four hours, a reason—of sorts—was proferred; the reporters hadn't gotten their visas, the whole team had to wait. Frustrated, puzzled, concerned, the players were later informed they would have to go to the office of the Czechoslovak Ice Hockey Union the following Monday. After waiting again a few hours for that meeting, they were told, "You're not going to London." This time no explanation was offered, nor much response to a number of questions the team asked, with some heat.

The players repaired to the Golden Pub, a small bar in Prague, but even after a few beers tensions didn't dispel. Loudly blaming the Minister of Foreign Affairs and the Minister of Information for their woes, they were further fired up by the news on the radio when it was announced that the team had decided not to go to London because of some sort of protest. As the discussions grew ever more heated, another group entered the bar who nobody had seen there before. First they met face to face with forward Vaclav Rozinak, who was about to go home. Catching his hand, one of the strangers asked where he was going. "That's none of your business," replied Rozinak. Another of the new group grasped Rozinak's jacket so hard that the buttons came off—which signaled a fracas that was all over in a few minutes. All the players were handcuffed and taken to a special bus.

None of the proud defending world champions knew yet they weren't dealing with a regular police force but with officers of the national state security agency, the KNB, forerunner of the KGB in Czechoslovakia. The confused players were put in two jails, still thinking they had been arrested for the fight in the bar. When Rozinak came back to his cell after fingerprinting, another inmate asked him, "How many fingers did they print?" When Rozinak said 10, the fellow told him: "I don't want to scare you, but you may not leave this cell at all. Only people who were brought here by the KNB give all their fingerprints."

Almost seven months later, on October 7, 1950, the players appeared in court on a suit that was styled a "process of anti-state group." For the first time, the players were informed they were guilty of espionage and were named as "state traitors." The main argument against them was the fact that in December of 1948, the players of LTC Praha (most of whom played for the national team) had discussed the possibility of defecting in Switzerland after the Spengler Cup had been played in Davos. The court claimed the entire national team wanted to defect after the World Championships in London.

Some questionable events had indeed taken place in Davos, but the players had never intended to hide anything. The trouble had started when an immigrant who called himself a member of the Committee of Free Czechoslovakia approached the most high-profile players, brothers Vladimir and Oldrich Zabrodsky, and suggested they persuade the rest of the team to defect and play in the British professional league. The world championship title (which Czechoslovakia had won in 1947 without Canada present) would be a great advertisement. A few hours later, the entire team gathered in Vladimir Zabrodsky's room at the Hotel Belvedere.

Everybody spoke out and it was decided that the entire team—not just a few—might defect. The next day, December 31, 1948, a few members of the team witnessed Vladimir Zabrodsky's conversation with the instigator. Zabrodsky asked for money, 60 or 80 thousand Swiss francs, but the two didn't agree to anything. Later that day, Zabrodsky suddenly suggested to the players that they should go home. When they decided to take a secret vote, the majority voted against defection.

The trip to Switzerland had been rather eventful—and in fact there had been several defections. One of the heads of the Czechoslovak delegation defected in Davos and, later, during an exhibition tour in Zurich, players Oldrich Zabrodsky and Miroslav Slama followed suit. At their hotel in Bern, Czechoslovak immigrants passionately tried to convince the players not to return to communist Czechoslovakia. The players, however, tried to avoid such conversations and even asked the Czechoslovak Embassy to protect them. In Zurich, on the way from the hotel to the bus on the last day of the trip, the players were physically separated from team management by a crowd of immigrants and police involvement was necessary.

None of the remaining Czechoslovakian players had ever seriously considered defection, though they'd had quite a few chances to do so: in Sweden in 1949 during the World Championships, in Vienna in 1950 as they prepared for the tournament in London. Always, the team had returned without incident. But these facts were not taken into consideration by the Czechoslovak Supreme Court and at 8 p.m. on October 7, 1950 the players were sentenced. Goaltender Bohumil Modry received 15 years in prison, forward Gustav Bubnik, 14 years; forward Stanislav Konopasek, 12 years; Vaclav Rozinak and Vladimir Kobranov, 10 years each. Seven other players were given sentences ranging from eight months to six years.

Most of the players spent five years in prison, after which their passion for the game—to say nothing of their lives—was seriously damaged. Modry, for example, arguably the greatest Czechoslovak goalie of all time, was released from prison at age 39 and couldn't go on with his brilliant career. He had been one of the LTC Praha players who made an historic trip to Moscow in 1948 for the first international games against Soviet hockey players. Now he was all but forgotten. During the World and European Championships in Czechoslovakia in 1959, nobody from the Czechoslovak Ice Hockey Union even invited him to watch the games. (Surprisingly, Soviet coaches Anatoli Tarasov and Arkady Chernyshev did. They brought Modry to their team bus and he sat on the Soviet bench at every game.)

In 1963, just a few months after Modry's death, Tarasov and Chernyshev were in Czechoslovakia again and invited Modry's widow, Erika, to their hotel. "I came into the room and saw Tarasov, Chernyshev and couple of high officials from the Czechoslovak Ice Hockey Union," she recalls.

"Tarasov introduced me to the officials and said: 'This is Mrs. Modry. Do you know who her husband was? He taught us how to play hockey and we will never forget that.'"

It remains uncertain why it was decided that Modry was the "main figure" in the potential defection plan—particularly in light of the fact that by 1950 he was no longer a member of the national team—but the official decision that he was the ringleader also profoundly affected 21-year-old Gustav Bubnik. Despite the difference in age, he was a close friend of Modry. It was the decision of the court that "Modry influenced the situation through the help of Bubnik." The young star forward was one of the few players who appealed the court decision. On December 22, 1950 the appeal of his 14-year sentence was declined, but Bubnik was able to talk to the court chairman right after that. "I remember him well," Bubnik says. "He wasn't afraid to talk to me. He said, 'You were used as an example for all Czechoslovak athletes. The decision wasn't made in the courtroom.'"

The toughest months for Bubnik were in prison in Bor. "The jail was right near the Plzen Winter Stadium," he recalls. "In the evenings I heard the sounds of the game. It was very depressing. Once, when depression was really heavy, I made a small figure of a hockey player out of fleece. I dyed him in the national team colors and sewed him into my pillow." Later, Bubnik had a chance to play again. He met Rozinak and Konopasek in prison and they were allowed to play a game against a team from Moravia. They built the rink, made the sticks and were ready to play. Then, just a few days before the event, Bubnik was granted his freedom. He was released on January 21, 1955.

After their sojourns in prison, many of the players did resume their careers. Bubnik played seven more seasons and later became a famous coach. Appointed coach of the Finnish national team in 1966, his team defeated the Czechoslovakian squad 3–1 at the World Championships in Vienna the next year—after which he received a number of telegrams from Czechoslovakia to the effect that, "The prison is still waiting for you!" Premysl Hajny became the coach of the Swiss club Servette and won a silver medal with his team. Stanislav Konopasek coached the Polish club GKS Katowice to a championship title. Zlatomir Cerveny worked with Olympia Ljubljana in Yugoslavia. Vladimir Kobranov and Vaclav Rozinak coached in Switzerland.

Ironically, many of the men who were once deemed "state traitors" dedicated their lives to promoting their homeland's hockey style all over Europe.

1950 VVS AIR FORCE MOSCOW

Igor Kuperman

FOR 40 YEARS, THIS STORY WAS COVERED by the darkness of secrecy. Only in the 1990s, after several years of glasnost and perestroika, have most of the details become public knowledge.

It all started in the middle of the 1940s. World War II was just over, but not a lot changed in the tough regime in the Soviet Union. The specter of Josef Stalin, styled "the Great Father of All Nations," still ruled people's lives—with both fear and love. And by then his son, Vasili, had ascended to very high office as a major-general and commander of the Military Air Forces of the Moscow Region. But Vasili Stalin was bored with his job and conceived the idea of creating his own fiefdom in the form of a sports club. Soon he was focusing more attention on this project than on his few teams of "pilots."

Vasili Stalin's new sports teams nominally represented the Military Air Forces of the Moscow Region and were known as VVS-MVO, or just VVS (*Voenno-Vozdushnye Sily*), and competed in soccer, hockey, volleyball, basketball, water polo, horse-racing etc. Finding top-class athletes wasn't a problem. Vasili deployed the despotic methods he had learned from his father's example; he simply stripped other teams and took their best players. Some were enlisted to fulfill mandatory military service. Others were promised apartments, cars, bigger salaries—all impressive perks in harsh postwar conditions.

With almost all the best sportsmen in the country, the VVS teams quickly rose to the top and became medal winners and champions. Only in soccer was Stalin less than successful. All the best Soviet players in that sport were concentrated in Central Red Army and Dynamo (police) clubs, and to "borrow" from them was impossible.

The hockey team was created in 1946, just before the first Soviet national championship was staged. Obtaining the best players could not be guaranteed for the simple reason that hockey was still so new in the USSR and nobody yet knew who the best players were, so the VVS team was made up mostly of the former bandy players at the Moscow Aviatechnical College. When Stalin decided the VVS players would wear jerseys with blue and yellow stripes, fans soon started to mock them by called them "mattresses." The team finished fifth in 1947 and seventh in 1948. Angry and disappointed, Vasili found a quick way to fix the problem. He extended invitations to four top players from Spartak and to few players from other teams. VVS finished second in 1949. Young and strong, they were poised to launch a dynasty, but catastrophe struck.

A regular-season game was scheduled in Sverdlovsk. Since a train took three days, the management (a.k.a. Vasili Stalin) opted to charter a military plane for January 7, 1950—their last flight. The plane crashed near Sverdlovsk at the Koltsovo airdrome.

There are conflicting stories of what happened. In one version, the pilot of the SI-47 aircraft tried six times to land in the dark amid blizzard conditions. He misjudged the location of the airdrome's field, noticed too late, tried to move the plane up but could not and crashed into the field. Another version stated that the plane's powerful landing lights were suddenly switched on in the darkness and blizzard. Thinking that the front of the plane was on fire, the players all moved to the rear, the pilot lost control and the plane fell from the sky. "I think this version is very close to the truth," said Nikolai Puchkov, a great Soviet goalie who became a member of the VVS after the crash. "Guys didn't like the flights. They were nervous." There were still other versions, but Colonel Vasilenko, then an air traffic controller who investigated the crash, clearly denied the idea that the crew wasn't sufficiently qualified, lacking flight experience in blizzard conditions. "All the pilots were members of a special division which served the government members," he said.

By Stalin's order, Boris Bocharnikov had been named the playing coach for the Ural Mountains road trip and was given a pair of good quality foreign skates. They were found at the crash site with blades twisted in mute, ugly testimony. No one survived. The 19 on board—11 players, a team doctor, a masseur and crew members; none survived—were buried near the site of the crash. Goalie Harijs

Mellups (the best in the country), defensemen Robert Shulmanis (added to VVS from Riga along with Mellups) and Boris Bocharnikov, goal scorers Ivan Novikov and Zdenek Zikmund (both also members of the Soviet national tennis team from 1944 to 1949, Zikmund having won six straight national titles in doubles with future hockey commentator Nikolai Ozerov), Yuri Tarasov (younger brother of Anatoli Tarasov) and Yuri Zhiburtovich were the best players lost in the crash.

Today there is a small plaque with the names of the 19 people interred near the site of the crash, but at the time there was absolutely no information in the newspapers about the disaster. Even players' immediate relatives weren't informed right away and knew nothing about it for quite a few days. Very few people in Moscow knew either. The team's fans heard only rumors.

On January 8, 1950, the day after the crash, two hockey games took place as scheduled at the outdoor Dynamo stadium in Moscow. In the middle of one, the announcer asked a few people to come to a room inside the arena. Former VVS players and the team's young reserves were told that Vasili Stalin would like to see them immediately. Within 15 minutes, the players arrived at the headquarters of the Military Air Forces of Moscow Region, where Stalin addressed them, head down, regarding the floor. "His face was black, he cried heavily and said just one phrase, 'The boys are dead'," recalls Nikolai Puchkov. The players were told to report immediately to Chelyabinsk—by train—for an upcoming game.

A few days later, VVS started to play again, but the censors prohibited writers from even mentioning the names of the new players. Only when Vsevolod Bobrov and Viktor Shuvalov scored were their names mentioned. The newspapers printed stories that whispered vague nothings like: "VVS won the game … The pilots scored the goal … The VVS goalie played well …" The name Zhiburtovich was sometimes mentioned—without a first name or initials—but this was Yuri's brother, Pavel. Yuri Zhiburtovich had been a little bit late for the flight that January morning. He ran across the airdrome at full speed and was barely in time to get on the plane.

Fans who attended a VVS game in Moscow a few days after the crash were surprised to see that the team looked different, but the preeminent players—Bobrov, Shuvalov and Alexander Vinogradov—were still on the ice. They'd been lucky. Star center Viktor Shuvalov had just been added to VVS from the Chelyabinsk team and Vasili Stalin didn't want him to go to Sverdlovsk and Chelyabinsk. "Chelyabinsk officials and fans will be very upset and unhappy if they see you in a VVS uniform," he told Shuvalov, who later became one of the outstanding forwards on the Soviet national team. Defenseman and team captain Alexander Vinogradov was suspended for two games for slashing and also didn't make the trip.

But the most tantalizing rumors surrounded the great Vsevolod Bobrov. How had he missed that flight? The most popular version of the story suggests that Bobrov was in a restaurant with friends the night before and couldn't get up on time the next morning.

Another asserts that Bobrov arrived at the airdrome on time and asked playing coach Boris Bocharnikov: "Why we are flying so early? There's still a few days before the game." When Bocharnikov said the main reason was to have a few more practices, Bobrov replied, "If somebody can't play, let them practice; I'll go by train," and left.

Another explanation arrived in 1953—from Bobrov himself. He only completed 12 pages when he was writing his memoirs, but fortunately he started his book with this episode.

"I came back home at 10 p.m. and soon went to bed. The flight was scheduled for 6 a.m. the next morning. I set up the alarm clock for 4 a.m. I really trusted this clock, it had worked perfectly for many years. … I don't know what happened. I suddenly woke up at 6:15 a.m. My clock had stopped during the night and the alarm didn't ring! That same evening, I took a train. Days later, I found out that this alarm clock saved my life!"

Stocked with new players, the VVS team continued to play its scheduled league games but finished the season in fourth place. The new talent simply wasn't able to replace the lost stars. Some sources, for example, indicated that Puchkov couldn't skate and his teammates had to take him onto the ice holding both of his hands. Puchkov laughed when he heard it. "It's a joke."

Before the start of the 1950–51 season, VVS was reinforced yet again. Five excellent players joined the team from all four Moscow clubs—Central Red Army, Dynamo, Spartak and the Soviet Wings—and VVS began its true reign. The team didn't lose a game during the 1950–51 season and became Soviet champions by beating their rival, the Central Red Army. Legendary coach Viktor Tikhonov was then a defenseman with the VVS team, while playing coach Bobrov was the best scorer in the Soviet league with 42 goals. After the last win, he said, "We did it for our dead comrades." They won again the next year, but it was more difficult. VVS was tied in points with the Central Red Army at the end of the schedule. A decisive game was scheduled for January 24, 1952. Bobrov (the best scorer again that season with 37 goals) scored twice and VVS won 3–2. In 1952–53, the VVS team finished one point ahead of Central Red Army. Bobrov was seriously injured that season and Shuvalov was the best scorer with 44 goals.

The VVS players really liked Vasili Stalin, but they were also afraid of him. Sometimes he told the players he had "just talked to my father, who was upset with the result of the game," which had predictable results on the players' emotions, when the truth was that Josef Stalin's interest in sports was only for its propaganda value both at home and abroad. He cared little for the day-to-day action of VVS or any other sports team.

"I spent three years watching Vasili Stalin closely," recalls Nikolai Puchkov. "He attended all our games, and was often in the dressing room before and after the game. I can't say anything bad about him. His face looked like his father. He was very emotional. He loved the players, and cared about us. He was an excellent pilot, and showed us his skills on the plane in the sky. Yes, he was a big drinker, and this fact created a lot of tension between him and the Ministry of Defense."

Viktor Shuvalov also recalls that, "Vasili was very friendly with us, always shook hands, asked about any kind of personal problems—and helped to solve them."

The younger Stalin was often emotional. Once, when VVS trailed Lokomotiv 5–1 and Bobrov scored five goals to pull out a 6–5 victory, an elated Stalin presented his star player with a gold watch. But he also possessed a mercurial temper. A few days before the accident in 1950, Vasili had fired VVS coach Matvei Goldin for the simple reason that when VVS lost a game to Dynamo, Goldin congratulated the opposing coach, an old friend, for the victory.

Stalin couldn't have known at the time his rash reaction had saved Goldin's life.

Shortly after Joseph Stalin died on March 5, 1953, his son was dismissed as commander of the Military Air Forces of Moscow Region. All VVS teams were immediatcly disbanded. Most of the hockey players joined the Central Red Army.

There is no information in any Soviet hockey publications as to why VVS, champions of 1951, 1952 and 1953, didn't participate in the next championship; that topic was strictly forbidden. Still, those who died in the plane crash were never forgotten by their fellow players. Whenever the Central Red Army team played in Sverdlovsk, the players put flowers on the grave of their fallen comrades.

THE ORIGINAL U.S. MIRACLE TEAM

Stan Fischler

IT SEEMS LIKE A CENTURY AGO, but the first "Miracle on Ice" happened in 1960. Some of the names—Ken Yackel, Bill Christian, John Mayasich—are a little dusty. Others such as Tommy Williams of the Washington Capitals still shine like new. Those who participated in those 1960 games will tell you that there never was, and may never be, an upset like the one the U.S. hockey team pulled in Squaw Valley, California.

"We were definitely underdogs," said coach Jack Riley, who had been selected to head the U.S. club after guiding the United States Military Academy hockey team at West Point. "We couldn't possibly win a gold medal. At least that's what they all said before we hit the ice." Riley's 1960 Olympians were to do more to bolster the prestige of American hockey than any other team since the 1938 Chicago Black Hawks, a club sprinkled with Americans that won the Stanley Cup. Their most formidable opponents would be the Russians and the Canadians. It was not believed to be even remotely possible for the Americans to topple either of these power teams.

The tournament began with three round-robin groups of three teams. The top two teams would advance from each group to play for the medals. The U.S. defeated Australia 12–1 and Czechoslovakia 7–5 to advance.

With six teams left in contention, coach Riley's first challenge was to prepare his club to face the Swedish national team, traditionally a strong-skating, hard-shooting club. The favored Swedes were routed 6–3. The U.S. then defeated Germany 9–1, setting the stage for a showdown with Canada.

The Canadians looked like the better team for much of the game, as they poured volley after volley at goalie Jack McCartan. "All I could see," said McCartan, "were streaks of green Canadian jerseys." McCartan made 39 saves, most of them difficult, and allowed only one goal. "He made one incredible save after another," said Riley. The Americans scored twice and won the match 2–1.

On Saturday, February 27, the Americans faced off against the Soviet team. More than 10,000 spectators jammed Blyth Arena for the contest while millions watched the game on television. After two periods, the clubs had battled to a 2–2 draw, but more importantly, the Americans proved that they could skate with the fleet Russians. For nearly 15 minutes of the final period, the rivals tested goalies McCartan and Nikolai Puchkov and neither gave an inch—until 14:59 of the period. Roger Christian and Tom Williams teamed up to feed the puck to Billy Christian, who found himself one-on-one with goalie Puchkov. "When the goalie came out of the net to cut down the angle," recalled coach Riley, "Billy outsmarted him and slid it in. That was it because McCartan wasn't going to let the Russians score again." The final score was United States 3, Soviet Union 2.

Only Czechoslovakia remained to blunt America's bid for a gold medal. And for a time it appeared that Riley's stickhandlers would blow it all on the final day of the championships. They were tied with the Czechs 3–3 after the first period, but fell behind 4–3 after 40 minutes. At that point a strange twist of fate helped the Americans. Nikolai Sologubov, a crack Russian defenseman, visited the Americans dressing room and offered Riley some advice. "He suggested that our players take some oxygen to restore our pep," Riley recalled. "As it turned out, some of our guys took his advice." Whether the oxygen did the trick or not will remain a point of debate for hockey historians as long as the 1960 Olympians are discussed. Whatever it was, the Americans stormed onto the ice and nearly knocked the Czechs off their skates.

Roger Christian alone accounted for three goals in the last period. He tied the score 4–4 at 5:50 of the period. Then Bill Cleary put the Americans ahead 5–4, following that with a power-play goal. Within a 38 second span, Roger Christian and Billy Cleary scored, and then Roger closed the scoring at 17:56 for the sixth and final goal of the period for Uncle Sam's skaters. The final score was 9–4 for the United States. America had won its first Olympic gold medal in hockey. "We had become a team of destiny," said Riley. "We won because of conditioning, spirit and a real desire to bring home the gold medal. The players had a deep belief in the old adage that there's no substitute for victory!"

THE REIGN OF THE RED:
1963–1971 SOVIET NATIONAL TEAM

John Sanful

AT THE 1963 WORLD CHAMPIONSHIPS in Stockholm, Sweden, the national team of the Soviet Union won the first of what would become nine consecutive gold medals. This unprecedented feat never has been equaled in the annals of international hockey history and is not likely to be matched. The period of Soviet domination from 1963 to 1971 marked a new era in hockey and launched an eastern European sports dynasty during a tension-wracked decade still chilled severely by the Cold War. It was the beginning of the legend that would become Soviet hockey and a period that eventually would change the way the game was played.

In addition to political tensions between east and west, the Cold War provided an opportunity for the Soviets to further their ideals through sports. A constant struggle to wage propaganda battles against the United States took place during this time with athletics often as the centerpiece of the battle. This emphasis on sports had been implemented during the 1940s by dictator Josef Stalin, who ruthlessly sought to conquer the hearts and minds of the world population through impressive, well-trained Soviet athletic programs. With its period of successive World Championship and Olympic victories between 1963 and 1971, Soviet ice hockey earned recognition throughout the world as the premier athletic program ever to compete in international hockey. This fact translated into social well-being for the

Soviet population, as hockey had become an essential staple in the life and athletic endeavors of the country. It also influenced how the Soviets—both athletes and the general population—were viewed by the rest of the world. With "the Big Red Machine" dominating its opposition, the Soviets were acknowledged both for their important contributions to the growth of the game and loathed because of their success. As legendary defenseman Viacheslav Fetisov recalls: "We played against the best professional teams and we beat them. We won the international tournaments we played in and it was always a road game for us. And people hated us because we were the Soviets."

The Soviet Union made a compelling enemy not only for the Americans, but for Canada, Czechoslovakia, Sweden and Finland, and many memorable matches with political implications took place during their championship reign. Even after the Czechs ended the Soviet streak in 1972, the anticipation of beating the USSR was always a key part of international hockey. Past Soviet successes were what made their defeat at the 1976 World Championships in Poland, where the Soviets lost to the Polish national team, such a shock. It is also what made the victory by the United States in 1980 so miraculous. Given the political tensions of the last four decades, the Soviets were a perfect enemy and their talent made them easy to hate.

Hockey long has been a game of dynasties, including the Montreal Canadiens of the 1950s and the New York Islanders and Edmonton Oilers of the 1980s. Dynasties recall legendary tales of competitions won and spark endless debates about who was the greatest of all time. The Soviet dynasty of 1963 to 1971 is one that often is overlooked. Because they were (technically) an amateur team, it is perhaps too easy to dismiss their accomplishments, but it cannot be denied that the Soviet style of this era changed the way the game was played, first in the USSR and later throughout the hockey world. As a result of this period of what legendary coach Anatoli Tarasov called "high collectiveness," the Russian philosophy of skating and passing was emblazoned on future generations of players like Viacheslav Fetisov, Igor Larionov, Sergei Makarov and even the current crop of Russian stars in the NHL. It heightened interest in the game domestically and made hockey second only to soccer as the Soviet Union's most popular national pastime. The USSR's period of domination also led to interest from NHL officials hoping to match their best against the Soviets and dispel the myth of the great Tarasovian philosophy. This desire helped to pave the way for the historic Summit Series in September of 1972 and eventually led to the introduction of Russian players to the NHL during the late 1980s and 1990s. Had the period of 1963 to 1971 not been as dominant, or resulted in only sporadic success, it is doubtful there ever would have been the amount of interest there was in "the Big Red Machine."

Led by the courage and playmaking skills of Konstantin Loktev, the all-around finesse of Anatoli Firsov and the relentless coaching style of Anatoli Tarasov, the Soviet string of nine World Championships (including two Olympic gold medals) from 1963 to 1971 clearly made them the best international team in the world. To better understand this so-called decade of gold requires an examination of the history of hockey in the motherland.

Soviet hockey began in earnest just prior to World War II with an intensive study program at the Moscow Institute for Physical Culture. Russians had been playing bandy (field hockey on ice) on the cold winter fields during the rule of Czar Nicholas II, and the popularity of the game managed to survive the 1917 Revolution. Hockey made very few inroads in the Soviet Union during the 1920s and 1930s despite its success in other eastern European countries, and the study of the sport truly did not begin until the introduction of the application of physical culture. Physical culture theoreticians contended that, to be good Communists, all Russians should be strong in both body and mind. A well-conditioned, healthy comrade was the spiritual embodiment of the ideal Soviet citizen. Exercise and adherence to the principles of the state were important above all else. Hockey was scrutinized carefully, debated and eventually played. The debate by Kremlin officials between bandy and hockey was intense, but in the end most agreed that hockey had the best chance of advancing the primary objective: establishing the Soviet sporting empire.

With the advent of the Cold War, the Soviets became interested in using spectator sports to promote their ideology. Kremlin officials set their sights squarely on competing against—and defeating—other countries (especially the United States) in matches of physical and athletic prowess on a grand scale. The policy of garnering gold medals (often called rekordsmenstvo) was handed down directly from Josef Stalin, who wholeheartedly endorsed the plan of using sports as a tool for ideological intrigue. The obvious outlets were the Olympics and World Championships. This was where the greatest emphasis could be put on competing collectively, winning gold medals and making strong statements to the rest of the global community.

During this period of physical culture, Anatoli Tarasov emerged as an important figure within the hockey ranks. As a former bandy player and student at the Moscow Physical Culture Institute, he was intrigued by the possibilities of his country's newly adopted sport. Indeed, Tarasov would remain fascinated with hockey until his death in 1995. At first a successful player, he later became an outstanding coach with the Red Army hockey club (CSKA) and led them to several Soviet hockey league championships. Tarasov was a tireless worker who practiced his players hard and expected nothing short of their best effort. Chosen by Soviet sports authorities to oversee the development of a national hockey team, Tarasov would come to be recognized as the architect of Soviet hockey.

With Anatoli Tarasov, one could only expect the unexpected. He devised training methods both on and off the ice that were considered radical at the time. Many years later, though, hockey programs from the NHL to youth hockey would implement guidelines based on the methods Tarasov had devised to keep his comrades in shape.

Since artificial ice surfaces were at a premium in the Soviet Union, Tarasov devoted much time to off-ice activities and a rigid dry land training program that included long distance running, soccer and swimming. Through his off-ice program, players were in peak physical condition and could skate forcefully with endurance. Once on the ice, they would practice like loyal party members, learning to incorporate their individual talents into a system that would help the overall goals of the team. The philosophy of passing and skating was what was stressed above all, with the understanding that effective skating would open up the ice and allow for the strategic setting up of plays in the opposition zone for prime scoring chances.

"For Tarasov, the most important aspects of the game were the development of skills and implementing tactics," says Igor Kuperman, former Soviet journalist and Russian

hockey authority. "They were essential. Tarasov's ideas helped put the Soviets on a level that never had been achieved before. He would make use of three different line combinations that were so different from each other that opponents did not know how to defend against them. That was important."

By 1953, Tarasov believed the Soviet national team was ready for formal international competition. However, shortly before the USSR was to make its debut at the World Championships, Vsevolod Bobrov suffered an injury. Bobrov was a legendary soccer star who was also the Soviets' best hockey player. Despite the loss of its superstar, Tarasov still believed that team good enough to compete for a gold medal, and he lobbied tirelessly for inclusion at the games. But the Kremlin would not allow it. Without Bobrov, Russian officials did not wish to risk embarrassment and the wrath of Josef Stalin. Stalin had been so angered by the Soviet soccer team's loss to Yugoslavia at the 1952 Olympics that he had not permitted the results of the game to be printed in Soviet newspapers. (It was not until after his death that Soviet citizens learned of the loss in 1952.) The debut of the USSR at the World Championships would have to wait until 1954 when Moscow Dynamo coach Arkady Chernyshev guided the Soviets to the gold medal in Stockholm with a 7–2 win over Canada's East York Lyndhursts in the final game. Only the Soviets themselves were not surprised by the victory that stunned the rest of the hockey world. They had been preparing for the big moment for a long time.

In 1956, the Soviet team made its debut at the Olympics and won another gold medal, but after a disappointing second-place finish behind Sweden on home ice in Moscow at the World Championships in 1957 (in a tournament that was boycotted by Canada and the United States because of Soviet action in Hungary), Tarasov was installed as head coach of the national team in place of Chernyshev. Still, the Soviets could not recapture their gold medal form. Tarasov's driven, often volatile personality began to interfere with the development of the national team and his feuds with players like Bobrov did not help matters. Soviet hockey head Leonid Khomenkov began pressing for the adaptation of the Canadian hockey model and hoped to enlist the help of coaches from Canada. This, he believed, would allow the Soviets to better compete with their western rivals at international competition. Tarasov saw things differently. He argued that if the Soviet Union was going to promote its Socialist ideals along the structures of physical culture, it was important to stay the course by working on the Russian rendering of hockey. To do anything less would be an admission of failure that he thought was not yet proven. After the third-place finish behind the United States and Canada and the Squaw Valley Olympics in 1960, Khomenkov again argued for some adaptation of the Canadian style of hockey. Again Tarasov argued in opposition. He was replaced as coach when Chernyshev was reinstalled in 1961, but his persistence would soon reap incredible dividends.

In 1963, Tarasov and Chernyshev were designated as co-coaches of the Soviet national team. The two only had been marginally successful individually, but in tandem this Soviet "Odd Couple" (Tarasov fiery and stubborn, Chernyshev diplomatic and laid back) worked together with great success. Beginning at the 1963 World Championships in Stockholm (where the USSR first had tasted success nine years before), the Soviets launched the

most prolific winning streak in international hockey history. The indomitable Soviet hockey legend would grow from the gold medal success in 1963, and while the victory that year could not help but make an impression on Tarasov, he was not as satisfied as his western counterparts. As he would later write: "Summing up the Stockholm Tournament, the foreign press moguls noted that our boys had been trained well for high speed skating and were very active. However, even then I could see that in skating at high speeds we could do much more than we were doing."

It was the relentless style of Tarasov that kept the Soviet teams improving upon their skills and tactics until they were virtually unbeatable. His manner would rub off on many of his players who would later go on to coach themselves, including Konstantin Loktev and Vladimir Yurzinov. Yurzinov was the leading scorer for the Soviets at the World Championships in 1963 and would go on to coach the Moscow Dynamo to the Soviet League championship in 1990. He also enjoyed a successful coaching career in Finland with TPS Turku, and later earned a silver medal for Russia at the 1998 Olympic Games in Nagano, Japan.

The development of hockey players in the Soviet Union was at its zenith during the golden years of 1963 to 1971. Pioneers in the sport like Vsevolod Bobrov and Viktor Shuvalov were old and out of the game, but their influence on the sport led to the development of key members of the 1960s teams. Sports schools had opened up all over the country and many boys (as young as seven) were playing hockey, with the philosophy of passing and skating ingrained in them so that when they might reach a league team or the national team they would be thoroughly schooled and know what to expect. This was the USSR's finest period in cultivating athletes, and while the Soviet system would continue to produce world-class athletes for another three decades after 1963, the players produced between 1963 and 1971 were among the greatest ever. The three players introduced to the national team during the 1960s who would arguably hold the highest significance were Anatoli Firsov, Valery Kharlamov and Vladislav Tretiak. Kharlamov and Tretiak came after the dynastic 1960s teams were well into their gold medal run, but Firsov was a key member of those great teams.

Anatoli Firsov is considered by many to be the greatest Soviet hockey player of all time. He was an exceptional athlete, blessed with great speed, instinctual offensive talent and heart. Tarasov first saw him play as a member of Spartak and immediately recognized his potential, enlisting him for both the Red Army and the national team. Firsov went on to enjoy a brilliant career as the player his teammates looked to in the clutch. He was a fluid hockey player whose artistry took Soviet hockey to a new level. As graceful as he was talented, Firsov was the player always watched most closely by opponents, drawing considerable praise (as well as penalties) from opponents in almost every international game he played.

Perhaps more than any other player, Firsov was the one who led Canada to press for the inclusion of professional players in international hockey. Canadian officials became particularly irked when Firsov scored six goals in a game as the Soviets defeated the Canadian national team 10–2 in Ottawa in an exhibition game on January 24, 1969. Many in Canada came to believe that the only way to compete with the Soviets—who were, after all, seasoned hockey men playing against young boys—was to employ the country's

top pros. Hockey Canada, created to handle Canadian hockey manners, petitioned the International Ice Hockey Federation to clarify the rules for amateur status and asked for professionals be used. Olympic President Avery Brundage (a staunch supporter of amateurism) asserted his influence when he told other international participants that any team that played against Canada would lose their Olympic eligibility. This was a punishment that the Soviet Union would not risk. In January of 1970, the IIHF ruled against the Canadians, who responded by boycotting officially sanctioned international events until 1976. In the meantime, this would touch off a period of intense negotiations that resulted in the Summit Series of 1972.

Even with the brilliance of Anatoli Firsov, what made the Soviet Union so formidable was the depth of its roster, which included stars like Konstantin Loktev, Boris Alexandrov, Alexander Ragulin, Slava Starshinov, Veniamin Almetov and Boris and Yevgeny Maiorov. The five-man A-Line unit of Loktev, Almetov, Alexandrov, Ragulin and Eduard Ivanov was the engine that led the Soviets from 1964 to 1967 until Firsov was ready to assume the mantle as a top-line player. In terms of the way they executed Tarasov's game plans, the A-Line can be seen as the unit that set the stage for other great Soviet combinations like the KLM line and the Green Unit of the 1980s of Krutov, Larionov, Makarov, Fetisov and Kasatonov. As Firsov and, shortly thereafter, other top athletes developed, the transition between the decades was smooth.

Another hallmark of the Soviet national team during its championship run from 1963 to 1971 was its adaptability. Tarasov was looking constantly for new and innovative ways to revise how the team approached opponents tactically. The fundamental premise, however, always remained true to his philosophy of passing and skating with the economic use of shots on goal. Every pass was intended to build on the previous one until finally someone was in a perfect position to receive a precision pass and score. Tarasov schooled his players to function as good Socialists because they all worked together and interacted with each other, their top priority being a commitment to implementing the system properly. There was no room for freelancing. And though he remained the singular voice in the Soviet hockey program, there was some sense of democracy among the players. They were participatory members of the program when it came to voting on which new players would be promoted to the national team and on determining whether or not to discipline a player for breaking any of the rules that they had all agreed upon. For Tarasov, it was important that his players feel some sense of participation in what they were doing but that he be the final arbiter in hockey decisions. This relationship was a key to World Championship success.

While always remaining true to his system, Tarasov was able to adapt his team's style to the teams they would play against. Czechoslovakia always had been among the top hockey playing nations in Europe, and the Czech national team was becoming more and more impressive during the late 1960s and into the 1970s. Tarasov understood the Czechoslovakian threat by 1965, and held lengthy discussions with his players, devising a plan for an all-out aggressive attack formulated to keep the Czechs off the puck and give them little room to set up any plays. The strategy was effective, as the Soviets continually managed to beat Czechoslovakia for the gold, with the Czechs forced to settle for silver four times and bronze twice at the World

Championships and Olympics between 1965 and 1971. After the Soviet invasion of 1968 crushed the democratic reforms of Alexander Dubcek in Czechoslovakia, the Czechs came to despise the USSR as much as the countries in the west. Hockey games between the two countries became battles of nationalist pride from that point, particularly for Czechoslovakia. The Czechoslovakian victory that ended the reign of the Soviet Union at the World Championships in 1972 was an emotional high not only for the Czech players involved but for the entire country.

Though the achievements of the Soviet Union between 1963 and 1971 were stunning, there were constant questions as to whether or not they were really the best hockey players in the world. In Canada, almost no one was willing to take the Soviets seriously. Canadians wanted to match their NHL stars against the Soviet players and put them in their place. The conventional wisdom held that because international hockey was played on a larger ice surface and because the Europeans—and the Soviets in particular—did not play a physical game, their players would be no match for the tough NHL players. Only the Soviet national team members, with the principles ingrained in them by Anatoli Tarasov, believed they had a chance. In truth, they were confident of a series victory when they stepped on the ice at the Montreal Forum on September 2, 1972.

If it were not for Paul Henderson's winning goal with 34 seconds remaining in the eighth game of the 1972 Summit Series, the Soviet hockey program no doubt would have earned even more distinction for their success between 1963 and 1971. There is also little question that had games with NHL teams been possible in the 1960s, as they were later in the Super Series of the 1970s and 1980s, that the Soviet players of that era would have made a much greater impression in North America. Those athletes were the complete model for Soviet society, combining skill, hard work and camaraderie—and owing it all to a scientific approach to sports. Their success against NHL competition in 1972 was anything but a fluke and their previous reign could be compared with the Montreal Canadiens teams that won the Stanley Cup five consecutive times from 1955–56 to 1959–60. That's how good "the Big Red Machine" was.

SUMMIT SERIES –1972
Frank Orr

SOMETIME, SOMEWHERE, a hockey confrontation could produce a higher level of play and competition, more drama and involve more sociology and politics than the 1972 Summit Series.

Of course, that could happen but not likely.

The first meeting of the national team of the old Soviet Union, always called the Russians, and the top NHL pros on Team Canada was of such spellbinding magnitude that hockey, called "a major part of the country's social fabric," has not been the same since Paul Henderson's goal at 19:26 of the third period of the eighth game gave Team Canada the slimmest victory possible.

After the four games in Canada, the Soviets had two wins, Canada one plus a tie. When the Soviets won the first game of four in Moscow for a 3–1–1 lead, the series appeared to be theirs. But the Canadians fought back to win the next three with Henderson scoring the winner in each.

Twenty-five years later, during the 1997 silver anniversary of the Summit, arguments continued to rage about the

influence of those 27 days in September, 1972.

A clash between the heavily favored Canadian team, which, for the first time in international play, included top NHL players, and the Soviet team, amateur hockey's best for two decades, was more complex than simple hockey.

The series became a battle between political philosophies, democracy versus communism, freedom against oppression, us versus them, even something beyond that.

"It was war and, yes, hell for us whether we wanted it or not," said center Phil Esposito, the best player in the series, the pivotal leader for the Canadians.

"The Canadians battled with the ferocity and intensity of a cornered animal," said Anatoli Tarasov who is considered to be the godfather of Soviet hockey, the fabled coach who guided its hockey program from its earliest days to world championship and Olympic domination.

"They believed the stories of their hockey superiority and which were not quite correct," Tarasov continued. "Our players were better conditioned physically and stronger in skills than the Canadian professionals. But we could not match them in heart and desire, always the strongest part of the Canadian game."

Some claim the series' influence on how hockey is played in Canada and the NHL was a slow evolution, each side learning from the other. But others say that when small Soviet forward Valeri Kharlamov held off two large Team Canada defenders with one arm and stickhandled the puck around them with the other hand on his stick for the goal that gave the Soviets the lead in the opening game, Canadian hockey never was the same again.

"Until then, NHL players never worked on their upper-body strength and seldom used off-ice training," said John Ferguson, assistant coach of Team Canada.

"Sure, a few jogged in the summer but, mostly, players came to training camp and skated themselves into condition. In 1972, we discovered that the Russians had superior upper-body strength to us. Within a couple of seasons most NHL teams hired conditioning specialists and off-ice training became important. We also looked at such basic skills as skating and passing and how we trained goalies."

Different playing styles injected much interest into the Summit. Team Canada stuck with the NHL approach of shooting the puck into the opposition's zone and then trying to regain it with physical forechecking. The Soviets used an approach learned from soccer of retaining the puck and passing it into scoring position.

"We believed in puck control in all areas of the ice; the NHL believed in territorial advantage, especially playing more in your zone than in their own zone," said Vladislav Tretiak, the brilliant Soviet goalie, 20 at the time.

"The NHL players fired many hard slap shots but we thought that was inefficient. We used short, quick passes to create a high-percentage shot on goal. To us, the man without the puck was the most dangerous because he could go to an open area to receive a pass."

Analysts of the series and its influence point to alterations in off-ice preparation by the Canadians, and changes in playing style by the Soviets.

"I have not noticed a big improvement in their teams since 1972 but they have picked up some things from our game," said Team Canada coach Harry Sinden, general manager of the Boston Bruins since 1972.

"I had played against them in 1958 (with the Whitby Dunlops, Canada's victorious entry in the World Championships) and a playing style was developing then that has been the basis of the Russian game ever since.

"Up to the time they played pro teams regularly, if the Russians had no play at the opposition's line, they would retreat with it and try again, instead of shooting it in and forechecking. Gradually, they changed.

"The Russians always skated with shorter, choppier strides which gave better balance and strong lateral movement. A basic difference—and this has changed very little—is that a Russian accelerates as he receives a pass and does not change strides while NHL players tend to slow down when the puck comes their way.

"After 1972, they slapped the puck more and instead of always trying to pass to the man in the slot in front of the net, they shot more from the sides. And, of course, they learned to play along the boards and in the corners, where we really had our edge in the big series.

"The 1972 series opened NHL and Canadian hockey minds considerably and in the next few years, all sorts of new ideas were tried, some retained, many discarded.

"We did not use just the good parts of Russian hockey. Canadian teams found that the Russians utilized interference as a tactic. Their 'pick' play was extremely frustrating to our guys."

The pick is when an attacking player not in possession of the puck skates directly at an opponent, frequently making contact with the defender, which allows the puck-carrier to advance unfettered.

"Deliberate picks had not been a big part of NHL play but after 1972, offensive interference became much more common in our game," Sinden added.

"I suppose the best thing about 1972 was the big picture. The wonderful play, the incredible drama, the enormous interest in all hockey countries led to a very large airing out, for the want of a better phrase, on the entire game of hockey, heavy thinking and serious discussions of even small aspects of the game."

While such top NHL stars as Esposito, Frank Mahovlich, Jean Ratelle, Rod Gilbert, Yvan Cournoyer, Brad Park and Serve Savard, exerted much influence, Canadian "foot soldiers," as they are called by NHL teams, spurred large shifts in the Russian approach. Forwards Wayne Cashman, Jean-Paul Parise, Ron Ellis and Pete Mahovlich, who excelled in the corners and along the boards, and defensemen Gary Bergman, Bill White and Pat Stapleton, strong defensively, were a major part of the Canadian triumph.

"We saw hockey as an open game to be played in a large area," said Russian center Alexander Maltsev. "The pros could reduce the space for smaller battles. The Canadians taught us the importance of controlling play along the boards and going after the puck in the corners much more eagerly than we had."

"After 1972, we looked for bigger defensemen so an Esposito could not set up his shop in front of our net and stay there," said goalie Tretiak.

The buildup for the Summit really began in 1954 when the first Soviet national team to enter the World Hockey Championships won the gold medal by defeating Canada, which was represented by a second-level senior amateur team. Until then, Canada sent low-ranked teams and easily handled the other countries in the global tournament. Strong senior teams won the world crown in 1955, 1958 and 1959. But a 1961 crown by the Trail Smoke Eaters was not repeated by Canada until 1994 when a team of NHL players won the gold medal. The Soviets won 28 of the 41 World and Olympic championships in that stretch.

Formation of Hockey Canada to foster the game's growth domestically and oversee international participation started negotiations for the Summit Series in 1969. Strong by then, the NHL Players' Association and its executive-director Alan Eagleson promised support of the top players for such a series. Eagleson played a large role in staging the Summit.

"The NHL first said that no NHL player would play for Canada," Eagleson remarked long after the series had ended. "But the players promised me they would defy any such order and the NHL [eventually] backed our idea."

But in 1972, the World Hockey Association, established as an NHL rival, became a reality. When Bobby Hull, the charismatic superstar of the Chicago Black Hawks, counted as a leader of the Canadian team, jumped to the new league, a controversy erupted.

The NHL decreed that if players who had signed with WHA teams were on the Team Canada roster, the NHL would withdraw its players. Hockey Canada was forced to agree with that edict and drop Hull, goalie Gerry Cheevers, defenseman J.C. Tremblay and center Derek Sanderson, setting off a loud protest in Canada.

The next blow to the Canadian team was a knee problem that kept defenseman Bobby Orr, the NHL's best player, out of the series.

Thirty-five Canadian players assembled in Toronto for training camp that began on August 14. The fact that no opponents were available for tune-up games was not viewed as a drawback because of supreme confidence in the ability of the team to handle the Soviets.

The surprise of the camp was the emergence of the forward line of veteran Toronto Maple Leafs wingers Henderson and Ellis flanking Bobby Clarke, an emerging star with the Philadelphia Flyers. As the training period progressed, the line played its way into a starting role.

While the Soviets scouted every Canadian practice, Team Canada checked out the comrades for only three days. On a trip to Moscow, the late Bob Davidson and the late John McLellan of the Leafs saw one workout and an exhibition game. They reported back that they were not impressed with the Soviets, especially goalie Tretiak, who surrendered eight goals in an intra-squad game. Tretiak had good reason not to be focused on his job: His wedding was the next day.

Summit interest had Canadians talking of little else as the opening game at the Montreal Forum on September 2 approached. Soviet practices after their arrival in Montreal were not impressive, some players wearing skates with blades that were welded in place.

But the Soviets showed two superb forward lines— Vladimir Petrov between Mikhailov and Kharlamov, the elegant Alekxander Yakushev and Vladimir Shadrin with a variety of linemates, often the brilliant Maltsev. His honeymoon over, Tretiak emerged as an extraordinary young goalie, wiping out the myth that the Soviets could not develop good netminders.

The atmosphere in the Forum that muggy September evening carried a tension that had been seldom equaled in the history of this fabled arena. The Soviets came away with a 7–3 win, scoring three goals in the concluding 10 minutes, to throw Team Canada's players, coaches and, in fact, an entire country into a state of shock.

Sinden made lineup changes for the second game in Toronto, sitting out several stars to upgrade the team's toughness. Splendid goaltending by Tony Esposito and a memorable shorthand clinching goal by Peter Mahovlich were crucial in a 4–1 Canadian victory.

Tretiak was magnificent in a 4–4 tie at Winnipeg in the third game, but in game four at Vancouver, the Soviets used careless penalties by the Canadians to build a 2–0 first period lead on their way to a 5–3 victory.

The Vancouver fans loudly booed Team Canada, especially in the third period when the players were struggling against the superior conditioning of the Soviets. That inspired Phil Esposito to deliver an impassioned speech in a post-game television interview that stamped him as the team's leader.

"To people across Canada, we're trying our best," Esposito said. "Everyone of us—35 guys that came out and played for Team Canada—we did it because we love our country and not for any other reason. They can throw the money out the window; we came because we love Canada. Even though we play in the United States … Canada is still our home and that's the only reason we've come [to play]. I don't think it's fair that we should be booed."

The players, seemingly abandoned by their own supporters, felt that Esposito's speech marked a turning point in their evolution as a team.

But more controversy awaited when the Canadians stopped in Stockholm for two exhibition games against the Swedish national team in an attempt to adjust to the larger European ice surface before the four games in Moscow. The games were very rough, with scorn heaped on Team Canada for rowdy tactics.

Before the first Moscow game, the Canadian team endured another crises. Veteran winger Vic Hadfield and youngsters Jocelyn Guevremont, Richard Martin and Gilbert Perreault—all of whom had seen little if any game action—left the team and returned to Canada.

However, 3,200 Canadian hockey fans accompanied the team to Moscow and their loud support boosted the players' outlook. But the first game in Moscow's dingy old Luzhniki arena placed Team Canada in an even deeper hole. Henderson's second goal of the game gave the Canadians a 4–1 lead early in the third period, but the Soviets scored four consecutive goals for a 5–4 win and a 3–1–1 lead in the eight-game series.

"We were having a rough time in Moscow with the defections, the lousy hotels, phone calls to the players' rooms in the middle of the night, the Russians snatching much of the food we had sent over for the team, especially the steaks and beer, and the terrible refereeing by the European officials," Sinden said.

"But a long cheer at the end of the first game in Moscow by the Canadian fans was a big lift for our spirits."

In game six, Canada produced three goals in 1:23 in the second period, then held on for a 3–2 win. That game contained the most controversial incident of the series when Clarke slashed Kharlamov on an already tender ankle, handicapping the Soviet star for the duration of the series.

In the seventh game, two goals by Esposito offset Russian scores by Yakushev and Petrov in the first period. The second was scoreless, then in the third, Rod Gilbert sent the Canadians ahead but Yakushev tied it again. At 17:54 of the third period, just when a tie appeared certain, a long pass from Serge Savard hit Henderson at center and while being knocked to the ice, he managed to unleash a shot that went between Tretiak's arm and body for a 4–3 win to tie the series.

The decisive game eight was preceded by a bitter fight over the officials. The Canadians were promised that German referees Franz Baader and Josef Kompalla would

not work again in the series. (Nicknamed "Badder and Worse" by the Canadians, the German officiating tandem had whistled 31 minutes of penalties—versus just four minutes for the Soviets—in game six.)

The seventh game had been officiated properly by Uve Dahlberg of Sweden and Rudy Bata of Czechoslovakia and the Canadians assumed they would handle game eight. But the Soviets threatened Dahlberg with a ban from IIHF work if he did not say he was ill. That meant Canada's choice, Bata, and the Soviets' pick, Kompalla, handled game eight.

Few Canadians who were alive on September 28, 1972, did not watch the game on TV or listen on radio, broadcast live in the afternoon. In schools across the country, classes were dropped to allow students to watch the game, many of them assembled in auditoriums or gymnasiums. Vehicle traffic on the streets was very light and few pedestrians were on the sidewalks.

The game started badly for Team Canada. Ridiculously cheap penalties left them two men short for more than a minute and Yakushev scored a power-play goal to send the Soviets ahead.

When Kompalla called an interference penalty on Canada's Jean-Paul Parise for an obviously imaginary foul, the rugged Canadian winger argued his way to a 10-minute misconduct. Parise rushed towards the official and raised his stick as if he were bringing it down on Kompalla's head but stopped it in time. He was ejected from the game.

Esposito tied the game on a power-play at 6:45 but the Soviets went ahead at 13:10 on a power-play goal by Vladimir Lutchenko. The Canadians pulled even again at 16:59 when Park scored. But then a Yakushev shot bounced off the wire mesh above the boards behind the Canadian net—Luzhniki did not have glass—into the slot where Shardrin drilled it home.

The Russians poured to the attack after that goal and only some big saves by goalie Dryden held them off until Bill White scored to tie it. But late in the second period, Yakushev and Valeri Vasiliev each scored to give the Russians a 5–3 lead.

In the third period Phil Esposito simply refused to allow Team Canada to lose. He scored at 2:27 and then at 12:56 he fought off two defenders for a shot that Tretiak stopped only to see Yvan Cournoyer knock in the rebound.

When the red light did not signify the tying goal, Alan Eagleson scrambled to ice level trying to make certain the goal counted. He was grabbed by soldiers serving as security in Luzhniki and when he engaged them in a shoving match, they started to drag Eagleson to the exit.

Several Canadian players, led by Pete Mahovlich, went to his rescue, swinging their sticks and wrestling him away from the soldiers. They led him across the ice to the safe haven of the Canadian bench. At mid-ice Eagleson, having tucked in his shirt and pushed his hair out his eyes, gave the Russian crowd his famous—and universally understood—one-finger salute.

Just when a tied series appeared certain—the Russians had announced that they would claim victory because on aggregate they had scored one more goal than Team Canada—Esposito and Henderson staged a grand finale.

In the final minute, a tired Esposito and Cournoyer stayed on the ice deep in the Russian zone while Henderson yelled for Pete Mahovlich to come off so he could get on the ice.

A Russian banged the puck around the boards, Cournoyer intercepted and tried to pass to Henderson but the puck was behind him. Reaching back to get it, Henderson did manage

a weak shot but fell and slid into the end boards. When two Russians mishandled the puck in the face-off circle, Esposito snared it and fired a shot that Tretiak stopped. But Henderson, regaining his feet and skating in front, secured the rebound and shot again. Tretiak made the stop but was down and helpless and Henderson's second try went over him into the net.

"Henderson has scored for Canada" were the words of fabled broadcaster Foster Hewitt on the telecast, creating a "where-were-you-when" moment shared by almost every Canadian. In Canada—where hockey towers over all other sports—the extended drama of September 1972, the quality of the Soviet team and the astonishing late-game heroics of Henderson and Esposito have forever set the Summit Series apart not just as great hockey but as an historic event that will resonate throughout the country as long as people care for the game.

1972 SUMMIT SERIES

CANADA

#	Pos.	Name		GP	G	A	PTS	PIM
7	C	Esposito	Phil	8	7	6	13	15
19	LW	Henderson	Paul	8	7	3	10	4
28	C	Clarke	Bobby	8	2	4	6	18
12	RW	Cournoyer	Yvan	8	3	2	5	2
5	RD	Park	Brad	8	1	4	5	2
10	LW	Hull	Dennis	4	2	2	4	4
22	LW	Parise	Jean-Paul	6	2	2	4	28
18	C	Ratelle	Jean	6	1	3	4	0
8	RW	Gilbert	Rod	6	1	3	4	9
2	LD	Bergman	Gary	8	0	3	3	13
6	RW	Ellis	Ron	8	0	3	3	8
17	RD	White	Bill	7	1	1	2	8
9	RW	Goldsworthy	Bill	3	1	1	2	4
27	LW	Mahovlich	Frank	6	1	1	2	0
33	C	Perreault	Gilbert	2	1	1	2	0
20	LW	Mahovlich	Pete	7	1	1	2	4
23	RD	Savard	Serge	5	0	2	2	0
14	LW	Cashman	Wayne	2	0	2	2	14
25	LD	Lapointe	Guy	7	0	1	1	6
15	C	Berenson	Red	2	0	1	1	0
21	C	Mikita	Stan	2	0	1	1	0
26	RD	Awrey	Don	2	0	0	0	0
29	G	Dryden	Ken	4	0	0	0	0
24	RW	Redmond	Mickey	1	0	0	0	0
3	LD	Stapleton	Pat	7	0	0	0	6
16	LD	Seiling	Rod	3	0	0	0	0
35	G	Esposito	Tony	4	0	0	0	0
11	LW	Hadfield	Vic	2	0	0	0	0

DID NOT PLAY: Orr, Glennie, Tallon, Johnston, Guevremont, Dionne, Martin.

SOVIET UNION

#	Pos.	Name		GP	G	A	PTS	PIM
15	LW	Yakushev	Alexander	8	7	4	11	4
19	C	Shadrin	Vladimir	8	3	5	8	0
17	LW	Kharlamov	Valeri	7	3	4	7	16
16	C	Petrov	Vladimir	8	3	4	7	10
25	LD	Liapkin	Yuri	6	1	5	6	0
13	RW	Mikhailov	Boris	8	3	2	5	9
10	C	Maltsev	Alexander	8	0	5	5	0
3	LD	Lutchenko	Vladimir	8	1	3	4	0
22	C	Anisin	Vyacheslav	7	1	3	4	2
18	RW	Vikulov	Vladimir	6	2	1	3	0
11	RW	Zimin	Yevgeny	2	2	1	3	0
9	LW	Blinov	Yuri	5	2	1	3	2
6	RD	Vasiljev	Valeri	5	1	2	3	6
7	RD	Tsygankov	Gennady	8	0	2	2	6
2	LD	Gusev	Alexander	6	1	0	1	2
24	LW	Bodunov	Alexander	3	1	0	1	0
23	RW	Lebedev	Yuri	3	1	0	1	2
5	LD	Ragulin	Alexander	6	0	1	1	4
4	RD	Kuzkin	Viktor	7	0	1	1	8
29	RW	Martynyuk	Alexander	1	0	0	0	0
30	RW	Volchkov	Alexander	1	0	0	0	0
20	G	Tretiak	Vladislav	8	0	0	0	0
8	C	Starshinov	Vyacheslav	1	0	0	0	0
21	RW	Solodukhin	Vyacheslav	1	0	0	0	0
26	RD	Poladjev	Yevgeny	3	0	0	0	0
12	LW	Mishakov	Yevgeny	6	0	0	0	11
14	LD	Shatalov	Yuri	2	0	0	0	0

1978 FINNISH NATIONAL UNDER-18 JUNIOR TEAM

Tom Ratschunas

THERE IS, OF COURSE, NO SUCH THING as a routine victory. Still, when Finland's under-18 team won the European Junior Championships in 1978, it was about as far from a run of the mill situation as possible. Expectations hadn't been high. Finland had never won in any team sport at the world or European level, and two brand-new and very young coaches didn't help to raise hopes. In fact, the federation's coaching director predicted a catastrophe when he checked the endeavors of Alpo Suhonen, the head coach at age 30, and his even younger assistant Rauno Korpi, 27, and their approach to leading the team. But then all the adversity was turned to the positive by the players and coaches and resulted in a happy ending indeed.

Since the tournament was first staged in 1968, the pecking order in the European Junior Championships had been remarkably stable. The Russians, Czechs and Swedes usually played for the medals with the Finns ensconced in fourth place. Only once, playing at home in Garmisch-Partenkirchen in 1969, had Germany placed fourth ahead of Finland. In 1974, led by Matti Hagman, the Finns captured their first set of medals when they placed third. Two years later, a second bronze medal was added with team leader Risto Siltanen playing wing. (A few years later, Siltanen switched to defense in a move that would lead all the way to the NHL.) With this history established, the two opening games of the 1978 European Junior Championships were seen as mere warmups for the medal battles to come. When the Finns blitzed the Swiss in game one with a 6–1 first period that featured six different goal scorers, it produced a backlash in concentration that allowed the team from the Alps to tally four unanswered goals in the second period before the Finns hit their stride again. A hat trick and an assist by Jarmo Makitalo led to the final result of 10–7. In game two, Norway was not allowed to find the Finns napping. Veli-Pekka Kinnunen (later to become a Memorial Cup winner in Canada with the Peterborough Petes) put the game out of reach for the Norwegians with a second-period hat trick, while a final tally of 11–1 gave the Finns the two wins they expected. From that point on, every victory meant a chance for a brighter medal.

For game three, the defending champions from Sweden and Finland were both missing players who had traveled to Canada for the World Junior Championships, which was being played at the same time. Finland was without the services of Reijo Ruotsalainen, while Sweden had lost three players, Thomas Steen (a future NHL stalwart with the Winnipeg Jets) and defensemen Tomas Jonsson (later with the Islanders) and Tommy Samuelsson. Three future legends for Sweden—Hakan Loob, Thomas Rundqvist and defenseman Anders Eldebrink—were not yet as formidable as they would become in a few years' time when all three were heading to the NHL. The tournament star for "the Three Crowns" was Ove Olsson, but against Finland his offensive threat was curtailed.

After two periods, Sweden was ahead of Finland 1–0 on a goal by Matti Pauna two minutes into the second frame. Swedish goalie Mikael Gustavsson was the star of the game, facing many more shots than his Finnish counterpart, but he couldn't prevent the Finns from turning the contest around with two markers in the final period. Veli-Pekka Kinnunen took a pass from Timo Blomqvist to tie things up seven and a half minutes before the final whistle. Kari Jalonen fed Ilkka Huura for the game winner, and the stage was set for Finland's most important game to date in the European junior tournament. If they could get past Czechoslovakia, the Finns would have their first shot at the title in the final game against the Soviets.

The Finns' young coaches had adopted a psychological approach to their team meetings to induce confidence in players unaccustomed to having the upper hand against Europe's top three. Before facing the Czechoslovakian team, the pregame session was about successful execution in any breakaways during the game. Based on the relative styles of the teams, Suhonen and Korpi predicted that Finland would very likely have such opportunities and the forwards were told to picture themselves in such situations and see in their mind's eye an effective conclusion.

The Czechoslovakian team was led by two Slovaks, Dusan Pasek and Igor Liba, playing on different lines. At this stage, Pasek was the tournament's scoring leader with nine points in three games and he was poised to power his team on again. And Pasek did score a goal—the final one of the game—but by that time Finland already had six, led by Jari Kurri with two at the end of the second period that gave his team a 5–0 stranglehold on the proceedings. The Czechs outscored the Finns in the final frame but could only close the gap by one goal as Finland skated off with a 6–2 victory. The mental preparation had worked; three of the six goals were on breakaways. Now the sky was the limit with the team playing for gold in front of their own fans.

Back in 1978, only a handful of scouts took the trouble to cross the Atlantic to check out the top talent in Europe (in contrast to the late 1990s, when more than 150 attend the European under-18 tournament), but one of these few was goaltending legend Jacques Plante, who was representing the Philadelphia Flyers. Alpo Suhonen was introduced to the former goalie and decided on the spur of the moment to invite him to a post-practice session to talk about the NHL and outline what was expected of young players with a dream of turning professional in North America. Plante, who loved the subtleties of hockey did better than that. He laced up his skates and got out on the ice.

Working with the goalies, he soon noticed something quite odd. From time to time, the puck disappeared. In those days, dark concrete just visible above the boards (plexiglass was not yet in use) tended to obscure a high shot momentarily—which considerably reduced the reaction time for the netminder. Holding a puck in his hand and moving backwards, Plante kept checking with Jari Paavola to determine where he lost sight of it. Together, they worked out exactly how far the goalie had to come out of his net so that eye contact with the puck was not lost. The tips and advice from Plante made a great impact on the young goalie, who was inspired to play his best hockey in the final game against the Soviets.

After Plante's presentation (during which terms like "scout" and "draft" and other NHL lore was explained) it was again Suhonen's turn to take charge of the proceedings. So far, the coaches had been very realistic in their appeals to the players' sentiments going into the games. Now the threshold was higher. A silver medal— already an historical first—was a certainty, but the message before the Soviet game contained three propositions:

1) I want to show with the way I play that I am a member of the best team in the tournament.

2) I want to win every one-on-one battle with a Soviet player.

3) I want to defeat the Soviets.

Suhonen went on to tell his players that if they lived in history, they couldn't create it, i.e. they had silver, but that shouldn't be enough any more. "Your emotions are still saturated, you have lots of energy remaining, this will help all of you along. We are going to do it!" As if to bear out his words, the final against the feared Soviets remains a classic in Finland to this day. Led by the play of center Jarmo Makitalo and his right winger Jari Kurri, as well as defenseman Juha Huikari, the Finns staged a series of comebacks that truly rattled their opponents until they succumbed. The big question before the game was how to decide the winner if the game was a tie, since both teams would be even in all the relevant criteria. The forceful Soviets won a victory in the directorate meeting that would turn out to be Pyrrhic. They were confident that should such a situation arise, it was safer to play one full overtime period and only go to sudden death if the game was still tied.

The Soviets took an early two-goal lead with Vladimir Shashov and Igor Funikov authoring the markers, but Jari Kurri reduced the deficit to a single goal and returned his team's confidence just one second before the first period ended. The teams traded goals in the second period, with Shashov scoring a second goal on another feed from Vladimir Krutov before Jussi Lepisto scored in the final minute of the period to narrow the margin again. The only goal in the third stanza added to the game's drama. With a little over three minutes remaining, Finland caught the Soviets for the first time to deadlock the proceedings at 3–3 when Juha Huikari completed a play by forwards Rauno Saarnio and Jarmo Makitalo.

In most of Europe, overtime and sudden death were unheard of outside the context of the NHL, and this was especially so in the Soviet Union. The Finnish juniors may not have participated in overtime themselves, but they had at least seen their older national role models in action in two postseason championships and thus had a small advantage in having a better grasp of what was to come.

The overtime stage of the game with the Soviets is still the mother of all extended playing time in Finnish hockey. Both teams rode an emotional roller coaster with wild turns of elation and grief. Soviet defenseman Evgeny Popikhin experienced the first high at the 13:43 mark when he scored an unassisted goal he thought was the game winner. Since the managers of the Soviet team had neglected to explain the system for deciding this game to the players, the first low came immediately afterward when Popikhin and his team had to go back to play. Three minutes later, Finland evened the score on a goal by Mika Laine. Still determined to be the day's hero, Popikhin combined with Mikail Panin to score his second goal of the overtime period at 18:17.

Finland was 20 seconds away from defeat when Suhonen pulled goalie Jari Paavola in favor of defenseman Juha Huikari and his trademark tool of a fierce shot from the blue line. Czechoslovakian referee Milan Barnet was not very well versed in this situation and consequently missed the fact that Huikari was on the ice a few seconds before Paavola was off it. Makitalo saw Huikari coming and risked feeding the puck to the blue line. Huikari was in full stride when he crossed the line and got to the puck and slammed a shot past goalie Dimitri Saprykhin for the equalizer.

The thriller that had tantalized the partisan crowd of 7,604 (8,000 counting the media and organizers) was brought to a speedy conclusion in the sudden-death period

that followed. The Soviets were at a rare psychological disadvantage against opponents who had come back so many times to snatch victory from them and they never got their momentum going at the start of period five. The ice was a flurry of blue of white as the Finns skated circles around their opponents in red. Defenseman Timo Blomqvist shot from the right and the puck bounced through the players in the slot towards the left, where Jari Kurri saw it coming. He all but threw himself forward to connect with the puck, which he steered in behind Saprykhin. It was just 1:42 of sudden death and the host nation had 20 brand-new heroes.

Finland's victory over the Soviets in 1978 is one that will long be remembered by those who witnessed it. The marathon contest lasted three hours and 25 minutes before the Finns were crowned European champions, and there is no doubt it put wind in the sails of Finnish hockey, though it would take another 10 years for the men's national team to achieve its first medal, a silver at the 1988 Calgary Olympics, when Timo Blomqvist, the only link to the 1978 juniors, became the first Finnish captain to mount the podium for a medal. (Another Olympian, Reijo Ruotsalainen, had been eligible in 1978 but missed the junior Europeans en route to an unprecedented participation in four world junior tournaments, a record that still stands.) The Olympic team coach in 1988 was Pentti Matikainen, whom Alpo Suhonen had switched from team captain to assistant coach the previous year while working with SaiPa Lappeenranta. It would be another seven years after that before Finland won a gold medal in 1995 at the World Championships in Stockholm, Sweden.

Alpo Suhonen was born in Valkeakoski near Tampere, but he honed his hockey skills in Pori with Karhut and Assat. He won the Finnish national championship with the latter in 1971 and aimed to become a sportswriter after his playing days, but there were no openings in Pori. He had spent many summers with his grandparents in Forssa (famous for its Koho sticks), and it was there that he found an opening as a playing coach.

His coaching career caught fire from the start. Within three years, he had brought two promotions to FoPS Forssa, from Division 2 to SM-Liiga, the national league, and prior to 1978 he served for two years as an assistant to Matti Vaisanen (who later became a legendary European scout for the Edmonton Oilers) for the 1976 European junior team that won a bronze medal and for the under-20 team that placed fourth in the 1977 World Junior Championships. He continued in Forssa until the European Junior Championships gold in 1978, after which he accepted an offer from the legendary Swiss team Ambri-Piotta.

Rauno Korpi, known later as "Tampere's Tarasov," could perhaps be better characterized as Finland's Scotty Bowman. He sustained a career-ending injury at age 18 playing for the Tappara Tampere juniors, at which time he took up coaching young players and graduated to assistant coach on Tappara's main team. From 1986 to 1988, Korpi crowned his years with Tappara by winning three consecutive national titles. Both coaches of the 1978 European junior champions were innovators and representatives of a modern coaching systems. Korpi's forte was the techniques pf physical preparation he learned as a student at the University of Jyvaskyla.

The crowd went wild when the final buzzer sounded in Helsinki on January 3, 1978, as did the players, who hurled their equipment in the air to sail down and freckle the ice. Suhonen was all superlatives after the game: "Fantastic

guys! This team is ahead of the national team in most aspects. They have a great attitude when it comes to determination, discipline in executing the game plan, the desire to win and in taking responsibility on the ice. These guys are destined to continue as winners, provided they will be availed of opportunities." Rauno Korpi reflected on the past: "In a way, this victory is one year late, as we had a much better team in Bremerhaven, Germany, last year. This just shows, though, that the team also has to function as an entity." A long line of well-wishers surrounded the coaches, shaking hands and clapping shoulders. In the middle of all the commotion, Suhonen reflected, more to himself than to anybody around him: "I guess this is my line of work. This is what I want to go on doing." And he smiled to himself.

THE 1980 U.S. OLYMPIC TEAM – I
THE BEST PREPARED TEAM IN THE WORLD

Kevin Allen

GIVEN THE THOUSANDS OF CRYPTIC WORDS that cascaded from coach Herb Brooks' mouth before the 1980 Olympics, his 15-word summation before the game against the Soviet Union didn't immediately seem profound.

After glancing down at notes on three-by-five cards, Brooks raised his eyes and said to his players: "You were born to be players. You were meant to be here. This moment is yours."

A few hours later, as all of America rejoiced in one of the most improbable upsets in sports history, U.S. players began to appreciate Brooks' message. Life changed dramatically for those players after team captain Mike Eruzione beat goalie Vladimir Myshkin with a 25-foot wrist shot to provide the U.S. squad with a 4–3 win against the seemingly-invincible Soviets. They had become instant American heroes, and their accomplishment would forever be remembered as the singular event that changed the face of hockey in America.

Their wild on-ice celebration was minor compared to what occurred across the nation after ABC announcer Al Michaels summed up the final seconds of the game with his now-famous line: "Do you believe in miracles? Ye-s-s-s!" The U.S. triumph at Lake Placid ranks with Bobby Thomson's pennant-clinching home run in 1951 and Joe Namath leading the New York Jets to a win against the Baltimore Colts in Super Bowl III as one of the most memorable moments in U.S. sports history, but in terms of raw emotion it was second to none.

"When I meet people they always tell me exactly where they were when we won the gold medal in 1980," said Steve Janaszak, the backup goaltender on the team. "And I always think, this was really big."

People wept, cars honked, strangers hugged, and groups in theaters, bars and airports around the country broke into spontaneous renditions of *God Bless America* and *The Star Spangled Banner*. In every tavern from Bangor, Maine to Nome, Alaska they raised their glass to toast the unlikely collection of college kids and ex-college players who had banded together under Brooks' stern tutelage to defeat the Russian bear. The country swelled with patriotism that day; for some it was the first time that they felt nationalistic pride since before the Vietnam War. Remember, America was angry entering the 1980s. People were frustrated by high inflation, unemployment and economic uncertainty on the home front, and disillusioned perhaps by the country's inability to control what was happening around the world. The Soviets had invaded Afghanistan. Iranian students had seized an embassy and held American citizens hostage. The cold war was entering its fourth decade. The world seemed to be spinning out of control and the Soviets were the symbol of all of America's international fears.

"I'm not going to say that Ronald Reagan rode our wave (to the presidency) a few months later," Janaszak said. "But suddenly people had something to latch onto in this country."

Americans fell in love with the 1980 U.S. players because they made them believe again that they were back in control, and that any level of accomplishment was possible.

Players probably didn't appreciate the magnitude of their accomplishment until they got away from Lake Placid, and realized that people just wanted to embrace them wherever they went. Americans didn't surrender this moment easily. Eruzione said the mail that arrived at his home was "like the scene out of the movie *Miracle on 34th Street*." Bag after bag of mail arrived at his home. About that time he began to think of Brooks' speeches and, in particular, the one before the Soviet game.

"He would say things to you that would always take you a while to figure out," Eruzione said. "But when you look back on it, you say: 'Oh, that's what he was talking about.' Like when he said 'You were meant to be here. This moment is yours.' I use that line all the time now when I speak. Yet at the time, I didn't know what he was talking about. But the more I think about it over the years, he is just so right about our accomplishment. We were meant to be."

The Soviets had certainly not seen the American bullet coming. By not allowing any of their players to play outside their country, they had been able to dominate the Olympics since 1964. They had expected to whip all challengers and their concern about the Americans was lessened when they pasted them 10–3 in an exhibition game at Madison Square Garden just a week before the Olympics. In hindsight, it was clear that the Soviets didn't heed the warning signs about the USA's strength early in the tournament. The Americans came from behind to tie Sweden 2–2 in the opener on defenseman Bill Baker's dramatic goal against goaltender Pelle Lindbergh with 27 seconds left. The tie was important to the Americans because they traditionally struggled against the Swedes. No American team had defeated the Swedes since Dave Christian's father, Bill, and uncle Roger had helped the USA win the Olympic gold medal in Squaw Valley in 1960.

Next up were the Czechs, who were led by a talented trio of brothers, Peter, Marian and Anton Stastny. Unknown to everyone, they were planning to defect to Canada and join the Quebec Nordiques after the Olympic Games.

"The Swedish game made us believe we could win," Eruzione said. "But the Czechs were the only team that was given a chance to challenge the Soviets, and we beat them 7–3. I think it was then the whole team thought: 'We can get to the medal round.'"

The Americans then defeated Norway, Romania and Germany to set the stage for the dramatic showdown with the Soviets. Although there had been discussion before the Olympics about trying to avoid the Soviets before the gold medal game, it was clear to players that Brooks had been preparing his team for the Soviets since the opening day of training camp. "I wanted my players to see that these Soviets were mortal," Brooks says now.

That wasn't easily accomplished because most of the

Russian players were Olympic veterans, and several of them probably could have been NHL stars had they been allowed to leave their country. Boris Mikhailov, Vladislav Tretiak, Alexander Maltsev, Vladimir Petrov, Vasili Vasiliev and Valeri Kharlamov were all members of the Soviet team that had played so well against Team Canada in the 1972 Summit Series. Canada needed a monumental goal by Paul Henderson with 34 seconds left in regulation to win that series 4–3–1.

To the Americans, the Soviets were superheros with special powers that allowed them to pass and skate better than everyone else on the planet. Brooks hated it when the American players applauded the Soviets before an exhibition game. He didn't believe his team could beat the Soviets as long as they viewed them as hockey gods. He began to talk about how Mikhailov looked like Stan Laurel from Laurel-and-Hardy movie fame. "You can beat Stan Laurel, can't you?" he would ask.

No one was quite sure whether every American player believed the Soviets could be beaten when the game started in 1980. The Soviets unleashed a furious offensive attack in the first period, badly out-shooting the Americans. But it was clear early in the game that goaltender Jim Craig was as hot as he had been throughout the tournament. With each big save Craig made, the Americans gained more confidence. "Once we knew we could keep the game close, we knew we had a chance to beat them," Brooks said.

The Americans were trailing 2–1 late in the first period when Mark Johnson scored the goal that seemed to ignite the team as if it was propelled by an Atlas rocket booster. Living up to his proud Olympic bloodline, Christian fired a long slapshot from the blue line. Tretiak was known for not surrendering any rebounds, but this shot bounced off his pads as if it were a rubber ball. Johnson, the son of 1976 U.S. Olympic coach Bob Johnson, was there to drive the puck past Tretiak for the tying goal with one second left in the period. Johnson's presence in the right place at the right time wasn't a surprise to anyone on the American team. Players called him Magic Johnson because of his puck wizardry, and they counted on him to lead them when the game was on the line. "Mark Johnson could always control the flow of the play on the ice," Janaszak said.

The U.S. dressing room was buzzing between periods, as players began realize that they had a chance to win the game. Fabled Soviet coach Viktor Tikhonov had shocked the Americans by lifting Tretiak after the second goal, and replacing him with Myshkin. The Americans presumed Tretiak, considered by many to be one of the top goaltenders in hockey history, would be back for the second period. They were shocked when the second period started with Myshkin between the pipes. It wasn't as if Myshkin was a shabby backup; he had blanked a team of NHL All-Stars 6–0 the year before. But he didn't pose the same psychological intimidation threat to the Americans as Tretiak did. Myshkin didn't seem invincible.

Even when the Americans trailed 3–2, they didn't panic. It was almost as if they knew they weren't done. Again it was Johnson playing the role of hero. He tied the game on a power-play goal at 8:39 of the third period. On the bench, players began to tell each other that the Soviets could be had. Brooks ordered shorter shifts in the third period to keep his troops fresh. When Brooks sent Eruzione off the bench for a shift two minutes after Johnson's goal, it had been long forgotten that Brooks considered cutting Eruzione before the tournament. Eruzione leaped off the

bench as if fired from a slingshot. In an instant, he was in the high slot, where Mark Pavelich found him with a centering pass. Eruzione then uncorked the shot that changed his life forever. It went through a screen and skipped past Myshkin. It wasn't the hardest shot of his life. "The thing had wings," Janaszak says. "It fluttered in."

The Soviets were stunned by the loss. The same team had beaten a National Hockey League All-Star team in the Challenge Cup the year before.

"It was probably the best team ever put together in the Soviet Union," said Detroit Red Wings defenseman Slava Fetisov, who was a youngster on the 1980 Soviet team. "We had prepared before the tournament to face the Czechs in the final round. But the Czechs didn't get in and we were pretty confident. We never thought of losing, never thought it could happen. That's why they call it a miracle because it could have happened only once in a lifetime."

Fetisov said Tikhonov made a "huge" mistake in pulling Tretiak because it provided the Americans with a psychological boost. "In our dressing room, nobody understood what was going on," Fetisov said. "Even Tikhonov always said that if Tretiak made one mistake, he was always unbeatable after that."

All that remained was for the Americans to play strong defensively for the final minutes, and they did so with Russian-like efficiency. Craig was playing so well that he probably seemed as intimidating to the Soviets as Tretiak had been to the Americans before the game started. When the game ended, the celebration befitted a champion. Sticks and gloves were thrown all over the ice and Craig was buried under a screaming pile of teammates. But even though the Americans had defeated the best team in the tournament, they really hadn't won anything. If they lost to Finland the next day, they wouldn't even receive a medal. The champagne that was sent to the team in honor of the win over the Soviets was declined for that reason. While America was celebrating the win over the Soviets, the American team was fretting about the Finns.

The Americans trailed in six of their seven games in that tournament, including the gold medal game against Finland. But they had come too far to allow the Finns to ruin their party. They came from behind to win 4–2 and complete the 1980 Miracle on Ice.

Years after the event, it's clear that the hockey world had badly underestimated the talent on the American team. Eruzione is usually considered the symbol of that American team because he scored the game winner. But he was actually a fourth-liner. History misrepresented the 1980 team as a team of overachievers, when in reality they were a talent-laden team.

Here's why the Americans won in 1980:

The team had NHL-caliber defenseman. The team's most well-known four of Ken Morrow, Mike Ramsey, Dave Christian and Jack O'Callahan combined to play 51 seasons in the NHL after the gold medal.

Craig was as sharp in goal as any American goaltender had ever been, including Jack McCartan who was phenomenal in 1960. "He had incredible focus during the few-week time frame," Janaszak said. "Every time I watch the tapes today, I'm amazed. He marshaled his resources to put everything he had into that time frame."

The U.S. center-ice trio of Johnson, Neal Broten and Mark Pavelich could all skate and were the equal of the centers iced by any opponent in the tournament.

Brooks brilliantly prepared his players for Lake Placid.

From the beginning, Brooks had designed the 1980 team to be able to play whatever style was necessary to win the gold medal, including a European style.

"He was driven to prove people wrong," Eruzione said. "He wanted to prove he could win when nobody thought we could. That we weren't too young, and that we could adapt to a European style when nobody thought we could. He just wanted to prove to everyone that he wasn't some lunatic."

The players weren't quite sure about the lunatic part until after the gold medal had been won. Brooks was a tough coach who ruled with a statesman's prose and a general's iron fist. He was a dictator/philosopher who controlled his team through a combination of intimidation and the ability to keep players guessing at all times. "He messed with our minds at every opportunity," said Ramsey, who was only 18 when he played for the gold medal team.

When he addressed players before a game, he did so with the same seriousness that a general might address his troops before a battle. Put a tunic on Brooks and he could have easily been a Roman captain addressing the Praetorian Guard. Put a helmet on him, he could have been Patton addressing the troops before the assault into Germany. He pushed his players' buttons every chance he had. "I was always looking for moments to solidify this team," Brooks said.

He questioned future NHL player Rob McClanahan's manhood in an effort to convince him to play with a charleyhorse in the game against Sweden. "When I reflect on the moments that unified our team," Janaszak said. "That one incident stands out head and shoulders above the rest."

At the time, players didn't view this as Brooks trying to bring them together. "As I recall, I think David Silk was going to go pop Herb," Janaszak said. "It was bordering on the edge of pandemonium in there."

McClanahan did play with the injury. "Here you had a guy who couldn't walk, and he played extremely well," Janaszak said.

Brooks did everything for a purpose, usually with the idea that the team would unify in their desire to hate him.

"If Herb came into my house today, it would still be uncomfortable," Eruzione said. "Not that I'm afraid of the guy, but you never know what Herb will do."

Brooks was driven for another reason in 1980. He had been one of the last cuts from the gold medal-winning 1960 U.S. team. When Brooks called home, his father told him: "Keep your mouth shut, thank everyone and come home." When he and his father watched the television as his former teammates won the gold medal at Squaw Valley, his dad said: "See, it looks like the coach made the right decision."

Brooks used to tell his players that there was method to his madness, and most of them see that today.

"They still have the respect and admiration for him, pushing the right buttons and making the right selections, keeping us in control of our emotions," Eruzione laughs. "There is still that other side that thinks he's flaky."

There were as many heroes as there were spots on USA's roster in 1980. O'Callahan severely injured his knee the week before the tournament and defied medical logic to play in Lake Placid. Brooks considered cutting him, but decided he was too crucial to the chemistry of the team. He was a very popular player. But the team's good chemistry also overshadowed the talent that was on the roster.

"There was a certain portrayal that this we were a bunch of college kids who got together one afternoon and drove out to Lake Placid in a van and won a gold medal," Steve Janaszak observed. "There was never enough appreciation of the talent level of players like Ramsey, or Morrow."

Morrow's contributions have been overlooked because he wasn't a high-scoring defenseman. Brooks had a policy against facial hair, but never said anything about Morrow's full beard, probably because no one could envision Morrow playing without one. "We needed a solid defense, and Morrow was the key guy for us," said Team USA assistant coach Craig Patrick, now the Pittsburgh Penguins' general manager. "He had great character and he was a steady, steady player. The players were all the same age, but he always seemed much older."

Eruzione said Morrow's value to the U.S. team was akin to Ray Bourque's value to the Boston Bruins. "People didn't realize how good he was until they watched the tape and said: 'Who's the big kid with the beard?'" Eruzione said.

Brooks was a superb strategist. Right before the Olympics he decided to switch Christian from forward to defense. "We wanted more mobility back there and it turned out to be one of the key moves of the tournament," Patrick says.

The net result of all of Brooks' moves was that the Americans were in the position to win the gold medal, and many shared in its reward. "This was very big for hockey in the United States," said Fox television analyst John Davidson, a former NHL player. "It led to a lot of kids growing up wanting to be hockey players, where previously those players were going to play baseball and basketball."

Youth hockey registrations were up seven percent over the next two years. Most of the U.S. Olympians were also rewarded with pro contracts. Mark Johnson, who had been offered a $10,000 signing bonus before the Olympics and told he would probably go the minor leagues, was given a $75,000 bonus and sent directly to the Pittsburgh Penguins. Other Olympians, particularly Morrow and Craig, received more lucrative NHL deals because of their Olympic performance. NHL general managers said afterward that the USA's performance at Lake Placid forced them to look at American players differently.

Surprisingly, Eruzione decided to hang up his skates, saying nothing he could do in hockey could top the feeling he felt when his shot crossed the goal line. Americans could relate to that because they knew the feeling as they watched from the living room. Most were misty-eyed as they watched the jubilant post-game celebration. Everyone remembers watching the television as Craig skated around the ice looking up into the stands, trying to find his father who had changed seats. When Craig wrapped himself in a blanket-sized U.S. flag, all of America felt its warmth.

1980 U.S. OLYMPIC TEAM SCORING

#	Pos	Name		Team	GP	G	A	PTS	PIM
24	LW	McClanahan	Rob	USA	7	5	3	8	2
25	LW	Schneider	Buzz	USA	7	5	3	8	4
23	RD	Christian	Dave	USA	7	0	8	8	6
16	C	Pavelich	Mark	USA	7	1	6	7	2
21	LW	Eruzione	Mike	USA	7	3	2	5	2
27	LW	Verchota	Phil	USA	7	3	2	5	8
8	RW	Silk	Dave	USA	7	2	3	5	0
28	RW	Harrington	John	USA	7	0	5	5	2
9	C	Broten	Neal	USA	7	2	1	3	2
11	RW	Christoff	Steve	USA	7	2	1	3	6
15	C	Wells	Mark	USA	7	2	1	3	0
3	RD	Morrow	Ken	USA	7	1	2	3	6
19	RW	Strobel	Eric	USA	7	1	2	3	2
5	LD	Ramsey	Mike	USA	7	0	2	2	8
10	C	Johnson	Mark	USA	7	5	6	11	6
6	RD	Baker	Bill	USA	7	1	0	1	4
17	LD	O'Callahan	Jack	USA	4	0	1	1	2
30	G	Craig	Jim	USA	7	0	0	0	0
20	LD	Suter	Bob	USA	7	0	0	0	6
1	G	Janaszak	Steve	USA		did not play			

THE 1980 U.S. OLYMPIC TEAM – II
HOW A GOLD MEDAL WINNER WAS BUILT

William J. Martin

HERB BROOKS was no better than third choice to coach America's 1980 Olympic hockey team. Born in East St. Paul, Minnesota, Brooks played at the University of Minnesota under former Chicago Black Hawks bruiser Johnny Mariucci, graduating in 1962 with the perfect major: psychology. Most know that Brooks was the last man cut from the 1960 gold medal Olympic team, but not that he played on the 1964 and 1968 USA Olympic teams, which finished fifth at Innsbruck and sixth at Grenoble. Watching the Russians dominate world play, Brooks studied the flow and tempo of their game. In 1972, he was named head coach at the University of Minnesota and won NCAA championships in 1974, 1976 and 1979. For his interview as a coaching candidate for the 1980 Olympic team, Brooks showed up with trademark preparation: loose-leaf binders of proposals, plans, options, and organizational flow charts. He won the job. Ethereal and enigmatic, the stone-faced hawk-eyed Brooks smiled as often as Georges Vezina gave up soft goals. Like most charismatic leaders, Brooks essentially was driven by the fear of failure, not the pursuit of glory.

For his assistant coach, Brooks chose Craig Patrick, a member of Hockey's Royal Family, grandson of Lester and son of Lynn, blood to Frank and Muzz. Craig grew up in Boston and played on two national championship teams at the University of Denver. He began his professional career in 1971 with the California Golden Seals and finished it as captain of the 1979 U.S. national team. Brooks told Patrick he was also giving him the title general manager "to improve your resume." Herb made no bones about Patrick's job — he wouldn't be treated well, "at least in front of the players." Patrick was to get close to the players and solve their problems, and tell Brooks "when a little thing might become a big thing." The soft-spoken young Patrick was the ideal assistant, forming a bond with the players while rooming with Herb on the road.

Brooks had contacted virtually every college hockey coach in America to track down prospects and called upon the NHL's Central Scouting Bureau to analyze them. He began with a pool of 400 hockey players who attended regional tryout camps in 1979. Prospects were given a 300-question psychological test — designed by a University of Minnesota psychology professor — that had nothing to do with hockey. Despite personal animosities engendered by their hard-fought college games, Brooks selected an advisory committee consisting of Boston University's Jack Parker, Harvard's Bill Cleary, Wisconsin's Bob Johnson, Colorado College's Jeff Sauer and New Hampshire's Charlie Holt. With the intense scrutiny of the committee, the 400 candidates were cut to 68 skaters who competed in Colorado Springs in July 1979. From this tryout, a 26-man touring squad was chosen. On September 1, 1979 the USA team left unnoticed for Oslo, Norway and a three-week European exhibition tour. Europe was followed by an exhausting four-month road trip across North America. To increase the level of competition, Brooks convinced the Central Hockey League to have its 18 games against his club count in the Central League's standings.

American college hockey's hotbed is located in a handful of states. Brooks believed the evil of geographical cliques had fractured previous U.S. national teams. He faced the same problem in 1980. Of the 20 Olympians, six colleges were represented but half the team was from Minnesota — eight players from the University of Minnesota and two from the University of Minnesota-Duluth. With five players from Boston University, a Minnesota-versus-Massachusetts factionalism loomed ominously. Wisconsin and Bowling Green had two players apiece, and North Dakota had one. Brooks went overboard to avoid favoring Minnesota: "I treated the players all the same — bad," he admits. Steve Janaszak, Brooks' goalie at Minnesota put it bluntly: "Every team I played on for five years had a common bond — 20 guys who hated Herb." Brooks' devotion to team over regionalism went over the top in a visit with Vice President Walter Mondale after the final 1980 game. Mondale, a former Minnesota senator, asked: "Where are the players from Minnesota?" Brooks replied, "We have no players from Minnesota, Mr. Vice President. We have only Americans."

Europeans emphasize the puck game; North Americans emphasize the game away from the puck. Brooks and Patrick combined these systems into a hybrid: "American Hockey," taking the physical toughness and aggressive forechecking of the North American game and merging it with the creative puck control of the highly-conditioned and wide-open European game. Practices started with 15 minutes of body-bending acrobatic stretches followed by puck-possession drills and ended with leg-numbing stops-and-starts the players called 'Herbies.' "American hockey" is embodied in Brooks' pithy catchphrases:

"Passes come from the heart, NOT from the stick."
"You don't punt on first down."
"Don't dump it in. That went out with short pants."
"In front of the net, it's Bloody Nose Alley."

Often Brooks' epigrams were pure Zen:
"Throw the puck back and weave, weave, weave. But don't just weave for the sake of weaving."
"Your play is an expression of yourself within a framework of friends."

And Brooks' metaphors are transcendent:
"Go up to the tiger, spit in his eye, then shoot him."
"We went to the well again, and the water was deeper, and the water was colder."

Brooks told his team over and over: "Gentlemen, you don't have enough talent to win on talent alone." He was right. Never was this more in evidence than in the team's 61st exhibition game, when USA played the Russians at Madison Square Garden — the same Russians who won two out of three from the NHL All-Stars in February 1979. In awe of the legendary Soviets, the Americans applauded as the Russian players were introduced on the Garden ice. Still in awe when the puck was dropped, the disorganized USA was dominated, outclassed, outshot 35–20, and outscored 10–3. "I gave them a bad plan," Brooks lamented over his tight-checking, physical game. "Senseless," he added, "not very smart." But the more shrewd observation was made by Russian coach Viktor Tikhonov: "Today we showed what we could do, but they did not." The Americans would show what they could do a week later when the 1980 Winter Olympics got under way in Lake Placid.

A bucolic resort in upstate New York founded in 1850,

Lake Placid was host to the 1932 Winter Olympics in which hockey was played outdoors next to the speed skating oval. Lake Placid got the 1980 Winter Games by default—no other city wanted them. Faced with Russians in Afghanistan, hostages in Iran, and rising inflation, America's self-esteem in 1980 had hit bottom. Seeded seventh out of 12 teams, hockey experts believed the USA had been put where it belonged. However, Bill Baker's goal with 27 seconds to give the U.S. a 2–2 in the opening game against Sweden and a 7–3 win over Czechoslovakia two nights later had the American players, if not the experts, beginning to believe in themselves. By the time they faced the Soviets in the medal round on February 22 an entire nation was beginning to believe in them too. In his pregame address, Brooks said, simply: "You were born to be a player. You were meant to be here."

With 10,000 fans crammed into the Lake Placid arena and millions more watching on television, Brooks' players proved they were meant to be there with a stunning 4–3 victory. At game's end the American players jumped over the boards, hugging and tackling each other in an unabashed ode to joy. For once, Brooks allowed his cast-iron expression to crack, bursting into a huge smile. He threw his right arm high into the air, and quickly left the rink—the moment belonged to his players. Brooks hid in the men's room, and when he finally snuck into a hallway, he saw hardened New York State Troopers standing guard, tears streaming down their faces. Back on the ice, the Soviets waited patiently for the traditional postgame handshakes. Strangely, the defeated Russian players—all proud and competitive athletes with their share of gold medals—were smiling.

Now only an elite Finnish team stood between America and the gold. On Saturday, at the last practice the team would ever have, Brooks told the players: "You're too young. You can't win this. Too young. Too damned young." Sunday morning, with countless new hockey fans watching anxiously on television, the Americans found themselves trailing the Finns 2–1 at the end of two periods. In his last locker-room speech, Brooks warned his team: "Twenty minutes, gentlemen. If it's not 20, you'll never live it down. This will haunt you the rest of your lives." The players knew he spoke the truth. In the final period, Phil Verchota tied the game at 2:25 and Rob McClanahan gave the USA the lead at 6:05. Mark Johnson added the final goal at 16:25. When the final buzzer sounded, an entire nation was drenched in tears of joy.

American hockey had reached its defining moment. Millions of Americans who had never watched a hockey game before watched the improbable triumph over the best teams in hockey by a bunch of college kids, average age 22. America's pride had suddenly been resurrected by an amateur hockey team. President Jimmy Carter telephoned Brooks and spoke for the nation in saying: "We're so proud." Goalie Jim Craig, draped in an American flag that two kids brought on the ice, searched the stands for his father who had switched seats.

At the medal ceremony, Al Michaels once again captured the moment: "No scriptwriter would ever dare." Each player grinned boyishly as he bent to receive his gold medal. Unselfishly, captain Mike Eruzione called all the players to the rostrum after the national anthem was sung. The USA had spit in the tiger's eye, and shot him dead.

THE 1980 U.S. OLYMPIC TEAM – III
LONG-TERM IMPACT, EPILOGUE AND "WHERE ARE THEY NOW?"

William J. Martin

ONLY TWO MEMBERS of the 1960 Squaw Valley gold medal team played in the NHL: goalie Jack McCartan and center Tommy Williams. Even by 1971–72, only a handful of Americans had made the NHL. In comparing the U.S. hockey talent between 1970 and 1979, Craig Patrick observed an amazing increase in the skill of American players in a decade. By 1997–98, 120 U.S.-born players were skating in the NHL, amazing proof of a quantum leap in the world-class quality of American hockey. Before 1980, American hockey had been a regional game confined to small geographical pockets. For Patrick, 1980 was the "coming-out party for American hockey," bringing American hockey players national and international respect. The 1980 gold medal was a shot heard round the world whose echoes still reverberate today.

In 1979–80, there were a total of 10,490 hockey teams registered in the United States. In 1981–82, team registrations rose to 11,094. In 1990, there were 14,969 registered teams and 205,441 registered players. In 1996–97, USA Hockey had registered 449,168 players and 29,479 teams. The registration of women hockey players enjoyed similar growth, increasing from 5,573 in 1990 to 23,000 in 1996, and that's before the impact of the 1998 USA women's gold at Nagano had made itself felt.

As the 20th anniversary of the Miracle on Ice approaches, a session of "Where-Are-They-Now" yields answers as diverse as the players on the Lake Placid roster:

GOALIES

Name	Age in 1980	Hometown	College
Jim Craig	22	North Easton, MA	Boston U.

Backbone of the team, playing every Olympic game, earning a 2.14 goals-against average. Spectacular in the 4–3 win over the Soviets as the U.S. team was outshot 39–16. Played in three NHL seasons, now an account manager in Easton, Massachusetts for a publisher of advertising materials.

Name	Age in 1980	Hometown	College
Steve Janaszak	22	White Bear Lake, MN	Minnesota

Played in three NHL games. Now a bond sales executive in New York.

DEFENSEMEN

Name	Age in 1980	Hometown	College
Bill Baker	22	Grand Rapids, MN	Minnesota

Played in three NHL seasons. Now an oral surgeon in Brainerd, Minnesota.

Name	Age in 1980	Hometown	College
Dave Christian	20	Warroad, MN	North Dakota

His father Billy and Uncle Roger starred on the 1960 gold medal team and operate Christian Brothers Hockey Equipment in Warroad, Minnesota. Switched to defense for Lake Placid, Christian played unselfishly and well. He led the team in Olympic assists with seven. Following a 14-year NHL career as a forward, Christian was appointed general manager and coach of a junior team in Fargo, North Dakota in 1998.

Name	Age in 1980	Hometown	College

Ken Morrow 22   Flint, MI   Bowling Green
Morrow joined the New York Islanders at the end of the 1979–80 season and won a Stanley Cup. He steadied the Islanders blue line through 1988–89, then coached at Flint in the International Hockey League, and now is the Islanders' director of pro scouting. Looking back, he says: "We didn't even sell out the arena for our first game. By the end, people were willing to trade their grandmother for a ticket."

Jack O'Callahan 21 Charlestown, MA   Boston U.
Played in seven solid NHL seasons. Now operates Beanpot Financial Services at the Chicago Mercantile Exchange. Assessing the gold medal victory, he says: "1980 took U.S. hockey center stage in the world, culminating in 1996 with the World Cup."

Mike Ramsey 18   Minneapolis, MN   Minnesota
Team's youngest player, just out of high school hockey, who said, "Brooks got inside our heads." Excelled in 17 NHL seasons. Now assistant coach, Buffalo Sabres.

Bob Suter   22   Madison, WI   Wisconsin
Returned to Wisconsin where he operates Gold Medal Sporting Goods in Madison.

FORWARDS

Neal Broten   19   Roseau, MN   Minnesota
The 5'9" center had a spectacular 17-year NHL career including a 105-point season with the North Stars. Now a horse rancher in River Falls, Wisconsin.

Steve Christoff 21   Richfield, MN   Boston U.
Played five NHL seasons. Now a pilot for Masaba Airlines, a Northwest Airlink in Minneapolis.

Mike Eruzione 25   Winthrop, MA   Boston U.
The ideal captain. Retired after winning the gold, believing nothing could equal the Olympic triumph. Consultant for the television movie "Miracle on Ice," starring Karl Malden as Herb Brooks. Now a member of the Boston University hockey coaching staff, director of development for BU Athletics, and a television hockey analyst.

John Harrington 22   Virginia, MN   Minn.-Duluth
Nicknamed "Bah" (as in Humbug), Harrington was always the last one to leave practice. Famous for his uncanny and rousing imitation of Brooks at the post-gold medal press conference: "Well, we were damned if we did and damned if we didn't. We looked like a bunch of monkeys screwing a football out there for a while but we rebounded, used our youth, took our hard hats and lunch pails to work, went right up to the tiger, spat in his eyes and punched him in the face." Harrington might now be the subject of his own players' parodies—he's the head hockey coach at St. John's University located in Collegeville, Minnesota.

Mark Johnson 21   Madison, WI   Wisconsin
Team MVP and leading Olympic scorer with 11 points, Brooks called him "the man who makes us go." His teammates nicknamed him "Magic." Eleven strong NHL seasons, then played in Austria. Now assistant coach at the University of Wisconsin, following in his father Badger Bob Johnson's footsteps.

Name	Age in 1980	Hometown	College

Rob McClanahan 21   St. Paul, MN   Minnesota
Five NHL seasons, now an investment broker in Minneapolis. Looking back, he says: "We were the best-conditioned team in the tournament and we had luck on our side."

Mark Pavelich 21   Eveleth, MN   Minn.-Duluth
Gutsy, diminutive center who played seven NHL seasons. Noted recluse, lives on Lake Superior in Lutsen, Minnesota, where he works as a home builder and fishing and hunting guide.

Buzz Schneider 24   Babbitt, MN   Minnesota
Only player on the 1980 squad who played in the 1976 Olympics. Now a semi-trailer sales executive in Shoreview, Minnesota.

Dave Silk   21   Scituate, MA   Boston U.
Seven National Hockey League seasons, played in Europe, now with Putnam Investments in Boston. "You can't explain to people what it felt like. You just can't," Silk says.

Eric Strobel   21   Rochester, MN   Minnesota
Strong, gifted skater. Of the final period of the Russian game he says, "I'll remember those 10 minutes forever." Now a telephone sales executive in Apple Valley, Minnesota.

Phil Verchota 22   Duluth, MN   Minnesota
Went on to captain the 1984 Olympic team at Sarajevo. Now a bank executive in St. Cloud, Minnesota.

Mark Wells 21   St. Clair Shores, MI   Bowling Green
Retired restaurant manager for a restaurant chain in Rochester Hills, Michigan.

COACHES

Herb Brooks 42   St. Paul, MN   Minnesota
Head coach. Now Minnesota-based scout for the Pittsburgh Penguins and old general manager, Craig Patrick. Coached in the NHL with Minnesota, New York Rangers and New Jersey between 1981 and 1993. Coached the 1998 French Olympic team at Nagano, starting a week before the Games because no funds were available. Herb wasn't thrilled about the 1998 Games. Lamenting the loss of hopes and dreams of amateurs, he mused: "There will never be another Miracle on Ice. Those were the times when people used to dream!"

Craig Patrick 33   Wellesley, MA   U. of Denver
Assistant coach. Now general manager, Pittsburgh Penguins.

Craig Patrick summed up America's surprise gold medal victory: "Herb Brooks had a master plan that turned out to be perfect." Crediting the players, Patrick added: "Those kids worked so hard for seven months with so much energy and so much devotion, they deserved the gold medal."

Indeed, they did.

MISSING JEWEL IN THE CROWNS: THE 1994 SWEDISH OLYMPIC TEAM

Tom Ratschunas

THE QUEST FOR THE OLYMPIC TITLE for "the Three Crowns" team of Sweden took almost 75 years. The Swedes were charter members in international ice hockey, participating in the first-ever Olympic tournament in 1920, but the top laurels always eluded them until the 1994 event in Lillehammer. In neighboring Norway, this missing gem in the nation's three crowns finally was added. The victory marked the first time since the 1948 soccer team that Sweden had won gold in an Olympic team event.

Selecting the "Dads"

For six months, Swedish coach Curt Lundmark planned the Olympic adventure while constantly under pressure from association president Rickard Fagerlund, who announced repeatedly via the media that it was high time for Sweden to win the gold medal at an Olympic tournament. Against this background it was not easy to be in Lundmark's shoes, as every setback for the national team during the early part of the season was aired in the press in heavy-handed fashion.

Lundmark endured. Progress was slow for him, as he was not building his team from established principles but a homemade formula, where the first ingredient was "Dads," at least three of them. This was his way of describing the need for some solid veterans to start assembling his team around. Three players, Hakan Loob, Tomas Jonsson and Mats Naslund, topped his list in this category. Another pair of veterans, Bengt-Ake Gustafsson and Thomas Rundqvist—both playing their first season in Austria—no longer seemed to have the necessary pace.

Loob's Farjestad team hit a slump in November and Hakan's mood mirrored his team. He did not feel motivated to play for the national team. Lundmark made long phone calls to Loob, having first promised himself not to hang up until he got a positive response. The argument presented was that playing in the Olympics would brighten up an otherwise miserable season. Loob made Lundmark promise that Lillehammer would be a positive experience and the deal was made. Loob then said that to justify his selection he would have to score 10 points. Lundmark replied that he didn't agree.

Mats Naslund was all for playing in the Olympics. He got his confirmation only after promising to be a "Dad" for the younger players, a role that he had left to others in his national team career up that point. Blueliner Tomas Jonsson, with his attitude and high work ethic, was the prototype for the "Dad" role. In his case, the problem was a run of injuries, but they did not prevent his participation. During the tournament he improved game by game and he was at his best in the finals, where he opened the scoring at the 6:10 mark of the first period. Lundmark was also lucky in his choice of goalies, selecting Tommy Salo from the Vasteras club and Hakan Algotsson from Vastra Frolunda Goteborg. Halfway through the tournament Algotsson became a father and traveled home to be with his wife. This elevated Salo to the number one goaltender. It also gave him peace of mind in the remaining games and provided him with the impetus to become a star. With the key pieces of the puzzle in place, Curt Lundmark went to Norway with a lot of optimism.

Sweden was only third in the opening round of the Olympics. The Slovaks, playing for the first time under their own flag, were a tough opponent for Sweden in a see-saw game. After veteran Peter Stastny had given Slovakia a 3–2 lead early in the second period, the Swedes rallied with two goals. A brilliant pass by Oto Hascak was converted by Roman Kontsek five minutes before the end to create a tie. Sweden still did not hit its stride in the second game versus Italy but won 4–1 thanks to three goals by its defensemen.

The next opponent, France, never was given a chance, as Roger Hansson opened the scoring after only 35 seconds. The 7–1 victory was the Olympic opener for Salo, who was cool and concentrated under fire, just as Lundmark had expected. The game also marked the awakening of young star Peter Forsberg, who had a goal and an assist. Team USA scored first in its encounter with Sweden, then Patrik Juhlin turned the tide with a hat trick and Roger Hansson added one marker to make it 4–1. The Americans still made a game of it until the last minute, when Loob got the clincher in the 6–4 affair. The last game in the first stage for Sweden was against Canada, with the Canucks coming out 3–2 winners. A late goal by Jonas Bergqvist was disallowed because his stick was too high. Corey Hirsch in the Canadian goal overshadowed Salo, who allowed two easy markers. As the international federation had set up a faulty schedule for the quarterfinals, Sweden, third in the group, benefited from this position by drawing Germany in the next round. So despite the loss, there were sunny faces in the Swedish camp.

Best form found in the playoff round

The quarterfinals are the worst part of any Olympic tournament format. The losers are eliminated with little to show for their efforts. The Swedish players were tense in the beginning of the game, reflecting Lundmark's nervousness. Lundmark knew that if his team lost he would be history. In the end, Germany posed little trouble to Sweden. The defensive-oriented game plan of the Germans finally faltered at 7:42 in the third period when Stefan Ornberg made it 2–0. As Algotsson had left the team to be present at the birth of his firstborn, Tommy Salo was in goal and responded with a 3–0 shutout victory that turned the tournament around for him.

In the semifinals against Russia (the Olympic title holders from Albertville) "the Three Crowns" team played its best hockey of the season. Early in the third period Sweden increased its lead to 4–1 thanks to Patrik Juhlin and it all seemed to be over. Then the Russians caught fire, with Sergei Berezin and Ravil Gusmanov scoring within nine seconds to test Sweden's nerves. In the dying seconds of the game Stefan Ornskog took the face-off and managed to prevent the Russians from getting an attack organized. The entire Swedish team played a great game, with all parts of the club doing a magnificent job. Special postgame compliments were given to the unproven fourth line of Jorgen Jonsson centering Niklas Eriksson and Andreas Dackell. The trio played solidly all over the ice without showing too much respect for the more experienced opposition.

The Swedish dream was realized in the dramatic finals. The deciding game of the tournament included everything one could wish from a hockey game. Canada was looking for its first Olympic gold since 1952—which had been won in Norway—and the Swedes were aiming for top place on the Olympic podium for the first time ever. A dramatic penalty shootout ended the game, which was tied 2–2 after

regulation time and a 10-minute, sudden-death overtime. Two Swedish players led the team effort. Peter Forsberg assisted on both regulation-time goals and was cool as a cucumber when converting both his penalty shots. The second and deciding one inspired the Swedish Postal Office to produce a memorial stamp with a bird's-eye view of Forsberg outmaneuvering Canadian goalie Corey Hirsch. Following a protest by Hirsch, a version of the stamp that was manufactured did not show his name on the back of the jersey. The other hero for the Swedes was goalie Tommy Salo, who made key saves in the shootout after playing a solid game.

Sweden had opened the scoring with a Tomas Jonsson shot from the blue line while on a power-play. For long periods the Swedes dominated through superior passing and faster skating. In the scoring department good opportunities were lost; even Forsberg failed on two occasions. The Canadians, true to their credo of never giving up, managed to turn the tables. Paul Kariya tied it up at 9:08 of the third period. Three-and-a-half minutes later, Canada went into the lead. The Swedish dream looked like it was going up in smoke. Then, with 2:10 remaining, Sweden got its chance. American referee Rob Hearne sent Canadian defenseman Brad Werenka off for a hooking offense on Mats Naslund. Only 21 seconds later the score was tied. Defenseman Magnus Svensson's shot from the blue line was deflected into the goal off a Canadian skate. The sudden-death period was characterized by little or no risk-taking, giving the goalies starring roles. Suddenly there was a penalty shootout, the first in Olympic or World Championship history to decide a gold medal.

The blow-by-blow showdown

Peter Nedved opened the proceedings with a shot into the top corner of the goal, leaving Salo without a chance. Sweden's first shooter was Hakan Loob, who did not give Hirsch much of a challenge. Learning from Nedved, Paul Kariya made it 2–0 by placing the puck in exactly the same corner. There was a lot of pressure on defenseman Magnus Svensson to open the scoring for Sweden, and he coped well outmaneuvering Hirsch and then lifting the puck over the goalie into the net. Dwayne Norris of Canada, Mats Naslund and then Canadian Greg Parks did not score. Tommy Salo stopped both Canadians with his pads. Then Peter Forsberg stepped on the ice. He started a feint, stopped it surprisingly and put the puck between Hirsch's pads. It was 2–2. A leg save by Salo prevented Canada from going ahead. The final penalty shot was taken by Roger Hansson. He had the chance to make history, but his shot went wide. The next stage was sudden-death penalty shots, one for each team until a decision was reached.

Sweden and Svensson started. He lost control and failed. Canada had the chance to decide again. Petr Nedved, in an effort to vary his shot, tried a low shot this time with a disastrous result. It was Forsberg again for the Swedes. He decided on a feint that Kent Nilsson displayed in the 1989 World Championships against the USA. At the crucial moment Forsberg almost lost the puck, but stretching, managed to put it under Hirsch's glove with the heel of the stick. It was a spectacular goal. But it was not over as Paul Kariya had the opportunity to even it up again. Salo was lured down on the ice by Kariya, who then shot high, only to be thwarted when Salo kicked his left leg up for a super stop. In that moment, a 75 year pursuit ended.

February 27, 1994 will always have a special meaning to sports and hockey people in Sweden. Even if Peter Forsberg and Tommy Salo stole the show in the closing stages of the event, the team as a whole will always have a special place in the hearts of the Swedish people.

From this team, special places in Swedish hockey history were taken by the three "Dads." They became true triple crown winners by having won the Stanley Cup, the World Championship gold and the Olympic gold. Tomas Jonsson won the Stanley Cup with the New York Islanders in 1982 and 1983 and the Worlds in 1991. Mats Naslund won the Stanley Cup with Montreal Canadiens in 1986 and the Worlds in 1991. Hakan Loob won the Stanley Cup with the Calgary Flames in 1989 and the World Championships in both 1987 and 1991.

THE 1998 CZECH OLYMPIC TEAM
Pavel Barta and Ivan Filippov

"THIS IS THE GREATEST DAY EVER in Czech hockey. Nothing else comes even close to it," said forward Martin Straka after his team won 1–0 over Russia in the Olympic final at Big Hat Arena on February 22, 1998. "When I saw the Czech flag and heard the national anthem, my whole hockey life was projected through my mind in one moment," Dominik Hasek revealed. Coach Slavomir Lener added: "Everyone is different. I thought about all the people we have made happy. About my family, friends and everybody back home who supported us and believed we can win." It was the first-ever Olympic gold for the Czech people. The former Czechoslovakian national team never had won it. Moreover, it was the first gold to be awarded to a team with NHL players on it.

Defenseman Petr Svoboda ("svoboda" translated to English means freedom) was only three years old in 1969, when Czechoslovakia's team achieved the most memorable victories in the country's history by twice defeating the Soviet Union at the World Championships in Stockholm, Sweden. The wins came less than a year after the Soviets rolled tanks into the center of Prague to crush the 1968 uprising known as the "Prague Spring."

"My parents still talk about the 1969 game. Beating Russians is still a big thing for that generation," said Svoboda, who defected in 1984 as a 18-year-old junior and started to play for the Montreal Canadiens in the NHL. He made his senior national team debut in Nagano 14 years later, scoring the only goal of the gold medal game when he rifled a shot past goalie Mikhail Shtalenkov at 8:08 of the third period. There was no politics involved in the game between the arch-rivals, not even in Svoboda's mind. This victory was as much about being proud to be a Czech after the split from Slovakia in 1993 as about beating the Russians. This was also about David and Goliath, about a team from a small country, a team who was not given much chance yet believed in itself.

After the semifinal victory over Canada, streets in Prague were flooded with joyous fans, many holding signs that read "Hasek for President." After the finals, the Czech celebrants added Svoboda's name to the ticket. The Czechs had several good chances, but it was Svoboda who finally broke through on a slap shot from the left point. There wouldn't be a better story to imagine at the end of the Czech road to glory than the winning goal being scored by "freedom!" At the news conference after the finals, goalie Dominik Hasek and assistant captain Robert Reichel

answered questions with broad grins on their faces. One of the questions was about money: "How much will you get for the Olympic win?" Reichel spoke into his microphone. "We don't care about money! We care about this!" As he said it, he held up the gold medal hanging on his neck and smiled.

The spirit of winning was evoked in 1996 when the Czech team won the World Championships in Vienna. It was the first title since 1985 and seventh overall, including six victories by the former Czechoslovakia, but the first-ever after the country split in two. The 1996 team had a mixture of players playing in the Czech Elite League, Sweden, Finland, Germany and the NHL. Robert Reichel, who had left the Calgary Flames to play with the Frankfurt Lions in the German League, brought to the team a spirit of national pride resulting in a unified, hard-working effort. The Czechs, led by head coach Ludek Bukac, went through the eight-game round robin unbeaten, including the 4–2 win in the final match against a strong Canadian team.

Three months later, another feast was expected. The Czechs had built a "dream team" for the World Cup of Hockey. Jaromir Jagr was on the team despite being ill prior to the start of the tournament. Petr Nedved was eligible to play for his homeland due to different rules, although he had dressed for Canada at the Olympics in Lillehammer two years earlier. Only Dominik Hasek turned down the invitation, saying he didn't play summer hockey. But Roman Turek was an easy choice after his great goaltending earlier during the World Championships in Vienna. The squad included 16 gold medalists from that championship but players never worked together. The Czechs finished the preliminary round with an 0–3–0 record, only four goals scored and 17 allowed. They were smoked 7–1 by Germany. "We haven't played as a team. We were like a puzzle no one could put together. We didn't find the road to heaven but the highway to hell," said Reichel, the captain.

After this fiasco, the Czech team played 11 games at different tournaments with a very disappointing record of 2–7–2. Ludek Bukac, who was very unpopular with some players, as well as with the media and the public, resigned. With just two months prior to the World Championships in Helsinki, Hlinka and Lener took over from him and started to prepare a new national team for the World Championship in Helsinki. Ivan Hlinka, the former Czech great who played briefly in the NHL with the Vancouver Canucks in the early 1980s, created a coaching tandem with the former assistant coach of Calgary—Slavomir Lener. Their team finished with a bronze medal in Helsinki and showed signs of the things to come. This coaching change was the turning point in the building of a team for the hockey tournament of the century in Nagano.

"Hockey experts in North America may not realize that many of the Czechs playing in Europe are as good or even better players then those who play for NHL teams," said Lener. "We learned from the World Cup disaster. Ivan and myself, we met individually with each player during the summer break and worked out a plan, hoping that the players will go for it. Still, we were not a team when we arrived in Nagano, but we gradually grew into it." The best team will win, not the team with the star players: this was the philosophy of the Czech coaches. Hlinka and Lener decided that if they were going to be successful in the Olympics, they had to change the players' attitudes. The best way to do that was to use Czech players playing in European leagues as the core. The objective was to get a mixture of experi-

ence and youth, talent and dedication on the team. To be on the team became a matter of honor.

"It's tough to predict if a guy would be in optimal shape when you have to name him to the team roster three months prior to the tournament," said Hlinka, after announcing 12 names of NHL players who had made his team in early December, 1997. That explains why the coaches turned down an idea to take more than the minimum. Those 12 players represented the lowest number of all teams seeded in the final Olympic round. The rosters of Canada and the U.S. were filled exclusively by NHL players; third goaltender Oleg Shevtsov was the only player on the Russian team who wasn't an NHLer; four Swedish players were picked from the domestic league, but only Jonas Jonsson had never played in the NHL. The Finns called up 14 NHL players, almost everybody they could. In comparison, about 40 Czechs skated at least once in the NHL during the 1997–98 season. Vaclav Prospal of the Ottawa Senators broke his leg and his national team spot was taken by Milan Hejduk, a flashy winger from Pardubice. Vladimir Vujtek of the Tampa Bay Lightning faced serious health problems just two weeks before the tournament and was replaced by Robert Lang of the Pittsburgh Penguins. There were only 11 NHLers on the Czech team by the time of the opening face-off against Finland on February 13.

"It really doesn't matter if you play in the NHL or not," said Jaromir Jagr. "Some guys have problems with their teams over here and the large ice rink in Nagano could be an advantage for European players. I hope we'll do much better than at the World Cup. That's why we all wanted to be at the Olympics. But the most important difference is Dominik will be there, too." "When I grew up it was always Olympics," said Dominik Hasek. "We knew nothing of the NHL. My heroes were always from my country and when they went to the Olympics it was a big thing. The times are changing. Now I know that to get the Stanley Cup is great and I would like to win one, but when I left to go to North America for another season last summer, nobody talked about the Stanley Cup and the NHL with me, they talked about the Olympics." Many hockey experts had said if Jagr scored one goal a game, Hasek would handle the rest. It sounded so simple, but it wasn't. And it was tough to figure out if the Czechs would surprise or disappoint. "The Olympics will be the best tournament ever in hockey. This really means a lot, if you consider the history. Our underdog status doesn't mean that I'll go play just for fun. It could be an advantage for us. And I believe we'll have a good team," added the Czech netminder.

The Czechs exceeded all pre-tournament predictions. The record shows that Dominik Hasek led his team to victory, posting shutouts against Finland in the opening game and Russia in the final, while adding a dramatic shootout victory over Canada en route to a 5–1–0 record and the Olympic gold. Hasek was great, especially when he faced 39 shots in the 4–1 quarterfinal win that sent the U.S. home. He was excellent during the late stages and in the dramatic shootout against Canada. But as good as Hasek was, his brilliance was not the only reason for the victory. He is entitled to receive the biggest share of the credit, but credit also must go to each and every player on the team. The coaching staff merits its well-deserved share too. They couldn't have done it without strong play from both the NHL stars and the players no one ever heard of before.

Defense was predicted as a weak link because the forwards wouldn't be able to help defensively. But offensive

stars like Jaromir Jagr sacrificed their scoring genius many times for strong backchecking. "Next time, they should write my number 68 with 'D' next to it on the roster list," joked the skilled right winger, who recorded one goal and four assists in six games. "We knew that Hasek is an excellent goalie," said coach Hlinka. "But the most important thought was that our players haven't come for breaking scoring records. They had character and worked hard for the team as if it was one body."

The Czech defensive crew emerged as the tournament's best. Not only did they make Hasek's job easier, they scored very important goals in the semifinals and finals. Richard Smehlik and offensive-minded Jiri Slegr were towers of strength. Frantisek Kucera, a rejected NHLer, and the rock-solid, unheralded banger Jaroslav Spacek completed the second pair. The third comprised Roman Hamrlik and veteran Petr Svoboda. "When I left Philadelphia, they saw me off saying that we could have the same chances for a win as the Jamaican bobsled team," said the author of the golden shot. "One of my Edmonton Oilers teammates left for a vacation in Mexico," added Hamrlik. "He said I would be free to join him one week later."

Vladimir Ruzicka, a 34-year-old with five seasons of NHL experience with the Edmonton Oilers, Boston Bruins and Ottawa Senators. He has scored 400 goals in the Czech league, but at Nagano, he skated and fought like a rookie trying to win a job in the NHL. He returned to the national team after eight years. He was so concerned about himself being in top-notch shape that he was taking extra practices with the Slavia Prague junior team before the Olympics. He was named team captain. In the first intermission of the quarterfinals against the U.S., with the Americans ahead 1-0, it was he who stood up and delivered an inspiring and elevating speech to his teammates. "There's no need to feel intimidated just because all the Americans play for NHL teams. We have a big chance to win and we can do it!" He scored the tying goal in the second period, while centering Jagr and Martin Straka. Ruzicka and Straka both scored three goals in the tournament.

Robert Reichel, renowned as another of the team's spiritual leaders, notched three key goals in the Olympics, including the game winner in the shootout against Canada. "I know most of his hockey history. I don't remember that he's ever missed on a penalty shot," said Lener, who coached Reichel on the national team and with Calgary while serving as an assistant coach between 1992 and 1995. Reichel centered a line called the Litvinov Mafia with his former schoolmates Robert Lang and sniper Martin Rucinsky. Forward Pavel Patera, a playmaker who topped all Czech league scorers in 1993–94 and 1994–95, always has been considered too weak to play in North America. At the 1997 World Championships in Helsinki, he led a line with Vladimir Vujtek and Martin Prochazka that collected 17 of 30 Czech goals. After Vujtek had to refuse an invitation to the Olympics, he was replaced by Jan Caloun and then Milan Hejduk on right wing. Patera scored the first goal on a power-play in the opening game with Finland and was the team's best scorer with five points, tying Jagr. He won a huge face-off in the semifinals against Canada's Theo Fleury that led to a goal by defenseman Jiri Slegr with 11:14 remaining in the game. He won one more face-off in the finals against Russia's Sergei Fedorov, another NHL multi-millionaire. The puck moved to Martin Prochazka who passed it back to the blue line. There was shooter Petr Svoboda, waiting with a loaded gun to finally end it all.

One line consisted entirely of players from the Czech national team. Power center Jiri Dopita, a former Boston Bruins prospect, proved to be strong and extremely difficult to knock off the puck. His backchecking was second to none. He showed he could play hardball when the heat is on. Josef Beranek, a 28-goal scorer with Philadelphia in the 1993–94 season, was another NHL castoff. The tall but not overly robust physical winger didn't mind getting involved and did not back down from anyone. David Moravec, the best scorer in the Czech league when the Olympic tournament was held, was virtually unknown on the other side of the ocean. He shifted to the side with Jagr, who skated on two lines after the playoffs started.

The Czechs came together to become a team in the truest sense of the word both on and off the ice. "I don't know how it came. It was as if it was by design. Yet it happened unexpectedly. All of a sudden we all held each other around the shoulders. The whole bench. We wanted to get closer, to share our feelings," said Martin Rucinsky about the emotion during the crucial moments of the semifinal shootout against Canada. What was happening at that moment wasn't just a symbol of team harmony but also a demonstration of team faith, energy and will. "At that moment we knew that we would not be defeated. I would have bet my life on it," said Robert Reichel.

The former Czechoslovakia was very close to Olympic gold medals on three occasions. In 1948, at St. Moritz, the national team tied Canada for the first time ever at such a big tournament, but it needed to win. The Czechs were stopped by the Soviet Union in 1976 at Innsbruck when they lost 4–3, allowing two goals in the closing minutes. They were even closer in 1984 at Sarajevo but lost 2–0 to the Soviets in the clinching game.

Assistant coach Ivan Hlinka was a great player in the 1970s. He had three World Championship titles and was a member of the 1976 Olympic team. But he never won more than a bronze medal as a coach, having finished third in the 1992, 1993 and 1997 World Championships and the 1992 Olympics. Hlinka is a tough man but he was one of those who was unable to stop his tears after the win. "I took it probably more emotionally, I coached a lot of guys who won the gold with us [in Nagano] at the 1991 Canada Cup, when I was at the national team's bench for the first time. Before we traveled to Nagano, we would consider the semi-finals as a big success. We lost to Russia in the preliminary round and had to face the toughest opponents we could imagine in the playoffs. But the hardest way you go, the more you grow up sometimes."

Eight hours after the win, the team boarded a charter flight for the Czech capital of Prague, where a national celebration was in full swing. The heroes were to be honored February 23 at a ceremony at Prague's Old Town Square. Win or lose, once the Czechs reached the Olympic finals, the trip was confirmed. The players were thrilled at the thought of sharing their greatest moment with hundreds of thousands of their countrymen.

It was the largest crowd to assemble in the national capital since November 1989, when the communist regime was overthrown. Like the 23 players, the nation was proud to be Czech, although not too many people believed the team could have reached something so special in Nagano. Any medal seemed to be a dream. But now the Czech hockey heroes will be remembered forever as 1998 Olympic champions, winners of the first dream tournament. Life goes on, but the memory remains.

CHAPTER 36

1998 U.S. Women's Gold Medal Team

The U.S. Team's Long Route from Underdog to Olympic Champion

Cammy Clark

CAMMI GRANATO can barely catch her breath and it has nothing to do with long shifts or hard practices. The 27-year-old captain of the U.S. women's gold medal-winning Olympic team has been racing from one commitment to the next at the same speed she chases down a loose puck in the corner.

Granato has been in such high demand since the Olympics that agent Kent Hughes needed to pull out her calendar in order to rattle off all her recent commitments.

She threw out the first pitch at the Chicago Cubs home opener. She was an awards presenter at the Nickelodeon Kid's Choice Awards Show hosted by Rosie O'Donnell in Los Angeles. There were speaking engagements for Merrill Lynch in New Jersey and New York, where she was flown between the two states via helicopter.

She was in Hawaii for an AT&T appearance. She already had made the phone company's TV commercial with her four brothers (in which Tony, of the San Jose Sharks, used to be the most famous Granato in the family).

"It's all so surreal," Cammi Granato said late one Sunday night in March from Boca Raton, Florida, where she was helping to charter her own foundation that will help children with cancer and athletic dreams.

"Winning the gold medal is the coolest feeling and most rewarding, then all the things happen to you," she said. "Twenty-four hours after winning the gold they took our picture for the Wheaties box. I never thought that I would be on a Wheaties box. It's unbelievable. I just have to smile.

"But the weirdest thing is that what I was doing was so wrong in everybody eyes when I was growing up. Now people commend you and are very excited and accepting. It's cool now for girls to play hockey. I don't know why the change of heart."

Granato has been fighting everything from stereotypes to the Canadians to get to the stand at Big Hat Arena in Nagano, Japan. It was all worth it when she bowed to receive the first Olympic gold medal ever put around a woman hockey player's neck.

It's a story of perseverance for all the women who competed in the first women's Olympic hockey tournament. It's also a story about the Americans, who had always played second-fiddle to the Canadians until winning the most important game ever in their up and coming sport.

The quest started in earnest in 1990, with the first IIHF Women's World Championships. The event was modest. It was held in Ottawa and attracted little media coverage. The Canadians beat the Americans 5–2 for the title to begin seven years of domination.

"We just didn't have the depth the Canadians had," Granato said.

The turning point for the Americans came during a midwinter day in 1996 when 50-year-old Ben Smith read a flyer that was sitting on his desk at Northeastern University, where he coached the men's hockey team. USA Hockey was looking for one good coach to lead the fledgling women's national team to the first women's Olympic tournament in Japan in 1998.

Smith's interest piqued immediately. "I'd be lying if I didn't say I wanted to get on board this program for selfish reasons," Smith said. "I was never good enough to be an Olympic athlete and I was only an assistant coach with the men's U.S. team in Calgary (in 1988). I thought it would be neat to give this a try."

Smith was named the first full-time coach of the American women's national team on June 6, 1996. But there was a bit of an adjustment on both sides.

Smith got on a bus in August with 40 girls trying out for the team and didn't exactly make a winning first impression. Smith asked how many of the girls liked hockey. When they all raised their hands, Smith said, "Good, I'm on the right bus."

Forward Karyn Bye thought, "Who is this clown?"

Smith's only previous experience coaching elite women was for two or three weeks during the summer of 1995 when he took an American team to Finland for a tournament. He also coached a team of 12-year-old girls in Gloucester, Massachusetts, sharing the job with his former wife. But it didn't take long for Smith to figure out how to handle his new team.

"With coach Smith, when he got in the driving seat, we knew good things were going to happen," Granato said. "We knew he had so much experience with the men's game. But he also realized that, 'Hey, these girls want to come to the rink every day.' They love hockey just as much any guys he's ever coached. We didn't have to sell him that we were totally committed. He could see it.

"He didn't want to get emotionally involved at first, but the way he cared for us and stuck up for us and cared for us, he's the type of coach you would go through the wall for."

Smith did not have to be sold on the women's level of commitment. "This group really struck me on how focused and how dedicated they were and how much they loved the game," Smith said. "It was like being an English professor, where everybody wanted to go to the Globe Theater (in London) to see Shakespeare. I had 20 eager students."

After all, his 20 eager students had spent years being ridiculed as young girls for playing a sport "meant for boys." Almost every one of those American girls had a story to tell about pretending to be a boy at one time or another to play hockey. Granato went by the name "Carl." Bye went by the initials, "K.L."

"They would get chased off the rinks, but they would tuck their hair up in their helmets and come back the next Saturday for a game," Smith said as a tone equally appropriate for a proud father. "They were not getting paid and they didn't think there was a pot of gold somewhere. They came because they love playing. That really distinguishes them and unites them and bonds them."

But the Canadian women also had similar stories and were also unquestionably dedicated. The next year the Americans made more sacrifices to dedicate more time to the national team.

Smith took over the women's team two months after they lost to Canada 4–1 in the gold medal game at the 1996 Pacific Rim Women's Hockey Championship in Vancouver. He didn't need his 1968 Harvard degree to figure out the biggest challenge facing the Americans for the Olympic gold was "psychological."

"I don't think they were very far from the Canadians in a physical sense, but in a psychological sense they were further behind than they wanted to admit," Smith said. "They were always finishing second and I wanted to erase that feeling as quickly as possible."

In the short duration of women's international hockey, Canada had ruled. Canada had won the first three Women's World Championships. Canada had won the first two Pacific Rim Hockey Championships. Canada had won the first 3-Nation's Tournament. The Americans were always seeing red and could probably recite *O Canada* in their sleep.

"I think there was definitely a difference in talent at the beginning," said U.S. Olympic captain Cammi Granato, who has played for the Americans in every major international competition. "Canada had a lot more depth. They had the stronger team. We never seemed to be able to touch them. But the gap was closing the last few years. I think we became pretty evenly matched, but the difference was Canada had the mental edge. They beat us over and over when it counted. There was a psychological barrier."

To conquer that barrier, it would take teamwork. Smith's team-building activities included visiting a haunted house for Halloween and rock climbing in the wilderness.

"It taught us to trust each other," Granato said.

That would be especially important when the Americans found themselves trailing 4–1 in the final period to the Canadians in the last round-robin game of the Olympics.

But first, Smith realized that it was not an overnight task for the Americans to erase seven years of being a bridesmaid when the goal was to be on the alter. In this case, the alter was the Olympic podium, where no women wearing black skates and shoulder pads had stood before.

Girls had been playing organized hockey for over 100 years, dating back to at least 1889, when the first documented game was held in Ottawa. Two years later, during the same season of the first Stanley Cup championship, a female team, "The Love-Me-Littles" played in a game at Queen's University in Kingston, Ontario in defiance of the school's Archbishop.

But it was not until the 1970s that the women's game blossomed across Canada, throughout Europe and in U.S. colleges in the Midwest and East. The international hockey scene is so new that the first World Championships were held when George Bush was midway through his U.S. presidency. Even bodychecking was allowed.

At that point, Canada was ahead of the rest of the world in the women's game. Canada beat Sweden 15–1, Germany 17–0 and Japan 18–0 in the round-robin portion of the 1990 World Championships. Canada edged Finland 6–5 in the semifinals to face the United States, which had defeated Sweden 10–3 in the other semifinal. The Americans beat Norway 17–0, Switzerland 16–3 and Finland 5–4 in the round-robin portion.

For the gold medal, the United States took a 2–0 lead, but Canada's athleticism took over and they scored five unanswered goals to capture the championship 5–2. Angela James, who was called the Wayne Gretzky of women's hockey, led the way for Canada with 11 goals and two assists in five games.

Two years later, in Tampere, Finland, Canada dominated the second Women's World Championships, trouncing the Americans 8–0 in the gold medal game. In 1994, the championships were in Lake Placid, New York, home of the American men's Olympic "Miracle on Ice" in 1980. But there would be no women's miracle, with Canada winning again in the gold medal game, this time 6–3 over the Americans.

The United States' commitment to women's hockey changed with the Olympics around the corner. Before Smith was hired, the national team simply met two to three weeks before an international tournament.

Smith said his first task was to "make sure I got off the bus with the best players. That's usually key to any good coach." So Smith and assistant coach Tom Mutch, also Smith's assistant at Northeastern, began scouring the United States for any hidden talent. But it turned out that USA Hockey hadn't missed anybody.

Smith made Walpole, Massachusetts the team's headquarters, holding several minicamps for the players to train and practice with the best. "I don't want to be negative or disrespectful but the talent on college teams is not that deep," Smith said. "Practices are not that demanding for the top players. When the athletes came here they fed off each other and pushed each other."

Smith also enlisted Mike Boyle, the strength and conditioning coach of the Boston Bruins, to help his players improve their fitness levels, which proved to be another key factor during the Olympics.

The 1997 Women's World Championships was the first major international tournament for Smith as head coach of the U.S. team. In the closest game ever between the two rivals, Canada needed overtime to beat the Americans 4–3 in the gold medal game before a partisan Canadian crowd of 3,000 at Kitchener Memorial Auditorium. About 200 accredited media were at that event, compared to only about 25 at the first World Championship in Ottawa.

While the Americans came away from that loss disheartened, they also came away knowing they were oh-so close to finally beating the Canadians.

In preparing for the Olympics, the Canadians got a later start than their American rivals. They didn't hire Olympic coach Shannon Miller full-time until June of 1997, a full year after Smith was on the job. In a move that many in Canada now question, the two rivals agreed to play 13 games as part of their pre-Olympic training. Miller didn't like the idea at first, but agreed to go along with it. In hindsight, it was a tour that gave the Americans confidence and led the Canadians to doubt themselves.

The Americans started with a pool of about 40 players. Goalie Erin Whitten, who had been a mainstay in goal for the Americans in their early years, didn't even make the team. She was beat out by Sarah Tueting and Sara DeCosta.

Smith had some tough decisions for the final 20, with young players like Katie King, Tara Mounsey, Laurie Baker and Angela Ruggiero emerging. The only two players from the 1990 tournament team who would make the Olympic roster were Granato and Lisa Brown-Miller, who had been only Lisa Brown at the time.

The 5'1" Brown-Miller missed her honeymoon to Alaska, leaving for training camp in Lake Placid one day after get-

ting married to John Miller on August 19, 1995.

The Canadians won the 13-game exhibition series 7–6, but the goals each team had scored were identical at 37. The Canadians were also embroiled in a controversy that only helped the American cause.

Angela James, a superstar for Canada in 1990 and 1992, had been used in a reduced role under coach Shannon Miller. She was finally cut from the Olympic team after Miller twice warned her she was on the bubble because of her defensive liabilities.

When James, 33, was cut, it led to a national outcry. James did not go quietly, saying "she hoped it wasn't the case that a personal relationship between management and a player" was a factor.

The Canadian Hockey Association launched an investigation into whether Miller had a sexual relationship with any of her players. It developed into a distraction that was drawn out for two weeks. In a press conference, Canadian Hockey Association president Murray Costello commented: "I've confirmed to my satisfaction that the evaluation process was done in a very detailed and diligent way. It's all well documented and I accept that. I've looked into the rumors of a personal relationship and I call them media allegations."

Miller, who had been a tough Calgary cop before she took the coaching job, conceded the ordeal affected her: "Day after day, 10 days, 14 days of it. I think eventually it does affect you."

Soon after the ordeal was over, the Canadians played the Americans on December 20 for the gold medal in the 3-Nations Tournament in Lake Placid. Miller considered it a dress rehearsal for the Olympics. The Americans, despite putting less importance on the game and even sitting out Granato and star defenseman Tara Mounsey, won 3–0. If goalie Manon Rheaume hadn't played so well for Canada, it could have been a total rout.

Miller told her team to "take that pain home with them for Christmas. The U.S. has felt that pain for years."

Following Christmas, Miller brought her squad on a retreat to Emerald Lake, British Columbia for a team building session. They went cross-country skiing and sang around a fire accompanied by a guitar. "We addressed some issues we needed to address," Miller observed at the time. "Silver medal at the 3-Nations tournament. Angela James. We had some closure."

The Americans continued a plan of a more physical attack designed to go after some of Canada's more soft players, notably Danielle Goyette. It was almost like the Americans were beating the Canadian team at their own game of psychological warfare. Come the Olympics, the Americans were on a roll and the Canadians were feeling the tremendous pressure of an entire nation *expecting* nothing less than a gold medal performance.

Granato simply said: "We picked the right time to peak."

The Americans had won four of the last six meetings between the two teams leading up to the Olympics. The Canadians never seemed to find a way to counter the more physical American attack.

At Nagano, the Americans easily beat China 5–0 and Sweden 7–1 in the first two games of the tournament. Finland gave the Americans a tough game that was tied 2–2 before the U.S. pulled away to win 4–2. The Americans then routed host Japan 10–0 to set up the last round-robin meeting with Canada.

Because both teams had locked up berths in the gold medal game, the only thing on the line in this final round-robin marchup was the psychological factor that goes with winning and losing. The United States fell behind 4–1. "We were so prepared for that tournament, that our confidence never swayed," Granato said. "Even when we were down 4–1, the team never got negative or down. We never lost our focus and never gave up. We never even thought of giving up. Our team just kept gaining momentum."

The Americans came back, scoring six unanswered goals in the final period to win 7–4 and give the Canadians plenty of reason to doubt themselves for the gold medal game three days later.

In the biggest game ever played in women's hockey, the Canadians came out flat while the Americans took a 2–0 lead. The Canadians fought back to 2–1 and were pushing for the game-tying goal in the third period. But Sandra Whyte scored into the empty net for the exclamation point of an eight-year odyssey to finally beat the Canadians when it counted.

Granato was shocked at the impact the U.S. win had back in the United States. Local rinks around the country have been flooded from parents inquiring how they can sign their little girls up for hockey. Granato chuckled, remembering all the times she was the "only" girl playing. "I still can't quite believe it," she said.

Granato plans to stick around for four more years and compete in the next Winter Olympics in 2002 when they will be in Salt Lake City. She can certainly afford it now with her slew of endorsements.

But while Granato has been pleased with the overwhelming response, she has one request for her agent. "She's been begging me to slow down," Hughes said. "She can't find time to train."

CHAPTER 37
Women's Championship Events

WOMEN'S WORLD CHAMPIONSHIPS

The first official IIHF Women's World Hockey Championships were held in 1990, three years after an unofficial women's world tournament had been held for the first time. Since 1990, the Women's World Championships have taken place every second year, though the last tournament prior to the 1998 Winter Olympics was held in 1997. Qualification for the World tournament begins at the Women's European Championships, where the top five teams earn the right to join Canada, the United States and the best team from Asia at the World event.

The eight nations participating at the Women's World Championships are split into two divisions with a round robin played within each group. After the round robin, the top two teams in both groups advance to one-game semifinals. Semifinals winners play for the overall championship while the losers play off for third place. The teams finishing third and fourth in the two round-robin groups use the same playoff format to decide fifth through eighth place.

Brief summaries of each IIHF Women's World Championship event follow below.

1987 (UNOFFICIAL)

The first Women's World Championships were held in Toronto from April 21 to April 26, 1987. It was not recognized as an official tournament by the International Ice Hockey Federation. Teams from Canada, the United States, Sweden, Switzerland, Japan and Holland were on hand, as well as a team representing the Canadian province of Ontario.

Though the Ontario team beat the United States in the semifinals before losing 4–0 to Canada in the title game, the provincial team was not assigned a ranking in the final standings, meaning that the United States was considered to be the second-place finisher after defeating Sweden 5–0 in what otherwise would have been the bronze medal game. Sweden was ranked third. Canada ran up a perfect record of 6–0 in winning the event.

1990

The first official Women's World Championships were held in Ottawa from March 19 to March 25, 1990. Eight nations were present at the tournament, with Canada, Sweden, West Germany and Japan playing in Group A while the United States, Finland, Switzerland and Norway comprised Group B. In the round-robin schedule, Canada beat Sweden 15–1, West Germany 17–0 and Japan 18–0 to top its group while the United States edged Finland 5–4 and crushed Switzerland 16–3 and Norway 17–0 to win Group B.

In the playoffs, teams from Group A crossed over to meet teams from Group B with a separate series of games to determine the medal winners and to round out the standings of the teams ranking five through eight. Canada narrowly defeated Finland 5–4 to advance to the gold medal game, while the Americans crushed Sweden 10–3. In the bronze medal game, Finland beat Sweden 6–3. The championship was won by Canada, who defeated the United States 5–2.

Among those leading the gold medal-winning Canadians were Angela James (11 goals) and Heather Ginzel (seven goals and five assists). Goaltenders Denis Caron (2.08 goals-against average in three games) and Cathy Phillips (1.15 in four) also starred. American Cindy Curley enjoyed the best individual performance of the tournament with 11 goals and 12 assists. Cammi Granato added nine goals to the U.S. total.

1992

China and Denmark each made their Women's World Championship debut in the tournament held in Tampere, Finland from April 20 to April 26, 1992. The two new countries played with Canada and Sweden in Group A, while Group B was made up of the United States, Finland, Switzerland and Norway as it had been in 1990. Once again the Canadians proved to be easily the best in their group, defeating Sweden 6–1, China 8–0 and Denmark 10–0. The United States, challenged only by Finland, edged the Finns 5–3, and crushed Norway 9–1 and the Swiss 13–0 to top Group B. In the semifinals, Canada beat Finland and the United States topped Sweden to set up another Canadian–American finals. This time Canada crushed the United States 8–0 to retain the World Championship, while Finland beat Sweden 5–4 to claim the bronze medal.

The 1992 Women's World Championships introduced Manon Rheaume to international play. The Canadian netminder was named to the tournament all-star team after allowing just two goals in the three games she played, although Sweden's Annica Ahlen was named best goalie at the event. Cammi Granato of the United States was named best forward after scoring eight goals in six games, while Canada's Geraldine Heaney was named best defenseman. Heaney was joined by American Ellen Weinberg as the all-star defensemen, while Granato, Canada's Angela James and Finland's Riikka Nieminen were the all-star forwards.

1994

Lake Placid, New York, was the sight of the 1994 Women's World Championships, but there would be no "Miracle on Ice" for the United States squad, who would lose only one game at the tournament again—the gold medal game against Team Canada.

As in past years, Canada breezed to the top of Group A with a 7–1 win over China, an 8–2 win over Sweden and a 12–0 whitewash of Norway. The Americans edged Finland 2–1, downed Switzerland 6–0 and crushed Germany 16–0 to finish atop Group B. When the teams crossed over to play the semifinals, Canada downed Finland 4–1, while the Americans humbled China 14–3. Finland then claimed its third bronze medal with an 8–1 drubbing of China. Canada downed the United States 6–3 to remain the World Champions.

As in 1992, Canada's Manon Rheaume was named the goaltender on the tournament all star team without being named best goalie. This year, the honor went to Erin Whitten of the United States. Best defenseman was once again Geraldine Heaney of Canada, while best forward was Riikka Nieminen. The flashy Finn had four goals and nine assists for 13 points in five games. Canada's Danielle Goyette led the tournament with nine goals and joined Nieminen as a forward on the all-star team along with American Karen Bye. Rounding out the all-star team were Canada's Therese Brisson and Kelly O'Leary of the United States, who were chosen for the defense.

1997

Russia made its debut at the Women's World Championships in 1997 and finished sixth among the eight teams taking part at the tournament played in six cities across southwestern Ontario. Russia tied Switzerland 3–3 for its only point in three games during the round-robin portion of the tournament, then beat Norway 2–1 in the playoffs before losing 3–1 to Sweden in the game to decide fifth and sixth place. Switzerland and Norway ranked seventh and eighth respectively.

For the fourth time in the four official Women's World Championships, Canada ran up a perfect record at the tournament to take the title. This year, however, it took overtime to defeat the Americans 4–3 in the gold medal game. Nancy Drolet scored the game winner for Canada to cap a three-goal performance. Canada had reached the gold medal game by defeating China 7–1, Russia 9–1 and Switzerland 6–0 to win Group A, then edging Finland 2–1 in the semifinals. The United States won Group B with wins of 10–0 over Sweden and 7–0 over Norway, but only managed a 3–3 tie with Finland before blanking China 6–0 in the semifinals. Finland shut out China 3–0 to win its fourth straight bronze medal at the Women's World Championships.

Among the top performers at the 1997 Women's World Championships were Finland's Riikka Nieminen (five goals and five assists), Canada's Hayley Wickenheiser (four goals and five assists) and Cammie Granato of the United States (five goals and three assists). All three were named all-star forwards at the event.

Canada's Cassie Campbell had two goals and six assists and earned a selection as an all-star defenseman, as did Kelly O'Leary of the United States. Rounding out the all-star team was goaltender Patricia Sautter of Switzerland.

WOMEN'S OLYMPICS 1998

Women's hockey made its debut at the Olympics Games in Nagano in 1998. Qualification for the event began at the Women's World Championships in 1997. The top five countries from the 1997 event qualified for the Olympics along with the host country, resulting in a six-team field comprising Canada, the United States, Finland, Sweden, China and Japan. As winners of every previous Women's World Championship (1990, 1992, 1994 and 1997) Canada was expected to bring home the first women's Olympic gold medal, but the tide clearly was turning in the months leading up to the tournament. A 13-game pre-Olympic series between the sport's two powers saw the Americans post an 6–7–0 record, but the United States defeated Canada handily at the 3-Nations Cup in Lake Placid prior to Christmas 1997 and seemed to be getting stronger as the Olympics approached.

Having won all of the medals available at the previous World Championships, Canada, the United States and Finland were clearly the class of the Women's Olympic tournament and proved it in their opening games as Canada beat Japan 13–0, the U.S. beat China 5–0 and Finland beat Sweden 6–0. Canada, however, struggled through its next three games, managing only a 2–0 win over China, a 5–3 win over Sweden and a 4–2 win over Finland, while the Americans ran up victories of 7–1, 4–2 and 10–0 over Sweden, Finland and Japan. Leslie Reddon was struggling in goal for the Canadians, though Manon Rheaume was proving solid. However, the two were not providing the type of clutch goaltending the Americans were receiving from their netminding duo of Sarah Tueting and Sara Decosta. This point was made clear when the

Canadians and Americans met to close out the preliminary round. Reddon allowed the U.S. to score six goals in a span of 11:53 late in the third period as the Americans turned a 4–1 deficit into a 7–4 victory and finished with a perfect 5–0 record. Canada was 4–1 but would have its chance for revenge in the gold medal game.

Meanwhile, Finland had proven to be the best of the rest, adding an 11–1 win over Japan and a 6–1 win over China to its 6–0 win over Sweden to finish the preliminary round with a record of 3–2. China, who had defeated Japan and Sweden by scores of 6–1 and 3–1, provided the opposition for Finland in the bronze medal game. The Finns were 4–1 winners behind a goal and an assist from Rikka Nieminen, who led the tournament in scoring with 12 points on seven goals and five assists.

Sarah Tueting and Manon Rheaume provided solid goaltending for their respective countries in the gold medal clash between the United States and Canada, but Tueting proved to be just a little bit better as the Americans carried a 2–0 lead into the game's final minutes. Danielle Goyette (who was the tournament's leading goal scorer with nine goals despite the death of her father shortly before the Olympics) put Canada on the scoreboard at 15:59 of the third period, but an empty-net goal at 19:52 sealed Canada's fate. While American captain Cammie Granato led her teammates in celebration, the Canadian women could not conceal the disappointment they felt in taking home a silver medal from the most important tournament of their lives.

WOMEN'S EUROPEAN CHAMPIONSHIPS

The first Women's European Championships were held in 1989 and have been staged every two years since, though the last tournament prior to the 1998 Winter Olympics was held in 1996. In 1993, a B Pool for the Women's European Championships was created. The country finishing last in the A Pool standings is relegated to the B Pool while the winner of B earns promotion to A.

Six teams play a round-robin schedule in the Women's European Championship A Pool in order to declare a winner. The top five countries earn a berth in the Women's World Championships. In the B Pool, eight countries are divided into two groups. After a round robin within each group, the teams from each group are paired for a one-game playoff to determine the final standings. The two first-place teams meet to determine top spot, the second-best teams meet to decide third place and so on.

WOMEN'S PACIFIC CHAMPIONSHIPS

The first Women's Pacific Championship was held in April of 1995. The annual tournament involves four countries—Canada, the United States, China and Japan. The first stage of the tournament is played in a round robin, after which the first-place team meets fourth place and second place meets third in the semifinals. Winners advance to the finals while the losers play for third place.

WOMEN'S CHAMPIONSHIP EVENTS
STANDINGS, AND LEADING SCORERS

WOMEN'S WORLD CHAMPIONSHIPS

1987 (UNOFFICIAL)

Rank	Team	GP	W	L	T	GF	GA	Pts
1	Canada	6	6	0	0	51		12
2	USA	6	5	1	0	61		10
3	Sweden	6	3	3	0	16		6
4	Switzerland	6	2	4	0	12		4
5	Japan	6	1	5	0	9		2
6	Holland	6	0	6	0	6		0

1990

Rank	Team	GP	W	L	T	GF	GA	Pts
1	Canada	5	5	0	0	61	8	10
2	USA	5	4	1	0	50	15	8
3	Finland	5	3	2	0	35	15	6
4	Sweden	5	2	3	0	25	35	4
5	Switzerland	5	3	2	0	23	39	6
6	Norway	5	1	4	0	16	45	2
7	W. Germany	5	2	3	0	16	33	4
8	Japan	5	0	5	0	11	47	0

1992

Rank	Team	GP	W	L	T	GF	GA	Pts
1	Canada	4	4	0	0	32	1	8
2	USA	4	3	1	0	27	12	6
3	Finland	4	3	1	0	32	13	6
4	Sweden	4	2	2	0	15	14	4
5	China	5	3	2	0	11	18	6
6	Norway	5	2	3	0	11	23	4
7	Denmark	5	1	4	0	7	24	2
8	Switzerland	5	0	5	0	6	36	0

1994

Rank	Team	GP	W	L	T	GF	GA	Pts
1	Canada	5	5	0	0	37	7	10
2	USA	5	4	1	0	41	10	8
3	Finland	5	3	2	0	40	8	6
4	China	5	1	3	1	17	34	3
5	Sweden	5	3	1	1	22	17	7
6	Norway	5	1	4	0	12	33	2
7	Switzerland	5	2	3	0	10	30	4
8	Germany	5	0	5	0	6	46	0

1997

Rank	Team	GP	W	L	T	GF	GA	Pts
1	Canada	5	5	0	0	28	6	10
2	USA	5	3	1	1	29	7	7
3	Finland	5	3	1	1	22	5	7
4	China	5	2	3	0	18	21	4
5	Sweden	5	2	2	1	12	19	5
6	Russia	5	1	3	1	9	22	3
7	Switzerland	5	1	3	1	8	27	3
8	Norway	5	0	4	1	3	22	1

OLYMPIC GAMES

Nagano, Japan • 1998 • Women

Rank	Team	GP	W	L	T	GF	GA	Pts
1	USA	5	5	0	0	33	7	10
2	Canada	5	4	1	0	28	12	8
3	Finland	5	3	2	0	27	10	6
4	China	5	2	3	0	10	15	4
5	Sweden	5	1	4	0	10	21	2
6	Japan	5	0	5	0	2	45	0

Bronze Medal game
Finland   4   China   1

Gold Medal game
USA   3   Canada   1

1998 Scoring Leaders

Player	Team	GP	G	A	PTS	PIM
Rikka Nieminen	Finland	6	7	5	12	4
Danielle Goyette	Canada	6	8	1	9	10
Karyn Bye	USA	6	5	3	8	4
Cammi Granato	USA	6	4	4	8	0
Katie King	USA	6	4	4	8	2
Gretchen Ulion	USA	6	3	5	8	4
H. Wickenheiser	Canada	6	2	6	8	4
Therese Brisson	Canada	6	5	2	7	6
Kirsi Hanninen	Finland	6	4	3	7	6
Laurie Baker	USA	6	4	3	7	6

Men's Olympic results are found on page 512.

WOMEN'S EUROPEAN CHAMPIONSHIPS

1989

Rank	Team	GP	W	L	T	GF	GA	Pts
1	Finland	3	3	0	0	56	0	6
2	Sweden	3	3	0	0	24	3	6
3	West Germany	3	2	1	0	17	5	4
4	Norway	3	2	1	1	18	6	3
5	Switzerland	3	2	1	1	24	15	3
6	Denmark	3	1	2	0	6	19	2
7	Czechoslovakia	3	0	3	0	0	55	0
8	Netherlands	3	0	3	0	1	43	0

1991

Rank	Team	GP	W	L	T	GF	GA	Pts
1	Finland	5	5	0	0	73	1	10
2	Sweden	5	4	1	0	54	4	8
3	Denmark	5	4	1	0	13	15	8
4	Norway	5	3	2	0	32	15	6
5	Switzerland	5	3	2	0	30	22	6
6	Germany	5	2	3	0	20	20	4
7	France	5	2	3	0	6	54	4
8	Czechoslovakia	5	0	4	1	4	31	1
9	Great Britain	5	1	3	1	5	28	3
10	Netherlands	5	0	5	0	2	49	0

1993 – A

Rank	Team	GP	W	L	T	GF	GA	Pts
1	Finland	3	3	0	0	33	6	6
2	Sweden	3	2	1	0	18	11	4
3	Norway	3	2	1	0	14	13	4
4	Germany	3	1	2	0	12	20	2
5	Switzerland	3	1	2	0	7	23	2
6	Denmark	3	0	3	0	5	16	0

WOMEN'S EUROPEAN CHAMPIONSHIPS

continued

1993 – B

Rank	Team	GP	W	L	T	GF	GA	Pts
7	Latvia	5	3	1	0	10	5	6
8	Czech Republic	5	2	1	1	8	6	5
9	France	5	2	2	0	13	9	4
10	Great Britain	5	1	2	1	4	11	3
11	Ukraine	5	1	3	0	1	5	2

1995 – A

Rank	Team	GP	W	L	T	GF	GA	Pts
1	Finland	5	5	0	0	61	2	10
2	Sweden	5	4	1	0	27	10	8
3	Switzerland	5	3	2	0	11	20	6
4	Norway	5	2	3	0	7	20	4
5	Germany	5	1	4	0	11	35	2
6	Latvia	5	0	5	0	5	35	0

1995 – B

Rank	Team	GP	W	L	T	GF	GA	Pts
1	Russia	3	3	0	0	37	1	6
2	Denmark	3	3	0	0	23	2	6
3	Czech Republic	3	2	1	0	15	11	4
4	Slovakia	3	1	1	1	9	8	3
5	France	3	1	2	0	9	23	2
6	Netherlands	3	1	1	1	11	12	3
7	Great Britain	3	0	3	0	4	25	0
8	Ukraine	3	0	3	0	2	28	0

1996 – A

Rank	Team	GP	W	L	T	GF	GA	Pts
1	Sweden	5	4	0	1	20	11	9
2	Russia	5	4	1	0	17	15	8
3	Finland	5	3	2	0	24	5	6
4	Norway	5	2	3	0	14	21	4
5	Switzerland	5	1	4	0	11	21	2
6	Germany	5	0	4	1	7	20	1

1996 – B

Rank	Team	GP	W	L	T	GF	GA	Pts
7	Denmark	4	4	0	0	16	4	8
8	Latvia	4	3	1	0	11	7	6
9	Czech Republic	4	2	1	1	19	12	5
10	Slovakia	4	2	2	0	11	12	4
11	France	4	2	2	0	16	15	4
12	Netherlands	4	1	2	1	15	15	3
13	Kazakhstan	4	1	3	0	10	15	2
14	Great Britain	4	0	4	0	6	24	0

PACIFIC WOMEN'S CHAMPIONSHIP

1995

Rank	Team	GP	W	L	T	GF	GA	Pts
1	USA	5	4	1	0	35	6	8
2	Canada	5	4	1	0	28	9	8
3	Chian	5	2	3	0	13	16	4
4	Japan	5	0	5	0	1	46	0

1996

Rank	Team	GP	W	L	T	GF	GA	Pts
1	Canada	5	5	0	0	38	3	10
2	USA	5	3	2	0	30	9	6
3	China	5	2	3	0	11	12	4
4	Japan	5	0	5	0	2	57	0

CHAPTER 38

2002 and 2006 Olympic Teams

Analysts Select Olympic Rosters for Hockey's Six Major Powers

U.S. AND CANADA: THE LESSONS OF NAGANO

Tim Wharnsby

EVERYONE KNEW how the 1998 men's Olympic hockey tournament was going to turn out: Canada and the United States would battle it out in the gold medal final. Sweden would take the bronze, right? Uhm, wrong.

Something not-so funny happened to the North American teams on the way to the medal podium. Another majestic Olympic hockey moment materialized. Another Miracle on Ice.

The Czech Republic, a team with just 11 NHLers on its roster, shocked all the favorites with one of the most memorable underdog performances the international hockey scene has witnessed.

The Czechs won the gold with a 1–0 win over the silver medalist Russians.

Finland took advantage of a weary bunch of Canadians 3–2 in the bronze medal game to make it a clean European sweep of the medals.

Yes, the 1998 Nagano Winter Games provided the first stage for full-scale participation by NHLers at an Olympics and the surprise and shocking ending made the first-time experience a wonderful moment.

The best team, not the best players, won the tournament.

"The hockey tournament was what we had predicted and hoped for," NHL commissioner Gary Bettman said. "From a pure hockey perspective, this has been a wonderful tournament.

"For anybody to suggest this was a good or bad thing because of how the United States or Canada fared, if your view was that this was all about having the U.S. win the gold medal, you didn't believe us when we said this was going to be a 'dream tournament' and not a 'dream team,'" he said, referring to lopsided Olympic basketball victories by Team USA's roster laden with NBA superstars. "You can't do something of this magnitude, you can't try to make the game grow, if your objective is to simply focus on one team winning."

After the experience of Nagano, hockey commentators in every major hockey nation will focus on how to select and prepare a winning team for the 2002 Winter Games in Salt Lake City. Just like Nagano, there will be great debate on the makeup of each country's roster.

But before we consider lineups for 2002 and 2006, a review of what happened at Nagano is required. Why did the Czech Republic succeed? Why did other top nations like the U.S. and Canada fail to earn a medal? What changes to the format of the Olympic tournament will be contemplated for 2002? Some hockey fans attribute the Czech Republic's shocking victory at Nagano simply to stellar goaltending coming at exactly the right time.

True, Dominik Hasek was as dominant a factor for the Czech Olympians as Mike Richter was for Team USA at the 1996 World Cup of Hockey. But the Czech Republic won in Nagano because out of the six top teams in the competition—Czech Republic, Russia, Finland, Canada, Sweden and the USA—they came together to become a team in the truest sense of the word.

That said, the Czechs certainly could not have won without Hasek. The Buffalo Sabres netminder posted two shutouts against Finland in the round robin and a third shutout, 1–0 victory over Russia, in the gold medal final. With a 5–1–0 record, Hasek sported a spectacular 0.97 goals-against average and .961 save percentage. He was brilliant in his team's 4–1 win over the U.S. in the quarterfinals. He stoned Canada in the shootout during the Czech Republic's 2–1 semifinal victory.

"As good as Hasek is, a lot of his success has to do with the fact he plays so differently than anyone else in the game," Red Wings coach Scotty Bowman said.

"He'll play without a stick, flop around, whatever it takes. The only other guy who played even a little like him was former Maple Leaf Mike Palmateer—and when he was on, he was really on. Hasek, though, defies description. He's not an angles goalie. He will back right into his net in order to give himself a longer look at a shot. But don't kid yourself, every move is calculated."

Hasek, however, was not the sole reason for the wild 150,000-strong celebration that took place in Prague's Old Town Square a couple days later to honor the conquering Czech heroes. Hasek afforded Czech coach Ivan Hlinka the luxury of being content to take Canada into a semifinal shootout, but the gold medal aura envelopes the whole Czech team, notably the team's top six blueliners: Jiri Slegr, Richard Smehlik, Frantisek Kucera, Jaroslav Spacek, Roman Hamrlik and Petr Svoboda.

Not only did this bunch provide air-tight defense, they provided most of the offense in the medal round. Slegr scored the Czechs' lone goal during regulation time in their semifinal shootout victory over Canada. Svoboda was good for the only goal the Czechs needed to down the Russians in the gold medal final. "I read in a lot of places (before the Olympics) that we had the worst defense," Svoboda said. "I read that we wouldn't be good enough. I don't mean to sound cocky, but we were out to prove people wrong. That was our approach." In the final, the Russians spent most of the game trying to fight through the Czech trap—without any success.

"The key was that we didn't give them the speed in the neutral zone," Hasek said.

Scotty Bowman, the NHL coach who has won more games than anyone else, warned before the first puck was dropped that the Czech Republic could be a sleeper in a

short tournament because of their one-two punch of Hasek and Jaromir Jagr who scored just once in six games but, like the rest of his teammates, was committed to defense.

"I have to admit the Czechs' overall level of play really surprised me, Hasek notwithstanding," Bowman said. "Guys like Jiri Slegr were vastly improved. Of course, Jaromir Jagr's performance is no surprise. He had a big tournament despite scoring just once. You could tell he was really in the mood to play and was dangerous all tournament, especially when the game was on the line."

Why couldn't the U.S. or Canada get the job done in the same circumstances? The U.S. lacked discipline on and off the ice and played too individualistically.

"The American players took a lot of flak for their early exit and a lot of it is deserved," Bowman said. "But Hasek was clearly the difference [in the 4–1 U.S. quarterfinal loss]. The thing that really hurt the Americans against the Czechs was that in the first five minutes they really poured it on but came out of it with nothing. They had three or four really good scoring opportunities but couldn't get the puck by him. Hasek pretty much ripped their hearts right out." Canada's Patrick Roy performed a similar role in shutting down the U.S. in Canada's previous 4–1 victory.

"We got frustrated when we couldn't score," U.S. coach Ron Wilson said. "That led to breakdowns in other areas."

"We knew we had great offensive players on the team and, sure, it was frustrating not to score the goals," center Mike Modano added. "But you have to play great defense too and we didn't do that."

Canada's downfall, on the other hand, has other contributing factors. First of all, the Czechs must be given credit for their golden performance. "I have never seen any Czech team play a better game," Team Canada associate coach Andy Murray said. "Their defensemen battled so hard. They blocked an incredible number of shots. I would say they played the game of their lives." But when Canada needed offense the most, not many scoring chances were mustered. The Canucks also made a glaring mistake in their own zone that led to Slegr's goal in the third period. And just as it seemed Canada was dominating the game, the buzzer sounded to end the 10-minute overtime.

Shootout time.

Hasek got the best of the five Canadian shooters—Theo Fleury, Ray Bourque, Joe Nieuwendyk, Eric Lindros and Brendan Shanahan. Czech Robert Reichel snuck a deadly accurate shot by Roy on his team's first attempt.

"That goal, I mean it hit both posts and went in," Roy said. "I couldn't believe it. I have to be honest with you. I thought I played it well. Reichel came at me and I backed up. I thought I was in the right spot but he had a great shot. It hit inside of the post, hit the other post and went in.

"It was a big break for them. You know the difference there is between that one and being in or out?" Roy asked as he held up his hand with the forefinger and thumb a centimeter apart.

That centimeter has been just part of the analysis of why Canada lost.

Bowman felt Canada simply did not have enough offense to win. Paul Kariya, who suffered a concussion 12 days before Canada's Olympic opener, and a healthy Joe Sakic (he missed the two medal round games because of a knee injury) would have helped.

"You take Teemu Selanne and Jaromir Jagr off their teams and they don't advance," Bowman said. "When Canada's team was named, I didn't think Canada could lose, but when I knew Kariya wasn't able to play, I said that could change the whole outlook. Sakic's injury just made it tougher." Others criticized head coach Marc Crawford for leaving Wayne Gretzky and Steve Yzerman off the shootout list.

Then there was the risky planned play that led to Slegr's goal in the third period that put the Czechs up 1–0. On the play, Theo Fleury attempted to swat the puck off a face-off in Canada's end to a breaking Rob Zamuner. Fleury, however, missed. The puck was kicked back to an uncovered Slegr, who beat Roy with a 60-foot drive.

Crawford said it was Fleury's call: "Players of that level need creative intelligence, you have to afford them the ability to do that," he said.

"It didn't cost us the game. We came back and tied it [on a goal by Trevor Linden]." In hindsight, Crawford saw problems with the U.S. and Canada understanding the larger-ice game and adjusting to it. There were problems attempting to play National Hockey League hockey in a non-NHL environment.

"Watching it now a little bit more, I see how creative the Europeans are when they attack the blue line," Crawford said. "They attack the blue line, they cut across, they have people coming late. They do a lot of passing to areas and have people going to the slot all the time.

"Those are things we don't do as well as they do right now. The general managers have talked about having a little bit more time so we can work on that type of element." The common theme of among NHL scouts, general managers and coaches is that neither Canada nor the U.S. need to alter the player selection process. The players selected will always be debated.

Instead, the teams should focus better on on-ice preparation. Bowman suggests a short training camp during the summer would help.

"In an event like this in which you are putting together a collection of players, you never really know what to expect," Bowman said. "It might be worthwhile to hold a training camp in the summer prior to the Olympics so the players can get to know each other. It might be wise to gather on a bigger ice surface. That Olympic-sized rink really had on an impact on how the North Americans performed." At the other end of the Olympic-sized rink, Jagr believes Canadians have spent too much time analyzing what transpired.

"We were just luckier than they were," Jagr said. "We played one game, the goalie [Hasek] was hot, too. There was nothing wrong with Canada's team."

Jagr linked Canada's scoring woes to an overabundance of centers in Crawford's lineup.

"I was listening to Don Cherry and he said there were nine centermen on the team. You know that's not going to help you," Jagr, said. "It's a different position. If you're a left winger, a right winger or center it's tough to switch. Especially in a big tournament like that. I don't know what I'd do if they put me at center." One center the hockey world felt sorry for was Wayne Gretzky, exiting his first and last Olympics without a medal of any color.

In fact, this was Gretzky's final performance on the international stage. The 37-year-old standout was devas-

tated at the tournament's outcome.

"You know, when I lost my first Stanley Cup, I thought it was the end of the world. But I knew I would get another shot at it," Gretzky said. "I don't want to be nostalgic but that was my last international competition as a player. I've enjoyed 19 years of it. There were some highs and lows, but for me that's it. Every time you put on a Canadian uniform and play for Team Canada, anything but gold is not acceptable. That's a pressure and a fact that our team lives with, that maybe no other country has. When you win, the roses are tremendous. When you lose, you have to stand up and take your lumps. And we're taking our lumps."

For NHLers like Gretzky, it was a weird feeling to be eliminated by a shootout. "We haven't gone through that feeling before," Gretzky said. "We've never experienced that as players before. You play a game seven, you go into overtime and keep going. This was a whole different feeling. We were in shock when we lost. We didn't know what happened. It was a tough loss for us to swallow. You keep it forever."

Will the shootout exist in 2002? All sorts of trial balloons were floating around Nagano, including suggestions to scrap the shootout, adopt a best two-of-three final like the World Cup and restructure the tournament to eliminate at least two teams before the quarterfinal matches to prevent round-robin games from being the glorified exhibitions that the matches proved to be in Nagano.

Will there be changes to the way the American and Canadian teams are selected for the 2002 Winter Games in Salt Lake City? Not likely.

Instead, Canada and the U.S. will look for ways to better prepare for the next Olympics.

Canada, for instance, is selecting its teams for the World Hockey Championships with an eye for young talent that might develop and play for Canada at the Olympics.

In 2002, Canada will be celebrating the 50th anniversary of its most recent Olympic gold medal.

"Canada will always have the depth over their American counterparts," Dallas Stars chief scout Craig Button said. "But it's tough to look down the road and forecast who will develop or peak at the right time. Who knew five years ago John LeClair would turn into the goal scorer he has become?" An Olympic medal will also take on more importance in North America the next time the Winter Games open. Like North American-born hockey players grow up dreaming about hoisting the Stanley Cup high, European hockey players are raised with their sights on winning an Olympic medal.

"Winning the bronze medal is a dream come true for me," Finland's Esa Tikkanen, a veteran NHLer, said. "When I was a little boy in Finland, I dreamed of one day going to the Olympics and winning a medal before I dreamed of going to the NHL and winning a Stanley Cup.

"In Canada, there is only one winner. In hockey life, only one team wins the Stanley Cup. But in the world, in the Olympics, there are three winners."

Projected rosters for both the Canadian and U.S. Olympic teams in 2002 and 2006 follow.

CANADA

Pos	2002 Name	Age	Pos	2006 Name	Age
G	Martin Brodeur	29	G	Martin Brodeur	33
G	Chris Osgood	29	G	Marc Denis	28
G	Felix Potvin	30	G	Roberto Luongo	26
D	Rob Blake	32	D	Chris Pronger	31
D	Chris Pronger	27	D	Scott Niedermayer	34
D	Adam Foote	30	D	Kyle McLaren	28
D	Scott Niedermayer	30	D	Ed Jovanovski	25
D	Darryl Sydor	29	D	Eric Brewer	26
D	Ed Jovanovski	29	D	Richard Jackman	27
D	Kyle McLaren	24	D	Derek Morris	27
F	Paul Kariya	27	F	Paul Kariya	31
F	Eric Lindros	29	F	Eric Lindros	33
F	Joe Sakic	32	F	Jeff Friesen	29
F	Keith Primeau	30	F	Mike Peca	32
F	Brendan Shanahan	33	F	Jarome Iginla	28
F	Trevor Linden	31	F	Ryan Smyth	30
F	Jeff Friesen	25	F	Eric Daze	30
F	Ryan Smyth	26	F	Joe Thornton	26
F	Jarome Iginla	24	F	Brendan Morrison	30
F	Eric Daze	26	F	Rob Niedermayer	31
F	Kris Draper	30	F	Vincent Lecavalier	25
F	Mike Peca	28	F	Rico Fata	26
F	Rob Niedermayer	27	F	Chris Gratton	30

U.S.A.

Pos	2002 Name	Age	Pos	2006 Name	Age
G	Mike Richter	35	G	Jim Carey	31
G	Mike Dunham	29	G	Brian Boucher	29
G	Guy Hebert	35	G	Jean-Marc Pelletier	28
D	Derian Hatcher	29	D	Derian Hatcher	33
D	Bryan Berard	25	D	Bryan Berard	29
D	Brian Leetch	34	D	Scott Lachance	33
D	Mathieu Schneider	32	D	Paul Mara	26
D	Scott Lachance	29	D	Nik Tselios	27
D	Paul Mara	22	D	Mike McBain	29
D	Deron Quint	26	D	Brad Winchester	25
F	Keith Tkachuk	30	F	Keith Tkachuk	34
F	Doug Weight	31	F	Jamie Langenbrunner	32
F	Bill Guerin	31	F	Steve Konowalchuk	33
F	Jeremy Roenick	32	F	Adam Deadmarsh	30
F	Tony Amonte	31	F	Brian Rolston	33
F	Adam Deadmarsh	26	F	David Legwand	25
F	John LeClair	32	F	Erik Rasmussen	29
F	Jamie Langenbrunner	28	F	Matt Cullen	29
F	Steve Konowalchuk	29	F	Tim Connolly	24
F	Bryan Smolinski	30	F	Ty Jones	27
F	Mike Modano	31	F	Chris Drury	29
F	Bill Lindsay	30	F	Marty Reasoner	30
F	Todd Marchant	29	F	Scott Gomez	26

RUSSIAN HOCKEY: TRADITIONAL STYLE MEETS A NEW CENTURY

Igor Kuperman

THOUGH THE 20TH CENTURY was filled with dramatic hockey events, the best was truly saved for last. Just 10 years before Nagano, at the 1988 Calgary Olympics, National Hockey League scouts and general managers were watching jealously the brilliant, seemingly effortless performance of the Soviet players as they won yet another gold medal. A rhetorical question—"Will these players ever be free to join our franchise?"—was on everybody's mind then.

A decade later a similar dilemma had Russian Hockey Federation officials concerned: "Will these players play for us at the Olympics or not?"

The "question of 1998" turned out to be less of an issue than the question in Calgary 10 years before. It didn't take long for most of the Russian NHLers to say "yes" to the Olympic team. Interestingly, coach Vladimir Yurzinov wasn't surprised by what turned out to be an overwhelmingly positive response. "They grew up watching the Soviet teams win almost every tournament," he said. "Later, they won many tournaments by themselves. And, how many of them have won something in the NHL? Very few....They're just thirsty for victories."

The present young generation of the Russian NHLers, as well as the next up-and-coming wave, both grew up in the 1970s and 1980s. The NHL was far away then. The Stanley Cup was just a legend behind the Iron Curtain. The Soviet national team, on the other hand, was just around the corner and the principles behind the Olympic ideals were still bright and attractive. So attractive that Sergei Nemchinov, for instance, spent a lot of sleepless nights after getting a contract offer from the New York Rangers in the summer of 1991.

The dream of Olympic gold had pursued him through the years and it was difficult to give away this dream just few months before Albertville '92. Even the Rangers scout's advice—"Sign the deal and you will be able to buy a lot of gold Olympic medals"—didn't make the choice easier. Russia is a unique country.

Without a doubt, the 2002 version of the Russian Olympic team will have the traditional features of all its predecessors—speed, skills and passing. With hockey's projected rule changes (against hooking, holding, interference, etc.), this combination could be lethal for many opponents, especially when keeping in mind the fact that Russian-trained hockey teams don't use the principle of "offensive" and "checking" lines. Yes, they would still like to use "plumbers" like Andrei Kovalenko and Andrei Nikolishin, but they will probably be more inserted in scoring lines than have their own "checking wall."

By 2002–03 season, the Russian Olympic team will be led by the grizzled veterans who have been significant stars in the NHL in the 1990s. Goaltender Nikolai Khabibulin, the third goalie at the 1992 Olympics, will be in his prime at age 29. The experienced, hard-hitting defense that will play in front of him will feature Boris Mironov, Alexei Zhitnik, Darius Kasparaitis, Sergei Gonchar and Sergei Zubov. The "just-over-30" stick magicians—Pavel Bure, Sergei Fedorov and Alexei

Zhamnov—will still be a serious threat to any team.

The supporting cast will have had a great chance to reach NHL stardom by the new century. You don't have to be a rocket scientist to foresee a great future for the likes of such defensemen as Oleg Tverdovsky and Andrei Zyuzin, forwards Sergei Samsonov and Alexei Morozov. And Morozov will already have the experience of the 1998 Olympics in Nagano.

By 2002 it will probably not be out of line to compare these youngsters to their great countrymen who shined at the end of 20th century. Samsonov's moves, his slick stickhandling and short, bulky body will always bring to mind another Sergei—Makarov. The wide strides and strength of Morozov will revive memories of 1972's star performer of Alexander Yakushev. The offensive rushes of Tverdovsky and Zyuzin will be similar to Viacheslav Fetisov's heroics.

This same group of young players will take charge in 2006 as well. However, a few valuable additions can be expected. Khabibulin will continue to guard the net but not as "the one and only." His backup, 6'4", 220-pound Denis Khlopotnov (drafted by Florida in 1996), will look as confident as most present NHL goalies of his size and stature. The defensive corps won't change much.

The desire to play will keep Zhitnik, Mironov, Gonchar and Kasparaitis in great shape despite having reached ages of 32 to 34. By then, such 1998 draftees as Vitali Vishnevsky and Dmitri Kalinin should be very noticeable defensemen in the NHL, to say the least. Vishnevsky, by the way, is already considered as the "second coming" of Darius Kasparaitis.

Pavel Bure will continue to fly all over the ice despite his age of 35. By then, he will probably be a captain of the team. Alexei Yashin and Alexei Kovalev, both 33, will keep terrorizing goalies, while 34-year-old Vyacheslav Kozlov will finally overcome his "philosophical differences" with the Russian Hockey Federation.

The young superstars who will be expected to make an impact on the 2006 team were all drafted in 1997. Fast and extremely skilled right winger Maxim Afinogenov will continue the tradition of great Russian wingers. Maxim Balmochnykh's appetite for hard work will surprise his North American teammates in the same way that Nemchinov's did 15 years ago when arrived with the Rangers. The playmaking skills of two-way center Roman Lyashenko will have made him a candidate (or maybe a winner) of the Selke Trophy as the best defensive forward in the league by 2006.

It is more than possible that some other names will appear in the Russian lineups in 2002 and 2006. In 1999, a fresh wave of Russian forwards will invade the NHL draft. Names like Denis Shvidky, Yevgeny Fedorov (no relation to Sergei), Alexander Buturlin and Fedor Fedorov and Dmitri Yashin (both younger brothers of present NHL superstars) will all become well known pretty soon.

Going further to predict the top picks for the 2001 or 2003 NHL Entry Draft, there will be few more names to remember but it is almost impossible to predict their future—especially when one considers that by the year 2006 about one hundred Russians will be playing in the NHL and only the best and proven players will make the Olympic team. Unless, one of today's 12-year-olds already deserved the comparison to Bure or Samsonov...

RUSSIA

2002

Pos	Name	Age
G	Nikolai Khabibulin	29
G	Denis Khlopotnov	24
G	Andrei Trefilov	33
D	Alexei Zhitnik	30
D	Sergei Zubov	32
D	Boris Mironov	30
D	Sergei Gonchar	28
D	Darius Kasparaitis	30
D	Andrei Zyuzin	24
D	Oleg Tverdovsky	26
F	Sergei Samsonov	24
F	Alexei Zhamnov	32
F	Dmitri Nabokov	25
F	Vyacheslav Kozlov	30
F	Sergei Fedorov	33
F	Andrei Kovalenko	32
F	Alexei Kovalev	29
F	Alexei Yashin	29
F	Alexei Morozov	25
F	Alexander Korolyuk	26
F	Pavel Bure	31
F	Andrei Nikolishin	29
F	Maxim Afinogenov	23

2006

Pos	Name	Age
G	Nikolai Khabibulin	33
G	Denis Khlopotnov	28
G	Alexander Fomichev	27
D	Alexei Zhitnik	34
D	Boris Mironov	34
D	Sergei Gonchar	32
D	Darius Kasparaitis	34
D	Andrei Zyuzin	28
D	Oleg Tverdovsky	30
D	Vitali Vishnevsky	26
D	Dmitri Kalinin	26
F	Sergei Samsonov	28
F	Dmitri Nabokov	29
F	Vyacheslav Kozlov	34
F	Alexei Kovalev	33
F	Alexei Yashin	33
F	Alexei Morozov	29
F	Alexander Korolyuk	30
F	Pavel Bure	35
F	Andrei Nikolishin	29
F	Maxim Afinogenov	27
F	Maxim Balmochnykh	27
F	Roman Lyashenko	27

SWEDEN: THE THREE CROWNS ENTER THE THIRD MILLENNIUM

Jan Stark

IT HAS BECOME MORE AND MORE APPARENT at the last couple of international competitions that the main thing a team must concentrate on is defense. The game is so tight and there is little difference between most of the players at the international level. For this reason it has become necessary to build a national team around great goaltending and mobile defensemen who are able to both attack and defend. (In other words, good skaters.) The selection process must focus on "team players" rather than good individuals. And, of course, teams always need to have goal scorers—players that in every situation have the mobility and the skill to find the net.

The Swedish Olympic team at Salt Lake City in 2002 will feature Tommy Salo in goal. This great player saved the Swedish team during both the Olympics in 1994 and the World Championships in 1998. He is always concentrated and cool in the net. He has the ability to wait for the opposition to make the move and then win the situation. By 2002, however, Salo may well be serving as backup to Johan Holmqvist, the new star of the Swedish league. Rookie of the year in 1998, Holmqvist should be the national team goaltender for many years to come. He's a stand-up goalie with a great glove hand.

Seven solid defenseman should provide the protection in front of Salo and Holmqvist in 2002. At age 32, Nicklas Lidstrom will be the oldest member of the team and an important team leader. His skating skill and hard, accurate shot should make him very important in power-play situations. Mattias Ohlund will be Lidstrom's successor in the

beginning of the next millennium. A good skater who is strong in front of his own net, a couple more seasons in the NHL should have Ohlund at the top of his game by 2002. Mattias Norstrom will be the team policeman. The type of team player who will still block shots even with a 5–0 lead and only seconds remaining, Norstrom can be counted on when the going gets rough. Another tough customer is Anders Eriksson. He's a defensive defenseman who can take care of business in front of both nets. He needs to improve his skating, but is afraid of nothing. Kim Johnsson was a pleasant surprise when he emerged as one of the best defensemen in the tournament at the 1998 World Championships. Though noted as a defensive defenseman, he can turn around a game with his long, accurate passes. Daniel Tjarnqvist proved himself to be one of the best young defensemen in the Swedish league in 1997–98. He's a good skater with a good shot, but will need to stop taking stupid penalties. If he's able to polish his game a bit more, he should be a pleasant surprise in 2002. Jonas Elofsson will be only 23 by the next Olympics, but he's already a kid who has played on championship teams with Farjestad in Sweden. Mobile and with good hands, he has the ability to set up plays very quickly, but needs to put on a few pounds to be more effective defensively.

Mats Sundin will be team captain in 2002 and the most important player on the roster. The talented center knows his way in every situation of the game and is ranked above Peter Forsberg in Sweden on the basis of his loyalty in every moment, on and off the ice. Which is not to say that Forsberg won't be a key player at Salt Lake City. By then, he may well be the best individual talent in the world. He has a complete set of skills and can do the most amazing things on the ice. Has has nerves of steel (remember his goal in the shootout to win the 1994 Olympics) and sees opportunities on the ice that nobody else sees. He has the mind of a chess player and—like Wayne Gretzky—is always two or three steps ahead of everybody else. Fredrik Modin is a winger who will find his right position at the side of Sundin. He's very good at passing defensemen on the outside and taking the shot in the stride.

Samuel Pahlsson has been called "the next Forsberg," but will struggle to live up to that type of billing. He'll center the second line in Salt Lake City and will get a lot of assists by setting up Per Prestberg. Prestberg was the goal-scoring sensation of the Swedish league in 1997–98 as "the man who emerged from the woods" to take on everybody. He's a scoring threat in any situation, but is most lethal when he's in the slot. Like Jonas Elofsson, Prestberg needs to add a few extra pounds to his body.

Daniel Sedin will be only 22 in 2002, but he's a big, strong kid with a hockey sense that could become like Forsberg's. Sedin's good both at setting up goals and score by himself and could be the sensation of the next Olympic tournament. His twin brother Henrik will play on his side and score when his brother sets him up. Strong and fearless, he can take the beating in front of the enemy net. Another tough player will be Marcus Nilson, a big, strong winger who loves the corners. He dives in them, digs hard and often comes out with the little black rubber. He has respect for nobody, which often costs him stupid penalties, and this will be something for him to improve on.

Johan Davidsson is a playmaker with good hands. He will be anchoring the third line as center and also play on the second power-play unit. Niklas Sundstrom takes the defensive responsibility, covering for others when they

make mistakes. The number-one penalty-killer, he always plays against the opponent's scoring line, and plays it well. Jörgen Jonsson teams up with Sundstrom on the number-one penalty-killing unit. He's a coach's dream player who always gives the maximum effort and always plays his best for the team. Mats Lindgren will be a key utility player who can adapt to any given situation. He can play wing or center and offensively or defensively, as is required. He's the perfect team player and a good skater with a good shot.

Many players from the 2002 Swedish Olympic team will be back to anchor the Tre Kronor in 2006. Johan Holmqvist will definitely be the top netminder by then and should be backed up by Johan Asplund. Asplund is currently the top junior goaltender in Sweden and played a major part when Sweden won the European Junior Championships in 1998. Like Holmqvist, he's a stand-up goaltender with a good glove hand.

Kim Johnsson, Daniel Tjarnqvist, Mattias Ohlund and Jonas Elofsson should all be back in 2006 and will likely be joined by Christian Backman, Rickard Borgqvist and Jonas Frogren. Backman is a powerful player with offensive strengths and a good playing sense. With his tremendous slap shot, he will no doubt anchor the power-play. Borgqvist is good around the net and is the kind of policeman who will fear nothing or no one.

The majority of the offensive roster from 2002 should also be back in 2006. The most noteworthy absence will be Mats Sundin, while Jorgen Jonsson and Mats Lindgren are also likely to be replaced. Newcomer Johan Forsander will add size to the roster as well as power to the attack. He's not afraid of the traffic in front of the net and has the ability to score in tight situations. Mikael Holmqvist is a magician with his stick, but lacks in the mental aspects of the game. This is something he has worked on and he should be ready by 2006. Kristian Huselius is a fearless player with good technical skills, but a tendency to "disappear" from games. If he's able to concentrate over the entire 60 minutes, he'll be playing on one of two power-play units in 2006.

SWEDEN

Pos	Name	Age	Pos	Name	Age
2002			**2006**		
G	Tommy Salo	31	G	Johan Holmqvist	28
G	Johan Holmqvist	24	G	Johan Asplund	26
D	Nicklas Lidstrom	32	D	Kim Johnsson	30
D	Mattias Ohlund	26	D	Daniel Tjarnqvist	30
D	Jonas Elofsson	23	D	Mattias Ohlund	30
D	Kim Johnsson	26	D	Jonas Elofsson	27
D	Mattias Norstrom	30	D	Christian Backman	26
D	Daniel Tjarnqvist	26	D	Rickard Borgqvist	26
D	Anders Eriksson	27	D	Jonas Frogren	26
F	Mats Sundin	31	F	Peter Forsberg	33
F	Peter Forsberg	29	F	Fredrik Modin	32
F	Daniel Sedin	22	F	Per Prestberg	31
F	Henrik Sedin	22	F	Samuel Pahlsson	29
F	Marcus Nilson	33	F	Niklas Sundstrom	31
F	Johan Davidsson	26	F	Johan Davidsson	30
F	Fredrik Modin	28	F	Marcus Nilson	28
F	Per Prestberg	27	F	Daniel Sedin	26
F	Niklas Sundstrom	27	F	Henrik Sedin	26
F	Jorgen Jonsson	30	F	Johan Forsander	28
F	Samuel Pahlsson	25	F	Mikael Holmqvist	27
F	Mats Lindgren	28	F	Kristian Huselius	27

FINLAND'S OLYMPIC FUTURE

Tom Ratschunas

FINLAND'S 2002 OLYMPIC TEAM is a natural extension of the bronze medal-winning team from Nagano in 1998. Half the team seem certain to be back for the next Olympics.

Those likely to be back at Salt Lake City in 2002 are Teemu Selanne, Saku Koivu, Jere Lehtinen, Ville Peltonen, Janne Niinimaa, Kimmo Rintanen, Sami Kapanen, Kimmo Timonen, Juha Lind and Aki-Petteri Berg. Janne Laukkanen is a borderline case based on age and fitness. The most notable changes will be in goal where a new generation will have taken over by 2002. Vesa Toskala and Mika Noronen are already stars in the Finnish League and Jani Hurme will have to decide if he wants to be an NHL goalie or return to be a part of the domestic scene. Hurme's rapid rise from the second level in Finland to the NHL is a potential a storybook plot, though, the start has been average.

The defense will have two solid injections of new blood in Jere Karalahti and Tony Lydman and perhaps a third in Kaj Linna who is not listed but may well develop into a solid contender based on the toughness he picked up when playing NCAA hockey in the United States.

The forwards are the most difficult category to predict. The criteria are more varied as the coaches will pick their own special choices for specific roles. Thus picking four lines of the best scorers will never be a possibility.

The returnees from Nagano are quite obvious. The next forward is clearly Olli Jokinen, who was upset by being overlooked for the tournament in Japan. The third overall choice in the 1997 NHL draft played just eight games for the Los Angeles Kings in 1997–98, but enjoyed a spectacular year at home, leading Finland to the World Junior Championship title and winning a national title with his club team, IFK Helsinki, before winning a silver medal at the World Championships in Switzerland. Behind Olli the current names mentioned for the next Olympics are Eero Somervuori, Tomi Kallio and Miika Elomo, who have skills to become key players by 2002 provided they maintain their current pace of development.

By the year 2006 Vesa Toskala and Mika Noronen should be in their prime with the third job goaltending open to speculation. The current sensation in the Helsinki area is Matti Kaltainen, who will have the frame of Ken Dryden.

The leader on the 2006 team should be Aki-Petteri Berg, who should retain his status of Olympian into the 2010 event as well. Although not listed, the durability of Toni Lydman should not be underestimated as he could be back on a defense that will be made up largely of new blueliners such as Ossi Vaananen, Harri Tikkanen, Mikko Jokela, Antti-Jussi Niemi, Markus Kankaanpera, Marko Kauppinen, Ilkka Mikkola and last but not least Pasi Petrilainen.

The offense will, of course include, names like Selanne and Koivu—if the wear and tear of their long careers has left them reasonably motivated and unscarred.

The biggest question mark for the future is diminutive winger Marko Ahosilta, who is cast in the Koivu mold and has to put a lot of work and determination into his career to cope physically on the highest level. The 2006 Olympic tournament will be when Olli Jokinen finally becomes the

captain and responsible for more than just his offensive prowess. The are also big expectations on another small player, centerman Teemu Laine from Jokerit Helsinki who will face the same challenges as Ahosilta. The role of the Teemu Selanne of his generation is the load that Jani Rita will have to cope with by this time, providing the scoring punch while Polish-born Tomek Valtonen will be shouldering the responsibility as the team's defensive anchor. Two younger brothers are expected to have reached stardom in their own right by 2006 in Teemu Elomo (brother of Miika) and Mikko-Sakari Koivu (brother of Saku). The remaining forwards listed will all have their offensive and defensive roles to play and their selection to the Olympic tournament will most certainly depend on the requirements of whoever is the coach and their willingness to perform according to the wishes of this coach.

FINLAND

2002			2006		
Pos	Name	Age	Pos	Name	Age
G	Jani Hurme	26	G	Matti Kaltainen	23
G	Mika Noronen	22	G	Mika Noronen	26
G	Vesa Toskala	24	G	Vesa Toskala	28
D	Kimmo Timonen	26	D	Aki-Petteri Berg	28
D	Aki-Petteri Berg	24	D	Ossi Vaananen	25
D	Toni Lydman	24	D	Harri Tikkanen	24
D	Jere Karalahti	26	D	Mikko Jokela	25
D	Janne Laukkanen	31	D	Antti-Jussi Niemi	28
D	Ilkka Mikkola	23	D	Markus Kankaanpera	25
D	Pasi Petrilainen	23	D	Marko Kauppinen	26
D	Janne Niinimaa	26	D	Ilkka Mikkola	27
			D	Pasi Petrilainen	27
F	Eero Somervuori	23	F	Mikko-Sakari Koivu	22
F	Teemu Selanne	31	F	Eero Somervuori	27
F	Saku Koivu	27	F	Niklas Hagman	26
F	Olli Jokinen	23	F	Olli Jokinen	27
F	Ville Peltonen	28	F	Ari Katavisto	25
F	Tomi Kallio	24	F	Teemu Laine	23
F	Antti Aalto	26	F	Teemu Normio	25
F	Juha Lind	27	F	Toni Koivisto	23
F	Jere Lehtinen	28	F	Tomek Valtonen	26
F	Jussi Tarvainen	25	F	Teemu Elomo	27
F	Miika Elomo	24	F	Jani Rita	24
F	Sami Kapanen	28	F	Tommi Hannus	25
F	Kimmo Rintanen	28	F	Pekka Saarenheimo	23
F	Kari Kalto	23	F	Marko Ahosilta	26
F	Juha Ylonen	29	F	Timo Vertala	27
			F	Niko Kapanen	27

CZECH SCIENCE-FICTION FOR 2002 & 2006

Pavel Barta and Ivan Filippov

DOMINIK HASEK DID NOT EXCLUDE the possibility of his participation at the next Olympic Games right after winning the gold medal in Nagano in 1998 even though he will be 37 in 2002. Most players at that age already are enjoying their pensions. Many players from the 1998 Czech team, like Jaromir Jagr, Robert Reichel and Martin Rucinsky, will be in their early 30s. Even if the IIHF were to change its rules of players eligibility it may not do much good for Bobby Holik. Holik was not available to play for the Czech team in 1998, as he had become an American citizen, even though he was born and raised in the Czech Republic (Czechoslovakia) and lived there until he was drafted into the NHL. Petr Nedved may not be eligible either as he dressed for Canada at the 1994 Olympics in Lillehammer. The burden of defending the Olympic gold will be on the shoulders of many players who did not participate in Nagano.

The next generation will be taking over by 2002, and they may well be able to do well again. Roman Turek will most likely replace Dominik Hasek on the 2002 Olympic team. He is a gold medalist from the World Championships in 1996 and currently is playing well in the NHL for the Dallas Stars. He will be only 32 years old in 2002 and will have four more years of NHL experience under his belt. He should be ready to step in. Another candidates for a goalie position could be Roman Cechmanek, a backup to Hasek in Nagano. The dark horse in the race for a number-one position is Martin Prusek, once called a younger copy of Hasek.

The defense will be led by gold medal-team members Jiri Slegr (who will be 31) and Roman Hamrlik, who at 28 should be at the peak of his career. The rest of defenders will be a mixture of NHL and elite European league blueliners such as Radim Bicanek, Stanislav Neckar, Libor Zabransky, Jan Srdinko, Michal Sykora, Pavel Kubina, Robert Schnabel, Marek Posmyk, Pavel Skrbek and Robert Kantor, an unsung hero from the Czech Elite League.

Robert Reichel should be called up as team captain and a penalty-shot specialist if the shootout survives into the new millennium. Jaromir Jagr will probably turn down the invitation due to the grind of the NHL schedule. If so, it will be a great loss because he could still make a big difference to the Czech team. The same applies to Pavel Patera. His quickness and ability to win key face-offs could serve the team well, but he will be well over 30 by 2002. Vaclav Prospal, who lost his spot on the 1998 team due to a broken leg, and his contemporaries like Radek Dvorak, Josef Marha, Michal Grosek, Radek Bonk and Vaclav Varada are names who will be the core troops of a team that will be led by Patrik Elias. He will be to this team what his predecessor Jiri Dopita was to the gold medal winners in 1998: the top power forward and scoring leader.

Bright new stars such as Yogi Svejkovsky, Jan Bulis and young talents like Patrik Stefan, Josef Vasicek and Michal Sivek should battle for the final spots. Petr Cajanek and former Tampa Bay prospect Marian Kacir are almost assured spots on the Czech team in 2002 as both will be the best players Czech Elite League. Petr Sykora (no relation to defenseman Michal), a member of the 1996 NHL All-Rookie Team, could help make his name world famous. He

could center another Petr Sykora who is the brother of defenseman Michal and was Detroit's second draft choice in 1997. There might be a controversy, however, between the Sykoras and comeback coach Ivan Hlinka which would end with the Sykoras on the sidelines.

The 2006 Olympics seem to be so far away that any contemplation about the roster is just that—blue-sky speculation. Let's start with the coaches: 51-year-old Slavomir Lener could take the bench-emperor job with the Czech national team after serving as the first-ever European head coach in the NHL with the expansion Tokyo Kamikaze. It wouldn't be the first Asian team he has coached. Lener led the national team of China in the 1984–85 season. His assistants will be Vladimir Ruzicka and Dominik Hasek. They will pick Tomas Vokoun as the number-one netminder after he breaks in with another NHL expansion team, the Martian Chronicles, at age 30. Five years younger, Michal Lanicek could be a solid backup. There will still be a tough but underrated defensive corps to call on. The squad could be led by Jaroslav Spacek and by Ladislav Benysek.

Vlastimil Kroupa and Pavel Trnka would battle for the seventh spot while 26-year-old Robert Prochazka and Tomas Zizka will be towers of power on defense. The third pair could be formed by Petr Buzek, a fair-to-middling NHLer, and Petr Svoboda, no relation to the 1998 gold medal-winning scorer but the son of former national team defenseman and 1985 World Champion Radek Svoboda. He could be called up not in memory of his father but because 24-year-old Rostislav Klesla will be found to be too big for North American-size ice rinks.

Patrik Stefan, 26, who by 2006 will be a franchise player in the NHL, could center the top Czech line with Milan Kraft, 26, and Michal Sivek, 27, but will have to sacrifice his offensive and playmaking skills to work for the team. Michal Bros, a non-NHLer and captain of the Czech Elite League team Vsetin that will have won its 16th consecutive championship title since 1995, centers the second line with teammate Jiri Hudler, who was once one of the best midget players back in 1998 despite being only 14 years old, and

Jan Bohac, 24. The third unit will be built around long-time national team forwards Tomas Plekanec, Pavel Brendl and Martin Podlesak. They will still be a promise for the future at 24, 25 and 26. Former offensive stars like Patrik Elias and Petr Sykora (no relation to the above Petr Sykoras) get slowly over the hill but will still be very valuable for the team. The three key goals will be scored by the eldest player: 35-year-old Robert Reichel who will be the team captain once again.

CZECH REPUBLIC

2002			2006		
Pos	Name	Age	Pos	Name	Age
G	Roman Turek	32	G	Tomas Vokoun	30
G	Petr Franek	27	G	Martin Prusek	31
G	Martin Prusek	27	G	Michal Lanicek	25
D	Jiri Slegr	31	D	Jaroslav Spacek	32
D	Roman Hamrlik	28	D	Ladislav Benysek	31
D	Jaroslav Spacek	28	D	Vlastimil Kroupa	31
D	Stanislav Neckar	27	D	Pavel Trnka	30
D	Libor Zabransky	29	D	Petr Buzek	29
D	Michal Sykora	29	D	Robert Prochazka	26
D	Marek Posmyk	24	D	Petr Svoboda	26
F	Robert Reichel	31	F	Robert Reichel	35
F	Pavel Patera	31	F	Patrik Elias	30
F	Vaclav Prospal	27	F	Petr Sykora	30
F	Radek Dvorak	25	F	Michal Bros	30
F	Radek Bonk	26	F	Patrik Stefan	26
F	Michal Grosek	27	F	Josef Marha	30
F	Josef Marha	26	F	Jaroslav Svejkovsky	30
F	Vaclav Varada	26	F	Michal Sivek	25
F	Petr Sykora	26	F	Jiri Hudler	22
F	Petr Sykora	24	F	Pavel Brendl	25
F	Jaroslav Svejkovsky	26	F	Martin Prolesak	26
F	Jan Bulis	24	F	Jan Bohac	24
F	Patrik Stefan	22	F	Milan Kraft	26

CHAPTER 39
Olympic, World and European Championships

OLYMPIC GAMES

THE INTERNATIONAL OLYMPIC COMMITTEE, together with the International Ice Hockey Federation, is responsible for Olympic hockey tournaments. The first tournament was held during the 1920 (Summer) Olympic Games. Later, in 1983, the IIHF decided to designate this tournament as a World Championship. The first Winter Olympic tournament took place in 1924.

Since 1924, hockey has been part of every Winter Olympic Games. Until 1992, the IIHF World Championships were combined with the Olympics (with the exception of 1972 and 1976). Beginning in 1992, a separate World Championship tournament has been held in Olympic years. In 1988, the IIHF allowed professional athletes to play at the Olympic hockey tournament. Women's hockey made its debut as an accredited medal sport at the 1998 Winter Olympics in Nagano, Japan.

There have been 18 Olympic tournaments between 1924 and 1998 (The 1920 tournament is officially considered to be the first World Championship rather than an Olympic competition). Here are the winning teams:

USSR/Unified Team - 8 1956, 1964, 1968, 1972, 1976, 1984, 1988, 1992
Canada - 5 1924, 1928, 1932, 1948, 1952
USA - 2 1960, 1980
Great Britain - 1 1936
Sweden - 1 1994
Czech Republic - 1 1998

EUROPEAN CHAMPIONSHIPS

THE FIRST EUROPEAN CHAMPIONSHIPS took place in 1910 organized by the *Ligue Internationale de Hockey sur Glace* that later became the International Ice Hockey Federation. Fourteen European Championships were staged as separate events from World Championships or the Olympic Games. The last separate European Championship tournament took place in 1932.

Beginning in 1933, the European Championships became part of the IIHF World Championships. Through 1970, the formula for determining European rankings was simple—the highest ranked European team at the World Championships become the European champion, the second-highest ranked European team the European silver medalist, etc. All games played by European teams were counted.

Beginning in 1971, games between European and North American teams weren't counted in calculating European standings. From 1982 to 1991, the system for determining the European Champion changed again, with only the results of the round-robin portion of the World Championships being employed to rank teams in contention for the European title. The last European Championship was held in conjunction with the World Championships in 1991.

The winners of the European Championships were presented with a substantial silver trophy. Prior to 1930, the players of the winning teams were awarded IIHF diplomas. From 1930 to 1991, players on the top three European teams were awarded gold, silver and bronze medals separate from those given to World winners.

There were 66 European Championships held between 1910 and 1991 (the results of the 1912 tournament were annulled). Here is the list of European Champions:

USSR - 27 1954, 1955, 1956, 1958, 1959, 1960, 1963, 1964, 1965, 1966, 1967, 1968, 1969, 1970, 1973, 1974, 1975, 1978, 1979, 1981, 1982 1983, 1985, 1986, 1987, 1989, 1991
Bohemia/Czechoslovakia - 14 1911, 1914, 1922, 1925, 1929, 1933, 1947, 1948, 1949, 1961, 1971, 1972, 1976, 1977
Sweden - 10 1921, 1923, 1928, 1932, 1951, 1952, 1953, 1957, 1962, 1990
Great Britain - 4 1910, 1936, 1937, 1938
Switzerland - 4 1926, 1935, 1939, 1950
Germany - 2 1930, 1934
Austria - 2 1927, 1931
France - 1 1924
Belgium –1 1913

WORLD CHAMPIONSHIPS

THE FIRST WORLD CHAMPIONSHIPS took place in 1920, during the (Summer) Olympics in Antwerp, Belgium. Prior to 1982, this 1920 tournament was considered an Olympic event, but in 1983 the International Ice Hockey Federation declared that this tournament was the first World Championship event. The decision was based on the fact that the 1920 event was an "exhibition" tournament held prior to the Olympic Games.

At the IIHF Congress in 1930, it was decided that the 1924 and 1928 Olympic tournaments would also gain the status of World Championships. At the same congress, the decision was made to hold the World Championships every year if at least one non-European country was represented. (There were no World Championships during the years of World War II).

Until 1972, Olympic tournaments incorporated the World Championships, but in 1972 and 1976 separate World and Olympic events were held for the first time. In 1980, 1984 and 1988, there were no World Championships apart for the Olympic Games, but since 1992, there have again been both World and Olympic tournaments held in Olympic years. Since 1976, the World Championships have been "open" to professional athletes.

There are four pools at the World Championships—A, B, C and D, with Pool A comprised of the world's top hockey nations. After every year, the last-place team from Pools

A, B and C is relegated to the group below, while the first-place team from Pools B, C and D is promoted to the group above. The team winning each pool of the World Championships receives a Cup, while players from the top three teams in each Pool receive gold, silver and bronze medals.

Beginning in 1998, the IIHF increased the number of teams in Pool A from 12 to 16. These 16 teams are divided into four groups. Each group plays a round-robin preliminary, with the top two teams from each group advancing to another round robin before the semifinals and finals are held. Pools B, C and D each consist of eight teams.

There have been 62 World Championships from 1920 to 1998. Here is the list of World Champions:

USSR/Russia - 23 1954, 1956, 1963, 1964, 1965, 1966, 1967, 1968, 1969, 1970, 1971, 1973, 1974, 1975, 1978, 1979, 1981, 1982, 1983, 1986, 1989, 1990, 1993
Canada - 21 1920, 1924, 1928, 1930, 1931, 1932, 1934, 1935, 1937, 1938, 1939, 1948, 1950, 1951, 1952, 1955, 1958, 1959, 1961, 1994, 1997
Czechoslovakia/Czech Republic - 7 1947, 1949, 1972, 1976, 1977, 1985, 1996
Sweden - 7 1953, 1957, 1962, 1987, 1991, 1992, 1998
USA - 2 1933, 1960
Great Britain - 1 1936
Finland - 1 1995

YEAR-BY-YEAR SUMMARIES

1910 EUROPEAN CHAMPIONSHIPS The decision to hold a European Championship was made as early as 1908, and one year later the first unofficial international tournament sponsored by the Ligue Internationale de Hockey sur Glace took place. The games were played in Chamonix, France during the second congress of the LIGH. The host nation began the tournament with a 4–2 victory over Germany and a 6–0 win against Belgium, but was beaten in the finals by the team from London, England.

The third LIGH Congress opened in Montreux, Switzerland on January 9, 1910 and it was here that the first official European Championships were held. As proposed by a Swiss delegate, the Oxford Canadians, a club made up of Canadian players attending the prestigious university, was admitted to the Ligue (and would be admitted as an autonomous association on November 20, 1911). Another team that featured many Canadian players represented Great Britain and claimed the European title, beating Germany 1–0, Switzerland 5–1 and tying Belgium 1–1, but the new European champions refused to play the Oxford club. France, which had done so well in 1909, did not compete at the 1910 tournament.

The games of the first official European Championships were played on natural ice on frozen Lake Geneva in the Swiss Alps and consisted of two 30-minute periods. The rink was surrounded by low boards and was smaller than required by the rules. It was not surprising that Great Britain proved the winner in 1910, as England was the first European country to develop hockey. The game was already being played in England by 1894, and Europe's first electrically refrigerated rink was build in London in 1903. That same year, the first national championship ever held in a European country was won by the London Canadians. The unofficial European Championship of 1909 had been won by the London Princes Club, which, like the Oxford Canadians, was made up mostly of students from Canada plus British military officer Major B.M. Patton. Four years later, Patton would become president of the *Ligue Internationale de Hockey sur Glace*. Another future federation president, Max Sillig, played for Switzerland at the 1910 tournament.

1911 EUROPEAN CHAMPIONSHIPS were held indoors on artificial ice for the first time when Berlin hosted the event. Berlin boasted three artificial ice rinks at the time and the tournament was staged at the Eistpalast. The Belgian team had also been practicing on artificial ice at the Antwerp Palais de Glace, while the Swiss had excellent natural rinks. In Bohemia, temperatures dropped below freezing in January, enabling the players from the country that would one day be known as the Czech Republic to get in three weeks of practice prior to making the trip to Germany. Money was raised in Bohemia to finance the team's journey to the European Championships, though the players were forced to contribute a large share of the finances.

The Bohemian players arrived in Berlin in a third-class coach on a special night train and played their first game at 4 p.m. on the day of their arrival. They scored a 13–0 win over Switzerland, then defeated their favored German hosts 4–1 that same evening. After a 3–0 win over Belgium, they were Europe's new champions. The surprise win by Bohemia was something of a sensation in the European hockey community, which numbered about 300 to 400 players at the time. LIGH president Louis Magnus praised the teamwork of the Bohemian players when he wrote in *Les Sports d'Hiver* that "It was especially interesting to see the game of a team and not that of individual players." On their homecoming in Prague, the Bohemian team was met at the railway station by hundreds of enthusiastic fans.

The LIGH Congress was held in Berlin on February 16–17 at the same time the championships were played. Russia was admitted as the Ligue's seventh member. The Russian delegation, however, arrived in Berlin without a clear idea of what type of hockey was being played. Bandy was still the game of choice in Russia and it was not surprising when the country was dropped from the LIGH membership on September 25, 1911 due to inactivity.

1912 EUROPEAN CHAMPIONSHIPS On March 14, 1911, the *Ligue Internationale de Hockey sur Glace* (LIGH) was renamed the International Ice Hockey Federation (IIHF) and officially adopted the Canadian rules for amateur play. All subsequent championships would be held according to those rules. Bohemia, the new European Champion in 1911, was awarded the honor of hosting the 1912 tournament in Prague.

When only Germany and the host nation con-

firmed their participation for the 1912 European Championships, it was decided to invite a team of German-born players from the DEHG Prague club as representatives of Austria. At the IIHF Congress, which was held concurrently with the tournament, Austria's membership was formalized, though this decision would soon have repercussions.

The games of the 1912 European Championships were well-attended with about 5,000 people jamming the small stadium of the Slavia club on Letna Street. (The arena was located near a water tower, which made it convenient to flood the rink). The teams featured seven-man lineups—a goaltender, two defencemen, a rover and three forwards—and countries were permitted to carry only two substitutes.

As in 1911, Bohemia emerged victorious, but their 1912 victory would be short-lived. Three days after the tournament ended, the German hockey club filed an unsuccessful protest against a goal scored by the champions. Since the decision of the panel of judges, which also acted as the IIHF Directorate, could not be appealed, another pretext was found to strip Bohemia of the title. Referring to the fact that Austria had not been eligible to enter the European Championships because it had not been made a member of the IIHF prior to the games, the Directorate canceled the results of the 1912 tournament.

1913 EUROPEAN CHAMPIONSHIPS Germany filed a protest against the participation of Bohemia prior to the 1913 European Championships in Munich. The protest was based on the fact that Austria was now a member of the IIHF and since Bohemia was a part of the Austro-Hungarian Empire, the inclusion of its team would in fact be giving Austria two spots in the tournament. Because only four teams were taking part in the event, and the former champions from Bohemia elicited great fan interest, Germany was convinced to withdraw its protest.

The games of the European Championships were played on a tiny ice surface this year, and, as a result, scores were very high. Both Bohemia and Belgium posted two wins and a tie, but Belgium was declared the winner based on a better goal differential. Of note, the 1913 tournament marked the first time teams wore numbers on their backs at the European Championships.

1914 EUROPEAN CHAMPIONSHIPS Prior to World War I, no European Championship event ever attracted more than four participants or lasted longer than three days. During this period, the players of Bohemia did not lose a single game, and in 1914 they celebrated their second official European Championship win, defeating both Belgium and Germany, the only other nations in the competition.

1920 WORLD CHAMPIONSHIPS A hockey tournament was held in Antwerp, Belgium in April of 1920 as a demonstration of winter sports in conjunction with the Olympic Games which would be staged later that summer. The Congress of the International Ice Hockey Federation used the occasion of this tournament to admit Canada and the United States as members, as the two North American countries would be participating in this event. Sixty-three years later, at the meetings of the IIHF Congress in the spring of 1983, this tournament was accorded the status of the first hockey World Championship.

The participation of teams from Canada and the U.S. helped to adjust the rules of both the IIHF and the Canadian game. There would be six players per side (the rover having been dropped at the IIHF Congress in March of 1912) and players could only be changed when the action was stopped. This tournament was played on a rink that was different in size from that prescribed by the IIHF rules. Seven nations were represented, but the first face-to-face confrontation of hockey players from the old and new worlds showed the overwhelming superiority of experienced North American players.

Canada was represented at the Olympic tournament by a club team (the Winnipeg Falcons) instead of a national squad, as would become the country's custom, and the Falcons won the tournament with three straight wins. Captain Frank Fredrickson later went on to fame in the Pacific Coast Hockey Association and the NHL and was inducted into the Hockey Hall of Fame. Moose Goheen of the American squad would also be accorded that honor in addition to winning a spot in the U.S. Hockey Hall of Fame.

The three teams beaten by Canada played for second and third place. The United States finished second and Czechoslovakia (formerly Bohemia) finished third despite scoring only one goal in three games. The tournament's format was flawed: Sweden played six games and won three, as many as Canada and the United States, but still finished out of the medals because of its loss to Czechoslovakia.

Playing for Switzerland at the tournament was IIHF president Max Sillig, the only president in the history of the sport to have taken part in the World Championships while holding office.

1921 EUROPEAN CHAMPIONSHIPS The impressive play of Sweden, which had ranked fourth in Antwerp in 1920 in the nation's first foray into international hockey, resulted in a decision by the IIHF to award Stockholm the honor of hosting the European Championships in 1921.

Teams would now be permitted to carry 11 players on their rosters. Games would still consist of two 30-minute periods.

Because only two nations participated at the 1921 European Championships, this event is the only tournament not to award a third prize. The sole game of the tournament was held on an open rink with electrical lighting and attracted some 6,000 spectators. The Swedish fans cheered enthusiastically as their team defeated Czechoslovakia 6–4 to win the European title.

1922 EUROPEAN CHAMPIONSHIPS Sweden and Czechoslovakia were joined by Switzerland when the European Championships were held in St. Moritz in 1922. The Czechoslovaks avenged their loss in 1921 with a pair of victories.

1923 EUROPEAN CHAMPIONSHIPS For the first time, five nations attended the European Championships with France competing for the first time since the unofficial tournament of 1909. The debutantes played well, losing only to the champions from Sweden. Czechoslovakia finished in third place.

1924 WINTER OLYMPICS AND WORLD CHAMPIONSHIPS This competition was played according to new rules that divided the game into three 20-minute periods. Matches were held in late January and early February during the International Week of Winter Sport that one year later was renamed the Winter Olympic Games

by the Congress of the International Olympic Committee.

The tournament was split into two groups with four teams in each. The top two ranking teams from each group went to the playoffs, thus the final standings included only the four play-off teams. A total of 255 goals were scored in the 16 games of the tournament, for an average of almost 16 goals per game. This level of output has never been matched.

The four years between this championship and the games in Antwerp in 1920 had done nothing to alter the balance of power between North America and Europe. Canada (represent-ed by the Toronto Granites) established a record that has never been beaten by scoring 110 goals in five games. Included in this total is an Olympic record 33–0 win over Switzerland that featured 18 goals in the first period. The United States was almost as dominant, sweeping its European opponents before dropping a 6–1 decision to Canada in the gold medal game.

1924 EUROPEAN CHAMPIONSHIPS For the first time, six nations entered the competition for the European Championships in 1924, including newcomers Spain and Italy. Still, only six games were played in total as Spain did not show up for its game with Sweden. The tournament was held in two stages, with Sweden, the winner of Group A, facing Group B winner France for the cham-pionship. France emerged with a 2–1 victory to earn IIHF diplomas awarded to the winners for the first time.

1925 EUROPEAN CHAMPIONSHIPS Prepar-ations for the 1925 European Championships in Czechoslovakia began as early as November of 1924, with several options developed in the event of warm weather. It was believed that holding the games on the Slavia rink at Letna would have the greatest financial and publicity impact, but despite the fact that it had been suf-ficiently cold in Prague before the New Year, the beginning of January was marked by a deep thaw. A stand-by rink was located, but, at the last moment, it too was covered by water.

Thus the Championships moved to a region in the Vysoke Tatry Mountains. The snow was removed from the ice of a small mountain lake, several benches were built on a bank and the resulting rink had markings painted on it. No posters or tickets were issued for the games and so attendance was sparse. Snowstorms repeated-ly forced the stoppage of play for snow removal.

The host Czechoslovaks did not allow a sin-gle goal in beating their three opponents and won the European Championship for the fourth time. Austria, which had entered the tournament for the first time in 12 years, finished second. The third-place Swiss team featured Carl Spengler, who had recently commissioned the Spengler Cup, a hockey trophy and tournament played annually in Davos, Switzerland in the last week of December.

1926 EUROPEAN CHAMPIONSHIPS In 1925, the International Ice Hockey Federation Congress established a minimum rink size of 18 meters (58 feet) wide by 50 meters (163.5 feet) long, with regulation size being 26 meters (85 feet) by 56 meters (184 feet). Body checking was introduced in the defensive zone. These new rules were applied at the 1926 European Championships which saw a record nine nation-al teams in attendance. Poland made its first appearance. Sweden was the sole former cham-pion not present this year, as Britain finally returned to the Championships 16 years after its

success at the first official tournament in 1910.

The 1926 event in Davos, Switzerland was a true hockey marathon, with the favorites playing seven games each and, on several occasions, two games in a day. While the nine teams were split into three groups of three, insufficient experience in organizing large tournaments resulted in standings only being determined for the four best teams. The playoffs were made up of the three group winners, with the fourth final-ist determined in a series of games involving the runners-up of the three groups. Two playoff rounds were needed after the first round robin ended in a three-way tie. Switzerland eventually emerged as the champion, which was a surprise because in the previous 15 years, the Swiss had only won one game in official tournaments.

Experts were unanimous in noting a higher standard of play among the top teams in 1926 when compared to previous years. Improved defensive play was noted in particular.

1927 EUROPEAN CHAMPIONSHIPS The host nation won the European Championships for the third year in a row, as Austria emerged victori-ous for the first time in a six-nation round-robin tournament. Belgium ranked second and added to its achievement with the Fair Play Cup estab-lished for the team with the fewest penalty min-utes. Hungary made its first appearance at the European Championships in 1927, but did not score a goal in losing all five games.

1928 WINTER OLYMPICS, WORLD AND EUROPEAN CHAMPIONSHIPS At the time, the 1928 tournament at the Winter Games in St. Moritz, Switzerland contested only the Olympic Championship, but two years later the IIHF Congress awarded it the status of both the World and European Championships, thus making it the first tournament to contest three champi-onship titles.

The United States was not present in 1928 and Canada was exempted from the preliminary games and awarded a bye directly into the medal round. The 10 European teams were split into three divisions, with the winner of each group also advancing to the medal round. Games were much closer than at previous Olympic tourna-ments, as warm weather often turned the natural ice surface to slush and thus reduced the advan-tage for strong skating teams.

Nevertheless, Canada's domination of inter-national competition continued. The Toronto Varsity Grads cruised to the gold by outscoring its European opponents 38–0 in three games.

1929 EUROPEAN CHAMPIONSHIPS Eight national teams competed at the 1929 European Championships, which marked the last time that games were played in two periods of 30 min-utes. Czechoslovakia won its fifth European title with a team comprised mainly of a new genera-tion of players, though veteran goalie Jan Peka played just as confidently as he had in 1913. Peka had been the national team goalie for near-ly a quarter of a century. This latest win by Czechoslovakia inspired the construction of the country's first artificial ice rink in Prague, which was opened on January 17, 1931.

Second place at the 1929 event in Budapest went to Poland, who also won the Fair Play Cup. Third place was determined in a playoff game for the first time this year, as semifinal losers Austria and Italy battled in a game won 4–2 by the Austrians.

1930 WORLD & EUROPEAN CHAMPIONSHIPS The International Ice Hockey Federation decid-

ed in 1930 to hold World and European Championships every year, if possible. It was ruled that in order for a tournament to gain World Championship status, at least one non-European team—Canada, the United States, or Japan—must be present. If such a World Championship was held in Europe, the highest-ranking European team would be declared European Champion.

The decision to play a World Championship in 1930 that was independent of the Winter Olympic Games marked a new stage in the development of hockey. The tournament broke all existing records with 12 countries taking part, including the first team from Japan. Canada was represented by a Toronto-based team sponsored by the C.C.M. sporting goods company that was touring Europe at the time. The Canadian team was once again exempt from preliminary competition and would play only in the finals.

The tournament began in Chamonix, but warm weather and poor ice conditions made it necessary to move the final games to Berlin. Germany scored a 2–1 victory over Switzerland on home ice to claim the 1930 European Championship, but dropped a 6–1 decision to Canada in the World Championship game. Austria beat Poland 2–0 in a game to determine third place among the European contestants. That game was played in Vienna, making this tournament the only one of its kind to be played in three different countries. The IIHF presented medals to the winners this year instead of the diplomas it had handed out in the past. Other firsts at this event included forward passing in the defensive zone and a new rule calling for three 15-minute periods.

1931 WORLD & EUROPEAN CHAMPIONSHIPS The World Championships now began to be held annually and each tournament marked a new stage in the search for an optimum system of determining the best team.

This time, the round-robin playoffs were pre-ceded by a complex set of preliminary games which involved all 10 countries including Canada (the Manitoba Grads), the United States national squad (which had not played games in Europe since 1924) and Romania, which was making its initial appearance in international hockey. This system produced the first four con-tenders for the medals: Canada, the U.S., Sweden and Czechoslovakia.

To increase the medal-round field to six teams, Austria, which had a win in the prelimi-naries, France, Romania and Poland (as the host nation) were given a second chance to qualify for the round-robin playoffs. Poland advanced with a 2–1 win over France, while Austria beat Romania 7–0.

The six-team final round of the 1931 World Championships saw Sweden play Canada to a 0–0 tie, which marked the first time a European team did not lose to the Canadian squad in inter-national tournament play. Still, with four wins and a tie, Canada won the gold medal and did not allow a single goal in the tournament. The United States finished second.

As in all combined World and European Championship events played before 1971, the European rankings were determined by the standings of European teams that had competed at the World Championships. Austria, third over-all behind Canada and the U.S., was declared the European Champion for the second time in its history. Austria also won the Fair Play Cup, which was sponsored by the U.S. Ambassador in Poland.

1932 WINTER OLYMPICS AND WORLD CHAMPIONSHIPS Many countries had applied to participate in the first major international ice hockey tournament to be held on the American continent, but the economics of the Great Depression prevented many national teams from traveling to the Winter Olympics in Lake Placid, New York. As a result, the four-nation hockey tournament would be the smallest field in Olympic history. Poland was the only nation to finish without a medal.

It was decided that the four Olympic hockey teams would compete in a double round robin, meaning each team would face its opponents twice. In addition to those 12 games, the IOC ruled that five exhibition games would be played on the days in which no official matches were scheduled. Among the participants in the exhibition games was a team from McGill University in Montreal, whose students had played in the first "modern" hockey game on March 3, 1875.

Two rinks were used to play the Olympic Games at Lake Placid, one indoors and one outdoors, which made it necessary for the players to keep adjusting from artificial to natural ice. All 12 games of the Olympic tournament were officiated by the same two referees, Lou Marsh of Canada and Donald P. Sands of the United States. In the first-round game between the U.S. and Germany, the audience decided that Sands was prejudiced against the visitors and forced the American referee to leave the ice. Lou Marsh conducted the rest of the game alone to the satisfaction of all.

Canada and the U.S. were evenly matched and well ahead of their European opponents. Overtime was required in both Canada–U.S. games, with Victor Lindqvist scoring the winning goal for a 2–1 victory by Canada's Winnipeg Hockey Club in the first game. (He later became a prominent international referee, officiating games at the 1962 and 1963 World Championships.) The second game ended in a 2–2 tie after three overtime periods. Attendance for that game was 7,000 in a rink that had just 3,000 seats. "We will never give away the Olympic gold to anybody," wrote Canadian newspapers after the tie with the U.S. clinched first place for Canada.

1932 EUROPEAN CHAMPIONSHIPS The last independent European Championship tournament drew nine national squads to Berlin in 1932, including Latvia which had joined the IIHF the year before.

Five teams advanced to the medal round. Sweden posted an undefeated record in final round play, finishing with two wins and two ties in four games. Games were low scoring, as Sweden tied 0–0 with second-place finisher Austria and 1–1 with the bronze medalists from Switzerland. Gustaf Johansson and Karl-Erik Furst were Sweden's top scorers with five and three goals respectively.

1933 WORLD & EUROPEAN CHAMPIONSHIPS Prague, with its considerable experience in organizing European Championships, hosted its first World Championship on the artificial ice of the new Stvanice winter stadium in 1933. The seventh World Championship tournament was the first to feature forward passing in any zone on the ice and ended in a surprise of historical importance, as a new champion emerged.

After winning six consecutive international tournaments (a record that would stand until 1969), Canada suffered its first loss in a World Championship game, as the Toronto National

"Sea Fleas" were defeated 2–1 in overtime by the United States in the final game of the tournament. The victory gave the Americans first place, while Canada settled for second.

Czechoslovakia's Jan Krasl (1899–1980) made his debut as a referee at this tournament. He had played 17 games for his national team at the World and European Championships between 1924 and 1930, and would finish his refereeing career at the 1955 World Championships.

1934 WORLD & EUROPEAN CHAMPIONSHIPS The 1934 World Championships were held in Milan, which had hosted the European Championships 10 years earlier. The same 12 nations that had competed in 1933 were present and played through a complex system of preliminary games and playoff rounds to establish the champion.

The medal round was made up from teams that had won the three different divisions from the second round of play, plus Germany (who had won a special playoff among the second-place teams). Canada, represented by the Saskatoon Quakers, regained its position as World Champions by beating the United States 2–1 in the final game.

1935 WORLD & EUROPEAN CHAMPIONSHIPS attracted a record field of 15 nations to Davos, Switzerland, though the United States was not among them. Holland made its first appearance on the international stage and won the Fair Play Cup which was sponsored by Bucharest's daily *Universul* newspaper. Only European teams were eligible for this award. The tournament involved 51 games played over nine days.

As in past years, the World Championships began with a series of preliminary games, though this year all teams took part regardless of their past success. The two top-ranking teams from each of the four subgroups then advanced to the next round. This format resembled the one adopted by the IIHF in 1979.

The eight top teams were divided into two groups and played a separate series of round-robin games. The two top teams from each group moved on to play for the medals, while the four bottom teams (two from each division) took part in a consolation round. The two semifinal games in the medal round matched the first-place team from one division against the second-place team from the other, with the winners playing for the gold medal. Canada emerged victorious for the eighth time, represented this year by the Winnipeg Monarchs whose roster included many players from the Olympic championship squad of 1932. The Swiss settled for the silver medal after losing to Canada in the final, were crowned European champions for the first time since 1926.

During the tournament, Czechoslovakia played a very competitive game against Canada, losing 2–1. Matej Buckna, of Czech origin, from the Canadian town of Trail, British Columbia, was a consultant for Czechoslovakia's team and a playing coach on contract for many years with LTC Prague. In 1948 he would take his club team to Moscow for the first series of games ever played between Czechoslovakia and the Soviet Union.

1936 WINTER OLYMPICS, WORLD AND EUROPEAN CHAMPIONSHIPS Teams from 15 countries competed at the 1936 Winter Olympics, including Italy, Japan and Latvia, who were all making their Olympic debut. Japan's goaltender, Teiji Honma, wore a face

mask for the first time in the history of World Championship play. Also for the first time, both the Canadians and Americans were defeated by European teams, as Canada failed to win the Olympic gold medal. Great Britain was the new hockey champion.

Coached by future IIHF president John "Bunny" Ahearne, the British team featured only one player (defenseman Carl Erhardt) who was a true Englishman. All his teammates were of British origin but had been raised and trained in Canada, as had the players who formed the core of the French team. Canada's delegation used this fact to argue for the disqualification of both France and England. After long negotiations, Canada withdrew its protest against Great Britain but not against France. The French team was permitted to take part, but almost refused to do so in its anger over the Canadian protest.

The games of the 1936 Olympics were played outdoors on natural ice. Snowstorms often forced the stoppage of play. The format of the tournament reflected past experience in planning World Championships. The first stage included four preliminary games. The two top-ranking teams from each subgroup then entered the semifinal round and formed two groups of four. Finally the two best teams from each semifinal played for the medals, counting the points won by the finalists during the previous stage. The loss by the U.S. to Italy in the elimination round was the biggest upset of the tournament, with the Italians scoring a 2–1 victory in overtime. The most important and surprising upset was Canada's loss to Great Britain during the semifinal round, as the 2–1 British victory over the Port Arthur Bearcats gave the team from the United Kingdom the gold medal.

The British players returned home in triumph, carrying not only their gold medals but the puck used to score the gold medal-winning goal against Canada. According to newspaper reports, it was bought by a London sports patron for a large sum of money.

1937 WORLD & EUROPEAN CHAMPIONSHIPS were held in Great Britain for the first time. The British had won the first European Championships in 1910 in addition to the 1936 Olympic tournament. The 1937 event in London featured 11 teams, including the debut of Norway. Teams were now permitted to use 14 players on their rosters and lineups usually included two goaltenders, three defenseman and three forward lines.

The format of the 1937 World tournament was virtually the same as it had been in 1935 except that results in the semifinal round would not be counted towards the final medal round. Canada (the Kimberly Dynamiters) returned to the top spot in the world by going undefeated at the tournament. Great Britain slipped to second. Switzerland finished third and won the Fair Play Cup. This prize to the team with the fewest penalties had been awarded since the early 1930s.

1938 WORLD & EUROPEAN CHAMPIONSHIPS In connection with the approaching 30th anniversary of the International Ice Hockey Federation, the Organizing Committee sent invitations for the 1938 World Championships to all 22 IIHF member countries. Teams from 15 nations attended the games in Prague, including newcomer Lithuania.

The host nation turned the World Championships into a festive occasion unequaled to that point in hockey history. Famous hockey players and organizers of the game came to the Czechoslovakian capital as

guests of honor of the IIHF. A special yearbook was issued for the 25th Congress, informing readers that Czechoslovakia had the most ice hockey clubs in Europe with 361, while Sweden had 116 and Poland 92. The greatest number of rinks with artificial ice had been built in Great Britain (21) and Germany (14).

"I played my first games at the World Championships in 1938," recalled Harijs Vitolinsh, a well-known Latvian player who was among the best defensemen during ice hockey's early years in the USSR. "I remember most our game with Norway. After regulation time the score was tied and Klavs, who was to become a referee after the war, scored two goals in the overtime period."

The organizing committee did not always act consistently when it came to ties. A game between Czechoslovakia and Sweden was not declared a tie until a period of overtime was played, while a game between Sweden and Austria was declared a tie after just three periods of regulation time.

Canada, Great Britain, Germany and the host Czechoslovaks all reached the final medal round, with Canada (the Sudbury Wolves) again claiming the World title. The Fair Play Cup was awarded to Austria.

1939 WORLD & EUROPEAN CHAMPIONSHIPS

Finland and Yugoslavia made their first appearance at the World Hockey Championships in 1939, the last such event prior to World War II. Team rosters were expanded to include 15 players. Canada was represented by the Trail Smoke Eaters, who breezed through the tournament with eight straight victories while allowing just one goal against.

The 1939 tournament was patterned on the format of the 1935 event, with the only difference being that results from the semifinal round would not be carried over into the final medal round. Canada, the United States, Switzerland and Czechoslovakia advanced to the final round, with the Czechoslovaks having to settle for the Fair Play Cup after finishing out of the medals.

As the two top contenders for the title of top European team, Switzerland and Czechoslovakia played to a scoreless tie in the medal round. An additional match was played between the two nations on March 5 in Basel, Switzerland, with the home team winning 2–0.

1947 WORLD & EUROPEAN CHAMPIONSHIPS

The first postwar congress of the IIHF was held in Brussels in April of 1946 and dates were set to resume the World Championships in 1947. Great Britain, Czechoslovakia and Switzerland all expressed a desire to host the tournament, but by early October of 1946 both Britain and Switzerland had abandoned the idea. With Czechoslovakia now confirmed as the host country, invitations to attend the 1947 World Championships were sent out from Prague on November 14, 1946.

The Congress in Brussels introduced some very important rule changes to international hockey. Three periods of 20 minutes, which had been introduced in Europe in 1945, were approved at the meetings in 1946 (35 years later than in Canada). Also approved was the modern size of 183 centimeters (6') by 122 centimeters (4') for the goalie net, plus a goal line and center-ice red line. One- and three-minute penalties were omitted from the rules and a penalty shot was introduced.

The 1947 tournament marked the first time that Canada did not attend the IIHF World Championships, and a split among organizing committees in the United States doomed the American team to fifth place, leaving only European teams to contend for the medals. Sweden's victory over Czechoslovakia was marked by a telegram of congratulations from Swedish King Gustav, but the team had hardly finished celebrating when they were upset by Austria in a loss that ultimately handed the gold medal back to the host nation.

Meanwhile, amateur hockey in the United States had developed a rift due to competition for control of the game between the Amateur Athletic Union and the Amateur Hockey Association of the United States. A mixed team had come to Prague for the 1947 World Championships, but in the middle of the tournament the IIHF passed a decision to break ties with Avery Brundage and the AAU in favor of AHAUS headed up by well-known hockey personality Walter Brown, who would later serve as president of the International Ice Hockey Federation. This demoralized an already divided U.S. team and resulted in the first finish out of the medals for an American team at the World Championships.

Canada's decision not to send a team to the World Championships in 1947 highlighted a growing rift between the Canadian Amateur Hockey Association and the International Ice Hockey Federation over IIHF policy. The dispute was solved later in the year when the IIHF agreed to alternate presidential terms between European and North American representatives.

1948 WINTER OLYMPICS, WORLD AND EUROPEAN CHAMPIONSHIPS

Because of the Second World War, there had been a 12-year break between Winter Olympic competitions. The Games at St. Moritz marked Canada's return to international competition for the first time since before the War, represented by the RCAF Flyers of Ottawa, a team made up of servicemen from the Royal Canadian Air Force.

The problems that had plagued the Americans at the 1947 World Championships produced grave complications in 1948, as two American teams arrived in Switzerland. One team was sent by AHAUS and was supported by the IIHF, while the other was sent by the AAU, which had represented the United States at all previous Winter Games and now used its old connections to gain support from the International Olympic Committee. Both American teams appeared on the ice for the opening ceremonies and police assistance was required to restore order. The IOC decided to disqualify both American teams, but passions later calmed down and the AAU team left for home, allowing the IOC to withdraw its suspension and let the AHAUS team play. In the end, the United States entry was "outlawed" by the IOC and was not counted in the final Olympic hockey standings (though it remained in the World Championships).

Problems also plagued the Olympic tournament on the ice, where warm weather played havoc with the schedule and made it necessary to begin some games at 7 a.m. Many games saw the winning team scoring in double digits, highlighting the differences in strength among the competing countries, but for the first time in a championship in which Canada competed, the winner was not decided until the final game. Because of a scoreless tie between Canada and Czechoslovakia, the two top medal contenders both finished the tournament without a loss. Canada ultimately claimed the Olympic title on the basis of goal differential. The results in 1948 proved that Czechoslovakia's World Championship in 1947 could not solely be attributed to Canada's absence, as it was generally agreed in St. Moritz that the Czechoslovak team was no weaker than Canada's and boasted a much stronger offense. Czechoslovakia's captain Vladimir Zabrodsky, who scored 27 goals in the tournament, was recognized as the Olympics' best forward.

The bronze medal in 1948 went to Switzerland, just as it had 20 years earlier when the Winter Olympics had also been staged in St. Moritz. Richard Torriani of Switzerland became the first hockey player to read the Olympic oath at the opening ceremony in 1948 on behalf of all the competitors.

1949 WORLD & EUROPEAN CHAMPIONSHIPS

were held in Sweden for the first time and ended in great success for Europe, particularly Czechoslovakia. The Czechoslovaks had won the world title with Canada absent in 1947, and tied the Canadian team at the 1948 Olympics before settling for the silver medal. Finally, in 1949, Czechoslovakia beat Canada for the first time with Stanislav Konopasek scoring the winning goal in a 3–2 victory. By capitalizing on goals by Josef Trousilek, Vaclav Rozinak and Konopasek, Czechoslovakia was a 3–0 winner in the decisive game with Sweden and became undisputed World Champions, while also winning the European title for the third time in a row.

The victory by Czechoslovakia was all the more significant due to the fact that a much younger team had come to Stockholm after a tragic plane crash on November 8, 1948 had taken the lives of the players who had won the 1947 title and the silver medal in St. Moritz. The entire team had been killed in the accident, including the outstanding Czechoslovak stars Ladislav Trojak, Vilibald Stovik, Miloslav Pokorny, Karel Stibor and Zdenek Jarkovsky.

Canada, which had lost to the United States at the 1933 World Championships and been beaten by a British team stocked with Canadian players at the 1936 Olympics, had now lost the world title to a European team for the first time. However, the Sudbury Wolves established a record that is not likely to be beaten at this level of competition when they defeated Denmark 47–0 in the first round of the tournament. Denmark was making its first appearance at the World Championships. The lopsided victory was accomplished despite a system that was designed to avoid unnecessary games between teams of clearly different calibers. Using a set-up that was an exact replica of the 1932 European Championships, organizers split the competition into three divisions with the two top teams from each group advancing to a round-robin final.

Finishing behind Czechoslovakia and Canada at this tournament was the United States, though it was learned during the IIHF Congress held in conjunction with the World Championships that the International Olympic Committee had broken relations with the IIHF as a direct result of the squabbling at the 1948 Olympics. Meanwhile, Sweden finished fourth behind the U.S. at the 1949 tournament and Swedish player Ake Andersson was named unanimously as the best player by a special panel of judges and awarded a gold watch by the *Dagens Nyheter* newspaper.

1950 WORLD & EUROPEAN CHAMPIONSHIPS

The defending World Champions from Czechoslovakia did not appear at the 1950 tournament in London. As a result, the number of competitors declined as did interest in the event.

Canada, represented by the Edmonton Mercurys, won by going undefeated throughout the tournament. The United States lost only to Canada and finished in second place. Norway finished last among the six teams that reached the medal round, but took home the Fair Play Cup. Belgium received a consolation prize by winning the playoff among the three nations ranked seventh to ninth.

Although it was not widely reported at the time, Czechoslovakia was absent from the 1950 World Championships because its entire team had been arrested by the Czechoslovakian KGB at the airport in Prague prior its scheduled departure for London. It was suspected that the players planned to defect, and all were given jail sentences of varying lengths. Czechoslovakia did not return to world play until the Olympics in 1952.

1951 WORLD & EUROPEAN CHAMPIONSHIPS

were split into two separate pools for the first time, with the weaker countries separated from the traditional powers. Czechoslovakia was again absent and because the American team sent to Paris wasn't first-rate, Canada had no trouble winning the world title once again. The Lethbridge Maple Leafs outscored their opposition 62–6 in winning all six of their games. Sweden claimed its fifth European Championship by finishing second overall behind Canada, though only edged out Switzerland based on a better goal differential.

In a Congress held at the same time as the World Championships, the IIHF decided to withdraw from participation in the Winter Olympics as a result of the ongoing feud that had started in 1948. This decision did not last long however and in August of the same year the IIHF made peace with the IOC at its Congress in Romania.

1952 WINTER OLYMPICS, WORLD AND EUROPEAN CHAMPIONSHIPS

As in 1948, the Olympic hockey tournament was staged as a single round-robin tournament with each team playing every other country once. With nine nations taking part, this meant each team played eight games. As in 1950, Canada was represented by the Edmonton Mercurys who won the gold medal with seven victories and a tie.

Only Sweden and the U.S. provided much opposition for Canada, as the Mercurys needed a goal with 20 seconds remaining to beat the Swedes 3–2. This proved to be the decisive victory in the tournament after Canada could only manage a 3–3 tie with the Americans despite outshooting them 58–13. The Olympic gold medal in 1952 was the fifth for Canada, an achievement not to be surpassed until 1984 by the USSR. No Canadian team has won the Olympic title since.

Czechoslovakia returned to international competition in 1952 and appeared to have won a bronze medal (and the European Championship) after a 4–0 victory over Sweden in their final game gave them the same record and goal differential as the Swedes. Newspapers had already reported Czechoslovakia's third-place finish when the organizing committee changed the European format and decided to hold an additional game to break the tie. Sweden then claimed the Olympic bronze medal and European title with a 5–3 victory.

1953 WORLD & EUROPEAN CHAMPIONSHIPS

The 1953 tournament was the only World Championship to be attended solely by European teams. Canada's decision not to par-

ticipate was explained this way by Canadian Amateur Hockey Association President W B George:"Every year we spend $10,000 to send a Canadian team over to Europe to play 40 exhibition games (plus the World Championships). All of these games are played to packed houses that only enrich European hockey coffers. In return we are subjected to constant, unnecessary abuse over our Canadian style of play."

With Canada and the United States absent, only four nations were included in the main group of the tournament, which copied the double round-robin format of the 1932 Olympics. Sweden won the World Championship for the first time, followed by West Germany (whose second place finish this year remains the best German finish ever). West Germany earned the silver medal despite a record of just one win and three losses because Czechoslovakia's players returned home without finishing the tournament as a gesture of mourning over the death of Czechoslovakian President Klement Gotvald. Third-place Switzerland was awarded the Fair Play Cup.

There was some talk that the Soviet Union would make its international hockey debut at the 1953 World Championships. Instead, hockey experts from the USSR—including legendary coach Anatoli Tarasov—were in Switzerland as observers. The Soviets would join IIHF competition in Stockholm in 1954.

1954 WORLD & EUROPEAN CHAMPIONSHIPS

The Soviet Union made an outstanding debut at the World Championships in 1954, winning the tournament handily. The only blemish on their undefeated record was a 1–1 tie with the host team from Sweden. Canada was represented by the East York Lyndhursts, a club that was not as strong as the Senior A amateur champions that had represented Canada in previous seasons. Still, the Lyndhursts had easily handled their opponents until meeting the Soviet Union's national team in the final game.

The day of the Canada–USSR game began with the sale of tickets for an additional match the following day, because if Canada beat the Soviets—a result that practically no one doubted—the team would be required to play off against Sweden to decide the European Championship. But the USSR Nationals surprised everyone. Their style of play was unfamiliar to the Canadians, as the Soviets appeared to pass too much, check too little, and skate too fast. They were thoroughly dominating in a 7–2 victory. An audience of 16,000 watched the historic game, including a correspondent for *Sport-Informations Dienst* named Gunther Sabetzki, future president of the International Ice Hockey Federation.

The 1954 World Championships marked the first time that the Directorate of the IIHF awarded prizes to the best players. The first winners were goaltender Don Lockhart (Canada), defenseman Lars Bjorn (Sweden) and forward Vsevolod Bobrov (USSR). An IIHF All-Star Team was also selected and, in addition to the player award winners, included: defencemen Vaclav Dubnik (Czechoslovakia), Tom Jamieson, Thomas Campbell, and Doug Chapman (all Canada); forwards Bill Shill, Eric Unger, Maurice Galand (all Canada), Vlastimil Bubnik, Vladimir Zabrodsky, Bronislav Danda (all Czechoslovakia),Victor Shuvalov (USSR) and Sven Johansson (Sweden).

1955 WORLD & EUROPEAN CHAMPIONSHIPS

were rotated between four cities and featured nine teams in the main pool. Canada was repre-

sented by the Penticton Vees, but the loss to the Soviets the previous year resulted in the addition of several players from other Canadian clubs. A problem arose before the championships when a passport check showed that 10 Canadian players listed hockey as their occupation. Vees president Clem Bird was quick to point out that all of these players had resumed their amateur status two years before.

Canada refused to take the Soviets lightly this year, studying the style of their play and sending scouts to observe the USSR's exhibition games. As a result, the Canadians went through the tournament without a loss in eight games, including a 5–0 win over the Soviets, to reclaim the World Championship. The USSR, whose players appeared to take the tournament a little too lightly, finished second with a record of 7–1.

1956 WINTER OLYMPICS, WORLD AND EUROPEAN CHAMPIONSHIPS

A special four-level Olympic Stadium was built at the Italian alpine resort of Cortina which would allow 12,000 spectators to view hockey action. IIHF president Bunny Ahearne declared the 1956 Olympic tournament the most representative in history, also serving to determine the Pool A World champion and the champion of Europe. The organizers returned to the two-stage formula and copied the format of the 1949 World Championships, with the two top teams from each of the three subgroups advancing to the round-robin final, while the remaining teams played in the consolation group.

West Germany's team was, in fact, a combined East–West squad.

The USSR was determined not to repeat the mistakes of 1955, and the Soviets swept through their first Olympic tournament without a defeat to win the gold medal. The United States took the silver, while the Kitchener-Waterloo Dutchmen of Canada lost to both the U.S. and USSR and settled for the bronze.

"There is one area," wrote the *New York Times*, "where the Russians have shown results bordering on the impossible and that area is ice hockey."

1957 WORLD & EUROPEAN CHAMPIONSHIPS

The decision to hold the 1957 World Championships in Moscow was in recognition of the achievements of Soviet hockey. When it was learned that Canada and the United States would be boycotting the tournament over Soviet involvement in Hungary, the USSR Nationals were unanimously declared the tournament favorite. The Soviet team, however, was attempting to integrate younger players onto its aging roster and this hurt its performance. While not losing a single game, the USSR could manage only ties against their main rivals (Sweden and Czechoslovakia) and watched the gold medal go to the Swedes while settling for second place.

The 1957 tournament was the last World Championship to be played on natural ice. Most games were held in the new Luzhniki Sports Palace, but the decisive USSR–Sweden game was played at the nearby Grand Sports Arena where some 50,000 spectators were in attendance. This remains the largest audience in hockey history.

1958 WORLD & EUROPEAN CHAMPIONSHIPS

All 28 games of the 1958 World Championships were held on the artificial ice of a rink set up at the Jordal Amfi Stadium in Oslo, Norway. Canada was represented by the Whitby Dunlops, a strong Ontario senior club that had defeated

the Soviet Union 7–2 in December of 1957 during a Canadian tour by the USSR national team.

The roster of the Whitby Dunlops was reinforced for the World Championships by adding six former professional players. Some had finished their pro careers one year before, while others had played pro hockey right up to the IIHF tournament. A dozen players already had previous experience playing against the USSR, including Jack McKenzie who had played for the Kitchener/Waterloo Dutchmen at the 1956 Olympics. Whitby's captain was Harry Sinden, who later gained fame as coach and general manager of the Boston Bruins. Sinden coached the Canadian team in the historic Canada-Russia Summit Series of 1972.

The Canadians in Oslo had little trouble taking the gold medal in 1958, winning all seven games and outscoring their opponents 82–6. Only the Soviets provided much opposition in a 4–2 victory for Canada.

1959 WORLD & EUROPEAN CHAMPIONSHIPS
in Czechoslovakia coincided with the 50th anniversary of hockey in that country. An unprecedented eight towns hosted the tournament, which was attended by 15 countries. This would be the last time that a championship played separately from the Olympics would be organized in two stages.

Canada was represented this year by the Belleville (Ontario) McFarlands and once again finished as World champions, losing only to the Czechs. The USSR took the silver medal. Czechoslovakia took the bronze.

1960 WINTER OLYMPICS, WORLD AND EUROPEAN CHAMPIONSHIPS
It had been 28 years since the Winter Olympics had last been staged in the United States, and the host nation's hockey team would capture its first Olympic gold medal and second World Championship with a victory in Squaw Valley, California. The Americans had been gradually building towards this victory by bringing good teams to the recent World Championships and had been quite open about their goal of winning at home in 1960. Five players on the gold medal team had won silver medals in 1956, and 10 had had previous experience at the World Championships.

Canada, represented by the Kitchener-Waterloo Dutchmen, lost only to the Americans in California and claimed the silver medal, but had now gone two Olympic Games in a row without winning gold. The Soviets claimed the European Championship for the third year in a row, but were forced to settle for the bronze medal overall for the first time since their debut on the world stage in 1954.

Australia competed for the first time and finished last among the nine nations.

1961 WORLD & EUROPEAN CHAMPIONSHIPS
marked the last time that games were held in the open air. A swimming pool in Lausanne provided the outdoor venue, with powerful freezing plants turning the water to ice. Diving platforms rose above the playing surface and proved an attractive perch for photographers. The warm March sun was a nuisance for players, who had to protect their eyes from the glare. The indoor rink in Geneva was also unusual, as it featured boards made of transparent plastic.

Beginning in 1961, the World Championships were played in three groups, which significantly increased the number of participating nations. A record 20 teams took part in Switzerland, including the first team from South Africa. The tournament was preceded by qualification

games to determine the final berths in Pool A and Pool B. Wins by both East and West Germany put each country in the A Pool, which resulted in a forfeit when the West Germans refused to play the East.

Canada was represented by the Trail Smoke Eaters, who were reinforced with six players from other teams. Trail had won the World Championship for Canada in 1939 and did so again with an undefeated record in 1961, though a tie with Czechoslovakia meant that first place was awarded only on the basis of a better goal differential. This was Canada's 19th win at the World Championships (a record that would be equaled by the Soviets in 1983). It would also prove to be the last win by a Canadian amateur team. Canada would not win the World Championships again until 1994.

The Soviet Union recorded its poorest finish to date in 1961, claiming the bronze medal as it had in 1960 but losing the European title when Czechoslovakia finished second. Despite losing the European title, the Soviet rebuilding program was nearing completion and the USSR national team that competed in Switzerland in 1961 had seven future World Champions on its roster.

1962 WORLD & EUROPEAN CHAMPIONSHIPS
In retaliation for the politically motivated boycott by the Canadians and Americans in 1957, the Soviet Union, Czechoslovakia and other Communist countries refused to participate in the 1962 IIHF World Championships at Colorado Springs, citing the American government's refusal to grant entry visas to East Germany's players and team management.

Canada, represented by the Galt Terriers, was upset by Sweden and finished in second place. The win marked Sweden's third gold medal. The United States took the bronze.

It was during these World Championships that Father David Bauer conceived the idea of establishing a permanent amateur Canadian national team to compete in the Olympics and World Championships.

1963 WORLD & EUROPEAN CHAMPIONSHIPS
Stockholm hosted the World Championships in 1963, nine years after the USSR had first triumphed in the Swedish city. Tournament games would be broadcast on Soviet television for the first time. There were 21 nations competing in three groups over 10 days in Sweden in 1963, including Bulgaria which was making its debut on the world stage. The tournament involved 64 games, a record at the time.

The 1963 World Championships produced one of the most dramatic tournaments on record, with the final outcome still in doubt for the four medal contenders heading into the final day. Both the USSR and Sweden were in contention for the gold medal. Canada could finish no higher than second.

The first game of the day featured the United States and East Germany, and while both were out of contention for the top prize, an East German win would make it easier for the Soviets to claim the gold, while an American win would mean the Soviets would have to beat Canada by 9–0 or better in their final game. A tie would mean that the USSR would have to beat Canada 1–0 or by a margin of two goals. The game did end 3–3, but no matter how the Soviets did against Canada, Sweden would still claim the gold medal with either a win or tie against Czechoslovakia.

A silver medal was on the line for Canada if it could beat the Soviets in the final game, but

the USSR was clearly the better team and held a 4–0 lead into the final minute. Canada (again represented by the Trail Smoke Eaters) managed to score two late goals, but the Soviets held on for the two-goal margin they needed in a 4–2 victory. When Czechoslovakia beat Sweden 3–2, the gold medal went to the USSR. The Swedes had to settle for the silver, while the Czechoslovaks took the bronze. Canada finished fourth and out of the medals for the first time. It was clear now that Canadian amateur club teams could no longer compete with the best Europeans. A permanent Canadian national team would wear the maple leaf in competition beginning in 1964.

Despite the fourth-place finish in 1963, Canadian goalie Seth Martin was among those selected as the best players at the World Championships. Swedish defenseman Roland Stolz and forward Miroslav Vlach of Czechoslovakia received similar honors.

1964 WINTER OLYMPICS, WORLD AND EUROPEAN CHAMPIONSHIPS
For the first time in international play, Canada was represented by a true national team at the 1964 Olympics in Innsbruck, Austria. Though many players would come and go, Canada would be represented by this national team for six years. Canada finished the 1964 Olympics with a 5–2 record, as did Czechoslovakia and Sweden, and the national team believed it had claimed the bronze medal over Sweden on the basis of a better goal differential. But 10 minutes before the medal presentations, IIHF president Bunny Ahearne overruled the pre-arranged IOC tie-breaking formula and announced a change that dropped Canada into fourth place. The Soviet Union won gold.

The Olympic tournament began with a qualification round designed to seed the teams into groups and resulted in several one-sided blowouts. West Germany had earned the right to represent the combined German team with a win over East Germany in a qualification series.

The best players honored at the tournament by the IIHF were goalie Seth Martin of Canada, defenseman Frantisek Tikal of Czechoslovakia and forward Boris Mayorov of the USSR. The coaches of the USSR team reversed the IIHF's selection of Mayorov and instead presented the award for best forward to Eduard Ivanov despite the fact that he was a defenseman. Ivanov was accepted as the official winner of the award in the IIHF record book.

1965 WORLD & EUROPEAN CHAMPIONSHIPS
Tampere, the second largest city in Finland, became the first Finnish city to host the World Championships in 1965. National teams from 15 countries played in the beautiful Gaahalli Ice Palace, Finland's first artificial rink.

Because the close competition in recent years had created situations whereby medal distribution depended only on how many goals had been scored, a new tie-breaking procedure was introduced in Tampere. It was decided that if two teams had an equal number of points, priority would be given to the winner of the game between the two. Only if two medal contenders played a tie game, or if there were more than two contenders would goal differential come into play.

In the event that goal differential was employed, the only games that would be counted would be those involving "the Big Quartet," as the teams from the USSR, Czechoslovakia, Sweden and Canada had begun to be known. This eliminated any advantage from running up lopsided scores against weak opponents as these

games would not be factored into any goal differential calculation.

However, no complex arithmetic was needed to crown a World Champion in 1965. The Soviets did not lose a single game and became the first European team to win the World Championships three years in a row. As a result, the Soviets were permitted to keep the World Championship Cup.

1966 WORLD & EUROPEAN CHAMPIONSHIPS

The USSR, Czechoslovakia and Canada finished 1–2–3 at the 1966 World Championships held in Ljubljana, Yugoslavia. Mild weather make hockey feel like a year-round sport with only the snow-capped peaks of the Alps in the distance serving as a reminder of winter.

In an attempt to increase audiences, tournament organizers decided to hold three separate tournaments for each of Pool A, Pool B and Pool C in the three Yugoslavian towns where hockey was most popular.

As had been decided in Tampere the year before, results of head-to-head games between two tied teams would be used to break any ties, but only when medals were at stake. In all other cases, goal differential would be used as it was when the United States was ranked ahead of Finland in the final standings.

The Soviet Union won the gold, finishing 6–0–1. Czechoslovakia finished second (6–1–0) while Canada ws third (5–2–0). The Soviet's one tie game came against fourth-place Sweden.

1967 WORLD & EUROPEAN CHAMPIONSHIPS

National teams from 21 countries assembled in Vienna for the 1967 World Championships, and the 66 games played set a new record. Rosters were increased to 18 players and tournament organizers had to cope with enormous logistical difficulties in providing accommodations and training facilities for the visiting teams. Proceeds from the games would only cover the expenses for the Pool A tournament, but dropping Pool B and Pool C would almost certainly result in severe setbacks for the game in a number of lesser hockey nations. The only logical option—and one suggested ten years earlier by then IIHF president Bunny Ahearne—was to organize three separate tournaments. This IIHF directors agreed to this new format in 1969.

The Soviet Union won its fifth consecutive World Championship in Vienna in 1967, claiming the title by the largest margin of victory (five points) in history. Canada's national team was bolstered by ex-pros Carl Brewer and Jack Bownass and had an excellent tournament before losing 6–0 to Sweden in the final game and settling for the bronze medal.

1968 WINTER OLYMPICS, WORLD AND EUROPEAN CHAMPIONSHIPS

marked the last time in which the Olympic, World, and European titles would all be decided in one event. Heading into the final game at Grenoble, Czechoslovakia needed a win against Sweden to claim the Olympic title, but had to settle for the silver medal after a 2–2 tie. Because the regulations stated that if a team from Europe won the Olympic title it would also be crowned European Champion, the tie with Sweden cost Czechoslovakia a unique opportunity to capture the Olympic, World and European crowns.

The Soviets won the Olympic gold medal for the second time in a row in 1968 and claimed their sixth consecutive World title, equaling Canada's record achievement of 1920 to 1932. The USSR had also gone 39 straight games without a loss dating back to 1963, matching another record set by Canada between 1936 and 1948. The Canadian national team won the bronze medal at Grenoble.

1969 WORLD & EUROPEAN CHAMPIONSHIPS

As proposed by the Swedish Hockey Union, the 1969 World Championships at Stockholm were played in two rounds. The top six countries would compete in a double round robin instead of the eight-team, single-round format of previous years, meaning each team would play 10 games instead of seven. The IIHF Council hoped the new format would increase competition, as the world title had been won by the Soviet Union for six straight years. Soviet coach Anatoli Tarasov disagreed. "I think our team will look better in the second round," he said. "As a matter of fact, the two-round system is to our advantage—our players rehabilitate faster and they know how to play with injuries. For this reason, it would be to our advantage if we had entry lists not for 19, but for 18 or even 17 players."

Despite Tarasov's talk, the USSR was lucky to win the gold medal in 1969. The Soviets, Sweden and Czechoslovakia all finished with identical 8–2 records and goal differential was needed to break the tie. If the Swedes had scored another goal in their 1–0 victory over Czechoslovakia in the final game, they would have been World Champions. Czechoslovakia would have claimed the gold if they could have tied the game. As it was, the Soviets, with an unprecedented seven rookies on the roster, won their seventh straight world title to establish a new international hockey record.

1970 WORLD & EUROPEAN CHAMPIONSHIPS

were scheduled for Canada, with games set for Winnipeg and Montreal. It was to be the first time that the tournament would be played in the country where hockey was born. In March of 1969, representatives of a new organization called Hockey Canada gathered in Toronto to select the best possible team to play at home.

Meanwhile, Canadian hockey officials were becoming more and more convinced that their top amateurs, even reinforced by ex-professionals, were unable to compete with the leading European national teams. Having won just three bronze medals with their own national team since 1964, Canadian representatives at the IIHF Congress in Stockholm in March of 1969 opened a discussion about the joint participation of amateurs and professionals. At the IIHF's summer congress in Switzerland in July, NHL president Clarence Campbell was among a 15-member Canadian delegation. He invited the six best players from teams in Pool B and Pool C to come to Canada and watch NHL games at the NHL's expense. A film about professional hockey was also shown with Canada's Prime Minister proposing to make the World Championships an open event.

Canada's emissaries were very successful. The IIHF agreed to make the rules of amateur hockey more consistent with those of the pro game and to allow nine professionals to play as an experiment for one year. It was also decided that amateur status would be given to any player who had left the pro game within six weeks of the World Championships instead of the previous standard of six months. However, meetings held in Geneva in January of 1970 produced so many reciprocal claims between the IIHF leadership and the Canadian organizing committee that the Canadians were finally prohibited from using professional players altogether. IOC president Avery Brundage was also strongly opposed to amateurs and professionals playing on the same sheet of ice. The Canadians reacted by withdrawing from all international hockey competition. Canada would not return to the IIHF World Championships until 1977.

As a result of the Canadian decision, the 1970 World Championships were hastily relocated to Stockholm, making the Swedish capital the first city to host the event two years in a row. Poland was brought up from Pool B to replace Canada, but managed just one tie in 10 games. The Soviet Union ran up a 9–1 record in winning the world title for the eighth year in a row.

1971 WORLD & EUROPEAN CHAMPIONSHIPS

A record-setting number of participants—22—competed in three World Pools in 1971. The main Pool A World Championships were held in Switzerland. Beginning with this year, points were counted separately for the World and European Championships. The results of games between European and North American teams at the World Championships would no longer count towards the European title. The Soviet Union won its ninth straight World title, but when games against the United States were eliminated, Czechoslovakia had the better record and so claimed the European gold for the 11th time. It was the first time since 1962 that a nation other than the USSR was crowned European Champion.

After playing in Pool B in 1970, the U.S. was back in Pool A at this tournament, but it turned out to be for only one year. By scoring just one goal in a 5–1 loss to West Germany in their final game, the Americans were relegated to Pool B again for the 1972 World Championships.

1972 WINTER OLYMPICS

The 1972 Olympics in Sapporo, marked the first major international hockey event to be held in Japan. The 1940 Winter Games had been scheduled for Sapporo, but were canceled due to World War II. The Soviet Union was triumphant once again in 1972 with four wins and a tie in five games. The surprise of the Olympics was the United States team. Seeded sixth in the tournament, and already relegated to Pool B for the upcoming World Championships, the Americans won the silver medal. The U.S. team featured two players who would go on fine professional careers in the World Hockey Association and the NHL: Robbie Ftorek and Mark Howe.

1972 WORLD & EUROPEAN CHAMPIONSHIPS

The 1972 tournament in Czechoslovakia was held in April and marked the first time the World and European Championships were conducted independently of the Olympics. This was a first step in bringing Canada back to the World Championships, as the separation from the Olympics made it possible to consider the participation of professional players. Allowing pros to play at the World Championships would now no longer have an impact on the Olympic movement, in much the same way soccer's World Cup did not affect the Olympics.

Twenty-five years after its first victory in Prague, Czechoslovakia once again used home-ice advantage to win the gold medal. Czechoslovakia's third World Championship equaled Sweden in this regard and snapped a Soviet winning streak that had reached 10 consecutive World and/or Olympic victories. The 1972 World Championships marked the first time that the Soviet squad was not led by longtime coaches Arkady Chernyshov and Anatoli Tarasov, as Vsevolod Bobrov made his international coaching debut.

It was at the 1972 tournament in Prague that final arrangements were made for the September series between the USSR and Canada's NHL professionals. Canadians had long believed their best pros would easily defeat Europe's amateur champions, but Team Canada was hard pressed to defeat the Soviets and had to rally to win the last three games in Moscow to take the eight-game series 4–3–1. Paul Henderson scored the decisive goal with 34 seconds left in the final game to give Canada a 6–5 victory.

1973 WORLD & EUROPEAN CHAMPIONSHIPS
were held in Moscow, and the USSR easily recaptured the title it had lost in Prague the year before. The tournament marked the first time since the European Championships in 1927 that the host nation won all of its games. The Soviets finished with a perfect record of 10–0.

Poland had made impressive strides by the 1973 World Championships. Under the guidance of Soviet coach Anatoli Yegorov, Poland had managed to land a place in Pool A but only recorded one win and one tie in 10 games played.

1974 WORLD & EUROPEAN CHAMPIONSHIPS
A drug-testing policy was introduced by the International Ice Hockey Federation at its congress in July of 1969 and first implemented at the Winter Olympics in Sapporo in 1972. Two years later, this drug testing suddenly made headlines at the Pool A tournament of the World Championships.

Drug testing required that two players were selected at random from each team after each game. A random test on the first day of the 1974 tournament in Helsinki following Sweden's 4–1 win over Poland showed that Ulf Nilsson from Sweden had used ephedrine, which was on the IOC's list of banned substances.

As a result, Poland was awarded the victory by a score of 5–0. This "win" ultimately allowed Poland to remain in Pool A. Later in the tournament, it was discovered the Finland's goalie Stig Wetzell had also taken ephedrine and the host nation's 5–2 upset of Czechoslovakia was reversed to a 5–0 defeat.

Once again in 1974, it was the Soviet Union that emerged as World Champions with nine wins in 10 games.

1975 WORLD & EUROPEAN CHAMPIONSHIPS
The format for the 1975 World Championships in Germany remained unchanged for the seventh consecutive year, but by this time the formula was satisfying neither spectators nor participants. The IIHF had become convinced that the results in the A Pool had become predictable, thereby hurting attendance.

Since the Canadians had withdrawn from the World tournament, the Soviets, Czechoslovaks and Swedes controlled the top places in the standings. The bottom teams in Pool A had managed very few victories. Poland, however, was showing noticeable improvement and finished fifth for the third year in a row in 1975 to once again avoid demotion to Pool B.

1976 WINTER OLYMPICS
marked the second time the Games were held in Innsbruck, Austria. The event had originally been awarded to Denver, Colorado, but was moved after disgruntled taxpayers protested the cost of staging an Olympics. Canada and Sweden did not take part.

The first round of competition served to divide the field into medal and consolation events. Influenza would prove to have a great effect on the outcome of the tournament as most of the players on the Czechoslovakian team took

sick. Frantisek Pospisil tested positive for a prohibited substance after traces of codeine were detected following a game between Poland and Czechoslovakia. Because of this positive test, the results of the game were reversed and entered into the records as a 1–0 win for Poland.

Despite these distractions, the last game of the tournament between the Soviet Union and Czechoslovakia proved to be a gem. The USSR trailed 2–0 midway through the second period when a pair of penalties left them two men short for two minutes. The Soviet penalty killers smothered the Czechoslovak attack, not allowing a single dangerous shot on goal during the two-man disadvantage.

The USSR eventually came from behind to tie the game 2–2 before the Czechoslovaks scored a go-ahead goal with nine minutes remaining in the third period. Taking advantage of a power-play, the Soviets tied the game with less than five minutes to play and then scored the eventual winner 24 seconds later.

The Soviet Union's gold medal represented the first time in Olympic hockey history that a team had won four consecutive Winter Games titles. Czechoslovakia took the silver medal while the West Germans were surprise winners of the bronze.

1976 WORLD & EUROPEAN CHAMPIONSHIPS
The appointment of Dr. Gunther Sabetzki to the position of president of the IIHF its July 1975 congress in Switzerland led to a declaration that professional players would be allowed to compete at the 1976 World Championships. This move was made to entice Canada back into the international fold, and Canada did return, but not until the following year.

The 1976 World Championships were held in Katowice, in recognition of Poland's improved play in recent years. Pool A was expanded to eight teams, which allowed the United States to avoid relegation to Pool B after a last-place finish in 1975. The second opening had been offered to Canada, but went instead to Pool B runner-up West Germany.

With eight teams in Pool A, a new format was devised that would split the nations into two groups of four after an opening round-robin series. The top four nations would then play a round-robin final, while the last four countries held a separate playoff. The United States used the new rules to advantage, employing seven pros from the NHL and World Hockey Association to break into the top four for the first time since 1962. The gold medal went to Czechoslovakia, who comfortably outdistanced the USSR with a record of 9–1.

1977 WORLD & EUROPEAN CHAMPIONSHIPS
Canada returned to the World Championships in 1977 after an eight-year absence. The tournament in Austria began two weeks later than other World Championships, but the April dates still meant the best Canadian professional players in both the NHL and WHA were competing in their league playoffs. Canada's team in 1977 was selected only from players on six NHL clubs that had failed to qualify for postseason play. Canada finished out of the medals in fourth place, but did beat the eventual champions from Czechoslovakia 8–2, which was the worst loss ever suffered by a gold medal-winning team.

The Soviet Union was able to beat Canada twice, but a loss to Czechoslovakia and two losses to the silver medalists from Sweden meant the that for the first time the USSR had to settle for the bronze medal in both the World and European Championships. Czechoslovakia's

victory gave them back-to-back world titles for the first time in history.

1978 WORLD & EUROPEAN CHAMPIONSHIPS
in Prague were staged from late April to early May, latest start date in the history of the event. This delayed start allowed the Canadian team to draw on players whose NHL clubs had been eliminated during the first round of the playoffs. Though the 20-man roster was assembled just nine days before the World Championships, Canada managed to win the bronze medal.

After two years of disappointment, the Soviet Union unveiled a roster that included nine newcomers. The Soviets managed to win the gold medal despite playing on the home ice of Czechoslovakia, the two-time defending World champions. The Soviet victory required a clutch 3–1 win over the host nation in the final game of the tournament.

Since the admittance of pro players to the World Championships, members of the same club team began to find themselves representing opposing national squads. This year in Prague, for example, two NHL players from the Minnesota North Stars defended Canada's colors, three played for Sweden and four were members of the United States team. Circumstances such as these had only previously been encountered in soccer's World Cup.

1979 WORLD & EUROPEAN CHAMPIONSHIPS
Over the preceding decade, the IIHF, seeking to further perfect the game, did much to make the amateur and professional rules more consistent. This included the termination of a two-minute penalty as soon as the team on the power-play scored, the elimination of icing for teams playing short-handed, and the introduction of delayed penalties. Other decisions adopted during the May 1978 congress that went into effect at the 1979 World Championships included making it necessary for the defending team to touch the puck before icing was called, abandoning the change of ends in the middle of the third period when games were played indoors, and increasing the rosters to 22.

A record 26 nations competed at the World Championships in 1979, with the eight teams in Pool A playing in Moscow. At the suggestion of the USSR Ice Hockey Federation, these eight teams were split into two groups of four based on the standings from the previous year. After a round-robin series for each group, the top two teams from each side would advance to the medal round with the points they gained in the first round counting towards the final standings. The format was, in fact, the same as it had been at the World Championships in 1935, and allowed for the tournament to be played in 14 days instead of 19.

Because the Soviets wanted the tournament concluded in time for May Day celebrations, the World Championships began one week earlier than the year before. As a result, Canada began the tournament with only a 19-man roster made up of young players whose teams had missed the NHL playoffs. The Canadians played poorly and finished fourth. As in 1973, the host Soviets won every game en route to the gold medal with the second-place Czechoslovakian team finishing well behind in the standings.

1980 WINTER OLYMPICS
No World and European Championships were played in this Olympic year. Unlike 1972 and 1976, no separate World Championships would be played following the Winter Games.

The gold medal victory by the United States

was quickly dubbed a "Miracle on Ice." Professionals were still not allowed to compete at the Olympics, and so Canada and the U.S. once again had to rely on amateur national teams. Canada would finish sixth, while the Americans became champions. Coach Herb Brooks, who had been the last player cut from the 1960 gold medal team, stocked his American team with an assortment of unknown college players who played a pre-Olympic schedule of 60 games. The team was 42–14–3 over 59 games, before being crushed 10–3 by the Soviet Union just three days before their first game in Lake Placid.

The USA began the Olympic tournament with a 2–2 tie against Sweden on defenseman Bill Baker's goal with 27 seconds remaining. Jim Craig starred in net, as he would throughout the tournament. The Americans then downed Czechoslovakia 7–3 and followed up with easy victories over Norway and Romania. In the final game of the round-robin division series, the U.S. fell behind West Germany 2–0 after one period, but rebounded for a 4–2 victory. Both the U.S. and Sweden finished the round robin with 4–0–1 records, but the Swedes were ranked on top due to a better goal differential. As a result, the Americans would have to take on the undefeated Soviets in the first game of the medal round just 13 days after their humiliating pre-Olympic defeat.

On February 22, 1980 a crowd of 10,000 jammed the Olympic Arena, while millions more Americans, turned on by their team's surprising success, tuned in at home. The Soviets built up leads of 1–0 and 2–1 during the first period, but a Mark Johnson goal as time expired sent the teams to the dressing room tied 2–2. Soviet coach Victor Tikhonov replaced legendary goaltender Vladislav Tretiak with back-up Vladimir Myshkin to start the second period. After 40 minutes, the Soviets led 3–2 and had outshot the Americans 30–10. In the third period, Johnson tied the game and captain Mark Eruzione put the U.S. ahead 4–3 with 10 minutes to go. Jim Craig made the lead hold up and an entire nation celebrated. The Americans faced Finland in the final game two days after the victory over the Soviet Union. A loss would have meant a silver medal, but the United States won gold with a 4–2 victory.

1981 WORLD & EUROPEAN CHAMPIONSHIPS
After settling for the silver medal at the 1980 Olympics, the Soviet Union returned to top spot at the 1981 World Championships, winning the title for the third time running. Sweden, enthusiastically cheered by their fans at home, won the silver medal for the eleventh time. The Netherlands achieved a record of sorts, as the team from Holland had jumped from Pool C to Pool A in just two seasons.

1982 WORLD & EUROPEAN CHAMPIONSHIPS
The format of the Pool A World Championships was changed again in 1982. All eight teams would play a round-robin series with the top four teams advancing to a medal round. As had been the case prior to 1979, teams would be credited with all the points they had accumulated in the first round, not just those gained against the other medal-round opponents. Only the results of the first round-robin series would be used to determine the European Champion.

By initially sending over a team stocked with junior players, Canada was able to wait until the first round of the NHL playoffs was finished before finalizing its roster. Wayne Gretzky, Bobby Clarke and Darryl Sittler helped give Canada its strongest team since returning to international competition in 1977, though the team only had time to practice once before play began.

The Soviet Union easily won the gold medal in Finland in 1982, and Czechoslovakia claimed the silver after tying the USSR 0–0 in the final game. The tie dropped Canada into third place, and resulted in protests by the Canadians that the Soviets had conspired to deny them a silver medal.

1983 WORLD & EUROPEAN CHAMPIONSHIPS
Unlike the preceding year's tournament, medal-round contenders at the World Championships in 1983 would only count the points they earned in the final round in order to determine medal standings. The four bottom teams that did not qualify for the medal round after the opening round robin would count all of their points in determining the ranking from fifth to eighth place. The IIHF congress also ruled that teams must provide a preliminary entry list of not less than 19 players, with the remaining three roster spots eligible to be filled during the course of the championships. These new rules were introduced in order to better balance the competition for medals. As in 1982, only the results of the initial round-robin series would be used to crown the European Champion.

In winning the 1983 World Championships, the Soviets claimed their 19th title, equaling Canada's record.

1984 WINTER OLYMPICS
The hockey competition at the 1984 Winter Olympics in Sarajevo comprised 12 teams competing in two separate divisions. Canada's Olympic team had posted a dismal 2–17–3 record in its last 22 exhibition games, and had seen players Mark Morrison and Don Dietrich disqualified after the Americans protested their former professional status. However, Russ Courtnall and Kirk Muller were added to the roster a week before the Olympics to boost the team's sagging offense.

Canada defeated the defending Olympic champions from the United States in the first game of the tournament and ran up four straight wins before losing to Czechoslovakia in the final game of their first-round schedule. Both nations advanced to the medal round, as did the Soviets and Swedes. Canada's weak offense eventually doomed the team to fourth place, while the USSR clinched the gold medal with a win over Czechoslovakia in the final game.

No World and European Championships were played in this Olympic year.

1985 WORLD & EUROPEAN CHAMPIONSHIPS
By winning the initial round-robin portion of the tournament, the Soviet Union was once again European Champion, but because results of the first round were no longer carried over into the medal round of play, losses to Canada and Czechoslovakia saw the USSR fall to third place overall. The Soviet team was playing without legendary goalie Vladislav Tretiak for the first time since 1969.

Czechoslovakia won the World Championship for the sixth time in 1985, making this their third victory on home ice. Canada finished second for the first time since 1962. The talented Canadian team still had a chance for the gold medal entering the final game of the tournament against the host nation, but was beaten 5–3.

Sweden's poor play was a surprising feature of the 1985 World Championships. The sixth-place finish of the Tre Kronor was the worst result for the Swedes since 1931.

1986 WORLD & EUROPEAN CHAMPIONSHIPS
were held in Moscow for the fourth time, and for the third time at home the Soviet Union won every game en route to the gold medal. However, the USSR did not clinch the title until the third period of the last game, when they beat Sweden 3–2. The Swedes were forced to play without star Peter Lindmark, the best goaltender of the tournament, who had been injured in a previous game.

The biggest surprise of the tournament was the poor showing of Czechoslovakia. The 1985 World Champions did not even qualify for the medal round and finished fifth. It was the first time since 1967 that Czechoslovakia finished out of the medals.

Canada finished third at the 1986 World Championships with a roster that included established NHL stars Denis Potvin and Brent Sutter, who made the tournament's second all-star team. Brett Hull made his international debut for the United States.

1987 WORLD & EUROPEAN CHAMPIONSHIPS
Sweden won the World Championships in Vienna in 1987, 25 years after its last world title. Both Sweden and the Soviet Union had one win and two ties during the medal round, but the Swedes claimed the gold medal with a better goal differential largely achieved in a 9–0 win over Canada on the last day of the tournament.

The 1987 World Championships were marred by a scandal relating to the eligibility of West Germany's Miroslav Sikora. The West Germans had been playing well and appeared to have a chance to reach the medal round after scoring victories over Canada and Finland. However, the Finns filed a protest because Sikora had played for Poland at the 1976 European Junior Championships. International Ice Hockey Federation rules at that time prohibited players from representing more than one country in official tournaments, but the Germans stated that they had obtained permission from the IIHF for Sikora to play.

The IIHF Directorate suspended Sikora after the Finnish protest and stripped West Germany of its two wins. The Germans protested this decision and filed a lawsuit in a Vienna court, which eventually ruled in favor of Germany and ordered the IIHF to reinstate the two victories or pay a substantial fine. The IIHF Directorate voted 11–2 to accept the court's decision regarding the West German victories, but Sikora remained suspended for the rest of the tournament. Meanwhile, the distracted West German team lost its three remaining games and failed to make the medal round.

Pool D made its debut on the World and European hockey scene in 1987.

1988 WINTER OLYMPICS
Several months before the start of the 1988 Olympic hockey tournament in Calgary, the decision was made to allowed teams to include professional players on their rosters. This made it possible for goalie Andy Moog, who was involved in a contract dispute with the Edmonton Oilers, to join the Canadian Olympic team. Oilers teammate Randy Gregg also joined the team, as did Brian Bradley of the Calgary Flames and Ken Yaremchuk of the Toronto Maple Leafs. Just a few days before the Olympics began, Tim Watters (Winnipeg Jets), Steve Tambellini (Vancouver Canucks) and Jim Peplinski (Calgary Flames) were also added to the roster. Despite these reinforcements, Canada wound up out of the medals with a fourth-place finish.

The Soviet Union dominated the tournament in Calgary, clinching the Olympic gold medal even before the last game (which they lost 2–1 to Finland). The Soviet team featured a 19-year-old rookie named Alexander Mogilny, who later went on to NHL stardom. The Finns took the silver in Calgary for their first Olympic medal.

No World and European Championships were played in this Olympic year.

1989 WORLD & EUROPEAN CHAMPIONSHIPS Sweden, who had won the last World Championships in 1987, were denied the title on home ice in 1989 by a Soviet team that was a perfect 10–0 during the tournament. The Swedes finished fourth. This year marked the last appearance together of the USSR's famous "Green Unit" of Viacheslav Fetisov, Alexei Kasatonov, Sergei Makarov, Igor Larionov and Vladimir Krutov. All five players joined NHL clubs the following season.

Canada won its fifth medal in the last six World Championships with a silver in Stockholm in 1989. In the middle of the tournament, a random drug test showed a positive result for Canadian defenseman Randy Carlyle. However, IIHF rules called for two samples to be taken from each player and a check of Carlyle's second sample 24 hours later cleared him of any wrongdoing.

The Americans weren't as lucky as Canada when it came to drug testing. The high levels of testosterone (a banned substance) found in the body of Corey Millen resulted in his suspension. Team USA officials tried to prove that this level was normal for Millen, but the IIHF did not reverse its decision.

1990 WORLD & EUROPEAN CHAMPIONSHIPS The USSR won the World Championships once again in Switzerland in 1990. The tournament featured great performances by two goaltenders. Arturs Irbe, who was named the tournament's best goalie, led the Soviets to the title while Czechoslovakia took the bronze medal on the strength of Dominik Hasek's play. Hasek was named to the tournament all-star team for the third year in a row. He moved to the NHL's Chicago Blackhawks the following year.

Norway returned to Pool A at the 1990 World Championships for the first time since 1965.

1991 WORLD & EUROPEAN CHAMPIONSHIPS in Finland marked the last time that eight nations competed in Pool A, as the decision was made to include 12 teams in subsequent years. More importantly, the IIHF decided that beginning in 1992, it would no longer award a separate European title as part of the World Championships.

Perhaps most significantly, the 1991 World Championships marked the last time Soviet players would wear the famous letters "CCCP" on their chests. The political breakup of the Soviet Union meant that the longtime hockey power would play as Russia after 1991. Political changes also saw the merging of East Germany and West Germany into one nation, and a new German team now appeared on the hockey scene.

Sweden won the World Championship in 1991, with Canada taking the silver medal. The USSR departed with a bronze medal.

1992 WINTER OLYMPICS After the breakup of the Soviet Union in January of 1992, the former Soviet Olympic committee decided to call its delegation to the Albertville Winter Games the "Unified Team" due to the fact that several ath-

letes in various sports were from former Soviet republics. Though the hockey team was comprised only of ethnic Russian players, it was known as the Unified Team as well and played with no logo on its uniform. No national anthem was played when the former Soviets won the gold medal in hockey. The Olympic anthem was played instead.

The 1992 Olympic hockey tournament used a playoff system for the first time in the postwar era. The one-game elimination playoff system included eight teams in the quarterfinals and saw the four teams with the best records in the preliminary round reach the semifinals. Led by Joe Juneau and Eric Lindros, Canada advanced to the finals, but a 3–1 victory by the Unified Team denied the country its first Olympic hockey gold medal since 1952. Still, a silver medal represented Canada's best finish since winning the bronze in 1968.

1992 WORLD CHAMPIONSHIPS Like the Olympics, the World Championships introduced a one-game elimination playoff system in 1992. After a preliminary round involving two groups of six teams, the top four teams from each group advanced to the playoffs. Canada and Russia were both victims of the new system, as hockey's two historic powers were knocked out in the quarterfinals.

Sweden advanced through the playoffs to clinch the World Championships for the second year in a row, marking the first time consecutive wins had been recorded by a team other than the Soviet Union since Czechoslovakia won in 1976 and 1977.

Greece, Israel, Luxembourg and Turkey each made their debut at the World Championships in 1992, appearing in Pool C, Group 2.

1993 WORLD CHAMPIONSHIPS Former international star Boris Mikhailov took over as coach of the Russian team, replacing Viktor Tikhonov who had ruled the Soviet/Russian squad for 15 years. Mikhailov's World Championship coaching debut was a success as Russia won the gold medal. The Russians defeated Sweden in the final game, denying the Swedes a third straight World Championship.

Though Canada finished fourth after losing the bronze medal game to Czechoslovakia, the tournament was dominated by the brilliant performance of 20-year-old Canadian center Eric Lindros. Lindros led the tournament in both goals and points. He was named best forward and voted to the all-star team.

The Czech Republic made its first appearance at the World Championships in 1993 (replacing Czechoslovakia), while national teams from Slovenia and three former Soviet republics— Latvia, Ukraine and Kazakhstan—made their first appearances in Pool C. Latvia, which took part in World and European Championships before World War II, returned to the international hockey scene for the first time in more than half a century.

1994 WINTER OLYMPICS The International Olympic Committee decided to have stage its Winter and Summer Games in different years, so the Winter Olympics in Lillehammer, Norway took place just two years after the previous competition in Albertville, France.

Russia, Slovakia and the Czech Republic each made their Olympic hockey debut in Norway.

The exciting tournament had a thrilling conclusion with a shootout in the final game between Sweden and Canada. The winning goal

by Peter Forsberg gave the Swedes their first Olympic championship. Three players on the Swedish team—Tomas Jonsson, Hakan Loob, and Mats Naslund—became the first players to win World, Olympic, and Stanley Cup titles in separate tournaments.

The loss to Sweden in the finals gave Canada its second consecutive Olympic silver medal. Russia lost to Finland in the third-place game and finished out of the medals for the first time in the history of Soviet/Russian Olympic hockey.

1994 WORLD CHAMPIONSHIPS For the first time since the Trail Smoke Eaters' victory in 1961, Canada won the World Championships in 1994. Avenging their loss to Sweden at the Olympics, the Canadians defeated Finland in a shoot-out when Luc Robitaille scored the winning goal. Canada's win was truly a team effort, as only Paul Kariya ranked among the top–10 leading scorers at the World Championships. Bill Ranford was spectacular in goal for Canada.

Great Britain returned to Pool A in 1994 for the first time since 1951. Slovakia, Belarus, Estonia and Croatia all made their debut in the Pool C World Championships.

1995 WORLD CHAMPIONSHIPS Finland won the World Championships for the first time in 1995, beating their rivals from Sweden in the gold-medal game. The Finns were led by the line of Jere Lehtinen, Saku Koivu and Ville Peltonen, all of whom were named to the tournament all-star team. For the second year in a row, Russia lost in the quarterfinals and did not have an opportunity to play for a medal.

For the first time in 20 years, the 1995 World Championships were played without the participation of NHL players. Because a long lockout delayed the start of their 1994–95 season, NHL teams were still playing and were unable to release their players go to represent their respective countries. Team Canada and the United States suffered the most from this situation.

Lithuania returned to the World tournament this year for the first time since 1938, competing in Pool C.

1996 WORLD CHAMPIONSHIPS A different team was crowned World champion for the fifth year in a row when the Czech Republic beat Canada in the gold medal game in Vienna in 1996. It was the first world title for players representing the Czech Republic. (Czechoslovakia last won in 1985).

The Czech Republic's victory came in the year in which Slovakia made its first appearance in Pool A. Like the Czech Republic, Slovakia was formerly a part of Czechoslovakia.

The growth of hockey on a world level and the changing political landscape saw 36 national teams play in Pools A, B, C and D in 1996.

1997 WORLD CHAMPIONSHIPS A new system was introduced for the World tournament in Finland in 1997. In the preliminaries, two groups of six teams each played round robins with the top three teams from each side advancing to a final group to play for the medals. The six remaining teams played off to determine rankings from seventh to 12th place.

The top six teams in the final group carried their points forward from the preliminary round. Each final-round team then played the three nations that had qualified for the finals from the other preliminary round group. The top two final-round teams then advanced to play in a best-of-three final, while the third- and fourth-place teams played one game for the bronze.

Sweden beat Canada in the first game of the finals, before the Canadians rallied to win two in a row and claim their 21st World Championship. Geoff Sanderson and Rob Blake had also been members of Canada's gold medal-winning team in 1994.

Latvia qualified for Pool A in 1997, returning to play with the world's top hockey nations for the first time since before World War II.

1998 WINTER OLYMPICS Qualification for the 1998 Olympics began in the fall of 1995. Hockey's six major nations (Canada, the Czech Republic, Finland, Russia, Sweden and the USA) were accorded six of eight berths in the final round at Nagano.

Based on the results of the 1995 Pool A World Championships, Italy and France were also admitted to the Olympics. Japan automatically qualified as the host country. These three nations were placed in an eight-team preliminary round.

To determine the five other preliminary round participants in Nagano, teams from 18 nations were put into four qualifying groups. The four winners of these groups were placed in two final qualifying groups along with the three teams that finished at the bottom of the standings at the Pool A World Championships in 1995 and the winner of 1995's Pool B tournament.

The first- and second-place finishers from each final qualifying group (Germany, Slovakia, Kazakhstan and Belarus) were promoted to take part in the Nagano Olympic tournament along with Austria, which won a playoff game between third-place teams.

The Olympic hockey tournament was played in two phases: a preliminary round and a final round. In the preliminary round Austria, Italy, Kazakhstan and Slovakia competed in Group A; Belarus, France, Germany and Japan competed in Group B. The winners of each group (Kazakhstan and Belarus) advanced to the final round to compete with Canada, the Czech Republic, Finland, Russia, Sweden and the United States.

Again divided into two groups of four, the eight top countries played a round robin to determine seedings for the quarterfinals. The quarterfinals, semifinals and finals were all single-game playoffs.

Beginning with the quarterfinals, the story of the Nagano Olympics was the sensational play of Czech goaltender Dominik Hasek. Despite being badly outshot, the defense held around Hasek and the entire Czech team gathered strength as the tournament progressed. They defeated the U.S. in the quarterfinals 4–1, got past Canada in the semifinals when Hasek stopped all five shots in a tie-breaking shootout and finally defeated Russia 1–0 to win the gold. Finland defeated Canada 4–2 to win the bronze medal.

1998 WORLD CHAMPIONSHIPS were expanded to include 16 countries. The teams were split into four groups of four, with a preliminary round robin played within each group to determine which eight nations would advance to play for the medals and which eight would be relegated to a consolation round.

The traditional hockey countries all advanced to the medal round with one exception. Though the Americans beat Switzerland 5–2 in their head-to-head matchup, both had identical records and Switzerland had a better goal-differential so the host nation moved on while the United States missed the medal round and eventually finished 12th. Switzerland continued its upset trend in the quarterfinal round, beating the Russians 4–2. Sweden, Finland and the Czech Republic also advanced, while Canada joined Russia, Belarus and Slovakia on the sidelines after dropping a must-win game 7–1 to a powerful Swedish team led by Peter Forsberg and Mats Sundin.

The semifinals were played in a two-game total-goals format with Finland beating the Czech Republic 6–3 on the round and Sweden downing the Swiss team 11–3. Hopes of a medal for the host nation were dashed when the Czechs beat Switzerland 4–0 to take third place. Sweden edged Finland 1–0 on a goal by Johan Tornberg in game one of a two-game total-goals final to win its first World Championship since 1992.

IIHF COUNTRY ABBREVIATIONS

Includes countries that were later renamed:
Bohemia
Commonwealth of Independent States,
Czechoslovakia,
East Germany,
Soviet Union,
West Germany

Andorra	AND
Australia	AUS
Austria	AUT
Azerbaijan	AZE
Belarus	BLR
Belgium	BEL
Bohemia	BOH
Brazil	BRA
Bulgaria	BUL
Commonwealth of Independent States	CIS
Canada	CAN
China	PRC
Chinese Taipei	TPE
Croatia	CRO
Czech Republic	CZE
Czechoslovakia	TCH
Denmark	DEN
East Germany	GDR
Estonia	EST
Finland	FIN
France	FRA
Germany	GER
Great Britain	GBR
Greece	GRE
Hong Kong	HKG
Hungary	HUN
Iceland	ISL
India	IND
israel	ISR
Italy	ITA
Japan	JAP
Kazakhstan	KAZ
Korea, South	KOR
Kuwait	KUW
Latvia	LAT
Lithuania	LIT
Luxembourg	LUX
Mexico	MEX
Netherlands	HOL
New Zealand	NZL
Norway	NOR
Korea, North	PRK
Poland	POL
Romania	ROM
Russia	RUS
Slovakia	SVK
Slovenia	SLO
South Africa	SAF
Soviet Union	URS
Spain	ESP
Sweden	SWE
Switzerland	SUI
Thailand	THA
Turkey	TUR
U.S.A.	USA
Ukraine	UKR
West Germany	FRG
Yugoslavia	YUG

WINTER OLYMPIC STANDINGS, RANKINGS, MEDAL ROUND GAME RESULTS, AND LEADING SCORERS

Cumulative Medal Rankings, 1924–1998

	G	S	B	TOTAL	LAST MEDAL
1. USSR/Russia*	8	2	1	11	Silver 98
2. Canada	5	4	2	11	Silver 94
3. USA	2	5	1	8	Gold 80
4. Sweden	1	2	4	7	Gold 94
5. Czechoslovakia/ Czech Republic	1	4	3	8	Gold 98
6. Great Britain	1	0	1	2	Gold 36
7. Finland	0	1	1	2	Bronze 94
8. W. Germany	0	0	2	76	Bronze 76
9. Switzerland	0	0	2	2	Bronze 48
10. Finland	0	0	1	1	**Bronze 98**

Soviet Union/Russia played as the Unified Team in 1992.

Antwerp, Belgium • 1920

(unofficial)

Hockey was played at the 1920 Summer Olympics in Antwerp, Belgium. This tournament is not counted in cumulative Winter Olympic Hockey statistics. The IIHF has declared it the first World Championship. Standings can be found on page 513.

1920 Final Rankings

1. Canada
2. USA
3. Czechoslovakia
4. Sweden
5. Switzerland

Chamonix, France • 1924

Group A

Team	GP	W	L	T	GF	GA	PTS
Canada	3	3	0	0	85	0	6
Sweden	3	2	1	0	18	25	4
Czech.	3	1	2	0	14	41	2
Switzerland	3	0	3	0	2	53	0

Group B

Team	GP	W	L	T	GF	GA	PTS
USA	3	3	0	0	52	0	6
Great Britain	3	2	1	0	34	16	4
France	3	1	2	0	9	42	2
Belgium	3	0	3	0	8	35	0

Final Round

Team	GP	W	L	T	GF	GA	PTS
Canada	3	3	0	0	47	3	6
USA	3	2	1	0	32	6	4
Great Britain	3	1	2	0	6	33	2
Sweden	3	0	3	0	3	46	0

1924 Final Rankings

1. Canada
2. USA
3. Great Britain
4. Sweden
5. Czechoslovakia
5. France
7. Switzerland
7. Belgium

St. Moritz, Switzerland • 1928

Group A

Team	GP	W	L	T	GF	GA	PTS
Great Britain	3	2	1	0	10	6	4
France	3	2	1	0	6	5	4
Belgium	3	2	1	0	9	10	4
Hungary	3	0	3	0	2	6	0

Group B

Team	GP	W	L	T	GF	GA	PTS
Sweden	2	1	0	1	5	2	3
Czech.	2	1	1	0	3	5	2
Poland	2	0	0	1	4	5	1

Group C

Team	GP	W	L	T	GF	GA	PTS
Switzerland	2	1	0	1	5	4	3
Austria	2	0	0	2	4	4	2
Germany	2	0	0	1	0	1	1

Final Round

Team	GP	W	L	T	GF	GA	PTS
Canada	3	3	0	0	38	0	6
Sweden	3	2	1	0	7	12	4
Switzerland	3	1	2	0	4	17	2
Great Britain	3	0	3	0	1	21	0

1928 Final Rankings

1. Canada
2. Sweden
3. Switzerland
4. Great Britain
5. France
5. Czechoslovakia
5. Austria
8. Belgium
8. Poland
11. Hungary

Lake Placid, New York, USA • 1932

Team	GP	W	L	T	GF	GA	PTS
Canada	6	5	0	1	32	4	11
USA	6	4	1	1	27	5	9
Germany	6	2	4	0	7	26	4
Poland	6	0	6	0	3	34	0

1932 Final Rankings

1. Canada
2. USA
3. Germany
4. Poland

Garmisch-Partenkirchen, Germany • 1936

Group A

Team	GP	W	L	T	GF	GA	PTS
Canada	3	3	0	0	24	3	6
Austria	3	2	1	0	11	7	4
Poland	3	1	2	0	11	12	2
Latvia	3	0	0	3	3	27	0

Group B

Team	GP	W	L	T	GF	GA	PTS
Germany	3	2	1	0	5	1	4
USA	3	2	1	0	5	2	4
Italy	3	1	2	0	2	5	2
Switzerland	3	1	2	0	1	5	2

Group C

Team	GP	W	L	T	GF	GA	PTS
Czech.	3	3	0	0	10	0	6
Hungary	3	2	1	0	14	5	4
France	3	1	2	0	4	7	2
Belgium	3	0	3	0	4	20	6

Group D

Team	GP	W	L	T	GF	GA	PTS
Great Britain	2	2	0	0	4	0	4
Sweden	2	1	1	0	2	1	2
Japan	2	0	2	0	0	5	0

Group A Semifinal Round

Team	GP	W	L	T	GF	GA	PTS
Great Britain	3	2	0	1	8	3	5
Canada	3	2	1	0	22	4	4
Germany	3	1	1	1	5	8	3
Hungary	3	0	0	3	2	22	0

Group B Semifinal Round

Team	GP	W	L	T	GF	GA	PTS
USA	3	3	0	0	5	1	6
Czech.	3	2	1	0	6	4	4

Team	GP	W	L	T	GF	GA	PTS
Sweden	3	1	2	0	3	6	2
Austria	3	0	3	0	1	4	0

Final Round

Team	GP	W	L	T	GF	GA	PTS
Great Britain	3	2	0	1	7	1	5
Canada	3	2	1	0	9	2	4
USA	3	1	1	1	2	1	3
Czech.	3	0	3	0	0	14	0

1936 Final Rankings

1. Great Britain
2. Canada
3. USA
4. Czechoslovakia
5. Germany
5. Sweden
7. Hungary
7. Austria

St. Moritz, Switzerland • 1948

Team	GP	W	L	T	GF	GA	PTS
Canada	7	6	0	1	57	2	13
Czech.	7	6	0	1	76	15	13
Switzerland	7	5	2	0	62	17	10
Sweden	7	4	3	0	53	23	8
Great Britain	7	3	4	0	36	43	6
Poland	7	2	5	0	25	74	4
Austria	7	1	6	0	31	64	2
Italy	7	0	7	0	23	125	0

1948 Final Rankings

1. Canada
2. Czechoslovakia
3. Switzerland
4. Sweden
5. Great Britain
6. Poland
7. Austria
8. Italy

Oslo, Norway • 1952

Team	GP	W	L	T	GF	GA	PTS
Canada	8	7	0	1	71	1	15
USA	8	6	1	1	43	21	13
Sweden	8	6	2	0	48	19	12
Czech.	8	6	2	0	47	18	12
Switzerland	8	4	4	0	40	40	8
Poland	8	2	5	1	21	56	5
Finland	8	2	6	0	21	60	4
W. Germany	8	1	6	1	21	53	3
Norway	8	0	8	0	15	46	0

1952 Final Rankings

1. Canada
2. USA
3. Sweden
4. Czechoslovakia
5. Switzerland
6. Poland
7. Finland
8. W. Germany
9. Norway

Cortina d'Ampezzo, Italy • 1956

Group A

Team	GP	W	L	T	GF	GA	PTS
Canada	3	3	0	0	30	1	6
W. Germany	3	1	1	1	9	6	3
Italy	3	0	1	2	5	7	2
Austria	3	0	2	1	2	32	1

Group B

Team	GP	W	L	T	GF	GA	PTS
Czech.	2	2	0	0	12	6	4
USA	2	1	1	0	7	4	2
Poland	2	0	2	0	3	12	0

Group C

Team	GP	W	L	T	GF	GA	PTS
Soviet Union	2	2	0	0	15	4	4
Sweden	2	1	1	0	7	10	2
Switzerland	2	0	2	0	8	16	0

Final Round

Team	GP	W	L	T	GF	GA	PTS
Soviet Union	5	5	0	0	25	5	10
USA	5	4	1	0	26	12	8
Canada	5	3	2	0	23	11	6
Sweden	5	1	3	1	10	17	3
Czech.	5	1	4	0	20	30	2
W. Germany	5	0	4	1	6	35	1

Consolation Round

Team	GP	W	L	T	GF	GA	PTS
Italy	3	3	0	0	21	7	6
Poland	3	2	1	0	12	10	4
Switzerland	3	1	2	0	12	8	2
Austria	3	0	3	0	9	19	0

1956 Final Rankings

1. Soviet Union
2. USA
3. Canada
4. Sweden
5. Czechoslovakia
6. W. Germany
7. Italy
8. Poland
9. Switzerland
10. Austria

1956 Scoring Leaders

Player	Team	GP	G	A	PTS	PIM
Jim Logan	Canada	8	7	5	12	2
Paul Knox	Canada	8	7	5	12	2
Vsevolod Bobrov	Soviet Union	7	9	2	11	4
Gerry Theberge	Canada	8	9	2	11	8
Jack McKenzie	Canada	8	7	4	11	4
John Mayasich	USA	7	7	3	10	2
Alexei Guryshev	Soviet Union	7	7	2	9	0
Vlastimil Bubnik	Czech.	7	5	4	9	14
George Scholes	Canada	8	5	3	8	2

Squaw Valley, California, USA • 1960

Group A

Team	GP	W	L	T	GF	GA	PTS
Canada	2	2	0	0	24	3	4
Sweden	2	1	1	0	21	5	2
Japan	2	0	2	0	1	38	0

Group B

Team	GP	W	L	T	GF	GA	PTS
Soviet Union	2	2	0	0	16	4	4
W. Germany	2	1	1	0	4	9	2
Finland	2	0	2	0	5	12	0

Group C

Team	GP	W	L	T	GF	GA	PTS
USA	2	2	0	0	19	6	4
Czech.	2	1	1	0	23	6	2
Austria	2	0	2	0	2	30	0

Final Round

Team	GP	W	L	T	GF	GA	PTS
USA	5	5	0	0	29	11	10
Canada	5	4	1	0	31	12	8
Soviet Union	5	2	2	1	24	19	5
Czech.	5	2	3	0	21	23	4
Sweden	5	1	3	1	19	19	3
W. Germany	5	0	5	0	5	45	0

Consolation Round

Team	GP	W	L	T	GF	GA	PTS
Finland	4	3	0	1	50	11	7
Japan	4	2	1	1	32	22	5
Austria	4	0	4	0	8	57	0

1960 Final Rankings
1. USA
2. Canada
3. Soviet Union
4. Czechoslovakia
5. Sweden
6. W. Germany
7. Finland
8. Japan
9. Austria

1960 Scoring Leaders

Player	Team	GP	G	A	PTS	PIM
Fred Etcher	Canada	7	9	12	21	0
Bobby Attersley	Canada	7	6	12	18	4
Bill Cleary	USA	7	7	7	14	2
Bill Christian	USA	7	2	11	13	2
G. Samolenko	Canada	7	8	4	12	0
Lars E. Lundvall	Sweden	7	8	4	12	2
Vaclav Panucek	Czech.	7	7	5	12	0
John Mayasich	USA	7	7	5	12	2
Nisse Nilsson	Sweden	7	7	5	12	4
V. Alexandrov	Soviet Union	7	7	5	12	8
Butch Martin	Canada	7	6	6	12	14
Ronald Petersson	Sweden	7	4	8	12	2

Innsbruck, Austria • 1964
Group A

Team	GP	W	L	T	GF	GA	PTS
Soviet Union	7	7	0	0	54	10	14
Sweden	7	5	2	0	47	16	10
Czech.	7	5	2	0	38	19	10
Canada	7	5	2	0	32	17	10
USA	7	2	5	0	29	33	4
Finland	7	2	5	0	10	31	4
W. Germany	7	2	5	0	13	49	4
Switzerland	7	0	7	0	9	57	0

Group B

Team	GP	W	L	T	GF	GA	PTS
Poland	7	6	1	0	40	13	12
Norway	7	5	2	0	40	19	10
Japan	7	4	2	1	35	31	9
Romania	7	3	3	1	31	28	7
Austria	7	3	3	1	24	28	7
Yugoslavia	7	3	3	1	29	37	7
Italy	7	2	5	0	24	42	4
Hungary	7	0	7	0	14	39	0

1964 Final Rankings
1. Soviet Union
2. Sweden
3. Czechoslovakia
4. Canada
5. USA
6. Finland
7. W. Germany
8. Switzerland
9. Poland
10. Norway
11. Japan
12. Romania
13. Austria
14. Yugoslavia
15. Italy
16. Hungary

1964 Scoring Leaders

Player	Team	GP	G	A	PTS	PIM
Sven Tumba	Sweden	7	8	3	11	0
Ulf Sterner	Sweden	7	6	5	11	4
Victor Yakushev	Soviet Union	7	7	3	10	0
Boris Mayorov	Soviet Union	7	7	3	10	0
Jiri Dolana	Czech.	7	7	3	10	0
Vy. Starshinov	Soviet Union	7	7	3	10	6
Josef Cerny	Czech.	7	5	5	10	2
A. Andersson	Sweden	7	7	2	9	8
K. Loktev	Soviet Union	7	4	5	9	8
Gary Dineen	Canada	7	3	6	9	10

Grenoble, France • 1968
Group A

Team	GP	W	L	T	GF	GA	PTS
Soviet Union	7	6	1	0	48	10	12
Czech.	7	5	1	1	33	17	11
Canada	7	5	2	0	28	15	10
Sweden	7	4	2	1	23	18	9
Finland	7	3	3	1	17	23	7
USA	7	2	4	1	23	28	5
W. Germany	7	1	6	0	13	39	2
E. Germany	7	0	7	0	13	48	0

Group B

Team	GP	W	L	T	GF	GA	PTS
Yugoslavia	5	5	0	0	33	9	10
Japan	5	4	1	0	27	12	8
Norway	5	3	2	0	15	15	6
Romania	5	2	3	0	22	23	4
Austria	5	1	4	0	12	27	2
France	5	0	5	0	9	32	0

1968 Final Rankings
1. Soviet Union
2. Czechoslovakia
3. Canada
4. Sweden
5. Finland
6. USA
7. W. Germany
8. E. Germany
9. Yugoslavia
10. Japan
11. Norway
12. Romania
13. Austria
14. France

1968 Scoring Leaders

Player	Team	GP	G	A	PTS	PIM
Anatoli Firsov	Soviet Union	7	12	4	16	4
Vladimir Vikulov	Soviet Union	7	2	10	12	2
Vyatch. Starshinov	Soviet Union	7	6	6	12	2
Victor Polupanov	Soviet Union	7	6	6	12	10
Josef Golonka	Czech.	7	4	6	10	8
Jan Hrbaty	Czech.	7	2	7	9	2
Fran Huck	Canada	7	4	5	9	10
Marshall Johnston	Canada	7	2	6	8	4
Jack Morrison	USA	7	2	6	8	10
V. Nedomansky	Czech.	7	5	2	7	4

Sapporo, Japan • 1972
Group A

Team	GP	W	L	T	GF	GA	PTS
Soviet Union	5	4	0	1	33	13	9
USA	5	3	2	0	18	15	6
Czech.	5	3	2	0	26	13	6
Sweden	5	2	2	1	17	13	5
Finland	5	2	3	0	14	24	4
Poland	5	0	5	0	9	39	0

Group B

Team	GP	W	L	T	GF	GA	PTS
W. Germany	4	3	1	0	22	10	6
Norway	4	3	1	0	16	14	6
Japan	4	2	1	1	17	16	5
Switzerland	4	0	2	2	9	16	2
Yugoslavia	4	0	3	1	9	17	1

1972 Final Rankings
1. Soviet Union
2. USA
3. Czechoslovakia
4. Sweden
5. Finland
6. Poland
7. W. Germany
8. Norway
9. Japan
10. Switzerland
11. Yugoslavia

1972 Scoring Leaders

Player	Team	GP	G	A	PTS	PIM
Valeri Kharlamov	Soviet Union	5	9	6	15	2
V. Nedomansky	Czech.	5	6	3	9	0
Vladimir Vikulov	Soviet Union	5	5	4	9	0
Craig Sarner	USA	5	4	5	9	0
Kevin Ahearn	USA	5	4	3	7	0
Alexander Maltsev	Soviet Union	5	4	3	7	0
Anatoli Firsov	Soviet Union	5	2	5	7	0
Yuri Blinov	Soviet Union	5	3	3	6	0
Jiri Kochta	Czech.	5	3	3	6	0
Richard Farda	Czech.	5	1	5	6	0

Innsbruck, Austria • 1976
Group A

Team	GP	W	L	T	GF	GA	PTS
Soviet Union	5	5	0	0	40	11	10
Czech.	5	3	2	0	17	10	6
W. Germany	5	2	3	0	21	24	4
Finland	5	2	3	0	19	18	4
USA	5	2	3	0	15	21	4
Poland	5	0	5	0	9	37	0

Group B

Team	GP	W	L	T	GF	GA	PTS
Romania	5	4	1	0	23	15	8
Austria	5	3	2	0	18	14	6
Japan	5	3	2	0	20	18	6
Yugoslavia	5	3	2	0	22	19	6
Switzerland	5	2	3	0	24	22	4
Bulgaria	5	0	5	0	19	38	0

1976 Final Rankings
1. Soviet Union
2. Czechoslovakia
3. W. Germany
4. Finland
5. USA
6. Poland
7. Romania
8. Austria
9. Japan
10. Yugoslavia
11. Switzerland
12. Bulgaria

1976 Scoring Leaders

Player	Team	GP	G	A	PTS	PIM
Vladimir Shadrin	Soviet Union	5	6	4	10	0
Alexander Maltsev	Soviet Union	5	5	5	10	0
Victor Shalimov	Soviet Union	5	5	5	10	2
Erich Kuhnhackl	W. Germany	5	5	5	10	10
Valeri Kharlamov	Soviet Union	5	3	6	9	6
Ernst Kopf	W. Germany	5	3	5	8	2
Vladimir Petrov	Soviet Union	5	4	3	7	8
A. Yakushev	Soviet Union	5	3	4	7	2
Bob Dobek	USA	5	3	4	7	4
Lorenz Funk	W. Germany	5	2	5	7	4
Victor Zhluktov	Soviet Union	5	3	4	7	0

Lake Placid, New York • 1980
Red Division

Team	GP	W	L	T	GF	GA	PTS
Soviet Union	5	5	0	0	51	11	10
Finland	5	3	2	0	26	18	6
Canada	5	3	2	0	28	12	6
Poland	5	2	3	0	15	23	4
Holland	5	1	3	1	16	43	3
Japan	5	0	4	1	7	36	1

Blue Division

Team	GP	W	L	T	GF	GA	PTS
Sweden	5	4	0	1	26	7	9
USA	5	4	0	1	25	10	9
Czech.	5	3	2	0	34	16	6
Romania	5	1	3	1	13	29	3
W. Germany	5	1	4	0	21	30	2
Norway	5	0	4	1	9	36	1

Final Round

Team	GP	W	L	T	GF	GA	PTS
USA	3	2	0	1	10	7	5
Soviet Union	3	2	1	0	16	8	4
Sweden	3	0	1	2	7	14	2
Finland	3	0	2	1	7	11	1

1980 Final Rankings
1. USA
2. Soviet Union
3. Sweden
4. Finland
5. Czechoslovakia
6. Canada
7. Poland
8. Holland
9. Romania
10. W. Germany
11. Norway
12. Japan

1980 Scoring Leaders

Player	Team	GP	G	A	PTS	PIM
Milan Novy	Czech.	6	7	8	15	0
Peter Stastny	Czech.	6	7	7	14	6
Jaroslav Pouzar	Czech.	6	8	5	13	8
Alexander Golikov	Soviet Union	7	6	5	13	6
Jukka Porvari	Finland	7	7	4	11	4
Boris Mikhailov	Soviet Union	7	6	5	11	2
Vladimir Krutov	Soviet Union	7	6	5	11	4
Sergei Makarov	Soviet Union	7	5	6	11	4
Marian Stastny	Czech.	6	5	6	11	4
Mark Johnson	USA	7	5	6	11	6

Sarajevo, Yugoslavia • 1984
Group A

Team	GP	W	L	T	GF	GA	PTS
Soviet Union	5	5	0	0	42	5	10
Sweden	5	3	1	1	34	15	7
W. Germany	5	3	1	1	27	17	7
Poland	5	1	4	0	16	37	2
Italy	5	1	4	0	15	31	2
Yugoslavia	5	1	4	0	8	37	2

Group B

Team	GP	W	L	T	GF	GA	PTS
Czech.	5	5	0	0	38	7	10
Canada	5	4	1	0	24	10	8
Finland	5	2	2	1	27	19	5
USA	5	1	2	2	16	17	4
Austria	5	1	4	0	13	37	2
Norway	5	0	4	1	15	43	1

Final Round

Team	GP	W	L	T	GF	GA	PTS
Soviet Union	3	3	0	0	16	1	6
Czech.	3	2	1	0	6	2	4
Sweden	3	1	2	0	3	12	2
Canada	3	0	3	0	0	10	0

Consolation Round

Team	GP	W	L	T	GF	GA	PTS
W. Germany	1	1	0	0	7	4	2
USA	1	1	0	0	7	4	2
Finland	1	0	1	0	4	7	0
Poland	1	0	1	0	4	7	0

1984 Final Rankings
1. Soviet Union
2. Czechoslovakia
3. Sweden
4. Canada
5. W. Germany
6. Finland
7. USA
8. Poland

1984 Scoring Leaders

Player	Team	GP	G	A	PTS	PIM
Erich Kuhnhackl	W. Germany	6	8	6	14	12
Peter Gradin	Sweden	7	9	4	13	6
N. Drozdetski	Soviet Union	7	10	2	12	2
V. Fetisov	Soviet Union	7	3	8	11	8
Petri Skriko	Finland	6	6	4	10	8
Vladimir Ruzicka	Czech.	7	4	6	10	4
R. Summanen	Finland	6	6	4	10	4
Darius Rusnak	Czech.	7	4	6	10	6
Jiri Hrdina	Czech.	7	4	6	10	10
Vincent Lukac	Czech.	7	4	5	9	2
Viktor Tjumenov	Soviet Union	6	0	9	9	2

Calgary, Canada • 1988
Group A

Team	GP	W	L	T	GF	GA	PTS
Finland	5	3	1	1	22	8	7
Sweden	5	2	0	3	23	10	7
Canada	5	3	1	1	17	12	7
Switzerland	5	3	2	0	19	10	6
Poland	5	0	4	1	3	13	1
France	5	1	4	0	10	41	0

Group B

Team	GP	W	L	T	GF	GA	PTS
Soviet Union	5	5	0	0	32	10	10
W. Germany	5	4	1	0	19	12	8
Czech.	5	3	2	0	23	14	6
USA	5	2	3	0	27	27	4
Austria	5	0	4	1	12	29	1
Norway	5	0	4	1	11	32	1

Final Round

Team	GP	W	L	T	GF	GA	PTS
Soviet Union	5	4	1	0	25	7	8
Finland	5	3	1	1	18	10	7
Sweden	5	2	1	2	15	16	6
Canada	5	2	2	1	17	14	5
W. Germany	5	1	4	0	8	26	2
Czech.	5	1	4	0	12	22	2

1988 Final Rankings
1. Soviet Union
2. Finland
3. Sweden
4. Canada
5. W. Germany
6. Czechoslovakia
7. USA
8. Switzerland
9. Austria
10. Poland
11. France
12. Norway

1988 Scoring Leaders

Player	Team	GP	G	A	PTS	PIM
Vladimir Krutov	Soviet Union	8	6	9	15	0
Igor Larionov	Soviet Union	8	4	9	13	4
V. Fetisov	Soviet Union	8	4	9	13	6
Corey Millen	USA	6	6	5	11	4
Dusan Pasek	Czech.	8	6	5	11	8
Sergei Makarov	Soviet Union	8	3	8	11	10
Erkki Lehtonen	Finland	8	4	6	10	2
Anders Eldebrink	Sweden	8	4	6	10	4
Igor Liba	Czech.	8	4	6	10	8
Gerd Truntschka	W. Germany	8	3	7	10	10
Raimo Helminen	Finland	7	2	8	10	4

Albertville, France • 1992
Group A

Team	GP	W	L	T	GF	GA	PTS
USA	5	4	0	1	18	7	9
Sweden	5	3	0	2	22	11	8
Finland	5	3	0	1	22	11	7
Germany	5	2	3	0	11	12	4
Italy	5	1	4	0	18	24	2
Poland	5	0	5	0	4	30	0

Group B

Team	GP	W	L	T	GF	GA	PTS
Canada	5	4	1	0	28	9	8
Unified Team*	5	4	1	0	32	10	8
Czechoslovakia	5	4	1	0	25	15	8
France	5	2	3	0	14	22	4
Switzerland	5	1	4	0	13	25	2
Norway	5	0	5	0	7	38	0

*Soviet Union/Russia played as Unified Team in 1992.

Medal Round

Canada	4	Germany	3
Czechoslovakia	3	Sweden	1
USA	4	France	1
Unified Team	6	Finland	1

Semifinals

Canada	4	Czechoslovakia	2
Unified Team	5	USA	2

Bronze Medal Game

Czechoslovakia	6	USA	1

Gold Medal Game

Unified Team	3	Canada	1

1992 Final Rankings
1. Unified Team
2. Canada
3. Czechoslovakia
4. USA
5. Sweden
6. Germany
7. Finland
8. France
9. Norway
10. Switzerland
11. Poland
12. Italy

1992 Scoring Leaders

Player	Team	GP	G	A	PTS
Joe Juneau	Canada	8	6	9	15
Andrei Khomutov	Unified	8	7	7	14
Robert Lang	Czech.	8	5	8	13
Teemu Selanne	Finland	8	7	4	11
Eric Lindros	Canada	8	5	6	11
H. Jarvenpaa	Finland	8	5	6	11
V. Bykov	Unified	8	4	7	11
Yuri Khmylev	Unified	8	4	6	10
Mika Nieminen	Finland	8	4	6	10
N. Borschevsky	Unified	8	7	2	9

Lillehammer, Norway • 1994
Group A

Team	GP	W	L	T	GF	GA	PTS
Finland	5	5	0	0	25	4	10
Germany	5	3	2	0	11	14	6
Czech. Rep.	5	3	2	0	16	11	6
Russia	5	3	2	0	20	14	6
Austria	5	1	4	0	13	28	2
Norway	5	0	5	0	5	19	0

Group B

Team	GP	W	L	T	GF	GA	PTS
Slovakia	5	3	0	2	26	14	8
Canada	5	3	1	1	17	11	7
Sweden	5	3	1	1	23	13	7
USA	5	1	1	3	21	17	5
Italy	5	1	4	0	15	31	2
France	5	0	4	1	11	27	1

Quarterfinals

Canada	3	Czech Rep.	2
Finland	6	USA	1
Sweden	3	Germany	0
Russia	3	Slovakia	2

Semifinals

Canada	5	Finland	3
Sweden	4	Russia	3

Bronze Medal Game

Finland	4	Russia	0

Gold Medal Game

Sweden	3	Canada	2

1994 Final Standings
1. Sweden
2. Canada
3. Finland
4. Russia
5. Czech Republic
6. Slovakia
7. Germany
8. USA
9. Italy
10. France
11. Norway
12. Austria

1994 Scoring Leaders

Player	Team	GP	G	A	PTS	PIM
Zigmund Palffy	Slovakia	8	3	7	10	8
Miroslav Satan	Slovakia	8	9	0	9	0
Peter Stastny	Slovakia	8	5	4	9	9
Hakan Loob	Sweden	8	4	5	9	2
Gates Orlando	Italy	7	3	6	9	41
Patrik Juhlin	Sweden	8	7	1	8	16
Jiri Kucera	Czech Rep.	8	6	2	8	4
Marty Dallman	Austria	7	4	4	8	8
Mika Nieminen	Finland	8	3	5	8	0
David Sacco	USA	8	3	5	8	12
Peter Forsberg	Sweden	8	2	6	8	6

Nagano, Japan • 1998 • Men
Preliminary Round
Group A

Team	GP	W	L	T	GF	GA	Pts
Kazakhstan	3	2	0	1	14	11	5
Slovakia	3	1	1	1	9	9	3
Italy	3	1	2	0	11	11	2
Austria	3	0	1	2	9	12	2

Group B

Team	GP	W	L	T	GF	GA	Pts
Belarus	3	2	0	1	14	4	5
Germany	3	2	1	0	7	9	4
France	3	1	2	0	5	8	2
Japan	3	0	2	1	5	10	1

Final Round
Group A

Team	GP	W	L	T	GF	GA	Pts
Canada	3	3	0	0	12	3	6
Sweden	3	2	1	0	11	7	4
USA	3	1	2	0	8	10	2
Belarus	3	0	3	0	4	15	0

Group B

Team	GP	W	L	T	GF	GA	Pts
Russia	3	3	0	0	15	6	6
Czech Rep.	3	2	1	0	12	4	4
Finland	3	1	2	0	11	9	2
Kazakhstan	3	0	3	0	6	25	0

Quarterfinals

Canada	4	Kazakhstan	1
Czech Republic	4	USA	1
Finland	2	Sweden	1
Russia	4	Belarus	1

Semifinals

Czech Republic	2	Canada	1
Russia	7	Finland	4

Bronze Medal game

Finland	3	Canada	2

Gold Medal game

Czech Republic	1	Russia	0

1998 Final Rankings, Men
1. Czech Republic
2. Russia
3. Finland
4. Canada
5–8. USA
5–8. Sweden
5–8. Belarus
5–8. Kazakhstan
9. Germany
10. Slovakia
11. France
12. Italy
13. Japan
14. Austria

1998 Scoring Leaders

Player	Team	GP	G	A	PTS	PIM
Teemu Selanne	Finland	5	4	6	10	8
Saku Koivu	Finland	6	2	8	10	4
Pavel Bure	Russia	6	9	0	9	2
Alex. Koreshkov	Kazakhstan	7	3	6	9	2
Phillipe Bozon	France	4	5	2	7	4
K. Shafranov	Kazakhstan	7	4	3	7	6
Dominik Lavoie	Austria	4	5	1	6	8
Jere Lehtinen	Finland	6	4	2	6	2
Alexei Yashin	Russia	6	3	3	6	0
Serge Poudrier	France	6	2	4	6	4
Sergei Fedorov	Russia	6	1	5	6	8

Women's Olympic results are found on page 489

WORLD AND EUROPEAN CHAMPIONSHIPS, POOL A
FINAL STANDINGS 1910–1998

European Championships

1910
Rank	Team	GP	W	L	T	GF	GA	Pts
1	Great Britain	3	2	0	1	7	2	5
2	Germany	3	2	1	0	14	6	4
3	Belgium	3	1	1	1	6	6	3
4	Switzerland	3	0	3	0	2	15	0

1911
Rank	Team	GP	W	L	T	GF	GA	Pts
1	Bohemia	3	3	0	0	20	1	6
2	Germany	3	2	1	0	17	4	4
3	Belgium	3	1	2	0	5	13	2
4	Switzerland	3	0	3	0	4	28	0

1912
Rank	Team	GP	W	L	T	GF	GA	Pts
1	Bohemia	2	1	0	1	7	2	3
2	Germany	2	1	0	1	6	3	3
3	Austria	2	0	2	0	1	9	0

1913
Rank	Team	GP	W	L	T	GF	GA	Pts
1	Belgium	3	2	0	1	25	7	5
2	Bohemia	3	2	0	1	15	6	5
3	Germany	3	1	2	0	18	16	2
4	Austria	3	0	3	0	5	34	0

1914
Rank	Team	GP	W	L	T	GF	GA	Pts
1	Bohemia	2	2	0	0	11	1	4
2	Germany	2	1	1	0	4	3	2
3	Belgium	2	0	2	0	2	13	0

1921
Rank	Team	GP	W	L	T	GF	GA	Pts
1	Sweden	1	1	0	0	6	4	2
2	Czechoslovakia	1	0	1	0	4	6	0

1922
Rank	Team	GP	W	L	T	GF	GA	Pts
1	Czechoslovakia	2	2	0	0	11	3	4
2	Sweden	2	1	1	0	9	3	2
3	Switzerland	2	0	2	0	1	15	0

1923
Rank	Team	GP	W	L	T	GF	GA	Pts
1	Sweden	4	4	0	0	23	6	8
2	France	4	3	1	0	13	8	6
3	Czechoslovakia	4	2	2	0	16	9	4
4	Belgium	4	1	3	0	5	18	2
5	Switzerland	4	0	4	0	7	23	0

1924
Rank	Team	GP	W	L	T	GF	GA	Pts
1	France	3	3	0	0	17	1	6
2	Sweden	3	2	1	0	8	4	4
3	Switzerland	2	1	1	0	14	6	2
4	Belgium	2	1	1	0	4	3	2
5	Spain	2	0	2	0	0	13	0
6	Italy	2	0	2	0	0	16	0

1925
Rank	Team	GP	W	L	T	GF	GA	Pts
1	Czechoslovakia	3	3	0	0	10	0	6
2	Austria	3	1	1	1	4	5	3
3	Switzerland	3	0	1	2	3	4	2
4	Belgium	3	0	2	1	1	9	1

1926
Rank	Team	GP	W	L	T	GF	GA	Pts
1	Switzerland	7	5	1	1	35	15	11
2	Czechoslovakia	7	5	2	0	18	8	10
3	Austria	7	4	2	1	14	13	9
4	Great Britain	7	3	4	0	26	19	6
5	France	4	2	2	0	5	6	4
6	Belgium	4	1	3	0	5	8	2
7	Poland	4	2	2	0	9	5	4
8	Italy	4	0	3	1	3	26	1
8	Spain	4	0	3	1	5	20	1

1927
Rank	Team	GP	W	L	T	GF	GA	Pts
1	Austria	5	5	0	0	13	2	10
2	Belgium	5	3	1	1	13	7	7
3	Germany	5	3	2	0	10	7	6
4	Poland	5	1	2	2	11	8	4
5	Czechoslovakia	5	1	3	1	7	6	3
6	Hungary	5	0	5	0	0	28	0

1929
Rank	Team	GP	W	L	T	GF	GA	Pts
1	Czechoslovakia	4	4	0	0	8	3	8
2	Poland	3	2	1	0	6	3	4
3	Austria	6	4	2	0	13	9	8
4	Italy	4	2	2	0	5	6	4
NR	Switzerland	3	1	2	0	2	6	2
NR	Finland							
NR	Hungary	4	0	3	1	2	7	1
NR	Germany	2	0	2	0	1	3	0
NR	Belgium	2	0	1	1	1	2	1

1932
Rank	Team	GP	W	L	T	GF	GA	Pts
1	Sweden	6	4	0	2	12	2	10
2	Austria	6	1	0	5	9	6	7
3	Switzerland	6	1	0	5	10	9	7
4	Germany	6	1	1	4	5	5	6
5	Czechoslovakia	6	1	4	1	10	10	3
6	France	5	3	0	2	11	4	8
7	Great Britain	5	3	1	1	11	9	7
8	Latvia	5	1	4	0	5	14	2
9	Romania	5	0	5	0	0	14	0

World Championships

Note: WR – World Ranking;
ER – European Ranking
For events that had separate prelimi-
nary and medal rounds, the results of
all games are combined in these
standings.

1920
WR	ER	Team	GP	W	L	T	GF	GA	Pts
1		Canada	3	3	0	0	29	1	6
2		USA	4	3	1	0	52	2	6
3		Czechoslovakia	3	1	2	0	1	31	2
4		Sweden	6	3	3	0	17	20	6
5		Switzerland	2	0	2	0	0	33	0

1930
WR	ER	Team	GP	W	L	T	GF	GA	Pts
1		Canada	1	1	0	0	6	1	2
2	1	Germany	5	4	1	0	14	11	8
3	2	Switzerland	3	2	1	0	6	4	4
4	3	Austria	3	2	1	0	5	3	4
5	4	Poland	3	1	2	0	6	5	2

1931
WR	ER	Team	GP	W	L	T	GF	GA	Pts
1		Canada	6	5	0	1	24	0	11
2		USA	6	5	1	0	22	3	10
3	1	Austria	8	4	4	0	14	16	8
4	2	Poland	7	2	4	1	6	11	5
5	3	Czechoslovakia	7	3	3	1	10	7	7
6	4	Sweden	6	2	3	1	4	7	5
7	5	Hungary	4	3	1	0	14	6	6
8	6	Great Britain	4	2	2	0	14	5	4
9	7	France	5	1	4	0	9	15	2
10	8	Romania	5	0	5	0	2	49	0

1933
WR	ER	Team	GP	W	L	T	GF	GA	Pts
1		USA	5	5	0	0	23	1	10
2		Canada	5	4	1	0	17	3	8
3	1	Czechoslovakia	8	6	2	0	17	12	12
4	2	Austria	8	4	4	0	14	13	8
5	3	Germany	6	3	2	1	13	8	7
5	3	Switzerland	6	3	2	1	10	11	7
7	5	Hungary	5	0	4	1	2	10	1
7	5	Poland	6	1	4	1	3	11	3
9	7	Romania	5	2	3	0	5	19	4

1934
WR	ER	Team	GP	W	L	T	GF	GA	Pts
1		Canada	4	4	0	0	19	2	8
2		USA	4	3	1	0	6	2	6
3	1	Germany	8	5	3	0	12	14	10
4	2	Switzerland	7	5	2	0	36	7	10
5	3	Czechoslovakia	6	3	3	0	8	4	6
6	4	Hungary	6	1	4	1	2	5	3
7	5	Austria	7	3	3	1	9	10	7
8	6	Great Britain	5	3	2	0	9	7	6
9	7	France	7	2	3	2	9	12	6
10	8	Romania	6	1	5	0	7	21	2
11	9	Belgium	3	1	2	0	5	23	2
12	10	France	5	1	4	0	4	19	2

1935

WR	ER	Team	GP	W	L	T	GF	GA	Pts
1		Canada	7	6	0	1	35	6	13
2	1	Switzerland	8	6	1	1	33	9	13
3	2	Great Britain	7	4	3	0	17	16	8
4	3	Czechoslovakia	8	5	3	0	34	11	10
5	4	Sweden	8	5	2	1	21	14	11
6	5	Austria	8	3	4	1	16	16	7
7	6	France	8	2	3	3	9	21	7
8	7	France	8	1	4	3	7	14	5
9	8	Germany	7	4	3	0	18	9	8
10	9	Poland	6	2	2	2	20	13	6

1937

WR	ER	Team	GP	W	L	T	GF	GA	Pts
1		Canada	9	9	0	0	60	4	18
2	1	Great Britain	9	8	1	0	50	3	16
3	2	Switzerland	8	4	3	1	27	13	9
4	3	Germany	9	3	5	1	13	32	7
5	4	Hungary	9	3	4	2	14	24	8
6	5	Czechoslovakia	8	4	2	2	22	9	10
7	6	France	9	2	7	0	8	54	4
8	7	Poland	9	3	6	0	16	24	6

1938

WR	ER	Team	GP	W	L	T	GF	GA	Pts
1		Canada	7	6	0	1	17	6	13
2	1	Great Britain	8	6	1	1	27	8	13
3	2	Czechoslovakia	7	4	2	1	9	6	9
4	3	Germany	8	3	5	0	12	9	6
5	4	Sweden	6	2	2	2	8	7	6
6	5	Switzerland	7	5	2	0	34	7	10

1939

WR	ER	Team	GP	W	L	T	GF	GA	Pts
1		Canada	8	8	0	0	42	1	16
2		USA	9	7	2	0	25	8	14
3	1	Switzerland	10	7	2	1	51	13	15
4	2	Czechoslovakia	10	3	5	2	37	11	8
5	3	Germany	10	6	2	2	32	22	14
6	4	Poland	7	3	4	0	17	19	6
7	5	Hungary	7	1	6	0	15	24	2
8	6	Great Britain	3	0	3	0	0	7	0
9	7	France	6	4	1	1	15	14	9
10	8	Latvia	6	3	3	0	16	24	6
11	9	Netherlands	4	1	3	0	3	20	2
12	10	Belgium	4	0	3	1	6	19	1
13	11	Yugoslavia	5	0	4	1	3	60	1
14	12	Finland	5	0	5	0	5	25	0

1947

WR	ER	Team	GP	W	L	T	GF	GA	Pts
1	1	Czechoslovakia	7	6	1	0	85	10	12
2	2	Sweden	7	5	1	1	55	15	11
3	3	Austria	7	5	2	0	49	32	10
4	4	Switzerland	7	4	2	1	47	22	9
5		USA	7	4	3	0	42	26	8
6	5	Poland	7	2	5	0	27	40	4
7	6	Romania	7	1	6	0	17	88	2
8	7	Belgium	7	0	7	0	15	104	0

1949

WR	ER	Team	GP	W	L	T	GF	GA	Pts
1	1	Czechoslovakia	7	5	2	0	42	12	10
2		Canada	7	4	1	2	74	10	10
3		USA	8	6	2	0	59	22	12
4	2	Sweden	7	4	2	1	42	15	9
5	3	Switzerland	8	4	3	1	48	32	9
6	4	Austria	7	1	6	0	30	60	2
7	5	Finland	7	2	4	0	27	36	4
8	6	Norway	5	2	3	0	22	27	4
9	7	Belgium	6	1	5	0	13	67	2
10	8	Denmark	3	0	3	0	4	80	0

1950

WR	ER	Team	GP	W	L	T	GF	GA	Pts
1		Canada	7	7	0	0	88	5	14
2		USA	7	5	2	0	49	29	10
3	1	Switzerland	7	4	3	0	57	46	8
4	2	Great Britain	7	4	3	0	25	32	8
5	3	Sweden	7	3	4	0	33	19	6
6	4	Norway	7	1	6	0	26	47	2
7	5	Belgium	4	2	2	0	15	60	4
8	6	Netherlands	4	1	3	0	7	33	2
9	7	France	4	0	4	0	3	32	0

1951

WR	ER	Team	GP	W	L	T	GF	GA	Pts
1		Canada	6	6	0	0	62	6	12
2	1	Sweden	6	4	1	1	33	14	9
3	2	Switzerland	6	4	1	1	28	12	9
4	3	Norway	6	2	4	0	10	27	4
5	4	Great Britain	6	1	4	1	18	42	3
6		USA	6	1	4	1	14	42	3
7	5	Finland	6	1	5	0	15	37	2

1953

WR	ER	Team	GP	W	L	T	GF	GA	Pts
1	1	Sweden	5	5	0	0	43	14	10
2	2	West Germany	6	1	5	0	23	46	2
3	3	Switzerland	5	1	4	0	13	36	2
NR		Czechoslovakia	4	3	1	0	32	15	6

1954

WR	ER	Team	GP	W	L	T	GF	GA	Pts
1	1	Soviet Union	7	6	0	1	37	10	13
2		Canada	7	6	1	0	59	12	12
3	2	Sweden	7	5	1	1	30	18	11
4	3	Czechoslovakia	7	4	3	0	41	21	8
5	4	West Germany	7	2	4	1	22	32	5
6	5	Finland	7	1	5	1	12	52	3
7	6	Switzerland	7	0	5	2	15	34	2
8	7	Norway	7	1	6	0	6	43	2

1955

WR	ER	Team	GP	W	L	T	GF	GA	Pts
1		Canada	8	8	0	0	66	6	16
2	1	Soviet Union	8	7	1	0	39	13	14
3	2	Czechoslovakia	8	5	2	1	63	22	11
4		USA	8	4	2	2	43	29	10
5	3	Sweden	8	3	3	2	31	16	8
6	4	West Germany	8	2	6	0	28	43	4
7	5	Poland	8	2	5	1	19	50	5
8	6	Switzerland	8	1	7	0	15	69	2
9	7	Finland	8	1	7	0	16	72	2

1957

WR	ER	Team	GP	W	L	T	GF	GA	Pts
1	1	Sweden	7	6	0	1	62	11	13
2	2	Soviet Union	7	5	0	2	77	9	12
3	3	Czechoslovakia	7	5	1	1	66	9	11
4	4	Finland	7	4	3	0	28	33	8
5	5	East Germany	7	3	4	0	23	48	6
6	6	Poland	7	2	5	0	25	45	4
7	7	Austria	7	0	6	1	8	61	1
8		Japan	7	0	6	1	11	84	1

1958

WR	ER	Team	GP	W	L	T	GF	GA	Pts
1		Canada	7	7	0	0	82	6	14
2	1	Soviet Union	7	5	1	1	44	15	11
3	2	Sweden	7	5	2	0	46	22	10
4	3	Czechoslovakia	7	3	2	2	21	21	8
5		USA	7	3	3	1	29	33	7
6	4	Finland	7	1	5	1	9	51	3
7	5	Norway	7	1	6	0	12	44	2
8	6	Poland	7	0	6	1	14	65	1

1959

WR	ER	Team	GP	W	L	T	GF	GA	Pts
1		Canada	8	7	1	0	60	9	14
2	1	Soviet Union	8	7	1	0	44	15	14
3	2	Czechoslovakia	8	6	2	0	46	22	10
4		USA	8	5	3	0	45	25	10
5	3	Sweden	8	3	4	1	27	26	7
6	4	Finland	8	1	6	1	20	44	3

1961

WR	ER	Team	GP	W	L	T	GF	GA	Pts
1		Canada	7	6	0	1	45	11	13
2	1	Czechoslovakia	7	6	0	1	33	9	13
3	2	Soviet Union	7	5	2	0	51	20	10
4	3	Sweden	7	4	3	0	33	27	8
5	4	East Germany	8	3	5	0	27	36	6
6		USA	7	1	5	1	24	43	3
7	5	Finland	7	1	5	1	19	43	3
8	6	West Germany	8	1	5	2	16	55	4

1962

WR	ER	Team	GP	W	L	T	GF	GA	Pts
1	1	Sweden	7	7	0	0	67	10	14
2		Canada	7	6	1	0	58	12	12
3		USA	7	5	2	0	54	23	10
4	2	Finland	7	3	4	0	32	42	6
5	3	Norway	7	3	4	0	32	54	6
6	4	West Germany	7	2	5	0	27	36	4
7	5	Switzerland	7	1	6	0	21	60	2
8	6	Great Britain	7	1	6	0	19	73	2

1963

WR	ER	Team	GP	W	L	T	GF	GA	Pts
1	1	Soviet Union	7	6	1	0	50	9	12
2	2	Sweden	7	6	1	0	44	10	12
3	3	Czechoslovakia	7	5	1	1	41	16	11
4		Canada	7	4	2	1	46	23	9
5	4	Finland	7	1	5	1	20	35	3
6	5	East Germany	7	1	5	1	16	43	3
7	6	West Germany	7	1	5	1	18	56	3
8		USA	7	1	5	1	21	64	3

1965

WR	ER	Team	GP	W	L	T	GF	GA	Pts
1	1	Soviet Union	7	7	0	0	51	13	14
2	2	Czechoslovakia	7	6	1	0	43	10	12
3	3	Sweden	7	4	2	1	33	17	9
4		Canada	7	4	3	0	28	21	8
5	4	East Germany	7	3	4	0	18	33	6
6		USA	7	2	5	0	22	44	4
7	5	Finland	7	1	5	1	14	27	3
8	6	Norway	8	1	7	0	17	60	2

1966

WR	ER	Team	GP	W	L	T	GF	GA	Pts
1	1	Soviet Union	7	6	0	1	55	7	13
2	2	Czechoslovakia	7	6	1	0	32	15	12
3		Canada	7	5	2	0	33	10	10
4	3	Sweden	7	3	3	1	26	17	7
5	4	East Germany	7	3	4	0	12	30	6
6		USA	7	2	5	0	18	39	4
7	5	Finland	7	2	5	0	18	43	4
8	6	Poland	7	0	7	0	11	44	0

1967

WR	ER	Team	GP	W	L	T	GF	GA	Pts
1	1	Soviet Union	7	7	0	0	58	9	14
2	2	Sweden	7	4	2	1	31	22	9
3		Canada	7	4	2	1	28	15	9
4	3	Czechoslovakia	7	3	2	2	29	18	8
5		USA	7	3	3	1	20	23	7
6	4	Finland	7	2	4	1	14	24	5
7	5	East Germany	7	1	5	1	14	38	3
8	6	West Germany	7	0	6	1	11	56	1

1969

WR	ER	Team	GP	W	L	T	GF	GA	Pts
1	1	Soviet Union	10	8	2	0	59	23	16
2	2	Sweden	10	8	2	0	45	19	16
3	3	Czechoslovakia	10	8	2	0	40	20	16
4		Canada	10	4	6	0	26	31	8
5	4	Finland	10	2	8	0	26	52	4
6		USA	10	0	10	0	23	74	0

1970

WR	ER	Team	GP	W	L	T	GF	GA	Pts
1	1	Soviet Union	10	9	1	0	68	11	18
2	2	Sweden	10	7	2	1	45	21	15
3	3	Czechoslovakia	10	5	4	1	47	30	11
4	4	Finland	10	5	5	0	31	40	10
5	5	East Germany	10	2	7	1	20	50	5
6	6	Poland	10	0	9	1	11	70	1

1971

WR	ER	Team	GP	W	L	T	GF	GA	Pts
1	1	Soviet Union	10	8	1	1	77	24	17
2	2	Czechoslovakia	10	7	2	1	44	20	15
3	3	Sweden	10	5	4	1	29	33	11
4	4	Finland	10	4	5	1	31	42	9
5	5	West Germany	12	3	8	1	32	69	7
6		USA	10	2	8	0	31	53	4

1972

WR	ER	Team	GP	W	L	T	GF	GA	Pts
1	1	Czechoslovakia	10	9	0	1	72	16	19
2	2	Soviet Union	10	7	1	2	78	17	16
3	3	Sweden	10	5	4	1	49	33	11
4	4	Finland	10	4	6	0	47	48	8
5	5	West Germany	10	2	8	0	21	76	4
6	6	Switzerland	10	1	9	0	19	96	2

1973

WR	ER	Team	GP	W	L	T	GF	GA	Pts
1	1	Soviet Union	10	10	0	0	100	18	20
2	2	Sweden	10	7	2	1	53	23	15
3	3	Czechoslovakia	10	6	3	1	48	20	13
4	4	Finland	10	3	6	1	24	39	7
5	5	Poland	10	1	8	1	14	76	3
6	6	West Germany	10	1	9	0	19	82	2

1974

WR	ER	Team	GP	W	L	T	GF	GA	Pts
1	1	Soviet Union	10	9	1	0	64	18	18
2	2	Czechoslovakia	10	7	3	0	57	20	14
3	3	Sweden	10	5	4	1	38	24	11
4	4	Finland	10	4	4	2	34	39	10
5	5	Poland	10	1	7	2	22	64	4
6	6	East Germany	10	1	8	1	21	71	3

1975

WR	ER	Team	GP	W	L	T	GF	GA	Pts
1	1	Soviet Union	10	10	0	0	90	23	20
2	2	Czechoslovakia	10	8	2	0	55	19	16
3	3	Sweden	10	5	5	0	51	34	10
4	4	Finland	10	5	5	0	36	34	10
5	5	Poland	10	2	8	0	18	78	4
6		USA	10	0	10	0	22	84	0

1976

WR	ER	Team	GP	W	L	T	GF	GA	Pts
1	1	Czechoslovakia	10	9	0	1	72	15	19
2	3	Soviet Union	10	6	3	1	50	23	13
3	2	Sweden	10	6	4	0	36	29	12
4		USA	10	3	6	1	25	47	7
5	4	Finland	10	3	4	3	40	38	9
6	5	West Germany	10	3	6	1	23	46	7
7	6	Poland	10	3	5	2	33	47	8
8	7	East Germany	10	2	7	1	19	53	5

1977

WR	ER	Team	GP	W	L	T	GF	GA	Pts
1	1	Czechoslovakia	10	7	2	1	54	32	15
2	2	Sweden	10	7	3	0	43	19	14
3	3	Soviet Union	10	7	3	0	77	24	14
4		Canada	10	6	3	1	47	35	13
5	4	Finland	10	5	5	0	45	43	10
6		USA	10	3	6	1	29	43	7
7	5	West Germany	10	2	7	1	23	58	5
8	6	Romania	10	1	9	0	20	84	2

1978

WR	ER	Team	GP	W	L	T	GF	GA	Pts
1	1	Soviet Union	10	9	1	0	61	26	18
2	2	Czechoslovakia	10	9	1	0	54	21	18
3		Canada	10	5	5	0	38	36	10
4	3	Sweden	10	4	6	0	39	37	8
5	4	West Germany	10	3	4	3	35	43	9
6		USA	10	2	6	2	38	58	6
7	5	Finland	10	2	6	2	37	44	6
8	6	East Germany	10	1	6	3	20	57	5

1979

WR	ER	Team	GP	W	L	T	GF	GA	Pts
1	1	Soviet Union	8	8	0	0	61	14	16
2	2	Czechoslovakia	8	4	2	2	32	32	10
3	3	Sweden	8	3	4	1	33	46	7
4		Canada	8	3	5	0	31	43	6
5	4	Finland	8	4	3	1	27	27	9
6	5	West Germany	8	3	4	1	32	31	7
7		USA	8	2	3	3	27	28	7
8	6	Poland	8	0	6	2	20	42	2

1981

WR	ER	Team	GP	W	L	T	GF	GA	Pts
1	1	Soviet Union	8	6	0	2	55	14	14
2	2	Sweden	8	5	2	1	24	30	11
3	3	Czechoslovakia	8	4	2	2	37	26	10
4		Canada	8	2	5	1	28	34	5
5		USA	8	4	3	1	39	43	9
6	4	Finland	8	3	3	2	37	32	8
7	5	West Germany	8	3	4	1	44	40	7
8	6	Netherlands	8	0	8	0	24	69	0

1982

WR	ER	Team	GP	W	L	T	GF	GA	Pts
1	1	Soviet Union	10	9	0	1	58	20	19
2	2	Czechoslovakia	10	5	3	2	38	20	12
3		Canada	10	5	3	2	40	30	12
4	3	Sweden	10	3	4	3	26	35	9
5	4	Finland	7	3	3	1	21	31	7
6	5	West Germany	7	2	4	1	19	30	5
7	6	France	7	1	5	1	20	44	3
8		USA	7	0	6	1	21	39	1

1983

WR	ER	Team	GP	W	L	T	GF	GA	Pts
1	1	Soviet Union	10	9	0	1	54	10	19
2	2	Czechoslovakia	10	6	2	2	40	21	14
3		Canada	10	6	4	0	35	30	12
4	3	Sweden	10	4	5	1	28	32	9
5	4	West Germany	10	5	4	1	31	34	11
6	5	East Germany	10	3	7	0	29	40	6
7	6	Finland	10	2	6	2	30	40	6
8	7	France	10	1	8	1	16	56	3

1985

WR	ER	Team	GP	W	L	T	GF	GA	Pts
1	2	Czechoslovakia	10	7	2	1	48	22	15
2		Canada	10	6	3	1	42	31	13
3	1	Soviet Union	10	8	2	0	64	16	16
4		USA	10	4	5	1	31	58	9
5	3	Finland	10	4	4	2	39	33	10
6	4	Sweden	10	4	6	0	37	40	8
7	5	West Germany	10	3	6	1	28	41	7
8	6	East Germany	10	0	8	2	16	64	2

1986

WR	ER	Team	GP	W	L	T	GF	GA	Pts
1	1	Soviet Union	10	10	0	0	50	15	20
2	2	Sweden	10	6	2	2	46	30	14
3		Canada	10	4	6	0	37	38	8
4	3	Finland	10	4	3	3	35	34	11
5	4	Czechoslovakia	10	5	4	1	38	21	11
6		USA	10	4	6	0	41	43	8
7	5	West Germany	10	2	7	1	23	52	5
8	6	Poland	10	1	8	1	26	63	3

1987

WR	ER	Team	GP	W	L	T	GF	GA	Pts
1	1	Sweden	10	5	3	2	44	22	12
2	2	Soviet Union	10	8	0	2	49	15	18
3	3	Czechoslovakia	10	6	2	2	32	24	14
4		Canada	10	3	5	2	25	29	8
5	4	Finland	10	5	4	1	32	31	11
6	5	West Germany	10	4	5	1	31	37	9
7		USA	10	4	6	0	38	49	8
8	6	Switzerland	10	0	10	0	25	69	0

1989

WR	ER	Team	GP	W	L	T	GF	GA	Pts
1	1	Soviet Union	10	10	0	0	47	16	20
2		Canada	10	7	3	0	57	29	14
3	2	Czechoslovakia	10	4	4	2	30	21	10
4	3	Sweden	10	4	4	2	34	32	10
5	4	Finland	10	5	4	1	35	27	11
6		USA	10	4	5	1	37	40	9
7	5	West Germany	10	1	7	2	22	41	4
8	6	Poland	10	1	9	0	12	76	2

1990

WR	ER	Team	GP	W	L	T	GF	GA	Pts
1	1	Soviet Union	10	8	1	1	53	13	17
2	2	Sweden	10	7	2	1	40	23	15
3	3	Czechoslovakia	10	5	4	1	36	30	11
4		Canada	10	6	3	1	43	32	13
5		USA	10	6	4	0	35	43	12
6	4	Finland	10	2	6	2	29	32	6
7	5	West Germany	10	1	8	1	19	42	3
8	6	Norway	10	1	8	1	21	61	3

1991

WR	ER	Team	GP	W	L	T	GF	GA	Pts
1	1	Sweden	10	5	0	5	43	29	15
2		Canada	10	5	2	3	39	30	13
3	2	Soviet Union	10	7	1	2	51	25	16
4		USA	10	3	5	2	35	51	4
5	3	Finland	10	6	3	1	35	21	13
6	4	Czechoslovakia	10	4	6	0	28	27	8
7	5	Switzerland	10	2	7	1	22	38	5
8	6	Germany	10	0	8	2	19	51	2

World Championships, *continued*

1992

Rank	Team	GP	W	L	T	GF	GA	Pts
1	Sweden	8	4	2	2	25	15	10
2	Finland	8	7	1	0	41	18	14
3	Czechoslovakia	8	6	2	0	33	13	12
4	Switzerland	8	3	3	2	18	21	8
5	Russia	6	4	1	1	23	12	9
6	Germany	6	4	2	0	31	17	8
7	USA	6	2	3	1	15	23	5
8	Canada	6	2	3	1	18	22	5
9	France	5	1	3	1	10	18	3
10	Norway	5	1	4	0	8	16	2
11	France	6	1	5	0	11	23	2
12	Poland	6	0	6	0	9	44	0

1993

Rank	Team	GP	W	L	T	GF	GA	Pts
1	Russia	8	5	2	1	27	16	11
2	Sweden	8	5	3	0	27	22	10
3	Czech Republic	8	6	1	1	33	10	13
4	Canada	8	6	2	0	41	17	12
5	Germany	6	4	2	0	21	17	8
6	USA	6	2	2	2	16	15	6
7	Finland	6	2	3	1	8	12	5
8	France	6	1	3	2	9	28	4
9	Austria	6	1	4	1	8	21	3
10	France	6	1	5	0	13	25	2
11	Norway	7	2	5	0	13	25	4
12	Switzerland	7	2	5	0	14	22	4

1994

Rank	Team	GP	W	L	T	GF	GA	Pts
1	Canada	8	7	1	0	35	19	14
2	Finland	8	6	1	1	48	11	13
3	Sweden	8	6	1	1	45	21	13
4	USA	8	4	4	0	24	35	8
5	Russia	6	4	2	0	31	10	8
6	France	6	3	3	0	19	22	6
7	Czech Republic	6	1	3	2	17	20	4
8	Austria	6	1	4	1	15	25	3
9	Germany	5	1	3	1	9	14	3
10	France	5	1	4	0	8	25	2
11	Norway	6	1	3	2	14	23	4
12	Great Britain	6	0	6	0	9	49	0

1995

Rank	Team	GP	W	L	T	GF	GA	Pts
1	Finland	8	6	1	1	34	15	13
2	Sweden	8	5	2	1	28	15	11
3	Canada	8	4	3	1	27	21	9
4	Czech Republic	8	4	4	0	17	16	8
5	Russia	5	4	1	0	18	12	8
6	USA	6	3	1	2	18	15	8
7	France	6	3	2	1	14	18	7
8	France	7	4	3	0	22	16	8
9	Germany	5	1	4	0	11	20	2
10	Norway	5	1	4	0	9	18	2
11	Austria	7	1	5	1	17	31	3
12	Switzerland	7	0	6	1	14	32	1

1996

Rank	Team	GP	W	L	T	GF	GA	Pts
1	Czech Republic	8	7	0	1	42	15	15
2	Canada	8	4	3	1	25	22	9
3	USA	8	5	2	1	22	22	11
4	Russia	8	5	2	1	31	17	11
5	Finland	6	2	2	2	24	18	6
6	Sweden	6	2	2	2	16	15	6
7	France	6	2	3	1	22	31	5
8	Germany	6	2	4	0	13	17	4
9	Norway	5	1	2	2	6	11	4
10	Slovakia	5	1	3	1	13	16	3
11	France	7	2	5	0	24	32	4
12	Austria	7	1	6	0	9	31	2

1997

Rank	Team	GP	W	L	T	GF	GA	Pts
1	Canada	11	7	3	1	36	22	15
2	Sweden	11	7	3	1	32	21	15
3	Czech Republic	9	6	3	0	30	20	12
4	Russia	9	4	3	2	28	24	10
5	Finland	8	5	3	0	29	15	10
6	USA	8	4	3	1	19	21	9
7	Latvia	8	4	2	2	37	23	10
8	France	8	3	4	1	28	28	7
9	Slovakia	8	3	4	1	20	23	7
10	France	8	2	6	0	20	43	4
11	Germany	8	2	6	0	10	30	4
12	Norway	8	0	7	1	13	32	1

1998

Rank	Team	GP	W	L	T	GF	GA	Pts
1	Sweden	10	9	0	1	38	9	19
2	Finland	10	4	3	3	26	14	11
3	Czech Republic	9	6	1	1	33	14	13
4	Switzerland	9	2	6	1	18	32	7
5–8	Russia	6	4	1	1	29	18	9
5–8	Canada	5	3	1	2	22	17	8
5–8	Slovakia	6	2	2	2	11	12	6
5–8	Belarus	6	2	4	0	17	23	4
9	Latvia	6	3	2	1	21	18	7
10	Italy	6	2	2	2	17	13	6
11	Germany	6	1	3	2	13	23	4
12	USA	6	1	4	1	10	19	3
13–16	France	3	1	2	0	5	12	2
13–16	Japan	3	0	3	0	7	19	0
13–16	Austria	3	0	3	0	3	15	0
13–16	Kazakhstan	3	0	3	0	6	19	0

CHAPTER 40
World Junior Championships
The Elite International Showcase for 18- and 19-year-old Players

IN 1973, THE SOVIET HOCKEY FEDERATION and the Czechoslovakian Ice Hockey Union proposed the creation of a World Junior Championship for players under the age of 20. The International Ice Hockey Federation supported the idea and, as a test, held an unofficial World Junior Championship tournament during the 1973–74 season. Three more unofficial tournaments took place before the first officially sanctioned World Junior Championship was held in 1976–77. A World Junior B Pool was created in 1979, then a C Pool in 1983 and a D Pool in 1996. The promotion-relegation system between the pools generally sees the winning team from B, C and D promoted up to the next level while the last-place team in A, B and C is dropped down.

Throughout the years, Canada and the former Soviet Union have been the most successful countries at the World Junior Championships, which are held annually in late December and early January. By 1998, the A Pool at the World Junior Championships had been expanded to include 10 teams divided into two groups of five. After round-robin games within each group, the top four teams advance to a playoff round while the two last-place teams play a two-game total-goals series to determine which team will be demoted to play in the B Pool the following year.

In the playoffs, the first-place team from each group crosses over to play the fourth-place team from the other group in the quarterfinals while the teams that finish second play the third-place team from the opposite group. The losers of the quarterfinals are paired off for one game each. The winners of those games then meet to determine fifth and sixth place, while the losers play off for seventh and eighth. Meanwhile, quarterfinals winners advance to the semifinals, with the winners advancing to the finals. The losers in the semifinals are paired to determine third and fourth place.

In the B Pool of the IIHF's World Junior Championships, eight teams are divided into two groups. After a round robin within these groups, the two last-place teams meet in a best-of-three series to determine which team will be relegated to the C Pool. Meanwhile, the three top teams from each group keep the points they've attained against the other advancing teams from their group and cross over to play another round-robin set with the teams of the other group. The winner of the tournament is determined by the team with the most total points after the second round robin.

The C Pool of the IIHF's World Junior Championships also comprises eight teams split into two divisions. After round-robin games within each group, teams are paired for a set of one-game playoffs to determine the final standings. The top teams from each group meet to establish first and second place, while the next two teams from each group play for third and fourth place, and so on. The same system applies to the D Pool.

Summaries of each Pool A World Junior Championship tournament follow:

1974 (UNOFFICIAL)
The first unofficial World Junior Championship was held in Leningrad, USSR in 1974 and marked the first contact for European teams with Canadian amateur hockey since 1969, when Canada severed its relationship with the International Ice Hockey Federation. The Peterborough Petes of the Ontario Hockey League represented Canada at the tournament, where the hosts were unstoppable. Seven future World and Olympic champions played for the Soviets as they cruised to the gold medal. Finland took silver while Canada finished third to claim the bronze. Viktor Khatulev of the USSR was the tournament's top scorer with three goals and six assists, though it was Sweden's Mats Ulander (seven goals, one assist) who was named best forward. Best defenseman was the Soviets' Vladimir Kucherenko while Canada's Frank Salive was best goaltender.

1975 (UNOFFICIAL)
For the first time ever, a world hockey championship was held on Canadian soil when Winnipeg and Brandon, Manitoba played host to the second edition of the unofficial World Junior Championships in 1975. The gold medal was not decided until the final game of the tournament when the Soviets beat Canada 4–3 and won the title again. Bryan Trottier (five goals and two assists) starred for the Canadian junior team, though the top scorer was Dale McMullin, who had three goals and five assists and was named to the tournament all-star team at forward along with Soviet players Boris Alexandrov and Viktor Khatulev (who was also named best player). Following the Soviets and Canada on the medal trail was Sweden, who won the bronze.

1976 (UNOFFICIAL)
The last unofficial World Junior Championship was held in Finland without the participation of the United States. The Soviets won again, making it three in a row. Canada finished second for the second straight year while Czechoslovakia earned a bronze medal. It was now obvious that this tournament had become a very important event on the international calendar. It was decided that the first IIHF-sanctioned World Junior Championships would take place the next year.

1977
The Soviet Union was the top team at the first official World Junior Championships in Banske, Czechoslovakia, finishing the 1977 tournament with a perfect record of 7–0. The Soviets scored 51 goals to set a record which would not be beaten until the Canadian junior team scored 54 goals in 1986. Still, it was Dale McCourt of the second-place Canadians who led the tournament with 18 points (10 goals and eight assists). Viacheslav Fetisov began his brilliant career by being named best defenseman. The host Czechs were bronze medal winners.

1978
Though it was not the final game, the main attraction at the 1978 World Junior Championships in Montreal was the game between Canada and the Soviet Union. Soviet defenseman Viacheslav Fetisov was matched against 16-year-old phenomenon Wayne Gretzky. The two would be named best defenseman and best forward of the tournament, and Gretzky would top the scoring parade with 17 points (eight goals and nine assists), but it was Fetisov and the Soviets who emerged as 3–2 winners. The Soviets later beat Sweden in the gold medal game, while Canada had to settle for a bronze medal on home ice.

1979
The 1979 World Junior Championships in Karlstad, Sweden brought together a large collection of future international and NHL stars. Soviets Alexei Kasatonov, Vladimir Krutov and Igor Larionov, Canadians Brian Propp and Brad McCrimmon, Americans Mike Ramsey, Neal Broten and Dave Christian, Finns Reijo Ruotsalainen and Jari Kurri, Swedes Pelle Lindbergh, Tomas Jonsson, Mats Naslund, Hakan Loob and Thomas Steen and Czechoslovakians Anton Stastny, Darius Rusnak, Jiri Lala, Dusan Pasek and Igor Liba all showed the promise of great futures at the top levels of the game. The Soviet Union made it three straight championships (and six in a row dating back to 1974) this year, with the Czechoslovakians taking the silver and the host Swedes the bronze. Canada tumbled into fifth place behind Finland. Vladimir Krutov of the USSR was the tournament's top scorer with eight goals and six assists and was named best forward while Soviet teammate Alexei Kasatonov was best defenseman. Best goaltender honors went to Sweden's Pelle Lindbergh who would later star in the NHL with the Philadelphia Flyers.

1980
The Soviet junior team won its fourth straight official World Junior Championship (and seventh in total, if the three unofficial championships in 1974, 1975 and 1976 are included) at Helsinki in 1980, with very difficult one-goal wins over Finland and Sweden. The Soviets' incredible winning run has been beaten only by Canada in the 1990s. In 1980, however, Canada would settle for a fifth-place finish. Finland (silver) and Sweden (bronze) rounded out the medal winners, while Czechoslovakia finished fourth. The United States finished seventh in its first appearance at the official tournament. For the second year in a row, Vladimir Krutov was the tournament's top scorer with seven goals and four assists. Finland's Jari Kurri also had 11 points (four goals and seven assists), but it was Krutov who was named best forward. Finns Reijo Ruotsalainen and Jari Paavola were selected as the tournament's best defenseman and best goaltender respectively.

1981

The Soviet domination of the World Junior Championships finally stopped in Bavaria, West Germany in 1981. The Swedes won the title behind the all-star performances of goaltender Lars Eriksson, defenseman Hakan Nordin and forwards Jan Erixon and Patrik Sundstrom. Eriksson was chosen as best goaltender while Sundstrom was tabbed as best forward. The tournament had very high scores, with an average of 10.3 goals scored in every game. The Czechoslovakians beat Austria by a record score of 21–4. Six players tied for the tournament scoring lead with nine points, Germany's Dieter Hegen leading the parade with eight goals. Ranking behind the Swedes at the tournament were the silver medal-winning Finns followed by the Soviet Union.

1982

Canada climbed on the world junior hockey throne in 1982, taking the gold medal with a record of 6–0–1 at the World Junior Championships in Minnesota. The team, coached by Dave King and Mike Keenan, beat the Soviets 7–0 en route to winning Canadian hockey's first world championship of any kind since the 1961 World Championship was won by the Trail Smoke Eaters. The Soviets slumped to fourth place this year, with Czechoslovakia (silver) and Finland (bronze) following Canada on the medal podium. The host Americans finished sixth. Defense made the difference for Canada, as Mike Moffat was named best goaltender and Gord Kluzak was tabbed as best defenseman. Mike Moller joined his teammates on the tournament all-star team after leading Canada with 14 points (five goals and nine assists). Leading the tournament was Finland's Raimo Summanen, who had seven goals and nine assists.

1983

After two years off of the top spot on the podium, the Soviet Union again won the gold medal at the World Junior Championships in 1983. The Soviet Juniors won all seven games on home ice in Leningrad, where the first unofficial version of the tournament had been staged nine years before. The Soviets scored 50 goals while allowing only 13, as Ilja Byakin was named the tournament's best defenseman and earned a spot on the all-star team. Matti Rautiainen of Finland was named best goaltender, though Dominik Hasek earned the berth on the all-star team after helping Czechoslovakia to earn the silver medal. Canada, led by Mario Lemieux, Dave Andreychuk and Steve Yzerman, finished third under the coaching of Dave King. Andreychuk (11 points) and Lemieux (10) each ranked among the scoring leaders, though the tournament's top scorer was Vladimir Ruzicka of Czechoslovakia with 12 goals and eight assists. However, Tomas Sandstrom of the fourth-place Swedes was tabbed as the tournament's best forward.

1984

The Soviet Union won the 1984 tournament in Nykoping, Sweden with a record of 6–0–1. The only team that did not lose to the Soviets was Canada, who managed a 3–3 tie but could finish no better than fourth with a record of 4–1–2. Following the USSR along the medal trail were Finland (silver) and Czechoslovakia (bronze). The Finns had a really good run for the title, but

finished one point behind the Soviets with a record of 6–1–0. Finnish center Raimo Helminen set a World Junior Championship record that would last for many years when he recorded 11 goals and 13 assists for 24 points in seven games. Not surprisingly, Helminen was named best forward and earned a berth on the tournament all-star team. Allan Perry became the first American to claim a Directorate Honor at the World Junior Championships when he was named the tournament's best goaltender despite his country's sixth-place finish.

1985

Canada won the World Junior Championships for just the second time in 1985 at a tournament held in Helsinki, Finland. As in 1982, the Canadians soundly defeated the Soviets (5–0) en route to the gold medal. The team was coached by Terry Simpson and consisted of many future NHLers such as Jeff Beukeboom, Brian Bradley, Adam Creighton, Stephane Richer, Wendel Clark, Shayne Corson, Bob Bassen and Claude Lemieux. The Canadians claimed top prize with a record of 5–0–2. Czechoslovakia was also 5–0–2 but settled for silver. The bronze medal went to the USSR. Craig Billington of Canada was named best goaltender, while Michal Pivonka of Czechoslovakia was best forward, though the tournament scoring leader was Esa Keskinen of Finland with 20 points (six goals, 14 assists). Fellow Finn Esa Tikkanen had 19 points. Honors for best defenseman went to Vesa Salo of Finland.

1986

The 1986 World Junior Championships, held in many cities across Southern Ontario, came to its dramatic peak in the final game. The Soviet Union beat Canada 4–1 to finish the tournament with a perfect record of 7–0 and reclaim the global title. The game attracted a lot of interest in Europe and was televised to the Soviet Union. Canada settled for a silver medal on home ice despite establishing a new scoring record with 54 goals. Two Canadians topped the tournament scoring parade, as Shayne Corson (seven goals, seven assists) and Joe Murphy (four goals, 10 assists) each had 14 points. Best forward at the tournament was another Canadian, Jim Sandlak, who had five goals and seven assists, the same totals as fellow Canadian Joe Nieuwendyk. The Soviets had the best defensive record, allowing just 14 goals against in seven games. Yevgeny Belosheikin was named best goaltender, while Mikhail Tatarinov was best defenseman.

1987

The last game of the 1987 World Junior Championships in Piestany, Czechoslovakia could have brought Canada the title. However, the game against the Soviet Union was halted prematurely due to a bench-clearing brawl. At the height of the on-ice melee, tournament officials doused all the lights in the arena, plunging the rink into darkness. The International Ice Hockey Federation suspended both teams. As a result, Finland won its first world junior title. Czechoslovakia finished second, while the United States claimed the bronze for its first medal in tournament history. Ulf Dahlen of Sweden was the top scorer with seven goals and eight assists, but it was Czechoslovakia's Robert Kron who was chosen as best forward. Finland's Markus Ketterer was best goaltender and Calle Johansson of Sweden was best defenseman.

1988

Canada rebounded from a disappointing finish in 1987, when a brawl with the Soviet Union cost them a chance at a gold medal, to win the 1988 World Junior Championships on Soviet ice in Moscow. In a dramatic game versus the host nation on January 1, 1988, the Canadians were outshot 40–16, but the brilliant goaltending of Jimmy Waite saved the day. Team Canada won the game 3–2 and later claimed the world title with a record of 6–0–1. The Soviets lost only to Canada and settled for a silver medal after posting a 6–1–0 record. The bronze medal went to Finland. Jimmy Waite was tabbed as the tournament's best goaltender. Teppo Numminen of Finland was best defenseman. Alexander Mogilny of the Soviet Union was named best forward after topping the scoring list with 18 points (eight goals and 10 assists). Canada's top scorer was Greg Hawgood, who just cracked the top 10 with a goal and eight assists.

1989

After failing to win gold on home ice in 1988, the Soviet Union took revenge at the World Junior Championships in Anchorage, Alaska in 1989. With a gold medal on the line on the last day of the tournament, the Soviets crushed Canada 7–2. The line of Pavel Bure, Sergei Fedorov (one goal) and Alexander Mogilny (three goals) was unstoppable against Team Canada. Canada fell into fourth place behind Sweden (silver) and Czechoslovakia (bronze). The United States could finish no better than fifth despite the fact that Jeremy Roenick (16 points) and Mike Modano (15) finished first and second in tournament scoring. Still, Pavel Bure (eight goals, six assists) was named best forward, while teammate Alexei Ivashkin was best goaltender. Rickard Persson of Sweden was selected as best defenseman.

1990

Once again, the Soviet Union and Canada collided for the title, which was not decided until the final game in Helsinki. Canada previously had rallied to beat the Soviets 6–4, but the USSR could win the gold medal with a win over Sweden on the last day. However, a Soviet line-up packed with future NHL stars could manage only a 3–3 tie. Both Canada and the Soviets finished the tournament with records of 5–1–1, but the gold went to the Canadians because of their head-to-head victory. Czechoslovakia finished third. The Czech team dominated the tournament awards with Robert Reichel winning the scoring title with 11 goals and 10 assists and earning a selection to the all-star team as well as the honor of best forward. Jaromir Jagr was second in scoring with 18 points and joined Reichel on the tournament all-star team. Canadian Dave Chyzowski (who was third in scoring with 13 points) rounded out the all-star forward line. Czechoslovakia's Jiri Slegr and the USSR's Alexander Godynyuk were the all-star defensemen, with Godynyuk tabbed as the tournament's best defenseman. Canada's Stephane Fiset was named best goaltender and chosen as an all-star.

1991

Eric Lindros led Team Canada to a gold medal on home ice in Saskatchewan at the World Junior Championships in 1991. He topped the team with six goals and 11 assists, but it was a goal by John Slaney that proved to be the key to victory. Slaney's goal gave Canada a 3–2 win

over the Soviet Union. Both countries finished the tournament with identical records of 5–1–1 for the second year in a row, but Canada earned the gold because of its head-to-head victory over the Soviets. Czechoslovakia finished just one point behind both countries with a 5–2–0 record to claim the bronze. Doug Weight of the fourth-place United States team topped the scoring parade with 19 points (five goals and 14 assists), while Pavel Bure of the Soviet Union led the tournament with 12 goals, but it was Eric Lindros who was picked as best forward. Jiri Slegr of Czechoslovakia was selected as best defenseman, while Switzerland's Pauli Jaks was best goaltender.

1992

A unique situation occurred during the 1992 World Junior Championships in Fussen, Germany. The Soviet team started the tournament under the named of the Soviet Union, but due to the official breakup of the country on January 1, 1992, finished the tournament under the name of the Commonwealth of Independent States. However, political upheaval did not prevent the hockey team from winning the title for the ninth time. Ten players from the winning team had great NHL careers ahead of them, while another five players would make the NHL as well. Sweden earned the silver medal, as Swedish players ranked 1–2–3–4 atop the tournament's scoring list. Michael Nylander led the way with 17 points and was chosen as best forward. Peter Forsberg (11 points) Markus Naslund (10) and Mikael Renberg (10) rounded out the top four scoring positions. American Mike Dunham was named best goaltender after leading the United States to a bronze medal. Canada's Scott Niedermayer was selected as best defenseman, although the two-time defending champion Canadians plummeted to sixth place at the tournament.

1993

Team Canada began its incredible run of five straight victories at the World Junior Championships with a gold medal at the 1993 tournament in Gavle, Sweden. Led by Paul Kariya and Chris Pronger, Canada had to defeat the host Swedes to claim gold. The silver medalists from Sweden received superb performances from two of their forwards. Peter Forsberg set a new tournament scoring record by registering seven goals and 24 assists for 31 points in just seven games. Markus Naslund accumulated 13 goals and 11 assists for 24 points. Forsberg was named best forward and was joined by Naslund and Kariya on the tournament all-star team. Janne Gronvall of Finland earned honors as best

defenseman. Canada's Manny Legace was best goaltender as the Canadians claimed the gold medal despite placing no players among the top 10 in scoring.

1994

As in 1993, the Swedes competed hard against Canada at the World Junior Championships in the Czech Republic but had to settle for a second-place finish in 1994 at 6–1–0. The gold medal went to Canada with a record of 6–0–1. The only team that did not lose to Team Canada was Russia, who managed a 3–3 tic. It was a real team effort by Canada, as no one from the country made the all-star team despite the fact that four Canadians cracked the top 10 in scoring, including Martin Gendron, who led the low-scoring tournament with seven goals and four assists. Niklas Sundstrom of Sweden, who also had 11 points (four goals, seven assists), was named best forward, while teammate Kenny Jonsson was best defenseman. Russia's Yevgeny Ryabchikov made the all-star team in goal, but it was Canada's Jamie Storr who was named best goaltender.

1995

On home ice in Red Deer, Alberta, Canada made it three gold medals in a row at the 1995 World Junior Championships. For the first time in tournament history, Canada ran up a perfect record of 7–0. Due to a labor dispute in the NHL, the regular season did not start until mid-January and several junior-aged players who normally might have been unavailable were able to join the Canadian team. Canadian players grabbed the top three spots in tournament scoring, with Marty Murray leading the pack with 15 points (six goals and nine assists). Jason Alllson also had 15 points on three goals and 12 assists, while Bryan McCabe had three goals and nine assists. McCabe was named the tournament's best defenseman, with Murray selected as best forward. Yevgeny Tarasov of the silver medal-winning Russians was named best goaltender. The bronze medal went to Sweden.

1996

Ten teams took part at the 1996 World Junior Championships in Boston (up from the traditional eight) and for the first time the teams were split into two groups. Canada finished with a 4–0 record to top Group A, then won its two playoff games, including a 4–1 victory over Sweden in the gold medal game. Canada's fourth straight tournament victory and ninth in all tied two records previously held by the former Soviet Union. Sweden settled for the silver

medal, while Russia took the bronze. Canada had brilliant performances at the tournament from Jose Theodore, who was named best goaltender, and Jarome Iginla, who was the scoring leader with five goals and seven assists (Germany's Florian Keller also had 12 points) and was named best forward. Honors for best defenseman went to Sweden's Mattias Ohlund.

1997

The road to a record-breaking fifth win in a row and tenth title overall was not an easy one for the Canadian team playing at the 1997 World Junior Championships in Geneva. Canada finished second behind the United States in its preliminary group with two ties and two wins. After victories in the quarterfinals and semifinals, the Canadian team faced the United States in the first all-North American finals in the history of the World Junior Championships. Canada beat Team USA 2–0 to claim the gold while the Americans settled for silver. Russia earned the bronze medal. The tournament was low-scoring. Slovakia's Radoslav Pavlikovsky, USA's Erik Rasmussen and Finland's Tommi Kallio sharing the lead with nine points apiece, though it was Russia's Alexei Morozov (one of four players to finish with eight points) who was tabbed as the tournament's best forward. Best defenseman was Joseph Corvo of the United States, while Canada's Marc Denis was best goaltender.

1998

The 1998 World Junior Championship was held in Helsinki and was dominated by the hosts from Finland. In the preliminary round, they went 3–0–1 to top Group A. After victories in the quarterfinals and semifinals, the Finns played Russia, who were undefeated with just one tie in the tournament. For the first time in the history of World Junior Championships, the final game went into overtime with Finland emerging with a 2–1 victory and just its second world junior title in history. Russia settled for the silver, with the bronze medal going to the surprising team from Switzerland. The five-time defending champions from Canada had trouble scoring throughout the tournament. After going 2–2 during the preliminaries, Team Canada dropped three straight playoff games, including a 6–3 loss to Kazakhstan that dropped the team into eighth place for its worst finish in tournament history. Olli Jokinen of Finland was named best forward of the tournament after he and American Jeff Farkas tied atop the scoring list with 10 points apiece. Best defenseman was Pavel Skrbek of the Czech Republic. Switzerland's David Aebischer was best goaltender.

WORLD JUNIOR CHAMPIONSHIPS POOL A STANDINGS AND RANKINGS

1974

Rank	Team	GP	W	L	T	GF	GA	Pts
1	Soviet Union	5	5	0	0	36	12	10
2	Finland	5	3	2	0	21	23	6
3	Canada	5	3	2	0	17	23	6
4	Sweden	5	2	3	0	32	21	4
5	USA	5	1	4	0	10	32	2
6	Czechoslovakia	5	1	4	0	19	24	2

1975

Rank	Team	GP	W	L	T	GF	GA	Pts
1	Soviet Union	5	5	0	0	22	8	10
2	Canada	5	4	1	0	27	10	8
3	Sweden	5	2	2	1	18	24	5
4	Czechoslovakia	5	1	2	2	9	11	4
5	Finland	5	1	3	1	10	14	3
6	USA	5	0	5	0	9	28	0

1976

Rank	Team	GP	W	L	T	GF	GA	Pts
1	Soviet Union	4	4	0	0	19	10	8
2	Canada	4	2	2	0	12	27	4
3	Czechoslovakia	4	2	2	0	12	10	4
4	Finland	4	1	3	0	12	14	2
5	Sweden	4	1	3	0	23	17	2

1977

Rank	Team	GP	W	L	T	GF	GA	Pts
1	Soviet Union	7	7	0	0	51	19	14
2	Canada	7	5	1	1	50	20	11
3	Czechoslovakia	7	4	2	1	32	17	9
4	Finland	7	4	3	0	35	29	8
5	Sweden	7	3	4	0	28	30	6
6	W. Germany	7	2	5	0	18	33	4
7	USA	7	1	5	1	25	45	3
8	Poland	7	0	6	1	12	58	1

1978

Rank	Team	GP	W	L	T	GF	GA	Pts
1	Soviet Union	7	6	1	0	50	16	12
2	Sweden	7	3	2	2	27	24	8
3	Canada	6	4	2	0	36	18	8
4	Czechoslovakia	6	2	3	1	21	31	5
5	USA	5	4	1	0	36	22	8
6	Finland	6	3	2	1	45	25	7
7	W. Germany	7	1	6	0	25	41	2
8	Switzerland	6	0	6	0	7	70	0

1979

Rank	Team	GP	W	L	T	GF	GA	Pts
1	Soviet Union	6	5	0	1	46	11	11
2	Czechoslovakia	6	3	1	2	19	23	8
3	Sweden	6	4	1	1	19	13	9
4	Finland	6	2	4	0	20	19	4
5	Canada	5	3	2	0	23	10	6
6	USA	5	2	3	0	21	23	4
7	W. Germany	5	1	4	0	17	26	2
8	Norway	5	0	5	0	6	46	0

1980

Rank	Team	GP	W	L	T	GF	GA	Pts
1	Soviet Union	5	5	0	0	24	9	10
2	Finland	5	4	1	0	29	8	8
3	Sweden	5	2	2	1	23	15	5
4	Czechoslovakia	5	2	3	0	28	27	4
5	Canada	5	3	2	0	25	18	6
6	W. Germany	5	2	3	0	15	28	4
7	USA	5	1	3	1	21	26	3
8	Switzerland	5	0	5	0	13	47	0

Note: For events that had separate preliminary and medal rounds, the results of all games are combined in these standings.

1981

Rank	Team	GP	W	L	T	GF	GA	Pts
1	Sweden	5	4	0	1	25	11	9
2	Finland	5	3	1	1	29	18	7
3	Soviet Union	5	3	2	0	36	14	6
4	Czechoslovakia	5	1	1	3	34	21	5
5	W. Germany	5	3	2	0	29	24	6
6	USA	5	2	3	0	19	27	4
7	Canada	5	1	3	1	26	25	3
8	Austria	5	0	5	0	9	67	0

1982

Rank	Team	GP	W	L	T	GF	GA	Pts
1	Canada	7	6	0	1	45	14	13
2	Czechoslovakia	7	5	1	1	44	17	11
3	Finland	7	5	2	0	47	29	10
4	Soviet Union	6	3	3	0	31	21	6
5	Sweden	7	4	3	0	42	26	8
6	USA	8	3	5	0	39	38	6
7	W. Germany	7	1	6	0	19	56	2
8	Switzerland	7	0	7	0	15	81	0

1983

Rank	Team	GP	W	L	T	GF	GA	Pts
1	Soviet Union	7	7	0	0	50	13	14
2	Czechoslovakia	7	5	1	1	43	22	11
3	Canada	7	4	2	1	39	24	9
4	Sweden	7	4	3	0	35	23	8
5	USA	7	3	4	0	28	29	6
6	Finland	7	3	4	0	35	29	6
7	W. Germany	7	1	6	0	12	46	2
8	Norway	7	0	7	0	13	69	0

1984

Rank	Team	GP	W	L	T	GF	GA	Pts
1	Soviet Union	7	6	0	1	47	17	13
2	Finland	7	6	1	0	44	21	12
3	Czechoslovakia	7	5	2	0	51	24	10
4	Canada	7	4	2	1	39	17	9
5	Sweden	7	3	4	0	27	25	6
6	USA	7	2	5	0	32	38	4
7	W. Germany	7	1	6	0	12	54	2
8	Switzerland	7	0	7	0	16	72	0

1985

Rank	Team	GP	W	L	T	GF	GA	Pts
1	Canada	7	5	0	2	44	14	12
2	Czechoslovakia	7	5	0	2	32	13	12
3	Soviet Union	7	5	2	0	38	17	10
4	Finland	7	4	1	2	42	20	10
5	Sweden	7	3	4	0	32	26	6
6	USA	7	2	5	0	23	37	4
7	W. Germany	7	0	6	1	9	44	1
8	Poland	7	0	6	1	10	59	1

1986

Rank	Team	GP	W	L	T	GF	GA	Pts
1	Soviet Union	7	7	0	0	42	14	14
2	Canada	7	5	2	0	54	22	10
3	USA	7	4	3	0	36	25	8
4	Czechoslovakia	7	4	3	0	30	20	8
5	Sweden	7	4	3	0	26	23	8
6	Finland	7	3	4	0	30	23	6
7	Switzerland	7	1	6	0	19	54	2
8	W. Germany	7	0	7	0	9	65	0

1987

Rank	Team	GP	W	L	T	GF	GA	Pts
1	Finland	7	5	1	1	45	23	11
2	Czechoslovakia	7	5	2	0	36	23	10
3	Sweden	7	4	2	1	45	11	9
4	USA	7	4	3	0	42	30	8
5	Poland	7	1	6	0	21	80	2
6	Switzerland	7	0	7	0	15	62	0
DQ	Canada	6	4	1	1	41	23	9
DQ	Soviet Union	6	2	3	1	27	20	5

1988

Rank	Team	GP	W	L	T	GF	GA	Pts
1	Canada	7	6	0	1	37	16	13
2	Soviet Union	7	6	1	0	44	18	12
3	Finland	7	5	1	1	36	20	11
4	Czechoslovakia	7	3	3	1	36	23	7
5	Sweden	7	3	3	1	36	24	7
6	USA	7	1	6	0	28	46	2
7	W. Germany	7	1	6	0	18	47	2
8	Poland	7	1	6	0	12	53	2

1989

Rank	Team	GP	W	L	T	GF	GA	Pts
1	Soviet Union	7	6	1	0	51	14	12
2	Sweden	7	6	1	0	39	14	12
3	Czechoslovakia	7	4	2	1	36	19	9
4	Canada	7	4	2	1	31	23	9
5	USA	7	3	3	1	41	25	7
6	Finland	7	2	4	1	29	37	5
7	Norway	7	1	6	0	14	56	2
8	W. Germany	7	0	7	0	13	66	0

1990

Rank	Team	GP	W	L	T	GF	GA	Pts
1	Canada	7	5	1	1	36	18	11
2	Soviet Union	7	5	1	1	50	23	11
3	Czechoslovakia	7	5	2	0	51	17	10
4	Finland	7	4	2	1	32	21	9
5	Sweden	7	4	2	1	38	29	9
6	Norway	7	2	5	0	25	51	4
7	USA	7	1	6	0	22	37	2
8	Poland	7	0	7	0	7	65	0

1991

Rank	Team	GP	W	L	T	GF	GA	Pts
1	Canada	7	5	1	1	40	18	11
2	Soviet Union	7	5	1	1	44	15	11
3	Czechoslovakia	7	5	2	0	44	19	10
4	USA	7	4	2	1	45	19	9
5	Finland	7	3	3	1	35	30	7
6	Sweden	7	3	4	0	32	29	6
7	Switzerland	7	1	6	0	5	48	2
8	Norway	7	0	7	0	8	75	0

1992

Rank	Team	GP	W	L	T	GF	GA	Pts
1	Russia	7	6	1	0	39	11	12
2	Sweden	7	5	1	1	41	24	11
3	USA	7	5	2	0	30	22	10
4	Finland	7	3	3	1	21	21	7
5	Czechoslovakia	6	3	3	0	26	20	6
6	Canada	7	2	3	2	19	30	6
7	Germany	7	1	6	0	15	42	2
8	Switzerland	8	1	7	0	23	44	2

1993

Rank	Team	GP	W	L	T	GF	GA	Pts
1	Canada	7	6	1	0	39	18	12
2	Sweden	7	6	1	0	53	15	12
3	Czech Republic	7	4	2	1	38	27	9
4	USA	7	4	3	0	32	23	8
5	Finland	7	3	3	1	32	22	7
6	Russia	7	2	3	2	26	20	6
7	Germany	7	1	6	0	16	37	2
8	Japan	7	0	7	0	9	83	0

1994

Rank	Team	GP	W	L	T	GF	GA	Pts
1	Canada	7	6	0	1	39	20	13
2	Sweden	7	6	1	0	35	16	12
3	Russia	7	5	1	1	23	17	11
4	Finland	7	4	2	1	24	24	6
5	Czech Republic	7	3	4	0	31	29	6
6	USA	7	1	5	1	20	33	3
7	Germany	7	1	6	0	10	26	2
8	Switzerland	7	1	5	1	10	27	3

1995

Rank	Team	GP	W	L	T	GF	GA	Pts
1	Canada	7	7	0	0	51	22	14
2	Russia	7	5	2	0	38	24	10
3	Sweden	7	4	2	1	35	21	9
4	Finland	7	3	3	1	31	30	7
5	USA	7	3	4	0	28	33	6
6	Czech Republic	7	3	4	0	43	26	6
7	Germany	7	1	6	0	17	55	2
8	Ukraine	7	1	6	0	12	44	2

1996

Rank	Team	GP	W	L	T	GF	GA	Pts
1	Canada	6	6	0	0	27	8	12
2	Sweden	7	4	2	1	26	13	9
3	Russia	7	4	2	1	32	19	9
4	Czech Republic	6	2	2	2	18	22	6
5	Finland	6	2	4	0	23	24	4
6	USA	6	3	3	0	21	27	6
7	Slovakia	6	2	1	3	24	23	7
8	Germany	6	1	3	2	19	27	4
9	Switzerland	6	1	4	1	16	24	3
10	Ukraine	6	1	5	0	12	31	2

1997

Rank	Team	GP	W	L	T	GF	GA	Pts
1	Canada	7	5	0	2	27	13	12
2	USA	6	4	1	1	23	9	9
3	Russia	6	4	1	1	26	9	9
4	Czech Republic	7	2	3	2	21	20	6
5	Finland	6	4	2	0	26	18	8
6	Slovakia	6	2	4	0	23	26	4
7	Switzerland	6	3	2	1	20	14	7
8	Sweden	6	2	3	1	20	18	5
9	Germany	6	1	5	0	14	34	2
10	Poland	6	0	6	0	7	46	0

1998

Rank	Team	GP	W	L	T	GF	GA	Pts
1	Finland	7	6	0	1	35	13	13
2	Russia	7	5	1	1	30	10	11
3	Switzerland	7	4	2	1	21	14	9
4	Czech Republic	7	3	3	1	24	22	7
5	USA	7	4	3	0	25	19	8
6	Sweden	7	3	4	0	25	13	6
7	Kazakhstan	7	2	5	0	16	51	4
8	Canada	7	2	5	0	13	18	4
9	Slovakia	6	3	3	0	26	18	6
10	Germany	6	0	6	0	4	41	0

CANADA CUP AND WORLD CUP OF HOCKEY
STANDINGS AND RANKINGS

Canada Cup

1976

Rank	Team	GP	W	L	T	GF	GA	Pts
1	Canada	7	5	1	1	33	14	11
2	Czechoslovakia	7	3	3	1	23	20	7
3	Soviet Union	5	2	2	1	23	14	5
4	Sweden	5	2	1	2	20	18	6
5	USA	5	1	3	1	14	21	3
6	Finland	5	1	4	0	16	42	2

1981

Rank	Team	GP	W	L	T	GF	GA	Pts
1	Soviet Union	7	5	1	1	32	15	11
2	Canada	7	5	1	1	37	22	11
3	Czechoslovakia	6	2	2	2	22	17	6
4	USA	6	2	3	1	18	23	5
5	Sweden	5	1	4	0	13	20	2
6	Finland	5	0	4	1	6	31	1

1984

Rank	Team	GP	W	L	T	GF	GA	Pts
1	Canada	8	5	2	1	37	27	11
2	Sweden	8	4	4	0	31	29	8
3	Soviet Union	6	5	1	0	24	10	10
4	USA	6	3	2	1	23	22	7
5	Czechoslovakia	5	0	4	1	10	21	1
6	W. Germany	5	0	4	1	13	29	1

1987

Rank	Team	GP	W	L	T	GF	GA	Pts
1	Canada	9	6	1	2	41	32	14
2	Soviet Union	9	5	3	1	42	32	11
3	Sweden	6	3	3	0	19	18	6
4	Czechoslovakia	6	2	3	1	15	20	5
5	USA	5	2	3	0	13	14	4
6	Finland	5	0	5	0	9	23	0

1991

Rank	Team	GP	W	L	T	GF	GA	Pts
1	Canada	8	6	0	2	33	14	14
2	USA	8	5	3	0	29	26	10
3	Finland	6	2	3	1	13	20	5
4	Sweden	6	2	4	0	13	21	4
5	Soviet Union	5	1	3	1	14	14	3
6	Czechoslovakia	5	1	4	0	11	18	2

World Cup of Hockey

1996

Rank	Team	GP	W	L	T	GF	GA	Pts
1	USA	7	6	1	0	37	18	12
2	Canada	8	5	3	0	26	26	10
3	Sweden	4	3	1	0	16	6	6
4	Russia	5	2	3	0	19	19	4
5	Finland	4	2	2	0	17	16	4
6	Germany	4	1	3	0	12	19	2
7	Slovakia	3	0	3	0	0	10	0
8	Czech Republic	3	0	3	0	4	17	0

Note: For events that had separate preliminary and medal rounds, the results of all games are combined in these standings.

CHAPTER 41

International "Open" Events

NHL Players and Teams versus European Opponents since 1972

BEGINNING WITH THE 1972 SUMMER SERIES between Team Canada and the Soviet national team, a variety of events were staged in either pre- or midseason that saw NHLers—playing either with their regular club teams or as part of national or all-star squads—playing their European counterparts.

Statistics for each of the events described here are included in player and goaltender data panels found in the Modern Player Register (Chapter 68) and the Goaltender Register (Chapter 69).

CANADA–RUSSIA 1972

For years, the best amateur teams in Canada were easily able to win World Championships and Olympic gold medals, but by the 1960s this was no longer true. Canada's top amateur clubs found themselves unable to compete with the Soviet Union and other top European countries and, denied the use of professional players by the International Ice Hockey Federation, Canada withdrew from international competition in 1970. Canadian fans were longing to see a series that would pit their best professionals against the best the Soviets had to offer. In September of 1972, they got their wish.

Most Canadians expected the 1972 Canada-Russia series to be a one-sided win for the NHL's best professionals. Certainly the Soviets had dominated World and Olympic play since 1962, but they were only amateurs! When Canadian hockey officials got a first-hand look at the Soviets' strange practice rituals and shabby equipment, the talk of a rout only increased. When Canada scored twice in the opening 6:32 of game one at the Montreal Forum on September 2, 1972 it appeared that Canadians had been correct.

"Until then," recalled Team Canada assistant coach John Ferguson, "NHL players never worked on their upper-body strength and seldom used off-ice training. Sure, a few jogged in the summer, but, mostly, players came to training camp and skated themselves into condition." This wasn't enough against the supremely fit Soviets. Team Canada wilted on that hot September night and the resulting 7–3 victory by the USSR sent shockwaves across Canada. Valeri Kharlamov scored twice that night, Vladimir Petrov, Boris Mikhailov and Alexander Yakushev had singles. A young goaltender named Vladislav Tretiak made 29 saves. Few Canadians knew those names at the start of September. By the end of the month they were as familiar as Esposito, Henderson, Cournoyer and Dryden.

Coach Harry Sinden shuffled his lineup for game two in Toronto and the result was a 4–1 Canadian victory, but Tretiak was magnificent in a 4–4 tie in game three at Winnipeg. Game four saw Team Canada take several careless penalties en route to a 5–3 loss. Canada's rugged style appeared graceless next to the smooth skating and slick passing of the Soviets and fans in Vancouver booed the Canadians loudly, inspiring Phil Esposito to deliver an impassioned speech in a postgame television interview: "To

people across Canada, we tried. We gave it our best and for the people that boo us, I am—all of us—are really disheartened and we're disillusioned and we're disappointed in some of the people. We cannot believe the ... booing we've gotten in our own building . We know we're trying [but] they've got a good team—let's face facts—but it 'doesn't mean we're not giving 150%. We certainly are. If the Russians boo their players like some of our Canadian fans—not all, just some—then I'll come back and apologize."

Esposito's speech marked a turning point in the Canadian squad's evolution as a team. "It was a war," Esposito would later say, "and yes, hell for us whether we wanted it or not."

Canada trailed 2–1–1 in the eight-game series and played two games in Sweden en route to Moscow in order to get familiar with the larger European ice surface. The games were rough, and much scorn was heaped on Team Canada for its rowdy tactics. Further controversy erupted after the team's arrival in Moscow when little-used players Vic Hadfield, Gilbert Perreault, Rick Martin and Jocelyn Guevremont elected to return home for their NHL training camps. But 3,200 Canadian fans had arrived in Moscow by then and they helped boost team morale. Especially after game five on September 22 when Team Canada let a 4–1 lead slip away in a 5–4 defeat.

"We were having a rough time in Moscow with the defections, lousy hotels, phone calls to the players' rooms in the middle of the night, the Russians snatching much of the food we had sent over for the team, especially the steaks and beer, and the terrible officiating by the European officials," recalls Harry Sinden. "But a long cheer at the end of the first game in Moscow by the Canadian fans was a big lift for our spirits."

Game six produced three goals within a span of 1:23 of the second period, with Paul Henderson's holding up as the game winner in a match that saw Team Canada overcome more blatantly pro-Soviet officiating for a 3–2 victory. This game contained the most controversial incident of the series when Bobby Clarke slashed Valeri Kharlamov on an already tender ankle and handicapped the star player's performance for the rest of the series. Henderson was again the hero in game seven when his goal at 17:54 of the third period gave Canada a 4–3 victory that evened the series at 3–3–1.

Few Canadians who were alive on September 28, 1972 missed game eight, as it was carried live on TV and radio in the mid-afternoon. Absenteeism was high at work places across the country and schools suspended classes to allow students to watch the game, many of them assembled in auditoriums or gymnasiums. The game started badly for Team Canada, with referee Josef Kompalla issuing cheap penalties that allowed the Soviets to score a pair of first-period power-play goals and build up a 5–3 lead through two. Goals by Phil Esposito and Yvan Cournoyer allowed Team Canada to tie the game midway through the third. In the dying moments, Paul Henderson corralled the rebound from a Phil Esposito shot, but his own shot was stopped by Tretiak. With 34 seconds left,

Henderson slipped his own rebound past the Soviet netminder. Team Canada had a thrilling 6–5 victory. An entire nation rejoiced.

"The Canadians battled with the ferocity of a cornered animal," marveled Anatoli Tarasov, godfather of Soviet hockey. "They believed the stories of their hockey superiority, which were not quite correct. Our players were better conditioned physically and stronger in skills than the Canadian professionals. But we could not match them in heart and desire."

CANADA–RUSSIA 1974

Most Canadians knew little about the opposition when Team Canada faced the Soviet Union in 1972. Many predicted an eight-game sweep for the Canadians. The country was shocked when the Soviets outclassed Canada in a 7–3 victory to open the series and the feeling was as much one of relief as of joy when Paul Henderson scored his winning goal with 34 seconds remaining in the final game. No one would be taking the Russians lightly in 1974. Back were many of the familiar names that had so impressed Canadian fans two years earlier: Tretiak, Yakushev, Maltsev, Mikhailov, Petrov and Kharlamov. Many in Canada knew these players better than the ones who would be representing them this time.

Team Canada 1974 was stocked with players from the World Hockey Association, the rival league which had sprung up to battle the NHL in 1972–73. Many had played in the NHL, but nobody was about to confuse Ralph Backstrom or Mike Walton with Phil Esposito. Bobby Hull—barred from playing for Canada in 1972 after his departure to the rival league—would be on hand this time, as would Gordie Howe, who had retired prior to the 1972 series but then returned to hockey in the WHA in order to play with sons Mark and Marty. Three members of Team Canada 1972 would be back to face the Soviets a second time: Pat Stapleton, Frank Mahovlich and Paul Henderson.

Canadian hockey fans had not entirely warmed to the World Hockey Association during its first two seasons, and the 1974 series was played as much to lend credibility to the WHA as it was to pit Canada against the Soviet Union. As such, the series did not elicit the same excitement, but Canadians did come around. The series opened in Quebec City on September 17 and Bobby Hull's goal with 5:42 remaining lifted Team Canada to a 3–3 tie. "I thought this would be just another game," said Gordie Howe afterwards, "but you put on a Canadian sweater and realize that it's not just another game. Too many Canadians are counting on it." Game two in Toronto resulted in a 4–1 Canadian victory (just as it had in 1972). The third game in Winnipeg was won 8–5 by the Soviets and a 5–5 tie in Vancouver meant that the two teams headed to Moscow with a win, a loss, and two ties apiece.

Tempers were on edge when the series resumed with game five on October 1 and the Soviets were 3–2 winners in a chippy game. "Oh, the Russians trip and hook, all right," com-

mented Gordie Howe. "But we're not angels, are we?" Two nights later the Soviets won 5–2 in a contest marred by a postgame punch-up that saw Rick Ley bloody the face of Valeri Kharlamov. The players were able to maintain their cool in game six, a contest Canada needed to win in order to salvage a tie in the series. Bobby Hull scored a late goal that appeared to give Canada a 5–4 victory, but the referee (Canadian Tom Brown) ruled that time had expired. Though Canada had received only two minor penalties in game seven, the Soviets announced that they would pull their team off the ice in game eight if the WHA players persisted in their dirty play. As it was, the Soviets rested several of their stars (including Vladislav Tretiak and Vladimir Petrov) and still beat a dispirited Canadian squad 3–2.

As had been the case in 1972, Alexander Yakushev was the Soviets' top scorer, netting five goals and adding three assists in seven games played. Vladimir Petrov (two goals, five assists) and Valeri Kharlamov (one and six) each contributed seven points. Bobby Hull was the series leader with seven goals and two assists and Andre Lacroix's six assists led the Canadians. The ageless Gordie Howe had three goals and four assists. Gerry Cheevers handled the bulk of Canada's goaltending, allowing 24 goals in seven games for a 3.43 goals-against average. He actually outperformed Vladislav Tretiak, who surrendered 25 goals in seven games for a 3.57 mark.

"My first idols," said Yakushev when the games were done, "were Boris Mayorov and Anatoli Firsov. When I was growing up, they were big in our game. After this series, I have another hero. Bobby Hull." Hull signed a photograph for his newest admirer and requested an autograph in return. "If I could," Hull admitted, "what I'd really like Yakushev to do is sign a contract with Winnipeg. God, but he's good."

SUPER SERIES

Various Super Series of midseason exhibition games were played North American arenas between Soviet and NHL teams were staged between 1975–76 and 1990–91.

The Soviet Union was represented by two teams, Central Red Army and the Soviet Wings in the first Super Series that took place during the 1975–76 NHL season. In subsequent years, the USSR sent over Spartak (1977–78), Soviet Wings (1978–79), the Red Army and Dynamo Moscow (1979–80), the Soviet national team (1982–83), Red Army and Dynamo Moscow (1985–86), Red Army and Dynamo Riga (1988–89), Khimik, Soviet Wings, Red Army and Dynamo Moscow (1989–90), and Khimik, Dynamo Moscow and Red Army (1990–91).

CANADA CUP

The Canada Cup was created in 1976 as an initiative of the NHL, the NHLPA and Hockey Canada. Staged before the start of the NHL regular season, the tournament offered hockey fans their first chance to see top NHL players representing their respective countries. All games were held in North America. The Canada Cup was held five times in total: 1976, 1981, 1984, 1987 and 1991. In four of the five tournaments, the six competing nations were Canada, Czechoslovakia, Finland, Sweden, USA and USSR. In 1984 Germany replaced Finland because of a higher finish in the previous IIHF World Championships. Canada won the event on each occasion except for 1981 when the USSR national team finished on top.

Summaries of each tournament follow.

CANADA CUP '76 Created by the NHL, the NHLPA and Hockey Canada in 1976, the Canada Cup heralded Canada's official return to international hockey after a boycott that had begun in 1970. The tournament included Canada, the United States and the top four hockey nations in Europe (the USSR, Czechoslovakia, Sweden and Finland) and gave NHL players a chance to represent their respective countries.

Team Canada's roster was built by Montreal Canadiens general manager Sam Pollock and coached by Scotty Bowman. It boasted one of the strongest lineups ever assembled, including Bobby Orr and Bobby Hull, who had missed the 1972 Canada-Russia Summit Series (Orr due to injuries and Hull because he had left the NHL for the World Hockey Association and thus had been ruled ineligible). The roster also included Phil Esposito, Guy Lafleur, Gilbert Perreault and Darryl Sittler. The Soviet Union, on the other hand, was a team in transition after losing to Czechoslovakia at the 1976 World tournament. Many familiar names from 1972 were gone, including long-time stars such as Valeri Kharlamov and Vladimir Petrov.

The tournament opened in Ottawa on September 2 with Team Canada scoring an easy 11–2 victory over Finland. Victories followed against the United States (4–2) and Sweden (4–0), but Canada's hopes of an undefeated tournament were dashed on September 9 with a 1–0 loss to Czechoslovakia. Vladimir Dzurilla earned the shutout, while Milan Novy scored the lone goal. Canada rebounded for a 3–1 win over the Soviets two nights later and finished the round-robin portion of the tournament in first place with a record of 4–1–0. The Czechs had dropped a surprising 2–1 decision to Sweden, but still advanced to face Canada in the finals on the strength of a 3–1–1 record.

Despite Dzurilla's initial success against Canada, he was pulled after allowing four goals in the first period in game one of the best-of-three finals. Jiri Holecek finished up in a 6–0 Canadian victory. Dzurilla then replaced Holecek after he surrendered two early goals in game two and was brilliant in a 4–4 tie through regulation time. At 11:03 of overtime, Darryl Sittler streaked down the left side of the Montreal Forum ice and, with a slight deke, slipped the puck past Dzurilla for the Canada Cup-winning goal.

The star of the tournament for Team Canada was Bobby Orr, who enjoyed a final turn in the spotlight before repeated knee injuries ended his brilliant career. Orr had two goals and seven assists for nine points in seven games (tying Viktor Zhluktov of the Soviet Union and teammate Denis Potvin for the scoring lead) and was named the tournament's Most Valuable Player.

CANADA CUP '81 After a five-year hiatus, the Canada Cup competition resumed in 1981 with Canada, the United States, Sweden, Finland, Czechoslovakia and the Soviet Union once again vying for international hockey supremacy. A total of 60 NHL players (22 Canadians, 22 Americans, 12 Swedes and four Finns) participated for their homelands.

As in 1976, the Soviet Union was in a rebuilding mode (after their Olympic loss to the United States in 1980). Only eight players remained from their 1976 Canada Cup squad, and just 11 players were back from the team that had defeated a group of NHL All-Stars at the Challenge Cup in 1979. Among the talented crop of Soviet newcomers were 21-year-olds Alexei Kasatonov, Igor Larionov and Vladimir Krutov. Viacheslav Fetisov made his Canada

Cup debut, while veteran Vladislav Tretiak once again tended goal.

Meanwhile, Team Canada had a young phenom of its own in Wayne Gretzky, who had set an NHL scoring record with 164 points in 1980–81. Gretzky headed up a Canadian roster that also featured Mike Bossy, Bryan Trottier, Clark Gillies and Denis Potvin of the two-time defending Stanley Cup champion New York Islanders. Goaltending duties were handled by Mike Liut. Canada waltzed through the round-robin portion of the tournament with only a 4–4 tie against Czechoslovakia blemishing a record that included a 7–3 victory over the Soviets in the final game on September 9. Despite the loss, the USSR held down second place with a record of 3–1–1. The Canada Cup format had been expanded to include a semifinals round this year, and Canada defeated the fourth-place United States 4–1 while the Soviets bounced the Czechs by the same score.

The one-game 1981 Canada Cup finals took place in Montreal on September 13 and saw the Soviet Union destroy Team Canada by a final score of 8–1. The Soviets frustrated Wayne Gretzky throughout and kept the tournament's leading scorer (12 points on five goals and seven assists) off the scoresheet, while Sergei Shepelev beat Mike Liut three times and Igor Larionov added two goals. Despite their victory, the Soviet team was not permitted to take home the Canada Cup trophy in a decision by Alan Eagleson that nearly sparked an international incident.

Vladislav Tretiak was named the Most Valuable Player of the Canada Cup tournament after the Soviets allowed just 15 goals in seven games. Behind Wayne Gretzky on the scoring list were Mike Bossy, Bryan Trottier, Guy Lafleur and Alexei Kasatonov, who all had 11 points. Bossy's eight goals topped the tournament, as did Kasatonov's 10 assists.

CANADA CUP '84 Though the 1984 Canada Cup took place just three years after the previous event, it featured a number of differences both on the ice and in its format. Among them was the debut of the West German squad, who replaced Finland by virtue of a fifth-place finish at the most recent World Championships. (Finland had finished seventh.) Another change saw Bryan Trottier jump the border, switching from Team Canada to the United States. Trottier's presence, along with Bob Carpenter, Joe Mullen, Rod Langway and Tom Barrasso (all bona fide NHL stars) gave the Americans their strongest lineup in Canada Cup history. The USA finished second behind the Soviet Union in the round robin with a record of 3–1–1.

In addition to the loss of Trottier, Team Canada had only five players return from its 1981 roster. Newcomers included Michel Goulet and Paul Coffey (who tied for second behind Wayne Gretzky in scoring with 11 points) and John Tonelli, whose gritty two-way play earned him the tournament's Most Valuable Player award. However, the Canadian team limped through the round robin with a record of 2–2–1 and finished fourth behind the USSR, the USA and Sweden (3–2–0).

As was the case in the first two Canada Cup tournaments, the USSR used the event to experiment with its roster. Soviet coach Viktor Tikhonov added 11 fresh faces to his club, including goaltender Alexander Tyzhnykh, who shared netminding duties with Vladimir Myshkin in the first post-Tretiak Canada Cup. Even without Viacheslav Fetisov, who was out with an injury, the Soviets became the first team

in tournament history to emerge from the round robin with a perfect record, capping off their 5–0–0 run with a 6–3 win over Canada on September 10. Three nights later, the two bitter rivals met in a one-game semifinals.

With Pete Peeters replacing Reggie Lemelin in goal, Canada battled the Soviets to a 2–2 tie through 60 minutes. At 12:29 of overtime, Mike Bossy tipped in a Paul Coffey shot and Canada had a 3–2 victory. One night before, the Swedes had crushed the Americans 9–2 to set up a Canada-Sweden final. As in 1976, the final of the 1984 Canada Cup was a best-of-three affair, though the series proved to be an anti-climax after the thrilling Canada–Russia game. Sweden featured such NHL stars as Kent Nilsson, Mats Naslund, Thomas Steen and Hakan Loob, but Team Canada swept the series with two victories by 5–2 and 6–5 scores.

CANADA CUP '87

The 1987 Canada Cup featured the emergence of Mario Lemieux as a true superstar. Teamed with Wayne Gretzky, Lemieux finally developed a work ethic to match his immense talent and the combination of hockey's two most gifted offensive players resulted in some of the most exciting games in the game's history.

Wayne Gretzky was late in accepting his invitation to join Team Canada after his Edmonton Oilers team won the Stanley Cup during the longest season in NHL history, but he arrived at training camp in the best shape of his life. Thirty-four other players also arrived at training camp and the reduction to a 23-man roster left such stars as Patrick Roy, Steve Yzerman, Cam Neely and Wendel Clark off the team.

The Soviet Union brought a veteran-laden lineup to the 1987 Canada Cup and was eager to regain its championship form after losing the most recent world title to Sweden. The Swedish squad would see eight national team members replaced by nine NHL stars during the Canada Cup, which only figured to make the team stronger. However, the 1984 Canada Cup finalists would not make it past the semifinals this year. The Americans were hurt by injuries to Mark Howe, Bryan Trottier and Neal Broten. Despite strong goaltending from John Vanbiesbrouck, the USA finished just 2–3–0 and was spared last place only by the 0–5–0 record of Finland, who had returned to the Canada Cup this year.

Canada was undefeated in the round robin, but only had managed a 4–4 tie with Czechoslovakia to open the tournament and a 3–3 tie with the Soviets in the final game. Canada faced the Czechs again in the semifinals and fell behind 2–0 after one period before rallying for a 5–3 victory. The USSR had lost 5–3 to Sweden during the round robin, but avenged that defeat with a 4–2 victory in the semifinals. Canada and the Soviets would meet for the Canada Cup championship.

Game one in the best-of-three finals was played at the Montreal Forum on September 11 and saw the Soviets defeat Canada 6–5 on Alexander Semak's overtime goal. Two nights later at Copps Coliseum in Hamilton, Mario Lemieux ended a classic game on a feed from Wayne Gretzky at 10:06 of the second overtime period for a 6–5 Canadian victory. With 1:26 remaining in the third and final game on September 15, Lemieux again converted a Gretzky pass for a 6–5 Canada Cup-winning victory. Lemieux had scored a tournament-leading 11 goals in nine games (including four game winners), while his 18 points were second behind Wayne Gretzky's tournament-record 21 points (on three goals and 18 assists).

CANADA CUP '91

"Anything less than winning is not acceptable," said Wayne Gretzky prior to the 1991 Canada Cup. The Great One would be back to help his country defend its 1987 championship, but he would not have his brilliant partner from that series. The back injury that had kept Mario Lemieux out for more than half the 1990–91 season sidelined him for the Canada Cup as well. However, hockey's next anointed superstar would be a member of Team Canada this year. Though he had refused to report to the Quebec Nordiques and was not yet a member of the NHL, 18-year-old Eric Lindros would contribute three goals and a tough, physical presence to Team Canada.

The 1991 Canada Cup witnessed a partial changing of the guard atop the hockey hierarchy, as Czechoslovakia fell to last place with a 1–4–0 record in the round robin (despite the presence of young Dominik Hasek) and the Soviet Union failed to reach the playoffs after going 1–3–1. The USSR had been on the decline since its last Olympic gold medal victory in 1988. With veteran national team members Vladimir Krutov and Igor Larionov allowed to join the NHL in 1989–90 and the subsequent defections of Alexander Mogilny and Sergei Fedorov, the Soviets no longer had complete access to their finest hockey resources.

Sweden edged the Soviet Union for fourth place in the round robin behind Mats Sundin's six points (two goals, four assists) before losing 4–0 to Canada in the semifinals. Christian Ruuttu, Petri Skriko and Esa Tikkanen led Finland into the playoffs for the first time in Canada Cup history before they lost 7–3 to the United States.

"There is no doubt this will be the best U.S. team ever," said American general manager Craig Patrick before the tournament. Led by Mike Modano, Brett Hull, Brian Leetch and Pat LaFontaine, and featuring solid goaltending by Mike Richter, Team USA lost only to Canada during the round robin, and it was looking for revenge in the playoffs. Canada scored a 4–1 victory over the Americans in game one of the finals, but the victory proved costly when a Gary

Suter cross-check put Wayne Gretzky out of action. Gretzky watched game two in civilian clothes and saw Mark Messier and Steve Larmer give Team Canada an early 2–0 lead. Jeremy Roenick and Kevin Miller evened the game 2–2 after two periods, but a shorthand goal by Larmer at 12:13 of the third and an empty-netter from Dirk Graham capped a 4–2 clinching victory. Despite missing the final game, Wayne Gretzky earned his fourth consecutive Canada Cup scoring title with 12 points in seven games on four goals and eight assists.

CHALLENGE CUP

In February of 1979, the Soviet national team played a three-game series against the NHL All-Star Team at Madison Square Garden in New York. This one-time series replaced the NHL All-Star Game that season. The winner of the series, the Soviets, was awarded a trophy named the NHL Challenge Cup.

RENDEZ-VOUS '87

In February of 1987, the NHL All-Star Game was replaced by a series in Quebec City that pitted the Soviet national team against a squad of NHL All-Stars. There was no winner of the two-game Rendez-Vous '87 series after each team won one game.

FRIENDSHIP TOUR

In September of both 1989 and 1990, two NHL teams traveled to the Soviet Union where they played a series of exhibition games against Soviet club teams. The Calgary Flames and Washington Capitals made the initial tour, while the Montreal Canadiens and Minnesota North Stars visited in 1990. Each NHL team played four different Soviet opponents.

WORLD CUP OF HOCKEY

The World Cup of Hockey was staged in August and September of 1996. The tournament was a successor to the Canada Cup and was organized by the NHL, the NHLPA and the IIHF. Like the Canada Cup, it was played before the NHL's regular season began, allowing top professional players to represent their countries. The eight best national teams in the world—Canada, USA, Russia, Czech Republic, Slovakia, Sweden, Finland and Germany—were divided into two groups, one playing in North America and the other in Europe. After a round robin within both groups, the top three teams from each advanced to the playoffs. All playoff games took place in North America. The teams that finished first in their groups received a bye in the first playoff round, advancing to the semifinals. Second and third-place teams played one game each, the winners advancing. Canada and the USA won their semifinals and met in a three-game finals won by Team USA two games to one. Goaltender Mike Richter was a standout for Team USA, receiving MVP honors.

CHAPTER 42

Other International Tournaments and Leagues

INTERNATIONAL HOCKEY places great emphasis on tournament play. National teams and club teams participate in a variety of annual events, some recently organized and some, like the Spengler Cup and the Izvestia/Baltica Cup, long established.

International leagues involving club teams are a relatively recent addition to the hockey scene. (Historically, league play had been confined to within each country.)

All are profiled here.

Also described is the European Junior Championships. This event acquires World Championship status in 1999. It is of particular interest because it is Europe's leading showcase for players under the age of 18. As a result, it is thoroughly scouted by NHL clubs looking to find talent in next year's Entry Draft.

ALPENLIGA

The Alpenliga was created in 1991 and has been held in every year since with the exception of 1994. The tournament includes participants from Austria, Italy and Slovenia and generally concludes in the first part of the season.

Eleven teams take part in the Alpenliga and play a quadruple round-robin schedule. The top eight teams then advance to the final round, where they are split into two groups of four. After a round robin within each group, the top teams from each group advance to play a two-game total-goals final.

ASIAN CUP

The International Ice Hockey Federation created the Asian Cup competition to broaden the scope of international hockey and to assist Asian nations in the staging of international games. The first tournament for Asian national teams took place in 1990 and was held annually until 1996 (except for 1991, when the tournament was canceled due to the Gulf War). The final tournament in January of 1996 matched the national teams of Kazakhstan, Japan, China and Korea in a round-robin series and was won by Kazakhstan.

ASIA-OCEANIA JUNIOR CHAMPIONSHIP

The Asia-Oceania Junior Championship for players under the age of 18 was held for the first time in 1983–84. The event was known as the Asian Junior Championships for its first two years, it acquired its current name in 1986. Tournaments generally are held in March. Currently, six nations take part play a round-robin series to determine a champion as well as silver and bronze medal winners.

ATLANTIC LEAGUE

In 1995–96, six club teams from France, Denmark and the Netherlands met in a new tournament called the Atlantic League. A winner was declared after a double round-robin schedule of games.

BALKAN LEAGUE

The first Balkan League tournament was held in 1994–95 and has become an annual event. Club teams from Romania, Yugoslavia and Bulgaria compete, with four teams playing a double round-robin schedule to determine the winner.

CALGARY CUP

The Calgary Cup took place in December 1986–January 1987 during the Pre-Olympic Week tournament in Calgary one year before the 1988 Winter Olympic Games. National teams from Canada, the United States, Czechoslovakia and the Soviet Union met in a round-robin series, with the two top teams playing off to decide a winner while the two bottom finishers met to determine third and fourth place. The event was won by Czechoslovakia.

CUP OF LOW COUNTRIES

The first tournament of the Cup of Low Countries was held in 1995–96 with the participation of clubs from the Netherlands and Belgium. Currently, the tournament involves 12 teams divided into two groups. After a double round robin within the groups, the teams from each group are paired for a one-game playoff to determine the final standings. The two first-place teams meet to determine top spot, the second-best teams meet to decide third place and so on.

DEUTSCHLAND CUP

Created in 1987 as a national team tournament by the German Ice Hockey Union, the Deutschland Cup usually is played in Stuttgart at the beginning of November. No tournament was held in 1989.

EAST EUROPEAN HOCKEY LEAGUE

The East European Hockey League was created in 1995–96 to allow club teams from the newly independent former Soviet republics to have full-time competition. The EEHL was strengthened in 1996–97 when the creation of the new Russian Hockey League excluded the top clubs from the Ukraine and Belarus. The EEHL is made up of teams from the Ukraine, Belarus, Latvia, Lithuania and a team from Poland.

Nine teams play a quadruple round-robin schedule to begin the EEHL, with the top eight clubs advancing to the playoffs. Quarterfinals and semifinals employ a best-of-three format while the finals and the series for third place are played as a best-of-five.

EUROPEAN CUP

The European Cup (or European Champions Cup) was created by the International Ice Hockey Federation in 1965 through the efforts of the German Ice Hockey Union—particularly those of future IIHF president Gunther Sabetzki. The object of the tournament was to determine the best club team in Europe. The first three tournaments, however, were held without the participation of the Soviet Union, whose teams later would dominate the event.

In the first two years of the European Cup tournament, the teams world play a four-game total-goals series. Until 1978–79, the event was played in a two-game total-goals format. After 1978–79, only the preliminary rounds used the total-goal format. The creation of the European Hockey League for the top clubs on the continent replaced the European Cup, which was held for the last time in 1996–97.

EUROPEAN JUNIOR CHAMPIONSHIPS

The idea of a European Junior Championships for players under the age of 19 was proposed by the Soviet Hockey Federation and the Czechoslovakian Ice Hockey Union. An initial unofficial tournament was held in 1967, with the tournament gaining official status the following year. (After the creation of the World Junior Championships for players under 20 in 1976–77, the age limit for participation in the European Junior Championships was lowered to 18. This lower age limit has resulted in the event being intensely scouted by representatives of NHL clubs looking to draft talented 18-year-old Europeans.) Pool B was created in 1969, with a C Pool added in 1978 and a D Pool in 1996. The promotion-relegation system between the pools generally sees the winning team from B, C and D promoted up to the next level while the last-place team in A, B and C is dropped down.

The European Junior Championships are held in March and April. Currently, the format of the A Pool sees eight countries divided into two groups. After an initial round robin within the groups, the teams that have finished last play a best-of-three series to determine the team that will be demoted to the B Pool.

The three top finishers from each group keep the points they have attained against the other advancing teams from their group and cross over to play a round-robin series against each of teams from the other group. The winner of the tournament is the team with the most total points after the second round robin. The same format is also employed in the B Pool.

The C Pool of the European Junior Championships also is comprised of eight teams split into two divisions. After round-robin games within each group, teams are paired for a set of one-game playoffs to determine the final standings. The top teams from each group meet to establish first and second place, while the next two teams from each group play for third and fourth place, and so on.

In the D Pool, eight teams are divided into two groups to play a round-robin series within each group. The top two teams from each group then advance (keeping any points they have gained against the other advancing team) to form a final group of four. After another round-robin series, the team with the most points is declared the winner. The two bottom teams from each group play a similar series to round out the final standings.

EUROPEAN HOCKEY LEAGUE

The International Ice Hockey Federation created a new tournament called the European Hockey League in 1996–97. The EHL is made up of the best clubs on the continent, including the national champions of European countries.

In 1997–98, the EHL included 24 clubs from 12 countries. Teams are divided into six divisions and play a double round-robin series (home-and-home games) within their divisions. After that, the six division winners and the two second-place teams with the best records advance to the playoffs. Teams play each other twice (home and away) in a total-goal quarterfinals with the four winners advancing to the final stage. At this stage in the tournament, teams play one-game semifinals with the winners advancing to a one-game final and the losers playing one game to determine third place.

FOUR NATION TOURNAMENT

The Four Nation Tournament was created by the International Ice Hockey Federation and originally allowed the best junior players from Europe's top hockey countries—the USSR (now Russia), Czechoslovakia (now represented by the Czech Republic), Sweden and Finland—to compete in tournaments for various age groups.

In 1977, the first Four Nation Tournament was held for players under the age of 20. The tournaments are held in late August/early September in order to help the country's national teams prepare for the upcoming season. The Four Nation Tournament for players under 18 was created in 1979 and is held annually at the beginning of February to serve as the last test before the European Junior Championships. A tournament for players under 16 was created in 1978, with an under–17 bracket added in 1990. These tourneys are played in early February. All Four Nation Tournaments are made up of round-robin games.

Since 1996, the Four Nation events have been transformed into Five and Six Nation tournaments with the participation of junior national teams of different ages from Slovakia, Germany, Canada and the United States.

GOODWILL GAMES

The Goodwill Games hockey tournament took place only once, in July-August of 1990 in the Tri-Cities area of Washington state. The top six national teams from Europe played together with Canadian and U.S. teams. The eight teams were divided into two groups, with the winner declared after a series of playoff games. The tournament was won by the Soviet Union despite the defection of Sergei Fedorov prior to the event.

IZVESTIA CUP

Created by the Soviet Hockey Federation in 1967, the Izvestia Cup was known as the Moscow International Tournament for its first two years. In 1969, it became known as the Izvestia Cup after its sponsor, a Soviet national newspaper. The tournament is played annually (except for 1991) in the middle of December. National teams from a variety of countries have participated, though in the mid-1970s, the WHA's Winnipeg Jets and Quebec Nordiques each played once. A team called the NHL Future Stars played in 1978.

In 1997, the *Izvestia* newspaper gave up its patronage of the tournament, which is now known as the Baltica Cup after the Baltica brewing company that sponsors the event.

JAPAN CUP

Created by the Japan Ice Hockey Federation, the Japan Cup was played in 1989 and 1990. Both tournaments were held in Tokyo in May. Three national teams (two from Europe and the hosts from Japan) played a double round-robin format to determine a winner. In 1989, the Soviet Union and Czechoslovakia were declared co-winners. Both teams had earned the same number of points and the organizing committee declined to count goal differential. The Soviets were sole winners in 1990.

KRAJALA CUP

Created by the Finnish Ice Hockey Union, the first Krajala Cup tournament was held in December of 1995. Since 1996, the event has been held in November. The Krajala Cup pits Europe's top four national teams in a round-robin tournament.

NISSAN CUP

The Nissan Cup was created by the Swiss Ice Hockey Union in 1988. The tournament is held in Switzerland in November or February and generally sees four top European national teams meet in a round-robin series.

PRAGOBANKA CUP

A round-robin tournament created by the Czech Republic's Ice Hockey Union in 1994, the Pragobanka Cup is an annual event for top European national teams. It is played in the Czech Republic in late August and early September.

RUDE PRAVO CUP

The Czechoslovak Ice Hockey Union created the Rude Pravo Cup in 1977. The first three tournaments (1977, 1978 and 1979) were played in September and involved the top national teams of Europe. The inaugural tournament of 1977 also included the Cincinnati Stingers of the World Hockey Association. In 1981–82 and 1982–83, the format of the Rude Pravo Cup was changed. The four best European teams—the Soviet Union, Czechoslovakia, Sweden and Finland—met throughout the season in a double round-robin (home-and-home) series. Both tournaments were won by the Soviets.

ST. PETERSBURG GRAND PRIX

The St. Petersburg Grand Prix was created by the Soviet Hockey Federation in 1975 when it was known as the International B-Team Tournament. The first tournament took place in Riga but has been held in St. Petersburg (previously known as Leningrad) since 1976. In 1982, the event was named the Leningradskaya Pravda Tournament due to the sponsorship of the *Leningradskaya Pravda* newspapers. It has been known as the St. Petersburg Grand Prix since 1992.

Europe's national B-teams usually have gathered for this tournament in April, with teams from Russia, the Czech Republic, Sweden and Finland having participated the most. A champion is declared through a round-robin format.

SPENGLER CUP

The Spengler Cup is the oldest European tournament for club teams. The cup was donated by Dr. Carl Spengler of Davos, Switzerland in 1923 with the understanding that Germany and Austria would represent themselves internationally with their best club teams. (At the time, those countries were banned from official International Ice Hockey Federation competitions in the wake of World War I.)

The Spengler Cup is played every year in Davos between Christmas and the New Year. Five teams participate in the tournament, with a select team from Canada usually included. Canada first competed at the Spengler Cup in 1984, though Canadians studying at Oxford University in England played in the tournament's early years. Canada's modern Spengler roster is built around Canadians playing professionally in European national leagues.

Each team at the Spengler plays a round-robin series after which the top two teams meet in the final game. The Rochester Americans of the American Hockey League were the first North American professional team to compete at the tournament when they took part in 1996.

SWEDEN CUP

The Sweden Cup was created by the Swedish Ice Hockey Association and was only held twice—in the Olympic years of 1980 and 1984. Top national teams played a round-robin tournament in Sweden in April. The 1980 tournament was won by the Soviet Union. Czechoslovakia won in 1984.

SWEDEN HOCKEY GAMES

The Sweden Hockey Games tournament was created by the Swedish Ice Hockey Union in 1991. Since then, top national teams have met annually in Sweden in February. Usually, the top European national teams (Russia, the Czech Republic, Sweden and Finland) plus Canada play this round-robin event in Stockholm.

VIKING CUP

Organized in 1981 by the Camrose Lutheran College (later named the Augustana University College), this tournament has been known as the Viking Cup since 1982 after the name of the host team—the Augustana Vikings. It is held every second year at Christmas time in the town of Camrose, Alberta.

The Viking Cup pits national and club junior teams from Europe against junior and university teams from North America. Eight teams are divided into two groups. After a round robin within each group, the top teams are given a bye through the first playoff round, while the second-place team from one group meets the third-place team from the other. Winners advance to meet the first-place teams in the semifinals. The semifinals winners meet for the championship while the two losing teams compete for third place. There is also a playoff series for the two teams that finish fourth in the initial round-robin section of the tournament.

WORLD HOCKEY CHALLENGE

The Quebec Esso Cup began in 1985–86 for teams of players under 17 years old. The tournament generally was held every second year in late December/early January. Canada was represented by five all-star teams—Ontario, Quebec, Atlantic, Western and Pacific—which participated along with an American team and three European national junior teams.

In 1992, the Quebec Esso Cup was replaced by the World Hockey Challenge. The format, however, remained the same. Ten junior teams are divided into two groups of five each. After a round robin within the groups, the top two teams from each group advance to the semifinals. Winners move on to the finals while the semifinals losers play to determine third place. The teams that finished third in the two round-robin groups meet to determine fifth and sixth place. The fourth and fifth-place finishers from the round robin also play off to round out the final standings.

CHAPTER 43

Other IIHF Championships

World Senior and Junior B–C–D Pools plus European and Asian Junior Championships

TEAMS ARE LISTED BY FINAL RANKING. W–L–T–Pts are calculated from all games played including preliminary, medal and consolation rounds. Often teams with superior W–L–T marks finish with inferior rankings due to early tournament losses that seed them in a lower bracket.

Ranking in Senior or Junior B, C or D events is sequential. As an example, if there are eight teams in Pool A, the top team in Pool B is ranked ninth.

Some final standings are missing. Research is ongoing to obtain them. In those instances, only rankings are published here.

IIHF three-letter abbreviations are use for country names. A list of these abbreviations is found on page 509.

World Championships, Pool B

1951

Rank	Team	GP	W	L	T	GF	GA	Pts
8	ITA	5	4	0	1	26	11	9
9	FRA	5	4	1	0	35	15	8
10	HOL	5	3	2	0	17	16	6
11	AUT	5	1	4	0	20	25	2
12	BEL	5	1	3	1	23	30	3
13	YUG	5	1	4	0	13	37	2

1952

10	GBR	5	4	1	0	28	10	8
11	AUT	5	3	1	1	32	19	7
12	ITA	5	3	2	0	26	21	6
13	HOL	5	1	3	1	19	26	3
14	BEL	5	1	3	1	17	24	3
15	FRA	5	1	3	1	19	41	3

1953

4	ITA	4	4	0	0	24	9	8
5	GBR	4	3	1	0	21	10	6
6	AUT	4	2	2	0	18	16	4
7	HOL	4	1	3	0	13	26	2
8	FRA	4	0	4	0	11	26	0

1955

10	ITA	4	4	0	0	50	4	8
11	AUT	4	3	1	0	15	9	6
12	HOL	4	2	2	0	18	20	4
13	YUG	4	1	3	0	9	23	2
14	BEL	4	0	4	0	8	44	0

1956

11	GDR	2	2	0	0	18	8	4
12	NOR	2	1	1	0	8	9	2
13	BEL	2	0	2	0	12	21	0

1959

13	ROM	2	2	0	0	12	4	4
14	HUN	2	1	1	0	5	9	2
15	AUT	2	0	2	0	4	8	0

1961

9	NOR	5	4	1	0	27	9	8
10	GBR	5	3	0	2	21	11	8
11	SUI	5	2	2	1	17	15	5
12	ITA	5	2	2	1	19	20	5
13	POL	5	1	4	0	13	17	2
14	AUT	5	1	4	0	10	35	2

1962

9	JAP	5	5	0	0	63	16	10
10	AUT	5	4	1	0	49	9	8
11	FRA	5	3	2	0	35	25	6
12	HOL	5	2	3	0	20	46	4
13	AUS	5	1	4	0	13	51	2
14	DEN	5	0	5	0	9	42	0

1963

9	NOR	6	5	1	0	35	15	10
10	SUI	6	4	1	1	28	10	9
11	ROM	6	4	1	1	29	17	9
12	POL	6	4	2	0	52	13	8
13	YUG	6	2	4	0	23	49	4
14	FRA	6	1	5	0	14	38	2
15	GBR	6	0	6	0	8	47	0

1964

9	POL	7	6	1	0	40	13	12
10	NOR	7	5	2	0	40	19	10
11	JAP	7	4	2	1	35	31	9
12	ROM	7	3	3	1	31	28	7
13	AUT	7	3	3	1	24	28	7
14	YUG	7	3	3	1	29	37	7
15	ITA	7	2	5	0	24	42	4
16	HUN	7	0	7	0	14	39	0

1965

9	POL	6	5	0	1	35	15	11
10	SUI	6	4	1	1	27	15	9
11	FRG	6	3	1	2	30	20	8
12	HUN	6	2	3	1	19	24	5
13	AUT	6	2	4	0	21	20	4
14	GBR	6	1	4	1	24	41	3
15	YUG	6	0	4	2	16	29	2
16	ITA	2	0	1	1	4	5	1
17	FRA	2	1	1	0	5	10	2

1966

9	FRG	7	7	0	0	34	12	14
10	ROM	7	5	1	1	29	16	11
11	YUG	7	4	1	2	25	23	10
12	NOR	7	4	3	0	28	17	8
13	AUT	7	3	4	0	25	30	6
14	SUI	7	2	5	0	24	26	4
15	HUN	7	1	6	0	19	30	2
16	GBR	7	0	6	1	15	45	1

1967

9	POL	7	5	0	2	32	13	12
10	ROM	7	5	0	2	34	18	12
11	NOR	7	0	2	5	35	38	5
12	YUG	7	2	1	4	36	31	8
13	ITA	7	2	3	2	26	31	6
14	AUT	6	2	3	1	21	29	5
15	SUI	7	1	4	2	25	37	4
16	HUN	7	0	4	3	28	40	3

1968

9	YUG	5	5	0	0	33	9	10
10	JAP	5	4	1	0	27	12	8
11	NOR	5	3	2	0	15	15	6
12	ROM	5	2	3	0	22	23	4
13	AUT	5	1	4	0	12	27	2
14	FRA	5	0	5	0	9	32	0

1969

7	GDR	7	7	0	0	62	13	14
8	POL	7	6	1	0	31	13	12
9	YUG	7	3	2	2	17	20	8
10	FRG	7	4	3	0	28	16	8
11	NOR	7	2	3	2	26	35	6
12	ROM	7	2	4	1	24	36	5
13	AUT	6	1	4	1	12	28	3
14	ITA	7	0	7	0	10	41	0

1970

7	USA	7	7	0	0	70	11	14
8	FRG	7	6	1	0	34	13	12
9	NOR	7	3	2	2	26	28	8
10	YUG	7	3	3	1	30	23	7
11	JAP	7	3	3	1	31	34	7
12	SUI	7	2	5	0	22	31	4
13	ROM	7	2	5	0	21	38	4
14	BUL	7	0	7	0	11	67	0

1971

7	SUI	7	6	0	1	31	14	13
8	POL	7	5	1	1	36	19	11
9	GDR	7	5	2	0	49	24	10
10	NOR	7	4	3	0	37	32	8
11	YUG	7	2	4	1	25	34	5
12	JAP	7	2	4	1	33	40	5
13	AUT	7	1	6	0	17	34	2
14	ITA	7	0	5	2	12	43	2

1972

7	POL	6	6	0	0	41	12	12
8	USA	6	5	1	0	39	22	10
9	GDR	6	4	2	0	31	18	8
10	ROM	6	3	3	0	25	26	6
11	JAP	6	1	4	1	20	49	3
12	YUG	6	1	5	0	25	28	2
13	NOR	6	0	5	1	15	41	1

1973

7	GDR	7	7	0	0	56	21	14
8	USA	7	5	1	1	52	23	11
9	YUG	7	4	1	2	36	22	10
10	ROM	7	4	2	1	24	20	9
11	JAP	7	2	5	0	23	28	4
12	AUT	7	2	5	0	21	44	4
13	SUI	7	2	5	0	26	44	4
14	ITA	7	0	7	0	18	54	0

1974

7	USA	7	7	0	0	40	14	14
8	YUG	7	4	1	2	41	27	10
9	FRG	7	5	2	0	34	28	10
10	JAP	7	4	3	0	31	31	8
11	HOL	7	2	4	1	33	37	5
12	ROM	7	2	4	1	30	29	5
13	NOR	7	1	5	1	18	31	3
14	AUT	7	0	6	1	12	42	1

1975

7	GDR	7	6	1	0	41	18	12
8	FRG	7	6	1	0	34	17	12
9	SUI	7	4	3	0	31	33	8
10	YUG	7	3	3	1	30	23	7
11	ROM	7	3	2	2	26	26	6
12	JAP	7	2	3	2	21	24	6
13	ITA	7	2	5	0	22	40	4
14	HOL	7	0	6	1	11	35	1

1976

9	ROM	7	5	1	1	40	23	11
10	JAP	7	5	2	0	34	17	10
11	NOR	7	4	3	0	29	21	8
12	SUI	7	4	3	0	25	28	8
13	YUG	7	4	3	0	37	26	8
14	HOL	7	3	4	0	22	30	6
15	ITA	7	2	4	1	23	41	5
16	BUL	7	0	7	0	23	47	0

1977

9	GDR	8	8	0	0	57	16	16
10	POL	8	6	2	0	39	22	12
11	JAP	8	5	2	1	30	21	11
12	NOR	8	3	2	3	28	30	9
13	SUI	8	4	4	0	35	33	8
14	HUN	8	3	5	0	27	46	6
15	YUG	8	2	5	1	30	36	5
16	HOL	8	1	5	2	23	39	4
17	AUT	8	0	7	1	19	45	1

1978

9	POL	7	6	0	1	51	19	13
10	JAP	7	5	1	1	26	17	11
11	SUI	7	4	2	1	42	32	9
12	ROM	7	3	3	1	41	29	7
13	HUN	7	3	4	0	21	36	6
14	NOR	7	2	4	1	29	34	5
15	ITA	7	1	5	1	32	41	3
16	YUG	7	1	6	0	14	48	2

1979

9	HOL	6	6	0	0	36	13	12
10	GDR	6	5	1	0	42	12	10
11	ROM	6	3	2	1	27	21	7
12	NOR	6	3	3	0	17	25	6
13	SUI	6	4	2	0	23	20	8
14	JAP	7	3	4	0	36	30	6
15	AUT	5	2	2	1	17	23	5
16	DEN	6	1	5	0	13	32	2
17	HUN	4	0	4	0	10	25	0
18	PRC	4	0	4	0	8	28	0

1981

9	ITA	7	6	0	1	38	18	13
10	POL	7	5	1	1	49	25	11
11	SUI	7	4	1	2	28	20	10
12	GDR	7	4	1	2	37	25	9
13	ROM	7	2	5	0	25	30	4
14	NOR	7	2	5	0	21	39	4
15	YUG	7	1	5	1	23	44	3
16	JAP	7	1	6	0	18	38	2

1982

9	GDR	7	6	0	1	48	25	13
10	AUT	7	4	2	1	33	26	9
11	POL	7	4	1	2	42	23	9
12	NOR	7	3	4	0	24	43	6
13	ROM	7	2	4	1	27	30	5
14	SUI	7	1	3	3	20	27	5
15	PRC	7	2	4	1	32	47	5
16	HOL	7	2	5	0	22	27	4

1983

9	USA	7	6	0	1	53	14	13
10	POL	7	5	1	1	43	19	11
11	AUT	7	3	0	4	41	27	10
12	NOR	7	4	3	0	29	28	8
13	JAP	7	2	3	2	23	31	6
14	SUI	7	1	4	2	25	35	4
15	ROM	7	1	5	1	20	48	3
16	YUG	7	0	6	1	18	50	1

1985

9	POL	7	6	0	1	37	13	13
10	SUI	7	5	1	1	29	13	11
11	ITA	7	5	2	0	29	22	10
12	AUT	7	3	4	0	18	24	6
13	JAP	7	3	4	0	31	36	6
14	HOL	7	3	4	0	36	25	6
15	NOR	7	2	5	0	28	38	4
16	HUN	7	0	7	0	17	54	0

Rank	Team	GP	W	L	T	GF	GA	Pts
1986								
9	SUI	7	6	1	0	38	20	12
10	ITA	7	4	3	0	21	18	8
11	GDR	7	4	3	0	25	21	8
12	FRA	7	3	4	0	22	25	6
13	HOL	7	3	4	0	25	32	6
14	AUT	7	3	4	0	24	27	6
15	YUG	7	3	4	0	24	25	6
16	JAP	7	2	5	0	15	26	4
1987								
9	POL	7	6	1	0	39	11	12
10	NOR	7	5	1	1	33	25	11
11	AUT	7	5	2	0	41	27	10
12	FRA	7	4	2	1	37	26	9
13	GDR	7	2	3	2	25	31	6
14	ITA	7	2	4	1	28	30	5
15	HOL	7	1	5	1	30	37	3
16	PRC	7	0	7	0	14	60	0
1989								
9	NOR	7	5	1	1	28	16	11
10	ITA	7	5	1	1	37	16	11
11	FRA	7	4	1	2	29	18	10
12	SUI	7	5	2	0	40	21	10
13	GDR	7	3	4	0	22	29	6
14	AUT	7	2	5	0	25	32	4
15	JAP	7	2	5	0	20	34	4
16	DEN	7	0	7	0	9	44	0
1990								
9	SUI	7	5	0	2	30	14	12
10	ITA	7	3	2	2	29	18	8
11	AUT	7	4	1	2	30	14	10
12	FRA	7	4	1	2	19	17	10
13	GDR	7	2	3	2	22	19	6
14	POL	7	3	2	2	25	16	8
15	JAP	7	0	6	1	13	41	1
16	HOL	7	0	6	1	14	43	1
1991								
9	ITA	7	7	0	0	49	10	14
10	NOR	7	5	2	0	26	13	10
11	FRA	7	5	2	0	28	18	10
12	POL	7	4	3	0	25	15	8
13	AUT	7	3	3	1	21	18	7
14	YUG	7	2	5	0	18	36	4
15	HOL	7	1	6	0	9	40	2
16	JAP	7	0	6	1	9	35	1
1992								
13	AUT	7	7	0	0	73	4	14
14	HOL	7	5	1	1	53	16	11
15	JAP	7	4	3	0	30	24	8
16	DEN	7	4	3	0	23	24	8
17	BUL	7	3	4	0	14	38	6
18	ROM	7	1	3	3	13	26	5
19	PRC	7	1	5	1	15	50	3
20	YUG	7	0	6	1	7	46	1
1993								
13	GBR	7	7	0	0	50	13	14
14	POL	7	6	1	0	71	12	12
15	HOL	7	5	2	0	47	20	10
16	DEN	7	4	3	0	38	24	8
17	JAP	7	3	4	0	34	31	6
18	ROM	7	2	5	0	20	44	4
19	PRC	7	1	6	0	12	79	2
20	BUL	7	0	7	0	9	58	0
1994								
13	SUI	7	6	0	1	52	9	13
14	LAT	7	6	1	0	61	9	12
15	POL	7	5	1	1	45	21	11
16	JAP	7	3	3	1	37	38	7
17	DEN	7	3	4	0	31	27	6
18	HOL	7	2	4	1	23	33	5
19	ROM	7	1	6	0	18	43	2
20	PRC	7	0	7	0	11	98	0
1995								
13	SVK	7	7	0	0	60	15	14
14	LAT	7	6	1	0	65	16	12
15	POL	7	4	3	0	29	30	8
16	HOL	8	3	5	0	22	41	6
17	DEN	6	3	3	0	28	25	6
18	JAP	7	2	5	0	26	45	4
19	GBR	7	2	5	0	19	35	4
20	ROM	7	1	6	0	15	57	2
1996								
13	LAT	7	6	0	1	41	16	13
14	SUI	7	5	1	1	37	13	11
15	BLR	7	5	2	0	29	18	10
16	GBR	7	4	2	1	29	23	9
17	POL	7	1	4	2	18	27	4
18	DEN	7	1	5	1	14	32	3
19	HOL	7	1	5	1	12	35	3
20	JAP	7	0	4	3	14	30	3
1997								
13	BLR	7	7	0	0	48	21	14
14	KAZ	7	5	1	1	31	21	11
15	SUI	7	3	2	2	26	22	8
16	AUT	7	2	2	3	22	22	7
17	POL	7	2	3	2	19	24	6
18	GBR	7	2	4	1	28	22	5
19	HOL	7	2	4	1	21	38	5
20	DEN	7	0	7	0	19	44	0

World Championships, Pool C

Rank	Team	GP	W	L	T	GF	GA	Pts
1961								
15	ROM	5	5	0	0	69	5	10
16	FRA	5	4	1	0	34	16	8
17	YUG	5	3	2	0	34	22	6
18	HOL	5	2	3	0	18	36	4
19	SAF	5	1	4	0	18	47	2
20	BEL	5	0	5	0	9	56	0
1963								
16	AUT	5	5	0	0	62	7	10
17	HUN	5	4	1	0	57	12	8
18	DEN	5	3	2	0	22	31	6
19	BUL	5	1	3	1	19	22	3
20	HOL	5	1	3	1	21	34	3
21	BEL	5	0	5	0	8	83	0
1966								
17	ITA	4	4	0	0	54	8	8
18	DEN	4	2	2	0	21	21	4
19	SAF	4	0	4	0	4	50	0
20	FRA							
1967								
17	JAP	4	4	0	0	46	8	8
18	BUL	4	2	2	0	17	17	4
19	DEN	4	2	2	0	18	23	4
20	FRA	4	1	3	0	18	21	2
21	HOL	4	1	3	0	19	49	2
1969								
15	JAP	5	4	1	0	36	10	8
16	SUI	5	4	1	0	41	9	8
17	HUN	5	0	2	3	26	39	3
18	HOL	5	2	2	1	24	40	5
19	BUL	5	2	2	1	21	28	5
20	DEN	5	0	4	1	10	32	1
1970								
15	AUT	6	5	0	1	44	9	11
16	ITA	6	0	0	6	27	27	6
17	HUN	6	3	2	1	35	15	7
18	FRA	6	4	1	1	32	15	9
19	DEN	6	1	3	2	21	27	4
20	HOL	6	1	3	2	19	37	4
21	BEL	6	0	5	1	15	63	1
1971								
15	ROM	7	6	0	1	70	12	13
16	FRA	7	6	1	0	45	19	12
17	HUN	7	5	1	1	58	27	11
18	GBR	7	3	3	1	47	39	7
19	BUL	7	2	4	1	36	32	5
20	DEN	7	2	5	0	33	30	4
21	HOL	7	2	5	0	31	30	4
22	BEL	7	0	7	0	7	138	0
1972								
14	AUT	6	5	0	1	21	12	11
15	ITA	6	4	1	1	31	13	9
16	HUN	6	2	2	2	31	24	6
17	BUL	6	3	3	0	20	19	6
18	PRC	6	2	2	2	19	20	6
19	HOL	6	1	5	0	13	25	2
20	DEN	6	1	5	0	11	33	2
1973								
15	NOR	7	7	0	0	53	14	14
16	HOL	7	5	2	0	52	21	10
17	HUN	7	5	2	0	44	24	10
18	BUL	7	3	3	1	29	28	7
19	PRC	7	2	3	2	21	28	6
20	FRA	7	3	4	0	23	29	6
21	DEN	7	0	5	2	22	58	2
22	GBR	7	0	6	1	18	60	1
1974								
15	SUI	7	6	1	0	63	4	12
16	ITA	7	5	1	1	42	14	11
17	BUL	7	4	2	1	39	18	9
18	HUN	7	3	1	3	38	22	9
19	FRA	7	4	3	0	37	25	8
20	PRC	7	1	4	2	16	38	4
21	AUS	7	1	6	0	13	74	2
22	PRK	7	0	6	1	12	65	1
1975								
15	NOR	6	5	0	1	43	3	11
16	BUL	6	4	1	1	40	17	9
17	AUT	6	3	2	1	32	16	7
18	HUN	6	3	2	1	44	21	7
19	FRA	6	2	2	2	32	22	6
20	DEN	6	1	5	0	26	32	2
21	BEL	6	0	6	0	5	111	0
1976								
17	AUT	10	7	2	1	70	25	15
18	HUN	10	6	3	1	74	30	13
19	FRA	10	4	4	2	46	40	10
20	DEN	10	2	8	0	42	56	4
21	GBR	4	0	4	0	6	44	0
1977								
18	ITA	6	5	0	1	64	6	11
19	DEN	6	5	0	1	61	15	11
20	BUL	6	4	2	0	47	25	8
21	FRA	6	3	3	0	37	24	6
22	ESP	6	1	5	0	17	61	2
23	BEL	6	1	5	0	24	89	2
24	GBR	6	1	5	0	17	47	2
1978								
17	HOL	7	6	0	1	74	17	13
18	AUT	7	5	1	1	65	31	11
19	DEN	7	4	2	1	59	25	9
20	PRC	7	4	3	0	47	30	8
21	BUL	7	3	3	1	27	30	7
22	FRA	7	3	4	0	46	39	6
23	ESP	7	1	6	0	26	84	2
24	BEL	7	0	7	0	13	101	0
1979								
19	YUG	7	7	0	0	83	10	14
20	ITA	7	6	1	0	64	17	12
21	FRA	7	5	2	0	59	27	10
22	BUL	7	4	3	0	35	28	8
23	ESP	7	2	5	0	25	48	4
24	GBR	7	2	5	0	23	68	4
25	KOR	7	1	5	1	16	67	3
26	AUS	7	0	6	1	13	53	1
1981								
17	AUT	7	7	0	0	43	5	14
18	PRC	7	6	1	0	46	14	12
19	HUN	7	4	2	1	38	22	9
20	DEN	7	3	3	1	36	27	7
21	FRA	7	3	4	0	48	36	6
22	BUL	7	3	4	0	22	32	6
23	PRK	7	1	6	0	18	66	2
24	GBR	7	0	7	0	11	60	0
1982								
17	JAP	7	7	0	0	70	14	14
18	YUG	7	5	2	0	59	20	10
19	DEN	7	4	2	1	35	20	9
20	FRA	7	4	3	0	56	30	8
21	HUN	7	4	3	0	43	29	8
22	BUL	7	2	4	1	29	30	5
23	ESP	7	1	6	0	26	50	2
24	KOR	7	0	7	0	11	136	0
1983								
17	HOL	7	7	0	0	78	11	14
18	HUN	7	5	2	0	50	25	10
19	PRC	7	4	2	1	28	23	9
20	DEN	7	4	3	0	24	26	8
21	FRA	7	3	3	1	41	25	7
22	BUL	7	1	5	1	20	36	3
23	ESP	7	1	5	1	17	55	3
24	PRK	7	1	6	0	15	72	2
1985								
17	FRA	7	6	0	1	54	13	13
18	YUG	7	6	1	0	36	13	12
19	PRC	7	5	1	1	45	22	11
20	ROM	7	4	3	0	51	29	8
21	DEN	7	3	4	0	16	23	6
22	BUL	7	2	5	0	27	45	4
23	PRK	7	1	6	0	18	56	2
24	ESP	7	0	7	0	9	55	0
1986								
17	NOR	6	5	0	1	55	11	11
18	PRC	6	4	0	2	42	10	10
19	BUL	6	4	2	0	21	30	8
20	ROM	6	3	3	0	33	20	6
21	DEN	6	4	2	0	32	18	8
22	HUN	6	2	3	1	31	27	5
23	PRK	6	1	4	1	14	27	3
24	ESP	6	1	4	1	19	47	3
1987								
17	JAP	7	5	1	1	61	13	11
18	DEN	7	5	1	1	47	23	11
19	ROM	7	5	1	1	48	22	11
20	YUG	7	3	0	4	60	23	10
21	HUN	7	3	4	0	33	28	6
22	PRK	7	2	5	0	13	45	4
23	BUL	7	1	5	1	21	40	3
24	BEL	7	0	7	0	8	97	0
1989								
17	HOL	7	7	0	0	48	15	14
18	YUG	7	6	1	0	55	14	12
19	PRC	7	4	2	1	31	29	9
20	HUN	7	3	3	1	32	30	7
21	BUL	7	3	3	1	35	35	7
22	PRK	7	2	5	0	26	40	4
23	KOR	7	1	5	1	26	46	3
24	AUS	7	0	7	0	14	58	0
1990								
17	YUG	8	7	0	1	57	16	15
18	DEN	8	7	1	0	55	14	14
19	PRC	8	4	3	1	34	29	9
20	ROM	8	4	3	1	36	27	9
21	PRK	8	5	3	0	28	34	10
22	BUL	8	4	4	0	31	38	8
23	HUN	8	2	5	1	33	28	5
24	BEL	8	1	7	0	16	67	2
25	KOR	8	0	8	0	21	58	0
1991								
17	DEN	8	7	0	1	71	13	15
18	PRC	8	6	1	1	44	24	13
19	ROM	8	6	2	0	51	22	12
20	BUL	8	4	3	1	35	26	9
21	GBR	8	4	3	1	45	25	9
22	HUN	8	3	4	1	37	32	7
23	PRK	8	2	5	1	29	35	5
24	KOR	8	1	7	0	19	64	2
25	BEL	8	0	8	0	11	101	0
1992								
13	GBR	5	5	0	0	62	10	10
14	PRK	5	3	2	0	22	28	6
15	AUS	5	2	2	1	24	23	5
16	HUN	5	2	3	0	18	33	4
17	BEL	5	2	3	0	17	24	4
18	KOR	5	0	4	1	18	43	1
19	ESP	5	5	0	0	114	5	10
20	SAF	5	4	1	0	49	17	8
21	GRE	5	3	2	0	36	31	6
22	ISR	5	1	3	1	22	42	3
23	LUX	5	1	3	1	20	73	3
24	TUR	5	0	5	0	10	83	0

1993

Rank	Team	GP	W	L	T	GF	GA	Pts
17	LAT	9	8	0	1	120	14	17
18	UKR	9	6	2	1	113	20	13
19	KAZ	9	6	3	0	91	19	12
20	SLO	9	7	2	0	100	19	14
21	HUN	5	3	2	0	36	31	6
22	PRK	5	3	2	0	30	26	6
23	AUS	5	2	3	0	19	51	4
24	BEL	5	2	3	0	19	74	4
25	KOR	6	2	4	0	23	63	4
26	ESP	6	1	5	0	21	46	2
27	ISR	7	2	5	0	30	97	4
28	SAF	5	0	5	0	8	100	0

1994

Rank	Team	GP	W	L	T	GF	GA	Pts
21	SVK	6	4	0	2	43	3	10
22	BLR	6	5	1	0	35	11	10
23	UKR	6	3	1	2	49	7	8
24	KAZ	6	3	1	2	52	12	8
25	SLO	6	2	4	0	26	27	4
26	HUN	6	1	5	0	14	47	2
27	BUL	6	0	6	0	3	115	0
28	EST	7	7	0	0	77	5	14
29	ESP	5	3	1	1	30	16	7
30	KOR	5	3	1	1	13	16	7
31	CRO	7	4	3	0	65	17	8
32	BEL	5	3	2	0	25	21	6
33	AUS	5	2	3	0	20	16	4
34	ISR	5	1	4	0	15	31	2
35	SAF	5	0	5	0	8	62	0

1995

Rank	Team	GP	W	L	T	GF	GA	Pts
21	BLR	4	3	1	0	14	8	6
22	KAZ	4	3	0	1	23	3	7
23	UKR	4	2	1	1	28	9	5
24	EST	4	3	1	0	22	16	6
25	PRC	4	2	2	0	13	26	4
26	HUN	4	1	3	0	15	20	2
27	SLO	4	2	2	0	28	15	4
28	YUG	4	1	3	0	13	31	2
29	BUL	4	0	4	0	4	32	0
30	CRO	6	5	0	1	50	17	11
31	LIT	6	5	0	1	48	13	11
32	ESP	6	4	2	0	42	19	8
33	KOR	6	3	3	0	42	19	6
34	BEL	6	2	3	1	30	27	5
35	ISR	6	3	3	0	31	22	6
36	AUS	6	3	3	0	31	31	6
37	SAF	6	1	5	0	14	47	2
38	GRE	4	0	3	1	9	56	1
39	NZL	4	0	4	0	7	53	0

1996

Rank	Team	GP	W	L	T	GF	GA	Pts
21	KAZ	7	6	1	0	51	10	12
22	UKR	7	6	1	0	40	13	12
23	SLO	7	5	2	0	41	19	10
24	HUN	7	2	3	2	34	31	6
25	EST	7	3	3	1	36	29	7
26	ROM	7	3	4	0	32	27	6
27	PRC	7	1	5	1	23	68	3
28	CRO	7	0	7	0	11	71	0

1997

Rank	Team	GP	W	L	T	GF	GA	Pts
21	UKR	5	4	0	1	21	6	9
22	SLO	5	3	2	0	25	13	6
23	EST	5	2	1	2	27	17	6
24	JAP	5	2	1	2	14	9	6
25	ROM	5	3	2	0	15	20	6
26	HUN	5	2	2	1	18	16	5
27	PRC	5	1	4	0	16	34	2
28	LIT	5	0	5	0	11	32	0

World Championships, Pool D

1987

Rank	Team	GP	W	L	T	GF	GA	Pts
25	AUS	6	5	0	1	176	6	11
26	KOR	6	4	1	1	130	16	9
27	NZL	6	2	4	0	42	142	4
28	HKG	6	0	6	0	1	185	0

1989

Rank	Team	GP	W	L	T	GF	GA	Pts
25	BEL	4	3	0	1	35	9	7
26	ROM	4	2	0	2	69	7	6
27	GBR	4	1	1	2	19	16	4
28	ESP	4	1	3	0	29	27	2
29	NZL	4	0	3	1	3	96	1

1990

Rank	Team	GP	W	L	T	GF	GA	Pts
26	GBR	4	4	0	0	57	7	8
27	AUS	4	0	2	2	10	34	2
28	ESP	4	0	2	2	11	37	2

1996

Rank	Team	GP	W	L	T	GF	GA	Pts
29	LIT	5	5	0	0	33	4	10
30	YUG	5	4	1	0	20	10	8
31	ESP	5	2	2	1	22	18	5
32	BEL	5	2	3	0	10	24	4
33	KOR	5	2	1	2	24	17	6
34	BUL	5	2	3	0	16	16	4
35	ISR	7	2	4	1	30	21	5
36	AUS	5	0	5	0	14	43	0

1997

Rank	Team	GP	W	L	T	GF	GA	Pts
29	CRO	5	3	1	1	16	9	7
30	KOR	5	4	1	0	19	9	8
31	ESP	5	2	3	0	21	19	4
32	YUG	5	1	2	2	13	18	4
33	ISR	5	2	3	0	18	25	4
34	AUS	5	1	3	1	20	25	3
35	BUL	5	2	1	2	17	15	6
36	BEL	5	2	3	0	12	16	4

World Junior Championships, Pool B

1979

Rank	Team	GP	W	L	T	GF	GA	Pts
9	SUI	4	4	0	0	32	11	8
10	FRA	4	3	1	0	26	13	6
11	POL	4	3	1	0	43	17	6
12	DEN	4	2	2	0	13	14	4
13	AUT	4	2	2	0	17	20	4
14	HOL	4	1	3	0	16	23	2
15	ITA	4	1	3	0	22	21	2
16	BEL	4	0	4	0	9	59	0

1980

Rank	Team	GP	W	L	T	GF	GA	Pts
9	AUT	4	4	0	0	33	9	8
10	POL	4	3	1	0	30	10	6
11	NOR	4	3	1	0	28	10	6
12	HOL	4	2	2	0	19	16	4
13	DEN	4	2	2	0	18	19	4
14	ITA	4	1	3	0	12	20	2
15	FRA	4	1	3	0	19	31	2
16	HUN	4	0	4	0	11	55	0

1981

Rank	Team	GP	W	L	T	GF	GA	Pts
9	SUI	5	4	0	1	34	10	9
10	NOR	5	3	0	2	32	18	8
11	POL	5	3	2	0	34	16	6
12	HOL	5	2	3	0	10	28	4
13	DEN	5	3	2	0	22	22	6
14	YUG	5	1	3	1	20	27	3
15	ITA	5	1	3	1	17	33	3
16	FRA	5	0	4	1	20	35	1

1982

Rank	Team	GP	W	L	T	GF	GA	Pts
9	NOR	4	4	0	0	18	9	8
10	AUT	4	3	1	0	21	13	6
11	JAP	4	3	1	0	23	13	6
12	DEN	4	2	2	0	22	18	4
13	FRA	4	2	2	0	18	16	4
14	ITA	4	0	3	1	9	19	1
15	HOL	4	1	2	1	12	19	3
16	YUG	4	0	4	0	12	28	0
9	SUI	5	4	1	0	29	14	8

1983

Rank	Team	GP	W	L	T	GF	GA	Pts
10	JAP	5	3	2	0	30	19	6
11	POL	5	4	1	0	29	17	8
12	AUT	5	2	3	0	23	25	4
13	FRA	5	2	2	1	32	21	5
14	HOL	5	2	2	1	32	35	5
15	DEN	5	1	3	1	17	41	3
16	ITA	5	0	4	1	18	38	1

1984

Rank	Team	GP	W	L	T	GF	GA	Pts
9	POL	5	4	0	1	29	18	9
10	AUT	5	4	1	0	22	17	8
11	JAP	5	2	1	2	30	21	6
12	NOR	5	2	3	0	29	21	4
13	HOL	5	3	1	1	22	20	7
14	FRA	5	2	3	0	28	25	4
15	ROM	5	1	4	0	15	33	2
16	DEN	5	0	5	0	9	29	0

1985

Rank	Team	GP	W	L	T	GF	GA	Pts
9	SUI	7	7	0	0	58	22	14
10	HOL	7	5	1	1	47	14	11
11	JAP	7	4	2	1	34	23	9
12	AUT	7	3	3	1	30	53	7
13	NOR	7	2	4	1	23	28	5
14	ITA	7	2	5	0	14	28	4
15	ROM	7	1	5	1	27	42	3
16	FRA	7	1	5	1	19	42	3

1986

Rank	Team	GP	W	L	T	GF	GA	Pts
9	POL	7	6	1	0	46	17	12
10	NOR	7	5	1	1	54	18	11
11	AUT	7	5	2	0	42	35	10
12	ROM	7	3	2	2	32	28	8
13	JAP	7	3	4	0	35	31	6
14	HOL	7	3	4	0	30	43	6
15	ITA	7	1	5	1	26	40	3
16	BUL	7	0	7	0	9	62	0

1987

Rank	Team	GP	W	L	T	GF	GA	Pts
9	FRG	5	4	0	1	48	11	9
10	NOR	5	3	1	1	38	25	7
11	JAP	5	3	2	0	28	24	6
12	AUT	5	1	3	1	14	36	3
13	FRA	5	3	1	1	21	16	7
14	ROM	5	2	3	0	25	36	4
15	HOL	5	1	3	1	25	30	3
16	ITA	5	0	4	1	14	35	1

1988

Rank	Team	GP	W	L	T	GF	GA	Pts
9	NOR	7	5	2	0	38	18	10
10	ROM	7	5	2	0	24	27	10
11	SUI	7	4	2	1	34	23	9
12	JAP	7	3	2	2	34	27	8
13	FRA	7	4	3	0	31	36	8
14	YUG	7	3	3	1	37	36	7
15	HOL	7	0	4	3	20	35	3
16	AUT	7	0	6	1	26	42	1

1989

Rank	Team	GP	W	L	T	GF	GA	Pts
9	POL	7	7	0	0	48	20	14
10	SUI	7	6	1	0	45	19	12
11	ROM	7	4	3	0	32	31	8
12	JAP	7	4	3	0	32	34	8
13	YUG	7	4	3	0	42	40	8
14	FRA	7	1	5	1	23	31	3
15	DEN	9	3	5	1	31	46	7
16	HOL	7	0	7	0	17	47	0
DNQ	ITA	2	0	2	0	4	6	0

1990

Rank	Team	GP	W	L	T	GF	GA	Pts
9	SUI	7	6	1	0	48	14	12
10	FRG	7	6	1	0	35	12	12
11	JAP	7	4	2	1	38	33	9
12	DEN	7	2	3	2	26	31	6
13	FRA	7	3	4	0	39	30	6
14	AUT	7	2	4	1	20	43	5
15	ROM	7	2	5	0	26	39	4
16	YUG	7	0	5	2	25	55	2

1991

Rank	Team	GP	W	L	T	GF	GA	Pts
9	GER	7	6	0	1	47	15	13
10	POL	7	6	1	0	53	17	12
11	FRA	7	4	1	2	42	19	10
12	JAP	7	4	2	1	34	22	9
13	ROM	7	2	4	1	23	43	5
14	HOL	7	1	5	1	16	41	3
15	AUT	7	1	6	0	13	48	2
16	DEN	7	1	6	0	22	45	2

1992

Rank	Team	GP	W	L	T	GF	GA	Pts
9	JAP	7	5	2	0	32	17	10
10	POL	7	5	2	0	42	19	10
11	NOR	7	5	2	0	45	17	10
12	FRA	7	5	2	0	31	15	10
13	ROM	7	4	3	0	23	26	8
14	HOL	7	2	5	0	14	38	4
15	AUT	7	2	5	0	16	29	4
16	PRK	7	0	7	0	12	54	0

1993

Rank	Team	GP	W	L	T	GF	GA	Pts
9	SUI	7	6	0	1	39	13	13
10	NOR	7	6	1	0	49	11	12
11	ITA	7	4	2	1	23	18	9
12	AUT	7	4	3	0	26	23	8
13	FRA	7	3	4	0	26	30	6
14	POL	7	1	5	1	17	28	3
15	ROM	7	1	5	1	16	37	3
16	HOL	7	1	6	0	10	46	2

1994

Rank	Team	GP	W	L	T	GF	GA	Pts
9	UKR	7	7	0	0	35	8	14
10	NOR	7	5	1	1	26	15	11
11	FRA	7	3	3	1	23	23	7
12	POL	7	3	4	0	15	26	6
13	ITA	7	2	4	1	20	22	5
14	AUT	7	1	3	3	21	27	5
15	JAP	7	2	5	0	19	27	4
16	ROM	7	1	4	2	21	32	4

1995

Rank	Team	GP	W	L	T	GF	GA	Pts
9	SUI	7	5	0	2	40	12	12
10	SVK	7	5	2	0	33	16	10
11	POL	7	4	2	1	26	22	9
12	FRA	7	5	2	0	25	14	10
13	NOR	7	2	4	1	26	27	5
14	AUT	7	2	4	1	20	31	5
15	JAP	7	1	5	1	17	44	3
16	ITA	7	1	6	0	16	37	2

1996

Rank	Team	GP	W	L	T	GF	GA	Pts
11	POL	6	6	0	0	47	7	12
12	LAT	6	5	1	0	27	20	10
13	NOR	6	3	3	0	18	16	6
14	HUN	6	3	3	0	24	20	6
15	ITA	6	2	4	0	13	27	4
16	JAP	6	1	5	0	13	31	2
NR	FRA	5	3	2	0	18	14	6
NR	AUT	5	0	5	0	10	35	0

1997

Rank	Team	GP	W	L	T	GF	GA	Pts
11	KAZ	7	6	0	1	39	15	13
12	LAT	7	5	1	1	28	19	11
13	FRA	7	4	1	2	22	18	10
14	NOR	7	2	2	3	33	23	7
15	UKR	7	3	3	1	26	18	7
16	JAP	7	2	3	2	24	17	6
17	HUN	7	1	6	0	14	44	2
18	ITA	7	0	7	0	12	46	0

World Junior Championships, Pool C

1983

Rank	Team	GP	W	L	T	GF	GA	Pts
17	ROM	6	6	0	0	49	9	12
18	BUL	6	3	3	0	16	18	6
19	HUN	6	3	3	0	21	30	6
20	AUS	6	0	6	0	12	41	0

1984

Rank	Team	GP	W	L	T	GF	GA	Pts
17	ITA	5	4	0	1	41	14	9
18	BUL	5	3	1	1	24	12	7
19	HUN	5	3	1	1	34	18	7
20	ESP	5	2	2	1	21	29	5
21	BEL	5	3	2	0	26	18	6
22	GBR	5	2	3	0	22	36	4
23	AUS	5	1	4	0	19	37	2
NR	ITA–2	5	0	5	0	7	30	0

Rank	Team	GP	W	L	T	GF	GA	Pts
1985								
17	BUL	5	5	0	0	28	17	10
18	HUN	5	4	1	0	35	12	8
19	BEL	5	2	2	1	32	27	5
20	DEN	5	2	2	1	20	24	5
21	GBR	5	1	4	0	10	37	2
22	ESP	5	0	5	0	18	26	0
1986								
17	FRA	5	4	0	1	52	13	9
18	DEN	5	3	0	2	29	16	8
19	GBR	5	3	2	0	20	32	6
20	PRC	5	2	3	0	23	27	4
21	HUN	5	1	4	0	16	32	2
22	BEL	5	0	4	1	14	34	1
1987								
17	YUG	5	5	0	0	56	12	10
18	DEN	5	4	1	0	44	24	8
19	GBR	5	3	2	0	25	21	6
20	BUL	5	2	3	0	21	23	4
21	ESP	5	1	4	0	19	34	2
22	AUS	5	0	5	0	5	56	0
1988								
17	DEN	7	7	0	0	59	11	14
18	ITA	7	6	1	0	27	17	12
19	BUL	7	5	2	0	39	16	10
20	GBR	7	3	3	1	21	27	7
21	ESP	7	2	4	1	19	45	5
22	HUN	7	2	5	0	14	28	4
23	PRK	7	1	4	2	20	29	4
24	BEL	7	0	7	0	8	34	0
1989								
17	AUT	4	3	0	1	21	14	7
18	ITA	4	2	0	2	22	14	6
19	PRK	4	2	2	0	17	20	4
20	GBR	4	0	2	2	15	19	2
21	BUL	4	0	3	1	12	20	1
1990								
17	HOL	6	5	1	0	40	17	10
18	PRK	6	4	1	1	27	14	9
19	ITA	6	5	1	0	35	10	10
20	BUL	6	2	3	1	25	31	5
21	KOR	6	3	3	0	25	39	6
22	GBR	6	1	5	0	17	31	2
23	HUN	6	0	6	0	19	46	0
1991								
17	PRK	7	6	1	0	50	18	12
18	ITA	7	6	1	0	57	11	12
19	YUG	7	5	1	1	77	21	11
20	GBR	7	4	3	0	45	20	8
21	KOR	7	3	3	1	55	28	7
22	BUL	7	2	5	0	34	48	4
23	HUN	7	1	6	0	28	46	2
24	GRE	7	0	7	0	4	158	0
1992								
17	ITA	3	3	0	0	17	6	6
18	DEN	4	3	1	0	30	9	6
19	GBR	4	1	3	0	22	19	2
20	ESP	4	3	1	0	19	15	6
21	HUN	4	2	2	0	13	18	4
22	KOR	3	0	3	0	8	18	0
23	YUG	3	1	1	1	11	16	3
24	BUL	3	0	2	1	2	21	1
25	GRE	Disqualified						
1993								
17	UKR	4	4	0	0	46	6	8
18	DEN	4	2	1	1	26	18	5
19	HUN	4	2	1	1	30	19	5
20	BUL	4	1	2	1	16	32	3
21	GBR	4	2	1	1	19	14	5
22	PRK	4	0	2	2	11	28	2
23	ESP	4	1	2	1	17	26	3
24	KOR	4	0	3	1	12	34	1
1994								
17	SVK	4	4	0	0	55	3	8
18	LAT	4	3	1	0	56	9	6
19	DEN	4	3	1	0	15	31	6
20	GBR	4	2	2	0	21	27	4
21	HUN	4	2	2	0	25	19	4
22	HOL	4	1	3	0	8	33	2
23	ESP	4	1	3	0	7	30	2
24	BUL	4	0	4	0	10	45	0
1995								
17	LAT	4	4	0	0	34	8	8
18	HUN	4	3	1	0	24	8	6
19	DEN	4	3	1	0	18	13	6
20	BLR	4	2	2	0	15	12	4
21	ESP	4	2	2	0	9	19	4
22	ROM	4	1	3	0	8	20	2
23	HOL	4	1	3	0	10	25	2
24	GBR	4	0	4	0	9	22	0
25	KAZ	5	3	0	2	47	10	8
26	SLO	5	3	0	2	40	15	8
27	EST	5	2	1	2	24	25	6
28	LIT	5	2	3	0	29	30	4
29	CRO	5	0	2	3	10	21	3
30	YUG	5	0	4	1	13	62	1
1996								
17	KAZ	4	4	0	0	31	16	8
18	SLO	4	3	1	0	27	11	6
19	DEN	4	3	1	0	23	9	6
20	BLR	4	2	2	0	27	16	4
21	GBR	4	2	2	0	17	16	4
22	ROM	4	1	3	0	12	29	2
23	HOL	4	1	3	0	10	21	2
24	ESP	4	0	4	0	5	34	0
1997								
19	BLR	4	4	0	0	34	4	8
20	SLO	4	3	1	0	24	14	6
21	DEN	4	3	1	0	32	12	6
22	GBR	4	2	2	0	17	14	4
23	AUT	4	2	2	0	9	13	4
24	ROM	4	1	3	0	9	21	2
25	CRO	4	1	3	0	5	25	2
26	HOL	4	0	4	0	10	37	0

World Junior Championships, Pool D

Rank	Team	GP	W	L	T	GF	GA	Pts
1996								
25	CRO	3	3	0	0	22	4	6
26	EST	3	2	1	0	24	5	4
27	YUG	3	2	1	0	15	9	4
28	LIT	3	1	2	0	25	12	2
29	BUL	3	1	2	0	14	35	2
30	SAF	3	0	3	0	3	38	0
1997								
27	EST	4	4	0	0	46	11	8
28	LIT	4	3	1	0	49	12	6
29	YUG	4	3	1	0	26	13	6
30	ESP	4	2	2	0	18	16	4
31	ISR	4	2	2	0	20	26	4
32	BUL	4	1	3	0	12	27	2
33	SAF	4	1	3	0	8	37	2
34	MEX	4	0	4	0	8	45	0

European Junior Championships, (Under 18) Pool A

Rank	Team	GP	W	L	T	GF	GA	Pts
1968								
1	TCH	6	6	0	0	47	14	12
2	URS	7	6	1	0	52	15	12
3	SWE	7	4	2	1	71	20	9
4	FIN	5	2	3	0	26	21	4
5	POL	7	2	3	2	41	53	6
6	GDR	7	2	5	0	21	62	4
NR	FRG	1	0	1	0	0	1	0
NR	NOR	2	0	2	0	1	35	0
NR	BUL	2	0	2	0	1	13	0
NR	SUI	2	0	2	0	2	13	0
NR	FRA	2	0	1	1	7	22	1
1969								
1	URS	5	4	0	1	46	12	9
2	SWE	5	4	1	0	37	17	8
3	TCH	5	3	1	1	28	8	7
4	FRG	5	1	4	0	15	33	2
5	FIN	5	1	4	0	18	32	2
6	POL	5	1	4	0	11	53	2
1970								
1	URS	5	5	0	0	41	11	10
2	TCH	5	4	1	0	26	12	8
3	SWE	5	3	2	0	44	10	6
4	FIN	5	2	3	0	13	19	4
5	FRG	5	1	4	0	11	33	2
6	SUI	5	0	5	0	8	58	0
1971								
1	URS	5	5	0	0	46	5	10
2	SWE	5	3	1	1	46	15	7
3	TCH	5	3	1	1	40	19	7
4	FIN	5	2	3	0	30	31	4
5	FRG	5	1	4	0	10	45	2
6	NOR	5	0	5	0	7	64	0
1972								
1	SWE	5	5	0	0	32	10	10
2	URS	5	4	1	0	30	14	8
3	TCH	5	3	2	0	37	14	6
4	FIN	5	2	3	0	19	24	4
5	FRG	5	1	4	0	19	42	2
6	NOR	5	0	5	0	11	44	0
1973								
1	URS	5	5	0	0	53	8	10
2	SWE	5	3	1	1	45	16	7
3	TCH	5	3	1	1	27	19	7
4	FIN	5	2	3	0	18	35	4
5	SUI	5	1	4	0	12	47	2
6	FRG	5	0	5	0	14	44	0
1974								
1	SWE	5	5	0	0	56	9	10
2	URS	5	4	1	0	45	11	8
3	FIN	5	3	2	0	23	25	6
4	TCH	5	2	3	0	27	26	4
5	POL	5	1	4	0	15	44	2
6	SUI	5	0	5	0	10	61	0
1975								
1	URS	5	4	1	0	32	8	8
2	TCH	5	4	1	0	25	13	8
3	SWE	5	4	1	0	36	17	8
4	FIN	5	1	3	1	10	19	3
5	POL	5	1	4	0	14	34	2
6	FRG	5	0	4	1	13	39	1
1976								
1	URS	6	5	0	1	34	12	11
2	SWE	6	3	2	1	28	14	7
3	FIN	5	2	3	0	14	22	4
4	TCH	6	4	2	0	28	23	8
5	FRG	5	2	3	0	24	35	4
6	POL	5	1	4	0	22	40	2
7	SUI	5	0	5	0	13	47	0
1977								
1	SWE	6	6	0	0	58	7	12
2	TCH	6	5	1	0	49	13	10
3	URS	6	4	2	0	49	19	8
4	FIN	6	3	3	0	31	38	6
5	SUI	6	1	4	1	21	52	3
6	FRG	6	1	4	1	14	45	3
7	POL	6	0	6	0	11	59	0
8	ROM							
1978								
1	FIN	6	6	0	0	37	17	12
2	URS	6	5	1	0	37	11	10
3	SWE	6	3	3	0	30	13	6
4	TCH	6	2	4	0	25	19	4
5	POL	6	4	2	0	23	28	8
6	SUI	6	3	3	0	34	38	6
7	FRG	6	1	5	0	17	47	2
8	NOR	6	0	6	0	15	45	0
1979								
1	TCH	5	5	0	0	33	7	10
2	FIN	5	4	1	0	45	8	8
3	URS	5	3	2	0	25	11	6
4	SWE	5	2	3	0	19	17	4
5	POL	5	3	2	0	19	12	6
6	SUI	5	2	3	0	21	21	4
7	FRG	5	1	4	0	14	32	2
8	ITA	5	0	5	0	0	68	0
1980								
1	URS	5	5	0	0	42	9	10
2	TCH	5	4	1	0	35	12	8
3	SWE	5	3	2	0	18	15	6
4	FIN	5	2	3	0	20	23	4
5	FRG	5	3	2	0	26	30	6
6	POL	5	2	3	0	18	30	4
7	SUI	5	1	4	0	16	30	2
8	NOR	5	0	5	0	13	39	0
1981								
1	URS	5	4	0	1	56	8	9
2	TCH	5	3	0	2	45	10	8
3	SWE	5	3	1	1	39	20	7
4	FIN	5	2	3	0	26	21	4
5	SUI	5	2	2	1	18	28	5
6	POL	5	2	3	0	13	50	4
7	FRG	5	1	3	1	9	33	3
8	AUT	5	0	5	0	4	40	0
1982								
1	SWE	5	5	0	0	44	12	10
2	TCH	5	4	1	0	46	12	8
3	URS	5	3	2	0	28	19	6
4	FIN	5	2	3	0	20	27	4
5	SUI	5	1	3	1	16	26	3
6	FRG	5	0	3	2	9	23	2
7	FRA	5	0	4	1	11	79	1
8	POL	Did Not Play						
1983								
1	URS	5	5	0	0	44	13	10
2	FIN	5	4	1	0	30	10	8
3	TCH	5	3	2	0	33	14	6
4	SWE	5	2	3	0	29	20	4
5	FRG	5	3	2	0	27	28	6
6	FRA	5	1	3	1	16	43	3
7	SUI	5	1	4	0	12	35	2
8	NOR	5	0	4	1	14	42	1
1984								
1	URS	5	5	0	0	50	11	10
2	TCH	5	4	1	0	35	9	8
3	SWE	5	3	2	0	41	13	6
4	FIN	5	2	3	0	18	22	4
5	FRG	5	3	2	0	29	33	6
6	SUI	5	2	3	0	23	34	4
7	FRA	5	1	4	0	11	30	2
8	HOL	5	0	5	0	9	64	0
1985								
1	SWE	5	4	0	1	39	5	9
2	URS	5	4	0	1	21	5	9
3	TCH	5	3	2	0	38	15	6
4	NOR	5	1	3	1	11	31	3
5	FIN	5	2	2	1	34	23	5
6	FRG	5	2	2	1	20	16	5
7	SUI	5	1	3	1	15	26	3
8	FRA	5	0	5	0	10	67	0
1986								
1	FIN	5	4	0	1	51	14	9
2	SWE	5	2	1	2	34	17	6
3	TCH	5	2	1	2	28	14	6
4	URS	5	1	1	3	27	23	5
5	FRG	5	3	2	0	19	26	6
6	SUI	5	2	2	1	21	27	5
7	NOR	5	1	3	1	19	28	3
8	ROM	5	0	5	0	12	62	0
1987								
1	SWE	7	6	1	0	51	5	12
2	TCH	7	6	1	0	48	16	12
3	URS	7	6	1	0	43	16	12
4	FIN	7	4	3	0	41	21	8
5	SUI	7	1	4	2	14	46	4
6	POL	7	1	4	2	13	55	4
7	NOR	7	1	5	1	13	37	3
8	FRG	7	0	6	1	13	40	1

Rank	Team	GP	W	L	T	GF	GA	Pts
1988								
1	TCH	6	5	1	0	42	13	10
2	FIN	6	5	1	0	49	12	10
3	URS	6	4	1	1	44	11	9
4	SWE	6	3	2	1	46	22	7
5	NOR	6	2	4	0	22	40	4
6	SUI	6	1	5	0	13	55	2
7	ROM	6	1	4	1	12	54	3
8	POL	6	1	4	1	14	35	3
1989								
1	URS	6	6	0	0	45	7	12
2	TCH	6	5	1	0	61	18	10
3	FIN	6	3	2	1	50	14	7
4	SWE	6	3	2	1	39	25	7
5	FRG	6	2	4	0	18	42	4
6	SUI	6	1	5	0	14	69	2
7	NOR	3	0	3	0	11	33	0
8	ROM	3	0	3	0	2	32	0
1990								
1	SWE	8	7	0	1	49	16	15
2	URS	8	6	2	0	56	15	12
3	TCH	8	6	1	1	57	16	13
4	FIN	8	4	4	0	34	33	8
5	NOR	8	2	6	0	31	57	4
6	POL	8	1	7	0	24	75	2
7	FRG	6	2	4	0	19	40	4
8	SUI	6	1	5	0	13	31	2
1991								
1	TCH	6	5	0	1	50	8	11
2	URS	6	5	0	1	42	13	11
3	FIN	6	4	2	0	47	15	8
4	SWE	6	3	3	0	53	22	6
5	GER	6	2	4	0	18	60	4
6	NOR	6	1	5	0	19	65	2
7	POL	5	2	3	0	23	33	4
8	FRA	5	0	5	0	7	43	0
1992								
1	TCH	6	6	0	0	39	13	12
2	SWE	6	3	1	2	23	12	8
3	RUS	6	4	2	0	28	11	8
4	FIN	6	3	2	1	38	10	7
5	GER	6	1	3	2	16	28	4
6	POL	6	1	5	0	11	58	2
7	NOR	6	2	4	0	19	29	4
8	SUI	6	1	4	1	18	31	3
1993								
1	SWE	8	8	0	0	69	13	16
2	RUS	8	5	2	1	50	21	11
3	CZE	8	6	2	0	97	12	12
4	FIN	8	4	3	1	27	27	9
5	NOR	8	1	6	1	16	74	3
6	GER	8	0	7	1	5	64	1
7	POL	6	2	3	1	32	45	5
8	ITA	6	1	4	1	23	63	3
1994								
1	SWE	5	4	0	1	38	11	9
2	RUS	5	3	0	2	25	15	8
3	CZE	5	3	1	1	31	11	7
4	FIN	5	2	3	0	19	21	4
5	SUI	5	2	2	1	20	20	5
6	GER	5	2	3	0	26	25	4
7	NOR	5	0	3	2	12	33	2
8	POL	5	0	4	1	10	45	1
1995								
1	FIN	5	4	1	0	24	11	8
2	GER	5	2	1	2	17	15	6
3	SWE	5	3	1	1	22	17	7
4	RUS	5	3	2	0	20	13	6
5	CZE	5	3	1	1	37	11	7
6	SUI	5	2	3	0	15	16	4
7	BLR	5	0	4	1	11	36	1
8	NOR	5	0	4	1	8	35	1
1996								
1	RUS	5	3	0	2	26	12	8
2	FIN	5	4	0	1	17	9	9
3	SWE	5	3	2	0	23	12	6
4	SUI	5	2	3	0	16	22	4
5	CZE	5	3	1	1	25	8	7
6	GER	5	2	3	0	14	26	4
7	SVK	5	1	4	0	17	24	2
8	BLR	5	0	5	0	12	37	0
1997								
1	FIN	6	5	0	1	31	8	11
2	SWE	6	4	0	2	27	15	10
3	SUI	6	3	3	0	18	21	6
4	RUS	6	2	2	2	28	23	6
5	CZE	6	2	3	1	22	23	5
6	SVK	6	1	5	0	14	28	2
7	UKR	6	3	3	0	13	25	6
8	GER	6	1	5	0	12	22	2

European Junior Championships, (Under 18) Pool B

Rank	Team	GP	W	L	T	GF	GA	Pts
1969								
7	SUI							
8	HUN							
9	YUG							
10	AUT							
1970								
7	NOR							
8	HOL							
9	POL							
10	ROM							
11	AUT							
12	YUG							
13	HUN							
1971								
7	ROM							
8	POL							
9	DEN							
10	HUN							
11	BUL							
7	SUI							
1972								
8	POL							
9	YUG							
10	ROM							
11	ITA							
12	HUN							
13	AUT							
14	DEN							
15	HOL							
16	FRA							
1973								
7	POL	5	5	0	0	53	12	10
8	ITA	5	3	1	1	28	26	7
9	YUG	5	2	0	3	26	19	7
10	ROM	5	3	2	0	33	20	6
11	FRA	5	2	3	0	21	31	4
12	AUT	5	1	2	2	19	24	4
13	NOR	5	1	1	3	27	19	5
14	DEN	5	1	4	0	14	41	2
15	BUL	4	1	3	0	7	26	2
16	HOL	4	0	3	1	8	18	1
1974								
7	FRG							
8	ROM							
9	BUL							
10	NOR							
11	DEN							
12	YUG							
13	AUT							
14	FRA							
15	HUN							
16	ITA							
1975								
7	SUI	4	4	0	0	45	11	8
8	BUL	4	2	1	1	26	16	5
9	YUG	4	2	1	1	18	23	5
10	ROM	4	0	1	3	17	18	3
11	NOR	4	2	1	1	12	13	5
12	DEN	4	1	3	0	12	24	2
13	AUT	4	1	2	1	13	27	3
14	FRA	4	0	3	1	15	26	1
1976								
8	ROM							
9	YUG							
10	AUT							
11	NOR							
12	DEN							
13	FRA							
14	ITA							
15	HUN							
16	ESP							
1977								
8	NOR							
9	YUG							
10	DEN							
11	AUT							
12	ITA							
13	FRA							
14	HOL							
15	ESP							
1978								
9	ITA	5	3	1	1	21	16	7
10	FRA	5	2	1	2	23	13	6
11	ROM	4	2	0	2	28	15	6
12	YUG	4	2	2	0	14	13	4
13	AUT	4	2	1	1	27	14	5
14	HOL	4	1	3	0	11	14	2
15	DEN	4	2	2	0	23	13	4
16	BEL	4	0	4	0	4	53	0
1979								
9	NOR	4	4	0	0	21	5	8
10	ROM	4	3	1	0	20	9	6
11	YUG	4	3	1	0	16	16	6
12	FRA	4	2	2	0	15	12	4
13	HOL	4	2	2	0	19	19	4
14	HUN	4	0	3	1	15	25	1
15	AUT	4	1	2	1	19	20	3
16	DEN	4	0	4	0	5	33	0
1980								
9	AUT	4	3	1	0	22	18	6
10	YUG	4	2	1	1	18	18	5
11	BUL	4	3	1	0	19	14	6
12	ROM	4	1	3	0	21	17	2
13	FRA	4	3	1	0	24	20	6
14	ITA	4	1	2	1	15	19	3
15	HUN	4	1	3	0	25	22	2
16	HOL	4	1	3	0	17	33	2
1981								
9	FRA	5	5	0	0	28	14	10
10	NOR	5	4	1	0	34	12	8
11	YUG	5	3	2	0	22	21	6
12	ITA	5	2	3	0	23	21	4
13	ROM	5	3	2	0	35	23	6
14	DEN	5	2	3	0	44	29	4
15	BUL	5	1	4	0	22	37	2
16	HUN	5	0	5	0	10	61	0
1982								
9	NOR	5	5	0	0	45	8	10
10	AUT	5	3	2	0	27	18	6
11	HOL	5	3	2	0	24	18	6
12	DEN	5	1	3	1	8	18	3
13	ROM	5	3	2	0	27	23	6
14	BUL	5	1	2	2	16	21	4
15	ITA	5	2	2	1	25	28	5
16	YUG	5	0	5	0	10	48	0
1983								
9	HOL	5	5	0	0	36	14	10
10	DEN	5	4	1	0	34	15	8
11	ROM	5	3	2	0	33	33	6
12	ITA	5	1	3	1	22	35	3
13	AUT	5	3	2	0	34	23	6
14	POL	5	2	3	0	37	24	4
15	BUL	5	1	3	1	12	31	3
16	HUN	5	0	5	0	16	49	0
1984								
9	NOR	6	5	0	1	36	15	11
10	POL	6	5	1	0	50	20	10
11	AUT	6	3	3	0	29	36	6
12	ROM	6	2	4	0	36	52	4
13	DEN	6	4	2	0	38	26	8
14	BUL	6	1	4	1	20	33	3
15	YUG	6	2	4	0	21	34	4
16	ITA	6	0	4	2	19	33	2
1985								
9	ROM	5	5	0	0	29	10	10
10	POL	5	4	1	0	27	16	8
11	BUL	5	3	2	0	23	18	6
12	HOL	5	2	3	0	19	27	4
13	DEN	5	3	2	0	25	24	6
14	AUT	5	2	3	0	20	21	4
15	YUG	5	1	4	0	16	25	2
16	HUN	5	0	5	0	12	30	0
1986								
9	POL	5	5	0	0	52	9	10
10	DEN	5	4	1	0	27	27	8
11	FRA	5	2	3	0	18	25	4
12	BUL	5	2	3	0	23	26	4
13	ITA	5	2	2	1	16	20	5
14	YUG	5	2	3	0	22	31	4
15	AUT	5	1	3	1	13	25	3
16	HOL	5	1	4	0	17	25	2
1987								
9	ROM	6	5	1	0	40	20	10
10	DEN	6	4	2	0	35	22	8
11	ITA	6	3	3	0	26	22	6
12	FRA	6	2	4	0	23	33	4
13	YUG	5	4	1	0	31	18	8
14	AUT	5	1	4	0	11	27	2
15	GBR	5	0	5	0	11	42	0
NR	BUL	3	2	1	0	15	8	4
1988								
9	FRG	6	6	0	0	35	9	12
10	AUT	6	4	1	1	25	10	9
11	YUG	6	3	2	1	25	27	7
12	DEN	6	2	4	0	16	23	4
13	ITA	6	2	2	2	22	24	6
14	FRA	6	3	3	0	38	20	6
15	HOL	6	1	5	0	18	46	2
16	GBR	6	0	4	2	17	37	2
1989								
9	POL	5	5	0	0	44	7	10
10	FRA	5	4	1	0	29	15	8
11	AUT	5	2	2	1	24	18	5
12	DEN	5	2	2	1	18	19	5
13	HOL	5	2	2	1	20	26	5
14	ITA	5	2	3	0	21	26	4
15	YUG	5	1	3	1	18	31	3
16	BUL	5	0	5	0	11	43	0
1990								
9	FRA	7	5	0	2	51	16	12
10	ITA	7	5	1	1	45	20	11
11	ROM	7	4	0	3	34	21	11
12	YUG	7	3	2	2	26	31	8
13	AUT	7	3	4	0	25	26	6
14	DEN	7	2	4	1	34	33	5
15	HOL	7	1	5	1	16	40	3
16	ESP	7	0	7	0	21	65	0

Rank	Team	GP	W	L	T	GF	GA	Pts
1991								
9	SUI	5	5	0	0	34	6	10
10	YUG	5	3	2	0	24	17	6
11	DEN	5	3	2	0	23	17	6
12	ITA	5	3	2	0	20	17	6
13	AUT	5	3	2	0	29	21	6
14	ROM	5	2	3	0	18	24	4
15	ESP	5	1	4	0	10	28	2
16	HOL	5	0	5	0	13	41	0
1992								
9	ITA	6	4	0	2	20	12	10
10	DEN	6	5	1	0	36	25	10
11	AUT	6	3	3	0	22	14	6
12	ROM	6	2	4	0	32	31	4
13	FRA	6	4	1	1	49	16	9
14	ESP	6	1	5	0	13	34	2
15	GBR	6	1	4	1	19	37	3
16	YUG	6	2	4	0	24	46	4
1993								
9	SUI	7	7	0	0	58	8	14
10	HUN	7	6	1	0	40	14	12
11	FRA	7	5	2	0	39	13	10
12	AUT	7	3	3	1	22	30	7
13	ROM	7	2	5	0	23	39	4
14	DEN	7	2	5	0	13	26	4
15	ESP	7	1	5	1	18	48	3
16	GBR	7	1	6	0	17	52	2
1994								
9	BLR	5	3	1	1	27	18	7
10	HUN	5	4	1	0	35	12	8
11	DEN	5	3	2	0	31	17	6
12	AUT	5	3	2	0	21	21	6
13	ITA	5	3	1	1	17	9	7
14	ROM	5	1	3	1	13	22	3
15	FRA	5	1	3	1	19	24	3
16	ESP	5	0	5	0	7	47	0
1995								
9	SVK	5	5	0	0	58	3	10
10	POL	5	4	1	0	30	21	8
11	DEN	5	3	2	0	26	27	6
12	HUN	5	1	3	1	16	38	3
13	ITA	5	3	2	0	21	25	6
14	FRA	5	2	2	1	19	19	5
15	ROM	5	1	4	0	11	28	2
16	AUT	5	0	5	0	13	33	0
1996								
9	UKR	5	5	0	0	26	12	10
10	DEN	5	4	1	0	32	19	8
11	FRA	5	3	2	0	25	17	6
12	NOR	5	2	3	0	17	18	4
13	POL	5	3	2	0	41	18	6
14	ITA	5	2	3	0	16	22	4
15	HUN	5	1	4	0	15	21	2
16	ROM	5	0	5	0	11	56	0
1997								
9	NOR	6	3	1	2	20	15	8
10	POL	6	4	1	1	27	19	9
11	HUN	7	3	1	3	27	23	9
12	BLR	6	3	2	1	23	25	7
13	DEN	6	3	3	0	25	21	6
14	FRA	7	1	5	1	25	34	3
15	ITA	5	2	3	0	24	23	4
16	SLO	5	1	4	0	15	26	2

European Junior Championships, (Under 18) Pool C

Rank	Team	GP	W	L	T	GF	GA	Pts
1978								
17	HUN	4	2	0	2	21	13	6
18	BUL	4	1	2	1	17	13	3
19	ESP	4	1	2	1	11	23	3
1979								
17	BUL	4	4	0	0	33	6	8
18	ESP	4	2	2	0	16	23	4
19	GBR	4	0	4	0	6	26	0
1980								
17	DEN	4	4	0	0	51	5	8
18	BEL	4	1	3	0	13	30	2
19	GBR	4	1	3	0	12	41	2
1981								
17	HOL	4	4	0	0	44	8	8
18	GBR	4	1	2	1	18	26	3
19	BEL	4	0	3	1	8	36	1
1982								
17	HUN	4	2	1	1	29	22	5
18	ESP	4	2	2	0	22	25	4
19	GBR	4	1	2	1	20	24	3
1983								
17	YUG							
18	GBR							
19	BEL							
20	ESP							
1984								
17	HUN	6	5	1	0	44	28	10
18	GBR	6	4	2	0	45	34	8
19	BEL	6	3	3	0	39	30	6
20	ESP	6	0	6	0	17	53	0
1985								
17	ITA	4	3	1	0	20	14	6
18	BEL	4	2	2	0	14	12	4
19	GBR	4	1	3	0	17	25	2
1986								
17	GBR	4	3	1	0	17	11	6
18	HUN	4	2	2	0	9	12	4
19	ESP	4	1	3	0	12	15	2
1987								
17	HOL	4	4	0	0	30	7	8
18	HUN	4	2	2	0	20	14	4
19	BEL	4	0	4	0	4	33	0
1988								
17	BUL	3	3	0	0	15	5	6
18	ESP	3	2	1	0	22	11	4
19	HUN	3	1	2	0	14	11	2
20	BEL	3	0	3	0	9	33	0
1989								
17	ESP	4	3	0	1	19	13	7
18	GBR	4	2	1	1	15	10	5
19	HUN	4	0	4	0	12	23	0
1990								
17	GDR	3	3	0	0	35	4	6
18	HUN	3	2	1	0	16	14	4
19	GBR	3	1	2	0	7	20	2
20	BUL	3	0	3	0	7	27	0
1991								
17	GBR	3	3	0	0	28	5	6
18	BUL	3	2	1	0	29	9	4
19	HUN	3	1	2	0	18	16	2
20	BEL	3	0	3	0	2	47	0
1992								
17	HUN	3	3	0	0	34	1	6
18	HOL	3	2	1	0	17	17	4
19	BUL	3	1	2	0	9	18	2
20	BEL	3	0	3	0	6	30	0
1993								
17	BLR	4	3	0	1	16	9	7
18	SVK	4	3	1	0	54	6	6
19	SLO	4	2	1	1	18	13	5
20	UKR	4	3	1	0	56	11	6
21	LAT	4	2	2	0	21	14	4
22	LIT	4	1	3	0	10	35	2
23	EST	4	2	2	0	38	20	4
24	HOL	4	1	3	0	14	24	2
25	BUL	4	0	4	0	4	99	0
1994								
17	SVK	6	6	0	0	111	14	12
18	LAT	6	5	1	0	85	15	10
19	SLO	6	4	2	0	39	22	8
20	UKR	6	3	3	0	67	16	6
21	EST	6	4	2	0	27	56	8
22	GBR	6	3	3	0	29	55	6
23	LIT	6	2	4	0	25	50	4
24	CRO	6	1	5	0	23	46	2
25	HOL	4	0	4	0	9	57	0
26	BUL	4	0	4	0	2	86	0
1995								
17	UKR	5	4	1	0	51	12	8
18	LAT	5	4	1	0	33	7	8
19	SLO	5	4	1	0	38	11	8
20	GBR	5	2	3	0	22	21	4
21	EST	5	1	4	0	9	38	2
22	ESP	5	0	5	0	2	66	0
23	LIT	5	5	0	0	69	10	10
24	CRO	5	4	1	0	61	9	8
25	HOL	4	2	2	0	16	14	4
26	YUG	4	1	3	0	17	25	2
27	ISR	4	2	2	0	22	26	4
28	BUL	4	1	3	0	27	20	2
29	TUR	4	0	4	0	3	111	0
1996								
17	SLO	4	4	0	0	36	6	8
18	AUT	4	2	1	1	17	9	5
19	LAT	4	3	1	0	34	8	6
20	EST	4	1	1	2	12	17	4
21	GBR	4	2	1	1	28	12	5
22	LIT	4	1	3	0	20	40	2
23	CRO	4	1	3	0	17	27	2
24	ESP	4	0	4	0	2	47	0
1997								
17	GBR	4	4	0	0	20	6	8
18	LAT	4	2	1	1	21	10	5
19	EST	4	3	1	0	15	17	6
20	AUT	4	2	1	1	13	8	5
21	ROM	4	2	2	0	13	10	4
22	LIT	4	1	3	0	10	22	2
23	CRO	4	1	3	0	5	12	2
24	HOL	4	0	4	0	6	18	0

European Junior Championships, (Under 18) Pool D

Rank	Team	GP	W	L	T	GF	GA	Pts
1996								
25	HOL	3	3	0	0	62	4	6
26	YUG	2	1	1	0	10	8	2
27	ISR	2	1	1	0	6	9	2
28	BUL	3	1	2	0	26	21	2
29	TUR	2	0	2	0	1	63	0
1997								
25	YUG	5	5	0	0	114	5	10
26	ESP	5	3	1	1	39	26	7
27	BUL	5	3	2	0	22	26	6
28	ISR	5	2	2	1	30	27	5
29	ISL	5	1	4	0	17	48	2
30	TUR	5	0	5	0	6	96	0

Asian Junior Championships

Rank	Team	GP	W	L	T	GF	GA	Pts
1984								
1	JAP	6	6	0	0	64	9	12
2	PRC	6	4	2	0	48	24	8
3	KOR	4	0	4	0	5	36	0
4	AUS	4	0	4	0	2	50	0
1985								
1	JAP	4	4	0	0	34	8	8
2	KOR	4	1	2	1	23	23	3
3	AUS	4	0	3	1	6	32	1

Asian-Oceanic Junior Championships

Rank	Team	GP	W	L	T	GF	GA	Pts
1986								
1	JAP	6	5	1	0	65	14	10
2	PRC	6	4	1	1	25	26	9
3	KOR	6	1	4	1	15	43	3
4	AUS	6	1	5	0	18	40	2
1987								
1	PRK	4	3	1	0	31	9	6
2	PRC	4	3	1	0	17	9	6
3	JAP	4	3	1	0	22	8	6
4	AUS	4	1	3	0	14	35	2
5	KOR	4	0	4	0	9	32	0
1988								
1	PRC	6	5	0	1	50	13	11
2	JAP	6	4	1	1	59	19	9
3	KOR	6	2	4	0	42	53	4
4	AUS	6	0	6	0	14	80	0
1989								
1	JAP	4	3	0	1	32	14	7
2	KOR	4	2	2	0	19	26	4
3	PRC	4	0	3	1	16	27	1
1990								
1	JAP	6	6	0	0	86	4	12
2	PRC	6	4	2	0	48	19	8
3	KOR	6	2	4	0	42	35	4
4	AUS	6	0	6	0	5	123	0
1991								
1	JAP	4	3	0	1	62	6	7
2	PRC	4	3	0	1	49	11	7
3	PRK	4	2	2	0	18	11	4
4	KOR	4	1	3	0	31	20	2
5	MEX	4	0	4	0	3	115	0
1992								
1	JAP	4	3	0	1	36	3	7
2	PRC	4	2	2	0	20	16	4
3	PRK	4	3	0	1	22	6	7
4	KOR	4	1	3	0	12	25	2
5	AUS	4	0	4	0	11	51	0
1993								
1	KAZ	4	4	0	0	88	0	8
2	JAP	4	3	1	0	65	9	6
3	KOR	4	2	2	0	31	24	4
4	PRC	4	1	3	0	26	27	2
5	AUS	4	0	4	0	1	151	0
1994								
1	KAZ	4	4	0	0	66	3	8
2	KOR	4	2	1	1	42	16	5
3	JAP	4	2	1	1	42	23	5
4	PRC	4	1	3	0	26	20	2
5	AUS	4	0	4	0	0	114	0
1995								
1	JAP	3	2	1	0	14	7	4
2	KAZ	3	2	1	0	15	10	4
3	PRC	3	1	2	0	6	16	2
4	KOR	3	1	2	0	12	14	2
1996								
1	KAZ	3	3	0	0	32	8	6
2	KOR	3	2	1	0	13	14	4
3	JAP	3	1	2	0	11	13	2
4	PRC	3	0	3	0	4	25	0
1997								
1	JAP	3	3	0	0	20	8	6
2	KAZ	3	2	1	0	15	11	4
3	KOR	3	1	2	0	18	15	2
4	PRC	3	0	3	0	7	26	0

CHAPTER 44

European Club Teams

Top Teams Playing in Europe's Various National Leagues

PROFILES OF LEADING European club teams follow. National titles and second- and third-place ranking are determined by play-off results. Playoff structures vary in European leagues. Some schedule a bronze medal series or game between semifinal losers to determine a third-place finisher. Others, like the National Hockey League, do not.

Club profiles are arranged alphabetically within each country. Because team names in some national leagues carry the names of corporate sponsors, name changes are frequent. Previous names are listed in each club's profile.

The following leagues sort club names by home city: Austria, Czech Republic, Germany, Italy, Slovakia and Switzerland.

The following leagues sort clubs by team name: Finland, Norway, Russia and Sweden.

AUSTRIA

SAMINA VEU FELDKIRCH
Founded: 1945
Previous Names: VEU Feldkirch
Arena: Vorarlberghalle
Capacity: 5,800
National Title: 1982, 1983, 1984, 1990, 1994, 1995, 1996, 1997, 1998
2nd place: 1970, 1986
3rd place: 1971, 1989
Top Goalies: Peter Mohr, Erich Nagele, Michael Rudman
Top Defensemen: Jeffery Geiger, Walter Schneider, Konrad Dorn, Erwin Langer, Karl Heinzle
Top Forwards: Kelly Greenbank, Alexander Barinev, Herbert Mortl, Richard Grenier, Brian Hill, Walter Znenahlik, Thomas Rundqvist, Bengt-Ake Gustafsson, Gerhard Puschnik, Rick Nasheim
Top Coaches: Josef Koller, Kelly Greenbank, Ralph Krueger

KLAGENFURTER AC
Founded: 1926
Previous Names: KAC - Die Karntner
Arena: Eissporthalle Klagenfurt
Capacity: 5,500
National Title: 1934, 1935, 1952, 1955, 1960, 1964, 1965, 1966, 1967, 1968, 1969, 1970, 1971, 1972, 1973, 1974, 1976, 1977, 1979, 1980, 1985, 1986, 1987, 1988, 1991
2nd place: 1978, 1982, 1983, 1996, 1997, 1998
3rd place: 1975
Top Goalies: Walter Gollob, Robert Mak, Karl Pregl, Johann Schaunig, Michael Puschacher
Top Defensemen: Johann Fritz, Walter Schneider, Herbert Gasser, Robin Doyle, Martin Krainz
Top Forwards: Rudolf Konig, Herbert Pok, Josef Puschnig, Edward Lebler, Thomas Cijan, Adelbert Saint John, Alexander Sadjina, Walter Konig, Helmut Koren, Dieter Kkalt, Manfred Muhr
Top Coaches: Yuri Baulin, Adelbert Saint John, Rudolf Sindelar, Bill Gilligan

HERAKLITH-VSV VILLACH
Founded: 1925
Previous Names: Villacher SV
Arena: Stadthalle Villach
Capacity: 4,500
National Title: 1981, 1992, 1993
2nd place: 1984, 1989, 1990, 1991, 1995
3rd place: 1983, 1988
Top Goalies: Arno Cuder, Kurt Muller, Gerhard Thomasser
Top Defensemen: Jeffery Geiger, Helmut Petrik, Reinhard Dossi, Engelbert Linder
Top Forwards: Richard Cunningham, Leopold Sivec, Peter Raffl, Richard Grenier, Adelbert Saint John, Kelly Glowa, Wolfgang Kromp
Top Coaches: Bart Crashley, Hermann Knoll, Ron Kennedy

CE WIEN
Founded: 1922
Previous Names: Wiener EV
Arena: Albert-Schultz-Eishalle
Capacity: 3,000
National Title: 1923, 1924, 1925, 1926, 1927, 1928, 1929, 1930, 1931, 1933, 1937, 1947, 1948, 1962
2nd place: 1972, 1980, 1981, 1987, 1988
3rd place: 1966, 1979, 1982
Top Goalies: Hermann Weiss, Friedrich Holzer, Friedrich Prohaska, Brian Stankiewicz
Top Defensemen: Hans Trauttenberg, Josef Schwitzer, Robin Sadler, Walter Schneider, Johann Schuller, Timo Blomqvist
Top Forwards: Friedrich Demmer, Josef Gobl, Karl Kirchberger, Adolf Bachura, Gregory Holst, Richard Cunningham, Kurt Harand, Bill Gilligan, Peter Znenahlik
Top Coaches: Karel Fako, Walter Znenahlik, Ken Tyler

EC GRAZ
Founded: 1949
Previous Names: ATSE Eggenberg, ATSE Graz
Arena: Eisstadion Liebenau
Capacity: 4,500
National Title: 1975, 1978
2nd place: 1971, 1973, 1977, 1992, 1993, 1994
3rd place: 1969, 1970, 1974, 1976,
Top Goalies: Karl Ettinger, Manfred Suppan, Franz Schilcher
Top Defensemen: Herbert Platzer, Werner Schilcher
Top Forwards: Max Moser, Bill Klatt, Franz Voves, Dieter Kalt
Top Coaches: Miroslav Kubera, Anatoli Kozlov, Frantisek Tikal

CZECH REPUBLIC

HC PETRA VSETIN
Founded: 1905
Previous Names: SK Vsetin, Bruslarsky klub Vsetin, Sokol Vsetin, Zbrojovka Vsetin, HC Dadak Vsetin
Arena: Zimni Stadion

Capacity: 5,400
National Title: 1995, 1996, 1997, 1998
Top Goalies: Roman Cechmanek
Top Defensemen: Antonin Stavjana, Bedrich Scerban, Alexei Yashkin, Jiri Veber
Top Forwards: Rostislav Vlach, Oto Hascak, Tomas Kapusta, Jiri Dopita. Tomas Srsen, Andrei Galkin
Top Coaches: Horst Valasek

HC SPARTA PRAHA
Founded: 1909
Previous Names: Sokol Sparta, Sokol Bratrstvi Sparta, Sokol Sparta Sokolovo, Spartak Sokolovo, Sparta CKD Praha
Arena: Zimni Stadion
Capacity: 14,080
National Title: 1953, 1954, 1990, 1993
2nd place: 1937, 1957, 1963, 1967, 1974, 1988
3rd place: 1956, 1961, 1965, 1968, 1977, 1978, 1987, 1996, 1997
Top Goalies: Jan Peka, Jiri Holecek, Jaromir Sindel, Petr Briza
Top Defensemen: Jaroslav Pusbauer, Josef Trousilek, Karel Gut, Frantisek Tikal, Karel Masopust, Josef Horesovsky, Otakar Vejvoda, Leo Gudas
Top Forwards: Karel Pesek-Kada, Josef Malecek, Karel Kozeluh, Miloslav Charouzd, Valdimir Zabrodsky, Jan Starsi, Stanislav Konopasek, Jiri Kochta, Jan Havel, Jiri Hrdina, Pavel Richter, David Volek, Jiri Dolezal, Rostislav Vlach, Tomas Jelinek, Richard Zemlicka, Petr Hrbek
Top Coaches: Vladimir Zabrodsky, Karel Gut, Ludek Bukac, Pavel Wohl

HC VITKOVICE
Founded: 1928
Previous Names: SSK Vitkovice, CSK Vitkovice, Vitkovicke zelezarny, Banik Vitkovice, VZKG Ostrava, TJ Vitkovice
Arena: Zimni Stadion
Capacity: 10,000
National Title: 1952, 1981
2nd place: 1950, 1951, 1953, 1983, 1993, 1997
3rd place: 1958, 1979, 1998
Top Goalies: Josef Mikolas, Jaromir Sindel
Top Defensemen: Vaclav Bubnik, Jan Lidral, Jan Kasper, Jaroslav Lycka, Milan Figala, Antonin Planovsky, Milos Holan, Richard Smehlik
Top Forwards: Zbynek Neuwirth, Vladimir Stransky, Miroslav Vlach, Jaroslav Vlk, Jaroslav Mec, Frantisek Cernik, Ladislav Svozil, Mirislav Frycer, Vladimir Vujtek
Top Coaches: Vladimir Bouzek, Vaclav Bubnik, Jan Soukup, Vladimir Vujtek Sr.

HC ZELEZARNY TRINEC
Founded: 1929
Previous Names: 1.HK Trinec, KS Zalozik, SK Zelezarny Trinec, TZ VRSR Trinec, TZ Trinec
Arena: Zimni Stadion
Capacity: 5,500
2nd place: 1998

Top Goalies: Radovan Biegl, Robert Horyna
Top Defensemen: Jiri Kuntos, Lubomir Sekeras, Antonin Planovsky, Petr Pavlas
Top Forwards: Roman Kontsek, Jozef Dano, Richard Kral, Roman Kadera,

HC IDP POJISTOVNA PARDUBICE
Founded: 1926
Previous Names: LTC a Rapid Pardubice, Slavia, Dynamo, Tesla Pardubice, HC Pardubice, HC Pojistovna IB Pardubice
Arena: Zimni Stadion
Capacity: 9,393
National Title: 1973, 1987, 1989
2nd place: 1975, 1976, 1994
3rd place: 1960, 1974, 1983, 1984, 1986
Top Goalies: Vladimir Nadrchal, Miroslav Lacky, Jiri Crha, Dominik Hasek
Top Defensemen: Frantisek Panchartek, Karel Vohralik, Vladimir Bezdicek, Jan Levinsky, Frantisek Musil, Stanislav Meciar
Top Forwards: Stanislav Pryl, Ludvik Kopecky, Milan Koks, Jiri Dolana, Vladimir Martinec, Jiri Novak, Bohuslav Stastny, Vladimir Veith, Josef Palecek, Jiri Jiroutek, Ladislav Lubina, Evzen Musil, Otakar Janecky, Jiri Sejba
Top Coaches: Bohumil Rejda, Horymir Sekera, Karel Franek, Vladimir Martinec

HC VELVANA KLADNO
Founded: 1924
Previous Names: SK Kladno, Sokol, Sokol SONP, Banik, SONP, Poldi SONP, Poldi, HC Kladno, HC Poldi Kladno
Arena: Zimni Stadion
Capacity: 8,600
National Title: 1959, 1975, 1976, 1977, 1978, 1980
2nd place: 1982
3rd place: 1972, 1981, 1994
Top Goalies: Jiri Kulicek, Miroslav Termer, Miroslav Krasa, Milan Hnilicka
Top Defensemen: Stanislav Bacilek, Frantisek Pospisil, Frantisek Kaberle, Bohumil Cermak, Otakar Vejvoda, Jaroslav Vins, Jan Neliba, Miloslav Horava, Drahomir Kadlec, Libor Prochazka
Top Forwards: Ludvik Kopecky, Jaroslav Volf, Jaroslav Jirik, Josef Vimmer, Bohumil Prosek, Lubomur Bauer, Eduard Novak, Zdenek Nedved, Milan Novy, Vaclav Sykora, Jiri Dudacek, Vladimir Kames, Jaromir Jagr, Martin Prochazka, Pavel Patera
Top Coaches: Vlastimil Sykora, Bohumil Prosek, Jaroslav Volf, Frantisek Pospisil

HC CESKE BUDEJOVICE
Founded: 1928
Previous Names: AC Stadion Ceske Budejovice, Sokol Stadion, ZSJ OD, SKP, Slavoj, Motor Ceske Budejovice
Arena: Zimni Stadion
Capacity: 7,100
National Title: 1951
2nd place: 1981
3rd place: 1937, 1946, 1953, 1995
Top Goalies: Ladslav Gula, Petr Briza, Roman Turek
Top Defensemen: Jan Lidral, Karel Masopust, Miroslav Dvorak, Frantisek Suchanek, Frantisek Joun, Ladislav Kolda, Petr Misek, Stanislav Neckar
Top Forwards: Vlastimil Hajsman, Josef hejna, Jaroslav Pouzar, Norbert Kral, Vladimir Caldr, Jaroslav Korbela, Jiri Lala, Tomas Jelinek, Vaclav Marik, Radek Toupal, Roman Horak, Lubos Rob, Lubomir Rybovic, Radek Belohlav
Top Coaches: Vaclav Cerveny, Karel Prazak, Zdenek Uher

HC SLAVIA PRAHA
Founded: 1900
Previous Names: SK Slavia, Sokol Slavia, Dynamo Slavia, Dynamo, Slavia, Slavia IPS Praha
Arena: Zimni Stadion
Capacity: 5,100
Top Goalies: Josef Gruss, Radek Toth
Top Defensemen: Jan Fleischmann, Jan Palous, Otakar Vindys, Jaroslav Puspbauer, Miloslav Horava, Andrei Yakovenko, Martin Maskarinec
Top Forwards: Jaroslav Jarkovsky, Jaroslav Jirkovsky, Mila Fleischmann, Josef Sroubek, Alois Cetkovsky, Vladimir Ruzicka, Viktor Ujcik, Ivo Prorok, Tomas Kucharcik, Jan Benda, Jiri Dolezal
Top Coaches: Frantisek Tikal, Jan Havel

HC CHEMOPETROL LITVINOV
Founded: 1945
Previous Names: SK Stalinovy zavody Horni Litvinov, Sokol Stalinovy zavody, Jiskra Stalinovy zavody, CHZ Litvinov, HC CHZ Litvinov
Arena: Zimni Stadion
Capacity: 7,500
2nd place: 1978, 1984, 1991, 1996
3rd place: 1982, 1990, 1992
Top Goalies: Miroslav Kapoun, Petr Franek
Top Defensemen: Jiri Bubla, Eduard Uvira, Arnold Kadlec, Kamil Prachar, Jiri Slegr, Petr Svoboda
Top Forwards: Josef Ulrych, Jaroslav Walter, Ivan Hlinka, Milos Tarant, Vladimir Ruzicka, Petr Rosol, Petr Klima, Jindrich Korkment, Josef Beranek, Kamil Kastak, Robert Reichel, Robert Lang, Jan Caloun, Jan Alinc
Top Coaches: Gustav Bubnik, Josef Ulrych, Josef beranek Sr., Ivan Hlinka

AC ZPS ZLIN
Founded: 1928
Previous Names: SK Bata Zlin, Sokol Botostroj Zlin, Sokol Svit Gottwaldov, Spartak a Jiskra Gottwaldov, TJ Gottwaldov, SK Zlin
Arena: Zimni Stadion
Capacity: 8,300
2nd place: 1995
3rd place: 1985
Top Goalies: Jiri Kralik, Jiri Svoboda, Roman Cechmanek
Top Defensemen: Jaroslav Sima, Jan Zajicek, Antonin Stavjana, Ludek Cajka, Petr Pavlas, Roman Hamrlik
Top Forwards: Rostislav Vlach, Zdenek Cech, Karel Heim, Radim Radevic, Tomas Kapusta, Radek Bonk, Michal Grosek, Jaroslav Otevrel, Roman Meluzin, David Bruk
Top Coaches: Horst Valasek, Zdenek Uher

HC KERAMIKA PLZEN
Founded: 1929
Previous Names: SK Viktoria Plzen, Sokol Plzen IV, Leninovy zavody, Spartak, TJ Skoda Plzen, HC Skoda Plzen, HC Interconex Plzen, HC ZKZ Plzen
Arena: Zimni Stadion
Capacity: 8,719
2nd place: 1958, 1959, 1992
3rd place: 1957
Top Goalies: Jiri Svoboda, Josef Hovora, Rudolf Pejchar
Top Defensemen: Stanislav Sventek, Vladimir Bednar, Jiri Neubauer, Milan Kajkl, Josef Reznicek, Vitezslav Duris, Milan Tichy
Top Forwards: Miloslav Sasek, Frantisek

Cerny, Miroslav Klapac, Pavel Huml, Bohuslav Ebermann, Jiri Kucera, Martin Straka, Radek Kampf
Top Coaches: Miloslav Vins, Jan Radic, Zdenek Haber

HC BECHEROVKA KARLOVY VARY
Founded: 1923
Previous Names: Dynamo Karlovy Vary, HC Slavia Becherovka Karlovy Vary
Arena: Zimni Stadion
Capacity: 3,700
Top Goalies: Vaclav Furbacher
Top Defensemen: Petr Pavlas
Top Forwards: Jan Lipiansky, Tomas Klimt, Ondrej Steiner, Martin Streit

HC DUKLA JIHLAVA
Founded: 1956
Previous Names: UDA Praha, Tankista Praha, Kridla vlasti v Olomouci, Dukla Jihlava
Arena: Zimni Stadion
Capacity: 9,200
National Title: 1967, 1968, 1969, 1970, 1971, 1972, 1974, 1982, 1983, 1984, 1985, 1991
2nd place: 1966, 1973, 1977, 1979, 1980, 1986, 1987
3rd place: 1962, 1964, 1975, 1976, 1988, 1992
Top Goalies: Marcel Sakac, Jiri Crha, Jiri Kralik, Jaromir Sindel
Top Defensemen: Jan Suchy, Frantisek Panchartek, Vladimir Bednar, Josef Horesovsky, Jiri Bubla, Milan Kajkl, Miroslav Dvorak, Petr Adamik, Milan Chalupa, Jan Neliba, Frantisek Kaberle, Eduard Uvira, Karel Horacek, Jaroslav Benak, Radoslav Svoboda, Frantisek Musil, Bedrich Scerban, Drahomir Kadlec
Top Forwards: Jiri Holik, Jaroslav Holik, Jan Klapac, Jiri Kochta, Josef Augusta, Jan Hrbaty, Bohuslav Ebermann, Frantisek Vyborny, Jiri Novak, Igor Liba, Petr Rosol, Jiri Sejba, Jiri Kucera, Oldrich Valek, Libor Dolana, Michal Pivonka, Robert Holik, Petr Kankovsky
Top Coaches: Jaroslav Pitner, Stanislav Nevesely, Jaroslav Holik

HC BOHEMEX TRADE OPAVA
Founded: 1945
Previous Names: HC Opava, Sokol KP, Slavoj, Tatran, TJ Slezan Opava, TJ Slezan OSP, Slezan STS, HC Slezan Opava, Slezan Bohemex Trade Opava
Arena: Zimni Stadion
Capacity: 5,500
Top Goalies: Rostislav Haas
Top Defensemen: Milos Hrubes, Ales Flasar, Martin Bakula, Petr Tejkl
Top Forwards: Juraj Jurik, Martin Filip, Radim Radevic, Petr Fabian

FINLAND

HIFK HELSINKI
Founded: 1897
Arena: Helsingin Jaahalli
Capacity: 8,000
National Title: 1969, 1970, 1974, 1980, 1983, 1998
2nd place: 1973, 1975, 1986
3rd place: 1955, 1959, 1971, 1972, 1982, 1987, 1988, 1992
Top Goalies: Stig Wetzell, Jorma Virtanen, Sakari Lindfors
Top Defensemen: Lalli Partinen, Juha Rantasila, Heikki Riihiranta, Pekka Rautakallio, Pertti Lehtonen, Simo Saarinen

Top Forwards: Esa Peltonen, Juhani Tamminen, Harri Linnonmaa, Matti Murto, Anssi Melametsa, Matti Hagman, Christian Ruuttu, Ilkka Sinisalo, Esa Tikkanen, Mika Kortelainen, Jari Laukkanen, Sami Kapanen, Ville Peltonen,
Top Coaches: Seppo Liitsola, Pentti Matikainen, Harri Rindell

HPK HAMEENLINNA
Founded: 1929
Arena: Hameenlinnan Jaahalli
Capacity: 5,000
2nd place: 1952, 1993
3rd place: 1954, 1991, 1997
Top Goalies: Kari Rosenberg
Top Defensemen: Janne Laukkanen, Kai Rautio
Top Forwards: Jarkko Varvio, Teppo Kivela, Pekka Peltola, Risto Jalo, Juha Virtanen, Marko Palo
Top Coaches: Hannu Jortikka, Pentti Matikainen

ILVES TAMPERE
Founded: 1931
Arena: Tampereen Jaahalli
Capacity: 8,044
National Title: 1936, 1937, 1938, 1945, 1946, 1947, 1950, 1951, 1952, 1957, 1958, 1960, 1962, 1966, 1972, 1985
2nd place: 1935, 1948, 1949, 1965, 1968, 1969, 1970, 1990, 1998
3rd place: 1934, 1939, 1941, 1943, 1963, 1964, 1967, 1974, 1975, 1983, 1989
Top Goalies: Juhani Lahtinen, Markus Mattsson, Jukka Tammi, Jarmo Myllys
Top Defensemen: Aarne Honkavaara, Yrjo Hakala, Matti Lampainen, Hannu Helander, Jarmo Wasama, Jyrki Lumme, Risto Siltanen, Ville Siren
Top Forwards: Juhani Wahlsten, Matti Harju, Raimo Kilpio, Lasse Oksanen, Jorma Peltonen, Matti Rautiainen, Seppo Ahokainen, Risto Jalo, Juha Jarvenpaa, Veikko Suominen, Ari Haanpaa, Raimo Helminen, Mikko Makela, Raimo Summanen
Top Coaches: Seppo hiitela, Sakari Pietila

JOKERIT HELSINKI
Founded: 1967
Arena: Hartwall Arena
Capacity: 13,700
National Title: 1973, 1992, 1994, 1996, 1997
2nd place: 1971, 1983, 1995
3rd place: 1998
Top Goalies: Jorma Valtonen, Hannu Kamppuri, Rauli Sohlman, Markus Ketterer
Top Defensemen: Ilpo Koskela, Jouko Oystila, Seppo Suoraniemi, Timo Saari, Markus Lehto, Nikolai Makarov, Waltteri Immonen, Janne Niinimaa, Mika Stromberg
Top Forwards: Timo Sutinen, Henry Leppa, Lauri Mononen, Timo Turunen, Jorma Peltonen, Veli-Pekka Ketola, Jari Lindgren, Hannu Kapanen, Arto Sirvio, Anssi Melametsa, Jari Kurri, Teemu Selanne, Juha Lind, Antti Tormanen, Juha Ylonen, Otakar Janecky, Timo Saarikoski, Petri Varis
Top Coaches: Reino Ruotsalainen, Boris Mayorov, Hannu Aravirta

JYP JYVASKYLA
Founded: 1977
Previous Names: JyP HT Jyvaskyla
Arena: Jyvaskylan Jaahalli
Capacity: 4,812
2nd place: 1989, 1992
3rd place: 1993
Top Goalies: Ari-Pekka Siekkinen

Top Defensemen: Ari Kankaanpera, Harri Laurila
Top Forwards: Antero Lehtonen, Risto Kurkinen, Lasse Nieminen, Toni Koivunen, Jussi Tarvainen, Jari Lindroos
Top Coaches: Hannu Aravirta

KALPA KUOPIO
Founded: 1929
Previous Names: KuPS Kuopio
Arena: Kuopion Jaahalli
Capacity: 5,004
2nd place: 1991
Top Goalies: Pasi Kuivalainen
Top Defensemen: Kimmo Tominen, Vesa Salo
Top Forwards: Jouni Rinne, Petro Koivunen, Kim Ahlroos, Mikko Kontilla, Pekka Tirkkonen, Sami Kapanen
Top Coaches: Esko Nokelainen, Juha Junno

KIEKKO-ESPOO ESPOO
Founded: 1984
Arena: Matinkylan Jaahalli
Capacity: 2,675
Top Goalies: Ari-Pekka Siekkinen
Top Defensemen: Teemu Sillanpaa, Veli-Pekka Kautonen
Top Forwards: Hannu Jarvenpaa, Marko Palo, Juha Ikonen, Tero Lehtera
Top Coaches: Harri Rindell

LUKKO RAUMA
Founded: 1936
Arena: Rauman Jaahalli
Capacity: 5,500
National Title: 1963
2nd place: 1961, 1966, 1988
3rd place: 1965, 1969, 1994, 1996
Top Goalies: Jarmo Myllys
Top Defensemen: Jarmo Kuusisto, Jouni Peltonen, Tuomas Gronman, Pasi Huura
Top Forwards: Teppo Rastio, Matti Keinonen, Jorma Peltonen, Jorma Vehmanen, Jouni Rinne, Ismo Villa, Jari Torkki, Esa Keskinen, Ari Vuori, Matti Forss, Mika Valila, Mika Alatalo
Top Coaches: Jorma Peltonen, Matti Keinonen, Vaclav Sykora

SAIPA LAPPEENRANTA
Founded: 1948
Arena: Lappeenrannan Jaahalli
Capacity: 5,500
3rd place: 1966
Top Goalies: Jussi Markkanen
Top Defensemen: Vesa Ruotsalainen, Antti Tuomenoksa
Top Forwards: Petri Skriko, Ari Santanen, Ari Saarinen, Vesa Viitakoski, Juha Jokiharju
Top Coaches: Alpo Suhonen, Pentti Matikainen

TAPPARA TAMPERE
Founded: 1942
Previous Names: TBK Tampere
Arena: Tampereen Jaahalli
Capacity: 8,044
National Title: 1953, 1954, 1955, 1959, 1961, 1964, 1975, 1977, 1979, 1982, 1984, 1986, 1987, 1988
2nd place: 1958, 1960, 1963, 1974, 1976, 1978, 1981
3rd place: 1946, 1947, 1948, 1950, 1951, 1956, 1957, 1962, 1973, 1990
Top Goalies: Antti Leppanen, Hannu Kamppuri, Markus Mattsson
Top Defensemen: Kalevi Numminen, Pekka Marjamaki, Hannu Haapalainen, Lasse Litma, Pertti Valkeapaa, Timo Jutila, Jari Gronstrand, Teppo Numminen, Pekka Laksola

Top Forwards: Seppo Liitsola, Seppo Ahokainen, Jukka Porvari, Pertti Koivulahti, Jorma Sevon, Antero Lehtonen, Jorma Vehmanen, Timo Susi, Jukka Alkula, Martti Jarkko, Janne Ojanen, Vesa Viitakoski, Valeri Krykov, Jarkko Varvio
Top Coaches: Kalevi Numminen, Rauno Korpi

TPS TURKU
Founded: 1922
Arena: Turkuhalli, Elysee Arena
Capacity: 11,820
National Title: 1956, 1976, 1989, 1990, 1991, 1993, 1995
2nd place: 1943, 1955, 1957, 1967, 1977, 1982, 1985, 1994, 1996, 1997
3rd place: 1953, 1978, 1979, 1981,
Top Goalies: Lasse Kiili, Urpo Ylonen, Markus Ketterer, Jouni Rokama
Top Defensemen: Seppo Lindstrom, Timo Nummelin, Seppo Suoraniemi, Hannu Virta, Jouko Narvanmaa, Petteri Lehto, Aki-Petteri Berg, Toumas Gronman, Marko Kiprusoff
Top Forwards: Juhani Wahlsten, Juhani Tamminen, Seppo Repo, Reijo Leppanen, Martti Jarkko, Antero Lehtonen, Arto Javanainen, Jukka Vilander, Ari Vuori, Kari Jalonen, Saku Koivu, Jere Lehtinen, Esa Keskinen, Marko Jantunen, Reijo Mikkolainen
Top Coaches: Raimo Maattanen, Hannu Jortikka, Vladimir Yurzinov

ASSAT PORI
Founded: 1932
Previous Names: Karhut Pori
Arena: Porin Jaahalli
Capacity: 7,000
National Title: 1965, 1971, 1978
2nd place: 1979, 1980, 1984
3rd place: 1976, 1995
Top Goalies: Jorma Valtonen, Kari Takko, Antero Kivela, Pasi Kuivalainen
Top Defensemen: Antti Heikkila, Pekka Rautakallio, Tapio Flinck, Harry Nikander, Risto Tuomi, Tapio Levo, Vesa Salo, Olli Kaski
Top Forwards: Raimo Kilpio, Veli-Pekka Ketola, Ismo Villa, Kari Makkonen, Matti Ruisma, Arto Javanainen, Jari Korpisalo, Rauli Raitanen
Top Coaches: Lasse Heikkila, Antti Heikkila

GERMANY

AUGSBURGER PANTHERS
Founded: 1937
Previous Names: HC Augsburg, Augsburger ERV, Augsburger EV
Arena: Curt-Frenzel-Stadion
Capacity: 7,774
Top Goalies: Vladimir Dzurilla, Franz Funk, Petri Ylonen
Top Defensemen: Paul Ambros, Jozef Capla, Rainer Blum, Udo Kiessling, Dieter Medicus, Leonhard Waitl
Top Forwards: Ernst Hofner, Ernst Kopf, Holger Meitinger, Daniel Held
Top Coaches: Xaver Unsinn, Hans Rampf, Mike Daski

BERLIN CAPITALS
Founded: 1987
Previous Names: Berliner SC Preussen
Arena: Eissporthalle Berlin
Capacity: 6,412
Top Goalies: Klaus Merk
Top Defensemen: Dieter Medicus, Tom O'Regan
Top Forwards: Andreas Brockmann, Axel

Kammerer, Uli Egen, Andrzej Zabawa, Georg Holzmann, Christian Brittig, Jurgen Rumrich, John Chabot
Top Coaches: Lorenz Funk, Olle Ost, Peter Ustorf

EHC EISBAREN BERLIN
Founded: 1948
Previous Names: VOPO Berlin, SC Dynamo Berlin, EHC Dynamo Berlin
Arena: Sportforum Berlin-Hohenschonhausen
Capacity: 5,000
2nd place: 1998
Top Goalies: Rene Bielke, Mario Brunetta
Top Defensemen: Roland Peters, Joachim Lempio, Reinhard Fengler
Top Forwards: Harald Kuhnke, Frank Proske, Jiri Dopita, Thomas Steen, Peter-John Lee, Andrew Kim, Daniel Held
Top Coaches: Joachim Ziesche, Hartmut Nickel

DUSSELDORFER EG
Founded: 1935
Arena: Eisstadion an der Brehmstrasse
Capacity: 10,283
National Title: 1967, 1972, 1975, 1990, 1991, 1992, 1993, 1996
2nd place: 1969, 1971, 1973, 1980, 1981, 1986, 1989, 1994
3rd place: 1937, 1938, 1939, 1944, 1966, 1976, 1987
Top Goalies: Rainer Makatsch, Erich Weishaupt, Helmut de Raaf
Top Defensemen: Otto Schneitberger, Robert Murray, Jorg Hiemer, Uli Hiemer, Rick Amann, Harald Krull, Udo Kiessling, Horst-Peter Kretschmer, Andreas Niederberger, Peter Andersson
Top Forwards: Peter Hejma, Hermann Hinterstocker, Martin Hinterstocker, Walter Koberle, Ralph Kruger, Roy Roedger, Walter Stadler, Gerd Truntschka, Dieter Hegen, Chris Valentine, Manfred Wolf, Peter-John Lee, Thomas Brandl, Gord Sherven, Benoit Doucet, Bernd Truntschka
Top Coaches: Hans Rampf, Xaver Unsinn, Gerhard Kiessling, Hans Zach

FRANKFURT LIONS
Founded: 1960
Previous Names: Eintracht Frankfurt, Frankfurter ESC
Arena: Eissporthalle am Ratsweg
Capacity: 6,946
Top Goalies: Jukka Tammi
Top Defensemen: Jorg Hiemer, Jerzy Potz, Greg Thomson, Jaroslav Mucha, Sergei Shendelev
Top Forwards: Ulrich Egen, Jiri Lala, Daniel Held, Robert Reichel, Ilja Vorobjev
Top Coaches: Jorma Siitarinen, Ladislav Olejnik

HC KASSEL HUSKIES
Founded: 1971
Previous Names: EC Kassel
Arena: Kasseler Eissporthalle
Capacity: 6,100
2nd place: 1997
Top Goalies: Pavel Cagas
Top Defensemen: Venci Sebek, Alexander Engel
Top Forwards: Pekka Peltola, Bruce Eakin, Mike Millar, Roger Hansson, Petr Kwasigroch, Robert Burakovsky
Top Coaches: Ross Yates

KAUFBEURER ADLER
Founded: 1946
Previous Names: ESV Kaufbeuren
Arena: Eisstadion Am Berliner Platz
Capacity: 4,560
Top Goalies: Gerhard Hegen, Erich Weishaupt
Top Defensemen: Alfred Lutzenberger, Dieter Medicus, Stefan Metz, Manfred Schuster, Erich Goldmann
Top Forwards: Alfred Hynek, Daniel Held, Dale Derkatch, Martin Hinterstocker, Walter Koberle, Vladimir Martinec, Joachim Morz, Andreas Volland, Dieter Hegen
Top Coaches: Xaver Unsinn, Markus Egen, Florian Strida, Richard Pergl

KOLNER HAIE
Founded: 1936
Previous Names: Kolner EK, Kolner EC
Arena: Eisstadion an der Lentstrasse
Capacity: 7,204
National Title: 1977, 1979, 1984, 1986, 1987, 1988, 1995
2nd place: 1991, 1993, 1996
3rd place: 1978, 1982, 1985, 1989, 1990
Top Goalies: Rainer Makatsch, Helmut de Raaf, Siegmund Suttner, Josef Heiss
Top Defensemen: Peter Gailer, Uwe Krupp, Jurg Hiemer, Uli Hiemer, Udo Kiessling, Harald Krull, Manfred Schuster, Karsten Mende, Herbert Hohenberger
Top Forwards: Peter Hejma, Franz Hofherr, Walter Koberle, Erich Kuhnhackl, Marcus Kuhl, Holger Meitinger, Rainer Philipp, Miroslav Sikora, Gerd Truntschka, Sergei Berezin, Peter Draisaitl, Andreas Lupzig, Thomas Brandl, Dieter Hegen, Helmut Steiger
Top Coaches: Gerhard Kiessling, Jozef Golonka, Hardy Nilsson

KREFELD PINGUINE
Founded: 1936
Previous Names: Krefelder EV
Arena: Rheinlandhalle
Capacity: 6,714
National Title: 1952
2nd place: 1954, 1955, 1977
3rd place: 1953, 1975
Top Goalies: Ulrich Jansen, Rene Bielke, Karel Lang
Top Defensemen: Karl Bierschel, Bruno Guttowski, Manfred Kramarczyk, Harald Kadow, Harald Krull, Paul Langner, Otto Schneitberger, Petri Liimatainen, Jayson Meyer
Top Forwards: Horst Ludwig, Dick Devloe, Holger Meitinger, Anton Pohl, Andrei Kovalev, Reemt Pyka, Chris Lindberg, Peter Ihnacak
Top Coaches: Hans-Goerg Pescher, Engelbert Holderied, Mark Zettel

EV LANDSHUT
Founded: 1948
Arena: Stadtische Eissportaanlage Landshut
Capacity: 7,000
National Title: 1970, 1983
2nd place: 1974, 1976, 1984, 1995
3rd place: 1967, 1968, 1973, 1977
Top Goalies: Bernhard Englbrecht, Josef Schramm, Siegmund Suttner, Petr Briza
Top Defensemen: Michael Eibl, Robert Murray, Udo Kiessling, Rick Amann, Klaus Auhuber, Eduard Uvira, Mike Heidt
Top Forwards: Jiri Kochta, Erich Kuhnhackl, Henryk Pytrel, Alois Schloder, Gerd Truntschka, Hans Zach, Mike Bullard, Georg Franz, Wally Schreiber, Helmut Steiger, Marco Sturm

Top Coaches: Karel Gut, Jaroslav Pitner, Bernie Johnston

ADLER MANNHEIM
Founded: 1938
Previous Names: Mannheimer ERC
Arena: Eisstadion am Friedrichspark
Capacity: 8,200
National Title: 1980, 1997, 1998
2nd place: 1982, 1983, 1985, 1987
3rd place: 1959, 1963, 1965, 1981, 1984, 1988
Top Goalies: Josef Schlickenrieder, Erich Weishaupt, Mike Rosati
Top Defensemen: Hans Maier, Rainer Blum, Peter Gailer, Bruno Guttowski, Robert Murray, Andreas Pokorny, Joachim Reil, Harold Kreis,
Top Forwards: Kurt Sepp, Marcus Kuhl, Jiri Lala, Holger Meitinger, Paul Messier, Peter Obresa, Roy Roedger, Andreas Volland, Manfred Wolf, Ross Yates, Jochen Hecht, Alexander Serikow, Dieter Kalt, Paul Beraldo
Top Coaches: Ladislav Olejnik, Heinz Weisenbach, Lance Nethery

NURNBERG ICE TIGERS
Founded: 1980
Previous Names: EHC 80 Nurnberg
Arena: Eisstadion Nurnberg
Capacity: 4,200
Top Goalies: Bernd Englbrecht, Boo Ahl
Top Defensemen: Daniel Kunce, Torsten Kienass
Top Forwards: Klaus Birk, Jiri Dolezal, Thomas Sterflinger,
Top Coaches: Jan Eysselt, Jozef Golonka

ECR REVIER LOWEN
Founded: 1987
Previous Names: EC Ratingen, Ratinger Lowen
Arena: Arena Oberhausen
Capacity: 9,425
Top Goalies: Joakim Persson, Marc Seliger
Top Defensemen: Marco Rentzsch, Peter Ekroth
Top Forwards: Andrei Fuchs, Boris Fuchs, Axel Kammerer, Jeff Lazaro
Top Coaches: Alexander Barinev, Bill Lochead

STAR BULLS ROSENHEIM
Founded: 1978
Previous Names: SB DJK Rosenheim, SB Rosenheim
Arena: Kathrein-Stadion Rosenheim
Capacity: 6,300
National Title: 1982, 1985, 1989
2nd place: 1988, 1990, 1992
3rd place: 1983, 1986, 1991
Top Goalies: Rainer Makatsch, Karl Friesen, Klaus Dalpiaz, Klaus Merk
Top Defensemen: Oldrich Machac, Jamie Masters, Rainer Blum, Horst-Peter Kretschmer
Top Forwards: Ron Fischer, Ernst Hofner, Holger Meitinger, Joachim Merz, Jaroslav Pouzar, Franz Reindl, Vladimir Vacatko, Hans Zach, Raimond Hilger, Micahel Pohl
Top Coaches: Pavel Wohl, Jan Starsi, Ernst Hofner

SCHWENNINGEN WILD WINGS
Founded: 1927
Previous Names: Schwenninger ERC
Arena: Eissportzentrum am Bauchenberg
Capacity: 5,200
Top Goalies: Mattias Hoppe
Top Defensemen: Brian Young, Mike Heidt, Harald Krull, Gord Hynes, Daniel Nowak

Top Forwards: George Fritz, Tony Currie, Daniel Held, Markus Berwanger, Ralph Kruger, Wally Schreiber, Mark MacKay
Top Coaches: Peter Ustorf, Billy Flint, Robert Burns

WEDEMARK SCORPIONS
Previous Names: ESC Wedemark
Arena: Icehouse Wedemark
Capacity: 4,000
Top Goalies: Francois Gravel
Top Defensemen: Anthony Circelli, Dmitri Frolov, Serge Poudrier
Top Forwards: Mark Jooris, Emilio Iovio, Gary Leeman
Top Coaches: Kevin Gaudet

GREAT BRITAIN

AYR SCOTTISH EAGLES
Founded: 1996
Arena: Centrum Arena
Capacity: 2,745
National Title: 1998
Top Goalies: Sven Rampf
Top Defensemen: Angelo Catenaro, Frantisek Prochazka, Ryan Kummu
Top Forwards: Jiri Lala, Jamie Steer, Markus Berwanger, Mark Cupolo
Top Coaches: Jim Lynch

BASINGSTOKE BISON
Founded: 1988
Previous Names: Basingstoke Beavers
Arena: The Ice Rink & Lido
Capacity: 2,000
Top Goalies: Richard Gallace
Top Defensemen: Russ Parent, Steve Brown
Top Forwards: Don Yewchin, Gary Douville, Rick Fera, Richard Little, Merv Priest, Kevin Conway, Blake Knox
Top Coaches: Peter Woods

BRACKNELL BEES
Founded: 1987
Arena: John Nike Leisuresport Complex
Capacity: 3,100
Top Goalies: Mark Bernard
Top Defensemen: Shayne McCosh, Matt Cote
Top Forwards: Jamie Craiper, Darin Fridgen, Dale Junkin, Peter Romeo, Joe Ferraccioli, Wayde Bucsis, Brian Pellerin
Top Coaches: Jim Fuyarchuk

CARDIFF DEVILS
Founded: 1986
Arena: Wales National Ice Rink
Capacity: 2,800
National Title: 1990, 1993, 1994
2nd place: 1998
Top Goalies: Stevie Lyle, Frank Caprice
Top Defensemen: Kip Noble, Stephen Cooper, Ian Cooper, Jason Stone, Shannon Hope
Top Forwards: Nicky Chinn, John Lawless, Ivan Matulik, Ken Hodge, Vezio Sacratini, Doug McCarthy, Steve Moria, Randy Smith
Top Coaches: John Lawless, Paul Heavey

MANCHESTER STORM
Founded: 1995
Arena: Nynex Arena
Capacity: 17,500
Top Goalies: John Finnie
Top Defensemen: Jeff Lindsay, Stephen Cooper, Jeff Sebastian
Top Forwards: Nick Poole, Craig Woodcroft, Brad Zavisha, Mike Morin, Brad Rubachuk
Top Coaches: John Lawless

NEWCASTLE COBRAS
Founded: 1947
Previous Names: Durham Wasps
Arena: Newcastle Arena
Capacity: 7,000
National Title: 1987, 1988, 1991, 1992
2nd place: 1983
Top Goalies: Mika Rautio
Top Defensemen: Ian Cooper, Stephen Cooper, Jeff MacLeod, Paul Dixon, Chris Norton
Top Forwards: John Ciotti, Dave Anderson, Anthony Johnson, Stephen Johnson, Jamie Craiper, Kelly Askew, Mike Bodnarchuk, Justin Duberman, Rick Brebant, Ralf Hantschke, Markku Kyllonen
Top Coaches: Rick Brebant

NOTTINGHAM PANTHERS
Founded: 1939
Arena: The Ice Stadium
Capacity: 2,850
National Title: 1989
2nd place: 1960, 1992, 1996, 1997
Top Goalies: Trevor Robins
Top Defensemen: Darren Durdle, Darryl Olsen, Chris Kelland, Mike Bishop, Garth Premak
Top Forwards: Rick Brebant, Marty Dallman, Derek Laxdal, Paul Adey, Neil Morgan
Top Coaches: Mike Blaisdell

SHEFFIELD STEELERS
Founded: 1991
Arena: Sheffield Arena
Capacity: 8,500
National Title: 1995, 1996, 1997
2nd place: 1994
3rd place: 1998
Top Goalies: Piero Greco
Top Defensemen: Rob Wilson, Chris Kelland, Mike O'Connor
Top Forwards: Nicky Chinn, Frank Kovacs, Tony Hand, Ken Priestlay, Jamie Leach, Tim Cranston, Jason Lafreniere, David Longstaff, Scott Neil
Top Coaches: Alex Dampier, Clyde Tuyl

ITALY

HC BOLZANO
Previous Names: HC Bolzano Ozo, HC Bolzano Coca-Cola, HC Bolzano Wurth, HC Forst Bolzano
Arena: Stadio del Ghiaccio
National Title: 1963, 1973, 1977, 1978, 1979, 1982, 1983, 1984, 1985, 1988, 1990, 1995, 1996, 1997, 1998
2nd place: 1954, 1955, 1960, 1964, 1965, 1974, 1975, 1976, 1981, 1987, 1991, 1993, 1994
3rd place: 1958, 1959, 1967, 1972, 1980, 1986, 1989
Top Goalies: Giorgio Tigliani, Mike Zanier, Jim Corsi, Roberto Romano
Top Defensemen: Gino Pasqualotto, Norbert Gasser, Robert Oberrauch, John Bellio
Top Forwards: Kent Nilsson, Ronnie Roberts, Ron Chipperfield, Martin Pavlu, Michael Mair, Lucio Topatigh, Rudi Hiti, Martin Pavlu, Bruno Zarrillo, Sergei Vostrikov, Igor Maslennikov, Gaetano Orlando
Top Coaches: Ron Chipperfield, Albert Da Rin, Rudi Hiti, Bob Manno, Ron Ivany, Gosta Johansson

SG BRUNICO
Arena: Stadio del Ghiaccio
2nd place: 1982

3rd place: 1981
Top Goalies: Reinhard Oberjakober
Top Defensemen: Martin Crepaz, Vyacheslav Uvayev
Top Forwards: Rick Bragnalo, Tony Cassolato, Thomas Tinkhauser, Krzysztof Bialynicki, Maurizio Mansi, Vladimir Yeremin, Alexander Gschliesser
Top Coaches: Jaroslav Pavlu, Nikolai Kazakov

HOCKEY COMO
Previous Names: IC Como Hockey Promolinea
Arena: Stadio del Ghiaccio
Top Defensemen: Petr Adamik, Maurizio Zanini
Top Forwards: Larry Marson, Tom Milani, Rudi Hiti, Giancarlo Bonino, Dominic Amodeo, Fabio Sguazzero

SG CORTINA
Previous Names: SG Cortina Rex, SG Cortina Doria,
Arena: Stadio del Ghiaccio
National Title: 1932, 1957, 1959, 1961, 1962, 1964, 1965, 1966, 1967, 1968, 1970, 1971, 1972, 1974, 1975
2nd place: 1958, 1963, 1969, 1973, 1978
3rd place: 1953, 1955, 1960, 1976
Top Defensemen: Gerry Ciarcia, Vladimir Kostka
Top Forwards: Ivan Zanatta, Albert Da Rin, Gianfranco Da Rin, Ruggero Savaris, Jiri Novak
Top Coaches: Slavomir Barton, Anton Haucvic

HC COURMAOSTA LIONS
Previous Names: HC Courmayer Aosta, HC Aosta MEGA Supermercati
Arena: Stadio del Ghiaccio
3rd place: 1994, 1995
Top Goalies: Corrado Micalef
Top Defensemen: Dave Larson, Bill Stewart
Top Forwards: Alexei Tkachuk, Alexander Barkov, Jason Lafreniere, Jim Camazzola

HC FASSA
Previous Names: HC Fassa-Canazei
Arena: Palazza del Ghiaccio
2nd place: 1989
3rd place: 1997
Top Defensemen: Craig Norwich, Bob Manno, Andrei Sapozhnikov
Top Forwards: Mustafa Besic, Giovanni Marchetti, Fred Perlini, Mark Stuckey, Jan Stopczyk, Kim Gellert, Petr Rosol
Top Coaches: Mike Fedorko, Len Semplice

HC GARDENA
Previous Names: HC Val Gardena Recoaro, HC Gardena Cinzano Vermouth, IIC Gardena Finstral
Arena: Stadio del Ghiaccio
National Title: 1969, 1976, 1980, 1981,
2nd place: 1966, 1967, 1970, 1971, 1977, 1979, 1983,
3rd place: 1964, 1965, 1968, 1975, 1978, 1996
Top Goalies: Jim Corsi, Jorma Valtonen, Nick Sanza,
Top Defensemen: Erwin Kostner, Ivo Insam, Georg Comploi, Dave Tomassoni
Top Forwards: Fabrizio Kasslatter, Edmund Rabanser, Adolf Insam, Lasse Oksanen, Adolf Insam, Kim Gellert, Gary Leeman, Roland Ramoser
Top Coaches: Dave Chambers, Ron Ivany, Zdenek Blaha, Walter Piccolruaz

LATSCHER SC
Previous Names: SC Laces
Arena: Stadio del Ghiaccio
Top Defensemen: Michael Stocker
Top Forwards: Patrick Lochi, Peter Sirotak

HC MERANO
Previous Names: HC Merano Lancia
Arena: Stadio del Ghiaccio
National Title: 1986
2nd place: 1980, 1984, 1988
3rd place: 1973, 1979
Top Goalies: Marco Capone, David Delfino
Top Defensemen: John Bellio, Bob Manno, Dave Tomassoni, Mike Amodeo
Top Forwards: Pat O'Banion, Frank Nigro, Grant Goegan, Mark Morrison, Tom Milani, Cary Farelli, Dan D'Alvise, Norbert Prunster, Scott Mcleod, John Vecchiarelli
Top Coaches: Bryan Lefley, Mike Daski

HC MILANO 24
Arena: Stadio del Ghiaccio
2nd place: 1996, 1997
Top Goalies: Mike Zanier
Top Defensemen: Mike De Angelis, Bob Nardella, Larry Rucchin
Top Forwards: Frank Di Muzio, Anthony Iob, Vezio Sacratini, Santino Pellegrino, John Tucker
Top Coaches: Rico Rossi

SV RENON
Previous Names: SV Renon Finstral
Arena: Stadio del Ghiaccio
Top Defensemen: Achim Vinatzer, Christian Tauferer
Top Forwards: Steve Smith, Dave Jensen, Stefan Mair, Jiri Vitek, Emanuel Scelfo

NORWAY

FRISK-ASKER IF ASKER
Arena: Askerhallen
Capacity: 2,000
National Title: 1975, 1979
Top Goalies: Kare Ostensen, Tore Wahlberg, Vern Mott
Top Defensemen: Thor Martinsen, Nils Nilsen,
Top Forwards: Olav Dalsoren, Morten Sethereng, Georg Smefjell, Morten Johansen, Vidar Johansen, Carl Gunnar Gundersen, Pal Martinsen, Allan Butler, Henrik Aaby

FURUSET ISHOCKEY IF OSLO
Arena: Furuset Ishall
Capacity: 2,300
National Title: 1949, 1951, 1952, 1954, 1980, 1983, 1990
Top Goalies: Torbjorn Orskaug
Top Defensemen: Petter Salsten, Cato Tom Andersen, Tommy Jakobsen, Oystein Jarlsbo, Leif Solheim, Jorgen Salsten, Jan Roar Fagerli
Top Forwards: Geir Hoff, Ole Eskild Dahlstrom, Sigurd Thinn, Sven Lien, Oyvind Solheim, Bjorn Skaare, Rob Doroshuk, Knut Walbye, Pal Dahlstrom

LILLEHAMMER IK
Arena: Kristins Hall
Capacity: 3,194
National Title: 1994
Top Goalies: Mattis Haakensen
Top Defensemen: Johnny Nilsen, Morgan Andersen, Svein Enok Norstebo
Top Forwards: Vegar Barlie, Per Age Skroder, Lars Bergseng, Geir Hoff

LORENSKOG IK
Arena: Lorenskog Ishall
Capacity: 2,800
Top Goalies: Jan Tore Kjaer
Top Defensemen: Bjorn Hermansen, Fredrik Trygg, Arne Billkvam
Top Forwards: Stein Lajord, Geir Dalene, Andrew Syverud, Jarle Gundersen, John Opsahl

MANGLERUD/STAR IL OSLO
Arena: Manglerud Ishall
Capacity: 900
National Title: 1977, 1978
Top Goalies: Jorn Goldstein, Steve Allmann
Top Defensemen: Rune Molberg, Per Erik Ingjer, Trond Abrahamsen, Erik Nerell
Top Forwards: Tom Roymark, Roar Ovstedal, Kjell Thorkildsen, Jarle Friis, Cato Andersen, Henrik Aaby, Knut Walbye, Marius Trygg

IHK SPARTA SARPSBORG
Arena: Sparta Amfi
Capacity: 4,020
National Title: 1984, 1989
Top Goalies: Tommy Skaarberg, Jarl Eriksen
Top Defensemen: Kim Sogaard, Arne Billkvam, Timo Blomqvist
Top Forwards: Stephen Foyn, Per Christian Knold, Geir Myhre, Bjorn Freddy Bekkerud, Igor Mishukov, Sivert Andersson, Roy Johansen
Top Coaches: Stephen Foyn

STJERNEN HOCKEY FREDRIKSTAD
Previous Names: IL Stjernen Fredrikstad
Arena: Stjernehallen
Capacity: 3,500
National Title: 1981, 1986,
Top Goalies: Pal Gjermundsen
Top Defensemen: Morgan Andersen, Per Oyvind Myhrene
Top Forwards: Orjan Lovdal, Morten Finstad, Rune Gulliksen, Trond Magnussen, Lars Hakon Andersen, Oldrich Valek

STORHAMAR IL HAMAR
Arena: Hamar OL-Amfi
Capacity: 6,000
National Title: 1995, 1996, 1997, 1998
Top Goalies: Jorma Virtanen, Svein Harald Arnesen
Top Defensemen: Age Ellingsen, Petter Salsten
Top Forwards: Erik Kristiansen, Tom Erik Olsen, Pal Martinsen, Rune Gulliksen, Ole Eskild Dahlstrom, Petter Thoresen, Peter Madach
Top Coaches: Lennart Ahlberg

TRONDHEIM IK
Arena: Leangen Ishall
Capacity: 3,000
Top Goalies: Jim Marthinsen
Top Defensemen: Jan Roar Fagerli, Svein Enok Norstebo, Magne Nordnes
Top Forwards: Pal Martinsen, Bjorn Anders Dahl, Dallas Gaume, Rune Gulliksen, Geir Myhre
Top Coaches: Peter Woods

VALERENGA ISHOCKEY OSLO
Founded: 1948
Previous Names: Valerengens IF Oslo
Arena: Jordal Amfi
Capacity: 6,300
National Title: 1960, 1962, 1963, 1965, 1966, 1967, 1968, 1969, 1970, 1971, 1973, 1982, 1985, 1987, 1988, 1991, 1992, 1993, 1998

Top Goalies: Jim Marthinsen
Top Defensemen: Jon Magne Karlstad, Oyvind Losamoen, Tor Helge Eikeland, Thor Gundersen, Pal Kristiansen
Top Forwards: Petter Thoresen, Ilkka Kaarna, Per Skjerwen Olsen, Roy Jansen, Arne Mikkelsen, Svein Normann Hansen, Arne Billkvam, Roy Johansen, Steinar Bjolbakk, Oystein Olsen, Maruis Rath, Einar Bruno Larsen, Espen Knutsen

RUSSIA

TORPEDO YAROSLAVL
Founded: 1959
Arena: Sports Palace Avtodizel
Capacity: 4,300
National Title: 1997
3rd place: 1998
Top Goalies: Sergei Kostyukhin
Top Defensemen: Vladimir Koltsov, Sergei Lukichev, Vladimir Kryuchkov, Dmitri Krasotkin, Dmitri Yushkevich
Top Forwards: Sergei Zaitsev, Alexander Zybin, Mikhail Vasiljev, Alexei Gorshkov, Igor Maslennikov, Anatoli Lvov, Andrei Tarasenko
Top Coaches: Sergei Nikolayev

LADA TOGLIATTI
Founded: 1976
Previous Name: Torpedo Togliatti
Arena: Sports Palace Volgar
Capacity: 3,500
National Title: 1994, 1996
2nd place: 1993, 1995, 1997
European Cup Title: 1996–97
Top Goalies: Sergei Nikolayev
Top Defensemen: Oleg Davydov, Igor Nikitin, Vladimir Tarasov
Top Forwards: Sergei Vostrikov, Igor Maslennikov, Anatoli Yemelin, Ivan Svintsitsky, Yuri Zlov, Vyacheslav Bezukladnikov,
Top Coaches: Gennady Tsygurov

DYNAMO MOSCOW
Founded: 1946
Arena: Sports Palace Luzhniki
Capacity: 11,000
National Title: 1947, 1954, 1990, 1991, 1992, 1993, 1995
2nd place: 1950, 1951, 1959, 1960, 1962, 1963, 1964, 1971, 1972, 1977, 1978, 1979, 1980, 1985, 1986, 1987, 1994, 1996
3rd place: 1948, 1949, 1952, 1953, 1955, 1956, 1957, 1958, 1966, 1967, 1968, 1969, 1974, 1976, 1981, 1982, 1983, 1988
Top Goalies: Vladimir Chinov, Boris Zaitsev, Alexander Pashkov, Vladimir Myshkin, Mikhail Shtalenkov, Andrei Trefilov
Top Defensemen: Pavel Zhiburtovich, Vitali Davydov, Valeri Vasiljev, Vasili Pervukhin, Zinetula Bilyaletdinov, Darius Kasparaitis, Sergei Gonchar, Alexander Karpovtsev
Top Forwards: Valentin Kuzin, Alexabder Uvarov, Yuri Krylov, Vladimir Yurzinov, Alexander Maltsev, Alexander Golikov, Vladimir Golikov, Sergei Svetlov, Sergei Yashin, Anatoli Semenov, Alexei Zhamnov, Alexei Kovalev, Alexei Yashin
Top Coaches: Arkadi Chernyshev, Yuri Moiseyev, Vladimir Yurzinov

KRYLJA SOVETOV MOSCOW (SOVIET WINGS)
Founded: 1947
Arena: Sports Palace Krylja Sovetov
Capacity: 5,800

National Title: 1957, 1974
2nd place: 1955, 1956, 1958, 1975
3rd place: 1950, 1951, 1954, 1959, 1960, 1973, 1978, 1989, 1991, 1993
European Cup Title: 1974–75
Top Goalies: Boris Zapryagayev, Yevgeny Yerkin, Alexander Pashkov, Alexander Sidelnikov, Vladimir Myshkin, Oleg Bratash
Top Defensemen: Alfred Kuchevsky, Sergei Babinov, Yuri Shatalov, Dmitri Mironov, Oleg Tverdovsky
Top Forwards: Alexei Guryshev, Mikhail Bychkov, Nikolai Khlystov, Igor Dmitriyev, Vyacheslav Anisin, Yuri Lebedev, Alexander Bodunov, Sergei Kapustin, Viktor Tyumenev, Sergei Nemchinov, Yuri Khmylev, Sergei Priakin
Top Coaches: Vladimir Yegorov, Boris Kulagin, Igor Tuzik, Igor Dmitriyev

KHIMIK VOSKRESENSK
Founded: 1953
Previous Name: Khimik Moscow
Arena: Sports Palace Khimik
Capacity: 4,500
2nd place: 1989
3rd place: 1965, 1970, 1984, 1990
Top Goalies: Valeri Zubarev, Alexander Pashkov
Top Defensemen: Alexander Ragulin, Yuri Liapkin, Alexander Smirnov, Sergei Selyanin, Igor Ulanov
Top Forwards: Yuri Morozov, Valeri Nikitin, Valentin Kozin, Alexander Golikov, Vladimir Golikov, Vladimir Lavrentjev, Igor Larionov, Alexander Chernykh, Valeri Kamensky, Dmitri Kvartalnov, German Titov, Valeri Bragin, Leonid Trukhno, Valeri Zelepukin, Vyacheslav Kozlov, Sergei Berezin,
Top Coaches: Nikolai Epshtein, Yuri Morozov, Vladimir Vasiljev

CSKA MOSCOW (CENTRAL RED ARMY)
Founded: 1946
Previous Names: CDKA Moscow, CDSA Moscow, CSK MO Moscow
Arena: Sports Palace CSKA
Capacity: 6,000
National Title: 1948, 1949, 1950, 1955, 1956, 1958, 1959, 1960, 1961, 1963, 1964, 1965, 1966, 1968, 1970, 1971, 1972, 1973, 1975, 1977, 1978, 1979, 1980, 1981, 1982, 1983, 1984, 1985, 1986, 1987, 1988, 1989
2nd place: 1947, 1952, 1953, 1954, 1957, 1967, 1969, 1974, 1976, 1990, 1992
3rd place: 1962
European Cup Title: 1968–69, 1969–70, 1970–71, 1971–72, 1972–73, 1973–74, 1975–76, 1977–78, 1978–79, 1979–80, 1980–81, 1981–82, 1982–83, 1983–84, 1984–85, 1985–86, 1986–87, 1987–88, 1988–89, 1989–90
Top Goalies: Grigory Mkrtychan, Nikolai Puchkov, Vladislav Tretiak, Yevgeny Belosheikin, Nikolai Khabibulin
Top Defensemen: Alexander Vinogradov, Dmitri Ukolov, Genrikh Sidorenkov, Nikolai Sologubov, Ivan Tregubov, Alexander Ragulin, Eduard Ivanov, Viktor Kuzkin, Igor Romishevsky, Vladimir Lutchenko, Gennady Tsygankov, Alexander Gusev, Sergei Babinov, Viacheslav Fetisov, Alexei Kasatonov, Sergei Starikov, Igor Stelnov, Igor Kravchuk, Alexei Gusarov, Vladimir Malakhov, Sergei Zubov, Vladimir Konstantinov, Boris Mironov
Top Forwards: Vsevolod Bobrov,

Viktor Shuvalov, Yevgeny Babich, Konstantin Loktev, Veniamin Alexandrov, Alexander Almetov, Anatoli Firsov, Vladimir Vikulov, Viktor Polupanov, Yevgeny Mishakov, Boris Mikhailov, Vladimir Petrov, Valeri Kharlamov, Viktor Zhluktov, Boris Alexandrov, Helmut Balderis, Sergei Kapustin, Sergei Makarov, Nikolai Drozdetsky, Vladimir Krutov, Igor Larionov, Andrei Khomutov, Vyacheslav Bykov, Valeri Kamensky, Sergei Fedorov, Pavel Bure, Alexander Mogilny, Vyacheslav Kozlov, Andrei Kovalenko
Top Coaches: Anatoli Tarasov, Viktor Tikhonov

SPARTAK MOSCOW
Founded: 1946
Arena: Sports Palace Sokolniki
Capacity: 4,710
National Title: 1962, 1967, 1969, 1976
2nd place: 1948, 1965, 1966, 1968, 1970, 1973, 1981, 1982, 1983, 1984, 1991
3rd place: 1947, 1963, 1964, 1972, 1975, 1979, 1980, 1986, 1992
Top Goalies: Viktor Zinger, Viktor Krivolapov, Viktor Doroschenko
Top Defensemen: Valeri Kuzmin, Alexei Makarov, Viktor Blinov, Dmitri Kitayev, Yevgeny Paladjev, Yuri Lyapkin, Sergei Korotkov, Vladimir Tyurikov, Ilja Byakin
Top Forwards: Vyacheslav Starshinov, Boris Mayorov, Yevgeny Mayorov, Viktor Yaroslavtsev, Yevgeny Zimin, Alexander Martynyuk, Alexander Yakushev, Vladimir Shadrin, Viktor Shalimov, Sergei Shepelev, Sergei Kapustin, Alexander Kozhevnikov, Viktor Tyumenev, Igor Boldin, Nikolai Borschevsky, Vitali Prokhorov, Alexander Selivanov
Top Coaches: Alexander Igumnov, Alexander Novokreschenov, Vsevolod Bobrov, Boris Mayorov, Boris Kulagin

SKA ST. PETERSBURG
Founded: 1946
Previous Names: ODO Leningrad, LDO Leningrad, SKVO Leningrad, SKA Leningrad
Arena: Sports Palace Yubileiny
Capacity: 6,500
3rd place: 1971, 1987
Top Goalies: Vladimir Shepovalov
Top Defensemen: Valeri Yegorov, Alexei Gusarov, Igor Yevdokimov, Svyatoslav Khalizov, Marat Davydov
Top Forwards: Belyai Bekyashev, Igor Grigorjev, Valentin Panyukhin, Yuri Glazov, Sergei Solodukhin, Vyacheslav Solodukhin, Alexander Andreyev, Nikolai Drozdetsky, Vyacheslav Lavrov
Top Coaches: Nikolai Puchkov, Valeri Shilov, Boris Mikhailov

KRISTALL ELEKTROSTAL
Founded: 1949
Previous Names: Khimik Elektrostal, DK imeni Karla Marksa Elektrostal, SK Elektrostal
Arena: Sports Palace Kristall
Capacity: 4,000
Top Goalies: Yevgeny Yerkin
Top Defensemen: Valeri Nazarov
Top Forwards: Igor Grebennikov, Viktor Pryazhnikov, Yuri Paramoshkin, Anatoli Ionov
Top Coaches: Vladimir Marinichev

TORPEDO NIZHNY NOVGOROD
Founded: 1946
Previous Name: Torpedo Gorky
Arena: Sports Palace GAZ
Capacity: 4,300
2nd place: 1961
Top Goalies: Viktor Konovalenko, Sergei Fadeyev
Top Defensemen: Vladimir Solodov, Vyacheslav Zhidkov, Vladimir Astafjev, Yuri Fedorov, Alexander Kulikov
Top Forwards: Lev Khalaichev, Robert Sakharovsky, Igor Chistovsky, Alexei Mishin, Vladimir Kovin, Mikhail Varnakov, Alexander Skvortsov
Top Coaches: Dmitri Boginov, Alexander Prilepsky, Nikolai Karpov, Yuri Morozov

SALAVAT YULAYEV UFA
Founded: 1961
Arena: Ice Sports Palace
Capacity: 4,200
3rd place: 1995, 1996, 1997
Top Goalies: Viktor Cherednik, Vladimir Tikhomirov
Top Defensemen: Anatoli Shalayev, Irek Gimayev, Sergei Gimayev, Andrei Yakhanov, Andrei Zyuzin
Top Forwards: Mikhail Anferov, Nikolai Zavarukhin Sr., Vladimir Bykov, Robert Murduskin, Ramil Yuldashev, Dmitri Denisov, Boris Timofeyev, Rail Muftiyev, Denis Afinogenov
Top Coaches: Valeri Nikitoin, Marat Azamatov, Rafail Ishmatov

METALLURG MAGNITOGORSK
Founded: 1950
Arena: Ice Sports Palace imeni I.H.Romazana
Capacity: 3,000
2nd place: 1998
3rd place: 1995
Top Goalies: Albert Shirgaziyev
Top Defensemen: Igor Zemlyanoi, Sergei Tertyshny, Yevgeny Shalygin, Valeri Nikulin
Top Forwards: Sergei Gomolyako, Sergei Devyatkov, Sergei Osipov, Igor Varitsky
Top Coaches: Valeri Postnikov

AK BARS KAZAN
Founded: 1955
Previous Names: SK imeni Uritskogo Kazan, Itil Kazan
Arena: Sports Palace
Capacity: 3,600
National Title: 1998
Top Goalies: Sergei Abramov
Top Defensemen: Rafik Yakubov, Vladislav Makarov
Top Forwards: Mikhail Sarmatin, Eduard Kudermetov, Almaz Garifullin, Alexei Chupin, Sergei Zolotov, Andrei Makarov
Top Coaches: Yuri Moiseyev

AVANGARD OMSK
Founded: 1950
Previous Names: Spartak Omsk, Aeroflot Omsk, Kauchuk Omsk, Khimik Omsk, Shinnik Omsk
Arena: Sports Complex Irtysh
Capacity: 5,200
3rd place: 1996
Top Goalies: Sergei Kharmtsov
Top Defensemen: Viktor Blinov, Sergei Korobkin, Konstantin Maslyukov
Top Forwards: Sergei Berdnikov, Nikolai Marinenko, Sergei Yelakov, Igor Belyaevsky
Top Coaches: Leonid Kiselev

TRAKTOR CHELYABINSK
Founded: 1947
Previous Names: Dzerzhinets Chelyabinsk, Avangard Chelyabinsk
Arena: Sports Palace Yunost
Capacity: 3,500
3rd place: 1977, 1993, 1994
Top Goalies: Leonid Gerasimov, Sergei Mylnikov, Andrei Zuyev
Top Defensemen: Nikolai Makarov, Sergei Babinov, Sergei Starikov, Oleg Davydov, Andrei Sapozhnikov
Top Forwards: Viktor Shuvalov, Anatoli Kartayev, Nikolai Shorin, Valeri Belousov, Petr Prorodin, Valeri Yevstifeyev, Sergei Makarov, Sergei Khrischev, Anatoli Chistyakov, Valeri Karpov, Igor Varitsky
Top Coaches: Anatoli Kostryukov, Gennady Tsygurov, Valeri Belousov

KRISTALL SARATOV
Founded: 1960
Previous Names: Avangard Saratov, Energetik Saratov
Arena: Sports Palace Kristall
Capacity: 5,010
Top Goalies: Vladimir Myshkin, Alexander Kulikov, Sergei Babariko
Top Defensemen: Sergei Borisov, Vladimir Kuplinov, Viktor Shevelev, Vladimir Krikunov
Top Forwards: Boris Mikhailov, Vladimir Golubovich, Alexander Barinev, Vadimir Semenov, Valeri Chekalkin, Nikolai Stakanov, Petr Malkov, Andrei Korolev, Sergei Zhebrovsky
Top Coaches: Robert Cherenkov

METALLURG NOVOKUZNETSK
Founded: 1949
Arena: Sports Palace Metallurg
Capacity: 8,050
Top Goalies: Vladimir Shepovalov
Top Defensemen: Yuri Zuyev
Top Forwards: Oleg Korolenko, Yuri Moiseyev, Anatoli Motovilov, Igor Samochernov, Vladislav Morozov

SIBIR NOVOSIBIRSK
Founded: 1949
Previous Name: Dynamo Novosibirsk
Arena: Sports Ice Palace Sibir
Capacity: 8,300
Top Goalies: Viktor Doroschenko
Top Defensemen: Alexei Volchenkov, Alexander Fatkullin, Arkadi Bagayev, Sergei Selyanin
Top Forwards: Vitali Stain, Vladimir Kungurtsev, Viktor Zhuchok, Georgy Uglov, Gennady Kapkaikin, Boris Barabanov, Vladimir Melenchuk, Yuri Klemeshov
Top Coaches: Vitali Stain

DYNAMO-ENERGIYA YEKATERINBURG
Founded: 1948
Previous Names: Spartak Sverdlovsk, Avtomobilist Sverdlovsk, Avtomobilist Yekaterinburg, Spartak Yekaterinburg
Arena: Sports Ice Palace
Capacity: 3,800
Top Goalies: Valeri Zubarev, Viktor Puchkov, Alexander Semenov
Top Defensemen: Alexander Kartsev, Alexander Baldin, Yuri Glotov, Alexander Astashev, Viktor Kuznetsov, Ilja Byakin, Andrei Martemjanov, Pavel Velizhanin
Top Forwards: Rem Mendubayev, Valeri Chekalkin, Viktor Kutergin, Vitali Krayev, Arkadi Rudakov,

Sergei Shepelev, Nikolai Narimanov, Mikhail Malko, Oleg Starkov, Leonid Trukhno, Vladimir Yeremin, Dmitri Popov
Top Coaches: Sergei Mitin

MOLOT-PRIKAMJE PERM
Founded: 1948
Previous Names: Perm, SK imeni Sverdlova Perm, Molot Perm
Arena: Universal Sports Palace Molot
Capacity: 6,000
Top Goalies: Valeri Yerokhin
Top Defensemen: Yuri Pepelyaev, Vasili Spiridonov, Igor Ulanov
Top Forwards: Sergei Shitkovsky, Alexander Gulyavtsev, Dmitri Romanov

SEVERSTAL CHEREPOVETS
Founded: 1956
Previous Name: Metallurg Cherepovets
Arena: Sports Palace Almaz
Capacity: 3,500
Top Defensemen: Andrei Kozyrev
Top Forwards: Igor Starkovsky, Igor Nikulin, Igor Petrov, Vladimir Kochin, Mikhail Ivanov
Top Coaches: Vladimir Golev

RUBIN TYMEN
Founded: 1959
Arena: Sports Palace Rubin
Capacity: 4,000
Top Goalies: Andrei Vasilevsky
Top Defensemen: Vladimir Kapulovsky, Viktor Arkhipov
Top Forwards: Nikolai babenko, Eduard Valiullin, Igor Latyshev
Top Coaches: Alexander Kuzmin

CSK VVS SAMARA
Founded: 1992
Arena: Sports Palace CSK VVS
Capacity: 3,000
Top Goalies: Alexei Sharnin
Top Defensemen: Oleg Yushin
Top Forwards: Aidar Musakayev, Alexei Klimantov, Zakhar Gataulin, Vladimir Yelovikov
Top Coaches: Alexander Astashev

SLOVAKIA

DUKLA TRENCIN
Founded: 1962
Previous Names: ASVS Trencin
Arena: Zimni Stadion
Capacity: 6,150
National Title: 1992, 1994, 1997
2nd place: 1989, 1990, 1995, 1996
3rd place: 1991, 1993
Top Goalies: Eduard Hartmann, Igor Murin
Top Defensemen: Stanislav Medrik, Ernest Bokros, Lubomir Sekeras, Robert Svehla, Milos Holan
Top Forwards: Miroslav Miklosovic, Marian Horvath, Lubomir Kolnik, Oto Hascak, Roman Kontsek, Branislav Janos, Zigmund Palffy, Zdeno Ciger, Jozef Dano, Miroslav Satan, Robert Petrovicky, Jan Pardavy, Marian Hossa
Top Coaches: Julius Supler, Frantisek Hossa

HC KOSICE
Founded: 1967
Previous Names: Dukla Kosice, VSZ Kosice
Arena: Zimni Stadion
Capacity: 5,081
National Title: 1986, 1988, 1995, 1996
2nd place: 1985, 1994, 1997, 1998
3rd place: 1989, 1992

Top Goalies: Jiri Holecek, Pavol Svitana, Pavol Svarny, Jaromir Dragan
Top Defensemen: Frantisek Gregor, Vladimir Sandrik, Juraj Bakos, Peter Slanina, Mojmir Bozik, Jergus Baca, Miroslav Marcinko, Jan Varholik, Stanislav Jasecko
Top Forwards: Frantisek Kollath, Jan Faith, Jan Sterbak, Bedrich Brunclik, Vincent Lukac, Igor Liba, Vladimir Svitek, Jan Vodila, Jozef Lukac, Miroslav Ihnacak, Petr Ihnacak, Milan Stas, Zdenek Nedved, Vlastimil Plavucha, Rene Pucher, Lubomir Rybovic, Peter Bondra
Top Coaches: Jan Faith, Bedrich Brunclik

HC MARTIMEX ZTS MARTIN
Founded: 1932
Previous Names: Slavia Martin, Sokol Martin, SK Martin, ZTS Martin, Hutnik Martin, Martimex ZTS Martin, HC Martimex Martin
Arena: Zimni Stadion
Capacity: 3,000
3rd place: 1994
Top Forwards: Jaroslav Markovic, Karol Ondreicka, Marian Uharcek, Peter Bartos, Jaroslav Torok, Ladislav Majercik, Michal Beran
Top Coaches: Frantisek Hossa

MHC PLASTIKA NITRA
Founded: 1931
Previous Names: AC Nitra, Sokol Nitra, Komunalny podnik Nitra, Spojene zavody Nitra, Slavoj Nitra, Slovan Nitra, Start Nitra, Plastika Nitra, HC Nitra
Arena: Zimni Stadion
Capacity: 4,000
Top Goalies: Ivan Harvanek
Top Defensemen: Tibor Turan
Top Forwards: Zigmund Palffy, Jozef Dano, Jozef Stumpel, Vladimir Beres, Ivan Ciernik
Top Coaches: Julius Cernicky

HC SK SLOVAN HARVARD BRATISLAVA
Founded: 1921
Previous Names: 1.CsSK, SK Bratislava, Sokol NV Bratislava, Slovan Bratislava, HC Slovan Bratislava
Arena: Zimni Stadion
Capacity: 8,000
National Title: 1979, 1998
2nd place: 1949, 1960, 1961, 1962, 1964, 1965, 1970, 1972
3rd place: 1963, 1966, 1969, 1973, 1980, 1996
Top Goalies: Vladimir Dzurilla, Marcel Sakac
Top Defensemen: Lubomir Ujvary, Milan Kuzela, Frantisek Gregor, Jozef Bukovinsky, Lubomir Rohacik, Eduard Uvira, Rudolf Tajcnar
Top Forwards: Jan Starsi, Stefan Kordiak, Jaroslav Walter, Milan Mrukvia, Vaclav Nedomansky, Ivan Grandtner, Jozef Golonka, Julius Haas, Darius Rusnak, Dusan Pasek, Marian Stastny, Peter Stastny, Anton Stastny, Ivan Dornic, Jan Jasko, Jozef Petho, Dusan Pohorelec, Karol Rusznyak, Jozef Voskar
Top Coaches: Ladislav Horsky, Jan Starsi, Jaroslav Walter, Dusan Ziska

HC SKP POPRAD-TATRY
Founded: 1926
Previous Names: SK Visoke Tatry, Karpatenverein Poprad, HC Poprad, HC Tatry, Tatranske pily Poprad, Tatran poprad, Lokomotiva Poprad Tatrapily, Lokomotiva

Vagonka Stavbar, Lokomotiva Stavbar,
Pozemne stavby SKP PS Poprad
Arena: Zimni Stadion
Capacity: 4,200
3rd place: 1995, 1997
Top Goalies: Jaroslav Landsman
Top Defensemen: Miroslav Turan,
Miroslav Javin
Top Forwards: Stanislav Horansky, Anton
Lach, Arne Krotak, Roman Stantien,
Slavomir Pavlicko
Top Coaches: Julius Supler

HK 32 LIPTOVSKY MIKULAS
Founded: 1932
Previous Names: Sokol Liptovsky Mikulas,
HG Liptovsky Mikulas, SK Liptovsky
Mikulas, SK Bata Liptovsky Mikulas,
Sokol Partizan Liptovsky Mikulas,
Iskra Liptovsky Mikulas,
Partizan Liptovsky Mikulas
Arena: Zimni Stadion
Capacity: 3,820
Top Defensemen: Juraj Kledrowetz,
Rudolf Zaruba
Top Forwards: Jan Pich, Jan Gazo,
Anton Kalousek

HK 36 SKALICA
Founded: 1947
Previous Names: Sokol Tekla Skalica,
Tatran Skalica, ZVL Skalica
Arena: Zimni Stadion
Capacity: 3,000
Top Goalies: Pavol Rybar
Top Defensemen: Stanislav Meciar
Top Forwards: Ivan Hrtus, Zdenek Jurasek
Top Coaches: Jiri Macelis

HK VTJ SPISSKA NOVA VES
Founded: 1932
Previous Names: AC Spisska Nova Ves,
Lokomotiva Spisska Nova Ves, Zeleznicar
Stavbar Spisska Nova Ves, Start Spisska
Nova Ves, HK Spisska Nova Ves
Arena: Zimni Stadion
Capacity: 5,000
Top Goalies: Eduard Hartmann
Top Defensemen: Stanislav Jasecko,
Miroslav Marcinko, Martin Strbak
Top Forwards: Marian Horvath,
Miroslav Farkasovsky, Anton Bartanus,
Rudolf Vercik, Vladimir Svitek

HK ZVOLEN
Founded: 1927
Previous Names: ZTC Zvolen, HC Zvolen,
ZTK Zlolen, ZZTK Zvolen, Lokomotiva
Zvolen, Tatran Bucina Zvolen, Lokomotiva
Bucina Zvolen
Arena: Zimni Stadion
Capacity: 5,000
Top Goalies: Jan Beno, Miroslav Michalek
Top Defensemen: Ladislav Cierny,
Peter Hricina
Top Forwards: Jozef Golonka,
Dusan Pohorelec, Andrej Podkonicky,
Peter Slamiar
Top Coaches: Bretislav Guryca

SWEDEN

AIK SOLNA
Founded: 1921
Arena: Globe Arena
Capacity: 13,850
National Title: 1934, 1935, 1938,
1946, 1947, 1982, 1984
2nd place: 1930, 1936, 1940,
1968, 1978, 1981
Top Goalies: Kjell Svensson,

Leif Holmqvist, Pelle Lindbergh,
Rolf Ridderwall
Top Defensemen: Bert-Ola Nordlander,
Bo Ericson, Mats Thelin, Mattias Norstrom
Top Forwards: Lars-Eric Ericsson,
Bengt Lundholm, Rolf Edberg,
Leif Holmgren, Ulf Nilsson, Ulf Isaksson,
Anders Hakansson, Mats Ulander,
Pelle Eklund, Thomas Gradin
Top Coaches: Erling Lindstrom,
Anders Parmstrom, Timo Lahtinen

BRYNAS IF GAVLE
Founded: 1955
Arena: Gavlerinken
Capacity: 6,200
National Title: 1964, 1966, 1967, 1968,
1970, 1971, 1972, 1976, 1977, 1980, 1993
2nd place: 1965, 1969, 1975, 1995
Top Goalies: William Lofqvist, Ake
Lilljebjorn, Michael Sundlov
Top Defensemen: Stig Ostling, Stig Salming,
Borje Salming, Mats Kihlstrom
Top Forwards: Lars-Goran Nilsson, Tord
Lundstrom, Hakan Wickberg, Hans Lindberg,
Stefan Karlsson, Inge Hammarstrom, Lars-
Gunnar Lundberg, Lars-Eric Ericsson, Mats
Naslund, Tomas Sandstrom, Andreas Dackell
Top Coaches: Tommy Sandlin

DJURGARDENS IF STOCKHOLM
Founded: 1921
Arena: Globe Arena
Capacity: 13,850
National Title: 1926, 1950, 1954, 1955,
1958, 1959, 1960, 1961, 1962, 1963,
1983, 1989, 1990, 1991
2nd place: 1923, 1924, 1927, 1956,
1957, 1979, 1984, 1985, 1992, 1998
Top Goalies: Yngve Johansson,
Rolf Ridderwall
Top Defensemen: Lars Bjorn, Roland Stoltz,
Leif Svensson, Tomas Jonsson,
Thomas Eriksson, Mikael Thelven,
Tommy Albelin, Arto Blomsten, Kenneth
Kennholt, Marcus Ragnarsson
Top Forwards: Gosta Johansson,
Sven-Tumba Johansson, Hans Tvilling,
Stig Tvilling, Carl Goran Oberg, Hans Mild,
Bjorn Palmqvist, Anders Hedberg,
Hakan Sodergren, Kent Nilsson, Jens Ohling,
Mats Sundin, Charles Bergman
Top Coaches: Arne Stromberg,
Bert-Ola Nordlander, Eilert Maatta,
Leif Boork, Lars Falk

FARJESTADS BK KARLSTAD
Founded: 1932
Arena: Farjestads Ishall
Capacity: 4,700
National Title: 1981, 1986,
1988, 1997, 1998
2nd place: 1976, 1977, 1983,
1987, 1990, 1991
Top Goalies: Lennart Andersson,
Peter Lindmark
Top Defensemen: Karl-Johan Sundqvist,
Lars Zetterstrom, Tommy Samuelsson,
Peter Loob, Hakan Nordin,
Fredrik Olausson, Roger Johansson
Top Forwards: Ulf Sterner, Bengt-Ake
Gustafsson, Anders Steen, Hakan Loob,
Thomas Rundqvist, Magnus Roupe,
Kent-Erik Andersson, Jorgen Jonsson,
Peter Ottosson, Magnus Arvedson
Top Coaches: Per Backman,
Conny Evensson

HV 71 JONKOPING
Founded: 1971
Arena: Rosenlundshallen

Capacity: 4,500
National Title: 1995
Top Goalies: Boo Ahl, Peter Aslin
Top Defensemen: Fredrik Stillman,
Lars Ivarsson, Kenneth Kennholt,
Per Gustafsson
Top Forwards: Peter Eriksson,
Anders Huusko, Erik Huusko,
Johan Lindbom, Johan Davidsson,
Esa Keskinen, Patrik Kjellberg
Top Coaches: Sune Bergman

LEKSANDS IF
Founded: 1919
Arena: Leksands Isstadion
Capacity: 6,900
National Title: 1969, 1973, 1974, 1975
2nd place: 1959, 1964, 1971, 1972, 1989
Top Goalies: Christer Abrahamsson,
Goran Hogosta, Peter Aslin, Ake Lilljebjorn
Top Defensemen: Ake Lallas,
Vilgot Larsson, Thommy Abrahamsson,
Roland Bond, Lars-Erik Sjoberg,
Ulf Weinstock, Tomas Jonsson,
Magnus Svensson
Top Forwards: Nils Nilsson, Sigurd Broms,
Folke Bengtsson, Mats Ahlberg,
Dan Soderstrom, Dan Labraaten, Per-Olov
Brasar, Hans Jax, Roland Eriksson,
Jonas Bergqvist, Thomas Steen,
Marcus Thuresson,
Top Coaches: Per-Agne Carlstrom,
Roland Bond, Wayne Fleming

LULEA HF
Founded: 1977
Arena: Ishallen Delfinen
Capacity: 6,000
National Title: 1996
2nd place: 1993, 1997
Top Goalies: Robert Skoog, Jarmo Myllys
Top Defensemen: Robert Nordmark,
Lars Lindgren, Mattias Ohlund,
Roger Akerstom
Top Forwards: Johan Stromwall,
Mikael Renberg, Lars-Gunnar Pettersson,
Lars Edstrom, Stefan Nilsson
Top Coaches: Lars Bergstrom

MALMO IF
Founded: 1956
Previous Names: Malmo FF
Arena: Malmo Isstadion
Capacity: 5,800
National Title: 1992, 1994
Top Goalies: Roger Nordstrom,
Peter Lindmark
Top Defensemen: Peter Andersson,
Timo Blomqvist, Mats Lusth, Robert Svehla
Top Forwards: Robert Burakovsky,
Roger Hansson, Mats Naslund,
Peter Sundtsrom, Daniel Rydmark,
Raimo Helminen, Matti Pauna,
Hakan Ahlund
Top Coaches: Timo Lahtinen

MODO HK ORNSKOLDSVIK
Founded: 1938
Previous Names: Alfredshem IK,
MoDo AIK Ornskoldsvik
Arena: Kempehallen
Capacity: 6,500
National Title: 1979
2nd place: 1994
Top Goalies: Fredrik Andersson
Top Defensemen: Nils Johansson,
Kjell-Rune Milton, Lars Lindgren,
Tomas Jonsson, Anders Eriksson
Top Forwards: Andres Hedberg,
Hakan Nygren, Thomas Gradin, Lars Molin,
Mikko Leinonen, Markus Naslund,

Peter Forsberg, Niklas Sundstrom
Top Coaches: Tommy Sandlin,
Kent Forsberg, Leif Boork

SODERTALJE SK
Founded: 1922
Arena: Scaniarinken
Capacity: 7,500
National Title: 1925, 1931, 1941,
1944, 1953, 1956, 1985
2nd place: 1928, 1929, 1932, 1937, 1942,
1945, 1946, 1951, 1960, 1973, 1986
Top Goalies: Carl Abrahamsson, Thord
Flodqvist, Kjell Svensson
Top Defensemen: Sven Thunman, Eilert
Maatta, Bjorn Johansson, Mats Waltin,
Bo Ericson, Anders Eldebrink,
Mats Kihlstrom
Top Forwards: Erik Johansson,
Mats Hysing, Stig Carlsson, Gote Blomqvist,
Ronald Pettersson, Stig-Goran Johansson,
Thom Eklund, Anders Kallur,
Dick Yderstrom, Kjell-Arne Wickstrom
Top Coaches: Kjell Svensson

VASTERAS IK
Founded: 1924
Previous Names: Vasteras SK
Arena: Rocklundahallen
Capacity: 6,100
2nd place: 1925, 1926
Top Goalies: Tomy Salo
Top Defensemen: Peter Popovic,
Leif Rohlin, Robert Nordmark,
Lars Ivarsson, Nicklas Lidstrom
Top Forwards: Uno Ohrlund,
Lars Pettersson, Patrik Juhlin,
Fredrik Nilsson
Top Coaches: Mikael Lundstrom

VASTRA FROLUNDA HC GOTEBORG
Founded: 1939
Previous Names: Vastra Frolunda IF Goteborg
Arena: Scandinavium
Capacity: 11,900
National Title: 1965
2nd place: 1962, 1966, 1967,
1970, 1980, 1996
Top Goalies: Goran Hogosta,
Hakan Algotsson
Top Defensemen: Gert Blome,
Arne Carlsson, Lars-Erik Sjoberg,
Thommie Bergman, Lars-Erik Esbjors,
Ronnie Sundin, Arto Blomsten
Top Forwards: Ronald Pettersson,
Ulf Sterner, Lars-Eric Lundvall,
Leif Henriksson, Mats linds, Finn Lundstrom,
Thomas Sjogren, Daniel Alfredsson
Top Coaches: Arne Stromberg, Leif Boork

SWITZERLAND

HC AMBRI-PIOTTA
Founded: 1937
Arena: Eisbahn Valascia
Capacity: 7,500
3rd place: 1987, 1988
Top Goalies: Danilo Morandi, Pauli Jaks
Top Defensemen: Ueli Hofmann,
Jakob Kolliker, Beat Ruedi
Top Forwards: Dale McCourt, Bixio Celio,
Urs Bartschi, Guido Lindemann,
John Fritsche, Dmitri Kvartalnov,
Igor Chibirev
Top Coaches: Alexander Yakushev

SC BERN
Founded: 1931

Arena: Eisstadion Allmend
Capacity: 16,855
National Title: 1959, 1965, 1974, 1975,
1977, 1979, 1989, 1991, 1992, 1997
2nd place: 1990, 1996
Top Goalies: Edi Grubauer, Paul Wyss,
Rene Kiener, Renato Tosio
Top Defensemen: Emil Handschin,
Ueli Hofmann, Rolf Tschanz, Timo Jutila,
Sven Leuenberger, Reijo Ruotsalainen,
Martin Rauch
Top Forwards: Bruno Wittwer,
Thomas Vrabec, Gaetan Boucher,
Patrick Howald, Gil Montandon,
Gaetano Orlando
Top Coaches: Jean-Paul Cadieux, Xaver
Unsinn, Craig Sarner, Bryan Lefley

HC LA CHAUX-DE-FONDS
Founded: 1919
Arena: Patinoire de Melezes
Capacity: 7,000
National Title: 1968, 1969, 1970,
1971, 1972, 1973
Top Goalies: Gerald Rigolet,
Top Defensemen: Gaston Furrer,
Charles Henzen, Rene Huguenin,
Top Forwards: Reto Delnon, Rolf Diethelm,
Guy Dubuis, Willi Pfister, Daniel Piller,
Michel Turler, Toni Neininger,
Bruno Wittwer, Jan Alston,
Top Coaches: Jan Soukup, Jean Cusson

HC DAVOS
Founded: 1921
Previous Names: EHC Davos
Arena: Eisstadion Davos
Capacity: 7,600
National Title: 1926, 1927, 1929, 1930,
1931, 1932, 1933, 1934, 1935, 1937, 1938,
1939, 1941, 1942, 1943, 1944, 1945, 1946,
1947, 1948, 1950, 1958, 1960, 1984, 1985,
2nd place: 1986, 1998
Top Goalies: Jean Ayer, Danilo Morandi,
Martin Riesen
Top Defensemen: Emil Handschin,
Samuel Balmer, Beat Ruedi,
Fausto Mazzoleni, Valeri Shiryaev
Top Forwards: Ferdinand Cattini,
Hans Cattini, Richard Torriani,
Albert Geromini, Walter Durst,
Otto Schlapfer, Fritz Naef, Herbert Kessler,
Jorg Eberle, Dan Hodgson, Christian Weber,
Jacques Soguel, Ken Yaremchuk
Top Coaches: Richard Torriani,
Stu Robertson, Herb Brooks, Dan Hober

HC FRIBOURG-GOTTERON
Founded: 1937
Arena: Patinoire Communale St-Leonard
Capacity: 7,500
2nd place: 1983, 1992, 1993, 1994
Top Goalies: Gerald Rigolet,
Top Defensemen: Rolf Tschanz,
Samuel Balmer, Patrice Brasey
Top Forwards: Reto Delnon, Alfred Luthi,
Vyacheslav Bykov, Andrei Khomutov,
Mario Rottaris, Gil Montandon
Top Coaches: Paul-Andre Cadieux,
Kjell Larsson

EHC KLOTEN
Founded: 1934
Arena: Schluefweg
Capacity: 7,579
National Title: 1967, 1993,
1994, 1995, 1996
2nd place: 1972, 1987, 1988

3rd place: 1986
Top Goalies: Reto Pavoni
Top Defensemen: Fausto Mazzoleni,
Anders Eldebrink, Greg Brown
Top Forwards: Urs Bartschi, Urs Lott,
Ueli Luthi, Peter Schlagenhauf,
Charles Berglund, Kent Nilsson,
Manuele Celio, Jorg Eberle, Andy Ton,
Felix Hollenstein, Mikael Johansson,
Roman Wager
Top Coaches: G. von Arx, Otto Schlapfer,
Andy Murray, Conny Evensson,
Wayne Fleming

HC LUGANO
Founded: 1940
Arena: Pista La Resega
Capacity: 8,000
National Title: 1986, 1987, 1988, 1990
2nd place: 1985, 1989, 1991,
Top Goalies: Alfio Molina, Gerald Rigolet,
Lars Weibel
Top Defensemen: Aldo Zenhausern,
Samuel Balmer, Sandro Bertaggia,
Luigi Riva, Mats Waltin, Kari Eloranta,
Tommy Sjodin
Top Forwards: Arnold Lortscher,
Thomas Vrabec, Alfred Luthi, Jorg Eberle,
Kent Nilsson, Patrick Howald, Andy Ton,
Stephane Lebeau
Top Coaches: Beat Ruedi,
John Slettvoll, Mats Waltin

SC RAPPERSWIL-JONA
Founded: 1945
Arena: Eishalle Lido
Capacity: 6,000
Top Defensemen: Pekka Rautakallio
Top Forwards: Serge Soguel,
Gilles Thibaudeau
Top Coaches: Otto Schubiger,
Pekka Rautakallio

EV ZUG
Founded: 1967
Arena: Kunsteisbahn Zug AG
Capacity: 7,650
2nd place: 1995, 1997, 1998
Top Goalies: Gerald Rigolet
Top Defensemen: Dino Kessler,
Andre Kunzi, Andreas Ritsch, Patrick Sutter
Top Forwards: Ivan Hlinka, Ken
Yaremchuk, Arnold Lortscher, Ueli Luthi,
Misko Antisin, Philipp Neuenschwander
Top Coaches: Bjorn Kinding, Andy Murray

ZURCHER SCHLITTSCHUH-CLUB
Founded: 1930
Arena: Hallenstadion AG
Capacity: 11,500
National Title: 1936, 1949, 1961
Top Goalies: Hans Banninger
Top Defensemen: Rolf Tschanz,
Reto Sturzenegger, Peter Wespi,
Robert Nordmark
Top Forwards: Richard Torriani,
Hans Keller, Herbert Kessler, Otto Schubiger,
Otto Schlapfer, Heini Lohrer, Urs Lott,
Fran Huck, Arnold Lortscher,
Andy Ton, Milan Novy
Top Coaches: Pavel Wohl, Alpo Suhonen

SC HERISAU
Founded: 1942
Arena: Eishalle Sportzentrum Herisau
Capacity: 4,000
Top Forwards: Jorg Eberle, Claude Vilgrain
Top Coaches: Giovanni Conte

CHAPTER 45

Leading National Leagues

Final Standings, 1992–93 to 1997–98, for Major European and Japanese National Leagues

INTERNATIONAL HOCKEY usually evokes images of players wearing the uniforms of their national teams, but in almost all hockey countries, a national league also flourishes. Club teams are supported in Europe and Asia in the same way that NHL clubs are followed by their fans in North America.

European leagues often consist of two or more division, with promotion and relegation between these divisions determined by results each season.

Top division standings are provided here for the following 16 countries: Austria, Czech Republic, Denmark, Finland, France, Germany, Great Britain, the Netherlands, Italy, Japan, Norway, Poland, Russia, Slovakia, Sweden and Switzerland

AUSTRIA

1992–93

Team	GP	W	L	T	GF	GA	PTS
VSV Villach	20	11	6	3	82	66	29
EC Graz	20	8	5	7	74	61	26
EK Zell am See	20	10	7	3	66	65	24
IEV Innsbruck	20	8	7	5	69	62	21
KAC Klagenfurt	20	8	7	5	75	71	21
VEU Feldkirch	20	2	15	3	64	105	9

Note: Alpenliga bonus points included

1993–94

Team	GP	W	L	T	GF	GA	PTS
EC Graz	18	10	6	2	67	50	25
EC Villach SV	18	8	6	4	66	61	20
VEU Feldkirch	18	7	8	3	54	62	19
Klagenfurter AC	18	5	10	3	53	67	14

1994–95
1ST TO 6TH PLACE

Team	GP	W	L	T	GF	GA	PTS
VEU Feldkirch	10	9	0	1	55	20	20
Klagenfurter AC	10	7	2	1	64	34	18
VSV Villach	10	5	4	1	45	31	15
ECO Graz	10	5	4	1	42	33	13
EC Ehrwald	10	1	9	0	26	62	2
EHC Lustenau	10	1	9	0	21	73	2

Bonus points included

7TH TO 10TH PLACE

Team	GP	W	L	T	GF	GA	PTS
SV Kapfenberg	12	6	5	1	60	51	14
CE Wien	12	5	5	2	65	63	14
EV Zeltweg	12	6	5	1	62	70	13
Pinzgauer Eisbaren	12	4	6	2	54	57	10

1995–96

Team	GP	W	L	T	GF	GA	PTS
VEU Feldkirch	28	23	2	3	170	63	49
Klagenfurter AC	28	17	6	5	137	78	39
VSV Villach	28	15	5	8	151	80	38
CE Wien	28	12	8	8	130	97	32
EHC Lustenau	28	11	15	2	108	116	24
SV Kapfenberg	28	7	15	6	78	127	20
ECO Graz	28	4	19	5	67	164	13
EV Zeltweg	28	3	21	3	75	201	9

1996–97

Team	GP	W	L	T	GF	GA	PTS
EC P. Kapfenberg	4	3	1	0	20	13	6
CE Wien	4	3	1	0	29	14	6
EC Graz	4	0	3	0	14	36	0

1997–98

Team	GP	W	L	T	GF	GA	PTS
VEU Feldkirch	18	10	5	3	65	46	27
Klagenfurter AC	18	10	5	3	74	66	26
VSV Villach	18	10	6	2	74	62	23
EV Wien	18	8	8	1	83	68	21
EC Graz	18	5	12	1	79	85	11

Note: Alpenliga bonus points included

CZECHOSLOVAKIA

1992–93

Team	GP	W	L	T	GF	GA	PTS
HC Litvinov	40	25	12	3	168	126	53
HC Sparta Praha	40	22	9	9	150	108	53
HK Dukla Trencin	40	21	15	4	167	146	46
SSK Vitkovice	40	20	16	4	174	147	44
HC Ceske Budejovice	40	18	14	8	142	122	44
SONP Poldi Kladno	40	21	18	1	135	142	43
HC Kosice	40	19	18	3	137	140	41
AC ZP Zlin	40	17	18	5	126	120	39
HC Dukla Jihlava	40	17	19	4	137	143	38
HC Olomouc	40	16	20	4	131	150	36
SKP Poprad	40	16	21	3	124	149	35
HC Pardubice	40	14	23	4	123	161	31
Slovan Bratislava	40	12	21	7	115	145	31
HC Skoda Plzen	40	12	26	2	125	153	26

CZECH REPUBLIC

1993–94

Team	GP	W	L	T	GF	GA	PTS
HC Kladno	44	24	12	8	182	151	56
HC Ceske Budejovice	44	23	15	6	163	120	52
SSK Vitkovice	44	19	14	11	162	138	49
AC ZPS Zlin	44	21	16	7	154	163	49
HC Sparta Praha	44	21	17	6	162	129	48
HC Pardubice	44	22	18	4	142	128	48
HC Olomouc	44	19	18	7	116	123	45
HC CHP Litvinov	44	18	18	8	161	154	44
HC Skoda Plzen	44	15	21	8	132	140	38
HC Dukla Iglau	44	16	22	6	131	143	38
HC Hradec Kralove	44	12	21	11	133	163	35
HC Vajgar J. Hradec	44	10	28	6	107	193	26

1994–95

Team	GP	W	L	T	GF	GA	PTS
HC Vsetin	44	23	13	8	141	107	54
HC Kladno	44	24	14	6	178	142	54
HC Olomouc	44	19	15	10	130	124	48
AC ZPS Zlin	44	20	16	8	158	149	48
HC Skoda Plzen	44	16	14	14	118	112	46
HC Ceske Budejovice	44	18	18	8	142	124	46
HC Slavia Praha	44	18	19	7	133	164	43
HC CHP Litvinov	44	18	20	6	149	143	42
HC Sparta Praha	44	16	19	9	123	129	41
HC Vitkovice	44	18	21	5	144	156	41
HC Pardubice	44	13	20	11	134	151	37
HC Dukla Jihlava	44	12	28	4	117	166	28

1995–96

Team	GP	W	L	T	GF	GA	PTS
HC Sparta Praha	40	27	10	3	152	108	57
HC Petra Vsetin	40	24	9	7	149	85	55
HC Ceske Budejovice	40	20	11	9	120	85	49
Chemopetrol Litvinov	40	21	12	7	155	117	49
AC ZPS Zlin	40	20	14	6	126	111	46
Slavia Praha	40	18	17	5	148	140	41
HC Olomouc	40	16	18	6	112	109	40
HC Kladno	40	17	18	5	127	131	39
HC Vitkovice	40	13	16	11	105	121	37
HC Dukla Jihlava	40	13	18	9	115	142	35
ZKZ Plzen	40	12	21	7	103	134	31
HC Zelezarny Trinec	40	12	22	6	128	162	30
Pojistovna Pardubice	40	12	24	4	103	128	28
Kometa BVV Brno	40	9	26	5	95	165	23

1996–97

Team	GP	W	L	T	GF	GA	PTS
HC Petra Vsetin	52	34	11	7	198	120	75
HC Sparta Praha	52	28	13	11	227	168	67
HC Vitkovice	52	25	15	12	160	120	62
HC Zelezarny Trinec	52	23	19	10	175	152	56
Pojistovna Pardubice	52	25	22	5	170	164	55
Poldi Kladno	52	21	19	12	132	152	54
HC Ceske Budejovice	52	20	20	12	149	145	52
HC Slavia Praha	52	21	21	10	166	167	52
Chemopetrol Litvinov	52	20	20	12	171	185	52
ZRS Zlin	52	22	24	6	179	179	50
ZKZ Plzen	52	19	24	9	155	172	47
HC Olomouc	52	16	25	11	122	155	43
HC Dukla Jihlava	52	13	29	10	140	187	36
Slezan Opava	52	10	35	7	125	203	27

1997–98

Team	GP	W	L	T	GF	GA	PTS
HC Petra Vsetin	52	33	13	6	181	116	72
HC Vitkovice	52	31	14	7	174	142	69
HC Zelezarny Trinec	52	29	12	11	189	156	69
HC Sparta Praha	52	27	15	10	176	117	64
HC ZKZ Plzen	52	24	17	11	160	146	59
HC Slavia Praha	52	22	18	12	152	132	56
Chemopetrol Litvinov	52	22	18	12	167	128	56
Pojistovna Pardubice	52	22	22	8	158	149	52
HC Dukla Jihlava	52	21	22	9	137	139	51
HC Ceske Budejovice	52	19	23	10	149	149	48
HC ZPS Barum Zlin	52	20	24	8	166	183	48
HC Velvana Kladno	52	11	31	10	124	194	32
HC B. Karlovy Vary	52	9	31	12	130	202	30
HC B. Trade Opava	52	7	37	8	101	211	22

DENMARK

1992–93

Team	GP	W	L	T	GF	GA	PTS
Esbjerg IK	10	8	1	1	61	41	32
Herning IK	10	6	3	1	64	44	28
Rungsted IK	10	4	5	1	48	46	21
Rodovre SIK	10	3	7	0	41	68	19
AAB Aalborg	10	3	5	2	48	50	17
Hellerup IK	10	3	6	1	44	57	17

Note: Points include results from Preliminary Round

1993–94

Team	GP	W	L	T	GF	GA	PTS
Esbjerg IK	18	14	1	3	123	61	31
Herning IK	18	13	3	2	114	61	28
AAB Aalborg	18	9	5	4	94	69	22
Rungsted	18	9	6	3	91	76	21
Frederikshavn	18	9	8	1	95	99	19
Odense	18	7	9	2	79	93	16
Hvidovre	18	6	10	2	73	88	14
Rodovre	18	5	9	4	69	89	14
HIK Gentofte	18	3	13	2	67	111	8
Vojens	18	3	14	1	55	114	7

1994–95

Team	GP	W	L	T	GF	GA	PTS
1ST TO 6TH PLACE							
Herning IK	36	31	2	3	281	104	49
Esbjerg IK	36	26	6	4	218	109	42
Rungsted IK	36	21	10	5	207	139	34
AAB Aalborg	36	15	11	9	159	138	32
Fredrikshavn IK	36	14	17	5	143	171	25
Vojens IK	36	15	20	1	183	198	23
7TH TO 10TH PLACE							
Odense IK	36	13	19	4	157	169	23
Hellerup IK	36	11	17	8	110	134	22
Rodovre SIK	36	7	22	7	109	225	17
Hvidovre IK	36	1	31	4	79	254	5

Note: Special count of points in effect after double round robin

1995–96

Team	GP	W	L	T	GF	GA	PTS
Esbjerg IK	36	26	5	5	205	103	44
Herning IK	36	26	7	3	200	115	43
Rungsted IK	36	17	12	7	171	145	32
Hvidovre IK	36	19	13	4	178	165	31
Vojens IK	36	17	16	3	178	170	28
Odense IK	36	12	15	9	146	165	25
Rodovre SIK	36	11	18	8	118	145	22
Fredrikshavn IK	36	10	19	7	133	173	20
Hellerup IK	36	9	22	5	119	184	16
AAB Aalborg	36	5	27	4	111	197	11

1996–97

Team	GP	W	L	T	GF	GA	PTS
Herning IK	27	18	6	3	144	74	39
Esbjerg IK	27	17	9	1	134	103	35
Rungsted IK	27	16	9	2	135	98	34
Vojens IK	27	16	9	2	131	107	34
Rodovre SIK	27	11	9	7	100	99	29
Hvidovre IK	27	13	12	2	94	96	28
Gentofte IC	27	11	14	2	121	137	24
AAB Aalborg	27	10	16	1	82	128	21
Fredrikshavn IK	27	8	17	2	92	121	18
Odense IK	27	4	23	0	75	145	8

1ST TO 6TH PLACE

	GP	W	L	T	GF	GA	PTS
Herning IK	15	12	2	1	94	36	25
Vojens IK	15	8	4	3	67	72	19
Esbjerg IK	15	8	5	2	82	57	18
Rundsted IK	15	6	8	1	86	70	13
Rodovre SIK	15	4	11	0	60	91	8
Hvidovre IK	15	3	11	1	46	91	7

7TH TO 14TH PLACE

	GP	W	L	T	GF	GA	PTS
Gentofte IC	14	12	2	0	97	37	27
Fredrikshavn IK	14	11	2	1	90	34	26
Odense IK	14	11	2	1	85	42	24
AAB Aalberg	14	10	4	0	84	41	21
KSF Kobnhavn	14	4	9	1	41	71	12
Arhus IK	14	3	9	2	55	117	8
Gladaxe SF	14	2	12	0	37	83	6
Herlev IK	14	1	12	1	36	99	4

Note: Bonus points included

1997–98

Team	GP	W	L	T	GF	GA	PTS
Herning	10	6	1	3	51	27	15
Esbjerg	10	7	2	1	45	35	15
Rungsted	10	5	4	1	38	40	11
Frederikshavn	10	4	6	0	41	43	8
Vojens	10	3	6	1	38	45	7
Rodovre	10	2	8	0	25	48	4

FINLAND

1992–93

Team	GP	W	L	T	GF	GA	PTS
TPS Turku	48	28	12	8	178	138	64
Jokerit Helsinki	48	28	13	7	184	133	63
IFK Helsinki	48	25	17	6	168	160	56
HPK Hameenlinna	48	25	19	4	178	137	54
Lukko Rauma	48	23	17	8	165	138	54
JyP HT Jyvaskyla	48	25	19	4	171	146	54
Assat Pori	48	22	8	18	180	152	52
Ilves Tampere	48	20	20	8	150	155	48
Tappara Tampere	48	19	21	8	172	155	46
KalPa Kuopio	48	17	26	5	159	185	39
Kiekko-Espoo	49	12	29	7	122	193	31
Reipas Lahti	48	6	39	3	125	260	15

1993–94

Team	GP	W	L	T	GF	GA	PTS
TPS Turku	48	34	14	0	227	124	68
Assat Pori	48	25	16	7	185	148	57
Jokerit Helsinki	48	26	18	4	181	131	56
Lukko Rauma	48	26	18	4	165	142	56
JyP HT Jyvaskyla	48	26	18	4	157	135	56
Ilves Tampere	48	21	18	9	153	144	51
Tappara Tampere	48	23	20	5	175	175	51
IFK Helsinki	48	23	21	4	167	161	50
HPK Hameenlinna	48	23	22	3	167	170	49
KalPa Kuopio	48	16	27	5	143	170	37
Kiekko-Espoo	48	13	30	5	138	197	31
Reipas Lahti	48	6	40	2	119	280	14

1994–95

Team	GP	W	L	T	GF	GA	PTS
Jokerit Helsinki	50	34	10	6	202	122	74
Lukko Rauma	50	29	12	9	210	134	67
IFK Helsinki	50	32	15	3	203	141	67
TPS Turku	50	30	17	3	219	149	63
JyP HT Jyvaskyla	50	22	20	8	164	181	52
Assat Pori	50	20	19	11	164	166	51
Kiekko-Espoo	50	20	26	4	154	169	44
KalPa Kuopio	50	17	25	8	154	195	42
HPK Hameenlinna	50	16	27	7	170	197	39
Tappara Tampere	50	16	30	4	154	221	36
TuTo Turku	50	18	32	0	152	227	36
Ilves Tampere	50	12	33	5	152	196	29

1995–96

Team	GP	W	L	T	GF	GA	PTS
Jokerit Helsinki	50	31	8	11	190	91	73
TPS Turku	50	33	12	5	216	141	71
Lukko Rauma	50	25	16	9	205	177	59
Tappara Tampere	50	24	19	7	172	131	55
HPK Hameenlinna	50	23	20	7	160	151	53
IFK Helsinki	50	21	19	10	142	158	52
Assat Pori	50	22	23	5	140	160	49
Ilves Tampere	50	18	25	7	153	183	43
Kiekko-Espoo	50	18	26	6	131	164	42
Jyp HT Jyvaskyla	50	13	26	11	132	155	37
KalPa Kuopio	50	13	27	10	126	162	36
TuTo Hockey Turku	50	12	32	6	140	204	30

1996–97

Team	GP	W	L	T	GF	GA	PTS
Jokerit Helsinki	50	35	11	4	192	116	74
TPS Turku	50	32	11	7	191	105	71
HPK Hameenlinna	50	28	15	7	191	143	63
Ilves Tampere	50	26	17	7	183	147	59
JyP HT Jyvaskyla	50	25	19	6	163	136	56
Kiekko-Espoo	50	21	20	9	154	163	51
Assat Pori	50	19	21	10	171	182	48
Tappara Tampere	50	18	24	8	139	171	44
IFK Helsinki	50	17	25	8	159	171	42
Lukko Rauma	50	16	29	5	136	170	37
SaiPa Lapeenranta	50	13	29	8	118	181	34
KalPa Kuopio	50	8	37	5	116	228	21

1997–98

Team	GP	W	L	T	GF	GA	PTS
TPS Turku	48	30	12	6	162	111	66
IFK Helsinki	48	29	14	5	179	115	63
Ilves Tampere	48	27	15	6	184	138	60
Jokerit Helsinki	48	24	19	5	139	137	53
Tappara Tampere	48	22	19	7	157	147	51
SaiPa Lapeenranta	48	21	20	7	135	142	49
Assat Pori	48	20	20	8	163	156	48
Kiekko-Espoo	48	20	22	6	153	139	46
Lukko Rauma	48	20	22	6	131	143	46
HPK Hameenlinna	48	18	25	5	148	181	41
JyP HT Jyvaskyla	48	17	28	3	135	167	37
KalPa Kuopio	48	6	38	4	91	201	16

FRANCE

1992–93

1ST TO 4TH PLACE

Team	GP	W	L	T	GF	GA	PTS
HC Rouen	12	12	0	0	80	27	24
HC Chamonix	12	4	8	0	42	55	8
HC Reims	12	4	8	0	46	66	8
HC Amiens	12	4	8	0	39	59	8

5TH TO 10TH PLACE

	GP	W	L	T	GF	GA	PTS
ASGA Angers	10	7	2	1	81	32	15
HC Anglet	10	7	3	0	57	40	14
LBL Grenoble	10	7	3	0	53	41	14
OHC Viri-Essonne	10	4	4	2	54	58	10
CS Morzine	10	2	8	0	37	72	4
Hockey Gap	10	1	8	1	27	66	3

11TH TO 16TH PLACE

	GP	W	L	T	GF	GA	PTS
SEPF Dunkerque	10	7	1	2	54	26	16
HC Megeve	10	6	4	1	47	37	13
SC Saint Gervais	10	5	5	0	56	51	10
CS Villard-de-Lans	10	3	3	4	40	46	10
NG Nantes	10	4	5	1	54	54	9
Valenciennes	10	0	8	2	37	74	2

1993–94

STAGE ONE

GROUP A

Team	GP	W	L	T	GF	GA	PTS
HC Rouen	6	6	0	0	78	12	12
ASGA Angers	6	4	2	0	36	20	8
CS Morzine	6	2	4	0	16	55	4
SC Saint Gervais	6	0	6	0	9	52	0

GROUP B

Team	GP	W	L	T	GF	GA	PTS
HC Chamonix	6	6	0	0	39	13	12
Hockey Gap	6	3	3	0	25	33	6
HC Anglet	6	2	4	0	33	33	4
CS Villard-de-Lans	6	1	5	0	29	47	2

GROUP C

Team	GP	W	L	T	GF	GA	PTS
HC Amiens	6	6	0	0	64	14	12
OHC Viry Essonne	6	3	3	0	34	37	6
HG Nantes	6	3	3	0	21	39	6
SEPF Dunkerque	6	0	6	0	15	44	0

GROUP D

Team	GP	W	L	T	GF	GA	PTS
LBL Grenoble	6	4	2	0	28	20	8
SP Brest	6	3	2	1	23	22	7
HC Reims	6	3	2	1	30	18	7
HC Megeve	6	1	5	0	12	33	2

STAGE TWO

1ST TO 8TH PLACE

Team	GP	W	L	T	GF	GA	PTS
HC Rouen	14	12	1	1	118	36	25
HC Chamonix	14	8	4	2	70	47	18
HC Amiens	14	8	5	1	86	57	17
ASGA Angers	14	7	5	2	69	57	16
SP Brest	14	6	6	2	61	68	14
LBL Grenoble	14	5	7	2	59	74	12
OHC Viry Essonne	14	3	9	2	62	106	8
Hockey Gap	14	1	13	0	46	126	2

9TH TO 16TH PLACE

Team	GP	W	L	T	GF	GA	PTS
HC Reims	14	13	0	1	130	36	27
CS Villard-de-Lans	14	9	4	1	69	62	19
HC Anglet	14	8	4	2	78	75	18
SEPF Dunkerque	14	7	3	4	75	62	18
HC Megeve	14	5	8	1	50	83	11
HG Nantes	14	4	10	0	47	78	8
CS Morzine	14	2	10	2	44	71	6
SC Saint Gervais	14	2	11	1	43	79	5

STAGE THREE

1ST TO 4TH PLACE

Team	GP	W	L	T	GF	GA	PTS
HC Rouen	6	5	1	0	35	15	10
HC Amiens	6	4	2	0	25	24	8
HC Chamonix	6	3	3	0	23	18	6
ASGA Angers	6	0	6	0	12	38	0

5TH TO 8TH PLACE

Team	GP	W	L	T	GF	GA	PTS
SP Brest	6	5	0	1	40	20	11
OHC Viry Essonne	6	4	1	1	38	31	9
LBL Grenoble	6	2	4	0	26	24	4
Hockey Gap	6	0	6	0	18	47	0

1994–95

Team	GP	W	L	T	GF	GA	PTS
HC Rouen	28	22	4	2	159	66	46
HGA Brest	28	16	8	4	147	82	36
HC Chamonix	28	15	10	3	106	107	33
CSG Grenoble	28	15	10	3	89	90	33
HCFB Reims	28	12	11	5	104	92	29
HCS Amiens	28	11	14	3	103	108	25
ASGA Angers	28	5	19	4	81	141	14
OHC Viry	28	3	23	2	81	184	8

1995–96

Team	GP	W	L	T	GF	GA	PTS
HC Rouen	28	22	5	1	172	77	45
HG Brest	28	19	5	4	142	70	42
HCS Amiens	28	13	10	5	108	101	31
HC Reims	28	10	9	9	111	105	29
CSG Grenoble	28	10	13	5	101	109	25
HC Chamonix	28	10	13	5	101	97	25
ASG Angers	28	8	15	5	84	112	21
OHC Viry	28	2	24	2	78	226	6

1996–97

1ST TO 6TH PLACE

Team	GP	W	L	T	GF	GA	PTS
Les Albatros Brest	10	6	2	2	43	29	14
HCS Amiens	10	6	3	1	36	35	13
HC Reims	10	5	4	1	30	32	11
Rouen HC	10	4	4	2	36	28	10
CSG Grenoble	10	3	4	3	32	31	9
ASG Angers	10	1	8	1	26	48	3

7TH TO 12TH PLACE

Team	GP	W	L	T	GF	GA	PTS
OHC Viry	10	8	2	0	49	29	16
HC Bordeaux	10	7	3	0	69	31	14
HC Lyon	10	6	4	0	51	40	12
HC Gap	10	4	4	2	41	45	10
HC Megeve	10	2	6	2	47	57	6
Epinal	10	1	9	0	36	91	2

1997–98

Team	GP	W	L	T	GF	GA	PTS
CSG Grenoble	18	17	1	0	86	47	44
HCS Amiens	18	12	4	2	102	51	35
HC Lyon	18	13	4	1	87	64	34
Rouen HC	18	10	7	1	78	60	27
HC Reims	18	8	8	2	62	53	26
HC Chamonix	18	9	8	1	73	62	24
ASGA Angers	18	10	8	0	84	64	23
HC Bordeaux	18	5	12	1	64	108	12
OHC Viry-Essonne	18	3	14	1	47	105	11
HC Anglet	18	2	15	1	50	119	5

Note: Includes bonus points from stage one

GERMANY

1992–93

Team	GP	W	L	T	GF	GA	PTS
Dusseldorfer EG	44	31	5	8	190	108	70
Kolner EC	44	23	11	10	152	117	56
Krefeld EV	44	23	14	7	165	118	53
EC Hedos Munchen	44	21	15	8	143	111	50
Mannheimer ERC	44	20	18	6	151	139	46
BSC Preussen Berlin	44	17	16	11	136	141	45
ESV Kaufbeuren	44	16	19	9	144	153	41
EC Ratingen	44	14	19	11	145	165	39
Schwenninger ERC	44	15	21	8	130	155	38
EV Landshut	44	14	22	8	126	160	36
EHC Freiburg	44	12	24	8	140	164	32
Eisbaren Berlin	44	8	30	6	118	207	22

1993–94

Team	GP	W	L	T	GF	GA	PTS
Dusseldorfer EG	44	33	9	2	182	92	68
EC Hedos Munchen	44	30	11	3	189	108	63
Krefelder EV	44	23	11	10	167	121	56
EV Landshut	44	26	14	4	142	113	56
Kolner EC	44	26	15	3	117	100	55
BSC Preussen Berlin	44	23	16	5	168	128	51
Mannheimer ERC	44	19	20	5	156	140	43
ESV Kaufbeuren	44	14	27	3	120	169	31
SB Rosenheim	44	12	27	5	108	163	29
Schwenninger ERC	44	11	26	7	115	175	29
Eisbaren Berlin	44	11	31	2	119	214	24
EC Ratingen	44	9	30	5	126	207	23

1994–95

Team	GP	W	L	T	GF	GA	PTS
Berliner SC Preussen	44	33	11	0	228	127	66
EV Landshut	44	31	10	3	187	98	64
Adler Mannheim	44	29	9	6	164	108	64
Dusseldorfer EG	44	29	11	4	196	128	62
Krefelder EV	44	29	12	3	203	127	61
Kolner Haie	44	28	14	2	185	125	58
EC Kassel Huskies	44	22	18	4	145	138	48
Star Bulls Rosenheim	44	20	17	7	131	124	47
SERC Wild Wings	44	18	19	7	174	148	43
Frankfurt Lions	44	16	23	5	110	140	37
Kaufbeurer Adler	44	12	25	7	138	181	31
EHC 80 Nurnberg	44	11	24	9	151	187	31
Augsburg EV	44	12	25	7	137	189	31
EC Hannover	44	13	27	4	120	177	30
Ratingen Lowen	44	9	30	5	102	214	23
Fuchse Sachsen	44	8	31	5	89	182	21
EHC Eisbaren Berlin	44	10	32	2	136	229	22

1995–96

Team	GP	W	L	OTL	T	GF	GA	PTS
Koln Sharks	50	37	9	1	4	261	129	79
Preussen Berlin Devils	50	35	8	2	7	219	107	79
Dusseldorf	50	36	10	1	4	228	127	77
Landschut	50	38	11	0	1	222	127	77
Schwenningen Wild Wings	50	30	14	2	6	214	150	68
Mannheim Eagles	50	29	14	2	7	195	163	67
Krefeld Penguins	50	26	19	1	5	169	154	58
Frankfurt Lions	50	22	23	3	5	189	182	52
Kassel Huskies	50	19	19	2	12	149	148	52
Ratingen Lions	50	21	26	3	3	181	195	48
Nurnberger Ice Tigers	50	16	26	2	8	143	179	42
Augsburg Panthers	50	17	27	2	6	163	180	42
Rosenheim Star Bulls	50	16	28	3	6	158	195	41
Riessersee	50	16	30	1	4	147	213	37
Kaufbeuren Eagles	50	13	31	1	6	145	228	33
EC Hannover	50	12	34	0	4	138	251	28
Eisbaren Berlin	50	11	36	2	3	125	236	27
Saxonia Foxes	50	9	38	0	3	126	236	21

Note: one point awarded for an Overtime Loss (OTL)

1996–97

Team	GP	W	L	OTL	T	GF	GA	PTS
Adler Mannheim	50	35	10	1	5	212	123	76
Kolner Haie	50	36	12	2	2	235	142	76
Kassel Huskies	50	27	19	1	4	190	167	59
Eisbaren Berlin	50	26	20	1	4	177	163	57
Berlin Capitals	50	23	21	3	6	162	149	55
Star Bulls Rosenheim	50	20	28	5	2	171	209	47
Landshut	48	29	16	3	3	202	122	64
Krefeld Pinguine	48	28	18	3	2	198	166	61
Dusseldorf	48	28	18	0	2	164	138	58
Schwenningen Wild Wings	48	23	24	5	1	200	191	52
Augsburg Panthers	48	21	22	1	5	176	181	48
Frankfurt Lions	48	21	23	1	4	136	142	47
Kaufbeurer Adler	48	17	28	3	3	166	252	40
Wedemark Scorpions	48	12	35	3	1	150	231	28
Nurnberg Ice Tigers	48	9	33	1	6	149	229	25
Ratinger Lowen	48	9	37	2	2	136	219	22

Note: one point awarded for an Overtime Loss (OTL)

1997–98

Team	GP	W	L	OTL	T	GF	GA	PTS
EHC Eisbaren Berlin	48	27	15	1	6	179	139	61
Frankfurt Lions	48	27	15	1	6	160	126	61
Kolner Haie	48	26	16	2	6	160	147	60
Adler Mannheim	48	26	19	3	3	170	145	58
Dusseldorfer EG	48	27	20	2	1	166	164	57
EV Landshut	48	25	19	2	4	148	118	56
Hannover Scorpions	44	22	16	2	6	160	142	52
Berlin Capitals	44	19	18	4	7	136	119	49
Schwenningen Wild Wings	44	19	20	3	5	157	148	46
Kassel Huskies	44	19	22	4	3	140	128	45
Krefeld Pinguine	44	18	20	1	6	126	141	43
Nurnberg Ice Tigers	44	18	22	2	4	158	154	42
Augsburger Panther	44	16	26	2	2	122	160	36
ECR Revier Lowen	44	14	26	1	4	132	184	33
Star Bulls Rosenheim	44	6	35	0	3	105	204	15

Note: one point awarded for an Overtime Loss (OTL)

GREAT BRITAIN

1992–93

Team	GP	W	L	T	GF	GA	PTS
Cardiff Devils	36	28	6	2	319	187	58
Murrayfields Racers	36	20	14	2	299	207	42
Nottingham Panthers	36	19	15	2	256	236	40
Whitley Warriors	36	18	17	1	262	286	37
Bracknell Bees	36	15	17	4	190	194	34
Billingham Bombers	36	14	18	4	275	303	32
Humberside Seahawks	36	15	20	1	198	223	31
Fife Flyers	36	15	20	1	193	232	31
Nor. & Peterborough	36	14	21	1	238	272	29
Durham Wasps	36	12	22	2	201	232	26

1993–94

Team	GP	W	L	T	GF	GA	PTS
Cardiff Devils	44	39	5	0	422	220	78
Sheffield Steelers	44	28	12	4	313	198	60
Fife Flyers	44	27	15	2	304	192	56
Nottingham Panthers	44	26	16	2	288	224	54
Murrayfield Racers	44	27	15	2	358	286	51
Durham Wasps	44	24	18	2	316	284	50
Whitley Warriors	44	22	18	4	282	298	48
Humberside Hawks	44	18	22	4	301	308	40
Basingstoke Beavers	44	12	25	6	255	344	30
Bracknell Bees	44	11	30	3	220	320	25
Peterborough Pirates	44	9	32	3	239	398	21
Billingham Bombers	44	5	39	0	238	491	10

Note: Fife had points deducted.

1994–95

Team	GP	W	L	T	GF	GA	PTS
Sheffield Steelers	44	35	5	4	334	183	74
Cardiff Devils	44	32	8	4	366	217	68
Nottingham Panthers	44	32	8	4	372	213	68
Edinburgh Racers	44	25	14	5	335	289	55
Durham Wasps	44	22	19	3	264	242	47
Fife Flyers	44	20	20	4	271	242	44
Basingstoke Beavers	44	20	22	2	271	279	42
Humberside Hawks	44	17	21	6	331	330	40
Peterborough Pirates	44	12	27	5	248	368	29
Whitley Warriors	44	10	30	4	242	372	24
Miton Keynes Kings	44	9	31	4	248	363	22
Bracknell Bees	44	6	35	3	189	373	15

GROUP A

Team	GP	W	L	T	GF	GA	PTS
Sheffield Steelers	6	4	2	0	35	24	8
Nottingham Panthers	6	3	9	0	35	25	6
Fife Flyers	6	3	3	0	29	37	6
Humberside Hawks	6	2	4	0	28	42	4

GROUP B

Team	GP	W	L	T	GF	GA	PTS
Edinburgh Racers	6	4	1	1	42	37	9
Cardiff Devils	6	3	1	2	46	30	8
Basingstoke Beavers	6	2	3	1	33	38	5
Durham Wasps	6	0	4	2	23	39	2

1995–96

Team	GP	W	L	T	GF	GA	PTS
Sheffield Steelers	36	27	4	5	268	122	59
Cardiff Devils	36	26	7	3	271	140	55
Durham Wasps	36	22	10	4	213	158	48
Nottingham Panthers	36	19	12	5	214	174	43
Humberside Hawks	36	16	16	4	202	235	36
Fife Flayers	36	14	16	6	209	238	34
Basingstoke Biston	36	11	20	5	146	190	27
Newcastle Warriors	36	10	22	4	167	256	24
Milton Keynes Kings	36	7	22	7	186	237	21
Slough Jets	36	5	28	3	172	298	13

1990–97

Team	GP	W	L	OTL	T	GF	GA	PTS
Cardiff Devils	42	30	8	1	3	208	130	64
Sheffield Steelers	42	27	9	2	4	168	127	60
Ayr Scottish Eagles	42	21	15	0	6	171	157	48
Nottingham Panthers	42	21	18	2	1	160	147	45
Newcastle Cobras	42	17	18	5	2	158	172	41
Bracknell Bees	42	15	24	1	2	169	202	33
Manchester Storm	42	14	24	1	3	142	191	32
Basingstoke Bisons	42	11	25	3	3	152	202	28

Note: one point awarded for an Overtime Loss (OTL)

1997–98

Team	GP	W	L	OTL	T	GF	GA	PTS
Ayr Scottish Eagles	28	20	5	1	2	117	69	43
Manchester Storm	28	18	6	3	1	123	80	40
Cardiff Devils	28	15	9	2	2	99	79	34
Nottingham Panthers	28	14	11	3	0	95	99	31
Bracknell Bees	28	14	12	1	1	95	115	30
Sheffield Steelers	28	11	12	2	3	103	101	27
Basington Bisons	28	5	13	4	6	80	116	20
Newcastle Cobras	28	6	19	2	1	66	119	15

NETHERLANDS

1992–93

Team	GP	W	L	T	GF	GA	PTS
Smoke Eaters Geleen	24	17	6	1	142	71	35
Pandas Rotterdam	24	15	7	2	119	85	32
Flame Guards Nijmegen	24	15	8	1	137	88	31
Trappers Tilburg	24	14	10	0	150	96	28
Flyers Heerenveen	24	11	11	2	132	104	24
Pro Badge Utrecht	24	9	15	0	109	158	18
Gjaltema Rams Assen	24	0	24	0	53	240	0

1st to 4th Place

Team	GP	W	L	T	GF	GA	PTS
Smoke Eaters Geleen	6	3	1	2	22	17	12
Flame Guards Nijmegen	6	3	2	1	27	24	9
Pandas Rotterdam	6	2	3	1	18	22	8
Trappers Tilburg	6	1	3	2	14	18	5

5th to 9th Place

Team	GP	W	L	T	GF	GA	PTS
Flyers Heerenveen	16	15	1	0	159	41	30
Pro Badge Utrecht	16	11	5	0	112	82	22
Gjaltema Rams Assen	16	7	9	0	81	105	14
GM HYS Den Haag	16	4	11	1	68	122	9
Lions Dordrecht	16	2	13	1	56	126	5

1993–94

Team	GP	W	L	T	GF	GA	PTS
Smoke Eaters Geleen	18	18	0	0	242	21	36
Flame Guards Nijmegen	18	14	4	0	142	48	26
Pandas Rotterdam	18	13	5	0	135	44	26
Trappers Tilburg	18	13	5	0	154	45	26
Assen Stars	18	9	8	1	76	133	19
Dordrecht Lions	18	8	9	1	90	123	17
Red Eagles Den Bosch	18	5	12	1	56	134	11
Groenewegen	18	4	14	0	65	150	8
Utrecht	18	3	15	0	45	177	6
Eindhoven	18	1	16	1	50	180	3

Final Round

Team	GP	W	L	T	GF	GA	PTS
Smoke Eaters Geleen	12	10	2	0	72	36	24
Flame Guards Nijmegen	12	6	5	1	59	59	16
Trappers Tilburg	12	6	5	1	53	48	14
Pandas Rotterdam	12	1	11	0	24	65	4

1994–95

Team	GP	W	L	T	GF	GA	PTS
Tilberg Trappers	24	22	1	1	220	52	45
Smoke Eaters Geleen	24	17	5	2	189	74	36
Fulda Tigers Nijmegen	24	17	6	1	118	92	35
CP & A Eindhoven	24	13	10	1	124	136	27
Pandas Rotterdam	24	7	17	0	98	151	14
Heerenveen Flyers	24	2	20	2	70	159	6
Dordrecht Lions	24	2	21	1	68	223	5

1995–96

Team	GP	W	L	T	GF	GA	PTS
Tilburg Trappers	20	16	1	3	123	36	35
Fulda Tigers Nijmegen	20	16	3	1	145	58	33
Flyers Heerenveen	20	8	9	3	71	78	19
Smoke Eaters Geleen	20	6	8	6	72	66	18
Kemphanen Eindhoven	20	3	12	5	57	139	11
Loons Dordrecht	20	2	18	0	48	139	4

1996–97

Team	GP	W	L	T	GF	GA	PTS
Flyers Heerenveen	14	13	1	0	84	24	26
Fulda Tigers Nijmegen	14	11	3	0	100	33	22
Tilburg Trappers	14	10	3	1	74	34	21
Smoke Eaters Geleen	14	6	7	1	59	64	11
Kemphanen Eindhoven	14	5	9	0	52	59	10
Phantoms Deume	14	5	9	0	38	89	10
MBB Builders Utrecht	14	4	10	0	54	81	8
Jordens Lions Dordrecht	14	1	13	0	43	120	2

1st to 4th Place

Team	GP	W	L	T	GF	GA	PTS
Fulda Tigers Nijmegen	6	5	1	0	37	19	10
Tilburg Trappers	6	3	2	1	27	22	7
Flyers Heerenveen	6	2	3	1	11	18	5
Smoke Eaters Geleen	6	1	5	0	21	37	2

1997–98

Team	GP	W	L	T	GF	GA	PTS
Tilburg Trappers	24	21	3	0	200	48	42
Tigers Nijmegen	24	19	4	1	162	85	39
Flyers Heerenveen	24	16	7	1	178	64	33
MBB Builders Utrecht	24	13	8	3	107	104	29
Wolves Den Haag	24	6	17	1	85	194	13
C.M./IJCK Eindhoven	24	5	19	0	70	188	10
H'wood Phantoms Deume	24	1	23	0	72	191	2

ITALY

1992–93

Team	GP	W	L	T	GF	GA	PTS
Lion Hockey Milano	16	14	2	0	117	48	33
HC Bolzano	16	12	1	3	102	51	31
HC Alleghe	16	8	5	3	75	71	23
HC Gardena	16	7	6	3	64	77	19
HC Asiago	16	6	7	3	78	74	18
SG Brunico	16	6	9	1	77	100	16
HC Varese	16	6	9	1	59	76	15
HC Fassa	16	3	11	2	54	86	8
HC Fiemme	16	2	14	0	69	112	5

Note: Alpenliga bonus points included

1993–94

Team	GP	W	L	T	GF	GA	PTS
Hockey Milano	20	16	3	1	148	77	54
HC Bolzano	20	15	4	1	125	69	52
HC Varese	20	15	3	2	99	59	45
Saima Milano	20	11	7	2	98	77	39
HC Courmaosta	20	10	6	4	109	82	39
HC Alleghe	20	6	12	2	77	79	34
HC Fassa	20	9	10	1	99	94	26
HC Gardena	20	6	10	4	85	97	23
HC Fiemme	20	6	12	2	76	106	22
HC Asiago	20	6	14	0	79	110	17
SC Brunico	20	0	19	1	52	197	3

Note: Alpenliga bonus points included

1994–95

Team	GP	W	L	T	GF	GA	PTS
HC Bolzano Wurth	36	26	9	1	215	115	53
Shimano Varese	36	23	10	3	169	111	49
HC Courmaosta	36	17	12	7	139	120	41
Saima Milano	36	16	16	4	141	149	36
Hockey Devils Milano	36	14	16	6	156	165	34
HC Gardena	36	15	17	4	158	166	34
HC Alleghe	36	15	17	4	110	130	34
SG Brunico	36	15	19	2	143	176	32
HC Fassa Wuber	36	13	21	2	162	183	28
HC Asiago	36	8	25	3	117	195	19

1995–96

Team	GP	W	L	T	GF	GA	PTS
HC Bolzano	32	26	3	3	214	105	55
HC 24 Milano	32	19	9	4	171	123	42
HC Gardena	32	19	9	4	154	114	42
Varese Hockey	32	19	10	3	138	94	41
HC Fassa	32	12	17	3	126	163	27
HC Asiago	32	12	19	1	111	114	25
SG Brunico	32	10	18	4	120	140	24
HC Alleghe	32	11	19	2	101	148	24
Devils Milano	32	4	28	0	110	214	8

1996–97

Team	GP	W	L	T	GF	GA	PTS
HC 24 Milano	10	8	2	0	84	31	16
HC Bolzano	10	8	2	0	70	45	16
SHC Fassa	10	6	3	1	53	44	13
HC Merano	10	4	6	0	34	34	8
SG Brunico	10	3	6	1	40	65	7
HC Gardena	10	0	10	0	26	88	0

1997–98

Team	GP	W	L	T	GF	GA	PTS
HC Bolzano	20	16	4	0	114	63	79
HC Asiago	20	13	6	1	84	63	68
SHC Fassa	20	11	8	1	78	89	60
HC Merano	20	10	10	0	97	91	54
HC Gardena	20	8	12	0	84	93	48
SG Brunico	20	2	18	0	55	113	34

Note: Includes bonus points from stage one

JAPAN

1992–93

Team	GP	W	L	T	GF	GA	PTS
Kokudo Tokyo	30	22	1	7	124	56	51
Oji Seishi Tomakomai	30	20	8	2	142	78	42
Seibu Tetsudo Tokyo	30	19	8	3	97	58	41
Jujo Seishi Kushiro	30	10	18	2	79	117	22
Yukijirushi Sapporo	30	7	19	4	58	95	18
Furukawa Denko Nikko	30	2	26	2	52	148	6

1993–94

Team	GP	W	L	T	GF	GA	PTS
Kokudo Tokyo	30	24	5	1	146	66	49
Shin-Oji Seishi Tomakomai	30	22	6	2	136	76	46
Seibu Tetsudo Tokyo	30	15	11	4	90	89	34
Nippon-Seishi Kushiro	30	12	17	1	95	121	25
Yukijushi Sapporo	30	6	19	5	69	109	17
Furukawa Denko Nikko	30	3	24	3	58	127	9

1994–95

Stage One

Team	GP	W	L	T	GF	GA	PTS
Kokudo Tokyo	15	13	1	1	59	25	27
New Oji Tomakomai	15	8	5	2	67	47	18
Seibu Tetsudo Tokyo	15	8	6	1	56	42	17
Nippon Paper Kushiro	15	7	7	1	52	50	15
Yukijrushi Sapporo	15	6	8	1	36	48	13
Furukawa Denko Nikko	15	0	15	0	23	81	0

Stage Two

Team	GP	W	L	T	GF	GA	PTS
Seibu Tetsudo Tokyo	15	12	3	0	76	38	24
New Oji Tomakomai	15	12	3	0	72	42	24
Kokudo Tokyo	15	9	6	0	68	48	18
Nippon Paper Kushiro	15	7	8	0	51	59	14
Yukijrushi Sapporo	15	4	10	1	35	70	19
Furukawa Denko Nikko	15	0	14	1	27	72	1

1995–96

Stage One

Team	GP	W	L	T	GF	GA	PTS
New Oji Tamakomai	20	15	3	2	101	55	32
Kokudo Keikadu Tokyo	20	12	4	4	76	54	28
Seibu Tetsudo Tokyo	20	13	7	0	88	76	26
Furukawa Denko Nikko	20	7	12	1	60	85	15
Yukijrushi Sapporo	20	4	13	3	59	99	11
Nippon Paper Kushiro	20	3	15	2	70	85	8

Stage Two

Team	GP	W	L	T	GF	GA	PTS
Seibu Tetsudo Tokyo	20	17	2	1	95	48	35
Kokudo Keikadu Tokyo	20	16	3	1	109	58	33
New Oji Tamakomai	20	10	10	0	84	76	20
Furukawa Denko Nikko	20	7	13	0	63	98	14
Nippon Paper Kushiro	20	6	14	0	70	86	12
Yukijrushi Sapporo	20	3	17	0	52	107	6

1996–97

Team	GP	W	L	T	GF	GA	PTS
New Oji Tomakomai	30	22	4	4	152	92	48
Seibu Tetsudo Tokyo	30	16	9	5	128	102	37
Kokudo Kaikadu Tokyo	30	18	12	0	105	72	36
Yukijushi Sapporo	30	10	18	2	78	116	22
Nippon Paper Kushiro	30	8	19	3	83	125	19
Furukawa Denko Nikko	30	8	20	2	71	110	18

1997–98

Team	GP	W	L	T	GF	GA	PTS
Kokudo Tokyo	40	24	12	4	149	119	52
Oji Tomakomai	40	22	14	4	165	129	48
Snow Brand	40	19	15	6	125	124	44
Seibu Tetsudo Tokyo	40	18	19	3	160	151	39
Furukawa Denko Nikko	40	16	23	1	110	139	33
Cranes Kushiro	40	11	27	2	120	167	24

NORWAY

1992–93

Team	GP	W	L	T	GF	GA	PTS
Storhamar Hamar	14	10	4	0	78	30	20
Valerengen	14	7	5	2	47	41	16
Stjernen Fredrikstad	14	8	5	1	67	54	17
Furuset Oslo	14	8	4	2	49	36	18
Lillehammer	14	8	6	0	63	52	16
Viking Stavanger	14	7	7	0	51	52	14
Sparta Sarpsborg	14	5	8	1	62	63	11

1993–94

Team	GP	W	L	T	GF	GA	PTS
VIF Hockey Oslo	14	10	2	2	66	37	24
Storhamar IL Hamar	14	9	4	1	67	49	23
Lillehammer	14	7	5	2	43	36	19
Stjernen Fredrikstad	14	7	6	1	66	56	16
Trondheim IHK	14	7	6	1	45	62	15
Sparta Sarpsborg	14	5	9	0	49	72	10
Manglerud Star	14	4	9	1	46	60	9
Viking Stavanger	14	3	11	0	36	62	6

Note: Bonus Points included

1994–95

Team	GP	W	L	T	GF	GA	PTS
Storhamar IL Hamar	28	21	2	5	195	52	47
VIF Hockey Oslo	28	18	6	4	134	91	40
Lillehammer IK	28	17	7	4	117	97	38
Spektrum Flyers Oslo	28	15	10	3	118	87	33
Stjernen Fredrikstad	28	13	12	3	134	125	29
Viking Stavanger	28	7	19	2	88	128	16
Trondheim IK	28	7	20	1	79	138	15
Sparta Sarpsborg	28	2	24	2	70	217	6

1995–96

Team	GP	W	L	T	GF	GA	PTS
VIF Hockey Oslo	28	21	7	0	135	86	42
Stjernen Fredrikstad	28	19	7	2	140	94	40
Storhamar Hamar	28	20	8	0	128	56	40
Spektrum Flyers Oslo	28	18	9	1	132	90	37
Lillehammer IHK	28	13	13	2	101	101	28
TIK Trondheim	28	8	18	2	87	108	18
Frisk Asker	18	5	11	1	69	154	11
Viking Stavanger	28	3	23	2	90	193	8

GROUP A

Team	GP	W	L	T	GF	GA	PTS
Storhamar Hamar	4	4	0	0	19	8	8
VIF Hockey Oslo	4	2	2	0	15	15	4
TIK Trondheim	4	0	4	0	9	20	0

GROUP B

Team	GP	W	L	T	GF	GA	PTS
Stjernen Fredrikstad	4	3	1	0	18	16	6
Lillehammer IHK	4	2	2	0	16	17	4
Spektrum Flyers Oslo	4	1	3	0	14	15	2

1996–97

Team	GP	W	L	T	GF	GA	PTS
Storhamar Hamar	36	33	1	2	252	58	68
Valerenga Oslo	36	27	9	0	214	99	54
TIK Trondheim	36	22	12	2	144	107	46
Frisk Asker	36	21	14	1	170	123	43
Stjernen Fredrikstad	36	20	14	2	153	133	42
Lillehammer IHK	36	17	16	3	158	160	37
Manglerud Star Oslo	36	13	21	2	127	179	28
Lorenskog	36	8	27	1	115	216	17
Furuset Oslo	36	6	27	3	96	211	15
Hasle Loren Oslo	36	5	31	0	88	231	10

1997–98

Team	GP	W	L	T	GF	GA	PTS
Valerengen Oslo	44	34	8	2	240	94	70
Storhamar Hamar	44	32	9	3	213	92	67
IL Stjernen	44	23	17	4	172	149	50
Sparta Sarpsborg	44	23	18	3	165	152	49
Frisk Asker	44	21	16	7	183	147	49
Lillehammer IHK	44	22	17	5	163	139	49
Manglerud Star Oslo	44	18	23	3	172	179	39
TIK Trondheim	44	15	24	5	159	181	35
Furuset Oslo	44	13	28	3	155	218	29
Lorenskog IHK	44	1	42	1	79	350	3

POLAND

1992–93
1ST TO 6TH PLACE

Team	GP	W	L	T	GF	GA	PTS
Unia Oswiecin	28	20	4	4	173	85	44
Podhale Nowy Targ	28	19	5	4	148	66	42
Polonia Bytom	28	17	6	5	118	71	39
Naprzod Katowice	28	16	9	3	111	90	35
STS Sanok	28	11	16	1	78	96	23
Gornik Katowice	28	10	15	3	107	126	23

7TH TO 10TH PLACE

Team	GP	W	L	T	GF	GA	PTS
Tysovia Tychy	24	10	10	4	88	73	24
Towimor Torun	24	8	15	1	83	104	17
Cracovia Krakow	24	8	15	1	76	122	17
Stoczniowec	24	0	24	0	37	184	0

1993–94

Team	GP	W	L	T	GF	GA	PTS
Podhale Nowy Targ	30	29	0	1	213	57	59
KS Unia Oswiecin	30	18	10	2	141	88	38
Naprzod Janow	30	17	12	1	129	108	35
BTH PoloniaBylom	30	14	16	0	96	141	28
Gornik 1920 Katowice	28	14	12	2	138	95	30
MKH TysoviaTychy	28	12	12	4	90	75	28
STS Sanok	28	11	11	6	85	93	28
KS Towimor Torun	28	10	15	3	125	131	23
KC Cracovia Krakow	28	6	19	3	60	116	15
Stoczniowec Gdansk	28	2	26	0	55	228	4

1994–95

Team	GP	W	L	T	GF	GA	PTS
Podhale Nowy Targ	32	25	2	5	196	77	55
KS Unia Oswiecim	32	23	6	3	202	78	49
KKH Katowice	32	21	8	3	182	86	45
Naprzod Janow	32	16	9	7	152	95	39
TTH Metron Torun	32	15	11	6	131	121	36
MHKS Polonia Bytom	32	11	18	3	97	167	25
Stoczniowec Gdansk	32	16	11	5	138	131	37
MkH Tysovia	32	16	14	2	122	101	34
STS Autosan Sanok	32	16	14	2	140	122	34
SMS PZHL Sosnowiec	32	8	23	1	77	159	17
BTH Bydgoszcz	32	4	27	1	65	165	9
Cracowia Krakow	32	1	29	2	85	285	4

1995–96
1ST TO 6TH PLACE

Team	GP	W	L	T	GF	GA	PTS
KS Unia Oswiecin	20	19	1	0	109	50	38
Podhale Nowy Targ	20	16	4	0	114	66	32
KKH Katowice	20	8	11	1	77	73	17
TTH Metrom Torun	20	7	12	1	59	73	15
STS Autosan Sanok	20	6	14	0	76	105	12
SMS PZHL Sosnowiec	20	3	17	0	48	116	6

7TH TO 13TH PLACE

Team	GP	W	L	T	GF	GA	PTS
Naprzod Janow	20	16	1	3	122	44	35
Stoczniowec Gdansk	20	15	4	1	106	59	31
MKH Tysovia Tychy	20	11	9	0	87	81	22
Cracowia Krakow	20	4	12	4	48	96	12
Polisa Bydgoszcz	20	5	14	1	60	95	11
MHKS Polonia Bytom	20	3	14	3	59	107	9

1996–97
1ST TO 6TH PLACE

Team	GP	W	L	T	GF	GA	PTS
Podhale Nowy Targ	40	31	9	0	215	99	62
KKH Katowice	40	28	10	2	168	120	58
KS Unia Oswiecin	40	26	13	1	186	105	53
STS Autosan Sanok	40	14	23	3	134	166	31
TTH Metron Torun	40	11	26	3	99	193	25
Naprzod Katowice	40	5	34	1	99	218	11

7TH TO 13TH PLACE

Team	GP	W	L	T	GF	GA	PTS
Stoczniowec Danzig	24	20	3	1	147	73	41
KS Cracovia Krakow	24	19	4	1	132	60	39
MHKS Polonia Bytom	24	16	8	0	110	80	32
MKH Tysovia Tychy	24	8	15	1	91	161	17
Polisa Bydgozcz	24	8	16	0	79	99	16
Optimus Krynica	24	7	16	1	92	111	15
SMS PZHL Sosnowiec	24	3	19	2	78	145	8

1997–98
1ST TO 6TH PLACE

Team	GP	W	L	T	GF	GA	PTS
Podhale Nowy Targ	30	22	5	3	106	70	47
Unia Oswiecin	30	17	10	3	106	78	37
STS Autosan Sanok	30	16	12	2	118	92	34
Hortex Katowice	30	15	14	1	103	83	31
Optimus Krynica	30	10	20	0	91	122	20
Stoczniowec Gdansk	30	5	24	1	83	162	11

7TH TO 13TH PLACE

Team	GP	W	L	T	GF	GA	PTS
Cracowia Krakow	24	21	3	0	129	72	42
TTH Metron Torun	24	18	6	0	118	75	36
TTS Tychy	24	16	7	1	137	90	33
SMS Sosnowiec 1	24	12	12	0	137	95	24
Naprzod Janow	24	9	13	2	93	83	20
Polonia Bytom	24	6	17	1	83	134	13
SMS Sosnowiec 2	24	0	24	0	43	191	0

RUSSIA/C.I.S.

1992–93
WESTERN DIVISION

Team	GP	W	L	T	GF	GA	PTS
Dynamo Moscow	42	26	7	9	141	83	61
Krylja Sovetov Moscow	42	25	13	4	127	93	54
Spartak Moscow	42	22	14	6	133	109	50
SKA St. Petersburg	42	22	15	5	125	115	49
Torpedo Yaroslavl	42	20	16	6	126	106	46
Pardaugava Riga	42	19	15	8	142	125	6
Sokol-Eskulap Kiev	42	18	17	7	141	119	43
Khimik Voskresensk	42	18	17	7	117	125	43
Metallurg Cherepovets	42	19	20	3	111	123	41
Dynamo Minsk	42	10	24	8	90	124	28
Kristall Saratov	42	8	28	6	92	179	22
CSKA Moscow	42	7	28	7	92	136	21

EASTERN DIVISION

Team	GP	W	L	T	GF	GA	PTS
Lada Togliatti	42	31	8	3	165	87	65
Traktor Chelyabinsk	42	28	9	5	175	112	61
Avangard Omsk	42	21	11	10	160	130	52
Salavat Yulayev Ufa	42	22	14	6	147	150	50
Ust-Kamenogorsk	42	23	17	2	177	146	48
Metallurg Magnitogorsk	42	20	15	7	147	120	47
Avto. Yekaterinburg	42	19	15	9	136	130	45
Nizhny Novgorod	42	13	21	8	96	115	34
Itil Kazan	42	14	24	4	126	156	32
Molot Perm	42	13	27	2	110	178	28
Metallurg Novokuznetsk	42	10	27	5	95	156	25
Avto. Karaganda	42	6	31	5	96	195	17

1993–94

Team	GP	W	L	T	GF	GA	PTS
Lada Togliatti	46	33	6	7	189	82	73
Dynamo Moscow	46	30	8	8	197	126	68
Traktor Chelyabinsk	46	32	11	3	187	120	67
Salavat Yulayev Ufa	46	28	12	6	171	104	62
Metallurg Magnitogorsk	46	28	13	5	180	144	61
Torpedo Yaroslavl	46	28	15	3	181	96	59
Itil Kazan	46	25	17	4	138	118	54
Spartak Moscow	46	24	17	5	163	142	53
Ust-Kamenogorsk	46	25	20	1	174	153	51
Krylja Sovetov Moscow	46	22	19	5	140	110	49
Khimik Voskresensk	46	20	17	9	130	122	49
Paradaugava Riga	46	21	19	6	153	155	48
SKA St. Petersburg	46	20	18	8	125	96	48
CSKA Moscow	46	21	20	5	111	121	47
Nizhny Novgorod	46	17	18	11	116	125	45
Avangard Omsk	46	21	22	3	140	133	45
Sokol Kiev	46	18	20	8	120	143	44
Metallurg Cherepovets	46	17	26	3	124	157	37
Tivali Minsk	46	14	27	5	118	152	33
Metallurg Novokuznetsk	46	10	28	8	106	158	28
Avto. Yekaterinburg	46	9	31	6	111	205	24
Stroitel Karaganda	46	10	34	2	109	205	22
Molot Perm	46	8	34	4	95	181	20
Kristall Saratov	46	7	36	3	103	233	17

1994–95
WESTERN DIVISION

Team	GP	W	L	T	GF	GA	PTS
Torpedo Yaroslavl	52	33	15	4	152	96	70
Krylja Sovetov Moscow	52	30	14	8	173	120	68
Dynamo Moscow	52	30	16	6	172	107	66
Nizhny Novgorod	52	26	16	10	137	111	62
Itil Kazan	52	27	18	7	150	123	61
CSKA Moscow	52	25	20	7	150	114	57
SKA St.Petersburg	52	26	21	5	127	122	57
Khimik Voskresensk	52	23	21	8	122	125	54
Spartak Moscow	52	23	24	5	132	154	51
Severstal Cherepovets	52	20	28	4	11	151	44
Kristall Elektrostal	52	17	31	4	112	157	38
Tivali Minsk	52	13	31	8	102	151	34
Sokol Kiev	52	12	30	10	104	142	34
Paradaugava Riga	52	14	34	4	99	168	32

1994–95 *continued*

EASTERN DIVISION

Team	GP	W	L	T	GF	GA	PTS
Lada Togliatti	52	41	7	4	229	83	86
Avangard Omsk	52	36	8	8	220	100	80
Metallurg Magnitogorsk	52	37	12	3	260	134	77
Salavat Yulayev Ufa	52	31	10	11	219	126	73
Traktor Chelyabinsk	52	26	21	5	177	146	57
Molot Perm	52	27	22	3	144	140	57
Ust-Kamenogorsk	52	24	24	4	173	171	52
Avto. Yekaterinburg	52	18	22	12	126	137	48
CSK VVS Samara	52	19	26	7	161	169	45
Kristall Saratov	52	19	28	5	134	173	43
Rubin Tyumen	52	18	30	4	155	205	40
Sibir Novosibirsk	52	14	35	3	158	273	31
Metallurg Novokuznetsk	52	11	33	8	125	185	30
Stroitel Karaganda	52	3	46	3	99	338	9

1995–96

1ST TO 14TH PLACE

Team	GP	W	L	T	GF	GA	PTS
Lada Togliatti	26	21	3	2	122	50	48
Dynamo Moscow	26	18	5	3	79	53	46
Avangard Omsk	26	16	6	4	87	54	42
Salavat Yzlayev Ufa	26	17	6	3	80	46	42
Metallurg Magnitogorsk	26	14	10	2	70	55	37
Torpedo Yaroslavl	26	15	10	1	70	55	37
AK Bars Kazan	26	14	8	4	68	56	36
Kristall Elektrostal	26	10	12	4	73	76	27
Severstal Cherepovets	26	7	16	3	62	83	22
SKA St.Petersburg	26	9	15	2	64	67	22
Rubin Tyumen	26	7	16	3	63	104	18
Molot Perm	26	6	18	2	74	95	17
Kristall Saratov	26	6	19	1	55	127	15
Spartak Moscow	26	5	21	0	69	117	11

15TH TO 28TH PLACE

Team	GP	W	L	T	GF	GA	PTS
CSKA Moscow	26	19	4	3	85	32	45
Nizhny Novgorod	26	17	5	4	74	43	44
Krylja Sovetov Moscow	26	18	8	0	89	41	43
Khimik Voskresensk	26	15	9	2	74	66	37
Avto. Yekaterinburg	26	15	10	1	70	55	36
Metallurg Novokuznetsk	26	13	11	2	67	64	35
Sokol Kiev	26	11	8	7	59	59	32
Ust-Kamenogorsk	26	11	12	3	84	84	31
Traktor Chelyabinsk	26	10	12	4	49	42	27
Sibir Novosibirsk	26	12	13	1	70	72	26
Neftekhimik Nizhnekamsk	26	10	13	3	58	65	25
CSK VVS Samara	26	9	16	1	50	77	23
Bulat Karaganda	26	4	22	0	62	124	10
Tivali Minsk	26	2	23	1	39	106	6

Bonus points included

1996–97

WESTERN DIVISION

Team	GP	W	L	T	GF	GA	PTS
AK Bars Kazan	24	17	4	3	77	40	37
Torpedo Yaroslavl	24	16	4	4	65	31	36
HC CSKA Moscow	24	12	7	5	58	58	29
Krylja Sovetov Moscow	24	12	9	3	83	61	27
Dynamo Moscow	24	12	9	3	60	55	27
Spartak Moscow	24	11	10	3	62	63	25
Khimik Voskresensk	24	9	9	6	65	63	24
Neftekhimik Nizhnekamsk	24	10	10	4	47	49	24
Severstal Cherepovets	24	6	8	10	56	59	22
SKA St.Petersburg	24	7	12	5	46	59	19
Nizhny Novgorod	24	6	14	4	47	64	16
Dizelist Penza	24	6	15	3	52	81	15
Kristall Elektrostal	24	4	17	3	44	79	11

EASTERN DIVISION

Team	GP	W	L	T	GF	GA	PTS
Lada Togliatti	24	20	2	2	116	43	42
Rubin Tyumen	24	15	6	3	81	61	33
Metallurg Magnitogorsk	24	15	6	3	81	50	33
Avangard Omsk	24	14	7	3	75	47	31
Salavat Yzlayev Ufa	24	14	9	1	83	58	29
Traktor Chelyabinsk	24	10	8	6	60	56	26
Kristal Saratov	24	10	13	1	76	87	21
Metallurg Novokuznetsk	24	8	12	4	65	81	20
CSK VVS Samara	24	9	14	1	65	72	19
Sibir Novosibirsk	24	8	14	2	62	106	18
SKA Amur	24	6	13	5	62	84	17
Spartak Yekaterinburg	24	6	17	1	68	104	13
Molot Perm	24	5	19	0	50	95	10

1996–97 *continued*

SECOND HALF

Team	GP	W	L	T	GF	GA	PTS
Lada Togliatti	38	30	5	3	146	63	63
AK Bars Kazan	38	25	8	5	113	78	55
Torpedo Yaroslavl	38	24	8	6	120	62	54
Metallurg Magnitogorsk	38	23	11	4	134	91	50
Avangard Omsk	38	19	12	7	126	84	45
Dynamo Moscow	38	17	14	7	105	88	41
Salavat Yulayev Ufa	38	17	15	6	116	97	40
Rubin Tyumen	38	17	16	5	114	106	39
Krylja Sovetov Moscow	38	17	17	4	112	105	38
Severstal Cherepovets	38	14	14	10	95	92	38
Traktor Chelyabinsk	38	13	16	9	82	95	35
Chimik Voskresensk	38	13	17	8	97	114	34
HC CSKA Moscow	38	12	16	10	83	104	34
Neftekhimik Nizhnekamsk	38	12	17	9	65	85	33
Kristall Saratov	38	14	20	4	102	125	32
CSK VVS Samara	38	14	20	4	85	114	32
Spartak Moscow	38	13	20	5	95	119	31
SKA St.Petersburg	38	8	23	7	85	116	23
Metallurg Novokuznetsk	38	7	23	8	77	122	22
Sibir Novosibirsk	38	8	25	5	78	170	21

1997–98

WESTERN DIVISION

Team	GP	W	L	T	GF	GA	PTS
Torpedo Yaroslavl	26	19	4	3	74	37	41
Dynamo Moscow	26	17	4	5	83	40	39
Lada Togliatti	26	16	4	6	75	42	38
Severstal Cherepovets	26	16	6	4	60	43	36
Spartak Moscow	26	13	8	5	81	61	31
SKA St. Petersburg	26	12	10	4	55	52	28
Neftekhimik Nizhnekamsk	26	10	12	4	64	61	24
CSKA Moscow	26	11	14	1	57	67	23
Krylja Sovetov Moscow	26	11	14	1	57	66	23
Khimik Voskresensk	26	8	12	6	60	72	22
Nizhny Novgorod	26	9	13	4	48	57	22
HC CSKA Moscow	26	6	17	3	44	82	15
Kristall Elektrostal	26	6	18	2	47	78	14
Dizelist Penza	26	2	20	4	43	90	8

EASTERN DIVISION

Team	GP	W	L	T	GF	GA	PTS
Ak Bars Kazan	26	22	3	1	96	40	45
Metallurg Magnitogorsk	26	19	2	5	109	42	43
Avangard Omsk	26	14	7	5	78	50	33
Molot-Prikamje Perm	26	12	7	7	82	71	31
CSK VVS Samara	26	12	11	3	59	60	27
Rubin Tyumen	26	11	10	5	85	79	27
Salavat Yulayev Ufa	26	11	11	4	70	63	26
Mechel Chelyabinsk	26	9	10	7	51	57	25
Traktor Chelyabinsk	26	8	11	7	60	68	23
SKA-Amur Khabarovsk	26	8	13	5	64	78	21
Metallurg Novokuznetsk	26	7	13	6	56	76	20
Kristall Saratov	26	6	14	6	54	78	18
Dynamo-E. Yekaterinburg	26	6	19	1	40	88	13
Sibir Novosibirsk	26	4	18	4	41	95	12

SECOND HALF

Team	GP	W	L	T	GF	GA	PTS
Ak Bars Kazan	46	36	7	3	158	79	75
Metallurg Magnitogorsk	46	31	5	10	173	82	72
Torpedo Yaroslavl	46	33	7	6	130	60	72
Lada Togliatti	46	32	7	7	165	71	71
Dynamo Moscow	46	30	10	6	151	91	66
Avangard Omsk	46	28	13	5	139	86	61
Severstal Cherepovets	46	27	12	7	110	81	61
Molot-Prikamje Perm	46	21	18	7	150	130	49
Spartak Moscow	46	20	17	9	128	115	49
SKA St.Petersburg	46	20	19	7	107	105	47
Neftekhimik Nizhnekamsk	46	19	22	5	126	121	43
Rubin Tyumen	46	17	22	7	137	152	41
SKA-Amur Khabarovsk	46	17	22	7	112	138	41
Khimik Voskresensk	46	16	23	7	101	126	39
CSK VVS Samara	46	16	24	6	92	117	38
Traktor Chelyabinsk	46	14	22	10	99	129	38
CSKA Moscow	46	17	26	3	107	137	37
Krylja Sovetov Moscow	46	17	27	2	99	132	36
Salavat Yulayev Ufa	46	15	25	6	108	128	36
Mechel Chelyabinsk	46	13	25	8	84	125	34

SLOVAKIA

1992–93

Note: Slovakia was a part of Czechoslovakia in 1992–93

1993–94

Team	GP	W	L	T	GF	GA	PTS
HK Dukla Trencin	36	25	7	4	151	88	54
HC Kosice	36	22	7	7	164	93	51
HC Slovan Bratislava	36	21	9	6	124	93	48
HC Martimex Martin	36	14	12	10	106	100	38
HC Nitra	36	16	14	6	108	102	38
HC AKP Poprad	36	15	17	4	106	111	34
HK Spisska Nova Ves	36	11	17	8	94	122	30
HC TJ ZPA Presov	36	11	19	6	96	131	28
HC Liptovsky Mikulas	36	11	20	5	109	133	27
ZTK Zvolen	36	4	28	4	91	176	12

1994–95

Team	GP	W	L	T	GF	GA	PTS
HK Dukla Trencin	36	27	4	5	188	82	59
HC Kosice	36	26	5	5	188	96	57
HC Slovan Bratislava	36	23	11	2	167	117	48
SKP PS Poprad	36	19	13	4	128	106	42
HK Liptovsky Mikulas	36	14	18	4	107	130	46
Martimex Martin	36	12	18	6	94	110	42
HC Dragon Presov	36	9	16	11	92	131	29
HK Spartak Dubnica	36	9	23	4	83	153	22
HC Nitra	36	8	22	6	87	147	22
HK Spisska Nova Ves	36	7	24	5	83	145	19

1995–96

Team	GP	W	L	T	GF	GA	PTS
HC Kosice	36	25	6	5	173	88	55
HK Dukla Trencin	36	20	10	6	139	94	46
HC Martimex Martin	36	18	11	7	112	95	43
PS SKP Poprad	36	18	13	5	127	98	41
HC Slovan Bratislava	36	18	13	5	127	123	41
AC Nitra	36	14	17	5	98	101	33
HK Sparta Dubnica	36	12	17	7	96	121	31
HC Liptovsky Mikulas	36	12	19	5	111	130	29
Iskra Banska Bystrica	36	9	21	6	80	124	24
HC Dragon Presov	36	7	26	3	75	164	17

1996–97

Team	GP	W	L	T	GF	GA	PTS
HK Dukla Trencin	36	27	6	3	151	100	57
HC Kosice	36	24	10	2	154	112	50
HC Slovan Bratislava	36	21	10	5	150	108	47
SKP PS Poprad	36	18	10	8	146	112	44
Martimex Martin	36	19	11	6	111	92	44
HK Liptovsky Mikulas	36	12	20	4	117	144	28
VTJ Spisska Nova Ves	36	12	20	4	111	140	28
Spartak Dubnica	36	9	21	6	116	161	24
Plastika Nitra	36	8	24	4	106	143	20
Iskra Banska Bystrica	36	6	24	6	97	147	18

1997–98

Team	GP	W	L	T	GF	GA	PTS
HC Slovan Bratislava	36	28	6	2	170	72	58
HC Kosice	36	27	7	2	174	87	56
HC SKP PS Poprad	36	18	11	7	122	106	43
HK Dukla Trencin	36	19	13	4	117	103	42
HKM Zvolen	36	15	19	2	92	112	32
HK 36 Skalica	36	13	18	5	100	124	31
Martimex ZTS Martin	36	12	18	6	112	120	30
VTJ Spisska Nova Ves	36	10	20	6	93	121	26
MHC Plastika Nitra	36	8	20	6	81	144	24
HK Liptovsky Mikulas	36	7	25	4	87	159	18

SWEDEN

1992–93

Team	GP	W	L	T	GF	GA	PTS
Vasteras IK	40	21	9	10	136	101	52
Brynas IF Gaevle	40	20	12	8	149	124	48
Malmo IF	40	21	14	5	152	130	47
Farjestads BK Karlstad	40	19	16	5	158	133	43
MoDo HK Ornskoldsvik	40	17	17	6	145	140	40
Lulea HF	40	16	7	7	142	134	39
Leksands IF	40	17	19	4	137	137	38
Djurgardens Stockholm	40	15	17	8	97	110	38
HV 71 Jonkoping	40	13	19	8	123	149	34
Rogle BK Angelholm	40	13	20	7	119	140	33

1993–94

Team	GP	W	L	T	GF	GA	PTS
Leksands IF	40	22	12	6	141	112	50
Brynas IF	40	22	14	4	131	107	48
Malmo IF	40	19	13	8	164	143	46
Frolund HC	40	18	14	8	122	117	44
Djurgadens Stockholm	40	17	15	8	132	123	42
Rogle BK	40	17	16	7	160	157	41
Vasteras IK	40	15	17	8	140	137	38
MoDo Hockey Domsjo	40	17	19	4	141	151	38
HV 71 Jonkoping	40	15	18	7	111	118	37
Lulea HF	40	12	22	6	131	168	30
Farjestads BK	22	7	11	4	66	73	18
IF Bjorkloven	22	5	15	2	57	90	12

1994–95

Team	GP	W	L	T	GF	GA	PTS
Djurgardens Stockholm	40	24	9	7	139	96	55
Malmo IF	40	20	7	13	130	105	53
Lulea HF	40	21	9	10	164	116	52
Leksand IF	40	21	13	6	155	132	48
Brynas Gavle	40	17	15	8	119	127	42
Farjestad Karlstad	40	17	17	6	128	135	40
Vasteras IK	40	15	18	7	145	137	37
HV 71 Jonkoping	40	12	19	9	117	143	33
AIK Solna Stockholm	40	11	21	8	111	146	30
MoDo Domsjo	40	8	22	10	121	140	26
Vastra Frolunda	22	6	11	5	63	70	17
Rogle Angelholm	22	5	16	1	49	93	11

1995–96

Team	GP	W	L	T	GF	GA	PTS
Lulea HF	40	22	12	6	153	109	50
Vastra Frolunda Goteborg	40	20	10	10	130	95	50
Farjestad BK Karlstad	40	20	14	6	150	117	46
HV 71 Jonkoping	40	18	14	8	156	132	44
Djurgardens Stockholm	40	17	14	9	122	119	43
MoDo Ornskoldsvik	40	15	13	12	127	133	42
Leksands IF	40	15	15	10	123	117	40
Malmo IF	40	15	18	7	129	147	37
AIK Solna Stockholm	40	11	18	11	96	126	33
Vasteras IK	40	12	22	6	123	163	30

1996–97

Team	GP	W	L	T	GF	GA	PTS
Leksands IF	50	28	15	7	166	132	63
Lulea HF	50	26	16	8	150	121	60
Farjestad BK Karlstad	50	26	16	8	148	132	60
Djurgardens Stockholm	50	27	18	5	186	135	59
AIK Solna Stockholm	50	23	17	10	149	131	56
HV 71 Jonkoping	50	22	19	9	178	159	53
Vastra Frolunda Goteborg	50	17	16	17	134	133	51
Malmo IF	50	20	20	10	171	154	50
Brynas Gavle	50	21	21	8	155	144	50
MoDo Ornskoldsvik	50	17	27	6	136	167	40
Sodertalje SK	50	15	28	7	122	179	37
Vasteras IK	50	5	34	11	133	241	21

1997–98

Team	GP	W	L	T	GF	GA	PTS
Djurgardens Stockholm	46	27	13	6	148	110	60
Farjestads BK Karlstad	46	24	12	10	154	112	58
Leksands IF	46	24	14	8	165	143	56
Frolunda HC Goteborg	46	17	14	15	136	107	49
Brynas IF	46	21	19	6	138	131	48
Modo Ornskoldsvik	46	20	20	6	129	123	46
HV 71 Jonkoping	46	19	19	8	127	145	46
Lulea HF	46	15	18	13	112	125	43
Malmo IF	46	17	21	8	134	121	42
Vasteras IK	46	15	22	9	102	146	39
AIK Solna Stockholm	46	13	26	7	93	134	33
Sodertalje SK	46	10	24	12	110	151	32

SWITZERLAND

1992–93

Team	GP	W	L	T	GF	GA	PTS
EHC Kloten	36	27	8	1	173	91	55
HC Fribourg	36	25	7	4	171	100	54
SC Bern	36	21	11	4	160	123	46
HC Lugano	36	21	14	1	131	116	43
EV Zug	36	19	14	3	144	117	41
HC Ambri-Poitta	36	17	15	4	130	125	38
Zurcher SC	36	12	21	3	112	141	27
EHC Bief	36	12	21	3	121	167	27
HC Ajoie	36	9	26	1	103	178	19
EHC Chur	36	5	31	0	109	196	10

1993–94

Team	GP	W	L	T	GF	GA	PTS
HC Fribourg	36	29	4	3	195	83	61
EHC Kloten	36	21	7	8	137	90	50
HC Lugano	36	19	12	5	129	102	43
EV Zug	36	19	14	3	152	135	41
SC Bern	36	18	14	4	140	108	40
HC Ambri-Piotta	36	17	17	2	137	142	36
HC Davos	36	12	21	3	97	136	27
Zurcher SC	36	9	21	6	125	149	24
EHC Olten	36	8	24	4	96	176	20
EHC Biel	36	8	26	2	83	170	18

1994–95

Team	GP	W	L	T	GF	GA	PTS
EV Zug	36	22	10	4	152	125	48
HC Lugano	36	21	10	5	147	102	47
HC Ambri-Piotta	36	19	12	5	151	136	43
HC Davos	36	19	13	4	139	125	42
Fribourg-Gotteron	36	18	13	5	177	140	41
SC Bern	36	18	15	3	146	123	39
EHC Kloten	36	15	13	8	116	119	38
Zurcher SC	36	12	21	3	129	152	27
SC Rapperswil-Jona	36	8	25	3	102	165	19
EHC Biel	36	7	27	2	108	170	16

1995–96

Team	GP	W	L	T	GF	GA	PTS
SC Bern	36	21	11	4	139	98	46
EHC Kloten	36	20	10	6	109	83	46
SC Rapperswil-Jona	36	18	13	5	137	127	41
EV Zug	36	18	15	3	149	129	39
HC Davos	36	15	12	9	140	124	39
HC Ambri-Piotta	36	16	14	6	142	139	38
HC Lugano	36	16	16	4	129	114	36
Zurcher SC	36	16	17	3	119	140	35
Fribourg-Gotteron	36	11	17	8	114	116	30
HC Lausanne	36	4	30	2	71	179	10

1996–97

Team	GP	W	L	T	GF	GA	PTS
SC Bern	46	29	15	2	205	140	60
EV Zug	46	26	15	5	188	142	57
HC Davos	46	24	20	2	187	181	50
EHC Kloten	46	21	18	7	152	131	49
HC Lugano	46	22	19	5	166	153	49
Fribourg-Gotteron	46	20	19	7	167	154	47
SC Rapperswil-Jona	45	21	22	2	156	163	44
Zuricher SC	45	19	24	2	155	188	40
HC Ambri-Piotta	45	17	25	3	153	165	37
HC La Chaux-de-Fonds	45	11	33	1	131	243	23

1997–98

Team	GP	W	L	T	GF	GA	PTS
EV Zug	40	24	10	6	151	109	54
Fribourg-Gotteron	40	23	12	5	142	111	51
HC Davos	40	24	14	2	150	119	50
HC Ambri-Piotta	40	23	15	2	156	116	48
SC Bern	40	19	14	7	139	131	45
HC Lugano	40	17	16	7	140	127	41
EHC Kloten	40	16	17	7	125	120	39
SC Rapperswil-Jona	40	15	22	3	118	142	33
HC La Chaux-de-Fonds	40	12	22	6	128	164	30
Zuricher SC	40	12	23	5	109	141	29
SC Herisau	40	9	29	2	94	172	20

CHAPTER 46

League Champions Around the Globe

From New Zealand to Iceland, an All-time List of National Champions

AUSTRALIA

1992–93	New South Wales
1993–94	New South Wales
1994–95	New South Wales
1995–96	South Australia
1996–97	New South Wales
1997–98	New South Wales

AUSTRIA

1922–23	Wiener EV
1923–24	Wiener EV
1924–25	Wiener EV
1925–26	Wiener EV
1926–27	Wiener EV
1927–28	Wiener EV
1928–29	Wiener EV
1929–30	Wiener EV
1930–31	Wiener EV
1931–32	Potzleinsdorfer SK
1932–33	Wiener EV
1933–34	Klagenfurter AC
1934–35	Klagenfurter AC
1935–36	No championship
1936–37	Wiener EV
1937–38	EK Engelmann Wien
1938–39 to 1944–45	
	No championship
1945–46	EK Engelmann Wien
1946–47	Wiener EV
1947–48	Wiener EV
1948–49	Wiener EG
1949–50	Wiener EG
1950–51	Wiener EG
1951–52	Klagenfurter AC
1952–53	EV Innsbruck
1953–54	EV Innsbruck
1954–55	Klagenfurter AC
1955–56	EK Engelmann Wien
1956–57	EK Engelmann Wien
1957–58	EV Innsbruck
1958–59	EV Innsbruck
1959–60	Klagenfurter AC
1960–61	EV Innsbruck
1961–62	Wiener EVg
1962–63	EV Innsbruck
1963–64	Klagenfurter AC
1964–65	Klagenfurter AC
1965–66	Klagenfurter AC
1966–67	Klagenfurter AC
1967–68	Klagenfurter AC
1968–69	Klagenfurter AC
1969–70	Klagenfurter AC
1970–71	Klagenfurter AC
1971–72	Klagenfurter AC
1972–73	Klagenfurter AC
1973–74	Klagenfurter AC
1974–75	ATSE Graz
1975–76	Klagenfurter AC
1976–77	Klagenfurter AC
1977–78	ATSE Graz
1978–79	Klagenfurter AC
1979–80	Klagenfurter AC
1980–81	EC Villach
1981–82	VEU Feldkirch
1982–83	VEU Feldkirch
1983–84	VEU Feldkirch
1984–85	Klagenfurter AC
1985–86	Klagenfurter AC
1986–87	Klagenfurter AC
1987–88	Klagenfurter AC
1988–89	GEV Innsbruck
1989–90	VEU Feldkirch
1990–91	Klagenfurter AC
1991–92	EC BIC Villach
1992–93	EC BIC Villach
1993–94	VEU Feldkirch
1994–95	VEU Feldkirch
1995–96	VEU Feldkirch
1996–97	VEU Feldkirch
1997–98	VEU Feldkirch

BELARUS

1992–93	Dynamo Minsk
1993–94	Tivali Minsk
1994–95	Tivali Minsk
1995–96	Polimir Novopolotsk
1996–97	Polimir Novopolotsk
1997–98	Neman Grodno

BELGIUM

1911–12	Brussels IHSC
1912–13	Brussels IHSC
1913–14	CdP Bruxelles
1914–15 to 1918–19	
	No championship
1919–20	CdP Bruxelles
1920–21	CdP Bruxelles
1921–22	Brussels IHSC
1922–23	Brussels IHSC
1923–24	Le Puck Anvers
1924–25	Le Puck Anvers
1925–26	Le Puck Anvers
1926–27	Le Puck Anvers
1927–28	Le Puck Anvers
1928–29	CdP Anvers
1929–30 to 1932–33	
	No championship
1933–34	CdP Anvers
1934–35	CdP Anvers
1935–36	CdP Anvers
1936–37	CdP Anvers
1937–38	Brussels IHSC
1938–39	Brussels IHSC
1939–40	Brussels IHSC
1940–41	Brussels IHSC
1941–42	Brussels IHSC
1942–43	Brussels IHSC
1943–44	No championship
1944–45	Brussels IHSC
1945–46	Brussels IHSC
1946–47	Brussels IHSC
1947–48	Brussels IHSC
1948–49	Brussels IHSC
1949–50	Brabo Antwerpen
1950–51	No championship
1951–52	No championship
1952–53	No championship
1953–54	Brabo Antwerpen
1954–55 to 1958–59	
	No championship
1959–60	CPL Liege
1960–61	CPL Liege
1961–62	Brussels IHSC
1962–63	Brussels IHSC
1963–64	Brussels IHSC
1964–65	No championship
1965–66	No championship
1966–67	Brussels IHSC
1967–68	Brussels IHSC
1968–69	No championship
1969–70	Brussels IHSC
1970–71	Brussels IHSC
1971–72	Brussels IHSC
1972–73	No championship
1973–74	No championship
1974–75	Brussels IHSC
1975–76	Brussels IHSC
1976–77	Brussels IHSC
1977–78	Brussels IHSC
1978–79	Olympia Heist-op-den-Berg
1979–80	Olympia Heist-op-den-Berg
1980–81	HYC Herentals
1981–82	Brussels IHSC
1982–83	Olympia Heist-op-den-Berg
1983–84	HYC Herentals
1984–85	HYC Herentals
1985–86	Olympia Heist-op-den-Berg
1986–87	Olympia Heist-op-den-Berg
1987–88	Phantoms Deurne
1988–89	Olympia Heist-op-den-Berg
1989–90	Olympia Heist-op-den-Berg
1990–91	Olympia Heist-op-den-Berg
1991–92	Olympia Heist-op-den-Berg
1992–93	HYC Herentals
1993–94	HYC Herentals
1994–95	No championship
1995–96	HYC Herentals
1996–97	HYC Herentals
1997–98	HYC Herentals

BULGARIA

1951–52	Cerveno zname Sofia
1952–53	Udarnik Sofia
1953–54	Udarnik Sofia
1954–55	Torpedo Sofia
1955–56	Cerveno zname Sofia
1956–57	Cerveno zname Sofia
1957–58	No championship
1958–59	Cerveno zname Sofia
1959–60	Cerveno zname Sofia
1960–61	Cerveno zname Sofia
1961–62	Cerveno zname Sofia
1962–63	Cerveno zname Sofia
1963–64	CDNA Sofia
1964–65	CSKA Cerveno zname Sofia
1965–66	CSKA Cerveno zname Sofia
1966–67	CSKA Cerveno zname Sofia
1967–68	Metallurg Pernik
1968–69	CSKA Septemvriisko zname S
1969–70	Krakra Pernik
1970–71	CSKA Septemvriisko zname S
1971–72	CSKA Septemvriisko zname S
1972–73	CSKA Septemvriisko zname S
1973–74	CSKA Septemvriisko zname S
1974–75	CSKA Septemvriisko zname S
1975–76	Levski-Spartak Sofia
1976–77	Levski-Spartak Sofia
1977–78	Levski-Spartak Sofia
1978–79	Levski-Spartak Sofia
1979–80	Levski-Spartak Sofia
1980–81	Levski-Spartak Sofia
1981–82	Levski-Spartak Sofia
1982–83	CSKA Septemvriisko zname S
1983–84	CSKA Septemvriisko zname S
1984–85	Slavia Sofia
1985–86	CSKA Septemvriisko zname S
1986–87	Slavia Sofia
1987–88	Slavia Sofia
1988–89	Levski-Spartak Sofia
1989–90	Levski-Spartak Sofia
1990–91	Slavia Sofia

1991–92	DFS Levski-Spartak Sofia
1992–93	DFS Slavia Sofia
1993–94	DFS Slavia Sofia
1994–95	HC Levski Sofia
1995–96	Slavia SF Sofia
1996–97	Slavia SF Sofia
1997–98	Slavia SF Sofia

CHINA

1987–88	Changchun
1988–89	Harbin
1989–90	No championship
1990–91	Nei Menggol
1991–92	No championship
1992–93	Qiqihar
1993–94	Qiqihar
1994–95	Qiqihar
1995–96	Qiqihar A
1996–97	Qiqihar A
1997–98	Qiqihar A

CROATIA

1991–92	HK Zagreb
1992–93	HK Zagreb
1993–94	HK Zagreb
1994–95	Medvescak Zagreb
1995–96	HK Zagreb
1996–97	Medvescak Zagreb
1997–98	Medvescak Zagreb

CZECHOSLOVAKIA

1936–37	LTC Praha
1937–38	LTC Praha
1938–39 to 1944–45	No championship
1945–46	LTC Praha
1946–47	LTC Praha
1947–48	LTC Praha
1948–49	LTC Praha
1949–50	ATK Praha
1950–51	SKP Ceske Budejovice
1951–52	VZKG Ostrava
1952–53	Spartak Praha Sokolovo
1953–54	Spartak Praha Sokolovo
1954–55	RH Brno
1955–56	RH Brno
1956–57	RH Brno
1957–58	RH Brno
1958–59	SONP Kladno
1959–60	RH Brno
1960–61	RH Brno
1961–62	ZKL Brno
1962–63	ZKL Brno
1963–64	ZKL Brno
1964–65	ZKL Brno
1965–66	ZKL Brno
1966–67	Dukla Jihlava
1967–68	Dukla Jihlava
1968–69	Dukla Jihlava
1969–70	Dukla Jihlava
1970–71	Dukla Jihlava
1971–72	Dukla Jihlava
1972–73	Tesla Pardubice
1973–74	Dukla Jihlava
1974–75	SONP Kladno

1975–76	SONP Kladno
1976–77	Poldi SONP Kladno
1977–78	Poldi SONP Kladno
1978–79	Slovan Bratislava
1979–80	Poldi SONP Kladno
1980–81	TJ Vitkovice
1981–82	Dukla Jihlava
1982–83	Dukla Jihlava
1983–84	Dukla Jihlava
1984–85	Dukla Jihlava
1985–86	VSZ Kosice
1986–87	Tesla Pardubice
1987–88	VSZ Kosice
1988–89	Tesla Pardubice
1989–90	Sparta Praha
1990–91	Dukla Jihlava
1991–92	Dukla Trencin
1991–92	Dukla Trencin

CZECH REPUBLIC

1992–93	HC Sparta Praha
1993–94	HC Olomouc
1994–95	HC Dadak Vsetin
1995–96	HC Petra Vsetin
1996–97	HC Petra Vsetin
1997–98	HC Petra Vsetin

DENMARK

1954–55	Rungsted IK
1955–56	Kobenhavns SF
1956–57	No championship
1957–58	No championship
1958–59	No championship
1959–60	Kobenhavns SF
1960–61	Kobenhavns SF
1961–62	Kobenhavns SF
1962–63	Rungsted IK
1963–64	Kobenhavns SF
1964–65	Kobenhavns SF
1965–66	Kobenhavns SF
1966–67	Gladsaxe SF
1967–68	Gladsaxe SF
1968–69	Esbjerg IK
1969–70	Kobenhavns SF
1970–71	Gladsaxe SF
1971–72	Kobenhavns SF
1972–73	Herning IK
1973–74	Gladsaxe SF
1974–75	Gladsaxe SF
1975–76	Kobenhavns SF
1976–77	Herning IK
1977–78	Rodovre SIK
1978–79	Vojens IK
1979–80	Vojens IK
1980–81	Aalborg BK
1981–82	Vojens IK
1982–83	Rodovre SIK
1983–84	Herlev IK
1984–85	Rodovre SIK
1985–86	Rodovre SIK
1986–87	Herning IK
1987–88	Esbjerg IK
1988–89	Fredrikshavn IK
1989–90	Rodovre SIK
1990–91	Herning IK
1991–92	Herning IK
1992–93	Esbjerg IK
1993–94	Herning IK
1994–95	Herning IK
1995–96	Esbjerg IK

1996–97	Herning IK
1997–98	Herning IK

ESTONIA

1933–34	Kalev Tallinn
1934–35	No championship
1935–36	ASC Tartu
1936–37	Kalev Tallinn
1937–38	No championship
1938–39	ASC Tartu
1939–40	Sport Tallinn
1940–41 to 1991–92	No championship
1992–93	Kreenholm Narva
1993–94	Kreenholm Narva
1994–95	Kreenholm Narva
1995–96	Kreenholm Narva
1996–97	Valk–494 Tartu
1997–98	Kreenholm Narva

FINLAND

1927–28	Viipurin Reipas
1928–29	HJK Helsinki
1929–30	No championship
1930–31	TaPa Tampere
1931–32	HJK Helsinki
1932–33	HSK Helsinki
1933–34	HSK Helsinki
1934–35	HJK Helsinki
1935–36	Ilves Tampere
1936–37	Ilves Tampere
1937–38	Ilves Tampere
1938–39	KIF Helsinki
1939–40	No championship
1940–41	KIF Helsinki
1941–42	No championship
1942–43	KIF Helsinki
1943–44	No championship
1944–45	Ilves Tampere
1945–46	Ilves Tampere
1946–47	Ilves Tampere
1947–48	Tarmo Hameenlinna
1948–49	Tarmo Hameenlinna
1949–50	Ilves Tampere
1950–51	Ilves Tampere
1951–52	Ilves Tampere
1952–53	TBK Tampere
1953–54	TBK Tampere
1954–55	TBK Tampere
1955–56	TPS Turku
1956–57	Ilves Tampere
1957–58	Ilves Tampere
1958–59	Tappara Tampere
1959–60	Ilves Tampere
1960–61	Tappara Tampere
1961–62	Ilves Tampere
1962–63	Lukko Rauma
1963–64	Tappara Tampere
1964–65	Karhut Pori
1965–66	Ilves Tampere
1966–67	RU–38 Pori
1967–68	KooVee Tampere
1968–69	HIFK Helsinki
1969–70	HIFK Helsinki
1970–71	Assat Pori
1971–72	Ilves Tampere
1972–73	Jokerit Helsinki
1973–74	HIFK Helsinki
1974–75	Tappara Tampere
1975–76	TPS Turku

1976–77	Tappara Tampere
1977–78	Assat Pori
1978–79	Tappara Tampere
1979–80	HIFK Helsinki
1980–81	Karpat Oulu
1981–82	Tappara Tampere
1982–83	HIFK Helsinki
1983–84	Tappara Tampere
1984–85	Ilves Tampere
1985–86	Tappara Tampere
1986–87	Tappara Tampere
1987–88	Tappara Tampere
1988–89	TPS Turku
1989–90	TPS Turku
1990–91	TPS Turku
1991–92	Jokerit Helsinki
1992–93	TPS Turku
1993–94	Jokerit Helsinki
1994–95	TPS Turku
1995–96	Jokerit Helsinki
1996–97	Jokerit Helsinki
1997–98	HIFK Helsinki

FRANCE

1903–04	Patineurs de Paris
1904–05	Patineurs de Paris
1905–06	Patineurs de Paris
1906–07	Sporting Club Lyon
1907–08	Patineurs de Paris
1908–09	No championship
1909–10	No championship
1910–11	No championship
1911–12	Patineurs de Paris
1912–13	Patineurs de Paris
1913–14	Patineurs de Paris
1914–15 to 1918–19	No championship
1919–20	Ice Skating Club Paris
1920–21	Sports D'Hiver Paris
1921–22	Sports D'Hiver Paris
1922–23	HC Chamonix
1923–24	No championship
1924–25	HC Chamonix
1925–26	HC Chamonix
1926–27	HC Chamonix
1927–28	No championship
1928–29	HC Chamonix
1929–30	HC Chamonix
1930–31	HC Chamonix
1931–32	Stade Francais Paris
1932–33	Stade Francais Paris
1933–34	Rapides de Paris
1934–35	Stade Francais Paris
1935–36	Francais Volants de Paris
1936–37	Francais Volants de Paris
1937–38	Francais Volants de Paris
1938–39	HC Chamonix
1939–40	No championship
1940–41	No championship
1941–42	HC Chamonix
1942–43	No championship
1943–44	HC Chamonix
1944–45	No championship
1945–46	HC Chamonix

1946–47	No championship
1947–48	No championship
1948–49	HC Chamonix
1949–50	Racing Club de Paris
1950–51	Racing Club de Paris
1951–52	HC Chamonix
1952–53	Paris Universite Club
1953–54	HC Chamonix
1954–55	HC Chamonix
1955–56	Patineurs de Lyon
1956–57	ACBB Paris
1957–58	HC Chamonix
1958–59	HC Chamonix
1959–60	ACBB Paris
1960–61	HC Chamonix
1961–62	ACBB Paris
1962–63	HC Chamonix
1963–64	HC Chamonix
1964–65	HC Chamonix
1965–66	HC Chamonix
1966–67	HC Chamonix
1967–68	HC Chamonix
1968–69	HC Saint-Gervais
1969–70	HC Chamonix
1970–71	HC Chamonix
1971–72	HC Chamonix
1972–73	HC Chamonix
1973–74	HC Saint-Gervais
1974–75	HC Saint-Gervais
1975–76	HC Chamonix
1976–77	HC Gap
1977–78	HC Gap
1978–79	HC Chamonix
1979–80	ASG Tours
1980–81	CSG Grenoble
1981–82	CSG Grenoble
1982–83	HC Saint-Gervais
1983–84	CS Megeve
1984–85	HC Saint-Gervais
1985–86	HC Saint-Gervais
1986–87	HC Mont Blanc Megeve
1987–88	HC Mont Blanc Megeve
1988–89	Francais Volants de Paris
1989–90	HC Rouen
1990–91	CSG Grenoble
1991–92	HC Rouen
1992–93	HC Rouen
1993–94	HC Rouen
1994–95	HC Rouen
1995–96	SP Brest
1996–97	SP Brest
1997–98	CSG Grenoble

GERMANY

1911–12	Berliner SC
1912–13	Berliner SC
1913–14	Berliner SC
1914–15 to 1918–19	No championship
1919–20	Berliner SC
1920–21	Berliner SC
1921–22	MTV Munchen
1922–23	Berliner SC
1923–24	Berliner SC
1924–25	Berliner SC
1925–26	Berliner SC
1926–27	SC Riessersee Garmisch-Partenkirchen
1927–28	Berliner SC
1928–29	Berliner SC
1929–30	Berliner SC
1930–31	Berliner SC
1931–32	Berliner SC
1932–33	Berliner SC
1933–34	SC Brandenburg Berlin
1934–35	SC Riessersee Garmisch-Partenkirchen
1935–36	Berliner SC
1936–37	Berliner SC
1937–38	SC Riessersee Garmisch-Partenkirchen
1938–39	Engelmann Wien
1939–40	Wiener EG
1940–41	SC Riessersee Garmisch-Partenkirchen
1941–42	No championship
1942–43	No championship
1943–44	Berliner SC/SC Brandenburg
1944–45	No championship
1945–46	No championship
1946–47	SC Riessersee Garmisch-Partenkirchen
1947–48	SC Riessersee Garmisch-Partenkirchen
1948–49	EV Fussen
1949–50	SC Riessersee Garmisch-Partenkirchen
1950–51	Preussen Krefeld
1951–52	Krefelder EV
1952–53	EV Fussen
1953–54	EV Fussen
1954–55	EV Fussen
1955–56	EV Fussen
1956–57	EV Fussen
1957–58	EV Fussen
1958–59	EV Fussen
1959–60	SC Riessersee Garmisch-Partenkirchen
1960–61	EV Fussen
1961–62	EC Bad Tolz
1962–63	EV Fussen
1963–64	EV Fussen
1964–65	EV Fussen
1965–66	EC Bad Tolz
1966–67	Dusseldorfer EG
1967–68	EV Fussen
1968–69	EV Fussen
1969–70	EV Landshut
1970–71	EV Fussen
1971–72	Dusseldorfer EG
1972–73	EV Fussen
1973–74	Berliner SC
1974–75	Dusseldorfer EG
1975–76	Berliner SC
1976–77	Kolner EC
1977–78	SC Riessersee Garmisch-Partenkirchen
1978–79	Kolner EC
1979–80	Mannheimer ERC
1980–81	SC Riessersee Garmisch-Partenkirchen
1981–82	SB Rosenheim
1982–83	EV Landshut
1983–84	Kolner EC
1984–85	SB Rosenheim
1985–86	Kolner EC
1986–87	Kolner EC
1987–88	Kolner EC
1988–89	SB Rosenheim
1989–90	Dusseldorfer EG
1990–91	Dusseldorfer EG
1991–92	Dusseldorfer EG
1992–93	Dusseldorfer EG
1993–94	Hedos Munchen
1994–95	Kolner EC
1995–96	Dusseldorfer EG
1996–97	Adler Mannheim
1997–98	Adler Mannheim

GREAT BRITAIN

1897–98	Niagara
1898–99	Princes' Skating Club London
1899–00	Princes' Skating Club London
1900–01	Princes' Skating Club London
1901–02	Cambridge University
1902–03	London Canadians
1903–04	London Canadians
1904–05	Princes' Skating Club London
1905–06	Princes' Skating Club London
1906–07	Oxford Canadians
1907–08	Princes' Skating Club London
1908–09	Princes' Skating Club London
1909–10	Oxford Canadians
1910–11	Oxford Canadians
1911–12	Princes' Skating Club London
1912–13	Oxford Canadians
1913–14	Princes' Skating Club London
1914–15 to 1926–27	No championship
1927–28	United Services
1928–29	United Services
1929–30	London Lions
1930–31	London Lions
1931–32	Oxford University
1932–33	Oxford University
1933–34	Grosvenor House Canadians
1934–35	Streatham
1935–36	Wembley Lions
1936–37	Wembley Lions
1937–38	Harringay Racers
1938–39	Harringay Greyhounds
1939–40	Harringay Greyhounds
1940–41 to 1945–46	No championship
1946–47	Brighton Tigers
1947–48	Brighton Tigers
1948–49	Harringay Racers
1949–50	Streatham
1950–51	Nottingham Panthers
1951–52	Wembley Lions
1952–53	Streatham
1953–54	Nottingham Panthers
1954–55	Harringay Racers
1955–56	Nottingham Panthers
1956–57	Wembley Lions
1957–58	Brighton Tigers
1958–59	Paisley Pirates
1959–60	Brighton Tigers
1960–61 to 1974–75	No championship
1975–76	Ayr Bruins
1976–77	Fife Flyers
1977–78	Fife Flyers
1978–79	Murrayfield Racers
1979–80	Murrayfield Racers
1980–81	Murrayfield Racers
1981–82	Dundee Rockets
1982–83	Dundee Rockets
1983–84	Dundee Rockets
1984–85	Fife Flyers
1985–86	Murrayfield Racers
1986–87	Durham Wasps
1987–88	Durham Wasps
1988–89	Nottingham Panthers
1989–90	Cardiff Devils
1990–91	Durham Wasps
1991–92	Durham Wasps
1992–93	Cardiff Devils
1993–94	Cardiff Devils
1994–95	Sheffield Steelers
1995–96	Sheffield Steelers
1996–97	Sheffield Steelers
1997–98	Ayr Scottish Eagles

GREECE

1988–89	Aris Thessaloniki
1989–90	Aris Thessaloniki
1990–91	Aris Thessaloniki
1991–92	Aris Thessaloniki
1992–93	Ice Flyers Athens
1993–94 to 1997–98	No championship

HONG KONG

1995–96	Planet Hollywood
1996–97	Drahmala Jets
1997–98	Drahmala Jets

HUNGARY

1936–37	BKE Budapest
1937–38	BKE Budapest
1938–39	BKE Budapest
1939–40	BKE Budapest
1940–41	BBTE Budapest

1941–42	BKE Budapest
1942–43	BBTE Budapest
1943–44	BKE Budapest
1944 45	No championship
1945–46	BKE Budapest
1946–47	MTK Budapest
1947–48	MTK Budapest
1948–49	MTK Budapest
1949–50	BVM Budapest
1950–51	Budapesti Kinizsi
1951–52	BVM Budapest
1952–53	Budapesti Postas
1953–54	Budapesti Postas
1954–55	Budapesti Kinizsi
1955–56	Budapesti Kinizsi
1956–57	BVM Budapest
1957–58	Ujpesti Dozsa Budapest
1958–59	BVM Budapest
1959–60	Ujpesti Dozsa Budapest
1960–61	Ferencvarosi TC Budapest
1961–62	Ferencvarosi TC Budapest
1962–63	BVM Budapest
1963–64	Ferencvarosi TC Budapest
1964–65	Ujpesti Dozsa Budapest
1965–66	Ujpesti Dozsa Budapest
1966–67	Ujpesti Dozsa Budapest
1967–68	Ujpesti Dozsa Budapest
1968–69	Ujpesti Dozsa Budapest
1969–70	Ujpesti Dozsa Budapest
1970–71	Ferencvarosi TC Budapest
1971–72	Ferencvarosi TC Budapest
1972–73	Ferencvarosi TC Budapest
1973–74	Ferencvarosi TC Budapest
1974–75	Ferencvarosi TC Budapest
1975–76	Ferencvarosi TC Budapest
1976–77	Ferencvarosi TC Budapest
1977–78	Ferencvarosi TC Budapest
1978–79	Ferencvarosi TC Budapest
1979–80	Ferencvarosi TC Budapest
1980–81	Volan Szekesfehervar
1981–82	Ujpesti Dozsa Budapest
1982–83	Ujpesti Dozsa Budapest
1983–84	Ferencvarosi TC Budapest
1984 85	Ujpesti Dozsa Budapest
1985–86	Ujpesti Dozsa Budapest
1986–87	Ujpesti Dozsa Budapest
1987–88	Ujpesti Dozsa Budapest
1988–89	Ferencvarosi TC Budapest
1989–90	Lehel Jaszberenyi
1990–91	Ferencvarosi TC Budapest
1991–92	Ferencvarosi TC Budapest
1992–93	Ferencvarosi TC Budapest
1993–94	Ferencvarosi TC Budapest
1994–95	Ferencvarosi TC Budapest
1995–96	Dunaferr SE Dunaujvaros
1996–97	Ferencvarosi TC Budapest
1997–98	Dunaferr SE Dunaujvaros

ICELAND

1967–68	Skautafelag Akureyrar
1968–69	Skautafelag Akureyrar
1969–70	Skautafelag Reykjavikur
1970–71 to 1977–78	No championship
1978–79	Skautafelag Reykjavikur
1979–80	Skautafelag Akureyrar
1980–81	No championship
1981–82	Skautafelag Akureyrar
1982–83	Skautafelag Akureyrar
1983–84	Skautafelag Akureyrar
1984–85	Skautafelag Reykjavikur
1985–86	No championship
1986–87	Skautafelag Akureyrar
1987–88	Skautafelag Akureyrar
1988–89	No championship
1989–90	No championship
1990–91	No championship
1991 92	Skautafelag Akureyrar
1992–93	Skautafelag Akureyrar
1993–94	Skautafelag Akureyrar
1994–95	Skautafelag Akureyrar
1995–96	Skautafelag Akureyrar
1996–97	Skautafelag Akureyrar
1997–98	Skautafelag Akureyrar

ISRAEL

1989–90	HC Haifa
1990–91	HC Haifa
1991–92	No championship
1992–93	No championship
1993–94	HC Haifa
1994–95	HC Bat Yam
1995–96	Lions Jerusalem
1996–97	Lions Jerusalem
1997–98	Macabi Lod

ITALY

1924–25	HC Milano
1925–26	HC Milano
1926–27	HC Milano
1927–28	No championship
1928–29	No championship
1929–30	HC Milano
1930–31	HC Milano
1931–32	SG Cortina
1932–33	HC Milano
1933–34	HC Milano
1934–35	HC Diavoli Rosso-Neri
1935–36	HC Diavoli Rosso-Neri
1936–37	AMDG Milano
1937–38	AMDG Milano
1938–39	No championship
1939–40	No championship
1940–41	AMDG Milano
1941–42 to 1945–46	No championship
1946–47	HC Milano
1947–48	HC Milano
1948–49	HC Diavoli Rosso-Neri
1949–50	HC Milano
1950–51	HC Milano-Inter
1951–52	HC Milano-Inter
1952–53	HC Diavoli Rosso-Neri
1953–54	HC Milano-Inter
1954–55	HC Milano-Inter
1955–56	No championship
1956–57	SG Cortina
1957–58	Milan-Inter HC
1958–59	SG Cortina
1959–60	Diavoli HC Milano
1960–61	SG Cortina Rex
1961–62	SG Cortina Rex
1962–63	HC Bolzano Ozo
1963–64	SG Cortina Rex
1964–65	SG Cortina Rex
1965–66	SG Cortina Rex
1966–67	SG Cortina Rex
1967–68	SG Cortina Rex
1968–69	HC Val Gardena Recoaro
1969–70	SG Cortina Dorla
1970–71	SG Cortina Dorla
1971–72	SG Cortina Doria
1972–73	HC Bolzano Coca-Cola
1973–74	SG Cortina Doria
1974–75	SG Cortina Doria
1975–76	HC Gardena Cinzano Vermouth
1976–77	HC Bolzano Coca-Cola
1977–78	HC Bolzano Henkel
1078–79	HC Bolzano Despar
1979–80	HC Gardena Recoaro
1980–81	HC Gardena Finstral
1981–82	HC Bolzano Wurth
1982–83	HC Bolzano Wurth
1983–84	HC Bolzano Wurth
1984–85	HC Bolzano Wurth
1985–86	HC Merano Lancla
1986–87	AS Kronenburg Varese Hockey
1987–88	HC Bolzano Dival
1988–89	AS Kronenburg Varese Hockey
1989–90	HC Bolzano Lancia
1990–91	HC Saima Milano
1991–92	HC Devils Milan
1992–93	HC Devils Milan
1993–94	HC Devils Milan
1994–95	HC Bolzano Wurth
1995–96	HC Bolzano
1996–97	HC Bolzano
1997–98	HC Bolzano

JAPAN

1974–75	Kokudo Keikaku Tokyo
1975–76	Oji Seishi Tomakomai
1976–77	Oji Seishi Tomakomai
1977–78	Seibu Tetsudo Tokyo
1978 79	Seibu Tetsudo Tokyo
1979–80	Oji Seishi Tomakomai
1980–81	Oji Seishi Tomakomai
1981–82	Kokudo Keikaku Tokyo
1982–83	Oji Seishi Tomakomai
1983–84	Oji Seishi Tomakomai
1984–85	Oji Seishi Tomakomai
1985–86	Oji Seishi Tomakomai
1986–87	Oji Seishi Tomakomai
1987–88	Kokudo Keikaku Tokyo
1988–89	Oji Seishi Tomakomai
1989–90	Oji Seishi Tomakomai
1990–91	Oji Seishi Tomakomai
1991–92	Kokudo Keikaku Tokyo
1992–93	Kokudo Tokyo
1993–94	New Oji Tomakomai
1994–95	Kokudo Tokyo
1995–96	Seibu Tetsudo Tokyo
1996–97	Seibu Tetsudo Tokyo
1997–98	Kokudo Tokyo

KAZAKHSTAN

1992–93	Torpedo Ust-Kamenogorsk
1993–94	Torpedo Ust-Kamenogorsk
1994–95	Torpedo Ust-Kamenogorsk
1995–96	Torpedo Ust-Kamenogorsk
1996–97	Torpedo Ust-Kamenogorsk
1997–98	Torpedo Ust-Kamenogorsk

LATVIA

1931–32	Union Riga
1932–33	Union Riga
1933–34	ASK Riga
1934–35	ASK Riga
1935–36	ASK Riga
1936–37	Universitates Sports Riga
1937–38	ASK Riga
1938–39	ASK Riga
1939–40	Universitates Sports Riga
1940–41	No championship
1941–42	Universitates Sports Riga
1942–43	No championship
1943–44	Universitates Sports Riga
1944–45 to 1991–92	No championship
1992–93	Pardaugava Riga
1993–94	Hokeja Centrs Riga
1994–95	HK Nik's-Brih Riga
1995–96	HK Nik's-Brih Riga
1996–97	LB/Essamika Ogre
1997–98	HK Nik's-Brih Riga

LITHUANIA

1925–26	LFLS Kaunas
1926–27	LFLS Kaunas
1927–28	LFLS Kaunas
1928–29	STSK Kaunas
1929–30	No championship
1930–31	LFLS Kaunas
1931–32	LGSF Kaunas
1932–33	LGSF Kaunas
1933–34	LFLS Kaunas
1934–35	No championship
1935–36	No championship
1936–37	LGSF Kaunas
1937–38	Tauras Kaunas
1938–39	KJK Kaunas
1939–40	Tauras Kaunas
1940–41	Spartakus
1941–42	Tauras Kaunas
1942–43 to 1991–92	No championship
1992–93	Energija Elektrenai
1993–94	Energija Elektrenai
1994–95	Energija Elektrenai
1995–96	Energija Elektrenai
1996–97	Energija Elektrenai
1997–98	Energija Elektrenai

LUXEMBOURG

1993–94	Tornado Luxembourg
1994–95	No championship
1995–96	Tornado Luxembourg
1996–97	Tornado Luxembourg
1997–98	Tornado Luxembourg

NETHERLANDS

1937–38	HIJC den Haag
1938–39	HIJC den Haag
1939–40 to 1944–45	No championship
1945–46	HIJC den Haag
1946–47	TIJSC Tilburg
1947–48	HIJC den Haag
1948–49	No championship
1949–50	Ijsvogels Amsterdam
1950–51 to 1963–64	No championship
1964–65	HIJS Hokij den Haag
1965–66	HIJS Hokij den Haag
1966–67	HIJS Hokij den Haag
1967–68	HIJS Hokij den Haag
1968–69	HIJS Hokij den Haag
1969–70	SIJ den Bosch
1970–71	Tilburg Trappers
1971–72	Tilburg Trappers
1972–73	Tilburg Trappers
1973–74	Tilburg Trappers
1974–75	Tilburg Trappers
1975–76	Tilburg Trappers
1976–77	Feenstra Flyers Heerenveen
1977–78	Feenstra Flyers Heerenveen
1978–79	Feenstra Flyers Heerenveen
1979–80	Feenstra Flyers Heerenveen
1980–81	Feenstra Flyers Heerenveen
1981–82	Feenstra Flyers Heerenveen
1982–83	Feenstra Flyers Heerenveen
1983–84	Vissers Nijmegen
1984–85	Deko Builders Amsterdam
1985–86	Noorder Stores GIJS Gronin
1986–87	Pandas Rotterdam
1987–88	Spitman Nijmegen
1988–89	Turbana Pandas Rotterdam
1989–90	Gunco Pandas Rotterdam
1990–91	Peter Langhout Utrecht
1991–92	Pro Badge Utrecht
1992–93	Flame Guards Nijmegen
1993–94	Couwenberg Trappers Tilburg
1994–95	CVT Tilburg Trappers
1995–96	CVT Tilburg Trappers
1996–97	Fulda Tigers Nijmegen
1997–98	Van Heumen Tigers Nijmegen

NEW ZEALAND

1989–90	Auckland
1990–91	Auckland
1991–92	Auckland
1992–93	Auckland
1993–94	Auckland
1994–95	North Island
1995–96	North Island
1996–97	North Island
1997–98	Auckland

NORWAY

1934–35	SFK Trygg Oslo
1935–36	SK Grane Sandvika
1936–37	SK Grane Sandvika
1937–38	SFK Trygg Oslo
1938–39	SK Grane Sandvika
1939–40	SK Grane Sandvika
1940–41 to 1944–45	No championship
1945–46	Forward Oslo
1946–47	Stabaek IF Baerum
1947–48	SK Strong Oslo
1948–49	Furuset IF Oslo
1949–50	Gamlebyen IF Oslo
1950–51	Furuset IF Oslo
1951–52	Furuset IF Oslo
1952–53	Gamlebyen IF Oslo
1953–54	Furuset IF Oslo
1954–55	Gamlebyen IF Oslo
1955–56	Gamlebyen IF Oslo
1956–57	IK Tigrene Oslo
1957–58	Gamlebyen IF Oslo
1958–59	Gamlebyen IF Oslo
1959–60	Valerengens IF Oslo
1960–61	IK Tigrene Oslo
1961–62	Valerengens IF Oslo
1962–63	Valerengens IF Oslo
1963–64	Gamlebyen IF Oslo
1964–65	Valerengens IF Oslo
1965–66	Valerengens IF Oslo
1966–67	Valerengens IF Oslo
1967–68	Valerengens IF Oslo
1968–69	Valerengens IF Oslo
1969–70	Valerengens IF Oslo
1970–71	Valerengens IF Oslo
1971–72	Hasle/Loren IL Oslo
1972–73	Valerengens IF Oslo
1973–74	Hasle/Loren IL Oslo
1974–75	Frisk Asker
1975–76	Hasle/Loren IL Oslo
1976–77	IL Manglerud/Star Oslo
1977–78	IL Manglerud/Star Oslo
1978–79	Frisk Asker
1979–80	Furuset IF Oslo
1980–81	IL Stjernen Fredrikstad
1981–82	Valerengens IF Oslo
1982–83	Furuset IF Oslo
1983–84	IL Sparta Sarpsborg
1984–85	Valerengens IF Oslo
1985–86	IL Stjernen Fredrikstad
1986–87	Valerengens IF Oslo
1987–88	Valerengens IF Oslo
1988–89	IL Sparta Sarpsborg
1989–90	Furuset IF Oslo
1990–91	Valerengens IF Oslo
1991–92	Valerengens IF Oslo
1992–93	Valerengens IF Oslo
1993–94	Lillehammer IK
1994–95	Storhamar IL Hamar
1995–96	Storhamar IL Hamar
1996–97	Storhamar IL Hamar
1997–98	Valerengens IF Oslo

POLAND

1926–27	AZS Warszawa
1927–28	AZS Warszawa
1928–29	AZS Warszawa
1929–30	AZS Warszawa
1930–31	AZS Warszawa
1931–32	No championship
1932–33	Legia Warszawa & Pogon Lwo
1933–34	AZS Poznan
1934–35	Czarni Lwow
1935–36	No championship
1936–37	Cracovia Krakow
1937–38	No championship
1938–39	Dab Katowice
1939–40 to 1944–45	No championship
1945–46	Cracovia Krakow
1946–47	Cracovia Krakow
1947–48	No championship
1948–49	Cracovia Krakow
1949–50	KTH Krynica
1950–51	CWKS Warszawa
1951–52	CWKS Warszawa
1952–53	CWKS Warszawa
1953–54	CWKS Warszawa
1954–55	Legia Warszawa
1955–56	Legia Warszawa
1956–57	Legia Warszawa
1957–58	Gornik Katowice
1958–59	Legia Warszawa
1959–60	Gornik Katowice
1960–61	Legia Warszawa
1961–62	Gornik Katowice
1962–63	Legia Warszawa
1963–64	Legia Warszawa
1964–65	GKS Katowice
1965–66	Podhale Nowy Targ
1966–67	Legia Warszawa
1967–68	GKS Katowice
1968–69	Podhale Nowy Targ
1969–70	GKS Katowice
1970–71	Podhale Nowy Targ
1971–72	Podhale Nowy Targ
1972–73	Podhale Nowy Targ

1973–74	Podhale Nowy Targ
1974–75	Podhale Nowy Targ
1975–76	Podhale Nowy Targ
1976–77	Podhale Nowy Targ
1977–78	Podhale Nowy Targ
1978–79	Podhale Nowy Targ
1979–80	GKS Zaglebie Sosnowiec
1980–81	GKS Zaglebie Sosnowiec
1981–82	GKS Zaglebie Sosnowiec
1982–83	GKS Zaglebie Sosnowiec
1983–84	Polonia Bytom
1984–85	GKS Zaglebie Sosnowiec
1985–86	Polonia Bytom
1986–87	Podhale Nowy Targ
1987–88	Polonia Bytom
1988–89	Polonia Bytom
1989–90	Polonia Bytom
1990–91	Polonia Bytom
1991–92	Unia Oswiecim
1992–93	Podhale Nowy Targ
1993–94	Podhale Nowy Targ
1994–95	Podhale Nowy Targ
1995–96	Podhale Nowy Targ
1996–97	Podhale Nowy Targ
1997–98	Podhale Nowy Targ

ROMANIA

1924–25	Brasovia Brasov
1925–26	No championship
1926–27	HC Roman Bucuresti
1927–28	HC Roman Bucuresti
1928–29	HC Roman Bucuresti
1929–30	TC Roman Bucuresti
1930–31	TC Roman Bucuresti
1931–32	TC Roman Bucuresti
1932–33	TC Roman Bucuresti
1933–34	TC Roman Bucuresti
1934–35	TC Bucuresti
1935–36	HC Bragadiru Bucuresti
1936–37	TC Bucuresti
1937–38	Dragos Voda Cernauti
1938–39	No championship
1939–40	HC Rapid Bucuresti
1940–41	HC Juventus Bucuresti
1941–42	HC Rapid Bucuresti
1942–43	No championship
1943–44	Venus Bucuresti
1944–45	HC Juventus Bucuresti
1945–46	HC Juventus Bucuresti
1946–47	HC Ciocanul Bucuresti
1947–48	No championship

1948–49	Avintul Meircurea Ciuc
1949–50	Locomotiva RTA Tirgu Murcs
1950–51	Locomotiva RTA Tirgu Mures
1951–52	Avintul Meircurea Ciuc
1952–53	CCA Bucuresti
1953–54	Stiinta Kluz
1954–55	CCA Bucuresti
1955–56	CCA Bucuresti
1956–57	Recolta Miercurea Ciuc
1957–58	CCA Bucuresti
1958–59	CCA Bucuresti
1959–60	Vointa Miercurea Ciuc
1960–61	CCA Bucuresti
1961–62	CCA Bucuresti
1962–63	Vointa Miercurea Ciuc
1963–64	Steaua Bucuresti
1964–65	Steaua Bucuresti
1965–66	Steaua Bucuresti
1966–67	Steaua Bucuresti
1967–68	Dinamo Bucuresti
1968–69	Steaua Bucuresti
1969–70	Dinamo Bucuresti
1970–71	Steaua Bucuresti
1971–72	Dinamo Bucuresti
1972–73	Dinamo Bucuresti
1973–74	Steaua Bucuresti
1974–75	Steaua Bucuresti
1975–76	Steaua Bucuresti
1976–77	Steaua Bucuresti
1977–78	Steaua Bucuresti
1978–79	Dinamo Bucuresti
1979–80	Steaua Bucuresti
1980–81	Dinamo Bucuresti
1981–82	Steaua Bucuresti
1982–83	Steaua Bucuresti
1983–84	Steaua Bucuresti
1984–85	Steaua Bucuresti
1985–86	Steaua Bucuresti
1986–87	Steaua Bucuresti
1987–88	Steaua Bucuresti
1988–89	Steaua Bucuresti
1989–90	Steaua Bucuresti
1990–91	Steaua Bucuresti
1991–92	Steaua Bucuresti
1992–93	Steaua Kluz
1993–94	Steaua Bucuresti
1994–95	Steaua Bucuresti
1995–96	Steaua Bucuresti
1996–97	SC Miercurea Ciuc
1997–98	Steaua Bucuresti

RUSSIA/C.I.S
see also Soviet Union

1992–93	Dynamo Moscow
1993–94	Lada Togliatti
1994–95	Dynamo Moscow
1995–96	Lada Togliatti
1996–97	Torpedo Yaroslavl
1997–98	Ak Bars Kazan

SLOVENIA

1991–92	Acroni Jesenice
1992–93	Acroni Jesenice
1993–94	Acroni Jesenice
1994–95	Olimpija Hertz Ljubljana
1995–96	Olimpija Hertz Ljubljana
1996–97	Olimpija Hertz Ljubljana
1997–98	Olimpija Hertz Ljubljana

SOUTH AFRICA

1991–92	Flyers Roodenpoort
1992–93	Flyers Roodenpoort
1993–94	Flyers Roodenpoort
1994–95	Can-Ams Johannesburg
1995–96	Can-Ams Johannesburg
1996–97	Can-Ams Johannesburg
1997–98	Pretoria Capitals

SOUTH KOREA

1986–87	Yonsei University
1987–88	Yonsei University
1988–89	Korea University
1989–90	Yonsei University
1990–91	Yonsei University
1991–92	Yonsei University
1992–93	Yonsei University
1993–94	Yonsei University
1994–95	Seoktop Seoul
1995–96	Seoktop Seoul
1996–97	Yonsei University
1997–98	Halla Winia

SOVIET UNION

1946–47	Dynamo Moscow
1947–48	CDKA Moscow
1948–49	CDKA Moscow
1949–50	CDKA Moscow
1950–51	VVS MVO Moscow
1951–52	VVS MVO Moscow
1952–53	VVS MVO Moscow
1953–54	Dynamo Moscow
1954–55	CSK MO Moscow
1955–56	CSK MO Moscow
1956–57	Krylja Sovetov Moscow
1957–58	CSK MO Moscow
1958–59	CSK MO Moscow
1959–60	CSKA Moscow
1960–61	CSKA Moscow
1961–62	Spartak Moscow
1962–63	CSKA Moscow
1963–64	CSKA Moscow
1964–65	CSKA Moscow
1965–66	CSKA Moscow
1966–67	Spartak Moscow
1967–68	CSKA Moscow
1968–69	Spartak Moscow
1969–70	CSKA Moscow
1970–71	CSKA Moscow
1971–72	CSKA Moscow
1972–73	CSKA Moscow

1973–74	Krylja Sovetov Moscow
1974–75	CSKA Moscow
1975–76	Spartak Moscow
1976–77	CSKA Moscow
1977–78	CSKA Moscow
1978–79	CSKA Moscow
1979–80	CSKA Moscow
1980–81	CSKA Moscow
1981–82	CSKA Moscow
1982–83	CSKA Moscow
1983–84	CSKA Moscow
1984–85	CSKA Moscow
1985–86	CSKA Moscow
1986–87	CSKA Moscow
1987–88	CSKA Moscow
1988–89	CSKA Moscow
1989–90	Dynamo Moscow
1990–91	Dynamo Moscow
1991–92	Dynamo Moscow

SPAIN

1952–53	Atletico Madrid
1953–54	Club Alpine Nurin
1954–55 to 1971–72	No championship
1972–73	Real Sosiedad San Sebastia
1973–74	Real Sosiedad San Sebastia
1974–75	Txuri Urdin San Sebastian
1975–76	Txuri Urdin San Sebastian
1976–77	Casco Viejo Bolbao
1977–78	Casco Viejo Bolbao
1978–79	Casco Viejo Bolbao
1979–80	Txuri Urdin San Sebastian
1980–81	Casco Viejo Bolbao
1981–82	Vizcaya Bilbao
1982–83	CH Jaca
1983–84	CH Jaca
1984–85	Txuri Urdin San Sebastian
1985–86	HC Puigcerda
1986–87	No championship
1987–88	FC Barcelona
1988–89	HC Puigcerda
1989–90	Txuri Urdin San Sebastian
1990–91	CH Jaca
1991–92	Txuri Urdin San Sebastian
1992–93	Txuri Urdin San Sebastian
1993–94	CH Jaca
1994–95	Txuri Urdin San Sebastian
1995–96	CH Jaca
1996–97	FC Barcelona
1997–98	CH Majadahonda

SWEDEN

1921–22	IK Gota Stockholm
1922–23	IK Gota Stockholm
1923–24	IK Gota Stockholm
1924–25	Sodertalje SK
1925–26	Djurgardens IF Stockholm

Year	Champion	Year	Champion	Year	Champion	Year	Champion
1926–27	IK Gota Stockholm	1978–79	MoDo AIK Orskoldsvik	1954–55	EHC Arosa		**UKRAINE**
1927–28	IK Gota Stockholm			1955–56	EHC Arosa	1992–93	Sokol Kiev
1928–29	IK Gota Stockholm	1979–80	Brynas IF Gavle	1956–57	EHC Arosa	1993–94	ShVSM Kiev
1929–30	IK Gota Stockholm	1980–81	Farjestads BK Karlstad	1957–58	HC Davos	1994–95	Sokol Kiev
1930–31	Sodertalje SK			1958–59	SC Bern	1995–96	No championship
1931–32	Hammarby IF Stockholm	1981–82	AIK Solna	1959–60	HC Davos	1996–97	Sokol Kiev
		1982–83	Djurgardens IF Stockholm	1960–61	Zurcher SC	1997–98	Sokol Kiev
1932–33	Hammarby IF Stockholm			1961–62	EHC Visp		
		1983–84	AIK Solna	1962–63	HC Villars		**YUGOSLAVIA**
1933–34	AIK Solna	1984–85	Sodertalje SK	1963–64	HC Villars	1938–39	Ilirija Ljubljana
1934–35	AIK Solna	1985–86	Farjestads BK Karlstad	1964–65	SC Bern	1939–40	Ilirija Ljubljana
1935–36	Hammarby IF Stockholm			1965–66	GC Zurich	1940–41 to 1945–46	
		1986–87	IF Bjorkloven Umea	1966–67	EHC Kloten		No championship
1936–37	Hammarby IF Stockholm	1987–88	Farjestads BK Karlstad	1967–68	HC La Chaux-de-Fonds	1946–47	Mladost Zagreb
				1968–69	HC La Chaux-de-Fonds	1947–48	Partizan Belgrad
1937–38	AIK Solna	1988–89	Djurgardens IF Stockholm			1948–49	Mladost Zagreb
1938–39	No championship			1969–70	HC La Chaux-de-Fonds	1949–50	No championship
1939–40	IK Gota Stockholm	1989–90	Djurgardens IF Stockholm			1950–51	Partizan Belgrad
1940–41	Sodertalje SK			1970–71	HC La Chaux-de-Fonds	1951–52	Partizan Belgrad
1941–42	Hammarby IF Stockholm	1990–91	Djurgardens IF Stockholm			1952–53	Partizan Belgrad
				1971–72	HC La Chaux-de-Fonds	1953–54	Partizan Belgrad
1942–43	Hammarby IF Stockholm	1991–92	Malmo IF			1954–55	Partizan Belgrad
		1992–93	Brynas IF	1972–73	HC La Chaux-de-Fonds	1955–56	Zagreb
1943–44	Sodertalje SK	1993–94	Malmo IF			1956–57	HK Jesenice
1944–45	Hammarby IF Stockholm	1994–95	HV 71 Jonkoping	1973–74	SC Bern	1957–58	HK Jesenice
		1995–96	Lulea HF	1974–75	SC Bern	1958–59	HK Jesenice
1945–46	AIK Solna	1996–97	Farjestads BK Karlstad	1975–76	SC Langnau	1959–60	HK Jesenice
1946–47	AIK Solna			1976–77	SC Bern	1960–61	HK Jesenice
1947–48	IK Gota Stockholm	1997–98	Farjestads BK Karlstad	1977–78	EHC Biel	1961–62	HK Jesenice
1948–49	No championship			1978–79	SC Bern	1962–63	HK Jesenice
1949–50	Djurgardens IF Stockholm		**SWITZERERLAND**	1979–80	EHC Arosa	1963–64	HK Jesenice
		1915–16	HC Bern	1980–81	EHC Biel	1964–65	HK Jesenice
1950–51	Hammarby IF Stockholm	1916–17	HC Bern	1981–82	EHC Arosa	1965–66	HK Jesenice
		1917–18	HC Bern	1982–83	EHC Biel	1966–67	HK Jesenice
1951–52	No championship	1918–19	HC Bellerive Vevey	1983–84	HC Davos	1967–68	HK Jesenice
1952–53	Sodertalje SK	1919–20	HC Bellerive Vevey	1984–85	HC Davos	1968–69	HK Jesenice
1953–54	Djurgardens IF Stockholm	1920–21	HC Rosey Gstaad	1985–86	HC Lugano	1969–70	HK Jesenice
		1921–22	EHC St. Moritz	1986–87	HC Lugano	1970–71	HK Jesenice
1954–55	Djurgardens IF Stockholm	1922–23	EHC St. Moritz	1987–88	HC Lugano	1971–72	Olimpija Ljubljana
		1923–24	HC Rosey Gstaad	1988–89	SC Bern	1972–73	HK Jesenice
1955–56	Sodertalje SK	1924–25	HC Rosey Gstaad	1989–90	HC Lugano	1973–74	Olimpija Ljubljana
1956–57	Gavle GIK	1925–26	HC Davos	1990–91	SC Bern	1974–75	Olimpija Ljubljana
1957–58	Djurgardens IF Stockholm	1926–27	HC Davos	1991–92	SC Bern	1975–76	Olimpija Ljubljana
		1927–28	EHC St. Moritz	1992–93	EHC Kloten	1976–77	HK Jesenice
1958–59	Djurgardens IF Stockholm	1928–29	HC Davos	1993–94	EHC Kloten	1977–78	HK Jesenice
		1929–30	HC Davos	1994–95	EHC Kloten	1978–79	Olimpija Ljubljana
1959–60	Djurgardens IF Stockholm	1930–31	HC Davos	1995–96	EHC Kloten	1979–80	Olimpija Ljubljana
		1931–32	HC Davos	1996–97	SC Bern	1980–81	HK Jesenice
1960–61	Djurgardens IF Stockholm	1932–33	HC Davos	1997–98	EV Zug	1981–82	HK Jesenice
		1933–34	HC Davos			1982–83	Olimpija Ljubljana
1961–62	Djurgardens IF Stockholm	1934–35	HC Davos		**SLOVAKIA**	1983–84	Olimpija Ljubljana
		1935–36	Zurcher SC	1993–94	Dukla Trencin	1984–85	HK Jesenice
1962–63	Djurgardens IF Stockholm	1936–37	HC Davos	1994–95	HC Kosice	1985–86	Partizan Belgrad
		1937–38	HC Davos	1995–96	HC Kosice	1986–87	HK Jesenice
1963–64	Brynas IF Gavle	1938–39	HC Davos	1996–97	Dukla Trencin	1987–88	HK Jesenice
1964–65	Vastra Frolunda IF Goteborg	1939–40	No championship	1997–98	HC Slovan Harvard Bratislava	1988–89	Medvescak Zagreb
		1940–41	HC Davos			1989–90	Medvescak Zagreb
1965–66	Brynas IF Gavle	1941–42	HC Davos			1990–91	Medvescak Zagreb
1966–67	Brynas IF Gavle	1942–43	HC Davos		**TURKEY**	1991–92	Crvena Zvezda Belgrad
1967–68	Brynas IF Gavle	1943–44	HC Davos	1991–92	Belpa Ankara		
1968–69	Leksands IF	1944–45	HC Davos	1992–93	Ankara Buyuksehir Belediye	1992–93	Crvena Zvezda Belgrad
1969–70	Brynas IF Gavle	1945–46	HC Davos				
1970–71	Brynas IF Gavle	1946–47	HC Davos	1993–94	Ankara Buyuksehir Belediye	1993–94	Partizan BLP Belgrad
1971–72	Brynas IF Gavle	1947–48	HC Davos				
1972–73	Leksands IF	1948–49	Zurcher SC	1994–95	Ankara Buyuksehir Belediye	1994–95	Partizan BLP Belgrad
1973–74	Leksands IF	1949–50	HC Davos				
1974–75	Leksands IF	1950–51	EHC Arosa	1995–96	Kavaklidere Ankara	1995–96	Crvena Zve. Belgrad
1975–76	Brynas IF Gavle	1951–52	EHC Arosa	1996–97	Ankara Buyuksehir Belediye	1996–97	Crvena Zve. Belgrad
1976–77	Brynas IF Gavle	1952–53	EHC Arosa			1997–98	Vojvodina Novi Sad
1977–78	Skelleftea AIK	1953–54	EHC Arosa	1997–98	Istanbul Paten Kulubu		

V

OTHER
FACETS
OF THE
GAME

Third-period action in the pre-Zamboni era meant playing on a much-rutted rink. The Boston Bruins defend against the Rangers in this photo from February 17, 1938. The helmet-wearing defense pair by the far post are Eddie Shore (2) and Jack Portland (8).

CHAPTER 47

The Odd and the Unusual

Hockey's Share of Sporting Superstitions and Curiosities

Bob Duff

ROCKET RICHARD'S 50 GOALS IN 50 GAMES. Bobby Orr, airborne, moments after scoring the Stanley Cup-winning goal against St. Louis. The NHL's history is rich with tradition, filled with great players and teams and their tremendous achievements. Alongside the great moments, room must be made for the offbeat, the unusual and the often unbelievable events which color the history of this great game.

The fellow who scored a goal in his first NHL game but never played again. The winger who skated with a Stanley Cup winner a decade after he played his final regular-season game. The guy who bought a ticket to a game in Boston and finished the night in the Bruins net. The team which won a game without scoring a goal. And the goalie who lost one without allowing a goal.

Moe Roberts was an amateur netminder with the Boston Athletic Association when he was among the 4,000 fans who packed the Boston Arena on December 8, 1925 to watch the Boston Bruins play host to the Montreal Maroons. In the second period, Bruins goalie Doc Stewart suffered a gashed leg when he came out to challenge Montreal forward Babe Siebert. He couldn't continue. Roberts was called out of the crowd to don the pads and he filled in admirably, providing shutout goaltending for his 25 minutes of work and earning Boston a 3–2 win. Nearly 26 years later, Roberts was serving as a trainer for the Chicago Black Hawks when he was called on to make another relief appearance on November 25, 1951. Roberts, 46, took over for Harry Lumley to start the third period after the Chicago goalie was felled by a knee injury. Again, he supplied shutout netminding in a scoreless period of a game the Black Hawks lost 5–2 to Toronto.

The Montreal Maroons ran into a similar goalie crisis on January 8, 1930, but as luck would have it, the club carried two netminders. Flat Walsh was bedridden with flu, so coach Dunc Munro told him to stay home and let Clint Benedict mind the nets that night against the Montreal Canadiens—which Benedict did, until a Howie Morenz shot slammed into his face, breaking Benedict's nose and cutting him for seven stitches. With no other qualified netminder in the building, the Maroons roused Walsh from his sickbed. He took a taxi to the rink and the game was held up until his arrival. Trailing 1–0 when he arrived, Walsh played shutout goal the rest of the way (approximately 50 minutes) and the Maroons rallied for a 2–1 win. Later that season, when Benedict returned from his injury, he did so wearing a crude leather mask, making him the first NHL netminder to don facial protection.

Claude LaForge was the first Detroit Red Wing player to wear a mask. But he wasn't a goalie. LaForge, who had suffered a broken cheekbone with Hershey of the AHL, wasn't going to miss his chance when he was called up by Detroit a few days later. On December 28, 1961, LaForge, a left winger, played against Chicago wearing a goalie mask. There is a famous picture from that game of LaForge breaking in alone on Black Hawks goalie Glenn Hall, who isn't wearing a mask. The following season, Terry Sawchuk became the first Red Wings goalie to wear a mask.

Hall, who set an NHL record by starting 502 consecutive games from 1955 to 1962, was also known as the guy who vomited before every game. It became such a ritual with Hall that if he came to believe that if he didn't throw up, he didn't play well. The St. Louis Blues were readying to play the Philadelphia Flyers in game seven of their 1968 Stanley Cup quarterfinal series when Hall sought out coach Scotty Bowman, concerned that he hadn't coughed up his cookies. "He told me that if he didn't have it, I should pull him out of the game early," Bowman said. Bowman was momentarily panic stricken, but his personal nausea was relieved moments later when he saw a pair of goal pads sticking out of one of the washroom stalls. "He was throwing up," Bowman said of Hall, "and whenever he did that, he played a supreme game." Which is exactly what Hall did, blocking 26 shots in a 3–1 win.

Hall also had another superstition. He never fished the puck out the net after a goal was scored. "I wasn't the one who put it there," reasoned Hall. No one put it there when Ottawa and the Pittsburgh Pirates battled on December 5, 1925, but that didn't stop the Senators from posting a 1–0 victory when Pittsburgh forward Herb Drury threw his stick in the path of a shot by Senators defenseman George Boucher. Under NHL rules of the day, referee Lou Marsh immediately awarded a goal—marking the only time in NHL history that a game was played and a team won without a puck ever entering the net.

Mario Gosselin could probably relate to the frustration that Pittsburgh goalie Roy Worters must have felt that night. When Kelly Hrudey was injured in the third period of a Los Angeles-Edmonton game in 1989, Gosselin took over in the Kings net. The Oilers led 6–5 at the time and that was still the score when Gosselin was pulled for an extra attacker. The Oilers scored into the empty net, but just before the game ended, the Kings made it 7–6, meaning Gosselin, who was the goalie of record when the empty-net goal was scored, was charged with the loss, even though he didn't allow a single goal while he was in the net.

Giving the red light a workout was never a concern when Hardy Astrom was in goal for Don Cherry's Colorado Rockies in 1979–80. "First practice in Colorado, we were working on breakout drills. I shoot the puck at Hardy from the far blue line and it goes right through his legs," Cherry remembered. "'Fluke,' I figure, so I shoot another one.

Right through his legs again. 'Next drill,' I said. Actually, Hardy was a nice guy. He just had a weakness with pucks." Not that legendary goalies also haven't had their off days. Alex Connell set the NHL shutout streak of 461 minutes and 29 seconds in 1927–28 and he was working on another goose egg when his Ottawa Senators played the Montreal Maroons in 1930. Deadlocked in a scoreless battle with time running out, the Maroons' Babe Siebert made a desperate rush and fired a long shot into the Ottawa zone. It carried well over the Senators net, but as Connell turned to follow its path, the puck ricocheted off the chicken wire behind the net, hit Connell in the face and bounced into the net for the only goal of the game.

Brave performances in goal are the stuff of NHL lore, but Clarence (Dolly) Dolson made his biggest save long before he donned his pads in an NHL rink. Dolson, who played three seasons with Detroit, was fighting with Canadian troops in France during World War I and spotted a hand grenade as it bounced its way into the crowded trench. Dolson blocked the shot, scooped up the rebound and heaved it back towards the enemy. The hand grenade exploded in mid-air, a split-second after Dolson had tossed it aside. Fortunately for Dolson, who was awarded the Distinguished Conduct Medal for his heroics, it was against the rules of the game in those days for a goaltender to smother the puck.

Such intestinal fortitude is a required quality for NHL puckstoppers. Frank (Ulcers) McCool was just a rookie when he backstopped Toronto to a Stanley Cup win in 1945 after winning the Calder Trophy as NHL rookie of the year. He posted three shutouts in a seven-game finals verdict over Detroit. But it was his upset tummy which most people remember. He battled stomach ulcers his whole life and the pranksters on the Leafs roster enjoyed tormenting their goalie by hiding his medication. One day, McCool decided to get even. He arrived at Maple Leaf Gardens hours early for practice, asking an equipment attendant for a hammer. While the equipment handler continued about his work of organizing sticks outside the dressing room, he couldn't help but notice the thumping sound emanating from inside the room. Finally, curiosity got the better of him and he entered the room, only to find McCool carefully sliding nails through the lace loops in each player's skates, then nailing them to the bench.

McCool made his point, but Aurel Joliat wasn't as fortunate. The Montreal Canadiens thumped Ottawa 10–3 on February 11, 1925. The rout was already on when—in the midst of play—Joliat skated up to the timekeeper's bench. "How many assists you got me for?" asked Joliat, who was battling Ottawa's Cy Denneny and Toronto's Babe Dye for the scoring title. "Three," answered the astonished scorer. "Should be four," scolded an angry Joliat. "Three," the scorer said sternly. "Four," responded an angry Joliat, who then jumped back into the play, picked up the puck, raced in and scored. After the goal, he swooped past the penalty box and glared at the scorer before assuming his left wing position for the face-off.

There was no such dispute over Roly Huard's first—and last—NHL goal. When the injury bug bit the Toronto Maple Leafs, the Buffalo Bisons of the International League offered to loan Toronto the services of forward Huard for one game—a December 13, 1930 tilt with the Boston Bruins at Maple Leaf Gardens. Huard scored the opening goal in a 7–3 loss to the Bruins that night, then packed his gear and returned to Buffalo, never to appear in another NHL game. He is the only player in NHL history to play just one game and score a goal in that game. On the other hand, Dave Michayluk's NHL debut was uneventful, but his departure from the league was a dream come true. He played for Pittsburgh's 1992 Stanley Cup-winning squad, a decade after skating in his last regular-season game. Michayluk, assigned to the minors by Philadelphia in 1982, was called up when the Penguins were riddled with injuries during the 1992 playoffs. He produced a goal and an assist in seven games en route to the title. Michayluk never played another NHL game.

Not all debuts are so eventful. A budding amateur star turned professional in the late 1920s, but, as was often the case, found the monied ranks too tough. Realizing their error, the team moved quickly to deal the player before other teams caught on to the fact that he couldn't cut it. "Do I have to go?" asked the young player after he was told he'd been traded. "Yes, I'm afraid you have to," answered his manager. "Well, I'll tell you something right now," the youngster said. "I'll never turn pro again."

Rob Murray wasn't making his NHL debut when Winnipeg was playing in Detroit on November 19, 1992, but no one bothered to inform Jets teammate Teemu Selanne. When Murray scored, Selanne, thinking it was Murray's first NHL goal, fished the puck out of the net and presented it to him. "Teemu skated up and said 'Congratulations,'" Murray remembered. "I said 'Teemu, I have scored in the league before.'" "Well, I'm not taking the puck back to the referee," answered Selanne.

According to the record books, Joe Ironstone played his first NHL game for the New York Americans in 1926, but his first appearance on an NHL ice surface came about a year earlier. In the fall of 1924, Ottawa sold Clint Benedict to the Maroons and signed two amateurs—Ironstone and Alex Connell—to battle for the open spot in goal. Connell won the position and although Ironstone was on the roster, he didn't suit up for a single game. He was sitting on the bench in street clothes, watching the Canadiens and Senators battle one January night, when a brawl broke out and the benches emptied. Reluctantly, Ironstone joined the flow over the boards, taking his trusty goal stick with him. He stood at centre ice, wielding his club like a ninja warrior, ensuring no one would challenge him.

The following season, the Senators and Boston Bruins also engaged in a bench-clearing brawl. Police had to be called out to quell the riot and fans pelted the ice with bottles, papers, peanuts, coins—and an Eskimo Pie ice cream, which struck Bruins forward Stan Jackson square in the face. "It didn't seem to hurt him much," noted a report of the game in the *Montreal Gazette*.

Occasionally, the unkindest blow of all can come from a teammate. Kings forward Luc Robitaille was drilled into the net during a scramble in a Vancouver–Los Angeles game. Instinctively, he quickly turned and drilled the first player he saw with a cross-check. Unfortunately, it was teammate Dave Taylor. As Taylor groggily rose to his feet,

seeking revenge, Robitaille, in a state of panic, pointed at nearby Vancouver defenceman Doug Lidster. "It was him," Robitaille told Taylor, who immediately lunged at Lidster. Robitaille waited nearly two years before revealing what had really happened.

Joe Hall, an early NHL tough guy with the Canadiens, was another who acted instinctively when a whistle sounded during a Canadiens–Ottawa game in 1918. Hall quickly assumed his usual position in the penalty box. "What did you give him a penalty for?" Canadiens captain Newsy Lalonde demanded of referee Marsh. Marsh allowed that he had called no infraction and Lalonde posed the same query to judge of play Steve Vair. Again, his question was greeted with a shrug, so Lalonde told Hall to get out of the box. "Sorry about that Newsy," Hall said as he sheepishly returned to his position on the Canadiens defense. "Force of habit, I guess."

Marsh, also a writer for a Toronto newspaper, was one of the characters of the league. He once punched a fan during a game but used his wit to deal with a female heckler one night in New York. "If you we're my husband, you gray-haired bum, I'd give you poison," the shrill-voiced woman announced just prior to a face-off. Marsh skated over to where she was seated and said loudly: "Lady, if I was your husband, I'd take it."

Such cross words have started many an NHL altercation, but it was a crossword puzzle which left the Chicago Black Hawks in stitches during a train trip in the 1920s. Chicago defenseman Helge Bostrom was fond of crossword puzzles, while partner Amby Moran was partial to card games. Bostrom was working feverishly on a puzzle during one trek and was down to the last word. "Hey Amby," he asked his partner, interrupting their game of hearts. "What's a four-letter word meaning bird?" "Goose," answered Moran. "G-O-S-E." "Hurrah," Bostrom shouted. "It just fits."

Spelling might not be a required element for NHL success, but the fear of spells is an entirely different matter. Over the years, many players have worked overtime to ward off the affliction of the evil hoodoo. When he's on a hot streak, current Ottawa Senators goalie Ron Tugnutt wears the same clothes—right down to socks and underwear—to the rink on game day. "It's nothing disgusting, though," Tugnutt said. "I wash them."

The champion of the overtly superstitious had to be Laurie Scott, who played with Toronto and New York in the 1920s. Scott never shaved before a game and insisted on being the last player to leave the dressing room. He would cross his fingers and spit between them whenever passing a cemetery. And he always set his stick blades up in the same pattern in his locker. Scott once threatened to retire from the game when teammate Leo Reise turned his sticks around the other way.

It was probably a good thing that Scott no longer played for them when the Rangers traveled to Maple Leaf Gardens for a December 14, 1929 game against Toronto. Colonel John Hammond, president of the Rangers, hired the Curtis-Wright Corporation to transport his club to and from Toronto via airplane, marking the first time an NHL club had traveled to a league game by commercial airline.

Apparently, Colonel Hammond was not a superstitious man, considering that the Rangers departed for Toronto on Friday, December 13. For the record, Toronto won a 7–6 overtime decision.

New York's other NHL team of the era, the Americans, often played second fiddle to the Rangers. The Amerks employed many methods to convince fans to come see their games—entertaining crowds during intermissions with barrel jumping and dogsled races on the ice. In 1926, the Americans put players' names on the back of their jerseys, something that the NHL didn't make mandatory until the late 1970s. That same season, the club's public relations machine went over the top after signing Montreal amateur Rene Boileau. A January 22, 1926 press release billed Boileau as Rainey Drinkwater, a Native American. "It will be news to Rene Boileau to learn that he comes from the Cauhnawaga Indian reservation," noted the *Montreal Gazette*.

The NHL wasn't a big-money game in those days. Teams were limited by a $35,000 salary cap and signing players in midseason would challenge a budget. Charlie (Dinny) Dinsmore was a spare forward for three seasons with the NHL's Montreal Maroons in the mid-1920s. He was part of a Stanley Cup championship squad in 1926 but left the game in 1928 to take a job as a bond trader. While a lucrative occupation, Dinsmore found that playing the stock market didn't offer the same thrills as playing in the NHL, so he went to the Maroons in the midst of the 1929–30 season to inquire about getting his old job back. Team officials said that they had no more money to sign another player, but Dinsmore was insistent and finally a deal was struck. Dinsmore signed a contract which paid him one dollar for the remaining nine games. At a little more than a dime a game, it made him the lowest-paid player in NHL history. That was a dollar well spent and so was the buck which Detroit used to acquire Kris Draper from Winnipeg in 1993. "And you know what? I think it was even a Canadian dollar," said Draper, a checking-line center who played a key role in Detroit's 1997 Stanley Cup triumph.

At the other end of the financial scale, D'Arcy Coulson was the NHL's first million-dollar player—albeit through birthright, not wages. A defenseman with the Philadelphia Quakers in 1930–31, Coulson was the son of an Ottawa millionaire, perhaps explaining why his NHL career lasted just one season.

It was around the time that Coulson broke into the big leagues that legendary hockey innovator Frank Patrick—who, along with his brother Lester, helped revolutionize the way the game was played—predicted the time would come when NHLers commanded million-dollar stipends. In a 1930 interview, Patrick insisted that hockey would become a multi-million dollar business, with games being played in arenas capable of seating 20,000 fans. Patrick stated hockey would become a game "for not one coach, but two or three." He foresaw a day when all teams would carry two goalies, five defensemen and would use three forward lines throughout the game. "What happens when a player goes off-form?" he asked. "They yank him. Why shouldn't a goalkeeper in hockey be taken out for his understudy if he is having a bad night? You'll see it in hockey." You know something? He could be right.

CHAPTER 48

Home Ice Advantage

How and *Why* to Build a Backyard Rink

Jack Falla, Chief Executive Icemaker, The Bacon Street Omni, Natick, Massachusetts

THE FIRST THING YOU HAVE TO KNOW about building a backyard skating rink is that the Law of Hydrodynamics as amended for rink owners states that water seeking its own level will find it in your neighbor's yard. I learned this in the 1950s when, in my first effort to build a rink, I let the garden hose run all night in the backyard of my parents' home in Winchester, Massachusetts. The next morning I found not the hoped-for frozen pool but a river running though our lilacs and under our neighbor's grape arbor. My engineering failure was nothing compared to the diplomatic problem facing my parents, relationships with those neighbors being such that Whiffle balls hit into their yard were ruled automatic double plays. The summer after I'd flooded their yard we changed that rule to automatic side retired. My yard produced a generation of straight-away hitters but, alas, no supremely gifted skaters.

I didn't try to build a rink again until the 1980s when I had a home and children of my own. This time I succeeded. Though before I answer the questions of *How*, I have to deal with the matter of *Why*. When, as a boy, I made my first attempt to build a rink, no one asked me why. It surprised me that, upon seeing an adult building a rink, my friends assumed they knew why. Obviously, I was trying to construct a catapult to send my son and daughter soaring toward careers in hockey or figure skating. While I knew a rink would enhance their skating ability, I also knew that wasn't why I was building it, nor is it why my wife Barbara and I have continued to have a backyard rink for 15 years and counting, long after our children have moved (albeit not so far that they don't still log considerable ice time).

The question of why to build a rink has less to do with a career in hockey than with the pure joy of skating and playing. Or, as my daughter Tracey, then eight years old, said one morning when Barbara asked her if she wanted to sign up for figure skating lessons at the town rink: "No. I want to have my own fun. Not somebody else's fun." In the matter of personal recreation and casual sport, we find it more enjoyable to descend the evolutionary ladder, moving away from organization and mass participation toward individuality and spontaneity. A backyard rink is for pick-up hockey games wherein fairness and justice are built-in by the players, not tacked on by striped-shirted authority. It's a safe place for a child to take those first shuffling and hesitant learn-to-skate strides (as a generation of family and neighborhood children have, on our rink). It's a place for my solitary early morning skates and for our occasional Saturday night skating parties for family and friends where shinny with a frozen tennis ball is followed by a hot chocolate or a cold beer. We build our rink for the best reason of all. For the fun of it.

Backyard rinks are, by definition, makeshift affairs and chances are that no two are ever going to be exactly alike.

But here's one proven way to put up a low-cost rink that will provide you and your family with those two most precious commodities—ice time and fun.

Here's How...

As you read this, remember this one guiding principle: a backyard rink is essentially a corral of plywood with a plastic liner. Yes, we too know that Wayne Gretzky's father Walter built his rink by letting a sprinkler run all night in the backyard of the family home in Brantford, Ontario. We once visited the Gretzky house and rink, where it was obvious that Walter benefitted from a gentle natural depression in his yard—one that could collect water in a wide but shallow puddle—and from his location in southern Ontario which gets a lot colder than does my town of Natick, Massachusetts. What worked for the Gretzkys probably won't work for those of us south of Canada and the border states and for those of us with a sloped backyard.

Is Your Yard Suitable?

A rink requires a comparatively flat surface. My 56' x 33' rink has about an 11-inch variance from the deepest to the shallowest part. Thus, when I'm finished flooding, the water is about three to four inches deep at the shallowest end and about 14 to 16 inches at the deepest end. I suspect that much more than a 14-inch variance would mean too much water pressure on the boards, pressure that could warp or break the boards or rip the plastic liner. Once you select the flattest area of your yard, examine it for rocks or exposed roots or anything that might rip the liner. I let my grass grow extra long in the fall to provide a natural padding for the plastic.

Plywood and Plastic

Your main costs will be for plywood and plastic. Once built, the boards will last for years (we still have a few that date back to our rink's first season) but the plastic liner will get torn and ripped and is an annual expense. The best material to use as a plastic liner is a seamless 40' x 100' sheet of 6-mil clear industrial plastic available at most building supply stores or lumber yards. 40' x 100' is a standard industry size and the price will be roughly $150 (U.S.). You can get larger sheets but those will be either custom made or a special order and will cost a lot more.

We made our rink boards by buying 14 standard size (4' x 8') sheets of three-quarter-inch plywood and thirty 10-foot two-by-fours which serve as legs for the boards. We then had the dealer cut nine of the boards in half lengthwise, thus giving us eighteen sheets measuring 2' x 8'. The five remaining large sheets form the backstop behind our goal at the deep end of the rink, and the two-foot high boards form the low walls around the rest of the rink. The main function of the low boards is to hold the plastic in

place and to keep errant passes from sailing out of the rink. Of course, you could have four-foot high boards all the way around your rink or at each end (if you plan on having two goals) but that will add to your cost and labor and make snow removal more difficult.

We make our large boards by nailing one of the two-by-fours to each end of a 4' x 8' sheet of plywood in such a way that a two-foot length of two-by-four extends below the board (these will be the legs of the board that will go into the ground) and four feet of the two-by–four extends above the board (these will serve as posts on which you can nail a wire backstop to keep high shots and deflected pucks out of your neighbor's yard). We cut the remaining two-by-fours into three-foot lengths; these will be the legs of the lower boards. Nail one of these smaller legs to the end of each low (i.e. 2' x 8') board so that one 12-inch leg extends below the board. These legs will be adequate to hold the low boards in place, since these boards are under far less pressure than the larger boards at the deep end of the rink. (And you'll be surprised at how much easier it is to dig a one-foot hole than a two-foot hole.) Constructing the boards is a one-time job. Once you've made your set, you can save them from year to year.

Dig This...

The hardest part of the annual rink construction is digging the post holes and putting up the boards. Starting in the fall, well before the ground freezes, you will have to dig post holes and set the boards in place. Each hole for the big boards has to be at least two feet deep to allow the bottom of the board to be flush with the ground when the board is lowered into place. The holes for the low boards need to be only one-foot deep but the same principle applies—make sure the bottom of the board is flush with the ground. Depending on the hardness of the soil in your yard, you might consider buying a sharp narrow spade or renting a special fence post-hole digging tool for a weekend. These resemble two long narrow spades hinged together near their blades.

Obviously, one post hole can accommodate two board legs. The ends of each board should be touching each other to create the smoothest possible seam. As you lower each board into the ground and shovel the dirt back into the holes around the board legs, make sure you *tamp down the ground firmly* to secure each board in place. A thorough tamp down is crucial. Digging post holes is a demanding and tiring job and not something you want to do in one day unless you have a lot of help. I start in October and rarely dig more than two or three holes at one time.

An OK Corral

When the boards are in place you will have completed your "corral." But because the seams—the place where two boards meet—rarely will fit perfectly flush, you'll want to cover them with soft material to prevent the plastic from ripping on the rough edge of an exposed board or from being pushed out through a gap in the boards and ruptured by the pressure of the water. We employ old strips of carpeting but canvas or any other tough fabric would serve equally well.

Since your yard is probably uneven there will be some gaps where the bottom of a board is not perfectly flush with the ground. We fill these gaps with rags or old sheets. Put this material inside the rink where it will cushion the plastic liner and keep it from being pushed out under the boards by the water. Warning: don't put in your plastic liner until the day—indeed, until the very hour—that you're ready to flood. The longer the plastic is exposed the greater the chance it will be torn.

Fence It In

When your corral is finished, you might want to buy a roll of garden wire (chicken wire isn't strong enough) to nail to the two-by-fours above the high boards or that part of the rink we've come to call "the shooting end." (Or you could skip this step on the theory that nothing teaches a hockey player the value of shooting low more than a long tramp through the snow to retrieve the puck that he or she just shot over the boards.)

Flooding and Freezing

Don't get faked out by those first few frosty days of late fall or early winter. What you need to make ice is a three-day stretch of serious cold wherein night temperatures are no more than 5°F to 15°F (–10°C to –15°C) and day temperatures don't rise above freezing. The colder the better. Keep an eye on the long-range weather forecast. When you're certain that a frigid stretch is no more than a day away, you're ready to put in your plastic liner and flood your rink.

Roll out the plastic and staple it to the rink boards. Make sure the plastic liner extends far enough up the boards to be above the water level. We staple ours right to the top of the low boards and about two-and-a-half-feet up on the high boards. As soon as the plastic is in place, turn on the hose and let it run. Using one garden hose it takes us about 26 hours to fill our rink. If your outdoor faucet is frozen, simply pour warm water on it. Even on the coldest days, two pitchers of warm water will de-ice a faucet.

Check the rink frequently when flooding. Sometimes pressure from the rising water can start to pull the plastic off the boards and you have to restaple. Even at night, I go out every two or three hours with a flashlight, checking for problems. You won't (and shouldn't) sleep much on the night you flood.

First Ice

Now comes the easy part. Put the hose in the cellar (if you leave it out it will freeze) and wait for the water to freeze. But wait *patiently*. The water will skim over quickly but it may be three or four days—maybe longer—before the ice will be thick enough to skate on. I test mine by holding onto a low board and slowly transferring my weight to the ice until I hear it crack. If it doesn't crack, I put my entire weight on the ice and walk around. But the main point here is that you want to be wearing shoes—not skates—when you check the ice. A hole in your plastic liner made by the blade of an overeager skater is an impossible repair job.

A Goal

Once the ice is ready, you'll have a lot more fun on your rink if you can get or make a goal. We got an old one from a nearby rink that was going out of business. Be sure to take the goal off the ice every night or whenever you're not using it. If you leave the goal in place it will gradually sink into the ice, creating a dangerous and immovable obstacle. We simply slide our goal over to the low boards and tip it

out of the rink so that the crossbar lies on the ground. It's an easy matter to tilt it back onto the ice when we want to use it again.

Resurfacing

The First Commandment of a backyard rink as it applies to all skaters over 10 years old is: *If you skate you shovel.* After the ice has been used for a while and snow starts to build up on it, we scrape it clean with a plastic shovel (plastic shovels seem to glide more easily over the ice than do metal shovels). If you're going to skate more that day, don't resurface. Even in single-digit cold it takes water longer to freeze on natural ice than it does on artificial ice. An occasional scraping every hour or so will work fine.

Don't resurface until you're finished skating for the day. It's best to avoid resurfacing until late in the afternoon or at night. Temperatures are colder at these times and the angle of the sun—which can cause melting along the boards even in sub-freezing temperatures—isn't a factor. Shoveling the ice after a snowstorm is another matter. A snowblower (one light enough to lift over the low boards) is probably the best option, though we still use shovels and revel in the exercise.

Let There Be Lights

If you have an electrical outlet outdoors you might want to light your rink for night skating. We light ours using five 150-watt floodlights mounted on the garage and on the back porch roof.

Taking it Down

Sometime in March, as the sun moves through the equinox and temperatures rise, it will become obvious that skating is over for the season and it's time to take down the rink. It is the gloomiest job in the gloomiest month. We drain ours by using a dandelion picker (a three-foot wooden shaft with a notched metal tip) to jab holes in the shallow end. (Note: if you drain the rink from the deep end the greater volume of water might saturate the ground and end up—as ours did one year—flowing into your cellar.) Drain the rink gradually in dry weather over a period of about two to four days.

When the plastic is exposed, we use a pair of shears to slice it into roughly six-foot strips which can be folded in half, rolled up, tied with a string and stacked like cordwood pending the arrival of the trash collector or your trip to the dump. After the plastic is out, it's an easy matter to pull the tacks out of the material you used to seal the seams (be careful not to lose a tack in the grass or it could pierce next year's rink) and to take down the fencing above the high boards (we transfer ours directly into the garden where it serves as a trellis for peas).

It's easy to pull out the low boards and to store them in the garage. Fill in the post holes as you pull out each board. The high boards can present a storage problem because of the 10-foot two-by-fours attached to them. But we just lean ours against the back of the garage. Removing them is a two-person job. Throw a fistful of grass seed on the tamped down dirt above the post holes and, after a few mowings, you'll hardly be able to see where your rink had been.

The question we're asked most frequently is: doesn't the rink kill the grass? No. Indeed, the plastic liner serves as a kind of green house so that the grass that had been under the rink is often turning green ahead of the rest of the yard.

There's no sugarcoating it, a backyard rink is a lot of work. Is it worth it? It is on evenings after work when Barbara and I clomp down the wooden runway leading from the porch to the rink and, with the rink lights off, skate by the light of a rising full moon; or on a weekend when we look out the kitchen window and see a child shuffling in that special learning-to-skate awkwardness outlined against the red sky of a late winter afternoon.

CHAPTER 49

Early Artificial Ice

The Development of Refrigeration Allowed the Game to Spread

Donald M. Clark

MANY SCIENTISTS AND TECHNICAL PEOPLE were involved in the development of mechanical refrigeration—the initial step towards the creation of artificial ice rinks. The first man-made refrigeration was produced by the evaporation of ethyl ether into a partial vacuum and is credited to William Cullen of the University of Glasgow in 1748. In 1834, Jacob Perkins obtained a British patent on a volatile-liquid, closed-cycle system using a compressor. He built one successful machine but did not pursue his invention.

In 1844, Dr. John Gorrie in Apalachicola, Florida, developed a machine to provide ice and air conditioning for his hospital. He was granted a patent in 1850 on a closed-cycle air refrigerating machine which made ice. Another American, Alexander Twinning of Cleveland, produced the first commercial ice in 1856 by means of a vapor-compression machine. James Harrison in Australia became interested in refrigeration and, after surveying the machines of Gorrie and Twinning, developed the first vapor-compression machine for use in the brewing industry and for freezing meat for shipment to England. Harrison's machine, which was produced for several decades, employed ethyl ether as the refrigerant.

During the 1850s, Ferdinand Carre of France developed a second type of refrigeration machine. In his system, the refrigerant (normally a vapor) is absorbed in a suitable liquid. This solution is heated, driving off the refrigerant as a vapor, which then is condensed. Evaporation of the liquid produces the desired cooling. The refrigerant vapor is absorbed again in the liquid, thus completing the cycle. In 1859, Carre introduced ammonia as the refrigerant with ammonia-water as an absorbent. The successful combination was used throughout the world.

The basic principles on which refrigeration machines operate were developed prior to the end of the 19th century. Subsequent inventions involved only modifications and improvements in the machines and processes. The biggest changes were improving the compressors and finding a substitute for ammonia. Post-World War I found the discovery of halogenated hydrocarbons such as Freon 11, 12 and 22 which proved to be safer and superior to ammonia as a refrigerant.

Artificial ice rinks first appeared in the 1870s. William Newton constructed a building in New York suitable for skating in 1870. Using the invention of Matthew Bujac of New York, he produced ice by circulating ammonia gas, ether, and carbonic acid through tubes placed below the surface of the water. A mechanically refrigerated ice surface was constructed by Professor Gamgee at Chelsea, in Charing Cross, London, England in 1876. The 100-square-foot surface was built with copper pipes, and through these a mixture of glycerine and water was circulated after it had been chilled by ether. The pipes were covered with water.

In 1876 the Rusholm rink in Manchester, England used the Gamgee process successfully in a larger rink than the one at Chelsea. The rink ran for one year, being used by figure and public skaters. A few years later in 1879, a large rink was built in Southport, England. This 70' x 170' rink (12,000 square feet) operated continuously for 10 years until it closed in 1889 due to financial problems. Economics aside, as a piece of engineering, the ice sheet in Southport was the first successful large ice surface.

Thomas L. Rankin installed a mechanically frozen ice surface in 1879 in New York's Madison Square Garden. The installation had an ice surface of 6,000 square feet, about one-third the size of a modern hockey rink. The opening of Rankin's rink featured a gala ice carnival, a popular event at the time. During the late 1880s and early 1890s, several rinks were constructed in European cities like London, Paris, Nice, Berlin, Frankfurt and Munich. The Paris, London and Munich rinks were circular.

In conjunction with the 1893 World's Columbian Exposition in Chicago, a large (54' x 208') mechanically refrigerated ice rink that used brine was installed in a beautiful Mohammedan-styled building built by the Hercules Iron Works. This, the first full-size rink in the country, was never used; a fire occurred in the building as it was being finished and it was completely destroyed. San Francisco, hosting the annual Northern California Fair, built a rink in 1893–94 with an ice surface of 60' x 160'. A Hercules machine for cooling the brine was part of the equipment. On December 14, 1894, the Ice Palace at Lexington and 107th Street in New York was opened with a large ice surface of 20,000 square feet.

Less than two weeks after the opening of the Ice Palace in New York, the North Avenue Rink in Baltimore was opened its doors by staging a hockey game—believed to be the first hockey game in North America played on artificial ice—between Johns Hopkins University and the Baltimore Athletic Club. The *Baltimore Sun* edition of December 26 considered the refrigeration system to be newsworthy: "Over three and one-half miles of 1½-inch pipe are laid throughout the floor. This is covered with four inches of water which was frozen solid to 100 tons of ice in 37 hours. The refrigeration system is by means of compressed liquid ammonia allowed to expand in pipes running through a brine tank. The cold brine is then pumped through the pipes in the rink by force of a 60-ton engine. The water is thus frozen to a solid mass of clear ice."

Pittsburgh's Schenley Park Casino rink was constructed in 1895. A full-size rink that employed direct expansion for the first time, the rink was a popular home for amateur hockey in the late 1890s. After a few years of operation the rink was closed, later reopening as the Duquesne Gardens. The reopened rink changed to the brine system. The famous St. Nicholas Arena, built by and for the elite of New York, was opened in March 1896. The ice surface measured 80' x 180' and the brine for the refrigeration was

cooled by two 40-ton ammonia refrigerating machines. College and amateur hockey games were played in the building until it was destroyed by fire in 1918. In October 1896, the Brooklyn Ice Palace on Claremont Avenue opened, giving New York three artificial ice rinks. Maintained by two Buffalo compressors, the ice surface measured 85' x 155'. What was reported to be the largest sheet of artificial ice in the world opened in January 1896, in the Convention Hall in Washington, D.C. The rink's surface measured 155' x 205'.

By 1899, St. Louis and Philadelphia had built artificial ice rinks. The St. Louis rink operated next to a commercial ice plant and used its ice-making equipment. St. Louis organized a four-team local hockey league and held a four-team tournament in conjunction with the 1904 World's Fair. Teams involved included those from Minnesota, Michigan and St. Louis. Cleveland's first rink, known as the Elysium, was built in 1908 and was the first to place the pipes in concrete. The Elysium operated continuously until 1943. Albany, New York constructed an artificial ice rink in 1906, but it was short-lived.

The Boston Arena, built in 1909, had an ice surface of 90' x 242'. The rink played an important part in the development of hockey and figure skating in the Boston area. The building was destroyed by fire in 1918 and rebuilt within a few years. In 1909, a large rink also was constructed in Chicago at the Marchfield Avenue Station.

Between 1911 and 1918, rinks with artificial ice were built in New Haven, Syracuse, San Francisco, San Diego, St. Louis, Portland, Seattle and Spokane. The latter three cities, at one time or another, along with Vancouver, Victoria and New Westminster, were members of the Pacific Coast Hockey Association, a major-league circuit from 1912 through 1924. In the early 1920s, rinks were built in Philadelphia and Milwaukee. Both of these installations had pipes embedded in concrete which in turn was covered with terrazzo paving. The Arena in Philadelphia had a system of heating brine which enabled the floor to be warmed up quickly so the ice could be removed.

Minnesota, a state known for hockey and skaters, did not have artificial ice until the Minneapolis Arena and Duluth Amphitheater were built in 1924. Despite the popularity of hockey in Upper Michigan, there was no artificial ice installation in "Copper Country" until after World War II. Many of the early rinks encountered financial problems and operated for only a few years.

Construction of mechanically refrigerated rinks in the colder Canadian climate trailed behind that in the United States. It was not until 1911 that an artificial ice rink had been built in the Dominion. The Patrick brothers, Lester and Frank, built rinks in Vancouver and Victoria, British Columbia, in 1911. In 1912, artificial ice was installed in Toronto, a first in Eastern Canada. By 1920, only four artificial ice rinks were running in all of Canada.

CHAPTER 50

Oldtimers' Hockey

Hockey for the Fun of It

Ted Barris

IN THE WINTER OF 1964, a group of doctors, lawyers and civil servants interested in playing pick-up hockey began renting the arena at St. Mary's University in Halifax regularly on Saturday afternoons. In 1966, a bunch of University of British Columbia business graduates started playing shinny on Wednesday nights in Vancouver. About the same time, a corps of inveterate hockey enthusiasts began gathering at the arena in Pointe-Claire, Quebec on Sunday nights. Nobody seemed interested in renting the ice after seven o'clock in the evening, so this ad hoc group of over-35-year-olds, calling themselves the Pointe-Claire Oldtimers' Hockey Club, started a six-team league of friendly competition.

In fact, it was Pointe-Claire defenseman and club organizer Bill Wilkinson who decided not to call it "hockey for seniors" and who coined the phrase "oldtimers' hockey." In addition to Sunday night hockey, in 1970 Wilkinson and the Pointe-Claire club inaugurated their own International Oldtimers' Invitational Tournament. Each year teams from Quebec, Ontario and the northern United States traveled to the Pointe-Claire area (near Montreal) to compete in a weekend tournament and to use up much of the ice time that nobody else wanted.

What these men's groups, and hundreds more like them, discovered almost simultaneously in Canada was that men born during or just after World War II were now approaching middle age. As kids, they had played hockey in the street, in driveways, on frozen ponds and creeks, and some organized house league and rep hockey. Some had even gone as far as semi-pro. But by about the age of 20 they had quit or been forced to quit because, unless they were destined for the NHL or amateur coaching, the game had no place for them. Marriage, jobs and families became the priorities in their lives, while sticks, skates and aging hockey equipment were discarded and forgotten.

But the coming of oldtimers' hockey "opened up a brand new world for these guys," says Gerry "Tubby" Aherne, one time backup goalie for the Toronto Maple Leafs. "Suddenly, their boyhood game, the game they'd grown up with, was theirs to play again. And it didn't matter how good or bad you were, whether you played all the time as a kid or for the first time as a 35-year-old, there was a competitive division in oldtimers for you."

What is "oldtimers' hockey?" It's the recreational side of the game that has evolved from street and pond hockey. It's adults picking up the hockey traditions and styles they enjoyed—or wish they had enjoyed—as youths. It's shinny, a little slower. It's house league play for the adult camaraderie. It's tournament competition, without the do-or-die pressure of the seventh game of the Stanley Cup finals. It's the most common form of hockey being played—in neighborhood arenas, on the frozen canal, at outdoor rinks, or even sometimes on the manicured ice surfaces of a Gardens, Forum, Stadium, Arena or Coliseum.

One of the alumni from those early tourneys in Pointe-Claire was a schoolteacher from Ennismore, just north of Peterborough, Ontario. In March of 1974, John Gouett teamed up with Gerry Aherne and organized a St. Michael's College oldtimers' hockey team to stage a barnstorming tour of Canada's western provinces. "During the spring break we played eight games in 10 days," Gouett recalled, "And while we were out there we asked everybody what they thought of oldtimer hockey and if they would come to a national tournament if we organized one."

The whirlwind western trip attracted numerous teams, plenty of small-town crowds and press, but most of all a positive response to their blue-sky idea of a national oldtimers' hockey association and tournament. That summer, Gouett quit teaching, assigned the family house and personal assets to guarantee a $15,000 line of credit and formed the Canadian Oldtimers' Hockey Association. He and Aherne got a $4,500 grant from Recreation Canada. They booked hotels and ice time, landed a few sponsors and arm-twisted enough players to make this national dream come true.

The result? At eight o'clock in the morning, on Friday, February 21, 1975, five referees dropped pucks at center ice in five different arenas in the Peterborough area, inaugurating the first national oldtimers' hockey tournament staged in Canada. Fifty-six teams (over 1,200 players) had arrived to play in four divisions based on age and players' hockey backgrounds. And while referee-in-chief Jim Orr managed to keep the games relatively safe, friendly and running on time (based essentially on a no body-contact rule) Aherne and Gouett had enough trophies, team photo sessions and postgame coolers of beer on hand to keep everybody happy.

Spectators flocked to the five arenas. Along with several hometown heroes to cheer for, such as 1950s Peterborough Petes stalwarts George Montague and Larry Babcock, there were plenty of bona fide former hockey stars to see again. The Grande Prairie Oldtimers, with an average age of 45, featured Garry "Duke" Edmundson, who had played for the 1951 Stanley Cup champion Montreal Canadiens. A Stanley Cup alumnus with the Detroit Red Wings, Marcel Pronovost arrived with the Toronto St. Michael's Oldtimers, while long-time Chicago Black Hawks right winger Chico Maki (then 35) appeared with the Simcoe Oldtimers. And the Yorkton Oldtime Terriers (from Saskatchewan) had no less than six former pros, including 1940s veteran Metro Prystai, who had played on a line with Gordie Howe and Ted Lindsay.

That First Annual National Oldtimers' Hockey Tournament did more than fill a few arenas with fans, bellies with beer, and hearts with nostalgia. It launched the fledgling COHA, which soon moved its office to Ottawa to officially become part of Fitness Canada; by 1980 it had 300 registered teams and by 1990 it had 3,000. It attracted sponsorship for the staging of annual tournaments in Canada, the U.S. and Europe. It gave writer/publisher Dave

Tatham the grist for a monthly publication—*Canadian Oldtimers' Hockey News*. But most important of all it demonstrated to adult men and women the universal appeal of returning to the game of their youth—playing hockey just for the fun of it.

Like the youthful rites of passage into the game—frozen toes, the Saturday morning practice and your goal written up in the weekly newspaper—oldtimers' hockey is attracting more adults than ever before. Adult recreational hockey (there are now more than 80,000 players registered in Canada) has become so widespread in North America that it's fair to say at any time of day or night somewhere in Canada or the U.S. a puck is sliding across the ice in an old-timers' hockey game.

Wherever the game was reintroduced to adults it found a natural home. One of those locations was a rink in Saskatoon's north end. In the fall of 1977 a Saturday afternoon meeting was called at the change shack adjacent to River Heights Elementary School. About 40 men ranging in age from their late–20s to their mid–40s gathered to talk about starting up an oldtimers' hockey team. A ready-mix concrete company sponsored the team with a set of sweaters and the River Heights Mixers oldtimers' hockey club was born.

Every Monday morning, at about the time the inhabitants of most London, Ontario offices are brewing their first cup of liquid inspiration, two of the six teams known as the Huff n' Puffs are taking to the ice at the Earl Nichols Arena on the south side of the city. The idea of an adult hockey scrimmage for retirees came from Al Finch and Ted Froats, who had a number of ex-air force buddies in southwestern Ontario. At first they rented the ice for an hour. As their numbers swelled, they paid for time at another arena. Today, Huff n' Puffs Hockey has attracted about 100 skaters and a handful of goalies who show up three times a week year round. None of the players is younger than 55 and most are in their 60s and 70s.

In the mid-1960s when the B.C. lower mainland had only three indoor hockey arenas to speak of and two hometown heroes to look up to (the legendary Fred "Cyclone" Taylor and Montreal Canadiens tough guy John Ferguson), organized adult hockey was nearly non-existent. About 1966, a handful of hockey-hungry grad students at UBC approached the management at the newly built Thunderbird Winter Sports Complex for some ice time. They got Wednesday nights at eight o'clock.

"It was pure shinny," remembers Keith Morrison. "Guys went out there, split into two more-or-less-even teams, went at it for an hour and a half, no referees, no whistles, just non-stop hockey." A decade later, with the phrase "oldtimers' hockey" steadily creeping into the hockey lexicon, Morrison and company were ready to establish a formal association. The ex-shinny players responded to a newspaper ad promoting the first Oldtimer Invitational tournament in nearby Port Coquitlam. They fit almost all the criteria. They were all over 35. They had adapted to no-slapshot, non-contact hockey. They trouble was, they had no name and no uniforms. Morrison's first *Hockey Newsletter* documents the solution:

"After 11 years of deliberation and procrastination, a Uniform Committee was struck. As usual [we] knew someone who could "get us a deal," which turned out to be the Atlanta Flames road uniform. Turning the Atlanta flaming "A" upside down gave us the flaming "V" crest. And a new name—the Vancouver Flames. Cost $20."

On summer evenings in July and August, die-hard hockey players, some clad in shorts and T-shirts, others in business clothes, leave the warm evening air for the chill of an arena in Brossard, Quebec across the Champlain Bridge from Montreal on the south shore of the St. Lawrence River. These 20-odd players chase pucks at Les 4 Glaces as members of various oldtimers' teams—the Rusty Blades, SWAT (Senior Westmount All-Star Team), the Montreal Old Puckers and even some from one of the original oldtimers' organizations in Montreal, the Fakawie Hockey League—all summer long.

"People think we're crazy to play hockey in the summertime," says Brook Ellis, who's been playing hockey since the days he was a high school student in the Toronto area in the 1950s. "I tell them summer hockey is a wonderful thing. When it's hot outside, it's great to walk into a nice cool rink, work up a sweat, then afterwards, when you're good and thirsty, have a cool drink. There isn't a game like it in the world. I feel sorry for the Americans who've only played baseball. They grow old and can't do it anymore. Canadian kids grow up into old men like us and can continue to play our game."

In the final days of the 1970 minor hockey season in east end Toronto, the tension of the bantam hockey playoffs got to the coaches of the two finalists. Dave Bayford and Bill Loreti were actually close friends, but in the excitement and pressure of the game the two coaches actually got into a fight in the penalty box. Following that game, they quit minor hockey forever, deciding instead to teach visually impaired or blind youngsters how to play hockey. The result was a team of young men—called the Ice Owls—80 percent of whose members are legally blind. Since 1972, the group has played regular games on Sunday mornings, competing in blind-players' tournaments across Canada and even in exhibition matches against NHL oldtimers and against sighted players in Helsinki, Leningrad and Kiev.

The evolution of the Ice Owls' hockey puck is a study in ingenuity. First they tried a tin can, then a tin can with marbles or ball bearings inside, a wooden puck and one with a chain attached to it. Another prototype used an empty plastic computer tape case rigged with a buzzer inside. It worked until snow and ice gummed up the buzzer or until the wear and tear shattered the plastic case. Ultimately, the blind oldtimers' team came up with a plastic wheel from a push-toy. They drilled a hole through to the hollow center of the wheel and inserted several steel piano tuning pegs; the combination of the hard plastic wheel clattering across the ice and the tuning pins rattling inside gave the Ice Owls a relatively lightweight, durable puck they could hear above any arena din.

On several occasions over the years, the Ice Owls oldtimers have played another oldtimers' institution—the Flying Fathers. In the early 1960s, North Bay broadcaster Terry Spearin got talking to local parish priest Brian McKee about the possibility of staging an adult hockey game to raise funds for the Catholic Youth Organization in town. On February 20, 1964 the 5,000-seat North Bay Memorial Gardens was nearly sold out to watch the broadcast team—the Statics—take on a number of ex-seminarians and priests from Sudbury, Sault Ste. Marie and Timmins, including Father Les Costello, who had played on the Toronto Maple Leafs Stanley Cup-winning team in 1948. During the lead up to the game, someone coined the phrase "the Flying Fathers." It stuck.

As their reputation for playing good oldtimer hockey

spread, the priests—playing these fun-matches on their own vacation time—adopted a seemingly never-ending repertoire of hockey shtick to spice up each game. They taunted referees with an assortment of cream pies and buckets of water. They confused their opposition by conducting pseudo-religious ordinations and blessings on the ice. For a time, they dressed up a member of their team in a nun's habit as Sister Mary Shooter and even brought a draft horse named Penance onto the ice in goalie pads to play net. Like the Harlem Globetrotters on ice, the Flying Fathers oldtimers' team has become one of the most sought-after, fund-raising phenomena in the world.

In their first 30 years of "playing and praying for a better world," the Flying Fathers accumulated many firsts as oldtimers, hockey players and ambassadors for Canada and the priesthood. They played nearly 1,000 games for charity and won nearly all of them. Their record is five games in one day. During one trip across Canada and the U.S., they played 16 games in 15 cities in 20 days, traveling 14,000 miles. The largest crowd they drew was 15,396 at Vancouver's Pacific Coliseum. A single game at the Montreal Forum in 1984 raised $50,000 for the Shriners Hospital. During a charity game at Maple Leaf Gardens in 1985, nearly 14,000 spectators watched the Flying Fathers play the Maple Leaf alumni. Leaf owner Harold Ballard turned over all gate receipts and proceeds from concessions that day, raising $240,000 for cancer research.

Each year between October and May, in addition to the thousands of oldtimers' house-league games, once-a-week senior recreational games, shinny matches and pick-up sessions across the continent, the calendar is full of weekend tourneys. Some are local. Many are national tournaments, sponsored by the Canadian Adult Recreational Hockey Association (formerly the COHA), including the Hub City in Saskatoon, the McMurtry Cup in Toronto, and the Monctonian. For those looking offshore, there are annual tour-and-play packages to Florida, Arizona, Nevada, Hawaii and Europe.

It's generally agreed by most oldtimers' hockey players, however, that the annual Snoopy's Senior World Hockey Tournament, organized by "Peanuts" cartoonist Charles M. Schulz, is an oldtimers' hockey mecca. Staged in mid-July in Santa Rosa (north of San Francisco), competition to get into the tourney is tough; of the 300 to 400 teams that apply to play, only 50 to 60 get in. All games take place at Redwood Empire Ice Arena, built in 1969 by Schulz for his figure-skating daughter and hockey-crazed sons.

"We used to sneak onto the St. Paul Academy rink and play under the light of the moon," says cartoonist Schulz about his childhood passion for hockey in Minnesota during the 1930s. "Nobody had pads. We used copies of *National Geographic* for shin pads."

And when there was nobody else around to play shinny with him, Schulz's mother would agree to play goal while he practiced his shot. In 1974, he launched Snoopy's Senior World Hockey Tournament at his own expense. Neither relentless press deadlines for his Peanuts cartoons nor quadruple heart bypass surgery a few years ago has prevented him, now in his 70s, from playing regularly for his Santa Rosa Diamond Icers.

Among the legendary teams to play against Schulz's Diamond Icers, the Mandai Memorials from Japan are a study in oldtimers' hockey dedication. In 1933, while Japanese colonial armies occupied northern China, a 24-year-old Japanese medical student named Toshihiko Shoji was training at the Manchurian Medical College. That autumn, as creeks and ponds froze, Shoji gathered a handful of his colleagues together. He described a winter game he had first seen during the 1920s, when an ice hockey team—the Battleford Millers—had visited Japan from western Canada to play exhibition games.

"We heated willow branches and bent them like field hockey sticks," explained Dr. Shoji. "And we used a small tennis ball for a puck. We used the rules explained in a hockey history book by the Spalding company." The Mandai hockey club was born. In 1975, long after those games in Manchuria had faded from memory, Dr. Shoji heard about the oldtimers' concept and formed the Mandai Memorial Ice Hockey Club with Japanese doctors in their 50s and 60s.

Until they got their skating legs back, Dr. Shoji and his teammates chose the opposition carefully. At first, they played inexperienced women's teams. Then in 1978 at the invitation of the Port Coquitlam Ambassadors, they headed to Canada. "Of course," said Shoji, "we lost." But then in 1981, the Memorials came to the Snoopy Tournament in the 60-plus division. "I think we have won only two or three games ever in this tournament," the doctor admitted, "but coming to Santa Rosa each year is a kind of medicine for each of us … motivation to keep in good health, to practice and think young."

CHAPTER 51

The Old Bootheel

It's Black, it's Round: the Hockey Puck as Never Seen Before

David Spaner

THEY'VE FLOWN INTO OUTER SPACE with an astronaut, been used to insult audiences by comedians, starred in movies and songs. Some Americans vow they can never see them, some Canadians see them in their dreams…

"I've had nightmares about pucks, but not while I'm sleeping," said Detroit Red Wings goalie Greg Stefan, once hospitalized for taking a puck in the throat. "I do get flashes though. You know, I'm just starting to fall asleep and then I jump, feeling something coming at me."

The puck first appeared as a flat disc on March 3, 1875. "A game of hockey will be played at the Victoria Skating Rink this evening between two nines from among the members," the *Montreal Gazette* announced. "Good fun can be expected, as some of the players are reputed to be exceedingly expert at the game.

"Some fears have been expressed on the part of the intending spectators that accidents were likely to occur through the ball flying about in a too lively manner, to the imminent danger of lookers-on… but we understand that the game will be played with a flat, circular piece of wood, thus preventing all danger of it leaving the surface of the ice."

Before that game, numerous items had been used as a puck, including lacrosse balls, fruit, frozen manure, tin cans and pieces of coal or wood. Most often, a rubber ball was used in the first organized hockey games in Montreal in the 1870s. But the owners of the Victoria Rink found that they were paying hundreds of dollars to replace windows shattered by the bouncing ball, so the top and bottom of the ball were sliced off to create a flat disc.

The players found the sliding flat object easier to play with and audiences found it more exciting to watch. Although wooden pucks were still experimented with, and all sorts of objects would continue to be used in pick-up games, by the 1890s the rubber puck was entrenched in organized hockey.

In one early Ontario Hockey Association game, a puck split in half as it was sailing toward the net, with one part falling into the goal and the other bounding into a corner of the rink. During the squabbling about whether it was a goal, referee Fred Waghorne pulled out the rule book which stated a puck was one-inch think. Waghorne ruled that the piece that had entered the goal wasn't a puck because it wasn't an inch think. The OHA backed Waghorne's decision and announced that pucks would now be one piece of rubber, rather than two cemented together.

The word "puck" appeared in print as early as 1891. "The ball (or 'puck,' as it is called) is a flat piece of india-rubber, circular in shape, about two inches thick, and with a diameter of about four inches," explained an article in a long-defunct publication called *Field*. "The game is played with, usually, seven a-side, and no striking with the stick is allowed, only pushing the 'puck' along the ice."

One bit of hockey lore says "puck" came into hockey use because it means a sprite or elf, darting about, disappearing and reappearing. The mischievous Puck of William Shakespeare's *A Midsummer Night's Dream* helped popularize the word. And the literate hockey-going public of the 1800s recognized the connection.

But the most likely explanation is that the word derived from the traditional Irish game of hurling. Hockey and its rules developed in the late 19th century in eastern Canada, then the home of a large, hurling-playing Irish diaspora, and it's easy to conclude the term "puck" was probably picked up from hurling to describe the ball being struck in hockey, which was called ice hurley by some.

Known as "the fastest grass sport in the world," hurling is a combination of lacrosse and field hockey played by 15-member teams on a rectangular field. In hurling, the "puck-out" is much like the soccer goal-kick, with the hurling goalkeeper putting the ball back into play by whacking it with a large stick. "Puck-in" describes a ball being returned from the sidelines. "Puck" was also used in hurling as a general term for striking the ball. "The rival hurlers … meet together in wild rivalry for a puck at the ever flying ball," noted a publication called *19th Century* in 1900.

"Puck," meaning to strike or smack, is also a popular Irish term apart from hurling, as in "Do you want a puck in the puss?" In Ulysses, James Joyce wrote: "Myler Keogh, Dublin's pet lamb, will meet sergeant-major Bennett, the Portobello bruiser. … God, that'd be a good pucking match to see."

Whatever its origin, National Hockey League Rule 25 states: "The puck shall be made of vulcanized rubber, or other approved material, one inch thick and three inches in diameter and shall weigh between five and a half ounces and six ounces."

The puck is a mixture of carbon black, raw rubber and sulphur. After it is mixed, the hot substance is dropped on to rollers which flatten it into sheets of rubber. They are rolled in a sausage shape, then cut, refrigerated and molded. NHL pucks have the league logo silk-screened on one side, the team emblem on the other. NHL teams keep the pucks in a freezer before games because that takes some of the bounce out.

In the 1920s the puck had sharp edges which could cut a player. These edges have long since been slightly beveled, but today's puck is hardly non-violent. Hockey has experimented with different colors and sizes but always returns to the vulcanized black pucks, which hold their shape and chip less than colored pucks.

While most pucks are slapped around in obscurity, some are in the Hall of Fame, including the three Bill Mosienko used to notch a hat trick in 21 seconds and the one Canadian astronaut Mark Garneau took aboard the space shuttle in 1984. And the puck has been featured in movies (1975's *Mystery of the Million Dollar Puck*) and songs (the "Puck Rock" compilation albums). The International Hockey Hall of Fame in Kingston, Ontario displays the square rubber

puck used in an 1886 game between Kingston's Queens University and Royal Military College.

John Qualls, of Grand Rapid, Michigan has amassed a collection of more than 1,500 pucks. Qualls' interest was piqued in the mid-1960s when Gordie Howe gave him an autographed puck. "I was down at the old Olympia and I met Gordie Howe. I thought all hockey pucks were the same, but then I saw the Detroit Red Wing crest, and I thought, 'That's neat.'"

There are other collectors. In 1972, a Canadian company obtained pucks that had been used in NHL games and mounted them on plaques, engraved with the puck's history. "There is a definite market for this," said businessman Reg Wright. "They are unique. Each one is different. They are like rare coins." Not rare enough, apparently, for people to buy them, and the plaques were discontinued.

While some pay homage to the puck, others—notably bruised goaltenders—have little affection for it. "I don't get to hold it or look at it too much," said Greg Stefan. "I feel it on my arm and that's about it."

But some can tell whether the puck is too big or too small, too soft or too hard. After a game in Philadelphia in 1985, Edmonton Oilers coach Glen Sather was irate. "Those pucks are horsecrap," he said. "They're the new ones the league approved. Sometimes you see the puck hit the post and come back warped.

"We used our old pucks for most of the year. The league kept sending us memos telling us to change but we didn't pay any attention. They are awful pucks."

The puck has taken blame for a lot of things, and comedian Don Rickles turned "you hockey puck" into a popular insult. But, mostly, the puck has been blamed for hockey's lack of success on U.S. television. Viewers can't see it.

"With your eyesight I'm surprised you can see the puck," Diane Keaton tells Woody Allen at a Rangers game in *Manhattan Murder Mystery*.

The World Hockey Association tried a flaming red puck in 1972, but the paint quickly peeled off. The league switched to a color called "superpuck blue" the following season, but these pucks went soft by the third period and bounced erratically.

Peter Rossi, a spokesman for the colored puck company, admitted that there had been some adverse response from the end users: "Geez, the players. They take one look at a puck that isn't black and they say, 'Hell, what is this?' So they're against it from the start."

J.C. Tremblay of the Quebec Nordiques, an outspoken advocate of the black puck, was enlisted by the league to try out its revamped colorized puck. "If we can find a puck Tremblay likes, we're in," said Rossi.

"I like the orange better than blue or red," Tremblay said. "It was very bad last year because the rubber was too soft. I called the president of the league about it and told him, 'This blue puck, it's no good.'"

The WHA had other big ideas such as a puck embedded with an electronic device so it would appear on screen as a red arrow. That faltered and colored pucks passed.

"It's a load of garbage," said NHL president Clarence Campbell, after the WHA's puck plan was unveiled. "The puck isn't invisible. I can see it plainly. You can see it. All right, it's less visible than a football, we can admit that."

After the demise of the WHA, the NHL would change its tune. In 1981, NHL president John Ziegler and other league executives met with Gary Berner, who had invented a fluorescent puck called the Berner High Visibility Ice Hockey Puck. "We're very open-minded to anything that will improve visibility, especially on television," said NHL vice president Brian O'Neill.

Then there's the question of the puck's nationality. "Pucks are called *les rondelles* in their native Canada," *TV Guide* reported, referring to the Quebec-French name.

By 1985 millions of Eastern European pucks had landed on North American shores. The European pucks were dangerously hard, said Canadian Ron Bruhm, president of Viceroy Rubber and Plastics. "We felt someone was going to be hurt in the future."

But it wasn't just European pucks that were battering more than goaltenders. In the 1980s, an American-produced puck which allegedly contained metal particles from worn-out steel-belted tires left shattered glass in its wake. The American Hockey League's Maine Mariners, for instance, had to replace 24 "shatterproof" panels at the ends of their rink before the pucks were recalled.

In the late 1980s, the NHL approached the Canadian Standards Association to discuss problems being caused by some pucks. "The pucks were breaking the polycarbonate shields around the rinks and the goaltenders were remarking these pucks had a different feel. Setting a standard is costly and the manufacturers were not anxious to disclose the content of their pucks," said the CSA's Tom Pashby.

Following a series of incidents involving pucks that broke or contained metal fragments or air bubbles, the Canadian Standards Association began calling for international standards in 1994. "We are thinking safety," said Tom Pashby. "We don't need to worry about shape or content. We don't care if they are made of cheese, so long as they don't break."

An electronically enhanced puck appeared in 1996 when the Fox network introduced FoxTrax. These high-tech discs appeared to be no different than a standard puck in the arena, but television audiences saw a puck surrounded by a blue glow that was supplemented by a red trail when shot or passed briskly. TV host David Letterman responded with "DaveTrax," a blue dot around his head, following him as he raced about the stage.

It's uncertain whether the glowing puck will maintain its luster or prove to be a passing fancy, joining other puck innovations in the dustbin of hockey history—ideas such as enlarging the puck. "Doesn't surprise me in the least," said Bobby Hull. "A goaltender probably thought of it."

CHAPTER 52

Youth Hockey Around the World

Pavel Barta, Ivan Filippov, Igor Kuperman,
Eero Lehti, Tom Ratschunas, Jan Stark and Eric Zweig

DON CHERRY ASIDE, many hockey experts maintain that Canada, while still producing more NHL players than any other country, is no longer producing the world's most skilled hockey players. A check of the NHL's top scorers in 1997–98 certainly reads like the roll call of the United Nations. Jaromir Jagr (Czech Republic), Peter Forsberg (Sweden) and Pavel Bure (Russia) finished 1–2–3, followed by Wayne Gretzky (Canada) and John LeClair (United States). But while Jagr, Forsberg, Bure and Finland's Teemu Selanne may well be the NHL's most talented performers, the fact remains that Canada was still the only nation to place three men (Gretzky, Ron Francis and Jason Allison) in the top 10 and no other country can match the 11 Canadians in the top 25. Then again, Canadians do make up 60 percent of the league, compared with about 20 percent each from Europe and the United States. The case can also be made that the likes of Gretzky, Francis, Adam Oates, and Steve Yzerman are all on the downside of their careers, but then players like Allison and Eric Lindros should still have their best years in front of them, and Paul Kariya takes a back seat to no one in terms of talent … provided that concussions do not cut short his career.

So perhaps it is not so much that Canadian hockey is in decline as it is the fact that the rest of the world has simply caught up. Perhaps this is why the United States could beat Canada at the World Cup of Hockey in 1996. Perhaps this is why Finland could win its first World Junior Championship in 1998. Perhaps this is why the Czech Republic became Olympic gold medalists for the first time in history at Nagano in 1998. But how did these countries do it? How did they develop the skills to play at the top?

When Robert Reichel, Martin Rucinsky, Robert Lang and Jiri Slegr were at in the same room at elementary school in Litvinov. Five other Olympic gold medalists from Nagano in 1998—Petr Svoboda, Josef Beranek, Jan Caloun, Vladimir Ruzicka and coach Ivan Hlinka—grew up in the same town, which is located less than 100 kilometers (60 miles) northwest of Prague. All of them have played in the NHL in addition to their international experience.

With a population of only about 30,000, Litvinov is the smallest city represented in the Czech Elite League, yet it has produced the highest number of NHL players by far. In the town of Litvinov, you either play hockey or you watch hockey. There's nothing else to do. Litvinov has a long history of developing boys into skilled hockey players. Tradition and quality coaching are the key ingredients. Over the years there has been an uninterrupted chain of people playing the game, a chain which has evolved into an obsession.

Other small towns also contributed to the Czech Republic's gold medal victory in 1998. Goalie hero Dominik Hasek was born in Pardubice. Jaromir Jagr hails from Hnidousy, a tiny village of just 134 people. Martin Prochazka comes from Kralupy, Roman Hamrlik from Otrokovice. Frantisek Kucera of Prague was the only member of the Olympic champions who hailed from a big city. All the others were discovered, and joined club teams, in their teens. Early morning trips to the rink, some of them very far away, are in the memories of all these Czech hockey heroes. These are the kind of memories that were shared by Canadian players for generations. But perhaps no longer. Facts such as these go a long way towards explaining why the Czechs, Finns and Swedes, like the Russians before them, have been able to make such strides in a game once dominated by Canada.

Minor hockey in Canada saw 507,000 young players enrolled in 1997–98. They played on approximately 30,000 teams in 2,300 minor hockey associations. It is estimated that as many as one million games and/or practices are held in an average year in Canada. The boom in minor hockey in the United States since the "Miracle on Ice" in 1980 has seen enrollment in minor hockey climb to 425,000 (most of them still in the traditional hockey areas, though the sport is growing in the South and West). The United States, however, with a population pushing 300 million has nearly 10 times as many people as Canada, which has a population of under 30 million. Russia has a population of 150 million and is home to two million hockey players, though only 40,000 are registered with the country's approximately 100 top sports clubs. The Czech Republic has over 50,000 minor hockey players from a population of 10.5 million, with another 100,000 unregistered players. Finland has 45,000 youth hockey players from a population of just over five million, while Sweden has 63,000 players from a population of under 10 million.

Players in most of the top hockey nations can begin to take up the game by the age of seven or eight. Canadians can start as young as four (though official games are not played until the age of six), while children in Sweden typically begin to play organized hockey by age nine. The Swedish Ice Hockey Association is that country's governing body, overseeing three different regions (North, Central and South) which are split into 23 districts. There are 848 sports clubs in Sweden within the 23 districts and each district can also be home to teams that are not affiliated with any of the 848 clubs.

Of the six nations surveyed, only the Czech Republic has no age requirements per se. "The only age rule in place," admits well-known Czech hockey journalist Pavel Barta, "requires the boys to attend grade school. It doesn't matter whether they were born in January or in December. All that matters is what grade they are in." The best hockey players in Russia can begin to take up the game at age seven. The country's top sports clubs operate special hockey schools

that will accept "gifted" pupils at that age.

Club teams represent the highest level of minor hockey in Russia. Clubs like the Central Red Army and Moscow Dynamo not only have teams in the elite league that have become well known to hockey fans in North America, but, in fact, have an entire system of teams right down through the youngest age levels. These clubs represent a specific area (such as Moscow) but a young player has freedom of movement within this top level.

For example, former Moscow-based journalist Igor Kuperman, who now works in hockey operations for the Phoenix Coyotes, tells the story of 10-year-old Alexei Zhamnov failing at a tryout for the Central Red Army and then, literally, walking down the street to the Dynamo cattle call, where he impressed the coaches enough to make the team. Zhamnov worked his way up the ranks within the Dynamo system until he was 22 and entered the NHL with the Winnipeg Jets.

The second level of youth hockey in Russia involves teams sponsored by local factories and industry. Though not its only purpose, this factory level can serve as almost a farm system for the elite club teams. Former Soviet star Vladimir Krutov was a 10-year-old good enough to be playing with the 12-year-olds at the factory level when he was recruited to join the Red Army. The lower rung of Russian youth hockey involves the Golden Puck Tournament. This nationwide event showcases players from ages 10 to 15 who are not affiliated with club or factory teams. It is an opportunity for the higher levels to uncover talented players who may have escaped their notice.

As in Russia, minor hockey in the United States falls into three distinct categories: House play (or house league), which is largely recreational; travel teams, which are more competitive; and selects, which comprise the all-stars. Generally, a league in any individual area will have teams at all three levels in the various age groups.

These leagues will conduct tryouts and players are placed at a level based on demonstrated skills. A panel of coaches from throughout the league makes the decisions. Movement of players to different teams, different leagues and different levels is permitted, but much of this movement is restricted by geography. Organizations (and parents) prefer to minimize travel time, as it is thought that a young player who has to travel long distances to get to games is less likely, in the long run, to enjoy playing.

Minor hockey in Finland is divided less along the lines of talent and more strictly in terms of a player's age. From eight to 11, there is absolutely no classification according to skill levels. Teams at this level play a friendly round-robin schedule of games within a system that is basically divided by region only. Not until the age of 12 do the individual regions begin to divide their players into different six- to eight-team leagues with a team placed in these leagues based on its success in previous years. As in Russia, club teams make up the highest leagues in Finland, and with the most successful players starting to move up together after the age of 12 the top talent usually finds its way onto club teams. When a child begins to demonstrate that he or she is clearly more talented than his or her teammates, it is the recommendation of the Finnish Ice Hockey Association that the coaches should discuss with the parents the possibility of this player moving up. In theory, the coaches and the parents make this decision together. If an outside opinion becomes necessary, most of the advanced clubs have a

so-called head of coaching in their organization who has the final word on such matters. "This is the way we feel it should go," says Eero Lehti, manager of youth hockey programs for the FIHA, "but I have my doubts about how well it works within each club." After age 15, there is only one level of competition for the players good enough to remain in the game. The best players of 16 or 17 years of age will be moved up to compete with older players if they prove to be more talented than their teammates. Players are quite free to move from team to team in Finland and can change teams as often as once every season if they desire. "When asked," says Lehti, "all the youth hockey clubs and their teams absolutely deny recruiting kids under the age of 14, but everybody knows it happens anyway. The main topic is how openly and with what ways or means or procedure does the recruiting take place."

In Canada, there are typically five or six levels of play (depending on geographic region) available to any player above the age of six. House league is generally at the bottom, followed by select teams and then a system of 'A' and 'B' ratings that advance all the way up to 'AAA'. Parents and/or the child are responsible for the decision to try out for higher levels. Coaches generally make the evaluations for their own team, though some regions are beginning to use independent evaluators. Residency rules are the basic determination as to who can play where in Canada, and how much a player can move from team to team varies from region to region. Toronto, for example, has many different teams, so a player can potentially have more to choose from, though the strength of individual hockey clubs can be a limiting factor. Many areas across Canada have only one team at the various different skill levels, so a child will play where his talent allows him. If a player does not make the team at the level he hopes to play, he is permitted to move to a different area, but only to a bordering geographic zone. In terms of division by age groups, children below the age of eight are classified as pre-novice in Canada; eight and nine as novice; 10 and 11, atom; 12 and 13, peewee; 14 and 15, bantam; and 16 and 17; midget. Players aged 18, 19 and 20 play either as juvenile or junior.

Major junior hockey is the top level of youth hockey in Canada, though the three major junior leagues are so focused on preparing players for pro careers that it is difficult to view them as the star atop Canada's minor hockey Christmas tree. Junior A or B is a more appropriate top class for the youth hockey system.

The United States breaks down its youth players along similar age lines, though the category names often differ.

As previously stated, the main factor in determining where a child will play in the Czech Republic is what grade he is in at school. "For those who have never had skates on their feet, it starts from scratch," explains Pavel Barta. "Others work from the level they are at." Regardless of skating skill, all players are entered in a preparation category, within which they are grouped according to skill level and the grade they belong to. Anything that would resemble an actual hockey game is not recommended until the second and third grades, and not until grade five is the preparation category abandoned. The more serious approach to youth hockey does not begin until a boy enters grade six.

Hockey players in sixth and seventh grade are classified as 'younger pupils' in the Czech Republic, while those in grades eight and nine are called 'older pupils.' Not until these years do players begin to compete in official leagues

organized by geographical regions. These top teams are called 'triple A' and play in a system that is organized Eero Lehti. By 15, age becomes the determinant as 15- and 16-year-olds will play 'adolescent' hockey. Very talented players can now be moved up an age group if such a move is deemed helpful to their development. Similar to North America, junior players range in age from 17 to 20. Since the fall of Communism, state subsidies for sport and culture have been all but eliminated. "The financial burden has been shifted from the state to the pockets of the parents, and only in Litvinov and some other places are youth teams still getting free ice time." Educational programs have survived due to the support of Elite League clubs and their sponsors and "there is a tendency to bring the most talented players to the same school classes in bigger cities and carry on as if nothing has changed."

Like the Czech Republic, 15 is a key age for hockey players in Russia, as this is the age in which a player might be recruited to leave home to further his career. The best 15-year-olds are aggressively scouted and invited to play for top clubs. Fifteen is also the age at which the youngest national teams are put together in Russia. The ages of 14 and 15 are keys years in Sweden, as two major district tournaments are held for those age groups. The latter is called TV-pucken and the playoffs in this tournament are broadcast throughout the country "so it can be said that the best 15-year-old players are identified by the hockey community in Sweden through television," says Swedish journalist Jan Stark. These 14- and 15-year-old tournaments are only for district teams, not for sports clubs. Sports clubs begin to play for national championships at age 16. By this age, top Swedish players may well have had to leave home to further their career. Further national junior championships for sports clubs are held at the age of 18 and 20.

In Canada, 16 is the age in which a child is permitted to leave home, but only to play major junior hockey. Younger players can also be promoted to this top level of minor hockey, but only in their hometown (meaning a 15-year-old Regina native could be called up to play for the Regina Pats, but not the Seattle Thunderbirds). Seventeen is the youngest age at which a player is permitted to leave home to play at other levels, however a case can be made to leave home earlier—though a boy will not be allowed to move simply for the chance to play better hockey. Wayne Gretzky, for example, was permitted to play in Toronto as a 14-year-old in order to escape growing resentment and harassment in his hometown of Brantford. It is up to the parent and child to reach a decision on leaving home, but any such case will be heard by an appeals committee.

In the United States, a player can leave home to play high school or midget hockey (which means an age range of 15 to 18). A player can also begin to play U.S. junior at this age and still retain his eligibility for the NCAA or Canadian major junior teams. Such advancement is often recommended for top players if they are obviously not receiving enough competition to further their development at home.

Finland has no specific requirements as to when a player can leave home. "If he/she lives in one of the major ice hockey cities [of which there are about 20]," explains Eero Lehti. "With all the necessary schools to attend, a player doesn't have to move anywhere. If he or she happens to live outside of these cities, it is quite necessary [although not obligatory to get to the top] for him or her to move to a city with a sports gymnasium to finish his/her school properly while at the same time practicing under good coaching."

At this point, there appears to be little more than cosmetic differences in the structure of youth hockey systems in the top hockey-playing countries. Where the differences between Canada and its international rivals become more apparent is in the handling of the very youngest players and in the amount of time allotted for practice at all age levels.

On the average, players from eight to 14 will play between 20 and 45 games a year in Finland (increasing by age), while players 15 and older can play between 50 and 80 games. Players under 11 will practice twice a week for up to 50 minutes each time. Players over 12 have 80-minute practices two or three times a week, while older players will practice for 80 minutes up to five times per week. Still, there are "too many games," says Eero Lehti. "Coaches and parents seem to be very eager to let the kids 'test their skills in real situations'. I know of a 12-year-old boys team that played 78 games two winters ago [1996]." In Canada the situation can be much worse.

While house league teams generally play only 15 to 20 games, top competitive teams can play as many as 130 games per year! Canadian Hockey, the sport's governing body, prefers a ratio of two practices to every one game, but officials admit this happens rarely. With so many teams and associations the practice-to-games ratio is extremely hard to police and, while younger children generally get more practice time than older ones, in reality most players get only one practice for every two games. This is seen as one of the key issues facing minor hockey in Canada, as games offer little opportunity to work on essential skills.

USA Hockey recommends a practice-to-games ratio of 3:1, but officials in the American hockey governing body admit that with top teams playing as many as 90 games in a year the ratio is more like 1:1. Parameters involving games and practices are not legislated by USA Hockey, so each local league has the say. Much is based on the importance of hockey in the region; for example more games will be played in Minneapolis than in Phoenix. The situation is similar in Sweden, where practice time has much to do with the availability of ice.

Stockholm is Sweden's largest city, as well as the largest of its 23 hockey districts, but "in Stockholm," says Jan Stark, "there are actually very few rinks when compared to the number of players." Still, a ratio of two practices for every game is maintained. "But on the other hand, in Ornskoldsvik (the hometown of Peter Forsberg) in the district of Angermanland they have more rinks which means more ice time and the ratio is about four to one."

Throughout minor hockey in the United States as much is done as possible to down-play the emphasis on winning, though a great deal of necessity depends on the parents and coaches. USA Hockey emphasizes such things as skill development, fair play and sportsmanship (what they call "life qualities"). *Fun*, *Safe* and *Rewarding* are considered to be the goals of hockey at the youth level. Similarly, Canadian Hockey lists fun and safety as its key concerns, but admits the emphasis an individual team places on winning is generally a reflection of the coach.

In Finland, "our main concern is how to educate our kids and youngsters into well-behaving citizens," says Eero Lahti. "The focus is totally on learning skills (individual technical skills and, especially, developing an understanding of the game) all the way from the age of six to the age of 18. Winning a game is just a result of an individual play-

er's skills in the continuously changing playing situations and of the cooperation of the six players inside the rink." Minor hockey in Russia has a similar aim.

"The emphasis is on winning," says Igor Kuperman, while agreeing that it is more accurate to state that the emphasis is on winning by developing highly skilled players as a top priority. Russian teams will play a *maximum* of 40 to 50 games per season and practice twice a day! Under the Communist regime, there used to be special classes in regular schools where practice time was built into the daily curriculum. This is no longer the case. Teams now practice in the early morning before school and in the late afternoon after school. Players will generally use public transit to get themselves to and from practice. Such dedication is expected of young Russian hockey players. As a boy, former star defenseman Vladimir Lutchenko (a member of the Soviet national team from 1969 to 1979) would travel two hours each way to attend practice! Practices in Russia stress skating and stick handling now, as they did then. There is also a lot of dry-land training away from the rink.

Not surprisingly, the demands of minor hockey in the Czech Republic are not unlike those in Russia, though, if anything, the Czech commitment is even more rigorous. Though interest in hockey is currently so high that sports clubs generally have more players than they can handle, traditional scouting practices include visiting public skating rinks or attending pre-school facilities in order to find physically well-developed children with a natural talent for playing games as young as age four!

"Whether they can skate or not is not an issue at all," says Pavel Barta. Once a prospective boy is identified, the scouts will give a questionnaire to his parents "in order to find out their physical measurements and see whether any of them were athletes with talents their child may have inherited." Children who are selected then form groups and start attending regular practices.

But, as we have seen, it is not until they reach grade one that Czech children truly begin their hockey career and not until they reach the second and third grade will they begin to play what is known as 'mini-hockey'. "Mini-hockey is played across the ice in one of the offensive zones with benches placed in the neutral zone," Barta explains. "This means two games can be played at the same time. Teams change lines at the same time in one-minute intervals." Beginning in 1998–99, mini-games and practices for grades one and two will use lighter pucks (four ounces), with regulation six-ounces pucks being introduced in the third grade. Absolutely no body contact will be allowed under any circumstances. These changes are designed to better develop skating and stickhandling skills. In grades four and five, young Czech players start playing on the full sheet of ice. "But they still do not form teams and do not play in leagues, just short tournaments. The most important thing at this level is to work on their skating and other skills without the distractions or compromises necessary to win games at any cost." When Czech players do finally play real league games in the sixth, seventh, eighth and ninth grades, they do not play more than about 30 games per season plus playoffs. Even the elite midget and junior players play only a 38-game season with a best-of-three playoff format involving eight teams.

"The duration and intensity of practices is proportional to the age level," Barta says. "The youngest players between the first and third grades practice on the ice for a maximum of 75 minutes up to three times per week, while fourth- and fifth-grade pupils practice up to four times a week. After that, teams practice six days a week with the length extending to about 90 minutes." Power and body training is also mandatory and is run during the regular season "which is from about mid-August to late-March." There are also dryland practices throughout the regular season and players participate in soccer, basketball, handball or rugby "to expand and develop skills that hockey practice alone cannot provide. It also helps to develop camaraderie and team cohesion." Players in the Czech Republic do not specialize at positions until they reach the 'older pupil' level (grades eight and nine).

The Czech Republic is not the only European nation that modifies the game to meet the needs of its youngest players. "The Finnish Ice Hockey Association has had special youth hockey rules since 1982," says Eero Lehti. "For those under 12 we have a so-called junior stick and a puck with a hole that weighs only half of what an official puck weighs." Finnish hockey players aged eight and nine play with smaller goalie nets and use just one-third of the ice, as they do in the Czech Republic. Body contact is not permitted until age 12, though "there is some pressure to move up the age or arrange special leagues where body contact will be permitted two years earlier." Body contact is not permitted in Sweden until the age of 14. Children at the entry level (age nine and 10) also play their games across the ice. In Russia, the youngest players practice on a cross-ice sheet, but games are always played on a full ice surface (though smaller nets are used as they are in Finland). Body contact is permitted at all ages in Russian hockey.

At the present time nothing has been done to modify the game for young players in the United States aside from restricting body checking until the peewee level (age 14), though consideration is being given to using lighter pucks. Canada has had an initiative program for novice and prenovice players in place for several years, but it is used by only about 20 percent of the country's 2,300 minor hockey associations. Canadian children can begin to play organized games as young as age six and only in recent years has the practice of using half the ice become more prominent. Smaller pucks and 'donut' pucks are now available for younger children in an effort to develop better shooting and puckhandling skills before muscles are developed enough to use regulation pucks. There is also a move towards the Finnish concept of making hockey sticks specifically for smaller children as opposed to cutting down larger sticks as has always been the case in the past.

No matter how a country chooses to structure its minor hockey system, no matter how much the game is tailored to meet the needs of its players, no matter how much practice time is guaranteed, it is the quality of coaching that ultimately makes the biggest difference.

Both USA Hockey and Canadian Hockey have similar programs in place to train coaches. The USA Hockey Coaches Education Clinic provides instruction for basic, intermediate and advanced levels and there are recommended levels a coach is expected to attain before moving up the ranks. Similarly in Canada, it is now thought that virtually any coach involved at even the game's lowest levels must have at least a minimum coaching certificate and more certification is required to coach at higher levels. Fathers are still the most common coaches among the younger age

groups in Canada. More and more professional coaches enter the ranks as the age of the players increase. By the major junior level, all coaches in Canada are professionals. The progression is similar in the United States, where parents do most of the coaching at the house play level, with more and more professionals becoming involved as a player approaches the junior level.

The screening of coaches has become more important in recent years. At the national level in Canada, all employees must meet the 10-step screening process provided by Volunteer Canada. This process has been recommended to every minor hockey association in the country, but the ultimate decision rests with the individual association and the Volunteer Canada guidelines have not been widely accepted. It is expected, however, that Ontario will mandate the process for minor hockey associations in that province. In the United States, as screening program for state associations has been set up by USA Hockey and is available for use by any that want it.

The training of coaches in Sweden is similar to the methods employed in Canada and the United States, with the 23 district associations taking the responsibility of educating their coaches. Most younger teams are coached by volunteers (i.e. parents). The system for training and educating coaches in Finland consists of five levels. All coaches up to level three are drawn from the parents of players. Level 1 in Finland is meant for instructors ("we'd rather call them instructors than coaches," says Eero Lehti) of children aged six to 13. To get a diploma an instructor has to have at least 100 hours of mandatory studies organized by the Finnish Ice Hockey Association or through regional educational sports organizations accepted by FIHA. There are also three different obligatory ice hockey clinics (as well as two separate clinics for coaching goalies)

Levels 2 to 5 are mainly open to coaches of youngsters and adults aged 14 and up. A coach certified to Level 2 has to collect 200 hours of study plus 80 hours worth of mandatory on-ice clinics. (Once again, a separate clinic is available for those who wish to instruct 14-year-old goalies). The various regions throughout Finland also have FIHA-approved hockey clinics for Level 2. To obtain a diploma at Level 3, a coach must put in 350 hours of mandatory study

through three on-ice clinics. A diploma at levels 4 and 5 requires the study of coaching as a profession. At Level 5 a degree from a department of physical education of a university is required.

The education of coaches is taken no less seriously in Russia and the Czech Republic. While volunteers are used to coach at the Golden Puck level in Russia, both factory and club level teams are all coached by professionals, most of whom are former hockey players. These professionals are trained at the highly-regarded Institute of Physical Culture, which graduates only 20 to 25 coaches per year from its elite two-year training course.

The Czech Republic trains coaches in a three-tiered system, with approximately 1,500 'C' license coaches at the entry level in 1998. Players with more than 200 games of experience in the Elite League or with a World Championship or Olympic medal are also entitled to hold a 'C' license.

After gaining at least two years of experience, coaches can apply for a 'B' license. If they pass the rigorous course at this level, they are eligible for professional work. Czech hockey registered 600 holders of this license in 1998. Only 186 coaches hold an 'A' license. In order to reach this top level on the coaching ladder one must have served as a head coach for an additional two years and be a graduate of the coaching college in the Faculty of Physical Training and Sports at the Charles University in Prague. Required subjects include anatomy, physiology, psychology and teaching technique.

Since the defeat of Team Canada by the United States at the World Cup of Hockey in 1996, Canadian fans, media and hockey officials have been taking a much more critical look at the development of young hockey players. Subsequent losses by both the men's and women's teams at the 1998 Nagano Olympics and the collapse of the World Junior Team after five straight gold medals have further eroded Canada's once-unshakable hockey self-confidence. Having first taught the game to the Europeans at the start of this century, it appears that both Canada and the United States could stand to take a few pointers from their international rivals as the century draws to a close

CHAPTER 53

The Evolution of Hockey Strategy

Stu Hackel, Harry Neale and Roger Neilson

Do you love the neutral zone trap? Do you loathe it? Remember this: In hockey, the only thing permanent is change. Infant hockey resembled rugby on ice. Evolving skills, rules, strategies and tools conspired to change that game into today's. In asking two respected and articulate voices, former coach/current CBC analyst Harry Neale and the innovative veteran coach Roger Neilson, to chronicle some developments that shaped the modern game, one is reminded just how simple the game once appeared.

"COACHES ALWAYS USED TO WRITE on the rink diagram board, 'Pass' in your zone, 'Skate' in the neutral zone and 'Shoot' in the offensive zone," smiles Neilson. "You get the puck in your end and make a pass, you skate through the neutral zone and shoot in the offensive zone. In some ways, that's not bad."

"When I played, and for years afterward," recalls Neale, "a winger was in trouble with his coach if he came off the boards 10 or 15 feet. In fact, some North American coaches would draw lines on the ice down the length of the rink and the wingers were never to go inside those lines."

No single force changed hockey more profoundly than the injection of European play. Today's hybrid of North American and European styles began taking shape in 1972, the moment Team Canada encountered the swirling Soviet Nationals—whose own style was adapted from the firewagon hockey of the 1950s Montreal Canadiens, filtered though soccer and developed in relative isolation. Neale can delineate the elements of the cross-pollination.

"Beginning in 1972, we saw the European clubs—especially the Soviets—turn a lost puck in the neutral zone into a play. We'd get caught with the three forwards going the wrong way and the defensemen standing still. They'd just blow right by. Today, the ability to regroup on a turnover in the neutral zone is a part of any successful NHL team's game plan. We call it 'the transition game.' NHL teams today practice what to do if they get the puck from their opponent on a bad pass or giveaway in the neutral zone. You didn't practice that 25 years ago. There was no plan."

"Another thing the Europeans taught us was for our forwards to not be so structured staying on their side of the ice. Their wingers criss-crossed, skated to the open ice, and hopefully, they'd get a pass. We painfully learned that was a difficult tactic to defend against."

"I watched European teams practice at a much higher tempo than we did. Our drills were specific—we'd do a three-on-two rush for 10 minutes, then we'd do a two-on-one. But they incorporated three, four or five things that we had separate drills for into one drill. The old 90 minute practice is a rarity now; today it's 45 or 55 minutes and the players don't stand around very much. We picked up from them that you play the game at a high tempo and you try to practice that way."

"Puck control has always been more important to Europeans than giving it up and trying to get it back. Don't shoot it in, turn it back if you don't like the looks of the rush. Control it in the offensive zone. I think cycling, which used to be called 'offensive puck control,' is a tactic we took directly from playing against Europeans—especially the Russians. We were confused by their puck control and cycling tactics. They'd control the puck in our end, often outside the scoring area, and then—bang!— it's in the scoring area. All the NHL coaches buy into it now, but we dump it in to get it back before we start cycling."

"Europeans were first in using the neutral zone as an offensive area of the rink. In North America, we used to think of it as a dead area. Now, more teams practice neutral zone play, trying to answer the question, 'What are we going to do going through the neutral zone to confuse the defensemen or make them make a wrong decision?' If we just come though the neutral zone in a straight line, the opposition doesn't have to be very bright to figure out who to cover. So neutral zone play has become vital to creating goal-scoring chances."

"The neutral zone trap is a European tactic—especially in Sweden and Finland. The Swedish teams trap better than anyone. I think it's a product of their bigger ice surface, which eliminates effective forechecking. Their coaches want their teams to play strong defensively and wait for turnovers, because other teams will get frustrated and try low percentage plays and you can pounce on the puck."

"I used to keep a stat in the early North American versus European series. They would pass the puck about 35 percent more than we did. The theory was that the puck is the fastest thing on the ice and if you move it quickly, you'll look like a faster team. If you watch a tape of most NHL games in the 1950s and now look at a game from the 1990s, there are many more passes today. The exception was the old Montreal Canadiens, who passed more often. You wonder whether the wider ice made it an even better tactic for Europeans."

And how has North American hockey influenced the Europeans?

"Toughness," Neale explains. "I remember speaking about the 1972 Summit Series with Anatoli Tarasov, who said, 'We had more skill than the Canadian team, we had more speed, we were in better shape, we had better teamwork. But we could not equal their tenacity or grit or do-what-you-have-to-do-to-win spirit.' That's one big area the Europeans have improved immensely. They are far more successful in one-on-one fights for the puck, where hockey skills are less important than desire. I'm not saying that the North Americans don't have the advantage in that department today, but it is not an automatic advantage."

"The European goaltenders are much better than they used to be. They've learned the angles, which are different over here because of the smaller ice surface. They also come out of the net and handle the puck, which they never did previously. The European goalies were always quick but they were never part of the play and now they are far more adventurous."

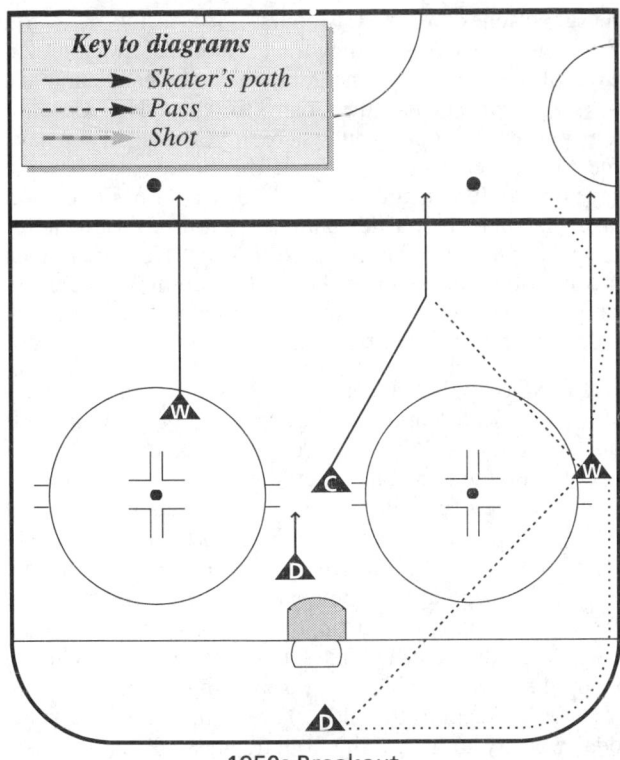

Key to diagrams
→ *Skater's path*
- - - → *Pass*
- - - → *Shot*

1950s Breakout

the power play, the best way to score was point shots. Then everyone realized if they take away the points, it forces you to go down low. Today everyone has access to video immediately. If you come up with a new play and put it in, if it works, in two weeks everyone will be using it."

And that is how it goes: innovation breed imitation, then calculation, then innovation again. It is a constant theme when Neale and Neilson discuss the various aspects of hockey's evolution.

Breakouts may be the most underappreciated aspect of the game. What is the key and how have they changed over time?

NEALE: Making that first pass is the secret to a good breakout. When I played in the Leafs organization in the 1950s, the common form of breakout was up to the wing at the hashmarks, or a little further. His job was to get the pass and either skate with it or move it to center. If he was checked he'd just tip it out. *(see 1950s Breakout diagram)*

NEILSON: The key was always to stop behind the net; we'd always say, "Get the net." Some teams then had their center circle back and some would have a defenseman in front and the guy would bring it out and the defenseman would pick for him. You might try to hit the wing, but there were many different set plays—D to D or up the middle. *(see Middle Breakout to Winger diagram)*

"I don't know if it's because losing a face-off is of less consequence on the big ice, but North American teams used to have a tremendous advantage on face-offs against European competition. I don't think that's true anymore. It didn't seem as if face-offs were so important for Europeans but it seems to have become a priority there. It's always been a priority here."

"It's harder to have good defensive zone coverage on Europe's wider rinks, but they play much better in their own zone now than they used to. I can't remember any Darius Kasparaitis or Ulf Samuelsson types from Europe 25 years ago. These two and Vladimir Konstantinov, when he played, have been among the best in the NHL. The Europeans produced more Fetisov and Ragulin types—big and strong, you couldn't push them around, good with the puck and they had good feet so you couldn't beat them— but they weren't robust and didn't aggressively go after the opposition. There are more hard-nosed European defensemen today who take you out with some enthusiasm. European coaches admired that in our defensemen and now encourage their own to play that way."

"It's harder to adopt an aggressive forechecking style on Europe's larger rinks than the smaller NHL rinks, and it has taken Europeans a bit longer to adapt to that part of the game. I don't think North American coaches have gotten their European players to dump-and-chase as often as North American forwards do today, and probably do too often, but now European forwards do use their speed to come up with loose pucks."

Apart from importing influences, the modern game has been shaped by the increased sophistication of coaching. Neilson's own development as a career coach is instructive: "For a guy like me, who was a junior B goalie, the way you learn about the game is from players, asking if they can try certain things, or from video—watching the teams' forechecking, breakout, the power play, whatever. You watch the video and something clicks in. I was watching video and it hit me—and I'm sure it hit others, too—that on

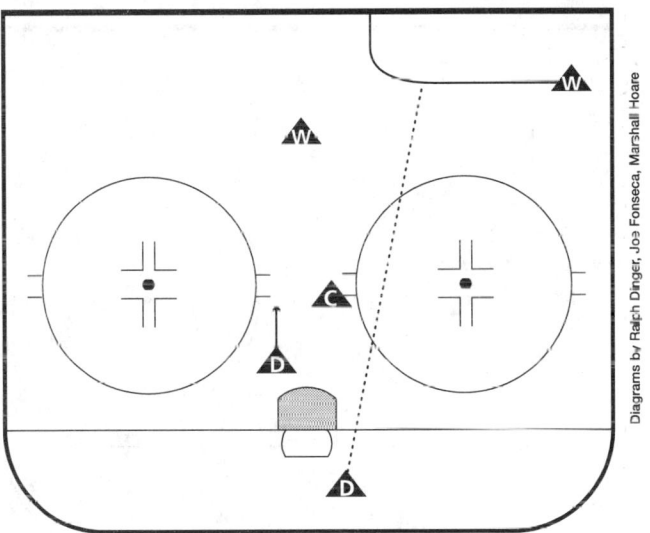

Middle Breakout to Winger

Diagrams by Ralph Dinger, Joe Fonseca, Marshall Hoare

NEALE: The better puckhandling defensemen back then—Red Kelly, Doug Harvey—would occasionally pass the puck up the middle to their center. *(see Middle Breakout to Center diagram)* It allows a team to break out with speed. That play is actually more common today than it used to be. Even today, if you make a mistake on that play, you're in an awful spot in your zone. Today, most defensemen make that pass to a wing cutting across. It's difficult to defend when people are moving into the holes. The defenders can't plug all the holes no matter what system they use. If the wing cuts across for a pass and someone fills his spot on the boards that he vacated, it gives the passer some options. *(see Modern Middle Breakout to Winger diagram)*

Was the idea of these breakouts to get an odd-man situation in the neutral zone or just gain the offensive zone?

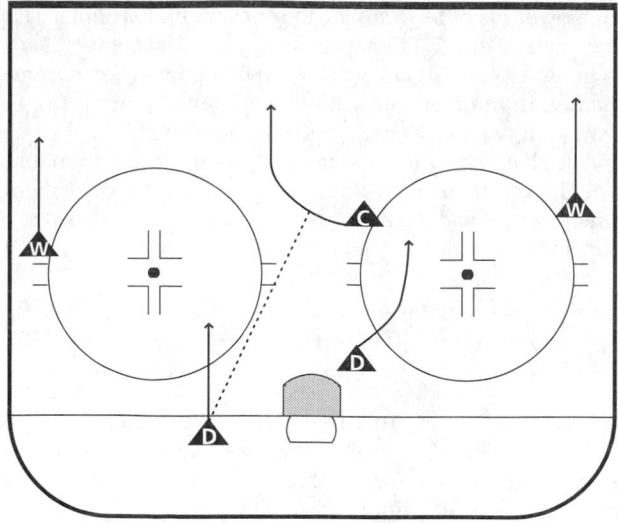

Middle Breakout to Center

NEILSON: You were hoping to bring the puck out, get it up and then get it in, but it's a good question. What are you trying to do? If you're just trying to get it out, why don't you just blast it out instead of wasting all that time? And I think that's basically what people are gradually realizing. Now there are a lot of players who really want to work it out. But I tell them, if you lose it one out of four times, you're in trouble.

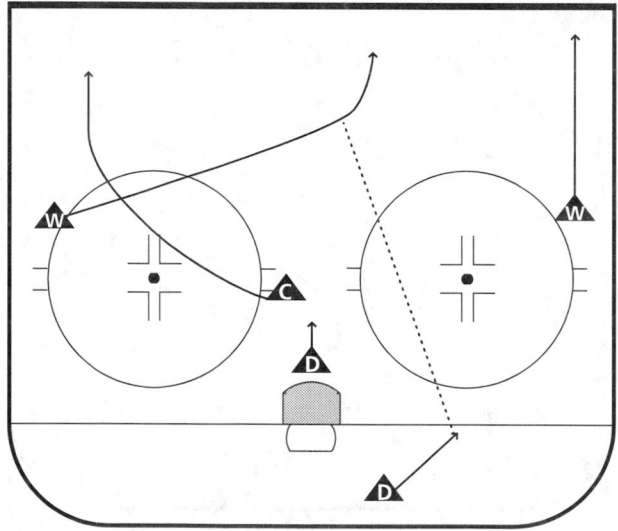

Modern Middle Breakout to Winger

NEALE: If you're an NHL defenseman, you're going to get hit after you pass the puck. If it bothers you, either you're going to pass it sooner, which will cause problems, or you're not going to go get it. A lot of times there just isn't a play, and the best thing you can do is just whack it off the boards into center or into the offensive zone. The purpose of the forecheck is to close off the options but European players are taught there are always options. Over here, because the players are faster, the rinks are smaller and the hits are harder, the options sometimes disappear. You don't have to be European to have problems reacting to the forecheck but it's probably more disconcerting for Europeans to admit to themselves, "I just have to get this thing out of here," because they are used to having options. It's one of the things a European defenseman has to learn: He's going to be confronted sooner when he gets the puck.

The good ones adapt. Of course, for a lot of North American defensemen, if they took the boards away, they'd be out of work. But even the good ones who can handle the puck well have to use the boards in the NHL. Coaches today prefer a safer breakout where, if you miss it, you have time to recover. Coming around the boards has become very popular. It's the toughest thing a winger has to do—to make that play in traffic—and it's a big adjustment for European wings who aren't used to big NHL defensemen pinching down on them as the puck is coming around. In Europe they come up the middle or carry it more often, especially after the "D to D" pass.

NEILSON: When I coached the Rangers in the early 1990s, I noticed teams were getting really good in their traps or contains. You might get through on two out of three, but on the third time, they'd bust through and pick it off. So we stopped setting up. A lot of teams believe in quick breakouts now. (see Quick Breakout diagram) Unless you're on the power-play, when you want things organized, you just keep going. If someone confronts you and you have no other play, you just put it up off the boards. When you do that, the other team's defenseman often pinches in to stop the puck. Pinching defensemen have been effective for years in keeping the play alive in the offensive zone. Today you try to negate the effectiveness of that defenseman pinching in. We call it counter-pinching where you just play that man. You have your center come over and the far wing, instead of heading up ice, comes over in a support position. It's an important play today. We even do drills for it. We practice that once a week. Once you get over the blue line, then your skaters fan out. If the defenseman is circling the net and he's confronted by a forechecker, he can just reverse it to his partner. But you really don't want guys to stop and let the trap set.

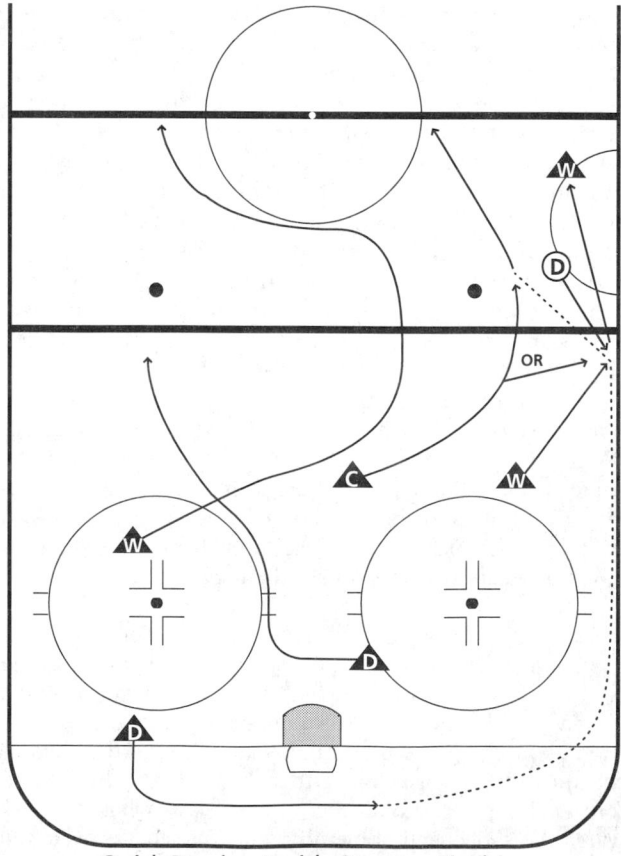

Quick Breakout with Counter-Pinching

What is your reaction after the trap has been set?

NEILSON: Teams want you to try a pass through the middle, so instead your defenseman flips it high into the other team's end. It's not a bad play because their defenseman may have difficulty playing a bouncing puck with forwards bearing down on him.

NEALE: One of the ways to break the trap is to start out like you're going into it. You pass to the defenseman back

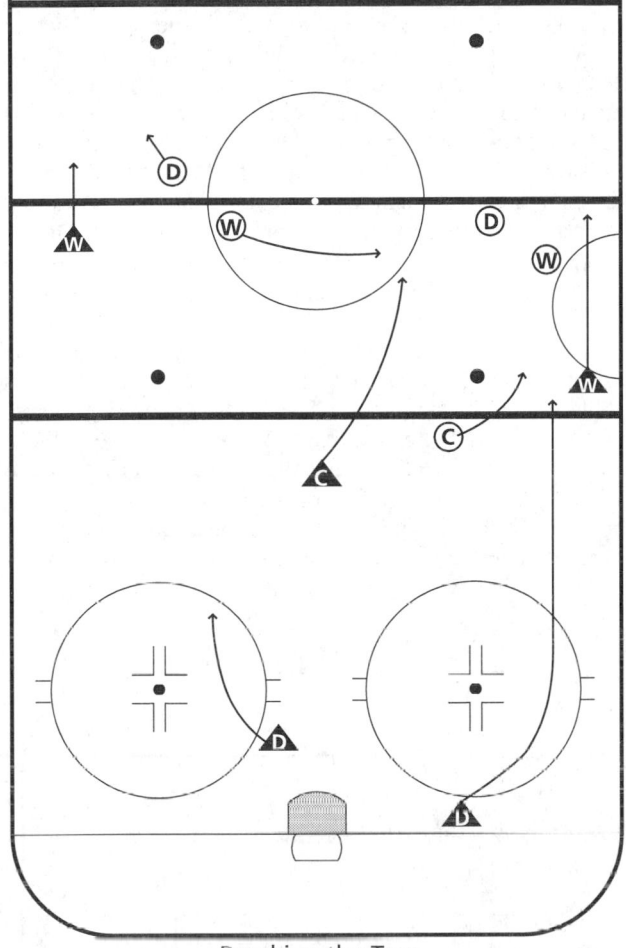

Breaking the Trap

on the far side and, if he can skate, he ought to be able to get into the neutral zone or to the red line without being seriously opposed and have the wing on his side of the rink to dump it to if he has to. You're not gaining the zone with any danger, but least you're out of your end. *(see Breaking the Trap diagram)*

To break the left wing lock, a defenseman has to join the rush to create an odd man situation in the neutral zone, jump past one of the two forecheckers to be the extra man. The first two forecheckers in the lock also have to pick up the defenseman on the rush, so they have a tough assignment—they're trying to forecheck and you can get knocked down forechecking, but to do their job properly, they can't afford to get knocked down. *(see Breaking the Left Wing Lock diagram)*

Gaining the offensive zone by dumping it in used to be a sin. Now it's almost standard.

NEALE: The main way teams used to gain the zone was to carry it in. Each team had at least one good stickhandler

on every line. Their job was to beat people with that skill. It was more of a one-on-one game. Bobby Hull, Gordie Howe, Rocket Richard and Guy Lafleur all fought off more checkers than anyone today. It was part of the game and they accepted it. They challenged the opposing defenseman and took their chances. The stars all had speed and big shots. If you weren't backing up fast enough, they'd blow right by you—and if you backed up too much because of their speed, they'd shoot it by you. Even though lots has changed, the good players today—Selanne, Kariya, Bure, Bondra, Sundin—all have those skills in abundance. They are fast and can handle the puck. We don't see as much stickhandling today because there's more emphasis on passing and, since players are bigger and faster, there is less time and space to be fancy.

NEILSON: In the old days teams played two-line hockey. The 1940s Leafs might have been the first team to play four lines and one of the first to shoot it in and go after it. That was a new kind of game, where you'd forecheck hard all the time. Hap Day, the Leaf coach, was a conditioning maniac, and he would drive those guys until they were sick at practice. You had to be tough, but it really helped the Leafs win Cups.

NEALE: But generally, until 20 or 30 years ago, the shoot-in was the last resort as opposed to one of the first. The Leafs may have been the exception. They played you wing-on-wing coming back and had the two defensemen standing up on the blue line. Their job was to bodycheck, block shots and take guys out. So the puck carrier had both his wings covered and two big defensemen waiting to meet

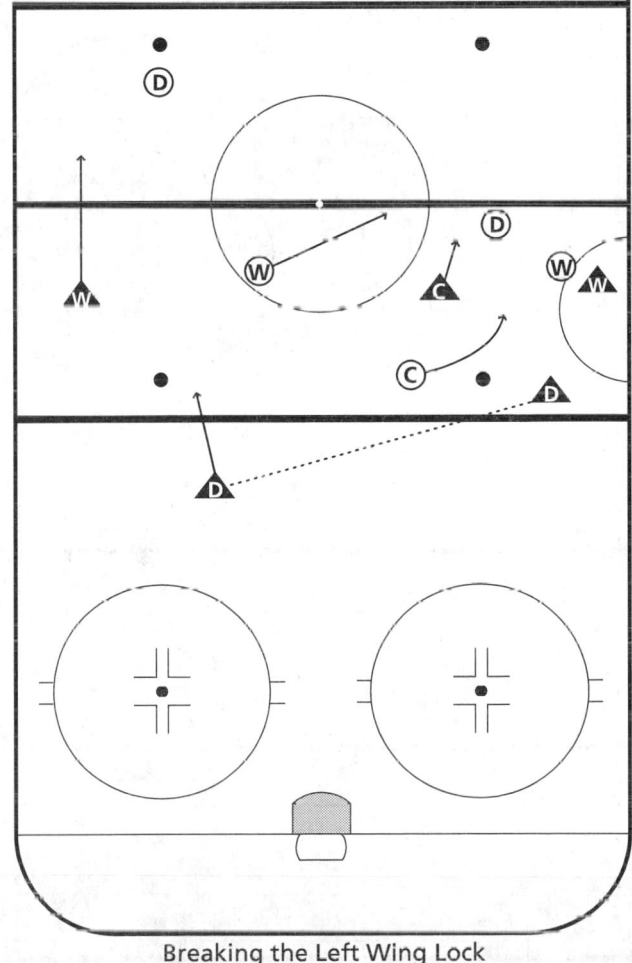

Breaking the Left Wing Lock

him. His best option was to pass it or dump it at the blue line. He could try to beat a defenseman into the zone, but that was like taking your life in your hands.

The theory on the shoot-in is that you're playing to dump the puck into a corner or hard around the boards so it ends up in the far corner, then you go in to forecheck and cause a giveaway. Coaches also like the shoot-in because it's a safe play, as opposed to stickhandling. If you lose it stickhandling, they could have all three forwards going the other way—four if a defenseman has joined.

NEILSON: There's so much emphasis today on counterattack that, conversely, there's a big emphasis on entries, making good decisions, sensing danger. Turnovers at the blue line are killers. The whole idea is that the puck must get in deep. You don't want to enter down the middle, because that's where everybody on the other team is. You want to pass wide, carry it wide, chip it through or shoot it in. *(see Wide Entry Even Strength diagram)* You want to bring it down the side and work it to the middle—even on the power-play. *(see Wide Entry on Power-Play diagram)* Teams used to come down the middle on the power-play, because the defensemen stood up at the blue line and the wings stayed with the offensive wings so they backed in. But now the penalty-killing wings stay high and the defensemen back off the line. So you don't want to go down the middle because the penalty killers are all there.

NEALE: The shoot-in is far less common in Europe. They can't forecheck as well on the big rinks, so they cross the blue line with the puck and then cause problems. We see

NHL players now shoot it in when they're three-on-three or two-on-two. If you did that in Europe, you'd be in trouble with your coach for not trying to cross over and confuse the defensemen, go wide to beat him, turn back and regroup, or look for a late man coming in hoping to beat the backcheckers into the zone. The most skilled NHL players—Gretzky, Kariya, Selanne—only shoot it in when they're tired, want a change or it's two against four and you wouldn't try to make a play.

In the last 15 years, the neutral zone has become an area where you try things offensively, instead of just a space you have to go though before you try them. When I coached in the WHA against touring European teams, I used to say, "They look like they pass it to nobody, but when the puck gets there, their guy is there." And, of course, that's always been Gretzky's feeling—go where the puck is going to, don't wait for it to go there. The WHA Winnipeg Jets were the first North American team to adopt that style. They had the best group of European players and Bobby Hull. They'd come into the neutral zone three abreast and by the time they got into the offensive zone, they'd be in different lanes than where they started. They produced all sorts of chances because it was hard to sort out who's got who. They'd jump into the holes, get a pass on the fly and cause tremendous problems for the defenders. The backcheckers wondered, "What do I do? Do chase that guy all over the ice? We'll have one hell of a traffic jam." We had to learn first how to defend against it—if you're backchecking and your wing cuts in the middle, you'd better wait and stay in your lane because somebody's coming there, and that's going to be your guy—then we found out it was a pretty good tactic and

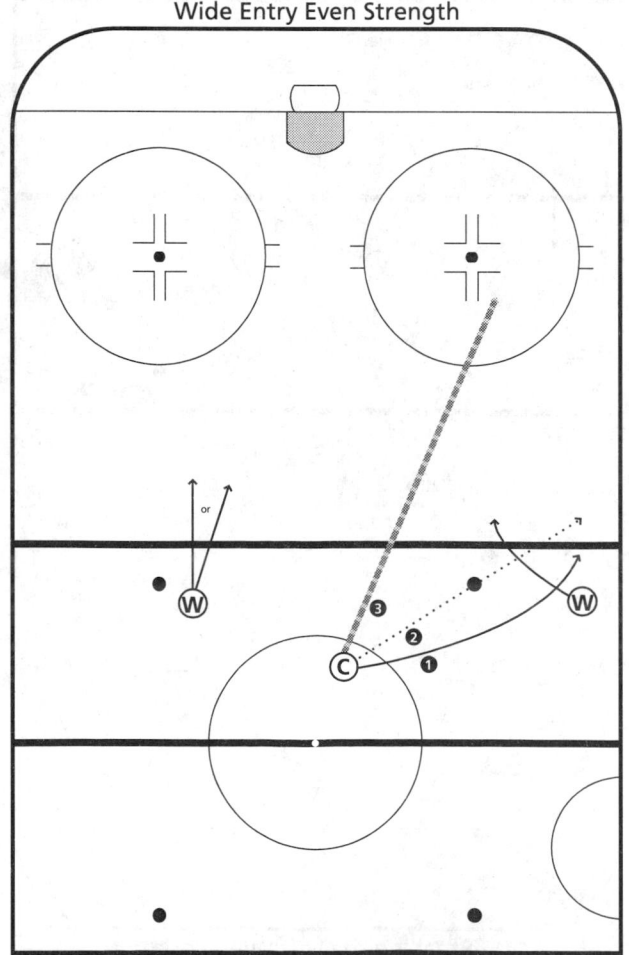

Wide Entry Even Strength

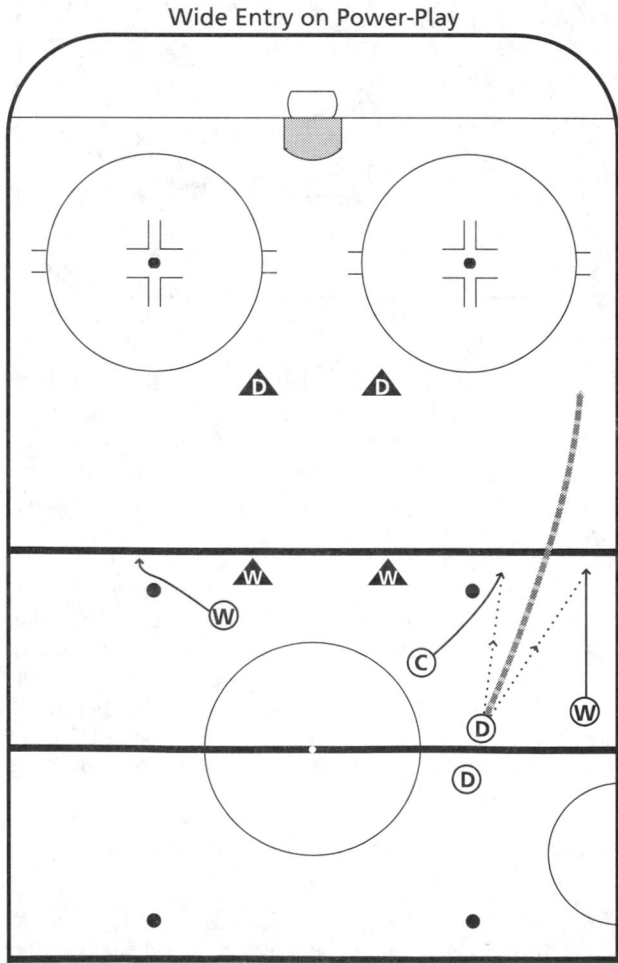

Wide Entry on Power-Play

started using it ourselves. You now see wings cut across, the defenseman jump up and go wide, the forwards criss-cross. Even if you're rushing through the neutral zone three-on-three, which is often the case, it's stupid to just be three across. You'd better cross over. Same thing two-on-two: do something to make the defensemen decide what to do, because some of them will make the wrong decision or be confused for a second, allowing you not only to get into the zone but toward the net.

NEILSON: The Europeans also brought regroups to the neutral zone. I don't think anyone in North America did that, where if you didn't like a play you turned back, or if you're changing on the go, you turned back until everybody got off. The Europeans were so good at it that you had to come up with a defense against it. That's where the traps, the Swedish one-three-one and all that came from. The fact that their rinks were so big was important because once they started to regroup, you couldn't chase them around. So you had to get into a zone defense.

Once you gain the zone, you go to the net.

NEILSON: Going to the net means two things: the guy without the puck goes to the net, and the guy with the puck puts it at the net. You used to see a lot of drop passes, where the puck carrier would leave it for a trailer and then either screen for him or go to the net for the rebound or a pass. That was great with two-line hockey, when you didn't have hard pressure from behind like today. Now coaches discourage that because you can drop it and a backchecker's there ready to take it the other way. Teams like New Jersey are very quick defensively coming back into the slot, so you can't afford to be putting the puck in there. Instead, you put the puck wide to bring it back in again. In the Middle Drive, a guy coming down the middle passes wide and goes through right to the middle of the net. The third guy can circle in behind him. *(see Middle Drive diagram)*

Middle Drive

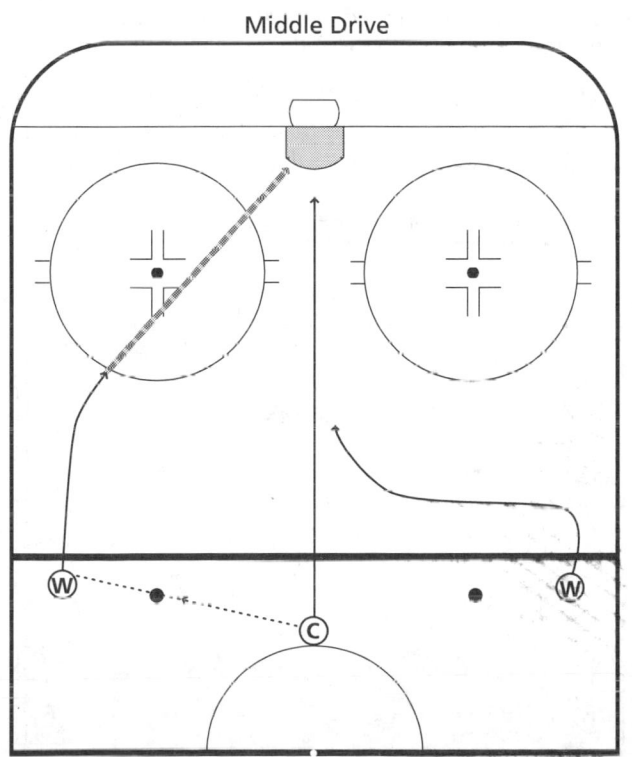

NEALE: North American hockey players are taught from Day 1—good things can happen if you go to the net. You can screen the shot, tip it in, grab the rebound. We used to call them "garbage goals." It seems like a derogatory term, but lots of big players score lots of goals because they go to the net without the puck. And you don't always have to be big—Dino Ciccarelli isn't big, but he plays big. It's a thankless task because you often have to get by someone from the other team. Once you get to the net, you have to stay there and take the pounding. Then the puck arrives and the question is, are your hands good enough to do something when you get them on the puck? Phil Esposito had the knack; often he was perfectly covered, but he got his hands free and could get the puck on net. Cam Neely, Clark Gillies, John LeClair—they somehow got impossible shots off while being held, tugged and grabbed.

And getting the puck on net has changed. In films from the 1950s and early 1960s, you don't see many slapshots from the outside. Most player wristed it toward the goal. Then everyone started to use the slapshot.

NEILSON: For years the slapshot was the only shot taken from the point. It was so much faster than the wrist shot. But now, more guys on the point take the wrist shot because there's no wind-up so it's easier to get it through when the opposition tries to take the point shots away. Against teams that wrist it in a lot, you can tell your defensemen, "Forget the guy parked in front of the net, you can play the puck. You can just step out and block the puck like a goalie."

NEALE: If going to the net for North Americans means going without the puck, for Europeans it means going there with the puck. Europeans want to make plays in the offensive zone involving multiple passes so at the end, when you go to the net, you're by yourself. You don't see them getting "garbage goals." Their idea is get the same chance without encountering all the physical resistance. There seem to be fewer European power forwards. They are the artists on the line, and when you pair them with a power forward you get a good result. One goes to the net, the other and gets them the puck.

Bobby Clarke is the first player I recall who regularly made the play to the net from behind the goal line.

NEILSON: When I coached Toronto, Darryl Sittler was also great at getting the puck behind the goal line off to one side of the net and making a quick pass out to Lanny McDonald going to the net. It concerned me because if the pass didn't work, the turnover would hurt us. I thought at first they were blind passes, but those two were pretty good at reading off each other. Then Gretzky started going behind the net and that was a pretty good play because all the defenders face the wrong way. Now most coaches discourage that play because it's too dangerous. If the pass doesn't work, you're looking at a three-on-two the other way. There also used to be a lot of pick plays coming out of the corner, where a player would almost run interference for the puck carrier. That's being penalized a lot today.

A recent tactic is cycling, which is quite important in today's game.

NEILSON: Cycling used to be called "offensive zone play." The purpose is to test the other team's coverage in the defensive zone. You try to get a guy open, get someone to lose their check, or sneak a defenseman in. Having your defensemen join the cycle has recently become a pretty important part of the game. To execute it properly, you have to get someone following up the puck carrier so he can hand off the puck to him. He can either come in from behind so the players are actually skating in a circle, or sort of like football, with reversals or misdirection plays. Your players have to read each other and know that it's starting so they can jump in. The whole idea of cycling is to always make safe passes, so you always put your passes toward the boards. You never turn around and throw it away from the boards into traffic. Hopefully you have a guy coming out of the cycle to get open and you just keep moving it around until someone does. If a guy on the other team reads it, and moves in to cut you off, you just put it off the boards. Teams practice cycling quite often today and you even see players do it on the power-play now, because if they can get a defenseman to chase the cycle, they can move the puck in and get a quick three-on-two.

Cycling may result from good forechecking, but there are different types of forechecking.

NEALE: A one-man forecheck is a defensive play and a two-man forecheck is an offensive play. The lines a coach sends out to execute a two-man forecheck can change the atmosphere of a game. If things aren't going too well and you're lulled into a kind of calm, that line may go out three out of six shifts. It gets the crowd and your team going. It's always a lot easier to go out on the ice after your teammates have had a good shift than if they've been in trouble the whole minute.

The traditional view of forechecking is it's a physical part of the game. We're going to run in, our first forechecker is going to take the puck carrier with the body and our second man gets the puck. It sounds good—except you have to get your two guys there before their second guy arrives. With the safe game coaches play today, there is often a second guy back with the puck carrier. So if you only use the old style, you won't get much forechecking done. *(see Two-Man Forecheck diagram)*

One-Man Forecheck

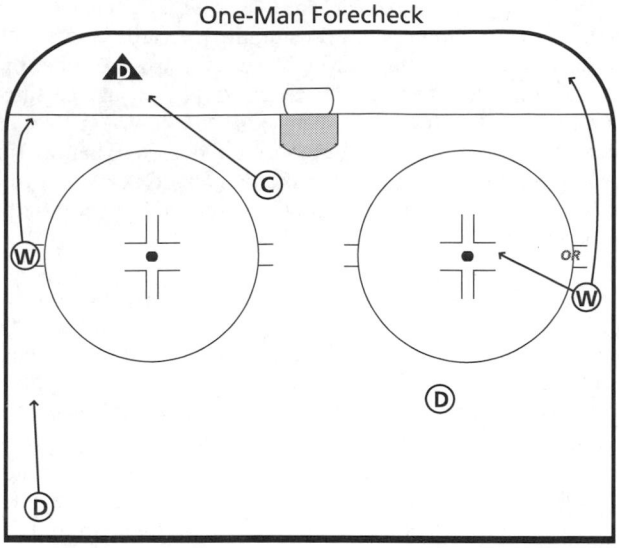

NEILSON: When you dump it in, the first thing you want is to pressure the puck carrier. *(see One-Man Forecheck diagram)* The other two guys must take away the boards, particularly the second guy, who is on the short boards so they can't use short corner reverse. The third guy is on the weak side and he's ready if it comes around the boards, or ready to move over into the slot and be the third man. That first guy denies them the net and flushes them out to the support and, if the defenseman pinches in, the third guy can back him up.

NEALE: Europeans use the "hurry principle" of forechecking. We'll hurry them into making a play and, because they can't take as much time as they'd like to survey all their options, they'll make a bad play. It's really a five-man exercise. The first man goes after the puck carrier and the second man has got to anticipate: if the puck squirts free, he gets it, or if the first pass was made, he hurries the second guy or tries to intercept. And the third forward hurries the third guy and so on. This is probably a consequence of the larger European ice surface, which made the traditional forecheck hard to execute.

NEILSON: Most teams now feel if you're going to forecheck, you've got to pinch in. That's been around for about 15 years. Before that, defensemen rarely pinched,

Two-Man Forecheck

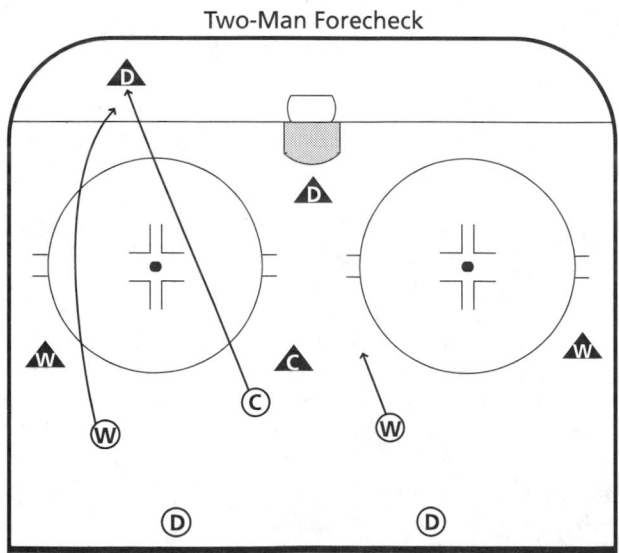

Man-on-Man (Pinching-in) Forecheck

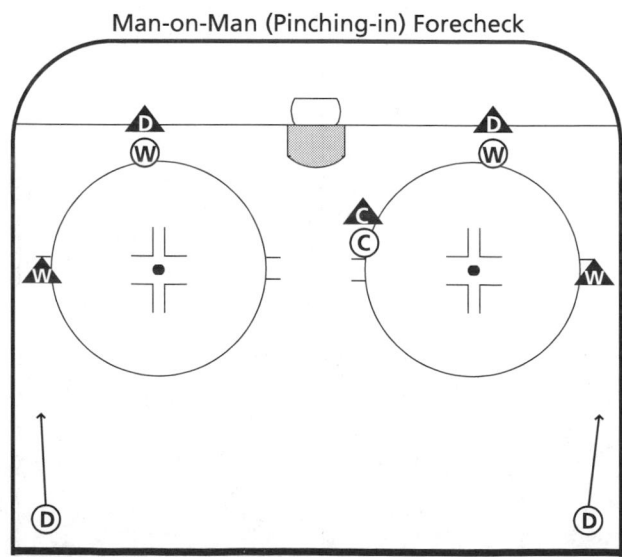

except if you were losing and had to take a chance. The Oilers brought pinching into the game on a more consistent basis. *(see Man-on-Man {Pinching-In} Forecheck diagram)* The whole Edmonton system was wings on their defensemen, the center on their center and the defensemen pinched on either side. The center could back up, but the main thing was that everyone had their man and you kept your man in front of you. They did that all the way down the rink, in the neutral zone as well. It was a wide-open system. I remember doing the video for them during the playoffs for their first Stanley Cup and there were many scoring chances for both sides. You had to have good skaters and lots of skill to execute that style. It was an exciting way to play.

NEALE: The left wing lock is a two-man forecheck with one guy high. It prevents the other team from getting an odd-man rush unless they bring a defenseman into it. It also allows your far side defenseman to pinch knowing he's got another guy back there. But it's just a way to keep a third guy high. The left wing is designated to stay high in the zone and seal off a breakout pass, although sometimes it's the center if the left wing is the first guy up the ice. They can get out of their end against that, but the best they can get is a three-on-three in the neutral zone. It's effective when you're protecting a lead. *(see Left Wing Lock diagram)*

These more complex offensive schemes have drastically changed defending in your zone.

NEILSON: The three-on-three down low coverage used to be strictly a man-on-man system; however, in today's game of cycling, picks and penalty calls, the man-on-man is too difficult to execute. The keys are—one: get to your man quickly; two: keep your stick in the passing lane; three: finish the check; four: the second man looks for puck; and, five: be sure to beat your man back to the net.

NEALE: The desired NHL style has long been to be physical in your own zone. When I take a guy in my own zone, I'm going to hit him, pin him against the glass or knock him down. Most defensemen were hitters 25–30 years ago. Teams still seem to want that, but with cycling and passing more prevalent, and forwards much quicker, it's harder to hit guys. So most teams now want one or two physical defensemen while the others play more of a European containment style. It combines both man-on-man and zone philosophies. You get to the forward quickly and under control. You may bump into him, but it's not to pin him, it's to tie him up so he can't go anywhere. If he passes the puck, you go with him. You don't give yourself up to make the hit, you seal off opportunities. On the "give and go," the approach was to take the play away by hitting the passer—if he gets the pass off and you knock him down, he can't get the return. But, if you go full out to hit him and miss, he can get around you for the return pass. In the containment approach, you take that away by having the defender stay with the man. They might execute the "give," but you can eliminate the "go." It's tough to do properly. With cycling, teams are willing to control the puck outside of the scoring area. So the defensive players have to be able to switch. They've got to talk to each other, yell "Switch!" or "I got him!" If not, when they cross over, they'll run into a traffic jam. The optimum today may be to split the difference. If you rely too much on containment, you may have trouble, because NHL teams love to play against defenses that never take you out.

One of the biggest changes in the defending has been on the two-on-one.

NEALE: The old theory was the goalie takes the shooter, the defenseman takes away the pass and the goalie cuts down the angle.

NEILSON: But today's shooters are way too good for that. Actually, when I coached junior, we always told the defenseman to force a pass, force them to make another play and we'd take our chances with it. I didn't like the guy just walking in, letting him shoot. Occasionally, the pass was made and the goalie looked bad. But in the traditional theory, you always wanted the defenseman to stand up in the middle.

NEALE: The only exception was if the shooter cut across the net, the defenseman had to chop him down. But the newest theory is the slide.

NEILSON: The purpose of the slide on the two-on-one is to take the pass away. You slide on the ice toward the puck and the only way the guy can get it through is if he flips it or dekes or tries to go around—and if he does any of those things, you've got a good chance of stopping him. And usually the guy can't shoot if the slide is done correctly.

Another recent development is the neutral zone trap.

NEALE: Today's neutral zone trap is a variation of the old one-man forecheck. When I was growing up in the Leaf organization, if you were a wing for the Leafs and had three forwards coming down and you got caught not being in front of one of them, you were sent to Pittsburgh. It was called a "one-man forecheck." The media called it "Kitty-Bar-The-Door," and the Leafs won Stanley Cups doing it. Executing the one-man forecheck was easier back then because so few wings crossed; it was easy to sort out who your man was. Now it's not so easy.

NEILSON: Punch Imlach was one of those coaches who drew lines down the sides of the rink. That was where wings were supposed to go. When he coached in Montreal

Left Wing Lock

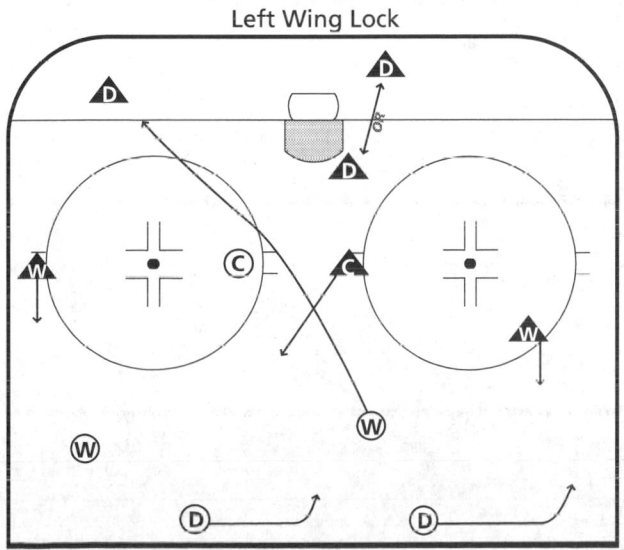

in the 1970s, Scotty Bowman was one of the first tell wings something different defensively, to lock the middle. I remember watching one game. Bob Gainey was backchecking his man and Scotty was screaming, "The middle! The middle!" A wing used to go back with his man, but Scotty wanted him to come over into the middle of the neutral zone and lock the middle to take away that pass. The defenseman's job became to watch the wide guys. It took the puck carrier's passing option away and so he'd be coming up facing four guys. *(see Backchecking – Locking the Middle diagram)* But that idea became obsolete. Back then, the defensemen tried to stay up at the blue line and the wings came back, so the other team would dump it in the end and the wing would have to come back and get the puck, making a breakout very difficult. It took another 10 years, but the next stage of that strategy was the trap. Not only did you lock the middle but you deny the puck carrier the red line. *(see Neutral Zone Trap diagram.)*

NEALE: Your first forechecker angles the puck carrier toward the boards and moves to cut him off before he gets out of the zone.

NEILSON: Your center has to mirror the movement of the far wing to force the puck carrier toward the boards. The near wing, who has backed off on the one-two-two, then jumps the puck carrier before center.

NEALE: The puck carrier's only options are—one: to beat you in a foot race, before you can cut him off at the blue line; two: chip it off the boards to his wing; or, three: pass it back into the middle to his center. If he beats you, your wing is there to jump him so he can't get to the blue line to dump it in; if he can't beat you and tries to chip it ahead, that same wing is there to intercept it; and if he tries to pass it back in the middle to his center…

NEILSON: …That can be picked off by the locking wing or the defenseman and lead to the counter-attack.

NEALE: The trap is designed to make the puck carrier think he can make one of those plays and then he can't make any of them. They get caught in the transition with their guys going to their net and four of your guys with the puck going the other way.

Some believe line matching is the biggest factor in a game's outcome.

NEILSON: My first year in Vancouver, Harry was coaching and I was an assistant. We hadn't been scoring. One night, we were playing Boston. I got the lineup, brought it back to Harry and I said, "Looks like they're starting their checking line." Harry brightens up and says, "Well, we can fool them. We'll start a line that can't score."

Backchecking – Locking The Middle

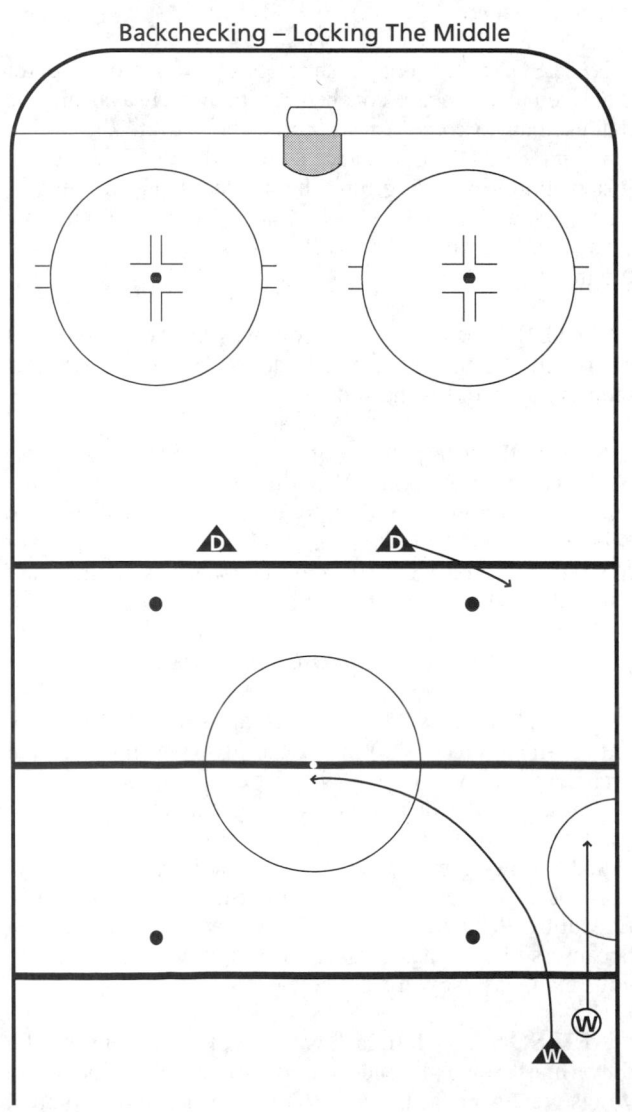

Neutral Zone Trap

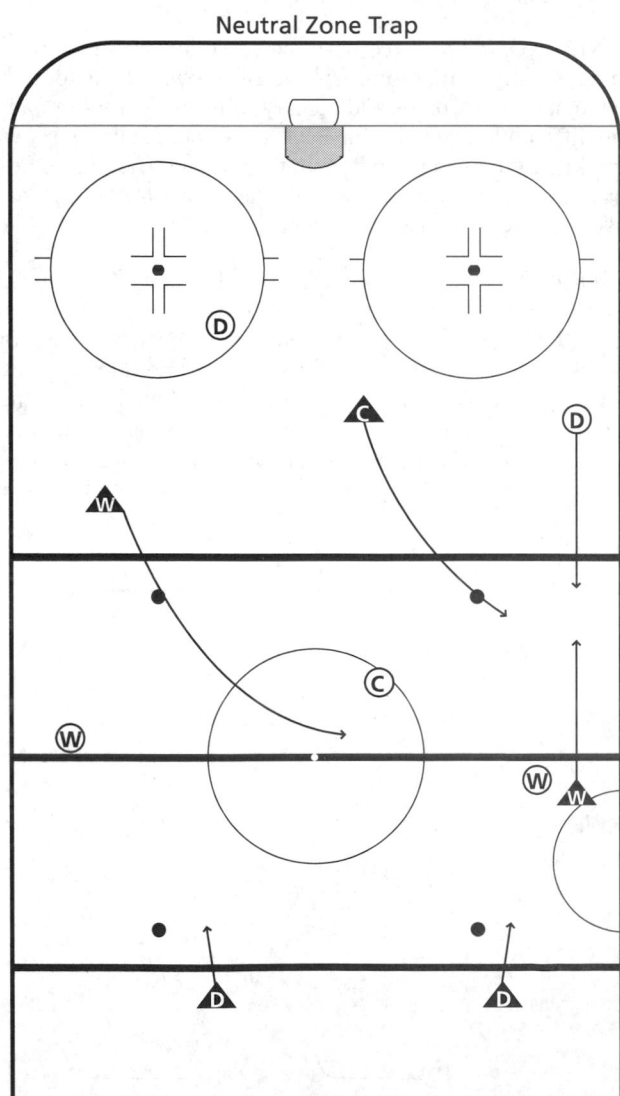

NEALE: When I began in hockey, the first lines played against each other, the second lines played against each other and so on. That was probably accidental. Both teams would start their best lines and they only had three. Shadowing, or matching certain individuals against others, is not new, however. For example, in the 1940s, the Leafs would send Bob Davidson out to check Maurice Richard. In the 1960s, Montreal used Claude Provost to shadow Bobby Hull. Chicago always used Eric Nesterenko against top forwards. Even recently, when Joel Otto played for Calgary, he always went against Mark Messier. But line matching has become more prevalent than shadowing in the last two decades. When I started to coach there was no rule giving the home team the last change. I think that was a product of all kinds of jockeying to get the match-up. That rule is a product of line matching.

NEILSON: Changing on the go has become more of an art than it used to be. Previously, teams just changed. Now teams have plays for it and they change every 40 seconds. When they're killing penalties, they change every 20 seconds. It's become very important because the game has gotten so fast and intense. You've got to have good shoot-ins when you're changing on the go— especially in the second period when it's a long way back to your bench. You've always got to put it in on your bench side. If you put it in the far corner, they'll come up the other side and you're done. Teams have that long play they'll use to burn you. One tactic you see is that the first guy coming on goes directly to the far side to prevent that long play. That turns them back into the middle and second guy goes after the puck carrier and the third guy locks the middle. *(see Changing on the Go diagram)*

NEALE: Most often, matching involves putting out a defensive unit against an offensive line. Quite often now, you also see a certain defense pair matched against the top forward line, or matching your fifth and sixth defensemen against the opposition's weaker lines, figuring that is the best time to use them.

Sometimes you'll see a team put its best line against yours. You may take a little offense away from the opposition because their coach warns them to be careful. I love when the best players go against each other because it makes for a good game. Effective matchups are really more possible when you are familiar with the opposition, and never more important than in the playoffs. If you can neutralize a player or a line, it may give you a chance to win.

NEILSON: There are some important considerations when you are matching. There can be big advantages in getting a top line out against a line that doesn't check so well. But if they have a tough line and you have a tough line also, you may not want his tough line out against your top line— they might rough your guys up. On the other hand, sometimes you may want them out because your line is so much better than theirs. You've got to keep in mind the players don't really like matching. Let's say you send your top line out for a face-off and then the other team changes on the fly

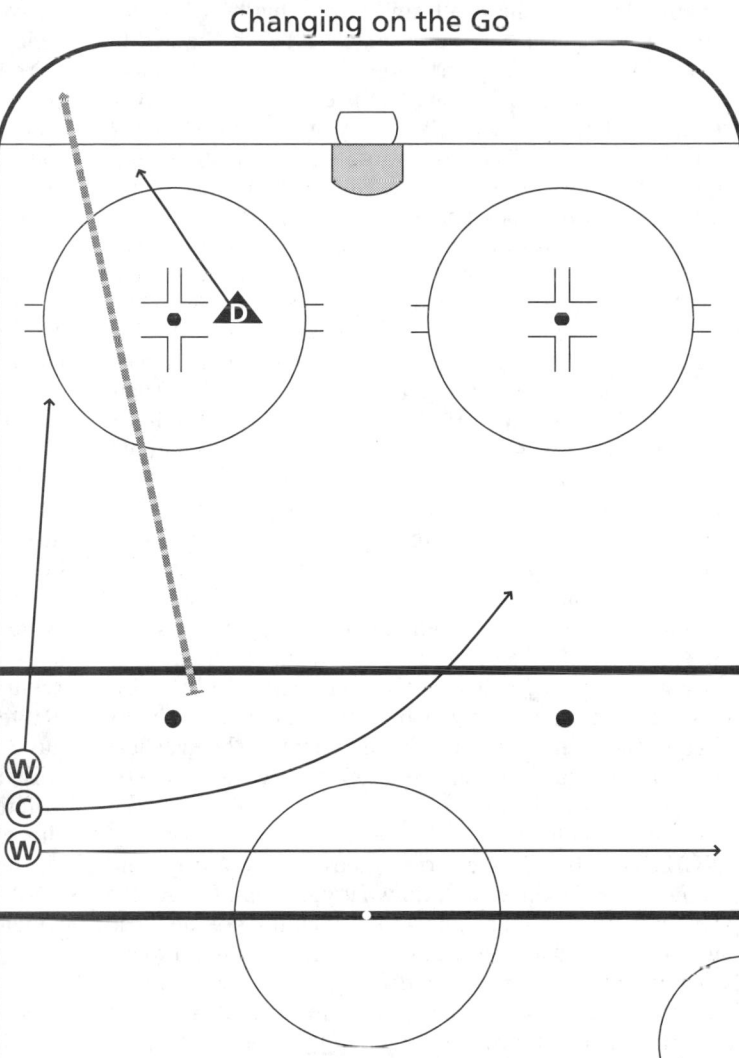

Changing on the Go

and gets their checkers out. If you're trying to keep your top guys away from their checkers and your guys just got out there, it's hard for them to come off. So you've got to weigh how important it is to get away from that checking line. And sometimes your matchups at the beginning of the game might be completely different than at the end of the game. You might want to go power against power but then, if you get a lead, you might want checkers against their power. And if you're ahead and you can get them to put their checkers on against your power, that's good, because it keeps their scorers off the ice. But if the matches aren't working or it's costing your team momentum, no matter what your plan was, a coach has to be ready to say, "It's not working, we're not going to match any more." I don't think you can be stubborn about that. Matching can be overrated, but it seems to me if you can get your guys on against the other team because of size or skill or whatever—without disrupting your team—you should do it.

Ken Dryden wrote in The Game *that he asked Habs coach Scotty Bowman what a coach's most important job was, and Scotty replied: "To get the right players on the ice."*

NEALE: The minute some coaches see a matchup they don't like, they may change the line, put the player on another line, or double-shift him on two lines. To get away from matchups, Scotty will play a guy on two different lines and force you to come up with a scheme to go against both

of them. He knows he can't always pull his best line off every time he sees the checkers come out. This makes it difficult for you to get any more than one matchup. If you think you're going to be able to match two lines against two, if the other guy doesn't want you to, you'll have a tough time doing it. Then you're going to have to decide which is the one you're going to work hard to get. When Scotty coached the Penguins, he'd "hide" Mario Lemieux, play him out of position or on a different line, so the other coach couldn't get the matchup out against him. If you are going to try matching lines against Scotty, you are going to have to have two lines ready to play against him. If you want to check Fedorov, you put someone out, he might pull Fedorov off and your guy is left with someone else. Then he comes right back with Fedorov, and you've got to have a second unit to go against him. Or he may not pull him off that first time. So you have to be comfortable with two units. It's a real test of the will of a coach who goes against a match-up coach, because you can't get everything you want—even when you are at home. Eventually he settles into something he likes and so do you. And that's the scariest thing about matchups, when your matchups are the same as the other guy's. Then you say, "Wait a minute, here … Is he right?'—especially when it's a guy like Scotty, who loves to match and does it way better than anyone. I used to kid Scotty, "Tell me the truth. You'd rather win the matchup than win the game." It's not true, of course, but it is very important to him.

NEILSON: If the other coach doesn't care about your matchups, you might as well do what you want. But sometimes they're more concerned with not letting you do what you want, rather than trying to get what they want. So when the game begins, especially when you're on the road and the other team has last change, you can make it look like you're trying to get a certain matchup, but you're just pretending to want that. They'll take a line off to keep them away from your guys and put them on again later and you can put out who you really want against them.

NEALE: I've often thought that the matchup some coaches want is not the line that starts after a whistle, it's the one coming out. Roger is a matchup coach if there ever was one, and in 1982 when he coached us to the finals in Vancouver, he drove Chicago nuts in the Conference championships. He faked the matchup he wanted. He put a line out against Denis Savard's line and Bob Pulford thought that was the line Roger wanted. So he changed Savard's line and put him out on the next shift, or changed him on the fly and Roger would have the line out there that he actually wanted all along. But to do that, he had to have two lines he trusted. And if have that, the other guy simply can't get away from two lines.

NEILSON: When you're matching on the road, you can usually only get one matchup you want. If you try for more than one, you're just going to screw yourself up. One coach last year came into Philly and changed after every face-off to get his matchups. So our feeling was, we're going to make him change all the time because we're going to catch him on one of those changes. Still, it can favor a lesser team whose coach has convinced them that by matching we'll throw the other team off. If you can sell your team on that, you've got something in your favor. If you can get the other coach to take off his scorers when you put on your checkers, you'll see the faces of his players as they skate by to the bench and they're all put off.

You don't see a lot of double-shifting guys in recent years. It's a faster game with a lot of three-line hockey and you need four lines to double-shift a guy. You don't see four-line hockey now because often the fourth line isn't good enough. You have to have tough guys who are really good checkers on your fourth line. If you have a good fourth line, you can do it.

NEALE: European teams never engaged in matchups. They put their three five-man units out and you coped with them any way you wanted. The Russians were the first I ever saw employing complete units of five and they stuck with them.

NEILSON: You knew who was coming on, you'd put your guys out and they didn't care. I think they felt, "We're just going to worry about ourselves." I'd watch them practice and they'd have a power-play unit at each end against penalty killers and after a few minutes they would just switch and the penalty-killing unit would add a guy and go on the power-play and the power-play unit would kill penalties. Each group of five was capable playing both special teams. That was pretty good. They had a lot of skilled guys. They had great chemistry within their units and that's why they wanted to use them all. They composed their lines differently, each one having a checker, a playmaker and a shooter, each group was complete within itself and I can see advantages to that. We do it completely differently, having whole lines who are offensive or defensive. Who knows which method is best?

NEALE: North American coaches recently have begun using five-man units sporadically. Most notable was Detroit's "Russian Five" in 1997. The difference is, when you played against Russia's five-man units, although one was better than the others, they were all trying to play the same way. When you played Detroit and you are trying to check "the Russian Five," you face a group that plays a completely different style than Scotty's other groups. There have been others in the NHL: Kevin Constantine did it in 1994 when he had Larionov, Makarov and Ozolinsh on the Sharks and again at times with Pittsburgh in 1997–98. When the Rangers won the Cup in 1994, Mike Keenan used a five-man unit with Messier's line and Leetch's defense tandem. These units are allowed to play a different style and coaches want that weapon, although injuries, penalties, guys playing below their capability can prevent it. But first, you have to believe in that theory before you assemble five-man units that you really like and want to use.

Winning face-offs always has been important, but the execution has changed.

NEILSON: Teeder Kennedy of the 1940s Leafs was one of the first great face-off artists and I once asked him to help the Leafs with face-offs in the 1970s. But the game was different. He had all these little plays based on how the other team was lined up. He might tell his wing on the boards to jump through and he'd flip it ahead to him right off the draw. Back then, wings lined up along the boards in the defensive zone. By the time he worked with us, big shots from the point meant you had to get out quickly to block that shot so we had stopped lining up that way.

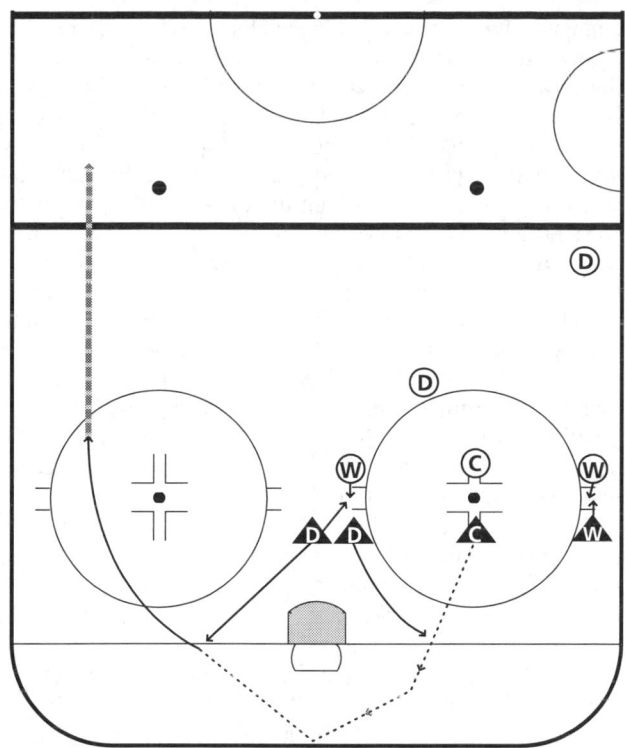

Penalty-Killing Defensive Zone Face-off Strategy

comes back and grabs the puck while the others block the forwards and he'll bang it off the boards. Sometime the guy blocking in the slot will just hold the forward up to allow the guy with the puck some time, then come over to get the puck off the boards so he can clear it.

NEALE: Every team has a set of rules if they lose it in their zone. The strategy for the defense has long been to try to take away the point shot. The defensive wings charge the point men. For a long time, the offensive team would try to make them fight their way through, using football-style blocks. But today, we see a lot of obstruction-interference penalties for that.

Coaches have developed many set offensive plays if they win the draw. The first—and simplest—was probably just drawing it back to the point for a shot.

NEILSON: When I was in Chicago, we had Doug Wilson on the point and he had a big shot. So we'd put two men in the slot and get the puck back to him and he'd fire. The two guys would go to the net for a rebound. *(see Power-Play – Offensive Zone Face-off Strategy diagram)*

NEALE: Roger had an offensive play when he coached the Leafs where Lanny McDonald would be on his off wing along the boards. Darryl Sittler would tie up the other center and get the puck behind him. Lanny would come over and just slap it or take a step and shoot it. It was impossible for the guy lined up with McDonald to stay with him. The only way to stop him was with your defenseman lined up in the slot, who was going to go out to block the point shot. He had to take Lanny on the way out to the point. But Tiger Williams was there to try to tie that guy up. It became known as "the Lanny McDonald face-off play" and is still used today. *(see Lanny McDonald Face-off Play diagram)*

NEILSON: Wayne Gretzky still does this one: in the offensive zone, his team won't put anyone along the boards and if no one from the other team is there either, he'll put it there and then go get it himself and make a play. Most teams now put someone on the boards when Gretzky's facing off, but once in a while he'll get that play. *(see Wayne Gretzky Face-off Play diagram)*

NEALE: In the four-men-up face-off, you bring one defenseman up and put him about three or four feet off the

NEALE: One of the first strategic plays I recall on face-offs was the defenseman taking the draw in the defensive zone. He'd draw it back to a more skilled guy who could use his imagination to get the puck out of the zone. Until the early 1960s, you'd also see the defenseman taking the face-off just run through the opposition center on the drop. His own center would be behind him and he'd come up and get the puck. Then face-off interference became a minor penalty and they put the lines in and made them line up.

NEILSON: There's a lot more strategy on penalty-killing face-offs today. *(see Penalty-Killing – Defensive Zone Face-off Strategy diagram)* Teams are putting their defensemen on the slot side of the circle and the wing on the boards side. As soon as the puck is dropped, the forwards start moving toward the puck, and if the penalty-killing center can draw it back, one of the defensemen

Power-Play Offensive Zone Face-off Strategy

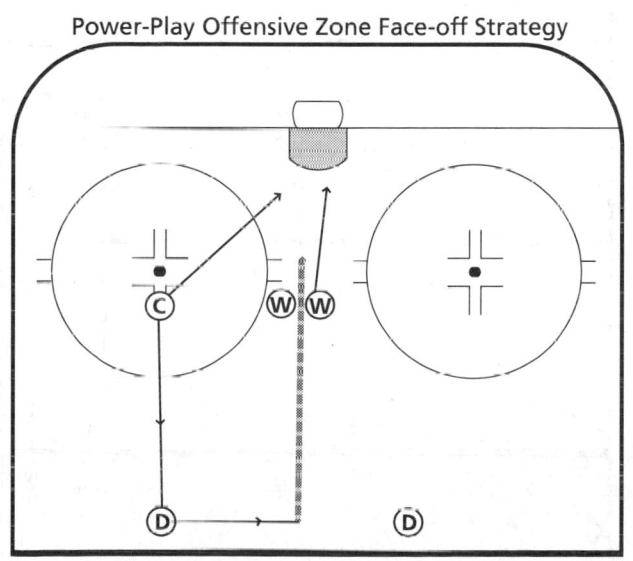

Lanny McDonald Face-off Play

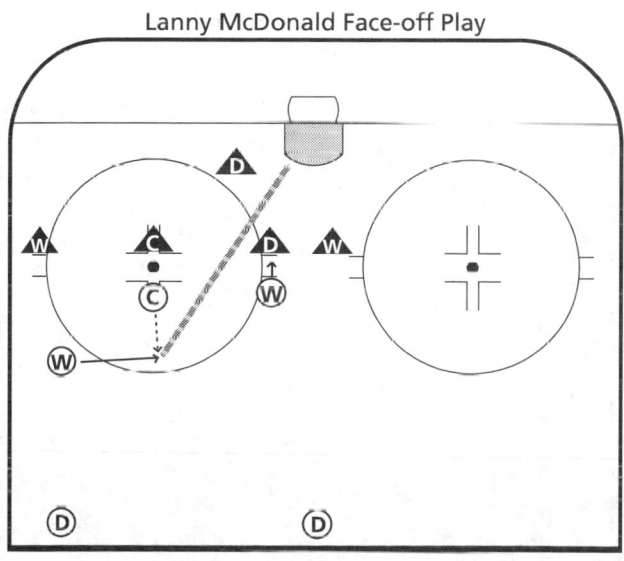

Wayne Gretzky Face-off Play

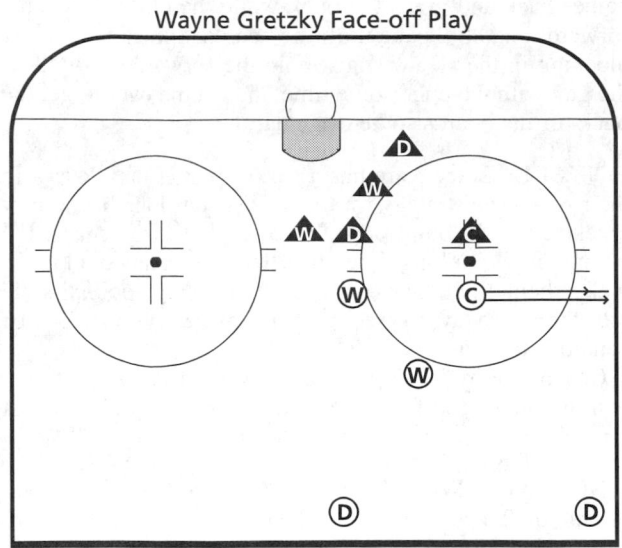

line and usually on the outside. The other defenseman is inside the blue line in the middle of the zone. It gives you more guys to recover the puck if the draw is not cleanly won. If the face-off is scrambled and it's on the board side, the "up" defenseman steps in and gets it back to the "back" defenseman for the shot. If it goes to the other side, he hustles back to his position. This has become very popular on the power-play. *(see Four-Men-Up Face-off diagram)*

In the neutral zone we see plays after a draw where one defenseman throws it to the other defenseman while the wings cross over and look for a pass. At the end of periods, you'll see teams sending out two centers and then they'll try to get the other team's centerman thrown out by cheating on the face-off. Turning the bottom hand over is a new tactic, the theory being you get more leverage. The downside is the other team knows where you are going with it. But some guys do it all the time—although sometimes their tactic is to tie your stick up and kick it somewhere. So it doesn't mean that they always try drawing it back.

Power-plays are one area where coaches have significant input into offensive strategy.

NEALE: At one time on the power-play, your defenseman's job was to move it to the forwards quickly. That

Four-Men-Up Faceoff

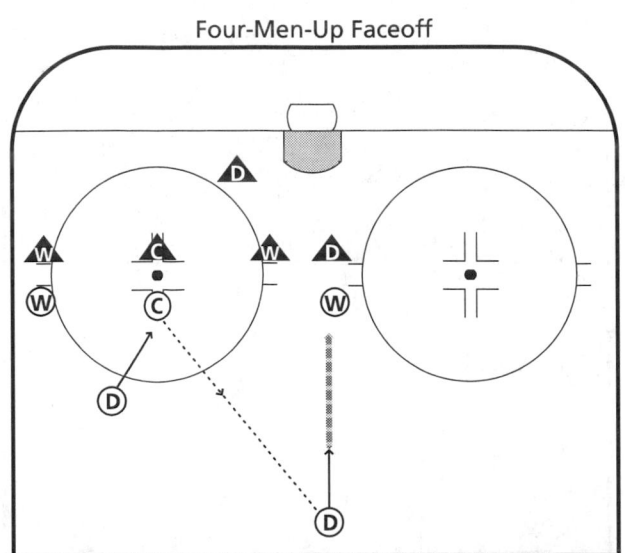

changed when teams put specialists on the point. Max Bentley may have been the first forward to play the point on the power-play. Andy Bathgate and Bernie Geoffrion did it later. They all had great shots—Geoffrion the best—but the others were great stickhandlers and passers. The theory was, when the puck was iced, Bentley would go back, get it and lead a smart rush, getting the puck to one of their forwards on the fly. With Geoffrion, Montreal would gain the zone and get it back to "Boomer," who'd get it on net. In those days, only two or three guys on each team had exceptional shots. Now only two or three don't and some defensemen shoot harder than forwards. Doug Harvey played back there with Geoffrion and, like Bentley, he could skate with it, get it to forwards in more dangerous positions or give it to Geoffrion, so they had options. Then you started to see guys like Camille Henry who became adept at tip-ins, redirecting the point shot into the net.

Since Bobby Orr's time, teams want a strong skater and passer to quarterback the power-play, making good passes to the forwards and joining the play as a fourth forward. He, or someone on the power-play, has a big shot when the team sets up. Traditionally, it came from the point, but it can be from wherever your trigger man works best. The Orr-era Bruins worked the puck to Phil Esposito in the slot. He was big, hard to move, had a great release and the ability to move around and find the opening in the middle of the box. Mike Bossy and Jari Kurri had that same ability. Brett Hull

1970s Power-Play Entry

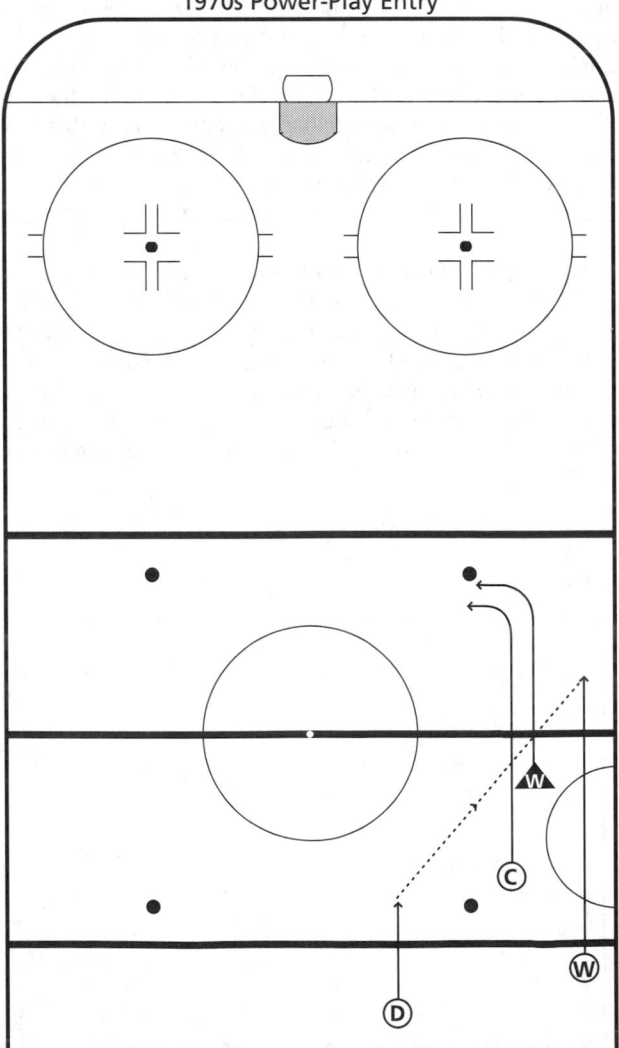

has it, too. He gets on the off wing between the dot and the top of the circle, looks for the one-time pass from the other side and just wires it.

NEILSON: Going back 15 or 20 years, we never used shoot-ins on the power-play. One entry on the power-play *(see 1970s Power-Play Entry diagram)* was you'd have your breakout and you'd end up with a guy coming down the boards with another guy trailing him and the puck carrier would cut in toward the middle and the penalty killer would go with him. The trailer would be open and you'd pass to him. Then teams started to clog up that area around the blue line. They'd pounce right on you. The way to beat that was to shoot it in. But today you've got to be careful because some goalies shoot it out like a third penalty-killing defenseman.

When goalies started to stop the shoot-in behind the net, teams countered with various things to keep it away from the goalie. Al MacInnis and Brent Severyn could fake the ring-around and put the puck on net. That kept the goalie anchored in the crease. Teams tried other things. The diagonal shoot-in off the glass was a bit risky because it comes off the boards bouncing and its easier for the penalty killers to recover and ice it. The softer cross-corner dump-ins were also a problem because it's the furthest point away from where the puck is, so its hard to recover unless you've got a guy going hard to that corner. It's much better to dump it into your corner because you keep yourself in the play.

Some skilled players still don't like dumping it in, but coaches like it because you recover a high percentage. Today's standard power-play involves shooting it in, but it starts in your own zone, with the defenseman behind your net. *(see Modern Power-Play diagram)* The center circles back, the other "D" is in the corner and he starts up. One wing is at the boards at the near blue line and as the breakout starts, he cuts across for a potential pass up the middle. The other wing is at the far blue line cutting the opposite way and he delays for a potential pass blue line to blue line. The timing is important here. As the defenseman moves out, if everyone is running their routes properly, he's got lots of options. As soon as you get the red line, you shoot it in. The idea is that you ring it around behind the net and you can get three guys on the puck. And you should always recover it because the other team can't afford to send more than two men in to recover it, so they're outmanned. And often, if they've sent two men in, they're in a bad position. So you can start to work it around for the shot you want.

NEALE: The favored NHL play is still the point shot. You want to shoot from the middle of the rink so you may have to pass it around a little to get the shooter in position, and then two or three forwards go to the net. The shot might go in, be screened, be tipped in or there might be a rebound to put it in. The ultimate objective for the European power-play was, and still is, to make a perfect play for a tap-in. They'll pass the puck and move around much more, trying to get a goalmouth pass where the guy just taps it in. The theory is if we pass the puck quickly enough, those four guys can't be five places. It was a big play in the WHA with Nilsson, Hedberg and Hull in Winnipeg and then the Stastnys in Quebec.

Penalty killers once stayed on the full two minutes, ragging the puck and hoisting it down the ice. Today they are on for 20 seconds.

NEALE: Going back to the "Original Six" days, you had guys whose main job was to kill penalties. They might only see the ice when their team was shorthanded. In the 1960s, coaches started using two sets of penalty-killing forwards, changing them midway through the kill. As coaches started to play more of their bench, these guys also had defensive responsibilities at even strength. Today, you sometimes see three sets, taking 20-second shifts.

Gretzky and Kurri may have been the first big offensive stars to be part of the penalty-killing. The last thing I'd say to my forwards when we saw them out there was "Be careful of the shorthand goal"—and already I'd be taking the edge off the power-play. There have always been different

Modern Power-Play Breakout and Entry

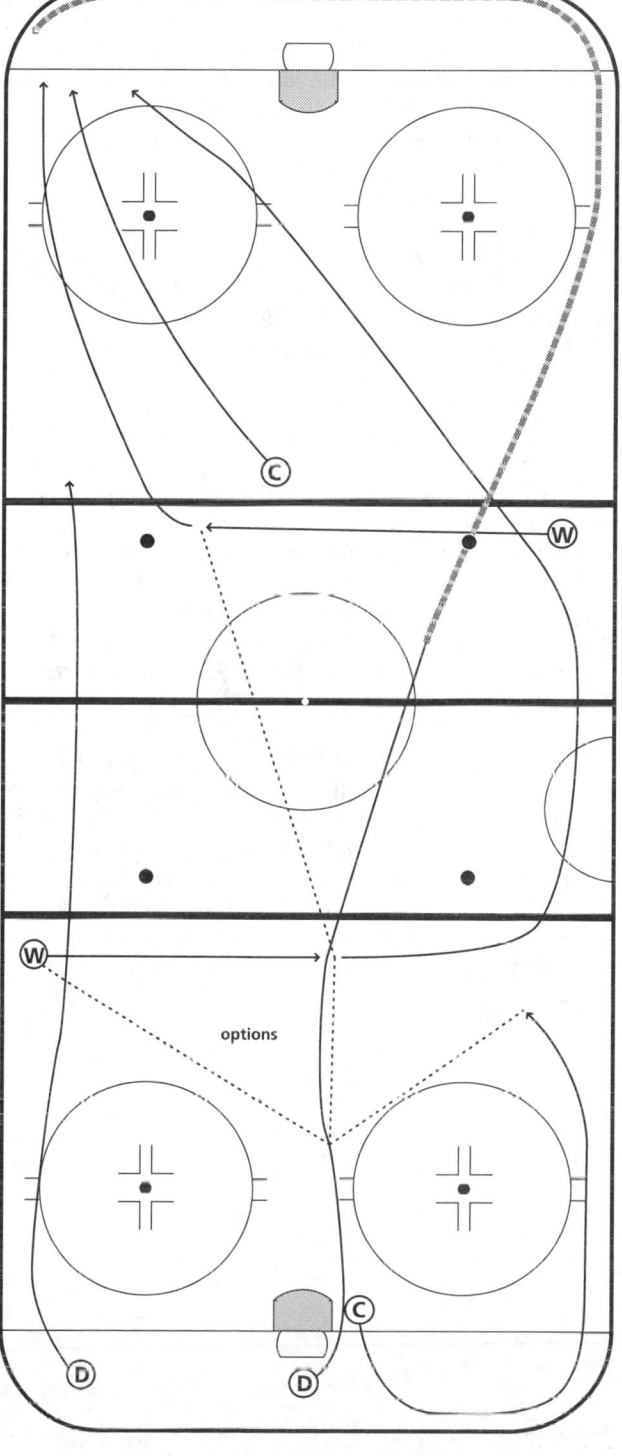

theories about penalty-killing. Some coaches have liked the penalty killers to forecheck, to keep the puck out the offensive zone as long as possible. But they had to be careful not to get caught. The first guy would circle and come back and the second guy would circle, but if you could beat the first guy, you had three or four against their three and could easily move down the ice with control. Other coaches were more cautious and tried not to get caught by backing their players off.

The way these two theories appear today is this—one: we're going to force you in all three zones, or two: we're going to passively force you but when you get into the neutral zone, you're going to find four of us lined up.

You might try to stickhandle past us and you'll get by sometimes but when you don't, it's a shorthand breakaway or a two-on-one. Some teams employ both strategies. The active penalty kill is all the rage today: force them in the end with one guy, force the puck carrier in the neutral zone, don't let them just walk to the red line, make them do something before the red line so they can't shoot it in. We'll always have three guys back there. And if you don't get to forecheck—let's say you're changing your players—then you just line up at the blue line.

Once they gain the zone, the defense forms the "box," which originated in the late 1950s or early 1960s. Roger points out, "the main object of the box, once you're in it, is to take away the points," so perhaps the box developed after big shots from the point became more of a factor.

NEILSON: Teams eventually learned if they sat in the box for the full two minutes, there was a good chance they'd get scored on. So they began to use more pressure. Immediately upon entry or after a face-off, or if the puck is fumbled, one guy goes after the puck carrier and everyone else killing the penalty puts pressure on their man. So there's pressure all over. Of course when everyone is putting pressure on, you're just a fraction of a second away from being caught at it. *(see Penalty-Killing with Pressure diagram)*

NEALE: You can be aggressive in your zone when the puck is up for grabs or rolling, but once they get clear possession, you can't run into the corner and get it. When they get clear possession, you're a bit less aggressive. Your emphasis then is to take away the point shot. When they've got a big point shooter like Al MacInnis on the point, you key on him. You want one guy always within a stick's length of him. You want to make it hard to get the puck to

him or make it hard to get his shot through. If he passes it, then you've done the job because you've made the best shooter pass it. Scotty had another approach he began using in Montreal. If the big shooter gets the shot off, even if it's challenged, the other guys get back and he's got to get that shot through a forest of skates, sticks and legs. The goalie's job is to get the high shots and the other guys stop the low shots from getting through.

European teams rarely forecheck on penalty-killing. They put four guys in the neutral zone, force a play or pass, wait for a mistake and ice it and make you start over again. They weren't very aggressive in the box, their theory being that the rink is so wide that if you get beaten being aggressive, you've got a mile and a half to get back to where you're supposed to be.

But really, the best penalty killer on any team is the goalie. If a team is sitting at the top of the penalty-killing list, it's not just the penalty killers, it's also the goalie, who has taken some goals away from the offense.

Among this dialogue's lessons is that, like a shark, the game cannot remain still. Where will hockey go from here? Will the convergence of North American and European styles continue? Will the complex sophistication of coaching methods advance even further? Will the future demand more speed, making a game that is fast already somehow faster? It's a long way from rugby on ice.

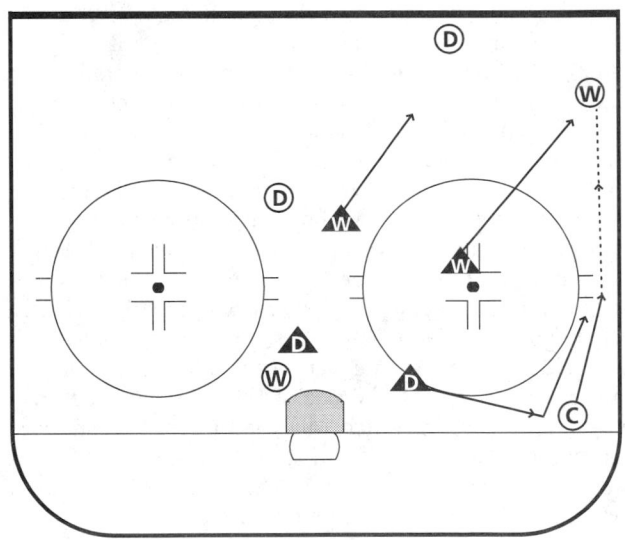

Penalty-Killing with Pressure

CHAPTER 54

Life in the Dressing Room

One of Hockey's Most Astute Observers on the Game's Inner Sanctum

Billy Harris

A VERY SMALL PERCENTAGE of the world's population ever visits, let alone uses, a dressing room. Actors and actresses use a dressing room to change into a particular character. Athletic teams use a dressing room to change into a uniform. The room itself has no character and no personality until you add players, a training staff and a coach. Then it becomes a team's inner sanctum. Players come together. Strategies are plotted. Differences are resolved. When things are going well, there can be no place you'd rather be. When they are not, you would rather be any place else.

As a youngster, one might use a change room to put on or remove the appropriate equipment before or after your games or practices. When the day's activity is done the young player heads home, carrying his or her gear. For several years, I carried my hockey equipment from home and boarded a streetcar that would take me to the Ravina Gardens, Varsity Arena, Icelandia or the Royals—the four indoor arenas that serviced Toronto's youth hockey community. Once you arrived at the arena, you were directed to a dressing room. After the game you reversed the procedure. This all took place during the 1940s before the city sprawled into the distant reaches of suburbia.

During the winter months many minor hockey games still were played outdoors, and in my case outdoor games were played at Withrow Park in Toronto's Riverdale neighborhood. For outdoor games I usually would change into my hockey equipment in the family living room, walk to the park carrying my stick and skates, and use the change room there to put on my skates. And then one day, it happened! Not only did I make the Junior B Weston Dukes, but—just as importantly—I was given my own spot in a permanent dressing room. At this particular magic moment, I no longer was responsible for transporting my equipment to and from the arena. That responsibility was assumed by a trainer. I no longer had to buy my own sticks, skates or any other hockey gear. After a practice or a game, I hung up my equipment and left the dressing room with both arms empty.

After playing our home games for two years at the Weston Arena, I then moved into a new dressing room in the northeast corner of Maple Leaf Gardens when I became a member of the Toronto Marlboros. (That particular room is used now as a lounge by Leafs wives and girlfriends.) Three years later, in 1955, I turned professional. This time I only had to move about 30 yards south to my new dressing room, which had housed the Toronto Maple Leafs since 1931. I had visited the Leafs dressing room nine years before as a 10-year-old on March 2, 1946. My uncle had won a "guess-the-score" contest and, as a result, I was able to attend a Leafs home game as a guest of Ed Fitkin, who was sports director for radio station CHUM and would later become public relations director for the Leafs. Mr. Fitkin picked me up at my house on Sparkhall Avenue and then we watched the Leafs defeat Chicago 9–4. After the game I

was taken into the dressing room. The players were all in a hurry. They were adjusting ties and they all wore fedoras. And then the dressing room was empty. The equipment had been packed in trunks and was on its way to Union Station. The players were heading to the station to catch the train for an out-of-town Sunday game. Almost 10 years later, on Saturday, October 8, 1955, the Toronto Maple Leafs dressing room became my dressing room.

The entrance to the Maple Leafs dressing room has been in exactly the same location since 1931. However, the interior has gone through many changes over the years. In 1955, once inside the door you would pass the entrance to a long narrow storage room on your right and then a left turn brought you into view of the main dressing room area. The room, almost square, had a wooden floor and the players' benches extended along the east and west walls. To the left there was a small medical room and in the far corners there were the washrooms and showers. There was also a stick rack with about 20 slots holding each player's sticks. Directly opposite the stick rack was a similar, smaller structure with 20 slots that served as our mail boxes. Overhead, above the players' bench on the east wall, were plaques depicting the names, management, wins, and losses of each Leafs team since 1931. On the north wall just outside the medical rooms was a plaque with the names of Leafs who had made all-star teams and another one with the players who had won individual awards. These historic plaques gave this otherwise very plain room its character.

This was our room for 35 games, practices and playoffs. For the other 35 games of our schedule we used the visitors room seven times a year in Montreal, Chicago, Boston, New York and Detroit. These five dressing rooms on the road were the epitome of "no frills." The visitors' room at the "G-aa-den" in Boston and at the Olympia in Detroit were both quite small. In Boston, the dressing room was not only small and antiquated but also frequented by rodents. It carried a putrid odor when the circus came to town. The small dressing room in Detroit was both adjacent to and separated from the ice by a spectator lobby. The visitors room on the north side of the old Madison Square Garden was large and spacious. At the Stadium in Chicago, the dressing room was adequate but we had to climb 13 steps four times per game to get to ice level. The Montreal Forum had the nicest visitors dressing room and it was just a few steps from the ice surface. Thirty-five times a year we entered these bare rooms just prior to a game. Within a half-hour after the game, the room was naked once again.

As a player, you share the room with your teammates. As a coach, the room becomes "yours." As a player, you listened. As a coach, you urged, lectured, badgered, pleaded, cajoled—whatever was necessary to arouse the athlete. The coach controls the dressing room, decides the time of meetings, decides when and if the media may enter, outlines his strategy, and by doing these things the dressing room

reflects his personality. In my first four years with the Leafs, the dressing room's personality changed annually. Between 1955 and 1958 we had four different coaches, starting with King Clancy and followed by Howie Meeker, Billy Reay and then Punch Imlach. I can remember just after Imlach became coach. Stafford Smythe made a rare appearance in the dressing room and told us that if we didn't start making some progress and start winning some games he would have no alternative except to trade players instead of replacing coaches.

I would describe the dressing room atmosphere on game nights from 1955 to 1965 as rather serious. There were always rumors that the coach had a couple of one-way train tickets direct to the minors for those who didn't take their jobs seriously. We had talented veterans like George Armstrong, Red Kelly, Ron Stewart, Bert Olmstead, Johnny Bower, Tim Horton and Allan Stanley, and we also had some mature young players. In those years each player negotiated his own contract in September. At age 20, you had the responsibility of haggling with a more experienced general manager over your salary and bonus clauses (both personal and team). Each year you negotiated one contract while the g.m. handled 35 such discussions and each year you tried not to repeat the negotiating errors you realized you made the year year before. There were no agents, and, as a player making major decisions on your own behalf, you became wise rather quickly. This is not to say that players didn't have fun before or after practice and that a lot of clowning around didn't take place. We seemed to have more fun when the team was playing well.

On a typical game day at Maple Leaf Gardens during the 1950s and 1960s, players would start arriving in the dressing room shortly after 10 a.m. The team meeting would begin at 11 o'clock and prior to its start, each player had two major responsibilities. The first was to go for a brief skate on the ice to make sure that your skates had been sharpened properly. The dress code was skates, suit or slacks and a blazer, plus shirt and tie.

The second responsibility was to "doctor" up at least three sticks and have them ready for game condition. The team meeting would just be a formality, discussing the visiting team's strengths and weaknesses and reviewing our own responsibilities. The only other thing we would do on game day was look after our tickets.

Good team chemistry seems to be a prerequisite for on-ice success. In the dressing room, which can become a refuge from the outside world, each player did his own thing. Bower, Pulford and Armstrong would head to the washroom for a cigarette; Olmstead would whittle away on his stick with his Swiss army knife; Eddie Shack, restless, would wander in and out of the medical room; Horton and Kelly would fall asleep. And then it would be time to exit through our dressing room door. Bower would lead us out to the ice where we would perform in front of 15,000 spectators and perhaps two million more on TV.

After most games, there was an entourage of visitors into our dressing room. They usually could be classified as well-wishers, hand-shakers or autograph-seekers. However, after one game, I can recall that we had only one visitor. In April of 1963 and April of 1964 we won the Stanley Cup, but in between—on January 18, 1964—the last-place Boston Bruins came to town and beat us 11–0. After the game, the dressing room was like a morgue. Then, perhaps the best hockey fan the Leafs ever had became the only visitor to enter the room. The late Wilf Snowden operated the special time clocks that kept track of individual player's ice time. He sauntered through the dressing room, sat down between Bobby Baun and myself and uttered, "those lucky buggers." I could hardly contain myself and responded: "Wilf, how can you call them lucky? They beat us 11–0."

Your hear many stories about dressing room characters. "Shackie" hadn't become one yet—Ed feared Imlach and those one-way train tickets. Later in his career, Eddie Shack became a very desirable tension-breaking character and was in demand, moving from Toronto to Los Angeles to Boston to Pittsburgh, and then back to Imlach in Buffalo. But my favorite story about a character in the dressing room involves Peter Mahovlich. The Montreal team was exhausted and resting prior to a Stanley Cup sudden-death overtime period and "not a creature was stirring." Peter quietly asked his reserved goalkeeper Ken Dryden, "do you have any nude pictures of your wife?" Ken, a little embarrassed, replied: "Of course not." Then Peter asked, "do you want to buy some?" Minutes later, Montreal scored to win another playoff game.

Nowhere else during my playing and coaching career did I ever experience the comfort and closeness I felt in the Maple Leafs dressing room. This is because I never spent as long a period in any other dressing room. As a coach for 12 years after my playing career, I never had a feeling of permanence—probably because I never spent more than three years as coach of the same team. That happened with the Laurentian Voyageurs, who played their home games at Sudbury's town arena. There, the Sudbury Wolves of the Ontario Hockey Association were the top team and, as a result, we used the visitors dressing room for three years. For the next three years, I coached in the World Hockey Association and in each of those years we were the number-two tenant. In year one, we were the Ottawa Nationals and played at the Ottawa Civic Centre. We did have a very comfortable dressing room though, as we played second fiddle to the junior Ottawa 67's. The next year, the Nationals became the Toronto Toros. We practiced at George Bell Arena in Toronto's west end and used the visitors dressing room. We played our games at Varsity Arena, where we were now second fiddle behind the University of Toronto Varsity Blues. Even though all are home games were at Varsity, not once did we practice there. The following season the Toros moved to a new location, but with home games now at Maple Leaf Gardens I don't have to tell you who the top tenant was. I was involved in designing the Toros dressing room in the northwest corner of the Gardens. Today, the old Toros room houses visiting NHL teams.

During my three years as a coach in Europe I really experienced the life of the gypsy. In 1971, I moved to Stockholm in September and coached the Swedish national team. I met the players on a Thursday. Friday we flew to Kosice, Czechoslovakia. Saturday we began an eight-day training camp. After returning to Sweden, the players reported to their respective elite teams in the Swedish League. For the next two months I scouted the league and it was my responsibility to select the 18 best players to represent Sweden at the 1972 Olympics in Sapporo, Japan.

I visited a lot of dressing rooms during this time but did not have my own. For our training period in Sapporo, we did not have a permanent dressing room and our games were played at different venues. We played Finland for the silver medal at nine o'clock in the morning. The group that really earned their keep during this time was the training staff, who were constantly packing and unpacking.

When I coached the Italian national team for two years, the feeling of impermanency continued. Once again it was my job to scout the elite first division teams and select an all-star squad that would become the national team that represent Italy at the IIHF's C Pool World Championships. Only two of the elite teams played under a roof—the other 10 played on outdoor surfaces. The Italian coaching experience was very challenging, especially in the dressing room. The national team was composed of 10 Italian players and 10 players of German ancestry. The Italians, naturally, communicated in Italian and the Germans in German. Very few players spoke or understood much English, though some could converse in French. For two years I coached through an interpreter.

I can remember just prior to the C Pool gold medal game in Copenhagen against Denmark that I purposely kept my pep talk very brief, just emphasizing one major offensive tactic and one defensive tactic. My pregame speech lasted about 25 seconds, then my interpreter, Juliano, had to tell the players in their language just what I had said. He spoke for five minutes. When I asked him what he said, he told me that he knew I had forgotten a few things that he thought they should be reminded of. To this day I do not know the content of his translation. Language had not presented a serious problem for me in Sweden because most players there had learned English as a second language in school. But there was one exception—Borje Salming. Borje had been born and raised in northern Sweden, just south of Lapland, and spoke only Swedish.

Late in my coaching career I was with the Sudbury Wolves of the OHL. Several players were high school students and we would practice and have team meetings after school hours. On several occasions I would have one of the dozen meddling owners phone me at home prior to supper, questioning some of the comments I had made a few hours earlier. The team trainer was a human tape recorder. There is a strong belief in the sporting fraternity that things said and done in a dressing room should be strictly "off the record." I do not necessarily find this totally true, but I do believe that all players should use discretion when discussing dressing room events.

In the modern parlance, hockey players refer to their inner sanctum simply as "the room." Character players and team leaders are said to be "good in the room." On reflection, the only room that has provided real memories for me—mostly pleasant—was the one at Maple Leaf Gardens. All the others I visited as a player and a coach appear as a blur on my mental computer. The last memorable occasion in my room took place on April 25, 1964. We had defeated Detroit 4–0 in game seven to win our third consecutive Stanley Cup title. For some reason, I was in no hurry to leave the room (not knowing at the time that I never would again be in there for a playoff game). I hadn't played much during the series, but because of injuries Imlach was forced to use me on left wing with Dave Keon and George Armstrong for games six and seven. In those two games I was +4 —not bad for a "weak defensive player." I was busy taking photos and socializing with teammates, experiencing a combined feeling of total exhaustion and total satisfaction. The next thing I knew, the room was empty and the Stanley Cup was sitting by itself on a small white table. I was surrounded by the plaques with the names of former Leafs—Clancy, Conacher, Primeau, Apps, Schriner, Kennedy, Broda, Klukay, Bentley, Barilko ... I was alone but enjoying the company. I left the dressing room and carried the Stanley Cup over to the Westbury Hotel, where Bobby Baun was hosting a party.

I was traded to Detroit in May of 1965. Twenty-six years later, I returned to my dressing room for the first time. The Toronto Maple Leafs Alumni were playing an oldtimers' game against the Montreal Alumni. It was March of 1991. As Leaf alumni, we were assigned the Maple Leafs dressing room to change. I felt like an intruder or a trespasser. My room was somebody else's now.

CHAPTER 55
Black Hockey History

William Humber

JACKIE ROBINSON'S DEBUT with baseball's minor-league Montreal Royals in 1946 changed sports forever. Until then athletes of black African descent had largely been banned from most mainstream sporting leagues in North America. Robinson experienced racial abuse not only from spectators but his on-field rivals, and some players on his future major-league team, the Brooklyn Dodgers, asked to be traded rather than take the field with him.

During the next decade the National Football League and its rival the All-American Conference, as well as the Canadian Football League, and the National Basketball Association integrated their lineups. The National Hockey League did not follow suit until 1958 but it alone of the big sporting leagues claimed that it never had any restrictions. It could point to the participation of black athletes in many levels of organized amateur and professional hockey since the past century.

Why, then, were there no blacks in the NHL until 1958? At first glance the answer was simple. Hockey players until the 1970s were drawn largely from Canada and that country's black population was tiny. Moreover, some suggested there might be cultural reasons that precluded even Canada's limited black population from playing the game. The NHL, strongly rooted in Canada, could claim that it shared the Canadian tradition of open-mindedness on matters of race so if there ever were black hockey players good enough to play in the NHL, they'd get their chance.

Herb Carnegie, however, has cast doubt upon the NHL's professed heritage of fair hiring. As well, the celebration at the 1998 All-Star Game of the 40th anniversary of Willie O'Ree's NHL debut raised additional questions about the atmosphere encountered by pioneering black players.

Even today, this atmosphere can, at times, turn foul. Several black players were subject to racial taunts in NHL games in 1997–98. The most notable was Chris Simon's on-ice slur against Mike Grier of the Edmonton Oilers. Grier, an American black and son of a National Football League administrator, had already found his somewhat unique identity a significant issue in the United States. Perhaps because of this he worked as a volunteer in the Hockey in Harlem program that brought the game to under-privileged children in New York.

Few could understand how Simon, an Ojibway native from Wawa, Ontario could be so insensitive to the reality of another minority member of the NHL. "That's what was strange to me, that it was someone who has his background and his race," Grier said. In any case Simon, who apologized directly and quickly to Grier, was suspended.

So What's the Truth?

Any fair study of black hockey participation must begin with the national origins of its players. As noted, until recently they were almost overwhelmingly Canadian. In the mid 1960s, for instance, the six-team NHL had only one non-Canadian (Boston Bruin Tommy Williams from Duluth, Minnesota.) Statistically, until that time the odds had never favored a large number of black players. Canada's black population as late as the 1950s comprised just over one-tenth of one percent of the national total. There were only 120 NHL jobs, meaning that if all players were Canadian, the entire black population of Canada would have been a single candidate along with four other applicants for one statistical position.

The background of NHL players has changed dramatically in the last 20 years, but even this has not necessarily helped the chances of black athletes because it has been due to the influx of players from American colleges, Russia, Sweden, the Czech Republic and other European countries. Only in the United States has there been historically substantial black communities and these have hardly been hockey hotbeds. Other sports such as basketball, football and baseball offered better infrastructure and more apparent opportunities. By the start of the 1997 season, 22 blacks had played in the NHL.

The Early Days of Hockey

Hockey's initial era of mass fascination occurred in the 1890s when what was an almost folksy game suddenly attained organizational and promotional support.

At the same time, however, the number of blacks in Canada was plunging due to the return of many former slaves to the United States. A populace that numbered over 60,000 (nearly two percent of the national total) prior to the American Civil War had tumbled to just over 16,000 by 1911, a number that amounted to one-fifth of one percent of the country's total. Despite this, members of that remaining population played the game. It was an early indicator that they felt themselves to be a part of the emerging identity of the new country.

In 1899 Hipple "Hippo" Galloway, the son of Mr. and Mrs. William Galloway, long-time residents of Alder Street in Dunnville, Ontario, played for the Woodstock team in the Central Ontario Hockey Association. A Woodstock paper under the headline *Colored Hockey Players* noted: "Galloway is a right good sport and thoroughly game player. He withstood all kinds of punishment in Hamilton last week and fairly won his spurs. The colored player is proverbially cool and collected, so essential to hockey." Galloway's hockey record is largely unknown, although there are references to a two-goal night in Hamilton and a couple of excellent passes to set up goals in Paris, Ontario.

Galloway was not alone. Charley Lightfoot of the Stratford team was a second black player in the league and accorded recognition as one of the better players in the Central Ontario Hockey Association. This was the darkest era of Jim Crow legislation and imposed segregation in the United States. Despite Canada's more liberal heritage, the shameful parroting of American models led to Galloway's banishment that summer from an Ontario baseball league because an American import objected to his presence. Galloway left Canada to barnstorm with a black baseball

team and a local sportswriter cried: "An effort should be made to keep Hippo in town. Our hockey team needs him."

The Colored Hockey League

At the same time a Colored Hockey League was formed in Atlantic Canada, replicating the Negro Baseball Leagues in the United States. It is unclear whether players were forced to develop a separate institution because of racial exclusion or if they felt, like many other minorities in Canada, the need for their own association as a means of retaining a community identity.

The Colored Hockey League of the Maritimes formed in 1900 included teams from Africville (the Seasides), Dartmouth (the Jubilees), Halifax (the Eurekas), Truro (the Victorias) and Amherst (the Royals). It was a Nova Scotia-based league but at least one other province, Prince Edward Island, had an all-black team featuring five members of the Mills family and two others that played all-white teams on the island and black teams in Nova Scotia.

Most fans were white and paid admission of 25 or 35 cents. Crowds often numbering 1,200 expected not only good hockey but occasional self-mockery or clowning, and would show their contempt if they were not forthcoming.

Exhibitions by black hockey teams in Nova Scotia continued well into the 1920s and their playing innovations included a rule allowing the goalie to fall to the ice to block a shot before such legislation entered the NHL rule book.

Bud Kelly

No other part of Canada had the size and proximity of a black population to support the kind of league found in Nova Scotia. Yet so powerful was the metaphor of hockey to the Canadian experience that black children were determined to play the game.

In the first two decades of the 20th century Fred "Bud" Kelly was, according to Frank Selke, "the best Negro hockey player I ever saw." Kelly claimed that his first pair of skates were two whiskey flasks that he found on his father's Ingersoll farm and tied to a pair of shoes. Gliding across the snow gave him his first taste of skating.

In 1916 Kelly was a member of Selke's seven-man 118th Battalion hockey team based out of London, Ontario, which played at the intermediate level of the Ontario Hockey Association. While a member of Peterborough's OHA senior team, he was scouted by Bruce Redpath, manager of the NHL's Toronto St. Pats (later the Maple Leafs). In a game against Toronto Varsity, Kelly flubbed a breakaway opportunity deliberately set up to see if Kelly could put the puck in the net. "I was so flabbergasted by the fact that neither defenseman even laid a glove on me that I just stopped and let the puck roll off my stick," Kelly recalled. The St. Pats never contacted him.

Kelly believed that race did not play a part in his lost opportunity and in fact suggested that so-called amateur hockey held better rewards than the NHL. Small-town entrepreneurs would make payments under the table and find players jobs in the off-season. Kelly worked as a chauffeur for the McClary family in London, a position he held for a half-century.

George Barnes and the St. Catharines Orioles

Another outstanding black player of that era was George Barnes, who played in the 1920s for Cayuga at the intermediate level in the Ontario Hockey Association. Barnes was part of a local community descended from black slaves.

According to Dunnville historian E.G. Hastings: "In a contest in Cayuga on December 30, 1929, with Caledonia as the visiting team, Barnes was involved in an incident in which an Indian player on the Caledonia team, Wid Green, received a severed muscle in the groin and succumbed from loss of blood. I was the referee at this game and it was recorded as the first known hockey fatality in the OHA."

In 1937 an all-black team, the St. Catharines Orioles, played in the Niagara District Hockey League against white teams. They were affiliated with a local quarry operator, Walker Brothers. It's unclear whether black players were barred from other teams or if they chose to form their own team as an outgrowth of local community life.

St. Catharines' black population had numbered in the thousands prior to the American Civil War but declined slowly as former fugitive slaves returned to the United States after the war. Nevertheless it still had 700 members in the 1930s and its hockey team was largely made up of ancestors of one of the community's founding members in the 1850s, Adam Nicholson.

To its credit, organized hockey did not practice the out-front, deliberate, exclusionary and all-encompassing policy of baseball. Further evidence of this was the career of Sam Bright, a nephew of George Barnes, who played in the late 1940s and early 1950s for the Fort Erie Spears of the Niagara District Hockey League. Pay and the level of play in senior hockey were often comparable or better than those of the National Hockey League.

As for the NHL, its own practices are somewhat more ambiguous, and its role more sinister, in regard to the black hockey player.

Herbie Carnegie

It has been argued that the absence in the 1930s and 1940s of a black hockey player on the superstar level of baseball players such as Satchel Paige or Josh Gibson refutes any notion that the NHL practiced discriminatory hiring. The experience of at least one player challenges that assumption.

In what is now the North York portion of what is now known as the megacity of Toronto, the best black player of his era, Herb Carnegie, played pond hockey with his brother Ossie. In the early 1930s he entered his first organized hockey competition at Lansing Public School. His father, born in Jamaica, cautioned him against his boyhood dream by telling him: "They won't let any black boys in the National Hockey League."

Carnegie advanced through the-then tough high school circuit and played junior hockey, practicing regularly at Maple Leaf Gardens. One day his coach told him that the shadowy figure watching in the upper blues was Toronto Maple Leafs owner Conn Smythe and that Smythe had indicated he'd sign Carnegie immediately if only someone could make him white.

Carnegie has lived with the comment throughout his entire life. While others have corroborated the intent, Smythe himself never publicly spoke on this issue and there is no direct evidence that such a sentiment formed a part of official NHL policy.

It's unlikely, however, that the NHL ever contemplated being a leader among North American big-league sports in opening its doors to black athletes. The history of sports segregation had its roots in the Reconstruction period after the American Civil War. It was the time immediately before

hockey's rules were set down and the game began to grow. By the time the NHL was established in 1917, the separation of the races in sports was simply an accepted reality.

Carnegie may not have been a superstar on the level of banned baseball players but he was something special; a great skater and goal scorer who won most valuable player awards in the superior Quebec Senior League, from which an eventual teammate, Jean Beliveau, graduated, as did NHL legends Doug Harvey and Jacques Plante. Finally, in 1947 the New York Rangers invited him to their camp but Carnegie had to negotiate his way through the Ranger farm system before being offered a contract to play just below the NHL.

The Rangers may have been imitating baseball's Brooklyn Dodgers, who had Jackie Robinson play a year of minor-league ball before his Brooklyn debut. They were not prepared to offer Carnegie a big league start and he opted to return to Quebec where the pay was better.

By failing to give Carnegie a big-league contract the NHL lost an historic opportunity to position itself as the one major league that had never discriminated.

Willie O'Ree

In some ways it was only a matter of time before a black player made the NHL. The NHL's black pioneer debuted in the city whose American League baseball team was the last to hire a black player. Both occurred around the same time. Willie O'Ree, ironically dubbed "King of the Near Miss" in a *Hockey Pictorial* profile in 1964, played his first game for the Boston Bruins on January 18, 1958. The near-miss label described his inability to score goals despite his great speed, which presented him with more opportunities than most hockey players.

Born in 1935 in Fredericton, New Brunswick, O'Ree played junior hockey in Kitchener in the mid-1950s before graduating to Quebec City's minor-league pro team. Called up by the Bruins in midseason, he managed only four goals in 45 games over two seasons. Nevertheless O'Ree made a career out of his average talent, particularly with the Los Angeles Blades of the Western Hockey League and later with San Diego in the 1960s.

At the time O'Ree said: "They've called me the Jackie Robinson of hockey, and I'm aware of being the first, and of the responsibilities, but I'm also aware that there have not been, and are not many, colored players able to play hockey, that there has never been the discrimination in this game there was in baseball, and that I didn't face any of the very real problems Robinson had to face."

In a later video documentary produced on his life, O'Ree did discuss a damaged right eye which restricted his playing ability and, more seriously, ugly incidents such as a racial taunting and butt-ending in the mouth from a Chicago Black Hawks player. It resulted in a fight and a vicious reaction from Chicago fans who were shocked that a black man would retaliate.

Other black players of O'Ree's era included Arthur Dorrington, a Canadian who signed with the Atlantic City Seagulls of the Eastern Amateur League in 1950, and O'Ree's Los Angeles teammate Stan Maxwell, the only other black player in organized hockey in the early 1960s.

Below the surface of NHL recognition were players like John Utendale. He played alongside Mark Messier's father Doug on the junior Edmonton Oil Kings, who went to the Western Canada finals in 1957. He later attended and played for the University of British Columbia.

Another pioneer hockey player, Windsor resident George "Kirk" Scott, was later memorialized in the International Afro-American Sports Hall of Fame. Scott, who attended Patterson Collegiate in Windsor in the late 1950s, was an acknowledged "rink rat" at the city arena who often came to school in need of rest. He played Junior B hockey in the Windsor area.

The Contemporary Scene

Mike Marson, who played 196 NHL games beginning in 1974, was the first of the contemporary black hockey players to enter the league following a long hiatus after O'Ree's career.

He recalled playing in Chicago where he was probably the only black person in the entire arena of 20,000 people: "A lot of people have never been faced with that type of difficulty or awareness. They miss the whole concept of what it's like to be the minority in a situation like that and the psychological setup you have to put yourself through going out on the ice night after night and the opposing teams are calling you whatever, and the guys are spitting in your face and then you're dealing with whatever goes on in the dressing room with your teammates."

Tony McKegney, with nearly 350 NHL regular season and playoff goals, including a 40-goal season in 1987–88 with the St. Louis Blues, was the first bona fide star of African-Canadian background. Born in Montreal, he was adopted by a family in Sarnia at the age of one and learned to play in the local system. "Sometimes I would wonder why I was trying to be a pro player when there were none to look up to. I'm proud of the fact that I was the first black to establish myself in the NHL [first appearing in 1978]. Now there are a few. I hope that helps youngsters who need someone to emulate."

The most successful black hockey player has been Grant Fuhr from Spruce Grove, Alberta, the number-one goalie for much of the Edmonton Oilers' Stanley Cup dynasty years of the 1980s when their superstar lineup included Wayne Gretzky, Mark Messier, Paul Coffey and Jari Kurri. It was a dazzling young team with great unity.

Gretzky could recall no instances of explicit racism on or off the ice and that black-white issues were raised only in the context of dressing room camaraderie. Fuhr was the first black to have his name on the Stanley Cup. Though Fuhr's career was interrupted by a suspension in the fall of 1990 after he admitted to substance abuse, it resumed successfully with Toronto and St. Louis.

Other significant black personalities have included John Paris from Windsor, Nova Scotia, the first black head coach in professional hockey who led the Atlanta Knights to the International Hockey League championship in 1994, and Anson Carter, a member of Canada's World Championship team of NHL players in 1997.

Carter's parents were both natives of Barbados and part of the great immigration boom of the modern era. They at first attempted to discourage his hockey playing because the sport was too rough, but despite being behind his Scarborough mates in skating ability he eventually surpassed them. Carter went on to a university career with the Michigan State University Spartans and was a member of Canada's 1994 World Junior champs.

CHAPTER 56
Sermon from the Rock
Alex Faulkner and Newfoundland Hockey
Mark Paddock

IF A STANLEY CUP CONTENDER was searching for a skilled and confident center in the early 1960s, then the island of Newfoundland was probably one of the very last places it would have looked. There were good reasons for this: The province had no professional or major junior hockey teams; it had a small population, well under half a million; it was far away, unknown and unscouted—heck, it didn't even join the Canadian Amateur Hockey Association until 1965. But the most compelling reason may have been this: No Newfoundlander had played in the NHL. Ever.

Sure, Hall of Famer Moose Watson was born in St. John's (the island's capital), but that was in 1898—and he played his whole career in the senior league in Ontario. So, yeah, there were plenty of reasons why Alex Faulkner shouldn't have been a Detroit Red Wing. But he was.

The simple fact that he was the first Newfoundlander to break NHL ice guaranteed Alex a special place in his fellow islanders' hearts. Still, that alone doesn't start to explain the near reverence, the misty nostalgia "the blond bomber" conjures up even today. You see, Alex became—and not by his own choice—something like a sociopolitical symbol.

When Premier Joey Smallwood guided Newfoundland into the Dominion of Canada in 1949, he did so largely by perpetrating the myth that it was too poor, sick and needy to stand on its own, which was partly responsible for the low esteem mainland Canadians would accord their new fellow countrymen. Faulkner's sudden ascent as a playoffs hero with Detroit in 1963 gave his people a much-needed burst of defiant pride. Finally, one of "our boys" had proved everyone wrong, had set every Newfie joke back on its ear.

The Faulkner story isn't just about one man, though. It's about two. In fact, it's about a whole family. Alex's older brother George was actually the first Newfoundlander to play professionally; younger brother Jack was the third to turn pro; the other two, Lindy and Seth, distinguished themselves in provincial senior hockey even though Seth had to stop early because of a badly broken leg.

The clan originated in Bishop's Falls, a small logging town in central Newfoundland where the boys were out playing shinny as soon as the ponds and the nearby Exploits River froze over in winter. George Faulkner recalls that their father would clear the ice on the river at night, then wake his sons before school the next day so they could get out for an early game. Local carpenters made them wooden goals; burlap sacks functioned as netting. "We used whatever we could get" as a puck, George remembers, but it was usually a thin slice of birch, skittish and hard to control.

These games may have been little but free-for-alls, but George believes they were crucial.

"We didn't know what we were doing; we didn't know the fundamentals. But we were out there doing them, especially skating and stickhandling. When you got the puck, you liked to keep it."

Moreover, with goalies who didn't wear pads, the boys rarely took shots. Playing a game of possession, they learned offense naturally.

Alex became a young star thanks to outstanding offensive skills—he could do everything well and with great intensity—and his first hint of big-league potential came in the late 1950s when the Boston Bruins came to the province to play exhibitions, including one against the young player's club in Grand Falls:

"We were waiting for the face-off, and Cal Gardner asked me, Have you ever considered going to the mainland?' I had no idea how I looked playing hockey, and I had no aspirations of playing [professionally]. Playing in the NHL was not something I grew up dreaming about because the dream was too far-fetched."

Still, if Alex needed proof you could go to the mainland and succeed, he didn't have to look far past George, who had gone to a junior tryout with the Quebec Citadelles in 1951 as the result of some luck and a break. Citadelles owner Frank Byrne had a brother who coached senior hockey in Grand Falls. Joe Byrne arranged for George and three other Newfoundlanders to attend Quebec's training camp and George earned a place at center on the Junior B squad. He stayed home for the next year to work (in a pulp and paper mill), but he went back to play Junior A for the Citadelles in 1953, this time on left wing. The Quebec Frontenacs bought and merged with the Citadelles during the season, and the revamped Frontenacs stormed to the provincial league title.

George subsequently signed a B-form with the New York Rangers (which meant he had an automatic invitation to their training camp in 1954) but Montreal decided he was too good to play for a rival and obtained his rights. He attended three straight training camps with the Canadiens from 1954 to 1956, only to be denied a spot every time by the team's tremendous depth. And he wasn't the first Newfoundlander to reach that point: Copper Leyte (who played junior with Jean Beliveau) also attended three Montreal camps in the early 1950s. But, unlike Leyte, George turned pro with the Shawinigan Falls Cataracts, Montreal's affiliate in the Quebec Hockey League, and played there from 1954–55 to 1957–58.

He probably would have made the Rangers—a losing team—but George harbors no bitterness: "I didn't let it bother me. If they weren't going to deal me, so what? I had my four years [in the QHL]. I didn't regret anything. Being with the Canadiens and the success they had, it was pretty hard to break into that."

Still, he had some close calls. In the 1955–56 season, Montreal's Dickie Moore cracked a bone in his wrist. Instead of calling up George, another left wing, the team called up right winger Claude Provost (who had played for the Jr. Canadiens). And he stayed—for 1,005 games and nine Stanley championships. "I get tormented once in a while about it," admits Alex. "Why call up Provost, who

wasn't a left winger?" Still, George is a more placid soul than his brother and says he understands the decision.

George actually had another chance that season but of a different kind: "When Dick Irvin Sr. left Montreal and went to Chicago to coach in 1955, he wanted to take a whole line—me, Claude Provost and Connie Broden—but the Canadiens wouldn't let us go. They called us the Kid Line. We were pretty good, quick and fast."

His career in Shawinigan was hardly a loss, though. The Cataracts won the league title in his rookie season as George shone in the spotlight, recording seven goals and five assists in 13 playoff matches. Then Shawinigan faced off against the Edmonton Flyers—Western Hockey League champs—for the Edinburgh Trophy. George's squad defeated Glenn Hall, Johnny Bucyk, Norm Ullman and the rest of a talent-heavy team in six intense games. One highlight for George was a two-goal game against Hall. "[The championship] was a big thing for me. I was the first Newfoundlander to turn pro. I was doing what I liked to do and doing fairly well."

The Canadiens organization molded George into a superbly fit two-way player. "George was the best all-around player who ever played hockey in Newfoundland," states Alex, repeating a view that is widely held by the province's hockey fans. "He could play any position. I often said jokingly that I'd like to put a set of pads on him for just one game. He probably would have had a shutout." Don Johnson, former president of the Newfoundland Amateur Hockey Association and the CAHA, remembers him as a great skater. "If he had to jump three steps sideways and two backwards, George was the best in the business."

George returned home in 1958 and accepted a post as athletic director in Harbour Grace, a small town in Conception Bay. With strong financial backing from future premier Frank Moores, he formed the most famous team in the province's hockey history to date, the Conception Bay All-Stars, who immediately became known as the CeeBees. Alex and Lindy came on board in year one and George moved to defense so he could get a better view (he was the playing coach). In the next 10 years, the high-scoring CeeBees made it to nine provincial finals and won four titles. Fate intervened for George again in 1965. At a coaching clinic in New Brunswick, he was spotted in a pickup game by Father David Bauer, manager of Canada's national team. He wanted George to join up. George consulted with Moores, who told him, "You gotta go," and he stayed with the Nationals through the 1966 World Championships in Yugoslavia.

Though they weren't as talented as the top European clubs, the Canadians were still undefeated in the tournament as they entered their third-last game against the Czechs, which they lost 2–1 when Czechoslovakia scored in the last minute. The referee disallowed two Canadian goals—one for no apparent reason except that the goal judge hadn't turned the light on, the other on a dubious penalty call—and hit Canada with 11 of the game's 15 penalties. Afterwards, the furious Canadians voted to go home but then changed their minds out of respect for Bauer. "It's time we quit the farce and play our own hockey," fumed coach Jack McLeod.

Canada lost its next game 3–0 to the USSR before beating Sweden to finish third and claim the bronze medal. With six markers, George led the team in goal-scoring at the tournament. Since he had not voted to go home after the Czech debacle, he was "very happy and very pleased about

[the medal]." Once more he had gone where no Newfoundlander had gone before.

By creating the CeeBees—and recruiting Alex—George indirectly paved the way for the start of his brother's career in the pros. In late 1960, the CeeBees played an exhibition match against a St. John's senior team coached by ex-Maple Leaf Howie Meeker. Alex performed brilliantly, as usual—the previous season, the St. John's *Evening Telegram* reported that he had scored over 100 goals in exhibitions—but he didn't know he had a special observer. King Clancy, then Toronto's assistant manager, was visiting his old buddy Howie and promptly had a team representative call the Faulkners. The Leafs wanted both Alex and George, but the latter wasn't interested in leaving the province again. Alex flew to Toronto alone to practice with the Leafs.

So nervous before the flight that he couldn't eat anything but a couple of soft-boiled eggs, Alex was soon put at ease by the Leafs: "You have never seen a finer bunch of gentlemen on one team than what was on that Maple Leaf team," he recalls with obvious respect. "They were fantastic to me. The first guy I ever skated with in practice was Red Kelly. He said to me, 'Don't ever let the opposition think that they're any better than you are.' Afterwards, I had a chat with [coach and g.m.] Punch Imlach, and he said, 'If you spend a year and a half in the American League, my bet is that you can play up here.'"

Toronto gave him a five-game tryout with Rochester in the American Hockey League and he signed a contract after his third game, in January 1961. With three centers ahead of him on the depth chart, he spent more time practicing than playing that season, but he needed it—the schedule was far longer and the pace a lot faster than in Newfoundland hockey. He laughs as he recounts that when his coach blew the whistle in practice to indicate that they all should slow down, he had to skate full steam ahead to keep up.

By his second season, the bomber was ready to explode. He earned a regular shift, and only a late-season injury—John Ferguson broke his nose in a surprise attack—prevented him from setting a team record for assists. He also played his first and only game with the Leafs in November but rarely saw the ice.

Then, in the summer of 1962, Toronto didn't keep him on its protected list and Detroit bought him. "I was more than happy about that, because Toronto had Dave Keon, Red Kelly, Bob Pulford and Billy Harris as their centers. I wasn't going to beat out any of them." Detroit's top two centers (Alex Delvecchio and Norm Ullman) were more than good themselves, but Alex was impressive enough to make the third line. Alex played regularly in 1962–63 with Larry Jeffrey and Bruce McGregor.

His game was toughened up again by this level of play. Alex recalls Gordie Howe, for example, who was notorious for his take-no-prisoners attitude. One day, the Wings played an exhibition against their AHL affiliate, Pittsburgh, and Alex's line dressed for the AHLers: "Gordie was going around his net with the puck, and I came up behind him, raised his stick and took the puck. He immediately stopped and knocked me down. When I fell, his stick was close to my head, and he took a knock at it, cutting me. When we were going on the bus afterwards, he grabbed my head and twisted it so he could see my cut. 'How many (stitches) did I get you for?' he said. 'Just three,' I said. With a grin, he said, 'Shucks, I thought I had you for more than that.'" In the playoffs, Andre Pronovost replaced Larry Jeffrey on

Alex's line, and almost any Newfoundlander over 40 can tell you what happened during those 11 games; unlike George's triumphs, virtually everyone could watch them on television. Alex scored three goals against Chicago's Glenn Hall (who might have been suffering from bad memories of George in 1955) in the six-game semifinals and two of them were game-winners, including the clincher in game six. Then he scored two goals in the finals against Toronto, one of which won game three in Detroit's only win in the series.

The irony is that Alex's line was a checking unit. Fast skaters with relentless styles, their job was to force turnovers. He recalls that Chicago scored one goal against his line; Toronto couldn't do it while he was on the ice.

When he came home that summer, Newfoundland proclaimed Alex Faulkner Day as a special holiday: "It was huge. I was scared to death. It was too big for me to handle. It didn't fit my personality, being this big celebrity. I was just playing hockey. But I've often said that it wouldn't have mattered who that first Newfoundlander was, the same thing would have happened. Looking back at it now, it was a fantastic time. We had a parade in central Newfoundland that went for miles and miles. In St. John's, they closed the schools and we had a ticker-tape parade downtown. We did the same thing in Conception Bay."

Premier Smallwood presented him with gold cufflinks; his wife received a gold locket.

The next season (1963–64) quickly brought Alex back down to earth. He broke his hand after nine games, missed six weeks, played three games, then destroyed his ankle ligaments. "Larry Jeffrey speared me accidentally in practice. I never could push off with that foot until the next year." He tried to play during the playoffs, but he wasn't effective. Detroit lost an agonizing seven-game final to Toronto.

No Newfoundlander has come as close to winning the Stanley Cup since.

Detroit wanted him to start 1964–65 in Pittsburgh, but Alex wasn't interested in the rigors of minor-league travel that kept him away from home for long periods and he went back to the CeeBees for two years. He thought that a new team might want him when the NHL's expansion plans were announced, so he agreed to play for Detroit's Central Hockey League affiliate in Memphis. He had a remarkable season, losing the scoring title by only two points—and he claims the official scorers missed four—yet he wasn't drafted by any expansion club, "which is a mystery we didn't understand then or now."

Alex finished his career in the pros with three fine seasons in San Diego (the Red Wings' Western League team). He had recommended his brother Jack to the Wings and the younger Faulkner made the San Diego roster for two years, one with Alex. "I had great years out there," Alex says. "All the travel was by train and it was run just as professionally as the National League. I made more money than I had in the NHL." With bonuses, his NHL salary had never exceeded $14,500 a year.

At 5'9" and 160 pounds, Alex was hardly a giant, but he played fearlessly—"I could always play to the best of my ability, regardless of where it was and who it was against"—while avoiding confrontations. Once, in a WHL game against Portland, he flattened notorious fighter Mad Dog Madigan with a check. Furious, Madigan was looking for a brawl. Alex's response? "You know I'm not fool enough to fight you. But the next time you're in the corner with the puck, I'll be in there after it."

Both George and Alex remained so devoted to hockey that they continued to play at the senior level in Newfoundland into their 40s. They competed successfully in many oldtimers' events, most notably winning gold medals at tournaments in Denmark (1978) and Florida (1979) with Jack. Now in his early 60s, Alex plays in two Bishop's Falls leagues and tries to attend at least one oldtimers' hockey tournament a year: "I still look forward to it, but the grind is starting to wane a little bit. Sometimes in the middle of winter, when there's a snowstorm on, you think twice about going. But I always go and always feel better about going."

Aware that his legend in Newfoundland is even bigger now than it was during his career, Alex keeps a humorous slant on it: "I know without question that I was never as good as most Newfoundlanders think I was. But, what odds, let 'em think it."

CHAPTER 57

The Other Guy's Barn

Grand and Not-So-Grand Hockey Arenas

Frank Orr

URING FEBRUARY OF 1999, the Toronto Maple Leafs will move their home base to the Air Canada Centre, located near the city's waterfront, a slapshot away from SkyDome, the big ballpark with its trademark retractable roof. The Leafs will vacate Maple Leaf Gardens, the team's home since 1931, and the last of the great old arenas that supplied the game of hockey with much of its history and folklore will be abandoned.

Maple Leaf Gardens will not be razed because the building was declared a historic site, a decision which prevents its unique architectural features from being obliterated. In addition, the St. Michael's Majors of the Ontario Hockey League will bring junior hockey action back to the Gardens in 1998–99.

Because they have not played anywhere else since 1931, to think of viewing a Leaf home game in Toronto except at the Gardens will be an adjustment for the team's devoted fans. To see a Montreal Canadiens game that was not played in the Montreal Forum but at the Molson Centre, a Boston Bruins match at FleetCenter, not the musty confines of the old Boston Garden, and to watch the Blackhawks in Chicago in the cavernous new United Center, not in the incredible din of Chicago Stadium, brings a pang of regret and nostalgia.

However, the precedent is strong for the shift to new facilities with no diminution of interest. Detroit Red Wings supporters survived a late 1970s switch from the dilapidated Olympia to Joe Louis Arena. While the sightlines for their rabid fans suffered when the New York Rangers made their 1967 switch from the intimate old to the spacious new Madison Square Garden, the sellout sign has been used every game night, even though the team had a yawning gap—1940 to 1994—between Stanley Cup triumphs.

"Those of us who have been around the game for a long time figured the old rinks of the 'Original Six' teams were the only places where the game could be played and appreciated properly, or so it seemed," commented Harry Sinden, president and general manager of the Boston Bruins since 1972, who guided the team from one of the top 'character buildings,' Boston Garden, to the new FleetCenter.

"But those were the places where our hockey memories from an early age were formed, the magic names and if you said, say, the words Boston and Bruins together, Boston Garden simply popped up.

"The team, the town and the rink were inseparable in your thoughts. Fortunately, there are good examples of how it doesn't take long for that caliber of identity to become established. The Philadelphia Flyers came to the NHL in the 1967 expansion and when the team became a contender in the early 1970s and won the Stanley Cup a couple of times, Philly, The Spectrum and the Flyers meant something in hockey.

"To compete in the NHL with today's economics, the old houses simply were not adequate. We must have a building with the posh appointments people want in entertainment facilities these days—plenty of private luxury boxes, clean restrooms in abundance, high-quality concessions, comfortable seats—to generate the revenue to have a competitive team on the ice."

Ed Snider, chairman of the Flyers and the man who built the franchise into a model hockey business, claims he likely always will be homesick for the Spectrum, even when checking the revenue generated by the CoreStates Center, the 19,500-seat arena opened in 1996.

"I loved watching hockey games in the Spectrum, I suppose, because that's where the team had its first success and the atmosphere was so electric," Snider said. "Of course, our fans are the same in the new building and as time goes by, I likely will feel the same way as I did about the old spot, especially if we win another Cup."

Since the NHL was founded as a four-team league in 1917—the Montreal Wanderers ceased operations six game into the season when their arena burned—the NHL has had 35 teams that played in 41 different cities and performed in a total of 63 arenas up to the end of the 1997–98 season.

Add 13 cities and arenas, never on the permanent lists, that hosted neutral site games earlier in the 1990s and the totals climb to 54 towns and 76 buildings.

The hockey houses range from the tiny Jubilee Rink with a natural ice surface and 3,250 seats where the Montreal Canadiens played a few games in their first season (1917–18) to the 28,000-seat ThunderDome, home to the Tampa Bay Lightning for a couple of seasons until the new Ice Palace was completed.

The 1990s are the boom years in the construction of arenas. From 1993 to the end of the 1997–98 season, 12 new arenas with NHL clubs as major tenants were opened in Anaheim, Boston, Buffalo, Chicago, Montreal, Ottawa, Philadelphia, St. Louis, San Jose, Tampa Bay, Vancouver and Washington.

By the end of the century, additional new houses should be completed in Toronto, Carolina (Raleigh), Florida (Miami), Denver and Los Angeles. The four-team expansion will see new facilities in Columbus, Nashville, St. Paul and Atlanta.

Thus, the 30-team NHL will be playing its games in 21 buildings less than 10 years old. In addition to the from-the-ground-up edifices, the Edmonton Coliseum, Calgary's Canadian Airlines Saddledome and Madison Square Garden in New York have had recent upgrades at a cost close to their original construction value.

While the final decade of the century produces the splendid stages on which the modern NHL drama is played, the first decade was when the first modest indoor arenas were built. The major step in that direction was the perfecting of the early freezing plants to make artificial ice and remove the game from the whims of nature.

The first artificial ice rinks suitable for hockey in North

America were built in the 1890s. (See story on page 564.)

These massive American ice plants inspired the Patricks, often called hockey's "royal family," to launch a daring plan that had an enormous influence on establishing the NHL. Frank and Lester Patrick already were important hockey names in the east as members of the fabled Renfrew Millionaires and other teams in the pro game's early days. But is was as administrators and coaches that they most effectively shaped all levels of the early game.

When the Patricks sold their large lumber operation and had money to invest, they came up with the idea of their own hockey league in B.C. in which they would own all teams and, most importantly, the arenas, including the largest indoor rink in the world in Vancouver.

The Patricks planned to stock their teams by raiding those in eastern Canada, enticing the players west by doubling salaries. On a honeymoon trip to Boston, Lester Patrick checked out the artificial ice plants and recruited players for his Pacific Coast Hockey Association, including the game's top star at the time, Cyclone Taylor.

The Patricks constructed a 4,000-seat arena in Victoria, B.C., at a cost of $110,000, while their 10,500-seat building in Vancouver budgeted at $210,000 wound up costing $275,000 to finish. Ground was broken in April 1911 and the buildings were ready for the opening games of the new league in December of that year.

The Patricks did two things: they provoked a challenge series between their league champion and the top team in the fledgling National Hockey Association, which was struggling for stability in the east; and the success of their artificial ice arenas in B.C. eventually inspired construction of similar rinks in the east.

Eastern promoters had sneered at the creation of the western league and the building of "expensive" arenas. But the success of the league in its early stages and the obvious advantages of an ice surface independent of the weather changed that outlook.

The first eastern freezing plant was in the Westmount Arena, located a block from the site of the Montreal Forum. The building was constructed in 1898 and artificial ice installed in 1914. The rink was home to the Canadiens and Wanderers in the NHL until destroyed by fire in 1918.

Mutual Street Arena in Toronto that year added artificial ice and March playoff games between other pro teams played on natural ice were occasionally shifted to Toronto if spring came early. The rink in Hamilton and the new Auditorium in Ottawa added artificial surfaces with crowds of 10,000 attending many games of the Ottawa Senators.

Due to its long cold winters, hockey-mad Montreal lagged behind in the acquisition of artificial ice. But when the Canadiens were forced by warm weather to switch their opening game in the 1923–24 season to Hamilton, postpone two other games and win the Stanley Cup with a "home" game in Ottawa, plans to construct the original Forum were completed quickly.

The first of the great NHL arenas was completed in 159 days to be ready for the opening of the 1924–25 season. The original plan was to have the Forum house only a new NHL expansion team called the Montreal Maroons, but when the building opened for hockey, it was the Canadiens on the ice for the first game.

Boston was granted a franchise, too, the Bruins playing in the old Boston Arena.

That launched the largest NHL growth period in teams and arenas until the six-team expansion in 1967. The Pittsburgh Pirates and the New York Americans joined the NHL in the 1925–26 season, the last season of operation for the Pacific Coast league.

In 1925, fabled promoter Tex Rickard built the second Madison Square Garden in New York and the NHL sold a franchise, called the Americans, to bootlegging baron William Dwyer to play in the new arena.

The next season, the New York Rangers shared MSG with the Americans while the Chicago Black Hawks and Detroit Cougars joined the NHL. The Cougars played their NHL first season in the small rink in Windsor, Ontario until construction on Detroit's Olympia was completed. The Black Hawks started NHL life in the 6,000-seat Chicago Coliseum, which was constructed for livestock shows, the smell in the building revealing strongly its previous tenants. They moved to the very loud Chicago Stadium in 1929.

Of the fabled, enduring hockey houses, construction of Maple Leaf Gardens in Toronto supplies the most illustrious folklore. Playing in the Mutual Street Arena, the Toronto team started life in the NHL in 1917, becoming the St. Patrick's in 1919.

Builder of the first New York Rangers roster for the 1926–27 NHL debut by that team, Conn Smythe was sacked before the season opened. He returned to his hometown, Toronto, with a vow to build a team that would be better than the Rangers and scraped together enough money from a variety of backers to buy the St. Pats and change the name to the Maple Leafs during the 1926–27 season.

As Smythe slowly built the Leafs towards contender status, heavy hockey interest dictated the need for a new, large arena because the 8,000-seat Mutual Street building was packed every night and potential customers were turned away at the door.

But the 1929 stock market crash and the start of the Depression seemed to rule out the raising of money to build a large arena. Smythe was undaunted by such odds and in a daring gamble he found a way to start construction.

Despite backing by a few financiers who were not wiped out in the crash and modest support from a bank, Smythe was well short of the revenue needed to start construction on land he had purchased at Church and Carlton streets in downtown Toronto.

In reality, Smythe's assistant Frank Selke, a former labor union executive, rescued the arena project. At a time when construction work was very scarce, Selke convinced the business managers of the 24 unions who would be involved in construction of Maple Leaf Gardens to take 20 percent of their salaries in shares in the new building. When the unions agreed that 80 percent of a salary was better than nothing, the contractors signed on, too, followed by the banks and investors.

Although Maple Leaf Gardens was constructed in just five months in 1931, opening on schedule in November, the job was done well. Sixty-seven years later the basic structure of the building remains intact, the only changes in that time being cosmetic, with increased seating, escalators and private boxes added.

Replaced by the magnificent Kiel Centre in 1994, the Arena in St. Louis was another building with a hectic history. Built at a cost of $2 million, the structure at the time was a brilliant architectural achievement, its roof span construction used on the Houston Astrodome indoor stadium almost four decades later. The arena's seating capacity of 21,000 was the largest indoors in the U.S.

The Arena opened in 1929 as permanent home for the

National Dairy Show. But the cows moved on a year later when the building went bankrupt. It was reopened in 1932 for minor-league hockey. The ice melted on one game day because the electric company pulled the plug when the bill was not paid.

When the Senators failed in Ottawa, the team was moved to St. Louis as the Eagles for the 1934–35 season, then disbanded. The minor pro St. Louis Flyers lasted until 1941 and the building had no hockey for six years.

In the late 1940s, the Wirtz family, owner of the Black Hawks, bought the Arena and posted a minor pro team there. The Black Hawks, who were attracting small crowds in Chicago, played a few NHL games in St. Louis, where they also failed to draw big crowds.

When the NHL expanded by six teams, as a favor to the Wirtz clan the league stipulated that St. Louis would be granted a franchise if its owners took the deadbeat arena, too. The Salomon family bought the franchise and a building, spending more than the $2 million original construction cost on improvements.

With Scotty Bowman as coach, the Blues rounded up an aging but effective team, slowly won over the fans and by playoff time, were playing to full houses. The Blues went to the Stanley Cup finals in their first three seasons to turn St. Louis into a good hockey town.

The team fell on hard times in the 1970s and was close to leaving town in 1978 when, at the last minute, the Ralston-Purina Corporation bought the team, the Arena was renamed the Checkerdome after a leading product of the owner and the team climbed the ladder again.

The Blues were close to moving again when Ralston-Purina dumped the franchise during the early 1980s recession but California promoter Harry Ornest purchased the franchise for a song, resurrected the Arena name again and the Blues had another good run in the 1980s. Strong local ownership took over from Ornest, the Kiel Center was built and another grand old hockey house bit the dust.

To older fans who grew up on the "Original Six" teams, many new arenas have a "cookie cutter" sameness to them in spite of their architectural differences, the variety of materials used in their construction, the array of amenities provided for fans.

The shorter neutral zones and egg-shaped ends of the Boston Garden and Memorial Auditorium in Buffalo demanded a slightly different style of hockey than the standard 200' x 85' surfaces of many other rinks.

A trip to the old Olympia in Detroit was memorable because the building housed what appeared to be the longest, steepest escalator in the world, the Mount Everest of rolling staircases that carried fans to the upper reaches of the building where Gordie Howe played the first 25 seasons of his extraordinary 32-year big league career.

Who can forget the incredible opening face-off din in the Chicago Stadium, which in reality was built like a steel tube running straight up to the third deck, which itself was high and seemed to tower over the ice surface? When Al Melgard played the world's largest unified organ with 25 keyboards, 883 stops and 40,000 pipes, you felt its vibrations on your feet as much as you heard its enormous sound in the Stadium.

Then there were the fans in the top level at Madison Square Garden, the most abrasive, perhaps crudest spectators in sports, berating opposition players with chants based on the players' foibles and vices. A writer once suggested that the last expedition planned by anthropologist Margaret Meade, who specialized in the study of primitive cultures, was going to be made in the MSG gallery.

Of course, with a few years under the seats and contending teams on the ice, the new buildings take on a collection individual characteristics that set them apart. After all, would the Montreal Forum be regarded as a hockey shrine if the Canadiens had not won 22 of their 24 Stanley Cup championships on its ice surface? Every arena was new sometime.

CHAPTER 58

Hockey Trading Cards

The Oldest—and Certainly the Most Volatile—Hockey Hobby

Kevin Allen

COLLECTORS WHO PLACE NEW HOCKEY CARDS in plastic sheets to keep them in pristine condition shudder when they hear the Parkhurst cement mixer story.

Back in the 1950s Parkhurst officials were looking for a method of achieving a better mix of cards in each pack. Their solution was to dump freshly manufactured Parkhurst cards in the cement mixer and give them a few wild whirls.

"A lot of cards probably got wrecked, but back then they didn't care," said Ken Whitmell, who worked for Parkhurst Products Inc. when they acquired permission to use the Parkhurst trademark in 1991–92. "The cards in the middle of the mixer came out in mint condition, and those on the outside probably got dinged up a little from banging around on the sides of the steel drum."

Today's collectors, especially those folks who have plunked down hundreds of dollars to purchase "dinged-up" Parkhurst cards, hate that story. But it shows conclusively that the hockey card manufacturers of yesteryear could never have envisioned that their innocent, relatively low-budget business venture would mature into a multi-faceted, multi-million-dollar industry. Plenty of modern collectors tear open their packs and immediately consult the Beckett Price Guide to see how much their insert cards are worth. Today's collector could find a $100 autographed card, or a $40 insert card, in his pack. That certainly would have been a bizarre thought for many folks before World War II who found hockey cards in packages of cigarettes, candy and gum. Sometimes they simply threw cards away after looking at them.

To appreciate the rich, colorful tradition of hockey cards, consider that there were hockey cards before there was even a National Hockey League. Cigarette companies began issuing hockey cards throughout Canada in 1910, seven years before the NHL debuted. The 1910–11 Sweet Caporal 45-card postcard set, printed by British American Tobacco company and included in Imperial Tobacco cigarettes, featured players from the National Hockey Association, which was the forerunner of the NHL. Many players featured did eventually play prominent roles in the NHL, including George Vezina, Newsy Lalonde and Art Ross. Vezina's card, if it's in top condition, can fetch $4,000 in the marketplace. That same 1910–11 season featured another set, now called the C56 set. The cards were in color, and small by today's standards.

Three different cigarette companies issued cards from 1910 to 1913 with the hope of spiking their sales. In the 1920s candy companies began to insert cards in packages to increase sales, and in the 1930s gum companies, in particular O-Pee-Chee and World Wide Gum, began to use cards to boost their products in the marketplace. The cards still remaining from that era are quite valuable in the collecting marketplace. For example, a Champs cigarette card of Howie Morenz is valued at $4,000 today.

Some of the prized hockey cards from the pre-World War II era are those from "redemption sets." Some manufacturers would give away prizes—such as skates and hockey sticks—for collectors who could send in a complete set of their hockey cards. Manufacturers obviously hoped consumers would buy more of their product while in a frenzy to complete their set. The short-printed cards from those sets, regardless of how little notoriety the player had, are now extremely valuable today. The Bert Corbeau card from the 1923 V145s is valued by some at $15,000. "It's just impossible to find," said Al Muir, an editor at Beckett. "It's believed that was the card that was printed in short quantity so you couldn't turn in those complete sets. A Sprague Cleghorn card from the 1924–25 Maple Crispette set can fetch $10,000 for the same reason."

Today's older collectors seem to have a special fondness for the Beehive photos, first issued in 1933. Kids in that era would tear the labels off the Beehive corn syrup bottles and send them in for the photo cards. Hall of Famer Gordie Howe collected these cards as a child in Saskatchewan and still laments that a relative threw away his collection. Bobby Hull was a Beehive collector and is fond of telling stories of rummaging through neighbors' garbage looking for the corn syrup labels. Beehive stopped issuing cards briefly in 1944 because of the war, but returned with a new series of photos postwar. They issued those photos until 1963. A third set of Beehives was issued from 1964 to 1967.

The modern era of collecting starts with the introduction of the 1951–52 Parkhurst set. Topps hockey cards debuted as a test in 1954–55. Topps didn't seem convinced that this was an effective method of selling chewing gum. The company didn't issue card sets in 1955–56 or 1956–57, but then came back in 1957–58 with a set. As a general rule in the 1950s, Topps issued cards of players from American teams and Parkhurst issued cards of players from the Montreal Canadiens and Toronto Maple Leafs. Starting in the 1960–61 season, Parkhurst also began to issue cards for players from the Detroit Red Wings. Topps covered the remaining teams.

After the 1963–64 season, Parkhurst decided NHL licensing fees were too high and left the hockey card business. Starting in 1964–65, Topps began issuing cards of players from every team. Once Parkhurst left, Topps seemed to take advantage of its situation as the lone provider of hockey cards. Topps designs in the 1960s were unique, but at some point in that decade the company's editing process became shoddy. Today, card designers take three to six weeks to finalize one card design. "When Topps had no competition, the (design) process probably took 10 minutes," said Ted Taylor, a collector, writer and public relations guru in the industry for many years. "Topps could put anything out and we had to buy it. I think they got lazy."

Evidence supports that contention. The attractive 1968–69 set lost some of its luster because many of the cards were cut unevenly. Also, Frank Mahovlich's head is

pasted on another player's body. "They didn't even bother to put it on straight," said Beckett's Al Muir. "They did that with eight or 10 cards that year."

Topps had no qualms about using three- and four-year old photographs, and occasionally Topps used the same photo of a player two years in a row. Nothing illustrates the company's sloppiness more than the Boston cards from the 1971–72 set. The Bruins' players obviously put their jerseys and gloves on over street clothes for the photo shoot. Topps didn't even bother to crop out the dress slacks underneath. You see Phil Esposito's plaid pants on the card.

Today's cards are standardized at 2½" x 3½", but they haven't always been that size. Parkhurst's 1952–53 cards were 1¹⁵/₁₆" x 2¹⁵/₁₆". The following year, Parkhurst went to a 2½" x 3⅝" card. There have been variations on that, including the 1964–65 Topps set. That 110-card set had oversized cards of 2½" x 4¹¹/₁₆", that have been nicknamed "Tall Boys" by collectors. That set in mint condition today sells for about $6,000. One reason why it's valuable is 1964 youngsters didn't seem to like the design and didn't take very good care of those cards. As oversized cards, they didn't fit well in boxes. Most of the 1964–65 cards that still exist have damaged corners. Corner sharpness is crucial to fetching top dollar for older cards.

No other card of that size was issued until 1993–94 when Fleer introduced a set called Power Play. One major reason why companies are reluctant to vary from standardized card sizes is that most collectors now have special plastic sheets, boxes and card sleeves that fit only regular sized cards. Unlike yesteryear when collectors put cards in the spokes of bicycles, or taped them to their walls, today's collectors go to great lengths to protect their treasures.

Most hockey cards issued through the years have featured vertical action. "The last horizontal set that worked was the 1956 Topps baseball set," Taylor said. "The market has never taken to horizontal cards. Hockey is a vertical sport. Unless you are a swimmer, or a knocked-out boxer, horizontal doesn't work."

Although purists criticize Topps' work in those days, some 1960s sets are extremely popular with older collectors. The 66-card 1966–67 set is valued at about $4,000, primarily because it boasts Bobby Orr's rookie card. His card is valued at $2,000. In a rare creative effort, Topps designed these cards like television sets. The wood grain boarders made it difficult to keep those cards in perfect condition. It's difficult to find these cards today without scratches on the boarders. That also explains the high price. This set design also illustrates the fickle nature of collectors. Some people love the design and others hate it. Some call it the "floating heads" set because the players' heads seemed to be pasted into the television set.

At the time, Topps' cards had French and English on the back of cards so they could be distributed in both Canada and the United States. In 1966–67, Topps issued a special "American only" test set with no French. That also included the Orr rookie card. That set is far more valuable because few are known to exist. O-Pee-Chee started to make hockey cards again in 1968–69. O-Pee-Chee used the Topps design, but always had more cards in the set, a reflection of hockey's popularity in Canada. That makes those O-Pee-Chee sets very popular with collectors of rookie cards. For example, the 1970–71 O-Pee-Chee sets had rookie cards for Bobby Clarke and Darryl Sittler. The 1970–71 Topps set did not. The 1971–72 set had rookie cards of Marcel Dionne and Guy Lafleur. The Topps set did not. Beginning

in 1974–75, O-Pee-Chee and Topps sets became nearly identical, except for the color of the back of the card. O-Pee-Chee did issue World Hockey Association sets from 1974 to 1978, while Topps did not.

Most serious collectors look at the early 1980s with fondness because that's the last period older cards were found for inexpensive prices. No price guide existed and many Americans were more than willing to trade hockey cards for baseball cards, or sell hockey for next to nothing. Before Muir worked for Beckett, he toured in a band. He remembers finding incredible bargains at flea markets in the U.S. in the 1980s.

"Baseball cards were always on display, but dealers almost always had hockey stuff buried away," Muir said. "They were only too happy to get rid of it. (With no) price guides for hockey at the time, to most people, they were worthless. But it was in 100-card-for $1 stacks that I picked up my (Phil) Esposito rookie card, plus rookies of Lafleur and (Ken) Dryden, plus early Orr cards, even stuff as far back as 1954–55. The fact that names such as Howe, (Alex) Delvecchio and (Terry) Sawchuk didn't have the cachet in the States they had in Canada meant bargains were not tough to find."

It wasn't until Wayne Gretzky was traded from Edmonton to Los Angeles in 1988 that the hockey trading card market gained legitimacy south of the Canadian border. The 1988–89 Topps card with Gretzky (holding) a Kings jersey seemed to signal the start of the rising card price. "Those bargains stopped soon after," Muir said.

The Beckett price guide debuted in 1990, and let everyone in on the secret that older hockey cards could be sold at higher prices in various parts of the country. Dr. James Beckett, who owns a Ph.D in statistics, made a name for himself as one of the leading authorities on baseball card collecting. He had started his own baseball price guide in 1984 and a hockey guide was another logical step. "His hockey guide had a very profound effect," said Fleer's Steve Charendoff, a long-time collector. "It brought stability to an industry that previously had none."

Another event helped fuel interest in hockey cards. The *Wall Street Journal* published an article about how a Billy Ripken baseball card with a vulgar message written on his bat had managed to creep into a card set. The story explained how the card had risen dramatically in value. It also included examples of other older cards that were also skyrocketing in value.

"The article told how some cards had outperformed every stock in the market," said NHL Players' Association collectibles boss Michael Merhab, who was working for the Upper Deck Company at the time. "All of a sudden you have all these guys reading the *Wall Street Journal* saying 'maybe I should buy trading cards instead of stocks.' There were people who didn't know hockey was a major sport, but they were buying cards. That was happening in football and basketball as well."

Investors scrambled to buy older hockey sets with the hope of selling them to adult collectors in the midst of a nostalgic craving. The vintage hockey card market seemed like an untapped mother lode.

"There were stockbrokers on Wall Street definitely buying cards," observed Michel Vaillancourt, owner of House of Hockey, a Tampa business specializing in buying and selling older cards. "They were looking to make quick money. Some did. Some didn't."

Hockey card collecting was no longer a kid's game. NHL

player Darren Turcotte owned two card stores and former NHL 50-goal scorer Brian Bellows bought cases of cards as investments. Patrick Roy, the winningest playoff goaltender in NHL history, frequently talked about becoming an avid collector. NHL coaching legend Scotty Bowman was quoted as saying he and his son had bought a pile of Brett Hull rookie cards as an investment. PGA golfer Craig Stadler admitted he had started to put money into the collecting world. The industry's credibility was at an all-time high in the early 1990s.

The logic behind the rising prices of hockey cards was based on the same principle of antique collecting. Most cards produced in years gone by were destroyed in the spokes of bicycles, chewed up by family pets or thrown away by parents after the children moved away. The theory: cards tucked away in the attic were rare, hence valuable. As had happened in baseball card collecting, a player's first card—called his rookie card—took on greater value.

Following the marketplace closely, companies lined up to obtain licenses to print hockey cards. After having nothing but Topps and O-Pee-Chee since the 1963–64 season, the hockey world welcomed Score, Upper Deck and Pro Set as trading card licensees in 1990–91. By coincidence, the new card companies debuted at a time when the league was rich in promising youngsters. The rookie cards of Jaromir Jagr, Jeremy Roenick, Pavel Bure and Eric Lindros came out in 1990–91. Teemu Selanne's rookie card came out in 1991–92. It was clear that big-name rookies could drive sales to record heights.

In that first year, these companies were printing cards as if they had a license to print money. In a sense, they did. Consumers were buying up every product that hit the marketplace, and companies were scrambling to push new products out the door. (Pro Set even acquired the rights to use the Parkhurst trademark on cards). Topps came out with Bowman hockey cards and O-Pee-Chee offered a premier edition that skyrocketed in price before it even arrived in dealers' hands. "It was selling for $8 or $10 for a pack because it seemed like there was none available," Vaillancourt remembered. "It was like that with a lot of products, especially when they first came out. And then prices would start to fall and dealers ended up with cases of (high-priced) cards they couldn't sell."

Collectors' pursuit of rookie cards prompted Score to sign Eric Lindros to an exclusive contract to appear in their sets even before he signed a NHL contract. Upper Deck attempted to sign exclusives with national junior teams in an attempt to feature players before they landed in the NHL.

Other companies complained about the exclusive contract, and the NHL Players' Association and league officials also didn't like the fact that too much emphasis was being placed on players who weren't yet in the league. The new rule: no exclusive deals with draft picks and limits on the number of non-NHL players who could appear in sets.

Complicating the situation was the fact that Classic, an unlicensed company, was giving potential draft picks huge amounts of money to be photographed to appear in their sets. Roman Hamrlik, for example, received more than $150,000 from Classic after he was the first over-all pick in the 1991 draft. "People thought they were going to put their kids through college by buying a case of cards and putting

it away for 20 years," said Charendoff, who worked for Classic at the time. "The trouble is if everyone does that then it becomes a house of cards and it comes tumbling down. And that's exactly what happened."

The idea that cards will have higher value in the future is predicated on scarcity. But non-stop press runs in the early 1990s, coupled with everyone hoarding cards, made it clear that scarcity wouldn't be a problem in the 21st century. Card companies then decided to create their own scarcity by including insert cards that had limited production. By 1992–93, the hockey card market was awash in insert cards. Collectors began to look at opening packs like they were entering a lottery. Would they be lucky enough to get a high-priced insert card? That worked for a while, but even that idea soon became stale.

In 1992, Fleer was awarded a license to issue hockey cards. By 1993–94, Pro Set's financial problems caused it to lose its license to print hockey cards. Leaf Brands joined the fray. The following year, O-Pee-Chee announced that 1994–95 would be its last year of printing hockey cards. Pinnacle Topps announced in 1996 that it was quitting the hockey business after 42 consecutive years of making cards. By 1997, Fleer was in Chapter 11 bankruptcy and out of the hockey card business. Pacific Trading Cards received a license to issue trading cards in 1997–98.

"When O-Pee-Chee stopped making cards, that's what really sounded the death knell for the hobby," Whitmell said. "People thought: 'Wow! I've been collecting O-Pee-Chee since the 1960s.' That's when it hit people that the industry was in trouble."

Collectors in Canada seemed to lament O-Pee-Chee's passing more than Americans grieved about Topps' decision to quit the hockey business. "There was just a minor sentimental ripple when Topps left," Muir said. "It wasn't as if Topps left the baseball market. There was some dismay about O-Pee-Chee, but not surprise. They had become the out-of-step grandfatherly company. O-Pee-Chee didn't speak to the modern collector. That's why it went the way of the dinosaur."

Merhab says the industry knew in the 1990s that boom period wouldn't last forever. "I can remember (former Upper Deck executive) Jay McCracken saying that this ship is going to hit an iceberg," Merhab says. "Nobody was saying it was right around the corner, but everyone was saying we have to watch this."

In 1998, the hockey card industry was still trying to stabilize. Efforts were being made to attract young collectors back in the marketplace and take advantage of hockey's growing popularity by catering to new fans. The wild investor mentality is reduced, but not erased in hockey cards.

"In the last questionnaire I saw, they asked what was the number-one reason for collecting hockey cards. The answers were heavily weighted toward investment," Merhab says. "The day someone shows me research in which people say they collect because they love players, or love hockey, then we can all say all of the investors are gone."

No one believes the industry will ever regain its lost innocence. The days of cement mixer collation and holding cards together with a rubber band have gone the way of scooters and toy tops. Even the youngest collector today is taught early that rubber bands damage a cards' edges.

CHAPTER 59

From Hollywood Hockey to Puck Rock

Pop Culture Cross-Pollenization: Hockey on Film, Television and Disc

David Spaner

Near the end of Jacques Plante's career, the ex-Canadiens legend was hired to appear in an action sequence in the movie *Face-off*. The script called for him to allow a goal on a breakaway, but as he stood before 5,000 extras at Maple Leaf Gardens, the proud Plante stopped the puck shot by a skater in a Vancouver Canucks uniform. The cameras rolled for a second take and again the goaltender wouldn't permit himself to let the puck pass. The filmmakers, growing impatient, shot a third take, and still the shooter couldn't score. An announcement was made over the Gardens' public-address system: "Ladies and gentlemen, the story calls for Vancouver to score a goal and Mr. Plante is going to permit it." The scene was shot a fourth time and finally Plante allowed a goal.

Hockey and the movies have always been just such an uneasy mix. Boxing and baseball have been the subject of more than their share of memorable films, from *Body and Soul* and *Bang the Drum Slowly* to *Raging Bull* and *Field of Dreams*. But hockey has long been regarded as too marginal a sport to warrant much Hollywood attention. It's only been with NHL expansion and the increased influence of Canadians in Hollywood that hockey's profile has been raised enough to feature it with some frequency in movies and television. Meanwhile in Canada, where hockey's mythology rivals Hollywood's south of the border, a "puck rock" genre of pop music is also flourishing.

Early attempts at capturing the sport on film were low-budget productions made primarily to cash in on an interest in all things ice-related that grew out of Sonja Henie's immense popularity in the late 1930s. Henie arrived in Hollywood after winning the gold medal for figure skating at the 1936 Winter Olympics and she skated her way through a series of feature films. Perhaps because of hockey's rough-and-tumble nature, the handful of pictures made about it had simple plots that often involved gangsters, romance and the heroes overcoming adversity to win the big game. *The Game That Kills* (1937) starred Rita Hayworth as a trainer's daughter. In *Idol of the Crowds* (1937), John Wayne left the family farm to play hockey and tangle with hoodlums. *It's a Pleasure* (1945) featured Henie romancing a hockey star.

The first hockey movie, *The King of Hockey*, was the prototype for these early efforts. Made by Warner Brothers in 1936 for about $125,000, it grossed between $400,000 and $600,000 according to producer Bryan Foy. Foy got the idea for the film after visiting a skating rink behind the old Warner lot on Sunset Boulevard in Hollywood.

The movie, whose rather nondescript working title was *The Shrinking Violet*, starred Wayne Morris—who would go on to leading roles in Warner Brothers' "A" pictures such as *Kid Galahad*—and Dick Purcell.

"We signed some hockey players from either UCLA or [the University of] Southern California," Foy recalled. "Purcell and Morris didn't need much help in the hockey scenes. They were good skaters." The screenwriter could have used some help with the dialogue, though, as the script was littered with such groaners as "We're down two points," and references to "fouls" and the "penalty cage." The plot follows Gabby Dugan (played by Purcell) as he moves from the college ranks to the pros. Along the way there are rumors of involvement with gamblers, on-ice fisticuffs, an injury which practically blinds Gabby, and in the end rehabilitation and victory. *The King of Hockey* made a minor comeback in the 1950s and 1960s when it was part of a package of old Warner movies sold to television.

After this initial flirtation with Hollywood, hockey would virtually disappear from theater screens for more than three decades. Sportswriter Oscar Madison (played by Walter Matthau) made a passing reference in 1968's *The Odd Couple*, when he tells his friend Felix Unger (Jack Lemmon): "You think you're impossible to live with. For our tenth wedding anniversary I took Blanche to the New York Rangers–Detroit Red Wings hockey game. She got hit by a puck. I still can't figure out why she left me. That's how impossible I am." (The game also got a mention in Matthau's 1973 film *The Laughing Policeman*.) And the massive 1970 hit *Love Story*, directed by Canadian Arthur Hiller, saw Ali McGraw in love with a Harvard hockey player portrayed by Ryan O'Neal.

The game itself didn't take center ice until the following year, with the first Canadian attempt at a hockey feature. Based on a book by Scott Young, *Face-off* told the story of a top Toronto Maple Leaf draft choice (played by Art Hindle) who falls for a pop singer, gets a swelled head and runs into problems with referees and his coach. Real NHL players George Armstrong and Derek Sanderson made acting cameos, while others such as Bobby Hull and Jacques Plante appeared in action sequences.

Face-off was followed by another Canadian feature, *Paperback Hero* (1973), in which a hockey player (Keir Dullea) winds up in a Wild West gunfight with police. That same year, Frank Mahovlich made a cameo appearance as himself in *Enuff is Enuff*, a Quebec-made film about a family that takes to the road.

The game got its big cinematic break in 1977. *Slap Shot* reunited actor Paul Newman with director George Roy Hill (they had teamed to make *Butch Cassidy and the Sundance Kid* and *The Sting*). The film succeeds largely due to the charismatic and athletic Newman, who who had previously played a boxer (in *Somebody Up There Likes Me*), a pool shark (*The Hustler*) and a race-car driver (*Winning*). Newman convincingly portrayed the internal tensions of aging Reggie Dunlop, the playing coach of the Charlestown Chiefs, a minor-league team based on the Johnstown Jets of the North American Hockey League.

Partially because there have been few other hockey films that compare with *Slap Shot*'s production values, the bawdy comedy has become a part of sport's lore. To this day fans

recite bits of dialogue and revel in the antics of the battling Hanson brothers, who continue to make personal appearances at hockey rinks more than 20 years later. However, at the time the movie was criticized by hockey fans, and fans of Paul Newman, for the large helpings of violence and profanity that were in fact accurate reflections of the gritty life in minor-league hockey.

"Well, that has to be their problem," the actor would respond years later. "Hey, it was advertised as a locker-room picture and it was a locker-room picture and it was true to its origins. What I don't like is gratuitous language thrown into a film to make it rakish. When George Roy Hill gave me the script, he thought I would worry about the writing. And I said, 'Are you kidding? It's the most original thing I've read in I can't think how long. Of course I'll do it.'"

Slap Shot's popularity hardly unleashed torrent of hockey movies. *Ice Castles*, released in 1979, starred Robby Benson in a melodramatic tale about a hockey player's relationship with a figure skater who is blinded in an accident. A couple of notable Canadian efforts came out in the early 1980s: *The Hounds of Notre Dame* (1980) about a championship hockey team at a Saskatchewan high school, and *The Sweater* (1981), an animated short—made by the National Film Board and based on the short story by Quebec novelist Roch Carrier—about what happens to a boy in small-town Quebec in the 1940s when his mother sends to Eaton's department store for a Canadiens sweater, but a jersey of the hated Toronto Maple Leafs arrives in the mail.

In 1985, the cinematic depiction of hockey reached its nadir with *Youngblood*. Based on the dubious notion that skilled players must become goons to survive in hockey, the film starred Rob Lowe as Dean Youngblood, who comes from upstate New York to play junior hockey in the city of Hamilton, Ontario. Depressed because "It's been pretty hard to meet people I can talk to up here," he spends most of his time in the town's *one* movie theater before returning home, where his father (played by ex-Leaf and Blackhawk Eric Nesterenko) teaches him how to fight. Then he's back to Canada, a better player because he's now a pugilist. The film also starred Patrick Swayze and Keanu Reeves, in his movie debut. The following year saw the release of *Touch and Go*, a romantic comedy starring Michael Keaton as a hockey player.

By the 1990s, the NHL was spreading its wings across the continent and puck-related productions became more commonplace. An independent Canadian feature called *Perfectly Normal* (1990) featured a goalie on a brewery's industrial-league team. At mid decade, the action-adventure genre hooked up with hockey in *Sudden Death*, a Jean-Claude Van Damme vehicle about a hostage-taking during a Stanley Cup final series game between the Chicago Blackhawks and Pittsburgh Penguins. *The Cutting Edge*, released in 1992, used the well-worn premise of a romance between a figure skater (Moira Kelly) and a hockey player (D.B. Sweeney).

As the 1990s went on, the hockey jersey struck a new pop-culture chord as rap performers and hiphop fans began wearing them. Meanwhile, following in the tradition of SCTV alumni Rick Moranis and Dave Thomas (*Strange Brew*) and John Candy (*Canadian Bacon*), Toronto-raised comedian Mike Myers parlayed his Saturday Night Live sketch character, Wayne Campbell, into a pair of successful films, *Wayne's World* and *Wayne's World 2*, both of which featured hockey prominently. Myers's character, who lives in the Chicago suburb of Aurora, Illinois, wears Chicago Blackhawks boxer shorts, hangs out at Stan Mikita's Donuts and plays street hockey with his sidekick, Garth (played by Dana Carvey).

Myers often dons a Toronto Maple Leafs jersey when he appears on U.S. talk shows. "I'm definitely a shameless homer," he said after the 1993 playoffs. "I cried when the Leafs got knocked out of the Stanley Cup playoffs. I literally bawled my eyes out like a child. And when they scored in overtime to beat Detroit I took my flags out of the closet and waved them from the windows of my L.A. house."

The 1997 movie *Les Boys*, a comedy about garage-league hockey, set a box-office record for Quebec-made films. This movie is included in the English language filmography that follows that accompanies this article because there is a popular dubbed version. A sequel is in the works. Proof of hockey's increased profile is the number of passing references in such major films as *Batman and Robin* (1997), in which the Dynamic Duo confronts Mr. Freeze's "hockey team from Hell"; 1992's *Lethal Weapon 3*, in which Mel Gibson disrupts a Los Angeles Kings game in pursuit of a criminal; and *The Last Seduction* (1994), in which Linda Fiorentino plots murder with a pick-up hockey player.

Woody Allen's 1994 comedy *Manhattan Murder Mystery* opens at a New York Ranger game. "I've done a number of basketball things over the years because whenever I think of going to [Madison Square] Garden I think of basketball," Allen said. "I changed it once to a hockey game … just to get a little bit of variation." In a later Allen picture, 1996's *Everyone Says I Love You*, Alan Alda, Goldie Hawn and Drew Barrymore debate personal matters in their Manhattan apartment while family members play hockey around them.

The Disney studio was responsible for the most popular hockey movie since *Slap Shot* with *The Mighty Ducks* in 1992. Emilio Estevez played the reluctant coach of a motley youth team in a story reminiscent of the old *Bad News Bears* baseball movies. Like the original *Bad News Bears*, *The Mighty Ducks* spawned a pair of sequels. In 1993–94, the Disney corporation was granted an NHL franchise, the Mighty Ducks of Anaheim.

A detail that made *The Mighty Ducks* pictures stand out from others of the genre was their artful casting. Traditional celluloid hockey teams were composed largely of English-speaking Canadians, with a few Americans and Quebeçois thrown in for good measure. In Disney's world, players come in a range of sizes, shapes, ethnic backgrounds—and genders (the Mighty Ducks team included female players).

Women have primarily played minor roles in hockey movies, usually as a player's romantic interest. Another Disney movie, *Freaky Friday* (1976) had Jodie Foster as a member of her school's field hockey team. The 1984 Canadian movie, *Hockey Night*, starred Megan Follows as a girl who makes it onto a boys' ice hockey team as a goalie. With the recent boom in women's hockey, it may only be a matter of time before the game gets its answer to *A League of Their Own*, the Penny Marshall-directed film about women baseball players.

Looking ahead, in 1998 Burt Reynolds will star in *Mystery Alaska* as the coach of a small-town hockey team that plays an exhibition game against the New York Rangers. A new CTV series called *Power Play* is set to air during the 1998–99 season. It's set in Hamilton, Ontario and deals with a small-market team's struggles to survive in big-time hockey.

Hockey's small-screen heritage goes back to 1952 when

"Hockey Night in Canada" debuted on the Canadian Broadcasting Corporation, telecasting games from Maple Leaf Gardens and the Montreal Forum. Canadian comedy team Johnny Wayne and Frank Shuster performed their hockey sketch for an American audience on The Ed Sullivan Show in 1958. The bit involved brawling, yet highbrow, hockey players, and it ended with four players pulling out musical instruments to form a string quartet in the penalty box.

Wayne and Shuster had been lampooning on-ice action on their weekly CBC radio show as far back as the 1940s. Once a year the Mimico Mice, a two-player team, would face-off against the Toronto Maple Leafs, complete with authentic sound effects from Maple Leaf Gardens and Foster Hewitt calling the play-by-play, using the names of actual Maple Leaf players of the era.

"He'd go, 'Wayne passes to Shuster, and Shuster goes down the ice.' We'd lose about 110–0. Sometimes we got one goal for neatness," Shuster said. "I still bump into people who say, 'How are the Mimico Mice doing?'"

"We loved hockey anyway," Shuster says. "I played pick-up games and sold Eskimo Pies at Maple Leaf Gardens when I was in high school. Johnny was a regular at the games. He considered himself the number one Maple Leafs fan."

Wayne Gretzky has hosted "Saturday Night Live" and appeared on The Young and the Restless. Jay Thomas had a recurring role on Cheers as an ex-Boston Bruin goaltender named Eddie LeBec and Matt LeBlanc's character on Friends has frequently expressed devotion to the New York Rangers. Canadian actor Michael J. Fox grew up playing hockey and in his sitcom Spin City his character drinks from a Rangers mug and frequently carries a hockey stick. Perhaps basking in the afterglow on the Rangers' 1994 Cup championship, a club pennant was prominently displayed in the detective squadroom of NYPD Blue for several seasons.

Hockey's finest moment in a U.S. sitcom came in a Seinfeld episode titled "The Face Painter." In this episode, Elaine (Julia Louis-Dreyfus) re-evaluates her relationship with a New Jersey Devils fan because he insists on painting his face in the Devils' colors when he goes to games.

The first made-for-TV movie to involve hockey was also Meryl Streep's film debut. The Deadliest Season (1977) starred Michael Moriarty (who would later star in the series Law and Order) as a defenseman who is charged with manslaughter after an on-ice incident.

The most ambitious project ever produced for CBC television was the 13-part series He Shoots, He Scores! which arrived in 1986 to much fanfare. A bilingual cast shot scenes in both English and French. The soap opera-like storyline followed a young Quebeçois hockey player from junior hockey to the major-league Quebec Nationals. True to the miniseries pattern, the series featured a vast array of characters, and hockey action blended liberally with sexual intrigue and double-dealing. The action sequences were filmed meticulously. "The hockey scenes must be perfect," said director Jean-Guy Lord. "We have a public to whom we cannot pass off peanuts as cashews." The Nationals' uniforms also looked an awful lot like those of the NHL's Quebec Nordiques, so real-life footage could be intercut with the staged sequences.

Three TV films took their stories from real-life events. ABC television's Miracle On Ice (1981) starred Karl Malden as Herb Brooks, coach of the gold medal-winning 1980 U.S. Olympic hockey team. Canada's CBC presented Net Worth during its 1995–96 season. Based on the book by David Cruise and Alison Griffiths, it told of the ill-fated attempt in 1957–58 to establish an NHL players' association. Aidan Devine and Kevin Connelly starred as Ted Lindsay and Gordie Howe, while veteran actor Al Waxman (Cagney & Lacey, King of Kensington) played Red Wings general manager Jack Adams. Director Atom Egoyan (Exotica and The Sweet Hereafter) teamed up with writer Paul Gross (Due South) to dramatize the troubled life story of Brian "Spinner" Spencer in Gross Misconduct, a made-for-TV movie originally broadcast in 1992.

Canadian pop music has found hockey to be a rich source of material. The earliest example was the Secrets' 1966 recording, "Clear the Track, Here Comes Shack," about Toronto Maple Leafs favorite Eddie Shack. Songs have also been written about Bill Barilko (the Tragically Hip's "Fifty-Mission Cap"), Wayne Gretzky ("Gretzky Rocks" by The Pursuit of Happiness) and Wendel Clark ("The Ballad of Wendel Clark", parts I and II, by the Rheostatics).

Canadian celebrities have produced novelty recordings (Bruno Gerussi's "Signin' with the NHL" and Alan Thicke's "Wondrous Bobby") but more polished efforts by Canadian performers have included Jane Siberry's "Hockey", Tom Cochrane's "Big League" and Tommy Hunter's "Pandemonium." In 1974's "Raised on Robbery," Joni Mitchell describes a barfly "sitting in the lounge of the Empire Hotel" who had "a little money riding on the Maple Leafs." The song goes on to proclaim, "Look at those jokers / Glued to that damn hockey game." Stompin' Tom Connors' "The Hockey Song" is particularly well-known to fans: "Oh, the good old hockey game / Is the best game you can name / And the best game you can name / Is the good old hockey game."

Vancouver's venerable DOA, Canada's best-known punk band, has often combined hockey and music, both in song ("Overtime," "Beat 'Em Bust 'Em," "Give 'Em the Lumber") and in the video of their cover of the old Bachman-Turner Overdrive song "Takin' Care of Business," which features the band playing hockey with a team of suit-wearing businessmen. DOA even travels with street-hockey gear, taking on all challengers.

In "Give 'Em the Lumber," DOA mourns the state of the Canadian game: "Quebec and Winnipeg are gone / Canadian hockey hits the swan song."

Sometimes the band's hockey obsession gets in the way of less pleasant pursuits, such as rehearsing. "We had a table hockey set where we practiced," says DOA's Joe Keighley. "Sometimes we were supposed to start practice at 4 o'clock, but we wouldn't start until 6 or 7. We'd start a table hockey tournament."

The band also ices a hockey team, DOA Murder Squad, which sports a 14–2 record playing food-bank benefit games against radio-station teams and others in the Vancouver area. "When we started doing the hockey team people started saying DOA has gone from punk rock to puck rock," says Keighley, noting that the term "puck rock" now is the basis of a fanzine and two compilation albums called Puck Rock Classics. The compilations include such tracks as "Gump Worsley's Lament" (Huevos Rancheros), "What's Wrong with Lumme" (Glenn Ford and the Piers), "Of Orange Pucks and Mighty Ducks" (Mr. Nobody), "I'm Gonna Play Hockey" (Hanson Brothers), "Ode to Gino" (JP5) and "Our Stanley Cup" (the Smugglers).

Other bands have also formed hockey teams and the Vancouver group NoMeansNo created the Hanson Brothers—named after the Slap Shot characters—who have

released two albums containing several hockey songs with titles like Gross Misconduct and Sudden Death.

The most famous piece of hockey music was written by a Vancouver-born, classically trained musician named Dolores Claman, who fell into commercial jingle writing because of a lack of "legitimate" work. In 1968, the CBC commissioned her to write a new theme song for Hockey Night in Canada.

"I was given this message: Make it like the theme to an adventure show," she recalls. "And that's what I had in mind. I was thinking about how great people feel when a goal is scored, rather than something to march along with, which is [the sort of tune] they used to have. It was kind of goose-pimple raising, something to raise your spirit, and it worked."

The tune has been recorded by pop bands such as the Shuffle Demons and even included in an opera.

"The more the merrier," Claman says. "I think it's great." She adds that she's pleased to know French- and English-speaking Canadians share an enthusiasm for the song. "In Canada, hockey is a kind of link. The song wasn't regional. It was for all of Canada.

"It was a job. But it seemed to be just right. It wears well, but I never knew it would last this long."

Hockey Discography

"Clear the Track, Here Comes Shack" (The Secrets), 1966
"Pandemonium" (Tommy Hunter), 1972
"The Hockey Song" (Stompin' Tom Connors), 1973
"Raised on Robbery" (Joni Mitchell), 1974
"Signin' with the NHL" (Bruno Gerussi), 1978
"The Ballad of Wendel Clark, Parts I and II" (Rheostatics), 1987
"Hockey Night in Canada Theme" (Shuffle Demons), 1988
"Big League" (Tom Cochrane),1988
"Hockey" (Jane Siberry), 1989
Gross Misconduct (Hanson Brothers album), 1992
"Fifty-mission Cap" (Tragically Hip), 1992
"The Hockey Song" (Jughead), 1992
"Overtime" (DOA), 1993
"Rock 'em Sock 'em Techno" (Don Cherry with BKS), 1993
Puck Rock, Volume 1 (hockey compilation album), 1994
"Gretzky Rocks" (Pursuit of Happiness), 1995
"Bust 'Em Beat 'Em" (DOA), 1995
Sudden Death (Hanson Brothers album), 1996
"The Puck Drops Here" (Greg Godovitz and Andy Curran), 1996
"Give 'Em the Lumber" (DOA), 1998
Puck Rock Classics, Volume 2 (compilation album)

Hockey Filmography

The King of Hockey, 1936
Olympic Honeymoon, 1937
Idol of the Crowds, 1937
The Game that Kills, 1937
I See Ice, 1938
Duke of West Point, 1938
Hell's Kitchen, 1939
It's a Pleasure, 1945
Tournament Tempo, 1946
White Lightning, 1953
The Odd Couple, 1968
Love Story, 1970
Face-off, 1971
Paperback Hero, 1973
Enuff is Enuff, 1973
The Laughing Detective, 1973
Mystery of the Million-Dollar Puck, 1975
Slap Shot, 1977
Telefon, 1977
The Deadliest Season (TV), 1977
Ice Castles, 1979
Oliver's Story, 1979
The Boy Who Drank Too Much (TV), 1979
Hounds of Notre Dame, 1980
The Sweater, 1981
Miracle on Ice (TV), 1981
Hockey Fever, 1983
Strange Brew, 1983
Hockey Night, 1984
Youngblood, 1985
Generation (TV), 1985
Touch and Go, 1986
He Shoots, He Scores (TV), 1986
The Accused, 1988
Perfectly Normal,1990
The Cutting Edge, 1992
Gross Misconduct (TV), 1992
The Mighty Ducks, 1992
Wayne's World, 1992
Manhattan Murder Mystery, 1993
Lethal Weapon 3, 1993
Wayne's World 2, 1993
D2: The Mighty Ducks, 1994
The Final Seduction, 1994
Net Worth (TV), 1995
Canadian Bacon, 1995
Sudden Death, 1995
D3: The Mighty Ducks, 1996
Happy Gilmore, 1996
Everyone Says I Love You, 1996
Batman and Robin, 1997
Les Boys, 1997
Power Play (TV), 1998
Mystery Alaska, 1998

CHAPTER 60
Table Hockey

The Complete History of the Most Realistic Mechanical Sports Game ever Devised

Don Munro Jr. and Rob Raven

TOY HOCKEY GAMES have been part of the Canadian scene since the days of the Great Depression. While these games can be divided into several categories (including board games, magnetic hockey, air hockey, bumper hockey and knock hockey), the image that usually comes to mind when one thinks of table top hockey is that of a miniature ice rink with players mounted on small spikes spinning and moving with the twist of their steel rods.

The earliest type of these mechanical hockey games was built by Donald H. Munro, Sr. in his Toronto home in 1932–33. Made of wood and scrap metal found in his neighborhood, Munro built his first game as a Christmas present for his children at a time when he could not afford to buy gifts. Soon after, Munro built a handful of these games on consignment for the Eaton's department store in Toronto. They turned out to be an instant success. These early games, referred to as "the wooden game" by collectors, were produced every year until 1955. During this period of 22 years, many improvements were made in the playing quality and appearance.

Despite these many improvements, the early wooden hockey games bore only a passing resemblance to the on-ice game. Players, for example, were simply wooden pegs with wire loops that moved back and forth like pinball flippers. Still, these games were exceedingly popular. One of the main reasons for this popularity was the design of the hump or high area in the center of the playing surface. This innovation allowed the puck (actually a metal ball) to roll to either end of the game and made it possible for both players to be actively involved at the same time (one on offense and one on defense). Until this time, bagatelle games (and even modern day pinball games) all were played on a single slope enabling only one player at a time to participate.

Due to their size (about 14 by 36 inches), the early Munro wooden games were sold mainly in department stores and through mail order catalogs, though occasionally they would be carried in sporting goods and hardware stores. The games sold for between four and five dollars during the 1930s. The first recorded price was listed in the 1939–40 *Eaton's Fall & Winter Catalogue* where the Munro Standard Model was advertised for $4.95. The number of games produced in these early years would range from a few hundred to a few thousand.

In the 1940s, the Munro Standard Model was expanded to include a DeLuxe version where the ball would roll out of the net after a goal and into a small cup mounted at each end of the game. A Club Model, with a heavier wooden frame and stronger wire parts, was introduced for the many Boys Clubs that existed in Canada at this time. In 1945–46, Munro's partner, Stewart Molson Robertson, manufactured games in Rochester, New York under Munro's American patent, but despite the popularity of the games in Canada, the venture proved unsuccessful in the United States. Sales in Canada were increasing to several thousand games per year, and by 1954, the last full year in which these wooden games were made, prices were $8.95 for the Standard Game, $10.95 for the DeLuxe and $14.95 for the Club. The DeLuxe was by far the most popular model.

During the era of the wooden game, three different mechanical hockey games surfaced. The first was built by Gotham Pressed Metal Products of The Bronx, New York, who displayed their version of "Ice Hockey" in their 1937 catalog. Like the Munro game, Gotham's playing surface featured a hump in the center to keep the puck (again a metal ball) moving from side to side. However, the Gotham game featured only one player at either end who both guarded the goal and pivoted in a complete circle to shoot the puck into the other end.

A second competitor to Munro was introduced by the Reliable Toy Company of Toronto in 1953. Patterned after the Munro Game, the "Foster Hewitt Hockey Game" was made of plastic and came equipped with figures shaped like miniature hockey players molded out of die-cast metal. The game was comparatively small (approximately 12" x 24") and was sold for only a few years before being replaced by the more modern-style games.

The first of these modern-style games (and the challenger that finally ended Munro's wooden era) was introduced by the Eagle Toy Company of Montreal in 1954. Eagle's National Hockey Game was endorsed by the Montreal Canadiens and was an immediate success for several reasons. It was the first Canadian game to feature players printed in color on flat tin cutouts shaped like real hockey players who stood on a surface that resembled ice. Eagle's game was decorated with team pennants from the NHL and was the first Canadian game to feature metal rods that allowed its players to pivot a complete 360 degrees. The Eagle game measured 16" x 36" and sold for $10.95. Soon, both Munro and Eagle were issuing similar games that not only had rods to allowed the players to spin but also had slots that let them slide up and down the ice surface.

The innovation that led to metal rods and slots had actually be introduced in Sweden during the 1930s. Aristospel A.B. of Stockholm manufactured the game, which was sold to several European countries. A Canadian patent was issued in 1941, but although the design of the Swedish game was unique at the time, it was a difficult and costly game to manufacture. Not until 1954 would a Canadian company (Cresta Limited of Toronto) introduce and manufacture the Swedish-style game. Also in 1954, K & B Toys of Burlington, Ontario copied the Cresta game and issued their own version under the name "3 Star Hockey." K & B was only in business until 1957, while Cresta lasted until 1958. Neither proved able to compete with Eagle and Munro, who had both unveiled their own rod-and-slot hockey games at the Montreal Toy Show in January of 1956. From that point on, Munro and Eagle produced nearly all of the hockey games sold in Canada and the United States.

Over the years, Munro and Eagle were the undisputed leaders in designing and creating models that year after year became more realistic in their appearance. The games also played better through such innovations as goal lights, period timers, puck droppers, and "glass" above the boards. Three-dimensional players were first introduced by Munro back in 1964, and while both Munro and Eagle experiment with the design of their players, the flat tin men remained the most popular. In 1971, safety concerns forced a switch to plastic men with self-adhesive team labels that customers applied themselves. Eagle's games had the official endorsement of the NHL and could replicate exactly the uniforms of its teams. Munro relied on the endorsement of top stars like Bobby Orr and Bobby Hull for their games and could only approximate the NHL uniforms.

The televising of NHL games during the 1950s and the league's expansion in 1967 greatly enlarged the North American market for table top hockey games. Whereas thousands of games had been sold previously, the numbers were now beginning to reach the hundreds of thousands and were climbing every year. To meet the rising demand, both Munro Games and Eagle Toys were sold to U.S. companies in September of 1968—Munro to Servotronics and Eagle to Coleco. Their dominance of the Canadian and American markets would continue—with games growing larger (24" x 34") and prices ranging up to 30 and 40 dollars during the 1970s—until the advent of video games relegated table hockey to a "second choice" toy item.

By the late 1980s, a resurgence of table hockey occurred with Irwin Toys acquiring Coleco's tooling and companies like Stiga (a Swedish firm that had long been selling their games in Europe), Playtoy/Remco, Radio Shack, and Kevin Sports developing new games in North America. A Wayne Gretzky-endorsed game was introduced by Kevin Sports in 1990, selling for $120. Bubble top hockey games of the type found in bars, arenas, and other venues have also become very popular. In recent years, a deluxe table hockey game made in Greenwich, New York ("TableHockey" by Rick Benej) retails for about $700 U.S.

The rebirth of table top hockey games has made the collecting of these games (both old and new) a popular hobby. For both the serious and casual collector, these games often bring back many vivid childhood memories from finding a hockey game under the tree at Christmas to picking out favorite teams, playing "seasons" or tournaments for the miniature replica Stanley Cup, or simply arguing about whether or not the puck went in. Many parents today watch their sons and daughters glued to a monitor while they play video or computer games and feel sad to see their children miss out of the marvelous and dynamic interaction of the old mechanical hockey games.

Table hockey collectors often search for a specific childhood game or games which did not survive their growth into adulthood. "My mother threw it out," is the popular refrain. Many serious collectors strive to obtain all the significant landmark games from years gone by. Collecting can also include trying to find lost pieces from old games, such as players or entire teams, missing nets, trophies, pucks, rods, springs, overhead gondolas, or original boxes. Often, these game pieces are very specific to the manufacturer. For example, the original Eagle nets in 1954 were made of green mesh, but by 1957 they were all tin to be followed by white plastic nets in 1959. Munro games at one point featured three different pucks: a standard wooden puck, a magnetic puck (for better control with tin players) and a puck with a steel ball bearing in the middle.

The range of players from these old games can be mind-boggling, with flat tin players, tin players with separate plastic and/or metal sticks, 3-D tin players, 3-D plastic players, flat plastic players, and more. Players in specific uniforms have also become highly collectible, with the 1967 Oakland Seals and the purple-clad Los Angeles Kings becoming much sought-after. With Eagle Toys having held exclusive rights to produce NHL uniforms, players from their games have been most in demand. Because it was the last game to carry the NHL's endorsement, team sets from the Wayne Gretzky game have also become highly collectable (particularly for relocated teams such as the Winnipeg Jets, Quebec Nordiques, Minnesota North Stars and Hartford Whalers).

The value of an old hockey game is directly influenced by four key factors: initial popularity of the game, rarity, condition/completeness, and the importance of the game in the evolution of table top hockey. Games in their original box with all their original parts can sell for upwards of $100. Many collectors will only purchase games in the best condition because they feel that repairs compromise authenticity. Others value the rarity of the game or its historical significance moreso than the shape they find it in. However, to any collector who is also a player, the real thrill is to play the game again and recapture the past pleasures and glories of youth.

For these "grown up kids," there are a number of tournaments available every year, including the Johnny GoodGuy Tournament in Brampton, Ontario, the Ontario Table Hockey Championships in Hamilton, and the Upper Canada Cup in Toronto. The Toronto-area also features at least two leagues: the Metro Toronto Table Hockey League in Thornhill and the National Tabletop Association in Brampton. Other Canadian tournaments include the Windsor Cup Classic in Windsor, Ontario and the Canadian Open Championship in Hull, Quebec. There is also the U.S. Nationals in Warwick, Illinois and the Hubbard Hall Face Off Tournament in Greenwich, New York. In Sweden, an annual tournament is played on the Stiga game and a World Championship is played every second year with players from as many as 20 different countries (including Canada and the United States) competing for world supremacy.

CHAPTER 61

Hockey Computer and Video Games

Tom Hoffarth

EVEN BEFORE THE FIRST FACE-OFF at the highly anticipated dream team competition at the 1998 Nagano
Winter Olympics, you could have found Japanese
fans who never had seen a National Hockey League game,
yet knew all about Dominik Hasek's acrobatics, Pavel
Bure's speed and the velocity of Brett Hull's slapshot.

They played hockey on their computers.

"Young people love playing hockey games; they open the
door to the NHL from PlayStation," Atsuo Kasamatsu, executive director of the NHL Fan Club in Japan and the father
of two avid players, admitted to a newspaper reporter.

One of the most popular sports genres with video players
worldwide, computer hockey games have heightened the
interest of the game with younger fans in the last decade—
maybe even more than television and satellite dishes.
Industry figures claim that video hockey accounted for 2.2
percent of the 48 million total games sold in 1997, which
may not seem like a substantial quantity. But the quality of
the games compared to other sport re-creation technology
far surpasses the industry standards.

How good is it? Tomorrow, you might not be able to tell
if the hockey game on the television set is the real deal or
someone playing a video game. Computer technology has
come as far and as fast as a slapshot from the other side of
the rink that continues to pick up speed as it approaches the
target. As a result, those who program these ever-popular
games are just as baffled as you about what the next step
will be with these cutting-edge toys for kids of all ages.

Artificial intelligence is the real buzzword here. It's the
thing that computer-game companies like Electronic Arts,
Acclaim, Virgin Interactive, Sony and Midway commit
hours of research time to. The goal is to produce a hockey
game that's as real as possible for consumer platforms like
Sony PlayStation, Nintendo 64 and Sega Saturn (for the
younger crowd) and the standard desktop personal computer (for the adult player who also can use a modem and transfer information over the Internet to play opponents online).

But then again, that's just the half of it.

"Our biggest challenge is to bring a balance of reality and
entertainment," said Dave Warfield, the senior associate producer of EA's popular series of NHL games. "In the past, the
emphasis was all about fun, getting shots off, making hits.
Over the last few years, the feedback from the game players
has dictated that we include as much realism as possible—
add team strategy, forechecking, zone setups. That's exciting,
but through all that, we can't lose sight of the fun element."

The genesis for video hockey goes back beyond the Sega
Genesis many grew up with. The boom of video games in
the early 1980s did not include many hockey titles, *per se*.
As a child, many pre-video players can recall playing
games like table hockey or Strat-o-matic dice-games, eventually graduating to the new and exciting dawn of the Atari
2600 "pong" game. For those with a little imagination, this
was the first computer hockey, although the model definitely was more like tennis, because of the way the white dot
would deflect off the paddles. Maybe that's a stretch for

some. Mattel's Intellivision then can be credited with introducing the sport as a computer form of entertainment.
Atari's first hockey try was a two-on-two version, followed
by games like "Blades of Steel" and "Mutant Hockey
League" on the Sega Genesis system.

Then came EA's "NHL '93." It set a standard of realism
and entertainment that everyone—including EA's own
game designers—has been trying to match since. By spring
1998, more than half-a-dozen NHL-licensed and approved
games were on the market worldwide each trying to outdo
the other. Prices of today's products range from $40 to $60.

It only made the hockey games as a whole that much
more superior to other sports games. *PC Gamer* magazine
named EA's "NHL '98" the best sports game of the year
during its annual reader survey. CNET.com, an online marketing tool of the Internet, did the same. *Computer Game
World* magazine regularly lists at least two NHL video
games among its top 10 monthly surveys of sports games.

While most hockey video games have become sophisticat-
ed enough to offer many of the same options, the difference
is in the philosophy of those who produce and program each
game, which can take more than a year to develop. With the
trend toward using actual NHL players (although the
gamers can create their own "players" by other means), the
task for the programmer in charge of the artificial intelligence is to take all 650-plus NHL players each year and
break down their game. That can lead to as many as 40
attributes—speed, stickhandling, shot accuracy, offensive
and defensive awareness, for example. Bodychecking is
another key element in the world of 3D animated physics—
all players are programmed to their actual height and
weight and according to what actually would happen if they
were to check players bigger or smaller than themselves.
From there, each quality is assigned a numerical value
between 1 and 100. To help determine those numbers, game
producers who in the past relied on general statistics that
were available in any bookstore or magazine rack have
become much more practical. What could be more lifelike
than the players and coaches themselves? EA used the help
of 1998 Canadian Olympic coach Marc Crawford and
Avalanche star Peter Forsberg on its "NHL '98" game. It
incorporated the motion animation of Florida goalie John
Vanbiesbrouck's butterfly saves, stack pads and numerous
moves to depict his cyber-double.

Crawford marveled at how his actual game strategy could
be transferred to another dimension.

"When playing hockey, the keys to victory depend on
how well teams change their offensive and defensive strategy, depending on what type of situation they're up
against," said Crawford, who also coached the 1998
Canadian Olympic team. "Teams play a different strategy
when they they are down by a goal or up by a goal. Or on
the power-play or when killing a penalty, teams have to recognize their opponents' strengths and weakness and take
advantage of them. In working with the EA Sports development team, we have a game to a point where it is now

possible to have complete control over what type of strategy a team utilizes. It is amazing to think that interactive sports games have come so far as to simulate exactly what happens on the real ice."

Once the information is compiled, the video game lead programmer takes it all into consideration when deciding how to control the physics of this virtual environment—i.e., how will the puck bounce off the boards when hit by a certain player a particular way. Add to that factors such as state-of-the-art motion capture to make the players look real—the polygonal players have digitized faces that come straight from actual photographs.

The result is a technological orchestration that allows both the programmer and game player to share in creating a virtual game on the TV screen. During the course of a typical video game session, the computer will make hundreds of split-second decisions about the players on the ice that are being controlled by the gamers as well. And that's where the fun begins.

"If a real player is skating down the wing, he's thinking about whether to pass or shoot, and that's one rating factored in by itself," EA's Warfield said. "Next, he sizes up whether it's a three-on-two or two-on-one situation, or whether he wants to cycle the puck or crash the net. Is he in the neutral zone or the offensive end? If it's a funnel play, the computer will tell if a player will move into a prime scoring area. Which player will decide to get in the way of the goalie while his teammate tries to get in the offensive area? All these decisions are programmed in based on what likely would happen in a real contest. And that's very important to the people who buy the games."

To get another sense of what a typical video hockey game is about, consider the elements that go into "NHL Power Play '98," developed by Vancouver-based Radical Entertainment and published by Virgin Interactive.

On the game packaging, it is explained this way: "Claude Lemieux doesn't check like Brind'Amour in real life—and he doesn't in NHL Power Play, either. Our Patrick Roy doesn't make glove saves like the Dominator and you'll have a tough time beating our Beezer through the five hole. We use actual styles and ability to deliver the most realistic game."

And that's what makes all the difference.

"I think the real test is whether you're willing to play with the games that you make," said Ferdie Espedido, who produced "NHL Power Play '98." "In the past, I think we played a lot of the competitors' games, but now we find our games much better and that's the one most of us play all the time. And that's the way it should be, right? Why would you expect anyone else to play your game if you aren't willing to play it yourself?

"You need to find a happy medium for everyone. Just like in real life."

A PlayStation control pad allows the users to do dozens of specific things for each player. For example: press the square button on the right side, and the player on the screen shoots a wrist shot (if he's on offense), a hook and knee-sliding block (if he's on defense) or makes a save-and-smother action (if the goalie has the puck). Another button does things like drop passes, fake shots, flip passes or line changes, deflect and poke check, body check, skate backward or dive on defense.

To start a typical game, gamers go through a checklist, starting with the decision on the level of competition (some allow for amateur, pro or All-Star) and in what format to play (exhibition, regular season, tournament, playoffs or

world tournament), plus the length of the periods (five, 10, 15 or 20 minutes). They then activate or deactivate various elements of the game such as penalties (which, if left on, can occur for hooking, slashing, tripping, interference, cross-checking, boarding, elbowing, holding and a penalty shot), offsides, fatigue (which will determine whether a player becomes less efficient the more he is on the ice), line changes (can be done manually or automatic), plus coaching (allowing the player to determine offensive and defensive strategies instead of the computer).

Sometimes the players on the ice will even fight. Just like in real life.

Fighting is strictly monitored by the NHL and NHLPA, both on the ice and in the computer environment. See what happens when two aggressive players knock into each other. Or don't use that element and play a slightly different game. This is how the "NHL Power Play" instruction booklet describes how fighting works on its game: "In these extreme situations (when two players become agitated), tempers will occasionally flare up in an expression of this aggression. Although the NHL and NHLPA in no way endorses fighting, it has been included as an option to offer full simulation of the sport."

Explained Ferdie Espedido: "The NHL only will allow a certain amount of fighting in these games. We're not saying fighting doesn't happen, but we have programmed that factor into each player—what are the odds of him fighting in certain real-life situations. There are those who are still the enforcers, but most of the time you'll see them playing on the fourth lines."

Although video game makers try to let parents know about the animated violence rating on the box, "NHL Power Play" refers those who want to know to an 800-number. "NHL '98" may offer the most elaborate controls for fighting once fisticuffs get under way. For example, one button allows for a jab, another to throw a hook, a third to unload a haymaker and a fourth to grab an opponent's sweater.

"The NHL went through a period where they wouldn't permit fighting at all on their games, but we convinced them that's what the fans demanded," said EA's Warfield. "They're more on-board now. They just don't want us to portray an ugly side or take it too far. In a true hockey fight, it's a lot of grappling. We kind of went for the 'arcade-type' punching. I think we do have to be careful of the image of the game. Again, it's finding that balance, and what the artificial intelligence tweaking can do."

And if realism seems to be too real, there are always those games trying to lean the other way. "NHL Open Ice," for example, a product of Midway Games for GT Interactive, allows for some spectacular events you'd never see on NHL ice. How about Bure spinning three times in the air about 30 feet above the ice, then launching a shot of such power that the puck and the net catch fire? Or an option button where the goalies can have regular or supersized heads? The popular "Wayne Gretzky 3D Hockey," followed up by "Wayne Gretzky's 3D Hockey '98," has similar features for those who enjoy playing on Nintendo 64 systems, where graphics often take on a life of their own.

Another interesting aspects of how far video games have come—and hockey video games in particular—is how television production has adapted to the game's presence to maintain a fresh, contemporary look. Whereas television once might have dictated how video games were presented, the reverse is more true these days. So while video game programmers try all they can to recreate the real-life effects,

TV producers are constantly trying to duplicate graphic enhancements. And, for better or worse, we have things like the glowing puck that Fox Television introduced on its weekly games. The intent is to make it easier for those at home to follow the puck. The reaction from fans who've followed the puck for years on TV without any help has been mixed.

Additionally, camera angles can be adjusted on most all games, allowing the gamer—not the programmer—to choose from a high, low, up, down, left, right or overhead shot. A video game has a huge advantage over TV in that regard. The most common angle on the video screen is an angle that shows the action from a vertical, or north-to-south, overhead. Logistical restrictions prevent TV from covering a game any other way except to pan right to left from mid-ice.

"Since the beginning of video games, NHL fans are used to playing what they're used to seeing," said Warfield. "They have to have an attachment. We try to look like TV, but in our case, our camera doesn't have to be in a particular location, and the beauty is they can move to any height at any time in the game, and game players love to see that new perspective. Without those limitations, we can go deeper into a game with all this data we can store in the computers."

It follows that replays also are available to the game player, again from all angles, to heighten the excitement and duplicate another realistic quality. And, to circumvent the technological boundaries, real life NHL broadcasters like Jim Hughson and Daryl Reaugh have been employed to make calls on the "NHL '98" game. Broadcasters who are affiliated with video games must go into a recording studio and repeat hundreds of phrases that they'd say during an actual hockey game. When a similar play occurs in a video game, the computer inside is able to retrieve that sound bite and incorporate it as if it happened as part of the flow. With today's (and tomorrow's) technology so advanced, broadcasters actually can call a game as if they were sitting in the living room watching the action.

The cost of making video hockey games increases every year because of increasingly complex technology as companies have to continue to hire the top programmers and audio people from around the world to improve the product. But companies who sell them in large quantities try to keep the prices relatively constant as the competition heightens. They then try to make up for the extra costs by selling a greater volume of games.

Personal computer requirements for hockey games continue to become more demanding as the information expands and allows enthusiasts to compete online with other players. Around North America, PC users have caught on to the fantasy league craze, using DOS-based software that brings a statistical realism to computer screens. Lancaster, Pennsylvania-based APBA has a strong following of PC users.

As for the future of video games, Espedido figures they will always be "more complex to build. As developers we have to keep our ear to the public and access the market. Do they want more realism or more fanfare?"

Warfield predicts that "the realism only will get better and better. The audio will continue to improve. There will be a point when you wear things like virtual reality wrap goggles so you feel as if you're on the ice as well, playing right along with everyone else."

From a gamer's viewpoint, the result could be as dramatic as those who've learned how to, say, operate real airplanes based on their constant playing with joysticks on video games.

The more a gamer learns the Xs and Os involved in the sport of hockey, the more chance he or she will grow up that much more ahead of the game as a player or a coach. At some point, parents may realize that all that time their children are spending in front of the video screen actually will pay off. Could video hockey games be part of the required training for real players? We should be able to answer that in the very near future.

CHAPTER 62

Glossary of Hockey Terms and Phrases

Andrew Podnieks

ACL • anterior cruciate ligament. A knee ligament, commonly injured in hockey

Albert • a player who is not very good (used to disparage a friend). Taken from a character in a popular Canadian television commercial who begins as an awkward novice and grows up to become a pro hockey star.

Allan Cup • trophy awarded to the top Senior hockey team in Canada

All the way • a face-off taking place in the defensive zone after an off-side play is being brought back "all the way"

All-star • a player who is among the best of the best

Altercation • a fight or shoving match

Alternate captain • sometimes called an "assistant captain." Player who wears an "A" on his jersey and acts as an on-ice leader in conjunction with, or in the absence of, the captain. There are usually two or three alternate captains per team.

Amateur • an athlete who does not receive compensation of any kind for his or her play

Assist • credit given to a player who passes the puck to a teammate, making it possible for the teammate to score a goal. A maximum of two players are credited with assists on each goal. Each assist counts as one point on a player's scoring record.

Assistant captain • see alternate captain

Assistant coach • any coach who assists the head coach. Some assistant coaches are behind the bench during games, assisting with line changes or working exclusively with defensemen; others conduct discrete parts of practices, review videotapes of games or work with the goaltenders.

Attacking zone • the part of the ice inside the opponent's blue line

Avco Cup • championship trophy of the World Hockey Association, named after the finance company that sponsored it

Backchecking • a forward skating deep into his own zone to check an opponent off the puck or prevent him from getting a scoring change

Backhand • a shot or pass using the back part of the blade, often while the shooter's back is to the net

Backliner • a defenseman

Backup • a team's substitute goalie. Since 1964–65, teams have been required to maintain two goalies in uniform and full equipment for every game

Banana blade • a very severely hooked stick blade, popular in the late 1960s but no longer legal

Bandy • a European game similar to hockey, popular in Northern Europe in the latter part of the 19th century and the early 20th century. Still played today.

Beantowners • colloquial name for the Boston Bruins

Beehive • a photograph of a hockey player, produced between the late 1940s and late 1960s. They were obtained by collecting labels from any of several products produced by the St. Lawrence Starch company, the most popular of which was Beehive Golden Corn Syrup.

Bench boss • a coach

Bench minor • a two-minute penalty given for an infraction by a player (or the coach or training staff) on the bench (as opposed to on the ice), usually for too many men on the ice or for unsportsmanlike conduct. Bench minors are served by one of the players on the ice (other than a goalie) when the foul was called.

Between the pipes • the goaltender's position in the net

Biscuit • the puck

Blade • the curved part of the stick used for shooting. Also, the sharpened runner on the skate.

Blazing speed • quality possessed by a fast skater

bleu, blanc et rouge • colloquial name for Montreal Canadiens, derived from the colors—blue, white and red—of their uniforms that were, in turn, derived from the colors of the national flag of France.

Blocked shot • a shot prevented from reaching the net by a player other than the goaltender

Blocker • the padded glove in which a goaltender holds his stick. So called because it has a large, flat rigid surface used to block shots.

Blue and White • nickname for the Toronto Maple Leafs

Blue line • one of two blue lines that divide the ice into three zones

Blueliner • a defenseman

Boarding • hitting an opponent violently into the boards, usually from behind. Punishable by a two-minute penalty.

Boards • wooden (or fiberglass) structure which surrounds the playing surface

Bodychecking • using one's body to impede an opponent.

Bonuses • payments incorporated into players' contracts, awarded for attainment of individual goals (for instance, scoring 100 points) or team objectives (finishing in first place)

Bootheel • early slang for the puck

Box • formation adopted by a team in its own zone while shorthanded. Also, short for the penalty box

Breakaway • a play in which a puck carrier moves in alone on the opposing goalie, having left the defenders and his teammates behind

Breakout • movement of the puck by a team out of its end into the attacking zone

Broadway Blueshirts • nickname for the New York Rangers

Brouhaha • a fight or scuffle

Bush league • pejorative term for amateur or low-level play

Butt end • the taped knob at the top of the stick, dangerous when used to hit a player

Butterfly • a goaltending style in which the goalie keeps his knees together and his feet slightly apart, enabling him to drop quickly to his knees to make a save and subsequently regain his feet

Cage • the net

Call-up • a player is transferred, or recalled, from a Junior or minor pro team to the NHL team that owns his rights

Camp by the side of the net • to position oneself beside the net and just outside the goal crease and wait for a pass or rebound

Cannonading blast • term made popular by Hockey Night in Canada announcer Danny Gallivan to describe a hard slapshot

Captain • the leader of a team and the only player who is supposed to have on-ice discussions with the referee over penalty calls and rule interpretations

Catching glove • glove used exclusively by the goalie to catch the puck (also known as a trapper)

Caught up ice • a situation in which a player is out of position in his team's offensive zone after play has moved well back into his team's defensive zone

Center • one of the three forward positions, and the player who usually takes face-offs

Center line • a red line which divides the rink in half

Change on the fly • to substitute players while the play continues

Charging • taking two or more strides before hitting a player. Usually results in a two-minute penalty.

Check • to take a man off the puck or away from the play

Checker • a player whose greatest skill is to prevent the opposing team's best players from scoring

Checking line • a forward line whose primary role is to play defensively

Chest pad • piece of equipment worn by goalies to protect their chest

Chippy • adjective for play which is dirty, particularly when sticks are being used illegally

Chops • the teeth or mouth

Chukker • old-time slang for a period (from the polo term)

Clear the puck • to shoot the puck out of one's defensive zone

Clutch-and-grab • defensive style of hockey often employed by slower

teams to prevent faster teams from using their speed

Coach • person who directs the team during games and practices, prepares strategy and decides which players will take part in games

Coach's Corner • popular between-periods segment of Hockey Night in Canada, featuring former NHL coach Don Cherry and studio host Ron MacLean

Coincidental penalties • penalties assessed simultaneously to players on opposite teams, during which neither team plays shorthanded

Color commentator • a TV or radio announcer who adds lively anecdotes and analysis of the game

Concussion • injury caused by one or more violent blows to the head or upper body, resulting in unconsciousness or disorientation. Effects of a concussion are cumulative, and can result in severe brain damage.

Conditional draft choice • in a trade, a draft choice in an unspecified round. The round in which the pick is made is determined by a factor such as the trading team's finish in the standings.

Contain • to keep an opponent in its own zone or to prevent the opponent from attacking with any consistent momentum

Cooler • the penalty box

Corners • rounded-off part of the rink between the goal line and end boards. Where hardworking players ("grinders") earn their money.

Cover • to check; that is, to watch a player on the other team closely so that he can't create or cash in on a scoring chance

Cowpie • slang for the puck

Crease • see goal crease

Crossbar • top bar that joins the two goal posts

Cross-check • to make contact with an opponent while holding one's stick with both hands. Subject to a two- or five-minute penalty.

Cup • short form for hockey's greatest prize, the Stanley Cup. Always written with a capital "C."

cup • plastic (or metal) insert in an athletic support, used to protect the genitals. Never written with a capital "C."

Curve • the warp in the blade of a stick

Cutting down the angle • goaltending technique in which the goalie skates slightly out of his crease to reduce the amount of net that a shooter can see

Cycling the puck • movement of the puck along the boards by one or more players in the offensive corners

D • short for defense. A pass from one defenseman to the other is known as a D-to-D pass.

Debatable call • a controversial call by an official

Defenseman • one of two players on the ice whose primary role is to guard the defensive zone

Defensive specialist • forward known for his ability to prevent goal-scoring chances for the other team

Defensive zone • that area inside a team's blue line

Deflection • a redirection of the puck, accidental or intentional, after a shot or pass has been made

Defunct team • a team that is no longer in the league. NHL examples include the Hamilton Tigers and Oakland Seals

Deke • a quick fake by a puck carrier, meant to trick an opponent out of position

Delay of game • a minor infraction, subject to a two-minute penalty. Given to a player who shoots the puck out of the rink, holds the puck, or does something to stop the play unnecessarily.

Delayed offside • a situation in which an attacker is offside, but the whistle is delayed because the defending team has possession of the puck and has the opportunity to move the puck out of its end

Delayed penalty • a penalty that is not called against a player until his team takes control of the puck

Dental work • euphemism for a player losing a tooth (or teeth) and being forced to leave the ice to be taken care of

Dig • to use one's body and stick to get the puck away from an opponent, usually along the boards

Dinged • hit by the puck

Disk • the puck

Dive • a player falling intentionally to make a routine check look like an infraction worthy of a penalty

Diver • a player suspected of taking dives. Philadelphia Flyer great Bill Barber was one of the first NHLers to be called a diver.

Done like dinner • catch phrase coined by Toronto Maple Leaf winger

Tiger Williams to describe a team that is either badly beaten or severely overmatched

Double minor • a pair of minor penalties assessed against one player, to be served consecutively

Down a man • a team playing shorthanded by one player

Draft-eligible • a player who is 18 or older and who has not yet been selected by a team at the NHL Entry Draft

Drawing a penalty • getting the referee to call a penalty against an opponent, whether through hard work or acting

Drop pass • a pass made by one player leaving the puck behind him to be picked up by a teammate skating behind him

Drop the gloves • to get into a fight

Dump and chase • strategy by which a team shoots the puck into the attacking zone, then skates in aggressively after it

Elbow pad • protective equipment worn on the elbows

Elbowing • hitting an opponent illegally with one's elbow. Subject to a two-minute penalty.

Empty-net goal • a goal scored into an undefended goal, usually in the dying minutes of a game, when the losing team has pulled its goalie for an extra attacker. Empty-net goals count against a team, but are not counted when calculating an individual goalie's goals-against average.

End-to-end action • exciting play with infrequent whistles and both teams getting many scoring chances

Enforcer • a player who fights frequently

"...et le but!" • French exclamation equivalent to "He scores!" Literally means "and the goal!"

Facemask • protective mask, worn by goalies, that covers the face and much of the head

Face-off • dropping of the puck to start play

Face-off circle • painted on the ice in red, in which face-offs take place

Face-off dot • solid red dots painted on the ice where face-offs take place

Face-off specialist • a player who is effective at winning face-offs

Fan • a spectator, or a supporter of a particular team

Fan (on a shot) • to miss the puck completely, or to fail to hit it cleanly, when trying to shoot

Feed • (verb) to pass the puck; (noun) a pass. A player who "takes a feed" has received a pass.

Fence • term used by some oldtimers to describe the glass Plexiglas segments that surround the rink, because until the 1950s many arenas had chain-link fencing or chicken wire where the glass is today

Finish a check • to check a man so well as to eliminate him altogether from the play

Fire wagon hockey • a fast-paced, wide-open, offensive style of play

Fisticuffs • fighting

Five hole • the area between a goalie's legs

Five-on-three • a situation in which a team has a two-man advantage, with five skaters on the ice to the other team's three

Five-on-five • term most often used after a penalty has expired to indicate that both teams are back at even strength

Floater • term for a player who can score but is unable or unwilling to put in a total effort (by backchecking or going into the corners)

Flying Frenchmen • nickname for the Montreal Canadiens

Forechecking • checking the other team in its own zone in an attempt to create scoring chances

Forehand • a player's natural side to shoot from (opposite to backhand)

Forward • one of three players on the ice—a center, left winger or right winger—whose primary role is to attack and attempt to score

Four-on-four • both teams having a man in the penalty box

Four-pointer • a game between division or conference rivals, resulting in a four-point swing in the standings depending on which team wins

Free agent • a player whose contract has expired and who is free to sign with any other team

Freeze the puck • to pin the puck against the boards to force an official to stop play

Futures • short for "future considerations"

Gallery Gods • fans with seats in the cheap upper balcony of the old Boston Garden. Also applied to other arenas.

Game-day skate • a light workout held the morning of a game

Game misconduct • a penalty that involves the ejection of a player from the game and a fine. The case is also referred to the commissioner, who

may decide to levy greater penalties (fines or suspensions). The penalized player's team does not play shorthanded.

Garbage goal • a goal of little aesthetic quality. The term gained currency during Phil Esposito's heyday, as many of his goals were scored on deflections or when the goalie was screened.

Give and go • a play in which one player passes the puck to a teammate, skates into the open, and receives a pass from the player he has just passed to

Glass • First introduced in the early 1950s, an unbreakable barrier of transparent panes placed atop the boards to protect the spectators. Glass replaced wire mesh.

Glove hand • a goalie's catching hand

Glove pass • use of the glove by a skater to direct the puck away from an opponent (illegal except in the defensive zone)

Glove side • the side of the net protected by the goaltender's catching glove. Opposite of the stick side.

Go-ahead goal • a goal that breaks a tie

Goal • the movement of the puck across the red (goal) line, into the net. Teams get one point for each goal. The player who shoots the puck into the net, or who was the last member of the scoring team to touch the puck, is credited with the goal in his scoring statistics.

Goal crease • area of the ice, painted blue, in front of the goal net. Players other than the goaltender are not permitted to skate or stand inside the crease unless the puck enters it first.

Goal judge • a minor official who sits directly behind the net. He determines whether the puck has entered the goal and turns on the red goal light to signal when it does.

Goal light • a red light located behind each net and illuminated by the goal judge when he sees that the puck has crossed the goal line into the net.

Goal line • a thin red line painted across the ice, 13 feet from the end boards, across which the puck must pass completely to count as a goal. Also used to determine when icing has occurred.

Goal mouth • the area immediately in front of the net, roughly corresponding to the goal crease.

Goal suck • pejorative for a player who stations himself well ahead of the play for a breakaway or an easy scoring chance

Goaler • antiquated term for goaltender

Goal post • one of two vertical posts, painted red and joined at the top by a crossbar. A shot that hits one of the posts or the crossbar without entering the net does not count as a goal, or as a shot on goal.

Goals against • number of goals allowed by a team

Goals-against average • ratio of goals allowed by a goaltender or team per 60 minutes played. Rounded to two decimal places.

Goaltender • player whose role it is to defend the net, by using any part of his body or his stick. Goaltenders use a wider stick than the other players, and are the only players allowed to use their hands to handle the puck.

Go down low • to play in the corners of the offensive zone

Golden helmet • in some European leagues, the player who leads his team in scoring wears a different colored helmet (gold). Similar to the yellow jersey worn by the overall leader in the Tour de France bicycle race.

Gondola • the broadcast area at Maple Leaf Gardens from 1931 until the late 1980s. It was suspended from the arena's ceiling, like a balloon gondola, and was made famous by longtime Leaf announcer Foster Hewitt.

Gone • slang for a player ejected from a game as in, "You're gone!"

Goon • a player, usually a winger, who has limited skills and whose primary job is to fight or to intimidate his opponents

Go upstairs • to shoot the puck toward the top of the net

Gretzky's office • the area directly behind the net. So called because Wayne Gretzky would often station himself behind the opponent's net and pass to a teammate in front of the net or bring the puck quickly from behind the net and stuff it in (a "wraparound" goal)

Grinder • a hard-working player who is better known for his checking than his scoring

Groin injury • a pull or tear to the muscles around the inner thigh and pelvis. Skating requires almost constant use of these muscles, so this injury is very common, and very debilitating, to hockey players.

Gross misconduct • a penalty that the referee can give to any player, coach, manager or trainer guilty of gross misconduct of any kind. The player, coach, manager or trainer is ejected and fined. The infraction is reviewed by the commissioner to determine if supplementary discipline is required. The penalized team does not play shorthanded.

Habs • short for "habitants," a nickname for the Montreal Canadiens

Hacker • a player who, in the absence of skill or speed, relies on hooking or slashing opponents with his stick

Had his head down • describes a puck carrier caught looking at the puck rather than watching what's going on around him, thus becoming an easy target for a bodycheck

Hall of Famer • a player who has been inducted into the Hockey Hall of Fame. An active player who displays skills equal to those already in the Hall of Fame is described as a "future Hall of Famer."

Hand pass • a glove pass

Handcuffed • describes a player who can't quite get his stick on the puck

Hat • colloquial term for the helmet

Hat trick • three goals scored by one player. If the player scores three goals uninterrupted by teammates' or opponents' scores, it's called a natural hat trick.

Headmanning the puck • passing the puck forward on an offensive rush

Heads-up play • a smart, intelligent play

Heel • part of the stick where the shaft curves into the blade

Helmet • protective headgear worn by all players

Hemmed in • describes a team unable to get the puck out of its own zone because of aggressive forechecking by the opposition

"He shoots, he scores" • catch phrase coined by broadcaster Foster Hewitt

Hickory • old-time slang for hockey stick

High heat • a hard shot to the top of the net

High sticking • raising the stick above shoulder level. Referee's stop play and call a penalty if the guilty player has struck an opponent with a high stick.

Hip check • using the hip to check an opponent

Hockey card • a collectible card with a player's photograph on it

Hockey Night in Canada • title of the Canadian Broadcasting Corporation's Saturday-night broadcasts of hockey games. Series began on radio before making its television premiere in 1952, making it North America's longest-running TV sports program.

Hockeyist • old-time slang for a hockey player

Holding • using the hands or arms to impede a player's progress. Subject to a two-minute penalty.

Home-and-home • a pair of back-to-back games, often on consecutive nights, between the same two opponents, one at each team's home arena

Hooking • using the stick to impede a player's progress, resulting in a two-minute penalty

Hot Stove League • a longtime radio, and later television, segment aired between periods on Hockey Night in Canada, during which the evening's game, as well as larger hockey issues, were discussed. On the TV version, the illusion of a small-town atmosphere was created by gathering the panelists around a potbellied stove on a set that looked like an old-fashioned general store. The segment has recently been revived as the "Satellite Hot Stove League," linking commentators in different cities via satellite, without the wood-burning appliance.

Hyperbaric chamber • a large piece of medical equipment in which a person sits and breathes pressurized oxygen. Injured players who spend time in a hyperbaric chamber recover more quickly because an increased amount of oxygen is forced into their tissues.

The "I" • short for the International Hockey League

Ice cleaner • precursor to the Zamboni, usually a large shovel or small wagon with water and ice scraping capabilities

Ice time • minutes played by a skater in a game

Icing • shooting the puck from behind the center red line across the other team's goal line. After the puck is iced, play stops and a face-off is held in the defensive zone of the team that iced the puck.

Illegal stick • one which is too long, has too wide a blade, or too severe a hook, resulting in confiscation of the stick and a two-minute penalty

In alone • a puck carrier on a breakaway who has only the goalie to beat

In back of the net • term used by broadcasters when they really mean "behind the net"

In the zone • describes a hot goalie

Insurance goal • a goal that widens a team's lead to two or three goals, usually late in the third period of a close game

Intentional offside • a play on which a player has deliberately put himself offside (by preceding the puck into the offensive zone or by accepting a two-line pass). The resulting face-off is held in the offside team's defensive zone rather than in the neutral zone.

Interference • checking a player who does not have the puck. Subject to a two-minute penalty

Intermission • a 15-minute break between periods (17 minutes in the modern NHL), during which the ice is resurfaced

Iron • a goal post or crossbar

Jockstrap • athletic supporter

Judge of play • a second referee, utilized in games played in the 1910s and 1920s

Junior hockey • organized hockey, based primarily in Canada, played by young men under the age of 20. The highest tier of Junior hockey is known as major Junior, and is the greatest supplier of players selected at the NHL's annual Entry Draft.

Katie-bar-the-door • a strategy that emphasizes goal prevention above all else

Keeping one's head up • paying attention to the play rather than merely focusing on the puck.

Kick save • save made by the goalie kicking the puck away from the goal mouth

Killing a penalty • preventing the opposition from scoring while they are on a power-play

Knee-on-knee hit • a dangerous bodycheck in which the knees of the checker and the player being checked collide

"Last minute to play in the game/period" • announcement made over the arena public-address system to inform fans there is one minute remaining in the period

Leave the puck • generally when a player skates in a manner indicating he has the puck when in fact he left it behind for a teammate to get (similar to a drop pass)

Left-wing lock • a defensive system. On an offensive rush, the left winger (and sometimes the right winger) hangs back at the blue line rather than forechecking, to prevent the defensive team from carrying the puck out of their own zone.

Lie (of a stick) • the angle at which a stick's blade is set to its shaft

Line change • substitution of players, usually the forward line

Linesman • one of two on-ice officials, subordinate to the referee, who watch for icing, offsides and some infractions; they also conduct most face-offs

Lineup • 1) the starting lineup, a list of the six players who are to be on the ice for the opening face-off; 2) the list of players in uniform who are eligible to participate in a game

Loafing • outdated term. In the early days of hockey, a player holding the puck with no intention of creating a scoring chance could be given a penalty for "loafing with the puck."

Looking for blood • a player seeking revenge for an earlier check against him or a teammate

Loose puck • a puck that is in open ice and controlled by neither team

Lowering the boom • dropping one's shoulder to administer a clean, hard check on an opponent

Lunchpail player • a player, also known as a grinder, whose skill level is not high but who plays with intensity and determination

Major penalty • a five-minute penalty

Mapleos • nickname for the Toronto Maple Leafs, current in the 1940s and 1950s

Marked man • someone who has upset his opponents and who will, in turn, be checked or antagonized

Marker • a goal

Match penalty • a form of misconduct penalty given when a player deliberately attempts to injure an opponent. The player is ejected from the game and his team plays shorthanded for five minutes.

Matching lines • a coach's attempt to put a particular line on the ice (normally a checking line) against certain players on the opposing team (usually their best scoring line)

Melee • a large brawl or shoving match

Memorial Cup • trophy awarded to the top team in major junior hockey.

Midget hockey • level of Canadian amateur hockey played by boys 17 and under. There's nothing midget about them as top 16- and 17-year-olds often top six feet.

Minor penalty • a two-minute penalty

Minors • professional leagues of lesser caliber than the NHL. The top minor leagues are the American and International leagues.

Minutes played • the number of minutes played by a goaltender, in a single game or over the length of the season, is an officially published statistic. Teams often keep tabs of the amount of time each skater is on the ice, but these records are not kept by the league.

Misconduct • a 10-minute penalty

"Move it!" • what the referee says when the puck is trapped along the boards by two or more players but he is as yet unwilling to blow his whistle to stop play

Mucker • a grinder

Netcam • a small television camera placed inside the goal net to provide a close-up view of the action for TV audiences, as well as to help video goal judges determine whether a goal has been legally scored

Netminder • a goalie

Neutral zone • the area between the blue lines

Neutral-zone trap • checking system used in the neutral zone designed to prevent the attacking team from entering the attacking zone at top speed.

Nobody • a player of little skill

Off-ice official • one of a number of people who assist in the conduct of a game. They include goal judges, game and penalty timekeepers, the official scorer and the video goal judge.

Official scorer • the off-ice official who keeps track of all goals, assists, goalie substitutions and penalties

Offside • describes a player who illegally enters the attacking zone before the puck. Play is stopped and a face-off is held. Offside is also called when a player accepts an offside (or two-line) pass.

Offside pass • a pass across two lines

Off wing • describes a left winger skating down the right-hand side of the ice, or vice versa. Also called the "wrong wing."

On the tape • a pass that hits the intended receiver right on the stick blade, which is wrapped in a protective layer of tape

One-on-one • a puck carrier who skates in on goal with only one defender between him and the goalie

One-timer • a shot, usually a slap shot, taken immediately after receiving a pass, without stopping the puck and setting up

Out-of-town scoreboard • a scoreboard, or series of scoreboards, dedicated to displaying the scores of games being played elsewhere around the league

Overskating the puck • skating past the puck without gaining possession of it

Overtime • sudden-death play that occurs if the game is tied after the three 20-minute periods that make up regulation time. In regular season play, a single five-minute overtime period is played, and if no goal is scored, the game enters the standings as a tie. During the playoffs, overtime periods are 20 minutes each, and play continues until the first goal is scored.

Pad save • a save made by the goalie using his leg pads

Paddle • the goal stick

Penalty • punishment for a rule infraction, requiring a player to leave the ice for a prescribed length of time

Penalty bench • the penalty box

Penalty box • the area where penalized players must remain for the duration of all penalties except game misconducts

Penalty-killing • attempt by a shorthanded team to prevent the opposition from scoring

Penalty minutes • statistical category, technically "penalties in minutes" (PIM), which tallies the amount of time a player or team is penalized

Penalty shot • a free shot on goal awarded by the referee for infractions such as tripping a man on a clear breakaway; putting a hand on the puck in the crease; or dislodging the net with less than two minutes to play in a period

Penalty-shot circle • from 1934–35 to 1940–41 penalty shots were taken from inside a circle in front of each net. The center of the circle was 38 feet from the goal line.

Penalty-shot line • a line 28 feet from the net; from 1941–42 to 1945–46 "minor" and "major" penalty shots were called; minor penalty shots were taken from this line.

Penalty timekeeper • off-ice official who ensures a player has served his entire penalty before he is allowed back onto the ice

Period • one of three 20-minute segments in a regulation game

Pest • a player, usually a checker, who antagonizes opponents either with his play or words

Peter Puck • an animated cartoon character, created by broadcaster Brian McFarlane, who appeared in a series of short animated films that

explained the game, primarily to children and new fans in the United States in the early 1970s

Pick • term borrowed from basketball. Positioning oneself in an opponent's way to give a puck-carrying teammate more room to skate

Pine(s) • the players' bench. A player who is benched or seeing little action is "riding the pines."

Pins • slang for a player's legs

Pipes • the goal posts

Playing the man • a player, usually a defenseman, checking the puck carrier, allowing the puck to be retrieved by a teammate

Playing the puck • a goalie leaving his net to handle the puck, whether to pass it or to clear the zone

Playmaker • a player whose greatest skill is passing the puck and setting up scoring chances

Playoff hockey • used to describe particularly intense, close-checking action whether it occurs in the regular season or the playoffs.

Plugger • a lunchpail player

Plus–minus • a statistic that attempts to express a player's defensive value. A player is awarded a "plus" each time he's on the ice when his team scores an even-strength or shorthanded goal. He is charged with a "minus" for each even-strength or shorthanded goal the other team scores when he's on the ice. A player's "plus–minus" rating is the number left over when the minuses are subtracted from the pluses.

Point man • a player, usually a defenseman, whose job while his team is forechecking or on the power-play is to keep the puck from leaving the offensive zone and to shoot the puck directly at the goalie

Point • area just inside the offensive blue line, usually near the boards

Point-blank • describes a shot taken extremely close to the net

Poke check • a sweeping move with the stick, often by the goalie, to knock the puck away from an opponent

Policeman • an enforcer

Pond • slang for ice

Pot • to score a goal

Power forward • a forward who is big and strong, who is equally capable of scoring or playing physically. Likely to have high totals in goals and assists as well as penalty minutes.

Power-play • situation in which one team has more men on the ice than their opponents, because the other team has been penalized

Press box • a facility set aside for reporters to watch games and prepare their reports for newspapers or magazines

Prexy • old-time slang for president, such as "NHL prexy Clarence Campbell"

Prospect • a young player who shows potential of succeeding in the NHL

Puck • a black, round disk made of vulcanized rubber, one inch thick and three inches in diameter

Puck-chasers • old-time slang for players

Puck control • maintaining possession of the puck for an extended time

Pull the goalie • to remove the goalie for an extra skater; usually done at the end of a game or when a delayed penalty is about to be called

Quick release • the ability to shoot the puck quickly with little time to prepare or aim

Quinella • scoring every type of goal in a single game: even-strength, power play, shorthanded, penalty shot and empty net, Mario Lemieux accomplished this feat on New Year's Eve 1988 versus New Jersey.

Ragging the puck • skating around with the puck to waste time, usually when killing a penalty

Railbird • a fan who has a seat right along the boards. In earlier eras, railbirds sitting along the side boards had to pay close attention to the game as weren't protected by any sort of glass or wire screen.

Real-Time Scoring • Computer based scoring program introduced into the NHL in 1997 that records all traditional statistics (goals, assists, penalties, saves, shots on goal, plus–minus) while also recording and generating new categories of information such as time on ice, hits, blocked shots, takeaways, giveaways and face-offs.

Rebound • a puck that caroms off the goalie back into play after a save

Recalled • a player who has been summoned from a minor-league or junior team to play for his NHL club

Red • by far the most common nickname in hockey (i.e., Ralph "Red" Almas, John "Red" Doran, Lloyd "Red" Doran, Mervyn "Red" Dutton, Dudley "Red" Garrett, Clifford "Red" Goupille, Robert "Red" Hamill, Bill "Red" Hay, George "Red" Henry, Bob "Red" Heron, Reginald "Red" Horner, Walter "Red" Jackson, John "Red" Keating, Leonard "Red" Kelly, Roy "Red" Storey, William "Red" Stuart, George "Red" Sullivan)

Red light • light used to signal a goal. Ineffective goaltenders are often tagged with "Red-Light" as a derisive nickname.

Red line • can refer either to the center line or to one of the two goal lines

Referee • the head official in a game

Retaliation penalty • a penalty assessed when a player is seen retaliating for a check, legal or not, by an opponent

Richard Riot • riot that broke out on the night of March 17, 1955, after a Montreal Canadiens–Detroit Red Wings game was suspended because of extreme fan unrest. Named after Montreal's Maurice "Rocket" Richard, who'd been suspended from this and all remaining Canadiens games after a stick-swinging incident in a game against Boston.

Rossmen • nickname for the Boston Bruins when they were managed by Art Ross

Roughing • minor shoving or fighting, subject to a two-minute penalty

Rover • a seventh on-ice position, eliminated from the National Hockey Association in 1911. The rover's duties combined those of the defensemen and forwards. The Pacific Coast Hockey Association, a rival league to the NHA and, later, the NHL, kept the rover until 1922.

Run interference • see pick

Rut (in the ice) • a flaw or imperfection in the ice. On-ice officials will frequently make impromptu repairs to the ice surface to make it safer for the players.

Save percentage • a statistic calculated by dividing the number of saves a goalie makes by the total number of shots on goal he faces. Expressed to three decimal places (eg., .912).

Scramble • a crowd in front of the net, made up of players from both teams, during which the puck is not controlled by anyone

Scratch • a player who is on a team's roster, but is not in uniform for a game, either because of injury or the coach's decision. A player who misses a game but is not injured is called a "healthy scratch."

Screening • blocking the goalie's view of the play

Screen shot • a shot taken while the goalie is screened

Second season • the playoffs

Semi-pro • a league in which some players receive a salary, but not on a consistent or full-time basis

Senior hockey • level of amateur hockey, in decline since the 1960s, for players 20 and up. Canada's top Senior team, winners of the Allan Cup, would often represent their country in the Olympics or at world championships

Shadow • to closely check a skilled opponent

Sheet • an ice rink

Shin pad • protective gear worn by all players to prevent injury to the shins and lower leg

Shinny • an informal, wide-open version of hockey

Shooting percentage • statistic calculated by dividing the number of goals a player (or team) scores by the number of shots taken. Expressed as a percentage to one decimal place (e.g. 12.5%).

Shootout • a tie breaking method, used in international and minor pro hockey, in which teams take penalty shots

Short side • the side of the net nearer a shooter

Shorthanded • state of a team which has fewer players on the ice than its opponent because one or more of its players have been penalized

Shot on goal • any shot that is stopped by the goalie that otherwise would have gone in (thus, a shot that hits the post, or is wide of the net, is not counted as a shot on goal)

Shutout • a game in which a goalie does not allow any goals

Simon pure • old-time term for an amateur player who never accepted pay for play.

Sin bin • the penalty box

Sixth attacker • extra skater who comes onto the ice late the game after the goalie has been pulled

Skater • a non-goaltender (i.e., a defenseman or forward)

Slapper • a slap shot

Slap shot • the hardest shot a player can generate, requiring a full windup with the stick

Slap Shot • famous 1977 movie that starred Paul Newman and which satirized hockey

Slashing • an infraction assessed when a player swings his stick violently at an opponent

Slot • the area directly in front of the net, from the crease to the top of the face-off circles

Slow whistle • situation in which an official takes longer than would be expected to stop play

Smother the puck • goaltending technique whereby a goalie freezes the puck and forces a play stoppage

Smythemen • old-time nickname for the Toronto Maple Leafs, who were owned and managed for many years by Conn Smythe

Snap shot • a quick wrist shot

Sniper • a talented goal scorer.

Soft goal • a goal the goalie should probably have saved

Sophomore jinx • a drop-off in a player's performance in his second year

Spearing • jabbing an opponent viciously, usually in the stomach, with the blade of the stick. Subject to a major penalty and a game misconduct. Attempting to spear (without making contact with an opponent) results in a double minor.

Spin-a-rama • a 360-degree turn, while carrying the puck, to evade an opponent. Term was coined by Montreal Canadiens announcer Danny Gallivan, who often called it a "Savardian spin-a-rama" after Habs defenseman Serge Savard.

Splendiferous • a Danny Gallivanism to describe an outstanding play

Splitting the defense • a puck carrier deking between the two defenseman to move in on goal

Standup goalie • a goaltender who stays on his feet and keeps his pads together. The opposite of a butterfly goalie.

Stick check • to take the puck from an opponent by reaching in quickly with the stick and poking it away

Stick • (noun) traditionally, a hook-shaped piece of wood, no more than five feet long, used by players to shoot, pass or handle the puck. Today, the shafts of many sticks are made of graphite or clad in aluminum, but the blade is still made of wood.

Stick • (verb) to use the blade of the stick on an opponent

Stick side • the side of the net protected by the goalie's stick and blocker

Stickhandling • controlling the puck by shifting it quickly from one side of the blade to the other

Stickwork • illegal use of the stick for interference and infractions such as hooking, slashing or holding

Stone • to make a great save as in "stone the shooter"

Sudden death • a form of overtime in which the first team to score is declared the winner

a Sutter • a noun, used to describe a player who exhibits the combination of determination, heart and skill displayed amply by the six Sutter brothers who played in the NHL from the 1970s to the 1990s

Tailenders • outmoded term for the last-place team in the league

Take a run • to charge a player

Take one for the team • incur a cheap hit from an opponent and draw a penalty, rather than retaliate and risk a penalty of one's own

Take the body • to check aggressively with the body rather than the stick

Target • the net

Third jersey • a sweater that is distinct from the team's usual home and road jerseys, usually reserved for special occasions.

Three Star selections • naming of the three best players in an NHL game. Originally named for a brand of Esso gasoline. In a playoff game on March 23, 1944, Rocket Richard scored five goals against Toronto and was named the first, second and third star of the game.

Three-on-one • a situation in which three members of the offensive team enter the attacking zone with only one defender between them and the goal.

Tie up your man • check your man closely and take him out of the play

Time of the goal (or penalty) • time of a goal or penalty is determined by subtracting the time left on the official clock from the length of the period (usually 20:00, although regular-season overtime periods are 5:00). Thus the time of a goal scored with one minute left in a period is 19:00, and is recorded as such on the score sheet. Under international

rules, the clock starts at 0:00 and counts forward to 20:00, so no such calculation is needed.

Time-out • a stoppage in play called by one of the teams rather than by an official. Teams are allowed one 30-second time-out per game, and can only be called by the coach.

Tip-in • a goal scored by deflecting the puck into the net

Toe • the very tip of the blade of a stick

Too many men on the ice • a bench minor penalty assessed when a team has more players on the ice than it's entitled to

Top shelf • the upper part of the net

Trailer • a player who skates into the offensive zone behind, or "trailing," the puck carrier

Trap • a defensive style of play in which forechecking or carrying the puck is downplayed, and in which all five skaters attempt to prevent the opposition from crossing into its offensive zone

Trapper • the goalie's catching glove

Tripping • a minor infraction in which one player knocks down an opponent with his stick or knee. Subject to a two-minute penalty.

Turn turtle • to cover one's face and curl up on the ice to avoid engaging in a hockey fight

turnover • one team gaining possession of the puck by forcing the other team into making an error

Tuuk • style of skate blade introduced in the late 1970s, in which most of the blade is encased in a hard plastic shell

Twig • slang for the stick

Twine • slang for the net

Two-line pass • an offside pass that crosses both the blue line and center red line untouched

Two-on-one • situation in which two attackers enter the offensive zone with only one defender between them and the goalie

Two-way player • a player who is equally adept at scoring and playing defensively

Underdog • the team that is expected to lose a game.

Unsportsmanlike conduct • a type of minor penalty which can be assessed whenever the referee sees behavior detrimental to the reputation of the game

Upstairs • the top part of the net. Also, when a referee confers with the video goal judge, whose booth is located above the ice surface, he is said to be "going upstairs."

Video goal judge • an official who reviews videotape so that he can advise the referee whether an infraction occurred that would require a goal to be disallowed

Visor • transparent plastic face guard, attached to the front of the helmet

Wall • the boards and glass

Wave • a cheer in which one section of fans stands and lifts its arms, then sits down just as the next section follows suit. This continues around the arena.

Weak side • the side of the offensive or defensive zone where the fewest number of players are positioned

Whistle • a stoppage in play

Whistle-tooter • a referee

Winger • player who plays one of the two outside forward positions, left wing or right wing

Wraparound • a play in which the puck carrier starts behind the other team's goal line and swings quickly in front of the net to stuff the puck into the net or take a quick forehand shot. So called because the player seems to wrap his stick and arms around the net.

Wrister • a wrist shot

Zamboni • brand name of ice-resurfacing machine developed by Frank Zamboni of Paramount, California in the late 1940s. Zamboni equipment is so widely used (22 of the NHL's 26 teams use a Zamboni) that the brand name has become a generic term for all ice-resurfacing machines. Also used as a verb: "We need seven minutes to zamboni the ice."

Zebra • slang for official

VI

STATISTICAL
AND
BIOGRAPHICAL
REGISTERS

Maurice "Rocket" Richard was the first NHLer
to score 50 goals in a season. His mark stood
for 16 years before Boom Boom Geoffrion scored
50 in 1960–61. It would be another five seasons
before 50 would be surpassed by Bobby Hull
who finished the 1965-66 season with 54 goals.
A new NHL award—the Maurice Richard Trophy—
will be awarded to the league's top goal
scorer for the first time in 1999.

CHAPTER 63

The Evolution of NHL Statistics

The NHL's First Full-Time Statistician Reflects on the Growth of the Numbers Game

Ron Andrews

IN THE BEGINNING of the National Hockey League in 1917–18 there were goals for each player; nothing more. Team standings were also available—games played, wins, losses, "draws" (ties), goals scored and goals scored against. That was it.

Today, with the manipulation of some keys on any personal computer or laptop, descriptions of NHL teams and players abound with endless numbers and facts.

But, how did the league get from point A in 1917–18 to today's myriad of information? Not easily, and often with painstaking patience.

In the league's first season, no assists were given on goals. And, for the next few seasons, assists were handed out sparingly. However, in 1935–36 for some inexplicable reason three assists could be awarded on a goal, hence the record for most points by both teams in one game. That was set February 18, 1936, when Montreal Maroons and New York Americans played to an 8–8 tie in which there were 52 points awarded. The record, however, was surpassed several times in the 1980s when NHL goal-scoring reached an all-time high.

In the early years of the league, there was no official statistician. Elmer Ferguson, sports editor of the defunct *Montreal Herald*, kept a record of players for the league and sent the statistics to the Montreal bureau of news organizations such as The Canadian Press and United Press International. From there, the information was sent to members of the organizations and would appear once a week in newspapers and be received by radio stations throughout North America.

The NHL office in Montreal was sent a telegram after each game by the official scorer listing the goals, assists and penalties. The "official game documents"—score sheet, penalty sheet and referee's report, which listed the lineup for the game of both teams—then would be mailed to Montreal by the official scorer.

By 1955, all six teams had statisticians who were responsible for shots by individuals, saves by goaltenders and players on ice when goals were scored. Although the sheet showed goals scored—either power-play or shorthand—these statistics were not readily available.

At the end of a season, Ferguson would be responsible for producing—on a Gestetner duplicating machine—final statistics, which included league standings and individual players' records, including goals, assists, points and penalty minutes. But for some reason, there was no record of games played by the players. Nor was there any compilation of the goaltending statistics for a regular season, only the Stanley Cup Playoffs. Oddly, penalties for all players were shown, broken down into minors, majors and match penalties. The first time regular-season games played were accredited to a player's record was in 1941–42, although games played were noted in season-by-season lists of individual scoring champions in publications of that era.

While the league began operating in 1917–18, it didn't hire a public relations director until the fall of 1946 after Clarence Campbell had been appointed NHL president to succeed Red Dutton. One of the first moves Campbell made was to name Ken McKenzie as publicity director for the league. This marked the first time statistical information was controlled from the NHL office, rather than by someone not employed by the league.

McKenzie, however, believed that hockey needed its own publication, much like *The Sporting News*—which dealt mainly with Major League Baseball—and with Campbell's approval, he joined in a partnership with long-time friend Will Cote to start *The Hockey News*. Using the mailing list of the NHL, *The Hockey News* published its first issue in September of 1947 and began to flourish.

At the same time, writers and broadcasters throughout North America demanded more detailed statistics from the NHL. After the 1962–63 season, McKenzie announced he was leaving the league to devote all his time to *The Hockey News*. With that development, Campbell decided the NHL needed a full-time publicity director and statistician to replace McKenzie.

It was a dream come true for anyone interested in hockey statistics, especially the writer of this article.

Polio had prevented me from playing hockey, but I possessed a passion for the game and, like most Canadian youngsters, I kept annual scrapbooks on the sport. A mutual friend put me in touch with a well-known Toronto radio broadcaster, the late Wes McKnight, who advised me that, instead of collecting scrapbooks of pictures and articles, I should concentrate on something original and different, such as statistical information.

I pored over the summaries of games in the Toronto newspapers, looking for something of note that wasn't included. Somehow, I came up with the idea of how often teams scored goals with their opponents shorthanded. I realized this was not a part of the game statistics, although the story of the game would mention that a player was in the penalty box when the opposing team scored. Until then, which was in the mid-1950s, this information was not available on a regular basis from the NHL. By this time, I was a junior editor at the Canadian Press wire service and I was compiling season-by-season power-play and penalty-killing statistics.

A few phone calls to writers explaining what I had accumulated brought positive results, to the point where the writers were sent the statistical data and it was being used. When I became one of the CP reporters for the Toronto Maple Leafs games in 1957–58, I used my own power-play and penalty-killing statistics in articles, which meant the statistics became available across the country.

My extreme enthusiasm for hockey continued to the point where many friends and co-workers were telling me that I should be with the NHL but my answer was simple:

"Ken McKenzie has been there for many years; he isn't old and he isn't going to leave."

Three Toronto newspaper reporters phoned me from the NHL's annual meeting in June, 1963, to inform me that McKenzie was leaving the league, and they asked me when I was going to get my resume to the league.

With the full support of the late Jack Sullivan, who was CP's sports editor at the time, I drafted a resume and, unknown to me at the time, "Sully" sent letters to the six NHL governors supporting my application.

At the time of the Hockey Hall of Fame induction ceremonies in August, I received a call from Clarence Campbell telling me to meet him at Toronto's Royal York Hotel that afternoon. When the interview was finished, I was the new public relations director and statistician for the league. I began on the Tuesday after Labor Day.

I had, with a lot of help from many people, turned a hobby into a career.

Compiling statistics is one thing; interpreting them is altogether different. The writing experience I gained at CP allowed me to produce a concise summary of the previous week's highlights in a release which was used by journalists and broadcasters. Special attention was paid to such things as milestone events by players, team winning and losing streaks, and oddities. And, the statistical section of the release contained power-play and shorthand figures, both individual and team.

Working overnight Sunday became a regular routine because time was of the essence. Something in the release could be outdated by the time it reached members of the news media. In that era, few games were played on Mondays or Tuesdays—with only six teams in the league—so the information still would be relevant by the time the media received it, as long as the releases were at the post office early Monday morning.

The statistical information for teams and players was recorded by hand in a large ledger book for the entire season, giving game-by-game statistics in chronological and cumulative order on a game-by-game basis, e.g.:

DATE	TEAM vs TEAM	PLAYER	GP	G	A	PTS	PIM	PPG	SHG
Dec 5	Det. 2 at Chi. 3	G. Howe	1	0(18)	0(20)	0(38)	0(6)	0(2)	0(3)

The first figures represent what the player did in that game; the bracketed numbers are for season-to-date.

While the release was being prepared, an enthusiastic office boy would run the envelopes through the addressing machine and then the stamp machine. He then would scurry off with the bag of mail to the main post office in Montreal for delivery.

The age of modern technology began to invade NHL Headquarters in 1965 when a photocopy machine was installed, thereby doing away with the Gestetner printer and making the reproduction of the releases for mail distribution much faster.

The compilation of the statistics, however, continued to be a manual function, requiring two people to work overnight Sunday to update weekend figures—midweek statistics were entered into the "big book" the day after games—and to prepare the release.

Step number two in upgrading the dissemination of the releases was the acquisition by the league of a Bell Canada TWX machine, a teleprinter which included a punched-tape reader. This provided a means of typing to the tape and then feeding the tape through the machine to the six NHL teams

on a conference call. That call was made first thing Monday morning and enabled the teams to service the media in their area that same day.

The mailing list still had to be maintained for non-NHL cities in North America. It had expanded from about 500 in 1963 to more than 1,000 two years later, including a trickle of requests from the European media.

In addition to the weekly releases, there were quarterly reports comprising team comparisons and individual statistics such as shooting percentages, the number of shots and goals scored; goaltender save percentages, shots and goals against; and team winning, undefeated, losing and winless streaks. Also included were the plus–minus statistics for individuals. General managers employed this information for contract negotiations and considered it confidential. In 1963, however, they agreed that the figures could be released. The statistic—it is part of the aforementioned Statistics Sheet—shows the players on ice for both teams when a goal is scored.

The league leader in the plus figure in 1963–64 was defenseman Pierre Pilote of Chicago. He was on the ice for 139 Black Hawk goals and 88 by the opposition. The net figure is based on even-strength goals, meaning power-play goals are not included. Pilote was on the ice for 41 Chicago power-play goals, giving him a net offensive total of 98. Defensively, he was on the ice for 88 goals against, 20 of which were opposition power-play goals, a net of 68. Subtracting the defensive total of 68 from the offensive total of 98 gave him a +30.

The highest plus any player attained was +124 by Boston's great defenseman Bobby Orr in 1970–71. Orr was on the ice for 258 of the Bruins' 399 goals. Of Orr's total, 79 were power-play goals, giving him an offensive net of 179. Boston's opponents scored 207 goals. Orr was on the ice for 85, 30 of which were power-play goals, giving him a defensive net of 55 and his over-all plus of 124.

Many players today have bonus clauses in their contracts for a high plus rating, so it has become more than an informational statistic.

The expansion of the NHL from six to 12 teams in 1967–68, meant "double the pleasure, double the fun" for the statistical bureau. Now two "big books" were required, one for the "Original Six" teams in the East Division and the other for the new West Division teams: California Seals, Los Angeles Kings, Minnesota North Stars, Philadelphia Flyers, Pittsburgh Penguins and St. Louis Blues.

I was then able to hire an assistant, Norm Jewison, who had worked part-time at the office while attending college in Montreal.

Even with 12 teams, the statistical information still was compiled manually and required both of us to work overnight Sunday to have the release ready first thing Monday morning. This routine continued until Buffalo and Vancouver were awarded franchises in 1970, bringing to 14 the total teams in the league. That season, the statistical information became computerized, albeit at a primitive level. An accounting firm located in the business district of Montreal, a few blocks away from the NHL offices, supplied the computer, which was a monster to say the least. The TWX machine was still the primary method of dispensing information to the 14 teams, but the computer enabled the tabulation of the statistics to be done by a key-punch operator who then produced the TWX tape that was used to distribute the statistics to the teams.

This method wasn't without its trials and tribulations.

The outdated telegram-method of receiving game reports had been replaced by TWX reports, sent in after each game by the teams' public relations directors. Jewison and I would gather all the reports for the week's games and take them to the computer center Sunday night to be keypunched into the system. One early Monday morning, there was a blizzard in Montreal. We got back to the underground parking lot but had to walk a couple of blocks from there to get to the Sun Life Building, where the NHL offices were located.

I thought I had the TWX tape safely covered in a cardboard box, but suddenly a gust of wind opened the box and the tape began to blow down the street. Jewison told me to make sure no more escaped from the box as he retrieved the flying tape. If the tape had broken, we would have had to go back to the computer center and start over. Fortunately, Jewison saved the tape and we were able to complete our mission.

At that time, the TWX system was a dial-up (long distance) connection service whereby all clubs had to stay on the line. If someone disconnected, the whole procedure would have to be restarted. Sometimes, the release didn't get to all the clubs until late Monday night. The system later ran on special Datapac phone lines which meant that local calling replaced the long distance method, eliminating the problems encountered on the conference calls.

But the two "big books" still had to be manually updated and Jewison and I would alternate weekends where we'd take the books home in a big burlap bag and bring the statistics up to date. In 1971, that was no longer necessary because the computer provided up-to-date information. It was the beginning of the end for manual compilation of statistics.

The league moved swiftly during the next few years to update its computer system, beginning in 1975, when its first in-house system was installed and the continual process of upgrading began.

While this was happening, there was still the task of updating past history, of taking advantage of the files tucked away in filing cabinets in the office. To this end, Carol Randall, an enthusiastic woman, was hired as a researcher in 1972. At a young age she was inflicted with polio, which required braces on both legs and the partial loss of the use of one arm. But she was a determined person, full of vibrant life and an inspiration to everyone.

Randall was able to go into the files and, for the first time in league history, provide such material as the longest team winning, undefeated, winless and losing streaks. Records were verified and established in many areas which were previously unknown.

Randall also tabulated, year-by-year, a list of shutouts by goaltenders and began the arduous task of compiling netminders' wins, losses and ties, dating back to 1917–18. In 1964–65, the NHL introduced a two-goaltender system for each team. Prior to that, the home team had to provide a backup netminder if the visiting team's goalie was injured during the game. The two-goaltender system then required a new statistic—minutes played—which meant the base for goals-against averages changed from games played to minutes played. Converting active goalies' averages based on minutes played rather than games was not too difficult. Randall, however, completed the conversion for all goalies in NHL history by poring through previous season statistics and adding minutes played to create the new goals-against averages. In addition, by going through game reports, she was able to make a complete list of all penalty shots from the inception of that rule in 1934.

Prior to the 1976–77 season, with the league comprising 18 teams, it became obvious that the statistical department needed another person. Benny Ercolani was hired, bringing to five the number of people in the department, including a secretary, plus the office boy who was still responsible for printing the weekly release and putting it into the mail. That list had grown to more than 2,500, three hundred of which were news media people in Europe.

At first, Ercolani assisted Randall in research, but his penchant for statistics soon surfaced and he began to take some of the load off me, allowing me to spend more time dealing with the media and the public relations department, which by now was located in New York. I had one major creed during my 19 years in the NHL: unless absolutely necessary, don't make reporters call back for information. The office was organized so that the requested material was available immediately on the initial phone call.

The improvement of the league's computer system continued and by 1983 all teams and the NHL's New York office had IBM personal computers and modems for dial-up-based communications with the league's mainframe computer.

Norm Jewison left the NHL's Montreal office in the summer of 1977 to become public relations director for the Vancouver Canucks and Carol Randall returned to her New Brunswick home in 1980. They were replaced by Mike Griffin and Roger Leblond, respectively. When I left the league in 1982, Ercolani replaced me as the league statistician and Gary Meagher became managing director, public relations.

The statistical department was moved to Toronto in July, 1991, and all departments of the league were serviced by the intricate computer system, including the Montreal, New York and Toronto offices.

One of the most important documents of the league is the *NHL Guide and Record Book*. It lists the amateur and professional record of every player currently in the NHL. It also has the team and individual records for every category possible. Originally, the *Guide* was a "Who's Who in Hockey," authored by Jim Hendy, a native of Cleveland, who compiled lifetime records of professional players, both at the NHL and minor-league levels.

When Ken McKenzie joined the league as public relations director in 1946, he added several categories to the work done by Hendy and came up with the first *NHL Guide*. Because his was virtually a one-man operation, he didn't have time to search game reports for past records that had never been compiled. In 1964, I realized that the accomplishments of former players were not duly recognized. So, during that summer, I searched the filed game reports for the players who had scored at least 200 goals in their careers and I was able to tabulate their games played and figure out a goals-per-game average for the 35 players who had scored at least 200 goals. The range was from Maurice Richard's 544 career goals to Hooley Smith's 200. When games played were figured into the mix, it showed that Babe Dye, who played for Toronto, Chicago and the New York Americans during an 11-season career, had the best average. He scored 202 goals in only 269 games, a percentage of .751. The following summer, the same research was completed for for assists and points.

Information such as complete Stanley Cup playoff records, including teams' all-time records against other clubs; All-Star Game team and individual records; junior and Entry Draft histories; career records of former players

and much more was added to the *Guide*. The addition of new features and information combined with the fact that the NHL had expanded from six teams in 1966–67 to 21 teams in 1979–80 meant that the *Guide* had to grow. The number of pages increased from 292 in the 1966–67 edition—the last book of the six-team era—to 872 in 1980–81.

In 1981–82 and 1982–83, the information contained in the *Guide* required more pages than could be bound efficiently into one book. To remedy the situation, the *Guide* was split into two separate volumes, each retaining the original 5" x 7" format. One volume was titled the *NHL Guide* while the other was known as the *NHL Record Book*. This split edition proved confusing to users so the format was redesigned in early 1984.

The current 8½" x 11" size was adopted for the 1984–85 season, reducing the number of pages to 352. Photographs were added in 1984–85 as the book achieved wide distribution in bookstores for the first time. Production of the new edition, titled the *NHL Official Guide & Record Book*, is handled by Dan Diamond and Associates of Toronto using statistics and research provided by the NHL. By 1998, the big *Guide* had grown to 464 pages and, with expansion to 30 teams set for the next two seasons, this number can only increase.

Original material, researched manually, is still an integral part of the publication. The computer, however, has enabled the editors to include much more detailed statistics, such as the career record of every player since 1917–18—playoffs and Stanley Cup championships included—to the point where the *NHL Official Guide & Record Book* is considered one of the most comprehensive publications in all professional sports, attracting readers from around the world.

For most of the league's history, the recording of game statistics has been accomplished by hand. Scorers sitting in the press box would record the events as they happened on the ice—goals, assists, saves, penalties, shots on goal, plus–minus—using pen and paper. A computer eventually organized this information, but the initial recording was done by hand.

And then it all changed. In the 1997–98 season—as a result of an alliance between the league and the IBM Corporation—all information about the NHL, its games and its players was recorded by scorers outfitted with laptop computers perched in the press boxes of NHL arenas. The NHL and its statistics had entered the 21st century. For the first time, face-offs, time on ice, hits, takeaways, giveaways, blocked shots and missed shots were recorded. The results were distributed to teams, media and broadcasters as the more traditional statistics of goals, assists, penalties and saves had been for so long.

Such recording is done on a scoring program known as the Real-Time Scoring System for Hockey developed by the IBM Sports Solution Development team based on a hockey scoring prototype in turn developed by the SQRA Corporation, a computer software development company based in Saanich, British Columbia. For the 1998–99 season the information developed from the Real-Time Scoring System for Hockey will be available on the internet on the NHL site www.nhl.com.

Also for the 1997–98 season, the Elias Sports Bureau became the official statistical consultant to the National Hockey League, bringing its unique perspective and resources to the world of hockey statistics. Elias is now developing and maintaining a database of NHL statistical history dating back to 1917. Its resources are available to NHL teams, league officials and the media 24 hours a day seven days a week.

And for the 1998 season the big news in the statistical world of hockey sits before you—*Total Hockey*. For the first time the statistical record of every player in NHL history is at your fingertips.

From the one-man operation of Elmer Ferguson to the wind-blown tapes of Montreal to today's place in the fast lane on the information superhighway, NHL statistics have come a long, long way.

CHAPTER 64

Adjusted Scoring

Total Hockey's New Statistical Categories

Dan Diamond

HOW CAN YOU ACCURATELY COMPARE Howie Morenz and Bobby Hull? Doug Bentley and Paul Kariya? Defensemen Dit Clapper and Raymond Bourque? It is a rare privilege for a fan to have followed the game long enough and closely enough to have naked-eye comparisons of superstars from different eras clearly fixed in his or her mind. Most of us don't have the benefit of sufficient years following the sport to be able to do this on our own. Instead we rely on written accounts and statistics, but how accurate are these as a basis for comparison? The game of hockey has undergone an unending series of fundamental changes. The length of the season, the size of players, the equipment they wear, the ice they skate on and the rules of hockey continue to evolve, making cross-era comparison chancy at best.

In preparing *Total Hockey* we set out to create a reliable method of comparing players from disparate eras. These resulting new statistical categories have been named Adjusted Scoring. In the player registers that follow, three Adjusted Scoring statistics are included: Adjusted Goals (**AG**), Adjusted Assists (**AA**) and Adjusted Points (**APts**).

Adjusted Average (**AAvg**) is a similar comparative statistic that has been created to evaluate goaltenders. (*See page 1601.*)

In each of these new statistical categories the object is the same: to place every NHL player's numbers on an equalized footing to facilitate comparison from season to season and era to era. Adjusted Scoring statistics have been calculated for each season in a player's NHL career. These, in turn have been totaled to provide career Adjusted Goals, Adjusted Assists and Adjusted Points. It is these adjusted totals that make for fascinating comparisons between players. Many of these are outlined in Chapter 65, Statistical Twins, beginning on the facing page.

Adjusted Scoring statistics take into account the following: 1) the average number of goals scored per game in each season, and 2) the length of the NHL regular-season schedule.

The same method is used to calculate all three.

Using Adjusted Goals as an example, since the NHL began play in the 1917–18 season, 212,811 goals have been scored in 32,765 games, for an average of 6.4951 goals per game. The average number of goals scored per game has also been calculated for each of the NHL's 81 seasons. The average of these individual season averages is 6.1725 goals per game. We have chosen to use this average-of-the-averages figure, rather than the higher grand total average because we feel it removes an unfair weighting toward recent seasons when the number of games on the NHL schedule has been at an all-time high. For the purposes of adjusting averages, we feel that the individual season average for 1927–28 (3.80) is as important a number as the season average for 1997–98 (5.2758). The fact that the NHL schedule consisted of 220 games in 1927–28 and 1,066 games in 1997–98 has no bearing. The players in each era

play the games that are on the schedule. Salary considerations notwithstanding, players in the 1920s would have been pleased to play an 82-game season and, I suspect, players today—particularly in the midst of a long road trip—wouldn't be displeased if modern NHL teams played just 44 games per season.

Each season's average number of goals scored per game is then factored against the overall average of individual season averages (6.1725). If the individual season average is less than this figure, goals that season were, in fact, harder to come by than the overall figure. Therefore each goal scored is more valuable (i.e., worth more than 1.00) than the baseline overall average. Conversely, in seasons in which goals are plentiful, each goal scored is worth less than 1.00.

Some concrete examples: Defense was king in 1952–53. Only 4.7905 goals were scored per game. Therefore each goal scored that year has been factored to represent 1.2885 Adjusted Goals. By comparison, goals were plentiful in 1981–82 with 8.0095 scored per game. Each goal scored this season represents .7706 Adjusted Goals. (These two sample seasons are of particular interest. In 1952–53 Gordie Howe scored 49 goals; in 1981–82 Wayne Gretzky scored 92. Both are single-season career highs for these two great scorers. Howe' 49 goals adjust to 78; Gretzky's 92 become 74.)

To further remove bias from our formula, we harness the power of the computer to remove each player's individual goals scored total from the calculation of the average number of goals per game in the season being adjusted. In the modern era, with so many players and so many goals scored, an individual total has little impact on the factoring, but in the early years a top scorers' output can skew the numbers. (Using 1917–18 as an example, a total of 341 goals were scored in the NHL. Joe Malone scored 44 of them.)

The result of all of this number crunching is a factoring that is unique to each player for each season.

What about length of schedule? The NHL has played schedules ranging in length from 18 to 84 games. We have factored every player's scoring stats to today's standard of 82 games. This is done by expressing each individual's games played as a percentage of a full schedule. This percentage is applied to the 82-game baseline, resulting in an equivalent number of games played out of 82. The actual number of games played is then factored against the out-of-82 number, resulting in a multiplier that is applied to the factored scoring total. An example: Nels Stewart played 100 percent of the 36 scheduled games in 1925–26, scoring 34 goals. If he played today, he would have played 100% of 82 games or 2.28 times more games (and, presumably, more goals) than were available to him in 1925–26.

Combining these factors of weighted goals and schedule length results in a powerful new statistical tool. Does it clearly decide who's number one? Of course not, but it provides plenty of ammunition for the discussion.

CHAPTER 65

Statistical Twins

Top Players Compared Across Eras Using Adjusted Scoring Statistics

Eric Zweig

WHO'S BETTER? It's the oldest argument in sports. Most fans feel that certain eras of NHL play are golden while others are not. Adjusted scoring stats attempt to resolve this debate, revealing cross-era connections between some of the game's greatest players.

MARIO LEMIEUX • JEAN BELIVEAU

There are many who rate him as the greatest center of all time and certainly his characteristics and record give support to this opinion. He was a big, strong man who could never be crowded off the puck and the bully boys of the league soon found that trying to body him was like hitting a truck in motion. He was a graceful skater and his long, sweeping strides gave deception to his speed. His stickhandling was superb.

Charles Coleman wrote this description of Jean Beliveau in *The Trail of the Stanley Cup Volume 3* (1976). It can most certainly be applied to Mario Lemieux as well. But if the two great French-Canadian stars were remarkably similar in their on-ice style, statistically, Lemieux appears much more dominant. However, when their numbers are adjusted to reflect the differences in their eras, Lemieux and Beliveau's totals are actually quite close. For example, Lemieux's best goal-scoring season (85 in 1988–89) translates into 73 adjusted goals, while Beliveau's 47 in 1955–56 adjust to 70. Overall, Lemieux's 10 best seasons range between 35 and 73 adjusted goals while Beliveau's stretch from 35 to 70. In terms of points, Lemieux's adjusted totals top 100 seven times with a high of 154 and Beliveau's five times with a high of 122.

When compared to the rest of the NHL at the time they were both playing, the statistical differences between Beliveau and Lemieux remain quite close with again only a slight edge going to Lemieux. He led the NHL in goals three times. Beliveau did it twice. Lemieux led or shared the lead in assists three times. Beliveau did it twice. Lemieux won the Hart Trophy as the most valuable player in the NHL three times. Beliveau won it twice. Beliveau holds an advantage over Lemieux in terms of all-star honors, having earned a total of 10 selections to either the First or Second Team to Lemieux's eight. Then again, Beliveau played 20 years to Lemieux's 12 and while he did battle a variety of injuries over his career, health issues certainly did not effect Beliveau they way they did Lemieux. No superstar, with the possible exception of Bobby Orr, ever had to overcome as much physical adversity as Lemieux.

Of course, Mario Lemieux won the Art Ross Trophy as the NHL scoring leader six times and Beliveau only won it once, but then Beliveau played on 10 Stanley Cup winners to Lemieux's two. Then again, Beliveau arrived in the NHL with a Montreal Canadiens team that already featured future Hall of Famers like Maurice Richard, Doug Harvey, Jacques Plante and others, while Lemieux had to wait years before the team became a serious contender.

BOBBY ORR
• CYCLONE TAYLOR • PAUL COFFEY

The most obvious comparison to Bobby Orr is Eddie Shore. Both were the greatest offensive defensemen of their eras, and two of the greatest NHL players of all time. Both are multiple Hart Trophy winners. Both quickly led the Bruins out of obscurity after their arrival in Boston and both helped the team become a league power while winning the Stanley Cup twice. But while Orr relied solely on his speed and skill to dominate the game, Shore added a nasty mean streak to his arsenal. The two were very different players.

In order to find a worthy historical match for Orr's talents, it is necessary to go outside of the NHL. Cyclone Taylor played his entire career in leagues that either predated or rivaled the NHL, but he can easily by considered the Bobby Orr of his day. Or, perhaps Orr should be considered the Cyclone Taylor of his day. Taylor began his career as a forward and a rover in the era of seven-man hockey, but was moved back to defense (then known as point and cover point) when he joined the Ottawa Senators in 1907–08. The reason for the switch? None of the other Ottawa forwards could keep up with him! Senators management reasoned that by moving Taylor to cover point, he would be free to lead the rush whenever he wanted and would still be more than able to handle his defensive responsibilities. The move worked. Taylor became the top-scoring defenseman in hockey and the Senators won the Stanley Cup in 1909. Had there been a Norris Trophy in his day, Taylor no doubt would have won that too.

Taylor's signing in Renfrew gave the National Hockey Association instant credibility in 1909–10. He would confer similar respectability on the Pacific Coast Hockey Association when he signed with the Vancouver Millionaires in 1912–13. In this way, Taylor was perhaps more like Bobby Hull than Bobby Orr. It was in the PCHA that Taylor's offensive exploits were best on display. He led the league in goal-scoring on three occasions and points five times. However, he was now being used as a center and rover and was no longer playing much defense.

Like Taylor, a young Orr revolutionized the hockey pay structure when he signed a two-year deal worth $75,000 in 1966 at a time when the Boston Bruins had first offered $8,000 plus a $5,000 signing bonus. Orr then changed the way the game was played by hearkening back to an era when defensemen like Cyclone Taylor could be counted on to lead the offense. In that regard, no one had ever been better. Orr collected goals, assists and points at a rate no defenseman had ever approached, leading the league in scoring twice and finishing as runner up behind teammate Phil Esposito four times. He established records for defenseman that appeared unbeatable when he had 46 goals and 135 points in 1974–75. Had his career not been cut short by a series of serious knee injuries, Bobby Orr way

well have established career numbers that would never be surpassed.

But, of course, records are made to be broken and Orr's were surpassed, and by a defenseman who was also not only a tremendous scorer but a gifted skater. Paul Coffey arrived in Edmonton in 1980–81 and, like Orr and Esposito in Boston, Wayne Gretzky and Coffey would help make the Oilers the greatest offensive team in hockey. Coffey set new records with 48 goals and 138 points in 1985–86 and has gone on to become hockey's all-time top-scoring defenseman. Longevity is an important factor in determining the best of all time, but how do Coffey's totals compare to Orr's when the relative ease or difficulty of goal-scoring in their different eras is factored in? In terms of Total Hockey's adjusted goals statistic, Coffey's best three goal-scoring seasons of 48 (1985–86), 40 (1983–84) and 37 (1984–85) work out to 39, 32 and 30 respectively. Orr's top three seasons of 46 (1974–75), 37 (1971–72) and 37 again (1970–71) calculate out at 43, 40 and 39.

And so, Orr must be ranked as modern hockey's greatest goal-scoring defenseman—a statement that comes as no surprise—and a worthy successor to a legend of the game like Cyclone Taylor.

STEVE YZERMAN • MAX BENTLEY

Both Steve Yzerman and Max Bentley are high-scoring centers who were at their best offensively when their teams weren't yet good enough to capitalize on their talents. Both later played for powerful clubs that were Stanley Cup champions, and while they were still important contributors to those teams' attack, both were no longer their team's main offensive threat. Yzerman has done all of this while playing for the Detroit Red Wings, while Bentley took the trade route to make it to the top.

Bentley joined the Chicago Black Hawks during the 1940–41 season and quickly established himself as one of the league's best scorers. He ranked third in the NHL scoring race with 70 points in his third season of 1942–43, just two points behind second-place Bill Cowley and three back of his teammate and brother Doug Bentley. Still, Chicago didn't make the playoffs that year. After missing the next two seasons due to military service, Max Bentley was back in Chicago in 1945–46 and led the NHL in scoring that year. He won a second straight scoring title in 1946–47, but the Black Hawks missed the playoffs that year too. On November 4, 1947, the Black Hawks traded Bentley (and Cy Thomas) to Toronto for five Maple Leafs. Bentley helped his new team win the Stanley Cup that year and repeat as champions in 1948–49. He played on a third Stanley Cup champion in Toronto in 1950–51.

Yzerman joined the Red Wings in 1983–84 and established club rookie records with 39 goals and 87 points. By 1986–87, he had become the youngest captain in team history at age 21 and went on to lead the team in scoring for seven straight years. He topped 100 points six years in a row, including 1988–89 when he had 65 goals and 90 assists for 155 points.

During this time, Detroit had some good years and some bad, but by 1992–93 the Red Wings were finally beginning to establish themselves as a league power. Yzerman's numbers were in decline, but with a better supporting cast the team got stronger. Detroit reached the Stanley Cup finals in 1994–95, set an NHL record with 62 wins in 1995–96, and finally won the Stanley Cup in 1996–97. The Red Wings repeated as champions in 1997–98.

Yzerman was never a scoring champion like Bentley, but he compensates for the imbalance by having better overall statistics. Even when the differences between their eras are considered, Yzerman's adjusted goals totals come out better than Bentley's—though the numbers become fairly close. Yzerman's best five seasons range between 43 and 56 adjusted goals and his top adjusted points totals are 90, 101, 103 and 120. Bentley comes in at 34 to 48 and 83, 94, 102 and 105.

PAUL KARIYA • DOUG BENTLEY

Blazing speed. Scoring skill. Showmanship. All attributes of a star hockey player and all found in abundance in Paul Kariya. At just 5'11" and 175 pounds, Kariya lacks only size but his other talents have more than offset that shortcoming. Almost a half-century before Kariya was even born, the same things were being said of another left winger: Doug Bentley.

At only 5'8" and 145 pounds, Doug Bentley joined the Chicago Black Hawks in 1939–40 and, like Kariya when he joined the Mighty Ducks more than 50 years later, quickly established the fact that he could play with the big boys. In just his fourth season, Bentley led the NHL in scoring and was named to the First All-Star Team for the first of three times. He also added a Second Team All-Star selection in 1948–49. In an eight-season span between 1942–43 and 1949–50, Bentley finished among the top 10 scorers in the NHL on six occasions, adding two second-place finishes to his 1942–43 scoring title.

Kariya's success has come even faster than Bentley's, scoring 50 goals 1995–96 in just his second NHL season and finishing eighth in the league scoring race with 108 points. (By way of comparison, Bentley's best adjusted goals season works out to 49, while his top adjusted points equal 107. Kariya's are 49 and 96) Kariya has added the Lady Byng Trophy to his First All-Star Team selections, which is something Bentley never accomplished even though his penalty totals were always low.

Like Kariya with teammate Teemu Selanne, Bentley usually enjoyed the good fortune of having at least one other talented scorer alongside him. In fact, the Pony Line of Bentley, his brother Max, and Bill Mosienko was the most dangerous scoring trio in the NHL in 1946–47. Bentley later played with scoring star Roy Conacher, but his Black Hawks teams were generally weak and he never had a chance to play for a Stanley Cup winner. It's too soon yet to know about Kariya.

In 1950, Bentley was named Chicago's greatest player to that point in team history. Kariya is already the most popular player in Mighty Ducks history and the Anaheim star certainly shows early indications of one day joining Bentley in the Hockey Hall of Fame.

RAYMOND BOURQUE • DIT CLAPPER

Though Dit Clapper began as a right wing before moving back to defense, he is a worthy match for Raymond Bourque. Both are career-long Boston Bruins who rank among the greats of the game. Bourque became the first player who wasn't a goaltender to win the Calder Trophy and a spot on the First All-Star Team in the same year when he entered the NHL in 1979–80. He has gone on to become one of the greatest defensemen in hockey history. He has been awarded the Norris Trophy more than anyone other than Bobby Orr and Doug Harvey and has garnered more all-star selections than any player but Gordie Howe.

Bourque trails only Paul Coffey for the most points ever scored by a defenseman, is the leading scorer in the history of the Bruins, and was just the fifth player in NHL history to top 1,000 career assists. He lacks only a Stanley Cup victory on his impressive resume.

Clapper was not the rookie sensation that Bourque was, but in his second season he helped the Bruins win the Stanley Cup. His nine goals and two assists in 40 games in 1928–29 seem paltry, but, in a year in which George Hainsworth recorded 22 shutouts in 44 games, Clapper's numbers actually ranked among some of the better offensive totals in the lowest-scoring season in NHL history. His production translates into 36 adjusted goals and 54 adjusted points in an 82-game regular season. When forward passing was permitted in the offensive zone and scoring numbers soared during the 1929–30 season, Clapper recorded 41 goals in 44 games for the second-best total in the NHL that season (behind linemate Cooney Weiland's 43 goals) and the third-highest total in league history prior to Rocket Richard's 50 goals in 1944–45. Clapper's 1929–30 total translates into 83 adjusted goals. His 22 goals (54 adjusted goals) in 1930–31 earned him a spot on the Second All-Star Team, an honor he received again when he scored 21 times (45 adjusted goals) in 1934–35.

So, though he did it as a forward, Clapper clearly demonstrated his offensive skill and was recognized at the time as one of the NHL's best players. But he earned his greatest accolades after being moved to defense. Clapper had played 10 years on right wing before being converted into a defenseman in 1937–38, and in just his second season at his new position he was named to the First All-Star Team after helping the Bruins to win another Stanley Cup title. Clapper was named to the First All-Star Team in each of the next two years as well, and was named to the Second All-Star team after his 17th NHL season of 1943–44. Clapper went on to play 20 years with the Bruins and, like Bourque, was a longtime captain of the team, wearing the "C" from 1932–33 to 1937–38 and from 1939–40 until 1945–46.

BRAD PARK • EARL SEIBERT

Brad Park had all the skills of a great defenseman. He could skate, shoot, pass and hit, and at 6'0" and 200 pounds he had size and strength. His teams in New York and Boston were always Stanley Cup contenders. Brad Park was indeed a great defenseman—but he was never the greatest.

Seven times in his career, Park was named to the postseason all-star team, including five selections to the First-Team, and yet someone else was always better. Three of the five times Park was selected to the First Team, he finished behind fellow First Teamer Bobby Orr in voting for the Norris Trophy, whom he would replace on the Boston blue line in 1975–76. Even then the two other times he was named to the First All-Star Team, he lost the Norris Trophy to Denis Potvin. (Park was also the runner-up behind Orr in Norris Trophy voting as a Second Team All-Star in 1971.)

Like Brad Park, Earl Seibert had all the skills of a great defenseman. He could skate, shoot, pass and hit, and at 6'2" and 198 pounds he had size and strength. His teams in New York and Chicago were Stanley Cup champions (in 1933 and 1938 respectively). Earl Seibert was indeed a great defenseman—but he was never the greatest.

Seibert was chosen as an all-star 10 consecutive times between 1934–35 and 1943–44 but, like Park, someone always seemed to be better. There was no Norris Trophy in this era but Eddie Shore won the Hart Trophy as NHL MVP four times, and defensemen Babe Seibert, Ebbie Goodfellow, Tom Anderson and Babe Pratt all won the Hart Trophy as well in years in which Seibert was an all-star. Only in 1942–43 might Seibert have actually been the NHL's best defenseman. However, that year fellow First Team All-Star Jack Stewart helped the Detroit Red Wings win the Stanley Cup while Second Teamer Flash Hollett led all blueliners with 19 goals, tying what was then the NHL record for a defenseman, so even then Seibert is no lock.

In addition to constantly being the second-best defenseman in the game, Park and Seibert are also similar in that both were traded in the prime of their careers and both played out the string with the Detroit Red Wings. Park's offensive numbers appear more impressive than Seibert's but when adjusted statistics are used to take account of the differences in their eras, their totals are much more in line. Park's seven best seasons range from 12 to 26 adjusted goals while Seibert's stretch from 10 to 29. Their best years for adjusted assists are 50 for Park and 42 for Seibert, though Park's best adjusted points total is 76 to only 56 for Seibert.

CHRIS CHELIOS • ART COULTER

While other greats of their era may have been flashier and garnered more attention, Chris Chelios and Art Coulter are a pair of great defensemen who were consistently rock-solid. Coulter made his NHL debut when he played part of the 1931–32 season with the Chicago Black Hawks, just as Chelios would debut late in the year with the Montreal Canadiens in 1983–84. Both began to make a name for themselves during their first full season and helped their teams record unexpected Stanley Cup triumphs the following year—Coulter in 1934 and Chelios in 1986.

Coulter was named to the all-star team after the 1934–35 season, but was then traded to the New York Rangers for future Hall of Famer Earl Seibert the next year. It was with his new team that Coulter really established himself as one of the game's best defenseman. He was named captain in 1937–38 and was an all-star three years in a row despite competition from such greats as Eddie Shore, Dit Clapper, Ebbie Goodfellow, Earl Seibert and Babe Siebert. He helped the Rangers win the Stanley Cup in 1940 and to finish in first place in the 1941–42 standings. He then entered the U.S. Coast Guard for service during World War II.

Except for the military stint, Chelios' career follows a similar pattern to Coulter's. Chelios was an all-star (and also won the Norris Trophy, which didn't exist in Coulter's time) in 1988–89, but was then traded to the Chicago Blackhawks for Denis Savard. Chelios has not enjoyed the Stanley Cup success in Chicago that Coulter had in New York, but, like Coulter, since his trade he has become recognized as one of the game's best despite the presence of other great defensemen like Raymond Bourque, Paul Coffey, Brian Leetch, Scott Stevens and Al MacInnis.

Chelios is an effective offensive defenseman, but it is his tough play and defensive skills that have made him one of the best in the game. Statistically, Chelios appears more dominant than Coulter. His high penalty minutes give a much more obvious indication of his toughness, but no one in Coulter's era racked up the kind of penalties players do today. Coulter, in his time, was considered a major physical presence whose aggressive play and rough bodychecks left opponents black and blue. Chelios would appear to have the

offensive advantage, but the adjusted goals statistic shows that Coulter's totals of four and five goals in his best seasons would work out to 10 or 11 goals in a standard 82-game season, putting his numbers much more in line with those of Chelios (10 to 17).

AL MACINNIS/DOUG WILSON • FLASH HOLLETT

Doug Wilson and Al MacInnis rank among the top defenseman of the 1980s and 1990s. Both are best known for their booming slapshots which made them a dangerous part of the offense as well as good defensive players. Though Wilson never led NHL defensemen in scoring, his best season of 39 goals and 85 points in 1981–82 resulted in his winning the Norris Trophy. MacInnis became just the fourth defenseman in history to top 100 points when he led all blueliners with 103 in 1989–90. He has been an all-star many times, but has never won the Norris Trophy.

Good as Wilson and MacInnis have been, both have tended to be overshadowed by the other great defensemen of their day. Wilson had to contend with Denis Potvin, Rod Langway and Mark Howe, as well as Paul Coffey and Raymond Bourque, while MacInnis has usually taken a back seat behind such stars as Coffey, Bourque, Chris Chelios and Brian Leetch. In the 1930s and 1940s, Flash Hollett suffered a similar fate.

In an era dominated by future Hall of Fame defensemen like Eddie Shore, Dit Clapper, Babe Siebert, Earl Seibert, Art Coulter and Babe Pratt, it is easy to overlook Flash Hollett. People usually do. But none of the defensive stars of his day was more gifted offensively than Hollett. An excellent rushing defensemen, Hollett was an adept playmaker, but goal scoring was his specialty. His 19 goals in 1941–42 and 1942–43 tied the NHL record for scoring by a defenseman established by Harry Cameron in 1921–22.

Hollett was named to the Second All-Star Team in 1942–43, but the Boston Bruins traded him to the Detroit Red Wings during the 1943–44 season. Hollett was a First Team All-Star in Detroit in 1944–45 after scoring 20 goals to establish a record for defensemen that would last until Bobby Orr scored 21 in 1968–69. Hollett was hampered by injuries during the 1945–46 season and never played in the NHL again.

When the differences in scoring from the eras in which they play are considered, Hollett, MacInnis and Wilson are remarkably similar in terms of their offensive talent. Each has over 200 career adjusted goals, with MacInnis enjoying five seasons of more than 20 adjusted goals and Wilson topping out with 31. Hollett tops 20 on six occasions with a high of 33 adjusted goals.

BRETT HULL • BILL COOK

To compare Brett Hull to Bobby would be unfair. Brett has been a great goal scorer but he's never been the game's dominant superstar the way Bobby Hull was. There are other great players from the history of the NHL who are a better match for Brett's talents—like Bill Cook.

Bill Cook was also a member of a famous hockey-playing family (his brother Bun was a long-time teammate and a fellow member of the Hockey Hall of Fame) and like Brett Hull, Bill Cook was a right winger with a hard, accurate shot. Both are considered good enough skaters, and both could pass the puck, but what makes them both great is their ability to put the puck in the net and to do it often.

Both Hull and Cook began their pro careers in western Canada before becoming NHL stars, though Cook was a lot more successful with Saskatoon (where he twice led his league in goals and points) than Hull ever was with the Calgary Flames. Cook entered the NHL with the New York Rangers in 1926–27 and promptly led the league with 33 goals in a 44-game schedule. Cook had only four assists that season, but his 37 points also led the league. He would lead, or tie for the NHL lead, in goals twice more in his career and won a second scoring title in 1932–33. He was an all-star four years in a row between 1930–31 and 1933–34.

Hull's success did not come as quickly as Cook's, but when it did come it was impressive. He led the NHL with 72 goals in 1989–90, 86 goals in 1990–91 (the third highest single-season total in history) and 72 goals in 1991–92. He was also a First Team All-Star in each of those seasons. Though he has never led the league in points, he did finish second behind Wayne Gretzky in 1990–91 and his Hart Trophy win that year as the NHL's most valuable player can easily counter Cook's two scoring titles. Of course, he has nothing to counter Cook's Stanley Cup victories in 1928 and 1933. Then again, Cook's top goal-scoring total of 34 is less than half of Hull's best year.

But how do these totals compare when the differences in their eras are factored in? Well, Cook's 34 goals in 48 games in 1931–32 work out to 74 in an average 82-game season. The adjusted goals total for Hull's 86-goal season works out to 80, so Hull still has the advantage. But wait! Cook's league-leading 33 goals in 44 games in 1926–27 were recorded during one of the most difficult seasons for goal-scoring in NHL history. His adjusted goal total for that year is a whopping 99! Over their whole careers, though, Cook's and Hull's numbers are remarkably close with Cook ranging between 29 and 74 adjusted goals in the next best years during his prime and Hull coming in at 35 to 64.

BRENDAN SHANAHAN/KEITH TKACHUK • CHARLIE CONACHER

No one has led the NHL in scoring with more goals than assists since Bobby Hull had 54 and 43 in 1964–65. For that reason, it's a bit difficult to find a modern player who compares with Charlie Conacher—a man who led the NHL in goals five times and points twice. Goal-scoring specialists from the 1980s and 1990s like Brett Hull, Cam Neely and Tim Kerr never had enough assists with their goals to take a serious run at the scoring title—though because of their combination of scoring and toughness, Neely and Kerr would be good choices to pair with Conacher.

"The Big Bomber," as Conacher was known, had a powerful shot but was also shifty around the net and could score on a deke just as well as with a bullet-like blast. At 6'1" and 200 pounds, Conacher was a big man who netted quite a few penalties (though his totals seem low by modern standards) to go along with his goals. For that reason, Brendan Shanahan is a good fit among active players. He is one of only four players (Gary Roberts, Kevin Stevens, Keith Tkachuk) to top 50 goals and 200 penalty minutes in the same season and is the best choice among those four because he has managed to maintain his goal-scoring ability over a longer time.

It's true Shanahan has never, and almost certainly will never, lead the league in scoring, but he has managed to crack the top 10 (1993–94) and has often led his own team, at least, in goals and points. Plus, in his best scoring years, Shanahan,

like Conacher, always recorded more goals than assists.

If Kevin Stevens had managed to maintain his pace of the early 1990s, he'd have been a good choice as the match for Charlie Conacher. Stevens scored more goals than Shanahan ever has and he finished as high as second in the NHL in scoring in 1991–92 (though he did have more assists than goals that year). Eventually, Keith Tkachuk will likely prove the best match of all. Tkachuk has managed to lead the league in goals and seems like a threat to reach the top 10 in scoring for many years to come. A Stanley Cup victory would help too. Both Conacher and Shanahan managed that.

Of course, there is one way in which it appears Conacher will always stand alone. Though goal-scoring in the NHL has been down in recent years, it is not nearly as low as it was during Conacher's heyday in the early 1930s. When his best totals from that era are reworked into adjusted goals, Conacher's career-high 36 goals in 47 games in 1934–35 calculate out at 78 goals in an average 82-game schedule. His 31 goals in 37 games when he first led the league in 1930–31 translate into 77 goals and he tops 70 again twice more. Good luck matching those totals these days!

ADAM OATES • JOE PRIMEAU

Two of the greatest playmakers of their eras, the talents of Adam Oates and Joe Primeau were often undervalued during their careers. Oates was at his best during the prime years of Mario Lemieux and the later days of Wayne Gretzky, while Primeau had to contend with Howie Morenz and Frank Boucher. As a result, both players only made one appearance on the postseason all-star team despite putting up impressive statistics over several seasons. Primeau, known as "Gentleman Joe," also took home the Lady Byng Trophy in 1931–32 and was the runner-up each of the next two seasons. Oates finished second in voting for the honor four straight years between 1992–93 and 1995–96.

Oates entered the NHL with the Red Wings in 1985–86 but did not become a star until his trade to St. Louis in 1989. With the Blues, Oates was paired with Brett Hull and his passing skills helped make Hull the NHL's top goal scorer three years in a row. After a trade to Boston, Oates established career highs with 45 goals, 97 assists and 142 points in 1992–93. The following season, his passing skills helped Cam Neely score 50 goals in just 44 games. Oates himself ranked among the top 10 scorers six years in a row between 1989–90 and 1994–95 and finished as high as third three times.

Primeau joined the Toronto Maple Leafs in 1927–28, but played only briefly for two seasons before being teamed with Charlie Conacher and Busher Jackson. The young threesome was dubbed the Kid Line and while Conacher and Jackson took most of the accolades for their goal-scoring prowess, it was Primeau's playmaking abilities and backchecking skill that made their exploits possible. Primeau cracked the top 10 in scoring three times in four years between 1930–31 and 1933–34, finishing as the runner-up behind Busher Jackson in 1931–32 and behind Charlie Conacher in 1933–34.

When the statistics of both players are compared, Oates would seem to have a considerable edge but when the relatively difficulty of scoring goals during the 1930s is taken into account, the numbers become much more even. When looking at adjusted goals, Primeau's modest totals of 13, 11, 14 and 10 goals between 1931–32 and 1934–35 work out to 28, 26, 31 and 21. When the same relative weight is given to Primeau's assists, his best six years average out at 80 per year. Oates' 45 goals in 1992–93 come to 38 adjusted

goals—which still provides him with a clear advantage—but his 97 assists would be only 67. (His 90 assists in 1990–91 adjust to 69.) There is another way in which Primeau comes out on top. The Leafs reached the Stanley Cup final four times during his seven full seasons as a player in Toronto and won it in 1932. Oates has yet to taste Stanley Cup champagne.

DOUG GILMOUR
• SYL APPS • TED KENNEDY

Syl Apps. Teeder Kennedy. Doug Gilmour. All three were gifted offensive centers and all-around talents who served as captain of the Toronto Maple Leafs. But all three were known for more than just their ability on the ice. All three had that intangible leadership quality that brought out the best in others around them.

Apps was a great athlete who represented Canada in as a pole-vaulter competition at the 1936 Olympics. He joined the Maple Leafs in 1936–37 and won the Calder Trophy as rookie of the year. He played his entire 10-year career in Toronto, leading the club in scoring three times and cracking the top 10 in the NHL six times. He was Maple Leafs captain from 1940–41 until 1947–48 (except for the two years he missed due to military service) and led the Leafs to three Stanley Cup titles.

Kennedy became a regular with the Maple Leafs while Apps was in the army in 1943–44. He was not the sheer talent that Apps was and was never a smooth skater, but made up for any deficiency with bulldog tenacity and sheer determination. He led he Leafs in scoring twice during his 12 full seasons in Toronto and ranked among the top 10 in the NHL four times. Kennedy played on five Stanley Cup-winners in Toronto and was captain of the team from 1948–49 until 1954–55 when he retired after winning the Hart Trophy as the NHL's most valuable player. (Kennedy made a brief comeback in 1956–57.)

Unlike Apps and Kennedy, Doug Gilmour did not play his entire career in Toronto, nor did he ever win the Stanley Cup with the Maple Leafs. In terms of natural ability, he is probably closer to Apps than Kennedy, but because of his small size, he too had to work hard to become an NHL star. Gilmour spent only four full seasons in Toronto, and parts of two others, but led the club in scoring three times and twice ranked among the league's top 10. He was the driving force behind the Leafs teams that reached the Conference championship in 1992–93 and 1993–94 and just missed becoming the first Leaf since Kennedy to win the Hart Trophy when he finished as the runner-up behind Mario Lemieux. Gilmour was captain of the Leafs from 1994–95 until 1996–97. His overall statistics appear much better than his two predecessors, but when the differences in the eras in which they played are factored in, the numbers are very interesting. Kennedy's best seasons increase from 60 and 61 points to 81 and 84 adjusted points, while Apps increases from 45 and 50 to 104 and 105. Gilmour's 127- and 111-point campaigns fall right in the middle at 92 and 90.

MARCEL DIONNE • CY DENNENY

When Marcel Dionne retired after the 1988–89 season, he ranked second in NHL history behind Gordie Howe with 731 goals, third behind Wayne Gretzky and Howe with 1,040 assists and third in points behind Gretzky and Howe with 1,771 points. He now ranks third in goals and still sits third in points, and so is clearly one of the greatest offen-

sive players in hockey history. Throughout his career, however, someone always seemed to be better than Dionne.

Though his eight 100-point seasons are bettered only by Wayne Gretzky (15) and Mario Lemieux (10), and his six 50-goal seasons have been topped only by Gretzky and Mike Bossy (nine each), Dionne only won the Art Ross Trophy once. Even then, he actually shared the scoring title with Wayne Gretzky, though Dionne was awarded the Trophy for scoring 53 goals to Gretzky's 51. Dionne finished second in scoring three times in his career and was in the top 10 on four other occasions.

When he retired after the 1928–29 season, Cy Denneny ranked first in NHL history with 246 goals and 315 points. Both totals remained NHL records until being surpassed by Howie Morenz during the 1930s. But while Cy Denneny had been the NHL's best career scorer, someone else always seemed to have a better year than he did.

In the NHL's first season of 1917–18, Denneny scored 36 goals in just 20 games, but finished second in the scoring race behind Joe Malone who had 44 goals. Over the next eight seasons, Denneny would finish second in scoring four more times. His only scoring title came in 1923–24 when he had 23 points in 24 games for the lowest total ever to lead the NHL. With the differences in their eras factored in, Denneny and Dionne have comparable career statistics, with Denneny's totals of 775 adjusted goals and 757 adjusted assists resulting in 1,532 adjusted points while Dionne has 653, 784 and 1,437.

Despite similar scoring statistics, there is one significant way in which Marcel Dionne and Cy Denneny differ. Dionne never came close to winning the Stanley Cup during his years with the Detroit Red Wings, Los Angeles Kings and New York Rangers. Denneny played on four Stanley Cup winners with the Ottawa Senators between 1919–20 and 1926–27 and won a fifth title as a player/assistant coach with the Boston Bruins in 1928–29.

JARI KURRI • FRANK NIGHBOR

Frank Nighbor was one of the most popular players of his day. Skilled on the ice, gracious away from the rink and widely admired, Nighbor was like the Wayne Gretzky of the 1910s and early 1920s. However, while he could be one of the game's best goal scorers, Nighbor was also one of the game's best defensive forwards. He was such an effortless skater—both forward and backwards—and so effective at using his poke check to break up opposition rushes that fans had trouble deciding if he was better on offense or defense. No one has ever said that about Wayne Gretzky … but they have said similar things about one of his former teammates.

Jari Kurri was a top goal scorers during his prime. He had more than 50 goals four years in a row, including a high of 71 in 1984–85 and a league-leading 68 in 1985–86. Yet even with all of that offense, Kurri was known as one of the best defensive forwards in the NHL. He was runner-up to Bobby Clarke for the Selke Trophy in 1982–83 and the feeling is he probably would have won the award several times if only he hadn't scored so many goals! Such is Kurri's defensive prowess that even as his goal-scoring declined he could be a useful player. His willingness to become a grinder instead of a sniper was clearly demonstrated with the Colorado Avalanche in 1997–98.

Like Kurri, Frank Nighbor was a league-leading goal scorer who could take care of business in his own end. He also became more of a defensive specialist in the latter stages of his career and, if anything, that dual ability was even more rare in his era than it is today. Nighbor's lone goal-scoring title actually came in the National Hockey Association (forerunner of the NHL) when he had 41 goals in 19 games in 1916–17 to tie Joe Malone for the NHA lead. This is the same Joe Malone who scored 44 goals in 20 games in the first NHL season the following year. Injuries limited Nighbor to just 11 goals in 10 games in 1917–18, but over the next three seasons he consistently ranked among the NHL's best scorers and his play helped the Ottawa Senators win the Stanley Cup four times in the 1920s (after having previously won the Stanley Cup with Vancouver in 1915). Kurri won the Stanley Cup five times in Edmonton. Kurri was also a five-time all-star with the Oilers and while there were no all-star teams in Nighbor's day, he was the first winner of the Hart Trophy as the NHL's most valuable player in 1923–24. He also won the first Lady Byng Trophy honor the following year (and again in 1925–26). Kurri won the Lady Byng Trophy in 1984–85. The two remain remarkably similar when the differences in their eras are accounted for, with Kurri rating 42, 47, 55 and 58 adjusted goals in his best seasons and Nighbor's top NHL totals coming in at 41, 49, 61 and 67.

MARK MESSIER • MAURICE RICHARD • NEWSY LALONDE

Team leadership is the tie that binds Mark Messier and Maurice Richard. The Rocket was the heart and soul of the Montreal Canadiens. He was both the team's scoring leader and inspirational leader during the 1940s and 1950s and the team captain from 1956 until 1960. Richard's exploits are legendary. The first player to score 50 goals in one season; the first to score 500 in his career; a member of eight Stanley Cup champions in 18 years.

The Rocket's burning eyes and jet black hair were visual symbols of the fire that burned inside him and his fierce temper is as legendary as his goal-scoring ability. He was the idol of Canadiens fans across Quebec like no other hockey player has ever been to anyone.

Though Messier has surpassed Richard's career total of 544 goals, he is in no way the pure scorer that the Rocket was, but then few have been. Richard's best season (50 goals in 50 games in 1944–45) works out to an adjusted goal total of 71 and he tops 50 adjusted goals in six other seasons. Messier scored 50 goals in 1981–82, but his adjusted total for that season is just 40. Still, he is a much more complete offensive player than Richard ever was. And like the Rocket, Messier's fierce determination has made him one of the great captains in NHL history, though it has rarely spilled over into the scenes of violence associated with Richard's worst moments.

Messier played under the shadow of Wayne Gretzky while winning his first four Stanley Cup championships in Edmonton, though it was Messier who won the Conn Smythe Trophy as playoff MVP when the Oilers won their first Stanley Cup title in 1985. Messier emerged as the team leader after Gretzky was traded to Los Angeles, winning the Hart Trophy in 1989–90 and leading the Oilers to a fifth Stanley Cup. But it was in New York that his reputation as a great team leader was sealed. He was signed by the Rangers in 1992 and promptly won the Hart Trophy for the second time after leading New York to a first-place finish. But it was the promise of the Stanley Cup that brought Messier to New York and he delivered two years later. Messier guaranteed the Rangers would beat New Jersey in game six of the 1994

conference championship, then made it come true with three goals in a 4–2 win. Later, he scored what proved to be the Stanley Cup-winning goal when the Rangers beat Vancouver in seven games and became the first Rangers captain in 54 years to hold the Cup aloft.

While Messier's passion for the game makes him a good match for Maurice Richard, there is really only one other player in the game's history who's overall on-ice performance can be compared with the Rocket. That player is Newsy Lalonde. Lalonde's career included many stops other than Montreal, but that is about the only way in which these two great French-Canadian stars differed.

Like Richard, Lalonde was both the greatest and most colorful hockey player of his era. He led four different professional leagues in scoring and almost always served as captain of his team. In the short seasons of his day, Lalonde's best year was 1920–21 when he collected 36 goals. His best adjusted goals total for his years in the NHL is 89, and he tops 80 twice more, but, like Richard, Lalonde was as well known for his temper as his goal-scoring prowess. He could be a vicious fighter and went after opponents, spectators and even teammates on occasion. His fans would flock to the rink to cheer him, but he was just as likely to fill the arena full of spectators who despised him.

Lalonde played with the Canadiens in the National Hockey Association and the NHL between 1910 and 1922 and later coached the team in the early 1930s. When Richard came along in the 1940s, Lalonde recognized him as a kindred spirit. He was a big fan of the Rocket and remained a lifelong fan of the Canadiens and a familiar presence at the Montreal Forum until his death in 1970.

PHIL ESPOSITO • NELS STEWART

Big and burly, but with deceptive speed and almost impossible to knock off the puck. Add to that an almost uncanny ability to put the puck where he wanted and you're going to wind up with a great goal scorer. It certainly worked that way for Nels Stewart. And it worked out that way, too, for Phil Esposito.

Nels Stewart displayed a knack for scoring while playing with Cleveland of the United States Amateur Hockey Association in the early 1920s and was added to the roster of the Montreal Maroons for the 1925–26 NHL season. The Maroons had entered the NHL just the season before and had finished with a weak 9–19–2 record. Stewart promptly led the NHL in scoring with 34 goals in 36 games in his first season with Montreal and the Maroons won the Stanley Cup in just their second year of existence.

Phil Esposito's rise to fame was at least somewhat similar to Stewart's. He demonstrated he could be an effective offensive player during his early years with the Chicago Black Hawks, but it was not until his 1967–68 trade to Boston (perennial last-place finishers at the time) that Esposito truly blossomed. In his second year with the Bruins, he led the NHL in scoring and in his third season he helped Boston to win the Stanley Cup. In his prime with the Maroons, Stewart centered Babe Siebert and Hooley Smith on the S-Line. The threesome was considered one of the most dangerous lines in the NHL for their combination of rough play and scoring power. In his prime with Boston, the Bruins were one of the NHL's most physical teams and Esposito centered Ken Hodge and Wayne Cashman on the NHL's top-scoring trio.

In his best years, Esposito dominated the NHL scoring statistics, leading the league in points five times and in goals six years in a row. He was the first player to top 100 points in a season (in 1968–69) and set a single-season record with 76 goals and 152 points in 1970–71. Stewart was not the playmaker that Esposito was and never had a stretch to equal Espo's string of scoring titles, but then he never played with Bobby Orr either! Still, Stewart ranked among the NHL's best scorers throughout his career and was known as "Old Poison" for the deadly accuracy of his shot. He was the only player of his era to top 300 goals and retired after the 1939–40 season as the NHL's all-time leading goal scorer with 324.

While Esposito may have been more dominant in his era than Stewart was in his, both are two-time winners of the Hart Trophy (Stewart in 1925–26 and 1929–30 and Esposito in 1968–69 and 1973–74). Both players were also traded in their prime—Esposito from Boston to New York in 1975–76 and Stewart from the Maroons to the Bruins in 1932–33. (He also played for the New York Americans.) But how does a player who scored 39 goals in his best season compare with a man who had more than 60 on four occasions and tops out at 76? Well, when the differences in the relative ease of scoring in their eras are factored in, Stewart's 39 goals in 44 games in 1929–30 come out as 78 adjusted goals in an average 82-game season, nearly the equal of Esposito's 76 goals in 78 games in 1970–71 which become 81 adjusted goals. But Stewart gets even better! His 21 goals in 44 games in 1928–29 (the lowest-scoring season in NHL history) works out to 86 adjusted goals. His 27 goals in 41 games the year before calculate at 84. Most amazing of all, Stewart's 34 goals in 36 games for the Maroons in 1925–26 result in the whopping total of 110 adjusted goals! So, even though Esposito may have had more years atop the NHL leader board, it appears Stewart was actually a more imposing goal scorer. His lifetime total for adjusted goals works out to 825 compared to Esposito's career total of 754.

And just where does the NHL's leading goal scorer of the 1920s and 1930s rank when compared to the all-time greats? Well, his 825 adjusted goals are not only more than Esposito's, they also rank well ahead of Bobby Hull's 742 adjusted goals. Howie Morenz, who's career total of 270 goals was the best before Stewart, comes closer but falls short with an adjusted total of 764. Cy Denneny (whose 246 goals were the most before Morenz) comes close with 775 adjusted goals. Even Maurice Richard (the first player to pass Stewart's actual career total of 324) also comes up short of Stewart with 778 adjusted goals. Wayne Gretzky's all-time leading total of 885 goals (through 1997–98) is actually factored down to an identical 778. Then there is Gordie Howe. Of all the players in NHL history, only Gordie Howe, whose 801 lifetime goals yield an adjusted total of 1,065, comes out ahead of Nels Stewart.

BOBBY HULL • HOWIE MORENZ

Both compiled impressive statistics, leading their teams in goals and points on an almost annual basis, winning league scoring titles, all-star selections, Hart Trophy honors and Stanley Cup championships. Yet both Howie Morenz and Bobby Hull were even more than the sum of their statistical parts. Others might have had better seasons now and then, but year in and year out Morenz and Hull were the players the fans of their day wanted to see.

Morenz joined the Montreal Canadiens in 1923–24 and

was an immediate sensation. He was the eighth-leading scorer in the NHL during his rookie season, but was the top goal scorer in the playoffs as the Canadiens won the Stanley Cup. Morenz and the Canadiens remained a league power throughout the 1920s and into the 1930s. He was clearly a gifted goal scorer, but what made Morenz stand out was his outstanding speed. To this day, there are oldtimers who claim Morenz was the fastest skater they ever saw. Like Hull, who was christened "the Golden Jet" for his blazing speed and blonde good looks, Morenz' skating skill led to all sorts of speed-related nicknames: "the Canadien Comet," "the Hurtling Habitant," "the Mitchell Meteor," and, best-known of all, "the Stratford Streak." Morenz was also known as "the Babe Ruth of hockey" for his box-office appeal in the United States. More than any other single player, Morenz made hockey a viable attraction in the new American expansion cities of New York, Detroit and Chicago in the late 1920s and into the years of the Great Depression.

Like Morenz, Bobby Hull put fans in the stands. His arrival in Chicago in 1957–58 came at a time when the Black Hawks had missed the playoffs 11 times in 12 years and were regularly attracting crowds of only 4,000 to 5,000 at the 18,000-seat Chicago Stadium. By his third season, Hull had won his first scoring title and in 1960–61 he helped the Black Hawks win their first Stanley Cup title since 1938. His powerful slapshot was like nothing hockey had ever seen before and the oldtimers claimed he was the fastest player in the game since the days of Howie Morenz. Chicagoans were now jamming their home arena and the team was a huge draw on the road as well. Hull and the Black Hawks remained a league power throughout the 1960s and into the 1970s.

Of course, even though Morenz led the Canadiens in goals and points for seven straight years between 1925–26 and 1931–32, and Hull led the Black Hawks in goals 12 times and points six times between 1959–60 and 1971–72, neither player had to lead their teams single-handedly. The Canadiens had a great supporting cast including future Hall of Famers George Vezina, and then George Hainsworth, in goal, Sylvio Mantha to anchor the defense and Aurel Joliat to help lead the attack. Hull's Black Hawks had Glenn Hall, Pierre Pilote and Stan Mikita, among others. Still, it was Hull and Morenz who were the heart and soul of their teams, yet neither would play their entire careers in the cities where they became famous. Hull, of course, signed with the World Hockey Association in 1972–73. His presence gave the fledgling new league instant credibility and for seven seasons he ranked among the offensive leaders in the WHA. Hull did return to the NHL for a final, brief appearance in 1979–80. As for Morenz, he had suffered numerous injuries over his career, and though none had ever caused him to miss much action the cumulative effect began to slow him down by 1933–34. The following season, he was traded to Chicago. Morenz played with the Black Hawks and the New York Rangers over the next two seasons, but returned to Montreal for a final year in 1936–37. He suffered a badly broken leg on January 28, 1937 and it was obvious he would never be able to play hockey again. He died while still in hospital on March 8.

So, who was better?

Hull won three scoring titles and Morenz only won two, but Morenz won the Hart Trophy three times and Hull only twice so there's not much to chose from there. Hull was definitely the more dominant goal scorer, leading the NHL

seven times while Morenz only did it once even though his 270 career goals were the record in his day. Hull topped 50 goals five times at a time when no one in NHL history had reached the milestone more than once and set single-season league scoring records with 54 goals in 1965–66 and 58 more in 1968–69. Morenz' best season was 40 goals in 44 games in 1929–30, but in terms of adjusted goals, that total translates into 80 goals in an average 82-game season. Hull's best adjusted goals total is 67. Morenz was in his prime during an era when goals were harder to come by than at any other time in NHL history and his adjusted totals get even better. His 27 goals in 30 games in 1924–25 work out to 97, while his 33 goals in 43 games in 1927–28 is 104! As for their career totals, Hull's 610 NHL goals become 742 adjusted goals, while the 270 scored by Morenz jump to 764 to again rank him among the all-time leaders. In terms of playmaking skills, Morenz factors out much better with 904 adjusted assists in his career compared to Hull's 563.

WAYNE GRETZKY • FRANK BOUCHER/BILL COWLEY/ ELMER LACH/STAN MIKITA

So, who compares to Wayne Gretzky? No one really. No one has ever had the statistical dominance in hockey that he has had. Gretzky has won the Art Ross Trophy a record 10 times and has actually led the NHL in scoring 11 times when his tie with Marcel Dionne in his first season of 1979–80 is included. Gordie Howe and Mario Lemieux led the NHL in scoring six times.

He has also won the Hart Trophy as most valuable player a record nine times. Gretzky has led the NHL in goals scored five times, a total matched only by Charlie Conacher, Rocket Richard and Gordie Howe and exceeded by just Phil Esposito (six times) and Bobby Hull (seven). Gretzky also holds both the single-season and career records for most goals scored, yet he has always maintained he is not a goal scorer.

What Gretzky is, is the greatest passer in history, with more assists than any other player has ever had points. Whether or not you agree that he is the best player of all time, you have to admit he's pretty unique. Gretzky has led or shared the NHL lead in assists 15 times. Bobby Orr had the NHL lead in assists five times. No one else has ever done it more than three times. Yet if we go by his own guidelines, and say that Gretzky is a playmaker and not a goal scorer, there are at least some players with historical similarities.

The earliest days of the NHL were dominated by goal scorers (assists were not officially tabulated in the first season of 1917–18) and it was not until Sweeny Schriner in 1935–36 that a player led the league in points with more assists (26) than goals (19). This is not to say that hockey hadn't produced any great playmakers until that year. It had. And one of the first was Frank Boucher.

Boucher centered brothers Bill and Bun Cook after all three entered the NHL with the New York Rangers in 1926–27. Over the next nine years, Boucher ranked among the top 10 in scoring eight times and became the first player to lead the NHL in assists three times. He also played on Stanley Cup champions in 1928 and 1933 and won the Lady Byng Trophy seven times in eight years. Boucher was the first player in NHL history to top 100 career assists and his 252 assists when he retired in 1937–38 made him the

NIIL's all-time leader. (Boucher added 10 more assists during a brief comeback in 1943–44.)

When the scoring differences of his era are factored in, Boucher's best seasons of 151 and 131 adjusted assists approach Gretzky's best years and actually top his best adjusted total of 110 assists. Boucher's highest adjusted single-season point totals (191 and 175) are also comparable to Gretzky's real numbers and better than his leading total of 154 adjusted points.

Boucher was surpassed as the NHL's career assist leader when Bill Cowley of the Boston Bruins recorded his 263rd assist during the 1943–44 season. Cowley had established himself as the NHL's premier passer when he led the league in assists for the first of three times in 1938–39. That year, he had 34 assists in just 34 games to become the first player in NHL history to average at least one assist per game. He then added 11 assists in 12 playoff games as the Bruins won the Stanley Cup. Cowley led the NHL in both assists and points in 1940–41 when the Bruins again won the Stanley Cup and he won the Hart Trophy.

Cowley established a career high with 72 points on 27 goals and 45 assists when he won the Hart and Art Ross trophies again in 1942–43, and would have obliterated those totals in 1943–44 if injuries had not cut short his season. In a year that saw Herb Cain set a new NHL scoring record with 83 points (in a 50-game schedule), Cowley had 31 goals and 40 assists for 71 points in just 36 games. His scoring average of 1.97 points-per-game that year is the highest ever by anyone with at least 50 points who is not Wayne Gretzky or Mario Lemieux! Cowley's best adjusted assist total of 84 compares favorably with Gretzky.

When Cowley retired after the 1946–47 season, he was the NHL's all-time leader in both points (548) and assists (353). His records would hold until being surpassed by the NHL's next great playmaker—Elmer Lach.

Elmer Lach entered the NHL in 1940–41 and was one of the league's top scorers by 1942–43. In 1943–44, he was teamed with Toe Blake and Rocket Richard on the Punch Line and again finished in the top 10 in scoring as the Canadiens won the Stanley Cup for the first time in 13 years. In 1944–45, Lach's playmaking skills helped Richard score 50 goals in 50 games. Lach established an NHL record with 54 assists that season (90 adjusted assists), while he, Richard and Blake finished 1–2–3 in the NHL scoring race. Lach added the Hart Trophy to his scoring title for that season. In 1945–46, Lach again led the NHL in assists as the Canadiens won another Stanley Cup. He won a second scoring title in 1947–48.

Several serious injuries began to limit Lach's effectiveness, but in 1951–52 he was again the NHL's assist leader and ranked third overall in the scoring race. Lach also passed Bill Cowley as the NHL's all-time leader in assists and points that season. In 1953, he scored the Stanley Cup-winning goal for the Canadiens. When Lach retired after the 1953–54 season, Rocket Richard had surpassed his points total but his 408 assists were the best in NHL history.

Lach's assists would remain a record for four seasons until surpassed by Gordie Howe, who would eventually up his total to a what once seemed an insurmountable 1,049. Gretzky would, of course, obliterate that record and others have or will pass it too. But despite his prolific assist totals, Howe also led the league in that category just three times. Another three-time assist leader is Stan Mikita, who began his career by piling up both prolific point and penalty-minute totals before settling down to become a Lady Byng

Trophy winner. In fact, Mikita was the first player ever to win three major trophies in one season when he won the Art Ross, the Hart and the Lady Byng in 1966–67. He then won all three awards again in 1967–68. Not even Wayne Gretzky has matched that hat trick!

ALL-TIME ADJUSTED SCORING LEADERS

Top 10 All-Time Career Adjusted Goals

1,065	Gordie Howe
825	Nels Stewart
778	Wayne Gretzky
778	Maurice Richard
775	Cy Denneny
764	Howie Morenz
758	Aurel Joliat
754	Phil Esposito
742	Bobby Hull
658	Jean Beliveau

Top 10 All-Time Career Adjusted Assists

1,429	Wayne Gretzky
1,199	Gordie Howe
1,000	Frank Boucher
985	Aurel Joliat
904	Howie Morenz
878	Stan Mikita
877	Alex Delvecchio
823	Paul Coffey
791	Hooley Smith
790	Ron Francis

Top 10 All-Time Career Adjusted Points

2,264	Gordie Howe
2,207	Wayne Gretzky
1,743	Aurel Joliat
1,668	Howie Morenz
1,532	Cy Denneny
1,531	Phil Esposito
1,503	Nels Stewart
1,493	Stan Mikita
1,453	Alex Delvecchio
1,437	Marcel Dionne

Single-Season Adjusted Goals

ALL-TIME
140	Babe Dye	1924-25	Toronto

ACTIVE
80	Brett Hull	1990-91	St. Louis

Single-Season Adjusted Assists

ALL-TIME
214	Cy Denneny	1924-25	Ottawa

ACTIVE
110	Wayne Gretzky	1985-86	Edmonton

Single-Season Adjusted Points

ALL-TIME
311	Cy Denneny	1924-25	Ottawa

ACTIVE
154	Wayne Gretzky	1981-82	Edmonton

CHAPTER 66

Team Degeneration

Why Does a Good Team Suddenly Go Bad?

Jeff Z. Klein and Karl-Eric Reif

EVERY HOCKEY SEASON is a fresh start, and every year, each team begins the season with optimism. For the players and fans of an elite team, there's the expectation of another year of excellence and excitement, a chance to repeat as champions or to grab the brass ring they just missed at the end of last year's ride. For the teams in the middle of the pack, there's the promise of moving up to join the top clubs and their own shot at winning it all—this new coach, or that new player, and once you're in the playoffs, hey, anything can happen. Even for the bottom-feeders there's the enthusiasm born of confidence that this year can't be worse than last. There's bound to be new guys in uniform, a high draft pick who should step right in, kids who were ineffective last year another year older and ready to take charge.

Every season is a fresh start, a new journey. It's like the launching of a cruise ship. Whether you're among the revelers on board, or just waving a cheery bon voyage amid the confetti and streamers on the dock, there's cause for celebration, and every confidence that good times are just ahead. Well, everyone who watched the Titanic sail out of Southampton thought it could go all the way, too.

A sudden and unexpected downturn in a team's fortunes has traditionally been regarded with superstitious wonder. Year-end postmortems usually yield more guesswork and excuses than real explanations, but through statistical analysis there is insight to be gained into what suddenly makes good teams go bad, and bad teams get radically worse. As we'll see, one factor—a drop-off on defense—underlies almost each of the clubs on this list.

First, let's take a look at the 20 most precipitous single-season declines in the history of major-league hockey.

Fourteen of the "Downturn 20" played seasons that ranged in length from 12 to 36 games and that's too small a sample from which to safely draw any conclusions. The short seasons of hockey's early era made every game vitally important. But given those abbreviated schedules and the tiny rosters teams used before the 1930s, the loss of one key player to injury or illness for just a couple of weeks could put his team's whole season on ice, as could a player's last-minute departure, jumping to another team in a rival league. The loss of a key performer is just what happened to most of the teams on this list. While short seasons are every bit as valid as long ones for most statistical comparisons, they can't be included here.

No, what we need are longer seasons to examine, to see whether something less simple, less obvious, undermined the year for teams that had expected better. Happily for professional hockey statisticians, the 1926–27 season provides a handy cutoff point. With the absorption of the Western Hockey League, the NHL that year went to a 44-game schedule, eight games longer than the season previous and 14 games longer than that of 1924–25. No other league up to that time had ever played more than a 30-game slate. Using the 44-game schedule as our minimum, here are the largest one-season drop-offs of the modern era. We've extended the list to 24 places because several recent teams came close to, but just missed, qualifying among the 20 most badly decayed.

Largest Single-Season Declines in Winning Percentage

	Team	League	Season	W-L-T	Pct	Season	W-L-T	Pct	Pts
1	MTL W	NHA	1909–10	11–1–0	.917	-> 1910–11	7–9–0	.438	–479
2	VIC	PCHA	1913–14	10–5–0	.667	-> 1914–15	4–13–0	.235	–431
3	MTL C	NHA	1913–14	13–7–0	.650	-> 1914–15	6–14–0	.300	–350
4	PORT	PCHA	1915–16	13–5–0	.722	-> 1916–17	9–15–0	.375	–347
5	OTT	NHA/L	1916–17	15–5–0	.750	-> 1917–18	9–13–0	.409	–341
6	NYR	NHL	1941–42	29–17–2	.625	-> 1942–43	11–31–8	.300	–325
7	REG	WCHL	1923–24	17–11–2	.600	-> 1924–25	8–20–0	.286	–314
8	TOR	NHL	1917–18*	13–9–0**	.591	-> 1918–19	5–13–0	.278	–313
9	OTT	NHA	1910–11*	13–3–0	.812	-> 1911–12	9–9–0	.500	–312
10	OTT	NHL	1929–30	21–15–8	.568	-> 1930–31	10–30–4	.273	–295
11	MTL W	NHA	1914–15	14–6–0**	.700	-> 1915–16	10–14–0	.417	–283
12	MTL C	NHL	1924–25	17–11–2	.600	-> 1925–26	11–24–1	.319	–281
13	CHI	NHL	1926–27	19–22–3	.466	-> 1927–28	7–34–3	.193	–273
14	DET	NHL	1969–70	40–21–5	.625	-> 1970–71	22–45–11	.353	–272
15	CHI	NHL	1952–53	27–28–15	.493	-> 1953–54	12–51–7	.221	–272
16	BOS	NHL	1930–31	28–10–6	.705	-> 1931–32	15–21–12	.438	–267
17	VAN	PCHA	1914–15*	13–4–0	.765	-> 1915–16	9–9–0	.500	–265
18	HAM/NYA	NHL	1924–25	19–10–1	.650	-> 1925–26	12–20–4	.389	–261
19	TOR B	NHL	1924–25	19–11–0	.633	-> 1925–26	12–21–3	.375	–258
20	TOR B	NHA	1913–14*	13–7–0	.650	-> 1914–15	8–12–0	.400	–250

* won Stanley Cup.   ** includes one victory in forfeited unplayed game

Largest Single-Season Declines in Winning Percentage

(minimum 44-game schedule)

	Team	League	Season	W-L-T	Pct	Season	W-L-T	Pct	Pts
1	NYR	NHL	1941–42	29–17–2	.625	->1942–43	11–31–8	.300	–325
2	OTT	NHL	1929–30	21–15–8	.568	->1930–31	10–30–4	.273	–295
3	CHI	NHL	1926–27	19–22–3	.466	->1927–28	7–34–3	.193	–273
4	DET	NHL	1969–70	40–21–5	.625	->1970–71	22–45–11	.353	–272
5	CHI	NHL	1952–53	27–28–15	.493	->1953–54	12–51–7	.221	–272
6	BOS	NHL	1930–31	28–10–6	.705	->1931–32	15–21–12	.438	–267
7	DET	NHL	1936–37*	25–14–9	.615	->1937–38	12–25–11	.365	–250
8	MTL M	NHL	1936–37	22–17–9	.552	->1937–38	12–30–6	.312	–240
9	TOR	WHA	1974–75	43–33–2	.564	->1975–76	24–52–5	.327	–237
10	WPG	NHL	1984–85	43–27–10	.600	->1985–86	26–47–7	.369	–231
11	PIT Pi	NHL	1927–28	19–17–8	.523	->1928–29	9–27–8	.295	–228
12	DET	NHL	1995–96	62–13–7	.799	->1996–97	*38–26–18	.573	–226
13	LA	NHL	1980–81	43–24–13	.619	->1981–82	24–41–15	.394	–225
14	MTL C	NHL	1946–47	34–16–10	.650	->1947–48	20–29–11	.425	–225
15	CHI	NHL	1982–83	47–23–10	.650	->1983–84	30–42–8	.425	–225
16	ST.L B	NHL	1980–81	45–18–17	.669	->1981–82	32–40–8	.450	–219
17	NYR	NHL	1983–84	42–29–9	.581	->1984–85	26–44–10	.388	–193
18	LA	WHA	1972–73	37–35–6	.513	->1973–74	25–53–0	.321	–192
19	PIT Pe	NHL	1981–82	31–36–13	.469	->1982–83	18–53–9	.281	–188
20	QUE N	NHL	1988–89	27–46–7	.381	->1989–90	12–61–7	.194	–188
21	NYR	NHL	1991–92	50–25–5	.656	->1992–93	34–39–11	.470	–186
22	BOS	NHL	1995–96	40–31–11	.555	->1996–97	26–47–9	.372	–183
23	WPG	NHL	1992–93	40–37–7	.518	->1993–94	24–51–9	.339	–179
24	NYR	NHL	1993–94*	52–24–8	.667	->1994–95	22–23–3	.490	–177

* won Stanley Cup.

What happened to these once-excellent teams? Did the arena hit an iceberg?

Let's examine the wartime Rangers, who sit in the silt at the very bottom of this Bermuda Triangle of sunken teams. World War II took a tremendous toll on hockey, as scores of NHL regulars and minor-league stars entered military service, and the quality of play plummeted. By the start of the 1942–43 season, 90 NHL players had signed up for or been drafted into the war effort—enough to fill the rosters of all six teams. The Montreal Canadiens were least affected, maintaining most of their prewar lineup and running roughshod through the eviscerated NHL.

The war hit New York, on the other hand, harder than any other club. Stanley Cup champions in 1940, and a first-place team with a .625 winning percentage in 1941–42, the 1942–43 Rangers were without their entire second line of Neil and Mac Colville and Alex Shibicky; two of their best defensemen, Art Coulter and Bill Juzda; and most damaging of all, their fine goaltender, Sugar Jim Henry. In losing Henry, Coulter, and Neil Colville, the Blueshirts were deprived of three future Hall of Famers. On top of that, New York had, at the start of the season, traded another eventual Hall of Fame defenseman, Babe Pratt, to Toronto, for rearguard Dudley "Red" Garrett, who later that year was killed in combat. The first-place Rangers plunged to last in the NHL; by the next season, New York was struggling so badly the ream requested—but was denied—a leave of absence from the league.

Regardless of the worthiness of the cause for the players' absence, in the context of hockey the key factor is that the men lost to the Rangers were primarily defensive players. The Rangers still had their top scoring line of Phil Watson, Bryan Hextall and Lynn Patrick, and the drop in the team's offensive output was noticeable but not crippling. The loss of their goaltender and their top three defensemen, however, proved devastating. The Rangers' goals-against average soared from 2.98 in 1941–42 to 5.06 in 1942–43.

Ottawa, the second team on the list, paid the price for performing the biggest favor ever to benefit the Toronto Maple Leafs: trading them King Clancy. The leprechaun-sized Hall of Fame defenseman, one of the very best ever to play the game, was second in scoring among NHL blueliners in 1929–30, but he brought even more to his own zone than he did to the attack. Ottawa's offense dulled a bit without Clancy's puck-rushing abilities, but without his defensive skills Ottawa's goals-against mushroomed. A pattern is quickly forming. One team lost half a roster, the other just one key figure, but in each case it was their defenses that collapsed and caused them to sink in the standings.

To see how often defensive troubles are the stumbling block resulting in a team's plunge in the standings, we've charted the offensive production and defensive record for each of the teams on the list of worst single-season declines. Because of the fluctuations in length of season and league-wide scoring levels, however, raw numbers don't provide a clear picture. To put these teams on a consistent scale, we convert each club's numbers to a percentage by which their offense and defense were better or worse than the league average for the season of decline and for the one that preceded it.

Whether goals-for or goals-against, a figure better than the league average gets a plus, and a figure worse than the league average is prefaced with a minus.

For example, the 29–17–2 Rangers of 1941–42 scored a league-high 177 goals that year, or, with overtime figured in, 3.59 goals per game—18.5 percent better than the NHL average of about 3.03, as you'll see under the column headed "% +/ GF/gm." They allowed 143 goals, or 2.90 per game—4.3 percent better than that league-wide average of 3.03, and shown in the adjacent column, headed "% +/ GA/gm." The 11–31–8 skeleton crew of 1942–43, however, scored 161 times—3.20 goals per game, 11.1 percent less than that season's NHL average of roughly 3.60, and surrendered a league high 253 goals—5.03 per game, or 39.7 percent worse than the NHL average.

The last two columns display the difference between the percentages in those two seasons. New York, 18.5 percent better on offense than the NHL as a whole in 1941–42, and 11.1 percent worse in 1942–43, drops 29.6 percentage points from its first-place campaign to their basement finish the next year. Better on defense than the league average by 4.3 percent in 1941–42 and worse by 39.7 percent in 1942–43, their fall is represented by a difference of 44 percentage points.

Change in Goals For and Goals Against by Teams with Biggest Single-Season Declines

(minimum 44-game schedule)

	Team	League	Season	% +/- GF/gm	% +/- GA/gm	Season	% +/- GF/gm	% +/- GA/gm	dif % GF/gm	dif % GA/gm
1	NYR	NHL	1941–42	+18.5	+4.3	->1942–43	−11.1	−39.7	−29.6	−44.0
2	OTT	NHL	1929–30	+4.6	+10.5	->1930–31	−12.9	−35.9	−17.5	−46.4
3	CHI	NHL	1926–27	+29.8	−30.9	->1927–28	−16.6	−64.2	−46.5	−33.4
4	DET	NHL	1969–70	+11.4	+9.9	->1970–71	−14.2	−26.5	−25.6	−36.3
5	CHI	NHL	1952–53	+0.8	−4.4	->1953–54	−20.9	−43.9	−21.7	−39.5
6	BOS	NHL	1930–31	+35.9	+14.5	->1931–32	+0.7	−3.4	−35.2	−17.9
7	DET	NHL	1936–37*	+8.5	+13.6	->1937–38	−18.5	−9.5	−27.0	−23.1
8	MTL M	NHL	1936–37	+6.1	+7.4	->1937–38	16.6	23.0	22.7	30.4
9	TOR	WHA	1974–75	+21.8	+6.1	->1975–76	+10.8	−31.6	−11.0	−37.7
10	WPG	NHL	1984–85	+15.0	−6.6	->1985–86	−6.9	−17.4	−21.9	−10.9
11	PIT Pi	NHL	1927–28	−20.0	+9.2	->1928–29	−29.2	−23.1	−9.2	−32.3
12	DET	NHL	1995–96	+26.8	+29.4	->1996–97*	+4.9	+18.3	−21.9	−11.1
13	LA	NHL	1980–81	+9.6	+5.7	->1901–82	−2.2	−15.0	−11.8	−20.7
14	MTL C	NHL	1046 47	0.4	+27.2	>1947 48	16.3	+3.0	−15.9	−23.4
15	CHI	NHL	1982–83	+9.3	+13.3	>1983–84	−12.0	+1.2	−21.3	−12.1
16	St.L B	NHL	1980–81	+14.5	+8.6	->1981–82	−1.9	−8.7	−16.4	−17.3
17	NYR	NHL	1983–84	−0.7	+7.9	->1984–85	−5.3	−10.8	−4.6	−18.7
18	LA	WHA	1972–73	−7.4	+10.6	->1973–74	−15.0	−20.6	−7.6	−31.2
19	PIT Pe	NHL	1981–82	−3.4	−5.0	->1982–83	−16.9	−27.4	−13.5	−22.4
20	QUE	NHL	1988–89	−10.8	−14.7	->1989–90	−18.2	−38.7	−7.4	−24.0
21	NYR	NHL	1991–92	+16.0	+11.1	->1992–93	−0.5	−0.8	−16.5	−11.9
22	BOS	NHL	1995–96	+9.3	−4.3	->1996–97	−2.0	−25.7	−11.3	−21.4
23	WPG	NHL	1992–93	+5.9	−5.2	->1993–94	−10.9	−26.5	−16.8	−21.3
24	NYR	NHL	1993–94*	+10.2	+14.9	->1994–95	−2.4	+5.9	−12.6	−9.0

* won Stanley Cup.

Average rate of change in goals for: −18.6%
Average rate of change in goals against: −24.8%

Every team on the list fell off both in scoring goals and preventing them, but twice as many—16 out of the 24 teams here—show a more severe decline on defense than on offense. And the average amount of decline on defense is significantly larger than that on offense. Obviously, a major drop-off in either scoring goals or stopping them threatens a team's ability to compete, and a decline in both pretty much guarantees it. But it seems safe to conclude that when a team really goes sour in its own end, when a team loses one or more critical defensive players through trade, injury, or what have you and doesn't address that loss—it's time to don your Mae West and lower the lifeboats.

The 1970–71 Detroit Red Wings are another case in point. They show the most abrupt one-season downturn of any team since the advent of the center red line and in any

season of 60 games or more. They too were paying the price for mishandling their defense. Carl Brewer—chef, pilot, scholar, union activist, and by far Detroit's best blueliner—retired, at least from the Red Wings, and former Calder and Conn Smythe Trophy-winning goalie Roger Crozier was traded to Buffalo. Detroit's only answer to Brewer's absence was to experiment with 42-year-old Gordie Howe on defense. And although Roy Edwards and Jimmy Rutherford were capable netminders, they weren't close to Crozier's level; he'd been dealt for young winger Tom Webster, who actually led the Wings in scoring that year but wasn't a devotee of backchecking. Only the Golden Seals gave up more goals that year than did the Red Wings, who finished dead last, behind first-year expansion clubs Buffalo and Vancouver.

Similar forces were at play for the 1928–29 Pittsburgh Pirates. Much of the roster was the same as the fine Pirate team of 1927–28: Hib Milks, Harry Darragh and Baldy Cotton still played up front. Roger Smith, Herb Drury and Johnny MacKinnon were still present and accounted for on the blue line, but the biggest difference was found between the pipes where journeyman Joe Miller was a replacement for future Hall of Famer Roy Worters who had held out for a raise before the season started. The Pirates, suffering financially, let him go to the last-place New York Americans, receiving the rights to Miller as compensation. Worters immediately carried the Amerks back into Stanley Cup contention, earning the Hart Trophy as league MVP in 1928–29. Pittsburgh floundered, trading veteran forwards for veteran forwards but never strengthening themselves in goal or defense. They fell only 9.2 percent on the attack, but plunged 32.3 percent on defense and ended up in last place themselves.

Detroit appears twice more on this list, and both are interesting exceptions to the absent-defensive-star rule. The 1936–37 edition of the Red Wings were a dreadnought, leading the NHL in offense and defense en route to the best record in the league and a second straight Stanley Cup championship. More seemed in store as Detroit headed into 1937–38 with a virtually identical cast. But 1936–37 had been a last kick at the can for many of Detroit's best players, particularly their great little forward line of Larry Aurie and Hall of Famers Marty Barry and Herbie Lewis. All of them barely 30, they seemed to age overnight; the Red Wings faded badly at both ends of the ice, followed their Cup triumph with a last-place finish, and all three retired within two years.

The 1996–97 Red Wings went the opposite way. Among the league's regular-season elite since 1991–92, winners of three straight division titles, and posting the NHL's best record for two years in a row, the Wings nonetheless fell short in the playoffs. Twice they were victims of huge opening-round upsets. In 1994–95 they reached the Stanley Cup finals only to be swept aside in four games by New Jersey. In 1996–97 they seemed finally to have learned that regular-season success is no guarantee of playoff glory. With a roster identical to the previous year's, but for the one significant acquisition of grinding goal scorer Brendan Shanahan, who took over the team scoring lead, the Red Wings paced themselves for a playoff run. There was plenty of cushion for a fall—Detroit had won at a nearly .800 clip in 1995–96—and importantly, their decline on defense was the third-smallest on this list. Having left something in the tank this time for the playoff drive, Red Wings finally kissed the Cup in 1996–97—the only team on the list that stooped to conquer.

CHAPTER 67

Presence in Scoring

Can Top Offensive Players Prevail Without Talented Linemates?

Jeff Z. Klein and Karl-Eric Reif

REMEMBER WARREN YOUNG? How about B.J. MacDonald? For those of you who don't recall, they were journeyman NHL players who exist in the chronicles of major-league hockey mainly as the answers to trivia questions, having produced "who is he?" one-year-wonder scoring seasons in the 1980s. MacDonald was a solid scorer in all seven of his WHA campaigns, but the 46 goals he posted for Edmonton in 1979–80 represented more than half his career total in four NHL seasons, and better than any of his seasons in the WHA. Young, a minor-league tough-guy, scored 40 goals for Pittsburgh—more than half his career total—in 1984–85. It was no coincidence that both of these big seasons came when they were skating alongside Wayne Gretzky or Mario Lemieux respectively.

Hockey is full of stories like that. A transcendent offensive player enhances the production of the others on his line, and that of the whole team. Stay-at-home defensemen who never cross their own blue line pick up assists on goals the offensive star scores going end-to-end. Even Edmonton goalie Grant Fuhr was credited with 14 assists in 1983–84, which probably were due at least in some small part to the 87 goals and 205 points Gretzky rang up that year.

It begs the question: if an offensive genius like Gretzky or Lemieux can lift third-line wingers to 40-goal years, how much could they accomplish with a true marksman like Bobby or Brett Hull, like Gordie Howe, or Maurice Richard, or Peter Bondra skating alongside? Fortunately for them, Gretzky met Jari Kurri, and Lemieux made the acquaintance of Jaromir Jagr. And it raises another question: how much, then, does being saddled with linemates who aren't gifted finishers hurt a great offensive player?

Gretzky and Kurri, Lemieux and Jagr, Guy Lafleur and Jacques Lemaire, Mike Bossy and Bryan Trottier—all through the history of the game, great goal scorers have combined with great playmakers to produce great offensive

Individual Presence in Team Goal-Scoring NHL, 1917–18 to 1997–98

	PLAYER, TEAM	SEASON	SCHEDULE	GP	G	TEAM GF	PRESENCE
1	Dye, Tor	1924–25	30	29	38	90	.756
2	Joe Malone, Que B	1919 20	24	24	39	91	.750
3	Joe Malone, Mtl C	1917–18	22	20	44	115	.682
4	Vic Ripley, Chi	1928–29	44	34	11	33	.647
5	Nels Stewart, Mtl M	1925–26	36	36	34	91	.596
6	Joe Malone, Ham	1920–21	24	20	30	92	.581
7	Aurel Joliat, Mtl C	1924–25	30	24	29	93	.566
8	Cy Denneny, Ott	1917–18	22	22	36	102	.545
9	Cy Denneny, Ott	1920–21	24	24	34	97	.540
10	Herberts, Bos	1924–25	30	30	17	49	.531
11	Cy Denneny, Ott	1924–25	30	28	27	83	.517
12	Babe Dye, Tor	1923–24	24	19	17	59	.511
13	Babe Dye, Tor	1922–23	24	22	26	82	.506
14	Punch Broadbent, Mtl M	1924–25	30	30	15	45	.500
15	Cy Denneny, Ott	1923–24	24	21	22	74	.484

seasons. Detroit's Production Line of Lindsay, Abel and Howe, the Big, Bad Bruins of Orr and Esposito—the list goes on and on. But what about players who had to carry their team alone?

Such a player has the additional burden of getting all the attention and the abuse from opposing defensemen, yet fights through it to get himself open for a pass—that comes on a bounce, or skitters 10 feet behind him, or never comes at all. He weaves through the sticks and elbows to dish a perfect feed to the open man, who flips it right into the goalie's midsection, or fires it five feet wide, or fans on it completely. We'll never know how much more these lone stars might have accomplished had they been surrounded by more talent, but we can at least try to recognize the achievements of the players who did the biggest job with the least help. At first blush it seems it should be a simple matter to identify players who fit that description, but as it turns out it's a rather thorny statistical challenge. Why that's so will become evident momentarily.

Some of the people on the following lists were players who, although playing for a team that did provide decent offensive support, still stood head and shoulders above their teammates. But there have been teams that, at least for that season, have had to rely heavily on one star player to score or set up their goals. These 'workhorse' star players are spotlighted here.

We call this quality 'presence,' and what it measures is the degree to which a player helped his team's attack while he was in the lineup. Because the criteria for awarding assists have differed from one season to the next, this study of presence will be confined to goal-scoring and will use the following formula:

$$\frac{\text{player's goals per game} \times \text{scheduled games}}{\text{team's goals} - \text{player's goals}}$$

For example, in the 80-game NHL season of 1989–90, Boston's Cam Neely played in 76 games and scored 55 times—.724 goals per game. We've chosen to use Neely's goals-per-game average, rather than simply his goal total, to better express what Neely meant to the Bruin offense when he was actually in the lineup—he can't be blamed for goals he or the rest of the B's failed to score while he was unavailable. The Bruins as a team scored 289 goals that year, and we'll subtract Neely's 55 to see how the rest of the team did without him. So we get this equation:

$$\frac{.724 \times 80}{289 - 55} = \frac{57.89}{234} = .2474$$

Neely's presence figure is .247, which you can think of as saying that when he was in the lineup, Neely's goal production amounted to 24.7 percent of that produced by the rest of the Bruins combined.

At left is a list of players with the largest single-season presence in goal scoring in NHL history.

A quick glance reveals that every player on the list qualified during the NHL's first dozen years. It should come as no surprise to those familiar with the game's early history that presence figures for every outstanding scorer of hockey's Mesozoic era are far higher, and consistently higher, than those for players from the early 1930s onward. Tiny rosters, with one line of starters getting an enormous share of the ice time, and just a handful of subs seeing but a few minutes a game if they played at all, ensured that the highest-scoring forward on nearly every team in every season until the late 1920s would appear on an all-time list of presence leaders, and that few latter-day players could hope to crack the top 100.

Most of the men who appear on this list earned their place as legends. Babe Dye, Aurel Joliat and Punch Broadbent were some of the most extraordinary and most colorful players of their day. Joe Malone, Cy Denneny and Nels Stewart, equally superb and all fascinating stories, were each the NHL's career scoring leader at some point in their great careers. All of them won a place in the Hall of Fame.

Presence figures for players from the NHL's early rival leagues and from leagues prior to World War I are often even higher. Didier Pitre, the great forward of the early-era Montreal Canadiens, registered the highest presence figure ever, .903, for the 1911–12 Habs, who then competed in the National Hockey Association, the forerunner of the NHL. In Montreal's 18 games, Pitre scored 28 of the Canadiens' 59 goals, or nearly as many as every other Habitant put together. His 1914–15 figure of .857 is the second-highest ever. Other legendary players from the pro game's early days, such as Pacific Coast Hockey Association stars Cyclone Taylor, Tom Dunderdale and Frank Foyston, all put up single-season presence marks higher than Dye's NHL best-ever .756.

The presence figures for today's players are drastically lower, and it's important to understand why that is and what it means. In major-league hockey in the NHA era—1909–10 through 1916–17 the figure was .446. From 1926–27, the first year of the NHL's monopoly, to 1930–31, the figure was .317. During the five NHL seasons played during World War II, the figure was .203, and in the expansion era—1967–68 through 1978–79—it had dropped to .186. Era by era, almost year by year, as rosters became larger, line changes became more frequent, and more players contributed to their team's offense—as the contributions of every team's one or two big guns were overwhelmed by the combined efforts of a larger number of lesser scorers—the presence figures for the top scorers fell. Until, that is, just the last couple of seasons.

It's also important to remember that through the years, with every expansion, it had been defense that has suffered, allowing more lower-echelon players to produce more offense in support of their team's big point-producers. Dilution thins defense. As the number of teams expands, offense inflates.

Through the game's history, that effect has been so pronounced, and so constant, it's been like an immutable law of physics. But here in the 1990s, in just the last few years, this trend has reversed as defense has reasserted itself.

With a 30-team NHL on the horizon, there aren't enough gifted goal scorers to go around. Few teams have more than one top scoring line. Until the early 1990s, through the decades of the game's modern era, most teams—even weaker ones—gave their opponents more offense than that to worry about. A defense couldn't shadow just one forward and be confident they'd shut down the entire attack.

How many teams today can boast the one-two punch of a Sakic and a Forsberg, a Selanne and a Kariya, a Lindros and a LeClair? With only one or two big scorers on most rosters today, teams count on their best offensive players—their 'go-to guys'—more heavily than at any time since the Roaring Twenties. Big scorers of the last few seasons now dominate the list of modern-day presence leaders.

We used the 1931–32 season as a cut-off point for assembling that list—a somewhat subjective choice, but not an arbitrary one. It was that season in which elements of modern hockey like forward passing, larger rosters, and frequent line changes were recent developments, and it's that season that shows the most pronounced demarcation in the gradual diminution of the average presence figure. In the mid-1980s, the list of the top 15 presence marks since 1931–32 included five players from the 1930s, two from the 1940s, two from the 1950s, two from the 1960s, three from the 1970s, and one from the 1980s. The updated top 15 now includes seven players who posted their numbers in the 1990s. In order to provide a bit more perspective, we've extended the list of the biggest modern performances in presence to 25 places.

Individual Presence in Team Goal-Scoring NHL and WHA, 1931–32 to 1997–98

	PLAYER, TEAM	LEAGUE	SEASON	SCHEDULE	GP	G	TEAM GF	PRESENCE
1	Brett Hull, St.L	NHL	1990–91	80	78	86	310	.394
2	Teemu Selanne, Ana.	NHL	1997–98	82	73	52	205	.382
3	Brett Hull, St.L	NHL	1991–92	80	73	70	279	.367
4	Real Cloutier, Que N	WHA	1978–79	80	77	75	288	.366
5	Cam Neely, Bos	NHL	1993–94	84	49	50	289	.359
6	Peter Bondra, Wsh	NHL	1995–96	82	67	52	234	.350
7	Maurice Richard, Mtl C	NHL	1950–51	70	65	42	173	.345
8	Mario Lemieux, Pit Pe	NHL	1988–89	80	76	85	347	.342
9	Peter Bondra, Wsh	NHL	1994–95	48	47	34	136	.340
10	Bill Cook, NYR	NHL	1931–32	48	48	34	134	.340
11	Peter Bondra, Wsh	NHL	1997–98	82	76	52	219	.336
12	Maurice Richard, Mtl C	NHL	1949–50	70	70	43	172	.333
13	Mario Lemieux, Pit Pe	NHL	1992–93	84	60	69	367	.324
14	Leroy Goldsworthy, Mtl C	NHL	1934–35	48	33	20	110	.323
15	Brett Hull, St.L	NHL	1989–90	80	80	72	295	.323
16	Marty Barry, Bos	NHL	1933–34	48	48	27	111	.321
17	Alexander Mogilny, Buf	NHL	1992–93	84	77	76	335	.320
18	Tod Sloan, Tor	NHL	1955–56	70	70	37	153	.319
19	Bobby Hull, Wpg	WHA	1974–75	78	78	77	322	.314
20	Bobby Hull, Chi	NHL	1965–66	70	65	54	240	.313
21	Maurice Richard, Mtl C	NHL	1946–47	60	60	45	189	.312
22	Teemu Selanne, Wpg	NHL	1992–93	84	84	76	322	.309
23	Charlie Conacher, Tor	NHL	1931–32	48	44	34	155	.307
24	Charlie Conacher, Tor	NHL	1934–35	48	47	36	157	.304
25	Pavel Bure, Van	NHL	1993–94	84	76	60	279	.303

The sudden appearance on this list of 13 entries recorded since 1988–89 indicates a sea-change in the basic condition of the NHL.

Many of the players here did have some help in reaching this list. Not always the sort of help they'd get from a team deep from top to bottom in scoring talent, but the sort of help every goal scorer dreams of—a great playmaker to skate with all season long. This confirms that a player's statistics can never be evaluated out of the context of his team, or out of the context of the season in which he played, but almost every player here was the one and only guy his team could really count on to produce goals, whether he put them in off nifty passes or whether he had to create scoring plays entirely on his own.

Brett Hull tops the modern presence list with two of the top three performances by this measure, and holds a third berth with the first of the three straight monster goal-scoring years he posted in St. Louis from 1989–90 through 1991–92.

As deadly as Hull's aim was, and for all terror he inspired in NHL netminders, the affable, outspoken hippie-dippy goal scorer would be the first to acknowledge the playmaking abilities of his centermen in those seasons—namely Adam Oates, one the finest pure passers in hockey, and late in that third year, Craig Janney.

Oates had been traded to Boston in 1992, and it's no coincidence he was centering for Cam Neely when Neely reached the fourth spot on the list. Nobody was along for the ride here, picking up points by accident; it took the combination of a superb playmaker like Oates and fearsome goal-getters like Hull and Neely to register remarkable numbers like these.

In 1997–98, Oates, now in Washington, helped Peter Bondra to another appearance on the list. Bondra, a brilliant sniper, earned two earlier rankings with the help of Michal Pivonka. "Peter the Great" has clearly been the creator of offense for the defense-minded Capitals; now that Bondra, the pure goal scorer, is paired with Oates, the pure passer, he may start adding single-season presence marks to this list annually.

Mario Lemieux, Pavel Bure and Teemu Selanne are three recent stars who show up here on the strength of their own unaccompanied prodigious skills. Lemieux was the set-up man and the finisher in Pittsburgh in 1988–89, helping minor-league marksman Rob Brown to a career-best 49-goal season and still potting 76 himself. By 1992–93, *le Magnifique* had a little more support, with crash-bang wingers Kevin Stevens and Rick Tocchet at the apex of their careers and helping dig the puck out for Mario. They were good, but Lemieux was awesome. He complained long and loudly about the guys assigned to shadow him defensively, but they never seemed to shut him down or even slow him down.

Bure, though, was really on his own in generating offense for the 1993–94 Canucks. Conscientious forwards Cliff Ronning and Geoff Courtnall checked well and made some plays as Bure's linemates, but only the Russian Rocket was consistently on target. Bure not only led the NHL in goals that season, he was the offensive spark that carried Vancouver all the way to the Stanley Cup finals—and he topped all playoff goal scorers that year as well.

Selanne, however, had the most remarkable year of anyone on this list. In his rookie season of 1992–93 he was the ultimate lone wolf scorer, recording more goals than any other Winnipeg Jet forward had points. He had nearly as many points as the next two Jet forwards combined. Now in Anaheim, and despite the absence of immensely talented linemate Paul Kariya for most of the 1997–98 season, Selanne scored 52 goals for a Mighty Ducks roster that generated only 153 goals from every other player in the lineup. His .382 presence figure ranks second in the modern era only to Brett Hull's best year.

Almost every other player here arrived as part of some great offensive combination. Real Cloutier, Marc Tardif and Serge Bernier, talented second-liners in the NHL, were all-stars as WHA linemates.

Rocket Richard, one of the deadliest shooters and most compelling players in the game's history, had superb passers like Buddy O'Connor, Toe Blake and Elmer Lach as linemates in the seasons he appears on the list. Ranger great Bill Cook was the business end of a great line featuring brother Bun and Hall of Fame playmaker Frank Boucher. Alexander Mogilny had the best season of his career skating alongside a sensational Pat LaFontaine in Buffalo. "The Golden Jet," Bobby Hull, had exceptional pivots like Stan Mikita and Phil Esposito to work with in Chicago, and the extraordinary Swedish stars Ulf Nilsson and Anders Hedberg in Winnipeg. "The Big Bomber," Charlie Conacher, teamed with Busher Jackson and the fabulous playmaker Joe Primeau to form Toronto's Kid Line, one of the best ever assembled. And Charlie Simmer completed the Triple Crown line of the Los Angeles Kings, with Dave Taylor and the marvelous Marcel Dionne.

Most of the players on both the all-time and modern lists are among the game's deadliest snipers, but an appearance on this list doesn't necessarily stamp a player as one of the great scorers of all time—merely that he was by far the best goal scorer, on what may have been an otherwise ineffective offensive side, in that one particular season.

Vic Ripley and Jimmy Herberts—obscure players in comparison to most on these lists were—remembered by Hall of Fame defenseman and hockey raconteur King Clancy with respect. Clancy remembered Herberts, in an era of smaller men, as an unusually large, strong player with a hard, heavy shot, who didn't come to major-league hockey until he was almost 30. Herberts had several good years for Boston and Toronto before finishing up in Detroit.

Clancy recalled Ripley as a capable forward with a peculiar way of snapping off a shot, using a lot of wrist action to make the puck veer and dip unpredictably. Ripley earned a spot on the all-time single-season presence list with just 11 goals in 33 games for the 1928–29 Black Hawks. This Chicago squad was the most anemic offensive side in history. Even in the lowest-scoring season in the history of major-league hockey, Chicago's team total of 33 goals in 44 games was pathetic.

Three players younger fans may not know appear on the modern list. Leroy Goldsworthy, another hefty physical specimen, was one of the very few American-born players of his time, a native of Two Harbors, Minnesota. His 20 goals in 33 games with the mediocre Canadiens of 1934–35 was by far the best production in a nine-year NHL career that saw him play for six different teams.

Tod Sloan, a rambunctious little center who spent 10 years with the Leafs and three more in Chicago, also had a career year when he made the list. Sloan at the time was centering Toronto's excellent checking line, flanked by George Armstrong and Dick Duff.

Marty Barry enjoyed the first few seasons of his Hall of Fame career centering Boston's top line between Harry Oliver and Perk Galbraith, then starred with Dit Clapper on his wing before being dealt to Detroit. Barry promptly teamed with Larry Aurie and Herbie Lewis to lead Red Wings to back-to-back Stanley Cup triumphs.

CHAPTER 68

The Rival Big Leagues

Competing Leagues and Their Attempts to Ice the Best Players in the World

David Spaner

Total Hockey's Player and Goaltender Registers (beginning on page 647) include everyone who has played even one shift in the NHL, but other leagues deemed worthy of major-league status are acknowledged by the addition of a second total line titled "Other Major League Totals" added to the individual data panels of the appropriate players. The criteria for "major-league" status and the major leagues themselves are described here.

WAYNE GRETZKY still has something to shoot for. The NHL's all-time leading goal scorer entered the 1998–99 season with 931 big-league goals. Gordie Howe, however, remains major-league hockey's all-time goal-scoring leader with 975.

Several years ago, Major League Baseball formed a committee to determine which leagues should be included to determine a player's overall major-league statistics. Hockey is long overdue in acknowledging the accomplishments of its earliest stars who played either before, or alongside, the NHL. Stars such as Cyclone Taylor, whose amazing feats have been left more to fantasy than fact, or fellow Hall of Famer Tommy Smith, whose scoring feats would be legendary if not for the fact that he played only 10 games in the NHL. Even outstanding hockey pioneers like Newsy Lalonde and Joe Malone scored the majority of their goals in major hockey leagues that predate the NHL.

What separates many of the early pre-NHL big-league circuits from professional minor league was their attempt to ice the best players in the world. Even at their best, the American Hockey League and the rest of the minors were professional feeder leagues that did not challenge the NHL for hockey's star players. Hockey's other major leagues presented players such as Taylor and Lalonde, Smith and Malone, Gordie Howe and Bobby Hull. Even the NHL, in its own way, admitted that these leagues were 'big time' when it ruled Wayne Gretzky was ineligible for its rookie of the year award because he had played in the World Hockey Association.

In addition to the above-mentioned mandate of attempting to ice the best players in the world, other criteria that give these leagues their major-league status included their willingness to pay top professional salaries and their desire to go after the Stanley Cup.

The most recent example of major-league hockey outside the NHL is the World Hockey Association. The WHA arrived on the scene in 1972 and, although its teams were never permitted to challenge for the Stanley Cup, the league had a mandate to outbid the NHL for players.

Toronto Maple Leafs goalie Bernie Parent was the first to jump, to the Miami Screaming Eagles, but the signing that signaled the WHA's big-league aspirations was Bobby Hull. Then the highest-paid player in the NHL at $100,000 a season, the Chicago Black Hawk signed a 10-year, $2.75-million contract with the Winnipeg Jets. Howe, Frank Mahovlich and others followed and the war would not end until 1979, when the NHL absorbed WHA teams in Quebec, Edmonton, Hartford and Winnipeg.

Since the WHA closed up shop, there have been faltering attempts to form rival leagues, but the NHL has reigned without opposition. Long before there was an NHL, however, there was big-league hockey and, when the stats of hockey's other big leagues—the National Hockey Association, Pacific Coast Hockey Association, Western Hockey League (to name just a few)—as well as those of the World Hockey Association, are added to players' NHL totals there are some considerable changes to the record book. Howe jumps from 801 goals to 975 to reclaim the all-time goal-scoring lead. Bobby Hull rises to third spot, his goals increasing from 610 to 913 including a record-tying nine 50-goal seasons. Frank Mahovlich, WHA goals included, now has 622 to surpass all but Hull among left wingers. Cyclone Taylor, who never played in the NHL, totaled 228 goals in 209 major-league games even though he spent much of his early career as a defenseman. Tommy Smith was scoreless in his 10 NHL games, but his other major-league totals are an impressive 345 goals in only 200 games. Newsy Lalonde, who led four leagues in scoring and five leagues in goals scored, goes from 124 NHL goals to 449 big-league goals, the most of any player of his era including Joe Malone, whose 143 NHL goals become 343 in total major-league play.

Hockey's first major professional league was also the game's first all-pro circuit, although there had been many instances of individual players being paid in the many amateur associations that flourished before the International (Pro) Hockey League was formed in 1904. The IHL, which operated until 1907, was the first league to attempt to be an umbrella for the world's best hockey players. Baseball was the dominant professional sport in turn-of-the-century North America, and the success of its professional leagues was a role model for the IHL. Like the formative leagues of North America's other major sports, the IHL included towns that would soon be too small for big-time hockey. The league was formed by Jack "Doc" Gibson, a dentist who had played hockey in Ontario before settling in the copper mining town of Houghton, Michigan. It was a five-team circuit near the Great Lakes, including Pittsburgh, Sault Ste. Marie (Ontario), Sault Ste. Marie (Michigan), Calumet (Michigan), and Houghton. At first, players were paid $15 to $40 a week, with stars receiving far more. Taylor, for instance, received $400 to play the final four games of the 1905–06 season.

"The towns in the International Hockey League will see the best hockey in the world this winter. There is no doubt about the quality being better than will be seen anywhere else," said the *Soo Evening News*. Through the IHL's brief history there would be rumors of cities about to join,

including Chicago, Columbus, Detroit and Toronto. With the exception of Pittsburgh, however, it would remain small-town, but it was big league. Its champions would never be permitted to play for the Stanley Cup, but the caliber of the short-lived IHL is reflected in the Hockey Hall of Fame membership of 15 of the league's 97 players: Taylor, Lalonde, Smith, Jimmy Gardner, Joe Hall, Jack Laviolette, Didier Pitre, Oliver Seibert, Bruce Stuart, Hod Stuart, George McNamara, Marty Walsh, Riley Hern, Hugh Lehman and Jack Gibson. As well, Gibson and Joe Linder are members of the United States Hockey Hall of Fame.

By 1907 many individual Canadian teams had gone professional and were providing too much competition for the towns of the IHL. The Manitoba Hockey League was recognized as professional as early as the 1906–07 season and boasted such stars as Art Ross and Joe Hall. Both players were added to the roster of the league's Kenora Thistles in January of 1907 and, along with fellow future Hockey Hall of Famers Tommy Phillips, Si Griffis, Tom Hooper, and Billy McGimsie, helped beat the Montreal Wanderers to become the smallest town ever to boast of winning a Stanley Cup championship.

The Eastern Canada Amateur Hockey Association had also played a key role in the demise of the IHL by deciding in 1906 to sign professionals to play alongside amateurs. Teams were merely required to state which players were being paid. The Montreal Victorias and Montreal Hockey Club chose to remain fully amateur until dropping out in 1908–09. After their departure the league became fully professional and the 'Amateur' was dropped from its name. The ECHA iced a four-team circuit with the Montreal Wanderers, Montreal Shamrocks, Ottawa Senators and Quebec Bulldogs.

Rivaling Canada's other pro leagues for talent in 1907–08 was the Ontario Professional Hockey League. With franchises in Toronto, Brantford, Guelph and Berlin (which would become Kitchener), and later Galt, St. Catharines and Waterloo, the OPHL was designed to minimize travel expenses and teams went from town to town on electric streetcars which caused the circuit to be dubbed the Trolley League. Still, the league was able to attract stars like Newsy Lalonde, who topped all scorers with 29 goals in nine games in the first season of 1907–08 and led Toronto to a league title and an unsuccessful Stanley Cup challenge against the Montreal Wanderers. Over the years, other future Hall of Famers like Tommy Smith, Joe Malone and Hugh Lehman would all suit up for OPHL teams and, before the league folded in 1911, teams from Galt and Berlin would also challenge for the Stanley Cup.

By 1908–09, the Manitoba Hockey League was in its final season as a professional loop and, despite the presence of the OPHL, the league recognized as hockey's best was the Eastern Canada Hockey Association. That season, IHL veteran Marty Walsh paced the ECHA in scoring and Ottawa, led by Walsh and former IHL star Cyclone Taylor, won the Stanley Cup. But the ECHA lasted just one season before changing its name to the Canadian Hockey Association prior to the 1909–10 campaign.

"BROKE UP ECHA MADE NEW LEAGUE," headlined the November 26, 1909, *Montreal Gazette*. At a meeting in Montreal, the ECHA member teams resigned from the league and a half-hour later most of them reconstituted themselves as the Canadian Hockey Association, which included the Ottawa Senators, the Montreal Shamrocks, Quebec, the Nationals and All-Montreal who replaced the Montreal Wanderers. The Wanderers were ousted based on their insistence on playing home games at the Jubilee Rink instead of the larger Montreal Arena. (Wanderers' owner P.J. Doran also owned the Jubilee.)

Instead of disappearing, the Wanderers emerged as a charter member of the CHA's new rival, the National Hockey Association. Other NHA teams included the Montreal Canadiens, the Renfrew Millionaires, Cobalt and Haileybury. The two leagues engaged in a spirited bidding war, with Lester Patrick signed by Renfrew for an unheard of sum of $3,000. Lester's less experienced brother Frank received $2,000. Other former ECHA stars like Cyclone Taylor also jumped (signing with Renfrew as well for a reported $5,250). The hockey war resulted in dwindling CHA attendance.

Back on October 14, 1909, league vice president L.N. Bate, of the Ottawa club, had stated that the CHA was in for the long haul, and would not compromise. "The Canadian league will entertain no proposition for such," he said. "We will continue as at present constituted. The people of Ottawa have show unmistakably that they are with the Ottawa club, and we do not intend to retreat one step."

However, in January 1910, the CHA would fold, unable to stave off the NHA, and Ottawa and the Montreal Shamrocks were admitted to the rival league. "The bewildered public which has always found it hard to decide which is the Canadian and which is the National Association will have more reason for bewilderment today," stated the January 15 *Montreal Gazette*, "for the game that Shamrocks and Ottawa will play in Ottawa tonight will be neither a National or a Canadian Association game. It will be the first game in the new combination, which is likely to be christened tomorrow the National Canadian Hockey Association." But it was more absorption than amalgamation, and all traces of the CHA would disappear into the NHA—the league that would prove to be the precursor of the NHL.

Having successfully fought off the CHA challenge and recognized as being a cut above the OPHL, the NHA was soon competing with two other major leagues. In 1910–11 the Interprovincial Professional Hockey League was formed with teams in New Brunswick and Nova Scotia. Beginning in 1911–12, the league was known as the Maritime Professional Hockey League and its champion that year would play the NHA's Quebec Bulldogs for the Stanley Cup. Unfortunately for the East Coast, the Moncton Victorias were defeated 9–3 and 8–0. The following year, the Sydney Millionaires were also humbled by the Bulldogs when they were beaten 14–3 and 6–2. World War I doomed the MPHL after the 1913–14 season but among those to skate in the circuit were Louis Berlinquette (a member of the Montreal Canadiens both before and after his season in Moncton), Tommy Smith, and other future Hall of Famers George McNamara and Jack Walker.

When the Maritime Professional Hockey League dropped out of the Stanley Cup scene, the Pacific Coast Hockey Association was only too ready to take its place. The PCHA had been formed on December 7, 1911 when brothers Frank and Lester Patrick had surprised the hockey world by launching what would quickly become the NHA's greatest rival for hockey supremacy. The first artificial ice surfaces in Canada would be constructed in Victoria and Vancouver with the downtown Vancouver facility boasting a capacity of 10,000. The league recruited from the East, signing such notables as Harry Hyland and Newsy Lalonde,

to fill out the rosters of the teams in Vancouver, Victoria and New Westminster.

Lalonde arrived in Vancouver a day before the PCHA was unveiled to the public. "Lalonde will play hockey for Frank Patrick's Vancouver team in the new Coast League and turned down some flattering offers while away," said the *Vancouver Province* of December 7, 1911. "He looks for some great sport out here this winter and predicts that the hockey will rank far and above that which will be seen in the East."

The PCHA decided to raid the eastern NHA clubs, and Cyclone Taylor who, along with Lalonde seemed to be an attraction for every early major league, moved to Vancouver in 1912–13, where he would become a legendary fixture for decades. By 1914 the NHA and PCHA began meeting in a Stanley Cup series, with Toronto downing Victoria in three straight games in the initial battle. Before the 1914–15 season, the PCHA's New Westminster franchised moved to Portland which became the first American city in a league competing for the Stanley Cup. But it was Vancouver's year, becoming the first PCHA team to win the Cup when Taylor, Frank Nighbor, Mickey MacKay and Hugh Lehman led the Millionaires to a three-game sweep of the NHA champion Ottawa Senators.

"You have a great team here," said Frank Shaughnessy, manager of the Senators. "They outplayed us in all departments. … I have got to hand it to the Vancouver team. They surely earned the championship."

After Vancouver's victory, the PCHA was riding high and it added the Seattle Metropolitans and continued raiding NHA clubs. The NHA responded by announcing PCHA players were now free agents. "WILL FIGHT PATRICKS," the *Montreal Gazette* proclaimed, and NHA clubs signed Nighbor, Bert Lindsay and other western stars. The 1915–16 season ended with the PCHA champion Portland Rosebuds falling to the Canadiens in the Stanley Cup final. One year later, Seattle would represent the PCHA and become the first American team to win the Stanley Cup when they beat the Canadiens in four games.

In 1917–18 the NHA turned into the National Hockey League and the new league continued the NHA's relationship with the PCHA. On ice, the NHL champions from Toronto beat Vancouver three game to two for the Stanley Cup. Off-ice, the NHL's Montreal Wanderers squabbled with the Vancouver Millionaires over future Hall of Famer Gordie Roberts' contract before the Montreal club withdrew forever from the hockey scene. For the next few years, the NHL and PCHA would continue to bicker, then battle for hockey supremacy at the end of the season. It wasn't until 1921–22 that another major professional organization entered the mix, a Prairie circuit called the Western Canada Hockey League.

The Edmonton Eskimos, Calgary Tigers, Regina Capitals and Saskatoon Sheiks featured such stars as Herb Gardiner, Red Dutton, Dick Irvin, Bill Cook and Art Gagne. In the WCHL's inaugural season, Regina won its title and met PCHA champion Vancouver for the right to play the NHL champ for the Stanley Cup. After Regina surprised Vancouver 2–1 in the opening game of a best-of-three series, the *Regina Leader* gushed: "They have placed prairie hockey on the major hockey map and brought Regina to the front as one of the greatest sporting cities in the Dominion." That was as close to a final as a Saskatchewan club would come, with Vancouver coming back to win the series before losing the Cup to Toronto.

The next season, the PCHA, WCHL and NHL ratified a working agreement, with an PCHA-WCHL interlocking schedule approved. In the spring of 1923, the NHL's Ottawa Senators met both the PCHA's Vancouver Maroons and the WCHL's Edmonton Eskimos before being declared Stanley Cup champions. In 1924, the PCHA's Seattle franchise dissolved and Vancouver and Victoria joined the WCHL, ending 13 years of PCHA history. The WCHL, with franchises in Calgary, Saskatoon, Victoria, Edmonton, Vancouver and Regina, featured an array of future Hall of Famers including George Hainsworth, Duke Keats, Frank Boucher, Eddie Shore, Dick Irvin and Bill and Bun Cook.

The 1924–25 season saw the Victoria Cougars—with Frank Fredrickson, Jack Walker, Harry Holmes and Frank Foyston—top the Montreal Canadiens for the Stanley Cup.

The small city of Victoria went hockey berserk that March. When the Cougars stopped Howie Morenz and the Canadiens to win hockey's "world series," as it was called, Habs' manager Leo Dandurand told the *Victoria Colonist*: "That the Eastern teams must improve their standard of playing if they hope to wrest the world hockey laurels from the West next year or in future years." Victoria's victory, however, proved to be the league's swan song.

The next season, the Regina franchise was transferred to Portland and the WCHL changed its name to the Western Hockey League. But the NHL was making its move for hockey hegemony, planning to expand into large U.S. cities and offering big salaries. Crowds declined in the West. In the 1925–26 season, Victoria would again make it to the Cup final, this time losing in Montreal to the Maroons. It was the last time the Cup was contested by a non-NHL team. After the season, PCHA president Frank Patrick announced that WHL players were for sale.

The next season, Bill Cook and Dick Irvin, who had tied for the 1925–26 WHL goal-scoring title, would finish 1–2 in the NHL's scoring race. Calgary's star defenseman Herb Gardiner, 35 years old, would sign with the Montreal Canadiens and win the Hart Trophy. Saskatoon goaltender George Hainsworth would also move to the Habs and win the Vezina Trophy for the next three seasons. Lester Patrick was brought to New York to coach the newly franchised Rangers, who would win the Stanley Cup in just their second season of 1927–28 with a core of WHL players (the Cook brothers and Frank Boucher). The Chicago Black Hawks were stocked with former Portland Rosebuds. The new Detroit franchise, which would eventually be known as the Red Wings, was called the Cougars because the Victoria Cougars moved en masse to the Motor City. Detroit's 1926–27 roster included seven members of the 1925 Cup-winning Cougars: Frank Foyston, Clem Loughlin, Harry Holmes, Jack Walker, Slim Halderson, Harry Meeking, and Frank Fredrickson.

A year earlier, as the Victoria players left the ice after losing a hard-fought 2–0 game to be eliminated from the Stanley Cup final, Montreal spectators had stood on their seats and roared their approval with waves of applause for the West's best. Major-league hockey would not return to Western Canada until the 1970s, but the Stanley Cup would remain in the West for a little while longer in that spring of 1926. Cougars owner, coach, and manager Lester Patrick had left the Stanley Cup in Victoria. Asked why he hadn't taken it to Montreal for the final, a confident Patrick said: "What's the use? It just means carting it all across the continent to pack it back again."

CHAPTER 69

Introduction to the Player Registers

Ralph Dinger and James Duplacey

THE PLAYER REGISTER in *Total Hockey* has been divided into three sections that reflect both the availability of statistics through the 80-year history of the National Hockey League and the global growth of the league and the sport.

The Pre-Expansion Register (Chapter 71) is set in two columns. It contains the complete statistical history of every player who played in the NHL from 1917–18 to 1966–67, the year before the league's first major expansion.

The Modern Register (Chapter 73) contains the complete statistical history of every player who played in the NHL after 1966–67, up to and including the 1997–98 season. Players whose careers spanned the two eras, beginning before and ending after 1966–67, are entered in both registers. Their complete data panels are located in the Modern Register, while their names and the page where their statistical information can be found are listed alphabetically in the Pre-Expansion Register.

The Goaltender Register (Chapter 75) contains the complete statistical record for every goaltender who played in the NHL from 1917–18 to 1997–98. Painstaking research by the *Total Hockey* staff and historian Ernie Fitzsimmons corrected numerous statistical errors and compiled the most thorough record of wins, losses and ties ever collected. There are some very interesting twists and turns in the Goaltenders Register. From 1917–18 to 1964–65, NHL rules permitted teams to dress only one goaltender for a game. If that goalie was injured and was unable to resume play, a replacement goaltender was used in his place. The home team was responsible for ensuring that a substitute goaltender was on hand. Often these goalies were minor league, senior or junior league netminders and this chance-of-a-lifetime opportunity would prove to be their only NHL appearance. This explains the one-game NHL careers of such well-travelled goalies as Claude Cyr, Nick Damore and Mickey Murray.

Other teams preferred to have their trainer serve as the substitute goaltender, accounting for the NHL careers of Lefty Wilson, Julian Klymkiw and Dan Olesevich. Another interesting addition to the Goaltender Register is the inclusion of all forwards and defensemen, who were forced by circumstances to take a turn in the crease. Until the 1941–42 season, goaltenders served their own penalties, requiring a player to take his place. This accounts for famous hockey names such as Charlie Conacher, King Clancy and Sprague Cleghorn finding their way into both the Player and Goaltender registers. Injuries to Frank Brophy forced Quebec Bulldogs' defenseman Harry Mummery to don the pads three times in single season. All of these players, complete with detailed notes and their entire statistical career, can be found in the pages of the Goaltender Register.

In the early years of the game, statistics were not recorded with the same accuracy and thoroughness that they are today. Even core stats such as games played, assists and penalty minutes were rarely compiled accurately. Adding to the confusion were wildly differing accounts of the statistics that were tabulated. Game sheets for the first four seasons of league play weren't kept reliably, creating confusion as to the accuracy of early statistics. Bob Duff, a reporter for the *Windsor Star*, was hired to research the early years of the NHL. Through exhaustive research that included reading newspaper game coverage from every NHL city and cross-checking them with other source reports, Duff has been able to compile an entirely new set of statistics for the first four years of the NHL, including the awarding of assists for every player who participated in the league's inaugural season.

During the course of this research, *Total Hockey* has also discovered that nine players thought to have played in the NHL actually did not. Conversely, *Total Hockey* has also added four players to the Pre-Expansion Player Register. Such errors were common in the ice age of pro sports. In those days, every game report was handwritten, usually in pencil and often with a shaky hand in chilly arenas. Through careful examination of the game sheets and hours spent combing through old newspapers, *Total Hockey* has compiled what we feel is the definitive player register. Of course, not all statistics in this primitive era could be found, especially for minor and senior leagues. But wherever possible, we have included team names and leagues with the notation "Statistics Not Available," insuring that reader can follow a player's movement from amateur to pro, even though accurate numbers were impossible to obtain.

Similar difficulties were encountered as European statistics were being compiled. Statistics for some countries, such as France and Italy, are difficult to find, as are statistical records for many second division teams. And while the "Statistics Not Available" notation is used frequently, *Total Hockey* international editor Igor Kuperman and his research team were able to fill in many of the gaps, giving fans the first real opportunity to trace a player's pre- and post-NHL career in Europe.

There are other "firsts" in the Pre-Expansion and Modern Player Registers. Complete statistical data for all the major pro leagues of the 1920s, 1930s and 1940s, including the International-American Hockey League, the Canadian-American Hockey League, the American Hockey Association and the Canadian Pro Hockey League are printed for the first time. Complete statistics for the Eastern Amateur Hockey League, which served as a training ground for numerous future NHL stars, have been included in *Total Hockey* for the first time. Complete trade notes, amateur draft, professional player draft and general player draft information for the WHA has also been included.

Total Hockey also includes the game's the first comprehensive trade register. Every NHL trade from 1917–18 to 1997–98 has been charted, including various dispersal, waiver and supplemental drafts. The Pre-Expansion Register also includes complete free agent signings and trade notes for the Pacific Coast Hockey Association, the Western Canadian Hockey League and the Western Hockey League from 1917–18 to 1925–26.

A list of those players deleted or added to the Pre-Expansion Player Register follows:

DELETED PLAYERS

Carr (no first name) was actually Ed Carpenter. His name was misread on the game sheet. **Tom Coulter** attended training camp but broke his leg. He never played an NHL game. **Tom Cowan:** There is no evidence that this player existed. **Bob McKinnon** is actually Alex McKinnon, who played in the late 1920s. **Earl Lachance** dressed for the Canadiens in 1924-25, but never played. **Price** (no first name) is probably Morley Bruce. Again, his name was misread on the game sheet. **Glenn Smith** and Glenn Grafton Smith are the same player. **Paul Stevens** should be Phil Stevens, a player with Boston and the Canadiens. **Sammy Robert** is actually Sammy Hebert, a spare goaltender with Toronto and Ottawa.

ADDED PLAYERS

Charles Pletsch's name had been was misspelled as "Flesch." **Bob Blake** played 12 games for Boston in 1935–36 that were originally credited to Mickey Blake. **Gord Spence** played three games for the Toronto St. Pats in 1925-26. (**Frederick**) **Henry Harris** had always been confused with Fred Harris, who previously had been credited with (Frederick) Henry's stats.

CHAPTER 70

Using the Pre-Expansion Player Register

James Duplacey

THE PRE-EXPANSION REGISTER begins on page 647. It contains the complete statistical history of every player who played in the NHL from 1917–18 to 1966–67, the year before the league's first major expansion. Players whose careers straddle the 1967–68 expansion are listed in full in the Modern Player Register (Chapter 73).

Here are notes on the various statistical categories used in the Pre-Expansion Player Register:

Biographical Information – This field contains the player's name, given names (if that name is different than the name by which he is commonly known. For example, King Clancy's given names were Francis Michael, Tod Sloan's given names were Aloysius Martin), nicknames, position (**C** – center, **RW** – right wing, **LW** – left wing, **F** – forward, **D** – defense), shooting side (**R** – right, **L** – left), height in feet and inches, weight in pounds, date of birth (month/day/year), place of birth (city/town and province/state for North America, city/town and country for all others) and date of death. If only the birth year is known, it is included. If the death date is not known, the date is represented by "Deceased." If any other biographical information is not known, the appropriate field is left blank. If the player is a member of the Hockey Hall of Fame (**HHOF**) and/or the United States Hockey Hall of Fame (**USHOF**), it is noted here.

Season – From 1917–18 through 1966–67, the hockey season started in the fall and ended the following spring and is represented as, for example, 1966–67. For players who retired or did not play for three or more seasons but later returned to the game, those years are represented as two four-digit dates, for example, 1964–1967.

Club – This field gives information as to which team or teams the player performed with during the season. If statistics for a particular team or season could not be located, the club name has been included with an added note of explanation.

League – This field contains the league name or abbreviated league name for each team line. If a player was with his country's national team, "Nat-Team" is listed in the league column. If a player was with a team that played an exhibition season only, the league field has been left blank, but a note of explanation has been included in his trade notes located at the end of his data panel. In total, over 100 leagues from around the world were researched for the *Total Hockey* project. A full list of the leagues found in *Total Hockey* and their abbreviations can be found on page 1878.

GP – Games Played – Games in which a player appears on the ice during a game. Players who are dressed but do not step on the ice during play are not credited with a game played.

G – Goals scored – A goal is credited to the last player from the scoring team to touch the puck before it completely crosses the goal line. A player may not direct the puck into the net with a skate or deflect a puck into the net with his stick above the height of the crossbar of the goal net.

A – Assists – An assist is awarded to any player, or players, taking part in the play immediately preceding the goal. From 1917-18 to 1926-27, only one assist was awarded for a goal. From 1930-31 to 1935-36, as many as three assists could be awarded per goal. From 1936–37 to 1966–67, no more than two assists were awarded for each goal.

Pts – Points – Any player credited with a goal or an assist receives one point.

AG – Adjusted goals – *(See page 626)*

AA – Adjusted assists – *(See page 626)*

APts – Adjusted points – *(See page 626)*

PIM – Penalties in minutes – Number of minutes a player is penalized during a season. Before the NHL was established from 1903–04 to 1913–14, penalties were either two, three or five minutes in length, charged at the discretion of the referee. From 1914–15 to 1916–17, all penalties were five minutes in duration. After the NHL was formed (from 1917–18 to 1921–22), penalties were either three minutes or five minutes in duration depending on the nature of the offense. In 1922–23, penalties were two, three or five minutes in duration, again depending on the infraction. Beginning in 1923–24, players were penalized two minutes for a minor penalty, five minutes a major penalty and 10 minutes for major fouls. The 10-minute misconduct was introduced in 1937–38 and the game misconduct and gross misconduct penalty were introduced in ensuing years.

NHL Totals – A total of a player's complete NHL career.

Other Major League Totals – This field includes the total of all the other major leagues a player performed in from 1893 to 1967. *(See Chapter 68, page 642)* To be categorized as major a league must fall into one of the following three categories: it must have been professional, challenged for the Stanley Cup and/or competed with other major leagues to sign the top hockey talent of the day. Under these criteria, the following leagues are categorized as major: the International Pro League (1904 to 1907), the Eastern Canada Amateur Hockey Association (1906 to 1908), the Manitoba Hockey League (1906 to 1909), the Ontario Professional Hockey League (1907 to 1911), the Eastern Canada Hockey Association (1908–09), the Canadian Hockey Association (1909–10), the National Hockey Association (1909 to 1917), the Maritime Professional Hockey League (1911 to 1914), the Pacific Coast Hockey Association (1911 to 1925), the Western Canada Hockey League (1921 to 1925), the Western Hockey League (1925–26) and the World Hockey Association (1972 to 1979).

Award and All-Star Notes – (located beneath a players' total lines) This field contains details of all-star selections and major trophies and awards won for the NHL, the minor leagues, Canadian major junior hockey and the NCAA and CIAU. Also included are IIHF World Championship and IIHF World Junior Championship awards and all-star selections as well as NHL appearances in the NHL All-Star Game.

Trade Notes – This field contains NHL trade notes for every player from 1917–18 to the end of their major professional careers. WHA trade notes are included for every player in the Pre-Expansion Register who played in the WHA after the conclusion of his NHL career. Trade notes and free agent signings for every player who played in the NHL and the PCHA, WCHL and the WHL from 1917–18 to 1926–27 have also been included. Special notes concerning injuries and other oddities and curiosities are indicated by a bullet (•)

CHAPTER 71

Pre-Expansion Player Register

Career Records for Players whose Last NHL Appearance was Prior to 1967-68

ABBOTT, REG — Reg Abbott
C – L. 5'11", 164 lbs. b: Winnipeg, Man., 2/4/1930.

Season	Club	League	GP	G	A	Pts	AG	AA	APts	PIM	GP	G	A	Pts	PIM
1948-49	Brandon Wheat Kings	MJHL	39	16	16	32	....	....	....	6	23	12	7	19	9
1949-50	Brandon Wheat Kings	MJHL	36	*27	27	*54	....	....	....	24	13	12	8	20	6
1950-51	Victoria Cougars	PCHL	70	14	24	38	....	....	....	29	12	3	*9	12	8
1951-52	Victoria Cougars	PCHL	57	16	27	43	....	....	....	30	13	3	6	9	7
1952-53	**Montreal Canadiens**	**NHL**	3	0	0	0	0	0	0	0					
	Victoria Cougars	WHL	65	22	22	44	....	....	....	18					
1953-54	Victoria Cougars	WHL	69	7	17	24	....	....	....	24	3	0	2	2	
1954-55	Pittsburgh Hornets	AHL	3	0	0	0	....	....	....	34	12	7	4	11	2
	Windsor Bulldogs	OHA Sr.	48	22	34	56	....	....	....	20					
1955-56	Windsor Bulldogs	OHA Sr.	48	20	24	44	....	....	....	25					
1956-57	Windsor Bulldogs	OHA Sr.	52	21	26	47	....	....	....	18	8	3	1	4	2
1957-58	Windsor Bulldogs	NOHA	35	6	12	18	....	....	....	10	12	5	1	6	4
1958-59	Windsor Bulldogs	NOHA	8	1	1	2	....	....	....	4					
1959-60			DID NOT PLAY												
1960-61	Winnipeg Maroons	SSHL	....	....	....	....	....	....	....		20	24	9	23	5
1961-62	Winnipeg Maroons	SSHL	....	....	....	....	....	....	....		11	7	10	17	0
1962-63	Winnipeg Maroons	SSHL	11	5	21	26	....	....	....	4	15	6	13	19	9
1963-64	Winnipeg Maroons	SSHL	11	9	10	19	....	....	....	2					
	Clinton Comets	EHL	10	2	3	5	....	....	....	6					
1964-65	Winnipeg Maroons	SSHL	6	6	6	12	....	....	....	2					
	Canada	WEC-A	7	2	2	4	....	....	....	0					
	NHL Totals		**3**	**0**	**0**	**0**	**0**	**0**	**0**	**0**					

ABEL, CLARENCE — Clarence "Taffy" Abel   USHOF
D – L. 6'1", 225 lbs. b: Sault Ste. Marie, MI, 5/28/1900. d: 8/1/1964.

Season	Club	League	GP	G	A	Pts	AG	AA	APts	PIM	GP	G	A	Pts	PIM
1918-19	Michigan Soo Nationals	TBSHL	STATISTICS NOT AVAILABLE												
1919-20	Michigan Soo Wildcats	TBSHL	8	3	1	4	....	....	....	26	....	....	....	....	....
1920-21	Michigan Soo Wildcats	TBSHL	STATISTICS NOT AVAILABLE												
1921-22	Michigan Soo Wildcats	TBSHL	STATISTICS NOT AVAILABLE												
1922-23	St. Paul Athletic Club	USAHA	18	3	0	3	....	....	....	....	4	0	0	0	....
1923-24	St. Paul Athletic Club	USAHA	3	1	0	1	....	....	....	....	8	0	0	0	....
	United States	Olympics	5	15	0	15	....	....	....	....					
1924-25	St. Paul Athletic Club	USAHA	39	8	0	8	....	....	....	....					
1925-26	Minneapolis Millers	CHL	35	12	9	21	....	....	....	56	3	0	1	1	6
1926-27	**New York Rangers**	**NHL**	44	8	4	12	23	34	57	78	2	0	1	1	8
1927-28	**New York Rangers**	**NHL**	23	0	1	1	0	8	8	28	9	1	0	1	14
1928-29	**New York Rangers**	**NHL**	44	2	1	3	8	9	17	41	6	0	0	0	8
1929-30	**Chicago Black Hawks**	**NHL**	38	3	3	6	6	10	16	42	2	0	0	0	10
1930-31	**Chicago Black Hawks**	**NHL**	43	0	1	1	0	4	4	45	9	0	0	0	8
1931-32	**Chicago Black Hawks**	**NHL**	48	3	3	6	0	0	14	34	2	0	0	0	2
1932-33	**Chicago Black Hawks**	**NHL**	47	0	4	4	0	11	11	63					
1933-34	**Chicago Black Hawks**	**NHL**	46	2	1	3	4	3	7	28	8	0	0	0	8
	NHL Totals		**333**	**18**	**18**	**26**	**47**	**87**	**134**	**359**	**38**	**1**	**1**	**2**	**58**

Signed as a free agent by **NY Rangers**, August 14, 1926. Traded to **Chicago** by **NY Rangers** for $15,000, April 15, 1929.

ABEL, GERRY — Gerry Abel
LW – L. 6'2", 168 lbs. b: Detroit, MI, 12/25/1944.

Season	Club	League	GP	G	A	Pts	AG	AA	APts	PIM	GP	G	A	Pts	PIM
1964-65	Hamilton Red Wings	OHA	27	3	13	16	....	....	....	31					
	Memphis Wings	CHL	8	2	2	4	....	....	....	0					
1965-66	Weyburn Red Wings	SJHL	STATISTICS NOT AVAILABLE												
	Memphis Wings	CHL	12	0	1	1	....	....	....	0					
1966-67	**Detroit Red Wings**	**NHL**	1	0	0	0	0	0	0	0					
	Memphis Wings	CHL	44	2	9	11	....	....	....	20	6	0	1	1	2
	Pittsburgh Hornets	AHL	2	0	2	2	....	....	....	0					
1967-68	Fort Worth Wings	CHL	52	3	14	17	....	....	....	35	6	1	2	3	2
	NHL Totals		**1**	**0**	**0**	**0**	**0**	**0**	**0**	**0**					

ABEL, SID — Sid "Boot Nose" Abel   HHOF
C – L. 5'11", 170 lbs. b: Melville, Sask., 2/22/1918.

Season	Club	League	GP	G	A	Pts	AG	AA	APts	PIM	GP	G	A	Pts	PIM
1936-37	Saskatoon Wesleys	City Jr.	STATISTICS NOT AVAILABLE												
1937-38	Flin Flon Bombers	City Sr.	23	12	16	28	....	....	....	13	8	4	*4	8	17
1938-39	**Detroit Red Wings**	**NHL**	15	1	1	2	2	2	4	0	6	1	1	2	2
	Pittsburgh Hornets	AHL	41	21	24	45	....	....	....	27					
1939-40	**Detroit Red Wings**	**NHL**	24	1	5	6	2	10	12	4	5	0	3	3	21
	Indianapolis Capitals	AHL	21	7	11	18	....	....	....	10					
1940-41	**Detroit Red Wings**	**NHL**	47	11	22	33	22	40	62	29	9	2	4	2	
1941-42	**Detroit Red Wings**	**NHL**	48	18	31	49	31	47	78	45	12	4	2	6	8
1942-43	**Detroit Red Wings**	**NHL**	49	18	24	42	26	31	57	33	10	5	8	13	4
1943-44	Montreal RCAF	QSHL	7	5	4	9	....	....	....	12					
	Montreal Canada Car	City Sr.	2	1	0	1	....	....	....	4					
1944-45	Montreal RCAF	City Sr.	4	6	8	14	....	....	....	4					
	Lachine Rapides	QPHL	2	2	2	4	....	....	....	0					
1945-46	**Detroit Red Wings**	**NHL**	7	0	2	2	0	4	4	0	3	0	0	0	
1946-47	**Detroit Red Wings**	**NHL**	60	19	29	48	26	42	68	29	3	1	1	2	2
1947-48	**Detroit Red Wings**	**NHL**	60	14	30	44	20	44	64	69	10	0	3	3	16
1948-49	**Detroit Red Wings**	**NHL**	60	28	26	54	45	42	87	49	11	3	3	6	6
1949-50	**Detroit Red Wings**	**NHL**	69	34	35	69	48	45	91	46	14	6	2	8	6
1950-51	**Detroit Red Wings**	**NHL**	69	23	38	61	31	50	81	30	6	4	3	7	0
1951-52	**Detroit Red Wings**	**NHL**	62	17	36	53	24	47	71	32	7	2	2	4	12
1952-53	**Chicago Black Hawks**	**NHL**	39	5	4	9	8	6	14	6	1	0	0	0	0
1953-54	**Chicago Black Hawks**	**NHL**	3	0	0	0	0	0	0	4					
	NHL Totals		**612**	**189**	**283**	**472**	**283**	**410**	**693**	**376**	**97**	**28**	**30**	**58**	**79**

NHL 2nd All-Star Team (1942, 1951) • NHL 1st All-Star Team (1949, 1950) • Won Hart Trophy (1949)

Played in NHL All-Star Game (1949, 1950, 1951)

Traded to **Chicago** by **Detroit** for cash, July 22, 1952.

ACHTYMICHUK, GENE — Gene "Acky" Achtymichuk
C – L. 5'11", 170 lbs. b: Lamont, Alta., 9/7/1932.

Season	Club	League	GP	G	A	Pts	AG	AA	APts	PIM	GP	G	A	Pts	PIM
1949-50	Edmonton Canadians	AJHL	....	*27	16	*43	....	....	....	2					
1950-51	Crows Nest Pass	WCJHL	40	37	27	64	....	....	....	22	14	10	17	27	4
1951-52	**Montreal Canadiens**	**NHL**	1	0	0	0	0	0	0	0					
	Crows Nest Pass	WCJHL	44	53	33	86	....	....	....	63					
1952-53	Buffalo Bisons	AHL	50	7	4	11	....	....	....	18					
1953-54	Victoria Cougars	WHL	65	11	21	32	....	....	....	25	5	1	0	1	0
1954-55	Victoria Cougars	WHL	69	18	19	37	....	....	....	18	5	0	1	1	0
1956-57	**Montreal Canadiens**	**NHL**	3	0	0	0	0	0	0	0					
	Quebec Aces	QHL	82	26	41	67	....	....	....	40	10	2	4	6	4
1957-58	**Montreal Canadiens**	**NHL**	16	3	5	8	4	5	9	2					
	Montreal Royals	QHL	54	14	30	52	....	....	....	28					
1958-59	**Detroit Red Wings**	**NHL**	12	0	0	0	0	0	0	0					
	Edmonton Flyers	WHL	39	16	17	33	....	....	....	30	3	0	1	1	0
1959-60	Edmonton Flyers	WHL	67	20	51	71	....	....	....	44	4	1	3	4	4
1960-61	Sudbury Wolves	EPHL	37	5	28	33	....	....	....	16					
	Edmonton Flyers	WHL	25	6	14	20	....	....	....	2					
1961-62	Portland Buckaroos	WHL	68	17	56	73	....	....	....	10	3	0	2	2	0
1962-63	Knoxville Knights	EHL	68	30	*96	126	....	....	....	29	5	1	5	6	4
1963-64	Knoxville Knights	EHL	72	30	*88	118	....	....	....	42	8	4	4	8	4
1964-65	Long Island Ducks	EHL	71	30	*83	113	....	....	....	28	15	3	9	12	8
1965-66	Long Island Ducks	FHI	72	34	*83	117	....	....	....	62	12	6	10	16	8
	Portland Buckaroos	WHL	....	....	....	....	....	....	....		3	0	0	0	0
1966-67	Long Island Ducks	EHL	71	13	45	58	....	....	....	82	3	0	0	0	
1967-68	Long Island Ducks	EHL	35	6	12	18	....	....	....	24					
1968-69	Edmonton Monarchs	ASHL	....	9	9	18	....	....	....	11	....	1	5	6	2
	NHL Totals		**32**	**3**	**5**	**8**	**4**	**5**	**9**	**2**	....	....	....	....	....

EHL 2nd All-Star Team (1964) • EHL North 1st All-Star Team (1965, 1966)

Traded to **Detroit** by **Montreal** with Claude Laforge and Bud MacPherson for cash, June 3, 1958. Traded to **Portland** (WHL) by **Detroit** (Edmonton-WHL) for Gord Haworth, August, 1961.

• ADAM, DOUGLAS Douglas Adam

LW – L. 5'11", 165 lbs. b: Toronto, Ont., 9/7/1923.

Season	Club	League	GP	G	A	Pts	AG	AA	APts	PIM	GP	G	A	Pts	PIM
			REGULAR SEASON								PLAYOFFS				
1941-42	Toronto Marlboros	OHA	17	6	1	7	....	....	....	6	2	0	0	0	2
1942-43			MILITARY SERVICE												
1943-44			MILITARY SERVICE												
1944-45			MILITARY SERVICE												
1945-46	Hollywood Wolves	PCHL	10	0	4	4	....	....	....	8	4	1	0	1	0
1946-47	Toronto Credit Jewellers	City Sr.	....	27	16	43	....	....	....	14	....	....	....	....	....
1947-48	Tacoma Rockets	PCHL	57	34	25	59	....	....	....	57	5	6	1	7	4
1948-49	Tacoma Rockets	PCHL	68	24	30	54	....	....	....	45	6	5	1	6	4
1949-50	**New York Rangers**	**NHL**	**4**	**0**	**1**	**1**	**0**	**1**	**1**	**0**	....	....	....	....	....
	Tacoma Rockets	PCHL	63	*53	26	79	....	....	....	68	5	3	2	5	6
1950-51	Tacoma Rockets	PCHL	68	31	19	50	....	....	....	68	6	2	0	2	4
1951-52	Tacoma Rockets	PCHL	53	31	26	57	....	....	....	43	6	0	0	0	0
1952-53	Tacoma Rockets	WHL	70	*39	31	70	....	....	....	74	....	....	....	....	....
1953-54	Seattle–Saskatoon	WHL	63	18	20	38	....	....	....	30	12	4	1	5	12
1954-55	Vancouver Canucks	WHL	29	14	7	21	....	....	....	20	....	....	....	....	....
	New Westminster Royals	WHL	36	16	15	31	....	....	....	33	....	....	....	....	....
1955-56	New Westminster Royals	WHL	55	16	20	36	....	....	....	36	4	1	0	1	5
1956-57	Charlotte Clippers	EHL	63	*65	49	114	....	....	....	46	13	*11	7	18	16
1957-58	Charlotte Checkers	EHL	55	44	33	77	....	....	....	32	14	7	10	*17	8
1958-59	Philadelphia Ramblers	EHL	64	39	38	77	....	....	....	66	....	....	....	....	....
1959-60	Philadelphia Ramblers	EHL	64	46	43	89	....	....	....	114	4	1	2	3	20
	Louisville Rebels	IHL	....	....	....	....	....	....	....	....	1	0	0	0	0
1960-61	Philadelphia Ramblers	EHL	41	16	23	39	....	....	....	24	3	1	0	1	2
	NHL Totals		**4**	**0**	**1**	**1**	**0**	**1**	**1**	**0**	....	....	....	....	....

PCHL Northern 1st All-Star Team (1950) • EHL 1st All-Star Team (1957, 1958, 1960) • EHL 2nd All-Star Team (1959)

• ADAMS, JACK Jack (John James) Adams HHOF

C – R. 5'9", 175 lbs. b: Fort William, Ont., 6/14/1895. d: 5/1/1968.

Season	Club	League	GP	G	A	Pts	AG	AA	APts	PIM	GP	G	A	Pts	PIM
1914-15	Fort William Maple Leafs	NMHL	....	....	....	....	....	....	....	....	2	4	0	4	3
1915-16	Calumet Miners	NMHL	STATISTICS NOT AVAILABLE												
1916-17	Peterborough 247th	Inter-Sr.	STATISTICS NOT AVAILABLE												
1917-18	Sarnia Sailors	OHA Sr.	6	15	0	15	....	....	....	....	....	....	....	....	....
	Toronto Arenas	**NHL**	**8**	**0**	**0**	**0**	**0**	**0**	**0**	**31**	**2**	**1**	**0**	**1**	**6**
1918-19	**Toronto Arenas**	**NHL**	**18**	**3**	**3**	**6**	**10**	**28**	**38**	**47**	....	....	....	....	....
1919-20	Vancouver Millionaires	PCHA	22	9	6	15	....	....	....	18	2	0	0	0	0
1920-21	Vancouver Millionaires	PCHA	24	17	12	29	....	....	....	60	7	5	1	6	8
1921-22	Vancouver Millionaires	PCHA	24	*26	4	*30	....	....	....	24	9	7	0	7	25
1922-23	**Toronto St. Pats**	**NHL**	**23**	**19**	**9**	**28**	**65**	**83**	**148**	**42**	....	....	....	....	....
1923-24	**Toronto St. Pats**	**NHL**	**22**	**13**	**3**	**16**	**54**	**53**	**107**	**49**	....	....	....	....	....
1924-25	**Toronto St. Pats**	**NHL**	**27**	**21**	**8**	**29**	**74**	**109**	**183**	**66**	**2**	**1**	**0**	**1**	**7**
1925-26	**Toronto St. Pats**	**NHL**	**36**	**21**	**5**	**26**	**66**	**58**	**124**	**52**	....	....	....	....	....
1926-27	**Ottawa Senators**	**NHL**	**40**	**5**	**1**	**6**	**14**	**8**	**22**	**66**	**6**	**0**	**0**	**0**	**2**
	NHL Totals		**174**	**82**	**29**	**111**	**283**	**339**	**622**	**353**	**10**	**2**	**0**	**2**	**15**
	Other Major League Totals		70	52	22	74	....	....	....	102	18	12	1	13	33

PCHA 1st All-Star Team (1921, 1922) • Won Lester Patrick Trophy (1966)

Signed as a free agent by **Toronto Arenas**, February 9, 1918. Traded to **Vancouver** (PCHA) by **Toronto** for cash, December 7, 1919. Traded to **Toronto St. Pats** by **Vancouver** (PCHA) for Corbett Denneny, December 22, 1922. Traded to **Ottawa** by **Toronto** for cash, August, 1926.

• ADAMS, JOHN John "Jack" Adams

LW – L. 5'10", 163 lbs. b: Calgary, Alta., 5/5/1920.

Season	Club	League	GP	G	A	Pts	AG	AA	APts	PIM	GP	G	A	Pts	PIM
1936-37	Calgary Canadians	City Jr.	1	0	0	0	....	....	....	0	....	....	....	....	....
1937-38	Calgary K of C	City Sr.	11	4	5	9	....	....	....	2	1	0	0	0	0
1938-39	Vancouver Lions	PCHL	29	5	13	18	....	....	....	16	2	0	1	1	2
1939-40	Vancouver Lions	PCHL	40	12	12	24	....	....	....	16	5	1	1	2	4
1940-41	**Montreal Canadiens**	**NHL**	**42**	**6**	**12**	**18**	**12**	**22**	**34**	**11**	**3**	**0**	**0**	**0**	**0**
1941-42			MILITARY SERVICE												
1942-43	Calgary RCAF	City Sr.	22	19	12	31	....	....	....	15	8	5	6	11	4
1943-44	Vancouver RCAF	City Sr.	9	4	3	7	....	....	....	11	....	....	....	....	....
	Vancouver Seahawks	City Sr.	....	....	....	....	....	....	....	....	3	2	2	4	4
1944-45			MILITARY SERVICE												
1945-46	Montreal Royals	QSHL	4	2	1	3	....	....	....	5	....	....	....	....	....
	Buffalo Bisons	AHL	19	2	2	4	....	....	....	0	9	4	4	8	4
1946-47	Houston Huskies	USHL	20	3	5	8	....	....	....	6	....	....	....	....	....
1947-48	New Westminster Royals	PCHL	52	20	13	33	....	....	....	36	5	0	0	0	2
1948-49	New Westminster Royals	PCHL	41	8	8	16	....	....	....	21	12	1	2	3	8
	NHL Totals		**42**	**6**	**12**	**18**	**12**	**22**	**34**	**11**	**3**	**0**	**0**	**0**	**0**

Traded to **Montreal** by **Vancouver** (PCHL) for cash, May 13, 1940. Traded to **Buffalo** (AHL) by **Montreal** with Moe White for Murdo MacKay, January 14, 1945.

• ADAMS, STEW Stew (Stewart) Adams

LW – L. 5'10", 165 lbs. b: Calgary, Alberta, 10/16/1904. d: 5/18/1978.

Season	Club	League	GP	G	A	Pts	AG	AA	APts	PIM	GP	G	A	Pts	PIM
1922-23	Calgary Canadians	City Jr.	12	3	5	8	....	....	....	8	....	....	....	....	....
1923-24	Calgary Canadians	City Jr.	STATISTICS NOT AVAILABLE												
1924-25	Calgary Canadians	City Jr.	STATISTICS NOT AVAILABLE												
1925-26	Minneapolis Millers	CHL	5	1	0	1	....	....	....	3	....	....	....	....	....
1926-27	Minneapolis Millers	AHA	32	2	4	6	....	....	....	15	6	1	0	1	2
1927-28	Minneapolis Millers	AHA	38	4	3	7	....	....	....	24	8	1	0	1	8
1928-29	Minneapolis Millers	AHA	40	11	8	19	....	....	....	41	4	0	0	0	4
1929-30	**Chicago Black Hawks**	**NHL**	**24**	**4**	**6**	**10**	**8**	**19**	**27**	**16**	**2**	**0**	**0**	**0**	**6**
	Minneapolis Millers	AHA	16	8	4	12	....	....	....	4	....	....	....	....	....
1930-31	**Chicago Black Hawks**	**NHL**	**37**	**5**	**13**	**18**	**12**	**47**	**59**	**18**	**9**	**3**	**3**	**6**	**8**
	London Panthers	IAHL	3	1	0	1	....	....	....	2	....	....	....	....	....
1931-32	**Chicago Black Hawks**	**NHL**	**26**	**0**	**5**	**5**	**0**	**14**	**14**	**26**	....	....	....	....	....
1932-33	**Toronto Maple Leafs**	**NHL**	**19**	**0**	**2**	**2**	**0**	**5**	**5**	**0**	....	....	....	....	....
	Syracuse Stars	IAHL	36	11	22	33	....	....	....	48	6	0	1	1	6
1933-34	Minneapolis Millers	CHL	43	*22	8	30	....	....	....	40	3	0	3	3	....
1934-35	Calgary Tigers	NWHL	8	5	6	11	....	....	....	13	....	....	....	....	....
1935-36	Calgary Tigers	NWHL	29	11	7	18	....	....	....	16	....	....	....	....	....
	NHL Totals		**106**	**9**	**26**	**35**	**20**	**85**	**105**	**60**	**11**	**3**	**3**	**6**	**14**

Traded to **Chicago** by **Minneapolis** (AHA) for Tom Westwick and $15,000, January 4, 1930. Traded to **Toronto** by **Chicago** for cash, November 3, 1932. Traded to **Montreal Maroons** (Windsor-IAHL) by **Toronto** (Syracuse-IAHL) for Al Huggins, November 1, 1933.

• AHLIN, TONY Tony Ahlin

LW – L. 5'11", 176 lbs. b: Eveleth, MN, 12/12/1914.

Season	Club	League	GP	G	A	Pts	AG	AA	APts	PIM	GP	G	A	Pts	PIM
			REGULAR SEASON								PLAYOFFS				
1932-33	Eveleth Rangers	CHL	40	4	15	19	....	....	....	29	3	1	0	1	0
1933-34	Duluth Hornets	CHL	30	16	12	28	....	....	....	20	....	....	....	....	....
1934-35	Eveleth Rangers	CHL	46	12	9	21	....	....	....	36	....	....	....	....	....
1935-36	Kansas City Greyhounds	AHA	47	15	9	24	....	....	....	34	....	....	....	....	....
1936-37	Kansas City Greyhounds	AHA	48	7	19	26	....	....	....	34	3	0	1	1	2
1937-38	**Chicago Black Hawks**	**NHL**	**1**	**0**	**0**	**0**	**0**	**0**	**0**	**0**	....	....	....	....	....
	Kansas City Greyhounds	AHA	47	6	18	24	....	....	....	29	....	....	....	....	....
1938-39	Kansas City Greyhounds	AHA	48	12	13	25	....	....	....	33	....	....	....	....	....
1939-40	Kansas City Greyhounds	AHA	41	10	15	25	....	....	....	16	....	....	....	....	....
1940-41	Kansas City Americans	AHA	1	0	0	0	....	....	....	2	....	....	....	....	....
1941-42	Rivervale Skeeters	EHL	56	20	13	33	....	....	....	45	7	1	4	5	0
	NHL Totals		**1**	**0**	**0**	**0**	**0**	**0**	**0**	**0**	....	....	....	....	....

• AILSBY, LLOYD Lloyd Ailsby

D – L. 5'11", 194 lbs. b: Lac Pelletier, Sask., 5/11/1917. Deceased.

Season	Club	League	GP	G	A	Pts	AG	AA	APts	PIM	GP	G	A	Pts	PIM
1934-35	Moose Jaw CPR	City Jr.	6	3	3	6	....	....	....	0	6	4	1	5	2
1935-36	Regina Caps	RCHL	16	5	2	7	....	....	....	6	2	0	0	0	0
1936-37	New York Rovers	EHL	47	11	21	32	....	....	....	8	3	2	5	7	2
1937-38	New York Rovers	EHL	56	28	22	50	....	....	....	6	....	....	....	....	....
1938-39	New York Rovers	EHL	53	17	13	30	....	....	....	38	....	....	....	....	....
1939-40	Philadelphia Rockets	AHL	52	11	19	30	....	....	....	24	....	....	....	....	....
1940-41	Philadelphia Rockets	AHL	56	8	13	21	....	....	....	28	....	....	....	....	....
1941-42	Cornwall Flyers	QSHL	39	9	7	16	....	....	....	20	5	0	1	1	2
1942-43			MILITARY SERVICE												
1943-44	Moose Jaw Victorias	SSHL	9	3	5	8	....	....	....	0	....	....	....	....	....
	Ottawa Commandos	QSHL	8	0	2	2	....	....	....	4	3	2	2	4	4
1944-45	Ottawa Senators	QSHL	18	6	8	14	....	....	....	26	2	0	0	0	4
1945-46	St. Paul Saints	USHL	53	4	19	23	....	....	....	23	6	0	3	3	0
1946-47	New Haven Ramblers	AHL	63	4	16	20	....	....	....	36	3	0	2	2	0
1947-48	St. Paul Saints	USHL	65	7	26	33	....	....	....	4	....	....	....	....	....
1948-49	St. Paul Saints	USHL	66	5	32	37	....	....	....	14	7	0	3	3	0
1949-50	St. Paul Saints	USHL	68	5	32	37	....	....	....	32	3	0	3	3	0
1950-51	St. Paul Saints	USHL	47	8	17	25	....	....	....	8	4	0	1	1	4
1951-52	**New York Rangers**	**NHL**	**3**	**0**	**0**	**0**	**0**	**0**	**0**	**2**	....	....	....	....	....
	New York Rovers	EHL	27	1	12	13	....	....	....	14	....	....	....	....	....
1952-53	Seattle Bombers	WHL	61	7	15	22	....	....	....	22	5	1	1	2	0
1953-54	Seattle Bombers	WHL	34	0	5	5	....	....	....	6	....	....	....	....	....
	Nelson Maple Leafs	WIHL	18	4	12	16	....	....	....	4	8	3	5	8	6
1954-55			DID NOT PLAY												
1955-56	Johnstown Jets	EHL	36	3	18	21	....	....	....	27	4	0	2	2	2
1956-57	Johnstown Jets	EHL	46	6	23	29	....	....	....	16	6	0	1	1	0
1957-58	Johnstown Jets	EHL	....	....	....	....	....	....	....	....	6	0	1	1	8
	NHL Totals		**3**	**0**	**0**	**0**	**0**	**0**	**0**	**2**	....	....	....	....	....

USHL 2nd All-Star Team (1946, 1948, 1950) • USHL 2nd All-Star Team (1949, 1951) • EHL 1st All-Star Team (1957)

• ALBRIGHT, CLINT Clint "The Professor" Albright

C – L. 6'2", 180 lbs. b: Winnipeg, Man., 2/28/1926.

Season	Club	League	GP	G	A	Pts	AG	AA	APts	PIM	GP	G	A	Pts	PIM
1944-45	Winnipeg Monarchs	City Jr.	8	10	6	16	....	....	....	8	17	*14	11	*25	22
1945-46	Winnipeg Monarchs	City Jr.	6	5	3	8	....	....	....	12	21	12	7	19	17
1946-47	University of Manitoba	Wpg-Sr.	4	*8	7	15	....	....	....	0	....	....	....	....	....
	Winnipeg Flyers	MHL Sr.	10	11	6	17	....	....	....	16	5	6	0	6	8
1947-48	Winnipeg Flyers	MHL Sr.	16	17	12	29	....	....	....	21	7	2	3	5	16
1948-49	**New York Rangers**	**NHL**	**59**	**14**	**5**	**19**	**22**	**8**	**30**	**19**	....	....	....	....	....
1949-50	Winnipeg Monarchs	MHL Sr.	STATISTICS NOT AVAILABLE												
1950-51	St. Paul Saints	USHL	62	21	19	40	....	....	....	36	4	1	1	2	4
	NHL Totals		**59**	**14**	**5**	**19**	**22**	**8**	**30**	**19**	....	....	....	....	....

• ALDCORN, GARY Gary Aldcorn

LW – L. 5'11", 170 lbs. b: Shaunavon, Sask., 3/7/1935.

Season	Club	League	GP	G	A	Pts	AG	AA	APts	PIM	GP	G	A	Pts	PIM
1951-52	Winnipeg Monarchs	MJHL	20	9	7	16	....	....	....	....	....	....	....	....	....
1952-53	Winnipeg Monarchs	MJHL	35	18	24	42	....	....	....	16	4	2	0	2	2
1953-54	Winnipeg Monarchs	MJHL	36	23	14	37	....	....	....	37	5	4	2	6	2
1954-55	Toronto Marlboros	OHA	47	27	22	49	....	....	....	57	13	5	6	11	*37
1955-56	Winnipeg Warriors	WHL	67	22	12	34	....	....	....	66	14	5	2	7	2
1956-57	**Toronto Maple Leafs**	**NHL**	**22**	**5**	**1**	**6**	**7**	**1**	**8**	**4**	....	....	....	....	....
	Rochester Americans	AHL	42	13	10	23	....	....	....	28	10	1	4	5	2
1957-58	**Toronto Maple Leafs**	**NHL**	**59**	**10**	**14**	**24**	**13**	**15**	**28**	**12**	....	....	....	....	....
	Rochester Americans	AHL	11	2	10	12	....	....	....	22	....	....	....	....	....
1958-59	**Toronto Maple Leafs**	**NHL**	**5**	**0**	**3**	**3**	**0**	**3**	**3**	**2**	....	....	....	....	....
	Rochester Americans	AHL	66	37	42	79	....	....	....	52	5	0	2	2	0
1959-60	**Detroit Red Wings**	**NHL**	**70**	**22**	**29**	**51**	**27**	**30**	**57**	**32**	**6**	**1**	**2**	**3**	**4**
1960-61	**Detroit Red Wings**	**NHL**	**49**	**2**	**6**	**8**	**2**	**6**	**8**	**16**	....	....	....	....	....
	Boston Bruins	**NHL**	**21**	**2**	**3**	**5**	**2**	**3**	**5**	**12**	....	....	....	....	....
1961-62	Winnipeg Maroons	SSHL	DID NOT PLAY – COACHING												
1962-63	Winnipeg Maroons	SSHL	3	1	3	4	....	....	....	2	....	....	....	....	....
1963-64	Winnipeg Maroons	SSHL	DID NOT PLAY – COACHING												
1964-65	Winnipeg Olympics	SSHL	4	5	3	8	....	....	....	2	....	....	....	....	....
	Canada	WEC-A	7	4	2	6	....	....	....	8	....	....	....	....	....
	NHL Totals		**226**	**41**	**56**	**97**	**51**	**58**	**109**	**78**	**6**	**1**	**2**	**3**	**4**

AHL 1st All-Star Team (1959)

Claimed by **Toronto** from **Pittsburgh** (AHL) in Inter-League Draft, June 5, 1956. Traded to **Detroit** by **Toronto** with Barry Cullen for Frank Rggeveen and Johnny Wilson, June 9, 1959. Traded to **Boston** by **Detroit** with Murray Oliver and Tom McCarthy for Vic Stasiuk and Leo Labine, January, 1961.

• ALEXANDRE, ART   Art Alexandre

LW – R. 5'5", 150 lbs.   b: St. Jean, Quebec, 3/2/1909.   d: 1976.

			REGULAR SEASON								PLAYOFFS				
Season	Club	League	GP	G	A	Pts	AG	AA	APts	PIM	GP	G	A	Pts	PIM
1930-31	Montreal St. Francois	City Sr	STATISTICS NOT AVAILABLE												
	Montreal CPR	City Sr.	STATISTICS NOT AVAILABLE												
1931-32	**Montreal Canadiens**	**NHL**	**10**	**0**	**2**	**2**	**0**	**6**	**6**	**8**	**4**	**0**	**0**	**0**	**0**
	Montreal Sr. Canadiens	City Sr.	11	6	2	8	....	....	....	2	2	0	1	1	0
1932-33	**Montreal Canadiens**	**NHL**	**1**	**0**	**0**	**0**	**0**	**0**	**0**	**0**	....	....	....	....	....
	Providence Reds	Can-Am	47	10	24	34	....	....	....	18	2	0	0	0	0
1933-34	Providence Reds	Can-Am	37	2	3	5	....	....	....	19	2	0	0	0	2
1934-35	Providence–Quebec	Can-Am	42	6	8	14	....	....	....	19	3	0	0	0	8
1935-36	Springfield Indians	Can-Am	47	13	16	29	....	....	....	32	3	0	1	1	2
1936-37	Kansas City Greyhounds	AHA	1	0	0	0	....	....	....	0	....	....	....	....	....
1937-38	Montreal Concordia	Mtl-Sr.	22	9	6	15	....	....	....	23	1	0	1	1	0
	NHL Totals		**11**	**0**	**2**	**2**	**0**	**6**	**6**	**8**	**4**	**0**	**0**	**0**	**0**

Traded to **Providence** (Can-Am) by **Montreal Canadiens** for cash, May 8, 1932.

• ALLEN, GEORGE   George Allen

LW/D – L. 5'10", 162 lbs.   b: Bayfield, N.B., 7/27/1914.   Deceased.

Season	Club	League	GP	G	A	Pts	AG	AA	APts	PIM	GP	G	A	Pts	PIM
1935-36	North Battleford Beavers	City Sr.	21	10	5	15	....	....	....	10	3	2	1	*3	4
1936-37	North Battleford Beavers	City Sr.	26	15	9	24	....	....	....	26	4	4	1	5	4
1937-38	Sudbury Frood Tigers	NOHA	4	2	0	2	....	....	....	8	....	....	....	....	....
	New Haven Eagles	AHL	35	9	13	22	....	....	....	20	2	0	0	0	0
1938-39	**New York Rangers**	**NHL**	**19**	**6**	**6**	**12**	**13**	**11**	**24**	**10**	**7**	**0**	**0**	**0**	**4**
	Philadelphia Ramblers	AHL	33	23	11	34	....	....	....	15	3	1	0	1	0
1939-40	**Chicago Black Hawks**	**NHL**	**48**	**10**	**12**	**22**	**21**	**24**	**45**	**26**	**2**	**0**	**0**	**0**	**0**
1940-41	**Chicago Black Hawks**	**NHL**	**44**	**14**	**17**	**31**	**28**	**31**	**59**	**22**	**5**	**2**	**2**	**4**	**10**
1941-42	**Chicago Black Hawks**	**NHL**	**43**	**7**	**13**	**20**	**12**	**20**	**32**	**31**	**3**	**1**	**1**	**2**	**0**
1942-43	**Chicago Black Hawks**	**NHL**	**47**	**10**	**14**	**24**	**14**	**18**	**32**	**26**	....	....	....	....	....
1943-44	**Chicago Black Hawks**	**NHL**	**45**	**17**	**24**	**41**	**21**	**29**	**50**	**36**	**9**	**5**	**4**	**9**	**8**
1944-45			MILITARY SERVICE												
1945-46	**Chicago Black Hawks**	**NHL**	**44**	**11**	**15**	**26**	**17**	**28**	**45**	**16**	**4**	**0**	**0**	**0**	**4**
1946-47	**Montreal Canadiens**	**NHL**	**49**	**7**	**14**	**21**	**9**	**20**	**29**	**12**	**11**	**1**	**3**	**4**	**6**
	Buffalo Bisons	AHL	3	1	1	2	....	....	....	4	....	....	....	....	....
1947-48	Cleveland Barons	AHL	68	15	34	49	....	....	....	30	9	2	5	7	6
1948-49	Cleveland Barons	AHL	28	2	3	5	....	....	....	26	....	....	....	....	....
	Minneapolis Millers	USHL	37	7	6	13	....	....	....	6	....	....	....	....	....
1949-50			DID NOT PLAY												
1950-51	Regina Caps	WCSHL	50	9	18	27	....	....	....	26	....	....	....	....	....
	NHL Totals		**339**	**82**	**115**	**197**	**135**	**181**	**316**	**179**	**41**	**9**	**10**	**19**	**32**

AHL 2nd All-Star Team (1939)

Traded to **Chicago** by **NY Rangers** for cash, May 17, 1939. Traded to **Montreal** by **Chicago** for Paul Bibeault with both teams holding rights of recall, September 23, 1946. • Players returned to original teams, June 2, 1947.

• ALLEN, KEITH   Keith "Bingo" Allen   HHOF

D – L. 5'10", 190 lbs.   b: Saskatoon, Sask., 8/21/1923.

Season	Club	League	GP	G	A	Pts	AG	AA	APts	PIM	GP	G	A	Pts	PIM
1940-41	Saskatoon Quakers	City Jr.	10	4	0	4	....	....	....	2	14	5	1	6	8
1941-42	Washington Eagles	EHL	60	13	11	24	....	....	....	27	8	0	1	1	0
1942-43	Buffalo Bisons	AHL	55	1	14	15	....	....	....	29	7	1	0	1	0
1943-44	Saskatoon Navy	City Sr.	15	9	7	16	....	....	....	12	1	0	0	0	0
1944-45	Saskatoon Navy	City Sr.	5	0	1	1	....	....	....	0	....	....	....	....	....
1945-46	Saskatoon Elks	City Sr.	33	5	4	9	....	....	....	42	3	1	0	1	6
1946-47	Springfield Indians	AHL	61	2	8	10	....	....	....	23	2	0	0	0	0
1947-48	Springfield Indians	AHL	51	2	12	14	....	....	....	12	....	....	....	....	....
1948-49	Springfield Indians	AHL	68	3	28	31	....	....	....	28	3	1	0	1	4
1949-50	Springfield Indians	AHL	69	3	17	20	....	....	....	30	2	0	2	2	0
1950-51	Springfield Indians	AHL	70	8	34	42	....	....	....	18	3	0	0	0	0
1951-52	Syracuse Warriors	AHL	67	4	17	21	....	....	....	24	....	....	....	....	....
1952-53	Syracuse Warriors	AHL	64	1	18	19	....	....	....	24	2	0	0	0	0
1953-54	**Detroit Red Wings**	**NHL**	**10**	**0**	**4**	**4**	**0**	**5**	**5**	**2**	**5**	**0**	**0**	**0**	**0**
	Sherbrooke Saints	QHL	3	0	1	1	....	....	....	4	....	....	....	....	....
	Syracuse Warriors	AHL	47	6	17	23	....	....	....	14	....	....	....	....	....
1954-55	**Detroit Red Wings**	**NHL**	**18**	**0**	**0**	**0**	**0**	**0**	**0**	**6**	....	....	....	....	....
	Edmonton Flyers	WHL	34	4	12	16	....	....	....	10	9	0	2	2	6
1955-56	Brandon Regals	WHL	69	0	13	13	....	....	....	40	....	....	....	....	....
1956-57	Seattle Americans	WHL	41	0	6	6	....	....	....	0	....	....	....	....	....
1957-58	Seattle Americans	WHL	DID NOT PLAY – COACHING												
	NHL Totals		**28**	**0**	**4**	**4**	**0**	**5**	**5**	**8**	**5**	**0**	**0**	**0**	**0**

AHL 2nd All-Star Team (1953) • Won Lester Patrick Trophy (1988)

Played in NHL All-Star Game (1954)

Traded to **Detroit** by **Syracuse** (AHL) for cash, February, 1954.

• ALLEN, VIV   Viv "Squee" Allen

RW – R. 5'6", 140 lbs.   b: Bayfield, N.B., 9/9/1916.   Deceased.

Season	Club	League	GP	G	A	Pts	AG	AA	APts	PIM	GP	G	A	Pts	PIM
1936-37	North Battleford Beavers	SSHL	21	5	3	8	....	....	....	9	4	1	1	2	0
1937-38	Creighton Eagles	City Sr.	15	4	6	10	....	....	....	16	4	0	1	1	4
1938-39	Lethbridge Maple Leafs	ASHL	16	9	6	15	....	....	....	20	7	4	2	6	13
1939-40	Rivervale Skeeters	EHL	60	26	47	63	....	....	....	28	....	....	....	....	....
1940-41	**New York Americans**	**NHL**	**6**	**0**	**1**	**1**	**0**	**2**	**2**	**0**	....	....	....	....	....
	Springfield Indians	AHL	29	5	7	12	....	....	....	6	3	0	3	3	0
1941-42	Pittsburgh Hornets	AHL	51	20	30	50	....	....	....	10	....	....	....	....	....
1942-43	Pittsburgh Hornets	AHL	47	6	32	38	....	....	....	18	2	0	1	1	0
	Washington Lions	AHL	1	0	0	0	....	....	....	0	....	....	....	....	....
1943-44	Pittsburgh Hornets	AHL	12	4	0	4	....	....	....	5	....	....	....	....	....
	Saskatoon Quakers	SSHL	8	3	6	9	....	....	....	4	4	5	2	7	2
	Philadelphia Falcons	EHL	4	2	1	3	....	....	....	2	....	....	....	....	....
1944-45	Cornwallis Navy	City Sr.	7	1	2	3	....	....	....	2	....	....	....	....	....
1945-46	Pittsburgh Hornets	AHL	2	0	0	0	....	....	....	0	....	....	....	....	....
	Dallas Texans	USHL	34	21	17	38	....	....	....	10	....	....	....	....	....
1946-47	Dallas Texans	USHL	58	*34	18	52	....	....	....	14	6	0	0	0	4
1947-48	Dallas Texans	USHL	61	16	27	43	....	....	....	19	....	....	....	....	....
1948-49	Dallas Texans	USHL	24	7	6	13	....	....	....	6	4	0	1	1	0
1949-50	Saskatoon Quakers	WCSHL	13	2	6	8	....	....	....	4	....	....	....	....	....
	NHL Totals		**6**	**0**	**1**	**1**	**0**	**2**	**2**	**0**	....	....	....	....	....

Signed as a free agent by **NY Americans**, October 15, 1940. Traded to **Pittsburgh** (AHL) by **NY Americans** with Glenn Brydson for Phil McAtee and Peanuts O'Flaherty, October 8, 1941.

• ALLUM, BILL   Bill Allum

D – L. 5'11", 194 lbs.   b: Winnipeg, Man., 10/9/1916.   d: 3/14/1992.

			REGULAR SEASON								PLAYOFFS				
Season	Club	League	GP	G	A	Pts	AG	AA	APts	PIM	GP	G	A	Pts	PIM
1934-35	Winnipeg Rangers	City Jr.	10	0	1	1	....	....	....	16	....	....	....	....	....
1935-36	Winnipeg Rangers	City Jr.	6	3	1	4	....	....	....	6	2	0	0	0	2
1936-37	Canada Packers	Wpg-Sr.	11	1	1	2	....	....	....	12	3	1	1	2	0
1937-38	New York Rovers	EHL	56	2	5	7	....	....	....	47	....	....	....	....	....
1938-39	New York Rovers	EHL	51	6	14	20	....	....	....	59	....	....	....	....	....
	Philadelphia Ramblers	AHL	2	0	0	0	....	....	....	0	9	0	1	1	2
1939-40	**Chicago Black Hawks**	**NHL**	**1**	**0**	**0**	**0**	**0**	**0**	**0**	**0**	....	....	....	....	....
	Philadelphia Rockets	AHL	54	6	9	15	....	....	....	53	....	....	....	....	....
1940-41	**New York Rangers**	**NHL**	**1**	**0**	**1**	**1**	**0**	**2**	**2**	**0**	....	....	....	....	....
	Philadelphia Rockets	AHL	55	3	10	13	....	....	....	54	....	....	....	....	....
1941-42	Buffalo Bisons	AHL	56	2	11	13	....	....	....	53	....	....	....	....	....
	New Haven Eagles	AHL	....	....	....	....	....	....	....	....	2	1	0	1	2
1942-43	Buffalo Bisons	AHL	54	2	16	18	....	....	....	31	9	*5	2	7	2
1943-44	Winnipeg Navy	City Sr.	10	0	2	2	....	....	....	4	....	....	....	....	....
	Cornwallis Navy	City Sr.	1	0	1	1	....	....	....	....	6	2	0	2	6
1944-45	Winnipeg Navy	City Sr.	1	0	0	0	....	....	....	0	....	....	....	....	....
	Cornwallis Navy	City Sr.	10	0	4	4	....	....	....	0	....	....	....	....	....
1945-46	Buffalo–St. Louis	AHL	59	5	13	18	....	....	....	10	....	....	....	....	....
1946-47	St. Louis–Cleveland	AHL	68	1	16	17	....	....	....	56	4	1	0	1	2
1947-48	Minneapolis Millers	USHL	63	0	13	13	....	....	....	34	10	0	1	1	2
1948-49	Owen Sound Mercurys	OHA Sr.	DID NOT PLAY – COACHING												
1949-50	Owen Sound Mercurys	OHA Sr.	42	3	12	15	....	....	....	47	....	....	....	....	....
1950-51	Owen Sound Mercurys	OHA Sr.	DID NOT PLAY – COACHING												
1951-52	Owen Sound Mercurys	OHA Sr.	48	9	18	27	....	....	....	35	12	1	9	10	6
1952-53	Owen Sound Mercurys	OHA Sr.	46	5	23	28	....	....	....	30	11	2	4	6	4
	NHL Totals		**2**	**0**	**1**	**1**	**0**	**2**	**2**	**0**	....	....	....	....	....

EHL 1st All-Star Team (1939) • USHL 2nd All-Star Team (1948)

Signed as a free agent by **NY Rangers**, October 12, 1937. Traded to **Buffalo** (AHL) by **NY Rangers** for cash, September 11, 1941.

• AMADIO, DAVE   — *see page 830*

• ANDERSON, BILL   Bill "Red" Anderson

D – R. 6', 190 lbs.   b: Tillsonburg, Ont., 12/13/1912.   Deceased.

Season	Club	League	GP	G	A	Pts	AG	AA	APts	PIM	GP	G	A	Pts	PIM
1933-34	Simcoe Juniors	OHA	STATISTICS NOT AVAILABLE												
1934-35	London Tecumseh's	IAHL	39	1	1	2	....	....	....	10	5	0	0	0	0
1935-36			DID NOT PLAY – INJURED												
1936-37	Cleveland Barons	AHL	1	0	0	0	....	....	....	0	....	....	....	....	....
	Minneapolis Millers	AHA	15	1	0	1	....	....	....	23	....	....	....	....	....
1937-38	St. Paul Saints	AHA	34	4	8	12	....	....	....	72	....	....	....	....	....
1938-39	St. Paul Saints	AHA	48	6	9	15	....	....	....	85	3	0	1	1	10
1939-40	Tulsa Oilers	AHA	48	3	19	22	....	....	....	91	....	....	....	....	....
1940-41	Tulsa Oilers	AHA	14	0	0	0	....	....	....	22	....	....	....	....	....
	Detroit Holzbaugh	MOHL	20	3	5	8	....	....	....	11	7	0	1	1	2
1941-42	Johnstown Bluebirds	EHL	59	10	32	42	....	....	....	100	4	1	1	2	6
1942-43	Boston Olympics	EHL	37	5	10	15	....	....	....	54	8	2	1	3	8
	Boston Bruins	**NHL**	....	....	....	....	....	....	....	....	**1**	**0**	**0**	**0**	**0**
	NHL Totals		**0**	**0**	**0**	**0**	**0**	**0**	**0**	**0**	**1**	**0**	**0**	**0**	**0**

EHL First All-Star Team (1942)

• ANDERSON, DALE   Dale Anderson

D – L. 6'3", 190 lbs.   b: Regina, Sask., 3/5/1932.

Season	Club	League	GP	G	A	Pts	AG	AA	APts	PIM	GP	G	A	Pts	PIM
1950-51	Prince Albert Mintos	SJHL	36	6	7	13	....	....	....	*129	6	0	4	4	*16
1951-52	Prince Albert Mintos	SJHL	49	13	38	51	....	....	....	217	5	3	4	7	24
1952-53	Vancouver Canucks	WHL	3	0	3	3	....	....	....	8	....	....	....	....	....
	Nelson Maple Leafs	WIHL	29	3	9	12	....	....	....	71	3	0	0	0	6
1953-54	Saskatoon Quakers	WHL	3	1	1	2	....	....	....	6	....	....	....	....	....
	Moose Jaw Millers	SSHL	33	3	20	23	....	....	....	*115	8	0	1	1	29
1954-55	Saskatoon Quakers	WHL	12	1	3	4	....	....	....	29	....	....	....	....	....
	Sault Ste. Marie Indians	NOHA	30	2	7	9	....	....	....	64	7	1	2	3	14
1955-56	Sault Ste. Marie Indians	NOHA	59	11	17	28	....	....	....	*184	7	0	5	5	26
1956-57	**Detroit Red Wings**	**NHL**	**13**	**0**	**0**	**0**	**0**	**0**	**0**	**6**	**2**	**0**	**0**	**0**	**0**
	Springfield Indians	AHL	40	4	16	20	....	....	....	121	....	....	....	....	....
1957-58	Springfield Indians	AHL	70	4	18	22	....	....	....	99	13	1	2	3	18
1958-59	Springfield Indians	AHL	18	2	4	6	....	....	....	36	....	....	....	....	....
1959-60	Vancouver Canucks	WHL	52	2	28	30	....	....	....	63	11	2	8	10	16
1960-61	Vancouver Canucks	WHL	61	1	17	18	....	....	....	105	9	0	0	0	10
1961-62	Vancouver Canucks	WHL	25	0	12	12	....	....	....	45	....	....	....	....	....
1962-63	Springfield Indians	AHL	52	3	5	8	....	....	....	42	....	....	....	....	....
1963-64	Vancouver Canucks	WHL	70	5	20	25	....	....	....	76	....	....	....	....	....
1964-65			DID NOT PLAY												
1965-66	Saskatoon Quakers	SSHL	30	12	32	44	....	....	....	53	11	2	9	11	22
1966-67	Saskatoon Quakers	SSHL	33	17	22	39	....	....	....	45	14	3	9	12	*36
	Portland Buckaroos	WHL	....	....	....	....	....	....	....	....	1	0	0	0	0
1967-68	Saskatoon Quakers	SSHL	....	3	12	15	....	....	....	51	....	2	6	8	8
	NHL Totals		**13**	**0**	**0**	**0**	**0**	**0**	**0**	**6**	**2**	**0**	**0**	**0**	**0**

• ANDERSON, DOUG Doug "Andy" Anderson

C – L. 5'7", 157 lbs. b: Edmonton, Alta., 10/20/1927.

Season	Club	League	GP	G	A	Pts	AG	AA	APts	PIM	P GP	P G	P A	P Pts	P PIM
			REGULAR SEASON								PLAYOFFS				
1946-47	Edmonton Canadians	City Jr.	6	4	4	8	....	....	....	2	....	....	....	....	....
1947-48	Edmonton Flyers	WCSHL	40	15	35	50	....	....	....	10	24	11	29	*40	6
1948-49	Edmonton Flyers	WCSHL	40	16	31	47	....	....	....	20	9	2	2	4	6
1949-50	Edmonton Flyers	WCSHL	45	18	44	62	....	....	....	28	6	1	5	6	7
1950-51	Edmonton Flyers	WCSHL	51	16	30	46	....	....	....	20	7	1	5	6	0
1951-52	Victoria Cougars	PCHL	67	14	33	47	....	....	....	10	13	4	4	8	10
1952-53	Victoria Cougars	WHL	70	18	50	68	....	....	....	14	....	....	....	....	....
	Montreal Canadiens	**NHL**	....	....	....	....	....	....	....	....	**2**	**0**	**0**	**0**	**0**
1953-54	Buffalo Bisons	AHL	7	0	2	2	....	....	....	4	....	....	....	....	....
	Victoria Cougars	WHL	60	7	15	22	....	....	....	10	....	....	....	....	....
1954-55	Victoria Cougars	WHL	51	15	28	43	....	....	....	4	3	0	0	0	0
1955-56	Victoria Cougars	WHL	62	23	40	63	....	....	....	24	9	3	2	5	4
1956-57	Victoria Cougars	WHL	70	22	42	64	....	....	....	22	3	1	0	1	0
1957-58	Victoria Cougars	WHL	26	4	9	13	....	....	....	2	....	....	....	....	....
1958-59	Victoria Cougars	WHL	67	16	32	48	....	....	....	12	3	0	2	2	0
1959-60	Victoria Cougars	WHL	70	10	22	32	....	....	....	2	11	2	2	4	0
1960-61	Victoria Cougars	WHL	70	6	30	36	....	....	....	12	5	1	4	5	0
1961-62	Portland Buckaroos	WHL	54	4	22	26	....	....	....	2	7	1	2	3	7
1962-63	Portland Buckaroos	WHL	60	5	6	11	....	....	....	0	....	....	....	....	....
	NHL Totals		**0**	**0**	**0**	**0**	**0**	**0**	**0**	**0**	**2**	**0**	**0**	**0**	**0**

• ANDERSON, TOM Tom "Cowboy" Anderson

LW/D – L. 5'10", 180 lbs. b: Edinburgh, Scotland, 7/9/1910. d: 9/15/1971.

Season	Club	League	GP	G	A	Pts	AG	AA	APts	PIM	P GP	P G	P A	P Pts	P PIM
1929-30	Drumheller Miners	ASHL	16	6	3	9	....	....	....	18	2	0	0	0	0
1930-31	Philadelphia Arrows	Can-Am	38	7	8	15	....	....	....	89	....	....	....	....	....
1931-32	Philadelphia Arrows	Can-Am	25	5	6	11	....	....	....	36	....	....	....	....	....
1932-33	Philadelphia Arrows	Can-Am	45	11	24	35	....	....	....	49	5	2	*4	6	5
1933-34	Philadelphia Arrows	Can-Am	40	20	25	45	....	....	....	46	2	0	2	2	4
1934-35	**Detroit Red Wings**	**NHL**	**27**	**5**	**2**	**7**	**11**	**4**	**15**	**16**	....	....	....	....	....
	Detroit Olympics	IAHL	15	5	8	13	....	....	....	14	5	1	0	1	2
1935-36	**New York Americans**	**NHL**	**24**	**3**	**2**	**5**	**7**	**5**	**12**	**20**	**5**	**0**	**0**	**0**	**6**
1936-37	**New York Americans**	**NHL**	**45**	**10**	**15**	**25**	**22**	**35**	**57**	**24**	....	....	....	....	....
	Cleveland Falcons	AHL	4	1	1	2	....	....	....	17	....	....	....	....	....
	New York Americans	**NHL**	**45**	**4**	**21**	**25**	**8**	**44**	**52**	**22**	**6**	**1**	**4**	**5**	**2**
	New Haven Eagles	AHL	6	0	0	0	....	....	....	15	....	....	....	....	....
1938-39	**New York Americans**	**NHL**	**47**	**13**	**27**	**40**	**27**	**51**	**78**	**14**	**2**	**0**	**0**	**0**	**0**
1939-40	**New York Americans**	**NHL**	**48**	**12**	**19**	**31**	**26**	**38**	**64**	**22**	**3**	**1**	**3**	**4**	**0**
1940-41	**New York Americans**	**NHL**	**35**	**3**	**12**	**15**	**6**	**22**	**28**	**8**	....	....	....	....	....
1941-42	**Brooklyn Americans**	**NHL**	**48**	**12**	**29**	**41**	**21**	**44**	**65**	**64**	....	....	....	....	....
1942-43	Calgary Currie Army	City Sr.	16	5	11	16	....	....	....	26	10	0	6	6	18
1943-44	Calgary Currie Army	City Sr.	16	2	6	8	....	....	....	21	2	0	2	2	2
1944-45	Calgary Currie Army	City Sr.	11	1	3	4	....	....	....	32	3	0	0	0	8
1945-46	Providence Reds	AHL	47	3	17	20	....	....	....	12	2	1	0	1	0
1946-47	Hollywood Wolves	PCHL	60	9	22	31	....	....	....	42	7	2	1	3	6
	NHL Totals		**319**	**62**	**127**	**189**	**128**	**243**	**371**	**190**	**16**	**2**	**7**	**9**	**8**

NHL 1st All-Star Team (1942) • Won Hart Trophy (1942)

Played in NHL All-Star Game (1939)

Traded to **Detroit** by **Philadelphia** (Can-Am) for cash, May 8, 1934. Traded to **NY Americans** by **Detroit** for cash, October 11, 1935. Rights transferred to **Chicago** from **Brooklyn** in Special Dispersal Draw, September 11, 1943.

• ANDREA, PAUL — *see page 836*

• ANDREWS, LLOYD Lloyd "Shrimp" Andrews

LW – L. b: Tillsonburg, Ont., 1899. Deceased.

Season	Club	League	GP	G	A	Pts	AG	AA	APts	PIM	P GP	P G	P A	P Pts	P PIM
1921-22	Niagara Falls Cataracts	OHA Sr.	STATISTICS NOT AVAILABLE												
	Toronto St. Pats	**NHL**	**11**	**0**	**0**	**0**	**0**	**0**	**0**	**0**	**7**	**2**	**0**	**2**	**5**
1922-23	**Toronto St. Pats**	**NHL**	**23**	**5**	**4**	**9**	**16**	**36**	**52**	**10**	....	....	....	....	....
1923-24	**Toronto St.Pats**	**NHL**	**12**	**2**	**1**	**3**	**8**	**17**	**25**	**0**	....	....	....	....	....
1924-25	**Toronto St. Pats**	**NHL**	**7**	**1**	**0**	**1**	**3**	**0**	**3**	**0**	....	....	....	....	....
1925-26			DID NOT PLAY												
1926-27	New Haven Eagles	Can-Am	32	17	*11	28	....	....	....	11	4	*4	0	*4	4
1927-28	New Haven Eagles	Can-Am	39	15	9	24	....	....	....	25	....	....	....	....	....
1928-29	Philadelphia Arrows	Can-Am	39	10	4	14	....	....	....	12	....	....	....	....	....
1929-30	Philadelphia Arrows	Can-Am	40	24	19	43	....	....	....	30	2	1	0	1	2
1930-31	Philadelphia Arrows	Can-Am	40	15	14	29	....	....	....	24	....	....	....	....	....
1931-32	Philadelphia Arrows	Can-Am	39	8	15	23	....	....	....	16	....	....	....	....	....
1932-33	St. Paul Saints	AHA	12	1	4	5	....	....	....	2	....	....	....	....	....
	Hibbing Maroons	CHL	34	13	16	29	....	....	....	10	....	....	....	....	....
1933-34	Hibbing Miners	CHL	43	18	16	34	....	....	....	28	6	*3	1	4	0
	NHL Totals		**53**	**8**	**5**	**13**	**27**	**53**	**80**	**10**	**7**	**2**	**0**	**2**	**5**

Signed as a free agent by **Toronto St. Pats**, January 23, 1922.

• ANGOTTI, LOU — *see page 837*

• ANSLOW, BERT Bert "Hub" Anslow

C – L. 6', 173 lbs. b: Pembroke, Ont., 3/23/1926.

Season	Club	League	GP	G	A	Pts	AG	AA	APts	PIM	P GP	P G	P A	P Pts	P PIM
1939-40	Pembroke Lumber Kings	Ott-Jr.	....	....	....	....	....	....	....	....	4	5	0	5	....
1940-41	Pembroke Dairy	Ott-Jr.	4	4	0	4	....	....	....	....	....	....	....	....	....
1941-42	Pembroke Maple Leafs	Ott-Jr.	....	....	....	....	....	....	....	....	5	6	1	7	....
1942-43	Pembroke All-Stars	Ott-Jr.	....	....	....	....	....	....	....	....	3	4	0	4	....
1943-44	Pembroke All-Stars	Ott-Jr.	....	....	....	....	....	....	....	....	5	7	4	11	....
1944-45			MILITARY SERVICE												
1945-46	Pembroke Lumber Kings	Ott-Sr.	17	31	14	45	....	....	....	27	12	13	*18	31	6
1946-47	New York Rovers	EHL	49	24	13	37	....	....	....	36	9	1	1	2	5
1947-48	**New York Rangers**	**NHL**	**2**	**0**	**0**	**0**	**0**	**0**	**0**	**0**	....	....	....	....	....
	New Haven Ramblers	AHL	3	0	0	0	....	....	....	0	....	....	....	....	....
	New York Rovers	EHL	16	17	15	32	....	....	....	32	....	....	....	....	....
	New York Rovers	QSHL	44	22	25	47	....	....	....	49	3	1	4	5	4
1948-49	Tacoma Rockets	PCHL	66	18	42	60	....	....	....	58	4	0	1	1	0
1949-50	St. Paul Saints	USHL	55	24	24	48	....	....	....	58	....	....	....	....	....
	New Haven Ramblers	AHL	14	3	3	6	....	....	....	6	....	....	....	....	....
1950-51	Kansas City Royals	USHL	26	5	8	13	....	....	....	18	....	....	....	....	....
	Calgary Stampeders	WCSHL	16	6	11	17	....	....	....	6	....	....	....	....	....
1951-52	Pembroke Lumber Kings	NOHA	43	32	42	74	....	....	....	26	24	*18	10	*28	16
1952-53	Pembroke Lumber Kings	NOHA	35	22	32	54	....	....	....	32	1	0	1	1	0
1953-54	Hamilton Tigers	OHA Sr.	42	17	15	32	....	....	....	56	....	....	....	....	....
1954-55	Pembroke Lumber Kings	NOHA	48	10	19	29	....	....	....	10	6	0	1	1	4
1955-56	Petawawa Army	City Sr.	5	0	5	5	....	....	....	....	4	0	3	3	....
1956-57			DID NOT PLAY												
1957-58			DID NOT PLAY												
1958-59	Deep River Diggers	OVSHL	12	3	3	6	....	....	....	....	7	8	4	12	....
1959-60	Pembroke Cleaners	Ott-Sr.	5	2	2	4	....	....	....	0	2	1	1	2	2
	NHL Totals		**2**	**0**	**0**	**0**	**0**	**0**	**0**	**0**	....	....	....	....	....

• APPS SR., SYL Syl Apps Sr.

C – L. 6', 185 lbs. b: Paris, Ont., 1/18/1915.

Season	Club	League	GP	G	A	Pts	AG	AA	APts	PIM	P GP	P G	P A	P Pts	P PIM
1935-36	Hamilton Tigers	City Jr.	19	22	16	*38	....	....	....	10	9	12	*7	*19	4
	Toronto Dominions	OHA Sr.	1	0	1	1	....	....	....	0	....	....	....	....	....
1936-37	**Toronto Maple Leafs**	**NHL**	**48**	**16**	***29**	**45**	**35**	**69**	**104**	**10**	**2**	**0**	**1**	**1**	**0**
1937-38	**Toronto Maple Leafs**	**NHL**	**47**	**21**	***29**	**50**	**45**	**60**	**105**	**9**	**7**	**1**	**4**	**5**	**0**
1938-39	**Toronto Maple Leafs**	**NHL**	**44**	**15**	**25**	**40**	**32**	**47**	**79**	**4**	**10**	**2**	**6**	**8**	**2**
1939-40	**Toronto Maple Leafs**	**NHL**	**27**	**13**	**17**	**30**	**28**	**34**	**62**	**5**	**10**	**5**	**2**	**7**	**2**
1940-41	**Toronto Maple Leafs**	**NHL**	**41**	**20**	**24**	**44**	**40**	**44**	**84**	**6**	**7**	**3**	**2**	**5**	**2**
1941-42	**Toronto Maple Leafs**	**NHL**	**38**	**18**	**23**	**41**	**31**	**35**	**66**	**0**	**13**	**5**	**9**	**14**	**2**
1942-43	**Toronto Maple Leafs**	**NHL**	**29**	**23**	**17**	**40**	**33**	**22**	**55**	**2**	....	....	....	....	....
1943-44			MILITARY SERVICE												
1944-45			MILITARY SERVICE												
1945-46	**Toronto Maple Leafs**	**NHL**	**40**	**24**	**16**	**40**	**37**	**30**	**67**	**2**	....	....	....	....	....
1946-47	**Toronto Maple Leafs**	**NHL**	**54**	**25**	**24**	**49**	**34**	**34**	**68**	**6**	**11**	**5**	**1**	**6**	**0**
1947-48	**Toronto Maple Leafs**	**NHL**	**55**	**26**	**27**	**53**	**38**	**40**	**78**	**12**	**9**	**4**	**4**	**8**	**0**
	NHL Totals		**423**	**201**	**231**	**432**	**353**	**415**	**768**	**56**	**69**	**25**	**29**	**54**	**8**

Won Calder Trophy (1937) • NHL Second All-Star Team (1938, 1941, 1943) • NHL First All-Star Team (1939, 1942) • Won Lady Byng Trophy (1942)

Played in NHL All-Star Game (1939, 1947)

• ARBOUR, AL — *see page 838*

• ARBOUR, AMOS Amos "Butch" Arbour

LW – L. 5'8", 160 lbs. b: Victoria Harbour, Ontario. Deceased.

Season	Club	League	GP	G	A	Pts	AG	AA	APts	PIM	P GP	P G	P A	P Pts	P PIM
1914-15	Victoria Harbour Station	OHA	STATISTICS NOT AVAILABLE												
1915-16	Montreal Canadiens	NHA	20	5	0	5	....	....	....	6	4	3	0	3	11
1916-17	Toronto 228th Battalion	NHA	10	13	2	15	....	....	....	6	....	....	....	....	....
1917-18			MILITARY SERVICE												
1918-19	**Montreal Canadiens**	**NHL**	**1**	**0**	**0**	**0**	**0**	**0**	**0**	**0**	....	....	....	....	....
1919-20	**Montreal Canadiens**	**NHL**	**22**	**21**	**5**	**26**	**49**	**34**	**83**	**13**	....	....	....	....	....
1920-21	**Montreal Canadiens**	**NHL**	**22**	**14**	**3**	**17**	**36**	**26**	**62**	**40**	....	....	....	....	....
1921-22	**Hamilton Tigers**	**NHL**	**23**	**9**	**6**	**15**	**25**	**38**	**63**	**8**	....	....	....	....	....
1922-23	**Hamilton Tigers**	**NHL**	**23**	**6**	**1**	**7**	**20**	**9**	**29**	**6**	....	....	....	....	....
1923-24	**Toronto St.Pats**	**NHL**	**20**	**1**	**2**	**3**	**4**	**35**	**39**	**4**	....	....	....	....	....
	NHL Totals		**111**	**51**	**17**	**68**	**134**	**142**	**276**	**71**	....	....	....	....	....
	Other Major League Totals		30	18	2	20	....	....	....	12	4	3	0	3	11

Signed as a free agent by **Montreal Canadiens**, January 23, 1919. Traded to **Hamilton** by **Montreal Canadiens** with Cully Wilson and Harry Mummery for Sprague Cleghorn, November 26, 1921. Traded to **Toronto St. Pats** by **Hamilton** with Bert Corbeau and George Carey for Ken Randall and cash, December 13, 1923.

• ARBOUR, JACK Jack Arbour

D – L. 5'8", 172 lbs. b: Waubaushene, Ontario, 3/7/1899. Deceased.

			REGULAR SEASON								PLAYOFFS				
Season	Club	League	GP	G	A	Pts	AG	AA	APts	PIM	GP	G	A	Pts	PIM
1919-20	Calgary Wanderers	Big 4	12	3	0	3	....	....	....	17	1	0	0	0	0
1920-21	Calgary Tigers	Big 4	15	2	3	5	....	....	....	15	....	....	....	....	....
1921-22	Calgary Tigers	WCHL	14	2	2	4	....	....	....	8	....	....	....	....	....
1922-23	Calgary Tigers	WCHL	5	0	1	1	....	....	....	2	....	....	....	....	....
1923-24	Seattle Metropolitans	PCHA	28	3	2	5	....	....	....	16	2	1	0	1	2
1924-25	Calgary Tigers	WCHL	3	0	0	0	....	....	....	0	....	....	....	....	....
1925-26			DID NOT PLAY – INJURED												
1926-27	**Detroit Cougars**	**NHL**	**37**	**4**	**1**	**5**	**12**	**8**	**20**	**46**	....	....	....	....	....
1927-28	Detroit Olympics	Can-Pro	42	12	6	18	....	....	....	77	2	0	0	0	2
1928-29	**Toronto Maple Leafs**	**NHL**	**10**	**1**	**0**	**1**	**4**	**0**	**4**	**10**	....	....	....	....	....
	London–Windsor	Can-Pro	30	7	3	10	....	....	....	33	8	0	0	0	18
1929-30	Windsor Bulldogs	IAHL	41	8	5	13	....	....	....	57	....	....	....	....	....
1930-31	Windsor Bulldogs	IAHL	46	7	16	23	....	....	....	34	6	3	1	4	*13
1931-32	Windsor Bulldogs	IAHL	45	9	9	18	....	....	....	74	6	0	0	0	2
1932-33	Windsor Bulldogs	IAHL	43	5	9	14	....	....	....	39	6	0	0	0	4
1933-34	Seattle Seahawks	NWHL	34	5	4	9	....	....	....	24	....	....	....	....	....
1934-35	Portland Buckaroos	NWHL	32	11	9	20	....	....	....	12	3	0	0	0	2
1935-36	Portland Buckaroos	PCHL	39	6	4	10	....	....	....	41	3	0	1	1	6
1936-37	Spokane Clippers	PCHL	13	1	2	3	....	....	....	12	....	....	....	....	....
1937-38	Spokane Clippers	PCHL	9	0	1	1	....	....	....	2	....	....	....	....	....
1938-39	Spokane Clippers	PCHL	2	0	0	0	....	....	....	0	....	....	....	....	....
	NHL Totals		**47**	**5**	**1**	**6**	**16**	**8**	**24**	**56**	....	....	....	....	....
	Other Major League Totals		50	5	5	10	....	....	....	26	2	1	0	1	2

Signed as a free agent by **Calgary** (WCHL), November 4, 1921. Traded to **Seattle** (PCHA) by **Calgary** (WCHL) with Ed Fisher for cash, November 4, 1925. Signed as a free agent by **Calgary** (WCHL), January 1, 1925. Traded to **Detroit Cougars** by **Calgary** (WHL) for cash, October 27, 1926. Rights traded to **Toronto** by **Detroit Cougars** with $12,500 for Jimmy Herberts, April 8, 1928.

• ARBOUR, JOHN *— see page 839*

• ARBOUR, TY Ty (Ernest J.) Arbour

LW – L. 5'7", 160 lbs. b: Waubaushene, Ontario, 6/29/1896. Deceased.

			REGULAR SEASON								PLAYOFFS				
Season	Club	League	GP	G	A	Pts	AG	AA	APts	PIM	GP	G	A	Pts	PIM
1919-20	Midland Aces	OHA Sr.	STATISTICS NOT AVAILABLE												
1920-21	Brandon Wheat Kings	MHL Sr.	12	11	4	15	....	....	....	4	....	....	....	....	....
1921-22	Edmonton Eskimos	WCHL	24	27	6	33	....	....	....	22	2	0	0	0	0
1922-23	Edmonton Eskimos	WCHL	30	18	9	27	....	....	....	10	4	0	1	1	0
1923-24	Edmonton Eskimos	WCHL	30	13	5	18	....	....	....	12	....	....	....	....	....
1924-25	Vancouver Maroons	WCHL	27	15	5	20	....	....	....	12	....	....	....	....	....
1925-26	Vancouver Maroons	WCHL	30	10	6	16	....	....	....	6	....	....	....	....	....
1926-27	**Pittsburgh Pirates**	**NHL**	**41**	**7**	**8**	**15**	**20**	**69**	**89**	**10**	....	....	....	....	....
1927-28	**Pittsburgh Pirates**	**NHL**	**7**	**0**	**0**	**0**	**0**	**0**	**0**	**0**	....	....	....	....	....
	Chicago Black Hawks	**NHL**	**32**	**5**	**5**	**10**	**15**	**42**	**57**	**32**	....	....	....	....	....
1928-29	**Chicago Black Hawks**	**NHL**	**44**	**3**	**4**	**7**	**12**	**37**	**49**	**32**	....	....	....	....	....
1929-30	**Chicago Black Hawks**	**NHL**	**42**	**10**	**8**	**18**	**20**	**26**	**46**	**26**	**2**	**1**	**0**	**1**	**0**
1930-31	**Chicago Black Hawks**	**NHL**	**41**	**3**	**3**	**6**	**7**	**11**	**18**	**12**	**9**	**1**	**0**	**1**	**6**
1931-32			DID NOT PLAY												
1932-33	Buffalo Bisons	IAHL	17	2	1	3	....	....	....	4	....	....	....	....	....
1933-34	Edmonton Eskimos	NWHL	33	18	8	26	....	....	....	2	1	0	0	0	0
	NHL Totals		**207**	**28**	**28**	**56**	**74**	**185**	**259**	**112**	**11**	**2**	**0**	**2**	**6**
	Other Major League Totals		111	73	25	98	....	....	....	56	6	0	1	1	0

WCHL 2nd All-Star Team (1922)

Signed as a free agent by **Edmonton** (WCHL), November 23, 1921. Traded to **Vancouver** (WCHL) by **Edmonton** (WCHL) for cash, November 10, 1924. Traded to **Pittsburgh** by **Vancouver** (WHL) for cash, October 0, 1026. Traded to **Chicago** by **Pittsburgh** to complete three-team transaction that sent Bert McCaffrey to Pittsburgh and Ed Rodden to Toronto, November 7, 1927. Traded to **Pittsburgh** (IAHL) by **Chicago** for cash, October 21, 1931

• ARMSTRONG, BOB Bob Armstrong

D – R. 6'1", 190 lbs. b: Toronto, Ont., 4/7/1931. Deceased.

			REGULAR SEASON								PLAYOFFS				
Season	Club	League	GP	G	A	Pts	AG	AA	APts	PIM	GP	G	A	Pts	PIM
1948-49	Stratford Kroehlers	OHA	37	6	5	11	....	....	....	33	3	0	1	1	2
1949-50	Stratford Kroehlers	OHA	46	10	12	22	....	....	....	50	....	....	....	....	....
1950-51	Stratford Kroehlers	OHA	52	13	16	29	....	....	....	87	3	2	1	3	9
	Boston Bruins	**NHL**	**2**	**0**	**0**	**0**	**0**	**0**	**0**	**2**	....	....	....	....	....
1951-52	Hershey Bears	AHL	67	6	15	21	....	....	....	61	5	0	0	0	4
	Boston Bruins	**NHL**	....	....	....	....	....	....	....	....	**5**	**0**	**0**	**0**	**2**
1952-53	**Boston Bruins**	**NHL**	**55**	**0**	**8**	**8**	**0**	**11**	**11**	**45**	**11**	**1**	**1**	**2**	**10**
1953-54	**Boston Bruins**	**NHL**	**64**	**2**	**10**	**12**	**3**	**14**	**17**	**81**	**4**	**0**	**1**	**1**	**0**
1954-55	**Boston Bruins**	**NHL**	**57**	**1**	**3**	**4**	**1**	**4**	**5**	**38**	**5**	**0**	**0**	**0**	**2**
1955-56	**Boston Bruins**	**NHL**	**68**	**0**	**12**	**12**	**0**	**15**	**15**	**122**	....	....	....	....	....
1956-57	**Boston Bruins**	**NHL**	**57**	**1**	**15**	**16**	**1**	**17**	**18**	**79**	**10**	**0**	**3**	**3**	**10**
1957-58	**Boston Bruins**	**NHL**	**47**	**1**	**4**	**5**	**1**	**4**	**5**	**66**	....	....	....	....	....
	Springfield Indians	AHL	26	5	11	16	....	....	....	37	13	5	8	13	*31
1958-59	**Boston Bruins**	**NHL**	**60**	**1**	**9**	**10**	**1**	**10**	**11**	**50**	**7**	**0**	**2**	**2**	**4**
1959-60	**Boston Bruins**	**NHL**	**69**	**5**	**14**	**19**	**6**	**14**	**20**	**96**	....	....	....	....	....
1960-61	**Boston Bruins**	**NHL**	**54**	**0**	**10**	**10**	**0**	**10**	**10**	**72**	....	....	....	....	....
1961-62	**Boston Bruins**	**NHL**	**9**	**2**	**1**	**3**	**2**	**1**	**3**	**20**	....	....	....	....	....
	Hull-Ottawa Canadiens	EPHL	61	6	28	34	....	....	....	116	13	1	3	4	10
1962-63	Rochester Americans	AHL	70	1	28	29	....	....	....	89	2	1	0	1	4
	NHL Totals		**542**	**13**	**86**	**99**	**15**	**100**	**115**	**671**	**42**	**1**	**7**	**8**	**28**

Played in NHL All-Star Game (1960)

• ARMSTRONG, GEORGE *— see page 840*

• ARMSTRONG, MURRAY Murray Armstrong

C – L. 5'10", 170 lbs. b: Manor, Sask., 1/1/1916.

			REGULAR SEASON								PLAYOFFS				
Season	Club	League	GP	G	A	Pts	AG	AA	APts	PIM	GP	G	A	Pts	PIM
1931-32	Regina Pats	City Jr.	3	1	0	1	....	....	....	0	3	1	1	2	0
1932-33	Regina Pats	City Jr.	3	0	0	0	....	....	....	7	15	9	2	11	39
1933-34	Regina Pats	City Jr.	2	4	2	6	....	....	....	0	4	2	1	3	4
1934-35	Regina Vics	SSHL	22	9	6	15	....	....	....	15	6	2	1	3	2
1935-36	New York Rovers	EHL	32	15	23	38	....	....	....	18	7	1	2	3	0
1936-37	Syracuse Stars	AHL	43	14	21	35	....	....	....	8	8	4	6	10	6
1937-38	**Toronto Maple Leafs**	**NHL**	**9**	**0**	**0**	**0**	**0**	**0**	**0**	**0**	**3**	**0**	**0**	**0**	**0**
	Syracuse Stars	AHL	35	7	31	38	....	....	....	10	5	3	1	4	0
1938-39	**Toronto Maple Leafs**	**NHL**	**3**	**0**	**1**	**1**	**0**	**2**	**2**	**0**	....	....	....	....	....
	Syracuse Stars	AHL	50	27	27	54	....	....	....	10	3	1	1	2	0
1939-40	**New York Americans**	**NHL**	**47**	**16**	**20**	**36**	**35**	**40**	**75**	**12**	**3**	**0**	**0**	**0**	**0**
1940-41	**New York Americans**	**NHL**	**48**	**10**	**14**	**24**	**20**	**26**	**46**	**6**	....	....	....	....	....
1941-42	**Brooklyn Americans**	**NHL**	**45**	**6**	**22**	**28**	**10**	**33**	**43**	**15**	....	....	....	....	....
1942-43	Regina Army	SSHL	24	29	32	61	....	....	....	36	5	5	12	17	4
1943-44	**Detroit Red Wings**	**NHL**	**28**	**12**	**22**	**34**	**15**	**27**	**42**	**4**	**5**	**0**	**2**	**2**	**0**
1944-45	**Detroit Red Wings**	**NHL**	**50**	**15**	**24**	**39**	**21**	**39**	**60**	**31**	**14**	**4**	**2**	**6**	**2**
1945-46	**Detroit Red Wings**	**NHL**	**40**	**8**	**18**	**26**	**12**	**34**	**46**	**4**	**5**	**0**	**2**	**2**	**0**
1946-47	Buffalo Bisons	AHL	19	10	8	18	....	....	....	4	....	....	....	....	....
	Dallas Texans	USHL	42	15	31	46	....	....	....	10	6	0	3	3	0
1947-48	Regina Pats	SJHL	DID NOT PLAY – COACHING												
	NHL Totals		**270**	**67**	**121**	**188**	**113**	**201**	**314**	**72**	**30**	**4**	**6**	**10**	**2**

EHL 2nd All-Star Team (1936) • Won Herman W. Paterson Cup (USHL - MVP) (1947) • Won Lester Patrick Trophy (1977)

Claimed by **Toronto** from **Philadelphia** (Can-Am) in Inter-League Draft, May 7, 1936. Traded to **NY Americans** by **Toronto** with Buzz Boll, Busher Jackson and Doc Romnes for Sweeney Schriner, May 15, 1939. Rights transferred to **Detroit** from **Brooklyn** in Special Dispersal Draw, September 11, 1943.

• ARMSTRONG, NORM Norm "Red" Armstrong

D – L. 5'11", 205 lbs. b: Owen Sound, Ont., 10/17/1938. d: 7/23/1974.

			REGULAR SEASON								PLAYOFFS				
Season	Club	League	GP	G	A	Pts	AG	AA	APts	PIM	GP	G	A	Pts	PIM
1958-59	Sarnia Steeplejacks	OHA Jr.	STATISTICS NOT AVAILABLE												
	Woodstock Athletics	OHA Sr.	STATISTICS NOT AVAILABLE												
1960-61	Charlotte Clippers	EHL	64	8	13	21	....	....	....	192	....	....	....	....	....
1961-62	Charlotte Checkers	EHL	1	0	1	1	....	....	....	0	....	....	....	....	....
	Philadelphia Ramblers	EHL	66	17	30	47	....	....	....	212	3	0	1	1	6
1962-63	**Toronto Maple Leafs**	**NHL**	**7**	**1**	**1**	**2**	**1**	**1**	**2**	**2**	....	....	....	....	....
	Rochester Americans	AHL	18	1	6	7	....	....	....	30	....	....	....	....	....
	Sudbury Wolves	EPHL	44	14	23	37	....	....	....	144	8	2	3	5	21
1963-64	Rochester Americans	AHL	67	17	13	30	....	....	....	112	2	0	1	1	4
1964-65	Rochester Americans	AHL	70	32	14	46	....	....	....	123	10	2	3	5	17
1965-66	Rochester Americans	AHL	67	14	26	40	....	....	....	146	12	0	0	0	12
1966-67	Tulsa Oilers	CHL	11	2	5	7	....	....	....	8	....	....	....	....	....
	Rochester Americans	AHL	57	13	34	47	....	....	....	77	....	....	....	....	....
1967-68	Rochester Americans	AHL	54	13	25	38	....	....	....	112	1	0	0	0	6
1968-69	Rochester Americans	AHL	74	29	40	69	....	....	....	133	....	....	....	....	....
1969-70	Rochester Americans	AHL	70	30	45	75	....	....	....	117	....	....	....	....	....
1970-71	Rochester Americans	AHL	44	13	17	30	....	....	....	101	....	....	....	....	....
	Springfield Kings	AHL	10	0	16	16	....	....	....	15	3	0	0	0	6
1971-72	Baltimore Clippers	AHL	68	9	15	24	....	....	....	61	18	2	2	4	19
1972-73	Rochester Americans	AHL	45	4	5	9	....	....	....	22	5	0	1	1	2
	NHL Totals		**7**	**1**	**1**	**2**	**1**	**1**	**2**	**2**	....	....	....	....	....

Traded to **Springfield** (AHL) by **Toronto** for Don Westbrooke, February, 1971. Claimed by **Baltimore** (AHL) from **LA Kings** in Reverse Draft, June 8, 1971. • Died of injuries suffered in an industrial accident, July 23, 1074.

• ARUNDEL, JOHN John Arundel

D – L. 5'11", 181 lbs. b: Winnipeg, Man., 11/4/1027.

			REGULAR SEASON								PLAYOFFS				
Season	Club	League	GP	G	A	Pts	AG	AA	APts	PIM	GP	G	A	Pts	PIM
1944-45	St. Michael's Majors	OHA	10	3	5	8	....	....	....	10	1	0	1	1	0
1945-46	Oshawa Generals	OHA	27	10	8	18	....	....	....	7	12	2	8	10	6
1946-47	Winnipeg Monarchs	MJHL	13	8	9	17	....	....	....	8	7	5	2	7	8
1947-48	Winnipeg Monarchs	MJHL	23	23	26	49	....	....	....	8	16	*15	11	*26	4
1948-49	Sydney Millionaires	CBSHL	60	12	29	41	....	....	....	00	0	0	0	0	0
1949-50	**Toronto Maple Leafs**	**NHL**	**3**	**0**	**0**	**0**	**0**	**0**	**0**	**9**	....	....	....	....	....
	Pittsburgh Hornets	AHL	34	0	8	8	....	....	....	17	....	....	....	....	....
	Los Angeles Monarchs	PCHL	32	3	10	13	....	....	....	17	17	1	7	8	28
1950-51	St. Michael's Monarchs	OHA Sr.	29	6	9	15	....	....	....	36	9	1	2	3	14
1951-52	Saint John Beavers	MMHL	85	10	21	31	....	....	....	143	15	1	6	7	26
1952-53	Ottawa Senators	QSHL	55	5	14	19	....	....	....	87	11	2	5	7	6
1953-54	Ottawa Senators	QHL	58	4	4	8	....	....	....	44	22	3	4	7	18
1954-55	Ottawa Senators	QHL	25	1	5	6	....	....	....	18	....	....	....	....	....
	Sudbury Wolves	NOHA	21	2	7	9	....	....	....	2	....	....	....	....	....
	NHL Totals		**3**	**0**	**0**	**0**	**0**	**0**	**0**	**9**	....	....	....	....	....

• ASHBEE, BARRY *— see page 842*

• ASHWORTH, FRANK Frank Ashworth

C – L. 5'8", 155 lbs. b: Moose Jaw, Sask., 10/16/1927.

			REGULAR SEASON								PLAYOFFS				
Season	Club	League	GP	G	A	Pts	AG	AA	APts	PIM	GP	G	A	Pts	PIM
1943-44	New York Rovers	EHL	17	10	1	11	....	....	....	16	....	....	....	....	....
	Brooklyn Crescents	EHL	30	15	19	34	....	....	....	7	11	3	6	9	10
1944-45	Moose Jaw Canucks	SJHL	16	*22	13	35	....	....	....	26	21	17	*27	*44	24
1945-46	Moose Jaw Canucks	SJHL	16	*30	20	*50	....	....	....	17	4	5	5	10	4
1946-47	**Chicago Black Hawks**	**NHL**	**18**	**5**	**4**	**9**	**7**	**6**	**13**	**2**	....	....	....	....	....
	Kansas City Pla-Mors	USHL	47	17	23	40	....	....	....	47	....	....	....	....	....
1947-48	Kansas City Pla-Mors	USHL	66	19	27	46	....	....	....	40	25	6	12	18	28
1948-49	Hershey Bears	AHL	8	0	0	0	....	....	....	2	....	....	....	....	....
	Tulsa Oilers	USHL	58	36	60	96	....	....	....	27	7	3	5	8	14
1949-50	Tulsa Oilers	USHL	70	28	50	78	....	....	....	44	....	....	....	....	....
1950-51			DID NOT PLAY – SUSPENDED												
1951-52	Calgary Stampeders	PCHL	55	22	26	48	....	....	....	60	....	....	....	....	....
1952-53	Calgary Stampeders	WHL	70	15	26	41	....	....	....	66	5	3	3	6	0
1953-54	Calgary Stampeders	WHL	67	24	42	66	....	....	....	28	18	5	11	16	21
1954-55	Calgary–Vancouver	WHL	51	5	7	12	....	....	....	20	5	0	1	1	2
1955-56			DID NOT PLAY												
1956-57	Calgary Stampeders	WHL	48	11	20	31	....	....	....	33	3	0	1	1	0
	NHL Totals		**18**	**5**	**4**	**9**	**7**	**6**	**13**	**2**	....	....	....	....	....

USHL 2nd All-Star Team (1949)

• ASMUNDSON, OSCAR

Oscar "Ossie" Asmundson
C – R. 5'11", 170 lbs. b: Red Deer, Alta., 11/17/1908.

			REGULAR SEASON								PLAYOFFS				
Season	Club	League	GP	G	A	Pts	AG	AA	APts	PIM	GP	G	A	Pts	PIM
1928-29	Victoria Cubs	PCHL	29	2	2	4	....	....	....	6	....	....	....	....	....
1929-30	Victoria Cubs	PCHL	35	8	3	11	....	....	....	40	....	....	....	....	....
1930-31	Tacoma–Vancouver	PCHL	30	10	2	12	....	....	....	36	4	1	0	1	4
1931-32	Bronx Tigers	Can-Am	40	15	16	31	....	....	....	61	1	0	0	0	0
1932-33	**New York Rangers**	**NHL**	**48**	**5**	**10**	**15**	**12**	**26**	**38**	**20**	**8**	**0**	**2**	**2**	**4**
1933-34	**New York Rangers**	**NHL**	**46**	**2**	**6**	**8**	**4**	**16**	**20**	**8**	**1**	**0**	**0**	**0**	**0**
1934-35	**Detroit Red Wings**	**NHL**	**3**	**0**	**0**	**0**	**0**	**0**	**0**	**0**	....	....	....	....	....
	St. Louis Eagles	**NHL**	**11**	**4**	**7**	**11**	**8**	**16**	**24**	**2**	....	....	....	....	....
	Detroit Olympics	IAHL	18	8	8	16	....	....	....	20	....	....	....	....	....
1935-36	New Haven Eagles	Can-Am	25	4	11	15	....	....	....	26	....	....	....	....	....
1936-37	**New York Americans**	**NHL**	**1**	**0**	**0**	**0**	**0**	**0**	**0**	**0**	....	....	....	....	....
	New Haven Eagles	AHL	44	12	23	35	....	....	....	32	....	....	....	....	....
1937-38	**Montreal Canadiens**	**NHL**	**2**	**0**	**0**	**0**	**0**	**0**	**0**	**0**	....	....	....	....	....
	New Haven Eagles	AHL	44	13	26	39	....	....	....	57	2	0	0	0	0
1938-39	Cleveland Falcons	AHL	22	1	4	5	....	....	....	2	....	....	....	....	....
1939-40	Cleveland Barons	AHL	39	14	18	32	....	....	....	24	....	....	....	....	....
1940-41	Cleveland Barons	AHL	48	8	22	30	....	....	....	33	9	3	3	6	15
1941-42	Philadelphia Rockets	AHL	57	13	35	48	....	....	....	38	....	....	....	....	....
	Providence Reds	AHL	2	0	0	0	....	....	....	0	....	....	....	....	....
1942-43	Washington Lions	AHL	41	9	19	28	....	....	....	22	....	....	....	....	....
1943-44	Coast Guard Cutters	....	28	15	23	38	....	....	....	8	12	11	15	*26	....
	NHL Totals		**111**	**11**	**23**	**34**	**24**	**58**	**82**	**30**	**9**	**0**	**2**	**2**	**4**

Traded to **NY Rangers** by **Vancouver** (PCHL) for cash, October 25, 1931. Traded to **Detroit** by **NY Rangers** for cash, October 1, 1934. Signed as a free agent by **St. Louis** after securing release from **Detroit**, February 6, 1935. Signed as a free agent by **NY Americans**, February 14, 1937. Traded to **Montreal Canadiens** by **NY Americans** for cash, October 28, 1937. Traded to **Cleveland** (AHL) by **Montreal Canadiens** for cash, November, 1938.
• **Coast Guard Cutters** played exhibition season only in 1943-44.

• ATANAS, WALT

Walt "Ants" Atanas
RW – R. 5'8", 174 lbs. b: Hamilton, Ont., 12/22/1923. d: 8/8/1991.

Season	Club	League	GP	G	A	Pts	AG	AA	APts	PIM	GP	G	A	Pts	PIM
1942-43	Hamilton Whizzers	OHA	23	*37	12	49	....	....	....	21	5	1	1	2	10
1943-44	Buffalo Bisons	AHL	46	16	19	35	....	....	....	33	9	6	7	13	2
1944-45	**New York Rangers**	**NHL**	**49**	**13**	**8**	**21**	**18**	**13**	**31**	**40**	....	....	....	....	....
1945-46	Cleveland Barons	AHL	31	10	10	20	....	....	....	30	....	....	....	....	....
	Minneapolis Millers	USHL	22	11	10	21	....	....	....	46	....	....	....	....	....
1946-47	Minneapolis Millers	USHL	51	10	19	29	....	....	....	40	3	1	0	1	4
1947-48	Minneapolis Millers	USHL	66	25	38	63	....	....	....	59	10	6	2	8	8
1948-49	Minneapolis Millers	USHL	64	35	20	55	....	....	....	15	....	....	....	....	....
1949-50	Minneapolis Millers	USHL	69	24	28	52	....	....	....	49	7	*7	4	11	10
1950-51	Buffalo Bisons	AHL	61	19	26	45	....	....	....	23	4	0	0	0	8
1951-52	Buffalo Bisons	AHL	11	2	2	4	....	....	....	4	....	....	....	....	....
	Victoria Cougars	PCHL	36	21	8	29	....	....	....	32	13	3	6	9	11
1952-53	Vancouver Canucks	WHL	68	28	24	52	....	....	....	28	9	1	1	2	14
1953-54	Springfield Indians	QHL	18	7	15	22	....	....	....	24	....	....	....	....	....
	Syracuse Warriors	AHL	28	9	19	28	....	....	....	14	....	....	....	....	....
1954-55	Springfield Indians	AHL	62	29	45	74	....	....	....	66	4	0	1	1	2
1955-56	Springfield Indians	AHL	56	24	28	52	....	....	....	49	....	....	....	....	....
1956-57	North Bay Trappers	NOHA	52	15	31	46	....	....	....	35	13	4	5	9	6
	NHL Totals		**49**	**13**	**8**	**21**	**18**	**13**	**31**	**40**	....	....	....	....	....

Claimed by **NY Rangers** from **Buffalo** (AHL) in Inter-League Draft, May 12, 1944.

• AUBUCHON, OSSIE

Ossie Aubuchon
LW – L. 5'10", 175 lbs. b: St. Hyacinthe, Que., 1/1/1917.

Season	Club	League	GP	G	A	Pts	AG	AA	APts	PIM	GP	G	A	Pts	PIM
1934-35	Montreal Victorias	City Jr.	....	....	....	....	....	....	....	....	1	0	0	0	0
1935-36	Montreal Jr. Canadiens	City Jr.	1	1	0	1	....	....	....	0	....	....	....	....	....
	Montreal Sr. Canadiens	City Jr.	17	0	3	3	....	....	....	4	....	....	....	....	....
1936-37	Montreal Sr. Canadiens	City Jr.	17	7	2	9	....	....	....	16	....	....	....	....	....
1937-38	Brighton Tigers	Britain	....	19	12	31	....	....	....	....	....	....	....	....	....
1938-39	Brighton Tigers	Britain	....	30	14	44	....	....	....	....	....	....	....	....	....
1939-40	Pittsburgh Hornets	AHL	37	4	19	23	....	....	....	6	9	1	2	3	4
1940-41	Cleveland–New Haven	AHL	48	7	12	19	....	....	....	14	8	1	1	2	2
1941-42	Providence Reds	AHL	52	14	19	33	....	....	....	27	....	....	....	....	....
1942-43	**Boston Bruins**	**NHL**	**3**	**3**	**0**	**3**	**4**	**0**	**4**	**0**	**6**	**1**	**0**	**1**	**0**
	Providence Reds	AHL	45	29	35	64	....	....	....	9	....	....	....	....	....
1943-44	**Boston Bruins**	**NHL**	**9**	**1**	**0**	**1**	**1**	**0**	**1**	**0**	....	....	....	....	....
	New York Rangers	**NHL**	**38**	**15**	**12**	**27**	**19**	**14**	**33**	**4**	....	....	....	....	....
1944-45	Buffalo Bisons	AHL	57	13	17	30	....	....	....	9	2	0	0	0	0
1945-46	Hershey–St. Louis	AHL	35	9	10	19	....	....	....	14	....	....	....	....	....
1946-47	Shawinigan Cataracts	QSHL	10	6	1	7	....	....	....	2	....	....	....	....	....
	St. Hyacinthe Gaulois	QPHL	37	26	32	58	....	....	....	10	4	0	2	2	0
	NHL Totals		**50**	**19**	**12**	**31**	**24**	**14**	**38**	**4**	**6**	**1**	**0**	**1**	**0**

Traded to **Boston** by **Providence** (AHL) for cash, March 8, 1943. Traded to **NY Rangers** by **Boston** for cash, November, 1943.

• AURIE, LARRY

Larry "Little Dempsey" Aurie
RW – R. 5'6", 148 lbs. b: Sudbury, Ont., 2/8/1905. d: 12/11/1952.

			REGULAR SEASON								PLAYOFFS				
Season	Club	League	GP	G	A	Pts	AG	AA	APts	PIM	GP	G	A	Pts	PIM
1921-22	Sudbury Cub Wolves	NOHA	4	5	2	7	....	....	....	2	2	2	1	3	0
1922-23	St. Michael's Majors	OHA	7	*16	4	*20	....	....	....	....	3	2	0	2	....
1923-24	Sudbury Wolves	NOHA	STATISTICS NOT AVAILABLE												
1924-25	Sudbury Wolves	NOHA	STATISTICS NOT AVAILABLE												
1925-26	Galt Terriers	OHA Sr.	20	11	4	15	....	....	....	35	2	0	0	0	0
1926-27	London Panthers	Can-Pro	32	14	7	21	....	....	....	38	4	4	0	4	4
1927-28	**Detroit Cougars**	**NHL**	**44**	**13**	**3**	**16**	**40**	**25**	**65**	**43**	....	....	....	....	....
1928-29	**Detroit Cougars**	**NHL**	**35**	**1**	**1**	**2**	**4**	**9**	**13**	**26**	**2**	**1**	**0**	**1**	**2**
1929-30	**Detroit Cougars**	**NHL**	**43**	**14**	**5**	**19**	**28**	**16**	**44**	**28**	....	....	....	....	....
1930-31	**Detroit Falcons**	**NHL**	**41**	**12**	**6**	**18**	**29**	**22**	**51**	**23**	....	....	....	....	....
1931-32	**Detroit Falcons**	**NHL**	**48**	**12**	**8**	**20**	**26**	**22**	**48**	**18**	**2**	**0**	**0**	**0**	**0**
1932-33	**Detroit Red Wings**	**NHL**	**45**	**12**	**11**	**23**	**28**	**29**	**57**	**25**	**4**	**1**	**0**	**1**	**4**
1933-34	**Detroit Red Wings**	**NHL**	**48**	**16**	**19**	**35**	**36**	**51**	**87**	**36**	**9**	**3**	**7**	**10**	**2**
1934-35	**Detroit Red Wings**	**NHL**	**48**	**17**	**29**	**46**	**36**	**65**	**101**	**24**	....	....	....	....	....
1935-36	**Detroit Red Wings**	**NHL**	**44**	**16**	**18**	**34**	**40**	**44**	**84**	**17**	**7**	**1**	**2**	**3**	**2**
1936-37	**Detroit Red Wings**	**NHL**	**45**	***23**	**20**	**43**	**50**	**47**	**97**	**20**	....	....	....	....	....
1937-38	**Detroit Red Wings**	**NHL**	**47**	**10**	**9**	**19**	**21**	**18**	**39**	**19**	....	....	....	....	....
1938-39	**Detroit Red Wings**	**NHL**	**1**	**1**	**0**	**1**	**2**	**0**	**2**	**0**	....	....	....	....	....
	Pittsburgh Hornets	AHL	39	8	19	27	....	....	....	16	....	....	....	....	....
1939-40	Pittsburgh Hornets	AHL	39	12	12	29	....	....	....	12	9	3	8	11	4
1940-41	Pittsburgh Hornets	AHL	6	0	3	3	....	....	....	2	....	....	....	....	....
1941-42	Pittsburgh Hornets	AHL	DID NOT PLAY – COACHING												
1942-43	Pittsburgh Hornets	AHL	DID NOT PLAY – COACHING												
1943-44	Pittsburgh Hornets	AHL	1	0	0	0	....	....	....	0	....	....	....	....	....
	NHL Totals		**489**	**147**	**129**	**276**	**340**	**348**	**688**	**279**	**24**	**6**	**9**	**15**	**10**

NHL First All-Star Team (1937) • AHL Second All-Star Team (1939)

Played in NHL All-Star Game (1934)

Signed as a free agent by **London** (Can-Pro), November 14, 1926. Claimed by **Detroit** from **London** (Can-Pro) in Inter-League Draft, September 26, 1927.

• AWREY, DON

— see page 845

• AYRES, VERN

Vern Ayres
D – L. 6'2", 220 lbs. b: Toronto, Ont., 4/27/1909. d: 2/18/1968.

Season	Club	League	GP	G	A	Pts	AG	AA	APts	PIM	GP	G	A	Pts	PIM
1927-28	Parkdale Canoe Club	OHA	9	3	1	4	....	....	....	....	1	0	0	0	....
1928-29			DID NOT PLAY												
1929-30	Toronto Young Rangers	OHA	STATISTICS NOT AVAILABLE												
1930-31	**New York Americans**	**NHL**	**26**	**2**	**1**	**3**	**5**	**4**	**9**	**54**	....	....	....	....	....
	New Haven Eagles	Can-Am	8	1	0	1	....	....	....	22	....	....	....	....	....
1931-32	**New York Americans**	**NHL**	**45**	**2**	**4**	**6**	**4**	**11**	**15**	**82**	....	....	....	....	....
1932-33	**New York Americans**	**NHL**	**48**	**0**	**3**	**3**	**0**	**8**	**8**	**97**	....	....	....	....	....
1933-34	**Montreal Canadiens**	**NHL**	**17**	**0**	**0**	**0**	**0**	**0**	**0**	**19**	....	....	....	....	....
	Quebec Castors	Can-Am	29	0	4	4	....	....	....	52	....	....	....	....	....
1934-35	**St. Louis Eagles**	**NHL**	**47**	**2**	**2**	**4**	**4**	**4**	**8**	**60**	....	....	....	....	....
1935-36	**New York Rangers**	**NHL**	**28**	**0**	**4**	**4**	**0**	**10**	**10**	**38**	....	....	....	....	....
	Philadelphia	AHL	20	4	6	10	....	....	....	26	4	0	0	0	8
1936-37	Philadelphia Ramblers	AHL	45	4	7	11	....	....	....	44	6	0	0	0	2
1937-38	Philadelphia Ramblers	AHL	44	1	11	12	....	....	....	34	5	0	1	1	2
1938-39	Hershey Bears	AHL	52	3	5	8	....	....	....	19	5	0	1	1	0
1939-40	Pittsburgh Hornets	AHL	54	0	10	10	....	....	....	37	1	0	2	2	2
1940-41	St. Louis Flyers	AHA	38	1	7	8	....	....	....	20	9	0	2	2	2
1941-42	St. Louis Flyers	AHA	45	2	9	11	....	....	....	36	3	1	0	1	6
	NHL Totals		**211**	**6**	**14**	**20**	**13**	**37**	**50**	**350**	....	....	....	....	....

Traded to **Montreal Maroons** by **NY Americans** for $6,000, June 1, 1933. Traded to **St. Louis** by **Montreal Maroons** with Normie Smith to complete transaction that sent Al Shields to Montreal Maroons (September 20, 1934), October 22, 1934. Claimed by **NY Rangers** from **St. Louis** in Dispersal Draft, October 15, 1935.

• BABANDO, PETE

Pete Babando
LW – L. 5'9", 187 lbs. b: Braeburn, PA, 5/10/1925.

Season	Club	League	GP	G	A	Pts	AG	AA	APts	PIM	GP	G	A	Pts	PIM
1943-44	Galt Kists	OHA	6	2	0	2	....	....	....	10	....	....	....	....	....
1944-45	Galt Red Wings	OHA	19	13	10	23	....	....	....	30	4	1	2	3	2
1945-46	Boston Olympics	EHL	32	25	10	35	....	....	....	50	12	8	8	16	10
1946-47	Hershey Bears	AHL	51	19	26	45	....	....	....	81	11	2	0	2	0
1947-48	**Boston Bruins**	**NHL**	**60**	**23**	**11**	**34**	**34**	**16**	**50**	**52**	**5**	**1**	**1**	**2**	**2**
1948-49	**Boston Bruins**	**NHL**	**58**	**19**	**14**	**33**	**30**	**22**	**52**	**34**	**4**	**0**	**0**	**0**	**2**
1949-50	**Detroit Red Wings**	**NHL**	**56**	**6**	**6**	**12**	**8**	**8**	**16**	**25**	**8**	**2**	**2**	**4**	**2**
1950-51	**Chicago Black Hawks**	**NHL**	**70**	**18**	**19**	**37**	**24**	**24**	**48**	**36**	....	....	....	....	....
1951-52	**Chicago Black Hawks**	**NHL**	**49**	**11**	**14**	**25**	**15**	**18**	**33**	**29**	....	....	....	....	....
1952-53	**Chicago Black Hawks**	**NHL**	**29**	**5**	**5**	**10**	**8**	**7**	**15**	**14**	....	....	....	....	....
	New York Rangers	**NHL**	**29**	**4**	**4**	**8**	**6**	**6**	**12**	**4**	....	....	....	....	....
1953-54	Buffalo Bisons	AHL	63	21	43	64	....	....	....	46	3	2	0	2	2
1954-55	Buffalo Bisons	AHL	59	20	30	50	....	....	....	61	10	5	6	11	6
1955-56	Buffalo Bisons	AHL	59	26	19	45	....	....	....	65	5	1	1	2	2
1956-57	Buffalo Bisons	AHL	33	7	9	16	....	....	....	30	....	....	....	....	....
1957-58	North Bay Trappers	NOHA	16	9	8	17	....	....	....	44	....	....	....	....	....
1958-59	Whitby Dunlops	OHA Sr.	50	22	27	49	....	....	....	28	9	3	5	8	8
1959-60	Whitby Dunlops	OHA Sr.	53	28	34	62	....	....	....	48	10	8	3	11	12
1960-61	Clinton Comets	EHL	1	0	0	0	....	....	....	2	....	....	....	....	....
1961-62	Clinton Comets	EHL	67	43	68	111	....	....	....	37	6	2	3	5	4
1962-63	Clinton Comets	EHL	66	55	83	138	....	....	....	26	13	9	*22	*31	16
1963-64	Clinton Comets	EHL	68	26	65	91	....	....	....	34	15	12	11	*23	34
1964-65	Clinton Comets	EHL	61	37	65	102	....	....	....	26	11	8	6	14	2
1965-66	Clinton Comets	EHL	1	1	0	1	....	....	....	0	....	....	....	....	....
1966-67	Clinton Comets	EHL	71	39	49	88	....	....	....	101	9	2	4	6	4
	NHL Totals		**351**	**86**	**73**	**159**	**125**	**101**	**226**	**194**	**17**	**3**	**3**	**6**	**6**

EHL 2nd All-Star Team (1962) • EHL 1st All-Star Team (1963) • EHL North 2nd All-Star Team (1967)

Traded to **Detroit** by **Boston** with Claire Martin, Lloyd Durham and Jimmy Peters Sr. for Bill Quackenbush and Pete Horeck, August 16, 1949. Traded to **Chicago** by **Detroit** with Harry Lumley, Jack Stewart, Al Dewsbury and Don Morrison for Jim Henry, Bob Goldham, Gaye Stewart and Metro Prystai, July 13, 1950. Traded to **NY Rangers** by **Chicago** for cash, January 9, 1953. Traded to **Montreal** by **NY Rangers** with Eddie Slowinski for Ivan Irwin, August 8, 1953. Traded to **Buffalo** (AHL) by **Montreal** with Gaye Stewart and Eddie Slowinski for Jackie LeClair and cash, August, 1954.

• BACKOR, PETER Peter Backor

D – L. 6', 190 lbs. b: Fort William, Ont., 4/29/1919.

Season	Club	League	GP	G	A	Pts	AG	AA	APts	PIM	GP	G	A	Pts	PIM
			REGULAR SEASON								PLAYOFFS				
1938-39	Fort William Forts	TBSHL	23	9	6	15	....	....	....	6	....	....	....	....	....
1939-40	St. Catharines Saints	OHA Sr.	29	27	17	44	....	....	....	28	8	2	2	4	6
1940-41	St. Catharines Saints	OHA Sr.	31	14	9	23	....	....	....	20	12	2	7	9	12
1941-42	St. Catharines Saints	OHA Sr.	27	7	7	14	....	....	....	26	11	2	4	6	11
1942-43	St. Catharines Saints	OHA Sr.	20	7	12	19	....	....	....	24	4	3	1	4	11
1943-44	St. Catharines Saints	OHA Sr.	28	11	12	23	....	....	....	27	5	0	1	1	4
	Montreal Royals	QSHL	....	....	....	....	....	....	....	....	1	1	0	1	0
	Port Arthur Shipbuilders	TBSHL	....	....	....	....	....	....	....	....	9	1	1	2	4
1944-45	**Toronto Maple Leafs**	**NHL**	**36**	**4**	**5**	**9**	**5**	**8**	**13**	**6**	....	....	....	....	....
1945-46	Pittsburgh Hornets	AHL	61	5	26	31	....	....	....	65	6	1	1	2	4
1946-47	Hollywood Wolves	PCHL	16	5	5	10	....	....	....	24	....	....	....	....	....
	Pittsburgh Hornets	AHL	48	9	10	19	....	....	....	30	12	2	1	3	6
1947-48	Pittsburgh Hornets	AHL	68	14	39	53	....	....	....	63	2	0	0	0	0
1948-49	Pittsburgh Hornets	AHL	68	10	42	52	....	....	....	64	....	....	....	....	....
1949-50	Pittsburgh Hornets	AHL	63	8	29	37	....	....	....	34	....	....	....	....	....
1950-51	Pittsburgh Hornets	AHL	71	7	33	40	....	....	....	80	13	0	4	4	8
1951-52	Pittsburgh Hornets	AHL	57	3	18	21	....	....	....	49	11	0	0	0	10
1952-53	Pittsburgh Hornets	AHL	53	1	10	11	....	....	....	36	3	0	1	1	16
1953-54	Pittsburgh Hornets	AHL	45	3	11	14	....	....	....	21	5	0	0	0	4
1954-55	Sault Ste. Marie Indians	NOHA	34	6	8	14	....	....	....	24	6	3	0	3	6
1955-56	Sault Ste. Marie Indians	NOHA	2	0	1	1	....	....	....	0	2	0	0	0	2
	NHL Totals		**36**	**4**	**5**	**9**	**5**	**8**	**13**	**6**	....	....	....	....	....

AHL 1st All-Star Team (1946, 1948, 1949, 1950, 1951)

• BACKSTROM, RALPH — *see page 847*

• BAILEY, ACE Ace (Irvine) Bailey HHOF

RW – R. 5'10", 160 lbs. b: Bracebridge, Ont., 7/3/1903. d: 4/7/1992.

Season	Club	League	GP	G	A	Pts	AG	AA	APts	PIM	GP	G	A	Pts	PIM
1922-23	Toronto St. Mary's	OHA	4	2	1	3	....	....	....	....	4	2	1	3	....
1923-24	Toronto St. Mary's	OHA Sr.	8	10	0	10	....	....	....	....	....	....	....	....	....
1924-25	Peterborough Seniors	OHA Sr.	8	5	0	5	....	....	....	....	2	3	0	3	2
1925-26	Peterborough Seniors	OHA Sr.	9	9	2	11	....	....	....	2	2	2	1	*3	....
1926-27	**Toronto Maple Leafs**	**NHL**	**42**	**15**	**13**	**28**	**44**	**113**	**157**	**82**	....	....	....	....	....
1927-28	**Toronto Maple Leafs**	**NHL**	**43**	**9**	**3**	**12**	**28**	**25**	**53**	**72**	....	....	....	....	....
1928-29	**Toronto Maple Leafs**	**NHL**	**44**	**22**	**10**	***32**	**90**	**93**	**183**	**78**	**4**	**1**	**2**	**3**	**4**
1929-30	**Toronto Maple Leafs**	**NHL**	**43**	**22**	**21**	**43**	**44**	**69**	**113**	**69**	....	....	....	....	....
1930-31	**Toronto Maple Leafs**	**NHL**	**40**	**23**	**19**	**42**	**57**	**70**	**127**	**46**	**2**	**1**	**1**	**2**	**0**
1931-32	**Toronto Maple Leafs**	**NHL**	**41**	**8**	**5**	**13**	**17**	**14**	**31**	**62**	**7**	**1**	**0**	**1**	**4**
1932-33	**Toronto Maple Leafs**	**NHL**	**47**	**10**	**8**	**18**	**23**	**21**	**44**	**52**	**8**	**0**	**1**	**1**	**4**
1933-34	**Toronto Maple Leafs**	**NHL**	**13**	**2**	**3**	**5**	**4**	**8**	**12**	**11**	....	....	....	....	....
	NHL Totals		**313**	**111**	**82**	**193**	**307**	**413**	**720**	**472**	**21**	**3**	**4**	**7**	**12**

NHL Scoring Leader (1929)

Signed as a free agent by **Toronto St. Pats**, November 3, 1926. • Suffered career-ending head injury in game vs. Boston, December 12, 1933.

• BAILEY, BOB Bob "Bashin' Bob" Bailey

RW – R. 5'11", 180 lbs. b: Kenora, Ont., 5/29/1931.

Season	Club	League	GP	G	A	Pts	AG	AA	APts	PIM	GP	G	A	Pts	PIM
1947-48	Detroit–Windsor	IHL	22	2	7	9	....	....	....	14	8	0	0	0	10
1948-49	Kenora Thistles	City Sr.	14	5	10	15	....	....	....	*51	5	2	3	5	8
1949-50	Windsor Spitfires	OHA	48	10	17	27	....	....	....	66	11	1	5	6	20
1950-51	Stratford Kroehlers	OHA	53	21	45	66	....	....	....	109	3	1	0	1	2
1951-52	Stratford Kroehlers	OHA	DID NOT PLAY – INJURED												
	Toledo Mercury's	IHL	2	0	3	3	....	....	....	0	....	....	....	....	....
1952-53	Cleveland Barons	AHL	54	11	35	46	....	....	....	*115	10	2	2	4	33
1953-54	**Toronto Maple Leafs**	**NHL**	**48**	**2**	**7**	**9**	**3**	**9**	**12**	**70**	**5**	**0**	**2**	**2**	**4**
	Ottawa Senators	QHL	2	0	0	0	....	....	....	12	....	....	....	....	....
	Pittsburgh Hornets	AHL	7	2	3	5	....	....	....	10	....	....	....	....	....
1954-55	**Toronto Maple Leafs**	**NHL**	**32**	**4**	**2**	**6**	**6**	**3**	**9**	**52**	**1**	**0**	**0**	**0**	**0**
	Pittsburgh Hornets	AHL	26	9	19	28	....	....	....	23	5	0	8	8	*24
1955-56	**Toronto Maple Leafs**	**NHL**	**6**	**0**	**0**	**0**	**0**	**0**	**0**	**6**	....	....	....	....	....
	Pittsburgh Hornets	AHL	48	6	30	36	....	....	....	98	4	2	1	3	4
1956-57	Springfield Indians	AHL	40	11	33	44	....	....	....	83	....	....	....	....	....
	Detroit Red Wings	**NHL**	....	....	....	....	....	....	....	....	**5**	**0**	**2**	**2**	**2**
1957-58	**Chicago Black Hawks**	**NHL**	**28**	**3**	**6**	**9**	**4**	**6**	**10**	**38**	....	....	....	....	....
	Detroit Red Wings	**NHL**	**36**	**6**	**6**	**12**	**8**	**6**	**14**	**41**	**4**	**0**	**0**	**0**	**16**
1958-59	Cleveland Barons	AHL	64	28	41	69	....	....	....	153	7	4	3	7	16
1959-60	Cleveland–Buffalo	AHL	34	6	24	30	....	....	....	67	....	....	....	....	....
1960-61	Quebec Aces	AHL	38	6	11	17	....	....	....	91	....	....	....	....	....
1961-62	Pittsburgh Hornets	AHL	27	3	17	20	....	....	....	91	....	....	....	....	....
	San Francisco Seals	WHL	12	2	6	8	....	....	....	12	2	0	0	0	16
1962-63	San Francisco Seals	WHL	11	0	6	6	....	....	....	14	....	....	....	....	....
	Philadelphia Ramblers	EHL	50	26	65	91	....	....	....	64	3	0	3	3	10
1963-64	Philadelphia Ramblers	EHL	7	2	4	6	....	....	....	67	....	....	....	....	....
	Fort Wayne Komets	IHL	22	12	19	31	....	....	....	64	....	....	....	....	....
1964-65	Dayton Gems	IHL	54	31	56	87	....	....	....	102	....	....	....	....	....
1965-66	Dayton Gems	IHL	61	45	87	132	....	....	....	127	10	9	8	17	53
1966-67	Dayton Gems	IHL	35	13	36	49	....	....	....	59	4	3	1	4	8
1967-68	Dayton Gems	IHL	24	15	36	51	....	....	....	93	....	....	....	....	....
	NHL Totals		**150**	**15**	**21**	**36**	**21**	**24**	**45**	**207**	**15**	**0**	**4**	**4**	**22**

Traded to **Cleveland** (AHL) by **Detroit** with John Bailey for the rights to Lou Jankowski and Bill Dineen, June, 1951. Traded to **Toronto** by **Cleveland** (AHL) with Gerry Foley and Chuck Blair for $30,000, July, 1953. • Suspended by AHL for remainder of 1955 AHL playoffs for assaulting referee Jerry Olinski, April 2, 1950. Traded to **Springfield** (AHL) by **Toronto** for $15,000, July, 1956. Traded to **Detroit** by **Springfield** (AHL) for cash, September 22, 1956. Loaned to **Springfield** (AHL) by **Detroit** for 1956-57 season, September, 1956. Selected by **Chicago** from **Detroit** in Intra-League Draft, June 5, 1957. Traded to **Detroit** by **Chicago** with Jack McIntyre, Nick Mickoski and Hec Lalonde for Earl Reibel, Billy Dea, Lorne Ferguson and Bill Dineen, December 17, 1957. Traded to **Cleveland** (AHL) by **Detroit** for cash, July 31, 1958. Traded to **Buffalo** (AHL) by **Cleveland** (AHL) for Bill Dineen, October 20, 1959. Traded to **Montreal** by **Chicago** (Buffalo - AHL) with Glen Skov, the rights to Danny Lewicki, Terry Gray and Lorne Ferguson for Cec Hoekstra, Reggie Fleming, Ab McDonald and Bob Courcy, June 7, 1960.

• BALDWIN, DOUG Doug Baldwin

D – L. 6', 175 lbs. b: Winnipeg, Man., 11/2/1922.

Season	Club	League	GP	G	A	Pts	AG	AA	APts	PIM	GP	G	A	Pts	PIM
			REGULAR SEASON								PLAYOFFS				
1939-40	Winnipeg Rangers	MJHL	2	0	0	0	....	....	....	2	....	....	....	....	....
1940-41	Winnipeg Rangers	MJHL	17	12	5	17	....	....	....	35	13	3	3	6	10
1941-42	Winnipeg Falcons	MJHL	14	12	6	18	....	....	....	27	6	4	5	9	19
1942-43	Quebec Aces	QSHL	33	0	5	5	....	....	....	4	4	0	1	1	2
1943-44	Quebec Aces	QSHL	25	7	15	22	....	....	....	46	15	7	8	15	26
1944-45	Quebec Aces	QSHL	17	5	18	23	....	....	....	44	5	2	2	4	0
1945-46	**Toronto Maple Leafs**	**NHL**	**15**	**0**	**1**	**1**	**0**	**2**	**2**	**6**	....	....	....	....	....
	Pittsburgh Hornets	AHL	4	2	2	4	....	....	....	4	....	....	....	....	....
1946-47	**Detroit Red Wings**	**NHL**	**4**	**0**	**0**	**0**	**0**	**0**	**0**	**0**	....	....	....	....	....
	Kansas City Pla-Mors	USHL	43	8	16	24	....	....	....	57	12	1	6	7	23
1947-48	**Chicago Black Hawks**	**NHL**	**5**	**0**	**0**	**0**	**0**	**0**	**0**	**2**	....	....	....	....	....
	Kansas City Pla-Mors	USHL	58	21	42	63	....	....	....	70	4	0	0	0	0
1948-49	Kansas City Pla-Mors	USHL	38	10	27	37	....	....	....	28	....	....	....	....	....
	Cleveland Barons	AHL	21	3	4	7	....	....	....	14	....	....	....	....	....
1949-50	Kansas City Mohawks	USHL	70	12	36	48	....	....	....	58	3	1	0	1	2
1950-51			DID NOT PLAY												
1954-55	Grand Rapids Rockets	IHL	13	1	6	7	....	....	....	4	....	....	....	....	....
1955-56	Windsor Bulldogs	OHA Sr.	6	0	0	0	....	....	....	43	....	....	....	....	....
	Chatham Maroons	OHA Sr.	35	6	14	20	....	....	....	0	11	1	6	7	14
1956-57	Chatham Maroons	OHA Sr.	39	5	18	23	....	....	....	40	6	1	3	4	6
1957-58	Toledo Mercurys	IHL	63	6	22	28	....	....	....	39	....	....	....	....	....
1958-59	Toledo Mercurys	IHL	26	2	5	7	....	....	....	12	....	....	....	....	....
	Washington Presidents	EHL	11	1	6	7	....	....	....	10	....	....	....	....	....
	NHL Totals		**24**	**0**	**1**	**1**	**0**	**2**	**2**	**8**	....	....	....	....	....

USHL 1st All-Star Team (1947, 1948) • USHL 2nd All-Star Team (1950)

Traded to **Detroit** by **Toronto** with Ray Powell for Gerry Brown, September 21, 1946. Traded to **Chicago** by **Detroit** for cash, June, 1947.

• BALFOUR, EARL Earl "Spider" Balfour

LW – L. 6'1", 180 lbs. b: Toronto, Ont., 1/4/1933.

Season	Club	League	GP	G	A	Pts	AG	AA	APts	PIM	GP	G	A	Pts	PIM
1949-50	Toronto Marlboros	OHA	2	0	0	0	....	....	....	2	....	....	....	....	....
1950-51	Toronto Marlboros	OHA	53	10	16	26	....	....	....	53	13	6	4	10	16
1951-52	Toronto Marlboros	OHA	51	10	29	39	....	....	....	75	6	3	3	6	8
	Toronto Maple Leafs	**NHL**	**3**	**0**	**0**	**0**	**0**	**0**	**0**	**2**	**1**	**0**	**0**	**0**	**0**
1952-53	Pittsburgh Hornets	AHL	63	14	30	44	....	....	....	33	10	0	4	4	14
1953-54	**Toronto Maple Leafs**	**NHL**	**17**	**0**	**1**	**1**	**0**	**1**	**1**	**6**	....	....	....	....	....
	Pittsburgh Hornets	AHL	51	16	22	38	....	....	....	29	4	1	1	2	0
1954-55	Pittsburgh Hornets	AHL	63	17	31	48	....	....	....	42	10	2	*9	11	9
1955-56	**Toronto Maple Leafs**	**NHL**	**59**	**14**	**5**	**19**	**20**	**6**	**26**	**40**	**3**	**0**	**1**	**1**	**2**
1956-57	Rochester Americans	AHL	63	21	16	37	....	....	....	38	10	3	5	8	6
1957-58	**Toronto Maple Leafs**	**NHL**	**1**	**0**	**0**	**0**	**0**	**0**	**0**	**0**	....	....	....	....	....
	Rochester Americans	AHL	70	27	31	58	....	....	....	58	....	....	....	....	....
1958-59	**Chicago Black Hawks**	**NHL**	**70**	**10**	**8**	**18**	**13**	**8**	**21**	**10**	**6**	**0**	**2**	**2**	**0**
1959-60	**Chicago Black Hawks**	**NHL**	**70**	**3**	**5**	**8**	**4**	**5**	**9**	**16**	**4**	**0**	**0**	**0**	**0**
1960-61	**Chicago Black Hawks**	**NHL**	**68**	**3**	**3**	**6**	**4**	**3**	**7**	**4**	**12**	**0**	**0**	**0**	**2**
1961-62	Pittsburgh Hornets	AHL	64	19	19	38	....	....	....	28	....	....	....	....	....
1962-63	Pittsburgh Hornets	AHL	71	7	15	22	....	....	....	30	....	....	....	....	....
1963-64			REINSTATED AS AN AMATEUR												
1964-65	Galt Hornets	OHA Sr.	34	19	23	42	....	....	....	18	4	4	6	10	6
1965-66	Galt Hornets	OHA Sr.	42	22	28	50	....	....	....	33	....	....	....	....	....
1966-67	Galt Hornets	OHA Sr.	39	21	15	36	....	....	....	32	....	....	....	....	....
1967-68	Toronto Marlboros	OHA Sr.	36	22	22	44	....	....	....	12	....	....	....	....	....
1968-69	Orillia Terriers	OHA Sr.	37	4	13	17	....	....	....	10	....	....	....	....	....
	NHL Totals		**288**	**30**	**22**	**52**	**41**	**23**	**64**	**78**	**26**	**0**	**3**	**3**	**4**

Claimed by **Chicago** from **Toronto** in Intra-League Draft, June 6, 1958. Claimed by **Boston** from **Chicago** in Intra-League Draft, June, 1961.

• BALFOUR, MURRAY Murray Balfour

RW – R. 5'9", 178 lbs. b: Regina, Sask., 8/24/1936. d: 5/30/1965.

Season	Club	League	GP	G	A	Pts	AG	AA	APts	PIM	GP	G	A	Pts	PIM
1952-53	Regina Pats	WCJHL	31	2	4	6	....	....	....	38	7	0	1	1	10
1953-54	Regina Pats	WCJHL	35	7	5	12	....	....	....	*99	16	4	4	8	*45
1954-55	Regina Pats	WCJHL	38	10	16	26	....	....	....	*156	12	7	4	11	*30
1955-56	Regina Pats	WCJHL	34	24	18	42	....	....	....	*104	10	7	5	12	20
1956-57	Hull Ottawa Canadiens	Ott-Jr.	19	12	7	19	....	....	....	76	....	....	....	....	....
	Hull-Ottawa Canadiens	QHL	18	2	6	8	....	....	....	15	....	....	....	....	....
	Hull-Ottawa Canadiens	EOHL	14	5	10	15	....	....	....	41	....	....	....	....	....
	Montreal Canadiens	**NHL**	**2**	**0**	**0**	**0**	**0**	**0**	**0**	**2**	....	....	....	....	....
1957-58	**Montreal Canadiens**	**NHL**	**3**	**1**	**1**	**2**	**1**	**1**	**2**	**4**	....	....	....	....	....
	Montreal Royals	QHL	62	23	25	48	....	....	....	107	7	1	2	3	20
1958-59	Rochester Americans	AHL	67	14	23	37	....	....	....	*181	1	0	0	0	0
1959-60	**Chicago Black Hawks**	**NHL**	**61**	**18**	**12**	**30**	**22**	**12**	**34**	**55**	**4**	**1**	**0**	**1**	**0**
1960-61	**Chicago Black Hawks**	**NHL**	**70**	**21**	**27**	**48**	**26**	**27**	**53**	**123**	**11**	**5**	**5**	**10**	**14**
1961-62	**Chicago Black Hawks**	**NHL**	**49**	**15**	**15**	**30**	**18**	**15**	**33**	**72**	**12**	**1**	**1**	**2**	**15**
1962-63	**Chicago Black Hawks**	**NHL**	**65**	**10**	**23**	**33**	**12**	**24**	**36**	**75**	**6**	**0**	**2**	**2**	**12**
1963-64	**Chicago Black Hawks**	**NHL**	**41**	**2**	**10**	**12**	**3**	**11**	**14**	**36**	**7**	**2**	**2**	**4**	**4**
1964-65	**Boston Bruins**	**NHL**	**15**	**0**	**2**	**2**	**0**	**2**	**2**	**26**	....	....	....	....	....
	Hershey Bears	AHL	31	10	8	18	....	....	....	36	....	....	....	....	....
	NHL Totals		**306**	**67**	**90**	**157**	**82**	**92**	**174**	**393**	**40**	**9**	**10**	**19**	**45**

Traded to **Chicago** by **Montreal** for cash, June 9, 1959. Traded to **Boston** by **Chicago** with Mike Draper for Matt Ravlich and Jerry Toppazzini, June 9, 1964.

• BALON, DAVE — *see page 850*

• BALUIK, STANLEY Stanley Baluik

C – L. 5′8″, 160 lbs. b: Port Arthur, Ont., 10/5/1935.

			REGULAR SEASON								PLAYOFFS				
Season	Club	League	GP	G	A	Pts	AG	AA	APts	PIM	GP	G	A	Pts	PIM
1950-51	Fort William Canadians	NOHA	12	4	3	7	....	....	....	8	3	0	2	2	0
1951-52	Fort William Canadians	NOHA	30	25	14	39	....	....	....	39	....	....	....	....	....
1952-53	Fort William Canadians	NOHA	30	27	*33	60	....	....	....	40	6	0	5	5	4
1953-54	Fort William Canadians	NOHA	34	35	*50	*85	....	....	....	30	4	3	4	7	6
1954-55	Kitchener Canucks	OHA	49	20	*51	71	....	....	....	122	....	....	....	....	....
	Montreal Royals	QHL	2	0	0	0	....	....	....	0	....	....	....	....	....
1955-56	Kitchener Canucks	OHA	48	31	*73	*104	....	....	....	46	8	2	10	12	30
1956-57	Chicoutimi Sagueneens	QHL	68	16	20	36	....	....	....	36	10	1	3	4	12
1957-58	Victoria Cougars	WHL	32	13	15	28	....	....	....	45	....	....	....	....	....
	Springfield Indians	AHL	5	2	0	2	....	....	....	8	....	....	....	....	....
1958-59	Victoria Cougars	WHL	55	28	26	54	....	....	....	57	3	1	1	2	0
1959-60	**Boston Bruins**	**NHL**	**7**	**0**	**0**	**0**	**0**	**0**	**0**	**2**	....	....	....	....	....
	Providence Reds	AHL	65	23	57	80	....	....	....	60	5	2	3	5	2
1960-61	Providence Reds	AHL	71	26	37	63	....	....	....	67	....	....	....	....	....
1961-62	Providence Reds	AHL	69	25	56	81	....	....	....	55	3	1	0	1	6
1962-63	Providence Reds	AHL	72	23	58	81	....	....	....	52	6	2	3	5	4
1963-64	Providence Reds	AHL	65	27	41	68	....	....	....	55	3	1	2	3	4
	NHL Totals		**7**	**0**	**0**	**0**	**0**	**0**	**0**	**2**	....	....	....	....	....

Won Dudley "Red" Garrett Memorial Award (Top Rookie - AHL) (1960)

• BARBE, ANDY Andy Barbe

RW – R. 6′, 170 lbs. b: Coniston, Ont., 7/27/1923.

Season	Club	League	GP	G	A	Pts	AG	AA	APts	PIM	GP	G	A	Pts	PIM
1941-42	Falconbridge Falcons	Jr. B	8	3	3	6	....	....	....	6	2	0	0	0	10
1942-43			MILITARY SERVICE												
1943-44			MILITARY SERVICE												
1944-45	Sudbury Open Pit Miners	City Sr.	8	4	4	8	....	....	....	9	3	1	2	3	0
1945-46	Oakland Oaks	PCHL	40	11	11	22	....	....	....	76	2	1	0	1	0
1946-47	Los Angeles Monarchs	PCHL	54	55	39	94	....	....	....	55	11	*12	4	16	2
1947-48	Los Angeles Monarchs	PCHL	57	42	38	80	....	....	....	95	4	1	0	1	0
1948-49	Los Angeles Monarchs	PCHL	70	42	35	77	....	....	....	32	7	5	2	7	0
1949-50	Pittsburgh Hornets	AHL	64	25	8	33	....	....	....	12	....	....	....	....	....
1950-51	**Toronto Maple Leafs**	**NHL**	**1**	**0**	**0**	**0**	**0**	**0**	**0**	**2**	....	....	....	....	....
	Pittsburgh Hornets	AHL	67	23	28	51	....	....	....	20	13	9	5	14	0
1951-52	Pittsburgh Hornets	AHL	68	22	40	62	....	....	....	16	11	3	6	9	2
1952-53	Pittsburgh Hornets	AHL	29	14	21	35	....	....	....	4	6	2	3	5	14
1953-54	Pittsburgh Hornets	AHL	67	25	36	61	....	....	....	8	5	0	1	1	2
1954-55	Pittsburgh Hornets	AHL	57	19	20	39	....	....	....	10	7	0	2	2	2
	NHL Totals		**1**	**0**	**0**	**0**	**0**	**0**	**0**	**2**	....	....	....	....	....

PCHL Southern 1st All-Star Team (1949)

• BARILKO, BILL Bill "Bashin' Bill" Barilko

D – R. 5′11″, 180 lbs. b: Timmins, Ont., 3/25/1927. d: 8/26/1951.

Season	Club	League	GP	G	A	Pts	AG	AA	APts	PIM	GP	G	A	Pts	PIM
1944-45	Timmins Canadians	NOHA	STATISTICS NOT AVAILABLE												
	Porcupine Combines	NOHA	....	3	2	5	....	....	....	8	....	....	....	....	....
1945-46	Hollywood Wolves	PCHL	38	4	5	9	....	....	....	103	12	2	3	5	8
1946-47	**Toronto Maple Leafs**	**NHL**	**18**	**3**	**7**	**10**	**4**	**10**	**14**	**33**	**11**	**0**	**3**	**3**	**18**
	Hollywood Wolves	PCHL	47	9	2	11	....	....	....	69	....	....	....	....	....
1947-48	**Toronto Maple Leafs**	**NHL**	**57**	**5**	**9**	**14**	**7**	**13**	**20**	***147**	**9**	**1**	**0**	**1**	**17**
1948-49	**Toronto Maple Leafs**	**NHL**	**60**	**5**	**4**	**9**	**8**	**6**	**14**	**95**	**9**	**0**	**1**	**1**	**20**
1949-50	**Toronto Maple Leafs**	**NHL**	**59**	**7**	**10**	**17**	**9**	**13**	**22**	**85**	**7**	**1**	**1**	**2**	**18**
1950-51	**Toronto Maple Leafs**	**NHL**	**58**	**6**	**6**	**12**	**8**	**8**	**16**	**96**	**11**	**3**	**2**	**5**	**31**
	NHL Totals		**252**	**26**	**36**	**62**	**36**	**50**	**86**	**456**	**47**	**5**	**7**	**12**	**104**

Played in NHL All-Star Game (1947, 1948, 1949)

• Died in plane crash during late-summer fishing trip, August 26, 1951.

• BARKLEY, DOUG Doug Barkley

D – R. 6′2″, 185 lbs. b: Lethbridge, Alta., 1/6/1937.

Season	Club	League	GP	G	A	Pts	AG	AA	APts	PIM	GP	G	A	Pts	PIM
1955-56	Medicine Hat Tigers	WCJHL	44	19	10	29	....	....	....	85	5	0	2	2	0
1956-57	Calgary Stampeders	WHL	63	4	8	12	....	....	....	112	3	0	0	0	0
1957-58	**Chicago Black Hawks**	**NHL**	**3**	**0**	**0**	**0**	**0**	**0**	**0**	**0**	....	....	....	....	....
	Calgary Stampeders	WHL	31	3	5	8	....	....	....	72	14	2	1	3	37
	Buffalo Bisons	AHL	27	0	3	3	....	....	....	22	....	....	....	....	....
1958-59	Buffalo Bisons	AHL	55	2	5	7	....	....	....	59	8	0	0	0	12
1959-60	**Chicago Black Hawks**	**NHL**	**3**	**0**	**0**	**0**	**0**	**0**	**0**	**2**	....	....	....	....	....
	Calgary Stampeders	WHL	55	7	18	25	....	....	....	82	....	....	....	....	....
1960-61	Buffalo Bisons	AHL	66	9	28	37	....	....	....	106	4	0	1	1	10
1961-62	Calgary Stampeders	WHL	70	25	49	74	....	....	....	82	7	2	3	5	17
1962-63	**Detroit Red Wings**	**NHL**	**70**	**3**	**24**	**27**	**4**	**25**	**29**	**78**	**11**	**0**	**3**	**3**	**16**
1963-64	**Detroit Red Wings**	**NHL**	**67**	**11**	**21**	**32**	**14**	**23**	**37**	**115**	**14**	**0**	**5**	**5**	**33**
1964-65	**Detroit Red Wings**	**NHL**	**67**	**5**	**20**	**25**	**6**	**22**	**28**	**122**	**5**	**0**	**1**	**1**	**14**
1965-66	**Detroit Red Wings**	**NHL**	**43**	**5**	**15**	**20**	**6**	**15**	**21**	**65**	....	....	....	....	....
	NHL Totals		**253**	**24**	**80**	**104**	**30**	**85**	**115**	**382**	**30**	**0**	**9**	**9**	**63**

WHL 1st All-Star Team (1962)

Traded to **Detroit** by **Chicago** for Len Lunde and John McKenzie, June 5, 1962. • Suffered career-ending eye injury in game vs. Chicago, January 30, 1966.

• BARRY, ED Ed Barry

LW – L. 5′10″, 180 lbs. b: Wellesley, MA, 10/12/1919.

			REGULAR SEASON								PLAYOFFS				
Season	Club	League	GP	G	A	Pts	AG	AA	APts	PIM	GP	G	A	Pts	PIM
1939-40	Northwestern University	Ivy	STATISTICS NOT AVAILABLE												
1940-41	Boston Olympics	EHL	25	3	6	9	....	....	....	24	4	2	1	3	5
1941-42	Boston Olympics	EHL	45	19	6	25	....	....	....	40	6	4	0	4	13
1942-43	Boston Olympics	EHL	7	8	2	10	....	....	....	22	....	....	....	....	....
	Coast Guard Cutters	EHL	31	20	17	37	....	....	....	17	12	8	6	14	13
1943-44	Coast Guard Cutters	....	37	22	20	42	....	....	....	28	12	8	9	17	8
1944-45			MILITARY SERVICE												
1945-46	Boston Olympics	EHL	48	26	25	51	....	....	....	57	8	4	7	11	4
1946-47	Boston Olympics	EHL	32	21	15	36	....	....	....	61	....	....	....	....	....
	Boston Bruins	**NHL**	**19**	**1**	**3**	**4**	**1**	**4**	**5**	**2**	....	....	....	....	....
1947-48	Boston Olympics	EHL	20	17	8	25	....	....	....	69	....	....	....	....	....
	Boston Olympics	QSHL	40	18	10	28	....	....	....	47	....	....	....	....	....
1948-49	Boston Olympics	QSHL	23	15	13	28	....	....	....	43	....	....	....	....	....
1949-50	Boston Olympics	EHL	13	10	2	12	....	....	....	23	....	....	....	....	....
1950-51	Boston Olympics	EHL	DID NOT PLAY – COACHING												
	NHL Totals		**19**	**1**	**3**	**4**	**1**	**4**	**5**	**2**	....	....	....	....	....

EHL 2nd All-Star Team (1946)

• **Coast Guard Cutters** played exhibiton schedule only in 1943-44. Signed as a free agent by **Boston**, January 9, 1947.

• BARRY, MARTY Marty Barry HHOF

C – L. 5′11″, 175 lbs. b: Quebec City, Que., 12/8/1905. d: 8/20/1969.

Season	Club	League	GP	G	A	Pts	AG	AA	APts	PIM	GP	G	A	Pts	PIM
1925-26	Montreal St. Anthony	City Sr.	STATISTICS NOT AVAILABLE												
1926-27	Montreal Bell Telephone	City Sr.	STATISTICS NOT AVAILABLE												
1927-28	**New York Americans**	**NHL**	**9**	**1**	**0**	**1**	**3**	**0**	**3**	**2**	....	....	....	....	....
	Philadelphia Arrows	Can-Am	33	11	3	14	....	....	....	70	....	....	....	....	....
1928-29	New Haven Eagles	Can-Am	35	*19	10	*29	....	....	....	54	2	0	1	1	2
1929-30	**Boston Bruins**	**NHL**	**44**	**18**	**15**	**33**	**36**	**49**	**85**	**34**	**6**	**3**	**3**	***6**	**14**
1930-31	**Boston Bruins**	**NHL**	**44**	**20**	**11**	**31**	**49**	**40**	**89**	**26**	**5**	**1**	**1**	**2**	**4**
1931-32	**Boston Bruins**	**NHL**	**48**	**21**	**17**	**38**	**45**	**48**	**93**	**22**	....	....	....	....	....
1932-33	**Boston Bruins**	**NHL**	**47**	**24**	**13**	**37**	**57**	**34**	**91**	**40**	**5**	**2**	**2**	**4**	**6**
1933-34	**Boston Bruins**	**NHL**	**48**	**27**	**12**	**39**	**61**	**32**	**93**	**12**	....	....	....	....	....
1934-35	**Boston Bruins**	**NHL**	**48**	**20**	**20**	**40**	**43**	**45**	**88**	**33**	**4**	**0**	**0**	**0**	**2**
1935-36	**Detroit Red Wings**	**NHL**	**48**	**21**	**19**	**40**	**52**	**46**	**98**	**16**	**7**	**2**	**4**	**6**	**6**
1936-37	**Detroit Red Wings**	**NHL**	**47**	**17**	**27**	**44**	**37**	**64**	**101**	**6**	**10**	**4**	**7**	**11**	**2**
1937-38	**Detroit Red Wings**	**NHL**	**48**	**9**	**20**	**29**	**19**	**41**	**60**	**34**	....	....	....	....	....
1938-39	**Detroit Red Wings**	**NHL**	**48**	**13**	**28**	**41**	**27**	**53**	**80**	**4**	**6**	**3**	**1**	**4**	**0**
1939-40	**Montreal Canadiens**	**NHL**	**30**	**4**	**10**	**14**	**9**	**20**	**29**	**2**	....	....	....	....	....
	Pittsburgh Hornets	AHL	6	2	0	2	....	....	....	0	7	2	1	3	4
1940-41	Minneapolis Millers	AHA	32	10	10	20	....	....	....	8	3	1	0	1	0
1941-42	Minneapolis Millers	AHA	DID NOT PLAY – COACHING												
	NHL Totals		**509**	**195**	**192**	**387**	**438**	**472**	**910**	**231**	**43**	**15**	**18**	**33**	**34**

NHL 1st All-Star Team (1937) • Won Lady Byng Trophy (1937)

Played in NHL All-Star Game (1937)

Claimed by **Boston** from **NY Americans** in Intra-League Draft, May 13, 1929. Traded to **Detroit** by **Boston** with Art Giroux for Cooney Weiland and Walt Buswell, June 30, 1935. Signed as a free agent by **Montreal**, November 2, 1939.

• BARRY, RAY Ray Barry

C – L. 5′11″, 170 lbs. b: Boston, MA, 10/4/1928.

Season	Club	League	GP	G	A	Pts	AG	AA	APts	PIM	GP	G	A	Pts	PIM
1946-47	Edmonton Caps	City Jr.	7	5	2	7	....	....	....	2	3	2	1	3	0
1947-48	St. Michael's Majors	OHA	31	9	28	37	....	....	....	8	....	....	....	....	....
1948-49	Sherbrooke–Boston	QSHL	63	18	61	79	....	....	....	18	12	2	*10	12	6
1949-50	Sherbrooke Saints	QSHL	59	21	40	61	....	....	....	47	21	5	9	14	26
1950-51	Edmonton Flyers	City Sr.	60	28	40	68	....	....	....	38	8	5	5	10	0
1951-52	**Boston Bruins**	**NHL**	**18**	**1**	**2**	**3**	**1**	**3**	**4**	**6**	....	....	....	....	....
	Hershey Bears	AHL	49	17	29	46	....	....	....	20	4	1	1	2	2
1952-53	Calgary Stampeders	WHL	53	15	25	40	....	....	....	16	5	2	2	4	0
1953-54	Calgary Stampeders	WHL	70	17	24	41	....	....	....	20	23	5	11	16	12
1954-55	Calgary Stampeders	WHL	68	25	28	53	....	....	....	17	9	1	4	5	0
1955-56	Calgary Stampeders	WHL	65	23	43	66	....	....	....	13	8	3	8	11	0
1956-57	Calgary Stampeders	WHL	61	11	37	48	....	....	....	26	3	1	2	3	0
1957-58	Red Deer Rustlers	ASHL	DID NOT PLAY – COACHING												
	NHL Totals		**18**	**1**	**2**	**3**	**1**	**3**	**4**	**6**	....	....	....	....	....

Signed as a free agent by **Boston**, October 3, 1950.

• BARTLETT, JIM Jim Bartlett

LW – L. 5'9", 165 lbs. b: Verdun, Que., 5/27/1932.

Season	Club	League	GP	G	A	Pts	AG	AA	APts	PIM	Playoffs GP	G	A	Pts	PIM
			REGULAR SEASON								PLAYOFFS				
1949-50	Verdun Maple Leafs	QJHL	6	0	0	0	....	....	....	4	1	0	0	0	0
1950-51	Verdun LaSalle	QJHL	38	8	8	16	....	....	....	67	3	1	0	1	7
1951-52	St. Jerome Eagles	QJHL	44	25	31	56	....	....	....	167	....	....	....	....	....
	Boston Olympics	EHL	14	2	6	8	....	....	....	39	2	1	0	1	4
1952-53	Cincinnati Mohawks	IHL	49	32	30	62	....	....	....	122	9	4	5	9	22
1953-54	Matane Red Rockets	QPHL	61	43	29	72	....	....	....	*139	....	....	....	....	....
1954-55	**Montreal Canadiens**	**NHL**	**2**	**0**	**0**	**0**	**0**	**0**	**0**	**4**	**2**	**0**	**0**	**0**	**0**
	Chicoutimi Sagueneens	QHL	58	28	28	56	....	....	....	150	7	1	4	5	20
1955-56	**New York Rangers**	**NHL**	**12**	**0**	**1**	**1**	**0**	**1**	**1**	**8**	....	....	....	....	....
	Providence Reds	AHL	50	28	19	47	....	....	....	110	9	3	5	8	27
1956-57	Providence Reds	AHL	63	21	22	43	....	....	....	105	4	1	0	1	27
1957-58	Providence Reds	AHL	59	25	21	46	....	....	....	86	5	2	1	3	11
1958-59	**New York Rangers**	**NHL**	**70**	**11**	**9**	**20**	**14**	**10**	**24**	**118**	....	....	....	....	....
1959-60	**New York Rangers**	**NHL**	**44**	**8**	**4**	**12**	**10**	**4**	**14**	**48**	....	....	....	....	....
	Springfield Indians	AHL	21	7	3	10	....	....	....	12	8	5	3	8	15
1960-61	**Boston Bruins**	**NHL**	**63**	**15**	**9**	**24**	**18**	**9**	**27**	**95**	....	....	....	....	....
1961-62	Providence Reds	AHL	62	31	34	65	....	....	....	80	3	0	1	1	8
1962-63	Providence Reds	AHL	67	28	38	66	....	....	....	87	6	1	2	3	10
1963-64	Providence Reds	AHL	72	26	39	65	....	....	....	75	3	2	1	3	4
1964-65	Providence Reds	AHL	71	22	36	58	....	....	....	92	....	....	....	....	....
1965-66	Providence Reds	AHL	68	19	26	45	....	....	....	70	....	....	....	....	....
1966-67	Baltimore Clippers	AHL	67	30	21	51	....	....	....	24	13	3	3	6	10
1967-68	Baltimore Clippers	AHL	71	22	29	51	....	....	....	71	....	....	....	....	....
1968-69	Baltimore Clippers	AHL	73	25	23	48	....	....	....	40	4	1	0	1	10
1969-70	Baltimore Clippers	AHL	65	30	28	58	....	....	....	34	5	2	1	3	2
1970-71	Baltimore Clippers	AHL	63	14	25	39	....	....	....	51	6	0	1	1	4
1971-72	Columbus Seals	IHL	14	4	6	10	....	....	....	23	....	....	....	....	....
	Baltimore Clippers	AHL	11	8	2	10	....	....	....	12	18	6	5	11	14
1972-73	Baltimore Clippers	AHL	72	24	16	40	....	....	....	31	....	....	....	....	....
	NHL Totals		**191**	**34**	**23**	**57**	**42**	**24**	**66**	**273**	**2**	**0**	**0**	**0**	**0**

Claimed by **NY Rangers** from **Montreal** in Intra-League Draft, June, 1955. Claimed by **Boston** from **NY Rangers** in Intra-League Draft, June 8, 1960. Traded to **Providence** (AHL) by **Boston** for cash, August, 1961.

• BARTON, CLIFF Cliff Barton

RW – R. 5'7", 155 lbs. b: Sault Ste. Marie, MI, 9/3/1907. d: 9/14/1969.

Season	Club	League	GP	G	A	Pts	AG	AA	APts	PIM	Playoffs GP	G	A	Pts	PIM
1926-27	Port Arthur West End	TBJHL	STATISTICS NOT AVAILABLE												
1927-28	Port Arthur Ports	TBSHL	21	13	6	19	....	....	....	15	....	....	....	....	....
1928-29	Port Arthur Ports	TBSHL	20	10	8	18	....	....	....	12	2	0	0	0	2
1929-30	**Pittsburgh Pirates**	**NHL**	**39**	**4**	**2**	**6**	**8**	**6**	**14**	**4**	....	....	....	....	....
1930-31	**Philadelphia Quakers**	**NHL**	**43**	**6**	**7**	**13**	**15**	**25**	**40**	**18**	....	....	....	....	....
1931-32	Pittsburgh Yellowjackets	IAHL	39	2	3	5	....	....	....	39	....	....	....	....	....
	Springfield Indians	Can-Am	2	0	0	0	....	....	....	0	....	....	....	....	....
1932-33	Buffalo Bisons	IAHL	40	1	2	3	....	....	....	12	5	0	0	0	0
1933-34	Buffalo Bisons	IAHL	44	19	8	27	....	....	....	18	6	2	1	3	4
1934-35	Buffalo Bisons	IAHL	44	18	8	26	....	....	....	43	....	....	....	....	....
1935-36	Buffalo Bisons	IAHL	47	12	17	20	....	....		32	5	0	0	0	4
1936-37	Philadelphia Ramblers	AHL	34	7	11	18	....	....	....	10	6	2	0	2	2
1937-38	Philadelphia Ramblers	AHL	47	13	19	32	....	....	....	11	5	0	1	1	0
1938-39	Philadelphia Ramblers	AHL	52	21	28	49	....	....	....	16	9	3	3	6	6
1939-40	**New York Rangers**	**NHL**	**3**	**0**	**0**	**0**	**0**	**0**	**0**	**0**	....	....	....	....	....
	Philadelphia Rockets	AHL	51	9	19	28	....	....	....	6	....	....	....	....	....
1940-41	Hershey Bears	AHL	6	1	1	2	....	....	....	0	....	....	....	....	....
	St. Louis Flyers	AHA	43	6	8	14	....	....	....	12	9	3	3	6	0
1941-42	St. Louis Flyers	AHA	50	26	22	48	....	....	....	22	3	0	0	0	2
1942-43	New Haven–Washington	AHL	34	8	21	29	....	....	....	0	....	....	....	....	....
1943-44	Pittsburgh Hornets	AHL	42	6	15	21	....	....	....	6	....	....		....	....
	NHL Totals		**85**	**10**	**9**	**19**	**23**	**31**	**54**	**22**	....	....	....	....	....

Transferred to **Philadelphia** after **Pittsburgh** franchise relocated, September 27, 1930. Claimed by **NY Rangers** from **Philadelphia** in Dispersal Draft, September 26, 1931. Traded to **Hershey** (AHL) by **NY Rangers** for cash, April 4, 1940.

• BATHGATE, ANDY — see page 856

• BATHGATE, FRANK Frank Bathgate

C – R. 5'10", 162 lbs. b: Winnipeg, Man., 2/14/1930.

Season	Club	League	GP	G	A	Pts	AG	AA	APts	PIM	Playoffs GP	G	A	Pts	PIM
1947-48	Guelph Biltmores	OHA	29	4	5	9	....	....	....	6	....	....	....	....	....
1948-49	Guelph Biltmores	OHA	45	16	22	38	....	....	....	34	....	....	....	....	....
1949-50	Guelph Biltmores	OHA	42	15	30	45	....	....	....	77	26	10	17	27	21
1950-51	Charlottetown Islanders	MMHL	75	35	58	93	....	....	....	47	15	*9	*10	*19	26
1951-52	Vancouver Canucks	PCHL	13	0	3	3	....	....	....	2	....	....	....	....	....
	Sydney Millionaires	MMHL	68	25	40	65	....	....	....	46	....	....	....	....	....
1952-53	**New York Rangers**	**NHL**	**2**	**0**	**0**	**0**	**0**	**0**	**0**	**2**	....	....	....	....	....
	Shawinigan Cataracts	QSHL	54	22	31	53	....	....	....	10	....	....	....	....	....
1953-54	Vancouver Canucks	WHL	5	0	3	3	....		....	7	....	....	....	....	....
	Windsor Bulldogs	OHA Sr.	42	20	39	59	....	....	....	81	3	0	1	1	4
1954-55	Windsor Bulldogs	OHA Sr.	45	18	31	49	....		....	76	12	6	2	8	16
1955-56	Windsor Bulldogs	OHA Sr.	48	23	30	53	....	....	....	82	....	....	....	....	....
1956-57	Windsor Bulldogs	OHA Sr.	52	16	37	53	....	....	....	67	12	6	6	12	31
1957-58	Windsor Bulldogs	OHA Sr.	59	33	37	70	....	....	....	99	13	3	11	14	20
1958-59	Windsor Bulldogs	OHA Sr.	21	4	10	14	....	....	....	10	....	....	....	....	....
	Belleville McFarlands	OHA Sr.	10	7	7	14	....	....	....	....	....	....	....	....	....
	Kingston CKLC's	OHA Sr.	18	7	7	14	....	....	....	2		....	....	....	....
1959-60	Chatham Maroons	OHA Sr.	51	13	25	38	....			12	19	7	12	19	20
1960-61	Chatham Maroons	OHA Sr.	....	6	11	17	....	....	....	4	....	....	....	....	....
1961-62	Waterloo Tigers	OHA Sr.	....	3	10	13	....	....	....	10	....	....	....	....	....
	NHL Totals		**2**	**0**	**0**	**0**	**0**	**0**	**0**	**2**	....	....	....	....	....

• BAUER, BOBBY Bobby Bauer HHOF

RW – R. 5'6", 150 lbs. b: Waterloo, Ont., 2/16/1915. d: 9/16/1964.

Season	Club	League	GP	G	A	Pts	AG	AA	APts	PIM	Playoffs GP	G	A	Pts	PIM
1933-34	St. Michael's Majors	OHA	10	4	2	6	....	....	....	0	2	0	1	1	0
1934-35	Kitchener Greenshirts	OHA	11	12	6	18	....	....	....	0	3	1	2	3	2
1935-36	Boston Cubs	Can-Am	48	15	13	28	....	....	....	8	....	....	....	....	....
1936-37	**Boston Bruins**	**NHL**	**1**	**1**	**0**	**1**	**2**	**0**	**2**	**0**	**1**	**0**	**0**	**0**	**0**
	Providence Reds	AHL	41	14	4	18	....	....	....	2	2	0	1	1	0
1937-38	**Boston Bruins**	**NHL**	**48**	**20**	**14**	**34**	**42**	**29**	**71**	**9**	**3**	**0**	**0**	**0**	**2**
1938-39	**Boston Bruins**	**NHL**	**48**	**13**	**18**	**31**	**27**	**34**	**61**	**4**	**12**	**3**	**2**	**5**	**0**
1939-40	**Boston Bruins**	**NHL**	**48**	**17**	**26**	**43**	**37**	**53**	**90**	**2**	**6**	**1**	**0**	**1**	**2**
1940-41	**Boston Bruins**	**NHL**	**48**	**17**	**22**	**39**	**34**	**40**	**74**	**2**	**11**	**2**	**2**	**4**	**0**
1941-42	**Boston Bruins**	**NHL**	**36**	**13**	**22**	**35**	**22**	**33**	**55**	**11**	....	....	....	....	....
1941-42	Ottawa RCAF	City Sr.	....	....	....	....	....	....	....	....	11	10	12	22	4
1942-43	Halifax RCAF	City Sr.	7	*12	8	20	....	....	....	0	12	9	10	19	0
1943-44			MILITARY SERVICE												
1944-45			MILITARY SERVICE												
1945-46	**Boston Bruins**	**NHL**	**39**	**11**	**10**	**21**	**17**	**19**	**36**	**4**	**10**	**4**	**3**	**7**	**2**
1946-47	**Boston Bruins**	**NHL**	**58**	**30**	**24**	**54**	**41**	**34**	**75**	**4**	**5**	**1**	**1**	**2**	**0**
1947-48	Kitchener Dutchmen	OHA Sr.	8	8	7	15	....	....	....	22	10	5	4	9	6
1948-49	Kitchener Dutchmen	OHA Sr.	31	17	21	38	....	....	....	13	12	4	4	8	0
1949-50	Kitchener Dutchmen	OHA Sr.	23	10	14	24	....	....	....	9	9	1	2	3	2
1950-51			DID NOT PLAY												
1951-52	**Boston Bruins**	**NHL**	**1**	**1**	**1**	**2**	**1**	**1**	**2**	**0**	....	....	....	....	....
	Kitchener Dutchmen	OHA Sr.	37	8	10	18	....	....	....	14	1	0	1	1	0
	NHL Totals		**327**	**123**	**137**	**260**	**223**	**243**	**466**	**36**	**48**	**11**	**8**	**19**	**6**

NHL 2nd All-Star Team (1939, 1940, 1941, 1947) • Won Lady Byng Trophy (1940, 1941, 1947)

Played in NHL All-Star Game (1939, 1947)

Claimed by **Boston** from **Syracuse** (IAHL) in Inter-League Draft, May 11, 1935.

• BAUN, BOB — see page 857

• BEATTIE, RED Red (John) Beattie

LW – L. 5'9", 170 lbs. b: Ibstock, England, 10/2/1907. Deceased.

Season	Club	League	GP	G	A	Pts	AG	AA	APts	PIM	Playoffs GP	G	A	Pts	PIM
1927-28	Edmonton Superiors	City Sr.	STATISTICS NOT AVAILABLE												
1928-29	Vancouver Lions	PCHL	26	5	0	5	....	....	....	24	2	0	0	0	2
1929-30	Vancouver Lions	PCHL	36	12	9	21	....	....	....	30	4	2	0	2	2
1930-31	Springfield Indians	Can-Am	7	8	6	14	....	....	....	4	....	....	....	....	....
	Boston Bruins	**NHL**	**32**	**10**	**11**	**21**	**24**	**40**	**64**	**25**	**4**	**0**	**0**	**0**	**0**
1931-32	**Boston Bruins**	**NHL**	**1**	**0**	**0**	**0**	**0**	**0**	**0**	**0**	....	....	....	....	....
1932-33	**Boston Bruins**	**NHL**	**48**	**8**	**12**	**20**	**19**	**32**	**51**	**12**	**5**	**0**	**0**	**0**	**2**
1933-34	**Boston Bruins**	**NHL**	**48**	**9**	**13**	**22**	**20**	**35**	**55**	**26**	....	....	....	....	....
1934-35	**Boston Bruins**	**NHL**	**48**	**9**	**18**	**27**	**19**	**40**	**59**	**27**	**4**	**1**	**0**	**1**	**2**
1935-36	**Boston Bruins**	**NHL**	**48**	**14**	**18**	**32**	**35**	**44**	**79**	**27**	**2**	**0**	**0**	**0**	**2**
1936-37	**Boston Bruins**	**NHL**	**48**	**8**	**7**	**15**	**17**	**16**	**33**	**10**	**3**	**1**	**0**	**1**	**0**
1937-38	**Boston Bruins**	**NHL**	**14**	**0**	**0**	**0**	**0**	**0**	**0**	**0**	....	....	....	....	....
	Detroit Red Wings	**NHL**	**11**	**1**	**2**	**3**	**2**	**4**	**6**	**0**	....	....	....	....	....
	Pittsburgh Hornets	AHL	2	0	0	0	....	....	....	0	....	....	....	....	....
	New York Americans	**NHL**	**19**	**3**	**4**	**7**	**6**	**8**	**14**	**5**	**6**	**2**	**2**	**4**	**2**
1938-39	**New York Americans**	**NHL**	**17**	**0**	**0**	**0**	**0**	**0**	**0**	**5**	....	....	....	....	....
	New Haven Eagles	AHL	13	1	3	4	....	....	....	2	....	....	....	....	....
1939-40			DID NOT PLAY												
1940-41			DID NOT PLAY												
1941-42	Vancouver Norvans	PCHL	21	15	9	24	....	....	....	6	3	1	0	1	2
1942-43	Victoria VMD	City Sr.	16	6	1	7	....	....	....	11	....	....	....	....	....
	NHL Totals		**334**	**62**	**85**	**147**	**142**	**219**	**361**	**137**	**24**	**4**	**2**	**6**	**8**

Rights awarded to **Boston** by NHL to settle contract dispute, December 12, 1930. Traded to **Detroit** by **Boston** for Gord Pettinger, December 19, 1937. Traded to **NY Americans** by **Detroit** for Joe Lamb, January 24, 1938.

• BECKETT, BOB Bob Beckett

C – L. 6', 185 lbs. b: Unionville, Ont., 4/8/1936.

Season	Club	League	GP	G	A	Pts	AG	AA	APts	PIM	Playoffs GP	G	A	Pts	PIM
1954-55	Galt Black Hawks	OHA	49	16	22	38	....	....	....	18	4	0	3	3	0
1955-56	Barrie Flyers	OHA	48	16	26	42	....	....	....	24	18	*16	8	*24	8
	Hershey Bears	AHL	1	0	1	1	....	....	....	0	....	....	....	....	....
1956-57	**Boston Bruins**	**NHL**	**18**	**0**	**3**	**3**	**0**	**3**	**3**	**2**	....	....	....	....	....
	Victoria Cougars	WHL	16	0	0	0	....	....	....	5	....	....	....	....	....
	Quebec Aces	QHL	26	9	15	24	....	....	....	6	10	4	3	7	11
1957-58	**Boston Bruins**	**NHL**	**9**	**0**	**0**	**0**	**0**	**0**	**0**	**2**	....	....	....	....	....
	Springfield Indians	AHL	62	17	16	33	....	....	....	40	13	4	4	8	13
1958-59	Quebec Aces	QHL	25	6	5	11	....	....	....	5	....	....	....	....	....
	Providence Reds	AHL	32	5	10	15	....	....	....	4	....	....	....	....	....
1959-60	Providence Reds	AHL	57	11	31	42	....	....	....	12	5	1	3	4	2
1960-61	Providence Reds	AHL	72	22	34	56	....	....	....	28	....	....	....	....	....
1961-62	**Boston Bruins**	**NHL**	**34**	**7**	**2**	**9**	**8**	**2**	**10**	**14**	....	....	....	....	....
	Providence Reds	AHL	27	13	15	28	....	....	....	21	3	1	1	2	0
1962-63	Providence Reds	AHL	62	12	25	37	....	....	....	34	6	0	2	2	2
1963-64	**Boston Bruins**	**NHL**	**7**	**0**	**1**	**1**	**0**	**1**	**1**	**0**	....	....	....	....	....
	Providence Reds	AHL	33	14	15	29	....	....	....	4	....	....	....	....	....
	NHL Totals		**68**	**7**	**6**	**13**	**8**	**6**	**14**	**18**	....	....	....	....	....

• BEDARD, JAMES James Bedard

D – L. 6', 180 lbs. b: Admiral, Sask., 11/19/1927.

			REGULAR SEASON								PLAYOFFS				
Season	Club	League	GP	G	A	Pts	AG	AA	APts	PIM	GP	G	A	Pts	PIM
1945-46	Moose Jaw Canucks	SJHL	10	0	3	3	....	....	....	20	4	1	0	1	8
1946-47	Moose Jaw Canucks	SJHL	26	11	2	13	....	....	....	*82	6	1	0	1	*18
1947-48	Moose Jaw Canucks	SJHL	25	12	5	17	....	....	....	60	5	0	0	0	*19
1948-49	Kansas City Pla-Mors	USHL	63	5	6	11	....	....	....	2	1	1	2	3	0
1949-50	**Chicago Black Hawks**	**NHL**	**5**	**0**	**0**	**0**	**0**	**0**	**0**	**2**	....	....	....	....	....
	Kansas City Pla-Mors	USHL	56	3	15	18	....	....	....	43	3	0	0	0	4
1950-51	**Chicago Black Hawks**	**NHL**	**17**	**1**	**1**	**2**	**1**	**1**	**2**	**6**	....	....	....	....	....
	Milwaukee Seagulls	USHL	50	4	16	20	....	....	....	59	....	....	....	....	....
1951-52	New Westminster Royals	PCHL	66	4	12	16	....	....	....	104	7	1	1	2	14
1952-53	New Westminster Royals	WHL	70	4	15	19	....	....	....	116	....	....	....	....	....
1953-54	New Westminster Royals	WHL	58	1	12	13	....	....	....	77	7	0	2	2	19
1954-55	New Westminster Royals	WHL	60	1	7	8	....	....	....	70	....	....	....	....	....
1955-56	Seattle Americans	WHL	15	1	0	1	....	....	....	29	....	....	....	....	....
	Penticton Vees	OSHL	40	2	13	15	....	....	....	96	....	....	....	....	....
1956-57	Vancouver Canucks	WHL	16	1	1	2	....	....	....	23	....	....	....	....	....
	Kelowna Packers	OSHL	27	1	6	7	....	....	....	18	7	0	2	2	4
1957-58	New Westminster Royals	WHL	12	0	2	2	....	....	....	4	....	....	....	....	....
	NHL Totals		**22**	**1**	**1**	**2**	**1**	**1**	**2**	**8**	....	....	....	....	....

• BEHLING, DICK Dick (Richard Charles) Behling

D – R. 6'1", 195 lbs. b: Kitchener, Ont., 3/16/1916. Deceased.

			REGULAR SEASON								PLAYOFFS				
Season	Club	League	GP	G	A	Pts	AG	AA	APts	PIM	GP	G	A	Pts	PIM
1934-35	Kitchener Greenshirts	OHA	7	1	0	1	....	....	....	4	....	....	....	....	....
1935-36	Kitchener Greenshirts	OHA	STATISTICS NOT AVAILABLE												
1936-37	Baltimore Orioles	EHL	48	9	5	14	....	....	....	16	3	1	2	3	2
1937-38	Baltimore Orioles	EHL	56	14	11	25	....	....	....	26	....	....	....	....	....
1938-39	Harringay Greyhounds	Britain	....	11	14	25	....	....	....	....	....	....	....	....	....
1939-40	Detroit Holtzbaugh	MOHL	35	9	7	16	....	....	....	22	1	0	0	0	0
1940-41	**Detroit Red Wings**	**NHL**	**3**	**0**	**0**	**0**	**0**	**0**	**0**	**0**	....	....	....	....	....
	Indianapolis Capitals	AHL	54	5	8	13	....	....	....	18	....	....	....	....	....
1941-42	Indianapolis Capitals	AHL	54	4	5	9	....	....	....	26	10	0	2	2	4
1942-43	**Detroit Red Wings**	**NHL**	**2**	**1**	**0**	**1**	**1**	**0**	**1**	**2**	....	....	....	....	....
	Indianapolis Capitals	AHL	22	1	4	5	....	....	....	10	....	....	....	....	....
1943-44			MILITARY SERVICE												
1944-45			MILITARY SERVICE												
1945-46	Indianapolis Capitals	AHL	17	0	3	3	....	....	....	4	5	0	0	0	0
1946-47	Hamilton Pats	OHA Sr.	14	3	4	7	....	....	....	6	3	0	0	0	0
1947-48	Kitchener Dutchmen	OHA Sr.	36	7	15	22	....	....	....	16	10	1	5	6	6
1948-49	Kitchener Dutchmen	OHA Sr.	39	1	13	14	....	....	....	20	12	4	3	7	6
1949-50	Kitchener Dutchmen	OHA Sr.	26	1	9	10	....	....	....	10	14	0	3	3	6
1950-51	Kitchener Dutchmen	OHA Sr.	23	2	9	11	....	....	....	4	....	....	....	....	....
	NHL Totals		**5**	**1**	**0**	**1**	**1**	**0**	**1**	**2**	....	....	....	....	....

EHL First All-Star Team (1938)

Signed as a free agent by **Detroit**, October 16, 1940.

• BEISLER, FRANK Frank Beisler

D – L. 6'2", 190 lbs. b: New Haven, CT, 10/18/1913.

			REGULAR SEASON								PLAYOFFS				
Season	Club	League	GP	G	A	Pts	AG	AA	APts	PIM	GP	G	A	Pts	PIM
1933-34	Hershey B'ars	EHL	25	3	1	4	....	....	....	23	6	1	0	1	8
1934-35	New Haven Eagles	Can-Am	41	3	1	4	....	....	....	32	....	....	....	....	....
1935-36	New Haven Eagles	Can-Am	46	4	5	9	....	....	....	38	....	....	....	....	....
1936-37	**New York Americans**	**NHL**	**1**	**0**	**0**	**0**	**0**	**0**	**0**	**0**	....	....	....	....	....
	New Haven Eagles	AHL	44	3	2	5	....	....	....	50	....	....	....	....	....
1937-38	New Haven Eagles	AHL	26	0	2	2	....	....	....	21	2	0	0	0	0
1938-39	Springfield Indians	AHL	53	1	1	2	....	....	....	75	3	0	1	1	2
1939-40	**New York Americans**	**NHL**	**1**	**0**	**0**	**0**	**0**	**0**	**0**	**0**	....	....	....	....	....
	Springfield Indians	AHL	50	3	8	11	....	....	....	37	3	0	2	2	2
1940-41	Springfield Indians	AHL	56	1	10	11	....	....	....	46	3	0	0	0	0
1941-42	Springfield Indians	AHL	42	2	6	8	....	....	....	25	5	0	0	0	0
1942-43	Buffalo Bisons	AHL	55	2	7	9	....	....	....	27	9	1	0	1	4
1943-44	Buffalo Bisons	AHL	25	3	4	7	....	....	....	15	....	....	....	....	....
1944-45			MILITARY SERVICE												
1945-46	Buffalo Bisons	AHL	4	0	1	1	....	....	....	0	....	....	....	....	....
1946-47	Buffalo Bisons	AHL	DID NOT PLAY – COACHING												
1947-48	Baltimore Clippers	EHL	DID NOT PLAY – COACHING												
	NHL Totals		**2**	**0**	**0**	**0**	**0**	**0**	**0**	**0**	....	....	....	....	....

EHL First All-Star Team (1934) • AHL Second All-Star Team (1941) • AHL First All-Star Team (1942, 1943)

• BELISLE, DANNY Danny Belisle

RW – R. 5'10", 164 lbs. b: South Porcupine, Ont., 5/9/1937.

			REGULAR SEASON								PLAYOFFS				
Season	Club	League	GP	G	A	Pts	AG	AA	APts	PIM	GP	G	A	Pts	PIM
1955-56	Guelph Biltmores	OHA	48	25	25	50	....	....	....	25	3	1	0	1	0
1956-57	Guelph Biltmores	OHA	52	36	30	66	....	....	....	70	10	6	10	16	21
1957-58	Trois-Rivieres Lions	QHL	55	24	31	55	....	....	....	32	....	....	....	....	....
	Providence Reds	AHL	7	2	2	4	....	....	....	2	....	....	....	....	....
1958-59	Vancouver Canucks	WHL	70	31	31	62	....	....	....	41	9	4	1	5	13
1959-60	Vancouver Canucks	WHL	68	24	24	48	....	....	....	27	11	*6	7	13	0
1960-61	**New York Rangers**	**NHL**	**4**	**2**	**0**	**2**	**2**	**0**	**2**	**0**	....	....	....	....	....
	Kitchener Beavers	EPHL	16	8	7	15	....	....	....	14	....	....	....	....	....
	Vancouver Canucks	WHL	51	30	17	47	....	....	....	17	9	0	2	2	0
1961-62	Los Angeles Blades	WHL	61	30	38	68	....	....	....	27	....	....	....	....	....
1962-63	San Francisco Seals	WHL	63	29	41	70	....	....	....	14	17	8	7	15	2
1963-64	Baltimore Clippers	AHL	13	1	2	3	....	....	....	4	....	....	....	....	....
	Vancouver Canucks	WHL	52	22	22	44	....	....	....	22	....	....	....	....	....
1964-65	Omaha Knights	CHL	6	2	6	8	....	....	....	2	....	....	....	....	....
	Quebec Aces	AHL	4	0	0	0	....	....	....	2	....	....	....	....	....
	Victoria Maple Leafs	WHL	53	23	24	47	....	....	....	40	12	2	5	7	6
1965-66	Memphis Wings	CHL	65	16	30	46	....	....	....	39	....	....	....	....	....
1966-67	California Seals	WHL	62	25	22	47	....	....	....	22	1	0	0	0	0
1967-68	Vancouver Canucks	WHL	66	15	20	35	....	....	....	8	....	....	....	....	....
1968-69	Jacksonville Rockets	EHL	71	39	49	85	....	....	....	26	4	2	1	3	0
1969-70	Barrie Flyers	OHA Sr.	7	1	2	3	....	....	....	16	....	....	....	....	....
	Columbus Checkers	IHL	58	32	43	75	....	....	....	21	....	....	....	....	....
1970-71	Des Moines Oak Leafs	IHL	41	8	21	29	....	....	....	10	....	....	....	....	....
1971-72	Des Moines Oak Leafs	IHL	DID NOT PLAY – COACHING												
	NHL Totals		**4**	**2**	**0**	**2**	**2**	**0**	**2**	**0**	....	....	....	....	....

Traded to **San Francisco** (WHL) by **LA Blades** (WHL) for Bob Solinger with NY Rangers holding rights of recall, July, 1962. Loaned to **Victoria** (WHL) by **NY Rangers** for remainder of 1964-65 season, December 12, 1964. Claimed by **Detroit** (Pittsburgh (AHL) from **NY Rangers** in Reverse Draft, June 9, 1965. Claimed by **Springfield** (AHL) from **Detroit** in Intra-League Draft, June, 1966.

• BELIVEAU, JEAN *— see page 862*

• BELL, BILLY Billy Bell

C/RW – R. 5'10", 180 lbs. b: Lachine, Que., 6/10/1891. d: 6/3/1959.

			REGULAR SEASON								PLAYOFFS				
Season	Club	League	GP	G	A	Pts	AG	AA	APts	PIM	GP	G	A	Pts	PIM
1911-12	Montreal Baillargeon	City Sr.	4	3	0	3	....	....	....	6	....	....	....	....	....
1912-13	Montreal Stars	City Sr.	5	3	0	3	....	....	....	16	....	....	....	....	....
	Montreal Westmounts	City Sr.	STATISTICS NOT AVAILABLE												
1913-14	Montreal Wanderers	NHA	2	1	0	1	....	....	....	0	....	....	....	....	....
1914-15	Ottawa Senators	NHA	11	1	0	1	....	....	....	17	....	....	....	....	....
1915-16	Montreal Wanderers	NHA	22	8	2	10	....	....	....	78	....	....	....	....	....
1916-17	Montreal Wanderers	NHA	13	11	1	12	....	....	....	47	....	....	....	....	....
1917-18	**Montreal Wanderers**	**NHL**	**2**	**1**	**0**	**1**	**2**	**0**	**2**	**0**	....	....	....	....	....
	Montreal Canadiens	**NHL**	**6**	**0**	**0**	**0**	**0**	**0**	**0**	**6**	....	....	....	....	....
1918-19	**Montreal Canadiens**	**NHL**	**1**	**0**	**0**	**0**	**0**	**0**	**0**	**0**	....	....	....	....	....
1919-20			DID NOT PLAY												
1920-21	**Montreal Canadiens**	**NHL**	**4**	**0**	**0**	**0**	**0**	**0**	**0**	**0**	....	....	....	....	....
1921-22	**Montreal Canadiens**	**NHL**	**6**	**1**	**0**	**1**	**3**	**0**	**3**	**0**	....	....	....	....	....
	Ottawa Senators	**NHL**	**17**	**1**	**2**	**3**	**3**	**12**	**15**	**4**	**1**	**0**	**0**	**0**	**0**
1922-23	**Montreal Canadiens**	**NHL**	**15**	**0**	**0**	**0**	**0**	**0**	**0**	**0**	**2**	**0**	**0**	**0**	**0**
1923-24	**Montreal Canadiens**	**NHL**	**10**	**0**	**0**	**0**	**0**	**0**	**0**	**0**	**5**	**0**	**0**	**0**	**0**
	NHL Totals		**61**	**3**	**2**	**5**	**8**	**12**	**20**	**10**	**8**	**0**	**0**	**0**	**0**
	Other Major League Totals		48	21	3	24	....	....	....	142	....	....	....	....	....

Rights retained by **Montreal Wanderers** after NHA folded, November 26, 1917. Claimed by **Montreal Canadiens** from **Montreal Wanderers** in Dispersal Draft, January 4, 1918. Loaned to **Ottawa** by **Montreal Canadiens** for remainder of 1921-22 season, January 6, 1922.

• BELL, HARRY Harry Bell

RW/D – R. 5'9", 176 lbs. b: Regina, Sask., 10/31/1925.

			REGULAR SEASON								PLAYOFFS				
Season	Club	League	GP	G	A	Pts	AG	AA	APts	PIM	GP	G	A	Pts	PIM
1943-44	Regina Commandos	SJHL	16	4	5	9	....	....	....	8	5	2	0	2	6
1944-45			MILITARY SERVICE												
1945-46	New York Rovers	EHL	35	9	11	20	....	....	....	16	....	....	....	....	....
1946-47	**New York Rangers**	**NHL**	**1**	**0**	**1**	**1**	**0**	**1**	**1**	**0**	....	....	....	....	....
	New York Rovers	EHL	26	6	7	13	....	....	....	8	....	....	....	....	....
	New Haven Ramblers	AHL	28	3	5	8	....	....	....	10	3	0	1	1	2
1947-48	New Haven Ramblers	AHL	66	10	15	25	....	....	....	61	4	0	0	0	10
1948-49	St. Paul Saints	USHL	60	9	21	30	....	....	....	77	7	1	4	5	2
1949-50	St. Paul Saints	USHL	63	14	15	29	....	....	....	57	3	0	0	0	4
1950-51	Tacoma Rockets	PCHL	62	14	26	40	....	....	....	25	6	0	3	3	2
1951-52	New York Rovers	EHL	34	11	10	21	....	....	....	28	....	....	....	....	....
1952-53	Regina Caps	SSHL	....	22	20	42	....	....	....	22	....	....	....	....	....
	NHL Totals		**1**	**0**	**1**	**1**	**0**	**1**	**1**	**0**	....	....	....	....	....

● BELL, JOE Joe Bell
LW – L. 5'9", 165 lbs. b: Portage la Prairie, Man., 11/27/1923.

Season	Club	League	REGULAR SEASON								PLAYOFFS				
			GP	G	A	Pts	AG	AA	APts	PIM	GP	G	A	Pts	PIM
1939-40	Portage Terriers	MJHL	1	0	1	1	....	....	....	0	....	....	....	....	....
1940-41	Portage Terriers	MJHL	16	17	13	30	....	....	....	14	5	5	2	7	12
1941-42	Portage Terriers	MJHL	18	*36	19	55	....	....	....	21	5	*13	5	*18	0
1942-43	**New York Rangers**	**NHL**	**15**	**2**	**5**	**7**	**3**	**6**	**9**	**6**	....	....	....	....	....
	Winnipeg Navy	City Sr.	9	4	5	9	....	....	....	2	4	2	2	4	8
1943-44	Winnipeg Navy	City Sr.	10	*17	6	*23	....	....	....	14	....	....	....	....	....
	Cornwallis Navy	City Sr.	1	5	2	7	....	....	....	....	11	12	15	27	*29
1944-45			MILITARY SERVICE												
1945-46	Hershey–New Haven	AHL	62	*46	31	77	....	....	....	26	3	1	1	2	4
1946-47	**New York Rangers**	**NHL**	**47**	**6**	**4**	**10**	**8**	**6**	**14**	**12**	....	....	....	....	....
	New Haven Ramblers	AHL	13	10	4	14	....	....	....	10	....	....	....	....	....
1947-48	Buffalo Bisons	AHL	66	30	27	57	....	....	....	64	8	4	0	4	4
1948-49	Buffalo Bisons	AHL	3	0	0	0	....	....	....	0	....	....	....	....	....
	Dallas Texans	USHL	55	37	38	75	....	....	....	40	4	4	1	5	2
1949-50	Cincinnati Mohawks	AHL	7	1	2	3	....	....	....	0	....	....	....	....	....
	Louisville Blades	USHL	53	31	25	56	....	....	....	8	....	....	....	....	....
1950-51	Seattle Ironmen	PCHL	63	*46	32	78	....	....	....	32	....	....	....	....	....
1951-52	Seattle Ironmen	PCHL	66	38	31	69	....	....	....	24	4	0	3	3	0
1952-53	Seattle Bombers	WHL	59	25	28	53	....	....	....	20	5	1	3	4	2
1953-54	Seattle Bombers	WHL	70	24	23	47	....	....	....	22	....	....	....	....	....
1954-55	Nelson Maple Leafs	WIHL	38	29	49	*78	....	....	....	58	9	5	3	8	*24
1955-56	Nelson Maple Leafs	WIHL	42	19	31	50	....	....	....	42	5	1	1	2	14
	NHL Totals		**62**	**8**	**9**	**17**	**11**	**12**	**23**	**18**	....	....	....	....	....

AHL First All-Star Team (1946) • USHL Second All-Star Team (1949) • PCHL First All-Star Team (1951)

Signed as a free agent by **NY Rangers**, October 30, 1942.

● BELLEFEUILLE, PETE Pete "The Fleeting Frenchman" Bellefeuille
RW – R. 5'10", 180 lbs. b: Trois-Rivieres, Quebec, 10/19/1901. Deceased.

Season	Club	League	REGULAR SEASON								PLAYOFFS				
			GP	G	A	Pts	AG	AA	APts	PIM	GP	G	A	Pts	PIM
1920-21	Quebec Voltigers	City Sr.	11	*17	0	17	....	....	....	....	4	0	1	1	....
1921-22	Quebec Voltigers	QPHL	STATISTICS NOT AVAILABLE												
1922-23	Trois-Rivieres Volants	QPHL	4	7	0	7	....	....	....	....	....	....	....	....	....
	Trois-Rivieres Violettes	Big 4	7	9	0	9	....	....	....	....	3	*4	0	4	....
1923-24	Iroquois Falls Paper	NOHA	8	*10	4	*14	....	....	....	12	....	....	....	....	....
1924-25	London AAA	OHA Sr.	11	9	4	13	....	....	....	27	....	....	....	....	....
1925-26	**Toronto St.Pats**	**NHL**	**36**	**14**	**2**	**16**	**44**	**23**	**67**	**22**	....	....	....	....	....
1926-27	**Toronto Maple Leafs**	**NHL**	**13**	**0**	**0**	**0**	**0**	**0**	**0**	**12**	....	....	....	....	....
	London Panthers	Can-Pro	6	4	0	4	....	....	....	4	....	....	....	....	....
	Detroit Cougars	**NHL**	**18**	**6**	**0**	**6**	**17**	**0**	**17**	**14**	....	....	....	....	....
1927-28	Detroit Olympics	Can-Pro	42	20	6	26	....	....	....	75	2	1	0	1	12
1928-29	**Detroit Cougars**	**NHL**	**1**	**1**	**0**	**1**	**4**	**0**	**4**	**0**	....	....	....	....	....
	Detroit Olympics	Can-Pro	42	19	5	24	....	....	....	43	2	1	0	1	2
1929-30	**Detroit Cougars**	**NHL**	**24**	**5**	**2**	**7**	**10**	**6**	**16**	**10**	....	....	....	....	....
	Detroit Olympics	IAHL	18	6	4	10	....	....	....	13	2	0	0	0	2
1930-31	Seattle Eskimos	PCHL	34	12	1	13	....	....	....	12	4	*2	0	2	6
1931-32	Syracuse Stars	IAHL	6	1	1	2	....	....	....	4	....	....	....	....	....
	Trois-Rivieres Renards	QPHL	24	8	10	18	....	....	....	29	....	....	....	....	....
1932-33			DID NOT PLAY												
1933-34	Quebec Beavers	Can-Am	1	0	0	0	....	....	....	0	....	....	....	....	....
	NHL Totals		**92**	**26**	**4**	**30**	**75**	**29**	**104**	**58**	....	....	....	....	....

Signed as a free agent by **Toronto St. Pats**, September 21, 1925. Traded to **Detroit Cougars** by **Toronto** for Slim Halderson, January 9, 1927.

● BELLEMER, ANDY Andy Bellemer
D – L. 5'11", 185 lbs. b: Penetanguishene, Ont., 7/3/1903. d: 4/12/1960.

Season	Club	League	REGULAR SEASON								PLAYOFFS				
			GP	G	A	Pts	AG	AA	APts	PIM	GP	G	A	Pts	PIM
1926-27	Windsor Hornets	Can-Pro	32	4	0	4	....	....	....	*88	....	....	....	....	....
1927-28	Windsor Hornets	Can-Pro	38	5	3	8	....	....	....	110	....	....	....	....	....
1928-29	Windsor Bulldogs	Can-Pro	41	3	1	4	....	....	....	76	8	0	0	0	9
1929-30	Windsor Bulldogs	IAHL	41	6	2	8	....	....	....	49	....	....	....	....	....
1930-31	Windsor Bulldogs	IAHL	47	6	5	11	....	....	....	*114	6	0	2	2	6
1931-32	Windsor–Cleveland	IAHL	41	2	5	7	....	....	....	108	....	....	....	....	....
1932-33	**Montreal Maroons**	**NHL**	**15**	**0**	**0**	**0**	**0**	**0**	**0**	**0**	....	....	....	....	....
	Cleveland Indians	IAHL	26	0	1	1	....	....	....	78	5	0	0	0	12
1933-34	Windsor–Syracuse	IAHL	42	2	3	5	....	....	....	79	6	1	0	1	*27
1934-35	Kansas City Greyhounds	AHA	41	4	4	8	....	....	....	59	2	0	0	0	2
1935-36	Cleveland–Rochester	IAHL	45	0	8	8	....	....	....	80	....	....	....	....	....
1936-37	Tulsa Oilers	AHA	46	9	6	15	....	....	....	64	....	....	....	....	....
1937-38	Tulsa Oilers	AHA	43	3	9	12	....	....	....	37	4	0	0	0	0
1938-39	Tulsa Oilers	AHA	48	2	13	15	....	....	....	65	8	1	0	1	10
1939-40	Tulsa Oilers	AHA	43	4	7	11	....	....	....	51	....	....	....	....	....
1940-41	Tulsa Oilers	AHA	48	3	7	10	....	....	....	67	....	....	....	....	....
1941-42	Tulsa Oilers	AHA	33	2	8	10	....	....	....	20	....	....	....	....	....
	Dallas Texans	AHA	15	2	5	7	....	....	....	24	....	....	....	....	....
1942-43	Research Colonels	Tor-Sr.	1	0	0	0	....	....	....	2	....	....	....	....	....
	NHL Totals		**15**	**0**	**0**	**0**	**0**	**0**	**0**	**0**	....	....	....	....	

AHA First All-Star Team (1937) • AHA Second All-Star Team (1938)

Traded to **Montreal Maroons** by **Windsor** (IAHL) for cash, November 28, 1932.

● BEND, LIN Lin (John Linthwaite) Bend
C – L. 5'10", 165 lbs. b: Poplar Point, Man., 12/20/1922. d: 4/10/1978.

Season	Club	League	REGULAR SEASON								PLAYOFFS				
			GP	G	A	Pts	AG	AA	APts	PIM	GP	G	A	Pts	PIM
1939-40	Portage Terriers	MJHL	1	0	0	0	....	....	....	0	....	....	....	....	....
1940-41	Portage Terriers	MJHL	10	16	15	31	....	....	....	10	6	4	2	6	2
1941-42	Portage Terriers	MJHL	17	27	*31	*58	....	....	....	24	15	22	15	37	13
1942-43	**New York Rangers**	**NHL**	**8**	**3**	**1**	**4**	**4**	**1**	**5**	**2**	....	....	....	....	....
	Winnipeg Army	City Sr.	7	3	1	4	....	....	....	4	....	....	....	....	....
1943-44			MILITARY SERVICE												
1944-45	Winnipeg Army	City Sr.	10	16	14	30	....	....	....	17	2	2	0	2	2
1945-46	St. Paul Saints	USHL	56	18	25	43	....	....	....	25	6	2	2	4	4
1946-47	New Haven Ramblers	AHL	64	18	17	35	....	....	....	18	3	2	2	4	2
1947-48	St. Paul Saints	USHL	66	22	27	49	....	....	....	25	....	....	....	....	....
1948-49	St. Paul Saints	USHL	66	29	35	64	....	....	....	20	7	2	3	5	0
1949-50	St. Paul Saints	USHL	70	21	23	44	....	....	....	34	3	1	1	2	2
1950-51	Kansas City Royals	USHL	39	10	11	21	....	....	....	24	....	....	....	....	....
	NHL Totals		**8**	**3**	**1**	**4**	**4**	**1**	**5**	**2**	....	....	....	....	....

Signed as a free agent by **NY Rangers**, October 30, 1942.

● BENNETT, FRANK Frank Bennett
LW/D – R. 5'11", 182 lbs. b: Toronto, Ontario, 3/4/1922.

Season	Club	League	REGULAR SEASON								PLAYOFFS				
			GP	G	A	Pts	AG	AA	APts	PIM	GP	G	A	Pts	PIM
1941-42	St. Michael's Majors	OHA	17	9	11	20	....	....	....	10	2	1	1	2	0
1942-43	St. Michael's Majors	OHA	20	7	10	17	....	....	....	8	6	3	4	7	4
1943-44	**Detroit Red Wings**	**NHL**	**7**	**0**	**1**	**1**	**0**	**1**	**1**	**2**	....	....	....	....	....
	Assumption College	Det-Sr.	STATISTICS NOT AVAILABLE												
1944-45	Providence Reds	AHL	52	7	23	30	....	....	....	4	....	....	....	....	....
1945-46	Providence Reds	AHL	3	0	2	2	....	....	....	2	....	....	....	....	....
	Shawinigan Cataracts	QSHL	38	1	11	12	....	....	....	15	4	0	0	0	2
1946-47	Shawinigan Cataracts	QSHL	40	2	5	7	....	....	....	25	4	1	1	2	0
1947-48	Shawinigan Cataracts	QSHL	19	0	7	7	....	....	....	9	....	....	....	....	....
	Dolbeau Castors	QPHL	STATISTICS NOT AVAILABLE												
	NHL Totals		**7**	**0**	**1**	**1**	**0**	**1**	**1**	**2**	....	....	....	....	....

● BENNETT, MAX Max Bennett
RW – R. 5'6", 157 lbs. b: Cobalt, Ont., 11/4/1912. d: 1/5/1972.

Season	Club	League	REGULAR SEASON								PLAYOFFS				
			GP	G	A	Pts	AG	AA	APts	PIM	GP	G	A	Pts	PIM
1931-32	Falconbridge Falcons	City Sr.	7	2	0	2	....	....	....	8	2	0	0	0	0
	Sudbury Wolves	NOHA	1	0	0	0	....	....	....	0	....	....	....	....	....
1932-33	Falconbridge Falcons	City Sr.	6	4	*3	*7	....	....	....	0	2	0	1	1	0
1933-34	Hamilton Tigers	OHA Sr.	23	*20	12	32	....	....	....	34	12	*11	3	*14	6
1934-35	Hamilton Tigers	OHA Sr.	18	19	7	26	....	....	....	17	6	0	1	1	2
1935-36	**Montreal Canadiens**	**NHL**	**1**	**0**	**0**	**0**	**0**	**0**	**0**	**0**	....	....	....	....	....
	Springfield Indians	Can-Am	44	6	9	15	....	....	....	25	3	1	0	1	0
1936-37	Springfield Indians	AHL	1	0	0	0	....	....	....	0	....	....	....	....	....
	Cleveland–Syracuse	AHL	31	9	9	18	....	....	....	18	9	3	4	7	6
1937-38	Syracuse Stars	AHL	44	20	15	35	....	....	....	18	8	2	*6	8	0
1938-39	Syracuse Stars	AHL	54	15	33	48	....	....	....	18	3	0	1	1	0
1939-40	Syracuse Stars	AHL	56	25	31	56	....	....	....	10	....	....	....	....	....
1940-41	Buffalo Bisons	AHL	55	12	31	43	....	....	....	22	....	....	....	....	....
1941-42	Buffalo Bisons	AHL	52	19	29	48	....	....	....	14	....	....	....	....	....
1942-43	Washington Lions	AHL	1	0	0	0	....	....	....	0	....	....	....	....	....
	Buffalo Bisons	AHL	56	20	24	44	....	....	....	19	9	4	5	9	6
1943-44	Pittsburgh Hornets	AHL	1	0	0	0	....	....	....	0	....	....	....	....	....
	Buffalo Bisons	AHL	54	22	30	52	....	....	....	17	9	1	6	7	2
1944-45	Pittsburgh Hornets	AHL	21	4	11	15	....	....	....	13	....	....	....	....	....
1945-46	Washington Lions	EHL	DID NOT PLAY – COACHING												
	NHL Totals		**1**	**0**	**0**	**0**	**0**	**0**	**0**	**0**	....	....	....	....	....

Signed as a free agent by **Montreal Canadiens**, May 27, 1935.

● BENOIT, JOE Joe Benoit
RW – R. 5'10", 160 lbs. b: St. Albert, Alta., 2/27/1916. d: 10/19/1981.

Season	Club	League	REGULAR SEASON								PLAYOFFS				
			GP	G	A	Pts	AG	AA	APts	PIM	GP	G	A	Pts	PIM
1935-36	Edmonton Athletics	City Jr.	8	8	2	10	....	....	....	4	3	0	0	0	2
1936-37	Trail Canadians	Kootenay	13	13	7	20	....	....	....	18	....	....	....	....	....
1937-38	Trail Smoke Eaters	Kootenay	20	26	6	32	....	....	....	21	5	5	3	8	8
1938-39	Trail Smoke Eaters	Kootenay	PLAYED EXHIBITION SEASON ONLY												
	Canada	WEC	7	6	3	9	....	....	....	....	....	....	....	....	....
1939-40	Trail Smoke Eaters	Kootenay	24	26	17	43	....	....	....	49	7	2	4	6	10
1940-41	**Montreal Canadiens**	**NHL**	**45**	**16**	**16**	**32**	**32**	**29**	**61**	**32**	**3**	**4**	**0**	**4**	**2**
1941-42	**Montreal Canadiens**	**NHL**	**46**	**20**	**16**	**36**	**34**	**24**	**50**	**27**	**3**	**1**	**0**	**1**	**5**
1942-43	**Montreal Canadiens**	**NHL**	**49**	**30**	**27**	**57**	**43**	**34**	**77**	**23**	**5**	**1**	**3**	**4**	**4**
1943-44			MILITARY SERVICE												
1944-45	Calgary Army	City Sr.	13	7	3	10	....	....	....	8	2	1	0	1	2
1945-46	**Montreal Canadiens**	**NHL**	**39**	**9**	**10**	**19**	**14**	**19**	**33**	**8**	....	....	....	....	....
1946-47	**Montreal Canadiens**	**NHL**	**6**	**0**	**0**	**0**	**0**	**0**	**0**	**4**	....	....	....	....	....
	Springfield Indians	AHL	34	9	10	19	....	....	....	4	2	0	0	0	0
1947-48			DID NOT PLAY												
1948-49	Montreal Royals	QSHL	1	0	0	0	....	....	....	0	....	....	....	....	....
	Spokane Flyers	Kootenay	DID NOT PLAY – COACHING												
	NHL Totals		**185**	**75**	**69**	**144**	**123**	**106**	**229**	**94**	**11**	**6**	**3**	**9**	**11**

Rights traded to **Montreal** by **Toronto** for Frankie Eddolls, June 7, 1940.

● BENSON, BILL Bill Benson
C – L. 5'11", 165 lbs. b: Winnipeg, Man., 7/29/1920.

Season	Club	League	REGULAR SEASON								PLAYOFFS				
			GP	G	A	Pts	AG	AA	APts	PIM	GP	G	A	Pts	PIM
1937-38	Winnipeg Monarchs	MJHL	20	7	10	17	....	....	....	2	5	1	3	4	0
1938-39	Winnipeg Monarchs	MJHL	21	18	12	30	....	....	....	2	7	6	3	9	2
1939-40	Winnipeg Monarchs	MJHL	24	19	*20	*39	....	....	....	16	7	5	4	9	2
1940-41	**New York Americans**	**NHL**	**22**	**3**	**4**	**7**	**6**	**7**	**13**	**4**	....	....	....	....	....
	Springfield Indians	AHL	22	3	6	9	....	....	....	4	....	....	....	....	....
1941-42	**Brooklyn Americans**	**NHL**	**45**	**8**	**21**	**29**	**14**	**32**	**46**	**31**	....	....	....	....	....
1942-43	Sydney Navy	City Sr.	3	3	4	7	....	....	....	0	....	....	....	....	....
	Winnipeg Navy	City Sr.	....	....	....	....	....	....	....	....	2	1	0	1	0
1943-44			MILITARY SERVICE												
1944-45			MILITARY SERVICE												
1945-46	Cleveland Barons	AHL	14	3	4	7	....	....	....	4	9	0	0	0	2
1946-47	Pittsburgh Hornets	AHL	64	20	22	42	....	....	....	26	12	4	3	7	4
1947-48	Pittsburgh Hornets	AHL	65	18	20	38	....	....	....	13	2	0	0	0	0
1948-49	Pittsburgh Hornets	AHL	67	18	22	40	....	....	....	24	....	....	....	....	....
1949-50	Pittsburgh Hornets	AHL	63	15	13	28	....	....	....	0	....	....	....	....	....
	NHL Totals		**67**	**11**	**25**	**36**	**20**	**39**	**59**	**35**	....	....	....	....	....

Signed as a free agent by **NY Americans**, October 11, 1940.

• BENSON, BOBBY Bobby Benson

D – L. 5′6″, 135 lbs. b: Winnipeg, Man., 5/18/1894. d: 9/7/1965.

			REGULAR SEASON								PLAYOFFS				
Season	Club	League	GP	G	A	Pts	AG	AA	APts	PIM	GP	G	A	Pts	PIM
1912-13	Winnipeg Strathconas	City Sr.	8	3	0	3	....	....	....	....	2	0	0	0	0
1913-14	Winnipeg Falcons	City Sr.	12	2	0	2	....	....	....	....	....	....	....	....	....
1914-15	Winnipeg Falcons	MHL Sr.	8	3	0	3	....	....	....	....	2	0	0	0	6
1915-16	Winnipeg Falcons	MHL Sr.	7	2	0	2	....	....	....	12	....	....	....	....	....
1916-17	Winnipeg 223rd Battalion	MHL Sr.	8	3	1	4	....	....	....	4	....	....	....	....	....
1917-18			MILITARY SERVICE												
1918-19			MILITARY SERVICE												
1919-20	Winnipeg Falcons	MHL Sr.	9	2	1	3	....	....	....	*26	6	0	5	5	*13
	Canada	WEC	3	0	1	1	....	....	....	....	....	....	....	....	....
1920-21	Saskatoon Crescents	SSHL	16	12	1	13	....	....	....	39	4	2	1	3	*12
1921-22	Saskatoon Crescents	WCHL	23	9	4	13	....	....	....	21	....	....	....	....	....
1922-23	Calgary Tigers	WCHL	27	7	1	8	....	....	....	22	....	....	....	....	....
1923-24	Calgary Tigers	WCHL	26	5	5	10	....	....	....	24	7	0	1	1	2
1924-25	Calgary Tigers	WCHL	9	0	1	1	....	....	....	4	....	....	....	....	....
	Boston Bruins	**NHL**	**8**	**0**	**1**	**1**	**0**	**13**	**13**	**4**	....	....	....	....	....
1925-26	Saskatoon Crescents	WHL	12	0	0	0	....	....	....	0	....	....	....	....	....
	Edmonton Eskimos	WHL	12	0	0	0	....	....	....	0	2	0	0	0	2
1926-27	Moose Jaw Maroons	PHL	32	6	4	10	....	....	....	65	....	....	....	....	....
1927-28	Winnipeg–Minneapolis	AHA	23	2	0	2	....	....	....	36	8	0	1	1	*31
1928-29	Minneapolis Millers	AHA	40	3	4	7	....	....	....	92	4	0	0	0	2
1929-30	Seattle Eskimos	PCHL	36	2	3	5	....	....	....	82	....	....	....	....	....
1930-31	Seattle Eskimos	PCHL	33	2	2	4	....	....	....	76	4	0	0	0	8
1931-32	Hollywood Stars	Cal-Pro	....	1	1	2	....	....	....	....	....	....	....	....	....
	NHL Totals		**8**	**0**	**1**	**1**	**0**	**13**	**13**	**4**	....	....	....	....	....
	Other Major League Totals		109	21	11	32	....	....	....	71	9	0	1	1	4

Signed as a free agent by **Saskatoon** (WCHL), November 14, 1921. Traded to **Calgary** (WCHL) by **Saskatoon** (WCHL) for Rube Brandow, November 27, 1922. Traded to **Montreal Maroons** by **Calgary** (WCHL) for cash, January 6, 1925. Traded to **Boston** by **Montreal Maroons** with Bernie Morris for Alf Skinner, January 6, 1925. Signed as a free agent by **Saskatoon** (WHL), October 27, 1925. Traded to **Edmonton** (WHL) by **Saskatoon** (WHL) for cash, January 17, 1926.

• BENTLEY, DOUG Doug Bentley HHOF

LW – L. 5′8″, 145 lbs. b: Delisle, Sask., 9/3/1916. d: 11/24/1972.

Season	Club	League	GP	G	A	Pts	AG	AA	APts	PIM	GP	G	A	Pts	PIM
1933-34	Saskatoon Wesleys	SJHL	STATISTICS NOT AVAILABLE												
1934-35	Regina Vics	SSHL	19	10	4	14	....	....	....	21	6	0	0	0	13
1935-36	Moose Jaw Millers	SSHL	20	3	3	6	....	....	....	30	....	....	....	....	....
1936-37	Moose Jaw Millers	SSHL	24	18	19	37	....	....	....	49	3	3	0	3	4
1937-38	Drumheller Miners	SSHL	21	25	18	43	....	....	....	20	6	6	*8	*14	6
1938-39	Drumheller Miners	SSHL	32	24	29	53	....	....	....	31	6	*7	0	7	6
1939-40	**Chicago Black Hawks**	**NHL**	**39**	**12**	**7**	**19**	**26**	**14**	**40**	**12**	**2**	**0**	**0**	**0**	**0**
1940-41	**Chicago Black Hawks**	**NHL**	**47**	**8**	**20**	**28**	**16**	**37**	**53**	**12**	**5**	**1**	**1**	**2**	....
1941-42	**Chicago Black Hawks**	**NHL**	**38**	**12**	**14**	**26**	**21**	**21**	**42**	**11**	**3**	**0**	**1**	**1**	**4**
1942-43	**Chicago Black Hawks**	**NHL**	**50**	**33**	**40**	**73**	**48**	**51**	**99**	**18**	....	....	....	....	....
1943-44	**Chicago Black Hawks**	**NHL**	**50**	**38**	**39**	**77**	**49**	**48**	**97**	**22**	**9**	**8**	**4**	**12**	**4**
1944-45	Laura Beavers	SSHL	STATISTICS NOT AVAILABLE												
1945-46	**Chicago Black Hawks**	**NHL**	**36**	**19**	**21**	**40**	**29**	**39**	**68**	**16**	**4**	**0**	**2**	**2**	**0**
1946-47	**Chicago Black Hawks**	**NHL**	**52**	**21**	**34**	**55**	**29**	**49**	**78**	**18**	....	....	....	....	....
1947-48	**Chicago Black Hawks**	**NHL**	**60**	**20**	**37**	**57**	**29**	**55**	**84**	**16**	....	....	....	....	....
1948-49	**Chicago Black Hawks**	**NHL**	**58**	**23**	**43**	**66**	**37**	**70**	**107**	**38**	....	....	....	....	....
1949-50	**Chicago Black Hawks**	**NHL**	**64**	**20**	**33**	**53**	**27**	**42**	**69**	**28**	....	....	....	....	....
1950-51	**Chicago Black Hawks**	**NHL**	**44**	**9**	**23**	**32**	**12**	**30**	**42**	**20**	....	....	....	....	....
1951-52	**Chicago Black Hawks**	**NHL**	**8**	**2**	**3**	**5**	**3**	**4**	**7**	**4**	....	....	....	....	....
	Saskatoon Quakers	PCHL	35	11	14	25	....	....	....	12	13	6	6	12	4
1952-53	Saskatoon Quakers	WHL	70	22	23	45	....	....	....	37	13	6	3	9	14
1953-54	**New York Rangers**	**NHL**	**20**	**2**	**10**	**12**	**3**	**14**	**17**	**2**	....	....	....	....	....
	Saskatoon Quakers	WHL	42	8	13	21	....	....	....	18	....	....	....	....	....
1954-55	Saskatoon Quakers	WHL	61	14	23	37	....	....	....	52	....	....	....	....	....
1955-56	Saskatoon–Brandon	WHL	60	7	26	33	....	....	....	21	....	....	....	....	....
1956-57			DID NOT PLAY												
1957-58	Saskatoon-St. Paul	WHL	19	11	16	27	....	....	....	0	....	....	....	....	....
1958-59	Saskatoon Quakers	WHL	DID NOT PLAY – COACHING												
1959-60	Saskatoon Quakers	WHL	DID NOT PLAY – COACHING												
1960-61	Saskatoon Quakers	WHL	DID NOT PLAY – COACHING												
1961-62	Los Angeles Blades	WHL	8	0	2	2	....	....	....	2	....	....	....	....	....
	NHL Totals		**566**	**219**	**324**	**543**	**329**	**474**	**803**	**217**	**23**	**9**	**8**	**17**	**8**

NHL First All-Star Team (1943, 1944, 1947) • NHL Scoring Leader (1943) • NHL Second All-Star Team (1949)

Played in NHL All-Star Game (1947, 1948, 1949, 1950, 1951)

• Sat out entire 1944-45 season after being refused permission to leave Canada because of war-time travel ban, September, 1944. Traded to **NY Rangers** by **Chicago** for cash, June 30, 1953.

• BENTLEY, MAX Max "Dispy-Doodle-Dandy" Bentley HHOF

C – L. 5′10″, 155 lbs. b: Delisle, Sask., 3/1/1920. d: 1/19/1984.

			REGULAR SEASON								PLAYOFFS				
Season	Club	League	GP	G	A	Pts	AG	AA	APts	PIM	GP	G	A	Pts	PIM
1937-38	Drumheller Miners	SSHL	26	28	15	*43	....	....	....	10	5	*7	1	*8	2
1938-39	Drumheller Miners	SSHL	32	29	24	53	....	....	....	16	6	5	3	8	6
1939-40	Saskatoon Quakers	ASHL	31	*37	14	51	....	....	....	4	4	1	1	2	2
1940-41	Providence Reds	AHL	9	4	2	6	....	....	....	0	....	....	....	....	....
	Kansas City Americans	AHA	5	5	5	10	....	....	....	0	....	....	....	....	....
	Chicago Black Hawks	**NHL**	**36**	**7**	**10**	**17**	**14**	**18**	**32**	**6**	**4**	**1**	**3**	**4**	**2**
1941-42	**Chicago Black Hawks**	**NHL**	**39**	**13**	**17**	**30**	**22**	**26**	**48**	**2**	**3**	**2**	**0**	**2**	**0**
1942-43	**Chicago Black Hawks**	**NHL**	**47**	**26**	**44**	**70**	**37**	**57**	**94**	**2**	....	....	....	....	....
1943-44	Calgary Currie Army	City Sr.	15	*18	13	*31	....	....	....	*26	2	3	4	7	0
1944-45	Calgary Currie Army	City Sr.	12	14	14	28	....	....	....	24	3	3	2	*5	0
1945-46	**Chicago Black Hawks**	**NHL**	**47**	**31**	**30**	***61**	**48**	**57**	**105**	**6**	**4**	**1**	**0**	**1**	**4**
1946-47	**Chicago Black Hawks**	**NHL**	**60**	**29**	**43**	***72**	**40**	**62**	**102**	**12**	....	....	....	....	....
1947-48	**Chicago Black Hawks**	**NHL**	**6**	**3**	**3**	**6**	**4**	**4**	**8**	**4**	....	....	....	....	....
	Toronto Maple Leafs	**NHL**	**53**	**23**	**25**	**48**	**34**	**37**	**71**	**10**	**9**	**4**	***7**	**11**	**0**
1948-49	**Toronto Maple Leafs**	**NHL**	**60**	**19**	**22**	**41**	**30**	**35**	**65**	**18**	**9**	**4**	**3**	**7**	**2**
1949-50	**Toronto Maple Leafs**	**NHL**	**69**	**23**	**18**	**41**	**31**	**23**	**54**	**14**	**7**	**3**	**3**	**6**	**0**
1950-51	**Toronto Maple Leafs**	**NHL**	**67**	**21**	**41**	**62**	**29**	**54**	**83**	**34**	**11**	**2**	***11**	***13**	**4**
1951-52	**Toronto Maple Leafs**	**NHL**	**69**	**24**	**17**	**41**	**34**	**22**	**56**	**40**	**4**	**1**	**0**	**1**	**2**
1952-53	**Toronto Maple Leafs**	**NHL**	**36**	**12**	**11**	**23**	**18**	**15**	**33**	**16**	....	....	....	....	....
1953-54	**New York Rangers**	**NHL**	**57**	**14**	**18**	**32**	**21**	**24**	**45**	**15**	....	....	....	....	....
1954-55	Saskatoon Quakers	WHL	40	24	17	41	....	....	....	23	....	....	....	....	....
1955-56	Saskatoon Quakers	WHL	10	2	2	4	....	....	....	20	....	....	....	....	....
1956-57	Saskatoon Jr. Quakers	SJHL	DID NOT PLAY – COACHING												
1957-58	Saskatoon Jr. Quakers	SJHL	DID NOT PLAY – COACHING												
1958-59	Saskatoon Quakers	WHL	26	6	12	18	....	....	....	2	....	....	....	....	....
	NHL Totals		**646**	**245**	**299**	**544**	**362**	**434**	**796**	**179**	**51**	**18**	**27**	**45**	**14**

Won Lady Byng Trophy (1943) • NHL First All-Star Team (1946) • NHL Scoring Leader (1946, 1947) • Won Hart Trophy (1946) • NHL Second All-Star Team (1947)

Played in NHL All-Star Game (1947, 1948, 1949, 1951)

Traded to **Toronto** by **Chicago** with Cy Thomas for Gus Bodnar, Bud Poile, Gaye Stewart, Ernie Dickens and Bob Goldham, November 2, 1947. Traded to **NY Rangers** by **Toronto** for cash, August 11, 1953.

• BENTLEY, REGGIE Reggie Bentley

LW – L. 5′8″, 155 lbs. b: Delisle, Sask., 5/3/1914.

Season	Club	League	GP	G	A	Pts	AG	AA	APts	PIM	GP	G	A	Pts	PIM
1935-36	Saskatoon Standards	SSHL	19	7	0	7	....	....	....	16	....	....	....	....	....
1936-37	Saskatoon Quakers	SSHL	20	7	2	9	....	....	....	4	....	....	....	....	....
1937-38	Moose Jaw Millers	SSHL	24	14	9	23	....	....	....	14	6	6	3	9	4
1938-39	Drumheller Miners	ASHL	32	21	10	31	....	....	....	52	6	4	1	5	9
1939-40	Drumheller Miners	ASHL	32	23	8	31	....	....	....	27	....	....	....	....	....
1940-41	Saskatoon Quakers	ASHL	30	14	5	19	....	....	....	2	4	0	0	0	0
1941-42	Kansas City Americans	AHA	50	16	16	32	....	....	....	16	6	3	4	7	0
1942-43	**Chicago Black Hawks**	**NHL**	**11**	**1**	**2**	**3**	**1**	**3**	**4**	**2**	....	....	....	....	....
1943-44	Moose Jaw Victorias	SSHL	2	2	3	5	....	....	....	0	....	....	....	....	....
	Calgary Currie Army	City Sr.	14	7	2	9	....	....	....	6	2	0	0	0	0
1944-45	Calgary Currie Army	City Sr.	10	1	1	2	....	....	....	2	2	0	1	1	0
1945-46	New Westminster Royals	PCHL	57	30	27	57	....	....	....	18	....	....	....	....	....
1946-47	New Westminster Royals	PCHL	60	41	30	71	....	....	....	14	4	2	1	3	0
1947-48	Saskatoon Quakers	WCSHL	45	28	22	50	....	....	....	17	....	....	....	....	....
1948-49	Saskatoon Quakers	WCSHL	48	22	18	40	....	....	....	4	....	....	....	....	....
	Spokane Spartans	Kootenay	....	....	....	....	....	....	....	....	4	4	3	7	0
1949-50	Saskatoon Quakers	WCSHL	50	15	14	29	....	....	....	14	4	1	0	1	0
1950-51	Saskatoon Quakers	WCSHL	40	12	13	25	....	....	....	8	12	2	1	3	0
1951-52	Yorkton Legionaires	SSHL	30	20	23	43	....	....	....	4	7	3	5	8	0
	NHL Totals		**11**	**1**	**2**	**3**	**1**	**3**	**4**	**2**	....	....	....	....	....

• BERENSON, RED — *see page 866*

• BERGDINON, FRED Fred Bergdinon

RW – L. 6′1″, 170 lbs. b: Minneapolis, MN, 1906. Deceased.

Season	Club	League	GP	G	A	Pts	AG	AA	APts	PIM	GP	G	A	Pts	PIM
1925-26	**Boston Bruins**	**NHL**	**2**	**0**	**0**	**0**	**0**	**0**	**0**	**0**	....	....	....	....	....
	NHL Totals		**2**	**0**	**0**	**0**	**0**	**0**	**0**	**0**	....	....	....	....	....

• BERGMAN, GARY — *see page 869*

• BERLINQUETTE, LOUIS Louis Berlinquette

LW – L. 5′11″, 175 lbs. b: Papineau, Quebec, 1887. Deceased.

Season	Club	League	GP	G	A	Pts	AG	AA	APts	PIM	GP	G	A	Pts	PIM
1908-09	Haileybury Seniors	City Sr.	8	9	0	9	....	....	....	19	....	....	....	....	....
1909-10	Haileybury Hockey Club	NHA	1	2	0	2	....	....	....	0	....	....	....	....	....
1910-11	Galt Professionals	OPHL	5	0	0	0	....	....	....	....	3	4	0	4	....
1911-12	Montreal Canadiens	NHA	4	0	0	0	....	....	....	5	....	....	....	....	....
1911-12	Moncton Victorias	MPHL	9	7	0	7	....	....	....	15	2	0	0	0	5
1912-13	Montreal Canadiens	NHA	16	4	0	4	....	....	....	14	....	....	....	....	....
1913-14	Montreal Canadiens	NHA	20	4	9	13	....	....	....	14	2	0	0	0	0
1914-15	Montreal Canadiens	NHA	20	2	1	3	....	....	....	40	....	....	....	....	....
1915-16	Montreal Canadiens	NHA	19	2	2	4	....	....	....	19	1	0	0	0	0
1916-17	Montreal Canadiens	NHA	20	7	4	11	....	....	....	36	5	0	0	0	8
1917-18	**Montreal Canadiens**	**NHL**	**20**	**2**	**1**	**3**	**5**	**0**	**5**	**12**	**2**	**0**	**0**	**0**	**0**
1918-19	**Montreal Canadiens**	**NHL**	**18**	**5**	**4**	**9**	**17**	**38**	**55**	**12**	**10**	**1**	**3**	**4**	**9**
1919-20	**Montreal Canadiens**	**NHL**	**24**	**8**	**9**	**17**	**18**	**62**	**80**	**36**	....	....	....	....	....
1920-21	**Montreal Canadiens**	**NHL**	**24**	**12**	**9**	**21**	**31**	**81**	**112**	**24**	....	....	....	....	....
1921-22	**Montreal Canadiens**	**NHL**	**24**	**13**	**5**	**18**	**36**	**31**	**67**	**10**	....	....	....	....	....
1922-23	**Montreal Canadiens**	**NHL**	**24**	**2**	**3**	**5**	**7**	**27**	**34**	**4**	**2**	**0**	**1**	**1**	**0**
1923-24	Saskatoon Quakers	WCHL	29	9	6	15	....	....	....	9	....	....	....	....	....
1924-25	**Montreal Maroons**	**NHL**	**29**	**4**	**2**	**6**	**14**	**26**	**40**	**22**	....	....	....	....	....
1925-26	**Pittsburgh Pirates**	**NHL**	**30**	**0**	**0**	**0**	**0**	**0**	**0**	**8**	**2**	**0**	**0**	**0**	**0**
1926-27	Quebec Castors	Can-Am	19	3	3	6	....	....	....	31	....	....	....	....	....
	NHL Totals		**193**	**46**	**33**	**79**	**128**	**265**	**393**	**128**	**16**	**1**	**4**	**5**	**9**
	Other Major League Totals		143	37	22	59	....	....	....	152	13	4	0	4	13

Rights retained by **Montreal Canadiens** after NHA folded, November 26, 1917. Traded to **Saskatoon** (WCHL) by **Montreal Canadiens** for cash, November 1, 1923. Traded to **Montreal Maroons** by **Saskatoon** (WCHL) for cash, November 26, 1924. Traded to **Pittsburgh** by **Montreal Maroons** for cash, November 10, 1925.

• BESLER, PHIL   Phil Besler

RW – R. 5′11″, 180 lbs.   b: Melville, Sask., 12/9/1913.   Deceased.

			REGULAR SEASON								PLAYOFFS				
Season	Club	League	GP	G	A	Pts	AG	AA	APts	PIM	GP	G	A	Pts	PIM
1929-30	Melville Millionaires	SSHL	20	3	0	3	....	....	....	25	2	0	0	0	0
1930-31	Melville Millionaires	SSHL	20	4	2	6	....	....	....	37	....	....	....	....	....
1931-32	Melville Millionaires	SSHL	DID NOT PLAY – INJURED												
1932-33	Humboldt Indians	SSHL	17	7	5	12	....	....	....	6	....	....	....	....	....
1933-34	Prince Albert Mintos	SSHL	21	*31	4	35	....	....	....	12	4	2	1	3	2
1934-35	Boston Cubs	Can-Am	38	6	3	9	....	....	....	30	3	*2	0	2	13
1935-36	**Boston Bruins**	**NHL**	**8**	**0**	**0**	**0**	**0**	**0**	**0**	**0**	....	....	....	....	....
	Boston Cubs	Can-Am	29	4	6	10	....	....	....	25	....	....	....	....	....
1936-37	Vancouver–Portland	PCHL	28	13	6	19	....	....	....	27	3	1	0	1	2
1937-38	Portland Buckaroos	PCHL	38	*24	3	27	....	....	....	26	2	0	1	1	6
1938-39	**Chicago Black Hawks**	**NHL**	**17**	**1**	**3**	**4**	**2**	**6**	**8**	**16**	....	....	....	....	....
	Pittsburgh Hornets	AHL	9	1	1	2	....	....	....	2	....	....	....	....	....
	Cleveland Falcons	AHL	2	0	0	0	....	....	....	0	....	....	....	....	....
	Detroit Red Wings	**NHL**	**5**	**0**	**1**	**1**	**0**	**2**	**2**	**2**	....	....	....	....	....
	Providence Reds	AHL	2	0	0	0	....	....	....	0	5	0	0	0	0
1939-40	Omaha Knights	AHA	48	20	16	36	....	....	....	57	9	3	2	5	*26
1940-41	Omaha Knights	AHA	47	15	15	30	....	....	....	26	....	....	....	....	....
1941-42	Omaha Knights	AHA	49	17	15	32	....	....	....	36	8	0	3	3	17
	NHL Totals		**30**	**1**	**4**	**5**	**2**	**8**	**10**	**18**	....	....	....	....	....

Signed as a free agent by **Chicago**, September 29, 1938. Traded to **Detroit** by **Chicago** for Charley Mason, January 27, 1939.

• BESSONE, PETE   Pete Bessone   USHOF

D – L. 5′11″, 200 lbs.   b: New Bedford, MA, 1/13/1913.   Deceased.

Season	Club	League	GP	G	A	Pts	AG	AA	APts	PIM	GP	G	A	Pts	PIM
1935-36	Paris Stade Francais	France	STATISTICS NOT AVAILABLE												
1936-37	Pittsburgh Yellowjackets	EHL	47	6	4	10	....	....	....	53	....	....	....	....	....
1937-38	**Detroit Red Wings**	**NHL**	**6**	**0**	**1**	**1**	**0**	**2**	**2**	**6**	....	....	....	....	....
	Pittsburgh Hornets	AHL	16	1	1	2	....	....	....	4	1	0	0	0	0
	Detroit Pontiacs	MOHL	15	6	2	8	....	....	....	38	....	....	....	....	....
1938-39	Pittsburgh Hornets	AHL	53	3	8	11	....	....	....	87	....	....	....	....	....
1939-40	Pittsburgh Hornets	AHL	54	4	8	12	....	....	....	100	9	0	2	2	20
1940-41	Pittsburgh Hornets	AHL	17	0	3	3	....	....	....	22	....	....	....	....	....
1941-42	Pittsburgh Hornets	AHL	53	2	18	20	....	....	....	102	....	....	....	....	....
1942-43	Pittsburgh–Cleveland	AHL	55	10	16	26	....	....	....	92	2	0	0	0	4
1943-44	Cleveland Barons	AHL	50	6	20	26	....	....	....	89	11	0	1	1	6
1944-45	Cleveland Barons	AHL	60	6	26	32	....	....	....	100	12	1	2	3	18
1945-46	Cleveland Barons	AHL	50	2	14	16	....	....	....	88	8	0	0	0	9
1946-47	Providence Reds	AHL	54	4	9	13	....	....	....	94	....	....	....	....	....
1947-48	Paris Racing Club	France	DID NOT PLAY – COACHING												
1948-49	Paris Racing Club	France	DID NOT PLAY – COACHING												
1949-50	Springfield Indians	AHL	4	0	0	0	....	....	....	2	....	....	....	....	....
	NHL Totals		**6**	**0**	**1**	**1**	**0**	**2**	**2**	**6**	....	....	....	....	....

EHL Second All-Star Team (1937)

Signed as a free agent by **Detroit**, January 15, 1938. Traded to **Pittsburgh** (AHL) by **Detroit** for cash, October 5, 1939.

• BETTIO, SAM   Sam (Silvio Angelo) Bettio

LW – L. 5′8″, 175 lbs.   b: Copper Cliff, Ont., 12/1/1928.

Season	Club	League	GP	G	A	Pts	AG	AA	APts	PIM	GP	G	A	Pts	PIM
1945-46	Copper Cliff Redmen	City Sr.	8	2	3	5	....	....	....	0	3	7	2	9	0
1946-47	Copper Cliff Redmen	City Sr.	9	*10	6	16	....	....	....	10	5	*7	*7	*14	8
1947-48	Hershey Bears	AHL	21	3	3	6	....	....	....	8	....	....	....	....	....
	Boston Olympics	EHL	8	8	5	13	....	....	....	10	....	....	....	....	....
	Boston Olympics	QSHL	22	11	14	25	....	....	....	31	....	....	....	....	....
1948-49	Hershey Bears	AHL	58	15	25	40	....	....	....	18	11	3	4	7	4
1949-50	**Boston Bruins**	**NHL**	**44**	**9**	**12**	**21**	**12**	**15**	**27**	**32**	....	....	....	....	....
	Hershey Bears	AHL	23	7	10	17	....	....	....	8	....	....	....	....	....
1950-51	Hershey Bears	AHL	57	19	42	61	....	....	....	28	6	2	4	6	0
1951-52	Hershey Bears	AHL	64	18	37	55	....	....	....	27	5	2	0	2	13
1952-53	Hershey Bears	AHL	63	21	43	64	....	....	....	24	3	2	1	3	2
1953-54	Victoria Cougars	WHL	68	24	39	63	....	....	....	49	5	1	1	2	2
1954-55	Buffalo Bisons	AHL	53	13	31	44	....	....	....	27	10	4	8	12	6
1955-56	Buffalo Bisons	AHL	61	14	17	31	....	....	....	37	2	1	1	2	0
1956-57	Buffalo Bisons	AHL	62	38	29	67	....	....	....	40	....	....	....	....	....
1957-58	Buffalo Bisons	AHL	70	19	34	53	....	....	....	39	....	....	....	....	....
1958-59	Sudbury Wolves	NOHA	19	13	15	28	....	....	....	....	5	4	0	4	4
1959-60	Sudbury Wolves	EPHL	67	45	56	101	....	....	....	39	14	7	7	14	23
1960-61	Sudbury Wolves	EPHL	65	37	50	87	....	....	....	99	....	....	....	....	....
1961-62	Sudbury Wolves	EPHL	35	12	22	34	....	....	....	41	6	1	7	8	2
	NHL Totals		**44**	**9**	**12**	**21**	**12**	**15**	**27**	**32**	....	....	....	....	....

• BEVERLEY, NICK   — *see page 873*

• BIONDA, JACK   Jack (John Arthur) Bionda

D – L. 6′, 180 lbs.   b: Hunstville, Ont., 9/18/1933.

Season	Club	League	GP	G	A	Pts	AG	AA	APts	PIM	GP	G	A	Pts	PIM
1951-52	Toronto Marlboros	OHA	13	1	1	2	....	....	....	20	2	1	1	2	2
1952-53	Toronto Marlboros	OHA	50	2	11	13	....	....	....	116	7	0	1	1	8
1953-54	Toronto Marlboros	OHA	56	16	19	35	....	....	....	107	15	2	2	4	32
1954-55	Soo Greyhounds	NOHA	20	1	5	6	....	....	....	30	....	....	....	....	....
1955-56	**Toronto Maple Leafs**	**NHL**	**13**	**0**	**1**	**1**	**0**	**1**	**1**	**18**	....	....	....	....	....
	Pittsburgh Hornets	AHL	46	7	9	16	....	....	....	*190	4	0	2	2	12
1956-57	**Boston Bruins**	**NHL**	**35**	**2**	**3**	**5**	**3**	**3**	**6**	**43**	**10**	**0**	**1**	**1**	**14**
	Springfield Indians	AHL	21	2	12	14	....	....	....	65	....	....	....	....	....
1957-58	**Boston Bruins**	**NHL**	**42**	**1**	**4**	**5**	**1**	**4**	**5**	**50**	....	....	....	....	....
	Springfield Indians	AHL	15	0	4	4	....	....	....	22	11	0	4	4	18
1958-59	**Boston Bruins**	**NHL**	**3**	**0**	**1**	**1**	**0**	**1**	**1**	**2**	**1**	**0**	**0**	**0**	**0**
	Providence Reds	AHL	66	9	17	26	....	....	....	144	....	....	....	....	....
1959-60	Victoria Cougars	WHL	68	6	19	25	....	....	....	85	11	0	3	3	10
1960-61	Portland Buckaroos	WHL	69	7	29	36	....	....	....	102	14	2	4	6	27
1961-62	Portland Buckaroos	WHL	70	2	25	27	....	....	....	121	7	1	3	4	25
1962-63	Portland Buckaroos	WHL	70	12	28	40	....	....	....	99	7	0	5	5	2
1963-64	Portland Buckaroos	WHL	63	5	14	19	....	....	....	79	5	0	1	1	6
1964-65	Portland Buckaroos	WHL	16	0	3	3	....	....	....	26	6	0	1	1	2
1965-66	Portland Buckaroos	WHL	72	3	24	27	....	....	....	100	14	1	6	7	14
1966-67	Portland Buckaroos	WHL	41	2	7	9	....	....	....	24	....	....	....	....	....
	NHL Totals		**93**	**3**	**9**	**12**	**4**	**9**	**13**	**113**	**11**	**0**	**1**	**1**	**14**

Claimed by **Boston** from **Toronto** in Intra-League Draft, June 6, 1956. Traded to **Springfield** (AHL) by **Boston** with Norm Defelice for Don Simmons, January, 1957.

• BLACK, STEPHEN   Stephen Black

LW – L. 6′, 185 lbs.   b: Fort William, Ont., 3/31/1927.

Season	Club	League	GP	G	A	Pts	AG	AA	APts	PIM	GP	G	A	Pts	PIM
1943-44	Port Arthur Flyers	TBJHL	10	4	2	6	....	....	....	8	6	3	6	9	0
1944-45	Port Arthur Flyers	TBJHL	11	17	8	25	....	....	....	4	3	2	0	2	0
	Port Arthur Bruins	TBJHL	....	....	....	....	....	....	....	....	5	2	3	5	2
1945-46	Port Arthur Flyers	TBJHL	6	11	10	21	....	....	....	0	5	7	5	12	4
1946-47	Oakland Oaks	PCHL	60	43	36	79	....	....	....	79	....	....	....	....	....
1947-48	St. Louis Flyers	AHL	58	11	18	29	....	....	....	29	....	....	....	....	....
1948-49	St. Louis Flyers	AHL	62	24	47	71	....	....	....	59	7	0	5	5	12
1949-50	**Detroit Red Wings**	**NHL**	**69**	**7**	**14**	**21**	**9**	**18**	**27**	**53**	**13**	**0**	**0**	**0**	**13**
1950-51	**Detroit Red Wings**	**NHL**	**5**	**0**	**0**	**0**	**0**	**0**	**0**	**2**	....	....	....	....	....
	Chicago Black Hawks	**NHL**	**39**	**4**	**6**	**10**	**5**	**8**	**13**	**22**	....	....	....	....	....
	Indianapolis Capitals	AHL	8	1	2	3	....	....	....	13	....	....	....	....	....
	Milwaukee Seagulls	USHL	9	4	6	10	....	....	....	11	....	....	....	....	....
1951-52	St. Louis Flyers	AHL	37	9	21	30	....	....	....	34	....	....	....	....	....
1952-53	Calgary Stampeders	WHL	45	21	16	37	....	....	....	61	5	4	3	7	2
1953-54	Calgary Stampeders	WHL	43	21	33	54	....	....	....	29	25	5	6	11	6
	NHL Totals		**113**	**11**	**20**	**31**	**14**	**26**	**40**	**77**	**13**	**0**	**0**	**0**	**13**

Played in NHL All-Star Game (1950)

Traded to **Detroit** by **St. Louis** (AHL) with Bill Brennan for Fern Gauthier, Cliff Simpson and Ed Nicholson, September, 1950. Traded to **Chicago** by **Detroit** with Lee Fogolin for Bert Olmstead and Vic Stasiuk, December 2, 1950.

• BLACKBURN, DON   — *see page 876*

• BLADE, HANK   Hank Blade

LW – L. 5′11″, 190 lbs.   b: Peterborough, Ont., 4/28/1920.

Season	Club	League	GP	G	A	Pts	AG	AA	APts	PIM	GP	G	A	Pts	PIM
1939-40	Ottawa Montagnards	City Sr.	20	5	0	5	....	....	....	8	7	0	0	0	0
1940-41	Ottawa Montagnards	City Sr.	20	12	5	17	....	....	....	2	....	....	....	....	....
	Ottawa Car Bombers	City Sr.	....	....	....	....	....	....	....	....	2	4	3	7	4
1941-42	Ottawa RCAF	City Sr.	16	7	10	17	....	....	....	6	5	0	1	1	0
1942-43	Ottawa RCAF	City Sr.	19	10	13	23	....	....	....	6	17	7	*9	16	10
	Vancouver RCAF	City Sr.	14	14	6	20	....	....	....	6	....	....	....	....	....
1943-44	Vancouver Seahawks	City Sr.	....	....	....	....	....	....	....	....	3	*4	2	6	4
1944-45	Ottawa Depot #17	City Sr.	12	*22	21	*43	....	....	....	8	....	....	....	....	....
	Ottawa Senators	QSHL	2	1	3	4	....	....	....	0	....	....	....	....	....
1945-46	Kansas City Pla-Mors	USHL	46	29	36	65	....	....	....	16	12	7	8	15	4
	Ottawa Senators	QSHL	5	0	2	2	....	....	....	6	....	....	....	....	....
1946-47	**Chicago Black Hawks**	**NHL**	**18**	**1**	**3**	**4**	**1**	**4**	**5**	**2**	....	....	....	....	....
	Kansas City Pla-Mors	USHL	38	23	24	47	....	....	....	17	12	4	7	11	4
1947-48	**Chicago Black Hawks**	**NHL**	**6**	**1**	**0**	**1**	**1**	**0**	**1**	**0**	....	....	....	....	....
	Pittsburgh Hornets	AHL	7	1	2	3	....	....	....	6	....	....	....	....	....
	Kansas City Pla-Mors	USHL	51	29	41	70	....	....	....	32	7	0	3	3	0
1948-49	Kansas City Pla-Mors	USHL	54	27	36	63	....	....	....	19	2	0	0	0	0
1949-50	Kansas City Mohawks	USHL	66	27	48	75	....	....	....	27	3	0	0	0	0
1950-51	Milwaukee Seagulls	USHL	63	26	48	74	....	....	....	34	....	....	....	....	....
1951-52	Calgary Stampeders	PCHL	62	14	27	41	....	....	....	24	....	....	....	....	....
1952-53	Calgary Stampeders	WHL	22	3	6	9	....	....	....	32	....	....	....	....	....
1953-54	Simcoe Gunners	OHA Sr.B	DID NOT PLAY – COACHING												
	NHL Totals		**24**	**2**	**3**	**5**	**2**	**4**	**6**	**2**	....	....	....	....	....

Won Herman W. Paterson Cup (USHL - MVP) (1951)

• BLAINE, GARY   Gary Blaine

RW – R. 5′11″, 190 lbs.   b: St. Boniface, Man., 4/19/1933.

Season	Club	League	GP	G	A	Pts	AG	AA	APts	PIM	GP	G	A	Pts	PIM
1950-51	Winnipeg Canadians	MJHL	33	13	14	27	....	....	....	45	....	....	....	....	....
1951-52	St. Boniface Canadians	MJHL	35	14	18	32	....	....	....	45	5	3	1	4	0
1952-53	St. Boniface Canadians	MJHL	17	16	15	31	....	....	....	50	25	*23	16	*39	31
1953-54	Montreal Royals	QHL	54	11	20	31	....	....	....	24	11	2	6	8	6
1954-55	**Montreal Canadiens**	**NHL**	**1**	**0**	**0**	**0**	**0**	**0**	**0**	**0**	....	....	....	....	....
	Montreal Royals	QHL	53	18	31	40	....	....	....	56	14	5	*11	*16	2
1955-56	Trois-Rivieres Lions	QHL	22	6	6	12	....	....	....	4	....	....	....	....	....
	Winnipeg Warriors	WHL	40	9	12	21	....	....	....	20	....	....	....	....	....
1956-57	Chicoutimi Sagueneens	QHL	12	2	6	8	....	....	....	2	....	....	....	....	....
	Buffalo Bisons	AHL	43	13	14	27	....	....	....	20	....	....			
1957-58	Quebec Aces	QHL	62	23	38	61	....	....	....	28	13	3	5	8	12
1958-59	Vancouver Canucks	WHL	67	16	19	35	....	....	....	60	8	1	2	3	10
1959-60	Soo Thunderbirds	EPHL	70	20	37	57	....	....	....	54	....	....	....	....	....
	NHL Totals		**1**	**0**	**0**	**0**	**0**	**0**	**0**	**0**	....	....	....	....	....

• BLAIR, ANDY   Andy Blair

C – L. 6′1″, 180 lbs.   b: Winnipeg, Man., 2/27/1908.   d: 12/27/1977.

Season	Club	League	GP	G	A	Pts	AG	AA	APts	PIM	GP	G	A	Pts	PIM
1923-24	University of Manitoba	MHL Sr.	6	4	2	6	....	....	....	2	1	0	0	0	0
1924-25	University of Manitoba	MJHL	9	14	4	18	....	....	....	4	8	10	1	11	6
1925-26	University of Manitoba	MJHL	1	0	0	0	....	....	....	0	....	....	....	....	....
	University of Manitoba	MHL Sr.	4	5	1	6	....	....	....	0	....	....	....	....	....
1926-27	University of Manitoba	MJHL	1	1	1	2	....		....	....	....	....	....	....	....
	Winnipeg Rangers	MHL Sr.	1	0	0	0	....	....	....	0	....	....	....	....	
1927-28	University of Manitoba	MHL Sr.	10	10	10	20	....	....	....	14	7	3	2	5	*18
	Winnipeg CPR	MHL Sr.	4	3	2	5	....	....	....	2	....	....	....	....	....
1928-29	**Toronto Maple Leafs**	**NHL**	**44**	**12**	**15**	**27**	**48**	**141**	**189**	**41**	**4**	***3**	**0**	***3**	**2**
1929-30	**Toronto Maple Leafs**	**NHL**	**42**	**11**	**10**	**21**	**22**	**32**	**54**	**27**	....	....	....	....	
1930-31	**Toronto Maple Leafs**	**NHL**	**44**	**11**	**8**	**19**	**27**	**29**	**56**	**32**	**2**	**1**	**0**	**1**	**0**
1931-32	**Toronto Maple Leafs**	**NHL**	**48**	**9**	**14**	**23**	**19**	**39**	**58**	**35**	**7**	**2**	**2**	**4**	**6**
1932-33	**Toronto Maple Leafs**	**NHL**	**43**	**6**	**9**	**15**	**14**	**24**	**38**	**38**	**9**	**0**	**2**	**2**	**4**
1933-34	**Toronto Maple Leafs**	**NHL**	**47**	**14**	**9**	**23**	**31**	**24**	**55**	**35**	**5**	**0**	**2**	**2**	**16**
1934-35	**Toronto Maple Leafs**	**NHL**	**45**	**6**	**14**	**20**	**13**	**31**	**44**	**22**	**2**	**0**	**0**	**0**	**2**
1935-36	**Toronto Maple Leafs**	**NHL**	**45**	**5**	**4**	**9**	**12**	**10**	**22**	**60**	**9**	**0**	**0**	**0**	**2**
1936-37	**Chicago Black Hawks**	**NHL**	**44**	**0**	**3**	**3**	**0**	**7**	**7**	**33**	....	....	....	....	....
	NHL Totals		**402**	**74**	**86**	**160**	**186**	**337**	**523**	**323**	**38**	**6**	**6**	**12**	**32**

Played in NHL All-Star Game (1934)

Traded to **Chicago** by **Toronto** for cash, May 7, 1936.

• BLAIR, CHUCK
Chuck Blair
RW – R. 5'10", 175 lbs. b: Edinburgh, Scotland, 7/23/1928.

Season	Club	League	GP	G	A	Pts	AG	AA	APts	PIM	GP	G	A	Pts	PIM
			REGULAR SEASON								PLAYOFFS				
1946-47	Oshawa Generals	OHA	28	19	22	41	....	....	....	6	....	....	....	....	....
1947-48	Oshawa Generals	OHA	33	18	20	38	....	....	....	24	6	0	1	1	13
1948-49	**Toronto Maple Leafs**	**NHL**	**1**	**0**	**0**	**0**	**0**	**0**	**0**	**0**	....	....	....	....	....
	Toronto Marlboros	OHA Sr.	36	21	14	35	....	....	....	47	23	10	10	20	16
1949-50	Toronto Marlboros	OHA Sr.	39	21	23	44	....	....	....	36	14	5	4	9	4
1950-51	Pittsburgh Hornets	AHL	71	27	16	43	....	....	....	41	13	6	1	7	8
1951-52	Pittsburgh Hornets	AHL	57	13	25	38	....	....	....	22	11	1	2	3	6
1952-53	Pittsburgh Hornets	AHL	48	17	18	35	....	....	....	16	10	2	3	5	10
1953-54	Cleveland Barons	AHL	59	23	15	38	....	....	....	2	9	4	3	7	2
1954-55	Buffalo Bisons	AHL	59	12	17	29	....	....	....	8	10	5	0	5	0
1955-56	Buffalo Bisons	AHL	56	17	16	33	....	....	....	20	5	3	1	4	4
1956-57	Buffalo Bisons	AHL	64	19	18	37	....	....	....	22	....	....	....	....	....
1957-58	Calgary Stampeders	WHL	65	25	23	48	....	....	....	31	14	2	9	11	0
1958-59	Calgary Stampeders	WHL	35	19	15	34	....	....	....	6	8	4	0	4	4
1959-60	Quebec Aces	AHL	48	8	12	20	....	....	....	8	....	....	....	....	....
1960-61	Clinton Comets	EHL	61	21	41	62	....	....	....	12	4	0	1	1	0
1961-62	Fort Erie Meteors	OHA Sr.	DID NOT PLAY – COACHING												
	NHL Totals		**1**	**0**	**0**	**0**	**0**	**0**	**0**	**0**	....	....	....	....	....

Traded to **Cleveland** (AHL) by **Toronto** with $30,000 for Bob Bailey and Gerry Foley, June, 1953. Traded to **NY Rangers** by **Buffalo** (AHL) with Gord Pennell for Pete Conacher, June, 1956.

• BLAIR, GEORGE
George "Dusty" Blair
C – R. 5'8", 160 lbs. b: South Porcupine, Ont., 9/15/1929.

Season	Club	League	GP	G	A	Pts	AG	AA	APts	PIM	GP	G	A	Pts	PIM
1947-48	Oshawa Generals	OHA	36	17	13	30	....	....	....	17	6	0	3	3	5
1948-49	Oshawa Generals	OHA	46	23	26	49	....	....	....	15	2	1	1	2	0
1949-50	Los Angeles Monarchs	PCHL	44	18	14	32	....	....	....	10	....	....	....	....	....
	Pittsburgh Hornets	AHL	17	1	3	4	....	....	....	2	....	....	....	....	....
1950-51	**Toronto Maple Leafs**	**NHL**	**2**	**0**	**0**	**0**	**0**	**0**	**0**	**0**	....	....	....	....	....
	St. Michael's Monarchs	OHA Sr.	23	11	13	24	....	....	....	4	19	8	7	15	4
1951-52	Pittsburgh Hornets	AHL	4	0	0	0	....	....	....	0	....	....	....	....	....
	Saint John Beavers	MMHL	60	31	33	64	....	....	....	6	15	9	9	18	2
1952-53	Ottawa Senators	QSHL	3	0	1	1	....	....	....	0	....	....	....	....	....
	Smith Falls Rideaus	OHA Sr.	45	22	*43	65	....	....	....	11	21	5	*17	22	10
1953-54	Ottawa Senators	QHL	71	28	43	71	....	....	....	0	22	*9	*12	*21	0
1954-55	Buffalo Bisons	AHL	64	18	31	49	....	....	....	6	10	3	1	4	0
1955-56	Providence Reds	AHL	55	18	16	34	....	....	....	6	9	1	12	13	0
1956-57	Providence Reds	AHL	59	9	24	33	....	....	....	4	5	1	1	2	2
1957-58	Calgary Stampeders	WHL	69	11	31	42	....	....	....	11	14	3	4	7	2
1958-59	Calgary Stampeders	WHL	53	14	13	27	....	....	....	4	8	3	1	4	0
1959-60	Calgary Stampeders	WHL	69	6	27	33	....	....	....	7	....	....	....	....	....
1960-61	Soo Thunderbirds	EPHL	66	11	23	34	....	....	....	20	10	1	1	2	0
1961-62	Soo Thunderbirds	EPHL	67	9	28	37	....	....	....	8	....	....	....	....	....
1962-63	Clinton Comets	EHL	65	17	44	61	....	....	....	4	13	2	9	11	0
1963-64	New Haven Blades	EHL	21	2	7	9	....	....	....	0	....	....	....	....	....
	Clinton Comets	EHL	15	1	3	4	....	....	....	0	....	....	....	....	....
1964-65	Nashville Dixie Flyers	EHL	66	13	42	55	....	....	....	14	13	4	8	12	0
	NHL Totals		**2**	**0**	**0**	**0**	**0**	**0**	**0**	**0**	....	....	....	....	....

Won Vimy Trophy (MVP - QHL) (1954)

Traded to **Chicago** (Buffalo - AHL) by **Toronto** with Frank Sullivan and Jackie LeClair for Brian Cullen, May 4, 1954.

• BLAKE, BOB
Bob (Louis Robert) Blake
LW – L. 6', 200 lbs. b: Ashfield, WI, 8/16/1916.

Season	Club	League	GP	G	A	Pts	AG	AA	APts	PIM	GP	G	A	Pts	PIM
1934-35	Boston Cubs	Can-Am	44	5	7	12	....	....	....	28	3	0	0	0	4
1935-36	Hibbing Miners	CHL	42	10	12	22	....	....	....	74	6	*3	1	4	8
1935-36	**Boston Bruins**	**NHL**	**12**	**0**	**0**	**0**	**0**	**0**	**0**	**0**	....	....	....	....	....
	Boston Cubs	Can-Am	37	7	10	17	....	....	....	38	....	....	....	....	....
1936-37	Minneapolis Millers	AHA	48	13	24	37	....	....	....	13	6	2	*7	9	0
1937-38	Minneapolis Millers	AHA	48	17	26	43	....	....	....	40	7	2	*4	*6	0
1938-39	Cleveland Barons	IAHL	53	9	11	20	....	....	....	14	9	0	2	2	2
1939-40	Cleveland – Pittsburgh	IAHL	50	9	9	18	....	....	....	12	....	....	....	....	....
1940-41	Minneapolis Millers	AHA	19	4	9	13	....	....	....	8	....	....	....	....	....
	Buffalo Bisons	AHL	33	1	6	7	....	....	....	20	....	....	....	....	....
1941-42	Buffalo Bisons	AHL	56	6	15	21	....	....	....	58	....	....	....	....	....
1942-43	Buffalo Bisons	AHL	42	3	14	17	....	....	....	28	9	1	3	4	2
1943-44			MILITARY SERVICE												
1944-45			MILITARY SERVICE												
1945-46	Buffalo Bisons	AHL	10	1	2	3	....	....	....	2	12	0	4	4	0
1946-47	Buffalo Bisons	AHL	63	6	11	17	....	....	....	57	4	0	2	2	0
1947-48	Buffalo Bisons	AHL	5	0	0	0	....	....	....	0	....	....	....	....	....
	Houston Huskies	USHL	49	12	20	32	....	....	....	29	12	2	2	4	10
1948-49	Buffalo Bisons	AHL	63	8	10	18	....	....	....	32	....	....	....	....	....
1949-50	Cincinnati Mohawks	AHL	49	4	15	19	....	....	....	33	....	....	....	....	....
1950-51	N. Haven–Buffalo–Cleve.	AHL	53	7	11	18	....	....	....	22	....	....	....	....	....
	NHL Totals		**12**	**0**	**0**	**0**	**0**	**0**	**0**	**0**	....	....	....	....	....

Signed as a free agent by **Boston**, October, 1934. Traded to **Minneapolis** by **Boston** for cash, September, 1936.

• BLAKE, MICKEY
Mickey (Francis) Blake
LW/D – L. 5'10", 186 lbs. b: Barriefield, Ont., 10/31/1912. Deceased.

Season	Club	League	GP	G	A	Pts	AG	AA	APts	PIM	GP	G	A	Pts	PIM
			REGULAR SEASON								PLAYOFFS				
1932-33	Windsor Bulldogs	IAHL	38	3	2	5	....	....	....	26	6	2	0	2	6
	Montreal Maroons	**NHL**	**1**	**0**	**0**	**0**	**0**	**0**	**0**	**0**	....	....	....	....	....
1933-34	Quebec Beavers	Can-Am	40	6	3	9	....	....	....	36	....	....	....	....	....
1934-35	**St. Louis Eagles**	**NHL**	**8**	**1**	**1**	**2**	**2**	**2**	**4**	**2**	....	....	....	....	....
	Detroit Olympics	IAHL	25	0	0	0	....	....	....	26	5	1	0	1	0
1935-36	**Toronto Maple Leafs**	**NHL**	**1**	**0**	**0**	**0**	**0**	**0**	**0**	**2**	....	....	....	....	....
	Syracuse Stars	IAHL	43	17	17	34	....	....	....	27	3	0	0	0	0
1936-37	Syracuse Stars	AHL	47	7	19	26	....	....	....	20	9	1	2	3	2
1937-38	Syracuse Stars	AHL	25	2	4	6	....	....	....	14	8	0	0	0	2
1938-39	Cleveland Falcons	AHL	47	7	12	19	....	....	....	20	8	0	0	0	0
1939-40	Pittsburgh Hornets	AHL	55	3	11	14	....	....	....	26	9	0	0	0	6
1940-41	Pittsburgh Hornets	AHL	56	18	14	32	....	....	....	28	6	0	2	2	0
1941-42	Pittsburgh Hornets	AHL	48	9	11	20	....	....	....	14	....	....	....	....	....
1942-43	Kingston Frontenacs	Ott-Sr.	16	6	3	9	....	....	....	2	4	1	0	1	2
	NHL Totals		**10**	**1**	**1**	**2**	**2**	**2**	**4**	**4**	....	....	....	....	....

IAHL Second All-Star Team (1936)

Traded to **St. Louis** by **Montreal Maroons** for cash, October 12, 1934. Traded to **Detroit** by **St. Louis** with $3,500 for George Patterson, November 28, 1934. • Detroit held option on services and returned Blake to St. Louis after 1934-35 season. Claimed by **Toronto** from **St. Louis** in Dispersal Draft, October 15, 1935.

• BLAKE, TOE
Toe (Hector) Blake **HHOF**
LW – L. 5'10", 165 lbs. b: Victoria Mines, Ont., 8/21/1912. d: 5/17/1995.

Season	Club	League	GP	G	A	Pts	AG	AA	APts	PIM	GP	G	A	Pts	PIM
1929-30	Cochrane Dunlops	City Sr.	7	3	0	3	....	....	....	4	....	....	....	....	....
1930-31	Sudbury Cub Wolves	NOHA	6	3	1	4	....	....	....	12	2	0	0	0	6
	Sudbury Industries	City Sr.	8	7	1	8	....	....	....	10	1	1	2	4	....
1931-32	Sudbury Cub Wolves	NOHA	3	*5	0	5	....	....	....	4	....	....	....	....	....
	Falconbridge Falcons	City Sr.	10	*8	1	9	....	....	....	18	2	1	0	1	2
1932-33	Hamilton Tigers	OHA Sr.	22	9	4	13	....	....	....	26	2	0	0	0	2
1933-34	Hamilton Tigers	OHA Sr.	23	19	14	33	....	....	....	28	12	*8	6	*14	8
1934-35	**Montreal Maroons**	**NHL**	**8**	**0**	**0**	**0**	**0**	**0**	**0**	**0**	**1**	**0**	**0**	**0**	**0**
	Hamilton Tigers	OHA Sr.	18	15	11	26	....	....	....	48	....	....	....	....	....
1935-36	Providence Reds	Can-Am	33	12	11	23	....	....	....	65	7	2	3	5	2
	Montreal Canadiens	**NHL**	**11**	**1**	**2**	**3**	**2**	**5**	**7**	**28**	....	....	....	....	....
1936-37	**Montreal Canadiens**	**NHL**	**43**	**10**	**12**	**22**	**22**	**28**	**50**	**12**	**5**	**1**	**0**	**1**	**0**
1937-38	**Montreal Canadiens**	**NHL**	**43**	**17**	**16**	**33**	**36**	**33**	**69**	**33**	**3**	**3**	**1**	**4**	**2**
1938-39	**Montreal Canadiens**	**NHL**	**48**	**24**	**23**	***47**	**51**	**43**	**94**	**10**	**3**	**1**	**1**	**2**	**2**
1939-40	**Montreal Canadiens**	**NHL**	**48**	**17**	**19**	**36**	**37**	**38**	**75**	**48**	....	....	....	....	....
1940-41	**Montreal Canadiens**	**NHL**	**48**	**12**	**20**	**32**	**24**	**37**	**61**	**49**	**3**	**0**	**3**	**3**	**5**
1941-42	**Montreal Canadiens**	**NHL**	**48**	**17**	**28**	**45**	**29**	**43**	**72**	**19**	**3**	**0**	**3**	**3**	**2**
1942-43	**Montreal Canadiens**	**NHL**	**48**	**23**	**36**	**59**	**33**	**46**	**79**	**26**	**5**	**4**	**3**	**7**	**0**
1943-44	**Montreal Canadiens**	**NHL**	**41**	**26**	**33**	**59**	**33**	**40**	**73**	**10**	**9**	**7**	**11**	**18**	**2**
1944-45	**Montreal Canadiens**	**NHL**	**49**	**29**	**38**	**67**	**40**	**63**	**103**	**25**	**6**	**0**	**2**	**2**	**5**
1945-46	**Montreal Canadiens**	**NHL**	**50**	**29**	**21**	**50**	**45**	**39**	**84**	**2**	**9**	***7**	**6**	**13**	**5**
1946-47	**Montreal Canadiens**	**NHL**	**60**	**21**	**29**	**50**	**29**	**42**	**71**	**6**	**11**	**2**	***7**	**9**	**0**
1947-48	**Montreal Canadiens**	**NHL**	**32**	**9**	**15**	**24**	**13**	**22**	**35**	**4**	....	....	....	....	....
1948-49	Buffalo Bisons	AHL	18	1	3	4	....	....	....	0	....	....	....	....	....
1949-50	Valleyfield Braves	QSHL	43	12	15	27	....	....	....	15	3	0	1	1	0
1950-51	Valleyfield Braves	QSHL	DID NOT PLAY – COACHING												
	NHL Totals		**577**	**235**	**292**	**527**	**394**	**479**	**873**	**272**	**58**	**25**	**37**	**62**	**23**

NHL Second All-Star Team (1938, 1946) • NHL First All-Star Team (1939, 1940, 1945) • NHL Scoring Leader (1939) • Won Hart Trophy (1939) • Won Lady Byng Trophy (1946)

Played in NHL All-Star Game (1937, 1939)

Signed as a free agent by **Montreal Maroons**, February 21, 1935. Traded to **Montreal Canadiens** by **Montreal Maroons** with Bill Miller and Ken Gravel for Lorne Chabot, February 13, 1936.

• BLINCO, RUSS
Russ "Beaver" Blinco
C – L. 5'10", 171 lbs. b: Grand'Mere, Que., 3/12/1908. Deceased.

Season	Club	League	GP	G	A	Pts	AG	AA	APts	PIM	GP	G	A	Pts	PIM
1928-29	Grand'Mere Maroons	ECHL	5	4	0	4	....	....	....	2	....	....	....	....	....
1929-30	Brooklyn Cresents	USAHA	STATISTICS NOT AVAILABLE												
1930-31	Brooklyn Cresents	USAHA	STATISTICS NOT AVAILABLE												
1931-32	Brooklyn Crescents	USAHA	STATISTICS NOT AVAILABLE												
1932-33	Windsor Bulldogs	IAHL	28	13	10	23	....	....	....	12	6	2	3	5	2
	Springfield Indians	Can-Am	13	2	2	4	....	....	....	....	....	....	....	....	....
1933-34	**Montreal Maroons**	**NHL**	**31**	**14**	**9**	**23**	**31**	**24**	**55**	**2**	**4**	**0**	**1**	**1**	**0**
	Windsor Bulldogs	IAHL	16	6	5	11	....	....	....	4	....	....	....	....	....
1934-35	**Montreal Maroons**	**NHL**	**48**	**13**	**14**	**27**	**28**	**31**	**59**	**4**	**7**	**2**	**2**	**4**	**2**
1935-36	**Montreal Maroons**	**NHL**	**46**	**13**	**10**	**23**	**32**	**24**	**56**	**10**	**3**	**0**	**0**	**0**	**0**
1936-37	**Montreal Maroons**	**NHL**	**48**	**6**	**12**	**18**	**13**	**28**	**41**	**2**	**5**	**1**	**0**	**1**	**2**
1937-38	**Montreal Maroons**	**NHL**	**47**	**10**	**9**	**19**	**21**	**18**	**39**	**4**	....	....	....	....	....
1938-39	**Chicago Black Hawks**	**NHL**	**48**	**3**	**12**	**15**	**6**	**22**	**28**	**2**	....	....	....	....	....
	NHL Totals		**268**	**59**	**66**	**125**	**131**	**147**	**278**	**24**	**19**	**3**	**3**	**6**	**4**

NHL Rookie of the Year (1934)

Played in NHL All-Star Game (1937)

Traded to **Montreal Maroons** (Windsor-IAHL) by **NY Rangers** after Springfield (Can-Am) franchise folded, December 18, 1932. Traded to **Chicago** by **Montreal Maroons** with Baldy Northcott and Earl Robinson for $30,000, September 15, 1938.

• BODNAR, GUS Gus (August) Bodnar
C – R. 5'11", 160 lbs. b: Fort William, Ont., 4/24/1923.

			REGULAR SEASON								PLAYOFFS				
Season	Club	League	GP	G	A	Pts	AG	AA	APts	PIM	GP	G	A	Pts	PIM
1940-41	Fort William Rangers	TBJHL	18	13	8	21	....	....	....	12	2	0	0	0	0
1941-42	Fort William Rangers	TBJHL	16	20	16	36	....	....	....	22	3	*5	4	9	2
1942-43	Fort William Rangers	TBJHL	9	10	*29	*39	....	....	....	9	3	2	3	5	2
1943-44	**Toronto Maple Leafs**	**NHL**	**50**	**22**	**40**	**62**	**28**	**49**	**77**	**18**	**5**	**0**	**0**	**0**	**0**
1944-45	**Toronto Maple Leafs**	**NHL**	**49**	**8**	**36**	**44**	**11**	**59**	**70**	**18**	**13**	**3**	**1**	**4**	**4**
1945-46	**Toronto Maple Leafs**	**NHL**	**49**	**14**	**23**	**37**	**21**	**43**	**64**	**14**	....	....	....	....	....
1946-47	**Toronto Maple Leafs**	**NHL**	**39**	**4**	**6**	**10**	**5**	**9**	**14**	**10**	**1**	**0**	**0**	**0**	**0**
	Pittsburgh Hornets	AHL	15	10	9	19	....	....	....	10	9	2	2	4	4
1947-48	Pittsburgh Hornets	AHL	6	2	3	5	....	....	....	0	....	....	....	....	....
	Chicago Black Hawks	**NHL**	**46**	**13**	**22**	**35**	**19**	**32**	**51**	**23**	....	....	....	....	....
1948-49	**Chicago Black Hawks**	**NHL**	**59**	**19**	**26**	**45**	**30**	**42**	**72**	**14**	....	....	....	....	....
1949-50	**Chicago Black Hawks**	**NHL**	**70**	**11**	**28**	**39**	**15**	**36**	**51**	**6**	....	....	....	....	....
1950-51	**Chicago Black Hawks**	**NHL**	**44**	**8**	**12**	**20**	**11**	**15**	**26**	**8**	....	....	....	....	....
1951-52	**Chicago Black Hawks**	**NHL**	**69**	**14**	**26**	**40**	**20**	**34**	**54**	**26**	....	....	....	....	....
1952-53	**Chicago Black Hawks**	**NHL**	**66**	**16**	**13**	**29**	**25**	**18**	**43**	**26**	**7**	**1**	**1**	**2**	**2**
1953-54	**Chicago Black Hawks**	**NHL**	**45**	**6**	**15**	**21**	**9**	**20**	**29**	**20**	....	....	....	....	....
	Boston Bruins	**NHL**	**14**	**3**	**3**	**6**	**5**	**4**	**9**	**10**	**1**	**0**	**0**	**0**	**0**
1954-55	**Boston Bruins**	**NHL**	**67**	**4**	**4**	**8**	**6**	**5**	**11**	**14**	**5**	**0**	**1**	**1**	**4**
	NHL Totals		**667**	**142**	**254**	**396**	**205**	**366**	**571**	**207**	**32**	**4**	**3**	**7**	**10**

Won Calder Memorial Trophy (1944)

Played in NHL All-Star Game (1951)

Traded to **Chicago** by **Toronto** with Bud Poile, Gaye Stewart, Ernie Dickens and Bob Goldham for Max Bentley and Cy Thomas, November 2, 1947. Traded to **Boston** by **Chicago** for Jerry Toppazzini, February 16, 1954.

• BOESCH, GARTH Garth Boesch
D – R. 6', 180 lbs. b: Milestone, Sask., 10/7/1920. d: 5/14/1998.

			REGULAR SEASON								PLAYOFFS				
Season	Club	League	GP	G	A	Pts	AG	AA	APts	PIM	GP	G	A	Pts	PIM
1937-38	Notre Dame Hounds	SJHL	6	5	0	5	....	....	....	4	2	0	0	0	0
1938-39	Notre Dame Hounds	SJHL	9	5	1	6	....	....	....	4	....	....	....	....	....
1939-40	Notre Dame Hounds	SJHL	12	7	4	11	....	....	....	12	....	....	....	....	....
1940-41	Regina Rangers	SSHL	32	10	7	17	....	....	....	26	8	1	2	3	10
1941-42	Regina Rangers	ASHL	31	12	8	20	....	....	....	36	3	0	0	0	6
	Lethbridge Maple Leafs	SSHL	....	....	....	....	....	....	....	....	9	2	2	4	2
1942-43	Lethbridge Bombers	ASHL	22	8	8	16	....	....	....	40	3	2	0	2	2
1943-44			MILITARY SERVICE												
1944-45	Winnipeg RCAF	City Sr.	1	0	1	1	....	....	....	0	4	2	1	3	13
1945-46	Pittsburgh Hornets	AHL	43	15	9	24	....	....	....	16	6	0	4	4	8
1946-47	**Toronto Maple Leafs**	**NHL**	**35**	**4**	**5**	**9**	**5**	**7**	**12**	**47**	**11**	**0**	**2**	**2**	**6**
1947-48	**Toronto Maple Leafs**	**NHL**	**45**	**2**	**7**	**9**	**3**	**10**	**13**	**52**	**8**	**2**	**1**	**3**	**2**
1948-49	**Toronto Maple Leafs**	**NHL**	**59**	**1**	**10**	**11**	**2**	**16**	**18**	**43**	**9**	**0**	**2**	**2**	**6**
1949-50	**Toronto Maple Leafs**	**NHL**	**58**	**2**	**6**	**8**	**3**	**8**	**11**	**63**	**6**	**0**	**0**	**0**	**4**
	NHL Totals		**197**	**9**	**28**	**37**	**13**	**41**	**54**	**205**	**34**	**2**	**5**	**7**	**18**

Played in NHL All-Star Game (1948, 1949)

Claimed by **NY Americans** from **Seattle** (PCHL) in Inter-League Draft, June 27, 1941.
• Refused permission to leave Canada for NY Americans training camp because of war-time travel restrictions, September, 1941. Rights transferred to **Toronto** from **Brooklyn** in Special Dispersal Draw, September 11, 1943.

• BOILEAU, MARC Marc Boileau
C – L. 5'11", 170 lbs. b: Pointe Claire, Que., 9/3/1932.

			REGULAR SEASON								PLAYOFFS				
Season	Club	League	GP	G	A	Pts	AG	AA	APts	PIM	GP	G	A	Pts	PIM
1950-51	Verdun LaSalle	QJHL	45	5	8	13	....	....	....	6	3	0	1	1	0
1951-52	St. Jerome Eagles	QJHL	36	17	17	34	....	....	....	16	....	....	....	....	....
1952-53	Kitchener Greenshirts	OHA	20	10	19	29	....	....	....	38	....	....	....	....	....
	Montreal Jr. Canadiens	QJHL	17	3	7	10	....	....	....	5	....	....	....	....	....
1953-54	Cincinnati Mohawks	IHL	38	12	21	33	....	....	....	13	11	1	1	2	0
1954-55			DID NOT PLAY – SUSPENDED												
1955-56	Saint John Beavers	NBSHL	....	22	43	65	....	....	....	66	20	6	3	9	18
1956-57	Indianapolis Chiefs	IHL	60	25	32	57	....	....	....	50	8	2	3	5	2
1957-58	Indianapolis Chiefs	IHL	63	26	*61	87	....	....	....	64	11	*8	5	13	7
1958-59	Seattle Totems	WHL	67	17	30	47	....	....	....	52	12	*10	7	17	10
1959-60	Seattle Totems	WHL	68	32	45	77	....	....	....	54	4	0	0	0	5
1960-61	Seattle Totems	WHL	70	42	31	73	....	....	....	49	11	5	4	9	14
1961-62	**Detroit Red Wings**	**NHL**	**54**	**5**	**6**	**11**	**6**	**6**	**12**	**8**	....	....	....	....	....
	Hershey Bears	AHL	14	7	8	15	....	....	....	6	....	....	....	....	....
1962-63	Los Angeles Blades	WHL	66	17	45	62	....	....	....	77	3	0	3	3	2
1963-64	Los Angeles Blades	WHL	69	12	32	44	....	....	....	35	12	3	3	6	33
1964-65	Los Angeles Blades	WHL	60	12	23	35	....	....	....	62	....	....	....	....	....
1965-66	Los Angeles Blades	WHL	72	10	29	39	....	....	....	48	....	....	....	....	....
1966-67			DID NOT PLAY – RETIRED												
1967-68	Seattle Totems	WHL	66	6	31	37	....	....	....	41	9	3	2	5	4
1968-69	Seattle Totems	WHL	73	14	30	44	....	....	....	42	2	0	0	0	0
1969-70	Seattle Totems	WHL	73	16	28	44	....	....	....	65	6	1	0	1	8
1970-71	Fort Wayne Komets	IHL	67	19	40	59	....	....	....	35	2	0	1	1	0
1971-72	Fort Wayne Komets	IHL	66	11	44	55	....	....	....	27	6	0	6	6	4
1972-73	Fort Wayne Komets	IHL	2	0	0	0	....	....	....	0	....	....	....	....	....
1973-74	Pittsburgh Penguins	AHL	DID NOT PLAY – COACHING												
	NHL Totals		**54**	**5**	**6**	**11**	**6**	**6**	**12**	**8**	....	....	....	....	....

IHL First All-Star Team (1958) • WHL Second All-Star Team (1960)

• Suspended by **Montreal** for refusing assignment to **Cincinnati** (IHL), September, 1954. Traded to **Detroit** (Seattle-WHL) by **Indianapolis** (IHL) for cash, September, 1958. Traded to **LA Blades** (WHL) by **Seattle** (WHL) with Frank Arnett for Jim Powers, Terry Slater and Jim Hay, July, 1962.

• BOILEAU, RENE Rene "Rainy Drinkwater" Boileau
C – L. 5'10", 160 lbs. b: Pointe Claire, Quebec, 5/18/1904.

			REGULAR SEASON								PLAYOFFS				
Season	Club	League	GP	G	A	Pts	AG	AA	APts	PIM	GP	G	A	Pts	PIM
1923-24	Pointe Claire Maple Leafs	Mtl-Sr.	STATISTICS NOT AVAILABLE												
1924-25	Montreal K of C	City Sr.	STATISTICS NOT AVAILABLE												
1925-26	Montreal Columbus	City Sr.	4	0	0	0	....	....	....	0	....	....	....	....	....
	New York Americans	**NHL**	**7**	**0**	**0**	**0**	**0**	**0**	**0**	**0**	....	....	....	....	....
1926-27	Niagara Falls Cataracts	Can-Pro	18	4	0	4	....	....	....	8	....	....	....	....	....
1927-28	New Haven Eagles	Can-Am	36	5	3	8	....	....	....	51	....	....	....	....	....
1928-29	St. Louis Flyers	AHA	36	4	0	4	....	....	....	28	....	....	....	....	....
1929-30	St. Louis Flyers	AHA	30	2	1	3	....	....	....	46	....	....	....	....	....
1930-31	St. Louis Flyers	AHA	37	3	0	3	....	....	....	43	....	....	....	....	....
1931-32	Trois-Rivieres Renards	ECHA	4	0	0	0	....	....	....	6	....	....	....	....	....
1932-33			DID NOT PLAY												
1933-34	Verdun Maple Leafs	City Sr.	5	1	0	1	....	....	....	10	2	0	0	0	0
	NHL Totals		**7**	**0**	**0**	**0**	**0**	**0**	**0**	**0**	....	....	....	....	....

Signed as a free agent by **NY Americans** (Niagara Falls—Can-Pro), January 15, 1926.

• BOIVIN, LEO — *see page 881*

• BOLL, FRANK Frank "Buzz" Boll
LW – L. 5'10", 166 lbs. b: Filmore, Sask., 3/6/1911. d: 1/1/1990.

			REGULAR SEASON								PLAYOFFS				
Season	Club	League	GP	G	A	Pts	AG	AA	APts	PIM	GP	G	A	Pts	PIM
1928-29	Weyburn Wanderers	City Jr.	....	....	....	....	....	....	....	....	3	0	2	2	0
1929-30	Regina Pats	SJHL	2	1	0	1	....	....	....	0	....	....	....	....	....
1930-31	Weyburn Beavers	SSHL	20	12	4	16	....	....	....	16	....	....	....	....	....
1931-32	Toronto Marlboros	OHA Sr.	20	14	4	18	....	....	....	17	2	1	1	2	2
	Syracuse Stars	IAHL	9	3	0	3	....	....	....	4	1	0	0	0	4
1932-33	Syracuse Stars	IAHL	38	9	6	15	....	....	....	16	6	1	2	3	2
	Toronto Maple Leafs	**NHL**	....	....	....	....	....	....	....	....	**1**	**0**	**0**	**0**	**0**
1933-34	**Toronto Maple Leafs**	**NHL**	**42**	**12**	**8**	**20**	**27**	**21**	**48**	**21**	**5**	**0**	**0**	**0**	**9**
1934-35	**Toronto Maple Leafs**	**NHL**	**47**	**14**	**4**	**18**	**30**	**9**	**39**	**4**	**6**	**0**	**0**	**0**	**0**
1935-36	**Toronto Maple Leafs**	**NHL**	**44**	**15**	**13**	**28**	**37**	**31**	**68**	**14**	**9**	**7**	**3**	**10**	**2**
1936-37	**Toronto Maple Leafs**	**NHL**	**25**	**6**	**3**	**9**	**13**	**7**	**20**	**12**	**2**	**0**	**0**	**0**	**0**
1937-38	**Toronto Maple Leafs**	**NHL**	**44**	**14**	**11**	**25**	**30**	**23**	**53**	**18**	**7**	**0**	**0**	**0**	**2**
1938-39	**Toronto Maple Leafs**	**NHL**	**11**	**0**	**0**	**0**	**0**	**0**	**0**	**0**	....	....	....	....	....
	Syracuse Stars	AHL	7	2	2	4	....	....	....	6	....	....	....	....	....
1939-40	**New York Americans**	**NHL**	**47**	**5**	**10**	**15**	**11**	**20**	**31**	**18**	**1**	**0**	**0**	**0**	**0**
1940-41	**New York Americans**	**NHL**	**47**	**12**	**14**	**26**	**24**	**26**	**50**	**16**	....	....	....	....	....
1941-42	**Brooklyn Americans**	**NHL**	**48**	**11**	**15**	**26**	**19**	**23**	**42**	**23**	....	....	....	....	....
1942-43	**Boston Bruins**	**NHL**	**43**	**25**	**27**	**52**	**36**	**34**	**70**	**20**	....	....	....	....	....
1943-44	**Boston Bruins**	**NHL**	**39**	**19**	**25**	**44**	**24**	**30**	**54**	**2**	....	....	....	....	....
	NHL Totals		**437**	**133**	**130**	**263**	**251**	**224**	**475**	**148**	**31**	**7**	**3**	**10**	**13**

Played in NHL All-Star Game (1934)

Traded to **NY Americans** by **Toronto** with Busher Jackson, Doc Romnes, Jim Fowler and Murray Armstrong for Sweeney Schriner, May 15, 1939. Rights transferred to **Boston** from **Brooklyn** in Special Dispersal Draw, October 9, 1942.

• BOLTON, HUGH Hugh (Tug) Bolton
D – L. 6'3", 186 lbs. b: Toronto, Ont., 4/15/1929.

			REGULAR SEASON								PLAYOFFS				
Season	Club	League	GP	G	A	Pts	AG	AA	APts	PIM	GP	G	A	Pts	PIM
1945-46	Toronto Young Rangers	OHA	24	5	5	10	....	....	....	6	1	0	0	0	0
1946-47	Toronto Young Rangers	OHA	15	7	2	9	....	....	....	16	....	....	....	....	....
1947-48	Toronto Marlboros	OHA	32	3	13	16	....	....	....	42	....	....	....	....	....
	Toronto Marlboros	OHA Sr.	2	0	1	1	....	....	....	0	....	....	....	....	....
1948-49	Toronto Marlboros	OHA	18	5	2	7	....	....	....	24	10	3	2	5	4
	Toronto Marlboros	OHA Sr.	....	....	....	....	....	....	....	....	14	1	1	2	33
1949-50	**Toronto Maple Leafs**	**NHL**	**2**	**0**	**0**	**0**	**0**	**0**	**0**	**2**	....	....	....	....	....
	Toronto Marlboros	OHA Sr.	38	9	31	40	....	....	....	35	2	0	0	0	2
1950-51	**Toronto Maple Leafs**	**NHL**	**13**	**1**	**3**	**4**	**1**	**4**	**5**	**4**	....	....	....	....	....
	Pittsburgh Hornets	AHL	9	2	4	6	....	....	....	6	13	1	3	4	6
1951-52	**Toronto Maple Leafs**	**NHL**	**60**	**3**	**13**	**16**	**4**	**17**	**21**	**73**	**3**	**0**	**0**	**0**	**4**
1952-53	**Toronto Maple Leafs**	**NHL**	**9**	**0**	**0**	**0**	**0**	**0**	**0**	**10**	....	....	....	....	....
	Pittsburgh Hornets	AHL	35	1	9	10	....	....	....	58	6	2	0	2	7
1953-54	**Toronto Maple Leafs**	**NHL**	**9**	**0**	**0**	**0**	**0**	**0**	**0**	**10**	**5**	**0**	**1**	**1**	**4**
	Ottawa Senators	QHL	24	2	15	17	....	....	....	10	....	....	....	....	
1954-55	**Toronto Maple Leafs**	**NHL**	**69**	**2**	**19**	**21**	**3**	**24**	**27**	**55**	**4**	**0**	**3**	**3**	**6**
1955-56	**Toronto Maple Leafs**	**NHL**	**67**	**4**	**16**	**20**	**6**	**20**	**26**	**65**	**5**	**0**	**1**	**1**	**0**
1956-57	**Toronto Maple Leafs**	**NHL**	**6**	**0**	**0**	**0**	**0**	**0**	**0**	**2**	....	....	....	....	....
1957-58	Rochester Americans	AHL	5	0	1	1	....	....	....	2	....	....	....	....	....
	NHL Totals		**235**	**10**	**51**	**61**	**14**	**65**	**79**	**221**	**17**	**0**	**5**	**5**	**14**

Played in NHL All-Star Game (1956)

• BONIN, MARCEL Marcel Bonin
RW/LW – L. 5'10", 170 lbs. b: Montreal, Que., 9/12/1932.

			REGULAR SEASON								PLAYOFFS				
Season	Club	League	GP	G	A	Pts	AG	AA	APts	PIM	GP	G	A	Pts	PIM
1949-50	Joliette Cyclones	QPHL	STATISTICS NOT AVAILABLE												
1950-51	Trois Rivieres Flambeaux	QJHL	44	30	43	73	....	....	....	73	8	1	6	7	7
	Shawinigan Cataracts	QSHL	2	0	1	1	....			0	....	....	....	....	....
1951-52	Quebec Aces	QSHL	60	15	36	51	....	....	....	131	20	4	14	18	50
1952-53	**Detroit Red Wings**	**NHL**	**37**	**4**	**9**	**13**	**6**	**12**	**18**	**14**	**5**	**0**	**1**	**1**	**0**
	Quebec Aces	QSHL	4	0	2	2	....	....	....	9	....	....	....	....	....
	St. Louis Flyers	AHL	24	7	23	30	....	....	....	4	....	....	....	....	....
1953-54	**Detroit Red Wings**	**NHL**	**1**	**0**	**0**	**0**	**0**	**0**	**0**	**0**	....	....	....	....	....
	Sherbrooke Saints	QHL	17	10	11	21	....	....	....	38	....	....	....	....	....
	Edmonton Flyers	WHL	43	16	33	49	....	....	....	53	13	5	6	11	30
1954-55	**Detroit Red Wings**	**NHL**	**69**	**16**	**20**	**36**	**23**	**26**	**49**	**53**	**11**	**0**	**2**	**2**	**4**
1955-56	**Boston Bruins**	**NHL**	**67**	**9**	**9**	**18**	**13**	**11**	**24**	**49**	....	....	....	....	....
1956-57	Quebec Aces	QHL	68	20	*60	80	....	....	....	88	10	5	9	*14	14
1957-58	**Montreal Canadiens**	**NHL**	**66**	**15**	**24**	**39**	**20**	**26**	**46**	**37**	**9**	**0**	**1**	**1**	**2**
1958-59	**Montreal Canadiens**	**NHL**	**57**	**13**	**30**	**43**	**16**	**32**	**48**	**38**	**11**	**10**	**5**	**15**	**4**
	Rochester Americans	AHL	7	3	5	8	....	....	....	4	....	....	....	....	....
1959-60	**Montreal Canadiens**	**NHL**	**59**	**17**	**34**	**51**	**21**	**35**	**56**	**59**	**8**	**1**	**4**	**5**	**12**
1960-61	**Montreal Canadiens**	**NHL**	**65**	**16**	**35**	**51**	**20**	**36**	**56**	**45**	**6**	**0**	**1**	**1**	**29**
1961-62	**Montreal Canadiens**	**NHL**	**33**	**7**	**14**	**21**	**8**	**14**	**22**	**41**	....	....	....	....	....
	NHL Totals		**454**	**97**	**175**	**272**	**127**	**192**	**319**	**336**	**50**	**11**	**14**	**25**	**51**

QHL First All-Star Team (1957)

Played in NHL All-Star Game (1954, 1957, 1958, 1959, 1960)

Traded to **Boston** by **Detroit** with Lorne Davis, Terry Sawchuk and Vic Stasiuk for Gilles Boisvert, Real Chevrefils, Norm Corcoran, Warren Godfrey and Ed Sandford, June 3, 1955. Claimed by **Montreal** from **Boston** in Intra-League Draft, June, 1957.

			REGULAR SEASON								PLAYOFFS				
Season	Club	League	GP	G	A	Pts	AG	AA	APts	PIM	GP	G	A	Pts	PIM

• BOONE, BUDDY Buddy (Carl) Boone

RW – R. 5'7", 158 lbs. b: Kirkland Lake, Ont., 9/11/1932.

Season	Club	League	GP	G	A	Pts	AG	AA	APts	PIM	GP	G	A	Pts	PIM
1949-50	St. Catharines Teepees	OHA	45	13	17	30	....	....	....	75	5	4	1	5	10
1950-51	St. Catharines Teepees	OHA	53	28	27	55	....	....	....	94	9	7	4	11	8
1951-52	St. Catharines Teepees	OHA	45	43	23	66	....	....	....	38	14	*8	4	12	4
1952-53	St. Louis Flyers	AHL	64	13	26	39	....	....	....	20	....	....	....	....	....
1953-54	Edmonton Flyers	WHL	28	3	5	8	....	....	....	22	....	....	....	....	....
	Quebec Aces	QHL	35	6	14	20	....	....	....	57	23	10	9	19	20
1954-55	Springfield Indians	AHL	63	30	31	61	....	....	....	38	4	2	0	2	0
1955-56	Springfield Indians	AHL	31	11	12	23	....	....	....	24	....	....	....	....	....
1956-57	Springfield Indians	AHL	57	24	22	46	....	....	....	45	....	....	....	....	....
	Boston Bruins	**NHL**	....	....	....	....	....	....	....	....	**10**	**1**	**0**	**1**	**12**
1957-58	**Boston Bruins**	**NHL**	**34**	**5**	**3**	**8**	**6**	**3**	**9**	**28**	**12**	**1**	**1**	**2**	**13**
	Springfield Indians	AHL	33	13	16	29	....	....	....	34	....	....	....	....	....
1958-59	Quebec Aces	QHL	20	5	6	11	....	....	....	14	....	....	....	....	....
	Providence Reds	AHL	28	7	10	17	....	....	....	16	....	....	....	....	....
1959-60	Kingston Frontenacs	EPHL	69	25	29	54	....	....	....	33	....	....	....	....	....
1960-61	Kingston Frontenacs	EPHL	51	24	23	47	....	....	....	26	....	....	....	....	....
	Winnipeg Warriors	WHL	13	7	7	14	....	....	....	10	....	....	....	....	....
1961-62	San Francisco Seals	WHL	62	30	27	57	....	....	....	22	2	0	0	0	0
1962-63	Vancouver Canucks	WHL	69	44	36	80	....	....	....	24	7	3	0	3	4
1963-64	Vancouver Canucks	WHL	66	38	25	63	....	....	....	18	....	....	....	....	....
1964-65	Vancouver Canucks	WHL	54	22	24	46	....	....	....	29	5	2	0	2	2
1965-66	Los Angeles Blades	WHL	58	17	19	36	....	....	....	6	....	....	....	....	....
1966-67	Los Angeles Blades	WHL	45	14	13	27	....	....	....	16	....	....	....	....	....
1967-68			DID NOT PLAY – RETIRED												
1968-69	Des Moines Oak Leafs	IHL	59	20	22	42	....	....	....	20	....	....	....	....	....
1969-70	Des Moines Oak Leafs	IHL	8	1	1	2	....	....	....	2	....	....	....	....	....
	NHL Totals		**34**	**5**	**3**	**8**	**6**	**3**	**9**	**28**	**22**	**2**	**1**	**3**	**25**

WHL First All-Star Team (1963) • WHL Second All-Star Team (1964)

• BOOTHMAN, GEORGE George Boothman

C/D – R. 6'2", 175 lbs. b: Calgary, Alta., 9/25/1916.

Season	Club	League	GP	G	A	Pts	AG	AA	APts	PIM	GP	G	A	Pts	PIM
1938-39	Calgary Stampeders	ASHL	4	0	0	0	....	....	....	0	....	....	....	....	....
1939-40	Turner Valley Oilers	ASHL	9	0	1	1	....	....	....	0	....	....	....	....	....
1940-41	Nelson Maple Leafs	Kooteney	29	6	11	17	....	....	....	30	2	0	1	1	0
1941-42	Sydney Millionaires	CBSHL	41	15	15	30	....	....	....	48	7	0	1	1	12
1942-43	**Toronto Maple Leafs**	**NHL**	**9**	**1**	**1**	**2**	**1**	**1**	**2**	**4**	....	....	....	....	....
	Providence Reds	AHL	35	7	18	25	....	....	....	18	2	0	1	1	2
1943-44	**Toronto Maple Leafs**	**NHL**	**49**	**16**	**18**	**34**	**20**	**22**	**42**	**14**	**5**	**2**	**1**	**3**	**2**
1944-45	Buffalo Bisons	AHL	41	12	29	41	....	....	....	25	6	4	0	4	2
1945-46	Buffalo–New Haven	AHL	50	12	15	27	....	....	....	19	12	5	6	11	0
1946-47	Dallas Texans	USHL	4	1	2	3	....	....	....	2	....	....	....	....	....
1947-48	San Diego Skyhawks	PCHL	56	18	18	36	....	....	....	17	14	3	3	6	14
1948-49	Milwaukee Clarks	IHL	32	13	20	33	....	....	....	26	8	4	4	8	17
1949-50	Milwaukee Clarks	EHL	6	0	3	3	....	....	....	2	....	....	....	....	....
	NHL Totals		**58**	**17**	**19**	**36**	**21**	**23**	**44**	**18**	**5**	**2**	**1**	**3**	**2**

IHL Southern Division Second All-Star Team (1949)

Loaned to **Providence** (AHL) by **Toronto** with Jack Forsey for loan of Buck Jones and Ab Demarco, February 3, 1943. Traded to **Providence** (AHL) by **Toronto** with Don Webster for Bill Ezinicki, October 13, 1944.

• BOSTROM, HELGE Helge Bostrom

D – L. 5'8", 185 lbs. b: Winnipeg, Man., 1/9/1894.

Season	Club	League	GP	G	A	Pts	AG	AA	APts	PIM	GP	G	A	Pts	PIM
1916-17	Winnipeg Monarchs	MHL Sr.	3	0	0	0	....	....	....	4	....	....	....	....	....
1917-18	Winnipeg Ypres	City Sr.	9	0	0	0	....	....	....	12	5	0	0	0	14
1918-19	Winnipeg Ypres	City Sr.	7	0	0	0	....	....	....	12	....	....	....	....	....
1919-20	Moose Jaw Maple Leafs	SSHL	11	2	3	5	....	....	....	26	2	*2	*1	*3	4
1920-21	Moose Jaw Maple Leafs	SSHL	15	5	2	7	....	....	....	26	4	1	0	1	0
1921-22	Edmonton Eskimos	WCHL	1	0	0	0	....	....	....	0	2	0	0	0	0
1922-23	Edmonton Eskimos	WCHL	22	2	1	3	....	....	....	20	3	0	0	0	0
1923-24	Vancouver Maroons	PCHA	30	3	0	3	....	....	....	24	7	2	1	3	2
1924-25	Vancouver Maroons	PCHA	28	7	4	11	....	....	....	18	....	....	....	....	....
1925-26	Vancouver Maroons	PCHA	29	0	1	1	....	....	....	28	....	....	....	....	....
1926-27	Minneapolis Millers	AHA	35	4	2	6	....	....	....	45	6	0	0	0	6
1927-28	Minneapolis Millers	AHA	36	10	3	13	....	....	....	39	8	0	0	0	22
1928-29	Minneapolis Millers	AHA	39	5	3	8	....	....	....	74	4	1	0	1	8
1929-30	**Chicago Black Hawks**	**NHL**	**20**	**0**	**1**	**1**	**0**	**3**	**3**	**8**	**2**	**0**	**0**	**0**	**0**
	Minneapolis Millers	AHA	12	2	1	3	....	....	....	14	....	....	....	....	....
1930-31	**Chicago Black Hawks**	**NHL**	**42**	**2**	**2**	**4**	**5**	**7**	**12**	**32**	**9**	**0**	**0**	**0**	**16**
1931-32	**Chicago Black Hawks**	**NHL**	**14**	**0**	**0**	**0**	**0**	**0**	**0**	**4**	**2**	**0**	**0**	**0**	**0**
1932-33	**Chicago Black Hawks**	**NHL**	**20**	**1**	**0**	**1**	**2**	**0**	**2**	**14**	....	....	....	....	....
	St. Paul–Tulsa	AHA	22	2	6	8	....	....	....	10	4	0	1	1	6
1933-34	Oklahoma City Warriors	AHA	48	5	8	13	....	....	....	48	....	....	....	....	....
1934-35	Philadelphia Arrows	Can-Am	15	0	5	5	....	....	....	10	....	....	....	....	....
	Syracuse Stars	IAHL	23	2	2	4	....	....	....	10	....	....	....	....	....
1935-36	Kansas City Greyhounds	AHA	25	0	1	1	....	....	....	18	....	....	....	....	....
	NHL Totals		**96**	**3**	**3**	**6**	**7**	**10**	**17**	**58**	**13**	**0**	**0**	**0**	**16**
	Other Major League Totals		53	5	1	6	....	....	....	44	12	2	1	3	2

Signed as a free agent by **Edmonton** (WCHL), January 8, 1922. Traded to **Vancouver** (PCHA) by **Edmonton** (WCHL) for cash, October 2, 1923. Signed as a free agent by **Minneapolis** (AHA), October 21, 1926. Traded to **Chicago** by **Minneapolis** (AHA) for Bob Burns, December, 1929. Traded to **St. Paul** (AHA) by **Chicago** for Art Wiebe, December 1932.

			REGULAR SEASON								PLAYOFFS				
Season	Club	League	GP	G	A	Pts	AG	AA	APts	PIM	GP	G	A	Pts	PIM

• BOUCHARD, BUTCH Butch (Emile) Bouchard HHOF

D – R. 6'2", 205 lbs. b: Montreal, Que., 9/11/1920.

Season	Club	League	GP	G	A	Pts	AG	AA	APts	PIM	GP	G	A	Pts	PIM
1938-39	Verdun Maple Leafs	Mtl-Jr.	9	1	1	2	....	....	....	20	10	0	2	2	12
1939-40	Verdun Maple Leafs	Mtl-Jr.	STATISTICS NOT AVAILABLE												
1940-41	Montreal Jr. Canadiens	Mtl-Jr.	31	2	8	10	....	....	....	60	....	....	....	....	....
	Providence Reds	AHL	12	3	1	4	....	....	....	8	3	0	1	1	8
1941-42	**Montreal Canadiens**	**NHL**	**44**	**0**	**6**	**6**	**0**	**9**	**9**	**38**	**3**	**1**	**1**	**2**	**0**
1942-43	**Montreal Canadiens**	**NHL**	**45**	**2**	**16**	**18**	**3**	**20**	**23**	**47**	**5**	**0**	**1**	**1**	**4**
1943-44	**Montreal Canadiens**	**NHL**	**39**	**5**	**14**	**19**	**6**	**17**	**23**	**52**	**9**	**1**	**3**	**4**	**4**
1944-45	**Montreal Canadiens**	**NHL**	**50**	**11**	**23**	**34**	**15**	**37**	**52**	**34**	**6**	**3**	**4**	**7**	**4**
1945-46	**Montreal Canadiens**	**NHL**	**45**	**7**	**10**	**17**	**11**	**19**	**30**	**52**	**9**	**2**	**1**	**3**	**17**
1946-47	**Montreal Canadiens**	**NHL**	**60**	**5**	**7**	**12**	**7**	**10**	**17**	**60**	**11**	**0**	**3**	**3**	**21**
1947-48	**Montreal Canadiens**	**NHL**	**60**	**4**	**6**	**10**	**6**	**9**	**15**	**78**	....	....	....	....	....
1948-49	**Montreal Canadiens**	**NHL**	**27**	**3**	**3**	**6**	**5**	**5**	**10**	**42**	**7**	**0**	**0**	**0**	**6**
1949-50	**Montreal Canadiens**	**NHL**	**69**	**1**	**7**	**8**	**1**	**9**	**10**	**88**	**5**	**0**	**2**	**2**	**2**
1950-51	**Montreal Canadiens**	**NHL**	**52**	**3**	**10**	**13**	**4**	**13**	**17**	**80**	**11**	**1**	**1**	**2**	**2**
1951-52	**Montreal Canadiens**	**NHL**	**60**	**3**	**9**	**12**	**4**	**12**	**16**	**45**	**11**	**0**	**2**	**2**	**14**
1952-53	**Montreal Canadiens**	**NHL**	**58**	**2**	**8**	**10**	**3**	**11**	**14**	**55**	**12**	**1**	**1**	**2**	**6**
1953-54	**Montreal Canadiens**	**NHL**	**70**	**1**	**10**	**11**	**2**	**14**	**16**	**89**	**11**	**2**	**1**	**3**	**4**
1954-55	**Montreal Canadiens**	**NHL**	**70**	**2**	**15**	**17**	**3**	**19**	**22**	**81**	**12**	**0**	**1**	**1**	**37**
1955-56	**Montreal Canadiens**	**NHL**	**36**	**0**	**0**	**0**	**0**	**0**	**0**	**22**	**1**	**0**	**0**	**0**	**0**
	NHL Totals		**785**	**49**	**144**	**193**	**70**	**204**	**274**	**863**	**113**	**11**	**21**	**32**	**121**

NHL Second All-Star Team (1944) • NHL First All-Star Team (1945, 1946, 1947)

Played in NHL All-Star Game (1947, 1948, 1950, 1951, 1952, 1953)

• BOUCHARD, DICK Dick Bouchard

RW – R. 5'8", 155 lbs. b: Lettelier, Man., 12/2/1934.

Season	Club	League	GP	G	A	Pts	AG	AA	APts	PIM	GP	G	A	Pts	PIM
1953-54	Quebec Frontenacs	QJHL	63	21	29	50	....	....	....	43	8	9	8	17	4
1954-55	Quebec Frontenacs	QJHL	45	25	33	58	....	....	....	52	18	*11	11	22	18
	New York Rangers	**NHL**	**1**	**0**	**0**	**0**	**0**	**0**	**0**	**0**	....	....	....	....	....
1955-56	Winnipeg Warriors	WHL	2	0	0	0	....	....	....	0	....	....	....	....	....
	Shawinigan Cataracts	QHL	54	10	22	32	....	....	....	28	11	2	6	8	8
1956-57	Shawinigan Cataracts	QHL	65	15	30	45	....	....	....	27	....	....	....	....	....
1957-58	Shawinigan Cataracts	QHL	63	23	38	61	....	....	....	60	14	4	6	10	6
1958-59	Rochester Americans	AHL	43	2	11	13	....	....	....	19	....	....	....	....	....
1959-60			REINSTATED AS AN AMATEUR												
1960-61	St. Paul Saints	IHL	35	9	14	23	....	....	....	24	10	6	4	10	16
1961-62	St. Paul Saints	IHL	57	27	31	58	....	....	....	48	11	6	2	8	8
1962-63	St. Paul Saints	IHL	65	31	34	65	....	....	....	29	....	....	....	....	....
1963-64	St. Paul Rangers	CHL	29	6	11	17	....	....	....	16	....	....	....	....	....
	NHL Totals		**1**	**0**	**0**	**0**	**0**	**0**	**0**	**0**	....	....	....	....	....

• BOUCHARD, EDMOND Edmond Bouchard

LW/D – L. 5'10", 185 lbs. b: St. Etienne, Quebec, 5/24/1892. d: 7/18/1955.

Season	Club	League	GP	G	A	Pts	AG	AA	APts	PIM	GP	G	A	Pts	PIM
1916-17	Quebec Montagnais	City Sr.	9	16	5	21	....	....	....	....	....	....	....	....	....
1917-18	Quebec Montagnais	QCHL	11	*27	6	*33	....	....	....	....	....	....	....	....	....
1918-19	Quebec Montagnais	QCHL	6	*21	0	*21	....	....	....	....	4	*8	0	*8	3
1919-20	Quebec Crescents	QCHL	1	1	0	1	....	....	....	0	....	....	....	....	....
	Montreal Hochelaga	City Sr.	10	12	*8	20	....	....	....	18	5	*10	*3	*13	9
1920-21	Quebec Voltigers	QCHL	5	6	0	6	....	....	....	....	4	*4	0	*4	....
1921-22	**Montreal Canadiens**	**NHL**	**18**	**1**	**5**	**6**	**3**	**31**	**34**	**4**	....	....	....	....	....
1922-23	**Hamilton Tigers**	**NHL**	**24**	**5**	***12**	**17**	**16**	**113**	**129**	**32**	....	....	....	....	....
1923-24	**Hamilton Tigers**	**NHL**	**20**	**5**	**0**	**5**	**20**	**0**	**20**	**2**	....	....	....	....	....
1924-25	**Hamilton Tigers**	**NHL**	**29**	**2**	**2**	**4**	**7**	**26**	**33**	**14**	....	....	....	....	....
1925-26	**New York Americans**	**NHL**	**34**	**3**	**1**	**4**	**9**	**11**	**20**	**10**	....	....	....	....	....
1926-27	**New York Americans**	**NHL**	**38**	**2**	**1**	**3**	**6**	**8**	**14**	**12**	....	....	....	....	....
	Niagara Falls Cataracts	Can-Pro	4	2	1	3	....	....	....	19	....	....	....	....	....
1927-28	**New York Americans**	**NHL**	**39**	**1**	**0**	**1**	**3**	**0**	**3**	**27**	....	....	....	....	....
1928-29	**New York Americans**	**NHL**	**6**	**0**	**0**	**0**	**0**	**0**	**0**	**2**	....	....	....	....	....
	Pittsburgh Pirates	**NHL**	**12**	**0**	**0**	**0**	**0**	**0**	**0**	**2**	....	....	....	....	....
	New Haven Eagles	Can-Am	25	5	4	9	....	....	....	45	....	....	....	....	....
1929-30	New Haven Eagles	Can-Am	38	18	3	21	....	....	....	58	....	....	....	....	....
1930-31	Buffalo Majors	AHA	40	23	12	35	....	....	....	44	....	....	....	....	....
	Pittsburgh Yellowjackets	IAHL	8	0	0	0	....	....	....	6	....	....	....	....	....
1931-32	Buffalo Majors	AHA	24	3	2	5	....	....	....	30	....	....	....	....	....
	St. Louis Flyers	AHA	3	1	0	1	....	....	....	2	....	....	....	....	....
	Duluth Hornets	AHA	18	2	1	3	....	....	....	20	8	1	1	2	10
	NHL Totals		**220**	**19**	**21**	**40**	**64**	**189**	**253**	**105**	....	....	....	....	....

Signed as a free agent by **Montreal Canadiens**, January 2, 1922. Traded to **Hamilton** by **Montreal Canadiens** for Joe Malone and Bert Corbeau, December 22, 1922. Transferred to **NY Americans** after NHL club purchased **Hamilton** franchise, September 26, 1925. Traded to **Pittsburgh** by **NY Americans** with Jesse Spring for Tex White, February 15, 1929.

• BOUCHER, BILLY Billy Boucher

RW – R. 5'7", 155 lbs. b: Ottawa, Ont., 11/10/1899. Deceased.

Season	Club	League	GP	G	A	Pts	AG	AA	APts	PIM	GP	G	A	Pts	PIM
1916-17	Ottawa Munitions	City Sr.	10	1	0	1	....	....	....	6	....	....	....	....	....
1917-18	Ottawa Munitions	City Sr.	6	*5	0	*5	....	....	....	24	1	1	0	1	0
1918-19	Ottawa Munitions	City Sr.	8	6	*3	9	....	....	....	18	....	....	....	....	....
1919-20	Ottawa Munitions	City Sr.	8	4	0	4	....	....	....	....	5	*11		4	*15	....
1920-21	Iroquois Falls Paper	NOHA	5	5	0	5	....	....	....	....	....	....	....	....	....
1921-22	**Montreal Canadiens**	**NHL**	**24**	**17**	**5**	**22**	**47**	**31**	**78**	**18**	....	....	....	....	....
1922-23	**Montreal Canadiens**	**NHL**	**24**	**23**	**4**	**27**	**80**	**36**	**116**	***52**	**2**	**1**	**0**	**1**	**2**
1923-24	**Montreal Canadiens**	**NHL**	**23**	**16**	**6**	**22**	**68**	**110**	**178**	**33**	**5**	**6**	**2**	**8**	***14**
1924-25	**Montreal Canadiens**	**NHL**	**30**	**18**	**13**	**31**	**63**	**183**	**246**	***92**	**6**	**2**	**1**	**3**	**17**
1925-26	**Montreal Canadiens**	**NHL**	**34**	**8**	**5**	**13**	**25**	**58**	**83**	**112**	....	....	....	....	....
1926-27	**Montreal Canadiens**	**NHL**	**21**	**4**	**0**	**4**	**12**	**0**	**12**	**14**	....	....	....	....	....
	Boston Bruins	**NHL**	**14**	**2**	**0**	**2**	**6**	**0**	**6**	**12**	**8**	**0**	**0**	**0**	**2**
1927-28	**New York Americans**	**NHL**	**43**	**5**	**2**	**7**	**15**	**17**	**32**	**58**	....	....	....	....	....
1928-29	New Haven Eagles	Can-Am	38	11	1	12	....	....	....	117	2	0	0	0	4
1929-30	New Haven Eagles	Can-Am	32	8	7	15	....	....	....	54	....	....	....	....	....
1930-31	New Haven Eagles	Can-Am	38	20	8	28	....	....	....	98	....	....	....	....	....
1931-32	Bronx Tigers	Can-Am	39	3	4	7	....	....	....	25	1	0	0	0	0
1932-33	Quebec Granites	ECHA	DID NOT PLAY – COACHING												
	NHL Totals		**213**	**93**	**35**	**128**	**316**	**435**	**751**	**391**	**21**	**9**	**3**	**12**	**35**

Signed as a free agent by **Montreal Canadiens**, December 13, 1921. Traded to **Boston** by **Montreal Canadiens** for Carson Cooper with both teams holding rights of recall, January 17, 1927. • Players returned to original teams, May 27, 1927. Traded to **NY Americans** by **Montreal Canadiens** for cash, October 17, 1927.

• BOUCHER, CLARENCE
Clarence (Also known as Bowcher) Boucher
D – L. 6'1", 195 lbs. b: North Bay, Ontario, 11/1/1896. Deceased.

			REGULAR SEASON								PLAYOFFS				
Season	Club	League	GP	G	A	Pts	AG	AA	APts	PIM	GP	G	A	Pts	PIM
1919-20	Sudbury Cub Wolves	NOHL	STATISTICS NOT AVAILABLE												
	Sudbury Wolves	NOHA	6	3	1	4	....	....	....	6	7	1	2	3	*20
1920-21	Cleveland Indians	USAHA	STATISTICS NOT AVAILABLE												
	Sudbury Wolves	NOHA	9	7	3	10	....	....	....	40	....	....	....	....	....
1921-22	Sudbury Wolves	NOHA	9	9	5	14	....	....	....	*39	....	....	....	....	....
1922-23	Iroquois Falls Paper	NOHA	STATISTICS NOT AVAILABLE												
1923-24	Iroquois Falls Paper	NOHA	8	0	0	0	....	....	....	*22	....	....	....	....	....
1924-25	Sudbury Wolves	NOHA	STATISTICS NOT AVAILABLE												
1925-26	Galt Terriers	OHA Sr.	16	4	3	7	....	....	....	*37	2	0	1	1	2
1926-27	**New York Americans**	**NHL**	**11**	**0**	**1**	**1**	**0**	**8**	**8**	**4**	....	....	....	....	....
	Niagara Falls Cataracts	Can-Pro	12	4	0	4	....	....	....	27	....	....	....	....	....
1927-28	**New York Americans**	**NHL**	**36**	**2**	**1**	**3**	**6**	**8**	**14**	**129**	....	....	....	....	....
	Niagara Falls Cataracts	Can-Pro	10	1	1	2	....	....	....	17	....	....	....	....	....
1928-29	New Haven Eagles	Can-Am	40	3	2	5	....	....	....	79	2	0	0	0	4
	NHL Totals		**47**	**2**	**2**	**4**	**6**	**16**	**22**	**133**	....	....	....	....	....

Signed as a free agent by **NY Americans**, July 14, 1926.

• BOUCHER, FRANK
Frank "Raffles" Boucher **HHOF**
C – L. 5'9", 185 lbs. b: Ottawa, Ont., 10/7/1901. d: 12/12/1977.

			REGULAR SEASON								PLAYOFFS				
Season	Club	League	GP	G	A	Pts	AG	AA	APts	PIM	GP	G	A	Pts	PIM
1916-17	Ottawa New Edinburghs	City Jr.	9	11	0	11	....	....	....	....	2	*6	0	*6	....
1917-18	Ottawa New Edinburghs	City Jr.	4	1	0	1	....	....	....	0	....	....	....	....	....
	Ottawa Munitions	City Sr.	1	0	0	0	....	....	....	0	1	0	0	0	0
1918-19	Ottawa New Edinburghs	City Sr.	7	1	2	3	....	....	....	5	....	....	....	....	....
1919-20			MILITARY SERVICE												
1920-21	Lethbridge Vets	ASHL	STATISTICS NOT AVAILABLE												
1921-22	**Ottawa Senators**	**NHL**	**24**	**8**	**2**	**10**	**22**	**12**	**34**	**4**	**1**	**0**	**0**	**0**	**0**
1922-23	Vancouver Maroons	PCHA	29	11	9	20	....	....	....	2	6	2	1	3	4
1923-24	Vancouver Maroons	PCHA	28	15	5	20	....	....	....	10	7	3	1	4	2
1924-25	Vancouver Maroons	WCHL	27	16	12	28	....	....	....	6	....	....	....	....	....
1925-26	Vancouver Maroons	WHL	29	15	7	22	....	....	....	14	....	....	....	....	....
1926-27	**New York Rangers**	**NHL**	**44**	**13**	**15**	**28**	**38**	**131**	**169**	**17**	**2**	**0**	**0**	**0**	**4**
1927-28	**New York Rangers**	**NHL**	**44**	**23**	**12**	**35**	**72**	**103**	**175**	**15**	**9**	***7**	**1**	***8**	**2**
1928-29	**New York Rangers**	**NHL**	**44**	**10**	***16**	**26**	**40**	**151**	**191**	**8**	**6**	**1**	**0**	**1**	**0**
1929-30	**New York Rangers**	**NHL**	**42**	**26**	***36**	**62**	**52**	**120**	**172**	**16**	**3**	**1**	**1**	**2**	**0**
1930-31	**New York Rangers**	**NHL**	**44**	**12**	**27**	**39**	**29**	**100**	**129**	**20**	**4**	**0**	**2**	**2**	**0**
1931-32	**New York Rangers**	**NHL**	**48**	**12**	**23**	**35**	**26**	**65**	**91**	**18**	**7**	**3**	***6**	**9**	**0**
1932-33	**New York Rangers**	**NHL**	**46**	**7**	***28**	**35**	**16**	**75**	**91**	**4**	**8**	**2**	**2**	**4**	**6**
1933-34	**New York Rangers**	**NHL**	**48**	**14**	**30**	**44**	**31**	**82**	**113**	**4**	**2**	**0**	**0**	**0**	**0**
1934-35	**New York Rangers**	**NHL**	**48**	**13**	**32**	**45**	**28**	**72**	**100**	**2**	**4**	**0**	**3**	**3**	**0**
1935-36	**New York Rangers**	**NHL**	**48**	**11**	**18**	**29**	**27**	**44**	**71**	**2**	....	....	....	....	....
1936-37	**New York Rangers**	**NHL**	**44**	**7**	**13**	**20**	**15**	**31**	**46**	**5**	**9**	**2**	**3**	**5**	**0**
1937-38	**New York Rangers**	**NHL**	**18**	**0**	**1**	**1**	**0**	**2**	**2**	**2**	....	....	....	....	....
1938-39	New York Rovers	EHL	DID NOT PLAY – COACHING												
1939-40	**New York Rangers**	**NHL**	DID NOT PLAY – COACHING												
1940-41	**New York Rangers**	**NHL**	DID NOT PLAY – COACHING												
1941-42	**New York Rangers**	**NHL**	DID NOT PLAY – COACHING												
1942-43	**New York Rangers**	**NHL**	DID NOT PLAY – COACHING												
1943-44	**New York Rangers**	**NHL**	**15**	**4**	**10**	**14**	**5**	**12**	**17**	**2**	....	....	....	....	....
	NHL Totals		**557**	**160**	**263**	**423**	**401**	**1000**	**1401**	**119**	**55**	**16**	**18**	**34**	**12**
	Other Major League Totals		113	57	33	90	....	....	....	32	13	5	2	7	6

PCHA First All-Star Team (1923) • PCHA All-Star Team (1924) • WCHL All-Star Team (1925) • Won Lady Byng Trophy (1928, 1929, 1930, 1931, 1933, 1934, 1935) • NHL Second All-Star Team (1931) • NHL First All-Star Team (1933, 1934, 1935) • Won Lester Patrick Trophy (1993)

Played in NHL All-Star Game (1937)

Signed as a free agent by **Ottawa**, December 6, 1921. Traded to **Vancouver** (PCHA) by **Ottawa** for cash, September 19, 1922. Traded to **NY Rangers** by **Vancouver** (WHL) for $15,000, September 28, 1926.

• BOUCHER, GEORGE
George "Buck" Boucher **HHOF**
D – L. 5'9", 169 lbs. b: Ottawa, Ont., 8/19/1896. d: 10/17/1960.

			REGULAR SEASON								PLAYOFFS				
Season	Club	League	GP	G	A	Pts	AG	AA	APts	PIM	GP	G	A	Pts	PIM
1913-14	Ottawa New Edinburghs	City Sr.	5	1	0	1	....	....	....	....	....	....	....	....	....
1914-15	Ottawa New Edinburghs	City Sr.	15	12	0	12	....	....	....	....	....	....	....	....	....
1915-16	Ottawa Senators	NHA	19	9	1	10	....	....	....	62	....	....	....	....	....
1916-17	Ottawa Senators	NHA	18	10	3	13	....	....	....	27	2	1	0	1	3
1917-18	**Ottawa Senators**	**NHL**	**21**	**9**	**8**	**17**	**22**	**0**	**22**	**46**	....	....	....	....	....
1918-19	**Ottawa Senators**	**NHL**	**17**	**4**	**2**	**6**	**14**	**19**	**33**	**32**	**7**	**3**	**0**	**3**	**12**
1919-20	**Ottawa Senators**	**NHL**	**23**	**9**	**8**	**17**	**20**	**55**	**75**	**55**	**5**	**2**	**0**	**2**	**3**
1920-21	**Ottawa Senators**	**NHL**	**23**	**11**	**8**	**19**	**28**	**72**	**100**	**53**	**5**	**2**	**0**	**2**	**9**
1921-22	**Ottawa Senators**	**NHL**	**23**	**13**	**12**	**25**	**36**	**77**	**113**	**12**	**2**	**0**	**0**	**0**	**4**
1922-23	**Ottawa Senators**	**NHL**	**23**	**15**	**9**	**24**	**51**	**83**	**134**	**44**	**8**	**2**	**1**	**3**	**8**
1923-24	**Ottawa Senators**	**NHL**	**21**	**14**	**5**	**19**	**59**	**90**	**149**	**28**	**2**	**0**	**1**	**1**	**4**
1924-25	**Ottawa Senators**	**NHL**	**28**	**15**	**4**	**19**	**52**	**53**	**105**	**80**	....	....	....	....	....
1925-26	**Ottawa Senators**	**NHL**	**36**	**8**	**4**	**12**	**25**	**46**	**71**	**64**	**2**	**0**	**0**	**0**	**10**
1926-27	**Ottawa Senators**	**NHL**	**40**	**8**	**3**	**11**	**23**	**25**	**48**	**115**	**6**	**0**	**0**	**0**	**43**
1927-28	**Ottawa Senators**	**NHL**	**43**	**7**	**5**	**12**	**21**	**42**	**63**	**70**	**2**	**0**	**0**	**0**	**4**
1928-29	**Ottawa Senators**	**NHL**	**29**	**3**	**1**	**4**	**12**	**9**	**21**	**60**	....	....	....	....	....
	Montreal Maroons	**NHL**	**12**	**1**	**1**	**2**	**4**	**9**	**13**	**10**	....	....	....	....	....
1929-30	**Montreal Maroons**	**NHL**	**37**	**2**	**6**	**8**	**4**	**19**	**23**	**50**	**3**	**0**	**0**	**0**	**2**
1930-31	**Montreal Maroons**	**NHL**	**30**	**0**	**0**	**0**	**0**	**0**	**0**	**25**	....	....	....	....	....
1931-32	**Chicago Black Hawks**	**NHL**	**43**	**1**	**5**	**6**	**2**	**14**	**16**	**50**	**2**	**0**	**1**	**1**	**0**
1932-33	Boston Cubs	Can-Am	9	0	0	0	....	....	....	8	....	....	....	....	....
1933-34	**Ottawa Senators**	**NHL**	DID NOT PLAY – COACHING												
	NHL Totals		**449**	**120**	**81**	**201**	**373**	**613**	**986**	**802**	**44**	**9**	**3**	**12**	**99**
	Other Major League Totals		37	19	4	23	....	....	....	89	2	1	0	1	3

Rights retained by **Ottawa** after NHA folded, November 26, 1917. Traded to **Montreal Maroons** by **Ottawa** for Joe Lamb, February 14, 1929. Claimed on waivers by **Chicago** from **Montreal Maroons**, November 27, 1931.

• BOUCHER, ROBERT
Robert "Shorty" Boucher
C – R. 5'8", 142 lbs. b: Ottawa, Ont., 2/14/1904. d: 6/10/1931.

			REGULAR SEASON								PLAYOFFS				
Season	Club	League	GP	G	A	Pts	AG	AA	APts	PIM	GP	G	A	Pts	PIM
1916-17	Ottawa New Edinburghs	City Jr.	9	1	0	1	....	....	....	....	....	....	....	....	....
1917-18	Ottawa Mutchmore	City Jr.	STATISTICS NOT AVAILABLE												
	Ottawa New Edinburghs	City Jr.	1	0	0	0	....	....	....	0	....	....	....	....	....
1918-19	Ottawa Creighton	City Jr.	STATISTICS NOT AVAILABLE												
1919-20	Ottawa New Edinburghs	City Sr.	4	0	0	0	....	....	....	0	....	....	....	....	....
1920-21	Ottawa New Edinburghs	City Sr.	1	1	0	1	....	....	....	....	....	....	....	....	....
	Iroquois Falls Eskimos	Ott-Sr.	1	0	1	1	....	....	....	....	....	....	....	....	....
1921-22	Ottawa New Edinburghs	City Sr.	1	0	0	0	....	....	....	0	....	....	....	....	....
1922-23	Iroquois Falls Eskimos	Ott-Sr.	STATISTICS NOT AVAILABLE												
1923-24	**Montreal Canadiens**	**NHL**	**12**	**0**	**0**	**0**	**0**	**0**	**0**	**0**	....	....	....	....	....
	Ottawa Gunners	City Sr.	7	4	1	5	....	....	....	....	....	....	....	....	....
1924-25	Vancouver Maroons	WCHL	19	1	0	1	....	....	....	3	....	....	....	....	....
1925-26	Edmonton Eskimos	WHL	29	2	1	3	....	....	....	16	....	....	....	....	....
1926-27	London Panthers	Can-Pro	32	8	2	10	....	....	....	39	4	0	0	0	2
1927-28	Toronto Falcons	Can-Pro	1	0	0	0	....	....	....	2	....	....	....	....	....
	Quebec Castors	Can-Am	23	3	0	3	....	....	....	18	6	1	0	1	10
1928-29	Newark Bulldogs	Can-Am	5	0	0	0	....	....	....	2	....	....	....	....	....
	NHL Totals		**12**	**0**	**0**	**0**	**0**	**0**	**0**	**0**	....	....	....	....	....
	Other Major League Totals		48	3	1	4	....	....	....	19	....	....	....	....	....

Signed as a free agent by **Montreal Canadiens**, January 25, 1924. Traded to **Vancouver** (PCHA) by **Montreal Canadiens** for Charlie Cotch, March 26, 1924. Traded to **Edmonton** (WHL) by **Vancouver** (WHL) for cash, November 16, 1925. Signed as a free agent by **London** (Can-Pro), November 2, 1926.

• BOUDRIAS, ANDRE
— *see page 888*

• BOURCIER, CONRAD
Conrad Bourcier
C – L. 5'7", 145 lbs. b: Montreal, Que., 5/28/1915. Deceased.

			REGULAR SEASON								PLAYOFFS				
Season	Club	League	GP	G	A	Pts	AG	AA	APts	PIM	GP	G	A	Pts	PIM
1934-35	Verdun Maple Leafs	Mtl-Jr.	10	5	12	17	....	....	....	0	6	*6	4	*10	4
1935-36	**Montreal Canadiens**	**NHL**	**6**	**0**	**0**	**0**	**0**	**0**	**0**	**0**	....	....	....	....	....
	Pittsburgh Yellowjackets	IAHL	9	2	2	4	....	....	....	2	....	....	....	....	....
	Verdun Maple Leafs	Mtl-Sr.	10	5	1	6	....	....	....	4	....	....	....	....	....
1936-37	Verdun Maple Leafs	Mtl-Sr.	STATISTICS NOT AVAILABLE												
1937-38	Verdun Maple Leafs	Mtl-Sr.	21	4	6	10	....	....	....	8	8	4	*6	10	12
1938-39	Verdun Maple Leafs	Mtl-Sr.	22	10	9	19	....	....	....	16	2	0	0	0	0
1939-40	Verdun Bulldogs	QPHL	41	21	32	53	....	....	....	30	2	1	0	1	2
1940-41	Verdun Maple Leafs	QSHL	32	12	12	24	....	....	....	17	....	....	....	....	....
1941-42	Montreal Cyclones	QPHL	7	8	4	12	....	....	....	12	....	....	....	....	....
1942-43			MILITARY SERVICE												
1943-44			MILITARY SERVICE												
1944-45	Montreal Cyclones	QPHL	....	14	11	25	....	....	....	....	....	....	....	....	....
	Cornwall Cookies	QPHL	1	0	0	0	....	....	....	0	....	....	....	....	....
1945-46	St. Hyacinthe Saints	QPHL	8	4	6	10	....	....	....	6	4	2	0	2	0
1946-47	Verdun Eagles	QPHL	47	40	28	68	....	....	....	24	....	....	....	....	....
1947-48			DID NOT PLAY – RETIRED												
1948-49	Montreal Hydro	City Sr.	12	10	*13	*23	....	....	....	....	....	....	....	....	....
	NHL Totals		**6**	**0**	**0**	**0**	**0**	**0**	**0**	**0**	....	....	....	....	....

• BOURCIER, JEAN
Jean Bourcier
LW – L. 5'11", 175 lbs. b: Montreal, Que., 1/3/1911.

			REGULAR SEASON								PLAYOFFS				
Season	Club	League	GP	G	A	Pts	AG	AA	APts	PIM	GP	G	A	Pts	PIM
1933-34	Verdun Maple Leafs	Mtl-Sr.	16	15	6	21	....	....	....	2	2	0	1	1	0
1934-35	Verdun Maple Leafs	Mtl-Sr.	20	*22	18	*40	....	....	....	4	....	....	....	....	....
1935-36	**Montreal Canadiens**	**NHL**	**9**	**0**	**1**	**1**	**0**	**2**	**2**	**0**	....	....	....	....	....
	Pittsburgh Yellowjackets	IAHL	18	8	5	13	....	....	....	4	....				
	Verdun Maple Leafs	Mtl-Sr.	10	11	8	19	....	....	....	2	....	....	....	....	....
1936-37	Verdun Maple Leafs	Mtl-Sr.	STATISTICS NOT AVAILABLE												
1937-38	Verdun Maple Leafs	Mtl-Sr.	22	16	13	29	....	....	....	0	8	0	3	3	14
1938-39	Verdun Maple Leafs	Mtl-Sr.	21	10	3	13	....	....	....	10	2	1	0	1	0
1939-40	Verdun Bulldogs	QPHL	39	22	20	42	....	....	....	8	2	2	2	4	0
1940-41	Verdun Maple Leafs	QSHL	13	5	4	9	....	....	....	0	....	....	....	....	....
	NHL Totals		**9**	**0**	**1**	**1**	**0**	**2**	**2**	**0**	....	....	....	....	....

Signed as a free agent by **Montreal Canadiens**, October 11, 1935.

• BOURGEAULT, LEO
Leo Bourgeault
D – L. 5'6", 165 lbs. b: Sturgeon Falls, Ont., 1/17/1903. Deceased.

			REGULAR SEASON								PLAYOFFS				
Season	Club	League	GP	G	A	Pts	AG	AA	APts	PIM	GP	G	A	Pts	PIM
1921-22	North Bay Trappers	NOHA	4	4	1	5	....	....	....	....	8	6	3	9	....
1922-23	North Bay Trappers	NOHA	STATISTICS NOT AVAILABLE												
1923-24	Guelph Royals	OHA Sr.	STATISTICS NOT AVAILABLE												
1924-25	Saskatoon Crescents	WCHL	19	3	0	3	....	....	....	8	....	....	....	....	....
1925-26	Saskatoon Crescents	WHL	30	5	2	7	....	....	....	18	2	0	0	0	8
1926-27	**Toronto St.Pats**	**NHL**	**22**	**0**	**0**	**0**	**0**	**0**	**0**	**44**	....	....	....	....	....
	New York Rangers	**NHL**	**20**	**2**	**1**	**3**	**6**	**8**	**14**	**28**	**2**	**0**	**0**	**0**	**4**
1927-28	**New York Rangers**	**NHL**	**37**	**7**	**0**	**7**	**21**	**0**	**21**	**7**	**9**	**0**	**0**	**0**	**8**
1928-29	**New York Rangers**	**NHL**	**44**	**2**	**3**	**5**	**8**	**27**	**35**	**59**	**6**	**0**	**0**	**0**	**0**
1929-30	**New York Rangers**	**NHL**	**44**	**7**	**6**	**13**	**14**	**19**	**33**	**54**	**3**	**1**	**1**	**2**	**6**
1930-31	**New York Rangers**	**NHL**	**10**	**0**	**1**	**1**	**0**	**4**	**4**	**12**	....	....	....	....	....
	Ottawa Senators	**NHL**	**28**	**0**	**4**	**4**	**0**	**14**	**14**	**28**	....	....	....	....	....
1931-32	Bronx Tigers	Can-Am	40	10	9	19	....	....	....	87	2	0	0	0	4
1932-33	**Ottawa Senators**	**NHL**	**35**	**1**	**1**	**2**	**2**	**3**	**5**	**18**	....	....	....	....	....
	Montreal Canadiens	**NHL**	**15**	**1**	**1**	**2**	**2**	**3**	**5**	**9**	**2**	**0**	**0**	**0**	**0**
1933-34	**Montreal Canadiens**	**NHL**	**48**	**4**	**3**	**7**	**9**	**8**	**17**	**10**	**2**	**0**	**0**	**0**	**0**
1934-35	**Montreal Canadiens**	**NHL**	**4**	**0**	**0**	**0**	**0**	**0**	**0**	**0**	....	....	....	....	....
	Quebec Castors	Can-Am	43	13	14	27	....	....	....	34	3	1	0	1	2
1935-36	Springfield Indians	Can-Am	2	1	0	1	....	....	....	0	2	0	2	2	0
	NHL Totals		**307**	**24**	**20**	**44**	**62**	**86**	**148**	**269**	**24**	**1**	**1**	**2**	**18**
	Other Major League Totals		49	8	2	10	....	....	....	26	2	0	0	0	8

Signed as a free agent by **Saskatoon** (WCHL), November 27, 1924. Traded to **Toronto St. Pats** by **Saskatoon** (WHL) with Corbett Denneny and Laurie Scott for cash, October 18, 1926. Traded to **NY Rangers** by **Toronto St. Pats** for cash, January, 1927. Traded to **Ottawa** by **NY Rangers** for cash, December 7, 1930. Traded to **Montreal Canadiens** by **Ottawa** with Harold Starr and future considerations (Nick Wasnie, March 23, 1933) for Marty Burke, February, 1933.

			REGULAR SEASON								PLAYOFFS				
Season	**Club**	**League**	**GP**	**G**	**A**	**Pts**	**AG**	**AA**	**APts**	**PIM**	**GP**	**G**	**A**	**Pts**	**PIM**

• BOWMAN, RALPH
Ralph "Scotty" Bowman
D – L. 5'11", 190 lbs. b: Winnipeg, Man., 6/20/1911. d: 10/17/1990.

Season	Club	League	GP	G	A	Pts	AG	AA	APts	PIM	GP	G	A	Pts	PIM
1929-30	Parkdale Canoe Club	OHA	8	1	1	2	....	....	....	20	3	0	0	0	2
1930-31	Niagara Falls Cataracts	OHA	7	10	1	11	....	....	....	2	2	1	0	1	0
1931-32	Niagara Falls Cataracts	OHA Sr.	18	1	1	2	....	....	....	28	2	0	0	0	8
1932-33	Niagara Falls Cataracts	OHA Sr.	19	3	0	3	....	....	....	49	5	1	0	1	2
1933-34	**Ottawa Senators**	**NHL**	**46**	**0**	**2**	**2**	**0**	**5**	**5**	**64**	....	....	....	....	....
1934-35	**St. Louis Eagles**	**NHL**	**31**	**2**	**2**	**4**	**4**	**4**	**8**	**51**	....	....	....	....	....
	Detroit Red Wings	**NHL**	**13**	**1**	**3**	**4**	**2**	**7**	**9**	**21**	....	....	....	....	....
1935-36	**Detroit Red Wings**	**NHL**	**48**	**3**	**2**	**5**	**7**	**5**	**12**	**44**	**7**	**2**	**1**	**3**	**2**
1936-37	**Detroit Red Wings**	**NHL**	**37**	**0**	**1**	**1**	**0**	**2**	**2**	**24**	**10**	**0**	**1**	**1**	**4**
1937-38	**Detroit Red Wings**	**NHL**	**45**	**0**	**2**	**2**	**0**	**4**	**4**	**26**	....	....	....	....	....
1938-39	**Detroit Red Wings**	**NHL**	**43**	**2**	**3**	**5**	**4**	**6**	**10**	**26**	**5**	**0**	**0**	**0**	**0**
1939-40	**Detroit Red Wings**	**NHL**	**11**	**0**	**2**	**2**	**0**	**4**	**4**	**4**	....	....	....	....	....
	Indianapolis Capitals	AHL	12	1	2	3	....	....	....	8	5	0	0	0	0
1940-41	Pittsburgh Hornets	AHL	48	1	4	5	....	....	....	14	5	0	0	0	0
1941-42	Philadelphia Rockets	AHL	55	3	6	9	....	....	....	92	....	....	....	....	....
	Providence Reds	AHL	2	0	0	0	....	....	....	0	....	....	....	....	....
1942-43	Washington–Hershey	AHL	47	1	14	15	....	....	....	14	....	....	....	....	....
	NHL Totals		**274**	**8**	**17**	**25**	**17**	**37**	**54**	**260**	**22**	**2**	**2**	**4**	**6**

Transferred to **St. Louis** after **Ottawa** franchise relocated, September 22, 1934. Traded to **Detroit** by **St. Louis** with Syd Howe for Ted Graham and $50,000, February 11, 1934. Traded to **Buffalo** (AHL) by **Detroit** for cash, October 24, 1940.

• BOWNASS, JACK
Jack Bownass
D – L. 6'1", 190 lbs. b: Winnipeg, Man., 7/27/1930.

Season	Club	League	GP	G	A	Pts	AG	AA	APts	PIM	GP	G	A	Pts	PIM
1947-48	Winnipeg Black Hawks	MJHL	1	0	0	0	....	....	....	0	....	....	....	....	....
1948-49	Winnipeg Black Hawks	MJHL	29	3	2	5	....	....	....	16	....	....	....	....	....
1949-50	Winnipeg Black Hawks	MJHL	36	3	7	10	....	....	....	76	6	1	1	2	12
1950-51	Sarnia–Windsor	IHL	46	6	7	13	....	....	....	101	3	0	0	0	4
1951-52	Shawinigan Cataracts	QSHL	49	0	3	3	....	....	....	84	....	....	....	....	....
1952-53	Chicoutimi Sagueneens	QSHL	38	2	4	6	....	....	....	59	....	....	....	....	....
1953-54	Sherbrooke Saints	QHL	71	9	17	26	....	....	....	111	5	1	0	1	4
1954-55	Montreal Royals	QHL	56	5	27	32	....	....	....	88	14	1	2	3	8
1955-56	Seattle Americans	WHL	65	10	22	32	....	....	....	131	....	....	....	....	....
1956-57	Trois-Rivieres Lions	QHL	62	7	16	23	....	....	....	75	4	0	4	4	4
1957-58	**Montreal Canadiens**	**NHL**	**4**	**0**	**1**	**1**	**0**	**1**	**1**	**0**	....	....	....	....	....
	Montreal Royals	QHL	61	3	31	34	....	....	....	120	7	0	6	6	21
1958-59	**New York Rangers**	**NHL**	**35**	**1**	**2**	**3**	**1**	**2**	**3**	**20**	....	....	....	....	....
	Buffalo Bisons	AHL	21	3	9	12	....	....	....	26	....	....	....	....	....
1959-60	**New York Rangers**	**NHL**	**37**	**2**	**5**	**7**	**2**	**5**	**7**	**34**	....	....	....	....	....
	Springfield Indians	AHL	16	0	0	0	....	....	....	37	....	....	....	....	....
1960-61	Kitchener Beavers	EPHL	70	1	36	37	....	....	....	110	7	0	4	4	12
1961-62	**New York Rangers**	**NHL**	**4**	**0**	**0**	**0**	**0**	**0**	**0**	**4**	....	....	....	....	....
	Kitchener Beavers	EPHL	62	6	40	46	....	....	....	119	7	2	0	2	0
1962-63	Los Angeles Blades	WHL	67	4	24	28	....	....	....	55	3	0	1	1	0
1963-64	Baltimore Clippers	AHL	15	0	4	4	....	....	....	27	....	....	....	....	....
	Los Angeles Blades	WHL	53	2	19	21	....	....	....	65	....	....	....	....	....
1964-65			REINSTATED AS AN AMATEUR												
1965-66	Winnipeg Rangers	MJHL	DID NOT PLAY – COACHING												
1966-67	Canada	Nat-Tm.	STATISTICS NOT AVAILABLE												
	Canada	WEC-A	7	0	2	2	....	....	....	12	....	....	....	....	....
1967-68	Canada	Nat-Tm.	STATISTICS NOT AVAILABLE												
1968-69	Ottawa Nationals	OHA Sr.	4	0	0	0	....	....	....	2	....	....	....	....	....
	Canada	WEC-A	4	0	0	0	....	....	....	4	....	....	....	....	....
1969-70	Canada	Nat-Tm.	STATISTICS NOT AVAILABLE												
1970-71	Jacksonville Rockets	EHL	8	0	0	0	....	....	....	2	....	....	....	....	....
	NHL Totals		**80**	**3**	**8**	**11**	**3**	**8**	**11**	**58**	....	....	....	....	....

IHL Second All-Star Team (1951) • QHL First All-Star Team (1958)

Loaned to **Seattle** (WHL) by **Montreal** for 1955-56 season, November, 1955. Claimed by **NY Rangers** from **Montreal** in Intra-League Draft, June 3, 1958.

• BOYD, BILL
Bill Boyd
RW – R. 5'10", 185 lbs. b: Belleville, Ont., 5/15/1898. d: 11/17/1940.

Season	Club	League	GP	G	A	Pts	AG	AA	APts	PIM	GP	G	A	Pts	PIM
1916-17	Hamilton Tigers	OHA Sr.	STATISTICS NOT AVAILABLE												
1917-18	Hamilton Tigers	OHA Sr.	5	11	0	11	....	....	....	....	....	....	....	....	....
1918-19			MILITARY SERVICE												
1919-20	Hamilton Tigers	OHA Sr.	6	9	1	10	....	....	....	....	2	0	2	2	....
1920-21	Halifax Wanderers	City Sr.	6	6	1	7	....	....	....	16	2	0	0	0	6
1921-22	Hamilton Tigers	OHA Sr.	9	8	8	16	....	....	....	....	....	....	....	....	....
1922-23	Milwaukee Sea Gulls	USAHA	....	9	0	9	....	....	....	....	....	....	....	....	....
1923-24	Minneapolis Rangers	USAHA	20	1	0	1	....	....	....	....	....	....	....	....	....
1924-25	Minneapolis Millers	USAHA	39	4	0	4	....	....	....	....	....	....	....	....	....
1925-26	Minneapolis Millers	CHL	34	11	2	13	....	....	....	30	3	0	0	0	4
1926-27	**New York Rangers**	**NHL**	**41**	**4**	**1**	**5**	**12**	**8**	**20**	**40**	....	....	....	....	....
1927-28	**New York Rangers**	**NHL**	**43**	**4**	**0**	**4**	**12**	**0**	**12**	**11**	**9**	**0**	**0**	**0**	**2**
1928-29	**New York Rangers**	**NHL**	**11**	**0**	**0**	**0**	**0**	**0**	**0**	**5**	....	....	....	....	....
1929-30	**New York Americans**	**NHL**	**43**	**7**	**6**	**13**	**14**	**19**	**33**	**16**	....	....	....	....	....
	NHL Totals		**138**	**15**	**7**	**22**	**38**	**27**	**65**	**72**	**9**	**0**	**0**	**0**	**2**

Signed as a free agent by **NY Rangers**, November 9, 1926. Claimed by **NY Americans** from **Springfield** (Can-Am) in Inter-League Draft, May 13, 1929.

• BOYD, IRWIN
Irwin "Yank" Boyd
RW – R. 5'10", 152 lbs. b: Ardmore, PA, 11/13/1908.

Season	Club	League	GP	G	A	Pts	AG	AA	APts	PIM	GP	G	A	Pts	PIM
1925-26	Toronto Canoe Club	OHA	7	5	1	6	....	....	....	....	....	....	....	....	....
	Toronto Canoe Club	OHA Sr.	2	3	0	3	....	....	....	....	....	....	....	....	....
1926-27	Toronto 1st Battalion	OHA Sr.	4	0	2	2	....	....	....	0	....	....	....	....	....
1927-28	Toronto CCM	City Sr.	STATISTICS NOT AVAILABLE												
1928-29	Toronto CCM	City Sr.	STATISTICS NOT AVAILABLE												
1929-30	Boston Tigers	Can-Am	40	24	12	36	....	....	....	90	5	2	2	4	8
1930-31	Boston Tigers	Can-Am	39	17	14	31	....	....	....	71	9	1	4	5	6
1931-32	**Boston Bruins**	**NHL**	**30**	**10**	**10**	**20**	**21**	**28**	**49**	**31**	....	....	....	....	....
	Boston Cubs	Can-Am	20	10	10	20	....	....	....	31	....	....	....	....	....
1932-33	Philadelphia Arrows	Can-Am	48	21	22	43	....	....	....	43	5	2	3	5	0
1933-34	Philadelphia Arrows	Can-Am	40	14	20	34	....	....	....	26	2	0	1	1	2
1934-35	**Detroit Red Wings**	**NHL**	**42**	**2**	**3**	**5**	**4**	**7**	**11**	**14**	....	....	....	....	....
	Detroit Olympics	IAHL	9	4	6	10	....	....	....	6	....	....	....	....	....
1935-36	London Techumsehs	IAHL	42	19	14	33	....	....	....	36	2	3	0	3	0
1936-37	New Haven Eagles	AHL	42	12	14	26	....	....	....	24	....	....	....	....	....
1937-38	New Haven Eagles	AHL	38	3	9	12	....	....	....	6	2	1	1	2	0
	Providence Reds	AHL	1	0	0	0	....	....	....	0	....	....	....	....	....
1938-39	St. Paul Saints	AHA	45	14	40	54	....	....	....	31	3	1	0	1	2
1939-40	St. Paul Saints	AHA	46	26	22	48	....	....	....	27	7	5	3	8	2
1940-41	St. Paul Saints	AHA	30	8	8	16	....	....	....	9	4	0	0	0	0
1941-42	St. Paul Saints	AHA	47	6	20	26	....	....	....	18	2	0	0	0	0
1942-43	**Boston Bruins**	**NHL**	**20**	**6**	**5**	**11**	**8**	**6**	**14**	**6**	**5**	**0**	**1**	**1**	**4**
1943-44	**Boston Bruins**	**NHL**	**5**	**0**	**1**	**1**	**0**	**1**	**1**	**0**	....	....	....	....	....
	Providence Reds	AHL	38	6	27	33	....	....	....	12	....	....	....	....	....
1944-45	Providence Reds	AHL	1	0	1	1	....	....	....	0	....	....	....	....	....
	NHL Totals		**97**	**18**	**19**	**37**	**33**	**42**	**75**	**51**	**5**	**0**	**1**	**1**	**4**

Traded to **Philadelphia** (Can-Am) by **Boston** for cash, October, 1932. Traded to **Detroit** by **Philadelphia** (Can-Am) for cash, May 8, 1934. Signed as a free agent by **Boston**, December 18, 1942.

• BOYER, WALLY
— see page 892

• BRACKENBOROUGH, JOHN
John "Spider" Brackenborough
LW/C – L. 5'11", 170 lbs. b: unknown. d: 7/8/1993.

Season	Club	League	GP	G	A	Pts	AG	AA	APts	PIM	GP	G	A	Pts	PIM
1915-16	Ottawa Grand Trunk	City Sr.	4	2	0	2	....	....	....	....	....	....	....	....	....
1916-17			MILITARY SERVICE												
1917-18			MILITARY SERVICE												
1918-19			MILITARY SERVICE												
1919-20	Depot Harbour	City Sr.	STATISTICS NOT AVAILABLE												
1920-21	North Bay Trappers	NOHA	6	6	5	11	....	....	....	4	....	....	....	....	....
1921-22	North Bay Trappers	NOHA	6	7	3	10	....	....	....	6	....	....	....	....	....
1922-23	Hamilton Tigers	OHA Sr.	12	20	8	*28	....	....	....	....	2	1	*2	*3	....
1923-24	Hamilton Tigers	OHA Sr.	10	13	*12	25	....	....	....	....	2	1	*2	3	....
1924-25			DID NOT PLAY – INJURED												
1925-26	**Boston Bruins**	**NHL**	**7**	**0**	**0**	**0**	**0**	**0**	**0**	**0**	....	....	....	....	....
	NHL Totals		**7**	**0**	**0**	**0**	**0**	**0**	**0**	**0**	....	....	....	....	....

• Lost sight and use of right eye in game vs. University of Toronto, February 28, 1924. Signed as a free agent by **Boston**, November 16, 1925.

• BRADLEY, BARTON
Barton Bradley
C – L. 5'8", 150 lbs. b: Fort William, Ont., 7/29/1930.

Season	Club	League	GP	G	A	Pts	AG	AA	APts	PIM	GP	G	A	Pts	PIM
1946-47	Port Arthur Bruins	TBJHL	6	5	6	11	....	....	....	7	7	5	4	9	4
1947-48	Port Arthur Bruins	TBJHL	9	9	9	18	....	....	....	7	5	4	3	7	2
1948-49	Port Arthur Bruins	TBJHL	12	10	*20	30	....	....	....	28	5	2	*9	*11	12
1949-50	**Boston Bruins**	**NHL**	**1**	**0**	**0**	**0**	**0**	**0**	**0**	**0**	....	....	....	....	....
	Hershey Bears	AHL	61	16	19	35	....	....	....	8	....	....	....	....	....
1950-51	Tulsa Oilers	USHL	64	27	37	64	....	....	....	32	9	3	3	6	30
1951-52	Tacoma Rockets	PCHL	70	37	39	76	....	....	....	28	7	2	8	10	2
1952-53	Tacoma Rockets	WHL	70	26	47	73	....	....	....	28	....	....	....	....	....
1953-54	Seattle Bombers	WHL	27	7	19	26	....	....	....	8	....	....	....	....	....
1954-55	Victoria–New Westminster	WHL	47	12	15	27	....	....	....	9	1	0	0	0	0
1955-56	Seattle Americans	WHL	68	22	28	50	....	....	....	37	....	....	....	....	....
1956-57	Seattle Americans	WHL	63	10	16	26	....	....	....	19	6	1	1	2	7
1957-58	Belleville McFarlands	EOHL	50	30	34	64	....	....	....	32	13	*9	11	20	....
1958-59	Belleville McFarlands	EOHL	48	21	29	50	....	....	....	18	....	....	....	....	....
	Canada	WEC-A	8	5	5	10	....	....	....	8	....	....	....	....	....
1959-60	Belleville McFarlands	EOHL	53	12	30	42	....	....	....	8	12	3	5	8	8
	NHL Totals		**1**	**0**	**0**	**0**	**0**	**0**	**0**	**0**	....	....	....	....	....

• BRANIGAN, ANDY
Andy Branigan
D – L. 5'11", 190 lbs. b: Winnipeg, Man., 4/11/1922. d: 4/13/1995.

Season	Club	League	GP	G	A	Pts	AG	AA	APts	PIM	PO GP	PO G	PO A	PO Pts	PO PIM
1939-40	Winnipeg Monarchs	MJHL	23	0	1	1				38	7	5	0	5	14
1940-41	**New York Americans**	**NHL**	**6**	**1**	**0**	**1**	**2**	**0**	**2**	**5**					
	Springfield Indians	AHL	50	2	6	8				21	3	0	0	0	4
1941-42	**Brooklyn Americans**	**NHL**	**21**	**0**	**2**	**2**	**0**	**3**	**3**	**26**					
	Springfield Indians	AHL	1	0	0	0				0					
1942-43	Winnipeg RCAF	City Sr.	13	4	1	5				*26	17	4	3	7	*38
1943-44	Winnipeg RCAF	City Sr.	1	0	1	1				6					
1944-45	Winnipeg RCAF	City Sr.	9	2	1	3				18					
	Rockcliffe RCAF	City Sr.	4	0	2	2				8					
1945-46	Indianapolis Capitals	AHL	62	4	17	21				71	5	0	1	1	0
1946-47	Hershey Bears	AHL	62	6	9	15				42	11	1	2	3	8
1947-48	Hershey Bears	AHL	63	1	11	12				91	2	0	0	0	6
1948-49	Hershey Bears	AHL	68	5	14	19				54	11	0	2	2	10
1949-50	Hershey Bears	AHL	66	1	15	16				73					
1950-51	Hershey Bears	AHL	64	6	9	15				114	6	0	0	0	8
1951-52	Hershey Bears	AHL	66	6	19	25				110	5	1	1	2	10
1952-53	Hershey Bears	AHL	51	5	4	9				71					
1953-54	Hershey Bears	AHL	68	3	22	25				124	11	0	1	1	10
1954-55	Providence Reds	AHL	61	2	12	14				114					
1955-56	Providence Reds	AHL	64	5	17	22				103	9	2	5	7	14
1956-57	Providence Reds	AHL	46	2	10	12				46	5	0	0	0	6
1957-58	Providence Reds	AHL	67	2	6	8				61	1	0	0	0	0
1958-59	Washington Presidents	EHL	63	5	16	21				82					
1959-60	New York Rovers	EHL	48	2	10	12				73					
	NHL Totals		**27**	**1**	**2**	**3**	**2**	**3**	**5**	**31**					

AHL Second All-Star Team (1956)

Signed as a free agent by **NY Americans**, October 15, 1940. Rights transferred to **Detroit** from **Brooklyn** in Special Dispersal Draw, September 11, 1943.

• BRAYSHAW, RUSS
Russ "Buster" Brayshaw
LW – L. 5'10", 170 lbs. b: Saskatoon, Sask., 1/17/1918.

Season	Club	League	GP	G	A	Pts	AG	AA	APts	PIM	PO GP	PO G	PO A	PO Pts	PO PIM
1937-38	Saskatoon Quakers	SSHL	16	2	1	3				4	5	0	0	0	0
1938-39	Moose Jaw Millers	SSHL	22	10	2	12				8	10	1	2	3	6
1939-40	Moose Jaw Millers	SSHL	32	9	8	17				29	7	1	1	2	4
1940-41	Moose Jaw Millers	SSHL	30	11	11	22				14					
1941-42	Moose Jaw Millers	SSHL	28	9	15	24				16	9	5	3	8	4
1942-43	Victoria VMD	City Sr.	18	16	15	31				16					
	New Westminster Spitfires	PCHL	1	0	0	0				2	6	4	5	9	8
1943-44	Seattle Ironmen	City Sr.	2	1	1	2				0					
	New Westminster Spitfires	PCHL	19	17	15	32				25	18	*24	9	33	14
1944-45	**Chicago Black Hawks**	**NHL**	**43**	**5**	**9**	**14**	**7**	**14**	**21**	**24**					
1945-46	Cleveland Barons	AHL	57	24	24	48				37	5	1	1	2	0
1946-47	Providence–St. Louis	AHL	59	18	20	38				29					
1947-48	St. Louis Flyers	AHL	7	2	2	4				6					
	Tulsa Oilers	USHL	52	22	21	43				12	2	0	0	0	0
1948-49	Seattle–Vancouver	PCHL	20	5	11	16				20					
	Saskatoon Quakers	WCSHL	12	2	7	9				16					
	NHL Totals		**43**	**5**	**9**	**14**	**7**	**14**	**21**	**24**					

• BRENNAN, DOUG
Doug Brennan
D – L. 5'11", 180 lbs. b: Peterborough, Ont., 1/10/1905.

Season	Club	League	GP	G	A	Pts	AG	AA	APts	PIM	PO GP	PO G	PO A	PO Pts	PO PIM
1925-26	Peterborough Seniors	OHA Sr.	STATISTICS NOT AVAILABLE												
1926-27	Winnipeg Maroons	AHA	7	2	0	2				10					
	Kenora Thistles	NOHA	18	9	1	10				21					
1927-28	Winnipeg Maroons	AHA	26	2	0	2				8					
1928-29	Vancouver Lions	PCHL	35	8	4	12				61	3	1	0	1	6
1929-30	Vancouver Lions	PCHL	32	11	4	15				58	4	1	0	1	*10
1930-31	Vancouver Lions	PCHL	29	8	1	9				93					
1931-32	**New York Rangers**	**NHL**	**38**	**4**	**3**	**7**	**8**	**8**	**16**	**40**	**7**	**1**	**0**	**1**	**10**
1932-33	**New York Rangers**	**NHL**	**48**	**5**	**4**	**9**	**12**	**11**	**23**	**94**	**8**	**0**	**0**	**0**	**11**
1933-34	**New York Rangers**	**NHL**	**37**	**0**	**0**	**0**	**0**	**0**	**0**	**18**	**1**	**0**	**0**	**0**	**0**
	Windsor Bulldogs	IAHL	7	1	0	1				0					
1934-35	Philadelphia Arrows	Can-Am	22	3	3	6				14					
	Vancouver Lions	NWHL	12	1	4	5				10	8	0	1	1	4
1935-36	Springfield Indians	Can-Am	42	2	3	5				8	3	0	1	1	8
	NHL Totals		**123**	**9**	**7**	**16**	**20**	**19**	**39**	**152**	**16**	**1**	**0**	**1**	**21**

Traded to **NY Rangers** by **Vancouver** (PCHL) for cash, October 30, 1931. • Suspended by Can-Am for attack on referee Norm Shay, January 20, 1936.

• BRENNAN, TOM
Tom Brennan
RW – R. 5'9", 155 lbs. b: Philadelphia, PA, 1/22/1922.

Season	Club	League	GP	G	A	Pts	AG	AA	APts	PIM	PO GP	PO G	PO A	PO Pts	PO PIM
1938-39	Montreal Victorias	QJHL	12	11	7	18				15	2	1	1	2	14
1939-40	Montreal Westmounts	QJHL	11	9	6	15				7	2	2	0	2	0
1940-41	Montreal Jr. Canadiens	QJHL	10	5	10	15				10	4	*6	1	*7	0
1941-42	Montreal Sr. Canadiens	QSHL	5	2	0	2				2					
1942-43	Philadelphia Falcons	EHL	44	34	34	68				28	12	8	6	14	16
1943-44	**Boston Bruins**	**NHL**	**21**	**2**	**1**	**3**	**2**	**1**	**3**	**2**					
	Boston Olympics	EHL	30	36	25	61				58	11	10	4	14	19
1944-45	**Boston Bruins**	**NHL**	**1**	**0**	**1**	**1**	**0**	**2**	**2**	**0**					
	Boston Olympics	EHL	46	53	55	*108				42	10	13	17	30	15
1945-46			DID NOT PLAY – INJURED												
1946-47	Valleyfield Braves	QSHL	13	4	2	6				16					
	Boston Olympics	EHL	32	15	21	36				35	6	3	3	6	0
1947-48	Boston Olympics	QSHL	13	3	4	7				4					
	Boston Olympics	EHL	5	3	1	4				2					
1948-49	Halifax St. Mary's	MMHL	49	26	35	61				56	16	7	6	13	12
1949-50	Halifax St. Mary's	MMHL	61	23	34	57				12	17	7	14	21	16
	Boston Olympics	EHL	1	0	0	0				0					
1950-51	Saint John Beavers	MMHL	53	24	42	66				78					
1951-52	Saint John Beavers	MMHL	1	0	0	0				0					
	Joliette Cyclones	QPHL	DID NOT PLAY – COACHING												
	NHL Totals		**22**	**2**	**2**	**4**	**2**	**3**	**5**	**2**					

EHL Second All-Star Team (1943) • EHL First All-Star Team (1944, 1945) • Won John Carlin Trophy (Top Scorer - EHL) (1945)

• Suffered career-ending eye injury in game vs. Joliette, November 29, 1953.

• BRENNEMAN, JOHN
— see page 896

• BRETTO, JOE
Joe "Moose" Bretto
D – L. 6'1", 248 lbs. b: Hibbing, MN, 11/29/1913.

Season	Club	League	GP	G	A	Pts	AG	AA	APts	PIM	PO GP	PO G	PO A	PO Pts	PO PIM
1932-33	Hibbing Maroons	CHL	40	7	9	16				96					
1933-34	Hibbing Miners	CHL	29	10	5	15				*141	6	0	1	1	14
	Boston Cubs	Can-Am	4	0	0	0				2					
1934-35	Boston Cubs	Can-Am	7	0	0	0				8					
	Minneapolis Millers	Can-Am	42	3	4	7				*86	5	3	2	5	*8
1935-36	Windsor Bulldogs	IAHL	45	6	7	13				32	8	1	0	1	8
1936-37	Cleveland Falcons	AHL	47	2	8	10				41					
1937-38	Cleveland Falcons	AHL	1	0	0	0				15					
	Minneapolis Millers	AHA	38	8	11	19				70	7	2	2	4	*22
1938-39	St. Paul Saints	AHA	44	8	8	16				39	3	0	*6	6	0
1939-40	St. Paul Saints	AHA	46	14	12	26				66	7	1	6	7	8
1940-41	St. Paul Saints	AHA	48	5	10	15				64	4	1	0	1	2
1941-42	St. Paul Saints	AHA	29	6	5	11				44					
1942-43			DID NOT PLAY – RETIRED												
1943-44			DID NOT PLAY – RETIRED												
1944-45	**Chicago Black Hawks**	**NHL**	**3**	**0**	**0**	**0**	**0**	**0**	**0**	**4**					
1945-46	St. Paul Saints	USHL	3	0	1	1				0					
	NHL Totals		**3**	**0**	**0**	**0**	**0**	**0**	**0**	**4**					

AHA First All-Star Team (1938, 1940) • AHA Second All-Star Team (1939, 1941, 1942)

Traded to **Cleveland** (AHL) by **Chicago** for cash, November 14, 1944. • Suspended for remainder of 1944-45 season by **Cleveland** (AHL) for refusing to report, November 19, 1944.

• BREWER, CARL
— see page 896

• BRIDEN, ARCHIE
Archie "Bones" Briden
LW – L. 5'8", 170 lbs. b: Renfrew, Ontario, 7/16/1898. Deceased.

Season	Club	League	GP	G	A	Pts	AG	AA	APts	PIM	PO GP	PO G	PO A	PO Pts	PO PIM
1914-15	Haileybury Rexalls	NOHA	STATISTICS NOT AVAILABLE												
1915-16	Cleveland Indians	USAHA	STATISTICS NOT AVAILABLE												
1916-17	Toronto 228th Battalion	NHA	13	2	2	4				27					
1917-18			MILITARY SERVICE												
1918-19			MILITARY SERVICE												
1919-20	Edmonton Eskimos	Big 4	12	10	8	18				21	2	*2	0	2	4
1920-21	Edmonton Eskimos	Big 4	15	18	7	25				12					
1921-22	Seattle Metropolitans	PCHA	24	1	2	3				12	2	0	0	0	3
1922-23	Seattle Metropolitans	PCHA	38	7	3	10				27					
1923-24	Victoria Cougars	PCHA	12	9	1	10				4					
1924-25	Edmonton Eskimos	WCHL	28	17	6	23				33					
1925-26	Calgary Tigers	WHL	26	14	2	16				10					
1926-27	**Boston Bruins**	**NHL**	**16**	**2**	**2**	**4**	**6**	**17**	**23**	**8**					
	Detroit Cougars	**NHL**	**26**	**3**	**0**	**3**	**9**	**0**	**9**	**28**					
1927-28	Philadelphia Arrows	Can-Am	37	13	3	16				26					
1928-29	Philadelphia Arrows	Can-Am	40	12	5	17				46					
1929-30	**Pittsburgh Pirates**	**NHL**	**30**	**4**	**3**	**7**	**8**	**10**	**18**	**20**					
	London Panthers	IAHL	16	3	0	3				14	2	0	0	0	2
1930-31	London Panthers	IAHL	12	0	2	2				16					
	Cleveland Indians	IAHL	34	8	11	19				20	6	2	3	5	2
1931-32	Cleveland Indians	IAHL	48	6	10	16				16					
	NHL Totals		**72**	**9**	**5**	**14**	**23**	**27**	**50**	**50**					
	Other Major League Totals		141	50	16	66				113	2	0	0	0	3

PCHA Second All-Star Team (1923) • PCHA First All-Star Team (1924)

Signed as a free agent by **Seattle** (PCHA), November 7, 1921. Traded to **Victoria** (PCHA) by **Seattle** (PCHA) for cash, January 17, 1924. Traded to **Edmonton** (WCHL) by **Victoria** (WCHL) with Roy Rickey for Ty Arbour, November 6, 1924. Traded to **Calgary** (WHL) by **Edmonton** (WHL) for Ernie Anderson, November 18, 1925. Traded to **Boston** by **Calgary** (WHL) for cash, August 30, 1926. Traded to **Detroit Cougars** by **Boston** with Duke Keats for Harry Meeking and Frank Fredrickson, January 7, 1927. Traded to **NY Rangers** by **Detroit Cougars** with Harry Meeking for Stan Brown, October 10, 1927. Traded to **Pittsburgh** by **NY Rangers** (Philadelphia—Can-Am) for cash, November, 1929. Traded to **London** (IAHL) by **Pittsburgh** for cash, January 21, 1930. Traded to **Cleveland** (IAHL) by **London** (IAHL) for Don Goodwillie, Roy Colquhoun and future considerations (Ed Kuntz), December 12, 1930.

• BRINK, MILT
Milt "Curly" Brink
C – R. 5'10", 165 lbs. b: Hibbing, MN, 11/26/1910. Deceased.

Season	Club	League	GP	G	A	Pts	AG	AA	APts	PIM	PO GP	PO G	PO A	PO Pts	PO PIM
1931-32	Boston Cubs	Can-Am	4	1	0	1				0	1	0	0	0	0
1932-33	Eveleth Rangers	CHL	38	9	14	23				6	3	0	1	1	7
1933-34	Eveleth Rangers	CHL	41	17	*17	34				10	3	2	1	3	2
1934-35	Eveleth Rangers	CHL	35	12	18	30				10					
1935-36	Kansas City Greyhounds	AHA	45	9	20	29				4					
1936-37	**Chicago Black Hawks**	**NHL**	**5**	**0**	**0**	**0**	**0**	**0**	**0**	**0**					
	Kansas City Greyhounds	AHA	2	0	1	1				0					
	Minneapolis Millers	AHA	11	0	2	2				4					
1937-38	St. Paul Saints	AHA	48	8	26	34				6					
1938-39	Wichita Skyhawks	AHA	5	0	1	1				0					
1939-40	Portage Lakes Lakers	City Sr.	24	19	11	30									
	NHL Totals		**5**	**0**	**0**	**0**	**0**	**0**	**0**	**0**					

• BRISSON, GERRY Gerry Brisson

RW – L. 5'9", 155 lbs. b: St. Boniface, Man., 9/3/1937.

Season	Club	League	GP	G	A	Pts	AG	AA	APts	PIM	GP	G	A	Pts	PIM
			REGULAR SEASON								PLAYOFFS				
1951-52	Winnipeg Excelsiors	Midget	....	8	*11	19	....	....	....	8	....	....	....	....	....
1952-53	Winnipeg Excelsiors	Midget	STATISTICS NOT AVAILABLE												
1953-54	Winnipeg Canadiens	MJHL	1	0	0	0	....	....	....	0	....	....	....	....	....
1954-55	Winnipeg Canadiens	MJHL	29	20	21	41	....	....	....	14	....	....	....	....	....
1955-56	St. Boniface Canadiens	MJHL	21	*30	19	49	....	....	....	45	10	*12	5	*15	2
1956-57	St. Boniface Canadiens	MJHL	22	21	19	40	....	....	....	60	7	4	6	10	2
1957-58	Peterborough Petes	OHA	52	28	23	51	....	....	....	34	5	3	0	3	2
	Winnipeg Warriors	WHL	1	1	0	1	....	....	....	0	....	....	....	....	....
	Montreal Royals	QHL	2	0	0	0	....	....	....	0	....	....	....	....	....
1958-59	Winnipeg Warriors	WHL	62	38	45	83	....	....	....	20	7	5	0	5	2
1959-60	Winnipeg Warriors	WHL	66	24	32	56	....	....	....	20	....	....	....	....	....
1960-61	Winnipeg Warriors	WHL	70	29	26	55	....	....	....	35	....	....	....	....	....
1961-62	Spokane Comets	WHL	70	44	39	83	....	....	....	60	16	7	9	16	16
1962-63	**Montreal Canadiens**	**NHL**	**4**	**0**	**2**	**2**	**0**	**2**	**2**	**4**	....	....	....	....	....
	Spokane Comets	WHL	66	26	21	47	....	....	....	44	....	....	....	....	....
1963-64	Quebec Aces	AHL	12	0	1	1	....	....	....	6	....	....	....	....	....
	San Francisco Seals	WHL	50	18	25	43	....	....	....	15	11	6	2	8	4
1964-65	Seattle Totems	WHL	63	19	19	38	....	....	....	35	7	0	1	1	2
1965-66	San Francisco Seals	WHL	65	22	15	37	....	....	....	23	3	0	0	0	0
1966-67	California Seals	WHL	7	1	1	2	....	....	....	2	....	....	....	....	....
	NHL Totals		**4**	**0**	**2**	**2**	**0**	**2**	**2**	**4**	....	....	....	....	....

WHL Prairie Division First All-Star Team (1959)

• BROADBENT, HARRY Harry "Punch" Broadbent **HHOF**

RW – R. 5'7", 183 lbs. b: Ottawa, Ont., 7/13/1892. d: 3/6/1971.

Season	Club	League	GP	G	A	Pts	AG	AA	APts	PIM	GP	G	A	Pts	PIM
1909-10	Ottawa Cliffsides	City Sr.	....	....	....	....	....	....	....	....	3	1	0	1	6
1910-11	Ottawa Cliffsides	City Sr.	6	14	0	14	....	....	....	....	1	1	0	1	0
1911-12	Ottawa New Edinburghs	City Sr.	STATISTICS NOT AVAILABLE												
1912-13	Ottawa Senators	NHA	20	20	0	20	....	....	....	15	....	....	....	....	....
1913-14	Ottawa Senators	NHA	17	6	7	13	....	....	....	61	....	....	....	....	....
1914-15	Ottawa Senators	NHA	20	24	3	27	....	....	....	115	5	3	0	3	....
1915-16			MILITARY SERVICE												
1916-17			MILITARY SERVICE												
1917-18			MILITARY SERVICE												
1918-19	**Ottawa Senators**	**NHL**	**8**	**4**	**3**	**7**	**14**	**28**	**42**	**12**	**5**	**2**	**3**	**5**	**42**
1919-20	**Ottawa Senators**	**NHL**	**21**	**19**	**6**	**25**	**44**	**41**	**85**	**40**	**4**	**0**	**0**	**0**	**3**
1920-21	**Ottawa Senators**	**NHL**	**9**	**4**	**1**	**5**	**10**	**9**	**19**	**10**	**7**	**2**	**2**	**4**	**4**
1921-22	**Ottawa Senators**	**NHL**	**24**	***32**	***14**	***46**	**93**	**91**	**184**	**28**	**2**	**0**	**1**	**1**	**8**
1922-23	**Ottawa Senators**	**NHL**	**24**	**14**	**0**	**14**	**47**	**0**	**47**	**32**	**8**	***6**	**1**	***7**	***12**
1923-24	**Ottawa Senators**	**NHL**	**22**	**9**	**4**	**13**	**37**	**71**	**108**	**44**	**2**	**0**	**0**	**0**	**4**
1924-25	**Montreal Maroons**	**NHL**	**30**	**15**	**4**	**19**	**52**	**53**	**105**	**75**	....	....	....	....	....
1925-26	**Montreal Maroons**	**NHL**	**36**	**12**	**5**	**17**	**37**	**58**	**95**	**112**	**8**	**2**	**0**	**2**	***36**
1926-27	**Montreal Maroons**	**NHL**	**42**	**9**	**5**	**14**	**26**	**43**	**69**	**88**	**2**	**0**	**0**	**0**	**0**
1927-28	**Ottawa Senators**	**NHL**	**43**	**3**	**2**	**5**	**9**	**17**	**26**	**62**	**2**	**0**	**0**	**0**	**0**
1928-29	**New York Americans**	**NHL**	**44**	**1**	**4**	**5**	**4**	**37**	**41**	**59**	**2**	**0**	**0**	**0**	**2**
	NHL Totals		**303**	**122**	**48**	**170**	**373**	**448**	**821**	**562**	**42**	**12**	**7**	**19**	**111**
	Other Major League Totals		57	50	10	60	....	....	....	191	5	3	0	3	0

NHL Scoring Leader (1922)

Signed as a free agent by **Ottawa**, January 21, 1919. Rights transferred to **Hamilton** by **NHL** with Sprague Cleghorn, December 30, 1920. • Broadbent and Cleghorn refused to report. Rights traded to **Montreal Canadiens** by **Hamilton** for cash, January 4, 1921. • Broadbent refused to report. Rights returned to **Ottawa** by **NHL**, February 21, 1921. Traded to **Montreal Maroons** by **Ottawa** with Clint Benedict for cash, October 20, 1924. Traded to **Ottawa** by **Montreal Maroons** for Hooley Smith and cash, September, 1927. Traded to **NY Americans** by **Ottawa** for cash, June, 1928.

• BRODEN, CONNIE Connie (Connell) Broden

C – L. 5'8", 160 lbs. b: Montreal, Que., 4/6/1932.

Season	Club	League	GP	G	A	Pts	AG	AA	APts	PIM	GP	G	A	Pts	PIM
1949-50	Montreal Jr. Royals	QJHL	36	7	19	26	....	....	....	14	3	0	1	1	0
1950-51	Montreal Jr. Royals	QJHL	29	15	12	27	....	....	....	15	....	....	....	....	....
	Montreal Royals	QSHL	1	0	0	0	....	....	....	0	....	....	....	....	....
1951-52	Montreal Jr. Canadiens	QJHL	39	16	24	40	....	....	....	18	18	10	7	17	16
1952-53	Cincinnati Mohawks	IHL	57	29	38	67	....	....	....	39	9	4	3	7	8
1953-54	Cincinnati Mohawks	IHL	59	32	37	69	....	....	....	34	11	3	2	5	14
1954-55	Shawinigan Cataracts	QHL	62	27	35	62	....	....	....	25	13	5	7	12	15
1955-56	**Montreal Canadiens**	**NHL**	**3**	**0**	**0**	**0**	**0**	**0**	**0**	**2**	....	....	....	....	....
	Shawinigan Cataracts	QHL	61	17	40	57	....	....	....	45	11	2	8	10	8
1956-57	Shawinigan Cataracts	QHL	68	20	29	49	....	....	....	32	....	....	....	....	....
	Montreal Canadiens	**NHL**	....	....	....	....	....	....	....	....	**6**	**0**	**1**	**1**	**0**
1957-58	Whitby Dunlops	OHA Sr.	7	5	9	14	....	....	....	0	....	....	....	....	....
	Canada	WEC-A	7	12	7	*19	....	....	....	6	....	....	....	....	....
	Montreal Canadiens	**NHL**	**3**	**2**	**1**	**3**	**3**	**1**	**4**	**0**	**1**	**0**	**0**	**0**	**0**
1958-59	Hull-Ottawa Canadiens	EOHL	26	11	12	23	....	....	....	40	7	0	4	4	20
	NHL Totals		**6**	**2**	**1**	**3**	**3**	**1**	**4**	**2**	**7**	**0**	**1**	**1**	**0**

Won William Northey Trophy (Top Rookie - QHL) (1955)

• BROPHY, BERNIE Bernie Brophy

LW – L. 5'8", 165 lbs. b: Collingwood, Ont., 8/9/1905. Deceased.

Season	Club	League	GP	G	A	Pts	AG	AA	APts	PIM	GP	G	A	Pts	PIM
			REGULAR SEASON								PLAYOFFS				
1924-25	Fort Pitt Hornets	USAHA	17	4	0	4	....	....	....	....	5	0	0	0	....
1925-26	**Montreal Maroons**	**NHL**	**10**	**0**	**0**	**0**	**0**	**0**	**0**	**0**	....	....	....	....	....
1926-27	Providence Reds	Can-Am	10	3	0	3	....	....	....	8	....	....	....	....	....
	Detroit Olympics	AHA	1	0	0	0	....	....	....	0	....	....	....	....	....
	Duluth Hornets	AHA	1	0	0	0	....	....	....	0	....	....	....	....	....
1927-28	Providence Reds	Can-Am	33	9	2	11	....	....	....	31	....	....	....	....	....
1928-29	**Detroit Cougars**	**NHL**	**37**	**2**	**4**	**6**	**8**	**37**	**45**	**23**	**2**	**0**	**0**	**0**	**2**
	Detroit Olympics	Can-Pro	10	3	4	7	....	....	....	12	....	....	....	....	....
1929-30	**Detroit Cougars**	**NHL**	**15**	**2**	**0**	**2**	**4**	**0**	**4**	**2**	....	....	....	....	....
	Detroit Olympics	IAHL	25	14	5	19	....	....	....	26	3	0	0	0	6
1930-31	Detroit Olympics	IAHL	35	11	5	16	....	....	....	38	....	....	....	....	....
1931-32	Cleveland Indians	IAHL	46	15	13	28	....	....	....	60	....	....	....	....	....
1932-33	Cleveland Indians	IAHL	23	13	5	18	....	....	....	20	....	....	....	....	....
1933-34	London Tecumseh's	IAHL	37	9	5	14	....	....	....	19	6	4	0	4	4
1934-35	London Tecumseh's	IAHL	34	12	10	22	....	....	....	20	5	1	*4	5	0
1935-36	Windsor Bulldogs	IAHL	41	6	6	12	....	....	....	11	5	0	1	1	0
	NHL Totals		**62**	**4**	**4**	**8**	**12**	**37**	**49**	**25**	**2**	**0**	**0**	**0**	**2**

Signed as a free agent by **Montreal Maroons**, January 4, 1926. Signed as a free agent by **Montreal Canadiens** after release by **Montreal Maroons**, February 10, 1927. Signed as a free agent by **Montreal Maroons**, September, 1928. Traded to **Detroit Cougars** by **Montreal Maroons** for cash, October 23, 1928. Traded to **Cleveland** (IAHL) by **Detroit Falcons** for cash, November 3, 1931. • Suspended for life by IAHL after leaving team during 1935-36 playoffs, March, 1936.

• BROWN, ADAM Adam Brown

LW – L. 5'9", 175 lbs. b: Johnstone, Scotland, 2/4/1920. Deceased.

Season	Club	League	GP	G	A	Pts	AG	AA	APts	PIM	GP	G	A	Pts	PIM
1937-38	Hamilton Bengal Cubs	OHA	8	5	1	6	....	....	....	24	....	....	....	....	....
1938-39	Stratford Majors	OHA Sr.	25	11	4	15	....	....	....	45	2	1	1	2	2
1939-40	Guelph Biltmores	OHA	20	21	7	28	....	....	....	22	3	2	5	7	2
1940-41	Omaha Knights	AHA	48	18	18	36	....	....	....	33	....	....	....	....	....
1941-42	**Detroit Red Wings**	**NHL**	**28**	**6**	**9**	**15**	**10**	**14**	**24**	**15**	**10**	**0**	**2**	**2**	**4**
	Indianapolis Capitals	AHL	29	11	19	30	....	....	....	22	....	....	....	....	....
1942-43	Indianapolis Capitals	AHL	55	34	51	85	....	....	....	47	3	3	2	5	5
	Detroit Red Wings	**NHL**	....	....	....	....	....	....	....	....	**6**	**1**	**1**	**2**	**2**
1943-44	**Detroit Red Wings**	**NHL**	**50**	**24**	**18**	**42**	**30**	**22**	**52**	**56**	**5**	**0**	**0**	**0**	**8**
1944-45	Barriefield Bears	City Sr.	....	21	9	30	....	....	....	14	....	....	....	....	....
1945-46	**Detroit Red Wings**	**NHL**	**48**	**20**	**11**	**31**	**31**	**20**	**51**	**27**	**5**	**1**	**1**	**2**	**0**
1946-47	**Detroit Red Wings**	**NHL**	**22**	**8**	**5**	**13**	**11**	**7**	**18**	**30**	....	....	....	....	....
	Chicago Black Hawks	**NHL**	**42**	**11**	**25**	**36**	**15**	**36**	**51**	**57**	....	....	....	....	....
1947-48	**Chicago Black Hawks**	**NHL**	**32**	**7**	**10**	**17**	**10**	**15**	**25**	**41**	....	....	....	....	....
1948-49	**Chicago Black Hawks**	**NHL**	**58**	**8**	**12**	**20**	**13**	**19**	**32**	**69**	....	....	....	....	....
1949-50	**Chicago Black Hawks**	**NHL**	**25**	**2**	**2**	**4**	**3**	**3**	**6**	**16**	....	....	....	....	....
	Kansas City Mohawks	USHL	5	2	8	10	....	....	....	0	....	....	....	....	....
	St. Louis Flyers	AHL	24	13	11	24	....	....	....	9	2	1	0	1	0
1950-51	**Chicago Black Hawks**	**NHL**	**53**	**10**	**12**	**22**	**13**	**15**	**28**	**61**	....	....	....	....	....
1951-52	**Boston Bruins**	**NHL**	**33**	**8**	**9**	**17**	**11**	**12**	**23**	**6**	....	....	....	....	....
	Hershey Bears	AHL	30	14	16	30	....	....	....	22	5	0	1	1	0
1952-53	Hershey Bears	AHL	62	11	25	36	....	....	....	23	3	0	0	0	0
1953-54	Quebec Aces	QHL	70	23	32	55	....	....	....	58	12	3	2	5	12
1954-55	Sudbury Wolves	NOHA	29	15	13	28	....	....	....	8	....	....	....	....	....
	NHL Totals		**391**	**104**	**113**	**217**	**147**	**163**	**310**	**378**	**26**	**2**	**4**	**6**	**14**

AHL First All-Star Team (1943)

Signed as a free agent by **Detroit**, October 3, 1940. Traded to **Chicago** by **Detroit** with Ray Powell for Leo Reise and Pete Horeck, December, 1946. Traded to **Boston** by **Chicago** for cash, August 20, 1951.

• BROWN, ARNIE *— see page 901*

• BROWN, CONNIE Connie (Cornelius) Brown

C – L. 5'7", 168 lbs. b: Vankleek Hill, Ont., 1/11/1917.

Season	Club	League	GP	G	A	Pts	AG	AA	APts	PIM	GP	G	A	Pts	PIM
1933-34	Ottawa St. Malachy's	City Jr.	16	11	9	20	....	....	....	17	....	....	....	....	....
1934-35	Ottawa Jr. Rideaus	City Jr.	12	11	*23	34	....	....	....	8	13	15	*10	25	2
	Ottawa Rideaus	City Sr.	1	1	0	1	....	....	....	0	....	....	....	....	....
1935-36	Ottawa Senators	City Sr.	19	3	7	10	....	....	....	8	4	1	1	2	2
1936-37	Cornwall Flyers	Ott-Sr.	23	16	12	*28	....	....	....	21	6	0	2	2	4
1937-38	Cornwall Flyers	Ott-Sr.	24	14	*36	*50	....	....	....	14	17	12	*13	*25	14
1938-39	**Detroit Red Wings**	**NHL**	**2**	**1**	**0**	**1**	**2**	**0**	**2**	**0**	....	....	....	....	....
	Pittsburgh Hornets	AHL	53	11	34	45	....	....	....	38	....	....	....	....	....
1939-40	**Detroit Red Wings**	**NHL**	**36**	**8**	**3**	**11**	**17**	**6**	**23**	**2**	**5**	**2**	**1**	**3**	**0**
	Indianapolis Capitals	AHL	15	9	10	19	....	....	....	11	....	....	....	....	....
1940-41	**Detroit Red Wings**	**NHL**	**3**	**1**	**2**	**3**	**2**	**4**	**6**	**0**	**9**	**0**	**2**	**2**	**0**
	Indianapolis Capitals	AHL	50	16	28	44	....	....	....	17	....	....	....	....	....
1941-42	**Detroit Red Wings**	**NHL**	**9**	**0**	**3**	**3**	**0**	**5**	**5**	**4**	....	....	....	....	....
	Indianapolis Capitals	AHL	44	19	34	53	....	....	....	19	10	6	5	11	5
1942-43	**Detroit Red Wings**	**NHL**	**23**	**5**	**16**	**21**	**7**	**20**	**27**	**6**	....	....	....	....	....
	Indianapolis Capitals	AHL	38	12	25	37	....	....	....	6	7	2	6	8	2
1943-44	Petawawa Grenades	Ott-Sr.	1	0	4	4	....	....	....	0	....	....	....	....	....
1944-45	Ottawa Engineers	City Sr.	....	....	....	....	....	....	....	....	3	2	2	4	4
1945-46	Ottawa Senators	QSHL	36	12	39	51	....	....	....	16	9	5	5	10	10
	Ottawa Quarter-Masters	City Sr.	....	8	*20	*28	....	....	....	....	4	*8	8	16	....
1946-47	Ottawa Senators	QSHL	18	7	11	18	....	....	....	8	8	1	2	3	4
1947-48	Valleyfield Braves	QSHL	40	20	36	56	....	....	....	34	6	4	2	6	2
1948-49	Valleyfield Braves	QSHL	63	41	47	88	....	....	....	22	4	0	2	2	0
1949-50	Glace Bay Miners	CBSHL	70	31	47	78	....	....	....	38	10	6	*13	*19	0
1950-51	Ottawa Army	ECSHL	37	20	28	48	....	....	....	16	3	5	2	7	2
1951-52	Hull Volants	ECSHL	29	9	21	30	....	....	....	0	5	0	*10	10	0
	NHL Totals		**73**	**15**	**24**	**39**	**28**	**35**	**63**	**12**	**14**	**2**	**3**	**5**	**0**

• BROWN, FRED

Fred "Baldy" Brown
LW – L. 5'8", 155 lbs. b: Kingston, Ont., 9/15/1900. Deceased.

Season	Club	League	GP	G	A	Pts	AG	AA	APts	PIM	GP	G	A	Pts	PIM
1923-24	Brockville Indians	OHA	STATISTICS NOT AVAILABLE												
1924-25	Hamilton Rowing Club	OHA Sr.	8	*10	3	*13	....	....	....	....	....	....	....	....	....
1925-26	Windsor Hornets	OHA Sr.	20	15	4	19	....	....	....	8	....	....	....	....	....
1926-27	Windsor Hornets	Can-Pro	29	9	3	12	....	....	....	16	....	....	....	....	....
1927-28	**Montreal Maroons**	**NHL**	**19**	**1**	**0**	**1**	**3**	**0**	**3**	**0**	**9**	**0**	**0**	**0**	**0**
	Windsor-Stratford	Can-Pro	29	11	7	18	....	....	....	8	....	....	....	....	....
1928-29	Kitchener Dutchmen	Can-Pro	40	15	6	21	....	....	....	56	3	0	0	0	2
1929-30	Niagara Falls Cataracts	IAHL	16	2	0	2	....	....	....	25	....	....	....	....	....
	Windsor Bulldogs	IAHL	24	3	3	6	....	....	....	18	....	....	....	....	....
1930-31	Syracuse Stars	IAHL	48	15	7	22	....	....	....	39	....	....	....	....	....
	NHL Totals		**19**	**1**	**0**	**1**	**3**	**0**	**3**	**0**	**9**	**0**	**0**	**0**	**0**

Traded to **Stratford** (Can-Pro) by **Montreal Maroons** for cash, April 23, 1928. Traded to **Windsor** (IAHL) by **Montreal Maroons** (Niagara Falls-IAHL) with Honey Kuntz for Fred Elliot, November 25, 1929.

• BROWN, GEORGE

George Brown HHOF
C – L. 5'11", 185 lbs. b: Winnipeg, Man., 5/17/1912.

Season	Club	League	GP	G	A	Pts	AG	AA	APts	PIM	GP	G	A	Pts	PIM
1930-31	Winnipeg Elmwood	MJHL	10	5	0	5	....	....	....	22	3	1	*1	*2	6
1931-32	Winnipeg Monarchs	City Jr.	12	5	1	6	....	....	....	*40	4	1	0	1	*15
1932-33	Winnipeg Monarchs	MHL Sr.	STATISTICS NOT AVAILABLE												
1933-34	Montreal Royals	City Sr.	16	6	5	11	....	....	....	*36	2	0	0	0	4
1934-35	Verdun Maple Leafs	Mtl-Sr.	20	18	19	37	....	....	....	22	....	....	....	....	....
1935-36	Verdun Maple Leafs	Mtl-Sr.	22	19	*23	*42	....	....	....	48	7	4	4	8	22
1936-37	**Montreal Canadiens**	**NHL**	**27**	**4**	**6**	**10**	**9**	**14**	**23**	**10**	**4**	**0**	**0**	**0**	**0**
1937-38	**Montreal Canadiens**	**NHL**	**34**	**1**	**7**	**8**	**2**	**14**	**16**	**14**	**3**	**0**	**0**	**0**	**2**
	New Haven Eagles	AHL	10	1	4	5	....	....	....	2	2	0	0	0	0
1938-39	**Montreal Canadiens**	**NHL**	**18**	**1**	**9**	**10**	**2**	**17**	**19**	**10**	....	....	....	....	....
	New Haven Eagles	AHL	35	10	7	17	....	....	....	27	....	....	....	....	....
1939-40	Springfield Indians	AHL	12	0	5	5	....	....	....	10	....	....	....	....	....
	Syracuse Stars	AHL	11	1	2	3	....	....	....	2	....	....	....	....	....
	Hershey Bears	AHL	7	0	0	0	....	....	....	0	....	....	....	....	....
1940-41	St. Jerome Papermakers	QPHL	13	8	7	15	....	....	....	12	4	1	0	1	6
1941-42	Montreal Sr. Canadiens	QPHL	38	3	6	9	....	....	....	83	6	0	1	1	16
1942-43	Montreal Sr. Canadiens	QPHL	24	3	5	8	....	....	....	32	4	1	0	1	8
	NHL Totals		**79**	**6**	**22**	**28**	**13**	**45**	**58**	**34**	**7**	**0**	**0**	**0**	**2**

Rights traded to **Montreal Maroons** by **NY Rangers** for Eddie Wares, October 30, 1935. Rights traded to **Montreal Canadiens** by **Montreal Maroons** for Gerry Carson, October 7, 1936. • Suspended by **Montreal** for refusing assignment to **New Haven** (AHL), November 26, 1939. Traded to **Boston** by **Montreal** for cash, November 29, 1939.

• BROWN, GERRY

Gerry Brown
LW – L. 5'9", 170 lbs. b: Edmonton, Alta., 7/7/1917.

Season	Club	League	GP	G	A	Pts	AG	AA	APts	PIM	GP	G	A	Pts	PIM
1933-34	Edmonton Southsides	City Jr.	9	4	2	6	....	....	....	4	3	1	0	1	0
1934-35	Edmonton Southsides	City Jr.	11	10	3	*13	....	....	....	15	6	1	*3	4	4
1935-36	Edmonton Dominions	City Sr.	13	*13	5	*18	....	....	....	12	3	0	0	0	5
1936-37	Edmonton Dominions	ASHL	26	21	18	39	....	....	....	28	6	3	3	6	2
1937-38	Earls Court Rangers	Britain	....	19	11	30	....	....	....	....	....	....	....	....	....
1938-39	Earls Court Rangers	Britain	45	34	13	47	....	....	....	....	....	....	....	....	....
1939-40	Cornwall Royals	QSHL	30	16	15	31	....	....	....	23	5	1	2	3	2
1940-41	Cornwall Flyers	QSHL	36	18	22	40	....	....	....	35	4	1	1	2	0
	Montreal Concordia	QSHL	2	0	0	0	....	....	....	0	....	....	....	....	....
1941-42	**Detroit Red Wings**	**NHL**	**13**	**4**	**4**	**8**	**7**	**6**	**13**	**0**	**12**	**2**	**1**	**3**	**4**
	Indianapolis Capitals	AHL	42	10	26	36	....	....	....	25	....	....	....	....	....
1942-43	Washington–Indianapolis	AHL	37	3	10	13	....	....	....	5	3	0	1	1	2
1943-44			MILITARY SERVICE												
1944-45			MILITARY SERVICE												
1945-46	**Detroit Red Wings**	**NHL**	**10**	**0**	**1**	**1**	**0**	**2**	**2**	**2**	....	....	....	....	....
	Indianapolis Capitols	AHL	48	28	25	53	....	....	....	22	5	0	1	1	4
1946-47	Buffalo Bisons	AHL	64	29	30	59	....	....	....	48	4	1	1	2	0
1947-48	Buffalo Bisons	AHL	67	25	43	68	....	....	....	45	8	2	3	5	8
1948-49	Hershey Bears	AHL	68	16	36	52	....	....	....	31	11	3	6	9	2
1949-50	Hershey Bears	AHL	70	19	35	54	....	....	....	16	....	....	....	....	....
1950-51	Hershey Bears	AHL	67	21	36	57	....	....	....	31	6	1	0	1	2
1951-52	Hershey Bears	AHL	68	26	28	54	....	....	....	38	5	1	3	4	0
1952-53	Ottawa Generals	OHA	DID NOT PLAY – COACHING												
	NHL Totals		**23**	**4**	**5**	**9**	**7**	**8**	**15**	**2**	**12**	**2**	**1**	**3**	**4**

Traded to **Toronto** by **Detroit** for Doug Baldwin and Ray Powell, September 21, 1946. Traded to **Montreal** by **Toronto** with John Mahaffy for Dutch Hiller and Vic Lynn, September 21, 1946.

• BROWN, HAROLD

Harold Brown
RW – L. 5'10", 160 lbs. b: Brandon, Man., 9/14/1920.

Season	Club	League	GP	G	A	Pts	AG	AA	APts	PIM	GP	G	A	Pts	PIM
1938-39	Portage Terriers	MJHL	17	5	4	9	....	....	....	4	2	0	0	0	0
1939-40	Portage–Brandon	MJHL	15	5	4	9	....	....	....	6	3	2	0	2	2
1940-41	Flin Flon Bombers	SSHL	32	25	20	45	....	....	....	12	3	0	1	1	0
1941-42	Flin Flon Bombers	SSHL	32	26	20	46	....	....	....	12	3	2	0	2	4
1942-43	Nanaimo Navy	City Sr.	19	*30	11	41	....	....	....	15	2	3	1	4	2
1943-44	Nanaimo Navy	PCHL	19	*30	8	*38	....	....	....	6	....	....	....	....	....
1944-45	Calgary Navy	City Sr.	4	1	1	2	....	....	....	2	....	....	....	....	....
1945-46	**New York Rangers**	**NHL**	**13**	**2**	**1**	**3**	**3**	**2**	**5**	**2**	....	....	....	....	....
	St. Paul Saints	USHL	39	20	17	37	....	....	....	4	6	1	2	3	2
1946-47	New Haven Ramblers	AHL	14	8	4	12	....	....	....	0	....	....	....	....	....
	St. Paul Saints	USHL	48	28	18	46	....	....	....	4	....	....	....	....	....
1947-48	St. Paul Saints	USHL	66	43	24	67	....	....	....	10	....	....	....	....	....
1948-49	St. Paul Saints	USHL	65	38	39	77	....	....	....	8	7	*6	2	8	0
1949-50	St. Paul Saints	USHL	70	30	24	54	....	....	....	16	3	1	1	2	0
1950-51	Denver Falcons	USHL	56	16	17	33	....	....	....	2	5	2	0	2	0
1951-52	Calgary Stampeders	PCHL	32	20	8	28	....	....	....	2	....	....	....	....	....
	Kamloops Elks	OSHL	27	16	15	31	....	....	....	24	....	....	....	....	....
1952-53	Calgary Stampeders	WHL	19	5	4	9	....	....	....	0	....	....	....	....	....
	Kamloops Elks	OSHL	27	18	11	29	....	....	....	0	12	3	1	4	0
	NHL Totals		**13**	**2**	**1**	**3**	**3**	**2**	**5**	**2**	....	....	....	....	....

USHL Second All-Star Team (1947, 1949) • USHL First All-Star Team (1948)

• BROWN, STAN

Stan Brown
D – L. 5'10", 150 lbs. b: North Bay, Ont., 5/9/1898. d: 7/6/1987.

Season	Club	League	GP	G	A	Pts	AG	AA	APts	PIM	GP	G	A	Pts	PIM
1915-16	Berlin Union Jacks	OHA	STATISTICS NOT AVAILABLE												
1916-17	Toronto St. Pats	OHA Sr.	8	3	0	3	....	....	....	....	....	....	....	....	....
1917-18	St. Michael's Majors	OHA	STATISTICS NOT AVAILABLE												
1918-19	Toronto Dentals	OHA Sr.	7	10	6	16	....	....	....	....	2	0	0	0	0
1919-20	Toronto Dentals	OHA Sr.	6	1	0	1	....	....	....	....	....	....	....	....	....
1920-21	University of Toronto	OHA Sr.	9	5	3	8	....	....	....	....	8	7	*7	*14	....
1922-23	Soo Greyhounds	NOHA	8	2	*5	7	....	....	....	6	7	4	3	7	*8
1923-24	Soo Greyhounds	NOHA	8	4	5	9	....	....	....	6	7	1	1	2	8
1924-25	Soo Greyhounds	NOHA	STATISTICS NOT AVAILABLE												
1925-26	Soo Greyhounds	Can-Pro	19	3	5	8	....	....	....	8	....	....	....	....	....
1926-27	**New York Rangers**	**NHL**	**24**	**6**	**2**	**8**	**17**	**17**	**34**	**14**	**2**	**0**	**0**	**0**	**0**
	Detroit Greyhounds	AHA	6	0	0	0	....	....	....	2	....	....	....	....	....
1927-28	**Detroit Cougars**	**NHL**	**24**	**2**	**0**	**2**	**6**	**0**	**6**	**4**	....	....	....	....	....
	Windsor Hornets	Can-Pro	10	3	1	4	....	....	....	2	....	....	....	....	....
1928-29	Windsor Bulldogs	Can Pro	40	9	4	13	....	....	....	14	8	0	2	2	8
1929-30	Windsor Bulldogs	IAHL	41	13	10	23	....	....	....	22	....	....	....	....	....
1930-31	Windsor Bulldogs	IAHL	44	15	6	21	....	....	....	28	6	0	1	1	2
1931-32	Windsor Bulldogs	IAHL	47	6	15	21	....	....	....	26	6	1	0	1	2
1932-33	Windsor Bulldogs	IAHL	44	6	5	11	....	....	....	26	6	0	2	2	4
1933-34	Windsor Bulldogs	IAHL	32	0	1	1	....	....	....	0	....	....	....	....	....
1934-35	Windsor Bulldogs	IAHL	1	0	0	0	....	....	....	0	....	....	....	....	....
1935-38			DID NOT PLAY												
1938-39	Flin Flon Bombers	ASHL	....	16	12	28	....	....	....	....	....	....	....	....	....
1939-40	Flin Flon Bombers	ASHL	....	19	14	33	....	....	....	16	....	....	....	....	....
	NHL Totals		**48**	**8**	**2**	**10**	**23**	**17**	**40**	**18**	**2**	**0**	**0**	**0**	**0**

Signed as a free agent by **Detroit** (AHA), November 10, 1926. Signed as a free agent by **NY Rangers** after **Detroit** (AHA) franchise folded, November 23, 1926. Traded to **Detroit Cougars** by **NY Rangers** for Harry Meeking and Archie Briden, October 10, 1927. Traded to **Windsor** (Can-Pro) by **Detroit Cougars** for cash, February 13, 1928.

• BROWN, WAYNE

Wayne "Weiner" Brown
RW – L. 5'8", 150 lbs. b: Deloro, Ont., 11/16/1930.

Season	Club	League	GP	G	A	Pts	AG	AA	APts	PIM	GP	G	A	Pts	PIM
1948-49	St. Catharines Teepees	OHA	46	9	13	22	....	....	....	35	5	0	1	1	0
1949-50	St. Catharines Teepees	OHA	47	23	17	40	....	....	....	58	5	0	0	0	0
1950-51	St. Catharines Teepees	OHA	51	29	23	52	....	....	....	80	9	5	3	8	12
1951-52	Tacoma Rockets	PCHL	70	28	30	58	....	....	....	36	6	1	0	1	2
1952-53	Tacoma Rockets	WHL	70	27	24	51	....	....	....	37	....	....	....	....	....
1953-54	Seattle Bombers	WHL	70	*49	32	81	....	....	....	24	....	....	....	....	....
	Boston Bruins	**NHL**	....	....	....	....	....	....	....	....	**4**	**0**	**0**	**0**	**2**
1954-55	Victoria Cougars	WHL	3	1	1	2	....	....	....	2	....	....	....	....	....
1955-56	Victoria Cougars	WHL	70	21	26	47	....	....	....	25	9	3	2	5	0
1956-57	Victoria Cougars	WHL	70	27	30	57	....	....	....	14	3	1	1	2	2
1957-58	Belleville McFarlands	EOHL	48	26	24	50	....	....	....	22	13	10	7	17	14
1958-59	Belleville McFarlands	EOHL	46	24	29	53	....	....	....	46	....	....	....	....	....
	Canada	WEC-A	5	2	1	3	....	....	....	7	....	....	....	....	....
1959-60	Belleville McFarlands	EOHL	48	23	28	51	....	....	....	6	13	3	4	7	4
1960-1966			DID NOT PLAY												
1966-67	Belleville Mohawks	OHA Sr.	35	14	20	34	....	....	....	24	....	....	....	....	....
1967-68	Belleville Mohawks	OHA Sr.	39	14	24	38	....	....	....	2	....	....	....	....	....
1968-69	Belleville Mohawks	OHA Sr.	25	8	21	29	....	....	....	2	....	....	....	....	....
1969-70	Belleville Mohawks	OHA Sr.	20	2	9	11	....	....	....	12	....	....	....	....	....
1970-71	Belleville Mohawks	OHA Sr.	DID NOT PLAY – COACHING												
1971-72	Belleville Quints	OHA Sr.	6	0	2	2	....	....	....	0	....	....	....	....	....
	NHL Totals		**0**	**0**	**0**	**0**	**0**	**0**	**0**	**0**	**4**	**0**	**0**	**0**	**2**

• BROWNE, CECIL

Cecil Browne
LW – L. 6', 165 lbs. b: St. James, Manitoba, 2/13/1896. d: 8/13/1986.

Season	Club	League	GP	G	A	Pts	AG	AA	APts	PIM	GP	G	A	Pts	PIM
1914-15	Winnipeg Strathconas	MJHL	5	15	5	20	....	....	....	6	....	....	....	....	....
1915-16	Winnipeg Strathconas	MJHL	6	12	4	16	....	....	....	8	....	....	....	....	....
	Winnipeg Monarchs	MHL Sr.	1	1	1	2	....	....	....	6	....	....	....	....	....
1916-17	Winnipeg Monarchs	MHL Sr.	8	9	*6	15	....	....	....	4	....	....	....	....	....
1917-18	Winnipeg Vimy	MHL Sr.	10	7	*9	16	....	....	....	10	....	....	....	....	....
1918-19			MILITARY SERVICE												
1919-20	Moose Jaw Maple Leafs	SSHL	12	20	3	23	....	....	....	14	2	*2	0	2	4
1920-21	Regina Victorias	SSHL	15	14	3	17	....	....	....	15	4	2	*3	5	0
1921-22	Regina Victorias	SSHL	6	7	2	9	....	....	....	2	1	*2	0	2	0
1922-23	Winnipeg Winnipegs	MHL Sr.	10	9	2	11	....	....	....	14	....	....	....	....	....
1923-24	Selkirk Fishermen	MHL Sr.	11	5	4	9	....	....	....	4	10	8	3	11	16
1924-25	Selkirk Fishermen	MHL Sr.	12	12	2	14	....	....	....	22	2	0	0	0	8
1925-26	Winnipeg Maroons	AHA	25	8	2	10	....	....	....	40	5	2	0	2	4
1926-27	Winnipeg Maroons	AHA	35	*24	6	*30	....	....	....	84	3	1	0	1	6
1927-28	**Chicago Black Hawks**	**NHL**	**13**	**2**	**0**	**2**	**6**	**0**	**6**	**4**	....	....	....	....	....
1928-29	Seattle Eskimos	PCHL	33	23	6	29	....	....	....	22	5	2	2	4	12
1929-30	Seattle Eskimos	PCHL	33	12	10	*22	....	....	....	36	....	....	....	....	....
	NHL Totals		**13**	**2**	**0**	**2**	**6**	**0**	**6**	**4**	....	....	....	....	....

• BRUCE, GORDIE

Gordie Bruce
LW – L. 5'11", 190 lbs. b: Ottawa, Ont., 5/9/1919. Deceased.

Season	Club	League	GP	G	A	Pts	AG	AA	APts	PIM	GP	G	A	Pts	PIM
1937-38	Sudbury Wolves	NOHA	STATISTICS NOT AVAILABLE												
	Sudbury Frood Tigers	NOHA	1	0	0	0	....	....	....	4	....	....	....	....	....
	Canada	WEC	7	3	2	5	....	....	....	....	....	....	....	....	....
1938-39	North Bay Trappers	NOHA	45	23	44	*67	....	....	....	....	2	*4	*3	*7	6
1939-40	Hershey Bears	AHL	50	10	20	30	....	....	....	13	5	2	3	5	6
1940-41	**Boston Bruins**	**NHL**	**8**	**0**	**1**	**1**	**0**	**2**	**2**	**2**	**2**	**0**	**0**	**0**	**0**
	Hershey Bears	AHL	46	23	19	41	....	....	....	39	10	*4	5	*9	6
1941-42	**Boston Bruins**	**NHL**	**15**	**4**	**8**	**12**	**7**	**12**	**19**	**11**	**5**	**2**	**3**	**5**	**4**
	Hershey Bears	AHL	38	19	13	32	....	....	....	34	....	....	....	....	....
1942-43	Montreal Army	QSHL	13	14	5	19	....	....	....	6	....	....	....	....	....
	Ottawa Commandos	QSHL	....	....	....	....	....	....	....	....	10	1	1	2	2
1943-44	Ottawa Commandos	QSHL	8	3	3	6	....	....	....	10	....	....	....	....	....
1944-45			MILITARY SERVICE												
1945-46	**Boston Bruins**	**NHL**	**5**	**0**	**0**	**0**	**0**	**0**	**0**	**0**	....	....	....	....	....
1946-47	Hershey Bears	AHL	57	35	28	63	....	....	....	44	10	6	9	15	0
1947-48	Hershey Bears	AHL	67	27	25	52	....	....	....	32	2	1	0	1	0
1948-49	Hershey Bears	AHL	62	22	23	45	....	....	....	34	11	*7	9	*16	2
1949-50	Hershey Bears	AHL	58	16	21	37	....	....	....	31	....	....	....	....	....
1950-51	Glace Bay Miners	CBSHL	59	7	10	17	....	....	....	52	10	*7	2	9	16
	NHL Totals		**28**	**4**	**9**	**13**	**7**	**14**	**21**	**13**	**7**	**2**	**3**	**5**	**4**

• BRUCE, MORLEY Morley Bruce

D/C – R. 5'9", 170 lbs. b: North Gower, Ontario, 3/7/1894. d: 11/25/1959.

			REGULAR SEASON								PLAYOFFS				
Season	Club	League	GP	G	A	Pts	AG	AA	APts	PIM	GP	G	A	Pts	PIM
1913-14	Ottawa New Edinburghs	City Sr.	6	2	0	2	....	....	....	....	....	....	....	....	....
1914-15	Ottawa Aberdeens	City Sr.	2	2	0	2	....	....	....	....	....	....	....	....	....
1915-16	Ottawa New Edinburghs	City Sr.	10	7	0	7	....	....	....	52	....	....	....	....	....
1916-17	Ottawa Munitions	City Sr.	....	....	....	....	....	....	....	....	7	0	0	0	3
1917-18	**Ottawa Senators**	**NHL**	**7**	**0**	**0**	**0**	**0**	**0**	**0**	**0**	....	....	....	....	....
1918-19			MILITARY SERVICE												
1919-20	**Ottawa Senators**	**NHL**	**24**	**1**	**1**	**2**	**2**	**7**	**9**	**2**	**5**	**0**	**0**	**0**	**0**
1920-21	**Ottawa Senators**	**NHL**	**21**	**3**	**1**	**4**	**7**	**9**	**16**	**23**	**7**	**0**	**0**	**0**	**2**
1921-22	**Ottawa Senators**	**NHL**	**22**	**4**	**1**	**5**	**11**	**6**	**17**	**2**	**1**	**0**	**0**	**0**	**0**
	NHL Totals		**74**	**8**	**3**	**11**	**20**	**22**	**42**	**27**	**13**	**0**	**0**	**0**	**2**

Signed as a free agent by **Ottawa**, December 7, 1917.

• BRUNETEAU, EDDIE Eddie Bruneteau

RW – R. 5'9", 172 lbs. b: St. Boniface, Man., 8/1/1919.

Season	Club	League	GP	G	A	Pts	AG	AA	APts	PIM	GP	G	A	Pts	PIM
1936-37	Winnipeg Rangers	MJHL	16	17	6	23	....	....	....	6	1	1	0	1	5
1937-38	Duluth Zephyrs	TBSHL	27	*26	11	37	....	....	....	10	....	....	....	....	....
1938-39	Duluth Zephyrs	TBSHL	10	7	1	8	....	....	....	6	....	....	....	....	....
	Duluth Zephyrs	USHL	12	8	2	10	....	....	....	12	....	....	....	....	....
1939-40	Omaha Knights	AHA	37	13	15	28	....	....	....	16	9	2	0	2	0
1940-41	**Detroit Red Wings**	**NHL**	**11**	**1**	**1**	**2**	**2**	**2**	**4**	**2**	**3**	**0**	**0**	**0**	**0**
	Omaha Knights	AHA	18	3	2	5	....	....	....	6	....	....	....	....	....
	Indianapolis Capitals	AHL	13	3	4	7	....	....	....	6	....	....	....	....	....
1941-42	Quebec Aces	QSHL	30	10	5	15	....	....	....	17	15	12	6	18	0
1942-43	Quebec Aces	QSHL	31	20	17	37	....	....	....	0	4	0	2	2	0
1943-44	**Detroit Red Wings**	**NHL**	**2**	**0**	**1**	**1**	**0**	**1**	**1**	**0**	....	....	....	....	....
	Quebec Aces	QSHL	25	14	27	41	....	....	....	6	15	10	*16	*26	4
1944-45	**Detroit Red Wings**	**NHL**	**42**	**12**	**13**	**25**	**16**	**21**	**37**	**6**	**14**	**5**	**2**	**7**	**0**
	Quebec Aces	QSHL	2	1	4	5	....	....	....	0	....	....	....	....	....
1945-46	**Detroit Red Wings**	**NHL**	**46**	**17**	**12**	**29**	**26**	**22**	**48**	**11**	**4**	**1**	**0**	**1**	**0**
1946-47	**Detroit Red Wings**	**NHL**	**60**	**9**	**14**	**23**	**12**	**20**	**32**	**14**	**4**	**1**	**4**	**5**	**0**
1947-48	**Detroit Red Wings**	**NHL**	**18**	**1**	**1**	**2**	**1**	**1**	**2**	**2**	**6**	**0**	**0**	**0**	**0**
	Indianapolis Capitals	AHL	42	19	19	38	....	....	....	16	....	....	....	....	....
1948-49	**Detroit Red Wings**	**NHL**	**1**	**0**	**0**	**0**	**0**	**0**	**0**	**0**	....	....	....	....	....
	Indianapolis Capitals	AHL	61	20	18	38	....	....	....	16	2	0	0	0	0
1949-50	Omaha Knights	USHL	69	43	40	83	....	....	....	16	7	5	3	8	0
1950-51	Omaha Knights	USHL	56	39	27	66	....	....	....	10	10	6	5	*11	0
1951-52	Indianapolis Capitals	AHL	56	20	21	41	....	....	....	0	....	....	....	....	....
1952-53	Milwaukee Clarks	IHL	43	23	28	51	....	....	....	2	....	....	....	....	....
1953-54	Sherbrooke Saints	QHL	71	4	35	39	....	....	....	4	5	2	3	5	0
	NHL Totals		**180**	**40**	**42**	**82**	**57**	**67**	**124**	**35**	**31**	**7**	**6**	**13**	**0**

USHL Second All-Star Team (1950, 1951) • IHL Second All-Star Team (1953)

Traded to **Detroit** by **Duluth** (USHL) for cash, October 2, 1939. Signed as a free agent by **Quebec** (QSHL), December 12, 1941. Traded to **Detroit** by **Quebec** (QSHL) for Bob Thorpe, November 16, 1944.

• BRUNETEAU, MUD Mud (Modere) Bruneteau

RW – R. 5'11", 185 lbs. b: St. Boniface, Man., 11/28/1914. d: 4/15/1982.

Season	Club	League	GP	G	A	Pts	AG	AA	APts	PIM	GP	G	A	Pts	PIM
1931-32	Winnipeg K of C	MJHL	9	2	2	4	....	....	....	4	....	....	....	....	....
1932-33	Winnipeg K of C	MJHL	11	4	4	8	....	....	....	10	3	3	0	3	2
1933-34	Winnipeg Falcons	MHL Sr.	15	13	4	17	....	....	....	11	1	1	0	1	0
1934-35	Detroit Olympics	IAHL	38	10	6	16	....	....	....	26	5	0	2	2	0
1935-36	**Detroit Red Wings**	**NHL**	**24**	**2**	**0**	**2**	**5**	**0**	**5**	**2**	**7**	**2**	**2**	**4**	**4**
	Detroit Olympics	IAHL	23	8	9	17	....	....	....	17	....	....	....	....	....
1936-37	**Detroit Red Wings**	**NHL**	**42**	**9**	**7**	**16**	**19**	**16**	**35**	**18**	**10**	**2**	**0**	**2**	**6**
1937-38	**Detroit Red Wings**	**NHL**	**24**	**3**	**6**	**9**	**6**	**12**	**18**	**16**	....	....	....	....	....
	Pittsburgh Hornets	AHL	4	1	4	5	....	....	....	2	2	1	0	1	2
1938-39	**Detroit Red Wings**	**NHL**	**20**	**3**	**7**	**10**	**6**	**13**	**19**	**0**	**6**	**0**	**0**	**0**	**0**
1939-40	**Detroit Red Wings**	**NHL**	**48**	**10**	**14**	**24**	**21**	**28**	**49**	**10**	**5**	**3**	**2**	**5**	**0**
1940-41	**Detroit Red Wings**	**NHL**	**45**	**11**	**17**	**28**	**22**	**31**	**53**	**12**	**9**	**2**	**1**	**3**	**2**
	Pittsburgh Hornets	AHL	4	1	4	5	....	....	....	2	....	....	....	....	....
1941-42	**Detroit Red Wings**	**NHL**	**48**	**14**	**19**	**33**	**24**	**29**	**53**	**8**	**12**	**5**	**1**	**6**	**6**
1942-43	**Detroit Red Wings**	**NHL**	**50**	**23**	**22**	**45**	**33**	**28**	**61**	**2**	**9**	**5**	**4**	**9**	**0**
1943-44	**Detroit Red Wings**	**NHL**	**39**	**35**	**18**	**53**	**45**	**22**	**67**	**4**	**5**	**1**	**2**	**3**	**2**
1944-45	**Detroit Red Wings**	**NHL**	**43**	**23**	**24**	**47**	**32**	**39**	**71**	**6**	**14**	**3**	**2**	**5**	**2**
1945-46	**Detroit Red Wings**	**NHL**	**28**	**6**	**4**	**10**	**9**	**7**	**16**	**2**	....	....	....	....	....
	Indianapolis Capitals	AHL	14	6	10	16	....	....	....	0	5	1	2	3	0
1946-47	Omaha Knights	USHL	16	6	4	10	....	....	....	2	3	0	1	1	0
1947-48	Omaha Knights	USHL	6	4	2	6	....	....	....	2	....	....	....	....	....
1948-49	Omaha Knights	USHL	DID NOT PLAY – COACHING												
	NHL Totals		**411**	**139**	**138**	**277**	**222**	**225**	**447**	**80**	**77**	**23**	**14**	**37**	**22**

• BRYDGE, BILL Bill Brydge

D – R. 5'9", 195 lbs. b: Renfrew, Ontario, 10/22/1901. d: 11/2/1949.

Season	Club	League	GP	G	A	Pts	AG	AA	APts	PIM	GP	G	A	Pts	PIM
1921-22	Iroquois Falls Paper	NOHA	....	....	....	....	....	....	....	....	4	*4	2	*6	*12
1922-23	Iroquois Falls Paper	NOHA	STATISTICS NOT AVAILABLE												
1923-24	Port Arthur Bearcats	MHL Sr.	16	2	5	7	....	....	....	8	2	0	0	0	2
1924-25	Port Arthur Bearcats	MHL Sr.	20	13	4	17	....	....	....	9	9	3	1	4	24
1925-26	Port Arthur Bearcats	MHL Sr.	20	9	3	12	....	....	....	18	3	*2	0	*2	8
1926-27	**Toronto Maple Leafs**	**NHL**	**41**	**6**	**3**	**9**	**17**	**25**	**42**	**76**	....	....	....	....	....
1927-28	Detroit Olympics	Can-Pro	41	5	4	9	....	....	....	91	2	0	0	0	8
1928-29	**Detroit Cougars**	**NHL**	**31**	**2**	**2**	**4**	**8**	**18**	**26**	**59**	**2**	**0**	**0**	**0**	**4**
	Detroit Olympics	Can-Pro	12	6	0	6	....	....	....	24	....	....	....	....	....
1929-30	**New York Americans**	**NHL**	**41**	**2**	**6**	**8**	**4**	**19**	**23**	**64**	....	....	....	....	....
1930-31	**New York Americans**	**NHL**	**43**	**2**	**5**	**7**	**5**	**18**	**23**	**70**	....	....	....	....	....
1931-32	**New York Americans**	**NHL**	**48**	**2**	**8**	**10**	**4**	**22**	**26**	**77**	....	....	....	....	....
1932-33	**New York Americans**	**NHL**	**48**	**4**	**15**	**19**	**9**	**40**	**49**	**60**	....	....	....	....	....
1933-34	**New York Americans**	**NHL**	**48**	**6**	**7**	**13**	**13**	**19**	**32**	**44**	....	....	....	....	....
1934-35	**New York Americans**	**NHL**	**47**	**2**	**6**	**8**	**4**	**13**	**17**	**29**	....	....	....	....	....
1935-36	**New York Americans**	**NHL**	**21**	**0**	**0**	**0**	**0**	**0**	**0**	**27**	....	....	....	....	....
	NHL Totals		**368**	**26**	**52**	**78**	**64**	**174**	**238**	**506**	**2**	**0**	**0**	**0**	**4**

Signed as a free agent by **Toronto St. Pats**, October 13, 1926. Traded to **Detroit Cougars** by **Toronto** for Art Duncan, July, 1927. Traded to **NY Americans** by **Detroit** for $5000, November 22, 1929.

• BRYDSON, GLENN Glenn "Swampy" Brydson

RW – R. 5'10", 170 lbs. b: Swansea, Ontario, 11/7/1910. Deceased.

			REGULAR SEASON								PLAYOFFS				
Season	Club	League	GP	G	A	Pts	AG	AA	APts	PIM	GP	G	A	Pts	PIM
1926-27	Toronto Canoe Club	OHA	2	1	0	1	....	....	....	....	....	....	....	....	....
1927-28	Toronto Canoe Club	OHA	9	3	0	3	....	....	....	....	3	*3	0	3	....
1928-29	Toronto Canoe Club	OHA	9	5	1	6	....	....	....	....	3	5	0	5	....
1929-30	Montreal AAA	City Sr.	10	3	0	3	....	....	....	12	2	0	0	0	4
1930-31	**Montreal Maroons**	**NHL**	**14**	**0**	**0**	**0**	**0**	**0**	**0**	**4**	**2**	**0**	**0**	**0**	**0**
	Montreal AAA	City Sr.	11	5	*4	*9	....	....	....	22	....	....	....	....	....
1931-32	**Montreal Maroons**	**NHL**	**47**	**12**	**13**	**25**	**26**	**36**	**62**	**44**	**4**	**0**	**0**	**0**	**4**
1932-33	**Montreal Maroons**	**NHL**	**48**	**11**	**17**	**28**	**26**	**45**	**71**	**26**	**2**	**0**	**0**	**0**	**0**
1933-34	**Montreal Maroons**	**NHL**	**37**	**4**	**5**	**9**	**9**	**13**	**22**	**19**	**1**	**0**	**0**	**0**	**0**
	Windsor Bulldogs	IAHL	2	1	1	2	....	....	....	0	....	....	....	....	....
1934-35	**St. Louis Eagles**	**NHL**	**48**	**11**	**18**	**29**	**23**	**40**	**63**	**45**	....	....	....	....	....
1935-36	**New York Rangers**	**NHL**	**30**	**4**	**12**	**16**	**10**	**29**	**39**	**7**	....	....	....	....	....
	Chicago Black Hawks	**NHL**	**22**	**6**	**4**	**10**	**15**	**10**	**25**	**32**	**2**	**0**	**0**	**0**	**4**
1936-37	**Chicago Black Hawks**	**NHL**	**34**	**7**	**7**	**14**	**15**	**16**	**31**	**20**	....	....	....	....	....
1937-38	**Chicago Black Hawks**	**NHL**	**19**	**1**	**3**	**4**	**2**	**6**	**8**	**6**	....	....	....	....	....
	New Haven Eagles	AHL	25	6	9	15	....	....	....	17	2	0	0	0	*12
1938-39	New Haven Eagles	AHL	51	8	25	33	....	....	....	18	....	....	....	....	....
1939-40	New Haven–Indianapolis	AHL	39	9	16	25	....	....	....	19	....	....	....	....	....
1940-41	Springfield Indians	AHL	54	20	36	56	....	....	....	28	3	1	2	3	0
1941-42	Pittsburgh Hornets	AHL	45	8	17	25	....	....	....	2	....	....	....	....	....
1942-43	Kingston Frontenacs	OHA Sr.	2	1	3	4	....	....	....	0	4	1	3	4	2
	NHL Totals		**299**	**56**	**79**	**135**	**126**	**195**	**321**	**203**	**11**	**0**	**0**	**0**	**8**

Signed as a free agent by **Montreal Maroons**, February 4, 1931. Traded to **Ottawa** by **Montreal Maroons** to complete transaction that sent Alex Connell to Montreal (October 3, 1934), October 22, 1934. Claimed by **NY Rangers** from **St. Louis** in Dispersal Draft, October 15, 1935. Traded to **Chicago** by **NY Rangers** for Howie Morenz, January 26, 1936. Traded to **New Haven** (AHL) by **Chicago** for cash, January 9, 1938.

• BRYDSON, GORD Gord Brydson

C/RW – R. 5'7", 150 lbs. b: Toronto, Ont., 1/3/1907. Deceased.

Season	Club	League	GP	G	A	Pts	AG	AA	APts	PIM	GP	G	A	Pts	PIM
1923-24	Toronto Canoe Club	OHA	8	1	1	2	....	....	....	8	....	....	....	....	....
1924-25	Toronto Canoe Club	OHA	8	8	*11	*19	....	....	....	....	2	1	0	1	....
1925-26	Toronto Canoe Club	OHA	9	13	2	15	....	....	....	....	....	....	....	....	....
	Toronto Canoe Club	OHA Sr.	1	0	0	0	....	....	....	0	....	....	....	....	....
1926-27	Chicago Cardinals	AHA	32	10	3	13	....	....	....	23	....	....	....	....	....
1927-28	Hamilton Tigers	Can-Pro	42	30	3	33	....	....	....	59	....	....	....	....	....
1928-29	Buffalo Bisons	Can-Pro	42	18	5	23	....	....	....	42	....	....	....	....	....
1929-30	**Toronto Maple Leafs**	**NHL**	**8**	**2**	**0**	**2**	**4**	**0**	**4**	**8**	....	....	....	....	....
	London Panthers	IAHL	32	18	8	26	....	....	....	8	2	1	0	1	2
1930-31	Chicago Shamrocks	AHA	47	*35	12	*47	....	....	....	54	....	....	....	....	....
1931-32	Chicago Shamrocks	AHA	46	9	9	18	....	....	....	35	3	2	1	3	0
1932-33	Detroit Olympics	IAHL	41	4	14	18	....	....	....	57	....	....	....	....	....
	NHL Totals		**8**	**2**	**0**	**2**	**4**	**0**	**4**	**8**	....	....	....	....	....

Rights awarded to **Stratford** (Can-Pro) by NHL President Frank Calder, October 14, 1927. Traded to **Hamilton** (Can-Pro) by **Stratford** (Can-Pro) for Dutch Cain, October 27, 1927. Traded to **Buffalo** (Can-Pro) by **Hamilton** (Can-Pro) for cash, October 25, 1928. Traded to **Toronto** by **Buffalo** (Can-Pro) for Carl Voss and Wes King, November 10, 1929. Traded to **London** (IAHL) by **Toronto** for cash, December 6, 1929. Signed as a free agent by **Chicago** (AHA), November 4, 1930. Traded to **Detroit** (IAHL) by **Chicago** (AHA) for cash, October 6, 1932.

• BUCHANAN, AL Al Buchanan

LW – L. 5'8", 160 lbs. b: Winnipeg, Man., 5/17/1927.

Season	Club	League	GP	G	A	Pts	AG	AA	APts	PIM	GP	G	A	Pts	PIM
1944-45	Winnipeg Monarchs	MJHL	6	5	5	10	....	....	....	0	16	9	4	13	8
1945-46	Winnipeg Monarchs	MJHL	9	7	0	7	....	....	....	0	7	2	1	3	0
1946-47	Winnipeg Monarchs	MJHL	15	16	9	25	....	....	....	11	6	1	4	5	7
1947-48	Toronto Marlboros	OHA Sr.	34	22	24	46	....	....	....	0	5	0	0	0	0
1948-49	**Toronto Maple Leafs**	**NHL**	**3**	**0**	**1**	**1**	**0**	**2**	**2**	**2**	....	....	....	....	....
	Toronto Marlboros	OHA Sr.	37	21	16	37	....	....	....	33	23	4	11	15	*41
1949-50	**Toronto Maple Leafs**	**NHL**	**1**	**0**	**0**	**0**	**0**	**0**	**0**	**0**	....	....	....	....	....
	Toronto Marlboros	OHA Sr.	35	21	24	45	....	....	....	21	14	*7	4	11	4
1950-51	Toronto Marlboros	OHA Sr.	32	14	19	33	....	....	....	25	3	1	1	2	2
1951-52	Saint John Beavers	MMHL	77	21	33	54	....	....	....	44	3	1	1	2	0
1952-53	Kitchener Dutchmen	OHA Sr.	46	20	21	41	....	....	....	24	11	1	2	3	8
1953-54			DID NOT PLAY – INJURED												
1954-55	Niagara Falls Cataracts	OHA Sr.	36	8	10	18	....	....	....	10	....	....	....	....	....
	NHL Totals		**4**	**0**	**1**	**1**	**0**	**2**	**2**	**2**	....	....	....	....	....

• BUCHANAN, BUCKY Bucky (Ralph) Buchanan

C/RW – R. 5'9", 172 lbs. b: Bout De L'Isle, Que., 12/28/1922.

Season	Club	League	GP	G	A	Pts	AG	AA	APts	PIM	GP	G	A	Pts	PIM
1940-41	Montreal Jr. Canadiens	QJHL	7	1	3	4	....	....	....	6	3	2	2	4	0
1941-42	Montreal Jr. Canadiens	QJHL	STATISTICS NOT AVAILABLE												
1942-43	Montreal Royals	QJHL	15	8	6	14	....	....	....	8	....	....	....	....	....
	Montreal Navy	City Sr.	10	4	7	11	....	....	....	11	5	3	2	5	0
	Toronto Navy	OHA Sr.	....	....	....	....	....	....	....	....	2	0	2	2	0
1943-44	Montreal Navy	City Sr.	15	10	8	18	....	....	....	10	4	*7	4	11	4
1944-45	Montreal Navy	City Sr.	13	*17	13	30	....	....	....	10	5	4	6	10	2
1945-46	San Francisco Shamrocks	PCHL	40	*50	25	75	....	....	....	27	....	....	....	....	....
1946-47	San Francisco Shamrocks	PCHL	57	*66	27	93	....	....	....	45	....	....	....	....	....
1947-48	Shawinigan Cataracts	QSHL	47	43	35	78	....	....	....	23	7	4	1	5	2
1948-49	**New York Rangers**	**NHL**	**2**	**0**	**0**	**0**	**0**	**0**	**0**	**0**	....	....	....	....	....
1948-49	Shawinigan Cataracts	QSHL	33	21	25	46	....	....	....	8	7	2	3	5	12
1949-50	Shawinigan Cataracts	QSHL	60	36	49	85	....	....	....	2	....	....	....	....	....
1950-51	Shawinigan Cataracts	QSHL	52	28	36	64	....	....	....	30	....	....	....	....	....
1951-52	Shawinigan Cataracts	QSHL	59	23	33	56	....	....	....	0	....	....	....	....	....
1952-53	Chicoutimi Sagueneens	QSHL	60	31	42	73	....	....	....	33	20	9	6	15	4
1953-54	Chicoutimi Sagueneens	QHL	63	29	34	63	....	....	....	18	7	2	2	4	2
1954-55	Quebec Aces	QHL	55	11	31	42	....	....	....	12	8	1	5	6	8
1955-56	Quebec Aces	QHL	52	10	17	27	....	....	....	2	7	3	0	3	2
1956-57	Quebec Aces	QHL	17	1	6	7	....	....	....	8	....	....	....	....	....
	Kingston CKLC's	OHA Sr.	30	26	22	48	....	....	....	12	5	2	2	4	0
1957-58	Pembroke Lumber Kings	EOHL	29	11	14	25	....	....	....	14	....	....	....	....	....
	NHL Totals		**2**	**0**	**0**	**0**	**0**	**0**	**0**	**0**	....	....	....	....	....

Won Vimy Trophy (MVP - QSHL) (1948, 1950) • QHL First All-Star Team (1953)

• BUCHANAN, MIKE Mike Buchanan
D – L. 6'1", 185 lbs. b: Sault Ste. Marie, Ont., 3/1/1932.

Season	Club	League	GP	G	A	Pts	AG	AA	APts	PIM	PO GP	PO G	PO A	PO Pts	PO PIM
1947-48	Ottawa St. Pats	OJHL	20	3	9	12	....	....	....	6	2	0	0	0	0
1948-49	St. Michael's Majors	OHA	16	0	0	0	....	....	....	14	....	....	....	....	....
1949-50	Guelph–Galt	OHA	42	2	4	6	....	....	....	65	4	0	0	0	2
1950-51	Galt Black Hawks	OHA	52	6	15	21	....	....	....	86	3	0	3	3	7
1951-52	Galt Black Hawks	OHA	46	15	25	40	....	....	....	98	3	0	1	1	4
	Chicago Black Hawks	**NHL**	**1**	**0**	**0**	**0**	**0**	**0**	**0**	**0**	....	....	....	....	....
	St. Louis Flyers	AHL	2	0	0	0	....	....	....	0	....	....	....	....	....
1952-53	Fort Wayne Komets	IHL	43	2	6	8	....	....	....	80	....	....	....	....	....
1953-54	Fort Wayne Komets	IHL	39	1	10	11	....	....	....	62	....	....	....	....	....
1954-55	University of Michigan	WCHA	....	3	7	10	....	....	....	48	....	....	....	....	....
1955-56	University of Michigan	WCHA	....	0	1	1	....	....	....	18	....	....	....	....	....
1956-57			DID NOT PLAY												
1957-58	Wembley–Paisley	Britain	24	3	7	10	....	....	....	32	....	....	....	....	....
	NHL Totals		**1**	**0**	**0**	**0**	**0**	**0**	**0**	**0**	....	....	....	....	....

NCAA West First All-American Team (1955)

• BUCHANAN, RON
— see page 906

• BUCYK, JOHN
— see page 907

• BUKOVICH, TONY Tony Bukovich
LW/C – L. 5'11", 160 lbs. b: Painesdale, MI, 8/30/1917.

Season	Club	League	GP	G	A	Pts	AG	AA	APts	PIM	PO GP	PO G	PO A	PO Pts	PO PIM
1939-40	Painesdale Pontiac Chiefs	MOHL	24	16	*17	33	....	....	....	....	....	....	....	....	....
1940-41	Painesdale Pontiac Chiefs	MOHL	STATISTICS NOT AVAILABLE												
1941-42	Fort Worth Rangers	AHA	47	1	4	5	....	....	....	6	5	0	0	0	0
1942-43	Windsor Colonial Tools	MOHL	7	10	6	16	....	....	....	2	7	10	*13	23	4
1943-44	**Detroit Red Wings**	**NHL**	**3**	**0**	**1**	**1**	**0**	**1**	**1**	**0**	....	....	....	....	....
	Indianapolis Capitals	AHL	6	1	0	1	....	....	....	5	....	....	....	....	....
1944-45	**Detroit Red Wings**	**NHL**	**14**	**7**	**2**	**9**	**10**	**3**	**13**	**6**	**6**	**0**	**1**	**1**	**0**
	Indianapolis Capitals	AHL	32	22	18	40	....	....	....	43	....	....	....	....	....
1945-46	Indianapolis Capitals	AHL	59	25	28	53	....	....	....	68	5	2	3	5	2
1946-47	Indianapolis Capitals	AHL	49	20	23	43	....	....	....	43	....	....	....	....	....
1947-48	Cleveland Barons	AHL	7	4	2	6	....	....	....	2	3	1	1	2	4
	Minneapolis Millers	USHL	10	4	4	8	....	....	....	11	....	....	....	....	....
	NHL Totals		**17**	**7**	**3**	**10**	**10**	**4**	**14**	**6**	**6**	**0**	**1**	**1**	**0**

• BULLER, HY Hy "The Blueline Blaster" Buller
D – L. 5'11", 183 lbs. b: Montreal, Que., 3/15/1926. Deceased.

Season	Club	League	GP	G	A	Pts	AG	AA	APts	PIM	PO GP	PO G	PO A	PO Pts	PO PIM
1941-42	Saskatoon Quakers	SJHL	8	3	5	8	....	....	....	*27	6	6	2	8	*28
1942-43	New York Rovers	EHL	41	11	14	25	....	....	....	61	9	1	2	3	14
1943-44	**Detroit Red Wings**	**NHL**	**7**	**0**	**3**	**3**	**0**	**4**	**4**	**4**	....	....	....	....	....
	Indianapolis Capitals	AHL	46	6	12	18	....	....	....	51	5	2	1	3	2
1944-45	**Detroit Red Wings**	**NHL**	**2**	**0**	**0**	**0**	**0**	**0**	**0**	**2**	....	....	....	....	....
	Hershey Bears	AHL	41	5	17	22	....	....	....	44	11	1	2	3	6
1945-46	Hershey Bears	AHL	59	8	19	27	....	....	....	61	3	0	0	0	2
1946-47	Hershey Bears	AHL	63	12	32	44				56	11	3	3	6	8
1947-48	Hershey–Cleveland	AHL	67	15	33	48	....	....	....	86	8	1	2	3	2
1948-49	Cleveland Barons	AHL	62	7	30	37	....	....	....	44	5	0	7	7	6
1949-50	Cleveland Barons	AHL	43	10	19	29	....	....	....	32	9	0	3	3	10
1950-51	Cleveland Barons	AHL	66	16	41	57	....	....	....	31	11	1	4	5	11
1951-52	**New York Rangers**	**NHL**	**68**	**12**	**23**	**35**	**17**	**30**	**47**	**96**	....	....	....	....	....
1952-53	**New York Rangers**	**NHL**	**70**	**7**	**18**	**25**	**11**	**25**	**36**	**73**	....	....	....	....	....
1953-54	**New York Rangers**	**NHL**	**41**	**3**	**14**	**17**	**5**	**19**	**24**	**40**	....	....	....	....	....
	Saskatoon Quakers	WHL	27	4	10	14	....	....	....	36	6	0	3	3	2
	NHL Totals		**188**	**22**	**58**	**80**	**33**	**78**	**111**	**215**	....	....	....	....	....

EHL Second All-Star Team (1943) • AHL First All-Star Team (1949, 1951) • NHL Second All-Star Team (1952)

Played in NHL All-Star Game (1952)

Traded to **NY Rangers** by **Cleveland** (AHL) with Wally Hergesheimer for Ed Reigle, Jack Gordon, Fred Shero, Fern Perreault and cash, May 14, 1951. Traded to **Montreal** by **NY Rangers** for Dick Gamble and the rights to Ed Dorohoy, June 8, 1954.

• BURCH, BILLY Billy Burch HHOF
C/LW – L. 6', 200 lbs. b: Yonkers, N.Y., 11/20/1900. d: 11/30/1950.

Season	Club	League	GP	G	A	Pts	AG	AA	APts	PIM	PO GP	PO G	PO A	PO Pts	PO PIM
1919-20	Toronto Canoe Club	OHA	....	....	....	....	....			....	12	*42	*12	*54	....
1920-21	Toronto Aura Lee	OHA Sr.	10	12	2	14	....	....	....	....	....	....	....	....	....
1921-22	Toronto Aura Lee	OHA Sr.	9	13	*10	*23	....	....	....	....	2	2	1	3	....
1922-23	New Haven Westminsters	USAHA	....	4	0	4	....	....	....	....	....	....	....	....	....
	Hamilton Tigers	**NHL**	**10**	**6**	**2**	**8**	**20**	**18**	**38**	**2**	....	....	....	....	....
1923-24	**Hamilton Tigers**	**NHL**	**24**	**16**	**2**	**18**	**68**	**35**	**103**	**4**	....	....	....	....	....
1924-25	**Hamilton Tigers**	**NHL**	**27**	**20**	**4**	**24**	**71**	**53**	**124**	**10**	....	....	....	....	....
1925-26	**New York Americans**	**NHL**	**36**	**22**	**3**	**25**	**70**	**34**	**104**	**33**	....	....	....	....	....
1926-27	**New York Americans**	**NHL**	**43**	**19**	**8**	**27**	**56**	**69**	**125**	**40**	....	....	....	....	....
1927-28	**New York Americans**	**NHL**	**32**	**10**	**2**	**12**	**31**	**17**	**48**	**34**	....	....	....	....	....
1928-29	**New York Americans**	**NHL**	**44**	**11**	**5**	**16**	**44**	**46**	**90**	**45**	**2**	**0**	**0**	**0**	**0**
1929-30	**New York Americans**	**NHL**	**35**	**7**	**3**	**10**	**14**	**10**	**24**	**22**	....	....	....	....	....
1930-31	**New York Americans**	**NHL**	**44**	**14**	**8**	**22**	**34**	**29**	**63**	**35**	....	....	....	....	....
1931-32	**New York Americans**	**NHL**	**48**	**7**	**15**	**22**	**15**	**42**	**57**	**20**	....	....	....	....	....
1932-33	**Boston Bruins**	**NHL**	**23**	**3**	**1**	**4**	**7**	**3**	**10**	**4**	....	....	....	....	....
	Chicago Black Hawks	**NHL**	**24**	**2**	**0**	**2**	**5**	**0**	**5**	**2**	....	....	....	....	....
	NHL Totals		**390**	**137**	**53**	**190**	**435**	**356**	**791**	**251**	**2**	**0**	**0**	**0**	**0**

Won Hart Trophy (1925) • Won Lady Byng Trophy (1927)

Signed as a free agent by **Hamilton**, January 30, 1923. Transferred to **NY Americans** after NHL club purchased **Hamilton** franchise, September 25, 1925. Traded to **Boston** by **NY Americans** for cash, April 13, 1932. Traded to **Chicago** by **Boston** for Vic Ripley, January 17, 1933.

• BURCHELL, FRED Fred "Skippy" Burchell
C – L. 5'6", 143 lbs. b: Montreal, Que., 1/9/1931. d: 6/4/1998.

Season	Club	League	GP	G	A	Pts	AG	AA	APts	PIM	PO GP	PO G	PO A	PO Pts	PO PIM
1947-48	Montreal Jr. Royals	QJHL	2	3	0	3	....	....	....	0	10	1	5	6	0
1948-49	Montreal Jr. Royals	QJHL	47	10	25	35	....	....	....	15	25	8	14	22	19
1949-50	Montreal Jr. Royals	QJHL	1	0	1	1	....	....	....	0	....	....	....	....	....
	Montreal Royals	QSHL	2	0	0	0	....	....	....	0	....	....	....	....	....
	Laval Nationals	Mtl-Jr.	34	22	*54	76	....	....	....	47	7	4	5	9	4
1950-51	Montreal Nationales	QJHL	45	48	*76	*124	....	....	....	46	3	0	1	1	6
	Montreal Canadiens	**NHL**	**2**	**0**	**0**	**0**	**0**	**0**	**0**	**0**	....	....	....	....	....
1951-52	Johnstown Jets	EHL	56	37	56	93	....	....	....	71	8	2	*12	*14	12
1952-53	Montreal Royals	QSHL	52	18	38	56	....	....	....	41	11	0	0	0	9
1953-54	**Montreal Canadiens**	**NHL**	**2**	**0**	**0**	**0**	**0**	**0**	**0**	**2**	....	....	....	....	....
	Montreal Royals	QHL	66	31	59	90	....	....	....	34	11	2	8	10	6
1954-55	Montreal Royals	QHL	61	19	41	60	....	....	....	50	13	2	2	4	6
1955-56	Montreal Royals	QHL	5	1	3	4	....	....	....	4	....	....	....	....	....
	Winnipeg Warriors	WHL	61	11	47	58	....	....	....	48	14	7	*12	19	8
1956-57	Winnipeg Warriors	WHL	66	17	40	57	....	....	....	22	....	....	....	....	....
1957-58	Rochester Americans	AHL	70	20	40	60	....	....	....	65	....	....	....	....	....
1958-59	Montreal Royals	QHL	59	11	41	52	....	....	....	31	8	*7	2	9	4
1959-60	Montreal Royals	EPHL	67	12	58	70	....	....	....	44	13	7	8	15	2
1960-61	Montreal Royals	EPHL	68	13	61	74	....	....	....	12	....	....	....	....	....
1961-62	Quebec Aces	AHL	67	21	57	78	....	....	....	14	....	....	....	....	....
1962-63	Quebec Aces	AHL	69	17	55	72	....	....	....	12	....	....	....	....	....
1963-64	Quebec Aces	AHL	58	4	30	34	....	....	....	10	8	1	2	3	0
1964-65	Verdun Pirates	QSHL	STATISTICS NOT AVAILABLE												
1965-66	Jersey Devils	EHL	2	1	0	1	....	....	....	2	....	....	....	....	....
	NHL Totals		**4**	**0**	**0**	**0**	**0**	**0**	**0**	**2**	....	....	....	....	....

EHL First All-Star Team (1952) • QHL First All-Star Team (1954)

• BUREGA, BILL Bill Burega
D – L. 6', 195 lbs. b: Winnipeg, Man., 3/13/1932.

Season	Club	League	GP	G	A	Pts	AG	AA	APts	PIM	PO GP	PO G	PO A	PO Pts	PO PIM
1949-50	Winnipeg Monarchs	MJHL	28	3	2	5	....	....	....	45	12	0	4	4	16
1950-51	Winnipeg Monarchs	MJHL	36	10	11	21	....	....	....	59	29	3	6	9	*79
1951-52	Winnipeg Canadians	MJHL	36	4	8	12	....	....	....	111	11	1	1	2	33
1952-53	Glace Bay Miners	MMHL	72	6	10	16				*163	11	0	1	1	15
1953-54	Quebec–Ottawa	QHL	41	0	5	5	....	....	....	115	7	0	0	0	8
	Pittsburgh Hornets	AHL	5	0	1	1	....	....	....	4	....	....	....	....	....
1954-55	Pittsburgh Hornets	AHL	57	2	5	7	....	....	....	140	10	0	2	2	*24
1955-56	**Toronto Maple Leafs**	**NHL**	**4**	**0**	**1**	**1**	**0**	**1**	**1**	**4**	....	....	....	....	....
	Winnipeg Warriors	WHL	67	2	18	20	....	....	....	151	14	2	4	6	*33
1956-57	Winnipeg Warriors	WHL	70	1	14	15	....	....	....	197	....	....	....	....	....
1957-58	Buffalo Bisons	AHL	56	0	7	7	....	....	....	136	....	....	....	....	....
1958-59	Saskatoon Quakers	WHL	62	2	10	12	....	....	....	104	....	....	....	....	....
1959-60	Soo Thunderbirds	EPHL	2	0	0	0	....	....	....	6	....	....	....	....	....
	Spokane Comets	WHL	65	4	14	18	....	....	....	162	....	....	....	....	....
1960-61	Calgary Stampeders	WHL	67	3	32	35	....	....	....	73	5	1	1	2	6
1961-62	Los Angeles Blades	WHL	70	1	14	15	....	....	....	142	....	....	....	....	....
1962-63	Los Angeles Blades	WHL	70	1	11	12	....	....	....	142	3	0	2	2	6
1963-64	Los Angeles Blades	WHL	51	0	7	7	....	....	....	75	12	0	3	3	31
1964-65	Vancouver Canucks	WHL	70	3	10	13	....	....	....	161	5	0	1	1	10
1965-66	Kingston Aces	OHA Sr.	12	1	10	11	....	....	....	40	....	....	....	....	....
1966-67	Kingston Aces	OHA Sr.	38	4	19	23	....	....	....	84	....	....	....	....	....
1967-68	Kingston Aces	OHA Sr.	40	1	14	15	....	....	....	86	....	....	....	....	....
1968-69	Kingston Aces	OHA Sr.	1	0	0	0	....	....	....	6	....	....	....	....	....
1969-70	Kingston Aces	OHA Sr.	25	1	9	10	....	....	....	61	....	....	....	....	....
	NHL Totals		**4**	**0**	**1**	**1**	**0**	**1**	**1**	**4**	....	....	....	....	....

Traded to **Buffalo** (AHL) by **Toronto** for cash, June, 1957.

• BURKE, EDDIE Eddie "Shanty" Burke
RW/C – R. 5'8", 175 lbs. b: Toronto, Ont., 6/3/1907. Deceased.

Season	Club	League	GP	G	A	Pts	AG	AA	APts	PIM	PO GP	PO G	PO A	PO Pts	PO PIM
1921-22	Toronto St. Mary's	OHA	STATISTICS NOT AVAILABLE												
1922-23	Toronto St. Mary's	OHA	6	5	*3	8	....	....	....	....	7	*7	1	*8	....
1923-24	Toronto St. Mary's	OHA	8	7	4	11	....	....	....	21	....	....	....	....	....
1924-25	Soo Greyhounds	NOHA	DID NOT PLAY – INJURED												
1925-26	Soo Greyhounds	NOHA	26	1	0	1	....	....	....	16	....	....	....	....	....
1926-27	Toronto Marlboros	OHA Sr.	STATISTICS NOT AVAILABLE												
1927-28	Boston Tigers	Can-Am	39	12	1	13	....	....	....	54	2	1	0	1	4
1928-29	Boston Tigers	Can-Am	34	3	3	6	....	....	....	55	4	1	0	1	4
1929-30	Boston Tigers	Can-Am	40	14	9	23	....	....	....	60	5	0	0	0	4
1930-31	Boston Tigers	Can-Am	40	20	18	38	....	....	....	60	9	4	3	7	12
1931-32	**Boston Bruins**	**NHL**	**16**	**3**	**0**	**3**	**6**	**0**	**6**	**12**	....	....	....	....	....
	Boston Tigers	Can-Am	28	9	5	14	....	....	....	47	5	2	1	3	5
1932-33	**New York Americans**	**NHL**	**15**	**2**	**0**	**2**	**5**	**0**	**5**	**4**	....	....	....	....	....
	Philadelphia Arrows	Can-Am	21	9	11	20	....	....	....	28	....	....	....	....	....
1933-34	**New York Americans**	**NHL**	**46**	**20**	**10**	**30**	**45**	**27**	**72**	**24**	....	....	....	....	....
1934-35	**New York Americans**	**NHL**	**29**	**4**	**10**	**14**	**8**	**22**	**30**	**15**	....	....	....	....	....
1935-36	Syracuse Stars	IAHL	47	11	32	43	....	....	....	18	3	1	1	2	2
1936-37	Syracuse Stars	AHL	21	0	7	7	....	....	....	9	9	0	0	0	0
	NHL Totals		**106**	**29**	**20**	**49**	**64**	**49**	**113**	**55**	....	....	....	....	....

Traded to **NY Americans** by **Boston** for cash, October 25, 1932.

			REGULAR SEASON								PLAYOFFS				
Season	Club	League	GP	G	A	Pts	AG	AA	APts	PIM	GP	G	A	Pts	PIM

• BURKE, MARTY Marty Burke

D – L. 5'8", 160 lbs. b: Toronto, Ont., 1/28/1905. Deceased.

Season	Club	League	GP	G	A	Pts	AG	AA	APts	PIM	GP	G	A	Pts	PIM
1923-24	Toronto St. Mary's	OHA	5	4	1	5	....	....	....	8	....	....	....	....	....
	Toronto St. Mary's	OHA Sr.	2	0	0	0	....	....	....	....	....	....	....	....	....
1924-25	Stratford Indians	OHA Sr.	18	1	4	5	....	....	....	*52	2	0	0	0	2
1925-26	Stratford Indians	OHA Sr.	20	3	4	7	....	....	....	34	....	....	....	....	....
1926-27	Port Arthur Ports	TBSHL	20	3	1	4	....	....	....	*65	2	1	0	1	*4
1927-28	**Montreal Canadiens**	**NHL**	**11**	**0**	**0**	**0**	**0**	**0**	**0**	**10**	....	....	....	....	....
	Pittsburgh Pirates	**NHL**	**35**	**2**	**1**	**3**	**6**	**8**	**14**	**51**	**2**	**1**	**0**	**1**	**2**
1928-29	**Montreal Canadiens**	**NHL**	**44**	**4**	**2**	**6**	**16**	**18**	**34**	**68**	**3**	**0**	**0**	**0**	**8**
1929-30	**Montreal Canadiens**	**NHL**	**44**	**2**	**11**	**13**	**4**	**36**	**40**	**71**	**6**	**0**	**1**	**1**	**6**
1930-31	**Montreal Canadiens**	**NHL**	**44**	**2**	**5**	**7**	**5**	**18**	**23**	**91**	**10**	**1**	**2**	**3**	**10**
1931-32	**Montreal Canadiens**	**NHL**	**48**	**3**	**6**	**9**	**6**	**17**	**23**	**50**	**4**	**0**	**0**	**0**	**12**
1932-33	**Montreal Canadiens**	**NHL**	**29**	**2**	**5**	**7**	**5**	**13**	**18**	**36**	....	....	....	....	....
	Ottawa Senators	**NHL**	**16**	**0**	**0**	**0**	**0**	**0**	**0**	**10**	....	....	....	....	....
1933-34	**Montreal Canadiens**	**NHL**	**45**	**1**	**4**	**5**	**2**	**11**	**13**	**28**	**2**	**0**	**1**	**1**	**2**
1934-35	**Chicago Black Hawks**	**NHL**	**47**	**2**	**2**	**4**	**4**	**4**	**8**	**29**	**2**	**0**	**0**	**0**	**2**
1935-36	**Chicago Black Hawks**	**NHL**	**40**	**0**	**3**	**3**	**0**	**7**	**7**	**49**	**2**	**0**	**0**	**0**	**2**
1936-37	**Chicago Black Hawks**	**NHL**	**41**	**1**	**3**	**4**	**2**	**7**	**9**	**28**	....	....	....	....	....
1937-38	**Chicago Black Hawks**	**NHL**	**12**	**0**	**0**	**0**	**0**	**0**	**0**	**8**	....	....	....	....	....
	Montreal Canadiens	**NHL**	**38**	**0**	**5**	**5**	**0**	**10**	**10**	**31**	....	....	....	....	....
1938-39	Saskatoon Quakers	SSHL	DID NOT PLAY – COACHING												
	NHL Totals		**494**	**19**	**47**	**66**	**50**	**149**	**199**	**560**	**31**	**2**	**4**	**6**	**44**

Loaned to **Pittsburgh** by **Montreal Canadiens** for remainder of 1927-28 season for the loan of Charles Langlois, December 16, 1927. Traded to **Ottawa** by **Montreal Canadiens** with future considerations (Nick Wasnie, March 23, 1933) for Harold Starr and Leo Bourgeault, February 15, 1933. Traded to **Montreal Canadiens** by **Ottawa** for Nick Wasnie, March 23, 1933. Traded to **Chicago** by **Montreal Canadiens** with Lorne Chabot and Howie Morenz for Leroy Goldsworthy, Lionel Conacher and Roger Jenkins, October 3, 1934. Traded to **Montreal Canadiens** by **Chicago** for Bill MacKenzie, December 10, 1937.

• BURMEISTER, ROY Roy Burmeister

LW – L. 5'10", 155 lbs. b: Collingwood, Ont., 8/12/1906. Deceased.

Season	Club	League	GP	G	A	Pts	AG	AA	APts	PIM	GP	G	A	Pts	PIM
1924-25	Owen Sound Greys	OHA	17	8	8	16	....	....	....	....	8	3	0	3	0
1925-26	Niagara Falls Cataracts	OHA Sr.	19	3	5	8	....	....	....	2	....	....	....	....	....
1926-27	Niagara Falls Cataracts	Can-Pro	22	6	3	9	....	....	....	4	....	....	....	....	....
1927-28	Niagara Falls Cataracts	Can-Pro	39	6	1	7	....	....	....	18	....	....	....	....	....
1928-29	New Haven Eagles	Can-Am	35	1	1	2	....	....	....	8	2	0	0	0	0
1929-30	**New York Americans**	**NHL**	**40**	**1**	**1**	**2**	**2**	**3**	**5**	**0**	....	....	....	....	....
	New Haven Eagles	Can-Am	6	1	1	2	....	....	....	40	....	....	....	....	....
1930-31	**New York Americans**	**NHL**	**11**	**0**	**0**	**0**	**0**	**0**	**0**	**0**	....	....	....	....	....
	New Haven Eagles	Can-Am	32	12	14	26	....	....	....	18	....	....	....	....	....
1931-32	New Haven Eagles	Can-Am	26	9	7	16	....	....	....	16	....	....	....	....	....
	New York Americans	**NHL**	**16**	**3**	**2**	**5**	**6**	**6**	**12**	**2**	....	....	....	....	....
1932-33	New Haven Eagles	Can-Am	28	6	0	6	....	....	....	10	....	....	....	....	....
	Boston Cubs	Can-Am	21	4	3	7	....	....	....	9	7	2	1	3	0
1933-34	Windsor–London	IAHL	40	2	1	3	....	....	....	11	....	....	....	....	....
1934-35	Philadelphia Arrows	Can-Am	48	12	22	34	....	....	....	13	....	....	....	....	....
1935-36	St. Louis Flyers	AHA	48	14	19	33	....	....	....	11	8	1	*3	4	0
1936-37	St. Paul Saints	AHA	42	8	19	27	....	....	....	2	3	0	1	1	0
1937-38	St. Paul Saints	AHA	47	6	10	16	....	....	....	4	....	....	....	....	....
1938-39	Kansas City Greyhounds	AHA	47	8	7	15	....	....	....	0	....	....	....	....	....
	NHL Totals		**67**	**4**	**3**	**7**	**8**	**9**	**17**	**2**	....	....	....	....	....

Traded to **Boston** (Boston—Can-Am) by **NY Americans** (New Haven—Can-Am) for Connie King, February 12, 1933. Traded to **NY Rangers** by **Boston** with Vic Ripley for Albert Siebert, December 18, 1933.

• BURNETT, KELLY Kelly Burnett

C – L. 5'10", 160 lbs. b: Lachine, Que., 6/16/1926.

Season	Club	League	GP	G	A	Pts	AG	AA	APts	PIM	GP	G	A	Pts	PIM
1943-44	Montreal Jr. Canadiens	QJHL	15	11	12	23	....	....	....	0	3	3	3	6	0
	Montreal Noordyn	City Sr.	4	2	0	2	....	....	....	0	....	....	....	....	....
1944-45	Montreal Jr. Canadiens	QJHL	13	*20	6	26	....	....	....	4	9	6	5	11	2
1945-46	Barrie Flyers	OHA	3	5	1	6	....	....	....	2	....	....	....	....	....
	Montreal Jr. Canadiens	QJHL	12	10	6	16	....	....	....	2	11	8	*13	21	8
1946-47	Victoriaville Tigers	QPHL	50	40	*75	*115	....	....	....	18	2	1	3	4	0
1947-48	Victoriaville Tigers	QPHL	50	36	*71	*107	....	....	....	8	14	*11	9	*20	0
1948-49	Sherbrooke Saints	QSHL	63	37	38	75	....	....	....	40	12	4	7	11	2
1949-50	Springfield Indians	AHL	67	27	49	76	....	....	....	14	2	0	1	1	0
1950-51	Springfield Indians	AHL	68	26	48	74	....	....	....	12	3	0	0	0	0
1951-52	Syracuse Warriors	AHL	68	25	43	68	....	....	....	10	....	....	....	....	....
1952-53	Syracuse Warriors	AHL	56	23	53	76	....	....	....	16	4	1	3	4	0
	New York Rangers	**NHL**	**3**	**1**	**0**	**1**	**2**	**0**	**2**	**0**	....	....	....	....	....
1953-54	Syracuse Warriors	AHL	45	8	29	37	....	....	....	12	....	....	....	....	....
1954-55	Montreal Royals	QHL	62	30	46	*76	....	....	....	12	14	4	4	8	0
1955-56	Montreal Royals	QHL	58	25	40	65	....	....	....	22	12	3	2	5	4
1956-57	Montreal Royals	QHL	67	22	35	57	....	....	....	28	4	3	1	4	0
1957-58	Montreal Royals	QHL	55	32	36	68	....	....	....	14	7	2	6	8	0
1958-59	Montreal Royals	QHL	57	16	28	44	....	....	....	6	8	2	*5	7	2
1959-60	Montreal Royals	EPHL	66	23	30	53	....	....	....	26	7	3	4	7	2
1960-61	Montreal Royals	EPHL	3	0	1	1	....	....	....	0	....	....	....	....	....
	NHL Totals		**3**	**1**	**0**	**1**	**2**	**0**	**2**	**0**	....	....	....	....	....

AHL Second All-Star Team (1953) • QHL First All-Star Team (1955, 1957) • Won President's Cup (Scoring Champion - QHL) (1955) • Won Vimy Trophy (MVP - QHL) (1955)

• BURNS, BOBBY Bobby Burns

LW – L. 5'10", 155 lbs. b: Gore Bay, Ont., 4/4/1905.

Season	Club	League	GP	G	A	Pts	AG	AA	APts	PIM	GP	G	A	Pts	PIM
1924-25	Owen Sound Greys	OHA	17	17	*11	28	....	....	....	....	9	2	3	5	4
1925-26	Preston Riversides	OHA Sr.	20	8	0	8	....	....	....	8	....	....	....	....	....
1926-27	Chicago Cardinals	AHA	33	6	3	9	....	....	....	20	....	....	....	....	....
1927-28	**Chicago Black Hawks**	**NHL**	**1**	**0**	**0**	**0**	**0**	**0**	**0**	**0**	....	....	....	....	....
	Duluth Hornets	AHA	39	9	1	10	....	....	....	38	5	0	0	0	6
1928-29	**Chicago Black Hawks**	**NHL**	**7**	**0**	**0**	**0**	**0**	**0**	**0**	**6**	....	....	....	....	....
1929-30	**Chicago Black Hawks**	**NHL**	**12**	**1**	**0**	**1**	**2**	**0**	**2**	**2**	....	....	....	....	....
	Minneapolis Millers	AHA	25	7	4	11	....	....	....	25	....	....	....	....	....
1930-31	Chicago Shamrocks	AHA	46	16	10	26	....	....	....	54	....	....	....	....	....
1931-32	Chicago Shamrocks	AHA	29	7	2	9	....	....	....	30	....	....	....	....	....
	St. Louis Flyers	AHA	13	3	0	3	....	....	....	12	....	....	....	....	....
1932-33	Kansas City Greyhounds	AHA	27	11	4	15	....	....	....	28	....	....	....	....	....
1933-34	Oklahoma City Warriors	AHA	47	16	12	28	....	....	....	30	....	....	....	....	....
1934-35	Oklahoma City Warriors	AHA	48	17	19	36	....	....	....	35	....	....	....	....	....
1935-36	Oklahoma–Minneapolis	AHA	48	20	20	40	....	....	....	33	....	....	....	....	....
1936-37	St. Louis Flyers	AHA	46	25	19	44	....	....	....	34	6	4	3	7	9
1937-38	St. Louis Flyers	AHA	43	11	22	33	....	....	....	24	7	0	1	1	5
1938-39	St. Louis Flyers	AHA	45	15	23	38	....	....	....	46	7	2	3	5	2
	NHL Totals		**20**	**1**	**0**	**1**	**2**	**0**	**2**	**8**	....	....	....	....	....

AHA Second All-Star Team (1936) • AHA First All-Star Team (1937)

NHL rights transferred to **Detroit** from **Chicago Shamrocks** (AHA) after AHA club owners purchased Detroit (NHL and IAHL) franchises, September 2, 1932.

• BURNS, CHARLIE — *see page 909*

• BURNS, NORM Norm Burns

C – R. 6', 195 lbs. b: Youngstown, Alta., 2/20/1918. d: 2/23/1995.

Season	Club	League	GP	G	A	Pts	AG	AA	APts	PIM	GP	G	A	Pts	PIM
1938-39	Sherbrooke Saints	QPHL	STATISTICS NOT AVAILABLE												
1939-40	Atlantic City Seagulls	EHL	49	22	28	50	....	....	....	14	....	....	....	....	....
	Rivervale Skeeters	EHL	14	10	8	18	....	....	....	0	....	....	....	....	....
1940-41	Washington Eagles	EHL	64	*67	26	*93	....	....	....	35	2	3	0	3	4
1941-42	**New York Rangers**	**NHL**	**11**	**0**	**4**	**4**	**0**	**6**	**6**	**2**	....	....	....	....	....
	New Haven Eagles	AHL	35	27	32	59	....	....	....	13	2	0	0	0	0
1942-43	Montreal RCAF	QSHL	25	12	14	26	....	....	....	10	9	2	1	3	6
1943-44	Toronto RCAF	OHA Sr.	11	3	5	8	....	....	....	4	....	....	....	....	....
	Toronto Fuels	City Sr.	....	11	11	22	....	....	....	0	4	10	7	17	0
1944-45			MILITARY SERVICE												
1945-46	St. Paul Saints	USHL	54	30	22	52	....	....	....	28	5	0	0	0	0
1946-47	New Haven–Cleveland	AHL	42	23	23	46	....	....	....	10	4	0	0	0	0
1947-48	Minneapolis Millers	USHL	57	23	27	50	....	....	....	8	10	1	2	3	0
1948-49	Washington–Springfield	AHL	39	5	21	26	....	....	....	4	....	....	....	....	....
	NHL Totals		**11**	**0**	**4**	**4**	**0**	**6**	**6**	**2**	....	....	....	....	....

EHL First All-Star Team (1941) • Won John Carlin Trophy (Top Scorer - EHL) (1941)

Claimed by **NY Rangers** from **Minneapolis** (AHA) in Inter-League Draft, June 27, 1941.

• BURRY, BERT Bert Burry

D – L. 5'9", 180 lbs. b: Toronto, Ont., 1909. Deceased.

Season	Club	League	GP	G	A	Pts	AG	AA	APts	PIM	GP	G	A	Pts	PIM
1927-28	Toronto Marlboros	OHA Sr.	2	0	0	0	....	....	....	....	....	....	....	....	....
1931-32	Springfield Indians	Can-Am	19	0	1	1	....	....	....	20	....	....	....	....	....
1932-33	**Ottawa Senators**	**NHL**	**4**	**0**	**0**	**0**	**0**	**0**	**0**	**0**	....	....	....	....	....
	Hibbing Maroons	CHL	7	0	0	0	....	....	....	6	....	....	....	....	....
1934-35			STATISTICS NOT AVAILABLE												
1935-36			STATISTICS NOT AVAILABLE												
1936-37	Ottawa Senators	City Sr.	8	0	0	0	....	....	....	2	....	....	....	....	....
	NHL Totals		**4**	**0**	**0**	**0**	**0**	**0**	**0**	**0**	....	....	....	....	....

• BURTON, CUMMY Cummy Burton

RW – R. 5'10", 170 lbs. b: Sudbury, Ont., 5/12/1936.

Season	Club	League	GP	G	A	Pts	AG	AA	APts	PIM	GP	G	A	Pts	PIM
1952-53	Windsor Spitfires	OHA	54	7	4	11	....	....	....	88	....	....	....	....	....
1953-54	Hamilton Tiger Cubs	OHA	58	30	25	55	....	....	....	100	7	0	1	1	10
1954-55	Hamilton Tiger Cubs	OHA	28	6	10	16	....	....	....	54	3	1	1	2	6
1955-56	Hamilton Tiger Cubs	OHA	38	31	30	61	....	....	....	50	....	....	....	....	....
	Detroit Red Wings	**NHL**	**3**	**0**	**0**	**0**	**0**	**0**	**0**	**0**	**3**	**0**	**0**	**0**	**0**
1956-57	Edmonton Flyers	WHL	57	14	15	29	....	....	....	83	8	3	4	7	16
1957-58	**Detroit Red Wings**	**NHL**	**26**	**0**	**1**	**1**	**0**	**1**	**1**	**12**	....	....	....	....	....
	Edmonton Flyers	WHL	35	10	11	21	....	....	....	26	5	3	2	5	8
1958-59	**Detroit Red Wings**	**NHL**	**14**	**0**	**1**	**1**	**0**	**1**	**1**	**9**	....	....	....	....	....
	Seattle Totems	WHL	50	16	25	41	....	....	....	60	....	....	....	....	....
1959-60	Sudbury Wolves	EPHL	64	26	32	58	....	....	....	44	10	1	5	6	6
1960-61	Sudbury Wolves	EPHL	62	15	21	36	....	....	....	49	....	....	....	....	....
1961-62	Sudbury Wolves	EPHL	63	18	31	49	....	....	....	59	1	0	2	2	0
1962-63	Edmonton Flyers	WHL	42	4	10	14	....	....	....	24	3	0	0	0	7
	Pittsburgh Hornets	AHL	3	0	0	0	....	....	....	0	....	....	....	....	....
1963-64	Charlotte Checkers	EHL	35	15	31	46	....	....	....	28	3	0	1	1	0
1964-1967			DID NOT PLAY – RETIRED												
1967-68	Florida Rockets	EHL	52	7	20	27	....	....	....	23	....	....	....	....	....
	NHL Totals		**43**	**0**	**2**	**2**	**0**	**2**	**2**	**21**	**3**	**0**	**0**	**0**	**0**

• BUSH, EDDIE
Eddie Bush
D – R. 6'1", 195 lbs. b: Collingwood, Ont., 7/11/1918. d: 5/31/1984.

Season	Club	League	GP	G	A	Pts	AG	AA	APts	PIM	GP	G	A	Pts	PIM
			REGULAR SEASON								PLAYOFFS				
1936-37	Guelph Indians	OHA	10	7	3	10	....	....	....	24	5	2	1	3	8
1937-38	Guelph Indians	OHA	14	8	4	12	....	....	....	41	9	7	*6	13	12
1938-39	**Detroit Red Wings**	**NHL**	**8**	**0**	**0**	**0**	**0**	**0**	**0**	**0**	....	....	....	....	....
	Pittsburgh Hornets	AHL	16	1	2	3	....	....	....	18	....	....	....	....	....
	Kansas City Greyhounds	AHA	25	4	13	17	....	....	....	69	....	....	....	....	....
1939-40	Indianapolis Capitals	AHL	41	7	10	17	....	....	....	49	2	0	0	0	2
1940-41	Indianapolis–Providence	AHL	56	10	13	23	....	....	....	93	4	2	0	2	11
1941-42	Providence Reds	AHL	36	12	24	36	....	....	....	62	....	....	....	....	....
	Detroit Red Wings	**NHL**	**18**	**4**	**6**	**10**	**7**	**9**	**16**	**40**	**12**	**1**	**6**	**7**	**23**
1942-43	Toronto RCAF	OHA Sr.	8	0	2	2	....	....	....	25	3	0	3	3	*40
1943-44	Dartmouth RCAF	City Sr.	3	1	3	4	....	....	....	4	....	....	....	....	....
1944-45	Dartmouth RCAF	City Sr.	4	1	1	2	....	....	....	6	....	....	....	....	....
1945-46			MILITARY SERVICE												
1946-47	St. Louis–Providence	AHL	60	12	25	37	....	....	....	*182	....	....	....	....	....
1947-48	Philadelphia Rockets	AHL	68	24	48	72	....	....	....	163	....	....	....	....	....
1948-49	Philadelphia–Cleveland	AHL	67	5	21	26	....	....	....	113	1	0	0	0	4
1949-50	Cincinnati Mohawks	AHL	8	0	2	2	....	....	....	12	....	....	....	....	....
	Louisville Blades	USHL	8	0	7	7	....	....	....	28	....	....	....	....	....
	Sherbrooke Saints	QSHL	31	7	18	25	....	....	....	89	18	6	9	15	*43
1950-51	Collingwood Shipbuilders	Tor-Sr.	DID NOT PLAY – COACHING												
1951-52	Quebec Aces	QSHL	9	0	1	1	....	....	....	0	....	....	....	....	....
	NHL Totals		**26**	**4**	**6**	**10**	**7**	**9**	**16**	**40**	**12**	**1**	**6**	**7**	**23**

AHL Second All-Star Team (1948)

Traded to **Providence** (AHL) by **Detroit** with Cecil Dillon for Harold Jackson, December 15, 1940. Traded to **Detroit** by **Providence** (AHL) for Buck Jones, Bob Whitelaw and future considerations, February 12, 1942. Traded to **St. Louis** (AHL) by **Detroit** for cash, August 17, 1946.

• BUSWELL, WALT
Walt Buswell
D – L. 5'11", 170 lbs. b: Montreal, Que., 11/6/1907. d: 10/16/1991.

Season	Club	League	GP	G	A	Pts	AG	AA	APts	PIM	GP	G	A	Pts	PIM
1929-30	Montreal CPR	City Sr.	STATISTICS NOT AVAILABLE												
1930-31	St. Francis Xavier	Mtl. Sr.	STATISTICS NOT AVAILABLE												
1931-32	Chicago Shamrocks	AHA	48	9	5	14	....	....	....	39	4	0	1	1	4
1932-33	**Detroit Red Wings**	**NHL**	**46**	**2**	**4**	**6**	**5**	**11**	**16**	**16**	**4**	**0**	**0**	**0**	**4**
1933-34	**Detroit Red Wings**	**NHL**	**47**	**1**	**2**	**3**	**2**	**5**	**7**	**8**	**9**	**0**	**1**	**1**	**2**
1934-35	**Detroit Red Wings**	**NHL**	**47**	**1**	**3**	**4**	**2**	**7**	**9**	**32**	....	....	....	....	....
	Detroit Olympics	IAHL	2	0	0	0	....	....	....	0	....	....	....	....	....
1935-36	**Montreal Canadiens**	**NHL**	**44**	**0**	**2**	**2**	**0**	**5**	**5**	**34**	....	....	....	....	....
1936-37	**Montreal Canadiens**	**NHL**	**44**	**0**	**4**	**4**	**0**	**9**	**9**	**30**	**5**	**0**	**0**	**0**	**2**
1937-38	**Montreal Canadiens**	**NHL**	**48**	**2**	**15**	**17**	**4**	**31**	**35**	**24**	**3**	**0**	**0**	**0**	**0**
1938-39	**Montreal Canadiens**	**NHL**	**46**	**3**	**7**	**10**	**6**	**13**	**19**	**10**	**3**	**2**	**0**	**2**	**2**
1939-40	**Montreal Canadiens**	**NHL**	**46**	**1**	**3**	**4**	**2**	**6**	**8**	**10**	....	....	....	....	....
1940-41	Joliette Cyclones	QPHL	12	3	5	8	....	....	....	2	3	1	6	7	4
	NHL Totals		**368**	**10**	**40**	**50**	**21**	**87**	**108**	**164**	**24**	**2**	**1**	**3**	**10**

Played in NHL All-Star Game (1937, 1939)

NHL rights transferred to **Detroit** from **Chicago Shamrocks** (AHA) after AHA club owners purchased Detroit (NHL and IAHL) franchises, September 2, 1932. Traded to **Boston** by **Detroit** with Cooney Weiland for Marty Barry and Art Giroux, July 11, 1935. Traded to **Montreal Canadiens** by **Boston** with Jean Pusie and cash for Roger Jenkins, July 13, 1935.

• BUTLER, DICK
Dick Butler
RW – R. 5'7", 175 lbs. b: Delisle, Sask., 6/2/1926.

Season	Club	League	GP	G	A	Pts	AG	AA	APts	PIM	GP	G	A	Pts	PIM
1944-45	Moose Jaw Canucks	SJHL	16	18	16	34	....	....	....	41	11	9	*7	16	14
1945-46	Moose Jaw Canucks	CJHL	15	21	17	38			....	22	4	8	2	10	6
1946-47	Kansas City Pla-Mors	USHL	59	19	31	50	....	....	....	48	12	7	1	8	13
1947-48	**Chicago Black Hawks**	**NHL**	**7**	**2**	**0**	**2**	**3**	**0**	**3**	**0**	....	....	....	....	....
	Kansas City Pla-Mors	USHL	49	16	22	38	....	....	....	26	7	1	2	3	2
1948-49	Hershey Bears	AHL	6	1	0	1	....	....	....	0	....	....	....	....	....
	Tulsa Oilers	USHL	57	42	41	83	....	....	....	35	7	2	5	7	0
1949-50	Tulsa Oilers	USHL	70	37	36	73	....	....	....	22	....	....	....	....	....
1950-51	Tulsa Oilers	USHL	61	23	27	50	....	....	....	13	9	0	5	5	6
1951-52	Calgary Stampeders	PCHL	13	2	2	4	....	....	....	21	....	....	....	....	....
1952-53	Spokane Flyers	WIHL	55	24	45	69	....	....	....	71	9	1	4	5	12
1953-54	Vernon Canadiens	OSHL	53	27	38	65	....	....	....	57	5	3	3	6	12
	NHL Totals		**7**	**2**	**0**	**2**	**3**	**0**	**3**	**0**	....	....	....	....	....

USHL First All-Star Team (1949)

• BUTTREY, GORD
Gord Buttrey
LW/RW – L. 6'1", 180 lbs. b: Regina, Sask., 3/17/1926.

Season	Club	League	GP	G	A	Pts	AG	AA	APts	PIM	GP	G	A	Pts	PIM
1941-42	Regina Abbotts	SJHL	3	0	0	0	....	....	....	0	5	0	0	0	0
1942-43	Regina Abbotts	SJHL	13	7	5	12	....	....	....	4	4	0	0	0	4
1943-44	**Chicago Black Hawks**	**NHL**	**10**	**0**	**0**	**0**	**0**	**0**	**0**	**0**	....	....	....	....	....
	Providence Reds	AHL	26	2	4	6	....	....	....	18	....	....	....	....	....
	Philadelphia Falcons	EHL	....	....	....	....	....	....	....	....	9	1	1	2	0
1944-45	Saskatoon Navy	SJHL	9	9	10	19	....	....	....	8	5	*9	2	11	9
1945-46	Saskatoon Quakers	SSHL	23	3	3	6	....	....	....	2	3	1	0	1	0
	Portland Eagles	PCHL	5	1	1	2	....	....	....	0	....	....	....	....	....
1946-47	Saskatoon Quakers	SSHL	37	7	14	21	....	....	....	27	3	0	0	0	0
1947-48	Edmonton Flyers	WCSHL	14	0	3	3	....	....	....	10	....	....	....	....	....
1948-49	Milwaukee Clarks	IHL	21	9	8	17	....	....	....	48	8	5	5	10	19
1949-50	Milwaukee Clarks	EHL	51	20	22	42	....	....	....	62	14	3	1	4	15
1950-51	Atlantic City Seagulls	EHL	54	26	40	66	....	....	....	25	13	1	4	5	2
1951-52	Atlantic City Seagulls	EHL	65	33	38	71	....	....	....	33	....	....	....	....	....
1952-53	Troy Bruins	IHL	59	28	33	61	....	....	....	42	6	2	1	3	2
1953-54	Troy Bruins	IHL	64	29	34	63	....	....	....	23	3	4	1	5	0
1954-55	Troy Bruins	IHL	60	19	28	47	....	....	....	69	11	3	4	7	14
1955-56	Troy–Indianapolis	IHL	53	16	17	33	....	....	....	34	....	....	....	....	....
	NHL Totals		**10**	**0**	**0**	**0**	**0**	**0**	**0**	**0**	....	....	....	....	....

EHL Second All-Star Team (1951)

Traded to **Providence** (AHL) by **Chicago** with Hec Highton and $10,000 for Mike Karakas, January 7, 1944.

• BYERS, GORD
Gord Byers
D – R. 5'10", 182 lbs. b: Eganville, Ont., 3/11/1930.

Season	Club	League	GP	G	A	Pts	AG	AA	APts	PIM	GP	G	A	Pts	PIM
1947-48	Copper Cliff Redmen	NOHA	8	0	2	2	....	....	....	10	3	1	1	2	2
1948-49	St. Catharines Teepees	OHA	29	2	2	4	....	....	....	63	5	0	1	1	11
1949-50	St. Catharines Teepees	OHA	41	5	17	22	....	....	....	102	5	0	1	1	8
	Boston Bruins	**NHL**	**1**	**0**	**1**	**1**	**0**	**1**	**1**	**0**	....	....	....	....	....
	Boston Olympics	EHL	2	0	1	1	....	....	....	6	5	0	2	2	9
1950-51	Tulsa–Kansas City	USHL	61	6	7	13	....	....	....	67	....	....	....	....	....
1951-52	Boston Olympics	EHL	50	0	5	5	....	....	....	100	....	....	....	....	....
1952-53	Troy Uncle Sam Trojans	EHL	56	3	13	16	....	....	....	103	....	....	....	....	....
1953-54	Chatham–Niagara Falls	OHA Sr.	43	1	10	11	....	....	....	133	6	2	1	3	18
1954-55	Sudbury Wolves	NOHA	14	0	1	1	....	....	....	20	....	....	....	....	....
1955-56			DID NOT PLAY												
1956-57	Sudbury Wolves	NOHA	5	1	0	1	....	....	....	10	....	....	....	....	....
	NHL Totals		**1**	**0**	**1**	**1**	**0**	**1**	**1**	**0**	....	....	....	....	....

• CAFFERY, JACK
Jack Caffery
C – R. 6', 165 lbs. b: Kingston, Ont., 6/30/1934. Deceased.

Season	Club	League	GP	G	A	Pts	AG	AA	APts	PIM	GP	G	A	Pts	PIM
1950-51	St. Michael's Majors	OHA	1	0	0	0	....	....	....	0	....	....	....	....	....
1951-52	St. Michael's Majors	OHA	1	2	1	3	....	....	....	0	1	0	0	0	0
1952-53	St. Michael's Majors	OHA	56	37	39	76	....	....	....	38	17	7	10	17	9
1953-54	St. Michael's Majors	OHA	54	25	34	59	....	....	....	40	8	5	8	13	11
1954-55	**Toronto Maple Leafs**	**NHL**	**3**	**0**	**0**	**0**	**0**	**0**	**0**	**0**	....	....	....	....	....
	Pittsburgh Hornets	AHL	55	15	11	26	....	....	....	52	9	2	2	4	4
1955-56	Pittsburgh Hornets	AHL	58	18	22	40	....	....	....	62	4	1	0	1	0
1956-57	**Boston Bruins**	**NHL**	**47**	**2**	**2**	**4**	**3**	**2**	**5**	**20**	**10**	**1**	**0**	**1**	**4**
1957-58	**Boston Bruins**	**NHL**	**7**	**1**	**0**	**1**	**1**	**0**	**1**	**2**	....	....	....	....	....
	Springfield Indians	AHL	46	13	22	35	....	....	....	22	13	2	3	5	10
1958-59			PLAYED PROFESSIONAL BASEBALL												
1959-60			PLAYED PROFESSIONAL BASEBALL												
1960-61	Springfield Indians	AHL	38	6	10	16	....	....	....	10	8	1	3	4	0
1961-62			PLAYED PROFESSIONAL BASEBALL												
1962-63			PLAYED PROFESSIONAL BASEBALL												
1963-64	Greensboro Generals	EHL	38	2	14	16	....	....	....	21	....	....	....	....	....
	NHL Totals		**57**	**3**	**2**	**5**	**4**	**2**	**6**	**22**	**10**	**1**	**0**	**1**	**4**

Claimed by **Boston** from **Toronto** (Pittsburgh - AHL) in Intra-League Draft, June 5, 1956.

• CAHAN, LARRY
— see page 916

• CAHILL, CHUCK
Chuck Cahill
RW – R. 5'10", 180 lbs. b: Summerside, PEI, 1/4/1904. d: 6/5/1954.

Season	Club	League	GP	G	A	Pts	AG	AA	APts	PIM	GP	G	A	Pts	PIM
1924-25	Summerside Crystals	PEI Sr.	STATISTICS NOT AVAILABLE												
1925-26	**Boston Bruins**	**NHL**	**31**	**0**	**1**	**1**	**0**	**11**	**11**	**4**	....	....	....	....	....
1926-27	**Boston Bruins**	**NHL**	**1**	**0**	**0**	**0**	**0**	**0**	**0**	**0**	....	....	....	....	....
	New Haven Eagles	Can-Am	26	10	1	11	....	....	....	35	4	0	0	0	15
1927-28	New Haven Eagles	Can-Am	28	8	1	9	....	....	....	24	....	....	....	....	....
1928-29	Philadelphia Arrows	Can-Am	36	9	1	10	....	....	....	38	....	....	....	....	....
1929-30	Philadelphia Arrows	Can-Am	39	18	13	31	....	....	....	60	2	0	0	0	2
1930-31	Buffalo Bisons	Can-Am	37	6	1	7	....	....	....	30	6	0	2	2	0
	NHL Totals		**32**	**0**	**1**	**1**	**0**	**11**	**11**	**4**	....	....	....	....	....

Signed as a free agent by **Boston**, December 1, 1925. Traded to **New Haven** (Can-Am) by **Boston** for cash, January 31, 1927.

• CAIN, FRANCIS
Francis "Dutch" Cain
D – R. 5'8", 175 lbs. b: Newmarket, Ont., 3/22/1899. Deceased.

Season	Club	League	GP	G	A	Pts	AG	AA	APts	PIM	GP	G	A	Pts	PIM
1920-21	Newmarket Redmen	OHA Sr.	10	2	1	3	....	....	....	....	....	....			
1921-22	Toronto St. Mary's	OHA	STATISTICS NOT AVAILABLE												
1922-23	Toronto Aura Lee	OHA Sr.	10	3	5	8	....	....	....	....	....	....	....	....	
1923-24	Soo Greyhounds	NOHA	4	3	0	3	....	....	....	2	6	1	1	2	6
1924-25	**Montreal Maroons**	**NHL**	**28**	**4**	**0**	**4**	**14**	**0**	**14**	**27**	....	....	....	....	....
1925-26	**Montreal Maroons**	**NHL**	**10**	**0**	**0**	**0**	**0**	**0**	**0**	**0**	....	....	....	....	....
	Toronto St. Pats	**NHL**	**23**	**0**	**0**	**0**	**0**	**0**	**0**	**8**	....	....	....	....	....
1926-27	Hamilton–Niagara Falls	Can-Pro	32	6	4	10	....	....	....	14	....	....	....	....	....
1927-28	Toronto Falcons	IAHL	20	3	2	5	....	....	....	25	2	0	0	0	0
1928-29	Niagara Falls–Buffalo	Can-Pro	41	11	4	15	....	....	....	33	....	....	....	....	....
1929-30	Buffalo Bisons	IAHL	41	3	7	10	....	....	....	22	7	2	*3	5	8
1930-31	Buffalo Bisons	IAHL	42	3	6	9	....	....	....	18	6	1	0	1	0
1931-32	Buffalo Bisons	IAHL	25	1	1	2	....	....	....	13	6	0	0	0	0
1932-33	St. Louis Flyers	AHA	23	1	1	2	....	....	....	16	....	....	....	....	....
	Tulsa Oilers	AHA	2	0	0	0	....	....	....	0	....	....	....	....	....
	NHL Totals		**61**	**4**	**0**	**4**	**14**	**0**	**14**	**35**	....	....	....	....	....

Signed as a free agent by **Montreal Maroons**, October 23, 1924. Claimed on waivers by **Toronto St. Pats** from **Montreal Maroons**, January 7, 1926. Traded to **Toronto** (Can-Pro) by **Hamilton** (Can-Pro) for Ken Randall, January 26, 1927.

			REGULAR SEASON								PLAYOFFS				
Season	**Club**	**League**	**GP**	**G**	**A**	**Pts**	**AG**	**AA**	**APts**	**PIM**	**GP**	**G**	**A**	**Pts**	**PIM**

• CAIN, HERB Herb Cain

LW – L. 5'11", 180 lbs. b: Newmarket, Ont., 12/24/1912. d: 2/15/1982.

Season	Club	League	GP	G	A	Pts	AG	AA	APts	PIM	GP	G	A	Pts	PIM
1931-32	Newmarket Redmen	OHA	7	*7	*2	*9	....	....	....	6	6	*11	0	11	....
1932-33	Hamilton Tigers	OHA Sr.	22	14	5	19	....	....	....	20	5	3	3	6	2
1933-34	**Montreal Maroons**	**NHL**	**30**	**4**	**5**	**9**	**9**	**13**	**22**	**14**	**4**	**0**	**0**	**0**	**0**
	Hamilton Tigers	OHA Sr.	11	4	2	6	....	....	....	17	....	....	....	....	....
1934-35	**Montreal Maroons**	**NHL**	**44**	**20**	**7**	**27**	**43**	**16**	**59**	**13**	**7**	**1**	**0**	**1**	**2**
	Windsor Bulldogs	IAHL	6	1	3	4	....	....	....	6	....	....	....	....	....
1935-36	**Montreal Maroons**	**NHL**	**48**	**5**	**13**	**18**	**12**	**31**	**43**	**16**	**3**	**0**	**1**	**1**	**0**
1936-37	**Montreal Maroons**	**NHL**	**42**	**13**	**17**	**30**	**28**	**40**	**68**	**18**	**5**	**1**	**1**	**2**	**0**
1937-38	**Montreal Maroons**	**NHL**	**47**	**11**	**19**	**30**	**23**	**39**	**62**	**10**	....	....	....	....	....
1938-39	**Montreal Canadiens**	**NHL**	**45**	**13**	**14**	**27**	**27**	**26**	**53**	**26**	**3**	**0**	**0**	**0**	**2**
1939-40	**Boston Bruins**	**NHL**	**48**	**21**	**10**	**31**	**46**	**20**	**66**	**30**	**6**	**1**	**3**	**4**	**2**
1940-41	**Boston Bruins**	**NHL**	**41**	**8**	**10**	**18**	**16**	**18**	**34**	**6**	**11**	**3**	**2**	**5**	**5**
	Hershey Bears	AHL	1	1	0	1	....	....	....	0	....	....	....	....	....
1941-42	**Boston Bruins**	**NHL**	**34**	**8**	**10**	**18**	**14**	**15**	**29**	**2**	**5**	**1**	**0**	**1**	**0**
1942-43	**Boston Bruins**	**NHL**	**45**	**18**	**18**	**36**	**26**	**23**	**49**	**19**	**7**	**4**	**2**	**6**	**0**
1943-44	**Boston Bruins**	**NHL**	**48**	**36**	**46**	***82**	**46**	**56**	**102**	**4**	....	....	....	....	....
1944-45	**Boston Bruins**	**NHL**	**50**	**32**	**13**	**45**	**45**	**21**	**66**	**16**	**7**	**5**	**2**	**7**	**0**
1945-46	**Boston Bruins**	**NHL**	**48**	**17**	**12**	**29**	**26**	**22**	**48**	**4**	**9**	**0**	**2**	**2**	**2**
1946-47	Hershey Bears	AHL	59	36	30	66	....	....	....	19	11	*9	6	15	9
1947-48	Hershey Bears	AHL	49	19	19	38	....	....	....	25	2	0	1	1	0
1948-49	Hershey Bears	AHL	49	25	35	60	....	....	....	10	11	4	6	10	6
1949-50	Hershey Bears	AHL	41	12	14	26	....	....	....	8	....	....	....	....	....
	NHL Totals		**570**	**206**	**194**	**400**	**361**	**340**	**701**	**178**	**67**	**16**	**13**	**29**	**13**

NHL Second All-Star Team (1944) • NHL Scoring Leader (1944)

• **Montreal Canadiens** protested Cain's contract with **Montreal Maroons**, claiming they owned his rights, October 3, 1934. NHL rights transferred to **Montreal Canadiens** by **NHL** after ruling by NHL President Frank Calder, October 3, 1934. NHL rights traded to **Montreal Maroons** by **Montreal Canadiens** with Lionel Conacher for the rights to Nels Crutchfield, October, 1934. Traded to **Montreal Canadiens** by **Montreal Maroons** for cash, September 24, 1938. Traded to **Boston** by **Montreal Canadiens** for Charlie Sands, November 1, 1939.

• CALLADINE, NORM Norm Calladine

C – R. 5'9", 155 lbs. b: Peterborough, Ont., 7/30/1916.

Season	Club	League	GP	G	A	Pts	AG	AA	APts	PIM	GP	G	A	Pts	PIM
1938-39	Baltimore Orioles	EHL	51	33	*41	74	....	....	....	4	....	....	....	....	....
1939-40	Baltimore Orioles	EHL	61	*53	41	94	....	....	....	12	9	5	*7	*12	0
1940-41	Philadelphia Rockets	AHL	52	8	24	32	....	....	....	4	....	....	....	....	....
1941-42	Providence Reds	AHL	56	32	23	55	....	....	....	6	....	....	....	....	....
1942-43	Providence Reds	AHL	51	16	35	51	....	....	....	7	2	0	0	0	0
	Boston Bruins	**NHL**	**3**	**0**	**1**	**1**	**0**	**1**	**1**	**0**	....	....	....	....	....
1943-44	**Boston Bruins**	**NHL**	**49**	**16**	**27**	**43**	**20**	**33**	**53**	**8**	....	....	....	....	....
1944-45	**Boston Bruins**	**NHL**	**11**	**3**	**1**	**4**	**4**	**2**	**6**	**0**	....	....	....	....	....
	Boston Olympics	EHL	2	0	3	3	....	....	....	0	....	....	....	....	....
	Hershey Bears	AHL	14	4	8	12	....	....	....	0	11	3	4	7	0
1945-46	Hershey Bears	AHL	5	0	2	2	....	....	....	0	....	....	....	....	....
	Washington Lions	EHL	22	13	6	19	....	....	....	0	12	9	7	16	0
	NHL Totals		**63**	**19**	**29**	**48**	**24**	**36**	**60**	**8**	....	....	....	....	....

EHL First All-Star Team (1939, 1940)

Traded to **Providence** (AHL) by **NY Rangers** for cash, September 11, 1941. Traded to **Boston** by **Providence** (AHL) for cash, March 8, 1943.

• CALLIGHEN, PATSY Patsy (Francis Charles) Callighen

D – L. 5'6", 175 lbs. b: Toronto, Ont., 2/13/1906.

Season	Club	League	GP	G	A	Pts	AG	AA	APts	PIM	GP	G	A	Pts	PIM
1922-23	Toronto St. Andrews	OHA	7	5	*5	10	....	....	....	....	....	....	....	....	....
1923-24	Toronto St. Mary's	OHA	8	2	4	6	....	....	....	....	....	....	....	....	....
	Toronto St. Mary's	OHA Sr.	2	2	0	2	....	....	....	....	....	....	....	....	....
1924-25	Owen Sound Greys	OHA	17	6	7	13	....	....	....	....	9	4	4	8	*23
1925-26	Owen Sound Greys	OHA	11	9	4	13	....	....	....	....	8	4	4	8	11
1926-27	Springfield Indians	Can-Am	31	5	2	7	....	....	....	*83	6	0	0	0	*27
1927-28	**New York Rangers**	**NHL**	**36**	**0**	**0**	**0**	**0**	**0**	**0**	**32**	**9**	**0**	**0**	**0**	**0**
	Springfield Indians	Can-Am	7	1	1	2	....	....	....	20	....	....	....	....	....
1928-29	Springfield Indians	Can-Am	39	2	2	4	....	....	....	*124	....	....	....	....	....
1929-30	Springfield Indians	Can-Am	37	10	6	16	....	....	....	63	....	....	....	....	....
1930-31	Springfield Indians	Can-Am	38	14	8	22	....	....	....	108	7	3	1	4	16
1931-32	Springfield Indians	Can-Am	40	1	5	6	....	....	....	74	....	....	....	....	....
1932-33	Quebec Castors	Can-Am	43	3	4	7	....	....	....	52	....	....	....	....	....
1933-34	Cleveland Indians	IAHL	43	5	12	17	....	....	....	92	....	....	....	....	....
1934-35	Cleveland Falcons	IAHL	44	3	4	7	....	....	....	67	2	1	0	1	2
1935-36	Cleveland–London	IAHL	46	2	6	8	....	....	....	70	2	0	1	1	2
	NHL Totals		**36**	**0**	**0**	**0**	**0**	**0**	**0**	**32**	**9**	**0**	**0**	**0**	**0**

Traded to **London** (IAHL) by **Cleveland** (IAHL) for Alvin Groh, December, 1935.

• CAMERON, BILLY Billy Cameron

RW – L. 5'11", 160 lbs. b: Timmins, Ont., 12/5/1896. Deceased.

Season	Club	League	GP	G	A	Pts	AG	AA	APts	PIM	GP	G	A	Pts	PIM
1914-15	Cleveland Hockey Club	USAHA	STATISTICS NOT AVAILABLE												
	Buckingham Seniors	City Sr.	7	3	0	3	....	....	....	....	....	....	....	....	....
1915-16	Buckingham Seniors	City Sr.	STATISTICS NOT AVAILABLE												
1916-17	Pittsburgh AA	USAHA	40	12	0	12	....	....	....	....	....	....	....	....	....
1917-18	Ottawa Ordinance Corps	City Sr.	STATISTICS NOT AVAILABLE												
1918-19			MILITARY SERVICE												
1919-20			MILITARY SERVICE												
1920-21	Quebec Royal Rifles	City Sr.	7	5	0	5	....	....	....	....	4	1	0	1	....
1921-22	Timmins Seniors	NOHA	STATISTICS NOT AVAILABLE												
1922-23	Porcupine Gold Miners	NOHA	....	....	....	....	....	....	....	....	1	1	0	1	....
1923-24	**Montreal Canadiens**	**NHL**	**18**	**0**	**0**	**0**	**0**	**0**	**0**	**2**	**6**	**0**	**0**	**0**	**0**
1924-25			DID NOT PLAY												
1925-26	**New York Americans**	**NHL**	**21**	**0**	**0**	**0**	**0**	**0**	**0**	**0**	....	....	....	....	....
1926-27	St. Paul Saints	AHA	31	3	1	4	....	....	....	22	....	....	....	....	....
1927-28	Kitchener Millionaires	Can-Pro	25	1	0	1	....	....	....	34	4	0	0	0	18
1928-29	Toronto Millionaires	Can-Pro	32	3	1	4	....	....	....	39	2	0	0	0	2
1929-30	Hamilton Tigers	IAHL	1	0	0	0	....	....	....	0	....	....	....	....	....
	Buffalo Bisons	IAHL	1	0	0	0	....	....	....	0	....	....	....	....	....
	NHL Totals		**39**	**0**	**0**	**0**	**0**	**0**	**0**	**2**	**6**	**0**	**0**	**0**	**0**

Signed as a free agent by **Montreal Canadiens**, December 21, 1923. Signed as a free agent by **NY Americans**, November 1, 1925.

• CAMERON, CRAIG — *see page 918*

			REGULAR SEASON								PLAYOFFS				
Season	**Club**	**League**	**GP**	**G**	**A**	**Pts**	**AG**	**AA**	**APts**	**PIM**	**GP**	**G**	**A**	**Pts**	**PIM**

• CAMERON, HARRY Harry "Cammie" Cameron HHOF

D – R. 5'10", 155 lbs. b: Pembroke, Ont., 2/6/1890. d: 10/20/1953.

Season	Club	League	GP	G	A	Pts	AG	AA	APts	PIM	GP	G	A	Pts	PIM
1910-11	Pembroke Debaters	Ott-Sr.	6	8	1	9	....	....	....	....	2	4	0	4	....
1911-12	Port Arthur Ports	NOHA	12	6	0	6	....	....	....	....	2	2	0	2	....
1912-13	Toronto Blueshirts	NHA	20	9	0	9	....	....	....	20	....	....	....	....	....
1913-14	Toronto Blueshirts	NHA	19	15	4	19	....	....	....	22	5	1	2	3	6
1914-15	Toronto Blueshirts	NHA	17	12	8	20	....	....	....	43	....	....	....	....	....
1915-16	Toronto Blueshirts	NHA	24	8	3	11	....	....	....	70	....	....	....	....	....
1916-17	Toronto 228th Battalion	NHA	14	7	4	11	....	....	....	32	....	....	....	....	....
	Montreal Wanderers	NHA	6	2	1	3	....	....	....	9	....	....	....	....	....
1917-18	**Toronto Arenas**	**NHL**	**21**	**17**	**10**	**27**	**43**	**0**	**43**	**28**	**7**	**4**	**3**	**7**	**12**
1918-19	**Toronto Arenas**	**NHL**	**7**	**6**	**3**	**9**	**21**	**28**	**49**	**24**	....	....	....	....	....
	Ottawa Senators	**NHL**	**7**	**5**	**1**	**6**	**17**	**9**	**26**	**23**	**5**	**6**	**0**	**6**	**6**
1919-20	**Toronto St. Pats**	**NHL**	**7**	**3**	**0**	**3**	**7**	**0**	**7**	**6**	....	....	....	....	....
	Montreal Canadiens	**NHL**	**16**	**12**	**5**	**17**	**27**	**34**	**61**	**36**	....	....	....	....	....
1920-21	**Toronto St. Patricks**	**NHL**	**24**	**18**	**9**	**27**	**47**	**81**	**128**	**35**	**2**	**0**	**0**	**0**	**2**
1921-22	**Toronto St. Patricks**	**NHL**	**24**	**18**	**17**	**35**	**50**	**112**	**162**	**22**	**6**	**0**	**4**	**4**	**19**
1922-23	**Toronto St. Patricks**	**NHL**	**22**	**9**	**6**	**15**	**30**	**54**	**84**	**21**	....	....	....	....	....
1923-24	Saskatoon Crescents	WCHL	29	10	10	20	....	....	....	16	....	....	....	....	....
1924-25	Saskatoon Crescents	WCHL	28	13	7	20	....	....	....	21	2	1	0	1	0
1925-26	Saskatoon Crescents	WHL	30	9	3	12	....	....	....	12	2	0	0	0	0
1926-27	Saskatoon Shieks	PHL	31	26	19	45	....	....	....	20	4	1	0	1	4
1927-28	Minneapolis Millers	AHA	19	2	3	5	....	....	....	32	....	....	....	....	....
1928-29	St. Louis Flyers	AHA	34	14	3	17	....	....	....	30	....	....	....	....	....
1929-30	St. Louis Flyers	AHA	46	14	6	20	....	....	....	34	....	....	....	....	....
1930-31	St. Louis Flyers	AHA	37	4	3	7	....	....	....	30	....	....	....	....	....
1931-32			DID NOT PLAY												
1932-33	Saskatoon Crescents	NWHL	9	0	0	0	....	....	....	4	....	....	....	....	....
	NHL Totals		**128**	**88**	**51**	**139**	**242**	**318**	**560**	**195**	**20**	**10**	**7**	**17**	**39**
	Other Major League Totals		187	85	40	125	....	....	....	245	9	2	2	4	6

Rights not retained by **Montreal Wanderers** after NHA folded, November 26, 1917. Signed as a free agent by **Toronto Arenas**, December 5, 1917. Loaned to **Ottawa** by **Toronto Arenas** to complete earlier transaction that sent Rusty Crawford to Toronto (December 14, 1919), January 19, 1919. Returned to **Toronto Arenas** by **Ottawa**, November 25, 1919. Traded to **Montreal Canadiens** by **Toronto St. Pats** for Goldie Prodgers, January 14, 1920. Traded to **Toronto St. Pats** by **Montreal Canadiens** for cash, November 27, 1921. Claimed on waivers by **Saskatoon** (WCHL) from **Toronto St. Pats**, November 9, 1923.

• CAMERON, SCOTTY Scotty (Angus) Cameron

C – L. 6'2", 175 lbs. b: Prince Albert, Sask., 11/5/1921. d: 4/12/1993.

Season	Club	League	GP	G	A	Pts	AG	AA	APts	PIM	GP	G	A	Pts	PIM
1939-40	Regina Abbots	SJHL	11	6	5	11	....	....	....	16	2	*4	1	5	4
1940-41	Regina Rangers	SSHL	32	20	20	40	....	....	....	9	8	3	5	8	8
1941-42	New York Rovers	EHL	6	0	0	0	....	....	....	0	....	....	....	....	....
1942-43	**New York Rangers**	**NHL**	**35**	**8**	**11**	**19**	**11**	**14**	**25**	**0**	....	....	....	....	....
	Montreal RCAF	QSHL	....	....	....	....	....	....	....	....	2	0	2	2	0
1943-44	Montreal Canada Car	City Sr.	5	3	1	4	....	....	....	0	....	....	....	....	....
	Montreal RCAF	QSHL	4	0	0	0	....	....	....	2	....	....	....	....	....
	Montreal RCAF	City Sr.	3	1	3	4	....	....	....	2	4	4	*9	13	4
1944-45	Montreal RCAF	City Sr.	3	1	3	4	....	....	....	2	4	4	*9	13	4
1945-46			MILITARY SERVICE												
1946-47	New Haven Ramblers	AHL	64	11	18	29	....	....	....	16	3	0	1	1	0
1947-48	New Haven Ramblers	AHL	64	13	23	36	....	....	....	6	3	0	1	1	0
1948-49	St. Paul Saints	USHL	57	14	30	44	....	....	....	6	7	1	6	7	0
1949-50	St. Paul Saints	USHL	70	7	31	38	....	....	....	8	3	0	3	3	2
1950-51	Yorkton Legionaires	SSHL	19	15	13	28	....	....	....	6	10	4	4	8	8
	Regina Caps	WCSHL	9	1	3	4	....	....	....	2	....	....	....	....	....
	NHL Totals		**35**	**8**	**11**	**19**	**11**	**14**	**25**	**0**	....	....	....	....	....

Claimed by **NY Rangers** from **Philadelphia** (AHA) in Inter-League Draft, June 27, 1941.

• CAMPBELL, DAVE Dave Campbell

D – L. 6', 200 lbs. b: Lachute, Que., 4/27/1896. Deceased.

Season	Club	League	GP	G	A	Pts	AG	AA	APts	PIM	GP	G	A	Pts	PIM
1915-16	Laval University	Mtl-Sr.	9	2	0	2	....	....	....	20	1	0	0	0	0
1916-17			MILITARY SERVICE												
1917-18			MILITARY SERVICE												
1918-19	Montreal Nationale	City Sr.	9	4	8	12	....	....	....	15	....	....	....	....	....
1919-20	Laval University	Mtl-Sr.	10	2	3	5	....	....	....	18	....	....	....	....	....
1920-21	**Montreal Canadiens**	**NHL**	**2**	**0**	**0**	**0**	**0**	**0**	**0**	**0**	....	....	....	....	....
1921-22			REINSTATED AS AN AMATEUR												
1922-23	Montreal Nationale	City Sr.	5	0	0	0	....	....	....	0	....	....	....	....	....
1923-24	Montreal Nationale	City Sr.	10	4	0	4	....	....	....	....	....	....	....	....	....
1924-25	Montreal Nationale	QAHA	14	2	0	2	....	....	....	....	....	....	....	....	....
1925-26	Montreal Nationale	QAHA	9	6	0	6	....	....	....	10	....	....	....	....	....
1926-27	Montreal Victorias	QAHA	4	2	0	2	....	....	....	16	....	....	....	....	....
1927-28	Philadelphia Arrows	Can-Am	19	0	0	0	....	....	....	30	....	....	....	....	....
	Montreal Electric	City Sr.	STATISTICS NOT AVAILABLE												
1928-29	Montreal AAA	City Sr.	DID NOT PLAY – COACHING												
	NHL Totals		**2**	**0**	**0**	**0**	**0**	**0**	**0**	**0**	....	....	....	....	....

Signed as a free agent by **Montreal Canadiens**, February 26, 1921. • Amateur status revoked by CAHA, February 21, 1923.

• CAMPBELL, DON Don Campbell

LW – L. 5'10", 175 lbs. b: Drumheller, Alta., 7/12/1925.

Season	Club	League	GP	G	A	Pts	AG	AA	APts	PIM	GP	G	A	Pts	PIM
1941-42	Portage Terriers	MJHL	14	2	0	2	....	....	....	2	4	0	1	1	0
1942-43	Portage Terriers	MJHL	11	2	2	4	....	....	....	14	....	....	....	....	....
1943-44	Portage Terriers	MJHL	1	0	0	0	....	....	....	0	2	0	0	0	2
	Chicago Black Hawks	**NHL**	**17**	**1**	**3**	**4**	**1**	**4**	**5**	**8**	....	....	....	....	....
1944-45			MILITARY SERVICE												
1945-46	Vancouver–Seattle	PCHL	49	21	27	48	....	....	....	31	3	0	1	1	0
1946-47	Seattle Ironmen	PCHL	37	7	10	17	....	....	....	16	10	2	2	4	6
1947-48	Portland Eagles	PCHL	5	0	2	2	....	....	....	4	....	....	....	....	....
1948-49	Portland Penguins	PCHL	17	0	1	1	....	....	....	15	....	....	....	....	....
1949-50	Kamloops Elks	OSHL	45	24	28	52	....	....	....	61	7	2	4	6	4
1950-51	Calgary Stampeders	WCSHL	7	1	0	1	....	....	....	10	....	....	....	....	....
	Kamloops Elks	OSHL	41	24	27	51	....	....	....	24	6	6	4	10	6
1951-52	Kamloops Elks	OSHL	27	11	12	33	....	....	....	24	....	....	....	....	....
1952-53			DID NOT PLAY												
1953-54	Kimberley Dynamiters	WIHL	38	18	20	38	....	....	....	41	9	3	3	6	12
	NHL Totals		**17**	**1**	**3**	**4**	**1**	**4**	**5**	**8**	....	....	....	....	....

• CAMPBELL, EARL Earl "Spiff" Campbell

D – L. 5'11", 166 lbs. b: Buckingham, Que., 7/23/1900. d: 2/11/1953.

Season	Club	League	GP	G	A	Pts	AG	AA	APts	PIM	GP	G	A	Pts	PIM
			REGULAR SEASON								PLAYOFFS				
1918-19	Ottawa New Edinburghs	City Sr.	3	0	0	0	....	....	....	0	....	....	....	....	....
	Ottawa Aberdeens	City Sr.	5	0	1	1	....	....	....	3	....	....	....	....	....
1919-20	Hull Volants	Ott-Sr.	8	8	0	8	....	....	....	....	....	....	....	....	....
1920-21	Hull Volants	Ott-Sr.	STATISTICS NOT AVAILABLE												
1921-22	Saskatoon Quakers	WCHL	20	7	4	11	....	....	....	19	....	....	....	....	....
1922-23	Saskatoon Quakers	WCHL	10	2	2	4	....	....	....	8	....	....	....	....	....
	Edmonton Eskimos	WCHL	14	3	2	5	....	....	....	6	4	0	0	0	0
1923-24	Edmonton Eskimos	WCHL	5	0	2	2	....	....	....	4	....	....	....	....	....
	Ottawa Senators	**NHL**	**18**	**4**	**1**	**5**	**16**	**17**	**33**	**6**	**2**	**0**	**0**	**0**	**0**
1924-25	**Ottawa Senators**	**NHL**	**30**	**0**	**0**	**0**	**0**	**0**	**0**	**0**	....	....	....	....	....
1925-26	**New York Americans**	**NHL**	**29**	**1**	**0**	**1**	**3**	**0**	**3**	**6**	....	....	....	....	....
1926-27	Hamilton Tigers	Can-Pro	26	4	0	4	....	....	....	22	2	1	0	1	0
1927-28	Stratford–Hamilton	Can-Pro	16	1	0	1	....	....	....	4	....	....	....	....	....
1928-29	Kitchener Dutchmen	Can-Pro	29	4	2	6	....	....	....	37	....	....	....	....	....
	NHL Totals		**77**	**5**	**1**	**6**	**19**	**17**	**36**	**12**	**2**	**0**	**0**	**0**	**0**
	Other Major League Totals		49	12	10	22	....	....	....	37	4	0	0	0	0

WCHL All-Star Team (1923)

Signed as a free agent by **Saskatoon** (WCHL), November 28, 1921. Traded to **Edmonton** (WCHL) by **Saskatoon** (WCHL) for cash, January 23, 1923. Loaned to **Ottawa** by **Edmonton** (WCHL) for 1923-24 season, December 23, 1923. Traded to **Ottawa** by **Edmonton** (WCHL) for cash, April, 1924. Signed as a free agent by **NY Americans**, September 18, 1925.

• CAMPEAU, TOD Tod (Jean-Guy) Campeau

C – L. 5'11", 170 lbs. b: St. Jerome, Que., 6/4/1923.

Season	Club	League	GP	G	A	Pts	AG	AA	APts	PIM	GP	G	A	Pts	PIM
1940-41	Concordia College	Mtl-Jr.	1	0	0	0	....	....	....	0	....	....	....	....	....
1941-42	Concordia College	Mtl-Jr.	STATISTICS NOT AVAILABLE												
1942-43	Montreal Jr. Canadiens	Mtl-Jr.	14	11	*21	32	....	....	....	0	7	6	5	11	17
	Montreal Sr. Canadiens	Mtl-Sr.	1	0	0	0	....	....	....	0	....	....	....	....	....
1943-44	**Montreal Canadiens**	**NHL**	**2**	**0**	**0**	**0**	**0**	**0**	**0**	**0**	....	....	....	....	....
	Montreal Vickers	City Sr.	12	*13	13	26	....	....	....	7	....	....	....	....	....
	Montreal Royals	QSHL	20	18	12	30	....	....	....	8	7	3	5	8	2
1944-45	Pittsburgh Hornets	AHL	6	1	2	3	....	....	....	2	....	....	....	....	....
	Valleyfield Braves	IHL	22	16	23	39	....	....	....	10	14	8	9	17	13
1945-46	Valleyfield Braves	QSHL	40	28	*50	*78	....	....	....	45	....	....	....	....	....
1946-47	Montreal Royals	QSHL	39	22	31	53	....	....	....	44	9	3	9	12	12
1947-48	**Montreal Canadiens**	**NHL**	**14**	**2**	**2**	**4**	**3**	**3**	**6**	**4**	....	....	....	....	....
	Buffalo Bisons	AHL	31	10	9	19	....	....	....	6	8	0	1	1	6
1948-49	**Montreal Canadiens**	**NHL**	**26**	**3**	**7**	**10**	**5**	**11**	**16**	**12**	**1**	**0**	**0**	**0**	**0**
	Dallas Texans	USHL	30	16	28	44	....	....	....	13	....	....	....	....	....
1949-50	Cincinnati Mohawks	AHL	68	22	41	63	....	....	....	53	....	....	....	....	....
1950-51	Cincinnati Mohawks	AHL	68	13	41	54	....	....	....	36	....	....	....	....	....
1951-52	Sherbrooke Saints	QSHL	51	20	29	49	....	....	....	32	11	2	9	11	14
1952-53	Sherbrooke Saints	QSHL	60	19	49	68	....	....	....	48	7	1	4	5	6
1953-54	Sherbrooke Saints	QHL	13	1	1	2	....	....	....	0	....	....	....	....	....
	Providence Reds	AHL	44	10	26	36	....	....	....	16	....	....	....	....	....
1954-55	Ottawa Senators	QHL	12	3	4	7	....	....	....	15	....	....	....	....	....
	Moncton Flyers	MSHL	29	12	34	46	....	....	....	35	20	10	10	34	9
1955-56	Chicoutimi Sagueneens	QHL	57	5	13	18	....	....	....	36	2	0	0	0	2
1956-57	Dalhousie Rangers	NNBHL	....	38	45	83	....	....	....	75	....	....	....	....	....
	NHL Totals		**42**	**5**	**9**	**14**	**8**	**14**	**22**	**16**	**1**	**0**	**0**	**0**	**0**

• CARBOL, LEO Leo Carbol

D – R. 5'11", 170 lbs. b: Ottawa, Ont., 6/5/1910.

Season	Club	League	GP	G	A	Pts	AG	AA	APts	PIM	GP	G	A	Pts	PIM
1929-30	Seattle Eskimos	PCHL	1	0	0	0	....	....	....	0	....	....	....	....	....
1930-31	Minneapolis Millers	AHA	44	5	5	10	....	....	....	*110	....	....	....	....	....
1931-32	Buffalo Majors	AHA	19	2	0	2	....	....	....	30	....	....	....	....	....
	St. Louis Flyers	AHA	7	0	1	1	....	....	....	4	....	....	....	....	....
1932-33	Detroit Olympics	IAHL	23	0	3	3	....	....	....	40	....	....	....	....	....
	St. Louis Flyers	AHA	19	2	2	4	....	....	....	40	4	0	0	0	8
1933-34	St. Louis Flyers	AHA	48	3	2	5	....	....	....	65	7	0	0	0	10
1934-35	St. Louis Flyers	AHA	48	6	7	13	....	....	....	69	6	0	1	1	*32
1935-36	St. Louis Flyers	AHA	46	2	5	7	....	....	....	63	8	1	0	1	8
1936-37	St. Louis Flyers	AHA	47	2	7	9	....	....	....	82	6	0	1	1	*16
1937-38	St. Louis Flyers	AHA	48	6	15	21	....	....	....	62	7	0	1	1	10
1938-39	St. Louis Flyers	AHA	48	3	15	18	....	....	....	67	7	1	2	3	10
1939-40	St. Louis Flyers	AHA	48	6	17	23	....	....	....	53	5	1	1	2	2
1940-41	St. Louis Flyers	AHA	43	3	19	22	....	....	....	58	9	1	*6	7	6
1941-42	St. Louis Flyers	AHA	48	5	11	16	....	....	....	69	2	0	0	0	10
1942-43	**Chicago Black Hawks**	**NHL**	**6**	**0**	**1**	**1**	**0**	**1**	**1**	**4**	....	....	....	....	....
1943-44			MILITARY SERVICE												
1944-45			MILITARY SERVICE												
1945-46	St. Louis Flyers	AHL	1	0	0	0	....	....	....	0	....	....	....	....	....
	NHL Totals		**6**	**0**	**1**	**1**	**0**	**1**	**1**	**4**	....	....	....	....	....

AHA First All-Star Team (1935, 1939, 1941, 1942) • AHA Second All-Star Team (1938)

NHL rights transferred to **Detroit** from **Chicago Shamrocks** (AHA) after AHA club owners purchased Detroit (IAHL and NHL) franchises, September 2, 1932. Traded to **Chicago** by **St. Louis** (AHA) for cash, October 9, 1942.

• CAREY, GEORGE George Carey

RW – R. 5'6", 140 lbs. b: Scotland. Deceased.

Season	Club	League	GP	G	A	Pts	AG	AA	APts	PIM	GP	G	A	Pts	PIM
			REGULAR SEASON								PLAYOFFS				
1911-12	Quebec Bulldogs	NHA	1	0	0	0	....	....	....	0	....	....	....	....	....
1912-13	Shawinigan Seniors	City Sr.	STATISTICS NOT AVAILABLE												
1913-14	Quebec St. Pats	City Sr.	7	7	0	7	....	....	....	....	....	....	....	....	....
1914-15	Quebec YMCA	City Sr.	9	16	0	16	....	....	....	....	....	....	....	....	....
1915-16	Quebec Sons of Ireland	City Sr.	8	17	0	17	....	....	....	....	2	*6	0	*6	....
1916-17	Quebec Bulldogs	NHA	17	8	9	17	....	....	....	11	....	....	....	....	....
1917-18	**Montreal Wanderers**	**NHL**	DID NOT PLAY – SUSPENDED												
1918-19			MILITARY SERVICE												
1919-20	**Quebec Bulldogs**	**NHL**	**20**	**11**	**9**	**20**	**25**	**62**	**87**	**6**	....	....	....	....	....
1920-21	**Hamilton Tigers**	**NHL**	**20**	**6**	**1**	**7**	**15**	**9**	**24**	**8**	....	....	....	....	....
1921-22	**Hamilton Tigers**	**NHL**	**23**	**3**	**2**	**5**	**8**	**12**	**20**	**6**	....	....	....	....	....
1922-23	**Hamilton Tigers**	**NHL**	**5**	**1**	**0**	**1**	**3**	**0**	**3**	**0**	....	....	....	....	....
	Calgary Tigers	WCHL	16	3	4	7	....	....	....	0	....	....	....	....	....
1923-24	**Toronto St. Pats**	**NHL**	**4**	**0**	**0**	**0**	**0**	**0**	**0**	**0**	....	....	....	....	....
	NHL Totals		**72**	**21**	**12**	**33**	**51**	**83**	**134**	**20**	....	....	....	....	....
	Other Major League Totals		34	11	13	24	....	....	....	11	....	....	....	....	....

Transferred to **Montreal Wanderers** from **Quebec** in Dispersal Draft, November 26, 1917. • Suspended by **Montreal Wanderers** for refusing to report to NHL club, November 29, 1917. Transferred to **Quebec** by **NHL** after Quebec franchise returned to NHL, November 25, 1919. Transferred to **Hamilton** after **Quebec** franchise relocated, November 2, 1920. Loaned to **Calgary** (WCHL) by **Hamilton**, January 16, 1923. Traded to **Toronto St. Pats** by **Hamilton** with Amos Arbour and Bert Corbeau for Ken Randall and cash, December 14, 1923.

• CARLETON, WAYNE — *see page 921*

• CARPENTER, EDDIE Eddie Carpenter

D – R. 6', 170 lbs. b: Hartford, MI, 6/15/1890. d: 4/30/1963.

Season	Club	League	GP	G	A	Pts	AG	AA	APts	PIM	GP	G	A	Pts	PIM
1909-10	Port Arthur Lake City	NOHA	STATISTICS NOT AVAILABLE												
1910-11	Port Arthur Lake City	NOHL	....	....	....	....	....	....	....	....	3	1	0	1	9
1911-12	Port Arthur Lake City	NOHA	STATISTICS NOT AVAILABLE												
1912-13	Moncton Victorias	MPHL	14	6	0	6	....	....	....	17	....	....	....	....	....
1913-14	New Glascow Black Foxes	MPHL	19	8	0	8	....	....	....	37	2	0	0	0	7
1914-15	Toronto Blue Shirts	NHA	19	1	0	1	....	....	....	63	....	....	....	....	....
1915-16	Seattle Metropolitans	PCHA	18	6	4	10	....	....	....	17	....	....	....	....	....
1916-17	Seattle Metropolitans	PCHA	24	5	3	8	....	....	....	19	4	0	0	0	3
1917-18			MILITARY SERVICE												
1918-19			MILITARY SERVICE												
1919-20	**Quebec Bulldogs**	**NHL**	**24**	**8**	**4**	**12**	**18**	**27**	**45**	**24**	....	....	....	....	....
1920-21	**Hamilton Tigers**	**NHL**	**21**	**2**	**1**	**3**	**5**	**9**	**14**	**7**	....	....	....	....	....
	NHL Totals		**45**	**10**	**5**	**15**	**23**	**36**	**59**	**31**	....	....	....	....	....
	Other Major League Totals		94	26	7	33	....	....	....	153	6	0	0	0	10

Signed as a free agent by **Montreal Canadiens**, December 15, 1919. Traded to **Quebec** by **Montreal Canadiens** for Goldie Prodgers, December 22, 1919. Transferred to **Hamilton** after **Quebec** franchise relocated, November 2, 1920.

• CARR, AL Al "Red" Carr

LW – L. 5'8", 178 lbs. b. Winnipeg, Man., 12/20/1916.

Season	Club	League	GP	G	A	Pts	AG	AA	APts	PIM	GP	G	A	Pts	PIM
1931-32	Winnipeg Falcons	MHL Jr.	4	0	0	0	....	....	....	12	1	0	0	0	0
1932-33	Winnipeg Falcons	MJHL	10	0	2	2	....	....	....	20	....	....	....	....	....
1933-34	Winnipeg Falcons	MJHL	STATISTICS NOT AVAILABLE												
1934-35	Nelson Maple Leafs	Kootenay	DID NOT PLAY – SUSPENDED												
1935-36	Trail Smoke Eaters	Kootenay	14	5	1	6	....	....	....	11	8	*7	2	9	4
1936-37	Nelson Maple Leafs	Kootenay	14	6	5	11	....	....	....	*20	3	1	0	1	*12
1937-38	Nelson Maple Leafs	Kootenay	24	19	16	35	....	....	....	43	2	0	1	1	2
1938-39	Nelson Maple Leafs	Kootenay	10	12	6	18	....	....	....	43	3	3	0	3	8
1939-40	Nelson Maple Leafs	Kootenay	23	12	7	19	....	....	....	29	7	0	3	3	*14
1940-41	Braborne Barons	Inter-Sr.	STATISTICS NOT AVAILABLE												
1941-42	Nanaimo Clippers	Inter-Sr.	27	20	16	36	....	....	....	*54	7	6	2	8	6
1942-43	Nanaimo Clippers	Inter-Sr.	20	12	8	20	....	....	....	9	3	0	1	1	2
1943-44	**Toronto Maple Leafs**	**NHL**	**5**	**0**	**1**	**1**	**0**	**1**	**1**	**2**	....	....	....	....	....
	Providence Reds	AHL	2	0	0	0	....	....	....	0	....	....	....	....	....
	Toronto Staffords	OHA Sr.	....	2	0	2	....	....	....	0	....	....	....	....	....
1944-45	Providence Reds	AHL	2	0	0	0	....	....	....	0	....	....	....	....	....
	Toronto Staffords	OHA Sr.	4	3	7	10	....	....	....	0	....	....	....	....	....
1945-46	Portland Eagles	PCHL	54	43	49	92	....	....	....	91	8	7	3	*10	15
1946-47	Portland–Westminster	PCHL	58	19	42	61	....	....	....	34	4	1	2	3	0
1947-48	Westminster–Tacoma	PCHL	33	7	14	21	....	....	....	22	....	....	....	....	....
1948-49	Milwaukee Clarks	IHL	32	19	27	46	....	....	....	39	4	0	1	1	0
1949-50	Nanaimo Clippers	OSHL	31	14	31	45	....	....	....	33	8	2	2	4	6
1950-51	Nanaimo Clippers	OSHL	45	18	41	59	....	....	....	42	9	3	*9	12	8
1951-52	Nanaimo Clippers	OSHL	41	15	17	32	....	....	....	33	6	2	3	5	2
	NHL Totals		**5**	**0**	**1**	**1**	**0**	**1**	**1**	**2**	....	....	....	....	....

• CARR, LORNE   Lorne Carr

RW – R. 5'8", 161 lbs.   b: Stoughton, Sask., 7/2/1910.

			REGULAR SEASON								PLAYOFFS				
Season	Club	League	GP	G	A	Pts	AG	AA	APts	PIM	GP	G	A	Pts	PIM
1929-30	Calgary Canadians	City Jr.	STATISTICS NOT AVAILABLE												
1930-31	Vancouver Lions	PCHL	32	5	4	9	....	....	....	2	4	0	0	0	0
1931-32	Buffalo Bisons	IAHL	40	5	9	14	....	....	....	10	6	2	0	2	4
1932-33	Buffalo Bisons	IAHL	44	22	18	40	....	....	....	13	6	2	1	3	4
1933-34	Syracuse Stars	IAHL	18	8	4	12	....	....	....	6	6	0	1	1	2
	New York Rangers	**NHL**	14	0	0	0	0	0	0	0	....	....	....	....	....
	Philadelphia Arrows	Can-Am	9	4	2	6	....	....	....	0	....	....	....	....	....
1934-35	**New York Americans**	**NHL**	48	17	14	31	36	31	67	14	....	....	....	....	....
1935-36	**New York Americans**	**NHL**	44	8	10	18	20	24	44	4	5	1	1	2	0
1936-37	**New York Americans**	**NHL**	48	18	16	34	39	38	77	22	....	....	....	....	....
1937-38	**New York Americans**	**NHL**	48	16	7	23	34	14	48	12	6	3	1	4	2
1938-39	**New York Americans**	**NHL**	46	19	18	37	40	34	74	16	2	0	0	0	0
1939-40	**New York Americans**	**NHL**	48	8	17	25	17	34	51	17	3	0	0	0	0
1940-41	**New York Americans**	**NHL**	48	13	19	32	26	35	61	10	....	....	....	....	....
1941-42	**Toronto Maple Leafs**	**NHL**	47	16	17	33	27	26	53	4	13	3	2	5	6
1942-43	**Toronto Maple Leafs**	**NHL**	50	27	33	60	39	42	81	15	6	1	2	3	0
1943-44	**Toronto Maple Leafs**	**NHL**	50	36	38	74	46	46	92	9	5	0	1	1	0
1944-45	**Toronto Maple Leafs**	**NHL**	47	21	25	46	29	41	70	7	13	2	2	4	5
1945-46	**Toronto Maple Leafs**	**NHL**	42	5	8	13	8	15	23	2	....	....	....	....	....
	NHL Totals		580	204	222	426	361	380	741	132	53	10	9	19	13

NHL First All-Star Team (1943, 1944)

Traded to **NY Rangers** by **Buffalo** (IAHL), April 8, 1933. Traded to **Syracuse** (IAHL) by **NY Rangers**, January 30, 1934. Traded to **NY Americans** by **Syracuse** (IAHL) for Ron Martin, January 30, 1934. Traded to **Toronto** by **Brooklyn** for the loan of Red Heron, Gus Marker and Nick Knott, October 30, 1941.

• CARRIGAN, GENE   Gene Carrigan

C – L. 6'1", 200 lbs.   b: Edmonton, Alta., 7/5/1907.   d: 3/15/1944.

Season	Club	League	GP	G	A	Pts	AG	AA	APts	PIM	GP	G	A	Pts	PIM
1926-27	Edmonton Eskimos	PCHL	19	0	0	0	....	....	....	4	....	....	....	....	....
1927-28	Hollywood Millionaires	Cal-Pro	STATISTICS NOT AVAILABLE												
1928-29	Springfield Indians	Can-Am	39	10	1	11	....	....	....	23	....	....	....	....	....
	Victoria–Portland	PCHL	12	0	0	0	....	....	....	0	....	....	....	....	....
1929-30	Springfield Indians	Can-Am	38	*28	24	52	....	....	....	22	....	....	....	....	....
1930-31	**New York Rangers**	**NHL**	33	2	0	2	5	0	5	13	....	....	....	....	....
	Springfield Indians	Can-Am	13	5	10	15	....	....	....	10	7	4	4	8	2
1931-32	London Tecumsehs	IAHL	48	19	9	28	....	....	....	27	6	0	0	0	5
1932-33	London Tecumsehs	IAHL	41	19	14	33	....	....	....	23	6	2	3	5	2
1933-34	Detroit Olympics	IAHL	43	17	18	35	....	....	....	19	4	2	3	5	0
	Detroit Red Wings	**NHL**	....	....	....	....	....	....	....	....	4	0	0	0	0
1934-35	**St. Louis Eagles**	**NHL**	4	0	1	1	0	2	2	0	....	....	....	....	....
1934-35	Boston Cubs	Can-Am	42	19	*37	56	....	....	....	18	3	1	1	2	2
1935-36	Boston Cubs	Can-Am	18	3	7	10	....	....	....	4	....	....	....	....	....
	Detroit Olympics	IAHL	28	5	13	18	....	....	....	11	6	0	4	4	2
1936-37	Springfield Indians	AHL	45	6	11	17	....	....	....	18	3	0	0	0	0
1937-38	Springfield–New Haven	AHL	38	2	9	11	....	....	....	18	4	0	0	0	0
1938-39	St. Paul Saints	AHA	47	28	26	54	....	....	....	13	3	1	0	1	0
1939-40	St. Paul Saints	AHA	47	16	36	52	....	....	....	19	7	2	3	5	2
1940-41	St. Paul Saints	AHA	48	5	15	20	....	....	....	18	4	0	0	0	0
1941-42	Fort Worth Rangers	AHA	43	11	11	22	....	....	....	19	5	0	3	3	4
	NHL Totals		37	2	1	3	5	2	7	13	4	0	0	0	0

AHA Second All-Star Team (1939)

Claimed by **NY Rangers** from **Hollywood** (Cal-Pro) in Inter-League Draft, May 14, 1928. Traded to **Chicago** (London-IAHL) by **NY Rangers** for cash, October 27, 1931. Traded to **Detroit** by **Chicago** (London-IAHL) for Frank Weight and Leroy Goldsworthy, October 20, 1933. Traded to **Boston** by **Detroit** for George Patterson, October 10, 1934. Traded to **Detroit** by **Boston** for Lorne Duguid, December 29, 1935. Loaned to **St. Louis** by **Boston** to replace injured Frank Jerwa, January 18, 1935. • Returned to **Boston** by **St. Louis**, January 30, 1935.

• CARROLL, GEORGE   George Carroll

D – R. 6'2", 210 lbs.   b: Moncton, N.B., 6/3/1897.   d: 8/1/1939.

Season	Club	League	GP	G	A	Pts	AG	AA	APts	PIM	GP	G	A	Pts	PIM
1913-14	Moncton Machinists	City Sr.	7	6	0	6	....	....	....	....	1	1	0	1	0
1914-15	Moncton St. Bernard's	City Sr.	2	0	0	0	....	....	....	....	....	....	....	....	....
1915-16	Moncton St. Bernard's	City Sr.	2	1	0	1	....	....	....	....	....	....	....	....	....
1916-17	Moncton St. Bernard's	City Sr.	2	5	0	5	....	....	....	....	....	....	....	....	....
1917-18			MILITARY SERVICE												
1918-19	Moncton Victorias	City Sr.	2	1	0	1	....	....	....	....	....	....	....	....	....
1919-20	Moncton Victorias	City Sr.	6	3	4	7	....	....	....	*27	11	16	6	22	*25
1920-21	Moncton Victorias	City Sr.	9	5	0	5	....	....	....	*31	2	0	0	0	0
1921-22	Moncton Victorias	City Sr.	13	12	0	12	....	....	....	*64	....	....	....	....	....
1922-23	Moncton Victorias	City Sr.	9	1	0	1	....	....	....	35	2	1	0	1	4
1923-24	Moncton Victorias	City Sr.	16	10	0	10	....	....	....	*63	....	....	....	....	....
1924-25	**Montreal Maroons**	**NHL**	4	0	0	0	0	0	0	0	....	....	....	....	....
	Boston Bruins	**NHL**	11	0	0	0	0	0	0	9	....	....	....	....	....
	Moncton Victorias	City Sr.	3	1	1	2	....	....	....	2	....	....	....	....	....
1925-26	Sunny Brae Rovers	City Sr.	DID NOT PLAY – COACHING												
	NHL Totals		15	0	0	0	0	0	0	9	....	....	....	....	....

Signed as a free agent by **Montreal Maroons**, November 13, 1924. Traded to **Boston** by **Montreal Maroons** with Stan Jackson for the rights to Ernie Parkes, December 19, 1924.

• CARRUTHERS, DWIGHT   *— see page 925*

• CARSE, BILL   Bill Carse

C – L. 5'8", 165 lbs.   b: Edmonton, Alta., 5/29/1914.

			REGULAR SEASON								PLAYOFFS				
Season	Club	League	GP	G	A	Pts	AG	AA	APts	PIM	GP	G	A	Pts	PIM
1932-33	Edmonton Canadiens	City Jr.	STATISTICS NOT AVAILABLE												
1933-34	Edmonton Athletic Club	City Jr.	9	6	2	8	....	....	....	2	2	*4	0	4	4
1934-35	Edmonton Eskimos	NWHL	28	19	13	32	....	....	....	27	....	....	....	....	....
1935-36	Vancouver–Edmonton	NWHL	39	17	8	25	....	....	....	33	7	0	0	0	4
1936-37	Vancouver Lions	PCHL	40	*29	9	*38	....	....	....	40	3	1	0	1	2
1937-38	Philadelphia Ramblers	AHL	48	15	25	40	....	....	....	26	5	1	2	3	0
1938-39	**New York Rangers**	**NHL**	1	0	1	1	0	2	2	0	6	1	1	2	0
	Philadelphia Ramblers	AHL	54	24	33	57	....	....	....	22	5	1	4	5	0
1939-40	**Chicago Black Hawks**	**NHL**	48	10	13	23	21	26	47	10	2	1	0	1	0
1940-41	**Chicago Black Hawks**	**NHL**	32	5	15	20	10	27	37	12	2	0	0	0	0
1941-42	**Chicago Black Hawks**	**NHL**	43	13	14	27	22	21	43	16	3	1	1	2	0
1942-43	Victoria Army	PCHL	20	21	*23	*44	....	....	....	8	5	4	6	10	0
1943-44	Nanaimo Army	City Sr.	3	0	3	3	....	....	....	0	....	....	....	....	....
1944-45			DID NOT PLAY												
1945-46	Vancouver Canucks	PCHL	56	38	43	81	....	....	....	22	10	*6	7	13	2
1946-47			DID NOT PLAY												
1947-48	Vancouver Canucks	PCHL	63	19	40	59	....	....	....	44	13	4	10	14	4
1948-49	Vancouver Canucks	PCHL	70	29	*64	93	....	....	....	12	3	1	2	3	0
1949-50	Vancouver Canucks	PCHL	41	9	13	22	....	....	....	2	....	....	....	....	....
1950-51	Vancouver Canucks	PCHL	DID NOT PLAY – COACHING												
	NHL Totals		124	28	43	71	53	76	129	38	13	3	2	5	0

PCHL Northern First All-Star Team (1949)

Traded to **NY Rangers** by **Vancouver** (PCHL) for cash, October 12, 1937. Traded to **Chicago** by **NY Rangers** for cash, May 17, 1939.

• CARSE, BOB   Bob Carse

LW – L. 5'9", 170 lbs.   b: Edmonton, Alta., 7/19/1919.

Season	Club	League	GP	G	A	Pts	AG	AA	APts	PIM	GP	G	A	Pts	PIM
1935-36	Edmonton Athletic Club	City Jr.	12	1	6	7	....	....	....	9	....	....	....	....	....
1936-37	Edmonton Athletic Club	City Jr.	STATISTICS NOT AVAILABLE												
1937-38	Edmonton Athletic Club	City Jr.	STATISTICS NOT AVAILABLE												
1938-39	Edmonton Athletic Club	City Jr.	12	12	9	21	....	....	....	8	11	10	7	17	12
1939-40	**Chicago Black Hawks**	**NHL**	22	3	5	8	6	10	16	11	2	0	0	0	0
	Providence Reds	AHL	31	5	12	17	....	....	....	9	6	3	2	5	2
1940-41	**Chicago Black Hawks**	**NHL**	43	9	9	18	18	16	34	9	5	0	0	0	2
1941-42	**Chicago Black Hawks**	**NHL**	33	7	16	23	12	24	36	10	3	0	2	2	0
	Kansas City Pla-Mors	USHL	18	9	13	22	....	....	....	9	....	....	....	....	....
1942-43	**Chicago Black Hawks**	**NHL**	47	10	22	32	14	28	42	6	....	....	....	....	....
1943-44	Calgary Currie Barracks	City Sr.	16	8	12	20	....	....	....	16	2	0	5	5	0
1944-45			MILITARY SERVICE												
1945-46	Edmonton Flyers	WCJHL	36	32	46	78	....	....	....	18	8	5	5	*10	8
1946-47	Cleveland Barons	AHL	62	27	61	88	....	....	....	16	4	0	0	0	0
1947-48	**Montreal Canadiens**	**NHL**	22	3	3	6	4	4	8	16	....	....	....	....	....
	Cleveland Barons	AHL	43	21	21	54	....	....	....	14	9	4	5	9	4
1948-49	Cleveland Barons	AHL	65	18	18	65	....	....	....	28	5	1	3	4	4
1949-50	Cleveland Barons	AHL	69	30	52	82	....	....	....	23	9	3	4	7	4
	NHL Totals		167	32	55	87	54	82	136	52	10	0	2	2	2

AHL Second All-Star Team (1939) • AHL First All-Star Team (1947, 1950)

Signed as a free agent by **Montreal**, October 14, 1947. Traded to **Cleveland** (AHL) by **Montreal** for future considerations, December 16, 1947.

• CARSON, BILL   Bill "Doc" Carson

C – L. 5'8", 158 lbs.   b: Bracebridge, Ont., 11/25/1900.   Deceased.

Season	Club	League	GP	G	A	Pts	AG	AA	APts	PIM	GP	G	A	Pts	PIM
1919-20	University of Toronto	OHA Sr.	3	6	1	7	....	....	....	....	6	*9	*4	*13	....
1920-21	University of Toronto	OHA Sr.	10	13	3	16	....	....	....	....	8	*16	2	*18	....
1921-22	University of Toronto	OHA Sr.	9	15	3	18	....	....	....	....	....	....	....	....	....
1922-23	University of Toronto	OHA Sr.	11	8	10	18	....	....	....	....	....	....	....	....	....
1923-24	Toronto Granites	OHA Sr.	5	9	2	11	....	....	....	....	....	....	....	....	....
1924-25	Stratford Indians	OHA Sr.	20	*29	8	*37	....	....	....	41	2	0	*2	2	3
1925-26	Stratford Indians	OHA Sr.	17	19	3	22	....	....	....	41	....	....	....	....	....
1926-27	**Toronto Maple Leafs**	**NHL**	40	16	6	22	47	51	98	41	....	....	....	....	....
1927-28	**Toronto Maple Leafs**	**NHL**	32	20	6	26	62	51	113	36	....	....	....	....	....
1928-29	**Toronto Maple Leafs**	**NHL**	24	7	6	13	28	55	83	45	....	....	....	....	....
	Boston Bruins	**NHL**	19	4	2	6	16	18	34	10	5	2	0	2	8
1929-30	**Boston Bruins**	**NHL**	44	7	4	11	14	13	27	24	6	1	0	1	6
1930-31	London Techumsehs	IAHL	7	0	1	1	....	....	....	2	....	....	....	....	....
1931-32			DID NOT PLAY – RETIRED												
1932-33			DID NOT PLAY – RETIRED												
1933-34	New Haven Eagles	Can-Am	33	7	4	11	....	....	....	6	....	....	....	....	....
	NHL Totals		159	54	24	78	167	188	355	156	11	3	0	3	14

Signed as a free agent by **Toronto St. Pats**, April 16, 1926. Traded to **Boston** by **Toronto** for cash, January 24, 1928.

• CARSON, FRANK Frank "Frosty" Carson

RW – R. 5'7", 165 lbs. b: Bracebridge, Ont., 1/12/1902. d: 5/29/1967.

Season	Club	League	GP	G	A	Pts	AG	AA	APts	PIM	PO GP	PO G	PO A	PO Pts	PO PIM
1919-20	Stratford Midgets	OHA	5	10	8	18	....	....	....	....	6	16	11	27	....
1920-21	Stratford Midgets	OHA	8	*20	9	29	....	....	....	....	13	33	15	48	....
1921-22	Stratford Midgets	OHA	4	10	5	15	....	....	....	6	4	9	3	12	....
	Stratford Indians	OHA Sr.	4	7	2	9	....	....	....	2	8	8	4	12	16
1922-23	Stratford Indians	OHA Sr.	10	*21	9	*30	....	....	....	8	9	13	*10	23	20
1923-24	Stratford Indians	OHA Sr.	12	19	10	*29	....	....	....	14	2	*3	*2	*5	0
1924-25	Stratford Indians	OHA Sr.	20	18	8	26	....	....	....	38	2	*2	0	*2	*4
1925-26	Stratford Indians	OHA Sr.	12	6	6	12	....	....	....	16	....	....	....	....	....
	Montreal Maroons	**NHL**	**16**	**2**	**1**	**3**	**6**	**11**	**17**	**6**	**8**	**0**	**0**	**0**	**0**
1926-27	**Montreal Maroons**	**NHL**	**44**	**2**	**3**	**5**	**6**	**25**	**31**	**12**	**2**	**0**	**0**	**0**	**2**
1927-28	**Montreal Maroons**	**NHL**	**21**	**0**	**1**	**1**	**0**	**8**	**8**	**10**	**9**	**0**	**0**	**0**	**0**
	Stratford Nationals	Can-Pro	13	6	1	7	....	....	....	18	5	3	*4	*7	4
1928-29	Windsor Bulldogs	Can-Pro	41	17	*12	29	....	....	....	60	8	4	1	5	18
1929-30	Windsor Bulldogs	IAHL	41	*31	14	*45	....	....	....	65	....	....	....	....	....
1930-31	**New York Americans**	**NHL**	**44**	**6**	**7**	**13**	**15**	**25**	**40**	**36**	....	....	....	....	....
1931-32	**Detroit Falcons**	**NHL**	**31**	**10**	**14**	**24**	**21**	**39**	**60**	**31**	**2**	**0**	**0**	**0**	**2**
	New Haven Eagles	Can-Am	15	6	3	9	....	....	....	28	....	....	....	....	....
1932-33	**Detroit Red Wings**	**NHL**	**45**	**12**	**13**	**25**	**28**	**34**	**62**	**35**	**4**	**0**	**1**	**1**	**0**
1933-34	**Detroit Red Wings**	**NHL**	**47**	**10**	**9**	**19**	**22**	**24**	**46**	**36**	**6**	**0**	**1**	**1**	**5**
	NHL Totals		**248**	**42**	**48**	**90**	**98**	**166**	**264**	**166**	**31**	**0**	**2**	**2**	**9**

Signed as a free agent by **Montreal Maroons**, January 26, 1926. Traded to **NY Americans** by **Montreal Maroons** (Windsor-IAHL) with Mike Neville, Hap Emms and Red Dutton for $35,000, May 14, 1930. Traded to **Detroit** by **NY Americans** with Hap Emms for Bert McInenly and Tom Filmore, August, 1931.

• CARSON, GERRY Gerry "Stub" Carson

D – L. 5'10", 175 lbs. b: Parry Sound, Ont., 10/10/1905. d: 11/1/1956.

Season	Club	League	GP	G	A	Pts	AG	AA	APts	PIM	PO GP	PO G	PO A	PO Pts	PO PIM
1926-27	Grimsby Peach Kings	OHA Sr.	STATISTICS NOT AVAILABLE												
1927-28	Philadelphia Arrows	Can-Am	37	7	4	11	....	....	....	38	....	....	....	....	....
1928-29	**Montreal Canadiens**	**NHL**	**26**	**0**	**0**	**0**	**0**	**0**	**0**	**4**	....	....	....	....	....
	New York Rangers	**NHL**	**14**	**0**	**0**	**0**	**0**	**0**	**0**	**5**	**5**	**0**	**0**	**0**	**0**
1929-30	**Montreal Canadiens**	**NHL**	**35**	**1**	**0**	**1**	**2**	**0**	**2**	**8**	**6**	**0**	**0**	**0**	**0**
	Providence Reds	Can-Am	6	1	0	1	....	....	....	19	....	....	....	....	....
1930-31	Providence Reds	Can-Am	38	4	2	6	....	....	....	84	2	0	0	0	14
1931-32	Providence Reds	Can-Am	40	9	5	14	....	....	....	77	5	1	0	1	8
1932-33	**Montreal Canadiens**	**NHL**	**48**	**5**	**2**	**7**	**12**	**5**	**17**	**53**	**2**	**0**	**0**	**0**	**2**
1933-34	**Montreal Canadiens**	**NHL**	**48**	**5**	**1**	**6**	**11**	**3**	**14**	**51**	**2**	**0**	**0**	**0**	**2**
1934-35	**Montreal Canadiens**	**NHL**	**48**	**0**	**5**	**5**	**0**	**11**	**11**	**56**	**2**	**0**	**0**	**0**	**4**
1935-36	**Montreal Canadiens**	**NHL**	DID NOT PLAY – INJURED												
1936-37	**Montreal Maroons**	**NHL**	**42**	**1**	**3**	**4**	**2**	**7**	**9**	**28**	**5**	**0**	**0**	**0**	**4**
	NHL Totals		**261**	**12**	**11**	**23**	**27**	**26**	**53**	**205**	**22**	**0**	**0**	**0**	**12**

Loaned to **NY Rangers** by **Montreal Canadiens** for remainder of 1929-30 season, February 15, 1929. Traded to **Providence** (Can-Am) by **Montreal Canadiens** with cash and the loan of Jean Pusie for Johnny Gagnon, October 21, 1930. • Missed entire 1935-36 season after undergoing knee surgery, September, 1935. Traded to **Montreal Maroons** by **Montreal Canadiens** for the rights to George Brown, October 7, 1936.

• CARTER, BILLY Billy Carter

C – L. 5'11", 155 lbs. b: Cornwall, Ont., 12/2/1937.

Season	Club	League	GP	G	A	Pts	AG	AA	APts	PIM	PO GP	PO G	PO A	PO Pts	PO PIM
1954-55	Hochelaga Indians	QJHL	36	25	35	60	....	....	....	6	....	....	....	....	....
1955-56	Montreal Jr. Canadiens	QJHL	STATISTICS NOT AVAILABLE												
1956-57	Hull-Ottawa Canadiens	Ott-Jr.	28	14	17	31	....	....	....	21	....	....	....	....	....
	Hull-Ottawa Canadiens	EOHL	16	7	7	14	....	....	....	6	....	....	....	....	....
	Rochester Americans	AHL	1	0	0	0	....	....	....	0	....	....	....	....	....
1957-58	Hull-Ottawa Canadiens	Ott-Jr.	27	15	29	44	....	....	....	26	....	....	....	....	....
	Hull-Ottawa Canadiens	EOHL	34	14	38	52	....	....	....	2	....	....	....	....	....
	Montreal Royals	QHL	1	0	0	0	....	....	....	0	....	....	....	....	....
	Montreal Canadiens	**NHL**	**1**	**0**	**0**	**0**	**0**	**0**	**0**	**0**	....	....	....	....	....
	Rochester Americans	AHL	1	0	0	0	....	....	....	0	....	....	....	....	....
1958-59	Rochester Americans	AHL	69	7	19	26	....	....	....	10	5	0	0	0	0
1959-60	Hull-Ottawa Canadiens	EPHL	70	42	60	102	....	....	....	2	7	1	4	5	2
1960-61	**Boston Bruins**	**NHL**	**8**	**0**	**0**	**0**	**0**	**0**	**0**	**2**	....	....	....	....	....
	Hull-Ottawa Canadiens	EPHL	60	27	32	59	....	....	....	6	14	4	5	9	6
1961-62	**Montreal Canadiens**	**NHL**	**7**	**0**	**0**	**0**	**0**	**0**	**0**	**4**	....	....	....	....	....
	Hull-Ottawa Canadiens	EPHL	62	26	47	73	....	....	....	17	13	6	8	14	0
1962-63	Hull-Ottawa Canadiens	EPHL	72	27	50	77	....	....	....	12	3	0	0	0	0
1963-64	Quebec Aces	AHL	36	2	9	11	....	....	....	2	....	....	....	....	....
	Seattle Totems	WHL	16	3	4	7	....	....	....	0	....	....	....	....	....
1964-65	Seattle Totems	WHL	16	0	2	2	....	....	....	0	....	....	....	....	....
	Memphis Wings	CHL	41	6	20	26	....	....	....	0	6	1	4	5	0
1965-66	Buffalo Bisons	AHL	71	16	45	61	....	....	....	2	....	....	....	....	....
1966-67	Buffalo Bisons	AHL	71	14	38	52	....	....	....	8	....	....	....	....	....
1967-68	Omaha Knights	CHL	67	9	30	39	....	....	....	6	....	....	....	....	....
	Buffalo Bisons	AHL	2	0	0	0	....	....	....	0	....	....	....	....	....
1968-69	Denver Spurs	WHL	74	16	49	65	....	....	....	4	....	....	....	....	....
	NHL Totals		**16**	**0**	**0**	**0**	**0**	**0**	**0**	**6**	....	....	....	....	....

Claimed by **Boston** from **Montreal** in Intra-League Draft, June, 1960. Traded to **Montreal** by **Boston** for cash, November, 1961. Traded to **Detroit** (Memphis-CHL) by **Seattle** (WHL) for Chuck Holmes, December, 1964.

• CARVETH, JOE Joe Carveth

RW – R. 5'10", 180 lbs. b: Regina, Sask., 3/21/1918. d: 8/15/1985.

Season	Club	League	GP	G	A	Pts	AG	AA	APts	PIM	PO GP	PO G	PO A	PO Pts	PO PIM
1935-36	Regina Green Shirts	City Jr.	6	*7	0	7	....	....	....	0	....	....	....	....	....
1936-37	Regina Jr. Aces	City Jr.	6	6	*7	*13	....	....	....	2	2	2	1	3	0
	Regina Aces	City Sr.	1	0	0	0	....	....	....	0	3	0	0	0	0
1937-38	Detroit Pontiacs	MOHL	27	9	16	25	....	....	....	57	3	0	0	0	0
1938-39	Detroit Pontiacs	MOHL	27	19	*25	44	....	....	....	25	7	3	5	8	4
1939-40	Indianapolis Capitals	AHL	11	2	2	4	....	....	....	0	....	....	....	....	....
1940-41	**Detroit Red Wings**	**NHL**	**19**	**2**	**1**	**3**	**4**	**2**	**6**	**2**	....	....	....	....	....
1941-42	**Detroit Red Wings**	**NHL**	**29**	**6**	**11**	**17**	**10**	**17**	**27**	**2**	**9**	**4**	**0**	**4**	**0**
	Indianapolis Capitals	AHL	29	8	17	25	....	....	....	9	....	....	....	....	....
1942-43	**Detroit Red Wings**	**NHL**	**43**	**18**	**18**	**36**	**26**	**23**	**49**	**6**	**10**	**6**	**2**	**8**	**4**
1943-44	**Detroit Red Wings**	**NHL**	**46**	**21**	**35**	**56**	**27**	**43**	**70**	**6**	**5**	**2**	**1**	**3**	**8**
	Indianapolis Capitals	AHL	1	1	1	2	....	....	....	2	....	....	....	....	....
1944-45	**Detroit Red Wings**	**NHL**	**50**	**26**	**28**	**54**	**36**	**46**	**82**	**6**	**14**	**5**	**6**	**11**	**2**
1945-46	**Detroit Red Wings**	**NHL**	**48**	**17**	**18**	**35**	**26**	**34**	**60**	**10**	**5**	**0**	**1**	**1**	**0**
1946-47	**Boston Bruins**	**NHL**	**51**	**21**	**15**	**36**	**29**	**21**	**50**	**18**	**5**	**2**	**1**	**3**	**0**
1947-48	**Boston Bruins**	**NHL**	**22**	**8**	**9**	**17**	**12**	**13**	**25**	**2**	....	....	....	....	....
	Montreal Canadiens	**NHL**	**35**	**1**	**10**	**11**	**1**	**15**	**16**	**6**	....	....	....	....	....
1948-49	**Montreal Canadiens**	**NHL**	**60**	**15**	**22**	**37**	**24**	**35**	**59**	**8**	**7**	**0**	**1**	**1**	**8**
1949-50	**Montreal Canadiens**	**NHL**	**11**	**1**	**1**	**2**	**1**	**1**	**2**	**2**	....	....	....	....	....
	Detroit Red Wings	**NHL**	**60**	**13**	**17**	**30**	**17**	**22**	**39**	**13**	**14**	**2**	**4**	**6**	**6**
1950-51	**Detroit Red Wings**	**NHL**	**30**	**1**	**4**	**5**	**1**	**5**	**6**	**0**	....	....	....	....	....
	Indianapolis Capitals	AHL	37	18	30	48	....	....	....	9	3	0	0	0	0
1951-52	Cleveland Barons	AHL	40	9	15	24	....	....	....	18	....	....	....	....	....
	Vancouver Canucks	PCHL	19	4	12	16	....	....	....	4	....	....	....	....	....
1952-53	Chatham Maroons	OHA Sr.	47	45	39	84	....	....	....	38	....	....	....	....	....
	Toledo Mercury's	IHL	8	2	3	5	....	....	....	0	5	0	4	4	6
1953-54	Chatham Maroons	OHA Sr.	55	16	26	42	....	....	....	105	6	3	1	4	4
	NHL Totals		**504**	**150**	**189**	**339**	**214**	**277**	**491**	**81**	**69**	**21**	**16**	**37**	**28**

Played in NHL All-Star Game (1950)

Signed as a free agent by **Detroit**, October 5, 1939. Traded to **Boston** by **Detroit** for Roy Conacher, August, 1946. Traded to **Montreal** by **Boston** for Jimmy Peters and John Quilty, December 16, 1947. Traded to **Detroit** by **Montreal** for Calum McKay, November 11, 1949.

• CASHMAN, WAYNE *— see page 927*

• CERESINO, RAY Ray Ceresino

RW – R. 5'9", 160 lbs. b: Port Arthur, Ont., 4/24/1929.

Season	Club	League	GP	G	A	Pts	AG	AA	APts	PIM	PO GP	PO G	PO A	PO Pts	PO PIM
1944-45	Port Arthur Bruins	TBJHL	10	17	6	23	....	....	....	2	8	6	4	10	....
1945-46	Port Arthur Bruins	TBJHL	6	10	9	19	....	....	....	0	7	6	*11	*17	0
1946-47	Oshawa Generals	OHA	28	24	29	53	....	....	....	4	5	0	6	6	2
1947-48	Oshawa Generals	OHA	1	0	0	0	....	....	....	0	5	2	2	4	0
1948-49	**Toronto Maple Leafs**	**NHL**	**12**	**1**	**1**	**2**	**2**	**2**	**4**	**2**	....	....	....	....	....
	Pittsburgh Hornets	AHL	47	22	16	38	....	....	....	14	....	....	....	....	....
1949-50	Cleveland Barons	AHL	47	17	24	41	....	....	....	22	9	3	2	5	5
1950-51	Cleveland Barons	AHL	52	21	27	48	....	....	....	11	11	4	3	7	2
1951-52	Cleveland Barons	AHL	14	3	1	4	....	....	....	0	....	....	....	....	....
	Seattle Ironmen	PCHL	44	13	15	28	....	....	....	18	2	0	1	1	0
1952-53	Cleveland Barons	AHL	64	23	35	58	....	....	....	12	11	2	1	3	0
1953-54	Cleveland Barons	AHL	57	14	22	36	....	....	....	9	6	1	1	2	2
1954-55	Providence Reds	AHL	22	4	10	14	....	....	....	2	....	....	....	....	....
	Montreal Royals	QHL	3	0	0	0	....	....	....	0	....	....	....	....	....
1955-56	Victoria Cougars	WHL	21	1	4	5	....	....	....	2	....	....	....	....	....
1956-57	Sault Ste. Marie Indians	NOHA	43	9	20	29	....	....	....	4	....	....	....	....	....
	NHL Totals		**12**	**1**	**1**	**2**	**2**	**2**	**4**	**2**	....	....	....	....	....

Traded to **Cleveland** (AHL) by **Toronto** with Harry Taylor and the loan of Tod Sloan for Bob Solinger, September 6, 1949. Traded to **Providence** (AHL) by **Cleveland** (AHL) for cash, June 19, 1954.

• CHAD, JOHN John Chad

RW – R. 5'10", 167 lbs. b: Provost, Alta., 9/16/1919. d: 10/11/1970.

Season	Club	League	GP	G	A	Pts	AG	AA	APts	PIM	PO GP	PO G	PO A	PO Pts	PO PIM
1937-38	Saskatoon Chiefs	City Jr.	STATISTICS NOT AVAILABLE												
1938-39	Edmonton Athletic Club	City Jr.	....	*15	*15	*30	....	....	....	0	11	*11	9	*20	10
1939-40	**Chicago Black Hawks**	**NHL**	**22**	**8**	**3**	**11**	**17**	**6**	**23**	**11**	**2**	**0**	**0**	**0**	**0**
	Providence Reds	AHL	31	14	8	22	....	....	....	8	6	0	3	3	0
1940-41	**Chicago Black Hawks**	**NHL**	**45**	**7**	**18**	**25**	**14**	**33**	**47**	**16**	**5**	**0**	**0**	**0**	**2**
1941-42	Regina Rangers	SSHL	25	16	7	23	....	....	....	10	3	1	0	1	16
1942-43	Calgary RCAF	City Sr.	23	20	21	41	....	....	....	32	7	7	4	11	*22
1943-44	Calgary Combines	City Sr.	9	2	1	3	....	....	....	4	....	....	....	....	....
1944-45	Calgary RCAF	City Sr.	9	5	6	11	....	....	....	6	....	....	....	....	....
1945-46	**Chicago Black Hawks**	**NHL**	**13**	**0**	**1**	**1**	**0**	**2**	**2**	**2**	**3**	**0**	**1**	**1**	**0**
1946-47	Providence Reds	AHL	63	32	43	75	....	....	....	12	....	....	....	....	....
1947-48	Providence Reds	AHL	67	41	53	94	....	....	....	8	5	0	1	1	0
1948-49	Providence Reds	AHL	55	32	46	78	....	....	....	8	8	3	6	9	0
1949-50	Providence Reds	AHL	70	36	54	90	....	....	....	4	4	1	3	4	0
1950-51	Providence Reds	AHL	34	13	19	32	....	....	....	2	....	....	....	....	....
1951-52	Saskatoon Quakers	PCHL	67	35	47	82	....	....	....	6	13	7	10	17	0
1952-53	Saskatoon Quakers	WHL	70	26	34	60	....	....	....	20	13	7	4	11	0
	NHL Totals		**80**	**15**	**22**	**37**	**31**	**41**	**72**	**29**	**10**	**0**	**1**	**1**	**2**

PCHL First All-Star Team (1952)

Signed as a free agent by **Chicago**, October 18, 1939.

• CHALMERS, BILL
Bill "Chick" Chalmers
C – L. 6′, 180 lbs. b: Stratford, Ont., 1/24/1934. d: 12/7/1994.

			REGULAR SEASON								PLAYOFFS				
Season	Club	League	GP	G	A	Pts	AG	AA	APts	PIM	GP	G	A	Pts	PIM
1951-52	Guelph Biltmores	OHA	53	11	17	28	....	....	....	12	22	3	5	8	6
1952-53	Guelph Biltmores	OHA	33	13	12	25	....	....	....	8	....	....	....	....	....
1953-54	Guelph Biltmores	OHA	22	11	17	28	....	....	....	21	....	....	....	....	....
	Galt Black Hawks	OHA	39	12	14	26	....	....	....	20	....	....	....	....	....
	New York Rangers	**NHL**	**1**	**0**	**0**	**0**	**0**	**0**	**0**	**0**	....	....	....	....	....
1954-55	Vancouver Canucks	WHL	17	2	3	5	....	....	....	4	....	....	....	....	....
	Kelowna Packers	OSHL	37	14	25	39	....	....	....	10	4	2	1	3	2
1955-56	Chatham Maroons	OHA Sr.	45	13	12	25	....	....	....	29	11	3	6	9	8
1956-57	Troy Bruins	IHL	1	0	0	0	....	....	....	0	....	....	....	....	....
	Chatham Maroons	OHA Sr.	3	0	2	2	....	....	....	2	....	....	....	....	....
	Soo Greyhounds	NOHA	40	8	11	19	....	....	....	6	9	3	0	3	0
1957-58	Louisville Rebels	IHL	64	23	*58	81	....	....	....	4	11	2	4	6	0
1958-59	Louisville Rebels	IHL	53	34	49	83	....	....	....	14	11	3	7	10	4
1959-60	Louisville Rebels	IHL	68	41	*93	*134	....	....	....	4	6	3	0	3	0
1960-61	Omaha Knights	IHL	70	35	69	104	....	....	....	15	8	2	7	9	0
1961-62	Omaha Knights	IHL	68	29	73	102	....	....	....	18	7	3	5	8	2
1962-63	Omaha Knights	IHL	68	28	59	87	....	....	....	16	7	3	5	8	2
1963-64	Toledo Blades	IHL	70	32	62	94	....	....	....	20	13	2	*15	*17	2
1964-65	Toledo Blades	IHL	64	27	63	90	....	....	....	12	4	5	1	6	0
1965-66	Toledo Blades	IHL	70	28	65	93	....	....	....	31	....	....	....	....	....
1966-67	Toledo Blades	IHL	72	34	67	101	....	....	....	20	10	5	8	13	8
1967-68	Toledo Blades	IHL	70	22	45	67	....	....	....	14	....	....	....	....	....
1968-69	Des Moines Oak Leafs	IHL	64	6	32	38	....	....	....	12	....	....	....	....	....
1969-70	Toledo Blades	IHL	51	18	42	60	....	....	....	20	3	1	0	1	2
1970-71	Toledo Blades	IHL	35	6	14	20	....	....	....	12	....	....	....	....	....
	Greensboro Generals	EHL	20	2	17	19	....	....	....	0	9	1	3	4	2
	NHL Totals		**1**	**0**	**0**	**0**	**0**	**0**	**0**	**0**	....	....	....	....	....

IHL 2nd All-Star Team (1960, 1961, 1967) • Won George H. Wilkinson Trophy (Top Scorer - IHL) (1960) • IHL First All-Star Team (1962) • Won James Gatschene Memorial Trophy (MVP - IHL) (1965)

Traded to **Des Moines** (IHL) by **Toledo** (IHL) with Terry Kerr for John Annable, August, 1968. Traded to **Toledo** (IHL) by **Des Moines** for Bob Regis, November, 1969. Traded to **Greensboro** (EHL) by **Des Moines** (IHL) for cash, January, 1971.

• CHAMBERLAIN, MURPH
Murph (Edwin Groves) "Old Hardrock" Chamberlain
LW – L. 5′11″, 165 lbs. b: Shawville, Que., 2/14/1915. d: 5/8/1971.

			REGULAR SEASON								PLAYOFFS				
Season	Club	League	GP	G	A	Pts	AG	AA	APts	PIM	GP	G	A	Pts	PIM
1932-33	Ottawa Primroses	OJHL	11	7	2	9	....	....	....	19	4	3	1	4	6
1933-34	Ottawa New Edinburghs	City Sr.	STATISTICS NOT AVAILABLE												
1934-35	Noranda Copper Kings	NOHA	13	6	5	11	....	....	....	10	....	....	....	....	....
1935-36	South Porcupine Porkies	NOHA	8	7	0	7	....	....	....	33	2	0	1	1	*11
1936-37	Sudbury Frood Mines	NOHA	15	12	3	15	....	....	....	38	15	*17	3	20	*39
1937-38	**Toronto Maple Leafs**	**NHL**	**43**	**4**	**12**	**16**	**8**	**25**	**33**	**51**	**5**	**0**	**0**	**0**	**2**
1938-39	**Toronto Maple Leafs**	**NHL**	**48**	**10**	**16**	**26**	**21**	**30**	**51**	**32**	**10**	**2**	**5**	**7**	**4**
1939-40	**Toronto Maple Leafs**	**NHL**	**40**	**5**	**17**	**22**	**11**	**34**	**45**	**63**	**3**	**0**	**0**	**0**	**0**
1940-41	**Montreal Canadiens**	**NHL**	**45**	**10**	**15**	**25**	**20**	**27**	**47**	**75**	**3**	**0**	**2**	**2**	**11**
1941-42	**Montreal Canadiens**	**NHL**	**26**	**6**	**3**	**9**	**10**	**5**	**15**	**30**	....	....	....	....	....
	Brooklyn Americans	**NHL**	**11**	**6**	**9**	**15**	**10**	**14**	**24**	**16**	....	....	....	....	....
	Springfield Indians	AHL	3	2	1	3	....	....	....	0	....	....	....	....	....
1942-43	**Boston Bruins**	**NHL**	**45**	**9**	**24**	**33**	**13**	**31**	**44**	**67**	**6**	**1**	**1**	**2**	**12**
1943-44	**Montreal Canadiens**	**NHL**	**47**	**15**	**32**	**47**	**19**	**39**	**58**	**85**	**9**	**5**	**3**	**8**	**12**
1944-45	**Montreal Canadiens**	**NHL**	**32**	**2**	**12**	**14**	**3**	**19**	**22**	**38**	**6**	**1**	**1**	**2**	**10**
1945-46	**Montreal Canadiens**	**NHL**	**40**	**12**	**14**	**26**	**18**	**26**	**44**	**42**	**9**	**4**	**2**	**6**	**18**
1946-47	**Montreal Canadiens**	**NHL**	**49**	**10**	**10**	**20**	**13**	**14**	**27**	**97**	**11**	**1**	**3**	**4**	**19**
1947-48	**Montreal Canadiens**	**NHL**	**30**	**6**	**3**	**9**	**9**	**4**	**13**	**62**	....	....	....	....	....
1948-49	**Montreal Canadiens**	**NHL**	**54**	**5**	**8**	**13**	**8**	**13**	**21**	**111**	**4**	**0**	**0**	**0**	**8**
1949-50	Sydney Millionaires	CBHL	DID NOT PLAY – COACHING												
	NHL Totals		**510**	**100**	**175**	**275**	**163**	**281**	**444**	**769**	**66**	**14**	**17**	**31**	**96**

Traded to **Montreal** by **Toronto** for $7,500, May 12, 1940. Loaned to **Brooklyn** by **Montreal** for the loan of Red Heron, February 10, 1942. Loaned to **Boston** by **Montreal** for 1942-43 season for cash, September, 1942.

• CHAMPAGNE, ANDRE
Andre Champagne
LW – L. 6′, 190 lbs. b: Ottawa, Ont., 9/19/1943.

			REGULAR SEASON								PLAYOFFS				
Season	Club	League	GP	G	A	Pts	AG	AA	APts	PIM	GP	G	A	Pts	PIM
1959-60	St. Michael's Majors	OHA	1	0	0	0	....	....	....	0	....	....	....	....	....
1960-61	St. Michael's Majors	OHA	47	11	12	23	....	....	....	59	18	7	2	9	22
1961-62	St. Michael's College	Tor-Jr.	29	14	18	32	....	....	....	79	3	1	4	5	26
1962-63	Neil McNeil Maroons	OHA	24	16	32	48	....	....	....	61	16	11	14	25	*67
	Toronto Maple Leafs	**NHL**	**2**	**0**	**0**	**0**	**0**	**0**	**0**	**0**	....	....	....	....	....
	Rochester Americans	AHL	....	....	....	....	....	....	....	....	1	0	0	0	0
1963-64	Toronto Marlboros	OHA	47	31	40	71	....	....	....	105	9	6	10	16	38
	Rochester Americans	AHL	3	0	0	0	....	....	....	0	....	....	....	....	....
1964-65	Tulsa Oilers	CHL	60	24	41	65	....	....	....	118	12	3	4	7	*43
1965-66	Rochester Americans	AHL	1	0	0	0	....	....	....	0	....	....	....	....	....
	Tulsa Oilers	CHL	65	16	49	65	....	....	....	38	11	1	5	6	4
1966-67	Tulsa Oilers	CHL	10	1	2	3	....	....	....	6	....	....	....	....	....
1967-68	Rochester Americans	AHL	48	2	5	7	....	....	....	14	....	....	....	....	....
1968-69	Rochester Americans	AHL	69	7	12	19	....	....	....	78	....	....	....	....	....
1969-70	Rochester Americans	AHL	24	3	5	8	....	....	....	25	....	....	....	....	....
	NHL Totals		**2**	**0**	**0**	**0**	**0**	**0**	**0**	**0**	....	....	....	....	....

• CHAPMAN, ART
Art Chapman
C – L. 5′10″, 170 lbs. b: Winnipeg, Man., 5/29/1906. d: 1/1/1963.

			REGULAR SEASON								PLAYOFFS				
Season	Club	League	GP	G	A	Pts	AG	AA	APts	PIM	GP	G	A	Pts	PIM
1922-23	Winnipeg Tigers	MJHL	8	8	2	10	....	....	....	2	....	....	....	....	....
1923-24	Winnipeg Tigers	MJHL	STATISTICS NOT AVAILABLE												
	Winnipeg Tigers	MHL Sr.	1	1	0	1	....	....	....	0	....	....	....	....	....
1924-25	Winnipeg Falcons	MHL Sr.	8	5	0	5	....	....	....	0	....	....	....	....	....
1925-26	Port Arthur Ports	TBSHL	19	13	2	15	....	....	....	17	9	3	1	4	6
1926-27	Port Arthur Ports	TBSHL	20	19	10	29	....	....	....	16	2	0	0	0	0
1927-28	Springfield Indians	Can-Am	39	14	5	19	....	....	....	6	4	1	1	2	6
1928-29	Providence Reds	Can-Am	39	14	*14	28	....	....	....	5	6	0	1	1	4
1929-30	Providence Reds	Can-Am	39	*26	19	45	....	....	....	22	3	*5	0	5	6
1930-31	**Boston Bruins**	**NHL**	**44**	**7**	**7**	**14**	**17**	**25**	**42**	**22**	**5**	**0**	**1**	**1**	**7**
1931-32	**Boston Bruins**	**NHL**	**48**	**11**	**14**	**25**	**23**	**39**	**62**	**18**	....	....	....	....	....
1932-33	**Boston Bruins**	**NHL**	**46**	**3**	**6**	**9**	**7**	**16**	**23**	**19**	**5**	**0**	**0**	**0**	**2**
1933-34	**Boston Bruins**	**NHL**	**21**	**2**	**5**	**7**	**4**	**13**	**17**	**7**	....	....	....	....	....
	New York Americans	**NHL**	**25**	**3**	**7**	**10**	**7**	**19**	**26**	**8**	....	....	....	....	....
1934-35	**New York Americans**	**NHL**	**47**	**9**	***34**	**43**	**19**	**77**	**96**	**4**	....	....	....	....	....
1935-36	**New York Americans**	**NHL**	**48**	**10**	***28**	**38**	**25**	**69**	**94**	**14**	**5**	**0**	**3**	**3**	**0**
1936-37	**New York Americans**	**NHL**	**43**	**8**	**23**	**31**	**17**	**54**	**71**	**36**	....	....	....	....	....
1937-38	**New York Americans**	**NHL**	**45**	**2**	**27**	**29**	**4**	**56**	**60**	**8**	**6**	**0**	**1**	**1**	**0**
1938-39	**New York Americans**	**NHL**	**45**	**3**	**19**	**22**	**6**	**36**	**42**	**2**	**2**	**0**	**0**	**0**	**0**
1939-40	**New York Americans**	**NHL**	**26**	**4**	**6**	**10**	**9**	**12**	**21**	**2**	**3**	**1**	**0**	**1**	**0**
1940-41	**New York Americans**	**NHL**	DID NOT PLAY – COACHING												
1941-42	**Brooklyn Americans**	**NHL**	DID NOT PLAY – COACHING												
1942-43	Buffalo Bisons	AHL	45	9	19	28	....	....	....	12	....	....	....	....	....
1943-44	Buffalo Bisons	AHL	1	0	0	0	....	....	....	0	....	....	....	....	....
	NHL Totals		**438**	**62**	**176**	**238**	**138**	**416**	**554**	**140**	**26**	**1**	**5**	**6**	**9**

NHL Second All-Star Team (1937)

Played in NHL All-Star Game (1937)

Claimed by **Boston** from **Providence** (Can-Am) in Inter-League Draft, May 13, 1929. Traded to **NY Americans** by **Boston** with Bob Gracie for Lloyd Gross and George Patterson, January 11, 1934.

• CHECK, LUDE
Lude (Ludic) Check
LW – L. 5′10″, 165 lbs. b: Brandon, Man., 5/22/1919.

			REGULAR SEASON								PLAYOFFS				
Season	Club	League	GP	G	A	Pts	AG	AA	APts	PIM	GP	G	A	Pts	PIM
1936-37	Brandon Wheat Kings	MJHL	15	13	6	19	....	....	....	16	4	4	0	4	0
1937-38	Brandon Wheat Kings	MJHL	15	19	13	32	....	....	....	16	5	3	3	6	4
1938-39	Regina Aces	City Sr.	39	19	6	25	....	....	....	12	....	....	....	....	....
1939-40	Regina Aces	City Sr.	32	15	10	25	....	....	....	12	7	0	1	1	6
1940-41	New York Rovers	EHL	64	21	20	41	....	....	....	10	3	1	0	1	0
1941-42	Sydney Millionaires	CBSHL	40	29	22	51	....	....	....	24	7	5	4	9	12
1942-43	Quebec Aces	QSHL	34	20	13	33	....	....	....	26	4	1	1	2	2
1943-44	Quebec Aces	QSHL	25	*28	18	46	....	....	....	14	15	15	10	25	6
	Detroit Red Wings	**NHL**	**1**	**0**	**0**	**0**	**0**	**0**	**0**	**0**	....	....	....	....	....
1944-45	**Chicago Black Hawks**	**NHL**	**26**	**6**	**2**	**8**	**8**	**3**	**11**	**4**	....	....	....	....	....
1945-46	Ottawa Senators	QSHL	39	31	29	60	....	....	....	29	9	6	5	11	6
1946-47	Ottawa Senators	QSHL	40	22	19	41	....	....	....	36	11	5	2	7	4
1947-48	Ottawa Senators	QSHL	46	17	23	40	....	....	....	35	26	*16	11	27	15
1948-49	Ottawa Senators	QSHL	59	26	30	56	....	....	....	29	23	8	10	18	8
1949-50	Ottawa Senators	QSHL	51	14	15	29	....	....	....	8	2	0	0	0	0
1950-51	Ottawa Senators	QSHL	38	11	9	20	....	....	....	16	11	2	4	6	4
	NHL Totals		**27**	**6**	**2**	**8**	**8**	**3**	**11**	**4**	....	....	....	....	....

Signed as a free agent by **Montreal**, October 24, 1944. Loaned to **Detroit** by **Montreal** as an emergency injury replacement, March 11, 1944. Traded to **Chicago** by **Montreal** for cash with Montreal retaining right of repurchase, October 26, 1944. Loaned to **Ottawa** (QSHL) by **Montreal** with Jim McFadden as compensation for Montreal's signing of Mike McMahon, October 24, 1945.

• CHERRY, DICK
— *see page 934*

• CHERRY, DON
Don Cherry
D – L. 5′11″, 180 lbs. b: Kingston, Ont., 2/5/1934.

			REGULAR SEASON								PLAYOFFS				
Season	Club	League	GP	G	A	Pts	AG	AA	APts	PIM	GP	G	A	Pts	PIM
1951-52	Windsor Spitfires	OHA	18	0	3	3	....	....	....	30	....	....	....	....	....
	Barrie Flyers	OHA	18	2	3	5	....	....	....	30	....	....	....	....	....
1952-53	Barrie Flyers	OHA	56	5	3	8	....	....	....	66	15	1	1	2	28
1953-54	Barrie Flyers	OHA	55	10	14	24	....	....	....	61	....	....	....	....	....
1954-55	Hershey Bears	AHL	63	7	13	20	....	....	....	125	....	....	....	....	....
	Boston Bruins	**NHL**	....	....	....	....	....	....	....	....	**1**	**0**	**0**	**0**	**0**
1955-56	Hershey Bears	AHL	58	3	22	25	....	....	....	102	....	....	....	....	....
1956-57	Hershey Bears	AHL	64	5	20	25	....	....	....	197	7	2	0	2	27
1957-58	Springfield Indians	AHL	65	9	17	26	....	....	....	83	13	1	1	2	10
1958-59	Springfield Indians	AHL	70	6	22	28	....	....	....	118	....	....	....	....	....
1959-60	Trois-Rivieres Lions	EPHL	23	3	4	7	....	....	....	12	7	0	1	1	2
	Springfield Indians	AHL	46	2	11	13	....	....	....	45	1	0	0	0	2
1960-61	Kitchener Beavers	EPHL	70	13	26	39	....	....	....	78	7	0	3	3	23
1961-62	Springfield Indians	AHL	11	1	3	4	....	....	....	10	....	....	....	....	....
	Sudbury Wolves	EPHL	55	9	20	29	....	....	....	62	5	3	2	5	10
1962-63	Spokane Comets	WHL	68	9	13	22	....	....	....	68	....	....	....	....	....
1963-64	Rochester Americans	AHL	70	5	11	16	....	....	....	106	2	0	0	0	4
1964-65	Rochester Americans	AHL	62	4	8	12	....	....	....	56	10	0	1	1	34
1965-66	Tulsa Oilers	CHL	17	1	2	3	....	....	....	28	....	....	....	....	....
	Rochester Americans	AHL	56	5	11	16	....	....	....	61	12	2	5	7	14
1966-67	Rochester Americans	AHL	72	6	24	30	....	....	....	61	13	1	2	3	16
1967-68	Rochester Americans	AHL	68	6	15	21	....	....	....	74	11	1	1	2	2
1968-69	Rochester Americans	AHL	43	7	11	18	....	....	....	20	....	....	....	....	....
	Vancouver Canucks	WHL	33	0	6	6	....	....	....	29	8	2	2	4	6
1969-70			DID NOT PLAY												
1970-71			DID NOT PLAY												
1971-72	Rochester Americans	AHL	19	1	4	5	....	....	....	8	....	....	....	....	....
	NHL Totals		**0**	**0**	**0**	**0**	**0**	**0**	**0**	**0**	**1**	**0**	**0**	**0**	**0**

Won Jack Adams Award (1976)

Traded to **Springfield** (AHL) by **Boston** for cash, September, 1957. Traded to **Detroit** by **Springfield** (AHL) for cash, November, 1961. Traded to **Montreal** by **Detroit** for cash, September 13, 1962. Rights transferred to **Toronto** when NHL club purchased **Spokane** (WHL) franchise, June, 1963.

• CHEVREFILS, REAL Real Chevrefils
LW – L. 5'10", 180 lbs. b: Timmins, Ont., 5/2/1932. d: 1/8/1981.

Season	Club	League	GP	G	A	Pts	AG	AA	APts	PIM	Playoffs GP	G	A	Pts	PIM
1948-49	Barrie Flyers	OHA	43	13	13	26	....	....	....	36	15	*14	9	23	24
1949-50	Barrie Flyers	OHA	48	27	32	59	....	....	....	95	9	6	7	13	16
1950-51	Barrie Flyers	OHA	54	52	51	103	....	....	....	104	12	*14	11	25	16
1951-52	**Boston Bruins**	**NHL**	**33**	**8**	**17**	**25**	**11**	**22**	**33**	**8**	**7**	**1**	**1**	**2**	**6**
	Hershey Bears	AHL	34	20	28	48	....	....	....	14	....	....	....	....	....
1952-53	**Boston Bruins**	**NHL**	**69**	**19**	**14**	**33**	**29**	**19**	**48**	**44**	**7**	**0**	**1**	**1**	**6**
1953-54	**Boston Bruins**	**NHL**	**14**	**4**	**1**	**5**	**6**	**1**	**7**	**2**	....	....	....	....	....
1954-55	**Boston Bruins**	**NHL**	**64**	**18**	**22**	**40**	**26**	**28**	**54**	**30**	**5**	**2**	**1**	**3**	**4**
1955-56	**Detroit Red Wings**	**NHL**	**38**	**3**	**4**	**7**	**4**	**5**	**9**	**24**	....	....	....	....	....
	Boston Bruins	**NHL**	**25**	**11**	**8**	**19**	**16**	**10**	**26**	**10**	....	....	....	....	....
1956-57	**Boston Bruins**	**NHL**	**70**	**31**	**17**	**48**	**43**	**20**	**63**	**38**	**10**	**2**	**1**	**3**	**4**
1957-58	**Boston Bruins**	**NHL**	**44**	**9**	**9**	**18**	**12**	**10**	**22**	**21**	**1**	**0**	**0**	**0**	**0**
	Springfield Indians	AHL	15	7	8	15	....	....	....	0	11	0	3	3	2
1958-59	**Boston Bruins**	**NHL**	**30**	**1**	**5**	**6**	**1**	**5**	**6**	**8**	....	....	....	....	....
	Providence Reds	AHL	6	1	1	2	....	....	....	0	....	....	....	....	....
	Quebec Aces	OHL	12	2	7	9	....	....	....	6	....	....	....	....	....
1959-60	Sudbury Wolves	EPHL	65	23	36	59	....	....	....	26	14	6	6	12	4
1960-61	Kingston Frontenacs	EPHL	37	16	20	36	....	....	....	16	....	....	....	....	....
	Winnipeg Warriors	WHL	19	6	7	13	....	....	....	2	....	....	....	....	....
1961-62	Los Angeles Blades	WHL	69	22	32	54	....	....	....	12	....	....	....	....	....
1962-63	San Francisco Seals	WHL	6	1	1	2	....	....	....	0	....	....	....	....	....
	Windsor Bulldogs	OHA Sr.	42	25	48	73	....	....	....	18	10	0	11	11	7
1963-64	Windsor Bulldogs	IHL	48	19	22	41	....	....	....	8	6	2	2	4	2
	NHL Totals		**387**	**104**	**97**	**201**	**148**	**120**	**268**	**185**	**30**	**5**	**4**	**9**	**20**

NHL Second All-Star Team (1957)

Played in NHL All-Star Game (1955, 1957)

Traded to **Detroit** by **Boston** with Ed Sandford, Norm Corcoran, Gilles Boisvert and Warren Godfrey for Marcel Bonin, Terry Sawchuk, Vic Stasiuk and Lorne Davis, June 3, 1955. Traded to **Boston** by **Detroit** with Jerry Toppazzini for Lorne Ferguson and Murray Costello, January 17, 1956.

• CHISHOLM, ART Art Chisholm
C – L. 5'9", 160 lbs. b: Arlington, MA, 11/11/1939.

Season	Club	League	GP	G	A	Pts	AG	AA	APts	PIM	Playoffs GP	G	A	Pts	PIM
1954-55	Arlington North Shore	H.S.	8	8	4	12	....	....	....	....	2	0	0	0	0
1955-56	Arlington North Shore	H.S.	STATISTICS NOT AVAILABLE												
1956-57	Arlington North Shore	H.S.	STATISTICS NOT AVAILABLE												
1957-58	Northeastern University	ECAC	DID NOT PLAY – FRESHMAN												
1958-59	Northeastern University	ECAC	24	*40	24	64	....	....	....		....	....	....	....	....
1959-60	Northeastern University	ECAC	24	25	31	56	....	....	....		....	....	....	....	....
1960-61	Northeastern University	ECAC	25	35	26	61	....	....	....		....	....	....	....	....
	Boston Bruins	**NHL**	**3**	**0**	**0**	**0**	**0**	**0**	**0**	**0**	....	....	....	....	....
	NHL Totals		**3**	**0**	**0**	**0**	**0**	**0**	**0**	**0**	....	....	....	....	....

Signed as a free agent by **Boston** to a 3-game amatour try-out contract, March 15, 1961.

• CHISHOLM, LEX Lex (Alexander) Chisholm
C/RW – R. 5'11", 175 lbs. b: Galt, Ont., 4/1/1915 d: 8/6/1981.

Season	Club	League	GP	G	A	Pts	AG	AA	APts	PIM	Playoffs GP	G	A	Pts	PIM
1933-34	Galt Terrier Pups	OHA	16	11	14	25	....	....	....	23	2	1	1	2	2
1934-35	Oshawa Generals	City Jr.	12	14	5	19	....	....	....	17	....	....	....	....	....
	Oshawa Chevies	City Sr.	1	0	0	0	....	....	....	0	....	....	....	....	....
1935-36	Oshawa Chevies	City Sr.	12	2	5	7	....	....	....	19	....	....	....	....	....
1936-37	Oshawa G-Men	OHA Sr.	9	1	0	1	....	....	....	4	....	....	....	....	....
1937-38	Oshawa G-Men	OHA Sr.	13	9	10	19	....	....	....	10	2	1	0	1	4
1938-39	Syracuse Stars	AHL	3	1	1	2	....	....	....	0	3	0	0	0	0
	Oshawa G-Men	OHA Sr.	19	15	*28	*43	....	....	....	24	7	2	5	7	15
1939-40	**Toronto Maple Leafs**	**NHL**	**28**	**6**	**8**	**14**	**13**	**16**	**29**	**11**	....	....	....	....	....
1940-41	**Toronto Maple Leafs**	**NHL**	**26**	**4**	**0**	**4**	**8**	**0**	**8**	**8**	**3**	**1**	**0**	**1**	**0**
	Pittsburgh Hornets	AHL	2	0	1	1	....	....	....	2	....	....	....	....	....
1941-42	Halifax Army	City Sr.	MILITARY SERVICE												
1942-43	Toronto Army Diggers	OHA Sr.	5	6	9	15	....	....	....	8	4	6	1	7	4
	NHL Totals		**54**	**10**	**8**	**18**	**21**	**16**	**37**	**19**	**3**	**1**	**0**	**1**	**0**

• CHOUINARD, GENE Gene "Noisy" Chouinard
D – L. 5'6", 160 lbs. b: Ottawa, Ont., 1/5/1907. d: 1/29/1951.

Season	Club	League	GP	G	A	Pts	AG	AA	APts	PIM	Playoffs GP	G	A	Pts	PIM
1921-22	Ottawa Montagnards	City Sr.	14	7	*9	16	....	....	....	14	7	2	4	6	3
1922-23	Ottawa Montagnards	City Sr.	9	*8	3	*11	....	....	....	14	2	0	0	0	0
1923-24	Ottawa Montagnards	City Sr.	10	2	1	3	....	....	....	....	6	4	0	4	0
1924-25	Ottawa Montagnards	City Sr.	16	12	1	13	....	....	....	....	7	2	2	4	16
1925-26	Eveluth-Hibbing Rangers	USAHA	19	0	0	0	....	....	....	0	....	....	....	....	....
1926-27	Niagara Falls–Stratford	Can-Pro	27	3	3	6	....	....	....	16	1	0	0	0	0
1927-28	**Ottawa Senators**	**NHL**	**8**	**0**	**0**	**0**	**0**	**0**	**0**	**0**	....	....	....	....	....
	Quebec Castors	Can-Am	2	0	0	0	....	....	....	0	....	....	....	....	....
	Waterville Maine	Inter-Sr.	5	0	1	1	....	....	....	2	2	0	0	0	0
1928-29	New Haven Eagles	Can-Am	22	4	1	5	....	....	....	8	2	0	0	0	4
1929-30	New Haven Eagles	Can-Am	40	4	7	11	....	....	....	60	....	....	....	....	
1930-31	New Haven Eagles	Can-Am	40	7	11	18	....	....	....	56	....	....	....	....	....
1930-31	Bronx Tigers	Can-Am	39	5	7	12	....	....	....	40	2	1	1	2	4
1932-33	Quebec Castors	Can-Am	20	3	5	8	....	....	....	16	....	....	....	....	....
1933-34	New Haven Eagles	Can-Am	40	8	12	20	....	....	....	25	....	....	....	....	....
1934-35	Tulsa Oilers	AHA	48	11	13	24	....	....	....	11	5	1	0	1	8
	London Tecumsehs	IAHL	1	0	0	0	....	....	....	0	....	....	....	....	....
1935-36	Tulsa Oilers	AHA	36	1	7	8	....	....	....	10	3	0	0	0	5
1936-37	Perth Blue Wings	Ott-Sr.	DID NOT PLAY – COACHING												
1937-38	Perth Cresents	Ott-Sr.	1	0	0	0	....	....	....	0	....	....	....	....	....
	NHL Totals		**8**	**0**	**0**	**0**	**0**	**0**	**0**	**0**	....	....	....	....	....

• CHRYSTAL, BOB Bob Chrystal
D – L. 6', 180 lbs. b: Winnipeg, Man., 4/3/1930.

Season	Club	League	GP	G	A	Pts	AG	AA	APts	PIM	Playoffs GP	G	A	Pts	PIM
1948-49	Brandon Wheat Kings	MJHL	30	2	10	12	....	....	....	72	25	5	2	7	*57
1949-50	Brandon Wheat Kings	MJHL	36	9	13	22	....	....	....	*89	6	3	2	5	6
1950-51	Denver Falcons	USHL	64	7	13	20	....	....	....	71	5	0	5	5	10
1951-52	Cleveland Barons	AHL	68	3	16	19	....	....	....	109	5	0	0	0	6
1952-53	Cleveland Barons	AHL	63	5	17	22	....	....	....	87	11	4	4	8	24
1953-54	**New York Rangers**	**NHL**	**64**	**5**	**5**	**10**	**8**	**7**	**15**	**44**	....	....	....	....	....
1954-55	**New York Rangers**	**NHL**	**68**	**6**	**9**	**15**	**9**	**11**	**20**	**68**	....	....	....	....	....
1955-56	Saskatoon Quakers	WHL	48	5	5	10	....	....	....	67	3	0	2	2	8
1956-57	Brandon Regals	WHL	70	8	20	28	....	....	....	52	9	3	2	5	12
1957-58	Saskatoon-St. Paul Regals	WHL	69	9	23	32	....	....	....	87	....	....	....	....	....
1958-59	Winnipeg Warriors	WHL	59	14	17	31	....	....	....	54	7	0	1	1	7
	NHL Totals		**132**	**11**	**14**	**25**	**17**	**18**	**35**	**112**	....	....	....	....	....

USHL Second All-Star Team (1951) • WHL Prairie Division First All-Star Team (1957, 1958)

Traded to **NY Rangers** by **Cleveland** (AHL) for Steve Krafcheck and cash, June, 1953. Claimed by **Chicago** from **NY Rangers** in Intra-League Draft, June 4, 1957.

• CHURCH, JACK Jack Church
D – R. 5'11", 180 lbs. b: Kamsack, Sask., 5/24/1915. d: 1/5/1996.

Season	Club	League	GP	G	A	Pts	AG	AA	APts	PIM	Playoffs GP	G	A	Pts	PIM
1933-34	Regina Maple Leafs	City Jr.	3	0	0	0	....	....	....	*10	2	0	0	0	*10
	Regina Vics	City Sr.	16	0	1	1	....	....	....	42	1	0	0	0	6
1934-35	Toronto Dominions	OHA Sr.	16	2	2	4	....	....	....	73	3	0	1	1	8
1935-36	Toronto Dominions	City Sr.	16	0	*12	12	....	....	....	*78	....	....	....	....	....
	Toronto Dukes	City Sr.	16	3	1	4	....	....	....	*70	3	1	0	1	12
1936-37	Syracuse Stars	AHL	48	2	4	6	....	....	....	*93	9	1	0	1	10
1937-38	Syracuse Stars	AHL	43	3	2	5	....	....	....	47	8	0	0	0	8
1938-39	**Toronto Maple Leafs**	**NHL**	**3**	**0**	**2**	**2**	**0**	**4**	**4**	**2**	**1**	**0**	**0**	**0**	**0**
	Syracuse Stars	AHL	52	3	12	15	....	....	....	45	3	0	0	0	5
1939-40	**Toronto Maple Leafs**	**NHL**	**31**	**1**	**4**	**5**	**2**	**8**	**10**	**62**	**10**	**1**	**1**	**2**	**6**
1940-41	**Toronto Maple Leafs**	**NHL**	**11**	**0**	**1**	**1**	**0**	**2**	**2**	**22**	**5**	**0**	**0**	**0**	**8**
1941-42	**Toronto Maple Leafs**	**NHL**	**27**	**0**	**3**	**3**	**0**	**5**	**5**	**30**	....	....	....	....	....
	Brooklyn Americans	**NHL**	**15**	**1**	**3**	**4**	**2**	**5**	**7**	**10**	....	....	....	....	....
1942-43	Cornwall Army	OHA Sr.	33	6	12	18	....	....	....	*102	6	1	2	3	10
1943-44			MILITARY SERVICE												
1944-45			MILITARY SERVICE												
1945-46	**Boston Bruins**	**NHL**	**43**	**2**	**6**	**8**	**3**	**11**	**14**	**28**	**9**	**0**	**0**	**0**	**4**
1946-47	New Haven Ramblers	AHL	64	7	11	18	....	....	....	83	3	0	0	0	2
1947-48	Providence Reds	AHL	64	1	17	18	....	....	....	67	5	0	2	2	6
	NHL Totals		**130**	**4**	**19**	**23**	**7**	**35**	**42**	**154**	**25**	**1**	**1**	**2**	**18**

AHL First All-Star Team (1939)

Traded to **Brooklyn** by **Toronto** for cash, February 2, 1942. Rights transferred to **Boston** from **Brooklyn** in Special Dispersal Draw, September 11, 1943. Traded to **NY Rangers** by **Boston** for $5,000, September 17, 1946.

• CIESLA, HANK Hank Ciesla
C – L. 6'2", 190 lbs. b: St. Catharines, Ont., 10/15/1934. Deceased.

Season	Club	League	GP	G	A	Pts	AG	AA	APts	PIM	Playoffs GP	G	A	Pts	PIM
1950-51	St. Catharines Teepees	OHA	1	0	1	1	....	....		0	1	0	0	0	0
1951-52	St. Catharines Teepees	OHA	41	14	25	39	....	....	....	27	14	5	7	12	14
1952-53	St. Catharines Teepees	OHA	56	19	24	43	....	....	....	43	1	0	0	0	0
1953-54	St. Catharines Teepees	OHA	59	39	30	69	....	....	....	66	15	6	7	13	8
1954-55	St. Catharines Teepees	OHA	45	*57	49	*106	....	....	....	36	11	7	8	15	23
1955-56	**Chicago Black Hawks**	**NHL**	**70**	**8**	**23**	**31**	**12**	**29**	**41**	**22**	....	....	....	....	....
1956-57	**Chicago Black Hawks**	**NHL**	**70**	**10**	**8**	**18**	**14**	**9**	**23**	**28**	....	....	....	....	....
1957-58	**New York Rangers**	**NHL**	**60**	**2**	**6**	**8**	**3**	**6**	**9**	**16**	**6**	**0**	**2**	**2**	**0**
1958-59	**New York Rangers**	**NHL**	**69**	**6**	**14**	**20**	**8**	**15**	**23**	**21**	....	....	....	....	....
1959-60	Rochester Americans	AHL	64	27	44	71	....	....	....	31	11	3	7	10	14
1960-61	Rochester Americans	AHL	70	30	44	74	....	....		23	....	....	....	....	....
1961-62	Cleveland Barons	AHL	70	25	38	63	....	....	....	22	6	4	3	7	6
1962-63	Cleveland Barons	AHL	72	*42	56	98			....	41	7	3	8	11	8
1963-64	Pittsburgh Hornets	AHL	69	18	38	56	....	....	....	46	5	1	3	4	8
1964-65	Buffalo Bisons	AHL	49	8	8	16	....	....	....	34	....	....	....	....	....
	NHL Totals		**269**	**26**	**51**	**77**	**37**	**59**	**96**	**87**	**6**	**0**	**2**	**2**	**0**

AHL Second All-Star Team (1963)

Traded to **Chicago** by **NY Rangers** for Ron Murphy, June, 1957. Traded to **Toronto** by **NY Rangers** with Bill Kennedy for Noel Price, October 3, 1959. Traded to **Cleveland** (AHL) by **Toronto** for Bill Dineen and cash, August, 1961. Claimed by **Detroit** (Pittsburgh - AHL) from **Cleveland** (AHL) in Inter-League Draft, June, 1963. Traded to **Chicago** (Buffalo - AHL) by **Detroit** (Pittsburgh - AHL) for Jerry Topazzini, October 10, 1964.

• CLANCY, KING King (Francis Michael) Clancy
D – L. 5'7", 155 lbs. b: Ottawa, Ont., 2/25/1903. d: 11/8/1986.

Season	Club	League	GP	G	A	Pts	AG	AA	APts	PIM	Playoffs GP	G	A	Pts	PIM
1917-18	Ottawa Munitions	City Jr.	4	2	0	2	....	....	....	....	....	....	....	....	....
	Ottawa St. Joseph's	H.S.	....	....	....	....	....	....	....	....	2	3	0	3	....
1918-19	Ottawa St. Brigids	City Sr.	8	0	1	1	....	....	....	3	1	0	0	0	6
1919-20	Ottawa St. Brigids	City Sr.	8	1	0	1			....	....	....	....	....	....	....
1920-21	Ottawa St. Brigids	City Sr.	11	6	0	6	....	....	....	....	6	*5	1	*6	12
1921-22	**Ottawa Senators**	**NHL**	**24**	**4**	**6**	**10**	**11**	**38**	**49**	**21**	**2**	**0**	**0**	**0**	**2**
1922-23	**Ottawa Senators**	**NHL**	**24**	**3**	**1**	**4**	**10**	**9**	**19**	**20**	**8**	**1**	**0**	**1**	**2**
1923-24	**Ottawa Senators**	**NHL**	**24**	**9**	***8**	**17**	**37**	**150**	**187**	**18**	**2**	**0**	**0**	**0**	**4**
1924-25	**Ottawa Senators**	**NHL**	**29**	**14**	**5**	**19**	**49**	**67**	**116**	**61**	....	....	....	....	....
1925-26	**Ottawa Senators**	**NHL**	**35**	**8**	**4**	**12**	**25**	**46**	**71**	**80**	**2**	**1**	**0**	**1**	**8**
1926-27	**Ottawa Senators**	**NHL**	**43**	**9**	**10**	**19**	**26**	**86**	**112**	**78**	**6**	**1**	**1**	**2**	**14**
1927-28	**Ottawa Senators**	**NHL**	**39**	**8**	**7**	**15**	**24**	**59**	**83**	**73**	**2**	**0**	**0**	**0**	**6**
1928-29	**Ottawa Senators**	**NHL**	**44**	**13**	**2**	**15**	**53**	**18**	**71**	**89**	....	....	....	....	....
1929-30	**Ottawa Senators**	**NHL**	**44**	**17**	**23**	**40**	**34**	**76**	**110**	**83**	**2**	**0**	**1**	**1**	**2**
1930-31	**Toronto Maple Leafs**	**NHL**	**44**	**7**	**14**	**21**	**17**	**51**	**68**	**63**	**2**	**1**	**0**	**1**	**0**
1931-32	**Toronto Maple Leafs**	**NHL**	**48**	**10**	**9**	**19**	**21**	**25**	**46**	**61**	**7**	**2**	**1**	**3**	**14**
1932-33	**Toronto Maple Leafs**	**NHL**	**48**	**13**	**12**	**25**	**31**	**32**	**63**	**79**	**9**	**0**	**3**	**3**	**14**
1933-34	**Toronto Maple Leafs**	**NHL**	**46**	**11**	**17**	**28**	**24**	**46**	**70**	**62**	**3**	**0**	**0**	**0**	**8**
1934-35	**Toronto Maple Leafs**	**NHL**	**47**	**5**	**16**	**21**	**11**	**36**	**47**	**53**	**7**	**1**	**0**	**1**	**8**
1935-36	**Toronto Maple Leafs**	**NHL**	**47**	**5**	**10**	**15**	**12**	**24**	**36**	**61**	**9**	**2**	**2**	**4**	**10**
1936-37	**Toronto Maple Leafs**	**NHL**	**6**	**1**	**0**	**1**	**2**	**0**	**2**	**4**	....	....	....	....	....
	NHL Totals		**592**	**137**	**144**	**281**	**387**	**763**	**1150**	**906**	**61**	**9**	**8**	**17**	**92**

NHL First All-Star Team (1931, 1934) • NHL Second All-Star Team (1932, 1933)

Played in NHL All-Star Game (1934, 1937)

Signed as a free agent by **Ottawa**, December 14, 1921. Traded to **Toronto** by **Ottawa** for Art Smith, Eric Pettinger and $35,000, October 11, 1930.

• CLAPPER, DIT
Dit (Aubrey Victor) Clapper **HHOF**
RW/D – R. 6'2", 195 lbs. b: Newmarket, Ont., 2/9/1907. d: 1/21/1978.

Season	Club	League	GP	G	A	Pts	AG	AA	APts	PIM	PO GP	PO G	PO A	PO Pts	PO PIM
			REGULAR SEASON								PLAYOFFS				
1925-26	Toronto Parkdale	OHA	2	0	0	0	....	....	....	0	....	....	....	....	....
1926-27	Boston Tigers	Can-Am	29	6	1	7	....	....	....	57	....	....	....	....	....
1927-28	**Boston Bruins**	**NHL**	**40**	**4**	**1**	**5**	**12**	**8**	**20**	**20**	**2**	**0**	**0**	**0**	**2**
1928-29	**Boston Bruins**	**NHL**	**40**	**9**	**2**	**11**	**36**	**18**	**54**	**48**	**5**	**1**	**0**	**1**	**0**
1929-30	**Boston Bruins**	**NHL**	**44**	**41**	**20**	**61**	**83**	**66**	**149**	**48**	**6**	**4**	**0**	**4**	**4**
1930-31	**Boston Bruins**	**NHL**	**43**	**22**	**8**	**30**	**54**	**29**	**83**	**50**	**5**	**2**	**4**	**6**	**4**
1931-32	**Boston Bruins**	**NHL**	**48**	**17**	**22**	**39**	**36**	**62**	**98**	**21**	....	....	....	....	....
1932-33	**Boston Bruins**	**NHL**	**48**	**14**	**14**	**28**	**33**	**37**	**70**	**42**	**5**	**1**	**1**	**2**	**2**
1933-34	**Boston Bruins**	**NHL**	**48**	**10**	**12**	**22**	**22**	**32**	**54**	**6**	....	....	....	....	....
1934-35	**Boston Bruins**	**NHL**	**48**	**21**	**16**	**37**	**45**	**36**	**81**	**21**	**3**	**1**	**0**	**1**	**0**
1935-36	**Boston Bruins**	**NHL**	**44**	**12**	**13**	**25**	**30**	**31**	**61**	**14**	**2**	**0**	**1**	**1**	**0**
1936-37	**Boston Bruins**	**NHL**	**48**	**17**	**8**	**25**	**37**	**19**	**56**	**25**	**3**	**2**	**0**	**2**	**5**
1937-38	**Boston Bruins**	**NHL**	**46**	**6**	**9**	**15**	**13**	**18**	**31**	**24**	**3**	**0**	**0**	**0**	**12**
1938-39	**Boston Bruins**	**NHL**	**42**	**13**	**13**	**26**	**27**	**24**	**51**	**22**	**12**	**0**	**1**	**1**	**6**
1939-40	**Boston Bruins**	**NHL**	**44**	**10**	**18**	**28**	**21**	**36**	**57**	**25**	**5**	**0**	**2**	**2**	**2**
1940-41	**Boston Bruins**	**NHL**	**48**	**8**	**18**	**26**	**16**	**33**	**49**	**24**	**11**	**0**	**5**	**5**	**4**
1941-42	**Boston Bruins**	**NHL**	**32**	**3**	**12**	**15**	**5**	**18**	**23**	**31**	....	....	....	....	....
1942-43	**Boston Bruins**	**NHL**	**38**	**5**	**18**	**23**	**7**	**23**	**30**	**12**	**9**	**2**	**3**	**5**	**9**
1943-44	**Boston Bruins**	**NHL**	**50**	**6**	**25**	**31**	**7**	**30**	**37**	**13**	....	....	....	....	....
1944-45	**Boston Bruins**	**NHL**	**46**	**8**	**14**	**22**	**11**	**23**	**34**	**16**	**7**	**0**	**0**	**0**	**0**
1945-46	**Boston Bruins**	**NHL**	**30**	**2**	**3**	**5**	**3**	**6**	**9**	**0**	**4**	**0**	**0**	**0**	**0**
1946-47	**Boston Bruins**	**NHL**	**6**	**0**	**0**	**0**	**0**	**0**	**0**	**0**	....	....	....	....	....
1947-48	**Boston Bruins**	**NHL**	DID NOT PLAY – COACHING												
	NHL Totals		**833**	**228**	**246**	**474**	**498**	**549**	**1047**	**462**	**82**	**13**	**17**	**30**	**50**

NHL Second All-Star Team (1931, 1935, 1944) • NHL First All-Star Team (1939, 1940, 1941)

Played in NHL All-Star Game (1937, 1939)

Traded to **Boston** by **Boston Olympics** (Can-Am) for cash, October 25, 1927.

• CLARK, NOBBY
Nobby (Patrick J.) Clark
D – R. 6'1", 190 lbs. b: Orillia, Ontario, 6/18/1897. Deceased.

Season	Club	League	GP	G	A	Pts	AG	AA	APts	PIM	PO GP	PO G	PO A	PO Pts	PO PIM
1922-23	Duluth Hornets	USAHA	20	5	0	5	....	....	....	....	....	....	....	....	....
1923-24	Eveleth Arrowheads	USAHA	11	1	0	1	....	....	....	....	....	....	....	....	....
1924-25	Eveleth Arrowheads	USAHA	38	6	0	6	....	....	....	....	4	0	0	0	....
1925-26	Hibbing-Eveleth Rangers	CHL	38	9	3	12	....	....	....	26	....	....	....	....	....
1926-27	Minneapolis Millers	AHA	36	7	5	12	....	....	....	46	6	0	0	0	4
1927-28	**Boston Bruins**	**NHL**	**5**	**0**	**0**	**0**	**0**	**0**	**0**	**0**	....	....	....	....	....
	New Haven Eagles	Can-Am	40	6	2	8	....	....	....	35	....	....	....	....	....
1928-29	Philadelphia Arrows	Can-Am	37	4	7	11	....	....	....	54	....	....	....	....	....
1929-1932			DID NOT PLAY – RETIRED												
1932-33	Hibbing Monarchs	CHL	12	1	6	7	....	....	....	4	....	....	....	....	....
	NHL Totals		**5**	**0**	**0**	**0**	**0**	**0**	**0**	**0**	....	....	....	....	....

Traded to **Boston** by **Minneapolis** (AHA) with Dutch Gainor for Red Stuart, cash and future considerations, October 24, 1927. Traded to **New Haven** (Can-Am) by **Boston** with Billy Coutu for cash, January 5, 1928

• CLEGHORN, ODIE
Odie (Ogilvie James) Cleghorn
RW/C – R. 5'9", 195 lbs. b: Montreal, Que., 9/19/1891. d: 7/13/1956.

Season	Club	League	GP	G	A	Pts	AG	AA	APts	PIM	PO GP	PO G	PO A	PO Pts	PO PIM
1908-09	Montreal Westmount	CAHL	STATISTICS NOT AVAILABLE												
1909-10	New York Wanderers	USAHA	8	*15	0	*15	....	....	....	....	....	....	....	....	....
1910-11	Renfrew Millionaires	NHA	16	20	0	20	....	....	....	66	....	....	....	....	....
1911-12	Montreal Wanderers	NHA	17	23	0	23	....	....	....	....	....	....	....	....	....
1912-13	Montreal Wanderers	NHA	19	18	0	18	....	....	....	44	....	....	....	....	....
1913-14	Montreal Wanderers	NHA	13	9	7	16	....	....	....	19	2	0	0	0	12
1914-15	Montreal Wanderers	NHA	15	21	5	26	....	....	....	39	2	0	0	0	12
1915-16	Montreal Wanderers	NHA	21	16	7	23	....	....	....	51	....	....	....	....	....
1916-17	Montreal Wanderers	NHA	18	28	4	32	....	....	....	49	....	....	....	....	....
1917-18			DID NOT PLAY												
1918-19	**Montreal Canadiens**	**NHL**	**18**	**21**	**6**	**27**	**79**	**58**	**137**	**33**	**10**	**8**	**1**	**9**	**9**
1919-20	**Montreal Canadiens**	**NHL**	**21**	**20**	**4**	**24**	**46**	**27**	**73**	**30**	....	....	....	....	....
1920-21	**Montreal Canadiens**	**NHL**	**21**	**5**	**4**	**9**	**13**	**35**	**48**	**8**	....	....	....	....	....
1921-22	**Montreal Canadiens**	**NHL**	**24**	**21**	**3**	**24**	**59**	**19**	**78**	**26**	....	....	....	....	....
1922-23	**Montreal Canadiens**	**NHL**	**24**	**19**	**7**	**26**	**65**	**64**	**129**	**14**	**2**	**0**	**0**	**0**	**2**
1923-24	**Montreal Canadiens**	**NHL**	**22**	**3**	**3**	**6**	**12**	**53**	**65**	**14**	**6**	**0**	**1**	**1**	**0**
1924-25	**Montreal Canadiens**	**NHL**	**30**	**3**	**2**	**5**	**10**	**26**	**36**	**14**	**5**	**0**	**1**	**1**	**0**
1925-26	**Pittsburgh Pirates**	**NHL**	**17**	**2**	**1**	**3**	**6**	**11**	**17**	**4**	**1**	**0**	**0**	**0**	**0**
1926-27	**Pittsburgh Pirates**	**NHL**	**3**	**0**	**0**	**0**	**0**	**0**	**0**	**0**	....	....	....	....	....
1927-28	**Pittsburgh Pirates**	**NHL**	**2**	**0**	**0**	**0**	**0**	**0**	**0**	**4**	....	....	....	....	....
	NHL Totals		**182**	**94**	**30**	**124**	**290**	**293**	**583**	**147**	**24**	**8**	**3**	**11**	**11**
	Other Major League Totals		119	135	23	158	....	....	....	268	4	0	0	0	24

Traded to **Montreal Wanderers** (NHA) by **Quebec** (NHA) for cash, January, 1911. • Granted Military Exemption in 1917-18 on condition that he not play hockey, 1917. Retained by **Montreal Wanderers** after NHA folded, November 26, 1917. Signed as a free agent by **Montreal Canadiens**, December 9, 1918. Released by **Montreal Canadiens** to assume coaching duties with **Pittsburgh Pirates**, September, 1925

• CLEGHORN, SPRAGUE
Sprague Cleghorn **HHOF**
D – L. 5'10", 190 lbs. b: Montreal, Que., 3/11/1890. d: 7/11/1956.

Season	Club	League	GP	G	A	Pts	AG	AA	APts	PIM	PO GP	PO G	PO A	PO Pts	PO PIM
1909-10	New York Wanderers	USAHA	8	7	0	7	....	....	....	....	....	....	....	....	....
1910-11	Renfrew Millionaires	NHA	12	5	0	5	....	....	....	27	....	....	....	....	....
1911-12	Montreal Wanderers	NHA	18	9	0	9	....	....	....	40	....	....	....	....	....
1912-13	Montreal Wanderers	NHA	19	12	0	12	....	....	....	46	....	....	....	....	....
1913-14	Montreal Wanderers	NHA	20	12	8	20	....	....	....	17	....	....	....	....	....
1914-15	Montreal Wanderers	NHA	19	21	*12	33	....	....	....	51	2	0	0	0	17
1915-16	Montreal Wanderers	NHA	8	9	4	13	....	....	....	22	....	....	....	....	....
1916-17	Montreal Wanderers	NHA	19	16	3	19	....	....	....	53	....	....	....	....	....
1917-18			DID NOT PLAY												
1918-19	**Ottawa Senators**	**NHL**	**18**	**7**	**9**	**16**	**25**	**89**	**114**	**27**	**5**	**2**	**2**	**4**	**12**
1919-20	**Ottawa Senators**	**NHL**	**21**	**16**	**5**	**21**	**37**	**34**	**71**	**85**	**5**	**0**	**1**	**1**	**4**
1920-21	**Ottawa Senators**	**NHL**	**3**	**2**	**3**	**5**	**5**	**26**	**31**	**9**	....	....	....	....	....
	Toronto St. Pats	**NHL**	**13**	**3**	**5**	**8**	**7**	**44**	**51**	**31**	**1**	**0**	**0**	**0**	**0**
	Ottawa Senators	**NHL**	....	....	....	....	....	....	....	....	**5**	**1**	**2**	**3**	**36**
1921-22	**Montreal Canadiens**	**NHL**	**24**	**17**	**9**	**26**	**47**	**57**	**104**	***80**	....	....	....	....	....
1922-23	**Montreal Canadiens**	**NHL**	**24**	**9**	**4**	**13**	**30**	**36**	**66**	**34**	**1**	**0**	**0**	**0**	**0**
1923-24	**Montreal Canadiens**	**NHL**	**23**	**8**	**3**	**11**	**33**	**53**	**86**	**39**	**6**	**2**	**1**	**3**	**2**
1924-25	**Montreal Canadiens**	**NHL**	**27**	**8**	**1**	**9**	**27**	**13**	**40**	**82**	**6**	**1**	**2**	**3**	**4**
1925-26	**Boston Bruins**	**NHL**	**28**	**6**	**5**	**11**	**18**	**58**	**76**	**49**	....	....	....	....	....
1926-27	**Boston Bruins**	**NHL**	**44**	**7**	**1**	**8**	**20**	**8**	**28**	**84**	**8**	**1**	**0**	**1**	**8**
1927-28	**Boston Bruins**	**NHL**	**37**	**2**	**2**	**4**	**6**	**17**	**23**	**14**	**2**	**0**	**0**	**0**	**0**
1928-29	Newark Bulldogs	Can-Am	3	0	0	0	....	....	....	0	....	....	....	....	....
1929-30	Providence Reds	Can-Am	DID NOT PLAY – COACHING												
	NHL Totals		**262**	**85**	**47**	**132**	**255**	**435**	**690**	**534**	**39**	**7**	**8**	**15**	**66**
	Other Major League Totals		115	84	27	111	....	....	....	256	2	0	0	0	17

Rights retained by **Montreal Wanderers** after NHA folded, November 26, 1917. Claimed by **Ottawa** from **Montreal Wanderers** in Dispersal Draft, January 4, 1918. Rights transferred to **Hamilton** by **NHL** with Punch Broadbent, December 30, 1920. • Broadbent and Cleghorn refused to report. Traded to **Toronto St. Pats** by **Hamilton** for future considerations, January 25, 1921. Signed as a free agent by **Ottawa** after securing his release from **Toronto St. Pats**, March 15, 1921. Rights transferred to **Hamilton Tigers** by **NHL**, April 6, 1921. Traded to **Montreal** by **Hamilton** for Harry Mummery and Amos Arbour, November 26, 1921. Traded to **Boston** by **Montreal** for $5,000, November 8, 1925.

• CLINE, BRUCE
Bruce Cline
RW – R. 5'7", 137 lbs. b: Massawippi, Que., 11/14/1931.

Season	Club	League	GP	G	A	Pts	AG	AA	APts	PIM	PO GP	PO G	PO A	PO Pts	PO PIM
1950-51	Quebec Citadelle	QJHL	46	11	20	31	....	....	....	4	23	6	8	14	13
1951-52	Quebec Citadelle	QJHL	50	20	30	50	....	....	....	19	15	5	5	10	9
1952-53	Valleyfield Braves	QSHL	59	15	9	24	....	....	....	10	4	1	2	3	0
1953-54	Valleyfield Braves	QHL	71	17	24	41	....	....	....	34	4	0	1	1	0
1954-55	Valleyfield Braves	QHL	62	13	42	55	....	....	....	2	....	....	....	....	....
1955-56	Providence Reds	AHL	64	27	30	57	....	....	....	18	9	3	3	6	9
1956-57	**New York Rangers**	**NHL**	**30**	**2**	**3**	**5**	**3**	**3**	**6**	**10**	....	....	....	....	....
	Providence Reds	AHL	36	14	21	35	....	....	....	13	5	2	1	3	2
1957-58	Providence Reds	AHL	70	19	40	59	....	....	....	27	5	0	7	7	4
1958-59	Buffalo Bisons	AHL	70	22	39	61	....	....	....	39	7	0	2	2	0
1959-60	Springfield Indians	AHL	70	25	50	75	....	....	....	9	10	5	5	10	0
1960-61	Springfield Indians	AHL	72	40	52	92	....	....	....	13	8	2	3	5	4
1961-62	Springfield Indians	AHL	70	38	40	78	....	....	....	21	11	5	2	7	6
1962-63	Springfield Indians	AHL	72	39	48	87	....	....	....	26	....	....	....	....	....
1963-64	Hershey Bears	AHL	64	26	20	46	....	....	....	6	6	0	3	3	2
1964-65	Hershey Bears	AHL	72	17	28	45	....	....	....	6	15	4	3	7	2
1965-66	Hershey Bears	AHL	53	19	26	45	....	....	....	2	3	0	1	1	0
1966-67	Hershey Bears	AHL	70	28	42	70	....	....	....	63	....	....	....	....	....
1967-68	Hershey Bears	AHL	40	7	16	23	....	....	....	17	5	2	3	5	2
	NHL Totals		**30**	**2**	**3**	**5**	**3**	**3**	**6**	**10**	....	....	....	....	....

Won Dudley "Red" Garrett Memorial Award (Top Rookie - AHL) (1956) • AHL First All-Star Team (1961) • AHL Second All-Star Team (1963)

Traded to **Montreal** by **Springfield** (AHL) with Ted Harris, Terry Gray, Wayne Larkin and Jeff Chasczewski for the loan of Gary Bergman, Wayne Boddy, Fred Hilts, Brian Smith, John Rodger and Lorne O'Donnell, June, 1963.

• CLUNE, WALLY
Wally Clune
D – R. 5'9", 150 lbs. b: Toronto, Ont., 2/20/1930. d: 2/3/1998.

Season	Club	League	GP	G	A	Pts	AG	AA	APts	PIM	PO GP	PO G	PO A	PO Pts	PO PIM
1947-48	St. Michael's Majors	OHA	32	3	5	8	....	....	....	37	....	....	....	....	....
1948-49	St. Michael's Majors	OHA	31	2	3	5	....	....	....	68	....	....	....	....	....
1949-50	Guelph Biltmores	OHA	44	7	10	17	....	....	....	68	26	2	6	8	*39
1950-51	Montreal Royals	QSHL	8	0	0	0	....	....	....	6	....	....	....	....	....
	Boston Olympics	EHL	50	10	19	29	....	....	....	112	6	0	1	1	16
1951-52	Montreal Royals	QSHL	57	3	11	14	....	....	....	84	7	0	2	2	6
1952-53	Montreal Royals	QSHL	43	1	13	14	....	....	....	67	16	0	3	3	21
1953-54	Victoria Cougars	WHL	64	8	6	14	....	....	....	69	5	1	0	1	2
1954-55	Victoria Cougars	WHL	69	7	17	24	....	....	....	85	5	0	2	2	8
1955-56	**Montreal Canadiens**	**NHL**	**5**	**0**	**0**	**0**	**0**	**0**	**0**	**6**	....	....	....	....	....
	Montreal Royals	QHL	53	2	9	11	....	....	....	110	13	0	3	3	*39
1956-57	Montreal Royals	QHL	54	1	6	7	....	....	....	105	3	0	0	0	0
1957-58	Montreal Royals	QHL	56	1	15	16	....	....	....	87	7	1	0	1	*30
1958-59	Montreal Royals	QHL	57	7	25	32	....	....	....	84	8	0	1	1	13
1959-60	Montreal Royals	EPHL	62	2	20	22	....	....	....	63	14	0	5	5	13
1960-61	Montreal Royals	EPHL	65	2	7	9	....	....	....	22	....	....	....	....	....
	NHL Totals		**5**	**0**	**0**	**0**	**0**	**0**	**0**	**6**	....	....	....	....	....

EHL First All-Star Team (1951)

Claimed by **Montreal** from **Montreal Royals** (QHL) in Intra-League Draft, June 10, 1956

• COFLIN, HUGH Hugh Coflin
D – L. 6', 190 lbs. b: Blaine Lake, Sask., 12/15/1928.

Season	Club	League	GP	G	A	Pts	AG	AA	APts	PIM	GP	G	A	Pts	PIM
			REGULAR SEASON								PLAYOFFS				
1946-47	Humboldt Indians	SJHL	22	7	4	11	....	....	....	4	....	....	....	....	....
1947-48	Moose Jaw Canucks	SJHL	26	8	11	19	....	....	....	34	5	1	2	3	8
1948-49	Moose Jaw Canucks	WCJHL	26	10	7	17	....	....	....	62	9	0	1	1	19
1949-50	Calgary Stampeders	WCSHL	50	6	11	17	....	....	....	*133	10	0	4	4	*35
1950-51	**Chicago Black Hawks**	**NHL**	**31**	**0**	**3**	**3**	**0**	**4**	**4**	**33**	....	....	....	....	....
	Milwaukee Seagulls	USHL	35	1	16	17	....	....	....	26	....	....	....	....	....
1951-52	Indianapolis Capitals	AHL	68	3	25	28	....	....	....	64	....	....	....	....	....
1952-53	Edmonton Flyers	WHL	23	1	4	5	....	....	....	55	....	....	....	....	....
1953-54	Edmonton Flyers	WHL	70	8	18	26	....	....	....	115	13	1	3	4	12
1954-55	Edmonton Flyers	WHL	44	5	25	30	....	....	....	78	9	0	2	2	18
1955-56	Edmonton Flyers	WHL	67	9	14	23	....	....	....	109	3	0	0	0	2
1956-57	Edmonton Flyers	WHL	57	6	20	26	....	....	....	77	8	1	0	1	8
1957-58	Edmonton Flyers	WHL	70	12	32	44	....	....	....	61	5	1	1	2	10
1958-59	Edmonton Flyers	WHL	61	9	25	34	....	....	....	61	3	0	1	1	0
1959-60	Edmonton Flyers	WHL	65	7	20	27	....	....	....	18	4	0	0	0	0
	NHL Totals		**31**	**0**	**3**	**3**	**0**	**4**	**4**	**33**	....	....	....	....	....

WHL Prairie Division First All-Star Team (1959)

Traded to **Detroit** by **Chicago** with $75,000 for George Gee, Jimmy Peters Sr., Clare Martin, Rags Raglin, Max McNab and Jim McFadden, August 20, 1951. Claimed on waivers by **Hershey** (AHL) from **Edmonton** (WHL), June, 1955. Traded to **Edmonton** (WHL) by **Hershey** (AHL) for Jimmy Uniac and Larry Zeidel, August, 1955.

• COLLINGS, NORM Norm "Dodger" Collings
F – L. 6'2", 175 lbs. b: Bradford, Ont., 5/6/1910.

Season	Club	League	GP	G	A	Pts	AG	AA	APts	PIM	GP	G	A	Pts	PIM
1928-29	West Toronto Redmen	OHA	2	1	0	1	....	....	....	....	3	2	0	2	....
1929-30	West Toronto Nationals	OHA	3	4	1	5	....	....	....	0	14	8	8	16	6
1930-31	Minneapolis Millers	AHA	25	3	1	4	....	....	....	2	....	....	....	....	....
1931-32	New Haven Eagles	Can-Am	37	6	5	11	....	....	....	10	2	1	0	1	0
1932-33	New Haven–Philadelphia	Can-Am	42	11	15	26	....	....	....	8	5	0	0	0	4
1933-34	Philadelphia Arrows	Can-Am	35	5	12	17	....	....	....	26	2	0	1	1	0
1934-35	**Montreal Canadiens**	**NHL**	**1**	**0**	**1**	**1**	**0**	**2**	**2**	**0**	....	....	....	....	....
	Philadelphia Arrows	Can-Am	44	7	15	22	....	....	....	29	....	....	....	....	....
1935-36	New Haven Eagles	Can-Am	34	3	9	12	....	....	....	15	....	....	....	....	....
1936-37			DID NOT PLAY												
1937-38	Tulsa Oilers	AHA	36	7	9	16	....	....	....	21	4	0	1	1	2
	NHL Totals		**1**	**0**	**1**	**1**	**0**	**2**	**2**	**0**	....	....	....	....	....

• COLLINS, GARY Gary (Ranleigh) Collins
C – L. 5'11", 185 lbs. b: Toronto, Ont., 9/27/1935.

Season	Club	League	GP	G	A	Pts	AG	AA	APts	PIM	GP	G	A	Pts	PIM
1951-52	Kitchener Greenshirts	OHA	30	9	3	12	....	....	....	4	4	0	0	0	4
1952-53	Kitchener Greenshirts	OHA	56	16	28	44	....	....	....	28	....	....	....	....	....
1953-54	Kitchener Greenshirts	OHA	59	28	36	64	....	....	....	14	4	2	1	3	2
1954-55	Toronto Marlboros	OHA	51	20	16	36	....	....	....	44	13	*10	2	12	*37
1955-56	Toronto Marlboros	OHA	48	16	45	61	....	....	....	55	11	2	10	12	22
1956-57	Rochester Americans	AHL	33	6	17	23	....	....	....	6	....	....	....	....	....
1957-58	Rochester-Providence	AHL	61	15	21	36	....	....	....	24	4	1	0	1	2
1958-59	New Westminster Royals	WHL	53	7	13	20	....	....	....	62	....	....	....	....	....
	Toronto Maple Leafs	**NHL**	....	....	....	....	....	....	....	....	**2**	**0**	**0**	**0**	**0**
1959-60	Rochester Americans	AHL	15	2	3	5	....	....	....	0	....	....	....	....	....
	Quebec Aces	AHL	49	7	16	23	....	....	....	12	....	....	....	....	....
1960-61	Quebec Aces	AHL	70	10	21	31	....	....	....	55	....	....	....	....	....
1961-62	Pittsburgh Hornets	AHL	36	2	9	11	....	....	....	25	....	....	....	....	....
	San Francisco Seals	WHL	16	0	2	2	....	....	....	10	....	....	....	....	....
1962-63	Trail Smoke Eaters	WIHL	DID NOT PLAY – COACHING												
1963-64			PLAYED PROFESSIONAL BASEBALL												
1964-65			PLAYED PROFESSIONAL BASEBALL												
1965-66	Galt Hornets	OHA Sr.	31	5	12	17	....	....	....	26	....	....	....	....	....
1966-67	Collingwood Georgians	OHA Sr.	32	2	13	15	....	....	....	12	....	....	....	....	....
1967-68	Collingwood Kings	OHA Sr.	18	3	11	14	....	....	....	8	....	....	....	....	....
	NHL Totals		**0**	**0**	**0**	**0**	**0**	**0**	**0**	**0**	**2**	**0**	**0**	**0**	**0**

Transferred to **Toronto** by **Chicago** as compensation for Chicago's signing of free agent Hank Ciesla, June, 1955. Loaned to **Rochester** (AHL) by **Providence** (AHL) for the loan of Ray Cyr for the remainder of 1957-58 season, January, 1958. Traded to **Montreal** (Quebec - AHL) by **Toronto** (Rochester - AHL) for cash, November, 1959.

• COLVILLE, MAC Mac Colville
RW/D – R. 5'9", 175 lbs. b: Edmonton, Alta., 1/8/1916.

Season	Club	League	GP	G	A	Pts	AG	AA	APts	PIM	GP	G	A	Pts	PIM
1933-34	Edmonton Athletic Club	City Jr.	9	8	1	9	....	....	....	12	2	1	*2	3	0
1934-35	New York Cresents	EHL	21	5	10	15	....	....	....	26	8	4	5	9	8
1935-36	**New York Rangers**	**NHL**	**18**	**1**	**4**	**5**	**2**	**10**	**12**	**6**	....	....	....	....	....
	Philadelphia Ramblers	Can-Am	16	3	15	18	....	....	....	26	4	2	2	4	0
1936-37	**New York Rangers**	**NHL**	**46**	**7**	**12**	**19**	**15**	**28**	**43**	**10**	**9**	**1**	**2**	**3**	**2**
1937-38	**New York Rangers**	**NHL**	**48**	**14**	**14**	**28**	**30**	**29**	**59**	**18**	**3**	**0**	**2**	**2**	**0**
1938-39	**New York Rangers**	**NHL**	**48**	**7**	**21**	**28**	**15**	**39**	**54**	**24**	**7**	**1**	**2**	**3**	**4**
1939-40	**New York Rangers**	**NHL**	**47**	**7**	**14**	**21**	**15**	**28**	**43**	**12**	**12**	**3**	**2**	**5**	**0**
1940-41	**New York Rangers**	**NHL**	**47**	**14**	**17**	**31**	**28**	**31**	**59**	**18**	**3**	**1**	**1**	**2**	**2**
1941-42	**New York Rangers**	**NHL**	**46**	**14**	**16**	**30**	**24**	**24**	**48**	**26**	**6**	**3**	**1**	**4**	**0**
1942-43	Ottawa Commandos	QSHL	19	7	7	14	....	....	....	19	23	13	14	27	25
	Ottawa Army	City Sr.	9	6	3	9	....	....	....	4	....	....	....	....	....
1943-44	Red Deer Wheelers	City Sr.	16	4	9	13	....	....	....	17	5	0	3	3	*14
1944-45			MILITARY SERVICE												
1945-46	**New York Rangers**	**NHL**	**39**	**7**	**6**	**13**	**11**	**11**	**22**	**8**	....	....	....	....	....
1946-47	**New York Rangers**	**NHL**	**14**	**0**	**0**	**0**	**0**	**0**	**0**	**8**	....	....	....	....	....
	New Haven Ramblers	AHL	45	1	9	10	....	....	....	28	2	0	0	0	2
1947-48	Vancouver Canucks	PCHL	DID NOT PLAY – COACHING												
1948-49	New Haven Ramblers	AHL	DID NOT PLAY – COACHING												
1949-50	New Haven Ramblers	AHL	DID NOT PLAY – COACHING												
1950-51	Edmonton Flyers	WCSHL	48	7	18	25	....	....	....	71	8	1	1	2	0
	NHL Totals		**353**	**71**	**104**	**175**	**140**	**200**	**340**	**130**	**40**	**9**	**10**	**19**	**14**

EHL First All-Star Team (1935)

Signed as a free agent by **NY Rangers**, October 18, 1935.

• COLVILLE, NEIL Neil Colville HHOF
C/D – R. 5'11", 175 lbs. b: Edmonton, Alta., 8/4/1914. d: 12/26/1987.

Season	Club	League	GP	G	A	Pts	AG	AA	APts	PIM	GP	G	A	Pts	PIM
1929-30	Edmonton Enarcos	City Jr.	12	1	0	1	....	....	....	....	....	....	....	....	....
1930-31	Edmonton Poolers	City Jr.	STATISTICS NOT AVAILABLE												
1931-32	Edmonton Poolers	City Jr.	....	7	3	10	....	....	....	....	....	....	....	....	....
1932-33	Edmonton Athletic Club	City Jr.	STATISTICS NOT AVAILABLE												
1933-34	Edmonton Athletic Club	City Jr.	9	*14	4	*18	....	....	....	13	2	*4	*2	*6	5
1934-35	New York Crescents	EHL	21	*24	11	*35	....	....	....	16	8	*8	4	12	2
1935-36	**New York Rangers**	**NHL**	**1**	**0**	**0**	**0**	**0**	**0**	**0**	**0**	....	....	....	....	....
	Philadelphia Ramblers	Can-Am	35	15	16	31	....	....	....	8	4	0	2	2	0
1936-37	**New York Rangers**	**NHL**	**45**	**10**	**18**	**28**	**22**	**42**	**64**	**33**	**9**	**3**	**3**	**6**	**0**
1937-38	**New York Rangers**	**NHL**	**45**	**17**	**19**	**36**	**36**	**39**	**75**	**11**	**3**	**0**	**1**	**1**	**0**
1938-39	**New York Rangers**	**NHL**	**47**	**18**	**19**	**37**	**38**	**36**	**74**	**12**	**7**	**0**	**2**	**2**	**2**
1939-40	**New York Rangers**	**NHL**	**48**	**19**	**19**	**38**	**41**	**38**	**79**	**22**	**12**	**2**	***7**	***9**	**18**
1940-41	**New York Rangers**	**NHL**	**48**	**14**	**28**	**42**	**28**	**52**	**80**	**28**	**3**	**1**	**1**	**2**	**0**
1941-42	**New York Rangers**	**NHL**	**48**	**8**	**25**	**33**	**14**	**38**	**52**	**37**	**6**	**0**	**5**	**5**	**6**
1942-43	Ottawa Commandos	QSHL	22	12	*30	42	....	....	....	32	12	*14	*14	*28	17
	Ottawa Army	City Sr.	12	11	12	23	....	....	....	4	....	....	....	....	....
1943-44			MILITARY SERVICE												
1944-45	**New York Rangers**	**NHL**	**4**	**0**	**1**	**1**	**0**	**2**	**2**	**2**	....	....	....	....	....
	Winnipeg RCAF	City Sr.	6	5	4	9	....	....	....	4	....	....	....	....	....
	Ottawa–Quebec	QSHL	5	1	2	3	....	....	....	0	7	2	5	7	4
1945-46	**New York Rangers**	**NHL**	**49**	**5**	**4**	**9**	**8**	**7**	**15**	**25**	....	....	....	....	....
1946-47	**New York Rangers**	**NHL**	**60**	**4**	**16**	**20**	**5**	**23**	**28**	**16**	....	....	....	....	....
1947-48	**New York Rangers**	**NHL**	**55**	**4**	**12**	**16**	**6**	**17**	**23**	**25**	**6**	**1**	**0**	**1**	**6**
1948-49	**New York Rangers**	**NHL**	**14**	**0**	**5**	**5**	**0**	**8**	**8**	**2**	....	....	....	....	....
	New Haven Ramblers	AHL	11	0	3	3	....	....	....	8	....	....	....	....	....
1949-50	New Haven Ramblers	AHL	17	3	4	7	....	....	....	13	....	....	....	....	....
	NHL Totals		**464**	**99**	**166**	**265**	**198**	**302**	**500**	**213**	**46**	**7**	**19**	**26**	**32**

EHL First All-Star Team (1935) • Won John Carlin Trophy (Top Scorer - EHL) (1935) • NHL Second All-Star Team (1939, 1940, 1948)

Played in NHL All-Star Game (1939, 1948)

Signed as a free agent by **NY Rangers**, October 18, 1935.

• COLWILL, LES Les Colwill
RW – R. 5'11", 170 lbs. b: Diwide, Sask., 1/1/1935.

Season	Club	League	GP	G	A	Pts	AG	AA	APts	PIM	GP	G	A	Pts	PIM
1951-52	Lethbridge Native Sons	WCJHL	28	11	7	18	....	....	....	0	4	5	2	7	0
1952-53	Lethbridge Native Sons	WCJHL	28	15	10	25	....	....	....	8	13	4	6	10	0
1953-54	Lethbridge Native Sons	WCJHL	36	37	35	72	....	....	....	4	4	1	1	2	4
1954-55	Lethbridge Native Sons	WCJHL	38	20	*32	52	....	....	....	23	11	4	*9	13	0
	Saskatoon Quakers	WHL	2	0	0	0	....	....	....	0	....	....	....	....	....
1955-56	Saskatoon Quakers	WHL	70	17	21	38	....	....	....	37	3	2	1	3	2
1956-57	Brandon Regals	WHL	68	29	26	55	....	....	....	23	9	4	3	7	6
1957-58	Saskatoon–St. Paul	WHL	70	35	27	62	....	....	....	30	....	....	....	....	....
1958-59	**New York Rangers**	**NHL**	**69**	**7**	**6**	**13**	**9**	**6**	**15**	**16**	....	....	....	....	....
1959-60	Vancouver–Calgary	WHL	66	17	22	39	....	....	....	10	....	....	....	....	....
	NHL Totals		**69**	**7**	**6**	**13**	**9**	**6**	**15**	**16**	....	....	....	....	....

• CONACHER, BRIAN — *see page 947*

• CONACHER, CHARLIE Charlie "The Big Bomber" Conacher HHOF
RW – R. 6'1", 195 lbs. b: Toronto, Ont., 12/20/1910. d: 12/30/1967.

Season	Club	League	GP	G	A	Pts	AG	AA	APts	PIM	GP	G	A	Pts	PIM
1926-27	North Toronto Juniors	OHA	9	9	1	10	....	....	....	....	1	0	0	0	0
	North Toronto Seniors	OHA Sr.	2	1	0	1	....	....	....	2	....	....	....	....	....
1927-28	Toronto Marlboros	OHA	9	11	0	11	....	....	....	....	13	*16	3	19	....
	Toronto Marlboros	OHA Sr.	1	2	0	2	....	....	....	0	....	....	....	....	....
1928-29	Toronto Marlboros	OHA Sr.	8	*18	3	*21	....	....	....	....	2	*7	0	7	....
1929-30	**Toronto Maple Leafs**	**NHL**	**38**	**20**	**9**	**29**	**40**	**29**	**69**	**48**	....	....	....	....	....
1930-31	**Toronto Maple Leafs**	**NHL**	**37**	***31**	**12**	**43**	**77**	**44**	**121**	**78**	**2**	**0**	**1**	**1**	**0**
1931-32	**Toronto Maple Leafs**	**NHL**	**44**	***34**	**14**	**48**	**74**	**39**	**113**	**66**	**7**	***6**	**2**	**8**	**0**
1932-33	**Toronto Maple Leafs**	**NHL**	**40**	**14**	**19**	**33**	**33**	**51**	**84**	**64**	**9**	**1**	**1**	**2**	**10**
1933-34	**Toronto Maple Leafs**	**NHL**	**42**	***32**	**20**	***52**	**72**	**54**	**126**	**38**	**5**	**3**	**2**	**5**	**0**
1934-35	**Toronto Maple Leafs**	**NHL**	**47**	***36**	**21**	***57**	**78**	**47**	**125**	**24**	**7**	**1**	***4**	**5**	**6**
1935-36	**Toronto Maple Leafs**	**NHL**	**44**	***23**	**15**	**38**	**58**	**36**	**94**	**74**	**9**	**3**	**2**	**5**	**12**
1936-37	**Toronto Maple Leafs**	**NHL**	**15**	**3**	**5**	**8**	**6**	**12**	**18**	**13**	**2**	**0**	**0**	**0**	**5**
1937-38	**Toronto Maple Leafs**	**NHL**	**19**	**7**	**9**	**16**	**15**	**18**	**33**	**6**	....	....	....	....	....
1938-39	**Detroit Red Wings**	**NHL**	**40**	**8**	**15**	**23**	**17**	**28**	**45**	**39**	**5**	**2**	**5**	**7**	**2**
1939-40	**New York Americans**	**NHL**	**47**	**10**	**18**	**28**	**21**	**36**	**57**	**41**	**3**	**1**	**1**	**2**	**8**
1940-41	**New York Americans**	**NHL**	**46**	**7**	**16**	**23**	**14**	**29**	**43**	**32**	....	....	....	....	....
	NHL Totals		**459**	**225**	**173**	**398**	**505**	**423**	**928**	**523**	**49**	**17**	**18**	**35**	**49**

NHL Second All-Star Team (1932, 1933) • NHL First All-Star Team (1934, 1935, 1936) • NHL Scoring Leader (1934, 1935)

Played in NHL All-Star Game (1934, 1937)

Traded to **Detroit** by **Toronto** for $16,000 with Detroit holding option of contract renewal, October 12, 1938. • Rights returned to **Toronto** by **Detroit** after NHL club failed to renew contract, July 1, 1939. Traded to **NY Americans** by **Toronto** for cash, September 22, 1939.

• CONACHER, JIM
Jim "Pencil" Conacher
C – L. 5'10", 155 lbs. b: Motherwell, Scotland, 5/5/1921.

			REGULAR SEASON								PLAYOFFS				
Season	Club	League	GP	G	A	Pts	AG	AA	APts	PIM	GP	G	A	Pts	PIM
1938-39	Toronto Young Rangers	OHA	8	2	1	3	....	....	....	0	3	0	1	1	0
1939-40	Toronto Young Rangers	OHA	16	13	9	22	....	....	....	8	2	2	0	2	0
1940-41	Oshawa Generals	OHA	16	17	15	32	....	....	....	8	17	8	13	21	12
1941-42	Omaha Knights	AHA	47	21	23	44	....	....	....	22	8	5	7	12	10
1942-43	Cornwall Army	QSHL	26	3	18	21	....	....	....	12	....	....	....	....	....
1943-44			MILITARY SERVICE												
1944-45			MILITARY SERVICE												
1945-46	**Detroit Red Wings**	**NHL**	**20**	**1**	**5**	**6**	**2**	**9**	**11**	**10**	**5**	**1**	**1**	**2**	**0**
	Indianapolis Capitals	AHL	32	17	30	47	....	....	....	6	....	....	....	....	....
1946-47	**Detroit Red Wings**	**NHL**	**33**	**16**	**13**	**29**	**22**	**19**	**41**	**2**	**5**	**2**	**1**	**3**	**2**
	Indianapolis Capitals	AHL	24	15	18	33	....	....	....	6	....	....	....	....	....
1947-48	**Detroit Red Wings**	**NHL**	**60**	**17**	**23**	**40**	**25**	**34**	**59**	**2**	**9**	**2**	**0**	**2**	**2**
1948-49	**Detroit Red Wings**	**NHL**	**4**	**1**	**0**	**1**	**2**	**0**	**2**	**2**	....	....	....	....	....
	Chicago Black Hawks	**NHL**	**55**	**25**	**23**	**48**	**40**	**37**	**77**	**41**	....	....	....	....	....
1949-50	**Chicago Black Hawks**	**NHL**	**66**	**13**	**20**	**33**	**17**	**25**	**42**	**14**	....	....	....	....	....
1950-51	**Chicago Black Hawks**	**NHL**	**52**	**10**	**27**	**37**	**13**	**35**	**48**	**16**	....	....	....	....	....
	Milwaukee Seagulls	USHL	9	2	4	6	....	....	....	2	....	....	....	....	....
1951-52	**Chicago Black Hawks**	**NHL**	**5**	**1**	**1**	**2**	**1**	**1**	**2**	**0**	....	....	....	....	....
	New York Rangers	**NHL**	**16**	**0**	**1**	**1**	**0**	**1**	**1**	**2**	....	....	....	....	....
1952-53	**New York Rangers**	**NHL**	**17**	**1**	**4**	**5**	**2**	**6**	**8**	**2**	....	....	....	....	....
	Buffalo Bisons	AHL	34	6	21	27	....	....	....	19	....	....	....	....	....
	NHL Totals		**328**	**85**	**117**	**202**	**124**	**167**	**291**	**91**	**19**	**5**	**2**	**7**	**4**

Traded to **Chicago** by **Detroit** with Bep Guidolin and Doug McCaig for George Gee and Bud Poile, October 24, 1948. Claimed on waivers by **NY Rangers** from **Chicago**, October 26, 1951.

• CONACHER, LIONEL
Lionel "The Big Train" Conacher **HHOF**
D – L. 6'2", 195 lbs. b: Toronto, Ont., 5/24/1901. d: 5/26/1954.

Season	Club	League	GP	G	A	Pts	AG	AA	APts	PIM	GP	G	A	Pts	PIM
1918-19	Toronto Aura Lee	OHA	STATISTICS NOT AVAILABLE												
1919-20	Toronto Canoe Club	OHA	....	....	....	....	....	....	....	....	12	21	9	30	....
1920-21	Toronto Aura Lee	OHA Sr.	10	3	2	5	....	....	....	....	....	....	....	....	....
1921-22	Toronto Aura Lee	OHA Sr.	20	7	2	9	....	....	....	....	2	2	0	2	0
1922-23	North Toronto Seniors	OHA Sr.	....	....	....	....	....	....	....	....	6	12	4	16	....
1923-24	Pittsburgh Yellowjackets	USAHA	20	12	4	16	....	....	....	....	13	*6	3	*9	....
1924-25	Pittsburgh Yellowjackets	USAHA	40	14	0	14	....	....	....	....	8	5	0	5	....
1925-26	**Pittsburgh Pirates**	**NHL**	**33**	**9**	**4**	**13**	**28**	**46**	**74**	**64**	**2**	**0**	**0**	**0**	**0**
1926-27	**Pittsburgh Pirates**	**NHL**	**9**	**0**	**0**	**0**	**0**	**0**	**0**	**12**	....	....	....	....	....
	New York Americans	**NHL**	**30**	**8**	**9**	**17**	**23**	**77**	**100**	**81**	....	....	....	....	....
1927-28	**New York Americans**	**NHL**	**35**	**11**	**6**	**17**	**34**	**51**	**85**	**82**	....	....	....	....	....
1928-29	**New York Americans**	**NHL**	**44**	**5**	**2**	**7**	**20**	**18**	**38**	**132**	**2**	**0**	**0**	**0**	**10**
1929-30	**New York Americans**	**NHL**	**40**	**4**	**6**	**10**	**8**	**19**	**27**	**73**	....	....	....	....	....
1930-31	**Montreal Maroons**	**NHL**	**36**	**4**	**3**	**7**	**10**	**11**	**21**	**57**	**2**	**0**	**0**	**0**	**2**
1931-32	**Montreal Maroons**	**NHL**	**45**	**7**	**9**	**16**	**15**	**25**	**40**	**60**	**4**	**0**	**0**	**0**	**2**
1932-33	**Montreal Maroons**	**NHL**	**47**	**7**	**21**	**28**	**16**	**56**	**72**	**61**	**2**	**0**	**1**	**1**	**0**
1933-34	**Chicago Black Hawks**	**NHL**	**48**	**10**	**13**	**23**	**22**	**35**	**57**	**87**	**8**	**2**	**0**	**2**	**4**
1934-35	**Montreal Maroons**	**NHL**	**38**	**2**	**6**	**8**	**4**	**13**	**17**	**44**	**7**	**0**	**0**	**0**	**14**
1935-36	**Montreal Maroons**	**NHL**	**46**	**7**	**7**	**14**	**17**	**17**	**34**	**65**	**3**	**0**	**0**	**0**	**0**
1936-37	**Montreal Maroons**	**NHL**	**47**	**6**	**19**	**25**	**13**	**45**	**58**	**64**	**5**	**0**	**1**	**1**	**2**
	NHL Totals		**498**	**80**	**105**	**185**	**210**	**413**	**623**	**882**	**35**	**2**	**2**	**4**	**34**

NHL Second All-Star Team (1933, 1937) • NHL First All-Star Team (1934)

Played in NHL All-Star Game (1934)

Signed as a free agent by **Pittsburgh**, November 11, 1925. Traded to **NY Americans** by **Pittsburgh** for Charlie Langlois and $2,000, December 16, 1926. Traded to **Montreal Maroons** by **NY Americans** for cash, November 5, 1930. Traded to **Chicago** by **Montreal Maroons** for Bill MacKenzie and Ted Graham, August, 1934. Traded to **Montreal Canadiens** by **Chicago** with Leroy Goldsworthy and Roger Jenkins for Lorne Chabot, Marty Burke and Howie Morenz, October 3, 1934. Traded to **Montreal Maroons** by **Montreal Canadiens** with the rights to Herb Cain for rights to Nels Crutchfield, October 3, 1934.

• CONACHER, PETE
Pete (Charles Jr.) Conacher
LW – L. 5'10", 165 lbs. b: Toronto, Ont., 7/29/1932.

Season	Club	League	GP	G	A	Pts	AG	AA	APts	PIM	GP	G	A	Pts	PIM
1949-50	Galt Black Hawks	OHA	48	25	27	52	....	....	....	22	....	....	....	....	....
1950-51	Galt Black Hawks	OHA	52	32	32	64	....	....	....	10	3	5	6	11	0
1951-52	Galt Black Hawks	OHA	51	53	67	120	....	....	....	33	3	3	3	6	0
	Chicago Black Hawks	**NHL**	**2**	**0**	**1**	**1**	**0**	**1**	**1**	**0**	....	....	....	....	....
1952-53	**Chicago Black Hawks**	**NHL**	**41**	**5**	**6**	**11**	**8**	**8**	**16**	**7**	**2**	**0**	**0**	**0**	**0**
	St. Louis Flyers	AHL	29	12	16	28	....	....	....	6	....	....	....	....	....
1953-54	**Chicago Black Hawks**	**NHL**	**70**	**19**	**9**	**28**	**29**	**12**	**41**	**23**	....	....	....	....	....
1954-55	**Chicago Black Hawks**	**NHL**	**18**	**2**	**4**	**6**	**3**	**5**	**8**	**2**	....	....	....	....	....
	New York Rangers	**NHL**	**52**	**10**	**7**	**17**	**14**	**9**	**23**	**10**	....	....	....	....	....
1955-56	**New York Rangers**	**NHL**	**41**	**11**	**11**	**22**	**16**	**14**	**30**	**10**	**5**	**0**	**0**	**0**	**0**
	Buffalo Bisons	AHL	18	17	15	32	....	....	....	6	....	....	....	....	....
1956-57	Buffalo Bisons	AHL	60	26	29	55	....	....	....	16	....	....	....	....	....
1957-58	**Toronto Maple Leafs**	**NHL**	**5**	**0**	**1**	**1**	**0**	**1**	**1**	**5**	....	....	....	....	....
	Buffalo Bisons	AHL	48	12	32	44	....	....	....	2	....	....	....	....	....
1958-59	Belleville McFarlands	EOHL	1	0	0	0	....	....	....	0	....	....	....	....	....
	Canada	WEC-A	8	7	3	10	....	....	....	2	....	....	....	....	....
1959-60	Buffalo Bisons	AHL	56	5	10	15	....	....	....	16	....	....	....	....	....
1960-61	Hershey Bears	AHL	69	11	24	35	....	....	....	4	8	1	2	3	4
1961-62	Hershey Bears	AHL	70	27	29	56	....	....	....	16	7	2	0	2	5
1962-63	Hershey Bears	AHL	70	29	24	53	....	....	....	6	15	5	4	9	0
1963-64	Hershey Bears	AHL	72	34	26	60	....	....	....	12	6	0	3	3	2
1964-65	Hershey Bears	AHL	63	34	24	58	....	....	....	10	15	8	2	10	4
1965-66	Hershey Bears	AHL	60	14	20	34	....	....	....	4	....	....	....	....	....
	NHL Totals		**229**	**47**	**39**	**86**	**70**	**50**	**120**	**57**	**7**	**0**	**0**	**0**	**0**

Traded to **NY Rangers** by **Chicago** with Bill Gadsby for Rich Lamoureux, Allan Stanley and Nick Mickoski, November 23, 1954. Traded to **Buffalo** (AHL) by **NY Rangers** for Chuck Blair and Gord Pennell, June, 1955. Traded to **Toronto** by **NY Rangers** for $15,000, June, 1957. Traded to **NY Rangers** by **Toronto** for $15,000, November 18, 1957. Traded to **Detroit** by **NY Rangers** (Buffalo - AHL) for Barry Cullen, August, 1960. Traded to **Hershey** (AHL) by **Detroit** with Marc Reaume and John McIntyre for Howie Young, June, 1961.

• CONACHER, ROY
Roy Conacher
LW – L. 6'2", 175 lbs. b: Toronto, Ont., 10/5/1916. d: 12/29/1984.

			REGULAR SEASON								PLAYOFFS				
Season	Club	League	GP	G	A	Pts	AG	AA	APts	PIM	GP	G	A	Pts	PIM
1933-34	West Toronto Nationals	OHA	6	0	1	1	....	....	....	0	....	....	....	....	....
1934-35	West Toronto Nationals	OHA	9	4	3	7	....	....	....	8	....	....	....	....	....
1935-36	West Toronto Nationals	OHA	10	*12	3	15	....	....	....	11	5	4	2	6	4
1936-37	Toronto Dominions	OHA Sr.	8	3	3	6	....	....	....	4	4	*3	0	*3	2
1937-38	Kirkland Lake Hurricanes	NOHA	12	12	11	23	....	....	....	2	1	1	0	1	0
1938-39	**Boston Bruins**	**NHL**	**47**	***26**	**11**	**37**	**56**	**20**	**76**	**12**	**12**	**6**	**4**	**10**	**12**
1939-40	**Boston Bruins**	**NHL**	**31**	**18**	**12**	**30**	**39**	**24**	**63**	**9**	**6**	**2**	**1**	**3**	**0**
1940-41	**Boston Bruins**	**NHL**	**41**	**24**	**14**	**38**	**49**	**26**	**75**	**7**	**11**	**1**	**5**	**6**	**0**
1941-42	**Boston Bruins**	**NHL**	**43**	**24**	**13**	**37**	**42**	**20**	**62**	**12**	**5**	**2**	**1**	**3**	**0**
1942-43	Saskatoon RCAF	City Sr.	20	13	8	21	....	....	....	2	3	2	2	4	0
1943-44	Dartmouth RCAF	City Sr.	3	*9	2	11	....	....	....	4	....	....	....	....	....
1944-45	Dartmouth RCAF	City Sr.	4	1	2	3	....	....	....	0	....	....	....	....	....
1945-46	**Boston Bruins**	**NHL**	**4**	**2**	**1**	**3**	**3**	**2**	**5**	**0**	**3**	**0**	**0**	**0**	**0**
1946-47	**Detroit Red Wings**	**NHL**	**60**	**30**	**24**	**54**	**41**	**34**	**75**	**6**	**5**	**4**	**4**	**8**	**2**
1947-48	**Chicago Black Hawks**	**NHL**	**52**	**22**	**27**	**49**	**32**	**40**	**72**	**4**	....	....	....	....	....
1948-49	**Chicago Black Hawks**	**NHL**	**60**	**26**	**42**	***68**	**41**	**68**	**109**	**8**	....	....	....	....	....
1949-50	**Chicago Black Hawks**	**NHL**	**70**	**25**	**31**	**56**	**34**	**40**	**74**	**16**	....	....	....	....	....
1950-51	**Chicago Black Hawks**	**NHL**	**70**	**26**	**24**	**50**	**35**	**31**	**66**	**16**	....	....	....	....	....
1951-52	**Chicago Black Hawks**	**NHL**	**12**	**3**	**1**	**4**	**4**	**1**	**5**	**0**	....	....	....	....	....
	NHL Totals		**490**	**226**	**200**	**426**	**376**	**306**	**682**	**90**	**42**	**15**	**15**	**30**	**14**

NHL First All-Star Team (1949) • Won Art Ross Trophy (1949)

Played in NHL All-Star Game (1949)

Traded to **Detroit** by **Boston** for Joe Carveth, August, 1946. Traded to **NY Rangers** by **Detroit** for Eddie Slowinski and future considerations, October 22, 1947. Conacher refused to report and transaction was voided. Traded to **Chicago** by **Detroit** for cash, November 1, 1947.

• CONN, HUGH
Hugh "Red" Conn
LW – L. 5'11", 180 lbs. b: Hartney, Man., 10/25/1904. Deceased.

Season	Club	League	GP	G	A	Pts	AG	AA	APts	PIM	GP	G	A	Pts	PIM
1925-26	Melville Millionaires	SSHL	17	8	*13	21	....	....	....	18	....	....	....	....	....
1926-27	Regina–Moose Jaw	PrHL	33	11	5	16	....	....	....	43	....	....	....	....	....
1927-28	Moose Jaw Maroons	PrHL	28	14	7	21	....	....	....	36	....	....	....	....	....
1928-29	Portland Buckaroos	PCHL	36	16	3	19	....	....	....	44	1	0	0	0	0
1929-30	Portland Buckaroos	PCHL	36	6	4	10	....	....	....	22	4	1	0	1	0
1930-31	Portland Buckaroos	PCHL	33	9	6	15	....	....	....	54	....	....	....	....	....
1931-32	Boston Cubs	Can-Am	40	8	11	19	....	....	....	43	5	2	0	2	13
1932-33	Philadelphia Arrows	Can-Am	42	15	16	31	....	....	....	38	3	0	0	0	0
1933-34	**New York Americans**	**NHL**	**48**	**4**	**17**	**21**	**9**	**46**	**55**	**12**	....	....	....	....	....
	Edmonton Eskimos	NWHL	1	0	0	0	....	....	....	0	....	....	....	....	....
1934-35	**New York Americans**	**NHL**	**48**	**5**	**11**	**16**	**11**	**24**	**35**	**10**	....	....	....	....	....
1935-36	Providence Reds	Can-Am	45	11	15	26	....	....	....	30	7	1	2	3	2
1936-37	Springfield Indians	AHL	42	9	6	15	....	....	....	26	5	1	2	3	2
1937-38	Vancouver Lions	PCHL	41	10	14	24	....	....	....	20	6	1	4	5	2
1938-39	Portland Buckaroos	PCHL	43	9	26	35	....	....	....	58	5	1	1	2	10
1939-40	Portland Buckaroos	PCHL	32	3	3	6	....	....	....	20	5	0	0	0	8
1940-41	Portland Buckaroos	PCHL	48	11	10	21	....	....	....	91	....	....	....	....	....
	NHL Totals		**96**	**9**	**28**	**37**	**20**	**70**	**90**	**22**	....	....	....	....	....

Traded to **Moose Jaw** (PrHL) by **Regina** (PrHL) for Lawrence Rose, January 27, 1927. Traded to **Montreal Canadiens** by **Springfield** (AHL) for Sammy Godin, September 30, 1937.

• CONNELLY, BERT
Bert (Albert Patrick) Connelly
LW – L. 5'11", 174 lbs. b: Montreal, Que., 4/22/1909. Deceased.

Season	Club	League	GP	G	A	Pts	AG	AA	APts	PIM	GP	G	A	Pts	PIM
1928-29	Moncton Eurekas	City Sr.	....	10	0	10	....	....	....	....	....	....	....	....	....
	Moncton CNR	City Sr.	....	7	0	7	....	....	....	....	....	....	....	....	....
1929-30	Montreal Columbus	City Sr.	10	0	0	0	....	....	....	11	....	....	....	....	....
1930-31	Verdun CPR	Mtl-Sr.	STATISTICS NOT AVAILABLE												
1931-32	Moncton Hawks	MSHL	24	10	4	14	....	....	....	44	9	2	1	3	8
1932-33	Moncton Hawks	MSHL	26	6	3	9	....	....	....	37	13	*7	0	7	14
1933-34	Moncton Hawks	MSHL	29	14	11	25	....	....	....	31	14	*10	5	*15	12
1934-35	**New York Rangers**	**NHL**	**47**	**10**	**11**	**21**	**21**	**24**	**45**	**23**	**4**	**1**	**0**	**1**	**0**
1935-36	**New York Rangers**	**NHL**	**25**	**2**	**2**	**4**	**5**	**5**	**10**	**10**	....	....	....	....	....
1936-37	Philadelphia Ramblers	AHL	43	9	12	21	....	....	....	35	3	0	0	0	0
1937-38	**Chicago Black Hawks**	**NHL**	**15**	**1**	**2**	**3**	**2**	**4**	**6**	**4**	**10**	**0**	**0**	**0**	**0**
	Springfield Indians	AHL	29	5	9	14	....	....	....	31	....	....	....	....	....
1938-39	Springfield Indians	AHL	45	15	12	27	....	....	....	30	3	0	0	0	0
1939-40	St. Paul Saints	AHA	46	24	25	49	....	....	....	53	7	4	2	6	21
1940-41	St. Paul Saints	AHA	46	16	11	27	....	....	....	31	4	0	0	0	4
1941-42	Fort Worth Rangers	AHA	49	27	32	59	....	....	....	36	5	3	0	3	6
1942-43	Montreal Royals	QSHL	14	3	5	8	....	....	....	2	....	....	....	....	....
1943-44	Montreal Canada Car	City Sr.	11	12	10	22	....	....	....	4	....	....	....	....	....
1944-45	Valleyfield Braves	QSHL	35	23	23	46	....	....	....	26	14	9	4	13	8
1945-46	St. Hyacinthe Saints	QPHL	17	13	10	23	....	....	....	33	4	1	2	3	2
	NHL Totals		**87**	**13**	**15**	**28**	**28**	**33**	**61**	**37**	**14**	**1**	**0**	**1**	**0**

AHA First All-Star Team (1942)

Signed as a free agent by **NY Rangers**, October 26, 1934. Signed as a free agent by **Chicago**, February 7, 1938.

• CONNELLY, WAYNE
— *see page 948*

• CONNOR, HARRY Harry Connor

LW – L. 6', 195 lbs. b: Ottawa, Ont., 12/3/1904. d: 3/2/1947.

			REGULAR SEASON								PLAYOFFS				
Season	Club	League	GP	G	A	Pts	AG	AA	APts	PIM	GP	G	A	Pts	PIM
1924-25	Ottawa Rideaus	City Sr.	15	8	1	9	....	....	....	....	3	0	0	0	0
1925-26	Guelph Royals	OHA Sr.	STATISTICS NOT AVAILABLE												
1926-27	Saskatoon Crescents	PCHL	32	22	14	36	....	....	....	*73	3	1	0	1	4
1927-28	**Boston Bruins**	**NHL**	**42**	**9**	**1**	**10**	**28**	**8**	**36**	**36**	**2**	**0**	**0**	**0**	**0**
1928-29	**New York Americans**	**NHL**	**43**	**6**	**2**	**8**	**24**	**18**	**42**	**83**	**2**	**0**	**0**	**0**	**2**
1929-30	**Ottawa Senators**	**NHL**	**25**	**1**	**2**	**3**	**2**	**6**	**8**	**22**	....	....	....	....	....
	Boston Bruins	**NHL**	**13**	**0**	**0**	**0**	**0**	**0**	**0**	**4**	**6**	**0**	**0**	**0**	**0**
1930-31	**Ottawa Senators**	**NHL**	**11**	**0**	**0**	**0**	**0**	**0**	**0**	**4**	....	....	....	....	....
	London Techumsehs	Can-Am	15	3	0	3	....	....	....	8	....	....	....	....	....
1931-32	Providence Reds	Can-Am	29	12	13	25	....	....	....	18	5	0	1	1	2
1932-33	Providence Reds	Can-Am	36	8	7	15	....	....	....	30	....	....	....	....	....
	Quebec Castors	Can-Am	11	3	4	7	....	....	....	24	....	....	....	....	....
	NHL Totals		**134**	**16**	**5**	**21**	**54**	**32**	**86**	**149**	**10**	**0**	**0**	**0**	**2**

Traded to **NY Americans** by **Boston** for Red Green, June, 1928. Claimed on waivers by **Ottawa** from **NY Americans** for $5,000, November 18, 1929. Traded to **Boston** by **Ottawa** for Bill Hutton, January 30, 1930. Traded to **Ottawa** by **Boston** for Bill Hutton, October 16, 1930.

• CONNORS, BOBBY Bobby Connors

LW/D – L. 5'9", 165 lbs. b: Scotland, 10/19/1904. d: 7/26/1931.

			REGULAR SEASON								PLAYOFFS				
Season	Club	League	GP	G	A	Pts	AG	AA	APts	PIM	GP	G	A	Pts	PIM
1923-24	Port Arthur Bearcats	MHL Sr.	16	4	1	5	....	....	....	5	2	0	0	0	0
1924-25	Port Arthur Bearcats	MHL Sr.	15	3	0	3	....	....	....	....	9	1	0	1	2
1925-26	Niagara Falls Cataracts	OHA Sr.	18	12	6	18	....	....	....	26	....	....	....	....	....
1926-27	**New York Americans**	**NHL**	**6**	**1**	**0**	**1**	**3**	**0**	**3**	**0**	....	....	....	....	....
	Niagara Falls Cataracts	Can-Pro	17	6	2	8	....	....	....	31	....	....	....	....	....
1927-28	Detroit Olympics	IAHL	38	14	10	24	....	....	....	*131	2	0	0	0	6
1928-29	**Detroit Cougars**	**NHL**	**41**	**13**	**3**	**16**	**53**	**27**	**80**	**68**	**2**	**0**	**0**	**0**	**10**
1929-30	**Detroit Cougars**	**NHL**	**31**	**3**	**7**	**10**	**6**	**23**	**29**	**42**	....	....	....	....	....
	Detroit Olympics	IAHL	15	9	5	14	....	....	....	29	3	1	0	1	13
1930-31	Seattle Eskimos	PCHL	27	9	1	10	....	....	....	88	....	....	....	....	....
	NHL Totals		**78**	**17**	**10**	**27**	**62**	**50**	**112**	**110**	**2**	**0**	**0**	**0**	**10**

Traded to **Detroit Cougars** by **NY Americans** for Frank Sheppard, September, 1928.
• Drowned near Port Arthur, Ontario on July 26,1931.

• CONVEY, EDDIE Eddie Convey

LW/C – L. 5'11", 165 lbs. b: Toronto, Ont., 12/16/1910. Deceased.

			REGULAR SEASON								PLAYOFFS				
Season	Club	League	GP	G	A	Pts	AG	AA	APts	PIM	GP	G	A	Pts	PIM
1927-28	St. Michael's Majors	OHA	6	12	*6	18	....	....	....	....	6	*7	*6	*13	....
1928-29	St. Michael's Majors	OHA	7	7	2	9	....	....	....	....	2	0	1	1	....
1929-30	Toronto Nationals	OHA Sr.	9	2	2	4	....	....	....	*33	2	0	0	0	2
1930-31	**New York Americans**	**NHL**	**2**	**0**	**0**	**0**	**0**	**0**	**0**	**0**	....	....	....	....	....
	New Haven Eagles	Can-Am	32	7	6	13	....	....	....	98	....	....	....	....	....
1931-32	**New York Americans**	**NHL**	**21**	**1**	**0**	**1**	**2**	**0**	**2**	**21**	....	....	....	....	....
	New Haven Eagles	Can-Am	23	5	11	16	....	....	....	28	2	1	1	2	0
1932-33	**New York Americans**	**NHL**	**13**	**0**	**1**	**1**	**0**	**3**	**3**	**12**	....	....	....	....	....
	New Haven Eagles	Can-Am	30	8	6	14	....	....	....	81	....	....	....	....	....
1933-34	Buffalo Bisons	IAHL	44	4	8	12	....	....	....	35	6	0	1	1	12
1934-35	Windsor Bulldogs	IAHL	44	*24	17	41	....	....	....	54	....	....	....	....	....
1935-36	Syracuse Stars	IAHL	45	20	19	39	....	....	....	58	2	2	0	2	0
1936-37	Syracuse Stars	AHL	48	12	37	49	....	....	....	82	9	2	4	6	*19
1937-38	Syracuse Stars	AHL	48	19	*33	52	....	....	....	42	8	2	3	5	0
1938-39	Syracuse Stars	AHL	54	14	25	39	....	....	....	30	3	1	1	2	0
1939-40	Syracuse Stars	AHL	53	17	33	50	....	....	....	24	....	....	....	....	....
1940-41	Pittsburgh Hornets	AHL	56	15	28	43	....	....	....	22	6	2	0	2	4
	NHL Totals		**36**	**1**	**1**	**2**	**2**	**3**	**5**	**33**	....	....	....	....	....

AHL Second All-Star Team (1938)

• COOK, BILL Bill Cook HHOF

RW – R. 5'10", 170 lbs. b: Brantford, Ont., 10/9/1896. d: 4/5/1986.

			REGULAR SEASON								PLAYOFFS				
Season	Club	League	GP	G	A	Pts	AG	AA	APts	PIM	GP	G	A	Pts	PIM
1919-20	Kingston Frontenacs	OHA Sr.	STATISTICS NOT AVAILABLE												
1920-21	Soo Greyhounds	City Sr.	13	12	6	18	....	....	....	....	....	....	....	....	....
	Soo Greyhounds	NOHA	9	*12	7	*19	....	....	....	48	5	1	6	6	....
1921-22	Soo Greyhounds	City Sr.	12	*20	8	*28	....	....	....	....	....	....	....	....	....
	Soo Greyhounds	NOHA	8	7	5	12	....	....	....	38	2	1	1	2	2
1922-23	Saskatoon Sheiks	WCHL	30	9	16	25	....	....	....	19	....	....	....	....	....
1923-24	Saskatoon Crescents	WCHL	30	*26	*14	*40	....	....	....	20	....	....	....	....	....
1924-25	Saskatoon Crescents	WCHL	27	22	10	32	....	....	....	79	2	0	0	0	4
1925-26	Saskatoon Crescents	WHL	30	*31	13	*44	....	....	....	26	2	2	....	....	....
1926-27	**New York Rangers**	**NHL**	**44**	***33**	**4**	***37**	**99**	**34**	**133**	**58**	**2**	**1**	**0**	**1**	**6**
1927-28	**New York Rangers**	**NHL**	**43**	**18**	**6**	**24**	**56**	**51**	**107**	**42**	**9**	**2**	**3**	**5**	**26**
1928-29	**New York Rangers**	**NHL**	**43**	**15**	**8**	**23**	**61**	**74**	**135**	**41**	**6**	**0**	**0**	**0**	**6**
1929-30	**New York Rangers**	**NHL**	**44**	**29**	**30**	**59**	**58**	**99**	**157**	**56**	**4**	**0**	**1**	**1**	**11**
1930-31	**New York Rangers**	**NHL**	**43**	**30**	**12**	**42**	**74**	**44**	**118**	**39**	**4**	**3**	**0**	**3**	**4**
1931-32	**New York Rangers**	**NHL**	**48**	***34**	**14**	**48**	**74**	**39**	**113**	**33**	**7**	**3**	**3**	**6**	**2**
1932-33	**New York Rangers**	**NHL**	**48**	***28**	**22**	***50**	**67**	**59**	**126**	**51**	**8**	**3**	**2**	**5**	**4**
1933-34	**New York Rangers**	**NHL**	**48**	**13**	**13**	**26**	**29**	**35**	**64**	**21**	**2**	**0**	**0**	**0**	**2**
1934-35	**New York Rangers**	**NHL**	**48**	**21**	**15**	**36**	**45**	**33**	**78**	**23**	**4**	**1**	**2**	**3**	**7**
1935-36	**New York Rangers**	**NHL**	**44**	**7**	**10**	**17**	**17**	**24**	**41**	**16**	....	....	....	....	....
1936-37	**New York Rangers**	**NHL**	**21**	**1**	**4**	**5**	**2**	**9**	**11**	**6**	....	....	....	....	....
1937-38	Cleveland Barons	AHL	5	0	0	0	....	....	....	5	1	0	0	0	0
	NHL Totals		**474**	**229**	**138**	**367**	**582**	**501**	**1083**	**386**	**46**	**13**	**11**	**24**	**68**
	Other Major League Totals		117	88	53	141	....	....	....	144	4	2	0	0	4

WCHL All-Star Team (1924, 1925) • WHL All-Star Team (1926) • NHL Scoring Leader (1927, 1933) • NHL First All-Star Team (1931, 1932, 1933) • NHL Second All-Star Team (1934)

Played in NHL All-Star Game (1934)

Signed as a free agent by **Saskatoon** (WCHL), August 24, 1922. Traded to **NY Rangers** by **Saskatoon** (WHL) for cash, October 18, 1926.

• COOK, BUD Bud (Alexander Leone) Cook

C – L. 5'10", 160 lbs. b: Kingston, Ont., 11/20/1907. d: 11/13/1993.

			REGULAR SEASON								PLAYOFFS				
Season	Club	League	GP	G	A	Pts	AG	AA	APts	PIM	GP	G	A	Pts	PIM
1924-25	Saskatoon Pats	City Jr.	6	5	1	*6	....	....	....	....	....	....	....	....	....
1925-26	Saskatoon Wesleys	City Jr.	10	7	*2	9	....	....	....	....	....	....	....	....	....
1926-27			DID NOT PLAY												
1927-28	Saskatoon Collegiate	City Jr.	3	1	0	1	....	....	....	0	....	....	....	....	....
1928-29	Oakland Shieks	Cal-Pro	20	13	7	20	....	....	....	33	....	....	....	....	....
1929-30	Oakland Shieks	Cal-Pro	24	24	*21	*45	....	....	....	34	....	....	....	....	....
1930-31	Providence Reds	Can-Am	33	16	11	27	....	....	....	61	2	0	1	1	4
1931-32	**Boston Bruins**	**NHL**	**28**	**4**	**4**	**8**	**8**	**11**	**19**	**14**	....	....	....	....	....
	Boston Cubs	Can-Am	7	1	2	3	....	....	....	9	....	....	....	....	....
1932-33	Boston Cubs	Can-Am	42	16	26	42	....	....	....	70	7	3	*4	*7	10
1933-34	**Ottawa Senators**	**NHL**	**18**	**1**	**0**	**1**	**2**	**0**	**2**	**8**	....	....	....	....	....
	Detroit Olympics	IAHL	26	11	6	17	....	....	....	30	6	3	0	3	17
1934-35	**St. Louis Eagles**	**NHL**	**4**	**0**	**0**	**0**	**0**	**0**	**0**	**0**	....	....	....	....	....
	Cleveland Falcons	IAHL	37	20	21	41	....	....	....	50	2	1	1	2	4
1935-36	Cleveland Falcons	IAHL	44	27	19	46	....	....	....	29	2	1	0	1	0
1936-37	Cleveland Barons	AHL	43	14	10	24	....	....	....	10	....	....	....	....	....
1937-38	Cleveland Falcons	AHL	43	13	27	40	....	....	....	46	2	0	0	0	2
1938-39	Providence Reds	AHL	DID NOT PLAY – INJURED												
1939-40	Cleveland Barons	AHL	54	14	15	29	....	....	....	27	....	....	....	....	....
1940-41	Cleveland Barons	AHL	54	9	22	31	....	....	....	26	9	1	5	6	13
1941-42	Cleveland Barons	AHL	54	8	32	40	....	....	....	32	5	0	2	2	4
1942-43	Cleveland Barons	AHL	51	5	21	26	....	....	....	28	4	0	1	1	0
1943-44	Cleveland Barons	AHL	4	2	3	5	....	....	....	2	....	....	....	....	....
	Coast Guard Clippers	....	31	16	18	34	....	....	....	2	8	7	5	12	6
1944-45			MILITARY SERVICE												
1945-46	Oakland Oaks	PCHL	37	17	30	47	....	....	....	30	2	3	2	5	0
	NHL Totals		**50**	**5**	**4**	**9**	**10**	**11**	**21**	**22**	....	....	....	....	....

AHL First All-Star Team (1938)

Traded to **Montreal Canadiens** by **Oakland** (Cal-Pro) for cash, February 18, 1930. Traded to **Boston** by **Montreal Canadiens** for cash, May 13, 1931. Traded to **Ottawa** by **Boston** with Perk Galbraith and Ted Saunders for Bob Gracie, October 4, 1933. Transferred to **St. Louis** after **Ottawa** franchise relocated, September 22, 1934. Traded to **Cleveland** (IAHL) by **St. Louis** for cash, November 29, 1934. • **Coast Guard Cutters** played exhibition season only in 1943-44.

• COOK, BUN Bun (Frederick Joseph) Cook HHOF

LW – L. 5'11", 180 lbs. b: Kingston, Ont., 9/18/1903. d: 3/19/1988.

			REGULAR SEASON								PLAYOFFS				
Season	Club	League	GP	G	A	Pts	AG	AA	APts	PIM	GP	G	A	Pts	PIM
1921-22	Soo Greyhounds	NOHA	3	2	1	3	....	....	....	2	....	....	....	....	....
1922-23	Soo Greyhounds	NOHA	8	2	3	5	....	....	....	10	5	2	2	4	4
1923-24	Soo Greyhounds	NOHA	8	3	3	6	....	....	....	10	7	1	0	1	8
1924-25	Saskatoon Crescents	WCHL	28	17	4	21	....	....	....	44	2	0	0	0	0
1925-26	Saskatoon Crescents	WHL	30	8	4	12	....	....	....	22	2	0	0	0	12
1926-27	**New York Rangers**	**NHL**	**44**	**14**	**9**	**23**	**41**	**77**	**118**	**42**	**2**	**0**	**0**	**0**	**6**
1927-28	**New York Rangers**	**NHL**	**44**	**14**	**14**	**28**	**43**	**121**	**164**	**45**	**9**	**2**	**1**	**3**	**10**
1928-29	**New York Rangers**	**NHL**	**43**	**13**	**5**	**18**	**53**	**46**	**99**	**70**	**6**	**1**	**0**	**1**	**12**
1929-30	**New York Rangers**	**NHL**	**43**	**24**	**18**	**42**	**48**	**59**	**107**	**55**	**4**	**2**	**0**	**2**	**2**
1930-31	**New York Rangers**	**NHL**	**44**	**18**	**17**	**35**	**44**	**62**	**106**	**72**	**4**	**0**	**0**	**0**	**2**
1931-32	**New York Rangers**	**NHL**	**45**	**14**	**20**	**34**	**30**	**56**	**86**	**43**	**7**	**6**	**2**	**8**	**12**
1932-33	**New York Rangers**	**NHL**	**48**	**22**	**15**	**37**	**52**	**40**	**92**	**35**	**8**	**2**	**0**	**2**	**4**
1933-34	**New York Rangers**	**NHL**	**48**	**18**	**15**	**33**	**40**	**40**	**80**	**36**	**2**	**0**	**0**	**0**	**2**
1934-35	**New York Rangers**	**NHL**	**48**	**13**	**21**	**34**	**28**	**47**	**75**	**26**	**4**	**2**	**0**	**2**	**0**
1935-36	**New York Rangers**	**NHL**	**26**	**4**	**5**	**9**	**10**	**12**	**22**	**12**	....	....	....	....	....
1936-37	**Boston Bruins**	**NHL**	**40**	**4**	**5**	**9**	**9**	**12**	**21**	**8**	....	....	....	....	....
1937-38	Providence Reds	AHL	19	0	1	1	....	....	....	4	4	0	0	0	2
1938-39	Providence Reds	AHL	11	1	3	4	....	....	....	4	....	....	....	....	....
1939-40	Providence Reds	AHL	1	0	0	0	....	....	....	0	2	0	0	0	0
1940-41	Providence Reds	AHL	1	0	0	0	....	....	....	0	....	....	....	....	....
1941-42	Providence Reds	AHL	2	0	1	1	....	....	....	0	....	....	....	....	....
1942-43	Providence Reds	AHL	3	1	1	2	....	....	....	4	....	....	....	....	....
	NHL Totals		**473**	**158**	**144**	**302**	**398**	**572**	**970**	**444**	**46**	**15**	**3**	**18**	**50**
	Other Major League Totals		58	25	8	33	....	....	....	66	4	0	0	0	12

NHL Second All-Star Team (1931)

Signed as a free agent by **Saskatoon** (WCHL), September 20, 1924. Traded to **NY Rangers** by **Saskatoon** (WHL) for cash, October 18, 1926. Traded to **Boston** by **NY Rangers** for cash, September 10, 1936. • Served as playing-coach in **Providence** (AHL), 1937-1943.

• COOK, LLOYD Lloyd "Farmer" Cook

D – L. 6', 170 lbs. b: Lynden, Ontario, 3/21/1890. d: 10/9/1964.

			REGULAR SEASON								PLAYOFFS				
Season	Club	League	GP	G	A	Pts	AG	AA	APts	PIM	GP	G	A	Pts	PIM
1914-15	Vancouver Millionaires	PCHA	17	11	6	17	....	....	....	15	3	3	0	3	9
1915-16	Vancouver Millionaires	PCHA	18	18	3	21	....	....	....	24	....	....	....	....	....
1916-17	Spokane Canaries	PCHA	23	13	9	22	....	....	....	32	....	....	....	....	....
1917-18	Vancouver Millionaires	PCHA	18	6	4	10	....	....	....	11	6	2	0	2	12
1918-19	Vancouver Millionaires	PCHA	20	8	6	14	....	....	....	22	2	1	0	1	0
1919-20	Vancouver Millionaires	PCHA	21	10	4	14	....	....	....	15	2	1	0	1	0
1920-21	Vancouver Millionaires	PCHA	24	12	9	21	....	....	....	18	7	3	1	4	2
1921-22	Vancouver Millionaires	PCHA	24	2	3	5	....	....	....	9	2	1	1	2	0
1922-23	Vancouver Maroons	PCHA	30	19	11	30	....	....	....	33	6	0	0	0	12
1923-24	Vancouver Maroons	PCHA	28	7	5	12	....	....	....	18	7	2	3	5	4
1924-25	**Boston Bruins**	**NHL**	**4**	**1**	**0**	**1**	**3**	**0**	**3**	**0**	....	....	....	....	....
1925-26	Culver City Pros	Cal-Pro	....	8	3	11	....	....	....	18	....	....	....	....	....
1926-27	Culver City Pros	Cal-Pro	STATISTICS NOT AVAILABLE												
1927-28	Los Angeles Richfields	Cal-Pro	22	13	2	15	....	....	....	18	....	....	....	....	....
1928-29	San Francisco Tigers	Cal-Pro	....	8	4	12	....	....	....	14	....	....	....	....	....
1929-30	San Francisco Tigers	Cal-Pro	....	4	3	7	....	....	....	....	....	....	....	....	....
1930-31	San Francisco Hawks	Cal-Pro	....	8	6	14	....	....	....	....	....	....	....	....	....
	NHL Totals		**4**	**1**	**0**	**1**	**3**	**0**	**3**	**0**	....	....	....	....	....
	Other Major League Totals		223	106	60	166	....	....	....	197	35	13	5	18	39

PCHA Second All-Star Team (1916, 1918, 1919) • PCHA First All-Star Team (1920, 1921, 1923)

Signed as a free agent by **Vancouver** (PCHA), December 25, 1917. Traded to **Boston** by **Vancouver** (WCHL) for cash, November 18, 1924.

• COOK, TOM
Tom Cook
C – L. 5'7", 140 lbs. b: Fort William, Ont., 5/7/1907. d: 10/2/1961.

Season	Club	League	GP	G	A	Pts	AG	AA	APts	PIM	GP	G	A	Pts	PIM
			REGULAR SEASON								PLAYOFFS				
1923-24	Fort William Dominions	TBJHL	STATISTICS NOT AVAILABLE												
1924-25	University of Manitoba	TBJHL	STATISTICS NOT AVAILABLE												
1925-26	Fort William Forts	TBSHL	19	7	4	11	....	....	....	26	3	0	0	0	6
1926-27	Fort William Forts	TBSHL	19	25	*12	*37	....	....	....	38	2	1	0	1	2
1927-28	Fort William Forts	TBSHL	20	*34	7	*41	....	....	....	29	2	0	0	0	2
1928-29	Tulsa Oilers	AHA	39	*22	11	*33	....	....	....	26	4	3	0	3	4
1929-30	**Chicago Black Hawks**	NHL	41	14	16	30	28	52	80	16	2	0	1	1	4
1930-31	**Chicago Black Hawks**	NHL	44	15	14	29	37	51	88	34	9	1	3	4	11
1931-32	**Chicago Black Hawks**	NHL	48	12	13	25	26	36	62	36	2	0	0	0	2
1932-33	**Chicago Black Hawks**	NHL	48	12	14	26	28	37	65	30	....	....	....	....	....
1933-34	**Chicago Black Hawks**	NHL	37	5	9	14	11	24	35	15	8	1	0	1	0
1934-35	**Chicago Black Hawks**	NHL	48	13	18	31	28	40	68	33	2	0	0	0	2
1935-36	**Chicago Black Hawks**	NHL	47	4	8	12	10	19	29	20	1	0	0	0	0
1936-37	**Chicago Black Hawks**	NHL	15	0	2	2	0	5	5	0	....	....	....	....	....
	Cleveland Barons	AHL	24	12	17	29	....	....	....	29	....	....	....	....	....
1937-38	New Haven Eagles	AHL	2	0	0	0	....	....	....	4	....	....	....	....	....
	Montreal Maroons	NHL	21	2	4	6	4	8	12	0	....	....	....	....	....
	NHL Totals		349	77	98	175	172	272	444	184	24	2	4	6	19

Claimed by **Chicago** from **Tulsa** (AHA) in Intra-League Draft, May 13, 1929. Traded to **Cleveland** (AHL) by **Chicago** for cash, January 15, 1937. Claimed by **Montreal Maroons** from **Cleveland** (AHL) in Inter-League Draft, May 9, 1937.

• COOPER, CARSON
Carson "Shovel-Shot" Cooper
RW – R. 5'7", 160 lbs. b: Cornwall, Ont., 7/17/1899. d: 7/4/1955.

Season	Club	League	GP	G	A	Pts	AG	AA	APts	PIM	GP	G	A	Pts	PIM
1918-19	Hamilton Tigers	OHA Sr.	7	1	1	2	....	....	....	....	....	....	....	....	....
1919-20	Hamilton Tigers	OHA Sr.	6	*18	2	20	....	....	....	....	2	2	0	*2	0
1920-21	Hamilton Tigers	OHA Sr.	10	*14	2	16	....	....	....	....	....	....	....	....	....
1921-22	Hamilton Tigers	OHA Sr.	10	*22	1	*23	....	....	....	....	....	....	....	....	....
1922-23	Hamilton Tigers	OHA Sr.	12	20	7	27	....	....	....	....	2	1	1	2	2
1923-24	Hamilton Tigers	OHA Sr.	10	*33	7	*40	....	....	....	....	2	*5	1	*6	....
1924-25	**Boston Bruins**	NHL	12	5	3	8	17	40	57	4	....	....	....	....	....
1925-26	**Boston Bruins**	NHL	36	28	3	31	90	34	124	10	....	....	....	....	....
1926-27	**Boston Bruins**	NHL	10	0	0	0	0	0	0	0	....	....	....	....	....
	Montreal Canadiens	NHL	14	9	3	12	26	25	51	16	3	0	0	0	0
1927-28	**Detroit Cougars**	NHL	43	15	2	17	46	17	63	32	....	....	....	....	....
1928-29	**Detroit Cougars**	NHL	43	18	9	27	73	83	156	14	2	0	0	0	2
1929-30	**Detroit Cougars**	NHL	44	18	18	36	36	59	95	14	....	....	....	....	....
1930-31	**Detroit Falcons**	NHL	44	14	14	28	34	51	85	10	....	....	....	....	....
1931-32	**Detroit Falcons**	NHL	48	3	5	8	6	14	20	11	2	0	0	0	0
1932-33	Detroit Olympics	IAHL	2	0	0	0	....	....	....	0	....	....	....	....	....
1933-34	Detroit Olympics	IAHL	37	11	6	17	....	....	....	16	6	1	1	2	2
1934-35	Detroit–Windsor	IAHL	31	6	9	15	....	....	....	4	3	0	0	0	2
	NHL Totals		294	110	57	167	328	323	651	111	7	0	0	0	2

Signed as a free agent by **Boston**, November 2, 1924. Traded to **Montreal Canadiens** by **Boston** for Billy Boucher with both teams holding right of recall, January 26, 1927. • Players returned to original teams May 22, 1927. Traded to **Detroit Cougars** by **Boston** for cash, May 22, 1927.

• COOPER, HAL
Hal (Harold Wallace) Cooper
RW – R. 5'5", 155 lbs. b: New Liskeard, Ont., 8/29/1915. Deceased.

Season	Club	League	GP	G	A	Pts	AG	AA	APts	PIM	GP	G	A	Pts	PIM
1931-32	Hamilton Victorias	OHA	3	1	2	3	....	....	....	4	3	2	0	2	2
1932-33	Hamilton Victorias	OHA	STATISTICS NOT AVAILABLE												
1933-34	Sudbury Wolves	City Sr.	8	7	3	10	....	....	....	17	2	1	*4	5	*7
1934-35	Falconbridge Falcons	City Sr.	8	8	2	10	....	....	....	10	2	0	1	1	0
1935-36	Falconbridge Falcons	City Sr.	10	7	7	14	....	....	....	12	3	1	2	3	0
1936-37	Falconbridge Falcons	City Sr.	14	7	3	10	....	....	....	16	4	*2	*4	*6	2
1937-38	Falconbridge Falcons	City Sr.	15	3	2	5	....	....	....	22	3	1	2	3	2
1938-39	Kirkland Lake Blue Devils	NOHA	8	7	12	19	....	....	....	10	9	4	7	11	6
1939-40	McIntyre Miners	City Sr.	15	*20	5	25	....	....	....	16	20	11	12	23	14
	Kirkland Lake Blue Devils	NOHA	15	20	5	25	....	....	....	16	....	....	....	....	....
1940-41	Niagara Falls Cataracts	OHA Sr.	32	21	20	41	....	....	....	22	3	0	2	2	2
1941-42	Niagara Falls Cataracts	OHA Sr.	25	12	13	25	....	....	....	13	7	7	0	7	7
1942-43	Niagara Falls Cataracts	OHA Sr.	22	5	16	21	....	....	....	8	2	2	1	3	2
1943-44	Providence Reds	AHL	51	23	21	44	....	....	....	6	....	....	....	....	....
1944-45	**New York Rangers**	NHL	8	0	0	0	0	0	0	2	....	....	....	....	....
	Hershey Bears	AHL	46	24	17	41	....	....	....	9	11	6	6	12	6
1945-46	Hershey Bears	AHL	41	12	8	20	....	....	....	4	....	....	....	....	....
1946-47	Houston Huskies	USHL	9	0	6	6	....	....	....	2	....	....	....	....	....
1947-48	Houston Huskies	USHL	DID NOT PLAY – INJURED												
1948-49	Hamilton Tigers	OHA Sr.	27	12	5	17	....	....	....	4	6	1	4	5	4
1949-50	Hamilton Tigers	OHA Sr.	13	0	1	1	....	....	....	11	....	....	....	....	....
	NHL Totals		8	0	0	0	0	0	0	2	....	....	....	....	....

Claimed by **NY Rangers** from **Providence** (AHL) in Inter-League Draft, May 12, 1939.

• COOPER, JOE
Joe Cooper
D – R. 6'2", 200 lbs. b: Winnipeg, Man., 12/14/1914. d: 4/3/1979.

Season	Club	League	GP	G	A	Pts	AG	AA	APts	PIM	GP	G	A	Pts	PIM
1931-32	Winnipeg K of C	MJHL	2	0	0	0	....	....	....	0	....	....	....	....	....
1932-33	Winnipeg K of C	MJHL	11	8	3	11	....	....	....	24	3	0	1	1	2
1933-34	Selkirk Fishermen	MJHL	13	12	3	15	....	....	....	28	5	3	*4	7	17
	Selkirk Fishermen	MHL Sr.	1	0	0	0	....	....	....	6	....	....	....	....	....
1934-35	New York Cresents	EHL	21	5	14	19	....	....	....	*70	7	5	0	5	*16
1935-36	**New York Rangers**	NHL	1	0	0	0	0	0	0	0	....	....	....	....	....
	Philadelphia Ramblers	Can-Am	48	5	10	15	....	....	....	86	4	1	0	1	6
1936-37	**New York Rangers**	NHL	48	0	3	3	0	7	7	42	9	1	1	2	12
1937-38	**New York Rangers**	NHL	46	3	2	5	6	4	10	56	3	0	0	0	4
1938-39	**Chicago Black Hawks**	NHL	17	3	3	6	6	6	12	10	....	....	....	....	....
	Philadelphia Ramblers	AHL	35	8	15	23	....	....	....	50	....	....	....	....	....
1939-40	**Chicago Black Hawks**	NHL	44	4	7	11	9	14	23	59	2	0	0	0	0
1940-41	**Chicago Black Hawks**	NHL	45	5	5	10	10	9	19	66	5	1	0	1	8
1941-42	**Chicago Black Hawks**	NHL	47	6	14	20	10	21	31	58	3	0	2	2	2
1942-43	Ottawa Commandos	QSHL	16	1	5	6	....	....	....	26	12	4	6	10	18
1943-44	**Chicago Black Hawks**	NHL	13	1	0	1	1	0	1	17	9	1	1	2	18
	Ottawa Commandos	QSHL	10	0	1	1	....	....	....	18	....	....	....	....	....
1944-45	**Chicago Black Hawks**	NHL	50	4	17	21	5	28	33	50	....	....	....	....	....
1945-46	**Chicago Black Hawks**	NHL	50	2	7	9	3	13	16	46	4	0	1	1	14
1946-47	**New York Rangers**	NHL	59	2	8	10	3	11	14	38	....	....	....	....	....
1947-48	Cleveland–Hershey	AHL	53	7	14	21	....	....	....	56	2	0	0	0	2
	NHL Totals		420	30	66	96	53	113	166	442	35	3	5	8	58

EHL First All-Star Team (1935) • Can-Am First All-Star Team (1936)

Signed as a free agent by **NY Rangers**, October 24, 1935. Traded to **Chicago** by **NY Rangers** for cash, January 16, 1939. Traded to **NY Rangers** by **Chicago** for cash, November 1, 1946. Traded to **Cleveland** (AHL) by **NY Rangers** with Ab DeMarco for cash, May 5, 1947.

• COPP, BOB
Bob Copp
D – L. 5'11", 180 lbs. b: Port Elgin, N.B., 11/15/1918.

Season	Club	League	GP	G	A	Pts	AG	AA	APts	PIM	GP	G	A	Pts	PIM
1934-35	Mount Allison University	MIAA	3	0	1	1	....	....	....	2	....	....	....	....	....
1935-36	Mount Allison University	MIAA	6	3	3	6	....	....	....	2	....	....	....	....	....
1936-37	Mount Allison University	MIAA	4	3	*4	7	....	....	....	6	1	0	0	0	0
	Amherst Pats	Mtn-Jr.	5	1	3	4	....	....	....	2	8	10	5	15	6
1937-38	Mount Allison University	MIAA	4	2	*7	*9	....	....	....	2	1	1	1	2	0
1938-39	University of Toronto	OQAA	DID NOT PLAY – INJURED												
1939-40	University of Toronto	OQAA	7	5	5	10	....	....	....	10	....	....	....	....	....
1940-41	Toronto Marlboros	OHA Sr.	31	4	2	6	....	....	....	19	17	4	4	8	8
1941-42	Toronto Marlboros	OHA Sr.	28	7	11	18	....	....	....	21	6	0	0	0	4
1942-43	**Toronto Maple Leafs**	NHL	38	3	9	12	4	11	15	24	....	....	....	....	....
	Halifax RCAF	City Sr.	....	....	....	....	....	....	....	....	7	1	3	4	0
1943-44	Ottawa Commandos	QSHL	2	2	1	3	....	....	....	2	....	....	....	....	....
1944-45	Uplands RCAF	Ott-Sr.	12	3	7	10	....	....	....	4	4	1	2	3	2
1945-46	Ottawa Senators	QSHL	35	11	19	30	....	....	....	46	5	0	1	1	4
	Ottawa RCAF	City Sr.	3	0	1	1	....	....	....	0	3	0	1	1	0
1946-47	Ottawa Senators	QSHL	28	2	8	10	....	....	....	32	11	1	1	2	8
1947-48	Ottawa Senators	QSHL	48	10	21	31	....	....	....	16	26	7	12	19	24
1948-49	Ottawa Senators	QSHL	60	21	34	55	....	....	....	15	23	9	10	19	10
1949-50	Ottawa Senators	QSHL	45	9	12	21	....	....	....	15	7	1	0	1	4
1950-51	**Toronto Maple Leafs**	NHL	2	0	0	0	0	0	0	2	....	....	....	....	....
	Ottawa Senators	QSHL	54	7	18	25	....	....	....	16	11	0	1	1	6
1951-52	Ottawa Senators	QSHL	4	0	0	0	....	....	....	0	....	....	....	....	....
1952-53	Ottawa Senators	QSHL	14	1	1	2	....	....	....	0	9	1	0	1	0
	Smith's Falls Rideaus	EOHL	32	1	14	15	....	....	....	6	....	....	....	....	....
1953-54	Ottawa Senators	QHL	42	0	5	5	....	....	....	8	21	0	1	1	6
1954-55	Ottawa Senators	QHL	27	0	4	4	....	....	....	6	....	....	....	....	....
	NHL Totals		40	3	9	12	4	11	15	26	....	....	....	....	....

• CORBEAU, BERT
Bert "Pig Iron" Corbeau
D – R. 5'11", 200 lbs. b: Penetanguishene, Ont., 2/9/1894. d: 9/22/1942.

Season	Club	League	GP	G	A	Pts	AG	AA	APts	PIM	GP	G	A	Pts	PIM
1913-14	Halifax Cresents	MPHL	22	5	0	5	....	....	....	31	....	....	....	....	....
1914-15	Montreal Canadiens	NHA	18	1	1	2	....	....	....	35	....	....	....	....	....
1915-16	Montreal Canadiens	NHA	23	7	0	7	....	....	....	*134	5	0	0	0	35
1916-17	Montreal Canadiens	NHA	19	7	5	12	....	....	....	87	6	4	0	4	9
1917-18	**Montreal Canadiens**	NHL	21	8	8	16	20	0	20	41	2	1	1	2	11
1918-19	**Montreal Canadiens**	NHL	16	2	3	5	7	28	35	54	10	1	1	2	20
1919-20	**Montreal Canadiens**	NHL	24	11	6	17	25	41	66	65	....	....	....	....	....
1920-21	**Montreal Canadiens**	NHL	24	12	1	13	31	9	40	*86	....	....	....	....	....
1921-22	**Montreal Canadiens**	NHL	22	3	7	10	8	44	52	26	....	....	....	....	....
1922-23	**Hamilton Tigers**	NHL	21	10	3	13	33	27	60	36	....	....	....	....	....
1923-24	**Toronto St. Pats**	NHL	24	8	6	14	33	110	143	*55	....	....	....	....	....
1924-25	**Toronto St. Pats**	NHL	30	4	3	7	14	40	54	67	2	0	0	0	0
1925-26	**Toronto St. Pats**	NHL	36	5	5	10	15	58	73	*121	....	....	....	....	....
1926-27	**Toronto Maple Leafs**	NHL	41	1	2	3	3	17	20	88	....	....	....	....	....
1927-28	Toronto Falcons	Can-Pro	41	5	2	7	....	....	....	*112	2	0	0	0	10
1928-29	London Panthers	Can-Pro	9	0	0	0	....	....	....	6	....	....	....	....	....
	NHL Totals		259	64	44	108	189	374	563	639	14	2	2	4	31
	Other Major League Totals		82	20	6	26	....	....	....	287	11	4	0	4	44

Rights retained by **Montreal Canadiens** after NHA folded, November 26, 1917. Traded to **Hamilton** by **Montreal Canadiens** with Edmond Bouchard for Joe Malone, October, 1922. Traded to **Toronto St. Pats** by **Hamilton** with George Carey and Amos Arbour for Ken Randall and cash, December 14, 1923.

• CORCORAN, NORM Norm Corcoran
C/RW – R. 5'10", 160 lbs. b: Toronto, Ont., 8/15/1931.

Season	Club	League	Regular Season								Playoffs				
			GP	G	A	Pts	AG	AA	APts	PIM	GP	G	A	Pts	PIM
1948-49	St. Michael's Majors	OHA	28	2	2	4	....	....	....	32	....	....	....	....	....
1949-50	St. Catharines TeePees	OHA	46	33	36	69	....	....	....	102	5	6	0	6	4
	Boston Bruins	**NHL**	**1**	**0**	**0**	**0**	**0**	**0**	**0**	**0**	....	....	....	....	....
	Boston Olympics	EHL	2	3	2	5	....	....	....	4	5	1	1	2	12
1950-51	Hershey Bears	AHL	68	17	24	41	....	....	....	96	2	0	0	0	0
1951-52	Hershey Bears	AHL	54	22	21	43	....	....	....	71	5	1	0	1	6
1952-53	**Boston Bruins**	**NHL**	**1**	**0**	**0**	**0**	**0**	**0**	**0**	**0**	....	....	....	....	....
	Hershey Bears	AHL	60	15	22	37	....	....	....	92	3	1	0	1	0
1953-54	Hershey Bears	AHL	69	22	36	58	....	....	....	70	11	5	7	12	18
1954-55	**Boston Bruins**	**NHL**	**2**	**0**	**0**	**0**	**0**	**0**	**0**	**2**	**4**	**0**	**0**	**0**	**6**
	Hershey Bears	AHL	61	16	30	46	....	....	....	90	....	....	....	....	....
1955-56	**Detroit Red Wings**	**NHL**	**2**	**0**	**0**	**0**	**0**	**0**	**0**	**0**	....	....	....	....	....
	Edmonton Flyers	WHL	35	12	15	27	....	....	....	48	....	....	....	....	....
	Chicago Black Hawks	**NHL**	**23**	**1**	**3**	**4**	**1**	**4**	**5**	**19**	....	....	....	....	....
1956-57	Trois-Rivieres Lions	QHL	49	16	25	41	....	....	....	72	4	2	1	3	4
	Springfield Indians	AHL	12	0	1	1	....	....	....	2	....	....	....	....	....
1957-58	Buffalo Bisons	AHL	67	14	37	51	....	....	....	26	....	....	....	....	....
1958-59	Trois-Rivieres Lions	QHL	58	13	32	45	....	....	....	51	6	0	0	0	2
1959-60	Quebec Aces	AHL	56	18	27	45	....	....	....	52	....	....	....	....	....
1960-61	Quebec Aces	AHL	61	22	35	57	....	....	....	57	....	....	....	....	....
1961-62	Pittsburgh Hornets	AHL	67	17	34	51	....	....	....	41	....	....	....	....	....
1962-63	Pittsburgh Hornets	AHL	25	1	1	2	....	....	....	4	....	....	....	....	....
	Edmonton Flyers	WHL	30	9	10	19	....	....	....	4	3	0	0	0	0
1963-64	Providence Reds	AHL	52	11	14	25	....	....	....	19	2	3	0	3	0
1964-65	Providence Reds	AHL	36	7	11	18	....	....	....	12	....	....	....	....	....
1965-66	Buffalo Bisons	AHL	31	2	4	6	....	....	....	14	....	....	....	....	....
	NHL Totals		**29**	**1**	**3**	**4**	**1**	**4**	**5**	**21**	**4**	**0**	**0**	**0**	**6**

Played in NHL All-Star Game (1955)

Traded to **Detroit** by **Boston** with Gilles Boisvert, Real Chevrefils, Warren Godfrey and Ed Sandford for Vic Stasiuk, Marcel Bonin, Lorne Davis and Terry Sawchuk, June 3, 1955. Claimed on waivers by **Chicago** from **NY Rangers**, January 17, 1956. Traded to **Toronto** by **Quebec** (AHL) for Guy Rousseau, June 1, 1961. Traded to **Pittsburgh** (AHL) by **Toronto** for cash, September, 1961.

• CORMIER, ROGER Roger Cormier
RW – R. 5'10", 167 lbs. b: Montreal, Que., 3/23/1905. d: 2/9/1971.

Season	Club	League	Regular Season								Playoffs				
			GP	G	A	Pts	AG	AA	APts	PIM	GP	G	A	Pts	PIM
1924-25	St. Francis Xavier	Mtl-Sr.	STATISTICS NOT AVAILABLE												
1925-26	**Montreal Canadiens**	**NHL**	**1**	**0**	**0**	**0**	**0**	**0**	**0**	**0**	....	....	....	....	....
	St. Francis Xavier	Mtl-Sr.	STATISTICS NOT AVAILABLE												
1926-27	Providence Reds	Can-Am	32	6	2	8	....	....	....	47	....	....	....	....	....
1927-28	Providence Reds	Can-Am	38	7	2	9	....	....	....	36	....	....	....	....	....
1928-29	Providence Reds	Can-Am	29	1	1	2	....	....	....	23	....	....	....	....	....
	Kitchener Dutchmen	Can-Pro	11	4	0	4	....	....	....	14	3	0	0	0	0
1929-30	Providence Reds	Can-Am	39	9	4	13	....	....	....	54	3	1	1	2	4
1930-31	Providence Reds	Can-Am	39	11	14	25	....	....	....	51	2	1	1	2	0
1931-32	Providence Reds	Can-Am	39	6	8	14	....	....	....	50	5	0	0	0	4
1932-33	Windsor Bulldogs	IAHL	44	8	12	20	....	....	....	70	5	2	2	4	12
1933-34	Cleveland Indians	IAHL	44	10	9	19	....	....	....	28	....	....	....	....	....
1934-35	Cleveland Falcons	IAHL	44	17	16	33	....	....	....	52	2	0	0	0	4
1935-36	Cleveland-Rochester	IAHL	41	8	5	13	....	....	....	23	....	....	....	....	....
1936-37			REINSTATED AS AN AMATEUR												
1937-38	Sherbrooke Red Raiders	QPHL	21	12	8	20	....	....	....	15	9	4	4	8	2
1938-39	Sherbrooke Red Raiders	QPHL	37	12	16	28	....	....	....	41	4	2	1	3	4
1939-40	Sherbrooke Red Raiders	QPHL	40	2	3	5	....	....	....	4	10	0	1	1	2
	NHL Totals		**1**	**0**	**0**	**0**	**0**	**0**	**0**	**0**	....	....	....	....	....

Signed as a free agent by **Montreal Canadiens**, January 15, 1926. Traded to **Windsor** (IAHL) by **Providence** (Can-Am) for Roy Hinsperger, October, 1932.

• CORRIGAN, CHUCK Chuck Corrigan
RW – R. 6'2", 192 lbs. b: Moosomin, Sask., 5/22/1916.

Season	Club	League	Regular Season								Playoffs				
			GP	G	A	Pts	AG	AA	APts	PIM	GP	G	A	Pts	PIM
1935-36	Toronto Goodyears	OHA Sr.	8	1	3	4	....	....	....	8	8	3	1	4	4
1936-37	Toronto Goodyears	OHA Sr.	9	4	1	5	....	....	....	8	5	1	1	2	6
1937-38	**Toronto Maple Leafs**	**NHL**	**3**	**0**	**0**	**0**	**0**	**0**	**0**	**0**	....	....	....	....	....
	Syracuse–Springfield	IAHL	42	8	2	10	....	....	....	17	....	....	....	....	....
1938-39	Springfield–Hershey	AHL	42	2	6	8	....	....	....	11	5	0	1	1	0
1939-40	Springfield Indians	AHL	54	12	31	43	....	....	....	14	3	0	1	1	0
1940-41	**New York Americans**	**NHL**	**16**	**2**	**2**	**4**	**4**	**4**	**8**	**2**	....	....	....	....	....
	Springfield Indians	AHL	22	3	1	4	....	....	....	7	3	0	1	1	0
1941-42	Springfield Indians	AHL	47	7	33	40	....	....	....	6	....	....	....	....	....
1942-43	Pittsburgh Hornets	AHL	52	17	25	42	....	....	....	10	2	0	1	1	5
1943-44	Pittsburgh Hornets	AHL	3	0	2	2	....	....	....	2	....	....	....	....	....
	Kingston Frontenacs	Ott-Sr.	13	7	8	15	....	....	....	10	....	....	....	....	....
1944-45			MILITARY SERVICE												
1945-46	Fort Worth Rangers	USHL	6	2	2	4	....	....	....	6	....	....	....	....	....
	St. Paul Saints	USHL	23	6	5	11	....	....	....	8	3	0	0	0	0
1946-47			DID NOT PLAY												
1947-48	Fresno Falcons	PCHL	65	36	37	73	....	....	....	24	9	4	4	8	16
1948-49	Fresno Falcons	PCHL	16	5	12	17	....	....	....	2	2	0	0	0	2
	NHL Totals		**19**	**2**	**2**	**4**	**4**	**4**	**8**	**2**	....	....	....	....	....

Signed as a free agent by **Toronto**, October 17, 1937. Signed as a free agent by **NY Americans**, January 30, 1941.

• CORRIVEAU, ANDRE Andre Corriveau
RW – L. 5'8", 135 lbs. b: Grand'Mere, Que., 5/15/1928.

Season	Club	League	Regular Season								Playoffs				
			GP	G	A	Pts	AG	AA	APts	PIM	GP	G	A	Pts	PIM
1944-45	Montreal Nationale	QJHL	10	2	4	6	....	....	....	4	....	....	....	....	....
1945-46	Montreal Nationale	QJHL	20	12	*16	28	....	....	....	8	4	2	0	2	2
1946-47	Montreal Nationale	MJHL	26	33	*46	*79	....	....	....	26	11	12	14	26	12
1947-48	Valleyfield Braves	QSHL	43	22	31	53	....	....	....	20	6	1	3	4	2
1948-49	Valleyfield Braves	QSHL	62	32	43	75	....	....	....	40	3	2	1	3	0
1949-50	Valleyfield Braves	QSHL	60	33	*54	*87	....	....	....	25	5	3	0	3	0
1950-51	Valleyfield Braves	QSHL	58	38	*51	*89	....	....	....	15	28	16	*27	*43	4
1951-52	Valleyfield Braves	QSHL	60	27	36	63	....	....	....	8	6	1	6	7	2
1952-53	Valleyfield Braves	QSHL	60	40	45	85	....	....	....	10	4	0	1	1	0
1953-54	**Montreal Canadiens**	**NHL**	**3**	**0**	**1**	**1**	**0**	**1**	**1**	**0**	....	....	....	....	....
	Valleyfield Braves	QHL	69	37	51	88	....	....	....	8	7	3	4	7	2
1954-55	Valleyfield Braves	QHL	56	31	32	63	....	....	....	28	....	....	....	....	....
1955-56	Montreal Royals	QHL	62	*37	40	77	....	....	....	2	11	1	7	8	2
1956-57	Montreal Royals	QHL	63	22	34	56	....	....	....	8	3	1	1	2	2
	NHL Totals		**3**	**0**	**1**	**1**	**0**	**1**	**1**	**0**	....	....	....	....	....

QHL Second All-Star Team (1953, 1954, 1955, 1957) • QHL First All-Star Team (1956) • Won Vimy Trophy (MVP - QHL) (1956)

• COSTELLO, LES Les Costello
LW – L. 5'8", 158 lbs. b: South Porcupine, Ont., 2/16/1928.

Season	Club	League	Regular Season								Playoffs				
			GP	G	A	Pts	AG	AA	APts	PIM	GP	G	A	Pts	PIM
1944-45	St. Michael's Majors	OHA	17	11	8	19	....	....	....	4	23	15	15	30	21
1945-46	St. Michael's Majors	OHA	24	17	23	40	....	....	....	17	11	8	10	18	12
1946-47	St. Michael's Majors	OHA	29	29	33	62	....	....	....	78	9	9	7	16	13
1947-48	Pittsburgh Hornets	AHL	68	32	22	54	....	....	....	40	2	0	0	0	2
	Toronto Maple Leafs	**NHL**	....	....	....	....	....	....	....	....	**5**	**2**	**2**	**4**	**2**
1948-49	**Toronto Maple Leafs**	**NHL**	**15**	**2**	**3**	**5**	**3**	**5**	**8**	**11**	....	....	....	....	....
	Pittsburgh Hornets	AHL	46	13	19	32	....	....	....	63	....	....	....	....	....
1949-50	Pittsburgh Hornets	AHL	70	18	31	49	....	....	....	69	....	....	....	....	....
	Toronto Maple Leafs	**NHL**	....	....	....	....	....	....	....	....	**1**	**0**	**0**	**0**	**0**
	NHL Totals		**15**	**2**	**3**	**5**	**3**	**5**	**8**	**11**	**6**	**2**	**2**	**4**	**2**

Played in NHL All-Star Game (1948)

• Retired from NHL to begin Seminary studies, May, 1950.

• COSTELLO, MURRAY Murray Costello
C – R. 6'3", 190 lbs. b: South Porcupine, Ont., 2/24/1934.

Season	Club	League	Regular Season								Playoffs				
			GP	G	A	Pts	AG	AA	APts	PIM	GP	G	A	Pts	PIM
1950-51	St. Michael's Majors	OHA	50	18	16	34	....	....	....	24	....	....	....	....	....
1951-52	St. Michael's Majors	OHA	51	16	27	43	....	....	....	18	8	5	8	13	4
1952-53	St. Michael's Majors	OHA	51	30	28	58	....	....	....	38	17	7	8	15	13
1953-54	Galt Black Hawks	OHA	3	1	0	1	....	....	....	0	....	....	....	....	....
	Chicago Black Hawks	**NHL**	**40**	**3**	**2**	**5**	**5**	**3**	**8**	**6**	....	....	....	....	....
	Hershey Bears	AHL	26	7	13	20	....	....	....	10	11	4	4	8	9
1954-55	**Boston Bruins**	**NHL**	**54**	**4**	**11**	**15**	**6**	**14**	**20**	**25**	**1**	**0**	**0**	**0**	**2**
1955-56	**Boston Bruins**	**NHL**	**41**	**6**	**6**	**12**	**9**	**7**	**16**	**19**	....	....	....	....	....
	Detroit Red Wings	**NHL**	**24**	**0**	**0**	**0**	**0**	**0**	**0**	**4**	**4**	**0**	**0**	**0**	**0**
1956-57	**Detroit Red Wings**	**NHL**	**3**	**0**	**0**	**0**	**0**	**0**	**0**	**0**	....	....	....	....	....
	Edmonton Flyers	WHL	65	19	26	45	....	....	....	37	7	0	2	2	12
1957-58			REINSTATED AS AN AMATEUR												
1958-59	Windsor Bulldogs	OHA Sr.	35	14	20	34	....	....	....	26	....	....	....	....	....
1959-60	Windsor Bulldogs	OHA Sr.	43	18	20	38	....	....	....	23	17	5	7	12	12
1960-61	Windsor Bulldogs	OHA Sr.	34	9	29	38	....	....	....	41	....	....	....	....	....
1961-62	Windsor Bulldogs	OHA Sr.	34	27	15	42	....	....	....	56	12	1	8	9	24
	NHL Totals		**162**	**13**	**19**	**32**	**20**	**24**	**44**	**54**	**5**	**0**	**0**	**0**	**2**

Traded to **Boston** by **Chicago** for Frank Martin, October 4, 1954. Traded to **Detroit** by **Boston** with Lorne Ferguson for Real Chevrefils and Jerry Toppazzini, January 17, 1956.

• COTCH, CHARLIE Charlie Cotch
LW – L. 5'11", 175 lbs. b: Sarnia, Ontario. Deceased.

Season	Club	League	Regular Season								Playoffs				
			GP	G	A	Pts	AG	AA	APts	PIM	GP	G	A	Pts	PIM
1921-22	London Tecumsehs	OHA Sr.	STATISTICS NOT AVAILABLE												
1922-23	Vancouver Maroons	PCHA	15	0	0	0	....	....	....	0	3	0	0	0	0
1923-24	Vancouver Maroons	PCHA	14	2	0	2	....	....	....	4	4	0	0	0	0
1924-25	**Hamilton Tigers**	**NHL**	**4**	**1**	**0**	**1**	**3**	**0**	**3**	**0**	....	....	....	....	....
	Toronto St. Pats	**NHL**	**7**	**0**	**0**	**0**	**0**	**0**	**0**	**0**	....	....	....	....	....
	NHL Totals		**11**	**1**	**0**	**1**	**3**	**0**	**3**	**0**	....	....	....	....	....
	Other Major League Totals		29	2	0	2	....	....	....	4	7	0	0	0	0

Signed as a free agent by **Vancouver** (PCHA), November 7, 1922. Traded to **Montreal Canadiens** by **Vancouver** (PCHA) for Bob Boucher, March 26, 1924. Rights traded to **Hamilton** by **Montreal Canadiens**, December 24, 1924. Signed as a free agent by **Toronto St. Pats**, February 9, 1925.

• COTTON, BALDY Baldy (William Harold) Cotton
LW – L. 5'10", 155 lbs. b: Nanticoke, Ont., 11/5/1902. Deceased.

Season	Club	League	Regular Season								Playoffs				
			GP	G	A	Pts	AG	AA	APts	PIM	GP	G	A	Pts	PIM
1919-20	Parkdale Canoe Club	OHA	6	3	0	3	....	....	....	0	....	....	....	....	....
1920-21	Toronto Maitlands	OHA	STATISTICS NOT AVAILABLE												
1921-22	Toronto Aura Lee	OHA	6	8	1	9	....	....	....	....	....	....	....	....	....
1922-23	Toronto Aura Lee	OHA	11	5	3	8	....	....	....	....	....	....	....	....	....
1923-24	Pittsburgh Yellowjackets	USAHA	20	7	0	7	....	....	....	0	13	2	3	5	....
1924-25	Pittsburgh Yellowjackets	USAHA	40	7	0	7	....	....	....	0	8	2	0	2	....
1925-26	**Pittsburgh Pirates**	**NHL**	**33**	**7**	**1**	**8**	**22**	**11**	**33**	**22**	**2**	**1**	**0**	**1**	**0**
1926-27	**Pittsburgh Pirates**	**NHL**	**37**	**5**	**0**	**5**	**14**	**0**	**14**	**17**	....	....	....	....	....
1927-28	**Pittsburgh Pirates**	**NHL**	**42**	**9**	**3**	**12**	**28**	**25**	**53**	**40**	**2**	**1**	**1**	**2**	**2**
1928-29	**Pittsburgh Pirates**	**NHL**	**32**	**3**	**2**	**5**	**12**	**18**	**30**	**38**	....	....	....	....	....
	Toronto Maple Leafs	**NHL**	**11**	**1**	**2**	**3**	**4**	**18**	**22**	**8**	**4**	**0**	**0**	**0**	**2**
1929-30	**Toronto Maple Leafs**	**NHL**	**41**	**21**	**17**	**38**	**42**	**56**	**98**	**47**	....	....	....	....	....
1930-31	**Toronto Maple Leafs**	**NHL**	**43**	**12**	**17**	**29**	**29**	**62**	**91**	**45**	**2**	**0**	**0**	**0**	**2**
1931-32	**Toronto Maple Leafs**	**NHL**	**48**	**5**	**13**	**18**	**11**	**36**	**47**	**41**	**7**	**2**	**2**	**4**	**8**
1932-33	**Toronto Maple Leafs**	**NHL**	**48**	**10**	**11**	**21**	**23**	**29**	**52**	**29**	**9**	**0**	**3**	**3**	**6**
1933-34	**Toronto Maple Leafs**	**NHL**	**47**	**8**	**14**	**22**	**18**	**38**	**56**	**46**	**5**	**0**	**2**	**2**	**0**
1934-35	**Toronto Maple Leafs**	**NHL**	**47**	**11**	**14**	**25**	**23**	**31**	**54**	**36**	**7**	**0**	**0**	**0**	**17**
1935-36	**New York Americans**	**NHL**	**45**	**7**	**9**	**16**	**17**	**22**	**39**	**27**	**5**	**0**	**1**	**1**	**9**
1936-37	**New York Americans**	**NHL**	**29**	**2**	**0**	**2**	**4**	**0**	**4**	**23**	....	....	....	....	....
	New Haven Eagles	AHL	18	4	8	12	....	....	....	48	....	....	....	....	....
	NHL Totals		**503**	**101**	**103**	**204**	**247**	**346**	**593**	**419**	**43**	**4**	**9**	**13**	**46**

Played in NHL All-Star Game (1934)

Signed as a free agent by **Pittsburgh Pirates**, September 26, 1925. Traded to **Toronto** by **Pittsburgh** for Gerald Lowrey and $10,000, February 12, 1929. Traded to **NY Americans** by **Toronto** for cash, October 9, 1935.

• COUGHLIN, JACK
Jack Coughlin

RW – R. 5'10", 170 lbs. b: Duro, Ont., 6/6/1892. Deceased.

			REGULAR SEASON								PLAYOFFS				
Season	Club	League	GP	G	A	Pts	AG	AA	APts	PIM	GP	G	A	Pts	PIM
1913-14	Ingersoll Seniors	OHA Sr.	STATISTICS NOT AVAILABLE												
1914-15			REINSTATED AS AN AMATEUR												
1915-16	Peterborough Electrics	OHA Sr.	STATISTICS NOT AVAILABLE												
	Houghton Seniors	USHA	STATISTICS NOT AVAILABLE												
1916-17	Toronto Blueshirts	NHA	8	2	0	2	....	....	....	3	....	....	....	....	....
1917-18	**Toronto Arenas**	**NHL**	**4**	**2**	**0**	**2**	**5**	**0**	**5**	**3**	....	....	....	....	....
1918-19			DID NOT PLAY												
1919-20	**Quebec Bulldogs**	**NHL**	**9**	**0**	**0**	**0**	**0**	**0**	**0**	**0**	....	....	....	....	....
	Montreal Canadiens	**NHL**	**3**	**0**	**0**	**0**	**0**	**0**	**0**	**0**	....	....	....	....	....
1920-21	**Hamilton Tigers**	**NHL**	**2**	**0**	**0**	**0**	**0**	**0**	**0**	**0**	....	....	....	....	....
	NHL Totals		**18**	**2**	**0**	**2**	**5**	**0**	**5**	**3**	....	....	....	....	....
	Other Major League Totals		8	2	0	2	....	....	....	3	....	....	....	....	....

Signed as a free agent by **Toronto Arenas**, December 5, 1917. Signed as a free agent by **Quebec**, January 13, 1920. Signed as a free agent by **Montreal Canadiens**, February 18, 1920. Traded to **Hamilton** by **Montreal Canadiens** with loan of Billy Coutu for Harry Mummery, Jack McDonald and Dave Ritchie, November 29, 1920.

• COULSON, D'ARCY
D'arcy Coulson

D – R. 5'11", 175 lbs. b: Sudbury, Ont., 2/17/1908.

			REGULAR SEASON								PLAYOFFS				
Season	Club	League	GP	G	A	Pts	AG	AA	APts	PIM	GP	G	A	Pts	PIM
1926-27	St. Michael's Majors	OHA	6	5	2	7	....	....	....	....	6	0	3	3	....
1927-28	Ottawa Shamrocks	City Sr.	15	5	2	7	....	....	....	....	1	0	0	0	0
1928-29	Ottawa Shamrocks	City Sr.	5	2	0	2	....	....	....	....	5	1	3	*4	8
1929-30	Ottawa Shamrocks	City Sr.	20	5	1	6	....	....	....	*89	6	2	1	3	26
	Chicago Shamrocks	City Sr.	7	0	6	6	....	....	....	23	....	....	....	....	....
1930-31	**Philadelphia Quakers**	**NHL**	**28**	**0**	**0**	**0**	**0**	**0**	**0**	**103**	....	....	....	....	....
1931-1934			DID NOT PLAY												
1934-35	Ottawa RCAF	City Sr.	3	0	0	0	....	....	....	0	5	0	0	0	18
1935-36	Ottawa RCAF	City Sr.	6	0	0	0	....	....	....	5	7	0	1	1	22
	NHL Totals		**28**	**0**	**0**	**0**	**0**	**0**	**0**	**103**	....	....	....	....	....

Claimed by **Montreal Canadiens** from **Philadelphia** in Dispersal Draft, November 26, 1931.

• COULTER, ART
Art Coulter **HHOF**

D – R. 5'11", 185 lbs. b: Winnipeg, Man., 5/31/1909. Deceased.

			REGULAR SEASON								PLAYOFFS				
Season	Club	League	GP	G	A	Pts	AG	AA	APts	PIM	GP	G	A	Pts	PIM
1928-29	Winnipeg Pilgrims	City Sr.	STATISTICS NOT AVAILABLE												
1929-30	Philadelphia Arrows	Can-Am	35	2	2	4	....	....	....	40	2	0	0	0	2
1930-31	Philadelphia Arrows	Can-Am	40	4	8	12	....	....	....	*109	....	....	....	....	....
1931-32	Philadelphia Arrows	Can-Am	26	9	4	13	....	....	....	42	....	....	....	....	....
	Chicago Black Hawks	**NHL**	**13**	**0**	**1**	**1**	**0**	**3**	**3**	**23**	**2**	**1**	**0**	**1**	**0**
1932-33	**Chicago Black Hawks**	**NHL**	**46**	**3**	**2**	**5**	**7**	**5**	**12**	**53**	....	....	....	....	....
1933-34	**Chicago Black Hawks**	**NHL**	**46**	**5**	**2**	**7**	**11**	**5**	**16**	**39**	**8**	**1**	**0**	**1**	**10**
1934-35	**Chicago Black Hawks**	**NHL**	**48**	**4**	**8**	**12**	**8**	**18**	**26**	**68**	**2**	**0**	**0**	**0**	**5**
1935-36	**Chicago Black Hawks**	**NHL**	**25**	**0**	**2**	**2**	**0**	**5**	**5**	**18**	....	....	....	....	....
	New York Rangers	**NHL**	**23**	**1**	**5**	**6**	**2**	**12**	**14**	**26**	....	....	....	....	....
1936-37	**New York Rangers**	**NHL**	**47**	**1**	**5**	**6**	**2**	**12**	**14**	**27**	**9**	**0**	**3**	**3**	**15**
1937-38	**New York Rangers**	**NHL**	**43**	**5**	**10**	**15**	**10**	**21**	**31**	**90**	....	....	....	....	....
1938-39	**New York Rangers**	**NHL**	**44**	**4**	**8**	**12**	**8**	**15**	**23**	**58**	**7**	**1**	**1**	**2**	**6**
1939-40	**New York Rangers**	**NHL**	**48**	**1**	**9**	**10**	**2**	**18**	**20**	**68**	**12**	**1**	**0**	**1**	**21**
1940-41	**New York Rangers**	**NHL**	**35**	**5**	**14**	**19**	**10**	**26**	**36**	**42**	**3**	**0**	**0**	**0**	**0**
1941-42	**New York Rangers**	**NHL**	**47**	**1**	**16**	**17**	**2**	**24**	**26**	**31**	**6**	**0**	**1**	**1**	**4**
1942-43	Coast Guard Clippers	EHL	37	13	20	33	....	....	....	32	10	4	1	5	8
1943-44	Coast Guard Clippers	....	26	10	13	23	....	....	....	10	12	6	8	14	8
	NHL Totals		**465**	**30**	**82**	**112**	**62**	**164**	**226**	**543**	**49**	**4**	**5**	**9**	**61**

NHL Second All-Star Team (1935, 1938, 1939, 1940) • EHL First All-Star Team (1943)

Played in NHL All-Star Game (1939)

Traded to **NY Rangers** by **Chicago** for Earl Seibert, January 15, 1936. • **Coast Guard Cutters** played exhibition season only in 1943-44.

• COURNOYER, YVAN
— see page 954

• COUTU, BILLY
Billy (Also known as Couture) "Beaver" Coutu

D – L. 5'11", 190 lbs. b: North Bay, Ont., 3/1/1892. Deceased.

			REGULAR SEASON								PLAYOFFS				
Season	Club	League	GP	G	A	Pts	AG	AA	APts	PIM	GP	G	A	Pts	PIM
1915-16	Michigan Soo Indians	City Sr.	STATISTICS NOT AVAILABLE												
1916-17	Montreal Canadiens	NHA	19	1	0	1	....	....	....	19	5	0	0	0	8
1917-18	**Montreal Canadiens**	**NHL**	**20**	**2**	**2**	**4**	**5**	**0**	**5**	**49**	**2**	**0**	**0**	**0**	**0**
1918-19	**Montreal Canadiens**	**NHL**	**17**	**1**	**2**	**3**	**3**	**19**	**22**	**21**	**10**	**0**	**2**	**2**	**8**
1919-20	**Montreal Canadiens**	**NHL**	**20**	**4**	**0**	**4**	**9**	**0**	**9**	**67**	....	....	....	....	....
1920-21	**Hamilton Tigers**	**NHL**	**24**	**8**	**4**	**12**	**20**	**35**	**55**	**74**	....	....	....	....	....
1921-22	**Montreal Canadiens**	**NHL**	**24**	**4**	**3**	**7**	**11**	**19**	**30**	**8**	....	....	....	....	....
1922-23	**Montreal Canadiens**	**NHL**	**24**	**5**	**2**	**7**	**16**	**18**	**34**	**37**	**1**	**0**	**0**	**0**	***12**
1923-24	**Montreal Canadiens**	**NHL**	**16**	**3**	**1**	**4**	**12**	**17**	**29**	**8**	**6**	**0**	**0**	**0**	**2**
1924-25	**Montreal Canadiens**	**NHL**	**28**	**3**	**2**	**5**	**10**	**26**	**36**	**49**	**6**	**1**	**0**	**1**	**14**
1925-26	**Montreal Canadiens**	**NHL**	**33**	**2**	**4**	**6**	**6**	**46**	**52**	**95**	....	....	....	....	....
1926-27	**Boston Bruins**	**NHL**	**40**	**1**	**1**	**2**	**3**	**8**	**11**	**35**	**7**	**1**	**0**	**1**	**4**
1927-28	New Haven Eagles	Can-Am	37	11	1	12	....	....	....	*108	....	....	....	....	....
1928-29	Newark Bulldogs	Can-Am	40	0	1	1	....	....	....	42	....	....	....	....	....
1929-30	Minneapolis Millers	AHA	47	8	2	10	....	....	....	*105	....	....	....	....	....
1930-31	Minneapolis Millers	AHA	33	0	1	1	....	....	....	46	....	....	....	....	....
1931-32	Providence Reds	IAHL	DID NOT PLAY – COACHING												
1932-33	Providence Reds	Can-Am	1	0	0	0	....	....	....	0	....	....	....	....	....
	NHL Totals		**246**	**33**	**21**	**54**	**95**	**188**	**283**	**443**	**32**	**2**	**2**	**4**	**40**
	Other Major League Totals		19	1	0	1	....	....	....	19	5	0	0	0	8

Rights retained by **Montreal Canadiens** after NHA folded, November 26, 1917. Loaned to **Hamilton** by **Montreal** for 1920-21 season with Jack Coughlin for Jack MacDonald, Dave Ritchie and Harry Mummery, November 29, 1920. Returned to **Montreal Canadiens** by **Hamilton**, November 15, 1921. Traded to **Boston** by **Montreal Canadiens** for Amby Moran, October 22, 1926. • Suspended for life by NHL for assault on referee Jerry LaFlamme, April 13, 1927. Traded to **New Haven** (Can-Am) by **Boston** for cash, January 5, 1928.

• COUTURE, GERRY
Gerry "Doc" Couture

RW – R. 6'2", 185 lbs. b: Saskatoon, Sask., 8/6/1925. Deceased.

			REGULAR SEASON								PLAYOFFS				
Season	Club	League	GP	G	A	Pts	AG	AA	APts	PIM	GP	G	A	Pts	PIM
1941-42	Saskatoon Quakers	City Jr.	8	*12	6	*18	....	....	....	0	6	*9	5	*14	0
1942-43	Saskatoon Quakers	City Jr.	8	14	10	*24	....	....	....	26	3	4	1	5	2
1943-44	Saskatoon Jr. Quakers	City Jr.	1	1	1	2	....	....	....	2	....	....	....	....	....
	U. of Saskatchewan	WCIAA	2	6	3	9	....	....	....	2	1	3	1	4	2
	Saskatoon Quakers	City Sr.	11	15	11	26	....	....	....	9	2	1	1	2	2
	Flin Flon Bombers	City Jr.	....	....	....	....	....	....	....	....	4	1	*3	4	10
1944-45	U. of Saskatchewan	WCIAA	9	19	10	29	....	....	....	14	2	1	1	2	0
	Moose Jaw Canucks	City Jr.	....	....	....	....	....	....	....	....	4	4	3	7	2
	Detroit Red Wings	**NHL**	....	....	....	....	....	....	....	....	**2**	**0**	**0**	**0**	**0**
1945-46	**Detroit Red Wings**	**NHL**	**43**	**3**	**7**	**10**	**5**	**13**	**18**	**18**	**5**	**0**	**2**	**2**	**0**
1946-47	**Detroit Red Wings**	**NHL**	**30**	**5**	**10**	**15**	**7**	**14**	**21**	**0**	**1**	**0**	**0**	**0**	**0**
	Indianapolis Capitals	AHL	34	24	18	42	....	....	....	21	....	....	....	....	....
1947-48	**Detroit Red Wings**	**NHL**	**19**	**3**	**6**	**9**	**4**	**9**	**13**	**2**	....	....	....	....	....
	Indianapolis Capitals	AHL	42	26	25	51	....	....	....	8	....	....	....	....	....
1948-49	**Detroit Red Wings**	**NHL**	**51**	**19**	**10**	**29**	**30**	**16**	**46**	**6**	**10**	**2**	**0**	**2**	**2**
1949-50	**Detroit Red Wings**	**NHL**	**69**	**24**	**7**	**31**	**32**	**9**	**41**	**21**	**14**	**5**	**4**	**9**	**2**
1950-51	**Detroit Red Wings**	**NHL**	**53**	**7**	**6**	**13**	**9**	**8**	**17**	**2**	**6**	**1**	**1**	**2**	**0**
1951-52	**Montreal Canadiens**	**NHL**	**10**	**0**	**1**	**1**	**0**	**1**	**1**	**4**	....	....	....	....	....
	Montreal Royals	QSHL	6	1	4	5	....	....	....	0	....	....	....	....	....
	Cleveland Barons	AHL	47	24	21	45	....	....	....	4	5	1	0	1	0
1952-53	**Chicago Black Hawks**	**NHL**	**70**	**19**	**18**	**37**	**29**	**25**	**54**	**22**	**7**	**1**	**0**	**1**	**0**
1953-54	**Chicago Black Hawks**	**NHL**	**40**	**6**	**5**	**11**	**9**	**7**	**16**	**14**	....	....	....	....	....
	Providence Reds	AHL	19	10	7	17	....	....	....	2	....	....	....	....	....
1954-55	Calgary Stampeders	WHL	70	33	49	82	....	....	....	8	9	5	6	*11	0
1955-56	Calgary Stampeders	WHL	66	32	50	82	....	....	....	10	8	3	7	10	8
1956-57	Calgary Stampeders	WHL	63	19	26	45	....	....	....	20	3	1	0	1	0
1957-58	Saskatoon–St. Paul	WHL	58	23	31	54	....	....	....	22	....	....	....	....	....
1958-59			REINSTATED AS AN AMATEUR												
1959-60	Saskatoon Quakers	SSHL	23	*26	*29	*55	....	....	....	26	7	7	*13	20	0
	NHL Totals		**385**	**86**	**70**	**156**	**125**	**102**	**227**	**89**	**45**	**9**	**7**	**16**	**4**

WHL First All-Star Team (1955)

Played in NHL All-Star Game (1950)

Traded to **Montreal** by **Detroit** for Bert Hirschfeld, June 19, 1951. Traded to **Chicago** by **Montreal** for cash, September 22, 1952.

• COUTURE, ROSIE
Rosie "Lola" Couture

RW – R. 5'11", 164 lbs. b: St. Bonfiace, Man., 7/24/1905. d: 3/1/1986.

			REGULAR SEASON								PLAYOFFS				
Season	Club	League	GP	G	A	Pts	AG	AA	APts	PIM	GP	G	A	Pts	PIM
1922-23	St. Boniface Canadians	MHL Jr.	7	6	2	8	....	....	....	4	....	....	....	....	....
1923-24	Winnipeg Argonauts	MHL Sr.	STATISTICS NOT AVAILABLE												
1924-25	Winnipeg Argonauts	MHL Sr.	8	7	2	9	....	....	....	6	....	....	....	....	....
1925-26	Winnipeg Argonauts	MHL Sr.	7	*9	*3	*12	....	....	....	4	2	3	0	3	2
1926-27	Winnipeg Winnipegs	MHL Sr.	8	*16	1	*17	....	....	....	6	5	4	1	5	2
1927-28	Winnipeg Maroons	AHA	39	14	6	20	....	....	....	20	....	....	....	....	....
1928-29	**Chicago Black Hawks**	**NHL**	**43**	**1**	**3**	**4**	**4**	**27**	**31**	**22**	....	....	....	....	....
1929-30	**Chicago Black Hawks**	**NHL**	**43**	**8**	**8**	**16**	**16**	**26**	**42**	**63**	**2**	**0**	**0**	**0**	**2**
1930-31	**Chicago Black Hawks**	**NHL**	**44**	**8**	**11**	**19**	**19**	**40**	**59**	**30**	**9**	**0**	**3**	**3**	**2**
1931-32	**Chicago Black Hawks**	**NHL**	**48**	**9**	**9**	**18**	**19**	**25**	**44**	**8**	**2**	**0**	**0**	**0**	**2**
1932-33	**Chicago Black Hawks**	**NHL**	**46**	**10**	**7**	**17**	**23**	**18**	**41**	**26**	....	....	....	....	....
1933-34	**Chicago Black Hawks**	**NHL**	**48**	**5**	**8**	**13**	**11**	**21**	**32**	**21**	**8**	**1**	**2**	**3**	**4**
1934-35	**Chicago Black Hawks**	**NHL**	**27**	**7**	**9**	**16**	**15**	**20**	**35**	**14**	**2**	**0**	**0**	**0**	**5**
1935-36	**Montreal Canadiens**	**NHL**	**10**	**0**	**1**	**1**	**0**	**2**	**2**	**0**	....	....	....	....	....
	Providence Reds	Can-Am	8	1	0	1	....	....	....	0	4	0	0	0	4
	London Techumsehs	IAHL	26	5	3	8	....	....	....	8	....	....	....	....	....
	NHL Totals		**309**	**48**	**56**	**104**	**107**	**179**	**286**	**184**	**23**	**1**	**5**	**6**	**15**

Traded to **Cleveland** (IAHL) by **Chicago** for cash, June, 1934. Traded to **Montreal Canadiens** by **Cleveland** (!AHL) for $2,500, October 21, 1935.

• COWLEY, BILL
Bill "Cowboy" Cowley **HHOF**

C – L. 5'10", 165 lbs. b: Bristol, Que., 6/12/1912. d: 12/31/1993.

			REGULAR SEASON								PLAYOFFS				
Season	Club	League	GP	G	A	Pts	AG	AA	APts	PIM	GP	G	A	Pts	PIM
1930-31	Ottawa Primrose	City Jr.	14	10	2	12	....	....	....	16	13	*13	4	*17	12
1931-32	Ottawa Jr. Shamrocks	City Jr.	2	2	1	3	....	....	....	2	3	4	*4	*8	2
	Ottawa Shamrocks	City Sr.	....	....	....	....	....	....	....	....	1	0	0	0	0
1932-33	Ottawa Shamrocks	City Sr.	14	7	6	13	....	....	....	24	4	1	0	1	4
1933-34	Halifax Wolverines	MSHL	38	*25	*25	*50	....	....	....	42	6	2	2	4	2
1934-35	**St. Louis Eagles**	**NHL**	**41**	**5**	**7**	**12**	**11**	**16**	**27**	**10**	....	....	....	....	....
	Tulsa Oilers	AHA	1	0	0	0	....	....	....	5	....	....	....	....	....
1935-36	**Boston Bruins**	**NHL**	**48**	**11**	**10**	**21**	**27**	**24**	**51**	**17**	**2**	**2**	**1**	**3**	**2**
1936-37	**Boston Bruins**	**NHL**	**46**	**13**	**22**	**35**	**28**	**52**	**80**	**4**	**3**	**0**	**3**	**3**	**0**
1937-38	**Boston Bruins**	**NHL**	**48**	**17**	**22**	**39**	**36**	**46**	**82**	**8**	**3**	**2**	**0**	**2**	**0**
1938-39	**Boston Bruins**	**NHL**	**34**	**8**	***34**	**42**	**17**	**64**	**81**	**2**	**12**	**3**	**11**	**14**	**2**
1939-40	**Boston Bruins**	**NHL**	**48**	**13**	**27**	**40**	**28**	**55**	**83**	**24**	**6**	**0**	**1**	**1**	**7**
1940-41	**Boston Bruins**	**NHL**	**46**	**17**	***45**	***62**	**34**	**84**	**118**	**16**	**2**	**0**	**0**	**0**	**0**
1941-42	**Boston Bruins**	**NHL**	**28**	**4**	**23**	**27**	**7**	**35**	**42**	**6**	**5**	**0**	**3**	**3**	**5**
1942-43	**Boston Bruins**	**NHL**	**48**	**27**	***45**	**72**	**39**	**58**	**97**	**10**	**9**	**1**	**7**	**8**	**4**
1943-44	**Boston Bruins**	**NHL**	**36**	**30**	**41**	**71**	**38**	**50**	**88**	**12**	....	....	....	....	....
1944-45	**Boston Bruins**	**NHL**	**49**	**25**	**40**	**65**	**35**	**66**	**101**	**12**	**7**	**3**	**3**	**6**	**0**
1945-46	**Boston Bruins**	**NHL**	**26**	**12**	**12**	**24**	**18**	**22**	**40**	**6**	**10**	**1**	**3**	**4**	**2**
1946-47	**Boston Bruins**	**NHL**	**51**	**13**	**25**	**38**	**18**	**36**	**54**	**16**	**5**	**0**	**2**	**2**	**0**
1947-48	Ottawa Army	OHA Sr.	DID NOT PLAY – COACHING												
1948-49	Vancouver Canucks	PCHL	....	....	....	....	....	....	....	....	....	....	....	....	....
	NHL Totals		**549**	**195**	**353**	**548**	**336**	**608**	**944**	**143**	**64**	**12**	**34**	**46**	**22**

NHL First All-Star Team (1938, 1941, 1943, 1944) • NHL Scoring Leader (1941) • Won Hart Trophy (1941, 1943) • NHL Second All-Star Team (1945)

Signed as a free agent by **St. Louis**, October 22, 1934. Claimed by **Boston** from **St. Louis** in Dispersal Draft, October 15, 1935.

• COX, DANNY
Danny "Silent Danny" Cox
LW – L. 5'10", 180 lbs. b: Little Current, Ont., 10/12/1903 d: 8/8/1982.

			REGULAR SEASON							PIM	PLAYOFFS				
Season	Club	League	GP	G	A	Pts	AG	AA	APts	PIM	GP	G	A	Pts	PIM
1922-23	Port Arthur Ports	TBSHL	16	*23	3	26	....	....	....	7	2	0	1	1	0
1923-24	Port Arthur Ports	TBSHL	16	12	*9	21	....	....	....	3	2	0	0	0	0
1924-25	Port Arthur Ports	TBSHL	20	12	4	16	....	....	....	7	10	8	3	11	0
1925-26	Port Arthur Ports	TBSHL	20	5	3	8	....	....	....	6	9	2	0	2	8
1926-27	**Toronto Maple Leafs**	**NHL**	**14**	**0**	**1**	**1**	**0**	**8**	**8**	**4**	....	....	....	....	....
	Hamilton Tigers	Can-Pro	19	7	2	9	....	....	....	6	2	1	1	2	0
1927-28	**Toronto Maple Leafs**	**NHL**	**41**	**9**	**6**	**15**	**28**	**51**	**79**	**27**	....	....	....	....	....
1928-29	**Toronto Maple Leafs**	**NHL**	**42**	**12**	**7**	**19**	**48**	**65**	**113**	**14**	**4**	**0**	**1**	**1**	**4**
1929-30	**Toronto Maple Leafs**	**NHL**	**18**	**1**	**4**	**5**	**2**	**13**	**15**	**18**	....	....	....	....	....
	Ottawa Senators	**NHL**	**24**	**3**	**2**	**5**	**6**	**6**	**12**	**20**	**2**	**0**	**0**	**0**	**0**
1930-31	**Ottawa Senators**	**NHL**	**44**	**9**	**12**	**21**	**22**	**44**	**66**	**12**	....	....	....	....	....
1931-32	**Detroit Falcons**	**NHL**	**47**	**4**	**6**	**10**	**8**	**17**	**25**	**23**	**2**	**0**	**0**	**0**	**2**
1932-33	**Ottawa Senators**	**NHL**	**47**	**4**	**7**	**11**	**9**	**18**	**27**	**8**	....	....	....	....	....
1933-34	**Ottawa Senators**	**NHL**	**29**	**0**	**4**	**4**	**0**	**11**	**11**	**0**	....	....	....	....	....
	New York Rangers	**NHL**	**13**	**5**	**0**	**5**	**11**	**0**	**11**	**2**	**2**	**0**	**0**	**0**	**0**
	Minneapolis Millers	CHL	48	21	24	45	....	....	....	8	5	0	1	1	4
	Quebec Castors	Can-Am	....	....	....	....	....	....	....	....	3	0	0	0	0
1935-36	Philadelphia Ramblers	Can-Am	48	*24	23	47	....	....	....	36	4	1	1	2	0
1936-37	Philadelphia Ramblers	AHL	42	12	15	27	....	....	....	18	6	0	1	1	14
1937-38	Seattle Seahawks	PCHL	38	7	7	14	....	....	....	6	4	0	0	0	4
1938-39	Seattle Seahawks	PCHL	39	11	13	24	....	....	....	18	7	3	1	4	9
1939-40	Wichita Skyhawks	AHA	31	10	19	29	....	....	....	4	....	....	....	....	....
1940-41	Seattle Olympics	PCHL	DID NOT PLAY – COACHING												
	NHL Totals		**319**	**47**	**49**	**96**	**134**	**233**	**367**	**128**	**10**	**0**	**1**	**1**	**6**

Can-Am Second All-Star Team (1936)

Signed as a free agent by **Toronto St. Pats**, October 13, 1926. Traded to **Ottawa** by **Toronto** with cash for Frank Nighbor, January 31, 1930. Claimed by **Detroit Falcons** from **Ottawa** for 1931-32 season in Dispersal Draft, September 26, 1931. Signed as a free agent by **NY Rangers** after securing release from **Ottawa** (January 30, 1934), February 3, 1934.

• CRASHLEY, BART — *see page 957*

• CRAWFORD, JACK
Jack Crawford
D – R. 5'11", 200 lbs. b: Dublin, Ont., 10/26/1916. d: 1/17/1979.

			REGULAR SEASON							PIM	PLAYOFFS				
Season	Club	League	GP	G	A	Pts	AG	AA	APts	PIM	GP	G	A	Pts	PIM
1934-35	St. Michael's College	Tor-Jr.	12	5	3	8	....	....	....	14	3	1	1	2	8
1935-36	West Toronto Nationals	Tor-Jr.	9	3	3	6	....	....	....	4	5	2	2	4	5
	McColl Frontenacs	Tor-Sr.	15	0	0	0	....	....	....	20	4	1	0	1	4
1936-37	Kirkland Lake Blue Devils	NOHA	9	6	4	10	....	....	....	20	4	0	1	1	8
1937-38	**Boston Bruins**	**NHL**	**2**	**0**	**0**	**0**	**0**	**0**	**0**	**0**	....	....	....	....	....
	Providence Reds	AHL	46	6	7	13	....	....	....	33	7	1	3	4	4
1938-39	**Boston Bruins**	**NHL**	**48**	**4**	**8**	**12**	**8**	**15**	**23**	**12**	**12**	**1**	**1**	**2**	**9**
1939-40	**Boston Bruins**	**NHL**	**35**	**1**	**4**	**5**	**2**	**8**	**10**	**26**	**6**	**0**	**0**	**0**	**0**
1940-41	**Boston Bruins**	**NHL**	**45**	**2**	**8**	**10**	**4**	**15**	**19**	**27**	**11**	**0**	**2**	**2**	**7**
1941-42	**Boston Bruins**	**NHL**	**43**	**2**	**9**	**11**	**3**	**14**	**17**	**37**	**5**	**0**	**1**	**1**	**4**
1942-43	**Boston Bruins**	**NHL**	**49**	**5**	**18**	**23**	**7**	**23**	**30**	**24**	**6**	**1**	**1**	**2**	**10**
1943-44	**Boston Bruins**	**NHL**	**34**	**4**	**16**	**20**	**5**	**19**	**24**	**8**	....	....	....	....	....
1944-45	**Boston Bruins**	**NHL**	**40**	**5**	**19**	**24**	**7**	**31**	**38**	**10**	**7**	**0**	**5**	**5**	**0**
1945-46	**Boston Bruins**	**NHL**	**48**	**7**	**9**	**16**	**11**	**17**	**28**	**10**	**10**	**1**	**2**	**3**	**4**
1946-47	**Boston Bruins**	**NHL**	**58**	**1**	**17**	**18**	**1**	**24**	**25**	**16**	**2**	**1**	**0**	**1**	**0**
1947-48	**Boston Bruins**	**NHL**	**45**	**3**	**11**	**14**	**4**	**16**	**20**	**10**	**4**	**0**	**1**	**1**	**2**
1948-49	**Boston Bruins**	**NHL**	**55**	**2**	**13**	**15**	**3**	**21**	**24**	**14**	**3**	**0**	**0**	**0**	**0**
1949-50	**Boston Bruins**	**NHL**	**46**	**2**	**8**	**10**	**3**	**10**	**13**	**8**	....	....	....	....	....
1950-51	Hershey Bears	AHL	35	1	10	11	....	....	....	14	5	0	2	2	0
1951-52	Hershey Bears	AHL	23	0	2	2	....	....	....	8	3	0	0	0	0
1952-53	Hershey Bears	AHL	DID NOT PLAY – COACHING												
	NHL Totals		**548**	**38**	**140**	**178**	**58**	**213**	**271**	**202**	**66**	**4**	**13**	**17**	**36**

NHL Second All-Star Team (1943) • NHL First All-Star Team (1946)

Signed as a free agent by **Boston**, October 26, 1937.

• CRAWFORD, RUSTY
Rusty (Russell) Crawford **HHOF**
LW – L. 5'11", 165 lbs. b: Cardinal, Ont., 11/7/1885. d: 12/19/1971.

			REGULAR SEASON							PIM	PLAYOFFS				
Season	Club	League	GP	G	A	Pts	AG	AA	APts	PIM	GP	G	A	Pts	PIM
1910-11	Saskatoon Wholesalers	City Sr.	STATISTICS NOT AVAILABLE												
1911-12	Saskatoon Wholesalers	City Sr.	....	....	....	....	....	....	....	....	2	0	0	0	*12
1912-13	Quebec Bulldogs	NHA	19	4	0	4	....	....	....	29	1	0	0	0	0
1913-14	Quebec Bulldogs	NHA	19	15	10	25	....	....	....	14	....	....	....	....	....
1914-15	Quebec Bulldogs	NHA	20	18	8	26	....	....	....	30	....	....	....	....	....
1915-16	Quebec Bulldogs	NHA	22	18	5	23	....	....	....	54	....	....	....	....	
1916-17	Quebec Bulldogs	NHA	19	11	6	17	....	....	....	62	....	....	....	....	....
1917-18	**Ottawa Senators**	**NHL**	**12**	**2**	**2**	**4**	**5**	**0**	**5**	**15**	....	....	....	....	....
	Toronto Arenas	**NHL**	**9**	**1**	**2**	**3**	**2**	**0**	**2**	**51**	**2**	**2**	**1**	**3**	**9**
1918-19	**Toronto Arenas**	**NHL**	**18**	**7**	**4**	**11**	**25**	**38**	**63**	**52**	....	....	....	....	....
1919-20	Saskatoon Crescents	City Sr.	12	3	3	6	....	....	....	14	....	....	....	....	....
1920-21	Saskatoon Crescents	City Sr.	14	11	7	18	....	....	....	12	4	2	2	4	4
1921-22	Saskatoon Sheiks	WCHL	24	8	8	16	....	....	....	29	....	....	....	....	....
1922-23	Saskatoon Sheiks	WCHL	19	7	6	13	....	....	....	10	....	....	....	....	....
	Calgary Tigers	WCHL	11	3	1	4	....	....	....	7	....	....	....	....	....
1923-24	Calgary Tigers	WCHL	26	4	4	8	....	....	....	21	7	1	1	2	6
1924-25	Calgary Tigers	WCHL	27	12	2	14	....	....	....	27	2	0	0	0	4
1925-26	Vancouver Maroons	WHL	14	0	0	0	....	....	....	8	....	....		....	....
1926-27	Minneapolis Millers	AHA	32	2	3	5	....	....	....	51	6	3	0	3	*13
1927-28	Minneapolis Millers	AHA	34	4	2	6	....	....	....	27	8	3	0	3	10
1928-29	Minneapolis Millers	AHA	40	9	3	12	....	....	....	33	4	0	0	0	0
1929-30	Minneapolis Millers	AHA	45	3	4	7	....	....	....	32	....	....	....	....	....
1930-31	Prince Albert Mintos	SSHL	DID NOT PLAY – COACHING												
	NHL Totals		**39**	**10**	**8**	**18**	**32**	**38**	**70**	**118**	**2**	**2**	**1**	**3**	**9**
	Other Major League Totals		220	100	50	150	....	....	....	291	10	1	1	2	10

Claimed by **Ottawa** from **Quebec** in Dispersal Draft, November 28, 1917. Signed as a free agent by **Toronto Arenas**, February 9, 1918. Signed as a free agent by **Ottawa**, December 2, 1919. Traded to **Toronto Arenas** by **Ottawa** for future considerations (Harry Cameron, January 19, 1920), December 14, 1918. Rights transferred to **Quebec** by **Toronto Arenas** when Quebec franchise returned to NHL, November 25, 1919. Reinstated as a amateur to sign with the **Saskatoon Crescents** (SSHL), December 29, 1919. Signed as a free agent by **Saskatoon** (WCHL), November 12, 1921. Traded to **Calgary** (WCHL) by **Saskatoon** (WCHL) for cash, February 10, 1923. Traded to **Vancouver** (WHL) by **Calgary** (WHL) for Curly Headley, November 3, 1925.

• CREIGHTON, DAVE
Dave Creighton
C – L. 6'1", 195 lbs. b: Port Arthur, Ont., 6/24/1930.

			REGULAR SEASON							PIM	PLAYOFFS				
Season	Club	League	GP	G	A	Pts	AG	AA	APts	PIM	GP	G	A	Pts	PIM
1946-47	Port Arthur Bruins	TBJHL	6	8	7	15	....	....	....	2	4	5	3	8	0
1947-48	Port Arthur Bruins	TBJHL	9	*19	*12	*31	....	....	....	4	22	*26	19	45	20
1948-49	**Boston Bruins**	**NHL**	**12**	**1**	**3**	**4**	**2**	**5**	**7**	**0**	**3**	**0**	**0**	**0**	**0**
	Hershey Bears	AHL	49	19	18	37	....	....	....	12	....	....	....	....	....
1949-50	**Boston Bruins**	**NHL**	**64**	**18**	**13**	**31**	**24**	**16**	**40**	**13**	....	....	....	....	....
1950-51	**Boston Bruins**	**NHL**	**56**	**5**	**4**	**9**	**7**	**5**	**12**	**4**	**5**	**0**	**1**	**1**	**0**
	Hershey Bears	AHL	11	2	5	7	....	....	....	0	....	....	....	....	....
1951-52	**Boston Bruins**	**NHL**	**49**	**20**	**17**	**37**	**28**	**22**	**50**	**18**	**7**	**2**	**1**	**3**	**2**
	Hershey Bears	AHL	19	9	15	24	....	....	....	4	....	....	....	....	....
1952-53	**Boston Bruins**	**NHL**	**45**	**8**	**8**	**16**	**12**	**11**	**23**	**14**	**11**	**4**	**5**	**9**	**10**
1953-54	**Boston Bruins**	**NHL**	**69**	**20**	**20**	**40**	**31**	**27**	**58**	**27**	**4**	**0**	**0**	**0**	**0**
1954-55	**Toronto Maple Leafs**	**NHL**	**14**	**2**	**1**	**3**	**3**	**1**	**4**	**8**	....	....	....	....	....
	Chicago Black Hawks	**NHL**	**49**	**7**	**7**	**14**	**10**	**9**	**19**	**6**	....	....	....	....	....
1955-56	**New York Rangers**	**NHL**	**70**	**20**	**31**	**51**	**29**	**39**	**68**	**43**	**5**	**0**	**0**	**0**	**4**
1956-57	**New York Rangers**	**NHL**	**70**	**18**	**21**	**39**	**25**	**24**	**49**	**42**	**5**	**2**	**2**	**4**	**2**
1957-58	**New York Rangers**	**NHL**	**70**	**17**	**35**	**52**	**22**	**38**	**60**	**40**	**6**	**3**	**3**	**6**	**2**
1958-59	**Toronto Maple Leafs**	**NHL**	**34**	**3**	**9**	**12**	**4**	**10**	**14**	**4**	**5**	**0**	**1**	**1**	**0**
	Rochester Americans	AHL	33	14	17	31	....	....	....	46	5	1	3	4	4
1959-60	**Toronto Maple Leafs**	**NHL**	**14**	**1**	**5**	**6**	**1**	**5**	**6**	**4**	....	....	....	....	....
	Rochester Americans	AHL	58	25	34	59	....	....	....	30	12	3	3	6	10
1960-61	Rochester Americans	AHL	71	30	42	72	....	....	....	31	....	....	....	....	....
1961-62	Buffalo Bisons	AHL	68	21	48	69	....	....	....	54	11	2	6	8	4
1962-63	Baltimore Clippers	AHL	71	24	48	72	....	....	....	14	3	1	2	3	25
1963-64	Baltimore Clippers	AHL	72	17	25	42	....	....	....	20	....	....	....	....	....
1964-65	Baltimore Clippers	AHL	62	23	28	51	....	....	....	10	5	2	2	4	6
1965-66	Baltimore–Providence	AHL	70	19	39	58	....	....	....	16	....	....	....	....	....
1966-67	Providence Reds	AHL	72	22	42	64	....	....	....	63	....	....	....	....	....
1967-68	Providence Reds	AHL	72	22	53	75	....	....	....	54	8	6	2	8	0
1968-69	Providence Reds	AHL	72	11	20	31	....	....	....	36	1	0	0	0	0
	NHL Totals		**616**	**140**	**174**	**314**	**198**	**212**	**410**	**223**	**51**	**11**	**13**	**24**	**20**

AHL Second All-Star Team (1968) • Won Les Cunningham Award (MVP - AHL) (1968)

Played in NHL All-Star Game (1952, 1953, 1954, 1955, 1956)

Traded to **Toronto** by **Boston** for Fern Flaman, July 20, 1954. Traded to **Chicago** by **Toronto** for cash, November 16, 1954. Traded to **Detroit** by **Chicago** with Jerry Toppazzini, John McCormack and Gord Hollingworth for Tony Leswick, John Wilson and Benny Woit, May 28, 1955. Traded to **NY Rangers** by **Detroit** with Bronco Horvath for Billy Dea and Aggie Kukulowicz, August 18, 1955. Claimed by **Montreal** from **NY Rangers** in Intra-League Draft, June 4, 1958. Claimed by **Toronto** from **Montreal** in Intra-league Draft, June, 1958. Traded to **Buffalo** (AHL) by **Toronto** for Dick Gamble, June, 1961. Traded to **Baltimore** (AHL) by **Buffalo** (AHL) for cash, July, 1962. Traded to **Providence** (AHL) by **Baltimore** (AHL) for Ed MacQueen, November 26, 1965.

• CREIGHTON, JIMMY
Jimmy Creighton
F – L. 5'9", 150 lbs. b: Brandon, Man., 11/18/1905. Deceased.

			REGULAR SEASON							PIM	PLAYOFFS				
Season	Club	League	GP	G	A	Pts	AG	AA	APts	PIM	GP	G	A	Pts	PIM
1925-26	Melville Millionaires	SSHL	14	15	2	17	....	....	....	6	....	....	....	....	....
1926-27	Brandon Wheat Kings	MHL Sr.	7	6	2	8	....	....	....	12	2	0	0	0	8
1927-28	Brandon Wheat Kings	MHL Sr.	16	11	3	14	....	....	....	29	....	....	....	....	....
1928-29	Port Arthur Ports	TBSHL	19	13	9	22	....	....	....	40	2	1	0	1	2
1929-30	Detroit Olympics	IAHL	23	10	8	18	....	....	....	24	....	....	....	....	....
1930-31	**Detroit Falcons**	**NHL**	**11**	**1**	**0**	**1**	**2**	**0**	**2**	**2**	....	....	....	....	....
	Detroit Olympics	IAHL	5	0	0	0	....	....	....	8	....	....	....	....	....
1931-32	Philadelphia Arrows	Can-Am	5	2	0	2	....	....	....	15	....	....	....	....	....
	Detroit Olympics	IAHL	3	0	0	0	....	....	....	0	....	....	....	....	....
	Boston Cubs	Can-Am	4	1	0	1	....	....	....	4	....	....	....	....	....
1932-33	Kansas City Greyhounds	AHA	10	1	3	4	....	....	....	9	....	....	....	....	....
	Duluth Hornets	AHA	1	0	0	0	....	....	....	2	....	....	....	....	....
	NHL Totals		**11**	**1**	**0**	**1**	**2**	**0**	**2**	**2**	....	....	....	....	....

Traded to **Detroit Cougars** by **Kansas City** (AHA) for cash, April 3, 1929. Traded to **NY Americans** by **Detroit Falcons** with Bert McInenly and Tommy Filmore for Hap Emms and Frank Carson, December 29, 1931.

• CRESSMAN, GLEN
Glen Cressman
C – R. 5'9", 155 lbs. b: Petersburg, Ont., 8/29/1934.

			REGULAR SEASON							PIM	PLAYOFFS				
Season	Club	League	GP	G	A	Pts	AG	AA	APts	PIM	GP	G	A	Pts	PIM
1951-52	Kitchener Greenshirts	OHA	3	0	3	3	....	....	....	0	4	0	2	2	0
1952-53	Kitchener Greenshirts	OHA	56	6	11	17	....	....	....	2	....	....	....	....	....
1953-54	Kitchener Greenshirts	OHA	59	20	28	48	....	....	....	10	4	0	1	1	0
1954-55	Toronto Marlboros	OHA	51	23	19	42	....	....	....	16	13	2	7	9	17
1955-56	Chicoutimi Sagueneens	QHL	64	12	18	30	....	....	....	7	5	0	1	1	0
1956-57	**Montreal Canadiens**	**NHL**	**4**	**0**	**0**	**0**	**0**	**0**	**0**	**2**	....	....	....	....	....
	Montreal Royals	QHL	34	11	13	24	....	....	....	4	4	0	0	0	2
	Rochester Americans	AHL	13	2	1	3	....	....	....	4	....	....	....	....	....
1957-58	Montreal Royals	QHL	64	14	21	35	....	....	....	8	7	0	2	2	0
1958-59	Chicoutimi Sagueneens	QHL	59	15	26	41	....	....	....	2	....	....	....	....	....
1959-60	Kingston Frontenacs	EPHL	62	13	22	35	....	....	....	6	....	....	....	....	....
1960-61	Montreal Royals	EPHL	47	5	9	14	....	....	....	6	....	....	....	....	....
1961-62	Knoxville Knights	EHL	46	13	17	30	....	....	....	8	8	2	2	4	0
1962-63	Knoxville Knights	EHL	68	34	36	70	....	....	....	6	5	0	0	0	2
1963-64	Knoxville Knights	EHL	72	27	47	74	....	....	....	23	8	3	2	5	4
1964-65	Knoxville Knights	EHL	71	43	40	83	....	....	....	24	10	6	4	10	0
1965-66	Knoxville Knights	EHL	72	26	43	69	....	....	....	4	3	0	0	0	0
	NHL Totals		**4**	**0**	**0**	**0**	**0**	**0**	**0**	**2**	....	....	....	....	....

• CRISP, TERRY — *see page 959*

• CROGHEN, MAURICE
Maurice "Moe" Croghen
D – L. 5'11", 185 lbs. b: Montreal, Que., 11/19/1914. Deceased.

Season	Club	League	GP	G	A	Pts	AG	AA	APts	PIM	GP	G	A	Pts	PIM
			REGULAR SEASON								**PLAYOFFS**				
1933-34	Montreal Jr. Royals	City Jr.	6	2	1	3	....	....	....	14	4	3	0	3	*19
1934-35	Verdun Maple Leafs	Mtl-Jr.	6	1	0	1	....	....	....	6	6	3	1	4	6
	Montreal Royals	City Sr.	20	2	0	2	....	....	....	14	7	0	2	2	6
1935-36	Verdun Maple Leafs	Mtl-Jr.	4	0	4	4	....	....	....	0	2	2	0	2	4
	Verdun Maple Leafs	Mtl-Sr.	1	0	0	0	....	....	....	0	7	0	0	0	0
1936-37	Quebec Aces	QSCHL	24	1	9	10	....	....	....	34	6	1	2	3	2
1937-38	**Montreal Maroons**	**NHL**	**16**	**0**	**0**	**0**	**0**	**0**	**0**	**4**	....	....	....	....	....
	Montreal Royals	City Sr.	1	0	0	0	....	....	....	0	....	....	....	....	....
1938-39	Springfield Indians	AHL	16	0	1	1	....	....	....	10	....	....	....	....	....
	Providence Reds	AHL	11	0	1	1	....	....	....	5	3	0	0	0	0
1939-40	Montreal Victorias	City Sr.	11	0	1	1	....	....	....	4	....	....	....	....	....
1940-41	Montreal Royals	City Sr.	20	1	1	2	....	....	....	27	....	....	....	....	....
	NHL Totals		**16**	**0**	**0**	**0**	**0**	**0**	**0**	**4**	....	....	....	....	....

Signed as a free agent by **Montreal Maroons**, October 27, 1937.

• CROSSETT, STAN
Stan Crossett
D – R. 6', 200 lbs. b: Tillsonburg, Ont., 4/18/1900. Deceased.

Season	Club	League	GP	G	A	Pts	AG	AA	APts	PIM	GP	G	A	Pts	PIM
1929-30	Port Hope Eagles	City Sr.	STATISTICS NOT AVAILABLE												
1930-31	**Philadelphia Quakers**	**NHL**	**21**	**0**	**0**	**0**	**0**	**0**	**0**	**10**	....	....	....	....	....
	NHL Totals		**21**	**0**	**0**	**0**	**0**	**0**	**0**	**10**	....	....	....	....	....

Signed as a free agent by **Philadelphia**, January 9, 1931.

• CROZIER, JOE
Joe Crozier
D – R. 6', 185 lbs. b: Winnipeg, Man., 2/19/1929.

Season	Club	League	GP	G	A	Pts	AG	AA	APts	PIM	GP	G	A	Pts	PIM
1947-48	Brandon Wheat Kings	MJHL	23	1	10	11	....	....	....	18	5	0	1	1	0
1948-49	Brandon Wheat Kings	MJHL	30	4	23	27	....	....	....	14	25	3	8	11	16
1949-50	San Francisco Shamrocks	PCHL	71	7	20	27	....	....	....	39	4	1	0	1	2
1950-51	Denver Falcons	USHL	9	1	2	3	....	....	....	6	....	....	....	....	....
	Vancouver Canucks	PCHL	46	2	15	17	....	....	....	24	....	....	....	....	....
1951-52	Quebec Aces	QSHL	60	2	24	26	....	....	....	60	20	1	5	6	18
1952-53	Quebec Aces	QSHL	60	6	14	20	....	....	....	40	22	1	12	13	15
1953-54	Quebec Aces	QHL	71	6	21	27	....	....	....	63	23	1	7	8	6
1954-55	Quebec Aces	QHL	59	5	21	26	....	....	....	34	8	3	1	4	8
1955-56	Quebec Aces	QHL	37	2	12	14	....	....	....	50	....	....	....	....	....
1956-57	Quebec Aces	QHL	67	7	30	37	....	....	....	61	10	1	2	3	6
1957-58	Quebec Aces	QHL	51	3	11	14	....	....	....	59	13	0	2	2	*30
	Springfield Indians	AHL	2	0	1	1	....	....	....	0	....	....	....	....	....
1958-59	Quebec Aces	OHL	42	1	12	13	....	....	....	26	....	....	....	....	....
	Providence Reds	AHL	3	0	0	0	....	....	....	8	....	....	....	....	....
1959-60	**Toronto Maple Leafs**	**NHL**	**5**	**0**	**3**	**3**	**0**	**3**	**3**	**2**	....	....	....	....	....
	Spokane Comets	WHL	45	1	10	11	....	....	....	50	....	....	....	....	....
	Rochester Americans	AHL	25	1	11	12	....	....	....	12	12	0	2	2	11
1960-61	Rochester Americans	AHL	35	1	13	14	....	....	....	14	....	....	....	....	....
1961-62	Charlotte Checkers	EHL	DID NOT PLAY – COACHING												
	NHL Totals		**5**	**0**	**3**	**3**	**0**	**3**	**3**	**2**	....	....	....	....	....

QHL Second All-Star Team (1954) • QHL First All-Star Team (1957)

• CRUTCHFIELD, NELS
Nels Crutchfield
C – L. 6'1", 175 lbs. b: Knowlton, Que., 7/12/1911. Deceased.

Season	Club	League	GP	G	A	Pts	AG	AA	APts	PIM	GP	G	A	Pts	PIM
1928-29	Shawinigan Cataracts	ECHA	24	8	1	9	....	....	....	39	....	....	....	....	....
1929-30	Shawinigan Cataracts	ECHA	24	5	4	9	....	....	....	38	....	....	....	....	....
1930-31	Shawinigan Cataracts	ECHA	12	6	4	10	....	....	....	6	....	....	....	....	....
1931-32	McGill University	Mtl-Sr.	12	7	6	13	....	....	....	*41	2	1	0	1	11
1932-33	McGill University	Mtl-Sr.	10	7	4	11	....	....	....	33	7	1	1	2	28
1933-34	McGill University	Mtl-Sr.	28	12	19	31	....	....	....	60	....	....	....	....	....
1934-35	**Montreal Canadiens**	**NHL**	**41**	**5**	**5**	**10**	**11**	**11**	**22**	**20**	**2**	**0**	**1**	**1**	**22**
	NHL Totals		**41**	**5**	**5**	**10**	**11**	**11**	**22**	**20**	**2**	**0**	**1**	**1**	**22**

Rights traded to **Montreal Canadiens** by **Montreal Maroons** for Lionel Conacher and the rights to Herb Cain, October 3, 1934. • Suffered career-ending injuries in automobile accident, September 28, 1935.

• CULLEN, BARRY
Barry (Charles) Cullen
RW – R. 6', 183 lbs. b: Ottawa, Ont., 6/16/1935.

Season	Club	League	GP	G	A	Pts	AG	AA	APts	PIM	GP	G	A	Pts	PIM
1953-54	St. Catharines Teepees	OHA	58	62	45	102	....	....	....	35	15	9	7	16	13
1954-55	St. Catharines Teepees	OHA	49	45	42	87	....	....	....	87	11	9	5	14	34
1955-56	**Toronto Maple Leafs**	**NHL**	**3**	**0**	**0**	**0**	**0**	**0**	**0**	**4**	....	....	....	....	....
	Winnipeg Warriors	WHL	67	38	34	72	....	....	....	72	14	7	6	13	14
1956-57	**Toronto Maple Leafs**	**NHL**	**51**	**6**	**10**	**16**	**8**	**12**	**20**	**30**	....	....	....	....	....
	Rochester Americans	AHL	7	4	4	8	....	....	....	6	....	....	....	....	....
1957-58	**Toronto Maple Leafs**	**NHL**	**70**	**16**	**25**	**41**	**21**	**27**	**48**	**37**	....	....	....	....	....
1958-59	**Toronto Maple Leafs**	**NHL**	**40**	**6**	**8**	**14**	**8**	**8**	**16**	**17**	**2**	**0**	**0**	**0**	**0**
1959-60	**Detroit Red Wings**	**NHL**	**55**	**4**	**9**	**13**	**5**	**9**	**14**	**23**	**4**	**0**	**0**	**0**	**2**
	Hershey Bears	AHL	7	2	2	4	....	....	....	0	....	....	....	....	....
1960-61	Buffalo Bisons	AHL	71	16	37	53	....	....	....	59	4	1	0	1	10
1961-62	Buffalo Bisons	AHL	69	*41	53	94	....	....	....	61	11	2	4	6	10
1962-63	Buffalo Bisons	AHL	53	20	23	43	....	....	....	20	13	3	3	6	14
1963-64	Buffalo Bisons	AHL	72	23	38	61	....	....	....	32	....	....	....	....	....
	NHL Totals		**219**	**32**	**52**	**84**	**42**	**56**	**98**	**111**	**6**	**0**	**0**	**0**	**2**

Won WHL Rookie of the Year Award (1956) • AHL First All-Star Team (1962)

Signed as a free agent by **Toronto**, June, 1955. Traded to **Detroit** by **Toronto** with Gary Aldcorn for Frank Roggeveen and Johnny Wilson, June 9, 1959. Traded to **Buffalo** (AHL) by **Detroit** (Hershey - AHL) for Pete Conacher, August, 1960.

• CULLEN, BRIAN
Brian Cullen
C – L. 5'10", 160 lbs. b: Ottawa, Ont., 11/11/1933.

Season	Club	League	GP	G	A	Pts	AG	AA	APts	PIM	GP	G	A	Pts	PIM
			REGULAR SEASON								**PLAYOFFS**				
1951-52	St. Catharines Teepees	OHA	54	30	31	61	....	....	....	25	14	7	6	13	4
	Buffalo Bisons	AHL	1	0	0	0	....	....	....	0	....	....	....	....	....
1952-53	St. Catharines Teepees	OHA	56	41	18	69	....	....	....	29	3	4	0	4	2
	Buffalo Bisons	AHL	3	1	5	6	....	....	....	0	....	....	....	....	....
1953-54	St. Catharines Teepees	OHA	59	*68	*93	*161	....	....	....	40	15	*12	*17	*29	18
1954-55	**Toronto Maple Leafs**	**NHL**	**27**	**3**	**5**	**8**	**4**	**6**	**10**	**6**	**4**	**1**	**0**	**1**	**0**
	Pittsburgh Hornets	AHL	36	11	25	36	....	....	....	20	....	....	....	....	....
1955-56	**Toronto Maple Leafs**	**NHL**	**21**	**2**	**6**	**8**	**3**	**7**	**10**	**8**	**5**	**1**	**0**	**1**	**2**
	Winnipeg Warriors	WHL	50	16	35	51	....	....	....	10	....	....	....	....	....
1956-57	**Toronto Maple Leafs**	**NHL**	**46**	**8**	**12**	**20**	**11**	**14**	**25**	**27**	....	....	....	....	....
	Rochester Americans	AHL	9	2	10	12	....	....	....	2	....	....	....	....	....
1957-58	**Toronto Maple Leafs**	**NHL**	**67**	**20**	**23**	**43**	**26**	**25**	**51**	**29**	....	....	....	....	....
1958-59	**Toronto Maple Leafs**	**NHL**	**59**	**4**	**14**	**18**	**5**	**15**	**20**	**10**	**10**	**1**	**0**	**1**	**0**
1959-60	**New York Rangers**	**NHL**	**64**	**8**	**21**	**29**	**10**	**21**	**31**	**6**	....	....	....	....	....
1960-61	**New York Rangers**	**NHL**	**42**	**11**	**19**	**30**	**13**	**19**	**32**	**6**	....	....	....	....	....
	Buffalo Bisons	AHL	15	6	6	12	....	....	....	9	4	0	0	0	0
1961-62	Buffalo Bisons	AHL	67	22	59	81	....	....	....	18	11	5	3	8	11
1962-63	Buffalo Bisons	AHL	31	5	17	22	....	....	....	23	5	1	0	1	0
	NHL Totals		**326**	**56**	**100**	**156**	**72**	**107**	**179**	**92**	**19**	**3**	**0**	**3**	**2**

Traded to **Toronto** by **Chicago** (Buffalo - AHL) for George Blair, Frank Sullivan and Jackie LeClair, May 4, 1954. Claimed by **NY Rangers** from **Toronto** in Intra-League Draft, June 9, 1959.

• CULLEN, RAY — *see page 962*

• CUNNINGHAM, BOB
Bob Cunningham
C – L. 5'11", 168 lbs. b: Welland, Ont., 2/26/1941.

Season	Club	League	GP	G	A	Pts	AG	AA	APts	PIM	GP	G	A	Pts	PIM
1958-59	Guelph Biltmores	OHA	54	19	27	46	....	....	....	25	10	1	6	7	8
1959-60	Guelph Biltmores	OHA	48	14	23	37	....	....	....	26	3	1	2	3	0
	Trois-Rivieres Lions	EPHL	3	1	3	4	....	....	....	2	5	1	1	2	0
1960-61	Guelph Biltmores	OHA	47	34	52	86	....	....	....	78	14	11	10	21	39
	New York Rangers	**NHL**	**3**	**0**	**1**	**1**	**0**	**1**	**1**	**0**	....	....	....	....	....
1961-62	**New York Rangers**	**NHL**	**1**	**0**	**0**	**0**	**0**	**0**	**0**	**0**	....	....	....	....	....
	Kitchener Beavers	EPHL	38	5	11	16	....	....	....	18	7	0	1	1	4
1962-63	Baltimore Clippers	AHL	57	9	17	26	....	....	....	21	3	0	1	1	0
1963-64	St. Paul Rangers	CHL	69	25	47	72	....	....	....	32	8	1	5	6	7
1964-65	St. Louis Braves	CHL	47	15	35	50	....	....	....	14	....	....	....	....	....
1965-66	Pittsburgh Hornets	AHL	65	10	21	31	....	....	....	14	3	0	0	0	0
1966-67	Baltimore Clippers	AHL	63	17	35	52	....	....	....	6	9	2	3	5	0
1967-68	Baltimore Clippers	AHL	71	13	30	43	....	....	....	8	....	....	....	....	....
1968-69	Denver Spurs	WHL	17	8	5	13	....	....	....	0	....	....	....	....	....
	Baltimore Clippers	AHL	46	5	12	17	....	....	....	22	....	....	....	....	....
1969-70	Denver Spurs	WHL	22	4	13	17	....	....	....	2	....	....	....	....	....
	Port Huron Flags	IHL	22	8	17	25	....	....	....	24	8	3	3	6	2
1970-71	Orillia Terriers	OHA Sr.	40	15	29	44	....	....	....	32	....	....	....	....	....
1971-72	Barrie Flyers	OHA Sr.	40	24	45	69	....	....	....	53	....	....	....	....	....
1972-73	Barrie Flyers	OHA Sr.	35	23	43	66	....	....	....	10	....	....	....	....	....
1973-74	Brantford Forresters	OHA Sr.	32	19	31	50	....	....	....	8	....	....	....	....	....
	NHL Totals		**4**	**0**	**1**	**1**	**0**	**1**	**1**	**0**	....	....	....	....	....

Traded to **Detroit** (Pittsburgh - AHL) by **NY Rangers** for Dunc McCallum, June, 1965. Claimed by **NY Rangers** (Baltimore - AHL) from **Detroit** in Reverse Draft, June, 1966.

• CUNNINGHAM, LES
Les Cunningham
C – L. 5'8", 165 lbs. b: Calgary, Alta., 10/4/1913.

Season	Club	League	GP	G	A	Pts	AG	AA	APts	PIM	GP	G	A	Pts	PIM
1931-32	Calgary Jimmies	City Jr.	12	3	2	5	....	....	....	15	3	1	0	1	6
1932-33	Regina Pats	City Jr.	3	3	0	3	....	....	....	0	15	6	0	6	12
1933-34	Saskatoon Elites	City Sr.	20	16	10	26	....	....	....	18	4	2	0	2	4
1934-35	Buffalo Bisons	IAHL	42	12	12	24	....	....	....	34	....	....	....	....	....
1935-36	Buffalo Bisons	IAHL	37	9	13	22	....	....	....	37	5	1	1	2	0
1936-37	**New York Americans**	**NHL**	**23**	**1**	**8**	**9**	**2**	**19**	**21**	**19**	....	....	....	....	....
	Cleveland Falcons	AHL	19	4	4	8	....	....	....	17	....	....	....	....	....
1937-38	Cleveland Falcons	AHL	48	19	28	47	....	....	....	55	2	1	2	3	0
1938-39	Cleveland Falcons	AHL	52	26	20	46	....	....	....	49	9	6	4	*10	0
1939-40	**Chicago Black Hawks**	**NHL**	**37**	**6**	**11**	**17**	**13**	**22**	**35**	**2**	**1**	**0**	**0**	**0**	**0**
1940-41	Cleveland Barons	AHL	56	22	*42	*64	....	....	....	10	9	3	4	7	2
1941-42	Cleveland Barons	AHL	56	25	35	60	....	....	....	23	5	4	2	6	4
1942-43	Cleveland Barons	AHL	55	35	47	82	....	....	....	24	4	2	2	4	0
1943-44	Cleveland Barons	AHL	52	26	52	78	....	....	....	13	11	6	4	10	0
1944-45	Cleveland Barons	AHL	56	35	45	80	....	....	....	4	11	3	8	11	2
1945-46	Cleveland Barons	AHL	62	33	44	77	....	....	....	10	7	4	6	10	5
1946-47	Cleveland Barons	AHL	61	8	29	37	....	....	....	11	....	....	....	....	....
1947-48	San Francisco Shamrocks	PCHL	39	15	24	39	....	....	....	27	3	0	5	5	2
1948-49	San Francisco Shamrocks	PCHL	9	4	4	8	....	....	....	14	....	....	....	....	....
1949-50	Brandon Wheat Kings	MJHL	DID NOT PLAY – COACHING												
	NHL Totals		**60**	**7**	**19**	**26**	**15**	**41**	**56**	**21**	**1**	**0**	**0**	**0**	**0**

AHL Second All-Star Team (1941, 1943, 1944) • AHL First All-Star Team (1942)

Traded to **NY Americans** by **Buffalo** (AHL) for Lloyd Klein, January 14, 1937. Traded to **Cleveland** (AHL) by **NY Americans** for cash, October, 1937. Claimed by **Chicago** from **Cleveland** (AHL) in Inter-League Draft, May 14, 1939. Traded to **Cleveland** (AHL) by **Chicago** for cash, May 12, 1940.

• CUPOLO, BILL Bill Cupolo
RW – R. 5'8", 170 lbs. b: Niagara Falls, Ont., 1/8/1924.

			REGULAR SEASON								PLAYOFFS				
Season	Club	League	GP	G	A	Pts	AG	AA	APts	PIM	GP	G	A	Pts	PIM
1942-43	Stratford Kroehlers	OHA	16	14	22	36	....	....	....	6	2	3	3	6	0
1943-44	Stratford Kroehlers	OHA	DID NOT PLAY – INJURED												
1944-45	**Boston Bruins**	**NHL**	**47**	**11**	**13**	**24**	**15**	**21**	**36**	**10**	**7**	**1**	**2**	**3**	**0**
1945-46	New Haven–Hershey	AHL	42	8	14	22	....	....	....	13	....	....	....	....	....
1946-47	Springfield Indians	AHL	50	8	12	20	....	....	....	38	2	0	0	0	2
1947-48	Springfield Indians	AHL	17	1	4	5	....	....	....	2	....	....	....	....	....
1948-49	Fort Worth Rangers	USHL	50	12	20	32	....	....	....	32	2	1	0	1	0
1949-50	San Diego–Seattle	PCHL	70	25	20	45	....	....	....	26	4	0	2	2	0
1950-51	Sydney Millionaires	CBSHL	49	20	28	48	....	....	....	54	11	4	5	9	11
1951-52	Sydney Millionaires	MMHL	41	12	19	31	....	....	....	42	....	....	....	....	....
	New Haven Tomahawks	EHL	29	19	10	29	....	....	....	25	9	3	2	5	2
1952-53	Washington Lions	EHL	13	4	2	6	....	....	....	12	....	....	....	....	....
	Kitchener–Chatham	OHA Sr.	41	12	16	28	....	....	....	36	....	....	....	....	....
1953-54	Chatham–Stratford	OHA Sr.	54	9	27	36	....	....	....	47	7	1	4	5	4
	NHL Totals		**47**	**11**	**13**	**24**	**15**	**21**	**36**	**10**	**7**	**1**	**2**	**3**	**0**

• CURRIE, HUGH Hugh Currie
D – R. 6', 190 lbs. b: Saskatoon, Sask., 10/22/1925.

Season	Club	League	GP	G	A	Pts	AG	AA	APts	PIM	GP	G	A	Pts	PIM
1943-44	Saskatoon Lions	SJHL	4	1	4	5	....	....	....	4	2	0	3	3	2
1944-45	Baltimore Orioles	EHL	47	3	15	18	....	....	....	44	11	2	4	6	18
1945-46	Dallas Texans	USHL	18	3	1	4	....	....	....	14	....	....	....	....	....
	Washington Lions	EHL	22	1	5	6	....	....	....	33	12	0	6	6	10
1946-47	Houston Huskies	USHL	36	4	8	12	....	....	....	30	....	....	....	....	....
	Tacoma Rockets	PCHL	18	5	8	13	....	....	....	44	....	....	....	....	....
1947-48	Buffalo Bisons	AHL	9	0	0	0	....	....	....	10	....	....	....	....	....
	Houston Huskies	USHL	52	5	7	12	....	....	....	67	12	1	0	1	2
1948-49	Houston Huskies	USHL	11	1	1	2	....	....	....	13	....	....	....	....	....
	San Diego Skyhawks	PCHL	51	4	11	15	....	....	....	52	14	2	6	8	30
1949-50	Louisville Blades	USHL	7	1	6	7	....	....	....	8	....	....	....	....	....
	Buffalo Bisons	AHL	54	3	25	28	....	....	....	64	5	0	0	0	13
1950-51	**Montreal Canadiens**	**NHL**	**1**	**0**	**0**	**0**	**0**	**0**	**0**	**0**	....	....	....	....	....
	Buffalo Bisons	AHL	57	9	56	65	....	....	....	54	4	0	1	1	2
1951-52	Buffalo Bisons	AHL	11	0	4	4	....	....	....	4	....	....	....	....	....
	Vancouver Canucks	PCHL	34	5	20	25	....	....	....	36	....	....	....	....	....
1952-53	Vancouver Canucks	WHL	68	3	25	28	....	....	....	77	9	2	5	7	10
1953-54	Springfield Indians	QHL	31	5	21	26	....	....	....	11	....	....	....	....	....
	Syracuse Warriors	AHL	41	2	13	15	....	....	....	26	....	....	....	....	....
1954-55	Springfield Indians	AHL	64	5	43	48	....	....	....	60	4	0	1	1	4
1955-56	Vancouver Canucks	WHL	69	6	30	36	....	....	....	36	15	0	3	3	6
1956-57	Vancouver Canucks	WHL	68	6	32	38	....	....	....	47	....	....	....	....	....
1957-58	Seattle Totems	WHL	70	11	32	43	....	....	....	78	11	1	1	2	10
1958-59	Vancouver Canucks	WHL	67	4	26	30	....	....	....	38	9	0	4	4	10
1959-60	Calgary Stampeders	WHL	66	1	25	26	....	....	....	30	....	....	....	....	....
1960-61	Victoria Cougars	WHL	70	1	16	17	....	....	....	39	5	0	1	1	0
1961-62	San Francisco Seals	WHL	7	0	1	1	....	....	....	2	....	....	....	....	....
	Vancouver Canucks	WHL	43	1	13	14	....	....	....	18	....	....	....	....	....
1962-63	Philadelphia Ramblers	EHL	65	2	50	52	....	....	....	31	3	1	0	1	2
1963-64	Edmonton Nuggets	ASHL	DID NOT PLAY – COACHING												
1964-65	Edmonton Nuggets	ASHL	DID NOT PLAY – COACHING												
1965-66	Edmonton Nuggets	ASHL	7	0	6	6	....	....	....	5	....	....	....	....	....
	NHL Totals		**1**	**0**	**0**	**0**	**0**	**0**	**0**	**0**	....	....	....	....	....

AHL Second All-Star Team (1951) • WHL Coast Division Second All Star Team (1957) • WHL Coast Division First All-Star Team (1958, 1959)

• CURRY, FLOYD Floyd "Busher" Curry
RW – R. 5'11", 174 lbs. b: Chapleau, Ont., 8/11/1925.

Season	Club	League	GP	G	A	Pts	AG	AA	APts	PIM	GP	G	A	Pts	PIM
1940-41	Kirkland Golden Gate	NOHA	20	9	4	13	....	....	....	5	....	....	....	....	....
1941-42	Oshawa Generals	OHA	24	11	15	26	....	....	....	20	12	9	10	19	15
1942-43	Oshawa Generals	OHA	22	22	24	46	....	....	....	16	10	8	5	13	8
1943-44	Oshawa Generals	OHA	26	22	26	48	....	....	....	13	10	4	7	11	6
1944-45			MILITARY SERVICE												
1945-46	Montreal Royals	QSHL	32	22	23	45	....	....	....	8	11	3	6	9	4
1946-47	Montreal Royals	QSHL	40	23	20	43	....	....	....	26	11	3	4	7	4
1947-48	**Montreal Canadiens**	**NHL**	**31**	**1**	**5**	**6**	**1**	**7**	**8**	**0**	....	....	....	....	....
	Buffalo Bisons	AHL	14	6	8	14	....	....	....	10	....	....	....	....	....
1948-49	Buffalo Bisons	AHL	67	24	19	43	....	....	....	12	....	....	....	....	....
	Montreal Canadiens	**NHL**	....	....	....	....	....	....	....	....	**2**	**0**	**0**	**0**	**2**
1949-50	**Montreal Canadiens**	**NHL**	**49**	**8**	**8**	**16**	**11**	**10**	**21**	**8**	**5**	**1**	**0**	**1**	**2**
	Buffalo Bisons	AHL	24	4	6	10	....	....	....	6	....	....	....	....	....
1950-51	**Montreal Canadiens**	**NHL**	**69**	**13**	**14**	**27**	**18**	**18**	**36**	**23**	**11**	**0**	**2**	**2**	**2**
1951-52	**Montreal Canadiens**	**NHL**	**64**	**20**	**18**	**38**	**28**	**23**	**51**	**10**	**11**	**4**	**3**	***7**	**6**
1952-53	**Montreal Canadiens**	**NHL**	**68**	**16**	**6**	**22**	**25**	**8**	**33**	**10**	**12**	**2**	**1**	**3**	**2**
1953-54	**Montreal Canadiens**	**NHL**	**70**	**13**	**8**	**21**	**20**	**11**	**31**	**22**	**11**	**4**	**0**	**4**	**4**
1954-55	**Montreal Canadiens**	**NHL**	**68**	**11**	**10**	**21**	**16**	**13**	**29**	**36**	**12**	**8**	**4**	**12**	**4**
1955-56	**Montreal Canadiens**	**NHL**	**70**	**14**	**18**	**32**	**20**	**22**	**42**	**10**	**10**	**1**	**5**	**6**	**12**
1956-57	**Montreal Canadiens**	**NHL**	**70**	**7**	**9**	**16**	**9**	**10**	**19**	**20**	**10**	**3**	**2**	**5**	**2**
1957-58	**Montreal Canadiens**	**NHL**	**42**	**2**	**3**	**5**	**3**	**3**	**6**	**8**	**7**	**0**	**0**	**0**	**2**
1958-59	Montreal Royals	QHL	57	9	13	22	....	....	....	40	8	1	3	4	2
	Rochester Americans	AHL	2	0	0	0	....	....	....	4	....	....	....	....	....
1959-60	Montreal Royals	EPHL	DID NOT PLAY – COACHING												
	NHL Totals		**601**	**105**	**99**	**204**	**151**	**125**	**276**	**147**	**91**	**23**	**17**	**40**	**38**

Played in NHL All-Star Game (1951, 1952, 1953, 1956, 1957)

• CUSHENAN, IAN Ian Cushenan
D – L. 6'2", 195 lbs. b: Hamilton, Ont., 11/29/1933.

Season	Club	League	GP	G	A	Pts	AG	AA	APts	PIM	GP	G	A	Pts	PIM
1952-53	St. Catharines Teepees	OHA	49	3	9	12	....	....	....	60	3	0	1	1	8
1953-54	St. Catharines Teepees	OHA	59	5	25	30	....	....	....	86	15	0	3	3	23
1954-55	Cleveland Barons	AHL	56	1	13	14	....	....	....	84	4	0	0	0	12
	Quebec Aces	QHL	6	0	2	2	....	....	....	4	....	....	....	....	....
1955-56	Cleveland Barons	AHL	63	2	16	18	....	....	....	113	8	0	3	3	*38
1956-57	**Chicago Black Hawks**	**NHL**	**11**	**0**	**0**	**0**	**0**	**0**	**0**	**13**	....	....	....	....	....
	Cleveland Barons	AHL	54	0	17	17	....	....	....	151	....	....	....	....	....
1957-58	**Chicago Black Hawks**	**NHL**	**61**	**2**	**8**	**10**	**3**	**9**	**12**	**67**	....	....	....	....	....
1958-59	**Montreal Canadiens**	**NHL**	**35**	**1**	**2**	**3**	**1**	**2**	**3**	**28**	....	....	....	....	....
1959-60	**New York Rangers**	**NHL**	**17**	**0**	**1**	**1**	**0**	**1**	**1**	**22**	....	....	....	....	....
	Springfield Indians	AHL	49	0	12	12	....	....	....	67	10	0	1	1	8
1960-61	Springfield Indians	AHL	71	5	41	46	....	....	....	81	8	2	3	5	18
1961-62	Buffalo Bisons	AHL	69	2	21	23	....	....	....	84	11	0	3	3	8
1962-63	Buffalo Bisons	AHL	72	3	29	32	....	....	....	97	13	1	6	7	34
1963-64	**Detroit Red Wings**	**NHL**	**5**	**0**	**0**	**0**	**0**	**0**	**0**	**4**	....	....	....	....	....
	Pittsburgh Hornets	AHL	56	4	16	20	....	....	....	77	5	0	3	3	9
1964-65	Buffalo Bisons	AHL	69	4	23	27	....	....	....	89	9	3	0	3	12
1965-66	Buffalo Bisons	AHL	69	0	13	13	....	....	....	66	....	....	....	....	....
	NHL Totals		**129**	**3**	**11**	**14**	**4**	**12**	**16**	**134**	....	....	....	....	....

AHL Second All-Star Team (1963)

Played in NHL All-Star Game (1958)

Traded to **Montreal** by **Chicago** for cash, June 9, 1959. Claimed by **NY Rangers** from **Montreal** in Intra-League Draft, June 10, 1959. Signed as a free agent by **Detroit**, August 5, 1963. Traded to **Chicago** by **Detroit** with John Miszuk and Art Stratton for Aut Erickson and Ron Murphy, June 9, 1964.

• DAHLSTROM, CULLY Cully (Carl S.) Dahlstrom USHOF
C – L. 5'11", 175 lbs. b: Minneapolis, MN, 7/3/1913.

Season	Club	League	GP	G	A	Pts	AG	AA	APts	PIM	GP	G	A	Pts	PIM
1932-33	Minneapolis Millers	CHL	27	3	9	12	....	....	....	27	7	1	0	1	0
1933-34	Minneapolis Millers	CHL	43	13	15	28	....	....	....	20	3	2	*4	*6	0
1934-35	St. Paul Saints	CHL	44	16	20	36	....	....	....	30	8	3	0	3	2
1935-36	St. Paul Saints	AHA	46	20	23	43	....	....	....	26	3	0	0	0	4
1936-37	St. Paul Saints	AHA	47	23	19	42	....	....	....	25	3	1	0	1	0
1937-38	**Chicago Black Hawks**	**NHL**	**48**	**10**	**9**	**19**	**21**	**18**	**39**	**11**	**10**	**3**	**1**	**4**	**2**
1938-39	**Chicago Black Hawks**	**NHL**	**48**	**6**	**14**	**20**	**13**	**26**	**39**	**2**	....	....	....	....	....
1939-40	**Chicago Black Hawks**	**NHL**	**45**	**11**	**19**	**30**	**24**	**38**	**62**	**15**	**2**	**0**	**0**	**0**	**0**
1940-41	**Chicago Black Hawks**	**NHL**	**40**	**11**	**14**	**25**	**22**	**26**	**48**	**6**	**5**	**3**	**3**	**6**	**2**
1941-42	**Chicago Black Hawks**	**NHL**	**33**	**13**	**14**	**27**	**22**	**21**	**43**	**6**	**3**	**0**	**0**	**0**	**0**
1942-43	**Chicago Black Hawks**	**NHL**	**38**	**11**	**13**	**24**	**16**	**16**	**32**	**10**	....	....	....	....	....
1943-44	**Chicago Black Hawks**	**NHL**	**50**	**20**	**22**	**42**	**25**	**27**	**52**	**8**	**9**	**0**	**4**	**4**	**0**
1944-45	**Chicago Black Hawks**	**NHL**	**40**	**6**	**13**	**19**	**8**	**21**	**29**	**0**	....	....	....	....	....
	NHL Totals		**342**	**88**	**118**	**206**	**151**	**193**	**344**	**58**	**29**	**6**	**8**	**14**	**4**

AHA First All-Star Team (1936) • Won Calder Trophy (1938)

Claimed by **Chicago** from **St. Paul** (AHA) in Inter-League Draft, May 9, 1937. Traded to **Seattle** (PCHL) by **Chicago** for cash, November 26, 1945.

• DALEY, FRANK Frank "Dapper Dan" Daley
LW/C – L. 5'11", 178 lbs. b: Port Arthur, Ont., 8/22/1909. d: 10/15/1968.

Season	Club	League	GP	G	A	Pts	AG	AA	APts	PIM	GP	G	A	Pts	PIM
1927-28	Fort William Forts	TBSHL	1	0	0	0	....	....	....	2	....	....	....	....	....
1928-29	Houghton Cougars	NMHL	34	8	5	13	....	....	....	45	5	1	0	1	0
	Detroit Cougars	**NHL**	**5**	**0**	**0**	**0**	**0**	**0**	**0**	**0**	**2**	**0**	**0**	**0**	**0**
1929-30	Detroit Olympics	IAHL	30	1	0	1	....	....	....	19	2	0	0	0	0
1930-31	Detroit Olympics	IAHL	47	4	8	12	....	....	....	52	....	....	....	....	....
1931-32	Cleveland Indians	IAHL	44	2	3	5	....	....	....	54	....	....	....	....	....
1932-33	Cleveland Indians	IAHL	39	14	8	22	....	....	....	45	....	....	....	....	....
1933-34	Windsor–London	IAHL	42	9	9	18	....	....	....	30	6	2	5	7	2
1934-35	Cleveland Falcons	IAHL	43	16	*25	41	....	....	....	44	2	0	0	0	0
1935-36	Cleveland Falcons	IAHL	48	17	*36	*53	....	....	....	45	2	0	0	0	2
1936-37	Cleveland–Springfield	AHL	32	6	7	13	....	....	....	15	4	0	1	1	0
1937-38	St. Louis Flyers	AHA	25	6	6	12	....	....	....	10	....	....	....	....	....
	Seattle Seahawks	PCHL	18	5	7	12	....	....	....	10	4	0	0	0	0
1938-39	Seattle Seahawks	PCHL	47	15	25	40	....	....	....	32	7	2	2	4	12
1939-40	Seattle Seahawks	PCHL	40	26	14	40	....	....	....	20	....	....	....	....	....
1940-41	Seattle Olympics	PCHL	47	28	31	59	....	....	....	32	2	0	0	0	0
1941-42	Philadelphia Rockets	AHL	56	16	35	51	....	....	....	12	....	....	....	....	....
1942-43	Hershey Bears	AHL	56	15	33	48	....	....	....	31	6	0	2	2	2
1943-44	Seattle Ironmen	City Sr.	5	11	6	17	....	....	....	18	....	....	....	....	....
	Hershey Bears	AHL	41	3	12	15	....	....	....	14	3	0	0	0	0
	NHL Totals		**5**	**0**	**0**	**0**	**0**	**0**	**0**	**0**	**2**	**0**	**0**	**0**	**0**

Traded to **Detroit Cougars** by **Houghton** (NMHL) for cash, February 23, 1929.

• DAME, NAPOLEON Napoleon "Bunny" Dame
LW – L. 5'9", 160 lbs. b: Edmonton, Alberta, 12/6/1913. Deceased.

Season	Club	League	GP	G	A	Pts	AG	AA	APts	PIM	GP	G	A	Pts	PIM
1931-32	Edmonton Canadiens	City Jr.	....	*14	2	*16	....	....	....	....	....	....	....	....	....
1932-33	Edmonton Canadiens	City Jr.	STATISTICS NOT AVAILABLE												
1933-34	Rossland Miners	Kootenay	18	14	5	19	....	....	....	5	....	....	....	....	....
1934-35	Rossland Miners	Kootenay	12	8	5	13	....	....	....	19	....	....	....	....	....
1935-36	Rossland Miners	Kootenay	16	7	9	16	....	....	....	15	2	1	1	2	0
1936-37	Trail Smoke Eaters	Kootenay	13	10	*12	22	....	....	....	6	3	0	0	0	0
1937-38	Trail Smoke Eaters	Kootenay	18	9	10	19	....	....	....	4	4	0	1	1	0
1938-39	Trail Smoke Eaters	Kootenay	PLAYED EXHIBITION SEASON ONLY												
	Canada	WEC	7	*8	4	*12	....	....	....	....	....	....	....	....	....
1939-40	Trail Smoke Eaters	Kootenay	27	28	34	62	....	....	....	14	7	4	4	8	6
1940-41	Trail Smoke Eaters	Kootenay	28	23	25	48	....	....	....	26	9	3	3	6	8
1941-42	**Montreal Canadiens**	**NHL**	**34**	**2**	**5**	**7**	**3**	**8**	**11**	**4**	....	....	....	....	....
1942-43			MILITARY SERVICE												
1943-44			MILITARY SERVICE												
1944-45	Calgary Currie Army	City Sr.	14	6	9	15	....	....	....	6	3	0	2	2	2
1945-46	Calgary Stampeders	WCSHL	36	23	31	54	....	....	....	14	15	9	8	17	5
1946-47	Calgary Stampeders	WCSHL	17	10	17	27	....	....	....	12	7	7	4	11	2
1947-48	Calgary Stampeders	WCSHL	46	14	22	36	....	....	....	22	11	4	4	8	8
1948-49	Calgary Stampeders	WCSHL	46	17	20	37	....	....	....	34	4	0	0	0	2
1949-50	Calgary Stampeders	WCSHL	44	14	15	29	....	....	....	23	11	1	2	3	4
	NHL Totals		**34**	**2**	**5**	**7**	**3**	**8**	**11**	**4**	....	....	....	....	....

Signed as a free agent by **Montreal**, October 30, 1941.

			REGULAR SEASON								PLAYOFFS				
Season	Club	League	GP	G	A	Pts	AG	AA	APts	PIM	GP	G	A	Pts	PIM

• DAMORE, HANK
Hank "Lou Costello" Damore
C – L. 5'6", 200 lbs. b: Niagara Falls, Ont., 7/17/1919.

Season	Club	League	GP	G	A	Pts	AG	AA	APts	PIM	GP	G	A	Pts	PIM
1935-36	Niagara Falls Cataracts	OHA	8	4	3	7	....	....	....	10	2	2	0	2	0
1936-37	Stratford Midgets	OHA	13	*19	7	*26	....	....	....	30	2	3	*2	*5	*17
1937-38	Stratford Midgets	OHA	14	13	17	30	....	....	....	*43	7	5	1	6	12
1938-39	Verdun Maple Leafs	QSHL	14	3	4	7	....	....	....	26	....	....	....	....	....
	Stratford Majors	MOHL	10	0	3	3	....	....	....	16	2	0	1	1	2
1939-40	Stratford Canadians	MOHL	38	18	16	34	....	....	....	40	4	3	3	6	10
1940-41	London Mohawks	OHA Sr.	18	3	5	8	....	....	....	28	....	....	....	....	....
1941-42	Detroit Mansfields	MOHL	17	11	26	37	....	....	....	8	....	....	....	....	....
	Toledo Babcocks	MOHL	....	....	....	....	....	....	....	....	7	5	*6	*11	*28
1942-43	Windsor Colonial Tool	City Sr.	15	17	*30	*47	....	....	....	*38	7	*16	10	*26	*14
1943-44	**New York Rangers**	**NHL**	**4**	**1**	**0**	**1**	**1**	**0**	**1**	**2**	....	....	....	....	....
	New Haven Eagles	EHL	12	*6	*16	*22	....	....	....	12	....	....	....	....	....
	Brooklyn Crescents	EHL	28	*34	*29	*63	....	....	....	26	11	8	12	20	6
1944-45	Washington Lions	EHL	1	1	0	1	....	....	....	0	....	....	....	....	....
	New York Rovers	EHL	39	19	41	60	....	....	....	40	12	8	9	17	14
	Baltimore Orioles	EHL	....	....	....	....	....	....	....	....	1	0	0	0	0
1945-46	Philadelphia Falcons	EHL	50	13	38	51	....	....	....	28	12	4	7	11	4
1946-47	Fresno Falcons	PCHL	59	25	55	80	....	....	....	30	2	0	2	2	0
1947-48	Los Angeles Monarchs	PCHL	43	12	23	35	....	....	....	30	....	....	....	....	....
	NHL Totals		**4**	**1**	**0**	**1**	**1**	**0**	**1**	**2**	....	....	....	....	....

EHL First All-Star Team (1944) • Won John Carlin Trophy (Top Scorer - EHL) (1944)

• DARRAGH, HAROLD
Harold "Howl" Darragh
LW – R. 5'10", 145 lbs. b: Ottawa, Ont., 9/13/1902. d: 10/28/1993.

Season	Club	League	GP	G	A	Pts	AG	AA	APts	PIM	GP	G	A	Pts	PIM
1919-20	Ottawa Gunners	City Sr.	7	4	0	4	....	....	....	....	....	....	....	....	....
1920-21	Ottawa Gunners	City Sr.	13	10	0	10	....	....	....	....	6	3	*6	9	3
1921-22	Ottawa Gunners	City Sr.	14	12	*7	19	....	....	....	0	6	*12	*7	*19	0
1922-23	Ottawa Gunners	City Sr.	1	0	0	0	....	....	....	0	....	....	....	....	....
	Pittsburgh Yellowjackets	USAHA	16	8	0	8	....	....	....	....	....	....	....	....	....
1923-24	Ottawa New Edinburghs	City Sr.	12	6	*4	10	....	....	....	....	2	0	0	0	....
1924-25	Pittsburgh Yellowjackets	USAHA	40	14	0	14	....	....	....	....	8	3	0	3	....
1925-26	**Pittsburgh Pirates**	**NHL**	**35**	**10**	**7**	**17**	**31**	**82**	**113**	**6**	**2**	**1**	**0**	**1**	**0**
1926-27	**Pittsburgh Pirates**	**NHL**	**42**	**12**	**3**	**15**	**35**	**25**	**60**	**4**	....	....	....	....	....
1927-28	**Pittsburgh Pirates**	**NHL**	**44**	**13**	**2**	**15**	**40**	**17**	**57**	**16**	**2**	**0**	**1**	**1**	**0**
1928-29	**Pittsburgh Pirates**	**NHL**	**43**	**9**	**3**	**12**	**36**	**27**	**63**	**6**	....	....	....	....	....
1929-30	**Pittsburgh Pirates**	**NHL**	**42**	**15**	**17**	**32**	**30**	**56**	**86**	**6**	....	....	....	....	....
1930-31	**Philadelphia Quakers**	**NHL**	**10**	**1**	**1**	**2**	**2**	**4**	**6**	**2**	....	....	....	....	....
	Boston Bruins	**NHL**	**25**	**2**	**4**	**6**	**5**	**14**	**19**	**4**	**5**	**0**	**1**	**1**	**2**
1931-32	**Toronto Maple Leafs**	**NHL**	**48**	**5**	**10**	**15**	**11**	**28**	**39**	**6**	**7**	**0**	**1**	**1**	**2**
1932-33	**Toronto Maple Leafs**	**NHL**	**19**	**1**	**2**	**3**	**2**	**5**	**7**	**0**	....	....	....	....	....
	Syracuse Stars	IAHL	24	7	13	20	....	....	....	4	6	2	0	2	0
1933-34	Syracuse Stars	IAHL	44	9	10	19	....	....	....	12	6	0	1	1	0
1934-35			DID NOT PLAY												
1935-36	Pittsburgh Yellowjackets	IAHL	41	7	14	21	....	....	....	4	....	....	....	....	....
	NHL Totals		**308**	**68**	**49**	**117**	**192**	**258**	**450**	**50**	**16**	**1**	**3**	**4**	**4**

Signed as a free agent by **Pittsburgh**, September 26, 1925. Transferred to **Philadelphia** after **Pittsburgh** franchise relocated, October 18, 1930. Traded to **Boston** by **Philadelphia** for Ron Lyons and Bill Hutton, December 8, 1930. Claimed on waivers by **Toronto** from **Boston**, June 8, 1931. Traded to **Syracuse** (IAHL) by **Toronto** for Bill Thoms, January 3, 1933.

• DARRAGH, JACK
Jack Darragh **HHOF**
RW – R. 5'10", 168 lbs. b: Ottawa, Ont., 12/4/1890. d: 6/25/1924.

Season	Club	League	GP	G	A	Pts	AG	AA	APts	PIM	GP	G	A	Pts	PIM
1909-10	Ottawa Cliffsides	City Sr.	....	....	....	....	....	....	....	....	3	4	0	4	0
1910-11	Ottawa Senators	NHA	16	18	0	18	....	....	....	36	2	0	0	0	6
1911-12	Ottawa Senators	NHA	17	15	0	15	....	....	....	10	....	....	....	....	....
1912-13	Ottawa Senators	NHA	20	15	0	15	....	....	....	16	....	....	....	....	....
1913-14	Ottawa Senators	NHA	20	23	5	28	....	....	....	69	....	....	....	....	....
1914-15	Ottawa Senators	NHA	18	11	2	13	....	....	....	32	5	3	0	3	....
1915-16	Ottawa Senators	NHA	21	16	5	21	....	....	....	41	....	....	....	....	....
1916-17	Ottawa Senators	NHA	20	26	5	31	....	....	....	25	2	2	0	2	3
1917-18	**Ottawa Senators**	**NHL**	**18**	**14**	**5**	**19**	**35**	**0**	**35**	**26**	....	....	....	....	....
1918-19	**Ottawa Senators**	**NHL**	**14**	**11**	**4**	**15**	**39**	**38**	**77**	**30**	**7**	**4**	**0**	**4**	**3**
1919-20	**Ottawa Senators**	**NHL**	**23**	**22**	**14**	**36**	**51**	**98**	**149**	**22**	**5**	**5**	***2**	***7**	**3**
1920-21	**Ottawa Senators**	**NHL**	**24**	**11**	**15**	**26**	**28**	**141**	**169**	**20**	**7**	***5**	**0**	**5**	**7**
1921-22			DID NOT PLAY – RETIRED												
1922-23	**Ottawa Senators**	**NHL**	**24**	**7**	**7**	**14**	**23**	**64**	**87**	**13**	**2**	**1**	**0**	**1**	**2**
1923-24	**Ottawa Senators**	**NHL**	**18**	**2**	**0**	**2**	**8**	**0**	**8**	**2**	**2**	**0**	**0**	**0**	**2**
	NHL Totals		**121**	**67**	**45**	**112**	**184**	**341**	**525**	**113**	**23**	**15**	**2**	**17**	**17**
	Other Major League Totals		132	124	17	141	....	....	....	229	9	5	0	5	9

Rights retained by **Ottawa** after NHA folded, November 26, 1917. • Died of peritonitis, June 25, 1924.

• DAVIDSON, BOB
Bob Davidson
LW – L. 5'11", 185 lbs. b: Toronto, Ont., 2/10/1912. Deceased.

Season	Club	League	GP	G	A	Pts	AG	AA	APts	PIM	GP	G	A	Pts	PIM
1929-30	Toronto Canoe Club	OHA	9	0	0	0	....	....	....	2	....	....	....	....	....
1930-31	Toronto Canoe Club	OHA	9	6	4	10	....	....	....	10	2	1	0	1	2
1931-32	Toronto Canoe Club	OHA	8	6	3	9	....	....	....	7	1	1	0	1	0
1932-33	Toronto Marlboros	OHA Sr.	21	8	8	16	....	....	....	15	2	2	0	2	4
1933-34	Toronto Marlboros	OHA Sr.	6	6	2	8	....	....	....	6	....	....	....	....	....
1934-35	**Toronto Maple Leafs**	**NHL**	**5**	**0**	**0**	**0**	**0**	**0**	**0**	**6**	....	....	....	....	....
	Syracuse Stars	IAHL	28	4	12	16	....	....	....	17	2	0	0	0	2
1935-36	**Toronto Maple Leafs**	**NHL**	**35**	**4**	**4**	**8**	**10**	**10**	**20**	**32**	**9**	**1**	**3**	**4**	**2**
	Syracuse Stars	IAHL	13	3	4	7	....	....	....	22	....	....	....	....	....
1936-37	**Toronto Maple Leafs**	**NHL**	**46**	**8**	**7**	**15**	**17**	**16**	**33**	**43**	**2**	**0**	**0**	**0**	**5**
1937-38	**Toronto Maple Leafs**	**NHL**	**48**	**3**	**17**	**20**	**6**	**35**	**41**	**52**	**7**	**0**	**2**	**2**	**10**
1938-39	**Toronto Maple Leafs**	**NHL**	**47**	**4**	**10**	**14**	**8**	**19**	**27**	**29**	**10**	**1**	**1**	**2**	**6**
1939-40	**Toronto Maple Leafs**	**NHL**	**48**	**8**	**18**	**26**	**17**	**36**	**53**	**56**	**10**	**0**	**3**	**3**	**16**
1940-41	**Toronto Maple Leafs**	**NHL**	**37**	**3**	**6**	**9**	**6**	**11**	**17**	**39**	**7**	**0**	**2**	**2**	**7**
1941-42	**Toronto Maple Leafs**	**NHL**	**37**	**6**	**20**	**26**	**10**	**30**	**40**	**39**	**13**	**1**	**2**	**3**	**20**
1942-43	**Toronto Maple Leafs**	**NHL**	**50**	**13**	**23**	**36**	**18**	**29**	**47**	**20**	**6**	**1**	**2**	**3**	**7**
1943-44	**Toronto Maple Leafs**	**NHL**	**47**	**19**	**28**	**47**	**24**	**34**	**58**	**21**	**5**	**0**	**0**	**0**	**4**
1944-45	**Toronto Maple Leafs**	**NHL**	**50**	**17**	**18**	**35**	**23**	**29**	**52**	**49**	**13**	**1**	**2**	**3**	**2**
1945-46	**Toronto Maple Leafs**	**NHL**	**41**	**9**	**9**	**18**	**14**	**17**	**31**	**12**	....	....	....	....	....
1946-47	St. Louis Flyers	AHL	DID NOT PLAY – COACHING												
	NHL Totals		**491**	**94**	**160**	**254**	**153**	**266**	**419**	**398**	**82**	**5**	**17**	**22**	**79**

• DAVIDSON, GORD
Gord Davidson
D – L. 5'11", 188 lbs. b: Stratford, Ont., 8/5/1918. Deceased.

Season	Club	League	GP	G	A	Pts	AG	AA	APts	PIM	GP	G	A	Pts	PIM
1935-36	Moose Jaw Canucks	SJHL	3	1	0	1	....	....	....	2	....	....	....	....	....
1936-37	Moose Jaw Canucks	SJHL	5	3	0	3	....	....	....	6	....	....	....	....	....
1937-38	Moose Jaw Canucks	SJHL	6	2	4	6	....	....	....	0	4	2	1	3	6
1938-39	Regina Aces	SSHL	27	1	3	4	....	....	....	22	....	....	....	....	....
1939-40	Regina Aces	SSHL	17	1	3	4	....	....	....	23	9	1	0	1	0
1940-41	Regina Rangers	SSHL	32	0	5	5	....	....	....	30	8	0	0	0	6
1941-42	New York Rovers	EHL	58	9	31	40	....	....	....	55	7	1	6	7	6
1942-43	**New York Rangers**	**NHL**	**35**	**2**	**3**	**5**	**3**	**4**	**7**	**4**	....	....	....	....	....
1943-44	**New York Rangers**	**NHL**	**16**	**1**	**3**	**4**	**1**	**4**	**5**	**4**	....	....	....	....	....
	Buffalo Bisons	AHL	30	2	15	17	....	....	....	19	9	1	6	7	2
1944-45	Buffalo Bisons	AHL	59	10	20	30	....	....	....	20	6	1	0	1	4
1945-46	Cleveland Barons	AHL	60	6	23	29	....	....	....	32	12	1	5	6	4
1946-47	Cleveland Barons	AHL	58	5	10	15	....	....	....	14	4	0	0	0	0
1947-48	Cleveland Barons	AHL	58	2	15	17	....	....	....	16	9	2	2	4	2
1948-49	Cleveland Barons	AHL	62	5	20	25	....	....	....	10	5	0	0	0	0
1949-50	Buffalo Bisons	AHL	67	4	19	23	....	....	....	25	1	0	0	0	0
1950-51	Springfield Indians	AHL	54	5	24	29	....	....	....	10	3	0	1	1	4
	NHL Totals		**51**	**3**	**6**	**9**	**4**	**8**	**12**	**8**	....	....	....	....	....

EHL First All-Star Team (1942) • AHL First All-Star Team (1945)

Traded to **Buffalo** (AHL) by **NY Rangers** with Roger Leger for Bob Dill, January 4, 1944.

• DAVIE, BOB
Bob "Pinkie" Davie
D – R. 6', 170 lbs. b: Beausejour, Man., 9/12/1912. d: 10/27/1990.

Season	Club	League	GP	G	A	Pts	AG	AA	APts	PIM	GP	G	A	Pts	PIM
1931-32	Winnipeg Monarchs	MJHL	12	1	2	3	....	....	....	36	4	1	0	1	4
1932-33	Boston Cubs	Can-Am	46	4	7	11	....	....	....	70	7	1	3	4	4
1933-34	**Boston Bruins**	**NHL**	**9**	**0**	**0**	**0**	**0**	**0**	**0**	**6**	....	....	....	....	....
	Boston Cubs	Can-Am	33	6	8	14	....	....	....	47	5	0	1	1	11
1934-35	**Boston Bruins**	**NHL**	**30**	**0**	**1**	**1**	**0**	**2**	**2**	**17**	....	....	....	....	....
	Boston Cubs	Can-Am	19	3	5	8	....	....	....	16	....	....	....	....	....
1935-36	**Boston Bruins**	**NHL**	**2**	**0**	**0**	**0**	**0**	**0**	**0**	**2**	....	....	....	....	....
	Boston–Springfield	Can-Am	28	2	8	10	....	....	....	35	....	....	....	....	....
1936-37	Minneapolis Millers	AHA	44	9	8	17	....	....	....	51	6	2	3	5	6
1937-38	Minneapolis Millers	AHA	10	1	3	4	....	....	....	10	....	....	....	....	....
	Springfield Indians	AHL	37	2	4	6	....	....	....	59	....	....	....	....	....
	NHL Totals		**41**	**0**	**1**	**1**	**0**	**2**	**2**	**25**	....	....	....	....	....

• DAVIES, BUCK
Buck (Kenneth George) Davies
C – L. 5'6", 162 lbs. b: Bowmanville, Ont., 8/10/1922.

Season	Club	League	GP	G	A	Pts	AG	AA	APts	PIM	GP	G	A	Pts	PIM
1941-42	Oshawa Generals	OHA	24	17	21	38	....	....	....	2	12	9	6	15	4
1942-43	Toronto Army Daggers	OHA Sr.	10	1	3	4	....	....	....	2	....	....	....	....	....
1943-44			MILITARY SERVICE												
1944-45			MILITARY SERVICE												
1945-46			MILITARY SERVICE												
1946-47	St. Paul Saints	USHL	58	19	45	64	....	....	....	26	....	....	....	....	....
1947-48	New Haven Ramblers	AHL	67	29	43	72	....	....	....	35	4	0	1	1	9
	New York Rangers	**NHL**	....	....	....	....	**-1**	**-1**	**-2**	....	**1**	**0**	**0**	**0**	**0**
1948-49	New Haven Ramblers	AHL	67	32	26	58	....	....	....	20	....	....	....	....	....
1949-50	Providence Reds	AHL	51	13	22	35	....	....	....	10	1	0	0	0	0
1950-51	Providence Reds	AHL	62	12	30	42	....	....	....	14	....	....	....	....	....
1951-52	Cleveland Barons	AHL	64	18	45	63	....	....	....	26	5	1	0	1	4
1952-53	Buffalo Bisons	AHL	59	9	20	29	....	....	....	25	....	....	....	....	....
1953-54	Providence Reds	AHL	56	22	27	49	....	....	....	26	....	....	....	....	....
1954-55	Providence Reds	AHL	56	17	32	49	....	....	....	42	....	....	....	....	....
1955-56	Providence Reds	AHL	34	12	14	26	....	....	....	40	9	2	1	3	0
1956-57	Providence Reds	AHL	60	18	25	43	....	....	....	76	5	0	0	0	4
1957-58	Providence Reds	AHL	58	7	15	22	....	....	....	33	1	0	0	0	0
1958-59	Washington Presidents	EHL	48	17	31	48	....	....	....	34	....	....	....	....	....
1959-60	Washington Presidents	EHL	64	27	36	63	....	....	....	40	....	....	....	....	....
1960-61	Philadelphia Ramblers	EHL	62	12	34	46	....	....	....	17	2	0	0	0	0
	NHL Totals		**0**	**0**	**0**	**0**	**-1**	**-1**	**-2**	**0**	**1**	**0**	**0**	**0**	**0**

Traded to **Providence** (AHL) by **NY Rangers** to complete transaction that sent Allan Stanley to NY Rangers (December, 1948), June, 1949.

• DAVIS, BOB
Bob "Friday" Davis
RW – R. 6', 202 lbs. b: Lachine, Quebec, 2/2/1899. d: 7/5/1970.

Season	Club	League	GP	G	A	Pts	AG	AA	APts	PIM	GP	G	A	Pts	PIM
1922-23	Eveleth Rangers	USAHA	19	3	0	3	....	....	....	....	....	....	....	....	....
1923-24	Fort William Forts	TBSHL	12	2	2	4	....	....	....	2	....	....	....	....	....
1924-25	Fort William Forts	TBSHL	19	2	2	4	....	....	....	....	....	....	....	....	....
1925-26	Fort William Forts	TBSHL	17	4	0	4	....	....	....	22	3	1	0	1	*12
1926-27	Fort William Forts	TBSHL	20	10	1	11	....	....	....	18	2	0	0	0	0
1927-28	Fort William Forts	TBSHL	21	10	3	13	....	....	....	12	2	0	0	0	2
1928-29	Duluth Hornets	AHA	40	6	3	9	....	....	....	79	....	....	....	....	....
1929-30	Duluth Hornets	AHA	48	7	4	11	....	....	....	61	4	0	0	0	2
1930-31	Duluth Hornets	AHA	48	7	8	15	....	....	....	68	4	0	1	1	4
1931-32	Duluth Hornets	AHA	48	10	6	16	....	....	....	64	8	1	0	1	8
1932-33	**Detroit Red Wings**	**NHL**	**3**	**0**	**0**	**0**	**0**	**0**	**0**	**0**	....	....	....	....	....
	Detroit Olympics	IAHL	22	1	1	2	....	....	....	26	....	....	....	....	....
1933-34	Montreal Lafontaine	City Sr.	16	5	7	12	....	....	....	2	....	....	....	....	....
1934-35	Montreal Lafontaine	City Sr.	19	2	4	6	....	....	....	4	....	....	....	....	....
1935-36	Fort William Wanderers	TBSHL	DID NOT PLAY – COACHING												
	NHL Totals		**3**	**0**	**0**	**0**	**0**	**0**	**0**	**0**	....	....	....	....	....

USHL Second All-Star Team (1947) • Won Outstanding Rookie Cup (Top Rookie - USHL) (1947)

Signed as a free agent by **Detroit**, December 5, 1932. Traded to **Buffalo** (IAHL) by **Detroit** with Tip O'Neil and John Newman for Gammy Lederman, September 24, 1933.

• DAVIS, LORNE Lorne Davis

RW – R. 5'11", 190 lbs. b: Regina, Sask., 7/20/1930.

Season	Club	League	GP	G	A	Pts	AG	AA	APts	PIM	Playoffs GP	G	A	Pts	PIM
			REGULAR SEASON								PLAYOFFS				
1947-48	Regina Pats	SJHL	28	8	5	13	....	....	....	7	5	1	1	2	2
1948-49	Regina Pats	WCJHL	26	16	12	28	....	....	....	36	7	5	3	8	4
1949-50	Regina Pats	WCJHL	40	25	17	42	....	....	....	22	9	6	1	7	8
1950-51	Montreal Royals	QSHL	50	14	17	31	....	....	....	4	7	5	1	6	4
	Victoria Cougars	PCHL	3	1	1	2	....	....	....	0	....	....	....	....	....
1951-52	**Montreal Canadiens**	**NHL**	**3**	**1**	**1**	**2**	**1**	**1**	**2**	**2**	....	....	....	....	....
	Vancouver Canucks	PCHL	15	11	10	21	....	....	....	4	....	....	....	....	....
	Buffalo Bisons	AHL	48	19	19	38	....	....	....	18	3	1	0	1	0
1952-53	Buffalo Bisons	AHL	64	33	34	67	....	....	....	49	....	....	....	....	....
	Montreal Canadiens	**NHL**	....	....	....	....	....	....	....	....	**7**	**1**	**1**	**2**	**2**
1953-54	**Montreal Canadiens**	**NHL**	**37**	**6**	**4**	**10**	**9**	**5**	**14**	**2**	**11**	**2**	**0**	**2**	**8**
	Montreal Royals	QHL	37	13	22	35	....	....	....	25	....	....	....	....	....
1954-55	Montreal Royals	QHL	1	0	2	2	....	....	....	0	....	....	....	....	....
	Chicago Black Hawks	**NHL**	**8**	**0**	**0**	**0**	**0**	**0**	**0**	**4**	....	....	....	....	....
	Detroit Red Wings	**NHL**	**22**	**0**	**5**	**5**	**0**	**6**	**6**	**2**	....	....	....	....	....
	Edmonton Flyers	WHL	29	11	5	16	....	....	....	10	9	*7	4	*11	2
1955-56	**Boston Bruins**	**NHL**	**15**	**0**	**1**	**1**	**0**	**1**	**1**	**0**	....	....	....	....	....
	Hershey Bears	AHL	45	19	21	40	....	....	....	42	....	....	....	....	....
1956-57	Hershey Bears	AHL	64	16	24	40	....	....	....	55	7	1	0	1	2
1957-58	Hershey Bears	AHL	68	18	16	34	....	....	....	36	11	0	0	0	12
1958-59	Providence Reds	AHL	70	22	24	46	....	....	....	65	....	....	....	....	....
1959-60	**Boston Bruins**	**NHL**	**10**	**1**	**1**	**2**	**1**	**1**	**2**	**10**	....	....	....	....	....
	Providence Reds	AHL	54	19	32	51	....	....	....	24	....	....	....	....	....
1960-61	Winnipeg Warriors	WHL	70	22	22	44	....	....	....	18	....	....	....	....	....
1961-62	Regina Capitals	SSHL	DID NOT PLAY – COACHING												
1962-63	Regina Capitals	SSHL	20	14	16	30	....	....	....	14	7	3	11	14	8
1963-64	Regina Capitals	SSHL	37	43	47	90	....	....	....	4	1	1	0	1	0
1964-65	Muskegon Zephyrs	IHL	67	20	39	59	....	....	....	30	....	....	....	....	....
1965-66	Regina Capitals	SSHL	11	8	17	25	....	....	....	2	....	....	....	....	....
	Canada	WEC-A	7	1	0	1	....	....	....	2	....	....	....	....	....
1966-67	Regina Capitals	SSHL	33	22	22	44	....	....	....	17	3	0	0	0	0
	NHL Totals		**95**	**8**	**12**	**20**	**11**	**14**	**25**	**20**	**18**	**3**	**1**	**4**	**10**

AHL Second All-Star Team (1953)

Played in NHL All-Star Game (1953)

Traded to **Chicago** by **Montreal** for Ike Hildebrand, October 14, 1954. Traded to **Detroit** by **Chicago** for Metro Prystai, November 9, 1954. Traded to **Boston** by **Detroit** with Terry Sawchuk, Vic Stasiuk and Marcel Bonin for Ed Sandford, Real Chevrifils, Norm Corcoran, Gilles Boisvert and Warren Godfrey, June, 1955.

• DAVISON, MURRAY Murray Davison

D – R. 6'2", 190 lbs. b: Brantford, Ont., 6/10/1938.

Season	Club	League	GP	G	A	Pts	AG	AA	APts	PIM	Playoffs GP	G	A	Pts	PIM
1955-56	Barrie Flyers	OHA	47	2	7	9	....	....	....	82	18	0	2	2	32
1956-57	Barrie Flyers	OHA	52	6	7	13	....	....	....	53	3	0	0	0	8
1957-58	Barrie Flyers	OHA	51	7	20	27	....	....	....	171	4	2	0	2	12
1958-59	Quebec Aces	QHL	3	0	0	0	....	....	....	0	....	....	....	....	....
	Kitchener Dutchmen	OHA Sr.	54	3	13	16	....	....	....	*125	11	1	3	4	*36
1959-60	Kitchener Dutchmen	OHA Sr.	48	0	11	11	....	....	....	63	8	2	4	6	4
1960-61	Cleveland Barons	AHL	1	0	0	0	....	....	....	0	4	0	0	0	0
	Greensboro Generals	EHL	64	4	37	41	....	....	....	106	9	0	4	4	10
1961-62	Cleveland Barons	AHL	65	1	6	7	....	....	....	53	6	0	0	0	0
1962-63	Springfield Indians	AHL	36	3	8	11	....	....	....	26	....	....	....	....	....
1963-64			DID NOT PLAY – SUSPENDED												
1964-65	Welland Wildcats	OHA Sr.	25	5	10	15	....	....	....	33	....	....	....	....	....
1965-66	**Boston Bruins**	**NHL**	**1**	**0**	**0**	**0**	**0**	**0**	**0**	**0**	....	....	....	....	....
	Oklahoma City Blazers	CHL	58	1	12	13	....	....	....	88	9	0	6	6	6
1966-67	Oklahoma City Blazers	CHL	41	0	6	6	....	....	....	83	5	1	0	1	8
1967-68	Oklahoma City Blazers	CHL	57	3	13	16	....	....	....	128	5	0	2	2	25
1968-69	Oklahoma City Blazers	CHL	28	1	3	4	....	....	....	63	7	0	1	1	21
1969-70	Oklahoma City Blazers	CHL	38	0	4	4	....	....	....	176	....	....	....	....	....
1970-71	Oklahoma City Blazers	CHL	1	0	0	0	....	....	....	0	....	....	....	....	....
	NHL Totals		**1**	**0**	**0**	**0**	**0**	**0**	**0**	**0**	....	....	....	....	....

Traded to **Springfield** (AHL) by **Cleveland** (AHL) with Wayne Larkin for Dick Mattiussi October 16, 1962.

• DAWES, ROBERT Robert Dawes

D/C – L. 6'1", 170 lbs. b: Saskatoon, Sask., 11/29/1924.

Season	Club	League	GP	G	A	Pts	AG	AA	APts	PIM	Playoffs GP	G	A	Pts	PIM
1942-43	Saskatoon Quakers	SJHL	7	7	6	13	....	....	....	20	3	3	1	4	0
1943-44	Oshawa Generals	OHA	26	8	19	27	....	....	....	32	10	2	4	6	4
1944-45	Saskatoon Falcons	SJHL	2	2	1	3	....	....	....	0	....	....	....	....	....
1945-46	New Haven Eagles	AHL	57	9	18	27	....	....	....	33	....	....	....	....	....
1946-47	**Toronto Maple Leafs**	**NHL**	**1**	**0**	**0**	**0**	**0**	**0**	**0**	**0**	....	....	....	....	....
	Springfield Indians	AHL	42	4	17	21	....	....	....	27	2	0	2	2	0
1947-48	Pittsburgh Hornets	AHL	68	13	31	44	....	....	....	35	2	1	1	2	5
1948-49	**Toronto Maple Leafs**	**NHL**	**5**	**1**	**0**	**1**	**2**	**0**	**2**	**0**	**9**	**0**	**0**	**0**	**2**
	Pittsburgh Hornets	AHL	55	16	35	51	....	....	....	31	....	....	....	....	....
1949-50	**Toronto Maple Leafs**	**NHL**	**11**	**1**	**2**	**3**	**1**	**3**	**4**	**2**	....	....	....	....	....
	Cleveland Barons	AHL	47	3	19	22	....	....	....	41	9	1	3	4	10
1950-51	**Montreal Canadiens**	**NHL**	**15**	**0**	**5**	**5**	**0**	**6**	**6**	**4**	**1**	**0**	**0**	**0**	**0**
	Buffalo–Cincinnati	AHL	25	6	6	12	....	....	....	10	....	....	....	....	....
	Seattle Ironmen	PCHL	20	2	11	13	....	....	....	10	....	....	....	....	....
1951-52	Montreal Royals	QSHL	5	0	0	0	....	....	....	2	....	....	....	....	....
	Buffalo Bisons	AHL	2	0	3	3	....	....	....	0	....	....	....	....	....
1952-53			DID NOT PLAY – INJURED												
1953-54	Galt Black Hawks	OHA	DID NOT PLAY – COACHING												
	Sudbury Wolves	NOHA	19	2	10	12	....	....	....	4	10	0	5	5	4
1954-55	New Westminster Royals	WHL	12	3	3	6	....	....	....	2	....	....	....	....	....
	Kelowna Packers	OSHL	51	12	23	35	....	....	....	34	4	1	3	4	0
1955-56	New Westminster Royals	WHL	56	8	25	33	....	....	....	47	4	2	1	3	0
1956-57	Kamloops Chiefs	OSHL	54	4	42	46	....	....	....	52	12	5	6	11	15
1957-58	Kamloops Chiefs	OSHL	48	11	35	46	....	....	....	36	15	0	5	5	2
1958-59	Johnstown Jets	EHL	37	14	23	37	....	....	....	24	12	4	6	10	8
1959-60	Johnstown Jets	EHL	50	19	40	59	....	....	....	8	13	0	*12	12	9
1960-61	Johnstown Jets	EHL	56	12	26	38	....	....	....	12	11	4	7	11	2
1961-62	Johnstown Jets	EHL	68	16	30	46	....	....	....	24	13	6	8	14	2
1962-63	Saskatoon Quakers	SSHL	27	12	23	35	....	....	....	14	6	2	7	9	2
1963-64	Saskatoon Quakers	SSHL	8	8	12	20	....	....	....	0	11	4	4	8	4
1964-65	Yorkton Terriers	SSHL	2	0	2	2	....	....	....	2	11	0	3	3	12
1965-66	Yorkton Terriers	SSHL	DID NOT PLAY – COACHING												
1966-67	Saskatoon Quakers	SSHL	16	2	11	13	....	....	....	4	14	1	9	10	2
	NHL Totals		**32**	**2**	**7**	**9**	**3**	**9**	**12**	**6**	**10**	**0**	**0**	**0**	**2**

Played in NHL All-Star Game (1949)

Traded to **Cleveland** (AHL) by **Toronto** with $40,000 and future considerations for Al Rollins, December, 1949. Traded to **Buffalo** (AHL) by **Cleveland** (AHL) for Joe McArthur, September 6, 1950. Traded to **Cincinnati** (AHL) by **Buffalo** (AHL) for cash, January, 1951. Traded to **Montreal** by **Cincinnati** (AHL) for Paul Masnick, February 13, 1951.

• DAY, HAP Hap (Clarence Henry) Day HHOF

D – L. 5'11", 175 lbs. b: Owen Sound, Ont., 6/14/1901. d: 2/17/1990.

Season	Club	League	GP	G	A	Pts	AG	AA	APts	PIM	Playoffs GP	G	A	Pts	PIM
1922-23	Hamilton Tigers	OHA Sr.	11	4	11	15	....	....	....	4	2	0	0	0	0
1923-24	Hamilton Tigers	OHA Sr.	10	6	11	17	....	....	....	....	2	1	1	2	....
1924-25	**Toronto St. Pats**	**NHL**	**26**	**10**	**12**	**22**	**35**	**168**	**203**	**33**	**2**	**0**	**0**	**0**	**0**
1925-26	**Toronto St. Pats**	**NHL**	**36**	**14**	**2**	**16**	**44**	**23**	**67**	**26**	....	....	....	....	....
1926-27	**Toronto Maple Leafs**	**NHL**	**44**	**11**	**5**	**16**	**32**	**43**	**75**	**50**	....	....	....	....	....
1927-28	**Toronto Maple Leafs**	**NHL**	**22**	**9**	**8**	**17**	**28**	**68**	**96**	**48**	....	....	....	....	....
1928-29	**Toronto Maple Leafs**	**NHL**	**44**	**6**	**6**	**12**	**24**	**55**	**79**	**84**	**4**	**1**	**0**	**1**	**4**
1929-30	**Toronto Maple Leafs**	**NHL**	**43**	**7**	**14**	**21**	**14**	**46**	**60**	**77**	....	....	....	....	....
1930-31	**Toronto Maple Leafs**	**NHL**	**44**	**1**	**13**	**14**	**2**	**47**	**49**	**56**	**2**	**0**	**3**	**3**	**7**
1931-32	**Toronto Maple Leafs**	**NHL**	**47**	**7**	**8**	**15**	**15**	**22**	**37**	**33**	**7**	**3**	**3**	**6**	**6**
1932-33	**Toronto Maple Leafs**	**NHL**	**47**	**6**	**14**	**20**	**14**	**37**	**51**	**46**	**9**	**0**	**1**	**1**	***21**
1933-34	**Toronto Maple Leafs**	**NHL**	**48**	**9**	**10**	**19**	**20**	**27**	**47**	**35**	**5**	**0**	**0**	**0**	**6**
1934-35	**Toronto Maple Leafs**	**NHL**	**45**	**2**	**4**	**6**	**4**	**9**	**13**	**38**	**7**	**0**	**0**	**0**	**4**
1935-36	**Toronto Maple Leafs**	**NHL**	**44**	**1**	**13**	**14**	**2**	**31**	**33**	**41**	**9**	**0**	**0**	**0**	**8**
1936-37	**Toronto Maple Leafs**	**NHL**	**48**	**3**	**4**	**7**	**6**	**9**	**15**	**20**	**2**	**0**	**0**	**0**	**0**
1937-38	**New York Americans**	**NHL**	**43**	**0**	**3**	**3**	**0**	**6**	**6**	**14**	**6**	**0**	**0**	**0**	**0**
	NHL Totals		**581**	**86**	**116**	**202**	**240**	**591**	**831**	**601**	**53**	**4**	**7**	**11**	**56**

Played in NHL All-Star Game (1934, 1937)

Signed as a free agent by **Toronto St. Pats**, December 9, 1924. Traded to **NY Americans** by **Toronto** for cash, September 23, 1937.

• DEA, BILLY — *see page 972*

• DEACON, DON Don Deacon

LW – L. 5'9", 190 lbs. b: Regina, Sask., 6/2/1913. Deceased.

Season	Club	League	GP	G	A	Pts	AG	AA	APts	PIM	Playoffs GP	G	A	Pts	PIM
1929-30	Regina Olympics	City Jr.	1	0	0	0	....	....	....	0	....	....	....	....	....
1930-31	Regina Pats	City Jr.	3	1	0	1	....	....	....	4	....	....	....	....	....
1931-32	Regina Pats	City Jr.	4	1	0	1	....	....	....	0	6	4	0	4	9
1932-33	Prince Albert Mintos	City Sr.	18	6	1	7	....	....	....	31	3	1	0	1	6
1933-34	Prince Albert Mintos	City Sr.	15	13	7	20	....	....	....	28	4	*3	0	*3	2
1934-35	Prince Albert Mintos	City Sr.	22	*26	10	36	....	....	....	44	4	*5	2	7	2
1935-36	Detroit Olympics	IAHL	44	14	17	31	....	....	....	70	6	1	4	5	7
1936-37	**Detroit Red Wings**	**NHL**	**4**	**0**	**0**	**0**	**0**	**0**	**0**	**2**	....	....	....	....	....
	Pittsburgh Hornets	AHL	40	14	15	29	....	....	....	18	5	2	2	4	14
1937-38	Pittsburgh Hornets	AHL	42	18	19	37	....	....	....	28	2	0	3	3	0
1938-39	**Detroit Red Wings**	**NHL**	**8**	**1**	**3**	**4**	**2**	**6**	**8**	**2**	**2**	**2**	**1**	**3**	**0**
	Pittsburgh Hornets	AHL	46	24	*41	*65	....	....	....	41	....	....	....	....	....
1939-40	**Detroit Red Wings**	**NHL**	**18**	**5**	**1**	**6**	**11**	**2**	**13**	**2**	....	....	....	....	....
	Indianapolis–Cleveland	AHL	39	13	25	38	....	....	....	16	....	....	....	....	....
1940-41	Cleveland Barons	AHL	53	15	15	30	....	....	....	46	9	1	5	6	10
1941-42	Cleveland Barons	AHL	49	13	14	27	....	....	....	15	1	1	0	1	0
1942-43	Calgary Currie Army	City Sr.	23	21	31	52	....	....	....	39	8	8	*7	*15	4
	NHL Totals		**30**	**6**	**4**	**10**	**13**	**8**	**21**	**6**	**2**	**2**	**1**	**3**	**0**

AHL First All-Star Team (1939, 1940)

Signed as a free agent by **Detroit**, October 11, 1934.

● DELMONTE, ARMAND
Armand "Dutch" Delmonte
RW – R. 5'10", 170 lbs. b: Timmins, Ont., 6/3/1927. Deceased.

			REGULAR SEASON								PLAYOFFS				
Season	Club	League	GP	G	A	Pts	AG	AA	APts	PIM	GP	G	A	Pts	PIM
1943-44	St. Catharines Falcons	OHA	23	8	4	12	....	....	....	32	6	4	0	4	4
1944-45	St. Catharines Falcons	OHA	21	17	14	31	....	....	....	36	5	2	2	4	4
1945-46	**Boston Bruins**	**NHL**	**1**	**0**	**0**	**0**	**0**	**0**	**0**	**0**	....	....	....	....	....
	Boston Olympics	EHL	46	30	20	50	....	....	....	58	12	2	3	5	15
1946-47	Boston Olympics	EHL	56	26	15	41	....	....	....	71	9	4	2	6	11
	Los Angeles Monarchs	PCHL	....	....	....	....	....	....	....	....	7	0	6	6	0
1947-48	St. Paul Saints	USHL	43	4	6	10	....	....	....	26	....	....	....	....	....
1948-49	St. Paul Saints	USHL	66	33	39	72	....	....	....	64	7	5	2	7	2
1949-50	St. Paul Saints	USHL	69	18	36	54	....	....	....	37	3	0	1	1	0
1950-51	St. Paul Saints	USHL	57	25	26	51	....	....	....	54	....	....	....	....	....
1951-52	Tacoma Rockets	PCHL	62	20	26	46	....	....	....	64	7	2	6	8	4
1952-53	Cleveland Barons	AHL	33	7	6	13	....	....	....	45	....	....	....	....	....
1953-54	Ottawa Senators	QHL	8	1	0	1	....	....	....	4	....	....	....	....	....
	Marion Barons	IHL	48	30	35	65	....	....	....	87	5	0	4	4	10
	NHL Totals		**1**	**0**	**0**	**0**	**0**	**0**	**0**	**0**	....	....	....	....	....

● DELORY, VALENTINE
Valentine Delory
LW – L. 5'10", 160 lbs. b: Toronto, Ont., 2/14/1927.

Season	Club	League	GP	G	A	Pts	AG	AA	APts	PIM	GP	G	A	Pts	PIM
1945-46	St. Catharines Falcons	OHA	23	7	15	22	....	....	....	21	4	0	4	4	0
1946-47	Hamilton Szabos	OHA	16	8	6	14	....	....	....	24	....	....	....	....	....
1947-48	New York Rovers	EHL	15	8	5	13	....	....	....	6	....	....	....	....	....
	New York Rovers	QSHL	39	9	12	21	....	....	....	14	3	1	0	1	0
1948-49	**New York Rangers**	**NHL**	**1**	**0**	**0**	**0**	**0**	**0**	**0**	**0**	....	....	....	....	....
	New York Rovers	EHL	57	19	34	53	....	....	....	12	....	....	....	....	....
1949-50	St. Paul Saints	USHL	2	0	0	0	....	....	....	0	....	....	....	....	....
	Tacoma Rockets	PCHL	1	0	0	0	....	....	....	0	....	....	....	....	....
	New York Rovers	EHL	47	*36	37	*73	....	....	....	20	12	7	8	*15	18
1950-51	St. Paul–Kansas City	USHL	62	14	18	32	....	....	....	21	....	....	....	....	....
1951-52	Boston Olympics	EHL	62	32	53	85	....	....	....	16	....	....	....	....	....
1952-53	Troy Uncle Sam Trojans	EHL	40	24	37	61	....	....	....	2	....	....	....	....	....
	Owen Sound Mercurys	OHA Sr.	7	1	3	4	....	....	....	2	....	....	....	....	....
	NHL Totals		**1**	**0**	**0**	**0**	**0**	**0**	**0**	**0**	....	....	....	....	....

EHL First All-Star Team (1950) • Won John Carlin Trophy (Top Scorer - EHL) (1950)

● DELVECCHIO, ALEX
— see page 976

● DEMARCO, AB SR.
Ab Sr. DeMarco
C – R. 6', 168 lbs. b: North Bay, Ont., 5/10/1916. Deceased.

Season	Club	League	GP	G	A	Pts	AG	AA	APts	PIM	GP	G	A	Pts	PIM
1936-37	Falconbridge Falcons	City Sr.	13	4	5	9	....	....	....	6	4	0	0	0	0
1937-38	Baltimore Orioles	EHL	56	25	27	52	....	....	....	12	....	....	....	....	....
1938-39	**Chicago Black Hawks**	**NHL**	**2**	**1**	**0**	**1**	**2**	**0**	**2**	**0**	....	....	....	....	....
	Providence Reds	AHL	53	6	12	18	....	....	....	8	5	0	0	0	2
1939-40	**Chicago Black Hawks**	**NHL**	**17**	**0**	**5**	**5**	**0**	**10**	**10**	**17**	**2**	**0**	**0**	**0**	**0**
	Providence Reds	AHL	20	5	9	14	....	....	....	16	....	....	....	....	....
1940-41	Providence Reds	AHL	55	20	34	54	....	....	....	13	4	0	3	3	5
1941-42	Providence Reds	AHL	52	23	38	61	....	....	....	17	....	....	....	....	....
1942-43	Providence Reds	AHL	39	27	39	66	....	....	....	9	....	....	....	....	....
	Toronto Maple Leafs	**NHL**	**4**	**0**	**1**	**1**	**0**	**1**	**1**	**0**	....	....	....	....	....
	Boston Bruins	**NHL**	**3**	**4**	**1**	**5**	**6**	**1**	**7**	**0**	**9**	**3**	**0**	**3**	**2**
1943-44	**Boston Bruins**	**NHL**	**3**	**0**	**0**	**0**	**0**	**0**	**0**	**0**	....	....	....	....	....
	New York Rangers	**NHL**	**36**	**14**	**19**	**33**	**18**	**23**	**41**	**2**	....	....	....	....	....
1944-45	**New York Rangers**	**NHL**	**50**	**24**	**30**	**54**	**33**	**49**	**82**	**10**	....	....	....	....	....
1945-46	**New York Rangers**	**NHL**	**50**	**20**	**27**	**47**	**31**	**51**	**82**	**20**	....	....	....	....	....
1946-47	**New York Rangers**	**NHL**	**44**	**9**	**10**	**19**	**12**	**14**	**26**	**4**	....	....	....	....	....
1947-48	Cleveland Barons	AHL	60	20	61	81	....	....	....	37	9	1	8	9	10
1948-49	Cleveland–Buffalo	AHL	64	23	37	60	....	....	....	40	....	....	....	....	....
1949-50	Buffalo Bisons	AHL	70	40	54	94	....	....	....	16	5	1	5	6	9
1950-51	Buffalo Bisons	AHL	64	37	*76	*113	....	....	....	35	4	0	3	3	0
1951-52	Buffalo Bisons	AHL	67	28	49	77	....	....	....	34	3	1	0	1	0
1952-53	North Bay Trappers	NOHA	40	20	37	57	....	....	....	38	7	0	5	5	2
1953-54	North Bay Trappers	NOHA	59	23	*69	*92	....	....	....	8	6	2	7	9	2
1954-55	North Bay Trappers	NOHA	50	19	34	53	....	....	....	4	13	4	*7	*11	24
1955-56	North Bay Trappers	NOHA	6	0	4	4	....	....	....	2	....	....	....	....	....
1956-57	North Bay Trappers	NOHA	4	1	1	2	....	....	....	0	....	....	....	....	....
1957-58	North Bay Trappers	NOHA	4	1	1	2	....	....	....	0	....	....	....	....	....
	NHL Totals		**209**	**72**	**93**	**165**	**102**	**149**	**251**	**53**	**11**	**3**	**0**	**3**	**2**

EHL Second All-Star Team (1938) • AHL Second All-Star Team (1950) • AHL First All-Star Team (1951) • Won John B. Sollenberger Trophy (Top Scorer - AHL) (1951) • Won Les Cunningham Award (MVP - AHL) (1951)

Signed as a free agent by **Chicago**, September 28, 1938. Traded to **Providence** (AHL) by **Chicago** for cash, May 14, 1940. Loaned to **Toronto** by **Providence** (AHL) with Alvin Jones for loan of Jack Forsey and George Boothman, February 3, 1943. Traded to **Boston** by **Providence** (AHL) for cash, March 8, 1943. Traded to **NY Rangers** by **Boston** for cash, November , 1943. Traded to **Detroit** by **NY Rangers** with Hank Goldup for Flash Hollett, June , 1946. • Rights returned to **NY Rangers** by **Detroit** when Hollett retired and transaction was voided, June, 1946. Traded to **Cleveland** (AHL) by **NY Rangers** with Joe Cooper for cah, May 5, 1947. Traded to **Washington** (AHL) by **Cleveland** (AHL) with Bryan Hextall for Dan Porteous, Frank Porteous and Eddie Bush, February, 1949.

● DEMERS, TONY
Tony Demers
RW – R. 5'9", 180 lbs. b: Chambly Basin, Que., 7/22/1917. d: 1997.

Season	Club	League	GP	G	A	Pts	AG	AA	APts	PIM	GP	G	A	Pts	PIM
1935-36	Montreal Lafontaine	City Jr.	1	1	0	1	....	....	....	2	....	....	....	....	....
1936-37	Southampton Kings	Britain	....	20	7	27	....	....	....	16	....	....	....	....	....
1937-38	**Montreal Canadiens**	**NHL**	**6**	**0**	**0**	**0**	**0**	**0**	**0**	**0**	....	....	....	....	....
	New Haven Eagles	AHL	5	0	0	0	....	....	....	0	2	0	0	0	0
	Lachine Rapides	QPHL	STATISTICS NOT AVAILABLE												
1938-39	Lachine Rapides	QPHL	29	24	12	36	....	....	....	39	6	2	2	4	7
1939-40	**Montreal Canadiens**	**NHL**	**14**	**2**	**3**	**5**	**4**	**6**	**10**	**2**	....	....	....	....	....
	Valleyfield Braves	QPHL	35	30	23	53	....	....	....	37	....	....	....	....	....
1940-41	**Montreal Canadiens**	**NHL**	**46**	**13**	**10**	**23**	**26**	**18**	**44**	**17**	**2**	**0**	**0**	**0**	**0**
1941-42	**Montreal Canadiens**	**NHL**	**7**	**3**	**4**	**7**	**5**	**6**	**11**	**4**	....	....	....	....	....
	Valleyfield V's	Mtl-Sr.	14	2	3	5	....	....	....	16	9	1	2	3	21
1942-43	**Montreal Canadiens**	**NHL**	**9**	**2**	**5**	**7**	**3**	**6**	**9**	**0**	....	....	....	....	....
	Montreal Army	QSHL	13	3	1	4	....	....	....	0	4	0	2	2	0
1943-44	**New York Rangers**	**NHL**	**1**	**0**	**0**	**0**	**0**	**0**	**0**	**0**	....	....	....	....	....
	Providence Reds	AHL	25	11	10	21	....	....	....	10	....	....	....	....	....
1944-45	Lachine Rapides	QPHL	11	2	3	5	....	....	....	12	....	....	....	....	....
1945-46	St-Hyacinthe Saints	QPHL	34	*50	29	*79	....	....	....	26	....	....	....	....	....
1946-47	Sherbrooke St. Xavier	QPHL	43	32	36	68	....	....	....	8	10	8	*15	*23	2
1947-48	Sherbrooke St. Xavier	QPHL	52	*62	46	108	....	....	....	24	10	6	6	12	9
1948-49	Sherbrooke Red Raiders	QSHL	60	53	58	111	....	....	....	29	10	*10	2	12	8
	NHL Totals		**83**	**20**	**22**	**42**	**38**	**36**	**74**	**23**	**2**	**0**	**0**	**0**	**0**

Won Vimy Trophy (MVP - QSHL) (1949)

Signed as a free agent by **Montreal Canadiens**, October 30, 1937. Loaned to **NY Rangers** by **Montreal** for the remainder of 1943-44 season to complete transaction that sent Phil Watson to Montreal, December, 1943.

● DENIS, JEAN-PAUL
Jean-Paul "Johnny" Denis
RW – R. 5'8", 170 lbs. b: Montreal, Que., 2/28/1924.

Season	Club	League	GP	G	A	Pts	AG	AA	APts	PIM	GP	G	A	Pts	PIM
1941-42	Montreal Concordias	City Jr.	12	11	6	17	....	....	....	2	2	2	2	4	0
1942-43	Montreal Concordias	City Jr.	20	13	9	22	....	....	....	13	4	1	0	1	2
1943-44	Montreal Concordias	City Jr.	10	4	4	8	....	....	....	14	5	3	1	4	6
	University of Montreal	City Sr.	2	0	1	1	....	....	....	0	....	....	....	....	....
1944-45	Hull Volants	Ott-Sr.	2	0	0	0	....	....	....	0	....	....	....	....	....
	Montreal Army	City Sr.	9	10	10	20	....	....	....	7	....	....	....	....	....
1945-46	Montreal Royals	QSHL	1	0	0	0	....	....	....	0	....	....	....	....	....
1946-47	**New York Rangers**	**NHL**	**6**	**0**	**1**	**1**	**0**	**1**	**1**	**0**	....	....	....	....	....
	New Haven Ramblers	AHL	26	9	3	12	....	....	....	14	....	....	....	....	....
	New York Rovers	EHL	16	6	15	21	....	....	....	15	....	....	....	....	....
	Montreal Royals	QSHL	1	0	0	0	....	....	....	0	1	0	0	0	0
1947-48	New Haven Ramblers	AHL	65	19	19	38	....	....	....	59	4	0	1	1	0
1948-49	New Haven Ramblers	AHL	63	24	23	47	....	....	....	108	....	....	....	....	....
1949-50	**New York Rangers**	**NHL**	**4**	**0**	**1**	**1**	**0**	**1**	**1**	**2**	....	....	....	....	....
	New Haven Ramblers	AHL	65	20	24	44	....	....	....	42	....	....	....	....	....
1950-51	Cincinnati Mohawks	AHL	61	22	31	53	....	....	....	109	....	....	....	....	....
1951-52	Cincinnati–Providence	AHL	38	17	19	36	....	....	....	57	6	2	0	2	11
1952-53	Providence Reds	AHL	57	21	17	38	....	....	....	74	....	....	....	....	....
1953-54	Quebec Aces	QHL	6	1	0	1	....	....	....	2	....	....	....	....	....
	Providence Reds	AHL	15	3	5	8	....	....	....	15	....	....	....	....	....
1954-55	Shawinigan Cataracts	QHL	42	18	25	43	....	....	....	46	13	3	8	11	25
1955-56	Shawinigan Cataracts	QHL	59	24	42	66	....	....	....	63	11	2	3	5	7
1956-57	Shawinigan Cataracts	QHL	62	19	33	52	....	....	....	57	....	....	....	....	....
1957-58	Shawinigan Cataracts	QHL	64	39	50	*89	....	....	....	68	8	1	7	8	2
1958-59	Montreal Royals	QHL	48	22	23	45	....	....	....	69	6	2	0	2	0
1959-60	Trois-Rivieres Lions	EPHL	69	30	40	70	....	....	....	51	7	4	1	5	6
1960-61	St. Paul Saints	IHL	67	41	52	93	....	....	....	52	13	8	6	14	9
1961-62	St. Paul Saints	IHL	64	32	56	88	....	....	....	49	11	*7	4	11	26
	NHL Totals		**10**	**0**	**2**	**2**	**0**	**2**	**2**	**2**	....	....	....	....	....

QHL First All-Star Team (1958) • Won President's Cup (Scoring Champion - QHL) (1958)

Traded to **Providence** (AHL) by **NY Rangers** with Zellio Toppazzini and Pat Egan for Jack Stoddard, December, 1951.

● DENIS, LULU
Lulu (Louis Gilbert) Denis
RW – R. 5'8", 140 lbs. b: Vonda, Sask., 6/7/1928.

Season	Club	League	GP	G	A	Pts	AG	AA	APts	PIM	GP	G	A	Pts	PIM
1945-46	Montreal Jr. Royals	QJHL	17	8	3	11	....	....	....	6	....	....	....	....	....
1946-47	Montreal Jr. Royals	QJHL	28	11	19	30	....	....	....	28	8	3	4	7	0
1947-48	Montreal Jr. Royals	QJHL	31	22	21	43	....	....	....	10	12	3	12	15	0
1948-49	Montreal Royals	QSHL	53	12	17	29	....	....	....	21	9	1	0	1	10
1949-50	**Montreal Canadiens**	**NHL**	**2**	**0**	**1**	**1**	**0**	**1**	**1**	**0**	....	....	....	....	....
	Montreal Royals	QSHL	57	24	23	47	....	....	....	51	6	1	1	2	2
1950-51	**Montreal Canadiens**	**NHL**	**1**	**0**	**0**	**0**	**0**	**0**	**0**	**0**	....	....	....	....	....
	Montreal Royals	QSHL	57	22	32	57	....	....	....	27	7	2	3	5	4
1951-52	Montreal Royals	QSHL	59	21	21	42	....	....	....	8	7	2	1	3	4
1952-53	Buffalo Bisons	AHL	2	1	0	1	....	....	....	0	....	....	....	....	....
	Montreal Royals	QHL	51	23	16	39	....	....	....	14	14	3	4	7	4
1953-54	Montreal Royals	QHL	68	16	36	52	....	....	....	14	11	0	6	6	4
1954-55	Montreal Royals	QHL	62	20	*47	67	....	....	....	8	4	0	0	0	2
1955-56	Montreal Royals	QHL	61	14	25	39	....	....	....	17	13	8	*10	*18	0
1956-57	Montreal Royals	QHL	68	22	26	48	....	....	....	34	4	0	1	1	0
1957-58	Montreal Royals	QHL	61	21	31	52	....	....	....	11	7	4	4	8	4
1958-59	Montreal Royals	QHL	61	15	31	46	....	....	....	39	8	3	3	6	4
1959-60	Montreal Royals	EPHL	67	22	31	53	....	....	....	33	14	2	3	5	4
1960-61	Montreal Royals	EPHL	34	8	9	17	....	....	....	6	....	....	....	....	....
	NHL Totals		**3**	**0**	**1**	**1**	**0**	**1**	**1**	**0**	....	....	....	....	....

QHL First All-Star Team (1955)

• DENNENY, CORB Corb Denneny

C – R. 5'8", 160 lbs. b: Cornwall, Ont., 1/25/1894. d: 1/16/1963.

Season	Club	League	GP	G	A	Pts	AG	AA	APts	PIM	GP	G	A	Pts	PIM
			REGULAR SEASON								PLAYOFFS				
1911-12	Cornwall Internationals	Ott-Sr	STATISTICS NOT AVAILABLE												
1912-13	Cobalt Mines	NOHA	STATISTICS NOT AVAILABLE												
1913-14	O'Brien Mines	NOHA	STATISTICS NOT AVAILABLE												
1914-15	Toronto Shamrocks	NHA	19	13	3	16	....	....	....	18	....	....	....	....	....
1915-16	Toronto Blueshirts	NHA	22	20	3	23	....	....	....	75	....	....	....	....	....
1916-17	Toronto Blueshirts	NHA	8	9	1	10	....	....	....	35	....	....	....	....	....
	Ottawa Senators	NHA	6	5	1	6	....	....	....	18	2	0	0	0	6
1917-18	**Toronto Arenas**	**NHL**	**21**	**20**	**9**	**29**	**51**	**0**	**51**	**14**	**7**	**3**	**1**	**4**	**3**
1918-19	**Toronto Arenas**	**NHL**	**17**	**8**	**3**	**11**	**28**	**28**	**56**	**15**	....	....	....	....	....
1919-20	**Toronto St. Pats**	**NHL**	**23**	**24**	***12**	**36**	**56**	**83**	**139**	**20**	....	....	....	....	....
1920-21	**Toronto St. Pats**	**NHL**	**20**	**19**	**7**	**26**	**49**	**62**	**111**	**29**	**2**	**0**	**0**	**0**	**4**
1921-22	**Toronto St. Pats**	**NHL**	**24**	**19**	**9**	**28**	**53**	**57**	**110**	**28**	**7**	**4**	***2**	**6**	**2**
1922-23	**Toronto St. Pats**	**NHL**	**1**	**1**	**0**	**1**	**3**	**0**	**3**	**0**	....	....	....	....	....
	Vancouver Maroons	PCHA	21	7	3	10	....	....	....	3	5	0	0	0	2
1923-24	**Hamilton Tigers**	**NHL**	**23**	**0**	**0**	**0**	**0**	**0**	**0**	**6**	....	....	....	....	....
1924-25	Saskatoon Crescents	WCHL	28	15	3	18	....	....	....	24	2	2	....	....	....
1925-26	Saskatoon Crescents	WHL	30	18	*16	34	....	....	....	12	2	0	....	....	....
1926-27	**Toronto Maple Leafs**	**NHL**	**29**	**7**	**1**	**8**	**20**	**8**	**28**	**24**	....	....	....	....	....
	Saskatoon Shieks	PrHL	4	0	2	2	....	....	....	0	4	2	0	2	4
1927-28	**Chicago Black Hawks**	**NHL**	**18**	**5**	**0**	**5**	**15**	**0**	**15**	**12**	....	....	....	....	....
	Saskatoon Shieks	PrHL	16	*15	6	21	....	....	....	10	....	....	....	....	....
1928-29	Minneapolis Millers	AHA	7	0	1	1	....	....	....	0	....	....	....	....	....
	Newark Bulldogs	Can-Am	27	11	7	18	....	....	....	36	....	....	....	....	....
1929-30	Minneapolis Millers	AHA	48	26	8	34	....	....	....	22	....	....	....	....	....
1930-31	Chicago Shamrocks	AHA	28	2	6	8	....	....	....	14	....	....	....	....	....
	NHL Totals		**176**	**103**	**41**	**144**	**275**	**238**	**513**	**148**	**16**	**7**	**3**	**10**	**9**
	Other Major League Totals		134	87	30	117	....	....	....	185	11	2	0	0	8

PCHA Second All-Star Team (1923) • WHL All-Star Team (1926)

Signed as a free agent by **Toronto Arenas**, December 5, 1917. Traded to **Vancouver** (WCHL) by **Toronto St. Pats** for Jack Adams, December 16, 1922. Traded to **Hamilton** by **Vancouver** (WCHL) for cash, December 14, 1923. Traded to **Saskatoon** (WCHL) by **Hamilton** for Carson Cooper, 1924. Traded to **Toronto St. Pats** by **Saskatoon** (PrHL) with Leo Bourgeault and Laurie Scott for cash, October 18, 1926. Rights returned to **Saskatoon** (PrHL) by **Toronto St. Pats** when terms of transaction were voided, February, 1927. Traded to **Chicago** by **Saskatoon** (PrHL) for cash, June, 1927. Traded to **Saskatoon** (PrHL) by **Chicago** with Nick Wasnie for Cally McCalmon and Earl Miller, January 11, 1928. Signed as a free agent by **Minneapolis** (AHA), October 28, 1929.

• DENNENY, CY Cy Denneny HHOF

LW – L. 5'7", 168 lbs. b: Farrow's Point, Ont., 12/23/1891. d: 10/12/1970.

Season	Club	League	GP	G	A	Pts	AG	AA	APts	PIM	GP	G	A	Pts	PIM
1914-15	Ontarios–Shamrocks	NHA	8	6	0	6	....	....	....	43	....	....	....	....	....
1915-16	Toronto Blueshirts	NHA	24	24	4	28	....	....	....	57	....	....	....	....	....
1916-17	Ottawa Senators	NHA	10	3	1	4	....	....	....	25	2	1	0	1	8
1917-18	**Ottawa Senators**	**NHL**	**20**	***36**	**10**	**46**	**97**	**0**	**97**	**80**	....	....	....	....	....
1918-19	**Ottawa Senators**	**NHL**	**18**	**18**	**6**	**24**	**67**	**58**	**125**	**55**	**7**	**5**	**3**	**8**	**9**
1919-20	**Ottawa Senators**	**NHL**	**24**	**16**	**6**	**22**	**37**	**41**	**78**	**31**	**5**	**0**	**2**	**2**	**3**
1920-21	**Ottawa Senators**	**NHL**	**24**	**34**	**5**	**39**	**92**	**44**	**136**	**10**	**7**	**4**	**2**	***6**	**15**
1921-22	**Ottawa Senators**	**NHL**	**22**	**27**	**12**	**39**	**77**	**77**	**154**	**20**	**2**	***2**	**0**	**2**	**4**
1922-23	**Ottawa Senators**	**NHL**	**24**	**21**	**10**	**31**	**73**	**93**	**166**	**20**	**8**	**3**	**1**	**4**	**6**
1923-24	**Ottawa Senators**	**NHL**	**21**	***22**	**1**	***23**	**96**	**17**	**113**	**10**	**2**	**2**	**0**	**2**	**10**
1924-25	**Ottawa Senators**	**NHL**	**28**	**27**	***15**	**42**	**97**	**214**	**311**	**16**	....	....	....	....	....
1925-26	**Ottawa Senators**	**NHL**	**36**	**24**	**12**	**36**	**76**	**144**	**220**	**18**	**2**	**0**	**0**	**0**	**4**
1926-27	**Ottawa Senators**	**NHL**	**42**	**17**	**6**	**23**	**50**	**51**	**101**	**16**	**6**	***5**	**0**	***5**	**0**
1927-28	**Ottawa Senators**	**NHL**	**44**	**3**	**0**	**3**	**9**	**0**	**9**	**12**	**2**	**0**	**0**	**0**	**0**
1928-29	**Boston Bruins**	**NHL**	**23**	**1**	**2**	**3**	**4**	**18**	**22**	**2**	**2**	**0**	**0**	**0**	**0**
	NHL Totals		**326**	**246**	**85**	**331**	**775**	**757**	**1532**	**290**	**43**	**21**	**8**	**29**	**51**
	Other Major League Totals		42	33	5	38	....	....	....	125	2	1	0	1	8

NHL Scoring Leader (1924)

Traded to **Ottawa** by **Toronto Blueshirts** for Sam Herbert and $750.00, January, 1917. Rights retained by **Ottawa** after NHA folded, November 26, 1917. Traded to **Boston** by **Ottawa** for cash, June, 1926.

• DENOIRD, GERRY Gerry Denoird

C – R. 5'10", 170 lbs. b: Toronto, Ontario, 8/4/1902. Deceased.

Season	Club	League	GP	G	A	Pts	AG	AA	APts	PIM	GP	G	A	Pts	PIM
1920-21	Toronto Aura Lee	OHA	3	1	0	1	....	....	....	0	....	....	....	....	....
1921-22	Toronto Aura Lee	OHA	6	10	0	10	....	....	....	0	....	....	....	....	....
1922-23	**Toronto St. Pats**	**NHL**	**15**	**0**	**0**	**0**	**0**	**0**	**0**	**0**	....	....	....	....	....
1923-24			REINSTATED AS AN AMATEUR												
1924-25	Toronto Aura Lee	OHA Sr.	2	1	0	1	....	....	....	0	....	....	....	....	....
	Toronto A.R. Clarke	City Sr.	STATISTICS NOT AVAILABLE												
	NHL Totals		**15**	**0**	**0**	**0**	**0**	**0**	**0**	**0**	....	....	....	....	....

Signed as a free agent by **Toronto St. Pats**, October 25, 1922.

• DESAULNIERS, GERARD Gerard Desaulniers

C – L. 5'11", 152 lbs. b: Shawinigan Falls, Quebec, 12/31/1928. Deceased.

Season	Club	League	GP	G	A	Pts	AG	AA	APts	PIM	GP	G	A	Pts	PIM
1947-48	Laval National	QJHL	32	21	27	48	....	....	....	26	20	*20	11	31	12
1948-49	Laval National	QJHL	48	41	34	75	....	....	....	57	9	2	11	13	14
	Montreal Royals	QSHL	3	0	0	0	....	....	....	0	8	0	4	4	2
1949-50	Montreal Royals	QSHL	59	21	34	55	....	....	....	49	6	2	2	4	4
1950-51	**Montreal Canadiens**	**NHL**	**3**	**0**	**1**	**1**	**0**	**1**	**1**	**2**	....	....	....	....	....
	Montreal Royals	QSHL	51	24	26	50	....	....	....	30	7	0	3	3	2
1951-52	Montreal Royals	QSHL	57	19	23	42	....	....	....	33	7	1	1	2	0
1952-53	**Montreal Canadiens**	**NHL**	**2**	**0**	**1**	**1**	**0**	**1**	**1**	**2**	....	....	....	....	....
	Montreal Royals	QSHL	45	13	22	35	....	....	....	18	16	3	10	13	4
1953-54	**Montreal Canadiens**	**NHL**	**3**	**0**	**0**	**0**	**0**	**0**	**0**	**0**	....	....	....	....	....
	Montreal Royals	QHL	66	11	26	37	....	....	....	31	11	4	4	8	0
1954-55	Shawinigan Cataracts	QHL	61	31	30	61	....	....	....	10	11	5	5	10	4
1955-56	Shawinigan Cataracts	QHL	62	14	23	37	....	....	....	35	11	7	3	10	0
1956-57	Shawinigan Cataracts	QHL	68	20	29	49	....	....	....	18	....	....	....	....	....
1957-58	Shawinigan Cataracts	QHL	58	14	24	38	....	....	....	12	14	4	7	11	6
1958-59	Trois-Rivieres Lions	QHL	60	17	24	41	....	....	....	12	8	6	1	7	0
1959-60	Trois-Rivieres Lions	EPHL	56	13	28	41	....	....	....	6	....	....	....	....	....
	NHL Totals		**8**	**0**	**2**	**2**	**0**	**2**	**2**	**4**	....	....	....	....	....

• DESILETS, JOFFRE Joffre Desilets

RW – R. 5'10", 170 lbs. b: Capreol, Ont., 4/16/1915. d: 11/30/1994.

Season	Club	League	GP	G	A	Pts	AG	AA	APts	PIM	GP	G	A	Pts	PIM
1929-30	Capreol Caps	Ott-Sr.	10	1	0	1	....	....	....	0	....	....	....	....	....
1930-31	Capreol Caps	Ott-Sr.	12	4	0	4	....	....	....	4	1	0	0	0	0
1931-32	Stratford Midgets	OHA	9	6	1	7	....	....	....	6	2	4	2	6	2
1932-33	Stratford Midgets	OHA	DID NOT PLAY – INJURED												
1933-34	Stratford Midgets	OHA	15	*34	13	*47	....	....	....	27	2	3	2	5	0
1934-35	Charlottetown Islanders	MSHL	20	10	13	23	....	....	....	16	....	....	....	....	....
	Saint John Beavers	NBSHL	17	*35	*27	*62	....	....	....	2	12	*14	7	21	12
1935-36	**Montreal Canadiens**	**NHL**	**38**	**7**	**6**	**13**	**17**	**14**	**31**	**0**	....	....	....	....	....
	London Tecumsehs	IAHL	9	1	2	3	....	....	....	4	2	0	0	0	0
1936-37	**Montreal Canadiens**	**NHL**	**48**	**7**	**12**	**19**	**15**	**28**	**43**	**17**	**5**	**1**	**0**	**1**	**0**
1937-38	**Montreal Canadiens**	**NHL**	**32**	**6**	**7**	**13**	**13**	**14**	**27**	**6**	**2**	**0**	**0**	**0**	**7**
1938-39	**Chicago Black Hawks**	**NHL**	**48**	**11**	**13**	**24**	**23**	**24**	**47**	**28**	....	....	....	....	....
1939-40	**Chicago Black Hawks**	**NHL**	**26**	**6**	**7**	**13**	**13**	**14**	**27**	**6**	....	....	....	....	....
	Providence Reds	AHL	22	7	8	15	....	....	....	8	1	0	0	0	2
1940-41	Cleveland Barons	AHL	53	15	29	44	....	....	....	13	5	1	0	1	4
1941-42	Cleveland Barons	AHL	56	24	24	48	....	....	....	26	4	2	0	2	0
1942-43	Victoria Army	City Sr.	19	21	12	33	....	....	....	16	23	*31	9	40	16
1943-44	Nanaimo Clippers	PCHL	14	7	3	10	....	....	....	10	....	....	....	....	....
	Vancouver Army	City Sr.	3	0	2	2	....	....	....	0	....	....	....	....	....
	Vernon Army	City Sr.	....	....	....	....	....	....	....	....	1	0	0	0	0
1944-45	Toronto Army	City Sr.	2	10	3	13	....	....	....	....	....	....	....	....	....
1945-46	New Haven Eagles	AHL	30	6	3	9	....	....	....	10	....	....	....	....	....
	Fort Worth Rangers	USHL	23	6	13	19	....	....	....	0	....	....	....	....	....
1946-47	Dallas Texans	USHL	49	16	23	39	....	....	....	8	....	....	....	....	....
1947-48	San Diego–Fresno	PCHL	53	5	21	26	....	....	....	16	9	4	2	6	0
1948-49	San Diego Skyhawks	PCHL	DID NOT PLAY – COACHING												
1949-50	Renfrew Lions	EOHL	12	0	1	1	....	....	....	2	....	....	....	....	....
1950-51	Renfrew Millionaires	EOHL	DID NOT PLAY – COACHING												
1951-52	Renfrew Millionaires	EOHL	16	3	4	7	....	....	....	2	....	....	....	....	....
	NHL Totals		**192**	**37**	**45**	**82**	**81**	**94**	**175**	**57**	**7**	**1**	**0**	**1**	**7**

AHL Second All-Star Team (1941, 1942)

Signed as a free agent by **Montreal Canadiens**, October 22, 1935. Traded to **Chicago** by **Montreal** for Lou Trudel, August 26, 1938. Traded to **Cleveland** (AHL) by **Chicago** for cash, May 12, 1940.

• DESJARDINS, VIC Vic Desjardins USHOF

C – R. 5'9", 160 lbs. b: S.S. Marie, MI, 7/4/1900. Deceased.

Season	Club	League	GP	G	A	Pts	AG	AA	APts	PIM	GP	G	A	Pts	PIM
1919-20	Michigan Soo Indians	USAHA	14	12	4	16	....	....	....	....	....	....	....	....	....
1920-21	Soo Greyhounds	NMHL	13	11	4	15	....	....	....	....	....	....	....	....	....
	Soo Greyhounds	NOHA	9	11	4	15	....	....	....	4	5	1	1	2	....
1921-22	Eveleth Rangers	USAHA	STATISTICS NOT AVAILABLE												
1922-23	Eveleth Rangers	USAHA	20	8	0	8	....	....	....	....	....	....	....	....	....
1923-24	Eveleth Rangers	USAHA	20	5	0	5	....	....	....	....	....	....	....	....	....
1924-25	Eveleth Arrowheads	USAHA	40	14	0	14	....	....	....	....	4	2	0	2	....
1925-26	Eveleth Rangers	CHL	38	18	4	22	....	....	....	40	....	....	....	....	....
1926-27	St. Paul Saints	AHA	34	13	4	17	....	....	....	30	....	....	....	....	....
1927-28	St. Paul Saints	AHA	40	20	*8	28	....	....	....	46	....	....	....	....	....
1928-29	St. Paul Saints	AHA	39	16	10	26	....	....	....	48	8	*4	1	*5	6
1929-30	St. Paul Saints	AHA	45	25	10	35	....	....	....	47	....	....	....	....	....
1930-31	**Chicago Black Hawks**	**NHL**	**39**	**3**	**12**	**15**	**7**	**44**	**51**	**11**	**9**	**0**	**0**	**0**	**0**
1931-32	**New York Rangers**	**NHL**	**48**	**3**	**3**	**6**	**6**	**8**	**14**	**16**	**7**	**0**	**0**	**0**	**0**
1932-33	St. Paul–Tulsa	AHA	31	16	12	28	....	....	....	10	4	*4	0	4	6
	Springfield Indians	Can-Am	13	5	9	14	....	....	....	4	....	....	....	....	....
1933-34	Tulsa Oilers	AHA	46	21	13	34	....	....	....	37	4	1	2	3	4
1934-35	Tulsa Oilers	AHA	46	16	18	34	....	....	....	37	5	2	*5	*7	4
1935-36	Tulsa Oilers	AHA	45	20	21	41	....	....	....	27	3	0	0	0	0
1936-37	Kansas City Greyhounds	AHA	48	13	16	29	....	....	....	37	3	1	0	1	0
1937-38	Kansas City Greyhounds	AHA	36	6	7	13	....	....	....	2	....	....	....	....	....
	NHL Totals		**87**	**6**	**15**	**21**	**13**	**52**	**65**	**27**	**16**	**0**	**0**	**0**	**0**

AHA First All-Star Team (1935) • AHA Second All-Star Team (1936)

Traded to **NY Rangers** by **Chicago** with Art Somers for Paul Thompson, September 27, 1931.

• DESLAURIERS, JACQUES Jacques Deslauriers

D – L. 6', 170 lbs. b: Montreal, Que., 9/3/1928.

Season	Club	League	GP	G	A	Pts	AG	AA	APts	PIM	GP	G	A	Pts	PIM
1945-46	Montreal Nationale	City Sr.	19	3	4	7	....	....	....	19	4	0	0	0	2
1946-47	Laval Nationale	Mtl-Jr.	27	7	12	19	....	....	....	47	12	2	7	9	11
1947-48	Laval Nationale	Mtl Jr.	32	6	8	14	....	....	....	24	20	2	11	13	39
1948-49	Dallas Texans	USHL	56	2	11	13	....	....	....	36	4	0	0	0	0
1949-50	Cincinnati Mohawks	AHL	52	0	4	4	....	....	....	18	....	....	....	....	....
1950-51	Valleyfield Braves	QSHL	53	2	13	15	....	....	....	32	21	2	4	6	12
1951-52	Valleyfield Braves	QSHL	60	7	9	16	....	....	....	22	6	1	0	1	2
1952-53	Valleyfield Braves	QSHL	60	8	17	25	....	....	....	18	4	0	0	0	6
1953-54	Valleyfield Braves	QHL	57	6	14	20	....	....	....	14	7	1	1	2	0
1954-55	Valleyfield Braves	QHL	61	7	25	32	....	....	....	40	....	....	....	....	....
1955-56	**Montreal Canadiens**	**NHL**	**2**	**0**	**0**	**0**	**0**	**0**	**0**	**0**	....	....	....	....	....
	Montreal Royals	QHL	63	4	21	25	....	....	....	26	13	2	2	4	12
1956-57	Montreal Royals	QHL	68	11	21	32	....	....	....	46	4	0	1	1	0
	Rochester Americans	AHL	2	0	1	1	....	....	....	0	....	....	....	....	....
1957-58	Chicoutimi Sagueneens	QHL	56	8	16	24	....	....	....	26	6	1	0	1	2
1958-59	Montreal Royals	QHL	51	5	15	20	....	....	....	32	8	0	2	2	4
1959-60	Montreal Royals	EPHL	52	3	9	12	....	....	....	44	14	0	5	5	4
	NHL Totals		**2**	**0**	**0**	**0**	**0**	**0**	**0**	**0**	....	....	....	....	....

QHL First All-Star Team (1956, 1957, 1959) • QHL Second All-Star Team (1958)

			REGULAR SEASON								PLAYOFFS				
Season	Club	League	GP	G	A	Pts	AG	AA	APts	PIM	GP	G	A	Pts	PIM

● DEWAR, TOM   Tom Dewar
D – L. 5'9", 170 lbs.   b: Frobisher, Sask., 6/10/1913.   Deceased.

Season	Club	League	GP	G	A	Pts	AG	AA	APts	PIM	GP	G	A	Pts	PIM
1931-32	Moose Jaw Cubs	SJHL	....	....	....	....				....	4	*4	*2	*6	*8
1932-33	Moose Jaw Cubs	SJHL	....	....	....	....				....	2	0	0	0	2
1933-34	Moose Jaw Cubs	SJHL	1	0	0	0				0					
1934-35	Moose Jaw Millers	SSHL	13	2	0	2				12					
	Saskatoon Standards	SSHL	24	4	6	10				20	2	0	0	0	4
1935-36	Prince Albert Mintos	SSHL	20	13	6	19				12	10	2	2	4	10
1936-37	Earls Court Royals	Britain	....	8	8	16				60					
1937-38	Moose Jaw Millers	SSHL	24	4	4	8				18	6	1	1	2	6
1938-39	Moose Jaw Millers	SSHL	30	8	5	13				18	8	0	0	0	0
1939-40	Calgary Stampeders	SSHL	32	6	11	17				6	8	2	1	3	2
1940-41	Calgary Stampeders	SSHL	30	4	12	16				10	8	2	0	2	2
1941-42	Calgary Stampeders	SSHL	29	2	6	8				4	6	0	2	2	8
1942-43	Calgary Buffalos	WCSHL	29	6	5	11				....					
1943-44	**New York Rangers**	**NHL**	**9**	**0**	**2**	**2**	**0**	**2**	**2**	**4**					
	Brooklyn Crescents	EHL	2	1	0	1				0					
	NHL Totals		**9**	**0**	**2**	**2**	**0**	**2**	**2**	**4**					

● DEWSBURY, AL   Al "Dews" Dewsbury
D – L. 6'2", 202 lbs.   b: Goderich, Ont., 4/12/1926.

Season	Club	League	GP	G	A	Pts	AG	AA	APts	PIM	GP	G	A	Pts	PIM
1943-44	Toronto Young Rangers	OHA	24	12	4	16				2					
	Toronto C.I.L.	OHA Sr.	....	10	6	16				12	7	2	3	5	2
	Hamilton Szabos	OHA									3	1	0	1	0
1944-45	Toronto Young Rangers	OHA	19	12	8	20				34	4	0	0	0	8
1945-46	Omaha Knights	USHL	41	6	6	12				28	7	1	2	3	0
1946-47	**Detroit Red Wings**	**NHL**	**23**	**2**	**1**	**3**	**3**	**1**	**4**	**12**	**2**	**0**	**0**	**0**	**4**
	Indianapolis Capitals	AHL	34	6	4	10				80					
1947-48	Indianapolis Capitals	AHL	10	0	4	4				34					
	Omaha Knights	USHL	32	11	7	18				57	3	0	2	2	9
	Detroit Red Wings	**NHL**									**1**	**0**	**0**	**0**	**0**
1948-49	Indianapolis Capitals	AHL	65	8	24	32				103	2	0	2	2	0
1949-50	**Detroit Red Wings**	**NHL**	**11**	**2**	**2**	**4**	**3**	**3**	**6**	**2**	**4**	**0**	**3**	**3**	**8**
	Indianapolis Capitals	AHL	30	15	22	37				75	8	2	5	7	16
1950-51	**Chicago Black Hawks**	**NHL**	**67**	**5**	**14**	**19**	**7**	**18**	**25**	**79**					
1951-52	**Chicago Black Hawks**	**NHL**	**69**	**7**	**17**	**24**	**10**	**22**	**32**	**99**					
1952-53	**Chicago Black Hawks**	**NHL**	**69**	**5**	**16**	**21**	**8**	**22**	**30**	**97**	**7**	**1**	**2**	**3**	**4**
1953-54	**Chicago Black Hawks**	**NHL**	**69**	**6**	**15**	**21**	**9**	**20**	**29**	**44**					
1954-55	**Chicago Black Hawks**	**NHL**	**2**	**0**	**1**	**1**	**0**	**1**	**1**	**10**					
	Montreal Royals	QHL	41	7	9	16				80	14	3	2	5	*34
1955-56	**Chicago Black Hawks**	**NHL**	**37**	**3**	**12**	**15**	**4**	**15**	**19**	**22**					
	Buffalo Bisons	AHL	31	8	18	26				48	5	0	3	3	4
1956-57	Buffalo–Hershey	AHL	59	6	31	37				101	5	0	0	0	2
1957-58	Hershey Bears	AHL	60	7	31	38				114	1	0	0	0	0
1958-59	Belleville McFarlands	EOHL	40	7	31	38				114					
	Canada	WEC-A	8	3	2	5				8					
	NHL Totals		**347**	**30**	**78**	**108**	**44**	**102**	**146**	**365**	**14**	**1**	**5**	**6**	**16**

AHL Second All-Star Team (1950)

Played in NHL All-Star Game (1951)

Traded to **Chicago** by **Detroit** with Harry Lumley, Jack Stewart, Don Morrison and Pete Babando for Jim Henry, Bob Goldham, Gaye Stewart and Metro Prystai, July 13, 1950. Loaned to **Montreal** (Montreal-QHL) by **Chicago** for remainder of 1954-55 season to complete transaction that sent Lorne Davis to Chicago, November 9, 1954. Returned to **Chicago** by **Montreal**, April, 1954. Traded to **Hershey** (AHL) by **Buffalo** (AHL) for Bob Hassard, February, 1957.

● DHEERE, MARCEL   Marcel "Ching" Dheere
LW – L. 5'7", 175 lbs.   b: St. Boniface, Man., 12/19/1920.

Season	Club	League	GP	G	A	Pts	AG	AA	APts	PIM	GP	G	A	Pts	PIM
1939-40	Treherne Juniors	MJHL				STATISTICS NOT AVAILABLE									
1940-41	Portland Buckaroos	PCHL	48	18	6	24				58					
1941-42	Montreal Sr. Canadiens	QSHL	37	7	3	10				67	6	0	0	0	2
1942-43	**Montreal Canadiens**	**NHL**	**11**	**1**	**2**	**3**	**1**	**3**	**4**	**2**	**5**	**0**	**0**	**0**	**6**
	Montreal Sr. Canadiens	QSHL	25	2	7	9				12					
1943-44	Montreal Canada Car	City Sr.	1	0	2	2				0					
	Montreal RCAF	QSHL	4	0	0	0				0					
1944-45						MILITARY SERVICE									
1945-46	Hull Volants	QSHL	28	10	9	19				15					
1946-47	Houston Huskies	USHL	58	20	28	48				22					
1947-48	Houston Huskies	USHL	18	8	9	17				4					
	Tulsa Oilers	USHL	38	15	15	30				10	2	0	0	0	0
1948-49	Tulsa Oilers	USHL	66	20	35	55				18	7	1	2	3	2
1949-50	Tulsa Oilers	USHL	6	1	3	4				2					
	St. Paul Saints	USHL	15	3	7	10				2	3	0	0	0	0
	Tacoma Rockets	PCHL	47	16	33	49				12	6	0	2	2	0
1950-51	Tacoma Rockets	PCHL	45	9	16	25				14					
1951-52	Vernon Canadians	OSHL	43	14	24	38				33					
1952-53	Melville Millionaires	SSHL	32	5	21	26				26	3	0	2	2	0
	NHL Totals		**11**	**1**	**2**	**3**	**1**	**3**	**4**	**2**	**5**	**0**	**0**	**0**	**6**

Traded to **Montreal** by **Portland** (PCHL) for cash, December 25, 1940.

● DIACHUK, EDWARD   Edward Diachuk
LW – L. 6'1", 185 lbs.   b: Vegreville, Alta., 8/16/1936.

Season	Club	League	GP	G	A	Pts	AG	AA	APts	PIM	GP	G	A	Pts	PIM
1953-54	Edmonton Oil Kings	WCJHL	27	4	5	9				17	8	1	3	4	2
1954-55	Edmonton Oil Kings	WCJHL	35	15	12	27				70	5	0	0	0	0
1955-56	Edmonton Oil Kings	WCJHL	15	12	8	20				31	6	2	2	4	5
	Edmonton Flyers	WHL	1	0	0	0				0					
1956-57	Edmonton Flyers	WHL	1	0	1	1				2					
1957-58	Penticton Vees	OSHL	39	11	9	20				84	5	0	0	0	6
	Edmonton Flyers	WHL	3	0	0	0				8					
1958-59	Edmonton Flyers	WHL	37	8	13	21				60	1	0	0	0	2
1959-60	Edmonton Flyers	WHL	64	15	12	27				94	4	0	0	0	18
1960-61	**Detroit Red Wings**	**NHL**	**12**	**0**	**0**	**0**	**0**	**0**	**0**	**19**					
	Edmonton Flyers	WHL	51	11	18	29				103					
1961-62	Sudbury Wolves	EPHL	28	4	9	13				46					
	Vancouver Canucks	WHL	19	2	3	5				20					
1962-63	Los Angeles Blades	WHL	55	9	7	16				50					
	NHL Totals		**12**	**0**	**0**	**0**	**0**	**0**	**0**	**19**					

Traded to **LA Blades** (WHL) by **Detroit** for cash, July, 1962.

● DICK, HARRY   Harry Dick
D – L. 5'11", 210 lbs.   b: Port Colborne, Ont., 11/22/1922.

Season	Club	League	GP	G	A	Pts	AG	AA	APts	PIM	GP	G	A	Pts	PIM
1938-39	Hershey Bears	EHL	6	0	0	0				0					
1939-40	Guelph Biltmores	OHA	20	4	4	8				33	3	2	1	3	0
	Atlantic City Sea Gulls	EHL	5	0	0	0				9	3	0	0	0	14
1940-41	Atlantic City Sea Gulls	EHL	62	13	32	45				*202	6	0	2	2	6
1941-42	Minneapolis Millers	AHA	48	8	14	22				*91					
	Philadelphia Rockets	AHL	2	0	0	0				6					
	Cleveland Barons	AHL	3	0	0	0				10					
	Atlantic City Sea Gulls	EHL									2	2	1	3	2
1942-43	Cleveland Barons	AHL	2	0	0	0				0					
1943-44					MILITARY SERVICE										
1944-45					MILITARY SERVICE										
1945-46	Kansas City Pla-Mors	USHL	51	17	19	36				107	12	1	2	3	*34
1946-47	**Chicago Black Hawks**	**NHL**	**12**	**0**	**1**	**1**	**0**	**1**	**1**	**12**					
	Kansas City Pla-Mors	USHL	40	6	14	20				80	11	4	3	7	12
1947-48	Tulsa Oilers	USHL	66	13	23	36				*191	2	0	0	0	19
1948-49	Washington Lions	AHL	64	8	17	25				118					
1949-50	Louisville Blades	USHL	68	14	32	46				137					
1950-51	Buffalo Bisons	AHL	67	6	35	41				*212	4	0	0	0	12
1951-52	Buffalo Bisons	AHL	54	3	22	25				119	2	0	0	0	5
1952-53	Vancouver Canucks	WHL	67	8	34	42				161	9	2	6	8	18
1953-54	Vancouver Canucks	WHL	54	4	15	19				116	12	3	2	5	*45
1954-55	Vancouver Canucks	WHL	69	10	23	33				*208	5	0	1	1	27
	NHL Totals		**12**	**0**	**1**	**1**	**0**	**1**	**1**	**12**					

● DICKENS, ERNIE   Ernie Dickens
D – L. 6', 175 lbs.   b: Winnipeg, Man., 6/25/1921.

Season	Club	League	GP	G	A	Pts	AG	AA	APts	PIM	GP	G	A	Pts	PIM
1937-38	Winnipeg Rangers	MJHL	22	2	1	3				*63	2	1	0	1	*12
1938-39	St. James Canadians	MJHL	18	6	7	13				*66	2	2	0	2	4
1939-40	Winnipeg Monarchs	MJHL	19	3	6	9				24	7	2	0	2	10
1940-41	Toronto Marlboros	OHA	15	2	7	9				50	12	3	8	11	10
	Toronto Marlboros	OHA Sr.	1	0	0	0				2					
1941-42	**Toronto Maple Leafs**	**NHL**	**10**	**2**	**2**	**4**	**3**	**3**	**6**	**6**	**13**	**0**	**0**	**0**	**4**
	Providence Reds	AHL	39	8	15	23				14					
1942-43	Toronto RCAF	OHA Sr.	10	4	7	11				10	13	4	2	6	15
1943-44	Toronto RCAF	OHA Sr.	10	1	9	10									
1944-45					MILITARY SERVICE										
1945-46	**Toronto Maple Leafs**	**NHL**	**15**	**1**	**3**	**4**	**2**	**6**	**8**	**6**					
	Pittsburgh Hornets	AHL	29	4	16	20				16	6	1	2	3	0
1946-47	Pittsburgh Hornets	AHL	64	11	40	51				21	12	1	1	2	6
1947-48	Pittsburgh Hornets	AHL	9	0	4	4				2					
	Chicago Black Hawks	**NHL**	**54**	**5**	**15**	**20**	**7**	**22**	**29**	**30**					
1948-49	**Chicago Black Hawks**	**NHL**	**59**	**2**	**3**	**5**	**3**	**5**	**8**	**14**					
1949-50	**Chicago Black Hawks**	**NHL**	**70**	**0**	**13**	**13**	**0**	**16**	**16**	**22**					
1950-51	**Chicago Black Hawks**	**NHL**	**70**	**2**	**8**	**10**	**3**	**10**	**13**	**20**					
1951-52	Calgary Stampeders	PCHL	69	14	34	48				20					
1952-53					DID NOT PLAY – RETIRED										
1953-54	Oshawa Truckmen	OHA Sr.				DID NOT PLAY – COACHING										
	NHL Totals		**278**	**12**	**44**	**56**	**18**	**62**	**80**	**98**	**13**	**0**	**0**	**0**	**4**

AHL First All-Star Team (1947)

Traded to **Chicago** by **Toronto** with Gus Bodnar, Bud Poile, Gaye Stewart and Bob Goldham for Max Bentley and Cy Thomas, November 2, 1947. Traded to **Calgary** (PCHL) by **Chicago** for Sid Finney, October 1, 1951.

● DICKENSON, HERB   Herb Dickenson
LW/RW – L. 5'11", 175 lbs.   b: Hamilton, Ont., 6/11/1931.

Season	Club	League	GP	G	A	Pts	AG	AA	APts	PIM	GP	G	A	Pts	PIM
1949-50	Guelph Biltmores	OHA	48	24	22	46				43	24	*18	8	26	8
1950-51	Guelph Biltmores	OHA	49	27	36	63				44	4	1	3	4	4
1951-52	**New York Rangers**	**NHL**	**37**	**14**	**13**	**27**	**20**	**17**	**37**	**8**					
	Cincinnati Mohawks	AHL	36	15	8	23				30					
1952-53	**New York Rangers**	**NHL**	**11**	**4**	**4**	**8**	**6**	**6**	**12**	**2**					
	NHL Totals		**48**	**18**	**17**	**35**	**26**	**23**	**49**	**10**					

• Suffered career-ending eye injury after being struck with puck prior to NY Rangers-Toronto game, November 5, 1952.

● DILL, BOB   Bob Dill   **USHOF**
D – L. 5'8", 185 lbs.   b: St. Paul, MN, 4/25/1920.   d: 4/16/1981.

Season	Club	League	GP	G	A	Pts	AG	AA	APts	PIM	GP	G	A	Pts	PIM
1938-39	Miami Clippers	TrHL	14	5	5	10				23					
1939-40					STATISTICS NOT AVAILABLE										
1940-41	Baltimore Orioles	EHL	56	24	12	36				130					
1941-42	Springfield Indians	AHL	50	8	13	21				106	5	3	2	5	0
1942-43	Buffalo Bisons	AHL	19	2	7	9				46					
	Coast Guard Clippers		29	15	20	35				48	11	6	4	10	22
1943-44	Buffalo Bisons	AHL	23	5	9	14				75					
	New York Rangers	**NHL**	**28**	**6**	**10**	**16**	**7**	**12**	**19**	**66**					
1944-45	**New York Rangers**	**NHL**	**48**	**9**	**5**	**14**	**12**	**8**	**20**	**69**					
1945-46	St. Paul Saints	USHL	30	11	11	22				62					
1946-47	St. Paul Saints	USHL	58	12	18	30				*154					
1947-48	St. Paul Saints	USHL	59	10	34	44				101					
1948-49	St. Paul Saints	USHL	63	15	29	44				134	7	4	1	5	10
1949-50	St. Paul Saints	USHL	59	12	33	45				116	3	0	1	1	6
1950-51	St. Paul 7-Ups	AAHL				DID NOT PLAY – COACHING										
1951-52	Springfield Indians	EHL	37	3	16	19				58					
	NHL Totals		**76**	**15**	**15**	**30**	**19**	**20**	**39**	**135**					

EHL Second All-Star Team (1943) • USHL First All-Star Team (1947, 1950)

Traded to **NY Rangers** by **Montreal** (Buffalo - AHL) for Gord Davidson and Roger Leger, January 4, 1944.

● DILLABOUGH, BOB   — see page 979

• DILLON, CECIL Cecil "Ceece" Dillon
RW – L. 5'11", 173 lbs. b: Toledo, OH, 4/26/1908. d: 11/14/1969.

Season	Club	League	GP	G	A	Pts	AG	AA	APts	PIM	GP	G	A	Pts	PIM
			REGULAR SEASON								PLAYOFFS				
1927-28	Owen Sound Greys	OHA Sr.	STATISTICS NOT AVAILABLE												
1928-29	Springfield Indians	Can-Am	33	4	3	7	....	....	....	18	....	....	....	....	....
1929-30	Springfield Indians	Can-Am	39	19	13	32	....	....	....	38	....	....	....	....	....
1930-31	**New York Rangers**	**NHL**	**25**	**7**	**3**	**10**	**17**	**11**	**28**	**8**	**4**	**0**	**1**	**1**	**2**
	Springfield Indians	Can-Am	14	9	15	24	....	....	....	10	....	....	....	....	....
1931-32	**New York Rangers**	**NHL**	**48**	**23**	**15**	**38**	**49**	**42**	**91**	**22**	**7**	**2**	**1**	**3**	**4**
1932-33	**New York Rangers**	**NHL**	**48**	**21**	**10**	**31**	**50**	**26**	**76**	**12**	**8**	**8**	**2**	**10**	**6**
1933-34	**New York Rangers**	**NHL**	**48**	**13**	**26**	**39**	**29**	**71**	**100**	**10**	**2**	**0**	**1**	**1**	**2**
1934-35	**New York Rangers**	**NHL**	**48**	**25**	**9**	**34**	**54**	**20**	**74**	**4**	**4**	**2**	**1**	**3**	**0**
1935-36	**New York Rangers**	**NHL**	**48**	**18**	**14**	**32**	**45**	**34**	**79**	**12**	....	....	....	....	....
1936-37	**New York Rangers**	**NHL**	**48**	**20**	**11**	**31**	**44**	**26**	**70**	**13**	**9**	**0**	**3**	**3**	**0**
1937-38	**New York Rangers**	**NHL**	**48**	**21**	**18**	**39**	**45**	**37**	**82**	**6**	**3**	**1**	**0**	**1**	**0**
1938-39	**New York Rangers**	**NHL**	**48**	**12**	**15**	**27**	**25**	**28**	**53**	**6**	**1**	**0**	**0**	**0**	**0**
1939-40	**Detroit Red Wings**	**NHL**	**44**	**7**	**10**	**17**	**15**	**20**	**35**	**12**	**5**	**1**	**0**	**1**	**0**
1940-41	Indianapolis–Providence	AHL	49	9	20	29	....	....	....	4	4	0	0	0	2
1941-42	Pittsburgh Hornets	AHL	51	13	23	36	....	....	....	2	....	....	....	....	....
	NHL Totals		**453**	**167**	**131**	**298**	**373**	**315**	**688**	**105**	**43**	**14**	**9**	**23**	**14**

NHL Second All-Star Team (1936, 1937) • NHL First All-Star Team (1938)

Played in NHL All-Star Game (1937)

Traded to **NY Rangers** by **Springfield** (Can-Am) for cash, January 1, 1931. Traded to **Detroit** by **NY Rangers** for cash, May 17, 1939. Traded to **Providence** (AHL) by **Detroit** with Eddie Bush for Harold Jackson, December 15, 1940.

• DINEEN, BILL Bill Dineen
RW – R. 5'11", 180 lbs. b: Arvida, Que., 9/18/1932.

Season	Club	League	GP	G	A	Pts	AG	AA	APts	PIM	GP	G	A	Pts	PIM
1949-50	St. Michael's Majors	OHA	43	15	18	33	....	....	....	43	5	2	3	5	4
1950-51	St. Michael's Majors	OHA	45	25	26	51	....	....	....	50	....	....	....	....	....
1951-52	St. Michael's Majors	OHA	47	21	30	51	....	....	....	37	8	3	3	6	0
1952-53	St. Michael's Majors	OHA	55	27	20	47	....	....	....	63	17	*13	7	20	18
1953-54	**Detroit Red Wings**	**NHL**	**70**	**17**	**8**	**25**	**26**	**11**	**37**	**34**	**12**	**0**	**0**	**0**	**2**
1954-55	**Detroit Red Wings**	**NHL**	**69**	**10**	**9**	**19**	**14**	**11**	**25**	**36**	**11**	**0**	**1**	**1**	**8**
1955-56	**Detroit Red Wings**	**NHL**	**70**	**12**	**7**	**19**	**17**	**9**	**26**	**30**	**10**	**1**	**0**	**1**	**8**
1956-57	**Detroit Red Wings**	**NHL**	**51**	**6**	**7**	**13**	**8**	**8**	**16**	**12**	**4**	**0**	**0**	**0**	**0**
1957-58	**Detroit Red Wings**	**NHL**	**22**	**2**	**4**	**6**	**3**	**4**	**7**	**2**	....	....	....	....	....
	Chicago Black Hawks	**NHL**	**41**	**4**	**9**	**13**	**5**	**10**	**15**	**8**	....	....	....	....	....
1958-59	Buffalo Bisons	AHL	49	8	19	27	....	....	....	17	11	3	5	8	10
1959-60	Buffalo Bisons	AHL	5	0	1	1	....	....	....	2	....	....	....	....	....
	Cleveland Barons	AHL	62	26	27	53	....	....	....	17	7	2	3	5	4
1960-61	Cleveland Barons	AHL	72	28	31	59	....	....	....	24	4	0	3	3	0
1961-62	Rochester Americans	AHL	70	19	19	38	....	....	....	20	2	0	0	0	2
1962-63	Quebec Aces	AHL	72	24	17	41	....	....	....	22	....	....	....	....	....
1963-64	Quebec Aces	AHL	61	27	25	52	....	....	....	26	9	3	3	6	0
1964-65	Seattle Totems	WHL	69	25	17	42	....	....	....	4	7	0	1	1	8
1965-66	Seattle Totems	WHL	71	23	16	39	....	....	....	10	....	....	....	....	....
1966-67	Seattle Totems	WHL	62	32	33	65	....	....	....	8	10	2	*7	9	4
1967-68	Seattle Totems	WHL	72	28	33	61	....	....	....	10	9	3	6	9	2
1968-69	Seattle Totems	WHL	74	9	10	25	....	....	....	0	4	0	0	0	0
1969-70	Denver Spurs	WHL	51	10	8	18	....	....	....	4	....	....	....	....	....
1970-71	Denver Spurs	WHL	16	5	6	11	....	....	....	4	....	....	....	....	....
	NHL Totals		**323**	**51**	**44**	**95**	**73**	**53**	**126**	**122**	**37**	**1**	**1**	**2**	**18**

WHL Second All-Star Team (1967)

Played in NHL All-Star Game (1954, 1955)

Rights traded to **Detroit** by **Cleveland** (AHL) with the rights to Lou Jankowski for Bob Bailey and John Bailey, June, 1951. Traded to **Chicago** by **Detroit** with Billy Dea, Lorne Ferguson and Earl Reibel for Nick Mikoski, Bob Bailey, Hec Lalande and Jack McIntyre, December 17, 1957. Traded to **Cleveland** (AHL) by **Buffalo** (AHL) for Bob Bailey, October 20, 1959.

• DINSMORE, CHUCK Chuck "Dinny" Dinsmore
C – L. 5'6", 155 lbs. b: Toronto, Ont., 7/23/1903. Deceased.

Season	Club	League	GP	G	A	Pts	AG	AA	APts	PIM	GP	G	A	Pts	PIM
1919-20	Toronto Aura Lee	OHA	6	0	0	0	....	....	....	....	....	....	....	....	....
1920-21	Toronto Aura Lee	OHA	3	0	0	0	....	....	....	....	....	....	....	....	....
1921-22	Toronto Aura Lee	OHA	6	1	0	1	....	....	....	....	....	....	....	....	....
1922-23	Toronto Aura Lee	OHA	1	0	0	0	....	....	....	....	....	....	....	....	....
	Toronto Aura Lee	OHA Sr.	8	2	1	3	....	....	....	....	....	....	....	....	....
1923-24	Toronto Aura Lee	OHA Sr.	9	4	6	10	....	....	....	....	....	....	....	....	....
1924-25	**Montreal Maroons**	**NHL**	**30**	**2**	**1**	**3**	**7**	**13**	**20**	**26**	....	....	....	....	....
1925-26	**Montreal Maroons**	**NHL**	**33**	**3**	**1**	**4**	**9**	**11**	**20**	**18**	**8**	**1**	**0**	**1**	**6**
1926-27	**Montreal Maroons**	**NHL**	**28**	**1**	**0**	**1**	**3**	**0**	**3**	**6**	....	....	....	....	....
1927-28	Montreal CNR	City Sr.	DID NOT PLAY – COACHING												
1928-29	Montreal CNR	City Sr.	DID NOT PLAY – COACHING												
1929-30	**Montreal Maroons**	**NHL**	**9**	**0**	**0**	**0**	**0**	**0**	**0**	**0**	**4**	**0**	**0**	**0**	**0**
	NHL Totals		**100**	**6**	**2**	**8**	**19**	**24**	**43**	**50**	**12**	**1**	**0**	**1**	**6**

Signed as a free agent by **Montreal Maroons**, November 18, 1924.

• DOAK, GARY see page 983

• DOHERTY, FRED Fred "Doc" Doherty
RW – L. 5'8", 160 lbs. b: Norwood, Ontario. Deceased.

Season	Club	League	GP	G	A	Pts	AG	AA	APts	PIM	GP	G	A	Pts	PIM
			REGULAR SEASON								PLAYOFFS				
1908-09	Guelph Professionals	OPHL	6	7	0	7	....	....	....	6	....	....	....	....	....
	Galt Professionals	OPHL	8	8	0	8	....	....	....	12	2	2	0	2	12
1909-10	Galt Professionals	OPHL	14	10	0	10	....	....	....	....	2	1	0	1	6
1910-11	Galt Professionals	OPHL	13	4	0	4	....	....	....	....	3	2	0	2	....
	Belleville Professionals	EOPHL	3	1	0	1	....	....	....	....	....	....	....	....	....
	Renfrew Creamery Kings	NHA	1	0	0	0	....	....	....	0	....	....	....	....	....
1911-12	Moncton Victorias	MPHL	16	16	0	16	....	....	....	31	2	0	0	0	2
1912-13	Toronto Blueshirts	NHA	1	0	0	0	....	....	....	0	....	....	....	....	....
	Moncton Victorias	MPHL	12	12	0	12	....	....	....	14	....	....	....	....	....
	Halifax Crescents	MPHL	1	0	0	0	....	....	....	0	....	....	....	....	....
1913-14	Toronto Ontarios	NHA	19	9	5	14	....	....	....	20	....	....	....	....	....
1914-15	Quebec Bulldogs	NHA	1	0	0	0	....	....	....	0	....	....	....	....	....
1915-16	Montreal Wanderers	NHA	1	0	0	0	....	....	....	0	....	....	....	....	....
1916-17			MILITARY SERVICE												
1917-18			MILITARY SERVICE												
1918-19	**Montreal Canadiens**	**NHL**	**2**	**0**	**0**	**0**	**0**	**0**	**0**	**0**	....	....	....	....	....
	NHL Totals		**2**	**0**	**0**	**0**	**0**	**0**	**0**	**0**	....	....	....	....	....
	Other Major League Totals		93	66	5	71	....	....	....	83	9	5	0	5	20

Signed as a free agent by **Montreal Canadiens**, December 13, 1918.

• DONNELLY, BABE Babe (James Joseph) Donnelly
D – L. 5'7", 180 lbs. b: Sault Ste. Marie, Ont., 12/22/1895. Deceased.

Season	Club	League	GP	G	A	Pts	AG	AA	APts	PIM	GP	G	A	Pts	PIM
1916-17	Toronto 227th Batallion	OHA Sr.	9	7	0	7	....	....	....	....	....	....	....	....	....
1917-18			MILITARY SERVICE												
1918-19			MILITARY SERVICE												
1919-20	Edmonton Eskimos	Big 4	11	3	1	4	....	....	....	6	2	0	1	1	2
1920-21	Soo Greyhounds	NOHA	9	3	4	7	....	....	....	18	5	2	3	5	....
	Soo Greyhounds	NMHL	14	8	4	12	....	....	....	....	....	....	....	....	....
1921-22	Soo Greyhounds	NOHA	8	9	3	12	....	....	....	12	2	1	1	2	*6
	Soo Greyhounds	NMHL	11	9	4	13	....	....	....	....	....	....	....	....	....
1922-23	Soo Greyhounds	NOHA	7	3	0	3	....	....	....	*25	7	3	2	5	*8
1923-24	Soo Greyhounds	NOHA	7	8	2	10	....	....	....	18	7	6	1	7	*21
1924-25	Soo Greyhounds	NOHA	STATISTICS NOT AVAILABLE												
1925-26	Soo Greyhounds	NOHA	32	8	2	10	....	....	....	40	....	....	....	....	....
1926-27	**Montreal Maroons**	**NHL**	**34**	**0**	**1**	**1**	**0**	**8**	**8**	**14**	**2**	**0**	**0**	**0**	**0**
	Stratford Nationals	Can-Pro	1	0	0	0	....	....	....	2	....	....	....	....	....
	Detroit Greyhounds	AHA	6	1	0	1	....	....	....	13	....	....	....	....	....
1927-28	Minneapolis Millers	AHA	26	1	2	3	....	....	....	32	....	....	....	....	....
1928-29	Philadelphia Arrows	Can-Am	22	1	1	2	....	....	....	20	....	....	....	....	....
1929-30	London Panthers	IAHL	12	4	1	5	....	....	....	16	....	....	....	....	....
	Toronto Millionaires	IAHL	3	0	0	0	....	....	....	2	....	....	....	....	....
1930-31	Buffalo Majors	AHA	39	5	9	14	....	....	....	90	....	....	....	....	....
1931-32	Buffalo Majors	AHA	16	4	2	6	....	....	....	21	....	....	....	....	....
	Tulsa Oilers	AHA	21	1	0	1	....	....	....	30	....	....	....	....	....
1932-33	Falconbridge Falcons	NOHA	DID NOT PLAY – COACHING												
1933-34	Falconbridge Falcons	NOHA	DID NOT PLAY – COACHING												
1934-35	Falconbridge Falcons	NOHA	5	0	1	1	....	....	....	8	2	1	0	1	0
1935-36	Streatham Redskins	Britain	....	3	7	10	....	....	....	18	....	....	....	....	....
1936-37	Streatham Redskins	Britain	DID NOT PLAY – COACHING												
	NHL Totals		**34**	**0**	**1**	**1**	**0**	**8**	**8**	**14**	**2**	**0**	**0**	**0**	**0**

Signed as a free agent by **Montreal Maroons** and loaned to **Detroit** (AHA), September 30, 1926. Rights traded to **London** (IAHL) by **Minneapolis** (AHA) for George Redding, October 24, 1929. Traded to **Toronto Milionaires** (IAHL) by **London** (IAHL) for George Hiller, December 16, 1929.

• DORAN, JOHN John (John Michael) "Red" Doran
D – L. 5'11", 195 lbs. b: Belleville, Ont., 5/24/1911. d: 2/11/1975.

Season	Club	League	GP	G	A	Pts	AG	AA	APts	PIM	GP	G	A	Pts	PIM
1929-30	West Toronto Nationals	OHA	4	2	0	2	....	....	....	2	7	2	1	3	14
1930-31	West Toronto Nationals	OHA	STATISTICS NOT AVAILABLE												
1931-32	Toronto Marlboros	OHA Sr.	7	0	0	0	....	....	....	8	....	....	....	....	....
1932-33	New Haven Eagles	Can-Am	41	4	2	6	....	....	....	38	....	....	....	....	....
1933-34	**New York Americans**	**NHL**	**39**	**1**	**4**	**5**	**2**	**11**	**13**	**40**					
	Quebec Castors	Can-Am	8	1	0	1	....	....	....	20	....	....	....	....	....
1934-35	Quebec Castors	Can-Am	44	7	11	18	....	....	....	*105	3	1	0	1	4
1935-36	**New York Americans**	**NHL**	**25**	**4**	**2**	**6**	**10**	**5**	**15**	**44**	**3**	**0**	**0**	**0**	**0**
1936-37	**New York Americans**	**NHL**	**21**	**0**	**1**	**1**	**0**	**2**	**2**	**10**	....	....	....	....	....
	New Haven–Pittsburgh	AHL	26	4	10	14	....	....	....	50	5	1	1	2	11
1937-38	**Detroit Red Wings**	**NHL**	**7**	**0**	**0**	**0**	**0**	**0**	**0**	**10**	....	....	....	....	....
	Pittsburgh–New Haven	AHL	37	4	12	16	....	....	....	38	2	0	0	0	2
1938-39	Providence–New Haven	AHL	40	2	10	12	....	....	....	87	5	1	1	2	8
1939-40	**Montreal Canadiens**	**NHL**	**6**	**0**	**3**	**3**	**0**	**6**	**6**	**6**	....	....	....	....	....
	Providence Reds	AHL	46	14	19	33	....	....	....	82	8	4	2	6	16
1940-41	Buffalo–Hershey	AHL	58	2	16	18	....	....	....	56	....	....	....	....	....
1941-42	Truro Bearcats	Hfx-Sr.	1	0	0	0	....	....	....	0	13	3	6	9	4
1942-43	Montreal Army	City Sr.	4	1	5	6	....	....	....	4	5	5	*7	*12	12
	NHL Totals		**98**	**5**	**10**	**15**	**12**	**24**	**36**	**110**	**3**	**0**	**0**	**0**	**0**

Traded to **Detroit** by **NY Americans** with $7,500 for Earl Robertson, May 9, 1937. Signed as a free agent by **Montreal**, October 9, 1939. Traded to **Buffalo** (AHL) by **Montreal** for cash, December 12, 1940.

• DORAN, LLOYD Lloyd "Red" Doran

C – L. 6′, 175 lbs. b: South Porcupine, Ont., 1/10/1921.

Season	Club	League	REGULAR SEASON GP	G	A	Pts	AG	AA	APts	PIM	PLAYOFFS GP	G	A	Pts	PIM
1940-41	Dome Porkies	NOHA	23	9	12	21	....	....	....	28	....	....	....	....	....
1941-42	Omaha Knights	AHA	39	6	18	24	....	....	....	25	8	4	3	7	*22
1942-43	Montreal Army	QSHL	30	9	16	25	....	....	....	46	7	2	1	3	10
1943-44	Kingston Army	OHA Sr.	11	8	14	22	....	....	....	14	....	....	....	....	....
1944-45			MILITARY SERVICE												
1945-46			MILITARY SERVICE												
1946-47	**Detroit Red Wings**	**NHL**	**24**	**3**	**2**	**5**	**4**	**3**	**7**	**10**	....	....	....	....	....
	Indianapolis Capitals	AHL	35	9	24	33	....	....	....	77	....	....	....	....	....
1947-48	Indianapolis Capitals	AHL	45	14	21	35	....	....	....	50	....	....	....	....	....
1948-49	St. Louis Flyers	AHL	67	19	55	74	....	....	....	39	7	3	5	8	0
1949-50	St. Louis Flyers	AHL	70	14	42	56	....	....	....	60	2	0	1	1	0
1950-51	Denver Falcons	USHL	12	3	2	5	....	....	....	6	....	....	....	....	....
	St. Louis–Cleveland	AHL	35	4	11	15	....	....	....	26	8	3	4	7	6
	NHL Totals		**24**	**3**	**2**	**5**	**4**	**3**	**7**	**10**	....	....	....	....	....

Signed as a free agent by **Detroit**, October 21, 1941. Traded to **St. Louis** (AHL) by **Detroit** with Red Almas, Tony Licari, Barry Sullivan and Thain Simon for Joe Lund and Hec Highton, September 9, 1948.

• DORATY, KEN Ken "Cagie" Doraty

F – R. 5′7″, 133 lbs. b: Stittsville, Ont., 6/23/1906. d: 4/4/1981.

Season	Club	League	GP	G	A	Pts	AG	AA	APts	PIM	GP	G	A	Pts	PIM
1923-24	Regina Pats	SJHL	6	5	2	7	....	....	....	0	5	3	3	6	0
1924-25	Regina Pats	SJHL	4	5	4	9	....	....	....	2	12	13	*7	*20	24
1925-26	Portland Rosebuds	PCHL	30	4	1	5	....	....	....	4	....	....	....	....	....
1926-27	**Chicago Black Hawks**	**NHL**	**18**	**0**	**0**	**0**	**0**	**0**	**0**	**0**	....	....	....	....	....
	Minneapolis Millers	AHA	7	0	0	0	....	....	....	0	....	....	....	....	....
1927-28	Kitchener Millionaires	Can-Pro	39	19	6	25	....	....	....	35	5	2	0	2	6
1928-29	Toronto Millionaires	Can-Pro	39	*26	5	31	....	....	....	42	2	1	1	2	2
1929-30	Cleveland Indians	IAHL	42	26	16	42	....	....	....	43	6	*5	0	5	*14
1930-31	Cleveland Indians	IAHL	48	25	24	49	....	....	....	43	6	1	4	5	6
1931-32	Cleveland Indians	IAHL	48	21	15	36	....	....	....	45	....	....	....	....	....
1932-33	**Toronto Maple Leafs**	**NHL**	**38**	**5**	**11**	**16**	**12**	**29**	**41**	**16**	**9**	**5**	**0**	**5**	**2**
	Syracuse Stars	IAHL	10	5	4	9	....	....	....	14	....	....	....	....	....
1933-34	**Toronto Maple Leafs**	**NHL**	**34**	**9**	**10**	**19**	**20**	**27**	**47**	**6**	**5**	**2**	**2**	**4**	**0**
	Buffalo Bisons	IAHL	4	0	0	0	....	....	....	2	....	....	....	....	....
1934-35	**Toronto Maple Leafs**	**NHL**	**11**	**1**	**4**	**5**	**2**	**9**	**11**	**0**	**1**	**0**	**0**	**0**	**0**
	Syracuse Stars	IAHL	30	12	17	29	....	....	....	37	2	0	1	1	0
	New Haven Eagles	Can-Am	1	0	0	0	....	....	....	0	....	....	....	....	....
1935-36	Syracuse–Cleveland	IAHL	46	*28	20	48	....	....	....	24	2	0	2	2	0
1936-37	Cleveland–Pittsburgh	AHL	44	14	15	29	....	....	....	21	5	1	0	1	4
1937-38	**Detroit Red Wings**	**NHL**	**2**	**0**	**1**	**1**	**0**	**2**	**2**	**2**	....	....	....	....	....
	Pittsburgh Hornets	AHL	48	12	17	29	....	....	....	22	2	0	0	0	0
1938-39	Seattle Seahawks	PCHL	48	25	17	42	....	....	....	23	7	1	2	3	6
	NHL Totals		**103**	**15**	**26**	**41**	**34**	**67**	**101**	**24**	**15**	**7**	**2**	**9**	**2**

IAHL Second All-Star Team (1936)

Played in NHL All-Star Game (1934)

Rights transferred to **Chicago** after NHL club purchased **Portland** (WHL) franchise, May 15, 1926. Traded to **Minneapolis** (AHA) by **Chicago** for Ed Rodden, January 24, 1927. Traded to **Kitchener** (Can-Pro) by **Minneapolis** (AHA) for cash, October, 1927. Traded to **Toronto** (Syracuse-IAHL) by **Cleveland** (IAHL) for cash, October 6, 1932. Traded to **Cleveland** (IAHL) by **Toronto** for cash, December, 1935. Signed as a free agent by **Detroit**, December 3, 1936.

• DORNHOEFER, GARY — *see page 988*

• DOROHOY, EDDIE Eddie "The Great Gabbo" Dorohoy

C/LW – L. 5′9″, 155 lbs. b: Medicine Hat, Alta., 3/13/1929.

Season	Club	League	GP	G	A	Pts	AG	AA	APts	PIM	GP	G	A	Pts	PIM
1946-47	Lethbridge Native Sons	AJHL	11	2	1	3	....	....	....	4	3	2	0	2	0
1947-48	Lethbridge Native Sons	AJHL	27	32	*49	81	....	....	....	22	6	6	*15	*21	9
1948-49	**Montreal Canadiens**	**NHL**	**16**	**0**	**0**	**0**	**0**	**0**	**0**	**6**	....	....	....	....	....
	Dallas Texans	USHL	34	19	21	40	....	....	....	76	4	2	2	4	0
1949-50	Cincinnati Mohawks	AHL	6	0	0	0	....	....	....	2	....	....	....	....	....
	Victoria Cougars	PCHL	31	15	16	31	....	....	....	25	....	....	....	....	....
1950-51	Victoria Cougars	PCHL	68	29	*58	*87	....	....	....	64	12	*6	8	*14	8
1951-52	Victoria Cougars	PCHL	68	29	*56	85	....	....	....	66	13	3	4	7	12
1952-53	Victoria Cougars	WHL	70	24	54	78	....	....	....	97	....	....	....	....	....
1953-54	Victoria Cougars	WHL	70	26	53	79	....	....	....	46	5	1	2	3	4
1954-55	Victoria Cougars	WHL	68	33	52	85	....	....	....	41	5	2	2	4	10
1955-56	Seattle Americans	WHL	69	18	41	59	....	....	....	131	....	....	....	....	....
1956-57	Seattle Americans	WHL	70	31	55	86	....	....	....	70	6	2	6	8	4
1957-58	Victoria Cougars	WHL	58	34	41	75	....	....	....	51	....	....	....	....	....
1958-59	Calgary Stampeders	WHL	64	35	*74	109	....	....	....	56	8	2	4	6	6
1959-60	Vancouver Canucks	WHL	33	17	21	38	....	....	....	30	....	....	....	....	....
1960-61	Vancouver Canucks	WHL	2	0	0	0	....	....	....	0	....	....	....	....	....
1961-62	Los Angeles–Vancouver	WHL	37	6	10	16	....	....	....	14	....	....	....	....	....
1962-63	Vancouver Canucks	WHL	6	0	2	2	....	....	....	0	....	....	....	....	....
	Knoxville Knights	EHL	20	7	20	27	....	....	....	2	5	1	2	3	0
1963-64	New Haven Blades	EHL	18	11	18	29	....	....	....	6	5	2	3	5	2
1964-65	Spokane Jets	WHL	47	20	50	70	....	....	....	118	....	....	....	....	....
	NHL Totals		**16**	**0**	**0**	**0**	**0**	**0**	**0**	**6**	....	....	....	....	....

PCHL Second All-Star Team (1952) • WHL Prairie Division First All-Star Team (1959) • Won Leader Cup (WHL Prairie Division - MVP) (1959)

Rights traded to **NY Rangers** by **Montreal** (Victoria-WHL) with Dick Gamble for Hy Buller with Montreal holding rights of recall if Dorohoy failed to make NY Rangers roster, June 8, 1954. Rights returned to **Montreal** by **NY Rangers** after training camp, September, 1954. Traded to **Victoria** (WHL) by **Montreal** for cash, August, 1955. Traded to **Victoria** (WHL) by **Seattle** (WHL) for Bill Davidson and Don Chiupka, September, 1957. Traded to **Calgary** (WHL) by **Victoria** (WHL) for George Ford, Enio Sclisizzi and Murray Wilkie, June, 1958.

• DOUGLAS, KENT — *see page 988*

• DOUGLAS, LES Les Douglas

C – L. 5′9″, 165 lbs. b: Perth, Ont., 12/5/1918.

Season	Club	League	REGULAR SEASON GP	G	A	Pts	AG	AA	APts	PIM	PLAYOFFS GP	G	A	Pts	PIM
1936-37	Perth Crescents	Ott-Jr.	12	*21	*19	*40	....	....	....	10	2	*3	*4	*7	0
1937-38	Perth Blue Devils	Ott-Jr.	8	*18	16	*34	....	....	....	10	14	*35	*18	*53	8
1938-39	Detroit Pontiacs	MOHL	27	*27	20	*47	....	....	....	25	7	5	4	9	13
1939-40	Indianapolis Capitols	AHL	54	15	19	34	....	....	....	20	5	0	3	3	0
1940-41	**Detroit Red Wings**	**NHL**	**18**	**1**	**2**	**3**	**2**	**4**	**6**	**2**	....	....	....	....	....
	Indianapolis Capitols	AHL	31	3	5	8	....	....	....	4	....	....	....	....	....
1941-42	Indianapolis Capitols	AHL	56	15	33	48	....	....	....	9	10	8	9	*17	6
1942-43	**Detroit Red Wings**	**NHL**	**21**	**5**	**8**	**13**	**7**	**10**	**17**	**4**	**10**	**3**	**2**	**5**	**2**
	Indianapolis Capitols	AHL	33	13	26	39	....	....	....	7	7	1	0	1	0
1943-44	Ottawa Commandos	QSHL	....	....	....	....	....	....	....	....	3	3	0	3	0
1944-45			MILITARY SERVICE												
1945-46	**Detroit Red Wings**	**NHL**	**1**	**0**	**0**	**0**	**0**	**0**	**0**	**0**	....	....	....	....	....
	Indianapolis Capitols	AHL	62	44	46	*90	....	....	....	35	5	1	2	3	2
1946-47	**Detroit Red Wings**	**NHL**	**12**	**0**	**2**	**2**	**0**	**3**	**3**	**2**	....	....	....	....	....
	Indianapolis Capitols	AHL	51	26	57	83	....	....	....	26	....	....	....	....	....
1947-48	Buffalo Bisons	AHL	68	27	50	77	....	....	....	23	8	2	3	5	0
1948-49	Buffalo Bisons	AHL	68	20	52	72	....	....	....	20	....	....	....	....	....
1949-50	Cleveland Barons	AHL	67	32	*68	*100	....	....	....	27	9	2	2	4	11
1950-51	Cleveland Barons	AHL	70	31	39	70	....	....	....	20	11	3	4	7	0
1951-52	Montreal Royals	QSHL	60	30	*50	80	....	....	....	20	7	3	7	10	2
	Buffalo Bisons	AHL	....	....	....	....	....	....	....	....	1	0	1	1	0
1952-53	Montreal Royals	QSHL	55	19	29	48	....	....	....	8	14	5	3	8	4
1953-54	Sarnia Sailors	OHA Sr.	22	8	15	23	....	....	....	6	....	....	....	....	....
1954-55			DID NOT PLAY												
1955-56	Kingston Goodyears	EOHL	27	8	12	20	....	....	....	52	1	0	0	0	0
	NHL Totals		**52**	**6**	**12**	**18**	**9**	**17**	**26**	**8**	**10**	**3**	**2**	**5**	**2**

AHL First All-Star Team (1946, 1950) • AHL Second All-Star Team (1947) • Won John B. Sollenberger Trophy (Top Scorer - AHL) (1950) • Won Les Cunningham Award (MVP - AHL) (1950) • Won Vimy Trophy (MVP - QSHL) (1952)

Traded to **Buffalo** (AHL) by **Detroit** with Harold Jackson for Jim McFadden, September, 1947.

• DOWNIE, DAVE Dave "Wildcat" Downie

C/RW – R. 5′8″, 168 lbs. b: Burke's Falls, Ont., 3/11/1909. Deceased.

Season	Club	League	GP	G	A	Pts	AG	AA	APts	PIM	GP	G	A	Pts	PIM
1925-26	Regina Falcons	City Jr.	8	7	3	10	....	....	....	4	3	2	1	3	*10
1926-27	Regina Falcons	City Jr.	6	6	1	*7	....	....	....	0	....	....	....	....	....
1927-28	Regina Monarchs	City Jr.	STATISTICS NOT AVAILABLE												
1928-29	Victoria–Portland	PCHL	35	7	12	19	....	....	....	61	2	0	0	0	8
1929-30	Portland Buckaroos	PCHL	27	6	0	6	....	....	....	37	4	*3	0	*3	0
1930-31	Portland Buckaroos	PCHL	34	*13	4	*17	....	....	....	78	....	....	....	....	....
1931-32	Syracuse Stars	IAHL	37	12	7	19	....	....	....	46	....	....	....	....	....
	Boston Cubs	Can-Am	8	1	0	1	....	....	....	12	....	....	....	....	....
1932-33	**Toronto Maple Leafs**	**NHL**	**11**	**0**	**1**	**1**	**0**	**3**	**3**	**2**	....	....	....	....	....
	Syracuse Stars	IAHL	34	15	12	27	....	....	....	52	6	1	2	3	*29
1933-34	Syracuse Stars	IAHL	26	12	10	22	....	....	....	31	6	0	0	0	0
1934-35	Syracuse Stars	IAHL	43	14	14	28	....	....	....	71	2	0	0	0	0
1935-36	Windsor Bulldogs	IAHL	43	15	15	30	....	....	....	*97	8	1	4	5	14
1936-37	Seattle Seahawks	PCHL	37	13	8	21	....	....	....	50	....	....	....	....	....
1937-38	Seattle Seahawks	PCHL	42	17	19	36	....	....	....	67	4	1	0	1	0
1938-39	Seattle Seahawks	PCHL	48	*35	29	64	....	....	....	32	7	3	2	5	9
1939-40	Seattle Seahawks	PCHL	40	22	*26	*48	....	....	....	26	....	....	....	....	....
1940-41	Seattle Olympics	PCHL	40	24	29	53	....	....	....	60	2	0	0	0	2
1941-42	Philadelphia Rockets	AHL	9	1	0	1	....	....	....	0	....	....	....	....	....
1942-43			DID NOT PLAY												
1943-44	Seattle Ironmen	City Sr.	9	*19	9	28	....	....	....	7	2	2	5	7	12
	Portland Oilers	City Sr.	....	....	....	....	....	....	....	....	4	7	1	8	2
	NHL Totals		**11**	**0**	**1**	**1**	**0**	**3**	**3**	**2**	....	....	....	....	....

Loaned to **Toronto** by **Syracuse** (IAHL), December 28, 1932.

• DRAPER, BRUCE Bruce Draper

C – L. 5′10″, 157 lbs. b: Toronto, Ont., 10/2/1940. d: 1/26/1968.

Season	Club	League	GP	G	A	Pts	AG	AA	APts	PIM	GP	G	A	Pts	PIM
1957-58	St. Michael's Majors	OHA	2	0	0	0	....	....	....	2	....	....	....	....	....
1958-59	St. Michael's Majors	OHA	48	24	25	49	....	....	....	58	15	5	7	12	24
1959-60	St. Michael's Majors	OHA	38	16	22	38	....	....	....	23	10	6	6	12	10
1960-61	St. Michael's Majors	OHA	46	44	33	77	....	....	....	77	19	10	*16	26	18
1961-62	Rochester Americans	AHL	70	25	40	65	....	....	....	31	2	0	0	0	0
1962-63	**Toronto Maple Leafs**	**NHL**	**1**	**0**	**0**	**0**	**0**	**0**	**0**	**0**	....	....	....	....	....
	Sudbury Wolves	EPHL	11	3	10	13	....	....	....	10	....	....	....	....	....
	Rochester Americans	AHL	55	8	18	26	....	....	....	12	2	0	1	1	0
1963-64	Denver Invaders	WHL	68	15	30	45	....	....	....	30	6	0	3	3	0
1964-65	Hershey Bears	AHL	42	12	20	32	....	....	....	10	15	7	3	10	6
1965-66	Hershey Bears	AHL	41	14	21	35	....	....	....	49	....	....	....	....	....
1966-67	Hershey Bears	AHL	2	1	0	1	....	....	....	0	....	....	....	....	....
	NHL Totals		**1**	**0**	**0**	**0**	**0**	**0**	**0**	**0**	....	....	....	....	....

Traded to **Hershey** (AHL) by **Toronto** with Gene Ubriaco for Les Duff, September, 1963. Loaned to **Denver** (WHL) by **Hershey** (AHL) with Hershey holding rights of recall, September, 1963.

• DRILLON, GORDIE   Gordie Drillon   HHOF

RW – R. 6'2", 178 lbs.   b: Moncton, N.B., 10/23/1914.   d: 10/22/1986.

Season	Club	League	GP	G	A	Pts	AG	AA	APts	PIM	GP	G	A	Pts	PIM
			REGULAR SEASON								PLAYOFFS				
1930-31	Moncton Athletics	City Jr.	6	*15	4	*19	....	....	....	....	2	*3	2	*5	12
	Moncton Aberdeens	H.S.	3	1	0	1	....	....	....	0	1	1	0	*1	....
1931-32	Moncton Wheelers	City Jr.	6	6	4	10	....	....	....	....	3	5	1	6	5
1932-33	Moncton Hawks	MSHL	4	13	3	16	....	....	....	0	2	*2	1	3	4
	Moncton Swift's	City Sr.	7	11	3	14	....	....	....	....	6	*13	4	*17	....
1933-34	Toronto Young Rangers	OHA	11	*20	*13	*33	....	....	....	4	2	*5	*3	*8	4
1934-35	Toronto Lions	OHA	11	17	9	26	....	....	....	2	5	2	1	3	6
	Toronto Dominions	OHA Sr.	11	12	6	18	....	....	....	2	3	2	1	3	4
1935-36	Pittsburgh Yellowjackets	EHL	40	22	12	34	....	....	....	4	8	3	2	5	0
1936-37	**Toronto Maple Leafs**	**NHL**	**41**	**16**	**17**	**33**	**35**	**40**	**75**	**2**	**2**	**0**	**0**	**0**	**0**
	Syracuse Stars	AHL	5	2	3	5	....	....	....	0	....	....	....	....	....
1937-38	**Toronto Maple Leafs**	**NHL**	**48**	***26**	**26**	***52**	**56**	**54**	**110**	**4**	**7**	***7**	**1**	**8**	**2**
1938-39	**Toronto Maple Leafs**	**NHL**	**40**	**18**	**16**	**34**	**38**	**30**	**68**	**15**	**10**	***7**	**6**	**13**	**4**
1939-40	**Toronto Maple Leafs**	**NHL**	**43**	**21**	**19**	**40**	**46**	**38**	**84**	**13**	**10**	**3**	**1**	**4**	**0**
1940-41	**Toronto Maple Leafs**	**NHL**	**42**	**23**	**21**	**44**	**46**	**39**	**85**	**2**	**7**	**3**	**2**	**5**	**2**
1941-42	**Toronto Maple Leafs**	**NHL**	**48**	**23**	**18**	**41**	**40**	**27**	**67**	**6**	**9**	**2**	**3**	**5**	**2**
1942-43	**Montreal Canadiens**	**NHL**	**49**	**28**	**22**	**50**	**40**	**28**	**68**	**14**	**5**	**4**	**2**	**6**	**0**
1943-44	Simcoe Army	OHA Sr.	MILITARY SERVICE												
1944-45	Dartmouth RCAF	City Sr.	1	0	1	1	....	....	....	0	....	....	....	....	....
	Valleyfield Braves	QPHL	8	11	4	15	....	....	....	0	14	8	6	14	2
1945-46	Halifax RCAF	City Sr.	3	7	8	15	....	....	....	4	....	....	....	....	....
1946-47	Charlottetown Legionaires	PEI Sr.	4	10	8	18	....	....	....	16	11	*41	12	*53	4
1947-48	North Sydney Victorias	CBSHL	2	0	1	1	....	....	....	0	....	....	....	....	....
1948-49	Grand Falls All-Stars	Nfld.	DID NOT PLAY – COACHING												
1949-50	Saint John Beavers	NBSHL	49	48	24	72	....	....	....	40	11	1	4	5	12
1950-51	Moncton Hawks	MMHL	DID NOT PLAY – COACHING												
	NHL Totals		**311**	**155**	**139**	**294**	**301**	**256**	**557**	**56**	**50**	**26**	**15**	**41**	**10**

NHL First All-Star Team (1938, 1939) • Won Lady Byng Trophy (1938) • NHL Scoring Leader (1938) • NHL Second All-Star Team (1942)

Played in NHL All-Star Game (1939)

Traded to **Montreal** by **Toronto** for cash, April, 1942.

• DROUILLARD, CLARENCE   Clarence "Clare" Drouillard

C – L. 5'7", 150 lbs.   b: Windsor, Ont., 3/2/1914.   Deceased.

Season	Club	League	GP	G	A	Pts	AG	AA	APts	PIM	GP	G	A	Pts	PIM
1932-33	Windsor Walkerton Tech	H.S.	3	3	*3	6	....	....	....	0	....	....	....	....	....
	Windsor Wanderers	MOHL	18	9	3	12	....	....	....	14	....	....	....	....	....
1933-34	St. Michael's Majors	OHA	11	14	11	25	....	....	....	4	3	*4	2	6	4
1934-35	Windsor Bulldogs	IAHL	44	7	15	22	....	....	....	12	....	....	....	....	....
1935-36	Windsor Bulldogs	IAHL	48	14	15	29	....	....	....	43	8	2	3	5	6
1936-37	Pittsburgh Hornets	AHL	48	15	16	31	....	....	....	28	5	0	1	1	2
1937-38	**Detroit Red Wings**	**NHL**	**10**	**0**	**1**	**1**	**0**	**2**	**2**	**0**	....	....	....	....	....
	Pittsburgh–Providence	AHL	36	6	12	18	....	....	....	21	7	1	5	6	0
1938-39	Hershey Bears	AHL	50	9	17	26	....	....	....	20	3	0	0	0	0
1939-40	Pittsburgh Hornets	AHL	56	12	25	37	....	....	....	22	9	3	4	7	6
1940-41	Pittsburgh–Buffalo	AHL	46	6	15	21	....	....	....	14	....	....	....	....	....
1941-42	Buffalo–Philadelphia	AHL	51	4	10	14	....	....	....	6	....	....	....	....	....
1942-43	Windsor Abars	City Sr.	11	9	14	23	....	....	....	2	7	9	2	11	0
1943-44	Windsor Gotfredson	MOHL	9	14	11	25	....	....	....	2	3	2	3	5	2
1944-45	Windsor Gotfredson	MOHL	2	2	0	2	....	....	....	2	2	4	4	8	0
	NHL Totals		**10**	**0**	**1**	**1**	**0**	**2**	**2**	**0**	....	....	....	....	....

Traded to **Detroit** by **Windsor** (IAHL) for Joe Bretto and cash, February 26, 1936.

• DROUIN, POLLY   Polly (Paul-Emile) Drouin

LW – L. 5'7", 160 lbs.   b: Verdun, Que., 1/25/1937.   d: 1/1/1968.

Season	Club	League	GP	G	A	Pts	AG	AA	APts	PIM	GP	G	A	Pts	PIM
1931-32	Ottawa Primrose	City Jr.	15	6	3	9	....	....	....	8	4	0	1	1	0
1932-33	Ottawa Primrose	City Jr.	13	5	3	8	....	....	....	6	4	2	1	3	6
1933-34	Hull Lasalle	QJHL	16	20	*18	*38	....	....	....	47	4	4	3	7	4
	Hull Lasalle Seniors	OHA Sr.	1	0	0	0	....	....	....	0	....	....	....	....	....
1934-35	**Montreal Canadiens**	**NHL**	**4**	**0**	**0**	**0**	**0**	**0**	**0**	**0**	....	....	....	....	....
	Ottawa Senators	QSHL	20	10	7	17	....	....	....	8	8	2	0	2	*20
1935-36	**Montreal Canadiens**	**NHL**	**30**	**1**	**8**	**9**	**2**	**19**	**21**	**19**	....	....	....	....	....
	Ottawa Senators	QSHL	12	7	7	14	....	....	....	12	....	....	....	....	....
1936-37	**Montreal Canadiens**	**NHL**	**4**	**0**	**0**	**0**	**0**	**0**	**0**	**0**	....	....	....	....	....
	New Haven Eagles	IHL	27	10	13	23	....	....	....	33	....	....	....	....	....
1937-38	**Montreal Canadiens**	**NHL**	**31**	**7**	**13**	**20**	**15**	**27**	**42**	**8**	**1**	**0**	**0**	**0**	**0**
1938-39	**Montreal Canadiens**	**NHL**	**28**	**7**	**11**	**18**	**15**	**20**	**35**	**2**	**3**	**0**	**1**	**1**	**5**
1939-40	**Montreal Canadiens**	**NHL**	**42**	**4**	**11**	**15**	**9**	**22**	**31**	**51**	**1**	**0**	**0**	**0**	**0**
	New Haven Eagles	AHL	7	1	6	7	....	....	....	0	....	....	....	....	....
1940-41	**Montreal Canadiens**	**NHL**	**21**	**4**	**7**	**11**	**8**	**13**	**21**	**0**	....	....	....	....	....
	New Haven Eagles	AHL	19	8	4	12	....	....	....	8	2	0	1	1	0
1941-42	Washington Lions	AHL	56	23	21	44	....	....	....	31	2	0	2	2	0
1942-43	Ottawa Commandos	QSHL	29	22	14	36	....	....	....	31	....	....	....	....	....
	Ottawa RCAF	QSHL	11	10	19	29	....	....	....	6	....	....	....	....	....
1943-44			MILITARY SERVICE												
1944-45			MILITARY SERVICE												
1945-46	Hull Volants	QSHL	13	8	13	21	....	....	....	10	....	....	....	....	....
	Ottawa QMG	City Sr.	....	....	....	....	....	....	....	....	4	6	*14	*20	....
1946-47	St-Hyacinthe Gaulois	QPHL	40	24	30	54	....	....	....	20	4	1	0	1	0
	NHL Totals		**160**	**23**	**50**	**73**	**49**	**101**	**150**	**80**	**5**	**0**	**1**	**1**	**5**

Played in NHL All-Star Game (1939)

Claimed by **Montreal Canadiens** from **St. Louis** in Dispersal Draft, October 13, 1945. Traded to **Washington** (AHL) by **Montreal** for cash, October 9, 1941.

• DRUMMOND, JIM   Jim Drummond

D – L. 5'9", 170 lbs.   b: Toronto, Ont., 10/20/1918.   d: 12/12/1950.

Season	Club	League	GP	G	A	Pts	AG	AA	APts	PIM	GP	G	A	Pts	PIM
			REGULAR SEASON								PLAYOFFS				
1937-38	Toronto Marlboros	OHA	12	3	5	8	....	....	....	8	6	0	4	4	6
1938-39	Oshawa Generals	OHA	14	7	12	19	....	....	....	14	16	6	10	16	19
	Oshawa G-Men	OHA Sr.	1	0	0	0	....	....	....	0	....	....	....	....	....
1939-40	Toronto Goodyears	OHA Sr.	28	5	13	18	....	....	....	18	11	0	1	1	6
1940-41	Toronto Marlboros	OHA Sr.	30	8	8	16	....	....	....	18	17	0	1	1	17
1941-42	Cornwall Flyers	QSHL	37	3	11	14	....	....	....	36	5	0	0	0	0
1942-43	Cornwall Flyers	QSHL	27	5	6	11	....	....	....	16	6	0	0	0	4
1943-44			MILITARY SERVICE												
1944-45	**New York Rangers**	**NHL**	**2**	**0**	**0**	**0**	**0**	**0**	**0**	**0**	....	....	....	....	....
	New York Rovers	EHL	12	2	5	7	....	....	....	7	....	....	....	....	....
	Hershey Bears	AHL	24	1	4	5	....	....	....	4	11	3	2	5	2
1945-46	Hershey Bears	AHL	55	4	11	15	....	....	....	16	3	0	1	1	0
1946-47	Cleveland Barons	AHL	53	5	17	22	....	....	....	26	4	0	0	0	2
1947-48	Philadelphia Rockets	AHL	23	4	7	11	....	....	....	10	....	....	....	....	....
1948-49	Philadelphia Rockets	AHL	24	0	6	6	....	....	....	15	....	....	....	....	....
	NHL Totals		**2**	**0**	**0**	**0**	**0**	**0**	**0**	**0**	....	....	....	....	....

Signed as a free agent by **NY Rangers**, December 5, 1944.

• DRURY, HERB   Herb Drury

D/RW – R. 5'7", 165 lbs.   b: Midland, Ontario, 3/2/1895.   Deceased.

Season	Club	League	GP	G	A	Pts	AG	AA	APts	PIM	GP	G	A	Pts	PIM
1914-15	Midland Seniors	OHA Sr.	1	2	0	2	....	....	....	....	....	....	....	....	....
1915-16	Port Colborne Seniors	OHA Sr.	1	0	0	0	....	....	....	0	....	....	....	....	....
1916-17	Pittsburgh AA	USAHA	6	1	0	1	....	....	....	....	....	....	....	....	....
1917-18	Pittsburgh AA	USAHA	12	10	0	10	....	....	....	....	....	....	....	....	....
1918-19			MILITARY SERVICE												
1919-20	United States	WEC-A	5	23	0	23	....	....	....	....	....	....	....	....	....
1920-21	Pittsburgh AA	USAHA	STATISTICS NOT AVAILABLE												
1921-22	Pittsburgh Stars	USAHA	STATISTICS NOT AVAILABLE												
1922-23	Pittsburgh Yellowjackets	USAHA	20	5	0	5	....	....	....	....	....	....	....	....	....
1923-24	Pittsburgh Yellowjackets	USAHA	2	2	0	2	....	....	....	....	13	5	0	5	....
	United States	Olympics	5	22	3	25	....	....	....	....	....	....	....	....	....
1924-25	Pittsburgh Yellowjackets	USAHA	33	7	0	7	....	....	....	....	8	4	0	4	....
1925-26	**Pittsburgh Pirates**	**NHL**	**33**	**6**	**2**	**8**	**18**	**23**	**41**	**40**	**2**	**1**	**0**	**1**	**0**
1926-27	**Pittsburgh Pirates**	**NHL**	**42**	**5**	**1**	**6**	**14**	**8**	**22**	**48**	....	....	....	....	....
1927-28	**Pittsburgh Pirates**	**NHL**	**44**	**6**	**4**	**10**	**18**	**34**	**52**	**44**	**2**	**0**	**1**	**1**	**0**
1928-29	**Pittsburgh Pirates**	**NHL**	**43**	**5**	**4**	**9**	**20**	**37**	**57**	**49**	....	....	....	....	....
1929-30	**Pittsburgh Pirates**	**NHL**	**27**	**2**	**0**	**2**	**4**	**0**	**4**	**12**	....	....	....	....	....
1930-31	**Philadelphia Quakers**	**NHL**	**24**	**0**	**2**	**2**	**0**	**7**	**7**	**10**	....	....	....	....	....
	NHL Totals		**213**	**24**	**13**	**37**	**74**	**109**	**183**	**203**	**4**	**1**	**1**	**2**	**0**

Signed as a free agent by **Pittsburgh**, September 26, 1925. Transferred to **Philadelphia** after **Pittsburgh** franchise relocated, October 18, 1930.

• DUBE, GILLES   Gilles Dube

LW – L. 5'10", 165 lbs.   b: Sherbrooke, Que., 6/2/1927.

Season	Club	League	GP	G	A	Pts	AG	AA	APts	PIM	GP	G	A	Pts	PIM
1945-46	Sherbrooke Randies	QPHL	7	1	3	4	....	....	....	0	....	....	....	....	....
1946-47	Montreal Jr. Canadiens	QJHL	12	16	16	32	....	....	....	8	2	1	2	3	2
1947-48	Sherbrooke St. Xavier	QPHL	43	31	41	72	....	....	....	44	8	6	10	16	13
1948-49	Sherbrooke Saints	QSHL	62	30	56	86	....	....	....	56	12	3	7	10	6
1949-50	**Montreal Canadiens**	**NHL**	**12**	**1**	**2**	**3**	**1**	**3**	**4**	**2**	....	....	....	....	....
	Cincinnati Mohawks	AHL	46	19	18	37	....	....	....	12	....	....	....	....	....
1950-51	Cincinnati Mohawks	AHL	62	16	26	42	....	....	....	29	....	....	....	....	....
1951-52	Sherbrooke Saints	QSHL	51	17	15	32	....	....	....	33	11	5	6	11	10
1952-53	Sherbrooke Saints	QSHL	60	21	32	53	....	....	....	55	7	3	2	5	14
1953-54	Sherbrooke Saints	QHL	72	17	45	62	....	....	....	68	5	1	5	6	4
	Detroit Red Wings	**NHL**	....	....	....	....					**2**	**0**	**0**	**0**	**0**
1954-55	Shawinigan Cataracts	QHL	56	18	41	59	....	....	....	30	13	1	7	8	7
1955-56	Shawinigan Cataracts	QHL	64	*37	*54	*91	....	....		68	11	3	5	8	2
1956-57	Shawinigan Cataracts	QHL	58	12	31	43	....	....	....	38	....	....	....	....	....
	NHL Totals		**12**	**1**	**2**	**3**	**1**	**3**	**4**	**2**	**2**	**0**	**0**	**0**	**0**

QHL First All-Star Team (1956) • Won President's Cup (Scoring Champion - QHL) (1956)

Loaned to **Sherbrooke** (QSHL) by **Montreal** for cash, September, 1951. Signed as a free agent by **Detroit** to three game try-out contract, April 10, 1954.

• DUFF, DICK   *— see page 993*

• DUFOUR, MARC   *— see page 994*

• DUGGAN, JACK   Jack (John Herbert) Duggan

LW – L. 5'8", 185 lbs.   b: Ottawa, Ontario, 12/17/1898.   Deceased.

Season	Club	League	GP	G	A	Pts	AG	AA	APts	PIM	GP	G	A	Pts	PIM
1917-18	Ottawa St. Brigids	City Sr.	11	5	0	5	....	....	....	9	....	....	....	....	....
1918-19	Ottawa Munitions	City Sr.	7	3	1	4	....	....	....	3	....	....	....	....	....
1919-20	Ottawa Munitions	City Sr.	8	8	0	8	....	....	....	....	5	5	*5	10	....
1920-21	Ottawa Munitions	City Sr.	8	8	0	8	....	....	....	....	1	0	1	1	0
1921-22	Ottawa Munitions	City Sr.	13	8	6	14	....	....	....	6	....	....	....	....	....
1922-23	Ottawa St. Pats	City Sr.	14	3	1	4	....	....	....	....	10	5	0	5	2
1923-24	Ottawa Montagnards	City Sr.	12	3	0	3	....	....	....	....	6	3	1	4	....
1924-25	Ottawa Montagnards	City Sr.	16	3	1	4	....	....	....	....	7	2	0	2	10
1925-26	**Ottawa Senators**	**NHL**	**27**	**0**	**0**	**0**	**0**	**0**	**0**	**0**	**2**	**0**	**0**	**0**	**0**
	Ottawa Canadiens	City Sr.	1	0	0	0	....	....	....	0	....	....	....	....	....
1926-27	London Panthers	Can-Pro	32	4	1	5	....	....	....	38	4	1	0	1	6
1927-28	London Panthers	Can-Pro	34	3	0	3	....	....	....	32	....	....	....	....	....
1928-29	Niagara Falls Cataracts	Can-Pro	42	2	1	3	....	....	....	53	....	....	....	....	....
	NHL Totals		**27**	**0**	**0**	**0**	**0**	**0**	**0**	**0**	**2**	**0**	**0**	**0**	**0**

Signed as a free agent by **Ottawa**, December 14, 1925. Traded to **Hamilton** (IAHL) by **Ottawa** for cash, November 7, 1929.

• DUGUID, LORNE Lorne Duguid

LW – L. 5'11", 185 lbs. b: Bolton, Ont., 4/4/1910. d: 5/21/1981.

			REGULAR SEASON								PLAYOFFS				
Season	Club	League	GP	G	A	Pts	AG	AA	APts	PIM	GP	G	A	Pts	PIM
1927-28	Montreal Victorias	QJHL	11	*10	0	*10	....	....	....	4	....	....	....	....	....
1928-29	Montreal Victorias	QJHL	10	*8	0	*8	....	....	....	14	....	....	....	....	....
1929-30	Montreal Victorias	QSHL	10	3	0	3	....	....	....	12	1	0	0	0	0
1930-31	Windsor Bulldogs	IAHL	48	22	19	41	....	....	....	13	6	3	2	5	6
1931-32	**Montreal Maroons**	**NHL**	**13**	**0**	**0**	**0**	**0**	**0**	**0**	**6**	....	....	....	....	....
	Windsor Bulldogs	IAHL	35	11	8	19	....	....	....	36	6	2	1	3	4
1932-33	**Montreal Maroons**	**NHL**	**48**	**4**	**7**	**11**	**9**	**18**	**27**	**38**	**2**	**0**	**0**	**0**	**4**
1933-34	**Montreal Maroons**	**NHL**	**5**	**0**	**1**	**1**	**0**	**3**	**3**	**0**	....	....	....	....	....
	Windsor Bulldogs	IAHL	38	13	9	22	....	....	....	34	....	....	....	....	....
1934-35	**Detroit Red Wings**	**NHL**	**34**	**3**	**3**	**6**	**6**	**7**	**13**	**9**	....	....	....	....	....
	Detroit Olympics	IAHL	17	12	5	17	....	....	....	0	....	....	....	....	....
1935-36	**Detroit Red Wings**	**NHL**	**5**	**0**	**0**	**0**	**0**	**0**	**0**	**0**	....	....	....	....	....
	Boston Bruins	**NHL**	**29**	**1**	**4**	**5**	**2**	**10**	**12**	**2**	....	....	....	....	....
	Detroit Olympics	IAHL	12	4	6	10	....	....	....	14	....	....	....	....	....
1936-37	**Boston Bruins**	**NHL**	**1**	**1**	**0**	**1**	**2**	**0**	**2**	**2**	....	....	....	....	....
	Providence Reds	AHL	47	20	21	41	....	....	....	16	3	2	0	2	2
1937-38	Cleveland Barons	AHL	48	22	27	49	....	....	....	22	2	1	1	2	0
1938-39	Pittsburgh Hornets	AHL	1	1	0	1	....	....	....	0	....	....	....	....	....
	Cleveland Barons	AHL	54	19	32	51	....	....	....	23	9	2	*7	9	4
1939-40	Cleveland–Pittsburgh	AHL	44	10	12	22	....	....	....	18	9	1	0	1	2
1940-41	Pittsburgh Hornets	AHL	48	7	21	28	....	....	....	12	6	1	0	1	4
	NHL Totals		**135**	**9**	**15**	**24**	**19**	**38**	**57**	**57**	**2**	**0**	**0**	**0**	**4**

AHL First All-Star Team (1938)

Signed as a free agent by **Montreal Maroons**, October 19, 1931. Traded to **Detroit** by **Montreal Maroons** for cash, October 28, 1934. Traded to **Boston** by **Detroit** for Gene Carrigan, December 29, 1935.

• DUKOWSKI, DUKE Duke (Laudas Joseph) Dukowski

D – L. 5'10", 185 lbs. b: Regina, Sask., 8/30/1902. Deceased.

Season	Club	League	GP	G	A	Pts	AG	AA	APts	PIM	GP	G	A	Pts	PIM
1916-17	Regina Vics	SSHL	3	0	1	1	....	....	....	0	....	....	....	....	....
1917-18	Regina Pats	SJHL	6	12	2	14	....	....	....	6	5	13	8	21	7
1918-19	Regina Pats	SJHL	10	*40	8	*48	....	....	....	6	8	*32	6	*38	12
1919-20	Regina Pats	SJHL	5	*14	1	*15	....	....	....	*16	....	....	....	....	....
	Regina Vics	SSHL	1	0	0	0	....	....	....	0	....	....	....	....	....
	Regina Braves	SSHL	1	1	0	1	....	....	....	0	....	....	....	....	....
1920-21	Regina Vics	SSHL	14	4	1	5	....	....	....	42	4	1	0	1	6
1921-22	Saskatoon-Moose Jaw	WCHL	21	13	2	15	....	....	....	19	....	....	....	....	....
1922-23	Regina Capitals	WCHL	29	6	0	6	....	....	....	20	2	0	1	1	2
1923-24	Regina Capitals	WCHL	30	8	3	11	....	....	....	39	2	0	0	0	6
1924-25	Regina Capitals	WCHL	27	13	4	17	....	....	....	86	....	....	....	....	....
1925-26	Portland Rosebuds	WHL	29	5	7	12	....	....	....	46	....	....	....	....	....
1926-27	**Chicago Black Hawks**	**NHL**	**28**	**3**	**2**	**5**	**9**	**17**	**26**	**16**	**2**	**0**	**0**	**0**	**0**
1927-28	Kansas City Pla-Mors	AHA	37	9	3	12	....	....	....	87	3	0	0	0	2
1928-29	Kansas City Pla-Mors	AHA	40	10	5	15	....	....	....	101	....	....	....	....	....
1929-30	**Chicago Black Hawks**	**NHL**	**44**	**7**	**10**	**17**	**14**	**32**	**46**	**42**	**2**	**0**	**0**	**0**	**6**
1930-31	**Chicago Black Hawks**	**NHL**	**25**	**1**	**3**	**4**	**2**	**11**	**13**	**28**	....	....	....	....	....
	New York Americans	**NHL**	**12**	**1**	**1**	**2**	**2**	**4**	**6**	**12**	....	....	....	....	....
1931-32	New Haven Eagles	Can-Am	40	6	9	15	....	....	....	102	2	0	1	1	6
1932-33	**New York Americans**	**NHL**	**48**	**4**	**7**	**11**	**9**	**18**	**27**	**43**	....	....	....	....	....
1933-34	**New York Americans**	**NHL**	**9**	**0**	**1**	**1**	**0**	**3**	**3**	**11**	....	....	....	....	....
	Chicago Black Hawks	**NHL**	**5**	**0**	**0**	**0**	**0**	**0**	**0**	**2**	....	....	....	....	....
	New York Rangers	**NHL**	**29**	**0**	**6**	**6**	**0**	**16**	**16**	**18**	**2**	**0**	**0**	**0**	**0**
	Syracuse Stars	IAHL	4	0	0	0	....	....	....	8	....	....	....	....	....
	NHL Totals		**200**	**16**	**30**	**46**	**36**	**101**	**137**	**172**	**6**	**0**	**0**	**0**	**6**
	Other Major League Totals		136	45	16	61	....	....	....	210	4	0	1	1	8

Signed as a free agent by **Saskatoon** (WCHL), November 17, 1921. Transferred to **Moose Jaw** (WCHL) after **Saskatoon** (WCHL) franchise relocated, February 1, 1922. Rights transferred to **Chicago** after NHL club purchased **Portland** (WHL) franchise, May 15, 1926. Claimed on waivers by **NY Americans** from **Chicago**, February 13, 1931. Loaned to **Chicago** by **NY Americans** for remainder of 1933-34 season, December 15, 1933. Recalled by **NY Americans** and traded to **NY Rangers** for cash, January 3, 1934.

• DUMART, WOODY Woody "Porky" Dumart **HHOF**

LW – L. 6', 190 lbs. b: Kitchener, Ont., 12/23/1916.

Season	Club	League	GP	G	A	Pts	AG	AA	APts	PIM	GP	G	A	Pts	PIM
1933-34	Kitchener Empires	OHA	12	8	3	11	....	....	....	12	3	1	*3	4	0
1934-35	Kitchener Greenshirts	OHA	17	17	11	*28	....	....	....	10	3	3	1	4	2
1935-36	**Boston Bruins**	**NHL**	**1**	**0**	**0**	**0**	**0**	**0**	**0**	**0**	....	....	....	....	....
	Boston Cubs	Can-Am	46	11	10	21	....	....	....	15	....	....	....	....	....
1936-37	**Boston Bruins**	**NHL**	**17**	**4**	**4**	**8**	**9**	**9**	**18**	**2**	**3**	**0**	**0**	**0**	**0**
	Providence Reds	AHL	32	4	7	11	....	....	....	10	....	....	....	....	....
1937-38	**Boston Bruins**	**NHL**	**48**	**13**	**14**	**27**	**27**	**29**	**56**	**6**	**3**	**0**	**0**	**0**	**0**
1938-39	**Boston Bruins**	**NHL**	**46**	**14**	**15**	**29**	**30**	**28**	**58**	**2**	**12**	**1**	**3**	**4**	**6**
1939-40	**Boston Bruins**	**NHL**	**48**	**22**	**21**	**43**	**48**	**42**	**90**	**16**	**6**	**1**	**0**	**1**	**0**
1940-41	**Boston Bruins**	**NHL**	**40**	**18**	**15**	**33**	**36**	**27**	**63**	**2**	**11**	**1**	**3**	**4**	**9**
1941-42	**Boston Bruins**	**NHL**	**35**	**14**	**15**	**29**	**24**	**23**	**47**	**8**	....	....	....	....	....
	Ottawa RCAF	City Sr.	....	....	....	....	....	....	....	....	19	*21	14	*35	10
1942-43	Ottawa RCAF	OHA Sr.	6	6	5	11	....	....	....	....	....	....	....	....	....
1943-44			MILITARY SERVICE												
1944-45			MILITARY SERVICE												
1945-46	**Boston Bruins**	**NHL**	**50**	**22**	**12**	**34**	**34**	**22**	**56**	**2**	**10**	**4**	**3**	**7**	**0**
1946-47	**Boston Bruins**	**NHL**	**60**	**24**	**28**	**52**	**33**	**40**	**73**	**12**	**5**	**1**	**1**	**2**	**8**
1947-48	**Boston Bruins**	**NHL**	**59**	**21**	**16**	**37**	**31**	**23**	**54**	**14**	**5**	**0**	**0**	**0**	**0**
1948-49	**Boston Bruins**	**NHL**	**59**	**11**	**12**	**23**	**17**	**19**	**36**	**6**	**5**	**3**	**0**	**3**	**0**
1949-50	**Boston Bruins**	**NHL**	**69**	**14**	**25**	**39**	**19**	**32**	**51**	**14**	....	....	....	....	....
1950-51	**Boston Bruins**	**NHL**	**70**	**20**	**21**	**41**	**27**	**27**	**54**	**7**	**6**	**1**	**2**	**3**	**0**
1951-52	**Boston Bruins**	**NHL**	**39**	**5**	**8**	**13**	**7**	**10**	**17**	**0**	**7**	**0**	**1**	**1**	**0**
1952-53	**Boston Bruins**	**NHL**	**62**	**5**	**9**	**14**	**8**	**12**	**20**	**2**	**11**	**0**	**2**	**2**	**0**
1953-54	**Boston Bruins**	**NHL**	**69**	**4**	**3**	**7**	**6**	**4**	**10**	**6**	**4**	**0**	**0**	**0**	**0**
1954-55	Providence Reds	AHL	15	2	2	4	....	....	....	0	....	....	....	....	....
	NHL Totals		**772**	**211**	**218**	**429**	**356**	**347**	**703**	**99**	**88**	**12**	**15**	**27**	**23**

NHL Second All-Star Team (1940, 1941, 1947)

Played in NHL All-Star Game (1947, 1948)

Signed as a free agent by **Boston**, October 9, 1935.

• DUNCAN, ART Art "Dunc" Duncan

D – R. 6'1", 190 lbs. b: Sault Ste. Marie, Ont., 7/4/1894. d: 4/13/1975.

Season	Club	League	GP	G	A	Pts	AG	AA	APts	PIM	GP	G	A	Pts	PIM
1915-16	Vancouver Millionaires	PCHA	17	7	4	11	....	....	....	25	....	....	....	....	....
1916-17	Toronto 228th Battalion	NHA	8	4	1	5	....	....	....	12	....	....	....	....	....
1917-18			MILITARY SERVICE												
1918-19	Vancouver Millionaires	PCHA	17	2	1	3	....	....	....	0	2	0	0	0	0
1919-20	Vancouver Millionaires	PCHA	22	5	9	14	....	....	....	3	2	0	0	0	0
1920-21	Vancouver Millionaires	PCHA	24	3	5	8	....	....	....	6	7	2	4	6	2
1921-22	Vancouver Millionaires	PCHA	24	5	9	14	....	....	....	25	9	3	0	3	6
1922-23	Vancouver Maroons	PCHA	25	15	6	21	....	....	....	8	6	3	2	5	0
1923-24	Vancouver Maroons	PCHA	30	*21	*10	*31	....	....	....	44	7	1	0	1	6
1924-25	Vancouver Maroons	WCHL	26	5	5	10	....	....	....	28	....	....	....	....	....
1925-26	Calgary Tigers	WHL	29	9	4	13	....	....	....	30	....	....	....	....	....
1926-27	**Detroit Cougars**	**NHL**	**34**	**3**	**2**	**5**	**9**	**17**	**26**	**26**	....	....	....	....	....
1927-28	**Toronto Maple Leafs**	**NHL**	**43**	**7**	**5**	**12**	**21**	**42**	**63**	**97**	....	....	....	....	....
1928-29	**Toronto Maple Leafs**	**NHL**	**39**	**4**	**4**	**8**	**16**	**37**	**53**	**53**	**4**	**0**	**0**	**0**	**4**
1929-30	**Toronto Maple Leafs**	**NHL**	**38**	**4**	**5**	**9**	**8**	**16**	**24**	**49**	....	....	....	....	....
1930-31	**Toronto Maple Leafs**	**NHL**	**2**	**0**	**0**	**0**	**0**	**0**	**0**	**0**	**1**	**0**	**0**	**0**	**0**
1931-32	**Toronto Maple Leafs**	**NHL**	DID NOT PLAY – COACHING												
	NHL Totals		**156**	**18**	**16**	**34**	**54**	**112**	**166**	**225**	**5**	**0**	**0**	**0**	**4**
	Other Major League Totals		222	76	54	130	....	....	....	181	33	9	6	15	14

PCHA Second All-Star Team (1919, 1923) • PCHA First All-Star Team (1920, 1922, 1924)

Signed as a free agent by **Vancouver** (PCHA), December 27, 1918. Traded to **Calgary** (WHL) by **Vancouver** (WHL) for Reg Mackay, October 16, 1925. Traded to **Chicago** by **Calgary** (WHL) for cash, May 15, 1926. Rights traded to **Detroit Cougars** by **Chicago** for Art Gagne and Gord Fraser, October 18, 1926. Traded to **Toronto** by **Detroit Cougars** for Bill Brydge, June, 1927.

• DUNLAP, FRANK Frank "Judge / Biff" Dunlap

RW/LW – L. 6', 185 lbs. b: Ottawa, Ont., 8/10/1924. d: 10/26/1993.

Season	Club	League	GP	G	A	Pts	AG	AA	APts	PIM	GP	G	A	Pts	PIM
1941-42	Ottawa St. Pats	City Jr.	....	....	....	....	....	....	....	....	7	9	8	17	4
1942-43	St. Michael's Majors	OHA	11	8	6	14	....	....	....	10	6	4	2	6	2
1943-44	St. Michael's Majors	OHA	15	11	14	25	....	....	....	20	12	6	8	14	10
	Toronto Maple Leafs	**NHL**	**15**	**0**	**1**	**1**	**0**	**1**	**1**	**2**	....	....	....	....	....
1944-45	Ottawa Commandos	QSHL	24	16	18	34	....	....	....	20	2	0	0	0	0
	Ottawa Navy	QSHL	7	4	8	12	....	....	....	9	....	....	....	....	....
1945-46	Hull Volants	QSHL	33	17	19	36	....	....	....	0	....	....	....	....	....
1946-47	Ottawa Senators	QSHL	17	7	5	12	....	....	....	4	1	0	0	0	0
	Ottawa Senators	City Sr.	1	1	3	4	....	....	....	0	....	....	....	....	....
1947-48	Pembroke Lumber Kings	OVSHL	14	10	12	22	....	....	....	2	5	4	1	5	2
	Renfrew Lions	OVSHL	....	....	....	....	....	....	....	....	5	1	4	5	0
	NHL Totals		**15**	**0**	**1**	**1**	**0**	**1**	**1**	**2**	....	....	....	....	....

• Played only home games in 1943-44 season while attending law school

• DUSSAULT, NORM Norm Dussault

C – L. 5'8", 165 lbs. b: Springfield, MA, 9/26/1925.

Season	Club	League	GP	G	A	Pts	AG	AA	APts	PIM	GP	G	A	Pts	PIM
1945-46	Baltimore Clippers	EHL	43	12	16	28	....	....	....	13	7	0	0	0	0
1946-47	Victoriaville Tigers	QPHL	42	35	36	71	....	....	....	39	5	2	1	3	6
1947-48	**Montreal Canadiens**	**NHL**	**28**	**5**	**10**	**15**	**7**	**15**	**22**	**4**	....	....	....	....	....
	Victoriaville Tigers	QPHL	31	24	24	48	....	....	....	9	....	....	....	....	....
1948-49	**Montreal Canadiens**	**NHL**	**47**	**9**	**8**	**17**	**14**	**13**	**27**	**6**	**2**	**0**	**0**	**0**	**0**
1949-50	**Montreal Canadiens**	**NHL**	**67**	**13**	**24**	**37**	**17**	**31**	**48**	**22**	**5**	**3**	**1**	**4**	**0**
1950-51	**Montreal Canadiens**	**NHL**	**64**	**4**	**20**	**24**	**5**	**26**	**31**	**15**	....	....	....	....	....
1951-52	Chicoutimi Sagueneens	QSHL	48	16	23	39	....	....	....	21	18	3	11	14	4
1952-53	Chicoutimi Sagueneens	QSHL	60	23	20	43	....	....	....	10	20	4	2	6	6
1953-54	Chicoutimi Sagueneens	QHL	68	25	34	59	....	....	....	14	5	0	2	2	0
1954-55	Chicoutimi Sagueneens	QHL	60	10	32	42	....	....	....	14	5	0	1	1	2
	NHL Totals		**206**	**31**	**62**	**93**	**43**	**85**	**128**	**47**	**7**	**3**	**1**	**4**	**0**

Traded to **Chicoutimi** (QSHL) by **Montreal** for cash, November 21, 1951.

• DUTTON, RED Red (Mervyn A.) Dutton **HHOF**

D – R. 6', 185 lbs. b: Russell, Man., 7/23/1898. d: 3/15/1987.

Season	Club	League	GP	G	A	Pts	AG	AA	APts	PIM	GP	G	A	Pts	PIM
1919-20	Winnipeg Winnipegs	MSHL	8	6	7	13	....	....	....	10	2	0	0	0	6
1920-21	Calgary Tigers	Big 4	15	5	3	8	....	....	....	*38	....	....	....	....	....
1921-22	Calgary Tigers	WCHL	22	16	5	21	....	....	....	*73	2	0	0	0	0
1922-23	Calgary Tigers	WCHL	18	2	4	6	....	....	....	24	....	....	....	....	....
1923-24	Calgary Tigers	WCHL	30	6	7	13	....	....	....	*54	7	1	1	2	7
1924-25	Calgary Tigers	WCHL	23	8	4	12	....	....	....	72	2	0	0	0	6
1925-26	Calgary Tigers	WHL	30	10	5	15	....	....	....	87	....	....	....	....	....
1926-27	**Montreal Maroons**	**NHL**	**44**	**4**	**4**	**8**	**12**	**34**	**46**	**108**	**2**	**0**	**0**	**0**	**4**
1927-28	**Montreal Maroons**	**NHL**	**42**	**7**	**6**	**13**	**21**	**51**	**72**	**94**	**9**	**1**	**0**	**1**	**27**
1928-29	**Montreal Maroons**	**NHL**	**44**	**1**	**3**	**4**	**4**	**27**	**31**	***139**	....	....	....	....	....
1929-30	**Montreal Maroons**	**NHL**	**43**	**3**	**13**	**16**	**6**	**42**	**48**	**98**	**4**	**0**	**0**	**0**	**2**
1930-31	**New York Americans**	**NHL**	**44**	**1**	**11**	**12**	**2**	**40**	**42**	**71**	....	....	....	....	....
1931-32	**New York Americans**	**NHL**	**47**	**3**	**5**	**8**	**6**	**14**	**20**	***107**	....	....	....	....	....
1932-33	**New York Americans**	**NHL**	**43**	**0**	**2**	**2**	**0**	**5**	**5**	**74**	....	....	....	....	....
1933-34	**New York Americans**	**NHL**	**48**	**2**	**8**	**10**	**4**	**21**	**25**	**65**	....	....	....	....	....
1934-35	**New York Americans**	**NHL**	**48**	**3**	**7**	**10**	**6**	**16**	**22**	**46**	....	....	....	....	....
1935-36	**New York Americans**	**NHL**	**46**	**5**	**8**	**13**	**12**	**19**	**31**	**69**	**3**	**0**	**0**	**0**	**0**
	NHL Totals		**449**	**29**	**67**	**96**	**73**	**269**	**342**	**871**	**18**	**1**	**0**	**1**	**33**
	Other Major League Totals		123	42	25	67	....	....	....	310	11	1	1	2	13

WCHL First All-Star Team (1922, 1924) • Won Lester Patrick Trophy (1993)

Played in NHL All-Star Game (1934)

Signed as a free agent by **Calgary** (WCHL), November 20, 1921. Traded to **Montreal Maroons** by **Calgary** (WHL) for cash, September 11, 1926. Traded to **NY Americans** by **Montreal Maroons** with Mike Neville, Hap Emms and Frank Carson for $35,000, May 14, 1930.

• DYCK, HENRY Henry Dyck

C/LW – L. 5'8", 155 lbs. b: Herbert, Sask., 9/5/1912. Deceased.

Season	Club	League	GP	G	A	Pts	AG	AA	APts	PIM	GP	G	A	Pts	PIM
			REGULAR SEASON								PLAYOFFS				
1930-31	Seattle Eskimos	PCHL	34	1	1	2	....	....	....	18	4	0	0	0	2
1931-32	Syracuse Stars	IAHL	2	0	0	0	....	....	....	0	....	....	....	....	....
	Hollywood Stars	Cal-Pro	....	13	12	25	....	....	....	....	....	....	....	....	....
1932-33	Saskatoon Crescents	WCHL	....	23	12	35	....	....	....	18	....	....	....	....	....
1933-34	Seattle Seahawks	NWHL	34	11	9	20	....	....	....	24	....	....	....	....	....
1934-35	Vancouver Lions	NWHL	32	11	8	19	....	....	....	20	8	0	1	1	6
1935-36	Vancouver–Edmonton	NWHL	41	17	6	23	....	....	....	8	....	....	....	....	....
1936-37	Spokane–Seattle	PCHL	10	2	0	2	....	....	....	2	....	....	....	....	....
1937-38	Tulsa Oilers	AHA	43	10	20	30	....	....	....	22	4	1	2	3	5
1938-39	Tulsa Oilers	AHA	48	16	18	34	....	....	....	31	8	4	1	5	0
1939-40	Kansas City Greyhounds	AHA	39	14	16	30	....	....	....	19	....	....	....	....	....
1940-41	Kansas City Americans	AHA	5	0	1	1	....	....	....	0	....	....	....	....	....
1941-42	Johnstown Bluebirds	EHL	58	46	40	86	....	....	....	32	7	11	5	16	2
1942-43	Buffalo–Washington	AHL	33	4	11	15	....	....	....	8	....	....	....	....	....
1943-44	**New York Rangers**	**NHL**	**1**	**0**	**0**	**0**	**0**	**0**	**0**	**0**	....	....	....	....	....
	Boston Olympics	EHL	1	1	0	1	....	....	....	0	9	7	8	15	4
	Toronto Staffords	OHA Sr.	....	23	18	41	....	....	....	14	11	15	12	*27	6
1944-45	Toronto Staffords	OHA Sr.	1	0	0	0	....	....	....	0	....	....	....	....	....
	NHL Totals		**1**	**0**	**0**	**0**	**0**	**0**	**0**	**0**	....	....	....	....	....

EHL First All-Star Team (1942)

Traded to **Vancouver** (NWHL) by **Seattle** (NWHL) for Sam McAdam, November, 1934.

• DYE, BABE Babe (Cecil) Dye **HHOF**

RW – R. 5'8", 150 lbs. b: Hamilton, Ont., 5/13/1898. d: 1/2/1962.

Season	Club	League	GP	G	A	Pts	AG	AA	APts	PIM	GP	G	A	Pts	PIM
1916-17	Toronto Aura Lee	OHA	8	*31	0	*31	....	....	....	....	....	....	....	....	....
1917-18	Toronto De Lasalle	OHA	STATISTICS NOT AVAILABLE												
1918-19	Toronto St. Pats	OHA Sr.	9	13	1	14	....	....	....	....	2	3	0	3	0
1919-20	**Toronto St. Pats**	**NHL**	**23**	**11**	**3**	**14**	**25**	**20**	**45**	**10**	....	....	....	....	....
1920-21	**Hamilton Tigers**	**NHL**	**1**	***2**	**0**	**2**	**5**	**0**	**5**	**0**	....	....	....	....	....
	Toronto St. Pats	**NHL**	**23**	***33**	**5**	**38**	**89**	**44**	**133**	**32**	**2**	**0**	**0**	**0**	**7**
1921-22	**Toronto St. Pats**	**NHL**	**24**	**31**	**7**	**38**	**90**	**44**	**134**	**39**	**7**	**11**	**1**	**12**	**5**
1922-23	**Toronto St. Pats**	**NHL**	**22**	***26**	**11**	***37**	**92**	**103**	**195**	**19**	....	....	....	....	....
1923-24	**Toronto St.Pats**	**NHL**	**19**	**17**	**2**	**19**	**72**	**35**	**107**	**23**	....	....	....	....	....
1924-25	**Toronto St. Pats**	**NHL**	**29**	***38**	**6**	***44**	**140**	**81**	**221**	**41**	**2**	**0**	**0**	**0**	**0**
1925-26	**Toronto St.Pats**	**NHL**	**31**	**18**	**5**	**23**	**57**	**58**	**115**	**26**	....	....	....	....	....
1926-27	**Chicago Black Hawks**	**NHL**	**41**	**25**	**5**	**30**	**74**	**43**	**117**	**14**	**2**	**0**	**0**	**0**	**2**
1927-28	**Chicago Black Hawks**	**NHL**	**10**	**0**	**0**	**0**	**0**	**0**	**0**	**0**	....	....	....	....	....
1928-29	**New York Americans**	**NHL**	**42**	**1**	**0**	**1**	**4**	**0**	**4**	**17**	**2**	**0**	**0**	**0**	**0**
1929-30	New Haven Eagles	Can-Am	34	11	4	15	....	....	....	16	....	....	....	....	....
1930-31	**Toronto Maple Leafs**	**NHL**	**6**	**0**	**0**	**0**	**0**	**0**	**0**	**0**	....	....	....	....	....
	St. Louis Flyers	AHA	DID NOT PLAY – COACHING												
1931-32	Chicago Shamrocks	AHA	DID NOT PLAY – COACHING												
	NHL Totals		**271**	**202**	**44**	**246**	**648**	**428**	**1076**	**221**	**15**	**11**	**1**	**12**	**14**

NHL Scoring Leader (1923, 1925)

Signed as a free agent by **Toronto St. Pats**, December 15, 1919. Loaned to **Hamilton** by **Toronto St. Pats**, December 4, 1920. Recalled by **Toronto St. Pats** from **Hamilton**, December 21, 1921. Traded to **Chicago** by **Toronto** for cash, October 18, 1926. Traded to **NY Americans** by **Chicago** for cash, June, 1928. Traded to **New Haven** (Can-Pro) by **NY Americans** for George Massecar, November 13, 1929. Signed as a free agent by **Toronto**, February, 1930.

• DYTE, JOHN John "Jack" Dyte

D – L. 6', b: New Liskeard, Ontario, 10/13/1918.

Season	Club	League	GP	G	A	Pts	AG	AA	APts	PIM	GP	G	A	Pts	PIM
1937-38	Barrie Colts	Jr. B	STATISTICS NOT AVAILABLE												
1938-39	Niagara Falls Cataracts	OHA Sr.	20	3	3	6	....	....	....	31	....	....	....	....	....
1939-40	Baltimore Orioles	EHL	57	8	18	26	....	....	....	57	9	0	2	2	6
1940-41	Baltimore Orioles	EHL	64	15	16	31	....	....	....	68	....	....	....	....	....
1941-42	Johnstown Bluebirds	EHL	60	15	21	36	....	....	....	88	7	4	4	8	8
1942-43	Montreal Royals	QSHL	13	1	1	2	....	....	....	20	....	....	....	....	....
1943-44	**Chicago Black Hawks**	**NHL**	**27**	**1**	**0**	**1**	**1**	**0**	**1**	**31**	....	....	....	....	....
	Providence–Buffalo	AHL	22	0	1	1	....	....	....	16	9	0	0	0	2
1944-45	Buffalo Bisons	AHL	52	2	8	10	....	....	....	56	6	0	0	0	2
1945-46	St. Louis Flyers	AHL	60	1	6	7	....	....	....	67	....	....	....	....	....
1946-47	New Liskeard Pioneers	City Sr.	DID NOT PLAY – COACHING												
1947-48	New Liskeard Pioneers	City Sr.	DID NOT PLAY – COACHING												
1948-49	North Sydney Victorias	CBSHL	58	6	18	24	....	....	....	65	6	3	1	4	4
	NHL Totals		**27**	**1**	**0**	**1**	**1**	**0**	**1**	**31**	....	....	....	....	....

EHL Second All-Star Team (1940) • EHL First All-Star Team (1941)

Signed as a free agent by **Chicago**, October 7, 1943. Traded to **Buffalo** (AHL) by **Chicago** for cash, June, 1944.

• EDDOLLS, FRANK Frank Eddolls

D – L. 5'8", 180 lbs. b: Lachine, Que., 7/5/1921. d: 8/13/1961.

Season	Club	League	GP	G	A	Pts	AG	AA	APts	PIM	GP	G	A	Pts	PIM
			REGULAR SEASON								PLAYOFFS				
1937-38	Verdun Jr. Maple Leafs	Mtl-Jr.	12	2	5	7	....	....	....	8	4	0	1	1	2
	Verdun Maple Leafs	Mtl-Sr.	1	0	0	0	....	....	....	0	....	....	....	....	....
1938-39	Verdun Jr. Maple Leafs	Mtl-Jr.	10	9	5	14	....	....	....	24	10	5	5	10	30
	Verdun Maple Leafs	Mtl-Sr.	1	0	0	0	....	....	....	0	....	....	....	....	....
1939-40	Oshawa Generals	OHA	15	13	8	21	....	....	....	8	7	3	5	8	8
1940-41	Oshawa Generals	OHA	16	9	12	21	....	....	....	31	17	5	*16	21	20
1941-42	Hershey Bears	AHL	54	8	11	19	....	....	....	30	10	0	1	1	8
1942-43	Montreal RCAF	QSHL	35	8	10	18	....	....	....	42	12	2	6	8	8
1943-44	Montreal RCAF	City Sr.	1	0	0	0	....	....	....	2	....	....	....	....	....
	Montreal Canada Car	City Sr.	1	0	0	0	....	....	....	0	....	....	....	....	....
	Montreal Services	City Sr.	3	0	0	0	....	....	....	0	....	....	....	....	....
1944-45	**Montreal Canadiens**	**NHL**	**43**	**5**	**8**	**13**	**7**	**13**	**20**	**20**	**3**	**0**	**0**	**0**	**0**
1945-46	**Montreal Canadiens**	**NHL**	**8**	**0**	**1**	**1**	**0**	**2**	**2**	**6**	**8**	**0**	**1**	**1**	**2**
	Buffalo Bisons	AHL	34	6	23	29	....	....	....	52	....	....	....	....	....
1946-47	**Montreal Canadiens**	**NHL**	**6**	**0**	**0**	**0**	**0**	**0**	**0**	**0**	**7**	**0**	**0**	**0**	**4**
	Buffalo Bisons	AHL	29	3	7	10	....	....	....	18	4	0	5	5	0
1947-48	**New York Rangers**	**NHL**	**58**	**6**	**13**	**19**	**9**	**19**	**28**	**16**	**2**	**0**	**0**	**0**	**0**
1948-49	**New York Rangers**	**NHL**	**34**	**4**	**2**	**6**	**6**	**3**	**9**	**10**	....	....	....	....	....
1949-50	**New York Rangers**	**NHL**	**58**	**2**	**6**	**8**	**3**	**8**	**11**	**20**	**11**	**0**	**1**	**1**	**4**
1950-51	**New York Rangers**	**NHL**	**68**	**3**	**8**	**11**	**4**	**10**	**14**	**24**	....	....	....	....	....
1951-52	**New York Rangers**	**NHL**	**42**	**3**	**5**	**8**	**4**	**6**	**10**	**18**	....	....	....	....	....
	Saskatoon Quakers	PCHL	12	3	6	9	....	....	....	6	....	....	....	....	....
	Cincinnati Mohawks	AHL	12	0	4	4	....	....	....	8	....	....	....	....	....
1952-53	Buffalo Bisons	AHL	50	5	25	30	....	....	....	24	....	....	....	....	....
1953-54	Buffalo Bisons	AHL	63	3	52	55	....	....	....	45	3	0	2	2	2
1954-55	**Chicago Black Hawks**	**NHL**	DID NOT PLAY – COACHING												
	NHL Totals		**317**	**23**	**43**	**66**	**33**	**61**	**94**	**114**	**31**	**0**	**2**	**2**	**10**

Won Vimy Trophy (MVP - QSHL) (1943) • AHL First All-Star Team (1954)

Played in NHL All-Star Game (1951)

Rights traded to **Toronto** by **Montreal** for the rights to Joe Benoit, June 7, 1940. Traded to **Montreal** by **Toronto** for the rights to Ted Kennedy, September, 1942. Traded to **NY Rangers** by **Montreal** with Buddy O'Connor for Hal Laycoe, Joe Bell and George Robertson, August 19, 1947. Traded to **Montreal** by **NY Rangers** for cash, October, 1952.

• EDMUNDSON, GARRY Garry "Duke" Edmundson

LW – L. 6', 173 lbs. b: Sexsmith, Alta., 5/6/1932.

Season	Club	League	GP	G	A	Pts	AG	AA	APts	PIM	GP	G	A	Pts	PIM
1948-49	Edmonton Athletic Club	City Jr.	....	5	10	15	....	....	....	14	....	....	....	....	....
1949-50	Edmonton Athletic Club	AJHL	....	19	13	32	....	....	....	11	....	....	....	....	....
1950-51	Regina Pats	WCJHL	23	12	6	18	....	....	....	38	12	11	8	19	13
1951-52	Kitchener Greenshirts	OHA	51	35	53	88	....	....	....	80	4	1	1	2	6
	Montreal Canadiens	**NHL**	**1**	**0**	**0**	**0**	**0**	**0**	**0**	**2**	**2**	**0**	**0**	**0**	**4**
1952-53	Montreal Royals	QSHL	12	4	3	7	....	....	....	8	12	3	4	7	16
1953-54	Cincinnati Mohawks	IHL	64	25	53	78	....	....	....	105	11	2	4	6	9
1954-55	Cincinnati Mohawks	IHL	60	24	32	56	....	....	....	86	9	3	6	9	20
1955-56	Cincinnati Mohawks	IHL	56	35	52	87	....	....	....	95	8	3	3	6	10
	Winnipeg Warriors	WHL	2	0	0	0	....	....	....	2	....	....	....	....	....
1956-57	Shawinigan Cataracts	QHL	3	0	1	1	....	....	....	16	....	....	....	....	....
	Cincinnati Mohawks	IHL	52	23	25	48	....	....	....	74	7	3	5	8	*28
1957-58	New Westminster Royals	WHL	69	21	43	64	....	....	....	*188	4	1	3	4	2
1958-59	Springfield Indians	AHL	62	17	27	44	....	....	....	113	....	....	....	....	....
1959-60	**Toronto Maple Leafs**	**NHL**	**39**	**4**	**6**	**10**	**5**	**6**	**11**	**47**	**9**	**0**	**1**	**1**	**4**
1960-61	**Toronto Maple Leafs**	**NHL**	**3**	**0**	**0**	**0**	**0**	**0**	**0**	**0**	....	....	....	....	....
	Rochester Americans	AHL	68	25	44	69	....	....	....	62	....	....	....	....	....
1961-62	San Francisco Seals	WHL	51	15	21	36				53	2	0	0	0	0
1962-63	San Francisco Seals	WHL	70	34	42	76	....	....	....	90	17	5	3	8	12
1963-64	San Francisco Seals	WHL	46	13	21	34	....	....	....	55	....	....	....	....	....
	NHL Totals		**43**	**4**	**6**	**10**	**5**	**6**	**11**	**49**	**11**	**0**	**1**	**1**	**8**

IHL First All-Star Team (1956) • IHL Second All-Star Team (1957)

Claimed by **Springfield** (AHL) from **Montreal** (New Westminster-WHL) in Inter-League Draft, June, 1958. Traded to **Toronto** by **Springfield** (AHL) for Frank Rogeveen, June, 1959.

• EGAN, PAT Pat "Box-Car" Egan

D – R. 5'10", 195 lbs. b: Blackie, Alta., 4/25/1918.

			REGULAR SEASON								PLAYOFFS				
Season	Club	League	GP	G	A	Pts	AG	AA	APts	PIM	GP	G	A	Pts	PIM
1935-36	Calgary Radios	City Jr.	6	1	2	3	....	....	....	*14	3	0	0	0	*11
1936-37	Nelson Maple Leafs	Kootenay	14	2	2	4	....	....	....	14	....	....	....	....	....
1937-38	Sudbury Frood Tigers	NOHA	11	0	0	0	....	....	....	19	2	0	1	1	0
1938-39	Seattle Seahawks	PCHL	44	9	11	20	....	....	....	*185	7	1	2	3	*25
1939-40	**New York Americans**	**NHL**	**10**	**4**	**3**	**7**	**9**	**6**	**15**	**6**	....	....	....	....	....
	Springfield Indians	AHL	47	12	11	23	....	....	....	74	3	0	0	0	10
1940-41	**New York Americans**	**NHL**	**39**	**4**	**9**	**13**	**8**	**16**	**24**	**51**	....	....	....	....	....
1941-42	**Brooklyn Americans**	**NHL**	**48**	**8**	**20**	**28**	**14**	**30**	**44**	***124**	....	....	....	....	....
1942-43	Montreal Army	City Sr.	19	6	8	14	....	....	....	56	7	0	0	0	*28
1943-44	**Detroit Red Wings**	**NHL**	**23**	**4**	**15**	**19**	**5**	**18**	**23**	**40**	....	....	....	....	....
	Boston Bruins	**NHL**	**25**	**11**	**13**	**24**	**14**	**16**	**30**	**55**	....	....	....	....	....
1944-45	**Boston Bruins**	**NHL**	**48**	**7**	**15**	**22**	**10**	**24**	**34**	***86**	**7**	**2**	**0**	**2**	**6**
1945-46	**Boston Bruins**	**NHL**	**41**	**8**	**10**	**18**	**12**	**19**	**31**	**32**	**10**	**3**	**0**	**3**	**8**
1946-47	**Boston Bruins**	**NHL**	**60**	**7**	**18**	**25**	**9**	**26**	**35**	**89**	**5**	**0**	**2**	**2**	**6**
1947-48	**Boston Bruins**	**NHL**	**60**	**8**	**11**	**19**	**12**	**16**	**28**	**81**	**5**	**1**	**1**	**2**	**2**
1948-49	**Boston Bruins**	**NHL**	**60**	**6**	**18**	**24**	**9**	**29**	**38**	**92**	**5**	**0**	**0**	**0**	**16**
1949-50	**New York Rangers**	**NHL**	**70**	**5**	**11**	**16**	**7**	**14**	**21**	**50**	**12**	**3**	**1**	**4**	**6**
1950-51	**New York Rangers**	**NHL**	**70**	**5**	**10**	**15**	**7**	**13**	**20**	**70**	....	....	....	....	....
1951-52	Cincinnati–Providence	AHL	68	9	30	39	....	....	....	149	15	2	5	7	49
1952-53	Providence Reds	AHL	26	6	9	15	....	....	....	48	....	....	....	....	....
1953-54	Providence Reds	AHL	70	10	19	29	....	....	....	127	....	....	....	....	....
1954-55	Providence Reds	AHL	59	6	28	34	....	....	....	*149	....	....	....	....	....
1955-56	Vancouver Canucks	WHL	70	4	22	26	....	....	....	*163	15	0	5	5	20
1956-57	Nelson Maple Leafs	WIHL	36	8	19	27	....	....	....	118	5	0	0	0	11
1957-58	Victoria Cougars	WHL	59	9	27	36	....	....	....	163	....	....	....	....	....
	Nelson Maple Leafs	WIHL	5	1	1	2	....	....	....	30	....	....	....	....	....
1958-59	Victoria Cougars	WHL	3	0	1	1	....	....	....	4	....	....	....	....	....
1959-60	Victoria Cougars	WHL	DID NOT PLAY – COACHING												
	NHL Totals		**554**	**77**	**153**	**230**	**116**	**227**	**343**	**776**	**44**	**9**	**4**	**13**	**44**

NHL Second All-Star Team (1942)

Played in NHL All-Star Game (1949)

Signed as a free agent by **NY Americans**, October 13, 1939. Rights transferred to **Detroit** from **Brooklyn** in Special Dispersal Draw, October 9, 1942. Traded to **Boston** by **Detroit** for Flash Hollett, January 5, 1944. Traded to **NY Rangers** by **Boston** for Billy Moe and the rights to Lorne Ferguson, October 7, 1949. Traded to **Providence** (AHL) by **NY Rangers** with Zellio Toppazzini and Jean-Paul Denis for Jack Stoddard, December, 1951.

• EHMAN, GERRY — *see page 1003*

• ELIK, BORIS Boris "Bo" Elik

LW – L. 5'11", 190 lbs. b: Geralton, Ont., 10/17/1929.

1949-50	Sunridge Beavers	Jr. B	STATISTICS NOT AVAILABLE												
1950-51	North Bay Black Hawks	EOHL	37	18	18	36	....	....	....	32	....	....	....	....	....
1951-52	North Bay Black Hawks	EOHL	31	13	8	21	....	....	....	45	11	3	5	8	19
1952-53	North Bay Trappers	NOHA	48	18	17	35	....	....	....	67	7	2	1	3	17
1953-54	North Bay Trappers	NOHA	33	12	18	30	....	....	....	33	4	2	1	3	18
1954-55	North Bay Trappers	NOHA	55	18	25	43	....	....	....	52	12	7	6	13	6
1955-56	North Bay Trappers	NOHA	55	20	23	43	....	....	....	50	8	5	2	7	8
	Cleveland Barons	AHL	1	0	1	1	....	....	....	0	....	....	....	....	....
1956-57	Cleveland Barons	AHL	61	40	40	80	....	....	....	82	12	4	6	10	8
1957-58	Cleveland Barons	AHL	70	31	37	68	....	....	....	129	7	0	4	4	4
1958-59	Rochester Americans	AHL	14	1	7	8	....	....	....	28	....	....	....	....	....
	Providence Reds	AHL	50	19	27	46	....	....	....	44	....	....	....	....	....
1959-60	Providence Reds	AHL	69	26	27	53	....	....	....	75	5	0	1	1	2
1960-61	Providence Reds	AHL	51	10	20	30	....	....	....	46	....	....	....	....	....
1961-62	Pittsburgh Hornets	AHL	64	21	19	40	....	....	....	112	....	....	....	....	....
1962-63	**Detroit Red Wings**	**NHL**	**3**	**0**	**0**	**0**	**0**	**0**	**0**	**0**	....	....	....	....	....
	Pittsburgh Hornets	AHL	7	0	0	0	....	....	....	0	....	....	....	....	....
	Edmonton Flyers	WHL	58	22	25	47	....	....	....	79	3	5	0	5	0
	NHL Totals		**3**	**0**	**0**	**0**	**0**	**0**	**0**	**0**	....	....	....	....	....

AHL First All-Star Team (1957) • Won Dudley "Red" Garrett Memorial Award (Top Rookie - AHL) (1957) • AHL Second All-Star Team (1958)

Traded to **Rochester** (AHL) by **Cleveland** (AHL) for Eddy Mazur, June, 1958.

• ELLIOT, FRED Fred Elliot

RW – R. 5'8", 165 lbs. b: Clinton, Ontario, 2/18/1903. Deceased.

1927-28	Toronto Falcons	Can-Pro	42	9	7	16	....	....	....	14	2	0	0	0	0
1928-29	**Ottawa Senators**	**NHL**	**43**	**2**	**0**	**2**	**8**	**0**	**8**	**6**	....	....	....	....	....
1929-30	Windsor Bulldogs	IAHL	3	0	1	1	....	....	....	4	....	....	....	....	....
	London Panthers	IAHL	5	1	0	1	....	....	....	16	....	....	....	....	....
	Niagara Falls Cataracts	IAHL	33	2	5	7	....	....	....	10	....	....	....	....	....
1930-31	London Panthers	IAHL	19	0	1	1	....	....	....	0	....	....	....	....	....
	Philadelphia Arrows	Can-Am	13	1	2	3	....	....	....	11	....	....	....	....	....
	Stratford Nationals	OPHL	1	0	0	0	....	....	....	0	....	....	....	....	....
	NHL Totals		**43**	**2**	**0**	**2**	**8**	**0**	**8**	**6**	....	....	....	....	....

Traded to **Windsor** (IAHL) by **Ottawa** for Fred Brown and Ed Kuntz, November 21, 1929. Traded to **Niagara Falls** (IAHL) by **London** (IAHL) for Steve Rice, December 7, 1929. Traded to **London** (IAHL) by **Windsor** (IAHL) with Lloyd Gross for Ian Morrison and Jack Smith, December 15, 1929.

• ELLIS, RON — *see page 1005*

• EMBERG, EDDIE Eddie Emberg

C – L. 5'10", 160 lbs. b: Montreal, Que., 11/18/1921.

			REGULAR SEASON								PLAYOFFS				
Season	Club	League	GP	G	A	Pts	AG	AA	APts	PIM	GP	G	A	Pts	PIM
1940-41	Verdun Maple Leafs	Mtl-Jr.	12	11	6	17	....	....	....	4	2	1	0	1	0
1941-42	Montreal Jr. Royals	Mtl-Jr.	12	11	9	20	....	....	....	4	2	*5	2	7	2
	Montreal Royals	QSHL	1	1	0	1	....	....	....	0	....	....	....	....	....
1942-43	Montreal RCAF	QSHL	26	7	10	17	....	....	....	0	12	1	2	3	0
	Montreal RCAF	City Sr.	8	4	12	16	....	....	....	0	1	0	0	0	0
1943-44	Montreal RCAF	QSHL	1	0	0	0	....	....	....	0	3	*7	2	9	2
1944-45	Montreal RCAF	City Sr.	3	3	2	5	....	....	....	0	....	....	....	....	....
	Quebec Aces	QSHL	12	5	3	8	....	....	....	7	7	6	4	*10	4
	Montreal Canadiens	**NHL**	....	....	....	....	....	....	....	....	**2**	**1**	**0**	**1**	**0**
1945-46	Quebec Aces	QSHL	31	19	7	26	....	....	....	18	6	2	2	4	0
1946-47	Valleyfield Braves	QSHL	40	23	*44	67	....	....	....	10	....	....	....	....	....
	Boston Olympics	EHL	....	....	....	....	....	....	....	....	2	4	1	5	2
1947-48	Ottawa Senators	QSHL	36	29	24	53	....	....	....	13	26	10	12	22	4
1948-49	Ottawa Senators	QSHL	62	31	53	84	....	....	....	27	17	5	5	10	8
1949-50	Ottawa Senators	QSHL	59	22	47	69	....	....	....	16	7	3	5	8	2
1950-51	Ottawa Senators	QSHL	58	19	41	60	....	....	....	16	5	0	3	3	0
1951-52	Ottawa Senators	QSHL	60	11	26	37	....	....	....	28	....	....	....	....	....
	NHL Totals		**0**	**0**	**0**	**0**	**0**	**0**	**0**	**0**	**2**	**1**	**0**	**1**	**0**

• EMMS, HAP Hap (Leighton) Emms

LW/D – L. 6', 190 lbs. b: Barrie, Ont., 1/12/1905. d: 10/22/1988.

1925-26	Brantford Seniors	OHA Sr.	STATISTICS NOT AVAILABLE												
1926-27	**Montreal Maroons**	**NHL**	**8**	**0**	**0**	**0**	**0**	**0**	**0**	**0**	....	....	....	....	....
	Stratford Nationals	Can-Pro	25	11	5	16	....	....	....	59	2	0	0	0	2
1927-28	**Montreal Maroons**	**NHL**	**10**	**0**	**1**	**1**	**0**	**8**	**8**	**10**	....	....	....	....	....
	Stratford Nationals	Can-Pro	29	8	5	13	....	....	....	56	5	1	0	1	*20
1928-29	Windsor Bulldogs	Can-Pro	42	21	5	26	....	....	....	104	8	*6	3	*9	30
1929-30	Windsor Bulldogs	IAHL	38	21	16	37	....	....	....	107	....	....	....	....	....
1930-31	**New York Americans**	**NHL**	**44**	**5**	**4**	**9**	**12**	**14**	**26**	**56**	....	....	....	....	....
1931-32	**New York Americans**	**NHL**	**13**	**1**	**0**	**1**	**2**	**0**	**2**	**11**	....	....	....	....	....
	Detroit Falcons	**NHL**	**20**	**5**	**9**	**14**	**11**	**25**	**36**	**27**	**2**	**0**	**0**	**0**	**2**
	New Haven Eagles	Can-Am	5	0	0	0	....	....	....	8	....	....	....	....	....
1932-33	**Detroit Red Wings**	**NHL**	**43**	**9**	**13**	**22**	**21**	**34**	**55**	**63**	**4**	**0**	**0**	**0**	**8**
1933-34	**Detroit Red Wings**	**NHL**	**45**	**7**	**7**	**14**	**15**	**19**	**34**	**51**	**8**	**0**	**0**	**0**	**2**
1934-35	**Boston Bruins**	**NHL**	**11**	**1**	**1**	**2**	**2**	**2**	**4**	**8**	....	....	....	....	....
	New York Americans	**NHL**	**28**	**2**	**2**	**4**	**4**	**4**	**8**	**19**	....	....	....	....	....
1935-36	**New York Americans**	**NHL**	**32**	**1**	**5**	**6**	**2**	**12**	**14**	**12**	....	....	....	....	....
1936-37	**New York Americans**	**NHL**	**46**	**4**	**8**	**12**	**9**	**19**	**28**	**48**	....	....	....	....	....
1937-38	**New York Americans**	**NHL**	**20**	**1**	**3**	**4**	**2**	**6**	**8**	**6**	....	....	....	....	....
	Pittsburgh Hornets	AHL	26	5	13	18	....	....	....	39	2	1	1	2	0
1938-39	Pittsburgh Hornets	AHL	55	9	26	25	....	....	....	62	....	....	....	....	....
1939-40	Omaha Knights	AHA	48	18	15	33	....	....	....	93	9	0	4	4	0
1940-41	Omaha Knights	AHA	27	7	11	18	....	....	....	31	....	....	....	....	....
1941-42	Omaha Knights	AHA	26	2	5	7	....	....	....	40	....	....	....	....	....
1942-43	Omaha Knights	AHA	23	2	5	7	....	....	....	40	....	....	....	....	....
1943-44			MILITARY SERVICE												
1944-45	St. Louis Flyers	AHL	2	0	0	0	....	....	....	0	....	....	....	....	....
	NHL Totals		**320**	**36**	**53**	**89**	**80**	**143**	**223**	**311**	**14**	**0**	**0**	**0**	**12**

Signed as a free agent by **Montreal Maroons**, November 10, 1926. Traded to **NY Americans** by **Montreal Maroons** (Windsor-IAHL) with Frank Carson, Red Dutton and Mike Neville for $35,000, May 14, 1930. Traded to **Detroit Falcons** by **NY Americans** with Frank Carson for Tommy Filmore and Bert McInenely, December 29, 1931. Signed as a free agent by **Boston** after securing release from **Detroit**, October 28, 1934. Traded to **NY Americans** by **Boston** with Obs Heximer for Red Jackson, December 13, 1938. Traded to **Detroit** by **NY Americans** for John Sorrell, February 13, 1938.

• ERICKSON, AUT — *see page 1007*

• ESPOSITO, PHIL — *see page 1010*

• EVANS, JACK
Jack "Tex" Evans
D – L. 6', 185 lbs. b: Morriston, South Wales, 4/21/1928. d: 11/10/1996.

Season	Club	League	GP	G	A	Pts	AG	AA	APts	PIM	GP	G	A	Pts	PIM
1947-48	Lethbridge Native Sons	WCJHL	23	10	21	31	....	....	....	58	6	5	3	8	8
	Lethbridge Maple Leafs	WCSHL	1	0	0	0	....	....	....	0	....	....	....	....	....
1948-49	**New York Rangers**	**NHL**	**3**	**0**	**0**	**0**	**0**	**0**	**0**	**4**	....	....	....	....	....
	Lethbridge Maple Leafs	WCSHL	48	7	10	17	....	....	....	124	3	0	0	0	8
1949-50	**New York Rangers**	**NHL**	**2**	**0**	**0**	**0**	**0**	**0**	**0**	**2**	....	....	....	....	....
	New Haven Ramblers	AHL	69	3	12	15	....	....	....	150	....	....	....	....	....
1950-51	**New York Rangers**	**NHL**	**49**	**1**	**0**	**1**	**1**	**0**	**1**	**95**	....	....	....	....	....
	Cincinnati Mohawks	AHL	16	3	3	6	....	....	....	56	....	....	....	....	....
1951-52	**New York Rangers**	**NHL**	**52**	**1**	**6**	**7**	**1**	**8**	**9**	**83**	....	....	....	....	....
1952-53	Saskatoon Quakers	WHL	68	9	22	31	....	....	....	179	13	0	3	3	16
1953-54	**New York Rangers**	**NHL**	**44**	**4**	**4**	**8**	**6**	**5**	**11**	**73**	....	....	....	....	....
	Saskatoon Quakers	WHL	27	2	3	5	....	....	....	49	....	....	....	....	....
1954-55	**New York Rangers**	**NHL**	**47**	**0**	**5**	**5**	**0**	**6**	**6**	**91**	....	....	....	....	....
	Saskatoon Quakers	WHL	22	2	4	6	....	....	....	16	....	....	....	....	....
	Victoria Cougars	WHL	....	....	....	....	....	....	....	....	1	0	0	0	2
1955-56	**New York Rangers**	**NHL**	**70**	**2**	**9**	**11**	**3**	**11**	**14**	**104**	**5**	**1**	**0**	**1**	**18**
1956-57	**New York Rangers**	**NHL**	**70**	**3**	**6**	**9**	**4**	**7**	**11**	**110**	**5**	**0**	**1**	**1**	**4**
1957-58	**New York Rangers**	**NHL**	**70**	**4**	**8**	**12**	**5**	**9**	**14**	**108**	**6**	**0**	**0**	**0**	**17**
1958-59	**Chicago Black Hawks**	**NHL**	**70**	**1**	**8**	**9**	**1**	**8**	**9**	**75**	**6**	**0**	**0**	**0**	**10**
1959-60	**Chicago Black Hawks**	**NHL**	**68**	**0**	**4**	**4**	**0**	**4**	**4**	**60**	**4**	**0**	**0**	**0**	**4**
1960-61	**Chicago Black Hawks**	**NHL**	**69**	**0**	**8**	**8**	**0**	**8**	**8**	**58**	**12**	**1**	**1**	**2**	**14**
1961-62	**Chicago Black Hawks**	**NHL**	**70**	**3**	**14**	**17**	**4**	**14**	**18**	**80**	**12**	**0**	**0**	**0**	**26**
1962-63	**Chicago Black Hawks**	**NHL**	**68**	**0**	**8**	**8**	**0**	**8**	**8**	**46**	**6**	**0**	**0**	**0**	**4**
1963-64	Buffalo Bisons	AHL	72	0	17	17	....	....	....	87	....	....	....	....	....
1964-65	Los Angeles Blades	WHL	69	2	13	15	....	....	....	91	....	....	....	....	....
1965-66	Vancouver Canucks	WHL	72	2	31	33	....	....	....	103	7	0	1	1	20
1966-67	California Seals	WHL	71	3	18	21	....	....	....	52	6	0	2	2	4
1967-68	San Diego Gulls	WHL	65	1	15	16	....	....	....	36	7	0	3	3	8
1968-69	San Diego Gulls	WHL	73	1	11	12	....	....	....	50	7	0	0	0	0
1969-70	San Diego Gulls	WHL	67	0	8	8	....	....	....	46	6	0	0	0	2
1970-71	San Diego Gulls	WHL	69	1	10	11	....	....	....	82	6	0	2	2	12
1971-72	San Diego Gulls	WHL	72	0	20	20	....	....	....	87	4	0	0	0	4
	NHL Totals		**752**	**19**	**80**	**99**	**25**	**88**	**113**	**989**	**56**	**2**	**2**	**4**	**97**

WHL First All-Star Team (1953)

Played in NHL All-Star Game (1961, 1962)

Claimed by **Chicago** from **NY Rangers** in Intra-League Draft, June 3, 1958. Claimed by **Boston** (Hershey - AHL) from **Chicago** in Reverse Draft, June, 1966. Traded to **San Diego** (WHL) by **Boston** for cash, October, 1967.

• EVANS, STEWART
Stewart "Stew" Evans
D – L. 5'10", 170 lbs. b: Ottawa, Ont., 6/19/1908. d: 6/9/1996.

Season	Club	League	GP	G	A	Pts	AG	AA	APts	PIM	GP	G	A	Pts	PIM
1928-29	Iroquois Falls Paper	NOHA	STATISTICS NOT AVAILABLE												
1929-30	Detroit Olympics	IAHL	38	8	11	19	....	....	....	113	3	1	0	1	7
1930-31	**Detroit Falcons**	**NHL**	**43**	**1**	**4**	**5**	**2**	**14**	**16**	**14**	....	....	....	....	....
1931-32	Detroit Olympics	IAHL	45	3	9	12	....	....	....	72	6	0	0	0	18
1932-33	**Detroit Red Wings**	**NHL**	**48**	**2**	**6**	**8**	**5**	**16**	**21**	**74**	**4**	**0**	**0**	**0**	**6**
1933-34	**Detroit Red Wings**	**NHL**	**17**	**0**	**0**	**0**	**0**	**0**	**0**	**20**					
	Montreal Maroons	**NHL**	**27**	**4**	**2**	**6**	**9**	**5**	**14**	**35**	**4**	**0**	**0**	**0**	**4**
1934-35	**Montreal Maroons**	**NHL**	**46**	**5**	**7**	**12**	**11**	**16**	**27**	**54**	**7**	**0**	**0**	**0**	**8**
1935-36	**Montreal Maroons**	**NHL**	**48**	**3**	**5**	**8**	**7**	**12**	**19**	**57**	**3**	**0**	**0**	**0**	**0**
1936-37	**Montreal Maroons**	**NHL**	**47**	**6**	**7**	**13**	**13**	**16**	**29**	**54**	**5**	**0**	**0**	**0**	**0**
1937-38	**Montreal Maroons**	**NHL**	**48**	**5**	**11**	**16**	**10**	**23**	**33**	**59**	....		....	....	....
1938-39	**Montreal Canadiens**	**NHL**	**43**	**2**	**7**	**9**	**4**	**13**	**17**	**58**	**3**	**0**	**0**	**0**	**2**
1939-40	Detroit Holzbaugh	MOHL	DID NOT PLAY – COACHING												
	NHL Totals		**367**	**28**	**49**	**77**	**61**	**115**	**176**	**425**	**26**	**0**	**0**	**0**	**20**

Signed as a free agent by **Detroit Cougars**, September 12, 1929. Traded to **Montreal Maroons** by **Detroit** for Ted Graham, January 2, 1934. Traded to **Montreal Canadiens** by **Montreal Maroons** for cash, September 14, 1938.

• EZINICKI, BILL
Bill "Wild Bill" Ezinicki
RW – R. 5'10", 170 lbs. b: Winnipeg, Man., 3/11/1924.

Season	Club	League	GP	G	A	Pts	AG	AA	APts	PIM	GP	G	A	Pts	PIM
1941-42	Winnipeg Rangers	MJHL	2	3	0	3	....	....	....	0	....	....	....	....	....
1942-43	Oshawa Generals	OHA	16	21	10	31	....	....	....	21	10	13	10	23	26
1943-44	Oshawa Generals	OHA	25	38	25	63	....	....	....	33	11	*13	3	16	*49
1944-45	**Toronto Maple Leafs**	**NHL**	**8**	**1**	**4**	**5**	**1**	**6**	**7**	**17**	....	....	....	....	....
1945-46	**Toronto Maple Leafs**	**NHL**	**24**	**4**	**8**	**12**	**6**	**15**	**21**	**29**	....	....	....	....	....
	Pittsburgh Hornets	AHL	27	9	12	21	....	....	....	23	....	....	....	....	....
1946-47	**Toronto Maple Leafs**	**NHL**	**60**	**17**	**20**	**37**	**23**	**29**	**52**	**93**	**11**	**0**	**2**	**2**	**30**
1947-48	**Toronto Maple Leafs**	**NHL**	**60**	**11**	**20**	**31**	**16**	**29**	**45**	**97**	**9**	**3**	**1**	**4**	**6**
1948-49	**Toronto Maple Leafs**	**NHL**	**52**	**13**	**15**	**28**	**20**	**24**	**44**	***145**	**9**	**1**	**4**	**5**	**20**
1949-50	**Toronto Maple Leafs**	**NHL**	**67**	**10**	**12**	**22**	**13**	**15**	**28**	***144**	**5**	**0**	**0**	**0**	**13**
1950-51	Pittsburgh Hornets	AHL	13	6	3	9	....	....	....	24	....	....	....	....	....
	Boston Bruins	**NHL**	**53**	**16**	**19**	**35**	**22**	**24**	**46**	**119**	**6**	**1**	**1**	**2**	**18**
1951-52	**Boston Bruins**	**NHL**	**28**	**5**	**5**	**10**	**7**	**6**	**13**	**47**	....	....	....	....	....
	Pittsburgh Hornets	AHL	16	4	9	13	....	....	....	53	11	3	1	4	*67
1952-53	Pittsburgh Hornets	AHL	41	15	13	28	....	....	....	*115	7	0	3	3	8
1953-54			PLAYED PRO GOLF												
1954-55	Ottawa Senators	QHL	18	5	6	11	....	....	....	39	....	....	....	....	....
	Vancouver Canucks	WHL	15	5	2	7	....	....	....	50	....	....	....	....	....
	New York Rangers	**NHL**	**16**	**2**	**2**	**4**	**3**	**3**	**6**	**22**	....	....	....		
1955-56			PLAYED PRO GOLF												
1956-57	Sudbury Wolves	NOHA	19	5	4	9	....	....	....	32	12	1	9	10	29
	NHL Totals		**368**	**79**	**105**	**184**	**111**	**151**	**262**	**713**	**40**	**5**	**8**	**13**	**87**

Played in NHL All-Star Game (1947, 1949)

Traded to **Toronto** by **Providence** (AHL) for George Boothman and Don Webster, October 13, 1944. Traded to **Boston** by **Toronto** with Vic Lynn for Fernie Flaman, Ken Smith and Phil Maloney, November 16, 1950. Traded to **Toronto** by **Boston** for cash, January 28, 1952. Traded to **Vancouver** (WHL) by **Toronto** with Phil Maloney and Hugh Barlow for $10,000, December 21, 1954. Traded to **NY Rangers** by **Vancouver** (WHL) for Jackie McLeod and cash, February 12, 1955. Traded to **Providence** (AHL) by **NY Rangers** with cash for Jean-Guy Gendron, May 8, 1955.

• FAHEY, TREVOR
Trevor Fahey
LW – L. 6'1", 175 lbs. b: New Waterford, N.S., 1/4/1944.

Season	Club	League	GP	G	A	Pts	AG	AA	APts	PIM	GP	G	A	Pts	PIM
1960-61	Guelph Royals	OHA	4	1	1	2	....	....	....	0	13	0	1	1	0
1961-62	Guelph Royals	OHA	26	3	2	5	....	....	....	0	....	....	....	....	....
1962-63	Guelph Royals	OHA	39	26	17	43	....	....	....	26	....	....	....	....	....
1963-64	Kitchener Rangers	OHA	35	17	11	28	....	....	....	23	....	....	....	....	....
1964-65	**New York Rangers**	**NHL**	**1**	**0**	**0**	**0**	**0**	**0**	**0**	**0**	....	....	....	....	....
	New York Rovers	EHL	72	30	25	55	....	....	....	41	....	....	....	....	....
1965-66	Minnesota Rangers	CHL	67	13	9	22	....	....	....	4	6	1	2	3	0
1966-67	Omaha Knights	CHL	54	8	5	13	....	....	....	22	7	0	2	2	8
1967-68	Toledo Blades	IHL	4	0	0	0	....	....	....	0	....	....	....	....	....
	Des Moines Oak Leafs	IHL	53	37	39	76	....	....	....	22	....	....	....	....	....
1968-69	Des Moines Oak Leafs	IHL	66	27	43	70	....	....	....	56	....	....	....	....	....
	Denver Spurs	WHL	5	1	1	2	....	....	....	0	....	....	....	....	....
1969-70	Des Moines–Fort Wayne	IHL	67	25	33	58	....	....	....	74	3	1	1	2	5
1970-71	St. Francis Xavier X-Men	AUAA	....	19	23	42	....	....	....	44	....	....	....	....	....
1971-72	St. Francis Xavier X-Men	AUAA	....	15	13	28	....	....	....	87	....	....	....	....	....
1972-73	St. Francis Xavier X-Men	AUAA	....	19	22	41	....	....	....	28	....	....	....	....	....
1973-74	St. Francis Xavier X-Men	AUAA	19	17	16	33	....	....	....	34	....	....	....	....	....
1974-75	Brandon University	CWUAA	DID NOT PLAY – COACHING												
	NHL Totals		**1**	**0**	**0**	**0**	**0**	**0**	**0**	**0**	....	....	....	....	....

IHL First All-Star Team (1969)

Traded to **LA Kings** by **NY Rangers** with Jim Murray and Ken Turlick for Barclay Plager, June 16, 1967.

• FALKENBERG, BOB — *see page 1013*

• FARRANT, WALT
Walt "Whitey" Farrant
RW – R. 5'10", 155 lbs. b: Toronto, Ont., 8/12/1912.

Season	Club	League	GP	G	A	Pts	AG	AA	APts	PIM	GP	G	A	Pts	PIM
1929-30	Parkdale Canoe Club	OHA	2	0	0	0	....	....	....	0	....	....	....	....	....
1930-31	Parkdale Canoe Club	OHA	9	*9	2	11	....	....	....	4	....	....	....	....	....
1931-32	Parkdale Canoe Club	OHA	10	*13	2	15	....	....	....	10	....	....	....	....	....
1932-33	Toronto Marlboros	OHA Sr.	19	8	8	16	....	....	....	10	2	0	0	0	0
1933-34	Toronto Marlboros	OHA Sr.	16	4	9	13	....	....	....	10	1	0	0	0	0
1934-35	Toronto All-Stars	City Sr.	2	1	0	1	....	....	....	2	....	....	....	....	....
	Toronto City Service	City Sr.	13	*14	9	23	....	....	....	4	7	*7	4	*11	4
1935-36	Rochester Cardinals	IAHL	46	26	19	45	....	....	....	12	....	....	....	....	....
	Springfield Indians	Can-Am	1	0	0	0	....	....	....	0	....	....	....	....	....
1936-37	New Haven–Providence	AHL	39	8	8	16	....	....	....	16	2	0	0	0	0
1937-38	Minneapolis Millers	AHA	47	18	20	38	....	....	....	25	5	2	3	5	5
1938-39	Minneapolis Millers	AHA	47	35	34	69	....	....	....	8	4	1	2	3	0
1939-40	Minneapolis Millers	AHA	48	29	35	64	....	....	....	9	3	1	1	2	0
1940-41	Minneapolis Millers	AHA	11	1	5	6	....	....	....	0	....	....	....	....	....
	Tulsa Oilers	AHA	36	15	12	27	....	....	....	0	....	....	....	....	....
1941-42	Toronto Marlboros	OHA Sr.	21	22	15	37	....	....	....	0	6	5	3	8	2
1942-43	Toronto Peoples Credit	City Sr.	STATISTICS NOT AVAILABLE												
1943-44	**Chicago Black Hawks**	**NHL**	**1**	**0**	**0**	**0**	**0**	**0**	**0**	**0**	....	....	....	....	....
	Toronto Peoples Credit	City Sr.	....	31	29	60	....	....	....	....	....	....	....	....	....
	NHL Totals		**1**	**0**	**0**	**0**	**0**	**0**	**0**	**0**					

AHA Second All-Star Team (1940)

Signed as a free agent by **NY Americans**, November, 1936. Loaned to **Chicago** by **Toronto** (City Sr.) as an emergency injury replacement, March, 1944.

• FASHOWAY, GORDIE
Gordie Fashoway
LW – L. 5'11", 190 lbs. b: Portage La Prairie, Man., 6/16/1926.

Season	Club	League	GP	G	A	Pts	AG	AA	APts	PIM	GP	G	A	Pts	PIM
1944-45	Winnipeg Monarchs	MJHL	8	4	3	7				4	8	8	2	10	16
	Winnipeg Army	City Sr.	....	....	....	....	....	....	....	....	2	0	0	0	0
1945-46	Winnipeg Monarchs	MJHL	8	10	4	14	....	....	....	12	7	6	1	7	0
1946-47	Harringay Racers	Britain	36	*63	22	85	....	....	....	44	3	*6	0	6	2
1947-48	New Westminster Royals	PCHL	60	47	36	83	....	....	....	50	5	4	6	10	32
1948-49	Kansas City Pla-Mors	USHL	64	13	22	35	....	....	....	42	2	1	0	1	0
1949-50	Kansas City Pla-Mors	USHL	66	*52	32	84	....	....	....	71	3	0	0	0	0
1950-51	**Chicago Black Hawks**	**NHL**	**13**	**3**	**2**	**5**	**4**	**3**	**7**	**14**	....	....	....	....	....
	Milwaukee Seagulls	USHL	10	4	9	13	....	....	....	4	....	....	....	....	....
	New Westminster Royals	PCHL	32	12	13	25	....	....	....	26	11	4	2	6	4
1951-52	New Westminster Royals	PCHL	70	*51	34	85	....	....	....	46	7	5	0	5	2
1952-53	New Westminster Royals	WHL	68	35	28	63	....	....	....	31	7	3	2	5	0
1953-54	New Westminster Royals	WHL	70	43	26	69	....	....	....	35	7	2	3	5	4
1954-55	New Westminster Royals	WHL	70	45	32	77	....	....	....	20	....	....	....	....	....
1955-56	New Westminster Royals	WHL	69	*47	32	79	....	....	....	16	4	0	1	1	0
1956-57	New Westminster Royals	WHL	70	41	25	66	....	....	....	36	11	*6	5	11	6
1957-58	New Westminster Royals	WHL	69	33	33	66	....	....	....	43	4	1	0	1	0
1958-59	New Westminster Royals	WHL	67	37	24	61	....	....	....	16	....	....	....	....	....
1959-60	Victoria Cougars	WHL	70	34	33	67	....	....	....	12	11	4	3	7	2
1960-61	Portland Buckaroos	WHL	66	42	32	74	....	....	....	8	14	6	*10	16	2
1961-62	Portland Buckaroos	WHL	60	29	27	56	....	....	....	14	7	3	3	6	10
1962-63	Portland Buckaroos	WHL	61	36	20	56	....	....	....	8	7	3	0	3	0
1963-64	Portland Buckaroos	WHL	1	0	0	0	....	....	....	0	....	....	....	....	....
	NHL Totals		**13**	**3**	**2**	**5**	**4**	**3**	**7**	**14**	....	....	....	....	....

USHL First All-Star Team (1950) • PCHL First All-Star Team (1952) • WHL Coast Division Second All-Star Team (1957, 1958, 1961) • Won Fred J. Hume Cup (WHL Most Gentlemanly Player) (1961)

Traded to **Quebec** (AHL) by **New Westminster** (WHL) for Claude Robert and cash, January, 1953. • Rights returned to **New Westminster** (WHL) by **Quebec** when Fashoway refused to report, January, 1953.

• FAULKNER, ALEX
Alex Faulkner
C – L. 5'8", 165 lbs. b: Bishop Falls, Nfld., 5/21/1936.

			REGULAR SEASON								PLAYOFFS				
Season	Club	League	GP	G	A	Pts	AG	AA	APts	PIM	GP	G	A	Pts	PIM
1956-57	Bishops Falls Seniors	Nfld.	12	*20	*17	*37	....	....	....	8	....	....	....	....	....
1957-58	Bishops Falls Seniors	Nfld.	12	*38	22	*60	....	....	....	9	....	....	....	....	....
1958-59	Conception Bay Cee Bees	Nfld.	STATISTICS NOT AVAILABLE												
1959-60	Conception Bay Cee Bees	Nfld.	STATISTICS NOT AVAILABLE												
1960-61	Conception Bay Cee Bees	Nfld.	STATISTICS NOT AVAILABLE												
	Rochester Americans	AHL	41	5	13	18	....	....	....	6	....	....	....	....	....
1961-62	**Toronto Maple Leafs**	**NHL**	**1**	**0**	**0**	**0**	**0**	**0**	**0**	**0**	....	....	....	....	....
	Rochester Americans	AHL	65	19	54	73	....	....	....	26	2	1	1	2	0
1962-63	**Detroit Red Wings**	**NHL**	**70**	**10**	**10**	**20**	**12**	**10**	**22**	**6**	**8**	**5**	**0**	**5**	**2**
1963-64	**Detroit Red Wings**	**NHL**	**30**	**5**	**7**	**12**	**7**	**8**	**15**	**9**	**4**	**0**	**0**	**0**	**0**
	Cincinnati Wings	CHL	11	4	8	12	....	....	....	6	....	....	....	....	....
	Pittsburgh Hornets	AHL	8	1	4	5	....	....	....	2	....	....	....	....	....
1964-65	Conception Bay Cee Bees	Nfld.	STATISTICS NOT AVAILABLE												
1965-66	Conception Bay Cee Bees	Nfld.	5	5	16	21	....	....	....	....	....	....	....	....	....
1966-67	Memphis Wings	CHL	70	28	*60	88	....	....	....	32	7	2	5	7	14
1967-68	San Diego Gulls	WHL	71	26	41	67	....	....	....	32	7	2	2	4	2
1968-69	San Diego Gulls	WHL	73	17	51	68	....	....	....	16	7	2	4	6	4
1969-70	San Diego Gulls	WHL	60	17	48	65	....	....	....	14	6	0	6	6	4
1970-71	San Diego Gulls	WHL	4	1	1	2	....	....	....	0	....	....	....	....	....
	St. John's Capitals	Nfld.	36	26	47	73	....	....	....	18	....	9	*21	*30	....
1971-72	St. John's Capitals	Nfld.	24	18	42	60	....	....	....	52	....	....	....	....	....
	NHL Totals		**101**	**15**	**17**	**32**	**19**	**18**	**37**	**15**	**12**	**5**	**0**	**5**	**2**

CHL Second All-Star Team (1967)

Signed as a free agent by **Toronto**, December, 1960. Claimed by **Detroit** from **Toronto** in Intra-League Draft, June 4, 1962.

• FERGUSON, JOHN
— *see page 1018*

• FERGUSON, LORNE
Lorne "Fergie" Ferguson
LW – L. 6', 175 lbs. b: Palmerston, Ont., 5/26/1930.

			REGULAR SEASON								PLAYOFFS				
Season	Club	League	GP	G	A	Pts	AG	AA	APts	PIM	GP	G	A	Pts	PIM
1947-48	Guelph Biltmores	OHA	35	28	11	39	....	....	....	87	....	....	....	....	....
1948-49	Guelph Biltmores	OHA	46	38	24	62	....	....	....	52	....	....	....	....	....
1949-50	**Boston Bruins**	**NHL**	**3**	**1**	**1**	**2**	**1**	**1**	**2**	**0**	....	....	....	....	....
	Tulsa Oilers	USHL	70	35	35	70	....	....	....	21	....	....	....	....	....
1950-51	**Boston Bruins**	**NHL**	**70**	**16**	**17**	**33**	**22**	**22**	**44**	**31**	**6**	**1**	**0**	**1**	**2**
1951-52	**Boston Bruins**	**NHL**	**27**	**3**	**4**	**7**	**4**	**5**	**9**	**14**	....	....	....	....	....
	Hershey Bears	AHL	8	5	1	6	....	....	....	2	....	....	....	....	....
1952-53	Hershey Bears	AHL	64	25	40	65	....	....	....	56	3	0	2	2	6
1953-54	Hershey Bears	AHL	70	*45	42	87	....	....	....	34	11	2	3	5	11
1954-55	**Boston Bruins**	**NHL**	**69**	**20**	**14**	**34**	**29**	**18**	**47**	**24**	**4**	**1**	**0**	**1**	**2**
1955-56	**Boston Bruins**	**NHL**	**63**	**15**	**12**	**27**	**22**	**15**	**37**	**30**	**10**	**1**	**2**	**3**	**12**
	Detroit Red Wings	**NHL**	....	....	....	....	....	....	....	....	....	....	....	....	....
1956-57	**Detroit Red Wings**	**NHL**	**70**	**13**	**10**	**23**	**18**	**12**	**30**	**26**	**5**	**1**	**0**	**1**	**6**
1957-58	**Detroit Red Wings**	**NHL**	**15**	**1**	**3**	**4**	**1**	**3**	**4**	**0**	....	....	....	....	....
	Chicago Black Hawks	**NHL**	**38**	**6**	**9**	**15**	**8**	**10**	**18**	**24**	....	....	....	....	....
1958-59	**Chicago Black Hawks**	**NHL**	**67**	**7**	**10**	**17**	**9**	**11**	**20**	**44**	**6**	**2**	**1**	**3**	**2**
1959-60	Buffalo Bisons	AHL	70	13	35	48	....	....	....	54	....	....	....	....	....
1960-61	Quebec Aces	AHL	13	1	1	2	....	....	....	2	....	....	....	....	....
	Kingston Frontenacs	EPHL	26	5	17	22	....	....	....	2	4	0	0	0	2
1961-62	Kingston Frontenacs	EPHL	48	9	15	24	....	....	....	35	2	0	0	0	14
1962-1965			DID NOT PLAY – RETIRED												
1965-66	Kingston Aces	OHA Sr.	12	6	4	10	....	....	....	8	....	....	....	....	....
1966-67	Kingston Aces	OHA Sr.	DID NOT PLAY – COACHING												
1967-68	Kingston Aces	OHA Sr.	10	8	4	12	....	....	....	2	....	....	....	....	....
1968-69			DID NOT PLAY												
1969-70	Belleville Mohawks	OHA Sr.	9	2	2	4	....	....	....	2	....	....	....	....	....
	NHL Totals		**422**	**82**	**80**	**162**	**114**	**97**	**211**	**193**	**31**	**6**	**3**	**9**	**24**

AHL Second All-Star Team (1954)

Traded to **Detroit** by **Boston** with Murray Costello for Real Chevrefils and Jerry Toppazzini, January 17, 1956. Traded to **Chicago** by **Detroit** with Earl Reibel, Billy Dea and Bill Dineen for Bob Bailey, Nick Mickoski, Jack McIntyre and Hec Lalande, December 17, 1957. Traded to **Montreal** by **Chicago** with Glen Skov, the rights to Danny Lewicki, Terry Gray and Bob Bailey for Cec Hoekstra, Reggie Fleming, Ab McDonald and Bob Courcy, June 7, 1960.

• FIELD, WILF
Wilf Field
D – R. 5'11", 185 lbs. b: Winnipeg, Man., 4/29/1915. d: 3/17/1979.

			REGULAR SEASON								PLAYOFFS				
Season	Club	League	GP	G	A	Pts	AG	AA	APts	PIM	GP	G	A	Pts	PIM
1933-34	Winnipeg Monarchs	MJHL	14	3	2	5	....	....	....	18	3	2	1	3	2
1934-35	Winnipeg Monarchs	MJHL	10	6	1	7	....	....	....	16	4	3	1	4	10
1935-36	Winnipeg Monarchs	MJHL	2	0	1	1	....	....	....	0	....	....	....	....	....
	Providence Reds	IAHL	42	0	1	1	....	....	....	5	7	0	0	0	8
1936-37	**New York Americans**	**NHL**	**2**	**0**	**0**	**0**	**0**	**0**	**0**	**0**	....	....	....	....	....
	New Haven Eagles	AHL	46	3	2	5	....	....	....	48	....	....	....	....	....
1937-38	Seattle Seahawks	PCHL	41	12	12	24	....	....	....	38	4	0	1	1	2
1938-39	**New York Americans**	**NHL**	**47**	**1**	**3**	**4**	**2**	**6**	**8**	**37**	**2**	**0**	**0**	**0**	**2**
1939-40	**New York Americans**	**NHL**	**45**	**1**	**3**	**4**	**2**	**6**	**8**	**28**	**3**	**0**	**0**	**0**	**0**
1940-41	**New York Americans**	**NHL**	**36**	**5**	**6**	**11**	**10**	**11**	**21**	**31**	....	....	....	....	....
1941-42	**Brooklyn Americans**	**NHL**	**41**	**6**	**9**	**15**	**10**	**14**	**24**	**23**	....	....	....	....	....
1942-43	Winnipeg RCAF	MHL Sr.	2	0	1	1	....	....	....	5	....	....	....	....	....
	Calgary RCAF Mustangs	ASHL	16	1	4	5	....	....	....	32	8	2	4	6	8
1943-44	Ottawa Commandos	QSHL	8	0	4	4	....	....	....	22	....	....	....	....	....
1944-45	**Montreal Canadiens**	**NHL**	**9**	**1**	**0**	**1**	**1**	**0**	**1**	**10**	....	....	....	....	....
	Chicago Black Hawks	**NHL**	**39**	**3**	**4**	**7**	**4**	**6**	**10**	**22**	....	....	....	....	....
1945-46	Buffalo Bisons	AHL	36	1	10	11	....	....	....	22	12	0	2	2	8
1946-47	Buffalo Bisons	AHL	62	2	14	16	....	....	....	34	4	0	0	0	4
1947-48	Buffalo Bisons	AHL	51	0	17	17	....	....	....	28	6	0	2	2	2
1948-49	Houston Huskies	USHL	64	6	18	24	....	....	....	34	....	....	....	....	....
1949-50	Buffalo Bisons	AHL	66	3	7	10	....	....	....	31	5	0	0	0	0
1950-51	Kansas City Royals	USHL	52	4	13	17	....	....	....	16	....	....	....	....	....
1951-52	Halifax Saints	MMHL	5	0	1	1	....	....	....	12	....	....	....	....	....
1952-53	Troy Uncle Sam Trojans	EHL	DID NOT PLAY – COACHING												
	NHL Totals		**219**	**17**	**25**	**42**	**29**	**43**	**72**	**151**	**5**	**0**	**0**	**0**	**2**

Signed as a free agent by **NY Americans**, November, 1936. Rights transferred to **Montreal** from **Brooklyn** in Special Dispersal Draw, September 11, 1943. Loaned to **Chicago** by **Montreal** for the remainder of the 1944-45 season, December 7, 1944.

• FIELDER, GUYLE
Guyle "Guy" Fielder
C – L. 5'9", 165 lbs. b: Potlach, ID, 11/21/1930.

			REGULAR SEASON								PLAYOFFS				
Season	Club	League	GP	G	A	Pts	AG	AA	APts	PIM	GP	G	A	Pts	PIM
1947-48	Prince Albert Mintos	SJHL	25	26	15	41	....	....	....	20	2	0	1	1	0
1948-49	Prince Albert Mintos	SJHL	20	17	*26	43	....	....	....	22	9	9	*14	23	4
	Lethbridge Native Sons	WCJHL	2	1	1	2	....	....	....	0	....	....	....	....	....
1949-50	Lethbridge Native Sons	WCJHL	39	47	*58	*105	....	....	....	19	10	2	7	9	14
1950-51	**Chicago Black Hawks**	**NHL**	**3**	**0**	**0**	**0**	**0**	**0**	**0**	**0**	....	....	....	....	....
	Lethbridge Native Sons	WCJHL	37	*44	*56	*100	....	....	....	6	7	3	5	8	8
1951-52	New Westminster Royals	PCHL	57	25	50	75	....	....	....	10	7	1	3	4	2
1952-53	St. Louis Flyers	AHL	62	22	*61	83	....	....	....	12	....	....	....	....	....
	Edmonton Flyers	WHL	3	0	1	1	....	....	....	0	....	....	....	....	....
	Detroit Red Wings	**NHL**	....	....	....	....	....	....	....	....	**4**	**0**	**0**	**0**	**0**
1953-54	Seattle Bombers	WHL	68	24	*64	*88	....	....	....	20	....	....	....	....	....
	Boston Bruins	**NHL**	....	....	....	....	....	....	....	....	**2**	**0**	**0**	**0**	**2**
1954-55	New Westminster Royals	WHL	70	20	*67	87	....	....	....	37	....	....	....	....	....
1955-56	Seattle Americans	WHL	70	18	61	79	....	....	....	42	....	....	....	....	....
1956-57	Seattle Americans	WHL	69	33	*89	*122	....	....	....	30	6	2	4	6	0
1957-58	**Detroit Red Wings**	**NHL**	**6**	**0**	**0**	**0**	**0**	**0**	**0**	**2**	....	....	....	....	....
	Seattle Totems	WHL	62	26	*85	*111	....	....	....	22	9	2	9	11	2
1958-59	Seattle Totems	WHL	69	24	*95	*119	....	....	....	18	12	4	9	13	4
1959-60	Seattle Totems	WHL	69	31	*64	*95	....	....	....	12	4	1	1	2	0
1960-61	Seattle Totems	WHL	69	24	*71	95	....	....	....	32	11	2	9	11	4
1961-62	Seattle Totems	WHL	69	21	52	73	....	....	....	46	2	0	0	0	0
1962-63	Seattle Totems	WHL	69	17	*80	*97	....	....	....	20	17	5	*17	*22	6
1963-64	Seattle Totems	WHL	66	17	*85	*102	....	....	....	34	....	....	....	....	....
	Quebec Aces	AHL	....	....	....	....	....	....	....	....	1	0	0	0	0
1964-65	Seattle Totems	WHL	70	14	*78	*92	....	....	....	38	7	0	7	7	2
1965-66	Seattle Totems	WHL	70	19	*75	94	....	....	....	10	....	....	....	....	....
1966-67	Seattle Totems	WHL	72	20	*71	*91	....	....	....	22	10	2	*7	9	12
1967-68	Seattle Totems	WHL	70	15	*55	70	....	....	....	26	9	6	5	11	2
1968-69	Seattle Totems	WHL	74	20	74	94	....	....	....	12	4	0	2	2	4
1969-70	Salt Lake Golden Eagles	WHL	55	8	58	66	....	....	....	20	....	....	....	....	....
1970-71	Salt Lake Golden Eagles	WHL	64	15	46	61	....	....	....	22	....	....	....	....	....
1971-72	Salt Lake Golden Eagles	WHL	30	5	22	27	....	....	....	4	....	....	....	....	....
	Portland Buckaroos	WHL	40	9	40	49	....	....	....	10	11	0	*10	10	2
1972-73	Portland Buckaroos	WHL	70	11	47	58	....	....	....	4	....	....	....	....	....
	NHL Totals		**9**	**0**	**0**	**0**	**0**	**0**	**0**	**2**	**6**	**0**	**0**	**0**	**2**

WHL Second All-Star Team (19) • Rookie of the Year - PCHL (1952) • AHL First All-Star Team (1953) • Won Dudley "Red" Garrett Memorial Award (Top Rookie - AHL) (1953) • WHL First All-Star Team (1954, 1960, 1963, 1964, 1967) • WHL Coast Division First All-Star Team (1957, 1958, 1959) • Won Leader Cup (WHL Coast Division - MVP) (1957, 1958, 1959) • Won Leader Cup (WHL - MVP) (Tied with Hank Bassen) (1960) • WHL Second All-Star Team (1961, 1965, 1966, 1968) • Won Leader Cup (WHL - MVP) (1964, 1967) • Won Fred J. Hume Cup (WHL Most Gentlemanly Player) (1966, 1967, 1969)

Traded to **Chicago** by **Detroit** with Steve Hrymnak and Red Almas for cash, September 23, 1952. Traded to **Boston** by **Detroit** for cash, September 24, 1953. Traded to **Detroit** by **Boston** for cash, June 15, 1957. Claimed by **Toronto** from **Seattle** (WHL) in Inter-League Draft, June, 1958. • Fielder refused to sign with Toronto and remained the property of Seattle. Traded to **Salt Lake** (WHL) by **Seattle** (WHL) for Bobby Schmautz, November, 1969. Traded to **Portland** (WHL) by **Salt Lake** (WHL) with the loan of Jake Rathwell for Fred Hilts and Lyle Bradley, January, 1972.

• FILLION, BOB
Bob Fillion
LW – L. 5'10", 170 lbs. b: Thetford Mines, Que., 7/12/1921.

			REGULAR SEASON								PLAYOFFS				
Season	Club	League	GP	G	A	Pts	AG	AA	APts	PIM	GP	G	A	Pts	PIM
1938-39	Verdun Maple Leafs	Mtl-Jr.	11	4	12	16	....	....	....	8	10	5	4	9	12
1939-40	Verdun Maple Leafs	Mtl-Jr.	11	10	6	16	....	....	....	6	....	....	....	....	....
	Verdun Maple Leafs	Mtl-Sr.	6	0	3	3	....	....	....	0	8	0	2	2	0
1940-41	Shawinigan Cataracts	QSHL	24	10	20	30	....	....	....	25	10	3	6	9	15
1941-42	Shawinigan Cataracts	QSHL	8	1	5	6	....	....	....	4	8	6	6	12	4
1942-43	Montreal Army	QSHL	33	4	13	17	....	....	....	8	7	1	3	4	2
1943-44	**Montreal Canadiens**	**NHL**	**41**	**7**	**23**	**30**	**9**	**28**	**37**	**14**	**3**	**0**	**0**	**0**	**0**
1944-45	**Montreal Canadiens**	**NHL**	**31**	**6**	**8**	**14**	**8**	**13**	**21**	**12**	**1**	**3**	**0**	**3**	**0**
1945-46	**Montreal Canadiens**	**NHL**	**50**	**10**	**6**	**16**	**15**	**11**	**26**	**12**	**9**	**4**	**3**	**7**	**6**
1946-47	**Montreal Canadiens**	**NHL**	**57**	**6**	**3**	**9**	**8**	**4**	**12**	**16**	**8**	**0**	**0**	**0**	**0**
1947-48	**Montreal Canadiens**	**NHL**	**32**	**9**	**9**	**18**	**13**	**13**	**26**	**8**	....	....	....	....	....
	Buffalo Bisons	AHL	18	9	9	18	....	....	....	4	....	....	....	....	....
1948-49	**Montreal Canadiens**	**NHL**	**59**	**3**	**9**	**12**	**5**	**14**	**19**	**14**	**7**	**0**	**1**	**1**	**4**
1949-50	**Montreal Canadiens**	**NHL**	**57**	**1**	**3**	**4**	**1**	**4**	**5**	**8**	**5**	**0**	**0**	**0**	**0**
1950-51	Sherbrooke Saints	QSHL	44	15	18	33	....	....	....	45	7	1	1	2	6
	NHL Totals		**327**	**42**	**61**	**103**	**59**	**87**	**146**	**84**	**33**	**7**	**4**	**11**	**10**

• FILLION, MARCEL
Marcel Fillion
LW – L. 5'7", 175 lbs. b: Thetford Mines, Que., 5/28/1923.

			REGULAR SEASON								PLAYOFFS				
Season	Club	League	GP	G	A	Pts	AG	AA	APts	PIM	GP	G	A	Pts	PIM
1940-41	Shawinigan Cataracts	QSHL	27	11	13	24	....	....	....	2	10	4	2	6	8
1941-42	Shawinigan Cataracts	QSHL	33	15	17	32	....	....	....	16	10	2	1	3	2
1942-43	Quebec Sea Gulls	City Sr.	....	....	....	....	....	....	....	....	10	*17	*23	*40	....
1943-44			DID NOT PLAY												
1944-45	**Boston Bruins**	**NHL**	**1**	**0**	**0**	**0**	**0**	**0**	**0**	**0**	....	....	....	....	....
	Boston Olympics	EHL	46	38	40	78	....	....	....	84	12	10	8	18	2
1945-46	Shawinigan Cataracts	QSHL	20	8	6	14	....	....	....	14	4	1	0	1	4
1946-47	Providence Reds	AHL	21	2	6	8	....	....	....	6	....	....	....	....	....
	Boston Olympics	EHL	27	19	6	25	....	....	....	18	9	7	*8	*15	14
1947-48	Boston Olympics	QSHL	48	25	32	57	....	....	....	22	....	....	....	....	....
	Boston Olympics	EHL	19	14	17	31	....	....	....	15	....	....	....	....	....
1948-49	Boston–Sherbrooke	QSHL	63	39	34	73	....	....	....	41	12	7	2	9	4
1949-50	Sherbrooke Saints	QSHL	60	21	29	50	....	....	....	24	6	0	0	0	2
1950-51	Sherbrooke Saints	QSHL	58	14	14	28	....	....	....	31	7	0	1	1	6
1951-52			DID NOT PLAY – RETIRED												
1952-53	Rimouski Renards	City Sr.	58	24	36	60	....	....	....	44	....	....	....	....	....
1953-54	Rimouski Renards	City Sr.	65	13	14	27	....	....	....	8	....	....	....	....	....
	NHL Totals		**1**	**0**	**0**	**0**	**0**	**0**	**0**	**0**	....	....	....	....	....

EHL Second All-Star Team (1945)

• FILMORE, TOMMY Tommy Filmore
RW – R. 5'11", 189 lbs. b: Thamesford, Ont.. Deceased.

Season	Club	League	GP	G	A	Pts	AG	AA	APts	PIM	GP	G	A	Pts	PIM
1926-27	London 12th Battery	OHA	....	....	....	....	....	....	....	....	13	*19	7	*26	....
1927-28	London Panthers	Can-Pro	40	19	7	26	....	....	....	18	....	....	....	....	....
1928-29	London–Detroit	Can-Pro	40	11	8	19	....	....	....	23	7	2	1	3	9
1929-30	Detroit Olympics	IAHL	42	18	16	34	....	....	....	34	3	1	0	1	0
1930-31	**Detroit Falcons**	**NHL**	**39**	**6**	**2**	**8**	**15**	**7**	**22**	**10**	....	....	....	....	....
1931-32	**Detroit Falcons**	**NHL**	**9**	**0**	**0**	**0**	**0**	**0**	**0**	**2**	....	....	....	....	....
	New York Americans	**NHL**	**31**	**8**	**6**	**14**	**17**	**17**	**34**	**12**	....	....	....	....	....
	Detroit Olympics	IAHL	11	2	1	3	....	....	....	4	....	....	....	....	....
1932-33	**New York Americans**	**NHL**	**34**	**1**	**4**	**5**	**2**	**11**	**13**	**9**	....	....	....	....	....
	Boston Bruins	**NHL**	**1**	**0**	**0**	**0**	**0**	**0**	**0**	**0**	....	....	....	....	....
	Boston Cubs	Can-Am	10	3	4	7	....	....	....	0	7	0	*4	4	4
1933-34	**Boston Bruins**	**NHL**	**3**	**0**	**0**	**0**	**0**	**0**	**0**	**0**	....	....	....	....	....
	Boston Cubs	Can-Am	35	16	11	27	....	....	....	10	5	2	1	3	6
1934-35	Quebec Beavers	Can-Am	15	3	4	7	....	....	....	6	3	1	0	1	10
1935-36	Providence Reds	Can-Am	42	10	7	17	....	....	....	6	7	1	*5	*6	6
1936-37	Springfield Indians	AHL	39	9	19	28	....	....	....	14	5	0	0	0	0
1937-38	Springfield Indians	AHL	37	16	14	30	....	....	....	19	....	....	....	....	....
1938-39	Springfield Indians	AHL	28	16	13	29	....	....	....	4	3	0	0	0	0
1939-40	Springfield Indians	AHL	39	16	20	36	....	....	....	6	3	3	1	4	7
1940-41			DID NOT PLAY												
1941-42	Fort Worth Rangers	AHA	1	0	0	0	....	....	....	0	....	....	....	....	....
	NHL Totals		**117**	**15**	**12**	**27**	**34**	**35**	**69**	**33**	....	....	....	....	....

Traded to **NY Americans** by **Detroit Falcons** with Bert McInenly and Jimmy Creighton for Hap Emms and Frank Carson, December 29, 1931. Traded to **Boston** by **NY Americans** for Lloyd Klein, February 12, 1933. Traded to **Montreal Canadiens** by **Boston** with cash for Tony Savage, November 5, 1934.

• FINKBEINER, LLOYD Lloyd Finkbeiner
LW/D – L. 5'10", 175 lbs. b: Guelph, Ont., 4/12/1920.

Season	Club	League	GP	G	A	Pts	AG	AA	APts	PIM	GP	G	A	Pts	PIM
1937-38	Guelph Indians	OHA	14	3	2	5	....	....	....	14	9	3	2	5	10
1938-39	Guelph Indians	OHA	14	2	1	3	....	....	....	23	2	0	0	0	4
1939-40	Detroit Pontiacs	MOHL	11	1	0	1	....	....	....	30	....	....	....	....	....
1940-41	**New York Americans**	**NHL**	**2**	**0**	**0**	**0**	**0**	**0**	**0**	**0**	....	....	....	....	....
	Springfield Indians	AHL	34	3	5	8	....	....	....	8	....	....	....	....	....
	Atlantic City Seagulls	EHL	6	0	0	0	....	....	....	0	....	....	....	....	....
1941-42			MILITARY SERVICE												
1942-43	Toronto Army Daggers	OHA Sr.	12	6	5	11	....	....	....	26	4	1	1	2	6
1943-44			MILITARY SERVICE												
1944-45	Montreal Royals	QSHL	2	0	0	0	....	....	....	0	....	....	....	....	....
1945-46	Buffalo Bisons	AHL	14	1	0	1	....	....	....	2	....	....	....	....	....
	Dallas Texans	USHL	42	13	8	21	....	....	....	28	....	....	....	....	....
1946-47	Dallas Texans	USHL	57	8	22	30	....	....	....	128	6	1	4	5	4
1947-48	Dallas Texans	USHL	66	9	18	27	....	....	....	78	....	....	....	....	....
1948-49	Houston Huskies	USHL	3	0	1	1	....	....	....	2	....	....	....	....	....
	Buffalo Bisons	AHL	63	7	14	21	....	....	....	95			....	....	....
1949-50	Buffalo Bisons	AHL	70	9	14	23	....	....	....	110	5	1	2	3	10
1950-51	Buffalo Bisons	AHL	64	6	20	26	....	....	....	86	4	1	1	2	10
1951-52	Buffalo Bisons	AHL	29	0	13	13	....	....	....	38	1	0	0	0	2
	Montreal Royals	QSHL	23	1	5	6	....	....	....	29	5	0	1	1	6
1952-53	Cincinnati Mohawks	IHL	48	5	26	31	....	....	....	87	9	2	5	7	32
1953-54	Stratford Indians	OHA Sr.	52	9	21	30	....	....	....	100	3	1	0	1	12
1954-55	Stratford Indians	OHA Sr.	50	2	16	18	....	....	....	103	7	1	6	7	8
1955-56	Stratford Indians	OHA Sr.	48	6	21	27	....	....	....	60	6	2	1	3	6
	NHL Totals		**2**	**0**	**0**	**0**	**0**	**0**	**0**	**0**	....			....	....

USHL Second All-Star Team (1948)

• FINNEY, SID Sid Finney
C – L. 5'11", 160 lbs. b: Banbridge, Ireland, 5/1/1920.

Season	Club	League	GP	G	A	Pts	AG	AA	APts	PIM	GP	G	A	Pts	PIM
1947-48	Calgary Buffalos	AJHL	15	6	8	14	....	....	....	9	8	2	2	4	0
1948-49	Calgary Buffalos	WCJHL	32	27	16	43	....	....	....	14	8	*9	3	12	2
1949-50	Calgary Stampeders	WCSHL	17	7	5	12	....	....	....	4	....	....	....	....	
1950-51	Calgary Stampeders	WCSHL	57	*44	37	*81	....	....	....	12	8	4	1	5	0
1951-52	**Chicago Black Hawks**	**NHL**	**35**	**6**	**5**	**11**	**8**	**6**	**14**	**0**	....	....	....	....	....
	St. Louis Flyers	AHL	23	8	5	13	....	....	....	2	....	....	....	....	....
1952-53	**Chicago Black Hawks**	**NHL**	**18**	**4**	**2**	**6**	**6**	**3**	**9**	**4**	**7**	**0**	**2**	**2**	**0**
	Calgary Stampeders	WHL	39	25	19	44	....	....	....	12	....	....	....	....	....
1953-54	**Chicago Black Hawks**	**NHL**	**6**	**0**	**0**	**0**	**0**	**0**	**0**	**0**	....	....	....	....	....
	Calgary Stampeders	WHL	47	29	33	62	....	....	....	9	25	*20	9	*29	4
1954-55	Calgary Stampeders	WHL	70	35	42	77	....	....	....	20	9	4	5	9	0
1955-56	Calgary Stampeders	WHL	69	43	36	79	....	....	....	24	8	7	4	11	0
1956-57	Calgary Stampeders	WHL	68	41	38	79	....	....	....	47	3	0	0	0	8
1957-58	Calgary Stampeders	WHL	58	*45	43	88	....	....	....	8	12	5	9	14	12
1958-59	Calgary Stampeders	WHL	60	29	30	59	....	....	....	24	8	1	5	6	2
1959-60	Calgary Stampeders	WHL	59	28	32	60	....	....	....	6	....	....	....	....	....
1960-61	Calgary Stampeders	WHL	59	26	42	68	....	....	....	12	5	2	4	6	0
1961-62	Calgary Stampeders	WHL	61	35	32	67	....	....	....	4	7	2	2	4	0
1962-63	Edmonton Flyers	WHL	65	23	42	65	....	....	....	16	3	1	3	4	0
1963-64	Portland Buckaroos	WHL	39	9	10	19	....	....	....	2	....	....	....	....	....
	Cincinnati Wings	CHL	13	3	3	6	....	....	....	4	....	....	....	....	....
1964-65			DID NOT PLAY												
1965-66	Drumheller Miners	ASHL	....	13	22	35	....	....		6	....	....	....	....	....
	NHL Totals		**59**	**10**	**7**	**17**	**14**	**9**	**23**	**4**	**7**	**0**	**2**	**2**	**0**

WHL Prairie Division First All-Star Team (1957, 1958) • Won Leader Cup (WHL Prairie Division - MVP) (1958)

Claimed by **Hershey** (AHL) from **Chicago**, June, 1958. Traded to **Edmonton** (WHL) by **Calgary** (WHL) for Gord Strato, September, 1961. Traded to **Portland** (WHL) by **Edmonton** (WHL) for Ken Laufman and Roger Leopold, November, 1963.

• FINNIGAN, ED Ed Finnigan
LW – L. 5'8", 170 lbs. b: Shawville, Que., 5/23/1913. Deceased.

Season	Club	League	GP	G	A	Pts	AG	AA	APts	PIM	GP	G	A	Pts	PIM
1927-28	North Bay Trappers	NOHA	12	3	13	16	....	....	....	....	2	0	0	0	0
1928-29	Ottawa Shamrocks	City Jr.	STATISTICS NOT AVAILABLE												
1929-30	Ottawa Rideaus	City Jr.	12	5	1	6	....	....	....	19	4	3	2	5	12
1930-31	Ottawa Rideaus	City Jr.	15	12	4	16	....	....	....	*49	2	0	1	1	10
	Ottawa Rideaus	City Sr.	....	....	....	....	....	....	....	....	12	*4	1	5	14
1931-32	Ottawa Rideaus	City Sr.	23	12	5	17	....	....	....	46	4	1	0	1	2
1932-33	Ottawa Rideaus	City Sr.	19	9	3	12	....	....	....	12	10	*6	3	*9	18
1933-34	Ottawa Edinburghs	City Sr.	20	14	7	21	....	....	....	28	10	7	6	13	16
1934-35	**St. Louis Eagles**	**NHL**	**12**	**1**	**1**	**2**	**2**	**2**	**4**	**2**	....	....	....	....	....
	Ottawa Senators	QSHL	20	15	*22	37	....	....	....	16	....	....	....	....	....
1935-36	**Boston Bruins**	**NHL**	**3**	**0**	**0**	**0**	**0**	**0**	**0**	**0**	....	....	....	....	....
	Boston Cubs	Can-Am	29	9	4	13	....	....	....	4	....	....	....	....	....
	Rochester Cardinals	IAHL	11	2	0	2	....	....	....	10	....	....	....	....	....
1936-37			DID NOT PLAY												
1937-38	Ottawa Senators	QSHL	22	10	9	19	....	....	....	8	4	1	1	2	0
1938-39			DID NOT PLAY												
1939-40	Ottawa RCAF	QSHL	2	2	0	2	....	....	....	2	....	....	....	....	....
1940-41	Hull Volants	QSHL	19	11	19	30	....	....	....	5	10	6	9	15	6
1941-42	Hull Volants	QSHL	12	7	13	20	....	....	....	0	7	5	3	8	2
1942-43	Hull–Ottawa	QSHL	18	6	10	16	....	....	....	0	....	....	....	....	....
1943-44	Ottawa Montagnards	City Sr.	13	*14	*16	*30	....	....	....	6	2	3	2	5	0
	Ottawa Canadiens	City Sr.	....	....	....	....	....	....	....	....	5	8	1	9	0
1944-45	Ottawa Commandos	QSHL	15	6	4	10	....	....	....	7	2	0	0	0	0
1945-46			DID NOT PLAY												
1946-47	Renfrew Lions	OVSHL	23	8	7	15	....	....	....	4	3	0	2	2	2
	NHL Totals		**15**	**1**	**1**	**2**	**2**	**2**	**4**	**2**	....	....	....	....	....

Claimed by **NY Americans** from **St. Louis** in Dispersal Draft, September 26, 1936. Traded to **Boston** by **NY Americans** for cash, September 26, 1936.

• FINNIGAN, FRANK Frank "The Shawville Express" Finnigan
RW – R. 5'9", 165 lbs. b: Shawville, Que., 7/9/1903. Deceased.

Season	Club	League	GP	G	A	Pts	AG	AA	APts	PIM	GP	G	A	Pts	PIM
1921-22	University of Ottawa	City Sr.	5	1	3	4	....	....	....	0	....	....	....	....	....
1922-23	Ottawa College	City Sr.	9	7	5	12	....	....	....	0	....	....	....	....	....
1923-24	Ottawa Montagnards	City Sr.	10	4	1	5	....	....	....	....	3	0	0	0	....
	Ottawa Senators	**NHL**	**2**	**0**	**0**	**0**	**0**	**0**	**0**	**0**	**2**	**0**	**0**	**0**	**2**
1924-25	**Ottawa Senators**	**NHL**	**29**	**0**	**0**	**0**	**0**	**0**	**0**	**20**	....	....	....	....	....
1925-26	**Ottawa Senators**	**NHL**	**36**	**2**	**0**	**2**	**6**	**0**	**6**	**24**	**2**	**0**	**0**	**0**	**0**
1926-27	**Ottawa Senators**	**NHL**	**36**	**15**	**1**	**16**	**44**	**8**	**52**	**52**	**6**	**3**	**0**	**3**	**0**
1927-28	**Ottawa Senators**	**NHL**	**38**	**20**	**5**	**25**	**62**	**42**	**104**	**34**	**2**	**0**	**1**	**1**	**6**
1928-29	**Ottawa Senators**	**NHL**	**44**	**15**	**4**	**19**	**61**	**37**	**98**	**71**	....	....	....	....	....
1929-30	**Ottawa Senators**	**NHL**	**43**	**21**	**15**	**36**	**42**	**49**	**91**	**46**	**1**	**0**	**0**	**0**	**4**
1930-31	**Ottawa Senators**	**NHL**	**44**	**9**	**8**	**17**	**22**	**29**	**51**	**40**	....	....	....	....	....
1931-32	**Toronto Maple Leafs**	**NHL**	**47**	**8**	**13**	**21**	**17**	**36**	**53**	**45**	**7**	**2**	**3**	**5**	**8**
1932-33	**Ottawa Senators**	**NHL**	**45**	**4**	**14**	**18**	**9**	**37**	**46**	**37**	....	....	....	....	....
1933-34	**Ottawa Senators**	**NHL**	**48**	**10**	**10**	**20**	**22**	**27**	**49**	**10**	....	....	....	....	....
1934-35	**St. Louis Eagles**	**NHL**	**34**	**5**	**5**	**10**	**11**	**11**	**22**	**10**	....	....	....	....	....
	Toronto Maple Leafs	**NHL**	**11**	**2**	**0**	**2**	**4**	**0**	**4**	**2**	**7**	**1**	**2**	**3**	**2**
1935-36	**Toronto Maple Leafs**	**NHL**	**40**	**2**	**6**	**8**	**5**	**14**	**19**	**10**	**9**	**0**	**3**	**3**	**0**
1936-37	**Toronto Maple Leafs**	**NHL**	**48**	**2**	**7**	**9**	**4**	**16**	**20**	**4**	**2**	**0**	**0**	**0**	**0**
	NHL Totals		**553**	**115**	**88**	**203**	**309**	**306**	**615**	**405**	**38**	**6**	**9**	**15**	**22**

Played in NHL All-Star Game (1934)

Signed as a free agent by **Ottawa**, February 21, 1924. Claimed by **Toronto** from **Ottawa** for 1931-32 season in Dispersal Draft, September 26, 1931. Transferred to **St. Louis** after **Ottawa** franchise relocated, September 30, 1934. Traded to **Toronto** by **St. Louis** for cash, February 13, 1935.

• FISHER, ALVIN Alvin Fisher
RW – R. 6'1", 175 lbs. b: Sault Ste. Marie, Ont.. Deceased.

Season	Club	League	GP	G	A	Pts	AG	AA	APts	PIM	GP	G	A	Pts	PIM
1919-20	Hamilton Tigers	OHA Sr.	4	0	1	1	....	....	....	....	2	0	0	0	0
1920-21	Soo Greyhounds	City Sr.	14	6	3	9	....	....	....	....	....	....	....	....	....
	Soo Greyhounds	NOHA	9	7	1	8	....	....	....	12	5	1	0	1	0
1921-22	Soo Greyhounds	City Sr.	12	2	5	7	....	....	....	....	....	....	....	....	
	Soo Greyhounds	NOHA	8	2	1	3	....	....	....	15	2	0	1	1	2
1922-23	Calgary Tigers	WCHL	18	5	3	8	....	....	....	10	....	....	....	....	....
1923-24	Seattle Metropolitans	PCHA	15	1	1	2	....	....	....	2	2	0	0	0	0
1924-25	**Toronto St. Pats**	**NHL**	**9**	**1**	**0**	**1**	**3**	**0**	**3**	**4**	....	....	....	....	....
	NHL Totals		**9**	**1**	**0**	**1**	**3**	**0**	**3**	**4**	....	....	....	....	....
	Other Major League Totals		33	6	4	10	....	....	....	12	2	0	0	0	0

Signed as a free agent by **Calgary** (WCHL), August 21, 1922. Traded to **Seattle** (PCHA) by **Calgary** with Jack Arbour for cash, August 21, 1923. Signed as a free agent by **Toronto St. Pats** after **Seattle** (PCHA) franchise folded, December 12, 1924.

• FISHER, DUNC
Dunc Fisher
RW – R. 5'7", 170 lbs. b: Regina, Sask., 8/30/1927.

Season	Club	League	REGULAR SEASON GP	G	A	Pts	AG	AA	APts	PIM	PLAYOFFS GP	G	A	Pts	PIM
1944-45	Regina Abbotts	SJHL	15	5	6	11	....	....	....	30	....	....	....	....	....
1945-46	Regina Abbotts	SJHL	18	19	13	32	....	....	....	22	5	5	2	7	2
1946-47	Regina Pats	SJHL	26	28	16	44	....	....	....	12	6	5	7	12	8
1947-48	New Haven Ramblers	AHL	68	25	34	59	....	....	....	29	4	2	1	3	0
	New York Rangers	**NHL**	....	....	....	....	....	....	....	....	**1**	**0**	**1**	**1**	**0**
1948-49	**New York Rangers**	**NHL**	**60**	**9**	**16**	**25**	**14**	**25**	**39**	**40**	....	....	....	....	....
1949-50	**New York Rangers**	**NHL**	**70**	**12**	**21**	**33**	**16**	**27**	**43**	**42**	**12**	**3**	**3**	**6**	**14**
1950-51	**New York Rangers**	**NHL**	**12**	**0**	**0**	**0**	**0**	**0**	**0**	**0**	....	....	....	....	....
	St. Paul Saints	USHL	2	0	1	1	....	....	....	0	....	....	....	....	....
	Boston Bruins	**NHL**	**53**	**9**	**20**	**29**	**12**	**26**	**38**	**20**	**6**	**1**	**0**	**1**	**0**
1951-52	**Boston Bruins**	**NHL**	**65**	**15**	**12**	**27**	**21**	**15**	**36**	**2**	**2**	**0**	**0**	**0**	**0**
1952-53	**Boston Bruins**	**NHL**	**7**	**0**	**1**	**1**	**0**	**1**	**1**	**0**	....	....	....	....	....
	Hershey Bears	AHL	55	29	24	53	....	....	....	2	3	0	3	3	0
1953-54	Hershey Bears	AHL	69	41	39	80	....	....	....	24	11	4	1	5	2
1954-55	Hershey Bears	AHL	62	28	35	63	....	....	....	36	....	....	....	....	....
1955-56	Hershey Bears	AHL	60	40	43	83	....	....	....	73	....	....	....	....	....
1956-57	Hershey Bears	AHL	64	40	38	78	....	....	....	59	7	6	3	9	0
1957-58	Hershey Bears	AHL	70	*41	47	88	....	....	....	56	11	6	7	13	0
1958-59	**Detroit Red Wings**	**NHL**	**8**	**0**	**0**	**0**	**0**	**0**	**0**	**0**	....	....	....	....	....
	Hershey Bears	AHL	62	19	32	51	....	....	....	28	13	4	9	13	12
1959-60	Hershey Bears	AHL	69	22	43	65	....	....	....	58	....	....	....	....	....
	NHL Totals		**275**	**45**	**70**	**115**	**63**	**94**	**157**	**104**	**21**	**4**	**4**	**8**	**14**

AHL Second All-Star Team (1954, 1955, 1956, 1957) • AHL First All-Star Team (1958)

Traded to **Boston** by **NY Rangers** for Ed Harrison and Zellio Toppazzini, November 16, 1950. Traded to **Detroit** by **Boston** for Don Poile and Hec Lalande, June 7, 1958.

• FISHER, JOE
Joe Fisher
RW – R. 6', 175 lbs. b: Medicine Hat, Alta., 7/4/1916.

Season	Club	League	GP	G	A	Pts	AG	AA	APts	PIM	GP	G	A	Pts	PIM
1934-35	Edmonton Athletic Club	City Jr.	9	0	3	3	....	....	....	7	....	....	....	....	....
1935-36	Coleman Canadians	ASHL	STATISTICS NOT AVAILABLE												
1936-37	Coleman Canadians	ASHL	STATISTICS NOT AVAILABLE												
1937-38	Kirkland Lake Blue Devils	NOHA	9	3	*14	17	....	....	....	6	2	*4	0	*4	0
1938-39	Pittsburgh Hornets	AHL	48	9	22	31	....	....	....	17	....	....	....	....	....
1939-40	**Detroit Red Wings**	**NHL**	**34**	**2**	**4**	**6**	**4**	**8**	**12**	**2**	**5**	**1**	**1**	**2**	**0**
	Indianapolis Capitals	AHL	17	7	16	23	....	....	....	9	....	....	....	....	....
1940-41	**Detroit Red Wings**	**NHL**	**27**	**5**	**8**	**13**	**10**	**15**	**25**	**11**	**5**	**1**	**0**	**1**	**6**
	Indianapolis Capitals	AHL	24	8	12	20	....	....	....	7	....	....	....	....	....
1941-42	**Detroit Red Wings**	**NHL**	**3**	**0**	**0**	**0**	**0**	**0**	**0**	**0**	**1**	**0**	**0**	**0**	**0**
	Indianapolis Capitals	AHL	41	21	18	39	....	....	....	15	10	4	4	8	2
1942-43	**Detroit Red Wings**	**NHL**	**1**	**1**	**0**	**1**	**1**	**0**	**1**	**0**	**1**	**0**	**0**	**0**	**0**
	Indianapolis Capitals	AHL	56	24	37	61	....	....	....	9	7	2	5	7	0
1943-44			MILITARY SERVICE												
1944-45	Winnipeg RCAF	City Sr.	4	3	2	5	....	....	....	0	3	2	2	4	5
1945-46	Calgary Stampeders	WCSHL	12	12	4	16	....	....	....	0	18	11	16	27	8
1946-47	Lethbridge Maple Leafs	WCSHL	35	15	44	59	....	....	....	22	7	4	3	7	12
1947-48	Regina Caps	WCSHL	32	17	24	41	....	....	....	2	1	2	0	2	0
1948-49	Regina Caps	WCSHL	1	0	0	0	....	....	....	0	7	2	6	8	2
1949-50	Medicine Hat Tigers	WCJHL	DID NOT PLAY – COACHING												
	NHL Totals		**65**	**8**	**12**	**20**	**15**	**23**	**38**	**13**	**12**	**2**	**1**	**3**	**6**

• FITZPATRICK, SANDY
— see page 1023

• FLAMAN, FERNIE
Fernie Flaman **HHOF**
D – R. 5'10", 190 lbs. b: Dysart, Sask., 1/25/1927.

Season	Club	League	GP	G	A	Pts	AG	AA	APts	PIM	GP	G	A	Pts	PIM
1942-43	Regina Abbots	MJHL	1	0	0	0	....	....	....	0	....	....	....	....	....
1943-44	Boston Olympics	EHL	32	12	7	19	....	....	....	31	12	2	6	8	14
	Brooklyn Crescents	EHL	11	5	9	14	....	....	....	12	....	....	....	....	....
1944-45	**Boston Bruins**	**NHL**	**1**	**0**	**0**	**0**	**0**	**0**	**0**	**0**	....	....	....	....	....
	Boston Olympics	EHL	46	16	27	43	....	....	....	75	10	3	5	8	13
1945-46	**Boston Bruins**	**NHL**	**1**	**0**	**0**	**0**	**0**	**0**	**0**	**0**	....	....	....	....	....
	Boston Olympics	EHL	45	11	23	34	....	....	....	80	12	2	7	9	11
1946-47	**Boston Bruins**	**NHL**	**23**	**1**	**4**	**5**	**1**	**6**	**7**	**41**	**5**	**0**	**0**	**0**	**8**
	Hershey Bears	AHL	38	4	8	12	....	....	....	64	....	....	....	....	....
1947-48	**Boston Bruins**	**NHL**	**56**	**4**	**6**	**10**	**6**	**9**	**15**	**69**	**5**	**0**	**0**	**0**	**12**
1948-49	**Boston Bruins**	**NHL**	**60**	**4**	**12**	**16**	**6**	**19**	**25**	**62**	**5**	**0**	**1**	**1**	**8**
1949-50	**Boston Bruins**	**NHL**	**69**	**2**	**5**	**7**	**3**	**6**	**9**	**122**	....	....	....	....	....
1950-51	**Boston Bruins**	**NHL**	**14**	**1**	**1**	**2**	**1**	**1**	**2**	**37**	....	....	....	....	....
	Toronto Maple Leafs	**NHL**	**39**	**2**	**6**	**8**	**3**	**8**	**11**	**64**	**9**	**1**	**0**	**1**	**8**
	Pittsburgh Hornets	AHL	11	1	6	7	....	....	....	24	....	....	....	....	....
1951-52	**Toronto Maple Leafs**	**NHL**	**61**	**0**	**7**	**7**	**0**	**9**	**9**	**110**	**4**	**0**	**2**	**2**	**18**
1952-53	**Toronto Maple Leafs**	**NHL**	**66**	**2**	**6**	**8**	**3**	**8**	**11**	**110**	....	....	....	....	....
1953-54	**Toronto Maple Leafs**	**NHL**	**62**	**0**	**8**	**8**	**0**	**11**	**11**	**84**	**2**	**0**	**0**	**0**	**0**
1954-55	**Boston Bruins**	**NHL**	**70**	**4**	**14**	**18**	**6**	**18**	**24**	**150**	**4**	**1**	**0**	**1**	**2**
1955-56	**Boston Bruins**	**NHL**	**62**	**4**	**17**	**21**	**6**	**21**	**27**	**70**	....	....	....	....	....
1956-57	**Boston Bruins**	**NHL**	**68**	**6**	**25**	**31**	**8**	**29**	**37**	**108**	**10**	**0**	**3**	**3**	**19**
1957-58	**Boston Bruins**	**NHL**	**66**	**0**	**15**	**15**	**0**	**16**	**16**	**71**	**12**	**2**	**2**	**4**	**10**
1958-59	**Boston Bruins**	**NHL**	**70**	**0**	**21**	**21**	**0**	**22**	**22**	**101**	**7**	**0**	**0**	**0**	**8**
1959-60	**Boston Bruins**	**NHL**	**60**	**2**	**18**	**20**	**2**	**18**	**20**	**112**	....	....	....	....	....
1960-61	**Boston Bruins**	**NHL**	**62**	**2**	**9**	**11**	**2**	**9**	**11**	**59**	....	....	....	....	....
1961-62	Providence Reds	AHL	65	3	33	36	....	....	....	95	3	0	1	1	6
1962-63	Providence Reds	AHL	68	4	17	21	....	....	....	65	6	0	2	2	0
1963-64	Providence Reds	AHL	22	1	5	6	....	....	....	21	3	0	1	1	4
1964-65	Providence Reds	AHL	DID NOT PLAY – COACHING												
	NHL Totals		**910**	**34**	**174**	**208**	**47**	**210**	**257**	**1370**	**63**	**4**	**8**	**12**	**93**

EHL First All-Star Team (1945, 1946) • NHL Second All-Star Team (1955, 1957, 1958)

Played in NHL All-Star Game (1952, 1955, 1956, 1957, 1958, 1959)

Traded to **Toronto** by **Boston** with Ken Smith and Phil Maloney for Bill Ezinicki, Leo Boivin, and Vic Lynn. November 16, 1950. Traded to **Boston** by **Toronto** for Dave Creighton, July 20, 1954.

• FLEMING, REGGIE
— see page 1024

• FOGOLIN, LIDIO
Lidio "Lee" Fogolin
D – L. 5'11", 195 lbs. b: Fort William, Ont., 2/27/1926.

Season	Club	League	GP	G	A	Pts	AG	AA	APts	PIM	GP	G	A	Pts	PIM
1942-43	Port Arthur Juniors	TBJHL	1	0	0	0	....	....	....	0	....	....	....	....	....
1943-44	Galt Kists	OHA	22	0	2	2	....	....	....	25	3	0	1	1	2
1944-45	Galt Red Wings	OHA	17	3	7	10	....	....	....	32	10	1	3	4	*25
1945-46	Galt Red Wings	OHA	27	13	24	37	....	....	....	51	5	1	1	2	8
1946-47	Omaha Knights	USHL	59	2	9	11	....	....	....	117	11	1	3	4	27
1947-48	Indianapolis Capitals	AHL	65	2	9	11	....	....	....	113	....	....	....	....	....
	Detroit Red Wings	**NHL**	....	....	....	....	....	....	....	....	**2**	**0**	**1**	**1**	**6**
1948-49	**Detroit Red Wings**	**NHL**	**43**	**1**	**2**	**3**	**2**	**3**	**5**	**59**	**9**	**0**	**0**	**0**	**4**
	Indianapolis Capitals	AHL	20	2	6	8	....	....	....	30	....	....	....	....	....
1949-50	**Detroit Red Wings**	**NHL**	**63**	**4**	**8**	**12**	**5**	**10**	**15**	**63**	**10**	**0**	**0**	**0**	**16**
1950-51	**Detroit Red Wings**	**NHL**	**19**	**0**	**1**	**1**	**0**	**1**	**1**	**16**	....	....	....	....	....
	Chicago Black Hawks	**NHL**	**35**	**3**	**10**	**13**	**4**	**13**	**17**	**63**	....	....	....	....	....
1951-52	**Chicago Black Hawks**	**NHL**	**69**	**0**	**9**	**9**	**0**	**12**	**12**	**96**	....	....	....	....	....
1952-53	**Chicago Black Hawks**	**NHL**	**70**	**2**	**8**	**10**	**3**	**11**	**14**	**79**	**7**	**0**	**1**	**1**	**4**
1953-54	**Chicago Black Hawks**	**NHL**	**68**	**0**	**1**	**1**	**0**	**1**	**1**	**95**	....	....	....	....	....
1954-55	**Chicago Black Hawks**	**NHL**	**9**	**0**	**1**	**1**	**0**	**1**	**1**	**16**	....	....	....	....	....
1955-56	**Chicago Black Hawks**	**NHL**	**51**	**0**	**8**	**8**	**0**	**10**	**10**	**88**	....	....	....	....	....
1956-57	Calgary Stampeders	WHL	61	1	9	10	....	....	....	84	3	0	0	0	2
	NHL Totals		**427**	**10**	**48**	**58**	**14**	**62**	**76**	**575**	**28**	**0**	**2**	**2**	**30**

Played in NHL All-Star Game (1950, 1951)

Traded to **Chicago** by **Detroit** with Steve Black for Bert Olmstead and Vic Stasiuk, December 10, 1950.

• FOLEY, GERRY
— see page 1027

• FOLK, BILL
Bill Folk
D – L. 5'11", 190 lbs. b: Regina, Sask., 7/11/1927.

Season	Club	League	GP	G	A	Pts	AG	AA	APts	PIM	GP	G	A	Pts	PIM
1944-45	Regina Abbotts	SJHL	16	1	2	3	....	....	....	54	....	....	....	....	....
1945-46	Regina Abbotts	SJHL	18	3	1	4	....	....	....	30	4	2	1	3	12
1946-47	Regina Caps	SJHL	29	7	5	12	....	....	....	40	6	2	0	2	10
1947-48	Boston Olympics	EHL	19	2	4	6	....	....	....	39	....	....	....	....	....
	Boston Olympics	QSHL	38	5	5	10	....	....	....	64	....	....	....	....	....
1948-49	Omaha Knights	USHL	62	4	14	18	....	....	....	84	4	0	2	2	6
1949-50	Omaha Knights	USHL	65	14	33	47	....	....	....	78	....	....	....	....	....
1950-51	Indianapolis Capitals	AHL	64	4	26	30	....	....	....	58	3	0	1	1	4
	Omaha Knights	USHL	....	....	....	....	....	....	....	....	6	*7	3	10	16
1951-52	**Detroit Red Wings**	**NHL**	**4**	**0**	**0**	**0**	**0**	**0**	**0**	**2**	....	....	....	....	....
	Indianapolis Capitals	AHL	50	4	14	18	....	....	....	56	....	....	....	....	....
1952-53	**Detroit Red Wings**	**NHL**	**8**	**0**	**0**	**0**	**0**	**0**	**0**	**2**	....	....	....	....	....
	Edmonton Flyers	WHL	56	9	19	28	....	....	....	74	15	1	7	8	24
1953-54	Edmonton Flyers	WHL	49	4	14	18	....	....	....	66	....	....	....	....	....
1954-55	Providence Reds	AHL	45	5	21	26	....	....	....	52	....	....	....	....	....
1955-56	Providence Reds	AHL	15	1	8	9	....	....	....	18	9	2	3	5	15
	Saskatoon Quakers	WHL	51	6	14	20	....	....	....	66	....	....	....	....	....
1956-57	Providence Reds	AHL	60	1	15	16	....	....	....	56	4	0	1	1	6
1957-58	Vancouver Canucks	WHL	68	7	21	28	....	....	....	72	11	1	9	10	18
1958-59	Winnipeg Warriors	WHL	56	7	25	32	....	....	....	61	7	0	6	6	6
1959-60	Winnipeg Warriors	WHL	56	4	32	36	....	....	....	53	....	....	....	....	....
1960-61	Spokane Comets	WHL	65	8	23	31	....	....	....	68	2	0	0	0	2
1961-62	Spokane Comets	WHL	2	0	1	1	....	....	....	4	....	....	....	....	....
1962-63			DID NOT PLAY												
1963-64			DID NOT PLAY												
1964-65	Regina Capitols	SSHL	8	3	6	9	....	....	....	6	5	1	1	2	9
1965-66	Regina Capitols	SSHL	6	0	8	8	....	....	....	10	....	....	....	....	....
	NHL Totals		**12**	**0**	**0**	**0**	**0**	**0**	**0**	**4**	....	....	....	....	....

• FONTEYNE, VAL
— see page 1029

• FONTINATO, LOU
Lou "Leapin' Louie" Fontinato
D – L. 6'1", 195 lbs. b: Guelph, Ont., 1/20/1932.

Season	Club	League	GP	G	A	Pts	AG	AA	APts	PIM	GP	G	A	Pts	PIM
1950-51	Guelph Biltmores	OHA	45	3	11	14	....	....	....	93	5	0	0	0	0
1951-52	Guelph Biltmores	OHA	48	6	15	21	....	....	....	152	23	1	4	5	*87
1952-53	Vancouver Canucks	WHL	65	3	18	21	....	....	....	169	9	1	3	4	12
1953-54	Vancouver–Saskatoon	WHL	63	4	14	18	....	....	....	147	6	0	1	1	25
1954-55	**New York Rangers**	**NHL**	**27**	**2**	**2**	**4**	**3**	**3**	**6**	**60**	....	....	....	....	....
	Saskatoon Quakers	WHL	35	4	6	10	....	....	....	55	....	....	....	....	....
1955-56	**New York Rangers**	**NHL**	**70**	**3**	**15**	**18**	**4**	**19**	**23**	***202**	**4**	**0**	**0**	**0**	**6**
1956-57	**New York Rangers**	**NHL**	**70**	**3**	**12**	**15**	**4**	**14**	**18**	**139**	**5**	**0**	**0**	**0**	**7**
1957-58	**New York Rangers**	**NHL**	**70**	**3**	**8**	**11**	**4**	**9**	**13**	***152**	**6**	**0**	**1**	**1**	**6**
1958-59	**New York Rangers**	**NHL**	**64**	**7**	**6**	**13**	**9**	**6**	**15**	**149**	....	....	....	....	....
1959-60	**New York Rangers**	**NHL**	**64**	**2**	**11**	**13**	**2**	**11**	**13**	**137**	....	....	....	....	....
1960-61	**New York Rangers**	**NHL**	**53**	**2**	**3**	**5**	**2**	**3**	**5**	**100**	....	....	....	....	....
1961-62	**Montreal Canadiens**	**NHL**	**54**	**2**	**13**	**15**	**2**	**13**	**15**	***167**	**6**	**0**	**1**	**1**	**23**
1962-63	**Montreal Canadiens**	**NHL**	**63**	**2**	**8**	**10**	**2**	**8**	**10**	**141**	....	....	....	....	....
	NHL Totals		**535**	**26**	**78**	**104**	**32**	**86**	**118**	**1247**	**21**	**0**	**2**	**2**	**42**

Traded to **Montreal** by **NY Rangers** for Doug Harvey, June 13, 1961. • Suffered career-ending neck injury in game vs. NY Rangers, March 9, 1963.

• FORSEY, JACK Jack Forsey
RW – R. 5'11", 170 lbs. b: Swift Current, Sask., 11/7/1914. Deceased.

			REGULAR SEASON								PLAYOFFS				
Season	Club	League	GP	G	A	Pts	AG	AA	APts	PIM	GP	G	A	Pts	PIM
1931-32	Calgary Jimmies	City Jr.	7	3	1	4	....	....	....	12	3	0	2	2	4
1932-33	Calgary Jimmies	City Jr.	5	4	*6	*10	....	....	....	6	....	....	....	....	....
1933-34	Nelson Red Wings	Kootenay	7	2	4	6	....	....	....	5	1	1	0	1	0
1934-35	Kimberley Dynamiters	Kootenay	7	3	5	8	....	....	....	7	3	3	2	5	4
1935-36	Kimberley Dynomiters	Kootenay	7	4	5	9	....	....	....	9	4	4	0	4	0
1936-37	Earls Court Rangers	Britain	....	39	20	59	....	....	....	8	....	....	....	....	....
1937-38	Earls Court Rangers	Britain	....	15	13	28	....	....	....	....	....	....	....	....	....
1938-39	Earls Court Rangers	Britain	....	34	18	53	....	....	....	....	....	....	....	....	....
1939-40	Sherbrooke Red Raiders	QPHL	41	29	54	83	....	....	....	45	9	8	*12	*20	4
1940-41	Cornwall Flyers	QSHL	36	14	17	31	....	....	....	16	4	2	0	2	2
1941-42	Providence Reds	AHL	52	19	27	46	....	....	....	10	....	....	....	....	....
1942-43	**Toronto Maple Leafs**	**NHL**	**19**	**7**	**9**	**16**	**10**	**11**	**21**	**10**	**3**	**0**	**1**	**1**	**0**
	Providence Reds	AHL	33	18	20	38	....	....	....	2	....	....	....	....	....
1943-44	Red Deer Wranglers	WCSHL	16	8	9	17	....	....	....	0	5	0	2	2	0
1944-45			MILITARY SERVICE												
1945-46	Tulsa Oilers	USHL	11	1	3	4	....	....	....	0	....	....	....	....	....
	Regina Caps	WCSHL	16	6	8	14	....	....	....	4	....	....	....	....	....
1946-47	Kimberley Dynamiters	Kootenay	36	18	24	42	....	....	....	8	4	3	3	6	0
1947-48	Saskatoon Quakers	WCSHL	7	2	1	3	....	....	....	0	....	....	....	....	....
1948-49	Kimberley Dynamiters	Kootenay	6	2	2	4	....	....	....	0	....	....	....	....	....
1949-50	Kamloops Elks	Kootenay	33	20	21	41	....	....	....	4	7	1	3	4	0
	NHL Totals		**19**	**7**	**9**	**16**	**10**	**11**	**21**	**10**	**3**	**0**	**1**	**1**	**0**

Loaned to **Providence** (AHL) by **Toronto** with George Boothman for rights to Alvin Jones and Ab DeMarco, February 3, 1943.

• FORSLUND, GUS Gus Forslund
RW – R. 5'10", 150 lbs. b: Umea, Sweden, 4/25/1908. Deceased.

Season	Club	League	GP	G	A	Pts	AG	AA	APts	PIM	GP	G	A	Pts	PIM
1926-27	Port Arthur Ports	TBSHL	16	1	1	2	....	....	....	2	....	....	....	....	....
1927-28	Fort William Forts	TBSHL	19	10	1	11	....	....	....	10	2	0	0	0	0
1928-29	Fort William Forts	TBSHL	DID NOT PLAY – INJURED												
1929-30	Duluth Hornets	AHA	48	9	5	14	....	....	....	32	4	0	*2	2	4
1930-31	Duluth Hornets	AHA	47	18	10	28	....	....	....	30	4	1	0	1	10
1931-32	Duluth Hornets	AHA	48	14	13	27	....	....	....	24	8	*5	1	*6	7
1932-33	**Ottawa Senators**	**NHL**	**48**	**4**	**9**	**13**	**9**	**24**	**33**	**2**	....	....	....	....	....
1933-34	Syracuse–Windsor	IAHL	43	8	12	20	....	....	....	12	....	....	....	....	....
1934-35	Philadelphia Arrows	Can-Am	48	20	32	52	....	....	....	15	....	....	....	....	....
1935-36	New Haven Eagles	Can-Am	48	16	17	33	....	....	....	26	....	....	....	....	....
1936-37	Fort William Wanderers	TBSHL	DID NOT PLAY – COACHING												
1937-38	Fort William Wanderers	TBSHL	1	2	0	2	....	....	....	0	....	....	....	....	....
1938-39	Duluth Zephyrs	TBSHL	11	8	13	21	....	....	....	....	....	....	....	....	....
	Duluth Zephyrs	USHL	26	18	13	31	....	....	....	7	....	....	....	....	....
1939-40	Geraldton Gold Miners	TBSHL	24	18	*21	*39	....	....	....	8	3	1	0	1	2
1940-41	Geraldton Gold Miners	TBSHL	12	6	3	9	....	....	....	2	4	0	1	1	0
	NHL Totals		**48**	**4**	**9**	**13**	**9**	**24**	**33**	**2**	....	....	....	....	....

Traded to **Windsor** (IAHL) by **Syracuse** (IAHL) with Mel Vail for Andy Bellemer. December, 1934.

• FORTIER, CHARLES Charles Fortier
. b: unknown. Deceased.

Season	Club	League	GP	G	A	Pts	AG	AA	APts	PIM	GP	G	A	Pts	PIM
1923-24	**Montreal Canadiens**	**NHL**	**1**	**0**	**0**	**0**	**0**	**0**	**0**	**0**	....	....	....	....	....
	NHL Totals		**1**	**0**	**0**	**0**	**0**	**0**	**0**	**0**	....	....	....	....	....

• FOSTER, HERB Herb Foster
LW – L. 5'10", 168 lbs. b: Brockville, Ont., 8/9/1913.

Season	Club	League	GP	G	A	Pts	AG	AA	APts	PIM	GP	G	A	Pts	PIM
1932-33	Atlantic City Sea Gulls	EHL	18	18	5	23	....	....	....	0	3	2	0	2	0
1933-34	Atlantic City Sea Gulls	EHL	19	20	6	26	....	....	....	10	5	4	3	7	4
1934-35	Atlantic City Sea Gulls	EHL	18	4	3	7	....	....	....	2	10	6	2	8	0
1935-36	Atlantic City Sea Gulls	EHL	40	*25	3	28	....	....	....	24	8	5	2	7	2
1936-37	Atlantic City Sea Gulls	EHL	48	*43	11	*54	....	....	....	12	3	*5	0	*5	0
1937-38	Atlantic City Sea Gulls	EHL	57	*39	32	*71	....	....	....	13	....	....	....	....	....
1938-39	Atlantic City Sea Gulls	EHL	52	*52	23	75	....	....	....	2	....	....	....	....	....
1939-40	Philadelphia Ramblers	AHL	54	21	22	43	....	....	....	14	....	....	....	....	....
1940-41	**New York Rangers**	**NHL**	**5**	**1**	**0**	**1**	**2**	**0**	**2**	**5**	....	....	....	....	....
	Philadelphia Ramblers	AHL	53	24	22	46	....	....	....	18	....	....	....	....	....
1941-42	Cleveland Barons	AHL	57	23	15	38	....	....	....	10	5	1	1	2	0
	Pittsburgh Hornets	AHL	1	0	0	0	....	....	....	0	....	....	....	....	....
1942-43	Washington Lions	AHL	57	18	29	47	....	....	....	12	....	....	....	....	....
1943-44	Kingston Frontenacs	OHA Sr.	14	12	15	27	....	....	....	2	....	....	....	....	....
1944-45			MILITARY SERVICE												
1945-46			MILITARY SERVICE												
1946-47	Shawinigan Cataracts	QSHL	37	13	11	24	....	....	....	29	3	0	1	1	4
1947-48	**New York Rangers**	**NHL**	**1**	**0**	**0**	**0**	**0**	**0**	**0**	**0**	....	....	....	....	....
	NY Rovers–Atlantic City	EHL	34	37	24	61	....	....	....	8	....	....	....	....	....
	New York Rovers	QSHL	21	7	5	12	....	....	....	0	4	3	1	4	0
1948-49			DID NOT PLAY												
1949-50	Atlantic City Sea Gulls	EHL	47	27	29	56	....	....	....	12	6	3	3	6	0
1950-51	Atlantic City Sea Gulls	EHL	DID NOT PLAY – COACHING												
	NHL Totals		**6**	**1**	**0**	**1**	**2**	**0**	**2**	**5**	....	....	....	....	....

EHL First All-Star Team (1933, 1934, 1937, 1938, 1939, 1948) • Won John Carlin Trophy (Top Scorer - EHL) (1937, 1938, 1939) • EHL Second All-Star Team (1950)

Traded to **Cleveland** (AHL) by **NY Rangers** for cash, September 9, 1941.

• FOSTER, YIP Yip (Harry) Foster
D – L. 6'6", 198 lbs. b: Guelph, Ont., 11/25/1907. Deceased.

			REGULAR SEASON								PLAYOFFS				
Season	Club	League	GP	G	A	Pts	AG	AA	APts	PIM	GP	G	A	Pts	PIM
1923-24	Toronto Canoe Club	OHA	1	0	0	0	....	....	....	....	....	....	....	....	....
1924-25	Toronto Aura Lee	OHA	8	7	4	11	....	....	....	....	10	4	4	8	....
1925-26	Toronto Aura Lee	OHA	7	2	1	3	....	....	....	....	....	....	....	....	....
1926-27	Toronto City Hall	City Sr.	STATISTICS NOT AVAILABLE												
1927-28	Springfield Indians	Can-Am	37	1	1	2	....	....	....	40	4	1	0	1	8
1928-29	Springfield Indians	Can-Am	38	5	1	6	....	....	....	83	....	....	....	....	....
1929-30	**New York Rangers**	**NHL**	**31**	**0**	**0**	**0**	**0**	**0**	**0**	**10**	....	....	....	....	....
	Boston Tigers	Can-Am	11	2	4	6	....	....	....	10	5	0	0	0	0
1930-31	Boston Tigers	Can-Am	36	7	13	20	....	....	....	80	9	3	5	8	*28
1931-32	**Boston Bruins**	**NHL**	**34**	**1**	**2**	**3**	**2**	**6**	**8**	**12**	....	....	....	....	....
1932-33	Boston Cubs	Can-Am	12	2	3	5	....	....	....	34	....	....	....	....	....
	Tulsa Oilers	AHA	24	4	3	7	....	....	....	23	4	0	1	1	4
1933-34	**Detroit Red Wings**	**NHL**	**6**	**0**	**0**	**0**	**0**	**0**	**0**	**2**	....	....	....	....	....
	Detroit Olympics	IAHL	37	4	8	12	....	....	....	35	6	0	1	1	4
1934-35	**Detroit Red Wings**	**NHL**	**12**	**2**	**0**	**2**	**4**	**0**	**4**	**8**	....	....	....	....	....
	Detroit Olympics	IAHL	30	7	2	9	....	....	....	27	5	0	2	2	6
1935-36	Detroit Olympics	IAHL	47	4	12	16	....	....	....	31	6	0	2	2	6
1936-37	Cleveland Barons	AHL	44	3	15	18	....	....	....	27	....	....	....	....	....
1937-38	Cleveland Barons	AHL	47	4	3	7	....	....	....	13	2	0	0	0	0
1938-39	Cleveland Barons	AHL	52	2	12	14	....	....	....	34	9	0	1	1	0
1939-40	Syracuse Stars	AHL	55	2	11	13	....	....	....	14	....	....	....	....	....
1940-41	Minneapolis Millers	AHA	47	4	5	9	....	....	....	10	3	0	0	0	0
1941-42	Minneapolis Millers	AHA	44	5	6	11	....	....	....	17	....	....	....	....	....
1942-43	Cleveland Barons	AHL	53	1	8	9	....	....	....	2	1	0	0	0	0
1943-44	Cleveland Barons	AHL	34	1	5	6	....	....	....	16	10	0	1	1	7
	NHL Totals		**83**	**3**	**2**	**5**	**6**	**6**	**12**	**32**	....	....	....	....	....

Rights traded to **NY Rangers** by **Toronto** for Eric Pettinger, October, 1927. Traded to **Boston** by **NY Rangers** with $15,000 for Bill Regan, February 17, 1930. Signed as a free agent by **Detroit**, October 17, 1933.

• FOWLER, JIMMY Jimmy "The Blonde Bouncer" Fowler
D – L. 5'11", 168 lbs. b: Toronto, Ont., 4/6/1915. d: 10/17/1985.

Season	Club	League	GP	G	A	Pts	AG	AA	APts	PIM	GP	G	A	Pts	PIM
1932-33	West Toronto Nationals	OHA	9	4	2	6	....	....	....	0	5	0	0	0	2
1933-34	Toronto Young Rangers	OHA	11	9	7	16	....	....	....	10	1	1	0	1	0
1934-35	Toronto City Service	City Sr.	11	3	3	6	....	....	....	4	7	2	6	8	8
	Toronto All-Stars	OHA Sr.	10	4	0	4	....	....	....	4	6	2	2	4	4
1935-36	Syracuse Stars	IAHL	45	10	15	25	....	....	....	23	3	1	0	1	0
1936-37	**Toronto Maple Leafs**	**NHL**	**48**	**7**	**11**	**18**	**15**	**26**	**41**	**22**	**2**	**0**	**0**	**0**	**0**
1937-38	**Toronto Maple Leafs**	**NHL**	**48**	**10**	**12**	**22**	**21**	**25**	**46**	**8**	**7**	**0**	**2**	**2**	**0**
1938-39	**Toronto Maple Leafs**	**NHL**	**39**	**1**	**6**	**7**	**2**	**11**	**13**	**9**	**9**	**0**	**1**	**1**	**2**
	Syracuse Stars	AHL	7	3	1	4	....	....	....	0	....	....	....	....	....
	NHL Totals		**135**	**18**	**29**	**47**	**38**	**62**	**100**	**39**	**18**	**0**	**3**	**3**	**2**

Signed as a free agent by **Toronto**, October 22, 1935. Traded to **NY Americans** by **Toronto** with Busher Jackson, Murray Armstrong, Buzz Boll and Doc Romnes for Sweeney Schriner, May 15, 1939.

• FOWLER, TOM Tom Fowler
C – L. 5'11", 165 lbs. b: Winnipeg, Man., 5/18/1924.

Season	Club	League	GP	G	A	Pts	AG	AA	APts	PIM	GP	G	A	Pts	PIM
1941-42	Winnipeg Monarchs	MJHL	5	0	0	0	....	....	....	0	3	0	0	0	2
1942-43	Winnipeg Monarchs	MJHL	13	4	12	16	....	....	....	0	8	3	3	6	2
1943-44	Winnipeg Monarchs	MJHL	10	9	*16	*25	....	....	....	12	3	5	1	6	2
	Winnipeg Esquires	MJHL	....	....	....	....	....	....	....	....	3	3	1	4	0
1944-45	Winnipeg Navy	City Sr.	16	10	7	17	....	....	....	12	6	3	1	4	6
1945-46	Kansas City Pla-Mors	USHL	54	12	33	45	....	....	....	34	12	1	5	6	2
1946-47	**Chicago Black Hawks**	**NHL**	**24**	**0**	**1**	**1**	**0**	**1**	**1**	**18**	....	....	....	....	....
	Kansas City Pla-Mors	USHL	22	8	10	18	....	....	....	14	....	....	....	....	....
1947-48	Tulsa Oilers	USHL	14	1	4	5	....	....	....	8	....	....	....	....	....
	Fort Worth Rangers	USHL	49	9	28	37	....	....	....	33	4	1	2	3	0
1948-49	Oakland Oaks	PCHL	63	29	57	86				32	3	0	1	1	0
1949-50	Oakland–Los Angeles	PCHL	66	19	32	51	....	....	....	23	17	2	*18	20	15
1950-51	St. Michael's Monarchs	OHA Sr.	32	9	19	28	....	....	....	32	9	2	2	4	4
1951-52	Saskatoon Quakers	PCHL	57	8	18	26	....	....	....	22	13	3	3	6	4
1952-53	Saskatoon Quakers	WHL	1	0	1	1	....	....	....	0	....	....	....	....	....
	Moose Jaw Millers	SSHL	32	25	*58	*83	....	....	....	8	10	6	6	12	4
	NHL Totals		**24**	**0**	**1**	**1**	**0**	**1**	**1**	**18**	....	....	....	....	....

PCHL Southern First All-Star Team (1949) • MVP - PCHL Southern Division (1949)

• FOYSTON, FRANK Frank Foyston HHOF

C/RW – L. 5′9″, 158 lbs. b: Minesing, Ont., 2/2/1891. d: 1/19/1966.

Season	Club	League	GP	G	A	Pts	AG	AA	APts	PIM	GP	G	A	Pts	PIM
1911-12	Toronto Eaton's	OHA Sr.	6	15	0	15	....	....	....	....	4	*5	0	*5	9
1912-13	Toronto Blueshirts	NHA	16	8	0	8	....	....	....	8	....	....	....	....	....
1913-14	Toronto Blueshirts	NHA	19	16	2	18	....	....	....	8	5	4	0	4	0
1914-15	Toronto Blueshirts	NHA	20	13	9	22	....	....	....	11	....	....	....	....	....
1915-16	Toronto Blueshirts	NHA	1	0	0	0	....	....	....	0	....	....	....	....	....
	Seattle Metropolitans	PCHA	18	9	4	13	....	....	....	6	....	....	....	....	....
1916-17	Seattle Metropolitans	PCHA	24	36	12	48	....	....	....	51	4	7	2	9	3
1917-18	Seattle Metropolitans	PCHA	13	9	5	14	....	....	....	9	2	0	0	0	3
1918-19	Seattle Metropolitans	PCHA	18	15	4	19	....	....	....	0	7	*12	1	*13	0
1919-20	Seattle Metropolitans	PCHA	22	*26	3	29	....	....	....	3	7	*9	2	*11	0
1920-21	Seattle Metropolitans	PCHA	23	*26	4	30	....	....	....	10	2	1	0	1	0
1921-22	Seattle Metropolitans	PCHA	24	16	7	23	....	....	....	25	2	0	0	0	3
1922-23	Seattle Metropolitans	PCHA	30	20	8	28	....	....	....	21	....	....	....	....	....
1923-24	Seattle Metropolitans	PCHA	30	17	6	23	....	....	....	8	2	1	0	1	0
1924-25	Victoria Cougars	WCHL	27	6	5	11	....	....	....	6	8	2	1	3	2
1925-26	Victoria Cougars	WHL	12	6	3	9	....	....	....	8	8	3	0	3	8
1926-27	**Detroit Cougars**	**NHL**	**41**	**10**	**5**	**15**	**29**	**43**	**72**	**16**	....	....	....	....	....
1927-28	**Detroit Cougars**	**NHL**	**23**	**7**	**2**	**9**	**21**	**17**	**38**	**16**	....	....	....	....	....
	Detroit Olympics	Can-Am	19	3	2	5	....	....	....	14	....	....	....	....	....
1928-29	Detroit Olympics	Can-Am	42	18	6	24	....	....	....	20	7	0	0	0	9
1929-30	Detroit Olympics	IAHL	31	2	1	3	....	....	....	6	3	0	0	0	0
1930-31			DID NOT PLAY – REFEREE												
1931-32	Bronx Tigers	Can-Am	DID NOT PLAY – COACHING												
	NHL Totals		**64**	**17**	**7**	**24**	**50**	**60**	**110**	**32**	....	....	....	....	....
	Other Major League Totals		297	223	72	295	....	....	....	174	47	39	6	45	19

PCHA First All-Star Team (1917, 1918, 1920, 1921, 1923, 1924) • PCHA MVP (1917) • PCHA Second All-Star Team (1919, 1922)

Signed as a free agent by **Seattle** (PCHA), December, 1915. Traded to **Victoria** (WCHL) by **Seattle** (PCHA) for cash, December 1, 1924. NHL rights transferred to **Detroit Cougars** after NHL club purchased **Victoria** (PCHA) franchise, May 15, 1926.

• FRAMPTON, BOB Bob Frampton

LW – L. 5′10″, 175 lbs. b: Toronto, Ont., 1/20/1929.

Season	Club	League	GP	G	A	Pts	AG	AA	APts	PIM	GP	G	A	Pts	PIM
1946-47	Montreal Jr. Royals	QJHL	27	22	9	31	....	....	....	25	8	4	4	8	4
1947-48	Montreal Jr. Royals	QJHL	27	19	27	46	....	....	....	40	7	3	2	5	11
1948-49	Montreal Jr. Royals	QJHL	46	32	33	65	....	....	....	44	25	*24	8	32	20
	Montreal Royals	QSHL	2	0	1	1	....	....	....	2	....	....	....	....	....
1949-50	**Montreal Canadiens**	**NHL**	**2**	**0**	**0**	**0**	**0**	**0**	**0**	**0**	**3**	**0**	**0**	**0**	**0**
	Cincinnati Mohawks	AHL	60	9	19	28	....	....	....	29	....	....	....	....	....
1950-51	Victoria Cougars	PCHL	52	20	21	41	....	....	....	40	12	2	5	7	2
1951-52	Victoria Cougars	PCHL	69	34	26	60	....	....	....	50	13	8	3	11	4
1952-53	Montreal Royals	QSHL	59	19	18	37	....	....	....	32	16	4	8	12	10
1953-54	Montreal Royals	QHL	55	12	18	30	....	....	....	18	8	0	1	1	16
1954-55	Montreal Royals	QHL	6	1	1	2	....	....	....	0	....	....	....	....	....
	NHL Totals		**2**	**0**	**0**	**0**	**0**	**0**	**0**	**0**	**3**	**0**	**0**	**0**	**0**

Claimed by **Chicago** from **Montreal Royals** (QHL) in Inter-League Draft, June 10, 1953.

• FRASER, ARCHIE Archie "Arch" Fraser

C – L. 5′11″, 160 lbs. b: Souris, Man., 2/9/1914. Deceased.

Season	Club	League	GP	G	A	Pts	AG	AA	APts	PIM	GP	G	A	Pts	PIM
1935-36	Yorkton Terriers	SSHL	17	5	7	12	....	....	....	4	3	0	1	1	4
1936-37	Yorkton Terriers	SSHL	24	14	11	25	....	....	....	20	7	1	*4	5	6
1937-38	Yorkton Terriers	SSHL	24	25	12	37	....	....	....	14	5	3	2	5	0
1938-39	Wembley Monarchs	Britain	....	29	13	42	....	....	....	....	....	....	....	....	....
1939-40	Yorkton Terriers	SSHL	27	20	20	40	....	....	....	6	5	3	0	3	8
1940-41	Yorkton Terriers	SSHL	31	18	19	37	....	....	....	8	8	3	5	8	2
1941-42	Yorkton Terriers	SSHL	32	17	17	34	....	....	....	10	....	....	....	....	....
1942-43	Yorkton Flyers	SSHL	24	11	9	20	....	....	....	10	....	....	....	....	....
1943-44	**New York Rangers**	**NHL**	**3**	**0**	**1**	**1**	**0**	**1**	**1**	**0**	....	....	....	....	....
	Moose Jaw Millers	SSHL	1	2	2	4	....	....	....	0	....	....	....	....	....
1944-45			MILITARY SERVICE												
1945-46			MILITARY SERVICE												
1946-47	Yorkton Terriers	Inter-Sr.	STATISTICS NOT AVAILABLE												
1947-48	Tacoma Rockets	PCHL	10	1	1	2	....	....	....	2	....	....	....	....	....
1948-49	Yorkton Terriers	Inter-Sr.	STATISTICS NOT AVAILABLE												
1949-50	Yorkton Terriers	Inter-Sr.	STATISTICS NOT AVAILABLE												
1950-51	Yorkton Legionaires	SSHL	2	1	1	2	....	....	....	0	9	6	6	12	2
1951-52	Yorkton Legionaires	SSHL	2	0	0	0	....	....	....	0	....	....	....	....	....
	NHL Totals		**3**	**0**	**1**	**1**	**0**	**1**	**1**	**0**	....	....	....	....	....

• FRASER, CHARLES Charles Fraser

D – L. b: Stellarton, N.S.. Deceased.

Season	Club	League	GP	G	A	Pts	AG	AA	APts	PIM	GP	G	A	Pts	PIM
1919-20	Stellarton Seniors	CBSHL	11	4	0	4	....	....	....	....	....	....	....	....	....
1920-21	Stellarton Seniors	CBSHL	3	0	0	0	....	....	....	6	2	0	0	0	3
1921-22	New Glasgow Black Foxes	MIHL	STATISTICS NOT AVAILABLE												
	Stellerton Seniors	CBSHL	....	....	....	....	....	....	....	....	6	4	0	4	....
1922-23	Stellerton Seniors	CBSHL	5	0	0	0	....	....	....	6	....	....	....	....	....
	Amherst Ramblers	MIHL	7	3	0	3	....	....	....	14	....	....	....	....	....
1923-24	**Hamilton Tigers**	**NHL**	**1**	**0**	**0**	**0**	**0**	**0**	**0**	**0**	....	....	....	....	....
	Amherst Ramblers	MIHL	15	3	3	6	....	....	....	22	....	....	....	....	....
1924-25	Stellerton Seniors	CBSHL	2	4	0	4	....	....	....	2	1	0	0	0	5
	NHL Totals		**1**	**0**	**0**	**0**	**0**	**0**	**0**	**0**	....	....	....	....	....

Signed as a free agent by **Hamilton**, December 14, 1923.

• FRASER, GORD Gord Fraser

D – L. 6′, 180 lbs. b: Pembroke, Ont., 1/3/1902. Deceased.

Season	Club	League	GP	G	A	Pts	AG	AA	APts	PIM	GP	G	A	Pts	PIM
1919-20	Calgary Wanderers	Big 4	10	2	1	3	....	....	....	20	2	1	0	1	0
1920-21	Calgary Tigers	Big 4	15	11	6	17	....	....	....	33	....	....	....	....	....
1921-22	Seattle Metropolitans	PCHA	24	5	2	7	....	....	....	32	2	0	0	0	0
1922-23	Seattle Metropolitans	PCHA	29	4	4	8	....	....	....	46	....	....	....	....	....
1923-24	Seattle Metropolitans	PCHA	30	14	3	17	....	....	....	*64	2	0	0	0	2
1924-25	Victoria Cougars	WCHL	28	9	3	12	....	....	....	64	8	2	1	3	16
1925-26	Victoria Cougars	WHL	7	1	0	1	....	....	....	12	8	2	0	2	24
1926-27	**Chicago Black Hawks**	**NHL**	**44**	**14**	**6**	**20**	**41**	**51**	**92**	**89**	**2**	**1**	**0**	**1**	**6**
1927-28	**Chicago Black Hawks**	**NHL**	**11**	**1**	**1**	**2**	**3**	**8**	**11**	**10**	....	....	....	....	....
	Detroit Cougars	**NHL**	**30**	**3**	**1**	**4**	**9**	**8**	**17**	**50**	....	....	....	....	....
1928-29	**Detroit Cougars**	**NHL**	**14**	**0**	**0**	**0**	**0**	**0**	**0**	**12**	....	....	....	....	....
	Detroit Olympics	Can-Pro	28	0	0	0	....	....	....	27	7	1	1	2	23
1929-30	**Montreal Canadiens**	**NHL**	**10**	**0**	**0**	**0**	**0**	**0**	**0**	**4**	....	....	....	....	....
	Pittsburgh Pirates	**NHL**	**30**	**6**	**4**	**10**	**12**	**13**	**25**	**37**	....	....	....	....	....
	Providence Reds	Can-Am	7	5	1	6	....	....	....	34	....	....	....	....	....
1930-31	**Philadelphia Quakers**	**NHL**	**5**	**0**	**0**	**0**	**0**	**0**	**0**	**22**	....	....	....	....	....
	Pittsburgh Yellowjackets	IAHL	38	7	3	10	....	....	....	75	....	....	....	....	....
1931-32	Pittsburgh Yellowjackets	IAHL	45	10	15	25	....	....	....	90	....	....	....	....	....
1932-33	London Tecumsehs	IAHL	44	3	8	11	....	....	....	60	6	0	0	0	16
1933-34	Seattle Sawhawks	NWHL	27	11	8	19	....	....	....	48	....	....	....	....	....
	London Tecumsehs	IAHL	6	0	0	0	....	....	....	4	....	....	....	....	....
1934-35	Portland Buckaroos	NWHL	32	10	7	17	....	....	....	66	3	1	0	1	10
1935-36	Pittsburgh Shamrocks	IAHL	15	4	2	6	....	....	....	14	....	....	....	....	....
1936-37	Baltimore Orioles	EHL	DID NOT PLAY – COACHING												
	NHL Totals		**144**	**24**	**12**	**36**	**65**	**80**	**145**	**224**	**2**	**1**	**0**	**1**	**6**
	Other Major League Totals		118	33	12	45	....	....	....	218	20	4	1	5	42

PCHA Second All-Star Team (1923) • PCHA First All-Star Team (1924)

Signed as a free agent by **Seattle** (PCHA), November, 1921. Traded to **Victoria** (WCHL) by **Seattle** (PCHA) for cash, December 1, 1924. NHL rights transferred to **Detroit Cougars** after NHL club purchased **Victoria** (WHL) franchise, May 15, 1926. Traded to **Chicago** by **Detroit Cougars** with Art Gagne for rights to Art Duncan, October 18, 1926. Traded to **Detroit** by **Chicago** with $5,000 for Duke Keats, December 16, 1927. Traded to **Montreal Canadiens** by **Detroit Cougars** for cash, October 10, 1929. Traded to **Pittsburgh** by **Montreal Canadiens** for Bert McCaffery, December 27, 1929. Transferred to **Philadelphia** after **Pittsburgh** franchise relocated, October 18, 1930.

• FRASER, HARVEY Harvey Fraser

C – R. 5′10″, 168 lbs. b: Soures, Man., 10/14/1918.

Season	Club	League	GP	G	A	Pts	AG	AA	APts	PIM	GP	G	A	Pts	PIM
1935-36	Yorkton Terriers	SSHL	17	12	5	17	....	....	....	8	3	*5	1	6	0
1936-37	Yorkton Terriers	SSHL	24	13	8	21	....	....	....	16	7	*5	1	*6	6
1937-38	Yorkton Terriers	SSHL	24	27	*24	*51	....	....	....	29	5	3	2	5	4
1938-39	Wembley Monarchs	Britain	....	18	15	33	....	....	....	....	....	....	....	....	....
1939-40	Yorkton Terriers	SSHL	31	32	17	49	....	....	....	14	5	3	1	4	10
1940-41	Yorkton Terriers	SSHL	30	26	18	44	....	....	....	16	9	*9	4	13	2
1941-42	Yorkton Terriers	SSHL	4	3	2	5	....	....	....	4	....	....	....	....	....
1942-43	Yorkton Flyers	SSHL	22	8	11	19	....	....	....	10	8	7	5	12	6
1943-44	Moose Jaw Victorias	SSHL	5	12	4	16	....	....	....	0	....	....	....	....	....
	New Westminster	PCHL	11	9	7	16	....	....	....	4	18	11	*17	*28	9
	Seattle Ironmen	PCHL	2	2	3	5	....	....	....	0	....	....	....	....	....
1944-45	**Chicago Black Hawks**	**NHL**	**21**	**5**	**4**	**9**	**7**	**6**	**13**	**0**	....	....	....	....	....
	Cleveland–Providence	AHL	21	13	17	30	....	....	....	8	12	1	3	4	4
1945-46	Cleveland–St. Louis	AHL	50	15	26	41	....	....	....	16	....	....	....	....	....
1946-47	St. Louis–Providence	AHL	64	28	25	53	....	....	....	21	....	....	....	....	....
1947-48	Providence Reds	AHL	64	45	52	97	....	....	....	12	5	1	2	3	4
1948-49	Providence Reds	AHL	68	34	55	89	....	....	....	16	14	5	3	8	6
1949-50	Providence Reds	AHL	52	20	30	50	....	....	....	4	3	0	2	2	4
1950-51	Hamilton Tigers	OHA Sr.	28	15	16	31	....	....	....	12	8	2	4	6	4
	NHL Totals		**21**	**5**	**4**	**9**	**7**	**6**	**13**	**0**	....	....	....	....	....

AHL Second All-Star Team (1949)

• FREDRICKSON, FRANK Frank Fredrickson HHOF

C – L. 5′11″, 180 lbs. b: Winnipeg, Man., 6/11/1895. d: 4/28/1979.

Season	Club	League	GP	G	A	Pts	AG	AA	APts	PIM	GP	G	A	Pts	PIM
1913-14	Winnipeg Falcons	MIHL	11	13	0	13	....	....	....	....	....	....	....	....	....
1914-15	Winnipeg Falcons	MIHL	8	10	0	10	....	....	....	....	1	1	0	1	2
1915-16	Winnipeg Falcons	MHL Sr.	6	*13	3	*16	....	....	....	14	....	....	....	....	....
1916-17	Winnipeg Falcons	MHL Sr.	8	*17	3	*20	....	....	....	*40	....	....	....	....	....
1917-18			MILITARY SERVICE												
1918-19			MILITARY SERVICE												
1919-20	Winnipeg Falcons	MHL Sr.	9	*22	5	*27	....	....	....	12	6	*22	5	*27	6
	Canada	Olympics	3	*10	10	11	....	....	....	....	....	....	....	....	....
1920-21	Victoria Cougars	PCHA	21	20	12	32	....	....	....	3	....	....	....	....	....
1921-22	Victoria Cougars	PCHA	24	15	10	25	....	....	....	26	....	....	....	....	....
1922-23	Victoria Cougars	PCHA	30	*39	*16	*55	....	....	....	26	2	2	0	2	4
1923-24	Victoria Cougars	PCHA	30	19	8	27	....	....	....	28	....	....	....	....	....
1924-25	Victoria Cougars	WCHL	28	22	8	30	....	....	....	43	8	6	3	9	8
1925-26	Victoria Cougars	WHL	30	16	8	24	....	....	....	89	8	2	3	5	16
1926-27	**Detroit Cougars**	**NHL**	**16**	**4**	**6**	**10**	**12**	**51**	**63**	**12**	....	....	....	....	....
	Boston Bruins	**NHL**	**28**	**14**	**7**	**21**	**41**	**60**	**101**	**33**	**8**	**2**	***4**	**6**	**22**
1927-28	**Boston Bruins**	**NHL**	**41**	**10**	**4**	**14**	**31**	**34**	**65**	**83**	**2**	**0**	**1**	**1**	**4**
1928-29	**Boston Bruins**	**NHL**	**12**	**1**	**3**	**4**	**4**	**27**	**31**	**24**	....	....	....	....	....
	Pittsburgh Pirates	**NHL**	**31**	**3**	**7**	**10**	**12**	**65**	**77**	**28**	....	....	....	....	....
1929-30	**Pittsburgh Pirates**	**NHL**	**9**	**4**	**7**	**11**	**8**	**23**	**31**	**20**	....	....	....	....	....
1930-31	**Detroit Falcons**	**NHL**	**24**	**1**	**2**	**3**	**2**	**7**	**9**	**6**	....	....	....	....	....
	Detroit Olympics	IAHL	6	0	1	1	....	....	....	2	....	....	....	....	....
1931-32	Winnipeg Winnipegs	MJHL	DID NOT PLAY – COACHING												
	NHL Totals		**161**	**37**	**36**	**73**	**110**	**267**	**377**	**206**	**10**	**2**	**5**	**7**	**26**
	Other Major League Totals		163	131	62	193	....	....	....	215	18	10	6	16	28

PCHA First All-Star Team (1921, 1922, 1923, 1924) • WHL First All-Star Team (1926)

Signed as a free agent by **Victoria** (PCHA), December 23, 1920. NHL rights transferred to **Detroit Cougars** after NHL club purchased **Victoria** (WHL) franchise, May 15, 1926. Traded to **Boston** by **Detroit Cougars** with Harry Meeking for Duke Keats and Archie Briden, January 7, 1927. Traded to **Pittsburgh** by **Boston** for Mickey MacKay and $12,000, December 21, 1928. Signed as a free agent by **Detroit Falcons**, November 24, 1930. Signed as a free agent by **Detroit Olympics** (IAHL) after clearing NHL waivers, February 13, 1931.

• FREW, IRV

Irv "Ranger" Frew
D – R. 5'10", 180 lbs. b: Kilsyth, Scotland, 8/16/1907. Deceased.

Season	Club	League	GP	G	A	Pts	AG	AA	APts	PIM	Playoffs GP	G	A	Pts	PIM
1926-27	Calgary Tigers	PrHL	27	0	0	0	....	....	....	8	2	0	0	0	0
1927-28	Stratford Nationals	Can-Pro	41	6	1	7	....	....	....	72	5	1	0	1	12
1928-29	Buffalo–Toronto	Can-Pro	44	3	1	4	....	....	....	77	2	0	0	0	12
1929-30	Cleveland Indians	IAHL	41	3	3	6	....	....	....	61	6	0	0	0	8
1930-31	Cleveland Indians	IAHL	45	3	5	8	....	....	....	59	6	0	0	0	6
1931-32	Cleveland Indians	IAHL	9	1	0	1	....	....	....	31	....	....	....	....	....
1932-33	Cleveland Indians	IAHL	19	2	0	2	....	....	....	56	....	....	....	....	....
	Quebec Beavers	Can-Am	26	1	2	3	....	....	....	57	....	....	....	....	....
1933-34	**Montreal Maroons**	**NHL**	**30**	**2**	**1**	**3**	**4**	**3**	**7**	**41**	**4**	**0**	**0**	**0**	**6**
	Quebec Beavers	Can-Am	14	3	1	4	....	....	....	16	....	....	....	....	....
1934-35	**St. Louis Eagles**	**NHL**	**48**	**0**	**2**	**2**	**0**	**4**	**4**	**89**	....	....	....	....	....
1935-36	**Montreal Canadiens**	**NHL**	**18**	**0**	**2**	**2**	**0**	**5**	**5**	**16**	....	....	....	....	....
	Springfield Indians	Can-Am	14	0	2	2	....	....	....	23	2	0	0	0	4
1936-37	Springfield Indians	AHL	45	5	6	11	....	....	....	65	5	0	0	0	11
1937-38	Springfield Indians	AHL	14	0	0	0	....	....	....	19	....	....	....	....	....
	Vancouver Lions	PCHL	10	0	1	1	....	....	....	25	6	0	0	0	*22
1938-39	Spokane Clippers	PCHL	45	1	7	8	....	....	....	106	....	....	....	....	....
1939-40	Springfield Indians	AHL	50	2	4	6	....	....	....	69	3	0	1	1	2
1940-41	St. Louis Flyers	AHA	39	6	5	11	....	....	....	37	9	1	0	1	17
	NHL Totals		**96**	**2**	**5**	**7**	**4**	**12**	**16**	**146**	**4**	**0**	**0**	**0**	**6**

AHA Second All-Star Team (1941)

Traded to **St. Louis** by **Montreal Maroons** with future considerations (Vern Ayres and Normie Smith, October 22, 1934) for Al Shields, September 20, 1934. Claimed by **Montreal Canadiens** from **St. Louis** in Dispersal Draft, October 15, 1935.

• FROST, HARRY

Harry Frost
RW – R. 5'11", 165 lbs. b: Kerr Lake, Ont., 8/17/1914.

Season	Club	League	GP	G	A	Pts	AG	AA	APts	PIM	Playoffs GP	G	A	Pts	PIM
1934-35	Sudbury Frood Tigers	NOHA	8	9	1	10	....	....	....	6	3	0	0	0	4
1935-36	Hershey B'ars	EHL	38	7	2	9	....	....	....	8	5	1	2	3	0
1936-37	Hershey B'ars	EHL	47	7	7	14	....	....	....	11	4	1	1	2	2
1937-38	Hershey B'ars	EHL	57	37	25	62	....	....	....	6	....	....	....	....	....
1938-39	**Boston Bruins**	**NHL**	**4**	**0**	**0**	**0**	**0**	**0**	**0**	**0**	**1**	**0**	**0**	**0**	**0**
	Hershey Bears	AHL	35	10	7	17	....	....	....	8	4	0	2	2	4
1939-40	Hershey Bears	AHL	52	12	18	30	....	....	....	6	6	1	2	3	0
1940-41	Hershey Bears	AHL	55	25	15	40	....	....	....	2	10	*4	3	7	0
1941-42	Philadelphia–Hershey	AHL	55	19	25	44	....	....	....	6	5	1	1	2	2
1942-43	Hershey Bears	AHL	56	*43	40	83	....	....	....	6	6	2	0	2	0
1943-44			MILITARY SERVICE												
1944-45			MILITARY SERVICE												
1945-46	Hershey Bears	AHL	39	9	6	15	....	....	....	8	3	0	1	1	4
1946-47	Springfield Indians	AHL	62	28	21	49	....	....	....	10	2	1	0	1	0
1947-48	Springfield Indians	AHL	67	21	23	44	....	....	....	19	....	....	....	....	....
1948-49	Fort Worth Rangers	USHL	6	2	3	5	....	....	....	2	....	....	....	....	....
	Springfield–Washington	AHL	55	25	14	39	....	....	....	2	....	....	....	....	....
1949-50	Louisville Blades	USHL	16	4	5	9	....	....	....	4	....	....	....	....	....
	Fresno Falcons	PCHL	42	9	7	16	....	....	....	2	....	....	....	....	....
	St. Louis Flyers	AHL	9	1	0	1	....	....	....	0	....	....	....	....	....
1950-51	Johnstown Jets	EHL	54	16	38	54	....	....	....	10	6	0	1	1	0
1951-52	Washington Lions	EHL	34	16	19	35	....	....	....	8	....	....	....	....	....
	NHL Totals		**4**	**0**	**0**	**0**	**0**	**0**	**0**	**0**	**1**	**0**	**0**	**0**	**0**

EHL First All-Star Team (1938) • AHL First All-Star Team (1941, 1942, 1943)

• FRYDAY, BOB

Bob Fryday
RW – R. 5'10", 155 lbs. b: Toronto, Ont., 12/5/1928.

Season	Club	League	GP	G	A	Pts	AG	AA	APts	PIM	Playoffs GP	G	A	Pts	PIM
1945-46	Toronto Marlboros	OHA	25	10	7	17				18	4	3	1	4	0
1946-47	Montreal Jr. Canadiens	QJHL	27	26	26	52	....	....	....	11	15	17	17	34	11
1947-48	Montreal Royals	QSHL	44	22	8	30	....	....	....	21	3	0	1	1	0
1948-49	Montreal Royals	QSHL	64	24	20	44	....	....	....	32	8	3	3	6	11
1949-50	**Montreal Canadiens**	**NHL**	**2**	**1**	**0**	**1**	**1**	**0**	**1**	**0**					
	Montreal Royals	QSHL	55	15	32	47	....	....	....	28	5	0	0	0	0
1950-51	Montreal Royals	QSHL	43	17	26	43	....	....	....	35	7	2	2	4	2
1951-52	**Montreal Canadiens**	**NHL**	**3**	**0**	**0**	**0**	**0**	**0**	**0**	**0**	....	....	....	....	....
	Montreal Royals	QSHL	51	15	15	30	....	....	....	32	6	1	0	1	2
	Cincinnati Mohawks	AHL	....	....	....	....	....	....	....	....	5	1	4	5	2
1952-53	Buffalo Bisons	AHL	57	18	13	31	....	....	....	6	....	....	....	....	....
	NHL Totals		**5**	**1**	**0**	**1**	**1**	**0**	**1**	**0**	....	....	....	....	....

• GADSBY, BILL

Bill "Gads" Gadsby **HHOF**
D – L. 6', 180 lbs. b: Calgary, Alta., 8/8/1927.

Season	Club	League	GP	G	A	Pts	AG	AA	APts	PIM	Playoffs GP	G	A	Pts	PIM
1943-44	Calgary Grills	City Jr.	9	4	1	5	....	....	....	4	....	....	....	....	....
1944-45	Edmonton Canadians	AJHL	STATISTICS NOT AVAILABLE												
1945-46	Edmonton Canadians	AJHL	....	14	12	26	....	....	....	....	....	....	....	....	....
1946-47	**Chicago Black Hawks**	**NHL**	**48**	**8**	**10**	**18**	**11**	**14**	**25**	**31**	....	....	....	....	....
	Kansas City Pla-Mors	USHL	12	2	3	5	....	....	....	8	....	....	....	....	....
1947-48	**Chicago Black Hawks**	**NHL**	**60**	**6**	**10**	**16**	**9**	**15**	**24**	**66**	....	....	....	....	....
1948-49	**Chicago Black Hawks**	**NHL**	**50**	**3**	**10**	**13**	**5**	**16**	**21**	**85**	....	....	....	....	....
1949-50	**Chicago Black Hawks**	**NHL**	**70**	**10**	**25**	**35**	**13**	**32**	**45**	**138**	....	....	....	....	....
1950-51	**Chicago Black Hawks**	**NHL**	**25**	**3**	**7**	**10**	**4**	**9**	**13**	**32**	....	....	....	....	....
1951-52	**Chicago Black Hawks**	**NHL**	**59**	**7**	**15**	**22**	**10**	**19**	**29**	**87**	....	....	....	....	....
1952-53	**Chicago Black Hawks**	**NHL**	**68**	**2**	**20**	**22**	**3**	**28**	**31**	**84**	**7**	**0**	**1**	**1**	**4**
1953-54	**Chicago Black Hawks**	**NHL**	**70**	**12**	**29**	**41**	**18**	**40**	**58**	**108**	....	....	....	....	....
1954-55	**Chicago Black Hawks**	**NHL**	**18**	**3**	**5**	**8**	**4**	**6**	**10**	**17**	....	....	....	....	....
	New York Rangers	**NHL**	**52**	**8**	**8**	**16**	**12**	**10**	**22**	**44**	....	....	....	....	....
1955-56	**New York Rangers**	**NHL**	**70**	**9**	**42**	**51**	**13**	**53**	**66**	**84**	**5**	**1**	**3**	**4**	**4**
1956-57	**New York Rangers**	**NHL**	**70**	**4**	**37**	**41**	**5**	**43**	**48**	**72**	**5**	**1**	**2**	**3**	**2**
1957-58	**New York Rangers**	**NHL**	**65**	**14**	**32**	**46**	**18**	**35**	**53**	**48**	**6**	**0**	**3**	**3**	**4**
1958-59	**New York Rangers**	**NHL**	**70**	**5**	**46**	**51**	**6**	**49**	**55**	**56**	....	....	....	....	....
1959-60	**New York Rangers**	**NHL**	**65**	**9**	**22**	**31**	**11**	**23**	**34**	**60**	....	....	....	....	....
1960-61	**New York Rangers**	**NHL**	**65**	**9**	**26**	**35**	**11**	**26**	**37**	**49**	....	....	....	....	....
1961-62	**Detroit Red Wings**	**NHL**	**70**	**7**	**30**	**37**	**8**	**30**	**38**	**88**	....	....	....	....	....
1962-63	**Detroit Red Wings**	**NHL**	**70**	**4**	**24**	**28**	**5**	**25**	**30**	**116**	**11**	**1**	**4**	**5**	***36**
1963-64	**Detroit Red Wings**	**NHL**	**64**	**2**	**16**	**18**	**3**	**18**	**21**	**80**	**14**	**0**	**4**	**4**	**22**
1964-65	**Detroit Red Wings**	**NHL**	**61**	**0**	**12**	**12**	**0**	**13**	**13**	**122**	**7**	**0**	**3**	**3**	**8**
1965-66	**Detroit Red Wings**	**NHL**	**58**	**5**	**12**	**17**	**6**	**12**	**18**	**72**	**12**	**1**	**3**	**4**	**12**
	NHL Totals		**1248**	**130**	**438**	**568**	**175**	**516**	**691**	**1539**	**67**	**4**	**23**	**27**	**92**

NHL Second All-Star Team (1953, 1954, 1957, 1965) • NHL First All-Star Team (1956, 1958, 1959)

Played in NHL All-Star Game (1953, 1954, 1956, 1957, 1958, 1959, 1960, 1965)

Traded to **NY Rangers** by **Chicago** with Pete Conacher for Allan Stanley, Nick Mickoski and Richard Lamoureux, November, 1954. Traded to **Detroit** by **NY Rangers** with Eddie Shack for Billy McNeil and Red Kelly, February 5, 1960. • Rights returned to NY Rangers by Detroit when Kelly refused to report, February 7, 1960. Traded to **Detroit** by **NY Rangers** for Les Hunt, June, 1961.

• GAGNE, ART

Art Gagne
RW – R. 5'7", 160 lbs. b: Ottawa, Ont., 10/11/1897. Deceased.

Season	Club	League	GP	G	A	Pts	AG	AA	APts	PIM	Playoffs GP	G	A	Pts	PIM
1914-15	Ottawa Aberdeens	City Sr.	3	1	0	1	....	....	....	....	1	0	0	0	....
	Ottawa Royal Canadians	City Sr.	5	2	0	2	....	....	....	....	2	0	0	0	....
1915-16	Ottawa Aberdeens	City Sr.	5	4	0	4	....	....	....	....	....	....	....	....	....
1916-17	Ottawa Grand Trunks	City Sr.	2	1	0	1	....	....	....	....	....	....	....	....	....
1916-17	Laval University	Mtl-Sr.	7	11	5	16	....	....	....	....	....	....	....	....	....
1917-18	Quebec Sons of Ireland	QCHL	4	9	1	10	....	....	....	....	1	1	0	1	0
1918-19	Quebec Montagnais	QSHL	5	7	0	7	....	....	....	....	3	5	0	5	9
1919-20	Quebec Montagnais	QSHL	STATISTICS NOT AVAILABLE												
1920-21	Edmonton Eskimos	Big 4	15	9	4	13	....	....	....	22	....	....	....	....	....
1921-22	Edmonton Eskimos	WCHL	20	15	7	22	....	....	....	24	2	0	....	....	....
1922-23	Edmonton Eskimos	WCHL	29	22	*21	*43	....	....	....	63	4	1	0	1	2
1923-24	Regina Capitals	WCHL	25	7	7	14	....	....	....	39	2	0	....	....	....
1924-25	Regina Capitals	WCHL	28	8	7	15	....	....	....	32	....	....	....	....	....
1925-26	Edmonton Eskimos	WHL	24	35	10	45	....	....	....	24	2	1	1	2	6
1926-27	**Montreal Canadiens**	**NHL**	**44**	**14**	**3**	**17**	**41**	**25**	**66**	**42**	**4**	**0**	**0**	**0**	**0**
1927-28	**Montreal Canadiens**	**NHL**	**44**	**20**	**10**	**30**	**62**	**85**	**147**	**75**	**2**	**1**	**1**	**2**	**4**
1928-29	**Montreal Canadiens**	**NHL**	**44**	**7**	**3**	**10**	**28**	**27**	**55**	**52**	**3**	**0**	**0**	**0**	**12**
1929-30	**Boston Bruins**	**NHL**	**6**	**0**	**1**	**1**	**0**	**3**	**3**	**6**	....	....	....	....	....
	Ottawa Senators	**NHL**	**33**	**6**	**4**	**10**	**12**	**13**	**25**	**32**	**2**	**1**	**0**	**1**	**4**
1930-31	**Ottawa Senators**	**NHL**	**44**	**19**	**11**	**30**	**47**	**40**	**87**	**60**	....	....	....	....	....
1931-32	**Detroit Falcons**	**NHL**	**13**	**1**	**1**	**2**	**2**	**3**	**5**	**0**	....	....	....	....	....
	Detroit Olympics	IAHL	20	6	7	13	....	....	....	18	6	0	1	1	2
1932-33	Edmonton Eskimos	WCHL	29	25	7	32	....	....	....	25	8	*6	1	*7	7
1933-34	Edmonton Eskimos	WCHL	33	18	*21	39	....	....	....	29	2	1	1	2	0
1934-35	Edmonton Eskimos	NWHL	28	20	12	32	....	....	....	18	....	....	....	....	....
1935-36	Edmonton–Seattle	NWHL	27	11	9	20	....	....	....	15	....	....	....	....	....
	NHL Totals		**228**	**67**	**33**	**100**	**192**	**196**	**388**	**257**	**11**	**2**	**1**	**3**	**20**
	Other Major League Totals		126	87	52	139	....	....	....	182	10	2	1	3	8

WCHL Second All-Star Team (1922) • WCHL First All-Star Team (1923) • WHL First All-Star Team (1926)

Signed as a free agent by **Edmonton** (WCHL), November 4, 1921. Traded to **Regina** (WCHL) by **Edmonton** (WCHL) for Emory Sparrow and $1,500, October 3, 1923. Signed as a free agent by **Edmonton** (WHL) after **Regina** (WHL) franchise folded, September, 1925. Traded to **Detroit Cougars** by **Edmonton** (WHL) for cash, October 5, 1926. Traded to **Chicago** by **Detroit Cougars** with Gord Fraser for rights to Art Duncan, October 15, 1926. Traded to **Montreal Canadiens** by **Chicago** for cash, October 18, 1926. Traded to **Boston** by **Montreal Canadiens** for cash, May 13, 1929. Traded to **Ottawa** by **Boston** for cash, December 21, 1929. Claimed by **Detroit Falcons** from **Ottawa** for 1931-32 season in Dispersal Draft, September 26, 1931. Traded to **Seattle** (NWHL) by **Edmonton** (NWHL) for Les Whittles, September, 1935. Signed as a free agent by **Edmonton** (NWHL), December, 1935.

• GAGNE, PIERRE

Pierre Gagne
LW – L. 6'1", 180 lbs. b: North Bay, Ont., 6/5/1940.

Season	Club	League	GP	G	A	Pts	AG	AA	APts	PIM	Playoffs GP	G	A	Pts	PIM
1958-59	Barrie Flyers	OHA	54	20	18	38	....	....	....	10	6	1	4	5	14
1959-60	Barrie Flyers	OHA	48	32	34	66				14	6	6	3	9	6
	Boston Bruins	**NHL**	**2**	**0**	**0**	**0**	**0**	**0**	**0**	**0**	....	....	....	....	....
1960-61	New York Rovers	EHL	45	10	19	29	....	....	....	31	....	....	....	....	....
1961-62	North Bay Trappers	EPHL	1	0	0	0	....	....	....	0	....	....	....	....	....
1961-62	Fort Wayne Komets	IHL	59	19	32	51	....	....	....	39	....	....	....	....	....
1963-64	University of Ottawa	OQAA	STATISTICS NOT AVAILABLE												
1964-65	Hull Volants	QSHL	STATISTICS NOT AVAILABLE												
1965-66	Hull Volants	QSHL	STATISTICS NOT AVAILABLE												
1966-67	Providence Reds	AHL	70	20	21	41	....	....	....	18	....	....	....	....	....
1967-68	Providence Reds	AHL	28	5	13	18	....	....	....	6	5	0	0	0	2
1968-69	Providence Reds	AHL	67	17	22	39	....	....	....	18	9	3	5	8	4
1969-70	Nashville Dixie Flyers	EHL	67	41	44	85	....	....	....	35	....	....	....	....	....
1970-71	Dalhousie University	AUAA	18	27	35	*62	....	....	....	16	....	....	....	....	....
1971-72	Dalhousie University	AUAA	18	10	*24	34	....	....	....	70	....	....	....	....	....
	NHL Totals		**2**	**0**	**0**	**0**	**0**	**0**	**0**	**0**	....	....	....	....	....

• GAGNON, JOHNNY Johnny "Black Cat" Gagnon

RW – R. 5'5", 140 lbs. b: Chicoutimi, Que., 6/8/1905. Deceased.

Season	Club	League	GP	G	A	Pts	AG	AA	APts	PIM	GP	G	A	Pts	PIM
			REGULAR SEASON								PLAYOFFS				
1922-23	Chicoutimi Bluets	Mtl-Sr.	7	0	0	0	....	....	....	....	1	0	0	0	....
	Quebec Bulldogs	Big 4	3	0	0	0	....	....	....	....	....	....	....	....	....
1923-24	Trois-Rivieres Renards	ECHA	9	2	0	2	....	....	....	....	....	....	....	....	....
1924-25	Trois-Rivieres Renards	ECHL	16	18	0	18	....	....	....	....	2	5	0	5	....
1925-26	Quebec Sons of Ireland	QAHA	10	5	0	5	....	....	....	....	6	4	0	4	....
1926-27	Quebec Beavers	Can-Am	32	*27	6	*33	....	....	....	54	2	0	0	0	5
1927-28	Providence Reds	Can-Am	39	20	4	24	....	....	....	80	....	....	....	....	....
1928-29	Providence Reds	Can-Am	39	7	3	10	....	....	....	50	6	*4	0	*4	10
1929-30	Providence Reds	Can-Am	39	21	17	38	....	....	....	72	3	2	*4	*6	6
1930-31	**Montreal Canadiens**	**NHL**	**41**	**18**	**7**	**25**	**44**	**25**	**69**	**43**	**10**	***6**	**2**	**8**	**8**
1931-32	**Montreal Canadiens**	**NHL**	**48**	**19**	**18**	**37**	**41**	**50**	**91**	**40**	**4**	**1**	**1**	**2**	**4**
1932-33	**Montreal Canadiens**	**NHL**	**48**	**12**	**23**	**35**	**28**	**62**	**90**	**64**	**2**	**0**	**2**	**2**	**0**
1933-34	**Montreal Canadiens**	**NHL**	**48**	**9**	**15**	**24**	**20**	**40**	**60**	**25**	**2**	**1**	**0**	**1**	**2**
1934-35	**Boston Bruins**	**NHL**	**24**	**1**	**1**	**2**	**2**	**2**	**4**	**9**	....	....	....	....	....
	Montreal Canadiens	**NHL**	**23**	**1**	**5**	**6**	**2**	**11**	**13**	**2**	**2**	**0**	**1**	**1**	**2**
1935-36	**Montreal Canadiens**	**NHL**	**48**	**7**	**9**	**16**	**17**	**22**	**39**	**42**	....	....	....	....	....
1936-37	**Montreal Canadiens**	**NHL**	**48**	**20**	**16**	**36**	**44**	**38**	**82**	**38**	**5**	**2**	**1**	**3**	**9**
1937-38	**Montreal Canadiens**	**NHL**	**47**	**13**	**17**	**30**	**27**	**35**	**62**	**9**	**3**	**1**	**3**	**4**	**2**
1938-39	**Montreal Canadiens**	**NHL**	**45**	**12**	**22**	**34**	**25**	**41**	**66**	**23**	**3**	**0**	**2**	**2**	**10**
1939-40	**Montreal Canadiens**	**NHL**	**10**	**4**	**5**	**9**	**9**	**10**	**19**	**0**	....	....	....	....	....
	New York Americans	**NHL**	**24**	**4**	**3**	**7**	**9**	**6**	**15**	**0**	**1**	**1**	**0**	**1**	**0**
1940-41	Shawinigan Cataracts	QSHL	33	15	26	41	....	....	....	58	10	3	*8	11	12
1941-42	North Sydney Victorias	NSSHL	23	5	11	16	....	....	....	6	6	2	4	6	4
1942-43	Providence Reds	AHL	50	9	10	19	....	....	....	12	....	....	....	....	....
1943-44	Providence Reds	AHL	DID NOT PLAY – COACHING												
1944-45	Providence Reds	AHL	9	0	5	5	....	....	....	0	....	....	....	....	....
	NHL Totals		**454**	**120**	**141**	**261**	**268**	**342**	**610**	**295**	**32**	**12**	**12**	**24**	**37**

Played in NHL All-Star Game (1937, 1939)

Traded to **Montreal Canadiens** by **Providece** (Can-Am) for Gerry Carson, the loan of Jean Pusie and cash, October 21, 1930. Traded to **Boston** by **Montreal Canadiens** for Joe Lamb, October 2, 1934. Traded to **Montreal Canadiens** by **Boston** for cash, January 9, 1935. Traded to **NY Americans** by **Montreal** for cash, January 3, 1940.

• GAINOR, NORM Norm "Dutch" Gainor

C – L. 6'1", 170 lbs. b: Calgary, Alta., 4/10/1904. d: 1/16/1962.

Season	Club	League	GP	G	A	Pts	AG	AA	APts	PIM	GP	G	A	Pts	PIM
1924-25	Crows Nest Pass	MHL Sr.	STATISTICS NOT AVAILABLE												
1925-26	Duluth Hornets	AHA	15	1	0	1	....	....	....	0	5	0	0	0	0
1926-27	Calgary Tigers	PrHL	23	16	11	27	....	....	....	38	2	0	0	0	0
1927-28	**Boston Bruins**	**NHL**	**42**	**8**	**4**	**12**	**24**	**34**	**58**	**35**	**2**	**0**	**0**	**0**	**6**
1928-29	**Boston Bruins**	**NHL**	**44**	**14**	**5**	**19**	**57**	**46**	**103**	**30**	**5**	**2**	**0**	**2**	**4**
1929-30	**Boston Bruins**	**NHL**	**42**	**18**	**31**	**49**	**36**	**103**	**139**	**39**	**3**	**0**	**0**	**0**	**0**
1930-31	**Boston Bruins**	**NHL**	**35**	**8**	**3**	**11**	**19**	**11**	**30**	**14**	**5**	**0**	**1**	**1**	**2**
1931-32	**New York Rangers**	**NHL**	**46**	**3**	**9**	**12**	**6**	**25**	**31**	**9**	**7**	**0**	**0**	**0**	**2**
1932-33	Springfield Indians	Can-Am	13	7	5	12	....	....	....	....	....	....	....	....	....
	Ottawa Senators	**NHL**	**2**	**0**	**0**	**0**	**0**	**0**	**0**	**0**	....	....	....	....	....
	Saskatoon Cresents	WCHL	21	10	11	21	....	....	....	4	....	....	....	....	....
1933-34	Calgary Tigers	NWHL	34	23	19	*42	....	....	....	24	5	2	0	2	2
1934-35	**Montreal Maroons**	**NHL**	**35**	**0**	**4**	**4**	**0**	**9**	**9**	**2**	....	....	....	....	....
1935-36	Calgary Tigers	NWHL	40	21	14	35	....	....	....	6	....	....	....	....	....
1936-37	Portland Buckaroos	PCHL	13	0	0	0	....	....	....	0	....	....	....	....	....
	NHL Totals		**246**	**51**	**56**	**107**	**142**	**228**	**370**	**129**	**22**	**2**	**1**	**3**	**14**

Traded to **Boston** by **Minneapolis** (AHA) with Nobby Clark for Red Stuart, cash and future considerations, October 24, 1927. Traded to **NY Rangers** by **Boston** for Joe Jerwa, June, 1931. Traded to **Ottawa** by **NY Rangers** for cash after Springfield (Can-Am) franchise folded (December 18, 1932), December 23, 1932. Traded to **Montreal Maroons** by **Calgary** (NWHL) for cash, October 22, 1934.

• GALBRAITH, PERCY Percy "Perk" Galbraith

LW/D – L. 5'10", 162 lbs. b: Toronto, Ont., 12/5/1898. d: 1/19/1961.

Season	Club	League	GP	G	A	Pts	AG	AA	APts	PIM	GP	G	A	Pts	PIM
1914-15	Winnipeg Winnipegs	MHL Sr.	8	2	2	4	....	....	....	6	....	....	....	....	....
1915-16	Winnipeg Victorias	MHL Sr.	2	3	1	4	....	....	....	2	....	....	....	....	....
1916-17			MILITARY SERVICE												
1917-18			MILITARY SERVICE												
1918-19			MILITARY SERVICE												
1919-20	Winnipeg Monarchs	MHL Sr.	7	6	1	7	....	....	....	6	....	....	....	....	....
1920-21	Eveleth Rangers	USAHA	STATISTICS NOT AVAILABLE												
1921-22	Eveleth Rangers	USAHA	STATISTICS NOT AVAILABLE												
1922-23	Eveleth Rangers	USAHA	20	4	0	4	....	....	....	....	....	....	....	....	....
1923-24	Eveleth Rangers	USAHA	21	9	2	11	....	....	....	....	....	....	....	....	....
1924-25	Eveleth Rangers	USAHA	38	10	0	10	....	....	....	....	4	0	0	0	0
1925-26	Eveleth-Hibbing Rangers	USAHA	37	6	5	11	....	....	....	40	....	....	....	....	....
1926-27	**Boston Bruins**	**NHL**	**42**	**9**	**8**	**17**	**26**	**69**	**95**	**26**	**8**	**3**	***3**	***6**	**2**
1927-28	**Boston Bruins**	**NHL**	**42**	**6**	**5**	**11**	**18**	**42**	**60**	**26**	**2**	**0**	**1**	**1**	**6**
1928-29	**Boston Bruins**	**NHL**	**38**	**2**	**1**	**3**	**8**	**9**	**17**	**44**	**5**	**0**	**0**	**0**	**2**
1929-30	**Boston Bruins**	**NHL**	**44**	**7**	**9**	**16**	**14**	**29**	**43**	**38**	**6**	**1**	**3**	**4**	**8**
1930-31	**Boston Bruins**	**NHL**	**43**	**2**	**3**	**5**	**5**	**11**	**16**	**28**	**5**	**0**	**0**	**0**	**6**
1931-32	**Boston Bruins**	**NHL**	**47**	**2**	**1**	**3**	**4**	**3**	**7**	**28**	....	....	....	....	....
1932-33	**Boston Bruins**	**NHL**	**47**	**1**	**2**	**3**	**2**	**5**	**7**	**28**	**5**	**0**	**0**	**0**	**0**
1933-34	**Boston Bruins**	**NHL**	**42**	**0**	**2**	**2**	**0**	**5**	**5**	**6**	....	....	....	....	....
	Ottawa Senators	**NHL**	**2**	**0**	**0**	**0**	**0**	**0**	**0**	**0**	....	....	....	....	....
1934-35	Eveleth Rangers	CHL	45	4	5	9	....	....	....	6	....	....	....	....	....
1935-36	Wichita Skyhawks	AHA	47	4	5	9	....	....	....	34	....	....	....	....	....
1936-37	Wichita Skyhawks	AHA	48	4	4	8	....	....	....	38	....	....	....	....	....
1937-38	St. Paul Saints	AHA	34	3	0	3	....	....	....	10	....	....	....	....	....
1938-39	St. Paul Saints	AHA	3	0	0	0	....	....	....	0	....	....	....	....	....
1939-40	St. Paul Saints	AHA	DID NOT PLAY – COACHING												
	NHL Totals		**347**	**29**	**31**	**60**	**77**	**173**	**250**	**224**	**31**	**4**	**7**	**11**	**24**

Rights traded to **Boston** by **St. Paul** (AHA) with the rights to Bill Hill for cash, January 3, 1926. Traded to **Ottawa** by **Boston** with Ted Saunders and Bud Cook for Bob Gracie, October 4, 1933.

• GALLAGHER, JOHN John (James) Gallagher

D – L. 5'11", 188 lbs. b: Kenora, Ont., 1/19/1909. d: 9/16/1981.

Season	Club	League	GP	G	A	Pts	AG	AA	APts	PIM	GP	G	A	Pts	PIM
			REGULAR SEASON								PLAYOFFS				
1928-29	Kenora Thistles	TBJHL	16	4	3	7	....	....	....	12	....	....	....	....	....
1929-30	Montreal AAA	City Sr.	10	3	0	3	....	....	....	25	2	0	0	0	0
	Montreal CPR	City Sr.	STATISTICS NOT AVAILABLE												
1930-31	**Montreal Maroons**	**NHL**	**35**	**4**	**2**	**6**	**10**	**7**	**17**	**35**	**2**	**0**	**0**	**0**	**0**
1931-32	**Montreal Maroons**	**NHL**	**19**	**1**	**0**	**1**	**2**	**0**	**2**	**18**	....	....	....	....	....
	Windsor Bulldogs	IAHL	29	6	4	10	....	....	....	48	6	2	1	3	13
1932-33	**Montreal Maroons**	**NHL**	**6**	**1**	**0**	**1**	**2**	**0**	**2**	**0**	....	....	....	....	....
	Detroit Red Wings	**NHL**	**35**	**3**	**6**	**9**	**7**	**16**	**23**	**48**	**4**	**1**	**1**	**2**	**4**
1933-34	**Detroit Red Wings**	**NHL**	**1**	**0**	**0**	**0**	**0**	**0**	**0**	**0**	....	....	....	....	....
1934-35	Windsor Bulldogs	IAHL	26	3	5	8	....	....	....	8	....	....	....	....	....
1935-36	Detroit Olympics	IAHL	44	4	3	7	....	....	....	40	6	3	0	3	2
1936-37	**New York Americans**	**NHL**	**9**	**0**	**0**	**0**	**0**	**0**	**0**	**8**	....	....	....	....	....
	Pittsburgh Hornets	AHL	29	6	6	12	....	....	....	20	5	0	0	0	0
	Detroit Red Wings	**NHL**	**11**	**1**	**0**	**1**	**2**	**0**	**2**	**4**	**10**	**1**	**0**	**1**	**17**
1937-38	**New York Americans**	**NHL**	**46**	**3**	**6**	**9**	**6**	**12**	**18**	**18**	**6**	**0**	**2**	**2**	**6**
1938-39	**New York Americans**	**NHL**	**43**	**1**	**5**	**6**	**2**	**9**	**11**	**22**	**2**	**0**	**0**	**0**	**0**
	NHL Totals		**205**	**14**	**19**	**33**	**31**	**44**	**75**	**153**	**24**	**2**	**3**	**5**	**27**

Traded to **Detroit** by **Montreal Maroons** for Reg Noble, December 9, 1932. Traded to **NY Americans** by **Detroit** for $6,000, October 7, 1936. Traded to **Detroit** by **NY Americans** for cash, November 29, 1936. Traded to **NY Americans** by **Detroit** for $6,000, October 7, 1937.

• GALLINGER, DON Don Gallinger

C – L. 6', 170 lbs. b: Port Colborne, Ont., 4/16/1925. d: 6/12/1990.

Season	Club	League	GP	G	A	Pts	AG	AA	APts	PIM	GP	G	A	Pts	PIM
1941-42	St. Catharines Teepees	OHA	STATISTICS NOT AVAILABLE												
1942-43	**Boston Bruins**	**NHL**	**48**	**14**	**20**	**34**	**20**	**25**	**45**	**16**	**9**	**3**	**1**	**4**	**10**
1943-44	**Boston Bruins**	**NHL**	**23**	**13**	**5**	**18**	**16**	**6**	**22**	**6**	....	....	....	....	....
	Toronto Bowsers	City Sr.	....	4	3	7	....	....	....	11	9	5	7	12	10
1944-45	Winnipeg RCAF	MHL Sr.	9	10	5	15	....	....	....	18	4	1	6	7	8
1945-46	**Boston Bruins**	**NHL**	**50**	**17**	**23**	**40**	**26**	**43**	**69**	**18**	**10**	**2**	**4**	**6**	**2**
1946-47	**Boston Bruins**	**NHL**	**47**	**11**	**19**	**30**	**15**	**27**	**42**	**12**	**4**	**0**	**0**	**0**	**7**
1947-48	**Boston Bruins**	**NHL**	**54**	**10**	**21**	**31**	**15**	**31**	**46**	**37**	....	....	....	....	....
1948-49			DID NOT PLAY – SUSPENDED												
	NHL Totals		**222**	**65**	**88**	**153**	**92**	**132**	**224**	**89**	**23**	**5**	**5**	**10**	**19**

• Suspended for life by NHL for gambling violations, March 9, 1948.

• GAMBLE, DICK Dick Gamble

LW – L. 6', 178 lbs. b: Moncton, N.B., 11/16/1928.

Season	Club	League	GP	G	A	Pts	AG	AA	APts	PIM	GP	G	A	Pts	PIM
1944-45	Moncton Bruins	City Jr.	3	*3	1	*4	....	....	....	2	10	*25	*9	*34	2
1945-46	Moncton Bruins	City Jr.	3	1	0	1	....	....	....	7	3	*6	3	*9	2
	Saint John Beavers	City Jr.	....	....	....	....	....	....	....	....	4	8	3	11	0
	Halifax St. Mary's	City Jr.	....	....	....	....	....	....	....	....	1	1	0	1	0
1946-47	Oshawa Generals	OHA	24	15	20	35	....	....	....	26	5	3	0	3	0
1947-48	Oshawa Generals	OHA	34	31	16	47	....	....	....	21	3	0	0	0	2
1948-49	Oshawa Generals	OHA	46	39	23	62	....	....	....	10	2	2	0	2	0
1949-50	Quebec Aces	QSHL	56	20	25	45	....	....	....	18	12	9	3	12	4
1950-51	Quebec Aces	QSHL	58	*46	34	80	....	....	....	44	19	10	8	18	14
	Montreal Canadiens	**NHL**	**1**	**0**	**0**	**0**	**0**	**0**	**0**	**0**	....	....	....	....	....
1951-52	**Montreal Canadiens**	**NHL**	**64**	**23**	**17**	**40**	**33**	**22**	**55**	**8**	**7**	**0**	**2**	**2**	**0**
1952-53	**Montreal Canadiens**	**NHL**	**69**	**11**	**13**	**24**	**17**	**18**	**35**	**26**	**5**	**1**	**0**	**1**	**2**
1953-54	**Montreal Canadiens**	**NHL**	**32**	**4**	**8**	**12**	**6**	**11**	**17**	**18**	....	....	....	....	....
	Montreal Royals	QHL	32	20	25	45	....	....	....	49	10	5	1	6	4
1954-55	**Chicago Black Hawks**	**NHL**	**14**	**2**	**0**	**2**	**3**	**0**	**3**	**6**	....	....	....	....	....
	Buffalo Bisons	AHL	45	38	21	59	....	....	....	26	10	4	4	8	6
	Montreal Canadiens	**NHL**	....	....	....	....	....	....	....	....	**2**	**0**	**0**	**0**	**2**
1955-56	**Montreal Canadiens**	**NHL**	**12**	**0**	**3**	**3**	**0**	**4**	**4**	**8**	....	....	....	....	....
	Quebec Aces	QHL	52	23	24	47	....	....	....	45	7	4	5	9	14
1956-57	Quebec Aes	QHL	63	35	14	49	....	....	....	28	10	4	4	8	8
1957-58	Buffalo Bisons	AHL	70	32	22	54	....	....	....	32	....	....	....	....	....
1958-59	Buffalo Bisons	AHL	70	31	30	61	....	....	....	24	11	2	2	4	14
1959-60	Buffalo Bisons	AHL	72	27	50	77	....	....	....	22	....	....	....	....	....
1960-61	Buffalo Bisons	AHL	72	40	36	76	....	....	....	18	4	2	0	2	6
1961-62	Rochester Americans	AHL	66	39	29	68	....	....	....	32	2	0	2	2	0
1962-63	Rochester Americans	AHL	70	35	22	57	....	....	....	16	2	0	1	1	0
1963-64	Rochester Americans	AHL	72	34	34	68	....	....	....	4	2	0	0	0	0
1964-65	Rochester Americans	AHL	70	48	29	77	....	....	....	16	10	5	8	13	6
1965-66	**Toronto Maple Leafs**	**NHL**	**2**	**1**	**0**	**1**	**1**	**0**	**1**	**0**	....	....	....	....	....
	Rochester Americans	AHL	71	*47	51	*98	....	....	....	22	12	2	*9	11	16
1966-67	**Toronto Maple Leafs**	**NHL**	**1**	**0**	**0**	**0**	**0**	**0**	**0**	**0**	....	....	....	....	....
	Rochester Americans	AHL	72	46	37	83	....	....	....	22	13	4	2	6	8
1967-68	Rochester Americans	AHL	67	20	22	42	....	....	....	77	4	0	1	1	8
1968-69	Rochester Americans	AHL	74	30	37	67	....	....	....	37	....	....	....	....	....
1969-70	Rochester Americans	AHL	8	1	4	5	....	....	....	6	....	....	....	....	....
	NHL Totals		**195**	**41**	**41**	**82**	**60**	**55**	**115**	**66**	**14**	**1**	**2**	**3**	**4**

AHL Second All-Star Team (1955, 1962, 1965, 1967) • AHL First All-Star Team (1961, 1966) • Won John B. Sollenberger Trophy (Top Scorer - AHL) (1966) • Won Les Cunningham Award (MVP - AHL) (1966)

Played in NHL All-Star Game (1953)

Signed as a free agent by **Montreal**, September 24, 1952. Traded to **Chicago** by **Montreal** for Bill Shevtz with Montreal holding rights of recall, October, 1954. Rights returned to **Montreal by Chicago**, November, 1954. Traded to **NY Rangers** by **Montreal** with Ed Dorohoy for Hy Buller, June 7, 1954. Traded to **Chicago** by **NY Rangers** for cash, October 9, 1954. Traded to **Montreal** by **Chicago** for cash, November 23, 1954. Traded to **Buffalo** (AHL) by **Montreal** for cash, July, 1957. Traded to **Toronto** by **Buffalo** (AHL) for Dave Creighton, July, 1961.

• GARDINER, HERB Herb Gardiner HHOF

D – L. 5'10", 190 lbs. b: Winnipeg, Man., 5/8/1891. d: 1/11/1972.

			REGULAR SEASON								PLAYOFFS				
Season	Club	League	GP	G	A	Pts	AG	AA	APts	PIM	GP	G	A	Pts	PIM
1919-20	Calgary Wanderers	Big 4	12	8	9	17	....	....	....	6	2	0	0	0	2
1920-21	Calgary Wanderers	Big 4	13	3	7	10	....	....	....	6	....	....	....	....	....
1921-22	Calgary Tigers	WCHL	24	4	1	5	....	....	....	6	2	0	0	0	0
1922-23	Calgary Tigers	WCHL	29	9	3	12	....	....	....	9	....	....	....	....	....
1923-24	Calgary Tigers	WCHL	22	5	5	10	....	....	....	4	7	3	1	4	10
1924-25	Calgary Tigers	WCHL	28	12	8	20	....	....	....	18	2	0	0	0	0
1925-26	Calgary Tigers	WHL	27	3	1	4	....	....	....	10	....	....	....	....	....
1926-27	**Montreal Canadiens**	**NHL**	**44**	**6**	**6**	**12**	**17**	**51**	**68**	**26**	**4**	**0**	**0**	**0**	**10**
1927-28	**Montreal Canadiens**	**NHL**	**44**	**4**	**3**	**7**	**12**	**25**	**37**	**26**	**2**	**0**	**1**	**1**	**4**
1928-29	**Chicago Black Hawks**	**NHL**	**13**	**0**	**0**	**0**	**0**	**0**	**0**	**0**	....	....	....	....	....
	Montreal Canadiens	**NHL**	....	....	....	....	....	....	....	....	**3**	**0**	**0**	**0**	**0**
1929-30	Philadelphia Arrows	Can-Am	1	0	0	0	....	....	....	0	....	....	....	....	....
1930-31	Philadelphia Arrows	Can-Am	DID NOT PLAY – COACHING												
1931-32	Philadelphia Arrows	Can-Am	1	0	0	0	....	....	....	0	....	....	....	....	....
1932-33	Philadelphia Arrows	Can-Am	DID NOT PLAY – COACHING												
1933-34	Philadelphia Arrows	Can-Am	DID NOT PLAY – COACHING												
1934-35	Philadelphia Arrows	Can-Am	12	0	0	0	....	....	....	0	....	....	....	....	....
1935-36	Philadelphia Ramblers	Can-Am	DID NOT PLAY – COACHING												
	NHL Totals		**101**	**10**	**9**	**19**	**29**	**76**	**105**	**52**	**9**	**0**	**1**	**1**	**14**
	Other Major League Totals		130	33	18	51	....	....	....	47	11	3	1	4	10

WCHL First All-Star Team (1923, 1925) • Won Hart Trophy (1927)

Signed as a free agent by **Calgary** (WCHL), November 4, 1921. Rights traded to **Montreal Canadiens** by **Calgary** for cash, October 20, 1926. Loaned to **Chicago** by **Montreal** for remainder of 1928-29 regular season for loan of Art Lesieur, January 9, 1929. Traded to **Boston** by **Montreal** for cash, June, 1929. Traded to **Philadelphia** (Can-Am) by **Boston** for cash, June, 1929.

• GARDNER, CAL Cal "Finger" Gardner

C – L. 6'1", 172 lbs. b: Transcona, Man., 10/30/1924.

			REGULAR SEASON								PLAYOFFS				
Season	Club	League	GP	G	A	Pts	AG	AA	APts	PIM	GP	G	A	Pts	PIM
1941-42	Winnipeg CUAC	City Jr.	9	6	3	9	....	....	....	11	....	....	....	....	....
1942-43	Winnipeg Esquires	City Jr.	15	18	9	27	....	....	....	37	6	8	5	13	2
	Winnipeg Rangers	MJHL	....	....	....	....	....	....	....	....	10	11	3	14	30
1943-44	Port Arthur Navy	TBSHL	10	18	*24	42	....	....	....	15	2	5	3	8	4
1944-45			MILITARY SERVICE												
1945-46	**New York Rangers**	**NHL**	**16**	**8**	**2**	**10**	**12**	**4**	**16**	**2**	....	....	....	....	....
	New York Rovers	EHL	40	*41	32	*73	....	....	....	28	....	....	....	....	....
1946-47	**New York Rangers**	**NHL**	**52**	**13**	**16**	**29**	**18**	**23**	**41**	**30**	....	....	....	....	....
1947-48	**New York Rangers**	**NHL**	**58**	**7**	**18**	**25**	**10**	**26**	**36**	**71**	**5**	**0**	**0**	**0**	**0**
1948-49	**Toronto Maple Leafs**	**NHL**	**53**	**13**	**22**	**35**	**20**	**35**	**55**	**35**	**9**	**2**	**5**	**7**	**0**
1949-50	**Toronto Maple Leafs**	**NHL**	**31**	**7**	**19**	**26**	**9**	**24**	**33**	**12**	**7**	**1**	**0**	**1**	**4**
1950-51	**Toronto Maple Leafs**	**NHL**	**66**	**23**	**28**	**51**	**31**	**36**	**67**	**42**	**11**	**1**	**1**	**2**	**4**
1951-52	**Toronto Maple Leafs**	**NHL**	**70**	**15**	**26**	**41**	**21**	**34**	**55**	**40**	**3**	**0**	**0**	**0**	**2**
1952-53	**Chicago Black Hawks**	**NHL**	**70**	**11**	**24**	**35**	**17**	**34**	**51**	**60**	**7**	**0**	**2**	**2**	**4**
1953-54	**Boston Bruins**	**NHL**	**70**	**14**	**20**	**34**	**21**	**27**	**48**	**62**	**4**	**1**	**1**	**2**	**0**
1954-55	**Boston Bruins**	**NHL**	**70**	**16**	**22**	**38**	**23**	**28**	**51**	**40**	**5**	**0**	**0**	**0**	**4**
1955-56	**Boston Bruins**	**NHL**	**70**	**15**	**21**	**36**	**22**	**26**	**48**	**57**	....	....	....	....	....
1956-57	**Boston Bruins**	**NHL**	**70**	**12**	**20**	**32**	**16**	**23**	**39**	**66**	**10**	**2**	**1**	**3**	**2**
1957-58	Springfield Indians	AHL	69	24	57	81	....	....	....	49	13	4	*12	16	4
1958-59	Providence Reds	AHL	68	24	39	63	....	....	....	73	....	....	....	....	....
1959-60	Kingston Frontenacs	EPHL	65	32	61	93	....	....	....	57	....	....	....	....	....
1960-61	Cleveland Barons	AHL	72	25	39	64	....	....	....	24	4	1	0	1	0
	NHL Totals		**696**	**154**	**238**	**392**	**220**	**320**	**540**	**517**	**61**	**7**	**10**	**17**	**20**

EHL First All-Star Team (1946) • Won John Carlin Trophy (Top Scorer - EHL) (1946) • AHL Second All-Star Team (1958)

Played in NHL All-Star Game (1948, 1949)

Traded to **Toronto** by **NY Rangers** with Bill Juzda, Rene Trudell and the rights to Frank Mathers for Wally Stanowski and Elwyn Morris, June, 1948. Traded to **Chicago** by **Toronto** with Roy Hannigan, Al Rollins and Gus Mortson for Harry Lumley, September 11, 1952. Traded to **Boston** by **Chicago** for cash, June 26, 1953.

• GARIEPY, RAY Ray "Rockabye Ray" Gariepy

D – L. 5'9", 180 lbs. b: Toronto, Ont., 9/4/1928.

			REGULAR SEASON								PLAYOFFS				
Season	Club	League	GP	G	A	Pts	AG	AA	APts	PIM	GP	G	A	Pts	PIM
1945-46	Barrie Flyers	OHA	28	3	6	9	....	....	....	79	....	....	....	....	....
1946-47	Barrie Flyers	OHA	31	8	16	24	....	....	....	*133	5	3	3	6	6
1947-48	Barrie Flyers	OHA	35	7	21	28	....	....	....	72	22	7	12	19	*63
1948-49	Buffalo Bisons	AHL	35	2	3	5	....	....	....	41	....	....	....	....	....
	Houston Huskies	USHL	36	3	10	13	....	....	....	45	....	....	....	....	....
1949-50	Buffalo Bisons	AHL	11	0	1	1	....	....	....	10	....	....	....	....	....
	Louisville Blades	USHL	54	3	14	17	....	....	....	87	....	....	....	....	....
1950-51	Hershey Bears	AHL	64	2	8	10	....	....	....	147	5	0	0	0	10
1951-52	Hershey Bears	AHL	57	2	7	9	....	....	....	111	5	1	0	1	2
1952-53	Hershey Bears	AHL	62	4	8	12	....	....	....	90	3	0	0	0	2
1953-54	**Boston Bruins**	**NHL**	**35**	**1**	**6**	**7**	**2**	**8**	**10**	**39**	....	....	....	....	....
	Hershey Bears	AHL	24	2	12	14	....	....	....	42	11	0	4	4	9
1954-55	Pittsburgh Hornets	AHL	56	2	20	22	....	....	....	90	10	0	2	2	8
1955-56	**Toronto Maple Leafs**	**NHL**	**1**	**0**	**0**	**0**	**0**	**0**	**0**	**4**	....	....	....	....	....
	Pittsburgh Hornets	AHL	54	1	13	14	....	....	....	95	4	0	3	3	11
1956-57	Owen Sound Mercury's	OHA Sr.	26	6	11	17	....	....	....	39	....	....	....	....	....
1957-58	Chatham Maroons	OHA Sr.	1	0	0	0	....	....	....	6	....	....	....	....	....
1958-1966			DID NOT PLAY – RETIRED												
1966-67	Collingwood Georgians	OHA Sr.	37	4	26	30	....	....	....	38	....	....	....	....	....
1967-68	Barrie Flyers	OHA Sr.	40	1	23	24	....	....	....	45	....	....	....	....	....
1968-69	Barrie Flyers	OHA Sr.	3	0	1	1	....	....	....	6	....	....	....	....	....
1969-70	Barrie Flyers	OHA Sr.	DID NOT PLAY – COACHING												
	NHL Totals		**36**	**1**	**6**	**7**	**2**	**8**	**10**	**43**	....	....	....	....	....

Traded to **Hershey** (AHL) by **Buffalo** (AHL) for Rollie McLenahan, June, 1950. Traded to **Toronto** by **Boston** for John Henderson, September 23, 1955. Traded to **Hershey** (AHL) by **Toronto** with Gil Mayer for cash, Jack Price for cash, Willie Marshall for cash, Bob Hassard and Bob Sollinger for cash, June, 1956.

• GARRETT, RED Red (Dudley) Garrett

D – L. 5'11", 190 lbs. b: Toronto, Ont., 7/24/1924. d: 11/25/1944.

			REGULAR SEASON								PLAYOFFS				
Season	Club	League	GP	G	A	Pts	AG	AA	APts	PIM	GP	G	A	Pts	PIM
1941-42	Toronto Marlboros	OHA	18	2	5	7	....	....	....	*61	2	1	1	2	6
1942-43	**New York Rangers**	**NHL**	**23**	**1**	**1**	**2**	**1**	**1**	**2**	**18**	....	....	....	....	....
	Providence Reds	AHL	6	0	0	0	....	....	....	2	....	....	....	....	....
	Sydney Navy	City Sr.	1	0	0	0	....	....	....	2	....	....	....	....	....
1943-44	Toronto Navy	OHA Sr.	13	0	1	1	....	....	....	12	....	....	....	....	....
	Cornwallis Navy	City Sr.	4	4	5	9	....	....	....	18	3	1	0	1	15
	NHL Totals		**23**	**1**	**1**	**2**	**1**	**1**	**2**	**18**	....	....	....	....	....

• Killed in action during escort run off the coast of Port-aux-Basques, Newfoundland, November 25, 1944.

• GAUDREAULT, ARMAND Armand Gaudreault

LW – L. 5'9", 155 lbs. b: Lac St. Jean, Que., 7/14/1921.

			REGULAR SEASON								PLAYOFFS				
Season	Club	League	GP	G	A	Pts	AG	AA	APts	PIM	GP	G	A	Pts	PIM
1940-41	Quebec Aces	QSHL	33	11	12	23	....	....	....	23	4	0	0	0	2
1941-42	Quebec Aces	QSHL	40	19	25	44	....	....	....	19	15	7	7	14	6
1942-43	Quebec Aces	QSHL	34	16	26	40	....	....	....	4	4	0	2	2	2
1943-44	Quebec Aces	QSHL	25	18	28	46	....	....	....	21	6	4	3	7	4
1944-45	**Boston Bruins**	**NHL**	**44**	**15**	**9**	**24**	**21**	**14**	**35**	**27**	**7**	**0**	**2**	**2**	**8**
1945-46	Hershey Bears	AHL	47	21	24	45	....	....	....	42	3	1	0	1	4
1946-47	Hershey Bears	AHL	61	23	31	54	....	....	....	34	11	3	3	6	10
	Quebec Aces	QSHL	1	0	0	0	....	....	....	0	....	....	....	....	....
1947-48	Hershey–Cleveland	AHL	17	10	11	21	....	....	....	6	2	1	0	1	15
	Sherbrooke Saints	QPHL	10	10	15	25	....	....	....	22	....	....	....	....	....
1948-49	Quebec Aces	QSHL	1	1	1	2	....	....	....	0	1	0	0	0	2
	Alma Eagles	QPHL	STATISTICS NOT AVAILABLE												
1949-50	Quebec Aces	QSHL	60	31	32	63	....	....	....	48	12	9	6	15	6
1950-51	Quebec Aces	QSHL	56	24	27	51	....	....	....	16	19	7	10	17	9
1951-52	Quebec Aces	QSHL	60	29	28	57	....	....	....	52	20	3	9	12	6
	NHL Totals		**44**	**15**	**9**	**24**	**21**	**14**	**35**	**27**	**7**	**0**	**2**	**2**	**8**

Signed as a free agent by **Boston**, November 2, 1944.

• GAUDREAULT, LEO Leo Gaudreault

LW/C – L. 5'10", 152 lbs. b: Chicoutimi, Que., 10/19/1905. d: 5/4/1909.

			REGULAR SEASON								PLAYOFFS				
Season	Club	League	GP	G	A	Pts	AG	AA	APts	PIM	GP	G	A	Pts	PIM
1921-22	Chicoutimi Bluets	QPHL	5	1	0	1	....	....	....	....	....	....	....	....	....
1922-23	Chicoutimi Bluets	QPHL	10	2	0	1	....	....	....	....	....	....	....	....	....
1923-24	Quebec Sons of Ireland	ECHA	12	3	0	3	....	....	....	....	....	....	....	....	....
1924-25	Montreal Nationale	ECHL	6	2	0	2	....	....	....	....	....	....	....	....	....
1925-26	Montreal Nationale	ECHL	STATISTICS NOT AVAILABLE												
1926-27	St. Francis Xavier	QPHL	STATISTICS NOT AVAILABLE												
1927-28	**Montreal Canadiens**	**NHL**	**32**	**6**	**2**	**8**	**18**	**17**	**35**	**24**	....	....	....	....	....
1928-29	**Montreal Canadiens**	**NHL**	**11**	**0**	**0**	**0**	**0**	**0**	**0**	**4**	....	....	....	....	....
	Providence Reds	Can-Am	28	2	0	2	....	....	....	45	6	0	0	0	14
1929-30	Providence Reds	Can-Am	39	7	12	19	....	....	....	64	3	1	0	1	0
1930-31	Providence Reds	Can-Am	40	22	20	42	....	....	....	44	2	1	2	3	8
1931-32	Providence Reds	Can-Am	40	13	15	28	....	....	....	22	5	1	0	1	6
1932-33	**Montreal Canadiens**	**NHL**	**24**	**2**	**2**	**4**	**5**	**5**	**10**	**2**	....	....	....	....	....
	Providence Reds	Can-Am	26	12	15	27	....	....	....	26	2	0	1	1	0
1933-34	Providence Reds	Can-Am	40	9	23	32	....	....	....	14	3	1	3	4	2
1934-35	Providence Reds	Can-Am	48	23	26	49	....	....	....	12	4	0	1	1	0
1935-36	Providence Reds	Can-Am	46	7	17	24	....	....	....	8	7	0	0	0	2
1936-37	Minneapolis Millers	AHA	42	8	15	23	....	....	....	20	6	2	5	7	2
	NHL Totals		**67**	**8**	**4**	**12**	**23**	**22**	**45**	**30**	....	....	....	....	....

Traded to **Providence** (Can-Am) by **Montreal Canadiens** for Armand Mondou, December 10, 1930. Signed as a free agent by **Montreal Canadiens**, September, 1932. Traded to **Providence** (Can-Am) by **Montreal** with Armand Mondou for Hago Harrington and Leo Murray, January, 1933.

• GAUTHIER, ART Art "Nosey" Gauthier

C – L. 5'8", 158 lbs. b: Espanola, Ont., 10/10/1904. Deceased.

			REGULAR SEASON								PLAYOFFS				
Season	Club	League	GP	G	A	Pts	AG	AA	APts	PIM	GP	G	A	Pts	PIM
1921-22	Iroquois Falls Eskimos	NOHA	....	....	....	....	....	....	....	....	7	5	5	10	....
1922-23	Iroquois Falls Eskimos	NOHA	STATISTICS NOT AVAILABLE												
1923-24	North Bay Trappers	NOHA	6	2	0	2	....	....	....	....	5	9	0	9	....
1924-25	Galt Terriers	OHA Sr.	20	7	10	17	....	....	....	34	....	....	....	....	....
1925-26	Galt Terriers	OHA Sr.	20	13	7	20	....	....	....	31	2	2	*2	4	0
1926-27	Galt Terriers	OHA Sr.	11	6	7	13	....	....	....	23	....	....	....	....	....
	Montreal Canadiens	**NHL**	**13**	**0**	**0**	**0**	**0**	**0**	**0**	**0**	**1**	**0**	**0**	**0**	**0**
1927-28	London Panthers	Can-Pro	23	8	3	11	....	....	....	22	....	....	....	....	....
1928-29	Toronto Ravinas	Can-Pro	38	10	5	15	....	....	....	24	2	0	1	1	2
1929-30	Hamilton Tigers	IAHL	21	2	1	3	....	....	....	6	....	....	....	....	....
	Niagara Falls Cataracts	IAHL	19	4	2	6	....	....	....	36	....	....	....	....	....
1930-31	Galt Terriers	OPHL	10	0	0	0	....	....	....	0	....	....	....	....	....
	London Tecumsehs	IAHL	1	0	0	0	....	....	....	0	....	....	....	....	....
	Buffalo Bisons	IAHL	22	3	0	3	....	....	....	8	6	0	0	0	0
1931-32	Buffalo Bisons	IAHL	23	2	1	3	....	....	....	0	....	....	....	....	....
	NHL Totals		**13**	**0**	**0**	**0**	**0**	**0**	**0**	**0**	**1**	**0**	**0**	**0**	**0**

Signed as a free agent by **Montreal Canadiens**, January 14, 1926. Traded to **Niagara Falls** (IAHL) by **Hamilton** (IAHL) for cash, November 4, 1929.

			REGULAR SEASON								PLAYOFFS				
Season	Club	League	GP	G	A	Pts	AG	AA	APts	PIM	GP	G	A	Pts	PIM

● GAUTHIER, FERN Fern Gauthier
RW – R. 5'11", 175 lbs. b: Chicoutimi, Que., 8/31/1919. d: 11/7/1992.

Season	Club	League	GP	G	A	Pts	AG	AA	APts	PIM	GP	G	A	Pts	PIM
1938-39	Shawinigan Cataracts	QPHL	30	1	7	8	....	....	....	11					
1939-40	Shawinigan Cataracts	QPHL	38	16	10	26	....	....	....	23					
1940-41	Shawinigan Cataracts	QSHL	31	27	26	53	....	....	....	33	10	6	5	11	2
1941-42	Shawinigan Cataracts	QSHL	32	30	21	51	....	....	....	22	10	7	4	11	6
	Washington Lions	AHL	7	0	0	0	....	....	....	0					
1942-43	Washington–Buffalo	AHL	49	12	13	25	....	....	....	15	6	0	0	0	2
1943-44	**New York Rangers**	**NHL**	33	14	10	24	18	12	30	0					
	Montreal Royals	QSHL	1	0	0	0	....	....	....						
1944-45	**Montreal Canadiens**	**NHL**	50	18	13	31	25	21	46	23	4	0	0	0	0
1945-46	**Detroit Red Wings**	**NHL**	30	9	8	17	14	15	29	6	5	3	0	3	2
	Indianapolis Capitals	AHL	14	4	8	12	....	....	....	0					
1946-47	**Detroit Red Wings**	**NHL**	40	1	12	13	1	17	18	2	3	1	0	1	0
	Indianapolis Capitals	AHL	16	7	17	24	....	....	....	6					
1947-48	**Detroit Red Wings**	**NHL**	35	1	5	6	1	7	8	2	10	1	1	2	5
	Indianapolis Capitals	AHL	32	16	17	33	....	....	....	4					
1948-49	**Detroit Red Wings**	**NHL**	41	3	2	5	5	3	8	2					
	Indianapolis Capitals	AHL	11	1	3	4	....	....	....	0					
1949-50	St. Louis Flyers	AHL	41	16	15	31	....	....	....	6					
1950-51	Sherbrooke Saints	QSHL	10	2	5	7	....	....	....	6					
	Quebec Aces	QSHL	25	6	19	25	....	....	....	8	19	4	4	8	4
1951-52	St. Laurent Castors	QPHL	....	33	32	65	....	....	....						
	NHL Totals		229	46	50	96	64	75	139	35	22	5	1	6	7

Loaned to **NY Rangers** by **Montreal** with Dutch Hiller, John Mahaffy, Charlie Sands and future considerations (Tony Demers, December, 1943) for the loan of Phil Watson, October 27, 1943. Traded to **Detroit** by **Montreal** to complete transaction that sent Billy Reay to Montreal (September 11, 1945), October 18, 1945. Traded to **St. Louis** (AHL) by **Detroit** with Cliff Simpson, Ed Nicholson and future considerations for Steve Black and Bill Brennan, September, 1949.

● GAUTHIER, JEAN — *see page 1044*

● GEE, GEORGE George Gee
C – L. 5'11", 180 lbs. b: Stratford, Ont., 6/28/1922. d: 1/14/1971.

Season	Club	League	GP	G	A	Pts	AG	AA	APts	PIM	GP	G	A	Pts	PIM
1940-41	Falconbridge Falcons	City Sr.	2	*6	0	6	....	....	....	2					
1941-42	Kansas City Americans	AHA	37	16	15	31	....	....	....	16	6	3	1	4	8
1942-43	Sudbury Frood Tigers	City Sr.	9	15	4	19	....	....	....	14	3	4	1	5	2
1943-44	Toronto Navy	OHA Sr.	11	1	1	2	....	....	....	0					
1944-45	Cornwallis Navy	City Sr.	22	*27	16	43	....	....	....	10	15	*17	10	27	13
1945-46	**Chicago Black Hawks**	**NHL**	35	14	15	29	21	28	49	12	4	1	1	2	4
	Kansas City Pla-Mors	USHL	14	13	9	22	....	....	....	15					
1946-47	**Chicago Black Hawks**	**NHL**	60	20	20	40	27	29	56	26					
1947-48	**Chicago Black Hawks**	**NHL**	60	14	25	39	20	37	57	18					
1948-49	**Chicago Black Hawks**	**NHL**	4	0	2	2	0	3	3	4					
	Detroit Red Wings	**NHL**	47	7	12	19	11	19	30	27	10	1	3	4	22
1949-50	**Detroit Red Wings**	**NHL**	69	17	21	38	23	27	50	42	14	3	*6	9	0
1950-51	**Detroit Red Wings**	**NHL**	70	17	20	37	23	26	49	19	6	0	1	1	0
1951-52	**Chicago Black Hawks**	**NHL**	70	18	31	49	25	40	65	39					
1952-53	**Chicago Black Hawks**	**NHL**	67	18	21	39	28	29	57	99	7	1	2	3	6
1953-54	**Chicago Black Hawks**	**NHL**	70	16	10	26	15	22	37	59					
1954-55	Windsor Bulldogs	OHA Sr.	31	25	32	57	....	....	....	36	12	4	11	15	19
1955-56	Windsor Bulldogs	OHA Sr.	44	24	18	42	....	....	....	36					
1956-57	Windsor Bulldogs	OHA Sr.	5	0	1	1	....	....	....	4	6	0	4	4	0
	NHL Totals		551	135	183	318	193	260	453	345	41	6	13	19	32

Played in NHL All-Star Game (1950)

Signed as a free agent by **Chicago**, November 10, 1941. Traded to **Detroit** by **Chicago** with Bud Poile for Jim Conacher, Bep Guidolin and Doug McCaig, October 25, 1948. Traded to **Chicago** by **Detroit** with Jim McFadden, Max McNab, Jimmy Peters Sr., Clare Martin and Rags Raglan for Hugh Coflin and $75,000, August 20, 1951. ● Died while playing for Detroit Old-Timers in game vs. Wyandotte Juniors, January 14, 1971.

● GENDRON, JEAN-GUY — *see page 1046*

● GEOFFRION, BERNIE — *see page 1046*

● GERAN, GERRY Gerry "Duke" Geran
C – R. 5'9", 180 lbs. b: Holyoke, MA, 8/3/1896. d: 1968.

Season	Club	League	GP	G	A	Pts	AG	AA	APts	PIM	GP	G	A	Pts	PIM
1915-16	Dartmouth College	Ivy	6	1	0	1	....	....	....	12					
1916-17	Dartmouth College	Ivy				DID NOT PLAY									
1917-18	**Montreal Wanderers**	**NHL**	1	0	0	0	0	0	0	0					
	Boston Navy	City Sr.	11	7	0	7	....	....	....						
1918-19	Boston AAA	USAHA			STATISTICS NOT AVAILABLE										
1919-20	Boston AAA	USAHA	3	4	0	4	....	....	....						
1920-21	Boston Shoe Traders	USAHA	6	3	0	3	....	....	....						
1921-22	Paris Volants	France	8	*88	0	*88	....	....	....						
1922-23	Boston AAA	USAHA	9	14	0	14	....	....	....		4	*4	0	*4	
1923-24	Boston AAA	USAHA	10	9	0	9	....	....	....		3	3	1	*4	
1924-25	Boston AAA	USAHA	19	13	0	13	....	....	....		4	0	0	0	0
1925-26	**Boston Bruins**	**NHL**	33	5	1	6	15	11	26	6					
1926-27	St. Paul Saints	AHA	12	1	1	2	....	....	....	0					
	NHL Totals		34	5	1	6	15	11	26	6	....	....	....	....	....

Signed as a free agent by **Montreal Wanderers**, December 3, 1917. Signed as a free agent by **Boston**, November 23, 1925. Traded to **St. Paul** (AHA) by **Boston** for cash, November 4, 1926.

● GERARD, EDDIE Eddie Gerard **HHOF**
LW/D – L. 5'9", 168 lbs. b: Ottawa, Ont., 2/22/1890. d: 12/7/1937.

Season	Club	League	GP	G	A	Pts	AG	AA	APts	PIM	GP	G	A	Pts	PIM
1910-11	Ottawa New Edinburghs	City Sr.	6	8	0	8	....	....	....						
1911-12	Ottawa New Edinburghs	City Sr.			STATISTICS NOT AVAILABLE										
1912-13	Ottawa New Edinburghs	City Sr.			STATISTICS NOT AVAILABLE										
1913-14	Ottawa Senators	NHA	11	6	7	13	....	....	....	34					
1914-15	Ottawa Senators	NHA	20	9	10	19	....	....	....	39	5	1	0	1	6
1915-16	Ottawa Senators	NHA	24	13	5	18	....	....	....	57					
1916-17	Ottawa Senators	NHA	19	17	9	26	....	....	....	37	2	1	0	1	3
1917-18	**Ottawa Senators**	**NHL**	20	13	7	20	33	0	33	26					
1918-19	**Ottawa Senators**	**NHL**	18	4	10	14	14	100	114	17	5	3	0	3	3
1919-20	**Ottawa Senators**	**NHL**	22	9	7	16	20	48	68	19	5	2	1	3	3
1920-21	**Ottawa Senators**	**NHL**	24	11	4	15	28	35	63	18	7	1	0	1	*53
1921-22	**Ottawa Senators**	**NHL**	21	7	11	18	19	71	90	16	2	0	0	0	8
	Toronto St. Pats	**NHL**	....	....	....	....	....	....	....		1	0	0	0	0
1922-23	**Ottawa Senators**	**NHL**	23	6	8	14	20	73	93	24	7	1	0	1	4
1923-24	**Montreal Canadiens**	**NHL**			DID NOT PLAY – COACHING										
	NHL Totals		128	50	47	97	134	327	461	120	27	7	1	8	71
	Other Major League Totals		74	45	31	76				167	7	2	0	2	9

Rights retained by **Ottawa** after NHA folded, November 26, 1917. Loaned to **Toronto St. Pats** by **Ottawa** as an emergency injury replacement, March 25, 1922.

● GETLIFFE, RAY Ray Getliffe
C/LW – L. 5'11", 175 lbs. b: Galt, Ont., 4/3/1914.

Season	Club	League	GP	G	A	Pts	AG	AA	APts	PIM	GP	G	A	Pts	PIM
1933-34	Stratford Midgets	OHA	13	26	*17	43	....	....	....	18	2	*6	1	*7	2
1934-35	Charlottetown Abbies	MSHL								29					
	St. John St. Peters	MSHL	17	*35	25	60	....	....	....	15	12	9	*14	*23	11
	St. John Beavers	NBSHL	2	1	1	2	....	....	....	6					
1935-36	**Boston Bruins**	**NHL**	1	0	0	0	0	0	0	2	2	0	0	0	0
	London Tecumsehs	IAHL	17	6	3	9	....	....	....	17					
	Boston Cubs	Can-Am	29	16	14	30	....	....	....	14					
1936-37	**Boston Bruins**	**NHL**	48	15	20	35	35	35	70	28	3	2	1	3	2
1937-38	**Boston Bruins**	**NHL**	36	11	13	24	23	27	50	16	3	0	1	1	2
1938-39	**Boston Bruins**	**NHL**	43	10	12	22	21	22	43	11	11	1	1	2	2
	Hershey Bears	AHL	4	1	4	5	....	....	....	2					
1939-40	**Montreal Canadiens**	**NHL**	46	11	12	23	24	24	48	29					
1940-41	**Montreal Canadiens**	**NHL**	39	15	10	25	30	18	48	25	3	1	1	2	0
1941-42	**Montreal Canadiens**	**NHL**	45	11	15	26	19	23	42	35	3	0	0	0	6
1942-43	**Montreal Canadiens**	**NHL**	50	18	26	44	26	36	62	26	5	0	1	1	8
1943-44	**Montreal Canadiens**	**NHL**	44	28	25	53	36	30	66	44	9	5	4	9	16
1944-45	**Montreal Canadiens**	**NHL**	41	16	7	23	22	11	33	34	6	0	1	1	0
	NHL Totals		393	136	137	273	236	226	462	250	45	9	10	19	30

Played in NHL All-Star Game (1939)

Signed as a free agent by **NY Rangers** and loaned to **London** (IAHL) for 1935-36 season, November 8, 1935. Traded to **Boston** by **NY Rangers** for cash, December 31, 1935. Walter Jackson loaned to **London** (IAHL) as compensation. Traded to **Montreal** by **Boston** with Charlie Sands for Herb Cain, November 2 10, 1939. Traded to **Detroit** by **Montreal** for Ray Getliffe and Roly Rossingnol, September 11, 1945. ● Getliffe decided to retire and Montreal received Fern Gauthier as compensation, October 18, 1945.

● GIESEBRECHT, GUS Gus Giesebrecht
C – L. 6', 177 lbs. b: Pembroke, Ont., 9/16/1918.

Season	Club	League	GP	G	A	Pts	AG	AA	APts	PIM	GP	G	A	Pts	PIM
1933-34	Ottawa St. Malachy's	City Jr.	15	6	11	17	....	....	....	4					
1934-35	Ottawa Senators	City Jr.	5	7	7	14	....	....	....	0					
	Pembroke Lumber Kings	Ott-Jr.	5	7	3	10	....	....	....						
	Pembroke Falcons	Ott-Sr.	4	4	4	8	....	....	....						
1935-36	Pembroke Lumber Kings	Ott-Jr.	8	*12	*12	*24	....	....	....	8	15	*28	*16	*44	4
1936-37	Pittsburgh Yellowjackets	EHL	47	12	18	30	....	....	....	11					
1937-38	Detroit Pontiacs	MOHL	28	23	25	48	....	....	....		3	2	1	3	0
	Pittsburgh Hornets	AHL	3	0	0	0	....	....	....	0	2	0	0	0	0
1938-39	**Detroit Red Wings**	**NHL**	28	10	10	20	21	19	40	2	6	0	2	2	0
	Pittsburgh Hornets	AHL		6	6	12	....	....	....	4					
1939-40	**Detroit Red Wings**	**NHL**	30	4	7	11	9	14	23	2	4	1	5	0	
	Indianapolis Capitals	AHL		10	9	19	....	....	....						
1940-41	**Detroit Red Wings**	**NHL**	43	7	18	25	14	33	47	7	9	2	1	3	0
1941-42	**Detroit Red Wings**	**NHL**	34	6	16	22	10	24	34	2	2	0	0	0	0
	Indianapolis Capitals	AHL		6	7	13	....	....	....	4		1	3	4	0
1942-43	Ottawa Canadians	OHA Sr.	18	18	15	33	....	....	....		8	5	4	9	4
1943-44	Kingston Frontenacs	OHA Sr.	11	8	20	28	....	....	....	12					
	Truro Bearcats	Hfx-Sr.	4	8	6	14	....	....	....						
1944-45					MILITARY SERVICE										
1945-46	Pembroke Lumber Kings	OVSHL	17	*35	*14	*49	....	....	....	17	11	*22	13	*35	2
1946-47	Pembroke Lumber Kings	OVSHL	24	*27	38	*65	....	....	....	6	8	*16	11	*27	2
	Ottawa Senators	QSHL					....	....	....		4	1	0	1	0
1947-48	Pembroke Lumber Kings	OVSHL	16	*21	*22	*43	....	....	....	12	5	2	*8	*10	2
1948-49	Pembroke Lumber Kings	OVSHL	9	8	*9	17	....	....	....	0	13	*14	7	*21	4
1949-50	Pembroke Lumber Kings	ECSHL	32	20	23	43	....	....	....	8	4	2	0	2	0
1950-51	Pembroke Lumber Kings	ECSHL	17	11	16	27	....	....	....		2	3	3	6	2
1951-52	Pembroke Lumber Kings	ECSHL	44	27	44	71	....	....	....	12	12	20	*13	*9	*22	2
	NHL Totals		135	27	51	78	54	90	144	13	17	2	3	5	0

• GILBERT, JEANNOT
Jeannot "Gil" Gilbert
C – L. 5'10", 170 lbs. b: Grande Baie, Que., 12/29/1940.

			REGULAR SEASON								PLAYOFFS				
Season	Club	League	GP	G	A	Pts	AG	AA	APts	PIM	GP	G	A	Pts	PIM
1959-60	Barrie Flyers	OHA	44	28	36	64	....	....	....	28	6	2	5	7	0
1960-61	Niagara Falls Flyers	OHA	48	36	28	64	....	....	....	21	7	2	8	10	0
	Kingston Frontenacs	EPHL	1	0	1	1	....	....	....	0	....	....	....	....	....
1961-62	Clinton Comets	EHL	67	38	51	89	....	....	....	33	6	4	1	5	0
	Kingston Frontenacs	EPHL	5	1	2	3	....	....	....	0	3	2	0	2	0
1962-63	**Boston Bruins**	**NHL**	**5**	**0**	**0**	**0**	**0**	**0**	**0**	**4**	....	....	....	....	....
	Kingston Frontenacs	EPHL	64	34	53	87	....	....	....	25	5	1	6	7	2
1963-64	Minneapolis Bruins	CHL	72	50	50	100	....	....	....	18	5	4	1	5	2
1964-65	**Boston Bruins**	**NHL**	**4**	**0**	**1**	**1**	**0**	**1**	**1**	**0**	....	....	....	....	....
	Providence Reds	AHL	64	25	30	55	....	....	....	16	....	....	....	....	....
1965-66	Hershey Bears	AHL	69	20	51	71	....	....	....	13	3	0	2	2	0
1966-67	Hershey Bears	AHL	72	26	57	83	....	....	....	48	5	0	2	2	0
1967-68	Hershey Bears	AHL	72	28	47	75	....	....	....	24	5	1	1	2	0
1968-69	Hershey Bears	AHL	71	35	65	100	....	....	....	13	11	3	3	6	10
1969-70	Hershey Bears	AHL	67	23	41	64	....	....	....	8	7	2	6	8	2
1970-71	Hershey Bears	AHL	56	14	28	42	....	....	....	8	4	0	2	2	4
1971-72	Hershey Bears	AHL	74	29	42	71	....	....	....	24	4	0	1	1	0
1972-73	Hershey Bears	AHL	71	31	58	89	....	....	....	8	7	3	8	11	2
1973-74	Quebec Nordiques	WHA	75	17	39	56	....	....	....	20	....	....	....	....	....
1974-75	Quebec Nordiques	WHA	58	7	21	28	....	....	....	12	11	3	6	9	2
	NHL Totals		**9**	**0**	**1**	**1**	**0**	**1**	**1**	**4**	....	....	....	....	....
	Other Major League Totals		133	24	60	84	....	....	....	32	11	3	6	9	2

EHL Rookie of the Year (1962) • AHL First All-Star Team (1969) • Won John B. Sollenberger Trophy (Top Scorer - AHL) (1969)

Claimed by **Pittsburgh** from **Boston** in Expansion Draft, June 6, 1967. Traded to **Hershey** (AHL) by **Pittsburgh** for Gene Ubriaco, October, 1967. Signed as a free agent by **Quebec** (WHA), August, 1973.

• GILBERT, ROD
— *see page 1049*

• GILLIE, FARRAND
Farrand "Bud" Gillie
LW/D – R. 5'10", 150 lbs. b: Cornwall, Ont., 5/11/1905. Deceased.

			REGULAR SEASON								PLAYOFFS				
Season	Club	League	GP	G	A	Pts	AG	AA	APts	PIM	GP	G	A	Pts	PIM
1927-28	Detroit Olympics	Can-Pro	10	0	0	0	....	....	....	0	....	....	....	....	....
1928-29	**Detroit Cougars**	**NHL**	**1**	**0**	**0**	**0**	**0**	**0**	**0**	**0**	....	....	....	....	....
	Detroit Olympics	Can-Pro	41	5	4	9	....	....	....	31	7	0	0	0	8
1929-30	Detroit Olympics	IAHL	42	9	7	16	....	....	....	38	3	0	0	0	0
1930-31	Detroit Olympics	IAHL	46	19	6	25	....	....	....	36	....	....	....	....	....
1931-32	Detroit Olympics	IAHL	48	16	10	26	....	....	....	31	6	0	0	0	8
1932-33	London Tecumsehs	IAHL	44	13	9	22	....	....	....	36	6	3	1	4	6
1933-34	London Tecumsehs	IAHL	44	11	5	16	....	....	....	26	6	2	2	4	2
1934-35	Windsor Bulldogs	IAHL	43	4	7	11	....	....	....	22	....	....	....	....	....
1935-36	Windsor–Rochester	IAHL	49	5	9	14	....	....	....	14	....	....	....	....	....
1936-37			DID NOT PLAY – INJURED												
1937-38	Cornwall Flyers	QSHL	24	8	9	17	....	....	....	18	17	7	6	13	*30
1938-39	Brighton Tigers	Britain	....	15	10	25	....	....	....	....	....	....	....	....	....
1939-40	Cornwall Flyers	QSHL	28	4	2	6	....	....	....	20	5	2	3	5	7
1940-41	Cornwall Flyers	QSHL	31	7	21	28	....	....	....	8	4	0	2	2	2
1941-42	Cornwall Flyers	QSHL	1	0	0	0	....	....	....	0	....	....	....	....	....
	NHL Totals		**1**	**0**	**0**	**0**	**0**	**0**	**0**	**0**	....	....	....	....	....

Transferred to **London** (IAHL) by **Detroit** as compensation for Detroit's signing of free agent Gord Brydson, October 24, 1932.

• GIRARD, KENNY
Kenny Girard
RW – R. 6', 184 lbs. b: Toronto, Ont., 12/8/1936.

			REGULAR SEASON								PLAYOFFS				
Season	Club	League	GP	G	A	Pts	AG	AA	APts	PIM	GP	G	A	Pts	PIM
1954-55	Toronto Marlboros	OHA	47	15	14	29	....	....	....	4	12	8	5	13	17
1955-56	Toronto Marlboros	OHA	41	20	12	32	....	....	....	4	11	7	9	16	0
1956-57	Toronto Marlboros	OHA	35	23	11	34	....	....	....	4	1	0	0	0	0
	Toronto Maple Leafs	**NHL**	**3**	**0**	**1**	**1**	**0**	**1**	**1**	**2**	....	....	....	....	....
1957-58	**Toronto Maple Leafs**	**NHL**	**3**	**0**	**0**	**0**	**0**	**0**	**0**	**0**	....	....	....	....	....
	Rochester Americans	AHL	52	13	10	23	....	....	....	2	....	....	....	....	....
	Shawinigan Cataracts	QHL	9	0	5	5	....	....	....	6	14	2	5	7	2
1958-59			PLAYED PRO GOLF												
1959-60	**Toronto Maple Leafs**	**NHL**	**1**	**0**	**0**	**0**	**0**	**0**	**0**	**0**	....	....	....	....	....
	Sudbury Wolves	EPHL	15	5	2	7	....	....	....	0	9	0	1	1	4
1960-61	Sudbury Wolves	EPHL	65	23	18	41	....	....	....	6	....	....	....	....	....
	Rochester Americans	AHL	9	0	3	3	....	....	....	0	....	....	....	....	....
1961-62	Pittsburgh Hornets	AHL	21	4	2	6	....	....	....	2	....	....	....	....	....
	San Francisco Seals	WHL	31	9	11	20	....	....	....	2	2	0	0	0	0
	NHL Totals		**7**	**0**	**1**	**1**	**0**	**1**	**1**	**2**	....	....	....	....	....

• GIROUX, ART
Art Giroux
RW – R. 5'10", 165 lbs. b: Winnipeg, Man., 6/6/1908. d: 6/5/1982.

			REGULAR SEASON								PLAYOFFS				
Season	Club	League	GP	G	A	Pts	AG	AA	APts	PIM	GP	G	A	Pts	PIM
1926-27	Saskatoon Shieks	PrHL	27	1	0	1	....	....	....	4	2	0	0	0	0
1927-28	Saskatoon Shieks	PrHL	19	6	1	7	....	....	....	2	....	....	....	....	....
1928-29	San Francisco–L.A.	Cal-Pro	....	7	1	8	....	....	....	....	....	....	....	....	....
1929-30	San Francisco Tigers	Cal-Pro	....	*34	10	44	....	....	....	59	....	....	....	....	....
1930-31	Providence Reds	Can-Am	39	16	7	23	....	....	....	41	2	0	0	0	4
1931-32	Providence Reds	Can-Am	36	11	10	21	....	....	....	25	5	3	1	4	2
1932-33	**Montreal Canadiens**	**NHL**	**40**	**5**	**2**	**7**	**12**	**5**	**17**	**14**	**2**	**0**	**0**	**0**	**0**
	Providence Reds	Can-Am	6	5	1	6	....	....	....	4	....	....	....	....	....
1933-34	Providence Reds	Can-Am	40	20	15	35	....	....	....	28	3	*7	1	*8	6
1934-35	**Boston Bruins**	**NHL**	**10**	**1**	**0**	**1**	**2**	**0**	**2**	**0**	....	....	....	....	....
	Boston Cubs	Can-Am	32	20	16	36	....	....	....	19	3	1	0	1	0
1935-36	**Detroit Red Wings**	**NHL**	**4**	**0**	**2**	**2**	**0**	**5**	**5**	**0**	....	....	....	....	....
	Detroit Olympics	IAHL	35	17	12	29	....	....	....	28	6	4	4	8	4
1936-37	Pittsburgh Hornets	AHL	47	21	7	28	....	....	....	26	5	3	0	3	2
1937-38	Providence Reds	AHL	43	12	10	22	....	....	....	13	7	3	5	8	2
1938-39	Providence Reds	AHL	51	23	24	47	....	....	....	4	5	1	1	2	0
1939-40	Providence Reds	AHL	54	17	23	40	....	....	....	21	8	2	2	4	0
1940-41	Providence Reds	AHL	48	20	19	39	....	....	....	12	4	1	1	2	0
1941-42	Cleveland Barons	AHL	54	18	22	40	....	....	....	18	5	1	0	1	2
1942-43	Cleveland Barons	AHL	53	13	11	24	....	....	....	22	2	0	0	0	0
1943-44	Providence–Pittsburgh	AHL	40	23	15	38	....	....	....	5	....	....	....	....	....
1944-45	Pittsburgh–St. Louis	AHL	44	18	17	35	....	....	....	8	....	....	....	....	....
	NHL Totals		**54**	**6**	**4**	**10**	**14**	**10**	**24**	**14**	**2**	**0**	**0**	**0**	**0**

AHL Second All-Star Team (1940)

Traded to **Montreal Canadiens** by **San Francisco** (Cal-Pro) for $5000, February 13, 1930. Traded to **Boston** by **Montreal Canadiens** for cash, October 18, 1934. Traded to **Detroit** by **Boston** with Marty Barry for Cooney Weiland and Walt Buswell, July 11, 1935.

• GLADU, JEAN-PAUL
Jean-Paul "J.P." Gladu
LW – L. 5'11", 180 lbs. b: St. Hyacinthe, Que., 6/20/1921.

			REGULAR SEASON								PLAYOFFS				
Season	Club	League	GP	G	A	Pts	AG	AA	APts	PIM	GP	G	A	Pts	PIM
1939-40	Verdun Maple Leafs	QJHL	11	5	3	8	....	....	....	4	4	5	0	5	0
1940-41	Shawinigan Cataracts	QSHL	36	27	44	68	....	....	....	42	10	4	3	7	6
1941-42	Shawinigan Cataracts	QSHL	28	13	24	37	....	....	....	37	10	3	10	13	0
1942-43	Quebec Sea Gulls	QPHL	....	....	....	....	....	....	....	....	10	13	20	33	....
1943-44	Quebec Sea Gulls	QPHL	STATISTICS NOT AVAILABLE												
1944-45	**Boston Bruins**	**NHL**	**40**	**6**	**14**	**20**	**8**	**23**	**31**	**2**	**7**	**2**	**2**	**4**	**0**
1945-46	Hershey–St. Louis	AHL	44	18	24	42	....	....	....	18	....	....	....	....	....
1946-47	St. Louis Flyers	AHL	62	30	19	49	....	....	....	48	....	....	....	....	....
1947-48	St. Louis Flyers	AHL	67	34	47	81	....	....	....	24	....	....	....	....	....
1948-49	St. Louis Flyers	AHL	67	51	34	85	....	....	....	28	7	3	0	3	0
1949-50	St. Louis Flyers	AHL	38	19	19	38	....	....	....	4	2	0	1	1	0
1950-51	St. Louis Flyers	AHL	66	25	25	50	....	....	....	10	....	....	....	....	....
1951-52	Cleveland Barons	AHL	26	7	15	22	....	....	....	4	....	....	....	....	....
	Providence Reds	AHL	40	24	18	42	....	....	....	26	15	*8	7	15	16
1952-53	Providence Reds	AHL	63	21	25	46	....	....	....	46	....	....	....	....	....
1953-54	Providence Reds	AHL	49	8	20	28	....	....	....	22	....	....	....	....	....
1954-55			DID NOT PLAY												
1955-56	Trois-Rivieres Lions	QHL	5	0	3	3	....	....	....	8	....	....	....	....	....
	NHL Totals		**40**	**6**	**14**	**20**	**8**	**23**	**31**	**2**	**7**	**2**	**2**	**4**	**0**

AHL Second All-Star Team (1948)

Traded to **St. Louis** (AHL) by **Boston** (Hershey - AHL) for cash, January, 1946. Traded to **Providence** (AHL) by **Cleveland** (AHL) with Joe Lund for Ken Davies and Vic Lynn, December 10, 1951.

• GLOVER, FRED
Fred Glover
C – R. 5'9", 170 lbs. b: Toronto, Ont., 1/5/1928.

			REGULAR SEASON								PLAYOFFS				
Season	Club	League	GP	G	A	Pts	AG	AA	APts	PIM	GP	G	A	Pts	PIM
1945-46	Galt Red Wings	OHA	20	20	9	29	....	....	....	16	5	1	2	3	4
1946-47	Galt Red Wings	OHA	32	34	26	60	....	....	....	67	9	6	2	8	21
1947-48	Omaha Knights	USHL	66	16	39	55	....	....	....	79	3	0	0	0	0
1948-49	Indianapolis Capitals	AHL	68	35	48	83	....	....	....	59	2	0	0	0	2
	Detroit Red Wings	**NHL**	....	....	....	....	....	....	....	....	**2**	**0**	**0**	**0**	**0**
1949-50	**Detroit Red Wings**	**NHL**	**7**	**0**	**0**	**0**	**0**	**0**	**0**	**0**	....	....	....	....	....
	Indianapolis Capitals	AHL	55	22	29	51	....	....	....	65	8	5	4	9	8
1950-51	Indianapolis Capitals	AHL	69	*48	36	84	....	....	....	106	3	0	1	1	8
	Detroit Red Wings	**NHL**	....	....	....	....	....	....	....	....	**6**	**0**	**0**	**0**	**0**
1951-52	**Detroit Red Wings**	**NHL**	**54**	**9**	**9**	**18**	**13**	**12**	**25**	**25**	....	....	....	....	....
	Indianapolis Capitals	AHL	10	5	6	11	....	....	....	8	....	....	....	....	....
1952-53	**Chicago Black Hawks**	**NHL**	**31**	**4**	**2**	**6**	**6**	**3**	**9**	**37**	....	....	....	....	....
	St. Louis Flyers	AHL	7	2	3	5	....	....	....	14	....	....	....	....	....
	Cleveland Barons	AHL	29	10	16	26	....	....	....	67	11	2	2	4	*36
1953-54	Cleveland Barons	AHL	55	23	42	65	....	....	....	117	9	*8	6	14	15
1954-55	Cleveland Barons	AHL	58	33	42	75	....	....	....	108	4	4	1	5	8
1955-56	Cleveland Barons	AHL	64	31	48	79	....	....	....	187	8	2	9	11	2
1956-57	Cleveland Barons	AHL	64	42	57	*99	....	....	....	111	12	6	8	*14	34
1957-58	Cleveland Barons	AHL	64	28	48	76	....	....	....	147	7	4	2	6	26
1958-59	Cleveland Barons	AHL	66	22	39	61	....	....	....	136	7	3	2	5	31
1959-60	Cleveland Barons	AHL	72	38	*69	*107	....	....	....	143	7	4	3	7	30
1960-61	Cleveland Barons	AHL	61	23	46	69	....	....	....	138	4	1	2	3	9
1961-62	Cleveland Barons	AHL	70	40	45	85	....	....	....	148	6	2	4	6	14
1962-63	Cleveland Barons	AHL	71	26	54	80	....	....	....	171	6	3	4	7	12
1963-64	Cleveland Barons	AHL	69	26	50	76	....	....	....	155	9	3	4	7	21
1964-65	Cleveland Barons	AHL	72	20	41	61	....	....	....	*208	....	....	....	....	....
1965-66	Cleveland Barons	AHL	47	8	28	36	....	....	....	74	12	0	3	3	41
1966-67	Cleveland Barons	AHL	60	25	35	60	....	....	....	107	5	1	1	2	10
1967-68	Cleveland Barons	AHL	70	13	32	45	....	....	....	132	....	....	....	....	....
	NHL Totals		**92**	**13**	**11**	**24**	**19**	**15**	**34**	**62**	**8**	**0**	**0**	**0**	**0**

AHL First All-Star Team (1951, 1955, 1957, 1960, 1962) • Won John B. Sollenberger Trophy (Top Scorer - AHL) (1957, 1960) • AHL Second All-Star Team (1958, 1964) • Won Les Cunningham Award (MVP - AHL) (1960, 1962, 1964)

Traded to **Chicago** by **Detroit** with Enio Sclisizzi for cash, August 14, 1952. Traded to **Cleveland** (AHL) by **Chicago** to complete transaction that sent Vic Lynn to Chicago (January 4, 1953), January 16, 1953.

• GLOVER, HOWIE
— *see page 1054*

• GODFREY, WARREN
— *see page 1055*

• GODIN, SAMMY
Sammy (Hogomer Gabriel) Godin
RW – R. 5'10", 156 lbs. b: Rockland, Ont., 9/20/1909. Deceased.

Season	Club	League	GP	G	A	Pts	AG	AA	APts	PIM	Playoffs GP	G	A	Pts	PIM
1926-27	Rockland Hockey Club	Inter-Sr.	STATISTICS NOT AVAILABLE												
1927-28	**Ottawa Senators**	**NHL**	**24**	**0**	**0**	**0**	**0**	**0**	**0**	**0**	....	....	....	....	....
1928-29	**Ottawa Senators**	**NHL**	**23**	**2**	**1**	**3**	**8**	**9**	**17**	**21**	....	....	....	....	....
	Niagara Falls	Can-Am	18	8	1	9	....	....	....	33	....	....	....	....	....
1929-30	Buffalo Bisons	IAHL	39	9	6	15	....	....	....	22	7	0	0	0	8
1930-31	Buffalo Bisons	IAHL	26	3	5	8	....	....	....	16	6	0	0	0	2
1931-32	Buffalo Bisons	IAHL	47	5	5	10	....	....	....	21	5	0	0	0	2
1932-33	Buffalo Bisons	IAHL	42	15	12	27	....	....	....	45	6	*4	0	4	8
1933-34	**Montreal Canadiens**	**NHL**	**36**	**2**	**2**	**4**	**4**	**5**	**9**	**15**	....	....	....	....	....
	Windsor Bulldogs	IAHL	9	0	0	0	....	....	....	2	....	....	....	....	....
1934-35	London–Buffalo	IAHL	44	13	10	23	....	....	....	40	5	0	2	2	2
1935-36	Buffalo Bisons	IAHL	48	19	18	37	....	....	....	14	5	2	1	3	0
1936-37	Vancouver Lions	PCHL	31	8	7	15	....	....	....	14	3	1	2	3	0
1937-38	Springfield Indians	AHL	3	0	1	1	....	....	....	2	....	....	....	....	....
	Minneapolis Millers	AHA	44	24	17	41	....	....	....	19	7	*5	1	*6	0
1938-39	Minneapolis Millers	AHA	9	2	4	6	....	....	....	4	....	....	....	....	....
	Kansas City Greyhounds	AHA	29	6	12	18	....	....	....	10	....	....	....	....	....
1939-40	Wichita Skyhawks	AHA	15	1	4	5	....	....	....	10	....	....	....	....	....
1940-41	Ottawa Canadians	City Sr.	8	1	1	2	....	....	....	2	....	....	....	....	....
	Hamilton Dofascos	City Sr.	13	1	2	3	....	....	....	20	....	....	....	....	....
1941-42	Ottawa Canadians	City Sr.	DID NOT PLAY – COACHING												
1942-43	Hamilton Majors	OHA Sr.	1	0	0	0	....	....	....	0	....	....	....	....	....
	NHL Totals		**83**	**4**	**3**	**7**	**12**	**14**	**26**	**36**	....	....	....	....	....

Signed as a free agent by **Ottawa**, December, 1928. Traded to **Buffalo** (IAHL) by **Ottawa** for cash, November, 1929. Traded to **Montreal Canadiens** by **Buffalo** (IAHL) for cash, October, 1933. Traded to **Springfield** (AHL) by **Montreal Canadiens** for Red Conn, September 30, 1937.

• GOEGAN, PETE
— *see page 1056*

• GOLDHAM, BOB
Bob "Golden Boy" Goldham
D – L. 6'2", 195 lbs. b: Georgetown, Ont., 5/12/1922. d: 11/6/1991.

Season	Club	League	GP	G	A	Pts	AG	AA	APts	PIM	Playoffs GP	G	A	Pts	PIM
1939-40	Toronto Marlboros	OHA	19	11	11	22	....	....	....	9	8	3	4	7	*30
1940-41	Toronto Marlboros	OHA	14	13	9	22	....	....	....	*55	12	11	13	24	*22
1941-42	Washington Lions	AHL	1	0	0	0	....	....	....	0	....	....	....	....	....
	Hershey Bears	AHL	34	7	10	17	....	....	....	44	....	....	....	....	....
	Toronto Maple Leafs	**NHL**	**19**	**4**	**7**	**11**	**7**	**11**	**18**	**25**	**13**	**2**	**2**	**4**	**31**
1942-43	Toronto Navy	OHA Sr.	12	0	6	6	....	....	....	29	....	....	....	....	....
	Victoria Navy	City Sr.	....	....	....	....	....	....	....	....	3	0	3	3	2
1943-44	Cornwallis Navy	City Sr.	8	6	*9	15	....	....	....	....	11	4	7	11	12
1944-45	Cornwallis Navy	City Sr.	12	2	9	11	....	....	....	4	2	0	1	1	4
1945-46	**Toronto Maple Leafs**	**NHL**	**49**	**7**	**14**	**21**	**11**	**26**	**37**	**44**	....	....	....	....	....
1946-47	**Toronto Maple Leafs**	**NHL**	**11**	**1**	**1**	**2**	**1**	**1**	**2**	**10**	....	....	....	....	....
1947-48	Pittsburgh Hornets	AHL	7	0	5	5	....	....	....	16	....	....	....	....	....
	Chicago Black Hawks	**NHL**	**38**	**2**	**9**	**11**	**3**	**13**	**16**	**38**	....	....	....	....	....
1948-49	**Chicago Black Hawks**	**NHL**	**60**	**1**	**10**	**11**	**2**	**16**	**18**	**43**	....	....	....	....	....
1949-50	**Chicago Black Hawks**	**NHL**	**67**	**2**	**10**	**12**	**3**	**13**	**16**	**57**	....	....	....	....	....
1950-51	**Detroit Red Wings**	**NHL**	**61**	**5**	**18**	**23**	**7**	**23**	**30**	**31**	**6**	**0**	**1**	**1**	**2**
1951-52	**Detroit Red Wings**	**NHL**	**69**	**0**	**14**	**14**	**0**	**18**	**18**	**24**	**8**	**0**	**1**	**1**	**8**
1952-53	**Detroit Red Wings**	**NHL**	**70**	**1**	**13**	**14**	**2**	**18**	**20**	**32**	**6**	**1**	**1**	**2**	**2**
1953-54	**Detroit Red Wings**	**NHL**	**69**	**1**	**15**	**16**	**2**	**20**	**22**	**50**	**12**	**0**	**2**	**2**	**2**
1954-55	**Detroit Red Wings**	**NHL**	**69**	**1**	**16**	**17**	**1**	**20**	**21**	**14**	**11**	**0**	**4**	**4**	**4**
1955-56	**Detroit Red Wings**	**NHL**	**68**	**3**	**16**	**19**	**4**	**20**	**24**	**32**	**10**	**0**	**3**	**3**	**4**
	NHL Totals		**650**	**28**	**143**	**171**	**43**	**199**	**242**	**400**	**66**	**3**	**14**	**17**	**53**

AHL Second All-Star Team (1942) • NHL Second All-Star Team (1955)

Played in NHL All-Star Game (1947, 1949, 1950, 1952, 1954, 1955)

Traded to **Chicago** by **Toronto** with Gus Bodnar, Bud Poile, Gaye Stewart and Ernie Dickens for Max Bentley and Cy Thomas, November 2, 1947. Traded to **Detroit** by **Chicago** with Jim Henry, Gaye Stewart and Metro Prystai for Al Dewsbury, Harry Lumley, Jack Stewart, Don Morrison and Pete Babando, July 13, 1950.

• GOLDSWORTHY, BILL
— *see page 1056*

• GOLDSWORTHY, LEROY
Leroy Goldsworthy
RW – R. 6', 165 lbs. b: Two Harbors, MN, 10/18/1906. d: 3/16/1980.

Season	Club	League	GP	G	A	Pts	AG	AA	APts	PIM	Playoffs GP	G	A	Pts	PIM
1924-25	Edmonton Victorias	City Sr.	1	0	0	0	....	....	....	0	3	0	0	0	2
1925-26	Edmonton Eskimos	WHL	11	0	0	0	....	....	....	0	....	....	....	....	....
1926-27	Springfield Indians	Can-Am	31	2	1	3	....	....	....	4	6	1	0	1	8
1927-28	Springfield Indians	Can-Am	38	8	5	13	....	....	....	32	4	2	0	2	2
1928-29	Springfield Indians	Can-Am	39	9	7	16	....	....	....	40	....	....	....	....	....
	New York Rangers	**NHL**	....	....	....	....	....	....	....	....	**1**	**0**	**0**	**0**	**0**
1929-30	**New York Rangers**	**NHL**	**44**	**4**	**1**	**5**	**8**	**3**	**11**	**16**	**4**	**0**	**0**	**0**	**2**
1930-31	**Detroit Falcons**	**NHL**	**12**	**1**	**0**	**1**	**2**	**0**	**2**	**2**	....	....	....	....	....
	Detroit Olympics	IAHL	9	4	0	4	....	....	....	4	....	....	....	....	....
	London Tecumsehs	IAHL	25	9	5	14	....	....	....	27	....	....	....	....	....
1931-32	Detroit Olympics	IAHL	47	16	9	25	....	....	....	16	6	2	0	2	2
1932-33	**Detroit Red Wings**	**NHL**	**25**	**3**	**6**	**9**	**7**	**16**	**23**	**6**	**2**	**0**	**0**	**0**	**0**
	Detroit Olympics	IAHL	17	12	2	14	....	....	....	22	....	....	....	....	....
1933-34	**Chicago Black Hawks**	**NHL**	**27**	**3**	**3**	**6**	**7**	**8**	**15**	**0**	**7**	**0**	**0**	**0**	**0**
	London Tecumsehs	IAHL	18	11	4	15	....	....	....	10	....	....	....	....	....
1934-35	**Chicago Black Hawks**	**NHL**	**7**	**0**	**0**	**0**	**0**	**0**	**0**	**2**	....	....	....	....	....
	Montreal Canadiens	**NHL**	**33**	**20**	**9**	**29**	**43**	**20**	**63**	**13**	**2**	**1**	**0**	**1**	**0**
	London Tecumsehs	IAHL	7	4	1	5	....	....	....	6	....	....	....	....	....
1935-36	**Montreal Canadiens**	**NHL**	**47**	**15**	**11**	**26**	**37**	**27**	**64**	**8**	....	....	....	....	....
1936-37	**Boston Bruins**	**NHL**	**47**	**8**	**6**	**14**	**17**	**14**	**31**	**8**	**3**	**0**	**0**	**0**	**0**
1937-38	**Boston Bruins**	**NHL**	**46**	**9**	**10**	**19**	**19**	**21**	**40**	**14**	**3**	**0**	**0**	**0**	**2**
1938-39	**New York Americans**	**NHL**	**48**	**3**	**11**	**14**	**6**	**20**	**26**	**10**	**2**	**0**	**0**	**0**	**0**
1939-40	Cleveland Barons	AHL	56	9	22	31	....	....	....	10	....	....	....	....	....
1940-41	Buffalo Bisons	AHL	56	6	18	24	....	....	....	8	....	....	....	....	....
1941-42	Dallas Texans	AHA	50	15	24	39	....	....	....	31	....	....	....	....	....
	NHL Totals		**336**	**66**	**57**	**123**	**146**	**129**	**275**	**79**	**24**	**1**	**0**	**1**	**4**
	Other Major League Totals		11	0	0	0	....	....	....	0	....	....	....	....	....

Traded to **NY Rangers** by **Edmonton** (WHL) for cash, October 19, 1926. Traded to **London** (IAHL) by **NY Rangers** for cash, October 29, 1930. Traded to **Detroit** by **London** (IAHL) for Harold Hicks, January 12, 1931. Traded to **Chicago** by **Detroit** with Frank Waite for Gene Carrigan, October 20, 1933. Traded to **London** (IAHL) by **Chicago** for cash, November 22, 1933. Traded to **Chicago** by **London** (IAHL) for Bill Kendall and $3,000, January 4, 1934. Traded to **Montreal Canadiens** by **Chicago** with Roger Jenkins and Lionel Conacher for Howie Morenz, Marty Burke and Lorne Chabot, October 3, 1934. Traded to **Chicago** by **Montreal Canadiens** for cash, October 17, 1934. Traded to **Montreal Canadiens** by **Chicago** for cash, December 9, 1934. Traded to **Boston** by **Montreal Canadiens** with Sammy McManus and $10,000 for Babe Siebert and Roger Jenkins, September 10, 1936. Traded to **NY Americans** by **Boston** with the loan of Art Jackson for 1938-39 season for cash, October 24, 1938.

• GOLDUP, HANK
Hank Goldup
LW – L. 5'11", 175 lbs. b: Kingston, Ont., 10/29/1918.

Season	Club	League	GP	G	A	Pts	AG	AA	APts	PIM	Playoffs GP	G	A	Pts	PIM
1935-36	Kingston Dunlop Forts	City Jr.	16	*29	14	43	....	....	....	....	....	....	....	....	....
1936-37	Toronto North Vocational	Jr. B	STATISTICS NOT AVAILABLE												
1937-38	Toronto Marlboros	OHA	14	*25	*16	*41	....	....	....	12	6	6	4	10	4
1938-39	Toronto Goodyears	OHA Sr.	16	18	11	29	....	....	....	18	13	6	9	15	12
1939-40	**Toronto Maple Leafs**	**NHL**	**21**	**6**	**4**	**10**	**13**	**8**	**21**	**2**	**10**	**5**	**1**	**6**	**4**
	Pittsburgh Hornets	AHL	17	12	12	24	....	....	....	4	....	....	....	....	....
1940-41	**Toronto Maple Leafs**	**NHL**	**26**	**10**	**5**	**15**	**20**	**9**	**29**	**9**	**7**	**0**	**0**	**0**	**0**
1941-42	**Toronto Maple Leafs**	**NHL**	**44**	**12**	**18**	**30**	**21**	**27**	**48**	**13**	**9**	**0**	**0**	**0**	**2**
1942-43	**Toronto Maple Leafs**	**NHL**	**8**	**1**	**7**	**8**	**1**	**9**	**10**	**4**	....	....	....	....	....
	New York Rangers	**NHL**	**36**	**11**	**20**	**31**	**16**	**25**	**41**	**33**	....	....	....	....	....
1943-44	Toronto Army Shamrocks	OHA Sr.	STATISTICS NOT AVAILABLE												
1944-45	**New York Rangers**	**NHL**	**48**	**17**	**25**	**42**	**23**	**41**	**64**	**25**	....	....	....	....	....
1945-46	**New York Rangers**	**NHL**	**19**	**6**	**1**	**7**	**9**	**2**	**11**	**11**	....	....	....	....	....
	New Haven Eagles	AHL	25	13	11	24	....	....	....	7	....	....	....	....	....
1946-47	Cleveland Barons	AHL	61	30	19	49	....	....	....	22	4	0	1	1	0
1947-48			DID NOT PLAY												
1948-49	Washington Lions	AHL	7	0	0	0	....	....	....	2	....	....	....	....	....
	Shawinigan Cataracts	QSHL	3	0	3	3	....	....	....	0	....	....	....	....	....
	Fenelon Falls Generals	Inter-Sr.	DID NOT PLAY – COACHING												
	NHL Totals		**202**	**63**	**80**	**143**	**103**	**121**	**224**	**97**	**26**	**5**	**1**	**6**	**6**

Traded to **NY Rangers** by **Toronto** with Red Garrett for Babe Pratt, November 27, 1942. Traded to **Detroit** by **NY Rangers** with Ab DeMarco for Flash Hollett, June 19, 1946. • Returned to **NY Rangers** by **Detroit** with Ab DeMarco when Flash Hollett decided to retire, June, 1946. Traded to **Cleveland** (AHL) by **NY Rangers** for cash, October 4, 1946.

• GOODEN, BILL
Bill Gooden
LW – L. 5'9", 175 lbs. b: Winnipeg, Man., 9/8/1923.

Season	Club	League	GP	G	A	Pts	AG	AA	APts	PIM	Playoffs GP	G	A	Pts	PIM
1940-41	Winnipeg Maroons	MJHL	7	8	2	10	....	....	....	6	3	4	0	4	2
1941-42	Portage Terriers	MJHL	18	15	22	37	....	....	....	25	15	22	15	37	31
1942-43	**New York Rangers**	**NHL**	**12**	**0**	**3**	**3**	**0**	**4**	**4**	**0**	....	....	....	....	....
	Niagara Falls Cataracts	OHA Sr.	22	11	12	23	....	....	....	21	2	0	0	0	4
1943-44	**New York Rangers**	**NHL**	**41**	**9**	**8**	**17**	**11**	**10**	**21**	**15**	....	....	....	....	....
1944-45	Hershey Bears	AHL	59	27	41	68	....	....	....	12	11	4	5	9	11
1945-46	Hershey–New Haven	AHL	56	19	16	35	....	....	....	24	....	....	....	....	....
1946-47	Springfield Indians	AHL	62	17	22	39	....	....	....	40	2	0	0	0	5
1947-48	Springfield Indians	AHL	68	32	36	68	....	....	....	14	....	....	....	....	....
1948-49	Fort Worth Rangers	USHL	5	4	0	4	....	....	....	2	....	....	....	....	....
	Springfield Indians	AHL	60	34	32	66	....	....	....	24	3	3	1	4	2
1949-50	Springfield Indians	AHL	67	29	37	66	....	....	....	23	2	1	0	1	0
1950-51	Springfield Indians	AHL	63	32	37	69	....	....	....	28	1	0	1	1	0
1951-52	Syracuse Warriors	AHL	65	21	25	46	....	....	....	33	....	....	....	....	....
1952-53	Syracuse Warriors	AHL	60	21	28	49	....	....	....	21	4	0	0	0	2
1953-54	Syracuse Warriors	AHL	41	15	20	35	....	....	....	6	....	....	....	....	....
1954-55	Vancouver Canucks	WHL	15	0	4	4	....	....	....	0	....	....	....	....	....
	Providence Reds	AHL	20	3	8	11	....	....	....	6	....	....	....	....	....
1955-56	Trois-Rivieres Lions	QHL	38	13	17	30	....	....	....	8	....	....	....	....	....
	Providence Reds	AHL	6	1	0	1	....	....	....	2	....	....	....	....	....
1956-57	Clinton Comets	EHL	25	7	10	17	....	....	....	4	....	....	....	....	....
	NHL Totals		**53**	**9**	**11**	**20**	**11**	**14**	**25**	**15**	....	....	....	....	....

AHL Second All-Star Team (1951)

Signed as a free agent by **NY Rangers**, October 30, 1942.

• GOODFELLOW, EBBIE   Ebbie Goodfellow   HHOF

C/D – L. 6′, 175 lbs.   b: Ottawa, Ont., 4/9/1907.   d: 9/10/1965.

			REGULAR SEASON								PLAYOFFS				
Season	Club	League	GP	G	A	Pts	AG	AA	APts	PIM	GP	G	A	Pts	PIM
1927-28	Ottawa Montagnards	City Sr.	15	7	2	9	....	....	....	....	6	*4	1	*5	....
1928-29	Detroit Olympics	Can-Pro	42	*26	8	*34	....	....	....	45	7	3	2	5	8
1929-30	**Detroit Cougars**	**NHL**	**44**	**17**	**17**	**34**	**34**	**56**	**90**	**54**	....	....	....	....	....
1930-31	**Detroit Falcons**	**NHL**	**44**	**25**	**23**	**48**	**62**	**85**	**147**	**32**	....	....	....	....	....
1931-32	**Detroit Falcons**	**NHL**	**48**	**14**	**16**	**30**	**30**	**45**	**75**	**56**	**2**	**0**	**0**	**0**	**0**
1932-33	**Detroit Red Wings**	**NHL**	**41**	**12**	**8**	**20**	**28**	**21**	**49**	**47**	**4**	**1**	**0**	**1**	**11**
1933-34	**Detroit Red Wings**	**NHL**	**48**	**13**	**13**	**26**	**29**	**35**	**64**	**45**	**9**	**4**	**3**	**7**	**12**
1934-35	**Detroit Red Wings**	**NHL**	**48**	**12**	**24**	**36**	**25**	**54**	**79**	**44**	....	....	....	....	....
1935-36	**Detroit Red Wings**	**NHL**	**48**	**5**	**18**	**23**	**12**	**44**	**56**	**69**	**7**	**1**	**0**	**1**	**4**
1936-37	**Detroit Red Wings**	**NHL**	**48**	**9**	**16**	**25**	**19**	**38**	**57**	**43**	**9**	**2**	**2**	**4**	**12**
1937-38	**Detroit Red Wings**	**NHL**	**30**	**0**	**7**	**7**	**0**	**14**	**14**	**13**	....	....	....	....	....
1938-39	**Detroit Red Wings**	**NHL**	**48**	**8**	**8**	**16**	**17**	**15**	**32**	**36**	**6**	**0**	**0**	**0**	**8**
1939-40	**Detroit Red Wings**	**NHL**	**43**	**11**	**17**	**28**	**24**	**34**	**58**	**31**	**5**	**0**	**2**	**2**	**9**
1940-41	**Detroit Red Wings**	**NHL**	**47**	**5**	**17**	**22**	**10**	**31**	**41**	**35**	**3**	**0**	**1**	**1**	**9**
1941-42	**Detroit Red Wings**	**NHL**	**9**	**2**	**2**	**4**	**3**	**3**	**6**	**2**	....	....	....	....	....
1942-43	**Detroit Red Wings**	**NHL**	**11**	**1**	**4**	**5**	**1**	**5**	**6**	**4**	....	....	....	....	....
	NHL Totals		**557**	**134**	**190**	**324**	**294**	**480**	**774**	**511**	**45**	**8**	**8**	**16**	**65**

NHL Second All-Star Team (1936) • NHL First All-Star Team (1937, 1940) • Won Hart Trophy (1940)

Played in NHL All-Star Game (1937, 1939)

Traded to **Detroit Falcons** by **NY Americans** for Johnny Sheppard and $12,500, October 14, 1928.

• GORDON, FRED   Fred Gordon

RW – R. 5′10″, 185 lbs.   b: Fleming, Sask., 5/6/1900.

Season	Club	League	GP	G	A	Pts	AG	AA	APts	PIM	GP	G	A	Pts	PIM
1921-22	Indian Head Tigers	RCHL	8	*10	0	10	....	....	....	8	1	*2	0	2	0
1922-23	Indian Head Tigers	RCHL	STATISTICS NOT AVAILABLE												
1923-24	Brandon Regals	MHL Sr.	12	4	5	9	....	....	....	5	2	0	0	0	2
1924-25	Saskatoon Crescents	WCHL	19	2	2	4	....	....	....	11	2	1	0	1	0
1925-26	Saskatoon Crescents	WHL	30	9	2	11	....	....	....	36	2	0	0	0	2
1926-27	**Detroit Cougars**	**NHL**	**38**	**5**	**5**	**10**	**14**	**43**	**57**	**28**	....	....	....	....	....
1927-28	**Boston Bruins**	**NHL**	**43**	**3**	**2**	**5**	**9**	**17**	**26**	**40**	**2**	**0**	**0**	**0**	**0**
1928-29	Minneapolis Millers	AHA	39	4	3	7	....	....	....	47	4	0	0	0	8
1929-30	Minneapolis Millers	AHA	40	4	7	11	....	....	....	102	....	....	....	....	....
1930-31	Minneapolis Millers	AHA	43	10	9	19	....	....	....	81	....	....	....	....	....
1931-32	Buffalo Majors	AHA	17	5	0	5	....	....	....	26	....	....	....	....	....
1932-33	Saskatoon Crescents	WCHL	3	0	0	0	....	....	....	0	....	....	....	....	....
1933-34	Kansas City Greyhounds	AHA	47	12	10	22	....	....	....	52	3	0	0	0	4
1934-35	Kansas City Greyhounds	AHA	21	1	2	3	....	....	....	16	....	....	....	....	....
1935-36			DID NOT PLAY – REFEREE												
1936-37	Tulsa Oilers	AHA	DID NOT PLAY – COACHING												
	NHL Totals		**81**	**8**	**7**	**15**	**23**	**60**	**83**	**68**	**2**	**0**	**0**	**0**	**0**
	Other Major League Totals		49	11	4	15	....	....	....	47	4	1	0	1	2

Traded to **Detroit Cougars** by **Saskatoon** (WHL) for cash, October 27, 1926. Traded to **Boston** by **Detroit Cougars** for Harry Meeking, May 22, 1927.

• GORDON, JACKIE   Jackie Gordon

C – R. 5′9″, 154 lbs.   b: Winnipeg, Man., 3/3/1928.

Season	Club	League	GP	G	A	Pts	AG	AA	APts	PIM	GP	G	A	Pts	PIM
1945-46	Winnipeg Rangers	City Jr.	STATISTICS NOT AVAILABLE												
1946-47	New York Rovers	EHL	54	37	40	77	....	....	....	6	7	4	5	9	0
1947-48	New Haven Ramblers	AHL	37	11	24	35	....	....	....	2	4	0	3	3	0
1948-49	**New York Rangers**	**NHL**	**31**	**3**	**9**	**12**	**5**	**14**	**19**	**0**	....	....	....	....	....
	New Haven Ramblers	AHL	36	10	28	38	....	....	....	14	....	....	....	....	....
1949-50	**New York Rangers**	**NHL**	**1**	**0**	**0**	**0**	**0**	**0**	**0**	**0**	**9**	**1**	**1**	**2**	**7**
	New Haven Ramblers	AHL	70	23	60	83	....	....	....	2	....	....	....	....	....
1950-51	**New York Rangers**	**NHL**	**4**	**0**	**1**	**1**	**0**	**1**	**1**	**0**	....	....	....	....	
	Cincinnati Mohawks	AHL	59	23	42	65	....	....	....	10	....	....	....	....	....
1951-52	Cleveland Barons	AHL	20	7	20	27	....	....	....	0	2	0	2	2	0
1952-53	Cleveland Barons	AHL	64	20	58	78	....	....	....	6	11	4	7	*11	0
1953-54	Cleveland Barons	AHL	70	31	71	102	....	....	....	20	9	5	*13	*18	4
1954-55	Cleveland Barons	AHL	67	17	50	67		....	....	22	4	1	3	4	0
1955-56	Cleveland Barons	AHL	54	26	43	69	....	....	....	33	6	5	4	9	2
1956-57	Cleveland Barons	AHL	33	4	14	18	....	....	....	0	12	2	2	4	2
1957-58	Cleveland Barons	AHL	51	6	18	24	....	....	....	10	6	1	2	3	2
1958-59	Cleveland Barons	AHL	38	3	5	8	....	....	....	0	....	....	....	....	....
1959-60	Cleveland Barons	AHL	8	0	1	1	....	....	....	0	....	....	....	....	....
1960-61	Cleveland Barons	AHL	5	0	0	0	....	....	....	0	....	....	....	....	....
1961-62	Cleveland Barons	AHL	DID NOT PLAY – COACHING												
	NHL Totals		**36**	**3**	**10**	**13**	**5**	**15**	**20**	**0**	**9**	**1**	**1**	**2**	**7**

EHL Second All-Star Team (1947)

Traded to **Cleveland** (AHL) by **NY Rangers** with Ed Reigle, Fred Shero, Fern Perreault and cash for Wally Hergesheimer and Hy Buller, May 14, 1951.

• GORMAN, ED   Ed Gorman

D – L. 6′, 180 lbs.   b: Buckingham, Ont., 9/25/1892.   d: 3/10/1963.

Season	Club	League	GP	G	A	Pts	AG	AA	APts	PIM	GP	G	A	Pts	PIM
1913-14	Buckingham Seniors	Mtl. Sr.	4	1	0	1	....	....	....	....	1	1	0	1	....
1914-15	Buckingham Seniors	Mtl. Sr.	8	3	0	3	....	....	....	....	4	1	0	1	....
1915-16	Pittsburgh Duquesne	City Sr.	STATISTICS NOT AVAILABLE												
1916-17	Pittsburgh AA	USAHA	39	13	0	13	....	....	....	....	....	....	....	....	....
1917-18	Pembroke Munitions	City Sr.	STATISTICS NOT AVAILABLE												
1918-19	Ottawa Royal Canadians	City Sr.	8	1	3	4	....	....	....	13	....	....	....	....	....
1919-20	Ottawa Munitions	City Sr.	7	1	0	1			....	19	5	3	5	8	....
1920-21	Ottawa St. Brigid's	City Sr.	11	6	0	6	....	....	....	....	6	2	1	3	*15
1921-22	Ottawa Montagnards	City Sr.	14	13	*9	*22	....	....	....	42	8	8	5	13	*15
1922-23	Ottawa Montagnards	City Sr.	9	4	3	7	....	....	....	20	2	1	0	1	4
1923-24	Ottawa Montagnards	City Sr.	12	4	0	4	....	....	....	....	6	*6	1	*7	....
1924-25	**Ottawa Senators**	**NHL**	**30**	**11**	**3**	**14**	**38**	**40**	**78**	**49**	....	....	....	....	....
1925-26	**Ottawa Senators**	**NHL**	**23**	**2**	**1**	**3**	**6**	**11**	**17**	**12**	**2**	**0**	**0**	**0**	**2**
1926-27	**Ottawa Senators**	**NHL**	**41**	**1**	**0**	**1**	**3**	**0**	**3**	**17**	**6**	**0**	**0**	**0**	**0**
1927-28	**Toronto Maple Leafs**	**NHL**	**19**	**0**	**1**	**1**	**0**	**8**	**8**	**30**	....	....	....	....	....
	Kitchener Millionaires	Can-Pro	12	4	1	5	....	....	....	20	5	0	0	0	14
	NHL Totals		**113**	**14**	**5**	**19**	**47**	**59**	**106**	**108**	**8**	**0**	**0**	**0**	**2**

Signed as a free agent by **Ottawa**, November 6, 1924. Traded to **Toronto** by **Ottawa** for cash, October 26, 1927. • Suspended by Toronto for refusing assignment to Toronto Ravinas (Can-Pro), February 10, 1928. Traded to **Kitchener** (Can-Pro) by **Toronto** for cash, February 13, 1928.

• GOTTSELIG, JOHNNY   Johnny Gottselig

LW – L. 5′11″, 158 lbs.   b: Odessa, Russia, 6/24/1905.   d: 5/15/1986.

Season	Club	League	GP	G	A	Pts	AG	AA	APts	PIM	GP	G	A	Pts	PIM
1922-23	Regina Pats	SJHL	5	5	0	5	....	....	....	0	....	....	....	....	....
1923-24	Regina Pats	SJHL	6	6	0	6	....	....	....	6	5	8	1	9	8
1924-25	Regina Pats	SJHL	5	*18	2	*20	....	....	....	0	4	13	2	15	2
	Regina Victorias	SSHL	1	1	0	1	....	....	....	2	....	....	....	....	....
1925-26	Regina Pats	SJHL	16	8	1	9	....	....	....	2	9	*8	0	8	2
1926-27	Regina Capitals	PrHL	32	23	7	30	....	....	....	21	2	1	0	1	0
1927-28	Winnipeg Maroons	AHA	39	15	4	19	....	....	....	24	....	....	....	....	....
1928-29	**Chicago Black Hawks**	**NHL**	**44**	**5**	**3**	**8**	**20**	**27**	**47**	**26**	....	....	....	....	....
1929-30	**Chicago Black Hawks**	**NHL**	**39**	**21**	**4**	**25**	**42**	**13**	**55**	**28**	**2**	**0**	**0**	**0**	**4**
1930-31	**Chicago Black Hawks**	**NHL**	**42**	**20**	**12**	**32**	**49**	**44**	**93**	**14**	**9**	**3**	**3**	**6**	**2**
1931-32	**Chicago Black Hawks**	**NHL**	**44**	**13**	**15**	**28**	**28**	**42**	**70**	**28**	**2**	**0**	**0**	**0**	**2**
1932-33	**Chicago Black Hawks**	**NHL**	**41**	**11**	**11**	**22**	**26**	**29**	**55**	**6**	....	....	....	....	....
1933-34	**Chicago Black Hawks**	**NHL**	**48**	**16**	**14**	**30**	**36**	**38**	**74**	**4**	**8**	**4**	**3**	**7**	**4**
1934-35	**Chicago Black Hawks**	**NHL**	**48**	**19**	**18**	**37**	**41**	**40**	**81**	**16**	**2**	**0**	**0**	**0**	**0**
1935-36	**Chicago Black Hawks**	**NHL**	**40**	**14**	**15**	**29**	**35**	**36**	**71**	**4**	**2**	**0**	**2**	**2**	**0**
1936-37	**Chicago Black Hawks**	**NHL**	**47**	**9**	**21**	**30**	**19**	**50**	**69**	**10**	....	....	....	....	....
1937-38	**Chicago Black Hawks**	**NHL**	**48**	**13**	**19**	**32**	**27**	**39**	**66**	**22**	**10**	**5**	**3**	***8**	**4**
1938-39	**Chicago Black Hawks**	**NHL**	**48**	**16**	**23**	**39**	**34**	**43**	**77**	**15**	....	....	....	....	....
1939-40	**Chicago Black Hawks**	**NHL**	**39**	**8**	**15**	**23**	**17**	**30**	**47**	**7**	**2**	**0**	**1**	**1**	**0**
1940-41	**Chicago Black Hawks**	**NHL**	**5**	**1**	**4**	**5**	**2**	**7**	**9**	**5**	....	....	....	....	....
	Kansas City Americans	AHA	13	9	6	15	....	....	....	2	8	3	1	4	2
1941-42	Kansas City Americans	AHA	40	25	35	60	....	....	....	22	6	2	5	7	2
1942-43	**Chicago Black Hawks**	**NHL**	**10**	**2**	**6**	**8**	**3**	**8**	**11**	**12**	....	....	....	....	....
1943-44	**Chicago Black Hawks**	**NHL**	**45**	**8**	**15**	**23**	**10**	**18**	**28**	**6**	**6**	**1**	**1**	**2**	**2**
1944-45	**Chicago Black Hawks**	**NHL**	**1**	**0**	**0**	**0**	**0**	**0**	**0**	**0**	....	....	....	....	....
1945-46	**Chicago Black Hawks**	**NHL**	DID NOT PLAY – COACHING												
	NHL Totals		**589**	**176**	**195**	**371**	**389**	**464**	**853**	**203**	**43**	**13**	**13**	**26**	**18**

NHL Second All-Star Team (1939)

Played in NHL All-Star Game (1937, 1939)

Claimed by **Chicago** from **Winnipeg** (AHA) in Inter-League Draft, May 14, 1928.

• GOUPILLE, RED   Red (Cliff) Goupille

D – L. 6′, 190 lbs.   b: Trois Rivieres, Que., 9/2/1915.

Season	Club	League	GP	G	A	Pts	AG	AA	APts	PIM	GP	G	A	Pts	PIM
1935-36	**Montreal Canadiens**	**NHL**	**4**	**0**	**0**	**0**	**0**	**0**	**0**	**0**	....	....	....	....	....
	Montreal Lafontaine	QSHL	22	7	11	18	....	....	....	54	....	....	....	....	....
1936-37	**Montreal Canadiens**	**NHL**	**4**	**0**	**0**	**0**	**0**	**0**	**0**	**0**	....	....	....	....	....
	New Haven Eagles	AHL	35	6	4	10	....	....	....	78	....	....	....	....	....
1937-38	**Montreal Canadiens**	**NHL**	**47**	**4**	**5**	**9**	**8**	**10**	**18**	**44**	**3**	**2**	**0**	**2**	**4**
1938-39	**Montreal Canadiens**	**NHL**	**18**	**0**	**2**	**2**	**0**	**4**	**4**	**24**	....	....	....	....	....
	New Haven Eagles	AHL	36	6	6	12	....	....	....	54	....	....	....	....	....
1939-40	**Montreal Canadiens**	**NHL**	**48**	**2**	**10**	**12**	**4**	**20**	**24**	**48**	....	....	....	....	....
1940-41	**Montreal Canadiens**	**NHL**	**48**	**3**	**6**	**9**	**6**	**11**	**17**	**81**	**2**	**0**	**0**	**0**	**0**
1941-42	**Montreal Canadiens**	**NHL**	**47**	**1**	**5**	**6**	**2**	**8**	**10**	**51**	**3**	**0**	**0**	**0**	**2**
1942-43	**Montreal Canadiens**	**NHL**	**6**	**2**	**0**	**2**	**3**	**0**	**3**	**8**	....	....	....	....	....
	Montreal Army	QSHL	22	3	5	8	....	....	....	37	7	0	3	3	20
1943-44			MILITARY SERVICE												
1944-45			MILITARY SERVICE												
1945-46	Hull Volants	QSHL	40	4	13	17	....	....	....	*95	....	....	....	....	....
1946-47	Sherbrooke Saints	QPHL	42	9	19	28	....	....	....	*112	10	4	7	11	10
1947-48	Sherbrooke St. Francis	QPHL	61	12	31	43	....	....	....	101	9	1	3	4	20
1948-49	Sherbrooke Saints	QSHL	63	6	16	22	....	....	....	90	12	1	1	2	24
1949-50	Sherbrooke Saints	QSHL	57	4	19	24	....	....	....	51	16	1	3	4	8
1950-51	Sherbrooke Saints	QSHL	59	1	15	16	....	....	....	54	7	0	0	0	6
	NHL Totals		**222**	**12**	**28**	**40**	**23**	**53**	**76**	**266**	**8**	**2**	**0**	**2**	**6**

Played in NHL All-Star Game (1939)

• GOYETTE, PHIL   — *see page 1061*

• GRABOSKI, TONY   Tony Graboski

LW/D – L. 5′10″, 178 lbs.   b: Timmins, Ont., 5/9/1916.

Season	Club	League	GP	G	A	Pts	AG	AA	APts	PIM	GP	G	A	Pts	PIM
1933-34	Oshawa Majors	OHA	16	6	6	12	....	....	....	16	3	0	1	1	8
1934-35	Oshawa Majors	OHA	13	3	7	10	....	....	....	6	2	1	2	3	2
1935-36	Sudbury Wolves	City Sr.	10	5	3	8	....	....	....	10	....	....	....	....	....
1936-37	Hershey B'ars	EHL	48	17	9	26	....	....	....	36	4	2	1	3	2
1937-38	Hershey B'ars	EHL	50	29	26	55	....	....	....	17	....	....	....	....	....
1938-39	Hershey Cubs	EHL	52	27	13	40	....	....	....	12	....	....	....	....	....
1939-40	Sydney Millionaires	CBSHL	34	*29	*27	*56	....	....	....	50	4	4	4	*8	*14
1940-41	**Montreal Canadiens**	**NHL**	**34**	**4**	**3**	**7**	**8**	**5**	**13**	**12**	**3**	**0**	**0**	**0**	**6**
	New Haven Eagles	AHL	10	3	4	7	....	....	....	4	....	....	....	....	....
1941-42	**Montreal Canadiens**	**NHL**	**23**	**2**	**5**	**7**	**3**	**8**	**11**	**8**	....	....	....	....	....
	Washington Lions	AHL	24	3	2	5	....	....	....	12	2	0	0	0	0
1942-43	**Montreal Canadiens**	**NHL**	**9**	**0**	**2**	**2**	**0**	**3**	**3**	**4**	....	....	....	....	....
	Washington–Hershey	AHL	38	8	26	34	....	....	....	10	6	0	0	0	2
1943-44			MILITARY SERVICE												
1944-45			MILITARY SERVICE												
1945-46	Ottawa Senators	QSHL	19	5	5	10	....	....	....	32	9	1	3	4	10
	NHL Totals		**66**	**6**	**10**	**16**	**11**	**16**	**27**	**24**	**3**	**0**	**0**	**0**	**6**

			REGULAR SEASON								PLAYOFFS				
Season	**Club**	**League**	**GP**	**G**	**A**	**Pts**	**AG**	**AA**	**APts**	**PIM**	**GP**	**G**	**A**	**Pts**	**PIM**

• GRACIE, BOB
Bob Gracie
C/LW – L. 5'9", 155 lbs. b: North Bay, Ont., 11/8/1910. d: 8/10/1963.

Season	Club	League	GP	G	A	Pts	AG	AA	APts	PIM	GP	G	A	Pts	PIM
1927-28	North Bay Trappers	NOHA	11	11	1	12	....	....	....	6	2	1	0	1	0
1928-29	Kirkland Lake Lakers	NOHA	6	*24	6	*30	....	....	....	4	4	3	3	6	2
1929-30	West Toronto Nationals	OHA	7	*17	6	*23	....	....	....	12	15	*17	7	*24	15
1930-31	Toronto Marlboros	OHA	10	4	*6	10	....	....	....	6	3	2	0	2	6
	Toronto Maple Leafs	**NHL**	**8**	**4**	**2**	**6**	**10**	**7**	**17**	**4**	**2**	**0**	**0**	**0**	**0**
1931-32	**Toronto Maple Leafs**	**NHL**	**48**	**13**	**8**	**21**	**28**	**22**	**50**	**29**	**7**	**3**	**1**	**4**	**0**
1932-33	**Toronto Maple Leafs**	**NHL**	**48**	**9**	**13**	**22**	**21**	**34**	**55**	**27**	**9**	**0**	**1**	**1**	**0**
1933-34	**Boston Bruins**	**NHL**	**24**	**2**	**6**	**8**	**4**	**16**	**20**	**8**	....	....	....	....	....
	New York Americans	**NHL**	**24**	**4**	**6**	**10**	**9**	**16**	**25**	**10**	....	....	....	....	....
1934-35	**New York Americans**	**NHL**	**14**	**2**	**1**	**3**	**4**	**2**	**6**	**4**	....	....	....	....	....
	New Haven Eagles	Can-Am	1	1	2	3	....	....	....	0	....	....	....	....	....
	Montreal Maroons	**NHL**	**32**	**10**	**8**	**18**	**21**	**18**	**39**	**11**	**7**	**0**	**2**	**2**	**2**
1935-36	**Montreal Maroons**	**NHL**	**48**	**11**	**14**	**25**	**27**	**34**	**61**	**31**	**3**	**0**	**1**	**1**	**0**
1936-37	**Montreal Maroons**	**NHL**	**47**	**11**	**25**	**36**	**24**	**59**	**83**	**18**	**5**	**1**	**2**	**3**	**2**
1937-38	**Montreal Maroons**	**NHL**	**48**	**12**	**19**	**31**	**25**	**39**	**64**	**32**	....	....	....	....	....
1938-39	**Montreal Canadiens**	**NHL**	**7**	**0**	**1**	**1**	**0**	**2**	**2**	**4**	....	....	....	....	....
	Chicago Black Hawks	**NHL**	**31**	**4**	**6**	**10**	**8**	**11**	**19**	**27**	....	....	....	....	....
	Cleveland Falcons	AHL	11	1	5	6	....	....	....	0	9	4	2	6	0
1939-40	Cleveland–Indianapolis	AHL	56	15	20	35	....	....	....	19	5	1	0	1	0
1940-41	Buffalo Bisons	AHL	56	22	26	48	....	....	....	2	....	....	....	....	....
1941-42	Buffalo–Hershey	AHL	52	18	16	34	....	....	....	4	7	2	3	5	0
1942-43	Hershey–Washington	AHL	57	27	36	63	....	....	....	4	....	....	....	....	....
1943-44	Pittsburgh Hornets	AHL	41	13	21	34	....	....	....	11	....	....	....	....	....
1944-45	Pittsburgh Hornets	AHL	58	40	55	*95	....	....	....	4	....	....	....	....	....
1945-46	Pittsburgh Hornets	AHL	4	4	4	8	....	....	....	0	....	....	....	....	....
	Hollywood Wolves	PCHL	16	7	7	14	....	....	....	13	....	....	....	....	....
1946-47	Hollywood Wolves	PCHL	2	4	0	4	....	....	....	10	....	....	....	....	....
1947-48	Fresno Falcons	PCHL	8	3	2	5	....	....	....	2	....	....	....	....	....
	NHL Totals		**379**	**82**	**109**	**191**	**181**	**260**	**441**	**205**	**33**	**4**	**7**	**11**	**4**

Signed as a free agent by **Toronto**, March 1, 1931. Traded to **Ottawa** by **Toronto** with $10,000 for Hec Kilrea, October 4, 1933. Traded to **Boston** by **Ottawa** for Perk Galbraith, Bud Cook and Ted Saunders, October 4, 1933. Traded to **NY Americans** by **Boston** with Art Chapman for Lloyd Gross and George Patterson, January 11, 1934. Traded to **Montreal Maroons** by **NY Americans** for cash, December 25, 1934. Traded to **Montreal Canadiens** by **Montreal Maroons** for cash, September 14, 1938. Traded to **Chicago** by **Montreal** for cash, November 25, 1938. Traded to **Indianapolis** (AHL) by **Cleveland** (AHL) with $30,000 for Don Deacon, February 5, 1940.

• GRAHAM, LETH
Leth Graham
LW – L. 5'9", 150 lbs. b: Ottawa, Ont.. Deceased.

Season	Club	League	GP	G	A	Pts	AG	AA	APts	PIM	GP	G	A	Pts	PIM
1912-13	Ottawa Stewartons	City Sr.	STATISTICS NOT AVAILABLE												
1913-14	Ottawa Senators	NHA	17	1	1	2	....	....	....	2	....	....	....	....	....
1914-15	Ottawa Senators	NHA	17	9	3	12	....	....	....	34	5	1	0	1	0
1915-16			MILITARY SERVICE												
1916-17			MILITARY SERVICE												
1917-18			MILITARY SERVICE												
1918-19			MILITARY SERVICE												
1919-20			DID NOT PLAY												
1920-21	**Ottawa Senators**	**NHL**	**14**	**0**	**0**	**0**	**0**	**0**	**0**	**0**	**1**	**0**	**0**	**0**	**0**
1921-22	**Ottawa Senators**	**NHL**	**1**	**2**	**0**	**2**	**5**	**0**	**5**	**0**	....	....	....	....	....
1922-23	**Hamilton Tigers**	**NHL**	**4**	**1**	**0**	**1**	**3**	**0**	**3**	**0**	....	....	....	....	....
1923-24	**Ottawa Senators**	**NHL**	**3**	**0**	**0**	**0**	**0**	**0**	**0**	**0**	....	....	....	....	....
1924-25	**Ottawa Senators**	**NHL**	**3**	**0**	**0**	**0**	**0**	**0**	**0**	**0**	....	....	....	....	....
1925-26	**Ottawa Senators**	**NHL**	**1**	**0**	**0**	**0**	**0**	**0**	**0**	**0**	....	....	....	....	....
	NHL Totals		**26**	**3**	**0**	**3**	**8**	**0**	**8**	**0**	**1**	**0**	**0**	**0**	**0**
	Other Major League Totals		34	10	4	14	....	....	....	36	5	1	0	1	0

Signed as a free agent by **Ottawa**, November 10, 1920. Signed as a free agent by **Hamilton**, November 15, 1922. Traded to **Ottawa** by **Hamilton** for cash, December 18, 1923.

• GRAHAM, TED
Ted Graham
D – L. 5'8", 170 lbs. b: Owen Sound, Ont., 1/30/1906. Deceased.

Season	Club	League	GP	G	A	Pts	AG	AA	APts	PIM	GP	G	A	Pts	PIM
1923-24	Owen Sound Greys	City Jr.	11	3	*7	10	....	....	....	....	15	7	4	11	....
1924-25	Stratford Indians	OHA Sr.	20	3	2	5	....	....	....	22	....	....	....	....	....
1925-26	London Ravens	OHA Sr.	20	4	3	7	....	....	....	6	4	0	1	1	2
1926-27	Chicago Cardinals	AHA	32	1	1	2	....	....	....	23	....	....	....	....	....
1927-28	**Chicago Black Hawks**	**NHL**	**19**	**1**	**0**	**1**	**3**	**0**	**3**	**8**	....	....	....	....	....
	Saskatoon Shieks	PrHL	12	3	5	8	....	....	....	7	....	....	....	....	....
1928-29	Tulsa Oilers	AHA	34	10	*15	25	....	....	....	38	4	1	0	1	4
1929-30	Tulsa Oilers	AHA	15	4	0	4	....	....	....	12	....	....	....	....	....
	Chicago Black Hawks	**NHL**	**26**	**1**	**2**	**3**	**2**	**6**	**8**	**23**	**2**	**0**	**0**	**0**	**8**
1930-31	**Chicago Black Hawks**	**NHL**	**42**	**0**	**7**	**7**	**0**	**25**	**25**	**38**	**9**	**0**	**0**	**0**	**12**
1931-32	**Chicago Black Hawks**	**NHL**	**48**	**0**	**3**	**3**	**0**	**8**	**8**	**40**	**2**	**0**	**0**	**0**	**2**
1932-33	**Chicago Black Hawks**	**NHL**	**47**	**3**	**8**	**11**	**7**	**21**	**28**	**57**	....	....	....	....	....
1933-34	**Montreal Maroons**	**NHL**	**19**	**2**	**1**	**3**	**4**	**3**	**7**	**10**	....	....	....	....	....
	Detroit Red Wings	**NHL**	**28**	**1**	**0**	**1**	**2**	**0**	**2**	**29**	**9**	**3**	**1**	**4**	**8**
1934-35	**Detroit Red Wings**	**NHL**	**24**	**0**	**2**	**2**	**0**	**4**	**4**	**26**	....	....	....	....	....
	St. Louis Eagles	**NHL**	**13**	**0**	**0**	**0**	**0**	**0**	**0**	**2**	....	....	....	....	....
	Detroit Olympics	IAHL	7	0	0	0	....	....	....	10	....	....	....	....	....
1935-36	**Boston Bruins**	**NHL**	**48**	**4**	**1**	**5**	**10**	**2**	**12**	**37**	**2**	**0**	**0**	**0**	**0**
1936-37	**Boston Bruins**	**NHL**	**1**	**0**	**0**	**0**	**0**	**0**	**0**	**0**	....	....	....	....	....
	New York Americans	**NHL**	**31**	**2**	**1**	**3**	**4**	**2**	**6**	**30**	....	....	....	....	....
	Providence Reds	AHL	7	0	0	0	....	....	....	0	....	....	....	....	....
1937-38	New Haven Eagles	AHL	29	0	2	2	....	....	....	14	2	0	0	0	0
	NHL Totals		**346**	**14**	**25**	**39**	**32**	**71**	**103**	**300**	**24**	**3**	**1**	**4**	**30**

Traded to **Chicago** by **London** (Can-Pro) for $2,250, December 14, 1926. Traded to **Moose Jaw** (PrHL) by **Chicago** for Ambrose Moran and future considerations, January 11, 1928. Traded to **Montreal Maroons** by **Chicago** with Bill MacKenzie for Lionel Conacher, October 1, 1933. Traded to **Detroit** by **Montreal Maroons** for Stew Evans, January 2, 1934. Traded to **St. Louis** by **Detroit** with Scott Bowman and $50,000 for Syd Howe, February 11, 1935. Claimed by **Boston** from **St. Louis** in Dispersal Draft, October 15, 1935. Traded to **NY Americans** by **Boston** for Walt Kalbfleish, December 19, 1936.

• GRANT, DANNY
— *see page 1062*

			REGULAR SEASON								PLAYOFFS				
Season	**Club**	**League**	**GP**	**G**	**A**	**Pts**	**AG**	**AA**	**APts**	**PIM**	**GP**	**G**	**A**	**Pts**	**PIM**

• GRAVELLE, LEO
Leo "The Gazelle" Gravelle
RW – R. 5'9", 160 lbs. b: Aylmer, Que., 6/10/1925.

Season	Club	League	GP	G	A	Pts	AG	AA	APts	PIM	GP	G	A	Pts	PIM
1944-45	St. Michael's Majors	OHA	17	*30	22	*52	....	....	....	6	22	*22	12	*34	8
1945-46	Montreal Royals	QSHL	34	21	21	42	....	....	....	20	11	*10	4	*14	4
1946-47	**Montreal Canadiens**	**NHL**	**53**	**16**	**14**	**30**	**22**	**20**	**42**	**12**	**6**	**2**	**0**	**2**	**2**
	Montreal Royals	QSHL	2	2	2	4	....	....	....	0	....	....	....	....	....
1947-48	**Montreal Canadiens**	**NHL**	**15**	**0**	**0**	**0**	**0**	**0**	**0**	**0**	....	....	....	....	....
	Buffalo Bisons	AHL	29	11	13	24	....	....	....	7	....	....	....	....	....
	Houston Huskies	USHL	24	14	15	29	....	....	....	7	12	4	3	7	0
1948-49	**Montreal Canadiens**	**NHL**	**36**	**4**	**6**	**10**	**6**	**9**	**15**	**6**	**7**	**2**	**1**	**3**	**0**
	Buffalo Bisons	AHL	25	6	4	10	....	....	....	20	....	....	....	....	....
1949-50	**Montreal Canadiens**	**NHL**	**70**	**19**	**10**	**29**	**26**	**13**	**39**	**18**	**4**	**0**	**0**	**0**	**0**
1950-51	**Montreal Canadiens**	**NHL**	**31**	**4**	**2**	**6**	**5**	**3**	**8**	**0**	....	....	....	....	....
	Detroit Red Wings	**NHL**	**18**	**1**	**2**	**3**	**1**	**3**	**4**	**6**	....	....	....	....	....
	Indianapolis Capitals	AHL	15	4	6	10	....	....	....	0	....	....	....	....	....
1951-52	Ottawa Senators	QSHL	59	18	26	44	....	....	....	17	7	3	2	5	0
1952-53	Ottawa Senators	QSHL	60	28	28	56	....	....	....	4	11	2	5	7	0
1953-54	Ottawa Senators	QHL	68	*45	41	86	....	....	....	6	22	*9	7	16	8
1954-55	Ottawa–Chicoutimi	QHL	45	13	14	27	....	....	....	6	7	2	1	3	0
1955-56	Montreal Royals	QHL	42	13	12	25	....	....	....	11	....	....	....	....	....
	NHL Totals		**223**	**44**	**34**	**78**	**60**	**48**	**108**	**42**	**17**	**4**	**1**	**5**	**2**

QHL First All-Star Team (1954)

Traded to **Detroit** by **Montreal** for Bert Olmstead, December 19, 1950.

• GRAY, ALEX
Alex "Peanuts" Gray
RW – R. 5'10", 170 lbs. b: Glasgow, Scotland, 6/21/1899. d: 4/10/1986.

Season	Club	League	GP	G	A	Pts	AG	AA	APts	PIM	GP	G	A	Pts	PIM
1922-23	Port Arthur Ports	TBSHL	14	18	8	26	....	....	....	10	2	0	1	1	0
1923-24	Port Arthur Ports	TBSHL	14	*20	5	*25	....	....	....	4	2	1	1	2	0
1924-25	Port Arthur Ports	TBSHL	20	*17	7	*24	....	....	....	9	10	11	4	15	4
1925-26	Port Arthur Ports	TBSHL	18	12	*9	21	....	....	....	14	9	4	1	5	0
1926-27	Port Arthur Ports	TBSHL	19	*27	6	33	....	....	....	31	9	1	0	1	0
1927-28	**New York Rangers**	**NHL**	**43**	**7**	**0**	**7**	**21**	**0**	**21**	**30**	**9**	**1**	**0**	**1**	**0**
1928-29	**Toronto Maple Leafs**	**NHL**	**7**	**0**	**0**	**0**	**0**	**0**	**0**	**2**	**4**	**0**	**0**	**0**	**0**
	Toronto Ravinas	Can-Pro	37	11	3	14	....	....	....	51	2	3	0	3	4
1929-30	Cleveland Indians	IAHL	42	21	12	33	....	....	....	54	6	4	*3	*7	4
1930-31	Cleveland Indians	IAHL	48	29	8	37	....	....	....	55	6	4	2	6	6
1931-32	Cleveland Indians	IAHL	48	16	10	26	....	....	....	35	....	....	....	....	....
1932-33	Cleveland–Windsor	IAHL	39	7	8	15	....	....	....	15	....	....	....	....	....
	NHL Totals		**50**	**7**	**0**	**7**	**21**	**0**	**21**	**32**	**13**	**1**	**0**	**1**	**0**

Traded to **Toronto** by **NY Rangers** with Lorne Chabot for Butch Keeling and John Ross Roach, October 17, 1928. Traded to **Toronto Ravinas** (Can-Pro) by **Toronto** for cash, November 28, 1928.

• GRAY, TERRY
— *see page 1064*

• GREEN, RED
Red (Redvers) Green **HHOF**
LW – L. 5'8", 148 lbs. b: Sudbury, Ont., 12/12/1899. Deceased.

Season	Club	League	GP	G	A	Pts	AG	AA	APts	PIM	GP	G	A	Pts	PIM
1917-18	Toronto De laSalle	OHA	STATISTICS NOT AVAILABLE												
1918-19	Parkdale Canoe Club	OHA	STATISTICS NOT AVAILABLE												
1919-20	Sudbury Wolves	NOHA	5	15	4	19	....	....	....	2	2	*13	3	16	2
1920-21	Port Colborne	OHA Sr.	STATISTICS NOT AVAILABLE												
1921-22	Sudbury Wolves	NOHA	9	*22	*9	*31	....	....	....	8	....	....	....	....	....
1922-23	Sudbury Wolves	NOHA	7	6	*5	*11	....	....	....	16	2	1	*2	*3	*4
1923-24	**Hamilton Tigers**	**NHL**	**23**	**11**	**0**	**11**	**46**	**0**	**46**	**20**	....	....	....	....	....
1924-25	**Hamilton Tigers**	**NHL**	**30**	**19**	**4**	**23**	**67**	**53**	**120**	**63**	....	....	....	....	....
1925-26	**New York Americans**	**NHL**	**35**	**13**	**4**	**17**	**41**	**46**	**87**	**42**	....	....	....	....	....
1926-27	**New York Americans**	**NHL**	**43**	**10**	**4**	**14**	**29**	**34**	**63**	**53**	....	....	....	....	....
1927-28	**New York Americans**	**NHL**	**40**	**6**	**1**	**7**	**18**	**8**	**26**	**67**	....	....	....	....	....
1928-29	**Detroit Cougars**	**NHL**	**2**	**0**	**0**	**0**	**0**	**0**	**0**	**0**	....	....	....	....	....
	Boston Bruins	**NHL**	**22**	**0**	**0**	**0**	**0**	**0**	**0**	**16**	**1**	**0**	**0**	**0**	**0**
	Providence Reds	Can-Am	7	2	1	3	....	....	....	4	....	....	....	....	....
1929-30	Duluth Hornets	AHA	48	14	3	17	....	....	....	81	3	0	0	0	10
1930-31	Duluth Hornets	AHA	42	8	2	10	....	....	....	60	3	0	0	0	0
1931-32	Tulsa Oilers	AHA	2	0	0	0	....	....	....	2	....	....	....	....	....
	NHL Totals		**195**	**59**	**13**	**72**	**201**	**141**	**342**	**261**	**1**	**0**	**0**	**0**	**0**

Signed as a free agent by **Hamilton**, November 13, 1923. Transferred to **NY Americans** after NHL club purchased **Hamilton** franchise, September 25, 1925. Traded to **Boston** by **NY Americans** for Harry Connor, December, 1928. Claimed on waivers by **Detroit Cougars** from **Boston**, February 16, 1929. Claimed on waivers by **Boston** from **Detroit Cougars**, March 4, 1929.

• GREEN, SHORTY
Shorty (Wilf) Green
RW – R. 5'10", 152 lbs. b: Sudbury, Ont., 7/17/1896. d: 4/19/1960.

Season	Club	League	GP	G	A	Pts	AG	AA	APts	PIM	GP	G	A	Pts	PIM
1916-17	Hamilton 227th	OHA Sr.	8	*17	0	*17	....	....	....	....	....	....	....	....	....
1917-18			MILITARY SERVICE												
1918-19	Hamilton Tigers	OHA Sr.	8	12	3	15	....	....	....	....	6	*8	3	*11	....
1919-20	Sudbury Wolves	NOHA	6	*23	4	*27	....	....	....	*16	7	*13	4	*17	8
1920-21	Sudbury Wolves	NOHA	4	4	2	6	....	....	....	7	....	....	....	....	....
1921-22	Sudbury Wolves	NOHA	9	5	4	9	....	....	....	9	....	....	....	....	....
1922-23	Sudbury Wolves	NOHA	7	3	1	4	....	....	....	16	1	0	1	1	2
1923-24	**Hamilton Tigers**	**NHL**	**22**	**7**	**2**	**9**	**29**	**35**	**64**	**19**	....	....	....	....	....
1924-25	**Hamilton Tigers**	**NHL**	**28**	**18**	**1**	**19**	**63**	**13**	**76**	**75**	....	....	....	....	....
1925-26	**New York Americans**	**NHL**	**32**	**6**	**4**	**10**	**18**	**46**	**64**	**40**	....	....	....	....	....
1926-27	**New York Americans**	**NHL**	**21**	**2**	**1**	**3**	**6**	**8**	**14**	**17**	....	....	....	....	....
1927-28	NY Americans	Can-Pro	DID NOT PLAY – COACHING												
1928-29	Duluth Hornets	AHA	DID NOT PLAY – COACHING												
1929-30	Duluth Hornets	AHA	2	0	0	0	....	....	....	2	....	....	....	....	....
1930-31	Duluth Hornets	AHA	1	0	0	0	....	....	....	8	....	....	....	....	....
	NHL Totals		**103**	**33**	**8**	**41**	**116**	**102**	**218**	**151**	....	....	....	....	....

Signed as a free agent by **Hamilton**, November 22, 1923. Transferred to **NY Americans** after NHL club purchased **Hamilton** franchise, September 25, 1925.

• GREEN, TED
— *see page 1065*

● **GRIGOR, GEORGE** George "Shorty" Grigor
C – R. 5'7", 150 lbs. b: Edinburgh, Scotland, 9/3/1916.

Season	Club	League	GP	G	A	Pts	AG	AA	APts	PIM	Playoffs GP	G	A	Pts	PIM
1934-35	Toronto Young Rangers	City Jr.	9	3	2	5	....	....	....	11	2	1	0	1	0
1935-36	Toronto Young Rangers	City Jr.	11	8	6	14	....	....	....	*25	2	0	0	0	0
	Toronto Dominions	City Sr.	16	3	4	7	....	....	....	16	....	....	....	....	....
1936-37	Toronto Dominions	City Sr.	9	1	3	4	....	....	....	12	3	0	1	1	4
1937-38			DID NOT PLAY												
1938-39	Niagara Falls Brights	OHA Sr.	20	4	11	15	....	....	....	*48	....	....	....	....	....
1939-40	Baltimore Orioles	EHL	59	21	23	44	....	....	....	58	9	2	*7	*9	9
1940-41	Baltimore Orioles	EHL	59	22	32	54	....	....	....	95	....	....	....	....	....
1941-42	Toronto Marlboros	OHA Sr.	25	9	12	21	....	....	....	*71	6	0	3	3	10
1942-43	Research Colonels	Tor-Sr.	10	6	15	21	....	....	....	6	....	....	....	....	....
1943-44	Toronto Staffords	OHA Sr.	....	14	*36	50	....	....	....	20	7	3	4	7	*35
	Chicago Black Hawks	**NHL**	**2**	**1**	**0**	**1**	**1**	**0**	**1**	**0**	**1**	**0**	**0**	**0**	**0**
1944-45	Toronto Staffords	OHA Sr.	8	1	4	5	....	....	....	8	....	....	....	....	....
	NHL Totals		**2**	**1**	**0**	**1**	**1**	**0**	**1**	**0**	**1**	**0**	**0**	**0**	**0**

Loaned to **Chicago** by **Toronto Staffords** (OHA Sr.) as an emergency injury replacement, March, 1944.

● **GRONSDAHL, LLOYD** Lloyd "Gabby" Gronsdahl
RW – R. 5'9", 170 lbs. b: Norquay, Sask., 5/10/1921.

Season	Club	League	GP	G	A	Pts	AG	AA	APts	PIM	Playoffs GP	G	A	Pts	PIM
1940-41	Regina Capitals	SJHL	16	7	11	18	....	....	....	6	4	*4	3	*7	2
1941-42	**Boston Bruins**	**NHL**	**10**	**1**	**2**	**3**	**2**	**3**	**5**	**0**	....	....	....	....	....
	Boston Olympics	EHL	43	29	14	43	....	....	....	11	1	0	1	1	0
1942-43	Toronto RCAF	OHA Sr.	5	6	0	6	....	....	....	10	13	*17	3	20	4
1943-44	Toronto RCAF	OHA Sr.	15	7	3	10	....	....	....	6	....	....	....	....	....
	Toronto Bowsers	City Sr.	....	5	6	11	....	....	....	4	13	12	14	26	4
1944-45			MILITARY SERVICE												
1945-46			MILITARY SERVICE												
1946-47	Hershey Bears	AHL	64	19	21	40	....	....	....	17	11	1	2	3	4
1947-48	Hershey Bears	AHL	66	11	11	22	....	....	....	7	2	1	0	1	2
1948-49	Tulsa Oilers	USHL	63	38	25	63	....	....	....	17	7	3	3	6	2
1949-50	Tulsa Oilers	USHL	60	20	23	43	....	....	....	21	....	....	....	....	....
1950-51	Tulsa Oilers	USHL	61	23	23	46	....	....	....	8	9	1	2	3	6
	NHL Totals		**10**	**1**	**2**	**3**	**2**	**3**	**5**	**0**	....	....	....	....	....

● **GROSS, LLOYD** Lloyd "Bomber" Gross
LW – L. 5'9", 175 lbs. b: Kitchener, Ont., 9/5/1905.

Season	Club	League	GP	G	A	Pts	AG	AA	APts	PIM	Playoffs GP	G	A	Pts	PIM
1925-26	Kitchener Greenshirts	OHA	11	7	*11	18	....	....	....	....	....	....	....	....	....
1926-27	**Toronto Maple Leafs**	**NHL**	**16**	**1**	**1**	**2**	**3**	**8**	**11**	**0**	....	....	....	....	....
	Kitchener Greenshirts	OHA Sr.	11	7	4	11	....	....	....	4	4	0	2	2	2
1927-28	Toronto Ravinas	Can-Pro	41	12	3	15	....	....	....	42	2	0	0	0	10
1928-29	Kitchener Dutchmen	Can-Pro	40	9	4	13	....	....	....	59	3	0	0	0	4
1929-30	Toronto Millionaires	IAHL	11	3	0	3	....	....	....	8	....	....	....	....	....
	Niagara Falls Cataracts	IAHL	12	6	3	9	....	....	....	7	....	....	....	....	....
	Buffalo Bisons	IAHL	19	9	4	13	....	....	....	34	....	....	....	....	....
1930-31	Buffalo Bisons	IAHL	47	13	15	28	....	....	....	57	6	2	1	3	2
1931-32	Buffalo Bisons	IAHL	48	*24	16	40	....	....	....	65	6	*3	2	5	4
1932-33	Buffalo Bisons	IAHL	42	*30	20	*50	....	....	....	83	6	*4	0	4	2
1933-34	**New York Americans**	**NHL**	**21**	**7**	**3**	**10**	**15**	**8**	**23**	**10**	....	....	....	....	....
	Boston Bruins	**NHL**	**6**	**1**	**0**	**1**	**2**	**0**	**2**	**6**	....	....	....	....	....
	Boston Cubs	Can-Am	3	1	1	2	....	....	....	0	....	....	....	....	....
	Detroit Red Wings	**NHL**	**13**	**1**	**1**	**2**	**2**	**3**	**5**	**2**	**1**	**0**	**0**	**0**	**0**
1934-35	**Detroit Red Wings**	**NHL**	**6**	**1**	**0**	**1**	**2**	**0**	**2**	**2**	....	....	....	....	....
	Detroit–Buffalo	IAHL	43	12	17	41	....	....	....	39	....	....	....	....	....
1935-36	Cleveland Falcons	IAHL	48	17	10	27	....	....	....	30	2	1	0	1	2
1936-37	Cleveland Barons	AHL	3	0	0	0	....	....	....	2	....	....	....	....	....
1937-38	Tulsa Oilers	AHA	48	24	20	44	....	....	....	36	3	0	0	0	0
1938-39	Tulsa Oilers	AHA	46	29	23	52	....	....	....	30	8	2	4	6	6
1939-40	Tulsa Oilers	AHA	45	13	24	37	....	....	....	24	....	....	....	....	....
1940-41	St. Paul Saints	AHA	48	12	20	32	....	....	....	22	4	0	0	0	5
1941-42	St. Paul Saints	AHA	50	8	9	17	....	....	....	33	2	0	0	0	0
	NHL Totals		**62**	**11**	**5**	**16**	**24**	**19**	**43**	**20**	**1**	**0**	**0**	**0**	**0**

AHA Second All-Star Team (1938, 1939)

Signed as a free agent by **Toronto**, March 7, 1927. Traded to **Niagara Falls** (IAHL) by **Toronto** (IAHL) with Fred Elliot for Ike Morrison, Harry Lott and Jim Smith, December 15, 1929. Traded to **Buffalo** (IAHL) by **Niagara Falls** (IAHL) with Gamey Lederman for Wilf McDonald, January 9, 1930. Claimed by **NY Rangers** from **Buffalo** (IAHL) in Inter-League Draft, May 13, 1933. Rights returned to **Buffalo** (IAHL) by **NY Rangers** when NHL club failed to complete terms of purchase, May 25, 1933. Traded to **NY Americans** by **Buffalo** (IAHL) for cash, October 11, 1933. Traded to **Boston** by **NY Americans** with George Patterson for Art Chapman and Bob Gracie, January 11, 1934. Traded to **Detroit** by **Boston** for cash, February 13, 1934.

● **GROSSO, DON** Don "Count" Grosso
LW/C – L. 5'11", 170 lbs. b: Sault Ste. Marie, Ont., 4/12/1915. d: 5/14/1985.

Season	Club	League	GP	G	A	Pts	AG	AA	APts	PIM	Playoffs GP	G	A	Pts	PIM
1933-34	Detroit Mundus	MOHL	10	8	1	9	....	....	....	17	6	3	0	3	8
1934-35	Sudbury Wolves	NOHA	7	3	0	3	....	....	....	4	5	1	2	3	2
1935-36	Falconbridge Falcons	NOHA	10	7	6	13	....	....	....	10	3	4	1	5	4
1936-37	Sudbury Frood Miners	NOHA	14	11	5	16	....	....	....	6	16	13	6	19	6
1937-38	Falconbridge Falcons	NOHA	13	*13	8	*21	....	....	....	2	3	1	2	3	6
1938-39	**Detroit Red Wings**	**NHL**	**1**	**1**	**1**	**2**	**2**	**2**	**4**	**0**	**3**	**1**	**2**	**3**	**7**
	Kirkland Lake Blue Devils	NOHA	0	*17	12	*29	....	....	....	2	9	*18	5	*23	2
1939-40	**Detroit Red Wings**	**NHL**	**29**	**2**	**3**	**5**	**4**	**6**	**10**	**11**	**5**	**0**	**0**	**0**	**0**
1940-41	**Detroit Red Wings**	**NHL**	**45**	**8**	**7**	**15**	**16**	**13**	**29**	**14**	**9**	**1**	**4**	**5**	**0**
1941-42	**Detroit Red Wings**	**NHL**	**48**	**23**	**30**	**53**	**40**	**46**	**86**	**13**	**12**	**8**	**6**	**14**	**29**
1942-43	**Detroit Red Wings**	**NHL**	**50**	**15**	**17**	**32**	**21**	**22**	**43**	**10**	**10**	**4**	**2**	**6**	**10**
1943-44	**Detroit Red Wings**	**NHL**	**42**	**16**	**31**	**47**	**20**	**38**	**58**	**13**	**5**	**1**	**0**	**1**	**0**
1944-45	**Detroit Red Wings**	**NHL**	**20**	**6**	**10**	**16**	**8**	**16**	**24**	**6**	....	....	....	....	....
	Chicago Black Hawks	**NHL**	**21**	**9**	**6**	**15**	**12**	**10**	**22**	**4**	....	....	....	....	....
1945-46	**Chicago Black Hawks**	**NHL**	**47**	**7**	**10**	**17**	**11**	**19**	**30**	**17**	**4**	**0**	**0**	**0**	**17**
1946-47	**Boston Bruins**	**NHL**	**33**	**0**	**2**	**2**	**0**	**3**	**3**	**2**	....	....	....	....	....
	Hershey Bears	AHL	25	8	14	22	....	....	....	34	11	4	6	10	2
1947-48	St. Louis Flyers	AHL	65	34	49	81	....	....	....	10	....	....	....	....	....
1948-49	St. Louis Flyers	AHL	63	10	45	55	....	....	....	17	7	0	2	2	4
1949-50	Soo Greyhounds	NOHA	DID NOT PLAY – COACHING												
1950-51	Soo Greyhounds	NOHA	DID NOT PLAY – COACHING												
1951-52	Soo Greyhounds	NOHA	4	0	1	1	....	....	....	0	8	2	2	4	12
	NHL Totals		**336**	**87**	**117**	**204**	**134**	**175**	**309**	**90**	**48**	**15**	**14**	**29**	**63**

Traded to **Chicago** by **Detroit** with Cully Simon and Byron McDonald for Earl Seibert, January 2, 1945. Traded to **Boston** by **Chicago** for cash, June, 1946. Traded to **St. Louis** (AHL) by **Boston** for cash, June 14, 1947.

● **GROSVENOR, LEN** Len Grosvenor
C/RW – R. 5'9", 172 lbs. b: Ottawa, Ont., 7/21/1905.

Season	Club	League	GP	G	A	Pts	AG	AA	APts	PIM	Playoffs GP	G	A	Pts	PIM
1925-26	Ottawa Rideaus	City Sr.	....	1	0	1	....	....	....	....	....	....	....	....	....
1926-27	Ottawa Rideaus	City Sr.	14	9	4	13	....	....	....	....	....	....	....	....	....
1927-28	**Ottawa Senators**	**NHL**	**43**	**1**	**2**	**3**	**3**	**17**	**20**	**18**	**2**	**0**	**0**	**0**	**2**
1928-29	**Ottawa Senators**	**NHL**	**42**	**3**	**2**	**5**	**12**	**18**	**30**	**16**	....	....	....	....	....
1929-30	**Ottawa Senators**	**NHL**	**15**	**0**	**3**	**3**	**0**	**10**	**10**	**19**	....	....	....	....	....
	London Panthers	IAHL	27	6	1	7	....	....	....	24	2	0	0	0	0
1930-31	**Ottawa Senators**	**NHL**	**33**	**5**	**4**	**9**	**12**	**14**	**26**	**25**	....	....	....	....	....
	London Tecumsehs	IAHL	9	4	1	5	....	....	....	9	....	....	....	....	....
1931-32	**New York Americans**	**NHL**	**12**	**0**	**0**	**0**	**0**	**0**	**0**	**0**	....	....	....	....	....
	Bronx Tigers	Can-Am	30	6	5	11	....	....	....	28	2	0	0	0	0
1932-33	**Montreal Canadiens**	**NHL**	**4**	**0**	**0**	**0**	**0**	**0**	**0**	**0**	**2**	**0**	**0**	**0**	**0**
	NHL Totals		**149**	**9**	**11**	**20**	**27**	**59**	**86**	**78**	**4**	**0**	**0**	**0**	**2**

Signed as a free agent by **Ottawa**, October 24, 1927. Loaned to **London** (IAHL) by **Ottawa**, December 26, 1929. Claimed by **NY Americans** from **Ottawa** for 1931-32 season in Dispersal Draft, September 26, 1931. Signed as a free agent by **Montreal Canadiens**, January 7, 1933.

● **GUIDOLIN, ALDO** Aldo Guidolin
RW/D – R. 6', 180 lbs. b: Forks of Credit, Ont., 6/6/1932.

Season	Club	League	GP	G	A	Pts	AG	AA	APts	PIM	Playoffs GP	G	A	Pts	PIM
1949-50	Guelph Biltmores	OHA	38	8	8	16	....	....	....	21	26	2	3	5	26
1950-51	Guelph Biltmores	OHA	38	7	11	18	....	....	....	35	5	0	1	1	0
1951-52	Guelph Biltmores	OHA	47	21	33	54	....	....	....	95	14	4	5	9	18
1952-53	**New York Rangers**	**NHL**	**30**	**4**	**4**	**8**	**6**	**6**	**12**	**24**	....	....	....	....	....
	Vancouver Canucks	WHL	3	2	0	2	....	....	....	4	....	....	....	....	....
	Valleyfield Braves	QSHL	24	3	5	8	....	....	....	29	....	....	....	....	....
1953-54	**New York Rangers**	**NHL**	**60**	**2**	**6**	**8**	**3**	**8**	**11**	**51**	....	....	....	....	....
1954-55	**New York Rangers**	**NHL**	**70**	**2**	**5**	**7**	**3**	**6**	**9**	**34**	....	....	....	....	....
1955-56	**New York Rangers**	**NHL**	**14**	**1**	**0**	**1**	**1**	**0**	**1**	**8**	....	....	....	....	....
	Providence Reds	AHL	51	5	26	31	....	....	....	111	8	4	3	7	11
1956-57	Providence Reds	AHL	34	8	16	24	....	....	....	28	5	1	1	2	6
1957-58	Providence Reds	AHL	59	0	10	22	....	....	....	64	5	1	2	3	12
1958-59	Springfield Indians	AHL	55	3	18	21	....	....	....	90	....	....	....	....	....
1959-60	Cleveland Barons	AHL	66	10	22	32	....	....	....	168	7	0	2	2	16
1960-61	Cleveland Barons	AHL	72	10	37	47	....	....	....	152	4	0	1	1	8
1961-62	Cleveland Barons	AHL	68	7	34	41	....	....	....	*177	6	1	2	3	10
1962-63	Baltimore Clippers	AHL	59	8	28	36	....	....	....	144	....	....	....	....	....
1963-64	Baltimore Clippers	AHL	72	7	17	24	....	....	....	165	....	....	....	....	....
1964-65	Baltimore Clippers	AHL	67	1	28	29	....	....	....	143	....	....	....	....	....
1965-66	Providence Reds	AHL	71	4	21	25	....	....	....	157	....	....	....	....	....
1966-67	Baltimore Clippers	AHL	64	3	14	17	....	....	....	108	9	0	1	1	20
1967-68	Baltimore Clippers	AHL	69	6	12	18	....	....	....	95	....	....	....	....	....
1968-69	Baltimore Clippers	AHL	72	0	8	8	....	....	....	60	....	....	....	....	....
	NHL Totals		**182**	**9**	**15**	**24**	**13**	**20**	**33**	**117**	....	....	....	....	....

AHL First All-Star Team (1961, 1962)

Traded to **Cleveland** (AHL) by **NY Rangers** with Ed Hoekstra for Art Stratton with NY Rangers holding rights of recall, June, 1959. Traded to **Baltimore** (AHL) by **NY Rangers** (Cleveland - AHL) for cash, August, 1962. Traded to **Providence** (AHL) by **Baltimore** (AHL) with Marcel Paille, Jim Mikol and Don McGregor for Ed Giacomin, May 18, 1965. Traded to **Baltimore** (AHL) by **Cleveland** (AHL) with Willie Marshall, Jim Bartlett and Ian Anderson for Ed Lawson and Kay Stephanson, June, 1966.

• GUIDOLIN, BEP
Bep (Armand) Guidolin
LW – L. 5'8", 175 lbs. b: Thorold, Ont., 12/9/1925.

			REGULAR SEASON								PLAYOFFS				
Season	Club	League	GP	G	A	Pts	AG	AA	APts	PIM	GP	G	A	Pts	PIM
1941-42	Oshawa Generals	OHA	21	4	13	17	....	....	....	38	11	0	3	3	22
1942-43	**Boston Bruins**	**NHL**	**42**	**7**	**15**	**22**	**10**	**19**	**29**	**43**	**9**	**0**	**4**	**4**	**12**
1943-44	**Boston Bruins**	**NHL**	**47**	**17**	**25**	**42**	**21**	**30**	**51**	**58**	....	....	....	....	....
1944-45	Newmarket Navy	City Sr.	12	4	11	15	....	....	....	20	....	....	....	....	....
1945-46	**Boston Bruins**	**NHL**	**50**	**15**	**17**	**32**	**23**	**32**	**55**	**62**	**10**	**5**	**2**	**7**	**13**
1946-47	**Boston Bruins**	**NHL**	**56**	**10**	**13**	**23**	**13**	**19**	**32**	**73**	**3**	**0**	**1**	**1**	**6**
1947-48	**Detroit Red Wings**	**NHL**	**58**	**12**	**10**	**22**	**17**	**15**	**32**	**78**	**2**	**0**	**0**	**0**	**4**
1948-49	**Detroit Red Wings**	**NHL**	**4**	**0**	**0**	**0**	**0**	**0**	**0**	**0**	....	....	....	....	....
	Chicago Black Hawks	**NHL**	**56**	**4**	**17**	**21**	**6**	**27**	**33**	**116**	....	....	....	....	....
1949-50	**Chicago Black Hawks**	**NHL**	**70**	**17**	**34**	**51**	**23**	**44**	**67**	**42**	....	....	....	....	....
1950-51	**Chicago Black Hawks**	**NHL**	**69**	**12**	**22**	**34**	**16**	**28**	**44**	**56**	....	....	....	....	....
1951-52	**Chicago Black Hawks**	**NHL**	**67**	**13**	**18**	**31**	**18**	**23**	**41**	**78**	....	....	....	....	....
1952-53	Syracuse Warriors	AHL	23	1	8	9	....	....	....	24	3	0	0	0	8
	Ottawa Senators	QSHL	43	9	24	33	....	....	....	54	....	....	....	....	....
1953-54	Ottawa Senators	QHL	71	18	38	56	....	....	....	*148	22	2	11	13	39
1954-55	Ottawa Senators	QHL	19	5	12	17	....	....	....	77	....	....	....	....	....
	North Bay Trappers	NOHA	20	8	12	20	....	....	....	40	13	2	6	8	36
1955-56	Val D'Or Miners	QSHL	DID NOT PLAY – COACHING												
	North Bay Trappers	NOHA	1	1	2	3	....	....	....	2	....	....	....	....	....
1956-57	Belleville McFarlands	EOHL	48	16	29	45	....	....	....	*156	10	4	3	7	12
1957-58	Windsor Bulldogs	NOHA	7	2	6	8	....	....	....	24	....	....	....	....	....
	Belleville McFarlands	EOHL	35	12	18	30	....	....	....	60	13	3	10	13	*32
1958-59	Kingston Merchants	EOHL	43	11	26	37	....	....	....	62	12	0	4	4	24
1959-60			DID NOT PLAY												
1960-61	Omaha–Indianapolis	IHL	64	14	33	47	....	....	....	63	....	....	....	....	....
	NHL Totals		**519**	**107**	**171**	**278**	**147**	**237**	**384**	**606**	**24**	**5**	**7**	**12**	**35**

• Youngest player (16 years, 11 months) to play regular-season NHL game, November, 1942.
Traded to **Detroit** by **Boston** for Billy Taylor, October 15, 1947. Traded to **Chicago** by **Detroit** with Jim Conacher and Doug McCaig for George Gee and Bud Poile, October 25, 1948.

• HADDON, LLOYD
Lloyd Haddon
D – L. 6', 195 lbs. b: Sarnia, Ont., 8/10/1938.

Season	Club	League	GP	G	A	Pts	AG	AA	APts	PIM	GP	G	A	Pts	PIM
1954-55	Hamilton Tiger Cubs	OHA	2	1	0	1	....	....	....	0	....	....	....	....	....
1955-56	Hamilton Tiger Cubs	OHA	34	5	1	6	....	....	....	4	....	....	....	....	....
1956-57	Hamilton Tiger Cubs	OHA	19	1	1	2	....	....	....	4	....	....	....	....	....
1957-58	Hamilton Tiger Cubs	OHA	52	9	19	28	....	....	....	32	15	7	8	15	10
1958-59	Hamilton Tiger Cubs	OHA	54	15	30	45	....	....	....	51	....	....	....	....	....
	Hershey Bears	AHL	1	0	0	0	....	....	....	0	....	....	....	....	....
	Edmonton Flyers	WHL	9	1	1	2	....	....	....	0	2	0	0	0	0
1959-60	**Detroit Red Wings**	**NHL**	**8**	**0**	**0**	**0**	**0**	**0**	**0**	**2**	**1**	**0**	**0**	**0**	**0**
	Edmonton Flyers	WHL	53	3	17	20	....	....	....	22	....	....	....	....	....
1960-61	Edmonton Flyers	WHL	68	15	20	35	....	....	....	25	....	....	....	....	....
1961-62	Edmonton Flyers	WHL	70	22	27	49	....	....	....	22	4	0	2	2	0
1962-63	Los Angeles Blades	WHL	70	19	32	51	....	....	....	4	3	1	3	4	0
1963-64	St. Louis Braves	CHL	72	14	49	63	....	....	....	24	6	1	2	3	2
1964-65	Los Angeles Blades	WHL	65	7	28	35	....	....	....	12	....	....	....	....	....
	NHL Totals		**8**	**0**	**0**	**0**	**0**	**0**	**0**	**2**	**1**	**0**	**0**	**0**	**0**

WHL First Alll-Star Team (1962)

Traded to **LA Blades** (WHL) by **Detroit** for cash, July, 1962. Traded to **Chicago** (St. Louis - AHL) by **LA Blades** (WHL) for Norm Johnson, Ron Leopold and Gord Veipava, August 12, 1963. Traded to **LA Blades** (WHL) by **St. Louis** (AHL) for cash, August 20, 1964.

• HADFIELD, VIC
— *see page 1075*

• HAGGARTY, JIM
Jim Haggarty
LW – L. 5'11", 167 lbs. b: Port Arthur, Ont., 4/14/1914.

Season	Club	League	GP	G	A	Pts	AG	AA	APts	PIM	GP	G	A	Pts	PIM
1932-33	Port Arthur Ports	TBJHL	12	*14	5	*19	....	....	....	4	2	0	0	0	0
1933-34	Port Arthur Ports	TBJHL	10	6	4	10	....	....	....	9	2	3	0	3	0
1934-35	Port Arthur Ports	TBSHL	16	11	2	13	....	....	....	21	3	*5	1	*6	5
1935-36	Wembley Monarchs	Britain	....	18	2	20	....	....	....	0	....	....	....	....	....
	Canada	Olympics	2	2	3	5	....	....	....	0	....	....	....	....	....
1936-37	Wembley Monarchs	Britain	....	29	14	43	....	....	....	6	....	....	....	....	....
1937-38	Wembley Monarchs	Britain	....	25	17	42	....	....	....	....	....	....	....	....	....
1938-39	Wembley Monarchs	Britain	....	12	20	32	....	....	....	....	....	....	....	....	....
1939-40	Montreal Royals	QSHL	28	7	8	15	....	....	....	0	6	1	3	4	2
1940-41	Montreal Royals	QSHL	21	8	10	18	....	....	....	4	22	9	9	18	22
1941-42	Montreal Royals	QSHL	36	24	14	38	....	....	....	12	....	....	....	....	....
	Montreal Canadiens	**NHL**	**5**	**1**	**1**	**2**	**2**	**2**	**4**	**0**	**3**	**2**	**1**	**3**	**0**
1942-43	Montreal RCAF	QSHL	35	15	17	32	....	....	....	6	12	8	1	9	4
1943-44			MILITARY SERVICE												
1944-45	Montreal RCAF	QSHL	5	9	11	20	....	....	....	2	....	....	....	....	....
	Valleyfield Braves	QPHL	9	7	2	9	....	....	....	0	....	....	....	....	....
1945-46	Montreal Royals	QSHL	....	....	....	....	....	....	....	....	3	1	0	1	0
1946-47	Montreal Royals	QSHL	36	15	17	32	....	....	....	8	10	3	0	3	2
1947-48	Montreal Royals	QSHL	48	20	42	62	....	....	....	12	3	0	0	0	0
1948-49	Montreal Royals	QSHL	29	17	30	47	....	....	....	8	9	1	7	8	0
1949-50	Montreal Royals	QSHL	8	1	6	7	....	....	....	0	....	....	....	....	....
	Valleyfield Braves	QSHL	24	2	6	8	....	....	....	0	....	....	....	....	....
	NHL Totals		**5**	**1**	**1**	**2**	**2**	**2**	**4**	**0**	**3**	**2**	**1**	**3**	**0**

Signed as a free agent by **Montreal**, March 3, 1942.

• HAIDY, GORD
Gord Haidy
RW – R. 5'11", 185 lbs. b: Winnipeg, Man., 4/11/1928.

			REGULAR SEASON								PLAYOFFS				
Season	Club	League	GP	G	A	Pts	AG	AA	APts	PIM	GP	G	A	Pts	PIM
1944-45	Windsor Spitfires	City Sr.	10	6	8	14	....	....	....	6	2	1	2	3	4
1945-46	Windsor Spitfires	IHL	15	9	6	15	....	....	....	22	....	....	....	....	....
1946-47	Windsor Spitfires	OHA	15	23	7	30	....	....	....	17	....	....	....	....	....
	Windsor Spitfires	IHL	26	31	25	56	....	....	....	35	6	*19	6	*25	8
1947-48	Windsor Spitfires	IHL	25	*32	11	43	....	....	....	48	....	....	....	....	....
	Windsor Spitfires	OHA	28	38	19	57	....	....	....	43	12	10	5	15	34
1948-49	Omaha Knights	USHL	6	3	4	7	....	....	....	0	....	....	....	....	....
	Indianapolis Capitals	AHL	48	14	10	24	....	....	....	51	2	0	0	0	0
1949-50	Indianapolis Capitals	AHL	47	20	10	30	....	....	....	32	8	5	1	6	4
	Detroit Red Wings	**NHL**	....	....	....	....	....	....	....	....	**1**	**0**	**0**	**0**	**0**
1950-51	Indianapolis Capitals	AHL	59	26	18	44	....	....	....	40	3	0	0	0	0
1951-52			DID NOT PLAY – SUSPENDED												
1952-53	New Westminster Royals	WHL	18	6	4	10	....	....	....	14	....	....	....	....	....
	Buffalo Bisons	AHL	10	0	0	0	....	....	....	4	....	....	....	....	....
1953-54	Windsor Bulldogs	OHA Sr.	54	*47	33	80	....	....	....	*191	4	2	1	3	8
1954-55	Windsor Bulldogs	OHA Sr.	48	30	30	60	....	....	....	88	12	2	*13	15	*27
1955-56	Windsor Bulldogs	OHA Sr.	48	23	27	50	....	....	....	114	....	....	....	....	....
1956-57	Windsor Bulldogs	OHA Sr.	52	28	30	58	....	....	....	62	11	5	11	16	*48
1957-58	Chatham Maroons	NOHA	58	22	25	47	....	....	....	91	....	....	....	....	....
1958-59	Windsor Bulldogs	NOHA	27	9	15	24	....	....	....	45	....	....	....	....	....
1959-60	Windsor Bulldogs	OHA Sr.	47	21	27	48	....	....	....	77	17	12	15	27	12
1960-61	Milwaukee–Indianapolis	IHL	14	5	6	11	....	....	....	8	....	....	....	....	....
	Windsor Bulldogs	WOHL	....	14	5	19	....	....	....	6	....	....	....	....	....
1961-62	Windsor Bulldogs	OHA Sr.	17	13	12	25	....	....	....	16	13	9	9	18	12
1962-63	Sarnia Rams	OHA Sr.	6	3	4	7	....	....	....	2	....	....	....	....	....
1963-64	Windsor Bulldogs	IHL	17	7	4	11	....	....	....	18	....	....	....	....	....
	NHL Totals		**0**	**0**	**0**	**0**	**0**	**0**	**0**	**0**	**1**	**0**	**0**	**0**	**0**

• HALDERSON, HAROLD
Harold "Slim" Halderson
D – R. 6'3", 200 lbs. b: Winnipeg, Man., 1/6/1900. d: 8/1/1965.

Season	Club	League	GP	G	A	Pts	AG	AA	APts	PIM	GP	G	A	Pts	PIM
1917-18	Winnipeg Ypres	MHL Sr.	7	5	6	11	....	....	....	4	4	4	3	*7	4
1918-19	Winnipeg Monarchs	MHL Sr.	9	3	5	8	....	....	....	4	....	....	....	....	....
1919-20	Winnipeg Falcons	MHL Sr.	9	10	*11	21	....	....	....	10	6	4	5	9	6
	Canada	Olympics	3	9	*2	11	....	....	....	....	....	....	....	....	....
1920-21	Saskatoon Crescents	SSHL	16	12	3	15	....	....	....	38	4	*8	0	*8	9
1921-22	Victoria Cougars	PCHA	23	7	3	10	....	....	....	13	....	....	....	....	....
1922-23	Victoria Cougars	PCHA	29	10	5	15	....	....	....	26	2	0	0	0	0
1923-24	Victoria Cougars	PCHA	30	6	2	8	....	....	....	50	....	....	....	....	....
1924-25	Victoria Cougars	WCHL	28	3	6	9	....	....	....	71	8	3	1	4	*20
1925-26	Victoria Cougars	WHL	23	3	1	4	....	....	....	51	7	2	0	2	18
1926-27	**Detroit Cougars**	**NHL**	**19**	**2**	**0**	**2**	**6**	**0**	**6**	**29**	....	....	....	....	....
	Toronto Maple Leafs	**NHL**	**25**	**1**	**2**	**3**	**3**	**17**	**20**	**36**	....	....	....	....	....
1927-28	Quebec Castors	Can-Am	40	13	5	18	....	....	....	71	6	1	1	2	14
1928-29	Newark Bulldogs	Can-Am	40	6	3	9	....	....	....	107	....	....	....	....	....
1929-30	Kansas City Pla-Mors	AHA	48	8	7	15	....	....	....	76	5	0	0	0	8
1930-31	Kansas City Pla-Mors	AHA	47	5	7	12	....	....	....	77	8	1	1	2	10
1931-32	Kansas City Pla-Mors	AHA	46	9	3	12	....	....	....	69	4	2	0	2	0
1932-33	Kansas City Greyhounds	AHA	26	1	4	5	....	....	....	30	....	....	....	....	....
	Wichita Blue Jays	AHA	24	7	2	9	....	....	....	40	....	....	....	....	....
1933-34	Tulsa Oilers	AHA	48	9	12	21	....	....	....	66	4	0	2	2	4
	Wichita Vikings	AHA	2	0	0	0	....	....	....	0	....	....	....	....	....
1934-35	Tulsa Oilers	AHA	48	6	13	19	....	....	....	65	5	1	2	3	2
1935-36	Tulsa Oilers	AHA	48	6	14	20	....	....	....	25	3	0	0	0	4
1936-37	Wichita Skyhawks	AHA	48	5	4	9	....	....	....	30	....	....	....	....	....
	NHL Totals		**44**	**3**	**2**	**5**	**9**	**17**	**26**	**65**	....	....	....	....	....
	Other Major League Totals		133	29	17	46	....	....	....	211	17	5	1	6	38

PCHA Second All-Star Team (1922) • PCHA First All-Star Team (1923) • AHA First All-Star Team (1936, 1937)

Signed as a free agent by **Victoria** (PCHA), October 5, 1921. Transferred to **Detroit Cougars** after NHL club purchased **Victoria** (WHL) franchise, May 15, 1926. Traded to **Toronto St. Pats** by **Detroit** for Pete Bellefuille, January 10, 1927.

● HALEY, LEN Len "Comet" Haley
RW – R. 5'6", 160 lbs. b: Edmonton, Alta., 9/15/1931.

Season	Club	League	GP	G	A	Pts	AG	AA	APts	PIM	GP	G	A	Pts	PIM
			REGULAR SEASON								PLAYOFFS				
1949-50	Medicine Hat Tigers	WCJHL	40	26	28	54	....	....	....	76	5	0	3	3	6
1950-51	Medicine Hat Tigers	WCJHL	40	37	30	67	....	....	....	53	5	3	3	6	14
	Omaha Knights	USHL	3	1	3	4	....	....	....	0	....	....	....	....	....
1951-52	Glace Bay Miners	MMHL	86	44	58	*102	....	....	....	71	5	2	1	3	4
1952-53	Edmonton Flyers	WHL	69	18	17	35	....	....	....	23	15	4	6	10	6
1953-54	Edmonton Flyers	WHL	70	17	25	42	....	....	....	40	13	3	4	7	18
1954-55	Edmonton–Saskatoon	WHL	68	20	23	43	....	....	....	43	....	....	....	....	....
1955-56	Saskatoon Quakers	WHL	68	17	22	39	....	....	....	95	3	1	3	4	4
1956-57	Brandon Regals	WHL	69	21	33	54	....	....	....	77	9	5	2	7	4
1957-58	Hershey Bears	AHL	70	30	19	49	....	....	....	34	11	4	4	8	4
1958-59	Hershey Bears	AHL	59	17	11	28	....	....	....	38	11	1	0	1	20
1959-60	**Detroit Red Wings**	**NHL**	**27**	**1**	**2**	**3**	**1**	**2**	**3**	**12**	**6**	**1**	**3**	**4**	**6**
	Edmonton Flyers	WHL	39	19	16	35	....	....	....	35	....	....	....	....	....
1960-61	**Detroit Red Wings**	**NHL**	**3**	**1**	**0**	**1**	**1**	**0**	**1**	**2**	....	....	....	....	....
	Edmonton Flyers	WHL	66	15	30	45	....	....	....	36	....	....	....	....	....
1961-62	San Francisco Seals	WHL	66	20	30	50	....	....	....	56	2	0	0	0	2
1962-63	San Francisco Seals	WHL	70	36	24	60	....	....	....	76	17	8	6	14	23
1963-64	San Francisco Seals	WHL	70	35	33	68	....	....	....	112	11	4	10	14	14
1964-65	San Francisco Seals	WHL	70	26	46	72	....	....	....	113	....	....	....	....	....
1965-66	Seattle Totems	WHL	69	27	39	66	....	....	....	89	....	....	....	....	....
1966-67	San Diego Gulls	WHL	69	13	33	46	....	....	....	71	....	....	....	....	....
1967-68	Tulsa Oilers	CHL	70	*34	46	80	....	....	....	67	11	*6	9	15	15
1968-69	Omaha Knights	CHL	70	16	25	41	....	....	....	63	7	2	4	6	0
	Edmonton Monarchs	ASHL	2	0	2	2	....	....	....	0	....	....	....	....	....
1969-70	New Haven Blades	EHL	39	12	31	43	....	....	....	16	11	5	3	8	16
1969-70	Grand Falls Cataracts	Nfld.	STATISTICS NOT AVAILABLE												
1970-71	Edmonton Monarchs	ASHL	....	23	26	49	....	....	....	76	....	....	....	....	....
1971-72	Edmonton Monarchs	ASHL	....	18	23	41	....	....	....	63	....	....	....	....	....
	NHL Totals		**30**	**2**	**2**	**4**	**2**	**2**	**4**	**14**	**6**	**1**	**3**	**4**	**6**

CHL First All-Star Team (1968)

Traded to **Saskatoon** (WHL) by **Detroit** (Edmonton-WHL) for cash, November, 1954. Claimed by **Hershey** (AHL) from **Brandon** (WHL) in Inter-League Draft, June 4, 1957. Traded to **Edmonton** (WHL) by **Hershey** (AHL) for Ray Kinasewich, September, 1959. Traded to **Montreal** (Seattle-WHL) by **San Francisco** (WHL) for Gary Brisson, November 1, 1965. Claimed by **Detroit** (Pittsburgh - AHL) from **Montreal** (Seattle-WHL) in Reverse Draft, June, 1966. Traded to **San Diego** (WHL) by **Detroit** for cash, June, 1966. Loaned to **Tulsa** (CHL) by **San Diego** for 1967-68 season, September, 1967. Traded to **NY Rangers** by **San Diego** for Bruce Carmichael, September, 1968. Traded to **Des Moines** (IHL) by **NY Rangers** (New Haven - AHL) for Nelson Tremblay, September, 1970.

● HALL, BOB Bob "Red" Hall
F – L. 5'8", 165 lbs. b: Oak Park, IL, 10/13/1899.

Season	Club	League	GP	G	A	Pts	AG	AA	APts	PIM	GP	G	A	Pts	PIM
1917-18	Brooklyn Crescents	AAHL	4	3	0	3	....	....	....	....	....	....	....	....	....
1918-19	Brooklyn Crescents	AAHL	7	11	3	14	....	....	....	8	....	....	....	....	....
	Brooklyn Crescents	City Sr.	4	0	3	3	....	....	....	2	....	....	....	....	....
1919-20	Dartmouth University	Ivy	STATISTICS NOT AVAILABLE												
1920-21	Dartmouth University	Ivy	STATISTICS NOT AVAILABLE												
1921-22	Dartmouth University	Ivy	STATISTICS NOT AVAILABLE												
1922-23	New York St. Nicholas	USAHA	....	2	0	2	....	....	....	....	....	....	....	....	....
1923-24	Boston AAA	USAHA	1	0	0	0	....	....	....	....	1	0	0	0	....
	Dartmouth University	Ivy	STATISTICS NOT AVAILABLE												
1924-25	Boston AAA	USAHA	8	2	0	2	....	....	....	....	....	....	....	....	....
	Boston Maples	USAHA	4	0	0	0	....	....	....	....	....	....	....	....	....
	Minneapolis Rockets	USAHA	6	0	0	0	....	....	....	0	....	....	....	....	....
1925-26	New York Athletic Club	EHL	STATISTICS NOT AVAILABLE												
	New York Americans	**NHL**	**8**	**0**	**0**	**0**	**0**	**0**	**0**	**0**	....	....	....	....	....
	NHL Totals		**8**	**0**	**0**	**0**	**0**	**0**	**0**	**0**	....	....	....	....	....

Signed as a free agent **NY Americans**, February 8, 1926.

● HALL, JOE Joe "Bad Joe" Hall **HHOF**
D – R. 5'10", 175 lbs. b: Staffordshire, England, 5/3/1882. d: 4/5/1919.

Season	Club	League	GP	G	A	Pts	AG	AA	APts	PIM	GP	G	A	Pts	PIM
1902-03	Brandon Regals	MHL Sr.	6	8	0	8	....	....	....	....	....	....	....	....	....
1903-04	Winnipeg Rowing Club	MHL Sr.	6	6	0	6	....	....	....	....	3	1	0	1	....
1904-05	Brandon Hockey Club	MHL Sr.	8	11	0	11	....	....	....	....	....	....	....	....	....
1905-06	Portage Lakes	IHL	20	33	0	33	....	....	....	*98	....	....	....	....	....
	Quebec Bulldogs	ECAHA	3	2	0	2	....	....	....	3	....	....	....	....	....
1906-07	Brandon Regals	MHL Sr.	9	14	0	14	....	....	....	....	2	5	0	5	....
1907-08	Montreal Shamrocks	ECAHA	8	9	0	9	....	....	....	17	....	....	....	....	....
1908-09	Montreal Wanderers	ECHA	5	10	0	10	....	....	....	18	....	....	....	....	....
	Winnipeg Maple Leafs	MHL	2	2	0	2	....	....	....	....	....	....	....	....	....
1909-10	Montreal Shamrocks	NHA	10	8	0	8	....	....	....	47	....	....	....	....	....
	Montreal Shamrocks	CHA	1	7	0	7	....	....	....	6	....	....	....	....	....
1910-11	Quebec Bulldogs	NHA	10	0	0	0	....	....	....	20	....	....	....	....	....
1911-12	Quebec Bulldogs	NHA	18	15	0	15	....	....	....	30	2	2	0	2	2
1912-13	Quebec Bulldogs	NHA	17	8	0	8	....	....	....	78	2	3	0	3	0
1913-14	Quebec Bulldogs	NHA	19	13	4	17	....	....	....	61	....	....	....	....	....
1914-15	Quebec Bulldogs	NHA	20	3	2	5	....	....	....	52	....	....	....	....	....
1915-16	Quebec Bulldogs	NHA	23	1	2	3	....	....	....	89	....	....	....	....	....
1916-17	Quebec Bulldogs	NHA	19	6	6	12	....	....	....	74	....	....	....	....	....
1917-18	**Montreal Canadiens**	**NHL**	**21**	**8**	**7**	**15**	**20**	**0**	**20**	**100**	**2**	**0**	**1**	**1**	**13**
1918-19	**Montreal Canadiens**	**NHL**	**16**	**7**	**2**	**9**	**25**	**19**	**44**	***135**	**10**	**0**	**0**	**0**	**26**
	NHL Totals		**37**	**15**	**9**	**24**	**45**	**19**	**64**	**235**	**12**	**0**	**1**	**1**	**39**
	Other Major League Totals		171	118	14	132	....	....	....	573	6	10	0	10	2

IHL First All-Star Team (1906)

Claimed by **Montreal Canadiens** from **Quebec** in Dispersal Draft, November 26, 1917.

● HALL, MURRAY — *see page 1078*

● HALL, WAYNE Wayne Hall
LW – L. 5'9", 165 lbs. b: Melita, Man., 5/22/1939.

Season	Club	League	GP	G	A	Pts	AG	AA	APts	PIM	GP	G	A	Pts	PIM
			REGULAR SEASON								PLAYOFFS				
1957-58	Flin Flon Bombers	SJHL	38	8	19	27	....	....	....	20	2	0	1	1	2
1958-59	Flin Flon Bombers	SJHL	45	36	48	84	....	....	....	24	11	5	10	15	16
1959-60	Trois-Rivieres Lions	EPHL	64	9	29	38	....	....	....	16	7	0	1	1	0
1960-61	**New York Rangers**	**NHL**	**4**	**0**	**0**	**0**	**0**	**0**	**0**	**0**	....	....	....	....	....
	Kitchener Dutchmen	EPHL	56	9	27	36	....	....	....	14	7	0	1	1	5
1961-62	Vancouver Canucks	WHL	61	12	30	42	....	....	....	4	....	....	....	....	....
1962-63	Seattle Totems	WHL	53	10	14	24	....	....	....	8	17	1	8	9	0
1963-64	St. Paul Rangers	CHL	72	15	28	43	....	....	....	14	10	3	4	7	0
1964-65	Providence Reds	AHL	23	4	13	17	....	....	....	14	....	....	....	....	....
	St. Louis Braves	CHL	24	3	9	12	....	....	....	4	....	....	....	....	....
	St. Paul Rangers	CHL	....	....	....	....	....	....	....	....	1	1	0	1	0
1965-66	Minneosta Rangers	CHL	60	17	35	52	....	....	....	10	7	1	2	3	2
1966-67	Omaha Knights	CHL	58	12	29	41	....	....	....	20	....	....	....	....	....
1967-68	Omaha Knights	CHL	65	18	23	41	....	....	....	0	....	....	....	....	....
1968-69	Omaha Knights	CHL	1	0	0	0	....	....	....	0	....	....	....	....	....
	Buffalo Bisons	AHL	54	5	18	23	....	....	....	16	6	0	0	0	2
	NHL Totals		**4**	**0**	**0**	**0**	**0**	**0**	**0**	**0**	....	....	....	....	....

● HALLIDAY, MILT Milt Halliday
LW – L. 5'10", 180 lbs. b: Ottawa, Ont., 9/21/1906. d: 8/16/1989.

Season	Club	League	GP	G	A	Pts	AG	AA	APts	PIM	GP	G	A	Pts	PIM
1924-25	Ottawa Gunners	City Sr.	16	7	1	8	....	....	....	....	....	....	....	....	....
1925-26	Ottawa Gunners	City Sr.	....	10	2	12	....	....	....	....	6	*3	0	*3	....
1926-27	**Ottawa Senators**	**NHL**	**38**	**1**	**0**	**1**	**3**	**0**	**3**	**2**	**6**	**0**	**0**	**0**	**0**
1927-28	**Ottawa Senators**	**NHL**	**13**	**0**	**0**	**0**	**0**	**0**	**0**	**2**	....	....	....	....	....
	London Panthers	Can-Pro	29	8	1	9	....	....	....	6	....	....	....	....	....
1928-29	**Ottawa Senators**	**NHL**	**16**	**0**	**0**	**0**	**0**	**0**	**0**	**0**	....	....	....	....	....
	Niagara Falls Cataracts	Can-Pro	25	4	1	5	....	....	....	10	....	....	....	....	....
1929-30	Hamilton Tigers	IAHL	41	12	3	15	....	....	....	10	....	....	....	....	....
1930-31	Pittsburgh Yellowjackets	IAHL	44	11	2	13	....	....	....	14	6	0	0	0	2
1931-32	Pittsburgh–Cleveland	IAHL	45	15	4	19	....	....	....	14	....	....	....	....	....
1932-33	Cleveland Falcons	IAHL	42	14	8	22	....	....	....	10	....	....	....	....	....
1933-34	Boston Cubs	Can-Am	39	9	9	18	....	....	....	8	5	2	1	3	0
1934-35	Boston Cubs	Can-Am	13	2	4	6	....	....	....	2	3	0	0	0	0
	Cleveland Falcons	IAHL	31	12	7	19	....	....	....	10	....	....	....	....	....
1935-36	Cleveland–Rochester	IAHL	45	5	8	13	....	....	....	6	....	....	....	....	....
1936-37			REINSTATED AS AN AMATEUR												
1937-38	Ottawa Montagnards	City Sr.	18	12	2	14	....	....	....	0	....	....	....	....	....
1938-39	Ottawa Montagnards	City Sr.	3	0	0	0	....	....	....	2	....	....	....	....	....
	NHL Totals		**67**	**1**	**0**	**1**	**3**	**0**	**3**	**4**	**6**	**0**	**0**	**0**	**0**

Signed as a free agent by **Ottawa**, October 24, 1926. Traded to **Hamilton** (IAHL) by **Ottawa** for cash, November 7, 1929.

● HAMEL, HERB Herb "Hap" Hamel
RW – R. 5'11", 155 lbs. b: New Hamburg, Ont., 6/8/1904. Deceased.

Season	Club	League	GP	G	A	Pts	AG	AA	APts	PIM	GP	G	A	Pts	PIM
1925-26	New Hamburg Seniors	OHA Sr.	STATISTICS NOT AVAILABLE												
1926-27	Stratford–Niagara Falls	Can-Pro	31	6	2	8	....	....	....	6	....	....	....	....	....
1927-28	Hamilton Tigers	Can-Pro	1	0	0	0	....	....	....	0	....	....	....	....	....
1928-29	Hamilton Tigers	Can-Pro	38	10	2	12	....	....	....	27	....	....	....	....	....
1929-30	Brantford Indians	Can-Pro	28	13	7	20	....	....	....	37	....	....	....	....	....
1930-31	**Toronto Maple Leafs**	**NHL**	**2**	**0**	**0**	**0**	**0**	**0**	**0**	**4**	....	....	....	....	....
	Stratford–Oshawa	OPHL	27	14	11	25	....	....	....	14	7	3	3	6	0
	NHL Totals		**2**	**0**	**0**	**0**	**0**	**0**	**0**	**4**	....	....	....	....	....

Loaned to **Toronto** by **Stratford** (OPHL), December 9, 1930

● HAMILL, RED Red (Robert George) Hamill
LW – L. 5'11", 180 lbs. b: Toronto, Ont., 1/11/1917. d: 1985.

Season	Club	League	GP	G	A	Pts	AG	AA	APts	PIM	GP	G	A	Pts	PIM
1936-37	Copper Cliff Redmen	NOHA	3	*10	2	12	....	....	....	10	....	....	....	....	....
	Copper Cliff Redmen	City Sr.	12	10	2	12	....	....	....	17	....	....	....	....	....
1937-38	**Boston Bruins**	**NHL**	**6**	**0**	**1**	**1**	**0**	**2**	**2**	**2**	....	....	....	....	....
	Providence Reds	AHL	40	8	9	17	....	....	....	31	7	2	2	4	*12
1938-39	**Boston Bruins**	**NHL**	**6**	**0**	**1**	**1**	**0**	**2**	**2**	**0**	**12**	**0**	**0**	**0**	**8**
	Hershey Bears	AHL	45	12	12	24	....	....	....	29	5	0	0	0	0
1939-40	**Boston Bruins**	**NHL**	**30**	**10**	**8**	**18**	**21**	**16**	**37**	**16**	**5**	**0**	**1**	**1**	**5**
	Hershey Bears	AHL	22	9	10	19	....	....	....	20	....	....	....	....	....
1940-41	**Boston Bruins**	**NHL**	**8**	**0**	**1**	**1**	**0**	**2**	**2**	**0**	....	....	....	....	....
	Hershey Bears	AHL	36	13	17	30	....	....	....	20	9	3	3	6	11
1941-42	**Boston Bruins**	**NHL**	**9**	**6**	**3**	**9**	**10**	**5**	**15**	**2**	....	....	....	....	....
	Hershey Bears	AHL	10	6	8	14	....	....	....	2	....	....	....	....	....
	Chicago Black Hawks	**NHL**	**34**	**18**	**9**	**27**	**31**	**14**	**45**	**21**	**3**	**0**	**1**	**1**	**0**
1942-43	**Chicago Black Hawks**	**NHL**	**50**	**28**	**16**	**44**	**40**	**20**	**60**	**44**	....	....	....	....	....
1943-44	Kingston Frontenacs	OHA Sr.	14	10	16	26	....	....	....	*28	....	....	....	....	....
1944-45			MILITARY SERVICE												
1945-46	**Chicago Black Hawks**	**NHL**	**38**	**20**	**17**	**37**	**31**	**32**	**63**	**23**	**4**	**1**	**0**	**1**	**7**
1946-47	**Chicago Black Hawks**	**NHL**	**60**	**21**	**19**	**40**	**29**	**27**	**56**	**12**	....	....	....	....	....
1947-48	**Chicago Black Hawks**	**NHL**	**60**	**11**	**13**	**24**	**16**	**19**	**35**	**18**	....	....	....	....	....
1948-49	**Chicago Black Hawks**	**NHL**	**57**	**8**	**4**	**12**	**13**	**6**	**19**	**16**	....	....	....	....	....
1949-50	**Chicago Black Hawks**	**NHL**	**59**	**6**	**2**	**8**	**8**	**3**	**11**	**6**	....	....	....	....	....
1950-51	**Chicago Black Hawks**	**NHL**	**2**	**0**	**0**	**0**	**0**	**0**	**0**	**0**	....	....	....	....	....
	Milwaukee Seagulls	USHL	52	7	27	34	....	....	....	47	....	....	....	....	....
1951-52	Galt Black Hawks	OHA	DID NOT PLAY – COACHING												
	NHL Totals		**419**	**128**	**94**	**222**	**199**	**148**	**347**	**160**	**24**	**1**	**2**	**3**	**20**

Signed as a free agent by **Boston**, October 26, 1937. Traded to **Chicago** by **Boston** for cash, December, 1941.

● HAMILTON, AL — *see page 1080*

● HAMILTON, CHUCK — *see page 1080*

• HAMILTON, JACK
Jack Hamilton
C – L. 5'7", 170 lbs. b: Trenton, Ont., 6/2/1925. Deceased.

Season	Club	League	REGULAR SEASON GP	G	A	Pts	AG	AA	APts	PIM	PLAYOFFS GP	G	A	Pts	PIM
1939-40	Toronto Young Rangers	OHA	13	0	0	0	....	....	....	0	2	0	0	0	0
1940-41	Toronto Young Rangers	OHA	7	2	0	2	....	....	....	0	5	0	0	0	0
1941-42	Toronto Young Rangers	OHA	17	9	8	17	....	....	....	9	6	2	5	7	0
1942-43	**Toronto Maple Leafs**	**NHL**	**49**	**4**	**22**	**26**	**6**	**28**	**34**	**60**	**6**	**1**	**1**	**2**	**0**
1943-44	**Toronto Maple Leafs**	**NHL**	**49**	**20**	**17**	**37**	**25**	**21**	**46**	**4**	**5**	**1**	**0**	**1**	**0**
1944-45	Cornwallis Navy	City Sr.	13	10	8	18	....	....	....	6	3	2	3	5	0
1945-46	**Toronto Maple Leafs**	**NHL**	**40**	**7**	**9**	**16**	**11**	**17**	**28**	**12**	....	....	....	....	....
	Pittsburgh Hornets	AHL	8	5	3	8	....	....	....	12	....	....	....	....	....
1946-47	Pittsburgh Hornets	AHL	64	27	41	68	....	....	....	63	12	3	5	8	13
1947-48	Pittsburgh Hornets	AHL	67	21	29	50	....	....	....	52	2	0	0	0	5
1948-49	Providence Reds	AHL	59	26	54	80	....	....	....	32	14	3	6	9	6
1949-50	Providence Reds	AHL	55	19	35	54	....	....	....	20	4	2	2	4	0
1950-51	Providence–St. Louis	AHL	67	33	44	77	....	....	....	39	....	....	....	....	....
1951-52	St. Louis Flyers	AHL	67	27	50	77	....	....	....	34	....	....	....	....	....
1952-53	New Westminster Royals	WHL	45	12	19	31	....	....	....	52	7	1	2	3	2
	Shawinigan Cataracts	QSHL	17	3	7	10	....	....	....	31	....	....	....	....	....
1953-54	New Westminster Royals	WHL	63	15	31	46	....	....	....	54	7	2	3	5	8
1954-55	Kitchener Dutchmen	OHA Sr.	40	7	30	37	....	....	....	22	10	5	9	14	6
1955-56	Owen Sound Mercurys	OHA Sr.	48	18	35	53	....	....	....	27	6	0	3	3	0
1956-57	Owen Sound Mercurys	OHA Sr.	8	0	5	5	....	....	....	16	....	....	....	....	....
	Troy Bruins	IHL	15	3	4	7	....	....	....	18	....	....	....	....	....
1957-58	North Bay Trappers	NOHA	10	0	4	4	....	....	....	14	....	....	....	....	....
	NHL Totals		**138**	**31**	**48**	**79**	**42**	**66**	**108**	**76**	**11**	**2**	**1**	**3**	**0**

AHL Second All-Star Team (1952)

Traded to **Providence** (AHL) by **Toronto** with cash to complete transaction that sent the rights to Danny Lewicki to Toronto, June, 1948.

• HAMILTON, REG
Reg Hamilton
D – L. 5'11", 180 lbs. b: Toronto, Ont., 4/29/1914. d: 6/12/1991.

Season	Club	League	REGULAR SEASON GP	G	A	Pts	AG	AA	APts	PIM	PLAYOFFS GP	G	A	Pts	PIM
1930-31	Toronto Marlboros	OHA	8	2	1	3	....	....	....	8	2	0	0	0	4
1931-32	Toronto Marlboros	OHA	10	5	3	8	....	....	....	10	4	0	0	0	*18
1932-33	Toronto Marlboros	OHA	10	3	3	6	....	....	....	*45	3	0	0	0	*12
1933-34	St. Michael's Majors	OHA	5	2	1	3	....	....	....	12	3	0	2	2	12
1934-35	Syracuse Stars	IAHL	40	4	4	8	....	....	....	38	2	0	0	0	2
1935-36	**Toronto Maple Leafs**	**NHL**	**7**	**0**	**0**	**0**	**0**	**0**	**0**	**0**	....	....	....	....	....
	Syracuse Stars	IAHL	40	4	19	23	....	....	....	86	3	0	1	1	2
1936-37	**Toronto Maple Leafs**	**NHL**	**39**	**3**	**7**	**10**	**6**	**16**	**22**	**32**	**2**	**0**	**1**	**1**	**2**
	Syracuse Stars	AHL	8	0	3	3	....	....	....	12	....	....	....	....	....
1937-38	**Toronto Maple Leafs**	**NHL**	**45**	**1**	**4**	**5**	**2**	**8**	**10**	**43**	**7**	**0**	**1**	**1**	**2**
1938-39	**Toronto Maple Leafs**	**NHL**	**48**	**0**	**7**	**7**	**0**	**13**	**13**	**54**	**10**	**0**	**2**	**2**	**4**
1939-40	**Toronto Maple Leafs**	**NHL**	**23**	**2**	**2**	**4**	**4**	**4**	**8**	**23**	**10**	**0**	**0**	**0**	**0**
1940-41	**Toronto Maple Leafs**	**NHL**	**45**	**3**	**12**	**15**	**6**	**22**	**28**	**59**	**7**	**1**	**2**	**3**	**13**
1941-42	**Toronto Maple Leafs**	**NHL**	**22**	**0**	**4**	**4**	**0**	**6**	**6**	**27**	....	....	....	....	....
1942-43	**Toronto Maple Leafs**	**NHL**	**48**	**4**	**17**	**21**	**6**	**22**	**28**	**68**	**6**	**1**	**1**	**2**	**9**
1943-44	**Toronto Maple Leafs**	**NHL**	**39**	**4**	**12**	**16**	**5**	**14**	**19**	**32**	**5**	**1**	**0**	**1**	**8**
1944-45	**Toronto Maple Leafs**	**NHL**	**50**	**3**	**12**	**15**	**4**	**19**	**23**	**41**	**13**	**0**	**0**	**0**	**6**
1945-46	**Chicago Black Hawks**	**NHL**	**48**	**1**	**7**	**8**	**2**	**13**	**15**	**31**	**4**	**0**	**1**	**1**	**2**
1946-47	**Chicago Black Hawks**	**NHL**	**10**	**0**	**3**	**3**	**0**	**4**	**4**	**2**	....	....	....	....	....
	Kansas City Pla-Mors	USHL	26	0	10	10	....	....	....	30	10	0	3	3	0
1947-48	Kansas City Pla-Mors	USHL	14	0	2	2	....	....	....	6	....	....	....	....	....
1948-49	Kansas City Pla-Mors	USHL	DID NOT PLAY – COACHING												
	NHL Totals		**424**	**21**	**87**	**108**	**35**	**141**	**176**	**412**	**64**	**3**	**8**	**11**	**46**

Traded to **Chicago** by **Toronto** for cash and future considerations, July 9, 1945.

• HAMPSON, TED
— see page 1081

• HANNA, JOHN
— see page 1083

• HANNIGAN, GORD
Gord Hannigan
C – L. 5'8", 155 lbs. b: Schumacher, Ont., 1/19/1929. d: 11/16/1966.

Season	Club	League	REGULAR SEASON GP	G	A	Pts	AG	AA	APts	PIM	PLAYOFFS GP	G	A	Pts	PIM
1947-48	St. Michael's Majors	OHA	32	14	13	27	....	....	....	55	....	....	....	....	....
1948-49	St. Michael's Majors	OHA	32	21	13	34	....	....	....	59	....	....	....	....	....
1949-50	Toronto Marlboros	OHA Sr.	25	6	12	18	....	....	....	19	14	2	4	6	14
1950-51	St. Michael's Monarchs	OHA Sr.	30	19	20	39	....	....	....	26	19	13	12	25	10
1951-52	Pittsburgh Hornets	AHL	67	24	26	50	....	....	....	80	11	2	5	7	15
1952-53	**Toronto Maple Leafs**	**NHL**	**65**	**17**	**18**	**35**	**26**	**25**	**51**	**51**	....	....	....	....	....
1953-54	**Toronto Maple Leafs**	**NHL**	**35**	**4**	**4**	**8**	**6**	**5**	**11**	**18**	**5**	**2**	**0**	**2**	**4**
1954-55	**Toronto Maple Leafs**	**NHL**	**13**	**0**	**2**	**2**	**0**	**3**	**3**	**8**	....	....	....	....	....
	Pittsburgh Hornets	AHL	35	9	16	25	....	....	....	19	10	1	7	8	16
1955-56	**Toronto Maple Leafs**	**NHL**	**48**	**8**	**7**	**15**	**12**	**9**	**21**	**40**	**4**	**0**	**0**	**0**	**4**
	Pittsburgh Hornets	AHL	17	10	10	20	....	....	....	20	....	....	....	....	....
1956-57	Rochester Americans	AHL	64	21	40	61	....	....	....	111	10	2	4	6	*37
1957-58	Edmonton Flyers	WHL	25	6	8	14	....	....	....	15	....	....	....	....	....
	NHL Totals		**161**	**29**	**31**	**60**	**44**	**42**	**86**	**117**	**9**	**2**	**0**	**2**	**8**

• HANNIGAN, PAT
— see page 1084

• HANNIGAN, RAY
Ray Hannigan
RW – R. 5'8", 155 lbs. b: Schumacher, Ont., 7/14/1927.

Season	Club	League	REGULAR SEASON GP	G	A	Pts	AG	AA	APts	PIM	PLAYOFFS GP	G	A	Pts	PIM
1944-45	South Porcupine Juniors	NOHA	....	15	3	18	....	....	....	2	....	....	....	....	....
1945-46	St. Michael's Majors	OHA	2	1	0	1	....	....	....	0	....	....	....	....	....
1946-47	St. Michael's Majors	OHA	22	13	8	21	....	....	....	21	9	11	2	13	6
1947-48	Toronto Marlboros	OHA Sr.	35	27	21	48	....	....	....	26	5	2	0	2	10
1948-49	**Toronto Maple Leafs**	**NHL**	**3**	**0**	**0**	**0**	**0**	**0**	**0**	**2**	....	....	....	....	....
	Toronto Marlboros	OHA Sr.	38	24	21	45	....	....	....	24	22	16	11	27	26
1949-50	Pittsburgh Hornets	AHL	64	30	21	51	....	....	....	14	....	....	....	....	....
1950-51	Pittsburgh Hornets	AHL	65	24	17	41	....	....	....	31	13	9	6	15	20
1951-52	Pittsburgh Hornets	AHL	49	17	18	35	....	....	....	56	10	4	1	5	11
1952-53	Edmonton Flyers	WHL	64	22	19	41	....	....	....	53	15	7	6	13	6
1953-54	Edmonton Flyers	WHL	66	30	31	61	....	....	....	29	13	3	7	10	11
1954-55	Edmonton Flyers	WHL	56	21	16	37	....	....	....	27	....	....	....	....	....
1955-56	Edmonton Oil Kings	WCJHL	DID NOT PLAY – COACHING												
	NHL Totals		**3**	**0**	**0**	**0**	**0**	**0**	**0**	**2**	....	....	....	....	....

Traded to **Chicago** by **Toronto** with Cal Gardner, Gus Mortson and Al Rollins for Harry Lumley, September 11, 1952. Loaned to **Edmonton** (WHL) by **Chicago**, September, 1952. Traded to **Edmonton** (WHL) by **Chicago** for Bill Brennan, June, 1953.

• HANSON, EMIL
Emil Hanson
RW/D – L. 5'8", 165 lbs. b: Camrose, Alberta, 11/18/1908. d: 1955.

Season	Club	League	REGULAR SEASON GP	G	A	Pts	AG	AA	APts	PIM	PLAYOFFS GP	G	A	Pts	PIM
1927-28	Augsburg College	USAHA	STATISTICS NOT AVAILABLE												
1928-29	Tulsa Oilers	AHA	1	0	0	0	....	....	....	0	....	....	....	....	....
1929-30	Tulsa Oilers	AHA	34	6	1	7	....	....	....	23	9	0	0	0	6
1930-31	Tulsa Oilers	AHA	47	5	9	14	....	....	....	64	4	1	1	2	2
1931-32	Tulsa Oilers	AHA	48	9	12	21	....	....	....	39	....	....	....	....	....
1932-33	**Detroit Red Wings**	**NHL**	**7**	**0**	**0**	**0**	**0**	**0**	**0**	**6**	....	....	....	....	....
	Detroit Olympics	IAHL	30	5	4	9	....	....	....	17	....	....	....	....	....
1933-34	Kansas City Greyhounds	AHA	48	6	11	17	....	....	....	25	3	1	1	2	4
1934-35	St. Paul Saints	CHL	46	17	14	31	....	....	....	50	8	3	1	4	8
1935-36	St. Paul Saints	AHA	46	7	16	23	....	....	....	36	5	1	0	1	2
1936-37	St. Paul Saints	AHA	46	6	5	11	....	....	....	23	3	1	0	1	4
1937-38	Wichita Skyhawks	AHA	47	6	9	15	....	....	....	20	4	1	0	1	2
1938-39	St. Paul Saints	AHA	43	11	14	25	....	....	....	14	3	0	0	0	0
1939-40	St. Paul Saints	AHA	46	4	9	13	....	....	....	20	7	1	2	3	0
1940-41	Minneapolis Millers	AHA	26	0	2	2	....	....	....	16	3	0	1	1	0
1941-42	Minneapolis Millers	AHA	46	4	4	8	....	....	....	10	....	....	....	....	....
	NHL Totals		**7**	**0**	**0**	**0**	**0**	**0**	**0**	**6**	....	....	....	....	....

AHA First All-Star Team (1936)

NHL rights transferred to **Detroit** from **Chicago Shamrocks** (AHA) after AHA club owners purchased Detroit (NHL and IAHL) franchises, September 2, 1932.

• HANSON, OSCAR
Oscar "Ossie" Hanson
C – L. 5'10", 175 lbs. b: Camrose, Alberta, 12/27/1908.

Season	Club	League	REGULAR SEASON GP	G	A	Pts	AG	AA	APts	PIM	PLAYOFFS GP	G	A	Pts	PIM
1932-33	St. Paul Saints	CHL	37	*22	*17	*39	....	....	....	63	4	2	0	2	4
1933-34	Oklahoma City Warriors	AHA	42	16	6	22	....	....	....	50	....	....	....	....	....
1934-35	St. Paul Saints	CHL	47	*29	*30	*59	....	....	....	53	8	7	5	12	8
1935-36	St. Paul Saints	AHA	47	*30	*30	*60	....	....	....	....	5	2	1	3	11
1936-37	St. Louis Flyers	AHA	47	*33	*29	*62	....	....	....	25	6	4	3	7	14
1937-38	St. Louis Flyers	AHA	22	12	14	26	....	....	....	13	....	....	....	....	....
	Chicago Black Hawks	**NHL**	**8**	**0**	**0**	**0**	**0**	**0**	**0**	**0**	....	....	....	....	....
	Cleveland Barons	AHL	21	3	3	6	....	....	....	0	2	0	0	0	0
1938-39	Minneapolis Millers	AHA	48	*37	*52	*89	....	....	....	38	4	4	0	4	6
1939-40	Minneapolis Millers	AHA	47	32	22	54	....	....	....	27	3	0	1	1	0
1940-41	Minneapolis Millers	AHA	37	12	12	24	....	....	....	20	3	0	0	0	0
1941-42	Minneapolis Millers	AHA	47	24	20	44	....	....	....	24	....	....	....	....	....
	NHL Totals		**8**	**0**	**0**	**0**	**0**	**0**	**0**	**0**	....	....	....	....	....

AHA First All-Star Team (1936, 1937, 1940)

Traded to **Chicago** by **St. Louis** (AHA) for cash, January 27, 1937. Traded to **Cleveland** (AHL) by **St. Louis** (AHA) for Walt Brenneman, January 25, 1938.

• HARMON, GLEN
Glen Harmon
D – L. 5'9", 165 lbs. b: Holland, Man., 1/2/1921.

Season	Club	League	REGULAR SEASON GP	G	A	Pts	AG	AA	APts	PIM	PLAYOFFS GP	G	A	Pts	PIM
1938-39	Brandon Elks	MJHL	17	2	5	7	....	....	....	47	13	3	3	6	28
1939-40	Brandon Elks	MJHL	23	4	10	14	....	....	....	67	3	1	0	1	0
1940-41	Winnipeg Rangers	MJHL	17	5	5	10	....	....	....	42	20	8	6	14	34
1941-42	Montreal Sr. Canadiens	QSHL	39	8	8	16	....	....	....	40	6	0	1	1	6
1942-43	**Montreal Canadiens**	**NHL**	**27**	**5**	**9**	**14**	**7**	**11**	**18**	**25**	**5**	**0**	**1**	**1**	**2**
	Montreal Sr. Canadiens	QSHL	20	5	8	13	....	....	....	35	....	....	....	....	....
1943-44	**Montreal Canadiens**	**NHL**	**43**	**5**	**16**	**21**	**6**	**19**	**25**	**36**	**9**	**1**	**2**	**3**	**4**
1944-45	**Montreal Canadiens**	**NHL**	**42**	**5**	**8**	**13**	**7**	**13**	**20**	**41**	**6**	**1**	**0**	**1**	**2**
1945-46	**Montreal Canadiens**	**NHL**	**49**	**7**	**10**	**17**	**11**	**19**	**30**	**28**	**9**	**1**	**4**	**5**	**0**
1946-47	**Montreal Canadiens**	**NHL**	**57**	**5**	**9**	**14**	**7**	**13**	**20**	**53**	**11**	**1**	**1**	**2**	**4**
1947-48	**Montreal Canadiens**	**NHL**	**56**	**10**	**4**	**14**	**15**	**6**	**21**	**52**	....	....	....	....	....
1948-49	**Montreal Canadiens**	**NHL**	**59**	**8**	**12**	**20**	**13**	**19**	**32**	**44**	**7**	**1**	**1**	**2**	**4**
1949-50	**Montreal Canadiens**	**NHL**	**62**	**3**	**16**	**19**	**4**	**20**	**24**	**28**	**5**	**0**	**1**	**1**	**21**
1950-51	**Montreal Canadiens**	**NHL**	**57**	**2**	**12**	**14**	**3**	**15**	**18**	**27**	**1**	**0**	**0**	**0**	**0**
1951-52	Montreal Royals	QSHL	55	5	20	25	....	....	....	33	5	3	4	7	2
1952-53	Montreal Royals	QSHL	58	5	17	22	....	....	....	26	16	5	4	9	4
1953-54	Montreal Royals	QHL	65	8	22	30	....	....	....	31	8	0	2	2	2
1954-55	Montreal Royals	QHL	62	5	22	27	....	....	....	64	14	2	5	7	6
	NHL Totals		**452**	**50**	**96**	**146**	**73**	**135**	**208**	**334**	**53**	**5**	**10**	**15**	**37**

NHL Second All-Star Team (1945, 1949)

Played in NHL All-Star Game (1949, 1950)

Claimed by **Montreal** from **Tulsa** (AHA) in Inter-League Draft, June, 27. 1941.

• HARMS, JOHN
John Harms
RW – R. 5'8", 160 lbs. b: Saskatoon, Sask., 4/25/1925.

Season	Club	League	REGULAR SEASON GP	G	A	Pts	AG	AA	APts	PIM	PLAYOFFS GP	G	A	Pts	PIM
1942-43	Saskatoon Quakers	SJHL	8	4	3	7	....	....	....	*28	3	2	*3	5	6
1943-44	**Chicago Black Hawks**	**NHL**	**1**	**0**	**0**	**0**	**0**	**0**	**0**	**0**	**4**	**3**	**0**	**3**	**2**
	Hershey Bears	AHL	52	10	10	20	....	....	....	35	7	2	1	3	6
1944-45	**Chicago Black Hawks**	**NHL**	**43**	**5**	**5**	**10**	**7**	**8**	**15**	**21**	....	....	....	....	....
	Providence Reds	AHL	3	0	4	4	....	....	....	0	....	....	....	....	....
1945-46	Kansas City Pla-Mors	USHL	45	26	25	51	....	....	....	73	12	2	2	4	14
1946-47	Kansas City Pla-Mors	USHL	60	21	34	55	....	....	....	80	12	3	9	12	9
1947-48	Kansas City Pla-Mors	USHL	66	29	40	69	....	....	....	56	7	2	6	8	0
1948-49	Kansas City Pla-Mors	USHL	57	19	48	67	....	....	....	64	2	0	0	0	0
1949-50	Kansas City Pla-Mors	USHL	64	15	27	42	....	....	....	38	3	2	0	2	2
1950-51	Regina Caps	SSHL	21	0	7	7	....	....	....	12	....	....	....	....	....
	Nelson Maple Leafs	WIHL	25	8	12	20	....	....	....	99	4	1	2	3	12
1951-52	Nelson Maple Leafs	WIHL	37	14	30	44	....	....	....	80	3	2	2	4	5
	Vernon Canadians	OSHL	1	0	0	0	....	....	....	0	....	....	....	....	....
1952-53	Vernon Canadians	OSHL	52	30	37	67	....	....	....	110	5	2	2	4	20
1953-54	Vernon Canadians	OSHL	55	27	23	50	....	....	....	113	5	1	3	4	4
1954-55	Vernon Canadians	OSHL	53	17	23	40	....	....	....	52	5	2	4	6	2
1955-56	Vernon Canadians	OSHL	39	16	25	41	....	....	....	58	....	....	....	....	....
1956-57	Vernon Canadians	OSHL	49	20	38	58	....	....	....	87	12	3	6	9	*26
1957-58	Vernon Canadians	OSHL	37	9	11	20	....	....	....	62	8	0	4	4	16
1958-59			DID NOT PLAY												
1959-60	Vernon Canadians	OSHL	41	7	28	35	....	....	....	136	12	2	7	9	22
1960-61	Vernon Canadians	OSHL	39	9	34	43	....	....	....	*131	....	....	....	....	....
	NHL Totals		**44**	**5**	**5**	**10**	**7**	**8**	**15**	**21**	**4**	**3**	**0**	**3**	**2**

USHL Second All-Star Team (1948)

• HARNOTT, WALTER
Walter "Happy" Harnott
LW – L. 5'10", 175 lbs. b: Montreal, Que., 9/24/1909. Deceased.

			REGULAR SEASON								PLAYOFFS				
Season	Club	League	GP	G	A	Pts	AG	AA	APts	PIM	GP	G	A	Pts	PIM
1928-29	Montreal Bell Telephone	City Sr.	2	1	1	2	....	....	....	2	....	....	....	....	....
1929-30	Montreal Columbus	City Sr.	10	2	0	2	....	....	....	2	....	....	....	....	....
1930-31	Montreal Columbus	City Sr.	9	3	0	3	....	....	....	6	2	0	0	0	6
1931-32	Boston Cubs	Can-Am	18	2	1	3	....	....	....	6	5	1	0	1	6
	Montreal AAA	City Sr.	8	4	1	5	....	....	....	12	....	....	....	....	....
1932-33	Boston Cubs	Can-Am	23	4	1	5	....	....	....	10	....	....	....	....	....
1933-34	**Boston Bruins**	**NHL**	**6**	**0**	**0**	**0**	**0**	**0**	**0**	**2**	....	....	....	....	....
	Boston Cubs	Can-Am	38	10	5	0	....	....	....	16	3	0	1	1	0
1934-35	Boston Cubs	Can-Am	40	11	15	0	....	....	....	20	3	1	0	1	0
	Syracuse Stars	IAHL	5	0	1	1	....	....	....	0	....	....	....	....	....
1935-36	Boston Cubs	Can-Am	22	3	4	7	....	....	....	14	....	....	....	....	....
	Calgary Tigers	NWHL	14	4	3	7	....	....	....	0	....	....	....	....	....
1936-37	St. Louis Flyers	AHA	7	1	0	1	....	....	....	2	....	....	....	....	....
1937-38	St. Paul Saints	AHA	34	12	15	27	....	....	....	4	....	....	....	....	....
	St. Louis Flyers	AHA	8	0	1	1	....	....	....	0	....	....	....	....	....
1938-39	St. Louis Flyers	AHA	47	16	25	41	....	....	....	31	7	3	4	7	2
1939-40	St. Louis Flyers	AHA	48	24	29	53	....	....	....	18	5	1	2	3	5
	Omaha Knights	AHA	....	....	....	....	....	....	....	....	3	1	1	2	0
1940-41	St. Louis Flyers	AHA	48	13	24	37	....	....	....	10	9	0	3	3	2
1941-42	St. Louis Flyers	AHA	42	7	10	17	....	....	....	8	3	0	0	0	2
1942-43	Montreal Royals	QSHL	9	0	2	2	....	....	....	2	....	....	....	....	....
	Montreal RCAF	City Sr.	7	2	3	5	....	....	....	2	2	4	1	5	2
1943-44	Montreal RCAF	City Sr.	4	0	0	0	....	....	....	0	2	0	0	0	0
1944-45	Montreal RCAF	City Sr.	12	6	*18	24	....	....	....	0	6	1	3	4	6
	Valleyfield Barves	QPHL	....	....	....	....	....	....	....	....	1	0	0	0	0
	NHL Totals		**6**	**0**	**0**	**0**	**0**	**0**	**0**	**2**	....	....	....	....	....

AHA Second All-Star Team (1940)

• **HARPER, TERRY** — *see page 1087*

• HARRINGTON, LELAND
Leland "Hago" Harrington
LW – L. 5'8", 163 lbs. b: Melrose, MA, 8/13/1904. d: 1959.

			REGULAR SEASON								PLAYOFFS				
Season	Club	League	GP	G	A	Pts	AG	AA	APts	PIM	GP	G	A	Pts	PIM
1923-24	Boston AA Unicorns	USAHA	12	9	0	9	....	....	....	....	5	2	0	2	....
1924-25	Boston AAA	USAHA	18	14	0	14	....	....	....	....	4	1	0	1	....
1925-26	**Boston Bruins**	**NHL**	**26**	**7**	**2**	**9**	**22**	**23**	**45**	**6**	....	....	....	....	....
1926-27	New Haven Eagles	Can-Am	32	21	4	25	....	....	....	36	4	2	1	3	0
1927-28	**Boston Bruins**	**NHL**	**22**	**1**	**0**	**1**	**3**	**0**	**3**	**7**	**2**	**0**	**0**	**0**	**0**
	New Haven Eagles	Can-Am	16	13	5	18	....	....	....	22	....	....	....	....	....
1928-29	Providence Reds	Can-Am	31	5	3	8	....	....	....	44	6	3	0	3	14
1929-30	Providence Reds	Can-Am	37	11	6	17	....	....	....	51	3	1	1	2	2
1930-31	Providence Reds	Can-Am	39	8	16	24	....	....	....	41	2	1	0	1	2
1931-32	Providence Reds	Can-Am	39	15	*20	35	....	....	....	44	5	3	1	4	0
1932-33	Providence Reds	Can-Am	22	11	12	23	....	....	....	20	....	....	....	....	....
	Montreal Canadiens	**NHL**	**24**	**1**	**1**	**2**	**2**	**3**	**5**	**2**	**2**	**1**	**0**	**1**	**2**
1933-34	Providence Reds	Can-Am	40	13	19	32	....	....	....	26	3	0	2	2	0
1934-35	Providence Reds	Can-Am	46	17	32	49	....	....	....	32	6	0	1	1	8
1935-36	Providence Reds	Can-Am	45	12	3	15	....	....	....	22	7	0	0	0	8
	NHL Totals		**72**	**9**	**3**	**12**	**27**	**26**	**53**	**15**	**4**	**1**	**0**	**1**	**2**

Traded to **Providence** (Can-Am) by **Boston** for cash, October, 1928. Traded to **Montreal Canadiens** by **Providence** (Can-Am) with Leo Murray for Leo Gaudreault and Armond Mondou, January, 1933.

• **HARRIS, BILLY** — *see page 1088*

• HARRIS, HENRY
Henry Harris
RW – L. 5'11", 185 lbs. b: Kenora, Ontario, 4/28/1906. Deceased.

			REGULAR SEASON								PLAYOFFS				
Season	Club	League	GP	G	A	Pts	AG	AA	APts	PIM	GP	G	A	Pts	PIM
1927-28	Regina Capitals	PrHL	23	2	2	4	....	....	....	12	....	....	....	....	....
1928-29	Seattle Eskimos	PCHL	36	8	3	11	....	....	....	*138	5	1	0	1	10
1929-30	Seattle Eskimos	PCHL	34	11	3	14	....	....	....	128	....	....	....	....	....
1930-31	**Boston Bruins**	**NHL**	**32**	**2**	**4**	**6**	**5**	**14**	**19**	**20**	....	....	....	....	....
	Boston Tigers	Can-Am	12	2	3	5	....	....	....	32	9	1	2	3	30
1931-32	Buffalo Majors	AHA	15	0	4	4	....	....	....	32	....	....	....	....	....
1932-33	Calgary Tigers	WCHL	30	6	6	12	....	....	....	65	6	0	2	2	9
1933-34	Calgary Tigers	NWHL	34	9	10	19	....	....	....	46	5	3	0	3	2
1934-35	Calgary Tigers	NWHL	22	5	5	10	....	....	....	22	....	....	....	....	....
	NHL Totals		**32**	**2**	**4**	**6**	**5**	**14**	**19**	**20**	....	....	....	....	....

Traded to **Boston** by **Seattle** for cash, February 4, 1930.

• **HARRIS, RON** — *see page 1089*

• **HARRIS, TED** — *see page 1089*

• HARRIS, THOMAS
Thomas "Smokey" Harris
LW – L. 5'11", 165 lbs. b: Port Arthur, Ontario, 10/11/1890. d: 6/4/1974.

			REGULAR SEASON								PLAYOFFS				
Season	Club	League	GP	G	A	Pts	AG	AA	APts	PIM	GP	G	A	Pts	PIM
1911-12	Vancouver Millionaires	PCHA	15	4	0	4	....	....	....	55	....	....	....	....	....
1912-13	Vancouver Millionaires	PCHA	16	14	6	20	....	....	....	61	....	....	....	....	....
1913-14	Vancouver Millionaires	PCHA	15	14	3	17	....	....	....	33	....	....	....	....	....
1914-15	Portland Rosebuds	PCHA	18	14	3	17	....	....	....	39	....	....	....	....	....
1915-16	Portland Rosebuds	PCHA	18	10	6	16	....	....	....	*75	4	*4	0	*4	*21
1916-17	Portland Rosebuds	PCHA	23	18	13	31	....	....	....	39	....	....	....	....	....
1917-18	Portland Rosebuds	PCHA	8	5	6	11	....	....	....	19	....	....	....	....	....
1918-19	Vancouver Millionaires	PCHA	20	19	6	25	....	....	....	0	2	2	0	2	3
1919-20	Vancouver Millionaires	PCHA	22	14	11	25	....	....	....	12	2	0	1	1	0
1920-21	Vancouver Millionaires	PCHA	24	15	*17	*32	....	....	....	6	7	*8	3	*11	12
1921-22	Vancouver Millionaires	PCHA	23	10	4	14	....	....	....	21	....	....	....	....	....
1922-23	Vancouver Maroons	PCHA	20	10	6	16	....	....	....	26	6	1	0	1	8
1923-24	Seattle Metropolitans	PCHA	30	8	*10	18	....	....	....	30	2	0	0	0	*8
1924-25	**Boston Bruins**	**NHL**	**6**	**3**	**1**	**4**	**10**	**13**	**23**	**8**	....	....	....	....	....
	Vancouver Maroons	WCHL	14	0	1	1	....	....	....	16	....	....	....	....	....
1925-26	Richfield Oil	Cal-Pro	....	6	3	9	....	....	....	24	....	....	....	....	....
1926-27	Edmonton Eskimos	PrHL	32	12	12	24	....	....	....	68	....	....	....	....	....
1927-28	Richfield Oil	Cal-Pro	STATISTICS NOT AVAILABLE												
1928-29	San Francisco Tigers	Cal-Pro	....	13	13	26	....	....	....	43	....	....	....	....	....
1929-30	Hollywood Millionaires	Cal-Pro	....	7	12	19	....	....	....	28	....	....	....	....	....
1930-31	San Francisco Hawks	Cal-Pro	....	8	10	18	....	....	....	....	....	....	....	....	....
1931-32	San Francisco Hawks	Cal-Pro	....	3	8	11	....	....	....	....	....	....	....	....	....
	NHL Totals		**6**	**3**	**1**	**4**	**10**	**13**	**23**	**8**	....	....	....	....	....
	Other Major League Totals		266	155	92	247	....	....	....	432	23	15	4	19	52

Traded to **Portland** (PCHA) by **Vancouver** (PCHA) for Ken Mallen, 1914. Transferred to **Vancouver** (PCHA) after **Portland** (PCHA) franchise folded, November 29, 1918. Traded to **Seattle** (PCHA) by **Vancouver** (PCHA) for cash, October 30, 1923. Traded to **Boston** by **Seattle** (PCHA) for cash, November 2, 1924. Traded to **Vancouver** (WCHL) by **Boston** for cash, December 21, 1924.

• HARRISON, ED
Ed Harrison
C/LW – L. 6', 165 lbs. b: Mimico, Ont., 7/25/1927.

			REGULAR SEASON								PLAYOFFS				
Season	Club	League	GP	G	A	Pts	AG	AA	APts	PIM	GP	G	A	Pts	PIM
1944-45	St. Michael's Majors	OHA	1	1	0	1	....	....	....	0	....	....	....	....	....
1945-46	St. Michael's Majors	OHA	22	16	14	30	....	....	....	8	11	11	8	19	4
1946-47	St. Michael's Majors	OHA	29	29	25	54	....	....	....	33	9	11	7	18	14
1947-48	**Boston Bruins**	**NHL**	**52**	**6**	**7**	**13**	**9**	**10**	**19**	**8**	**5**	**1**	**0**	**1**	**2**
1948-49	**Boston Bruins**	**NHL**	**59**	**5**	**5**	**10**	**8**	**8**	**16**	**20**	**4**	**0**	**0**	**0**	**0**
1949-50	**Boston Bruins**	**NHL**	**70**	**14**	**12**	**26**	**19**	**15**	**34**	**23**	....	....	....	....	....
1950-51	**Boston Bruins**	**NHL**	**9**	**1**	**0**	**1**	**1**	**0**	**1**	**0**	....	....	....	....	....
	New York Rangers	**NHL**	**4**	**1**	**0**	**1**	**1**	**0**	**1**	**2**	....	....	....	....	....
	Hershey Bears	AHL	48	24	14	38	....	....	....	23	6	1	6	7	0
1951-52	Cincinnati Mohawks	AHL	57	20	9	29	....	....	....	19	7	3	2	5	0
1952-53	Vancouver Canucks	WHL	5	0	1	1	....	....	....	0	....	....	....	....	....
	Syracuse Warriors	AHL	12	2	2	4	....	....	....	2	....	....	....	....	....
	Washington Lions	EHL	17	5	10	15	....	....	....	4	....	....	....	....	....
	Quebec Aces	QSHL	16	6	2	8	....	....	....	6	22	6	9	15	13
1953-54	Quebec Aces	QHL	33	3	2	5	....	....	....	4	....	....	....	....	....
	Sudbury Wolves	NOHA	13	8	3	11	....	....	....	0	11	5	3	8	2
1954-1960			DID NOT PLAY												
1960-61	Woodstock Athletics	OHA Sr.	....	12	11	2	....	....	....	2	....	....	....	....	....
1961-62	Woodstock Athletics	OHA Sr.	28	9	17	26	....	....	....	0	12	1	1	2	0
	NHL Totals		**194**	**27**	**24**	**51**	**38**	**33**	**71**	**53**	**9**	**1**	**0**	**1**	**2**

Traded to **NY Rangers** by **Boston** with Zellio Toppazzini for Dunc Fisher, November 16, 1950.

• HART, WILF
Wilf "Gizzy" Hart
LW – L. 5'9", 171 lbs. b: Weyburn, Sask., 6/1/1902. d: 6/22/1964.

			REGULAR SEASON								PLAYOFFS				
Season	Club	League	GP	G	A	Pts	AG	AA	APts	PIM	GP	G	A	Pts	PIM
1919-20	Weyburn Wanderers	SSHL	10	12	0	12	....	....	....	0	....	....	....	....	....
1920-21	Weyburn Wanderers	SSHL	11	2	2	4	....	....	....	0	....	....	....	....	....
1921-22	Moose Jaw Maple Leafs	SSHL	7	3	0	3	....	....	....	2	....	....	....	....	....
1922-23	Weyburn Wanderers	SSHL	10	17	6	23	....	....	....	4	5	*6	*2	*8	2
1923-24	Victoria Cougars	PCHA	29	15	1	16	....	....	....	10	....	....	....	....	....
1924-25	Victoria Cougars	WCHL	26	8	6	14	....	....	....	8	....	4	1	5	0
1925-26	Victoria Cougars	WHL	27	6	4	10	....	....	....	2	....	0	0	0	4
1926-27	**Detroit Cougars**	**NHL**	**2**	**0**	**0**	**0**	**0**	**0**	**0**	**0**	....	....	....	....	....
	Montreal Canadiens	**NHL**	**40**	**3**	**3**	**6**	**9**	**25**	**34**	**8**	**4**	**0**	**0**	**0**	**0**
	Windsor Hornets	Can-Pro	5	4	1	5	....	....	....	6	....	....	....	....	....
1927-28	**Montreal Canadiens**	**NHL**	**44**	**3**	**2**	**5**	**9**	**17**	**26**	**4**	**2**	**0**	**0**	**0**	**0**
1928-29	Providence Reds	Can-Am	38	13	1	14	....	....	....	14	....	....	....	....	....
1929-30	Providence Reds	Can-Am	39	24	12	36	....	....	....	28	3	2	3	5	0
1930-31	Providence Reds	Can-Am	37	25	13	38	....	....	....	16	2	1	1	2	0
1931-32	Providence Reds	Can-Am	40	21	17	38	....	....	....	29	5	2	*2	4	6
1932-33	**Montreal Canadiens**	**NHL**	**18**	**0**	**3**	**3**	**0**	**8**	**8**	**0**	**2**	**0**	**1**	**1**	**0**
	Providence Reds	Can-Am	46	7	9	16	....	....	....	60	....	....	....	....	....
1933-34	Providence Reds	Can-Am	40	13	9	22	....	....	....	12	3	0	*4	4	7
1934-35	Weyburn Beavers	SSHL	DID NOT PLAY – COACHING												
	NHL Totals		**104**	**6**	**8**	**14**	**18**	**50**	**68**	**12**	**8**	**0**	**1**	**1**	**0**
	Other Major League Totals		82	29	11	40	....	....	....	20	....	....	....	....	....

PCHA All Star Team (1924)

Signed as a free agent by **Victoria** (WCHL), October 24, 1923. Transferred to **Detroit Cougars** after NHL club purchased **Victoria** (WHL) franchise, May 15, 1926. Traded to **Montreal** by **Detroit Cougars** for cash, December 16, 1926.

• **HARVEY, DOUG** — *see page 1091*

• HASSARD, BOB Bob Hassard
C – R. 6', 167 lbs. b: Lloydminster, Sask., 3/26/1929.

Season	Club	League	GP	G	A	Pts	AG	AA	APts	PIM	GP	G	A	Pts	PIM
1945-46	Toronto Marlboros	OHA	23	4	8	12	....	....	....	6	4	2	3	5	0
1946-47	Toronto Marlboros	OHA	17	9	16	25	....	....	....	7	2	1	1	2	0
1947-48	Toronto Marlboros	OHA	31	19	16	35	....	....	....	18	....	....	....	....	....
	Toronto Marlboros	OHA Sr.	4	3	0	3	....	....	....	0	5	1	1	2	2
1948-49	Toronto Marlboros	OHA	35	33	36	69	....	....	....	28	1	1	0	1	0
	Toronto Marlboros	OHA Sr.	1	0	1	1	....	....	....	0	....	....	....	....	....
1949-50	**Toronto Maple Leafs**	**NHL**	**1**	**0**	**0**	**0**	**0**	**0**	**0**	**0**	....	....	....	....	....
	Toronto Marlboros	OHA Sr.	41	12	21	33	....	....	....	22	14	3	*10	13	4
1950-51	**Toronto Maple Leafs**	**NHL**	**12**	**0**	**1**	**1**	**0**	**1**	**1**	**0**	....	....	....	....	....
	Toronto Marlboros	OHA Sr.	28	19	17	36	....	....	....	12	....	....	....	....	....
1951-52	Pittsburgh Hornets	AHL	67	18	46	64	....	....	....	36	11	5	5	10	10
1952-53	**Toronto Maple Leafs**	**NHL**	**70**	**8**	**23**	**31**	**12**	**32**	**44**	**14**	....	....	....	....	....
1953-54	**Toronto Maple Leafs**	**NHL**	**26**	**1**	**4**	**5**	**2**	**5**	**7**	**4**	....	....	....	....	....
	Pittsburgh Hornets	AHL	46	15	24	39	....	....	....	44	5	3	1	4	8
1954-55	**Chicago Black Hawks**	**NHL**	**17**	**0**	**0**	**0**	**0**	**0**	**0**	**4**	....	....	....	....	....
	Pittsburgh Hornets	AHL	39	9	16	25	....	....	....	38	10	7	1	8	8
1955-56	Pittsburgh Hornets	AHL	64	22	48	70	....	....	....	47	4	1	3	4	4
1956-57	Hershey–Buffalo	AHL	61	12	19	31	....	....	....	20	....	....	....	....	....
1957-58	Buffalo Bisons	AHL	70	14	31	45	....	....	....	13	....	....	....	....	....
1958-59	Whitby Dunlops	EOHL	23	11	23	24	....	....	....	6	10	6	5	11	4
1959-60	Whitby Dunlops	OHA Sr.	43	15	23	38	....	....	....	16	11	2	4	6	2
	NHL Totals		**126**	**9**	**28**	**37**	**14**	**38**	**52**	**22**	....	....	....	....	....

Traded to **Chicago** by **Toronto** for cash, September 10, 1954.

• HAWORTH, GORD Gord "Red" Haworth
C – L. 5'10", 165 lbs. b: Drummondville, Que., 2/20/1932.

Season	Club	League	GP	G	A	Pts	AG	AA	APts	PIM	GP	G	A	Pts	PIM
1948-49	Victoriaville Tigers	QJHL	46	9	13	22	....	....	....	36	4	0	1	1	6
	Atlantic City Seagulls	EHL	7	0	1	1	....	....	....	2	....	....	....	....	....
1950-51	Quebec Citadelles	QJHL	46	27	30	57	....	....	....	43	23	10	8	18	22
1951-52	Quebec Citadelles	QJHL	46	31	51	82	....	....	....	49	15	7	6	13	18
1952-53	**New York Rangers**	**NHL**	**2**	**0**	**1**	**1**	**0**	**1**	**1**	**0**	....	....	....	....	....
	Valleyfield Braves	QSHL	53	9	21	30	....	....	....	26	4	0	1	1	2
1953-54	Valleyfield Braves	QHL	69	24	28	52	....	....	....	64	6	1	0	1	0
1954-55	Valleyfield Braves	QHL	60	16	32	48	....	....	....	33	....	....	....	....	....
1955-56	Springfield Indians	AHL	30	3	13	16	....	....	....	30	....	....	....	....	....
	Trois-Rivieres Lions	QHL	16	4	6	10	....	....	....	8	....	....	....	....	....
1956-57	Victoria Cougars	WHL	64	17	35	52	....	....	....	26	3	0	0	0	0
1957-58	Victoria Cougars	WHL	67	23	37	60	....	....	....	18	....	....	....	....	....
1958-59	Victoria Cougars	WHL	65	21	52	73	....	....	....	32	3	2	0	2	0
1959-60	Victoria Cougars	WHL	70	27	33	60	....	....	....	24	11	3	7	10	4
1960-61	Portland Buckaroos	WHL	68	18	47	65	....	....	....	24	14	3	3	6	0
1961-62	Sudbury Wolves	EPHL	63	14	41	55	....	....	....	32	5	2	1	3	4
1962-63	Los Angeles Blades	WHL	69	11	40	51	....	....	....	16	3	2	3	5	2
1963-64	Los Angeles Blades	WHL	68	17	36	53	....	....	....	24	12	2	7	9	4
1964-65	Los Angeles Blades	WHL	47	7	18	25	....	....	....	15	....	....	....	....	....
1965-66	Drummondville Eagles	QSHL	41	13	29	42	....	....	....	24	....	....	....	....	....
1966-67	Drummondville Eagles	QSHL	41	13	28	41	....	....	....	26	....	....	....	....	....
1967-68	Drummondville Eagles	QSHL	DID NOT PLAY – COACHING												
1968-69	Drummondville Eagles	QSHL	43	14	28	42	....	....	....	21	....	....	....	....	....
1969-70	Jacksonville Rockets	EHL	70	16	56	72	....	....	....	6	4	0	1	1	2
1970-71	Drummondville Rangers	QJHL	DID NOT PLAY – COACHING												
	NHL Totals		**2**	**0**	**1**	**1**	**0**	**1**	**1**	**0**	....	....	....	....	....

Traded to **Springfield** (AHL) by **Valleyfield** (QHL) for cash, September, 1955. Traded to **Victoria** (WHL) by **NY Rangers** for cash, September, 1956. Traded to **Detroit** by **Portland** (WHL) for Gene Achtymichuk, August, 1961. Traded to **LA Blades** (WHL) by **Detroit** for cash, July, 1962.

• HAY, BILL Bill "Red" Hay
C – L. 6'3", 190 lbs. b: Lumsden, Sask., 12/9/1935.

Season	Club	League	GP	G	A	Pts	AG	AA	APts	PIM	GP	G	A	Pts	PIM
1952-53	Regina Pats	WCJHL	29	14	17	31	....	....	....	22	7	0	2	2	0
1953-54	U. of Saskatchewan	WCIAA	5	4	1	5	....	....	....	4	....	....	....	....	....
1954-55	Regina Pats	WCJHL	33	16	31	47	....	....	....	68	14	8	2	10	6
1955-56	Colorado College	WIHA	DID NOT PLAY – FRESHMAN												
1956-57	Colorado College	WIHA	....	26	42	68	....	....	....	....	....	....	....	....	....
1957-58	Colorado College	WIHA	....	16	32	*48	....	....	....	23	....	....	....	....	....
1958-59	Calgary Stampeders	WHL	53	24	30	54	....	....	....	27	8	3	5	8	6
1959-60	**Chicago Black Hawks**	**NHL**	**70**	**18**	**37**	**55**	**22**	**38**	**60**	**31**	**4**	**1**	**2**	**3**	**2**
1960-61	**Chicago Black Hawks**	**NHL**	**69**	**11**	**48**	**59**	**13**	**49**	**62**	**45**	**12**	**2**	**5**	**7**	**20**
1961-62	**Chicago Black Hawks**	**NHL**	**60**	**11**	**52**	**63**	**13**	**53**	**66**	**34**	**12**	**3**	**7**	**10**	**18**
1962-63	**Chicago Black Hawks**	**NHL**	**64**	**12**	**33**	**45**	**15**	**35**	**50**	**36**	**6**	**3**	**2**	**5**	**6**
1963-64	**Chicago Black Hawks**	**NHL**	**70**	**23**	**33**	**56**	**31**	**37**	**68**	**30**	**7**	**3**	**1**	**4**	**4**
1964-65	**Chicago Black Hawks**	**NHL**	**69**	**11**	**26**	**37**	**14**	**28**	**42**	**36**	**14**	**3**	**1**	**4**	**4**
1965-66	**Chicago Black Hawks**	**NHL**	**68**	**20**	**31**	**51**	**24**	**31**	**55**	**20**	**6**	**0**	**2**	**2**	**4**
1966-67	**Chicago Black Hawks**	**NHL**	**36**	**7**	**13**	**20**	**9**	**13**	**22**	**12**	**6**	**0**	**1**	**1**	**4**
	NHL Totals		**506**	**113**	**273**	**386**	**141**	**284**	**425**	**244**	**67**	**15**	**21**	**36**	**62**

WCHA First All-Star Team (1957, 1958) • NCAA West First All-American Team (1957, 1958) • NCAA Championship All-Tournament Team (1957) • Won Calder Memorial Trophy (1960)

Played in NHL All-Star Game (1960, 1961)

Traded to **Chicago** by **Montreal** for cash, April, 1959. Claimed by **St. Louis** from **Chicago** in Expansion Draft, June 6, 1967.

• HAY, GEORGE George Hay HHOF
LW – L. 5'10", 155 lbs. b: Listowel, Ont., 1/10/1898. d: 7/13/1975.

Season	Club	League	GP	G	A	Pts	AG	AA	APts	PIM	GP	G	A	Pts	PIM
1914-15	Winnipeg Strathconas	MHL Sr.	7	4	0	4	....	....	....	....	....	....	....	....	....
1915-16	Winnipeg Monarchs	MHL Sr.	7	6	4	10	....	....	....	10	2	2	1	3	2
1916-17	Winnipeg Monarchs	MJHL	STATISTICS NOT AVAILABLE												
1917-18			MILITARY SERVICE												
1918-19			MILITARY SERVICE												
1919-20	Regina Vics	City Sr.	12	8	3	11	....	....	....	5	2	1	0	1	0
1920-21	Regina Vics	City Sr.	16	9	4	13	....	....	....	7	4	5	2	7	2
1921-22	Regina Capitals	WCHL	25	21	11	32	....	....	....	9	4	0	0	0	5
1922-23	Regina Capitals	WCHL	30	28	8	36	....	....	....	12	2	1	0	1	0
1923-24	Regina Capitals	WCHL	25	20	11	31	....	....	....	8	3	1	1	2	0
1924-25	Regina Capitals	WCHL	20	16	6	22	....	....	....	6	....	....	....	....	....
1925-26	Portland Rosebuds	WHL	30	*19	12	31	....	....	....	4	....	....	....	....	....
1926-27	**Chicago Black Hawks**	**NHL**	**35**	**14**	**8**	**22**	**41**	**69**	**110**	**12**	**2**	**1**	**2**	**3**	**2**
1927-28	**Detroit Cougars**	**NHL**	**42**	**22**	**13**	**35**	**68**	**112**	**180**	**20**	....	....	....	....	....
1928-29	**Detroit Cougars**	**NHL**	**39**	**11**	**8**	**19**	**44**	**74**	**118**	**14**	**2**	**1**	**0**	**1**	**0**
1929-30	**Detroit Cougars**	**NHL**	**44**	**18**	**15**	**33**	**36**	**49**	**85**	**8**	....	....	....	....	....
1930-31	**Detroit Falcons**	**NHL**	**44**	**8**	**10**	**18**	**19**	**36**	**55**	**24**	....	....	....	....	....
1931-32	Detroit Olympics	IAHL	48	10	9	19	....	....	....	26	6	0	0	0	2
1932-33	**Detroit Falcons**	**NHL**	**34**	**1**	**6**	**7**	**2**	**16**	**18**	**6**	**4**	**0**	**1**	**1**	**0**
	Detroit Olympics	IAHL	9	6	1	7	....	....	....	6	....	....	....	....	....
1933-34	**Detroit Red Wings**	**NHL**	**1**	**0**	**0**	**0**	**0**	**0**	**0**	**0**	....	....	....	....	....
	Detroit Olympics	IAHL	4	0	0	0	....	....	....	5	....	....	....	....	....
	NHL Totals		**239**	**74**	**60**	**134**	**210**	**356**	**566**	**84**	**8**	**2**	**3**	**5**	**2**
	Other Major League Totals		130	104	48	152	....	....	....	39	9	2	1	3	5

WCHL First All-Star Team (1922, 1923, 1924) • WHL First All-Star Team (1926)

Signed as a free agent by **Regina** (WCHL), December 1, 1921. Transferred to **Portland** (WHL) after **Regina** (WCHL) franchise relocated, September 1, 1925. Transferred to **Chicago** after NHL club purchased **Portland** (WHL) franchise, May 15, 1926. Traded to **Detroit Cougars** by **Chicago** with Percy Traub for $15,000, June, 1927.

• HAY, JIM Jim "Red Eye" Hay
D – R. 5'11", 185 lbs. b: Saskatoon, Sask., 5/15/1931.

Season	Club	League	GP	G	A	Pts	AG	AA	APts	PIM	GP	G	A	Pts	PIM
1947-48	Windsor Spitfires	OHA	29	10	15	25	....	....	....	40	10	2	0	2	10
	Detroit Auto Club	IHL	25	10	15	25	....	....	....	37	....	....	....	....	....
1948-49	Windsor Spitfires	OHA	48	9	8	17	....	....	....	74	4	0	0	0	2
	Saskatoon Quakers	SJHL	2	1	0	1	....	....	....	0	2	2	1	3	4
	Detroit Auto Club	IHL	10	5	3	8	....	....	....	5	6	2	2	4	4
1949-50	Windsor Spitfires	OHA	48	5	15	20	....	....	....	98	11	2	1	3	6
1950-51	Omaha Knights	USHL	64	24	22	46	....	....	....	150	4	1	2	3	4
1951-52	Indianapolis Capitals	AHL	68	7	15	22	....	....	....	129	....	....	....	....	....
1952-53	**Detroit Red Wings**	**NHL**	**42**	**1**	**4**	**5**	**2**	**6**	**8**	**2**	**4**	**0**	**0**	**0**	**2**
	Edmonton Flyers	WHL	26	2	1	3	....	....	....	49	....	....	....	....	....
1953-54	**Detroit Red Wings**	**NHL**	**12**	**0**	**0**	**0**	**0**	**0**	**0**	**0**	....	....	....	....	....
	Sherbrooke Saints	QHL	54	4	6	10	....	....	....	98	5	0	0	0	10
1954-55	**Detroit Red Wings**	**NHL**	**21**	**0**	**1**	**1**	**0**	**1**	**1**	**20**	**5**	**1**	**0**	**1**	**0**
	Quebec Aces	QHL	38	5	13	18	....	....	....	107	....	....	....	....	....
1955-56	Brandon Regals	WHL	70	7	7	14	....	....	....	158	....	....	....	....	....
1956-57	Edmonton Flyers	WHL	52	3	13	16	....	....	....	120	....	....	....	....	....
1957-58	Troy Bruins	IHL	64	14	29	43	....	....	....	*125	....	....	....	....	....
1958-59	Victoria Cougars	WHL	67	5	23	28	....	....	....	110	3	0	1	1	4
1959-60	Victoria Cougars	WHL	70	4	19	23	....	....	....	118	11	1	2	3	17
1960-61	Victoria Cougars	WHL	70	7	21	28	....	....	....	88	5	0	0	0	0
1961-62	San Francisco Seals	WHL	61	4	16	20	....	....	....	101	2	0	1	1	0
1962-63	Seattle Totems	WHL	70	9	21	30	....	....	....	109	17	2	5	7	10
1963-64	Seattle Totems	WHL	70	3	6	9	....	....	....	65	....	....	....	....	....
1964-65	Portland Buckaroos	WHL	64	2	15	17	....	....	....	115	10	0	4	4	14
1965-66	Portland Buckaroos	WHL	72	3	20	23	....	....	....	115	14	0	1	1	8
1966-67	Portland Buckaroos	WHL	51	1	9	10	....	....	....	49	....	....	....	....	....
1967-68	Portland Buckaroos	WHL	72	5	18	23	....	....	....	75	12	0	2	2	15
1968-69	Portland Buckaroos	WHL	74	0	23	23	....	....	....	71	10	0	2	2	17
1969-70	Salt Lake Golden Eagles	WHL	61	2	7	9	....	....	....	105	....	....	....	....	....
	Portland Buckaroos	WHL	....	....	....	....	....	....	....	....	3	1	1	2	6
1970-71	Salt Lake Golden Eagles	WHL	11	1	0	1	....	....	....	14	....	....	....	....	....
	Jersey Devils	EHL	18	1	6	7	....	....	....	37	....	....	....	....	....
1971-72	Jersey Devils	EHL	74	2	18	20	....	....	....	134	....	....	....	....	....
1972-73	Jersey Devils	EHL	DID NOT PLAY – COACHING												
	NHL Totals		**75**	**1**	**5**	**6**	**2**	**7**	**9**	**22**	**9**	**1**	**0**	**1**	**2**

USHL Second All-Star Team (1951)

Traded to **Montreal** (Seattle-WHL) by **LA Blades** (WHL) with Terry Slater and Jim Powers for Frank Arnett and Marc Boileau, July, 1962. Traded to **Portland** (WHL) by **Seattle** (WHL) for cash, October, 1964. Signed as a free agent by **Salt Lake** (WHL), November, 1969. Loaned to **Portland** (WHL) by **Salt Lake** (WHL) for the 1970 WHL playoffs, April, 1970.

• HAYNES, PAUL Paul Haynes

C – L. 5'10", 160 lbs. b: Montreal, Que., 3/1/1910. Deceased.

			REGULAR SEASON								PLAYOFFS				
Season	Club	League	GP	G	A	Pts	AG	AA	APts	PIM	GP	G	A	Pts	PIM
1928-29	Montreal Champetre	City Sr.	....	2	0	2	....	....	....	....	....	....	....	....	....
	Loyola College Warriors	Mtl-Sr.	STATISTICS NOT AVAILABLE												
1929-30	Montreal AAA	City Sr.	10	2	1	3	....	....	....	4	2	0	0	0	0
1930-31	**Montreal Maroons**	**NHL**	**19**	**1**	**0**	**1**	**2**	**0**	**2**	**0**	....	....	....	....	....
	Windsor Bulldogs	IAHL	27	11	16	27	....	....	....	16	6	4	*6	*10	2
1931-32	**Montreal Maroons**	**NHL**	**12**	**1**	**0**	**1**	**2**	**0**	**2**	**0**	**4**	**0**	**0**	**0**	**0**
	Windsor Bulldogs	IAHL	33	10	14	24	....	....	....	6	....	....	....	....	....
1932-33	**Montreal Maroons**	**NHL**	**48**	**16**	**25**	**41**	**38**	**67**	**105**	**18**	**2**	**0**	**0**	**0**	**2**
1933-34	**Montreal Maroons**	**NHL**	**44**	**5**	**4**	**9**	**11**	**11**	**22**	**18**	**4**	**0**	**1**	**1**	**2**
	Windsor Bulldogs	IAHL	4	0	0	0	....	....	....	0	....	....	....	....	....
1934-35	**Montreal Maroons**	**NHL**	**11**	**1**	**2**	**3**	**2**	**4**	**6**	**0**	....	....	....	....	....
	Boston Bruins	**NHL**	**37**	**4**	**3**	**7**	**8**	**7**	**15**	**8**	**3**	**0**	**0**	**0**	**0**
1935-36	**Montreal Canadiens**	**NHL**	**48**	**5**	**19**	**24**	**12**	**46**	**58**	**24**	....	....	....	....	....
1936-37	**Montreal Canadiens**	**NHL**	**47**	**8**	**18**	**26**	**17**	**42**	**59**	**24**	**5**	**2**	**3**	**5**	**0**
1937-38	**Montreal Canadiens**	**NHL**	**48**	**13**	**22**	**35**	**27**	**46**	**73**	**25**	**3**	**0**	**4**	**4**	**5**
1938-39	**Montreal Canadiens**	**NHL**	**47**	**5**	**33**	**38**	**10**	**62**	**72**	**27**	**3**	**0**	**0**	**0**	**4**
1939-40	**Montreal Canadiens**	**NHL**	**23**	**2**	**8**	**10**	**4**	**16**	**20**	**8**	....	....	....	....	....
1940-41	**Montreal Canadiens**	**NHL**	**7**	**0**	**0**	**0**	**0**	**0**	**0**	**12**	....	....	....	....	....
	New Haven Eagles	AHL	31	3	11	14	....	....	....	4	2	0	0	0	0
1941-42	Montreal Sr. Canadiens	QSHL	DID NOT PLAY – COACHING												
	NHL Totals		**391**	**61**	**134**	**195**	**133**	**301**	**434**	**164**	**24**	**2**	**8**	**10**	**13**

Played in NHL All-Star Game (1937, 1939)

Traded to **Boston** by **Montreal Maroons** for cash, December 28, 1934. Traded to **Montreal Canadiens** by **Boston** for Jack Riley, September 30, 1935.

• HEADLEY, FERN Fern "Curly" Headley

D – L. 5'11", 175 lbs. b: Crystal, ND, 3/2/1901. d: 5/4/1909.

Season	Club	League	GP	G	A	Pts	AG	AA	APts	PIM	GP	G	A	Pts	PIM
1922-23	Saskatoon Shieks	WCHL	10	2	0	2	....	....	....	4	....	....	....	....	....
1923-24	Saskatoon Crescents	WCHL	20	2	0	2	....	....	....	6	....	....	....	....	....
1924-25	**Boston Bruins**	**NHL**	**11**	**0**	**1**	**1**	**0**	**13**	**13**	**2**	....	....	....	....	....
	Montreal Canadiens	**NHL**	**16**	**1**	**0**	**1**	**3**	**0**	**3**	**4**	**5**	**0**	**0**	**0**	**0**
1925-26	Calgary Tigers	WHL	29	2	1	3	....	....	....	47	....	....	....	....	....
1926-27	Calgary Tigers	PHL	30	16	10	26	....	....	....	30	2	0	0	0	4
1927-28	Minneapolis Millers	AHA	37	6	5	11	....	....	....	37	8	0	0	0	0
1928-29	St. Louis Flyers	AHA	40	14	11	25	....	....	....	54	....	....	....	....	....
1929-30	St. Louis Flyers	AHA	48	5	6	11	....	....	....	47	....	....	....	....	....
1930-31	Chicago Shamrocks	AHA	47	5	8	13	....	....	....	44	....	....	....	....	....
1931-32	Chicago Shamrocks	AHA	47	6	5	11	....	....	....	50	4	0	0	0	5
1932-33	Wichita–Duluth	AHA	41	10	9	19	....	....	....	37	....	....	....	....	....
1933-34	Tulsa Oilers	AHA	32	6	2	8	....	....	....	34	4	0	0	0	4
1934-35	Tulsa Oilers	AHA	48	5	11	16	....	....	....	31	5	0	0	0	2
1935-36	Tulsa Oilers	AHA	43	1	4	5	....	....	....	33	3	0	0	0	4
1936-37	Kansas City Greyhounds	AHA	7	1	1	2	....	....	....	13	....	....	....	....	....
	Tulsa Oilers	AHA	18	0	0	0	....	....	....	6	....	....	....	....	....
1937-38			DID NOT PLAY												
1938-39	Wichita Skyhawks	AHA	33	6	7	13	....	....	....	36	....	....	....	....	....
	NHL Totals		**27**	**1**	**1**	**2**	**3**	**13**	**16**	**6**	**5**	**0**	**0**	**0**	**0**
	Other Major League Totals		59	6	1	7	....	....	....	57	....	....	....	....	....

AHA Second All-Star Team (1935)

Signed as a free agent by **Saskatoon** (WCHL), October 22, 1922. Traded to **Boston** by **Saskatoon** (WCHL) for cash, November 18, 1924. Loaned to **Montreal Canadiens** by **Boston** for remainder of 1925-26 season, January 14, 1925. Traded to **Vancouver** (WHL) by **Boston** for cash, October 29, 1925. Traded to **Calgary** (WHL) by **Vancouver** (WHL) for Rusty Crawford, November 3, 1925. Rights transferred to **Detroit** from **Chicago Shamrocks** (AHA) after AHA club owners purchased Detroit (NHL and IAHL) franchises, September 2, 1932.

• HEALEY, DICK Dick Healey

D – L. 5'10", 170 lbs. b: Vancouver, B.C., 3/12/1930.

Season	Club	League	GP	G	A	Pts	AG	AA	APts	PIM	GP	G	A	Pts	PIM
1955-56	Edmonton Oil Kings	WCJHL	35	3	9	12	....	....	....	69	6	0	0	0	6
1956-57	Red Deer Rustlers	Inter-Sr.	STATISTICS NOT AVAILABLE												
1957-58	Red Deer Rustlers	Inter-Sr.	STATISTICS NOT AVAILABLE												
1958-59	Red Deer Rustlers	Inter-Sr.	STATISTICS NOT AVAILABLE												
1959-60	Sudbury Wolves	EPHL	66	1	10	11	....	....	....	75	12	0	3	3	8
1960-61	**Detroit Red Wings**	**NHL**	**1**	**0**	**0**	**0**	**0**	**0**	**0**	**2**	....	....	....	....	....
	Sudbury Wolves	EPHL	30	1	8	9	....	....	....	35	....	....	....	....	....
	Edmonton Flyers	WHL	10	0	0	0	....	....	....	11	....	....	....	....	....
	Hershey Bears	AHL	16	0	2	2	....	....	....	6	7	1	0	1	2
1961-62	Soo Thunderbirds	EPHL	61	2	22	24	....	....	....	68	....	....	....	....	....
1962-63	Edmonton Flyers	WHL	2	0	1	1	....	....	....	0	....	....	....	....	....
1963-64	Lacombe Rockets	ASHL	STATISTICS NOT AVAILABLE												
1964-65	Lacombe Rockets	ASHL	STATISTICS NOT AVAILABLE												
1965-66	Lacombe Rockets	ASHL	....	6	8	14	....	....	....	36	....	....	....	....	....
1966-67	Edmonton Nuggets	ASHL	17	1	2	3	....	....	....	24	....	....	....	....	....
1967-68	Vermilion Tigers	Inter-Sr.	STATISTICS NOT AVAILABLE												
1968-69	Edmonton Monarchs	ASHL	....	3	35	38	....	....	....	37	....	0	7	7	10
	NHL Totals		**1**	**0**	**0**	**0**	**0**	**0**	**0**	**2**	....	....	....	....	....

• HEBENTON, ANDY Andy "Spuds" Hebenton

RW – L. 5'9", 180 lbs. b: Winnipeg, Man., 10/3/1929.

			REGULAR SEASON								PLAYOFFS				
Season	Club	League	GP	G	A	Pts	AG	AA	APts	PIM	GP	G	A	Pts	PIM
1947-48	Winnipeg Canadians	MJHL	24	21	13	34	....	....	....	15	6	5	3	8	6
1948-49	Winnipeg Canadians	MJHL	30	*30	13	43	....	....	....	34	10	*9	7	*16	10
1949-50	Cincinnati Mohawks	AHL	44	8	7	15	....	....	....	0	....	....	....	....	....
	Montreal Royals	QSHL	5	0	2	2	....	....	....	0	....	....	....	....	....
1950-51	Victoria Cougars	PCHL	56	16	16	32	....	....	....	12	12	*6	3	9	2
1951-52	Victoria Cougars	PCHL	67	31	25	56	....	....	....	81	13	6	6	12	5
1952-53	Victoria Cougars	WHL	70	27	24	51	....	....	....	46	....	....	....	....	....
1953-54	Victoria Cougars	WHL	70	21	24	45	....	....	....	29	5	3	1	4	0
1954-55	Victoria Cougars	WHL	70	46	34	80	....	....	....	20	5	1	1	2	2
1955-56	**New York Rangers**	**NHL**	**70**	**24**	**14**	**38**	**35**	**17**	**52**	**8**	**5**	**1**	**0**	**1**	**2**
1956-57	**New York Rangers**	**NHL**	**70**	**21**	**23**	**44**	**29**	**27**	**56**	**10**	**5**	**2**	**0**	**2**	**2**
1957-58	**New York Rangers**	**NHL**	**70**	**21**	**24**	**45**	**28**	**26**	**54**	**17**	**6**	**2**	**3**	**5**	**4**
1958-59	**New York Rangers**	**NHL**	**70**	**33**	**29**	**62**	**42**	**31**	**73**	**8**	....	....	....	....	....
1959-60	**New York Rangers**	**NHL**	**70**	**19**	**27**	**46**	**24**	**28**	**52**	**4**	....	....	....	....	....
1960-61	**New York Rangers**	**NHL**	**70**	**26**	**28**	**54**	**32**	**29**	**61**	**10**	....	....	....	....	....
1961-62	**New York Rangers**	**NHL**	**70**	**18**	**24**	**42**	**22**	**24**	**46**	**10**	**6**	**1**	**2**	**3**	**0**
1962-63	**New York Rangers**	**NHL**	**70**	**15**	**22**	**37**	**18**	**23**	**41**	**8**	....	....	....	....	....
1963-64	**Boston Bruins**	**NHL**	**70**	**12**	**11**	**23**	**16**	**12**	**28**	**8**	....	....	....	....	....
1964-65	Portland Buckaroos	WHL	70	34	40	74	....	....	....	16	10	*7	6	13	0
1965-66	Victoria Cougars	WHL	72	31	45	76	....	....	....	12	14	6	11	17	14
1966-67	Victoria Cougars	WHL	72	24	36	60	....	....	....	19	....	....	....	....	....
1967-68	Portland Buckaroos	WHL	70	16	29	45	....	....	....	10	12	3	4	7	0
1968-69	Portland Buckaroos	WHL	74	26	51	77	....	....	....	26	11	2	1	3	0
1969-70	Portland Buckaroos	WHL	72	36	42	78	....	....	....	9	11	2	7	9	0
1970-71	Portland Buckaroos	WHL	72	29	52	81	....	....	....	10	11	6	3	9	14
1971-72	Portland Buckaroos	WHL	72	30	34	64	....	....	....	12	11	3	4	7	2
1972-73	Portland Buckaroos	WHL	72	30	36	66	....	....	....	26	....	....	....	....	....
1973-74	Portland Buckaroos	WHL	78	28	44	72	....	....	....	16	10	2	4	6	2
1974-75	Seattle Totems	CHL	4	0	0	0	....	....	....	0	....	....	....	....	....
	Portland Buckaroos	WIHL	20	4	11	15	....	....	....	0	....	....	....	....	....
	NHL Totals		**630**	**189**	**202**	**391**	**246**	**217**	**463**	**83**	**22**	**6**	**5**	**11**	**8**

WHL First All-Star Team (1955, 1965, 1970) • Won Lady Byng Trophy (1957) • Won Fred J. Hume Cup (WHL Most Gentlemanly Player) (1965, 1970, 1971, 1972, 1973, 1974) • WHL Second All-Star Team (1971, 1973)

Played in NHL All-Star Game (1960)

Traded to **NY Rangers** by **Victoria** (WHL) for cash, June, 1955. Claimed by **Boston** from **NY Rangers** in Intra-League Draft, June 4, 1963. Traded to **Portland** (WHL) by **Boston** for cash, June 5, 1964. Traded to **Toronto** by **Boston** with Orland Kurtenbach and Pat Stapleton for Ron Stewart, June 8, 1965. Traded to **Portland** (WHL) by **Toronto** (Victoria-WHL) for Rick Charron, Brian Smith and Tom McVie, September, 1967.

• HEFFERNAN, FRANK Frank "Moose" Heffernan

D – L. 6', 210 lbs. b: Peterborough, Ontario. Deceased.

Season	Club	League	GP	G	A	Pts	AG	AA	APts	PIM	GP	G	A	Pts	PIM
1911-12	Ottawa College	City Sr.	STATISTICS NOT AVAILABLE												
1912-13	Toronto R & AA	OHA Sr.	6	2	0	2	....	....	....	0	4	2	0	2	....
1913-14	Toronto R & AA	OHA Sr.	6	4	0	4	....	....	....	....	2	0	0	0	....
1914-15	Toronto Victorias	OHA Sr.	6	5	0	5	....	....	....	....	4	0	0	0	....
1915-16	New York Crescents	USAHA	8	7	0	7	....	....	....	....	....	....	....	....	....
1916-17	Springhill Miners	NSSHL	2	6	0	6	....	....	....	....	....	....	....	....	....
	New York Crescents	USAHA	2	1	0	1	....	....	....	....	6	2	0	....	....
1917-18	New York Wanderers	USAHA	4	1	0	1	....	....	....	....	....	....	....	....	....
1918-19	Toronto St. Pats	OHA Sr.	9	6	3	9	....	....	....	....	1	1	0	1	....
1919-20	**Toronto St. Pats**	**NHL**	**19**	**0**	**1**	**1**	**0**	**7**	**7**	**10**	....	....	....	....	....
	NHL Totals		**19**	**0**	**1**	**1**	**0**	**7**	**7**	**10**	....	....	....	....	....

Signed as a free agent by **Toronto St. Pats**, December 8, 1919.

• HEFFERNAN, GERRY Gerry Heffernan

RW – R. 5'9", 160 lbs. b: Montreal, Que., 7/24/1916.

Season	Club	League	GP	G	A	Pts	AG	AA	APts	PIM	GP	G	A	Pts	PIM
1934-35	Montreal Jr. Royals	City Jr.	12	8	6	14	....	....	....	2	2	1	0	1	2
1935-36	Montreal Jr. Royals	City Jr.	9	5	3	8	....	....	....	2	2	3	1	4	0
	Montreal Royals	City Sr.	....	....	....	....	....	....	....	....	5	0	0	0	0
1936-37	Montreal Royals	City Sr.	21	6	15	21	....	....	....	12	5	2	0	2	2
1937-38	Harringay Greyhounds	Britain	18	18	12	30	....	....	....	....	....	....	....	....	....
1938-39	Montreal Royals	QSHL	21	12	10	22	....	....	....	35	20	11	*21	*32	22
1939-40	Montreal Royals	QSHL	29	11	19	30	....	....	....	38	13	5	11	16	11
1940-41	Montreal Royals	QSHL	33	15	18	33	....	....	....	24	22	8	7	15	8
1941-42	**Montreal Canadiens**	**NHL**	**40**	**5**	**15**	**20**	**9**	**23**	**32**	**15**	**2**	**2**	**1**	**3**	**0**
	Montreal Royals	QSHL	9	2	4	6	....	....	....	6	....	....	....	....	....
1942-43	Montreal Royals	QSHL	22	19	15	34	....	....	....	28	4	0	1	1	2
	Montreal Canadiens	**NHL**	....	....	....	....	....	....	....	....	**2**	**0**	**0**	**0**	**0**
1943-44	**Montreal Canadiens**	**NHL**	**43**	**28**	**20**	**48**	**36**	**24**	**60**	**12**	**7**	**1**	**2**	**3**	**8**
1944-45	Montreal Royals	QSHL	23	23	28	51	....	....	....	14	7	4	4	8	2
1945-46	Montreal Royals	QSHL	38	20	24	44	....	....	....	41	11	7	6	13	4
	NHL Totals		**83**	**33**	**35**	**68**	**45**	**47**	**92**	**27**	**11**	**3**	**3**	**6**	**8**

Signed as a free agent by **Montreal**, November 20, 1941.

• HEINRICH, LIONEL Lionel Heinrich

LW – L. 5'10", 180 lbs. b: Churchbridge, Sask., 4/20/1934.

Season	Club	League	GP	G	A	Pts	AG	AA	APts	PIM	GP	G	A	Pts	PIM
1951-52	Humboldt Indians	SJHL	45	3	3	6	....	....	....	65	10	1	1	2	12
1952-53	Humboldt Indians	SJHL	27	10	11	21	....	....	....	92	10	3	2	5	12
1953-54	Humboldt Indians	SJHL	42	19	21	40	....	....	....	96	5	2	1	3	4
	Melville Millionaires	SSHL	2	1	0	1	....	....	....	4	9	3	4	7	17
1954-55	Hershey Bears	AHL	54	8	15	23	....	....	....	45	....	....	....	....	....
1955-56	**Boston Bruins**	**NHL**	**35**	**1**	**1**	**2**	**1**	**1**	**2**	**33**	....	....	....	....	....
	Hershey Bears	AHL	15	0	1	1	....	....	....	22	....	....	....	....	....
1956-57	Victoria Cougars	WHL	69	2	11	13	....	....	....	96	3	1	0	1	9
1957-58	Quebec Aces	QHL	4	0	1	1	....	....	....	10	....	....	....	....	....
	Windsor Bulldogs	OHA Sr.	43	5	9	14	....	....	....	64	....	....	....	....	....
1958-59	Regina Capitals	SSHL	9	0	3	3	....	....	....	10	....	....	....	....	....
1959-60	Regina Capitals	SSHL	3	0	1	1	....	....	....	35	....	....	....	....	....
1960-61			DID NOT PLAY												
1961-62	Regina Capitals	SSHL	3	0	1	1	....	....	....	0	....	....	....	....	....
	NHL Totals		**35**	**1**	**1**	**2**	**1**	**1**	**2**	**33**	....	....	....	....	....

• HELLER, OTT
Ott (Eberhardt) Heller
D – R. 6', 190 lbs. b: Kitchener, Ont., 6/2/1910. Deceased.

Season	Club	League	GP	G	A	Pts	AG	AA	APts	PIM	GP	G	A	Pts	PIM
			REGULAR SEASON								PLAYOFFS				
1928-29	Kitchener Greenshirts	OHA	STATISTICS NOT AVAILABLE												
1929-30	Springfield Indians	Can-Am	26	6	2	8	....	....	....	32	....	....	....	....	....
1930-31	Springfield Indians	Can-Am	38	16	15	31	....	....	....	85	7	0	2	2	26
1931-32	New York Rangers	NHL	21	2	2	4	4	6	10	9	7	3	1	4	8
	Springfield Indians	Can-Am	21	7	7	14	....	....	....	30	....	....	....	....	....
1932-33	New York Rangers	NHL	40	5	7	12	12	18	30	31	8	3	0	3	10
1933-34	New York Rangers	NHL	48	2	5	7	4	13	17	29	2	0	0	0	0
1934-35	New York Rangers	NHL	47	3	11	14	6	24	30	31	4	0	1	1	4
1935-36	New York Rangers	NHL	43	2	11	13	5	27	32	40	....	....	....	....	....
1936-37	New York Rangers	NHL	48	5	12	17	11	28	39	42	9	0	0	0	11
1937-38	New York Rangers	NHL	48	2	14	16	4	29	33	68	3	0	1	1	2
1938-39	New York Rangers	NHL	48	0	23	23	0	43	43	42	7	0	1	1	10
1939-40	New York Rangers	NHL	47	5	14	19	11	28	39	26	12	0	3	3	12
1940-41	New York Rangers	NHL	48	2	16	18	4	29	33	42	3	0	1	1	4
1941-42	New York Rangers	NHL	35	6	5	11	10	8	18	22	6	0	0	0	0
1942-43	New York Rangers	NHL	45	4	14	18	6	18	24	14	....	....	....	....	....
1943-44	New York Rangers	NHL	50	8	27	35	10	33	43	29	....	....	....	....	....
1944-45	New York Rangers	NHL	45	7	12	19	10	19	29	26	....	....	....	....	....
1945-46	New York Rangers	NHL	34	2	3	5	3	6	9	14	....	....	....	....	....
	St. Paul Saints	USHL	16	2	5	7	....	....	....	4	6	0	1	1	4
1946-47	New Haven Ramblers	AHL	64	7	29	36	....	....	....	40	3	0	0	0	6
1947-48	New Haven Ramblers	AHL	67	6	25	31	....	....	....	40	4	1	0	1	6
1948-49	Indianapolis Capitals	AHL	55	6	21	27	....	....	....	24	2	0	0	0	4
1949-50	Indianapolis Capitals	AHL	30	0	1	1	....	....	....	6	4	0	0	0	2
1950-51	Indianapolis Capitals	AHL	48	4	12	16	....	....	....	34	2	0	1	1	2
1951-52	Indianapolis Capitals	AHL	48	4	15	19	....	....	....	40	....	....	....	....	....
1952-53	New Haven Nutmegs	EHL	21	2	6	8	....	....	....	14	....	....	....	....	....
	Kitchener Dutchmen	OHA Sr.	24	3	10	13	....	....	....	20	....	....	....	....	....
	Cleveland Barons	AHL	....	....	....	....	....	....	....	....	5	0	0	0	2
1953-54	Marion Barons	IHL	64	4	25	29	....	....	....	70	5	0	2	2	6
	Cleveland Barons	AHL	DID NOT PLAY – COACHING												
1954-55	Valleyfield Braves	QHL	18	0	3	3	....	....	....	4	....	....	....	....	....
	Cleveland Barons	AHL	6	0	1	1	....	....	....	2	3	0	1	1	4
1955-56	Chatham Maroons	OHA Sr.	7	0	2	2	....	....	....	10	....	....	....	....	....
	NHL Totals		647	55	176	231	100	329	429	465	61	6	8	14	61

NHL Second All-Star Team (1941) • AHL Second All-Star Team (1947) • AHL First All-Star Team (1948) • IHL Second All-Star Team (1954)

Signed as a free agent by **Springfield** (Can-Am), November 2, 1931. Traded to **NY Rangers** by **Springfield** (Can-Am) for cash, May 9, 1932.

• HELMAN, HARRY
Harry Helman
RW – R. 5'6", 145 lbs. b: Ottawa, Ontario, 8/28/1894.

Season	Club	League	GP	G	A	Pts	AG	AA	APts	PIM	GP	G	A	Pts	PIM
1919-20	Ottawa GWVA	City Sr.	7	4	0	4	....	....	....	....	....	....	....	....	....
1920-21	Ottawa Munitions	City Sr.	9	4	0	4	....	....	....	....	1	0	0	0	10
1921-22	Ottawa Munitions	City Sr.	11	4	3	7	....	....	....	21	....	....	....	....	....
1922-23	Ottawa Senators	NHL	24	0	0	0	0	0	0	5	4	0	0	0	0
1923-24	Ottawa Senators	NHL	17	1	0	1	4	0	4	2	....	....	....	....	....
1924-25	Ottawa Senators	NHL	1	0	0	0	0	0	0	0	....	....	....	....	....
1924-25			REINSTATED AS AN AMATEUR												
1925-26			DID NOT PLAY												
1926-27	Saskatoon Shieks	PrHL	5	0	0	0	....	....	....	8	....	....	....	....	....
	NHL Totals		42	1	0	1	4	0	4	7	4	0	0	0	0

Signed as a free agent by **Ottawa**, November 16, 1922.

• HEMMERLING, TONY
Tony (Elmer Charles) Hemmerling
LW – L. 5'11", 178 lbs. b: Landis, Sask., 5/15/1914. Deceased.

Season	Club	League	GP	G	A	Pts	AG	AA	APts	PIM	GP	G	A	Pts	PIM
1929-30	Biggar Nationals	SSHL	6	1	1	2	....	....	....	2	....	....	....	....	....
	Wilkie Outlaws	SJHL	....	....	....	....	....	....	....	....	2	1	0	1	6
1930-31	North Battleford Beavers	SSHL	15	3	8	11	....	....	....	20	4	2	0	2	8
1931-32	North Battleford Beavers	SSHL	20	11	5	16	....	....	....	24	....	....	....	....	....
1932-33	Saskatoon Quakers	SSHL	16	3	1	4	....	....	....	23	3	0	0	0	6
1933-34	Seattle Seahawks	NWHL	34	13	4	17	....	....	....	46	....	....	....	....	....
1934-35	Seattle Seahawks	NWHL	36	21	12	33	....	....	....	46	5	1	2	3	0
1935-36	Seattle Seahawks	NWHL	7	0	0	0	....	....	....	0	....	....	....	....	....
	New York Americans	NHL	3	0	0	0	0	0	0	0	....	....	....	....	....
	Rochester Cardinals	IAHL	11	2	5	7	....	....	....	2	....	....	....	....	....
	New Haven Eagles	Can-Am	18	4	6	10	....	....	....	8	....	....	....	....	....
1936-37	New York Americans	NHL	19	3	3	6	6	7	13	4	....	....	....	....	....
	New Haven Eagles	AHL	24	3	10	13	....	....	....	12	....	....	....	....	....
1937-38	New Haven Eagles	AHL	42	11	11	22	....	....	....	14	2	1	1	2	2
1938-39	New Haven Eagles	AHL	50	13	13	26	....	....	....	9	....	....	....	....	....
1939-40	New Haven Eagles	AHL	51	26	31	57	....	....	....	4	3	2	2	4	0
1940-41	Buffalo Bisons	AHL	56	14	10	24	....	....	....	22	....	....	....	....	....
1941-42	Buffalo Bisons	AHL	55	20	19	39	....	....	....	7	....	....	....	....	....
1942-43	Pittsburgh Hornets	AHL	42	17	19	30	....	....	....	16	2	0	0	0	0
1943-44	Pittsburgh Hornets	AHL	51	19	24	43	....	....	....	23	....	....	....	....	....
1944-45	Pittsburgh Hornets	AHL	57	31	33	64	....	....	....	6	....	....	....	....	....
1945-46	Pittsburgh Hornets	AHL	1	0	0	0	....	....	....	0	....	....	....	....	....
	Providence–Buffalo	AHL	14	4	3	7	....	....	....	2	....	....	....	....	....
	Dallas Texans	USHL	7	1	1	2	....	....	....	2	....	....	....	....	....
1946-47	Fresno Falcons	PCHL	5	4	1	5	....	....	....	0	....	....	....	....	....
1947-48	Oakland Oaks	PCHL	DID NOT PLAY – COACHING												
	NHL Totals		22	3	3	6	6	7	13	4	....	....	....	....	....

AHL Second All-Star Team (1940)

Traded to **Calgary** (NWHL) by **Seattle** (NWHL) for Jim Evans, December, 1935. Traded to **NY Americans** by **Calgary** (NWHL) for cash, December, 1935. Traded to **New Haven** (AHL) by **NY Americans** for cash, January, 1936. Traded to **Buffalo** (AHL) by **New Haven** (AHL) for cash, September, 1940. Traded to **Pittsburgh** (AHL) by **Buffalo** (AHL) for cash, September, 1942.

• HENDERSON, MURRAY
Murray "Moe" Henderson
D – L. 6', 180 lbs. b: Toronto, Ont., 9/5/1921.

Season	Club	League	GP	G	A	Pts	AG	AA	APts	PIM	GP	G	A	Pts	PIM
			REGULAR SEASON								PLAYOFFS				
1940-41	Toronto Young Rangers	OHA	15	5	0	5	....	....	....	8	5	2	0	2	8
1941-42	Toronto Marlboros	OHA Sr.	28	2	4	6	....	....	....	10	6	2	1	3	8
1942-43	Toronto RCAF	OHA Sr.	10	2	5	7	....	....	....	19	11	2	8	10	14
1943-44	Toronto RCAF	OHA Sr.	7	6	1	7	....	....	....	6	....	....	....	....	....
1944-45	Boston Bruins	NHL	5	0	1	1	0	2	2	4	7	0	1	1	2
	Boston Olympics	EHL	3	1	2	3	....	....	....	4	3	2	2	4	2
1945-46	Boston Bruins	NHL	48	4	11	15	6	20	26	30	10	1	1	2	4
1946-47	Boston Bruins	NHL	57	5	12	17	7	17	24	63	4	0	0	0	4
1947-48	Boston Bruins	NHL	49	6	8	14	9	12	21	50	3	1	0	1	5
1948-49	Boston Bruins	NHL	60	2	9	11	3	14	17	28	5	0	1	1	2
1949-50	Boston Bruins	NHL	64	3	8	11	4	10	14	42	....	....	....	....	....
1950-51	Boston Bruins	NHL	66	4	7	11	5	9	14	37	5	0	0	0	2
1951-52	Boston Bruins	NHL	56	0	6	6	0	8	8	51	7	0	0	0	4
1952-53	Hershey Bears	AHL	61	4	19	23	....	....	....	49	3	0	0	0	0
1953-54	Hershey Bears	AHL	69	7	25	32	....	....	....	85	11	0	3	3	12
1954-55	Hershey Bears	AHL	59	4	14	18	....	....	....	61	....	....	....	....	....
1955-56	Hershey Bears	AHL	9	0	3	3	....	....	....	8	....	....	....	....	....
	NHL Totals		405	24	62	86	34	92	126	305	41	2	3	5	23

AHL Second All-Star Team (1955)

Signed as a free agent by **Boston**, February 28, 1945.

• HENDERSON, PAUL
— see page 1098

• HENDRICKSON, JOHN
John "Jake" Hendrickson
D – R. 5'11", 175 lbs. b: Kingston, Ont., 12/5/1936.

Season	Club	League	GP	G	A	Pts	AG	AA	APts	PIM	GP	G	A	Pts	PIM
1954-55	Hamilton Tiger Cubs	OHA	38	1	7	8	....	....	....	15	3	0	0	0	0
1955-56	Hamilton Tiger Cubs	OHA	44	10	14	24	....	....	....	98	....	....	....	....	....
1956-57	Hamilton Tiger Cubs	OHA	46	6	9	15	....	....	....	120	4	0	0	0	2
	Springfield Indians	AHL	2	0	0	0	....	....	....	2	....	....	....	....	....
1957-58	Detroit Red Wings	NHL	1	0	0	0	0	0	0	0	....	....	....	....	....
	Edmonton Flyers	WHL	62	4	10	14	....	....	....	88	5	1	1	2	6
1958-59	Detroit Red Wings	NHL	3	0	0	0	0	0	0	2	....	....	....	....	....
	Springfield–Hershey	AHL	15	0	0	0	....	....	....	8	....	....	....	....	....
	Edmonton Flyers	WHL	35	5	10	15	....	....	....	39	2	0	0	0	0
1959-60	Seattle Totems	WHL	1	0	0	0	....	....	....	0	....	....	....	....	....
	Sudbury Wolves	EPHL	64	8	27	35	....	....	....	71	3	1	1	2	4
1960-61	Sudbury Wolves	EPHL	48	9	14	23	....	....	....	67	....	....	....	....	....
1961-62	Detroit Red Wings	NHL	1	0	0	0	0	0	0	2	....	....	....	....	....
	Sudbury Wolves	EPHL	69	18	22	40	....	....	....	98	4	1	3	4	6
1962-63	Calgary Stampeders	WHL	61	14	35	49	....	....	....	64	....	....	....	....	....
1963-64	St. Louis Braves	CHL	70	6	32	38	....	....	....	86	6	1	5	6	4
1964-65	St. Louis Braves	CHL	25	2	12	14	....	....	....	30	....	....	....	....	....
	Los Angeles Blades	WHL	14	2	4	6	....	....	....	12	....	....	....	....	....
1965-66	Los Angeles Blades	WHL	67	10	44	54	....	....	....	61	....	....	....	....	....
1966-67	Los Angeles Blades	WHL	57	3	25	28	....	....	....	63	....	....	....	....	....
1967-68	Port Huron Flags	IHL	22	4	12	16	....	....	....	20	....	....	....	....	....
1968-69	Des Moines–Fort Wayne	IHL	66	5	25	30	....	....	....	52	6	1	3	4	0
1969-70	Long Island Ducks	EHL	46	5	40	45	....	....	....	38	....	....	....	....	....
1970-71	Port Huron Flags	IHL	21	5	3	8	....	....	....	16	....	....	....	....	....
	NHL Totals		5	0	0	0	0	0	0	4	....	....	....	....	....

Traded to **LA Blades** (WHL) by **St. Louis** (AHL) for cash, February, 1965. Traded to **Des Moines** (IHL) by **Port Huron** (IHL) for cash, October, 1968. Traded to **Fort Wayne** (IHL) by **Des Moines** (IHL) with Ivan Robertson for Ron Hopkinson, January, 1970. Traded to **Long Island** (EHL) by **Fort Wayne** (IHL) for Ed Lawson, October, 1969. Traded to **Port Huron** (IHL) by **Long Island** (EHL) for cash, October, 1970.

• HENRY, CAMILLE
— see page 1099

• HERBERTS, JIMMY
Jimmy "Sailor" Herberts
C/RW – R. 5'10", 185 lbs. b: Cayuga, Ont., 10/31/1897. d: 12/5/1968.

Season	Club	League	GP	G	A	Pts	AG	AA	APts	PIM	GP	G	A	Pts	PIM
1922-23	Hamilton Tigers	OHA Sr.	12	3	2	5	....	....	....	....	2	1	0	1	8
1923-24	Eveleth Rangers	USAHA	19	3	0	3	....	....	....	....	....	....	....	....	....
1924-25	Boston Bruins	NHL	30	17	5	22	60	67	127	50	....	....	....	....	....
1925-26	Boston Bruins	NHL	36	26	5	31	83	58	141	47	....	....	....	....	....
1926-27	Boston Bruins	NHL	34	15	7	22	44	60	104	51	8	3	0	3	8
1927-28	Boston Bruins	NHL	12	8	3	11	24	25	49	22	....	....	....	....	....
	Toronto Maple Leafs	NHL	31	7	1	8	21	8	29	40	....	....	....	....	....
1928-29	Detroit Cougars	NHL	40	9	5	14	36	46	82	34	1	0	0	0	2
1929-30	Detroit Cougars	NHL	23	1	3	4	2	10	12	4	....	....	....	....	....
	London Panthers	IAHL	1	0	0	0	....	....	....	0	....	....	....	....	....
1930-31	Detroit Olympics	IAHL	44	14	11	25	....	....	....	34	....	....	....	....	....
1931-32	Detroit Olympics	IAHL	43	5	5	10	....	....	....	34	6	0	0	0	2
1932-33	Syracuse Stars	IAHL	2	0	0	0	....	....	....	0	....	....	....	....	....
	Windsor Bulldogs	IAHL	7	2	0	2	....	....	....	0	....	....	....	....	....
	NHL Totals		206	83	29	112	270	274	544	248	9	3	0	3	10

Signed as a free agent by **Boston**, November 2, 1924. Traded to **Toronto** by **Boston** with the rights to Eric Pettinger for $15,000, December 21, 1927. Traded to **Detroit Cougars** by **Toronto** for the rights to Jack Arbour and $12,500, June, 1928.

• HERCHENRATTER, ART Art Herchenratter
LW – L. 6', 185 lbs. b: Kitchener, Ont., 11/24/1917.

Season	Club	League	GP	G	A	Pts	AG	AA	APts	PIM	PO GP	PO G	PO A	PO Pts	PO PIM
1936-37	Kitchener Greenshirts	OHA	13	7	1	8	....	....	....	6	2	0	0	0	5
1937-38	Kitchener Greenshirts	OHA	11	4	6	10	....	....	....	0	....	....	....	....	....
1938-39	Detroit Holtzbaugh	MOHL	26	9	5	14	....	....	....	4	7	1	2	3	2
1939-40	Windsor Bulldogs	MOHL	40	*31	16	47	....	....	....	14	4	2	1	3	0
1940-41	**Detroit Red Wings**	**NHL**	**10**	**1**	**2**	**3**	**2**	**4**	**6**	**2**	....	....	....	....	....
	Indianapolis Capitols	AHL	39	1	6	7	....	....	....	6	....	....	....	....	....
1941-42	New Haven Eagles	AHL	13	4	1	5	....	....	....	4	....	....	....	....	....
	Omaha Knights	AHA	22	7	5	12	....	....	....	8	....	....	....	....	....
1942-43			MILITARY SERVICE												
1943-44	Truro Bearcats	NSSHL	3	2	1	3	....	....	....	0	....	....	....	....	....
1944-45			MILITARY SERVICE												
1945-46	Stratford Indians	OHA Sr.	2	0	0	0	....	....	....	0	5	0	5	5	0
1946-47	Springfield Indians	AHL	22	2	5	7	....	....	....	2	....	....	....	....	....
	Houston Huskies	USHL	15	6	7	13	....	....	....	4	....	....	....	....	....
1947-48	Kitchener Dutchmen	OHA Sr.	19	5	16	21	....	....	....	10	10	2	5	7	8
1948-49	Kitchener Dutchmen	OHA Sr.	32	7	10	17	....	....	....	14	4	0	0	0	0
1949-50	Kitchener Dutchmen	OHA Sr.	14	2	1	3	....	....	....	4	....	....	....	....	....
	NHL Totals		**10**	**1**	**2**	**3**	**2**	**4**	**6**	**2**	....	....	....	....	....

Signed as a free agent by **Detroit**, October 16, 1940.

• HERGERTS, FRED Fred Hergerts
C – R. 6'1", 190 lbs. b: Calgary, Alta., 1/29/1913.

Season	Club	League	GP	G	A	Pts	AG	AA	APts	PIM	PO GP	PO G	PO A	PO Pts	PO PIM
1930-31	Calgary Canadians	City Jr.	2	1	*2	*3	....	....	....	0	....	....	....	....	....
1931-32	Calgary Bronks	ASHL	20	9	*12	21	....	....	....	*50	3	*2	1	*3	2
1932-33	Drumheller Miners	ASHL	15	11	*9	20	....	....	....	12	5	1	1	2	2
1933-34	Syracuse–Cleveland	IAHL	40	1	3	4	....	....	....	11	6	1	0	1	2
1934-35	**New York Americans**	**NHL**	**19**	**2**	**4**	**6**	**4**	**9**	**13**	**2**	....	....	....	....	....
	Philadelphia Arrows	Can-Am	26	6	10	16	....	....	....	23	....	....	....	....	....
1935-36	**New York Americans**	**NHL**	**1**	**0**	**0**	**0**	**0**	**0**	**0**	**0**	....	....	....	....	....
	Detroit Olympics	IAHL	45	6	6	12	....	....	....	34	6	1	0	1	10
1936-37	Pittsburgh–Cleveland	AHL	48	4	15	19	....	....	....	47	5	0	0	0	0
1937-38	Kansas City Greyhounds	AHA	48	16	22	38	....	....	....	19	....	....	....	....	....
1938-39	St. Louis Flyers	AHA	39	16	36	52	....	....	....	40	2	0	1	1	0
1939-40	St. Louis Flyers	AHA	48	23	*48	*71	....	....	....	31	5	2	1	3	8
1940-41	St. Louis Flyers	AHA	48	11	*33	44	....	....	....	26	9	1	3	4	2
1941-42	St. Louis Flyers	AHA	44	15	13	28	....	....	....	22	3	1	1	2	0
1942-43	Hershey Bears	AHL	56	30	45	75	....	....	....	33	6	0	6	6	2
1943-44	Hershey Bears	AHL	53	19	31	50	....	....	....	43	7	2	4	6	2
1944-45	St. Louis Flyers	AHL	55	23	36	59	....	....	....	21	....	....	....	....	....
1945-46	St. Louis Flyers	AHL	58	9	32	41	....	....	....	34	....	....	....	....	....
1946-47	St. Louis Flyers	AHL	46	3	9	12	....	....	....	20	....	....	....	....	....
1947-48	Calgary Stampeders	WCSHL	45	2	12	14	....	....	....	78	11	3	4	7	6
1948-49	Nelson Maple Leafs	Kootenay	36	14	27	41	....	....	....	56	5	1	4	5	6
1949-50	Nelson Maple Leafs	Kootenay	DID NOT PLAY – COACHING												
1950-51	Nelson Maple Leafs	Kootenay	22	7	24	31	....	....	....	38	4	0	0	0	0
	NHL Totals		**20**	**2**	**4**	**6**	**4**	**9**	**13**	**2**	....	....	....	....	....

AHA First All-Star Team (1940)

Traded to **Detroit** (IAHL) by **NY Americans** with $7500 for Ed Wiseman, November 23, 1935.

• HERGESHEIMER, PHILIP Philip "Phantom" Hergesheimer
RW – R. 5'10", 175 lbs. b: Winnipeg, Man., 7/9/1914.

Season	Club	League	GP	G	A	Pts	AG	AA	APts	PIM	PO GP	PO G	PO A	PO Pts	PO PIM
1932-33	Winnipeg Falcons	MJHL	8	8	2	10	....	....	....	6	....	....	....	....	....
1933-34	Winnipeg Falcons	MJHL	14	9	6	15	....	....	....	21	1	0	0	0	0
1934-35	Boston Cubs	Can-Am	46	10	6	16	....	....	....	16	3	1	0	1	2
1935-36	Boston Cubs	Can-Am	27	2	7	9	....	....	....	10	....	....	....	....	....
	London Tecumsehs	IAHL	16	3	3	6	....	....	....	0	2	0	0	0	0
1936-37	Minneapolis Millers	AHA	48	23	26	49	....	....	....	22	6	1	4	5	4
1937-38	Cleveland Barons	AHL	47	*25	20	45	....	....	....	13	2	2	1	3	0
1938-39	Cleveland Falcons	AHL	64	*34	19	53	....	....	....	23	9	*7	1	*8	14
1939-40	**Chicago Black Hawks**	**NHL**	**42**	**9**	**11**	**20**	**19**	**22**	**41**	**6**	**1**	**0**	**0**	**0**	**0**
1940-41	**Chicago Black Hawks**	**NHL**	**48**	**8**	**16**	**24**	**16**	**29**	**45**	**9**	**5**	**0**	**0**	**0**	**2**
1941-42	**Chicago Black Hawks**	**NHL**	**23**	**3**	**11**	**14**	**5**	**17**	**22**	**2**	....	....	....	....	....
	Boston Bruins	**NHL**	**3**	**0**	**0**	**0**	**0**	**0**	**0**	**2**	....	....	....	....	....
	Hershey Bears	AHL	12	8	7	15	....	....	....	2	10	6	5	11	4
1942-43	**Chicago Black Hawks**	**NHL**	**9**	**1**	**3**	**4**	**1**	**4**	**5**	**0**	....	....	....	....	....
	Cleveland Barons	AHL	36	14	27	41	....	....	....	4	4	1	1	2	2
1943-44	Cleveland Barons	AHL	33	21	19	40	....	....	....	6	....	....	....	....	....
	Ottawa Commandos	QSHL	1	0	2	2	....	....	....	0	1	0	0	0	2
1944-45			MILITARY SERVICE												
1945-46	Cleveland Barons	AHL	54	21	27	48	....	....	....	4	12	6	10	*16	4
1946-47	Philadelphia Rockets	AHL	64	48	44	*92	....	....	....	20	....	....	....	....	....
1947-48	Philadelphia Rockets	AHL	57	42	31	73	....	....	....	6	....	....	....	....	....
1948-49	Philadelphia Rockets	AHL	67	38	28	66	....	....	....	14	....	....	....	....	....
1949-50	Cincinnati Mohawks	AHL	70	31	30	61	....	....	....	7	....	....	....	....	....
1950-51	Cincinnati Mohawks	AHL	54	6	13	19	....	....	....	8	....	....	....	....	....
1951-52	Kelowna Packers	OSHL	45	34	14	48	....	....	....	34	....	....	....	....	....
1952-53	Kelowna Packers	OSHL	54	20	26	46	....	....	....	10	4	2	2	4	2
1953-54	Kelowna Packers	OSHL	63	17	21	38	....	....	....	56	8	2	4	6	8
1954-55	Kamloops Elks	OSHL	40	10	8	18	....	....	....	18	9	2	0	2	2
	NHL Totals		**125**	**21**	**41**	**62**	**41**	**72**	**113**	**19**	**6**	**0**	**0**	**0**	**2**

AHA Second All-Star Team (1937) • AHL First All-Star Team (1939, 1944, 1947) • AHL Second All-Star Team (1948, 1949)

Traded to **Chicago** by **Cleveland** (AHL) for Charley Mason and future considerations, May 17, 1939. • Suspended by **Chicago** for refusing assignment to **Kansas City** (AHA), January 20, 1942. Traded to **Boston** by **Chicago** for cash with Chicago holding rights of recall, January 26, 1942. • Rights returned to **Chicago** by **Boston**, July 1, 1942.

• HERGESHEIMER, WALLY Wally Hergesheimer
RW – R. 5'8", 155 lbs. b: Winnipeg, Man., 1/8/1927.

Season	Club	League	GP	G	A	Pts	AG	AA	APts	PIM	PO GP	PO G	PO A	PO Pts	PO PIM
1943-44	Winnipeg Rangers	MJHL	2	2	1	3	....	....	....	2	....	....	....	....	....
1944-45	Winnipeg Rangers	MJHL	10	*20	10	*30	....	....	....	2	14	10	5	15	2
1945-46	Brandon Elks	MJHL	10	15	11	26	....	....	....	4	7	3	1	4	0
1946-47	Brandon Elks	MJHL	16	*25	14	39	....	....	....	8	19	22	9	31	8
1947-48	Minneapolis Millers	USHL	37	8	14	22	....	....	....	4	4	0	0	0	0
1948-49	San Francisco Shamrocks	PCHL	70	34	39	73	....	....	....	22	....	....	....	....	....
1949-50	Minneapolis Millers	USHL	69	43	37	80	....	....	....	22	7	5	5	10	0
1950-51	Cleveland Barons	AHL	71	42	41	83	....	....	....	8	11	*11	2	13	0
1951-52	**New York Rangers**	**NHL**	**68**	**26**	**12**	**38**	**37**	**15**	**52**	**6**	....	....	....	....	....
1952-53	**New York Rangers**	**NHL**	**70**	**30**	**29**	**59**	**47**	**41**	**88**	**10**	....	....	....	....	....
1953-54	**New York Rangers**	**NHL**	**66**	**27**	**16**	**43**	**42**	**22**	**64**	**42**	....	....	....	....	....
1954-55	**New York Rangers**	**NHL**	**14**	**4**	**2**	**6**	**6**	**3**	**9**	**4**	....	....	....	....	....
1955-56	**New York Rangers**	**NHL**	**70**	**22**	**18**	**40**	**32**	**22**	**54**	**26**	**5**	**1**	**0**	**1**	**0**
1956-57	**Chicago Black Hawks**	**NHL**	**41**	**2**	**8**	**10**	**3**	**9**	**12**	**12**	....	....	....	....	....
1957-58	Buffalo Bisons	AHL	70	26	21	47	....	....	....	18	....	....	....	....	....
1958-59	**New York Rangers**	**NHL**	**22**	**3**	**0**	**3**	**4**	**0**	**4**	**6**	....	....	....	....	....
	Buffalo Bisons	AHL	45	23	23	46	....	....	....	21	11	2	1	3	6
1959-60	Buffalo Bisons	AHL	72	25	29	54	....	....	....	13	....	....	....	....	....
1960-61	Calgary Stampeders	WHL	70	40	26	66	....	....	....	17	5	3	0	3	0
1961-62	Los Angeles Blades	WHL	66	21	44	65	....	....	....	6	....	....	....	....	....
	NHL Totals		**351**	**114**	**85**	**199**	**171**	**112**	**283**	**106**	**5**	**1**	**0**	**1**	**0**

USHL First All-Star Team (1950) • AHL Second All-Star Team (1951) • Won Dudley "Red" Garrett Memorial Award (Top Rookie - AHL) (1951)

Played in NHL All-Star Game (1953, 1956)

Traded to **Cleveland** (AHL) by **NY Rangers** for Bill Richardson, Neil Strain, Bob Jackson and Joe McArthur, September 5, 1950. Traded to **NY Rangers** by **Cleveland** (AHL) with Hy Buller for Ed Reigle, Jack Gordon, Fred Shero, Fern Perreault and cash, May 14, 1951. Traded to **Chicago** by **NY Rangers** for Red Sullivan, June 19, 1956. Traded to **Buffalo** by **Chicago** with Frank Martin for Ken Wharram, June, 1958. NHL rights transferred to **NY Rangers** from **Buffalo** after NHL club purchased AHL franchise, June, 1958.

• HERON, RED Red (Robert) Heron
C – L. 5'11", 170 lbs. b: Toronto, Ont., 12/31/1917.

Season	Club	League	GP	G	A	Pts	AG	AA	APts	PIM	PO GP	PO G	PO A	PO Pts	PO PIM
1932-33	Toronto Marlboros	OHA	9	4	1	5	....	....	....	4	3	0	0	0	2
1933-34	Toronto Native Sons	OHA	12	11	7	18	....	....	....	7	....	....	....	....	....
1934-35	West Toronto Nationals	OHA	12	3	1	4	....	....	....	14	....	....	....	....	....
1935-36	West Toronto Nationals	OHA	9	11	6	17	....	....	....	16	5	*6	*4	*10	2
	Toronto Goodyears	OHA Sr.	13	*16	1	17	....	....	....	4	6	4	2	6	9
1936-37	Toronto Goodyears	OHA Sr.	8	5	3	8	....	....	....	16	5	3	0	3	8
1937-38	Toronto Goodyears	OHA Sr.	16	*21	15	36	....	....	....	6	6	3	2	5	4
	Syracuse Stars	AHL	1	0	0	0	....	....	....	0	6	1	2	3	0
1938-39	**Toronto Maple Leafs**	**NHL**	**6**	**0**	**0**	**0**	**0**	**0**	**0**	**0**	**2**	**0**	**0**	**0**	**4**
	Syracuse Stars	AHL	46	12	14	26	....	....	....	26	3	0	1	1	10
1939-40	**Toronto Maple Leafs**	**NHL**	**42**	**11**	**12**	**23**	**24**	**24**	**48**	**12**	**9**	**2**	**0**	**2**	**2**
	Pittsburgh Hornets	AHL	4	3	3	6	....	....	....	0	....	....	....	....	....
1940-41	**Toronto Maple Leafs**	**NHL**	**35**	**9**	**5**	**14**	**18**	**9**	**27**	**12**	**7**	**0**	**2**	**2**	**0**
	Pittsburgh Hornets	AHL	2	2	0	2	....	....	....	0	....	....	....	....	....
1941-42	**Brooklyn Americans**	**NHL**	**11**	**0**	**1**	**1**	**0**	**2**	**2**	**2**	....	....	....	....	....
	Montreal Canadiens	**NHL**	**12**	**1**	**1**	**2**	**2**	**2**	**4**	**12**	**3**	**0**	**0**	**0**	**0**
	Pittsburgh Hornets	AHL	30	23	19	42	....	....	....	12	....	....	....	....	....
1942-43	Research Colonels	Tor-Sr.	12	22	12	34	....	....	....	4	....	....	....	....	....
1943-44	Toronto RCAF	OHA Sr.	15	6	10	16	....	....	....	12	....	....	....	....	....
	Toronto Staffords	OHA Sr.	....	9	5	14	....	....	....	4	9	9	5	14	8
1944-45	Rockcliffe RCAF	Ott-Sr.	....	....	....	....	....	....	....	....	2	0	2	2	0
	NHL Totals		**106**	**21**	**19**	**40**	**44**	**37**	**81**	**38**	**21**	**2**	**2**	**4**	**6**

Loaned to **Brooklyn** by **Toronto** with Nick Knott and Gus Marker for Lorne Carr, October 30, 1941. Loaned to **Montreal** by **Brooklyn** for the loan of Murph Chamberlain, February 13, 1942.

• HEXIMER, ORVILLE Orville "Obs" Heximer
LW/C – L. 5'7", 159 lbs. b: Niagara Falls, Ont., 2/16/1910.

Season	Club	League	GP	G	A	Pts	AG	AA	APts	PIM	PO GP	PO G	PO A	PO Pts	PO PIM
1926-27	Niagara Falls Cataracts	OHA	....	....	....	....	....	....	....	....	4	*2	*3	5	....
1928-29	Niagara Falls Cataracts	OHA	STATISTICS NOT AVAILABLE												
1929-30	**New York Rangers**	**NHL**	**19**	**1**	**0**	**1**	**2**	**0**	**2**	**4**	....	....	....	....	....
	Springfield Indians	Can-Am	14	13	6	19	....	....	....	18	....	....	....	....	....
1930-31	Springfield Indians	Can-Am	40	*36	*25	*61	....	....	....	70	7	4	0	4	4
1931-32	Springfield Indians	Can-Am	40	11	17	28	....	....	....	51	....	....	....	....	....
1932-33	**Boston Bruins**	**NHL**	**48**	**7**	**5**	**12**	**16**	**13**	**29**	**12**	**5**	**0**	**0**	**0**	**2**
1933-34	Boston Cubs	Can-Am	39	12	15	27	....	....	....	53	5	1	2	3	2
1934-35	**New York Americans**	**NHL**	**17**	**5**	**2**	**7**	**11**	**4**	**15**	**0**	....	....	....	....	....
	Boston–New Haven	Can-Am	25	13	13	26	....	....	....	18	....	....	....	....	....
1935-36	New Haven Eagles	Can-Am	39	15	10	25	....	....	....	35	....	....	....	....	....
1936-37	New Haven Eagles	AHL	42	9	12	21	....	....	....	39	....	....	....	....	....
1937-38	New Haven–Springfield	AHL	44	14	13	27	....	....	....	21	2	0	0	0	0
1938-39	St. Paul Saints	AHA	41	22	25	47	....	....	....	43	3	0	2	2	0
1939-40			DID NOT PLAY												
1940-41	Niagara Falls Brights	OHA Sr.	26	4	6	10	....	....	....	8	3	1	0	1	5
1941-42	Niagara Falls Weavers	OHA Sr.	18	0	1	1	....	....	....	2	7	0	3	3	15
	NHL Totals		**84**	**13**	**7**	**20**	**29**	**17**	**46**	**16**	**5**	**0**	**0**	**0**	**2**

Signed as a free agent by **NY Rangers**, December 10, 1929. Traded to **Boston** by **NY Rangers** for $10,000, August 22, 1932. Traded to **NY Americans** by **Boston** with Hap Emms for Walter Jackson, December 13, 1934. Traded to **New Haven** (Can-Am) by **NY Americans** for cash, October 21, 1935. Traded to **Springfield** (AHL) by **New Haven** (AHL) for Bob McCully, December 1, 1937.

• HEXTALL, BRYAN JR. — *see page 1101*

• HEXTALL, BRYAN SR. Bryan Sr. Hextall
RW – L. 5'10", 180 lbs. b: Grenfell, Sask., 7/31/1913. d: 7/25/1984.

Season	Club	League	GP	G	A	Pts	AG	AA	APts	PIM	GP	G	A	Pts	PIM
			REGULAR SEASON								PLAYOFFS				
1931-32	Winnipeg Monarchs	MJHL	4	0	0	0	....	....	....	0	1	2	0	2	0
1932-33	Portage Terriers	MJHL	12	10	*8	*18	....	....	....	6	2	0	0	0	4
1933-34	Portage Terriers	MJHL	7	6	4	10	....	....	....	8	....	....	....	....	....
	Vancouver Lions	NWHL	5	2	0	2	....	....	....	0	....	....	....	....	....
1934-35	Vancouver Lions	NWHL	32	14	10	24	....	....	....	27	8	0	0	0	*10
1935-36	Vancouver Lions	NWHL	40	*27	9	36	....	....	....	65	7	1	2	3	15
1936-37	Philadelphia Ramblers	AHL	18	*29	23	52	....	....	....	34	6	2	4	6	6
	New York Rangers	NHL	3	0	1	1	0	2	2	0	....	....	....	....	....
1937-38	New York Rangers	NHL	48	17	4	21	36	8	44	6	3	2	0	2	0
1938-39	New York Rangers	NHL	48	20	15	35	43	28	71	18	7	0	1	1	4
1939-40	New York Rangers	NHL	48	*24	15	39	52	30	82	52	12	4	3	7	11
1940-41	New York Rangers	NHL	48	*26	18	44	53	33	86	16	3	0	1	1	0
1941-42	New York Rangers	NHL	48	24	32	*56	42	49	91	30	6	1	1	2	4
1942-43	New York Rangers	NHL	50	27	32	59	39	41	80	28	....	....	....	....	....
1943-44	New York Rangers	NHL	50	21	33	54	27	40	67	41	....	....	....	....	....
1944-45	St. Catharines Saints	OHA Sr.	1	0	1	1	....	....	....	0	....	....	....	....	....
1945-46	New York Rangers	NHL	3	0	1	1	0	2	2	0	....	....	....	....	....
1946-47	New York Rangers	NHL	60	20	10	30	27	14	41	18	....	....	....	....	....
1947-48	New York Rangers	NHL	43	8	14	22	12	20	32	18	6	1	3	4	0
1948-49	Cleveland–Washington	AHL	57	18	23	41	....	....	....	16	....	....	....	....	....
	NHL Totals		449	187	175	362	331	267	598	227	37	8	9	17	19

NHL First All-Star Team (1940, 1941, 1942) • NHL Scoring Leader (1942) • NHL Second All-Star Team (1943)

• HEYLIGER, VIC Vic Heyliger USHOF
C – L. 5'9", 175 lbs. b: Boston, MA, 9/26/1919.

Season	Club	League	GP	G	A	Pts	AG	AA	APts	PIM	GP	G	A	Pts	PIM
1936-37	University of Michigan	NCAA	....	....	....	....	....	....	....	....	....	....	....	....	....
1937-38	Chicago Black Hawks	NHL	7	0	0	0	0	0	0	0	....	....	....	....	....
	St. Paul Saints	AHA	3	0	0	0	....	....	....	0	....	....	....	....	....
1938-39	Detroit Holzbaugh	MOHL	27	5	9	14	....	....	....	27	2	1	1	2	2
1939-40	University of Illinois	WIAA	DID NOT PLAY – COACHING												
1940-41	University of Illinois	WIAA	DID NOT PLAY – COACHING												
1941-42	University of Illinois	WIAA	DID NOT PLAY – COACHING												
1942-43	University of Illinois	WIAA	DID NOT PLAY – COACHING												
1943-44	Chicago Black Hawks	NHL	26	2	3	5	2	4	6	2	....	....	....	....	....
	NHL Totals		33	2	3	5	2	4	6	2	....	....	....	....	....

Signed as a free agent by **Chicago**, November 3, 1937. Signed as a free agent by **Chicago**, October 18, 1943.

• HICKE, BILL — see page 1102

• HICKS, HAROLD Harold "Hal" Hicks
D – L. 5'7", 170 lbs. b: Sillery, Quebec, 12/10/1900. Deceased.

Season	Club	League	GP	G	A	Pts	AG	AA	APts	PIM	GP	G	A	Pts	PIM
1924-25	Ottawa Rideaus	City Sr.	12	2	0	2	....	....	....	....	3	0	0	0	....
1925-26	Ottawa Rideaus	City Sr.	....	4	3	7	....	....	....	....	....	....	....	....	....
1926-27	Stratford Nationals	Can-Pro	31	5	4	9	....	....	....	76	2	0	0	0	0
1927-28	Stratford Nationals	Can-Pro	42	8	6	14	....	....	....	61	5	*4	1	5	8
1928-29	Montreal Maroons	NHL	44	2	0	2	8	0	8	27	....	....	....	....	....
1929-30	Detroit Cougars	NHL	30	3	2	5	6	6	12	35	....	....	....	....	....
	Detroit Olympics	IAHL	15	0	1	1	....	....	....	21	3	0	0	0	0
1930-31	Detroit Falcons	NHL	22	2	0	2	5	0	5	10	....	....	....	....	....
	London Techumsehs	IAHL	27	4	3	7	....	....	....	10	....	....	....	....	....
1931-32	London Tecumsehs	IAHL	47	3	9	12	....	....	....	53	6	0	1	1	2
1932-33	London Tecumsehs	IAHL	44	9	15	24	....	....	....	51	6	0	0	0	5
1933-34	London Tecumsehs	IAHL	15	1	1	2	....	....	....	8	....	....	....	....	....
	NHL Totals		96	7	2	9	19	6	25	72	....	....	....	....	....

Traded to **Montreal Maroons** by **Stratford** (IAHL) for cash, April 23, 1928. Traded to **Detroit Cougars** by **Montreal Canadiens** for $8,000, September 30, 1929. Traded to **London** (IAHL) by **Detroit** for Leroy Goldsworthy, January 12, 1931.

• HICKS, WAYNE — see page 1104

• HILDEBRAND, IKE Ike Hildebrand
RW – R. 5'7", 147 lbs. b: Winnipeg, Man., 5/27/1927.

Season	Club	League	GP	G	A	Pts	AG	AA	APts	PIM	GP	G	A	Pts	PIM
1945-46	Oshawa Generals	OHA	27	14	21	35	....	....	....	8	12	*21	11	*32	4
1946-47	Oshawa Generals	OHA	29	28	25	53	....	....	....	23	5	3	1	4	16
1947-48	Toronto Marlboros	OHA Sr.	35	29	37	66	....	....	....	29	5	2	0	2	6
1948-49	Los Angeles Monarchs	PCHL	45	17	19	36	....	....	....	32	7	1	5	6	17
1949-50	Los Angeles Monarchs	PCHL	63	24	36	60	....	....	....	28	17	6	8	14	20
1950-51	Kansas City Royals	USHL	63	*42	49	91	....	....	....	67	....	....	....	....	....
1951-52	Cleveland Barons	AHL	48	31	16	47	....	....	....	19	5	1	3	4	7
1952-53	Cleveland Barons	AHL	64	*38	34	72	....	....	....	40	11	1	1	2	11
1953-54	New York Rangers	NHL	31	6	7	13	9	9	18	12	....	....	....	....	....
	Vancouver Canucks	WHL	8	0	0	0	....	....	....	2	....	....	....	....	....
	Chicago Black Hawks	NHL	7	1	4	5	2	5	7	4	....	....	....	....	....
1954-55	Chicago Black Hawks	NHL	3	0	0	0	0	0	0	0	....	....	....	....	....
	Montreal Royals	QHL	53	17	25	42	....	....	....	27	14	1	6	7	14
1955-56	Cleveland Barons	AHL	54	9	19	28	....	....	....	43	8	1	1	2	10
1956-57	Pembroke Lumber Kings	EOHL	23	6	12	18	....	....	....	44	....	....	....	....	....
	Belleville McFarlands	EOHL	25	19	36	55	....	....	....	73	10	2	5	7	10
1957-58	Belleville McFarlands	EOHL	51	15	39	54	....	....	....	55	13	5	*19	24	2
1958-59	Belleville McFarlands	EOHL	46	30	36	66	....	....	....	31	....	....	....	....	....
	Canada	WEC-A	8	6	6	*12	....	....	....	4	....	....	....	....	....
1959-60	Belleville McFarlands	OHA Sr.	45	23	22	45	....	....	....	20	12	3	11	14	4
	NHL Totals		41	7	11	18	11	14	25	16	....	....	....	....	....

USHL First All-Star Team (1951) • AHL First All-Star Team (1953)

Traded to **Vancouver** (WHL) by **NY Rangers** for cash, January 7, 1954. Traded to **Chicago** by **Vancouver** (WHL) for cash, January 20, 1954. Traded to **Detroit** by **Chicago** for Lorne Davis, October 14, 1954.

• HILL, MEL Mel "Sudden Death" Hill
RW – R. 5'10", 175 lbs. b: Glenboro, Man., 2/15/1914. d: 4/11/1996.

Season	Club	League	GP	G	A	Pts	AG	AA	APts	PIM	GP	G	A	Pts	PIM
			REGULAR SEASON								PLAYOFFS				
1933-34	Saskatoon Wesleys	City Jr.	....	....	....	....	....	....	....	....	3	*4	0	4	0
1934-35	Sudbury Wolves	City Sr.	10	9	4	13	....	....	....	8	5	2	1	3	0
1935-36	Sudbury Frood Miners	City Sr.	10	7	6	13	....	....	....	15	....	....	....	....	....
1936-37	Sudbury Frood Miners	City Sr.	15	*18	5	23	....	....	....	10	16	9	*14	23	6
1937-38	Boston Bruins	NHL	6	2	0	2	4	0	4	2	1	0	0	0	0
	Providence Reds	AHL	40	13	10	23	....	....	....	0	7	4	2	6	0
1938-39	Boston Bruins	NHL	46	10	10	20	21	19	40	16	12	6	3	9	12
1939-40	Boston Bruins	NHL	38	9	11	20	19	22	41	19	3	0	0	0	0
1940-41	Boston Bruins	NHL	41	5	4	9	10	7	17	4	8	1	1	2	0
	Hershey Bears	AHL	5	1	5	6	....	....	....	4	....	....	....	....	....
	Springfield Indians	AHL	1	0	0	0	....	....	....	0	....	....	....	....	....
1941-42	Brooklyn Americans	NHL	47	14	23	37	24	35	59	10	....	....	....	....	....
1942-43	Toronto Maple Leafs	NHL	49	17	27	44	24	34	58	47	6	3	0	3	0
1943-44	Toronto Maple Leafs	NHL	17	9	10	19	11	12	23	6	....	....	....	....	....
1944-45	Toronto Maple Leafs	NHL	45	18	17	35	25	28	53	14	13	2	3	5	6
1945-46	Toronto Maple Leafs	NHL	35	5	7	12	8	13	21	10	....	....	....	....	....
	Pittsburgh Hornets	AHL	13	7	8	15	....	....	....	0	6	1	2	3	0
1946-47	Pittsburgh Hornets	AHL	62	26	36	62	....	....	....	42	12	3	6	9	6
1947-48	Pittsburgh Hornets	AHL	63	10	22	32	....	....	....	14	2	0	0	0	2
1948-49	Regina Caps	WCSHL	43	23	30	53	....	....	....	11	8	4	6	10	4
1949-50	Regina Caps	WCSHL	50	17	21	38	....	....	....	16	....	....	....	....	....
1950-51	Regina Caps	WCSHL	22	3	5	8	....	....	....	6	....	....	....	....	....
1951-52	Regina Caps	SSHL	17	7	11	18	....	....	....	16	3	1	0	1	4
	NHL Totals		324	89	109	198	146	170	316	128	43	12	7	19	18

Signed as a free agent by **Boston**, October 26, 1937. Traded to **Brooklyn** by **Boston** for cash, June 27, 1941. Rights transferred to **Toronto** from **Brooklyn** in Special Dispersal Draw, October 9, 1942.

• HILLER, DUTCH Dutch (Wilbert Carl) Hiller
LW – L. 5'8", 170 lbs. b: Kitchener, Ont., 5/11/1915.

Season	Club	League	GP	G	A	Pts	AG	AA	APts	PIM	GP	G	A	Pts	PIM
1933-34	Sudbury Wolves	City Sr.	8	7	0	7	....	....	....	15	2	*5	1	*6	2
1934-35	Sudbury Wolves	City Sr.	4	5	0	5	....	....	....	8	3	2	0	2	*8
1935-36	Sudbury Frood Miners	City Sr.	6	5	0	5	....	....	....	10	....	....	....	....	....
1936-37	Harringay Greyhounds	Britain	....	22	11	33	....	....	....	16	....	....	....	....	....
1937-38	New York Rangers	NHL	8	0	1	1	0	2	2	2	1	0	0	0	0
	New York Rovers	EHL	43	26	30	56	....	....	....	31	....	....	....	....	....
1938-39	New York Rangers	NHL	48	10	19	29	21	36	57	22	7	1	0	1	9
1939-40	New York Rangers	NHL	48	13	18	31	28	36	64	57	12	2	4	6	2
1940-41	New York Rangers	NHL	44	8	10	18	16	18	34	20	3	0	0	0	0
1941-42	Detroit Red Wings	NHL	7	0	0	0	0	0	0	0	....	....	....	....	....
	Boston Bruins	NHL	43	7	10	17	12	15	27	19	5	0	1	1	0
1942-43	Boston Bruins	NHL	3	0	0	0	0	0	0	0	....	....	....	....	....
	Montreal Canadiens	NHL	39	8	6	14	11	8	19	4	5	1	0	1	4
1943-44	New York Rangers	NHL	50	18	22	40	23	27	50	15	....	....	....	....	....
1944-45	Montreal Canadiens	NHL	48	20	16	36	28	26	54	20	6	1	1	2	4
1945-46	Montreal Canadiens	NHL	45	7	11	18	11	20	31	4	9	4	2	6	2
1946-47	Pittsburgh Hornets	AHL	64	13	16	29	....	....	....	37	12	2	3	5	12
1947-48	Kitchener Dutchmen	OHA Sr.	19	15	12	27	....	....	....	20	9	2	4	6	8
1948-49	Los Angeles Monarchs	PCHL	DID NOT PLAY – COACHING												
	NHL Totals		383	91	113	204	150	188	338	163	48	9	8	17	21

EHL Second All-Star Team (1938)

Traded to **Detroit** by **NY Rangers** for $5,000, April 8, 1941. Traded to **Boston** by **Detroit** with $5,000 for Pat McReavy, November 24, 1941. Traded to **Montreal** by **Boston** for cash, August, 1943. Loaned to **NY Rangers** by **Montreal** with John Mahaffy, Fern Gauthier, Charlie Sands and future considerations (Tony Demers, December, 1943) for the loan of Phil Watson, November, 1943. Traded to **Toronto** by **Montreal** with Vic Lynn for John Mahaffy and Gerry Brown, September 21, 1946.

• HILLMAN, FLOYD Floyd Hillman
D – L. 5'11", 170 lbs. b: Ruthven, Ont., 11/19/1933.

Season	Club	League	GP	G	A	Pts	AG	AA	APts	PIM	GP	G	A	Pts	PIM
1952-53	Oshawa Generals	OHA	56	7	13	20	....	....	....	94	4	1	0	1	4
1953-54	Kitchener Greenshirts	OHA	55	3	16	19	....	....	....	115	4	0	0	0	8
1954-55	Windsor Bulldogs	OHA Sr.	46	2	10	12	....	....	....	*131	12	1	3	4	27
1955-56	Victoria Cougars	WHL	30	2	4	6	....	....	....	69	....	....	....	....	....
	Hershey Bears	AHL	41	1	6	7	....	....	....	70	....	....	....	....	....
1956-57	Boston Bruins	NHL	6	0	0	0	0	0	0	10	....	....	....	....	....
	Quebec Aces	QHL	62	4	8	12	....	....	....	140	10	0	2	2	14
1957-58	Quebec Aces	QHL	23	0	5	5	....	....	....	49	13	0	2	2	15
	Springfield Indians	AHL	43	3	11	14	....	....	....	62	....	....	....	....	....
1958-59	Providence Reds	AHL	2	0	0	0	....	....	....	0	....	....	....	....	....
	Quebec Aces	QHL	59	1	18	19	....	....	....	149	....	....	....	....	....
1959-60	Providence Reds	AHL	72	4	27	31	....	....	....	132	5	0	1	1	10
1960-61	Providence Reds	AHL	39	0	8	8	....	....	....	53	....	....	....	....	....
	Kingston Frontenacs	EPHL	18	0	1	1	....	....	....	27	....	....	....	....	....
1961-62	San Francisco Seals	WHL	70	0	14	14	....	....	....	122	2	0	1	1	7
1962-63	Windsor Bulldogs	OHA Sr.	33	3	20	23	....	....	....	72	11	0	2	2	27
1963-64	Windsor Bulldogs	IHL	68	4	22	26	....	....	....	180	6	0	2	2	8
	NHL Totals		6	0	0	0	0	0	0	10	....	....	....	....	....

Traded to **Boston** by **Victoria** (WHL) for Arnott Whitney, December, 1955.

• HILLMAN, LARRY — see page 1106

• HILLMAN, WAYNE — see page 1107

• HIMES, NORMIE Normie Himes

C – R. 5'9", 145 lbs. b: Galt, Ontario, 4/1/1900. d: 9/14/1958.

			REGULAR SEASON								PLAYOFFS				
Season	Club	League	GP	G	A	Pts	AG	AA	APts	PIM	GP	G	A	Pts	PIM
1922-23	Galt Terriers	OHA Sr.	9	11	5	16	....	....	....	....	....	....	....	....	....
1923-24	Galt Terriers	OHA Sr.	12	9	3	12	....	....	....	6	....	....	....	....	....
1924-25	Galt Terriers	OHA Sr.	20	14	3	17	....	....	....	19	....	....	....	....	....
1925-26	Galt Terriers	OHA Sr.	20	13	6	19	....	....	....	13	2	2	0	2	1
1926-27	**New York Americans**	**NHL**	**42**	**9**	**2**	**11**	**26**	**17**	**43**	**14**	....	....	....	....	....
1927-28	**New York Americans**	**NHL**	**44**	**14**	**5**	**19**	**43**	**42**	**85**	**22**	....	....	....	....	....
1928-29	**New York Americans**	**NHL**	**44**	**10**	**0**	**10**	**40**	**0**	**40**	**25**	**2**	**0**	**0**	**0**	**0**
1929-30	**New York Americans**	**NHL**	**44**	**28**	**22**	**50**	**56**	**72**	**128**	**15**	....	....	....	....	....
1930-31	**New York Americans**	**NHL**	**44**	**15**	**9**	**24**	**37**	**33**	**70**	**18**	....	....	....	....	....
1931-32	**New York Americans**	**NHL**	**48**	**7**	**21**	**28**	**15**	**59**	**74**	**9**	....	....	....	....	....
1932-33	**New York Americans**	**NHL**	**48**	**9**	**25**	**34**	**21**	**67**	**88**	**12**	....	....	....	....	....
1933-34	**New York Americans**	**NHL**	**48**	**9**	**16**	**25**	**20**	**43**	**63**	**10**	....	....	....	....	....
1934-35	**New York Americans**	**NHL**	**40**	**5**	**13**	**18**	**11**	**29**	**40**	**2**	....	....	....	....	....
1935-36	New Haven Eagles	Can-Am	46	4	14	18	....	....	....	26	....	....	....	....	....
1936-37	New Haven Eagles	AHL	6	0	0	0	....	....	....	2	....	....	....	....	....
	NHL Totals		**402**	**106**	**113**	**219**	**269**	**362**	**631**	**127**	**2**	**0**	**0**	**0**	**0**

Played in NHL All-Star Game (1934)

Signed as a free agent by **NY Americans**, October 1, 1926.

• HIRSCHFELD, BERT Bert Hirschfeld

LW – L. 5'10", 165 lbs. b: Halifax, Nova Scotia, 3/1/1929. d: 7/3/1996.

Season	Club	League	GP	G	A	Pts	AG	AA	APts	PIM	GP	G	A	Pts	PIM
1946-47	Halifax St. Mary's	City Jr.	7	*13	*15	*28	....	....	....	0	7	8	*12	*20	2
1947-48	Halifax St. Mary's	City Jr.	25	16	*39	55	....	....	....	11	8	*19	8	*27	0
	Halifax Crescents	City Sr.	2	1	3	4	....	....	....	2	....	....	....	....	....
1948-49	Montreal Royals	QJHL	40	32	26	58	....	....	....	17	25	23	15	*38	15
	Montreal Royals	QSHL	1	0	0	0	....	....	....	0	....	....	....	....	....
1949-50	**Montreal Canadiens**	**NHL**	**13**	**1**	**2**	**3**	**1**	**3**	**4**	**2**	**5**	**1**	**0**	**1**	**0**
	Cincinnati Mohawks	AHL	53	22	12	34	....	....	....	2	....	....	....	....	....
	Montreal Royals	QSHL	8	1	1	2	....	....	....	0	....	....	....	....	....
1950-51	**Montreal Canadiens**	**NHL**	**20**	**0**	**2**	**2**	**0**	**3**	**3**	**0**	....	....	....	....	....
	Cincinnati Mohawks	AHL	42	15	8	23	....	....	....	2	....	....	....	....	....
1951-52	Indianapolis Capitals	AHL	67	23	38	61	....	....	....	8	....	....	....	....	....
1952-53	St. Louis Flyers	AHL	58	12	27	39	....	....	....	4	....	....	....	....	....
1953-54	Providence Reds	AHL	60	10	26	36	....	....	....	10	....	....	....	....	....
1954-55	Moncton Hawks	MSHL	....	29	27	56	....	....	....	10	24	*18	13	31	0
1955-56	New Haven Blades	EHL	1	0	2	2	....	....	....	0	....	....	....	....	....
	Moncton Hawks	NBSHL	....	12	40	52	....	....	....	31	8	1	2	3	2
1956-57	Campbellton Tigers	NNBSL	....	9	15	24	....	....	....	6	....	....	....	....	....
1957-58			DID NOT PLAY												
1958-59	Halifax Wolves	NSSHL	....	3	9	12	....	....	....	0	....	....	....	....	....
1959-60	Halifax Wolves	NSSHL	....	11	6	17	....	....	....	9	....	....	....	....	....
1960-61	Halifax Wolves	NSSHL	....	25	17	42	....	....	....	2	....	....	....	....	....
1961-62	Halifax Wolves	NSSHL	....	11	20	31	....	....	....	2	5	6	6	12	2
1962-63	Halifax Tartans	NSSHL	DID NOT PLAY – COACHING												
	NHL Totals		**33**	**1**	**4**	**5**	**1**	**6**	**7**	**2**	**5**	**1**	**0**	**1**	**0**

Traded to **Detroit** by **Montreal** for Doc Couture, June 19, 1951.

• HITCHMAN, LIONEL Lionel "Hitch" Hitchman

D – R. 6'1", 167 lbs. b: Toronto, Ont., 11/3/1901. d: 1/12/1969.

Season	Club	League	GP	G	A	Pts	AG	AA	APts	PIM	GP	G	A	Pts	PIM
1919-20	Toronto Aura Lee	OHA	4	0	0	0	....	....	....	0	....	....	....	....	....
1920-21	Toronto Aura Lee	OHA	3	1	0	1	....	....	....	4	....	....	....	....	....
1921-22	Ottawa New Edinburghs	City Sr.	8	2	1	3	....	....	....	14	....	....	....	....	....
1922-23	Ottawa New Edinburghs	City Sr.	16	5	1	6	....	....	....	30	3	0	0	0	*18
	Ottawa Senators	**NHL**	**3**	**0**	**1**	**1**	**0**	**9**	**9**	**12**	**7**	**1**	**0**	**1**	**4**
1923-24	**Ottawa Senators**	**NHL**	**24**	**2**	**6**	**8**	**8**	**110**	**118**	**24**	**2**	**0**	**0**	**0**	**4**
1924-25	**Ottawa Senators**	**NHL**	**12**	**0**	**0**	**0**	**0**	**0**	**0**	**2**	....	....	....	....	....
	Boston Bruins	**NHL**	**18**	**3**	**0**	**3**	**10**	**0**	**10**	**22**	....	....	....	....	....
1925-26	**Boston Bruins**	**NHL**	**36**	**7**	**4**	**11**	**22**	**40**	**62**	**70**	....	....	....	....	....
1926-27	**Boston Bruins**	**NHL**	**41**	**3**	**6**	**9**	**9**	**51**	**60**	**70**	**8**	**1**	**0**	**1**	**31**
1927-28	**Boston Bruins**	**NHL**	**44**	**5**	**3**	**8**	**15**	**25**	**40**	**87**	**2**	**0**	**0**	**0**	**2**
1928-29	**Boston Bruins**	**NHL**	**38**	**1**	**0**	**1**	**4**	**0**	**4**	**64**	**5**	**0**	**1**	**1**	**22**
1929-30	**Boston Bruins**	**NHL**	**39**	**2**	**7**	**9**	**4**	**23**	**27**	**58**	**6**	**1**	**0**	**1**	**14**
1930-31	**Boston Bruins**	**NHL**	**41**	**0**	**2**	**2**	**0**	**7**	**7**	**40**	**5**	**0**	**0**	**0**	**0**
1931-32	**Boston Bruins**	**NHL**	**48**	**4**	**3**	**7**	**8**	**8**	**16**	**36**	....	....	....	....	....
1932-33	**Boston Bruins**	**NHL**	**45**	**0**	**1**	**1**	**0**	**3**	**3**	**34**	**5**	**1**	**0**	**1**	**0**
1933-34	**Boston Bruins**	**NHL**	**27**	**1**	**0**	**1**	**2**	**0**	**2**	**4**	....	....	....	....	....
	Boston Cubs	Can-Am	4	0	0	0	....	....	....	2	....	....	....	....	....
	NHL Totals		**416**	**28**	**33**	**61**	**82**	**282**	**364**	**523**	**40**	**4**	**1**	**5**	**77**

Signed as a free agent by **Ottawa**, February 28, 1923. Traded to **Boston** by **Ottawa** for cash, January 10, 1925.

• HODGE, KEN — *see page 1109*

• HODGSON, TED Ted Hodgson

RW – R. 5'11", 185 lbs. b: Hobbema, Alta., 6/30/1945.

Season	Club	League	GP	G	A	Pts	AG	AA	APts	PIM	GP	G	A	Pts	PIM
1963-64	Estevan Bruins	SJHL	60	19	17	36	....	....	....	123	11	4	4	8	32
1964-65	Estevan Bruins	SJHL	55	37	38	75	....	....	....	148	6	3	4	7	20
	Minneapolis Bruins	CHL	2	0	0	0	....	....	....	2	5	0	0	0	0
1965-66	Estevan Bruins	SJHL	35	21	35	56	....	....	....	152	11	2	7	9	28
1966-67	**Boston Bruins**	**NHL**	**4**	**0**	**0**	**0**	**0**	**0**	**0**	**0**	....	....	....	....	....
	Buffalo Bisons	AHL	7	2	2	4	....	....	....	16	....	....	....	....	....
	Oklahoma City Blazers	CHL	53	5	7	12	....	....	....	101	9	2	1	3	10
1967-68	Oklahoma City Blazers	CHL	62	11	10	21	....	....	....	136	7	0	1	1	15
1968-69	Oklahoma City Blazers	CHL	44	12	20	32	....	....	....	56	12	0	1	1	25
1969-70	Salt Lake Golden Eagles	WHL	57	18	22	40	....	....	....	54	....	....	....	....	....
1970-71	Salt Lake Golden Eagles	WHL	60	8	13	21	....	....	....	90	....	....	....	....	....
1971-72	Salt Lake Golden Eagles	WHL	72	22	17	39	....	....	....	86	....	....	....	....	....
1972-73	Cleveland Crusaders	WHA	74	15	23	38	....	....	....	93	9	1	3	4	13
1973-74	Cleveland Crusaders	WHA	10	0	2	2	....	....	....	6	....	....	....	....	....
	Los Angeles Sharks	WHA	23	3	9	12	....	....	....	22	....	....	....	....	....
	Jacksonville Barons	AHL	46	4	13	17	....	....	....	42	....	....	....	....	....
1974-75	Philadelphia Firebirds	NAHL	71	10	26	36	....	....	....	39	3	0	1	1	4
1975-76	Roanoke Valley Rebels	SHL	54	11	14	25	....	....	....	32	6	1	3	4	2
1976-77	Oklahoma City Blazers	CHL	46	5	23	28	....	....	....	83	....	....	....	....	....
	NHL Totals		**4**	**0**	**0**	**0**	**0**	**0**	**0**	**0**	....	....	....	....	....
	Other Major League Totals		107	18	34	52	....	....	....	121	9	1	3	4	13

Traded to **NY Rangers** by **Salt Lake** (WHL) for cash, May 22, 1970. Traded to **Buffalo** by **NY Rangers** for cash, June, 1970. Selected by **Calgary-Cleveland** (WHA) in 1972 WHA General Player Draft, February 12, 1972. Traded to **LA Sharks** (WHA) by **Cleveland** (WHA) with Bill Young for Ron Ward, February, 1974. Selected by **Phoenix** (WHA) from **LA Sharks** (WHA) in WHA Expansion Draft, June, 1974.

• HOEKSTRA, CECIL Cecil "Cec" Hoekstra

C – L. 6', 175 lbs. b: Winnipeg, Man., 4/2/1935.

Season	Club	League	GP	G	A	Pts	AG	AA	APts	PIM	GP	G	A	Pts	PIM
1951-52	Weston Wildcats	Tor-Jr.	....	15	15	30	....	....	....	....	....	....	....	....	....
1952-53	St. Boniface Canadians	MJHL	31	11	17	28	....	....	....	10	24	7	20	27	2
1953-54	St. Catharines Teepees	OHA	59	24	35	59	....	....	....	8	14	4	8	12	0
1954-55	St. Catharines Teepees	OHA	49	30	50	80	....	....	....	24	11	5	7	12	11
	Montreal Royals	QHL	....	....	....	....	....	....	....	....	3	1	0	1	0
1955-56	Montreal Royals	QHL	34	6	5	11	....	....	....	8	....	....	....	....	....
	Winnipeg Warriors	WHL	28	1	9	10	....	....	....	4	14	0	0	0	2
1956-57	Winnipeg Warriors	WHL	69	21	12	33	....	....	....	16	....	....	....	....	....
1957-58	Montreal Royals	QHL	31	13	24	37	....	....	....	11	7	3	4	7	0
	Rochester Americans	AHL	13	1	2	3	....	....	....	0	....	....	....	....	....
1958-59	Rochester Americans	AHL	70	26	24	50	....	....	....	4	5	1	1	2	0
1959-60	**Montreal Canadiens**	**NHL**	**4**	**0**	**0**	**0**	**0**	**0**	**0**	**0**	....	....	....	....	....
	Rochester Americans	AHL	69	17	32	49	....	....	....	2	5	1	1	2	0
1960-61	Buffalo Bisons	AHL	68	6	16	22	....	....	....	14	4	0	0	0	0
1961-62	Pittsburgh Hornets	AHL	68	16	31	47	....	....	....	16	....	....	....	....	....
1962-63	Calgary Stampeders	WHL	67	14	31	45	....	....	....	10	....	....	....	....	....
1963-64	Cleveland Barons	AHL	72	23	28	51	....	....	....	12	9	3	7	10	0
1964-65	Cleveland Barons	AHL	20	2	3	5	....	....	....	6	....	....	....	....	....
1965-66	Cleveland Barons	AHL	70	21	26	47	....	....	....	10	12	2	6	8	6
1966-67	Cleveland Barons	AHL	59	20	34	54	....	....	....	10	2	0	0	0	0
1967-68	Cleveland Barons	AHL	72	24	36	60	....	....	....	14	....	....	....	....	....
1968-69	Cleveland Barons	AHL	73	15	26	41	....	....	....	8	5	0	2	2	2
1969-70	Cleveland Barons	AHL	72	8	20	28	....	....	....	0	....	....	....	....	....
1970-71	Galt Hornets	OHA Sr.	STATISTICS NOT AVAILABLE												
1971-72	Galt Hornets	OHA Sr.	3	0	1	1	....	....	....	4	....	....	....	....	....
	NHL Totals		**4**	**0**	**0**	**0**	**0**	**0**	**0**	**0**	....	....	....	....	....

Traded to **Montreal** by **Chicago** with Reggie Fleming, Ab McDonald and Bob Courcy for Terry Gray, Glen Skov, the rights to Danny Lewicki, Lorne Ferguson and Bob Bailey, June 7, 1960. Traded to **Pittsburgh** (AHL) by **Chicago** for cash, June, 1960. Traded to **Chicago** by **Pittsburgh** (AHL) for cash, September, 1961.

• HOFFINGER, VAL Val "Doc" Hoffinger

D – L. 5'6", 190 lbs. b: Seltz, Russia, 1/1/1901.

Season	Club	League	GP	G	A	Pts	AG	AA	APts	PIM	GP	G	A	Pts	PIM
1925-26	Saskatoon Empires	City Sr.	4	6	1	7	....	....	....	6	....	....	....	....	....
1926-27	Saskatoon Sheiks	PrHL	29	13	6	19	....	....	....	42	4	0	0	0	*8
1927-28	**Chicago Black Hawks**	**NHL**	**18**	**0**	**1**	**1**	**0**	**8**	**8**	**18**	....	....	....	....	....
	Saskatoon Sheiks	PrHL	16	5	1	6	....	....	....	14	....	....	....	....	....
1928-29	**Chicago Black Hawks**	**NHL**	**10**	**0**	**0**	**0**	**0**	**0**	**0**	**12**	....	....	....	....	....
	Hamilton–Kitchener	Can-Pro	25	3	3	6	....	....	....	28	....	....	....	....	....
	Duluth Hornets	AHA	6	0	1	1	....	....	....	4	....	....	....	....	....
1929-30	Hamilton–Kitchener	IAHL	42	4	3	7	....	....	....	74	....	....	....	....	....
1930-31	Syracuse Stars	IAHL	8	0	0	0	....	....	....	21	....	....	....	....	....
	Detroit Olympics	IAHL	39	4	6	10	....	....	....	68	....	....	....	....	....
1931-32	London Tecumsehs	IAHL	44	4	3	7	....	....	....	16	6	1	1	2	2
1932-33	London–Cleveland	IAHL	33	6	6	12	....	....	....	18	....	....	....	....	....
1933-34	Edmonton Eskimos	PrHL	5	0	0	0	....	....	....	0	....	....	....	....	....
1934-35	Oklahoma City Warriors	AHA	46	4	4	8	....	....	....	46	....	....	....	....	....
	NHL Totals		**28**	**0**	**1**	**1**	**0**	**8**	**8**	**30**	....	....	....	....	....

Loaned to **Kitchener** (Can-Pro) by **Chicago**, January 7, 1929. Traded to **Detroit** by **Chicago** for Rusty Hughes, December 7, 1931. Traded to **Cleveland** (IAHL) by **London** for cash, December, 1932.

• HOLLETT, FLASH
Flash (William) Hollett
D – L. 6', 180 lbs. b: North Sydney, N.S., 4/13/1912. Deceased.

			REGULAR SEASON								PLAYOFFS				
Season	Club	League	GP	G	A	Pts	AG	AA	APts	PIM	GP	G	A	Pts	PIM
1932-33	Syracuse Stars	IAHL	19	0	2	2	....	....	....	16	6	3	0	3	9
1933-34	**Toronto Maple Leafs**	**NHL**	4	0	0	0	0	0	0	4	....	....	....	....	....
	Ottawa Senators	**NHL**	30	7	4	11	15	11	26	21	....	....	....	....	....
	Buffalo Bisons	IAHL	13	5	4	9	....	....	....	8	....	....	....	....	....
1934-35	**Toronto Maple Leafs**	**NHL**	48	10	16	26	21	36	57	38	7	0	0	0	6
1935-36	**Toronto Maple Leafs**	**NHL**	11	1	4	5	2	10	12	8	....	....	....	....	....
	Syracuse Stars	IAHL	4	2	1	3	....	....	....	8	....	....	....	....	....
	Boston Bruins	**NHL**	6	1	2	3	2	5	7	2	....	....	....	....	....
	Boston Cubs	Can-Am	18	6	15	21	....	....	....	24	....	....	....	....	....
1936-37	**Boston Bruins**	**NHL**	48	3	7	10	6	16	22	22	3	0	0	0	2
1937-38	**Boston Bruins**	**NHL**	48	4	10	14	8	21	29	54	3	0	1	1	0
1938-39	**Boston Bruins**	**NHL**	44	10	17	27	21	32	53	35	12	1	3	4	2
1939-40	**Boston Bruins**	**NHL**	44	10	18	28	21	36	57	18	5	1	2	3	2
1940-41	**Boston Bruins**	**NHL**	41	9	15	24	18	27	45	23	11	3	4	7	8
	Hershey Bears	AHL	5	4	2	6	....	....	....	2	....	....	....	....	....
1941-42	**Boston Bruins**	**NHL**	48	19	14	33	33	21	54	21	5	0	1	1	2
1942-43	**Boston Bruins**	**NHL**	50	19	25	44	27	32	59	19	9	0	9	9	4
1943-44	**Boston Bruins**	**NHL**	25	9	7	16	11	8	19	4	....	....	....	....	....
	Detroit Red Wings	**NHL**	27	6	12	18	7	14	21	34	5	0	0	0	6
1944-45	**Detroit Red Wings**	**NHL**	50	20	21	41	28	34	62	39	14	3	4	7	6
1945-46	**Detroit Red Wings**	**NHL**	38	4	9	13	6	17	23	16	5	0	2	2	0
1946-47	Toronto Staffords	OHA Sr.	DID NOT PLAY – COACHING												
1947-48	Kitchener Dutchmen	OHA Sr.	15	6	11	17	....	....	....	24	....	....	....	....	....
1948-49	Toronto Marlboros	OHA Sr.	31	6	15	21	....	....	....	20	20	5	13	18	15
1949-50	Toronto Marlboros	OHA Sr.	42	7	27	34	....	....	....	29	14	1	8	9	14
	NHL Totals		**562**	**132**	**181**	**313**	**226**	**320**	**546**	**358**	**79**	**8**	**26**	**34**	**38**

NHL Second All-Star Team (1943) • NHL First All-Star Team (1945)

Loaned to **Ottawa** by **Toronto** for remainder of 1933-34 season, January 2, 1934. Traded to **Boston** by **Toronto** for $16,000, January 15 1936. Traded to **Detroit** by **Boston** for Pat Egan, January 5, 1944. Traded to **NY Rangers** by **Detroit** for Ab DeMArco and Hank Goldup, June 19, 1946.

• HOLLINGWORTH, GORD
Gord Hollingworth
D – L. 5'11", 170 lbs. b: Montreal, Que., 7/24/1933. Deceased.

1949-50	Montreal Jr. Canadiens	QJHL	35	0	3	3	....	....	....	30	28	0	4	4	69
1950-51	Montreal Jr. Canadiens	QJHL	45	2	16	18	....	....	....	122	9	2	1	3	*35
1951-52	Montreal Jr. Canadiens	QJHL	39	10	12	22	....	....	....	97	19	4	5	9	*43
1952-53	Montreal Jr. Canadiens	QJHL	45	6	11	17	....	....	....	106	7	0	1	1	15
	Montreal Royals	QSHL	1	0	0	0	....	....	....	0	....	....	....	....	....
1953-54	Montreal Royals	QHL	63	2	16	18	....	....	....	78	11	1	4	5	14
1954-55	**Chicago Black Hawks**	**NHL**	70	3	9	12	4	11	15	135	....	....	....	....	....
1955-56	**Detroit Red Wings**	**NHL**	41	0	2	2	0	2	2	28	3	0	0	0	2
1956-57	**Detroit Red Wings**	**NHL**	25	0	1	1	0	1	1	16	....	....	....	....	....
	Springfield Indians	AHL	22	2	9	11	....	....	....	28	....	....	....	....	....
1957-58	**Detroit Red Wings**	**NHL**	27	1	2	3	1	2	3	22	....	....	....	....	....
	Hershey Bears	AHL	39	0	9	9	....	....	....	93	11	1	1	2	20
1958-59	Cleveland Barons	AHL	65	6	15	21	....	....	....	102	7	0	4	4	6
1959-60	Hershey Bears	AHL	63	5	15	20	....	....	....	131	....	....	....	....	....
1960-61	Hershey Bears	AHL	67	3	13	16	....	....	....	76	5	0	1	1	13
1961-62	Hershey Bears	AHL	45	0	11	11	....	....	....	63	....	....	....	....	....
	NHL Totals		**163**	**4**	**14**	**18**	**5**	**16**	**21**	**201**	**3**	**0**	**0**	**0**	**2**

Played in NHL All-Star Game (1955)

Traded to **Chicago** by **Montreal** for $15,000, October 3, 1954. Traded to **Detroit** by **Chicago** with Jerry Toppazzini, John McCormack and Dave Creighton for Tony Leswick, Glen Skov, Johnny Wilson and Benny Woit, May 28, 1955. Traded to **Cleveland** (AHL) by **Detroit** with cash for Pete Goegan, February 20, 1958. Traded to **Hershey** (AHL) by **Cleveland** (AHL) with Claude Dufour for Gil Mayer, June, 1959.

• HOLMES, BILL
Bill Holmes
C – R. 6', 200 lbs. b: Portage la Prairie, Man., 3/9/1899. d: 3/14/1961.

1921-22	Brandon Wheat Kings	MHL Sr.	12	8	1	9	....	....	....	4	2	0	0	0	6
1922-23	Brandon Wheat Kings	MHL Sr.	16	16	2	18	....	....	....	19	....	....	....	....	....
1923-24	Brandon Wheat Kings	MHL Sr.	11	1	2	3	....	....	....	5	3	0	1	1	6
1924-25	Edmonton Eskimos	WCHL	6	0	0	0	....	....	....	0	....	....	....	....	....
1925-26	**Montreal Canadiens**	**NHL**	9	1	0	1	3	0	3	2	....	....	....	....	....
1926-27	**New York Americans**	**NHL**	1	0	0	0	0	0	0	0	....	....	....	....	....
	Niagara Falls Cataracts	Can-Pro	25	20	4	24	....	....	....	51	....	....	....	....	....
1927-28	Niagara Falls–London	Can-Pro	41	22	4	26	....	....	....	88	....	....	....	....	....
1928-29	New Haven Eagles	Can-Am	38	9	6	15	....	....	....	76	2	1	0	1	8
1929-30	**New York Americans**	**NHL**	42	5	4	9	10	13	23	33	....	....	....	....	....
1930-31	Syracuse Stars	IAHL	48	19	*37	56	....	....	....	61	....	....	....	....	....
1931-32	Cleveland Indians	IAHL	2	0	0	0	....	....	....	0	....	....	....	....	....
	Pittsburgh Yellowjackets	IAHL	4	1	0	1	....	....	....	2	....	....	....	....	....
	Buffalo Majors	IAHL	19	1	0	1	....	....	....	6	....	....	....	....	....
1932-33			DID NOT PLAY												
1933-34	Syracuse Stars	IAHL	16	3	2	5	....	....	....	4	....	....	....	....	....
1934-35	London Techumsehs	IAHL	6	1	1	2	....	....	....	6	....	....	....	....	....
	New Haven Eagles	Can-Am	39	11	19	30	....	....	....	11	....	....	....	....	....
1935-36	Pittsburgh Yellowjackets	EHL	21	1	4	5	....	....	....	8	....	....	....	....	....
	NHL Totals		**52**	**6**	**4**	**10**	**13**	**13**	**26**	**35**	....	....	....	....	....
	Other Major League Totals		6	0	0	0	....	....	....	0	....	....	....	....	....

Signed as a free agent by **Edmonton** (WCHL), November 13, 1924. Signed as a free agent by **Montreal Canadiens**, December 26, 1925. Signed as a free agent by **NY Americans**, January, 1927.

• HOLMES, CHUCK
Chuck Holmes
RW – R. 6', 185 lbs. b: Edmonton, Alta., 9/21/1934.

			REGULAR SEASON								PLAYOFFS				
Season	Club	League	GP	G	A	Pts	AG	AA	APts	PIM	GP	G	A	Pts	PIM
1951-52	Edmonton Oil Kings	WCJHL	1	1	0	1	....	....	....	2	....	....	....	....	....
1952-53	Edmonton Oil Kings	WCJHL	14	12	8	20	....	....	....	17	11	5	4	9	6
1953-54	Edmonton Oil Kings	WCJHL	35	32	36	68	....	....	....	41	10	7	15	22	12
1954-55	Edmonton Oil Kings	WCJHL	26	17	14	31	....	....	....	43	5	2	2	4	14
	Edmonton Flyers	WHL	8	1	2	3	....	....	....	0	9	2	1	3	2
1955-56	Edmonton Flyers	WHL	69	16	22	38	....	....	....	54	3	1	0	1	0
1956-57	Edmonton Flyers	WHL	65	18	23	41	....	....	....	35	8	1	3	4	8
1957-58	Edmonton Flyers	WHL	57	23	34	57	....	....	....	58	5	0	0	0	2
1958-59	**Detroit Red Wings**	**NHL**	15	0	3	3	0	3	3	6	....	....	....	....	....
	Edmonton Flyers	WHL	43	13	22	35	....	....	....	44	3	0	0	0	0
1959-60	Edmonton Flyers	WHL	64	22	37	59	....	....	....	33	4	0	1	1	2
1960-61	Edmonton Flyers	WHL	68	19	32	51	....	....	....	19	....	....	....	....	....
1961-62	**Detroit Red Wings**	**NHL**	8	1	0	1	1	0	1	4	....	....	....	....	....
	Edmonton Flyers	WHL	60	27	47	74	....	....	....	43	12	3	8	11	6
1962-63	Edmonton Flyers	WHL	39	14	23	37	....	....	....	39	3	1	2	3	10
	Pittsburgh Hornets	AHL	30	1	15	16	....	....	....	8	....	....	....	....	....
1963-64	Pittsburgh Hornets	AHL	37	8	14	22	....	....	....	28	....	....	....	....	....
1964-65	Memphis Wings	CHL	15	2	6	8	....	....	....	12	....	....	....	....	....
	Seattle Totems	WHL	42	11	13	24	....	....	....	41	7	3	1	4	12
1965-66	Portland Buckaroos	WHL	71	10	20	30	....	....	....	20	8	0	1	1	2
1966-67	Seattle Totems	WHL	71	14	13	27	....	....	....	44	10	5	2	7	13
1967-68	Seattle Totems	WHL	72	23	24	47	....	....	....	55	9	4	4	8	2
1968-69	Seattle Totems	WHL	74	25	38	63	....	....	....	40	4	0	1	1	0
1969-70	Seattle Totems	WHL	69	16	15	31	....	....	....	26	6	2	1	3	0
1970-71	Seattle Totems	WHL	44	11	18	29	....	....	....	31	....	....	....	....	....
	NHL Totals		**23**	**1**	**3**	**4**	**1**	**3**	**4**	**10**	....	....	....	....	....

WHL First All-Star Team (1968)

Traded to **Seattle** (WHL) by **Detroit** (Memphis-CHL) for Billy Carter with Detroit holding rights of recall, December, 1964. Traded to **Portland** (WHL) by **Detroit** for cash, July, 1965. Traded to **Seattle** (WHL) by **Portland** (WHL) for Gordie Sinclair, July, 1966.

• HOLMES, LOU
Lou Holmes
C/LW – L. 5'10", 150 lbs. b: Rushall, England, 1/29/1911.

1929-30	Edmonton Bruins	City Jr.	12	7	6	13	....	....	....	....	....	....	....	....	....
1930-31	Edmonton Bruins	City Jr.	STATISTICS NOT AVAILABLE												
1931-32	**Chicago Black Hawks**	**NHL**	41	1	4	5	2	11	13	6	2	0	0	0	2
1932-33	**Chicago Black Hawks**	**NHL**	18	0	0	0	0	0	0	0	....	....	....	....	....
	St. Paul–Tulsa	AHA	26	11	9	20	....	....	....	11	4	0	0	0	0
1933-34	Edmonton Eskimos	NWHL	34	15	8	23	....	....	....	11	2	3	0	3	2
1934-35	Edmonton Eskimos	NWHL	13	13	4	17	....	....	....	2	....	....	....	....	....
	Oklahoma City Warriors	AHA	21	6	6	12	....	....	....	10	....	....	....	....	....
1935-36	Edmonton Eskimos	NWHL	39	13	14	27	....	....	....	42	....	....	....	....	....
1936-37	Spokane Clippers	PCHL	35	16	5	21	....	....	....	24	3	0	1	1	0
1937-38	Spokane–Portland	PCHL	43	14	21	35	....	....	....	30	1	0	2	2	2
1938-39	Portland Buckaroos	PCHL	48	34	40	*74	....	....	....	26	5	4	4	*8	8
1939-40	Portland Buckaroos	PCHL	38	13	13	26	....	....	....	23	5	1	1	2	4
1940-41	Portland Buckaroos	PCHL	47	24	26	50	....	....	....	28	....	....	....	....	....
1941-42	St. Paul Saints	AHA	48	15	16	31	....	....	....	18	2	0	1	1	6
1942-43			MILITARY SERVICE												
1943-44			MILITARY SERVICE												
1944-45			MILITARY SERVICE												
1945-46	Edmonton All-Stars	Inter-Sr.	STATISTICS NOT AVAILABLE												
1946-47	Edmonton New Method	City Sr.	5	5	4	9	....	....	....	4	....	....	....	....	....
1947-48	Edmonton Flyers	WCSHL	36	8	17	25	....	....	....	0	....	....	....	....	....
1948-49	Edmonton Flyers	WCSHL	3	2	0	2	....	....	....	0	....	....	....	....	....
	NHL Totals		**59**	**1**	**4**	**5**	**2**	**11**	**13**	**6**	**2**	**0**	**0**	**0**	**2**

Traded to **Tulsa** (AHA) by **Chicago** for cash, May, 1932. Traded to **Chicago** by **St. Paul** (AHA) for Gerry Lowrey, November 9, 1932. Traded to **Tulsa** (AHA) by **Chicago** for the rights to Norm Locking, March 7, 1933.

• HOLOTA, JOHN
John Holota
C – L. 5'6", 160 lbs. b: Hamilton, Ont., 2/25/1921. d: 3/10/1951.

1939-40	Guelph Biltmores	OHA	20	14	14	28	....	....	....	8	3	3	4	7	0
1940-41	Guelph Biltmores	OHA	16	20	*21	41	....	....	....	7	5	3	9	12	4
1941-42	Omaha Knights	AHA	48	28	32	60	....	....	....	45	8	7	7	14	2
1942-43	**Detroit Red Wings**	**NHL**	12	2	0	2	3	0	3	0	....	....	....	....	....
	Indianapolis Capitals	AHL	13	8	15	23	....	....	....	5	....	....	....	....	....
	Toronto Army Daggers	OHA Sr.	2	4	2	6	....	....	....	0	4	0	1	1	0
1943-44	Toronto Army Daggers	OHA Sr.	....	30	30	*60	....	....	....	....	....	....	....	....	....
1944-45			MILITARY SERVICE												
1945-46	**Detroit Red Wings**	**NHL**	3	0	0	0	0	0	0	0	....	....	....	....	....
	Indianapolis Capitols	AHL	34	20	17	37	....	....	....	8	....	....	....	....	....
	Omaha Knights	USHL	17	17	12	29	....	....	....	2	7	2	3	5	6
1946-47	Cleveland Barons	AHL	64	*52	35	87	....	....	....	28	4	1	0	1	0
1947-48	Cleveland Barons	AHL	68	48	38	86	....	....	....	11	9	4	4	8	8
1948-49	Cleveland Barons	AHL	62	34	44	78	....	....	....	12	5	4	1	5	0
1949-50	Cleveland Barons	AHL	44	14	28	42	....	....	....	16	5	3	2	5	5
1950-51	New Haven Ramblers	AHL	25	10	9	19	....	....	....	12	....	....	....	....	....
	Portland Eagles	PCHL	18	6	11	17	....	....	....	0	....	....	....	....	....
	Denver Falcons	USHL	11	3	4	7	....	....	....	0	....	....	....	....	....
	NHL Totals		**15**	**2**	**0**	**2**	**3**	**0**	**3**	**0**	....	....	....	....	....

AHA Second All-Star Team (1942) • AHL First All-Star Team (1947)

• HOLWAY, ALBERT

Albert "Toots" Holway
D – L. 6'2", 190 lbs. b: Toronto, Ont., 9/24/1902. Deceased.

			REGULAR SEASON								PLAYOFFS				
Season	Club	League	GP	G	A	Pts	AG	AA	APts	PIM	GP	G	A	Pts	PIM
1920-21	Soo Greyhounds	NOHA	1	0	0	0				0					
1921-22	Soo Greyhounds	NOHA	STATISTICS NOT AVAILABLE												
1922-23	Soo Greyhounds	NOHA	STATISTICS NOT AVAILABLE												
1923-24	**Toronto St. Pats**	**NHL**	**6**	**1**	**0**	**1**	**4**	**0**	**4**	**0**					
1924-25	**Toronto St. Pats**	**NHL**	**25**	**2**	**2**	**4**	**7**	**26**	**33**	**20**	**2**	**0**	**0**	**0**	**0**
1925-26	**Toronto St. Pats**	**NHL**	**12**	**0**	**0**	**0**	**0**	**0**	**0**	**0**					
	Montreal Maroons	**NHL**	**17**	**0**	**0**	**0**	**0**	**0**	**0**	**6**	**6**	**0**	**0**	**0**	**2**
1926-27	**Montreal Maroons**	**NHL**	**13**	**0**	**0**	**0**	**0**	**0**	**0**	**2**					
	Stratford Nationals	Can-Pro	20	3	3	6				16	2	1	0	1	9
1927-28	Stratford Nationals	Can-Pro	40	3	5	8				65	5	3	0	3	11
1928-29	**Pittsburgh Pirates**	**NHL**	**40**	**4**	**0**	**4**	**16**	**0**	**16**	**20**					
1929-30	London Panthers	IAHL	42	8	7	15				66	2	0	0	0	2
1930-31	London Tecumsehs	IAHL	48	9	3	12				68					
1931-32	London Tecumsehs	IAHL	48	4	4	8				82	6	0	0	0	*26
1932-33	London Tecumsehs	IAHL	43	2	10	12				101	6	0	1	1	6
1933-34	London Tecumsehs	IAHL	44	3	3	6				39	6	0	0	0	2
1934-35	London Tecumsehs	IAHL	32	2	4	6				23	5	0	0	0	6
1935-36	Cleveland Falcons	IAHL	49	1	1	2				31	2	0	0	0	0
1936-37	Cleveland Barons	AHL	3	0	0	0				0					
	Seattle Seahawks	PCHL	26	0	0	0				6					
	NHL Totals		**113**	**7**	**2**	**9**	**27**	**26**	**53**	**48**	**8**	**0**	**0**	**0**	**2**

Signed as a free agent by **Toronto St. Pats**, February 15, 1924. Claimed on waivers by **Montreal Maroons** from **Toronto St. Pats**, December 28, 1926. Traded to **Pittsburgh** by **Montreal Maroons** for Duke McCurry, September 30, 1928. Traded to **London** (IAHL) by **Pittsburgh** for cash, October 22, 1929.

• HORECK, PETE

Pete Horeck
LW – L. 5'9", 158 lbs. b: Massey, Ont., 6/15/1923.

			REGULAR SEASON								PLAYOFFS				
Season	Club	League	GP	G	A	Pts	AG	AA	APts	PIM	GP	G	A	Pts	PIM
1941-42	Atlantic City Sea Gulls	EHL	59	24	30	54				66	14	2	5	7	6
1942-43	Cleveland–Providence	AHL	59	25	20	45				58	4	1	1	2	2
	Washington Lions	AHL	1	0	0	0				0					
1943-44	Cleveland Barons	AHL	54	*34	29	63				29	11	4	5	9	14
1944-45	**Chicago Black Hawks**	**NHL**	**50**	**20**	**16**	**36**	**28**	**26**	**54**	**44**					
1945-46	**Chicago Black Hawks**	**NHL**	**50**	**20**	**21**	**41**	**31**	**39**	**70**	**34**	**4**	**0**	**0**	**0**	**2**
1946-47	**Chicago Black Hawks**	**NHL**	**18**	**4**	**6**	**10**	**5**	**9**	**14**	**12**					
	Detroit Red Wings	**NHL**	**38**	**12**	**13**	**25**	**16**	**19**	**35**	**59**	**5**	**2**	**0**	**2**	**6**
1947-48	**Detroit Red Wings**	**NHL**	**50**	**12**	**17**	**29**	**17**	**25**	**42**	**44**	**10**	**3**	***7**	**10**	**12**
1948-49	**Detroit Red Wings**	**NHL**	**60**	**14**	**16**	**30**	**22**	**25**	**47**	**46**	**11**	**1**	**1**	**2**	**10**
1949-50	**Boston Bruins**	**NHL**	**34**	**5**	**5**	**10**	**7**	**6**	**13**	**22**					
1950-51	**Boston Bruins**	**NHL**	**66**	**10**	**13**	**23**	**13**	**17**	**30**	**57**	**4**	**0**	**0**	**0**	**13**
1951-52	**Chicago Black Hawks**	**NHL**	**60**	**9**	**11**	**20**	**13**	**14**	**27**	**22**					
1952-53	Sault Ste. Marie Indians	NOHA	19	4	8	12				18	3	0	1	1	7
1953-54	Sudbury Wolves	NOHA	12	3	5	8				25	11	2	4	6	18
1954-55	Sudbury Wolves	NOHA	38	18	18	36				42					
1955-56	Sault Ste. Marie Indians	NOHA	36	12	24	36				30	7	1	2	3	22
1956-57	Soo Greyhounds	NOHA	47	22	20	42				91	10	3	2	5	18
1957-58	Louisville Rebels	IHL	15	6	7	13				69					
	Chatham Maroons	OHA Sr.	15	7	4	11				34					
1958-59	Charlotte Clippers	EHL	DID NOT PLAY – COACHING												
1959-60	Charlotte Clippers	EHL	15	1	1	2				22					
	NHL Totals		**426**	**106**	**118**	**224**	**152**	**180**	**332**	**340**	**34**	**6**	**8**	**14**	**43**

Claimed by **Chicago** from **Cleveland** (AHL) in Inter-League Draft, May 12, 1944. Traded to **Detroit** by **Chicago** with Leo Reise for Adam Brown and Ray Powell, December 1946. Traded to **Boston** by **Detroit** with Bill Quackenbush for Pete Babando, Clare Martin, Lloyd Durham and Jimmy Peters, August 16, 1949. Traded to **Chicago** by **Boston** for cash, November 1, 1951.

• HORNE, GEORGE

George "Shorty" Horne
RW – R. 5'6", 165 lbs. b: Sudbury, Ontario, 6/27/1904. d: 7/31/1929.

			REGULAR SEASON								PLAYOFFS				
Season	Club	League	GP	G	A	Pts	AG	AA	APts	PIM	GP	G	A	Pts	PIM
1920-21	Sudbury Cub Wolves	NOHA	4	2	1	3					4	2	0	2	
1921-22	Sudbury Cub Wolves	NOHA	4	2	0	6				6	2	1	1	2	2
	Sudbury Wolves	NOHA									4	2	3	5	6
1922-23	North Bay Trappers	NOHA	STATISTICS NOT AVAILABLE												
1923-24	North Bay Trappers	NOHA	6	6	0	6					5	*13	0	*13	
1924-25	Grimsby Peach Kings	City Sr.	STATISTICS NOT AVAILABLE												
1925-26	**Montreal Maroons**	**NHL**	**13**	**0**	**0**	**0**	**0**	**0**	**0**	**2**					
1926-27	**Montreal Maroons**	**NHL**	**2**	**0**	**0**	**0**	**0**	**0**	**0**	**0**					
	Stratford–Niagara Falls	Can-Pro	22	6	4	10				24					
1927-28	Stratford Nationals	Can-Pro	40	*32	3	35				35	5	3	0	3	13
1928-29	**Toronto Maple Leafs**	**NHL**	**39**	**9**	**3**	**12**	**36**	**27**	**63**	**32**	**4**	**0**	**0**	**0**	**4**
	NHL Totals		**54**	**9**	**3**	**12**	**36**	**27**	**63**	**34**	**4**	**0**	**0**	**0**	**4**

Signed as a free agent by **Montreal Maroons**, October 8, 1925. Traded to **Toronto** by **Stratford** (Can-Pro) for cash, September, 1928. • Drowned in Sagatoski Lake, Ontario, July 31, 1929.

• HORNER, RED

Red (Reginald) Horner
D – R. 6', 190 lbs. b: Lynden, Ont., 5/28/1909.

			REGULAR SEASON								PLAYOFFS				
Season	Club	League	GP	G	A	Pts	AG	AA	APts	PIM	GP	G	A	Pts	PIM
1926-27	Toronto Marlboros	OHA	9	5	1	6					2	0	0	0	
1927-28	Toronto Marlboros	OHA	9	4	5	9				2	13	7	5	12	
	Toronto Marlboros	OHA Sr.	1	0	0	0				0					
1928-29	**Toronto Maple Leafs**	**NHL**	**22**	**0**	**0**	**0**	**0**	**0**	**0**	**30**	**4**	**1**	**0**	**1**	**2**
	Toronto Marlboros	OHA Sr.	2	0	0	0									
1929-30	**Toronto Maple Leafs**	**NHL**	**33**	**2**	**7**	**9**	**4**	**23**	**27**	**96**					
1930-31	**Toronto Maple Leafs**	**NHL**	**42**	**1**	**11**	**12**	**2**	**40**	**42**	**71**	**2**	**0**	**0**	**0**	**4**
1931-32	**Toronto Maple Leafs**	**NHL**	**42**	**7**	**9**	**16**	**15**	**25**	**40**	**97**	**7**	**2**	**2**	**4**	**20**
1932-33	**Toronto Maple Leafs**	**NHL**	**48**	**3**	**8**	**11**	**7**	**21**	**28**	***144**	**9**	**1**	**0**	**1**	**10**
1933-34	**Toronto Maple Leafs**	**NHL**	**40**	**11**	**10**	**21**	**24**	**27**	**51**	***146**	**5**	**1**	**0**	**1**	**6**
1934-35	**Toronto Maple Leafs**	**NHL**	**46**	**4**	**8**	**12**	**8**	**18**	**26**	***125**	**7**	**0**	**1**	**1**	**4**
1935-36	**Toronto Maple Leafs**	**NHL**	**43**	**2**	**9**	**11**	**5**	**22**	**27**	***167**	**9**	**1**	**2**	**3**	***22**
1936-37	**Toronto Maple Leafs**	**NHL**	**48**	**3**	**9**	**12**	**6**	**21**	**27**	***124**	**2**	**0**	**0**	**0**	**7**
1937-38	**Toronto Maple Leafs**	**NHL**	**47**	**4**	**20**	**24**	**8**	**41**	**49**	***82**	**7**	**0**	**1**	**1**	**14**
1938-39	**Toronto Maple Leafs**	**NHL**	**48**	**4**	**10**	**14**	**8**	**19**	**27**	***85**	**10**	**1**	**2**	**3**	***26**
1939-40	**Toronto Maple Leafs**	**NHL**	**31**	**1**	**9**	**10**	**2**	**18**	**20**	***87**	**9**	**0**	**2**	**2**	**55**
	NHL Totals		**490**	**42**	**110**	**152**	**89**	**275**	**364**	**1254**	**71**	**7**	**10**	**17**	**170**

Played in NHL All-Star Game (1934, 1937)

Signed as a free agent by **Toronto**, December 22, 1928.

• HORTON, TIM

— see page 1117

• HORVATH, BRONCO

— see page 1117

• HOWARD, JOHN FRANCIS

John Francis "Jack" Howard
D – L. 6', 190 lbs. b: London, Ont., 10/15/1911.

			REGULAR SEASON								PLAYOFFS				
Season	Club	League	GP	G	A	Pts	AG	AA	APts	PIM	GP	G	A	Pts	PIM
1933-34	Hamilton Tigers	OHA Sr.	23	5	1	6				28	12	2	1	3	18
1934-35	Hamilton Tigers	OHA Sr.	20	6	6	12				41	6	2	1	3	6
1935-36	Syracuse Stars	IAHL	48	5	6	11				48	3	0	0	0	0
1936-37	**Toronto Maple Leafs**	**NHL**	**2**	**0**	**0**	**0**	**0**	**0**	**0**	**0**					
	Syracuse Stars	AHL	46	6	9	15				46	9	2	0	2	2
1937-38	Syracuse Stars	AHL	47	6	9	15				32	8	0	3	3	4
1938-39	Syracuse Stars	AHL	23	1	0	1				10					
1939-40	St. Louis Flyers	AHL	45	9	5	14				18	5	0	2	2	2
1940-41	St. Louis Flyers	AHL	8	0	1	1				10					
	Springfield–Pittsburgh	AHL	36	0	8	8				24	6	0	0	0	8
1941-42	Pittsburgh Hornets	AHL	55	6	13	19				10					
1942-43	Pittsburgh Hornets	AHL	54	1	16	17				12	2	0	2	2	4
1943-44	Pittsburgh Hornets	AHL	38	3	12	15				16					
1944-45	Pittsburgh Hornets	AHL	26	1	6	7				16					
	NHL Totals		**2**	**0**	**0**	**0**	**0**	**0**	**0**	**0**					

Signed as a free agent by **Toronto**, October 22, 1935.

• HOWE, GORDIE

— see page 1121

• HOWE, SYD

Syd Howe HHOF
C/LW – L. 5'9", 165 lbs. b: Ottawa, Ont., 9/28/1911. d: 5/20/1976.

			REGULAR SEASON								PLAYOFFS				
Season	Club	League	GP	G	A	Pts	AG	AA	APts	PIM	GP	G	A	Pts	PIM
1927-28	Ottawa Gunners	City Jr.	STATISTICS NOT AVAILABLE												
1928-29	Ottawa Rideaus	City Sr.	15	7	1	8									
1929-30	**Ottawa Senators**	**NHL**	**12**	**1**	**1**	**2**	**2**	**3**	**5**	**0**	**2**	**0**	**0**	**0**	**0**
	London Panthers	IAHL	5	1	0	1				0					
	Ottawa Rideaus	City Sr.	11	8	1	9				9					
1930-31	**Philadelphia Quakers**	**NHL**	**44**	**9**	**11**	**20**	**22**	**40**	**62**	**20**					
1931-32	**Toronto Maple Leafs**	**NHL**	**3**	**0**	**0**	**0**	**0**	**0**	**0**	**0**					
	Syracuse Stars	IAHL	45	9	12	21				44					
1932-33	**Ottawa Senators**	**NHL**	**48**	**12**	**12**	**24**	**28**	**32**	**60**	**17**					
1933-34	**Ottawa Senators**	**NHL**	**42**	**13**	**7**	**20**	**29**	**19**	**48**	**18**					
1934-35	**St. Louis Eagles**	**NHL**	**36**	**14**	**13**	**27**	**30**	**29**	**59**	**23**					
	Detroit Red Wings	**NHL**	**14**	**8**	**12**	**20**	**17**	**27**	**44**	**11**					
1935-36	**Detroit Red Wings**	**NHL**	**48**	**16**	**14**	**30**	**40**	**34**	**74**	**26**	**7**	**3**	**3**	**6**	**2**
1936-37	**Detroit Red Wings**	**NHL**	**45**	**17**	**10**	**27**	**37**	**23**	**60**	**10**	**10**	**2**	**5**	**7**	**0**
1937-38	**Detroit Red Wings**	**NHL**	**48**	**8**	**19**	**27**	**17**	**39**	**56**	**14**					
1938-39	**Detroit Red Wings**	**NHL**	**48**	**16**	**20**	**36**	**34**	**37**	**71**	**11**	**6**	**3**	**1**	**4**	**4**
1939-40	**Detroit Red Wings**	**NHL**	**46**	**14**	**23**	**37**	**30**	**47**	**77**	**17**	**5**	**2**	**2**	**4**	**2**
1940-41	**Detroit Red Wings**	**NHL**	**48**	**20**	**24**	**44**	**40**	**44**	**84**	**8**	**9**	**1**	***7**	**8**	**0**
1941-42	**Detroit Red Wings**	**NHL**	**48**	**16**	**19**	**35**	**27**	**29**	**56**	**6**	**12**	**3**	**5**	**8**	**0**
1942-43	**Detroit Red Wings**	**NHL**	**50**	**20**	**35**	**55**	**28**	**45**	**73**	**10**	**7**	**1**	**2**	**3**	**0**
1943-44	**Detroit Red Wings**	**NHL**	**46**	**32**	**28**	**60**	**41**	**34**	**75**	**6**	**5**	**2**	**2**	**4**	**0**
1944-45	**Detroit Red Wings**	**NHL**	**46**	**17**	**36**	**53**	**23**	**59**	**82**	**6**	**7**	**0**	**0**	**0**	**2**
1945-46	**Detroit Red Wings**	**NHL**	**26**	**4**	**7**	**11**	**6**	**13**	**19**	**9**					
	Indianapolis Capitals	AHL	14	6	11	17				4	5	2	0	2	0
1946-47	Ottawa Senators	QSHL	24	19	21	40				4	11	2	1	3	0
	Ottawa Army	City Sr.	1	2	1	3				0					
1947-48	Ottawa Army	City Sr.	DID NOT PLAY – COACHING												
1948-49	Ottawa Army	City Sr.	1	0	0	0				0					
	NHL Totals		**698**	**237**	**291**	**528**	**451**	**554**	**1005**	**212**	**70**	**17**	**27**	**44**	**10**

NHL Second All-Star Team (1945)

Played in NHL All-Star Game (1939)

Loaned to **Philadelphia** by **Ottawa** for 1930-31 season, November, 1930. Claimed by **Toronto** from **Ottawa** for 1931-32 season in Dispersal Draft, September 26, 1931. Transferred to **St. Louis** after **Ottawa** franchise relocated, September 22, 1934. Traded to **Detroit** by **St. Louis** with Scotty Bowman and Ted Graham for $50,000, February 11, 1935.

• HOWE, VIC

Vic Howe
RW – R. 6', 172 lbs. b: Saskatoon, Sask., 11/2/1929.

			REGULAR SEASON								PLAYOFFS				
Season	Club	League	GP	G	A	Pts	AG	AA	APts	PIM	GP	G	A	Pts	PIM
1948-49	Windsor Hettche Spitfires	IHL	31	16	14	30				17	13	8	5	13	2
1949-50	Windsor Spitfires	OHA	41	9	11	20				15	11	2	6	8	6
1950-51	**New York Rangers**	**NHL**	**3**	**1**	**0**	**1**	**1**	**0**	**1**	**0**					
	New York Rovers	EHL	53	15	24	39				55	5	1	3	4	2
1951-52	Cincinnati Mohawks	AHL	2	0	1	1				0					
	New York Rovers	EHL	59	21	34	55				15					
1952-53	Saskatoon Quakers	WHL	1	0	0	0				2					
	Troy Uncle Sam Trojans	EHL	59	27	52	79				23					
1953-54	**New York Rangers**	**NHL**	**1**	**0**	**0**	**0**	**0**	**0**	**0**	**0**					
	Saskatoon Quakers	WHL	65	15	23	38				35	6	0	2	2	0
1954-55	**New York Rangers**	**NHL**	**29**	**2**	**4**	**6**	**3**	**5**	**8**	**10**					
	Saskatoon–Vancouver	WHL	22	3	6	9				2					
	Valleyfield Braves	QHL	6	1	1	2				4					
1955-56	Regina Regals	WHL	3	0	0	0				0					
	Nelson Maple Leafs	WIHL	29	10	12	22				12	5	1	0	1	2
1956-57	Harringay Racers	Britain	56	26	26	52				32					
1957-1961			DID NOT PLAY – RETIRED												
1961-62	Moncton Hawks	NBSHL		19	20	39				10	11	4	8	12	4
	NHL Totals		**33**	**3**	**4**	**7**	**4**	**5**	**9**	**10**					

• HOWELL, HARRY

— see page 1122

• HOWELL, RON
Ron Howell
D/LW – L. 6', 185 lbs. b: Hamilton, Ontario, 12/4/1935.

Season	Club	League	GP	G	A	Pts	AG	AA	APts	PIM	GP	G	A	Pts	PIM
			REGULAR SEASON								PLAYOFFS				
1952-53	Kitchener–Guelph	OHA	5	2	2	4	....	....	....	8	....	....	....	....	....
1953-54	Guelph Biltmores	OHA	54	20	26	46	....	....	....	48	3	0	0	0	2
1954-55	Guelph Biltmores	OHA	35	18	26	44	....	....	....	22	6	6	5	11	6
	New York Rangers	**NHL**	**3**	**0**	**0**	**0**	**0**	**0**	**0**	**0**	....	....	....	....	....
1955-56	Guelph Biltmores	OHA	36	21	40	61	....	....	....	24	3	0	0	0	0
	New York Rangers	**NHL**	**1**	**0**	**0**	**0**	**0**	**0**	**0**	**0**	....	....	....	....	....
1956-57	Kitchener Dutchmen	OHA Sr.	30	8	18	26	....	....	....	16	11	2	7	9	8
1957-58	Kitchener Dutchmen	OHA Sr.	30	19	22	41	....	....	....	16	16	5	3	8	16
1958-59	Vancouver Canucks	WHL	37	9	9	18	....	....	....	12	9	2	3	5	4
1959-60			PLAYED PRO FOOTBALL												
1960-61	Rochester Americans	AHL	22	4	1	5	....	....	....	2	....	....	....	....	....
1961-62			PLAYED PRO FOOTBALL												
1962-63	Kitchener Tigers	OHA Sr.	13	7	6	13	....	....	....	2	....	....	....	....	....
	Long Island Ducks	EHL	10	3	9	12	....	....	....	6	7	3	1	4	6
1963-64	Guelph Regals	OHA Sr.	7	1	3	4	....	....	....	13	....	....	....	....	....
	Long Island Ducks	EHL	28	7	7	14	....	....	....	15	5	2	2	4	0
	NHL Totals		**4**	**0**	**0**	**0**	**0**	**0**	**0**	**0**	....	....	....	....	....

• HRYMNAK, STEVE
Steve Hrymnak
D – L. 5'11", 178 lbs. b: Port Arthur, Ont., 3/3/1926.

Season	Club	League	GP	G	A	Pts	AG	AA	APts	PIM	GP	G	A	Pts	PIM
1942-43	Port Arthur Juniors	TBJHL	9	8	3	11	....	....	....	8	5	0	0	0	10
1943-44	Port Arthur Flyers	TBJHL	10	0	5	5	....	....	....	19	6	3	4	7	4
1944-45			MILITARY SERVICE												
1945-46	Port Arthur Flyers	TBJHL	4	5	4	9	....	....	....	4	5	4	6	10	8
1946-47	New York Rovers	EHL	53	0	7	7	....	....	....	52	7	0	0	0	7
1947-48	New Haven Ramblers	AHL	39	10	4	14	....	....	....	23	4	0	1	1	4
1948-49	New Haven Ramblers	AHL	55	10	11	21	....	....	....	28	....	....	....	....	....
1949-50	New Haven Ramblers	AHL	70	13	17	30	....	....	....	28	....	....	....	....	....
1950-51	St. Louis Flyers	AHL	57	11	11	22	....	....	....	32	....	....	....	....	....
1951-52	**Chicago Black Hawks**	**NHL**	**18**	**2**	**1**	**3**	**3**	**1**	**4**	**4**	....	....	....	....	....
	St. Louis Flyers	AHL	48	14	36	50	....	....	....	19	....	....	....	....	....
1952-53	St. Louis Flyers	AHL	64	14	27	41	....	....	....	31	....	....	....	....	....
	Detroit Red Wings	**NHL**	....	....	....	....	....	....	....	....	**2**	**0**	**0**	**0**	**0**
1953-54	Edmonton Flyers	WHL	69	13	17	30	....	....	....	41	13	3	4	7	5
1954-55	Edmonton Flyers	WHL	69	8	22	30	....	....	....	26	9	2	0	2	20
1955-56	Edmonton Flyers	WHL	69	8	17	25	....	....	....	26	3	0	0	0	0
1956-57	New Westminster Royals	WHL	52	6	13	19	....	....	....	34	....	....	....	....	....
1957-58	New Westminster Royals	WHL	48	9	18	27	....	....	....	36	4	0	1	1	6
	NHL Totals		**18**	**2**	**1**	**3**	**3**	**1**	**4**	**4**	**2**	**0**	**0**	**0**	**0**

Traded to **Detroit** by **Chicago** with Red Almas and Guyle Fielder for cash, September 23, 1952.

• HUARD, ROLLY
Rolly Huard
C – L. 5'10", 170 lbs. b: Ottawa, Ontario, 9/6/1902.

Season	Club	League	GP	G	A	Pts	AG	AA	APts	PIM	GP	G	A	Pts	PIM
1921-22	University of Ottawa	City Sr.	12	10	7	17	....	....	....	12	....	....	....	....	....
1922-23	Ottawa Montagnards	City Sr.	9	*8	4	12	....	....	....	2	2	0	0	0	0
1923-24	Ottawa Montagnards	City Sr.	12	4	2	6	....	....	....	....	6	*5	1	6	....
1924-25	Ottawa Montagnards	City Sr.	16	13	3	16	....	....	....	....	7	1	0	1	8
1925-26	Fort William Forts	TBSHL	20	13	4	17	....	....	....	18	3	0	0	0	2
1926-27	Windsor Hornets	Can-Pro	32	16	4	20	....	....	....	16	....	....	....	....	....
1927-28	Windsor Hornets	Can-Pro	42	21	7	28	....	....	....	8	....	....	....	....	....
1928-29	Buffalo Bisons	Can-Pro	42	18	8	26	....	....	....	12	....	....	....	....	....
1929-30	Buffalo Bisons	IAHL	40	8	6	14	....	....	....	16	7	1	1	2	10
1930-31	**Toronto Maple Leafs**	**NHL**	**1**	**1**	**0**	**1**	**2**	**0**	**2**	**0**	....	....	....	....	....
	Syracuse Stars	IAHL	10	1	2	3	....	....	....	0	....	....	....	....	....
	Buffalo Bisons	IAHL	20	5	4	9	....	....	....	6	....	....	....	....	....
1931-32	London Tecumsehs	IAHL	45	3	11	14	....	....	....	12	6	1	2	3	0
1932-33	St. Louis Flyers	AHA	45	15	17	32	....	....	....	2	4	0	0	0	2
1933-34	St. Louis Flyers	AHA	42	5	5	10	....	....	....	14	7	0	1	1	2
1934-35			DID NOT PLAY												
1935-36	Ottawa LaSalle	City Sr.	DID NOT PLAY – COACHING												
	NHL Totals		**1**	**1**	**0**	**1**	**2**	**0**	**2**	**0**	....	....	....	....	....

Signed as a free agent by **London** (Can-Pro), October 14, 1926. Loaned to **Toronto** by **Buffalo** (Can-Pro) as an emergency injury replacement, December 14, 1930. • One of only two players (Dean Morton) in NHL history to score a goal in only NHL game.

• HUCUL, FRED
— *see page 1125*

• HUDSON, RON
Ron Hudson
C – L. 5'8", 148 lbs. b: Calgary, Alta., 7/14/1911.

Season	Club	League	GP	G	A	Pts	AG	AA	APts	PIM	GP	G	A	Pts	PIM
1931-32	Truro Bearcats	Hfx-Sr.	16	6	3	9	....	....	....	25	5	0	1	1	0
1932-33	Charlottetown Abegweits	MSHL	25	5	1	6	....	....	....	27	2	0	0	0	2
1933-34	Charlottetown Abegweits	MSHL	23	6	8	14	....	....	....	16	3	1	0	1	0
1934-35	Halifax Wolverines	MSHL	20	6	3	9	....	....	....	14	....	....	....	....	....
	Halifax Wolverines	Big 3	4	1	0	1	....	....	....	0	14	*17	2	*19	10
1935-36	Detroit Olympics	IAHL	47	7	19	26	....	....	....	10	6	1	1	2	0
1936-37	Pittsburgh Hornets	AHL	45	9	7	16	....	....	....	27	5	1	1	2	2
1937-38	**Detroit Red Wings**	**NHL**	**32**	**5**	**2**	**7**	**10**	**4**	**14**	**2**	....	....	....	....	....
	Pittsburgh Hornets	AHL	14	3	5	8	....	....	....	8	2	0	0	0	0
1938-39	Providence Reds	AHL	51	16	22	38	....	....	....	7	5	1	3	4	0
1939-40	**Detroit Red Wings**	**NHL**	**1**	**0**	**0**	**0**	**0**	**0**	**0**	**0**	....	....	....	....	....
	Indianapolis Capitols	AHL	54	27	27	54	....	....	....	19	5	0	1	1	0
1940-41	Omaha Knights	AHA	47	23	29	*52	....	....	....	19	....	....	....	....	....
1941-42	Omaha Knights	AHA	44	19	23	42	....	....	....	4	3	1	1	2	0
1942-43			MILITARY SERVICE												
1943-44			MILITARY SERVICE												
1944-45	St. Louis Flyers	AHL	21	0	2	2	....	....	....	8	....	....	....	....	....
	NHL Totals		**33**	**5**	**2**	**7**	**10**	**4**	**14**	**2**	....	....	....	....	....

AHA First All-Star Team (1941)

Signed as a free agent by **Detroit**, October 15, 1935.

• HUGGINS, AL
Al "Chink" Huggins
LW – L. 6', 160 lbs. b: Toronto, Ont., 12/21/1910.

Season	Club	League	GP	G	A	Pts	AG	AA	APts	PIM	GP	G	A	Pts	PIM
1926-27	Toronto Canoe Club	OHA	9	0	0	0	....	....	....	0	....	....	....	....	....
1927-28	Montreal CPR	City Sr.	STATISTICS NOT AVAILABLE												
1928-29	Iroquois Falls Paper	NOHA	STATISTICS NOT AVAILABLE												
1929-30	Montreal AAA	City Sr.	7	3	0	3	....	....	....	16	2	*1	0	1	2
1930-31	**Montreal Maroons**	**NHL**	**20**	**1**	**1**	**2**	**2**	**4**	**6**	**2**	....	....	....	....	....
	Windsor Bulldogs	IAHL	27	1	0	1	....	....	....	27	6	1	0	1	4
1931-32	Windsor Bulldogs	IAHL	40	13	11	24	....	....	....	51	6	0	3	3	10
1932-33	Windsor–Detroit	IAHL	41	9	9	18	....	....	....	47	6	0	2	2	4
1933-34	Syracuse Stars	IAHL	43	14	23	37	....	....	....	24	6	0	3	3	4
1934-35	Syracuse Stars	IAHL	42	10	19	29	....	....	....	41	....	....	....	....	....
1935-36	Syracuse Stars	IAHL	DID NOT PLAY – COACHING												
1936-37	Syracuse Stars	AHL	DID NOT PLAY – COACHING												
1937-38	South Porcupine Porkies	NOHA	8	3	5	8	....	....	....	8	....	....	....	....	....
1938-39	South Porcupine Porkies	NOHA	DID NOT PLAY												
1939-40	South Porcupine Porkies	NOHA	15	5	1	6	....	....	....	18	5	1	2	3	*8
1940-41	South Porcupine Porkies	NOHA	22	8	8	16	....	....	....	18	....	....	....	....	....
1941-42	South Porcupine Porkies	NOHA	4	1	4	5	....	....	....	0	....	....	....	....	....
	NHL Totals		**20**	**1**	**1**	**2**	**2**	**4**	**6**	**2**	....	....	....	....	....

Traded to **Syracuse** (IAHL) by **Montreal Maroons** for Stew Adams, November 1, 1933.

• HUGHES, AL
Al Hughes
C/LW – R. 5'9", 165 lbs. b: Guelph, Ontario, 5/13/1901.

Season	Club	League	GP	G	A	Pts	AG	AA	APts	PIM	GP	G	A	Pts	PIM
1922-23	Hamilton Tigers	OHA Sr.	10	2	0	2	....	....	....	2	2	0	0	0	0
1923-24	Toronto AA Clarke	City Sr.	STATISTICS NOT AVAILABLE												
1924-25	Toronto AA Clarke	City Sr.	STATISTICS NOT AVAILABLE												
1925-26	New York Knickerbockers	USAHA	STATISTICS NOT AVAILABLE												
1926-27	Niagara Falls Cataracts	Can-Pro	14	2	0	2	....	....	....	8	....	....	....	....	....
1927-28	Niagara Falls Cataracts	Can-Pro	42	20	2	22	....	....	....	38	....	....	....	....	....
1928-29	New Haven Eagles	Can-Am	38	8	1	9	....	....	....	16	2	2	0	2	4
1929-30	New Haven Eagles	Can-Am	40	22	19	41	....	....	....	28	....	....	....	....	....
1930-31	**New York Americans**	**NHL**	**42**	**5**	**7**	**12**	**12**	**25**	**37**	**14**	....	....	....	....	....
1931-32	**New York Americans**	**NHL**	**18**	**1**	**1**	**2**	**2**	**3**	**5**	**8**	....	....	....	....	....
	New Haven Eagles	Can-Am	25	6	8	14	....	....	....	8	2	0	1	1	0
1932-33	St. Louis Flyers	AHA	44	14	15	29	....	....	....	20	4	1	1	2	0
1933-34	St. Louis Flyers	AHA	47	3	5	8	....	....	....	14	7	1	1	2	0
	NHL Totals		**60**	**6**	**8**	**14**	**14**	**28**	**42**	**22**	....	....	....	....	....

• HUGHES, JAMES
James "Rusty" Hughes
D – R. 5'9", 190 lbs. b: Webbwood, Ontario, 5/12/1906.

Season	Club	League	GP	G	A	Pts	AG	AA	APts	PIM	GP	G	A	Pts	PIM
1925-26	Winnipeg Maroons	CHL	24	1	3	4	....	....	....	18	5	2	*2	*4	0
1926-27	Winnipeg Maroons	AHA	10	2	0	2	....	....	....	2	....	....	....	....	....
	Windsor Hornets	Can-Pro	1	1	0	1	....	....	....	0	....	....	....	....	....
1927-28	Windsor–Niagara Falls	Can-Pro	34	0	2	2	....	....	....	51	....	....	....	....	....
1928-29	Buffalo Bisons	Can-Pro	40	4	1	5	....	....	....	79	....	....	....	....	....
1929-30	**Detroit Cougars**	**NHL**	**40**	**0**	**1**	**1**	**0**	**3**	**3**	**48**	....	....	....	....	....
1930-31	Detroit Olympics	IAHL	7	0	0	0	....	....	....	4	....	....	....	....	....
	Syracuse Stars	IAHL	39	1	2	3	....	....	....	75	....	....	....	....	....
1931-32	Syracuse Stars	IAHL	48	1	2	3	....	....	....	80	....	....	....	....	....
1932-33	St. Louis Flyers	AHA	44	1	0	1	....	....	....	38	4	0	1	1	6
1933-34	Syracuse Stars	IAHL	43	2	2	4	....	....	....	76	6	1	0	1	2
1934-35	Syracuse–Windsor	IAHL	42	0	4	4	....	....	....	59	....	....	....	....	....
1935-36	Windsor–Pittsburgh	IAHL	45	1	5	6	....	....	....	64	....	....	....	....	....
	NHL Totals		**40**	**0**	**1**	**1**	**0**	**3**	**3**	**48**	....	....	....	....	....

Claimed by **Detroit Cougars** from **Windsor** (Can-Pro) in Inter-League Draft, May 13, 1929. Traded to **Syracuse** (IAHL) by **Detroit** for Val Hoffinger, December 7, 1930.

• HULL, BOBBY
— *see page 1129*

• HULL, DENNIS
— *see page 1129*

• HUNT, FRED
Fred "Fritz" Hunt
RW – R. 5'8", 160 lbs. b: Brantford, Ont., 1/17/1918. Deceased.

Season	Club	League	GP	G	A	Pts	AG	AA	APts	PIM	GP	G	A	Pts	PIM
1933-34	Brantford Lions	OHA	16	5	3	8	....	....	....	14	....	....	....	....	....
1934-35	Brantford Lions	OHA	17	4	1	5	....	....	....	12	....	....	....	....	....
1935-36	St. Michaels Majors	OHA	9	2	9	11	....	....	....	12	4	1	1	2	11
1936-37	St. Michaels Majors	OHA	12	5	5	10	....	....	....	16	13	10	7	17	19
1937-38	Hershey B'ars	EHL	57	10	14	24	....	....	....	45	....	....	....	....	....
1938-39	Hershey B'ars	EHL	53	22	32	54	....	....	....	20	....	....	....	....	....
1939-40	Baltimore Orioles	EHL	59	31	37	68	....	....	....	52	8	2	5	7	2
1940-41	**New York Americans**	**NHL**	**15**	**2**	**5**	**7**	**4**	**9**	**13**	**0**	....	....	....	....	....
	Springfield Indians	AHL	40	17	27	44	....	....	....	38	3	0	1	1	2
1941-42	Springfield Indians	AHL	51	19	21	40	....	....	....	45	2	0	0	0	0
1942-43	Buffalo Bisons	AHL	50	27	30	57	....	....	....	52	9	5	3	8	2
1943-44	Buffalo Bisons	AHL	52	27	*53	80	....	....	....	39	9	5	*11	16	0
1944-45	**New York Rangers**	**NHL**	**44**	**13**	**9**	**22**	**18**	**14**	**32**	**6**	....	....	....	....	....
1945-46	Buffalo Bisons	AHL	62	27	43	70	....	....	....	32	12	5	*11	*16	6
1946-47	Buffalo Bisons	AHL	63	26	21	47	....	....	....	29	2	0	1	1	0
1947-48	Buffalo Bisons	AHL	40	12	20	32	....	....	....	0	8	4	3	7	4
1948-49	Buffalo–Hershey	AHL	61	20	28	48	....	....	....	9	9	3	2	5	0
	NHL Totals		**59**	**15**	**14**	**29**	**22**	**23**	**45**	**6**	....	....	....	....	....

Signed as a free agent by **NY Americans**, September 29, 1939. Rights transferred to **NY Rangers** from **Brooklyn** in Special Dispersal Draw, September 11, 1943.

• HURST, RON
Ron Hurst
RW – R. 5'9", 175 lbs. b: Toronto, Ont., 5/18/1931.

Season	Club	League	GP	G	A	Pts	AG	AA	APts	PIM	GP	G	A	Pts	PIM
			REGULAR SEASON								PLAYOFFS				
1946-47	Toronto Young Rangers	OHA	1	0	0	0	....	....	....	0	....	....	....	....	....
1947-48	Weston Dukes	Tor-Jr.	STATISTICS NOT AVAILABLE												
1948-49	Weston Dukes	Tor-Jr.	STATISTICS NOT AVAILABLE												
	Toronto Marlboros	OHA	....	....	....	....	....	....	....	....	9	3	8	11	7
1949-50	Toronto Marlboros	OHA	48	13	12	25	....	....	....	74	5	2	4	6	12
1950-51	Toronto Marlboros	OHA	51	15	13	28	....	....	....	127	12	8	3	11	36
1951-52	Saint John Beavers	MMHL	63	17	25	42	....	....	....	51	15	4	3	7	30
1952-53	Ottawa Senators	QSHL	8	2	1	3	....	....	....	4	....	....	....	....	....
	Charlottetown Islanders	MMHL	70	23	21	44	....	....	....	104	18	3	9	12	35
1953-54	Soo Greyhounds	NOHA	53	11	30	41	....	....	....	63	9	4	5	9	8
1954-55	Soo Greyhounds	NOHA	57	24	29	53	....	....	....	60	14	5	4	9	29
1955-56	**Toronto Maple Leafs**	**NHL**	**50**	**7**	**5**	**12**	**10**	**6**	**16**	**62**	**3**	**0**	**2**	**2**	**4**
	Pittsburgh Hornets	AHL	13	7	8	15	....	....	....	44	....	....	....	....	....
1956-57	**Toronto Maple Leafs**	**NHL**	**14**	**2**	**2**	**4**	**3**	**2**	**5**	**8**	....	....	....	....	....
	Rochester Americans	AHL	26	7	16	23	....	....	....	58	10	1	4	5	20
1957-58	Rochester Americans	AHL	59	12	22	34	....	....	....	120	....	....	....	....	....
1958-59	Hershey Bears	AHL	19	2	8	10	....	....	....	47	....	....	....	....	....
1959-60	Hershey Bears	AHL	43	7	7	14	....	....	....	175	....	....	....	....	....
	NHL Totals		**64**	**9**	**7**	**16**	**13**	**8**	**21**	**70**	**3**	**0**	**2**	**2**	**4**

Traded to **Hershey** (AHL) by **Toronto** with Wally Boyer and Mike Nykoluk for Willie Marshall, April 29, 1958.

• HUTCHINSON, RONALD
Ronald Hutchinson
C – L. 5'10", 165 lbs. b: Flin Flon, Man., 10/24/1936.

Season	Club	League	GP	G	A	Pts	AG	AA	APts	PIM	GP	G	A	Pts	PIM
1954-55	Flin Flon Bombers	SJHL	16	1	6	7	....	....	....	0	....	....	....	....	....
1955-56	Flin Flon Bombers	SJHL	47	32	29	61	....	....	....	4	12	2	1	3	6
1956-57	Flin Flon Bombers	SJHL	55	28	54	82	....	....	....	10	10	7	12	19	2
1957-58	Vancouver Canucks	WHL	66	22	21	43	....	....	....	23	11	2	7	9	11
1958-59	Vancouver Canucks	WHL	70	15	33	48	....	....	....	21	9	2	4	6	9
1959-60	Vancouver Canucks	WHL	70	12	26	38	....	....	....	25	11	0	3	3	0
1960-61	**New York Rangers**	**NHL**	**9**	**0**	**0**	**0**	**0**	**0**	**0**	**0**	....	....	....	....	....
	Vancouver Canucks	WHL	53	11	5	16	....	....	....	10	9	0	1	1	0
1961-62	Vancouver–Seattle	WHL	70	18	16	34	....	....	....	14	2	0	0	0	0
1962-63	Vancouver Canucks	WHL	68	12	23	35	....	....	....	36	7	0	3	3	2
1963-64	Vancouver Canucks	WHL	70	10	19	29	....	....	....	8	....	....	....	....	....
1964-65	Vancouver Canucks	WHL	2	0	0	0	....	....	....	0	....	....	....	....	....
	Charlotte Checkers	EHL	59	20	30	50	....	....	....	33	3	1	1	2	0
1965-66	Vancouver Canucks	WHL	41	10	7	17	....	....	....	8	....	....	....	....	....
1966-67	Vancouver Canucks	WHL	13	0	1	1	....	....	....	4	....	....	....	....	....
1968-69	Cranbrook Royals	WIHL	46	10	33	43	....	....	....	32	....	....	....	....	....
1969-70	Cranbrook Royals	WIHL	35	13	21	34	....	....	....	6	....	....	....	....	....
	NHL Totals		**9**	**0**	**0**	**0**	**0**	**0**	**0**	**0**	....	....	....	....	....

• HUTTON, BILL
Bill Hutton
D/RW – R. 5'11", 165 lbs. b: Calgary, Alta., 1/28/1910. Deceased.

Season	Club	League	GP	G	A	Pts	AG	AA	APts	PIM	GP	G	A	Pts	PIM
1928-29	Calgary Canadians	City Jr.	STATISTICS NOT AVAILABLE												
1929-30	**Boston Bruins**	**NHL**	**16**	**2**	**0**	**2**	**4**	**0**	**4**	**2**	....	....	....	....	....
	Ottawa Senators	**NHL**	**18**	**0**	**1**	**1**	**0**	**3**	**3**	**0**	**2**	**0**	**0**	**0**	**0**
	Philadelphia Arrows	Can-Am	6	1	1	2	....	....	....	0	....	....	....	....	....
1930-31	**Boston Bruins**	**NHL**	**9**	**0**	**0**	**0**	**0**	**0**	**0**	**2**	....	....	....	....	....
	Philadelphia Quakers	**NHL**	**21**	**1**	**1**	**2**	**2**	**4**	**6**	**4**	....	....	....	....	....
1931-32	Boston Cubs	Can-Am	6	0	0	0	....	....	....	2	....	....	....	....	
	Detroit–Syracuse	IAHL	8	0	0	0	....	....	....	0	....	....	....	....	....
	Duluth Hornets	AHA	2	0	0	0	....	....	....	0	....	....	....	....	....
1932-33	Calgary Tigers	NWHL	30	6	3	9	....	....	....	10	6	0	0	0	4
1933-34	Calgary Tigers	NWHL	32	11	1	12	....	....	....	25	5	2	0	2	2
1934-35	Vancouver Lions	NWHL	32	5	10	15	....	....	....	31	0	1	0	1	2
1935-36	Vancouver Lions	NWHL	40	4	7	11	....	....	....	10	7	0	0	0	2
1936-37	Spokane Clippers	PCHL	40	9	7	10	....	....	....	10	6	1	0	1	2
1937-38	Vancouver Lions	PCHL	42	4	5	9	....	....	....	24	6	1	1	2	4
1938-39	Vancouver Lions	PCHL	47	9	15	24	....	....	....	30	2	0	0	0	5
1939-40	Vancouver Lions	PCHL	39	7	3	10	....	....	....	28	5	1	3	4	4
1940-41	Vancouver Lions	PCHL	47	9	18	27	....	....	....	37	6	1	1	2	6
1941-42	Tulsa Oilers	AHA	50	5	8	13	....	....	....	12	2	1	0	1	0
1942-43	Vancouver St. Regis	PCHL	10	1	3	4	....	....	....	6	5	2	0	2	4
1943-44	Vancouver St. Regis	PCHL	23	5	7	12	....	....	....	6	3	0	0	0	2
1943-44	Seattle Bombers	City Sr.	2	1	2	3	....	....	....	0	....	....	....	....	....
	NHL Totals		**64**	**3**	**2**	**5**	**6**	**7**	**13**	**8**	**2**	**0**	**0**	**0**	**0**

Traded to **Ottawa** by **Boston** for Harry Connor, January 30, 1930. Traded to **Boston** by **Ottawa** for Harry Connor, October 16, 1930. Traded to **Philadelphia** by **Boston** with Ron Lyons for Harry Darragh, December 8, 1930. Traded to **Detroit** (IAHL) by **Philadelphia** for cash, February 24, 1931.

• HYLAND, HARRY
Harry Hyland **HHOF**
RW – R. 5'6", 156 lbs. b: Montreal, Que., 1/2/1889. d. 8/8/1969.

Season	Club	League	GP	G	A	Pts	AG	AA	APts	PIM	GP	G	A	Pts	PIM
1908-09	Montreal Shamrocks	ECHA	11	19	0	19	....	....	....	36	....	....	....	....	....
1909-10	Montreal Wanderers	NHA	11	24	0	24	....	....	....	23	1	3	0	3	3
1910-11	Montreal Wanderers	NHA	15	14	0	14	....	....	....	43	....	....	....	....	....
1911-12	New Westminster Royals	PCHA	15	26	0	26	....	....	....	44	....	....	....	....	....
1912-13	Montreal Wanderers	NHA	20	27	0	27	....	....	....	38	....	....	....	....	....
1913-14	Montreal Wanderers	NHA	18	30	12	42	....	....	....	18	....	....	....	....	....
1914-15	Montreal Wanderers	NHA	19	23	6	29	....	....	....	49	2	0	0	0	26
1915-16	Montreal Wanderers	NHA	20	14	0	14	....	....	....	69	....	....	....	....	....
1916-17	Montreal Wanderers	NHA	13	12	2	14	....	....	....	21	....	....			
	Montreal St. Ann's	City Sr.	....	3	1	4	....	....	....	....	....	....	....	....	....
1917-18	**Montreal Wanderers**	**NHL**	**4**	**6**	**1**	**7**	**15**	**0**	**15**	**6**	....	....	....	....	....
	Ottawa Senators	**NHL**	**13**	**8**	**1**	**9**	**20**	**0**	**20**	**59**	....	....	....	....	....
1918-19	McGill University	Mtl-Sr.	DID NOT PLAY – COACHING												
	NHL Totals		**17**	**14**	**2**	**16**	**35**	**0**	**35**	**65**	....	....	....	....	....
	Other Major League Totals		142	189	20	209	....	....	....	341	3	3	0	3	29

PCHA First All-Star Team (1912)

Rights retained by **Montreal Wanderers** after NHA folded, November 26, 1917. Claimed by **Ottawa** from **Montreal Wanderers** in Dispersal Draft, January 4, 1918.

• IMLACH, BRENT
Brent Imlach
F – L. 5'8", 160 lbs. b: Quebec City, Que., 11/16/1946.

Season	Club	League	GP	G	A	Pts	AG	AA	APts	PIM	GP	G	A	Pts	PIM
			REGULAR SEASON								PLAYOFFS				
1964-65	Toronto Marlboros	OHA	4	0	0	0	....	....	....	0	....	....	....	....	....
1965-66	Toronto Marlboros	OHA	45	23	18	41	....	....	....	15	14	0	5	5	4
	Toronto Maple Leafs	**NHL**	**2**	**0**	**0**	**0**	**0**	**0**	**0**	**0**	....	....	....	....	....
	Rochester Americans	AHL	1	0	0	0	....	....	....	2	....	....	....	....	....
1966-67	London Knights	OHA	46	3	15	18	....	....	....	10	....	....	....	....	....
	Toronto Maple Leafs	**NHL**	**1**	**0**	**0**	**0**	**0**	**0**	**0**	**0**	....	....	....	....	....
1967-68	U. of Western Ontario	OQAA	....	11	15	26	....	....	....	9	....	....	....	....	....
1968-69	U. of Western Ontario	OQAA	....	14	20	34	....	....	....	8	....	....	....	....	....
1969-70	University of Toronto	OQAA	....	3	10	13	....	....	....	8	....	....	....	....	....
1970-71	University of Toronto	OUAA	....	0	5	5	....	....	....	4	....	....	....	....	....
1971-72	York University	OUAA	....	16	22	38	....	....	....	28	....	....	....	....	....
	NHL Totals		**3**	**0**	**0**	**0**	**0**	**0**	**0**	**0**	....	....	....	....	....

Traded to **Buffalo** by **Toronto** with Floyd Smith for cash, August 31, 1970.

• INGARFIELD, EARL
— see page 1134

• INGOLDSBY, JOHNNY
Johnny "Ding" Ingoldsby
RW/D – R. 6'2", 210 lbs. b: Toronto, Ont., 6/21/1924. d: 8/10/1982.

Season	Club	League	GP	G	A	Pts	AG	AA	APts	PIM	GP	G	A	Pts	PIM
1942-43	**Toronto Maple Leafs**	**NHL**	**8**	**0**	**1**	**1**	**0**	**1**	**1**	**0**	....	....	....	....	....
	Providence Reds	AHL	24	10	12	22	....	....	....	2	2	0	0	0	0
1943-44	**Toronto Maple Leafs**	**NHL**	**21**	**5**	**0**	**5**	**6**	**0**	**6**	**15**	....	....	....	....	....
	Toronto CIL	City Sr.	....	4	3	7	....	....	....	0	....	....	....	....	....
1944-45			MILITARY SERVICE												
1945-46	Toronto Staffords	OHA Sr.	11	3	8	11	....	....	....	10	....	....	....	....	....
1946-47			REINSTATED AS AN AMATEUR												
1947-48	Owen Sound Mercurys	OHA Sr.	36	7	17	24	....	....	....	24	5	7	6	13	4
1948-49	Owen Sound Mercurys	OHA Sr.	37	17	14	31	....	....	....	27	4	0	1	1	0
1949-50	Owen Sound Mercurys	OHA Sr.	26	9	6	15	....	....	....	17	....	....	....	....	....
1950-51			DID NOT PLAY												
1951-52			DID NOT PLAY												
1952-53	New Haven Nutmegs	EHL	60	29	52	81	....	....	....	20	....	....			
1953-54	Marion Barons	IHL	61	19	18	37	....	....	....	30	5	0	1	1	10
1954-55	Grand Rapids Rockets	IHL	59	13	24	37	....	....	....	18	4	0	0	0	0
1955-56	Grand Rapids Rockets	IHL	58	16	30	46	....	....	....	18	....	....	....	....	....
1956-57	Huntington Hornets	IHL	60	18	10	28	....	....	....	6	4	3	1	4	0
1957-58	New Haven Blades	EHL	50	26	31	57	....	....	....	65	6	2	2	4	2
1958-59	New Haven Blades	EHL	64	15	23	38	....	....	....	8	....	....	....	....	....
1959-60	New Haven–Charlotte	EHL	40	8	15	23	....	....	....	18	....	....	....	....	....
	NHL Totals		**29**	**5**	**1**	**6**	**6**	**1**	**7**	**15**	....	....	....	....	....

• INGRAM, FRANK
Frank Ingram
RW – R. 5'8", 185 lbs. b: Craven, Sask., 9/17/1907.

Season	Club	League	GP	G	A	Pts	AG	AA	APts	PIM	GP	G	A	Pts	PIM
1922-23	Regina Pats	City Jr.	2	1	1	2	....	....	....	0	....	....	....	....	....
1923-24	Regina Pats	City Jr.	6	3	1	4	....	....	....	5	1	1	0	1	0
1924-25	Regina Pats	City Jr.	5	11	1	12	....	....	....	5	12	10	5	15	*29
1925-26	Regina Victorias	City Sr.	17	18	12	*30	....	....	....	13	9	*12	*8	*20	4
1926-27	Fort William Forts	TBSHL	6	1	0	1	....	....	....	5	....	....	....	....	....
	Regina Capitals	PrHL	14	3	3	6	....	....	....	2	2	0	0	0	2
1927-28	St. Paul Saints	AHA	40	5	6	11	....	....	....	46	....	....	....	....	....
1928-29	St. Paul Saints	AHA	40	20	4	24	....	....	....	69	8	2	*2	4	4
1929-30	**Chicago Black Hawks**	**NHL**	**37**	**6**	**10**	**16**	**12**	**32**	**44**	**28**	**2**	**0**	**0**	**0**	**0**
1930-31	**Chicago Black Hawks**	**NHL**	**43**	**17**	**4**	**21**	**42**	**14**	**56**	**37**	**9**	**0**	**1**	**1**	**2**
1931-32	**Chicago Black Hawks**	**NHL**	**21**	**1**	**2**	**3**	**2**	**6**	**8**	**4**	....	....	....	....	....
	Philadelphia Arrows	Can-Am	8	1	3	4	....	....	....	13	....	....	....	....	
	Pittsburgh Yellowjackets	IAHL	15	6	3	9	....	....	....	21	....	....	....	....	....
1932-33	Cleveland–Detroit	IAHL	36	10	9	19	....	....	....	49	....	....	....	....	....
	Boston Cubs	Can-Am	5	0	0	0	....	....	....	2	....	....	....	....	....
1933-34	Detroit Olympics	IAHL	11	0	1	1	....	....	....	6	....	....	....	....	....
	Oklahoma City Warriors	AHA	42	6	7	13				40	....	....	....	....	....
1934-35	Oklahoma City Warriors	AHA	45	21	21	42	....	....	....	26	....	....	....	....	....
1935-36	Oklahoma–Minneapolis	AHA	48	20	18	38	....	....	....	8	....	....	....	....	....
1936-37	St. Louis Flyers	AHA	44	4	17	21	....	....	....	6	6	0	0	0	0
1938-39	Kansas City Greyhounds	AHA	48	12	24	36	....	....	....	11	....	....	....	....	....
1938-39	Kansas City Greyhounds	AHA	16	1	3	4	....	....	....	4	....	....	....	....	....
1939-40	Wichita Skyhawks	AHA	6	0	2	2	....	....	....	2	....	....	....	....	....
	Portage Lakes Lakers	NOHA	24	9	11	20	....	....	....	....	....	....	....	....	....
	NHL Totals		**101**	**24**	**16**	**40**	**56**	**52**	**108**	**69**	**11**	**0**	**1**	**1**	**2**

AHA Second All-Star Team (1935, 1936)

Traded to **Chicago** by **St. Paul** (AHA) for cash, November, 1929.

• INGRAM, JOHN J.
John J. "Jack" Ingram
C – L. 5'11", 170 lbs. b: Halifax, N.S., 1894. d: 12/14/1957.

Season	Club	League	GP	G	A	Pts	AG	AA	APts	PIM	GP	G	A	Pts	PIM
1913-14	Moncton Corncobs	City Sr.	7	15	0	15	....	....	....	....	1	2	0	2	....
	Halifax Socials	MPHA	1	0	0	0	....	....	....	0	....	....	....	....	....
1914-15	Moncton Machinists	City Sr.	4	4	0	4	....	....	....	....	....	....			....
1915-16	Moncton St. Bernards	EXHIB	1	2	0	2	....	....	....		....	....	....	....	....
	Moncton Trojans	EXHIB	STATISTICS NOT AVAILABLE												
1916-17			DID NOT PLAY												
1917-18	Moncton St. Bernards	EXHIB	2	7	0	7	....	....	....	....	....	....	....	....	....
1918-19	Moncton Victorias	EXHIB	1	3	0	3	....	....	....	....	....	....	....	....	....
1919-20	Moncton Victorias	City Sr.	6	8	3	11	....	....	....	4	9	*23	4	*27	4
1920-21	Moncton Victorias	MIHL	9	*18	0	*18	....	....	....	6	2	4	0	4	2
1921-22	Moncton Victorias	MIHL	13	*24	0	*24	....	....	....	36	....	....	....	....	....
1922-23	Moncton Victorias	MIHL	12	18	0	18	....	....	....	30	....	....	....	....	
1923-24	Moncton Victorias	MIHL	16	12	0	12	....	....	....	19	....	....	....	....	....
1924-25	**Boston Bruins**	**NHL**	**1**	**0**	**0**	**0**	**0**	**0**	**0**	**0**	....	....	....	....	....
	Moncton Victorias	City Sr.	3	*7	0	*7	....	....	....	2	....	....	....	....	....
1925-26			DID NOT PLAY – REFEREE												
1926-27	Providence Reds	Can-Am	1	0	0	0	....	....	....	0	....	....	....	....	....
1927-28			DID NOT PLAY – REFEREE												
1928-29	Moncton Atlantics	NBSHL	12	7	3	10	....	....	....	16	2	1	0	1	2
1929-30	Moncton Atlantics	City Sr.	1	1	0	1	....	....	....	2	....	....	....	....	....
1930-31	Moncton Victorias	NBSHL	2	0	0	0	....	....	....	2	....	....	....	....	....
	NHL Totals		**1**	**0**	**0**	**0**	**0**	**0**	**0**	**0**	....	....	....	....	....

• INGRAM, RON   Ron Ingram

D – R. 5'11", 185 lbs.   b: Toronto, Ont., 7/5/1933.

			REGULAR SEASON								PLAYOFFS				
Season	Club	League	GP	G	A	Pts	AG	AA	APts	PIM	GP	G	A	Pts	PIM
1950-51	Toronto Marlboros	OHA	3	0	1	1	....	....	....	2	....	....	....	....	....
1951-52	Toronto Marlboros	OHA	40	8	15	23	....	....	....	27	5	1	0	1	6
1952-53	Toronto Marlboros	OHA	47	3	12	15	....	....	....	98	7	1	1	2	30
1953-54	Stratford Indians	OHA Sr.	54	10	13	23	....	....	....	113	12	3	6	9	34
1954-55	Stratford Indians	OHA Sr.	50	6	20	26	....	....	....	96	7	2	4	6	12
1955-56	Montreal Royals	QHL	54	3	6	9	....	....	....	95	12	2	1	3	24
1956-57	**Chicago Black Hawks**	**NHL**	**45**	**1**	**6**	**7**	**1**	**7**	**8**	**21**	....	....	....	....	....
	Cleveland Barons	AHL	18	0	4	4	....	....	....	18	12	3	5	8	31
1957-58	Buffalo Bisons	AHL	63	5	10	15	....	....	....	92	....	....	....	....	....
1958-59	Buffalo Bisons	AHL	58	3	14	17	....	....	....	57	11	0	6	6	38
1959-60	Buffalo Bisons	AHL	71	5	18	23	....	....	....	131	....	....	....	....	....
1960-61	Buffalo Bisons	AHL	72	5	18	23	....	....	....	108	4	1	0	1	16
1961-62	Buffalo Bisons	AHL	57	6	18	24	....	....	....	113	11	0	4	4	7
1962-63	Buffalo Bisons	AHL	65	3	29	32	....	....	....	113	12	1	5	6	32
	Chicago Black Hawks	**NHL**	....	....	....	....	....	....	....	....	**2**	**0**	**0**	**0**	**0**
1963-64	**Detroit Red Wings**	**NHL**	**50**	**3**	**6**	**9**	**4**	**7**	**11**	**50**	....	....	....	....	....
	New York Rangers	**NHL**	**16**	**1**	**3**	**4**	**1**	**3**	**4**	**8**	....	....	....	....	....
1964-65	**New York Rangers**	**NHL**	**3**	**0**	**0**	**0**	**0**	**0**	**0**	**2**	....	....	....	....	....
	Baltimore Clippers	AHL	63	12	31	43	....	....	....	92	5	0	0	0	10
1965-66	Baltimore Clippers	AHL	72	10	34	44	....	....	....	132	....	....	....	....	....
1966-67	Baltimore Clippers	AHL	59	4	31	35	....	....	....	65	8	1	3	4	12
1967-68	Buffalo Bisons	AHL	71	9	32	41	....	....	....	102	5	2	4	6	12
1968-69	Buffalo Bisons	AHL	62	4	33	37	....	....	....	97	6	0	3	3	8
1969-70	Seattle Totems	WHL	72	5	23	28	....	....	....	48	....	....	....	....	....
	NHL Totals		**114**	**5**	**15**	**20**	**6**	**17**	**23**	**81**	**2**	**0**	**0**	**0**	**0**

AHL First All-Star Team (1968) • AHL Second All-Star Team (1969)

Loaned to **Cleveland** (AHL) by **Chicago** for Ian Cushenean, September, 1956. Traded to **Detroit** by **Chicago** with Roger Crozier for Howie Young, June 5, 1963. Traded to **NY Rangers** by **Detroit** for Junior Langlois, February 14, 1964. Traded to **Seattle** (WHL) by **NY Rangers** (Buffalo - AHL) for cash, October, 1969.

• IRVIN, DICK   Dick Irvin   HHOF

C – L. 5'9", 162 lbs.   b: Hamilton, Ont., 7/19/1892.   d: 3/16/1957.

Season	Club	League	GP	G	A	Pts	AG	AA	APts	PIM	GP	G	A	Pts	PIM
1912-13	Winnipeg Strathconas	MHL Sr.	7	*32	0	*32	....	....	....	12	1	0	0	0	0
	Winnipeg Monarchs	MHL Sr.	2	5	0	5	....	....	....	....	....	....	....	....	....
1913-14	Winnipeg Strathconas	MHL Sr.	3	11	0	11	....	....	....	....	....	....	....	....	....
	Winnipeg Monarchs	MHL Sr.	7	*23	1	*24	....	....	....	....	....	....	....	....	....
1914-15	Winnipeg Monarchs	MHL Sr.	6	*23	3	*26	....	....	....	30	8	*27	0	*27	16
1915-16	Winnipeg Monarchs	MHL Sr.	8	*17	4	*21	....	....	....	38	2	7	1	8	2
1916-17	Portland Rosebuds	PCHA	23	35	10	45	....	....	....	24	....	....	....	....	....
1917-18	Winnipeg Yrpes	MHL Sr.	9	*29	8	*37	....	....	....	26	....	....	....	....	....
1918-19			MILITARY SERVICE												
1919-20	Regina Vics	SSHL	12	*32	4	*36	....	....	....	22	2	1	0	1	4
1920-21	Regina Vics	SSHL	11	19	5	24	....	....	....	12	4	*8	0	*8	4
1921-22	Regina Capitals	WCHL	20	21	7	28	....	....	....	17	4	*3	0	*3	2
1922-23	Regina Capitals	WCHL	25	9	4	13	....	....	....	12	2	1	0	1	0
1923-24	Regina Capitals	WCHL	29	15	8	23	....	....	....	33	2	0	2	2	4
1924-25	Regina Capitals	WCHL	28	13	5	18	....	....	....	38	....	....	....	....	....
1925-26	Portland Rosebuds	WHL	30	*31	5	36	....	....	....	29	....	....	....	....	....
1926-27	**Chicago Black Hawks**	**NHL**	**43**	***18**	**18**	**36**	**53**	**158**	**211**	**34**	**2**	**2**	**0**	**2**	**4**
1927-28	**Chicago Black Hawks**	**NHL**	**12**	**5**	**4**	**9**	**15**	**34**	**49**	**14**	....	....	....	....	....
1928-29	**Chicago Black Hawks**	**NHL**	**39**	**6**	**1**	**7**	**24**	**9**	**33**	**30**	....	....	....	....	....
	NHL Totals		**94**	**29**	**23**	**52**	**92**	**201**	**293**	**78**	**2**	**2**	**0**	**2**	**4**
	Other Major League Totals		155	124	39	163	....	....	....	153	8	4	2	6	6

PCHA Second All-Star Team (1917) • WCHL Second All-Star Team (1922) • WCHL First All-Star Team (1924)

Signed as a free agent by **Regina** (WCHL), December 27, 1921. Transferred to **Portland** (WHL) after **Regina** (WCHL) franchise relocated, September 1, 1925. NHL rights transferred to **Chicago** after NHL club purchased **Portland** (WHL) franchise, May 15, 1926.

• IRVINE, TED   *— see page 1135*

• IRWIN, IVAN   Ivan "Ivan the Terrible" Irwin

D – L. 6'2", 185 lbs.   b: Chicago, IL, 3/13/1927.

Season	Club	League	GP	G	A	Pts	AG	AA	APts	PIM	GP	G	A	Pts	PIM
1947-48	Boston Olympics	QSHL	40	1	3	4	....	....	....	30	....	....	....	....	....
	Boston Olympics	EHL	16	2	1	3	....	....	....	36	....	....	....	....	....
1948-49	Sherbrooke Saints	QSHL	55	1	8	9	....	....	....	124	12	1	2	3	*36
1949-50	Sherbrooke Saints	QSHL	7	1	0	1	....	....	....	30	....	....	....	....	....
	Cincinnati Mohawks	AHL	52	2	7	9	....	....	....	114	....	....	....	....	....
1950-51	Cincinnati Mohawks	AHL	62	3	14	17	....	....	....	145	....	....	....	....	....
1951-52	Cincinnati Mohawks	AHL	67	4	10	14	....	....	....	111	7	0	1	1	18
1952-53	**Montreal Canadiens**	**NHL**	**4**	**0**	**1**	**1**	**0**	**1**	**1**	**0**	....	....	....	....	....
	Victoria Cougars	WHL	58	5	20	25	....	....	....	116	....	....	....	....	....
1953-54	**New York Rangers**	**NHL**	**56**	**2**	**12**	**14**	**3**	**16**	**19**	**109**	....	....	....	....	....
	Vancouver Canucks	WHL	13	1	0	1	....	....	....	20	....	....	....	....	....
1954-55	**New York Rangers**	**NHL**	**60**	**0**	**13**	**13**	**0**	**17**	**17**	**85**	....	....	....	....	....
1955-56	**New York Rangers**	**NHL**	**34**	**0**	**1**	**1**	**0**	**1**	**1**	**20**	**5**	**0**	**0**	**0**	**8**
	Providence Reds	AHL	19	0	5	5	....	....	....	43	....	....	....	....	....
1956-57	Providence Reds	AHL	62	4	14	18	....	....	....	149	5	0	1	1	8
1957-58	**New York Rangers**	**NHL**	**1**	**0**	**0**	**0**	**0**	**0**	**0**	**0**	....	....	....	....	....
	Providence Reds	AHL	63	2	16	18	....	....	....	146	5	1	2	3	6
1958-59	Buffalo Bisons	AHL	63	3	12	15	....	....	....	106	11	0	3	3	16
1959-60	Buffalo Bisons	AHL	40	1	8	9	....	....	....	53	....	....	....	....	....
	NHL Totals		**155**	**2**	**27**	**29**	**3**	**35**	**38**	**214**	**5**	**0**	**0**	**0**	**8**

AHL Second All-Star Team (1957) • AHL First All-Star Team (1958, 1959)

Rights traded to **Montreal** by **Cincinnati** (AHL) for cash, October 3, 1951. Traded to **NY Rangers** by **Montreal** for Eddie Slowinski and Pete Babando, August 8, 1953.

• JACKSON, ART   Art Jackson

C – L. 5'8", 165 lbs.   b: Toronto, Ont., 12/15/1915.   d: 5/15/1971.

Season	Club	League	GP	G	A	Pts	AG	AA	APts	PIM	GP	G	A	Pts	PIM
1931-32	Toronto Marlboros	OHA	3	0	0	0	....	....	....	0	....	....	....	....	....
1932-33	Toronto Marlboros	OHA	9	7	5	*12	....	....	....	10	3	2	0	2	6
1933-34	St. Michael's Majors	OHA	12	23	13	36	....	....	....	6	3	*4	2	6	6
1934-35	**Toronto Maple Leafs**	**NHL**	**20**	**1**	**3**	**4**	**2**	**7**	**9**	**4**	**1**	**0**	**0**	**0**	**2**
	Syracuse Stars	IAHL	24	13	12	25	....	....	....	0	2	1	0	1	0
1935-36	**Toronto Maple Leafs**	**NHL**	**48**	**5**	**15**	**20**	**12**	**36**	**48**	**14**	**8**	**0**	**3**	**3**	**2**
	Syracuse Stars	IAHL	1	0	0	0	....	....	....	0	....	....	....	....	....
1936-37	**Toronto Maple Leafs**	**NHL**	**14**	**2**	**0**	**2**	**4**	**0**	**4**	**2**	....	....	....	....	....
	Syracuse Stars	AHL	30	17	21	38	....	....	....	38	9	1	3	4	0
1937-38	**Boston Bruins**	**NHL**	**48**	**9**	**3**	**12**	**19**	**6**	**25**	**24**	**3**	**0**	**0**	**0**	**0**
1938-39	**New York Americans**	**NHL**	**48**	**12**	**13**	**25**	**25**	**24**	**49**	**15**	**2**	**0**	**0**	**0**	**2**
1939-40	**Boston Bruins**	**NHL**	**46**	**7**	**18**	**25**	**15**	**36**	**51**	**6**	**5**	**1**	**2**	**3**	**0**
1940-41	**Boston Bruins**	**NHL**	**48**	**17**	**15**	**32**	**34**	**27**	**61**	**10**	**11**	**1**	**3**	**4**	**16**
1941-42	**Boston Bruins**	**NHL**	**47**	**6**	**18**	**24**	**10**	**27**	**37**	**25**	**5**	**0**	**1**	**1**	**0**
1942-43	**Boston Bruins**	**NHL**	**50**	**22**	**31**	**53**	**31**	**40**	**71**	**20**	**9**	**6**	**3**	**9**	**7**
1943-44	**Boston Bruins**	**NHL**	**49**	**28**	**41**	**69**	**36**	**50**	**86**	**8**	....	....	....	....	....
1944-45	**Boston Bruins**	**NHL**	**19**	**5**	**8**	**13**	**7**	**13**	**20**	**10**	....	....	....	....	....
	Toronto Maple Leafs	**NHL**	**31**	**9**	**13**	**22**	**12**	**21**	**33**	**6**	**8**	**0**	**0**	**0**	**0**
	NHL Totals		**468**	**123**	**178**	**301**	**207**	**287**	**494**	**144**	**52**	**8**	**12**	**20**	**29**

Traded to **Boston** by **Toronto** for cash and future considerations, September 23, 1937. Loaned to **NY Americans** by **Boston** with Leroy Goldsworthy for 1938-39 season, October 24, 1938. Traded to **Toronto** by **Boston** for $7,500 and future considerations (Bingo Kampman, October 29, 1945), December 24, 1944.

• JACKSON, HAROLD   Harold "Hal" Jackson

D – R. 6', 195 lbs.   b: Cedar Springs, Ont., 8/1/1918.   Deceased.

Season	Club	League	GP	G	A	Pts	AG	AA	APts	PIM	GP	G	A	Pts	PIM
1933-34	Windsor Wanderers	MOHL	19	1	3	4	....	....	....	10	....	....	....	....	....
1934-35	Windsor Wanderers	MOHL	26	5	3	8	....	....	....	31	5	0	0	0	6
1935-36	St. Michael's Majors	OHA	8	2	1	3	....	....	....	4	5	0	0	0	8
1936-37	**Chicago Black Hawks**	**NHL**	**38**	**1**	**3**	**4**	**2**	**7**	**9**	**6**	....	....	....	....	....
1937-38	**Chicago Black Hawks**	**NHL**	**3**	**0**	**0**	**0**	**0**	**0**	**0**	**0**	**1**	**0**	**0**	**0**	**2**
1938-39	Providence Reds	AHL	51	5	6	11	....	....	....	57	5	0	3	3	6
1939-40	Providence–Cleveland	AHL	47	5	7	12	....	....	....	38	8	1	1	2	4
1940-41	**Detroit Red Wings**	**NHL**	**1**	**0**	**0**	**0**	**0**	**0**	**0**	**0**	....	....	....	....	....
	Providence–Indianapolis	AHL	54	3	9	12	....	....	....	49	....	....	....	....	....
1941-42	Indianapolis Capitals	AHL	56	5	19	24	....	....	....	52	10	2	5	7	8
1942-43	**Detroit Red Wings**	**NHL**	**4**	**0**	**4**	**4**	**0**	**5**	**5**	**6**	**6**	**0**	**1**	**1**	**4**
	Indianapolis Capitals	AHL	53	9	16	25	....	....	....	30	4	0	3	3	14
1943-44	**Detroit Red Wings**	**NHL**	**50**	**7**	**12**	**19**	**9**	**14**	**23**	**76**	**5**	**0**	**0**	**0**	**11**
	Indianapolis Capitals	AHL	1	0	1	1	....	....	....	0	....	....	....	....	....
1944-45	**Detroit Red Wings**	**NHL**	**50**	**5**	**6**	**11**	**7**	**10**	**17**	**45**	**14**	**1**	**1**	**2**	**10**
1945-46	**Detroit Red Wings**	**NHL**	**36**	**3**	**4**	**7**	**5**	**7**	**12**	**36**	**5**	**0**	**0**	**0**	**6**
1946-47	**Detroit Red Wings**	**NHL**	**37**	**1**	**5**	**6**	**1**	**7**	**8**	**39**	....	....	....	....	....
1947-48	Buffalo Bisons	AHL	63	7	30	37	....	....	....	97	8	0	3	3	13
	NHL Totals		**219**	**17**	**34**	**51**	**24**	**50**	**74**	**208**	**31**	**1**	**2**	**3**	**33**

Traded to **Detroit** by **Providence** (AHL) for Cec Dillon and Ed Bush, December 15, 1940. Traded to **Buffalo** (AHL) by **Detroit** with Les Douglas for Jim McFadden, September, 1947.

• JACKSON, HARVEY   Harvey "Busher" Jackson   HHOF

LW – L. 5'11", 195 lbs.   b: Toronto, Ont., 1/19/1911.   d: 6/25/1966.

Season	Club	League	GP	G	A	Pts	AG	AA	APts	PIM	GP	G	A	Pts	PIM
1927-28	Toronto Marlboros	OHA	4	4	0	4	....	....	....	2	2	0	0	0	0
1928-29	Toronto Marlboros	OHA	9	10	4	14	....	....	....	0	3	*7	2	*9	....
1929-30	**Toronto Maple Leafs**	**NHL**	**31**	**12**	**6**	**18**	**24**	**19**	**43**	**29**	....	....	....	....	....
1930-31	**Toronto Maple Leafs**	**NHL**	**43**	**18**	**13**	**31**	**44**	**47**	**91**	**81**	**2**	**0**	**0**	**0**	**0**
1931-32	**Toronto Maple Leafs**	**NHL**	**48**	**28**	**25**	**53**	**61**	**71**	**132**	**63**	**7**	**5**	**2**	**7**	**13**
1932-33	**Toronto Maple Leafs**	**NHL**	**48**	**27**	**17**	**44**	**64**	**45**	**109**	**43**	**9**	**3**	**1**	**4**	**2**
1933-34	**Toronto Maple Leafs**	**NHL**	**38**	**20**	**18**	**38**	**45**	**48**	**93**	**38**	**5**	**1**	**0**	**1**	**8**
1934-35	**Toronto Maple Leafs**	**NHL**	**42**	**22**	**22**	**44**	**47**	**49**	**96**	**27**	**7**	**3**	**2**	**5**	**2**
1935-36	**Toronto Maple Leafs**	**NHL**	**47**	**11**	**11**	**22**	**27**	**27**	**54**	**19**	**9**	**3**	**2**	**5**	**4**
1936-37	**Toronto Maple Leafs**	**NHL**	**46**	**21**	**19**	**40**	**46**	**45**	**91**	**12**	**2**	**1**	**0**	**1**	**2**
1937-38	**Toronto Maple Leafs**	**NHL**	**48**	**17**	**17**	**34**	**36**	**35**	**71**	**18**	**6**	**1**	**0**	**1**	**8**
1938-39	**Toronto Maple Leafs**	**NHL**	**41**	**10**	**17**	**27**	**21**	**32**	**53**	**12**	**7**	**0**	**1**	**1**	**2**
1939-40	**New York Americans**	**NHL**	**43**	**12**	**8**	**20**	**26**	**16**	**42**	**10**	**3**	**0**	**1**	**1**	**2**
1940-41	**New York Americans**	**NHL**	**46**	**8**	**18**	**26**	**16**	**33**	**49**	**4**	....	....	....	....	....
1941-42	**Boston Bruins**	**NHL**	**26**	**5**	**7**	**12**	**9**	**11**	**20**	**18**	**5**	**0**	**1**	**1**	**0**
1942-43	**Boston Bruins**	**NHL**	**44**	**19**	**15**	**34**	**27**	**19**	**46**	**38**	**9**	**1**	**2**	**3**	**10**
1943-44	**Boston Bruins**	**NHL**	**42**	**11**	**21**	**32**	**14**	**25**	**39**	**25**	....	....	....	....	....
	NHL Totals		**633**	**241**	**234**	**475**	**507**	**522**	**1029**	**437**	**71**	**18**	**12**	**30**	**53**

NHL First All-Star Team (1932, 1934, 1935, 1937) • NHL Scoring Leader (1932) • NHL Second All-Star Team (1933)

Played in NHL All-Star Game (1934, 1937, 1939)

Traded to **NY Americans** by **Toronto** with Buzz Boll, Doc Romnes, Jim Fowler and Murray Armstrong for Sweeney Schriner, May 15, 1939. Traded to **Boston** by **NY Americans** for $7,500, January 4, 1942.

• JACKSON, JOHN   John "Jack" Jackson

D – R. 5'10", 185 lbs.   b: Windsor, Ont., 5/3/1925.

Season	Club	League	GP	G	A	Pts	AG	AA	APts	PIM	GP	G	A	Pts	PIM
1944-45	Montreal Jr. Royals	City Jr.	5	1	2	3	....	....	....	0	3	2	1	3	0
1945-46	Kansas City Pla-Mors	USHL	39	11	11	22	....	....	....	28	12	0	1	1	12
1946-47	**Chicago Black Hawks**	**NHL**	**48**	**2**	**5**	**7**	**3**	**7**	**10**	**38**	....	....	....	....	....
	Kansas City Pla-Mors	USHL	15	1	3	4	....	....	....	24	....	....	....	....	....
1947-48	Kansas City Pla-Mors	USHL	66	6	19	25	....	....	....	72	7	0	1	1	0
1948-49	Kansas City Pla-Mors	USHL	66	11	17	28	....	....	....	82	2	1	0	1	0
1949-50	Kansas City Mohawks	USHL	70	9	30	39	....	....	....	34	3	0	0	0	0
1950-51	New Haven Ramblers	AHL	22	0	2	2	....	....	....	10	....	....	....	....	....
	Denver Falcons	USHL	28	3	9	12	....	....	....	28	5	1	5	6	20
1951-52	Seattle Ironmen	PCHL	54	6	13	19	....	....	....	72	....	....	....	....	....
	NHL Totals		**48**	**2**	**5**	**7**	**3**	**7**	**10**	**38**	....	....	....	....	....

• JACKSON, LLOYD Lloyd Jackson

C – L. 5'9", 150 lbs. b: Ottawa, Ont., 1/7/1912.

Season	Club	League	GP	G	A	Pts	AG	AA	APts	PIM	GP	G	A	Pts	PIM
			REGULAR SEASON								PLAYOFFS				
1929-30	Ottawa Montagnards	City Jr.	12	8	*3	11	....	....	....	2	2	1	0	1	4
1930-31	Ottawa Montagnards	City Jr.	4	0	2	2	....	....	....	0	....	....	....	....	....
	New Glasgow Tigers	NSSHL	24	15	5	20	....	....	....	14	2	0	0	0	2
1931-32	New Haven Eagles	Can-Am	40	9	11	20	....	....	....	3	2	1	0	1	0
1932-33	New Haven Eagles	Can-Am	36	4	14	18	....	....	....	16	....	....	....	....	....
1933-34	Cleveland–Syracuse	IAHL	16	3	1	4	....	....	....	2	....	....	....	....	....
	Seattle Seahawks	NWHL	22	9	9	18	....	....	....	4	....	....	....	....	....
1934-35	New Haven Eagles	Can-Am	47	23	35	*58	....	....	....	10	....	....	....	....	....
1935-36	New Haven Eagles	Can-Am	47	17	28	45	....	....	....	3	....	....	....	....	....
1936-37	**New York Americans**	**NHL**	**14**	**1**	**1**	**2**	**2**	**2**	**4**	**0**	....	....	....	....	....
	New Haven Eagles	AHL	44	5	19	24	....	....	....	....	....	....	....	....	....
1937-38	Springfield Indians	AHL	40	5	11	16	....	....	....	2	....	....	....	....	....
1938-39	Springfield Indians	AHL	51	10	16	26	....	....	....	6	3	1	0	1	0
1939-40	Springfield Indians	AHL	54	10	22	32	....	....	....	2	3	1	0	1	0
1940-41	Tulsa Oilers	AHA	15	5	5	10	....	....	....	0	....	....	....	....	....
	Kansas City Americans	AHA	24	5	8	13	....	....	....	12	....	....	....	....	....
1941-42	Fort Worth Rangers	AHA	50	15	37	52	....	....	....	2	5	2	3	5	2
	NHL Totals		**14**	**1**	**1**	**2**	**2**	**2**	**4**	**0**	....	....	....	....	....

Can-Am First All-Star Team (1936)

• JACKSON, STAN Stan Jackson

LW – L. 6', 180 lbs. b: Parrsboro, N.S., 8/27/1898. d: 11/28/1955.

Season	Club	League	GP	G	A	Pts	AG	AA	APts	PIM	GP	G	A	Pts	PIM
1919-20	Amherst Ramblers	MSHL	2	1	0	1	....	....	....	5	....	....	....	....	....
1920-21	Amherst Ramblers	MSHL	10	13	0	13	....	....	....	10	2	1	0	1	2
1921-22	Amherst Ramblers	MSHL	8	9	0	9	....	....	....	10	....	....	....	....	....
	Toronto St. Pats	**NHL**	**1**	**0**	**0**	**0**	**0**	**0**	**0**	**0**	....	....	....	....	....
	Halifax Independents	City Sr.	1	0	0	0	....	....	....	0	....	....	....	....	....
	Stellerton Millionaires	MSHL	....	....	....	....	....	....	....	....	6	4	0	4	2
1922-23	Amherst Ramblers	MSHL	12	14	0	14	....	....	....	24	....	....	....	....	....
1923-24	**Toronto St. Pats**	**NHL**	**21**	**1**	**1**	**2**	**4**	**17**	**21**	**6**	....	....	....	....	....
1924-25	**Toronto St. Pats**	**NHL**	**1**	**0**	**0**	**0**	**0**	**0**	**0**	**0**	....	....	....	....	....
	Boston Bruins	**NHL**	**23**	**5**	**0**	**5**	**17**	**0**	**17**	**36**	....	....	....	....	....
1925-26	**Boston Bruins**	**NHL**	**28**	**3**	**3**	**6**	**9**	**34**	**43**	**30**	....	....	....	....	....
1926-27	New Haven Eagles	Can-Am	7	5	0	5	....	....	....	8	....	....	....	....	....
	Ottawa Senators	**NHL**	**8**	**0**	**0**	**0**	**0**	**0**	**0**	**2**	....	....	....	....	....
	London Panthers	Can-Pro	16	3	0	3	....	....	....	36	4	2	1	3	8
1927-28	London Panthers	Can-Pro	42	16	9	25	....	....	....	91	....	....	....	....	....
1928-29	London Panthers	Can-Pro	14	4	1	5	....	....	....	30	....	....	....	....	....
	Philadelphia Arrows	Can-Am	18	2	1	3	....	....	....	24	....	....	....	....	....
1929-30	Philadelphia Arrows	Can-Am	38	8	13	21	....	....	....	60	2	0	1	1	4
1930-31	Buffalo Bisons	IAHL	41	6	1	7	....	....	....	32	6	1	0	1	6
1931-32	Buffalo Bisons	IAHL	38	1	3	4	....	....	....	8	....	....	....	....	....
1932-33			DID NOT PLAY												
1933-34	Charlottetown Abegweits	MSHL	DID NOT PLAY – COACHING												
	NHL Totals		**85**	**9**	**4**	**13**	**30**	**51**	**81**	**74**	....	....	....	....	....

Signed as a free agent by **Toronto St. Pats**, December 23, 1921. Traded to **Boston** by **Toronto St. Pats** with George Carroll for the rights to Ernie Parkes, December 24, 1924. Traded to **Ottawa** by **Boston** for cash, January 18, 1927. Traded to **London** (Can-Pro) by **Boston** for cash, February, 1927. Traded to **Philadelphia** (Can-Am) by **London** (Can-Pro) for Fred Lowrey, January 18, 1929.

• JACKSON, WALTER Walter "Red" Jackson

LW – L. 5'8", 164 lbs. b: Instock, England, 6/3/1908.

Season	Club	League	GP	G	A	Pts	AG	AA	APts	PIM	GP	G	A	Pts	PIM
1927-28	Winnipeg CPR	City Sr.	9	4	1	5	....	....	....	8	....	....	....	....	....
1928-29	Winnipeg CPR	City Sr.	8	3	3	6	....	....	....	10	3	1	0	1	0
1929-30	Winnipeg Elmwoods	City Sr.	12	8	2	10	....	....	....	2	7	*5	3	*8	4
1930-31	Winnipeg Native Sons	City Sr.	4	2	2	4	....	....	....	2	....	....	....	....	....
	St. Louis Flyers	AHA	36	11	7	18	....	....	....	16	....	....	....	....	....
1931-32	St. Louis Flyers	AHA	48	8	5	13	....	....	....	24	....	....	....	....	....
1932-33	**New York Americans**	**NHL**	**34**	**10**	**2**	**12**	**23**	**5**	**28**	**6**	....	....	....	....	....
	New Haven Eagles	Can-Am	9	2	2	4	....	....	....	6	....	....	....	....	....
1933-34	**New York Americans**	**NHL**	**47**	**6**	**9**	**15**	**13**	**24**	**37**	**12**	....	....	....	....	....
1934-35	**New York Americans**	**NHL**	**1**	**0**	**0**	**0**	**0**	**0**	**0**	**0**	....	....	....	....	....
	Cleveland Falcons	IAHL	4	0	0	0	....	....	....	0	....	....	....	....	....
	Boston Cubs	Can-Am	29	11	19	30	....	....	....	2	3	1	0	1	0
1935-36	**Boston Bruins**	**NHL**	**2**	**0**	**0**	**0**	**0**	**0**	**0**	**0**	....	....	....	....	....
	London Tecumsehs	IAHL	4	0	3	3	....	....	....	0	....	....	....	....	....
	New Haven Eagles	Can-Am	24	7	4	11	....	....	....	4	....	....	....	....	....
1936-37	New Haven Eagles	Can-Am	1	0	0	0	....	....	....	0	....	....	....	....	....
	Minneapolis Millers	AHA	30	8	9	17	....	....	....	8	6	4	1	5	2
1937-38	St. Louis Flyers	AHA	22	2	5	7	....	....	....	14	....	....	....	....	....
	NHL Totals		**84**	**16**	**11**	**27**	**36**	**29**	**65**	**18**	....	....	....	....	....

Traded to **NY Americans** by **St. Louis** (AHA) for George Massecar, October 30, 1932. Traded to **Boston** by **NY Americans** for Obs Heximer and Hap Emms, December 13, 1934. Transferred to **London** (IAHL) by **Boston** as compensation for Boston's signing of Rey Getliffe, December 31, 1935.

• JACOBS, PAUL Paul Jacobs

D. b: unknown. Deceased.

Season	Club	League	GP	G	A	Pts	AG	AA	APts	PIM	GP	G	A	Pts	PIM
1917-18	Montreal Stars	City Sr.	9	10	1	11	....	....	....	15	....	....	....	....	....
1918-19	**Toronto Arenas**	**NHL**	**1**	**0**	**0**	**0**	**0**	**0**	**0**	**0**	....	....	....	....	....
	Montreal Stars	City Sr.	7	4	7	11	....	....	....	27	....	....	....	....	....
1919-20	Laval University	Mtl-Sr.	10	6	0	6	....	....	....	24	....	....	....	....	....
1920-21			DID NOT PLAY												
1921-22	Quebec Voltigeurs	QPHL	6	2	1	3									
1922-23	Cleveland Indians	USAHA	16	0	0	0	....	....	....	....	....	....	....	....	....
1923-24	Montreal Nationale	ECHA	8	0	0	0	....	....	....	....	....	....	....	....	....
1924-25	Cleveland Blues	USAHA	9	0	0	0	....	....	....	....	....	....	....	....	....
	NHL Totals		**1**	**0**	**0**	**0**	**0**	**0**	**0**	**0**	....	....	....	....	....

Signed as a free agent by **Toronto Arenas**, December 15, 1918.

• JAMES, GERRY Gerry James

RW – R. 5'11", 185 lbs. b: Regina, Sask., 10/22/1934.

Season	Club	League	GP	G	A	Pts	AG	AA	APts	PIM	GP	G	A	Pts	PIM
			REGULAR SEASON								PLAYOFFS				
1951-52	Toronto Marlboros	OHA	3	0	0	0	....	....	....	4	6	2	5	7	14
1952-53	Toronto Marlboros	OHA	49	19	15	34	....	....	....	131	7	0	1	1	20
1953-54	Toronto Marlboros	OHA	41	23	17	40	....	....	....	123	15	8	2	10	26
1954-55	**Toronto Maple Leafs**	**NHL**	**1**	**0**	**0**	**0**	**0**	**0**	**0**	**0**	....	....	....	....	....
	Toronto Marlboros	OHA	38	8	13	21	....	....	....	60	13	4	4	8	28
1955-56	**Toronto Maple Leafs**	**NHL**	**46**	**3**	**3**	**6**	**4**	**4**	**8**	**50**	**5**	**1**	**0**	**1**	**8**
1956-57	**Toronto Maple Leafs**	**NHL**	**53**	**4**	**12**	**16**	**5**	**14**	**19**	**90**	....	....	....	....	....
1957-58	**Toronto Maple Leafs**	**NHL**	**15**	**3**	**2**	**5**	**4**	**2**	**6**	**61**	....	....	....	....	....
	Rochester Americans	AHL	15	2	4	6	....	....	....	46	....	....	....	....	....
1958-59			PLAYED PRO FOOTBALL												
1959-60	**Toronto Maple Leafs**	**NHL**	**34**	**4**	**9**	**13**	**5**	**9**	**14**	**56**	**10**	**0**	**0**	**0**	**0**
1960-61	Winnipeg Warriors	WHL	26	2	7	9	....	....	....	50	....	....	....	....	....
1961-62			PLAYED PRO FOOTBALL												
1962-63	HC Davos	Switz.	DID NOT PLAY – COACHING												
1963-64	HC Davos	Switz.	DID NOT PLAY – COACHING												
1964-65	Yorkton Terriers	SSHL	36	11	31	42	....	....	....	89	11	0	4	4	33
1965-66	Yorkton Terriers	SSHL	29	11	22	33	....	....	....	*91	5	3	1	4	17
1966-67	Yorkton Terriers	SSHL	35	13	21	34	....	....	....	65	4	1	5	6	4
1967-1971			DID NOT PLAY												
1971-72	Yorkton Terriers	SSHL	40	8	30	38	....	....	....	143	....	....	....	....	....
	NHL Totals		**149**	**14**	**26**	**40**	**18**	**29**	**47**	**257**	**15**	**1**	**0**	**1**	**8**

• JAMIESON, JIM Jim Jamieson

D – L. 5'9", 170 lbs. b: Brantford, Ont., 3/21/1922.

Season	Club	League	GP	G	A	Pts	AG	AA	APts	PIM	GP	G	A	Pts	PIM
1940-41	Detroit Holzbaugh	MOHL	27	14	6	20	....	....	....	47	7	*5	*7	*12	15
1941-42			DID NOT PLAY – INJURED												
1942-43	Windsor Ford	MOHL	15	10	6	16	....	....	....	8	3	0	2	2	4
	New York Rovers	EHL	....	....	....	....	....	....	....	....	1	0	0	0	0
1943-44	**New York Rangers**	**NHL**	**1**	**0**	**1**	**1**	**0**	**1**	**1**	**0**	....	....	....	....	....
	New York Rovers	EHL	40	6	10	16	....	....	....	73	11	3	2	5	22
1944-45	Pasadena Panthers	PCHL	STATISTICS NOT AVAILABLE												
1945-46	Pasadena Panthers	PCHL	STATISTICS NOT AVAILABLE												
1946-47	Baltimore Orioles	EHL	50	9	23	32	....	....	....	29	9	2	2	4	8
1947-48			DID NOT PLAY												
1948-49	Milwaukee–Akron	IHL	18	4	5	9	....	....	....	28	2	0	0	0	0
1949-50	Brantford Nationals	OHA Sr.	DID NOT PLAY – COACHING												
1950-51	Brantford Nationals	OHA Sr.	DID NOT PLAY – COACHING												
1951-52	Brantford Redmen	OHA Sr.	13	1	1	2	....	....	....	6	....	....	....	....	....
	NHL Totals		**1**	**0**	**1**	**1**	**0**	**1**	**1**	**0**	....	....	....	....	....

EHL Second All-Star Team (1944) • EHL First All-Star Team (1947)

• JANKOWSKI, LOU Lou Jankowski

C/RW – R. 6', 180 lbs. b: Regina, Sask., 6/27/1931.

Season	Club	League	GP	G	A	Pts	AG	AA	APts	PIM	GP	G	A	Pts	PIM
1948-49	Oshawa Generals	OHA	34	7	5	12	....	....	....	27	2	0	0	0	0
1949-50	Oshawa Generals	OHA	45	20	32	52	....	....	....	31	....	....	....	....	....
1950-51	Oshawa Generals	OHA	49	*61	54	115	....	....	....	14	5	6	4	10	2
	Detroit Red Wings	**NHL**	**1**	**0**	**1**	**1**	**0**	**1**	**1**	**0**	....	....	....	....	....
1951-52	Indianapolis Capitals	AHL	51	18	18	36	....	....	....	13	....	....	....	....	....
1952-53	**Detroit Red Wings**	**NHL**	**22**	**1**	**2**	**3**	**2**	**3**	**5**	**0**	**1**	**0**	**0**	**0**	**0**
	Edmonton Flyers	WHL	10	3	1	4	....	....	....	0	....	....	....	....	....
	St. Louis Flyers	AHL	37	14	19	33	....	....	....	4	....	....	....	....	....
1953-54	**Chicago Black Hawks**	**NHL**	**68**	**15**	**13**	**28**	**23**	**18**	**41**	**7**	....	....	....	....	....
1954-55	**Chicago Black Hawks**	**NHL**	**36**	**3**	**2**	**5**	**4**	**3**	**7**	**8**	....	....	....	....	....
	Buffalo Bisons	AHL	11	8	8	16	....	....	....	2	10	0	7	7	0
1955-56	Buffalo Bisons	AHL	62	14	20	34	....	....	....	8	4	1	2	3	0
1956-57	Buffalo Bisons	AHL	64	13	24	37	....	....	....	17	....	....	....	....	....
1957-58	Buffalo Bisons	AHL	59	21	25	46				0	....	....	....	....	....
1958-59	Calgary Stampeders	WHL	54	*45	47	92	....	....	....	13	4	1	1	2	0
1959-60	Calgary Stampeders	WHL	70	*42	42	84	....	....	....	9	....	....	....	....	....
1960-61	Calgary Stampeders	WHL	69	*57	42	99	....	....	....	7	5	3	2	5	2
1961-62	Calgary Stampeders	WHL	64	44	40	84	....	....	....	13	7	2	4	6	0
1962-63	Calgary Stampeders	WHL	67	24	26	50				4					
1963-64	Denver Invaders	WHL	69	*41	44	85	....	....	....	10	6	5	2	7	2
1964-65	Victoria Cougars	WHL	69	30	27	57	....	....	....	16	12	3	2	5	2
1965-66	Victoria Cougars	WHL	68	32	32	64	....	....	....	10	14	4	2	6	8
1966-67	Victoria Cougars	WHL	67	22	37	59	....	....	....	4	....	....	....	....	....
1967-68	Phoenix Roadrunners	WHL	72	25	23	48	....	....	....	6	4	0	0	0	0
1968-69	Denver Spurs	WHL	19	2	3	5	....	....	....	0	....	....	....	....	....
	Amarillo Wranglers	CHL	46	14	11	25	....	....	....	2	....	....	....	....	....
	NHL Totals		**127**	**19**	**18**	**37**	**29**	**25**	**54**	**15**	**1**	**0**	**0**	**0**	**0**

WHL Prairie Division First All-Star Team (1959) • WHL First All-Star Team (1960, 1961, 1964) • Won Leader Cup (WHL - MVP) (1961) • WHL Second All-Star Team (1962) • Won Fred J. Hume Cup (WHL Most Gentlemanly Player) (1964)

Rights traded to **Detroit** by **Cleveland** (AHL) with the rights to Bob Bailey for Bob Bailey and John Bailey, June, 1951. Traded to **Chicago** by **Detroit** with Larry Zeidel and Larry Wilson for cash, August 12, 1953. Traded to **Phoenix** (WHL) by **Victoria** (WHL) for cash, September, 1967. Traded to **Denver** (WHL) by **Phoenix** (WHL) for cash, July, 1968.

• JARRETT, DOUG — see page 1139

• JARRETT, GARY — see page 1140

• JARVIS, JAMES
James "Bud" Jarvis
LW – L. 5'6", 165 lbs. b: Fort William, Ont., 12/7/1907.

			REGULAR SEASON								PLAYOFFS				
Season	Club	League	GP	G	A	Pts	AG	AA	APts	PIM	GP	G	A	Pts	PIM
1927-28	Port Arthur Ports	TBSHL	20	13	7	20	....	....	....	14	....	....	....	....	....
1928-29	Port Arthur Ports	TBSHL	17	13	5	18	....	....	....	10	2	1	1	2	0
1929-30	**Pittsburgh Pirates**	**NHL**	**44**	**11**	**8**	**19**	**22**	**26**	**48**	**32**	....	....	....	....	....
1930-31	**Philadelphia Quakers**	**NHL**	**44**	**5**	**7**	**12**	**12**	**25**	**37**	**30**	....	....	....	....	....
1931-32	Springfield Indians	Can-Am	39	4	5	9	....	....	....	24	....	....	....	....	....
1932-33	Buffalo Bisons	IAHL	37	11	6	17	....	....	....	14	6	0	3	3	0
1933-34	Buffalo Bisons	IAHL	44	12	3	15	....	....	....	25	6	0	3	3	2
1934-35	Buffalo Bisons	IAHL	44	8	11	19	....	....	....	16	....	....	....	....	....
1935-36	Buffalo Bisons	IAHL	48	13	9	22	....	....	....	20	5	0	1	1	0
1936-37	**Toronto Maple Leafs**	**NHL**	**24**	**1**	**0**	**1**	**2**	**0**	**2**	**0**	....	....	....	....	....
	Syracuse Stars	AHL	12	1	1	2	....	....	....	2	9	0	0	0	0
1937-38	Providence Reds	AHL	47	6	6	12	....	....	....	4	7	1	1	2	0
1938-39	Providence Reds	AHL	51	2	16	18	....	....	....	14	5	0	0	0	0
1939-40	Hershey Bears	AHL	50	18	17	35	....	....	....	10	6	1	0	1	2
1940-41	Geraldton Gold Miners	TBSHL	19	4	4	8	....	....	....	4	4	1	0	1	0
1941-42			MILITARY SERVICE												
1942-43			MILITARY SERVICE												
1943-44	Hershey Bears	AHL	31	8	14	22	....	....	....	2	7	1	1	2	0
	NHL Totals		**112**	**17**	**15**	**32**	**36**	**51**	**87**	**62**	....	....	....	....	....

Signed as a free agent by **Pittsburgh**, October 31, 1929. Transferred to **Philadelphia** after **Pittsburgh** franchise relocated, October 18, 1930. Claimed by **NY Rangers** from **Philadelphia** in Dispersal Draft, September 26, 1931. Signed as a free agent by **Toronto** after **Buffalo** (IAHL) franchise folded, September, 1936.

• JEFFREY, LARRY
— *see page 1142*

• JENKINS, ROGER
Roger "Broadway" Jenkins
RW/D – R. 5'11", 173 lbs. b: Appleton, WI, 11/18/1911.

			REGULAR SEASON								PLAYOFFS				
Season	Club	League	GP	G	A	Pts	AG	AA	APts	PIM	GP	G	A	Pts	PIM
1929-30	Edmonton Imperials	City Jr.	STATISTICS NOT AVAILABLE												
1930-31	**Chicago Black Hawks**	**NHL**	**10**	**0**	**1**	**1**	**0**	**4**	**4**	**2**	**3**	**0**	**0**	**0**	**0**
	London Tecumsehs	IAHL	8	0	0	0	....	....	....	6	....	....	....	....	....
	Toronto Maple Leafs	**NHL**	**21**	**0**	**0**	**0**	**0**	**0**	**0**	**12**	....	....	....	....	....
1931-32	Bronx Tigers	Can-Am	39	9	7	16	....	....	....	66	2	0	0	0	6
1932-33	**Chicago Black Hawks**	**NHL**	**46**	**3**	**10**	**13**	**7**	**26**	**33**	**42**	....	....	....	....	....
1933-34	**Chicago Black Hawks**	**NHL**	**48**	**2**	**2**	**4**	**4**	**5**	**9**	**37**	**8**	**0**	**0**	**0**	**0**
1934-35	**Montreal Canadiens**	**NHL**	**45**	**4**	**6**	**10**	**8**	**13**	**21**	**63**	**2**	**1**	**0**	**1**	**2**
1935-36	**Boston Bruins**	**NHL**	**40**	**2**	**6**	**8**	**5**	**14**	**19**	**51**	**2**	**0**	**1**	**1**	**2**
	Boston Cubs	Can-Am	5	2	2	4	....	....	....	9	....	....	....	....	....
1936-37	**Montreal Canadiens**	**NHL**	**10**	**0**	**0**	**0**	**0**	**0**	**0**	**8**	....	....	....	....	....
	Montreal Maroons	**NHL**	**1**	**0**	**0**	**0**	**0**	**0**	**0**	**0**	....	....	....	....	....
	New York Americans	**NHL**	**26**	**1**	**4**	**5**	**2**	**9**	**11**	**6**	....	....	....	....	....
1937-38	**Chicago Black Hawks**	**NHL**	**37**	**1**	**8**	**9**	**2**	**16**	**18**	**26**	**10**	**0**	***6**	**6**	**8**
1938-39	**Chicago Black Hawks**	**NHL**	**14**	**1**	**1**	**2**	**2**	**2**	**4**	**2**	....	....	....	....	....
	New York Americans	**NHL**	**27**	**1**	**1**	**2**	**2**	**2**	**4**	**4**	....	....	....	....	....
1939-40	Springfield Indians	AHL	50	8	18	26	....	....	....	29	2	0	0	0	0
1940-41	Hershey Bears	AHL	56	5	19	24	....	....	....	81	10	2	1	3	14
1941-42	Hershey Bears	AHL	55	9	28	37	....	....	....	110	10	3	5	8	12
1942-43	Hershey–Washington	AHL	57	10	33	43	....	....	....	90	6	0	1	1	2
1943-44	Seattle Ironmen	PCHL	16	16	19	35	....	....	....	45	2	1	3	4	2
	Portland Oilers	City Sr.	....	....	....	....	....	....	....	....	4	2	3	5	12
1944-45	Seattle Ironmen	PCHL	DID NOT PLAY – COACHING												
1945-46	Seattle Ironmen	PCHL	55	12	20	32	....	....	....	69	3	0	0	0	2
1946-47	Tacoma Rockets	PCHL	55	9	22	31	....	....	....	40	....	....	....	....	....
1947-48	Tacoma Rockets	PCHL	58	6	24	30	....	....	....	101	5	0	2	2	6
	NHL Totals		**325**	**15**	**39**	**54**	**32**	**91**	**123**	**253**	**25**	**1**	**7**	**8**	**12**

AHL First All-Star Team (1943)

Signed as a free agent by **Chicago**, October 28, 1930. Loaned to **Toronto** by **Chicago**, December 4, 1930. • Returned to **Chicago** by **Toronto**, February 3, 1931. Traded to **Montreal Canadiens** by **Chicago** with Leroy Goldsworthy, Lionel Conacher and Marty Burke for Lorne Chabot and Howie Morenz, October 3, 1934. Traded to **Boston** by **Montreal Canadiens** for Jean Pusie and Walt Buswell, July 13, 1935. Traded to **Montreal Canadiens** by **Boston** with Babe Siebert for Leroy Goldsworthy and Sammy McManus, September 10, 1936. Signed as a free agent by **Montreal Maroons** after securing release from **Montreal Canadiens**, December 17, 1936. Loaned to **NY Americans** by **Montreal Maroons** for cash, January 1, 1937. Signed as a free agent by **Chicago** after securing release from **Montreal Maroons**, November 20, 1937. Signed as a free agent by **NY Americans**, January 1, 1939. Traded to **Springfield** (AHL) by **NY Americans** for cash, October 2, 1939.

• JENNINGS, BILL
Bill Jennings
RW – R. 5'10", 165 lbs. b: Toronto, Ont., 6/28/1917.

			REGULAR SEASON								PLAYOFFS				
Season	Club	League	GP	G	A	Pts	AG	AA	APts	PIM	GP	G	A	Pts	PIM
1934-35	West Toronto Nationals	City Jr.	12	6	0	6	....	....	....	22	....	....	....	....	....
1935-36	Toronto Dominions	City Sr.	9	5	2	7	....	....	....	18	....	....	....	....	....
	West Toronto Nationals	OHA	8	7	4	11	....	....	....	0	5	1	3	4	*17
1936-37	Toronto Dominions	City Sr.	8	3	*5	8	....	....	....	10	8	2	1	3	15
1937-38	Toronto Goodyears	OHA Sr.	14	9	8	17	....	....	....	16	4	0	0	0	2
1938-39	Earls Court Rangers	Britain	....	18	11	29	....	....	....	....	....	....	....	....	....
1939-40	Detroit Holzbaugh Fords	MOHL	35	24	20	44	....	....	....	38	7	3	1	4	29
1940-41	**Detroit Red Wings**	**NHL**	**12**	**1**	**5**	**6**	**2**	**9**	**11**	**2**	**9**	**2**	**2**	**4**	**0**
	Indianapolis Capitols	AHL	40	16	17	33	....	....	....	20	....	....	....	....	....
1941-42	**Detroit Red Wings**	**NHL**	**16**	**2**	**1**	**3**	**3**	**2**	**5**	**6**	....	....	....	....	....
	Indianapolis Capitols	AHL	34	9	25	34	....	....	....	10	10	4	2	6	4
1942-43	**Detroit Red Wings**	**NHL**	**8**	**3**	**3**	**6**	**4**	**4**	**8**	**2**	....	....	....	....	....
	Indianapolis Capitols	AHL	49	23	33	56	....	....	....	5	7	2	5	7	2
1943-44	**Detroit Red Wings**	**NHL**	**33**	**6**	**11**	**17**	**7**	**13**	**20**	**10**	**4**	**0**	**0**	**0**	**0**
1944-45	**Boston Bruins**	**NHL**	**39**	**20**	**13**	**33**	**28**	**21**	**49**	**25**	**7**	**2**	**2**	**4**	**6**
	Indianapolis Capitols	AHL	3	1	1	2	....	....	....	....	....	....	....	....	....
1945-46	St. Louis–Hershey	AHL	54	24	22	46	....	....	....	14	....	....	....	....	....
	NHL Totals		**108**	**32**	**33**	**65**	**44**	**49**	**93**	**45**	**20**	**4**	**4**	**8**	**6**

Signed as a free agent by **Detroit**, October 16, 1940. Traded to **Boston** by **Detroit** for Pete Leswick, October 30, 1944.

• JEREMIAH, ED
Ed Jeremiah
RW/D – R. 5'9", 160 lbs. b: Worcester, MA, 11/4/1905. d: 8/15/1967.

			REGULAR SEASON								PLAYOFFS				
Season	Club	League	GP	G	A	Pts	AG	AA	APts	PIM	GP	G	A	Pts	PIM
1927-28	Dartmouth College	Ivy	4	5	0	5	....	....	....	....	....	....	....	....	....
1928-29	Dartmouth College	Ivy	17	2	0	2	....	....	....	....	....	....	....	....	....
1929-30	Dartmouth College	Ivy	13	4	0	4	....	....	....	....	....	....	....	....	....
1930-31	New Haven Eagles	Can-Am	36	3	5	8	....	....	....	42	....	....	....	....	....
1931-32	**New York Americans**	**NHL**	**9**	**0**	**1**	**1**	**0**	**3**	**3**	**0**	....	....	....	....	....
	Boston Bruins	**NHL**	**6**	**0**	**0**	**0**	**0**	**0**	**0**	**0**	....	....	....	....	....
	Boston Cubs	Can-Am	15	2	0	2	....	....	....	6	....	....	....	....	....
	New Haven Eagles	Can-Am	13	0	8	8	....	....	....	15	....	....	....	....	....
1932-33	New Haven Eagles	Can-Am	17	2	1	3	....	....	....	6	....	....	....	....	....
1933-34	Philadelphia Arrows	Can-Am	37	2	2	4	....	....	....	55	2	0	0	0	2
1934-35	Cleveland Falcons	IAHL	10	0	1	1	....	....	....	0	2	0	0	0	2
1935-36	Boston Olympics	USAHA	DID NOT PLAY – COACHING												
	NHL Totals		**15**	**0**	**1**	**1**	**0**	**3**	**3**	**0**	....	....	....	....	....

Traded to **Boston** by **NY Americans** for cash, February 1, 1932.

• JERWA, FRANK
Frank Jerwa
LW/D – L. 6'1", 179 lbs. b: Bankhead, Alta., 3/15/1909.

			REGULAR SEASON								PLAYOFFS				
Season	Club	League	GP	G	A	Pts	AG	AA	APts	PIM	GP	G	A	Pts	PIM
1928-29	Regina Pats	City Sr.	5	4	*2	6	....	....	....	4	....	....	....	....	....
	Vancouver Lions	NWHL	5	3	0	3	....	....	....	4	1	0	0	0	0
1929-30	Vancouver Lions	NWHL	36	10	5	15	....	....	....	42	4	0	0	0	2
1930-31	Vancouver Lions	NWHL	32	11	5	16	....	....	....	54	4	1	1	2	12
1931-32	**Boston Bruins**	**NHL**	**24**	**4**	**5**	**9**	**8**	**14**	**22**	**14**	....	....	....	....	....
	Boston Cubs	Can-Am	22	6	14	20	....	....	....	50	....	....	....	....	....
1932-33	**Boston Bruins**	**NHL**	**31**	**3**	**4**	**7**	**7**	**11**	**18**	**23**	....	....	....	....	....
	Boston Cubs	Can-Am	19	5	11	16	....	....	....	34	7	4	1	5	12
1933-34	**Boston Bruins**	**NHL**	**5**	**0**	**0**	**0**	**0**	**0**	**0**	**2**	....	....	....	....	....
	Boston Cubs	Can-Am	34	12	19	31	....	....	....	75	5	1	2	3	22
1934-35	**Boston Bruins**	**NHL**	**5**	**0**	**0**	**0**	**0**	**0**	**0**	**0**	....	....	....	....	....
	Boston Cubs	Can-Am	25	24	12	36	....	....	....	14	....	....	....	....	....
	St. Louis Eagles	**NHL**	**16**	**4**	**7**	**11**	**8**	**16**	**24**	**14**	....	....	....	....	....
1935-36	New Haven Eagles	Can-Am	45	19	21	40	....	....	....	41	....	....	....	....	....
1936-37	Springfield Indians	AHL	33	4	5	9	....	....	....	44	5	1	0	1	2
1937-38	Seattle Seahawks	PCHL	40	12	19	31	....	....	....	29	4	0	2	2	4
1938-39	Seattle Seahawks	PCHL	47	14	28	42	....	....	....	38	7	0	0	0	0
1939-40	Vancouver Lions	PCHL	22	5	8	13	....	....	....	36	5	2	0	2	*12
1940-41	Vancouver Lions	PCHL	44	27	20	47	....	....	....	33	6	1	1	2	*22
	NHL Totals		**81**	**11**	**16**	**27**	**23**	**41**	**64**	**53**	....	....	....	....	....

Can-Am Second All-Star Team (1936)

Traded to **Boston** by **Vancouver** (PCHL) for cash, April 15, 1931. Traded to **St. Louis** by **Boston** for Gerry Shannon, January 10, 1933.

• JERWA, JOE
Joe Jerwa
D – L. 6'2", 185 lbs. b: Bankhead, Alta., 1/22/1909. Deceased.

			REGULAR SEASON								PLAYOFFS				
Season	Club	League	GP	G	A	Pts	AG	AA	APts	PIM	GP	G	A	Pts	PIM
1927-28	Canmore Miners	ASHL	STATISTICS NOT AVAILABLE												
1928-29	Vancouver Lions	NWHL	35	8	5	13	....	....	....	72	3	0	1	1	6
1929-30	Vancouver Lions	NWHL	35	12	6	18	....	....	....	76	4	1	0	1	6
1930-31	**New York Rangers**	**NHL**	**33**	**4**	**7**	**11**	**10**	**25**	**35**	**72**	**4**	**0**	**0**	**0**	**4**
	Springfield Indians	Can-Am	9	8	0	8	....	....	....	26	....	....	....	....	....
1931-32	**Boston Bruins**	**NHL**	**11**	**0**	**0**	**0**	**0**	**0**	**0**	**8**	....	....	....	....	....
	Boston Cubs	Can-Am	31	7	15	22	....	....	....	116	5	2	*2	4	*27
1932-33	Boston Cubs	Can-Am	39	10	18	18	....	....	....	108	7	4	2	6	*22
1933-34	**Boston Bruins**	**NHL**	**2**	**0**	**0**	**0**	**0**	**0**	**0**	**2**	....	....	....	....	....
	Boston Cubs	Can-Am	36	4	8	12	....	....	....	*101	5	2	0	2	*28
1934-35	Boston Cubs	Can-Am	44	21	17	38	....	....	....	95	3	1	*5	*6	*20
1935-36	**New York Americans**	**NHL**	**47**	**9**	**12**	**21**	**22**	**29**	**51**	**65**	**5**	**2**	**3**	**5**	**2**
1936-37	**Boston Bruins**	**NHL**	**26**	**3**	**5**	**8**	**6**	**12**	**18**	**30**	....	....	....	....	....
	New York Americans	**NHL**	**20**	**6**	**8**	**14**	**13**	**19**	**32**	**27**	....	....	....	....	....
1937-38	**New York Americans**	**NHL**	**48**	**3**	**14**	**17**	**6**	**29**	**35**	**53**	**6**	**0**	**0**	**0**	**8**
1938-39	**New York Americans**	**NHL**	**47**	**4**	**12**	**16**	**8**	**22**	**30**	**52**	**2**	**0**	**0**	**0**	**2**
1939-40	Cleveland Barons	AHL	49	4	10	14	....	....	....	61	....	....	....	....	....
1940-41	Cleveland Barons	AHL	56	13	22	35	....	....	....	20	4	4	0	4	6
1941-42	Cleveland Barons	AHL	33	1	8	9	....	....	....	18	....	....	....	....	....
	NHL Totals		**234**	**29**	**58**	**87**	**65**	**136**	**201**	**309**	**17**	**2**	**3**	**5**	**16**

Traded to **NY Rangers** by **Vancouver** (PCHL) with Red Beattie for $25,000, May 6, 1930. Traded to **Boston** by **NY Rangers** for Norm Gainor, August 25, 1931. Traded to **NY Americans** by **Boston** with Nels Stewart for cash, September 28, 1935. • Rights returned to **Boston** by **NY Americans** after NY Americans failed to complete purchase agreement, May 27, 1936. Traded to **NY Americans** by **Boston** for the loan of Al Shields and future considerations (the rights Terry Reardon and Tom Cooper, October 17, 1937), January 25, 1937. Traded to **Cleveland** (AHL) by **NY Americans** for cash, October 12, 1939.

• JOANETTE, ROSARIO
Rosario "Kitouette" Joanette
C – R. 5'8", 165 lbs. b: Valleyfield, Que., 7/27/1919.

			REGULAR SEASON								PLAYOFFS				
Season	Club	League	GP	G	A	Pts	AG	AA	APts	PIM	GP	G	A	Pts	PIM
1939-40	Valleyfield Braves	City Sr.	26	3	8	11	....	....	....	2	4	2	1	3	6
1940-41	Valleyfield Braves	City Sr.	37	28	37	65	....	....	....	18	3	0	0	0	2
1941-42	Valleyfield V's	City Sr.	26	17	23	40	....	....	....	32	7	4	4	8	0
1942-43			MILITARY SERVICE												
1943-44			MILITARY SERVICE												
1944-45	**Montreal Canadiens**	**NHL**	**2**	**0**	**1**	**1**	**0**	**2**	**2**	**4**	....	....	....	....	....
	Valleyfield Braves	QPHL	37	*45	*56	*101	....	....	....	30	14	7	7	14	8
1945-46	Valleyfield Braves	QSHL	40	23	25	48	....	....	....	17	....	....	....	....	....
	Shawinigan Cataracts	QSHL	....	....	....	....	....	....	....	....	4	2	1	3	11
1946-47	Valleyfield Braves	QSHL	39	13	22	35	....	....	....	41	....	....	....	....	....
1947-48	Valleyfield Braves	QSHL	44	20	37	57	....	....	....	23	6	6	6	12	2
1948-49	Valleyfield Braves	QSHL	51	23	33	56	....	....	....	11	4	0	2	2	0
1949-50	Valleyfield Braves	QSHL	59	23	50	73	....	....	....	22	5	1	4	5	4
1950-51	Valleyfield Braves	QSHL	58	30	42	72	....	....	....	18	27	*18	15	33	10
1951-52	Valleyfield Braves	QSHL	55	18	31	49	....	....	....	14	6	0	4	4	0
1952-53	Valleyfield Braves	QSHL	58	18	34	52	....	....	....	6	4	0	1	1	2
1953-54	Valleyfield Braves	QHL	60	13	16	29	....	....	....	10	7	2	4	6	0
1954-55	Valleyfield Braves	QHL	53	13	37	50	....	....	....	11	....	....	....	....	....
1955-56	Trois-Rivieres Lions	QHL	32	2	10	12	....	....	....	2	....	....	....	....	....
	Cornwall Colts	EOHL	16	21	20	41	....	....	....	18	7	2	8	10	18
1956-57	Cornwall Chevies	EOHL	49	22	31	53	....	....	....	20	6	0	2	2	4
	NHL Totals		**2**	**0**	**1**	**1**	**0**	**2**	**2**	**4**	....	....	....	....	....

• JOHANSEN, BILL

Bill (also known as Johnson) Johansen
C/RW – R. 6', 163 lbs. b: Port Arthur, Ont., 7/27/1928.

Season	Club	League	GP	G	A	Pts	AG	AA	APts	PIM	Playoffs GP	G	A	Pts	PIM
1945-46	Fort William Rangers	TBJHL	8	1	5	6	....	....	....	4	....	....	....	....	....
1946-47	Fort William Rangers	TBJHL	6	7	7	14	....	....	....	2	3	1	2	3	2
1947-48	Fort William Rangers	TBJHL	9	14	5	19	....	....	....	0	2	1	0	1	2
1948-49	Toronto Marlboros	OHA Sr.	36	13	12	25	....	....	....	8	23	6	14	20	6
1949-50	**Toronto Maple Leafs**	**NHL**	**1**	**0**	**0**	**0**	**0**	**0**	**0**	**0**	....	....	....	....	....
	Toronto Marlboros	OHA Sr.	41	22	33	55	....	....	....	9	14	6	6	12	4
1950-51	Toronto Marlboros	OHA Sr.	32	14	24	38	....	....	....	8	3	1	2	3	0
1951-52	Ottawa Senators	QSHL	54	19	30	49	....	....	....	6	7	1	2	3	0
1952-53	Ottawa Senators	QSHL	60	16	24	40	....	....	....	19	7	0	1	1	2
1953-54	Ottawa Senators	QHL	67	16	35	51	....	....	....	23	22	6	9	15	8
1954-55	Providence Reds	AHL	23	5	8	13	....	....	....	10	....	....	....	....	....
	Ottawa Senators	QHL	27	5	12	17	....	....	....	6	....	....	....	....	....
1955-56	Providence Reds	AHL	53	8	27	35	....	....	....	14	9	3	4	7	4
1956-57	Providence Reds	AHL	49	7	18	25	....	....	....	14	5	0	1	1	2
1957-58	Vancouver Canucks	WHL	61	17	25	42	....	....	....	10	6	2	3	5	2
1958-59	Winnipeg Warriors	WHL	62	20	29	49	....	....	....	12	7	2	2	4	2
1959-60	Winnipeg Warriors	WHL	58	14	22	36	....	....	....	4	....	....	....	....	....
1960-61	Victoria Cougars	WHL	67	10	21	31	....	....	....	18	5	3	1	3	0
1961-62	Spokane Comets	WHL	67	14	23	37	....	....	....	8	8	3	2	5	0
1962-63	Spokane Comets	WHL	69	12	24	36	....	....	....	4	....	....	....	....	....
1963-63	Charlotte Checkers	EHL	17	16	10	26	....	....	....	6	....	....	....	....	....
1964-65	New York Rovers	EHL	62	20	33	53	....	....	....	4	....	....	....	....	....
	NHL Totals		**1**	**0**	**0**	**0**	**0**	**0**	**0**	**0**	....	....	....	....	....

• JOHNS, DON

— *see page 1146*

• JOHNSON, AL

Al Johnson
RW/C – R. 5'11", 180 lbs. b: Winnipeg, Man., 3/30/1935.

Season	Club	League	GP	G	A	Pts	AG	AA	APts	PIM	Playoffs GP	G	A	Pts	PIM
1951-52	St. Boniface Canadians	MJHL	....	8	15	23	....	....	....	....	....	....	....	....	....
1952-53	St. Boniface Canadians	MJHL	22	4	12	16	....	....	....	2	24	6	9	15	10
1953-54	St. Boniface Canadians	MJHL	36	13	*31	44	....	....	....	40	18	11	12	23	42
1954-55	Trois-Rivieres Flambeaux	QJHL	44	14	17	31	....	....	....	23	10	5	5	10	2
	Montreal Royals	QHL	2	0	1	1	....	....	....	2	....	....	....	....	....
1955-56	Souris Elks	Big 6	28	33	30	63	....	....	....	18	....	....	....	....	....
	Winnipeg Warriors	WHL	2	0	0	0	....	....	....	0	....	....	....	....	....
1956-57	**Montreal Canadiens**	**NHL**	**2**	**0**	**1**	**1**	**0**	**1**	**1**	**2**	....	....	....	....	....
	Cincinnati Mohawks	IHL	56	29	29	58	....	....	....	36	7	2	2	4	2
1957-58	Shawinigan Cataracts	QHL	57	15	28	43	....	....	....	18	14	8	10	18	2
1958-59	Spokane Spokes	WHL	68	30	33	63	....	....	....	28	4	0	0	0	7
1959-60	Spokane Spokes	WHL	69	29	27	56	....	....	....	28	....	....	....	....	....
1960-61	**Detroit Red Wings**	**NHL**	**70**	**16**	**21**	**37**	**20**	**21**	**41**	**14**	**11**	**2**	**2**	**4**	**6**
1961-62	**Detroit Red Wings**	**NHL**	**31**	**5**	**6**	**11**	**6**	**6**	**12**	**14**	....	....	....	....	....
	Hershey Bears	AHL	40	15	25	40	....	....	....	14	7	4	2	6	2
1962-63	**Detroit Red Wings**	**NHL**	**2**	**0**	**0**	**0**	**0**	**0**	**0**	**0**	....	....	....	....	....
	Pittsburgh Hornets	AHL	58	15	19	34	....	....	....	24	....	....	....	....	....
1963-64	Winnipeg Maroons	SSHL	6	6	4	10	....	....	....	2	....	....	....	....	....
1964-65	Winnipeg Maroons	SSHL	6	6	8	14	....	....	....	6	....	....	....	....	....
	Canada	WEC-A	7	4	2	6	....	....	....	6	....	....	....	....	....
1965-66	Canada	Nat-Tm.	STATISTICS NOT AVAILABLE												
1966-67			DID NOT PLAY – RETIRED												
1967-68	Fort Worth Wings	CHL	46	23	27	50	....	....	....	27	....	....	....	....	....
1968-69	Denver Spurs	WHL	71	27	22	49	....	....	....	10	....	....	....	....	....
	NHL Totals		**105**	**21**	**28**	**49**	**26**	**28**	**54**	**30**	**11**	**2**	**2**	**4**	**6**

WHL Coast Division Second All-Star Team (1959) • WHL First All-Star Team (1960)

Traded to **Detroit** by **Montreal** for cash and future considerations, June, 1960.

• JOHNSON, EARL

Earl Johnson
LW – L. 6', 185 lbs. b: Fort Francis, Ont., 6/28/1931.

Season	Club	League	GP	G	A	Pts	AG	AA	APts	PIM	Playoffs GP	G	A	Pts	PIM
1948-49	Windsor Spitfires	OHA	54	39	29	68	....	....	....	....	....	....	....	....	....
1949-50	Windsor Spitfires	OHA	42	18	18	36	....	....	....	6	2	1	0	1	0
	Detroit Hettche	IHL	39	18	16	34	....	....	....	....	....	....	....	....	....
1950-51	Windsor Spitfires	OHA	54	39	28	67	....	....	....	19	8	2	3	5	0
1951-52	Edmonton Flyers	PCHL	69	37	34	71	....	....	....	19	4	0	1	1	2
1952-53	Edmonton Flyers	WHL	70	26	34	60	....	....	....	26	15	10	7	17	20
1953-54	**Detroit Red Wings**	**NHL**	**1**	**0**	**0**	**0**	**0**	**0**	**0**	**0**	....	....	....	....	....
	Edmonton Flyers	WHL	19	5	0	5	....	....	....	6	....	....	....	....	....
	Sherbrooke Saints	QHL	50	18	22	40	....	....	....	41	5	4	2	6	2
1954-55	Vancouver Canucks	WHL	45	16	19	35	....	....	....	33	5	2	1	3	2
	Quebec Aces	QHL	21	12	6	18	....	....	....	18	....	....	....	....	....
1955-56	Springfield Indians	AHL	7	4	2	6	....	....	....	6	....	....	....	....	....
	Vancouver–Edmonton	WHL	42	15	10	25	....	....	....	44	3	0	1	1	2
1956-57	Vancouver Canucks	WHL	54	17	14	31	....	....	....	49	....	....	....	....	....
	Providence Reds	AHL	9	2	4	6	....	....	....	6	....	....	....	....	....
1957-58	Trois-Rivieres Lions	QHL	50	14	8	22	....	....	....	6	....	....	....	....	....
1958-59	Spokane Comets	WHL	67	40	32	72	....	....	....	30	4	0	1	1	4
1959-60	Spokane Comets	WHL	69	31	31	62	....	....	....	20	....	....	....	....	....
1960-61	Spokane Comets	WHL	70	32	30	62	....	....	....	40	4	0	0	0	0
1961-62	Pittsburgh Hornets	AHL	18	3	3	6	....	....	....	2	....	....	....	....	....
	Los Angeles Blades	WHL	31	9	8	17	....	....	....	0	....	....	....	....	....
1962-63	New Haven Blades	EHL	53	20	25	45	....	....	....	11	....	....	....	....	....
	NHL Totals		**1**	**0**	**0**	**0**	**0**	**0**	**0**	**0**	....	....	....	....	....

WHL Coast Division Second All-Star Team (1959)

• JOHNSON, IVAN

Ivan "Ching" Johnson — **HHOF**
D – L. 5'11", 210 lbs. b: Winnipeg, Man., 12/7/1898. d: 6/17/1979.

Season	Club	League	GP	G	A	Pts	AG	AA	APts	PIM	Playoffs GP	G	A	Pts	PIM
1919-20	Winnipeg Monarchs	MHL Sr.	7	6	3	9	....	....	....	10	....	....	....	....	....
1920-21	Eveleth Rangers	USAHA	STATISTICS NOT AVAILABLE												
1921-22	Eveleth Rangers	USAHA	STATISTICS NOT AVAILABLE												
1922-23	Eveleth Rangers	USAHA	20	4	0	4	....	....	....	....	....	....	....	....	....
1923-24	Minneapolis Millers	USAHA	20	9	3	12	....	....	....	....	....	....	....	....	....
1924-25	Minneapolis Rockets	USAHA	40	8	0	8	....	....	....	....	....	....	....	....	....
1925-26	Minneapolis Millers	USAHA	38	14	5	19	....	....	....	92	3	2	0	2	6
1926-27	**New York Rangers**	**NHL**	**27**	**3**	**2**	**5**	**9**	**17**	**26**	**66**	**2**	**0**	**0**	**0**	**8**
1927-28	**New York Rangers**	**NHL**	**42**	**10**	**6**	**16**	**31**	**51**	**82**	**146**	**9**	**1**	**1**	**2**	***46**
1928-29	**New York Rangers**	**NHL**	**8**	**0**	**0**	**0**	**0**	**0**	**0**	**14**	**6**	**0**	**0**	**0**	**26**
1929-30	**New York Rangers**	**NHL**	**30**	**3**	**3**	**6**	**6**	**10**	**16**	**82**	**4**	**0**	**0**	**0**	**14**
1930-31	**New York Rangers**	**NHL**	**44**	**2**	**6**	**8**	**5**	**22**	**27**	**77**	**4**	**1**	**0**	**1**	**17**
1931-32	**New York Rangers**	**NHL**	**47**	**3**	**10**	**13**	**6**	**28**	**34**	**106**	**7**	**2**	**0**	**2**	***24**
1932-33	**New York Rangers**	**NHL**	**48**	**8**	**9**	**17**	**19**	**24**	**43**	**127**	**8**	**1**	**0**	**1**	**14**
1933-34	**New York Rangers**	**NHL**	**48**	**2**	**6**	**8**	**4**	**16**	**20**	**86**	**2**	**0**	**0**	**0**	**4**
1934-35	**New York Rangers**	**NHL**	**29**	**2**	**3**	**5**	**4**	**7**	**11**	**34**	**4**	**0**	**0**	**0**	**2**
1935-36	**New York Rangers**	**NHL**	**47**	**5**	**3**	**8**	**12**	**7**	**19**	**58**	....	....	....	....	....
1936-37	**New York Rangers**	**NHL**	**35**	**0**	**0**	**0**	**0**	**0**	**0**	**2**	**9**	**0**	**1**	**1**	**4**
1937-38	**New York Americans**	**NHL**	**31**	**0**	**0**	**0**	**0**	**0**	**0**	**10**	**6**	**0**	**0**	**0**	**2**
1938-39	Minneapolis Millers	AHA	47	2	9	11	....	....	....	60	4	0	2	2	0
1939-40	Minneapolis Millers	AHA	48	0	4	4	....	....	....	26	3	0	0	0	2
1940-41	Washington Lions	AHL	DID NOT PLAY – COACHING												
	NHL Totals		**436**	**38**	**48**	**86**	**96**	**182**	**278**	**808**	**61**	**5**	**2**	**7**	**161**

NHL Second All-Star Team (1931, 1934) • NHL First All-Star Team (1932, 1933) • AHA Second All-Star Team (1939)

Played in NHL All-Star Game (1934)

Signed as a free agent by **NY Rangers**, September 2, 1926. Signed as a free agent by **NY Americans**, November 19, 1937.

• JOHNSON, JIM

— *see page 1147*

• JOHNSON, NORM

Norm Johnson
C – L. 5'10", 170 lbs. b: Moose Jaw, Sask., 11/27/1932.

Season	Club	League	GP	G	A	Pts	AG	AA	APts	PIM	Playoffs GP	G	A	Pts	PIM
1949-50	Moose Jaw Canucks	WCJHL	3	0	0	0	....	....	....	0	....	....	....	....	....
1950-51	Moose Jaw Canucks	WCJHL	39	6	9	15	....	....	....	24	....	....	....	....	....
1951-52	Moose Jaw Canucks	WCJHL	44	16	13	29	....	....	....	96	....	....	....	....	....
1952-53	Moose Jaw Canucks	WCJHL	33	25	16	41	....	....	....	42	9	4	3	7	8
1953-54	Moose Jaw Canadians	WCJHL	37	22	35	57	....	....	....	40	8	2	3	5	6
1954-55	Fort Wayne Komets	IHL	22	7	8	15	....	....	....	17	....	....	....	....	....
	Yorkton Terriers	WCSHL	....	....	....	....	....	....	....	....	6	1	1	2	4
1955-56	Brandon Regals	WHL	69	15	22	37	....	....	....	53	....	....	....	....	....
1956-57	Brandon Regals	WHL	70	32	46	78	....	....	....	75	9	2	7	9	2
1957-58	**Boston Bruins**	**NHL**	**15**	**2**	**3**	**5**	**3**	**3**	**6**	**8**	**12**	**4**	**0**	**4**	**6**
	Springfield Indians	AHL	52	8	33	41	....	....	....	46	....	....	....	....	....
1958-59	**Boston Bruins**	**NHL**	**39**	**2**	**17**	**19**	**3**	**18**	**21**	**25**	....	....	....	....	....
	Chicago Black Hawks	**NHL**	**7**	**1**	**0**	**1**	**1**	**0**	**1**	**8**	....	....	....	....	....
	Rochester Americans	AHL	14	3	4	7	....	....	....	8	5	1	2	3	13
1959-60	Calgary Stampeders	WHL	45	20	40	60	....	....	....	32	....	....	....	....	....
	Buffalo Bisons	AHL	23	5	12	17	....	....	....	10	....	....	....	....	....
	Chicago Black Hawks	**NHL**	....	....	....	....	....	....	....	....	**2**	**0**	**0**	**0**	**0**
1960-61	Calgary Stampeders	WHL	58	23	64	87	....	....	....	19	5	1	3	4	2
1961-62	Calgary Stampeders	WHL	69	29	*64	93	....	....	....	26	7	0	5	5	2
1962-63	Calgary Stampeders	WHL	69	22	43	65	....	....	....	27	....	....	....	....	....
1963-64	St. Paul Rangers	CHL	1	0	1	1	....	....	....	2	....	....	....	....	....
	Los Angeles Blades	WHL	70	33	53	86	....	....	....	38	12	5	14	19	18
1964-65	Los Angeles Blades	WHL	69	26	55	81	....	....	....	39	....	....	....	....	....
1965-66	Los Angeles Blades	WHL	71	23	54	77	....	....	....	34	....	....	....	....	....
1966-67	Los Angeles Blades	WHL	67	31	46	77	....	....	....	20	....	....	....	....	....
1967-68	Portland Buckaroos	WHL	72	23	40	63	....	....	....	24	12	1	9	10	14
1968-69	Portland Buckaroos	WHL	71	43	47	90	....	....	....	40	11	4	6	10	8
1969-70	Portland Buckaroos	WHL	71	34	62	96	....	....	....	34	11	7	10	17	24
1970-71	Portland Buckaroos	WHL	72	37	55	92	....	....	....	86	13	3	*11	14	29
1971-72	Spokane Jets	WIHL	DID NOT PLAY – COACHING												
	NHL Totals		**61**	**5**	**20**	**25**	**7**	**21**	**28**	**41**	**14**	**4**	**0**	**4**	**6**

WHL Prairie Division Second All-Star Team (1957) • WHL First All-Star Team (1961, 1962)

Claimed by **Boston** from **Springfield** (AHL) in Intra-League Draft, June, 1957. Claimed on waivers by **Chicago** from **Boston**, January 7, 1959. Loaned to **Montreal** (Rochester - AHL) by **Chicago** to complete transaction that sent Dollard St. Laurent to Chicago (June 3, 1958), February 20, 1959. Traded to **LA Blades** (WHL) by **Chicago** with Ron Leopold and Gord Vejprava for Lloyd Haddon, October, 1964. Traded to **Portland** (WHL) by **LA Blades** (WHL) for cash, July, 1967.

• JOHNSON, TOM Tom Johnson HHOF
D – L. 6', 180 lbs. b: Baldur, Man., 2/18/1928.

Season	Club	League	GP	G	A	Pts	AG	AA	APts	PIM	GP	G	A	Pts	PIM
			REGULAR SEASON								PLAYOFFS				
1946-47	Winnipeg Monarchs	MJHL	14	10	4	14	....	....	....	12	7	3	1	4	19
1947-48	**Montreal Canadiens**	**NHL**	**1**	**0**	**0**	**0**	**0**	**0**	**0**	**0**	....	....	....	....	....
	Montreal Royals	QSHL	16	0	4	4	....	....	....	10	....	....	....	....	....
1948-49	Buffalo Bisons	AHL	68	4	18	22	....	....	....	70	....	....	....	....	....
1949-50	Buffalo Bisons	AHL	58	7	19	26	....	....	....	52	5	0	0	0	20
	Montreal Canadiens	**NHL**	....	....	....	....	....	....	....	....	**1**	**0**	**0**	**0**	**0**
1950-51	**Montreal Canadiens**	**NHL**	**70**	**2**	**8**	**10**	**3**	**10**	**13**	**128**	**11**	**0**	**0**	**0**	**6**
1951-52	**Montreal Canadiens**	**NHL**	**67**	**0**	**7**	**7**	**0**	**9**	**9**	**76**	**11**	**1**	**0**	**1**	**2**
1952-53	**Montreal Canadiens**	**NHL**	**70**	**3**	**8**	**11**	**5**	**11**	**16**	**63**	**12**	**2**	**3**	**5**	**8**
1953-54	**Montreal Canadiens**	**NHL**	**70**	**7**	**11**	**18**	**11**	**15**	**26**	**85**	**11**	**1**	**2**	**3**	**30**
1954-55	**Montreal Canadiens**	**NHL**	**70**	**6**	**19**	**25**	**9**	**24**	**33**	**74**	**12**	**2**	**0**	**2**	**22**
1955-56	**Montreal Canadiens**	**NHL**	**64**	**3**	**10**	**13**	**4**	**12**	**16**	**75**	**10**	**0**	**2**	**2**	**8**
1956-57	**Montreal Canadiens**	**NHL**	**70**	**4**	**11**	**15**	**5**	**13**	**18**	**59**	**10**	**0**	**2**	**2**	**13**
1957-58	**Montreal Canadiens**	**NHL**	**66**	**3**	**18**	**21**	**4**	**20**	**24**	**75**	**2**	**0**	**0**	**0**	**0**
1958-59	**Montreal Canadiens**	**NHL**	**70**	**10**	**29**	**39**	**13**	**31**	**44**	**76**	**11**	**2**	**3**	**5**	**8**
1959-60	**Montreal Canadiens**	**NHL**	**64**	**4**	**25**	**29**	**5**	**26**	**31**	**59**	**8**	**0**	**1**	**1**	**4**
1960-61	**Montreal Canadiens**	**NHL**	**70**	**1**	**15**	**16**	**1**	**15**	**16**	**54**	**6**	**0**	**1**	**1**	**8**
1961-62	**Montreal Canadiens**	**NHL**	**62**	**1**	**17**	**18**	**1**	**17**	**18**	**45**	**6**	**0**	**1**	**1**	**0**
1962-63	**Montreal Canadiens**	**NHL**	**43**	**3**	**5**	**8**	**4**	**5**	**9**	**28**	....	....	....	....	....
1963-64	**Boston Bruins**	**NHL**	**70**	**4**	**21**	**25**	**5**	**23**	**28**	**33**	....	....	....	....	....
1964-65	**Boston Bruins**	**NHL**	**51**	**0**	**9**	**9**	**0**	**10**	**10**	**30**	....	....	....	....	....
	NHL Totals		**978**	**51**	**213**	**264**	**70**	**241**	**311**	**960**	**111**	**8**	**15**	**23**	**109**

NHL Second All-Star Team (1956) • NHL First All-Star Team (1959) • Won James Norris Trophy (1959)

Played in NHL All-Star Game (1952, 1953, 1956, 1957, 1958, 1959, 1960, 1963)

Claimed by **Boston** from **Montreal** in Waiver Draft, June 4, 1963.

• JOHNSON, VIRGIL Virgil Johnson USHOF
D – L. 5'9", 165 lbs. b: Minneapolis, MN, 3/4/1912. Deceased.

Season	Club	League	GP	G	A	Pts	AG	AA	APts	PIM	GP	G	A	Pts	PIM
1932-33	Minneapolis Millers	CHL	39	6	8	14	....	....	....	30	7	0	1	1	11
1933-34	Minneapolis Millers	CHL	36	9	13	22	....	....	....	21	3	0	2	2	2
1934-35	St. Paul Saints	CHL	45	6	13	19	....	....	....	38	8	2	*5	*7	8
1935-36	St. Paul Saints	AHA	47	9	20	29	....	....	....	14	5	0	1	1	4
1936-37	St. Paul Saints	AHA	48	4	15	19	....	....	....	35	3	0	2	2	4
1937-38	**Chicago Black Hawks**	**NHL**	**25**	**1**	**0**	**1**	**2**	**0**	**2**	**2**	**10**	**0**	**0**	**0**	**0**
	St. Paul Saints	AHA	24	2	6	8	....	....	....	14	....	....	....	....	....
1938-39	St. Paul Saints	AHA	48	5	12	17	....	....	....	22	3	1	0	1	0
1939-40	St. Paul Saints	AHA	45	6	16	22	....	....	....	15	7	0	1	1	6
1940-41	St. Paul Saints	AHA	48	6	15	21	....	....	....	14	4	0	0	0	4
1941-42	St. Paul Saints	AHA	49	8	17	25	....	....	....	18	2	1	0	1	0
1942-43	Hershey Bears	AHL	53	4	19	23	....	....	....	10	6	0	4	4	0
1943-44	**Chicago Black Hawks**	**NHL**	**48**	**1**	**8**	**9**	**1**	**10**	**11**	**23**	**9**	**0**	**3**	**3**	**4**
1944-45	**Chicago Black Hawks**	**NHL**	**2**	**0**	**1**	**1**	**0**	**2**	**2**	**2**	....	....	....	....	....
	Cleveland Barons	AHL	26	2	5	7	....	....	....	10	8	0	0	0	2
1945-46	Minneapolis Millers	USHL	53	9	17	26	....	....	....	12	....	....	....	....	....
1946-47	Minneapolis Millers	USHL	51	2	19	21	....	....	....	30	3	0	0	0	2
1947-1950			DID NOT PLAY												
1950-51	Minneapolis Jerseys	AAHL	18	2	19	21	....	....	....	2	3	0	2	2	0
1951-52	St. Paul Saints	AAHL	34	10	19	29	....	....	....	12	3	0	5	5	0
	NHL Totals		**75**	**2**	**9**	**11**	**3**	**12**	**15**	**27**	**19**	**0**	**3**	**3**	**4**

AHA First All-Star Team (1942)

Traded to **Chicago** by **St. Paul** (AHA) for cash, January 8, 1938.

• JOHNSTON, GEORGE George "Wingy" Johnston
RW – R. 5'8", 160 lbs. b: St. Charles, Man., 7/30/1920.

Season	Club	League	GP	G	A	Pts	AG	AA	APts	PIM	GP	G	A	Pts	PIM
1938-39	Duluth Zephyrs	TBSHL	11	5	2	7	....	....	....	14	....	....	....	....	....
1939-40	Saskatoon Quakers	SSHL	28	11	12	23	....	....	....	2	4	0	1	1	0
1940-41	Providence Reds	AHL	50	17	24	41	....	....	....	4	4	2	2	4	0
1941-42	**Chicago Black Hawks**	**NHL**	**2**	**2**	**0**	**2**	**3**	**0**	**3**	**0**	....	....	....	....	....
	Kansas City Americans	AHA	31	18	14	32	....	....	....	6	6	3	*9	12	0
1942-43	**Chicago Black Hawks**	**NHL**	**30**	**10**	**7**	**17**	**14**	**9**	**23**	**0**	....	....	....	....	....
1943-44	Vancouver RCAF	PCHL	10	12	5	17	....	....	....	2	....	....	....	....	....
1944-45	Moncton #4 Repairs	City Sr.	STATISTICS NOT AVAILABLE												
1945-46	**Chicago Black Hawks**	**NHL**	**16**	**5**	**4**	**9**	**8**	**7**	**15**	**2**	....	....	....	....	....
	Kansas City Pla-Mors	USHL	38	38	34	72	....	....	....	6	12	4	8	12	2
1946-47	**Chicago Black Hawks**	**NHL**	**10**	**3**	**1**	**4**	**4**	**1**	**5**	**0**	....	....	....	....	....
	Kansas City Pla-Mors	USHL	47	29	29	58	....	....	....	6	12	5	4	9	4
1947-48	Cleveland–New Haven	AHL	54	20	27	47	....	....	....	14	4	1	1	2	0
1948-49	New Haven Ramblers	AHL	39	14	23	37	....	....	....	2	....	....	....	....	....
	Tacoma Rockets	PCHL	28	17	14	31	....	....	....	4	6	0	5	5	0
1949-50	Tacoma Rockets	PCHL	70	46	44	90	....	....	....	64	5	0	2	2	0
1950-51	Tacoma Rockets	PCHL	70	27	31	58	....	....	....	17	6	1	2	3	0
1951-52	Tacoma Rockets	PCHL	70	32	45	77	....	....	....	8	7	2	4	6	0
1952-53	Tacoma Rockets	WHL	70	24	41	65	....	....	....	8	....	....	....	....	....
1953-54	Spokane Flyers	WIHL	66	35	39	74	....	....	....	45	5	2	4	6	0
1954-55	Spokane Flyers	WIHL	35	15	24	39	....	....	....	16	....	....	....	....	....
	NHL Totals		**58**	**20**	**12**	**32**	**29**	**17**	**46**	**2**	....	....	....	....	....

USHL First All-Star Team (1946, 1947) • PCHL Northern Second All-Star Team (1950) • PCHL Second All-Star Team (1952)

• JOHNSTONE, ROSS Ross Johnstone
D – L. 6', 185 lbs. b: Montreal, Que., 4/7/1926.

Season	Club	League	GP	G	A	Pts	AG	AA	APts	PIM	GP	G	A	Pts	PIM
1942-43	Toronto Marlboros	OHA	19	1	9	10	....	....	....	16	3	0	1	1	6
	Oshawa Generals	OHA	....	....	....	....	....	....	....	....	2	1	0	1	4
1943-44	**Toronto Maple Leafs**	**NHL**	**18**	**2**	**0**	**2**	**2**	**0**	**2**	**6**	**3**	**0**	**0**	**0**	**0**
	Providence Reds	AHL	6	1	0	1	....	....	....	2	....	....	....	....	....
1944-45	**Toronto Maple Leafs**	**NHL**	**24**	**3**	**4**	**7**	**4**	**6**	**10**	**8**	....	....	....	....	....
1945-46	Pittsburgh Hornets	AHL	56	1	7	8	....	....	....	23	....	....	....	....	....
1946-47	Springfield Indians	AHL	33	1	7	8	....	....	....	2	2	1	0	1	0
1947-48	Springfield Indians	AHL	68	2	19	21	....	....	....	10	....	....	....	....	....
1948-49	New Haven Ramblers	AHL	10	1	3	4	....	....	....	2	....	....	....	....	....
1949-50	Detroit Hettche	IHL	18	7	3	10	....	....	....	6	3	1	0	1	0
1950-51	Toronto Marlboros	OHA Sr.	31	7	6	13	....	....	....	36	3	1	1	2	0
1951-52	Atlantic City Seagulls	EHL	38	7	10	17	....	....	....	8	....	....	....	....	....
	NHL Totals		**42**	**5**	**4**	**9**	**6**	**6**	**12**	**14**	**3**	**0**	**0**	**0**	**0**

• JOLIAT, AUREL Aurel Joliat HHOF
LW – L. 5'7", 136 lbs. b: Ottawa, Ont., 8/29/1901. d: 6/2/1986.

Season	Club	League	GP	G	A	Pts	AG	AA	APts	PIM	GP	G	A	Pts	PIM
			REGULAR SEASON								PLAYOFFS				
1916-17	Ottawa New Edinburghs	City Jr.	8	2	0	2	....	....	....	....	2	0	0	0	....
1917-18	Ottawa Aberdeens	City Jr.	3	2	0	2	....	....	....	3	....	....	....	....	....
1918-19	Ottawa New Edinburghs	City Sr.	8	5	*3	8	....	....	....	9	....	....	....	....	....
1919-20	Ottawa New Edinburghs	City Sr.	7	*12	0	*12	....	....	....	....	....	....	....	....	....
1920-21	Iroquois Falls Flyers	NOHA	STATISTICS NOT AVAILABLE												
1921-22	Iroquois Falls Flyers	NOHA	STATISTICS NOT AVAILABLE												
1922-23	**Montreal Canadiens**	**NHL**	**24**	**13**	**9**	**22**	**44**	**83**	**127**	**31**	**2**	**1**	**1**	**2**	**8**
1923-24	**Montreal Canadiens**	**NHL**	**24**	**15**	**5**	**20**	**63**	**90**	**153**	**19**	**6**	**4**	***4**	**8**	**10**
1924-25	**Montreal Canadiens**	**NHL**	**24**	**29**	**11**	**40**	**105**	**153**	**258**	**85**	**5**	**2**	**2**	**4**	***21**
1925-26	**Montreal Canadiens**	**NHL**	**35**	**17**	**9**	**26**	**53**	**106**	**159**	**52**	....	....	....	....	....
1926-27	**Montreal Canadiens**	**NHL**	**43**	**14**	**4**	**18**	**41**	**34**	**75**	**79**	**4**	**1**	**0**	**1**	**10**
1927-28	**Montreal Canadiens**	**NHL**	**44**	**28**	**11**	**39**	**88**	**94**	**182**	**105**	**2**	**0**	**0**	**0**	**4**
1928-29	**Montreal Canadiens**	**NHL**	**44**	**12**	**5**	**17**	**48**	**46**	**94**	**59**	**3**	**1**	**1**	**2**	**10**
1929-30	**Montreal Canadiens**	**NHL**	**42**	**19**	**12**	**31**	**38**	**39**	**77**	**40**	**6**	**0**	**2**	**2**	**6**
1930-31	**Montreal Canadiens**	**NHL**	**43**	**13**	**22**	**35**	**32**	**81**	**113**	**73**	**10**	**0**	***4**	**4**	**12**
1931-32	**Montreal Canadiens**	**NHL**	**48**	**15**	**24**	**39**	**32**	**68**	**100**	**46**	**4**	**2**	**0**	**2**	**4**
1932-33	**Montreal Canadiens**	**NHL**	**48**	**18**	**21**	**39**	**42**	**56**	**98**	**53**	**2**	**2**	**1**	**3**	**2**
1933-34	**Montreal Canadiens**	**NHL**	**48**	**22**	**15**	**37**	**49**	**40**	**89**	**27**	**3**	**0**	**1**	**1**	**0**
1934-35	**Montreal Canadiens**	**NHL**	**48**	**17**	**12**	**29**	**36**	**27**	**63**	**18**	**2**	**1**	**0**	**1**	**0**
1935-36	**Montreal Canadiens**	**NHL**	**48**	**15**	**8**	**23**	**37**	**19**	**56**	**16**	....	....	....	....	....
1936-37	**Montreal Canadiens**	**NHL**	**47**	**17**	**15**	**32**	**37**	**35**	**72**	**30**	**5**	**0**	**3**	**3**	**2**
1937-38	**Montreal Canadiens**	**NHL**	**44**	**6**	**7**	**13**	**13**	**14**	**27**	**24**	....	....	....	....	....
	NHL Totals		**654**	**270**	**190**	**460**	**758**	**985**	**1743**	**757**	**54**	**14**	**19**	**33**	**89**

NHL First All-Star Team (1931) • NHL Second All-Star Team (1932, 1934, 1935) • Won Hart Trophy (1934)

Played in NHL All-Star Game (1934, 1937)

Rights traded to **Montreal Canadiens** by **Saskatoon** (WCHL) for Newsy Lalonde and $3,500, September 18, 1922.

• JOLIAT, RENE Rene (Bobby) Joliat
RW/D – L. 5'5", 140 lbs. b: Ottawa, Ontario, 4/25/1898. d: 8/10/1953.

Season	Club	League	GP	G	A	Pts	AG	AA	APts	PIM	GP	G	A	Pts	PIM
1916-17	Ottawa Grand Trunks	City Sr.	7	3	0	3	....	....	....	6	....	....	....	....	....
1917-18	Ottawa Grand Trunks	City Sr.	STATISTICS NOT AVAILABLE												
1918-19	Ottawa New Edinburghs	City Sr.	STATISTICS NOT AVAILABLE												
1919-20	Ottawa New Edinburghs	City Sr.	STATISTICS NOT AVAILABLE												
1920-21			DID NOT PLAY												
1921-22	Iroquois Falls Flyers	City Sr.	STATISTICS NOT AVAILABLE												
1922-23	Ottawa New Edinburghs	City Sr.	STATISTICS NOT AVAILABLE												
1923-24	Hull Volants	QSHL	STATISTICS NOT AVAILABLE												
1924-25	**Montreal Canadiens**	**NHL**	**1**	**0**	**0**	**0**	**0**	**0**	**0**	**0**	....	....	....	....	....
	Boston Maples	USAHA	2	2	0	2	....	....	....	0	....	....	....	....	....
1925-26			REINSTATED AS AN AMATEUR												
1926-1929			STATISTICS NOT AVAILABLE												
1929-30	Ottawa Shamrocks	City Sr.	15	0	0	0	....	....	....	20	6	0	0	0	4
	NHL Totals		**1**	**0**	**0**	**0**	**0**	**0**	**0**	**0**	....	....	....	....	....

Signed as a free agent by **Montreal Canadiens**, November 17, 1924.

• JONES, BUCK Buck (Alvin Bernard) Jones
D – R. 6', 180 lbs. b: Owen Sound, Ont., 8/17/1918.

Season	Club	League	GP	G	A	Pts	AG	AA	APts	PIM	GP	G	A	Pts	PIM
1936-37	Barrie Flyers	Jr. B	STATISTICS NOT AVAILABLE												
1937-38	Harringay Greyhounds	Britain	....	2	2	4	....	....	....	....	....	....	....	....	....
1938-39	**Detroit Red Wings**	**NHL**	**11**	**0**	**1**	**1**	**0**	**2**	**2**	**6**	**6**	**0**	**1**	**1**	**10**
	Pittsburgh Hornets	AHL	40	2	8	10	....	....	....	37	....	....	....	....	....
1939-40	**Detroit Red Wings**	**NHL**	**2**	**0**	**0**	**0**	**0**	**0**	**0**	**0**	....	....	....	....	....
	Indianapolis Capitals	AHL	56	6	6	12	....	....	....	70	5	0	2	2	12
1940-41	Indianapolis Capitals	AHL	54	4	5	9	....	....	....	78	....	....	....	....	....
1941-42	**Detroit Red Wings**	**NHL**	**21**	**2**	**1**	**3**	**3**	**2**	**5**	**8**	....	....	....	....	....
	Providence Reds	AHL	32	9	9	18	....	....	....	49	....	....	....	....	....
1942-43	Providence Reds	AHL	39	4	11	15	....	....	....	79	....	....	....	....	....
	Toronto Maple Leafs	**NHL**	**16**	**0**	**0**	**0**	**0**	**0**	**0**	**22**	**6**	**0**	**0**	**0**	**8**
1943-44	Kingston Army	OHA Sr.	4	0	3	3	....	....	....	6	....	....	....	....	....
1944-45			MILITARY SERVICE												
1945-46			MILITARY SERVICE												
1946-47	Tulsa Oilers	USHL	58	7	4	11	....	....	....	127	5	0	1	1	12
1947-48	Tulsa Oilers	USHL	65	3	6	9	....	....	....	47	2	0	0	0	2
1948-49	Hershey Bears	AHL	65	1	5	6	....	....	....	76	11	0	2	2	*17
1949-50	Hershey Bears	AHL	66	0	6	6	....	....	....	60	....	....	....	....	....
1950-51	Tulsa Oilers	USHL	57	0	10	10	....	....	....	72	6	0	4	4	4
1951-52	Tacoma Rockets	PCHL	70	1	3	4	....	....	....	140	6	0	0	0	14
1952-53	Tacoma Rockets	WHL	69	7	14	21	....	....	....	105	....	....	....	....	....
1953-54	Seattle Bombers	WHL	26	1	1	2	....	....	....	34	....	....	....	....	....
	Nelson Maple Leafs	WIHL	7	0	0	0	....	....	....	10	8	1	0	1	12
1954-55	Valleyfield Braves	QHL	19	0	3	3	....	....	....	4	....	....	....	....	....
	NHL Totals		**50**	**2**	**2**	**4**	**3**	**4**	**7**	**36**	**12**	**0**	**1**	**1**	**18**

Loaned to **Toronto** by **Providence** (AHL) with Ab Demarco for loan of Jack Forsey and George Boothman, February 3, 1943.

• JOYAL, EDDIE *— see page 1154*

• JUCKES, BING
Bing (Winston) Juckes
LW – L. 5'10", 165 lbs. b: Hamiota, Man., 6/14/1926.

Season	Club	League	GP	G	A	Pts	AG	AA	APts	PIM	GP	G	A	Pts	PIM
			REGULAR SEASON								PLAYOFFS				
1942-43	St. James Juniors	MJHL	1	1	0	1	....	....	....	0	1	0	0	0	0
1943-44	St. Catharines Falcons	OHA	19	7	5	12	....	....	....	17	4	0	0	0	2
1944-45	Winnipeg Rangers	MJHL	3	5	0	5	....	....	....	12	3	5	1	6	8
	Winnipeg Navy	City Sr.	9	4	5	9	....	....	....	15	6	3	1	4	*14
1945-46	Brandon Elks	MJHL	10	23	16	39	....	....	....	*31	7	*16	4	*20	19
	Providence Reds	AHL	5	1	1	2	....	....	....	6	....	....	....	....	....
1946-47	Lethbridge Maple Leafs	WCSHL	34	31	9	40	....	....	....	47	4	3	1	4	0
1947-48	**New York Rangers**	**NHL**	**2**	**0**	**0**	**0**	**0**	**0**	**0**	**0**	....	....	....	....	....
	New Haven Ramblers	AHL	55	27	19	46	....	....	....	18	2	1	0	1	4
1948-49	St. Paul Saints	USHL	65	40	44	84	....	....	....	53	7	2	4	6	20
1949-50	**New York Rangers**	**NHL**	**14**	**2**	**1**	**3**	**3**	**1**	**4**	**6**	....	....	....	....	....
	New Haven Ramblers	AHL	46	5	12	17	....	....	....	16	....	....	....	....	....
1950-51	Denver Falcons	USHL	58	25	21	46	....	....	....	56	5	1	2	3	2
1951-52	Calgary Stampeders	PCHL	33	12	18	30	....	....	....	16	....	....	....	....	....
1952-53	Yorkton Legionaires	SSHL	20	9	9	18	....	....	....	23	....	....	....	....	....
1953-54	Vernon Canadians	OSHL	30	29	16	45	....	....	....	29	....	....	....	....	....
1954-55	Brandon Wheat Kings	MHL Sr.	3	2	4	6	....	....	....	6	....	....	....	....	....
	NHL Totals		**16**	**2**	**1**	**3**	**3**	**1**	**4**	**6**	....	....	....	....	....

USHL First All-Star Team (1949)

Traded to **Denver** (USHL) by **NY Rangers** for cash, October 16, 1950.

• JUZDA, BILL
Bill "The Honest Brakeman" Juzda
D – R. 5'9", 190 lbs. b: Winnipeg, Man., 10/29/1920.

Season	Club	League	GP	G	A	Pts	AG	AA	APts	PIM	GP	G	A	Pts	PIM
1938-39	Winnipeg Elmwoods	MJHL	16	1	0	1	....	....	....	36	5	1	1	2	0
1939-40	Kenora Thistles	MJHL	24	3	6	9	....	....	....	29	9	2	3	5	20
1940-41	**New York Rangers**	**NHL**	**5**	**0**	**0**	**0**	**0**	**0**	**0**	**2**	....	....	....	....	....
	Philadelphia Rockets	AHL	52	7	14	21	....	....	....	47	....	....	....	....	....
1941-42	**New York Rangers**	**NHL**	**45**	**4**	**8**	**12**	**7**	**12**	**19**	**29**	**6**	**0**	**1**	**1**	**4**
1942-43	Buffalo Bisons	AHL	1	0	0	0	....	....	....	0	....	....	....	....	....
	Winnipeg RCAF	City Sr.	13	3	3	6	....	....	....	8	17	1	3	4	28
1943-44	Winnipeg RCAF	City Sr.	3	0	0	0	....	....	....	4	....	....	....	....	....
1944-45	Dartmouth RCAF	City Sr.	4	0	0	0	....	....	....	12	3	0	4	4	4
1945-46	**New York Rangers**	**NHL**	**32**	**1**	**3**	**4**	**2**	**6**	**8**	**17**	....	....	....	....	....
	Providence Reds	AHL	18	4	3	7	....	....	....	20	2	0	0	0	9
1946-47	**New York Rangers**	**NHL**	**45**	**3**	**5**	**8**	**4**	**7**	**11**	**60**	....	....	....	....	....
	New Haven Ramblers	AHL	16	2	4	6	....	....	....	20	....	....	....	....	....
1947-48	**New York Rangers**	**NHL**	**60**	**3**	**9**	**12**	**4**	**13**	**17**	**70**	**6**	**0**	**0**	**0**	**9**
1948-49	**Toronto Maple Leafs**	**NHL**	**38**	**1**	**2**	**3**	**2**	**3**	**5**	**23**	**9**	**0**	**2**	**2**	**8**
	Pittsburgh Hornets	AHL	7	0	3	3	....	....	....	4	....	....	....	....	....
1949-50	**Toronto Maple Leafs**	**NHL**	**62**	**1**	**14**	**15**	**1**	**18**	**19**	**68**	**7**	**0**	**0**	**0**	**16**
1950-51	**Toronto Maple Leafs**	**NHL**	**65**	**0**	**9**	**9**	**0**	**12**	**12**	**64**	**11**	**0**	**0**	**0**	**7**
1951-52	**Toronto Maple Leafs**	**NHL**	**46**	**1**	**4**	**5**	**1**	**5**	**6**	**65**	**3**	**0**	**0**	**0**	**2**
1952-53	Pittsburgh Hornets	AHL	59	1	15	16	....	....	....	108	10	0	1	1	11
1953-54			DID NOT PLAY												
1954-55	Brandon Wheat Kings	MHL Sr.	10	3	7	10	....	....	....	32	....	....	....	....	....
1955-56	Winnipeg Warriors	WHL	3	0	1	1	....	....	....	4	....	....	....	....	....
1956-57	Pine Falls Falcons	Inter-Sr.	DID NOT PLAY – COACHING												
	NHL Totals		**398**	**14**	**54**	**68**	**21**	**76**	**97**	**398**	**42**	**0**	**3**	**3**	**46**

AHL Second All-Star Team (1953)

Played in NHL All-Star Game (1948, 1949)

Traded to **Toronto** by **NY Rangers** with Cal Gardner, Rene Trudel and the rights to Frank Mathers for Wally Stanowski and Elwyn Morris, June, 1948.

• KABEL, BOB
Bob Kabel
C – R. 6', 183 lbs. b: Dauphin, Man., 11/11/1934.

Season	Club	League	GP	G	A	Pts	AG	AA	APts	PIM	GP	G	A	Pts	PIM
1952-53	Flin Flon Bombers	SJHL	47	26	12	38	....	....	....	54	11	5	2	7	4
1953-54	Flin Flon Bombers	SJHL	40	23	34	57	....	....	....	60	17	3	*14	17	37
1954-55	Saskatoon Wesleys	SJHL	46	19	21	40	....	....	....	62	5	1	1	2	17
	Saskatoon Quakers	WHL	1	0	0	0	....	....	....	2	....	....	....	....	....
1955-56	Vancouver Canucks	WHL	60	14	12	26	....	....	....	60	15	2	4	6	14
1956-57	Trois-Rivieres Lions	QHL	57	9	16	25	....	....	....	49	4	0	0	0	14
	Providence Reds	AHL	7	0	2	2	....	....	....	6	....	....	....	....	....
1957-58	Saskatoon–St. Paul	WHL	69	23	43	66	....	....	....	82	....	....	....	....	....
1958-59	Saskatoon Quakers	WHL	63	28	27	55	....	....	....	29	....	....	....	....	....
1959-60	**New York Rangers**	**NHL**	**44**	**5**	**11**	**16**	**6**	**11**	**17**	**32**	....	....	....	....	....
	Vancouver Canucks	WHL	25	9	4	13	....	....	....	22	....	....	....	....	....
1960-61	**New York Rangers**	**NHL**	**4**	**0**	**2**	**2**	**0**	**2**	**2**	**2**	....	....	....	....	....
	Springfield Indians	AHL	53	27	25	52	....	....	....	45	6	0	4	4	6
1961-62	Springfield Indians	AHL	50	8	28	36	....	....	....	26	11	1	5	6	12
1962-63	Vancouver Canucks	WHL	63	20	51	71	....	....	....	32	7	5	4	9	2
	Baltimore Clippers	AHL	3	0	0	0	....	....	....	0	....	....	....	....	....
1963-64	Vancouver Canucks	WHL	70	17	50	67	....	....	....	52	....	....	....	....	....
	St. Paul Rangers	CHL	....	....	....	....	....	....	....	....	4	1	3	4	0
1964-65	Vancouver Canucks	WHL	70	20	40	60	....	....	....	62	5	0	1	1	4
1965-66	Providence Reds	AHL	27	8	6	14	....	....	....	6	....	....	....	....	....
	Vancouver Canucks	WHL	42	9	9	18	....	....	....	14	....	....	....	....	....
1966-67	California Seals	WHL	47	9	9	18	....	....	....	20	4	0	0	0	2
1967-68	Phoenix Roadrunners	WHL	70	16	32	48	....	....	....	12	4	0	3	3	2
1968-69	Phoenix Roadrunners	WHL	68	14	33	47	....	....	....	20	....	....	....	....	....
1969-70	Salt Lake Golden Eagles	WHL	3	0	2	2	....	....	....	7	....	....	....	....	....
	NHL Totals		**48**	**5**	**13**	**18**	**6**	**13**	**19**	**34**	....	....	....	....	....

Traded to **Calfornia** (WHL) by **NY Rangers** (WHL) for Gerry Brisson with NY Rangers holding rights of recall, October, 1966. Traded to **Phoenix** (WHL) by **NY Rangers** for cash, September, 1967. Traded to **Salt Lake** (WHL) by **Phoenix** (WHL) for cash, May, 1969.

• KACHUR, ED
Ed Kachur
RW – R. 5'8", 170 lbs. b: Fort William, Ont., 4/22/1934.

Season	Club	League	GP	G	A	Pts	AG	AA	APts	PIM	GP	G	A	Pts	PIM
			REGULAR SEASON								PLAYOFFS				
1949-50	Fort William Canadians	TBJHL	16	5	5	10	....	....	....	54	10	1	1	2	10
1950-51	Fort William Canadians	TBJHL	14	5	3	8	....	....	....	32	6	3	3	6	12
1951-52	Fort William Canadians	TBJHL	29	38	22	60	....	....	....	96	12	4	0	4	*28
1952-53	Fort William Canadians	TBJHL	19	21	14	35	....	....	....	34	5	2	3	5	0
1953-54	Cincinnati Mohawks	IHL	63	32	26	58	....	....	....	61	11	2	2	4	2
1954-55	Shawinigan Cataracts	QHL	59	25	14	39	....	....	....	46	13	5	3	8	18
1955-56	Shawinigan Cataracts	QHL	64	31	34	65	....	....	....	91	11	6	5	11	16
1956-57	**Chicago Black Hawks**	**NHL**	**34**	**5**	**7**	**12**	**7**	**8**	**15**	**21**	....	....	....	....	....
	Shawinigan Cataracts	QHL	32	12	12	24	....	....	....	12	....	....	....	....	....
1957-58	**Chicago Black Hawks**	**NHL**	**62**	**5**	**7**	**12**	**6**	**8**	**14**	**14**	....	....	....	....	....
1958-59	Buffalo Bisons	AHL	68	15	17	32	....	....	....	26	11	*5	2	7	6
1959-60	Buffalo Bisons	AHL	57	19	10	29	....	....	....	10	....	....	....	....	....
1960-61	Soo Thunderbirds	EPHL	70	38	43	81	....	....	....	71	12	3	6	9	16
1961-62	Soo Thunderbirds	EPHL	70	22	32	54	....	....	....	65	....	....	....	....	....
1962-63	Buffalo Bisons	AHL	68	19	19	38	....	....	....	35	13	2	3	5	8
1963-64	Buffalo Bisons	AHL	64	13	14	27	....	....	....	10	....	....	....	....	....
1964-65	Los Angeles Blades	WHL	22	1	6	7	....	....	....	4	....	....	....	....	....
	Providence Reds	AHL	41	16	7	23	....	....	....	16	....	....	....	....	....
1965-66	Providence Reds	AHL	57	28	19	47	....	....	....	30	....	....	....	....	....
1966-67	Providence Reds	AHL	55	22	20	42	....	....	....	20	....	....	....	....	....
1967-68	Providence Reds	AHL	72	*47	29	76	....	....	....	30	8	3	2	5	8
1968-69	Providence Reds	AHL	71	26	26	52	....	....	....	24	9	1	4	5	6
1969-70	Providence Reds	AHL	21	9	4	13	....	....	....	2	....	....	....	....	....
1970-71	Thunder Bay Twins	USHL	15	17	10	27	....	....	....	25	....	....	....	....	....
1971-72	Johnstown Jets	EHL	25	18	11	29	....	....	....	6	....	....	....	....	....
	NHL Totals		**96**	**10**	**14**	**24**	**13**	**16**	**29**	**35**	....	....	....	....	....

QHL Second All-Star Team (1956) • AHL First All-Star Team (1968)

Traded to **Chicago** by **Montreal** with Forbes Kennedy for $50,000, May 24, 1956. Traded to **LA Blades** (WHL) by **Buffalo** (AHL) for cash, August 30, 1964. Traded to **Providence** (AHL) by **LA Blades** (WHL) for Harry Ottenbriet, December 2, 1964.

• KAISER, VERN
Vern Kaiser
LW – L. 6', 180 lbs. b: Preston, Ont., 9/28/1926.

Season	Club	League	GP	G	A	Pts	AG	AA	APts	PIM	GP	G	A	Pts	PIM
1941-42	Preston Riversides	City Jr.	STATISTICS NOT AVAILABLE												
	Calgary Navy	City Sr.	5	0	0	0	....	....	....	0	2	0	0	0	2
1942-43			MILITARY SERVICE												
1943-44			MILITARY SERVICE												
1944-45	Winnipeg Navy	City Sr.	4	0	1	1	....	....	....	10	6	0	2	2	8
1945-46	Washington–NY Rovers	EHL	46	5	6	11	....	....	....	83	12	0	0	0	*20
1946-47	Seattle Ironmen	PCHL	50	10	8	18	....	....	....	153	9	1	2	3	10
1947-48	Fort Worth Rangers	USHL	59	13	18	31	....	....	....	41	4	1	0	1	2
1948-49	Springfield Indians	AHL	61	25	17	42	....	....	....	32	3	1	1	2	4
1949-50	Springfield Indians	AHL	64	19	19	38	....	....	....	65	2	1	0	1	0
1950-51	**Montreal Canadiens**	**NHL**	**50**	**7**	**5**	**12**	**9**	**6**	**15**	**33**	**2**	**0**	**0**	**0**	**0**
	Buffalo Bisons	AHL	15	7	13	20	....	....	....	4	4	1	2	3	2
1951-52	Buffalo Bisons	AHL	58	24	26	50	....	....	....	67	2	0	1	1	2
1952-53	Buffalo Bisons	AHL	61	14	15	29	....	....	....	87	....	....	....	....	....
1953-54	Montreal–Springfield	QHL	43	14	22	36	....	....	....	27	....	....	....	....	....
	Syracuse Warriors	AHL	17	11	11	22	....	....	....	10	....	....	....	....	....
	NHL Totals		**50**	**7**	**5**	**12**	**9**	**6**	**15**	**33**	**2**	**0**	**0**	**0**	**0**

Traded to **Montreal** by **Springfield** (AHL) for Charles Gagnon and future considerations, April 18, 1950.

• KALBFLEISH, WALTER
Walter "Jake" Kalbfleish
D – R. 5'10", 175 lbs. b: New Hamburg, Ont., 12/18/1911. Deceased.

Season	Club	League	GP	G	A	Pts	AG	AA	APts	PIM	GP	G	A	Pts	PIM
1929-30	Niagara Falls Cataracts	OHA	6	1	1	2	....	....	....	*16	2	1	0	1	2
1930-31	Niagara Falls Cataracts	OHA	7	2	3	5	....	....	....	6	2	1	1	2	0
1931-32	Niagara Falls Cataracts	OHA Sr.	20	0	1	1	....	....	....	54	2	0	0	0	2
1932-33	Niagara Falls Cataracts	OHA Sr.	22	3	1	4	....	....	....	50	5	0	0	0	6
1933-34	**Ottawa Senators**	**NHL**	**22**	**0**	**4**	**4**	**0**	**11**	**11**	**20**	....	....	....	....	....
	Niagara Falls Cataracts	OHA Sr.	17	4	1	5	....	....	....	36	....	....	....	....	....
1934-35	**St. Louis Eagles**	**NHL**	**3**	**0**	**0**	**0**	**0**	**0**	**0**	**6**	....	....	....	....	....
	Buffalo Bisons	IAHL	28	3	3	6	....	....	....	30	....	....	....	....	....
1935-36	**New York Americans**	**NHL**	**4**	**0**	**0**	**0**	**0**	**0**	**0**	**2**	**5**	**0**	**0**	**0**	**2**
	Rochester Cardinals	IAHL	21	3	2	5	....	....	....	14	....	....	....	....	....
	Providence Reds	Can-Am	21	2	2	4	....	....	....	30	....	....	....	....	....
1936-37	**New York Americans**	**NHL**	**6**	**0**	**0**	**0**	**0**	**0**	**0**	**4**	....	....	....	....	....
	Boston Bruins	**NHL**	**1**	**0**	**0**	**0**	**0**	**0**	**0**	**0**	....	....	....	....	....
	Providence–New Haven	AHL	36	3	1	4	....	....	....	38	3	0	0	0	0
1937-38	Providence Reds	AHL	48	1	9	10	....	....	....	46	7	0	0	0	0
1938-39	Hershey Bears	AHL	45	4	4	8	....	....	....	42	3	0	0	0	0
1939-40	Hershey Bears	AHL	53	3	4	7	....	....	....	72	6	0	1	1	4
1940-41	Niagara Falls Brights	OHA Sr.	4	0	0	0	....	....	....	4	3	0	0	0	4
1941-42	Niagara Falls Weavers	OHA Sr.	27	2	3	5	....	....	....	34	7	0	0	0	8
1942-43	Niagara Falls Cataracts	OHA Sr.	5	0	2	2	....	....	....	6	1	0	0	0	0
	NHL Totals		**36**	**0**	**4**	**4**	**0**	**11**	**11**	**32**	**5**	**0**	**0**	**0**	**2**

Signed as a free agent by **Ottawa**, May 10, 1933. Transferred to **St. Louis** after **Ottawa** franchise relocated, September 22, 1934. Claimed by **NY Americans** from **St. Louis** in Dispersal Draft, October 15, 1936. Traded to **Boston** by **NY Americans** for Ted Graham, December 19, 1936.

• KALETA, ALEX
Alex "Sea Biscuit" Kaleta
LW – L. 6', 175 lbs. b: Canmore, Alta., 11/29/1919. d: 7/9/1987.

			REGULAR SEASON								PLAYOFFS				
Season	Club	League	GP	G	A	Pts	AG	AA	APts	PIM	GP	G	A	Pts	PIM
1938-39	Calgary Stampeders	ASHL	32	15	13	28	....	....	....	39	....	....	....	....	....
1939-40	Regina Aces	ASHL	32	19	20	39	....	....	....	33	9	4	6	10	10
1940-41	Lethbridge Maple Leafs	ASHL	24	20	*28	48	....	....	....	22	15	8	8	16	*26
1941-42	**Chicago Black Hawks**	**NHL**	**48**	**7**	**21**	**28**	**12**	**32**	**44**	**12**	**3**	**1**	**2**	**3**	**0**
1942-43	Calgary Currie Army	City Sr.	24	23	*35	*58	....	....	....	23	10	6	7	13	6
1943-44	Calgary Currie Army	City Sr.	15	8	15	23	....	....	....	24	2	*5	1	6	2
1944-45	Calgary Currie Army	City Sr.	16	14	12	26	....	....	....	16	3	1	2	3	*12
1945-46	**Chicago Black Hawks**	**NHL**	**49**	**19**	**27**	**46**	**29**	**51**	**80**	**17**	**4**	**0**	**1**	**1**	**2**
1946-47	**Chicago Black Hawks**	**NHL**	**57**	**24**	**20**	**44**	**33**	**29**	**62**	**37**	....	....	....	....	....
1947-48	**Chicago Black Hawks**	**NHL**	**52**	**10**	**16**	**26**	**15**	**23**	**38**	**40**	....	....	....	....	....
1948-49	**New York Rangers**	**NHL**	**56**	**12**	**19**	**31**	**19**	**30**	**49**	**18**	....	....	....	....	....
1949-50	**New York Rangers**	**NHL**	**67**	**17**	**14**	**31**	**23**	**18**	**41**	**40**	**10**	**0**	**3**	**3**	**0**
1950-51	**New York Rangers**	**NHL**	**58**	**3**	**4**	**7**	**4**	**5**	**9**	**26**	....	....	....	....	....
	Hershey Bears	AHL	5	0	2	2	....	....	....	6	....	....	....	....	....
1951-52	Saskatoon Quakers	PCHL	62	38	44	82	....	....	....	23	13	6	*13	19	4
1952-53	Saskatoon Quakers	WHL	70	26	*57	83	....	....	....	6	13	9	*14	*23	2
1953-54	Saskatoon Quakers	WHL	70	19	53	72	....	....	....	52	6	0	5	5	4
1954-55	Saskatoon Quakers	WHL	13	2	9	11	....	....	....	10	....	....	....	....	....
	NHL Totals		**387**	**92**	**121**	**213**	**135**	**188**	**323**	**190**	**17**	**1**	**6**	**7**	**2**

Traded to **NY Rangers** by **Chicago** with Emile Francis for Jim Henry, October 7, 1948.

• KAMINSKY, MAX
Max Kaminsky
C – L. 5'11", 160 lbs. b: Niagara Falls, Ont., 4/19/1913. d: 5/5/1961.

Season	Club	League	GP	G	A	Pts	AG	AA	APts	PIM	GP	G	A	Pts	PIM
1929-30	Niagara Falls Cataracts	OHA	6	9	*4	13	....	....	....	2	2	*5	1	*6	0
1930-31	Niagara Falls Cataracts	OHA	7	14	*15	*29	....	....	....	0	2	*3	0	*3	4
1931-32	Niagara Falls Cataracts	OHA Sr.	20	12	3	15	....	....	....	18	2	0	0	0	2
1932-33	Niagara Falls Cataracts	OHA Sr.	21	11	7	18	....	....	....	36	5	2	1	3	13
1933-34	**Ottawa Senators**	**NHL**	**38**	**9**	**17**	**26**	**20**	**46**	**66**	**14**	....	....	....	....	....
	Niagara Falls Cataracts	OHA Sr.	6	5	3	8	....	....	....	8	....	....	....	....	....
1934-35	**St. Louis Eagles**	**NHL**	**12**	**0**	**0**	**0**	**0**	**0**	**0**	**0**	....	....	....	....	....
	Boston Bruins	**NHL**	**38**	**12**	**15**	**27**	**25**	**33**	**58**	**4**	**4**	**0**	**0**	**0**	**0**
1935-36	**Boston Bruins**	**NHL**	**36**	**1**	**2**	**3**	**2**	**5**	**7**	**20**	....	....	....	....	....
1936-37	**Montreal Maroons**	**NHL**	**6**	**0**	**0**	**0**	**0**	**0**	**0**	**0**	....	....	....	....	....
	Providence–New Haven	AHL	21	3	5	8	....	....	....	4	....	....	....	....	....
1937-38	Springfield Indians	AHL	46	5	8	13	....	....	....	18	....	....	....	....	....
1938-39	Springfield Indians	AHL	46	7	14	21	....	....	....	8	3	0	1	1	2
1939-40	Springfield Indians	AHL	53	11	29	40	....	....	....	20	3	0	2	2	0
1940-41	Springfield Indians	AHL	40	13	9	22	....	....	....	9	3	2	0	2	0
1941-42	Springfield Indians	AHL	53	18	23	41	....	....	....	9	5	0	2	2	0
1942-43	Buffalo Bisons	AHL	42	10	36	46	....	....	....	6	9	2	*12	14	4
1943-44	Buffalo Bisons	AHL	42	7	29	36	....	....	....	17	9	4	2	6	2
1944-45	Pittsburgh Hornets	AHL	54	5	28	33	....	....	....	17	....	....	....	....	....
1945-46	Pittsburgh Hornets	AHL	DID NOT PLAY – COACHING												
	NHL Totals		**130**	**22**	**34**	**56**	**47**	**84**	**131**	**38**	**4**	**0**	**0**	**0**	**0**

AHL Second All-Star Team (1940)

Signed as a free agent by **Ottawa**, December 4, 1933. Transferred to **St. Louis** after **Ottawa** franchise relocated, September 22, 1934. Traded to **Boston** by **St. Louis** with Des Roche for Joe Lamb, December 4, 1934. Traded to **Montreal Maroons** by **Boston** for cash, December 7, 1936.

• KAMPMAN, RUDOLPH
Rudolph "Bingo" Kampman
D – R. 5'10", 187 lbs. b: Kitchener, Ont., 3/12/1914. d: 12/22/1987.

Season	Club	League	GP	G	A	Pts	AG	AA	APts	PIM	GP	G	A	Pts	PIM
1933-34	Kitchener Greenshirts	OHA	16	10	1	11	....	....	....	26	4	4	0	4	2
1934-35	Creighton Mines	City Sr.	STATISTICS NOT AVAILABLE												
1935-36	Creighton Mines	City Sr.	8	0	1	1	....	....	....	25	5	2	0	2	13
1936-37	Sudbury Frood Mines	City Sr.	14	2	3	5	....	....	....	27	13	2	4	6	14
	Kitchener Greenshirts	OHA Sr.	2	0	1	1	....	....	....	0	....	....	....	....	....
1937-38	**Toronto Maple Leafs**	**NHL**	**32**	**1**	**2**	**3**	**2**	**4**	**6**	**56**	**7**	**0**	**1**	**1**	**6**
	Syracuse Stars	AHL	12	2	1	3	....	....	....	4	....	....	....	....	....
1938-39	**Toronto Maple Leafs**	**NHL**	**41**	**2**	**8**	**10**	**4**	**15**	**19**	**52**	**10**	**1**	**1**	**2**	**20**
1939-40	**Toronto Maple Leafs**	**NHL**	**39**	**6**	**9**	**15**	**13**	**18**	**31**	**59**	**10**	**0**	**0**	**0**	**0**
1940-41	**Toronto Maple Leafs**	**NHL**	**39**	**1**	**4**	**5**	**2**	**7**	**9**	**53**	**7**	**0**	**0**	**0**	**0**
1941-42	**Toronto Maple Leafs**	**NHL**	**38**	**4**	**7**	**11**	**7**	**11**	**18**	**67**	**13**	**0**	**2**	**2**	**12**
1942-43	Halifax Army	City Sr.	8	4	3	7	....	....	....	18	4	0	1	1	14
	Ottawa Commandos	QSHL	....	....	....	....	....	....	....	....	13	3	4	7	14
1943-44	Halifax Cresents	City Sr.	2	0	1	1	....	....	....	2	....	....	....	....	....
	New Glascow Bombers	City Sr.	2	0	0	0	....	....	....	4	2	0	0	0	0
1944-45	Dartmouth RCAF	City Sr.	5	0	0	0	....	....	....	8	3	0	0	0	4
1945-46	Providence Reds	AHL	27	4	8	12	....	....	....	12	2	0	0	0	0
1946-47	St. Louis Flyers	AHL	45	4	14	18	....	....	....	44	....	....	....	....	....
1947-48	St. Louis Flyers	AHL	46	4	13	17	....	....	....	29	....	....	....	....	....
1948-49	Fresno Falcons	PCHL	69	6	14	20	....	....	....	82	3	0	0	0	4
1949-50	Fresno Falcons	PCHL	37	3	6	9	....	....	....	27	....	....	....	....	....
	Nanaimo Clippers	OSHL	9	2	2	4	....	....	....	14	8	1	0	1	8
1950-51	Kitchener Dutchmen	OHA Sr.	23	2	3	5	....	....	....	20	....	....	....	....	....
	NHL Totals		**189**	**14**	**30**	**44**	**28**	**55**	**83**	**287**	**47**	**1**	**4**	**5**	**38**

PCHL Southern First All-Star Team (1949)

Traded to **Boston** by **Toronto** to complete transaction that sent Art Jackson to Toronto, October 29, 1945. Returned to **Toronto** by **Boston** and loaned to Providence (AHL), November 6, 1945.

• KANE, FRANCIS
Francis "Red" Kane
D – L. 5'11", 186 lbs. b: Stratford, Ont., 1/19/1923.

Season	Club	League	GP	G	A	Pts	AG	AA	APts	PIM	GP	G	A	Pts	PIM
1941-42	Falconbridge Falcons	City Jr.	9	1	1	2	....	....	....	10	2	1	0	1	0
1942-43	Brantford Lions	OHA	20	3	3	6	....	....	....	42	10	1	3	4	18
1943-44	**Detroit Red Wings**	**NHL**	**2**	**0**	**0**	**0**	**0**	**0**	**0**	**0**	....	....	....	....	....
	Indianapolis Capitols	AHL	51	6	13	19	....	....	....	17	5	0	4	4	0
1944-45	Indianapolis Capitals	AHL	59	4	8	12	....	....	....	95	5	0	0	0	4
1945-46	St. Louis Flyers	AHL	5	0	0	0	....	....	....	10	....	....	....	....	....
	Tulsa Oilers	USHL	47	8	7	15	....	....	....	*127	13	0	0	0	14
1946-47	Fort Worth Rangers	USHL	59	3	13	16	....	....	....	69	8	0	0	0	12
1947-48	Fort Worth Rangers	USHL	57	8	15	23	....	....	....	61	4	0	3	3	0
1948-49	Fort Worth Rangers	USHL	62	2	22	24	....	....	....	116	2	1	1	2	2
1949-50	Oakland–Los Angeles	PCHL	51	4	7	11	....	....	....	88	16	1	8	9	43
1950-51	New Haven–Springfield	AHL	39	1	8	9	....	....	....	49	....	....	....	....	....
	Vancouver Canucks	PCHL	18	1	9	10	....	....	....	25	....	....	....	....	....
	NHL Totals		**2**	**0**	**0**	**0**	**0**	**0**	**0**	**0**	....	....	....	....	....

• KEATING, JACK
Jack Keating
LW – L. 5'7", 145 lbs. b: St. John, N.B., 2/12/1908. Deceased.

			REGULAR SEASON								PLAYOFFS				
Season	Club	League	GP	G	A	Pts	AG	AA	APts	PIM	GP	G	A	Pts	PIM
1925-26	Chatham Ironmen	NNBSL	12	2	1	3	....	....	....	0	2	0	0	0	0
1926-27	Saint John Fusiliers	City Sr.	12	10	3	13	....	....	....	26	2	1	0	1	2
1927-28	Saint John Fusiliers	City Sr.	12	15	*8	*23	....	....	....	*42	9	9	*5	*14	*20
1928-29	Saint John Fusiliers	City Sr.	12	12	*9	*21	....	....	....	16	2	1	0	1	4
1929-30	Saint John Beavers	City Sr.	11	9	6	15	....	....	....	35	6	2	0	2	8
1930-31	New Haven Eagles	Can-Am	39	9	2	11	....	....	....	49	....	....	....	....	....
1931-32	**New York Americans**	**NHL**	**22**	**5**	**3**	**8**	**11**	**8**	**19**	**6**	....	....	....	....	....
	New Haven Eagles	Can-Am	21	4	4	8	....	....	....	26	....	....	....	....	....
1932-33	**New York Americans**	**NHL**	**13**	**0**	**2**	**2**	**0**	**5**	**5**	**11**	....	....	....	....	....
	New Haven Eagles	Can-Am	39	12	8	20	....	....	....	71	....	....	....	....	....
1933-34	Buffalo Bisons	IAHL	43	8	4	12	....	....	....	21	6	0	0	0	2
1934-35	Providence Reds	Can-Am	46	16	19	35	....	....	....	27	6	*2	2	4	2
1935-36	Providence Reds	Can-Am	47	10	12	22	....	....	....	35	7	2	3	5	4
1936-37	Providence Reds	AHL	48	12	31	43	....	....	....	22	3	1	2	3	2
1937-38	Providence Reds	AHL	45	15	13	28	....	....	....	20	7	2	3	5	0
1938-39	Providence Reds	AHL	51	5	18	23	....	....	....	16	5	0	1	1	0
1939-40	Syracuse Stars	AHL	40	11	17	28	....	....	....	14	....	....	....	....	....
1940-41	Buffalo Bisons	AHL	3	0	0	0	....	....	....	0	....	....	....	....	....
	St. Paul Saints	AHA	34	5	3	8	....	....	....	6	4	0	1	1	6
1941-42	Saint John Beavers	NBSHL	7	*9	5	14	....	....	....	0	2	2	1	3	2
1942-43	Saint John Garrison	City Sr.	3	1	3	4	....	....	....	2	9	3	*6	*9	6
1943-44	Saint John Garrison	City Sr.	11	6	11	*17	....	....	....	2	5	*9	4	13	0
1944-45			DID NOT PLAY												
1945-46	Saint John Beavers	NBSHL	1	1	1	2	....	....	....	0	....	....	....	....	....
1946-47	Saint John Beavers	NBSHL	DID NOT PLAY – COACHING												
	NHL Totals		**35**	**5**	**5**	**10**	**11**	**13**	**24**	**17**	....	....	....	....	....

Signed as a free agent by **NY Americans**, October 22, 1930. Loaned to **Buffalo** (IAHL) by **NY Americans** for cash, January 9, 1934. Traded to **Providence** (Can-Am) by **NY Americans** with Gord Kuhn for cash, November 13, 1934. Loaned to **St. Paul** (AHA) by **Buffalo** (AHL), December 11, 1940.

• KEATING, JOHN
John "Red" Keating
LW – L. 6', 180 lbs. b: Kitchener, Ont., 10/9/1916.

Season	Club	League	GP	G	A	Pts	AG	AA	APts	PIM	GP	G	A	Pts	PIM
1934-35	Kitchener Greenshirts	OHA	14	11	10	21	....	....	....	4	2	1	0	1	0
1935-36	Kitchener Greenshirts	OHA	7	6	1	7	....	....	....	10	4	3	1	4	0
1936-37	Richmond Hawks	Britain	....	13	2	15	....	....	....	6	....	....	....	....	....
1937-38	Harringay Racers	Britain	....	*29	3	32	....	....	....	....	....	....	....	....	....
1938-39	**Detroit Red Wings**	**NHL**	**1**	**0**	**1**	**1**	**0**	**2**	**2**	**2**	....	....	....	....	....
	Pittsburgh Hornets	AHL	50	19	12	31	....	....	....	18	....	....	....	....	....
1939-40	**Detroit Red Wings**	**NHL**	**10**	**2**	**0**	**2**	**4**	**0**	**4**	**2**	....	....	....	....	....
	Indianapolis Capitals	AHL	32	8	12	20	....	....	....	4	5	1	2	3	0
1940-41	Indianapolis Capitals	AHL	53	21	18	39	....	....	....	6	....	....	....	....	....
1941-42	Indianapolis Capitals	AHL	55	19	25	44	....	....	....	14	10	*9	9	*18	0
1942-43	Indianapolis Capitals	AHL	7	4	4	8	....	....	....	0	....	....	....	....	....
1943-44			MILITARY SERVICE												
1944-45			MILITARY SERVICE												
1945-46	Indianapolis Capitals	AHL	14	8	3	11	....	....	....	0	5	1	1	2	0
	Hollywood Wolves	PCHL	8	5	2	7	....	....	....	6	....	....	....	....	....
1946-47	Los Angeles Monarchs	PCHL	55	36	26	62	....	....	....	16	10	3	3	6	26
1947-48	Los Angeles Monarchs	PCHL	45	41	19	60	....	....	....	26	....	....	....	....	....
	NHL Totals		**11**	**2**	**1**	**3**	**4**	**2**	**6**	**4**	....	....	....	....	....

• KEATS, DUKE
Duke (Gordon Blanchard) Keats **HHOF**
C – R. 5'11", 195 lbs. b: Montreal, Que., 3/1/1895. d: 1/16/1971.

Season	Club	League	GP	G	A	Pts	AG	AA	APts	PIM	GP	G	A	Pts	PIM
1913-14	Cobalt O'Brien Mines	NOHA	STATISTICS NOT AVAILABLE												
	North Bay Trappers	NOHA	3	2	0	2	....	....	....	18	4	*6	0	*6	....
1914-15			STATISTICS NOT AVAILABLE												
1915-16	Toronto Blueshirts	NHA	24	22	7	29	....	....	....	112	....	....	....	....	....
1916-17	Toronto Blueshirts	NHA	13	15	2	17	....	....	....	65	....	....	....	....	....
1917-18			MILITARY SERVICE												
1918-19			MILITARY SERVICE												
1919-20	Edmonton Eskimos	Big 4	12	*18	*14	*32	....	....	....	*41	2	*2	*2	*4	2
1920-21	Edmonton Dominions	Big 4	15	*23	6	*29	....	....	....	36	....	....	....	....	....
1921-22	Edmonton Eskimos	WCHL	25	*31	*24	*55	....	....	....	47	2	0	1	1	6
1922-23	Edmonton Eskimos	WCHL	25	24	13	37	....	....	....	*72	2	2	2	4	4
1923-24	Edmonton Eskimos	WCHL	29	19	12	31	....	....	....	41	....	....	....	....	....
1924-25	Edmonton Eskimos	WCHL	28	23	9	32	....	....	....	63	....	....	....	....	....
1925-26	Edmonton Eskimos	WHL	30	20	9	29	....	....	....	*134	2	0	1	1	9
1926-27	**Boston Bruins**	**NHL**	**17**	**4**	**7**	**11**	**12**	**60**	**72**	**20**	....	....	....	....	....
	Detroit Cougars	**NHL**	**25**	**12**	**1**	**13**	**35**	**8**	**43**	**32**	....	....	....	....	....
1927-28	**Detroit Cougars**	**NHL**	**5**	**0**	**2**	**2**	**0**	**17**	**17**	**6**	....	....	....	....	....
	Chicago Black Hawks	**NHL**	**32**	**14**	**8**	**22**	**43**	**68**	**111**	**55**	....	....	....	....	....
1928-29	**Chicago Black Hawks**	**NHL**	**3**	**0**	**1**	**1**	**0**	**9**	**9**	**0**	....	....	....	....	....
	Tulsa Oilers	AHA	39	*22	11	*33	....	....	....	18	4	0	1	1	10
1929-30	Tulsa Oilers	AHA	3	2	2	4	....	....	....	2	....	....	....	....	....
1930-31	Tulsa Oilers	AHA	43	14	10	24	....	....	....	44	4	0	1	1	6
1931-32			REINSTATED AS AN AMATEUR												
1932-33	Edmonton Eskimos	WCHL	25	8	7	15	....	....	....	*146	8	1	*4	5	0
1933-34	Edmonton Eskimos	NWHL	25	8	6	14	....	....	....	8	2	0	0	0	2
1934-35	Edmonton Eskimos	NWHL	DID NOT PLAY – COACHING												
	NHL Totals		**82**	**30**	**19**	**49**	**90**	**162**	**252**	**113**	....	....	....	....	....
	Other Major League Totals		174	154	76	230	....	....	....	534	6	2	4	6	19

WCHL First All-Star Team (1922, 1923, 1924, 1925) • WHL First All-Star Team (1926)

Signed as a free agent by **Toronto St. Pats**, December 9, 1919. Reinstated as an amateur and signed as a free agent by **Edmonton** (Big 4), December, 1919. Signed as a free agent by **Edmonton** (WCHL), November 4, 1921. Traded to **Boston** by **Edmonton** (WHL) for cash, September 4, 1926. Traded to **Detroit Cougars** by **Boston** with Archie Briden for Frank Frederickson and Harry Meeking, January 7, 1927. Traded to **Chicago** by **Detroit Cougars** for Gord Fraser and $5,000, December 16, 1927.

• KEELING, BUTCH
Butch (Melville Sydney) Keeling
LW – L. 5'11", 180 lbs. b: Owen Sound, Ont., 8/10/1905. Deceased.

			REGULAR SEASON								PLAYOFFS				
Season	Club	League	GP	G	A	Pts	AG	AA	APts	PIM	GP	G	A	Pts	PIM
1923-24	Owen Sound Greys	OHA	11	24	4	28	....	....	....	....	15	*37	9	*46	....
1924-25	Owen Sound Greys	OHA	16	22	8	30	....	....	....	....	9	*15	5	*20	12
1925-26	London Ravens	OHA Sr.	20	14	3	17	....	....	....	18	4	2	1	3	0
1926-27	**Toronto Maple Leafs**	**NHL**	**30**	**11**	**2**	**13**	**32**	**17**	**49**	**29**	....	....	....	....	....
	London Panthers	Can-Pro	12	13	1	14	....	....	....	25	....	....	....	....	....
1927-28	**Toronto Maple Leafs**	**NHL**	**43**	**10**	**6**	**16**	**31**	**51**	**82**	**52**	....	....	....	....	....
1928-29	**New York Rangers**	**NHL**	**43**	**6**	**3**	**9**	**24**	**27**	**51**	**35**	**6**	***3**	**0**	***3**	**2**
1929-30	**New York Rangers**	**NHL**	**43**	**19**	**7**	**26**	**38**	**23**	**61**	**34**	**4**	**0**	**3**	**3**	**8**
1930-31	**New York Rangers**	**NHL**	**44**	**13**	**9**	**22**	**32**	**33**	**65**	**35**	**4**	**1**	**1**	**2**	**0**
1931-32	**New York Rangers**	**NHL**	**48**	**17**	**3**	**20**	**36**	**8**	**44**	**38**	**7**	**2**	**1**	**3**	**12**
1932-33	**New York Rangers**	**NHL**	**47**	**8**	**6**	**14**	**19**	**16**	**35**	**22**	**8**	**0**	**2**	**2**	**8**
1933-34	**New York Rangers**	**NHL**	**48**	**15**	**5**	**20**	**33**	**13**	**46**	**20**	**2**	**0**	**0**	**0**	**0**
1934-35	**New York Rangers**	**NHL**	**47**	**15**	**4**	**19**	**32**	**9**	**41**	**14**	**4**	**2**	**1**	**3**	**0**
1935-36	**New York Rangers**	**NHL**	**46**	**13**	**5**	**18**	**32**	**12**	**44**	**22**	....	....	....	....	....
1936-37	**New York Rangers**	**NHL**	**48**	**22**	**4**	**26**	**48**	**9**	**57**	**18**	**9**	**3**	**2**	**5**	**2**
1937-38	**New York Rangers**	**NHL**	**38**	**8**	**9**	**17**	**17**	**18**	**35**	**12**	**3**	**0**	**1**	**1**	**2**
1938-39	Philadelphia Ramblers	AHL	48	6	13	19	....	....	....	16	9	2	1	3	5
1939-40	Kansas City Greyhounds	AHA	46	15	11	26	....	....	....	27	....	....	....	....	....
	NHL Totals		**525**	**157**	**63**	**220**	**374**	**236**	**610**	**331**	**47**	**11**	**11**	**22**	**34**

Traded to **Toronto St. Pats** by **London** (Can-Pro) for Pete Bellefeuille, December 27, 1926. Traded to **NY Rangers** by **Toronto** with John Ross Roach for Lorne Chabot and Alex Gray, October 17, 1928.

• KEENAN, LARRY
— *see page 1163*

• KELLER, RALPH
Ralph Keller
D – R. 5'9", 174 lbs. b: Wilkie, Sask., 2/6/1936.

			REGULAR SEASON								PLAYOFFS				
Season	Club	League	GP	G	A	Pts	AG	AA	APts	PIM	GP	G	A	Pts	PIM
1952-53	Prince Albert Mintos	SJHL	1	0	0	0	....	....	....	0	....	....	....	....	....
1953-54	Prince Albert Mintos	SJHL	48	7	21	28	....	....	....	83	15	1	1	2	34
1954-55	Prince Albert Mintos	SJHL	48	12	16	28	....	....	....	93	10	3	3	6	14
	Saskatoon Quakers	WHL	1	0	1	1	....	....	....	0	....	....	....	....	....
1955-56	Prince Albert Mintos	SJHL	50	20	35	55	....	....	....	56	12	6	7	13	12
	Saskatoon Quakers	WHL	4	0	0	0	....	....	....	2	3	0	0	0	2
1956-57	Vancouver Canucks	WHL	68	6	15	21	....	....	....	75	....	....	....	....	....
1957-58	Saskatoon–St. Paul	WHL	34	5	10	15	....	....	....	51	....	....	....	....	....
	Providence Reds	AHL	31	1	7	8	....	....	....	22	....	....	....	....	....
1958-59	Saskatoon Quakers	WHL	64	6	17	23	....	....	....	70	....	....	....	....	....
1959-60	Vancouver Canucks	WHL	70	12	19	31	....	....	....	102	11	2	4	6	16
1960-61	Vancouver Canucks	WHL	70	9	31	40	....	....	....	95	9	2	3	5	6
1961-62	Los Angeles Blades	WHL	70	17	38	55	....	....	....	136	....	....	....	....	....
1962-63	**New York Rangers**	**NHL**	**3**	**1**	**0**	**1**	**1**	**0**	**1**	**6**	....	....	....	....	....
	Baltimore Clippers	AHL	71	7	23	30	....	....	....	133	3	0	0	0	8
1963-64	Hershey Bears	AHL	61	5	20	25	....	....	....	102	6	1	2	3	10
1964-65	Hershey Bears	AHL	72	7	32	39	....	....	....	166	15	1	3	4	*38
1965-66	Hershey Bears	AHL	45	5	14	19	....	....	....	91	....	....	....	....	....
1966-67	Hershey Bears	AHL	69	11	33	44	....	....	....	109	5	0	4	4	6
1967-68	Hershey Bears	AHL	70	11	35	46	....	....	....	126	5	1	1	2	4
1968-69	Hershey Bears	AHL	74	9	46	55	....	....	....	104	11	3	4	7	*38
1969-70	Hershey Bears	AHL	62	13	21	34	....	....	....	94	7	1	3	4	21
1970-71	Hershey Bears	AHL	70	17	22	39	....	....	....	81	4	1	0	1	15
1971-72	Hershey Bears	AHL	67	8	26	34	....	....	....	100	4	0	1	1	2
1972-73	Hershey Bears	AHL	73	9	33	42	....	....	....	103	7	1	5	6	8
1973-74	Hershey Bears	AHL	74	8	23	31	....	....	....	99	10	2	1	3	6
	NHL Totals		**3**	**1**	**0**	**1**	**1**	**0**	**1**	**6**	....	....	....	....	....

WHL Second All-Star Team (1960) • WHL First All-Star Team (1961) • AHL First All-Star Team (1969)

Claimed by **Montreal** from **NY Rangers** in Intra-League Draft, June, 1963. Traded to **Hershey** (AHL) by **Montreal** for cash, August, 1963.

• KELLY, PETE
Pete Kelly
RW – R. 5'11", 170 lbs. b: St. Vital, Man., 5/22/1913.

			REGULAR SEASON								PLAYOFFS				
Season	Club	League	GP	G	A	Pts	AG	AA	APts	PIM	GP	G	A	Pts	PIM
1929-30	Montreal Victorias	City Jr.	10	3	0	3	....	....	....	4	....	....	....	....	....
1930-31	Montreal AAA	City Jr.	10	*7	0	*7	....	....	....	10	2	1	0	1	2
	Montreal AAA	City Sr.	....	....	....	....	....	....	....	....	1	0	0	0	0
1931-32	Montreal AAA	City Jr.	10	8	*9	*17	....	....	....	10	8	7	*5	*12	8
	Montreal AAA	City Sr.	....	....	....	....	....	....	....	....	1	0	0	0	0
1932-33	Montreal Royals	City Sr.	8	0	0	0	....	....	....	0	....	....	....	....	....
1933-34	Charlottetown Abegweits	MSHL	39	14	11	25	....	....	....	67	3	1	0	1	2
1934-35	**St. Louis Eagles**	**NHL**	**25**	**3**	**10**	**13**	**6**	**22**	**28**	**14**	....	....	....	....	....
	Charlottetown Abegweits	MSHL	20	16	11	*27	....	....	....	27	....	....	....	....	....
1935-36	**Detroit Red Wings**	**NHL**	**46**	**6**	**8**	**14**	**15**	**19**	**34**	**30**	**7**	**1**	**1**	**2**	**2**
1936-37	**Detroit Red Wings**	**NHL**	**47**	**5**	**4**	**9**	**11**	**9**	**20**	**12**	**8**	**2**	**0**	**2**	**0**
1937-38	**Detroit Red Wings**	**NHL**	**9**	**0**	**1**	**1**	**0**	**2**	**2**	**2**	....	....	....	....	....
	Pittsburgh Hornets	AHL	39	7	20	27	....	....	....	26	2	0	2	2	0
1938-39	**Detroit Red Wings**	**NHL**	**32**	**4**	**9**	**13**	**8**	**17**	**25**	**4**	**4**	**0**	**0**	**0**	**0**
	Pittsburgh Hornets	AHL	6	2	6	8	....	....	....	0	....	....	....	....	....
1939-40	Pittsburgh Hornets	AHL	54	20	20	40	....	....	....	22	9	2	5	7	9
1940-41	**New York Americans**	**NHL**	**11**	**3**	**5**	**8**	**6**	**9**	**15**	**2**	....	....	....	....	....
	Pittsburgh–Springfield	AHL	44	10	30	40	....	....	....	14	3	2	1	3	0
1941-42	**Brooklyn Americans**	**NHL**	**7**	**0**	**1**	**1**	**0**	**2**	**2**	**4**	....	....	....	....	....
	Springfield Indians	AHL	46	33	*44	*77	....	....	....	11	5	1	6	7	4
1942-43	Moncton RCAF	City Sr.	4	*9	6	*15	....	....	....	....	4	4	*8	*12	12
1943-44	Moncton Fliers	City Sr.	4	4	3	*7	....	....	....	0	....	....	....	....	....
	Charlottetown All-Stars	City Sr.	4	3	6	9	....	....	....	2	....	....	....	....	....
	Saint John Beavers	City Sr.	4	6	7	13	....	....	....	0	5	8	4	12	0
1944-45	Charlottetown #2	City Sr.	8	7	15	22	....	....	....	7	2	3	1	4	0
	New Glasgow Bombers	CBSHL	2	3	3	6	....	....	....	0	8	*16	9	*25	0
1945-46			MILITARY SERVICE												
1946-47	New Glasgow Bombers	CBSHL	16	14	14	28	....	....	....	....	5	2	1	3	0
1947-48	U. of New Brunswick	City Sr.	1	0	3	3	....	....	....	0	4	4	6	10	2
1948-49	U. of New Brunswick	City Sr.	3	2	1	3	....	....	....	0	5	*6	5	11	0
1949-50	U. of New Brunswick	City Sr.	5	7	5	12	....	....	....	4	1	0	0	0	0
1950-51	U. of New Brunswick	City Sr.	1	0	3	3	....	....	....	0	....	....	....	....	....
1952-53	U. of New Brunswick	City Sr.	DID NOT PLAY – COACHING												
	NHL Totals		**177**	**21**	**38**	**59**	**46**	**80**	**126**	**68**	**19**	**3**	**1**	**4**	**2**

AHL First All-Star Team (1942)

Signed as a free agent by **St. Louis**, November, 1934. Claimed by **NY Americans** from **St. Louis** in Dispersal Draft, October 15, 1935. Traded to **Detroit** by **NY Americans** for Carl Voss, October 16, 1935. Traded to **Pittsburgh** (AHL) by **Detroit** for cash, December 2, 1937. Traded to **NY Americans** by **Detroit** for Norm Schultz, December 31, 1940.

• KELLY, RED
Red (Leonard Patrick) Kelly **HHOF**
D/C – L. 5'11", 180 lbs. b: Simcoe, Ont., 7/9/1927.

			REGULAR SEASON								PLAYOFFS				
Season	Club	League	GP	G	A	Pts	AG	AA	APts	PIM	GP	G	A	Pts	PIM
1944-45	St. Michael's Majors	OHA	1	0	0	0	....	....	....	0	....	....	....	....	....
1945-46	St. Michael's Majors	OHA	26	13	11	24	....	....	....	18	11	1	0	1	7
1946-47	St. Michael's Majors	OHA	30	8	24	32	....	....	....	11	9	3	3	6	9
1947-48	**Detroit Red Wings**	**NHL**	**60**	**6**	**14**	**20**	**9**	**20**	**29**	**13**	**10**	**3**	**2**	**5**	**2**
1948-49	**Detroit Red Wings**	**NHL**	**59**	**5**	**11**	**16**	**8**	**17**	**25**	**10**	**11**	**1**	**1**	**2**	**10**
1949-50	**Detroit Red Wings**	**NHL**	**70**	**15**	**25**	**40**	**20**	**32**	**52**	**9**	**14**	**1**	**3**	**4**	**2**
1950-51	**Detroit Red Wings**	**NHL**	**70**	**17**	**37**	**54**	**23**	**48**	**71**	**24**	**6**	**0**	**1**	**1**	**0**
1951-52	**Detroit Red Wings**	**NHL**	**67**	**16**	**31**	**47**	**23**	**40**	**63**	**16**	**5**	**1**	**0**	**1**	**0**
1952-53	**Detroit Red Wings**	**NHL**	**70**	**19**	**27**	**46**	**29**	**38**	**67**	**8**	**6**	**0**	**4**	**4**	**0**
1953-54	**Detroit Red Wings**	**NHL**	**62**	**16**	**33**	**49**	**24**	**45**	**69**	**18**	**12**	**5**	**1**	**6**	**0**
1954-55	**Detroit Red Wings**	**NHL**	**70**	**15**	**30**	**45**	**22**	**39**	**61**	**28**	**11**	**2**	**4**	**6**	**17**
1955-56	**Detroit Red Wings**	**NHL**	**70**	**16**	**34**	**50**	**23**	**43**	**66**	**39**	**10**	**2**	**4**	**6**	**2**
1956-57	**Detroit Red Wings**	**NHL**	**70**	**10**	**25**	**35**	**14**	**29**	**43**	**18**	**5**	**1**	**0**	**1**	**0**
1957-58	**Detroit Red Wings**	**NHL**	**61**	**13**	**18**	**31**	**17**	**20**	**37**	**26**	**4**	**0**	**1**	**1**	**2**
1958-59	**Detroit Red Wings**	**NHL**	**67**	**8**	**13**	**21**	**10**	**14**	**24**	**34**	....	....	....	....	....
1959-60	**Detroit Red Wings**	**NHL**	**50**	**6**	**12**	**18**	**7**	**12**	**19**	**10**	....	....	....	....	....
	Toronto Maple Leafs	**NHL**	**18**	**6**	**5**	**11**	**7**	**5**	**12**	**8**	**10**	**3**	**8**	**11**	**2**
1960-61	**Toronto Maple Leafs**	**NHL**	**64**	**20**	**50**	**70**	**24**	**51**	**75**	**12**	**2**	**1**	**0**	**1**	**0**
1961-62	**Toronto Maple Leafs**	**NHL**	**58**	**22**	**27**	**49**	**27**	**27**	**54**	**6**	**12**	**4**	**6**	**10**	**0**
1962-63	**Toronto Maple Leafs**	**NHL**	**66**	**20**	**40**	**60**	**25**	**42**	**67**	**8**	**10**	**2**	**6**	**8**	**6**
1963-64	**Toronto Maple Leafs**	**NHL**	**70**	**11**	**34**	**45**	**14**	**38**	**52**	**16**	**14**	**4**	**9**	**13**	**4**
1964-65	**Toronto Maple Leafs**	**NHL**	**70**	**18**	**28**	**46**	**23**	**30**	**53**	**8**	**6**	**3**	**2**	**5**	**2**
1965-66	**Toronto Maple Leafs**	**NHL**	**63**	**8**	**24**	**32**	**10**	**24**	**34**	**12**	**4**	**0**	**2**	**2**	**0**
1966-67	**Toronto Maple Leafs**	**NHL**	**61**	**14**	**24**	**38**	**17**	**25**	**42**	**4**	**12**	**0**	**5**	**5**	**2**
1967-68	**Los Angeles Kings**	**NHL**	DID NOT PLAY – COACHING												
	NHL Totals		**1316**	**281**	**542**	**823**	**376**	**639**	**1015**	**327**	**164**	**33**	**59**	**92**	**51**

NHL Second All-Star Team (1950, 1956) • NHL First All-Star Team (1951, 1952, 1953, 1954, 1955, 1957) • Won Lady Byng Trophy (1951, 1953, 1954, 1961) • Won James Norris Trophy (1954)

Played in NHL All-Star Game (1950, 1951, 1952, 1953, 1954, 1955, 1956, 1957, 1958, 1960, 1961, 1962, 1963)

Traded to **NY Rangers** by **Detroit** with Billy McNeil for Bill Gadsby and Eddie Shack, February 5, 1960. • Transaction cancelled after Kelly refused to report, February 7, 1960. Traded to **Toronto** by **Detroit** for Marc Reaume, February 10, 1960. Rights traded to **LA Kings** by **Toronto** for Ken Block, June 8, 1967.

• KELLY, REGIS

Regis "Pep" Kelly
RW – R. 5'7", 152 lbs. b: North Bay, Ont., 1/17/1914. Deceased.

			REGULAR SEASON								PLAYOFFS				
Season	Club	League	GP	G	A	Pts	AG	AA	APts	PIM	GP	G	A	Pts	PIM
1932-33	Newmarket Redmen	OHA	17	14	5	19	....	....	....	....	19	*13	3	*16	16
1933-34	St. Michael's Majors	OHA	11	13	8	21	....	....	....	12	3	3	1	4	*15
1934-35	**Toronto Maple Leafs**	**NHL**	**47**	**11**	**8**	**19**	**23**	**18**	**41**	**14**	**7**	**2**	**0**	**2**	**4**
	Syracuse Stars	IAHL	1	0	0	0	....	....	....	0	....	....	....	....	....
1935-36	**Toronto Maple Leafs**	**NHL**	**42**	**11**	**8**	**19**	**27**	**19**	**46**	**24**	**9**	**2**	**3**	**5**	**4**
1936-37	**Toronto Maple Leafs**	**NHL**	**16**	**2**	**0**	**2**	**4**	**0**	**4**	**8**	....	....	....	....	....
	Chicago Black Hawks	**NHL**	**29**	**13**	**4**	**17**	**28**	**9**	**37**	**0**	....	....	....	....	....
1937-38	**Toronto Maple Leafs**	**NHL**	**43**	**9**	**10**	**19**	**19**	**21**	**40**	**25**	**7**	**2**	**2**	**4**	**2**
1938-39	**Toronto Maple Leafs**	**NHL**	**48**	**11**	**11**	**22**	**23**	**20**	**43**	**12**	**9**	**1**	**0**	**1**	**0**
1939-40	**Toronto Maple Leafs**	**NHL**	**34**	**11**	**9**	**20**	**24**	**18**	**42**	**15**	**6**	**0**	**1**	**1**	**0**
1940-41	**Chicago Black Hawks**	**NHL**	**21**	**5**	**3**	**8**	**10**	**5**	**15**	**7**	....	....	....	....	....
	Providence Reds	AHL	16	5	7	12	....	....	....	0	....	....	....	....	....
1941-42	**Brooklyn Americans**	**NHL**	**8**	**1**	**0**	**1**	**2**	**0**	**2**	**0**	....	....	....	....	....
	Buffalo–Springfield	AHL	52	17	24	41	....	....	....	5	....	....	....	....	....
1942-43	Pittsburgh Hornets	AHL	50	12	12	24	....	....	....	3	2	0	2	2	0
1943-44	Sudbury Open Pit Mines	NOHA	6	3	1	4	....	....	....	2	....	....	....	....	....
1944-45	Sudbury Open Pit Mines	NOHA	4	5	2	7	....	....	....	0	4	1	1	2	2
	Powassen Hawks	NOHA	....	7	3	10	....	....	....	....	....	....	....	....	....
	NHL Totals		**288**	**74**	**53**	**127**	**160**	**110**	**270**	**105**	**38**	**7**	**6**	**13**	**10**

Loaned to **Chicago** by **Toronto** for remainder of 1936-37 season for loan of Bill Kendall, December 29, 1936. Traded to **Chicago** by **Toronto** for cash, May 10, 1940. Traded to **Buffalo** (AHL) by **Chicago** for cash, October, 1941. Traded to **NY Americans** by **Buffalo** (AHL) for cash, October 19, 1941.

• KEMP, STAN

Stan "Bud" Kemp
D – R. 5'9", 165 lbs. b: Hamilton, Ont., 3/2/1924.

			REGULAR SEASON								PLAYOFFS				
Season	Club	League	GP	G	A	Pts	AG	AA	APts	PIM	GP	G	A	Pts	PIM
1942-43	Hamilton Whizzers	OHA	24	11	9	20	....	....	....	17	5	1	1	2	8
1943-44	Providence Reds	AHL	47	3	8	11	....	....	....	43	....	....	....	....	....
1944-45	Providence Reds	AHL	57	16	40	56	....	....	....	37	....	....	....	....	....
1945-46	Providence Reds	AHL	49	12	16	28	....	....	....	30	2	0	1	1	0
1946-47	Pittsburgh Hornets	AHL	64	3	11	14	....	....	....	64	12	1	0	1	13
1947-48	Pittsburgh Hornets	AHL	68	10	20	30	....	....	....	93	2	0	1	1	2
1948-49	**Toronto Maple Leafs**	**NHL**	**1**	**0**	**0**	**0**	**0**	**0**	**0**	**2**	....	....	....	....	....
	Pittsburgh Hornets	AHL	68	13	34	47	....	....	....	90	....	....	....	....	....
1949-50	Pittsburgh Hornets	AHL	70	11	17	28	....	....	....	82	....	....	....	....	....
1950-51	Hamilton Tigers	OHA Sr.	2	0	0	0	....	....	....	0	....	....	....	....	....
	Toronto Marlboros	OHA Sr.	22	3	8	11	....	....	....	46	3	0	0	0	6
1951-52	Hamilton–Brantford	OHA Sr.	48	9	22	31	....	....	....	95	7	0	2	2	14
1952-53	Brantford Redmen	OHA Sr.	48	6	20	26	....	....	....	73	5	1	3	4	10
1953-54	Hamilton Tigers	OHA Sr.	44	8	28	36	....	....	....	74	2	0	0	0	0
1954-55	Kitchener Dutchmen	OHA Sr.	49	15	17	32	....	....	....	74	10	1	3	4	18
1955-56	Stratford Indians	OHA Sr.	7	2	6	8	....	....	....	50	....	....	....	....	....
	Kitchener Dutchmen	OHA Sr.	44	5	22	27	....	....	....	0	10	3	2	5	16
1956-57	Stratford Indians	OHA Sr.	36	9	15	24	....	....	....	24	5	1	3	4	4
	NHL Totals		**1**	**0**	**0**	**0**	**0**	**0**	**0**	**2**	....	....	....	....	....

AHL Second All-Star Team (1949)

• KENDALL, BILL

Bill "Cowboy" Kendall
RW – R. 5'8", 168 lbs. b: Winnipeg, Man., 4/1/1910. Deceased.

			REGULAR SEASON								PLAYOFFS				
Season	Club	League	GP	G	A	Pts	AG	AA	APts	PIM	GP	G	A	Pts	PIM
1928-29	Winnipeg Elmwoods	City Jr.	5	1	0	1	....	....	....	0	3	0	0	0	0
1929-30	Winnipeg Elmwoods	City Jr.	8	6	1	7	....	....	....	4	2	0	1	1	4
1930-31	Winnipeg Elmwoods	MHL Sr.	3	1	0	1	....	....	....	0	....	....	....	....	....
	St. Louis Flyers	AHA	23	5	2	7	....	....	....	8	....	....	....	....	....
1931-32	St. Louis Flyers	AHA	47	4	4	8	....	....	....	41	....	....	....	....	....
1932-33	Wichita–Duluth	AHA	41	10	6	16	....	....	....	12	....	....	....	....	....
1933-34	**Chicago Black Hawks**	**NHL**	**21**	**3**	**0**	**3**	**7**	**0**	**7**	**0**	**2**	**0**	**0**	**0**	**0**
	London Tecumsehs	IAHL	26	5	6	11	....	....	....	10	6	0	4	4	4
1934-35	**Chicago Black Hawks**	**NHL**	**47**	**6**	**4**	**10**	**13**	**9**	**22**	**16**	**2**	**0**	**0**	**0**	**0**
1935-36	**Chicago Black Hawks**	**NHL**	**22**	**2**	**1**	**3**	**5**	**2**	**7**	**0**	**2**	**0**	**0**	**0**	**0**
	London Tecumsehs	IAHL	22	9	4	13	....	....	....	12	....	....	....	....	....
1936-37	**Chicago Black Hawks**	**NHL**	**17**	**3**	**0**	**3**	**6**	**0**	**6**	**6**	....	....	....	....	....
	Toronto Maple Leafs	**NHL**	**15**	**2**	**4**	**6**	**4**	**9**	**13**	**4**	....	....	....	....	....
1937-38	**Chicago Black Hawks**	**NHL**	**9**	**0**	**1**	**1**	**0**	**2**	**2**	**2**	....	....	....	....	....
	St. Louis Flyers	AHA	39	17	10	27	....	....	....	24	7	2	1	3	2
1938-39	St. Louis Flyers	AHA	48	27	27	54	....	....	....	47	7	3	4	7	5
1939-40	St. Louis Flyers	AHA	48	30	30	60	....	....	....	30	5	1	1	2	2
1940-41	St. Louis Flyers	AHA	30	23	12	35	....	....	....	11	9	1	2	3	4
1941-42	St. Louis Flyers	AHA	50	13	8	21	....	....	....	17	3	0	1	1	0
1942-43			MILITARY SERVICE												
1943-44			MILITARY SERVICE												
1944-45	St. Louis Flyers	AHL	60	15	31	46	....	....	....	4	....	....	....	....	....
1945-46	St. Louis Flyers	AHL	27	2	6	8	....	....	....	0	....	....	....	....	....
	NHL Totals		**131**	**16**	**10**	**26**	**35**	**22**	**57**	**28**	**6**	**0**	**0**	**0**	**0**

Traded to **London** (IAHL) by **Chicago** with $3000 for Leroy Goldsworthy, January 4, 1934. Traded to **Chicago** by **London** (IAHL) for the loan of Norm Locking, January 23, 1936. Loaned to **Toronto** by **Chicago** for remainder of 1936-37 season for loan of Regis Kelly, December 29, 1936.

• KENNEDY, FORBES — see page 1165

• KENNEDY, TED

Ted "Teeder" Kennedy **HHOF**
C – R. 5'11", 175 lbs. b: Humberstone, Ont., 12/12/1925.

			REGULAR SEASON								PLAYOFFS				
Season	Club	League	GP	G	A	Pts	AG	AA	APts	PIM	GP	G	A	Pts	PIM
1942-43	Port Colborne Sailors	OHA Sr.	23	23	*29	52	....	....	....	15	....	....	....	....	....
	Toronto Maple Leafs	**NHL**	**2**	**0**	**1**	**1**	**0**	**1**	**1**	**0**	....	....	....	....	....
1943-44	**Toronto Maple Leafs**	**NHL**	**49**	**26**	**23**	**49**	**33**	**28**	**61**	**2**	**5**	**1**	**1**	**2**	**4**
1944-45	**Toronto Maple Leafs**	**NHL**	**49**	**29**	**25**	**54**	**40**	**41**	**81**	**14**	**13**	***7**	**2**	**9**	**2**
1945-46	**Toronto Maple Leafs**	**NHL**	**21**	**3**	**2**	**5**	**5**	**4**	**9**	**4**	....	....	....	....	....
1946-47	**Toronto Maple Leafs**	**NHL**	**60**	**28**	**32**	**60**	**38**	**46**	**84**	**27**	**11**	**4**	**5**	**9**	**4**
1947-48	**Toronto Maple Leafs**	**NHL**	**60**	**25**	**21**	**46**	**37**	**31**	**68**	**32**	**9**	**8**	**6**	**14**	**0**
1948-49	**Toronto Maple Leafs**	**NHL**	**59**	**18**	**21**	**39**	**28**	**33**	**61**	**25**	**9**	**2**	***6**	**8**	**2**
1949-50	**Toronto Maple Leafs**	**NHL**	**53**	**20**	**24**	**44**	**27**	**31**	**58**	**34**	**7**	**1**	**2**	**3**	**8**
1950-51	**Toronto Maple Leafs**	**NHL**	**63**	**18**	***43**	**61**	**24**	**56**	**80**	**32**	**11**	**4**	**5**	**9**	**6**
1951-52	**Toronto Maple Leafs**	**NHL**	**70**	**19**	**33**	**52**	**27**	**43**	**70**	**33**	**4**	**0**	**0**	**0**	**4**
1952-53	**Toronto Maple Leafs**	**NHL**	**43**	**14**	**23**	**37**	**21**	**32**	**53**	**42**	....	....	....	....	....
1953-54	**Toronto Maple Leafs**	**NHL**	**67**	**15**	**23**	**38**	**23**	**31**	**54**	**78**	**5**	**1**	**1**	**2**	**2**
1954-55	**Toronto Maple Leafs**	**NHL**	**70**	**10**	**42**	**52**	**14**	**55**	**69**	**74**	**4**	**1**	**3**	**4**	**0**
1955-56			DID NOT PLAY – RETIRED												
1956-57	**Toronto Maple Leafs**	**NHL**	**30**	**6**	**16**	**22**	**8**	**19**	**27**	**35**	....	....	....	....	....
1957-58	Peterborough Petes	OHA	DID NOT PLAY – COACHING												
	NHL Totals		**696**	**231**	**329**	**560**	**325**	**451**	**776**	**432**	**78**	**29**	**31**	**60**	**32**

NHL Second All-Star Team (1950, 1951, 1954) • Won Hart Trophy (1955)

Played in NHL All-Star Game (1947, 1948, 1949, 1950, 1951, 1954)

Rights traded to **Toronto** by **Montreal** for rights to Frank Eddolls, March 6, 1943.

• KENNY, ERNEST

Ernest "Eddie" Kenny
D – L. 6'2", 195 lbs. b: Vermilion, Alta., 8/20/1907. d: 6/2/1970.

			REGULAR SEASON								PLAYOFFS				
Season	Club	League	GP	G	A	Pts	AG	AA	APts	PIM	GP	G	A	Pts	PIM
1927-28	Edmonton Elks	City Sr.	STATISTICS NOT AVAILABLE												
1928-29	Victoria Cubs	NWHL	35	1	3	4	....	....	....	96	....	....	....	....	....
1929-30	Victoria Cubs	PCHL	36	5	0	5	....	....	....	116	....	....	....	....	....
1930-31	Detroit Olympics	IAHL	17	0	0	0	....	....	....	54	....	....	....	....	....
	Tacoma Tigers	PCHL	10	0	0	0	....	....	....	48	....	....	....	....	....
	New York Rangers	**NHL**	**6**	**0**	**0**	**0**	**0**	**0**	**0**	**0**	....	....	....	....	....
1931-32	Portland Pirates	City Sr.	STATISTICS NOT AVAILABLE												
1932-33	Edmonton Eskimos	WCHL	28	7	6	13	....	....	....	94	8	3	0	3	18
1933-34	Edmonton Eskimos	NWHL	34	13	10	23	....	....	....	91	2	0	0	0	*10
1934-35	**Chicago Black Hawks**	**NHL**	**4**	**0**	**0**	**0**	**0**	**0**	**0**	**18**	....	....	....	....	....
	London–Windsor	IAHL	39	4	4	8	....	....	....	54	5	0	0	0	4
1935-36	London Tecumsehs	IAHL	46	2	4	6	....	....	....	85	2	0	0	0	2
1936-37	Oakland–Spokane	PCHL	39	4	2	6	....	....	....	86	6	0	0	0	*17
1937-38	Spokane Clippers	PCHL	41	9	5	14	....	....	....	94	....	....	....	....	....
1938-39	Spokane Clippers	PCHL	48	9	13	22	....	....	....	70	....	....	....	....	....
1939-40	Seattle Seahawks	PCHL	39	3	9	12	....	....	....	57	....	....	....	....	....
	NHL Totals		**10**	**0**	**0**	**0**	**0**	**0**	**0**	**18**	....	....	....	....	....

Traded to **NY Rangers** by **Tacoma** (PCHL) for cash, January 3, 1931. Traded to **Chicago** by **Edmonton** (NWHL) for cash, October 22, 1934.

• KEON, DAVE — see page 1166

• KILREA, BRIAN — see page 1170

• KILREA, HEC

Hec "Hurricane" Kilrea
LW – L. 5'8", 175 lbs. b: Blackburn, Ont., 6/11/1907. d: 10/8/1969.

			REGULAR SEASON								PLAYOFFS				
Season	Club	League	GP	G	A	Pts	AG	AA	APts	PIM	GP	G	A	Pts	PIM
1924-25	Ottawa Rideaus	City Sr.	16	5	*4	9	....	....	....	....	3	0	0	0	0
1925-26	**Ottawa Senators**	**NHL**	**35**	**5**	**0**	**5**	**15**	**0**	**15**	**12**	**2**	**0**	**0**	**0**	**0**
1926-27	**Ottawa Senators**	**NHL**	**42**	**11**	**7**	**18**	**32**	**60**	**92**	**48**	**6**	**1**	**1**	**2**	**4**
1927-28	**Ottawa Senators**	**NHL**	**43**	**19**	**4**	**23**	**59**	**34**	**93**	**66**	**2**	**1**	**0**	**1**	**0**
1928-29	**Ottawa Senators**	**NHL**	**38**	**5**	**7**	**12**	**20**	**65**	**85**	**36**	....	....	....	....	....
1929-30	**Ottawa Senators**	**NHL**	**44**	**36**	**22**	**58**	**72**	**72**	**144**	**72**	**2**	**0**	**0**	**0**	**4**
1930-31	**Ottawa Senators**	**NHL**	**44**	**14**	**8**	**22**	**34**	**29**	**63**	**44**	....	....	....	....	....
1931-32	**Detroit Falcons**	**NHL**	**47**	**13**	**3**	**16**	**28**	**8**	**36**	**28**	**2**	**0**	**0**	**0**	**0**
1932-33	**Ottawa Senators**	**NHL**	**47**	**14**	**8**	**22**	**33**	**21**	**54**	**26**	....	....	....	....	....
1933-34	**Toronto Maple Leafs**	**NHL**	**43**	**10**	**13**	**23**	**22**	**35**	**57**	**15**	**5**	**2**	**0**	**2**	**2**
1934-35	**Toronto Maple Leafs**	**NHL**	**46**	**11**	**13**	**24**	**23**	**29**	**52**	**16**	**6**	**0**	**0**	**0**	**4**
1935-36	**Detroit Red Wings**	**NHL**	**48**	**6**	**17**	**23**	**15**	**41**	**56**	**37**	**7**	**0**	**3**	**3**	**2**
1936-37	**Detroit Red Wings**	**NHL**	**48**	**6**	**9**	**15**	**13**	**21**	**34**	**20**	**10**	**3**	**1**	**4**	**2**
1937-38	**Detroit Red Wings**	**NHL**	**48**	**9**	**9**	**18**	**19**	**18**	**37**	**10**	....	....	....	....	....
1938-39	**Detroit Red Wings**	**NHL**	**48**	**8**	**9**	**17**	**17**	**17**	**34**	**8**	**6**	**1**	**2**	**3**	**0**
1939-40	**Detroit Red Wings**	**NHL**	**12**	**0**	**0**	**0**	**0**	**0**	**0**	**0**	....	....	....	....	....
	Indianapolis Capitols	AHL	41	6	21	27	....	....	....	6	5	0	1	1	9
1940-41	Indianapolis Capitals	AHL	46	5	9	14	....	....	....	6	....	....	....	....	....
1941-42	Indianapolis Capitals	AHL	56	13	10	23	....	....	....	15	10	0	0	0	6
1942-43	Indianapolis Capitals	AHL	55	9	10	19	....	....	....	11	7	2	1	3	2
	NHL Totals		**633**	**167**	**129**	**296**	**402**	**450**	**852**	**438**	**48**	**8**	**7**	**15**	**18**

Played in NHL All-Star Game (1934)

Signed as a free agent by **Ottawa**, November 12, 1925. Claimed by **Detroit Falcons** from **Ottawa** for 1931-32 season in Dispersal Draft, September 26, 1931. Traded to **Toronto** by **Ottawa** for cash, June, 1933. Traded to **Detroit** by **Toronto** for $7,000 and future considerations (Knucker Irvine, October, 1935), September 29, 1935.

● KILREA, KEN

Ken Kilrea
LW – L. 6', 170 lbs. b: Ottawa, Ont., 1/16/1919. d: 1/14/1990.

			REGULAR SEASON								PLAYOFFS				
Season	Club	League	GP	G	A	Pts	AG	AA	APts	PIM	GP	G	A	Pts	PIM
1935-36	University of Ottawa	OHA	9	*18	7	*25	....	....	....	9	7	*8	5	*13	14
1936-37	Detroit Pontiacs	MOHL	25	13	10	23	....	....	....	8	5	1	2	3	0
1937-38	Detroit Pontiacs	MOHL	28	*25	19	*44	....	....	....	4	3	0	2	2	2
1938-39	**Detroit Red Wings**	**NHL**	**1**	**0**	**0**	**0**	**0**	**0**	**0**	**0**	**3**	**1**	**1**	**2**	**4**
	Pittsburgh Hornets	AHL	51	14	28	42	....	....	....	21	....	....	....	....	....
1939-40	**Detroit Red Wings**	**NHL**	**40**	**10**	**8**	**18**	**21**	**16**	**37**	**4**	**5**	**1**	**1**	**2**	**0**
	Indianapolis Capitals	AHL	11	4	15	19	....	....	....	2	....	....	....	....	....
1940-41	**Detroit Red Wings**	**NHL**	**15**	**2**	**0**	**2**	**4**	**0**	**4**	**0**	**5**	**0**	**0**	**0**	**0**
	Indianapolis Capitals	AHL	34	9	18	27	....	....	....	7	....	....	....	....	....
1941-42	**Detroit Red Wings**	**NHL**	**21**	**3**	**12**	**15**	**5**	**18**	**23**	**4**	....	....	....	....	....
	Indianapolis Capitals	AHL	27	15	29	44	....	....	....	8	10	1	8	9	2
1942-43	Ottawa Commandos	QSHL	20	12	18	30	....	....	....	6	20	10	11	21	18
	Ottawa Canadians	City Sr.	2	1	3	4	....	....	....	0	....	....	....	....	....
	Ottawa Royal Canadians	City Sr.	11	23	*21	*44	....	....	....	0	....	....	....	....	....
1943-44	**Detroit Red Wings**	**NHL**	**14**	**1**	**3**	**4**	**1**	**4**	**5**	**0**	**2**	**0**	**0**	**0**	**0**
	Indianapolis Capitals	AHL	6	1	2	3	....	....	....	0	2	0	0	0	0
1944-45	Buffalo Bisons	AHL	51	19	46	65	....	....	....	14	6	3	*8	11	7
1945-46	New Haven Eagles	AHL	45	13	24	37	....	....	....	23	....	....	....	....	....
	Fort Worth Rangers	USHL	14	1	11	12	....	....	....	2	....	....	....	....	....
1946-47	Springfield Indians	AHL	14	3	1	4	....	....	....	2	....	....	....	....	....
	Fort Worth Rangers	USHL	33	18	21	39	....	....	....	16	9	2	6	8	2
1947-48	Philadelphia Rockets	AHL	63	15	35	50	....	....	....	20	....	....	....	....	....
1948-49	Philadelphia Rockets	AHL	64	15	8	43	....	....	....	32	....	....	....	....	....
1949-50	Ottawa Army	City Sr.	40	28	22	50	....	....	....	20	3	5	2	7	5
	Grand Rapids Rockets	IHL	4	2	1	3	....	....	....	0	8	3	8	11	4
1950-51	Ottawa Army	City Sr.	32	16	28	44	....	....	....	16	3	6	2	8	2
	Johnstown Jets	EHL	1	0	0	0	....	....	....	10	6	3	4	7	2
	NHL Totals		**91**	**16**	**23**	**39**	**31**	**38**	**69**	**8**	**15**	**2**	**2**	**4**	**4**

Signed as a free agent by **Detroit**, March 18, 1938.

● KILREA, WALLY

Wally Kilrea
RW/C – R. 5'7", 150 lbs. b: Ottawa, Ont., 2/18/1909.

			REGULAR SEASON								PLAYOFFS				
Season	Club	League	GP	G	A	Pts	AG	AA	APts	PIM	GP	G	A	Pts	PIM
1927-28	Ottawa Montagnards	City Sr.	15	5	3	8	....	....	....	....	6	1	1	2	....
1928-29	Ottawa Montagnards	City Sr.	12	5	*8	*13	....	....	....	....	....	....	....	....	....
1929-30	**Ottawa Senators**	**NHL**	**38**	**4**	**2**	**6**	**8**	**6**	**14**	**4**	**2**	**0**	**0**	**0**	**0**
	London Panthers	IAHL	3	0	0	0	....	....	....	0	....	....	....	....	....
1930-31	**Philadelphia Quakers**	**NHL**	**44**	**8**	**12**	**20**	**19**	**44**	**63**	**22**	....	....	....	....	....
1931-32	**New York Americans**	**NHL**	**48**	**3**	**8**	**11**	**6**	**22**	**28**	**18**	....	....	....	....	....
1932-33	**Ottawa Senators**	**NHL**	**32**	**4**	**5**	**9**	**9**	**13**	**22**	**14**	....	....	....	....	....
	Montreal Maroons	**NHL**	**19**	**1**	**7**	**8**	**2**	**18**	**20**	**2**	**2**	**0**	**0**	**0**	**0**
1933-34	**Montreal Maroons**	**NHL**	**45**	**3**	**1**	**4**	**7**	**3**	**10**	**7**	**4**	**0**	**0**	**0**	**0**
	Windsor Bulldogs	IAHL	3	0	0	0	....	....	....	2	....	....	....	....	....
1934-35	**Detroit Red Wings**	**NHL**	**3**	**0**	**0**	**0**	**0**	**0**	**0**	**0**	....	....	....	....	....
	Detroit Olympics	IAHL	33	11	16	27	....	....	....	23	5	1	*4	5	0
1935-36	**Detroit Red Wings**	**NHL**	**48**	**4**	**10**	**14**	**10**	**24**	**34**	**10**	**7**	**2**	**2**	**4**	**2**
	Detroit Olympics	IAHL	3	4	2	6	....	....	....	0	....	....	....	....	....
1936-37	**Detroit Red Wings**	**NHL**	**47**	**8**	**13**	**21**	**17**	**31**	**48**	**6**	**10**	**0**	**2**	**2**	**4**
1937-38	**Detroit Red Wings**	**NHL**	**5**	**0**	**0**	**0**	**0**	**0**	**0**	**4**	....	....	....	....	....
	Pittsburgh Hornets	AHL	44	6	11	17	....	....	....	28	2	0	0	0	0
1938-39	Hershey Bears	AHL	42	17	31	48	....	....	....	35	5	5	2	7	5
1939-40	Hershey Bears	AHL	56	12	29	41	....	....	....	18	10	2	5	7	4
1940-41	Hershey Bears	AHL	55	17	37	54	....	....	....	0	10	1	3	4	4
1941-42	Hershey Bears	AHL	56	12	35	47	....	....	....	14	10	4	2	6	2
1942-43	Hershey Bears	AHL	56	31	*68	*99	....	....	....	8	4	0	0	0	0
1943-44	Hershey Bears	AHL	33	15	30	45	....	....	....	8	....	....	....	....	....
	NHL Totals		**329**	**35**	**58**	**93**	**78**	**161**	**239**	**87**	**25**	**2**	**4**	**6**	**6**

AHL First All-Star Team (1943)

Loaned to **Philadelphia Quakers** by **Ottawa** for 1930-31 season, September, 1930. Claimed by **NY Americans** from **Ottawa** for 1931-32 season in Dispersal Draft, September 26, 1931. Traded to **Montreal Maroons** by **Ottawa** for cash, February, 1933. Traded to **Detroit** by **Montreal Maroons** for Gus Marker, September 23, 1934. Traded to **Hershey** (AHL) by **Detroit** for cash, June 23, 1938.

● KING, FRANK

Frank King
C – L. 5'11", 185 lbs. b: Toronto, Ont., 3/7/1929.

			REGULAR SEASON								PLAYOFFS				
Season	Club	League	GP	G	A	Pts	AG	AA	APts	PIM	GP	G	A	Pts	PIM
1947-48	Brandon Wheat Kings	MJHL	22	13	8	21	....	....	....	31	5	4	0	4	10
1948-49	Brandon Wheat Kings	MJHL	30	27	14	41	....	....	....	*78	25	*22	9	*31	11
1949-50	Minneapolis Millers	USHL	70	34	30	64	....	....	....	49	7	5	4	9	10
1950-51	**Montreal Canadiens**	**NHL**	**10**	**1**	**0**	**1**	**1**	**0**	**1**	**2**	....	....	....	....	....
	Cincinnati–Providence	AHL	42	8	18	26	....	....	....	36	....	....	....	....	....
	Seattle Ironmen	PCHL	3	1	1	2	....	....	....	3	....	....	....	....	....
1951-52	Quebec Aces	QSHL	36	4	4	8	....	....	....	24	8	1	1	2	10
1952-53	Halifax Atlantics	MMHL	72	38	40	78	....	....	....	92	15	7	8	15	31
1953-54	Sudbury Wolves	NOHA	45	14	11	25	....	....	....	26	1	0	0	0	0
1954-55	Vernon Canadians	OSHL	50	22	27	49	....	....	....	121	5	1	3	4	0
1955-56	Vernon Canadians	OSHL	56	40	34	74	....	....	....	115	....	....	....	....	....
1956-57	Vernon Canadians	OSHL	50	17	33	50	....	....	....	90	12	7	*13	*20	18
1957-58	Vernon Canadians	OSHL	54	38	29	67	....	....	....	111	4	1	1	2	13
1958-59	Vernon Canadians	OSHL	52	23	28	51	....	....	....	....	....	....	....	....	....
1959-60	Vernon Canadians	OSHL	12	11	8	19	....	....	....	2	13	11	9	20	24
	NHL Totals		**10**	**1**	**0**	**1**	**1**	**0**	**1**	**2**	....	....	....	....	....

● KINSELLA, RAY

Ray Kinsella
LW – L. 5'10", 162 lbs. b: Ottawa, Ont., 1/27/1911. d: 4/29/1996.

			REGULAR SEASON								PLAYOFFS				
Season	Club	League	GP	G	A	Pts	AG	AA	APts	PIM	GP	G	A	Pts	PIM
1928-29	Ottawa Post Office	City Sr.	STATISTICS NOT AVAILABLE												
	Ottawa CPR	City Sr.	STATISTICS NOT AVAILABLE												
1929-30	Ottawa Shamrocks	City Sr.	15	0	1	1	....	....	....	10	6	2	0	2	2
1930-31	**Ottawa Senators**	**NHL**	**14**	**0**	**0**	**0**	**0**	**0**	**0**	**0**	....	....	....	....	....
	Ottawa Rideaus	City Sr.	18	3	4	7	....	....	....	34	....	....	....	....	....
1931-32	Philadelphia Arrows	Can-Am	31	8	3	11	....	....	....	12	....	....	....	....	....
1932-33	Quebec–New Haven	Can-Am	32	5	5	10	....	....	....	22	....	....	....	....	....
1933-34	New Haven Eagles	Can-Am	40	6	15	21	....	....	....	15	....	....	....	....	....
1934-35	London Tecumsehs	IAHL	7	0	2	2	....	....	....	5	....	....	....	....	....
	Tulsa Oilers	AHA	43	11	16	27	....	....	....	27	5	0	0	0	0
1935-36			DID NOT PLAY – INJURED												
1936-37	Ottawa Senators	QSHL	19	7	7	14	....	....	....	7	....	....	....	....	....
1937-38	Ottawa Montagnards	City Sr.	17	2	9	11	....	....	....	12	....	....	....	....	....
	NHL Totals		**14**	**0**	**0**	**0**	**0**	**0**	**0**	**0**	....	....	....	....	....

● KIRK, BOBBY

Bobby "Cagey" Kirk
RW – R. 5'9", 180 lbs. b: Dough Grange, Ireland, 8/8/1909. d: 7/11/1970.

			REGULAR SEASON								PLAYOFFS				
Season	Club	League	GP	G	A	Pts	AG	AA	APts	PIM	GP	G	A	Pts	PIM
1927-28	Elmwood Millionairews	City Jr.	1	0	0	0	....	....	....	0	....	....	....	....	....
1928-29	Winnipeg Elmwoods	City Jr.	8	6	1	7	....	....	....	....	3	0	1	1	4
	Winnipeg CNR	MHL Sr.	5	0	1	1	....	....	....	4	....	....	....	....	....
1929-30	Winnipeg Elmwoods	City Jr.	5	*8	1	9	....	....	....	12	....	....	....	....	....
1930-31	Elmwood Millionaires	MHL Sr.	3	0	0	0	....	....	....	0	....	....	....	....	....
	St. Louis Flyers	AHA	32	9	3	12	....	....	....	12	....	....	....	....	....
1931-32	St. Louis Flyers	AHA	39	1	4	5	....	....	....	16	....	....	....	....	....
1932-33	Regina–Vancouver	WCJHL	29	10	2	12	....	....	....	14	2	0	0	0	0
1933-34	Vancouver Lions	NWHL	34	9	2	11	....	....	....	28	7	3	0	3	4
1934-35	Vancouver Lions	NWHL	32	*25	8	33	....	....	....	28	8	4	2	6	8
1935-36	Philadelphia Arrows	Can-Am	48	22	*29	*51	....	....	....	16	4	0	1	1	0
1936-37	Philadelphia Ramblers	AHL	34	7	15	22	....	....	....	8	6	2	1	3	0
1937-38	**New York Rangers**	**NHL**	**39**	**4**	**8**	**12**	**8**	**16**	**24**	**14**	....	....	....	....	....
	Philadelphia Ramblers	AHL	11	7	1	8	....	....	....	4	5	1	2	3	2
1938-39	Philadelphia Ramblers	AHL	49	14	36	50	....	....	....	12	9	2	6	8	2
1939-40	Philadelphia–Hershey	AHL	54	16	16	32	....	....	....	6	6	0	1	1	4
1940-41	Hershey Bears	AHL	52	19	26	45	....	....	....	6	10	*4	2	6	4
1941-42	Hershey Bears	AHL	57	17	29	46	....	....	....	18	10	1	4	5	0
1942-43	Vancouver RCAF	City Sr.	11	9	11	20	....	....	....	4	....	....	....	....	....
	NHL Totals		**39**	**4**	**8**	**12**	**8**	**16**	**24**	**14**	....	....	....	....	....

Can-Am First All-Star Team (1936)

Claimed by **NY Rangers** from **Vancouver** (PCHL) in Inter-League Draft, May 11, 1935.

● KIRKPATRICK, BOB

Bob Kirkpatrick
C – L. 5'10", 165 lbs. b: Regina, Sask., 12/1/1915.

			REGULAR SEASON								PLAYOFFS				
Season	Club	League	GP	G	A	Pts	AG	AA	APts	PIM	GP	G	A	Pts	PIM
1933-34	Regina Pats	SJHL	....	....	....	....	....	....	....	....	4	1	0	1	4
1934-35	Regina Aces	SSHL	19	5	6	11	....	....	....	6	3	0	0	0	4
1935-36	Prince Albert Mintos	SSHL	16	13	3	16	....	....	....	23	9	4	*2	6	4
1936-37	Earls Court Royals	Britain	....	30	21	51	....	....	....	26	....	....	....	....	....
1937-38	Lethbridge Maple Leafs	ASHL	23	23	17	40	....	....	....	16	2	1	2	3	2
1938-39	Lethbridge Maple Leafs	ASHL	31	21	*36	*57	....	....	....	36	10	*9	*10	*19	7
1939-40	Lethbridge Maple Leafs	ASHL	22	14	15	29	....	....	....	6	2	0	3	3	0
1940-41	Lethbridge Maple Leafs	ASHL	32	14	10	24	....	....	....	6	3	4	2	6	0
1941-42	New York Rovers	EHL	59	34	43	77	....	....	....	26	7	4	5	9	5
1942-43	**New York Rangers**	**NHL**	**49**	**12**	**12**	**24**	**17**	**15**	**32**	**6**	....	....	....	....	....
1943-44	Winnipeg Army	City Sr.	10	6	6	12	....	....	....	4	....	....	....	....	....
1944-45	Winnipeg Army	City Sr.	3	2	1	3	....	....	....	0	....	....	....	....	....
1945-46	St. Paul Saints	USHL	47	14	33	47	....	....	....	2	6	1	3	4	2
1946-47	St. Paul Saints	USHL	52	15	22	37	....	....	....	8	....	....	....	....	....
1947-48	Lethbridge Maple Leafs	ASHL	43	13	30	43	....	....	....	26	5	1	1	2	0
1948-49	Lethbridge Maple Leafs	ASHL	48	17	26	43	....	....	....	8	3	1	1	2	4
	NHL Totals		**49**	**12**	**12**	**24**	**17**	**15**	**32**	**6**	....	....	....	....	....

EHL Second All-Star Team (1942)

● KITCHEN, HOBIE

Hobie (Hobart Cleveland) Kitchen
D – L. 5'11", 187 lbs. b: Toronto, Ont., 2/0/1904. Deceased.

			REGULAR SEASON								PLAYOFFS				
Season	Club	League	GP	G	A	Pts	AG	AA	APts	PIM	GP	G	A	Pts	PIM
1921-22	Toronto Aura Lee	OHA	2	0	0	0	....	....	....	0	....	....	....	....	....
1922-23	Toronto Aura Lee	OHA	2	0	0	0	....	....	....	0	....	....	....	....	....
1923-24	Toronto St. Mary's	OHA Sr.	8	5	0	5	....	....	....	15	....	....	....	....	....
1924-25	Niagara Falls Cataracts	OHA Sr.	20	21	2	23	....	....	....	25	10	5	2	7	14
1925-26	**Montreal Maroons**	**NHL**	**30**	**5**	**2**	**7**	**15**	**23**	**38**	**16**	....	....	....	....	....
1926-27	**Detroit Cougars**	**NHL**	**17**	**0**	**2**	**2**	**0**	**17**	**17**	**42**	....	....	....	....	....
	New Haven Eagles	Can-Am	6	0	0	0	....	....	....	10	....	....	....	....	....
1927-28	Kitchener Millionaires	Can-Pro	9	0	0	0	....	....	....	40	....	....	....	....	....
1928-29	Niagara Falls Cataracts	Can-Pro	6	0	0	0	....	....	....	6	....	....	....	....	....
	NHL Totals		**47**	**5**	**4**	**9**	**15**	**40**	**55**	**58**	....	....	....	....	....

Signed as a free agent by **Montreal Maroons**, April 10, 1925. Signed as a free agent by **Detroit Cougars**, October 27, 1926.

● KLEIN, JIM

Jim "Dede" Klein
LW – L. 6', 185 lbs. b: Saskatoon, Sask., 1/13/1910. Deceased.

			REGULAR SEASON								PLAYOFFS				
Season	Club	League	GP	G	A	Pts	AG	AA	APts	PIM	GP	G	A	Pts	PIM
1924-25	Saskatoon Wesleys	City Jr.	7	5	*1	6	....	....	....	....	....	....	....	....	....
1925-26	Saskatoon Wesleys	City Jr.	12	*19	0	*19	....	....	....	....	4	*7	0	*7	2
1926-27	Saskatoon Wesleys	City Jr.	6	*6	1	*7	....	....	....	17	2	*3	0	*3	2
1927-28	Saskatoon Shieks	PrHL	27	*15	6	21	....	....	....	33	....	....	....	....	....
1928-29	**Boston Bruins**	**NHL**	**8**	**1**	**0**	**1**	**4**	**0**	**4**	**5**	....	....	....	....	....
	Minneapolis Millers	AHA	9	1	1	2	....			2	....	....	....	....	....
	Providence Reds	Can-Am	1	0	0	0	....	....	....	2	....	....	....	....	....
1929-30	Philadelphia Arrows	Can-Am	32	13	0	13	....	....	....	46	2	1	0	1	4
1930-31	Boston Tigers	Can-Am	10	7	3	10	....	....	....	12	8	*7	1	8	*32
	Syracuse Stars	IAHL	32	19	3	22	....	....	....	34	....	....	....	....	....
1931-32	**Boston Bruins**	**NHL**	**5**	**1**	**0**	**1**	**2**	**0**	**2**	**0**	....	....	....	....	....
	Boston Tigers	Can-Am	37	*22	19	*41	....	....	....	19	5	*4	*2	*6	6
1932-33	Boston Cubs	Can-Am	20	15	15	30	....	....	....	30					
	New York Americans	**NHL**	**15**	**2**	**2**	**4**	**5**	**5**	**10**	**4**	....	....	....	....	....
1933-34	**New York Americans**	**NHL**	**48**	**13**	**9**	**22**	**29**	**24**	**53**	**34**	....	....	....	....	....
1934-35	**New York Americans**	**NHL**	**29**	**7**	**3**	**10**	**15**	**7**	**22**	**9**	....	....	....	....	....
	New Haven Eagles	Can-Am	15	10	10	20	....	....	....	16	....	....	....	....	....
1935-36	**New York Americans**	**NHL**	**42**	**4**	**8**	**12**	**10**	**19**	**29**	**14**	**5**	**0**	**0**	**0**	**2**
	Rochester Cardinals	IAHL	4	3	1	4	....	....	....	0	....	....	....	....	....
1936-37	**New York Americans**	**NHL**	**14**	**2**	**1**	**3**	**4**	**2**	**6**	**2**	....	....	....	....	....
	New Haven–Cleveland	AHL	37	14	15	29	....	....	....	14	....	....	....	....	....
1937-38	**New York Americans**	**NHL**	**3**	**0**	**1**	**1**	**0**	**2**	**2**	**0**	....	....	....	....	....
	Pittsburgh Hornets	AHL	43	11	21	33	....	....	....	10	2	2	0	2	2
1938-39	Hershey Bears	AHL	49	17	15	32	....	....	....	32	5	0	1	1	4
1939-40	Hershey–Syracuse	AHL	52	16	21	37	....	....	....	8	....	....	....	....	....
1940-41	Buffalo Bisons	AHL	50	12	23	35	....	....	....	20	....	....	....	....	....
1941-42	Buffalo Bisons	AHL	55	20	22	42	....	....	....	20	....	....	....	....	....
1942-43	Buffalo Bisons	AHL	52	22	42	64	....	....	....	11	9	*5	10	*15	0
1943-44	Buffalo Bisons	AHL	47	23	22	45	....	....	....	22	9	1	4	5	0
1944-45	Pittsburgh Hornets	AHL	56	30	36	66	....	....	....	27	....	....	....	....	....
1945-46	Pittsburgh Hornets	AHL	8	1	5	6	....	....	....	2	....	....	....	....	....
	Hollywood Wolves	PCHL	33	24	12	36	....	....	....	14	12	10	6	16	8
1946-47	Saskatoon Quakers	WCSHL	35	12	17	29	....	....	....	30	3	1	1	2	2
1947-48	Tacoma Rockets	PCHL	46	28	27	55	....	....	....	32	5	0	1	1	0
	NHL Totals		**164**	**30**	**24**	**54**	**69**	**59**	**128**	**68**	**5**	**0**	**0**	**0**	**2**

Traded to **NY Americans** by **Boston** for Tom Filmore, February, 1933. Traded to **Cleveland** (AHL) by **NY Americans** for Les Cunningham, January 14, 1937.

• KLINGBEIL, IKE
Ike (Ernest R.) Klingbeil
D – L. 5'10", 180 lbs. b: Hancock, MI, 11/3/1908.

Season	Club	League	GP	G	A	Pts	AG	AA	APts	PIM	GP	G	A	Pts	PIM
			REGULAR SEASON								PLAYOFFS				
1932-33	University of Michigan	WIAA	STATISTICS NOT AVAILABLE												
1933-34	Detroit Mundus	MOHL	11	5	1	6	....	....	....	27	6	2	2	4	*24
1934-35	Detroit Farm Crest	MOHL	16	3	1	4	....	....	....	26	1	1	0	1	0
1935-36	Detroit Tool Shop	MOHL	5	2	0	2	....	....	....	4	....	....	....	....	....
1936-37	**Chicago Black Hawks**	**NHL**	**5**	**1**	**2**	**3**	**2**	**5**	**7**	**2**	....	....	....	....	....
	Portage Lakes Lakers	City Sr.	STATISTICS NOT AVAILABLE												
	NHL Totals		**5**	**1**	**2**	**3**	**2**	**5**	**7**	**2**	....	....	....	....	....

• KLUKAY, JOE
Joe "The Duke of Paducah" Klukay
LW – L. 6', 182 lbs. b: Sault Ste. Marie, Ont., 11/6/1922.

Season	Club	League	GP	G	A	Pts	AG	AA	APts	PIM	GP	G	A	Pts	PIM
1942-43	Stratford Kroehlers	OHA	14	11	18	29	....	....	....	11	2	4	4	8	0
	Toronto Maple Leafs	**NHL**	....	....	....	....	....	....	....	....	**1**	**0**	**0**	**0**	**0**
1943-44	Toronto Navy	City Sr.	25	14	13	27	....	....	....	19	....	....	....	....	....
1944-45	Cornwallis Navy	City Sr.	13	8	4	12	....	....	....	8	3	3	3	6	6
1945-46	Pittsburgh Hornets	AHL	57	26	23	49	....	....	....	20	6	4	1	5	2
1946-47	**Toronto Maple Leafs**	**NHL**	**55**	**9**	**20**	**29**	**12**	**29**	**41**	**12**	**11**	**1**	**0**	**1**	**0**
1947-48	**Toronto Maple Leafs**	**NHL**	**59**	**15**	**15**	**30**	**22**	**22**	**44**	**28**	**9**	**1**	**1**	**2**	**2**
1948-49	**Toronto Maple Leafs**	**NHL**	**45**	**11**	**10**	**21**	**17**	**16**	**33**	**11**	**9**	**2**	**3**	**5**	**4**
1949-50	**Toronto Maple Leafs**	**NHL**	**70**	**15**	**16**	**31**	**20**	**20**	**40**	**19**	**7**	**3**	**0**	**3**	**4**
1950-51	**Toronto Maple Leafs**	**NHL**	**70**	**14**	**16**	**30**	**19**	**21**	**40**	**16**	**11**	**4**	**3**	**7**	**0**
1951-52	**Toronto Maple Leafs**	**NHL**	**43**	**4**	**8**	**12**	**6**	**10**	**16**	**6**	**4**	**1**	**1**	**2**	**0**
1952-53	**Boston Bruins**	**NHL**	**70**	**13**	**16**	**29**	**20**	**22**	**42**	**20**	**11**	**1**	**2**	**3**	**9**
1953-54	**Boston Bruins**	**NHL**	**70**	**20**	**17**	**37**	**31**	**23**	**54**	**27**	**4**	**0**	**0**	**0**	**0**
1954-55	**Boston Bruins**	**NHL**	**10**	**0**	**0**	**0**	**0**	**0**	**0**	**4**	....	....	....	....	....
	Toronto Maple Leafs	**NHL**	**56**	**8**	**8**	**16**	**12**	**10**	**22**	**44**	**4**	**0**	**0**	**0**	**4**
1955-56	**Toronto Maple Leafs**	**NHL**	**18**	**0**	**1**	**1**	**0**	**1**	**1**	**2**	....	....	....	....	....
	Pittsburgh Hornets	AHL	47	24	26	50	....	....	....	40	4	4	1	5	8
1956-57	Windsor Bulldogs	OHA Sr.	52	23	30	53	....	....	....	80	12	6	4	10	9
1957-58	Windsor Bulldogs	NOHA	57	10	27	37	....	....	....	33	13	1	9	10	11
1958-59	Windsor Bulldogs	NOHA	49	21	21	42	....	....	....	25	....	....	....	....	....
1959-60			DID NOT PLAY												
1960-61	Windsor Bulldogs	OHA Sr.	33	12	37	49	....	....	....	10	....	....	....	....	....
1961-62	Windsor Bulldogs	OHA Sr.	33	12	20	32	....	....	....	32	13	1	7	8	6
1962-63	Windsor Bulldogs	OHA Sr.	12	3	9	12	....	....	....	2	10	1	7	8	2
1963-64	Windsor Bulldogs	IHL	1	0	1	1	....	....	....	0	....	....	....	....	....
	NHL Totals		**566**	**109**	**127**	**236**	**159**	**174**	**333**	**189**	**71**	**13**	**10**	**23**	**23**

Played in NHL All-Star Game (1947, 1948, 1949)

Traded to **Boston** by **Toronto** for cash, September 16, 1952. Traded to **Toronto** by **Boston** for Leo Boivin, November 9, 1954.

• KNIBBS, BILL
Bill Knibbs
C – L. 6'1", 180 lbs. b: Toronto, Ont., 1/24/1942.

Season	Club	League	GP	G	A	Pts	AG	AA	APts	PIM	GP	G	A	Pts	PIM
1959-60	Barrie Flyers	OHA	48	14	25	39	....	....	....	29	6	2	1	3	19
1960-61	Niagara Falls Flyers	OHA	48	22	35	57	....	....	....	31	7	4	1	5	2
1961-62	Niagara Falls Flyers	OHA	50	28	34	62	....	....	....	19	10	2	4	6	5
	Kingston Frontenacs	EPHL	1	0	0	0	....	....	....	0	7	1	2	3	0
1962-63	Kingston Frontenacs	EPHL	69	22	25	47	....	....	....	8	5	0	1	1	5
1963-64	Minneapolis Bruins	CHL	72	29	36	65	....	....	....	12	5	0	3	3	0
1964-65	**Boston Bruins**	**NHL**	**53**	**7**	**10**	**17**	**9**	**11**	**20**	**4**	....	....	....	....	....
	Minneapolis Bruins	CHL	16	11	8	19	....	....	....	10	....	....	....	....	....
1965-66	Baltimore Clippers	AHL	71	21	17	38	....	....	....	18	....	....	....	....	....
1966-67	Baltimore Clippers	AHL	70	16	17	33	....	....	....	24	9	2	2	4	4
1967-68	Buffalo Bisons	AHL	49	13	27	40	....	....	....	21	5	3	0	3	2
1968-69	Buffalo Bisons	AHL	68	13	38	51	....	....	....	38	6	2	3	5	0
1969-70	Buffalo Bisons	AHL	69	17	43	60	....	....	....	18	8	1	4	5	10
1970-71	Seattle Totems	WHL	39	14	17	31	....	....	....	4	....	....	....	....	....
	Omaha Knights	CHL	19	10	22	32	....	....	....	70	11	2	9	11	2
1971-72	Providence Reds	AHL	76	13	33	46	....	....	....	34	5	0	2	2	2
1972-73	Providence Reds	AHL	67	17	39	56	....	....	....	32	4	0	1	1	0
1973-74	Rochester Americans	AHL	38	9	25	34	....	....	....	6	....	....	....	....	....
1974-75	Rochester Americans	AHL	44	8	17	25	....	....	....	14	7	1	1	2	4
	NHL Totals		**53**	**7**	**10**	**17**	**9**	**11**	**20**	**4**	....	....	....	....	....

Claimed by **NY Rangers** from **Boston** in Intra-League Draft, June 9, 1965. Traded to **Rochester** (AHL) by **NY Rangers** with $20,000 for Bob Kelly, June, 1973.

• KNOTT, WILLIAM
William "Nick" Knott
D – L. 6'2", 200 lbs. b: Kingston, Ont., 7/23/1920. d: 4/12/1987.

Season	Club	League	GP	G	A	Pts	AG	AA	APts	PIM	GP	G	A	Pts	PIM
1938-39	Oshawa Generals	OHA	14	15	7	22	....	....	....	17	16	16	8	24	26
1939-40	Oshawa Generals	OHA	18	6	17	23	....	....	....	17	7	4	4	8	17
1940-41	Pittsburgh Hornets	AHL	30	7	11	18	....	....	....	20	6	2	3	5	6
1941-42	**Brooklyn Americans**	**NHL**	**14**	**3**	**1**	**4**	**5**	**2**	**7**	**9**	....	....	....	....	....
	Springfield Indians	AHL	38	13	28	41	....	....	....	74	5	0	3	3	2
1942-43	Cornwall Army	QSHL	32	17	26	43	....	....	....	51	6	1	1	2	22
1943-44			MILITARY SERVICE												
1944-45			MILITARY SERVICE												
1945-46	Tulsa Oilers	USHL	45	16	21	37	....	....	....	64	8	1	4	5	17
1946-47	Tulsa Oilers	USHL	57	10	29	39	....	....	....	120	5	1	1	2	14
1947-48	Tulsa Oilers	USHL	65	24	28	52	....	....	....	69	2	0	1	1	0
1948-49	Tulsa Oilers	USHL	56	31	24	55	....	....	....	79	6	2	3	5	4
1949-50	Tulsa Oilers	USHL	37	10	14	24	....	....	....	36	....	....	....	....	....
	NHL Totals		**14**	**3**	**1**	**4**	**5**	**2**	**7**	**9**	....	....	....	....	....

USHL Second All-Star Team (1946)

Loaned to **Brooklyn** by **Toronto** with Red Heron and Gus Marker for Lorne Carr, October 30, 1941.

• KNOX, PAUL
Paul Knox
RW – R. 5'10", 160 lbs. b: Toronto, Ontario, 11/23/1933.

Season	Club	League	GP	G	A	Pts	AG	AA	APts	PIM	GP	G	A	Pts	PIM
			REGULAR SEASON								PLAYOFFS				
1950-51	St. Michael's Majors	OHA	2	0	0	0	....	....	....	0	....	....	....	....	....
1951-52	St. Michael's Majors	OHA	34	12	14	26	....	....	....	10	....	....	....	....	....
1952-53	St. Michael's Majors	OHA	47	21	20	41	....	....	....	19	17	*13	7	20	2
1953-54	St. Michael's Majors	OHA	58	40	28	68	....	....	....	20	8	9	10	19	4
1954-55	**Toronto Maple Leafs**	**NHL**	**1**	**0**	**0**	**0**	**0**	**0**	**0**	**0**	....	....	....	....	....
	University of Toronto	OUAA	STATISTICS NOT AVAILABLE												
1955-56	Kitchener Dutchmen	OHA Sr.	48	19	24	43	....	....	....	6	10	6	4	10	2
	Canada	Olympics	8	7	7	*14	....	....	....	2	....	....	....	....	....
1956-57	Kitchener Dutchmen	OHA Sr.	52	18	22	40	....	....	....	30	10	8	5	13	0
1957-58	Kitchener Dutchmen	NOHA	....	....	....	....	....	....	....	....	1	0	0	0	0
1958-59	Kitchener Dutchmen	NOHA	3	2	0	2	....	....	....	0	11	3	2	5	5
	NHL Totals		**1**	**0**	**0**	**0**	**0**	**0**	**0**	**0**	....	....	....	....	....

• KOPAK, RUSS
Russ Kopak
C – L. 5'10", 158 lbs. b: Edmonton, Alta., 4/26/1924.

Season	Club	League	GP	G	A	Pts	AG	AA	APts	PIM	GP	G	A	Pts	PIM
1942-43	Regina Abbotts	SJHL	13	14	8	22	....	....	....	16	4	1	0	1	*13
1943-44	**Boston Bruins**	**NHL**	**24**	**7**	**9**	**16**	**9**	**11**	**20**	**0**	....	....	....	....	....
	Boston Olympics	EHL	19	20	24	44	....	....	....	4	9	4	5	9	11
1944-45	Boston Olympics	EHL	41	41	41	82	....	....	....	53	10	*15	10	25	6
1945-46	Fort Worth Rangers	USHL	56	21	31	52	....	....	....	23	....	....	....	....	....
1946-47	Fort Worth Rangers	USHL	59	22	25	47	....	....	....	30	9	0	2	2	2
1947-48	Fort Worth Rangers	USHL	44	15	28	43	....	....	....	23	....	....	....	....	....
1948-49	Fort Worth–Houston	USHL	66	17	33	50	....	....	....	14	2	0	0	0	0
1949-50	Seattle–Victoria	PCHL	72	13	20	33	....	....	....	21	....	....	....	....	....
	NHL Totals		**24**	**7**	**9**	**16**	**9**	**11**	**20**	**0**	....	....	....	....	....

EHL Second All-Star Team (1944, 1945)

• KOTANEN, DICK
Dick Kotanen
D – R. 5'11", 190 lbs. b: Port Arthur, Ont., 11/18/1925.

Season	Club	League	GP	G	A	Pts	AG	AA	APts	PIM	GP	G	A	Pts	PIM
1942-43	Port Arthur West-Enders	TBJHL	8	3	2	5	....	....	....	2	3	0	1	1	2
1943-44	Port Arthur West-Enders	TBJHL	11	3	4	7	....	....	....	6	4	0	3	3	4
	Port Arthur Shipbuilders	TBSHL	1	0	0	0	....	....	....	2	....	....	....	....	....
1944-45	Winnipeg Maroons	MJHL	4	1	1	2	....	....	....	0	2	0	1	1	2
	Winnipeg Army	City Sr.	9	0	2	2	....	....	....	2	2	0	0	0	2
1945-46	Brandon Elks	MJHL	8	2	3	5	....	....	....	2	7	1	2	3	16
1946-47	Port Arthur Bearcats	TBSHL	12	1	8	9	....	....	....	12	5	0	0	0	*8
1947-48	New York Rovers	EHL	17	3	6	9	....	....	....	10	....	....	....	....	....
	New York Rovers	QSHL	45	3	8	11	....	....	....	34	4	1	2	3	4
1948-49	New York Rovers	EHL	63	4	10	14	....	....	....	*52	....	....	....	....	....
1949-50	Regina Capitols	SSHL	49	5	5	10	....	....	....	102	....	....	....	....	....
	New York Rovers	EHL	1	0	0	0	....	....	....	0	12	0	0	0	22
1950-51	**New York Rangers**	**NHL**	**1**	**0**	**0**	**0**	**0**	**0**	**0**	**0**	....	....	....	....	....
	Sherbrooke Saints	QSHL	19	0	2	2	....	....	....	30	....	....	....	....	....
	New York Rovers	EHL	32	2	4	6	....	....	....	79	6	0	1	1	*37
1951-52	Trail Smoke Eaters	WIHL	33	4	14	18	....	....	....	110	10	3	4	7	20
1952-53	Seattle Bombers	WHL	2	1	1	2	....	....	....	0	....	....	....	....	....
	Kamloops Elks	OSHL	51	3	16	19	....	....	....	107	12	3	4	7	24
1953-54	Windsor Bulldogs	OHA Sr.	54	10	23	33	....	....	....	87	4	1	3	4	20
1954-55	Windsor–Chatham	OHA Sr.	46	3	18	21	....	....	....	77	....	....	....	....	....
	Pembroke Lumber Kings	NOHA	2	1	0	1	....	....	....	2	....	....	....	....	....
1955-56	Chatham Maroons	OHA Sr.	48	1	8	9	....	....	....	109	10	0	4	4	22
1956-57	Chatham Maroons	OHA Sr.	17	0	4	4	....	....	....	22	....	....	....	....	....
	Kingston CKLC's	EOHL	29	1	9	10	....	....	....	40	5	1	0	1	8
1957-58	North Bay Trappers	NOHA	42	1	13	14	....	....	....	32	....	....	....	....	....
	NHL Totals		**1**	**0**	**0**	**0**	**0**	**0**	**0**	**0**	....	....	....	....	....

• KOZAK, LES
Les Kozak
LW – L. 6', 185 lbs. b: Dauphin, Manitoba, 10/28/1940.

Season	Club	League	GP	G	A	Pts	AG	AA	APts	PIM	GP	G	A	Pts	PIM
1955-56	Melville Millionaires	SJHL	3	0	0	0	....	....	....	2	....	....	....	....	....
1956-57	Saskatoon Quakers	SJHL	1	0	0	0	....	....	....	0	....	....	....	....	....
	Toronto Marlboros	OHA	1	0	1	1	....	....	....	0	8	0	1	1	0
1957-58	St. Michael's Majors	OHA	38	9	15	24	....	....	....	10	3	0	0	0	0
1958-59	St. Michael's Majors	OHA	43	10	8	18	....	....	....	18	15	4	1	5	10
1959-60	St. Michael's Majors	OHA	42	18	17	35	....	....	....	34	10	2	2	4	10
1960-61			DID NOT PLAY												
1961-62	**Toronto Maple Leafs**	**NHL**	**12**	**1**	**0**	**1**	**1**	**0**	**1**	**2**	....	....	....	....	....
	Rochester Americans	AHL	45	14	9	23	....	....	....	31	....	....	....	....	....
	NHL Totals		**12**	**1**	**0**	**1**	**1**	**0**	**1**	**2**	....	....	....	....	....

• Entered Seminary in 1960 and missed the 1960-61 season while studying for the priesthood.
• Suffered career-ending head injury in game vs. Providence (AHL), February 23, 1962.

• KRAFTCHECK, STEPHEN
Stephen Kraftcheck
D – R. 5'11", 190 lbs. b: Tinturn, Ont., 3/3/1929. d: 8/10/1997.

Season	Club	League	GP	G	A	Pts	AG	AA	APts	PIM	GP	G	A	Pts	PIM
			REGULAR SEASON								PLAYOFFS				
1945-46	Hamilton Lloyds	OHA	2	0	0	0	....	....	....	2	....	....	....	....	....
	Hamilton Aerovox	Midget	STATISTICS NOT AVAILABLE												
1946-47	Hamilton Aerovox	Jr. B	STATISTICS NOT AVAILABLE												
1947-48	Hamilton Aerovox	Jr. B	STATISTICS NOT AVAILABLE												
1948-49	San Francisco Shamrocks	PCHL	70	11	22	33	....	....	....	82	....	....	....	....	....
1949-50	Cleveland Barons	AHL	70	7	37	44	....	....	....	46	8	0	3	3	12
1950-51	**Boston Bruins**	**NHL**	**22**	**0**	**0**	**0**	**0**	**0**	**0**	**8**	**6**	**0**	**0**	**0**	**7**
	Indianapolis Capitals	AHL	47	6	27	33	....	....	....	39	3	0	0	0	2
1951-52	**New York Rangers**	**NHL**	**58**	**8**	**9**	**17**	**11**	**12**	**23**	**30**	....	....	....	....	....
1952-53	**New York Rangers**	**NHL**	**69**	**2**	**9**	**11**	**3**	**12**	**15**	**45**	....	....	....	....	....
1953-54	Cleveland Barons	AHL	70	5	20	25	....	....	....	62	7	2	1	3	10
1954-55	Cleveland Barons	AHL	60	9	26	35	....	....	....	38	4	0	2	2	0
1955-56	Cleveland Barons	AHL	57	5	29	34	....	....	....	40	8	1	4	5	10
1956-57	Cleveland Barons	AHL	63	7	33	40	....	....	....	42	12	2	*11	13	8
1957-58	Cleveland Barons	AHL	66	15	34	49	....	....	....	53	7	0	3	3	4
1958-59	**Toronto Maple Leafs**	**NHL**	**8**	**1**	**0**	**1**	**1**	**0**	**1**	**0**	....	....	....	....	....
	Rochester Americans	AHL	60	2	37	39	....	....	....	42	5	0	2	2	4
1959-60	Rochester Americans	AHL	68	1	41	42	....	....	....	47	12	1	3	4	12
1960-61	Rochester Americans	AHL	71	3	37	40	....	....	....	26	....	....	....	....	....
1961-62	Rochester Americans	AHL	69	4	41	45	....	....	....	45	2	0	0	0	2
1962-63	Providence Reds	AHL	69	2	19	21	....	....	....	22	6	0	2	2	2
1963-64	Providence Reds	AHL	69	1	5	6	....	....	....	22	....	....	....	....	....
	NHL Totals		**157**	**11**	**18**	**29**	**15**	**24**	**39**	**83**	**6**	**0**	**0**	**0**	**7**

PCHL Southern First All-Star Team (1949) • AHL Second All-Star Team (1956, 1961) • AHL First All-Star Team (1957, 1958, 1959, 1960) • Won Eddie Shore Award (Outstanding Defenseman - AHL) (1959)

Traded to **Boston** by **Cleveland** (AHL) for cash, April 17, 1950. Loaned to **Indianapolis** (AHL) by **Boston** for the loan of Max Quakenbush, December 5, 1950. Traded to **NY Rangers** by **Boston** with Ed Reigle for $30,000, May 14, 1951. Traded to **Cleveland** (AHL) by **NY Rangers** with cash for Bob Chrystal, June, 1953. Traded to **Toronto** by **Cleveland** (AHL) for Ian Anderson, June, 1958. Traded to **Providence** (AHL) by **Toronto** (Rochester - AHL) for cash, June, 1962.

• KRAKE, SKIP
— see page 1182

• KROL, JOE
Joe Krol
LW – L. 5'11", 173 lbs. b: Winnipeg, Man., 8/13/1915. d: 10/26/1993.

Season	Club	League	GP	G	A	Pts	AG	AA	APts	PIM	GP	G	A	Pts	PIM
1932-33	Winnipeg K of C	City Jr.	11	6	3	9	....	....	....	18	3	1	1	2	2
1933-34	Selkirk Fishermen	Wpg-Jr.	14	3	3	6	....	....	....	43	5	0	2	2	13
1934-35	Winnipeg Monarchs	City Jr.	13	12	7	19	....	....	....	16	3	*6	2	*8	10
1935-36	New York Rovers	EHL	39	16	22	38	....	....	....	47	8	2	0	2	6
1936-37	**New York Rangers**	**NHL**	**1**	**0**	**0**	**0**	**0**	**0**	**0**	**0**	....	....	....	....	....
	Philadelphia Ramblers	AHL	48	10	17	27	....	....	....	26	6	0	1	1	2
1937-38	Philadelphia Ramblers	AHL	43	4	10	14	....	....	....	10	4	1	1	2	0
1938-39	**New York Rangers**	**NHL**	**1**	**1**	**1**	**2**	**2**	**2**	**4**	**0**	....	....	....	....	....
	Philadelphia Ramblers	AHL	54	24	30	54	....	....	....	34	8	2	3	5	4
1939-40	Philadelphia Rockets	AHL	52	7	11	18	....	....	....	23	....	....	....	....	....
1940-41	Hershey–Springfield	AHL	52	15	20	35	....	....	....	32	3	0	2	2	2
1941-42	**Brooklyn Americans**	**NHL**	**24**	**9**	**3**	**12**	**15**	**5**	**20**	**8**	....	....	....	....	....
	Springfield Indians	AHL	18	3	12	15	....	....	....	5	....	....	....	....	....
1942-43	Vancouver RCAF	City Sr.	19	14	16	30	....	....	....	32	2	0	1	1	0
	Winnipeg RCAF	City Sr.	....	....	....	....	....	....	....	....	3	0	1	1	2
1943-44	Winnipeg RCAF	City Sr.	9	4	3	7	....	....	....	8	....	....	....	....	....
	NHL Totals		**26**	**10**	**4**	**14**	**17**	**7**	**24**	**8**	....	....	....	....	....

EHL First All-Star Team (1930)

Signed as a free agent by **NY Rangers**, November, 1936. Traded to **Hershey** (AHL) by **NY Rangers** for cash, April 4, 1940. Traded to **NY Americans** (Springfield - AHL) by **Hershey** for cash, February 14, 1941.

• KRYZNOWSKI, EDWARD
Edward Kryznowski
D – L. 5'11", 175 lbs. b: Fort Francis, Ont., 11/14/1925.

Season	Club	League	GP	G	A	Pts	AG	AA	APts	PIM	GP	G	A	Pts	PIM
1947-48	University of Toronto	OUAA	18	10	12	22	....	....	....	....	....	....	....	....	....
1948-49	**Boston Bruins**	**NHL**	**36**	**1**	**3**	**4**	**2**	**5**	**7**	**10**	**5**	**0**	**1**	**1**	**2**
	Hershey Bears	AHL	18	0	8	8	....	....	....	6	....	....	....	....	....
1949-50	**Boston Bruins**	**NHL**	**57**	**6**	**10**	**16**	**8**	**13**	**21**	**12**	....	....	....	....	....
	Hershey Bears	AHL	10	1	1	2	....	....	....	4	....	....	....	....	....
1950-51	**Boston Bruins**	**NHL**	**69**	**3**	**6**	**9**	**4**	**8**	**12**	**10**	**6**	**0**	**0**	**0**	**2**
1951-52	**Boston Bruins**	**NHL**	**70**	**5**	**3**	**8**	**7**	**4**	**11**	**33**	**7**	**0**	**0**	**0**	**0**
1952-53	**Chicago Black Hawks**	**NHL**	**5**	**0**	**0**	**0**	**0**	**0**	**0**	**0**	....	....	....	....	....
	Providence Reds	AHL	51	5	26	31	....	....	....	19	....	....	....	....	....
1953-54	Providence Reds	AHL	70	2	14	16	....	....	....	37	....	....	....	....	....
1954-55	Hershey Bears	AHL	60	7	14	21	....	....	....	37	....	....	....	....	....
1955-56	Hershey Bears	AHL	64	9	26	35	....	....	....	53	....	....	....	....	....
	NHL Totals		**237**	**15**	**22**	**37**	**21**	**30**	**51**	**65**	**18**	**0**	**1**	**1**	**4**

Traded to **Chicago** by **Boston** with Vic Lynn for cash, August 14, 1952.

• KUHN, GORD
Gord "Doggie" Kuhn
RW – R. 5'7", 145 lbs. b: Truro, N.S., 11/19/1905. d: 7/29/1978.

Season	Club	League	GP	G	A	Pts	AG	AA	APts	PIM	GP	G	A	Pts	PIM
			REGULAR SEASON								PLAYOFFS				
1924-25	Truro Bearcats	Hfx-Sr.	8	15	0	15	....	....	....	....	7	2	2	4	4
1925-26	Truro Bearcats	Hfx-Sr.	STATISTICS NOT AVAILABLE												
1926-27	Windsor Maple Leafs	Hfx-Sr.	10	5	4	9	....	....	....	2	9	6	4	*10	2
1927-28	Truro Bearcats	Hfx-Sr.	11	10	*7	17	....	....	....	8	2	1	0	1	2
1928-29	Halifax Wolverines	City Sr.	12	13	3	16	....	....	....	25	10	*12	6	*18	6
1929-30	Truro Bearcats	NSSHL	17	*14	5	*19	....	....	....	39	10	*12	1	*13	6
1930-31	New Haven Eagles	Can-Am	36	5	5	10	....	....	....	48	....	....	....	....	....
1931-32	New Haven Eagles	Can-Am	40	16	6	22	....	....	....	52	....	....	....	....	....
1932-33	**New York Americans**	**NHL**	**12**	**1**	**1**	**2**	**2**	**3**	**5**	**4**	....	....	....	....	....
	New Haven Eagles	Can-Am	29	5	6	11	....	....	....	39	2	0	0	0	2
1933-34	Buffalo Bisons	IAHL	36	4	5	9	....	....	....	20	6	1	0	1	20
1934-35	Providence Reds	Can-Am	46	13	22	35	....	....	....	26	6	0	1	1	6
1935-36	Providence Reds	Can-Am	46	8	9	17	....	....	....	47	7	2	2	4	*10
1936-37	Providence Reds	AHL	45	17	13	30	....	....	....	34	3	1	1	2	7
1937-38	Providence Reds	AHL	48	9	18	27	....	....	....	44	7	0	4	4	4
1938-39	Providence Reds	AHL	52	13	9	22	....	....	....	13	5	0	2	2	0
1939-40	Syracuse Stars	AHL	47	4	9	13	....	....	....	11	....	....	....	....	....
	NHL Totals		**12**	**1**	**1**	**2**	**2**	**3**	**5**	**4**	....	....	....	....	....

Traded to **Providence** (Can-Am) by **NY Americans** with Jack Keating for cash, November 13, 1934.

• KUKULOWICZ, AGGIE
Aggie (Adolph) Kukulowicz
C – L. 6'3", 175 lbs. b: Winnipeg, Man., 4/2/1933.

Season	Club	League	GP	G	A	Pts	AG	AA	APts	PIM	GP	G	A	Pts	PIM
1950-51	Brandon Wheat Kings	MJHL	36	27	30	57	....	....	....	18	6	5	4	9	0
1951-52	Quebec Citadels	QJHL	50	24	35	59	....	....	....	54	15	3	*11	14	10
1952-53	**New York Rangers**	**NHL**	**3**	**1**	**0**	**1**	**2**	**0**	**2**	**0**	....	....	....	....	....
	Quebec Citadels	QJHL	46	13	24	37	....	....	....	109	9	6	2	8	4
1953-54	**New York Rangers**	**NHL**	**1**	**0**	**0**	**0**	**0**	**0**	**0**	**0**	....	....	....	....	....
	Saskatoon Quakers	WHL	70	14	27	41	....	....	....	38	6	0	1	1	2
1954-55	Saskatoon Quakers	WHL	57	12	25	37	....	....	....	31	....	....	....	....	....
1955-56	Brandon Regals	WHL	67	16	38	54	....	....	....	38	....	....	....	....	....
1956-57	New Westminster Royals	WHL	70	7	32	39	....	....	....	71	13	0	3	3	10
1957-58	Seattle Totems	WHL	67	5	23	28	....	....	....	61	9	2	2	4	15
1958-59	Saskatoon Quakers	WHL	9	1	6	7	....	....	....	0	....	....	....	....	....
	Quebec Aces	QHL	14	2	8	10	....	....	....	8	....	....	....	....	....
	Cornwall Chevies	EOHL	18	5	13	18	....	....	....	6	6	1	2	3	2
1959-60	St. Paul Saints	IHL	68	38	80	118	....	....	....	57	13	6	8	14	0
1960-61	St. Paul Saints	IHL	72	34	53	87	....	....	....	39	13	6	13	*19	19
1961-62	Minneapolis Millers	IHL	62	24	61	85	....	....	....	8	5	1	3	4	13
1962-63	Winnipeg Maroons	SSHL	10	3	12	15	....	....	....	0	....	....	....	....	....
	Yorkton Terriers	SSHL	39	11	15	26	....	....	....	12	12	7	2	9	2
1963-64	Winnipeg Maroons	SSHL	16	12	15	27	....	....	....	14	....	....	....	....	....
1964-65	Winnipeg Maroons	SSHL	6	2	3	5	....	....	....	0	....	....	....	....	....
1965-66	GKS Katowice	Poland	DID NOT PLAY – COACHING												
	NHL Totals		**4**	**1**	**0**	**1**	**2**	**0**	**2**	**0**	....	....	....	....	....

IHL Second All-Star Team (1960)

• KULLMAN, ARNIE
Arnie Kullman
C – L. 5'7", 170 lbs. b: Winnipeg, Man., 10/9/1927.

Season	Club	League	GP	G	A	Pts	AG	AA	APts	PIM	GP	G	A	Pts	PIM
1943-44	Winnipeg Rangers	MJHL	2	0	0	0	....	....	....	0	....	....	....	....	....
1944-45	Winnipeg Rangers	MJHL	10	11	6	17	....	....	....	12	4	4	1	5	0
1945-46	Brandon Elks	MJHL	4	4	3	7	....	....	....	4	7	4	3	7	0
1946-47	Stratford Kroehlers	OHA	28	29	15	44	....	....	....	26	2	0	1	1	2
1947-48	**Boston Bruins**	**NHL**	**1**	**0**	**0**	**0**	**0**	**0**	**0**	**0**	....	....	....	....	....
	Boston Olympics	QSHL	45	25	18	43	....	....	....	45	....	....	....	....	....
	Boston Olympics	EHL	17	4	5	9	....	....	....	24	....	....	....	....	....
1948-49	Hershey Bears	AHL	66	20	36	56	....	....	....	29	9	5	7	12	8
1949-50	**Boston Bruins**	**NHL**	**12**	**0**	**1**	**1**	**0**	**1**	**1**	**11**	....	....	....	....	....
	Hershey Bears	AHL	42	13	14	27	....	....	....	42	....	....	....	....	....
1950-51	Hershey Bears	AHL	69	32	33	65	....	....	....	52	4	3	2	5	4
1951-52	Hershey Bears	AHL	63	25	31	56	....	....	....	45	1	0	0	0	10
1952-53	Hershey Bears	AHL	64	25	39	64	....	....	....	22	3	0	1	1	4
1953-54	Hershey Bears	AHL	69	40	41	81	....	....	....	35	11	4	8	12	8
1954-55	Hershey Bears	AHL	62	23	48	71	....	....	....	67	....	....	....	....	....
1955-56	Hershey Bears	AHL	63	22	30	52	....	....	....	83	....	....	....	....	....
1956-57	Hershey Bears	AHL	57	18	24	42	....	....	....	53	7	0	1	1	29
1957-58	Hershey Bears	AHL	67	16	29	45	....	....	....	47	10	2	1	3	5
1958-59	Hershey Bears	AHL	59	10	17	27	....	....	....	70	13	2	4	6	16
1959-60	Hershey Bears	AHL	72	9	24	33	....	....	....	57	....	....	....	....	....
	NHL Totals		**13**	**0**	**1**	**1**	**0**	**1**	**1**	**11**	....	....	....	....	....

• KULLMAN, EDDIE
Eddie Kullman
RW – R. 5'7", 165 lbs. b: Winnipeg, Man., 12/12/1923. d: 1997.

Season	Club	League	GP	G	A	Pts	AG	AA	APts	PIM	GP	G	A	Pts	PIM
1941-42	Winnipeg Rangers	MJHL	18	14	5	19	....	....	....	9	....	....	....	....	....
1942-43	Winnipeg Rangers	MJHL	14	15	12	27	....	....	....	15	19	25	*20	45	16
1943-44	Winnipeg Rangers	MJHL	2	0	0	0	....	....	....	0	....	....	....	....	....
1944-45	Winnipeg Rangers	MJHL	1	0	0	0	....	....	....	0	....	....	....	....	....
1945-46	Winnipeg Rangers	MJHL	10	6	4	10	....	....	....	4	....	....	....	....	....
1946-47	Portland Eagles	PCHL	60	*56	46	102	....	....	....	135	12	3	7	10	6
1947-48	**New York Rangers**	**NHL**	**51**	**15**	**17**	**32**	**22**	**25**	**47**	**32**	**6**	**1**	**0**	**1**	**2**
	New Haven Ramblers	AHL	12	5	4	9	....	....	....	8	....	....	....	....	....
1948-49	**New York Rangers**	**NHL**	**18**	**4**	**5**	**9**	**6**	**8**	**14**	**14**	....	....	....	....	....
	Providence Reds	AHL	41	16	24	40	....	....	....	22	10	5	4	9	6
1949-50	Providence Reds	AHL	69	32	34	66	....	....	....	62	4	2	2	4	2
1950-51	**New York Rangers**	**NHL**	**70**	**14**	**18**	**32**	**19**	**23**	**42**	**88**	....	....	....	....	....
1951-52	**New York Rangers**	**NHL**	**64**	**11**	**10**	**21**	**15**	**13**	**28**	**59**	....	....	....	....	....
	Cincinnati Mohawks	AHL	7	3	1	4	....	....	....	4	....	....	....	....	....
1952-53	**New York Rangers**	**NHL**	**70**	**8**	**10**	**18**	**12**	**14**	**26**	**61**	....	....	....	....	....
1953-54	**New York Rangers**	**NHL**	**70**	**4**	**10**	**14**	**6**	**14**	**20**	**44**	....	....	....	....	....
1954-55	Saskatoon–Vancouver	WHL	53	9	21	30	....	....	....	52	5	0	2	2	6
	Windsor Bulldogs	OHA Sr.	3	0	1	1	....	....	....	6	....	....	....	....	....
	NHL Totals		**343**	**56**	**70**	**126**	**80**	**97**	**177**	**298**	**6**	**1**	**0**	**1**	**2**

Traded to **Providence** (AHL) by **NY Rangers** with Elwyn Morris, cash and future considerations (Ken Davies, June, 1949) for Allan Stanley, December, 1948. Traded to **NY Rangers** by **Providence** (AHL) for Orville LaValle and Sheldon Bloomer, August 16, 1950.

• KUNTZ, ALAN
Alan Kuntz
LW – L. 5'11", 165 lbs. b: Toronto, Ont., 6/4/1919. d: 3/7/1987.

			REGULAR SEASON								PLAYOFFS				
Season	**Club**	**League**	**GP**	**G**	**A**	**Pts**	**AG**	**AA**	**APts**	**PIM**	**GP**	**G**	**A**	**Pts**	**PIM**
1936-37	Ottawa Jr. Senators	City Jr.	4	2	1	3	....	....	....	0	4	0	1	1	0
1937-38	Ottawa Glebe Collegiate	City Jr.	STATISTICS NOT AVAILABLE												
1938-39	Guelph Indians	OHA	14	9	10	19	....	....	....	9	2	0	2	2	2
1939-40	Washington Eagles	EHL	41	22	27	49	....	....	....	2	4	1	0	1	2
1940-41	Philadelphia Rockets	AHL	48	11	14	25	....	....	....	23	....	....	....	....	....
1941-42	**New York Rangers**	**NHL**	**31**	**10**	**11**	**21**	**17**	**17**	**34**	**10**	**6**	**1**	**0**	**1**	**2**
	New Haven Eagles	AHL	21	5	9	14	....	....	....	2	....	....	....	....	....
1942-43	Montreal Army	QSHL	32	19	21	40	....	....	....	36	7	1	3	4	0
1944-45			MILITARY SERVICE												
1945-46	**New York Rangers**	**NHL**	**14**	**0**	**1**	**1**	**0**	**2**	**2**	**2**	....	....	....	....	....
	St. Paul Saints	USHL	39	7	9	16	....	....	....	24	6	2	2	4	6
1946-47	New Haven Ramblers	AHL	55	17	27	44	....	....	....	27	....	....	....	....	....
1947-48	Springfield Indians	AHL	62	24	34	58	....	....	....	22	....	....	....	....	....
1948-49	Vancouver Canucks	PCHL	64	42	38	80	....	....	....	14	3	1	0	1	4
1949-50	Vancouver Canucks	PCHL	70	37	46	83	....	....	....	33	12	2	5	7	0
1950-51	Ottawa Senators	QSHL	53	10	17	27	....	....	....	22	11	4	2	6	0
1951-52	Ottawa Senators	QSHL	59	25	37	62	....	....	....	7	7	4	6	10	0
1952-53	Ottawa Senators	QSHL	49	14	19	33	....	....	....	6	10	2	2	4	0
1953-54	Ottawa Senators	QHL	62	13	19	32	....	....	....	9	22	2	7	9	2
1954-55	Ottawa Senators	QHL	27	8	8	16	....	....	....	11	....	....	....	....	....
	Pembroke Lumber Kings	Ott-Sr.	22	11	15	26	....	....	....	2	6	3	2	5	0
1955-56	Brockville Macedonas	EOHL	37	4	21	25	....	....	....	22	2	0	0	0	14
	NHL Totals		**45**	**10**	**12**	**22**	**17**	**19**	**36**	**12**	**6**	**1**	**0**	**1**	**2**

PCHL Northern Second All-Star Team (1949)

• KURTENBACH, ORLAND
— *see page 1189*

• KURYLUK, MERVIN
Mervin Kuryluk
LW – L. 5'11", 185 lbs. b: Yorkton, Sask., 8/10/1937.

1954-55	Moose Jaw Canucks	WJHL	39	10	21	31	....	....	....	78	....	....	....	....	....
1955-56	Yorkton Terriers	SJHL	48	26	34	60	....	....	....	113	5	2	1	3	11
1956-57	Melville Millionaires	SJHL	50	31	35	66	....	....	....	135	....	....	....	....	....
	Calgary Stampeders	WHL	4	1	0	1	....	....	....	0	3	0	1	1	2
1957-58	Calgary Stampeders	WHL	59	12	16	28	....	....	....	44	14	1	3	4	10
1958-59	Saskatoon Quakers	WHL	59	15	33	48	....	....	....	34	....	....	....	....	....
1959-60	Soo Thunderbirds	EPHL	45	15	26	41	....	....	....	40	....	....	....	....	....
	Calgary Stampeders	WHL	22	5	9	14	....	....	....	16	....	....	....	....	....
1960-61	Soo Thunderbirds	EPHL	69	22	20	42	....	....	....	84	12	4	7	11	13
1961-62	Soo Thunderbirds	EPHL	65	36	26	62	....	....	....	130	....	....	....	....	....
	Chicago Black Hawks	**NHL**	....	....	....	....	....	....	....	....	**2**	**0**	**0**	**0**	**0**
	Buffalo Bisons	AHL	....	....	....	....	....	....	....	....	2	0	0	0	0
1962-63	St. Louis Braves	EPHL	61	22	53	75	....	....	....	60	....	....	....	....	....
1963-64	Buffalo Bisons	AHL	72	14	25	39	....	....	....	45	....	....	....	....	....
1964-65	Buffalo Bisons	AHL	1	1	0	1	....	....	....	0	....	....	....	....	....
	St. Louis Braves	CHL	58	9	31	40	....	....	....	66	....	....	....	....	....
	Los Angeles Blades	WHL	14	0	1	1	....	....	....	8	....	....	....	....	....
	NHL Totals		**0**	**0**	**0**	**0**	**0**	**0**	**0**	**0**	**2**	**0**	**0**	**0**	**0**

• KWONG, LARRY
Larry "King" Kwong
RW – R. 5'6", 150 lbs. b: Vernon, B.C., 6/17/1923.

1941-42	Trail Smoke Eaters	ASHL	29	9	13	22	....	....	....	10	3	0	0	0	0
1942-43	Nanaimo Clippers	City Sr.	11	6	6	12	....	....	....	0	3	0	1	1	2
1943-44	Vancouver St. Regis	PCHL	17	10	6	16	....	....	....	0	....	....	....	....	....
	Red Deer Wheelers	ASHL	2	0	0	0	....	....	....	0	5	1	2	3	0
1944-45			MILITARY SERVICE												
1945-46	Trail Smoke Eaters	Kootenay	19	12	8	20	....	....	....	12	5	6	0	6	8
1946-47	New York Rovers	EHL	47	19	18	37	....	....	....	15	9	7	3	10	0
1947-48	**New York Rangers**	**NHL**	**1**	**0**	**0**	**0**	**0**	**0**	**0**	**0**	....	....	....	....	....
	New York Rovers	EHL	17	13	16	29	....	....	....	5	....	....	....	....	....
	New York Rovers	QSHL	48	20	37	57	....	....	....	23	4	1	0	1	0
1948-49	Valleyfield Braves	QSHL	63	37	47	84	....	....	....	8	3	1	0	1	7
1949-50	Valleyfield Braves	QSHL	60	25	35	60	....	....	....	16	5	2	1	3	2
1950-51	Valleyfield Braves	QSHL	60	34	*51	85	....	....	....	35	28	7	21	28	6
1951-52	Valleyfield Braves	QSHL	60	38	28	66	....	....	....	16	6	1	5	6	0
1952-53	Valleyfield Braves	QSHL	56	10	22	32	....	....	....	6	3	0	2	2	0
1953-54	Valleyfield Braves	QHL	68	24	25	49	....	....	....	17	7	3	3	6	2
1954-55	Valleyfield Braves	QHL	50	24	30	54	....	....	....	8	....	....	....	....	....
1955-56	Trois-Rivieres Lions	QHL	29	3	6	9	....	....	....	10	....	....	....	....	....
	Troy Bruins	IHL	21	9	9	18	....	....	....	2	5	1	2	3	2
1956-57	Troy Bruins	IHL	9	1	0	1	....	....	....	0	....	....	....	....	....
	Cornwall Chevies	EOHL	33	14	15	29	....	....	....	22	6	5	1	6	0
1957-58	Nottingham Panthers	Britain	55	55	24	79	....	....	....	10	....	....	....	....	....
	NHL Totals		**1**	**0**	**0**	**0**	**0**	**0**	**0**	**0**	....	....	....	....	....

Won Vimy Trophy (MVP - QSHL) (1951)

• KYLE, BILL
Bill Kyle
C – R. 6'1", b: Dysart, Sask., 12/23/1924. d: 4/17/1968.

			REGULAR SEASON								PLAYOFFS				
Season	**Club**	**League**	**GP**	**G**	**A**	**Pts**	**AG**	**AA**	**APts**	**PIM**	**GP**	**G**	**A**	**Pts**	**PIM**
1939-40	Notre Dame Hounds	SJHL	5	1	0	1	....	....	....	2	....	....	....	....	....
1940-41	Dysart Devils	Jr. B	STATISTICS NOT AVAILABLE												
1941-42	Notre Dame Hounds	SJHL	11	6	5	11	....	....	....	6	5	2	3	5	4
1942-43	Regina Commandos	SJHL	12	10	10	20	....	....	....	14	6	*6	2	8	10
1943-44			MILITARY SERVICE												
1944-45			MILITARY SERVICE												
1945-46	Portland Eagles	PCHL	58	38	33	71	....	....	....	60	8	7	2	9	6
1946-47	Portland Eagles	PCHL	54	40	59	99	....	....	....	60	14	7	*10	*17	4
1947-48	Regina Caps	WCSHL	48	29	43	72	....	....	....	26	4	1	1	2	2
1948-49	Regina Caps	WCSHL	48	21	41	62	....	....	....	56	8	4	*10	*14	4
1949-50	**New York Rangers**	**NHL**	**2**	**0**	**0**	**0**	**0**	**0**	**0**	**0**	....	....	....	....	....
	Regina Caps	WCSHL	44	17	28	45	....	....	....	58	....	....	....	....	....
1950-51	**New York Rangers**	**NHL**	**1**	**0**	**3**	**3**	**0**	**4**	**4**	**0**	....	....	....	....	....
	Regina Caps	WCSHL	44	17	28	45	....	....	....	55	....	....	....	....	....
	New York Rovers	EHL	1	1	0	1	....	....	....	0	5	1	3	4	0
1951-52	Sherbrooke Saints	QSHL	60	20	31	51	....	....	....	36	11	1	2	3	2
1952-53	Regina Caps	SSHL	31	23	38	61	....	....	....	23	7	7	*8	15	4
1953-54	Regina Caps	SSHL	37	20	34	54	....	....	....	18	....	....	....	....	....
1954-55	Yorkton Terriers	City Sr.	DID NOT PLAY – COACHING												
1955-56	Brandon Regals	WHL	66	13	45	58	....	....	....	44	....	....	....	....	....
1955-56			DID NOT PLAY												
1956-57			DID NOT PLAY												
1957-58			DID NOT PLAY												
1958-59	Regina Caps	SSHL	9	6	10	16	....	....	....	2	....	....	....	....	....
1959-60	Regina Caps	SSHL	13	6	16	22	....	....	....	22	9	6	7	13	2
	NHL Totals		**3**	**0**	**3**	**3**	**0**	**4**	**4**	**0**	....	....	....	....	....

• KYLE, GUS
Gus Kyle
D – L. 6'1", 202 lbs. b: Dysart, Sask., 9/11/1923. d: 11/17/1996.

1940-41	Notre Dame Hounds	SJHL	17	7	8	15	....	....	....	29	2	0	0	0	2
1941-42	New York Rovers	EHL	57	5	17	22	....	....	....	89	7	1	2	3	18
1942-43	Ottawa Postal Corps	City Sr.	18	7	18	25	....	....	....	43	4	1	4	5	2
1943-44	Fredericton Army	City Sr.	5	*8	3	*11	....	....	....	....	....	....	....	....	....
	Saint John Beavers	City Sr.	1	1	0	1	....	....	....	0	1	2	0	2	0
1944-45	Saint John Beavers	City Sr.	....	....	....	....	....	....	....	....	6	5	0	5	14
1945-46	Saint John Beavers	City Sr.	9	4	5	9	....	....	....	16	10	6	5	*11	32
1946-47	Saint John Beavers	MSHL	39	24	41	65	....	....	....	115	6	4	6	10	8
1947-48	Regina Caps	WCSHL	43	15	20	35	....	....	....	*76	4	1	0	1	4
1948-49	Regina Caps	WCSHL	40	5	10	15	....	....	....	100	7	0	0	0	8
1949-50	**New York Rangers**	**NHL**	**70**	**3**	**5**	**8**	**4**	**6**	**10**	**143**	**12**	**1**	**2**	**3**	**30**
1950-51	**New York Rangers**	**NHL**	**64**	**2**	**3**	**5**	**3**	**4**	**7**	**92**	....	....	....	....	....
1951-52	**Boston Bruins**	**NHL**	**69**	**1**	**12**	**13**	**1**	**15**	**16**	***127**	**2**	**0**	**0**	**0**	**4**
1952-53	Calgary Stampeders	WHL	70	8	22	30	....	....	....	146	5	0	3	3	18
1953-54	Calgary Stampeders	WHL	69	10	17	27	....	....	....	94	19	0	8	8	29
1954-55	Calgary Stampeders	WHL	66	5	16	21	....	....	....	88	9	0	3	3	8
1955-56	Calgary Stampeders	WHL	7	0	3	3	....	....	....	10	....	....	....	....	....
	NHL Totals		**203**	**6**	**20**	**26**	**8**	**25**	**33**	**362**	**14**	**1**	**2**	**3**	**34**

Traded to **Boston** by **NY Rangers** with Penti Lund for Paul Ronty, September 20, 1951.

• LABADIE, MIKE
Mike Labadie
RW – R. 5'11", 170 lbs. b: St. Francis D'Assisi, Que., 8/17/1932.

1950-51	Quebec Citadelle	Jr. B	10	6	8	14	....	....	....	11	....	....	....	....	....
	Quebec Citadelle	QJHL	2	0	1	1	....	....	....	0	....	....	....	....	....
1951-52	Quebec Citadelle	QJHL	50	34	43	77	....	....	....	31	15	6	7	13	6
1952-53	Quebec Citadelle	QJHL	47	35	43	78	....	....	....	60	9	3	*8	11	9
	New York Rangers	**NHL**	**3**	**0**	**0**	**0**	**0**	**0**	**0**	**0**	....	....	....	....	....
1953-54	Quebec Aces	QHL	67	20	24	44	....	....	....	32	16	5	5	10	2
1954-55	Quebec Aces	QHL	55	19	38	57	....	....	....	11	8	1	5	6	4
1955-56	Quebec Aces	QHL	61	18	21	39	....	....	....	35	7	4	3	7	0
1956-57	Quebec Aces	QHL	65	18	34	52	....	....	....	22	10	2	1	3	0
1957-58	Quebec Aces	QHL	64	22	30	52	....	....	....	10	12	5	9	14	0
1958-59	Quebec Aces	QHL	10	4	3	7	....	....	....	2	....	....	....	....	....
	Cleveland Barons	AHL	59	23	35	58	....	....	....	16	7	0	2	2	2
1959-60	Cleveland Barons	AHL	72	24	22	46	....	....	....	20	7	1	5	6	2
1960-61	Quebec Aces	AHL	66	21	37	58	....	....	....	10	....	....	....	....	....
1961-62	Quebec Aces	AHL	56	17	22	39	....	....	....	8	....	....	....	....	....
1962-63	Quebec Aces	AHL	72	15	24	39	....	....	....	20	....	....	....	....	....
1963-64	Springfield Indians	AHL	70	31	34	65	....	....	....	12	....	....	....	....	....
1964-65	Springfield Indians	AHL	55	19	21	40	....	....	....	19	....	....	....	....	....
1965-66	Victoria Maple Leafs	WHL	72	8	21	29	....	....	....	14	14	4	3	7	4
1966-67	Victoria Maple Leafs	WHL	48	10	15	25	....	....	....	9	....	....	....	....	....
1967-68	Buffalo Bisons	AHL	70	23	30	53	....	....	....	16	5	1	3	4	2
1968-69	Buffalo Bisons	AHL	6	0	1	1	....	....	....	0	....	....	....	....	....
	NHL Totals		**3**	**0**	**0**	**0**	**0**	**0**	**0**	**0**	....	....	....	....	....

Won William Northey Trophy (Top Rookie - QHL) (1954)

Traded to **Cleveland** (AHL) by **Quebec** (AHL) for Ian Anderson, November 7, 1958.

• LABINE, LEO
Leo "The Lion" Labine
RW – R. 5'10", 170 lbs. b: Haileybury, Ont., 7/22/1931.

Season	Club	League	GP	G	A	Pts	AG	AA	APts	PIM	Playoffs GP	G	A	Pts	PIM
1949-50	St. Michaels Majors	OHA	47	20	22	42	....	....	....	77	5	1	2	3	13
1950-51	Barrie Flyers	OHA	52	32	46	78	....	....	....	143	12	13	13	*26	*36
1951-52	**Boston Bruins**	**NHL**	**15**	**2**	**4**	**6**	**3**	**5**	**8**	**9**	**5**	**0**	**1**	**1**	**4**
	Hershey Bears	AHL	53	23	23	46	....	....	....	88	5	0	1	1	20
1952-53	**Boston Bruins**	**NHL**	**51**	**8**	**15**	**23**	**12**	**21**	**33**	**69**	**7**	**2**	**1**	**3**	***19**
	Hershey Bears	AHL	16	7	3	10	....	....	....	33	3	1	2	3	8
1953-54	**Boston Bruins**	**NHL**	**68**	**16**	**19**	**35**	**24**	**26**	**50**	**57**	**4**	**0**	**1**	**1**	**8**
1954-55	**Boston Bruins**	**NHL**	**67**	**24**	**18**	**42**	**35**	**23**	**58**	**75**	**5**	**2**	**1**	**3**	**11**
1955-56	**Boston Bruins**	**NHL**	**68**	**16**	**18**	**34**	**23**	**22**	**45**	**104**	....	....	....	....	....
1956-57	**Boston Bruins**	**NHL**	**67**	**18**	**29**	**47**	**25**	**34**	**59**	**128**	**10**	**2**	**3**	**5**	***14**
1957-58	**Boston Bruins**	**NHL**	**62**	**7**	**14**	**21**	**9**	**15**	**24**	**60**	**11**	**0**	**2**	**2**	**10**
1958-59	**Boston Bruins**	**NHL**	**70**	**9**	**23**	**32**	**11**	**24**	**35**	**74**	**7**	**2**	**1**	**3**	**12**
1959-60	**Boston Bruins**	**NHL**	**63**	**16**	**28**	**44**	**20**	**29**	**49**	**58**	....	....	....	....	....
1960-61	**Boston Bruins**	**NHL**	**40**	**7**	**12**	**19**	**8**	**12**	**20**	**34**	....	....	....	....	....
	Detroit Red Wings	**NHL**	**24**	**2**	**9**	**11**	**2**	**9**	**11**	**32**	**11**	**3**	**2**	**5**	**4**
1961-62	**Detroit Red Wings**	**NHL**	**48**	**3**	**4**	**7**	**4**	**4**	**8**	**30**	....	....	....	....	....
	Sudbury Wolves	EPHL	9	10	10	20	....	....	....	18	5	0	4	4	4
1962-63	Los Angeles Blades	WHL	68	30	47	77	....	....	....	90	3	1	0	1	2
1963-64	Los Angeles Blades	WHL	70	31	46	77	....	....	....	56	12	*10	12	*22	10
1964-65	Los Angeles Blades	WHL	58	16	37	53	....	....	....	42	....	....	....	....	....
1965-66	Los Angeles Blades	WHL	71	33	30	63	....	....	....	33	....	....	....	....	....
1966-67	Los Angeles Blades	WHL	70	18	29	47	....	....	....	24	....	....	....	....	....
	NHL Totals		**643**	**128**	**193**	**321**	**176**	**224**	**400**	**730**	**60**	**11**	**12**	**23**	**82**

WHL First All-Star Team (1964)

Played in NHL All-Star Game (1955, 1956)

Traded to **Detroit** by **Boston** with Vic Stasiuk for Gary Aldcorn, Murray Oliver and Tom McCarthy, January, 1961.

• LABOSSIERRE, GORD
— see page 1191

• LABOVITCH, MAX
Max Labovitch
RW – R. 5'11", 165 lbs. b: Winnipeg, Man., 1/18/1924.

Season	Club	League	GP	G	A	Pts	AG	AA	APts	PIM	Playoffs GP	G	A	Pts	PIM
1941-42	Winnipeg Rangers	MJHL	17	13	8	21	....	....	....	14	....	....	....	....	....
1942-43			MILITARY SERVICE												
1943-44	**New York Rangers**	**NHL**	**5**	**0**	**0**	**0**	**0**	**0**	**0**	**4**	....	....	....	....	....
	New York Rovers	EHL	24	11	13	24	....	....	....	20	11	6	10	16	0
1944-45			MILITARY SERVICE												
1945-46	Fort Worth Rangers	USHL	13	0	3	3	....	....	....	10	....	....	....	....	....
1946-47	Los Angeles Ramblers	Calif-Sr.	42	24	20	44	....	....	....	21	....	....	....	....	....
1947-48	Toledo Mercurys	IHL	22	11	9	20	....	....	....	28	13	4	3	7	34
1948-49	Toledo Mercurys	IHL	18	6	6	12	....	....	....	4	12	4	5	9	20
1949-50	Toledo Buckeyes	IHL	49	12	30	42	....	....	....	73	8	1	3	4	12
	NHL Totals		**5**	**0**	**0**	**0**	**0**	**0**	**0**	**4**	....	....	....	....	....

• LABRIE, GUY
Guy Labrie
D – L. 6', 185 lbs. b: St. Charles Bellechase, Que., 8/11/1920.

Season	Club	League	GP	G	A	Pts	AG	AA	APts	PIM	Playoffs GP	G	A	Pts	PIM
1939-40	Quebec Beavers	QPHL	41	12	6	18	....	....	....	57	....	....	....	....	....
1940-41	Valleyfield Braves	QSHL	....	14	12	26	....	....	....	48	....	....	....	....	....
1941-42	Quebec Aces	QSHL	11	1	0	1	....	....	....	10	....	....	....	....	....
1942-43			DID NOT PLAY												
1943-44	**Boston Bruins**	**NHL**	**15**	**2**	**7**	**9**	**2**	**8**	**10**	**2**	....	....	....	....	....
	Boston Olympics	QSHL	26	24	14	38	....	....	....	8	10	1	10	11	4
1944-45	Boston Olympics	QSHL	9	6	8	14	....	....	....	10	....	....	....	....	....
	New York Rangers	**NHL**	**27**	**2**	**2**	**4**	**3**	**3**	**6**	**14**	....	....	....	....	....
1945-46	New Haven–Providence	AHL	58	4	16	20	....	....	....	37	....	....	....	....	....
1946-47	Quebec Aces	QSHL	17	1	2	3	....	....	....	18	2	1	1	2	0
1947-48	Quebec Aces	QSHL	45	6	18	24	....	....	....	42	10	2	4	6	21
1948-49	Quebec Aces	QSHL	48	6	8	14	....	....	....	64	3	0	0	0	0
1949-50	Sherbrooke Saints	QSHL	58	8	15	23	....	....	....	56	22	1	10	11	31
1950-51	Sherbrooke Saints	QSHL	47	3	18	21	....	....	....	56	7	1	3	4	2
1951-52	Sherbrooke Saints	QSHL	59	7	18	25	....	....	....	38	11	0	3	3	2
1952-53	Sherbrooke Saints	QSHL	56	11	15	26	....	....	....	38	4	1	1	2	2
1953-54	Riviere-du-Loop Wolves	QPHL	60	6	11	17	....	....	....	30	....	....	....	....	....
	NHL Totals		**42**	**4**	**9**	**13**	**5**	**11**	**16**	**16**	....	....	....	....	....

QHL Second All-Star Team (1953)

Traded to **NY Rangers** by **Boston** for $12,000, November 27, 1944. Traded to **New Haven** (AHL) by **NY Rangers** for cash, June, 1945. Traded to **Sherbrooke** (QSHL) by **Quebec** (QSHL) with Jim Planche for Herb Carnegie, July 2, 1949.

• LACH, ELMER
Elmer Lach **HHOF**
C – L. 5'10", 165 lbs. b: Nokomis, Sask., 1/22/1918.

Season	Club	League	GP	G	A	Pts	AG	AA	APts	PIM	Playoffs GP	G	A	Pts	PIM
1935-36	Regina Abbotts	SJHL	2	0	1	1	....	....	....	2	4	3	0	3	6
1936-37	Weyburn Beavers	SSHL	23	16	6	22	....	....	....	27	3	0	1	1	4
1937-38	Weyburn Beavers	SSHL	22	12	12	24	....	....	....	44	3	2	1	3	0
1938-39	Moose Jaw Millers	SSHL	29	17	*20	37	....	....	....	23	10	6	*4	*10	8
1939-40	Moose Jaw Millers	SSHL	30	15	29	44	....	....	....	20	8	5	*9	*14	12
1940-41	**Montreal Canadiens**	**NHL**	**43**	**7**	**14**	**21**	**14**	**26**	**40**	**16**	**3**	**1**	**0**	**1**	**0**
1941-42	**Montreal Canadiens**	**NHL**	**1**	**0**	**1**	**1**	**0**	**2**	**2**	**0**	....	....	....	....	....
1942-43	**Montreal Canadiens**	**NHL**	**45**	**18**	**40**	**58**	**26**	**51**	**77**	**14**	**5**	**2**	**4**	**6**	**6**
1943-44	**Montreal Canadiens**	**NHL**	**48**	**24**	**48**	**72**	**30**	**59**	**89**	**23**	**9**	**2**	**11**	**13**	**4**
1944-45	**Montreal Canadiens**	**NHL**	**50**	**26**	***54**	***80**	**36**	**90**	**126**	**37**	**6**	**4**	**4**	**8**	**2**
1945-46	**Montreal Canadiens**	**NHL**	**50**	**13**	***34**	**47**	**20**	**64**	**84**	**34**	**9**	**5**	**12**	**17**	**4**
1946-47	**Montreal Canadiens**	**NHL**	**31**	**14**	**16**	**30**	**19**	**23**	**42**	**22**	....	....	....	....	....
1947-48	**Montreal Canadiens**	**NHL**	**60**	**30**	**31**	***61**	**44**	**46**	**90**	**72**	....	....	....	....	....
1948-49	**Montreal Canadiens**	**NHL**	**36**	**11**	**18**	**29**	**17**	**29**	**46**	**59**	**1**	**0**	**0**	**0**	**4**
1949-50	**Montreal Canadiens**	**NHL**	**64**	**15**	**33**	**48**	**20**	**42**	**62**	**33**	**5**	**1**	**2**	**3**	**4**
1950-51	**Montreal Canadiens**	**NHL**	**65**	**21**	**24**	**45**	**29**	**31**	**60**	**48**	**11**	**2**	**2**	**4**	**2**
1951-52	**Montreal Canadiens**	**NHL**	**70**	**15**	***50**	**65**	**21**	**66**	**87**	**36**	**11**	**1**	**2**	**3**	**4**
1952-53	**Montreal Canadiens**	**NHL**	**53**	**16**	**25**	**41**	**25**	**35**	**60**	**56**	**12**	**1**	**6**	**7**	**6**
1953-54	**Montreal Canadiens**	**NHL**	**48**	**5**	**20**	**25**	**8**	**27**	**35**	**28**	**4**	**0**	**2**	**2**	**0**
	NHL Totals		**664**	**215**	**408**	**623**	**309**	**591**	**900**	**478**	**76**	**19**	**45**	**64**	**36**

NHL Second All-Star Team (1944, 1946) • NHL First All-Star Team (1945, 1948, 1952) • NHL Scoring Leader (1945) • Won Hart Trophy (1945) • Won Art Ross Trophy (1948)

Played in NHL All-Star Game (1948, 1952, 1953)

• LAFLEUR, ROLAND
Roland (Rene) Lafleur
LW – L. 5'9", 160 lbs. b: Ottawa, Ontario, 1899. Deceased.

Season	Club	League	GP	G	A	Pts	AG	AA	APts	PIM	Playoffs GP	G	A	Pts	PIM
1922-23	Ottawa Montagnards	City Sr.	9	*8	*0	*17	....	....	....	14	2	0	0	0	*7
1923-24	Ottawa Royal Canadians	City Sr.	12	3	0	3	....	....	....	....	....	....	....	....	....
1924-25	**Montreal Canadiens**	**NHL**	**1**	**0**	**0**	**0**	**0**	**0**	**0**	**0**	....	....	....	....	....
	Ottawa New Edinburghs	City Sr.	16	8	1	9	....	....	....	....	....	....	....	....	....
1925-26	Berlin Wanderers	City Sr.	STATISTICS NOT AVAILABLE												
1926-27	Ottawa Gunners	City Sr.	14	2	3	5	....	....	....	....	....	....	....	....	....
1927-28	Ottawa Rideaus	City Sr.	14	5	2	7	....	....	....	....	....	....	....	....	....
1928-29	Ottawa Lasalle	City Sr.	13	5	0	5	....	....	....	....	3	0	0	0	....
1929-30	Ottawa Lasalle	City Sr.	20	3	1	4	....	....	....	32	....	....	....	....	....
1930-31	Ottawa Lasalle	City Sr.	20	2	3	5	....	....	....	33	2	0	0	0	6
	NHL Totals		**1**	**0**	**0**	**0**	**0**	**0**	**0**	**0**	....	....	....	....	....

Signed as a free agent by **Montreal Canadiens**, November 17, 1924.

• LAFORCE, ERNIE
Ernie Laforce
D – L. 5'11", 175 lbs. b: Montreal, Que., 6/23/1916.

Season	Club	League	GP	G	A	Pts	AG	AA	APts	PIM	Playoffs GP	G	A	Pts	PIM
1937-38	Montreal Lafontaine	QPHL	3	0	0	0	....	....	....	2	....	....	....	....	....
1938-39	Verdun Maple Leafs	QSHL	18	4	4	8	....	....	....	14	2	0	0	0	4
1939-40	Verdun Bulldogs	QPHL	38	10	20	30	....	....	....	24	2	0	0	0	0
1940-41	Verdun Maple Leafs	QSHL	34	6	9	15	....	....	....	23	....	....	....	....	....
1941-42	Montreal St. Pats	QSHL	37	5	15	20	....	....	....	12	....	....	....	....	....
1942-43	**Montreal Canadiens**	**NHL**	**1**	**0**	**0**	**0**	**0**	**0**	**0**	**0**	....	....	....	....	....
	Montreal Royals	QSHL	32	1	15	16	....	....	....	18	4	0	2	2	0
1943-44	Montreal Canada Car	City Sr.	7	3	3	6	....	....	....	2	....	....	....	....	....
	Montreal Royals	QSHL	19	1	15	16	....	....	....	6	7	0	1	1	8
1944-45	Montreal Royals	QSHL	22	7	13	20	....	....	....	19	7	0	3	3	2
1945-46	Montreal Royals	QSHL	24	9	7	16	....	....	....	4	6	0	1	1	6
1946-47	Montreal Royals	QSHL	21	3	6	9	....	....	....	18	11	1	7	8	10
1947-48	Montreal Royals	QSHL	44	6	20	26	....	....	....	16	3	0	0	0	0
1948-49	Montreal Royals	QSHL	58	2	18	20	....	....	....	20	9	3	4	7	8
1949-50	Montreal Royals	QSHL	52	2	14	16	....	....	....	31	6	0	0	0	2
	NHL Totals		**1**	**0**	**0**	**0**	**0**	**0**	**0**	**0**	....	....	....	....	....

• LAFORGE, CLAUDE
— see page 1196

• LAFRANCE, ADIE
Adie (Adelard Henry) Lafrance
LW – L. 5'10", 165 lbs. b: Chapleau, Ont., 1/13/1912.

Season	Club	League	GP	G	A	Pts	AG	AA	APts	PIM	Playoffs GP	G	A	Pts	PIM
1929-30	Sudbury St. Louis	NOHA	8	4	1	5	....	....	....	0	....	....	....	....	....
1930-31	Sudbury St. Louis	NOHA	8	4	1	5	....	....	....	4	3	*4	0	*4	0
	Sudbury Wolf Cubs	NOHA	....	....	....	....	....	....	....	....	1	0	0	0	0
1931-32	Falconbridge Falcons	NOHA	9	3	4	7	....	....	....	2	2	0	0	0	0
	Sudbury Wolves	NOHA	3	2	0	2	....	....	....	0	....	....	....	....	....
1932-33	Sudbury Wolves	NOHA	7	4	2	6	....	....	....	10	2	1	0	1	2
1933-34	**Montreal Canadiens**	**NHL**	**3**	**0**	**0**	**0**	**0**	**0**	**0**	**2**	**2**	**0**	**0**	**0**	**0**
	Falconbridge Falcons	NOHA	8	5	1	6	....	....	....	12	2	1	0	1	2
1934-35	Quebec Beavers	Can-Am	46	4	4	8	....	....	....	10	3	0	0	0	2
1935-36	Springfield Indians	Can-Am	48	13	19	32	....	....	....	32	3	2	3	5	4
1936-37	Springfield Indians	AHL	30	9	10	19	....	....	....	11	2	0	0	0	0
1937-38	Springfield Indians	AHL	41	8	13	21	....	....	....	17	....	....	....	....	....
1938-39	Springfield Indians	AHL	54	11	26	37	....	....	....	23	3	0	0	0	0
	NHL Totals		**3**	**0**	**0**	**0**	**0**	**0**	**0**	**2**	**2**	**0**	**0**	**0**	**0**

• LAFRANCE, LEO
Leo Lafrance
LW – L. 5'8", 160 lbs. b: Allomette, Quebec, 11/3/1902.

Season	Club	League	GP	G	A	Pts	AG	AA	APts	PIM	Playoffs GP	G	A	Pts	PIM
1920-21	Sudbury Cub Wolves	NOHA	2	2	2	4	....	....	....	....	5	*7	*4	*11	....
1921-22	Iroquois Falls Eskimos	NOHA	....	....	....	....	....				7	7	*5	*12	....
1922-23	Iroquois Falls Paper	NOHA	STATISTICS NOT AVAILABLE												
1923-24	Iroquois Falls Flyers	NOHA	8	2	1	3	....	....	....	15	....	....	....	....	....
1924-25	Duluth Hornets	USAHA	31	6	0	6	....	....	....	....	....	....	....	....	....
1925-26	Duluth Hornets	CHL	40	8	2	10	....	....	....	28	8	1	1	2	12
1926-27	**Montreal Canadiens**	**NHL**	**4**	**0**	**0**	**0**	**0**	**0**	**0**	**0**	....	....	....	....	....
	Duluth Hornets	AHA	37	12	4	16	....	....	....	41	3	2	0	2	0
1927-28	**Montreal Canadiens**	**NHL**	**15**	**1**	**0**	**1**	**3**	**0**	**3**	**2**	....	....	....	....	....
	Chicago Black Hawks	**NHL**	**14**	**1**	**0**	**1**	**3**	**0**	**3**	**4**	....	....	....	....	....
	Kansas City Pla-Mors	AHA	13	1	0	1	....	....	....	8	3	0	0	0	2
1928-29	Tulsa Oilers	AHA	40	19	7	26	....	....	....	33	4	0	0	0	4
1929-30	Tulsa Oilers	AHA	DID NOT PLAY – INJURED												
1930-31	Tulsa Oilers	AHA	48	27	15	42	....	....	....	41	4	*3	0	3	6
1931-32	Tulsa Oilers	AHA	48	11	5	16	....	....	....	51	....	....	....	....	....
1932-33	Wichita Blue Jays	AHA	39	16	8	24	....	....	....	32	....	....	....	....	....
1933-34	Duluth Hornets	CHL	14	0	0	0	....	....	....	41	....	....	....	....	....
	Tulsa Oilers	AHA	31	6	10	16	....	....	....	35	4	1	0	1	0
1934-35	Minneapolis Millers	CHL	46	16	11	27	....	....	....	26	5	2	3	5	2
1935-36	Rochester Cardinals	IAHL	9	1	0	1	....	....	....	7	....	....	....	....	....
	Calgary–Seattle	NWHL	29	8	4	12	....	....	....	27	4	3	2	5	2
	NHL Totals		**33**	**2**	**0**	**2**	**6**	**0**	**6**	**6**	....	....	....	....	....

Loaned to **Chicago** by **Montreal Canadiens** for cash, December 30, 1927.

• LAFRENIERE, ROGER
see page 1197

			REGULAR SEASON								PLAYOFFS				
Season	Club	League	GP	G	A	Pts	AG	AA	APts	PIM	GP	G	A	Pts	PIM

• LALANDE, HEC Hec Lalande

C – L. 5'9", 150 lbs. b: North Bay, Ont., 11/24/1934.

Season	Club	League	GP	G	A	Pts	AG	AA	APts	PIM	GP	G	A	Pts	PIM
1952-53	Galt Black Hawks	OHA	56	9	24	33	....	....	....	65	11	6	6	12	27
1953-54	Galt Black Hawks	OHA	59	17	22	39	....	....	....	118	....	....	....	....	....
	Chicago Black Hawks	**NHL**	**2**	**0**	**0**	**0**	**0**	**0**	**0**	**0**	....	....	....	....	....
1954-55	Galt Black Hawks	OHA	49	31	48	79	....	....	....	93	4	5	0	5	8
	Buffalo Bisons	AHL	3	0	1	1	....	....	....	2	....	....	....	....	....
1955-56	**Chicago Black Hawks**	**NHL**	**65**	**8**	**18**	**26**	**12**	**22**	**34**	**70**	....	....	....	....	....
1956-57	**Chicago Black Hawks**	**NHL**	**50**	**11**	**17**	**28**	**15**	**20**	**35**	**38**	....	....	....	....	....
	Rochester Americans	AHL	13	5	2	7	....	....	....	17	....	....	....	....	....
1957-58	**Chicago Black Hawks**	**NHL**	**22**	**2**	**2**	**4**	**3**	**2**	**5**	**10**	....	....	....	....	....
	Detroit Red Wings	**NHL**	**12**	**0**	**2**	**2**	**0**	**2**	**2**	**2**	....	....	....	....	....
	Hershey Bears	AHL	11	7	7	14	....	....	....	12	11	3	4	7	10
1958-59	Hershey Bears	AHL	58	12	23	35	....	....	....	58	13	1	4	5	30
1959-60	Hershey Bears	AHL	61	14	28	42	....	....	....	71	....	....	....	....	....
1960-61	Hershey Bears	AHL	72	15	41	56	....	....	....	71	8	3	*7	*10	11
1961-62	Hershey Bears	AHL	64	21	36	57	....	....	....	19	7	0	2	2	0
1962-63	St. Louis Braves	EPHL	26	6	24	30	....	....	....	57	....	....	....	....	....
1963-64	Clinton Comets	EHL	62	27	75	102	....	....	....	33	15	11	10	21	11
1964-65	Clinton Comets	EHL	62	31	69	100	....	....	....	18	11	4	8	12	4
1965-66	Jersey Devils	EHL	36	8	25	33	....	....	....	2	....	....	....	....	....
1966-67	Jersey Devils	EHL	18	7	20	27	....	....	....	10	16	8	8	16	2
1967-68	Jersey Devils	EHL	2	1	0	1	....	....	....	0	....	....	....	....	....
	Belleville Monarchs	OHA Sr.	28	5	12	17	....	....	....	2	....	....	....	....	....
	NHL Totals		**151**	**21**	**39**	**60**	**30**	**46**	**76**	**120**	....	....	....	....	....

Traded to **Detroit** by **Chicago** with Nick Mikoski, Bob Bailey, Jack McIntyre for Bill Dineen, Billy Dea and Earl Reible, December 17, 1957. Traded to **Hershey** (AHL) by **Detroit** with Don Poile for Dunc Fisher, June 7, 1958.

• LALONDE, NEWSY Newsy (Edmond) Lalonde HHOF

C – R. 5'9", 168 lbs. b: Cornwall, Ont., 10/31/1888. d: 11/21/1971.

Season	Club	League	GP	G	A	Pts	AG	AA	APts	PIM	GP	G	A	Pts	PIM
1904-05	Cornwall Victorias	FAHL	2	1	0	1	....	....	....	....	....	....	....	....	....
1905-06	Woodstock Seniors	OHA Sr.	STATISTICS NOT AVAILABLE												
1906-07	Canadian Soo	IHL	18	29	4	33	....	....	....	27	....	....	....	....	....
1907-08	Portage la Prairie	MHL Sr.	1	0	0	0	....	....	....	0	....	....	....	....	....
	Toronto Professionals	OPHL	11	*29	0	*29	....	....	....	....	1	2	0	2	....
	Haileybury Silver Kings	TPHL	....	....	....	....	....	....	....	....	1	3	0	3	0
1908-09	Toronto Professionals	OPHL	11	29	0	29	....	....	....	*79	....	....	....	....	....
1909-10	Montreal Canadiens	NHA	6	*16	0	*16	....	....	....	40	....	....	....	....	....
	Renfrew Cremery Kings	NHA	5	*22	0	*22	....	....	....	16	....	....	....	....	....
1910-11	Montreal Canadiens	NHA	16	19	0	19	....	....	....	63	....	....	....	....	....
1911-12	Vancouver Millionaires	PCHA	15	*27	0	*27	....	....	....	51	....	....	....	....	....
1912-13	Montreal Canadiens	NHA	18	25	0	25	....	....	....	61	....	....	....	....	....
1913-14	Montreal Canadiens	NHA	14	22	5	27	....	....	....	23	2	0	0	0	2
1914-15	Montreal Canadiens	NHA	7	4	3	7	....	....	....	17	....	....	....	....	....
1915-16	Montreal Canadiens	NHA	24	*28	6	34	....	....	....	78	4	3	0	3	41
1916-17	Montreal Canadiens	NHA	18	27	5	32	....	....	....	53	6	2	0	2	13
1917-18	**Montreal Canadiens**	**NHL**	**14**	**23**	**7**	**30**	**60**	**0**	**60**	**51**	**2**	**4**	**2**	**6**	**17**
1918-19	**Montreal Canadiens**	**NHL**	**17**	***23**	***10**	***33**	**87**	**100**	**187**	**42**	**10**	**17**	**1**	**18**	**18**
1919-20	**Montreal Canadiens**	**NHL**	**23**	**37**	**9**	**46**	**89**	**62**	**151**	**34**	....	....	....	....	**0**
1920-21	**Montreal Canadiens**	**NHL**	**24**	**32**	**11**	***43**	**86**	**101**	**187**	**2**	....	....	....	....	....
1921-22	**Montreal Canadiens**	**NHL**	**20**	**9**	**5**	**14**	**25**	**31**	**56**	**20**	....	....	....	....	....
1922-23	Saskatoon Sheiks	WCHL	29	*30	4	34	....	....	....	44	....	....	....	....	....
1923-24	Saskatoon Crescents	WCHL	21	10	10	20	....	....	....	24	....	....	....	....	....
1924-25	Saskatoon Crescents	WCHL	22	8	6	14	....	....	....	42	2	0	0	0	4
1925-26	Saskatoon Crescents	WHL	3	0	0	0	....	....	....	2	2	0	0	0	2
1926-27	**New York Americans**	**NHL**	**1**	**0**	**0**	**0**	**0**	**0**	**0**	**2**	....	....	....	....	....
1927-28	Quebec Castors	Can-Am	1	0	0	0	....	....	....	0	....	....	....	....	....
1928-29	Niagara Falls Cataracts	Can-Pro	DID NOT PLAY – COACHING												
	NHL Totals		**99**	**124**	**42**	**166**	**347**	**294**	**641**	**151**	**12**	**21**	**3**	**24**	**35**
	Other Major League Totals		239	325	43	368	....	....	....	620	17	7	0	7	62

IHL Second All-Star Team (1907) • PCHA First All-Star Team (1912) • NHL Scoring Leader (1919, 1921) • WCHL First All-Star Team (1924)

Rights retained by **Montreal Canadiens** after NHA folded, November 26, 1917. Traded to **Saskatoon** (WCHL) by **Montreal Canadiens** for the rights to Aurel Joliat, September 18, 1922. Traded to **NY Americans** by **Saskatoon** (WHL) for cash, September 27, 1926.

• LAMB, JOE Joe Lamb

RW – R. 5'10", 170 lbs. b: Sussex, N.B., 6/18/1906. Deceased.

Season	Club	League	GP	G	A	Pts	AG	AA	APts	PIM	GP	G	A	Pts	PIM
1922-23	Sussex Dairy Kings	NBSHL	8	1	0	1	....	....	....	4	4	2	0	2	2
1923-24	Sussex Dairy Kings	NBSHL	6	3	4	7	....	....	....	2	6	4	1	5	2
1924-25	Sussex Dairy Kings	NBSHL	12	14	4	18	....	....	....	8	6	2	3	5	6
1925-26	Montreal Young Royals	City Jr.	....	....	....	....	....	....	....	....	....	....	....	....	....
1926-27	Montreal Victorias	ECHL	7	5	0	5	....	....	....	20	....	....	....	....	....
1927-28	Montreal Victorias	City Sr.	7	4	*4	8	....	....	....	6	....	....	....	....	....
	Montreal Royal Bank	City Sr.	8	5	1	6	....	....	....	30	....	....	....	....	....
	Montreal Maroons	**NHL**	**21**	**8**	**5**	**13**	**24**	**42**	**66**	**39**	**8**	**1**	**0**	**1**	**32**
1928-29	**Montreal Maroons**	**NHL**	**30**	**4**	**1**	**5**	**16**	**9**	**25**	**44**	....	....	....	....	....
	Ottawa Senators	**NHL**	**6**	**0**	**0**	**0**	**0**	**0**	**0**	**8**	....	....	....	....	....
1929-30	**Ottawa Senators**	**NHL**	**44**	**29**	**20**	**49**	**58**	**66**	**124**	***119**	**2**	**0**	**0**	**0**	**11**
1930-31	**Ottawa Senators**	**NHL**	**44**	**11**	**14**	**25**	**27**	**51**	**78**	**91**	....	....	....	....	....
1931-32	**New York Americans**	**NHL**	**48**	**14**	**11**	**25**	**30**	**31**	**61**	**71**	....	....	....	....	....
1932-33	**Boston Bruins**	**NHL**	**42**	**11**	**8**	**19**	**26**	**21**	**47**	**68**	**5**	**0**	**1**	**1**	**6**
1933-34	**Boston Bruins**	**NHL**	**48**	**10**	**15**	**25**	**22**	**40**	**62**	**47**	....	....	....	....	....
1934-35	**Montreal Canadiens**	**NHL**	**7**	**3**	**2**	**5**	**6**	**4**	**10**	**4**	....	....	....	....	....
	St. Louis Eagles	**NHL**	**31**	**11**	**12**	**23**	**23**	**27**	**50**	**19**	....	....	....	....	....
1935-36	**Montreal Maroons**	**NHL**	**35**	**0**	**3**	**3**	**0**	**7**	**7**	**12**	**3**	**0**	**0**	**0**	**2**
1936-37	**New York Americans**	**NHL**	**48**	**3**	**9**	**12**	**6**	**21**	**27**	**53**	....	....	....	....	....
1937-38	**New York Americans**	**NHL**	**25**	**1**	**0**	**1**	**2**	**0**	**2**	**20**	....	....	....	....	....
	Detroit Red Wings	**NHL**	**14**	**3**	**1**	**4**	**6**	**2**	**8**	**6**	....	....	....	....	....
	Pittsburgh Hornets	AHL	6	2	0	2	....	....	....	4	....	....	....	....	....
1938-39	Springfield Indians	AHL	51	11	16	27	....	....	....	72	3	0	1	1	4
1939-40	Springfield Indians	AHL	54	20	14	34	....	....	....	44	3	0	0	0	4
	NHL Totals		**443**	**108**	**101**	**209**	**246**	**321**	**567**	**601**	**18**	**1**	**1**	**2**	**51**

Signed as a free agent by **Montreal Maroons**, January 29, 1928. Traded to **Ottawa** by **Montreal Maroons** for George Boucher, February 14, 1929. Claimed by **NY Americans** from **Ottawa** for 1931-32 season in Dispersal Draft, September 26, 1931. Traded to **Boston** by **Ottawa** with $5,000 for Conney Weiland, October 17, 1932. Traded to **Montreal Canadiens** by **Boston** for John Gagnon, December 3, 1934. Traded to **Boston** by **Montreal Canadiens** for cash, December 4, 1934. Traded to **St. Louis** by **Boston** for Max Kaminsky and Des Roche, December 4, 1934. Claimed by **Montreal Maroons** from **St. Louis** in Dispersal Draft, October 15, 1935. Traded to **NY Americans** by **Montreal Maroons** with $10,000 for Carl Voss, September 6, 1936. Traded to **Detroit** by **NY Americans** for Red Beattie, January 24, 1938.

• LAMIRANDE, JEAN-PAUL Jean-Paul Lamirande

LW/D – R. 5'8", 170 lbs. b: Shawinigan Falls, Que., 8/21/1924. Deceased.

Season	Club	League	GP	G	A	Pts	AG	AA	APts	PIM	GP	G	A	Pts	PIM
1943-44	Montreal Army	City Sr.	2	0	0	0	....	....	....	0	2	0	0	0	2
1944-45	Montreal Army	City Sr.	14	3	5	8	....	....	....	10	3	0	0	0	2
1945-46	Montreal Royals	QSHL	36	6	8	14	....	....	....	60	9	2	2	4	22
1946-47	**New York Rangers**	**NHL**	**14**	**1**	**1**	**2**	**1**	**1**	**2**	**14**	....	....	....	....	....
	New Haven Ramblers	AHL	4	0	1	1	....	....	....	6	....	....	....	....	....
	St. Paul Saints	USHL	26	0	4	4	....	....	....	18	....	....	....	....	....
1947-48	**New York Rangers**	**NHL**	**18**	**0**	**1**	**1**	**0**	**1**	**1**	**6**	**6**	**0**	**0**	**0**	**4**
	New Haven Ramblers	AHL	46	7	20	27	....	....	....	22	....	....	....	....	....
1948-49	New Haven Ramblers	AHL	30	3	7	10	....	....	....	18	....	....	....	....	....
1949-50	**New York Rangers**	**NHL**	**16**	**4**	**3**	**7**	**5**	**4**	**9**	**6**	**2**	**0**	**0**	**0**	**0**
	New Haven Ramblers	AHL	52	26	31	57	....	....	....	16	....	....	....	....	....
1950-51	St. Louis Flyers	AHL	64	13	36	49	....	....	....	6	....	....	....	....	....
1951-52	Chicoutimi Sagueneens	QSHL	58	11	28	39	....	....	....	32	18	2	7	9	4
1952-53	Chicoutimi Sagueneens	QSHL	56	4	19	23	....	....	....	36	20	2	6	8	17
1953-54	Chicoutimi Sagueneens	QHL	68	5	22	27	....	....	....	65	7	0	0	0	4
1954-55	**Montreal Canadiens**	**NHL**	**1**	**0**	**0**	**0**	**0**	**0**	**0**	**0**	....	....	....	....	....
	Shawinigan Cataracts	QHL	60	3	29	32	....	....	....	59	11	2	4	6	8
1955-56	Trois-Rivieres–Shawinigan	QHL	58	6	16	22	....	....	....	44	11	1	2	3	10
1956-57	Quebec Aces	QHL	67	4	14	18	....	....	....	52	10	0	5	5	6
1957-58	Quebec Aces	QHL	45	3	16	19	....	....	....	24	13	1	2	3	6
	Canada	WEC-A	7	1	4	5	....	....	....	0	....	....	....	....	....
1958-59	Belleville McFarlands	EOHL	20	5	8	13	....	....	....	10	....	....	....	....	....
	Canada	WEC-A	8	1	0	1	....	....	....	0	....	....	....	....	....
1959-60	Windsor Bulldogs	OHA Sr.	49	6	16	22	....	....	....	50	14	0	4	4	2
1960-61	Kingston Frontenacs	EPHL	2	0	1	1	....	....	....	2	....	....	....	....	....
	Clinton Comets	EHL	52	6	27	33	....	....	....	22	4	0	1	1	7
	NHL Totals		**49**	**5**	**5**	**10**	**6**	**6**	**12**	**26**	**8**	**0**	**0**	**0**	**4**

QHL First All-Star Team (1953, 1955) • QHL Second All-Star Team (1956, 1957) • Named Best Defenseman at WEC-A (1959) • EHL Second All-Star Team (1961)

Traded to **Montreal** by **NY Rangers** for cash, September 25, 1954.

• LAMOUREUX, LEO Leo Lamoureux

D – L. 5'11", 175 lbs. b: Espanola, Ont., 10/1/1916. d: 1/11/1961.

Season	Club	League	GP	G	A	Pts	AG	AA	APts	PIM	GP	G	A	Pts	PIM
1934-35	Oshawa Generals	OHA	14	6	14	20	....	....	....	8	2	4	0	4	4
1935-36	Timmins Black Shirts	NOHA	14	10	11	21	....	....	....	19	....	....	....	....	....
1936-37	Kirkland Lake Blue Devils	NOHA	6	4	5	9	....	....	....	0	4	1	0	1	2
1937-38	Windsor Chryslers	MOHL	31	13	15	28	....	....	....	36	8	4	5	9	6
1938-39	Earls Court Rangers	Britain	....	9	7	16	....	....	....	....	....	....	....	....	....
1939-40	Cornwall Royals	QSHL	29	7	9	16	....	....	....	29	5	1	2	3	6
1940-41	Hamilton Dofascos	OHA Sr.	28	12	9	21	....	....	....	50	6	1	4	5	8
1941-42	**Montreal Canadiens**	**NHL**	**1**	**0**	**0**	**0**	**0**	**0**	**0**	**0**	....	....	....	....	....
	Washington Lions	AHL	55	5	19	24	....	....	....	40	2	0	2	2	0
1942-43	**Montreal Canadiens**	**NHL**	**46**	**2**	**16**	**18**	**3**	**20**	**23**	**53**	....	....	....	....	....
	Washington Lions	AHL	1	1	0	1	....	....	....	0	....	....	....	....	....
1943-44	**Montreal Canadiens**	**NHL**	**44**	**8**	**23**	**31**	**10**	**28**	**38**	**32**	**9**	**0**	**3**	**3**	**8**
1944-45	**Montreal Canadiens**	**NHL**	**49**	**2**	**22**	**24**	**3**	**36**	**39**	**58**	**6**	**1**	**1**	**2**	**2**
1945-46	**Montreal Canadiens**	**NHL**	**45**	**5**	**7**	**12**	**8**	**13**	**21**	**18**	**9**	**0**	**2**	**2**	**2**
1946-47	**Montreal Canadiens**	**NHL**	**50**	**2**	**11**	**13**	**3**	**16**	**19**	**14**	**4**	**0**	**0**	**0**	**4**
1947-48	Buffalo–Springfield	AHL	55	2	17	19	....	....	....	18	....	....	....	....	....
1948-49	Shawinigan Cataracts	QSHL	31	1	18	19	....	....	....	26	....	....	....	....	....
1949-50	Shawinigan Cataracts	QSHL	22	1	15	16	....	....	....	8	....	....	....	....	....
1950-51	Detroit Hettche	IHL	13	0	4	4	....	....	....	12	....	....	....	....	....
	Charlottetown Islanders	MMHL	1	0	1	1	....	....	....	2	....	....	....	....	....
1951-52	Charlottetown Islanders	MMHL	1	0	0	0	....	....	....	0	....	....	....	....	....
1952-53	North Bay Trappers	NOHA	8	0	4	4	....	....	....	6	....	....	....	....	....
1953-54			DID NOT PLAY – RETIRED												
1954-55			DID NOT PLAY – RETIRED												
1955-56	Indianapolis Chiefs	IHL	24	0	5	5	....	....	....	19	....	....	....	....	....
	NHL Totals		**235**	**19**	**79**	**98**	**27**	**113**	**140**	**175**	**28**	**1**	**6**	**7**	**16**

Signed as a free agent by **Montreal**, October 16, 1941.

• LANCIEN, JACK   Jack Lancien

D – L. 6′, 188 lbs.   b: Regina, Sask., 6/14/1923.

Season	Club	League	GP	G	A	Pts	AG	AA	APts	PIM	Playoffs GP	G	A	Pts	PIM
1945-46	Regina Pats	WCSHL	12	1	2	3	....	....	....	12	....	....	....	....	....
1946-47	**New York Rangers**	**NHL**	**1**	**0**	**0**	**0**	**0**	**0**	**0**	**0**	....	....	....	....	....
	New York Rovers	EHL	55	3	11	14	....	....	....	44	9	0	0	0	9
1947-48	New Haven Ramblers	AHL	68	7	20	27	....	....	....	64	4	0	1	1	4
	New York Rangers	**NHL**	....	....	....	....	....	....	....	....	**2**	**0**	**0**	**0**	**2**
1948-49	New Haven Ramblers	AHL	67	2	24	26	....	....	....	66	....	....	....	....	....
1949-50	**New York Rangers**	**NHL**	**43**	**1**	**4**	**5**	**1**	**5**	**6**	**27**	**4**	**0**	**1**	**1**	**0**
	New Haven Ramblers	AHL	26	2	7	9	....	....	....	17	....	....	....	....	....
	St. Paul Saints	USHL	4	0	2	2	....	....	....	4	....	....	....	....	....
1950-51	**New York Rangers**	**NHL**	**19**	**0**	**1**	**1**	**0**	**1**	**1**	**8**	....	....	....	....	....
	Cincinnati Mohawks	AHL	40	4	6	10	....	....	....	41	....	....	....	....	....
1951-52	Cincinnati Mohawks	AHL	61	2	4	6	....	....	....	43	7	0	1	1	4
1952-53	Vancouver Canucks	WHL	64	10	12	22	....	....	....	39	9	0	1	1	4
1953-54	Vancouver Canucks	WHL	70	9	24	33	....	....	....	54	12	0	4	4	8
1954-55	Vancouver Canucks	WHL	70	5	30	35	....	....	....	17	5	0	1	1	4
1955-56	Spokane Flyers	WIHL	44	7	32	39	....	....	....	13	10	1	9	10	2
1956-57	Spokane Flyers	WIHL	48	9	23	32	....	....	....	23	9	0	*10	10	0
1957-58	Spokane Flyers	WIHL	47	11	29	40	....	....	....	13	13	1	6	7	2
1958-59	Spokane Comets	WHL	31	1	12	13	....	....	....	6	4	0	1	1	0
	Trail Smoke Eaters	WIHL	5	1	3	4	....	....	....	0	....	....	....	....	....
1959-60	Spokane Comets	WHL	1	0	0	0	....	....	....	0	....	....	....	....	....
1960-61	Rossland Warriors	WIHL	4	1	1	2	....	....	....	....	....	....	....	....	....
	NHL Totals		**63**	**1**	**5**	**6**	**1**	**6**	**7**	**35**	**6**	**0**	**1**	**1**	**2**

• LANE, MYLES   Myles Lane   USHOF

D – L. 6′, 180 lbs.   b: Melrose, MA, 10/2/1905.   d: 1987.

Season	Club	League	GP	G	A	Pts	AG	AA	APts	PIM	Playoffs GP	G	A	Pts	PIM
1923-24	Boston Hockey Club	USAHA	4	0	0	0	....	....	....	....	....	....	....	....	....
1924-25	Boston Hockey Club	USAHA	1	1	0	1	....	....	....	....	....	....	....	....	....
1925-26	Dartmouth College	Ivy	8	20	0	20	....	....	....	....	....	....	....	....	....
1926-27	Dartmouth College	Ivy	4	10	0	10	....	....	....	....	....	....	....	....	....
1927-28	Dartmouth College	Ivy	5	20	0	20	....	....	....	....	....	....	....	....	....
1928-29	**New York Rangers**	**NHL**	**24**	**1**	**0**	**1**	**4**	**0**	**4**	**22**	....	....	....	....	....
	Boston Bruins	**NHL**	**19**	**1**	**0**	**1**	**4**	**0**	**4**	**2**	**5**	**0**	**0**	**0**	**0**
1929-30	**Boston Bruins**	**NHL**	**3**	**0**	**0**	**0**	**0**	**0**	**0**	**0**	**6**	**0**	**0**	**0**	**0**
1930-31			DID NOT PLAY												
1931-32	Boston Cubs	Can-Am	40	3	4	7	....	....	....	48	5	0	1	1	2
1932-33	Boston Cubs	Can-Am	39	3	10	13	....	....	....	45	7	0	2	2	10
1933-34	**Boston Bruins**	**NHL**	**25**	**2**	**1**	**3**	**4**	**3**	**7**	**17**	....	....	....	....	....
	Boston Cubs	Can-Am	16	3	2	5	....	....	....	8	....	....	....	....	....
	NHL Totals		**71**	**4**	**1**	**5**	**12**	**3**	**15**	**41**	**11**	**0**	**0**	**0**	**0**

Traded to **Boston** by **NY Rangers** for $7,5000, January 21, 1929.

• LANGELLE, PETE   Pete Langelle

C – L. 5′11″, 170 lbs.   b: Winnipeg, Man., 11/4/1917.

Season	Club	League	GP	G	A	Pts	AG	AA	APts	PIM	Playoffs GP	G	A	Pts	PIM
1935-36	Winnipeg Monarchs	City Jr.	15	5	4	9	....	....	....	6	....	....	....	....	....
1936-37	Winnipeg Monarchs	City Jr.	10	12	7	19	....	....	....	10	8	2	1	3	2
1937-38	Syracuse Stars	AHL	48	4	14	18	....	....	....	8	8	*5	4	*9	2
1938-39	**Toronto Maple Leafs**	**NHL**	**2**	**1**	**0**	**1**	**2**	**0**	**2**	**0**	**11**	**1**	**2**	**3**	**2**
	Syracuse Stars	AHL	51	10	13	23	....	....	....	8	....	....	....	....	....
1939-40	**Toronto Maple Leafs**	**NHL**	**39**	**7**	**14**	**21**	**15**	**28**	**43**	**2**	**10**	**0**	**3**	**3**	**0**
1940-41	**Toronto Maple Leafs**	**NHL**	**47**	**4**	**15**	**19**	**8**	**27**	**35**	**0**	**7**	**1**	**1**	**2**	**0**
1941-42	**Toronto Maple Leafs**	**NHL**	**48**	**10**	**22**	**32**	**17**	**33**	**50**	**9**	**13**	**3**	**3**	**6**	**2**
1942-43	Winnipeg RCAF	City Sr.	13	11	*17	*28	....	....	....	12	17	11	7	18	4
1943-44	Winnipeg RCAF	City Sr.	10	4	5	9	....	....	....	7	....	....	....	....	....
1944-45	Winnipeg RCAF	City Sr.	10	4	6	10	....	....	....	2	....	....	....	....	....
1945-46			MILITARY SERVICE												
1946-47	Pittsburgh Hornets	AHL	64	20	30	50	....	....	....	4	12	4	7	11	2
1947-48	Pittsburgh Hornets	AHL	67	21	37	58	....	....	....	8	2	0	0	0	0
1948-49	Pittsburgh Hornets	AHL	68	10	26	36	....	....	....	13	....	....	....	....	....
1949-50	Pittsburgh Hornets	AHL	47	8	15	23	....	....	....	7	....	....	....	....	....
1950-51	Pittsburgh Hornets	AHL	47	4	10	14	....	....	....	0	8	1	3	4	2
1951-52	Saint John Beavers	MMHL	72	16	18	34	....	....	....	35	15	3	4	7	4
1953-54	Pilot Mound Seniors	MHL Sr.	13	4	14	18	....	....	....	14	....	....	....	....	....
	NHL Totals		**136**	**22**	**51**	**73**	**42**	**88**	**130**	**11**	**41**	**5**	**9**	**14**	**4**

Signed as a free agent by **Toronto**, October 27, 1937.

• LANGLOIS, ALBERT   Albert "Junior" Langlois

D – L. 6′, 205 lbs.   b: Magog, Que., 11/6/1934.

Season	Club	League	GP	G	A	Pts	AG	AA	APts	PIM	Playoffs GP	G	A	Pts	PIM
1952-53	Quebec Citadelles	QJHL	9	0	0	0	....	....	....	0	....	....	....	....	....
1953-54	Quebec Frontenacs	QJHL	63	2	11	13	....	....	....	86	8	1	2	3	8
1954-55	Quebec Citadelle	QJHL	43	2	18	20	....	....	....	73	18	3	3	6	18
1955-56	Shawinigan Cataracts	QHL	64	8	6	14	....	....	....	48	11	2	4	6	14
1956-57	Shawinigan Cataracts	QHL	16	0	2	2	....	....	....	12	....	....	....	....	....
	Rochester Americans	AHL	47	5	24	29	....	....	....	64	10	0	4	4	18
1957-58	**Montreal Canadiens**	**NHL**	**1**	**0**	**0**	**0**	**0**	**0**	**0**	**0**	**7**	**0**	**1**	**1**	**4**
	Rochester Americans	AHL	68	0	11	11	....	....	....	88	....	....	....	....	....
1958-59	**Montreal Canadiens**	**NHL**	**48**	**0**	**3**	**3**	**0**	**3**	**3**	**26**	**7**	**0**	**0**	**0**	**4**
1959-60	**Montreal Canadiens**	**NHL**	**67**	**1**	**14**	**15**	**1**	**14**	**15**	**48**	**8**	**0**	**3**	**3**	**18**
1960-61	**Montreal Canadiens**	**NHL**	**61**	**1**	**12**	**13**	**1**	**12**	**13**	**56**	**5**	**0**	**0**	**0**	**6**
1961-62	**New York Rangers**	**NHL**	**69**	**7**	**18**	**25**	**8**	**18**	**26**	**90**	**6**	**0**	**1**	**1**	**2**
1962-63	**New York Rangers**	**NHL**	**60**	**2**	**14**	**16**	**2**	**15**	**17**	**62**	....	....	....	....	....
1963-64	**New York Rangers**	**NHL**	**44**	**4**	**2**	**6**	**5**	**2**	**7**	**32**	....	....	....	....	....
	Detroit Red Wings	**NHL**	**17**	**1**	**6**	**7**	**1**	**7**	**8**	**13**	**14**	**0**	**0**	**0**	**12**
	Baltimore Clippers	AHL	6	1	0	1	....	....	....	6	....	....	....	....	....
1964-65	**Detroit Red Wings**	**NHL**	**65**	**1**	**12**	**13**	**1**	**13**	**14**	**107**	**6**	**1**	**0**	**1**	**4**
1965-66	**Boston Bruins**	**NHL**	**65**	**4**	**10**	**14**	**5**	**10**	**15**	**54**	....	....	....	....	....
1966-67	Los Angeles Blades	WHL	59	6	34	40	....	....	....	97	....	....	....	....	....
	NHL Totals		**497**	**21**	**91**	**112**	**24**	**94**	**118**	**488**	**53**	**1**	**5**	**6**	**50**

QHL Second All-Star Team (1956)

Played in NHL All-Star Game (1959, 1960)

Traded to **NY Rangers** by **Montreal** for John Hanna, June 13, 1961. Traded to **Detroit** by **NY Rangers** for Ron Ingram, February 14, 1964. Traded to **Boston** by **Detroit** with Ron Harris, Parker MacDonald and Bob Dillabough for Ab McDonald, Bob McCord and Ken Stephenson, May 31, 1965.

• LANGLOIS, CHARLIE   Charlie Langlois

RW/D – R. 6′, 210 lbs.   b: Latbiniere, Que., 8/25/1894.   Deceased.

Season	Club	League	GP	G	A	Pts	AG	AA	APts	PIM	Playoffs GP	G	A	Pts	PIM
1916-17	Montreal Stars	City Sr.	10	2	*5	7	....	....	....	24	4	3	*2	*5	*15
1917-18	Montreal Lyalls	City Sr.	11	10	7	17	....	....	....	24	1	1	0	1	0
1918-19	Montreal Nationale	City Sr.	3	5	3	8	....	....	....	3	....	....	....	....	....
1919-20	Sudbury Wolves	NOHA	6	5	2	7	....	....	....	2	7	6	4	10	12
1920-21	Sudbury Wolves	NOHA	9	8	5	13	....	....	....	*61	....	....	....	....	....
1921-22	Sudbury Wolves	NOHA	8	1	2	3	....	....	....	21	....	....	....	....	....
1922-23	Sudbury Wolves	NOHA	7	1	1	2	....	....	....	6	2	0	0	0	0
1923-24	Sudbury Wolves	NOHA	STATISTICS NOT AVAILABLE												
1924-25	**Hamilton Tigers**	**NHL**	**30**	**6**	**1**	**7**	**21**	**13**	**34**	**59**	....	....	....	....	....
1925-26	**New York Americans**	**NHL**	**36**	**9**	**1**	**10**	**28**	**11**	**39**	**76**	....	....	....	....	....
1926-27	**New York Americans**	**NHL**	**9**	**2**	**0**	**2**	**6**	**0**	**6**	**8**	....	....	....	....	....
	Pittsburgh Pirates	**NHL**	**36**	**5**	**1**	**6**	**14**	**8**	**22**	**36**	....	....	....	....	....
1927-28	**Pittsburgh Pirates**	**NHL**	**8**	**0**	**0**	**0**	**0**	**0**	**0**	**8**	....	....	....	....	....
	Montreal Canadiens	**NHL**	**32**	**0**	**0**	**0**	**0**	**0**	**0**	**14**	**2**	**0**	**0**	**0**	**0**
1928-29	Providence Reds	Can-Am	37	3	0	3	....	....	....	26	5	0	0	0	*24
1929-30	Duluth Hornets	AHA	46	7	1	8	....	....	....	87	4	0	0	0	0
1930-31	Duluth Hornets	AHA	47	2	6	8	....	....	....	64	4	0	0	0	6
1931-32	Tulsa Oilers	AHA	30	1	2	3	....	....	....	73	....	....	....	....	....
	NHL Totals		**151**	**22**	**3**	**25**	**69**	**32**	**101**	**201**	**2**	**0**	**0**	**0**	**0**

Signed as a free agent by **Hamilton**, October 16, 1924. Transferred to **NY Americans** after NHL club purchased **Hamilton** franchise, September 26, 1925. Traded to **Pittsburgh** by **NY Americans** with $2,000 for Lionel Conacher, December 16, 1926. Loaned to **Montreal Canadiens** by **Pittsburgh** for remainder of 1927-28 season for the loan of Marty Burke, December 16, 1927.

• LAPERRIERE, JACQUES   *— see page 1205*

• LAPRADE, EDGAR   Edgar Laprade   HHOF

C – R. 5′8″, 160 lbs.   b: Port Arthur, Ont., 10/10/1919.

Season	Club	League	GP	G	A	Pts	AG	AA	APts	PIM	Playoffs GP	G	A	Pts	PIM
1935-36	Port Arthur Juniors	TBJHL	14	13	10	23	....	....	....	6	4	*4	*2	*6	2
1936-37	Port Arthur Juniors	TBJHL	18	*19	14	*33	....	....	....	2	3	*6	*3	*9	5
1937-38	Port Arthur Juniors	TBJHL	18	*23	11	*34	....	....	....	9	5	*6	0	*6	0
1938-39	Port Arthur Seniors	TBSHL	10	11	9	*40	....	....	....	7	19	*25	7	*32	10
1938-39	Port Arthur Bearcats	MJHL	....	7	4	11	....	....	....	....	....	....	....	....	....
1939-40	Port Arthur Bearcats	TBSHL	22	*20	15	35	....	....	....	8	3	*5	1	*6	2
1940-41	Port Arthur Bearcats	TBSHL	20	*26	*21	*47	....	....	....	7	12	*13	*10	*33	60
1941-42	Port Arthur Bearcats	TBSHL	15	18	*23	41	....	....	....	4	17	12	*21	*33	6
1942-43	Port Arthur Bearcats	TBSHL	8	7	10	17	....	....	....	0	3	7	4	11	4
1943-44	Winnipeg Army	City Sr.	6	10	3	13	....	....	....	0	....	....	....	....	....
1944-45	Barriefield Bears	City Sr.	....	19	*28	*47	....	....	....	2	4	5	8	13	0
1945-46	**New York Rangers**	**NHL**	**49**	**15**	**19**	**34**	**23**	**35**	**58**	**0**	....	....	....	....	....
1946-47	**New York Rangers**	**NHL**	**58**	**15**	**25**	**40**	**20**	**36**	**56**	**9**	....	....	....	....	....
1947-48	**New York Rangers**	**NHL**	**59**	**13**	**34**	**47**	**19**	**50**	**69**	**7**	**6**	**1**	**4**	**5**	**0**
1948-49	**New York Rangers**	**NHL**	**56**	**18**	**12**	**30**	**28**	**19**	**47**	**12**	....	....	....	....	....
1949-50	**New York Rangers**	**NHL**	**60**	**22**	**22**	**44**	**30**	**28**	**58**	**2**	**12**	**3**	**5**	**8**	**4**
1950-51	**New York Rangers**	**NHL**	**42**	**10**	**13**	**23**	**13**	**17**	**30**	**0**	....	....	....	....	....
1951-52	**New York Rangers**	**NHL**	**70**	**9**	**29**	**38**	**13**	**38**	**51**	**8**	....	....	....	....	....
1952-53	**New York Rangers**	**NHL**	**11**	**2**	**1**	**3**	**3**	**1**	**4**	**2**	....	....	....	....	....
1953-54	**New York Rangers**	**NHL**	**35**	**1**	**6**	**7**	**2**	**8**	**10**	**2**	....	....	....	....	....
1954-55	**New York Rangers**	**NHL**	**61**	**3**	**11**	**14**	**4**	**14**	**18**	**0**	....	....	....	....	....
	NHL Totals		**501**	**108**	**172**	**280**	**155**	**246**	**401**	**42**	**18**	**4**	**9**	**13**	**4**

Won Calder Memorial Trophy (1946) • Won Lady Byng Trophy (1950)

Played in NHL All-Star Game (1947, 1948, 1949, 1950)

Signed as a free agent by **NY Rangers**, October 15, 1945.

• LAPRAIRIE, BENJAMIN   Benjamin "Bun" LaPrairie

D – R. 5′10″, 160 lbs.   b: Hibbing, MN

Season	Club	League	GP	G	A	Pts	AG	AA	APts	PIM	Playoffs GP	G	A	Pts	PIM
1934-35	Chicago Baby Ruth	City Sr.	2	1	0	1	....	....	....	....	....	....	....	....	....
1935-36	Kansas City Greyhounds	AHA	47	0	0	0	....	....	....	6	....	....	....	....	....
1936-37	**Chicago Black Hawks**	**NHL**	**7**	**0**	**0**	**0**	**0**	**0**	**0**	**0**	....	....	....	....	....
	Minneapolis Millers	AHA	5	0	0	0	....	....	....	6	....	....	....	....	....
	NHL Totals		**7**	**0**	**0**	**0**	**0**	**0**	**0**	**0**	....	....	....	....	....

• LAROCHELLE, WILDOR   Wildor Larochelle

RW – R. 5′8″, 158 lbs.   b: Sorel, Que., 9/23/1906.   d: 3/21/1964.

Season	Club	League	GP	G	A	Pts	AG	AA	APts	PIM	Playoffs GP	G	A	Pts	PIM
1925-26	**Montreal Canadiens**	**NHL**	**33**	**2**	**1**	**3**	**6**	**11**	**17**	**10**	....	....	....	....	....
1926-27	**Montreal Canadiens**	**NHL**	**41**	**0**	**1**	**1**	**0**	**8**	**8**	**6**	**4**	**0**	**0**	**0**	**0**
1927-28	**Montreal Canadiens**	**NHL**	**40**	**3**	**1**	**4**	**9**	**8**	**17**	**30**	**2**	**0**	**0**	**0**	**0**
1928-29	**Montreal Canadiens**	**NHL**	**2**	**0**	**0**	**0**	**0**	**0**	**0**	**0**	....	....	....	....	....
	Providence Reds	Can-Am	39	8	4	12	....	....	....	50	6	0	1	1	8
1929-30	**Montreal Canadiens**	**NHL**	**44**	**14**	**11**	**25**	**28**	**36**	**64**	**28**	**6**	**1**	**0**	**1**	**12**
1930-31	**Montreal Canadiens**	**NHL**	**40**	**8**	**5**	**13**	**19**	**18**	**37**	**35**	**10**	**1**	**2**	**3**	**8**
1931-32	**Montreal Canadiens**	**NHL**	**48**	**18**	**8**	**26**	**39**	**22**	**61**	**16**	**4**	**2**	**1**	**3**	**4**
1932-33	**Montreal Canadiens**	**NHL**	**47**	**11**	**4**	**15**	**26**	**11**	**37**	**27**	**2**	**1**	**0**	**1**	**0**
1933-34	**Montreal Canadiens**	**NHL**	**48**	**16**	**11**	**27**	**36**	**29**	**65**	**27**	**2**	**1**	**1**	**2**	**0**
1934-35	**Montreal Canadiens**	**NHL**	**48**	**9**	**19**	**28**	**19**	**42**	**61**	**12**	**2**	**0**	**0**	**0**	**0**
1935-36	**Montreal Canadiens**	**NHL**	**13**	**0**	**2**	**2**	**0**	**5**	**5**	**6**	....	....	....	....	....
	Chicago Black Hawks	**NHL**	**27**	**2**	**1**	**3**	**5**	**2**	**7**	**8**	**2**	**0**	**0**	**0**	**0**
	Philadelphia Arrows	Can-Am	6	2	3	5	....	....	....	0	....	....	....	....	....
1936-37	**Chicago Black Hawks**	**NHL**	**43**	**9**	**10**	**19**	**19**	**23**	**42**	**6**	....	....	....	....	....
1937-38			DID NOT PLAY												
1938-39	New Haven Eagles	AHL	21	2	3	5	....	....	....	2	....	....	....	....	....
	NHL Totals		**474**	**92**	**74**	**166**	**206**	**215**	**421**	**211**	**34**	**6**	**4**	**10**	**24**

Signed as a free agent by **Montreal Canadiens**, November 23, 1925. Traded to **Chicago** by **Montreal Canadiens** for cash, December 21, 1935.

• LAROSE, CHARLES Charles "Bonner" Larose
LW – R. 5'8", 170 lbs. b: Ottawa, Ontario, 2/14/1901. d: 1/23/1961.

Season	Club	League	REGULAR SEASON								PLAYOFFS				
			GP	G	A	Pts	AG	AA	APts	PIM	GP	G	A	Pts	PIM
1917-18	Ottawa St. Brigids	City Sr.	8	0	0	0	....	....	....	16	....	....	....	....	....
1918-19			MILITARY SERVICE												
1919-20	Ottawa St. Pats	City Sr.	9	4	0	4	....	....	....	....	....	....	....	....	....
1920-21	Ottawa K of C	City Sr.	6	1	0	1	....	....	....	....	....	....	....	....	....
1921-22	Ottawa K of C	City Sr.	11	6	5	11	....	....	....	6	....	....	....	....	....
1922-23	Ottawa Royal Canadians	City Sr.	14	10	4	14	....	....	....	23	....	....	....	....	....
1923-24	Ottawa Royal Canadians	City Sr.	12	5	1	6	....	....	....	....	....	....	....	....	....
1924-25	Fort Pitt Hornets	USAHA	22	7	0	7	....	....	....	....	8	0	0	0	....
1925-26	St. Paul Saints	CHL	10	0	0	0	....	....	....	0	....	....	....	....	....
	Boston Bruins	**NHL**	**6**	**0**	**0**	**0**	**0**	**0**	**0**	**0**	....	....	....	....	....
1926-27	Boston Tigers	Can-Am	13	0	1	1	....	....	....	4	....	....	....	....	....
	New Haven Eagles	Can-Am	5	0	1	1	....	....	....	4	3	0	0	0	0
	NHL Totals		**6**	**0**	**0**	**0**	**0**	**0**	**0**	**0**	....	....	....	....	....

Signed as a free agent by **Boston**, February 19, 1926.

• LAROSE, CLAUDE — *see page 1208*

• LARSON, NORMAN Norman Larson
RW – R. 6', 175 lbs. b: Moose Jaw, Sask., 10/13/1920.

Season	Club	League	REGULAR SEASON								PLAYOFFS				
			GP	G	A	Pts	AG	AA	APts	PIM	GP	G	A	Pts	PIM
1937-38	Moose Jaw Canucks	SJHL	6	*14	5	*19	....	....	....	4	4	*8	*5	*13	0
1938-39	Moose Jaw Millers	SSHL	24	16	6	22	....	....	....	2	10	*8	2	*10	2
1939-40	Moose Jaw Millers	SSHL	26	23	9	32	....	....	....	4	8	*10	2	12	4
1940-41	**New York Americans**	**NHL**	**48**	**9**	**9**	**18**	**18**	**16**	**34**	**6**	....	....	....	....	....
1941-42	**Brooklyn Americans**	**NHL**	**40**	**16**	**9**	**25**	**27**	**14**	**41**	**6**	....	....	....	....	....
	Springfield Indians	AHL	5	3	3	6	....	....	....	0	4	1	2	3	0
1942-43	Port Arthur Shipbuilders	TBSHL	8	5	10	15	....	....	....	6	3	1	2	3	2
	Lakehead Army	TBSHL	1	2	3	5	....	....	....	0	....	....	....	....	....
1943-44	Port Arthur Shipbuilders	TBSHL	6	*20	3	*23	....	....	....	0	....	....	....	....	....
1944-45	Quebec Aces	QSHL	14	18	17	35	....	....	....	2	5	*7	3	*10	0
1945-46	New Haven–Hershey	AHL	62	36	53	89	....	....	....	20	3	2	0	2	0
1946-47	**New York Rangers**	**NHL**	**1**	**0**	**0**	**0**	**0**	**0**	**0**	**0**	....	....	....	....	....
	New Haven Ramblers	AHL	11	1	5	6	....	....	....	0	....	....	....	....	....
1947-48	Hershey Bears	AHL	19	4	1	5	....	....	....	0	....	....	....	....	....
1948-49	Hershey Bears	AHL	55	13	24	37	....	....	....	13	8	0	2	2	0
1949-50	Hershey Bears	AHL	68	20	35	55	....	....	....	8	....	....	....	....	....
1950-51	Calgary Stampeders	WCSHL	47	28	35	63	....	....	....	20	8	1	3	4	2
1951-52	Calgary Stampeders	PCHL	65	30	25	55	....	....	....	18	....	....	....	....	....
1952-53	Calgary Stampeders	WHL	1	0	0	0	....	....	....	0	....	....	....	....	....
	Kamloops Elks	OSHL	45	26	21	47	....	....	....	22	12	4	8	12	0
1953-54	Kimberley Dynamiters	WIHL	39	23	29	52	....	....	....	12	9	1	4	5	8
1954-55	Kimberley Dynamiters	WIHL	26	10	16	26	....	....	....	17	8	2	3	5	2
1955-56	Kimberley Dynamiters	WIHL	43	35	37	72	....	....	....	6	5	1	1	2	2
	NHL Totals		**89**	**25**	**18**	**43**	**45**	**30**	**75**	**12**	....	....	....	....	....

AHL Second All-Star Team (1946)

• LATREILLE, PHIL Phil Latreille
C/RW – R. 5'10", 185 lbs. b: Montreal, Que., 4/22/1938.

Season	Club	League	REGULAR SEASON								PLAYOFFS				
			GP	G	A	Pts	AG	AA	APts	PIM	GP	G	A	Pts	PIM
1956-57	Montreal D'arcy McGee	H.S.	10	*13	9	*22	....	....	....	....	....	....	....	....	....
1957-58	Middlebury College	ECAC 2	DID NOT PLAY – FRESHMAN												
1958-59	Middlebury College	ECAC 2	22	*57	33	*90	....	....	....	....	....	....	....	....	....
1959-60	Middlebury College	ECAC 2	23	*77	19	*96	....	....	....	....	....	....	....	....	....
1960-61	Middlebury College	ECAC 2	25	*80	28	*108	....	....	....	....	....	....	....	....	....
	New York Rangers	**NHL**	**4**	**0**	**0**	**0**	**0**	**0**	**0**	**2**	....	....	....	....	....
1961-62	Long Island Ducks	EHL	6	0	2	2	....	....	....	0	....	....	....	....	....
	NHL Totals		**4**	**0**	**0**	**0**	**0**	**0**	**0**	**2**	....	....	....	....	....

Signed as a free agent by **NY Rangers** to a five-game amateur tryout contract, March 10, 1961.

• LAUDER, MARTIN Martin "Harry" Lauder
D/C – L. 5'6", 165 lbs. b: Durham, Ontario, 1/26/1907.

Season	Club	League	REGULAR SEASON								PLAYOFFS				
			GP	G	A	Pts	AG	AA	APts	PIM	GP	G	A	Pts	PIM
1925-26	Owen Sound Greys	OHA	12	*18	*6	*24	....	....	....	....	8	*7	2	9	8
1926-27	Owen Sound Greys	OHA	15	23	*13	36	....	....	....	....	....	....	....	....	....
1927-28	**Boston Bruins**	**NHL**	**3**	**0**	**0**	**0**	**0**	**0**	**0**	**2**	....	....	....	....	....
	Providence Reds	Can-Am	16	3	1	4	....	....	....	8	....	....	....	....	....
1928-29	Hamilton Tigers	Can-Pro	36	8	5	13	....	....	....	52	....	....	....	....	....
1929-30	Hamilton Tigers	IAHL	40	19	11	30	....	....	....	39	....	....	....	....	....
1930-31	Syracuse Stars	IAHL	20	6	2	8	....	....	....	26	....	....	....	....	....
	Buffalo Bisons	IAHL	29	8	0	8	....	....	....	18	6	1	0	1	0
1931-32	Buffalo Bisons	IAHL	46	7	3	10	....	....	....	24	6	0	0	0	0
1932-33	Buffalo Bisons	IAHL	42	4	2	6	....	....	....	24	5	0	0	0	0
	NHL Totals		**3**	**0**	**0**	**0**	**0**	**0**	**0**	**2**	....	....	....	....	....

Signed as a free agent by **Boston**, October 2, 1927.

• LAVIOLETTE, JACK Jack Laviolette HHOF
D/RW – R. 5'11", 170 lbs. b: Belleville, Ont., 7/27/1879. d: 1/10/1960.

Season	Club	League	REGULAR SEASON								PLAYOFFS				
			GP	G	A	Pts	AG	AA	APts	PIM	GP	G	A	Pts	PIM
1903-04	Montreal Nationals	FAHL	6	8	0	8	....	....	....	....	....	....	....	....	....
1904-05	Michigan Soo Indians	IHL	4	15	0	15	....	....	....	24	....	....	....	....	....
1905-06	Michigan Soo Indians	IHL	17	15	0	15	....	....	....	28	....	....	....	....	....
1906-07	Michigan Soo Indians	IHL	19	10	7	17	....	....	....	34	....	....	....	....	....
1907-08	Montreal Shamrocks	ECAHA	6	1	0	1	....	....	....	36	....	....	....	....	....
1908-09	Montreal Shamrocks	ECHA	9	1	0	1	....	....	....	36	....	....	....	....	....
1909-10	Montreal Canadiens	NHA	11	3	0	3	....	....	....	26	....	....	....	....	....
1910-11	Montreal Canadiens	NHA	16	0	0	0	....	....	....	24	....	....	....	....	....
1911-12	Montreal Canadiens	NHA	17	7	0	7	....	....	....	10	....	....	....	....	....
1912-13	Montreal Canadiens	NHA	20	8	0	8	....	....	....	77	....	....	....	....	....
1913-14	Montreal Canadiens	NHA	20	7	9	16	....	....	....	30	2	0	1	1	0
1914-15	Montreal Canadiens	NHA	18	6	3	9	....	....	....	35	....	....	....	....	....
1915-16	Montreal Canadiens	NHA	18	8	3	11	....	....	....	62	4	0	0	0	6
1916-17	Montreal Canadiens	NHA	18	7	3	10	....	....	....	21	6	1	0	1	0
1917-18	**Montreal Canadiens**	**NHL**	**18**	**2**	**1**	**3**	**5**	**0**	**5**	**6**	**2**	**0**	**0**	**0**	**0**
	NHL Totals		**18**	**2**	**1**	**3**	**5**	**0**	**5**	**6**	**2**	**0**	**0**	**0**	**0**
	Other Major League Totals		193	88	25	113	....	....	....	443	12	1	1	2	6

IHL First All-Star Team (1905, 1907) • IHL Second All-Star Team (1906)

Rights retained by **Montreal Canadiens** after NHA folded, November 26, 1917.

• LAYCOE, HAL Hal Laycoe
D – L. 6'2", 185 lbs. b: Sutherland, Sask., 6/23/1922. d: 4/29/1997.

Season	Club	League	REGULAR SEASON								PLAYOFFS				
			GP	G	A	Pts	AG	AA	APts	PIM	GP	G	A	Pts	PIM
1939-40	Saskatoon Dodgers	SJHL	....	....	....	....	....	....	....	....	2	0	4	4	4
1940-41	Saskatoon Jr. Quakers	SJHL	11	12	11	23	....	....	....	13	10	6	8	*14	10
	Saskatoon Quakers	SSHL	1	0	0	0	....	....	....	0	....	....	....	....	....
1941-42	Saskatoon Quakers	SSHL	28	14	13	27	....	....	....	27	9	3	4	7	4
1942-43	Canadian Postal Corps	City Sr.	1	0	0	0	....	....	....	0	....	....	....	....	....
1943-44	Toronto Navy	City Sr.	14	6	5	11	....	....	....	4	....	....	....	....	....
1944-45	Winnipeg Navy	City Sr.	15	10	15	25	....	....	....	8	5	5	*8	*13	0
1945-46	**New York Rangers**	**NHL**	**17**	**0**	**2**	**2**	**0**	**4**	**4**	**6**	....	....	....	....	....
	New York Rovers	EHL	35	7	22	29	....	....	....	25	....	....	....	....	....
1946-47	**New York Rangers**	**NHL**	**58**	**1**	**12**	**13**	**1**	**17**	**18**	**25**	....	....	....	....	....
1947-48	**Montreal Canadiens**	**NHL**	**14**	**1**	**2**	**3**	**1**	**3**	**4**	**4**	....	....	....	....	....
	Buffalo Bisons	AHL	45	8	25	33	....	....	....	36	8	2	0	2	15
1948-49	**Montreal Canadiens**	**NHL**	**51**	**3**	**5**	**8**	**5**	**8**	**13**	**31**	**7**	**0**	**1**	**1**	**13**
	Buffalo Bisons	AHL	10	4	1	5	....	....	....	10	....	....	....	....	....
1949-50	**Montreal Canadiens**	**NHL**	**30**	**0**	**2**	**2**	**0**	**3**	**3**	**21**	**2**	**0**	**0**	**0**	**0**
1950-51	**Montreal Canadiens**	**NHL**	**38**	**0**	**2**	**2**	**0**	**3**	**3**	**25**	....	....	....	....	....
	Boston Bruins	**NHL**	**6**	**1**	**1**	**2**	**1**	**1**	**2**	**4**	**6**	**0**	**1**	**1**	**5**
1951-52	**Boston Bruins**	**NHL**	**70**	**5**	**7**	**12**	**7**	**9**	**16**	**61**	**7**	**1**	**1**	**2**	**11**
1952-53	**Boston Bruins**	**NHL**	**54**	**2**	**10**	**12**	**3**	**14**	**17**	**36**	**11**	**0**	**2**	**2**	**10**
1953-54	**Boston Bruins**	**NHL**	**58**	**3**	**16**	**19**	**5**	**22**	**27**	**29**	**2**	**0**	**0**	**0**	**0**
1954-55	**Boston Bruins**	**NHL**	**70**	**4**	**13**	**17**	**6**	**17**	**23**	**34**	**5**	**1**	**0**	**1**	**0**
1955-56	**Boston Bruins**	**NHL**	**65**	**5**	**5**	**10**	**7**	**6**	**13**	**16**	....	....	....	....	....
1956-57	New Westminster Royals	WHL	DID NOT PLAY – COACHING												
	NHL Totals		**531**	**25**	**77**	**102**	**36**	**107**	**143**	**292**	**40**	**2**	**5**	**7**	**39**

EHL Second All-Star Team (1946)

Traded to **Montreal** by **NY Rangers** with Joe Bell and George Robertson for Buddy O'Connor and Frank Eddolls, August 19, 1947. Traded to **Boston** by **Montreal** for Ross Lowe, February 14, 1951.

• LEACH, LARRY Larry Leach
C – L. 6'2", 175 lbs. b: Lloydminster, Sask., 6/18/1936.

Season	Club	League	REGULAR SEASON								PLAYOFFS				
			GP	G	A	Pts	AG	AA	APts	PIM	GP	G	A	Pts	PIM
1953-54	Humboldt Indians	SJHL	46	8	6	14	....	....	....	20	5	1	0	1	2
1954-55	Humboldt Indians	SJHL	47	6	9	15	....	....	....	8	10	0	1	1	4
1955-56	Humboldt Indians	SJHL	45	22	35	57	....	....	....	27	5	2	3	5	8
	Victoria Cougars	WHL	3	1	0	1	....	....	....	6	4	0	0	0	0
1956-57	Victoria Cougars	WHL	66	6	10	16	....	....	....	72	3	0	0	0	2
1957-58	Victoria Cougars	WHL	33	7	9	16	....	....	....	23	....	....	....	....	....
	Springfield Indians	AHL	35	1	9	10	....	....	....	8	13	3	1	4	12
1958-59	**Boston Bruins**	**NHL**	**29**	**4**	**12**	**16**	**5**	**13**	**18**	**26**	**7**	**1**	**1**	**2**	**8**
	Providence Reds	AHL	37	12	17	29	....	....	....	24	....	....	....	....	....
1959-60	**Boston Bruins**	**NHL**	**69**	**7**	**12**	**19**	**9**	**12**	**21**	**47**	....	....	....	....	....
	Portland Buckaroos	WHL	54	13	16	29	....	....	....	80	14	6	7	13	22
1961-62	**Boston Bruins**	**NHL**	**28**	**2**	**5**	**7**	**2**	**5**	**7**	**18**	....	....	....	....	....
	Providence Reds	AHL	25	8	11	19	....	....	....	33	....	....	....	....	....
1962-63	Providence Reds	AHL	52	22	24	46	....	....	....	56	....	....	....	....	....
1963-64	Providence Reds	AHL	60	12	30	42	....	....	....	43	3	1	1	2	16
1964-65	Portland Buckaroos	WHL	52	7	10	17	....	....	....	48	10	2	1	3	6
1965-66	Portland Buckaroos	WHL	72	18	23	41	....	....	....	57	3	0	0	0	6
1966-67	Portland Buckaroos	WHL	60	18	17	35	....	....	....	43	4	0	0	0	0
1967-68	Portland Buckaroos	WHL	72	21	20	41	....	....	....	48	11	1	0	1	8
1968-69	Portland Buckaroos	WHL	72	8	18	26	....	....	....	50	9	0	0	0	2
1969-70	Portland Buckaroos	WHL	72	6	17	23	....	....	....	44	11	0	2	2	12
1970-71	Portland Buckaroos	WHL	60	6	15	21	....	....	....	28	11	3	3	6	6
1971-72	Portland Buckaroos	WHL	54	15	21	36	....	....	....	32	6	0	0	0	6
1972-73	Portland Buckaroos	WHL	71	5	14	19	....	....	....	42	....	....	....	....	....
1973-74	Lloydminster Blazers	SJHL	DID NOT PLAY – COACHING												
	NHL Totals		**126**	**13**	**29**	**42**	**16**	**30**	**46**	**91**	**7**	**1**	**1**	**2**	**8**

Traded to **Portland** (WHL) by **Boston** for cash, May 1964. Claimed by **Chicago** from **Portland** (WHL) in Inter-League Draft, June, 1968. Traded to **Portland** (WHL) by **Chicago** for cash, October, 1968.

• LEBRUN, AL Al LeBrun
D – R. 6', 185 lbs. b: Timmins, Ont., 12/1/1940.

Season	Club	League	REGULAR SEASON								PLAYOFFS				
			GP	G	A	Pts	AG	AA	APts	PIM	GP	G	A	Pts	PIM
1957-58	Guelph Biltmores	OHA	34	0	1	1	....	....	....	16	....	....	....	....	....
1958-59	Guelph Biltmores	OHA	54	3	12	15	....	....	....	55	10	0	1	1	17
1959-60	Guelph Biltmores	OHA	48	5	13	18	....	....	....	74	5	1	0	1	8
1960-61	Guelph Royals	OHA	47	4	12	16	....	....	....	127	12	1	4	5	40
	New York Rangers	**NHL**	**4**	**0**	**2**	**2**	**0**	**2**	**2**	**4**	....	....	....	....	....
	Kitchener Beavers	EPHL	1	0	0	0	....	....	....	0	....	....	....	....	....
1961-62	Kitchener Beavers	EPHL	70	0	16	16	....	....	....	36	7	0	1	1	8
1962-63	Vancouver Canucks	WHL	55	5	8	13	....	....	....	31	....	....	....	....	....
1963-64			DID NOT PLAY – INJURED												
1964-65	St. Paul Rangers	CHL	66	11	15	26	....	....	....	52	11	1	1	2	9
1965-66	**New York Rangers**	**NHL**	**2**	**0**	**0**	**0**	**0**	**0**	**0**	**0**	....	....	....	....	....
	St. Paul Rangers	CHL	69	4	13	17	....	....	....	38	7	0	3	3	4
1966-67	Pittsburgh Hornets	AHL	26	1	8	9	....	....	....	24	....	....	....	....	....
	Los Angeles Blades	WHL	42	1	8	9	....	....	....	33	....	....	....	....	....
1967-68	Dallas Black Hawks	CHL	61	6	17	23	....	....	....	53	4	0	0	0	4
1968-69	Memphis South Stars	CHL	34	1	4	5	....	....	....	20	....	....	....	....	....
	San Diego Gulls	WHL	29	1	4	5	....	....	....	8	3	0	0	0	2
1969-70	San Diego Gulls	WHL	72	7	18	25	....	....	....	37	6	0	1	1	2
1970-71	San Diego Gulls	WHL	66	3	13	16	....	....	....	50	....	....	....	....	....
1971-72	San Diego Gulls	WHL	72	2	17	19	....	....	....	67	4	0	0	0	2
1972-73	San Diego Gulls	WHL	72	2	16	18	....	....	....	101	6	0	0	0	2
1973-74	San Diego Gulls	WHL	37	0	4	4	....	....	....	10	4	0	1	1	0
	NHL Totals		**6**	**0**	**2**	**2**	**0**	**2**	**2**	**4**	....	....	....	....	....

CHL First All-Star Team (1966) • Named CHL's Top Defenseman (1966) • CHL Second All-Star Team (1968)

• Missed entire 1963-64 season after undergoing spinal surgery. Claimed by **Detroit** from **NY Rangers** in Intra-League Draft, June 15, 1966. Traded to **Chicago** by **Detroit** with Murray Hall to complete transaction that sent Howie Young to Detroit, May 8, 1967. Claimed by **San Diego** (WHL) from **Chicago** in Reverse Draft, June, 1968.

• LeCLAIR, JACKIE Jackie Leclair

C – L. 5'10", 150 lbs. b: Quebec City, Que., 5/30/1929.

			REGULAR SEASON								PLAYOFFS				
Season	**Club**	**League**	**GP**	**G**	**A**	**Pts**	**AG**	**AA**	**APts**	**PIM**	**GP**	**G**	**A**	**Pts**	**PIM**
1946-47	Ottawa St. Pats	City Jr.	22	16	19	35	....	....	....	14	7	*21	*11	*32	2
1947-48	Lethbridge Native Sons	AJHL	16	12	29	41	....	....	....	20	6	7	6	13	20
1948-49	Quebec Citadelle	QJHL	36	21	27	48	....	....	....	30	13	4	9	13	4
1949-50	Ottawa Senators	QSHL	56	19	42	61	....	....	....	28	7	2	0	2	2
1950-51	Ottawa Senators	QSHL	56	20	22	42	....	....	....	43	7	0	1	1	0
1951-52	Quebec Aces	QSHL	57	25	29	54	....	....	....	22	16	7	6	13	11
1952-53	Ottawa Senators	QSHL	54	22	37	59	....	....	....	27	11	8	2	10	0
1953-54	Ottawa Senators	QHL	4	3	7	10	....	....	....	7	....	....	....	....	....
	Pittsburgh Hornets	AHL	52	14	17	31	....	....	....	11	4	0	1	1	2
1954-55	**Montreal Canadiens**	**NHL**	**59**	**11**	**22**	**33**	**16**	**28**	**44**	**12**	**12**	**5**	**0**	**5**	**2**
1955-56	**Montreal Canadiens**	**NHL**	**54**	**6**	**8**	**14**	**9**	**10**	**19**	**30**	**8**	**1**	**1**	**2**	**4**
	Montreal Royals	QHL	12	5	10	15	....	....	....	8	....	....	....	....	....
1956-57	**Montreal Canadiens**	**NHL**	**47**	**3**	**10**	**13**	**4**	**12**	**16**	**14**	....	....	....	....	....
	Chicoutimi Sagueneens	QHL	14	8	9	17	....	....	....	4	10	1	*10	11	0
1957-58	Chicoutimi Sagueneens	QHL	48	20	40	60	....	....	....	32	6	0	1	1	4
1958-59	Quebec Aces	QHL	61	22	42	64	....	....	....	54	....	....	....	....	....
1959-60	Quebec Aces	AHL	72	22	39	61	....	....	....	22	....	....	....	....	....
1960-61	Quebec Aces	AHL	72	22	34	56	....	....	....	12	....	....	....	....	....
1961-62	Quebec Aces	AHL	50	3	11	14	....	....	....	18	....	....	....	....	....
1962-63	Charlotte Checkers	EHL	67	31	67	98	....	....	....	32	10	7	9	16	0
1963-64	Charlotte Checkers	EHL	57	27	56	83	....	....	....	34	3	1	2	3	0
1964-65	Charlotte–New Haven	EHL	44	23	35	58	....	....	....	78	....	....	....	....	....
	Knoxville Knights	EHL	....	....	....	....	....	....	....	....	10	4	3	7	6
1965-66	New Haven Blades	EHL	63	32	64	96	....	....	....	87	3	1	0	1	0
1966-67	New Haven Blades	EHL	68	20	55	75	....	....	....	49	....	....	....	....	....
1967-68	Florida Rockets	EHL	62	34	65	99	....	....	....	12	5	0	5	5	4
	NHL Totals		**160**	**20**	**40**	**60**	**29**	**50**	**79**	**56**	**20**	**6**	**1**	**7**	**6**

EHL North Second All-Star Team (1966)

Played in NHL All-Star Game (1956)

Claimed by **Toronto** from **Ottawa** (QHL) in Inter-League Draft, June 10, 1953. Traded to **Chicago** (Buffalo - AHL) by **Toronto** with George Blair and Frank Sullivan for Brian Cullen, May 4, 1954. Traded to **Montreal** by **Buffalo** (AHL) with cash for Gaye Stewart, Eddie Slowinski and Pete Babando, August, 1954. Traded to **Chicoutimi** (QHL) by **Montreal** with Guy Rousseau and Jacques Deslauriers for Stan Smrke, October, 1957. Traded to **Florida** (EHL) by **New Haven** (AHL) for Russ McClenaghan, September, 1967.

• LEDUC, ALBERT Albert "Battleship" LeDuc

D – R. 5'9", 180 lbs. b: Valleyfield, Que., 11/22/1902. Deceased.

			REGULAR SEASON								PLAYOFFS				
Season	**Club**	**League**	**GP**	**G**	**A**	**Pts**	**AG**	**AA**	**APts**	**PIM**	**GP**	**G**	**A**	**Pts**	**PIM**
1923-24	Montreal Hochelaga	City Sr.	9	6	0	6	....	....	....	4	....	....	....	....	....
1924-25	Montreal Nationals	ECHL	11	9	0	9	....	....	....	....	....	....	....	....	....
1925-26	**Montreal Canadiens**	**NHL**	**32**	**10**	**3**	**13**	**31**	**34**	**65**	**62**	....	....	....	....	....
1926-27	**Montreal Canadiens**	**NHL**	**43**	**5**	**2**	**7**	**14**	**17**	**31**	**62**	**4**	**0**	**0**	**0**	**2**
1927-28	**Montreal Canadiens**	**NHL**	**42**	**8**	**5**	**13**	**24**	**42**	**66**	**73**	**2**	**1**	**0**	**1**	**5**
1928-29	**Montreal Canadiens**	**NHL**	**43**	**9**	**2**	**11**	**36**	**18**	**54**	**79**	**3**	**1**	**0**	**1**	**4**
1929-30	**Montreal Canadiens**	**NHL**	**44**	**6**	**8**	**14**	**12**	**26**	**38**	**90**	**6**	**1**	**3**	**4**	**8**
1930-31	**Montreal Canadiens**	**NHL**	**44**	**8**	**6**	**14**	**19**	**22**	**41**	**82**	**7**	**0**	**2**	**2**	**9**
1931-32	**Montreal Canadiens**	**NHL**	**41**	**5**	**3**	**8**	**11**	**8**	**19**	**60**	**4**	**1**	**1**	**2**	**2**
1932-33	**Montreal Canadiens**	**NHL**	**48**	**5**	**3**	**8**	**12**	**8**	**20**	**62**	**2**	**1**	**0**	**1**	**2**
1933-34	**Ottawa Senators**	**NHL**	**32**	**1**	**3**	**4**	**2**	**8**	**10**	**34**	....	....	....	....	....
	New York Rangers	**NHL**	**10**	**0**	**0**	**0**	**0**	**0**	**0**	**6**	....	....	....	....	....
1934-35	**Montreal Canadiens**	**NHL**	**4**	**0**	**0**	**0**	**0**	**0**	**0**	**4**	....	....	....	....	....
	Quebec Beavers	Can-Am	41	12	14	26	....	....	....	53	3	0	0	0	13
1935-36	Providence Reds	Can-Am	48	5	15	20	....	....	....	82	7	2	2	4	8
1936-37	Providence Reds	Can-Am	37	2	8	10	....	....	....	48	3	0	2	2	2
1937-38	Verdun Maple Leafs	QSHL	DID NOT PLAY – COACHING												
	NHL Totals		**383**	**57**	**35**	**92**	**161**	**183**	**344**	**614**	**28**	**5**	**6**	**11**	**32**

Can-Am Second All-Star Team (1936)

Signed as a free agent by **Montreal Canadiens**, April 16, 1925. Traded to **Ottawa** by **Montreal Canadiens** for cash with Montreal Canadiens retaining the rights of repurchase, October 22, 1933. Loaned to **NY Rangers** by **Ottawa** for remainder of 1933-34 season, February 15, 1934. Traded to **Montreal Canadiens** by **Ottawa** for cash, April 9, 1934. Signed as playing manager/coach of **Quebec Castors** (Can-Am) with Montreal retaining right of recall, October 24, 1934.

• LEE, BOBBY Bobby Lee

C – R. 5'10", 165 lbs. b: Verdun, Que., 12/28/1911. d: 12/31/1974.

			REGULAR SEASON								PLAYOFFS				
Season	**Club**	**League**	**GP**	**G**	**A**	**Pts**	**AG**	**AA**	**APts**	**PIM**	**GP**	**G**	**A**	**Pts**	**PIM**
1929-30	Queens University	Mtl-Sr.	9	3	0	3	....	....	....	0	....	....	....	....	....
1930-31	Montreal Columbus	City Jr.	9	4	0	4	....	....	....	8	....	....	....	....	....
1931-32	Queens University	OHA Sr.	STATISTICS NOT AVAILABLE												
1932-33	Queens University	OHA Sr.	STATISTICS NOT AVAILABLE												
1933-34	Montreal LaFontaine	City Sr.	15	6	2	8	....	....	....	10	....	....	....	....	....
1934-35	Montreal LaFontaine	City Sr.	18	9	6	15	....	....	....	24	....	....	....	....	....
	Baltimore Orioles	EHL	4	0	1	1	....	....	....	4	9	5	2	7	4
1935-36	Baltimore Orioles	EHL	40	19	20	39	....	....	....	45	8	4	6	10	15
1936-37	Brighton Tigers	Britain	....	32	21	53	....	....	....	22	....	....	....	....	....
1936-39	Earls Court Rangers	Britain	....	74	60	134	....	....	....	....	....	....	....	....	....
1937-38	Earls Court Rangers	Britain	....	23	13	36	....	....	....	20	....	....	....	....	....
1938-39	Earls Court Rangers	Britain	....	18	22	40	....	....	....	....	....	....	....	....	....
1939-40	Quebec Aces	QSHL	30	8	13	21	....	....	....	27	....	....	....	....	....
1940-41	Quebec Aces	QSHL	36	14	24	38	....	....	....	15	4	3	1	4	2
1941-42	Quebec Aces	QSHL	40	20	30	50	....	....	....	10	15	5	*15	*20	6
1942-43	**Montreal Canadiens**	**NHL**	**1**	**0**	**0**	**0**	**0**	**0**	**0**	**0**	....	....	....	....	....
	Montreal Royals	QSHL	33	14	20	34	....	....	....	26	4	1	0	1	2
	Montreal RCAF	QSHL	....	....	....	....	....	....	....	....	5	2	2	4	4
1943-44	Montreal RCAF	QSHL	7	1	4	5	....	....	....	2	....	....	....	....	....
	Montreal Canada Car	City Sr.	6	1	10	11	....	....	....	2	....	....	....	....	....
	Montreal RCAF	City Sr.	8	8	12	20	....	....	....	4	4	4	7	11	6
1944-45			MILITARY SERVICE												
1945-46			MILITARY SERVICE												
1946-47	Brighton Tigers	Britain	36	57	*54	*111	....	....	....	22	2	3	2	5	8
1947-48	Brighton Tigers	Britain	....	63	59	122	....	....	....	33	....	....	....	....	....
1948-49	Brighton Tigers	Britain	28	20	31	51	....	....	....	12	....	....	....	....	....
1949-50	Brighton Tigers	Britain	52	38	51	89	....	....	....	20	....	....	....	....	....
1950-51	Brighton Tigers	Britain	60	41	37	78	....	....	....	18	....	....	....	....	....
1951-52	Brighton Tigers	Britain	60	36	27	63	....	....	....	26	....	....	....	....	....
1952-53	Brighton Tigers	Britain	60	20	17	37	....	....	....	36	....	....	....	....	....
1953-54	Brighton Tigers	Britain	57	56	57	113	....	....	....	34	....	....	....	....	....
	NHL Totals		**1**	**0**	**0**	**0**	**0**	**0**	**0**	**0**	....	....	....	....	....

Won John Carlin Trophy (Top Scorer - EHL) (1936)

• LEGER, ROGER Roger Leger

D – R. 5'11", 200 lbs. b: L'Annonciation, Que., 3/26/1919. d: 4/7/1965.

			REGULAR SEASON								PLAYOFFS				
Season	**Club**	**League**	**GP**	**G**	**A**	**Pts**	**AG**	**AA**	**APts**	**PIM**	**GP**	**G**	**A**	**Pts**	**PIM**
1940-41	Joliette Cyclones	Mtl-Sr.	26	19	28	47	....	....	....	22	4	4	3	7	6
1941-42	Joliette Cyclones	Mtl-Sr.	30	29	24	53	....	....	....	62	....	....	....	....	....
1942-43	Ottawa Montagnards	City Sr.	14	2	0	2	....	....	....	0	....	....	....	....	....
1943-44	**New York Rangers**	**NHL**	**7**	**1**	**2**	**3**	**1**	**2**	**3**	**2**	....	....	....	....	....
	New York Rovers	EHL	3	4	1	5	....	....	....	4	....	....	....	....	....
	Buffalo Bisons	AHL	29	7	17	24	....	....	....	10	9	6	7	13	4
1944-45	Buffalo Bisons	AHL	54	19	36	55	....	....	....	36	6	0	4	4	12
1945-46	Buffalo Bisons	AHL	57	22	35	57	....	....	....	41	12	1	8	9	4
1946-47	**Montreal Canadiens**	**NHL**	**49**	**4**	**18**	**22**	**5**	**26**	**31**	**12**	**11**	**0**	**6**	**6**	**10**
	Buffalo Bisons	AHL	10	2	3	5	....	....	....	8	....	....	....	....	....
1947-48	**Montreal Canadiens**	**NHL**	**48**	**4**	**14**	**18**	**6**	**20**	**26**	**26**					....
1948-49	**Montreal Canadiens**	**NHL**	**28**	**6**	**7**	**13**	**9**	**11**	**20**	**10**	**5**	**0**	**1**	**1**	**2**
	Buffalo Bisons	AHL	10	1	2	3	....	....	....	6	....	....	....	....	....
	Dallas Texans	USHL	12	3	5	8	....	....	....	12	....	....	....	....	....
1949-50	**Montreal Canadiens**	**NHL**	**55**	**3**	**12**	**15**	**4**	**15**	**19**	**21**	**4**	**0**	**0**	**0**	**2**
	Cincinnati Mohawks	AHL	11	4	4	8	....	....	....	2	....	....	....	....	....
1950-51	Victoria Cougars	PCHL	68	17	43	60	....	....	....	84	12	1	4	5	8
1951-52	Victoria Cougars	PCHL	70	16	47	63	....	....	....	68	13	2	9	11	14
1952-53	Montreal Royals	QSHL	60	5	30	35	....	....	....	22	16	2	7	9	15
1953-54	Montreal Royals	QHL	61	8	29	37	....	....	....	50	11	1	5	6	2
1954-55	Shawinigan Cataracts	QHL	59	2	29	31	....	....	....	83	11	1	9	10	6
1955-56	Shawinigan Cataracts	QHL	45	4	17	21	....	....	....	29	10	0	0	0	0
	NHL Totals		**187**	**18**	**63**	**71**	**26**	**74**	**99**	**71**	**20**	**0**	**7**	**7**	**14**

AHL First All-Star Team (1945, 1946) • PCHL First All-Star Team (1951, 1952) • MVP - PCHL (1951) • QHL First All-Star Team (1953, 1954)

Traded to **Montreal** by **NY Rangers** with Gord Davidson for Bob Dill, January 4, 1944.

• LEIER, EDWARD Edward Leier

C – R. 5'11", 175 lbs. b: Poland, 11/3/1927.

			REGULAR SEASON								PLAYOFFS				
Season	**Club**	**League**	**GP**	**G**	**A**	**Pts**	**AG**	**AA**	**APts**	**PIM**	**GP**	**G**	**A**	**Pts**	**PIM**
1946-47	Winnipeg Rangers	MJHL	15	16	8	24	....	....	....	0	2	2	0	2	0
1947-48	Winnipeg Black Hawks	MJHL	19	12	10	22	....	....	....	2	....	....	....	....	....
	Winnipeg Nationals	City Sr.	2	3	2	5	....	....	....	0	....	....	....	....	....
1948-49	Saskatoon Quakers	WCSHL	25	3	17	20	....	....	....	4	....	....	....	....	....
1949-50	**Chicago Black Hawks**	**NHL**	**5**	**0**	**1**	**1**	**0**	**1**	**1**	**0**	....	....	....	....	....
	Kansas City Mohawks	USHL	59	19	21	40	....	....	....	2	3	1	1	2	0
1950-51	**Chicago Black Hawks**	**NHL**	**11**	**2**	**0**	**2**	**3**	**0**	**3**	**2**	....	....	....	....	....
	Milwaukee Seagulls	USHL	17	6	4	10	....	....	....	6	....	....	....	....	....
1951-52	Vancouver Canucks	PCHL	61	18	37	55	....	....	....	2	....	....	....	....	....
1952-53	Vancouver Canucks	WHL	59	10	27	37	....	....	....	0	0	1	1	2	0
1953-54	Springfield Indians	QHL	56	14	27	41	....	....	....	10	....	....	....	....	....
	Syracuse Warriors	AHL	17	5	6	11	....	....	....	2	....	....	....	....	....
1954-55	Springfield Indians	AHL	59	14	46	60	....	....	....	8	4	0	2	2	0
1955-56	Springfield Indians	AHL	62	9	48	57	....	....	....	14	....	....	....	....	....
	NHL Totals		**16**	**2**	**1**	**3**	**3**	**1**	**4**	**2**	....	....	....	....	....

• LEITER, BOBBY — see page 1224

• LEMIEUX, REAL — see page 1227

• LEPINE, HEC Hec Lepine

C – R. 5'11", 185 lbs. b: St. Anne de Bellevue, Que., 12/7/1897. d: 3/29/1951.

			REGULAR SEASON								PLAYOFFS				
Season	**Club**	**League**	**GP**	**G**	**A**	**Pts**	**AG**	**AA**	**APts**	**PIM**	**GP**	**G**	**A**	**Pts**	**PIM**
1922-23	Montreal Sr. Royals	City Sr.	4	14	0	14	....	....	....	....	....	....	....	....	....
1923-24	Montreal Hochelaga	City Sr.	7	*15	0	*15	....	....	....	0	....	....	....	....	....
1924-25	Montreal Nationale	ECHL	3	2	0	2	....	....	....	0	....	....	....	....	....
	Fort Pitt Hornets	USAHA	21	11	0	11	....	....	....	....	8	1	0	1	....
1925-26	**Montreal Canadiens**	**NHL**	**33**	**5**	**2**	**7**	**15**	**23**	**38**	**2**	....	....	....	....	....
1926-27	Providence Reds	Can-Am	28	6	1	7	....	....	....	28	....	....	....	....	....
	NHL Totals		**33**	**5**	**2**	**7**	**15**	**23**	**38**	**2**	....	....	....	....	....

Signed as a free agent by **Montreal Canadiens**, December 29, 1925.

● LEPINE, PIT
Pit (Alfred Pierre) Lepine
C – L. 5'11", 168 lbs. b: St. Anne de Bellevue, Que., 7/30/1901. d: 8/2/1955.

			REGULAR SEASON								PLAYOFFS				
Season	Club	League	GP	G	A	Pts	AG	AA	APts	PIM	GP	G	A	Pts	PIM
1922-23	Montreal Shamrocks	City Sr.	1	1	0	1	....	....	....	....	....	....	....	....	....
1922-23	Montreal Sr. Royals	City Sr.	4	2	0	2	....	....	....	....	....	....	....	....	....
1923-24	Montreal Hochelaga	City Sr.	9	3	0	3	....	....	....	2	....	....	....	....	....
1924-25	Montreal Nationale	ECHL	15	8	0	8	....	....	....	....	....	....	....	....	....
1925-26	**Montreal Canadiens**	**NHL**	**27**	**9**	**1**	**10**	**28**	**11**	**39**	**18**	....	....	....	....	....
	Montreal Nationale	ECHL	3	2	0	2	....	....	....	0	....	....	....	....	....
1926-27	**Montreal Canadiens**	**NHL**	**44**	**16**	**1**	**17**	**47**	**8**	**55**	**20**	**4**	**0**	**0**	**0**	**4**
1927-28	**Montreal Canadiens**	**NHL**	**20**	**4**	**1**	**5**	**12**	**8**	**20**	**6**	**1**	**0**	**0**	**0**	**0**
1928-29	**Montreal Canadiens**	**NHL**	**44**	**6**	**1**	**7**	**24**	**9**	**33**	**48**	**3**	**0**	**0**	**0**	**2**
1929-30	**Montreal Canadiens**	**NHL**	**44**	**24**	**9**	**33**	**48**	**29**	**77**	**47**	**6**	**2**	**2**	**4**	**6**
1930-31	**Montreal Canadiens**	**NHL**	**44**	**17**	**7**	**24**	**42**	**25**	**67**	**63**	**10**	**4**	**2**	**6**	**6**
1931-32	**Montreal Canadiens**	**NHL**	**48**	**19**	**11**	**30**	**41**	**31**	**72**	**42**	**3**	**1**	**0**	**1**	**4**
1932-33	**Montreal Canadiens**	**NHL**	**46**	**8**	**8**	**16**	**19**	**21**	**40**	**45**	**2**	**0**	**0**	**0**	**2**
1933-34	**Montreal Canadiens**	**NHL**	**48**	**10**	**8**	**18**	**22**	**21**	**43**	**44**	**2**	**0**	**0**	**0**	**0**
1934-35	**Montreal Canadiens**	**NHL**	**48**	**12**	**19**	**31**	**25**	**42**	**67**	**16**	**2**	**0**	**0**	**0**	**2**
1935-36	**Montreal Canadiens**	**NHL**	**32**	**6**	**10**	**16**	**15**	**24**	**39**	**4**	....	....	....	....	....
1936-37	**Montreal Canadiens**	**NHL**	**34**	**7**	**8**	**15**	**15**	**19**	**34**	**15**	**5**	**0**	**1**	**1**	**0**
1937-38	**Montreal Canadiens**	**NHL**	**47**	**5**	**14**	**19**	**10**	**29**	**39**	**24**	**3**	**0**	**0**	**0**	**0**
1938-39	New Haven Eagles	AHL	52	8	23	31	....	....	....	16	....	....	....	....	....
1939-40	**Montreal Canadiens**	**NHL**	DID NOT PLAY – COACHING												
	NHL Totals		**526**	**143**	**98**	**241**	**348**	**277**	**625**	**392**	**41**	**7**	**5**	**12**	**26**

Played in NHL All-Star Game (1937)

Signed as a free agent by **Montreal Canadiens**, November 13, 1925.

● LEROUX, GASTON
Gaston "Gus" Leroux
D – R. 6', 195 lbs. b: Montreal, Quebec, 1/9/1913.

			REGULAR SEASON								PLAYOFFS				
Season	Club	League	GP	G	A	Pts	AG	AA	APts	PIM	GP	G	A	Pts	PIM
1930-31	Montreal Sr. Canadiens	City Sr.	7	0	0	0	....	....	....	2	....	....	....	....	....
1931-32	Montreal St. Francois	City Sr.	STATISTICS NOT AVAILABLE												
1932-33	Banque Nationale	Mtl-Sr.	STATISTICS NOT AVAILABLE												
1933-34	Quebec Beavers	Can-Am	8	0	0	0	....	....	....	0	....	....	....	....	....
	Montreal LaFontaine	City Sr.	14	4	2	6	....	....	....	11	....	....	....	....	....
1934-35	Cleveland Falcons	IAHL	42	2	6	8	....	....	....	15	2	0	0	0	0
1935-36	**Montreal Canadiens**	**NHL**	**2**	**0**	**0**	**0**	**0**	**0**	**0**	**0**	....	....	....	....	....
	Windsor Bulldogs	IAHL	12	1	1	2	....	....	....	2	7	0	0	0	0
	Springfield Indians	Can-Am	23	1	3	4	....	....	....	20	....	....	....	....	....
1936-37	Sherbrooke Red Raiders	QPHL	STATISTICS NOT AVAILABLE												
1937-38	Sherbrooke Red Raiders	QPHL	21	8	5	13	....	....	....	5	9	1	4	5	8
1938-39	Sherbrcoke Red Raiders	QPHL	35	3	5	8	....	....	....	8	5	0	1	1	2
	NHL Totals		**2**	**0**	**0**	**0**	**0**	**0**	**0**	**0**	....	....	....	....	....

Signed as a free agent by **Montreal Canadiens**, October 24, 1935.

● LESIEUR, ART
Art Lesieur
D – R. 5'11", 191 lbs. b: Fall River, MA, 9/13/1907.

			REGULAR SEASON								PLAYOFFS				
Season	Club	League	GP	G	A	Pts	AG	AA	APts	PIM	GP	G	A	Pts	PIM
1927-28	Nashua Nationals	NEHL	23	3	2	5	....	....	....	20	4	1	*2	*3	6
	Providence Reds	Can-Am	1	0	0	0	....	....	....	2	....	....	....	....	....
1928-29	**Montreal Canadiens**	**NHL**	**15**	**0**	**0**	**0**	**0**	**0**	**0**	**0**	....	....	....	....	....
	Chicago Black Hawks	**NHL**	**2**	**0**	**0**	**0**	**0**	**0**	**0**	**0**	....	....	....	....	....
	Providence Reds	Can-Am	16	1	0	1	....	....	....	16	4	0	0	0	2
1929-30	Providence Reds	Can-Am	40	3	0	3	....	....	....	57	3	0	0	0	4
1930-31	**Montreal Canadiens**	**NHL**	**21**	**2**	**0**	**2**	**5**	**0**	**5**	**14**	**10**	**0**	**0**	**0**	**4**
	Providence Reds	Can-Am	19	3	3	6	....	....	....	26	....	....	....	....	....
1931-32	**Montreal Canadiens**	**NHL**	**24**	**1**	**2**	**3**	**2**	**6**	**8**	**12**	**4**	**0**	**0**	**0**	**0**
	Providence Reds	Can-Am	18	4	3	7	....	....	....	35	....	....	....	....	....
1932-33	Providence Reds	Can-Am	25	1	3	4	....	....	....	34	....	....	....	....	....
1933-34	Providence Reds	Can-Am	40	2	1	3	....	....	....	68	3	0	1	1	8
1934-35	Providence Reds	Can-Am	47	5	9	14	....	....	....	80	6	1	0	1	10
1935-36	**Montreal Canadiens**	**NHL**	**38**	**1**	**0**	**1**	**2**	**0**	**2**	**24**	....	....	....	....	....
1936-37	Providence Reds	AHL	48	3	7	10	....	....	....	54	3	0	0	0	2
1937-38	Providence Reds	AHL	47	6	10	16	....	....	....	36	7	0	1	1	8
1938-39	Providence Reds	AHL	54	5	7	12	....	....	....	53	5	0	0	0	4
1939-40	Providence Reds	AHL	54	6	7	13	....	....	....	26	8	0	0	0	4
1940-41	Pittsburgh Hornets	AHL	32	2	0	2	....	....	....	22	....	....	....	....	....
	NHL Totals		**100**	**4**	**2**	**6**	**9**	**6**	**15**	**50**	**14**	**0**	**0**	**0**	**4**

AHL Second All-Star Team (1938, 1939)

Signed as a free agent by **Montreal Canadiens**, October 30, 1930. Loaned to **Chicago** by **Montreal Canadiens** for remainder of 1928-29 season for the loan of Herb Gardiner, January 9, 1930. Traded to **Pittsburgh** (AHL) by **Providence** (AHL) for cash, October 15, 1940.

● LESWICK, JACK
Jack "Newsy" Leswick
C – R. 5'6", 155 lbs. b: Saskatoon, Sask., 1/1/1910. d: 8/7/1934.

			REGULAR SEASON								PLAYOFFS				
Season	Club	League	GP	G	A	Pts	AG	AA	APts	PIM	GP	G	A	Pts	PIM
1929-30	Drumheller Miners	ASHL	11	14	5	19	....	....	....	15	....	....	....	....	....
	Duluth Hornets	AHA	13	1	1	2	....	....	....	6	3	0	0	0	4
1930-31	Duluth Hornets	AHA	41	22	9	31	....	....	....	27	4	0	1	1	4
1931-32	Duluth Hornets	AHA	34	9	7	16	....	....	....	36	8	0	*5	5	4
1932-33	Wichita Blue Jays	AHA	41	*22	18	*40	....	....	....	76	....	....	....	....	....
1933-34	**Chicago Black Hawks**	**NHL**	**3**	**1**	**7**	**8**	**2**	**19**	**21**	**16**	....	....	....	....	....
	Kansas City Greyhounds	AHA	8	1	5	6	....	....	....	14	....	....	....	....	....
	NHL Totals		**3**	**1**	**7**	**8**	**2**	**19**	**21**	**16**	....	....	....	....	....

Signed as a free agent by **Chicago** (Duluth-AHA), January, 1930.

● LESWICK, PETE
Pete Leswick
C/RW – R. 5'7", 163 lbs. b: Saskatoon, Sask., 7/12/1918.

			REGULAR SEASON								PLAYOFFS				
Season	Club	League	GP	G	A	Pts	AG	AA	APts	PIM	GP	G	A	Pts	PIM
1935-36	Saskatoon Wesleys	SSHL	5	4	1	5	....	....	....	0	....	....	....	....	....
1936-37	**New York Americans**	**NHL**	**1**	**1**	**0**	**1**	**2**	**0**	**2**	**0**	....	....	....	....	....
	New Haven Eagles	AHL	21	4	3	7	....	....	....	0	....	....	....	....	....
1937-38	Seattle Seahawks	PCHL	42	20	10	30	....	....	....	22	3	0	0	0	2
1938-39	Kansas City Greyhounds	AHA	25	12	13	25	....	....	....	10	....	....	....	....	....
	Spokane Clippers	PCHL	20	7	3	10	....	....	....	9	....	....	....	....	....
1939-40	Kansas City Greyhounds	AHA	45	14	18	32	....	....	....	17	....	....	....	....	....
1940-41	Kansas City Americans	AHA	45	14	22	36	....	....	....	16	8	2	4	6	0
1941-42	Fort Worth Rangers	AHA	50	35	30	65	....	....	....	17	5	1	4	5	2
1942-43	Vancouver St. Regis	PCHL	3	6	1	7	....	....	....	2	5	3	2	5	4
1943-44	Portland Decleros	PCHL	5	16	2	18	....	....	....	8	....	....	....	....	....
	New Westminster	PCHL	....	....	....	....	....	....	....	....	15	15	*17	*32	12
1944-45	**Boston Bruins**	**NHL**	**2**	**0**	**0**	**0**	**0**	**0**	**0**	**0**	....	....	....	....	....
	Indianapolis Capitals	AHL	53	29	39	68	....	....	....	12	3	1	0	1	0
1945-46	Indianapolis Capitals	AHL	61	29	52	81	....	....	....	10	5	1	1	2	0
1946-47	Cleveland Barons	AHL	64	32	41	73	....	....	....	35	4	1	1	2	0
1947-48	Cleveland Barons	AHL	59	36	40	76	....	....	....	8	6	2	4	6	2
1948-49	Cleveland Barons	AHL	68	44	35	79	....	....	....	10	5	0	2	2	0
1949-50	Cleveland Barons	AHL	64	36	50	86	....	....	....	18	9	2	2	4	0
1950-51	Buffalo Bisons	AHL	11	6	5	11	....	....	....	0	....	....	....	....	....
	Seattle Ironmen	PCHL	49	14	21	35	....	....	....	6	....	....	....	....	....
1951-52	Halifax Saints	MMHL	70	32	36	68	....	....	....	6	9	3	4	7	4
	NHL Totals		**3**	**1**	**0**	**1**	**2**	**0**	**2**	**0**	....	....	....	....	....

AHA First All-Star Team (1942) • AHL Second All-Star Team (1944, 1947) • AHL First All-Star Team (1946, 1948, 1949, 1950)

Signed as a free agent by **NY Americans**, October 15, 1935. Signed as a free agent by **Boston**, October 12, 1944. Traded to **Detroit** by **Boston** for Bill Jennings, October 30, 1944. Traded to **Cleveland** (AHL) by **Detroit** for cash, September 10, 1946.

● LESWICK, TONY
Tony "Mighty Mouse" Leswick
RW/LW – R. 5'7", 160 lbs. b: Humboldt, Sask., 3/17/1923.

			REGULAR SEASON								PLAYOFFS				
Season	Club	League	GP	G	A	Pts	AG	AA	APts	PIM	GP	G	A	Pts	PIM
1939-40	Saskatoon Dodgers	SJHL	....	....	....	....	....	....	....	....	2	4	1	5	0
1940-41	Saskatoon Quakers	SJHL	11	15	10	25	....	....	....	34	14	8	*10	*18	16
	Saskatoon Quakers	SSHL	1	0	0	0	....	....	....	2	2	4	1	5	0
1941-42	Saskatoon Quakers	SSHL	32	21	21	42	....	....	....	45	9	3	5	8	4
1942-43	Cleveland Barons	AHL	52	14	26	40	....	....	....	43	4	3	3	6	4
	Victoria VMD	City Sr.	2	0	2	2	....	....	....	0	....	....	....	....	....
1943-44	Saskatoon Quakers	SSHL	18	26	*26	52	....	....	....	*50	4	3	2	5	18
	New Westminster	PCHL	19	25	11	36	....	....	....	10	2	0	2	2	0
1944-45	Winnipeg Navy	City Sr.	12	9	8	17	....	....	....	*33	6	7	2	9	12
1945-46	**New York Rangers**	**NHL**	**50**	**15**	**9**	**24**	**23**	**17**	**40**	**26**	....	....	....	....	....
1946-47	**New York Rangers**	**NHL**	**59**	**27**	**14**	**41**	**37**	**20**	**57**	**51**	....	....	....	....	....
1947-48	**New York Rangers**	**NHL**	**60**	**24**	**16**	**40**	**35**	**23**	**58**	**76**	**6**	**3**	**2**	**5**	**8**
1948-49	**New York Rangers**	**NHL**	**60**	**13**	**14**	**27**	**20**	**22**	**42**	**70**	....	....	....	....	....
1949-50	**New York Rangers**	**NHL**	**69**	**19**	**25**	**44**	**26**	**32**	**58**	**85**	**12**	**2**	**4**	**6**	**12**
1950-51	**New York Rangers**	**NHL**	**70**	**15**	**11**	**26**	**20**	**14**	**34**	**112**	....	....	....	....	....
1951-52	**Detroit Red Wings**	**NHL**	**70**	**9**	**10**	**19**	**13**	**13**	**26**	**93**	**8**	**3**	**1**	**4**	**22**
1952-53	**Detroit Red Wings**	**NHL**	**70**	**15**	**12**	**27**	**23**	**17**	**40**	**87**	**6**	**1**	**0**	**1**	**11**
1953-54	**Detroit Red Wings**	**NHL**	**70**	**6**	**18**	**24**	**9**	**24**	**33**	**90**	**12**	**3**	**1**	**4**	**18**
1954-55	**Detroit Red Wings**	**NHL**	**70**	**10**	**17**	**27**	**14**	**22**	**36**	**137**	**11**	**1**	**2**	**3**	**20**
1955-56	**Chicago Black Hawks**	**NHL**	**70**	**11**	**11**	**22**	**16**	**14**	**30**	**71**	....	....	....	....	....
1956-57	Edmonton Flyers	WHL	60	22	31	53	....	....	....	107	8	2	1	3	6
1957-58	**Detroit Red Wings**	**NHL**	**22**	**1**	**2**	**3**	**1**	**2**	**3**	**2**	**4**	**0**	**0**	**0**	**0**
	Edmonton Flyers	WHL	42	10	15	25	....	....	....	46	....	....	....	....	....
1958-59	Edmonton Flyers	WHL	36	3	13	16	....	....	....	27	....	....	....	....	....
1959-60	Vancouver Canucks	WHL	9	3	6	9	....	....	....	0	11	0	1	1	0
	NHL Totals		**740**	**165**	**159**	**324**	**237**	**220**	**457**	**900**	**59**	**13**	**10**	**23**	**91**

NHL Second All-Star Team (1950) • WHL Prairie Division Second All-Star Team (1957)

Played in NHL All-Star Game (1947, 1948, 1949, 1950, 1952, 1954)

Claimed by **NY Rangers** from **Cleveland** (AHL) in Inter-League Draft, June 14, 1945. Traded to **Detroit** by **NY Rangers** for Gaye Stewart, June 8, 1951. Traded to **Chicago** by **Detroit** with Glen Skov, John Wilson and Benny Woit for Jerry Toppazzini, John McCormack, Dave Creighton and Gord Hollingworth, May 28, 1955. Traded to **Detroit** by **Chicago** for cash, September 1, 1956.

● LEVANDOSKI, JOSEPH
Joseph Levandoski
RW – R. 5'11", 185 lbs. b: Cobalt, Ont., 3/17/1921.

			REGULAR SEASON								PLAYOFFS				
Season	Club	League	GP	G	A	Pts	AG	AA	APts	PIM	GP	G	A	Pts	PIM
1940-41	Guelph Biltmores	OHA	16	8	6	14	....	....	....	2	5	2	1	3	0
1941-42	Rivervale Skeeters	EHL	55	26	27	53	....	....	....	51	7	9	4	13	0
1942-43	New Haven–Hershey	AHL	54	17	22	39	....	....	....	31	6	2	0	2	0
1943-44	Petawawa Grenades	Ott-Sr.	6	0	3	3	....	....	....	4	....	....	....	....	....
1945-46	St. Paul Saints	USHL	55	12	23	35	....	....	....	23	6	1	0	1	4
1946-47	**New York Rangers**	**NHL**	**8**	**1**	**1**	**2**	**1**	**1**	**2**	**0**	....	....	....	....	....
	New Haven Ramblers	AHL	47	10	12	22	....	....	....	47	3	2	0	2	2
1947-48	St. Paul Saints	USHL	56	20	24	44	....	....	....	41	....	....	....	....	....
1948-49	St. Paul Saints	USHL	36	9	13	22	....	....	....	40	....	....	....	....	....
	Buffalo Bisons	AHL	23	6	8	14	....	....	....	6	....	....	....	....	....
1949-50	St. Paul Saints	USHL	61	12	15	27	....	....	....	44	3	1	1	2	4
1950-51	Kansas City Royals	USHL	64	9	31	40	....	....	....	108	....	....	....	....	....
1951-52	Sydney Millionaires	MMHL	81	17	26	43	....	....	....	85	....	....	....	....	....
1952-53	Calgary Stampeders	WHL	70	7	21	28	....	....	....	79	5	1	4	5	0
1953-54	Providence Reds	AHL	61	2	5	7	....	....	....	62	....	....	....	....	....
	Sherbrooke Saints	QHL	....	....	....	....	....	....	....	....	2	1	0	1	0
1954-55	Providence Reds	AHL	16	1	3	4	....	....	....	18	....	....	....	....	....
	Quebec Aces	QHL	36	2	11	13	....	....	....	42	8	0	2	2	12
1955-56	Quebec Aces	QHL	8	0	3	3	....	....	....	23	....	....	....	....	....
	Kingston Goodyears	EOHL	27	8	23	31	....	....	....	80	14	1	11	12	29
1956-57	Kingston CKLC's	EOHL	37	3	8	11	....	....	....	50	5	0	1	1	18
1957-58	Kingston CKLC's	EOHL	49	7	23	30	....	....	....	60	7	0	2	2	20
1958-59	Kingston Merchants	EOHL	12	2	0	2	....	....	....	12	....	....	....	....	....
	NHL Totals		**8**	**1**	**1**	**2**	**1**	**1**	**2**	**0**	....	....	....	....	....

USHL Second All-Star Team (1951)

Traded to **Quebec** (QHL) by **Providence** (AHL) for Pierre Brilliant, December 5, 1954.

● LEVINSKY, ALEX

Alex "Mine Boy" Levinsky
D – R. 5'10", 184 lbs. b: Syracuse, NY, 2/2/1910. d: 1990.

			REGULAR SEASON								PLAYOFFS				
Season	Club	League	GP	G	A	Pts	AG	AA	APts	PIM	GP	G	A	Pts	PIM
1928-29	Toronto Marlboros	OHA	8	4	1	5	....	....	....	....	3	0	*4	4	....
1929-30	University of Toronto	OHA	9	4	1	5	....	....	....	20	3	1	1	2	8
1930-31	Toronto Marlboros	OHA Sr.	10	3	0	3	....	....	....	16	3	0	0	0	8
	Toronto Maple Leafs	**NHL**	**8**	**0**	**1**	**1**	**0**	**4**	**4**	**2**	**2**	**0**	**0**	**0**	**0**
1931-32	**Toronto Maple Leafs**	**NHL**	**47**	**5**	**5**	**10**	**11**	**14**	**25**	**29**	**7**	**0**	**0**	**0**	**6**
1932-33	**Toronto Maple Leafs**	**NHL**	**48**	**1**	**4**	**5**	**2**	**11**	**13**	**61**	**9**	**1**	**0**	**1**	**14**
1933-34	**Toronto Maple Leafs**	**NHL**	**47**	**5**	**11**	**16**	**11**	**29**	**40**	**38**	**5**	**0**	**0**	**0**	**6**
1934-35	**New York Rangers**	**NHL**	**20**	**0**	**4**	**4**	**0**	**9**	**9**	**6**	....	....	....	....	....
	Chicago Black Hawks	**NHL**	**23**	**3**	**4**	**7**	**6**	**9**	**15**	**16**	**2**	**0**	**0**	**0**	**0**
1935-36	**Chicago Black Hawks**	**NHL**	**48**	**1**	**7**	**8**	**2**	**17**	**19**	**69**	**2**	**0**	**1**	**1**	**0**
1936-37	**Chicago Black Hawks**	**NHL**	**48**	**0**	**8**	**8**	**0**	**19**	**19**	**32**	....	....	....	....	....
1937-38	**Chicago Black Hawks**	**NHL**	**48**	**3**	**2**	**5**	**6**	**4**	**10**	**18**	**10**	**1**	**0**	**1**	**0**
1938-39	**Chicago Black Hawks**	**NHL**	**30**	**1**	**3**	**4**	**2**	**6**	**8**	**36**	....	....	....	....	....
	Philadelphia Ramblers	AHL	17	4	5	9	....	....	....	2	9	0	4	4	4
1939-40	Philadelphia Ramblers	AHL	53	3	13	16	....	....	....	22	....	....	....	....	....
	NHL Totals		**367**	**19**	**49**	**68**	**40**	**122**	**162**	**307**	**37**	**2**	**1**	**3**	**26**

Played in NHL All-Star Game (1934)

Signed as a free agent by **Toronto**, March 2, 1931. Traded to **NY Rangers** by **Toronto** for cash, April 11, 1934. Traded to **Chicago** by **NY Rangers** with $5,000 for Joe Cooper, January 16, 1939.

● LEWICKI, DANNY

Danny "Dashin' Danny" Lewicki
LW – L. 5'8", 147 lbs. b: Fort William, Ont., 3/12/1931.

Season	Club	League	GP	G	A	Pts	AG	AA	APts	PIM	GP	G	A	Pts	PIM
1945-46	Fort William K of C	TBJHL	3	1	1	2	....	....	....	2	....	....	....	....	....
1946-47	Fort William K of C	TBJHL	16	*14	4	*18	....	....	....	4	4	*7	3	10	0
1947-48	Stratford Columbus Club	OHA	9	*19	7	26	....	....	....	14	7	*12	7	*19	8
	Port Arthur Bruins	TBJHL	....	....	....	....	....	....	....	....	17	*21	19	*40	15
1948-49	Stratford Kroehlers	OHA	29	24	24	48	....	....	....	52	3	2	4	6	0
1949-50	Toronto Marlboros	OHA	32	36	36	72	....	....	....	62	5	1	4	5	10
	Toronto Marlboros	OHA Sr.	....	....	....	....	....	....	....	....	4	2	2	4	2
1950-51	**Toronto Maple Leafs**	**NHL**	**61**	**16**	**18**	**34**	**22**	**23**	**45**	**26**	**9**	**0**	**0**	**0**	**0**
1951-52	**Toronto Maple Leafs**	**NHL**	**51**	**4**	**9**	**13**	**6**	**12**	**18**	**26**	....	....	....	....	....
	Pittsburgh Hornets	AHL	6	3	4	7	....	....	....	6	....	....	....	....	....
1952-53	**Toronto Maple Leafs**	**NHL**	**4**	**1**	**3**	**4**	**2**	**4**	**6**	**2**	....	....	....	....	....
	Pittsburgh Hornets	AHL	56	19	42	61	....	....	....	27	10	*6	4	10	12
1953-54	**Toronto Maple Leafs**	**NHL**	**7**	**0**	**1**	**1**	**0**	**1**	**1**	**12**	....	....	....	....	....
	Pittsburgh Hornets	AHL	60	36	45	81	....	....	....	19	5	0	2	2	16
1954-55	**New York Rangers**	**NHL**	**70**	**29**	**24**	**53**	**43**	**31**	**74**	**8**	....	....	....	....	....
1955-56	**New York Rangers**	**NHL**	**70**	**18**	**27**	**45**	**26**	**34**	**60**	**26**	**5**	**0**	**3**	**3**	**0**
1956-57	**New York Rangers**	**NHL**	**70**	**18**	**20**	**38**	**25**	**23**	**48**	**47**	**5**	**0**	**1**	**1**	**2**
1957-58	**New York Rangers**	**NHL**	**70**	**11**	**19**	**30**	**14**	**21**	**35**	**26**	**6**	**0**	**0**	**0**	**6**
1958-59	**Chicago Black Hawks**	**NHL**	**58**	**8**	**14**	**22**	**10**	**15**	**25**	**4**	**3**	**0**	**0**	**0**	**0**
1959-60	Buffalo Bisons	AHL	62	14	41	55	....	....	....	56	....	....	....	....	....
1960-61	Quebec Aces	AHL	67	18	25	43	....	....	....	42	....	....	....	....	....
1961-62	Quebec Aces	AHL	65	27	28	55	....	....	....	18	....	....	....	....	....
1962-63	Quebec Aces	AHL	64	23	25	48	....	....	....	30	....	....	....	....	....
	NHL Totals		**461**	**105**	**135**	**240**	**148**	**164**	**312**	**177**	**28**	**0**	**4**	**4**	**8**

AHL Second All-Star Team (1954) • NHL Second All-Star Team (1955)

Played in NHL All-Star Game (1955)

Traded to **NY Rangers** by **Toronto** for cash, July 20, 1954. Claimed by **Chicago** from **NY Rangers** in Intra-League Draft, June 4, 1958. Traded to **Montreal** by **Chicago** with Glen Skov, Bob Bailey, Terry Gray and Lorne Ferguson for Cec Hoekstra, Reggie Fleming, Ab McDonald and Bob Courcy, June 7, 1960.

● LEWIS, DOUGLAS

Douglas Lewis
LW – L. 5'8", 155 lbs. b: Winnipeg, Man., 3/3/1921.

Season	Club	League	GP	G	A	Pts	AG	AA	APts	PIM	GP	G	A	Pts	PIM
1939-40	Kenora Thistles	MJHL	23	8	6	14	....	....	....	6	8	1	0	1	2
1940-41	Edmonton Athletic Club	City Jr.	....	....	....	....	....	....	....		5	3	0	3	4
1941-42	Springfield Indians	AHL	50	9	25	34	....	....	....	15	5	0	3	3	0
1942-43	Buffalo Bisons	AHL	55	9	27	36	....	....	....	21	7	0	4	4	7
1943-44	Winnipeg Navy	City Sr.	10	3	2	5	....	....	....	8	....	....	....	....	....
1943-44	Cornwallis Navy	City Sr.	2	2	4	6	....	....	....	2	1	1	1	2	0
1944-45	Buffalo Bisons	AHL	56	15	27	42	....	....	....	19	6	0	1	1	0
1945-46	Buffalo Bisons	AHL	62	20	32	52	....	....	....	8	2	0	0	0	0
1946-47	**Montreal Canadiens**	**NHL**	**3**	**0**	**0**	**0**	**0**	**0**	**0**	**0**	....	....	....	....	....
	Buffalo Bisons	AHL	55	10	25	35	....	....	....	16	4	0	1	1	0
1947-48	Buffalo Bisons	AHL	67	20	24	44	....	....	....	12	8	2	1	3	2
1948-49	Buffalo Bisons	AHL	64	22	16	38	....	....	....	23	....	....	....	....	....
1949-50	Buffalo Bisons	AHL	70	9	20	29	....	....	....	30	5	1	0	1	0
1950-51	Seattle Ironmen	PCHL	29	11	4	15	....	....	....	4	....	....	....	....	....
	Boston Olympics	EHL	17	5	1	6	....	....	....	6	....	....	....	....	....
1951-52	Halifax Saints	MMHL	46	10	8	18	....	....	....	0	....	....	....	....	....
	NHL Totals		**3**	**0**	**0**	**0**	**0**	**0**	**0**	**0**	....	....	....	....	....

● LEWIS, HERBIE

Herbie "The Duke of Duluth" Lewis **HHOF**
LW – L. 5'9", 163 lbs. b: Calgary, Alta., 4/17/1906. d: 1/20/1991.

Season	Club	League	GP	G	A	Pts	AG	AA	APts	PIM	GP	G	A	Pts	PIM
1922-23	Calgary Canadians	City Jr.	12	*17	7	*24	....	....	....	24	....	....	....	....	....
1923-24	Calgary Canadians	City Jr.	STATISTICS NOT AVAILABLE												
1924-25	Duluth Hornets	AHA	40	9	0	9	....	....	....	....	....	....	....	....	....
1925-26	Duluth Hornets	AHA	39	17	*11	*28	....	....	....	52	8	*3	1	*4	8
1926-27	Duluth Hornets	AHA	37	18	6	24	....	....	....	52	3	1	0	1	2
1927-28	Duluth Hornets	AHA	40	14	5	19	....	....	....	56	5	0	0	0	8
1928-29	**Detroit Cougars**	**NHL**	**36**	**9**	**5**	**14**	**36**	**46**	**82**	**33**	....	....	....	....	....
1929-30	**Detroit Cougars**	**NHL**	**44**	**20**	**11**	**31**	**40**	**36**	**76**	**36**	....	....	....	....	....
1930-31	**Detroit Falcons**	**NHL**	**43**	**15**	**6**	**21**	**37**	**22**	**59**	**38**	....	....	....	....	....
1931-32	**Detroit Falcons**	**NHL**	**48**	**5**	**14**	**19**	**11**	**39**	**50**	**21**	**2**	**0**	**0**	**0**	**0**
1932-33	**Detroit Red Wings**	**NHL**	**48**	**20**	**14**	**34**	**47**	**37**	**84**	**20**	**4**	**1**	**0**	**1**	**0**
1933-34	**Detroit Red Wings**	**NHL**	**43**	**16**	**15**	**31**	**36**	**40**	**76**	**15**	**9**	***5**	**2**	**7**	**2**
1934-35	**Detroit Red Wings**	**NHL**	**47**	**16**	**27**	**43**	**34**	**61**	**95**	**26**	....	....	....	....	....
1935-36	**Detroit Red Wings**	**NHL**	**45**	**14**	**23**	**37**	**35**	**56**	**91**	**25**	**7**	**2**	**3**	**5**	**0**
1936-37	**Detroit Red Wings**	**NHL**	**45**	**14**	**18**	**32**	**30**	**42**	**72**	**14**	**10**	**4**	**3**	**7**	**4**
1937-38	**Detroit Red Wings**	**NHL**	**42**	**13**	**18**	**31**	**27**	**37**	**64**	**12**	....	....	....	....	....
1938-39	**Detroit Red Wings**	**NHL**	**42**	**6**	**10**	**16**	**13**	**19**	**32**	**8**	**6**	**1**	**2**	**3**	**0**
1939-40	Indianapolis Capitals	AHL	26	1	6	7	....	....	....	6	3	1	2	3	0
1940-41	Indianapolis Capitals	AHL	2	1	0	1	....	....	....	0	....	....	....	....	....
1941-42	Indianapolis Capitals	AHL	DID NOT PLAY – COACHING												
	NHL Totals		**483**	**148**	**161**	**309**	**346**	**435**	**781**	**248**	**38**	**13**	**10**	**23**	**6**

Played in NHL All-Star Game (1934)

Claimed by **Detroit Cougars** from **Duluth** (AHA) in Inter-League Draft, May 14, 1928.

● LICARI, TONY

Tony Licari
RW – R. 5'7", 147 lbs. b: Ottawa, Ont., 4/9/1921.

Season	Club	League	GP	G	A	Pts	AG	AA	APts	PIM	GP	G	A	Pts	PIM
1937-1939	Ottawa Glebe Colligiate	City Jr.	STATISTICS NOT AVAILABLE												
1939-40	Perth Blue Wings	City Jr.	9	13	12	25	....	....	....	0	12	*15	12	*27	6
1940-41	Guelph Biltmores	OHA	12	10	16	26	....	....	....	4	5	8	4	12	2
1941-42	Dallas Texans	AHA	49	15	18	33	....	....	....	10	....	....	....	....	....
1942-43	Ottawa RCAF	City Sr.	19	19	17	36	....	....	....	0	15	11	11	22	4
1943-44	Vancouver RCAF	City Sr.	14	16	7	23	....	....	....	9	3	*4	1	5	0
1944-45	Ottawa #17 Depot	City Sr.	7	13	*22	35	....	....	....	2	....	....	....	....	....
1945-46			MILITARY SERVICE												
1946-47	**Detroit Red Wings**	**NHL**	**9**	**0**	**1**	**1**	**0**	**1**	**1**	**0**	....	....	....	....	....
	Indianapolis Capitals	AHL	52	21	28	49	....	....	....	6	....	....	....	....	....
1947-48	Indianapolis Capitals	AHL	65	20	39	59	....	....	....	10	....	....	....	....	....
1948-49	St. Louis Flyers	AHL	68	22	52	74	....	....	....	8	7	1	4	5	2
1949-50	Ottawa RCAF	City Sr.	40	28	29	57	....	....	....	22	5	4	3	7	4
1950-51	Ottawa Senators	QSHL	2	1	0	1	....	....	....	2	....	....	....	....	....
	Ottawa RCAF	City Sr.	40	23	28	51	....	....	....	14	7	*9	5	*14	6
1951-52	Harringay Racers	Britain	60	47	54	101	....	....	....	52	....	....	....	....	....
1952-53	Harringay Racers	Britain	51	45	57	102	....	....	....	28	....	....	....	....	....
1953-54	Harringay Racers	Britain	60	42	*67	109	....	....	....	30	....	....	....	....	....
1954-55	Pembroke Lumber Kings	NOHA	1	0	0	0	....	....	....	0	....	....	....	....	....
	NHL Totals		**9**	**0**	**1**	**1**	**0**	**1**	**1**	**0**	....	....	....	....	....

Traded to **St. Louis** (AHL) by **Detroit** with Red Almas, Lloyd Doran, Barry Sullivan and Thain Simon for Joe Lund and Hec Highton, September 9, 1948.

● LINDSAY, TED

Ted "Terrible Teddie" Lindsay **HHOF**
LW – L. 5'8", 163 lbs. b: Renfrew, Ont., 7/29/1925.

Season	Club	League	GP	G	A	Pts	AG	AA	APts	PIM	GP	G	A	Pts	PIM
1943-44	St. Michael's Majors	OHA Jr.	22	22	7	29	....	....	....	24	12	*13	6	*19	16
1944-45	**Detroit Red Wings**	**NHL**	**45**	**17**	**6**	**23**	**23**	**10**	**33**	**43**	**14**	**2**	**0**	**2**	**6**
1945-46	**Detroit Red Wings**	**NHL**	**47**	**7**	**10**	**17**	**11**	**19**	**30**	**14**	**5**	**0**	**1**	**1**	**0**
1946-47	**Detroit Red Wings**	**NHL**	**59**	**27**	**15**	**42**	**37**	**21**	**58**	**57**	**5**	**2**	**2**	**4**	**10**
1947-48	**Detroit Red Wings**	**NHL**	**60**	***33**	**19**	**52**	**49**	**28**	**77**	**95**	**10**	**3**	**1**	**4**	**6**
1948-49	**Detroit Red Wings**	**NHL**	**50**	**26**	**28**	**54**	**41**	**45**	**86**	**97**	**11**	**2**	***6**	**8**	**31**
1949-50	**Detroit Red Wings**	**NHL**	**60**	**23**	***55**	***78**	**31**	**71**	**102**	**141**	**13**	**4**	**4**	**8**	**16**
1950-51	**Detroit Red Wings**	**NHL**	**67**	**24**	**35**	**59**	**33**	**40**	**79**	**110**	**6**	**0**	**1**	**1**	**8**
1951-52	**Detroit Red Wings**	**NHL**	**70**	**30**	**39**	**69**	**43**	**51**	**94**	**123**	**8**	***5**	**2**	***7**	**8**
1952-53	**Detroit Red Wings**	**NHL**	**70**	**32**	**39**	**71**	**50**	**55**	**105**	**111**	**6**	**4**	**4**	**8**	**6**
1953-54	**Detroit Red Wings**	**NHL**	**70**	**26**	**36**	**62**	**40**	**49**	**89**	**110**	**12**	**4**	**4**	**8**	**14**
1954-55	**Detroit Red Wings**	**NHL**	**49**	**19**	**19**	**38**	**28**	**24**	**52**	**85**	**11**	**7**	**12**	**19**	**12**
1955-56	**Detroit Red Wings**	**NHL**	**67**	**27**	**23**	**50**	**40**	**29**	**69**	**161**	**10**	**6**	**3**	**9**	**22**
1956-57	**Detroit Red Wings**	**NHL**	**70**	**30**	***55**	**85**	**41**	**65**	**106**	***103**	**5**	**2**	**4**	**6**	**8**
1957-58	**Chicago Black Hawks**	**NHL**	**68**	**15**	**24**	**39**	**20**	**26**	**46**	**110**	....	....	....	....	....
1958-59	**Chicago Black Hawks**	**NHL**	**70**	**22**	**36**	**58**	**28**	**39**	**67**	***184**	**6**	**2**	**4**	**6**	**13**
1959-60	**Chicago Black Hawks**	**NHL**	**68**	**7**	**19**	**26**	**9**	**19**	**28**	**91**	**4**	**1**	**1**	**2**	**0**
1960-1964			DID NOT PLAY – RETIRED												
1964-65	**Detroit Red Wings**	**NHL**	**69**	**14**	**14**	**28**	**18**	**15**	**33**	**173**	**7**	**3**	**0**	**3**	**34**
	NHL Totals		**1068**	**379**	**472**	**851**	**542**	**612**	**1154**	**1808**	**133**	**47**	**49**	**96**	**194**

NHL First All-Star Team (1948, 1950, 1951, 1952, 1953, 1954, 1956, 1957) • NHL Second All-Star Team (1949) • Won Art Ross Trophy (1950)

Played in NHL All-Star Game (1947, 1948, 1949, 1950, 1951, 1952, 1953, 1954, 1955, 1956, 1957)

Traded to **Chicago** by **Detroit** with Forbes Kennedy and Glenn Hall for Johnny Wilson, Hank Bassen and Bill Preston, July, 1957. Traded to **Detroit** by **Chicago** for cash, October 14, 1964.

• LISCOMBE, CARL Carl "Lefty" Liscombe

LW – L. 5'7", 162 lbs. b: Perth, Ont., 5/17/1915.

Season	Club	League	GP	G	A	Pts	AG	AA	APts	PIM	GP	G	A	Pts	PIM
			REGULAR SEASON								PLAYOFFS				
1934-35	Hamilton Tigers	OHA Sr.	19	*22	6	*28	....	....	....	20	6	1	0	1	2
1935-36	Detroit Olympics	IAHL	47	12	8	20	....	....	....	37	6	1	1	2	4
1936-37	Pittsburgh Hornets	AHL	48	8	13	21	....	....	....	23	5	0	1	1	2
1937-38	**Detroit Red Wings**	**NHL**	**41**	**14**	**10**	**24**	**30**	**21**	**51**	**30**	....	....	....	....	....
	Pittsburgh Hornets	AHL	5	3	1	4	....	....	....	17	....	....	....	....	....
1938-39	**Detroit Red Wings**	**NHL**	**41**	**8**	**18**	**26**	**17**	**34**	**51**	**13**	**6**	**0**	**0**	**0**	**2**
1939-40	**Detroit Red Wings**	**NHL**	**25**	**2**	**7**	**9**	**4**	**14**	**18**	**4**	....	....	....	....	....
	Indianapolis Capitals	AHL	24	8	11	19	....	....	....	9	5	2	1	3	2
1940-41	**Detroit Red Wings**	**NHL**	**33**	**10**	**10**	**20**	**20**	**18**	**38**	**0**	**8**	**4**	**3**	**7**	**12**
	Indianapolis Capitals	AHL	19	4	5	9	....	....	....	7	....	....	....	....	....
1941-42	**Detroit Red Wings**	**NHL**	**47**	**13**	**17**	**30**	**22**	**26**	**48**	**14**	**12**	**6**	**6**	**12**	**2**
1942-43	**Detroit Red Wings**	**NHL**	**50**	**19**	**23**	**42**	**27**	**29**	**56**	**19**	**10**	**6**	**8**	**14**	**2**
1943-44	**Detroit Red Wings**	**NHL**	**50**	**36**	**37**	**73**	**46**	**45**	**91**	**17**	**5**	**1**	**0**	**1**	**2**
1944-45	**Detroit Red Wings**	**NHL**	**42**	**23**	**9**	**32**	**32**	**14**	**46**	**18**	**14**	**4**	**2**	**6**	**0**
1945-46	**Detroit Red Wings**	**NHL**	**44**	**12**	**9**	**21**	**18**	**17**	**35**	**2**	**4**	**1**	**0**	**1**	**0**
1946-47	St. Louis–Providence	AHL	63	35	32	67	....	....	....	16	....	....	....	....	....
1947-48	Providence Reds	AHL	68	*50	68	*118	....	....	....	10	5	1	1	2	2
1948-49	Providence Reds	AHL	68	*55	47	102	....	....	....	2	14	3	2	5	2
1949-50	Providence Reds	AHL	57	13	29	42	....	....	....	16	3	0	0	0	0
1950-51	Sarnia–Detroit	IHL	45	29	23	52	....	....	....	9	3	1	0	1	0
	Hamilton Tigers	OHA Sr.	4	0	0	0	....	....	....	0	....	....	....	....	....
1951-52	Detroit Hettche	IHL	45	35	31	66	....	....	....	14	....	....	....	....	....
1952-53	Chatham Maroons	OHA Sr.	14	4	7	11	....	....	....	2	....	....	....	....	....
1953-54	Chatham Maroons	OHA Sr.	12	0	0	0	....	....	....	4	....	....	....	....	....
	NHL Totals		**373**	**137**	**140**	**277**	**216**	**218**	**434**	**117**	**59**	**22**	**19**	**41**	**20**

AHL First All-Star Team (1948) • Won John B. Sollenberger Trophy (Top Scorer - AHL) (1948) • Won Les Cunningham Award (MVP - AHL) (1948, 1949) • AHL Second All-Star Team (1949) • IHL Second All-Star Team (1951)

Signed as a free agent by **Detroit**, September 24, 1935.

• LITZENBERGER, ED Ed "Litz" Litzenberger

C/RW – R. 6'1", 174 lbs. b: Neudorf, Sask., 7/15/1932.

Season	Club	League	GP	G	A	Pts	AG	AA	APts	PIM	GP	G	A	Pts	PIM
1949-50	Regina Pats	WCJHL	40	25	19	44	....	....	....	16	9	*11	4	15	4
1950-51	Regina Pats	WCJHL	40	*44	35	79	....	....	....	23	12	*14	16	*30	6
1951-52	Regina Pats	WCJHL	41	42	29	71	....	....	....	75	8	8	5	13	8
1952-53	**Montreal Canadiens**	**NHL**	**2**	**1**	**0**	**1**	**2**	**0**	**2**	**2**	....	....	....	....	....
	Montreal Royals	QSHL	59	26	24	50	....	....	....	42	16	8	4	12	15
1953-54	**Montreal Canadiens**	**NHL**	**3**	**0**	**0**	**0**	**0**	**0**	**0**	**0**	....	....	....	....	....
	Montreal Royals	QHL	67	31	39	70	....	....	....	44	11	4	5	9	6
1954-55	**Montreal Canadiens**	**NHL**	**29**	**7**	**4**	**11**	**10**	**5**	**15**	**12**	....	....	....	....	....
	Chicago Black Hawks	**NHL**	**44**	**16**	**24**	**40**	**23**	**31**	**54**	**28**	....	....	....	....	....
1955-56	**Chicago Black Hawks**	**NHL**	**70**	**10**	**29**	**39**	**14**	**36**	**50**	**36**	....	....	....	....	....
1956-57	**Chicago Black Hawks**	**NHL**	**70**	**32**	**32**	**64**	**44**	**37**	**81**	**48**	....	....	....	....	....
1957-58	**Chicago Black Hawks**	**NHL**	**70**	**32**	**30**	**62**	**43**	**33**	**76**	**63**	....	....	....	....	....
1958-59	**Chicago Black Hawks**	**NHL**	**70**	**33**	**44**	**77**	**42**	**47**	**89**	**37**	**6**	**3**	**5**	**8**	**8**
1959-60	**Chicago Black Hawks**	**NHL**	**52**	**12**	**18**	**30**	**15**	**18**	**33**	**15**	**4**	**0**	**1**	**1**	**4**
1960-61	**Chicago Black Hawks**	**NHL**	**62**	**10**	**22**	**32**	**12**	**22**	**34**	**14**	**10**	**1**	**3**	**4**	**2**
1961-62	**Detroit Red Wings**	**NHL**	**32**	**8**	**12**	**20**	**10**	**12**	**22**	**4**	....	....	....	....	....
	Toronto Maple Leafs	**NHL**	**37**	**10**	**10**	**20**	**12**	**10**	**22**	**14**	**10**	**0**	**2**	**2**	**4**
1962-63	**Toronto Maple Leafs**	**NHL**	**58**	**5**	**13**	**18**	**6**	**14**	**20**	**10**	**9**	**1**	**2**	**3**	**6**
1963-64	**Toronto Maple Leafs**	**NHL**	**19**	**2**	**0**	**2**	**3**	**0**	**3**	**0**	**1**	**0**	**0**	**0**	**10**
	Rochester Americans	AHL	33	15	14	29	....	....	....	26	2	1	1	2	2
1964-65	Rochester Americans	AHL	72	25	61	86	....	....	....	34	10	1	3	4	6
1965-66	Victoria Maple Leafs	WHL	23	7	17	24	....	....	....	26	....	....	....	....	....
	Rochester Americans	AHL	47	7	15	22	....	....	....	10	12	1	5	6	8
	NHL Totals		**618**	**178**	**238**	**416**	**236**	**265**	**501**	**283**	**40**	**5**	**13**	**18**	**34**

Won William Northey Trophy (Top Rookie - QHL) (1953) • QHL Second All-Star Team (1954) • Won Calder Memorial Trophy (1955) • NHL Second All-Star Team (1957)

Played in NHL All-Star Game (1955, 1957, 1958, 1959, 1962, 1963)

Traded to **Chicago** by **Montreal** for cash, December 10, 1954. Traded to **Detroit** by **Chicago** for Gerry Melnyk and Brian Smith, June, 1961. Claimed on waivers by **Toronto** from **Detroit**, December, 1961.

• LOCAS, JACQUES Jacques Locas

RW – R. 5'11", 175 lbs. b: Pointe aux Trembles, Que., 2/12/1926. Deceased.

Season	Club	League	GP	G	A	Pts	AG	AA	APts	PIM	GP	G	A	Pts	PIM
1943-44	Concordia Civics	Mtl-Jr.	13	8	7	15	....	....	....	8	5	3	0	3	2
1944-45	Concordia Civics	Mtl-Jr.	10	6	5	11	....	....	....	2	2	2	1	3	2
1945-46	Concordias Civics	Mtl-Jr.	20	*25	8	*33	....	....	....	31	5	*7	3	10	4
1946-47	Montreal Royals	QSHL	38	23	12	35	....	....	....	69	10	*11	3	14	12
1947-48	**Montreal Canadiens**	**NHL**	**56**	**7**	**8**	**15**	**10**	**12**	**22**	**66**	....	....	....	....	....
1948-49	**Montreal Canadiens**	**NHL**	**3**	**0**	**0**	**0**	**0**	**0**	**0**	**0**	....	....	....	....	....
	Dallas Texans	USHL	6	3	2	5	....	....	....	0	....	....	....	....	....
1949-50	Cincinnati Mohawks	AHL	62	8	15	23	....	....	....	36	....	....	....	....	....
1950-51	Montreal Royals	QSHL	22	15	7	22	....	....	....	63	7	2	2	4	10
1951-52	Montreal Royals	QSHL	41	11	15	26	....	....	....	44	7	0	1	1	0
1952-53	Sherbrooke Saints	QSHL	57	36	28	64	....	....	....	61	7	2	3	5	*24
1953-54	Chicoutimi Sagueneens	QHL	65	35	20	55	....	....	....	45	7	2	0	2	6
1954-55	Chicoutimi Sagueneens	QHL	46	24	14	38	....	....	....	36	....	....	....	....	....
1955-56	Chicoutimi Sagueneens	QHL	62	27	23	50	....	....	....	80	5	2	0	2	2
1956-57	Chicoutimi Sagueneens	QHL	67	33	13	46	....	....	....	54	10	5	2	7	*24
1957-58	Chicoutimi Sagueneens	QHL	64	*40	16	56	....	....	....	54	5	2	0	2	6
1958-59	Chicoutimi Sagueneens	QHL	61	*49	24	73	....	....	....	46	....	....	....	....	....
1959-60	Quebec Aces	AHL	39	9	8	17	....	....	....	20	....	....	....	....	....
	NHL Totals		**59**	**7**	**8**	**15**	**10**	**12**	**22**	**66**	....	....	....	....	....

QHL First All-Star Team (1958, 1959)

• LOCKING, NORM Norm Locking

LW/C – L. 6', 165 lbs. b: Owen Sound, Ont., 5/24/1911. d: 5/15/1995.

Season	Club	League	GP	G	A	Pts	AG	AA	APts	PIM	GP	G	A	Pts	PIM
			REGULAR SEASON								PLAYOFFS				
1931-32	Pittsburgh Yellowjackets	IAHL	29	2	0	2	....	....	....	12	....	....	....	....	....
1932-33	St. Paul–Tulsa	AHA	39	11	11	22	....	....	....	32	4	1	0	1	*10
1933-34	Cleveland Indians	IAHL	40	*24	10	34	....	....	....	21	....	....	....	....	....
1934-35	**Chicago Black Hawks**	**NHL**	**35**	**2**	**5**	**7**	**4**	**11**	**15**	**19**	....	....	....	....	....
1935-36	**Chicago Black Hawks**	**NHL**	**13**	**0**	**1**	**1**	**0**	**2**	**2**	**7**	....	....	....	....	....
	London Tecumsehs	IAHL	33	11	12	23	....	....	....	22	2	0	0	0	0
1936-37	Syracuse Stars	AHL	36	12	13	25	....	....	....	26	9	1	3	4	2
1937-38	Syracuse Stars	AHL	48	19	17	36	....	....	....	13	8	4	3	7	0
1938-39	Syracuse Stars	AHL	53	20	30	50	....	....	....	28	3	0	1	1	2
1939-40	Syracuse Stars	AHL	55	*31	32	*63	....	....	....	12	....	....	....	....	....
1940-41	Cleveland Barons	AHL	52	25	19	44	....	....	....	27	9	0	4	4	4
1941-42	Cleveland Barons	AHL	54	14	32	46	....	....	....	7	5	1	1	2	0
1942-43	Cleveland Barons	AHL	56	26	40	66	....	....	....	14	3	1	2	3	2
1943-44	Cleveland Barons	AHL	19	9	9	18	....	....	....	0	11	0	6	6	0
	NHL Totals		**48**	**2**	**6**	**8**	**4**	**13**	**17**	**26**	....	....	....	....	....

AHL First All-Star Team (1940, 1941) • AHL Second All-Star Team (1943)

Rights traded to **Chicago** by **Tulsa** (AHA) for Lou Holmes, March 7, 1933. Traded to **Cleveland** (IAHL) by **Chicago** for cash, November, 1933. Traded to **Chicago** by **Cleveland** (IAHL) for cash, November 1, 1934. Loaned to **London** (IAHL) by **Chicago** for Bill Kendall, January 23, 1936.

• LONG, STANLEY Stanley Long

D – L. 5'11", 190 lbs. b: Owen Sound, Ont., 11/6/1929. Deceased.

Season	Club	League	GP	G	A	Pts	AG	AA	APts	PIM	GP	G	A	Pts	PIM
1946-47	Barrie Flyers	OHA	14	1	1	2	....	....	....	29	5	0	1	1	4
1947-48	Barrie Flyers	OHA	34	9	25	34	....	....	....	60	22	10	14	24	56
1948-49	Barrie Flyers	OHA	42	11	39	50	....	....	....	89	15	4	11	15	17
1949-50	Barrie Flyers	OHA	48	19	37	56	....	....	....	112	9	1	8	9	12
	Buffalo Bisons	AHL	1	0	0	0	....	....	....	0	....	....	....	....	....
1950-51	Victoria Cougars	PCHL	62	9	15	24	....	....	....	77	12	2	4	6	16
	Montreal Royals	QSHL	5	0	0	0	....	....	....	9	....	....	....	....	....
1951-52	Buffalo Bisons	AHL	61	11	20	31	....	....	....	96	3	2	1	3	2
	Montreal Canadiens	**NHL**	....	....	....	....	....	....	....	....	**3**	**0**	**0**	**0**	**0**
1952-53	Victoria Cougars	WHL	51	9	19	28	....	....	....	55	....	....	....	....	....
1953-54	Buffalo Bisons	AHL	6	0	4	4	....	....	....	10	....	....	....	....	....
1954-55	Kitchener Canucks	OHA	DID NOT PLAY – COACHING												
	NHL Totals		**0**	**0**	**0**	**0**	**0**	**0**	**0**	**0**	**3**	**0**	**0**	**0**	**0**

• LONSBERRY, ROSS — *see page 1238*

• LORRAIN, ROD Rod Lorrain

RW – R. 5'5", 156 lbs. b: Buckingham, Que., 7/26/1914. d: 10/22/1980.

Season	Club	League	GP	G	A	Pts	AG	AA	APts	PIM	GP	G	A	Pts	PIM
1932-33	Hull-Lasalle Juniors	Ott-Jr.	11	5	2	7	....	....	....	2	....	....	....	....	....
1933-34	Hull-Lasalle Juniors	Ott-Jr.	11	*21	14	35	....	....	....	2	4	3	6	9	2
1934-35	Ottawa Senators	City Sr.	14	4	6	10	....	....	....	10	8	1	2	3	4
1935-36	**Montreal Canadiens**	**NHL**	**1**	**0**	**0**	**0**	**0**	**0**	**0**	**2**	....	....	....	....	....
	Ottawa Senators	QSHL	11	8	4	12	....	....	....	4	....	....	....	....	....
	Providence Reds	Can-Am	22	2	1	3	....	....	....	4	3	0	0	0	2
1936-37	**Montreal Canadiens**	**NHL**	**47**	**3**	**6**	**9**	**6**	**14**	**20**	**8**	**5**	**0**	**0**	**0**	**0**
1937-38	**Montreal Canadiens**	**NHL**	**48**	**13**	**19**	**32**	**27**	**39**	**66**	**14**	**3**	**0**	**0**	**0**	**0**
1938-39	**Montreal Canadiens**	**NHL**	**38**	**10**	**9**	**19**	**21**	**17**	**38**	**0**	**3**	**0**	**3**	**3**	**0**
	New Haven Eagles	AHL	9	1	3	4	....	....	....	0	....	....	....	....	....
1939-40	**Montreal Canadiens**	**NHL**	**41**	**1**	**5**	**6**	**2**	**10**	**12**	**6**	....	....	....	....	....
1940-41	St. Jerome Papermakers	QPHL	34	34	24	58	....	....	....	12	13	*10	6	*16	11
1941-42	**Montreal Canadiens**	**NHL**	**4**	**1**	**0**	**1**	**2**	**0**	**2**	**0**	....	....	....	....	....
	Washington Lions	AHL	34	4	15	19	....	....	....	0	2	2	0	2	0
1942-43	Washington Lions	AHL	49	8	20	28	....	....	....	8	....	....	....	....	....
1943-44	University of Montreal	OQAA	3	1	2	3	....	....	....	0	....	....	....	....	....
	Montreal Vickers	City Sr.	8	5	3	8	....	....	....	0	....	....	....	....	....
1944-45	Hull Volants	QSHL	11	2	9	11	....	....	....	0	....	....	....	....	....
	NHL Totals		**179**	**28**	**39**	**67**	**58**	**80**	**138**	**30**	**11**	**0**	**3**	**3**	**0**

Played in NHL All-Star Game (1939)

• LOUGHLIN, CLEM Clem (Clement) Loughlin

D – L. 6', 180 lbs. b: Carroll, Man., 11/15/1894. d: 2/8/1977.

Season	Club	League	GP	G	A	Pts	AG	AA	APts	PIM	GP	G	A	Pts	PIM
1910-11	Winnipeg Monarchs	MHL Sr.	1	0	0	0	....	....	....	....	....	....	....	....	....
1911-12	Winnipeg Monarchs	MHL Sr.	STATISTICS NOT AVAILABLE												
1912-13	Winnipeg Strathconas	City Sr.	8	3	0	3	....	....	....	....	2	1	0	1	0
1913-14	Winnipeg Monarchs	City Sr.	1	1	0	1	....	....	....	0	....	....	....	....	....
	Winnipeg Strathconas	MHL Sr.	12	6	0	6	....	....	....	....	....	....	....	....	....
1914-15	Winnipeg Monarchs	MHL Sr.	5	2	3	5	....	....	....	12	8	6	0	6	10
1915-16	Winnipeg Monarchs	MHL Sr.	8	1	1	2	....	....	....	6	2	0	0	0	0
1916-17	Portland Rosebuds	PCHA	24	3	1	4	....	....	....	43	....	....	....	....	....
1917-18	Portland Rosebuds	PCHA	16	2	0	2	....	....	....	6	....	....	....	....	....
1918-19	Victoria Cougars	PCHA	16	1	3	4	....	....	....	3	....	....	....	....	....
1919-20	Victoria Cougars	PCHA	22	2	2	4	....	....	....	18	....	....	....	....	....
1920-21	Victoria Cougars	PCHA	24	7	3	10	....	....	....	21	....	....	....	....	....
1921-22	Victoria Cougars	PCHA	24	6	3	9	....	....	....	6	....	....	....	....	....
1922-23	Victoria Cougars	PCHA	30	12	10	22	....	....	....	24	2	0	0	0	4
1923-24	Victoria Cougars	PCHA	30	10	7	17	....	....	....	26	....	....	....	....	....
1924-25	Victoria Cougars	WCHL	28	9	2	11	....	....	....	46	8	1	1	2	4
1925-26	Victoria Cougars	WHL	30	7	3	10	....	....	....	52	8	1	2	3	12
1926-27	**Detroit Cougars**	**NHL**	**34**	**7**	**3**	**10**	**20**	**25**	**45**	**40**	....	....	....	....	....
1927-28	**Detroit Cougars**	**NHL**	**43**	**1**	**2**	**3**	**3**	**17**	**20**	**21**	....	....	....	....	....
1928-29	**Chicago Black Hawks**	**NHL**	**24**	**0**	**1**	**1**	**0**	**9**	**9**	**16**	....	....	....	....	....
	Kitchener Millionaires	Can-Pro	18	3	1	4	....	....	....	21	3	0	0	0	8
1929-30	London Panthers	IAHL	40	5	2	7	....	....	....	37	2	0	0	0	0
1930-31	London Tecumsehs	IAHL	46	4	7	11	....	....	....	50	....	....	....	....	....
1931-32	London Tecumsehs	IAHL	42	0	0	0	....	....	....	2	6	0	0	0	0
1932-33	London Tecumsehs	IAHL	DID NOT PLAY – COACHING												
	NHL Totals		**101**	**8**	**6**	**14**	**23**	**51**	**74**	**77**	....	....	....	....	....
	Other Major League Totals		244	59	34	93	....	....	....	245	18	2	3	5	20

PCHA Second All-Star Team (1921, 1922, 1923) • PCHA First All-Star Team (1924)

Signed as a free agent by **Victoria** (PCHA) after **Portland** (PCHA) franchise folded, November 28, 1918. Transferred to **Detroit Cougars** after NHL club purchased **Victoria** (PCHA) franchise, May 15, 1926. Traded to **Chicago** by **Detroit Cougars** for cash, October 18, 1928. Signed as a free agent by **Toronto**, November 12, 1929. Traded to **London** (IAHL) by **Toronto** for cash, November 12, 1929.

• LOUGHLIN, WILF Wilf Loughlin

D/LW – L. 6'2", 200 lbs. b: Carroll, Manitoba, 2/28/1896. d: 6/25/1966.

			REGULAR SEASON								PLAYOFFS				
Season	Club	League	GP	G	A	Pts	AG	AA	APts	PIM	GP	G	A	Pts	PIM
1915-16	Winnipeg Monarchs	City Sr.	1	0	0	0				6					
1916-17	Winnipeg Monarchs	MHL Sr.	8	5	3	8				10					
1917-18	Winnipeg Vimy	MHL Sr.	10	10	4	14				12					
1918-19	Victoria Cougars	PCHA	7	1	3	4				0					
	Winnipeg Monarchs	MHL Sr.	8	12	3	15				6					
1919-20	Victoria Cougars	PCHA	20	4	1	5				19					
1920-21	Victoria Cougars	PCHA	24	8	5	13				15					
1921-22	Victoria Cougars	PCHA	24	8	3	11				27					
1922-23	Victoria Cougars	PCHA	27	0	0	0				9	2	0	0	0	0
1923-24	**Toronto St. Pats**	**NHL**	**14**	**0**	**0**	**0**	**0**	**0**	**0**	**2**					
1924-25	Regina Capitals	WCHL	18	0	0	0				6					
1925-26	Edmonton Eskimos	WHL	5	1	0	1				0					
	Winnipeg Maroons	AHA	3	0	0	0				0					
1926-27	Moose Jaw Maroons	PHL	5	0	0	0				0					
	NHL Totals		**14**	**0**	**0**	**0**	**0**	**0**	**0**	**2**					
	Other Major League Totals		125	22	12	34				76	2	0	0	0	0

PCHA Second All-Star Team (1921)

Signed as a free agent by **Victoria** (PCHA), February 18, 1919. Traded to **Toronto St. Pats** by **Victoria** (PCHA) for cash, October 24, 1923. Signed as a free agent by **Regina** (WCHL), October 21, 1924. Transferred to **Portland** (WHL) after **Regina** (WCHL) franchise relocated, September 1, 1925. Traded to **Edmonton** (WHL) by **Portland** (WHL) for cash, November 16, 1925.

• LOWE, NORM Norm "Odie" Lowe

C – R. 5'8", 140 lbs. b: Winnipeg, Man., 4/15/1928.

			REGULAR SEASON								PLAYOFFS				
Season	Club	League	GP	G	A	Pts	AG	AA	APts	PIM	GP	G	A	Pts	PIM
1945-46	Winnipeg Rangers	MJHL	10	6	5	11				16	2	1	0	1	2
1946-47	Lethbridge Native Sons	AJHL	11	10	*22	*32				8	3	*5	*7	*12	4
	Lethbridge Canadians	WCSHL	1	1	1	2				0					
1947-48	Winnipeg Canadians	MJHL	24	23	*28	*51				44	6	2	5	7	10
1948-49	New York Rovers	EHL	62	27	39	66				29					
1949-50	**New York Rangers**	**NHL**	**4**	**1**	**1**	**2**	**1**	**1**	**2**	**0**					
	New York Rovers	EHL	44	17	36	53				18	12	7	8	*15	6
1950-51	St. Paul Saints	USHL	63	12	24	36				16	4	0	0	0	2
1951-52	St. Paul Saints	AAHL	39	33	45	78				32					
	Moncton Hawks	MMHL	2	0	0	0				0					
1952-53	Nelson Maple Leafs	OSHL	45	24	34	58				22					
1953-54	Winnipeg Maroons	City Sr.	STATISTICS NOT AVAILABLE												
1954-55	Vernon Canadians	OSHL	54	17	28	45				28	5	2	4	6	0
1955-56	Vernon Canadians	OSHL	56	43	48	91				21					
1956-57	Vernon Canadians	OSHL	54	*61	*53	*114				52	12	9	7	16	6
1957-58	Vernon Canadians	OSHL	54	25	28	53				54	8	6	2	8	6
1958-59	Vernon Canadians	OSHL	54	38	33	71				28					
1959-60	Vernon Canadians	OSHL	45	35	44	79				16	13	*13	8	*21	2
1960-61	Vernon Canadians	OSHL	44	36	50	86				20					
1961-62	Vernon Canadians	OSHL	DID NOT PLAY – COACHING												
	NHL Totals		**4**	**1**	**1**	**2**	**1**	**1**	**2**	**0**					

• LOWE, ROSS Ross Lowe

D/LW – R. 6'2", 180 lbs. b: Oshawa, Ont., 9/21/1928. d: 8/8/1955.

			REGULAR SEASON								PLAYOFFS				
Season	Club	League	GP	G	A	Pts	AG	AA	APts	PIM	GP	G	A	Pts	PIM
1944-45	Oshawa Generals	OHA	17	3	0	3				20	3	1	1	2	0
1945-46	Oshawa Generals	OHA	23	19	10	29				40	12	9	7	16	13
1946-47	Oshawa Generals	OHA	13	5	4	9				11	5	2	0	2	2
1947-48	Oshawa Generals	OHA	36	21	16	37				80	6	1	2	3	30
1948-49	Hershey Bears	AHL	43	4	7	11				55	11	0	0	0	2
1949-50	**Boston Bruins**	**NHL**	**3**	**0**	**0**	**0**	**0**	**0**	**0**	**0**					
	Hershey Bears	AHL	57	7	15	22				76					
1950-51	**Boston Bruins**	**NHL**	**43**	**5**	**3**	**8**	**7**	**4**	**11**	**40**					
	Hershey–Buffalo	AHL	25	5	5	10				57	4	0	0	0	17
	Montreal Canadiens	**NHL**									**2**	**0**	**0**	**0**	**0**
1951-52	**Montreal Canadiens**	**NHL**	**31**	**1**	**5**	**6**	**1**	**6**	**7**	**42**					
1952-53	Buffalo Bisons	AHL	43	5	15	20				53					
1953-54	Victoria Cougars	WHL	66	15	23	38				101	5	0	1	1	10
1954-55	Springfield Indians	AHL	60	32	50	82				91	4	1	2	3	16
	NHL Totals		**77**	**6**	**8**	**14**	**8**	**10**	**18**	**82**	**2**	**0**	**0**	**0**	**0**

AHL First All-Star Team (1955) • Won Les Cunningham Award (MVP - AHL) (1955)

Traded to **Montreal** by **Boston** for Hal Laycoe, February 14, 1951. Claimed by **NY Rangers** from **Montreal** in Intra-League Draft, June 1, 1955.

• LOWREY, EDDIE Eddie Lowrey

C – R. 5'6", 160 lbs. b: Manotick, Ontario, 8/13/1891. Deceased.

			REGULAR SEASON								PLAYOFFS				
Season	Club	League	GP	G	A	Pts	AG	AA	APts	PIM	GP	G	A	Pts	PIM
1912-13	Ottawa Senators	NHA	13	4	0	4				14					
1913-14	Toronto Ontarios	NHA	16	1	3	4				13					
1914-15	Montreal Canadiens	NHA	1	0	0	0				0					
	Ottawa Senators	NHA	4	2	1	3				3	2	0	0	0	0
1915-16	Toronto Blueshirts	NHA	2	0	0	0				0					
1916-17	Ottawa Senators	NHA	20	3	0	3				0	2	0	0	0	0
1917-18	**Ottawa Senators**	**NHL**	**12**	**2**	**1**	**3**	**5**	**0**	**5**	**3**					
1918-19	**Ottawa Senators**	**NHL**	**10**	**0**	**1**	**1**	**0**	**9**	**9**	**3**					
1919-20	Ottawa Munitions	City Sr.	DID NOT PLAY – COACHING												
1920-21	**Hamilton Tigers**	**NHL**	**4**	**0**	**0**	**0**	**0**	**0**	**0**	**0**					
1921-22	Regina Capitals	WCHL	7	1	0	1				0					
	University of Ottawa	City Sr.	DID NOT PLAY – COACHING												
	NHL Totals		**26**	**2**	**2**	**4**	**5**	**9**	**14**	**6**					
	Other Major League Totals		63	11	4	15				30	4	0	0	0	0

EHL First All-Star Team (1947) • Won John Carlin Trophy (Top Scorer - EHL) (1947) • Won Calder Memorial Trophy (1949)

Rights retained by **Ottawa** after NHA folded, November 26, 1917. Signed as a free agent by **Hamilton**, December 12, 1920. Signed as a free agent by **Regina** (WCHL), December 1, 1921.

• LOWREY, FRED Fred "Frock" Lowrey

RW – R. 5'9", 155 lbs. b: Ottawa, Ont., 8/12/1902. d: 1/24/1968.

			REGULAR SEASON								PLAYOFFS				
Season	Club	League	GP	G	A	Pts	AG	AA	APts	PIM	GP	G	A	Pts	PIM
1917-18	Ottawa Landsdownes	City Jr.	1	0	0	0				0					
1918-19	Ottawa Military HQ	City Sr.	6	1	0	1				3					
1919-20	Ottawa Munitions	City Sr.	8	2	0	2					5	3	1	4	
1920-21	Quebec Royal Rifles	City Sr.	11	13	0	13					4	1	0	1	
1921-22	Ottawa Munitions	City Sr.	13	12	3	15				18					
1922-23	New Haven Westminsters	USAHA	9	15	0	*15									
1923-24	New Haven Bears	USAHA	12	7	0	7									
1924-25	**Montreal Maroons**	**NHL**	**28**	**0**	**0**	**0**	**0**	**0**	**0**	**6**					
1925-26	**Montreal Maroons**	**NHL**	**10**	**0**	**0**	**0**	**0**	**0**	**0**	**2**					
	Pittsburgh Pirates	**NHL**	**16**	**1**	**0**	**1**	**3**	**0**	**3**	**2**	**2**	**0**	**0**	**0**	**6**
1926-27	Quebec Beavers	Can-Am	9	0	1	1				0					
	New Haven Eagles	Can-Am	22	4	0	4				21	4	1	0	1	0
1927-28	Philadelphia Arrows	Can-Am	29	11	2	13				25					
1928-29	London Panthers	Can-Pro	22	2	0	2				0					
	Philadelphia Arrows	Can-Am	5	0	0	0				4					
1929-30	Niagara Falls Cataracts	IAHL	37	10	3	13				28					
1930-31	Pittsburgh Yellowjackets	IAHL	1	0	1	1				2					
	Buffalo Majors	AHA	5	0	0	0				0					
	Niagara Falls Cataracts	OPHL	26	11	2	13				6	5	2	3	5	0
1931-32	Philadelphia Arrows	Can-Am	13	1	1	2				4					
1932-33			REINSTATED AS AN AMATEUR												
1933-34	Ottawa Rideaus	City Sr.	10	4	0	4				10					
1934-35	Ottawa RCAF	City Sr.	8	10	0	10				8	5	1	0	1	4
1935-36	Ottawa RCAF	City Sr.	17	1	0	1				4					
1936-37	Trenton RCAF	City Sr.	DID NOT PLAY – COACHING												
	NHL Totals		**54**	**1**	**0**	**1**	**3**	**0**	**3**	**10**	**2**	**0**	**0**	**0**	**6**

Signed as a free agent by **Montreal Maroons**, November 3, 1924. Claimed on waivers by **Pittsburgh** from **Montreal Maroons**, January 12, 1926. Traded to **Toronto** by **London** (Can-Pro) for cash, October 29, 1929.

• LOWREY, GERRY Gerry Lowrey

LW – L. 5'8", 150 lbs. b: Ottawa, Ont., 2/14/1906. d: 10/20/1979.

			REGULAR SEASON								PLAYOFFS				
Season	Club	League	GP	G	A	Pts	AG	AA	APts	PIM	GP	G	A	Pts	PIM
1921-22	University of Ottawa	City Sr.	12	0	2	2				6					
1922-23	Iroquois Falls Eskimos	NOHA	STATISTICS NOT AVAILABLE												
1923-24	North Bay Trappers	NOHA	6	4	0	4				0	5	9	0	9	0
1924-25	London AAA	City Sr.	18	14	6	20				24					
1925-26	London Ravens	OHA Sr.	19	18	7	25				23	4	*6	1	*7	0
1926-27	London Panthers	Can-Pro	30	7	2	9				27	4	5	1	6	15
1927-28	**Toronto Maple Leafs**	**NHL**	**25**	**6**	**5**	**11**	**18**	**42**	**60**	**29**					
	Toronto Falcons	Can-Pro	19	10	4	14				57					
1928-29	**Toronto Maple Leafs**	**NHL**	**32**	**3**	**11**	**14**	**12**	**103**	**115**	**24**					
	Pittsburgh Pirates	**NHL**	**12**	**2**	**1**	**3**	**8**	**9**	**17**	**6**					
1929-30	**Pittsburgh Pirates**	**NHL**	**44**	**16**	**14**	**30**	**32**	**46**	**78**	**30**					
1930-31	**Philadelphia Quakers**	**NHL**	**43**	**13**	**14**	**27**	**32**	**51**	**83**	**27**					
1931-32	**Chicago Black Hawks**	**NHL**	**48**	**8**	**3**	**11**	**17**	**8**	**25**	**32**	**2**	**1**	**0**	**1**	**2**
1932-33	St. Paul Saints	AHA	14	6	1	7				16					
	Ottawa Senators	**NHL**	**7**	**0**	**0**	**0**	**0**	**0**	**0**	**0**					
	Quebec Castors	Can-Am	26	12	14	26				43					
1933-34	Quebec Castors	Can-Am	40	11	17	28				30					
1934-35	Quebec–Providence	Can-Am	52	21	23	44				64	6	2	2	4	6
1935-36	Providence Reds	Can-Am	45	5	14	19				26	7	0	2	2	2
1936-37	Providence Reds	AHL	40	3	16	19				17	3	1	0	1	0
1937-38			REINSTATED AS AN AMATEUR												
1938-39	Hull Volants	City Sr.	5	2	6	8				2	18	9	6	15	15
1939-40	Ottawa Camerons	City Sr.	15	13	8	21				12					
1940-41	Ottawa Montagnards	City Sr.	18	5	9	14				6					
1941-42	Ottawa Montagnards	City Sr.	1	0	0	0				0					
	NHL Totals		**211**	**48**	**48**	**96**	**119**	**259**	**378**	**148**	**2**	**1**	**0**	**1**	**2**

Signed as a free agent by **London** (Can-Pro), November 18, 1926. Traded to **Toronto** by **London** (Can-Pro) for Al Pudas, October 20, 1927. Traded to **Pittsburgh** by **Toronto** with $9,500 for Harold Cotton, February 12, 1929. Transferred to **Philadelphia** after **Pittsburgh** franchise relocated, September 27, 1930. Claimed by **Chicago** from **Philadelphia** in Dispersal Draft, September 21, 1931. Traded to **St. Paul** (AHA) by **Chicago** for Lou Holmes, November 9, 1932. Signed as a free agent by **Ottawa** after securing release from **St. Paul** (AHA), January 4, 1932. Signed as a free agent by **Quebec** (Can-Am) after being released by **Ottawa**, January 19, 1932.

• LUCAS, DAVE Dave Lucas

D – L. 6', 205 lbs. b: Downeyville, Ont., 3/22/1932.

			REGULAR SEASON								PLAYOFFS				
Season	Club	League	GP	G	A	Pts	AG	AA	APts	PIM	GP	G	A	Pts	PIM
1951-52	Lindsay Braves	Jr. B	STATISTICS NOT AVAILABLE												
1952-53	Washington Lions	EHL	62	2	14	16				43					
1953-54	Troy Bruins	IHL	63	5	15	20				129	3	0	0	0	4
1954-55	Troy Bruins	IHL	3	0	1	1				4					
	Washington Lions	EHL	48	7	27	34				95	8	3	5	8	9
1955-56	Washington Lions	EHL	64	10	14	24				132	4	1	1	2	0
1956-57	Johnstown Jets	EHL	62	12	28	40				100	6	1	2	3	4
1957-58	Johnstown Jets	EHL	64	11	36	47				55	6	0	3	3	4
1958-59	Johnstown Jets	EHL	61	10	24	34				50					
1959-60	Johnstown Jets	EHL	63	13	19	32				91	13	3	6	9	17
1960-61	Johnstown Jets	EHL	61	9	34	43				70	12	1	4	5	8
1961-62	Johnstown Jets	EHL	68	14	30	44				70	15	2	5	7	8
1962-63	**Detroit Red Wings**	**NHL**	**1**	**0**	**0**	**0**	**0**	**0**	**0**	**0**					
	Portland Buckaroos	WHL	1	0	0	0				0					
	Pittsburgh Hornets	AHL	1	0	1	1				0					
	Johnstown Jets	EHL	68	15	33	48				52	3	0	1	1	6
1963-64	Portland Buckaroos	WHL	2	0	0	0				0					
	Johnstown Jets	EHL	70	17	36	53				86	10	0	6	6	34
1964-65	Johnstown Jets	EHL	72	12	48	60				126	5	2	4	6	16
1965-66	Johnstown Jets	EHL	72	13	35	48				84	2	0	0	0	2
	Pittsburgh Hornets	AHL	5	0	0	0				2					
1966-67	Johnstown Jets	EHL	72	16	41	57				72	5	0	2	2	2
1967-68	Salem Rebels	EHL	DID NOT PLAY – COACHING												
1968-69	Salem Rebels	EHL	63	7	28	35				112					
	NHL Totals		**1**	**0**	**0**	**0**	**0**	**0**	**0**	**0**					

EHL Second All-Star Team (1956, 1957, 1958, 1960, 1963) • EHL First All-Star Team (1962, 1964) • EHL North Second All-Star Team (1965, 1966)

• LUND, PENTTI Pentti Lund

RW – R. 6', 185 lbs. b: Helsinki, Finland, 12/6/1925.

Season	Club	League	GP	G	A	Pts	AG	AA	APts	PIM	GP	G	A	Pts	PIM
			REGULAR SEASON								PLAYOFFS				
1942-43	Port Arthur West-Enders	TBJHL	9	5	11	16	....	....	....	4	3	3	3	6	5
1943-44	Port Arthur Navy	TBJHL	10	21	*24	*45	....	....	....	10	2	3	2	5	0
1944-45	Port Arthur Navy	TBJHL	9	*26	9	*35	....	....	....	9	5	5	2	7	0
1945-46	Boston Olympics	EHL	34	14	19	33	....	....	....	10	12	*13	6	19	7
1946-47	Boston Olympics	EHL	56	*49	43	*92	....	....	....	21	9	7	*8	*15	4
	Boston Bruins	**NHL**	....	....	....	....	....	....	....	....	**1**	**0**	**0**	**0**	**0**
1947-48	Hershey Bears	AHL	68	26	36	62	....	....	....	21	2	0	0	0	0
	Boston Bruins	**NHL**	....	....	....	....	....	....	....	....	**2**	**0**	**0**	**0**	**0**
1948-49	**New York Rangers**	**NHL**	**59**	**14**	**16**	**30**	**22**	**25**	**47**	**16**	....	....	....	....	....
1949-50	**New York Rangers**	**NHL**	**64**	**18**	**9**	**27**	**24**	**11**	**35**	**16**	**12**	**6**	**5**	**11**	**0**
1950-51	**New York Rangers**	**NHL**	**59**	**4**	**16**	**20**	**5**	**21**	**26**	**6**	....	....	....	....	....
1951-52	**Boston Bruins**	**NHL**	**23**	**0**	**5**	**5**	**0**	**6**	**6**	**0**	**2**	**1**	**0**	**1**	**0**
	Hershey Bears	AHL	7	1	1	2	....	....	....	5	....	....	....	....	....
1952-53	**Boston Bruins**	**NHL**	**54**	**8**	**9**	**17**	**12**	**12**	**24**	**2**	**2**	**0**	**0**	**0**	**0**
1953-54	Soo Greyhounds	NOHA	6	1	2	3	....	....	....	0	9	1	1	2	0
1954-55	Soo Greyhounds	NOHA	48	13	18	31	....	....	....	9	14	2	5	7	4
	NHL Totals		**259**	**44**	**55**	**99**	**63**	**75**	**138**	**40**	**19**	**7**	**5**	**12**	**0**

Traded to **NY Rangers** by **Boston** with Ray Manson to complete transaction that sent Grant Warwick to Boston, February 6, 1948. Traded to **Boston** by **NY Rangers** with Gus Kyle for Paul Ronty, September 20, 1951.

• LUNDE, LEN — *see page 1244*

• LUNDY, PAT Pat Lundy

C – R. 5'11", 170 lbs. b: Saskatoon, Sask., 5/31/1925.

Season	Club	League	GP	G	A	Pts	AG	AA	APts	PIM	GP	G	A	Pts	PIM
1942-43	Saskatoon Quakers	SJHL	8	11	4	15	....	....	....	4	3	4	*3	*7	4
1943-44	Saskatoon Navy	City Sr.	18	26	20	46	....	....	....	7	4	3	3	6	0
1944-45			MILITARY SERVICE												
1945-46	**Detroit Red Wings**	**NHL**	**4**	**3**	**2**	**5**	**5**	**4**	**9**	**2**	**2**	**1**	**0**	**1**	**0**
	Saskatoon Elks	WCSHL	34	19	22	41	....	....	....	24	3	0	0	0	0
1946-47	**Detroit Red Wings**	**NHL**	**59**	**17**	**17**	**34**	**23**	**24**	**47**	**10**	**5**	**0**	**1**	**1**	**2**
1947-48	**Detroit Red Wings**	**NHL**	**11**	**4**	**1**	**5**	**6**	**1**	**7**	**6**	**5**	**1**	**1**	**2**	**0**
	Indianapolis Capitals	AHL	39	17	28	45	....	....	....	20	....	....	....	....	....
1948-49	**Detroit Red Wings**	**NHL**	**15**	**4**	**3**	**7**	**6**	**5**	**11**	**4**	**4**	**0**	**0**	**0**	**0**
	Indianapolis Capitals	AHL	47	29	20	49	....	....	....	13	....	....	....	....	....
1949-50	Indianapolis Capitals	AHL	70	30	47	77	....	....	....	8	8	*7	7	*14	0
1950-51	**Chicago Black Hawks**	**NHL**	**61**	**9**	**9**	**18**	**12**	**12**	**24**	**9**	....	....	....	....	....
	Milwaukee Seagulls	USHL	9	7	6	13	....	....	....	0	....	....	....	....	....
1951-52	St. Louis Flyers	AHL	58	24	37	61	....	....	....	21	....	....	....	....	....
1952-53	Calgary Stampeders	WHL	68	25	24	49	....	....	....	20	5	1	5	6	0
1953-54	Calgary Stampeders	WHL	66	29	42	71	....	....	....	18	17	*15	10	*25	2
1954-55	Calgary Stampeders	WHL	65	28	33	61	....	....	....	10	9	3	3	6	2
1955-56	Brandon Regals	WHL	23	15	5	20	....	....	....	4	....	....	....	....	....
1956-57			REINSTATED AS AN AMATEUR												
1957-58			DID NOT PLAY												
1958-59	Regina Capitals	SSHL	8	13	10	23	....	....	....	2	....	....	....	....	....
1959-60	Regina Capitals	SSHL	22	*26	21	47	....	....	....	4	9	8	6	14	4
1960-61	Regina Capitals	SSHL	DID NOT PLAY – COACHING												
1961-62	Regina Capitals	SSHL	19	16	12	28	....	....	....	9	....	....	....	....	....
	NHL Totals		**150**	**37**	**32**	**69**	**52**	**46**	**98**	**31**	**16**	**2**	**2**	**4**	**2**

Traded to **Chicago** by **Detroit** for cash, October 1, 1950.

• LYNN, VIC Vic Lynn

LW/D – L. 5'10", 175 lbs. b: Saskatoon, Sask., 1/26/1925.

Season	Club	League	GP	G	A	Pts	AG	AA	APts	PIM	GP	G	A	Pts	PIM
1941-42	Saskatoon Quakers	SJHL	7	6	8	14	....	....	....	12	6	0	2	2	10
1942-43	New York Rovers	EHL	38	4	6	10	....	....	....	*122	10	3	3	6	30
1943-44	**Detroit Red Wings**	**NHL**	**3**	**0**	**0**	**0**	**0**	**0**	**0**	**4**	....	....	....	....	....
	Indianapolis Capitals	AHL	32	4	5	9	....	....	....	61	....	....	....	....	....
	Saskatoon Quakers	SSHL	....	....	....	....	....	....	....	....	4	2	0	2	13
1944-45	St. Louis Flyers	AHL	60	15	23	38	....	....	....	67	....	....	....	....	....
1945-46	**Montreal Canadiens**	**NHL**	**2**	**0**	**0**	**0**	**0**	**0**	**0**	**0**	....	....	....	....	....
	Buffalo Bisons	AHL	53	26	25	51	....	....	....	60	12	5	5	10	10
1946-47	**Toronto Maple Leafs**	**NHL**	**31**	**6**	**14**	**20**	**8**	**20**	**28**	**44**	**11**	**4**	**1**	**5**	**16**
1947-48	**Toronto Maple Leafs**	**NHL**	**60**	**12**	**22**	**34**	**17**	**32**	**49**	**53**	**9**	**2**	**5**	**7**	***20**
1948-49	**Toronto Maple Leafs**	**NHL**	**52**	**7**	**9**	**16**	**11**	**14**	**25**	**36**	**8**	**0**	**1**	**1**	**2**
1949-50	**Toronto Maple Leafs**	**NHL**	**70**	**7**	**13**	**20**	**9**	**16**	**25**	**39**	**7**	**0**	**2**	**2**	**2**
1950-51	Pittsburgh Hornets	AHL	16	2	4	6	....	....	....	17	....	....	....	....	....
	Boston Bruins	**NHL**	**56**	**14**	**6**	**20**	**19**	**8**	**27**	**69**	**5**	**0**	**0**	**0**	**2**
1951-52	**Boston Bruins**	**NHL**	**12**	**2**	**2**	**4**	**3**	**3**	**6**	**4**	....	....	....	....	....
	Providence–Cleveland	AHL	44	17	25	42	....	....	....	37	5	1	3	4	2
1952-53	Cleveland Barons	AHL	35	11	17	28	....	....	....	46	....	....	....	....	....
	Chicago Black Hawks	**NHL**	**29**	**0**	**10**	**10**	**0**	**14**	**14**	**23**	**7**	**1**	**1**	**2**	**4**
1953-54	**Chicago Black Hawks**	**NHL**	**11**	**1**	**0**	**1**	**2**	**0**	**2**	**2**	....	....	....	....	....
	Saskatoon Quakers	WHL	38	11	12	23	....	....	....	14	6	2	3	5	9
1954-55	Saskatoon Quakers	WHL	70	20	24	44	....	....	....	82	....	....	....	....	....
1955-56	Saskatoon Quakers	WHL	64	17	26	43	....	....	....	100	3	0	1	1	6
1956-57	Brandon Regals	WHL	61	10	21	31	....	....	....	137	9	2	7	9	8
1957-58	Saskatoon–St. Paul	WHL	38	13	19	32	....	....	....	49	....	....	....	....	....
	Sudbury Wolves	OHA Sr.	7	0	1	1	....	....	....	8	....	....	....	....	....
1958-59	Prince Albert Mintos	SJHL	DID NOT PLAY – COACHING												
	Saskatoon Quakers	WHL	20	3	8	11	....	....	....	20	....	....	....	....	....
1959-60	Saskatoon Quakers	SSHL	20	10	10	20	....	....	....	30	7	2	8	10	10
1960-61	Saskatoon Quakers	SSHL	DID NOT PLAY – COACHING												
1961-62	Saskatoon Quakers	SSHL	12	5	5	10	....	....	....	16	8	1	3	4	6
1962-63	Saskatoon Quakers	SSHL	18	5	13	18	....	....	....	24	....	....	....	....	....
1963-64	Saskatoon Quakers	SSHL	DID NOT PLAY – COACHING												
	NHL Totals		**326**	**49**	**76**	**125**	**69**	**107**	**176**	**274**	**47**	**7**	**10**	**17**	**46**

Played in NHL All-Star Game (1947, 1948, 1949)

Traded to **Montreal** (Buffalo - AHL) by **Detroit** for cash, October 14,1945. Traded to **Toronto** by **Montreal** with Dutch Hiller for John Mahaffy and Gerry Brown, September 21, 1946. Traded to **Boston** by **Toronto** with Bill Ezinicki and Leo Boivin for Fern Flaman, Ken Smith, and Phil Maloney, November 20, 1950. Traded to **Cleveland** (AHL) by **Boston** (Providence - AHL) with Joe Lund for Ken Davies and Jean Gladu with Boston retaining rights of recall, December 10, 1951. Traded to **Chicago** by **Boston** (Cleveland - AHL) for future considerations (Fred Glover, January 16, 1953), January 4, 1953.

• LYONS, RON Ron "Peaches" Lyons

LW – L. 5'11", 170 lbs. b: Portage la Prairie, Man., 2/15/1909.

Season	Club	League	GP	G	A	Pts	AG	AA	APts	PIM	GP	G	A	Pts	PIM
			REGULAR SEASON								PLAYOFFS				
1929-30	Portland Buckaroos	PCHL	35	4	1	5	....	....	....	4	4	1	0	1	4
1930-31	**Boston Bruins**	**NHL**	**14**	**0**	**0**	**0**	**0**	**0**	**0**	**19**	**5**	**0**	**0**	**0**	**0**
	Boston Tigers	Can-Am	7	2	3	5	....	....	....	33	....	....	....	....	....
	Philadelphia Quakers	**NHL**	**22**	**2**	**4**	**6**	**5**	**14**	**19**	**8**	....	....	....	....	....
1931-32	Boston Tigers	Can-Am	2	1	0	1	....	....	....	6	....	....	....	....	....
	Springfield Indians	Can-Am	31	7	7	14	....	....	....	24	....	....	....	....	....
1932-33	Windsor Bulldogs	IAHL	5	1	2	3	....	....	....	4	....	....	....	....	....
1933-34	Portland Buckaroos	NWHL	34	14	12	26	....	....	....	44	....	....	....	....	....
1934-35	Portland Buckaroos	NWHL	32	13	10	23	....	....	....	45	3	1	0	1	2
1935-36	Portland–Seattle	NWHL	31	3	4	7	....	....	....	4	....	....	....	....	....
1936-37	Seattle–Portland	PCHL	7	1	2	3	....	....	....	8	....	....	....	....	....
1937-38	Seattle–Portland	PCHL	7	0	0	0	....	....	....	0	....	....	....	....	....
	NHL Totals		**36**	**2**	**4**	**6**	**5**	**14**	**19**	**27**	**5**	**0**	**0**	**0**	**0**

Rights sold to **Boston** by **Portland** (PCHL) for $5,000, April 17, 1930. Traded to **Philadelphia** by **Boston** with Bill Hutton for Harold Darragh, December 8, 1930. Traded to **Boston** by **Philadelphia** for cash, February, 1931.

• MacDONALD, JACK Jack MacDonald

LW. b: unknown. d: 1/24/1958.

Season	Club	League	GP	G	A	Pts	AG	AA	APts	PIM	GP	G	A	Pts	PIM
1905-06	Quebec Bulldogs	ECAHA	3	0	0	0	....	....	....	0	....	....	....	....	....
	New Glasgow Cubs	CBSHL	....	....	....	....	....	....	....	....	2	2	0	2	....
1906-07	Quebec Bulldogs	ECAHA	9	10	0	10	....	....	....	13	....	....	....	....	....
1907-08	Quebec Bulldogs	ECAHA	9	9	0	9	....	....	....	14	....	....	....	....	....
1908-09	Quebec Bulldogs	ECHA	9	8	0	8	....	....	....	17	....	....	....	....	....
1909-10	Waterloo Professionals	OPHL	15	18	0	18	....	....	....	....	....	....	....	....	....
1910-11	Quebec Bulldogs	NHA	16	14	0	14	....	....	....	25	....	....	....	....	....
1911-12	Quebec Bulldogs	NHA	17	18	0	18	....	....	....	0	2	*9	0	*9	0
1912-13	Vancouver Millionaires	PCHA	16	11	4	15	....	....	....	9	....	....	....	....	....
1913-14	Toronto Ontarios	NHA	20	27	8	35	....	....	....	12	....	....	....	....	....
1914-15	Quebec Bulldogs	NHA	19	9	8	17	....	....	....	17	....	....	....	....	....
1915-16	Quebec Bulldogs	NHA	20	9	5	14	....	....	....	10	....	....	....	....	....
1916-17	Quebec Bulldogs	NHA	18	13	7	20	....	....	....	3	....	....	....	....	....
1917-18	**Montreal Wanderers**	**NHL**	**4**	**3**	**1**	**4**	**7**	**0**	**7**	**3**	**2**	**1**	**0**	**1**	**0**
	Montreal Canadiens	**NHL**	**8**	**9**	**1**	**10**	**22**	**0**	**22**	**12**	**2**	**1**	**0**	**1**	**0**
1918-19	**Montreal Canadiens**	**NHL**	**17**	**8**	**4**	**12**	**28**	**38**	**66**	**9**	**10**	**1**	**4**	**5**	**6**
1919-20	**Quebec Bulldogs**	**NHL**	**24**	**6**	**7**	**13**	**13**	**48**	**61**	**4**	....	....	....	....	....
1920-21	**Montreal Canadiens**	**NHL**	**6**	**0**	**1**	**1**	**0**	**9**	**9**	**0**	....	....	....	....	....
	Toronto St. Pats	**NHL**	**6**	**0**	**0**	**0**	**0**	**0**	**0**	**2**	....	....	....	....	....
1921-22	**Montreal Canadiens**	**NHL**	**3**	**0**	**0**	**0**	**0**	**0**	**0**	**0**	....	....	....	....	....
	NHL Totals		**68**	**26**	**14**	**40**	**70**	**95**	**165**	**30**	**14**	**3**	**4**	**7**	**6**
	Other Major League Totals		168	146	32	178	....	....	....	120	2	9	0	9	0

Claimed by **Montreal Wanderers** from **Quebec** in Dispersal Draft, November 26, 1917. Claimed by **Montreal Canadiens** from **Montreal Wanderers** in Dispersal Draft, January 4, 1918. Transferred to **Quebec** by **Montreal Canadiens** when Quebec franchise returned to NHL, November 25, 1919. Transferred to **Hamilton** after **Quebec** franchise relocated, November 2, 1920. Traded to **Montreal Canadiens** by **Hamilton** with Harry Mummery, Dave Ritchie for Jack Coughlin and the loan of Billy Coutu, November 29, 1920. Loaned to **Toronto St. Pats** by **Montreal Canadiens** for remainder of 1920-21 season, February 11, 1921.

• MacDONALD, KILBY Kilby MacDonald

LW – L. 5'11", 178 lbs. b: Ottawa, Ont., 9/6/1914. d: 5/11/1986.

Season	Club	League	GP	G	A	Pts	AG	AA	APts	PIM	GP	G	A	Pts	PIM
1930-31	Ottawa Montagnards	City Jr.	15	2	0	2	....	....	....	14	....	....	....	....	....
	Ottawa Montagnards	City Sr.	4	0	0	0	....	....	....	2	....	....	....	....	....
1931-32	Ottawa Montagnards	City Jr.	12	10	7	17	....	....	....	21	2	1	0	1	4
	Ottawa Montagnards	City Sr.	1	0	0	0	....	....	....	0	....	....	....	....	....
1932-33	Ottawa Montagnards	City Jr.	12	7	7	14	....	....	....	20	2	1	1	2	*12
	Ottawa Montagnards	City Sr.	1	0	0	0	....	....	....	0	....	....	....	....	....
1933-34	Lake Placid Seniors	NYSHL	STATISTICS NOT AVAILABLE												
1934-35	Kirkland Lake Blue Devils	NOHA	13	7	8	15	....	....	....	20	....	....	....	....	....
1935-36	Noranda Copper Kings	NOHA	16	14	10	24	....	....	....	48	2	*4	1	*5	4
1936-37	New York Rovers	EHL	45	21	22	43	....	....	....	24	3	3	3	6	0
1937-38	Philadelphia Ramblers	AHL	44	10	21	31	....	....	....	12	5	2	3	5	2
1938-39	Philadelphia Ramblers	AHL	49	18	37	55	....	....	....	48	9	4	4	8	0
1939-40	**New York Rangers**	**NHL**	**44**	**15**	**13**	**28**	**32**	**26**	**58**	**19**	**12**	**0**	**2**	**2**	**4**
1940-41	**New York Rangers**	**NHL**	**47**	**5**	**6**	**11**	**10**	**11**	**21**	**12**	**3**	**1**	**0**	**1**	**0**
1941-42	Hershey–Buffalo	AHL	58	28	30	58	....	....	....	18	....	....	....	....	....
1942-43	Montreal Army	QSHL	29	11	20	31	....	....	....	10	7	3	6	9	16
	Montreal Army	City Sr.	3	1	3	4	....	....	....	0	5	6	6	*12	12
1943-44	Montreal Army	City Sr.	4	0	0	0	....	....	....	0	....	....	....	....	....
	New York Rangers	**NHL**	**24**	**7**	**9**	**16**	**9**	**11**	**20**	**4**	....	....	....	....	....
1944-45	**New York Rangers**	**NHL**	**36**	**9**	**6**	**15**	**12**	**10**	**22**	**12**	....	....	....	....	....
1945-46	Hull Volants	QSHL	9	2	4	6	....	....	....	0	....	....	....	....	....
	NHL Totals		**151**	**36**	**34**	**70**	**63**	**58**	**121**	**47**	**15**	**1**	**2**	**3**	**4**

EHL First All-Star Team (1937) • AHL First All-Star Team (1939) • Won Calder Trophy (1940)

Traded to **Hershey** (AHL) by **NY Rangers** for cash with NY Rangers holding rights of recall, September 11, 1941.

• MacDONALD, LOWELL — *see page 1248*

• MacDONALD, PARKER — *see page 1248*

• MACDONNELL, MOYLAN
Moylan MacDonnell
D – R. 5'9", 145 lbs. b: Stoney Mountain, Man., 8/27/1889. Deceased.

Season	Club	League	GP	G	A	Pts	AG	AA	APts	PIM	PO GP	PO G	PO A	PO Pts	PO PIM
1909-10	New York Crescents	AHAA	8	7	0	7	....	....	....	....	....	....	....	....	....
1910-11	New York Crescents	AHAA	STATISTICS NOT AVAILABLE												
1911-12	New York Crecents	AHAA	STATISTICS NOT AVAILABLE												
1912-13	New York Irish Americans	AHAA	8	4	0	4	....	....	....	12	....	....	....	....	....
1913-14	New York Irish Americans	AHAA	4	2	0	2	....	....	....	....	....	....	....	....	....
1914-15	New York Hockey Club	AAHA	7	7	0	7	....	....	....	....	....	....	....	....	....
1915-16	New York Hockey Club	AAHL	8	6	0	6	....	....	....	....	....	....	....	....	....
1916-17			MILITARY SERVICE												
1917-18			MILITARY SERVICE												
1918-19			MILITARY SERVICE												
1919-20			DID NOT PLAY												
1920-21	**Hamilton Tigers**	**NHL**	**22**	**1**	**2**	**3**	**2**	**17**	**19**	**2**	....	....	....	....	....
	NHL Totals		**22**	**1**	**2**	**3**	**2**	**17**	**19**	**2**	....	....	....	....	....

Signed as a free agent by **Hamilton**, December 21, 1920.

• MACEY, HUBERT
Hubert "Hub" Macey
LW – L. 5'8", 178 lbs. b: Big River, Sask., 4/13/1921.

Season	Club	League	GP	G	A	Pts	AG	AA	APts	PIM	PO GP	PO G	PO A	PO Pts	PO PIM
1938-39	Portage Terriers	MJHL	18	12	3	15	....	....	....	12	3	2	2	4	0
1939-40	Portage Terriers	MJHL	21	14	7	21	....	....	....	14	4	2	2	4	0
1940-41	Portage Terriers	MJHL	19	18	10	28	....	....	....	6	6	5	2	7	2
	Winnipeg Rangers	MJHL	....	....	....	....	....	....	....	....	13	9	6	15	4
1941-42	**New York Rangers**	**NHL**	**9**	**3**	**5**	**8**	**5**	**8**	**13**	**0**	**1**	**0**	**0**	**0**	**0**
	New York Rovers	EHL	47	39	33	72	....	....	....	8	....	....	....	....	....
1942-43	**New York Rangers**	**NHL**	**9**	**3**	**3**	**6**	**4**	**4**	**8**	**0**	....	....	....	....	....
	Kingston Frontenacs	City Sr.	13	13	9	22	....	....	....	24	4	0	5	5	0
1943-44	Kingston Army	OHA Sr.	2	2	1	3	....	....	....	2	....	....	....	....	....
1944-45			MILITARY SERVICE												
1945-46			MILITARY SERVICE												
1946-47	**Montreal Canadiens**	**NHL**	**12**	**0**	**1**	**1**	**0**	**1**	**1**	**0**	**7**	**0**	**0**	**0**	**0**
	Buffalo Bisons	AHL	32	15	16	31	....	....	....	4	....	....	....	....	....
	Houston Huskies	USHL	9	4	4	8	....	....	....	0	....	....	....	....	....
1947-48	Houston Huskies	USHL	59	31	60	91	....	....	....	8	12	4	5	9	0
1948-49	Houston Huskies	USHL	14	6	9	15	....	....	....	0	....	....	....	....	....
	Springfield Indians	AHL	43	20	29	49	....	....	....	2	3	0	1	1	0
1949-50	Springfield Indians	AHL	48	10	26	36	....	....	....	2	2	0	1	1	0
1950-51	Vancouver Canucks	PCHL	19	6	5	11	....	....	....	2	....	....	....	....	....
	Tulsa Oilers	USHL	41	11	27	38	....	....	....	6	6	3	0	3	0
1951-52	Glace Bay Miners	MMHL	71	30	27	57	....	....	....	24	3	0	0	0	0
1952-53	Glace Bay Miners	MMHL	62	22	34	56	....	....	....	10	7	3	1	4	0
1953-54	Sault Ste. Marie Indians	NOHA	21	4	11	15	....	....	....	4	....	....	....	....	....
1954-55			DID NOT PLAY – RETIRED												
1955-56	Kingston Goodyears	EOHL	30	20	22	42	....	....	....	4	14	7	*13	20	2
1956-57	Kingston CKLC's	EOHL	44	23	28	51	....	....	....	28	5	3	0	3	0
	NHL Totals		**30**	**6**	**9**	**15**	**9**	**13**	**22**	**0**	**8**	**0**	**0**	**0**	**0**

EHL First All-Star Team (1942)

Traded to **Montreal** (Buffalo - AHL) by **NY Rangers** for cash, August, 1946. Traded to **Springfield** (AHL) by **Montreal** for Gordie Bell and Sid McNabney, December 21, 1948.

• MACGREGOR, BRUCE
— see page 1249

• MACKAY, CALUM
Calum "Baldy" MacKay
LW – L. 5'10", 178 lbs. b: Toronto, Ont., 1/1/1927.

Season	Club	League	GP	G	A	Pts	AG	AA	APts	PIM	PO GP	PO G	PO A	PO Pts	PO PIM
1943-44	Port Arthur Bruins	TBJHL	10	5	12	17	....	....	....	7	4	4	0	4	4
	Port Arthur Flyers	TBJHL	....	....	....	....	....	....	....	....	2	2	0	2	0
1944-45	Port Arthur Bruins	TBJHL	10	12	15	27	....	....	....	24	0	3	*7	10	....
1945-46	Port Arthur Bruins	TBJHL	3	3	4	7	....	....	....	9	6	*9	5	14	6
1946-47	Oshawa Generals	OHA	27	16	22	38	....	....	....	54	5	1	0	1	25
	Detroit Red Wings	**NHL**	**5**	**0**	**0**	**0**	**0**	**0**	**0**	**0**	....	....	....	....	....
1947-48	Omaha Knights	USHL	25	9	10	19	....	....	....	22	....	....	....	....	....
	Indianapolis Capitals	AHL	36	18	10	04	....	....	....	18	....	....	....	....	....
1948-49	**Detroit Red Wings**	**NHL**	**1**	**0**	**0**	**0**	**0**	**0**	**0**	**0**	....	....	....	....	....
	Indianapolis Capitals	AHL	65	26	48	74	....	....	....	34	2	0	0	0	0
1949-50	Indianapolis Capitals	AHL	14	6	5	11	....	....	....	16	....	....	....	....	....
	Montreal Canadiens	**NHL**	**52**	**8**	**10**	**18**	**11**	**13**	**24**	**44**	**5**	**0**	**1**	**1**	**2**
1950-51	**Montreal Canadiens**	**NHL**	**70**	**18**	**10**	**28**	**24**	**13**	**37**	**69**	**11**	**1**	**0**	**1**	**0**
1951-52	**Montreal Canadiens**	**NHL**	**12**	**0**	**1**	**1**	**0**	**1**	**1**	**8**	....	....	....	....	....
	Buffalo Bisons	AHL	47	20	21	41	....	....	....	45	3	1	0	1	0
1952-53	Buffalo Bisons	AHL	64	28	42	70	....	....	....	65	....	....	....	....	....
	Montreal Canadiens	**NHL**	....	....	....	....	....	....	....	....	**7**	**1**	**3**	**4**	**10**
1953-54	**Montreal Canadiens**	**NHL**	**47**	**10**	**13**	**23**	**15**	**18**	**33**	**54**	**3**	**0**	**1**	**1**	**0**
1954-55	**Montreal Canadiens**	**NHL**	**50**	**14**	**21**	**35**	**20**	**27**	**47**	**39**	**12**	**3**	**8**	**11**	**8**
1955-56	Montreal Royals	QHL	32	13	17	30	....	....	....	56	13	3	2	5	4
	NHL Totals		**237**	**50**	**55**	**105**	**70**	**72**	**142**	**214**	**38**	**5**	**13**	**18**	**20**

Played in NHL All-Star Game (1953)

Traded to **Montreal** by **Detroit** for Joe Carveth, November 11, 1949.

• MACKAY, DAVE
Dave MacKay
D – R. 6', 210 lbs. b: Edmonton, Alta., 1/14/1919.

Season	Club	League	GP	G	A	Pts	AG	AA	APts	PIM	PO GP	PO G	PO A	PO Pts	PO PIM
1937-38	University of Alberta	WCIAU	22	17	9	26	....	....	....	59	....	....	....	....	....
1938-39	University of Alberta	WCIAU	19	19	5	24	....	....	....	60	....	....	....	....	....
	Edmonton Oil Kings	City Sr.	9	3	1	4	....	....	....	8	....	....	....	....	....
1940-41	**Chicago Black Hawks**	**NHL**	**29**	**3**	**0**	**3**	**6**	**0**	**6**	**26**	**5**	**0**	**1**	**1**	**2**
	Providence Reds	AHL	....	2	5	7	....	....	....	6	....	....	....	....	....
1941-42	Nanaimo Clipprers	PCHL	27	3	0	3	....	....	....	26	5	0	1	1	2
1942-43	Nanaimo Clippers	PCHL	14	17	14	31	....	....	....	24	3	3	0	3	4
1943-44	Nanaimo Army	PCHL	14	8	4	12	....	....	....	33	....	....	....	....	....
1944-45			MILITARY SERVICE												
1945-46			MILITARY SERVICE												
1946-47			MILITARY SERVICE												
1947-48	New Westminster Royals	PCHL	13	3	11	14	....	....	....	47	5	1	1	2	14
1948-49	New Westminster Royals	PCHL	3	0	0	0	....	....	....	8	....	....	....	....	....
1949-50	Vernon Canadians	OSHL	43	13	9	22	....	....	....	86	4	2	1	3	8
1950-51	Vernon Canadians	OSHL	51	8	14	22	....	....	....	65	10	1	2	3	20
1951-52	Vernon Canadians	OSHL	5	0	1	1	....	....	....	4	....	....	....	....	....
1952-53	Vernon Canadians	OSHL	DID NOT PLAY – COACHING												
1953-54	Vernon Canadians	OSHL	43	5	25	30	....	....	....	51	....	....	....	....	....
	NHL Totals		**29**	**3**	**0**	**3**	**6**	**0**	**6**	**26**	**5**	**0**	**1**	**1**	**2**

• MACKAY, MICKEY
Mickey (Duncan) MacKay **HHOF**
C – L. 5'9", 162 lbs. b: Chelsey, Ont., 5/25/1894. d: 5/21/1940.

Season	Club	League	GP	G	A	Pts	AG	AA	APts	PIM	PO GP	PO G	PO A	PO Pts	PO PIM
1914-15	Vancouver Millionaires	PCHA	17	*33	11	44	....	....	....	9	3	4	2	6	9
1915-16	Vancouver Millionaires	PCHA	14	12	7	19	....	....	....	32	....	....	....	....	....
1916-17	Vancouver Millionaires	PCHA	23	22	11	33	....	....	....	37	....	....	....	....	....
1917-18	Vancouver Millionaires	PCHA	18	10	8	18	....	....	....	31	7	7	5	12	15
1918-19	Vancouver Millionaires	PCHA	17	9	9	18	....	....	....	9	....	....	....	....	....
1919-20	Calgary Columbus Club	Big 4	11	4	6	10	....	....	....	14	....	....	....	....	....
1920-21	Vancouver Millionaires	PCHA	21	10	8	18	....	....	....	15	7	0	4	4	0
1921-22	Vancouver Millionaires	PCHA	24	14	*12	26	....	....	....	20	9	1	0	1	6
1922-23	Vancouver Maroons	PCHA	30	28	12	40	....	....	....	38	6	3	0	3	16
1923-24	Vancouver Maroons	PCHA	28	*21	4	25	....	....	....	2	7	3	0	3	2
1924-25	Vancouver Maroons	WCHL	28	*27	6	33	....	....	....	17	....	....	....	....	....
1925-26	Vancouver Maroons	WHL	27	12	4	16	....	....	....	24	....	....	....	....	....
1926-27	**Chicago Black Hawks**	**NHL**	**34**	**14**	**8**	**22**	**41**	**69**	**110**	**23**	**2**	**0**	**0**	**0**	**0**
1927-28	**Chicago Black Hawks**	**NHL**	**36**	**17**	**4**	**21**	**53**	**34**	**87**	**23**	....	....	....	....	....
1928-29	**Pittsburgh Pirates**	**NHL**	**10**	**1**	**0**	**1**	**4**	**0**	**4**	**2**	....	....	....	....	....
	Boston Bruins	**NHL**	**30**	**8**	**2**	**10**	**32**	**18**	**50**	**18**	**3**	**0**	**0**	**0**	**2**
1929-30	**Boston Bruins**	**NHL**	**37**	**4**	**5**	**9**	**8**	**16**	**24**	**13**	**6**	**0**	**0**	**0**	**4**
	NHL Totals		**147**	**44**	**19**	**63**	**138**	**137**	**275**	**79**	**11**	**0**	**0**	**0**	**6**
	Other Major League Totals		247	198	92	290	....	....	....	234	39	18	11	29	48

PCHA First All-Star Team (1915) • PCHA Second All-Star Team (1916, 1918, 1921) • PCHA First All-Star Team (1917, 1919, 1922, 1923) • WCHL First All-Star Team (1925) • WHL First All-Star Team (1926)

• Re-instated as an amateur for 1919-20 season, November 23, 1919. Signed as a free agent by **Vancouver** (PCHA), November 2, 1920. Traded to **Chicago** by **Vancouver** (WHL) for cash, October 4, 1926. Traded to **Pittsburgh** by **Chicago** for cash, September, 1928. Traded to **Boston** by **Pittsburgh** with $12,000 for Frank Frederickson, December 21, 1928.

• MACKAY, MURDO
Murdo MacKay
RW/C – R. 5'11", 175 lbs. b: Fort William, Ont., 8/8/1917.

Season	Club	League	GP	G	A	Pts	AG	AA	APts	PIM	PO GP	PO G	PO A	PO Pts	PO PIM
1932-33	Fort William Forts	TBJHL	7	2	0	2	....	....	....	0	....	....	....	....	....
1933-34	Fort William Cubs	TBJHL	19	11	3	14	....	....	....	16	....	....	....	....	....
1934-35	Fort William Kams	TBJHL	10	8	3	11	....	....	....	6	....	....	....	....	....
1935-36	Fort William Kams	TBJHL	16	*23	9	*32	....	....	....	10	2	1	0	1	2
1936-37	New York Rovers	EHL	47	5	5	10	....	....	....	6	3	0	0	0	0
1937-38	New York Rovers	EHL	39	7	6	13	....	....	....	4	....	....	....	....	....
1938-39	New York Rovers	EHL	42	20	28	38	....	....	....	8	....	....	....	....	....
1939-40	New York Rovers	EHL	58	44	44	88	....	....	....	29	....	....	....	....	....
1940-41	Philadelphia Rockets	AHL	56	20	15	35	....	....	....	12	....	....	....	....	....
1941-42	Buffalo Bisons	AHL	56	21	20	41	....	....	....	17	....	....	....	....	....
1942-43	Nanaimo Navy	City Sr.	20	22	7	29	....	....	....	8	6	5	3	8	6
1943-44	Nanaimo Navy	PCHL	18	16	8	24	....	....	....	4	....	....	....	....	....
1944-45	Halifax Navy	City Sr.	12	8	6	14	....	....	....	0	6	3	1	4	0
1945-46	**Montreal Canadiens**	**NHL**	**5**	**0**	**1**	**1**	**0**	**2**	**2**	**0**	....	....	....	....	....
	Buffalo Bisons	AHL	58	32	31	63	....	....	....	18	12	5	8	13	2
1946-47	Buffalo Bisons	AHL	59	35	26	61	....	....	....	13	4	1	1	2	4
	Montreal Canadiens	**NHL**	....	....	....	....	....	....	....	....	**9**	**0**	**1**	**1**	**0**
1947-48	**Montreal Canadiens**	**NHL**	**14**	**0**	**2**	**2**	**0**	**3**	**3**	**0**	....	....	....	....	....
	Buffalo Bisons	AHL	55	37	39	70	....	....	....	15	8	4	4	8	0
1948-49	Buffalo Bisons	AHL	68	32	52	84	....	....	....	20	....	....	....	....	....
	Montreal Canadiens	**NHL**	....	....	....	....	....	....	....	....	**6**	**1**	**1**	**2**	**0**
1949-50	Buffalo Bisons	AHL	67	30	24	54	....	....	....	6	5	0	0	0	0
1950-51	Cleveland Barons	AHL	69	25	36	61	....	....	....	6	11	2	2	4	0
1951-52	Quebec Aces	QSHL	40	14	24	38	....	....	....	4	15	5	6	11	6
1952-53	Quebec Aces	QSHL	55	4	18	22	....	....	....	4	22	3	8	11	6
	NHL Totals		**19**	**0**	**3**	**3**	**0**	**5**	**5**	**0**	**15**	**1**	**2**	**3**	**0**

EHL Second All-Star Team (1940) • AHL First All-Star Team (1949)

Traded to **Buffalo** (AHL) by **NY Rangers** for cash, September 11, 1941. Traded to **Montreal** by **Buffalo** (AHL) for John Ellis Adams and Moe White, January 14, 1948. Transferred to **Quebec** (QSHL) by **Montreal** as compensation for Montreal's signing of free agent Dick Gamble, September 24, 1952.

• MACKELL, FLEMING
Fleming "Mac" Mackell
C – L. 5'7", 156 lbs. b: Montreal, Que., 4/30/1929.

Season	Club	League	GP	G	A	Pts	AG	AA	APts	PIM	PO GP	PO G	PO A	PO Pts	PO PIM
1944-45	Montreal Jr. Royals	QJHL	9	3	4	7	....	....	....	0	13	3	7	10	2
1945-46	St. Michael's Majors	OHA	24	25	25	50	....	....	....	29	11	13	9	22	*52
1946-47	St. Michael's Majors	OHA	28	*49	33	*82	....	....	....	71	9	10	10	20	*33
1947-48	**Toronto Maple Leafs**	**NHL**	**3**	**0**	**0**	**0**	**0**	**0**	**0**	**2**	....	....	....	....	....
	Pittsburgh Hornets	AHL	62	22	43	65	....	....	....	84	2	1	0	1	4
1948-49	**Toronto Maple Leafs**	**NHL**	**11**	**1**	**1**	**2**	**2**	**2**	**4**	**6**	**9**	**2**	**4**	**6**	**4**
	Pittsburgh Hornets	AHL	52	38	38	76	....	....	....	65	....	....	....	....	....
1949-50	**Toronto Maple Leafs**	**NHL**	**36**	**7**	**13**	**20**	**9**	**16**	**25**	**24**	**7**	**1**	**1**	**2**	**11**
	Pittsburgh Hornets	AHL	36	25	22	47	....	....	....	62	....	....	....	....	....
1950-51	**Toronto Maple Leafs**	**NHL**	**70**	**12**	**13**	**25**	**16**	**17**	**33**	**40**	**11**	**2**	**3**	**5**	**9**
1951-52	**Toronto Maple Leafs**	**NHL**	**32**	**2**	**8**	**10**	**3**	**10**	**13**	**16**	....	....	....	....	....
	Boston Bruins	**NHL**	**30**	**1**	**8**	**9**	**1**	**10**	**11**	**24**	**5**	**2**	**1**	**3**	**12**
1952-53	**Boston Bruins**	**NHL**	**65**	**27**	**17**	**44**	**42**	**24**	**66**	**63**	**11**	**2**	***7**	**9**	**7**
1953-54	**Boston Bruins**	**NHL**	**67**	**15**	**32**	**47**	**23**	**44**	**67**	**60**	**4**	**1**	**1**	**2**	**8**
1954-55	**Boston Bruins**	**NHL**	**60**	**11**	**24**	**35**	**16**	**31**	**47**	**76**	**4**	**0**	**1**	**1**	**0**
1955-56	**Boston Bruins**	**NHL**	**52**	**7**	**9**	**16**	**10**	**11**	**21**	**59**	....	....	....	....	....
1956-57	**Boston Bruins**	**NHL**	**65**	**22**	**17**	**39**	**30**	**20**	**50**	**73**	**10**	**5**	**3**	**8**	**4**
1957-58	**Boston Bruins**	**NHL**	**70**	**20**	**40**	**60**	**26**	**44**	**70**	**72**	**12**	**5**	**14**	**19**	**12**
1958-59	**Boston Bruins**	**NHL**	**57**	**17**	**23**	**40**	**22**	**24**	**46**	**28**	**7**	**2**	**6**	**8**	**8**
1959-60	**Boston Bruins**	**NHL**	**47**	**7**	**15**	**22**	**9**	**15**	**24**	**19**	....	....	....	....	....
1960-61	Quebec Aces	AHL	62	13	22	35	....	....	....	54	....	....	....	....	....
1961-62			DID NOT PLAY												
1962-63	Los Angeles Blades	WHL	29	10	21	31	....	....	....	26	3	1	1	2	2
1963-64	New Glasgow Rangers	MSHL	....	5	14	19	....	....	....	4	....	....	....	....	....
1964-65	New Glasgow Rangers	MSHL	....	49	*75	*124	....	....	....	85	....	....	....	....	....
1965-66	St. Hyacinthe Saints	QSHL	20	10	10	20	....	....	....	29	....	....	....	....	....
1966-67			DID NOT PLAY												
1967-68	St. John's Capitals	Nfld.	33	11	21	32	....	....	....	....	....	....	....	....	....
	NHL Totals		**665**	**149**	**220**	**369**	**209**	**268**	**477**	**562**	**80**	**22**	**41**	**63**	**75**

NHL First All-Star Team (1953)

Played in NHL All-Star Game (1947, 1948, 1949, 1954)

Traded to **Boston** by **Toronto** for Jim Morrison, January 9, 1952.

MACKELL, JACK
Jack MacKell
RW/D – R. 5'7", 150 lbs. b: Ottawa, Ontario, 4/12/1896. Deceased.

Season	Club	League	GP	G	A	Pts	AG	AA	APts	PIM	GP	G	A	Pts	PIM
			REGULAR SEASON								PLAYOFFS				
1915-16	Ottawa New Edinburghs	City Sr.	7	5	0	5	....	....	....	6	....	....	....	....	....
1916-17	Ottawa Munitions	City Sr.	10	7	0	7	....	....	....	48	....	....	....	....	....
1917-18	Ottawa Munitions	City Sr.	6	1	0	1	....	....	....	15	1	1	0	1	0
	Pembrooke Munitions	City Sr.	STATISTICS NOT AVAILABLE												
1918-19	Ottawa Munitions	City Sr.	7	*8	2	*10	....	....	....	39	....	....	....	....	....
1919-20	**Ottawa Senators**	**NHL**	**23**	**2**	**1**	**3**	**4**	**7**	**11**	**33**	**5**	**0**	**0**	**0**	**0**
1920-21	**Ottawa Senators**	**NHL**	**23**	**2**	**1**	**3**	**5**	**9**	**14**	**26**	**6**	**0**	**0**	**0**	**0**
	NHL Totals		**46**	**4**	**2**	**6**	**9**	**16**	**25**	**59**	**11**	**0**	**0**	**0**	**0**

Signed as a free agent by **Ottawa**, December 19, 1919.

MACKENZIE, BILL
Bill MacKenzie
D – R. 5'11", 175 lbs. b: Winnipeg, Man., 12/12/1911. d: 5/29/1990.

Season	Club	League	GP	G	A	Pts	AG	AA	APts	PIM	GP	G	A	Pts	PIM
1929-30	Winnipeg Elmwoods	City Jr.	9	7	1	8	....	....	....	10	2	1	0	1	6
1930-31	Winnipeg Elmwoods	City Jr.	11	8	6	14	....	....	....	6	12	6	3	9	2
1931-32	Montreal AAA	City Sr.	10	0	3	3	....	....	....	22	4	1	1	2	8
1932-33	**Chicago Black Hawks**	**NHL**	**36**	**4**	**4**	**8**	**9**	**11**	**20**	**13**	....	....	....	....	....
	Montreal Royals	City Sr.	12	7	4	11	....	....	....	33	4	0	0	0	15
1933-34	**Montreal Maroons**	**NHL**	**47**	**4**	**3**	**7**	**9**	**8**	**17**	**20**	**4**	**0**	**0**	**0**	**0**
1934-35	**Montreal Maroons**	**NHL**	**5**	**0**	**0**	**0**	**0**	**0**	**0**	**0**	....	....	....	....	....
	New York Rangers	**NHL**	**15**	**1**	**0**	**1**	**2**	**0**	**2**	**10**	**3**	**0**	**0**	**0**	**0**
	Windsor Bulldogs	IAHL	21	3	1	4	....	....	....	19	....	....	....	....	....
1935-36	Windsor Bulldogs	IAHL	42	10	8	18	....	....	....	52	8	0	1	1	6
1936-37	**Montreal Maroons**	**NHL**	**10**	**0**	**1**	**1**	**0**	**2**	**2**	**6**	....	....	....	....	....
	Montreal Canadiens	**NHL**	**39**	**4**	**3**	**7**	**9**	**7**	**16**	**22**	**5**	**1**	**0**	**1**	**0**
1937-38	**Montreal Canadiens**	**NHL**	**11**	**0**	**0**	**0**	**0**	**0**	**0**	**4**	....	....	....	....	....
	Chicago Black Hawks	**NHL**	**35**	**1**	**2**	**3**	**2**	**4**	**6**	**20**	**9**	**0**	**1**	**1**	**11**
1938-39	**Chicago Black Hawks**	**NHL**	**47**	**1**	**0**	**1**	**2**	**0**	**2**	**36**	....	....	....	....	....
1939-40	**Chicago Black Hawks**	**NHL**	**19**	**0**	**1**	**1**	**0**	**2**	**2**	**14**	....	....	....	....	....
	Providence Reds	AHL	21	6	7	13	....	....	....	30	7	1	2	3	5
1940-41	Cleveland Barons	AHL	56	7	10	17	....	....	....	34	9	1	1	2	4
1941-42	Cleveland Barons	AHL	56	5	12	17	....	....	....	20	5	0	0	0	0
1942-43	Cleveland Barons	AHL	42	6	8	14	....	....	....	18	4	0	2	2	2
1943-44			MILITARY SERVICE												
1944-45	Cleveland Barons	AHL	13	0	2	2	....	....	....	6	....	....	....	....	....
	NHL Totals		**264**	**15**	**14**	**29**	**33**	**34**	**67**	**145**	**21**	**1**	**1**	**2**	**11**

AHL Second All-Star Team (1940, 1943) • AHL First All-Star Team (1941, 1942)

Signed as a free agent by **Montreal Maroons** after securing release from **Chicago**, July 25, 1933. Loaned to **NY Rangers** by **Montreal Maroons** for remainder of 1934-35 season, January 29, 1935. Traded to **Montreal Canadiens** by **Montreal Maroons** for Paul Runge, December 3, 1936. Traded to **Chicago** by **Montreal Canadiens** for Marty Burke, December 10, 1937. Traded to **Cleveland** (AHL) by **Montreal Canadiens** with Bill Summerhill for Jim O'Neil, May 17, 1940.

MACKEY, REG
Reg MacKey
D – L. 5'7", 155 lbs. b: Ottawa, Ont., 5/7/1900. Deceased.

Season	Club	League	GP	G	A	Pts	AG	AA	APts	PIM	GP	G	A	Pts	PIM
1924-25	Calgary Tigers	WCHL	16	3	0	3	....	....	....	15	2	0	0	0	2
1925-26	Vancouver Maroons	WHL	29	8	0	8	....	....	....	23	....	....	....	....	....
1926-27	**New York Rangers**	**NHL**	**34**	**0**	**0**	**0**	**0**	**0**	**0**	**16**	**1**	**0**	**0**	**0**	**0**
1927-28	Boston Tigers	Can-Am	36	18	2	20	....	....	....	78	2	0	0	0	2
1928-29	Boston Tigers	Can-Am	33	15	4	19	....	....	....	68	4	1	1	2	8
1929-30	Boston Tigers	Can-Am	37	19	7	26	....	....	....	104	4	3	1	4	16
1930-31	Boston Tigers	Can-Am	40	6	9	15	....	....	....	80	8	1	1	2	6
1931-32			REINSTATED AS AN AMATEUR												
1932-33	Calgary Tigers	WCJHL	30	9	2	11	....	....	....	42	6	0	1	1	5
1933-34	Calgary Tigers	NWHL	3	0	0	0	....	....	....	0	....	....	....	....	....
	NHL Totals		**34**	**0**	**0**	**0**	**0**	**0**	**0**	**16**	**1**	**0**	**0**	**0**	**0**
	Other Major League Totals		45	11	0	11	....	....	....	38	2	0	0	0	2

Signed as a free agent by **Calgary** (WCHL), August 26, 1924. Traded to **Vancouver** (WHL) by **Calgary** (WHL) for Art Duncan, October 16, 1925. Traded to **NY Rangers** by **Vancouver** (WHL) for cash, October 9, 1926. Traded to **Boston** (Can-Am) by **NY Rangers** for cash, November 8, 1927.

MACKIE, HOWIE
Howie Mackie
RW/D – L. 5'10", 190 lbs. b: Kitchener, Ont., 8/30/1913. Deceased.

Season	Club	League	GP	G	A	Pts	AG	AA	APts	PIM	GP	G	A	Pts	PIM
1933-34	Kitchener Greenshirts	OHA Sr.	15	4	4	8	....	....	....	8	....	....	....	....	....
1934-35	Kitchener Greenshirts	OHA Sr.	STATISTICS NOT AVAILABLE												
1935-36	Hamilton Tigers	OHA Sr.	22	*24	11	35	....	....	....	21	9	*14	3	17	14
1936-37	**Detroit Red Wings**	**NHL**	**13**	**1**	**0**	**1**	**2**	**0**	**2**	**4**	**8**	**0**	**0**	**0**	**0**
	Pittsburgh Hornets	AHL	32	8	5	13	....	....	....	12	1	0	0	0	0
1937-38	**Detroit Red Wings**	**NHL**	**7**	**0**	**0**	**0**	**0**	**0**	**0**	**0**	....	....	....	....	....
	Pittsburgh Hornets	AHL	32	2	8	10	....	....	....	12	2	0	0	0	0
1938-39	Hershey Bears	AHL	53	12	18	30	....	....	....	8	5	1	2	3	0
1939-40	Hershey Bears	AHL	52	11	5	16	....	....	....	29	5	0	1	1	4
1940-41	Hershey Bears	AHL	43	15	19	34	....	....	....	19	10	0	2	2	4
1941-42	Hershey Bears	AHL	22	3	0	3	....	....	....	0	....	....	....	....	....
	Pittsburgh Hornets	AHL	1	0	0	0	....	....	....	0	....	....	....	....	....
	Philadelphia Rockets	AHL	33	14	15	29	....	....	....	12	....	....	....	....	....
1942-43	Pittsburgh Hornets	AHL	40	0	4	4	....	....	....	8	....	....	....	....	....
1943-44	Pittsburgh Hornets	AHL	29	2	10	12	....	....	....	21	....	....	....	....	....
1944-45	Pittsburgh Hornets	AHL	40	9	21	30	....	....	....	33	....	....	....	....	....
1945-46	Pittsburgh Hornets	AHL	31	5	9	14	....	....	....	31	4	0	0	0	0
	NHL Totals		**20**	**1**	**0**	**1**	**2**	**0**	**2**	**4**	**8**	**0**	**0**	**0**	**0**

MACKINTOSH, IAN
Ian MacKintosh
RW – R. 5'11", 175 lbs. b: Selkirk, Manitoba, 6/10/1927.

Season	Club	League	GP	G	A	Pts	AG	AA	APts	PIM	GP	G	A	Pts	PIM
1943-44	Winnipeg Rangers	MJHL	10	15	10	25	....	....	....	20	....	....	....	....	....
	Winnipeg St. James	MJHL	....	....	....	....	....	....	....	....	6	7	5	12	6
1944-45	Winnipeg Rangers	MJHL	7	8	5	13	....	....	....	5	4	0	5	5	0
	Winnipeg Navy	City Sr.	2	0	0	0	....	....	....	0	....	....	....	....	....
1945-46	New York Rovers	EHL	49	13	27	40	....	....	....	14	4	0	3	3	0
1946-47	New York Rovers	EHL	53	22	23	45	....	....	....	17	9	5	5	10	4
	New Haven Ramblers	AHL	3	2	0	2	....	....	....	0	....	....	....	....	....
1947-48	New Haven Ramblers	AHL	58	11	13	24	....	....	....	21	3	1	0	1	2
	New York Rovers	QSHL	3	0	0	0	....	....	....	0	....	....	....	....	....
1948-49	St. Paul Saints	USHL	63	20	26	46	....	....	....	20	7	3	8	*11	0
1949-50	St. Paul Saints	USHL	70	35	42	77	....	....	....	33	3	1	2	3	0
1950-51	St. Paul Saints	USHL	64	39	38	77	....	....	....	82	4	1	1	2	2
1951-52	Cincinnati Mohawks	AHL	68	19	25	44	....	....	....	12	7	2	0	2	0
1952-53	**New York Rangers**	**NHL**	**4**	**0**	**0**	**0**	**0**	**0**	**0**	**4**	....	....	....	....	....
	Vancouver Canucks	WHL	63	28	31	59	....	....	....	26	9	1	2	3	0
	NHL Totals		**4**	**0**	**0**	**0**	**0**	**0**	**0**	**4**	....	....	....	....	....

MACMILLAN, JOHN
John MacMillan
RW – L. 5'10", 185 lbs. b: Lethbridge, Alta., 10/25/1935.

Season	Club	League	GP	G	A	Pts	AG	AA	APts	PIM	GP	G	A	Pts	PIM
1952-53	Crows Nest Pass	AJHL	1	0	0	0	....	....	....	0	....	....	....	....	....
1953-54	Lethbridge Native Sons	WCJHL	28	5	9	14	....	....	....	12	4	0	0	0	2
1954-55	Lethbridge Native Sons	WCJHL	37	5	11	16	....	....	....	24	3	0	3	3	0
1955-56	Lethbridge Native Sons	WCJHL	45	27	27	54	....	....	....	34	9	4	6	10	6
1956-57	University of Denver	WCHA	DID NOT PLAY – FRESHMAN												
1957-58	University of Denver	WCHA	37	19	12	31	....	....	....	50	....	....	....	....	....
1958-59	University of Denver	WCHA	28	16	25	41	....	....	....	32	....	....	....	....	....
1959-60	University of Denver	WCHA	34	30	25	55	....	....	....	34	....	....	....	....	....
1960-61	**Toronto Maple Leafs**	**NHL**	**31**	**3**	**5**	**8**	**4**	**5**	**9**	**8**	**4**	**0**	**0**	**0**	**0**
	Rochester Americans	AHL	38	8	7	15	....	....	....	14	....	....	....	....	....
1961-62	Pittsburgh Hornets	AHL	33	6	10	16	....	....	....	25	....	....	....	....	....
	Toronto Maple Leafs	**NHL**	**31**	**1**	**0**	**1**	**1**	**0**	**1**	**8**	**3**	**0**	**0**	**0**	**0**
1962-63	**Toronto Maple Leafs**	**NHL**	**6**	**1**	**1**	**2**	**1**	**1**	**2**	**6**	**1**	**0**	**0**	**0**	**0**
	Rochester Americans	AHL	57	22	23	45	....	....	....	37	....	....	....	....	....
1963-64	**Toronto Maple Leafs**	**NHL**	**13**	**0**	**0**	**0**	**0**	**0**	**0**	**4**	....	....	....	....	....
	Detroit Red Wings	**NHL**	**20**	**0**	**3**	**3**	**0**	**3**	**3**	**6**	**4**	**0**	**1**	**1**	**2**
	Pittsburgh Hornets	AHL	31	4	8	12	....	....	....	8	5	1	1	2	0
1964-65	**Detroit Red Wings**	**NHL**	**3**	**0**	**1**	**1**	**0**	**1**	**1**	**0**	....	....	....	....	....
	Memphis Wings	CHL	61	17	20	37	....	....	....	43	....	....	....	....	....
	St. Paul Rangers	CHL	3	0	0	0	....	....	....	6	....	....	....	....	....
1965-66	Memphis Wings	CHL	64	12	14	26	....	....	....	29	....	....	....	....	....
1966-67	San Diego Gulls	WHL	71	20	26	46	....	....	....	76	....	....	....	....	....
1967-68	San Diego Gulls	WHL	72	12	32	44	....	....	....	61	7	0	0	0	4
1968-69	San Diego Gulls	WHL	74	22	38	60	....	....	....	55	7	3	0	3	4
1969-70	San Diego Gulls	WHL	71	19	48	67	....	....	....	35	6	4	3	7	0
1970-71	San Diego Gulls	WHL	72	12	23	35	....	....	....	31	6	0	0	0	2
	NHL Totals		**104**	**5**	**10**	**15**	**6**	**10**	**16**	**32**	**12**	**0**	**1**	**1**	**2**

WCHA Second All-Star Team (1960)

Played in NHL All-Star Game (1962, 1963)

Claimed on waivers by **Detroit** from **Toronto**, December 3, 1963.

MACNEIL, AL
— see page 1253

MacPHERSON, BUD
Bud (James Albert) MacPherson
D – L. 6'4", 200 lbs. b: Edmonton, Alta., 3/31/1927. d: 1988.

Season	Club	League	GP	G	A	Pts	AG	AA	APts	PIM	GP	G	A	Pts	PIM
1946-47	Oshawa Generals	OHA	11	1	0	1	....	....	....	8	2	0	1	1	7
1947-48	Edmonton Flyers	WCSHL	37	8	11	19	....	....	....	21	24	3	3	6	*67
1948-49	**Montreal Canadiens**	**NHL**	**3**	**0**	**0**	**0**	**0**	**0**	**0**	**2**	....	....	....	....	....
	Edmonton Flyers	ASHL	44	5	17	22	....	....	....	65	9	0	3	3	10
1949-50	Cincinnati Mohawks	AHL	41	2	9	11	....	....	....	38	....	....	....	....	....
1950-51	**Montreal Canadiens**	**NHL**	**62**	**0**	**16**	**16**	**0**	**21**	**21**	**40**	**11**	**0**	**2**	**2**	**8**
	Cincinnati Mohawks	AHL	6	0	0	0	....	....	....	10	....	....	....	....	....
1951-52	**Montreal Canadiens**	**NHL**	**54**	**2**	**1**	**3**	**3**	**1**	**4**	**24**	**11**	**0**	**0**	**0**	**0**
1952-53	**Montreal Canadiens**	**NHL**	**59**	**2**	**3**	**5**	**3**	**4**	**7**	**67**	**4**	**0**	**1**	**1**	**9**
1953-54	**Montreal Canadiens**	**NHL**	**41**	**0**	**5**	**5**	**0**	**7**	**7**	**41**	**3**	**0**	**0**	**0**	**4**
	Montreal Royals	QHL	5	0	2	2	....	....	....	12	....	....	....	....	....
	Buffalo Bisons	AHL	8	0	1	1	....	....	....	6	....	....	....	....	....
1954-55	**Montreal Canadiens**	**NHL**	**30**	**1**	**8**	**9**	**1**	**10**	**11**	**55**	....	....	....	....	....
1955-56	Montreal Royals	QHL	31	2	9	11	....	....	....	63	13	2	1	3	30
1956-57	**Montreal Canadiens**	**NHL**	**10**	**0**	**0**	**0**	**0**	**0**	**0**	**4**	....	....	....	....	....
	Montreal Royals	QHL	46	3	10	13	....	....	....	53	4	0	1	1	4
	Rochester Americans	AHL	7	0	3	3	....	....	....	12	....	....	....	....	....
1957-58	Edmonton Flyers	WHL	70	5	22	27	....	....	....	57	5	0	1	1	4
1958-59	Edmonton Flyers	WHL	63	3	13	16	....	....	....	54	3	1	1	2	12
	Hershey Bears	AHL	....	....	....	....	....	....	....	....	10	0	2	2	6
1959-60	Edmonton Flyers	WHL	62	7	12	19	....	....	....	20	4	0	1	1	4
1960-61	Edmonton Flyers	WHL	11	0	1	1	....	....	....	8	....	....	....	....	....
	NHL Totals		**259**	**5**	**33**	**38**	**7**	**43**	**50**	**233**	**29**	**0**	**3**	**3**	**21**

Played in NHL All-Star Game (1953)

Traded to **Chicago** by **Montreal** with Ken Mosdell and Eddie Mazur for $55,000 with Montreal holding rights of recall, May 17, 1956. • Returned to **Montreal** by **Chicago** after training camp, October 10, 1956.

• MAHAFFY, JOHN
John Mahaffy
C – L. 5'7", 165 lbs. b: Montreal, Que., 7/18/1919.

			REGULAR SEASON								PLAYOFFS				
Season	Club	League	GP	G	A	Pts	AG	AA	APts	PIM	GP	G	A	Pts	PIM
1934-35	Montreal Royals	QJHL	10	3	6	9	....	....	....	4	2	0	0	0	0
1935-36	Montreal Royals	QJHL	7	5	6	11	....	....	....	4	....	....	....	....	....
1936-37	Montreal Royals	QSHL	21	4	8	12	....	....	....	16	5	0	1	1	2
1937-38	Montreal Royals	QSHL	22	4	3	7	....	....	....	20	1	0	0	0	2
1938-39	Streatham Hockey Club	Britain	....	8	13	21	....	....	....	....	....	....	....	....	....
1939-40	Montreal Royals	QSHL	29	9	13	22	....	....	....	25	13	2	4	6	12
1940-41	Montreal Royals	QSHL	33	17	25	42	....	....	....	60	17	10	7	17	38
1941-42	Montreal Royals	QSHL	38	9	16	25	....	....	....	35	....	....	....	....	....
1942-43	**Montreal Canadiens**	**NHL**	**9**	**2**	**5**	**7**	**3**	**6**	**9**	**4**	....	....	....	....	....
	Montreal Army–Royals	QSHL	28	21	16	37	....	....	....	14	7	4	2	6	4
1943-44	**New York Rangers**	**NHL**	**28**	**9**	**20**	**29**	**11**	**24**	**35**	**0**	....	....	....	....	....
	Montreal Army	City Sr.	4	0	0	0	....	....	....	0	....	....	....	....	....
	Montreal Royals	QSHL	4	2	6	8	....	....	....	2	....	....	....	....	....
1944-45	Pittsburgh Hornets	AHL	37	17	23	40	....	....	....	10	....	....	....	....	....
	Montreal Royals	QSHL	3	5	4	9	....	....	....	4	....	....	....	....	....
	Montreal Canadiens	**NHL**	....	....	....	....	....	....	....	....	**1**	**0**	**1**	**1**	**0**
1945-46	Pittsburgh Hornets	AHL	58	28	36	64	....	....	....	35	6	4	2	6	10
1946-47	Buffalo Bisons	AHL	63	29	40	69	....	....	....	37	4	0	0	0	0
1947-48	Philadelphia Rockets	AHL	60	26	57	83	....	....	....	6	....	....	....	....	....
1948-49	Philadelphia Rockets	AHL	67	21	50	71	....	....	....	10	....	....	....	....	....
1949-50	Hershey Bears	AHL	69	23	36	59	....	....	....	13	....	....	....	....	....
1950-51	Hershey Bears	AHL	33	5	14	19	....	....	....	7	....	....	....	....	....
1951-52	Shawinigan Cataracts	QSHL	60	16	28	44	....	....	....	18	....	....	....	....	....
	NHL Totals		**37**	**11**	**25**	**36**	**14**	**30**	**44**	**4**	**1**	**0**	**1**	**1**	**0**

Loaned to **NY Rangers** by **Montreal** with Dutch Hiller, Fern Gauthier, Charlie Sands and future considerations (Tony Demers, December, 1943) for loan of Phil Watson, October 27, 1943.

• MAHOVLICH, FRANK
— *see page 1256*

• MAHOVLICH, PETE
— *see page 1257*

• MAILLEY, FRANK
Frank Mailley
D – L. 5'9", 182 lbs. b: Lachine, Quebec, 8/1/1916.

Season	Club	League	GP	G	A	Pts	AG	AA	APts	PIM	GP	G	A	Pts	PIM
1938-39	Miami Beach Pirates	TrHL	14	8	8	16	....	....	....	14	....	....	....	....	....
	Lachine Rapides	QSHL	1	0	0	0	....	....	....	0	....	....	....	....	....
1939-40	St. Hyacinthe Gaulois	QSHL	22	9	13	21	....	....	....	12	2	0	0	0	6
1940-41	Washington Eagles	EHL	65	18	27	45	....	....	....	30	2	1	2	3	0
1941-42	Washington Lions	AHL	56	6	20	26	....	....	....	15	2	0	0	0	0
1942-43	**Montreal Canadiens**	**NHL**	**1**	**0**	**0**	**0**	**0**	**0**	**0**	**0**	....	....	....	....	....
	Washington Lions	AHL	51	4	14	18	....	....	....	30					
1943-44			MILITARY SERVICE												
1944-45			MILITARY SERVICE												
1945-46	Quebec Aces	QSHL	6	0	0	0	....	....	....	4	6	0	0	0	0
	NHL Totals		**1**	**0**	**0**	**0**	**0**	**0**	**0**	**0**	....	....	....	....	....

• MAJEAU, FERN
Fern Majeau
C/LW – L. 5'9", 155 lbs. b: Verdun, Que., 5/3/1916. d: 6/21/1966.

Season	Club	League	GP	G	A	Pts	AG	AA	APts	PIM	GP	G	A	Pts	PIM
1934-35	Verdun Jr. Maple Leafs	Mtl-Jr.	10	9	12	21	....	....	....	12	5	*6	2	8	6
	Verdun Maple Leafs	Mtl-Sr.	1	0	0	0	....	....	....	2	....	....	....	....	....
1935-36	Verdun Jr. Maple Leafs	Mtl-Jr.	9	8	*8	*16	....	....	....	10	....	....	....	....	....
	Verdun Maple Leafs	Mtl-Sr.	5	0	3	3	....	....	....	0	7	2	2	4	2
1936-37	Verdun Maple Leafs	Mtl-Sr.	21	3	6	9	....	....	....	40	....	....	....	....	....
1937-38	Montreal Royals	Mtl-Sr.	12	4	5	9	....	....	....	8	1	0	1	1	0
1938-39	Lachine Rapides	QPHL	30	12	9	21	....	....	....	38	6	0	1	1	4
1939-40	Lachine Rapides	QPHL	41	17	25	42	....	....	....	54	9	8	6	14	4
1940-41	Verdun Maple Leafs	Mtl-Sr.	34	10	10	20				[illegible]	....	....	....	....	
1941-42	Montreal Pats	City Sr.	28	11	8	19	....	....	....	22	....	....	....	....	....
1942-43	Montreal Sr. Canadiens	QSHL	24	8	5	13	....	....	....	17	4	4	2	6	2
1943-44	**Montreal Canadiens**	**NHL**	**44**	**20**	**18**	**38**	**25**	**22**	**47**	**39**	**1**	**0**	**0**	**0**	**0**
1944-45	**Montreal Canadiens**	**NHL**	**12**	**2**	**6**	**8**	**3**	**10**	**13**	**4**	....	....	....	....	....
	Montreal Royals	QSHL	9	6	7	13	....	....	....	10	7	4	0	4	10
1945-46	Valleyfield Braves	QSHL	39	17	27	44	....	....	....	46	....	....	....	....	....
1946-47	Valleyfield Braves	QSHL	33	10	25	35	....	....	....	32	....	....	....	....	....
1947-48	Lachine Rapides	QPHL	53	23	32	55	....	....	....	42	6	3	3	6	2
1948-49	Montreal Hydro Quebec	QPHL	11	6	10	16	....	....	....	....	....	....	....	....	....
	NHL Totals		**56**	**22**	**24**	**46**	**28**	**32**	**60**	**43**	**1**	**0**	**0**	**0**	**0**

Signed as a free agent by **Montreal Canadiens**, October 28, 1943.

• MAKI, CHICO
— *see page 1259*

• MALONE, CLIFF
Cliff Malone
RW – R. 5'10", 155 lbs. b: Quebec City, Que., 9/4/1925.

Season	Club	League	GP	G	A	Pts	AG	AA	APts	PIM	GP	G	A	Pts	PIM
1943-44	Montreal Jr. Royals	QJHL	9	8	8	16	....	....	....	2	....	....	....	....	....
1944-45	Montreal Jr. Royals	QJHL	13	14	9	23	....	....	....	2	15	12	9	21	4
	Montreal RCAF	City Jr.	14	11	6	17	....	....	....	6	1	3	0	3	0
	Montreal Royals	City Sr.	2	0	0	0	....	....	....	0	1	0	0	0	2
1945-46	Montreal Royals	QSHL	....	....	....	....	....	....	....	....	2	1	0	1	0
1946-47	Montreal Royals	QSHL	31	16	19	35	....	....	....	6	11	4	4	8	12
1947-48	Montreal Royals	QSHL	46	18	49	67	....	....	....	21	3	1	0	1	2
1948-49	Montreal Royals	QSHL	64	35	60	95	....	....	....	40	9	3	4	7	10
1949-50	Montreal Royals	QSHL	60	21	36	57	....	....	....	55	6	2	1	3	4
1950-51	Montreal Royals	QSHL	60	25	24	49	....	....	....	54	7	0	4	4	2
1951-52	**Montreal Canadiens**	**NHL**	**3**	**0**	**0**	**0**	**0**	**0**	**0**	**0**	....	....	....	....	....
	Montreal Royals	QSHL	56	29	37	66	....	....	....	10	7	3	4	7	0
1952-53	Montreal Royals	QSHL	60	15	34	49	....	....	....	42	15	3	6	9	2
1953-54	Montreal Royals	QHL	13	0	3	3	....	....	....	8	....	....	....	....	....
	NHL Totals		**3**	**0**	**0**	**0**	**0**	**0**	**0**	**0**	....	....	....	....	....

• MALONE, JOE
Joe "Phantom" Malone   HHOF
C/LW – L. 5'10", 150 lbs. b: Quebec City, Que., 2/28/1890. d: 5/15/1969.

			REGULAR SEASON								PLAYOFFS				
Season	Club	League	GP	G	A	Pts	AG	AA	APts	PIM	GP	G	A	Pts	PIM
1907-08	Quebec Crescents	QJHL	STATISTICS NOT AVAILABLE												
1908-09	Quebec Bulldogs	ECHA	12	8	0	8	....	....	....	17	....	....	....	....	....
1909-10	Waterloo Professionals	OPHL	11	8	0	8	....	....	....	....	....	....	....	....	....
	Quebec Bulldogs	CHA	2	5	0	5	....	....	....	3	....	....	....	....	....
1910-11	Quebec Bulldogs	NHA	13	9	0	9	....	....	....	3	....	....	....	....	....
1911-12	Quebec Bulldogs	NHA	18	21	0	21	....	....	....	0	2	5	0	5	0
1912-13	Quebec Bulldogs	NHA	20	*43	0	*43	....	....	....	34	4	*9	0	*9	0
1913-14	Quebec Bulldogs	NHA	17	24	4	28	....	....	....	20	....	....	....	....	....
1914-15	Quebec Bulldogs	NHA	12	16	5	21	....	....	....	21	....	....	....	....	....
1915-16	Quebec Bulldogs	NHA	24	25	10	35	....	....	....	21	....	....	....	....	....
1916-17	Quebec Bulldogs	NHA	19	*41	7	48	....	....	....	12	....	....	....	....	....
1917-18	**Montreal Canadiens**	**NHL**	**20**	***44**	**4**	***48**	**122**	**0**	**122**	**30**	**2**	**0**	**0**	**0**	**0**
1918-19	**Montreal Canadiens**	**NHL**	**8**	**7**	**2**	**9**	**25**	**19**	**44**	**3**	**5**	**5**	**1**	**6**	**3**
1919-20	**Quebec Bulldogs**	**NHL**	**24**	***39**	**10**	***49**	**94**	**69**	**163**	**12**	....	....	....	....	....
1920-21	**Hamilton Tigers**	**NHL**	**20**	**28**	**9**	**37**	**75**	**81**	**156**	**6**	....	....	....	....	....
1921-22	**Hamilton Tigers**	**NHL**	**24**	**24**	**7**	**31**	**68**	**44**	**112**	**4**	....	....	....	....	....
1922-23	**Montreal Canadiens**	**NHL**	**20**	**1**	**0**	**1**	**3**	**0**	**3**	**2**	**2**	**0**	**0**	**0**	**0**
1923-24	**Montreal Canadiens**	**NHL**	**9**	**0**	**0**	**0**	**0**	**0**	**0**	**0**	....	....	....	....	....
	NHL Totals		**125**	**143**	**32**	**175**	**387**	**213**	**600**	**57**	**9**	**5**	**1**	**6**	**3**
	Other Major League Totals		148	200	26	226	....	....	....	131	6	14	0	14	0

NHL Scoring Leader (1918, 1920)

Claimed by **Montreal Canadiens** from **Quebec** in Dispersal Draft, November 26, 1917. Transferred to **Quebec** by **Montreal Canadiens** when Quebec franchise returned to NHL, November 25, 1919. Transferred to **Hamilton** after **Quebec** franchise relocated, November 2, 1920. • Suspended by **Hamilton** for refusing to report to training camp, December 6, 1922. Traded to **Montreal Canadiens** by **Hamilton** for Edmond Bouchard, December 27, 1922.

• MALONEY, PHIL
Phil Maloney
C – L. 5'8", 165 lbs. b: Ottawa, Ont., 10/6/1927.

Season	Club	League	GP	G	A	Pts	AG	AA	APts	PIM	GP	G	A	Pts	PIM
1945-46	Ottawa St. Pats	City Jr.	12	*18	9	*27	....	....	....	9	5	0	8	8	0
1946-47	Shawinigan Cataracts	QPHL	34	10	15	25	....	....	....	4	4	3	3	6	0
1947-48	Shawinigan Cataracts	QPHL	48	18	46	64	....	....	....	24	7	2	6	8	0
1948-49	Hershey Bears	AHL	64	29	50	79	....	....	....	21	11	5	6	11	2
1949-50	**Boston Bruins**	**NHL**	**70**	**15**	**31**	**46**	**20**	**40**	**60**	**6**	....	....	....	....	....
1950-51	**Boston Bruins**	**NHL**	**13**	**2**	**0**	**2**	**3**	**0**	**3**	**2**	....	....	....	....	....
	Toronto Maple Leafs	**NHL**	**1**	**1**	**0**	**1**	**1**	**0**	**1**	**0**	....	....	....	....	....
	Pittsburgh Hornets	AHL	54	13	23	36	....	....	....	14	5	2	0	2	2
1951-52	Pittsburgh Hornets	AHL	66	19	37	56	....	....	....	25	5	0	1	1	0
1952-53	**Toronto Maple Leafs**	**NHL**	**29**	**2**	**6**	**8**	**3**	**8**	**11**	**2**	....	....	....	....	....
	Pittsburgh Hornets	AHL	28	8	22	30	....	....	....	22	....	....	....	....	....
1953-54	Ottawa Senators	QHL	27	9	13	22	....	....	....	379	22	8	6	14	18
	Pittsburgh Hornets	AHL	35	7	11	18	....	....	....	20	....	....	....	....	....
1954-55	Vancouver Canucks	WHL	37	16	27	43	....	....	....	9	5	2	2	4	0
	Ottawa Senators	QHL	25	8	14	22	....	....	....	7	....	....	....	....	....
1955-56	Vancouver Canucks	WHL	70	37	58	*95	....	....	....	14	15	8	7	15	4
1956-57	Vancouver Canucks	WHL	70	43	55	98	....	....	....	8	....	....	....	....	....
1957-58	Vancouver Canucks	WHL	70	35	59	94	....	....	....	0	11	8	*17	*25	4
1958-59	Vancouver Canucks	WHL	13	8	9	17	....	....	....	2	....	....	....	....	....
	Chicago Black Hawks	**NHL**	**24**	**2**	**2**	**4**	**3**	**2**	**5**	**6**	**6**	**0**	**0**	**0**	**0**
1959-60	**Chicago Black Hawks**	**NHL**	**21**	**6**	**4**	**10**	**7**	**4**	**11**	**0**	....	....	....	....	....
	Buffalo Bisons	AHL	46	21	41	62	....	....	....	14	....	....	....	....	....
1960-61	Buffalo Bisons	AHL	71	37	65	102	....	....	....	27	4	0	3	3	0
1961-62	Vancouver Canucks	WHL	70	34	52	86	....	....	....	2	....	....	....	....	....
1962-63	Vancouver Canucks	WHL	64	29	61	90	....	....	....	8	7	2	7	9	0
1963-64	Vancouver Canucks	WHL	65	28	53	81	....	....	....	38	....	....	....	....	....
1964-65	Vancouver Canucks	WHL	69	29	52	81	....	....	....	18	5	1	5	6	0
1965-66	Vancouver Canucks	WHL	65	22	51	73	....	....	....	16	7	5	8	13	0
1966-67	Vancouver Canucks	WHL	72	17	49	66	....	....	....	42	8	1	6	7	0
1967-68	Vancouver Canucks	WHL	72	22	46	68	....	....	....	0	....	....	....	....	....
1968-69	Vancouver Canucks	WHL	65	4	24	28			....	19	2	0	0	0	0
1969-70	Vancouver Canucks	WHL	16	2	1	3	....	....	....	0	....	....	....	....	
	NHL Totals		**158**	**28**	**43**	**71**	**37**	**54**	**91**	**16**	**6**	**0**	**0**	**0**	**0**

WHL First All-Star Team (1956) • Won Leader Cup (WHL - MVP) (1956, 1962, 1963) • WHL Coast Division Second All-Star Team (1957, 1958) • AHL First All-Star Team (1961) • Won Les Cunningham Award (MVP - AHL) (1961) • WHL Second All-Star Team (1962, 1963) • Won Fred J. Hume Cup (WHL Most Gentlemanly Player) (1962, 1963, 1968)

Traded to **Toronto** by **Boston** with Fernie Flaman, Ken Smith and Leo Boivin for Bill Ezinicki and Vic Lynn, November 16, 1950. Claimed by **NY Rangers** from **Toronto** in Intra-League Draft, June 4, 1957. Traded to **Chicago** by **NY Rangers** for $7,500, December 31, 1958. Traded to **Vancouver** by **Chicago** (Buffalo - AHL) for cash, September, 1961.

• MANASTERSKY, TOM
Tom Manastersky
D – R. 5'9", 185 lbs. b: Montreal, Que., 3/7/1929.

Season	Club	League	GP	G	A	Pts	AG	AA	APts	PIM	GP	G	A	Pts	PIM
1945-46	Montreal Jr. Royals	QJHL	19	0	4	4	....	....	....	23	....	....	....	....	....
	Montreal Royals	QSHL	1	0	0	0	....	....	....	2	....	....	....	....	....
1946-47	Montreal Jr. Royals	QJHL	25	1	3	4	....	....	....	68	7	0	1	1	29
	Montreal Royals	QSHL	3	0	0	0	....	....	....	2	....	....	....	....	....
1947-48	Montreal Jr. Royals	QJHL	8	1	1	2	....	....	....	16	13	0	1	1	*38
1948-49	Montreal Jr. Royals	QJHL	30	2	5	7	....	....	....	63	25	3	9	12	*83
	Montreal Royals	QSHL	2	0	0	0	....	....	....	0	15	1	5	6	67
1949-50	Montreal Royals	QSHL	27	2	7	9	....	....	....	87	3	0	0	0	25
1950-51	**Montreal Canadiens**	**NHL**	**6**	**0**	**0**	**0**	**0**	**0**	**0**	**11**	....	....	....	....	....
	Cincinnati Mohawks	AHL	5	0	0	0	....	....	....	18	....	....	....	....	....
	Victoria Cougars	PCHL	18	1	1	2	....	....	....	45	....	....	....	....	....
	Montreal Royals	QSHL	1	0	0	0	....	....	....	0	....	....	....	....	....
	NHL Totals		**6**	**0**	**0**	**0**	**0**	**0**	**0**	**11**	....	....	....	....	....

• MANCUSO, GUS Gus (Felix) Mancuso

RW – L. 5'7", 160 lbs. b: Niagara Falls, Ont., 4/11/1914. Deceased.

Season	Club	League	GP	G	A	Pts	AG	AA	APts	PIM	GP	G	A	Pts	PIM
			REGULAR SEASON								PLAYOFFS				
1930-31	Niagara Falls Cataracts	OHA	3	1	2	3	....	....	....	0	....	....	....	....	....
1931-32	Niagara Falls Cataracts	OHA	4	1	0	1	....	....	....	2	5	*3	0	3	2
1932-33	Niagara Falls Cataracts	OHA	STATISTICS NOT AVAILABLE												
1933-34	Niagara Falls Cataracts	OHA	24	9	1	10	....	....	....	20	2	0	0	0	0
1934-35	Hershey B'ars	EHL	21	16	5	21	....	....	....	31	9	6	4	10	4
1935-36	Hershey B'ars	EHL	40	24	12	36	....	....	....	37	8	3	0	3	18
1936-37	Hershey B'ars	EHL	48	14	14	28	....	....	....	17	4	1	0	1	2
1937-38	**Montreal Canadiens**	**NHL**	**17**	**1**	**1**	**2**	**2**	**2**	**4**	**4**	....	....	....	....	....
	New Haven Eagles	AHL	32	6	4	0	....	....	....	17	2	0	1	1	0
1938-39	**Montreal Canadiens**	**NHL**	**2**	**0**	**0**	**0**	**0**	**0**	**0**	**0**	....	....	....	....	....
	New Haven Eagles	AHL	42	4	14	18	....	....	....	47	....	....	....	....	....
1939-40	**Montreal Canadiens**	**NHL**	**2**	**0**	**0**	**0**	**0**	**0**	**0**	**0**	....	....	....	....	....
	New Haven Eagles	AHL	47	9	20	29	....	....	....	41	3	0	1	1	0
1940-41	New Haven Eagles	AHL	56	17	25	42	....	....	....	12	2	0	0	0	2
1941-42	New Haven Eagles	AHL	46	19	29	48	....	....	....	24	2	0	0	0	0
1942-43	**New York Rangers**	**NHL**	**21**	**6**	**8**	**14**	**8**	**10**	**18**	**13**	....	....	....	....	....
	New Haven Eagles	AHL	30	10	16	26	....	....	....	13	....	....	....	....	....
1943-44			MILITARY SERVICE												
1944-45			MILITARY SERVICE												
1945-46	Providence Reds	AHL	15	3	5	8	....	....	....	4	....	....	....	....	....
	Hollywood Wolves	PCHL	6	2	4	6	....	....	....	0	4	3	0	3	10
1946-47	Hollywood Wolves	PCHL	59	27	17	44	....	....	....	33	7	1	1	2	9
1947-48	Los Angeles Monarchs	PCHL	51	17	15	32	....	....	....	15	4	0	2	2	2
1948-49	Los Angeles Monarchs	PCHL	22	3	3	6	....	....	....	11	....	....	....	....	....
	NHL Totals		**42**	**7**	**9**	**16**	**10**	**12**	**22**	**17**	....	....	....	....	....

EHL Second All-Star Team (1935) • EHL First All-Star Team (1936)

Signed as a free agent by **Montreal Canadiens**, October 30, 1937. Traded to **NY Rangers** by **Montreal** for cash, November 4, 1942.

• MANN, JACK Jack Mann

C – L. 5'7", 160 lbs. b: Winnipeg, Man., 7/27/1919.

Season	Club	League	GP	G	A	Pts	AG	AA	APts	PIM	GP	G	A	Pts	PIM
1937-38	Winnipeg Rangers	City Jr.	9	0	1	1	....	....	....	6	2	0	0	0	0
1938-39	St. James Canadians	Wpg-Jr.	17	7	7	14	....	....	....	10	2	0	3	3	2
1939-40	Nelson Maple Leafs	Kootenay	27	20	9	29	....	....	....	21	7	*7	2	*9	6
1940-41	Nelson Maple Leafs	Kootenay	27	*30	15	45	....	....	....	30	2	2	1	3	2
1941-42	Nanaimo Clippers	PCHL	26	*27	11	38	....	....	....	33	7	*7	2	*9	14
1942-43	Nanaimo Clippers	PCHL	19	16	12	28	....	....	....	8	3	1	0	1	0
1943-44	**New York Rangers**	**NHL**	**3**	**0**	**0**	**0**	**0**	**0**	**0**	**0**	....	....	....	....	....
	New York Rovers	EHL	30	19	13	32	....	....	....	9	10	5	3	8	9
	Brooklyn Crescents	EHL	2	0	0	0	....	....	....	5	....	....	....	....	....
1944-45	**New York Rangers**	**NHL**	**6**	**3**	**4**	**7**	**4**	**6**	**10**	**0**	....	....	....	....	....
	New York Rovers	EHL	39	16	31	47	....	....	....	29	6	5	3	8	4
	Philadelphia Falcons	EHL	2	1	0	1	....	....	....	0	....	....	....	....	....
1945-46	St. Paul Saints	USHL	36	12	11	23	....	....	....	6	6	0	4	4	0
1946-47	St. Paul Saints	USHL	6	1	2	3	....	....	....	0	....	....	....	....	....
1946-47	Fresno Falcons	PCHL	46	12	12	24	....	....	....	8	2	0	0	0	0
1947-48	Westminster–Portland	WHL	56	18	34	52	....	....	....	16	....	....	....	....	....
	NHL Totals		**9**	**3**	**4**	**7**	**4**	**6**	**10**	**0**	....	....	....	....	....

• MANN, NORM Norm Mann

RW/C – R. 5'10", 155 lbs. b: Bradford, England, 3/3/1914.

Season	Club	League	GP	G	A	Pts	AG	AA	APts	PIM	GP	G	A	Pts	PIM
1931-32	Newmarket Redmen	OHA	7	1	1	2	....	....	....	*12	5	1	2	3	2
1932-33	Newmarket Redmen	OHA	17	11	8	19	....	....	....	....	19	6	*7	13	14
1933-34	Toronto Marlboros	OHA Sr.	24	16	9	25	....	....	....	25	2	0	1	1	2
1934-35	Toronto British Consols	City Sr.	15	6	12	18	....	....	....	20	4	2	2	4	4
	Toronto All-Stars	OHA Sr.	6	2	4	6	....	....	....	10	4	2	1	3	0
1935-36	Syracuse Stars	IAHL	48	8	23	31	....	....	....	60	3	0	0	0	2
	Toronto Maple Leafs	**NHL**	....	....	....	....	....	....	....	....	**1**	**0**	**0**	**0**	**0**
1936-37	Syracuse Stars	AHL	46	17	24	41	....	....	....	47	9	3	5	8	11
1937-38	Philadelphia Ramblers	AHL	26	4	9	13	....	....	....	8	1	0	0	0	0
1938-39	**Toronto Maple Leafs**	**NHL**	**16**	**0**	**0**	**0**	**0**	**0**	**0**	**2**	....	....	....	....	....
	Syracuse Stars	AHL	43	11	20	31	....	....	....	42	3	1	0	1	0
1939-40	Providence Reds	AHL	36	11	16	27	....	....	....	25	8	3	5	8	6
1940-41	**Toronto Maple Leafs**	**NHL**	**15**	**0**	**3**	**3**	**0**	**5**	**5**	**2**	**1**	**0**	**0**	**0**	**0**
	Providence Reds	AHL	28	8	8	16	....	....	....	8	4	2	0	2	6
1941-42	Pittsburgh Hornets	AHL	41	16	36	52	....	....	....	11	....	....	....	....	....
1942-43	Pittsburgh Hornets	AHL	54	31	45	76	....	....	....	83	2	0	1	1	0
	Cleveland Barons	AHL	1	0	0	0	....	....	....	0	....	....	....	....	....
1943-44	Toronto Navy	OHA Sr.	23	8	27	35	....	....	....	10	....	....	....	....	....
1944-45	Toronto Navy	City Sr.	12	8	10	18	....	....	....	21	6	2	1	3	2
1945-46	Toronto Staffords	OHA Sr.	13	4	11	15	....	....	....	10	13	2	3	5	4
1946-47	Cleveland Barons	AHL	27	5	6	11	....	....	....	17	4	0	0	0	2
	NHL Totals		**31**	**0**	**3**	**3**	**0**	**5**	**5**	**4**	**2**	**0**	**0**	**0**	**0**

Signed as a free agent by **Toronto**, October 7, 1935. Claimed by **NY Rangers** from **Syracuse** (AHL) in Inter-League Draft, May 9, 1937. Traded to **Toronto** by **NY Rangers** for $4,000, November 15, 1938. Traded to **Pittsburgh** (AHL) by **Toronto** for cash, October 30, 1941.

• MANNERS, RENNISON Rennison Manners

C – L. 5'11", 160 lbs. b: Ottawa, Ontario, 2/5/1904. Deceased.

Season	Club	League	GP	G	A	Pts	AG	AA	APts	PIM	GP	G	A	Pts	PIM
1922-23	Pittsburgh Yellowjackets	USAHA	20	3	0	3	....	....	....	....	....	....	....	....	....
1923-24	Pittsburgh Yellowjackets	USAHA	7	1	0	1	....	....	....	....	2	0	1	1	....
1924-25	Fort Pitt Panthers	USAHA	19	7	0	7	....	....	....	....	8	4	0	4	....
1925-26	Fort Pitt Panthers		STATISTICS NOT AVAILABLE												
1926-27	Ottawa Montagnards	City Sr.	15	3	2	5	....	....	....	....	2	0	0	0	0
1927-28	Ottawa Montagnards	City Sr.	15	2	4	6	....	....	....	....	4	0	0	0	0
1928-29	Ottawa Montagnards	City Sr.	12	*8	2	10	....	....	....	....	....	....	....	....	....
1929-30	**Pittsburgh Pirates**	**NHL**	**33**	**3**	**2**	**5**	**6**	**6**	**12**	**14**	....	....	....	....	....
	London Panthers	IAHL	3	0	0	0	....	....	....	0	....	....	....	....	....
1930-31	**Philadelphia Quakers**	**NHL**	**4**	**0**	**0**	**0**	**0**	**0**	**0**	**0**	....	....	....	....	....
	Niagara Falls Cataracts	OPHL	27	9	8	17	....	....	....	23	2	0	0	0	2
1931-1933			REINSTATED AS AN AMATEUR												
1933-34	Ottawa Montagnards	City Sr.	10	2	2	4	....	....	....	4	3	1	0	1	0
	NHL Totals		**37**	**3**	**2**	**5**	**6**	**6**	**12**	**14**	....	....	....	....	....

Transferred to **Philadelphia** after **Pittsburgh** franchise relocated, September 26, 1930.

• MANSON, RAY Ray Manson

LW – L. 5'11", 180 lbs. b: St. Boniface, Man., 12/3/1926.

Season	Club	League	GP	G	A	Pts	AG	AA	APts	PIM	GP	G	A	Pts	PIM
			REGULAR SEASON								PLAYOFFS				
1943-44	St. Boniface Canadians	MJHL	10	8	3	11	....	....	....	2	9	3	3	6	0
1944-45	Winnipeg Esquires	MJHL	10	10	5	15	....	....	....	16	6	6	2	8	15
1945-46	Winnipeg Rangers	MJHL	10	10	5	15	....	....	....	13	2	1	0	1	2
1946-47	Brandon Elks	MJHL	16	22	*19	*41	....	....	....	10	7	*10	2	*12	5
1947-48	**Boston Bruins**	**NHL**	**1**	**0**	**0**	**0**	**0**	**0**	**0**	**0**	....	....	....	....	....
	Boston Olympics	EHL	20	20	17	37	....	....	....	6	....	....	....	....	....
	Boston Olympics	QSHL	46	24	22	46	....	....	....	10	....	....	....	....	....
1948-49	**New York Rangers**	**NHL**	**1**	**0**	**1**	**1**	**0**	**2**	**2**	**0**	....	....	....	....	....
	New York Rovers	QSHL	41	17	13	30	....	....	....	8	....	....	....	....	....
1949-50	New Haven Ramblers	AHL	70	11	15	26	....	....	....	26	....	....	....	....	....
1950-51	New Haven Ramblers	AHL	26	9	7	16	....	....	....	2	....	....	....	....	....
	St. Paul Saints	USHL	41	12	11	23	....	....	....	8	4	1	1	2	7
1951-52	Vancouver Canucks	PCHL	70	36	32	68	....	....	....	21	....	....	....	....	....
1952-53	Vancouver–Saskatoon	WHL	69	20	25	45	....	....	....	8	13	6	*14	20	0
1953-54	Saskatoon Quakers	WHL	70	28	42	70	....	....	....	22	6	1	3	4	0
1954-55	Saskatoon Quakers	WHL	58	27	27	54	....	....	....	2	....	....	....	....	....
1955-56	Brandon Regals	WHL	69	35	28	63	....	....	....	22	....	....	....	....	....
1956-57	Brandon Regals	WHL	70	40	43	83	....	....	....	18	8	2	5	7	0
	NHL Totals		**2**	**0**	**1**	**1**	**0**	**2**	**2**	**0**	....	....	....	....	....

WHL Prairie Division First All-Star Team (1957)

Traded to **NY Rangers** by **Boston** with Pentti Lund to complete transaction that sent Grant Warwick to Boston, February 6, 1949.

• MANTHA, GEORGES Georges Mantha

D/LW – L. 5'8", 165 lbs. b: Lachine, Que., 11/29/1908. d: 1/25/1990.

Season	Club	League	GP	G	A	Pts	AG	AA	APts	PIM	GP	G	A	Pts	PIM
1926-27	Montreal Victorias	QAHA	4	2	0	2	....	....	....	0	....	....	....	....	....
1927-28	Montreal Victorias	QAHA	STATISTICS NOT AVAILABLE												
	Montreal Bell Telephone	City Sr.	3	1	1	2	....	....	....	4	....	....	....	....	....
1928-29	**Montreal Canadiens**	**NHL**	**21**	**0**	**0**	**0**	**0**	**0**	**0**	**8**	**3**	**0**	**0**	**0**	**0**
	University of Montreal	City Sr.	3	0	1	1	....	....	....	2	....	....	....	....	....
	Montreal Bell Telephone	City Sr.	4	1	1	2	....	....	....	14	....	....	....	....	....
1929-30	**Montreal Canadiens**	**NHL**	**44**	**5**	**2**	**7**	**10**	**6**	**16**	**16**	**6**	**0**	**0**	**0**	**8**
1930-31	**Montreal Canadiens**	**NHL**	**44**	**11**	**6**	**17**	**27**	**22**	**49**	**25**	**10**	**5**	**1**	**6**	**4**
1931-32	**Montreal Canadiens**	**NHL**	**48**	**1**	**7**	**8**	**2**	**19**	**21**	**8**	**4**	**0**	**1**	**1**	**8**
1932-33	**Montreal Canadiens**	**NHL**	**43**	**3**	**6**	**9**	**7**	**16**	**23**	**10**	....	....	....	....	....
1933-34	**Montreal Canadiens**	**NHL**	**44**	**6**	**9**	**15**	**13**	**24**	**37**	**12**	....	....	....	....	....
1934-35	**Montreal Canadiens**	**NHL**	**42**	**12**	**10**	**22**	**25**	**22**	**47**	**14**	**2**	**0**	**0**	**0**	**4**
1935-36	**Montreal Canadiens**	**NHL**	**35**	**1**	**12**	**13**	**2**	**29**	**31**	**14**	....	....	....	....	....
1936-37	**Montreal Canadiens**	**NHL**	**47**	**13**	**14**	**27**	**28**	**33**	**61**	**17**	**5**	**0**	**0**	**0**	**0**
1937-38	**Montreal Canadiens**	**NHL**	**47**	**23**	**19**	**42**	**49**	**39**	**88**	**12**	**3**	**1**	**0**	**1**	**0**
1938-39	**Montreal Canadiens**	**NHL**	**25**	**5**	**5**	**10**	**10**	**9**	**19**	**6**	**3**	**0**	**0**	**0**	**0**
1939-40	**Montreal Canadiens**	**NHL**	**42**	**9**	**11**	**20**	**19**	**22**	**41**	**6**	....	....	....	....	....
1940-41	**Montreal Canadiens**	**NHL**	**6**	**0**	**1**	**1**	**0**	**2**	**2**	**0**	....	....	....	....	....
	New Haven Eagles	AHL	49	16	15	31	....	....	....	8	....	....	....	....	....
1941-42	Washington Lions	AHL	50	18	25	43	....	....	....	4	1	0	0	0	0
1942-43	Washington Lions	AHL	19	2	2	4	....	....	....	4	....	....	....	....	....
	NHL Totals		**488**	**89**	**102**	**191**	**192**	**243**	**435**	**148**	**36**	**6**	**2**	**8**	**24**

AHL Second All-Star Team (1941)

Played in NHL All-Star Game (1937, 1939)

Traded to **Washington** (AHL) by **Montreal** for cash, October 9, 1941.

• MANTHA, SYLVIO Sylvio Mantha HHOF

D – R. 5'10", 178 lbs. b: Montreal, Que., 4/14/1902. d: 8/7/1974.

Season	Club	League	GP	G	A	Pts	AG	AA	APts	PIM	GP	G	A	Pts	PIM
1922-23	Montreal Nationale	City Sr.	9	4	0	4	....	....	....	....	....	....	....	....	....
1923-24	**Montreal Canadiens**	**NHL**	**24**	**1**	**0**	**1**	**4**	**0**	**4**	**9**	**5**	**0**	**0**	**0**	**0**
1924-25	**Montreal Canadiens**	**NHL**	**30**	**2**	**0**	**2**	**7**	**0**	**7**	**16**	**6**	**0**	**0**	**0**	**2**
1925-26	**Montreal Canadiens**	**NHL**	**34**	**2**	**1**	**3**	**6**	**11**	**17**	**66**	....	....	....	....	....
1926-27	**Montreal Canadiens**	**NHL**	**43**	**10**	**5**	**15**	**29**	**43**	**72**	**77**	**4**	**1**	**0**	**1**	**0**
1927-28	**Montreal Canadiens**	**NHL**	**43**	**4**	**11**	**15**	**12**	**94**	**106**	**61**	**2**	**0**	**0**	**0**	**6**
1928-29	**Montreal Canadiens**	**NHL**	**44**	**9**	**4**	**13**	**36**	**37**	**73**	**56**	**3**	**0**	**0**	**0**	**0**
1929-30	**Montreal Canadiens**	**NHL**	**44**	**13**	**11**	**24**	**26**	**36**	**62**	**108**	**6**	**2**	**1**	**3**	**18**
1930-31	**Montreal Canadiens**	**NHL**	**44**	**4**	**7**	**11**	**10**	**25**	**35**	**75**	**10**	**2**	**1**	**3**	***26**
1931-32	**Montreal Canadiens**	**NHL**	**47**	**5**	**5**	**10**	**11**	**14**	**25**	**62**	**4**	**0**	**1**	**1**	**8**
1932-33	**Montreal Canadiens**	**NHL**	**48**	**4**	**7**	**11**	**9**	**18**	**27**	**50**	**2**	**0**	**1**	**1**	**2**
1933-34	**Montreal Canadiens**	**NHL**	**48**	**4**	**6**	**10**	**9**	**16**	**25**	**24**	**2**	**0**	**0**	**0**	**2**
1934-35	**Montreal Canadiens**	**NHL**	**47**	**3**	**11**	**14**	**6**	**24**	**30**	**36**	**2**	**0**	**0**	**0**	**2**
1935-36	**Montreal Canadiens**	**NHL**	**42**	**2**	**4**	**6**	**5**	**10**	**15**	**25**	....	....	....	....	....
1936-37	**Boston Bruins**	**NHL**	**4**	**0**	**0**	**0**	**0**	**0**	**0**	**2**	....	....	....	....	....
1937-38	Montreal Concordia	QSHL	DID NOT PLAY – COACHING												
	NHL Totals		**542**	**63**	**72**	**135**	**170**	**328**	**498**	**667**	**46**	**5**	**4**	**9**	**66**

NHL Second All-Star Team (1931, 1932)

Signed as a free agent by **Montreal Canadiens**, December 3, 1923. Signed as a free agent by **Boston**, February 11, 1937.

• MARACLE, BUD
Bud (Elmer) Maracle
LW – L. 5'11", 195 lbs. b: Ayr, Ont., 9/8/1904. Deceased.

Season	Club	League	GP	G	A	Pts	AG	AA	APts	PIM	GP	G	A	Pts	PIM
			REGULAR SEASON								PLAYOFFS				
1921-22	Haileybury High School	H.S.	....	....	....	....	....	....	....	....	4	3	*5	*8	....
1922-23	North Bay Trappers	NOHA	STATISTICS NOT AVAILABLE												
1923-24	North Bay Trappers	NOHA	6	*11	0	*11	....	....	....	....	5	11	0	11	....
1924-25	North Bay Trappers	NOHA	STATISTICS NOT AVAILABLE												
1925-26	Toronto Industrial	City Sr.	STATISTICS NOT AVAILABLE												
1926-27	Springfield Indians	Can-Am	32	5	1	6	....	....	....	44	6	2	1	3	4
1927-28	Springfield Indians	Can-Am	40	15	3	18	....	....	....	65	3	2	1	*3	0
1928-29	Springfield Indians	Can-Am	37	4	4	8	....	....	....	47	....	....	....	....	....
1929-30	Springfield Indians	Can-Am	31	5	4	9	....	....	....	22	....	....	....	....	....
1930-31	Springfield Indians	Can-Am	26	6	4	10	....	....	....	44	....	....	....	....	....
	New York Rangers	**NHL**	**11**	**1**	**3**	**4**	**2**	**11**	**13**	**4**	**4**	**0**	**0**	**0**	**0**
1931-32	Bronx Tigers	Can-Am	1	0	0	0	....	....	....	0	....	....	....	....	....
	Springfield Indians	Can-Am	27	3	9	12	....	....	....	14	....	....	....	....	....
1932-33			DID NOT PLAY – INJURED												
1933-34	New Haven Eagles	Can-Am	40	11	6	17	....	....	....	31	....	....	....	....	....
1934-35	New Haven–Philadelphia	Can-Am	43	14	10	24	....	....	....	22	....	....	....	....	....
1935-36	Tulsa Oilers	AHA	48	12	8	20	....	....	....	17	3	0	0	0	0
1936-37	Tulsa Oilers	AHA	42	3	10	13	....	....	....	12	....	....	....	....	....
1937-38			REINSTATED AS AN AMATEUR												
1938-39	Detroit Pontiacs	MOHL	22	3	5	8	....	....	....	2	7	1	0	1	6
	NHL Totals		**11**	**1**	**3**	**4**	**2**	**11**	**13**	**4**	**4**	**0**	**0**	**0**	**0**

Traded to **NY Rangers** by **Springfield** (Can-Am) for Gene Carrigan, February 12, 1931.
Traded to **Bronx** (Can-Am) by **NY Rangers** for cash, November 1, 1931.

• MARCETTA, MILAN — *see page 1265*

• MARCH, MUSH
Mush (Harold) March
RW – R. 5'5", 154 lbs. b: Silton, Sask., 10/18/1908. Deceased.

Season	Club	League	GP	G	A	Pts	AG	AA	APts	PIM	GP	G	A	Pts	PIM
1925-26	Regina Falcons	City Jr.	8	*10	*7	*17	....	....	....	2	3	3	*2	5	4
1926-27	Regina Falcons	City Jr.	5	*7	0	*7	....	....	....	4	....	....	....	....	....
1927-28	Regina Monarchs	SJHL	5	*13	*5	*18	....	....	....	*17	13	*39	3	*42	10
1928-29	**Chicago Black Hawks**	**NHL**	**35**	**3**	**3**	**6**	**12**	**27**	**39**	**6**	....	....	....	....	....
1929-30	**Chicago Black Hawks**	**NHL**	**43**	**8**	**7**	**15**	**16**	**23**	**39**	**48**	....	....	....	....	....
1930-31	**Chicago Black Hawks**	**NHL**	**44**	**11**	**6**	**17**	**27**	**22**	**49**	**36**	**9**	**3**	**1**	**4**	**11**
1931-32	**Chicago Black Hawks**	**NHL**	**48**	**12**	**10**	**22**	**26**	**28**	**54**	**59**	**2**	**0**	**0**	**0**	**2**
1932-33	**Chicago Black Hawks**	**NHL**	**48**	**9**	**11**	**20**	**21**	**29**	**50**	**38**	....	....	....	....	....
1933-34	**Chicago Black Hawks**	**NHL**	**48**	**4**	**13**	**17**	**9**	**35**	**44**	**26**	**8**	**2**	**2**	**4**	**6**
1934-35	**Chicago Black Hawks**	**NHL**	**48**	**13**	**17**	**30**	**28**	**38**	**66**	**48**	**2**	**0**	**0**	**0**	**0**
1935-36	**Chicago Black Hawks**	**NHL**	**48**	**16**	**19**	**35**	**40**	**46**	**86**	**42**	**2**	**2**	**3**	**5**	**0**
1936-37	**Chicago Black Hawks**	**NHL**	**37**	**11**	**6**	**17**	**24**	**14**	**38**	**31**	....	....	....	....	....
1937-38	**Chicago Black Hawks**	**NHL**	**41**	**11**	**17**	**28**	**23**	**35**	**58**	**16**	**9**	**2**	**4**	**6**	**12**
1938-39	**Chicago Black Hawks**	**NHL**	**46**	**10**	**11**	**21**	**21**	**20**	**41**	**29**	....	....	....	....	....
1939-40	**Chicago Black Hawks**	**NHL**	**45**	**9**	**14**	**23**	**19**	**28**	**47**	**49**	**2**	**1**	**0**	**1**	**2**
1940-41	**Chicago Black Hawks**	**NHL**	**44**	**8**	**9**	**17**	**16**	**16**	**32**	**16**	**4**	**2**	**3**	**5**	**0**
1941-42	**Chicago Black Hawks**	**NHL**	**48**	**6**	**26**	**32**	**10**	**40**	**50**	**22**	**3**	**0**	**2**	**2**	**4**
1942-43	**Chicago Black Hawks**	**NHL**	**50**	**7**	**29**	**36**	**10**	**37**	**47**	**46**	....	....	....	....	....
1943-44	**Chicago Black Hawks**	**NHL**	**48**	**10**	**27**	**37**	**13**	**33**	**46**	**16**	**4**	**0**	**0**	**0**	**4**
1944-45	**Chicago Black Hawks**	**NHL**	**38**	**5**	**5**	**10**	**7**	**8**	**15**	**12**	....	....	....	....	....
	NHL Totals		**759**	**153**	**230**	**383**	**322**	**479**	**801**	**540**	**45**	**12**	**15**	**27**	**41**

Played in NHL All-Star Game (1937)

• MARCON, LOU
Lou Marcon
D – R. 5'9", 168 lbs. b: Fort William, Ont., 5/28/1935.

Season	Club	League	GP	G	A	Pts	AG	AA	APts	PIM	GP	G	A	Pts	PIM
1951-52	Fort William Canadians	TBJHL	28	1	0	1	....	....	....	10	....	....	....	....	....
1952-53	Fort William Canadians	TBJHL	30	1	2	3	....	....	....	20	6	0	2	2	4
1953-54	Fort William Canadians	TBJHL	30	1	5	6	....	....	....	48	4	0	0	0	2
1954-55	Fort William Canadians	TBJHL	STATISTICS NOT AVAILABLE												
1955-56	Cincinnati Mohawks	IHL	59	2	22	24	....	....	....	113	8	1	1	2	8
1956-57	Cincinnati Mohawks	IHL	55	0	17	17	....	....	....	49	7	0	1	1	4
	Rochester Americans	AHL	2	0	0	0	....	....	....	0	....	....	....	....	....
1957-58	Montreal Royals	QHL	3	0	0	0	....	....	....	2	....	....	....	....	....
	Cincinnati Mohawks	IHL	64	7	31	38	....	....	....	89	4	0	1	1	2
1958-59	**Detroit Red Wings**	**NHL**	**21**	**0**	**1**	**1**	**0**	**1**	**1**	**12**	....	....	....	....	....
	Edmonton Flyers	WHL	47	1	6	7	....	....	....	66	....	....	....	....	....
1959-60	**Detroit Red Wings**	**NHL**	**38**	**0**	**3**	**3**	**0**	**3**	**3**	**30**	....	....	....	....	....
	Edmonton Flyers	WHL	15	0	9	9	....	....	....	28	4	0	0	0	*22
1960-61	Edmonton Flyers	WHL	55	7	11	18	....	....	....	91	....	....	....	....	....
1961-62	Edmonton Flyers	WHL	62	2	15	17	....	....	....	68	12	1	2	3	23
1962-63	**Detroit Red Wings**	**NHL**	**1**	**0**	**0**	**0**	**0**	**0**	**0**	**0**	....	....	....	....	....
	Edmonton Flyers	WHL	28	5	8	13	....	....	....	61	....	....	....	....	....
	Pittsburgh Hornets	AHL	35	0	3	3	....	....	....	105	....	....	....	....	....
1963-64	Pittsburgh Hornets	AHL	49	3	15	18	....	....	....	108	5	0	0	0	15
1964-65	Pittsburgh Hornets	AHL	62	2	11	13	....	....	....	190	4	0	1	1	6
1965-66	Memphis Wings	CHL	59	1	9	10	....	....	....	107	....	....	....	....	....
	Pittsburgh Hornets	AHL	11	0	2	2	....	....	....	25	3	0	0	0	12
1966-67	Memphis Wings	CHL	67	4	10	14	....	....	....	206	7	1	2	3	25
1967-68	Fort Worth Wings	CHL	66	0	7	7	....	....	....	157	13	0	0	0	32
1968-69	Thunder Bay Twins	USHL	59	2	22	24	....	....	....	113	8	1	1	2	8
1969-70			DID NOT PLAY												
1970-71			DID NOT PLAY												
1971-72	Thunder Bay Twins	USHL	DID NOT PLAY – COACHING												
1972-73	Thunder Bay Twins	USHL	22	1	5	6	....	....	....	20	....	....	....	....	....
	NHL Totals		**60**	**0**	**4**	**4**	**0**	**4**	**4**	**42**	....	....	....	....	....

IHL Second All-Star Team (1957) • IHL First All-Star Team (1958)

Claimed by **Detroit** from **Montreal** in Intra-League Draft, June, 1958.

• MARCOTTE, DON — *see page 1267*

• MARIO, FRANK
Frank Mario
C – L. 5'8", 170 lbs. b: Esterhazy, Sask., 2/25/1921. Deceased.

Season	Club	League	GP	G	A	Pts	AG	AA	APts	PIM	GP	G	A	Pts	PIM
			REGULAR SEASON								PLAYOFFS				
1939-40	Regina Abbots	SJHL	12	8	9	17	....	....	....	6	2	0	1	1	0
1940-41	Regina Rangers	SSHL	32	13	19	32	....	....	....	26	8	4	5	9	9
1941-42	**Boston Bruins**	**NHL**	**9**	**1**	**1**	**2**	**2**	**2**	**4**	**0**	....	....	....	....	....
	Hershey Bears	AHL	42	12	27	39	....	....	....	38	5	1	1	2	0
1942-43	Cornwall Army	Ott-Sr.	32	15	27	42	....	....	....	51	6	0	2	2	12
1943-44			MILITARY SERVICE												
1944-45	**Boston Bruins**	**NHL**	**44**	**8**	**18**	**26**	**11**	**29**	**40**	**24**	....	....	....	....	....
1945-46	Hershey Bears	AHL	37	6	24	30	....	....	....	29	3	1	0	1	2
1946-47	Hershey Bears	AHL	64	24	47	71	....	....	....	65	11	5	*13	*18	7
1947-48	Hershey Bears	AHL	68	30	36	66	....	....	....	32	2	1	0	1	0
1948-49	Hershey Bears	AHL	68	26	46	72	....	....	....	27	11	2	3	5	0
1949-50	Hershey Bears	AHL	48	9	25	34	....	....	....	25	....	....	....	....	....
1950-51	Hershey Bears	AHL	58	21	38	59	....	....	....	40	6	0	4	4	0
1951-52	Hershey Bears	AHL	68	15	38	53	....	....	....	26	5	0	4	4	0
1952-53	Quebec Aces	QSHL	55	8	22	30	....	....	....	30	22	3	9	12	2
1953-54	Cornwall Royals	QSHL	DID NOT PLAY – COACHING												
	NHL Totals		**53**	**9**	**19**	**28**	**13**	**31**	**44**	**24**	....	....	....	....	....

Signed as a free agent by **Boston**, October 21, 1941.

• MARIUCCI, JOHN
John Mariucci **HHOF, USHOF**
D – L. 5'10", 200 lbs. b: Eveleth, MN, 5/8/1916. d: 3/23/1987.

Season	Club	League	GP	G	A	Pts	AG	AA	APts	PIM	GP	G	A	Pts	PIM
1939-40	University of Minnesota	WIHA	STATISTICS NOT AVAILABLE												
1940-41	**Chicago Black Hawks**	**NHL**	**23**	**0**	**5**	**5**	**0**	**9**	**9**	**33**	**5**	**0**	**2**	**2**	**16**
	Providence Reds	AHL	17	3	3	6	....	....	....	15	....	....	....	....	....
1941-42	**Chicago Black Hawks**	**NHL**	**47**	**5**	**8**	**13**	**9**	**12**	**21**	**44**	**3**	**0**	**0**	**0**	**0**
1942-43	Coast Guard Clippers	EHL	45	23	23	46	....	....	....	67	12	4	8	12	14
1943-44	Coast Guard Clippers	....	34	11	16	27	....	....	....	*29	12	3	8	11	18
1944-45			MILITARY SERVICE												
1945-46	**Chicago Black Hawks**	**NHL**	**50**	**3**	**8**	**11**	**5**	**15**	**20**	**58**	**4**	**0**	**1**	**1**	**10**
1946-47	**Chicago Black Hawks**	**NHL**	**52**	**2**	**9**	**11**	**3**	**13**	**16**	**110**	....	....	....	....	....
1947-48	**Chicago Black Hawks**	**NHL**	**51**	**1**	**4**	**5**	**1**	**6**	**7**	**63**	....	....	....	....	....
1948-49	St. Louis Flyers	AHL	68	12	30	42	....	....	....	74	7	0	1	1	12
1949-50	Minneapolis Millers	USHL	67	8	24	32	....	....	....	87	7	0	2	2	23
1950-51	St. Paul Saints	USHL	59	2	28	30	....	....	....	85	4	0	0	0	0
1951-52	Minneapolis Millers	AAHL	39	18	31	49	....	....	....	45	....	....	....	....	....
1952-53	University of Minesota	WIHA	DID NOT PLAY – COACHING												
	NHL Totals		**223**	**11**	**34**	**45**	**18**	**55**	**73**	**308**	**12**	**0**	**3**	**3**	**26**

EHL First All-Star Team (1943) • Won Lester Patrick Trophy (1977)

• **Coast Guard Cutters** played exhibition season only in 1943-44. Traded to **St. Louis** (AHL) by **Chicago** for cash, September, 1948.

• MARKER, GUS
Gus (August) Marker
RW – R. 5'9", 162 lbs. b: Wetaskiwin, Alberta, 8/1/1907. Deceased.

Season	Club	League	GP	G	A	Pts	AG	AA	APts	PIM	GP	G	A	Pts	PIM
1928-29	Tulsa Oilers	AHA	36	10	5	15	....	....	....	39	4	1	0	1	2
1929-30	Tulsa Oilers	AHA	48	13	7	20	....	....	....	31	9	1	1	2	2
1930-31	Tulsa Oilers	AHA	48	21	11	32	....	....	....	42	4	1	1	2	8
1931-32	Tulsa Oilers	AHA	44	11	7	18	....	....	....	20	....	....	....	....	....
1932-33	**Detroit Red Wings**	**NHL**	**13**	**1**	**1**	**2**	**2**	**3**	**5**	**8**	....	....	....	....	....
	Detroit Olympics	IAHL	27	6	7	13	....	....	....	31	....	....	....	....	....
1933-34	**Detroit Red Wings**	**NHL**	**7**	**1**	**0**	**1**	**2**	**0**	**2**	**2**	**4**	**0**	**0**	**0**	**2**
	Detroit Olympics	IAHL	37	13	13	26	....	....	....	48	6	3	*6	*9	2
1934-35	**Montreal Maroons**	**NHL**	**44**	**11**	**4**	**15**	**23**	**9**	**32**	**18**	**7**	**1**	**1**	**2**	**4**
	Windsor Bulldogs	IAHL	3	1	2	3	....	....	....	2	....	....	....	....	....
1935-36	**Montreal Maroons**	**NHL**	**48**	**7**	**12**	**19**	**17**	**29**	**46**	**10**	**3**	**1**	**0**	**1**	**2**
1936-37	**Montreal Maroons**	**NHL**	**47**	**10**	**12**	**22**	**22**	**28**	**50**	**22**	**5**	**0**	**1**	**1**	**0**
1937-38	**Montreal Maroons**	**NHL**	**48**	**9**	**15**	**24**	**19**	**31**	**50**	**35**	....	....	....	....	....
1938-39	**Toronto Maple Leafs**	**NHL**	**29**	**9**	**6**	**15**	**19**	**11**	**30**	**11**	**10**	**2**	**2**	**4**	**0**
1939-40	**Toronto Maple Leafs**	**NHL**	**42**	**10**	**9**	**19**	**21**	**18**	**39**	**15**	**10**	**1**	**3**	**4**	**23**
1940-41	**Toronto Maple Leafs**	**NHL**	**27**	**4**	**5**	**9**	**8**	**9**	**17**	**10**	**7**	**0**	**0**	**0**	**5**
1941-42	**Brooklyn Americans**	**NHL**	**17**	**2**	**5**	**7**	**3**	**8**	**11**	**2**	....	....	....	....	....
	Springfield Indians	AHL	16	10	6	16	....	....	....	6	....	....	....	....	....
1942-43	Kingston Frontenacs	Ott Sr.	4	0	4	4	....	....	....	2	4	2	5	7	0
	NHL Totals		**322**	**64**	**69**	**133**	**136**	**146**	**282**	**133**	**40**	**5**	**7**	**12**	**36**

NHL rights transferred to **Detroit** from **Chicago Shamrocks** (AHA) after AHA club owners purchased Detroit (NHL and IAHL) franchises, September 2, 1932. Traded to **Montreal Maroons** by **Detroit** for Wally Kilrea, September 23, 1934. Traded to **Toronto** by **Montreal Maroons** for $4,000, November 3, 1938. Loaned to **Brooklyn** by **Toronto** with Red Heron and Nick Knott for Lorne Carr, October 30, 1941.

• MARKLE, JACK
Jack Markle
RW – R. 5'9", 155 lbs. b: Thessalon, Ont., 5/15/1907. d: 6/25/1956.

Season	Club	League	GP	G	A	Pts	AG	AA	APts	PIM	GP	G	A	Pts	PIM
1923-24	Owen Sound Greys	OHA	2	0	0	0	....	....	....	0	....	....	....	....	....
1925-26	Owen Sound Greys	OHA	12	4	1	5	....	....	....	....	8	5	0	5	7
1926-27	Owen Sound Greys	OHA	16	*31	8	*39	....	....	....	....	....	....	....	....	....
1927-28	London Panthers	Can-Pro	29	3	1	4	....	....	....	60	....	....	....	....	....
1928-29	Hamilton Tigers	Can-Pro	36	12	4	16	....	....	....	10	....	....	....	....	....
1929-29	Hamilton Tigers	IAHL	42	12	10	22	....	....	....	21	....	....	....	....	....
1930-31	Syracuse Stars	IAHL	48	18	20	38	....	....	....	4	....	....	....	....	....
1931-32	Syracuse Stars	IAHL	48	20	13	33	....	....	....	10	....	....	....	....	....
1932-33	Syracuse Stars	IAHL	30	8	16	24	....	....	....	6	6	1	2	3	0
1933-34	Syracuse Stars	IAHL	42	14	22	36	....	....	....	16	6	4	2	6	2
1934-35	Syracuse Stars	IAHL	44	23	20	*43	....	....	....	4	2	0	0	0	5
1935-36	**Toronto Maple Leafs**	**NHL**	**8**	**0**	**1**	**1**	**0**	**2**	**2**	**0**	....	....	....	....	....
	Syracuse Stars	IAHL	43	27	24	51	....	....	....	4	3	0	1	1	0
1936-37	Syracuse Stars	AHL	48	21	*39	*60	....	....	....	2	9	2	4	6	0
1937-38	Syracuse Stars	AHL	48	22	32	*54	....	....	....	8	8	*5	1	6	0
1938-39	Syracuse Stars	AHL	53	16	32	48	....	....	....	4	3	2	1	3	0
1939-40	Syracuse Stars	AHL	45	9	24	33	....	....	....	6	....	....	....	....	....
	NHL Totals		**8**	**0**	**1**	**1**	**0**	**2**	**2**	**0**	....	....	....	....	....

IAHL First All-Star Team (1936) • AHL Second All-Star Team (1938)

Loaned to **Toronto** by **Syracuse** (IAHL), January 20, 1936.

• MARKS, JACK Jack Marks
LW/D – L. 6', 180 lbs. b: Brantford, Ontario, 6/11/1885. d: 8/20/1945.

Season	Club	League	GP	G	A	Pts	AG	AA	APts	PIM	GP	G	A	Pts	PIM
			REGULAR SEASON								PLAYOFFS				
1904-05	Brockville Hockey Club	FAHL	8	6	0	6									
1905-06	Brockville Hockey Club	FAHL	6	1	0	1									
1906-07	New Glasgow Seniors	MIHL									1	0	0	0	2
	Canadian Soo	IHL	14	13	10	23				26					
1907-08	Brantford Professionals	OPHL	10	7	0	7									
	Toronto Professionals	OPHL									1	0	0	0	0
	Pittsburgh Lycums	WPHL	STATISTICS NOT AVAILABLE												
1908-09	Brantford Hockey Club	OPHL	7	6	0	6				16	2	0	0	0	3
1909-10	Brantford Hockey Club	OPHL	1	5	0	5									
1910-11	Chicago All-Americans	USAHA	STATISTICS NOT AVAILABLE												
1911-12	Quebec Bulldogs	NHA	10	4	0	4				10	2	0	0	0	2
1912-13	Quebec Bulldogs	NHA	19	18	0	18				39	1	2	0	2	0
1913-14	Quebec Bulldogs	NHA	20	9	6	15				32					
1914-15	Quebec Bulldogs	NHA	17	7	4	11				49					
1915-16	Quebec Bulldogs	NHA	23	12	0	12				40					
1916-17	Quebec Bulldogs	NHA	17	0	1	1				6					
1917-18	**Montreal Wanderers**	**NHL**	**1**	**0**	**0**	**0**	**0**	**0**	**0**	**0**					
	Toronto Arenas	**NHL**	**5**	**0**	**0**	**0**	**0**	**0**	**0**	**0**					
1918-19			DID NOT PLAY												
1919-20	**Quebec Bulldogs**	**NHL**	**1**	**0**	**0**	**0**	**0**	**0**	**0**	**4**					
	NHL Totals		**7**	**0**	**0**	**0**	**0**	**0**	**0**	**4**					
	Other Major League Totals		138	81	21	102				218	6	2	0	2	5

IHL Second All-Star Team (1907)

Rights retained by **Montreal Wanderers** after NHA folded, November 26, 1917. Claimed by **Montreal Canadiens** from **Montreal Wanderers** in Dispersal Draft, January 4, 1918. Loaned to **Toronto Arenas** by **Montreal Canadiens**, January 4, 1918. NHL rights transferred to **Quebec** from **Montreal Canadiens** when Quebec franchise returned to NHL, November 25, 1919.

• MAROTTE, GILLES — *see page 1269*

• MARQUESS, MARK Mark Marquess
RW – R. 5'8", 160 lbs. b: Bassano, Alta., 3/26/1924.

Season	Club	League	GP	G	A	Pts	AG	AA	APts	PIM	GP	G	A	Pts	PIM
1944-45	Moose Jaw Canucks	SJHL	15	19	*19	*38				4	20	*26	9	35	8
1945-46	Saskatoon Elks	WCSHL	4	0	2	2				4					
	Boston Olympics	EHL	36	18	22	40				10	12	7	6	13	2
1946-47	**Boston Bruins**	**NHL**	**27**	**5**	**4**	**9**	**7**	**6**	**13**	**6**	**4**	**0**	**0**	**0**	**0**
	Hershey Bears	AHL	27	10	13	23				14					
1947-48	Hershey Bears	AHL	63	21	27	48				25	2	0	1	1	2
1948-49	Hershey Bears	AHL	58	25	23	48				33	11	3	8	11	4
1949-50	Hershey Bears	AHL	70	12	22	34				38					
1950-51	Hershey Bears	AHL	57	9	27	36				32	5	1	2	3	2
1951-52	Tacoma Rockets	PCHL	70	17	38	55				67	7	6	2	8	8
1952-53	Tacoma Rockets	WHL	70	25	30	55				34					
1953-54	Seattle Bombers	WHL	70	28	23	51				48					
1954-55	Victoria Cougars	WHL	70	12	20	32				32	5	1	0	1	4
1955-56	Victoria–Vancouver	WHL	65	11	25	36				51	15	3	6	9	6
1956-57	Vernon–Kamloops	OSHL	39	15	28	43				23	5	0	3	3	2
1957-58	Kamloops Chiefs	OSHL	47	13	26	39				19	15	*8	4	12	6
	NHL Totals		**27**	**5**	**4**	**9**	**7**	**6**	**13**	**6**	**4**	**0**	**0**	**0**	**0**

• MARSHALL, BERT — *see page 1270*

• MARSHALL, DON — *see page 1271*

• MARSHALL, WILLIE Willie "The Whip" Marshall
C – L. 5'10", 165 lbs. b: Kirkland Lake, Ont., 12/1/1931.

Season	Club	League	GP	G	A	Pts	AG	AA	APts	PIM	GP	G	A	Pts	PIM
1948-49	St. Michael's Majors	OHA	32	13	18	31				14					
1949-50	St. Michael's Majors	OHA	48	39	27	66				32	5	6	1	7	10
1950-51	Toronto Marlboros	OHA	43	29	30	59				20					
	Guelph Biltmores	OHA	4	4	3	7				2					
	St. Michael's Majors	OHA	2	1	1	2				0	6	1	1	2	2
1951-52	Charlottetown Islanders	MMHL	84	50	44	94				89	4	0	2	2	0
1952-53	**Toronto Maple Leafs**	**NHL**	**2**	**0**	**0**	**0**	**0**	**0**	**0**	**0**					
	Pittsburgh Hornets	AHL	62	27	39	66				58	10	1	*8	9	13
1953-54	Pittsburgh Hornets	AHL	61	28	45	73				41	5	1	4	5	2
1954-55	**Toronto Maple Leafs**	**NHL**	**16**	**1**	**4**	**5**	**1**	**5**	**6**	**0**					
	Pittsburgh Hornets	AHL	46	23	25	48				37	10	*9	7	*16	6
1955-56	**Toronto Maple Leafs**	**NHL**	**6**	**0**	**0**	**0**	**0**	**0**	**0**	**0**					
	Pittsburgh Hornets	AHL	58	45	52	97				47	4	2	1	3	0
1956-57	Hershey Bears	AHL	64	35	59	94				18	7	3	7	10	4
1957-58	Hershey Bears	AHL	68	40	*64	*104				56	11	*10	9	*19	6
1958-59	**Toronto Maple Leafs**	**NHL**	**9**	**0**	**1**	**1**	**0**	**1**	**1**	**2**					
	Rochester–Hershey	AHL	56	29	32	61				10	9	*5	2	7	0
1959-60	Hershey Bears	AHL	72	38	40	78				99					
1960-61	Hershey Bears	AHL	56	25	44	69				36	7	3	5	8	2
1961-62	Hershey Bears	AHL	70	30	65	95				24	7	0	6	6	0
1962-63	Hershey Bears	AHL	72	36	56	92				12	15	3	7	10	10
1963-64	Providence Reds	AHL	72	33	50	83				18	3	2	3	5	0
1964-65	Providence Reds	AHL	69	12	44	56				12					
1965-66	Providence Reds	AHL	70	13	27	40				8					
1966-67	Baltimore Clippers	AHL	68	33	56	89				22	9	6	7	13	0
1967-68	Baltimore Clippers	AHL	51	24	41	65				2					
1968-69	Baltimore Clippers	AHL	74	26	52	78				18	4	1	2	3	0
1969-70	Baltimore Clippers	AHL	42	9	19	28				0	5	2	2	4	0
1970-71	Baltimore Clippers	AHL	64	15	40	55				0	6	0	1	1	0
1971-72	Rochester Americans	AHL	10	2	2	4				2					
	Toledo Hornets	IHL	46	15	32	47				89	4	0	2	2	0
	NHL Totals		**33**	**1**	**5**	**6**	**1**	**6**	**7**	**2**					

AHL First All-Star Team (1956, 1958) • Won John B. Sollenberger Trophy (Top Scorer - AHL) (1958) • AHL Second All-Star Team (1962)

Traded to **Hershey** (AHL) by **Toronto** for cash, July, 1956. Traded to **Toronto** by **Hershey** (AHL) for Mike Nykoluk, Wally Boyer and Ron Hurst, April 29, 1958. Traded to **Hershey** (AHL) by **Toronto** for Gerry Ehman, December, 1958. Traded to **Providence** (AHL) by **Hershey** (AHL) for Dan Poliziani, June, 1963. Traded to **Baltimore** (AHL) by **Providence** (AHL) with Aldo Guidolin and Jim Bartlett for Ken Stephanson, Ed Lawson and Mike Corbett, June, 1966.

• MARTIN, CLARE Clare Martin
D – R. 5'11", 180 lbs. b: Waterloo, Ont., 2/25/1922. Deceased.

Season	Club	League	GP	G	A	Pts	AG	AA	APts	PIM	GP	G	A	Pts	PIM
1940-41	Boston Olympics	EHL	9	0	1	1				4					
	Guelph Biltmores	OHA	16	4	4	8				28	5	1	4	5	6
1941-42	**Boston Bruins**	**NHL**	**13**	**0**	**1**	**1**	**0**	**2**	**2**	**4**	**5**	**0**	**0**	**0**	**0**
	Boston Olympics	EHL	43	11	18	29				31	1	0	1	1	0
1942-43	Ottawa Postal Corps	City Sr.	9	3	2	5				11					
1943-44	Montreal Royals	QSHL	3	0	2	2				4	6	1	1	2	0
1944-45	Halifax Navy	City Sr.									5	0	3	3	2
1945-46	Boston Olympics	EHL	51	19	22	41				26	12	4	10	14	2
1946-47	**Boston Bruins**	**NHL**	**6**	**3**	**0**	**3**	**4**	**0**	**4**	**0**	**5**	**0**	**1**	**1**	**0**
	Hershey Bears	AHL	42	4	11	15				38					
1947-48	**Boston Bruins**	**NHL**	**59**	**5**	**13**	**18**	**7**	**19**	**26**	**34**	**5**	**0**	**0**	**0**	**6**
1948-49	Hershey Bears	AHL	26	3	13	16				18	11	1	7	8	10
1949-50	**Detroit Red Wings**	**NHL**	**64**	**2**	**5**	**7**	**3**	**6**	**9**	**14**	**10**	**0**	**1**	**1**	**0**
1950-51	**Detroit Red Wings**	**NHL**	**50**	**1**	**6**	**7**	**1**	**8**	**9**	**12**	**2**	**0**	**0**	**0**	**0**
1951-52	**Chicago Black Hawks**	**NHL**	**31**	**1**	**2**	**3**	**1**	**3**	**4**	**8**					
	New York Rangers	**NHL**	**14**	**0**	**1**	**1**	**0**	**1**	**1**	**6**					
	Cincinnati Mohawks	AHL	17	0	3	3				10	7	1	1	2	12
1952-53	Kitchener Dutchmen	OHA Sr.	46	5	19	24				60	11	4	3	7	18
1953-54	Kitchener Dutchmen	OHA Sr.	37	9	16	25				36	8	1	0	1	5
1954-55	Kitchener Dutchmen	OHA Sr.	20	3	5	8				18	10	1	2	3	6
	NHL Totals		**237**	**12**	**28**	**40**	**16**	**39**	**55**	**78**	**27**	**0**	**2**	**2**	**6**

Traded to **Detroit** by **Boston** with Pete Babando, Lloyd Durham and Jimmy Peters Sr. for Bill Quackenbush and Pete Horeck, August 16, 1949. Traded to **Chicago** by **Detroit** with George Gee, Jimmy Peters Sr., Rags Raglin, Max McNab and Jim McFadden for Hugh Coflin and $75,000, August 20, 1951. Traded to **NY Rangers** by **Chicago** for cash, December 28, 1951.

• MARTIN, FRANK Frank Martin
D – L. 6'2", 190 lbs. b: Cayuga, Ont., 5/1/1933.

Season	Club	League	GP	G	A	Pts	AG	AA	APts	PIM	GP	G	A	Pts	PIM
1949-50	St. Catharines Teepees	OHA	44	5	13	18				44	5	1	3	4	10
1950-51	St. Catharines Teepees	OHA	43	5	15	20				53	9	2	2	4	2
1951-52	St. Catharines Teepees	OHA	54	25	30	55				40	12	1	2	3	6
1952-53	**Boston Bruins**	**NHL**	**14**	**0**	**2**	**2**	**0**	**3**	**3**	**6**	**6**	**0**	**1**	**1**	**2**
	Hershey Bears	AHL	41	5	4	9				14	3	0	1	1	0
1953-54	**Boston Bruins**	**NHL**	**68**	**3**	**17**	**20**	**5**	**23**	**28**	**38**	**4**	**0**	**1**	**1**	**0**
1954-55	**Chicago Black Hawks**	**NHL**	**66**	**4**	**8**	**12**	**6**	**10**	**16**	**35**					
1955-56	**Chicago Black Hawks**	**NHL**	**61**	**3**	**11**	**14**	**4**	**14**	**18**	**21**					
1956-57	**Chicago Black Hawks**	**NHL**	**70**	**1**	**8**	**9**	**1**	**9**	**10**	**12**					
1957-58	**Chicago Black Hawks**	**NHL**	**3**	**0**	**0**	**0**	**0**	**0**	**0**	**10**					
	Buffalo Bisons	AHL	52	2	20	22				14					
1958-59	Buffalo Bisons	AHL	65	4	26	30				20	8	0	6	6	5
1959-60	Buffalo Bisons	AHL	72	4	21	25				15					
1960-61	Quebec Aces	AHL	67	3	16	19				32					
1961-62	Quebec Aces	AHL	58	4	14	18				18					
1962-63	Quebec Aces	AHL	67	4	30	34				34					
1963-64	Quebec Aces	AHL	71	5	18	23				36	9	0	1	1	2
1964-65	Cleveland Barons	AHL	67	7	23	30				22					
	NHL Totals		**282**	**11**	**46**	**57**	**16**	**59**	**75**	**122**	**10**	**0**	**2**	**2**	**2**

AHL Second All-Star Team (1959)

Played in NHL All-Star Game (1955)

Traded to **Chicago** by **Boston** for Murray Costello, October 4, 1954. Traded to **Buffalo** by **Chicago** (AHL) with Wally Hergishimer for Ken Wharram, June, 1958. Traded to **Quebec** (AHL) by **Buffalo** (AHL) for cash, July, 1960.

• MARTIN, JACK Jack Martin
C – L. 5'11", 184 lbs. b: St. Catharines, Ont., 11/29/1940.

Season	Club	League	GP	G	A	Pts	AG	AA	APts	PIM	GP	G	A	Pts	PIM
1957-58	St. Michael's Majors	OHA	50	11	15	26				32	9	2	4	6	10
1958-59	Toronto Marlboros	OHA	51	15	14	29				62	5	3	0	3	13
1959-60	Toronto Marlboros	OHA	42	30	30	60				63	4	1	3	4	10
	Sudbury Wolves	EPHL									4	1	0	1	2
1960-61	**Toronto Maple Leafs**	**NHL**	**1**	**0**	**0**	**0**	**0**	**0**	**0**	**0**					
	Sudbury Wolves	EPHL	44	9	12	21				22					
1961-62	Soo Thunderbirds	EPHL	10	1	1	2				8					
	Pittsburgh Hornets	AHL	4	0	1	1				0					
	San Francisco Seals	WHL	28	3	6	9				12					
1962-63	Charlotte Checkers	EHL	67	32	33	65				57	10	2	6	8	4
1963-64	Nashville Dixie Flyers	EHL	71	47	60	107				10	2	1	0	1	2
1964-65	Knoxville Knights	EHL	67	39	69	108				8	10	5	5	10	4
	NHL Totals		**1**	**0**	**0**	**0**	**0**	**0**	**0**	**0**					

• MARTIN, PIT — *see page 1272*

• MARTIN, RON Ron Martin
RW – R. 5'6", 130 lbs. b: Calgary, Alta., 8/22/1909. d: 2/7/1971.

Season	Club	League	GP	G	A	Pts	AG	AA	APts	PIM	GP	G	A	Pts	PIM
1925-26	Calgary Canadiens	City Jr.	STATISTICS NOT AVAILABLE												
1926-27	Calgary Tigers	PrHL	32	13	5	18				20	2	1	0	1	0
1927-28	Kitchener–Niagara Falls	Can-Pro	35	13	5	18				20					
1928-29	Toronto–Buffalo	Can-Pro	43	11	2	13				26					
1929-30	Buffalo Bisons	IAHL	40	22	3	25				33	7	2	1	3	13
1930-31	Buffalo Bisons	IAHL	48	28	13	41				24	6	1	3	4	0
1931-32	Buffalo Bisons	IAHL	46	15	18	33				42	6	*3	2	5	2
1932-33	**New York Americans**	**NHL**	**47**	**5**	**7**	**12**	**12**	**18**	**30**	**6**					
1933-34	**New York Americans**	**NHL**	**47**	**8**	**9**	**17**	**18**	**24**	**42**	**30**					
1934-35	Syracuse Stars	IAHL	43	6	12	18				18	2	0	1	1	2
1935-36	Edmonton–Portland	NWHL	40	11	13	24				13	5	*4	1	5	0
1936-37	Portland Buckaroos	PCHL	39	9	9	18				10	3	*3	*3	*6	2
1937-38	Portland Buckaroos	PCHL	41	6	15	21				16	2	2	0	2	7
1938-39	Portland Buckaroos	PCHL	43	18	18	36				10	5	3	0	3	2
1939-40	Portland Buckaroos	PCHL	39	14	11	25				12	5	1	2	3	2
1940-41	Portland Buckaroos	PCHL	41	8	8	16				18					
1941-42			MILITARY SERVICE												
1942-43			MILITARY SERVICE												
1943-44	Portland Decleros	NMHL	16	12	13	25				2					
	Portland Oilers	NMHL									2	3	1	4	0
	NHL Totals		**94**	**13**	**16**	**29**	**30**	**42**	**72**	**36**					

Claimed by **Detroit** from **Buffalo** (IAHL) in Inter-League Draft, May 9, 1931. Traded to **NY Americans** by **Detroit** for Doug Young, October 18, 1931. Traded to **Syracuse** (IAHL) by **NY Americans** with future considerations for Lorne Carr, November 5, 1934.

• MASNICK, PAUL   Paul Masnick
C – R. 5'9", 165 lbs. b: Regina, Sask., 4/14/1931.

Season	Club	League	GP	G	A	Pts	AG	AA	APts	PIM	GP	G	A	Pts	PIM
1948-49	Regina Pats	WCJHL	26	7	10	17	....	....	....	4	7	1	1	2	0
1949-50	Regina Pats	WCJHL	40	44	43	87	....	....	....	62	9	9	14	23	4
1950-51	**Montreal Canadiens**	**NHL**	**43**	**4**	**1**	**5**	**5**	**1**	**6**	**14**	**11**	**2**	**1**	**3**	**4**
	Cincinnati Mohawks	AHL	19	5	7	12	....	....	....	15	....	....	....	....	....
1951-52	**Montreal Canadiens**	**NHL**	**15**	**1**	**2**	**3**	**1**	**3**	**4**	**2**	**6**	**1**	**0**	**1**	**12**
	Buffalo–Cincinnati	AHL	31	8	20	28	....	....	....	23	7	0	4	4	4
1952-53	**Montreal Canadiens**	**NHL**	**53**	**5**	**7**	**12**	**8**	**10**	**18**	**44**	**6**	**1**	**0**	**1**	**7**
	Montreal Royals	QSHL	10	6	6	12	....	....	....	10	....	....	....	....	....
1953-54	**Montreal Canadiens**	**NHL**	**50**	**5**	**21**	**26**	**8**	**29**	**37**	**57**	**10**	**0**	**4**	**4**	**4**
	Montreal Royals	QHL	14	3	14	17	....	....	....	9	....	....	....	....	....
1954-55	**Montreal Canadiens**	**NHL**	**11**	**0**	**0**	**0**	**0**	**0**	**0**	**0**	....	....	....	....	....
	Chicago Black Hawks	**NHL**	**11**	**1**	**0**	**1**	**1**	**0**	**1**	**8**	....	....	....	....	....
	Montreal Canadiens	**NHL**	**8**	**0**	**1**	**1**	**0**	**1**	**1**	**0**	....	....	....	....	....
	Montreal Royals	QHL	27	10	13	23	....	....	....	14	14	2	9	11	14
1955-56	Winnipeg Warriors	WHL	62	29	39	68	....	....	....	37	14	*11	9	20	14
1956-57	Rochester Americans	AHL	64	24	38	62	....	....	....	46	10	5	5	10	17
1957-58	**Toronto Maple Leafs**	**NHL**	**41**	**2**	**9**	**11**	**3**	**10**	**13**	**14**	....	....	....	....	....
1958-59	Saskatoon Quakers	WHL	64	24	51	75	....	....	....	48	....	....	....	....	....
1959-60	Winnipeg–Victoria	WHL	68	16	29	45	....	....	....	16	11	2	5	7	2
1960-61	Victoria Cougars	WHL	11	0	0	0	....	....	....	16	....	....	....	....	....
	St. Paul Saints	IHL	30	12	23	35	....	....	....	20	9	5	4	9	7
1961-62	St. Paul Saints	IHL	60	31	59	90	....	....	....	34	11	2	6	8	12
1962-63	St. Paul Saints	IHL	31	11	21	32	....	....	....	4	....	....	....	....	....
	NHL Totals		**232**	**18**	**41**	**59**	**26**	**54**	**80**	**139**	**33**	**4**	**5**	**9**	**27**

Traded to **Chicago** by **Montreal** for loan of Al Dewsbury for the remainder of 1954-55 season, November 9, 1954. Traded to **Montreal** by **Chicago** for cash, December 10, 1954. Traded to **Toronto** by **Montreal** for cash, September 30, 1957.

• MASON, CHARLEY   Charley "Dutch" Mason
RW – R. 5'10", 160 lbs. b: Seaforth, Ont., 2/1/1912. d: 5/17/1971.

Season	Club	League	GP	G	A	Pts	AG	AA	APts	PIM	GP	G	A	Pts	PIM
1929-30	U. of Saskatchewan	City Sr.	STATISTICS NOT AVAILABLE												
1930-31	Saskatoon Wesleys	City Jr.	3	0	1	1	....	....	....	0	....	....	....	....	....
	U. of Saskatchewan	City Sr.	7	4	1	5	....	....	....	4	....	....	....	....	....
1931-32	Saskatoon Wesleys	City Jr.	4	4	1	5	....	....	....	2	....	....	....	....	....
	Saskatoon Crescents	City Sr.	16	9	2	11	....	....	....	2	4	0	0	0	0
1932-33	Saskatoon Crescents	City Jr.	29	13	7	20	....	....	....	6	....	....	....	....	....
1933-34	Vancouver Lions	NWHL	33	22	8	30	....	....	....	8	7	3	1	4	2
1934-35	**New York Rangers**	**NHL**	**46**	**5**	**9**	**14**	**11**	**20**	**31**	**14**	**4**	**0**	**1**	**1**	**0**
1935-36	**New York Rangers**	**NHL**	**28**	**1**	**5**	**6**	**2**	**12**	**14**	**30**	....	....	....	....	....
	Philadelphia Arrows	IAHL	21	8	7	15	....	....	....	9	4	1	0	1	0
1936-37	Philadelphia Arrows	AHL	48	24	15	39	....	....	....	17	6	1	2	3	4
1937-38	**New York Americans**	**NHL**	**2**	**0**	**0**	**0**	**0**	**0**	**0**	**0**	....	....	....	....	....
	Philadelphia Ramblers	AHL	45	24	20	44	....	....	....	11	5	1	1	2	2
1938-39	**Detroit Red Wings**	**NHL**	**6**	**0**	**1**	**1**	**0**	**2**	**2**	**0**	....	....	....	....	....
	Chicago Black Hawks	**NHL**	**13**	**1**	**3**	**4**	**2**	**6**	**8**	**0**	....	....	....	....	....
	Pittsburgh Hornets	AHL	25	8	16	24	....	....	....	4	....	....	....	....	....
1939-40	Cleveland Barons	AHL	40	12	12	24	....	....	....	15	....	....	....	....	....
1940-41	Buffalo–Springfield	AHL	44	17	18	35	....	....	....	14					
1941-42	Providence–Philadelphia	AHL	59	7	22	29	....	....	....	12	....	....	....	....	....
1942-43			DID NOT PLAY												
1943-44	Saskatoon Huskies	SJHL	DID NOT PLAY – COACHING												
	NHL Totals		**95**	**7**	**18**	**25**	**15**	**40**	**55**	**44**	**4**	**0**	**1**	**1**	**0**

AHL First All-Star Team (1938)

Traded to **NY Rangers** by **Vancouver** (NWHL) for cash, September 27, 1934. Traded to **NY Americans** by **NY Rangers** (Philadelphia-Can-Am) for cash with NY Rangers holding rights of recall, October 7, 1937. Traded to **Detroit** by **NY Rangers** for cash, October 12, 1938. Traded to **Chicago** by **Detroit** for Phil Besler, January 27, 1939. Traded to **Cleveland** (AHL) by **Chicago** with future considerations for Phil Hergesheimer, May 17, 1939.

• MASSECAR, GEORGE   George Massecar
LW – L. 5'9", 165 lbs. b: Waterford, Ont., 7/10/1904. d: 7/14/1957.

Season	Club	League	GP	G	A	Pts	AG	AA	APts	PIM	GP	G	A	Pts	PIM
1925-26	Niagara Falls Cataracts	OHA Sr.	19	4	3	7	....	....	....	10	....	....	....	....	....
1926-27	Niagara Falls Cataracts	Can-Pro	24	9	3	12	....	....	....	16	....	....	....	....	....
1927-28	Niagara Falls Cataracts	Can-Pro	40	6	3	9	....	....	....	25	....	....	....	....	....
1928-29	New Haven Eagles	Can-Am	40	8	1	9	....	....	....	39	2	0	0	0	4
1929-30	**New York Americans**	**NHL**	**43**	**7**	**3**	**10**	**14**	**10**	**24**	**18**	....	....	....	....	....
1930-31	**New York Americans**	**NHL**	**43**	**4**	**7**	**11**	**10**	**25**	**35**	**16**	....	....	....	....	....
1931-32	**New York Americans**	**NHL**	**14**	**1**	**1**	**2**	**2**	**3**	**5**	**12**	....	....	....	....	....
	Bronx Tigers	Can-Am	21	5	2	7	....	....	....	16	2	0	0	0	4
1932-33	St. Louis Flyers	AHA	45	14	*21	35	....	....	....	14	4	*4	0	4	8
1933-34	Detroit Olympics	IAHL	44	10	12	22	....	....	....	13	6	1	1	2	0
1934-35	Buffalo Bisons	IAHL	43	9	7	16	....	....	....	4	....	....	....	....	....
1935-36	Buffalo Bisons	IAHL	48	10	11	21	....	....	....	12	5	1	0	1	0
	NHL Totals		**100**	**12**	**11**	**23**	**26**	**38**	**64**	**46**	....	....	....	....	....

Traded to **NY Americans** by **New Haven** (Can-Am) for Babe Dye, November 13, 1929. Traded to **St. Louis** (AHA) by **NY Americans** for Walter Jackson, October 30, 1932. Traded to **Detroit** by **St. Louis** (AHA) for cash, April 25, 1933. Traded to **Buffalo** (IAHL) by **Detroit** (IAHL) for cash, October 31, 1934. Transferred to **Cleveland** (IAHL) after **Buffalo** (IAHL) franchise folded, December 10, 1936. Refused to report and retired.

• MATHERS, FRANK   Frank Mathers   HHOF
D – L. 6'1", 182 lbs. b: Winnipeg, Man., 3/29/1924.

Season	Club	League	GP	G	A	Pts	AG	AA	APts	PIM	GP	G	A	Pts	PIM
1942-43	Winnipeg Rangers	MJHL	10	7	8	15	....	....	....	0	....	....	....	....	....
1943-44	Regina Commandos	SJHL	4	5	5	10	....	....	....	2	1	2	3	5	0
1944-45			MILITARY SERVICE												
1945-46	Ottawa Senators	QSHL	27	3	9	12	....	....	....	10	4	2	0	2	8
1946-47	Ottawa Senators	QSHL	36	5	7	12	....	....	....	27	10	5	1	6	12
1947-48	Ottawa Senators	QSHL	44	11	23	34	....	....	....	30	26	9	*14	*23	30
1948-49	**Toronto Maple Leafs**	**NHL**	**15**	**1**	**2**	**3**	**2**	**3**	**5**	**2**	....	....	....	....	....
	Pittsburgh Hornets	AHL	46	7	23	30	....	....	....	50	....	....	....	....	....
1949-50	**Toronto Maple Leafs**	**NHL**	**6**	**0**	**1**	**1**	**0**	**1**	**1**	**2**	....	....	....	....	....
	Pittsburgh Hornets	AHL	58	3	20	23	....	....	....	28	....	....	....	....	....
1950-51	Pittsburgh Hornets	AHL	70	7	17	24	....	....	....	74	13	2	10	12	6
1951-52	**Toronto Maple Leafs**	**NHL**	**2**	**0**	**0**	**0**	**0**	**0**	**0**	**0**	....	....	....	....	....
	Pittsburgh Hornets	AHL	66	5	43	48	....	....	....	59	8	1	0	1	8
1952-53	Pittsburgh Hornets	AHL	55	8	26	34	....	....	....	46	10	1	4	5	18
1953-54	Pittsburgh Hornets	AHL	69	9	43	52	....	....	....	73	5	0	2	2	12
1954-55	Pittsburgh Hornets	AHL	62	10	30	40	....	....	....	38	10	2	3	5	0
1955-56	Pittsburgh Hornets	AHL	64	12	51	63	....	....	....	61	4	1	2	3	2
1956-57	Hershey Bears	AHL	49	1	15	16	....	....	....	51	7	1	2	3	6
1957-58	Hershey Bears	AHL	64	1	28	29	....	....	....	42	11	1	5	6	4
1958-59	Hershey Bears	AHL	64	1	22	23	....	....	....	62	3	0	1	1	0
1959-60	Hershey Bears	AHL	57	2	12	14	....	....	....	24	....	....	....	....	....
1960-61	Hershey Bears	AHL	62	1	7	8	....	....	....	22	8	0	5	5	2
1961-62	Hershey Bears	AHL	13	0	3	3	....	....	....	6	7	0	1	1	6
1962-63	Hershey Bears	AHL	DID NOT PLAY – COACHING												
	NHL Totals		**23**	**1**	**3**	**4**	**2**	**4**	**6**	**4**	....	....	....	....	....

AHL First All-Star Team (1952, 1953, 1954, 1955, 1956) • AHL Second All-Star Team (1958) • Won Lester Patrick Trophy (1987)

Played in NHL All-Star Game (1948)

Traded to **Toronto** by **NY Rangers** with Cal Gardner, Bil Juzda and Rene Trudell for Wally Stanowski and Elwyn Morris, June, 1948.

• MATTE, JOE   Joe Matte
D – R. 5'11", 165 lbs. b: Bourget, Ont., 3/6/1893. d: 6/13/1961.

Season	Club	League	GP	G	A	Pts	AG	AA	APts	PIM	GP	G	A	Pts	PIM
1913-14	Montreal Hochelaga	City Sr.	5	3	0	3	....	....	....	....	....	....	....	....	....
1914-15	Montreal Gaite Canadiens	City Sr.	STATISTICS NOT AVAILABLE												
1915-16	Montreal La Casquette	City Sr.	12	4	0	4	....	....	....	6	1	3	0	3	0
1916-17	Montreal La Casquette	City Sr.	10	*9	0	9	....	....	....	12	....	....	....	....	....
1917-18	Montreal Hochelaga	City Sr.	11	*23	3	*26	....	....	....	9	3	*6	1	*7	....
1918-19	Hamilton Tigers	OHA Sr.	8	12	5	17	....	....	....	....	6	4	1	5	....
1919-20	**Toronto St. Pats**	**NHL**	**17**	**8**	**3**	**11**	**18**	**20**	**38**	**19**	....	....	....	....	....
	Hamilton Tigers	OHA Sr.	1	0	1	1	....	....	....	0	....	....	....	....	....
1920-21	**Hamilton Tigers**	**NHL**	**21**	**6**	**9**	**15**	**15**	**81**	**96**	**29**	....	....	....	....	....
1921-22	**Hamilton Tigers**	**NHL**	**21**	**3**	**3**	**6**	**8**	**19**	**27**	**6**	....	....	....	....	....
1922-23	Saskatoon Sheiks	WCHL	29	14	6	20	....	....	....	25	....	....	....	....	....
1923-24	Vancouver Maroons	PCHA	29	11	4	15	....	....	....	14	7	2	1	3	6
1924-25	Vancouver Maroons	WCHL	24	8	1	9	....	....	....	20	....	....	....	....	....
1925-26	**Boston Bruins**	**NHL**	**3**	**0**	**0**	**0**	**0**	**0**	**0**	**0**	....	....	....	....	....
	Montreal Canadiens	**NHL**	**0**	**0**	**0**	**0**	**0**	**0**	**0**	**0**	....	....	....	....	....
	NHL Totals		**68**	**17**	**15**	**32**	**41**	**120**	**161**	**54**	....	....	....	....	....
	Other Major League Totals		82	33	11	44	....	....	....	59	7	2	1	3	6

Signed as a free agent by **Toronto St. Pats**, January 16, 1920. Traded to **Hamilton** by **Toronto St. Pats** with Goldie Prodgers for cash, November 27, 1920. Traded to **Saskatoon** (WCHL) by **Hamilton** for cash, October 1, 1922. Traded to **Vancouver** (PCHA) by **Saskatoon** (WCHL) for cash, October 30, 1923. Signed as a free agent by **Boston**, December 5, 1925. Claimed on waivers by **Montreal Canadiens** by **Boston**, January 15, 1926.

• MATTE, ROLAND JOSEPH   Roland Joseph (Joe) Matte
D – R. 5'11", 178 lbs. b: Bourget, Ont., 3/15/1909. Deceased.

Season	Club	League	GP	G	A	Pts	AG	AA	APts	PIM	GP	G	A	Pts	PIM
1928-29	Ottawa Shamrocks	City Jr.	STATISTICS NOT AVAILABLE												
1929-30	**Detroit Cougars**	**NHL**	**12**	**0**	**1**	**1**	**0**	**3**	**3**	**0**	....	....	....	....	....
	Detroit Olympics	IAHL	26	0	0	0	....	....	....	6	....	....	....	....	....
1930-31	Pittsburgh Yellowjackets	IAHL	3	1	0	1	....	....	....	0	....	....	....	....	....
	Niagara Falls Cataracts	OPHL	25	9	1	10	....	....	....	45	5	2	0	2	10
	Detroit Olympics	IAHL	2	0	0	0	....	....	....	0	....	....	....	....	....
1931-32	Pittsburgh Yellowjackets	IAHL	48	4	4	8	....	....	....	82	....	....	....	....	....
1932-33	Cleveland Indians	IAHL	34	3	4	7	....	....	....	34	....	....	....	....	....
1933-34	Cleveland Indians	IAHL	1	0	0	0	....	....	....	0	....	....	....	....	....
	St. Louis Flyers	AHA	48	11	3	14	....	....	....	78	7	0	0	0	12
1934-35	St. Louis Flyers	AHA	48	14	10	24	....	....	....	50	6	1	1	2	10
1935-36	St. Louis Flyers	AHA	41	5	8	13	....	....	....	38	8	1	0	1	13
1936-37	St. Louis Flyers	AHA	41	5	8	13	....	....	....	36	6	1	0	1	4
1937-38	St. Louis Flyers	AHA	48	15	17	32	....	....	....	45	7	0	3	3	4
1938-39	St. Louis Flyers	AHA	40	13	15	28	....	....	....	28	7	2	1	3	4
1939-40	St. Louis Flyers	AHA	48	13	15	28	....	....	....	46	5	0	1	1	12
1940-41	Kansas City Americans	AHA	44	9	3	12	....	....	....	22	8	1	2	3	16
1941-42	Kansas City Americans	AHL	50	4	6	10	....	....	....	41	6	0	1	1	2
1942-43	**Chicago Black Hawks**	**NHL**	**12**	**0**	**2**	**2**	**0**	**3**	**3**	**8**	....	....	....	....	....
	Cleveland Barons	AHL	25	2	5	7	....	....	....	2	3	0	1	1	0
	NHL Totals		**24**	**0**	**3**	**3**	**0**	**6**	**6**	**8**	....	....	....	....	....

AHA First All-Star Team (1935, 1938, 1939, 1940) • AHA Second All-Star Team (1936, 1937)

Signed as a free agent by **Detroit Cougars**, September 12, 1929. Signed as a free agent by **Chicago**, September, 1942.

• MATZ, JOHNNY Johnny Matz

C – R. b: Nebraska, USA, 6/1/1891. d: 12/21/1969.

			REGULAR SEASON								PLAYOFFS				
Season	Club	League	GP	G	A	Pts	AG	AA	APts	PIM	GP	G	A	Pts	PIM
1919-20	Edmonton Hustlers	Big 4	12	11	3	14	....	....	....	8	....	....	....	....	....
1920-21	Edmonton Dominos	Big 4	16	1	2	3	....	....	....	9	....	....	....	....	....
1921-22	Edmonton Eskimos	WCHL	24	4	1	5	....	....	....	2	2	0	0	0	0
1922-23	Edmonton Eskimos	WCHL	4	0	0	0	....	....	....	4	....	....	....	....	....
	Saskatoon Sheiks	WCHL	24	4	3	7	....	....	....	6	....	....	....	....	....
1923-24	Saskatoon Crescents	WCHL	24	2	1	3	....	....	....	4	....	....	....	....	....
1924-25	**Montreal Canadiens**	**NHL**	**30**	**3**	**2**	**5**	**10**	**26**	**36**	**0**	**5**	**0**	**0**	**0**	**2**
1925-26			DID NOT PLAY – INJURED												
1926-27	Moose Jaw Maroons	PrHL	32	1	10	11	....	....	....	62	....	....	....	....	....
1927-28	Moose Jaw Maroons	PrHL	28	3	3	6	....	....	....	44	....	....	....	....	....
	NHL Totals		**30**	**3**	**2**	**5**	**10**	**26**	**36**	**0**	**5**	**0**	**0**	**0**	**2**
	Other Major League Totals		76	10	5	15	....	....	....	16	2	0	0	0	0

Signed as a free agent by **Edmonton** (WCHL), December 5, 1921. Traded to **Saskatoon** (WCHL) by **Edmonton** (WCHL) for Rube Brandow, January 1, 1923. Traded to **Montreal Canadiens** by **Saskatoon** (WCHL) for cash, November 25, 1924.

• MAXNER, WAYNE Wayne Maxner

LW – L. 5′11″, 180 lbs. b: Halifax, N.S., 9/27/1942.

			REGULAR SEASON								PLAYOFFS				
Season	Club	League	GP	G	A	Pts	AG	AA	APts	PIM	GP	G	A	Pts	PIM
1961-62	Niagara Falls Flyers	OHA	28	14	15	29	....	....	....	38	10	7	4	11	4
1962-63	Niagara Falls Flyers	OHA	50	32	*62	*94	....	....	....	48	23	*26	*23	*49	10
1963-64	Minneapolis Bruins	CHL	70	27	29	56	....	....	....	44	5	2	1	3	0
1964-65	**Boston Bruins**	**NHL**	**54**	**7**	**6**	**13**	**9**	**6**	**15**	**42**	....	....	....	....	....
	Minneapolis Bruins	CHL	16	8	11	19	....	....	....	20	....	....	....	....	....
1965-66	**Boston Bruins**	**NHL**	**8**	**1**	**3**	**4**	**1**	**3**	**4**	**6**	....	....	....	....	....
	San Francisco Seals	WHL	60	20	20	40	....	....	....	50	5	1	1	2	0
1966-67	California Seals	WHL	67	25	35	60	....	....	....	54	6	0	2	2	0
1967-68	Hershey Bears	AHL	54	13	20	33	....	....	....	16	2	0	0	0	2
1968-69			DID NOT PLAY – INJURED												
1969-70	Long Island Ducks	EHL	64	41	41	82	....	....	....	30	....	....	....	....	....
1970-71	Montreal Voyageurs	AHL	4	0	0	0	....	....	....	0	....	....	....	....	....
	Long Island Ducks	EHL	64	44	43	87	....	....	....	12	....	....	....	....	....
1971-72	Gander Flyers	Nfld.	45	52	59	*111	....	....	....	....	....	....	....	....	....
1972-73	Springfield Kings	AHL	4	0	1	1	....	....	....	2	....	....	....	....	....
	Long Island Ducks	EHL	35	19	39	58	....	....	....	2	....	....	....	....	....
1973-74	Windsor Spitfires	Jr. A	DID NOT PLAY – COACHING												
	NHL Totals		**62**	**8**	**9**	**17**	**10**	**9**	**19**	**48**	....	....	....	....	....

EHL North First All-Star Team (1971)

Traded to **Hershey** (AHL) by **Boston** for cash, June, 1968. • Missed entire 1968-69 season after breaking leg in the summer of 1968.

• MAXWELL, WALLY Wally Maxwell

C – L. 5′10″, 158 lbs. b: Ottawa, Ont., 8/24/1933.

			REGULAR SEASON								PLAYOFFS				
Season	Club	League	GP	G	A	Pts	AG	AA	APts	PIM	GP	G	A	Pts	PIM
1950-51	Toronto Marlboros	OHA	38	18	22	40	....	....	....	24	13	5	11	16	9
1951-52	Toronto Marlboros	OHA	53	28	49	77	....	....	....	42	6	5	2	7	6
1952-53	Toronto Marlboros	OHA	51	22	51	73	....	....	....	49	1	0	0	0	0
	Toronto Maple Leafs	**NHL**	**2**	**0**	**0**	**0**	**0**	**0**	**0**	**0**	....	....	....	....	....
1953-54	Toronto Marlboros	OHA	59	42	32	74	....	....	....	82	15	11	5	16	20
1954-55	University of Michigan	WCHA	DID NOT PLAY – FRESHMAN												
1955-56	University of Michigan	WCHA	....	7	4	11	....	....	....	8	....	....	....	....	....
1956-57	University of Michigan	WCHA	....	10	6	16	....	....	....	14	....	....	....	....	....
1957-58	Whitby Dunlops	EOHL	14	1	6	7	....	....	....	2	....	....	....	....	....
	Windsor Bulldogs	OHA Sr.	33	12	12	24	....	....	....	15	11	6	2	8	2
1958-59	Windsor Bulldogs	OHA Sr.	31	8	15	23	....	....	....	17	....	....	....	....	....
1959-60	Toledo—St. Louis	IHL	3	0	0	0	....	....	....	2	....	....	....	....	....
1960-61	Oakville Oaks	OHA Sr.	31	21	27	48	....	....	....	....	....	....	....	....	....
1961-62	Oakville Oaks	OHA Sr.	10	7	3	10	....	....	....	....	....	....	....	....	....
	NHL Totals		**2**	**0**	**0**	**0**	**0**	**0**	**0**	**0**	....	....	....	....	....

• MAYER, SHEP Shep Mayer

RW – R. 5′8″, 180 lbs. b: Sturgeon Falls, Ont., 9/11/1923.

			REGULAR SEASON								PLAYOFFS				
Season	Club	League	GP	G	A	Pts	AG	AA	APts	PIM	GP	G	A	Pts	PIM
1940-41	Sturgeon Falls Indians	NOHA	STATISTICS NOT AVAILABLE												
1941-42	Guelph Biltmores	OHA	23	9	8	17	....	....	....	34	11	8	7	15	20
1942-43	**Toronto Maple Leafs**	**NHL**	**12**	**1**	**2**	**3**	**1**	**3**	**4**	**4**	....	....	....	....	....
	Saskatoon RCAF	SSHL	16	6	3	9	....	....	....	27	3	2	0	2	4
1943-44			MILITARY SERVICE												
1944-45	RCAF Flyers	City Sr.	....	14	3	17	....	....	....	....	....	....	....	....	....
1945-46			MILITARY SERVICE												
1946-47	North Bay Rangers	NOHA	STATISTICS NOT AVAILABLE												
1947-48	Soo Indians	TBSHL	STATISTICS NOT AVAILABLE												
1948-49	Soo Indians	TBSHL	STATISTICS NOT AVAILABLE												
1949-50	Saskatoon Quakers	WCSHL	23	2	4	6	....	....	....	4	....	....	....	....	....
	Valleyfield Braves	QSHL	44	12	10	22	....	....	....	69	3	0	0	0	2
1950-51	Ottawa RCAF Flyers	ECSHL	34	12	9	21	....	....	....	20	7	5	8	13	14
	NHL Totals		**12**	**1**	**2**	**3**	**1**	**3**	**4**	**4**	....	....	....	....	....

• MAZUR, EDDIE Eddie "Spider" Mazur

D/LW – L. 6′2″, 186 lbs. b: Winnipeg, Man., 7/25/1929. d: 7/3/1995.

			REGULAR SEASON								PLAYOFFS				
Season	Club	League	GP	G	A	Pts	AG	AA	APts	PIM	GP	G	A	Pts	PIM
1947-48	Winnipeg Monarchs	MJHL	11	5	5	10	....	....	....	0	10	4	3	7	4
1948-49	Dallas Texans	USHL	66	10	20	30	....	....	....	48	4	1	1	2	0
1949-50	Victoria Cougars	PCHL	65	33	26	59	....	....	....	17	....	....	....	....	....
1950-51	Victoria Cougars	PCHL	70	43	30	73	....	....	....	41	12	4	6	10	8
	Montreal Canadiens	**NHL**	....	....	....	....	....	....	....	....	**2**	**0**	**0**	**0**	**0**
1951-52	Buffalo Bisons	AHL	60	19	18	37	....	....	....	55	1	0	1	1	2
	Montreal Canadiens	**NHL**	....	....	....	....	....	....	....	....	**5**	**2**	**0**	**2**	**4**
1952-53	Victoria Cougars	WHL	51	20	18	38	....	....	....	54	....	....	....	....	....
	Montreal Canadiens	**NHL**	....	....	....	....	....	....	....	....	**7**	**2**	**2**	**4**	**11**
1953-54	**Montreal Canadiens**	**NHL**	**67**	**7**	**14**	**21**	**11**	**19**	**30**	**95**	**11**	**0**	**3**	**3**	**7**
1954-55	**Montreal Canadiens**	**NHL**	**25**	**1**	**5**	**6**	**1**	**6**	**7**	**21**	....	....	....	....	....
	Montreal Royals	QHL	19	4	8	12	....	....	....	16	14	*8	5	13	27
1955-56	Winnipeg Warriors	WHL	70	34	30	64	....	....	....	72	14	6	11	17	16
1956-57	**Chicago Black Hawks**	**NHL**	**15**	**0**	**1**	**1**	**0**	**1**	**1**	**4**	....	....	....	....	....
	Rochester Americans	AHL	47	24	40	64	....	....	....	90	10	3	9	12	18
1957-58	Rochester Americans	AHL	59	22	25	47	....	....	....	67	....	....	....	....	....
1958-59	Cleveland Barons	AHL	70	34	44	78	....	....	....	54	7	2	2	4	8
1959-60	Cleveland Barons	AHL	61	29	24	53	....	....	....	79	7	2	4	6	24
1960-61	Cleveland Barons	AHL	72	30	39	69	....	....	....	73	4	1	0	1	17
1961-62	Cleveland Barons	AHL	70	24	24	48	....	....	....	44	6	0	0	0	4
1962-63	Providence Reds	AHL	72	18	33	51	....	....	....	72	4	1	0	1	8
1963-64	Providence Reds	AHL	64	23	33	56	....	....	....	56	3	1	4	5	6
1964-65	Victoria Maple Leafs	WHL	62	16	30	46	....	....	....	97	11	1	0	1	6
1965-66	Grand Forks Flyers	MHL Sr.	....	*22	*37	*59	....	....	....	23	....	....	....	....	....
	NHL Totals		**107**	**8**	**20**	**28**	**12**	**26**	**38**	**120**	**25**	**4**	**5**	**9**	**22**

PCHL Northern Second All-Star Team (1950) • PCHL Second All-Star Team (1951) • AHL Second All-Star Team (1957, 1959)

Played in NHL All-Star Game (1953)

Traded to **Chicago** by **Montreal** with Bud MacPherson and Ken Mosdell for $55,000 with Chicago holding option of recall, May 24,1956. Traded to **Cleveland** (AHL) by **Chicago** for Bo Elik, September 23, 1958. Traded to **Providence** (AHL) by **Cleveland** (AHL) for cash, September, 1962.

• McADAM, SAM Sam McAdam

C/LW – L. 5′8″, 175 lbs. b: Sterling, Scotland, 5/31/1908. Deceased.

			REGULAR SEASON								PLAYOFFS				
Season	Club	League	GP	G	A	Pts	AG	AA	APts	PIM	GP	G	A	Pts	PIM
1925-26	Tammany Tigers	Wpg-Jr.	1	1	0	1	....	....	....	4	....	....	....	....	....
1926-27	Winnipeg Winnipegs	MHL Sr.	5	0	1	1	....	....	....	4	1	0	0	0	0
1927-28	Elmwood Millionaires	Wpg-Jr.	5	5	*3	8	....	....	....	....	2	1	1	2	6
	Winnipeg CPR	City Sr.	6	*6	*4	*10	....	....	....	12	....	....	....	....	....
1928-29	Vancouver Lions	PCHL	36	10	5	15	....	....	....	24	3	1	0	1	4
1929-30	Vancouver Lions	PCHL	35	11	7	18	....	....	....	38	4	1	1	2	0
1930-31	**New York Rangers**	**NHL**	**5**	**0**	**0**	**0**	**0**	**0**	**0**	**0**	....	....	....	....	....
	Vancouver Lions	PCHL	12	0	0	0	....	....	....	30	1	0	0	0	0
	Detroit Olympics	IAHL	19	7	8	15	....	....	....	14	....	....	....	....	....
1931-32	Springfield Indians	IAHL	39	10	6	16	....	....	....	33	....	....	....	....	....
1932-33	Vancouver Maroons	WCJHL	29	15	13	28	....	....	....	113	2	4	1	5	0
1933-34	Vancouver Lions	WCJHL	32	14	13	27	....	....	....	22	7	*6	2	8	2
1934-35	Seattle Seahawks	NWHL	36	11	17	28	....	....	....	32	5	2	1	3	4
1935-36	Seattle Seahawks	NWHL	39	23	14	37	....	....	....	14	4	3	*4	*7	0
1936-37	Seattle–Vancouver	PCHL	40	18	9	27	....	....	....	12	1	1	0	1	0
1937-38	Seattle Seahawks	PCHL	41	14	12	26	....	....	....	19	4	0	2	2	0
1938-39	Spokane Clippers	PCHL	48	18	21	39	....	....	....	6	....	....	....	....	....
1939-40	Portland Buckaroos	PCHL	36	2	8	10	....	....	....	12	5	0	1	1	2
1940-41	Spokane Bombers	PCHL	47	9	14	23	....	....	....	21	4	0	1	1	6
1941-42	New Westminster Spitfires	PCHL	10	1	5	6	....	....	....	0	....	....	....	....	....
1942-43	Vancouver St. Regis	PCHL	2	0	1	1	....	....	....	0	....	....	....	....	....
1943-44	Vancouver St. Regis	PCHL	1	0	1	1	....	....	....	0	....	....	....	....	....
	NHL Totals		**5**	**0**	**0**	**0**	**0**	**0**	**0**	**0**	....	....	....	....	....

Traded to **NY Rangers** by **Vancouver** (PCHL) for $7,000, January 3, 1931.

• McANDREW, HAZEN Hazen McAndrew

D – L. 5′10″, 175 lbs. b: Mayo, Que., 8/7/1917. Deceased.

			REGULAR SEASON								PLAYOFFS				
Season	Club	League	GP	G	A	Pts	AG	AA	APts	PIM	GP	G	A	Pts	PIM
1935-36	Niagara Falls Cataracts	OHA	8	5	2	7	....	....	....	*24	2	0	0	0	4
1936-37	Toronto British Consols	City Jr.	12	8	1	9	....	....	....	36	6	3	0	3	14
	Niagara Falls Cataracts	OHA	....	....	....	....	....	....	....	....	4	0	0	0	2
1937-38	Harringay Greyhounds	Britain	....	4	0	4	....	....	....	....	....	....	....	....	....
1938-39	Harringay Greyhounds	Britain	....	5	5	10	....	....	....	....	....	....	....	....	....
	Ottawa Senators	City Sr.	9	0	0	0	....	....	....	10	....	....	....	....	....
1939-40	Niagara Falls Cataracts	OHA Sr.	3	1	1	2	....	....	....	4	....	....	....	....	....
	Atlantic City Seagulls	EHL	34	10	9	19	....	....	....	26	3	2	0	2	6
1940-41	Springfield Indians	AHL	7	1	3	4	....	....	....	21	3	0	0	0	6
	Niagara Falls Brights	OHA Sr.	28	2	3	5	....	....	....	*78	3	0	1	1	0
1941-42	**Brooklyn Americans**	**NHL**	**7**	**0**	**1**	**1**	**0**	**2**	**2**	**6**	....	....	....	....	....
	Hershey Bears	AHL	3	0	0	0	....	....	....	0	....	....	....	....	....
	Philadelphia–Springfield	AHL	45	3	6	9	....	....	....	24	5	0	1	1	9
1942-43	Niagara Falls Cataracts	OHA Sr.	24	9	10	19	....	....	....	*80	2	0	0	0	6
1943-44			MILITARY SERVICE												
1944-45			MILITARY SERVICE												
1945-46			MILITARY SERVICE												
1946-47	Springfield Indians	AHL	63	2	8	10	....	....	....	94	2	0	0	0	2
	Owen Sound Mercurys	OHA Sr.	3	0	1	1	....	....	....	6	....	....	....	....	....
1947-48			DID NOT PLAY												
1948-49	Springfield Indians	AHL	63	3	8	11	....	....	....	70	3	0	0	0	0
1949-50	Vancouver Canucks	PCHL	63	1	14	15	....	....	....	67	3	0	0	0	16
	NHL Totals		**7**	**0**	**1**	**1**	**0**	**2**	**2**	**6**	....	....	....	....	....

● McATEE, JUD
Jud (Jerome) McAtee
LW – L. 5'9", 170 lbs. b: Stratford, Ont., 2/5/1920.

Season	Club	League	GP	G	A	Pts	AG	AA	APts	PIM	GP	G	A	Pts	PIM
			REGULAR SEASON								PLAYOFFS				
1936-37	Stratford Miners	OHA	9	7	7	14	....	....	....	2	....	....	....	....	....
1937-38	Stratford Midgets	OHA	14	12	7	19	....	....	....	6	7	2	0	2	4
1938-39	Oshawa Generals	OHA	14	2	3	5	....	....	....	6	16	8	6	14	6
1939-40	Oshawa Generals	OHA	18	*25	*19	*44	....	....	....	12	7	9	4	13	8
1940-41	Indianapolis Capitals	AHL	54	11	13	24	....	....	....	6	....	....	....	....	....
1941-42	Indianapolis Capitals	AHL	54	16	23	39	....	....	....	4	10	3	3	6	0
1942-43	**Detroit Red Wings**	**NHL**	**1**	**0**	**0**	**0**	**0**	**0**	**0**	**0**	....	....	....	....	....
	Indianapolis Capitals	AHL	55	17	21	38	....	....	....	0	7	2	1	3	0
1943-44	**Detroit Red Wings**	**NHL**	**1**	**0**	**2**	**2**	**0**	**2**	**2**	**0**	....	....	....	....	....
	St. Catharines Saints	OHA Sr.	20	14	9	23	....	....	....	14	5	1	2	3	0
1944-45	**Detroit Red Wings**	**NHL**	**44**	**15**	**11**	**26**	**21**	**18**	**39**	**6**	**14**	**2**	**1**	**3**	**0**
1945-46	St. Louis Flyers	AHL	62	15	24	39	....	....	....	14	....	....	....	....	....
1946-47	St. Louis Flyers	AHL	64	12	22	34	....	....	....	6	....	....	....	....	....
	St. Louis–Hershey	AHL	58	6	15	21	....	....	....	10	2	1	0	1	0
1948-49	Tulsa Oilers	USHL	49	22	34	56	....	....	....	4	....	....	....	....	....
	Hershey Bears	AHL	15	0	1	1	....	....	....	2	6	0	0	0	0
1949-50	Tulsa Oilers	USHL	42	9	13	22	....	....	....	12	....	....	....	....	....
	NHL Totals		**46**	**15**	**13**	**28**	**21**	**20**	**41**	**6**	**14**	**2**	**1**	**3**	**0**

Signed as a free agent by **Detroit**, October 16, 1940.

● McATEE, NORM
Norm McAtee
C – L. 5'8", 165 lbs. b: Stratford, Ont., 6/28/1921.

Season	Club	League	GP	G	A	Pts	AG	AA	APts	PIM	GP	G	A	Pts	PIM
1936-37	Stratford Miners	Jr. B	5	3	2	5	....	....	....	0	....	....	....	....	....
1937-38	Stratford Midgets	Jr. B	14	9	8	17	....	....	....	6	7	2	1	3	0
1938-39	Oshawa Generals	OHA	13	6	4	10	....	....	....	0	16	10	8	18	5
1939-40	Oshawa Generals	OHA	18	17	18	35	....	....	....	9	7	1	*11	12	2
1940-41	Oshawa Generals	OHA	14	15	12	27	....	....	....	2	15	14	11	25	2
1941-42	Philadelphia–Hershey	AHL	20	9	15	24	....	....	....	6	....	....	....	....	....
	Omaha Knights	AHA	24	1	5	6	....	....	....	2	8	0	0	0	0
1942-43	Toronto RCAF	OHA Sr.	2	0	1	1	....	....	....	5	13	10	5	15	17
1943-44			MILITARY SERVICE												
1944-45			MILITARY SERVICE												
1945-46	Indianapolis–Hershey	AHL	61	12	31	43	....	....	....	15	....	....	....	....	....
1946-47	**Boston Bruins**	**NHL**	**13**	**0**	**1**	**1**	**0**	**1**	**1**	**0**	....	....	....	....	....
	Hershey Bears	AHL	40	5	7	12	....	....	....	2	2	0	0	0	0
1947-48	Hershey Bears	AHL	9	0	2	2	....	....	....	0	....	....	....	....	....
	Tulsa Oilers	USHL	57	14	20	34	....	....	....	9	2	0	0	0	0
1948-49	Washington Lions	AHL	64	14	28	42	....	....	....	13	....	....	....	....	....
1949-50	Sherbrooke Saints	QSHL	36	15	16	31	....	....	....	10	22	*16	*16	*22	8
1950-51	Sherbrooke Saints	QSHL	50	15	30	45	....	....	....	12	5	1	3	4	2
1951-52	Troy Bruins	IHL	33	11	17	28	....	....	....	29	7	0	4	4	4
1952-53	Troy Bruins	IHL	59	29	35	64	....	....	....	15	6	1	3	4	2
1953-54	Troy Bruins	IHL	62	20	48	68	....	....	....	22	3	0	2	2	0
	NHL Totals		**13**	**0**	**1**	**1**	**0**	**1**	**1**	**0**	....	....	....	....	....

● McAVOY, GEORGE
George McAvoy
D – L. 6', 185 lbs. b: Edmonton, Alta., 6/21/1931.

Season	Club	League	GP	G	A	Pts	AG	AA	APts	PIM	GP	G	A	Pts	PIM
1947-48	Edmonton Athletic Club	City Jr.	17	2	3	5	....	....	....	6	4	0	0	0	4
1948-49	Edmonton Athletic Club	City Jr.	17	6	9	15	....	....	....	41	....	....	....	....	....
1949-50	Laval Nationale	QJHL	36	2	6	8	....	....	....	73	7	1	1	2	15
1950-51	Montreal Jr. Canadiens	QJHL	41	7	12	19	....	....	....	54	9	1	1	2	18
1951-52	Halifax St. Mary's	MMHL	6	0	0	0	....	....	....	4	....	....	....	....	....
	Boston Olympics	EHL	61	4	18	22	....	....	....	153	4	0	2	2	9
1952-53	Penticton Vees	OSHL	44	9	5	14	....	....	....	*162	10	1	1	2	16
1953-54	Penticton Vees	OSHL	61	11	24	35	....	....	....	*265	10	1	5	6	12
1954-55	Penticton Vees	OSHL	53	8	26	34	....	....	....	122	....	....	....	....	....
	Canada	WEC-A	8	2	2	4	....	....	....	14	....	....	....	....	....
	Montreal Canadiens	**NHL**	....	....	....	....	....	....	....	....	**4**	**0**	**0**	**0**	**0**
1955-56	Providence Reds	AHL	60	4	19	23	....	....	....	131	9	1	7	8	25
1956-57	Providence Reds	AHL	64	3	27	30	....	....	....	141	5	1	0	1	9
1957-58	Providence Reds	AHL	25	2	10	12	....	....	....	45	5	0	0	0	10
1958-59	New Westminster Royals	WHL	11	0	4	4	....	....	....	18	....	....	....	....	....
	Cleveland Barons	AHL	59	6	24	30	....	....	....	99	7	0	3	3	14
1959-60	Cleveland Barons	AHL	72	6	21	27	....	....	....	124	7	0	0	0	14
1960-61	Calgary Stampeders	WHL	70	5	28	33	....	....	....	111	5	0	2	2	10
1961-62	Calgary Stampeders	WHL	70	5	30	35	....	....	....	113	7	0	2	2	13
1962-63	Calgary Stampeders	WHL	70	9	16	25	....	....	....	141	....	....	....	....	....
	NHL Totals		**0**	**0**	**0**	**0**	**0**	**0**	**0**	**0**	**4**	**0**	**0**	**0**	**0**

● McBRIDE, CLIFF
Cliff McBride
RW/D – R. 5'10", 180 lbs. b: Toronto, Ontario, 1/10/1909.

Season	Club	League	GP	G	A	Pts	AG	AA	APts	PIM	GP	G	A	Pts	PIM
1926-27	Iroquois Falls Eskimos	NOHA	....	....	....	....	....	....	....	....	6	15	3	18	8
1927-28	Fort William Forts	TBSHL	20	12	5	17	....	....	....	*81	2	0	0	0	2
1928-29	**Montreal Maroons**	**NHL**	**1**	**0**	**0**	**0**	**0**	**0**	**0**	**0**	....	....	....	....	....
	Windsor Bulldogs	Can-Am	20	3	1	4	....	....	....	29	....	....	....	....	....
1929-30	**Toronto Maple Leafs**	**NHL**	**1**	**0**	**0**	**0**	**0**	**0**	**0**	**0**	....	....	....	....	....
	London Panthers	IAHL	12	1	0	1	....	....	....	29	....	....	....	....	....
	Toronto Millionaires	IAHL	25	2	7	9	....	....	....	5	....	....	....	....	....
	Galt Terriers	Can-Pro	1	0	0	0	....	....	....	0	....	....	....	....	....
	Brantford Indians	Can-Pro	8	0	1	1	....	....	....	2	....	....	....	....	....
1930-31	Pittsburgh Yellowjackets	IAHL	4	0	0	0	....	....	....	8	....	....	....	....	....
	Cleveland Indians	IAHL	38	2	3	5	....	....	....	34	6	0	1	1	0
1931-32	Syracuse Stars	IAHL	46	4	5	9	....	....	....	54	....	....	....	....	....
1932-33			DID NOT PLAY – RETIRED												
1933-34	New Haven Eagles	Can-Am	39	7	8	15	....	....	....	51	....	....	....	....	....
1934-35	New Haven Eagles	Can-Am	44	13	11	24	....	....	....	32	....	....	....	....	....
1935-36	Springfield Indians	Can-Am	42	6	9	15	....	....	....	33	3	0	0	0	8
1936-37	Springfield Indians	AHL	45	1	9	10	....	....	....	77	5	1	0	1	4
1937-38	Springfield Indians	AHL	43	5	5	10	....	....	....	22	....	....	....	....	....
	NHL Totals		**2**	**0**	**0**	**0**	**0**	**0**	**0**	**0**	....	....	....	....	....

Traded to **Toronto** by **Montreal Maroons** for cash, October 23, 1929. Loaned to **London** (IAHL) by **Toronto**, November 12, 1929. Traded to **Toronto Millionaires** (IAHL) by **Toronto** for cash, February 6, 1930. Signed as a free agent by **Pittsburgh** (IAHL) after **Toronto Millionaires** (IAHL) franchise folded, October 30, 1930. Traded to **Cleveland** (IAHL) by **Pittsburgh** (IAHL) for Francis McGuire, November, 1930.

● McBURNEY, JIM
Jim McBurney
LW – L. 5'7", 150 lbs. b: Sault Ste. Marie, Ont., 6/3/1933.

Season	Club	League	GP	G	A	Pts	AG	AA	APts	PIM	GP	G	A	Pts	PIM
			REGULAR SEASON								PLAYOFFS				
1950-51	Soo Red Wings	NOHA	5	7	3	10	....	....	....	4	2	1	3	4	0
1951-52	Galt Black Hawks	OHA	47	35	31	66	....	....	....	27	3	2	1	3	0
1952-53	Galt Black Hawks	OHA	55	*61	35	*96	....	....	....	18	11	4	5	9	6
	Chicago Black Hawks	**NHL**	**1**	**0**	**1**	**1**	**0**	**1**	**1**	**0**	....	....	....	....	....
1953-54	Soo Greyhounds	NOHA	58	30	21	51	....	....	....	6	1	0	0	0	0
1954-55	Soo Greyhounds	NOHA	51	*33	13	46	....	....	....	6	14	*8	2	10	8
1955-56	Soo Greyhounds	NOHA	50	26	12	38	....	....	....	2	5	0	1	1	0
1956-57			DID NOT PLAY												
1957-58	Soo Greyhounds	NOHA	47	17	11	28	....	....	....	10	4	1	0	1	0
1958-59	Soo Greyhounds	NOHA	54	*49	29	78	....	....	....	4	3	1	1	2	2
	NHL Totals		**1**	**0**	**1**	**1**	**0**	**1**	**1**	**0**	....	....	....	....	....

● McCABE, STAN
Stan McCabe
LW – L. 5'6", 165 lbs. b: Ottawa, Ont., 6/16/1908. d: 6/2/1958.

Season	Club	League	GP	G	A	Pts	AG	AA	APts	PIM	GP	G	A	Pts	PIM
1924-25	Ottawa Gunners	City Jr.	6	1	0	1	....	....	....	....	....	....	....	....	....
1925-26	Ottawa Rideaus	City Jr.	15	10	0	10	....	....	....	....	....	....	....	....	....
1926-27	North Bay Trappers	NOHA	11	18	8	26	....	....	....	42	4	2	4	6	10
1927-28	Detroit Olympics	Can-Pro	41	15	4	19	....	....	....	31	2	0	0	0	4
1928-29	Detroit Olympics	Can-Pro	39	17	2	19	....	....	....	70	7	2	0	2	11
1929-30	**Detroit Cougars**	**NHL**	**25**	**7**	**3**	**10**	**14**	**10**	**24**	**23**	....	....	....	....	....
	Detroit Olympics	IAHL	17	7	3	10	....	....	....	39	....	....	....	....	....
1930-31	**Detroit Falcons**	**NHL**	**44**	**2**	**1**	**3**	**5**	**4**	**9**	**22**	....	....	....	....	....
1931-32	Detroit Olympics	IAHL	47	10	8	18	....	....	....	61	6	0	0	0	14
1932-33	**Montreal Maroons**	**NHL**	**1**	**0**	**0**	**0**	**0**	**0**	**0**	**0**	....	....	....	....	....
	Quebec Castors	Can-Am	47	11	19	30	....	....	....	46	....	....	....	....	....
1933-34	**Montreal Maroons**	**NHL**	**8**	**0**	**0**	**0**	**0**	**0**	**0**	**4**	....	....	....	....	....
	Quebec Castors	Can-Am	36	17	11	28	....	....	....	16	....	....	....	....	....
1934-35	Windsor Bulldogs	IAHL	15	0	3	3	....	....	....	4	....	....	....	....	....
	Philadelphia Arrows	Can-Am	19	6	6	12	....	....	....	14	....	....	....	....	....
1935-36	Pittsburgh Yellowjackets	IAHL	19	7	17	24	....	....	....	15	....	....	....	....	....
1936-37	Oakland–Spokane	PCHL	14	0	1	1	....	....	....	2	....	....	....	....	....
1937-38	Detroit Pontiacs	MOHL	23	10	7	17	....	....	....	4	3	0	0	0	0
1938-39	Detroit Pontiacs	MOHL	21	5	6	11	....	....	....	10	7	1	0	1	0
	NHL Totals		**78**	**9**	**4**	**13**	**19**	**14**	**33**	**49**	....	....	....	....	....

Signed as a free agent by **Detroit Cougars**, November 1, 1927. Claimed on waivers by **Montreal Maroons** from **Detroit**, November 14, 1932. Traded to **Quebec** (Can-Am) by **Montreal Maroons** for cash, November 27, 1932. Traded to **Montreal Maroons** by **Quebec** (Can-Am) for Paul Runge, December 6, 1933.

● McCAFFREY, BERT
Bert "Mac" McCaffrey
RW/D – R. 5'10", 180 lbs. b: Chesley, Ontario. d: 4/15/1955.

Season	Club	League	GP	G	A	Pts	AG	AA	APts	PIM	GP	G	A	Pts	PIM
1916-17	Toronto Riversides	OHA Sr.	8	9	0	9	....	....	....	....	2	1	0	1	4
1917-18	Toronto Crescents	OHA Sr.	9	*23	0	*23	....	....	....	....	....	....	....	....	....
1918-19	Toronto Dentals	OHA Sr.	6	7	1	8	....	....	....	....	2	0	0	0	....
1919-20	Parkdale Canoe Club	OHA Sr.	6	6	3	9	....	....	....	....	1	1	1	2	....
1920-21	Toronto Granites	OHA Sr.	10	1	3	4	....	....	....	....	2	0	2	2	....
1921-22	Toronto Granites	OHA Sr.	10	5	8	13	....	....	....	....	8	8	4	12	....
1922-23	Toronto Granites	OHA Sr.	12	10	4	14	....	....	....	....	8	6	2	8	8
1923-24	Toronto Granites	OHA Sr.	14	18	10	28	....	....	....	....	....	....	....	....	....
	Canada	Olympics	5	19	15	34	....	....	....	....	....	....	....	....	....
1924-25	**Toronto St. Pats**	**NHL**	**30**	**9**	**6**	**15**	**31**	**81**	**112**	**12**	**2**	**1**	**0**	**1**	**6**
1925-26	**Toronto St.Pats**	**NHL**	**36**	**14**	**7**	**21**	**44**	**82**	**126**	**42**	....	....	....	....	....
1926-27	**Toronto Maple Leafs**	**NHL**	**43**	**5**	**5**	**10**	**14**	**43**	**57**	**43**	....	....	....	....	....
1927-28	**Toronto Maple Leafs**	**NHL**	**9**	**1**	**1**	**2**	**3**	**8**	**11**	**9**	....	....	....	....	....
	Pittsburgh Pirates	**NHL**	**35**	**6**	**3**	**9**	**18**	**25**	**43**	**14**	....	....	....	....	....
1928-29	**Pittsburgh Pirates**	**NHL**	**42**	**1**	**0**	**1**	**4**	**0**	**4**	**34**	....	....	....	....	....
1929-30	**Pittsburgh Pirates**	**NHL**	**15**	**3**	**4**	**7**	**6**	**13**	**19**	**12**	....	....	....	....	....
	Montreal Canadiens	**NHL**	**28**	**1**	**3**	**4**	**2**	**10**	**12**	**26**	**6**	**1**	**1**	**2**	**6**
1930-31	**Montreal Canadiens**	**NHL**	**22**	**2**	**1**	**3**	**5**	**4**	**9**	**10**	....	....	....	....	....
	Providence Reds	Can-Am	20	6	2	8	....	....	....	24	2	2	1	3	2
1931-32	Philadelphia Arrows	Can-Am	35	7	9	16	....	....	....	26	....	....	....	....	....
1932-33	Philadelphia Arrows	Can-Am	7	1	0	1	....	....	....	2	....	....	....	....	....
	NHL Totals		**260**	**42**	**30**	**72**	**127**	**266**	**393**	**202**	**8**	**2**	**1**	**3**	**12**

Signed as a free agent by **Toronto St. Pats**, October 16, 1924. Traded to **Pittsburgh** by **Toronto** to complete three team transaction that sent Ty Arbour to Chicago and Ed Rodden to Toronto, November 7, 1927. Traded to **Montreal Canadiens** by **Pittsburgh** for Gord Fraser, December 24, 1929.

• McCAIG, DOUGLAS
Douglas McCaig
D – R. 6′, 190 lbs. b: Guelph, Ont., 2/24/1919.

Season	Club	League	GP	G	A	Pts	AG	AA	APts	PIM	GP	G	A	Pts	PIM
			REGULAR SEASON								PLAYOFFS				
1939-40	Detroit Holzbaugh	MOHL	34	7	6	13	....	....	....	43	12	1	1	2	18
1940-41	Indianapolis Capitals	AHL	27	1	1	2	....	....	....	14	....	....	....	....	....
	Detroit Holzbaugh	MOHL	11	1	4	5	....	....	....	12	....	....	....	....	....
1941-42	**Detroit Red Wings**	**NHL**	**9**	**0**	**1**	**1**	**0**	**2**	**2**	**6**	**2**	**0**	**0**	**0**	**6**
	Indianapolis Capitals	AHL	44	4	8	12	....	....	....	6	10	3	4	7	*13
1942-43	Toronto RCAF	City Sr.	7	2	4	6	....	....	....	12	12	4	2	6	*27
1943-44	Toronto RCAF	City Sr.	7	1	1	2	....	....	....	16	....	....	....	....	....
1944-45	Winnipeg RCAF	City Sr.	10	4	7	11	....	....	....	31	....	....	....	....	....
	Summerside RCAF	PEI Sr.	....	....	....	....	....	....	....	....	3	1	0	1	0
1945-46	**Detroit Red Wings**	**NHL**	**6**	**0**	**1**	**1**	**0**	**2**	**2**	**12**	....	....	....	....	....
	St. Louis–Indianapolis	AHL	43	4	12	16	....	....	....	55	5	0	1	1	12
1946-47	**Detroit Red Wings**	**NHL**	**47**	**2**	**4**	**6**	**3**	**6**	**9**	**62**	**5**	**0**	**1**	**1**	**4**
	Indianapolis Capitals	AHL	13	4	2	6	....	....	....	27	....	....	....	....	....
1947-48	**Detroit Red Wings**	**NHL**	**29**	**3**	**3**	**6**	**4**	**4**	**8**	**37**	....	....	....	....	....
1948-49	**Detroit Red Wings**	**NHL**	**1**	**0**	**0**	**0**	**0**	**0**	**0**	**0**	....	....	....	....	....
	Chicago Black Hawks	**NHL**	**55**	**1**	**3**	**4**	**2**	**5**	**7**	**60**	....	....	....	....	....
1949-50	**Chicago Black Hawks**	**NHL**	**63**	**0**	**4**	**4**	**0**	**5**	**5**	**49**	....	....	....	....	....
1950-51	**Chicago Black Hawks**	**NHL**	**53**	**2**	**5**	**7**	**3**	**6**	**9**	**29**	....	....	....	....	....
	Milwaukee Seagulls	USHL	6	1	1	2	....	....	....	4	....	....	....	....	....
1951-52	Edmonton Flyers	PCHL	70	4	7	11	....	....	....	*148	4	0	0	0	0
1952-53	Toledo Mercury's	IHL	59	7	12	19	....	....	....	73	5	0	0	0	4
1953-54	Toledo Mercury's	IHL	57	4	13	17	....	....	....	52	5	1	1	2	0
1954-55	Toledo Mercury's	IHL	34	1	8	9	....	....	....	25	....	....	....	....	....
1955-56	Fort Wayne Komets	IHL	38	11	15	26	....	....	....	39	....	....	....	....	....
1956-57	Fort Wayne Komets	IHL	DID NOT PLAY – COACHING												
	NHL Totals		**263**	**8**	**21**	**29**	**12**	**30**	**42**	**255**	**7**	**0**	**1**	**1**	**10**

AHL Second All-Star Team (1942) • IHL Second All-Star Team (1953, 1955)

Traded to **Chicago** by **Detroit** with Jim Conacher and Bep Guidolin for George Gee and Bud Poile, October 25, 1948. Traded to **Detroit** by **Chicago** for Max Quackenbush, September 18, 1951.

• McCALLUM, DUNC — *see page 1281*

• McCALMON, EDDIE
Eddie "Cally" McCalmon
RW – R. 5′8″, 170 lbs. b: Varney, Ontario, 5/30/1902. Deceased.

Season	Club	League	GP	G	A	Pts	AG	AA	APts	PIM	GP	G	A	Pts	PIM
1920-21	Lumsden Athletic Club	RCHL	10	21	0	21	....	....	....	3	3	6	0	6	....
1921-22	Regina Victorias	City Sr.	1	0	0	0	....	....	....	0	....	....	....	....	....
1922-23	Regina Victorias	City Sr.	STATISTICS NOT AVAILABLE												
1923-24	U. of Saskatchewan	RCHL	STATISTICS NOT AVAILABLE												
1924-25	U. of Saskatchewan	RCHL	5	2	*4	6	....	....	....	4	....	....	....	....	....
1925-26	U. of Saskatchewan	RCHL	STATISTICS NOT AVAILABLE												
1926-27	U. of Saskatchewan	RCHL	....	....	....	....	....	....	....	....	....	....	....	....	....
1927-28	**Chicago Black Hawks**	**NHL**	**23**	**2**	**0**	**2**	**6**	**0**	**6**	**8**	....	....	....	....	....
	Saskatoon Shieks	PrHL	12	8	0	8	....	....	....	2	....	....	....	....	....
1928-29	Tulsa Oilers	AHA	2	0	0	0	....	....	....	5	....	....	....	....	....
1929-30	Toronto Millionaires	Can-Pro	34	6	4	10	....	....	....	10	....	....	....	....	....
1930-31	**Philadelphia Quakers**	**NHL**	**16**	**3**	**0**	**3**	**7**	**0**	**7**	**6**	....	....	....	....	....
	NHL Totals		**39**	**5**	**0**	**5**	**13**	**0**	**13**	**14**	....	....	....	....	....

Traded to **Chicago** by **Saskatoon** (PrHL) with Earl Miller for Nick Wasnie and Corb Denneny, January 11, 1928. Signed as a free agent by **Toronto Millionaires** (Can-Pro), December 3, 1929. Signed as a free agent by **Philadelphia** after **Toronto Millionaires** franchise folded, December 15, 1930.

• McCARTHY, THOMAS
Thomas "Tom" McCarthy
RW – R. 5′11″, 165 lbs. b: Hamilton, Ontario. Deceased.

Season	Club	League	GP	G	A	Pts	AG	AA	APts	PIM	GP	G	A	Pts	PIM
1914-15	New York Irish-Americans	AAHL	8	5	0	5	....	....	....	....	....	....	....	....	....
1915-16	Brooklyn Crescents	AAHL	7	5	0	5	....	....	....	....	....	....	....	....	....
1916-17	Brooklyn Crescents	USAHA	12	14	0	14	....	....	....	....	....	....	....	....	....
1917-18	New York Wanderers	USAHA	10	4	0	4	....	....	....	....	....	....	....	....	....
1918-19	Hamilton Tigers	OHA Sr.	8	*19	3	22	....	....	....	....	6	4	2	6	....
1919-20	**Quebec Bulldogs**	**NHL**	**12**	**12**	**6**	**18**	**27**	**41**	**68**	**0**	....	....	....	....	....
1920-21	**Hamilton Tigers**	**NHL**	**22**	**10**	**1**	**11**	**25**	**9**	**34**	**10**	....	....	....	....	....
1921-22	Saskatoon Shieks	WCHL	7	1	0	1	....	....	....	0	....	....	....	....	....
1922-23	Seattle Metropolitans	PCHA	16	2	1	3	....	....	....	0	1	0	0	0	0
	NHL Totals		**34**	**22**	**7**	**29**	**52**	**50**	**102**	**10**	....	....	....	....	....
	Other Major League Totals		23	3	1	4	....	....	....	0	1	0	0	0	0

Signed as a free agent by **Quebec**, February 2, 1920. Transferred to **Hamilton** after **Quebec** franchise relocated, November 2, 1920.

• McCARTHY, THOMAS PATRICK
Thomas Patrick "Tom" McCarthy
LW – L. 6′1″, 191 lbs. b: Toronto, Ont., 9/15/1934.

Season	Club	League	GP	G	A	Pts	AG	AA	APts	PIM	GP	G	A	Pts	PIM
			REGULAR SEASON								PLAYOFFS				
1950-51	Toronto Marlboros	OHA	2	1	0	1	....	....	....	0	....	....	....	....	....
1951-52	Toronto Marlboros	OHA	3	2	3	5	....	....	....	0	....	....	....	....	....
	Weston Dukes	Jr. B	3	2	3	5	....	....	....	0	....	....	....	....	....
1952-53	Toronto Marlboros	OHA	56	13	12	25	....	....	....	56	7	0	0	0	2
1953-54	Toronto Marlboros	OHA	59	18	29	47	....	....	....	50	1	0	0	0	0
1954-55	Toronto–Guelph	OHA	37	23	29	52	....	....	....	55	6	2	5	7	21
1955-56	Saskatoon–Vancouver	WHL	67	24	22	46	....	....	....	64	15	7	5	12	9
1956-57	**Detroit Red Wings**	**NHL**	**3**	**0**	**0**	**0**	**0**	**0**	**0**	**0**	....	....	....	....	....
	Edmonton Flyers	WHL	42	18	19	37	....	....	....	108	8	2	2	4	2
1957-58	**Detroit Red Wings**	**NHL**	**18**	**2**	**1**	**3**	**3**	**1**	**4**	**4**	....	....	....	....	....
	Victoria–Edmonton	WHL	45	22	31	53	....	....	....	36	....	....	....	....	....
	Providence Reds	AHL	1	0	0	0	....	....	....	2	5	0	1	1	4
1958-59	**Detroit Red Wings**	**NHL**	**15**	**2**	**3**	**5**	**3**	**3**	**6**	**4**	....	....	....	....	....
	Hershey Bears	AHL	40	4	6	10	....	....	....	14	5	1	0	1	0
1959-60	Sudbury Wolves	EPHL	70	46	62	*108	....	....	....	86	4	*8	*12	*20	6
1960-61	**Boston Bruins**	**NHL**	**24**	**4**	**5**	**9**	**5**	**5**	**10**	**0**	....	....	....	....	....
	Sudbury Wolves	EPHL	45	30	24	54	....	....	....	60	....	....	....	....	....
1961-62	Kingston Frontenacs	EPHL	70	53	45	98	....	....	....	68	11	7	3	10	35
1962-63	Portland Buckaroos	WHL	66	27	37	64	....	....	....	61	7	4	4	8	0
1963-64	Portland Buckaroos	WHL	55	11	23	34	....	....	....	31	5	2	3	5	0
1964-65	Tulsa Oilers	CHL	68	*53	44	*97	....	....	....	110	12	3	7	10	29
1965-66	Cleveland Barons	AHL	72	33	34	67	....	....	....	27	12	7	5	*12	6
1966-67	Cleveland Barons	AHL	70	36	38	74	....	....	....	21	5	2	2	4	0
1967-68	Baltimore Clippers	AHL	70	34	49	83	....	....	....	52	....	....	....	....	....
1968-69	Rochester Americans	AHL	68	31	31	62	....	....	....	34	....	....	....	....	....
1969-70	Rochester Americans	AHL	24	5	8	13	....	....	....	24	....	....	....	....	....
1970-71	Orillia Terriers	OHA Sr.	39	22	38	60	....	....	....	14	....	....	....	....	....
1971-72	Orillia Terriers	OHA Sr.	5	0	3	3	....	....	....	0	....	....	....	....	....
1972-73	Orillia Terriers	OHA Sr.	24	6	15	21	....	....	....	22	....	....	....	....	....
	Brantford Forresters	OHA Sr.	12	9	12	21	....	....	....	5	....	....	....	....	....
	NHL Totals		**60**	**8**	**9**	**17**	**11**	**9**	**20**	**8**	....	....	....	....	....

CHL First All-Star Team (1965)

Rights traded to **NY Rangers** by **Toronto** for cash, September, 1954. Claimed by **Detroit** from **NY Rangers** in Waiver Draft, June 6, 1956. Traded to **Boston** by **Detroit** with Murray Oliver and Gary Aldcorn for Vic Stasiuk and Leo Labine, January, 1961. Traded to **Toronto** by **Boston** for cash, August, 1964. Claimed by **Montreal** from **Toronto** in Intra-League Draft, June, 1965.

• McCARTNEY, WALT
Walt McCartney
LW – L. 5′10″, 160 lbs. b: Regina, Sask., 4/26/1911. Deceased.

Season	Club	League	GP	G	A	Pts	AG	AA	APts	PIM	GP	G	A	Pts	PIM
1926-27	Indian Head Bengals	RCHL	6	2	0	2	....	....	....	0	....	....	....	....	....
1927-28	Weyburn Beavers	RCHL	9	4	2	6	....	....	....	2	....	....	....	....	....
1928-29	Weyburn Beavers	RCHL	20	15	4	19	....	....	....	0	2	0	0	0	2
1929-30	Weyburn Beavers	RCHL	20	5	5	10	....	....	....	8	6	1	0	1	0
1930-31	Weyburn Beavers	RCHL	20	11	0	11	....	....	....	10	....	....	....	....	....
1931-32	Weyburn Beavers	RCHL	17	*10	1	11	....	....	....	8	3	1	1	2	4
1932-33	**Montreal Canadiens**	**NHL**	**2**	**0**	**0**	**0**	**0**	**0**	**0**	**0**	....	....	....	....	....
	Quebec Beavers	Can-Am	12	0	0	0	....	....	....	4	....	....	....	....	....
1933-34	Vancouver Lions	NWHL	27	4	3	7	....	....	....	10	7	2	0	2	4
1934-35	Calgary Tigers	NWHL	14	12	2	14	....	....	....	2	....	....	....	....	....
1935-36	Calgary–Portland	NWHL	37	13	7	20	....	....	....	12	....	....	....	....	....
1936-37	Vancouver–Spokane	PCHL	32	6	10	16	....	....	....	16	6	*3	1	4	5
1937-38	Spokane Clippers	PCHL	42	6	7	13	....	....	....	19	....	....	....	....	....
1938-39	Portland Buckaroos	PCHL	45	21	19	40	....	....	....	49	5	2	1	3	6
1939-40	Portland Buckaroos	PCHL	37	14	9	23	....	....	....	26	5	2	0	2	6
1940-41	Portland–Seattle	PCHL	46	11	16	27	....	....	....	16	2	1	1	2	0
1941-42			DID NOT PLAY												
1942-43	Kingston Frontenacs	City Sr.	2	0	0	0	....	....	....	0	....	....	....	....	....
1943-44	Vancouver St. Regis	PCHL	3	0	0	0	....	....	....	0	....	....	....	....	....
	Portland Oilers	City Sr.	15	15	10	25	....	....	....	2	6	*11	1	*12	6
	NHL Totals		**2**	**0**	**0**	**0**	**0**	**0**	**0**	**0**	....	....	....	....	....

• McCORD, BOB — *see page 1283*

• McCORMACK, JOHN
John "Goose" McCormack
C – L. 6′, 185 lbs. b: Edmonton, Alta., 8/2/1925.

Season	Club	League	GP	G	A	Pts	AG	AA	APts	PIM	GP	G	A	Pts	PIM
1943-44	St. Michael's Majors	OHA	24	18	30	48	....	....	....	6	25	15	24	39	14
1944-45	St. Michael's Majors	OHA	15	18	23	41	....	....	....	6	9	10	*11	*21	8
1945-46	Tulsa Oilers	USHL	45	9	32	41	....	....	....	11	13	4	*12	*16	0
1946-47	Leaside Lions	Bantam	DID NOT PLAY – COACHING												
1947-48	**Toronto Maple Leafs**	**NHL**	**3**	**0**	**1**	**1**	**0**	**1**	**1**	**0**	....	....	....	....	....
1947-48	Toronto Marlboros	OHA Sr.	33	28	*49	*77	....	....	....	10	5	0	4	4	2
1948-49	**Toronto Maple Leafs**	**NHL**	**1**	**0**	**0**	**0**	**0**	**0**	**0**	**0**	....	....	....	....	....
	Toronto Marlboros	OHA Sr.	37	21	18	39	....	....	....	10	23	12	*19	31	2
1949-50	**Toronto Maple Leafs**	**NHL**	**34**	**6**	**5**	**11**	**8**	**6**	**14**	**0**	**6**	**1**	**0**	**1**	**0**
1949-50	Toronto Marlboros	OHA Sr.	29	17	33	50	....	....	....	14	....	....	....	....	....
1950-51	**Toronto Maple Leafs**	**NHL**	**46**	**6**	**7**	**13**	**8**	**9**	**17**	**2**	....	....	....	....	....
	Pittsburgh Hornets	AHL	17	4	12	16	....	....	....	0	13	6	9	15	2
1951-52	**Montreal Canadiens**	**NHL**	**54**	**2**	**10**	**12**	**3**	**13**	**16**	**4**	....	....	....	....	....
	Buffalo Bisons	AHL	8	5	3	8	....	....	....	0	....	....	....	....	....
1952-53	**Montreal Canadiens**	**NHL**	**59**	**1**	**9**	**10**	**2**	**12**	**14**	**9**	**9**	**0**	**0**	**0**	**0**
1953-54	**Montreal Canadiens**	**NHL**	**51**	**5**	**10**	**15**	**8**	**14**	**22**	**12**	**7**	**0**	**1**	**1**	**0**
	Buffalo Bisons	AHL	16	7	15	22	....	....	....	0	....	....	....	....	....
1954-55	**Chicago Black Hawks**	**NHL**	**63**	**5**	**7**	**12**	**7**	**9**	**16**	**8**	....	....	....	....	....
1955-56	Edmonton Flyers	WHL	37	6	9	15	....	....	....	6	....	....	....	....	....
	NHL Totals		**311**	**25**	**49**	**74**	**36**	**64**	**100**	**35**	**22**	**1**	**1**	**2**	**0**

Played in NHL All-Star Game (1953)

• Missed entire 1946-47 season when he retired from hockey to commence seminary studies, October 9, 1946. Traded to **Montreal** by **Toronto** for cash, September 23, 1951. Claimed on waivers by **Chicago** from **Montreal**, September 15, 1954. Traded to **Detroit** by **Chicago** with Dave Creighton, Gord Hollingworth and Jerry Toppazzini for Tony Leswick, Glen Skov, John Wilson and Benny Woit, May 28, 1955.

• McCREARY, BILL SR. — *see page 1285*

• McCREARY, KEITH — *see page 1285*

McCREEDY, JOHNNY

Johnny McCreedy
RW – R. 5'9", 160 lbs. b: Winnipeg, Man., 3/23/1911. d: 12/7/1979.

			REGULAR SEASON								PLAYOFFS				
Season	Club	League	GP	G	A	Pts	AG	AA	APts	PIM	GP	G	A	Pts	PIM
1935-36	Winnipeg Monarchs	City Jr.	14	10	*11	21	....	....	....	6	....	....	....	....	....
1936-37	Winnipeg Monarchs	City Jr.	9	7	9	16	....	....	....	2	8	*11	1	*12	4
1937-38	Trail Smoke Eaters	Kootenay	20	19	17	36	....	....	....	46	5	2	*7	9	0
1938-39	Trail Smoke Eaters	Kootenay	PLAYED EXHIBITION SEASON ONLY												
1939-40	Kirkland Lake Blue Devils	NOHA	15	8	3	11	....	....	....	6	20	*20	6	26	17
	Canada	WEC-A	7	4	3	7	....	....	....	....	....	....	....	....	....
1940-41	Sydney Millionaires	CBSHL	39	31	26	57	....	....	....	50	21	12	20	32	22
1941-42	**Toronto Maple Leafs**	**NHL**	**47**	**15**	**8**	**23**	**26**	**12**	**38**	**14**	**13**	**4**	**3**	**7**	**6**
1942-43	Toronto RCAF	City Sr.	12	9	13	22	....	....	....	12	11	8	8	16	9
1943-44	Brantford RCAF	OHA Sr.	MILITARY SERVICE												
1944-45	**Toronto Maple Leafs**	**NHL**	**17**	**2**	**4**	**6**	**3**	**6**	**9**	**11**	**8**	**0**	**0**	**0**	**10**
	NHL Totals		**64**	**17**	**12**	**29**	**29**	**18**	**47**	**25**	**21**	**4**	**3**	**7**	**16**

McCULLEY, BOB

Bob McCulley
RW/D – R. 6'2", 210 lbs. b: Stratford, Ontario, 2/8/1914.

Season	Club	League	GP	G	A	Pts	AG	AA	APts	PIM	GP	G	A	Pts	PIM
1930-31	Stratford Midgets	OHA	5	3	1	4	....	....	....	4	9	5	1	6	12
1931-32	Oshawa Generals	OHA	STATISTICS NOT AVAILABLE												
1932-33	Providence Reds	Can-Am	41	7	2	9	....	....	....	38	2	0	0	0	0
1933-34	Providence—New Haven	Can-Am	40	13	3	16	....	....	....	28	....	....	....	....	....
1934-35	**Montreal Canadiens**	**NHL**	**1**	**0**	**0**	**0**	**0**	**0**	**0**	**0**	....	....	....	....	....
	New Haven—Boston	Can-Am	35	9	9	18	....	....	....	21	3	0	0	0	2
1935-36	Boston—New Haven	Can-Am	47	18	8	26	....	....	....	22	....	....	....	....	....
1936-37	Springfield—Providence	Can-Am	38	8	9	17	....	....	....	20	5	1	2	3	2
1937-38	Springfield Indians	AHL	8	1	0	1	....	....	....	10	....	....	....	....	....
	New Haven Eagles	AHL	39	3	2	5	....	....	....	13	2	0	1	1	2
1938-39	New Haven Eagles	AHL	53	13	12	25	....	....	....	10	....	....	....	....	....
1939-40	New Haven Eagles	AHL	51	8	8	16	....	....	....	32	3	0	1	1	6
1940-41	Philadelphia Rockets	AHL	54	2	4	6	....	....	....	52	....	....	....	....	....
1941-42	Minneapolis Millers	AHA	17	2	2	4	....	....	....	10	....	....	....	....	....
	Providence Reds	AHL	20	1	3	4	....	....	....	9	....	....	....	....	....
	NHL Totals		**1**	**0**	**0**	**0**	**0**	**0**	**0**	**0**	....	....	....	....	....

Signed as a free agent by **Montreal Canadiens**, October 23, 1932. Traded to **Boston** (Can-Am) by **Montreal Canadiens** for Sheldon Buckles, December 2, 1934. Traded to **New Haven** (AHL) by **Springfield** (AHL) for Orville Heximer, December 1, 1938.

McCURRY, DUKE

Duke (Francis J.) McCurry
LW – L. 5'8", 160 lbs. b: Toronto, Ontario, 6/13/1900. d: 11/8/1965.

Season	Club	League	GP	G	A	Pts	AG	AA	APts	PIM	GP	G	A	Pts	PIM
1917-18	Toronto De LaSalle	OHA	STATISTICS NOT AVAILABLE												
1918-19	Parkdale Canoe Club	OHA	STATISTICS NOT AVAILABLE												
1919-20	Toronto Canoe Club	OHA	6	4	3	7	....	....	....	....	12	21	11	32	....
1920-21	Timmins Seniors	NOHA	STATISTICS NOT AVAILABLE												
1921-22	Timmins Seniors	NOHA	STATISTICS NOT AVAILABLE												
1922-23	Toronto Argonauts	OHA Sr.	12	7	6	13	....	....	....	....	....	....	....	....	....
1923-24	Pittsburgh Yellowjackets	USAHA	20	6	0	6	....	....	....	....	13	4	0	4	....
1924-25	Pittsburgh Yellowjackets	USAHA	37	6	0	6	....	....	....	....	8	2	0	2	....
1925-26	**Pittsburgh Pirates**	**NHL**	**36**	**13**	**4**	**17**	**41**	**46**	**87**	**32**	**2**	**0**	**2**	**2**	**4**
1926-27	**Pittsburgh Pirates**	**NHL**	**33**	**3**	**3**	**6**	**9**	**25**	**34**	**23**	....	....	....	....	....
1927-28	**Pittsburgh Pirates**	**NHL**	**44**	**5**	**3**	**8**	**15**	**25**	**40**	**60**	**2**	**0**	**0**	**0**	**0**
1928-29	**Pittsburgh Pirates**	**NHL**	**35**	**0**	**1**	**1**	**0**	**9**	**9**	**4**	....	....	....	....	....
1929-30			DID NOT PLAY												
1930-31	Pittsburgh Yellowjackets	IAHL	36	8	3	11	....	....	....	42	6	0	0	0	0
	NHL Totals		**148**	**21**	**11**	**32**	**65**	**105**	**170**	**119**	**4**	**0**	**2**	**2**	**4**

Signed as a free agent by **Pittsburgh**, September 26, 1925. Traded to **Montreal Maroons** by **Pittsburgh** for Albert Holway, September 30, 1929. Refused to report and sat out entire season. Signed as a free agent by **Pittsburgh** (IAHL), November 20, 1930.

McDONAGH, BILL

Bill McDonagh
LW – L. 5'9", 150 lbs. b: Rouyn, Que., 4/30/1928.

Season	Club	League	GP	G	A	Pts	AG	AA	APts	PIM	GP	G	A	Pts	PIM
1947-48	St. Michael's Majors	OHA	3	0	0	0	....	....	....	0	....	....	....	....	....
1948-49	Detroit Brights	IHL	29	19	20	39	....	....	....	25	2	1	0	1	0
1949-50	**New York Rangers**	**NHL**	**4**	**0**	**0**	**0**	**0**	**0**	**0**	**2**	....	....	....	....	....
	New Haven Ramblers	AHL	61	7	10	17	....	....	....	8	....	....	....	....	....
1950-51	St. Paul Saints	USHL	64	17	17	34	....	....	....	39	4	1	0	1	2
1951-52	Shawinigan Cataracts	QSHL	46	3	9	12	....	....	....	8	....	....	....	....	....
1952-53	Sydney Millionaires	MMHL	82	28	35	63	....	....	....	50	6	2	1	3	12
1953-54	Fredericton Caps	NBSHL	49	19	26	45	....	....	....	61	23	10	14	24	27
1954-55	Fredericton Caps	NBSHL	....	16	38	54	....	....	....	70	6	1	5	6	2
1955-56	Fredericton Caps	NBSHL	....	21	49	70	....	....	....	46	9	2	5	7	2
1956-57			DID NOT PLAY – SUSPENDED												
1957-58	Sudbury Wolves	OHA Sr.	16	3	5	8	....	....	....	6	....	....	....	....	....
	NHL Totals		**4**	**0**	**0**	**0**	**0**	**0**	**0**	**2**	....	....	....	....	....

IHL Northern Division Second All-Star Team (1949)

Traded to **NY Rangers** by **Detroit** for cash, June, 1949. • Suspended by Fredericton (NBSHL) for refusing to play in game vs. Saint John, March 7, 1956.

McDONALD, AB

— *see page 1286*

McDONALD, BUCKO

Bucko (Wilfred Kennedy) McDonald
D – L. 5'10", 205 lbs. b: Fergus, Ont., 10/31/1914. d: 7/21/1991.

			REGULAR SEASON								PLAYOFFS				
Season	Club	League	GP	G	A	Pts	AG	AA	APts	PIM	GP	G	A	Pts	PIM
1933-34	Buffalo Bisons	IAHL	41	3	1	4	....	....	....	14	6	1	0	1	0
1934-35	**Detroit Red Wings**	**NHL**	**15**	**1**	**2**	**3**	**2**	**4**	**6**	**8**	....	....	....	....	....
	Buffalo–Detroit	IAHL	32	6	3	9	....	....	....	28	....	....	....	....	....
1935-36	**Detroit Red Wings**	**NHL**	**47**	**4**	**6**	**10**	**10**	**14**	**24**	**32**	**7**	**3**	**0**	**3**	**10**
	Detroit Olympics	IAHL	1	0	0	0	....	....	....	0	....	....	....	....	....
1936-37	**Detroit Red Wings**	**NHL**	**47**	**3**	**5**	**8**	**6**	**12**	**18**	**20**	**10**	**0**	**0**	**0**	**2**
1937-38	**Detroit Red Wings**	**NHL**	**47**	**3**	**7**	**10**	**6**	**14**	**20**	**14**	....	....	....	....	....
1938-39	**Detroit Red Wings**	**NHL**	**14**	**0**	**0**	**0**	**0**	**0**	**0**	**2**	....	....	....	....	....
	Toronto Maple Leafs	**NHL**	**33**	**3**	**3**	**6**	**6**	**6**	**12**	**20**	**10**	**0**	**0**	**0**	**4**
1939-40	**Toronto Maple Leafs**	**NHL**	**34**	**2**	**5**	**7**	**4**	**10**	**14**	**13**	**1**	**0**	**0**	**0**	**0**
1940-41	**Toronto Maple Leafs**	**NHL**	**31**	**6**	**11**	**17**	**12**	**20**	**32**	**12**	**7**	**2**	**0**	**2**	**2**
1940-41	Providence Reds	AHL	17	3	4	7	....	....	....	26	....	....	....	....	....
1941-42	**Toronto Maple Leafs**	**NHL**	**48**	**2**	**19**	**21**	**3**	**29**	**32**	**24**	**9**	**0**	**1**	**1**	**2**
1942-43	**Toronto Maple Leafs**	**NHL**	**40**	**2**	**11**	**13**	**3**	**14**	**17**	**39**	**6**	**1**	**0**	**1**	**4**
	Providence Reds	AHL	9	0	5	5	....	....	....	2	....	....	....	....	....
1943-44	**Toronto Maple Leafs**	**NHL**	**9**	**2**	**4**	**6**	**2**	**5**	**7**	**8**	....	....	....	....	....
	New York Rangers	**NHL**	**41**	**5**	**6**	**11**	**6**	**7**	**13**	**14**	....	....	....	....	....
1944-45	**New York Rangers**	**NHL**	**40**	**2**	**9**	**11**	**3**	**14**	**17**	**0**	....	....	....	....	....
1945-46	Hull Volants	QSHL	39	13	15	28	....	....	....	6	....	....	....	....	....
	NHL Totals		**446**	**35**	**88**	**123**	**63**	**149**	**212**	**206**	**50**	**6**	**1**	**7**	**24**

NHL Second All-Star Team (1942)

Traded to **Detroit** by **Buffalo** (IAHL) for Gamey Lederman and Lloyd Gross, January 9, 1935. Traded to **Toronto** by **Detroit** for Bill Thoms and $10,000, December 19, 1934. Traded to **NY Rangers** by **Toronto** for cash, November, 1943.

McDONALD, BUTCH

Butch (Byron) McDonald
LW/C – L. 6', 185 lbs. b: Moose Jaw, Sask., 11/21/1916.

Season	Club	League	GP	G	A	Pts	AG	AA	APts	PIM	GP	G	A	Pts	PIM
1934-35	Moose Jaw Canucks	City Jr.	6	4	*4	8	....	....	....	2	6	4	*4	*8	*12
1935-36	Moose Jaw Canucks	City Jr.	STATISTICS NOT AVAILABLE												
1936-37	Pittsburgh Yellowjackets	EHL	47	16	20	36	....	....	....	30	....	....	....	....	....
1937-38	Pittsburgh–New Haven	AHL	43	0	2	2	....	....	....	2	1	0	0	0	0
1938-39	Minneapolis Millers	AHA	48	31	42	73	....	....	....	21	4	0	1	1	0
	Pittsburgh Hornets	AHL	1	1	0	1	....	....	....	0	....	....	....	....	....
1939-40	**Detroit Red Wings**	**NHL**	**37**	**1**	**6**	**7**	**2**	**12**	**14**	**2**	**5**	**0**	**2**	**2**	**10**
	Indianapolis Capitals	AHL	15	4	13	17	....	....	....	4	....	....	....	....	....
1940-41	Indianapolis Capitals	AHL	51	13	30	43	....	....	....	2	....	....	....	....	....
1941-42	Moose Jaw Canucks	SSHL	30	13	17	30	....	....	....	8	9	2	7	9	2
1942-43	Regina Army	RCHL	21	20	31	51	....	....	....	2	1	0	0	0	0
1943-44			MILITARY SERVICE												
1944-45	**Detroit Red Wings**	**NHL**	**3**	**1**	**1**	**2**	**1**	**2**	**3**	**0**	....	....	....	....	....
	Indianapolis Capitals	AHL	29	8	25	33	....	....	....	2	....	....	....	....	....
	Chicago Black Hawks	**NHL**	**26**	**6**	**13**	**19**	**8**	**21**	**29**	**0**	....	....	....	....	....
1945-46	Kansas City Pla-Mors	USHL	51	*39	*60	*99	....	....	....	5	12	2	8	10	0
1946-47	Kansas City Pla-Mors	USHL	51	16	*52	68	....	....	....	....	12	2	6	8	0
1947-48	Calgary Stampeders	WCSHL	47	21	*47	68	....	....	....	14	11	4	5	9	5
1948-49	Calgary Stampeders	WCSHL	47	17	*43	60	....	....	....	12	4	1	1	2	6
1949-50	Calgary Stampeders	WCSHL	10	4	7	11	....	....	....	0	....	....	....	....	....
1950-51	Calgary Stampeders	WCSHL	DID NOT PLAY – COACHING												
	NHL Totals		**66**	**8**	**20**	**28**	**11**	**35**	**46**	**2**	**5**	**0**	**2**	**2**	**10**

AHA First All-Star Team (1939) • USHL First All-Star Team (1946)

Traded to **Chicago** by **Detroit** with Don Grosso and Cully Simon for Earl Seibert, January, 1945.

McDONALD, JOHN

John "Jack" McDonald
RW – R. 5'11", 205 lbs. b: Swan River, Man., 11/24/1921. d: 1/24/1958.

Season	Club	League	GP	G	A	Pts	AG	AA	APts	PIM	GP	G	A	Pts	PIM
1938-39	Winnipeg St. John's	City Jr	STATISTICS NOT AVAILABLE												
1939-40	Portage Terriers	MJHL	21	21	5	26	....	....	....	12	4	4	0	4	2
1940-41	Portage Terriers	MJHL	19	29	11	40	....	....	....	6	6	5	3	8	5
1941-42	Portage Terriers	MJHL	17	29	17	46	....	....	....	10	5	6	6	12	5
1942-43	Flin Flon Bombers	SSHL	24	16	14	30	....	....	....	16	8	8	2	10	4
1943-44	**New York Rangers**	**NHL**	**43**	**10**	**9**	**19**	**13**	**11**	**24**	**6**	....	....	....	....	....
	NHL Totals		**43**	**10**	**9**	**19**	**13**	**11**	**24**	**6**	....	....	....	....	....

McDONALD, ROBERT

Robert McDonald
RW – L. 5'10", 170 lbs. b: Toronto, Ont., 1/4/1923.

Season	Club	League	GP	G	A	Pts	AG	AA	APts	PIM	GP	G	A	Pts	PIM
1941-42	Detroit Mansfields	MOHL	2	1	1	2	....	....	....	0	....	....	....	....	....
1942-43	Windsor Army	City Sr.	11	8	10	18	....	....	....	10	3	1	0	1	2
1943-44	**New York Rangers**	**NHL**	**1**	**0**	**0**	**0**	**0**	**0**	**0**	**0**	....	....	....	....	....
	New York Rovers	EHL	41	15	36	51	....	....	....	12	11	5	8	13	0
1944-45	New York Rovers	EHL	42	13	21	34	....	....	....	14	12	4	9	13	0
1945-46	Windsor Godfredson	IHL	15	10	*25	*35	....	....	....	10	2	0	1	1	0
1946-47	Detroit Auto Club	IHL	27	21	26	47	....	....	....	38	....	....	....	....	....
1947-48	Detroit Brights	IHL	27	14	11	25	....	....	....	4	2	0	1	1	4
1948-49	Detroit Brights	IHL	18	0	4	4	....	....	....	0	....	....	....	....	....
	NHL Totals		**1**	**0**	**0**	**0**	**0**	**0**	**0**	**0**	....	....	....	....	....

EHL Second All-Star Team (1944)

● McFADDEN, JIM — Jim McFadden
C – L. 5'7", 178 lbs. b: Belfast, Ireland, 4/15/1920.

Season	Club	League	GP	G	A	Pts	AG	AA	APts	PIM	GP	G	A	Pts	PIM
			REGULAR SEASON								PLAYOFFS				
1939-40	Carman Beavers	Inter-Sr.	STATISTICS NOT AVAILABLE												
	Portland Buckaroos	PCHL	6	2	1	3	....	....	....	6	4	3	1	4	0
1940-41	Portland Buckaroos	PCHL	47	20	14	34	....	....	....	37	....	....	....	....	....
1941-42	Montreal Sr. Canadiens	QSHL	27	8	6	14	....	....	....	12	5	0	1	1	4
1942-43	Winnipeg Army	City Sr.	12	14	10	24	....	....	....	6	....	....	....	....	....
1943-44	Winnipeg Army	City Sr.	8	7	2	9	....	....	....	2	....	....	....	....	....
1944-45	Winnipeg Army	City Sr.	17	*20	*21	*41	....	....	....	16	2	0	1	1	2
1945-46	Ottawa Senators	QSHL	30	25	32	57	....	....	....	57	9	1	8	9	6
1946-47	Ottawa Senators	QSHL	16	17	17	34	....	....	....	2	....	....	....	....	....
	Buffalo Bisons	AHL	31	19	15	34	....	....	....	37	4	2	0	2	2
	Detroit Red Wings	**NHL**	....	....	....	....	....	....	....	....	**4**	**0**	**2**	**2**	**0**
1947-48	**Detroit Red Wings**	**NHL**	**60**	**24**	**24**	**48**	**35**	**35**	**70**	**12**	**10**	**5**	**3**	**8**	**10**
1948-49	**Detroit Red Wings**	**NHL**	**55**	**12**	**20**	**32**	**19**	**32**	**51**	**10**	**8**	**0**	**1**	**1**	**6**
1949-50	**Detroit Red Wings**	**NHL**	**68**	**14**	**16**	**30**	**19**	**20**	**39**	**8**	**14**	**2**	**3**	**5**	**8**
1950-51	**Detroit Red Wings**	**NHL**	**70**	**14**	**18**	**32**	**19**	**23**	**42**	**10**	**6**	**0**	**0**	**0**	**2**
1951-52	**Chicago Black Hawks**	**NHL**	**70**	**10**	**24**	**34**	**14**	**31**	**45**	**14**	....	....	....	....	....
1952-53	**Chicago Black Hawks**	**NHL**	**70**	**23**	**21**	**44**	**36**	**29**	**65**	**29**	**7**	**3**	**0**	**3**	**4**
1953-54	**Chicago Black Hawks**	**NHL**	**19**	**3**	**3**	**6**	**5**	**4**	**9**	**6**	....	....	....	....	....
	Calgary Stampeders	WHL	37	27	28	55	....	....	....	16	18	10	12	22	4
1954-55	Calgary Stampeders	WHL	56	31	34	65	....	....	....	36	8	5	4	9	7
1955-56	Calgary Stampeders	WHL	64	23	37	60	....	....	....	26	8	4	4	8	4
1956-57	Calgary Stampeders	WHL	9	3	5	8	....	....	....	8	....	....	....	....	....
	NHL Totals		**412**	**100**	**126**	**226**	**147**	**174**	**321**	**89**	**49**	**10**	**9**	**19**	**30**

Won Calder Memorial Trophy (1948)

Played in NHL All-Star Game (1950)

Traded to **Montreal** by **Portland** (PCHL) for cash, December 25, 1940. Loaned to **Ottawa** (QSHL) by **Montreal** with Lude Check as compensation for Montreal's signing of Mike McMahon, October 24, 1945. Traded to **Buffalo** (AHL) by **Montreal** for cash, October 8, 1946. Traded to **Detroit** by **Buffalo** (AHL) for Les Douglas and Harold Jackson, March, 1947. Traded to **Chicago** by **Detroit** with George Gee, Max McNab, Jimmy Peters Sr., Clare Martin and Rags Raglan for Hugh Coflin and $75,000, August 20, 1951.

● McFADYEN, DON — Don McFadyen
C/LW – L. 5'9", 163 lbs. b: Grossfield, Alta., 3/24/1907.

Season	Club	League	GP	G	A	Pts	AG	AA	APts	PIM	GP	G	A	Pts	PIM
1929-30	Marquette University	WIHA	STATISTICS NOT AVAILABLE												
1930-31	Chicago Shamrocks	AHA	47	21	11	32	....	....	....	60	....	....	....	....	....
1931-32	Chicago Shamrocks	AHA	48	13	*17	30	....	....	....	40	4	0	1	1	4
1932-33	**Chicago Black Hawks**	**NHL**	**48**	**5**	**9**	**14**	**12**	**24**	**36**	**20**	....	....	....	....	....
1933-34	**Chicago Black Hawks**	**NHL**	**46**	**1**	**3**	**4**	**2**	**8**	**10**	**20**	**8**	**2**	**2**	**4**	**5**
1934-35	**Chicago Black Hawks**	**NHL**	**37**	**2**	**5**	**7**	**4**	**11**	**15**	**4**	**2**	**0**	**0**	**0**	**0**
1935-36	**Chicago Black Hawks**	**NHL**	**48**	**4**	**16**	**20**	**10**	**39**	**49**	**33**	**1**	**0**	**0**	**0**	**0**
	NHL Totals		**179**	**12**	**33**	**45**	**28**	**82**	**110**	**77**	**11**	**2**	**2**	**4**	**5**

Signed as a free agent by **Chicago** (AHA), June 24, 1930. Traded to **Chicago** by **Chicago Shamrocks** (AHA) for cash, September 2, 1932.

● McFARLANE, GORDON — Gordon "Red" McFarlane
RW/D – R. 6'2", 180 lbs. b: Snowflake, Manitoba, 7/18/1901. Deceased.

Season	Club	League	GP	G	A	Pts	AG	AA	APts	PIM	GP	G	A	Pts	PIM
1922-23	Calgary Fourex	City Sr.	STATISTICS NOT AVAILABLE												
1923-24	Seattle Metropolitans	PCHA	28	4	1	5	....	....	....	36	2	1	0	1	2
1924-25	Vancouver Maroons	WCHL	5	1	0	1	....	....	....	0	....	....	....	....	....
	Calgary Tigers	WCHL	21	6	1	7	....	....	....	24	2	0	0	0	0
1925-26	Calgary Tigers	WHL	27	6	1	7	....	....	....	22	....	....	....	....	....
1926-27	**Chicago Black Hawks**	**NHL**	**2**	**0**	**0**	**0**	**0**	**0**	**0**	**0**	....	....	....	....	....
	Springfield Indians	Can-Am	23	5	0	5	....	....	....	26	3	0	0	0	2
1927-28	Kitchener Millionaires	Can-Am	38	12	3	15	....	....	....	82	5	0	0	0	8
1928-29	Kitchener Dutchmen	Can-Pro	42	7	10	17	....	....	....	102	6	1	0	1	10
1929-30	Cleveland Indians	IAHL	42	9	7	16	....	....	....	97	3	0	0	0	4
1930-31	Cleveland Indians	IAHL	48	5	9	14	....	....	....	95	6	1	1	2	6
1931-32	Cleveland Indians	IAHL	26	5	5	10	....	....	....	44	....	....	....	....	....
1932-33	Cleveland Indians	IAHL	40	5	7	12	....	....	....	53	....	....	....	....	....
1933-34	Portland–Vancouver	NWHL	18	2	1	3	....	....	....	8	....	....	....	....	....
1934-35	Calgary–Vancouver	NWHL	28	8	5	13	....	....	....	35	5	0	0	0	4
1935-36	Calgary Tigers	NWHL	40	11	10	21	....	....	....	37	....	....	....	....	....
1936-37			DID NOT PLAY												
1937-38	Calgary Rangers	ASHL	26	9	16	25	....	....	....	37	6	2	1	3	10
	NHL Totals		**2**	**0**	**0**	**0**	**0**	**0**	**0**	**0**	....	....	....	....	....
	Other Major League Totals		81	17	3	20	....	....	....	82	4	1	0	1	2

Rights traded to **Seattle** (PCHA) by **Calgary** (WCHL) with Bill Binney for Bernie Morris, October 7, 1923. Signed as a free agent by **Seattle**, October, 15, 1923. Signed as a free agent by **Vancouver** (WCHL) after **Seattle** (PCHA) franchise folded, November 10, 1924. Traded to **Calgary** (WCHL) by **Vancouver** (WCHL) for cash, December 21, 1924. Traded to **Chicago** by **Calgary** (WHL) for cash, November 16, 1926.

● McGIBBON, IRV — Irv "Irv" McGibbon
RW – R. 6', 180 lbs. b: Antigonish, N.S., 10/11/1914. d: 2/1/1981.

Season	Club	League	GP	G	A	Pts	AG	AA	APts	PIM	GP	G	A	Pts	PIM
1934-35	Antigonish Bulldogs	CBSHL	....	21	12	*33	....	....	....	20	....	....	....	....	....
1935-36	Antigonish Bulldogs	CBSHL	....	14	8	22	....	....	....	34	....	....	....	....	....
1936-37	Antigonish Bulldogs	CBSHL	STATISTICS NOT AVAILABLE												
1937-38	Sydney Millionaires	CBSHL	STATISTICS NOT AVAILABLE												
1938-39	Sydney Millionaires	CBSHL	21	17	9	26	....	....	....	36	6	7	4	11	*21
1939-40	Glace Bay Miners	CBSHL	40	25	15	40	....	....	....	59	4	1	0	1	4
1940-41	Glace Bay Miners	CBSHL	42	16	7	23	....	....	....	75	4	0	0	0	4
1941-42	Montreal Sr. Canadiens	QSHL	24	5	4	9	....	....	....	18	....	....	....	....	....
	Washington Lions	EHL	23	3	9	12	....	....	....	13	2	0	0	0	0
1942-43	**Montreal Canadiens**	**NHL**	**1**	**0**	**0**	**0**	**0**	**0**	**0**	**2**	....	....	....	....	....
	New Glasgow Bombers	CBSHL									8	*4	5	9	9
1943-44			MILITARY SERVICE												
1944-45			MILITARY SERVICE												
1945-46	Pictou Royals	NSSHL	17	13	9	22	....	....	....	19	11	2	*15	*17	2
1946-47	Antigonish Bulldogs	CBSHL	16	16	13	29	....	....	....	....	....	....	....	....	....
1947-48	Antigonish Bulldogs	CBSHL	....	9	12	21	....	....	....	4	....	....	....	....	....
1948-49	Antigonish Bulldogs	CBSHL	....	33	*43	76	....	....	....	10	....	....	....	....	....
1949-50	Antigonish Bulldogs	CBSHL	DID NOT PLAY – COACHING												
	NHL Totals		**1**	**0**	**0**	**0**	**0**	**0**	**0**	**2**	....	....	....	....	....

Signed as a free agent by **Montreal**, October 16, 1941.

● McGILL, JACK — Jack McGill
LW – L. 5'10", 150 lbs. b: Ottawa, Ont., 11/3/1910. Deceased.

Season	Club	League	GP	G	A	Pts	AG	AA	APts	PIM	GP	G	A	Pts	PIM
			REGULAR SEASON								PLAYOFFS				
1928-29	Ottawa New Edinburghs	City Sr.	15	3	0	3	....	....	....	....	2	0	0	0	0
1929-30	Ottawa New Edinburghs	City Sr.	19	3	3	6	....	....	....	12	2	0	0	0	0
1930-31	McGill University	Mtl-Sr.	12	*6	0	6	....	....	....	29	4	6	0	6	*18
1931-32	McGill University	Mtl-Sr.	12	5	2	7	....	....	....	36	2	0	0	0	0
1932-33	McGill University	Mtl-Sr.	12	*12	6	*18	....	....	....	*45	3	0	2	2	8
1933-34	McGill University	Mtl-Sr.	12	9	8	17	....	....	....	24	4	2	4	6	6
1934-35	**Montreal Canadiens**	**NHL**	**44**	**9**	**1**	**10**	**19**	**2**	**21**	**34**	**2**	**2**	**0**	**2**	**0**
1935-36	**Montreal Canadiens**	**NHL**	**46**	**13**	**7**	**20**	**32**	**17**	**49**	**28**	....	....	....	....	....
1936-37	**Montreal Canadiens**	**NHL**	**44**	**5**	**2**	**7**	**11**	**5**	**16**	**9**	**1**	**0**	**0**	**0**	**0**
	NHL Totals		**134**	**27**	**10**	**37**	**62**	**24**	**86**	**71**	**3**	**2**	**0**	**2**	**0**

● McGILL, JOHN — John "Big Jack" McGill
C – L. 6'1", 180 lbs. b: Edmonton, Alta., 9/19/1921.

Season	Club	League	GP	G	A	Pts	AG	AA	APts	PIM	GP	G	A	Pts	PIM
1938-39	Edmonton Athletic Club	City Jr.	....	12	5	17	....	....	....	11	....	....	....	....	....
1939-40	Edmonton Athletic Club	City Jr.	STATISTICS NOT AVAILABLE												
1941-42	Boston Olympics	EHL	36	34	34	68	....	....	....	50	1	1	0	1	2
	Boston Bruins	**NHL**	**13**	**8**	**11**	**19**	**14**	**17**	**31**	**2**	**5**	**4**	**1**	**5**	**6**
1942-43	Ottawa Army Medics	City Sr.	11	9	6	15	....	....	....	10	....	....	....	....	....
	Ottawa Commandos	QSHL	10	4	6	10	....	....	....	18	4	0	2	2	17
1943-44	Winnipeg RCAF	City Sr.	1	0	0	0	....	....	....	0	....	....	....	....	....
1944-45	**Boston Bruins**	**NHL**	**14**	**4**	**2**	**6**	**5**	**3**	**8**	**0**	**7**	**3**	**3**	**6**	**0**
1944-45	Boston Olympics	EHL	7	4	13	17	....	....	....	22	1	2	0	2	5
	Boston Bruins	**NHL**	**46**	**6**	**14**	**20**	**9**	**26**	**35**	**21**	**10**	**0**	**0**	**0**	**0**
1946-47	**Boston Bruins**	**NHL**	**24**	**5**	**9**	**14**	**7**	**13**	**20**	**19**	**5**	**0**	**0**	**0**	**11**
	Hershey Bears	AHL	36	21	28	49	....	....	....	57	....	....	....	....	....
1947-48	Hershey Bears	AHL	64	21	47	68	....	....	....	82	2	0	2	2	2
1948-49	Houston Huskies	USHL	3	0	3	3	....	....	....	6	....	....	....	....	....
	Buffalo–Providence	AHL	53	27	47	74	....	....	....	68	14	2	*12	14	15
1949-50	Providence Reds	AHL	66	24	58	82	....	....	....	67	4	1	2	3	4
1950-51	Providence Reds	AHL	69	29	69	98	....	....	....	58	....	....	....	....	....
1951-52	Providence Reds	AHL	50	19	42	61	....	....	....	36	15	1	4	5	27
1952-53	Edmonton Flyers	WHL	13	1	1	2	....	....	....	30	....	....	....	....	....
1953-54	New Westminster Royals	WHL	7	2	2	4	....	....	....	8	5	1	0	1	4
	NHL Totals		**97**	**23**	**36**	**59**	**35**	**59**	**94**	**42**	**27**	**7**	**4**	**11**	**17**

Traded to **Buffalo** by **Boston** (Hershey - AHL) for Gerry Brown and Hal Jackson, September, 1948. Traded to **Providence** (AHL) by **Hershey** (AHL) for cash and the rights to Ferdinand Laliberte, November 2, 1948.

● McGREGOR, SANDY — Sandy (Donald) McGregor
RW – R. 5'11", 165 lbs. b: Toronto, Ont., 3/30/1939.

Season	Club	League	GP	G	A	Pts	AG	AA	APts	PIM	GP	G	A	Pts	PIM
1956-57	Toronto Marlboros	OHA	1	0	0	0	....	....	....	0	....	....	....	....	....
1957-58	Guelph Biltmores	OHA	32	7	10	17	....	....	....	2	....	....	....	....	....
1958-59	Guelph Biltmores	OHA	54	34	36	70	....	....	....	26	6	0	4	4	2
1959-60	Trois-Rivieres Lions	EPHL	58	11	6	17	....	....	....	14	7	0	1	1	4
1960-61	Kitchener Beavers	EPHL	62	11	26	37	....	....	....	30	7	1	0	1	4
1961-62	Kitchener Beavers	EPHL	70	24	33	57	....	....	....	65	7	3	0	3	8
1962-63	Baltimore Clippers	AHL	69	21	28	49	....	....	....	22	3	0	0	0	0
1963-64	**New York Rangers**	**NHL**	**2**	**0**	**0**	**0**	**0**	**0**	**0**	**2**	....	....	....	....	....
	Baltimore Clippers	AHL	55	15	12	27	....	....	....	10	....	....	....	....	....
1964-65	Baltimore Clippers	AHL	66	23	16	39	....	....	....	14	5	1	0	1	2
1965-66	Baltimore Clippers	AHL	55	8	8	16	....	....	....	22	....	....	....	....	....
1966-67	Baltimore Clippers	AHL	54	12	16	28	....	....	....	25	7	1	3	4	0
1967-68	Baltimore Clippers	AHL	72	29	27	56	....	....	....	22	....	....	....	....	....
1968-69	Baltimore Clippers	AHL	73	44	19	63	....	....	....	34	4	0	2	2	2
	NHL Totals		**2**	**0**	**0**	**0**	**0**	**0**	**0**	**2**	....	....	....	....	....

Traded to **Providence** (AHL) by **NY Rangers** with Jim Mikol, Marcel Paille and Aldo Guidolin for Ed Giacomin, May, 1965. Traded to **Baltimore** (AHL) by **Providence** (AHL) for Buzz Dechamps, May, 1965.

● McGUIRE, MICKEY — Mickey (Francis) McGuire
LW – L. 5'10", 158 lbs. b: Gravenhurst, Ont., 7/7/1898. Deceased.

Season	Club	League	GP	G	A	Pts	AG	AA	APts	PIM	GP	G	A	Pts	PIM
1920-21	Porcupine Gold Miners	NOHA	....	....	....	....	....	....	....	....	2	*3	0	*3	0
1921-22	Porcupine Gold Miners	NOHA	STATISTICS NOT AVAILABLE												
1922-23	Porcupine Gold Miners	NOHA	STATISTICS NOT AVAILABLE												
1923-24	Cleveland Indians	USAHA	20	11	5	16	....	....	....	....	8	1	1	2	....
1924-25	Cleveland Blues	USAHA	38	9	0	9	....	....	....	....	....	....	....	....	....
1925-26	Minneapolis Millers	CHL	29	6	5	11	....	....	....	58	3	2	1	3	8
1926-27	**Pittsburgh Pirates**	**NHL**	**32**	**3**	**0**	**3**	**9**	**0**	**9**	**6**	....	....	....	....	....
1927-28	**Pittsburgh Pirates**	**NHL**	**4**	**0**	**0**	**0**	**0**	**0**	**0**	**0**	....	....	....	....	....
	Windsor Hornets	Can-Pro	33	16	3	19	....	....	....	31	....	....	....	....	....
1928-29	Windsor–London	Can-Pro	39	6	1	7	....	....	....	32	....	....	....	....	....
1929-30	Cleveland Indians	IAHL	39	11	6	17	....	....	....	30	6	1	0	1	0
1930-31	Pittsburgh Yellowjackets	IAHL	43	7	4	11	....	....	....	33	5	1	1	2	2
1931-32	Cleveland Indians	IAHL	18	2	1	3	....	....	....	2	....	....	....	....	....
	NHL Totals		**36**	**3**	**0**	**3**	**9**	**0**	**9**	**6**	....	....	....	....	....

Signed as a free agent by **Pittsburgh**, October 7, 1926.

• McINENLY, BERT
Bert McInenly
LW/D – L. 5'9", 160 lbs. b: Quebec City, Que., 5/6/1906. d: 3/11/1984.

			REGULAR SEASON								PLAYOFFS				
Season	Club	League	GP	G	A	Pts	AG	AA	APts	PIM	GP	G	A	Pts	PIM
1924-25	Ottawa Rideaus	City Jr.	5	1	0	1	....	....	....	....	....	....	....	....	....
1925-26	Ottawa Shamrocks	City Sr.	15	8	2	10	....	....	....	....	....	....	....	....	....
1926-27	Berlin Mountaineers	NEHL	30	24	9	33	....	....	....	19	....	....	....	....	....
	Ottawa Shamrocks	City Jr.	2	2	1	3	....	....	....	....	....	....	....	....	....
1927-28	Ottawa Gunners	City Sr.	14	3	3	6	....	....	....	....	....	....	....	....	....
1928-29	Detroit Olympics	Can-Pro	41	5	0	5	....	....	....	....	7	3	0	3	26
1929-30	Detroit Olympics	Can-Pro	42	9	3	12	....	....	....	113	3	1	0	1	4
1930-31	**Detroit Falcons**	**NHL**	**44**	**3**	**5**	**8**	**7**	**18**	**25**	**48**	....	....	....	....	....
1931-32	**Detroit Falcons**	**NHL**	**17**	**0**	**1**	**1**	**0**	**3**	**3**	**16**	....	....	....	....	....
	New York Americans	**NHL**	**30**	**12**	**6**	**18**	**26**	**17**	**43**	**44**	....	....	....	....	....
1932-33	**Ottawa Senators**	**NHL**	**30**	**2**	**2**	**4**	**5**	**5**	**10**	**8**	....	....	....	....	....
1933-34	**Ottawa Senators**	**NHL**	**2**	**0**	**0**	**0**	**0**	**0**	**0**	**0**	....	....	....	....	....
	Boston Bruins	**NHL**	**7**	**0**	**0**	**0**	**0**	**0**	**0**	**4**	....	....	....	....	....
	Boston Cubs	Can-Am	26	4	9	13	....	....	....	36	5	0	1	1	25
1934-35	**Boston Bruins**	**NHL**	**33**	**2**	**1**	**3**	**4**	**2**	**6**	**24**	**4**	**0**	**0**	**0**	**2**
	Boston Cubs	Can-Am	15	2	3	5	....	....	....	29	....	....	....	....	....
1935-36	**Boston Bruins**	**NHL**	**3**	**0**	**0**	**0**	**0**	**0**	**0**	**0**	....	....	....	....	....
	Boston Cubs	Can-Am	40	4	10	14	....	....	....	24	....	....	....	....	....
1936-37	Providence Reds	AHL	46	5	4	9	....	....	....	61	3	1	1	2	2
1937-38	Springfield Indians	AHL	37	0	7	7	....	....	....	39	....	....	....	....	....
1938-39	Springfield Indians	AHL	51	4	7	11	....	....	....	69	3	0	0	0	0
1939-40	Syracuse Stars	AHL	56	2	13	15	....	....	....	26	....	....	....	....	....
1940-41	Buffalo Bisons	AHL	49	0	10	10	....	....	....	34	....	....	....	....	....
	NHL Totals		**166**	**19**	**15**	**34**	**42**	**45**	**87**	**144**	**4**	**0**	**0**	**0**	**2**

Traded to **NY Americans** by **Detroit Falcons** with Tommy Filmore and Jimmy Creighton for Hap Emms and Frank Carson, December 29, 1931. Traded to **Ottawa** by **NY Americans** for cash, October 19, 1932. Traded to **Boston** by **Ottawa** for cash, October 21, 1933.

• McINTYRE, JACK
Jack (John Archibald) McIntyre
D – L. 5'11", 170 lbs. b: Brussels, Ont., 9/8/1930.

Season	Club	League	GP	G	A	Pts	AG	AA	APts	PIM	GP	G	A	Pts	PIM
1947-48	St. Catharines Teepees	OHA	31	4	4	8	....	....	....	49	3	2	2	4	6
1948-49	St. Catharines Teepees	OHA	46	14	16	30	....	....	....	64	5	0	3	3	10
1949-50	St. Catharines Teepees	OHA	39	30	26	56	....	....	....	21	5	5	3	8	0
	Boston Bruins	**NHL**	**1**	**0**	**1**	**1**	**0**	**1**	**1**	**0**	....	....	....	....	....
	Boston Olympics	EHL	15	4	5	9	....	....	....	6	5	2	1	3	2
1950-51	Hershey Bears	AHL	64	28	36	64	....	....	....	19	6	1	0	1	0
	Boston Bruins	**NHL**	....	....	....	....	....	....	....	....	**2**	**0**	**0**	**0**	**0**
1951-52	**Boston Bruins**	**NHL**	**52**	**12**	**19**	**31**	**17**	**25**	**42**	**18**	**7**	**1**	**2**	**3**	**2**
	Hershey Bears	AHL	5	1	2	3	....	....	....	2	....	....	....	....	....
1952-53	**Boston Bruins**	**NHL**	**70**	**7**	**15**	**22**	**11**	**21**	**32**	**31**	**10**	**4**	**2**	**6**	**2**
1953-54	Hershey Bears	AHL	44	15	17	32	....	....	....	99	....	....	....	....	....
	Chicago Black Hawks	**NHL**	**23**	**8**	**3**	**11**	**12**	**4**	**16**	**4**	....	....	....	....	....
1954-55	**Chicago Black Hawks**	**NHL**	**65**	**16**	**13**	**29**	**23**	**17**	**40**	**40**	....	....	....	....	....
1955-56	**Chicago Black Hawks**	**NHL**	**46**	**10**	**5**	**15**	**14**	**6**	**20**	**14**	....	....	....	....	....
	Buffalo Bisons	AHL	27	17	19	36	....	....	....	10	5	0	5	5	17
1956-57	**Chicago Black Hawks**	**NHL**	**70**	**18**	**14**	**32**	**25**	**16**	**41**	**32**	....	....	....	....	....
1957-58	**Chicago Black Hawks**	**NHL**	**27**	**0**	**4**	**4**	**0**	**4**	**4**	**10**	....	....	....	....	....
	Detroit Red Wings	**NHL**	**41**	**15**	**7**	**22**	**20**	**8**	**28**	**4**	**4**	**1**	**1**	**2**	**0**
1958-59	**Detroit Red Wings**	**NHL**	**55**	**15**	**14**	**29**	**19**	**15**	**34**	**14**	....	....	....	....	....
	Hershey Bears	AHL	10	7	3	10	....	....	....	2	....	....	....	....	....
1959-60	**Detroit Red Wings**	**NHL**	**49**	**8**	**7**	**15**	**10**	**7**	**17**	**6**	**6**	**1**	**1**	**2**	**0**
	Hershey Bears	AHL	17	7	9	16	....	....	....	4	....	....	....	....	....
1960-61	Hershey Bears	AHL	72	32	25	57	....	....	....	32	8	4	2	6	0
1961-62	Pittsburgh Hornets	AHL	67	25	23	48	....	....	....	32	....	....	....	....	....
1962-63	Edmonton Flyers	WHL	53	25	25	50	....	....	....	20	3	1	2	3	2
	Pittsburgh Hornets	AHL	8	0	1	1	....	....	....	6	....	....	....	....	....
1963-64	Cincinnati Wings	CHL	12	0	4	4	....	....	....	12	....	....	....	....	....
	Guelph Regals	OHA Sr.	20	10	27	37	....	....	....	2	5	3	1	4	6
1964-65	Guelph Regals	OHA Sr.	29	22	20	42	....	....	....	10	7	5	4	9	4
1965-66	Guelph Regals	OHA Sr.	1	0	0	0	....	....	....	0	....	....	....	....	....
1966-67	Johnstown Jets	EHL	5	0	1	1	....	....	....	4	....	....	....	....	....
1967-68			DID NOT PLAY												
1968-69	Woodstock Athletics	OHA Sr.	33	11	15	26	....	....	....	22	....	....	....	....	....
	NHL Totals		**499**	**109**	**102**	**211**	**151**	**124**	**275**	**173**	**29**	**7**	**6**	**13**	**4**

Traded to **Chicago** by **Boston** for cash, January 21, 1954. Traded to **Detroit** by **Chicago** with Bob Bailey, Nick Mickoski and Hec Lalonde for Earl Reibel, Billy Dea, Lorne Ferguson and Bill Dineen, December 17, 1957.

• McKAY, DOUG
Doug McKay
LW – L. 5'9", 165 lbs. b: Hamilton, Ont., 5/28/1929.

Season	Club	League	GP	G	A	Pts	AG	AA	APts	PIM	GP	G	A	Pts	PIM
1947-48	Windsor Spitfires	OHA	33	18	32	50	....	....	....	25	12	1	4	5	21
	Detroit Brights	IHL	24	8	16	24	....	....	....	68	....	....	....	....	....
1948-49	Detroit Auto Club	IHL	6	2	4	6	....	....	....	26	6	1	3	4	36
	Windsor Spitfires	IHL	42	19	29	48	....	....	....	98	4	0	1	1	2
1949-50	Indianapolis Capitals	AHL	65	16	31	47	....	....	....	37	8	2	6	8	*21
	Detroit Red Wings	**NHL**	....	....	....	....	....	....	....	....	**1**	**0**	**0**	**0**	**0**
1950-51	Indianapolis Capitals	AHL	35	7	8	15	....	....	....	31	....	....	....	....	....
	Omaha Knights	USHL	10	4	5	9	....	....	....	26	10	2	1	3	24
1951-52	Indianapolis Capitals	AHL	50	2	8	10	....	....	....	35	....	....	....	....	....
1952-53	Vernon Canadians	OSHL	16	2	2	4	....	....	....	16	....	....	....	....	....
	Brantford Redmen	OHA Sr.	11	6	10	16	....	....	....	26	4	1	2	3	4
1953-54	Hamilton Tigers	OHA Sr.	2	0	0	0	....	....	....	4	....	....	....	....	....
	Vernon Canadians	OSHL	43	5	25	30	....	....	....	51	....	....	....	....	....
1954-55			DID NOT PLAY												
1955-56	Stratford Indians	OHA Sr.	27	8	14	22	....	....	....	59	7	2	3	5	22
1956-57	Stratford Indians	OHA Sr.	25	3	12	15	....	....	....	44	3	0	1	1	2
	NHL Totals		**0**	**0**	**0**	**0**	**0**	**0**	**0**	**0**	**1**	**0**	**0**	**0**	**0**

• McKENNEY, DON — *see page 1295*

• McKENNY, JIM — *see page 1295*

• McKENZIE, JOHN — *see page 1296*

• McKINNON, ALEX
Alex "Bob" McKinnon
RW – R. 5'8", 175 lbs. b: Sault Ste. Marie, Ont., 4/17/1895. d: 10/8/1949.

			REGULAR SEASON								PLAYOFFS				
Season	Club	League	GP	G	A	Pts	AG	AA	APts	PIM	GP	G	A	Pts	PIM
1916-17	Hamilton 227th Battalion	OHA Sr.	6	5	0	5	....	....	....	....	....	....	....	....	....
1917-18			MILITARY SERVICE												
1918-19			MILITARY SERVICE												
1919-20	Sudbury Wolves	NOHA	6	5	*10	*15	....	....	....	10	7	3	*7	10	8
1920-21	Sudbury Wolves	NOHA	9	7	5	12	....	....	....	19	....	....	....	....	....
1921-22	Sudbury Wolves	NOHA	9	10	8	18	....	....	....	18	....	....	....	....	....
1922-23	Sudbury Wolves	NOHA	4	1	2	3	....	....	....	6	2	*2	0	2	2
1923-24	Pittsburgh Yellowjackets	USAHA	20	9	0	9	....	....	....	....	13	4	0	4	....
1924-25	**Hamilton Tigers**	**NHL**	**30**	**8**	**2**	**10**	**27**	**26**	**53**	**45**	....	....	....	....	....
1925-26	**New York Americans**	**NHL**	**35**	**5**	**3**	**8**	**15**	**34**	**49**	**34**	....	....	....	....	....
1926-27	**New York Americans**	**NHL**	**42**	**2**	**1**	**3**	**6**	**8**	**14**	**29**	....	....	....	....	....
1927-28	**New York Americans**	**NHL**	**43**	**3**	**3**	**6**	**9**	**25**	**34**	**71**	....	....	....	....	....
1928-29	**Chicago Black Hawks**	**NHL**	**44**	**1**	**1**	**2**	**4**	**9**	**13**	**56**	....	....	....	....	....
1929-30	Sudbury Wolves	NOHA	DID NOT PLAY – COACHING												
	NHL Totals		**194**	**19**	**10**	**29**	**61**	**102**	**163**	**235**	....	....	....	....	....

Signed as a free agent by **Hamilton**, October 16, 1924. Transferred to **NY Americans** after NHL club purchased **Hamilton** franchise, September 26, 1925. Traded to **Chicago** by **NY Americans** for Rabbit McVeigh, October, 1928.

• McKINNON, JOHN
John McKinnon
D – R. 5'8", 170 lbs. b: Guysborough, N.S., 7/15/1902. d: 2/8/1969.

Season	Club	League	GP	G	A	Pts	AG	AA	APts	PIM	GP	G	A	Pts	PIM
1923-24	Cleveland Indians	USAHA	10	0	0	0	....	....	....	....	....	....	....	....	....
1924-25	Fort Pitt Hornets	USAHA	23	*24	0	*24	....	....	....	....	8	2	0	2	....
1925-26	**Montreal Canadiens**	**NHL**	**2**	**0**	**0**	**0**	**0**	**0**	**0**	**0**	....	....	....	....	....
	Minneapolis Millers	CHL	32	12	8	20	....	....	....	44	3	*3	1	*4	6
1926-27	**Pittsburgh Pirates**	**NHL**	**44**	**13**	**0**	**13**	**38**	**0**	**38**	**21**	....	....	....	....	....
1927-28	**Pittsburgh Pirates**	**NHL**	**43**	**3**	**3**	**6**	**9**	**25**	**34**	**71**	**2**	**0**	**0**	**0**	**4**
1928-29	**Pittsburgh Pirates**	**NHL**	**39**	**1**	**0**	**1**	**4**	**0**	**4**	**44**	....	....	....	....	....
1929-30	**Pittsburgh Pirates**	**NHL**	**41**	**10**	**7**	**17**	**20**	**23**	**43**	**42**	....	....	....	....	....
1930-31	**Philadelphia Quakers**	**NHL**	**39**	**1**	**1**	**2**	**2**	**4**	**6**	**46**	....	....	....	....	....
1931-32	Kansas City Pla-Mors	AHA	48	16	4	20	....	....	....	65	3	0	0	0	2
1932-33	Kansas City Greyhounds	AHA	32	7	4	11	....	....	....	32	4	0	0	0	2
1933-34	Oklahoma City Warriors	AHA	46	10	4	14	....	....	....	16	....	....	....	....	....
1934-35	Oklahoma City Warriors	AHA	43	3	4	7	....	....	....	15	....	....	....	....	....
1935-36	St. Louis Flyers	AHA	39	1	9	10	....	....	....	12	8	2	2	4	*16
1936-37	St. Louis Flyers	AHA	47	5	9	14	....	....	....	16	6	1	0	1	2
1937-38	St. Louis Flyers	AHA	7	0	0	0	....	....	....	2	....	....	....	....	....
1938-39	St. Louis Flyers	AHA	DID NOT PLAY – COACHING												
	NHL Totals		**208**	**28**	**11**	**39**	**73**	**52**	**125**	**224**	**2**	**0**	**0**	**0**	**4**

Signed as a free agent by **Montreal Canadiens**, November 23, 1925. Traded to **Pittsburgh** by **Montreal Canadiens** for cash, October 28, 1926. Transferred to **Philadelphia** after **Pittsburgh** franchise relocated, October 18, 1930. **Trail Smoke Eaters** played exhibition season only in 1960-61.

• McLEAN, FRED
Fred "Larry" McLean
D – L. 6'2", 200 lbs. b: Lakeville Corner, N.B., 3/16/1893. Deceased.

Season	Club	League	GP	G	A	Pts	AG	AA	APts	PIM	GP	G	A	Pts	PIM
1910-11	Fredericton Capitols	City Sr.	6	3	0	3	....	....	....	13	3	1	0	1	3
1911-12	Fredericton Capitols	City Sr.	2	2	0	2	....	....	....	0	1	1	0	1	0
1912-13	Fredericton Capitols	City Sr.	5	11	0	11	....	....	....	5	3	6	0	6	18
	Chatham Ironmen	NNBSL	4	3	0	3	....	....	....	0	....	....	....	....	....
1913-14	U. of New Brunswick	MIHL	3	5	0	5	....	....	....	12	1	5	0	5	0
	Fredericton Capitols	City Sr.	2	4	0	4	....	....	....	5	....	....	....	....	....
1914-15	Sydney Millionaires	EPHL	8	8	0	8	....	....	....	19	....	....	....		
1915-16	Maine Island Falls	NESHL	STATISTICS NOT AVAILABLE												
1916-17	Boston Arenas	USAHA	STATISTICS NOT AVAILABLE												
1917-18	Sydney Millionaires	CBSHL	6	8	7	15	....	....	....	8	6	2	4	6	3
1918-19	Sydney Millionaires	CBSHL	STATISTICS NOT AVAILABLE												
1919-20	Glace Bay Miners	CBSHL	4	7	4	*11	....	....	....	....	2	2	2	4	2
	Quebec Bulldogs	**NHL**	**9**	**0**	**0**	**0**	**0**	**0**	**0**	**2**	....	....	....	....	....
1920-21	**Hamilton Tigers**	**NHL**	**2**	**0**	**0**	**0**	**0**	**0**	**0**	**0**	....	....	....	....	....
	Fredericton Capitols	City Sr.	3	2	0	2	....	....	....	10	2	2	0	2	6
1921-22	U. of New Brunswick	MIHL	DID NOT PLAY – COACHING												
	NHL Totals		**11**	**0**	**0**	**0**	**0**	**0**	**0**	**2**	....	....	....	....	....

Signed as a free agent by **Quebec**, February 16, 1920. Transferred to **Hamilton** after **Quebec** franchise relocated, November 2, 1920.

• McLEAN, JACK
Jack McLean
C/RW – R. 5'8", 165 lbs. b: Winnipeg, Man., 1/31/1923.

Season	Club	League	GP	G	A	Pts	AG	AA	APts	PIM	GP	G	A	Pts	PIM
1939-40	Toronto Young Rangers	OHA	20	8	10	18	....	....	....	12	2	0	0	0	2
1940-41	Toronto Young Rangers	OHA	14	8	7	15	....	....	....	27	5	4	3	7	8
1941-42	Toronto Young Rangers	OHA	16	17	13	30	....	....	....	22	6	4	4	8	6
1942-43	**Toronto Maple Leafs**	**NHL**	**27**	**9**	**8**	**17**	**13**	**10**	**23**	**33**	**6**	**2**	**2**	**4**	**2**
1943-44	**Toronto Maple Leafs**	**NHL**	**32**	**3**	**15**	**18**	**4**	**18**	**22**	**30**	**3**	**0**	**0**	**0**	**6**
1944-45	**Toronto Maple Leafs**	**NHL**	**8**	**2**	**1**	**3**	**3**	**2**	**5**	**13**	**4**	**0**	**0**	**0**	**0**
1945-46	Toronto Staffords	OHA Sr.	11	9	6	15	....	....	....	14	6	2	1	3	6
1946-47	Ottawa Senators	QSHL	24	11	17	28	....	....	....	35	7	0	2	2	8
1947-48	Ottawa Senators	QSHL	41	26	14	40	....	....		50	24	6	7	13	36
	NHL Totals		**67**	**14**	**24**	**38**	**20**	**30**	**50**	**76**	**13**	**2**	**2**	**4**	**8**

• McLELLAN, JOHN John McLellan

C – L. 5'11", 150 lbs. b: South Porcupine, Ont., 8/6/1928. d: 10/27/1979.

			REGULAR SEASON								PLAYOFFS				
Season	Club	League	GP	G	A	Pts	AG	AA	APts	PIM	GP	G	A	Pts	PIM
1946-47	St. Michael's Majors	OHA	30	11	13	24	....	....	....	8	9	0	0	0	0
1947-48	Toronto Marlboros	OHA Sr.	36	16	26	42	....	....	....	45	5	1	2	3	8
1948-49	Toronto Marlboros	OHA Sr.	36	11	19	30	....	....	....	38	23	*16	15	*31	20
1949-50	Toronto Marlboros	OHA Sr.	36	12	20	32	....	....	....	41	14	3	7	10	14
1950-51	Pittsburgh Hornets	AHL	37	8	6	14	....	....	....	23	....	....	....	....	....
	Tulsa Oilers	USHL	14	9	5	14	....	....	....	16	9	4	1	5	9
1951-52	**Toronto Maple Leafs**	**NHL**	**2**	**0**	**0**	**0**	**0**	**0**	**0**	**0**	....	....	....	....	....
	Pittsburgh Hornets	AHL	60	21	22	43	....	....	....	43	11	1	1	2	12
1952-53	Pittsburgh Hornets	AHL	51	13	24	37	....	....	....	59	10	2	2	4	20
1953-54	Pittsburgh Hornets	AHL	55	8	16	24	....	....	....	72	2	0	0	0	0
1954-55	Cleveland Barons	AHL	60	30	31	61	....	....	....	97	4	1	1	2	4
1955-56	Cleveland Barons	AHL	61	12	12	24	....	....	....	72	5	3	1	4	8
1956-57	Cleveland Barons	AHL	57	20	13	33	....	....	....	83	12	*7	2	9	12
1957-58	Cleveland Barons	AHL	46	11	15	26	....	....	....	53	4	0	0	0	2
1958-59	Belleville McFarlands	EOHL	45	17	27	44	....	....	....	74	....	....	....	....	....
	Canada	WEC-A	7	4	*7	11	....	....	....	10	....	....	....	....	....
1959-60	Milwaukee Falcons	IHL	23	7	18	25	....	....	....	29	....	....	....	....	....
1960-61	Schmacher Flyers	NOHA	STATISTICS NOT AVAILABLE												
1961-62			DID NOT PLAY												
1962-63	Nashville Dixie Flyers	EHL	58	19	37	56	....	....	....	46	3	0	2	2	2
1963-64	Nashville Dixie Flyers	EHL	1	0	0	0	....	....	....	0	....	....	....	....	....
1964-65	Nashville Dixie Flyers	EHL	DID NOT PLAY – COACHING												
	NHL Totals		**2**	**0**	**0**	**0**	**0**	**0**	**0**	**0**	....	....	....	....	....

Traded to **Cleveland** (AHL) by **Toronto** with cash for Hugh Barlow, September 15, 1954.

• McLENAHAN, ROLLIE Rollie "Mighty Mite" McLenahan

D – L. 5'7", 169 lbs. b: Fredericton, N.B., 10/26/1921. d: 4/23/1984.

Season	Club	League	GP	G	A	Pts	AG	AA	APts	PIM	GP	G	A	Pts	PIM
1935-36	Marysville Royals	F'ton-Jr.	....	....	....	....	....	....	....	....	2	0	0	0	4
1936-37	Devon Northsiders	F'ton-Jr.	....	....	....	....	....	....	....	....	1	0	1	1	2
1937-38	Fredericton High School	H.S.	4	6	2	8	....	....	....	8	4	6	1	7	4
	Devon Northsiders	F'ton-Jr.	....	....	....	....	....	....	....	....	2	0	1	1	*4
1938-39	Fredericton Merchants	City Sr.	12	12	5	17	....	....	....	....	....	....	....	....	....
1939-40	Windsor Mills	OHA Sr.	....	....	....	....	....	....	....	....	2	0	0	0	2
1940-41	Guelph Biltmores	OHA	15	6	4	10	....	....	....	15	5	1	4	5	4
1941-42	Washington Eagles	EHL	57	19	25	44	....	....	....	55	8	3	4	7	20
1942-43	Sudbury Tigers	City Sr.	3	0	0	0	....	....	....	2	3	1	2	3	2
1943-44	Sudbury Tigers	City Sr.	8	5	4	9	....	....	....	*20	....	....	....	....	....
1944-45	Sudbury Tigers	City Sr.	6	7	6	13	....	....	....	10	7	0	4	4	12
1945-46	**Detroit Red Wings**	**NHL**	**9**	**2**	**1**	**3**	**3**	**2**	**5**	**10**	**2**	**0**	**0**	**0**	**0**
	Indianapolis Capitals	AHL	39	7	13	20	....	....	....	32	....	....	....	....	....
1946-47	Cleveland Barons	AHL	64	6	17	23	....	....	....	55	4	0	0	0	2
1947-48	Hershey Bears	AHL	58	7	18	25	....	....	....	59	2	0	1	1	4
1948-49	Hershey Bears	AHL	64	15	33	48	....	....	....	86	11	4	6	10	8
1949-50	Hershey Bears	AHL	67	25	35	60	....	....	....	49	....	....	....	....	....
1950-51	Buffalo Bisons	AHL	65	11	33	44	....	....	....	44	4	1	2	3	8
1951-51	Fredericton Capitals	NBSHL	19	*23	17	40	....	....	....	*35	....	....	....	....	....
1952-53	Fredericton Capitals	NBSHL	9	11	6	17	....	....	....	30	6	*5	*5	*10	8
	Sudbury Wolves	NOHA	36	27	34	61	....	....	....	31	7	3	5	8	0
1953-54	Cincinnati Mohawks	IHL	47	24	29	53	....	....	....	96	11	3	3	6	*20
1954-55	Cincinnati Mohawks	IHL	57	27	47	74	....	....	....	80	10	1	8	9	25
1955-56	Cincinnati Mohawks	IHL	58	*34	32	66	....	....	....	62	8	2	*7	9	0
1956-57	Cincinnati Mohawks	IHL	50	7	10	17	....	....	....	31	....	....	....	....	....
1957-58	Rochester Americans	AHL	DID NOT PLAY – COACHING												
	NHL Totals		**9**	**2**	**1**	**3**	**3**	**2**	**5**	**10**	**2**	**0**	**0**	**0**	**0**

AHL First All-Star Team (1950) • IHL First All-Star Team (1954, 1955, 1956)

Traded to **Chicago** by **Detroit** for cash, April, 1946. Traded to **Buffalo** (AHL) by **Hershey** (AHL) for Ray Gariepy, October 4, 1950.

• McLEOD, JACKIE Jackie (Robert John) McLeod

RW – R. 5'9", 150 lbs. b: Regina, Sask., 4/30/1930.

Season	Club	League	GP	G	A	Pts	AG	AA	APts	PIM	GP	G	A	Pts	PIM
1945-46	Notre Dame Hounds	SJHL	1	0	0	0	....	....	....	0	....	....	....	....	....
1946-47	Notre Dame Hounds	SJHL	24	8	9	17	....	....	....	10	....	....	....	....	....
1947-48	Moose Jaw Canucks	MJHL	13	5	12	17	....	....	....	4	5	*11	5	*16	4
1948-49	Moose Jaw Canucks	MJHL	26	19	20	39	....	....	....	25	7	4	2	6	10
1948-49	Moose Jaw Canucks	MJHL	14	6	16	22	....	....	....	10	....	....	....	....	....
1949-50	**New York Rangers**	**NHL**	**38**	**6**	**9**	**15**	**8**	**11**	**19**	**2**	**7**	**0**	**0**	**0**	**0**
1950-51	**New York Rangers**	**NHL**	**41**	**5**	**10**	**15**	**7**	**13**	**20**	**2**	....	....	....	....	....
1951-52	**New York Rangers**	**NHL**	**13**	**2**	**3**	**5**	**3**	**4**	**7**	**2**	....	....	....	....	....
	Cincinnati Mohawks	AHL	49	14	18	32	....	....	....	38	2	0	1	1	2
1952-53	**New York Rangers**	**NHL**	**3**	**0**	**0**	**0**	**0**	**0**	**0**	**2**	....	....	....	....	....
	Saskatoon Quakers	WHL	55	30	47	77	....	....	....	28	13	8	11	19	19
1953-54	Saskatoon Quakers	WHL	69	33	38	71	....	....	....	46	6	4	1	5	4
1954-55	**New York Rangers**	**NHL**	**11**	**1**	**1**	**2**	**1**	**1**	**2**	**4**	....	....	....	....	....
	Saskatoon–Vancouver	WHL	51	20	31	51	....	....	....	44	5	2	1	3	14
1955-56	Saskatoon Quakers	WHL	70	34	49	83	....	....	....	97	3	1	1	2	14
1956-57	Vancouver Canucks	WHL	41	30	19	49	....	....	....	30	....	....	....	....	....
1957-58	Vancouver Canucks	WHL	68	44	27	71	....	....	....	45	9	*14	4	18	8
1958-59	Saskatoon Quakers	WHL	63	27	26	53	....	....	....	44	....	....	....	....	....
1959-60	Calgary Stampeders	WHL	62	28	28	56	....	....	....	50	....	....	....	....	....
1960-61	Moose Jaw Canucks	SSHL	12	6	6	12	....	....	....	6	....	....	....	....	....
	Trail Smoke Eaters	....	17	14	13	27	....	....	....	21	....	....	....	....	....
	Canada	Nat-Tm.	19	14	*13	*27	....	....	....	21	....	....	....	....	....
	Canada	WEC-A	7	*10	4	14	....	....	....	6	....	....	....	....	....
1961-62	Moose Jaw Canucks	SSHL	29	27	25	52	....	....	....	36	....	....	....	....	....
	Canada	WEC-A	7	11	8	19	....	....	....	10	....	....	....	....	....
1962-63	Saskatoon Quakers	SSHL	31	37	*51	*88	....	....	....	22	1	0	0	0	2
	Canada	WEC-A	7	5	8	13	....	....	....	6	....	....	....	....	....
1963-64	Saskatoon Quakers	SSHL	40	*52	52	104	....	....	....	22	11	7	8	15	6
1964-65	Moose Jaw Canucks	SSHL	2	3	4	7	....	....	....	12	10	12	*12	24	10
1965-66	Canada	Nat-Tm.	DID NOT PLAY – COACHING												
	NHL Totals		**106**	**14**	**23**	**37**	**19**	**29**	**48**	**12**	**7**	**0**	**0**	**0**	**0**

Traded to **Vancouver** (WHL) by **NY Rangers** with cash for Bill Ezinicki, February 12, 1955. Claimed by **NY Rangers** from **Vancouver** (WHL) in Inter-League Draft, June, 1958. Traded to **Victoria** (WHL) by **Calgary** (WHL) for cash, September, 1960. • **Trail Smoke Eaters** played exhibition season only in 1960-61.

• McMAHON, MIKE JR. — *see page 1298*

• McMAHON, MIKE SR. Mike Sr. McMahon

D – L. 5'8", 215 lbs. b: Brockville, Ont., 2/1/1915. d: 12/3/1974.

			REGULAR SEASON								PLAYOFFS				
Season	Club	League	GP	G	A	Pts	AG	AA	APts	PIM	GP	G	A	Pts	PIM
1935-36	Brockville Magedomas	Ott-Sr.	17	11	8	19	....	....	....	27	5	3	4	7	8
1936-37	Cornwall Flyers	Ott-Sr.	17	7	*13	20	....	....	....	48	6	2	2	4	6
1937-38	Cornwall Flyers	Ott-Sr.	24	17	17	34	....	....	....	34	17	9	7	16	*46
1938-39	Cornwall Flyers	Ott-Sr.	38	20	34	54	....	....	....	*144	9	3	5	8	*22
1939-40	Cornwall Royals	QSHL	30	2	7	9	....	....	....	81	5	2	3	5	14
1940-41	Quebec Aces	QSHL	33	5	11	16	....	....	....	57	4	1	1	2	4
1941-42	Quebec Aces	QSHL	40	16	11	27	....	....	....	76	13	5	5	10	*32
1942-43	Quebec Aces	QSHL	33	6	24	30	....	....	....	73	4	1	2	3	20
	Ottawa Commandos	QSHL	....	....	....	....	....	....	....	....	2	0	2	2	0
	Montreal Royals	QSHL	....	....	....	....	....	....	....	....	1	0	0	0	2
	Montreal Canadiens	**NHL**	....	....	....	....	....	....	....	....	**5**	**0**	**0**	**0**	**14**
1943-44	**Montreal Canadiens**	**NHL**	**42**	**7**	**17**	**24**	**9**	**21**	**30**	***98**	**8**	**1**	**2**	**3**	**16**
1944-45	Montreal Royals	QSHL	10	6	16	22	....	....	....	58	7	1	2	3	8
1945-46	**Montreal Canadiens**	**NHL**	**13**	**0**	**1**	**1**	**0**	**2**	**2**	**2**	....	....	....	....	....
	Boston Bruins	**NHL**	**2**	**0**	**0**	**0**	**0**	**0**	**0**	**2**	....	....	....	....	....
	Buffalo Bisons	AHL	26	2	14	16	....	....	....	50	12	5	1	6	14
1946-47	Dallas Texans	USHL	13	1	3	4	....	....	....	43	....	....	....	....	....
	Buffalo Bisons	AHL	50	12	28	40	....	....	....	68	4	1	0	1	4
1947-48	Houston Huskies	USHL	39	7	11	18	....	....	....	91	....	....	....	....	....
	Buffalo Bisons	AHL	17	2	9	11	....	....	....	15	8	0	2	2	16
1948-49	Springfield Indians	AHL	16	2	4	6	....	....	....	14	....	....	....	....	....
	NHL Totals		**57**	**7**	**18**	**25**	**9**	**23**	**32**	**102**	**13**	**1**	**2**	**3**	**30**

Loaned to **Boston** by **Montreal** as compensation for Montreal's recall of Paul Bibeault, January 8, 1946. Returned to **Montreal** by **Boston**, January 17, 1946.

• McMANUS, SAMMY Sammy McManus

LW – L. 5'9", 160 lbs. b: Belfast, Ireland, 10/22/1911. Deceased.

Season	Club	League	GP	G	A	Pts	AG	AA	APts	PIM	GP	G	A	Pts	PIM
1928-29	Toronto Canoe Club	OHA	5	0	0	0	....	....	....	....	3	0	0	0	....
1929-30	Toronto Canoe Club	OHA	9	2	3	5	....	....	....	8	....	....	....	....	....
	Toronto Goodyears	City Sr.	STATISTICS NOT AVAILABLE												
1930-31	New Glasgow Tigers	CBSHL	24	7	10	17	....	....	....	28	2	0	0	0	0
1931-32	Fredericton Capitals	MSHL	24	11	10	21	....	....	....	18	2	0	0	0	0
1932-33	Moncton Hawks	MSHL	25	3	*5	8	....	....	....	43	13	2	4	6	8
1933-34	Moncton Hawks	MSHL	38	*25	23	48	....	....	....	47	15	8	9	17	12
1934-35	**Montreal Maroons**	**NHL**	**25**	**0**	**1**	**1**	**0**	**2**	**2**	**8**	**1**	**0**	**0**	**0**	**0**
	Windsor Bulldogs	IAHL	10	2	4	6	....	....	....	6	....	....	....	....	....
	New Haven Eagles	Can-Am	8	6	1	7	....	....	....	7	....	....	....	....	....
1935-36	Philadelphia Ramblers	Can-Am	43	19	21	40	....	....	....	22	4	0	2	2	2
1936-37	**Boston Bruins**	**NHL**	**1**	**0**	**0**	**0**	**0**	**0**	**0**	**0**	....	....	....	....	....
	Providence Reds	AHL	31	12	9	21	....	....	....	6	3	0	0	0	2
1937-38	Providence Reds	AHL	45	8	19	27	....	....	....	18	7	3	1	4	2
1938-39	Hershey Bears	AHL	36	12	19	31	....	....	....	10	5	1	2	3	2
1939-40	Pittsburgh–New Haven	AHL	53	5	21	26	....	....	....	12	9	2	5	7	4
1940-41	Kansas City Americans	AHA	44	15	23	38	....	....	....	19	8	2	3	5	6
1941-42	St. Louis Flyers	AHA	50	18	39	57	....	....	....	12	3	0	0	0	0
1942-43	Washington–New Haven	AHL	51	19	35	54	....	....	....	4	....	....	....	....	....
1943-44	Saint John Beavers	City Sr.	6	*7	8	*15	....	....	....	0	15	*36	21	*58	18
1944-45	Moncton RCAF Flyers	City Sr.	1	3	0	3	....	....	....	0	....	....	....	....	....
	Saint John Garrison	City Sr.	1	3	0	3	....	....	....	0	....	....	....	....	....
	Saint John Beavers	City Sr.	1	0	1	1	....	....	....	0	9	*20	13	*33	6
1945-46	Moncton Maroons	City Sr.	13	*27	15	*42	....	....	....	11	4	*15	3	*18	2
1946-47	Moncton Hawks	MSHL	32	37	34	71	....	....	....	13	9	*8	9	*17	2
	NHL Totals		**26**	**0**	**1**	**1**	**0**	**2**	**2**	**8**	**1**	**0**	**0**	**0**	**0**

Can-Am First All-Star Team (1936) • AHL Second All-Star Team (1938) • AHA Second All-Star Team (1942)

Signed as a free agent by **Montreal Maroons**, October 31, 1934. Traded to **NY Rangers** by **Montreal Maroons** for $10,000, October 26, 1935. Traded to **Montreal Maroons** by **NY Rangers** for cash, September, 1936. Traded to **Montreal Canadiens** by **Montreal Maroons** for the rights to Buddy O'Connor, September 10, 1936. Traded to **Boston** by **Montreal Canadiens** with Leroy Goldsworthy and $10,000 for Babe Siebert and Roger Jenkins, September 10, 1936.

• McNAB, MAX Max McNab

C – L. 6'2", 179 lbs. b: Watson, Sask., 6/21/1924.

Season	Club	League	GP	G	A	Pts	AG	AA	APts	PIM	GP	G	A	Pts	PIM
1942-43	Saskatoon Quakers	MJHL	4	7	8	15	....	....	....	6	2	1	2	3	0
1943-44			MILITARY SERVICE												
1944-45			MILITARY SERVICE												
1945-46	Saskatoon Elks	WCSHL	5	8	1	9	....	....	....	0	....	....	....	....	....
1946-47	Indianapolis Capitals	AHL	6	0	0	0	....	....	....	2	....	....	....	....	....
	Omaha Knights	USHL	37	20	19	39	....	....	....	15	11	6	6	12	0
	Detroit Metal Moldings	IHL	3	4	2	6	....	....	....	6	....	....	....	....	....
1947-48	**Detroit Red Wings**	**NHL**	**12**	**2**	**2**	**4**	**3**	**3**	**6**	**2**	**3**	**0**	**0**	**0**	**2**
	Omaha Knights	USHL	44	*44	32	76	....	....	....	10	3	3	2	5	0
1948-49	**Detroit Red Wings**	**NHL**	**51**	**10**	**13**	**23**	**16**	**21**	**37**	**14**	**10**	**1**	**0**	**1**	**2**
1949-50	**Detroit Red Wings**	**NHL**	**65**	**4**	**4**	**8**	**5**	**5**	**10**	**8**	**10**	**0**	**0**	**0**	**0**
1950-51	Indianapolis Capitals	AHL	70	36	48	84	....	....	....	36	3	1	2	3	2
	Detroit Red Wings	**NHL**	....	....	....	....	....	....	....	....	**2**	**0**	**0**	**0**	**0**
1951-52			DID NOT PLAY – INJURED												
1952-53	New Westminster Royals	WHL	68	28	32	60	....	....	....	4	7	2	0	2	0
1953-54	New Westminster Royals	WHL	67	22	39	61	....	....	....	8	6	2	1	3	2
1954-55	New Westminster Royals	WHL	70	32	49	81	....	....	....	4	....	....	....	....	....
1955-56	New Westminster Royals	WHL	70	29	32	61	....	....	....	19	4	1	1	2	0
1956-57	New Westminster Royals	WHL	56	19	28	47	....	....	....	2	13	4	*8	*12	4
1957-58	New Westminster Royals	WHL	67	24	50	74	....	....	....	14	4	0	1	1	0
1958-59	New Westminster Royals	WHL	65	26	32	58	....	....	....	4	....	....	....	....	....
	NHL Totals		**128**	**16**	**19**	**35**	**24**	**29**	**53**	**24**	**25**	**1**	**0**	**1**	**4**

USHL Second All-Star Team (1948) • Won Leader Cup (WHL - MVP) (1955)

• Missed entire 1951-52 season after undergoing operation to correct bulging disc in back.

• McNABNEY, SID Sid McNabney
C – L. 5'7", 150 lbs. b: Toronto, Ont., 1/15/1929.

			REGULAR SEASON								PLAYOFFS				
Season	Club	League	GP	G	A	Pts	AG	AA	APts	PIM	GP	G	A	Pts	PIM
1947-48	Barrie Flyers	OHA	33	14	14	28	....	....	....	36	22	5	10	15	20
1948-49	Barrie Flyers	OHA	45	27	37	64	....	....	....	91	15	8	11	19	36
1949-50	Buffalo Bisons	AHL	67	12	21	33	....	....	....	41	5	1	1	2	11
1950-51	Buffalo Bisons	AHL	70	28	42	70	....	....	....	35	4	2	3	5	8
	Montreal Canadiens	**NHL**	....	....	....	....	....	....	....	....	**5**	**0**	**1**	**1**	**2**
1951-52	Buffalo Bisons	AHL	57	19	23	42	....	....	....	51	3	0	0	0	2
	Edmonton Flyers	PCHL	4	5	1	6	....	....	....	2	....	....	....	....	....
1952-53	Syracuse Warriors	AHL	49	9	11	20	....	....	....	29	2	0	0	0	0
	NHL Totals		**0**	**0**	**0**	**0**	**0**	**0**	**0**	**0**	**5**	**0**	**1**	**1**	**2**

Rights traded to **Montreal** (Buffalo - AHL) by **Springfield** (AHL) with Gord Bell for Hub Macey, December 21, 1948.

• McNAMARA, HOWARD Howard "Hal" McNamara
D – L. 6', 240 lbs. b: Randolph, Ontario, 8/3/1893. d: 8/27/1937.

			REGULAR SEASON								PLAYOFFS				
Season	Club	League	GP	G	A	Pts	AG	AA	APts	PIM	GP	G	A	Pts	PIM
1908-09	Montreal Shamrocks	ECHA	10	4	0	4	....	....	....	61	....	....	....	....	....
	Canadian Soo	....	2	4	0	4	....	....	....	6	....	....	....	....	....
1909-10	Cobalt Silver Kings	NHA	6	0	0	0	....	....	....	15	....	....	....	....	....
	Berlin Professionals	OPHL	3	0	0	0	....	....	....	....	....	....	....	....	....
1910-11	Waterloo Professionals	OPHL	15	2	0	2	....	....	....	....	....	....	....	....	....
1911-12	Halifax Crescents	MPHL	11	4	0	4	....	....	....	26	....	....	....	....	....
1912-13	Toronto Tecumsehs	NHA	20	12	0	12	....	....	....	62	2	1	0	1	3
1913-14	Toronto Ontarios	NHA	20	7	6	13	....	....	....	36	....	....	....	....	....
1914-15	Toronto Shamrocks	NHA	18	4	1	5	....	....	....	67	....	....	....	....	....
1915-16	Montreal Canadiens	NHA	24	10	7	17	....	....	....	119	5	0	0	0	24
1916-17	228th Battalion	NHA	12	11	3	14	....	....	....	36	....	....	....	....	....
1917-18			MILITARY SERVICE												
1918-19			MILITARY SERVICE												
1919-20	**Montreal Canadiens**	**NHL**	**12**	**1**	**0**	**1**	**2**	**0**	**2**	**6**	....	....	....	....	....
	NHL Totals		**12**	**1**	**0**	**1**	**2**	**0**	**2**	**6**	....	....	....	....	....
	Other Major League Totals		139	54	17	71				422	7	1	0	1	27

Signed as a free agent by **Montreal Canadiens**, December 7, 1919.

• McNAUGHTON, GEORGE George McNaughton
RW/C – R. 5'9", 150 lbs. b: Gaspe, Quebec, 4/4/1897. Deceased.

			REGULAR SEASON								PLAYOFFS				
Season	Club	League	GP	G	A	Pts	AG	AA	APts	PIM	GP	G	A	Pts	PIM
1915-16	Quebec Sons of Ireland	QCHL	8	15	0	15	....	....	....	....	2	5	0	5	....
1916-17	Quebec Sons of Ireland	QCHL	10	15	2	17	....	....	....	....	3	2	1	3	3
1917-18	Quebec Sons of Ireland	QCHL	....	....	....	....	....	....	....	....	3	2	1	3	3
1918-19	Quebec Cresents	QCHL	STATISTICS NOT AVAILABLE												
1919-20	**Quebec Bulldogs**	**NHL**	**1**	**0**	**0**	**0**	**0**	**0**	**0**	**0**	....	....	....	....	....
	Winnipeg Virtlands	MHL Sr.	1	2	0	2	....	....	....	0	....	....	....	....	....
1920-21	La Tuque Warriors	QPHL	STATISTICS NOT AVAILABLE												
1921-22	Grand Mere Seniors	QCHL	STATISTICS NOT AVAILABLE												
1922-23	Quebec Sons of Ireland	QCHL	15	14	0	14	....	....	....	....	5	*7	0	*7	
1923-24	Quebec Sons of Ireland	ECHA	1	0	0	0	....	....	....	....	1	0	0	0	....
	NHL Totals		**1**	**0**	**0**	**0**	**0**	**0**	**0**	**0**	....	....	....	....	....

Signed as a free agent by **Quebec**, December 21, 1919.

• McNEILL, BILLY Billy McNeill
RW – R. 5'10", 175 lbs. b: Edmonton, Alta., 1/26/1936.

			REGULAR SEASON								PLAYOFFS				
Season	Club	League	GP	G	A	Pts	AG	AA	APts	PIM	GP	G	A	Pts	PIM
1951-52	Edmonton Oil Kings	WCJHL	49	23	25	48	....	....	....	45	9	4	*10	14	2
1952-53	Edmonton Oil Kings	WCJHL	36	15	15	30	....	....	....	59	10	5	3	8	12
	Edmonton Flyers	WHL	1	0	0	0	....	....	....	0	....	....	....	....	....
1953-54	Edmonton Oil Kings	WCJHL	35	21	39	60	....	....	....	47	10	10	18	28	23
1954-55	Edmonton Oil Kings	WCJHL	49	22	28	50	....	....	....	66	3	3	2	5	2
	Edmonton Flyers	WHL	3	1	1	2	....	....	....	0	....	....	....	....	....
1955-56	Edmonton Flyers	WHL	68	19	31	50	....	....	....	69	1	0	0	0	0
1956-57	**Detroit Red Wings**	**NHL**	**64**	**5**	**10**	**15**	**7**	**12**	**19**	**34**	....	....	....	....	....
	Edmonton Flyers	WHL	4	1	0	1	....	....	....	26	....	....	....	....	....
1957-58	**Detroit Red Wings**	**NHL**	**35**	**5**	**10**	**15**	**6**	**11**	**17**	**29**	**4**	**1**	**1**	**2**	**4**
	Edmonton Flyers	WHL	31	17	14	31	....	....	....	42	....	....	....	....	....
1958-59	**Detroit Red Wings**	**NHL**	**54**	**2**	**5**	**7**	**0**	**5**	**5**	**32**	....	....	....	....	....
	Edmonton Flyers	WHL	12	12	12	24	....	....	....	15	3	1	1	2	0
1959-60	**Detroit Red Wings**	**NHL**	**47**	**5**	**13**	**18**	**6**	**13**	**19**	**33**	....	....	....	....	....
1960-61	Edmonton Flyers	WHL	23	8	17	25	....	....	....	16	....	....	....	....	....
1961-62	Edmonton Flyers	WHL	26	13	28	41	....	....	....	68	12	7	4	11	19
1962-63	**Detroit Red Wings**	**NHL**	**42**	**3**	**7**	**10**	**4**	**7**	**11**	**12**	....	....	....	....	....
	Edmonton Flyers	WHL	22	5	19	24	....	....	....	8	3	0	3	3	0
1963-64	**Detroit Red Wings**	**NHL**	**15**	**1**	**1**	**2**	**1**	**1**	**2**	**2**	....	....	....	....	....
	Vancouver Canucks	WHL	24	4	20	24	....	....	....	4	....	....	....	....	....
	Pittsburgh Hornets	AHL	20	1	6	7	....	....	....	23	....	....	....	....	....
1964-65	Vancouver Canucks	WHL	68	29	59	88	....	....	....	86	5	2	4	6	0
1965-66	Vancouver Canucks	WHL	72	40	62	102	....	....	....	20	7	6	7	13	0
1966-67	Vancouver Canucks	WHL	6	3	5	8	....	....	....	4	....	....	....	....	....
1967-68	Vancouver Canucks	WHL	41	11	24	35	....	....	....	41	....	....	....	....	....
1968-69	Vancouver Canucks	WHL	22	3	2	5	....	....	....	10	....	....	....	....	....
	Rochester Americans	AHL	19	3	15	18	....	....	....	18	....	....	....	....	....
1969-70	Salt Lake Golden Eagles	WHL	24	6	16	22	....	....	....	4	....	....	....	....	....
1970-71	Salt Lake Golden Eagles	WHL	5	0	0	0	....	....	....	2	....	....	....	....	....
	San Diego Gulls	WHL	65	14	15	29	....	....	....	39	6	0	1	1	0
	NHL Totals		**257**	**21**	**46**	**67**	**27**	**49**	**76**	**142**	**4**	**1**	**1**	**2**	**4**

WHL First All-Star Team (1965, 1966) • Won Leader Cup (WHL - MVP) (1965, 1966)

Traded to **NY Rangers** by **Detroit** with Red Kelly for Eddie Shack and Bill Gadsby, February 4, 1960. • Kelly refused to report and deal was voided. Traded to **Vancouver** (WHL) by **Detroit** for Barrie Ross and future considerations, January, 1964. Traded to **Salt Lake** (CHL) by **Vancouver** (WHL) for Germain Gagnon and cash, August, 1969.

• McNEILL, STU Stu McNeill
C – R. 5'10", 170 lbs. b: Port Arthur, Ont., 9/25/1938.

			REGULAR SEASON								PLAYOFFS				
Season	Club	League	GP	G	A	Pts	AG	AA	APts	PIM	GP	G	A	Pts	PIM
1955-56	Port Arthur North Stars	TBJHL	30	16	23	39	....	....	....	2	9	3	4	7	2
1956-57	Port Arthur North Stars	TBJHL	30	27	28	55	....	....	....	0	8	3	4	7	0
1957-58	Hamilton Tiger Cubs	OHA	52	11	27	38	....	....	....	29	15	4	8	12	10
	Detroit Red Wings	**NHL**	**2**	**0**	**0**	**0**	**0**	**0**	**0**	**0**	....	....	....	....	....
1958-59	Hamilton Tiger Cubs	OHA	53	22	27	49	....	....	....	17	....	....	....	....	....
	Detroit Red Wings	**NHL**	**3**	**1**	**1**	**2**	**1**	**1**	**2**	**2**	....	....	....	....	....
1959-60	**Detroit Red Wings**	**NHL**	**5**	**0**	**0**	**0**	**0**	**0**	**0**	**0**	....	....	....	....	....
	Edmonton Flyers	WHL	59	10	17	27	....	....	....	4	4	0	1	1	0
	NHL Totals		**10**	**1**	**1**	**2**	**1**	**1**	**2**	**2**	....	....	....	....	....

• McREAVY, PAT Pat McReavy
C – R. 5'11", 165 lbs. b: Owen Sound, Ont., 1/16/1918.

			REGULAR SEASON								PLAYOFFS				
Season	Club	League	GP	G	A	Pts	AG	AA	APts	PIM	GP	G	A	Pts	PIM
1935-36	St. Michael's Majors	OHA	10	8	9	17	....	....	....	2	5	2	3	5	2
1936-37	Copper Cliff Redmen	NOHA	4	5	4	9	....	....	....	4	....	....	....	....	....
	Copper Cliff Redmen	City Sr.	14	7	7	14	....	....	....	12	....	....	....	....	....
1937-38	Sudbury Wolves	NOHA	1	0	1	1	....	....	....	0	....	....	....	....	....
	Canada	WEC-A	7	2	1	3	....	....	....	....	....	....	....	....	....
1938-39	**Boston Bruins**	**NHL**	**6**	**0**	**0**	**0**	**0**	**0**	**0**	**0**	....	....	....	....	....
	Providence Reds	AHL	47	11	16	17	....	....	....	23	5	0	1	1	0
1939-40	**Boston Bruins**	**NHL**	**2**	**0**	**0**	**0**	**0**	**0**	**0**	**2**	....	....	....	....	....
	Hershey Bears	AHL	53	16	17	33	....	....	....	8	6	2	3	5	2
1940-41	**Boston Bruins**	**NHL**	**7**	**0**	**1**	**1**	**0**	**2**	**2**	**2**	**11**	**2**	**2**	**4**	**5**
	Hershey Bears	AHL	51	21	25	46	....	....	....	2	2	1	0	1	0
1941-42	**Boston Bruins**	**NHL**	**6**	**0**	**1**	**1**	**0**	**2**	**2**	**0**	....	....	....	....	....
	Detroit Red Wings	**NHL**	**34**	**5**	**8**	**13**	**9**	**12**	**21**	**0**	**11**	**1**	**1**	**2**	**4**
1942-43	Montreal RCAF	City Sr.	14	2	4	6	....	....	....	8	....	....	....	....	....
	Toronto RCAF	OHA Sr.	1	0	1	1	....	....	....	0	....	....	....	....	....
1943-44	Montreal RCAF	QSHL	7	2	2	4	....	....	....	2	....	....	....	....	....
1944-45	Valleyfield Braves	QPHL	3	2	2	4	....	....	....	0	....	....	....	....	....
1945-46	St. Louis Flyers	AHL	46	22	28	50	....	....	....	11	....	....	....	....	....
1946-47	St. Louis Flyers	AHL	64	18	29	47	....	....	....	21	....	....	....	....	....
1947-48	Owen Sound Mercurys	OHA Sr.	27	20	28	48	....	....	....	2	5	3	7	10	0
1948-49	Owen Sound Mercurys	OHA Sr.	39	17	22	39	....	....	....	4	4	1	4	5	0
1949-50	Owen Sound Mercurys	OHA Sr.	42	26	25	51	....	....	....	6	....	....	....	....	....
1950-51	Owen Sound Mercurys	OHA Sr.	DID NOT PLAY – COACHING												
1951-52	Owen Sound Mercurys	OHA Sr.	1	0	0	0	....	....	....	0	....	....	....	....	....
	NHL Totals		**55**	**5**	**10**	**15**	**9**	**16**	**25**	**4**	**22**	**3**	**3**	**6**	**9**

Traded to **Detroit** by **Boston** for Dutch Hiller and $5,000, November 24, 1941. Traded to **Buffalo** (AHL) by **Detroit** for cash, November 5, 1945.

• McVEIGH, CHARLEY Charley "Rabbit" McVeigh
C/LW – L. 5'6", 145 lbs. b: Kenora, Ont., 3/29/1898. d: 5/7/1984.

			REGULAR SEASON								PLAYOFFS				
Season	Club	League	GP	G	A	Pts	AG	AA	APts	PIM	GP	G	A	Pts	PIM
1918-19	Kenora Thistles	NOHA	STATISTICS NOT AVAILABLE												
1919-20	Winnipeg Victorias	City Sr.	7	3	*12	15	....	....	....	12	....	....	....	....	....
1920-21	Moose Jaw Maple Leafs	City Sr.	15	9	5	14	....	....	....	19	4	0	2	2	2
1921-22	Regina Capitals	WCHL	19	15	6	21	....	....	....	8	6	1	0	1	0
1922-23	Regina Capitals	WCHL	30	10	2	12	....	....	....	20	2	0	0	0	0
1923-24	Regina Capitals	WCHL	26	10	0	10	....	....	....	6	2	0	0	0	0
1924-25	Regina Capitals	WCHL	28	9	5	14	....	....	....	8	....	....	....	....	....
1925-26	Portland Rosebuds	WHL	27	8	3	11	....	....	....	14	....	....	....	....	....
1926-27	**Chicago Black Hawks**	**NHL**	**43**	**12**	**4**	**16**	**35**	**34**	**69**	**23**	**2**	**0**	**0**	**0**	**0**
1927-28	**Chicago Black Hawks**	**NHL**	**43**	**6**	**7**	**13**	**18**	**59**	**77**	**10**	....	....	....	....	....
1928-29	**New York Americans**	**NHL**	**44**	**6**	**2**	**8**	**24**	**18**	**42**	**16**	**2**	**0**	**0**	**0**	**2**
1929-30	**New York Americans**	**NHL**	**40**	**14**	**14**	**28**	**28**	**46**	**74**	**32**	....	....	....	....	....
1930-31	**New York Americans**	**NHL**	**44**	**5**	**11**	**16**	**12**	**40**	**52**	**23**	....	....	....	....	....
1931-32	**New York Americans**	**NHL**	**40**	**12**	**15**	**27**	**26**	**42**	**68**	**16**	....	....	....	....	....
1932-33	**New York Americans**	**NHL**	**40**	**7**	**12**	**19**	**16**	**32**	**48**	**10**	....	....	....	....	....
1933-34	**New York Americans**	**NHL**	**48**	**15**	**12**	**27**	**33**	**32**	**65**	**4**	....	....	....	....	....
1934-35	**New York Americans**	**NHL**	**47**	**7**	**11**	**18**	**15**	**24**	**39**	**4**	....	....	....	....	....
1935-36	London Tecumsehs	IAHL	47	12	11	23	....	....	....	8	2	0	0	0	0
	NHL Totals		**397**	**84**	**88**	**172**	**207**	**327**	**534**	**138**	**4**	**0**	**0**	**0**	**2**
	Other Major League Totals		130	52	16	68	....	....	....	56	10	1	0	1	0

WCHL First All-Star Team (1923)

Signed as a free agent by **Regina**, December 28, 1921. Transferred to **Portland** (WCHL) after **Regina** (WCHL) franchise relocated, September 1, 1925. Rights transferred to **Chicago** after NHL club purchased **Portland** (WHL) franchise, May 15, 1926. Traded to **NY Americans** by **Chicago** for Alex McKinnon, October, 1928.

• McVICAR, JACK Jack "Slim" McVicar
D – R. 6', 160 lbs. b: Renfrew, Ontario, 6/4/1904. Deceased.

			REGULAR SEASON								PLAYOFFS				
Season	Club	League	GP	G	A	Pts	AG	AA	APts	PIM	GP	G	A	Pts	PIM
1925-26	Grimsby Peach Kings	Inter-Sr.	STATISTICS NOT AVAILABLE												
1926-27	Chicago Americans	AHA	6	0	0	0	....	....	....	2	....	....	....	....	....
	Quebec Castors	Can-Am	23	2	4	6	....	....	....	58	2	0	0	0	4
1927-28	Quebec Castors	Can-Am	39	5	4	9	....	....	....	42	6	1	1	2	8
1928-29	Newark Bulldogs	Can-Am	30	4	2	6	....	....	....	42	....	....	....	....	....
1929-30	Providence Reds	Can-Am	34	8	7	15	....	....	....	91	3	3	1	4	10
1930-31	**Montreal Maroons**	**NHL**	**40**	**2**	**4**	**6**	**5**	**14**	**19**	**35**	**2**	**0**	**0**	**0**	**2**
1931-32	**Montreal Maroons**	**NHL**	**48**	**0**	**0**	**0**	**0**	**0**	**0**	**28**	**4**	**0**	**0**	**0**	**0**
1932-33	Windsor Bulldogs	IAHL	10	0	1	1	....	....	....	25	....	....	....	....	....
	Providence Reds	Can-Am	36	7	4	11	....	....	....	64	2	1	1	2	2
1933-34	Providence Reds	Can-Am	36	3	3	6	....	....	....	24	3	0	0	0	12
	NHL Totals		**88**	**2**	**4**	**6**	**5**	**14**	**19**	**63**	**6**	**0**	**0**	**0**	**2**

Traded to **Montreal Maroons** by **Chicago** (AHA) for cash, January 1, 1927. Traded to **Providence** (Can-Am) by **Newark** (Can-Am) for cash, October 8, 1929. Traded to **Providence** (AHL) by **Montreal Maroons** for Harvey Rockburn, December, 1932.

• MEEKER, HOWIE Howie Meeker

RW – R. 5'9", 165 lbs. b: Kitchener, Ont., 11/4/1924.

			REGULAR SEASON								PLAYOFFS				
Season	Club	League	GP	G	A	Pts	AG	AA	APts	PIM	GP	G	A	Pts	PIM
1941-42	Stratford Kist	Jr. B	STATISTICS NOT AVAILABLE												
1942-43	Stratford Kroehlers	OHA	6	6	4	10	....	....	....	4	2	0	1	1	0
	Brantford Lions	OHA	....	....	....	....	....	....	....	....	2	0	1	1	4
1943-44			MILITARY SERVICE												
1944-45			MILITARY SERVICE												
1945-46	Stratford Indians	OHA Sr.	7	8	5	13	....	....	....	4	5	6	5	11	0
1946-47	**Toronto Maple Leafs**	**NHL**	55	27	18	45	37	26	63	76	11	3	3	6	6
1947-48	**Toronto Maple Leafs**	**NHL**	58	14	20	34	20	29	49	62	9	2	4	6	15
1948-49	**Toronto Maple Leafs**	**NHL**	30	7	7	14	11	11	22	56	....	....	....	....	....
1949-50	**Toronto Maple Leafs**	**NHL**	70	18	22	40	24	28	52	35	7	0	1	1	4
1950-51	**Toronto Maple Leafs**	**NHL**	49	6	14	20	8	18	26	24	11	1	1	2	14
1951-52	**Toronto Maple Leafs**	**NHL**	54	9	14	23	13	18	31	50	4	0	0	0	11
1952-53	**Toronto Maple Leafs**	**NHL**	25	1	7	8	2	10	12	26	....	....	....	....	....
1953-54	**Toronto Maple Leafs**	**NHL**	5	1	0	1	2	0	2	0	....	....	....	....	....
1954-55	Pittsburgh Hornets	AHL	2	0	0	0	....	....	....	2	....	....	....	....	....
1955-56	Pittsburgh Hornets	AHL	DID NOT PLAY – COACHING												
	NHL Totals		346	83	102	185	117	140	257	329	42	6	9	15	50

Won Calder Memorial Trophy (1947)

Played in NHL All-Star Game (1947, 1948, 1949)

• MEEKING, HARRY Harry "Hurricane Howie" Meeking

LW – L. 5'7", 160 lbs. b: Kitchener, Ont., 11/4/1894. d: 2/12/1972.

Season	Club	League	GP	G	A	Pts	AG	AA	APts	PIM	GP	G	A	Pts	PIM
1913-14	Toronto R and AA	OHA Sr.	4	5	0	5	....	....	....	....	2	2	0	2	4
1914-15	Toronto Victorias	OHA Sr.	6	16	0	16	....	....	....	....	4	2	0	2	....
1915-16	Toronto Blue Shirts	NHA	14	3	1	4	....	....	....	8	2	0	0	0	0
1916-17	Ottawa Signallers	City Sr.	8	7	0	7	....	....	....	....	....	....	....	....	....
1917-18	**Toronto Arenas**	**NHL**	21	10	9	19	25	0	25	28	7	4	2	6	21
1918-19	**Toronto Arenas**	**NHL**	15	7	4	11	25	38	63	32	....	....	....	....	....
1919-20	Victoria Cougars	PCHA	21	4	4	8	....	....	....	*51	....	....	....	....	....
1920-21	Victoria Cougars	PCHA	24	13	2	15	....	....	....	15	....	....	....	....	....
1921-22	Victoria Cougars	PCHA	24	2	4	6	....	....	....	33	....	....	....	....	....
1922-23	Victoria Cougars	PCHA	28	17	9	26	....	....	....	43	2	0	0	0	2
1923-24	Victoria Cougars	PCHA	29	8	5	13	....	....	....	34	....	....	....	....	....
1924-25	Victoria Cougars	WCHL	28	12	2	14	....	....	....	24	7	0	1	1	4
1925-26	Victoria Cougars	WHL	19	1	1	2	....	....	....	20	7	0	0	0	6
1926-27	**Detroit Cougars**	**NHL**	6	0	0	0	0	0	0	4	....	....	....	....	....
	Boston Bruins	**NHL**	23	1	0	1	3	0	3	2	7	0	0	0	0
	Windsor Bulldogs	Can-Pro	11	5	2	7	....	....	....	14	....	....	....	....	....
1927-28	New Haven Eagles	Can-Am	39	9	6	15	....	....	....	61	....	....	....	....	....
1928-29	Philadelphia Arrows	Can-Am	38	5	1	6	....	....	....	60	....	....	....	....	....
1929-30	Toronto Millionaires	IAHL	19	2	3	5	....	....	....	30	....	....	....	....	....
	London Tecumsehs	IAHL	6	1	1	2	....	....	....	6	....	....	....	....	....
	Kitchener Dutchmen	Can-Pro	2	1	0	1	....	....	....	0	....	....	....	....	....
	NHL Totals		65	18	13	31	53	38	91	66	14	4	2	6	21
	Other Major League Totals		187	60	28	88	....	....	....	228	18	0	1	1	12

PCHA Second All-Star Team (1922, 1923)

Signed as a free agent by **Toronto Arenas**, December 5, 1917. Traded to **Victoria** (PCHA) by **Toronto St. Pats** for cash, December 7, 1919. Rights transferred to **Detroit Cougars** after NHL club purchased **Victoria** (WHL) franchise, May 15, 1926. Traded to **Boston** by **Detroit Cougars** with Frank Frederickson for Duke Keats and Archie Briden, January 7, 1927. Traded to **Detroit Cougars** by **Boston** for Fred Gordon, May 22, 1927. Signed as a free agent by **Toronto Millionaires** (IAHL), November 17, 1929. Traded to **London** (IAHL) by **Toronto** (IAHL) for cash, December 1, 1929.

• MEGER, PAUL Paul Meger

LW – L. 5'7", 160 lbs. b: Watrous, Sask., 2/17/1929.

Season	Club	League	GP	G	A	Pts	AG	AA	APts	PIM	GP	G	A	Pts	PIM
1946-47	Barrie Flyers	OHA	31	13	14	27	....	....	....	20	5	3	2	5	9
1947-48	Barrie Flyers	OHA	36	30	30	60	....	....	....	28	21	14	20	34	20
1948-49	Barrie Flyers	OHA	40	33	42	75	....	....	....	79	15	7	7	14	18
1949-50	Buffalo Bisons	AHL	63	26	40	66	....	....	....	33	5	1	2	3	0
	Montreal Canadiens	**NHL**	....	....	....	....	....	....	....	....	2	0	0	0	2
1950-51	**Montreal Canadiens**	**NHL**	17	2	4	6	3	5	8	6	11	1	3	4	4
	Buffalo Bisons	AHL	46	34	35	69	....	....	....	16	....	....	....	....	....
1951-52	**Montreal Canadiens**	**NHL**	69	24	18	42	34	23	57	44	11	0	3	3	2
1952-53	**Montreal Canadiens**	**NHL**	69	9	17	26	14	24	38	38	5	1	2	3	4
1953-54	**Montreal Canadiens**	**NHL**	44	4	9	13	6	12	18	24	6	1	0	1	4
	Montreal Royals	QHL	23	13	17	30	....	....	....	28	....	....	....	....	....
1954-55	**Montreal Canadiens**	**NHL**	13	0	4	4	0	5	5	6	....	....	....	....	....
	NHL Totals		212	39	52	91	57	69	126	118	35	3	8	11	16

AHL Second All-Star Team (1950) • Won Dudley "Red" Garrett Memorial Award (Top Rookie - AHL) (1950) • AHL First All-Star Team (1951)

Played in NHL All-Star Game (1951, 1952, 1953)

• MEISSNER, DICK Dick Meissner

RW – R. 5'11", 200 lbs. b: Kindersley, Sask., 1/6/1940.

			REGULAR SEASON								PLAYOFFS				
Season	Club	League	GP	G	A	Pts	AG	AA	APts	PIM	GP	G	A	Pts	PIM
1956-57	Humboldt Indians	SJHL	51	9	13	22	....	....	....	8	4	0	1	1	0
1957-58	Estevan Bruins	SJHL	51	49	24	73	....	....	....	9	6	2	5	7	0
1958-59	Estevan Bruins	SJHL	46	46	43	89	....	....	....	37	14	*18	*14	*32	9
1959-60	**Boston Bruins**	**NHL**	60	5	6	11	6	6	12	22	....	....	....	....	....
1960-61	**Boston Bruins**	**NHL**	9	0	1	1	0	1	1	2	....	....	....	....	....
	Kingston Frontenacs	EPHL	58	26	22	48	....	....	....	19	5	1	2	3	0
1961-62	**Boston Bruins**	**NHL**	66	3	3	6	4	3	7	13	....	....	....	....	....
1962-63	Hershey Bears	AHL	70	28	26	54	....	....	....	18	15	8	6	14	10
1963-64	**New York Rangers**	**NHL**	35	3	5	8	4	5	9	0	....	....	....	....	....
	Baltimore Clippers	AHL	12	5	5	10	....	....	....	4	....	....	....	....	....
1964-65	**New York Rangers**	**NHL**	1	0	0	0	0	0	0	0	....	....	....	....	....
	Baltimore Clippers	AHL	69	35	42	77	....	....	....	21	5	3	1	4	0
1965-66	St. Louis Braves	CHL	62	27	12	39	....	....	....	23	5	2	1	3	0
1966-67	Los Angeles Blades	WHL	72	39	42	81	....	....	....	6	....	....	....	....	....
1967-68	Portland Buckaroos	WHL	6	1	1	2	....	....	....	2	....	....	....	....	....
	Baltimore Clippers	AHL	61	29	25	54	....	....	....	9	....	....	....	....	....
1968-69	Providence Reds	AHL	73	16	22	38	....	....	....	37	9	5	8	13	9
1969-70	Providence Reds	AHL	63	19	23	42	....	....	....	20	....	....	....	....	....
1970-71	Providence Reds	AHL	5	0	2	2	....	....	....	2	....	....	....	....	....
1971-72	Phoenix Roadrunners	WHL	14	4	4	8	....	....	....	11	....	....	....	....	....
	Seattle Totems	WHL	9	2	3	5	....	....	....	0	....	....	....	....	....
1972-73			DID NOT PLAY												
1973-74			DID NOT PLAY												
1974-75	Portland Buckaroos	WIHL	19	3	8	11	....	....	....	19	....	....	....	....	....
	NHL Totals		171	11	15	26	14	15	29	37	....	....	....	....	....

Traded to **NY Rangers** by **Boston** with Don McKenney for Dean Prentice, February 4, 1963. Traded to **Chicago** by **NY Rangers** with Dave Richardson, Tracy Pratt and Mel Pearson for John McKenzie and Ray Cullen, June, 1965. Selected by **Providence** (AHL) from **Chicago** in Reverse Draft, June, 1968. Traded to **Phoenix** (WHL) by **Providence** (AHL) with Adam Keller for Jim Patterson, August, 1971.

• MELNYK, GERRY — *see page 1305*

• MENARD, HILLARY Hillary "Minnie" Menard

LW – L. 5'8", 165 lbs. b: Timmins, Ont., 1/15/1934.

Season	Club	League	GP	G	A	Pts	AG	AA	APts	PIM	GP	G	A	Pts	PIM
1951-52	Barrie Flyers	OHA	42	20	16	36	....	....	....	64	....	....	....	....	....
1952-53	Barrie–Galt	OHA	55	23	19	42	....	....	....	143	10	11	7	18	9
1953-54	**Chicago Black Hawks**	**NHL**	1	0	0	0	0	0	0	0	....	....	....	....	....
	Galt Black Hawks	OHA	19	6	15	21	....	....	....	30	....	....	....	....	....
	Hamilton Tiger Cubs	OHA	4	0	0	0	....	....	....	0	....	....	....	....	....
	Guelph Biltmores	OHA	34	17	23	40	....	....	....	42	3	3	0	3	21
1954-55	Pembroke Lumber Kings	OVSHL	15	1	3	4	....	....	....	10	....	....	....	....	....
1955-56	Val D'Or Miners	Mtl-Sr.	STATISTICS NOT AVAILABLE												
1956-57	Belleville McFarlands	EOHL	51	*50	28	78	....	....	....	134	10	5	4	9	10
1957-58	Belleville McFarlands	EOHL	51	22	24	46	....	....	....	46	13	7	4	11	18
1958-59	Belleville McFarlands	EOHL	48	12	22	34	....	....	....	55	....	....	....	....	....
1959-60	New York Rovers	EHL	48	22	14	36	....	....	....	53	....	....	....	....	....
1960-61	Omaha Knights	IHL	55	18	30	48	....	....	....	88	....	....	....	....	....
	New York Rovers	EHL	2	0	0	0	....	....	....	0	....	....	....	....	....
1961-62	Omaha Knights	IHL	64	20	41	61	....	....	....	76	7	0	1	1	6
1962-63	Des Moines Oak Leaves	USHL	....	25	36	51	....	....	....	50	....	....	....	....	....
	Omaha Knights	IHL	7	4	2	6	....	....	....	16	7	6	2	8	8
1963-64	Des Moines Oak Leaves	IHL	39	11	22	33	....	....	....	49	....	....	....	....	....
1964-65	Des Moines Oak Leafs	IHL	1	0	0	0	....	....	....	0	....	....	....	....	....
1965-66	Des Moines Oak Leafs	IHL	3	1	0	1	....	....	....	2	....	....	....	....	....
1966-67	Belleville Mohawks	OHA Sr.	40	13	26	39	....	....	....	18	....	....	....	....	....
1967-68	Belleville Mohawks	OHA Sr.	34	22	11	33	....	....	....	23	....	....	....	....	....
	NHL Totals		1	0	0	0	0	0	0	0	....	....	....	....	....

• MENARD, HOWIE — *see page 1306*

• MERONEK, BILL Bill "Smiley" Meronek

C – L. 5'9", 155 lbs. b: Stoney Mountain, Man., 4/15/1917.

Season	Club	League	GP	G	A	Pts	AG	AA	APts	PIM	GP	G	A	Pts	PIM
1934-35	St. Boniface Canadians	MJHL	10	7	7	14	....	....	....	0	....	....	....	....	....
1935-36	Portage Terriers	MJHL	16	16	7	23	....	....	....	2	6	6	*6	12	6
1936-37	Portage Terriers	MJHL	16	*21	*20	*41	....	....	....	4	4	3	0	3	2
1937-38	Verdun Maple Leafs	Mtl-Sr.	20	10	10	20	....	....	....	4	8	4	3	7	0
1938-39	Verdun Maple Leafs	Mtl-Sr.	22	*17	17	34	....	....	....	9	2	0	1	1	0
1939-40	**Montreal Canadiens**	**NHL**	7	2	2	4	4	4	8	0	....	....	....	....	....
	Verdun Maple Leafs	QSHL	26	14	23	37	....	....	....	10	....	....	....	....	....
1940-41	Montreal Sr. Canadiens	QSHL	29	17	10	27	....	....	....	4	....	....	....	....	....
1941-42	Montreal Sr. Canadiens	QSHL	31	4	15	19	....	....	....	32	6	*8	6	*14	0
1942-43	Montreal Sr. Canadiens	QSHL	24	13	19	32	....	....	....	4	....	....	....	....	....
	Montreal Canadiens	**NHL**	12	3	6	9	4	8	12	0	1	0	0	0	0
1943-44	Montreal Noordyn	City Sr.	10	*13	13	26	....	....	....	6	....	....	....	....	....
	Montreal Royals	QSHL	19	12	16	28	....	....	....	0	7	6	4	10	0
1944-45	Montreal Royals	QSHL	23	16	*32	48	....	....	....	8	6	3	4	7	0
1945-46	Montreal Royals	QSHL	35	15	36	51	....	....	....	18	8	0	4	4	2
1946-47	Lachine Rapides	QPHL	49	39	63	102	....	....	....	14	10	4	7	11	10
1947-48	Lachine Rapides	QPHL	1	0	0	0	....	....	....	0	....	....	....	....	....
1948-49	Hull Volants	ECSHL	15	11	*27	*38	....	....	....	4	7	8	3	11	2
1949-50	Cornwall Calumets	ECSHL	15	7	17	24	....	....	....	6	....	....	....	....	....
	Hull Volants	ECSHL	10	5	10	15	....	....	....	0	13	7	11	18	0
	NHL Totals		19	5	8	13	8	12	20	0	1	0	0	0	0

Signed as a free agent by **Montreal**, February 1, 1943.

• MERRILL, HORACE Horace Merrill
D – L. 5'9", 176 lbs. b: Ottawa, Ontario, 11/30/1885. d: 12/24/1958.

Season	Club	League	GP	G	A	Pts	AG	AA	APts	PIM	GP	G	A	Pts	PIM
1910-11	Ottawa New Edinburghs	City Sr.	5	1	0	1	....	....	....	....	3	2	0	2	....
1911-12	Ottawa New Edinburghs	City Sr.	STATISTICS NOT AVAILABLE												
1912-13	Ottawa Senators	NHA	10	5	0	5	....	....	....	4	....	....	....	....	....
1913-14	Ottawa Senators	NHA	18	3	3	6	....	....	....	29	....	....	....	....	....
1914-15	Ottawa Senators	NHA	20	3	0	3	....	....	....	32	5	1	0	1	0
1915-16	Ottawa Senators	NHA	24	4	1	5	....	....	....	25	....	....	....	....	....
1916-17	Ottawa Senators	NHA	18	1	1	2	....	....	....	12	2	0	0	0	3
1917-18	**Ottawa Senators**	**NHL**	**3**	**0**	**0**	**0**	**0**	**0**	**0**	**3**	....	....	....	....	....
1918-19			DID NOT PLAY												
1919-20	**Ottawa Senators**	**NHL**	**5**	**0**	**0**	**0**	**0**	**0**	**0**	**0**	....	....	....	....	....
	NHL Totals		**8**	**0**	**0**	**0**	**0**	**0**	**0**	**3**	....	....	....	....	....
	Other Major League Totals		90	16	5	21	....	....	....	102	7	1	0	1	3

Signed as a free agent by **Ottawa**, February 20, 1918. Signed as a free ágent by **Ottawa**, November 28, 1919.

• METZ, DON Don Metz
RW – R. 5'10", 165 lbs. b: Wilcox, Sask., 1/10/1916.

Season	Club	League	GP	G	A	Pts	AG	AA	APts	PIM	GP	G	A	Pts	PIM
1935-36	St. Michael's Majors	OHA	10	9	4	13	....	....	....	5	5	3	0	3	8
	Toronto Goodyears	OHA Sr.	13	6	3	9	....	....	....	4	9	3	4	7	10
1936-37	Toronto Goodyears	OHA Sr.	9	3	2	5	....	....	....	6	5	0	2	2	6
1937-38	Toronto Goodyears	OHA Sr.	16	20	*22	*42	....	....	....	4	6	6	2	*8	2
1938-39	Toronto Goodyears	OHA Sr.	18	15	16	31	....	....	....	8	15	*16	8	*24	17
	Toronto Maple Leafs	**NHL**	....	....	....	....	....	....	....	....	**2**	**0**	**0**	**0**	**0**
1939-40	**Toronto Maple Leafs**	**NHL**	**10**	**1**	**1**	**2**	**2**	**2**	**4**	**4**	**2**	**0**	**0**	**0**	**0**
	Pittsburgh Hornets	AHL	32	13	25	38	....	....	....	10	7	2	2	4	4
1940-41	**Toronto Maple Leafs**	**NHL**	**31**	**4**	**10**	**14**	**8**	**18**	**26**	**6**	**7**	**1**	**1**	**2**	**2**
1941-42	**Toronto Maple Leafs**	**NHL**	**25**	**2**	**3**	**5**	**3**	**5**	**8**	**8**	**4**	**4**	**3**	**7**	**0**
1942-43	Regina Rangers	City Sr.	24	*43	26	*69	....	....	....	12	5	*10	4	14	6
1943-44	RCAF Seahawks	Van-Sr.	....	....	....	....	....	....	....	....	2	1	1	2	4
1944-45	**Toronto Maple Leafs**	**NHL**	....	....	....	....	....	....	....	....	**11**	**0**	**1**	**1**	**4**
1945-46	**Toronto Maple Leafs**	**NHL**	**7**	**1**	**0**	**1**	**2**	**0**	**2**	**0**	....	....	....	....	....
	Pittsburgh Hornets	AHL	44	22	29	51	....	....	....	8	6	3	4	7	2
1946-47	**Toronto Maple Leafs**	**NHL**	**40**	**4**	**9**	**13**	**5**	**13**	**18**	**10**	**11**	**2**	**3**	**5**	**4**
	Pittsburgh Hornets	AHL	24	19	17	36	....	....	....	4	....	....	....	....	....
1947-48	**Toronto Maple Leafs**	**NHL**	**26**	**4**	**6**	**10**	**6**	**9**	**15**	**2**	**2**	**0**	**0**	**0**	**2**
	Pittsburgh Hornets	AHL	3	0	1	1	....	....	....	0	....	....	....	....	....
1948-49	**Toronto Maple Leafs**	**NHL**	**33**	**4**	**6**	**10**	**6**	**9**	**15**	**12**	**3**	**0**	**0**	**0**	**0**
	Pittsburgh Hornets	AHL	17	5	7	12	....	....	....	4	....	....	....	....	....
	NHL Totals		**172**	**20**	**35**	**55**	**32**	**56**	**88**	**42**	**42**	**7**	**8**	**15**	**12**

Played in NHL All-Star Game (1947)

• METZ, NICK Nick Metz
LW – L. 5'11", 160 lbs. b: Wilcox, Sask., 2/16/1914. Deceased.

Season	Club	League	GP	G	A	Pts	AG	AA	APts	PIM	GP	G	A	Pts	PIM
1932-33	St. Michael's Majors	OHA	10	9	3	*12	....	....	....	14	2	0	*2	2	2
1933-34	St. Michael's Majors	OHA	12	18	15	33	....	....	....	10	3	*4	0	4	6
1934-35	**Toronto Maple Leafs**	**NHL**	**18**	**2**	**2**	**4**	**4**	**4**	**8**	**4**	**6**	**1**	**1**	**2**	**0**
	Syracuse Stars	IAHL	26	13	13	26	....	....	....	6	....	....	....	....	....
1935-36	**Toronto Maple Leafs**	**NHL**	**38**	**14**	**6**	**20**	**35**	**14**	**49**	**14**	....	....	....	....	....
1936-37	**Toronto Maple Leafs**	**NHL**	**48**	**9**	**11**	**20**	**19**	**26**	**45**	**19**	**2**	**0**	**0**	**0**	**0**
1937-38	**Toronto Maple Leafs**	**NHL**	**48**	**15**	**7**	**22**	**32**	**14**	**46**	**12**	**7**	**0**	**2**	**2**	**0**
1938-39	**Toronto Maple Leafs**	**NHL**	**47**	**11**	**10**	**21**	**23**	**19**	**42**	**15**	**10**	**3**	**3**	**6**	**6**
1939-40	**Toronto Maple Leafs**	**NHL**	**31**	**6**	**5**	**11**	**13**	**10**	**23**	**2**	**9**	**1**	**3**	**4**	**9**
1940-41	**Toronto Maple Leafs**	**NHL**	**47**	**14**	**21**	**35**	**28**	**39**	**67**	**10**	**7**	**3**	**4**	**7**	**0**
1941-42	**Toronto Maple Leafs**	**NHL**	**30**	**11**	**9**	**20**	**19**	**14**	**33**	**20**	**13**	**4**	**4**	**8**	**12**
1942-43	Nanaimo Army	City Sr.	1	1	2	3	....	....	....	0	13	3	3	6	10
1943-44	Nanaimo Army	PCHL	7	2	7	9	....	....	....	0	....	....	....	....	....
1944-45	**Toronto Maple Leafs**	**NHL**	**50**	**22**	**13**	**35**	**31**	**21**	**52**	**26**	**7**	**1**	**1**	**2**	**2**
1945-46	**Toronto Maple Leafs**	**NHL**	**41**	**11**	**11**	**22**	**17**	**20**	**37**	**4**	....	....	....	....	....
1946-47	**Toronto Maple Leafs**	**NHL**	**60**	**12**	**16**	**28**	**16**	**23**	**39**	**15**	**6**	**4**	**2**	**6**	**0**
1947-48	**Toronto Maple Leafs**	**NHL**	**60**	**4**	**8**	**12**	**6**	**12**	**18**	**8**	**9**	**2**	**0**	**2**	**2**
	NHL Totals		**518**	**131**	**119**	**250**	**243**	**216**	**459**	**149**	**76**	**19**	**20**	**39**	**31**

• MICHALUK, ART Art Michaluk
D – R. 6', 180 lbs. b: Canmore, Alta., 5/4/1923.

Season	Club	League	GP	G	A	Pts	AG	AA	APts	PIM	GP	G	A	Pts	PIM
1939-40	Canmore Zephyrs	AJHL	9	1	1	2	....	....	....	0	2	0	2	2	2
1940-41			MILITARY SERVICE												
1941-42			MILITARY SERVICE												
1942-43	Calgary RCAF Mustangs	City Sr.	21	3	2	5	....	....	....	24	8	1	1	2	8
1943-44			MILITARY SERVICE												
1944-45	Calgary RCAF Mustangs	ASHL	15	6	3	9	....	....	....	14	3	0	0	0	8
1945-46	Calgary Stampeders	WCSHL	35	5	9	14	....	....	....	24	18	0	3	3	16
1946-47	Calgary Stampeders	WCSHL	39	16	16	32	....	....	....	58	7	2	5	7	*15
1947-48	**Chicago Black Hawks**	**NHL**	**5**	**0**	**0**	**0**	**0**	**0**	**0**	**0**	....	....	....	....	....
	Pittsburgh–Providence	AHL	40	6	10	16	....	....	....	32	5	1	2	3	2
1948-49	Providence Reds	AHL	65	4	17	21	....	....	....	55	11	1	3	4	6
1949-50	Providence Reds	AHL	67	7	20	27	....	....	....	32	4	1	2	3	2
1950-51	Providence Reds	AHL	70	13	21	34	....	....	....	34	....	....	....	....	....
1951-52	Providence Reds	AHL	62	3	15	18	....	....	....	41	15	0	5	5	8
1952-53	Calgary Stampeders	WHL	70	10	26	36	....	....	....	22	5	0	2	2	8
1953-54	Calgary Stampeders	WHL	68	7	26	33	....	....	....	20	18	1	7	8	8
1954-55	Calgary Stampeders	WHL	70	8	22	30	....	....	....	24	9	0	7	7	10
1955-56	Calgary Stampeders	WHL	54	3	14	17	....	....	....	28	8	0	2	2	6
1956-57	Calgary Stampeders	WHL	51	2	12	14	....	....	....	15	3	0	2	2	2
1957-58	Calgary Stampeders	WHL	17	3	15	18	....	....	....	2	14	0	3	3	6
	NHL Totals		**5**	**0**	**0**	**0**	**0**	**0**	**0**	**0**	....	....	....	....	....

WHL First All-Star Team (1953, 1956) • WHL Prairie Division First All-Star Team (1957)

• MICHALUK, JOHN John Michaluk
F – L. 5'10", 155 lbs. b: Canmore, Alta., 11/2/1928.

Season	Club	League	GP	G	A	Pts	AG	AA	APts	PIM	GP	G	A	Pts	PIM
1948-49	Calgary Buffalos	WCJHL	30	26	17	43	....	....	....	24	8	6	5	11	8
	Calgary Stampeders	WCSHL	2	0	0	0	....	....	....	0	....	....	....	....	....
1949-50	Spokane Flyers	WIHL	58	21	15	36	....	....	....	27	4	1	2	3	0
1950-51	**Chicago Black Hawks**	**NHL**	**1**	**0**	**0**	**0**	**0**	**0**	**0**	**0**	....	....	....	....	....
	Milwaukee Seagulls	USHL	56	13	11	24	....	....	....	41	....	....	....	....	....
1951-52	Providence Reds	AHL	46	13	12	25	....	....	....	16	3	0	1	1	0
1952-53	Providence Reds	AHL	18	1	3	4	....	....	....	6	....	....	....	....	....
	Quebec Aces	QSHL	22	3	3	6	....	....	....	17	21	0	2	2	5
1953-54	Calgary Stampeders	WHL	66	7	9	16	....	....	....	8	20	2	7	9	8
1954-55	Calgary Stampeders	WHL	14	3	4	7	....	....	....	2	9	0	0	0	2
	NHL Totals		**1**	**0**	**0**	**0**	**0**	**0**	**0**	**0**	....	....	....	....	....

• MICKEY, LARRY — *see page 1309*

• MICKOSKI, NICK Nick "Broadway Nick" Mickoski
LW – L. 6'1", 183 lbs. b: Winnipeg, Man., 12/7/1927.

Season	Club	League	GP	G	A	Pts	AG	AA	APts	PIM	GP	G	A	Pts	PIM
1943-44	St.Catherines Falcons	OHA	26	4	6	10	....	....	....	50	6	0	0	0	17
1944-45	Canadian Ukrainian A.C.	MJHL	12	11	4	15	....	....	....	2	4	5	4	9	0
	Providence Reds	AHL	6	0	0	0	....	....	....	5	....	....	....	....	....
1945-46	St. James Canadians	MJHL	10	10	6	16	....	....	....	8	2	0	0	0	0
	Stratford Kroehlers	OHA	16	11	13	24	....	....	....	30	....	....	....	....	....
	New York Rovers	EHL	25	6	8	14	....	....	....	8	9	1	2	3	6
1946-47	New York Rovers	QSHL	30	25	16	41	....	....	....	16	....	....	....	....	....
	New York Rovers	EHL	10	9	16	25	....	....	....	10	....	....	....	....	....
1947-48	**New York Rangers**	**NHL**	....	....	....	....	....	....	....	....	**2**	**0**	**1**	**1**	**0**
	New Haven Ramblers	AHL	22	11	16	27	....	....	....	4	4	2	1	3	2
1948-49	**New York Rangers**	**NHL**	**54**	**13**	**9**	**22**	**20**	**14**	**34**	**20**	....	....	....	....	....
1949-50	**New York Rangers**	**NHL**	**45**	**10**	**10**	**20**	**13**	**13**	**26**	**10**	**12**	**1**	**5**	**6**	**2**
	New Haven Ramblers	AHL	23	12	17	29	....	....	....	7	....	....	....	....	....
1950-51	**New York Rangers**	**NHL**	**64**	**20**	**15**	**35**	**27**	**19**	**46**	**12**	....	....	....	....	....
1951-52	**New York Rangers**	**NHL**	**43**	**7**	**13**	**20**	**10**	**17**	**27**	**20**	....	....	....	....	....
	Cincinnati Mohawks	AHL	22	11	10	21	....	....	....	15	5	2	3	5	4
1952-53	**New York Rangers**	**NHL**	**70**	**19**	**16**	**35**	**29**	**22**	**51**	**39**	....	....	....	....	....
1953-54	**New York Rangers**	**NHL**	**68**	**19**	**16**	**35**	**29**	**22**	**51**	**22**	....	....	....	....	....
1954-55	**New York Rangers**	**NHL**	**18**	**0**	**14**	**14**	**0**	**18**	**18**	**6**	....	....	....	....	....
	Chicago Black Hawks	**NHL**	**52**	**10**	**19**	**29**	**14**	**24**	**38**	**42**	....	....	....	....	....
1955-56	**Chicago Black Hawks**	**NHL**	**70**	**19**	**20**	**39**	**28**	**25**	**53**	**52**	....	....	....	....	....
1956-57	**Chicago Black Hawks**	**NHL**	**70**	**16**	**20**	**36**	**22**	**23**	**45**	**24**	....	....	....	....	....
1957-58	**Chicago Black Hawks**	**NHL**	**28**	**5**	**6**	**11**	**6**	**6**	**12**	**20**	....	....	....	....	....
	Detroit Red Wings	**NHL**	**37**	**8**	**12**	**20**	**10**	**13**	**23**	**30**	**4**	**0**	**0**	**0**	**4**
1958-59	**Detroit Red Wings**	**NHL**	**66**	**11**	**15**	**26**	**14**	**16**	**30**	**20**	....	....	....	....	....
1959-60	**Boston Bruins**	**NHL**	**18**	**1**	**0**	**1**	**1**	**0**	**1**	**2**	....	....	....	....	....
	Providence Reds	AHL	48	29	22	51	....	....	....	6	5	2	5	7	4
1960-61	Winnipeg Warriors	WHL	69	25	24	49	....	....	....	16	....	....	....	....	....
1961-62	San Francisco Seals	WHL	70	31	48	79	....	....	....	24	2	1	1	2	0
1962-63	San Francisco Seals	WHL	68	41	54	95	....	....	....	20	17	5	11	16	6
1963-64	San Francisco Seals	WHL	68	20	37	57	....	....	....	28	11	2	10	12	4
1964-65	San Francisco Seals	WHL	60	13	33	46	....	....	....	24	....	....	....	....	....
1965-66			DID NOT PLAY												
1966-67	Grand Falls Cataracts	Nfld.	40	27	49	76	....	....	....	....	....	....	....	....	....
1967-68	Grand Falls Cataracts	Nfld.	40	34	56	90	....	....	....	....	....	....	....	....	....
1968-69	Grand Falls Cataracts	Nfld.	40	24	28	52	....	....	....	....	....	....	....	....	....
	NHL Totals		**703**	**158**	**185**	**343**	**223**	**232**	**455**	**319**	**18**	**1**	**6**	**7**	**6**

WHL First All-Star Team (1963)

Played in NHL All-Star Game (1956)

Traded to **Chicago** by **NY Rangers** with Allan Stanley and Rich Lamoureux for Bill Gadsby and Pete Conacher, November 23, 1954. Traded to **Detroit** by **Chicago** with Hec Lalonde, Bob Bailey and Jack McIntyre for Bill Dineen, Billy Dea, Lorne Ferguson and Earl Reibel, December 17, 1957. Traded to **Boston** by **Detroit** for Jim Morrison, August 25, 1959.

• MIGAY, RUDY Rudy Migay
C – L. 5'6", 150 lbs. b: Fort William, Ont., 11/18/1928.

Season	Club	League	GP	G	A	Pts	AG	AA	APts	PIM	GP	G	A	Pts	PIM
1944-45	Port Arthur Flyers	TBJHL	11	22	10	32	....	....	....	22	3	2	2	4	6
1945-46	Port Arthur Flyers	TBJHL	6	11	*17	*28	....	....	....	0	5	3	6	9	4
1946-47	St. Michael's Majors	OHA	28	25	18	43	....	....	....	15	9	2	11	13	0
1947-48	Port Arthur Bruins	TBJHL	7	12	8	20	....	....	....	12	24	17	*30	47	18
1948-49	Pittsburgh Hornets	AHL	64	21	31	52	....	....	....	38	....	....	....	....	....
1949-50	**Toronto Maple Leafs**	**NHL**	**18**	**1**	**5**	**6**	**1**	**6**	**7**	**8**	....	....	....	....	....
	Pittsburgh Hornets	AHL	44	11	25	36	....	....	....	31	....	....	....	....	....
1950-51	Pittsburgh Hornets	AHL	58	20	38	58	....	....	....	45	13	1	*15	*16	11
1951-52	**Toronto Maple Leafs**	**NHL**	**19**	**2**	**1**	**3**	**3**	**1**	**4**	**12**	....	....	....	....	....
	Pittsburgh Hornets	AHL	32	20	26	46	....	....	....	10	11	7	4	11	8
1952-53	**Toronto Maple Leafs**	**NHL**	**40**	**5**	**4**	**9**	**8**	**6**	**14**	**22**	....	....	....	....	....
1953-54	**Toronto Maple Leafs**	**NHL**	**70**	**8**	**15**	**23**	**12**	**20**	**32**	**60**	**5**	**1**	**0**	**1**	**4**
1954-55	**Toronto Maple Leafs**	**NHL**	**67**	**8**	**16**	**24**	**12**	**20**	**32**	**66**	**3**	**0**	**0**	**0**	**10**
1955-56	**Toronto Maple Leafs**	**NHL**	**70**	**12**	**16**	**28**	**17**	**20**	**37**	**52**	**5**	**0**	**0**	**0**	**6**
1956-57	**Toronto Maple Leafs**	**NHL**	**66**	**15**	**20**	**35**	**20**	**23**	**43**	**51**	....	....	....	....	....
1957-58	**Toronto Maple Leafs**	**NHL**	**48**	**7**	**14**	**21**	**9**	**15**	**24**	**18**	....	....	....	....	....
	Rochester Americans	AHL	15	5	8	13	....	....	....	18	....	....	....	....	....
1958-59	**Toronto Maple Leafs**	**NHL**	**19**	**1**	**1**	**2**	**1**	**1**	**2**	**4**	**2**	**0**	**0**	**0**	**0**
	Rochester Americans	AHL	51	24	58	82	....	....	....	100	3	1	0	1	6
1959-60	**Toronto Maple Leafs**	**NHL**	**1**	**0**	**0**	**0**	**0**	**0**	**0**	**0**	....	....	....	....	....
	Rochester Americans	AHL	50	16	48	64	....	....	....	50	12	3	*10	13	19
1960-61	Port Arthur Bearcats	TBSHL	DID NOT PLAY – COACHING												
1961-62	Port Arthur Bearcats	TBSHL	DID NOT PLAY – COACHING												
1962-63	Rochester Americans	AHL	2	1	1	2	....	....	....	4	....	....	....	....	....
1963-64	Denver Invaders	WHL	56	20	31	51	....	....	....	30	6	0	3	3	32
1964-65	Tulsa Oilers	CHL	50	5	26	31	....	....	....	53	....	....	....	....	....
1965-66	Tulsa Oilers	CHL	DID NOT PLAY – COACHING												
	NHL Totals		**418**	**59**	**92**	**151**	**83**	**112**	**195**	**293**	**15**	**1**	**0**	**1**	**20**

AHL First All-Star Team (1959) • Won Les Cunningham Award (MVP - AHL) (1959)

Played in NHL All-Star Game (1957)

• MIKITA, STAN — *see page 1310*

• MIKOL, JIM Jim Mikol
LW/D – R. 6', 175 lbs. b: Kitchener, Ont., 6/11/1938.

			REGULAR SEASON								PLAYOFFS				
Season	Club	League	GP	G	A	Pts	AG	AA	APts	PIM	GP	G	A	Pts	PIM
1956-57	Peterbourgh Petes	OHA	13	2	0	2	....	....	....	4	....	....	....	....	....
1957-58	Peterbourgh Petes	OHA	35	6	12	18	....	....	....	37	5	0	2	2	13
1958-59	North Bay Trappers	NOHA	48	3	11	14	....	....	....	47	....	....	....	....	....
1959-60	Johnstown Jets	EHL	64	11	14	25	....	....	....	101	13	2	5	7	18
1960-61	Cleveland Barons	AHL	70	12	22	34	....	....	....	116	4	0	0	0	0
1961-62	Cleveland Barons	AHL	70	32	48	80	....	....	....	89	6	1	4	5	12
1962-63	**Toronto Maple Leafs**	**NHL**	**4**	**0**	**1**	**1**	**0**	**1**	**1**	**2**	....	....	....	....	....
	Cleveland Barons	AHL	49	20	30	50	....	....	....	58	5	0	5	5	4
1963-64	Cleveland Barons	AHL	72	24	44	68	....	....	....	52	9	3	4	7	6
1964-65	**New York Rangers**	**NHL**	**30**	**1**	**3**	**4**	**1**	**3**	**4**	**6**	....	....	....	....	....
	St. Paul Rangers	CHL	33	14	33	47	....	....	....	30	11	1	7	8	12
1965-66	Providence Reds	AHL	72	24	26	50	....	....	....	35	....	....	....	....	....
1966-67	Providence Reds	AHL	31	8	9	17	....	....	....	8	....	....	....	....	....
1967-68	Providence Reds	AHL	63	19	30	49	....	....	....	30	8	1	3	4	12
1968-69	Cleveland Barons	AHL	72	20	35	55	....	....	....	27	5	0	0	0	0
1969-70	Cleveland Barons	AHL	68	8	19	27	....	....	....	18	....	....	....	....	....
	NHL Totals		**34**	**1**	**4**	**5**	**1**	**4**	**5**	**8**	....	....	....	....	....

Claimed by **Boston** from **Cleveland** (AHL) in Inter-League Draft, June 10, 1964. Claimed by **NY Rangers** from **Boston** in Intra-League Draft, June 10, 1964. Traded to **Providence** (AHL) by **NY Rangers** with Sandy McGregor, Marcel Paille and Aldo Guidolin for Ed Giacomin, May, 1965. Traded to **Montreal** by **Providence** (AHL) for Yves Locas, July, 1968. Traded to **Cleveland** (AHL) by **Montreal** with Bill Staub for Howie Glover, August, 1968.

• MILKS, HIB Hib (Hubert) Milks
LW/C – L. 5'11", 165 lbs. b: Eardley, Ont., 4/1/1902. d: 1/21/1949.

Season	Club	League	GP	G	A	Pts	AG	AA	APts	PIM	GP	G	A	Pts	PIM
1917-18	Ottawa Landsdownes	City Jr.	1	0	0	0	....	....	....	0	....	....	....	....	....
1918-19	Ottawa West Enders	City Jr.	STATISTICS NOT AVAILABLE												
1919-20	Ottawa Gunners	City Sr.	8	1	0	1	....	....	....	....	....	....	....	....	....
1920-21	Ottawa Gunners	City Sr.	13	6	0	6	....	....	....	....	6	6	2	8	....
1921-22	Ottawa Gunners	City Sr.	14	6	4	10	....	....	....	15	6	7	4	11	*18
1922-23	Pittsburgh Yellowjackets	USAHA	20	10	0	10	....	....	....	....	....	....	....	....	....
1923-24	Ottawa New Edinburghs	City Sr.	12	*16	0	*16	....	....	....	....	2	0	0	0	....
1924-25	Pittsburgh Yellowjackets	USAHA	39	12	0	12	....	....	....	....	8	2	0	2	0
1925-26	**Pittsburgh Pirates**	**NHL**	**36**	**14**	**5**	**19**	**44**	**58**	**102**	**17**	**2**	**0**	**0**	**0**	**0**
1926-27	**Pittsburgh Pirates**	**NHL**	**44**	**16**	**6**	**22**	**47**	**51**	**98**	**18**	....	....	....	....	....
1927-28	**Pittsburgh Pirates**	**NHL**	**44**	**18**	**3**	**21**	**56**	**25**	**81**	**32**	**2**	**0**	**0**	**0**	**2**
1928-29	**Pittsburgh Pirates**	**NHL**	**44**	**9**	**3**	**12**	**36**	**27**	**63**	**22**	....	....	....	....	....
1929-30	**Pittsburgh Pirates**	**NHL**	**41**	**13**	**11**	**24**	**26**	**36**	**62**	**36**	....	....	....	....	....
1930-31	**Philadelphia Quakers**	**NHL**	**44**	**17**	**6**	**23**	**42**	**22**	**64**	**42**	....	....	....	....	....
1931-32	**New York Rangers**	**NHL**	**48**	**0**	**4**	**4**	**0**	**11**	**11**	**12**	**7**	**0**	**0**	**0**	**0**
1932-33	**Ottawa Senators**	**NHL**	**16**	**0**	**3**	**3**	**0**	**8**	**8**	**0**	....	....	....	....	....
	NHL Totals		**317**	**87**	**41**	**128**	**251**	**238**	**489**	**179**	**11**	**0**	**0**	**0**	**2**

Signed as a free agent by **Pittsburgh**, September 26, 1925. Transferred to **Philadelphia** after **Pittsburgh** franchise relocated, October 18, 1930. Claimed by **NY Rangers** from **Philadelphia** in Dispersal Draft, September 26, 1931. Signed as a free agent by **Ottawa**, October 2, 1932.

• MILLAR, HUGH Hugh Millar
D – L. 5'9", 200 lbs. b: Edmonton, Alta., 4/3/1921.

Season	Club	League	GP	G	A	Pts	AG	AA	APts	PIM	GP	G	A	Pts	PIM
1938-39	Winnipeg Rangers	MJHL	21	5	7	12	....	....	....	14	....	....	....	....	....
1939-40	Winnipeg Rangers	MJHL	22	9	1	10	....	....	....	27	....	....	....	....	....
1940-41	Winnipeg Rangers	MJHL	14	8	3	11	....	....	....	23	20	12	7	19	23
1941-42	Omaha Knights	AHA	50	3	8	11	....	....	....	34	8	5	1	6	4
1942-43	Winnipeg Navy	City Sr.	12	11	6	17	....	....	....	10	5	*4	2	*6	4
1943-44	Winnipeg Navy	City Sr.	9	3	2	5	....	....	....	15	....	....	....	....	....
	Calgary Combines	City Sr.	2	0	0	0	....	....	....	4	3	1	1	2	2
1944-45	Cornwallis Navy	City Sr.	12	0	4	4	....	....	....	14	3	0	0	0	2
1944-45	Winnipeg Navy	City Sr.	2	0	0	0	....	....	....	2	....	....	....	....	....
1945-46	Indianapolis Capitals	AHL	50	6	26	32	....	....	....	26	5	0	1	1	2
1946-47	**Detroit Red Wings**	**NHL**	**4**	**0**	**0**	**0**	**0**	**0**	**0**	**0**	**1**	**0**	**0**	**0**	**0**
	Indianapolis Capitals	AHL	57	18	12	30	....	....	....	43	....	....	....	....	....
1947-48	Indianapolis Capitals	AHL	68	8	36	44	....	....	....	39	....	....	....	....	....
	NHL Totals		**4**	**0**	**0**	**0**	**0**	**0**	**0**	**0**	**1**	**0**	**0**	**0**	**0**

AHL Second All-Star Team (1946, 1948) • AHL First All-Star Team (1947)

• MILLER, BILL Bill Miller
C/D – R. 6', 160 lbs. b: Campbellton, N.B., 8/1/1908.

Season	Club	League	GP	G	A	Pts	AG	AA	APts	PIM	GP	G	A	Pts	PIM
1923-24	Campbellton Rink Rats	NNBSL	STATISTICS NOT AVAILABLE												
1924-25	Campbellton Tigers	NNBSL	6	5	2	7	....	....	....	2	....	....	....	....	....
1925-26	Campbellton Tigers	NNBSL	4	3	1	4	....	....	....	2	3	2	1	3	0
1926-27	Campbellton Tigers	NNBSL	2	2	0	2	....	....	....	0	....	....	....	....	....
	Mount Allison University	MIAA	2	*4	0	*4	....	....	....	3	....	....	....	....	....
1927-28	Campbellton Tigers	NNBSL	3	5	0	5	....	....	....	0	....	....	....	....	....
	Mount Allison University	MIAA	2	*5	0	*5	....	....	....	0	....	....	....	....	....
1928-29	Mount Allison University	MIAA	2	0	1	1	....	....	....	8	....	....	....	....	....
	Mount Allison Mounties	NBSHL	6	*13	1	*14	....	....	....	....	....	....	....	....	....
1929-30	Mount Allison University	MIAA	2	2	0	2	....	....	....	....	....	....	....	....	....
	Campbellton Tigers	NNBSL	3	3	1	4	....	....	....	2	....	....	....	....	....
1930-31	Campbellton Tigers	NNBSL	11	*28	11	*39	....	....	....	6	5	8	3	11	2
1931-32	Campbellton Tigers	NNBSL	23	*19	8	27	....	....	....	14	2	0	0	0	0
	Fredericton Capitals	City Sr.	5	0	3	3	....	....	....	2	....	....	....	....	....
1932-33	Moncton Hawks	MSHL	23	5	0	5	....	....	....	0	13	2	*7	9	4
1933-34	Moncton Hawks	MSHL	41	8	19	27	....	....	....	30	15	10	12	22	4
1934-35	**Montreal Maroons**	**NHL**	**22**	**3**	**0**	**3**	**6**	**0**	**6**	**2**	**7**	**0**	**0**	**0**	**0**
	Moncton Hawks	MSHL	20	*17	5	22	....	....	....	4	3	*5	2	7	0
	Moncton Hawks	Big 3	4	2	1	3	....	....	....	2	....	....	....	....	....
1935-36	**Montreal Maroons**	**NHL**	**8**	**0**	**0**	**0**	**0**	**0**	**0**	**0**	....	....	....	....	....
	New Haven Eagles	Can-Am	11	0	0	0	....	....	....	0	....	....	....	....	....
	Montreal Canadiens	**NHL**	**17**	**1**	**2**	**3**	**2**	**5**	**7**	**2**	....	....	....	....	....
1936-37	**Montreal Canadiens**	**NHL**	**48**	**3**	**1**	**4**	**6**	**2**	**8**	**12**	**5**	**0**	**0**	**0**	**0**
	NHL Totals		**95**	**7**	**3**	**10**	**14**	**7**	**21**	**16**	**12**	**0**	**0**	**0**	**0**

• Recalled from **New Haven** (Can-Am) by **Montreal Maroons** to coach in Tommy Gorman's absence, April 4, 1936. Traded to **Montreal Canadiens** by **Montreal Maroons** with Toe Blake and Ken Gravell for Lorne Chabot, February 13, 1936.

• MILLER, EARL Earl Miller
LW – L. 5'11", 180 lbs. b: Lumsden, Sask., 9/12/1905. Deceased.

Season	Club	League	GP	G	A	Pts	AG	AA	APts	PIM	GP	G	A	Pts	PIM
1923-24	Saskatoon Nutana	City Jr.	STATISTICS NOT AVAILABLE												
1924-25	U. of Saskatchewan	City Sr.	5	0	0	0	....	....	....	2	....	....	....	....	....
1925-26	U. of Saskatchewan	City Sr.	1	0	1	1	....	....	....	0	....	....	....	....	....
1926-27	Saskatoon Shieks	PrHL	20	4	2	6	....	....	....	14	4	*3	*1	*4	2
1927-28	**Chicago Black Hawks**	**NHL**	**21**	**1**	**1**	**2**	**3**	**8**	**11**	**32**	....	....	....	....	....
	Saskatoon Shieks	PrHL	12	5	4	9	....	....	....	32	....	....	....	....	....
1928-29	**Chicago Black Hawks**	**NHL**	**17**	**1**	**1**	**2**	**4**	**9**	**13**	**24**	....	....	....	....	....
	Kitchener Dutchmen	Can-Pro	22	9	6	15	....	....	....	75	....	....	....	....	....
1929-30	**Chicago Black Hawks**	**NHL**	**28**	**11**	**5**	**16**	**22**	**16**	**38**	**50**	**2**	**1**	**0**	**1**	**6**
1930-31	**Chicago Black Hawks**	**NHL**	**19**	**3**	**4**	**7**	**7**	**14**	**21**	**8**	**1**	**0**	**0**	**0**	**0**
	London Panthers	IAHL	4	0	3	3	....	....	....	4	....	....	....	....	....
1931-32	**Chicago Black Hawks**	**NHL**	**9**	**0**	**0**	**0**	**0**	**0**	**0**	**0**	....	....	....	....	....
	Toronto Maple Leafs	**NHL**	**15**	**3**	**3**	**6**	**6**	**8**	**14**	**10**	**7**	**0**	**0**	**0**	**0**
	Pittsburgh Yellowjackets	IAHL	22	3	2	5	....	....	....	14	....	....	....	....	....
1932-33	Syracuse Stars	IAHL	44	19	15	34	....	....	....	26	6	*4	0	4	6
1933-34	Syracuse Stars	IAHL	43	21	19	*40	....	....	....	54	6	1	3	4	14
1934-35	Buffalo Bisons	IAHL	39	7	9	16	....	....	....	39	....	....	....	....	....
1935-36	Buffalo Bisons	IAHL	17	0	3	3	....	....	....	4	....	....	....	....	....
	NHL Totals		**109**	**19**	**14**	**33**	**42**	**55**	**97**	**124**	**10**	**1**	**0**	**1**	**6**

Traded to **Chicago** by **Saskatoon** (PrHL) with Cally McCalmon for Corb Denneny and Nick Wasnie, January 11, 1928. Traded to **Toronto** by **Chicago** for cash, February 8, 1932.

• MILLER, JACK Jack Miller
C – L. 5'8", 155 lbs. b: Delisle, Sask., 9/16/1925.

Season	Club	League	GP	G	A	Pts	AG	AA	APts	PIM	GP	G	A	Pts	PIM
1941-42	Saskatoon Quakers	SJHL	8	2	1	3	....	....	....	2	2	0	0	0	0
1942-43	Prince Albert Blackhawks	SJHL	7	4	6	10	....	....	....	6	3	0	0	0	0
	Amprior RCAF	Ott-Sr.	8	6	7	13	....	....	....	2	2	1	1	2	0
1943-44	Amprior RCAF	Ott-Sr.	8	2	4	6	....	....	....	2	....	....	....	....	....
1944-45	Moose Jaw Canucks	SJHL	16	7	5	12	....	....	....	16	10	3	1	4	10
1945-46	Saskatoon Elks	WCSHL	30	12	11	23	....	....	....	6	....	....	....	....	....
1946-47	Los Angeles Ramblers	Kootenay	48	8	20	28	....	....	....	38	....	....	....	....	....
1947-48	Kansas City Pla-Mors	USHL	66	23	28	51	....	....	....	59	7	2	1	3	2
1948-49	Kansas City Pla-Mors	USHL	66	18	36	54	....	....	....	46	2	0	2	2	2
1949-50	**Chicago Black Hawks**	**NHL**	**6**	**0**	**0**	**0**	**0**	**0**	**0**	**0**	....	....	....	....	....
	Kansas City Pla-Mors	USHL	62	19	31	50	....	....	....	38	3	0	2	2	2
1950-51	**Chicago Black Hawks**	**NHL**	**11**	**0**	**0**	**0**	**0**	**0**	**0**	**4**	....	....	....	....	....
	Milwaukee Seagulls	USHL	44	22	14	36	....	....	....	47	....	....	....	....	....
1951-52	Calgary Stampeders	PCHL	39	10	15	25	....	....	....	19	....	....	....	....	....
1952-53	Spokane Flyers	OSHL	59	*45	50	95	....	....	....	68	9	5	0	5	18
1953-54	Vernon Canadians	OSHL	63	29	57	86	....	....	....	18	5	4	3	7	0
1954-55	Spokane Flyers	WIHL	32	21	30	51	....	....	....	40	4	2	2	4	2
1955-56	Spokane Flyers	WIHL	46	21	56	77	....	....	....	77	10	3	7	10	0
	NHL Totals		**17**	**0**	**0**	**0**	**0**	**0**	**0**	**4**	....	....	....	....	....

• MISZUK, JOHN — *see page 1316*

• MITCHELL, BILL Bill Mitchell
D – L. 5'11", 180 lbs. b: Port Dalhousie, Ont., 2/22/1930.

Season	Club	League	GP	G	A	Pts	AG	AA	APts	PIM	GP	G	A	Pts	PIM
1946-47	Stratford Kroehlers	OHA	27	5	12	17	....	....	....	16	2	0	1	1	2
1947-48	Stratford Kroehlers	OHA	34	4	10	14	....	....	....	41	2	0	1	1	0
	Kitchener Dutchmen	OHA Sr.	2	1	0	1	....	....	....	0	....	....	....	....	....
1948-49	Stratford Kroehlers	OHA	36	7	10	17	....	....	....	27	3	1	0	1	0
1949-50	Toronto Marlboros	OHA	46	7	12	19	....	....	....	46	5	2	0	2	4
1950-51	Kitchener Dutchmen	OHA Sr.	32	6	9	15	....	....	....	27	....	....	....	....	....
	Halifax St. Mary's	MMHL	3	0	0	0	....	....	....	0	....	....	....	....	....
	Moncton Hawks	MMHL	1	0	0	0	....	....	....	0	....	....	....	....	....
1951-52	Kitchener Dutchmen	OHA Sr.	47	18	20	38	....	....	....	40	5	0	1	1	4
1952-53	Kitchener Dutchmen	OHA Sr.	24	14	8	22	....	....	....	18	....	....	....	....	....
	Toledo Mercurys	IHL	15	3	9	12	....	....	....	4	5	1	1	2	10
1953-54	Toledo Mercurys	IHL	63	15	15	30	....	....	....	57	5	0	3	3	8
1954-55	Toledo Mercurys	IHL	60	18	30	48	....	....	....	55	3	1	1	2	4
1955-56	Toledo Mercurys	IHL	58	17	30	47	....	....	....	63	9	1	4	5	18
1956-57	Toledo Mercurys	IHL	60	12	31	43	....	....	....	36	5	3	3	6	6
1957-58	Toledo Mercurys	IHL	61	13	39	52	....	....	....	43	....	....	....	....	....
1958-59	Toledo Mercurys	IHL	60	12	33	45	....	....	....	50	....	....	....	....	....
	Fort Wayne Komets	IHL	....	....	....	....	....	....	....	....	11	0	7	7	6
1959-60	Toledo—St. Louis	IHL	55	11	26	37	....	....	....	34	....	....	....	....	....
1960-61	Chatham Maroons	OHA Sr.	....	16	*40	56	....	....	....	26	....	....	....	....	....
1961-62	Galt–Windsor	OHA Sr.	30	6	31	37	....	....	....	22	7	2	2	4	8
	Canada	WEC-A	6	0	1	1	....	....	....	19	....	....	....	....	....
	Toledo Mercurys	IHL	2	0	0	0	....	....	....	2	....	....	....	....	....
1962-63	Windsor Bulldogs	OHA Sr.	43	1	23	24	....	....	....	14	8	1	2	3	8
1963-64	Windsor Bulldogs	IHL	67	9	33	42	....	....	....	26	6	1	3	4	4
	Detroit Red Wings	**NHL**	**1**	**0**	**0**	**0**	**0**	**0**	**0**	**0**	....	....	....	....	....
	Cincinnati Wings	CHL	2	0	0	0	....	....	....	0	....	....	....	....	....
1964-65	Toledo Blades	IHL	48	5	21	26	....	....	....	42	4	0	1	1	2
1965-66	Fox Valley Volunteers	USHL	....	9	15	24	....	....	....	22	....	....	....	....	....
1966-67	University of Toledo	NCAA	DID NOT PLAY – COACHING												
	Toledo Blades	IHL	7	0	3	3	....	....	....	2	....	....	....	....	....
1967-68	Toledo Blades	IHL	39	4	12	16	....	....	....	26	....	....	....	....	....
1969-70	Toledo Blades	IHL	....	....	....	....	....	....	....	....	7	2	2	4	8
1970-71	Toledo Blades	IHL	2	0	0	0	....	....	....	2	....	....	....	....	....
	NHL Totals		**1**	**0**	**0**	**0**	**0**	**0**	**0**	**0**	....	....	....	....	....

IHL Second All-Star Team (1964)

Signed as a free agent by **Detroit**, February 22, 1964. • Served as playing/coach with **Toldeo**, 1968-1970.

• MITCHELL, HERB
Herb "Hap" Mitchell
LW – L. 5'10", 190 lbs. b: Meaford, Ontario, 1/4/1896. d: 1/12/1969.

			REGULAR SEASON								PLAYOFFS				
Season	Club	League	GP	G	A	Pts	AG	AA	APts	PIM	GP	G	A	Pts	PIM
1921-22	Hamilton Tigers	OHA Sr.	10	5	1	6	....	....	....	....	....	....	....	....	....
1922-23	Hamilton Tigers	OHA Sr.	12	8	8	16	....	....	....	....	2	1	0	1	8
1923-24	Hamilton Tigers	OHA Sr.	9	10	0	10	....	....	....	....	2	1	0	1	....
1924-25	**Boston Bruins**	**NHL**	**27**	**3**	**0**	**3**	**10**	**0**	**10**	**24**	....	....	....	....	....
1925-26	**Boston Bruins**	**NHL**	**26**	**3**	**0**	**3**	**9**	**0**	**9**	**14**	....	....	....	....	....
1926-27	New Haven Eagles	Can-Am	30	4	3	7	....	....	....	18	3	0	0	0	2
1927-28	Windsor Bulldogs	Can-Pro	10	0	1	1	....	....	....	2	....	....	....	....	....
1928-29	Windsor Bulldogs	OHA Sr.	DID NOT PLAY – COACHING												
	NHL Totals		**53**	**6**	**0**	**6**	**19**	**0**	**19**	**38**	....	....	....	....	....

Signed as a free agent by **Boston**, November 2, 1924.

• MITCHELL, RED
Red (William D.) Mitchell
D – R. 5'10", 185 lbs. b: Toronto, Ont., 9/6/1912.

Season	Club	League	GP	G	A	Pts	AG	AA	APts	PIM	GP	G	A	Pts	PIM
1930-31	Toronto Marlboros	OHA	2	0	0	0	....	....	....	2	1	0	0	0	0
1931-32	Toronto Marlboros	OHA	8	1	1	2	....	....	....	6	4	0	0	0	6
1932-33	Detroit Olympics	IAHL	19	0	0	0	....	....	....	54	....	....	....	....	....
	Kitchener Greenshirts	OHA Sr.	10	3	1	4	....	....	....	34	....	....	....	....	....
1933-34	Detroit Olympics	IAHL	43	2	2	4	....	....	....	26	6	1	1	2	0
1934-35	New Haven Eagles	Can-Am	46	1	4	5	....	....	....	75	....	....	....	....	....
1935-36	New Haven Eagles	Can-Am	37	2	4	6	....	....	....	49	....	....	....	....	....
1936-37	Minneapolis Millers	AHA	34	1	7	8	....	....	....	54	6	1	1	2	10
1937-38	Minneapolis Millers	AHA	46	3	9	12	....	....	....	70	7	0	1	1	8
1938-39	Minneapolis Millers	AHA	47	9	21	30	....	....	....	*87	4	0	2	2	0
1939-40	Minneapolis Millers	AHA	48	6	9	15	....	....	....	68	3	0	0	0	4
1940-41	Kansas City Americans	AHA	47	3	2	5	....	....	....	50	8	0	1	1	0
1941-42	**Chicago Black Hawks**	**NHL**	**1**	**0**	**0**	**0**	**0**	**0**	**0**	**4**	....	....	....	....	....
	Kansas City Americans	AHA	50	1	14	15	....	....	....	75	6	1	2	3	12
1942-43	**Chicago Black Hawks**	**NHL**	**42**	**1**	**1**	**2**	**1**	**1**	**2**	**47**	....	....	....	....	....
1943-44	Toronto Peoples Credit	City Sr.	STATISTICS NOT AVAILABLE												
1944-45	**Chicago Black Hawks**	**NHL**	**40**	**3**	**4**	**7**	**4**	**6**	**10**	**16**	....	....	....	....	....
1945-46	Kansas City Pla-Mors	USHL	49	2	27	29	....	....	....	47	12	0	4	4	6
1946-47	Kansas City Pla-Mors	USHL	60	8	31	39	....	....	....	72	12	1	6	7	6
1947-48	Providence Reds	AHL	10	1	1	2	....	....	....	6	....	....	....	....	....
	Kansas City Pla-Mors	USHL	54	6	12	18	....	....	....	47	7	1	1	2	5
	NHL Totals		**83**	**4**	**5**	**9**	**5**	**7**	**12**	**67**	....	....	....	....	....

• MOE, BILLY
Billy Moe **USHOF**
D – L. 5'11", 170 lbs. b: Danvers, MA, 10/2/1916.

Season	Club	League	GP	G	A	Pts	AG	AA	APts	PIM	GP	G	A	Pts	PIM
1939-40	Atlantic City Seagulls	EHL	34	2	3	5	....	....	....	19	....	....	....	....	....
	Baltimore Orioles	EHL	26	4	2	6	....	....	....	12	9	0	3	3	8
1940-41	Baltimore Orioles	EHL	49	6	6	12	....	....	....	71	....	....	....	....	....
1941-42	Philadelphia Rockets	AHL	54	5	19	24	....	....	....	30	....	....	....	....	....
1942-43	Hershey Bears	AHL	55	8	12	20	....	....	....	69	6	0	1	1	9
1943-44	Hershey Bears	AHL	47	9	22	31	....	....	....	48	6	0	2	2	8
1944-45	**New York Rangers**	**NHL**	**35**	**2**	**4**	**6**	**3**	**6**	**9**	**14**	....	....	....	....	....
	Hershey Bears	AHL	12	1	5	6	....	....	....	12	....	....	....	....	....
1945-46	**New York Rangers**	**NHL**	**48**	**4**	**4**	**8**	**6**	**7**	**13**	**14**	....	....	....	....	....
1946-47	**New York Rangers**	**NHL**	**59**	**4**	**10**	**14**	**5**	**14**	**19**	**44**	....	....	....	....	....
1947-48	**New York Rangers**	**NHL**	**59**	**1**	**15**	**16**	**1**	**22**	**23**	**31**	**1**	**0**	**0**	**0**	**0**
1948-49	**New York Rangers**	**NHL**	**60**	**0**	**9**	**9**	**0**	**14**	**14**	**60**	....	....	....	....	....
1949-50	Hershey Bears	AHL	55	2	20	22	....	....	....	29	....	....	....	....	....
1950-51	Hershey Bears	AHL	59	3	12	15	....	....	....	41	6	0	4	4	0
1951-52	Calgary Stampeders	PCHL	57	5	15	20	....	....	....	48	....	....	....	....	....
1952-53	Troy Uncle Sam Trojans	EHL	57	12	23	35	....	....	....	51	....	....	....	....	....
	NHL Totals		**261**	**11**	**42**	**53**	**15**	**63**	**78**	**163**	**1**	**0**	**0**	**0**	**0**

AHL First All-Star Team (1944)

• MOFFAT, RON
Ron (Robert) "Atlas" Moffat
LW – L. 5'11", 180 lbs. b: West Hope, N.D., 8/21/1905. d: 8/19/1960.

Season	Club	League	GP	G	A	Pts	AG	AA	APts	PIM	GP	G	A	Pts	PIM
1925-26	Saskatoon Crescents	WHL	8	0	0	0	....	....	....	2	....	....	....	....	....
1926-27	Saskatoon Shieks	PHL	29	12	5	17	....	....	....	6	4	0	0	0	2
1927-28	Saskatoon Shieks	PHL	28	12	*11	*23	....	....	....	18	....	....	....	....	....
1928-29	Tulsa Oilers	AHA	18	1	2	3	....	....	....	8	....	....	....	....	....
1929-30	Tulsa Oilers	AHA	48	14	5	19	....	....	....	45	9	2	0	2	4
1930-31	Tulsa Oilers	AHA	47	17	11	28	....	....	....	22	4	1	0	1	12
1931-32	Tulsa Oilers	AHA	41	11	1	12	....	....	....	34	....	....	....	....	....
1932-33	**Detroit Red Wings**	**NHL**	**24**	**1**	**1**	**2**	**2**	**3**	**5**	**6**	**4**	**0**	**0**	**0**	**0**
	Detroit Olympics	IAHL	22	7	2	9	....	....	....	16	....	....	....	....	....
1933-34	**Detroit Red Wings**	**NHL**	**5**	**0**	**0**	**0**	**0**	**0**	**0**	**2**	**3**	**0**	**0**	**0**	**0**
	Detroit Olympics	IAHL	38	17	10	27	....	....	....	25	6	*5	2	7	4
1934-35	**Detroit Red Wings**	**NHL**	**8**	**0**	**0**	**0**	**0**	**0**	**0**	**0**	....	....	....	....	....
	Detroit–Windsor	IAHL	37	11	15	26	....	....	....	41	5	3	1	4	5
1935-36	Windsor Bulldogs	IAHL	47	18	12	30	....	....	....	34	8	2	3	5	4
1936-37	Spokane Clippers	PCHL	40	15	5	20	....	....	....	36	6	2	0	2	0
1937-38	Seattle Seahawks	PCHL	42	12	20	32	....	....	....	36	4	0	0	0	2
1938-39	Spokane–Seattle	PCHL	43	15	12	27	....	....	....	16	....	....	....	....	....
1939-40	Seattle Seahawks	PCHL	6	0	0	0	....	....	....	0	....	....	....	....	....
	NHL Totals		**37**	**1**	**1**	**2**	**2**	**3**	**5**	**8**	**7**	**0**	**0**	**0**	**0**
	Other Major League Totals		8	0	0	0	....	....	....	2	....	....	....	....	....

IAHL Second All-Star Team (1936)

Signed as a free agent by **Saskatoon** (WHL), January 11, 1926. Transferred to **Saskatoon Shieks** (PrHL) after WHL folded, May 22, 1926. Signed as a free agent by **Detroit**, August 1, 1932. Traded to **Windsor** (IAHL) by **Detroit** for cash, October 18, 1935.

• MOHNS, DOUG
— see page 1318

• MOHNS, LLOYD
Lloyd "Dunc" Mohns
D – R. 5'9", 185 lbs. b: Petawawa, Ont., 7/31/1921.

Season	Club	League	GP	G	A	Pts	AG	AA	APts	PIM	GP	G	A	Pts	PIM
1939-40	Pembroke Lumber Kings	Ott-Jr.	8	3	4	7	....	....	....	2	2	0	0	0	0
1940-41	Pembroke Lumber Kings	Ott-Jr.	10	4	3	7	....	....	....	10	4	0	0	0	7
1941-42	Pembroke Lumber Kings	Ott-Jr.	12	2	2	4	....	....	....	16	6	3	2	7	4
1942-43	New York Rovers	EHL	3	1	0	1	....	....	....	0	10	2	0	2	14
	Petawawa Grenades	Ott-Sr.	8	9	1	10	....	....	....	4	7	3	0	3	0
	Vancouver Army	City Sr.	1	1	1	2	....	....	....	0	....	....	....	....	....
1943-44	**New York Rangers**	**NHL**	**1**	**0**	**0**	**0**	**0**	**0**	**0**	**0**	....	....	....	....	....
	New York Rovers	EHL	15	2	2	4	....	....	....	25	....	....	....	....	....
	Brooklyn Cresents	EHL	30	6	6	12	....	....	....	16	11	3	6	9	13
1944-45	Hershey Bears	AHL	26	3	1	4	....	....	....	27	....	....	....	....	....
	Philadelphia Falcons	EHL	1	0	0	0	....	....	....	12	....	....	....	....	....
	New York Rovers	EHL	22	4	8	12	....	....	....	31	5	1	1	2	6
1945-46	Pembroke Lumber Kings	Ott-Sr.	16	4	2	6	....	....	....	14	12	4	8	12	8
1946-47	Kirkland Lake Blue Devils	NOHA	STATISTICS NOT AVAILABLE												
1947-48	Oakland Oaks	PCHL	11	0	2	2	....	....	....	7	....	....	....	....	....
	Brantford Indians	OHA Sr.	9	1	0	1	....	....	....	8	....	....	....	....	....
1948-49	Brantford Indians	OHA Sr.	DID NOT PLAY – SUSPENDED												
	NHL Totals		**1**	**0**	**0**	**0**	**0**	**0**	**0**	**0**	....	....	....	....	....

• Suspened for two years by OHA Sr. (January 25, 1948) for attacking referee Frank Elliot in game vs. Owen Sound, January 20, 1948.

• MOLYNEAUX, LARRY
Larry Molyneaux
D – R. 5'11", 208 lbs. b: Sutton West, Ont., 7/9/1912.

Season	Club	League	GP	G	A	Pts	AG	AA	APts	PIM	GP	G	A	Pts	PIM
1931-32	Newmarket Redmen	OHA	7	1	1	2	....	....	....	6	6	3	0	3	....
1932-33	Springfield Indians	Can-Am	13	0	1	1	....	....	....	17	....	....	....	....	....
	Quebec Castors	Can-Am	33	2	2	4	....	....	....	40	....	....	....	....	....
1933-34	Quebec Castors	Can-Am	40	2	5	7	....	....	....	60	....	....	....	....	....
1934-35	New Haven Eagles	Can-Am	48	6	11	17	....	....	....	60	....	....	....	....	....
1935-36	Philadelphia Ramblers	Can-Am	48	2	10	12	....	....	....	54	....	....	....	....	....
1936-37	Philadelphia Ramblers	AHL	45	2	5	7	....	....	....	42	6	0	0	0	2
1937-38	**New York Rangers**	**NHL**	**2**	**0**	**0**	**0**	**0**	**0**	**0**	**2**	**3**	**0**	**0**	**0**	**8**
	Philadelphia Ramblers	AHL	47	0	8	8	....	....	....	45	5	0	0	0	0
1938-39	**New York Rangers**	**NHL**	**43**	**0**	**1**	**1**	**0**	**2**	**2**	**18**	**7**	**0**	**0**	**0**	**0**
	Philadelphia Ramblers	AHL	5	0	2	2	....	....	....	16	....	....	....	....	....
1939-40	Cleveland Barons	AHL	54	2	6	8	....	....	....	46	....	....	....	....	....
1940-41	Cleveland–Pittsburgh	AHL	34	1	5	6	....	....	....	22	9	0	0	0	14
	NHL Totals		**45**	**0**	**1**	**1**	**0**	**2**	**2**	**20**	**10**	**0**	**0**	**0**	**8**

AHL First All-Star Team (1938) • AHL Second All-Star Team (1940)

• MONDOU, ARMAND
Armand Mondou
LW – L. 5'10", 175 lbs. b: Yamaska, Que., 6/27/1905. d: 9/13/1976.

Season	Club	League	GP	G	A	Pts	AG	AA	APts	PIM	GP	G	A	Pts	PIM
1925-26	St. Francis Xavier	Mtl-Sr.	STATISTICS NOT AVAILABLE												
1926-27	Providence Reds	Can-Am	32	6	2	8	....	....	....	35	....	....	....	....	....
1927-28	Providence Reds	Can-Am	40	12	9	21	....	....	....	50	....	....	....	....	....
1928-29	Providence Reds	Can-Am	10	1	0	1	....	....	....	10	....	....	....	....	....
	Montreal Canadiens	**NHL**	**32**	**3**	**4**	**7**	**12**	**37**	**49**	**6**	**3**	**0**	**0**	**0**	**2**
1929-30	**Montreal Canadiens**	**NHL**	**44**	**3**	**5**	**8**	**6**	**16**	**22**	**24**	**6**	**1**	**1**	**2**	**6**
1930-31	**Montreal Canadiens**	**NHL**	**40**	**5**	**4**	**9**	**12**	**14**	**26**	**10**	**8**	**0**	**0**	**0**	**0**
1931-32	**Montreal Canadiens**	**NHL**	**47**	**6**	**12**	**18**	**13**	**33**	**46**	**22**	**4**	**1**	**2**	**3**	**2**
1932-33	**Montreal Canadiens**	**NHL**	**24**	**1**	**3**	**4**	**2**	**8**	**10**	**15**	....	....	....	....	....
	Providence Reds	Can-Am	23	9	8	17	....	....	....	14	....	....	....	....	....
1933-34	**Montreal Canadiens**	**NHL**	**48**	**5**	**3**	**8**	**11**	**8**	**19**	**4**	**1**	**0**	**1**	**1**	**0**
	Quebec Beavers	CAHL	1	1	1	2	....	....	....	0	....	....	....	....	....
1934-35	**Montreal Canadiens**	**NHL**	**46**	**9**	**15**	**24**	**19**	**33**	**52**	**6**	**2**	**0**	**1**	**1**	**0**
1935-36	**Montreal Canadiens**	**NHL**	**36**	**7**	**11**	**18**	**17**	**27**	**44**	**10**	....	....	....	....	....
1936-37	**Montreal Canadiens**	**NHL**	**7**	**1**	**1**	**2**	**2**	**2**	**4**	**0**	**5**	**0**	**0**	**0**	**0**
	New Haven Eagles	AHL	35	6	22	28	....	....	....	12	....	....	....	....	....
1937-38	**Montreal Canadiens**	**NHL**	**7**	**2**	**4**	**6**	**4**	**8**	**12**	**0**	....	....	....	....	....
1938-39	**Montreal Canadiens**	**NHL**	**34**	**3**	**7**	**10**	**6**	**13**	**19**	**2**	**3**	**1**	**0**	**1**	**2**
	New Haven Eagles	AHL	14	8	5	13	....	....	....	26	....	....	....	....	....
1939-40	**Montreal Canadiens**	**NHL**	**21**	**2**	**2**	**4**	**4**	**4**	**8**	**0**	....	....	....	....	....
	New Haven Eagles	AHL	21	6	15	21	....	....	....	4	3	0	0	0	2
	NHL Totals		**386**	**47**	**71**	**118**	**108**	**203**	**311**	**99**	**32**	**3**	**5**	**8**	**12**

Played in NHL All-Star Game (1939)

Traded to **Montreal Canadiens** by **Providence** (Can-Am) for Leo Gaudreault, December 19, 1928. Traded to **Providence** (Can-Am) by **Montreal Canadiens** with Leo Gaudreault for Hago Harington and Leo Murray with Montreal holding rights of recall, January, 1933.

• MOORE, DICKIE
— see page 1322

• MORAN, AMBY
Amby (Ambrose Jason) Moran
D – L. 6', 200 lbs. b: Winnipeg, Man., 4/3/1895. d: 4/8/1958.

Season	Club	League	GP	G	A	Pts	AG	AA	APts	PIM	GP	G	A	Pts	PIM
1919-20	Winnipeg Winnipegs	MHL Sr.	4	3	1	4	....	....	....	2	1	0	0	0	0
1920-21	Brandon Regals	MHL Sr.	12	12	4	16	....	....	....	16	6	9	1	10	4
1921-22	Regina Capitals	WCHL	25	7	2	9	....	....	....	18	4	1	0	1	0
1922-23	Regina Capitals	WCHL	28	15	8	23	....	....	....	37	2	0	1	1	0
1923-24	Regina Capitals	WCHL	14	2	0	2	....	....	....	6	....	....	....	....	....
1924-25	Regina Capitals	WCHL	6	0	0	0	....	....	....	8	....	....	....	....	....
	Vancouver Maroons	WCHL	15	10	1	11	....	....	....	26	....	....	....	....	....
1925-26	Vancouver Maroons	WHL	30	5	0	5	....	....	....	30	....	....	....	....	....
1926-27	**Montreal Canadiens**	**NHL**	**12**	**0**	**0**	**0**	**0**	**0**	**0**	**10**	....	....	....	....	....
	Moose Jaw Canucks	PrHL	11	7	0	7	....	....	....	10	....	....	....	....	....
	New Haven Eagles	Can-Am	6	0	0	0	....	....	....	18	....	....	....	....	....
1927-28	Moose Jaw Canucks	PrHL	12	3	2	5	....	....	....	35	....	....	....	....	....
	Chicago Black Hawks	**NHL**	**23**	**1**	**1**	**2**	**3**	**8**	**11**	**14**	....	....	....	....	....
1928-29	Tulsa Oilers	AHA	34	3	1	4	....	....	....	26	4	0	0	0	0
1929-30	Tulsa Oilers	AHA	4	0	0	0	....	....	....	0	....	....	....	....	....
	St. Louis Flyers	AHA	1	0	0	0	....	....	....	0	....	....	....	....	....
1930-31	St. Louis Flyers	AHA	6	1	0	1	....	....	....	0	....	....	....	....	
	Buffalo Majors	AHA	1	0	1	1	....	....	....	0	....	....	....	....	....
	NHL Totals		**35**	**1**	**1**	**2**	**3**	**8**	**11**	**24**	....	....	....	....	....
	Other Major League Totals		118	39	11	50	....	....	....	125	6	1	1	2	0

Signed as a free agent by **Regina** (WCHL), November 30, 1921. Traded to **Vancouver** (WCHL) by **Regina** (WCHL) for cash, January 10, 1925. Traded to **Boston** by **Vancouver** (WHL) for cash, September 4, 1926. Traded to **Montreal Canadiens** by **Boston** for Billy Coutu, October 22, 1926. Traded to **New Haven** (Can-Am) by **Montreal** for cash, January 27, 1927. Traded to **Chicago** by **Moose Jaw** (PrHL) for cash, January, 1929.

• MORENZ, HOWIE Howie "The Stratford Streak" Morenz **HHOF**

C – L. 5'9", 165 lbs. b: Mitchell, Ont., 6/21/1902. d: 3/8/1937.

			REGULAR SEASON								PLAYOFFS				
Season	Club	League	GP	G	A	Pts	AG	AA	APts	PIM	GP	G	A	Pts	PIM
1919-20	Stratford Midgets	OHA	5	14	4	18	....	....	....	....	7	14	12	26	....
1920-21	Stratford Midgets	OHA	8	19	*12	*31	....	....	....	....	13	*38	*18	*56	....
1921-22	Stratford Midgets	OHA	4	17	6	23	....	....	....	10	5	*17	*4	*21	....
	Stratford Indians	OHA Sr.	4	10	3	13	....	....	....	2	8	*15	*8	*23	*21
1922-23	Stratford Indians	OHA Sr.	10	15	*13	28	....	....	....	19	10	*28	7	*35	*36
1923-24	**Montreal Canadiens**	**NHL**	**24**	**13**	**3**	**16**	**54**	**53**	**107**	**20**	**6**	**7**	**2**	**9**	**10**
1924-25	**Montreal Canadiens**	**NHL**	**30**	**27**	**7**	**34**	**97**	**95**	**192**	**31**	**6**	**7**	**1**	**8**	**10**
1925-26	**Montreal Canadiens**	**NHL**	**31**	**23**	**3**	**26**	**73**	**34**	**107**	**39**	....	....	....	....	....
1926-27	**Montreal Canadiens**	**NHL**	**44**	**25**	**7**	**32**	**74**	**60**	**134**	**49**	**4**	**1**	**0**	**1**	**4**
1927-28	**Montreal Canadiens**	**NHL**	**43**	***33**	***18**	***51**	**104**	**157**	**261**	**66**	**2**	**0**	**0**	**0**	**12**
1928-29	**Montreal Canadiens**	**NHL**	**42**	**17**	**10**	**27**	**69**	**93**	**162**	**47**	**3**	**0**	**0**	**0**	**6**
1929-30	**Montreal Canadiens**	**NHL**	**44**	**40**	**10**	**50**	**80**	**32**	**112**	**72**	**6**	**3**	**0**	**3**	**10**
1930-31	**Montreal Canadiens**	**NHL**	**39**	**28**	**23**	***51**	**69**	**85**	**154**	**49**	**10**	**1**	***4**	**5**	**10**
1931-32	**Montreal Canadiens**	**NHL**	**48**	**24**	**25**	**49**	**52**	**71**	**123**	**46**	**4**	**1**	**0**	**1**	**4**
1932-33	**Montreal Canadiens**	**NHL**	**46**	**14**	**21**	**35**	**33**	**56**	**89**	**64**	**2**	**0**	**3**	**3**	**2**
1933-34	**Montreal Canadiens**	**NHL**	**39**	**8**	**13**	**21**	**18**	**35**	**53**	**21**	**2**	**1**	**1**	**2**	**0**
1934-35	**Chicago Black Hawks**	**NHL**	**48**	**8**	**26**	**34**	**17**	**58**	**75**	**21**	**2**	**0**	**0**	**0**	**0**
1935-36	**Chicago Black Hawks**	**NHL**	**23**	**4**	**11**	**15**	**10**	**27**	**37**	**20**	....	....	....	....	....
	New York Rangers	**NHL**	**19**	**2**	**4**	**6**	**5**	**10**	**15**	**6**	....	....	....	....	....
1936-37	**Montreal Canadiens**	**NHL**	**30**	**4**	**16**	**20**	**9**	**38**	**47**	**12**	....	....	....	....	....
	NHL Totals		**550**	**270**	**197**	**467**	**764**	**904**	**1668**	**563**	**47**	**21**	**11**	**32**	**68**

NHL Scoring Leader (1928, 1931) • Won Hart Trophy (1928, 1931, 1932) • NHL First All-Star Team (1931, 1932) • NHL Second All-Star Team (1933)

Played in NHL All-Star Game (1934)

Traded to **Chicago** by **Montreal Canadiens** with Lorne Chabot and Marty Burke for Leroy Goldsworthy, Lionel Conacher and Roger Jenkins, October 3, 1934. Traded to **NY Rangers** by **Chicago** for Glenn Brydson, January 26, 1936. Traded to **Montreal Canadiens** by **NY Rangers** for cash, September 1, 1936. • Suffered career-ending leg injury in game vs. Chicago, January 28, 1937.

• MORIN, PETE Pete Morin

LW – L. 5'6", 150 lbs. b: Lachine, Que., 12/8/1915. Deceased.

Season	Club	League	GP	G	A	Pts	AG	AA	APts	PIM	GP	G	A	Pts	PIM
1934-35	Montreal Victorias	City Jr.	1	1	0	1	....	....	....	6	....	....	....	....	....
1935-36	Montreal Victorias	City Jr.	STATISTICS NOT AVAILABLE												
1936-37	Montreal Royals	QSHL	21	17	5	22	....	....	....	15	5	3	1	4	4
1937-38	Montreal Royals	QSHL	22	4	4	8	....	....	....	14	1	0	0	0	0
1938-39	Montreal Royals	QSHL	17	7	12	19	....	....	....	16	20	*21	13	*34	6
1939-40	Montreal Royals	QSHL	29	14	20	34	....	....	....	4	13	5	10	15	7
1940-41	Montreal Royals	QSHL	35	17	19	36	....	....	....	17	22	*17	7	24	33
1941-42	**Montreal Canadiens**	**NHL**	**31**	**10**	**12**	**22**	**17**	**18**	**35**	**7**	**1**	**0**	**0**	**0**	**0**
	Montreal Royals	QSHL	11	3	1	4	....	....	....	4	....	....	....	....	....
1942-43	Montreal RCAF	QSHL	35	15	21	36	....	....	....	4	12	3	6	9	4
1943-44	Montreal RCAF	QSHL	7	1	1	2	....	....	....	2	....	....	....	....	....
1944-45	Lachine Rapides	QPHL	STATISTICS NOT AVAILABLE												
1945-46	Montreal Royals	QSHL	39	33	28	61	....	....	....	17	11	2	*12	*14	2
1946-47	Montreal Royals	QSHL	31	18	32	50	....	....	....	10	11	1	*15	*16	2
1947-48	Montreal Royals	QSHL	47	34	*57	*91	....	....	....	6	3	1	1	2	2
1948-49	Montreal Royals	QSHL	53	25	54	79	....	....	....	20	8	6	6	12	2
1949-50	Montreal Royals	QSHL	52	25	29	54	....	....	....	13	6	0	3	3	0
1950-51	Laval Nationale	QJHL	DID NOT PLAY – COACHING												
	NHL Totals		**31**	**10**	**12**	**22**	**17**	**18**	**35**	**7**	**1**	**0**	**0**	**0**	**0**

Won Vimy Trophy (MVP - QSHL) (1946)

Signed as a free agent by **Montreal**, November 28, 1941.

• MORRIS, BERNIE Bernie Morris

C/RW – R. 5'7", 145 lbs. b: Regina, Sask.. Deceased.

Season	Club	League	GP	G	A	Pts	AG	AA	APts	PIM	GP	G	A	Pts	PIM
1913-14	Regina Victorias	City Sr.	1	2	0	2	....	....	....	3	....	....	....	....	....
1914-15	Victoria Aristocrats	PCHA	10	7	3	10	....	....	....	0	....	....	....	....	....
1915-16	Seattle Metropolitans	PCHA	18	*23	9	32	....	....	....	27	....	....	....	....	....
1916-17	Seattle Metropolitans	PCHA	24	37	17	*54	....	....	....	17	4	*14	2	*16	0
1917-18	Seattle Metropolitans	PCHA	18	20	*12	32	....	....	....	9	2	1	0	1	0
1918-19	Seattle Metropolitans	PCHA	20	22	7	29	....	....	....	15	....	....	....	....	....
1919-20	Seattle Metropolitans	PCHA	....	....	....	....	....	....	....	....	5	0	*2	2	0
1920-21	Seattle Metropolitans	PCHA	24	11	13	24	....	....	....	3	2	1	0	1	0
1921-22	Seattle Metropolitans	PCHA	24	14	10	24	....	....	....	36	2	0	0	0	0
1922-23	Seattle Metropolitans	PCHA	29	21	5	26	....	....	....	30	....	....	....	....	....
1923-24	Calgary Tigers	WCHL	30	16	7	23	....	....	....	13	7	3	*5	*8	8
1924-25	Calgary Tigers	WCHL	7	2	0	2	....	....	....	2	....	....	....	....	....
	Boston Bruins	**NHL**	**6**	**2**	**0**	**2**	**7**	**0**	**7**	**0**	....	....	....	....	....
	Regina Capitals	WCHL	7	1	2	3	....	....	....	2	....	....	....	....	....
1925-26	Palais-De-Glace	Cal-Pro	10	10	*9	19	....	....	....	8	....	....	....	....	....
1926-27	Edmonton Eskimos	PrHL	27	18	6	24	....	....	....	28	....	....	....	....	....
1927-28	Detroit Olympics	Can-Pro	37	16	9	25	....	....	....	35	2	0	0	0	6
1928-29	Hamilton Tigers	Can-Pro	12	3	2	5	....	....	....	14	....	....	....	....	....
1929-30	Hamilton Tigers	IAHL	17	3	3	6	....	....	....	12	....	....	....	....	....
	NHL Totals		**6**	**2**	**0**	**2**	**7**	**0**	**7**	**0**	....	....	....	....	....
	Other Major League Totals		211	174	85	259	....	....	....	154	22	19	9	28	8

PCHA First All-Star Team (1916, 1917, 1918, 1919, 1922) • PCHA Second All-Star Team (1917, 1921, 1923)

Traded to **Calgary** (WCHL) by **Seattle** (PCHA) for Bill Binney and the rights to Gordon McFarland, October 7, 1923. Traded to **Montreal Maroons** by **Calgary** (WHL) for cash, January 3, 1925. Traded to **Boston** by **Montreal Maroons** with Bobby Benson for Alf Skinner, January 3, 1925. Signed as a free agent by **Regina** (WCHL) after release by **Boston**, February 10, 1925.

• MORRIS, ELWYN Elwyn "Moe" Morris

D – L. 5'8", 187 lbs. b: Toronto, Ont., 1/3/1921.

			REGULAR SEASON								PLAYOFFS				
Season	Club	League	GP	G	A	Pts	AG	AA	APts	PIM	GP	G	A	Pts	PIM
1937-38	Toronto Marlboros	OHA	10	6	3	9	....	....	....	0	6	3	0	3	2
1938-39	Toronto Marlboros	OHA	7	3	1	4	....	....	....	0	2	1	0	1	0
1939-40	Toronto Marlboros	OHA	19	13	16	29	....	....	....	9	5	1	0	1	0
1940-41	Toronto Marlboros	OHA	16	7	17	24	....	....	....	12	12	1	4	5	2
1941-42	Toronto Marlboros	OHA Sr.	20	2	9	11	....	....	....	17	6	0	2	2	0
1942-43	Toronto Navy	City Sr.	11	6	10	16	....	....	....	8	10	1	7	8	15
1943-44	**Toronto Maple Leafs**	**NHL**	**50**	**12**	**21**	**33**	**15**	**25**	**40**	**22**	**5**	**1**	**2**	**3**	**2**
1944-45	**Toronto Maple Leafs**	**NHL**	**29**	**0**	**2**	**2**	**0**	**3**	**3**	**18**	**13**	**3**	**0**	**3**	***14**
1945-46	**Toronto Maple Leafs**	**NHL**	**38**	**1**	**5**	**6**	**2**	**9**	**11**	**10**	....	....	....	....	....
	Pittsburgh Hornets	AHL	10	0	7	7	....	....	....	0	....	....	....	....	....
1946-47	Pittsburgh Hornets	AHL	64	2	15	17	....	....	....	45	12	0	2	2	6
1947-48	Pittsburgh Hornets	AHL	56	0	13	13	....	....	....	14	2	0	0	0	0
1948-49	**New York Rangers**	**NHL**	**18**	**0**	**1**	**1**	**0**	**2**	**2**	**8**	....	....	....	....	....
	Providence Reds	AHL	45	1	18	19	....	....	....	13	14	1	0	1	4
1949-50	Providence Reds	AHL	58	1	12	13	....	....	....	11	4	0	2	2	0
1950-51	Providence Reds	AHL	69	8	13	21	....	....	....	18	....	....	....	....	....
1951-52	Providence Reds	AHL	67	2	17	19	....	....	....	21	15	2	2	4	4
1952-53	Providence Reds	AHL	51	4	13	17	....	....	....	13	....	....	....	....	....
1953-54	Owen Sound Mercurys	OHA Sr.	52	9	28	37	....	....	....	12	10	0	7	7	2
1954-55	Stratford Indians	OHA Sr.	50	1	1	2	....	....	....	18	....	....	....	....	....
	NHL Totals		**135**	**13**	**29**	**42**	**17**	**39**	**56**	**58**	**18**	**4**	**2**	**6**	**16**

AHL Second All-Star Team (1947)

Traded to **NY Rangers** by **Toronto** with Wally Stanowski for Cal Gardner, the rights to Frank Mathers, Bill Juzda and Rene Trudell, June, 1948. Traded to **Providence** (AHL) by **NY Rangers** with Ed Kullman, cash and future considerations (Ken Davies, June, 1949) for Allan Stanley, December, 1949.

• MORRISON, DON Don Morrison

C – R. 5'10", 165 lbs. b: Saskatoon, Sask., 7/14/1923.

Season	Club	League	GP	G	A	Pts	AG	AA	APts	PIM	GP	G	A	Pts	PIM
1944-45	Winnipeg RCAF	City Sr.	STATISTICS NOT AVAILABLE												
1945-46	Omaha Knights	USHL	46	32	24	56	....	....	....	8	7	2	0	2	4
1946-47	Omaha Knights	USHL	59	32	44	*76	....	....	....	11	11	6	*12	*18	0
1947-48	**Detroit Red Wings**	**NHL**	**40**	**10**	**15**	**25**	**15**	**22**	**37**	**6**	**3**	**0**	**1**	**1**	**0**
	Indianapolis Capitals	AHL	27	12	16	28	....	....	....	9	....	....	....	....	....
1948-49	**Detroit Red Wings**	**NHL**	**13**	**0**	**1**	**1**	**0**	**2**	**2**	**0**	....	....	....	....	....
	Indianapolis Capitals	AHL	48	20	29	49	....	....	....	25	2	0	1	1	0
1949-50	Indianapolis Capitals	AHL	57	21	38	59	....	....	....	14	8	3	4	7	0
1950-51	**Chicago Black Hawks**	**NHL**	**59**	**8**	**12**	**20**	**11**	**15**	**26**	**6**	....	....	....	....	....
1951-52	St. Louis Flyers	AHL	65	17	43	60	....	....	....	18	....	....	....	....	....
	NHL Totals		**112**	**18**	**28**	**46**	**26**	**39**	**65**	**12**	**3**	**0**	**1**	**1**	**0**

USHL First All-Star Team (1947)

Traded to **Chicago** by **Detroit** with Harry Lumley, Jack Stewart, Al Dewsbury and Pete Babando for Jim Henry, Bob Goldham, Gaye Stewart and Metro Prystai, July 13, 1950.

• MORRISON, JIM — *see page 1325*

• MORRISON, JOHN John "Crutchy" Morrison

LW – R. 5'8", 163 lbs. b: Selkirk, Man., 3/4/1895. Deceased.

Season	Club	League	GP	G	A	Pts	AG	AA	APts	PIM	GP	G	A	Pts	PIM
1913-14	Selkirk Fishermen	MHL Jr.	10	5	0	5	....	....	....	....	....	....	....	....	....
1914-15	Selkirk Fishermen	MHL Sr.	STATISTICS NOT AVAILABLE												
1915-16	Winnipeg 61st Battalion	City Sr.	8	7	2	9	....	....	....	8	5	2	0	2	6
1916-17			MILITARY SERVICE												
1917-18			MILITARY SERVICE												
1918-19			MILITARY SERVICE												
1919-20	Selkirk Fishermen	MSHL	9	6	5	11	....	....	....	6	....	....	....	....	....
1920-21	Winnipeg Falcons	MSHL	10	9	4	13	....	....	....	2	....	....	....	....	....
1921-22	Selkirk Fishermen	MSHL	5	10	2	12	....	....	....	4	....	....	....	....	....
	Edmonton Eskimos	WCHL	17	8	2	10	....	....	....	4	2	0	0	0	0
1922-23	Edmonton Eskimos	WCHL	26	10	2	12	....	....	....	5	3	1	0	1	0
1923-24	Edmonton Eskimos	WCHL	23	1	2	3	....	....	....	2	....	....	....	....	....
1924-25	Edmonton Eskimos	WCHL	27	5	2	7	....	....	....	11	....	....	....	....	....
1925-26	**New York Americans**	**NHL**	**18**	**0**	**0**	**0**	**0**	**0**	**0**	**0**	....	....	....	....	....
1926-27	Regina Capitals	PrHL	30	20	6	26	....	....	....	18	2	1	0	1	2
1927-28	Duluth Hornets	AHA	32	7	3	10	....	....	....	8	5	0	0	0	2
1928-29	Duluth Hornets	AHA	37	10	3	13	....	....	....	10	....	....	....	....	....
1929-30	St. Paul Saints	AHA	45	9	4	13	....	....	....	10	....	....	....	....	....
1930-31	Buffalo Majors	AHA	42	6	12	18	....	....	....	2	....	....	....	....	....
1931-32	Buffalo Majors	AHA	24	3	2	5	....	....	....	6	....	....	....	....	....
	Duluth Hornets	AHA	16	2	0	2	....	....	....	2	7	0	0	0	0
	NHL Totals		**18**	**0**	**0**	**0**	**0**	**0**	**0**	**0**	....	....	....	....	....
	Other Major League Totals		93	24	8	32	....	....	....	22	5	1	0	1	0

Signed as a free agent by **Edmonton** (WCHL), January 9, 1922. Traded to **NY Americans** by **Edmonton** (WCHL) with Joe Simpson and Roy Rickey for cash, September 18, 1925.

• MORRISON, ROD Rod Morrison

RW – R. 5'9", 160 lbs. b: Saskatoon, Sask., 10/7/1925.

Season	Club	League	GP	G	A	Pts	AG	AA	APts	PIM	GP	G	A	Pts	PIM
1942-43	Saskatoon Quakers	SJHL	8	3	6	9	....	....	....	0	3	2	*3	5	0
1943-44	Indianapolis Capitals	AHL	54	13	10	23	....	....	....	4	5	0	0	0	0
1944-45	Saskatoon Falcons	SSHL	8	7	3	10	....	....	....	6	2	2	1	3	0
1945-46	Omaha Knights	USHL	36	8	7	15	....	....	....	8	7	1	1	2	2
1946-47	Indianapolis Capitals	AHL	37	7	17	24	....	....	....	6	....	....	....	....	....
1947-48	**Detroit Red Wings**	**NHL**	**34**	**8**	**7**	**15**	**12**	**10**	**22**	**4**	**3**	**0**	**0**	**0**	**0**
	Indianapolis Capitals	AHL	26	5	10	15	....	....	....	16	....	....	....	....	....
1948-49	Indianapolis Capitals	AHL	65	22	29	51	....	....	....	34	2	0	0	0	0
1949-50	Indianapolis Capitals	AHL	69	27	31	58	....	....	....	15	8	4	5	9	0
1950-51	Indianapolis Capitals	AHL	68	14	33	47	....	....	....	14	3	2	1	3	0
	NHL Totals		**34**	**8**	**7**	**15**	**12**	**10**	**22**	**4**	**3**	**0**	**0**	**0**	**0**

			REGULAR SEASON								PLAYOFFS				
Season	Club	League	GP	G	A	Pts	AG	AA	APts	PIM	GP	G	A	Pts	PIM

• MORTSON, GUS

Gus "Old Hardrock" Mortson
D – L. 5'11", 190 lbs. b: New Liskeard, Ont., 1/24/1925.

Season	Club	League	GP	G	A	Pts	AG	AA	APts	PIM	GP	G	A	Pts	PIM
1943-44	St. Michael's Majors	OHA	25	5	11	16	....	....	....	16	12	2	2	4	12
1944-45	St. Michael's Majors	OHA	17	6	12	18	....	....	....	18	20	7	9	16	20
1945-46	Tulsa Oilers	USHL	51	19	29	48	....	....	....	47	13	1	5	6	12
1946-47	**Toronto Maple Leafs**	**NHL**	**60**	**5**	**13**	**18**	**7**	**19**	**26**	***133**	**11**	**1**	**3**	**4**	**22**
1947-48	**Toronto Maple Leafs**	**NHL**	**58**	**7**	**11**	**18**	**10**	**16**	**26**	**118**	**5**	**1**	**2**	**3**	**2**
1948-49	**Toronto Maple Leafs**	**NHL**	**60**	**2**	**13**	**15**	**3**	**21**	**24**	**85**	**9**	**2**	**1**	**3**	**8**
1949-50	**Toronto Maple Leafs**	**NHL**	**68**	**3**	**14**	**17**	**4**	**18**	**22**	**125**	**7**	**0**	**0**	**0**	**18**
1950-51	**Toronto Maple Leafs**	**NHL**	**60**	**3**	**10**	**13**	**4**	**13**	**17**	***142**	**11**	**0**	**1**	**1**	**4**
1951-52	**Toronto Maple Leafs**	**NHL**	**65**	**1**	**10**	**11**	**1**	**13**	**14**	**106**	**4**	**0**	**0**	**0**	**8**
1952-53	**Chicago Black Hawks**	**NHL**	**68**	**5**	**18**	**23**	**8**	**25**	**33**	**88**	**7**	**1**	**1**	**2**	**6**
1953-54	**Chicago Black Hawks**	**NHL**	**68**	**5**	**13**	**18**	**8**	**18**	**26**	***132**	....	....	....	....	....
1954-55	**Chicago Black Hawks**	**NHL**	**65**	**2**	**11**	**13**	**3**	**14**	**17**	**133**	....	....	....	....	....
1955-56	**Chicago Black Hawks**	**NHL**	**52**	**5**	**10**	**15**	**7**	**12**	**19**	**87**	....	....	....	....	....
1956-57	**Chicago Black Hawks**	**NHL**	**70**	**5**	**18**	**23**	**7**	**21**	**28**	***147**	....	....	....	....	....
1957-58	**Chicago Black Hawks**	**NHL**	**67**	**3**	**10**	**13**	**4**	**11**	**15**	**62**	....	....	....	....	....
1958-59	**Detroit Red Wings**	**NHL**	**36**	**0**	**1**	**1**	**0**	**1**	**1**	**22**	....	....	....	....	....
	Buffalo Bisons	AHL	29	3	9	12	....	....	....	46	11	3	3	6	12
1959-60	Buffalo Bisons	AHL	72	10	32	42	....	....	....	37	....	....	....	....	....
1960-61			DID NOT PLAY												
1961-62			DID NOT PLAY												
1962-63	Chatham Maroons	OHA Sr.	36	11	14	25	....	....	....	46	9	1	1	2	6
1963-64	Chatham Maroons	IHL	29	2	14	16	....	....	....	60	....	....	....	....	....
1964-65	Oakville Oaks	OHA Sr.	31	7	18	25	....	....	....	78	11	1	5	6	18
	Buffalo Bisons	AHL	3	0	3	3	....	....	....	0	....	....	....	....	....
1965-66	Oakville Oaks	OHA Sr.	27	7	15	22	....	....	....	48	....	....	....	....	....
1966-67	Oakville Oaks	OHA Sr.	13	3	3	6	....	....	....	8	....	....	....	....	....
	NHL Totals		**797**	**46**	**152**	**198**	**66**	**202**	**268**	**1380**	**54**	**5**	**8**	**13**	**68**

NHL First All-Star Team (1950) • AHL Second All-Star Team (1960)

Played in NHL All-Star Game (1947, 1948, 1950, 1951, 1952, 1953, 1954, 1956)

Traded to **Chicago** by **Toronto** with Ray Hannigan, Al Rollins and Cal Gardner for Harry Lumley, September 11, 1952. Traded to **Detroit** by **Chicago** for future considerations, June, 1958. Claimed on waivers by **NY Rangers** (Buffalo - AHL) from **Detroit**, January 17, 1959.

• MOSDELL, KENNY

Kenny Mosdell
C – L. 6'1", 170 lbs. b: Montreal, Que., 7/13/1922.

Season	Club	League	GP	G	A	Pts	AG	AA	APts	PIM	GP	G	A	Pts	PIM
1939-40	Montreal Jr. Royals	QJHL	12	7	9	16	....	....	....	4	2	0	0	0	0
	Montreal Royals	QSHL	1	0	0	0	....	....	....	2	....	....	....	....	....
1940-41	Montreal Jr. Royals	QJHL	12	7	10	17	....	....	....	18	14	6	*14	20	13
	Montreal Royals	QSHL	1	0	1	1	....	....	....	0	....	....	....	....	....
1941-42	**Brooklyn Americans**	**NHL**	**41**	**7**	**9**	**16**	**12**	**14**	**26**	**16**	....	....	....	....	....
	Springfield Indians	AHL	1	0	0	0	....	....	....	0	....	....	....	....	....
1942-43	Lachine RCAF	QSHL	35	17	19	35	....	....	....	52	12	8	3	11	23
1943-44	Montreal RCAF	QSHL	7	3	7	10	....	....	....	13	....	....	....	....	....
	Montreal Fairchild	City Sr.	6	7	6	13	....	....	....	5	....	....	....	....	....
1944-45	**Montreal Canadiens**	**NHL**	**31**	**12**	**6**	**18**	**16**	**10**	**26**	**16**	....	....	....	....	....
1945-46	**Montreal Canadiens**	**NHL**	**13**	**2**	**1**	**3**	**3**	**2**	**5**	**8**	**9**	**4**	**1**	**5**	**6**
	Buffalo Bisons	AHL	43	21	23	44	....	....	....	46	....	....	....	....	....
1946-47	**Montreal Canadiens**	**NHL**	**54**	**5**	**10**	**15**	**7**	**14**	**21**	**50**	**4**	**2**	**0**	**2**	**4**
1947-48	**Montreal Canadiens**	**NHL**	**23**	**1**	**0**	**1**	**1**	**0**	**1**	**19**	....	....	....	....	....
1948-49	**Montreal Canadiens**	**NHL**	**60**	**17**	**9**	**26**	**27**	**14**	**41**	**50**	**7**	**1**	**1**	**2**	**4**
1949-50	**Montreal Canadiens**	**NHL**	**67**	**15**	**12**	**27**	**20**	**15**	**35**	**42**	**5**	**0**	**0**	**0**	**12**
1950-51	**Montreal Canadiens**	**NHL**	**66**	**13**	**18**	**31**	**18**	**23**	**41**	**24**	**11**	**1**	**1**	**2**	**4**
1951-52	**Montreal Canadiens**	**NHL**	**44**	**5**	**11**	**16**	**7**	**14**	**21**	**19**	**2**	**1**	**0**	**1**	**0**
1952-53	**Montreal Canadiens**	**NHL**	**63**	**5**	**14**	**19**	**8**	**19**	**27**	**27**	**7**	**3**	**2**	**5**	**4**
1953-54	**Montreal Canadiens**	**NHL**	**67**	**22**	**24**	**46**	**34**	**33**	**67**	**64**	**11**	**1**	**0**	**1**	**4**
1954-55	**Montreal Canadiens**	**NHL**	**70**	**22**	**32**	**54**	**32**	**41**	**73**	**82**	**12**	**2**	**7**	**9**	**8**
1955-56	**Montreal Canadiens**	**NHL**	**67**	**13**	**17**	**30**	**19**	**21**	**40**	**48**	**9**	**1**	**1**	**2**	**2**
1956-57	**Chicago Black Hawks**	**NHL**	**25**	**2**	**4**	**6**	**3**	**5**	**8**	**10**	....	....	....	....	....
1957-58	**Montreal Canadiens**	**NHL**	**2**	**0**	**1**	**1**	**0**	**1**	**1**	**0**	....	....	....	....	....
	Montreal Royals	QHL	62	27	42	69	....	....	....	51	7	3	6	9	2
1958-59	Rochester Americans	AHL	2	0	0	0	....	....	....	0	....	....	....	....	....
	Montreal Royals	QHL	55	20	40	60	....	....	....	77	6	1	4	5	9
	Montreal Canadiens	**NHL**	....	....	....	....	....	....	....	....	**3**	**0**	**0**	**0**	**0**
1959-60	Montreal Royals	EPHL	61	26	36	62	....	....	....	50	14	3	3	6	12
	NHL Totals		**693**	**141**	**168**	**309**	**207**	**226**	**433**	**475**	**80**	**16**	**13**	**29**	**48**

NHL First All-Star Team (1954) • NHL Second All-Star Team (1955) • QHL Second All-Star Team (1959)

Played in NHL All-Star Game (1951, 1952, 1953, 1954, 1955)

Signed as a free agent by **Brooklyn**, October 28, 1941. Rights transferred to **Montreal** from **Brooklyn** in Special Dispersal Draw, September 11, 1943. Traded to **Chicago** by **Montreal** with Eddie Mazur and Bud MacPherson for $55,000 with Montreal holding right of recall, May 17, 1956. Returned to **Montreal** by **Chicago**, September 20, 1957.

• MOSIENKO, BILL

Bill "Mosie" Mosienko **HHOF**
RW – R. 5'8", 160 lbs. b: Winnipeg, Man., 11/2/1921. d: 7/9/1994.

Season	Club	League	GP	G	A	Pts	AG	AA	APts	PIM	GP	G	A	Pts	PIM
1939-40	Winnipeg Monarchs	City Jr.	24	21	8	29	....	....	....	14	7	8	3	11	2
1940-41	Providence Reds	AHL	36	14	19	33	....	....	....	8	....	....	....	....	....
	Kansas City Americans	AHA	7	2	2	4	....	....	....	0	8	4	1	5	2
1941-42	**Chicago Black Hawks**	**NHL**	**12**	**6**	**8**	**14**	**10**	**12**	**22**	**4**	**3**	**2**	**0**	**2**	**0**
	Kansas City Americans	AHA	33	12	19	31	....	....	....	9	....	....	....	....	....
1942-43	**Chicago Black Hawks**	**NHL**	**2**	**2**	**0**	**2**	**3**	**0**	**3**	**0**	....	....	....	....	....
	Quebec Aces	QSHL	8	5	3	8	....	....	....	2	4	2	2	4	2
1943-44	**Chicago Black Hawks**	**NHL**	**50**	**32**	**38**	**70**	**41**	**46**	**87**	**10**	**8**	**2**	**2**	**4**	**6**
1944-45	**Chicago Black Hawks**	**NHL**	**50**	**28**	**26**	**54**	**39**	**42**	**81**	**0**	....	....	....	....	....
1945-46	**Chicago Black Hawks**	**NHL**	**40**	**18**	**30**	**48**	**28**	**57**	**85**	**12**	**4**	**2**	**0**	**2**	**2**
1946-47	**Chicago Black Hawks**	**NHL**	**59**	**25**	**27**	**52**	**34**	**39**	**73**	**2**	....	....	....	....	....
1947-48	**Chicago Black Hawks**	**NHL**	**40**	**16**	**9**	**25**	**23**	**13**	**36**	**0**	....	....	....	....	....
1948-49	**Chicago Black Hawks**	**NHL**	**60**	**17**	**25**	**42**	**27**	**40**	**67**	**6**	....	....	....	....	....
1949-50	**Chicago Black Hawks**	**NHL**	**69**	**18**	**28**	**46**	**24**	**36**	**60**	**10**	....	....	....	....	....
1950-51	**Chicago Black Hawks**	**NHL**	**65**	**21**	**15**	**36**	**29**	**19**	**48**	**18**	....	....	....	....	....
1951-52	**Chicago Black Hawks**	**NHL**	**70**	**31**	**22**	**53**	**44**	**29**	**73**	**10**	....	....	....	....	....
1952-53	**Chicago Black Hawks**	**NHL**	**65**	**17**	**20**	**37**	**26**	**28**	**54**	**8**	**7**	**4**	**2**	**6**	**7**
1953-54	**Chicago Black Hawks**	**NHL**	**65**	**15**	**19**	**34**	**23**	**26**	**49**	**17**	....	....	....	....	....
1954-55	**Chicago Black Hawks**	**NHL**	**64**	**12**	**15**	**27**	**17**	**19**	**36**	**24**	....	....	....	....	....
1955-56	Winnipeg Warriors	WHL	64	22	23	45	....	....	....	37	14	6	*12	18	4
1956-57	Winnipeg Warriors	WHL	61	27	26	53	....	....	....	25	....	....	....	....	....
1957-58	Winnipeg Warriors	WHL	65	38	36	74	....	....	....	43	7	1	0	1	6
1958-59	Winnipeg Warriors	WHL	63	42	46	88	....	....	....	55	7	1	3	4	10
1959-60	Winnipeg Warriors	WHL	DID NOT PLAY – COACHING												
	NHL Totals		**711**	**258**	**282**	**540**	**368**	**406**	**774**	**121**	**22**	**10**	**4**	**14**	**15**

NHL Second All-Star Team (1945, 1946) • Won Lady Byng Trophy (1945) • WHL Prairie Division First All-Star Team (1957, 1958, 1959)

Played in NHL All-Star Game (1947, 1949, 1950, 1952, 1953)

• MOTTER, ALEX

Alex Motter
C – L. 6', 175 lbs. b: Melville, Sask., 6/20/1913. d: 10/18/1996.

Season	Club	League	GP	G	A	Pts	AG	AA	APts	PIM	GP	G	A	Pts	PIM
1930-31	Melville Millionaires	SJHL	20	4	4	8	....	....	....	12	....	....	....	....	....
1931-32	Regina Pats	City Jr.	3	1	1	2	....	....	....	0	6	*3	0	*3	0
1932-33	Regina Pats	City Jr.	3	2	1	3	....	....	....	2	15	2	2	4	12
1933-34	Prince Albert Mintos	SSHL	22	17	*19	*36	....	....	....	22	4	0	1	1	2
1934-35	**Boston Bruins**	**NHL**	**3**	**0**	**0**	**0**	**0**	**0**	**0**	**0**	**4**	**0**	**0**	**0**	**0**
	Boston Cubs	Can-Am	42	14	11	25	....	....	....	34	3	1	2	3	0
1935-36	**Boston Bruins**	**NHL**	**23**	**1**	**4**	**5**	**2**	**10**	**12**	**4**	**2**	**0**	**0**	**0**	**0**
1935-36	Boston Cubs	Can-Am	15	2	8	10	....	....	....	13	....	....	....	....	....
1936-37	Providence Reds	AHL	43	11	14	25	....	....	....	26	3	0	1	1	0
1937-38	**Detroit Red Wings**	**NHL**	**32**	**5**	**17**	**22**	**10**	**35**	**45**	**6**	....	....	....	....	....
	Providence Reds	AHL	17	6	6	12	....	....	....	4	....	....	....	....	....
1938-39	**Detroit Red Wings**	**NHL**	**44**	**5**	**11**	**16**	**10**	**20**	**30**	**17**	**4**	**0**	**1**	**1**	**0**
1939-40	**Detroit Red Wings**	**NHL**	**37**	**7**	**12**	**19**	**15**	**24**	**39**	**28**	**5**	**1**	**1**	**2**	**15**
	Providence Reds	AHL	16	5	49	16	....	....	....	....	....	....	....	....	....
1940-41	**Detroit Red Wings**	**NHL**	**48**	**13**	**12**	**25**	**26**	**22**	**48**	**18**	**9**	**1**	**3**	**4**	**4**
1941-42	**Detroit Red Wings**	**NHL**	**19**	**2**	**4**	**6**	**3**	**6**	**9**	**20**	**12**	**1**	**3**	**4**	**20**
1942-43	**Detroit Red Wings**	**NHL**	**50**	**6**	**4**	**10**	**8**	**5**	**13**	**42**	**5**	**0**	**1**	**1**	**2**
	Cleveland Barons	AHL	2	1	1	2	....	....	....	0	....	....	....	....	....
1943-44	Coast Guard Clippers	....	33	12	21	34	....	....	....	12	12	4	10	14	9
1944-45			MILITARY SERVICE												
1945-46	Cleveland Barons	AHL	23	1	7	8	....	....	....	18	12	4	2	6	4
1946-47	Springfield Indians	AHL	61	6	14	20	....	....	....	50	2	1	0	1	0
1947-48	Philadelphia Rockets	AHL	63	6	22	28	....	....	....	55	....	....	....	....	....
	NHL Totals		**256**	**39**	**64**	**103**	**74**	**122**	**196**	**135**	**41**	**3**	**9**	**12**	**41**

Traded to **Detroit** by **Boston** for Clarence Drouillard and cash, December 22, 1937. Loaned to **Cleveland** (AHL) by **Detroit** as an injury replacement for Dick Adolph, October 23, 1942. • **Coast Guard Cutters** played exhibition season only in 1943-44. Traded to **Cleveland** (AHL) by **Detroit** for cash, October 25, 1945.

• MULOIN, WAYNE

— *see page 1329*

• MUMMERY, HARRY

Harry "Mum" Mummery
D – L. 5'11", 220 lbs. b: Chicago, IL, 8/25/1889. d: 12/7/1945.

Season	Club	League	GP	G	A	Pts	AG	AA	APts	PIM	GP	G	A	Pts	PIM
1910-11	Brandon Hockey Club	MHL Sr.	5	1	0	1	....	....	....	....	....	....	....	....	....
1911-12	Moose Jaw Canadians	City Sr.	STATISTICS NOT AVAILABLE												
1912-13	Quebec Bulldogs	NHA	19	5	0	5	....	....	....	*87	2	1	0	1	0
1913-14	Quebec Bulldogs	NHA	20	8	5	13	....	....	....	29	....	....	....	....	....
1914-15	Quebec Bulldogs	NHA	20	7	4	11	....	....	....	88	....	....	....	....	....
1915-16	Quebec Bulldogs	NHA	23	2	1	3	....	....	....	84	....	....	....	....	....
1916-17	Montreal Canadiens	NHA	20	4	2	6	....	....	....	82	6	0	0	0	18
1917-18	**Toronto Arenas**	**NHL**	**18**	**3**	**3**	**6**	**7**	**0**	**7**	**41**	**7**	**1**	***7**	**8**	**38**
1918-19	**Toronto Arenas**	**NHL**	**13**	**2**	**0**	**2**	**7**	**0**	**7**	**35**	....	....	....	....	....
1919-20	**Quebec Bulldogs**	**NHL**	**24**	**9**	**9**	**18**	**20**	**62**	**82**	**42**	....	....	....	....	....
1920-21	**Montreal Canadiens**	**NHL**	**24**	**15**	**5**	**20**	**39**	**44**	**83**	**68**	....	....	....	....	....
1921-22	**Hamilton Tigers**	**NHL**	**21**	**4**	**2**	**6**	**11**	**12**	**23**	**40**	....	....	....	....	....
1922-23	**Hamilton Tigers**	**NHL**	**7**	**0**	**0**	**0**	**0**	**0**	**0**	**4**	....	....	....	....	....
	Saskatoon Sheiks	WCHL	4	0	0	0	....	....	....	2	....	....	....	....	....
	NHL Totals		**107**	**33**	**19**	**52**	**84**	**118**	**202**	**230**	**7**	**1**	**7**	**8**	**38**
	Other Major League Totals		106	26	12	38	....	....	....	372	8	1	0	1	18

NHL rights returned to **Quebec** (NHA) by **Montreal Canadiens** (NHA) prior to formation of NHL, November, 1917. Claimed by **Toronto Arenas** from **Quebec** in Dispersal Draft, November 26, 1917. Transferred to **Quebec** by **Toronto Arenas** when Quebec franchise returned to NHL, November 25, 1919. Transferred to **Hamilton** after **Quebec** franchise relocated, November 2, 1920. Traded to **Montreal Canadiens** by **Hamilton** with Jack McDonald and Dave Ritchie for Jack Couglin and the loan of Billy Coutu for 1920-21 season, November 29, 1920. Traded to **Hamilton** by **Montreal Canadiens** with Amos Arbour for Sprague Cleghorn, November 26, 1921. Traded to **Saskatoon** (WCHL) by **Hamilton** for cash, February 8, 1923.

• MUNRO, DUNC — Dunc Munro

D – L. 5'8", 190 lbs. b: Moray, Scotland, 1/19/1901. d: 1/3/1958.

Season	Club	League	GP	G	A	Pts	AG	AA	APts	PIM	GP	G	A	Pts	PIM
1920-21	Toronto Granites	OHA Sr.	8	4	5	9	....	....	....	....	2	1	0	1	....
1921-22	Toronto Granites	OHA Sr.	10	4	6	10	....	....	....	....	8	5	4	9	....
1922-23	Toronto Granites	OHA Sr.	12	7	7	14	....	....	....	....	2	2	0	2	4
1923-24	Toronto Granites	OHA Sr.	15	9	5	14	....	....	....	....	....	....	....	....	....
	Canada	Olympics	5	18	4	22	....	....	....	2	....	....	....	....	....
1924-25	**Montreal Maroons**	**NHL**	**27**	**5**	**1**	**6**	**17**	**13**	**30**	**14**	....	....	....	....	....
1925-26	**Montreal Maroons**	**NHL**	**33**	**4**	**6**	**10**	**12**	**70**	**82**	**55**	**6**	**1**	**0**	**1**	**6**
1926-27	**Montreal Maroons**	**NHL**	**43**	**6**	**5**	**11**	**17**	**43**	**60**	**42**	**2**	**0**	**0**	**0**	**4**
1927-28	**Montreal Maroons**	**NHL**	**43**	**5**	**2**	**7**	**15**	**17**	**32**	**35**	**9**	**0**	**2**	**2**	**8**
1928-29	**Montreal Maroons**	**NHL**	**1**	**0**	**0**	**0**	**0**	**0**	**0**	**0**	....	....	....	....	....
1929-30	**Montreal Maroons**	**NHL**	**40**	**7**	**2**	**9**	**14**	**6**	**20**	**10**	**4**	**2**	**0**	**2**	**4**
1930-31	**Montreal Maroons**	**NHL**	**4**	**0**	**1**	**1**	**0**	**4**	**4**	**0**	....	....	....	....	....
1931-32	**Montreal Canadiens**	**NHL**	**48**	**1**	**1**	**2**	**2**	**3**	**5**	**14**	**4**	**0**	**0**	**0**	**2**
	NHL Totals		**239**	**28**	**18**	**46**	**77**	**156**	**233**	**170**	**25**	**3**	**2**	**5**	**24**

Signed as a free agent by **Montreal Maroons**, October 30, 1924. • Suffered minor heart attack and missed rest of season, November 15, 1928. • Named playing coach/manager by **Montreal Maroons**, September 23, 1929. Signed as a free agent by **Montreal Canadiens**, November 6, 1931.

• MUNRO, GERRY — Gerry Munro

D – L. 5'10", 175 lbs. b: Sault Ste. Marie, Ont., 11/28/1897. Deceased.

Season	Club	League	GP	G	A	Pts	AG	AA	APts	PIM	GP	G	A	Pts	PIM
1919-20	Soo Greyhounds	NMHL	2	2	0	2	....	....	....	2	....	....	....	....	....
	Soo Greyhounds	NOHA	3	5	1	6	....	....	....	2	....	....	....	....	....
1920-21	Soo Greyhounds	NMHL	10	5	2	7	....	....	....	....	....	....	....	....	....
	Soo Greyhounds	NOHA	4	2	0	2	....	....	....	4	5	*5	1	6	....
1921-22	Soo Greyhounds	NMHL	10	1	1	2	....	....	....	....	....	....	....	....	....
	Soo Greyhounds	NOHA	7	0	1	1	....	....	....	11	2	0	0	0	2
1922-23	Sudbury Wolves	NOHA	8	3	1	4	....	....	....	10	2	0	0	0	4
1923-24	Sudbury Mines	NOHA	STATISTICS NOT AVAILABLE												
1924-25	**Montreal Maroons**	**NHL**	**29**	**1**	**0**	**1**	**3**	**0**	**3**	**22**	....	....	....	....	....
1925-26	**Toronto St. Pats**	**NHL**	**4**	**0**	**0**	**0**	**0**	**0**	**0**	**0**	....	....	....	....	....
1926-27	Detroit Greyhounds	AHA	5	1	0	1	....	....	....	0	....	....	....	....	....
	Chicago Cardinals	AHA	10	0	2	2	....	....	....	8	....	....	....	....	....
	Winnipeg Maroons	AHA	20	2	2	4	....	....	....	20	3	0	0	0	0
1927-28	Kansas City Pla-Mors	AHA	22	3	1	4	....	....	....	37	....	....	....	....	....
1928-29	Kansas City Pla-Mors	AHA	30	1	0	1	....	....	....	12	....	....	....	....	....
1929-30	Kansas City Pla-Mors	AHA	48	2	1	3	....	....	....	34	4	2	0	2	7
1930-31	Minneapolis Millers	AHA	43	5	5	10	....	....	....	58	....	....	....	....	....
	NHL Totals		**33**	**1**	**0**	**1**	**3**	**0**	**3**	**22**	....	....	....	....	....

Signed as a free agent by **Montreal Maroons**, October 31, 1924. Traded to **Toronto St. Pats** by **Montreal Maroons** for cash, October 23, 1925. Signed as a free agent by **Minneapolis** (AHA), November 3, 1930.

• MURDOCH, MURRAY — Murray Murdoch

LW – L. 5'10", 180 lbs. b: Lucknow, Ont., 5/19/1904.

Season	Club	League	GP	G	A	Pts	AG	AA	APts	PIM	GP	G	A	Pts	PIM
1923-24	University of Manitoba	MHL Sr.	8	9	5	14	....	....	....	0	1	0	1	0	0
1924-25	Winnipeg Tiger Falcons	MHL Sr.	18	12	2	14	....	....	....	2	....	....	....	....	....
1925-26	Winnipeg Maroons	CHL	34	9	2	11	....	....	....	12	5	0	1	1	0
1926-27	**New York Rangers**	**NHL**	**44**	**6**	**4**	**10**	**17**	**34**	**51**	**12**	**2**	**0**	**0**	**0**	**0**
1927-28	**New York Rangers**	**NHL**	**44**	**7**	**3**	**10**	**21**	**25**	**46**	**14**	**9**	**2**	**1**	**3**	**12**
1928-29	**New York Rangers**	**NHL**	**44**	**8**	**6**	**14**	**32**	**55**	**87**	**18**	**6**	**0**	**0**	**0**	**2**
1929-30	**New York Rangers**	**NHL**	**44**	**13**	**13**	**26**	**26**	**42**	**68**	**22**	**4**	**3**	**0**	**3**	**6**
1930-31	**New York Rangers**	**NHL**	**44**	**7**	**7**	**14**	**17**	**25**	**42**	**8**	**4**	**0**	**2**	**2**	**0**
1931-32	**New York Rangers**	**NHL**	**48**	**5**	**16**	**21**	**11**	**45**	**56**	**32**	**7**	**0**	**2**	**2**	**2**
1932-33	**New York Rangers**	**NHL**	**48**	**5**	**11**	**16**	**12**	**29**	**41**	**23**	**8**	**3**	***4**	**7**	**2**
1933-34	**New York Rangers**	**NHL**	**48**	**17**	**10**	**27**	**38**	**27**	**65**	**29**	**2**	**0**	**0**	**0**	**0**
1934-35	**New York Rangers**	**NHL**	**48**	**14**	**15**	**29**	**30**	**33**	**63**	**14**	**4**	**0**	**2**	**2**	**4**
1935-36	**New York Rangers**	**NHL**	**48**	**2**	**9**	**11**	**5**	**22**	**27**	**9**	....	....	....	....	....
1936-37	**New York Rangers**	**NHL**	**48**	**0**	**14**	**14**	**0**	**33**	**33**	**16**	**9**	**1**	**1**	**2**	**0**
1937-38	Philadelphia Ramblers	AHL	44	4	9	13	....	....	....	4	5	0	1	1	4
1938-39	Yale University	Ivy	DID NOT PLAY – COACHING												
	NHL Totals		**508**	**84**	**108**	**192**	**209**	**370**	**579**	**197**	**55**	**9**	**12**	**21**	**28**

Won Lester Patrick Trophy (1974)

Signed as a free agent by **NY Rangers**, September 2, 1926.

• MURPHY, RON — see page 1333

• MURRAY, ALLAN — Allan Murray

D – L. 5'7", 165 lbs. b: Stratford, Ontario, 11/10/1908.

Season	Club	League	GP	G	A	Pts	AG	AA	APts	PIM	GP	G	A	Pts	PIM
1927-28	South Porcupine Porkies	NOHA	STATISTICS NOT AVAILABLE												
1928-29	Buffalo Bisons	Can-Pro	28	2	1	3	....	....	....	27	....	....	....	....	....
1929-30	Buffalo Bisons	IAHL	37	1	0	1	....	....	....	54	....	....	....	....	....
1930-31	Buffalo Bisons	IAHL	46	0	3	3	....	....	....	42	4	0	0	0	2
1931-32	Buffalo Bisons	IAHL	46	2	7	9	....	....	....	39	6	0	0	0	2
1932-33	Buffalo Bisons	IAHL	43	1	7	8	....	....	....	48	6	0	0	0	4
1933-34	**New York Americans**	**NHL**	**39**	**1**	**1**	**2**	**2**	**3**	**5**	**20**	....	....	....	....	....
	Syracuse Stars	IAHL	9	1	0	1	....	....	....	28	....	....	....	....	....
1934-35	**New York Americans**	**NHL**	**43**	**2**	**1**	**3**	**4**	**2**	**6**	**36**	....	....	....	....	....
1935-36	**New York Americans**	**NHL**	**48**	**1**	**0**	**1**	**2**	**0**	**2**	**33**	**5**	**0**	**0**	**0**	**2**
1936-37	**New York Americans**	**NHL**	**40**	**0**	**2**	**2**	**0**	**5**	**5**	**22**	....	....	....	....	....
1937-38	**New York Americans**	**NHL**	**47**	**0**	**1**	**1**	**0**	**2**	**2**	**34**	**6**	**0**	**0**	**0**	**6**
1938-39	**New York Americans**	**NHL**	**18**	**0**	**0**	**0**	**0**	**0**	**0**	**8**	....	....	....	....	....
1939-40	**New York Americans**	**NHL**	**36**	**1**	**4**	**5**	**2**	**8**	**10**	**10**	**3**	**0**	**0**	**0**	**0**
	NHL Totals		**271**	**5**	**9**	**14**	**10**	**20**	**30**	**163**	**14**	**0**	**0**	**0**	**8**

Signed as a free agent by **NY Americans**, February 20, 1933.

• MURRAY, LEO — Leo Murray

C/LW – L. 5'9", 165 lbs. b: Portage La Prairie, Man., 2/15/1906. Deceased.

Season	Club	League	GP	G	A	Pts	AG	AA	APts	PIM	GP	G	A	Pts	PIM
1924-25	Montreal Ste. Anne	ECHL	12	8	0	8	....	....	....	....	....	....	....	....	....
1925-26	Montreal Columbus Club	QAHA	8	5	0	5	....	....	....	15	....	....	....	....	....
1926-27	Quebec Castors	Can-Am	32	13	4	17	....	....	....	36	2	0	0	0	2
1927-28	Quebec Castors	Can-Am	39	10	5	15	....	....	....	69	6	1	0	1	12
1928-29	Newark Bulldogs	Can-Am	40	6	3	9	....	....	....	78	....	....	....	....	....
1929-30	Providence Reds	Can-Am	22	3	3	6	....	....	....	47	....	....	....	....	....
1930-31	Detroit Olympics	IAHL	27	3	5	8	....	....	....	18	....	....	....	....	....
	Philadelphia Arrows	Can-Am	15	5	1	6	....	....	....	27	....	....	....	....	....
1931-32	Providence Reds	Can-Am	39	17	11	28	....	....	....	65	5	2	*2	4	2
1932-33	**Montreal Canadiens**	**NHL**	**6**	**0**	**0**	**0**	**0**	**0**	**0**	**2**	....	....	....	....	....
	Providence Reds	Can-Am	42	16	14	30	....	....	....	51	2	1	1	2	0
1933-34	Providence Reds	Can-Am	40	9	12	21	....	....	....	60	3	0	0	0	9
1934-35	Providence Reds	Can-Am	39	2	10	12	....	....	....	32	6	1	0	1	6
1935-36	Springfield Indians	Can-Am	16	2	6	8	....	....	....	12	3	0	1	1	0
	NHL Totals		**6**	**0**	**0**	**0**	**0**	**0**	**0**	**2**	....	....	....	....	....

Signed as a free agent by **Quebec** (Can-Am), November 3, 1926. Rights traded to **Providence** (Can-Am) by **Newark** (Can-Am) for cash, October 8, 1929. Signed as a free agent by **NY Americans**, October 22, 1930. Traded to **Montreal Canadiens** by **Providence** (Can-Am) with Hago Harrington for Leo Gaudreault and Armand Mondou, January, 1933.

• MYLES, VIC — Vic Myles

D – R. 6'1", 208 lbs. b: Fairlight, Sask., 11/12/1915.

Season	Club	League	GP	G	A	Pts	AG	AA	APts	PIM	GP	G	A	Pts	PIM
1931-32	Moose Jaw Cubs	City Jr.	....	....	....	....	....	....	....	....	4	0	0	0	4
1932-33	Moose Jaw Cubs	City Jr.	....	....	....	....	....	....	....	....	2	0	0	0	2
1933-34	Moose Jaw Crescents	SSHL	20	9	2	11	....	....	....	38	3	0	1	1	*7
1934-35	North Battleford Beavers	SSHL	20	4	3	7	....	....	....	*45	6	4	*4	*8	16
1935-36	North Battleford Beavers	SSHL	16	10	9	19	....	....	....	38	3	2	0	2	2
1936-37	North Battleford Beavers	SSHL	25	2	10	12	....	....	....	*74	4	1	*4	5	6
1937-38	Moose Jaw Cresents	SSHL	23	9	17	26	....	....	....	*63	6	4	2	6	*8
1938-39	Moose Jaw Millers	SSHL	29	12	12	24	....	....	....	42	10	2	2	4	*14
1939-40	Philadelphia Rockets	AHL	50	7	8	15	....	....	....	60	....	....	....	....	....
1940-41	New Haven Eagles	AHL	55	5	9	14	....	....	....	96	....	....	....	....	....
1941-42	New Haven Eagles	AHL	56	8	19	27	....	....	....	88	....	....	....	....	....
1942-43	New Haven Eagles	AHL	4	0	3	3	....	....	....	8	....	....	....	....	....
	New York Rangers	**NHL**	**45**	**6**	**9**	**15**	**8**	**11**	**19**	**57**	....	....	....	....	....
1943-44	Moose Jaw–Flin Flon	SSHL	18	10	14	24	....	....	....	26	10	*9	6	*15	*34
1944-45			MILITARY SERVICE												
1945-46	Tulsa Oilers	USHL	53	22	26	48	....	....	....	56	13	7	6	13	*27
1946-47	St. Paul Saints	USHL	58	14	27	41	....	....	....	73	....	....	....	....	....
1947-48	Regina Capitals	WCSHL	47	11	8	19	....	....	....	62	4	3	2	5	6
1948-49	Regina Capitals	WCSHL	45	12	10	22	....	....	....	87	8	1	7	8	6
1949-50	Saskatoon Quakers	WCSHL	50	7	15	22	....	....	....	99	5	0	0	0	10
1950-51	Regina Capitals	WCSHL	28	6	11	17	....	....	....	39	....	....	....	....	....
1951-52	Moose Jaw Canucks	WCSHL	DID NOT PLAY – COACHING												
	NHL Totals		**45**	**6**	**9**	**15**	**8**	**11**	**19**	**57**	....	....	....	....	....

Traded to **NY Rangers** by **New Haven** (AHL) for cash, November 17, 1942.

• NATTRASS, RALPH — Ralph Nattrass

D – R. 6', 185 lbs. b: Gainsboro, Sask., 5/26/1925.

Season	Club	League	GP	G	A	Pts	AG	AA	APts	PIM	GP	G	A	Pts	PIM
1943-44	Moose Jaw Canucks	SJHL	2	2	2	4	....	....	....	0	....	....	....	....	....
1944-45	Moose Jaw Canucks	SJHL	16	7	5	12	....	....	....	53	21	9	5	14	*37
1945-46	Kansas City Pla-Mors	USHL	50	4	20	24	....	....	....	75	12	2	5	7	20
1946-47	**Chicago Black Hawks**	**NHL**	**35**	**4**	**5**	**9**	**5**	**7**	**12**	**34**	....	....	....	....	....
	Kansas City Pla-Mors	USHL	17	1	5	6	....	....	....	22	....	....	....	....	....
1947-48	**Chicago Black Hawks**	**NHL**	**60**	**5**	**12**	**17**	**7**	**17**	**24**	**79**	....	....	....	....	....
1948-49	**Chicago Black Hawks**	**NHL**	**60**	**4**	**10**	**14**	**6**	**16**	**22**	**99**	....	....	....	....	....
1949-50	**Chicago Black Hawks**	**NHL**	**68**	**5**	**11**	**16**	**7**	**14**	**21**	**96**	....	....	....	....	....
1950-51	Cincinnati Mohawks	AHL	55	0	30	30	....	....	....	84	....	....	....	....	....
	NHL Totals		**223**	**18**	**38**	**56**	**25**	**54**	**79**	**308**	....	....	....	....	....

Traded to **Montreal** by **Chicago** for cash, October 4, 1950.

• NEILSON, JIM — see page 1342

• NESTERENKO, ERIC — see page 1343

• NEVILLE, MIKE — Mike Neville

C – R. 5'9", 168 lbs. b: Toronto, Ont., 10/11/1904. Deceased.

Season	Club	League	GP	G	A	Pts	AG	AA	APts	PIM	GP	G	A	Pts	PIM
1921-22	Grand'Mere Maroons	QPHL	8	7	0	7	....	....	....	....	....	....	....	....	....
1922-23	Quebec Sons Of Ireland	QPHL	8	2	0	2	....	....	....	....	5	1	0	1	....
1923-24	Trois-Rivieres Lions	QPHL	10	2	0	2	....	....	....	....	....	....	....	....	....
1924-25	London AAA	OHA Sr.	8	5	4	9	....	....	....	2	....	....	....	....	....
	Toronto St. Pats	**NHL**	**12**	**1**	**0**	**1**	**3**	**0**	**3**	**4**	**2**	**0**	**0**	**0**	**0**
1925-26	**Toronto St.Pats**	**NHL**	**33**	**3**	**3**	**6**	**9**	**34**	**43**	**8**	....	....	....	....	....
1926-27	Hamilton Tigers	Can-Pro	32	15	4	19	....	....	....	38	2	0	0	0	0
1927-28	Hamilton–Stratford	Can-Pro	40	18	9	27	....	....	....	25	5	2	2	4	4
1928-29	Windsor Bulldogs	IAHL	38	14	7	21	....	....	....	18	8	2	*5	7	6
1929-30	Windsor Bulldogs	IAHL	39	11	17	28	....	....	....	20	....	....	....	....	....
1930-31	**New York Americans**	**NHL**	**19**	**1**	**0**	**1**	**2**	**0**	**2**	**2**	....	....	....	....	....
	New Haven Eagles	Can-Am	12	1	3	4	....	....	....	10	....	....	....	....	....
	London Panthers	IAHL	19	2	5	7	....	....	....	15	....	....	....	....	....
1931-32	London Tecumseh's	IAHL	48	10	11	21	....	....	....	25	5	0	0	0	2
1932-33	London Tecumseh's	IAHL	42	9	8	17	....	....	....	15	6	1	2	3	0
1933-34	Cleveland–Syracuse	IAHL	41	3	3	6	....	....	....	13	5	0	1	1	0
1934-35	Calgary–Portland	NWHL	24	6	6	12	....	....	....	6	....	....	....	....	....
1935-36	Rochester Cardinals	IAHL	39	2	2	4	....	....	....	4	....	....	....	....	....
	NHL Totals		**64**	**5**	**3**	**8**	**14**	**34**	**48**	**14**	**2**	**0**	**0**	**0**	**0**

Signed as a free agent by **Toronto St. Pats**, January 14, 1925. Traded to **NY Americans** by **Montreal Maroons** (Windsor-IAHL) with Frank Carson, Red Dutton and Hap Emms for $35,000, April 14, 1930. Traded to **London** (IAHL) by **NY Americans** for cash, January 28, 1931.

• NEVIN, BOB — see page 1344

• NEWMAN, JOHN
John Newman
C/LW – L. 5'8", 155 lbs. b: Ottawa, Ontario, 4/24/1910. d: 4/17/1967.

			REGULAR SEASON								PLAYOFFS				
Season	Club	League	GP	G	A	Pts	AG	AA	APts	PIM	GP	G	A	Pts	PIM
1928-29	Ottawa Shamrocks	City Jr.	STATISTICS NOT AVAILABLE												
1929-30	Detroit Olympics	IAHL	41	9	11	20	....	....	....	29	2	0	0	0	4
1930-31	**Detroit Falcons**	**NHL**	**8**	**1**	**1**	**2**	**2**	**4**	**6**	**0**	....	....	....	....	....
	Detroit Olympics	IAHL	21	3	5	8	....	....	....	30	....	....	....	....	....
1931-32	Detroit Olympics	IAHL	46	10	8	18	....	....	....	32	6	2	0	2	12
1932-33	Detroit Olympics	IAHL	34	7	6	13	....	....	....	25	....	....	....	....	....
1933-34	Buffalo Bisons	IAHL	43	5	2	7	....	....	....	16	6	0	2	2	2
1934-35	Buffalo–Cleveland	IAHL	39	7	11	18	....	....	....	4	....	....	....	....	....
1935-36	Buffalo Bisons	IAHL	47	5	14	19	....	....	....	10	5	0	2	2	0
1936-37	Seattle Seahawks	PCHL	26	4	4	8	....	....	....	5	....	....	....	....	....
1937-38	Detroit Pontiacs	MOHL	28	10	12	22	....	....	....	23	3	2	1	3	4
1938-39	Detroit Pontiacs	MOHL	27	9	6	15	....	....	....	4	7	3	2	5	0
1939-40	Detroit Pontiacs	MOHL	23	9	2	11	....	....	....	11	....	....	....	....	....
	NHL Totals		**8**	**1**	**1**	**2**	**2**	**4**	**6**	**0**	....	....	....	....	....

Signed as a free agent by **Detroit Cougars**, September 12, 1929. Traded to **Buffalo** (IAHL) by **Detroit** with Bob Davis and Tip O'Neil for Gammy Lederman, September 24, 1933.

• NICHOLSON, AL
Al Nicholson
LW – L. 6'1", 180 lbs. b: Estevan, Sask., 4/26/1936.

Season	Club	League	GP	G	A	Pts	AG	AA	APts	PIM	GP	G	A	Pts	PIM
1952-53	Humboldt Indians	SJHL	40	6	9	15	....	....	....	24	12	3	1	4	2
1953-54	Humboldt Indians	SJHL	47	18	22	40	....	....	....	59	5	1	0	1	10
1954-55	Humboldt Indians	SJHL	38	37	34	71	....	....	....	52	10	6	7	13	8
1955-56	**Boston Bruins**	**NHL**	**14**	**0**	**0**	**0**	**0**	**0**	**0**	**4**	....	....	....	....	....
	Hershey Bears	AHL	38	9	15	24	....	....	....	32	....	....	....	....	....
1956-57	**Boston Bruins**	**NHL**	**5**	**0**	**1**	**1**	**0**	**1**	**1**	**0**	....	....	....	....	....
	Hershey Bears	AHL	55	22	27	49	....	....	....	51	3	0	0	0	2
1957-58	Springfield Indians	AHL	61	14	19	33	....	....	....	38	13	0	2	2	10
1958-59	Victoria Cougars	WHL	69	36	51	87	....	....	....	78	3	1	1	2	0
1959-60	Victoria–Winnipeg	WHL	71	21	34	55	....	....	....	22	....	....	....	....	....
1960-61	Winnipeg Warriors	WHL	70	15	33	48	....	....	....	51	....	....	....	....	....
1961-62	San Francisco Seals	WHL	70	25	35	60	....	....	....	8	2	1	1	2	0
1962-63	San Francisco Seals	WHL	70	27	35	62	....	....	....	4	17	5	9	14	6
1963-64	San Francisco Seals	WHL	69	24	30	54	....	....	....	31	11	6	8	14	4
1964-65	San Francisco Seals	WHL	70	28	30	58	....	....	....	37	....	....	....	....	....
1965-66	San Francisco Seals	WHL	70	23	28	51	....	....	....	23	7	1	0	1	0
1966-67	San Diego Gulls	WHL	72	25	27	52	....	....	....	24	....	....	....	....	....
1967-68	San Diego Gulls	WHL	72	28	33	61	....	....	....	23	7	3	2	5	4
1968-69	San Diego Gulls	WHL	74	22	33	55	....	....	....	49	7	3	5	8	4
1969-70	San Diego Gulls	WHL	72	28	25	53	....	....	....	14	6	1	5	6	10
1970-71	San Diego Gulls	WHL	72	28	44	72	....	....	....	27	6	2	1	3	8
1971-72	San Diego Gulls	WHL	72	26	36	62	....	....	....	26	4	0	0	0	2
	NHL Totals		**19**	**0**	**1**	**1**	**0**	**1**	**1**	**4**	....	....	....	....	....

Claimed by **Pittsburgh** (AHL) from **Boston** in Reverse Draft, June 12, 1966. Traded to **San Diego** (WHL) by **Pittsburgh** (AHL), June 12, 1966.

• NICHOLSON, EDWARD
Edward Nicholson
D – L. 5'8", 180 lbs. b: Portsmouth, Ont., 9/9/1923.

Season	Club	League	GP	G	A	Pts	AG	AA	APts	PIM	GP	G	A	Pts	PIM
1945-46	Kingston Athletic Club	OHA Sr.	STATISTICS NOT AVAILABLE												
1946-47	Indianapolis Capitals	AHL	57	4	10	14	....	....	....	79	....	....	....	....	....
1947-48	**Detroit Red Wings**	**NHL**	**1**	**0**	**0**	**0**	**0**	**0**	**0**	**0**	....	....	....	....	....
	Indianapolis Capitals	AHL	65	5	16	21	....	....	....	63	....	....	....	....	....
1948-49	Indianapolis Capitals	AHL	65	3	24	27	....	....	....	46	2	0	0	0	0
1949-50	St. Louis Flyers	AHL	70	12	19	31	....	....	....	20	2	0	0	0	2
1950-51	St. Louis Flyers	AHL	68	8	24	32	....	....	....	37	....	....	....	....	....
1951-52	St. Louis Flyers	AHL	50	2	11	13	....	....	....	23	....	....	....	....	....
	NHL Totals		**1**	**0**	**0**	**0**	**0**	**0**	**0**	**0**	....	....	....	....	....

Signed as a free agent by **Detroit**, March 20, 1948. Traded to **St. Louis** (AHL) by **Detroit** with Fern Gauthier, Cliff Simpson and future considerations for Steve Black and Bill Brennan, September, 1949.

• NICHOLSON, HICKEY
Hickey (John Ivan) Nicholson
LW – L. 5'10", 170 lbs. b: Charlottetown, P.E.I., 9/9/1914. d: 11/22/1956.

Season	Club	League	GP	G	A	Pts	AG	AA	APts	PIM	GP	G	A	Pts	PIM
1929-30	Charlottetown Abegweits	PEI Sr.	8	6	1	7	....	....	....	28	4	*3	0	3	2
	Moncton Atlantics	City Sr.	1	1	1	2	....	....	....	0	....	....	....	....	....
1930-31	Charlottetown Abegweits	PEI Sr.	11	8	3	11	....	....	....	....	1	0	0	0	2
1931-32	Charlottetown Abegweits	MSHL	24	6	3	9	....	....	....	18	....	....	....	....	....
1932-33	Charlottetown Abegweits	MSHL	10	0	2	2	....	....	....	12	4	2	0	2	4
1933-34	Charlottetown Abegweits	MSHL	39	12	7	19	....	....	....	43	3	2	2	4	4
1934-35	Charlottetown Abegweits	MSHL	19	8	15	23	....	....	....	34	6	1	0	1	14
	Charlottetown Abegweits	Big 3	4	2	1	3	....	....	....	4	....	....	....	....	....
1935-36	Richmond Hawks	Britain	....	8	8	16	....	....	....	40	....	....	....	....	....
1936-37	Harringay Racers	Britain	....	9	8	17	....	....	....	30	....	....	....	....	....
1937-38	**Chicago Black Hawks**	**NHL**	**2**	**1**	**0**	**1**	**2**	**0**	**2**	**0**	....	....	....	....	....
	Kansas City Greyhounds	AHA	47	11	17	28	....	....	....	26	....	....	....	....	....
1938-39	Kansas City Greyhounds	AHA	48	10	35	51	....	....	....	33	....	....	....	....	....
1939-40	Kansas City Greyhounds	AHA	47	14	14	28	....	....	....	33	....	....	....	....	....
1940-41	Halifax Army	City Sr.	4	6	2	8	....	....	....	2	....	....	....	....	....
	NHL Totals		**2**	**1**	**0**	**1**	**2**	**0**	**2**	**0**	....	....	....	....	....

• NIGHBOR, FRANK
Frank "The Pembroke Peach" Nighbor **HHOF**
C – R. 5'9", 160 lbs. b: Pembroke, Ont., 1/26/1893. d: 4/13/1966.

Season	Club	League	GP	G	A	Pts	AG	AA	APts	PIM	GP	G	A	Pts	PIM
1910-11	Pembroke Debaters	Ott-Sr.	STATISTICS NOT AVAILABLE												
1911-12	Port Arthur Bearcats	NOHL	STATISTICS NOT AVAILABLE												
1912-13	Toronto Blueshirts	NHA	19	25	0	25	....	....	....	9	....	....	....	....	....
1913-14	Vancouver Millionaires	PCHA	11	10	5	15	....	....	....	6	....	....	....	....	....
1914-15	Vancouver Millionaires	PCHA	17	23	7	30	....	....	....	12	3	4	*6	*10	6
1915-16	Ottawa Senators	NHA	23	19	5	24	....	....	....	26	....	....	....	....	....
1916-17	Ottawa Senators	NHA	19	*41	2	43	....	....	....	18	2	1	0	1	6
1917-18	**Ottawa Senators**	**NHL**	**10**	**11**	**8**	**19**	**28**	**0**	**28**	**6**	....	....	....	....	....
1918-19	**Ottawa Senators**	**NHL**	**18**	**18**	**9**	**27**	**67**	**89**	**156**	**30**	**2**	**0**	***2**	**2**	**3**
1919-20	**Ottawa Senators**	**NHL**	**23**	**26**	**15**	**41**	**61**	**106**	**167**	**18**	**5**	***6**	**1**	***7**	**2**
1920-21	**Ottawa Senators**	**NHL**	**24**	**19**	**10**	**29**	**49**	**91**	**140**	**10**	**7**	**1**	***4**	**5**	**2**
1921-22	**Ottawa Senators**	**NHL**	**20**	**8**	**10**	**18**	**22**	**64**	**86**	**4**	**2**	**2**	**1**	**3**	**4**
1922-23	**Ottawa Senators**	**NHL**	**22**	**11**	**7**	**18**	**37**	**64**	**101**	**16**	**8**	**1**	***2**	**3**	**10**
1923-24	**Ottawa Senators**	**NHL**	**20**	**10**	**3**	**13**	**41**	**53**	**94**	**14**	**2**	**0**	**1**	**1**	**2**
1924-25	**Ottawa Senators**	**NHL**	**26**	**5**	**2**	**7**	**17**	**26**	**43**	**18**	....	....	....	....	....
1925-26	**Ottawa Senators**	**NHL**	**35**	**12**	***13**	**25**	**37**	**157**	**194**	**40**	**2**	**0**	**0**	**0**	**2**
1926-27	**Ottawa Senators**	**NHL**	**38**	**6**	**6**	**12**	**17**	**51**	**68**	**26**	**6**	**1**	**1**	**2**	**0**
1927-28	**Ottawa Senators**	**NHL**	**42**	**8**	**5**	**13**	**24**	**42**	**66**	**46**	**2**	**0**	**0**	**0**	**2**
1928-29	**Ottawa Senators**	**NHL**	**30**	**1**	**4**	**5**	**4**	**37**	**41**	**22**	....	....	....	....	....
1929-30	**Ottawa Senators**	**NHL**	**19**	**0**	**0**	**0**	**0**	**0**	**0**	**0**	....	....	....	....	....
	Toronto Maple Leafs	**NHL**	**22**	**2**	**0**	**2**	**4**	**0**	**4**	**2**	....	....	....	....	....
1930-31	Buffalo Bisons	IAHL	1	0	0	0	....	....	....	0	....	....	....	....	....
1931-1933	Buffalo Bisons	IAHL	DID NOT PLAY – COACHING												
	NHL Totals		**349**	**137**	**92**	**229**	**408**	**780**	**1188**	**252**	**36**	**11**	**12**	**23**	**27**
	Other Major League Totals		89	118	19	137	....	....	....	71	5	5	6	11	12

PCHA First All-Star Team (1915) • Won Hart Trophy (1924) • Won Lady Byng Trophy (1925, 1926)

Signed as a free agent by **Ottawa**, December 22, 1917. Traded to **Toronto** by **Ottawa** for Danny Cox and cash, January 31, 1930.

• NOBLE, REG
Reg Noble **HHOF**
C/D – L. 5'8", 180 lbs. b: Collingwood, Ont., 6/23/1896. d: 1/19/1962.

Season	Club	League	GP	G	A	Pts	AG	AA	APts	PIM	GP	G	A	Pts	PIM
1915-16	St. Michael's Majors	OHA	....	....	....	....	....	....	....	....	6	*9	0	*9	....
	Toronto Riversides	OHA Sr.	10	14	0	14	....	....	....	....	4	*6	0	*6	....
1916-17	Toronto Blueshirts	NHA	14	9	3	12	....	....	....	51	....	....	....	....	....
	Montreal Canadiens	NHA	6	4	0	4	....	....	....	15	2	0	0	0	3
1917-18	**Toronto Arenas**	**NHL**	**20**	**30**	**10**	**40**	**80**	**0**	**80**	**35**	**7**	**3**	**2**	**5**	**22**
1918-19	**Toronto Arenas**	**NHL**	**17**	**10**	**4**	**14**	**36**	**38**	**74**	**43**	....	....	....	....	....
1919-20	**Toronto St. Pats**	**NHL**	**24**	**24**	**9**	**33**	**56**	**62**	**118**	**51**	....	....	....	....	....
1920-21	**Toronto St. Pats**	**NHL**	**24**	**19**	**8**	**27**	**49**	**72**	**121**	**54**	**2**	**0**	**0**	**0**	**0**
1921-22	**Toronto St. Pats**	**NHL**	**24**	**17**	**11**	**28**	**47**	**71**	**118**	**19**	**7**	**0**	**1**	**1**	**21**
1922-23	**Toronto St. Pats**	**NHL**	**24**	**12**	**10**	**22**	**40**	**93**	**133**	**41**	....	....	....	....	....
1923-24	**Toronto St.Pats**	**NHL**	**23**	**12**	**3**	**15**	**50**	**53**	**103**	**23**	....	....	....	....	....
1924-25	**Toronto St. Pats**	**NHL**	**3**	**1**	**0**	**1**	**3**	**0**	**3**	**4**	....	....	....	....	....
	Montreal Maroons	**NHL**	**27**	**7**	**6**	**13**	**24**	**81**	**105**	**58**	....	....	....	....	....
1925-26	**Montreal Maroons**	**NHL**	**33**	**9**	**9**	**18**	**28**	**106**	**134**	**96**	**8**	**1**	**1**	**2**	**12**
1926-27	**Montreal Maroons**	**NHL**	**43**	**3**	**3**	**6**	**9**	**25**	**34**	**112**	**2**	**0**	**0**	**0**	**2**
1927-28	**Detroit Cougars**	**NHL**	**44**	**6**	**8**	**14**	**18**	**68**	**86**	**63**	....	....	....	....	....
1928-29	**Detroit Cougars**	**NHL**	**43**	**6**	**4**	**10**	**24**	**37**	**61**	**52**	**2**	**0**	**0**	**0**	**2**
1929-30	**Detroit Cougars**	**NHL**	**43**	**6**	**4**	**10**	**12**	**13**	**25**	**72**	....	....	....	....	....
1930-31	**Detroit Falcons**	**NHL**	**44**	**2**	**5**	**7**	**5**	**18**	**23**	**42**	....	....	....	....	....
1931-32	**Detroit Falcons**	**NHL**	**48**	**3**	**3**	**6**	**6**	**8**	**14**	**72**	**2**	**0**	**0**	**0**	**0**
1932-33	**Detroit Falcons**	**NHL**	**5**	**0**	**0**	**0**	**0**	**0**	**0**	**6**	....	....	....	....	....
	Montreal Maroons	**NHL**	**20**	**0**	**0**	**0**	**0**	**0**	**0**	**16**	**2**	**0**	**0**	**0**	**2**
1933-34	Cleveland Indians	IAHL	40	2	3	5	....	....	....	43	....	....	....	....	....
	NHL Totals		**509**	**167**	**97**	**264**	**487**	**745**	**1232**	**859**	**32**	**4**	**4**	**8**	**61**
	Other Major League Totals		20	13	3	16	....	....	....	66	2	0	0	0	3

Rights not retained by **Montreal Canadiens** after NHA folded, November 26, 1917. Signed as a free agent by **Toronto Arenas**, December 5, 1917. Traded to **Montreal Maroons** by **Toronto St. Pats** for $8,000, December 9, 1924. Traded to **Detroit Cougars** by **Montreal Maroons** for $7,500, October 4, 1927. Traded to **Montreal Maroons** by **Detroit Falcons** for John Gallagher, December 9, 1932.

• NOLAN, PADDY
Paddy (Patrick) Nolan
LW/D – L. 5'8", 170 lbs. b: Charlottetown, PEI, 12/1/1897. d: 4/12/1957.

Season	Club	League	GP	G	A	Pts	AG	AA	APts	PIM	GP	G	A	Pts	PIM
1915-16	Glace Bay Miners	CBSHL	8	16	4	20	....	....	....	....	4	9	0	9	....
1916-17	Glace Bay Miners	CBSHL	1	1	1	2	....	....	....	....	1	*3	0	3	....
	New Glasgow Black Foxes	CBSHL	2	2	0	2	....	....	....	12	....	....	....	....	....
1917-18	Glace Bay Miners	CBSHL	8	10	2	12	....	....	....	5	6	4	2	6	2
1918-19	Glace Bay Miners	CBSHL	STATISTICS NOT AVAILABLE												
1919-20	New Glasgow Black Foxes	MIHL	6	6	0	6	....	....	....	....	....	....	....	....	....
1920-21	Stellerton Seniors	CBSHL	4	7	3	10	....	....	....	....	2	0	1	1	3
1921-22	**Toronto St. Pats**	**NHL**	**2**	**0**	**0**	**0**	**0**	**0**	**0**	**0**	....	....	....	....	....
	New Glasgow Black Foxes	MIHL	6	4	0	4	....	....	....	12	7	4	0	4	....
1922-23	Stellerton Professionals	MIHL	12	15	0	15	....	....	....	30	3	6	0	6	5
1923-24	Stellerton Professionals	MIHL	16	10	0	10	....	....	....	23	....	....	....	....	....
1924-25	New Glasgow Colts	CBSHL	2	6	0	6	....	....	....	0	....	....	....	....	....
	Stellerton Professionals	MIHL	....	....	....	....	....	....	....	....	2	2	0	2	0
1925-26			REINSTATED AS AN AMATEUR												
1926-27	New Glasgow Colts	CBSHL	STATISTICS NOT AVAILABLE												
1927-28			DID NOT PLAY												
1928-29	New Glasgow Chevrolets	CBSHL	....	5	5	10	....	....	....	....	....	....	....	....	....
1929-30	New Glasgow Colts	CBSHL	15	12	0	12	....	....	....	11	3	2	0	2	....
1930-31	New Glasgow High	H.S.	DID NOT PLAY – COACHING												
	New Glasgow Tigers	CBSHL	2	2	0	2	....	....	....	0	....	....	....	....	....
	NHL Totals		**2**	**0**	**0**	**0**	**0**	**0**	**0**	**0**	....	....	....	....	....

Signed as a free agent by **Toronto St. Pats**, December 23, 1921.

• NORTHCOTT, BALDY
Baldy (Lawrence) Northcott
D/LW – L. 6', 184 lbs. b: Calgary, Alta., 9/7/1908. d: 11/7/1986.

			REGULAR SEASON								PLAYOFFS				
Season	Club	League	GP	G	A	Pts	AG	AA	APts	PIM	GP	G	A	Pts	PIM
1928-29	North Bay Trappers	NOHA	STATISTICS NOT AVAILABLE												
	Montreal Maroons	**NHL**	**5**	**0**	**0**	**0**	**0**	**0**	**0**	**0**	....	....	....	....	....
1929-30	**Montreal Maroons**	**NHL**	**43**	**10**	**1**	**11**	**20**	**3**	**23**	**6**	**4**	**0**	**0**	**0**	**4**
1930-31	**Montreal Maroons**	**NHL**	**22**	**7**	**3**	**10**	**17**	**11**	**28**	**15**	**2**	**0**	**1**	**1**	**0**
	Windsor Bulldogs	IAHL	21	12	6	18	....	....	....	18	....	....	....	....	....
1931-32	**Montreal Maroons**	**NHL**	**48**	**19**	**6**	**25**	**41**	**17**	**58**	**33**	**4**	**1**	**2**	**3**	**4**
1932-33	**Montreal Maroons**	**NHL**	**48**	**22**	**21**	**43**	**52**	**56**	**108**	**30**	**2**	**0**	**0**	**0**	**4**
1933-34	**Montreal Maroons**	**NHL**	**47**	**20**	**13**	**33**	**45**	**35**	**80**	**27**	**4**	**2**	**0**	**2**	**0**
1934-35	**Montreal Maroons**	**NHL**	**47**	**9**	**14**	**23**	**19**	**31**	**50**	**44**	**7**	***4**	**1**	***5**	**0**
1935-36	**Montreal Maroons**	**NHL**	**48**	**15**	**21**	**36**	**37**	**51**	**88**	**41**	**3**	**0**	**0**	**0**	**0**
1936-37	**Montreal Maroons**	**NHL**	**46**	**15**	**14**	**29**	**33**	**33**	**66**	**18**	**5**	**1**	**1**	**2**	**2**
1937-38	**Montreal Maroons**	**NHL**	**46**	**11**	**12**	**23**	**23**	**25**	**48**	**50**	....	....	....	....	....
1938-39	**Chicago Black Hawks**	**NHL**	**46**	**5**	**7**	**12**	**10**	**13**	**23**	**9**	....	....	....	....	....
1939-40	Winnipeg Rangers	MJHL	DID NOT PLAY – COACHING												
	NHL Totals		**446**	**133**	**112**	**245**	**297**	**275**	**572**	**273**	**31**	**8**	**5**	**13**	**14**

NHL First All-Star Team (1933)

Played in NHL All-Star Game (1937)

Traded to **Chicago** by **Montreal Maroons** with Earl Robinson and Russ Blinco for $30,000, September 15, 1938.

• NYKOLUK, MIKE
Mike Nykoluk
RW – R. 5'11", 212 lbs. b: Toronto, Ont., 12/11/1934.

			REGULAR SEASON								PLAYOFFS				
Season	Club	League	GP	G	A	Pts	AG	AA	APts	PIM	GP	G	A	Pts	PIM
1953-54	Toronto Marlboros	OHA	59	19	28	47	....	....	....	12	15	2	4	6	4
1954-55	Toronto Marlboros	OHA	47	14	25	39	....	....	....	23	13	3	7	10	17
1955-56	Winnipeg Warriors	WHL	70	10	25	35	....	....	....	18	14	10	*12	*22	7
1956-57	**Toronto Maple Leafs**	**NHL**	**32**	**3**	**1**	**4**	**4**	**1**	**5**	**20**	....	....	....	....	....
	Rochester Americans	AHL	28	9	13	22	....	....	....	30	9	3	2	5	4
1957-58	Rochester Americans	AHL	69	14	37	51	....	....	....	45	....	....	....	....	....
1958-59	Hershey Bears	AHL	66	15	38	53	....	....	....	60	13	*5	4	9	15
1959-60	Hershey Bears	AHL	71	13	32	45	....	....	....	55	....	....	....	....	....
1960-61	Hershey Bears	AHL	71	10	24	34	....	....	....	14	8	1	5	6	0
1961-62	Hershey Bears	AHL	59	4	20	24	....	....	....	13	7	1	2	3	12
1962-63	Hershey Bears	AHL	72	7	36	43	....	....	....	21	15	1	9	10	2
1963-64	Hershey Bears	AHL	72	9	63	72	....	....	....	39	6	1	3	4	0
1964-65	Hershey Bears	AHL	71	11	55	66	....	....	....	29	15	2	11	13	6
1965-66	Hershey Bears	AHL	67	10	53	63	....	....	....	14	3	0	1	1	0
1966-67	Hershey Bears	AHL	72	16	*68	84	....	....	....	26	5	0	4	4	4
1967-68	Hershey Bears	AHL	72	19	*66	85	....	....	....	30	5	2	6	8	0
1968-69	Hershey Bears	AHL	74	15	55	70	....	....	....	14	11	0	8	8	0
1969-70	Hershey Bears	AHL	72	16	57	73	....	....	....	12	7	0	2	2	2
1970-71	Hershey Bears	AHL	71	14	39	53	....	....	....	33	4	0	3	3	0
1971-72	Hershey Bears	AHL	62	13	30	43	....	....	....	20	4	0	2	2	4
	NHL Totals		**32**	**3**	**1**	**4**	**4**	**1**	**5**	**20**	....	....	....	....	....

AHL Second All-Star Team (1967) • Won Les Cunningham Award (MVP - AHL) (1967) • AHL First All-Star Team (1968)

Traded to **Hershey** (AHL) by **Toronto** with Wally Boyer and Ron Hurst for Willie Marshall, June, 1958

• OATMAN, RUSSELL
Russell Oatman
LW – L. 5'10", 195 lbs. b: Tilsonburg, Ont., 2/19/1905. d: 10/25/1964.

			REGULAR SEASON								PLAYOFFS				
Season	Club	League	GP	G	A	Pts	AG	AA	APts	PIM	GP	G	A	Pts	PIM
1924-25	Minneapolis Rockets	USAHA	27	4	0	4	....	....	....	....	....	....	....	....	....
1925-26	Victoria Cougars	PCHA	30	8	4	12	....	....	....	38	8	1	0	1	32
1926-27	**Detroit Cougars**	**NHL**	**14**	**3**	**0**	**3**	**9**	**0**	**9**	**12**	....	....	....	....	....
	Montreal Maroons	**NHL**	**25**	**8**	**4**	**12**	**23**	**34**	**57**	**30**	**2**	**0**	**0**	**0**	**0**
	Windsor Hornets	Can-Pro	1	0	0	0	....	....	....	0	....	....	....	....	....
1927-28	**Montreal Maroons**	**NHL**	**43**	**7**	**4**	**11**	**21**	**34**	**55**	**36**	**9**	**1**	**0**	**1**	**18**
1928-29	**Montreal Maroons**	**NHL**	**11**	**1**	**0**	**1**	**4**	**0**	**4**	**12**	....	....	....	....	....
	New York Rangers	**NHL**	**27**	**1**	**1**	**2**	**4**	**9**	**13**	**10**	**4**	**0**	**0**	**0**	**0**
1929-30	Hamilton Tigers	IAHL	7	2	0	2	....	....	....	8	....	....	....	....	....
	Niagara Falls Cataracts	IAHL	20	6	2	8	....	....	....	2	....	....	....	....	....
	NHL Totals		**120**	**20**	**9**	**29**	**61**	**77**	**138**	**100**	**15**	**1**	**0**	**1**	**18**

Signed as a free agent by **Victoria** (WHL), October 25, 1925. Rights transferred to **Detroit Cougars** after NHL club purchased **Victoria** (WHL) franchise, May 15, 1926. Traded to **Montreal Maroons** by **Detroit Cougars** for cash, January, 1927. Traded to **NY Rangers** by **Montreal Maroons** for cash, December 12, 1928. Traded to **Niagara Falls** (IAHL) by **Hamilton** (IAHL) for future considerations (Lloyd McIntyre), January 30, 1930.

• O'BRIEN, ELLARD
Ellard "Obie" O'Brien
D – L. 6'3", 183 lbs. b: St. Catharines, Ont., 5/27/1930.

			REGULAR SEASON								PLAYOFFS				
Season	Club	League	GP	G	A	Pts	AG	AA	APts	PIM	GP	G	A	Pts	PIM
1948-49	St. Catharines Teepees	OHA	25	9	8	17	....	....	....	20	5	3	3	6	2
1949-50	St. Catharines Teepees	OHA	48	58	43	101	....	....	....	79	5	1	2	3	13
	Boston Olympics	EHL	3	1	2	3	....	....	....	0	5	0	1	1	0
1950-51	Tulsa Oilers	USHL	57	33	28	61	....	....	....	38	2	0	1	1	11
1951-52	Hershey Bears	AHL	54	13	28	41	....	....	....	22	5	0	1	1	2
1952-53	Hershey Bears	AHL	61	16	32	48	....	....	....	38	3	0	1	1	2
1953-54	Hershey Bears	AHL	63	20	31	51	....	....	....	23	11	5	9	14	6
1954-55	Hershey Bears	AHL	62	31	38	69	....	....	....	28	....	....	....	....	....
1955-56	**Boston Bruins**	**NHL**	**2**	**0**	**0**	**0**	**0**	**0**	**0**	**0**	....	....	....	....	....
	Hershey Bears	AHL	49	12	14	26	....	....	....	71	....	....	....	....	....
1956-57	Hershey Bears	AHL	64	20	35	55	....	....	....	78	7	1	3	4	4
1957-58	Hershey Bears	AHL	65	23	48	71	....	....	....	46	11	4	11	15	6
1958-59	Hershey Bears	AHL	63	16	26	42	....	....	....	48	13	4	3	7	18
1959-60	Quebec Aces	AHL	67	9	19	28	....	....	....	36	....	....	....	....	....
1960-61	Quebec Aces	AHL	68	8	7	15	....	....	....	25	....	....	....	....	....
1961-62	Philadelphia Ramblers	EHL	60	23	32	55	....	....	....	12	3	0	0	0	4
	NHL Totals		**2**	**0**	**0**	**0**	**0**	**0**	**0**	**0**	....	....	....	....	....

• O'CONNOR, BUDDY
Buddy (Hubert) O'Connor **HHOF**
C – R. 5'8", 142 lbs. b: Montreal, Que., 6/21/1916. d: 8/24/1977.

			REGULAR SEASON								PLAYOFFS				
Season	Club	League	GP	G	A	Pts	AG	AA	APts	PIM	GP	G	A	Pts	PIM
1934-35	Montreal Jr. Royals	City Jr.	10	*15	7	*22	....	....	....	4	2	1	1	2	0
	Montreal Royals	City Sr.	....	....	....	....	....	....	....	....	4	1	0	1	2
1935-36	Montreal Royals	City Sr.	22	14	10	24	....	....	....	6	8	6	5	*11	6
1936-37	Montreal Royals	City Sr.	19	10	*17	27	....	....	....	27	5	0	4	*4	2
1937-38	Montreal Royals	City Sr.	22	9	14	23	....	....	....	10	1	0	0	0	0
1938-39	Montreal Royals	City Sr.	22	13	*23	*36	....	....	....	28	18	14	15	29	17
1939-40	Montreal Royals	City Sr.	29	16	25	41	....	....	....	6	13	*13	11	*24	8
1940-41	Montreal Royals	QSHL	35	15	*38	43	....	....	....	12	22	8	*21	*29	8
1941-42	**Montreal Canadiens**	**NHL**	**36**	**9**	**16**	**25**	**15**	**24**	**39**	**4**	**3**	**0**	**1**	**1**	**0**
	Montreal Royals	QSHL	9	1	5	6	....	....	....	4	....	....	....	....	....
1942-43	**Montreal Canadiens**	**NHL**	**50**	**15**	**43**	**58**	**21**	**55**	**76**	**2**	**5**	**4**	**5**	**9**	**0**
1943-44	**Montreal Canadiens**	**NHL**	**44**	**12**	**42**	**54**	**15**	**51**	**66**	**6**	**8**	**1**	**2**	**3**	**2**
1944-45	**Montreal Canadiens**	**NHL**	**50**	**21**	**23**	**44**	**29**	**37**	**66**	**2**	**2**	**0**	**0**	**0**	**0**
1945-46	**Montreal Canadiens**	**NHL**	**45**	**11**	**11**	**22**	**17**	**20**	**37**	**2**	**9**	**2**	**3**	**5**	**0**
	Montreal Royals	QSHL	2	0	1	1	....	....	....	0	2	0	2	2	0
1946-47	**Montreal Canadiens**	**NHL**	**46**	**10**	**20**	**30**	**13**	**29**	**42**	**6**	**8**	**3**	**4**	**7**	**0**
1947-48	**New York Rangers**	**NHL**	**60**	**24**	**36**	**60**	**35**	**53**	**88**	**8**	**6**	**1**	**4**	**5**	**0**
1948-49	**New York Rangers**	**NHL**	**46**	**11**	**24**	**35**	**17**	**38**	**55**	**0**	....	....	....	....	....
1949-50	**New York Rangers**	**NHL**	**66**	**11**	**22**	**33**	**15**	**28**	**43**	**4**	**12**	**4**	**2**	**6**	**4**
1950-51	**New York Rangers**	**NHL**	**66**	**16**	**20**	**36**	**22**	**26**	**48**	**0**	....	....	....	....	....
1951-52	Cincinnati Mohawks	AHL	65	11	43	54	....	....	....	4	4	2	3	5	2
1952-53	Cincinnati Mohawks	IHL	1	0	0	0	....	....	....	0	....	....	....	....	....
	NHL Totals		**509**	**140**	**257**	**397**	**199**	**361**	**560**	**34**	**53**	**15**	**21**	**36**	**6**

NHL Second All-Star Team (1948) • Won Lady Byng Trophy (1948) • Won Hart Trophy (1948) • AHL Second All-Star Team (1952)

Played in NHL All-Star Game (1949)

Rights traded to **Montreal Maroons** by **Montreal Canadiens** for Sammy McManus, September 10, 1936. Traded to **Montreal Canadiens** by **Montreal Maroons** for cash, September 24, 1938. Traded to **NY Rangers** by **Montreal** with Frank Eddolls for Hal Laycoe, Joe Bell and George Robertson, August 19, 1947.

• ODROWSKI, GERRY
— see page 1358

• O'FLAHERTY, PEANUTS
Peanuts (John Benedict) O'Flaherty
RW – R. 5'7", 154 lbs. b: Toronto, Ont., 4/10/1918.

			REGULAR SEASON								PLAYOFFS				
Season	Club	League	GP	G	A	Pts	AG	AA	APts	PIM	GP	G	A	Pts	PIM
1934-35	St. Michaels Majors	OHA	12	10	6	16	....	....	....	10	3	1	0	1	0
1935-36	West Toronto Nationals	City Jr.	10	6	*14	*20	....	....	....	4	5	4	*4	8	9
1936-37	Toronto Dominions	OHA Sr.	9	*7	*5	*12	....	....	....	4	11	4	4	8	6
1937-38	Toronto Marlboros	OHA	12	20	10	30	....	....	....	16	6	5	4	9	6
	Toronto Goodyears	OHA Sr.	....	....	....	....	....	....	....	....	2	2	1	3	....
1938-39	Toronto Goodyears	OHA Sr.	20	*23	12	35	....	....	....	12	15	13	9	*22	6
1939-40	Toronto Goodyears	OHA Sr.	29	*41	35	*76	....	....	....	18	11	*11	8	*19	8
1940-41	**New York Americans**	**NHL**	**10**	**4**	**0**	**4**	**8**	**0**	**8**	**0**	....	....	....	....	....
	Pittsburgh–Springfield	AHL	35	12	20	32	....	....	....	4	6	1	2	3	2
1941-42	**Brooklyn Americans**	**NHL**	**11**	**1**	**1**	**2**	**2**	**2**	**4**	**0**	....	....	....	....	....
	Springfield Indians	AHL	42	18	*44	62	....	....	....	14	5	5	1	6	0
1942-43	Pittsburgh Hornets	AHL	36	10	27	37	....	....	....	6	2	1	0	1	0
1943-44	Pittsburgh Hornets	AHL	2	1	2	3	....	....	....	0	....	....	....	....	....
	Toronto RCAF	OHA Sr.	8	7	7	14	....	....	....	2	....	....	....	....	....
	Toronto Peoples Credit	City Sr.	STATISTICS NOT AVAILABLE												
1944-45			MILITARY SERVICE												
1945-46	Pittsburgh Hornets	AHL	61	24	45	69	....	....	....	24	6	4	3	7	2
1946-47	Pittsburgh Hornets	AHL	64	33	35	68	....	....	....	24	12	0	5	5	4
1947-48	Pittsburgh Hornets	AHL	50	16	20	36	....	....	....	12	....	....	....	....	....
1948-49	Pittsburgh Hornets	AHL	67	24	25	49	....	....	....	22	....	....	....	....	....
1949-50	Pittsburgh Hornets	AHL	69	10	15	25	....	....	....	2	....	....	....	....	....
1950-51	St. Michael's Monarchs	OHA Sr.	28	7	12	19	....	....	....	40	16	1	6	7	10
1951-52	Saint John Beavers	MMHL	45	5	9	14	....	....	....	50	10	1	3	4	2
1952-53	Ottawa Senators	QSHL	DID NOT PLAY – COACHING												
1953-54	Soo Greyhounds	NOHA	4	0	0	0	....	....	....	2	....	....	....	....	....
1954-55	Soo Greyhounds	NOHA	3	0	0	0	....	....	....	0	....	....	....	....	....
1955-56	Sudbury Wolves	NOHA	8	0	1	1	....	....	....	4	....	....	....	....	....
1956-57			DID NOT PLAY – COACHING												
1957-58	Sudbury Wolves	NOHA	DID NOT PLAY – COACHING												
1958-59	Sudbury Wolves	NOHA	1	0	0	0	....	....	....	0	....	....	....	....	....
	NHL Totals		**21**	**5**	**1**	**6**	**10**	**2**	**12**	**0**	....	....	....	....	....

Traded to **NY Americans** by **Toronto** (Pittsburgh - AHL) with Phil McAtee for Viv Allen and Glenn Brydson, September, 1940.

• O'GRADY, GEORGE
George O'Grady
D – L. 5'8", 175 lbs. b: Montreal, Quebec. Deceased.

			REGULAR SEASON								PLAYOFFS				
Season	Club	League	GP	G	A	Pts	AG	AA	APts	PIM	GP	G	A	Pts	PIM
1911-12	Montreal Garnets	City Sr.	6	5	0	5	....	....	....	2	2	0	0	0	0
1912-13	Montreal Garnets	City Sr.	11	4	0	4	....	....	....	*33	....	....	....	....	....
1913-14	Montreal Wanderers	NHA	12	1	2	3	....	....	....	8	....	....	....	....	....
1914-15	Montreal Wanderers	NHA	2	1	0	1	....	....	....	0	1	0	0	0	0
1915-16	Montreal Wanderers	NHA	2	0	1	1	....	....	....	4	....	....	....	....	....
1916-17	Montreal Stars	City Sr.	....	....	....	....	....	....	....	....	....	....	....	....	....
1917-18	**Montreal Wanderers**	**NHL**	**4**	**0**	**0**	**0**	**0**	**0**	**0**	**0**	....	....	....	....	....
	NHL Totals		**4**	**0**	**0**	**0**	**0**	**0**	**0**	**0**	....	....	....	....	....
	Other Major League Totals		16	2	3	5	....	....	....	12	1	0	0	0	0

Rights retained by **Montreal Wanderers** after NHA folded, November 26, 1917.

• OLIVER, HARRY
Harry "Pee Wee" Oliver **HHOF**
RW – R. 5'8", 155 lbs. b: Selkirk, Man., 10/26/1898. d: 6/16/1985.

			REGULAR SEASON								PLAYOFFS				
Season	Club	League	GP	G	A	Pts	AG	AA	APts	PIM	GP	G	A	Pts	PIM
1918-19	Selkirk Fishermen	MHL Sr.	9	15	9	24	....	....	....	6	....	....	....	....	....
1919-20	Selkirk Fishermen	MHL Sr.	10	7	6	13	....	....	....	4	....	....	....	....	....
1920-21	Calgary Canadians	Big 4	16	14	6	20	....	....	....	11	....	....	....	....	....
1921-22	Calgary Tigers	WCHL	20	10	4	14	....	....	....	7	2	1	0	1	0
1922-23	Calgary Tigers	WCHL	29	25	7	32	....	....	....	10	....	....	....	....	....
1923-24	Calgary Tigers	WCHL	27	22	12	34	....	....	....	14	7	2	2	4	4
1924-25	Calgary Tigers	WCHL	24	20	*13	*33	....	....	....	23	2	0	0	0	0
1925-26	Calgary Tigers	WHL	30	13	12	25	....	....	....	14	....	....	....	....	....
1926-27	**Boston Bruins**	**NHL**	**42**	**18**	**6**	**24**	**53**	**51**	**104**	**17**	**8**	**4**	**2**	***6**	**4**
1927-28	**Boston Bruins**	**NHL**	**43**	**13**	**5**	**18**	**40**	**42**	**82**	**20**	**2**	**2**	**0**	**2**	**4**
1928-29	**Boston Bruins**	**NHL**	**43**	**17**	**6**	**23**	**69**	**55**	**124**	**24**	**5**	**1**	**1**	**2**	**8**
1929-30	**Boston Bruins**	**NHL**	**40**	**16**	**5**	**21**	**32**	**16**	**48**	**12**	**6**	**2**	**1**	**3**	**6**
1930-31	**Boston Bruins**	**NHL**	**44**	**16**	**14**	**30**	**39**	**51**	**90**	**18**	**4**	**0**	**0**	**0**	**2**
1931-32	**Boston Bruins**	**NHL**	**44**	**13**	**7**	**20**	**28**	**19**	**47**	**22**	....	....	....	....	....
1932-33	**Boston Bruins**	**NHL**	**47**	**11**	**7**	**18**	**26**	**18**	**44**	**10**	**5**	**0**	**0**	**0**	**0**
1933-34	**Boston Bruins**	**NHL**	**48**	**5**	**9**	**14**	**11**	**24**	**35**	**6**	....	....	....	....	....
1934-35	**New York Americans**	**NHL**	**47**	**7**	**9**	**16**	**15**	**20**	**35**	**4**	....	....	....	....	....
1935-36	**New York Americans**	**NHL**	**45**	**9**	**16**	**25**	**22**	**39**	**61**	**12**	**5**	**1**	**2**	**3**	**0**
1936-37	**New York Americans**	**NHL**	**20**	**2**	**1**	**3**	**4**	**2**	**6**	**2**	....	....	....	....	....
	NHL Totals		**463**	**127**	**85**	**212**	**339**	**337**	**676**	**147**	**35**	**10**	**6**	**16**	**24**
	Other Major League Totals		130	90	48	138	....	....	....	68	11	3	2	5	4

WCHL First All-Star Team (1924, 1925)

Signed as a free agent by **Calgary** (WCHL), December 22, 1921. Traded to **Boston** by **Calgary** (WHL) for cash, September 4, 1926. Traded to **NY Americans** by **Boston** for cash, November 2, 1934.

• OLIVER, MURRAY
— *see page 1361*

• OLMSTEAD, BERT
Bert Olmstead **HHOF**
LW – L. 6'1", 180 lbs. b: Scepter, Sask., 9/4/1926.

Season	Club	League	GP	G	A	Pts	AG	AA	APts	PIM	GP	G	A	Pts	PIM
1944-45	Moose Jaw Canucks	SJHL	16	0	3	3	....	....	....	8	21	12	8	20	26
1945-46	Moose Jaw Canucks	SJHL	18	24	19	43	....	....	....	32	12	2	9	11	15
1946-47	Kansas City Pla-Mors	USHL	60	27	15	42	....	....	....	34	12	2	3	5	4
1947-48	Kansas City Pla-Mors	USHL	66	26	26	52	....	....	....	42	7	1	4	5	0
1948-49	**Chicago Black Hawks**	**NHL**	**9**	**0**	**2**	**2**	**0**	**3**	**3**	**4**	....	....	....	....	....
	Kansas City Pla-Mors	USHL	52	33	44	77	....	....	....	54	2	0	1	1	0
1949-50	**Chicago Black Hawks**	**NHL**	**70**	**20**	**29**	**49**	**27**	**37**	**64**	**40**	....	....	....	....	....
1950-51	**Chicago Black Hawks**	**NHL**	**15**	**2**	**1**	**3**	**3**	**1**	**4**	**0**	....	....	....	....	....
	Milwaukee Seagulls	USHL	12	8	7	15	....	....	....	11	....	....	....	....	....
	Montreal Canadiens	**NHL**	**39**	**16**	**22**	**38**	**22**	**28**	**50**	**50**	**11**	**2**	**4**	**6**	**9**
1951-52	**Montreal Canadiens**	**NHL**	**69**	**7**	**28**	**35**	**10**	**36**	**46**	**49**	**11**	**0**	**1**	**1**	**4**
1952-53	**Montreal Canadiens**	**NHL**	**69**	**17**	**28**	**45**	**26**	**39**	**65**	**83**	**12**	**2**	**2**	**4**	**4**
1953-54	**Montreal Canadiens**	**NHL**	**70**	**15**	**37**	**52**	**23**	**51**	**74**	**85**	**11**	**0**	**1**	**1**	**19**
1954-55	**Montreal Canadiens**	**NHL**	**70**	**10**	***48**	**58**	**14**	**63**	**77**	**103**	**12**	**0**	**4**	**4**	**21**
1955-56	**Montreal Canadiens**	**NHL**	**70**	**14**	***56**	**70**	**20**	**71**	**91**	**94**	**10**	**4**	**10**	**14**	**8**
1956-57	**Montreal Canadiens**	**NHL**	**64**	**15**	**33**	**48**	**20**	**39**	**59**	**74**	**10**	**0**	***9**	**9**	**13**
1957-58	**Montreal Canadiens**	**NHL**	**57**	**9**	**28**	**37**	**12**	**31**	**43**	**71**	**9**	**0**	**3**	**3**	**0**
1958-59	**Toronto Maple Leafs**	**NHL**	**70**	**10**	**31**	**41**	**13**	**33**	**46**	**74**	**12**	**4**	**2**	**6**	**13**
1959-60	**Toronto Maple Leafs**	**NHL**	**53**	**15**	**21**	**36**	**19**	**21**	**40**	**63**	**10**	**3**	**4**	**7**	**0**
1960-61	**Toronto Maple Leafs**	**NHL**	**67**	**18**	**34**	**52**	**22**	**35**	**57**	**84**	**3**	**1**	**2**	**3**	**10**
1961-62	**Toronto Maple Leafs**	**NHL**	**56**	**13**	**23**	**36**	**16**	**23**	**39**	**10**	**4**	**0**	**1**	**1**	**0**
	NHL Totals		**848**	**181**	**421**	**602**	**247**	**511**	**758**	**884**	**115**	**16**	**43**	**59**	**101**

NHL Second All-Star Team (1953, 1956)

Played in NHL All-Star Game (1953, 1956, 1957, 1959)

Traded to **Detroit** by **Chicago** with Vic Stasiuk for Lee Fogolin and Steve Black, December 10, 1950. Traded to **Montreal** by **Detroit** for Leo Gravelle, December 19, 1950. Claimed by **Toronto** from **Montreal** in Intra-League Draft, June 4, 1958.

• OLSON, DENNIS
Dennis Olson
C – R. 6', 182 lbs. b: Kenora, Ont., 11/9/1934.

Season	Club	League	GP	G	A	Pts	AG	AA	APts	PIM	GP	G	A	Pts	PIM
1951-52	Port Arthur Flyers	TBJHL	30	16	15	31	....	....	....	18	3	0	1	1	0
1952-53	Port Arthur Flyers	TBJHL	30	24	23	47	....	....	....	39	8	3	4	7	2
1953-54	Port Arthur North Stars	TBJHL	36	31	22	53	....	....	....	43	5	4	2	6	12
1954-55	Troy Bruins	IHL	57	9	24	33	....	....	....	36	11	1	6	7	7
1955-56	Troy Bruins	IHL	60	31	39	70	....	....	....	76	5	0	2	2	9
1956-57	New Westminster Royals	WHL	70	25	14	39	....	....	....	23	13	5	2	7	6
1957-58	**Detroit Red Wings**	**NHL**	**4**	**0**	**0**	**0**	**0**	**0**	**0**	**0**	....	....	....	....	....
	Seattle–Victoria	WHL	62	30	27	57	....	....	....	16	....	....	....	....	....
	Edmonton Flyers	WHL	1	0	0	0	....	....	....	0	....	....	....	....	....
1958-59	Springfield Indians	AHL	68	21	23	44	....	....	....	20	....	....	....	....	....
1959-60	Trois-Rivieres Lions	EPHL	6	1	1	2	....	....	....	2	....	....	....	....	....
	Springfield Indians	AHL	61	14	29	43	....	....	....	13	10	1	5	6	4
1960-61	Kitchener Beavers	EPHL	54	31	31	62	....	....	....	57	....	....	....	....	....
	Springfield Indians	AHL	17	1	7	8	....	....	....	2	8	4	6	*10	0
1961-62	Springfield Indians	AHL	70	24	22	46	....	....	....	30	11	4	3	7	4
1962-63	Springfield Indians	AHL	72	25	33	58	....	....	....	20	....	....	....	....	....
1963-64	Springfield Indians	AHL	72	20	33	53	....	....	....	16	....	....	....	....	....
1964-65	Springfield Indians	AHL	72	21	34	55	....	....	....	30	....	....	....	....	....
	NHL Totals		**4**	**0**	**0**	**0**	**0**	**0**	**0**	**0**					

Won WHL Coast Division Rookie of the Year Award (1957)

Traded to **Springfield** (AHL) by **Detroit** with Bill McCreary Sr. and Hank Bassen for Gerry Ehman, April, 1958.

• O'NEILL, JIM
Jim "Peggy" O'Neill
C/RW – R. 5'8", 160 lbs. b: Semans, Sask., 4/3/1913. Deceased.

			REGULAR SEASON								PLAYOFFS				
Season	Club	League	GP	G	A	Pts	AG	AA	APts	PIM	GP	G	A	Pts	PIM
1930-31	Saskatoon Wesleys	SJHL	4	*6	2	*8	....	....	....	2	....	....	....	....	....
1931-32	Saskatoon Wesleys	SJHL	4	3	0	3	....	....	....	5	....	....	....	....	....
	Saskatoon Crescents	SSHL	18	6	3	9	....	....	....	22	4	0	1	1	12
1932-33	Boston Cubs	Can-Am	46	13	17	30	....	....	....	63	7	1	3	4	8
1933-34	**Boston Bruins**	**NHL**	**23**	**2**	**2**	**4**	**4**	**5**	**9**	**15**	....	....	....	....	....
	Boston Cubs	Can-Am	12	6	5	11	....	....	....	19	....	....	....	....	....
1934-35	**Boston Bruins**	**NHL**	**48**	**2**	**11**	**13**	**4**	**24**	**28**	**35**	**4**	**0**	**0**	**0**	**9**
1935-36	**Boston Bruins**	**NHL**	**48**	**2**	**11**	**13**	**5**	**27**	**32**	**49**	**2**	**1**	**1**	**2**	**4**
1936-37	**Boston Bruins**	**NHL**	**21**	**0**	**2**	**2**	**0**	**5**	**5**	**6**	....	....	....	....	....
	Providence Reds	AHL	15	2	7	9	....	....	....	14	3	0	1	1	2
1937-38	Cleveland Barons	AHL	38	5	24	29	....	....	....	66	2	0	0	0	0
1938-39	Cleveland Barons	AHL	41	4	18	22	....	....	....	29	9	2	6	8	0
1939-40	Cleveland Barons	AHL	56	7	20	27	....	....	....	35	....	....	....	....	....
1940-41	**Montreal Canadiens**	**NHL**	**12**	**0**	**3**	**3**	**0**	**5**	**5**	**0**	**3**	**0**	**0**	**0**	**0**
	New Haven Eagles	AHL	40	7	17	24	....	....	....	40	....	....	....	....	....
1941-42	**Montreal Canadiens**	**NHL**	**4**	**0**	**1**	**1**	**0**	**2**	**2**	**4**	....	....	....	....	....
	Washington Lions	AHL	41	7	33	40	....	....	....	22	2	0	0	0	6
1942-43	Washington–Hershey	AHL	55	19	50	69	....	....	....	52	6	3	1	4	2
1943-44	Hershey Bears	AHL	54	20	33	53	....	....	....	18	7	0	6	6	2
1944-45	Hershey Bears	AHL	55	14	32	46	....	....	....	16	11	2	7	9	4
1945-46	Hershey Bears	AHL	52	5	26	31	....	....	....	33	3	0	0	0	2
	NHL Totals		**156**	**6**	**30**	**36**	**13**	**68**	**81**	**109**	**9**	**1**	**1**	**2**	**13**

Traded to **Montreal** by **Boston** (Cleveland - AHL) for Bill Summerhill and Bill MacKenzie, May 17, 1940. Traded to **Hershey** (AHL) by **Washington** (AHL) for Bob Gracie, November, 1942.

• O'NEILL, TOM
Tom "Windy" O'Neill
RW – R. 5'10", 155 lbs. b: Deseronto, Ont., 9/28/1923. Deceased.

Season	Club	League	GP	G	A	Pts	AG	AA	APts	PIM	GP	G	A	Pts	PIM
1941-42	St. Michael's Majors	OHA	18	6	6	12	....	....	....	28	2	0	0	0	0
1942-43	St. Michael's Majors	OHA	16	5	9	14	....	....	....	34	5	3	3	6	4
1943-44	**Toronto Maple Leafs**	**NHL**	**33**	**8**	**7**	**15**	**10**	**8**	**18**	**29**	**4**	**0**	**0**	**0**	**6**
1944-45	**Toronto Maple Leafs**	**NHL**	**33**	**2**	**5**	**7**	**3**	**8**	**11**	**24**	....	....	....	....	....
1945-46	Quebec Aces	QSHL	39	6	14	20	....	....	....	33	5	0	1	1	0
1946-47	Halifax Crescents	MSHL	32	25	21	46	....	....	....	49	4	0	0	0	0
1947-48	Halifax Crescents	MSHL	26	14	16	30	....	....	....	36	4	0	4	4	0
1948-49	Halifax St. Mary's	MSHL	22	4	2	6	....	....	....	18	7	0	0	0	10
	NHL Totals		**66**	**10**	**12**	**22**	**13**	**16**	**29**	**53**	**4**	**0**	**0**	**0**	**6**

• O'REE, WILLIE
Willie O'Ree
LW/RW – L. 5'10", 175 lbs. b: Fredericton, N.B., 10/15/1935.

Season	Club	League	GP	G	A	Pts	AG	AA	APts	PIM	GP	G	A	Pts	PIM
1951-52	Fredericton Merchants	City Sr.	6	10	4	14	....	....	....	2	8	10	5	15	18
	Fredericton Jr. Capitals	NBJHL	3	2	0	2	....	....	....	0	....	....	....	....	....
1952-53	Fredericton Jr. Capitals	NBJHL	12	15	3	18	....	....	....	6	4	5	0	5	2
	Fredericton Capitals	NBSHL	2	2	0	2	....	....	....	0	....	....	....	....	....
1953-54	Fredericton Capitals	NBSHL	23	7	11	18	....	....	....	15	25	*15	10	25	10
1954-55	Quebec Frontenacs	QJHL	43	27	17	44	....	....	....	41	17	7	6	13	10
1955-56	Kitchener Canucks	OHA	41	30	28	58	....	....	....	38	8	4	3	7	6
1956-57	Quebec Aces	QHL	68	22	12	34	....	....	....	80	10	3	3	6	10
1957-58	**Boston Bruins**	**NHL**	**2**	**0**	**0**	**0**	**0**	**0**	**0**	**0**	....	....	....	....	....
	Springfield Indians	AHL	6	0	0	0	....	....	....	0	....	....	....	....	....
	Quebec Aces	QHL	57	13	19	32	....	....	....	43	9	4	2	6	8
1958-59	Quebec Aces	QHL	56	9	21	30	....	....	....	74	....	....	....	....	....
1959-60	Kingston Frontenacs	EPHL	50	21	25	46	....	....	....	41	....	....	....	....	....
1960-61	**Boston Bruins**	**NHL**	**43**	**4**	**10**	**14**	**5**	**10**	**15**	**26**	....	....	....	....	....
	Hull-Ottawa Canadiens	EPHL	16	10	9	19	....	....	....	21	....	....	....	....	....
1961-62	Hull-Ottawa Canadiens	EPHL	12	1	2	3	....	....	....	18	....	....	....	....	....
	Los Angeles Blades	WHL	54	28	26	54	....	....	....	57	....	....	....	....	....
1962-63	Los Angeles Blades	WHL	64	25	26	51	....	....	....	41	3	2	3	5	2
1963-64	Los Angeles Blades	WHL	60	17	18	35	....	....	....	45	12	4	8	12	10
1964-65	Los Angeles Blades	WHL	70	*38	21	59	....	....	....	75	....	....	....	....	....
1965-66	Los Angeles Blades	WHL	62	33	33	66	....	....	....	30	....	....	....	....	....
1966-67	Los Angeles Blades	WHL	68	34	26	60	....	....	....	58	....	....	....	....	....
1967-68	San Diego Gulls	WHL	66	21	33	54	....	....	....	54	7	2	2	4	6
1968-69	San Diego Gulls	WHL	70	38	41	79	....	....	....	63	7	3	3	6	12
1969-70	San Diego Gulls	WHL	66	24	22	46	....	....	....	50	6	6	3	9	4
1970-71	San Diego Gulls	WHL	66	18	15	33	....	....	....	47	6	4	1	5	14
1971-72	San Diego Gulls	WHL	48	16	17	33	....	....	....	42	4	0	1	1	2
1972-73	New Haven Nighthawks	AHL	50	21	24	45	....	....	....	41	....	....	....	....	....
	San Diego Gulls	WHL	18	6	5	11	....	....	....	18	6	1	4	5	2
1973-74	San Diego Gulls	WHL	73	30	28	58	....	....	....	89	4	3	3	6	0
1974-75	San Diego Charms	Cal-Sr.	STATISTICS NOT AVAILABLE												
1975-76	San Diego Charms	Cal-Sr.	STATISTICS NOT AVAILABLE												
1976-77			DID NOT PLAY												
1977-78			DID NOT PLAY												
1978-79	San Diego Hawks	PCL	53	21	25	46	....	....	....	37	....	....	....	....	....
	NHL Totals		**45**	**4**	**10**	**14**	**5**	**10**	**15**	**26**	....	....	....	....	....

WHL Second All-Star Team (1969)

Traded to **Montreal** by **Boston** with Stan Maxwell for Cliff Pennington and Terry Gray, June, 1961. Traded to **LA Blades** (WHL) by **Montreal** for cash, November, 1961. Traded to **San Diego** (WHL) by **LA Blades** (WHL) for cash, July, 1971.

ORLANDO, JIMMY Jimmy Orlando
D – L. 5'11", 185 lbs. b: Montreal, Que., 2/27/1916.

Season	Club	League	GP	G	A	Pts	AG	AA	APts	PIM	GP	G	A	Pts	PIM
			REGULAR SEASON								PLAYOFFS				
1932-33	Montreal Victorias	City Jr.	11	2	0	2	....	....	....	33	....	....	....	....	....
1933-34	Montreal Victorias	City Jr.	8	0	4	4	....	....	....	44	2	0	0	0	8
	Montreal Vics	City Sr.	1	0	0	0	....	....	....	0	....	....	....	....	....
1934-35	Montreal Victorias	City Jr.	2	3	2	5	....	....	....	8	....	....	....	....	....
	Montreal Vics	City Sr.	7	0	0	0	....	....	....	18	....	....	....	....	....
1935-36	Rochester Cardinals	IAHL	12	0	0	0	....	....	....	18	....	....	....	....	....
	Montreal Sr. Canadiens	City Sr.	19	1	6	7	....	....	....	49	....	....	....	....	....
1936-37	**Detroit Red Wings**	**NHL**	**9**	**0**	**1**	**1**	**0**	**2**	**2**	**8**	....	....	....	....	....
	Pittsburgh Hornets	AHL	36	0	5	5	....	....	....	61	5	0	0	0	5
1937-38	**Detroit Red Wings**	**NHL**	**6**	**0**	**0**	**0**	**0**	**0**	**0**	**4**	....	....	....	....	....
	Pittsburgh Hornets	AHL	45	0	7	7	....	....	....	*82	2	0	0	0	0
1938-39	Springfield Indians	AHL	54	7	9	16	....	....	....	106	3	0	0	0	8
1939-40	**Detroit Red Wings**	**NHL**	**48**	**1**	**3**	**4**	**2**	**6**	**8**	**54**	**5**	**0**	**0**	**0**	**15**
1940-41	**Detroit Red Wings**	**NHL**	**48**	**1**	**10**	**11**	**2**	**18**	**20**	**99**	**9**	**0**	**2**	**2**	**31**
1941-42	**Detroit Red Wings**	**NHL**	**48**	**1**	**7**	**8**	**2**	**11**	**13**	**111**	**12**	**0**	**4**	**4**	**45**
1942-43	**Detroit Red Wings**	**NHL**	**40**	**3**	**4**	**7**	**4**	**5**	**9**	**99**	**10**	**0**	**3**	**3**	**14**
1943-44			MILITARY SERVICE												
1944-45			MILITARY SERVICE												
1945-46	Valleyfield Braves	QSHL	40	3	19	22	....	....	....	52	....	....	....	....	....
	Ottawa Senators	QSHL	....	....	....	....	....	....	....	....	9	1	3	4	22
1946-47	Valleyfield Braves	QSHL	35	5	8	13	....	....	....	69	....	....	....	....	....
1947-48	Montreal Royals	QSHL	39	3	14	17	....	....	....	*124	3	0	0	0	4
1948-49	Montreal Royals	QSHL	45	3	20	23	....	....	....	*164	8	2	1	3	18
1949-50	Montreal Royals	QSHL	1	0	0	0	....	....	....	0	....	....	....	....	....
	Valleyfield Braves	QSHL	30	2	11	13	....	....	....	52	5	0	1	1	24
1950-51	Valleyfield Braves	QSHL	53	1	11	12	....	....	....	107	16	0	6	6	24
	NHL Totals		**199**	**6**	**25**	**31**	**10**	**42**	**52**	**375**	**36**	**0**	**9**	**9**	**105**

AHL Second All-Star Team (1939)

ORR, BOBBY — *see page 1364*

OUELETTE, EDDIE Eddie Ouelette
C – L. 5'8", 172 lbs. b: Ottawa, Ont., 3/9/1911.

Season	Club	League	GP	G	A	Pts	AG	AA	APts	PIM	GP	G	A	Pts	PIM
1928-29	Windsor-Walkerton Tech	City Jr.	STATISTICS NOT AVAILABLE												
1929-30	Toronto Millionaires	IAHL	18	3	5	8	....	....	....	15	....	....	....	....	....
1930-31	Pittsburgh Yellowjackets	IAHL	44	2	5	7	....	....	....	26	6	0	0	0	2
1931-32	Pittsburgh–Windsor	IAHL	39	9	4	13	....	....	....	26	6	0	0	0	2
1932-33	Windsor Bulldogs	IAHL	43	7	10	17	....	....	....	63	6	2	0	2	4
1933-34	Cleveland–London	IAHL	42	9	19	28	....	....	....	15	6	2	0	2	6
1934-35	London Tecumsehs	IAHL	44	15	*25	40	....	....	....	50	5	1	2	3	4
1935-36	**Chicago Black Hawks**	**NHL**	**43**	**3**	**2**	**5**	**7**	**5**	**12**	**11**	**1**	**0**	**0**	**0**	**0**
1936-37	Portland Buckaroos	PCHL	39	18	8	26	....	....	....	50	3	0	1	1	8
1937-38	Portland Buckaroos	PCHL	42	12	20	32	....	....	....	63	2	2	0	2	4
1938-39	Portland Buckaroos	PCHL	48	32	30	62	....	....	....	64	5	3	4	7	10
1939-40	Portland Buckaroos	PCHL	37	13	10	23	....	....	....	53	4	2	2	4	0
1940-41	Portland Buckaroos	PCHL	47	21	22	43	....	....	....	59	....	....	....	....	....
1941-42	Lachine Flyers	QPHL	18	4	5	9	....	....	....	12	2	0	0	0	2
	NHL Totals		**43**	**3**	**2**	**5**	**7**	**5**	**12**	**11**	**1**	**0**	**0**	**0**	**0**

Signed as a free agent by **Toronto Millionaires** (IAHL), January 20, 1930. Signed as a free agent by **Pittsburgh** (IAHL) after **Toronto** (IAHL) franchise folded, October 30, 1930.

OUELETTE, GERRY Gerry Ouelette
RW – R. 5'9", 170 lbs. b: Grand Falls, N.B., 11/1/1938.

Season	Club	League	GP	G	A	Pts	AG	AA	APts	PIM	GP	G	A	Pts	PIM
1958-59	Waterloo Siskins	Jr. B	STATISTICS NOT AVAILABLE												
1959-60	Kingston Frontenacs	EPHL	64	35	42	77	....	....	....	23	....	....	....	....	....
1960-61	**Boston Bruins**	**NHL**	**34**	**5**	**4**	**9**	**6**	**4**	**10**	**0**	....	....	....	....	....
	Kingston Frontenacs	EPHL	21	13	5	18	....	....	....	4	3	1	2	3	0
1961-62	Kingston Frontenacs	EPHL	32	15	10	25	....	....	....	11	....	....	....	....	....
	Providence Reds	AHL	34	8	14	22	....	....	....	4	....	....	....	....	....
1962-63	Kingston Frontenacs	EPHL	61	31	42	73	....	....	....	10	....	....	....	....	....
1963-64	Minneapolis Bruins	CHL	69	32	47	79	....	....	....	4	5	0	2	2	2
1964-65	Minneapolis Bruins	CHL	57	24	36	60	....	....	....	8	5	1	3	4	0
	San Francisco Seals	WHL	7	1	0	1	....	....	....	0	....	....	....	....	....
1965-66	Buffalo Bisons	AHL	72	11	21	32	....	....	....	6	....	....	....	....	....
1966-67	Buffalo Bisons	AHL	66	17	20	37	....	....	....	8	....	....	....	....	....
1967-68	Buffalo Bisons	AHL	66	18	32	50	....	....	....	6	5	0	6	6	2
1968-69	Buffalo Bisons	AHL	74	25	37	62	....	....	....	12	6	4	1	5	4
1969-70	Buffalo Bisons	AHL	67	26	46	72	....	....	....	10	11	2	7	9	2
1970-71	Omaha Knights	CHL	71	23	*58	81	....	....	....	14	11	5	*13	*18	0
1971-72	Campbellton Tigers	NNBSL	DID NOT PLAY – COACHING												
1972-73	Campbellton Tigers	NNBSL	DID NOT PLAY – COACHING												
1973-74	Campbellton Tigers	NNBSL	DID NOT PLAY – COACHING												
1974-75	Campbellton Tigers	NNBSL	....	5	9	14	....	....	....	0	....	....	....	....	....
1975-76	Campbellton Tigers	NNBSL	....	10	16	26	....	....	....	4	....	....	....	....	....
	NHL Totals		**34**	**5**	**4**	**9**	**6**	**4**	**10**	**0**	....	....	....	....	....

Claimed by **Buffalo** (AHL) from **Boston** in Reverse Draft, June, 1965.

OWEN, GEORGE George Owen USHOF
D – L. 5'11", 190 lbs. b: Hamilton, Ont., 2/12/1901. d: 3/4/1986.

Season	Club	League	GP	G	A	Pts	AG	AA	APts	PIM	GP	G	A	Pts	PIM
			REGULAR SEASON								PLAYOFFS				
1918-19	Newton-Mass High	H.S.	STATISTICS NOT AVAILABLE												
1919-20	Harvard University	Ivy	DID NOT PLAY – FRESHMAN												
1920-21	Harvard University	Ivy	11	10	0	10	....	....	....	....	....	....	....	....	....
1921-22	Harvard University	Ivy	DID NOT PLAY												
1922-23	Harvard University	Ivy	STATISTICS NOT AVAILABLE												
1923-24	Boston Hockey Club	USAHA	12	*10	0	*10	....	....	....	....	....	....	....	....	....
1924-25	Harvard University	Ivy	DID NOT PLAY – COACHING												
1925-26	Boston AA Unicorns	USAHA	....	....	....	....	....	....	....	....	2	0	2	2	....
1926-27	Boston University Club	City Sr.	STATISTICS NOT AVAILABLE												
1927-28	Boston University Club	City Sr.	STATISTICS NOT AVAILABLE												
1928-29	**Boston Bruins**	**NHL**	**27**	**5**	**4**	**9**	**20**	**37**	**57**	**48**	**5**	**0**	**0**	**0**	**0**
1929-30	**Boston Bruins**	**NHL**	**42**	**9**	**4**	**13**	**18**	**13**	**31**	**31**	**6**	**0**	**2**	**2**	**6**
1930-31	**Boston Bruins**	**NHL**	**38**	**12**	**13**	**25**	**29**	**47**	**76**	**33**	**5**	**2**	**3**	**5**	**13**
1931-32	**Boston Bruins**	**NHL**	**42**	**12**	**10**	**22**	**26**	**28**	**54**	**29**	....	....	....	....	....
1932-33	**Boston Bruins**	**NHL**	**34**	**6**	**2**	**8**	**14**	**5**	**19**	**10**	**5**	**0**	**0**	**0**	**6**
1933-34	Michigan Tech Spartans	WIAA	DID NOT PLAY – COACHING												
	NHL Totals		**183**	**44**	**33**	**77**	**107**	**130**	**237**	**151**	**21**	**2**	**5**	**7**	**25**

Rights traded to **Boston** by **Toronto** for Eric Pettinger and the rights to Hugh Plaxton, January 10, 1929.

PALANGIO, PETER Peter Palangio
LW – L. 5'11", 175 lbs. b: North Bay, Ont., 9/10/1908.

Season	Club	League	GP	G	A	Pts	AG	AA	APts	PIM	GP	G	A	Pts	PIM
1926-27	North Bay Trappers	NOHA	11	*25	10	*35	....	....	....	24	4	*9	3	*12	4
	Montreal Canadiens	**NHL**	**6**	**0**	**0**	**0**	**0**	**0**	**0**	**0**	**4**	**0**	**0**	**0**	**0**
1927-28	**Detroit Cougars**	**NHL**	**14**	**3**	**0**	**3**	**9**	**0**	**9**	**8**	....	....	....	....	....
	Windsor Bulldogs	IAHL	28	16	1	17	....	....	....	18	....	....	....	....	....
1928-29	**Montreal Canadiens**	**NHL**	**2**	**0**	**0**	**0**	**0**	**0**	**0**	**0**	....	....	....	....	....
	Kitchener Dutchmen	IAHL	37	17	7	24	....	....	....	26	3	1	0	1	4
1929-30	London Panthers	IAHL	44	11	6	17	....	....	....	36	2	0	0	0	0
1930-31	London Tecumsehs	IAHL	3	2	0	2	....	....	....	0	....	....	....	....	....
	Syracuse Stars	IAHL	41	18	12	30	....	....	....	12	....	....	....	....	....
1931-32	Syracuse Stars	IAHL	43	12	5	17	....	....	....	18	....	....	....	....	....
1932-33	St. Louis Flyers	AHA	43	21	14	35	....	....	....	38	4	0	1	1	2
1933-34	St. Louis Flyers	AHA	48	21	9	30	....	....	....	22	7	*3	1	*4	6
1934-35	St. Louis Flyers	AHA	47	34	19	53	....	....	....	8	6	*4	3	*7	11
1935-36	St. Louis Flyers	AHA	48	22	20	42	....	....	....	38	8	*5	1	*6	8
1936-37	**Chicago Black Hawks**	**NHL**	**30**	**8**	**9**	**17**	**17**	**21**	**38**	**16**	....	....	....	....	....
1937-38	**Chicago Black Hawks**	**NHL**	**19**	**2**	**1**	**3**	**4**	**2**	**6**	**4**	**3**	**0**	**0**	**0**	**0**
	St. Louis Flyers	AHA	25	8	13	21	....	....	....	9	7	3	0	3	2
1938-39	Tulsa Oilers	AHA	34	12	18	30	....	....	....	16	8	1	3	4	2
1939-40	Tulsa Oilers	AHA	46	21	27	48	....	....	....	14	....	....	....	....	....
1940-41	Tulsa Oilers	AHA	48	12	21	33	....	....	....	17	....	....	....	....	....
1941-42	Dallas Texans	AHA	49	22	29	51	....	....	....	6	....	....	....	....	....
1942-43	Hershey–Pittsburgh	AHL	34	6	19	25	....	....	....	4	2	1	0	1	2
1943-44	Sudbury Open Pit Miners	NOHA	1	0	1	1	....	....	....	0	....	....	....	....	....
1944-45	North Bay Merchants	NOHA	....	*23	*12	*35	....	....	....	....	....	....	....	....	....
	NHL Totals		**71**	**13**	**10**	**23**	**30**	**23**	**53**	**28**	**7**	**0**	**0**	**0**	**0**

AHA First All-Star Team (1935, 1936)

Signed as a free agent by **Montreal Canadiens**, February, 1927. Loaned to **Windsor** (IAHL) by **Montreal Canadiens** for remainder of 1927-28 season, February 13, 1928. Loaned to **Detroit Cougars** by **Windsor** (IAHL) for Stan Brown, February 13, 1928. Traded to **London** (IAHL) by **Montreal Canadiens** for cash, November 11, 1929. Traded to **Syracuse** (IAHL) by **London** (IAHL) for cash, November 28, 1930. Traded to **St. Louis** (AHA) by **Syracuse** (IAHL) for cash, October 19, 1932. Traded to **Chicago** by **St. Louis** (AHA) for $25,000, December 19, 1936. Traded to **Tulsa** (AHA) by **Chicago** for cash, October 24, 1938.

PALAZZARI, ALDO Aldo Palazzari
RW – L. 5'7", 168 lbs. b: Eveleth, MN, 7/25/1918.

Season	Club	League	GP	G	A	Pts	AG	AA	APts	PIM	GP	G	A	Pts	PIM
1938-39	Eveleth Rangers	USHL	30	25	13	38	....	....	....	24	5	2	2	4	2
1939-40	University of Illinois	WIAA	STATISTICS NOT AVAILABLE												
1940-41	University of Illinois	WIAA	STATISTICS NOT AVAILABLE												
1941-42	Akron Clippers	USHL	12	2	5	7	....	....	....	10	2	1	2	3	6
	University of Illinois	WIAA	STATISTICS NOT AVAILABLE												
1942-43	Akron Clippers	USHL	....	....	....	....	....	....	....	....	....	....	....	....	....
1943-44	**Boston Bruins**	**NHL**	**24**	**6**	**3**	**9**	**7**	**4**	**11**	**4**	....	....	....	....	....
	Boston Olympics	EHL	17	15	17	32	....	....	....	14	....	....	....	....	....
	New York Rangers	**NHL**	**11**	**2**	**0**	**2**	**2**	**0**	**2**	**0**	....	....	....	....	....
	NHL Totals		**35**	**8**	**3**	**11**	**9**	**4**	**13**	**4**	....	....	....	....	....

Traded to **NY Rangers** by **Boston** for cash, February 22, 1944. • Suffered career-ending eye injury during NY Rangers training camp, October 18, 1944.

PANAGABKO, ED Ed Panagabko
C – L. 5'8", 170 lbs. b: Norquay, Sask., 5/17/1934. d: 1/18/1979.

Season	Club	League	GP	G	A	Pts	AG	AA	APts	PIM	GP	G	A	Pts	PIM
1951-52	Humboldt Indians	SJHL	43	31	19	50	....	....	....	20	9	11	3	14	6
1952-53	Humboldt Indians	SJHL	33	24	27	51	....	....	....	2	12	5	7	12	4
1953-54	Humboldt Indians	SJHL	32	10	20	30	....	....	....	27	5	2	2	4	10
	Seattle Bombers	WHL	1	0	0	0	....	....	....	0	....	....	....	....	....
	Melville Millionaires	SSHL	....	....	....	....	....	....	....	....	4	1	1	2	2
1954-55	Grand Rapids Rockets	IHL	60	25	35	60	....	....	....	53	4	2	2	4	2
1955-56	**Boston Bruins**	**NHL**	**28**	**0**	**3**	**3**	**0**	**4**	**4**	**38**	....	....	....	....	....
	Hershey Bears	AHL	41	16	25	41	....	....	....	52	....	....	....	....	....
1956-57	**Boston Bruins**	**NHL**	**1**	**0**	**0**	**0**	**0**	**0**	**0**	**0**	....	....	....	....	....
	Hershey Bears	AHL	58	13	19	32	....	....	....	44	7	0	2	2	8
1957-58	Hershey Bears	AHL	61	12	14	26	....	....	....	24	10	0	0	0	6
1958-59	Providence Reds	AHL	69	13	36	49	....	....	....	50	....	....	....	....	....
1959-60	Providence Reds	AHL	49	7	21	28	....	....	....	25	5	5	2	7	2
1960-61	Providence Reds	AHL	68	20	32	52	....	....	....	45	....	....	....	....	....
1961-62	Portland–Los Angeles	WHL	69	24	52	76	....	....	....	37	....	....	....	....	....
1962-63	San Francisco Seals	WHL	70	31	47	78	....	....	....	42	17	3	11	14	2
1963-64	San Francisco Seals	WHL	67	15	29	44	....	....	....	35	11	8	9	17	6
1964-65	San Francisco Seals	WHL	70	21	43	64	....	....	....	59	....	....	....	....	....
1965-66			DID NOT PLAY												
1966-67	San Diego Gulls	WHL	57	9	22	31	....	....	....	14	....	....	....	....	....
1967-68	San Diego Gulls	WHL	44	2	2	4	....	....	....	29	7	0	1	1	0
	NHL Totals		**29**	**0**	**3**	**3**	**0**	**4**	**4**	**38**	....	....	....	....	....

Traded to **San Francisco** (WHL) by **Boston** for cash, July, 1962.

• PAPIKE, JOE   Joe Papike
RW – R. 6', 175 lbs.   b: Eveleth, MN, 3/28/1915.   d: 5/28/1967.

			REGULAR SEASON								PLAYOFFS				
Season	Club	League	GP	G	A	Pts	AG	AA	APts	PIM	GP	G	A	Pts	PIM
1932-33	Eveleth Rangers	CHL	37	13	7	20	....	....	....	6	3	1	1	2	4
1933-34	Eveleth Rangers	CHL	43	13	6	19	....	....	....	17	3	0	1	1	2
1934-35	Baltimore Orioles	EHL	20	7	3	10	....	....	....	10	9	2	5	7	0
1935-36	Wichita Skyhawks	AHA	47	11	9	20	....	....	....	19	....	....	....	....	....
1936-37	Wichita Skyhawks	AHA	48	22	15	37	....	....	....	6	....	....	....	....	....
1937-38	Wichita Skyhawks	AHA	47	22	22	44	....	....	....	12	4	0	0	0	0
1938-39	Wichita Skyhawks	AHA	44	12	12	24	....	....	....	2	....	....	....	....	....
1939-40	Kansas City Greyhounds	AHA	38	12	19	31	....	....	....	12	....	....	....	....	....
1940-41	**Chicago Black Hawks**	**NHL**	**9**	**2**	**2**	**4**	**4**	**4**	**8**	**2**	**5**	**0**	**2**	**2**	**0**
	Kansas City Americans	AHA	39	20	23	43	....	....	....	15	....	....	....	....	....
1941-42	**Chicago Black Hawks**	**NHL**	**9**	**1**	**0**	**1**	**2**	**0**	**2**	**0**	....	....	....	....	....
	Kansas City Americans	AHA	34	22	24	46	....	....	....	6	6	2	5	7	4
1942-43			MILITARY SERVICE												
1943-44			MILITARY SERVICE												
1944-45	**Chicago Black Hawks**	**NHL**	**2**	**0**	**1**	**1**	**0**	**2**	**2**	**2**	....	....	....	....	....
1945-46			DID NOT PLAY												
1946-47	Duluth Coolerators	TBSHL	8	11	7	18	....	....	....	0	....	....	....	....	....
	NHL Totals		**20**	**3**	**3**	**6**	**6**	**6**	**12**	**4**	**5**	**0**	**2**	**2**	**0**

AHA Second All-Star Team (1938, 1941)

• PAPPIN, JIM   — *see page 1369*

• PARGETER, GEORGE   George Pargeter
LW – L. 5'7", 168 lbs.   b: Calgary, Alta., 2/24/1923.

Season	Club	League	GP	G	A	Pts	AG	AA	APts	PIM	GP	G	A	Pts	PIM
1942-43	Red Deer Wheelers	ASHL	24	18	9	27	....	....	....	8	....	....	....	....	....
1943-44	Red Deer Wheelers	ASHL	16	5	6	11	....	....	....	8	5	2	*6	*8	7
1944-45	Buffalo Bisons	AHL	53	25	14	39	....	....	....	12	6	3	5	8	0
1945-46	New Haven Eagles	AHL	48	21	15	36	....	....	....	6	....	....	....	....	....
	Fort Worth Rangers	USHL	14	8	4	12	....	....	....	0	....	....	....	....	....
1946-47	**Montreal Canadiens**	**NHL**	**4**	**0**	**0**	**0**	**0**	**0**	**0**	**0**	....	....	....	....	....
	Springfield–Buffalo	AHL	58	14	24	38	....	....	....	21	4	0	1	1	0
1947-48	Houston Huskies	USHL	26	11	16	27	....	....	....	2	....	....	....	....	....
	Buffalo Bisons	AHL	33	3	4	7	....	....	....	2	8	1	1	2	0
1948-49	Buffalo Bisons	AHL	66	31	34	65	....	....	....	18	....	....	....	....	....
1949-50	Buffalo Bisons	AHL	68	21	23	44	....	....	....	9	5	1	0	1	2
1950-51	Buffalo Bisons	AHL	63	20	24	44	....	....	....	6	4	0	1	1	0
1951-52	Buffalo Bisons	AHL	51	7	15	22	....	....	....	8	3	0	0	0	0
1952-53	Seattle Bombers	WHL	69	16	33	49	....	....	....	4	5	2	0	2	0
1953-54	Calgary Stampeders	WHL	67	20	15	35	....	....	....	4	25	7	10	17	2
1954-55	Calgary Stampeders	WHL	70	17	19	36	....	....	....	10	9	2	2	4	0
	NHL Totals		**4**	**0**	**0**	**0**	**0**	**0**	**0**	**0**	....	....	....	....	....

• PARISE, JEAN-PAUL   — *see page 1370*

• PARKES, ERNIE   Ernie Parkes
RW – R. 5'10", 150 lbs.   b: Vancouver, B.C., 11/4/1904.   d: 7/7/1948.

Season	Club	League	GP	G	A	Pts	AG	AA	APts	PIM	GP	G	A	Pts	PIM
1914-15	Toronto Argonauts	OHA Sr.	2	3	0	3	....	....	....	....	....	....	....	....	....
1915-16	Toronto Argonauts	OHA Sr.	10	13	0	13	....	....	....	....	2	0	0	0	0
1916-17	Toronto Riversides	OHA Sr.	7	6	0	6	....	....	....	....	2	0	0	0	3
1917-18	Kitchener Greenshirts	OHA Sr.	9	29	0	29	....	....	....	....	5	8	0	8	....
1918-19	Kitchener Greenshirts	OHA Sr.	9	7	*8	15	....	....	....	....	....	....	....	....	....
1919-20	Kitchener Greenshirts	OHA Sr.	8	*22	*6	*28	....	....	....	....	2	1	1	2	....
1920-21	Kitchener Greenshirts	OHA Sr.	7	6	2	8	....	....	....	....	1	1	0	1	....
1921-22	Vancouver Millionaires	PCHA	24	8	3	11	....	....	....	0	9	0	1	1	0
1922-23	Vancouver Millionaires	PCHA	30	11	4	15	....	....	....	2	6	2	1	3	2
1923-24	Vancouver Millionaires	PCHA	30	3	1	4	....	....	....	2	6	1	0	1	0
1924-25	**Montreal Maroons**	**NHL**	**17**	**0**	**0**	**0**	**0**	**0**	**0**	**2**	....	....	....	....	....
	NHL Totals		**17**	**0**	**0**	**0**	**0**	**0**	**0**	**2**	....	....	....	....	....
	Other Major League Totals		84	22	8	30	....	....	....	4	21	3	2	5	2

PCHA Second All-Star Team (1923)

Signed as a free agent by **Vancouver** (PCHA) November 16, 1921. Signed as a free agent by **Toronto St. Pats**, December 8, 1924. Traded to **Boston** by **Toronto St. Pats** for cash, December 8, 1924. Traded to **Montreal Maroons** by **Boston** for George Carroll, December 20, 1924.

• PARSONS, GEORGE   George Parsons
LW – L. 5'11", 174 lbs.   b: Toronto, Ont., 6/28/1914.   Deceased.

Season	Club	League	GP	G	A	Pts	AG	AA	APts	PIM	GP	G	A	Pts	PIM
1930-31	Toronto Native Sons	City Jr.	9	4	2	6	....	....	....	4	2	0	0	0	0
1931-32	Toronto Nationals	OHA	10	11	2	13	....	....	....	11	3	0	1	1	2
1932-33	Toronto Nationals	OHA	9	8	2	10	....	....	....	10	5	*3	1	*4	8
1933-34	Toronto Young Rangers	OHA	6	13	9	22	....	....	....	8	1	0	1	1	0
1934-35	Toronto Cities Service	City Sr.	13	*14	4	*18	....	....	....	15	7	4	4	8	*17
	Toronto All-Stars	OHA Sr.	13	13	1	14	....	....	....	10	6	3	1	4	2
1935-36	Syracuse Stars	IAHL	48	20	17	37	....	....	....	18	3	0	0	0	0
1936-37	**Toronto Maple Leafs**	**NHL**	**5**	**0**	**0**	**0**	**0**	**0**	**0**	**0**	....	....	....	....	....
	Syracuse Stars	AHL	43	26	11	37	....	....	....	32	9	3	3	6	0
1937-38	**Toronto Maple Leafs**	**NHL**	**30**	**5**	**6**	**11**	**10**	**12**	**22**	**6**	**7**	**3**	**2**	**5**	**11**
	Syracuse Stars	AHL	17	6	8	14	....	....	....	17	....	....	....	....	....
1938-39	**Toronto Maple Leafs**	**NHL**	**43**	**7**	**7**	**14**	**15**	**13**	**28**	**14**	....	....	....	....	....
	NHL Totals		**78**	**12**	**13**	**25**	**25**	**25**	**50**	**20**	**7**	**3**	**2**	**5**	**11**

Signed as a free agent by **Toronto**, October 22, 1935. • Suffered career-ending eye injury during game vs. Chicago, March 4, 1939.

• PATRICK, LESTER   Lester "The Silver Fox" Patrick
D – R. 6'1", 180 lbs.   b: Drummondville, Que., 12/31/1883.   d: 6/1/1960.

			REGULAR SEASON								PLAYOFFS				
Season	Club	League	GP	G	A	Pts	AG	AA	APts	PIM	GP	G	A	Pts	PIM
1903-04	Brandon Hockey Club	NWHL	....	....	....	....	....	....	....	....	2	0	0	0	....
1904-05	Westmount Academy	CAHL	8	4	0	4	....	....	....	....	....	....	....	....	....
1905-06	Montreal Wanderers	ECAHA	9	17	0	17	....	....	....	26	2	3	0	3	3
1906-07	Montreal Wanderers	ECAHA	9	11	0	11	....	....	....	11	6	10	0	10	32
1907-08	Nelson Seniors	BCHL	....	....	....	....	....	....	....	....	2	1	0	1	....
1908-09	Nelson Seniors	BCHL	STATISTICS NOT AVAILABLE												
1909-10	Renfrew Creamery Kings	NHA	12	23	0	23	....	....	....	25	....	....	....	....	....
1910-11	Nelson Seniors	BCHL	STATISTICS NOT AVAILABLE												
1911-12	Victoria Aristocrats	PCHA	16	10	0	10	....	....	....	9	....	....	....	....	....
1912-13	Victoria Aristocrats	PCHA	15	14	5	19	....	....	....	12	3	4	0	4	....
1913-14	Victoria Aristocrats	PCHA	9	5	5	10	....	....	....	0	3	2	0	2	....
1914-15	Victoria Aristocrats	PCHA	17	12	5	17	....	....	....	15	....	....	....	....	....
1915-16	Victoria Aristocrats	PCHA	18	13	11	24	....	....	....	27	....	....	....	....	....
1916-17	Spokane Canaries	PCHA	23	10	11	21	....	....	....	15	....	....	....	....	....
1917-18	Seattle Metropolitans	PCHA	17	2	8	10	....	....	....	15	2	0	1	1	0
1918-19	Victoria Cougars	PCHA	9	2	5	7	....	....	....	0	....	....	....	....	....
1919-20	Victoria Cougars	PCHA	11	2	2	4	....	....	....	3	....	....	....	....	....
1920-21	Victoria Cougars	PCHA	5	2	3	5	....	....	....	13	....	....	....	....	....
1921-22	Victoria Cougars	PCHA	2	0	0	0	....	....	....	0	....	....	....	....	....
1922-23			DID NOT PLAY												
1923-24			DID NOT PLAY												
1924-25			DID NOT PLAY												
1925-26	Victoria Cougars	WHL	23	5	8	13	....	....	....	20	1	0	0	0	2
1926-27	**New York Rangers**	**NHL**	**1**	**0**	**0**	**0**	**0**	**0**	**0**	**2**	....	....	....	....	....
	NHL Totals		**1**	**0**	**0**	**0**	**0**	**0**	**0**	**2**	....	....	....	....	....
	Other Major League Totals		186	111	63	174	....	....	....	165	15	16	1	17	34

PCHA First All-Star Team (1913, 1915, 1916, 1917) • PCHA Second All-Star Team (1918, 1920)

• Named coach and general manager of **NY Rangers** replacing Conn Smythe and Frank Carroll, October 27, 1926.

• PATRICK, LYNN   Lynn Patrick   HHOF
C/LW – L. 6'1", 192 lbs.   b: Victoria, B.C., 2/3/1912.   d: 1/26/1980.

Season	Club	League	GP	G	A	Pts	AG	AA	APts	PIM	GP	G	A	Pts	PIM
1933-34	Montreal Royals	City Sr.	15	5	3	8	....	....	....	4	2	0	0	0	0
1934-35	**New York Rangers**	**NHL**	**48**	**9**	**13**	**22**	**19**	**29**	**48**	**17**	**4**	**2**	**2**	**4**	**0**
1935-36	**New York Rangers**	**NHL**	**48**	**11**	**14**	**25**	**27**	**34**	**61**	**29**	....	....	....	....	....
1936-37	**New York Rangers**	**NHL**	**45**	**8**	**16**	**24**	**17**	**38**	**55**	**23**	**9**	**3**	**0**	**3**	**2**
1937-38	**New York Rangers**	**NHL**	**48**	**15**	**19**	**34**	**32**	**39**	**71**	**24**	**3**	**0**	**1**	**1**	**2**
1938-39	**New York Rangers**	**NHL**	**35**	**8**	**21**	**29**	**17**	**39**	**56**	**25**	**7**	**1**	**1**	**2**	**0**
1939-40	**New York Rangers**	**NHL**	**48**	**12**	**16**	**28**	**26**	**32**	**58**	**34**	**12**	**2**	**2**	**4**	**4**
1940-41	**New York Rangers**	**NHL**	**48**	**20**	**24**	**44**	**40**	**44**	**84**	**12**	**3**	**1**	**0**	**1**	**14**
1941-42	**New York Rangers**	**NHL**	**47**	**32**	**22**	**54**	**56**	**33**	**89**	**18**	**6**	**1**	**0**	**1**	**0**
1942-43	**New York Rangers**	**NHL**	**50**	**22**	**39**	**61**	**31**	**50**	**81**	**28**	....	....	....	....	....
1943-44			MILITARY SERVICE												
1944-45			MILITARY SERVICE												
1945-46	**New York Rangers**	**NHL**	**38**	**8**	**6**	**14**	**12**	**11**	**23**	**30**	....	....	....	....	....
1946-47	New Haven Ramblers	AHL	16	2	6	8	....	....	....	16	3	1	0	1	2
1947-48	New Haven Ramblers	AHL	DID NOT PLAY – COACHING												
	NHL Totals		**455**	**145**	**190**	**335**	**277**	**349**	**626**	**240**	**44**	**10**	**6**	**16**	**22**

NHL First All-Star Team (1942) • NHL Second All-Star Team (1943) • Won Lester Patrick Trophy (1989)

• PATRICK, MUZZ   Muzz (Murray) Patrick
D – L. 6'2", 200 lbs.   b: Victoria, B.C., 6/28/1915.   d: 7/23/1998.

Season	Club	League	GP	G	A	Pts	AG	AA	APts	PIM	GP	G	A	Pts	PIM
1934-35	New York Crescents	EHL	21	3	3	0	....	....	....	16	6	2	3	5	9
1935-36	New York Rovers	EHL	40	3	8	11	....	....	....	31	8	2	2	4	15
1936-37	Philadelphia Ramblers	AHL	48	2	11	13	....	....	....	62	6	0	1	1	2
1937-38	Philadelphia Ramblers	AHL	48	3	6	9	....	....	....	37	5	2	0	2	6
	New York Rangers	**NHL**	**1**	**0**	**2**	**2**	**0**	**4**	**4**	**0**	**3**	**0**	**0**	**0**	**2**
1938-39	**New York Rangers**	**NHL**	**48**	**1**	**10**	**11**	**2**	**19**	**21**	**64**	**7**	**1**	**0**	**1**	**17**
1939-40	**New York Rangers**	**NHL**	**46**	**2**	**4**	**6**	**4**	**8**	**12**	**44**	**12**	**3**	**0**	**3**	**13**
1940-41	**New York Rangers**	**NHL**	**47**	**2**	**8**	**10**	**4**	**15**	**19**	**21**	**3**	**0**	**0**	**0**	**2**
1941-42			MILITARY SERVICE												
1942-43			MILITARY SERVICE												
1943-44			MILITARY SERVICE												
1944-45			MILITARY SERVICE												
1945-46	**New York Rangers**	**NHL**	**24**	**0**	**2**	**2**	**0**	**4**	**4**	**4**	....	....	....	....	....
	Providence Reds	AHL	2	0	1	1	....	....	....	0	....	....	....	....	....
1946-47	St. Paul Saints	USHL	7	0	0	0	....	....	....	0	....	....	....	....	....
1947-48	St. Paul Saints	USHL	DID NOT PLAY – COACHING												
1948-49	Tacoma Rockets	PCHL	DID NOT PLAY – COACHING												
1949-50	Tacoma Rockets	PCHL	8	0	0	0	....	....	....	12	....	....	....	....	....
	NHL Totals		**166**	**5**	**26**	**31**	**10**	**50**	**60**	**133**	**25**	**4**	**0**	**4**	**34**

• PATTERSON, GEORGE
George "Paddy" Patterson
LW/RW – R. 6'1", 176 lbs. b: Kingston, Ont., 5/22/1906. d: 1/20/1977.

			REGULAR SEASON								PLAYOFFS				
Season	Club	League	GP	G	A	Pts	AG	AA	APts	PIM	GP	G	A	Pts	PIM
1925-26	Kingston Frontenacs	Ott-Jr.	STATISTICS NOT AVAILABLE												
1926-27	Hamilton Tigers	Can-Pro	23	14	3	17	....	....	....	30	....	....	....	....	....
	Toronto Maple Leafs	**NHL**	**17**	**4**	**2**	**6**	**12**	**17**	**29**	**17**	....	....	....	....	....
1927-28	**Toronto Maple Leafs**	**NHL**	**12**	**1**	**0**	**1**	**3**	**0**	**3**	**14**	....	....	....	....	....
	Montreal Canadiens	**NHL**	**16**	**0**	**1**	**1**	**0**	**8**	**8**	**0**	....	....	....	....	....
	Toronto Ravinas	Can-Pro	16	7	0	7	....	....	....	37	....	....	....	....	....
1928-29	**Montreal Canadiens**	**NHL**	**44**	**4**	**5**	**9**	**16**	**46**	**62**	**34**	**3**	**0**	**0**	**0**	**2**
1929-30	**New York Americans**	**NHL**	**39**	**13**	**4**	**17**	**26**	**13**	**39**	**24**	....	....	....	....	....
1930-31	**New York Americans**	**NHL**	**44**	**8**	**6**	**14**	**19**	**22**	**41**	**67**	....	....	....	....	....
1931-32	**New York Americans**	**NHL**	**20**	**6**	**0**	**6**	**13**	**0**	**13**	**26**	....	....	....	....	....
	New Haven Eagles	Can-Am	25	17	10	27	....	....	....	33	2	2	0	2	12
1932-33	**New York Americans**	**NHL**	**41**	**12**	**7**	**19**	**28**	**18**	**46**	**26**	....	....	....	....	....
1933-34	**New York Americans**	**NHL**	**13**	**3**	**0**	**3**	**7**	**0**	**7**	**6**	....	....	....	....	....
	Boston Bruins	**NHL**	**10**	**0**	**1**	**1**	**0**	**3**	**3**	**2**	....	....	....	....	....
	Boston Tiger Cubs	Can-Am	17	7	3	10	....	....	....	15	5	0	2	2	2
1934-35	**Detroit Red Wings**	**NHL**	**7**	**0**	**0**	**0**	**0**	**0**	**0**	**0**	....	....	....	....	....
	St. Louis Eagles	**NHL**	**21**	**0**	**1**	**1**	**0**	**2**	**2**	**2**	....	....	....	....	....
	Detroit–Buffalo	IAHL	28	10	9	19	....	....	....	58	....	....	....	....	....
1935-36	Buffalo Bisons	IAHL	48	7	11	18	....	....	....	31	1	0	0	0	2
1936-37	Minneapolis Millers	AHA	35	19	17	36	....	....	....	35	6	*8	2	*10	6
1937-38	Minneapolis Millers	AHA	48	25	34	*59	....	....	....	46	7	1	*4	5	0
1938-39	Cleveland Barons	AHL	53	11	5	16	....	....	....	20	9	1	1	2	0
1939-40	New Haven Eagles	AHL	54	25	27	52	....	....	....	42	3	2	2	4	2
1940-41	New Haven Eagles	AHL	45	19	33	52	....	....	....	33	2	0	0	0	0
1941-42	New Haven Eagles	AHL	28	9	16	25	....	....	....	18	2	0	1	1	2
1942-43	New Haven–Indianapolis	AHL	49	19	31	50	....	....	....	8	7	1	4	5	0
1943-44	Hershey Bears	AHL	48	15	31	46	....	....	....	16	7	1	1	2	4
1944-45	Hershey–Providence	AHL	54	26	33	59	....	....	....	9	....	....	....	....	....
	NHL Totals		**284**	**51**	**27**	**78**	**124**	**129**	**253**	**218**	**3**	**0**	**0**	**0**	**2**

AHA Second All-Star Team (1937) • AHA First All-Star Team (1938)

Traded to **Toronto St. Pats** by **Hamilton** (Can-Pro) for Al Pudas, February 1, 1927. Traded to **Montreal Canadiens** by **Toronto** for cash, February 8, 1928. Traded to **Boston** by **Montreal Canadiens** for cash, May 13, 1929. Claimed on waivers by **NY Americans** from **Boston**, October 23, 1929. Traded to **Boston** by **NY Americans** with Lloyd Gross for Art Chapman and Bob Gracie, January 11, 1934. Traded to **Detroit** by **Boston** for Gene Carrigan, October 10, 1934. Traded to **St. Louis** by **Detroit** for Mickey Blake and $3,500 with Detroit holding right of recall, November 29, 1934. Returned to **Detroit**, December 24, 1934.

• PAUL, BUTCH
Butch (Arthur) Paul
C – R. 5'11", 160 lbs. b: Rocky Mountain House, Alta., 9/11/1943. d: 3/25/1966.

Season	Club	League	GP	G	A	Pts	AG	AA	APts	PIM	GP	G	A	Pts	PIM
1963-64	Edmonton Oil Kings	SJHL	12	11	15	26	....	....	....	15	....	....	....	....	....
	Cincinnati Wings	CHL	1	0	1	1	....	....	....	5	....	....	....	....	....
1964-65	**Detroit Red Wings**	**NHL**	**3**	**0**	**0**	**0**	**0**	**0**	**0**	**0**	....	....	....	....	....
	Charlotte Checkers	EHL	30	27	14	41	....	....	....	50	....	....	....	....	....
	Pittsburgh Hornets	AHL	30	7	16	23	....	....	....	16	4	1	0	1	2
1965-66	Memphis Wings	CHL	68	13	47	60	....	....	....	44	....	....	....	....	....
	NHL Totals		**3**	**0**	**0**	**0**	**0**	**0**	**0**	**0**	....	....	....	....	....

• Died of injuries suffered in an automobile accident, March 25, 1966.

• PAULHUS, ROLLIE
Rollie "Tubby" Paulhus
D – L. 5'8", 185 lbs. b: Montreal, Quebec, 9/1/1902. Deceased.

Season	Club	League	GP	G	A	Pts	AG	AA	APts	PIM	GP	G	A	Pts	PIM
1924-25	Verdun Maple Leafs	Mtl-Sr.	STATISTICS NOT AVAILABLE												
1925-26	**Montreal Canadiens**	**NHL**	**33**	**0**	**0**	**0**	**0**	**0**	**0**	**0**	....	....	....	....	....
1926-27	Providence Reds	Can-Am	29	5	3	8	....	....	....	74	....	....	....	....	....
1927-28	Providence Reds	Can-Am	39	15	3	18	....	....	....	76	....	....	....	....	....
1928-29	Providence Reds	Can-Am	38	5	2	7	....	....	....	108	2	0	0	0	2
1929-30	Providence Reds	Can-Am	8	0	0	0	....	....	....	6	....	....	....	....	....
	London Panthers	IAHL	2	0	0	0	....	....	....	0	....	....	....	....	....
	New Haven Eagles	Can-Am	10	0	1	1	....	....	....	20	....	....	....	....	....
	Windsor Bulldogs	IAHL	1	0	0	0	....	....	....	0	....	....	....	....	....
1930-31	Philadelphia Arrows	Can-Am	29	0	3	3	....	....	....	63	....	....	....	....	....
1931-32	Philadelphia Arrows	Can-Am	22	1	1	2	....	....	....	26	....	....	....	....	....
	Cleveland Indians	IAHL	8	0	0	0	....	....	....	2	....	....	....	....	....
	NHL Totals		**33**	**0**	**0**	**0**	**0**	**0**	**0**	**0**	....	....	....	....	....

Signed as a free agent by **Montreal Canadiens**, November 16, 1925. Traded to **London** (Can-Am) by **Providence** (Can-Am) for cash, January 27, 1930 Traded to **Providence** (Can-Am) by **London** (Can-Am) for cash, February 5, 1930. Traded to **New Haven** (Can-Am) by **Providence** (Can-Am) for cash, February 10, 1930.

• PAVELICH, MARTY
Marty Pavelich
LW – L. 5'11", 168 lbs. b: Sault Ste. Marie, Ont., 11/6/1927.

Season	Club	League	GP	G	A	Pts	AG	AA	APts	PIM	GP	G	A	Pts	PIM
1944-45	Galt Red Wings	OHA	21	8	12	20	....	....	....	10	9	7	5	12	6
1945-46	Galt Red Wings	OHA	25	22	26	48	....	....	....	18	5	2	1	3	5
1946-47	Galt Red Wings	OHA	28	22	28	50	....	....	....	32	9	4	5	9	6
1947-48	**Detroit Red Wings**	**NHL**	**41**	**4**	**8**	**12**	**6**	**12**	**18**	**10**	**10**	**2**	**2**	**4**	**6**
	Indianapolis Capitals	AHL	26	3	14	17	....	....	....	21	....	....	....	....	....
1948-49	**Detroit Red Wings**	**NHL**	**60**	**10**	**16**	**26**	**16**	**25**	**41**	**40**	**9**	**0**	**1**	**1**	**8**
1949-50	**Detroit Red Wings**	**NHL**	**65**	**8**	**15**	**23**	**11**	**19**	**30**	**58**	**14**	**4**	**2**	**6**	**13**
	Indianapolis Capitals	AHL	6	2	3	5	....	....	....	2	....	....	....	....	....
1950-51	**Detroit Red Wings**	**NHL**	**67**	**9**	**20**	**29**	**12**	**26**	**38**	**41**	**6**	**0**	**1**	**1**	**2**
1951-52	**Detroit Red Wings**	**NHL**	**68**	**17**	**19**	**36**	**24**	**25**	**49**	**54**	**8**	**2**	**2**	**4**	**2**
1952-53	**Detroit Red Wings**	**NHL**	**64**	**13**	**20**	**33**	**20**	**28**	**48**	**49**	**6**	**2**	**1**	**3**	**7**
1953-54	**Detroit Red Wings**	**NHL**	**65**	**9**	**20**	**29**	**14**	**27**	**41**	**57**	**12**	**2**	**2**	**4**	**4**
1954-55	**Detroit Red Wings**	**NHL**	**70**	**15**	**15**	**30**	**22**	**19**	**41**	**59**	**11**	**1**	**3**	**4**	**12**
1955-56	**Detroit Red Wings**	**NHL**	**70**	**5**	**13**	**18**	**7**	**16**	**23**	**38**	**10**	**0**	**1**	**1**	**14**
1956-57	**Detroit Red Wings**	**NHL**	**64**	**3**	**13**	**16**	**4**	**15**	**19**	**48**	**5**	**0**	**0**	**0**	**6**
	NHL Totals		**634**	**93**	**159**	**252**	**136**	**212**	**348**	**454**	**91**	**13**	**15**	**28**	**74**

Played in NHL All-Star Game (1950, 1952, 1954, 1955)

• PAYER, EVARISTE
Evariste Payer
C/LW – L. 5'6", 150 lbs. b: Rockland, Ont., 12/12/1887. Deceased.

Season	Club	League	GP	G	A	Pts	AG	AA	APts	PIM	GP	G	A	Pts	PIM
1909-10	Rockland Seniors	Ott-Sr.	STATISTICS NOT AVAILABLE												
1910-11	Montreal Canadiens	NHA	5	0	0	0	....	....	....	3	....	....	....	....	....
1911-12	Montreal Canadiens	NHA	4	1	0	1	....	....	....	0	....	....	....	....	....
	Montreal Hochelega	City Sr.	7	6	0	6	....	....	....	6	....	....	....	....	....
1912-13	Montreal Champetre	City Sr.	12	13	0	13	....	....	....	15	1	1	0	1	0
1913-14	Montreal Champetre	City Sr.	10	10	0	10	....	....	....	20	....	....	....	....	....
1914-15			MILITARY SERVICE												
1915-16			MILITARY SERVICE												
1916-17			MILITARY SERVICE												
1917-18	**Montreal Canadiens**	**NHL**	**1**	**0**	**0**	**0**	**0**	**0**	**0**	**0**	....	....	....	....	....
	Rockland Seniors	Ott-Sr.	STATISTICS NOT AVAILABLE												
	NHL Totals		**1**	**0**	**0**	**0**	**0**	**0**	**0**	**0**	....	....	....	....	....
	Other Major League Totals		9	1	0	1	....	....	....	3	....	....	....	....	....

Signed as a free agent by **Montreal Canadiens**, January 29, 1918.

• PEARSON, MEL
— see page 1377

• PEER, BERT
Bert Peer
RW – R. 5'11", 175 lbs. b: Port Credit, Ont., 11/12/1910.

Season	Club	League	GP	G	A	Pts	AG	AA	APts	PIM	GP	G	A	Pts	PIM
1934-35	British Consols	Tor-Sr.	12	7	3	10	....	....	....	2	4	2	0	2	6
	Oakville Villans	OHA Sr.	14	9	3	12	....	....	....	20	2	0	2	2	0
1935-36	Oakville Villans	OHA Sr.	15	10	4	14	....	....	....	15	2	1	0	1	2
	British Consols	Tor-Sr.	14	11	3	14	....	....	....	19	5	0	1	1	26
1936-37	Harringay Racers	Britain	....	38	22	60	....	....	....	26	....	....	....	....	....
1937-38	Harringay Racers	Britain	....	19	8	27	....	....	....	....	....	....	....	....	....
1938-39	Valleyfield Braves	QPHL	36	25	24	49	....	....	....	61	11	5	6	11	8
1939-40	**Detroit Red Wings**	**NHL**	**1**	**0**	**0**	**0**	**0**	**0**	**0**	**0**	....	....	....	....	....
	Omaha Knights	AHA	34	14	17	31	....	....	....	14	9	1	*7	8	19
	Ottawa Senators	QSHL	8	0	2	2	....	....	....	0	....	....	....	....	....
1940-41	Omaha Knights	AHA	32	8	14	22	....	....	....	13	....	....	....	....	....
1941-42	Fort Worth Rangers	AHA	50	*38	40	*78	....	....	....	31	5	3	4	7	7
1942-43	Toronto Navy	OHA Sr.	10	3	15	18	....	....	....	4	10	7	9	16	8
1943-44			MILITARY SERVICE												
1944-45			MILITARY SERVICE												
1945-46	Tulsa Oilers	USHL	11	7	8	15	....	....	....	4	13	5	4	9	2
	Valleyfield Braves	QSHL	16	6	9	15	....	....	....	4	....	....	....	....	....
1946-47	Hamilton Tigers	OHA Sr.	24	16	17	33	....	....	....	2	7	3	3	6	0
1947-48	Hamilton Tigers	OHA Sr.	35	6	13	19	....	....	....	10	20	1	4	5	8
	NHL Totals		**1**	**0**	**0**	**0**	**0**	**0**	**0**	**0**	....	....	....	....	....

AHA Second All-Star Team (1942)

• PEIRSON, JOHNNY
Johnny Peirson
RW – R. 5'11", 170 lbs. b: Winnipeg, Man., 7/21/1925.

Season	Club	League	GP	G	A	Pts	AG	AA	APts	PIM	GP	G	A	Pts	PIM
1943-44	Montreal Jr. Canadiens	City Jr.	15	1	2	3	....	....	....	4	3	2	0	2	8
1944-45			MILITARY SERVICE												
1945-46	McGill University	Mtl-Sr.	6	13	5	18	....	....	....	....	....	....	....	....	....
1946-47	**Boston Bruins**	**NHL**	**5**	**0**	**0**	**0**	**0**	**0**	**0**	**0**	....	....	....	....	....
	Boston Olympics	EHL	10	5	10	15	....	....	....	24	....	....	....	....	....
	Hershey Bears	AHL	26	11	11	22	....	....	....	32	11	3	2	5	10
1947-48	**Boston Bruins**	**NHL**	**15**	**4**	**2**	**6**	**6**	**3**	**9**	**0**	**5**	**2**	**3**	**5**	**0**
	Hershey Bears	AHL	36	14	26	40	....	....	....	39	....	....	....	....	....
1948-49	**Boston Bruins**	**NHL**	**59**	**22**	**21**	**43**	**35**	**33**	**68**	**45**	**5**	**3**	**1**	**4**	**4**
1949-50	**Boston Bruins**	**NHL**	**57**	**27**	**25**	**52**	**37**	**32**	**69**	**49**	....	....	....	....	....
1950-51	**Boston Bruins**	**NHL**	**70**	**19**	**19**	**38**	**26**	**24**	**50**	**43**	**2**	**1**	**1**	**2**	**2**
1951-52	**Boston Bruins**	**NHL**	**68**	**20**	**30**	**50**	**28**	**39**	**67**	**30**	**7**	**0**	**2**	**2**	**4**
1952-53	**Boston Bruins**	**NHL**	**49**	**14**	**15**	**29**	**21**	**21**	**42**	**32**	**11**	**3**	**6**	**9**	**2**
1953-54	**Boston Bruins**	**NHL**	**68**	**21**	**19**	**40**	**32**	**26**	**58**	**55**	**4**	**0**	**0**	**0**	**2**
1954-55			DID NOT PLAY – RETIRED												
1955-56	**Boston Bruins**	**NHL**	**33**	**11**	**14**	**25**	**16**	**17**	**33**	**10**	....	....	....	....	....
1956-57	**Boston Bruins**	**NHL**	**68**	**13**	**26**	**39**	**18**	**30**	**48**	**41**	**10**	**0**	**3**	**3**	**12**
1957-58	**Boston Bruins**	**NHL**	**53**	**2**	**2**	**4**	**3**	**2**	**5**	**10**	**5**	**0**	**1**	**1**	**0**
	NHL Totals		**545**	**153**	**173**	**326**	**222**	**227**	**449**	**315**	**49**	**9**	**17**	**26**	**26**

Played in NHL All-Star Game (1950, 1951)

• PENNINGTON, CLIFF
Cliff Pennington
C – R. 6', 170 lbs. b: Winnipeg, Man., 4/18/1940.

Season	Club	League	GP	G	A	Pts	AG	AA	APts	PIM	GP	G	A	Pts	PIM
1955-56	St. Boniface Canadians	MJHL	1	1	1	2	....	....	....	0	4	1	0	1	2
1956-57	St. Boniface Canadians	MJHL	30	28	27	55	....	....	....	2	7	3	1	4	0
1957-58	Flin Flon Bombers	SJHL	47	32	39	71	....	....	....	8	12	*12	5	17	0
1958-59	Flin Flon Bombers	SJHL	48	*62	50	*112	....	....	....	4	11	14	9	23	4
	Winnipeg Warriors	WHL	5	4	1	5	....	....	....	0	....	....	....	....	....
1959-60	Kitchener Dutchmen	OHA Sr.	47	23	28	51	....	....	....	5	6	4	6	10	0
	Canada	Olympics	5	0	2	2	....	....	....	4	....	....	....	....	....
	Winnipeg Warriors	WHL	2	1	1	2	....	....	....	2	....	....	....	....	....
	Flin Flon Bombers	SJHL	....	....	....	....	....	....	....	....	1	0	0	0	0
1960-61	**Montreal Canadiens**	**NHL**	**4**	**1**	**0**	**1**	**1**	**0**	**1**	**0**	....	....	....	....	....
	Hull-Ottawa Canadiens	EPHL	65	33	*69	*102	....	....	....	10	14	4	*11	15	0
1961-62	**Boston Bruins**	**NHL**	**70**	**9**	**32**	**41**	**11**	**32**	**43**	**2**	....	....	....	....	....
1962-63	**Boston Bruins**	**NHL**	**27**	**7**	**10**	**17**	**9**	**10**	**19**	**4**	....	....	....	....	....
	Kingston Frontenacs	EPHL	39	21	41	62	....	....	....	6	5	2	*9	*11	0
1963-64	San Francisco Seals	WHL	26	6	15	21	....	....	....	4	....	....	....	....	....
	Quebec Aces	AHL	43	11	19	30	....	....	....	2	7	1	1	2	0
1964-65	Verdun Pirates	QSHL	STATISTICS NOT AVAILABLE												
1965-66	Los Angeles Blades	WHL	36	6	8	14	....	....	....	6	....	....	....	....	....
1966-67	Florida Rockets	EHL	64	37	49	86	....	....	....	2	....	....	....	....	....
1967-68	Nashville Dixie Flyers	EHL	68	49	66	115	....	....	....	18	4	3	3	6	0
1968-69	Nashville Dixie Flyers	EHL	72	59	58	117	....	....	....	26	14	6	11	17	4
1969-70	Des Moines Oak Leafs	IHL	72	43	57	100	....	....	....	6	3	1	2	3	0
1970-71	Des Moines–Flint	IHL	54	22	42	64	....	....	....	8	....	....	....	....	....
1971-72	Jacksonville-St. Petes	EHL	66	25	56	81	....	....	....	61	2	1	2	3	2
1972-73	Sun Coast Suns	EHL	48	25	47	72	....	....	....	10	....	....	....	....	....
1973-74	Sun Coast Suns	SHL	5	0	5	5	....	....	....	0	....	....	....	....	....
	NHL Totals		**101**	**17**	**42**	**59**	**21**	**42**	**63**	**6**	....	....	....	....	....

EHL South First All-Star Team (1969) • IHL First All-Star Team (1970) • Won James Gatschene Memorial Trophy (MVP - IHL) (1970)

Traded to **Boston** by **Montreal** with Terry Gray for Willie O'Ree and Stan Maxwell, June, 1961.

• PERREAULT, FERN   Fern Perreault

LW – L. 5'11", 174 lbs.   b: Chambly Basin, Que., 3/31/1927.

Season	Club	League	GP	G	A	Pts	AG	AA	APts	PIM	GP	G	A	Pts	PIM
			REGULAR SEASON								PLAYOFFS				
1944-45	Montreal Nationale	QJHL	11	3	2	5	....	....	....	8	....	....	....	....	....
1945-46	Montreal Nationale	QJHL	20	8	10	18	....	....	....	18	4	3	0	3	4
1946-47	New York Rovers	EHL	44	11	13	24	....	....	....	15	8	0	0	0	2
1947-48	**New York Rangers**	**NHL**	**2**	**0**	**0**	**0**	**0**	**0**	**0**	**0**	....	....	....	....	....
	New York Rovers	EHL	21	12	13	25	....	....	....	26	....	....	....	....	....
	New York Rovers	QSHL	35	6	17	23	....	....	....	18	4	1	1	2	4
1948-49	Tacoma Rockets	PCHL	70	37	40	77	....	....	....	67	6	5	2	7	9
1949-50	**New York Rangers**	**NHL**	**1**	**0**	**0**	**0**	**0**	**0**	**0**	**0**	....	....	....	....	....
	New Haven Ramblers	AHL	65	25	24	49	....	....	....	23	....	....	....	....	....
1950-51	Cincinnati Mohawks	AHL	70	26	30	56	....	....	....	16	....	....	....	....	....
1951-52	Cleveland Barons	AHL	27	9	14	23	....	....	....	18	....	....	....	....	....
	Montreal Royals	QSHL	28	7	12	19	....	....	....	14	7	1	2	3	8
1952-53	Chicoutimi Sagueneens	QSHL	45	5	18	23	....	....	....	26	20	9	10	19	18
1953-54	Chicoutimi Sagueneens	QHL	68	18	41	59	....	....	....	18	7	0	3	3	2
1954-55	Shawinigan Cataracts	QHL	57	17	37	54	....	....	....	42	12	3	4	7	10
1955-56	Chicoutimi Sagueneens	QHL	64	17	33	50	....	....	....	46	5	2	1	3	4
1956-57	Chicoutimi Sagueneens	QHL	67	22	39	61	....	....	....	48	10	*8	5	13	8
1957-58	Chicoutimi Sagueneens	QHL	50	30	23	53	....	....	....	42	6	1	0	1	6
1958-59	Montreal Royals	QHL	61	25	30	55	....	....	....	34	8	1	*5	6	4
1959-60	Montreal Royals	EPHL	30	6	3	9	....	....	....	14	....	....	....	....	....
	NHL Totals		**3**	**0**	**0**	**0**	**0**	**0**	**0**	**0**	....	....	....	....	....

PCHL Northern First All-Star Team (1949)

Traded to **Cleveland** (AHL) by **NY Rangers** with Ed Reigle, Jack Gordon, Fred Shero and cash for Hy Buller and Wally Hergesheimer, May 14, 1951.

• PETERS, FRANK   Frank "Frosty" Peters

D – R. 5'11", 160 lbs.   b: Rouses Point, NY, 6/5/1905.   Deceased.

Season	Club	League	GP	G	A	Pts	AG	AA	APts	PIM	GP	G	A	Pts	PIM
1922-23	Edmonton Yeomen	City Jr.	STATISTICS NOT AVAILABLE												
1923-24	Crow's Nest Pass	RMSHL	STATISTICS NOT AVAILABLE												
1924-25	Boston Maples	USAHA	7	2	0	2	....	....	....	....	....	....	....	....	....
1925-26	Eveleth-Hibbing Rangers	CHL	30	0	1	1	....	....	....	7	....	....	....	....	....
1926-27	Eveluth-Hibbing Rangers	CHL	STATISTICS NOT AVAILABLE												
1927-28	Philadelphia Arrows	Can-Am	18	3	0	3	....	....	....	22	....	....	....	....	....
	Windsor Hornets	Can-Pro	8	0	0	0	....	....	....	10	....	....	....	....	....
1928-29	Philadelphia Arrows	Can-Am	38	4	3	7	....	....	....	93	....	....	....	....	....
1929-30	Philadelphia Arrows	Can-Am	39	10	5	15	....	....	....	*135	2	0	0	0	0
1930-31	**New York Rangers**	**NHL**	**43**	**0**	**0**	**0**	**0**	**0**	**0**	**59**	**4**	**0**	**0**	**0**	**2**
1931-32	Detroit Olympics	IAHL	48	1	11	12	....	....	....	75	6	0	0	0	4
1932-33	Philadelphia Arrows	Can-Am	46	3	1	4	....	....	....	103	3	0	0	0	2
1933-34	Philadelphia Arrows	Can-Am	40	2	2	4	....	....	....	61	2	0	0	0	2
	NHL Totals		**43**	**0**	**0**	**0**	**0**	**0**	**0**	**59**	**4**	**0**	**0**	**0**	**2**

Traded to **NY Rangers** by **Philadelphia** (Can-Am) for cash, February 18, 1930. Traded to **Detroit** by **NY Rangers** for cash, October 19, 1931. Traded to **NY Rangers** by **Detroit** for Sparky Vail, September, 1932. Traded to **Philadelphia** (Can-Am) by **NY Rangers** for George Nichols, September, 1932.

• PETERS, GARRY   — *see page 1382*

• PETERS, JIMMY JR.   — *see page 1383*

• PETERS, JIMMY SR.   Jimmy Sr. Peters

RW – R. 5'11", 165 lbs.   b: Montreal, Que., 10/2/1922.

Season	Club	League	GP	G	A	Pts	AG	AA	APts	PIM	GP	G	A	Pts	PIM
1940-41	Montreal Jr. Canadiens	QJHL	11	7	8	15	....	....	....	6	16	4	10	14	22
	Montreal Sr. Canadiens	QSHL	1	0	0	0	....	....	....	0	....	....	....	....	....
1941-42	Philadelphia–Springfield	AHL	43	12	18	30	....	....	....	4	4	1	1	2	0
1942-43	Montreal Army	City Sr.	5	3	5	8	....	....	....	4	....	....	....	....	....
	Montreal Army	QSHL	27	16	18	34	....	....	....	15	3	0	1	1	4
1943-44	Montreal Army	City Sr.	2	0	0	0	....	....	....	0	....	....	....	....	....
	Kingston Army	OHA Sr.	10	13	16	28	....	....	....	10	....	....	....	....	....
1944-45			MILITARY SERVICE												
1945-46	**Montreal Canadiens**	**NHL**	**47**	**11**	**19**	**30**	**17**	**35**	**52**	**10**	**9**	**3**	**1**	**4**	**6**
	Montreal Royals	QSHL	1	1	0	1	....	....	....	0	....	....	....	....	....
1946-47	**Montreal Canadiens**	**NHL**	**60**	**11**	**13**	**24**	**15**	**19**	**34**	**27**	**11**	**1**	**2**	**3**	**10**
1947-48	**Montreal Canadiens**	**NHL**	**22**	**1**	**3**	**4**	**1**	**4**	**5**	**6**	....	....	....	....	....
	Boston Bruins	**NHL**	**37**	**12**	**15**	**27**	**17**	**22**	**39**	**38**	**5**	**1**	**2**	**3**	**2**
1948-49	**Boston Bruins**	**NHL**	**60**	**16**	**15**	**31**	**25**	**24**	**49**	**8**	**4**	**0**	**1**	**1**	**0**
1949-50	**Detroit Red Wings**	**NHL**	**70**	**14**	**16**	**30**	**19**	**20**	**39**	**20**	**8**	**0**	**2**	**2**	**0**
1950-51	**Detroit Red Wings**	**NHL**	**68**	**17**	**21**	**38**	**23**	**27**	**50**	**14**	**6**	**0**	**0**	**0**	**0**
1951-52	**Chicago Black Hawks**	**NHL**	**70**	**15**	**21**	**36**	**21**	**27**	**48**	**16**	....	....	....	....	....
1952-53	**Chicago Black Hawks**	**NHL**	**69**	**22**	**19**	**41**	**34**	**27**	**61**	**16**	**7**	**0**	**1**	**1**	**4**
1953-54	**Chicago Black Hawks**	**NHL**	**46**	**6**	**4**	**10**	**9**	**5**	**14**	**21**	....	....	....	....	....
	Detroit Red Wings	**NHL**	**25**	**0**	**4**	**4**	**0**	**5**	**5**	**10**	**10**	**0**	**0**	**0**	**0**
1954-55	Windsor Bulldogs	OHA Sr.	46	25	31	56	....	....	....	62	12	10	7	17	2
1955-56	Windsor Bulldogs	OHA Sr.	48	12	37	49	....	....	....	72	....	....	....	....	....
	NHL Totals		**574**	**125**	**150**	**275**	**181**	**215**	**396**	**186**	**60**	**5**	**9**	**14**	**22**

Played in NHL All-Star Game (1950)

Signed as a free agent by **Brooklyn**, October 28, 1941. Rights transferred to **Buffalo** from **Brooklyn** in Special Dispersal Draw, October 9, 1942. Claimed by **Montreal** from **Buffalo** (AHL) in Inter-League Draft, June 14, 1945. Traded to **Boston** by **Montreal** with John Quilty for Joe Carveth, December 17, 1947. Traded to **Detroit** by **Boston** with Pete Babando, Clare Martin, Lloyd Durham for Bill Quakenbush and Pete Horeck, August 16, 1949. Traded to **Chicago** by **Detroit** with George Gee, Clare Martin, Rags Raglin, Max McNab and Jim McFadden for Hugh Coflin and $75,000, August 20, 1951. Traded to **Detroit** by **Chicago** for future considerations, January 25, 1954.

• PETTINGER, ERIC   Eric "Cowboy" Pettinger

LW/C   L. 6', 175 lbs.   b: Regina, Sask., 12/14/1904.   d: 12/24/1968.

Season	Club	League	GP	G	A	Pts	AG	AA	APts	PIM	GP	G	A	Pts	PIM
			REGULAR SEASON								PLAYOFFS				
1921-22	Regina Pats	City Jr.	5	4	1	5	....	....	....	2	8	1	0	1	*12
1922-23	Regina Pats	City Jr.	4	5	1	6	....	....	....	0	6	2	1	3	*8
	Regina Victorias	RCHL	1	0	0	0	....	....	....	0	....	....	....	....	....
1923-24	Regina Pats	City Jr.	6	8	3	11	....	....	....	*14	5	6	2	8	6
	Regina Victorias	RCHL	3	0	0	0	....	....	....	0	....	....	....	....	....
1924-25	Regina Victorias	RCHL	9	*9	*4	*13	....	....	....	4	4	3	1	4	4
1925-26	Regina Victorias	RCHL	17	17	10	27	....	....	....	24	9	7	4	11	6
1926-27	Fort William Forts	TBSHL	20	7	5	12	....	....	....	37	2	*2	*1	*3	0
1927-28	Fort William Forts	TBSHL	17	22	10	32	....	....	....	12	2	0	0	0	0
1928-29	**Boston Bruins**	**NHL**	**17**	**0**	**0**	**0**	**0**	**0**	**0**	**17**	....	....	....	....	....
	Toronto Maple Leafs	**NHL**	**25**	**3**	**3**	**6**	**12**	**27**	**39**	**24**	**4**	**1**	**0**	**1**	**8**
1929-30	**Toronto Maple Leafs**	**NHL**	**43**	**4**	**9**	**13**	**8**	**29**	**37**	**40**	....	....	....	....	....
1930-31	**Ottawa Senators**	**NHL**	**13**	**0**	**0**	**0**	**0**	**0**	**0**	**2**	....	....	....	....	....
	London Panthers	IAHL	36	9	5	14	....	....	....	44	....	....	....	....	....
1931-32	London Tecumsehs	IAHL	48	21	12	33	....	....	....	46	6	0	1	1	8
1932-33	London Tecumsehs	IAHL	43	20	21	41	....	....	....	54	6	0	0	0	9
1933-34	London Tecumsehs	IAHL	43	11	12	23	....	....	....	41	6	4	3	7	0
1934-35	London Tecumsehs	IAHL	44	10	15	25	....	....	....	45	5	4	0	4	5
1935-36	London Techumsehs	IAHL	47	23	19	42	....	....	....	43	2	0	2	2	2
1936-37	Pittsburgh–Cleveland	AHL	12	1	0	1	....	....	....	0	....	....	....	....	....
	Portland Buckaroos	PCHL	1	0	0	0	....	....	....	0	....	....	....	....	....
	NHL Totals		**98**	**7**	**12**	**19**	**20**	**56**	**76**	**83**	**4**	**1**	**0**	**1**	**8**

IAHL First All-Star Team (1936)

Signed as a free agent by **NY Rangers**, September, 1927. Rights traded to **Toronto** by **NY Rangers** for the rights to Yip Foster, October, 1927. Traded to **Boston** by **Toronto** with $15,000 for the rights to Jim Herberts, December 21, 1927. Traded to **Toronto** by **Boston** with the rights to Hugh Plaxton for the rights to George Owen, January 10, 1929. Traded to **Ottawa** by **Toronto** with Art Smith and $35,000 for King Clancy, October 11, 1930. Traded to **London** (IAHL) by **Ottawa** for cash, October 31, 1932.

• PETTINGER, GORD   Gord "Gosh" Pettinger

C – L. 6', 175 lbs.   b: Regina, Sask., 11/17/1911.

Season	Club	League	GP	G	A	Pts	AG	AA	APts	PIM	GP	G	A	Pts	PIM
1928-29	Regina Pats	City Jr.	6	*5	1	6	....	....	....	2	6	6	0	6	4
1929-30	Regina Pats	City Jr.	3	*2	*2	*4	....	....	....	4	....	....	....	....	....
1930-31	Vancouver Lions	NWHL	33	5	5	10	....	....	....	10	4	0	1	1	0
1931-32	Bronx Tigers	Can-Am	39	14	18	32	....	....	....	34	2	0	*2	2	6
1932-33	**New York Rangers**	**NHL**	**34**	**1**	**2**	**3**	**2**	**5**	**7**	**18**	**8**	**0**	**0**	**0**	**0**
	Springfield Indians	Can-Am	13	7	5	12	....	....	....	12	....	....	....	....	....
1933-34	**Detroit Red Wings**	**NHL**	**48**	**3**	**14**	**17**	**7**	**38**	**45**	**14**	**7**	**1**	**0**	**1**	**2**
	Detroit Olympics	IAHL	1	0	0	0	....	....	....	0	....	....	....	....	....
1934-35	**Detroit Red Wings**	**NHL**	**13**	**2**	**3**	**5**	**4**	**7**	**11**	**2**	....	....	....	....	....
	London Tecumsehs	IAHL	44	10	15	25	....	....	....	45	5	4	0	4	5
1935-36	**Detroit Red Wings**	**NHL**	**30**	**8**	**7**	**15**	**20**	**17**	**37**	**6**	**7**	**2**	**2**	**4**	**0**
	Detroit Olympics	IAHL	18	9	16	25	....	....	....	10	....	....	....	....	....
1936-37	**Detroit Red Wings**	**NHL**	**48**	**7**	**15**	**22**	**15**	**35**	**50**	**13**	**10**	**0**	**2**	**2**	**2**
1937-38	**Detroit Red Wings**	**NHL**	**12**	**1**	**3**	**4**	**2**	**6**	**8**	**4**	....	....	....	....	....
	Boston Bruins	**NHL**	**35**	**7**	**10**	**17**	**15**	**21**	**36**	**10**	**3**	**0**	**0**	**0**	**0**
1938-39	**Boston Bruins**	**NHL**	**48**	**11**	**14**	**25**	**23**	**26**	**49**	**8**	**12**	**1**	**1**	**2**	**7**
1939-40	**Boston Bruins**	**NHL**	**24**	**2**	**6**	**8**	**4**	**12**	**16**	**2**	....	....	....	....	....
	Hershey Bears	AHL	29	9	12	21	....	....	....	0	5	1	1	2	4
1940-41	Hershey Bears	AHL	52	13	28	41	....	....	....	4	6	2	*6	8	2
1941-42	Hershey Bears	AHL	56	12	38	50	....	....	....	8	10	2	8	10	2
1942-43			MILITARY SERVICE												
1943-44			MILITARY SERVICE												
1944-45	Hershey–Cleveland	AHL	43	6	15	21	....	....	....	4	....	....	....	....	....
1945-46	Regina Capitals	WCSHL	8	2	6	8	....	....	....	0	....	....	....	....	....
	NHL Totals		**292**	**42**	**74**	**116**	**92**	**167**	**259**	**77**	**47**	**4**	**5**	**9**	**11**

Signed as a free agent by **NY Rangers**, October 29, 1930. Traded to **Detroit** by **NY Rangers** for cash, October 23, 1933. Traded to **Boston** by **Detroit** for Red Beattie, December 19, 1937.

• PHILLIPS, BATT   Batt (William J.) Phillips

C – L. 5'10", 163 lbs.   b: Carleton Place, Ont., 9/23/1902.   d. 1/10/1978.

Season	Club	League	GP	G	A	Pts	AG	AA	APts	PIM	GP	G	A	Pts	PIM
1925-26	Brandon Regals	Wpg-Sr.	15	12	3	15	....	....	....	14	....	....	....	....	....
1926-27	**Montreal Maroons**	**NHL**	**1**	**0**	**0**	**0**	**0**	**0**	**0**	**0**	....	....	....	....	....
	Kenora Thistles	TBSHL	19	15	5	20	....	....	....	15	....	....	....	....	....
1927-28	Winnipeg Maroons	AHA	10	1	0	1	....	....	....	8	....	....	....	....	....
1928-29	Vancouver Lions	PCHL	32	10	9	19	....	....	....	81	3	1	1	2	4
1929-30	**Montreal Maroons**	**NHL**	**27**	**1**	**1**	**2**	**2**	**3**	**5**	**6**	**4**	**0**	**0**	**0**	**2**
	Vancouver Lions	PCHL	11	5	1	6	....	....	....	10	....	....	....	....	....
	Windsor Bulldogs	IAHL	1	1	0	1	....	....	....	0	....	....	....	....	....
1930-31	Windsor Bulldogs	IAHL	35	6	17	23	....	....	....	20	6	2	1	3	2
1931-32	Windsor Bulldogs	IAHL	47	7	14	21	....	....	....	37	6	0	0	0	7
1932-33	Philadelphia Arrows	Can-Am	47	10	24	34	....	....	....	47	5	0	0	0	0
1933-34	Windsor Bulldogs	IAHL	13	3	1	4	....	....	....	6	....	....	....	....	....
	Quebec Castors	Can-Am	31	4	4	8	....	....	....	6	....	....	....	....	....
1934-35	Quebec Castors	Can-Am	39	4	16	20	....	....	....	4	3	0	0	0	0
1934-35	Cleveland Falcons	IAHL	2	0	0	0	....	....	....	2	....	....	....	....	....
1935-36			REINSTATED AS AN AMATEUR												
1936-37	Carleton Place Seniors	Ott-Sr.	6	1	7	8	....	....	....	2	5	4	5	*9	4
1937-38	Carleton Place Seniors	Ott-Sr.	14	7	10	17	....	....	....	4	4	2	4	6	0
1938-39	Carleton Place Seniors	Ott-Sr.	DID NOT PLAY – COACHING												
1939-40	Carleton Place Seniors	Ott-Sr.	11	3	9	12	....	....	....	4	3	0	0	0	0
	NHL Totals		**28**	**1**	**1**	**2**	**2**	**3**	**5**	**6**	**4**	**0**	**0**	**0**	**2**

Traded to **Montreal Maroons** by **Vancouver** (PCHL) for $10,000, December 17, 1929. Traded to **Philadelphia** (Can-Am) by **Montreal Maroons** for cash, October 22, 1932.

• PHILLIPS, CHARLIE Charlie Phillips
D – L. 5'11", 200 lbs. b: Toronto, Ont., 5/10/1917.

Season	Club	League	GP	G	A	Pts	AG	AA	APts	PIM	Playoffs GP	G	A	Pts	PIM
1936-37	Toronto Lions	City Jr.	12	8	2	10	....	....	....	14	....	....	....	....	....
1937-38	Moncton Maroons	MSHL	29	24	9	33	....	....	....	*90	11	9	3	12	*37
1938-39	Saint John Beavers	....	34	16	16	32	....	....	....	*60	13	7	9	16	20
1939-40	Glace Bay Miners	CBSHL	40	8	7	15	....	....	....	33	4	1	0	1	2
1940-41	Glace Bay Miners	CBSHL	43	6	14	20	....	....	....	51	4	1	0	1	10
1941-42	Glace Bay Miners	CBSHL	40	29	33	62	....	....	....	*97	7	*6	5	*11	*18
1942-43	**Montreal Canadiens**	**NHL**	**17**	**0**	**0**	**0**	**0**	**0**	**0**	**6**	....	....	....	....	....
	Washington Lions	AHL	10	5	3	8	....	....	....	14	....	....	....	....	....
1943-44	Kingston Frontenacs	Ott-Sr.	14	1	5	6	....	....	....	17	....	....	....	....	....
1944-45	Providence Reds	AHL	4	0	0	0	....	....	....	0	....	....	....	....	....
1945-46	Lachine Rapides	QPHL	3	0	0	0	....	....	....	0	4	2	2	4	2
1946-47	Montreal Royals	QSHL	1	0	0	0	....	....	....	0	....	....	....	....	....
	Lachine Rapides	QPHL	14	4	4	8	....	....	....	4	....	....	....	....	....
	Washington Lions	EHL	14	9	7	16	....	....	....	21	9	4	3	7	9
1947-48	Glace Bay Miners	CBSHL	47	17	17	34	....	....	....	105	4	2	1	3	4
	Moncton Hawks	MSHL	....	....	....	....	....	....	....	....	1	1	0	1	0
1948-49	Saint John Beavers	MSHL	48	20	20	40	....	....	....	57	7	2	0	2	4
1949-50	Glace Bay Miners	CBSHL	66	11	29	40	....	....	....	31	10	1	3	4	6
1950-51	Moncton Hawks	MMHL	19	5	2	7	....	....	....	4	....	....	....	....	....
	Kentville Wildcats	NSSHL	DID NOT PLAY – COACHING												
	NHL Totals		**17**	**0**	**0**	**0**	**0**	**0**	**0**	**6**	....	....	....	....	....

• **Saint John Beavers** played exhibition season only in 1938-39.

• PHILLIPS, MERYN J. Meryn J. "Bill" Phillips
C – R. 5'7", 160 lbs. b: Richmond Hill, Ont., 5/24/1899. Deceased.

Season	Club	League	GP	G	A	Pts	AG	AA	APts	PIM	Playoffs GP	G	A	Pts	PIM
1919-20	Soo Greyhounds	NOHA	2	1	1	2	....	....	....	2	....	....	....	....	....
	Soo Greyhounds	NMHL	5	5	3	8	....	....	....	....	....	....	....	....	....
1920-21	Soo Greyhounds	NOHA	9	8	*9	17	....	....	....	38	5	4	*3	*7	....
	Soo Greyhounds	NOHL	13	11	11	22	....	....	....	....	....	....	....	....	....
1921-22	Soo Greyhounds	NOHA	8	9	6	15	....	....	....	22	2	....	1	....	2
	Soo Greyhounds	NMHL	12	10	*14	24	....	....	....	....	....	....	....	....	....
1922-23	Soo Greyhounds	NOHA	12	*19	*20	*39	....	....	....	22	7	*10	1	11	*8
	Soo Greyhounds	NOHA	8	*8	3	*11	....	....	....	12	7	*10	1	*11	*8
1923-24	Soo Greyhounds	NOHA	8	6	*8	*14	....	....	....	10	7	5	*6	11	8
1923-24	Soo Greyhounds	NOHA	STATISTICS NOT AVAILABLE												
1924-25	Soo Greyhounds	NOHA	STATISTICS NOT AVAILABLE												
1925-26	Soo Greyhounds	NOHA	20	9	4	13	....	....	....	32	....	....	....	....	....
	Montreal Maroons	**NHL**	**12**	**3**	**1**	**4**	**9**	**11**	**20**	**6**	**8**	**4**	**1**	**5**	**4**
1926-27	**Montreal Maroons**	**NHL**	**43**	**15**	**1**	**16**	**44**	**8**	**52**	**45**	**2**	**0**	**0**	**0**	**0**
1927-28	**Montreal Maroons**	**NHL**	**40**	**7**	**5**	**12**	**21**	**42**	**63**	**33**	**9**	**2**	**1**	**3**	**9**
1928-29	**Montreal Maroons**	**NHL**	**42**	**6**	**5**	**11**	**24**	**46**	**70**	**41**	....	....	....	....	....
1929-30	**Montreal Maroons**	**NHL**	**44**	**13**	**10**	**23**	**26**	**32**	**58**	**48**	**4**	**0**	**0**	**0**	**2**
1930-31	**Montreal Maroons**	**NHL**	**43**	**6**	**1**	**7**	**15**	**4**	**19**	**38**	**1**	**0**	**0**	**0**	**2**
	Windsor Bulldogs	IAHL	3	3	1	4	....	....	....	0	....	....	....	....	....
1931-32	**Montreal Maroons**	**NHL**	**46**	**1**	**1**	**2**	**2**	**3**	**5**	**11**	**4**	**0**	**0**	**0**	**2**
1932-33	**Montreal Maroons**	**NHL**	**2**	**0**	**0**	**0**	**0**	**0**	**0**	**0**	....	....	....	....	....
	New York Americans	**NHL**	**30**	**1**	**7**	**8**	**2**	**18**	**20**	**10**	....	....	....	....	....
	NHL Totals		**302**	**52**	**31**	**83**	**143**	**164**	**307**	**232**	**28**	**6**	**2**	**8**	**19**

Signed as a free agent by **Montreal Maroons**, February 17, 1926. Signed as a free agent by **NY Americans**, November 21, 1932.

• PICARD, NOEL — *see page 1386*

• PICKETTS, HAL Hal Picketts
RW – R. 6', 183 lbs. b: Asquith, Sask., 4/22/1909.

Season	Club	League	GP	G	A	Pts	AG	AA	APts	PIM	Playoffs GP	G	A	Pts	PIM
1927-28	Saskatoon Hilltops	City Jr.	1	0	1	1	....	....	....	0	5	1	1	2	13
	Saskatoon Tigers	City Sr.	2	0	0	0	....	....	....	0	....	....	....	....	....
1928-29	Saskatoon Hilltops	City Jr.	STATISTICS NOT AVAILABLE												
1929-30	Biggar Nationals	City Sr.	10	4	0	4	....	....	....	8	....	....	....	....	....
1930-31	North Battleford Beavers	City Sr.	19	7	3	10	....	....	....	18	4	2	1	*3	6
1931-32	Bronx Tigers	Can-Am	37	2	0	2	....	....	....	30	2	0	0	0	0
1932-33	New Haven Eagles	Can-Am	46	8	3	11	....	....	....	90	....	....	....	....	....
1933-34	**New York Americans**	**NHL**	**48**	**3**	**1**	**4**	**7**	**3**	**10**	**32**	....	....	....	....	....
1934-35	Buffalo Bisons	IAHL	30	8	2	10	....	....	....	30	....	....	....	....	....
1935-36	Rochester–London	IAHL	43	4	3	7	....	....	....	32	2	0	0	0	4
1936-37	Spokane Clippers	PCHL	32	7	1	8	....	....	....	53	6	1	0	1	6
1937-38	Spokane Clippers	PCHL	34	3	2	5	....	....	....	42	....	....	....	....	....
1938-39			REINSTATED AS AN AMATEUR												
1939-40	Yorkton–Saskatoon	SSHL	21	4	4	8	....	....	....	21	5	0	0	0	6
1940-41	Yorkton Terriers	SSHL	31	4	9	13	....	....	....	16	9	2	2	4	18
	NHL Totals		**48**	**3**	**1**	**4**	**7**	**3**	**10**	**32**	....	....	....	....	....

• PIDHIRNY, HARRY Harry Pidhirny
C – L. 5'11", 155 lbs. b: Toronto, Ont., 3/5/1928.

Season	Club	League	GP	G	A	Pts	AG	AA	APts	PIM	Playoffs GP	G	A	Pts	PIM
1944-45	Toronto Young Rangers	OHA	20	11	3	14	....	....	....	4	5	3	3	6	0
1945-46	Toronto Young Rangers	OHA	25	9	13	22	....	....	....	0	2	2	0	2	0
1946-47	Toronto Young Rangers	OHA	14	11	8	19	....	....	....	5	....	....	....	....	....
1947-48	Galt Rockets	OHA	36	22	26	48	....	....	....	23	8	*11	8	19	5
1948-49	Philadelphia Rockets	AHL	68	19	20	39	....	....	....	13	....	....	....	....	....
1949-50	Springfield Indians	AHL	70	21	28	49	....	....	....	6	2	0	0	0	0
1950-51	Springfield Indians	AHL	64	30	28	58	....	....	....	8	1	0	0	0	0
1951-52	Syracuse Warriors	AHL	56	25	23	48	....	....	....	4	....	....	....	....	....
1952-53	Syracuse Warriors	AHL	63	34	30	64	....	....	....	2	4	2	1	3	0
1953-54	Syracuse Warriors	AHL	51	31	12	43	....	....	....	4	....	....	....	....	....
1954-55	Springfield Indians	AHL	64	23	27	50	....	....	....	14	4	2	0	2	0
1955-56	Springfield Indians	AHL	63	32	39	71	....	....	....	16	....	....	....	....	....
1956-57	Springfield Indians	AHL	60	23	28	51	....	....	....	8	....	....	....	....	....
1957-58	**Boston Bruins**	**NHL**	**2**	**0**	**0**	**0**	**0**	**0**	**0**	**0**	....	....	....	....	....
	Springfield Indians	AHL	68	20	28	48	....	....	....	6	13	0	4	4	0
1958-59	Springfield Indians	AHL	70	21	*60	81	....	....	....	26	....	....	....	....	....
1959-60	Springfield Indians	AHL	69	31	36	67	....	....	....	10	10	5	6	11	0
1960-61	Springfield Indians	AHL	71	34	37	71	....	....	....	19	8	*5	5	*10	0
1961-62	San Francisco Seals	WHL	66	24	34	58	....	....	....	12	2	1	2	3	0
1962-63	Providence Reds	AHL	53	13	22	35	....	....	....	4	4	0	1	1	2
1963-64	Baltimore Clippers	AHL	62	10	20	30	....	....	....	4	....	....	....	....	....
1964-65	Baltimore Clippers	AHL	72	8	11	19	....	....	....	12	5	0	0	0	2
1965-66	Baltimore Clippers	AHL	47	1	4	5	....	....	....	6	....	....	....	....	....
1966-67	Springfield Indians	AHL	DID NOT PLAY – COACHING												
1967-68	Muskegon Mohawks	IHL	36	15	23	38	....	....	....	4	9	5	2	7	0
1968-69	Syracuse Blazers	EHL	DID NOT PLAY – COACHING												
1969-70	Barrie Flyers	OHA Sr.	4	1	1	2	....	....	....	0	....	....	....	....	....
	NHL Totals		**2**	**0**	**0**	**0**	**0**	**0**	**0**	**0**	....	....	....	....	....

AHL Second All-Star Team (1959)

• PIKE, ALF Alf "The Embalmer" Pike
LW/C – L. 6', 187 lbs. b: Winnipeg, Man., 9/15/1917.

Season	Club	League	GP	G	A	Pts	AG	AA	APts	PIM	Playoffs GP	G	A	Pts	PIM
1935-36	Winnipeg Monarchs	City Jr.	14	10	11	21	....	....	....	20	....	....	....	....	....
1936-37	Winnipeg Monarchs	City Jr.	14	10	10	20	....	....	....	21	8	2	*10	*12	*21
1937-38	New York Rovers	EHL	45	16	23	39	....	....	....	58	....	....	....	....	....
1938-39	New York Rovers	EHL	25	9	4	13	....	....	....	12	....	....	....	....	....
	Philadelphia Ramblers	AHL	3	1	1	2	....	....	....	0	9	4	2	6	4
1939-40	**New York Rangers**	**NHL**	**47**	**8**	**9**	**17**	**17**	**18**	**35**	**38**	**12**	**3**	**1**	**4**	**6**
1940-41	**New York Rangers**	**NHL**	**48**	**6**	**13**	**19**	**12**	**24**	**36**	**23**	**3**	**0**	**1**	**1**	**2**
1941-42	**New York Rangers**	**NHL**	**34**	**8**	**19**	**27**	**14**	**29**	**43**	**16**	**6**	**1**	**0**	**1**	**4**
1942-43	**New York Rangers**	**NHL**	**41**	**6**	**16**	**22**	**8**	**20**	**28**	**48**	....	....	....	....	....
1943-44	Winnipeg RCAF	City Sr.	9	3	4	7	....	....	....	10	....	....	....	....	....
1944-45	Winnipeg RCAF	City Sr.	9	5	2	7	....	....	....	20	....	....	....	....	....
1945-46	**New York Rangers**	**NHL**	**33**	**7**	**9**	**16**	**11**	**17**	**28**	**18**	....	....	....	....	....
1946-47	**New York Rangers**	**NHL**	**31**	**7**	**11**	**18**	**9**	**16**	**25**	**2**	....	....	....	....	....
1947-48	Winnipeg Nationals	City Sr.	11	5	1	6	....	....	....	17	....	....	....	....	....
1948-49	Winnipeg Nationals	TBSHL	2	2	4	6	....	....	....	4	....	....	....	....	....
1949-50	Guelph Biltmores	OHA	DID NOT PLAY – COACHING												
	NHL Totals		**234**	**42**	**77**	**119**	**71**	**124**	**195**	**145**	**21**	**4**	**2**	**6**	**12**

• PILOTE, PIERRE — *see page 1387*

• PITRE, DIDIER Didier "Cannonball" Pitre HHOF
RW/D – R. 5'11", 185 lbs. b: Valleyfield, Quebec, 9/1/1883. d: 7/29/1934.

Season	Club	League	GP	G	A	Pts	AG	AA	APts	PIM	Playoffs GP	G	A	Pts	PIM
1903-04	Montreal Nationals	FAHL	2	1	0	1	....	....	....	0	....	....	....	....	....
1904-05	Montreal Nationals	CAHL	2	0	0	0	....	....	....	0	....	....	....	....	....
	American Soo Indians	IHL	13	11	0	11	....	....	....	6	....	....	....	....	....
1905-06	American Soo Indians	IHL	22	*41	0	*41	....	....	....	29	....	....	....	....	....
1906-07	American Soo Indians	IHL	23	25	11	36	....	....	....	28	....	....	....	....	....
1907-08	Montreal Shamrocks	ECAHA	10	3	0	3	....	....	....	15	....	....	....	....	....
	Edmonton Eskimos	City Sr.	....	....	....	....	....	....	....	....	2	0	0	0	0
1908-09	Edmonton Eskimos	City Sr.	STATISTICS NOT AVAILABLE												
	Renfrew Creamery Kings	FAHL	STATISTICS NOT AVAILABLE												
1909-10	Montreal Canadiens	NHA	12	10	0	10	....	....	....	5	....	....	....	....	....
1910-11	Montreal Canadiens	NHA	16	19	0	19	....	....	....	22	....	....	....	....	....
1911-12	Montreal Canadiens	NHA	18	27	0	27	....	....	....	40	....	....	....	....	....
1912-13	Montreal Canadiens	NHA	17	24	0	24	....	....	....	80	....	....	....	....	....
1913-14	Vancouver Millionaires	PCHA	15	14	2	16	....	....	....	12	....	....	....	....	....
1914-15	Montreal Canadiens	NHA	20	30	4	34	....	....	....	15	....	....	....	....	....
1915-16	Montreal Canadiens	NHA	24	24	*15	*39	....	....	....	42	5	*4	0	4	18
1916-17	Montreal Canadiens	NHA	20	22	2	24	....	....	....	47	6	7	0	7	32
1917-18	**Montreal Canadiens**	**NHL**	**20**	**17**	**6**	**23**	**43**	**0**	**43**	**29**	**2**	**0**	**0**	**0**	**13**
1918-19	**Montreal Canadiens**	**NHL**	**17**	**14**	**4**	**18**	**51**	**38**	**89**	**15**	**10**	**2**	**6**	**8**	**6**
1919-20	**Montreal Canadiens**	**NHL**	**23**	**14**	**12**	**25**	**32**	**83**	**115**	**6**	....	....	....	....	....
1920-21	**Montreal Canadiens**	**NHL**	**23**	**15**	**1**	**16**	**39**	**9**	**48**	**23**	....	....	....	....	....
1921-22	**Montreal Canadiens**	**NHL**	**23**	**2**	**4**	**6**	**5**	**25**	**30**	**12**	....	....	....	....	....
1922-23	**Montreal Canadiens**	**NHL**	**23**	**1**	**2**	**3**	**3**	**18**	**21**	**0**	**2**	**0**	**0**	**0**	**0**
	NHL Totals		**129**	**63**	**29**	**91**	**173**	**173**	**346**	**85**	**14**	**2**	**6**	**8**	**19**
	Other Major League Totals		210	250	34	284	....	....	....	341	11	11	0	11	50

IHL First All-Star Team (1906, 1907)

Rights retained by **Montreal Canadiens** after NHA folded, November 26, 1917.

• PLAGER, BOB — *see page 1389*

• PLAMONDON, GERRY Gerry Plamondon
LW – L. 5'8", 170 lbs. b: Sherbrooke, Que., 1/5/1925.

Season	Club	League	GP	G	A	Pts	AG	AA	APts	PIM	GP	G	A	Pts	PIM
			REGULAR SEASON								PLAYOFFS				
1943-44	Montreal Jr. Canadiens	QJHL	15	*21	7	28	....	....	....	2	3	*6	1	7	0
	Montreal Canada Car	City Sr.	11	6	6	12	....	....	....	0	....	....	....	....	....
1944-45	Pittsburgh Hornets	AHL	4	2	2	4	....	....	....	10	....	....	....	....	....
	Valleyfield Braves	QSHL	23	14	20	34	....	....	....	8	14	*14	7	*21	2
1945-46	**Montreal Canadiens**	**NHL**	**6**	**0**	**2**	**2**	**0**	**4**	**4**	**2**	**1**	**0**	**0**	**0**	**0**
	Valleyfield Braves	QSHL	39	*40	28	68	....	....	....	12	....	....	....	....	....
1946-47	Montreal Royals	QSHL	26	15	15	30	....	....	....	21	11	5	4	9	4
1947-48	**Montreal Canadiens**	**NHL**	**3**	**1**	**1**	**2**	**1**	**1**	**2**	**0**	....	....	....	....	....
	Montreal Royals	QSHL	46	*51	22	73	....	....	....	16	3	0	1	1	0
1948-49	**Montreal Canadiens**	**NHL**	**27**	**5**	**5**	**10**	**8**	**8**	**16**	**8**	**7**	**5**	**1**	**6**	**0**
	Montreal Royals	QSHL	36	34	25	59	....	....	....	24	....	....	....	....	....
1949-50	**Montreal Canadiens**	**NHL**	**37**	**1**	**5**	**6**	**1**	**6**	**7**	**0**	**3**	**0**	**1**	**1**	**2**
	Cincinnati Mohawks	AHL	20	8	9	17	....	....	....	6	....	....	....	....	....
1950-51	**Montreal Canadiens**	**NHL**	**1**	**0**	**0**	**0**	**0**	**0**	**0**	**0**	....	....	....	....	....
	Cincinnati Mohawks	AHL	70	21	29	50	....	....	....	43	....	....	....	....	....
1951-52	Montreal Royals	QSHL	60	23	29	52	....	....	....	21	7	3	1	4	0
1952-53	Montreal Royals	QSHL	57	18	22	40	....	....	....	6	16	2	4	6	2
1953-54	Matane Red Rockets	QPHL	68	18	43	61	....	....	....	16	....	....	....	....	....
1954-55	Trois-Rivieres Flambeaux	QJHL	DID NOT PLAY – COACHING												
1955-56	Chicoutimi Sagueneens	QHL	7	1	1	2	....	....	....	12	....	....	....	....	....
1956-57	Cornwall Chevies	EOHL	50	7	24	31	....	....	....	20	6	0	0	0	10
1957-58	Pembroke Lumber Kings	EOHL	50	12	21	33	....	....	....	18	12	1	4	5	6
	NHL Totals		**74**	**7**	**13**	**20**	**10**	**19**	**29**	**10**	**11**	**5**	**2**	**7**	**2**

• PLAXTON, HUGH Hugh Plaxton
LW – L. 5'10", 184 lbs. b: Barrie, Ont., 5/16/1904. Deceased.

Season	Club	League	GP	G	A	Pts	AG	AA	APts	PIM	GP	G	A	Pts	PIM
1921-22	University of Toronto	OHA Sr.	3	0	0	0	....	....	....	....	....	....	....	....	....
1922-23	University of Toronto	OHA Sr.	6	11	3	14	....	....	....	....	1	0	0	0	0
1923-24	University of Toronto	OHA Sr.	8	*18	3	*21	....	....	....	10	5	1	2	3	8
1924-25	University of Toronto	OHA Sr.	8	4	2	6	....	....	....	....	6	5	2	7	....
1925-26	Toronto Grads	OHA Sr.	DID NOT PLAY												
1926-27	Toronto Grads	OHA Sr.	9	*31	7	*38	....	....	....	11	13	*21	5	*26	26
1927-28	Toronto Grads	....	12	20	*10	30	....	....	....	....	....	....	....	....	....
	Canada	Olympics	3	*12	2	14	....	....	....	....	....	....	....	....	....
1928-1932			DID NOT PLAY												
1932-33	**Montreal Maroons**	**NHL**	**15**	**1**	**2**	**3**	**2**	**5**	**7**	**4**	....	....	....	....	....
	Windsor Bulldogs	IAHL	10	1	1	2	....	....	....	4	....	....	....	....	....
	Vancouver Maroons	WCHL	8	0	0	0	....	....	....	0	....	....	....	....	....
	NHL Totals		**15**	**1**	**2**	**3**	**2**	**5**	**7**	**4**	....	....	....	....	....

• **University of Toronto** played exhibition season only in 1927-28. • Did not play from 1928 to 1932 while practicing law in Ontario. Rights traded to **Toronto** by **Boston** with Eric Pettinger for the rights to George Owen, January 10, 1929.

• PLETSCH, CHARLES Charles Pletsch
D. b: Chesley, Ont., 1893.

Season	Club	League	GP	G	A	Pts	AG	AA	APts	PIM	GP	G	A	Pts	PIM
1920-21	Markdale Seniors	Inter-Sr.	STATISTICS NOT AVAILABLE												
	Hamilton Tigers	**NHL**	**1**	**0**	**0**	**0**	**0**	**0**	**0**	**0**	....	....	....	....	....
	NHL Totals		**1**	**0**	**0**	**0**	**0**	**0**	**0**	**0**	....	....	....	....	....

Signed as a free agent by **Hamilton**, December 31, 1920.

• PODOLSKY, NELS Nels Podolsky
LW – L. 5'10", 170 lbs. b: Winnipeg, Man., 12/19/1925.

Season	Club	League	GP	G	A	Pts	AG	AA	APts	PIM	GP	G	A	Pts	PIM
1942-43	Montreal Jr. Royals	QJHL	4	2	2	4	....	....	....	6	8	2	1	3	0
	Montreal Royals	QSHL	1	0	0	0	....	....	....	0	....	....	....	....	....
1943-44	Galt Kists	OHA	26	25	16	41	....	....	....	54	3	1	0	1	4
1944-45	Halifax Navy	City Sr.	3	0	0	0	....	....	....	6	....	....	....	....	....
	Cornwallis Navy	City Sr.	MILITARY SERVICE												
1945-46	Omaha Knights	USHL	44	9	13	22	....	....	....	64	7	2	3	5	4
1946-47	Indianapolis Capitals	AHL	61	8	7	15	....	....	....	96	....	....	....	....	....
1947-48	Indianapolis Capitals	AHL	68	25	30	55	....	....	....	57	....	....	....	....	....
1948-49	**Detroit Red Wings**	**NHL**	**1**	**0**	**0**	**0**	**0**	**0**	**0**	**0**	**7**	**0**	**0**	**0**	**4**
	Indianapolis Capitals	AHL	64	26	30	56	....	....	....	92	2	1	0	1	0
1949-50	Indianapolis Capitals	AHL	52	18	24	42	....	....	....	67	8	1	4	5	8
1950-51	Indianapolis Capitals	AHL	19	3	4	7	....	....	....	13	1	0	0	0	0
1951-52	Edmonton Flyers	PCHL	59	14	16	30	....	....	....	112	2	0	1	1	0
1952-53	St. Louis Flyers	AHL	18	2	6	8	....	....	....	39	....	....	....	....	....
	Shawinigan Cataracts	QSHL	47	15	19	34	....	....	....	93	....	....	....	....	....
1953-54	Sherbrooke Saints	QHL	64	15	25	40	....	....	....	67	5	0	1	1	4
1954-55	Troy Bruins	IHL	60	16	18	34	....	....	....	156	11	1	4	5	9
1955-56	Troy Bruins	IHL	60	17	17	34	....	....	....	147	5	0	0	0	4
1956-57	Troy Bruins	IHL	52	9	14	23	....	....	....	105	....	....	....	....	....
1957-58	Soo Greyhounds	NOHA	35	4	9	13	....	....	....	54	4	0	0	0	10
	NHL Totals		**1**	**0**	**0**	**0**	**0**	**0**	**0**	**0**	**7**	**0**	**0**	**0**	**4**

• POETA, TONY Tony Poeta
RW – L. 5'5", 168 lbs. b: North Bay, Ont., 3/4/1933.

Season	Club	League	GP	G	A	Pts	AG	AA	APts	PIM	GP	G	A	Pts	PIM
1950-51	Galt Black Hawks	OHA	51	17	13	30	....	....	....	35	3	0	0	0	0
1951-52	Galt Black Hawks	OHA	51	27	28	55	....	....	....	31	3	4	0	4	2
	Chicago Black Hawks	**NHL**	**1**	**0**	**0**	**0**	**0**	**0**	**0**	**0**	....	....	....	....	....
1952-53	Galt–Barrie	OHA	54	29	34	63	....	....	....	49	15	10	9	19	27
1953-54	Cleveland Barons	AHL	2	0	0	0	....	....	....	2	5	1	0	1	2
	Marion Barons	IHL	55	29	35	64	....	....	....	37	5	3	3	6	6
1954-55	Valleyfield Braves	QHL	11	1	1	2	....	....	....	0	....	....	....	....	....
	North Bay Trappers	NOHA	42	8	11	19	....	....	....	10	13	0	1	1	17
1955-56	North Bay Trappers	NOHA	25	5	4	9	....	....	....	8	....	....	....	....	....
	Stratford Indians	OHA Sr.	24	3	8	11	....	....	....	4	7	0	0	0	0
1956-57			REINSTATED AS AN AMATEUR												
1957-58	North Bay Trappers	NOHA	26	1	4	5	....	....	....	9	....	....	....	....	....
	Belleville McFarlands	OHA Sr.	7	1	1	2	....	....	....	2	....	....	....	....	....
1958-59	North Bay Trappers	NOHA	54	15	22	37	....	....	....	31	....	....	....	....	....
1959-60	Greensboro–Johnstown	EHL	13	0	6	6	....	....	....	5	....	....	....	....	....
	Milwaukee Falcons	IHL	29	6	9	15	....	....	....	35	....	....	....	....	....
	NHL Totals		**1**	**0**	**0**	**0**	**0**	**0**	**0**	**0**	....	....	....	....	....

• POILE, BUD Bud (Norman Robert) Poile HHOF
RW – R. 6', 189 lbs. b: Fort William, Ont., 2/10/1924.

Season	Club	League	GP	G	A	Pts	AG	AA	APts	PIM	GP	G	A	Pts	PIM
1940-41	Fort William Rangers	TBJHL	17	25	10	35	....	....	....	14	2	3	2	5	4
1941-42	Fort William Rangers	TBJHL	18	*36	29	*65	....	....	....	*55	3	*5	*7	*12	11
	Fort William Forts	TBSHL	1	0	2	2	....	....	....	0	....	....	....	....	....
	Port Arthur Bearcats	TBSHL	....	....	....	....	....	....	....	....	6	1	2	3	2
1942-43	**Toronto Maple Leafs**	**NHL**	**48**	**16**	**19**	**35**	**23**	**24**	**47**	**24**	**6**	**2**	**4**	**6**	**4**
1943-44	**Toronto Maple Leafs**	**NHL**	**11**	**6**	**8**	**14**	**7**	**10**	**17**	**9**	....	....	....	....	....
	Toronto RCAF	OHA Sr.	8	5	9	14	....	....	....	8	....	....	....	....	....
1944-45			MILITARY SERVICE												
1945-46	**Toronto Maple Leafs**	**NHL**	**9**	**1**	**8**	**9**	**2**	**15**	**17**	**0**	....	....	....	....	....
1946-47	**Toronto Maple Leafs**	**NHL**	**59**	**19**	**17**	**36**	**26**	**24**	**50**	**19**	**7**	**2**	**0**	**2**	**2**
1947-48	**Toronto Maple Leafs**	**NHL**	**4**	**2**	**0**	**2**	**3**	**0**	**3**	**0**	....	....	....	....	....
	Chicago Black Hawks	**NHL**	**54**	**23**	**29**	**52**	**34**	**43**	**77**	**17**	....	....	....	....	....
1948-49	**Chicago Black Hawks**	**NHL**	**4**	**0**	**0**	**0**	**0**	**0**	**0**	**2**	....	....	....	....	....
	Detroit Red Wings	**NHL**	**56**	**21**	**21**	**42**	**33**	**33**	**66**	**6**	**10**	**0**	**1**	**1**	**2**
1949-50	**New York Rangers**	**NHL**	**27**	**3**	**6**	**9**	**4**	**8**	**12**	**8**	....	....	....	....	....
	Boston Bruins	**NHL**	**39**	**16**	**14**	**30**	**21**	**18**	**39**	**6**	....	....	....	....	....
1950-51	Tulsa Oilers	USHL	60	15	38	53	....	....	....	48	9	5	6	11	4
1951-52	Glace Bay Miners	MMHL	84	33	60	93	....	....	....	69	2	0	0	0	0
1952-53	Edmonton Flyers	WHL	70	20	29	49	....	....	....	62	15	0	7	7	12
1953-54	Edmonton Flyers	WHL	49	12	39	51	....	....	....	34	13	3	9	12	0
1954-55	Edmonton Flyers	WHL	3	1	2	3	....	....	....	0	....	....	....	....	....
1955-56	Edmonton Flyers	WHL	DID NOT PLAY – COACHING												
	NHL Totals		**311**	**107**	**122**	**229**	**153**	**175**	**328**	**91**	**23**	**4**	**5**	**9**	**8**

NHL Second All-Star Team (1948) • Won Lester Patrick Trophy (1989)

Played in NHL All-Star Game (1947, 1948)

Traded to **Chicago** by **Toronto** with Gus Bodnar, Gaye Stewart, Ernie Dickens and Bob Goldham for Max Bentley and Cy Thomas, November 2, 1947. Traded to **Detroit** by **Chicago** with George Gee for Jim Conacher, Bep Guidolin and Doug McCaig, October 25, 1948. Traded to **NY Rangers** by **Detroit** for cash, August 16, 1949. Traded to **Boston** by **NY Rangers** for cash, December 22, 1949.

• POILE, DON Don Poile
C – L. 5'11", 160 lbs. b: Fort William, Ont., 6/1/1932.

Season	Club	League	GP	G	A	Pts	AG	AA	APts	PIM	GP	G	A	Pts	PIM
1949-50	Fort William Hurricanes	TBJHL	12	8	2	10	....	....	....	8	5	1	0	1	4
1950-51	Fort William Hurricanes	TBJHL	21	2	7	9	....	....	....	14	12	7	7	14	12
1951-52	Fort William Hurricanes	TBJHL	30	30	36	66	....	....	....	46	21	*13	*18	*31	29
1952-53	Milwaukee Chiefs	IHL	56	42	34	76	....	....	....	14	....	....	....	....	....
	Edmonton Flyers	WHL	....	....	....	....	....	....	....	....	2	0	0	0	0
1953-54	Edmonton Flyers	WHL	70	26	33	59	....	....	....	16	13	2	2	4	8
1954-55	**Detroit Red Wings**	**NHL**	**4**	**0**	**0**	**0**	**0**	**0**	**0**	**0**	....	....	....	....	....
	Edmonton Flyers	WHL	52	16	29	45	....	....	....	21	9	5	1	6	0
1955-56	Edmonton Flyers	WHL	70	22	29	51	....	....	....	63	3	2	0	2	2
1956-57	Edmonton Flyers	WHL	69	31	25	56	....	....	....	54	8	3	2	5	14
1957-58	**Detroit Red Wings**	**NHL**	**62**	**7**	**9**	**16**	**9**	**10**	**19**	**12**	**4**	**0**	**0**	**0**	**0**
	Edmonton Flyers	WHL	2	1	3	4	....	....	....	0	....	....	....	....	....
1958-59	Edmonton Flyers	WHL	51	18	29	47	....	....	....	19	3	1	0	1	4
	Hershey Bears	AHL	4	0	0	0	....	....	....	0	....	....	....	....	....
1959-60	Edmonton Flyers	WHL	70	20	34	54	....	....	....	28	4	0	1	1	12
1960-61	Edmonton Flyers	WHL	60	22	21	43	....	....	....	21	....	....	....	....	....
1961-62	Edmonton Flyers	WHL	63	23	27	50	....	....	....	20	12	7	7	14	2
	NHL Totals		**66**	**7**	**9**	**16**	**9**	**10**	**19**	**12**	**4**	**0**	**0**	**0**	**0**

Won WHL Rookie of the Year Award (1954)

Played in NHL All-Star Game (1954)

Traded to **Hershey** (AHL) by **Detroit** with Hec Lalande for Dunc Fisher, June 7, 1958.

• POIRIER, GORDIE Gordie Poirier
C – L. 5'6", 160 lbs. b: Maple Creek, Sask., 10/27/1914.

Season	Club	League	GP	G	A	Pts	AG	AA	APts	PIM	GP	G	A	Pts	PIM
1931-32	Montreal Columbus	City Jr.	10	6	2	8	....	....	....	14	....	....	....	....	....
1932-33	St. Francis Xavier	Mtl-Sr.	11	4	0	4	....	....	....	15	2	1	0	1	6
1933-34	Montreal Sr. Canadiens	City Sr.	15	1	1	2	....	....	....	8	4	1	2	3	0
1934-35	Montreal Sr. Canadiens	City Sr.	20	7	11	18	....	....	....	20	2	1	1	2	0
1935-36			DID NOT PLAY												
1936-37	Brighton Tigers	Britain	....	25	9	34	....	....	....	36	....	....	....	....	....
1937-38	Brighton Tigers	Britain	....	18	18	36	....	....	....	10	....	....	....	....	....
1938-39	Brighton Tigers	Britain	....	23	20	43	....	....	....	....	....	....	....	....	....
1939-40	**Montreal Canadiens**	**NHL**	**10**	**0**	**0**	**0**	**0**	**0**	**0**	**0**	....	....	....	....	....
	St. Hyacinthe Gaulois	QPHL	36	37	43	80	....	....	....	22	....	....	....	....	....
1940-41	Ottawa–Montreal	QSHL	29	8	23	31	....	....	....	16	8	0	5	5	10
1941-42	Ottawa Senators	QSHL	40	21	19	40	....	....	....	12	8	1	4	5	13
1942-43	Ottawa Commandos	QSHL	32	17	14	31	....	....	....	19	22	13	5	18	10
1942-43	Ottawa Army	City Sr.	10	15	16	31	....	....	....	5	....	....	....	....	....
1943-44	Ottawa Commandos	QSHL	8	2	6	7	....	....	....	6	....	....	....	....	....
1944-45			MILITARY SERVICE												
1945-46	Ottawa GMC's	OVSHL	....	9	13	2	....	....	....	....	4	6	10	16	
	Ottawa Senators	QSHL	29	12	16	28	....	....	....	9	5	1	2	3	0
1946-47	Brighton Tigers	Britain	36	28	32	60	....	....	....	35	2	3	1	4	0
1947-48	Brighton Tigers	Britain	47	31	31	62	....	....	....	44	....	....	....	....	....
	NHL Totals		**10**	**0**	**0**	**0**	**0**	**0**	**0**	**0**	....	....	....	....	....

• POLICH, JOHN John Polich
RW – R. 6'2", 200 lbs. b: Hibbing, MN, 7/8/1916.

Season	Club	League	GP	G	A	Pts	AG	AA	APts	PIM	GP	G	A	Pts	PIM
1938-39	Loyola College	Calif-Sr.	STATISTICS NOT AVAILABLE												
1939-40	**New York Rangers**	**NHL**	**1**	**0**	**0**	**0**	**0**	**0**	**0**	**0**	....	....	....	....	....
	Philadelphia Rockets	AHL	53	11	22	33	....	....	....	56	....	....	....	....	....
1940-41	**New York Rangers**	**NHL**	**2**	**0**	**1**	**1**	**0**	**2**	**2**	**0**	....	....	....	....	....
	Philadelphia Rockets	AHL	50	10	31	41	....	....	....	53	....	....	....	....	....
1941-42			REINSTATED AS AN AMATEUR												
1942-43	Los Angeles Monarchs	Calif-Sr.	DID NOT PLAY – COACHING												
1943-44	Los Angeles Monarchs	Calif-Sr.	DID NOT PLAY – COACHING												
1944-45	Los Angeles Monarchs	PCHL	DID NOT PLAY – COACHING												
1945-46	Los Angeles Monarchs	PCHL	34	11	14	25	....	....	....	86	7	2	1	3	14
1946-47	Los Angeles Monarchs	PCHL	50	25	37	62	....	....	....	37	10	6	5	11	9
1947-48	Los Angeles Monarchs	PCHL	53	17	30	47	....	....	....	59	4	3	0	3	6
	NHL Totals		**3**	**0**	**1**	**1**	**0**	**2**	**2**	**0**	....	....	....	....	....

Signed as a free agent by **NY Rangers**, October 13, 1939. Traded to **Pittsburgh** (AHL) by **NY Rangers**, September 11, 1941. • Refused to report and retired from professional play, October 10, 1941.

REGULAR SEASON | PLAYOFFS

• POLIZIANI, DANIEL
Daniel Poliziani
RW – R. 5′11″, 158 lbs. b: Sydney, N.S., 1/8/1935.

Season	Club	League	GP	G	A	Pts	AG	AA	APts	PIM	GP	G	A	Pts	PIM
1952-53	St. Catharines Teepees	OHA	54	9	13	22	....	....	....	18	3	0	2	2	2
1953-54	St. Catharines Teepees	OHA	20	3	6	9	....	....	....	10	....	....	....	....	....
	Barrie Flyers	OHA	35	24	27	51	....	....	....	29	....	....	....	....	....
1954-55	Barrie Flyers	OHA	34	18	38	56	....	....	....	105	....	....	....	....	....
	Cleveland Barons	AHL	2	1	0	1	....	....	....	0	....	....	....	....	....
1955-56	Cleveland Barons	AHL	5	2	1	3	....	....	....	0	....	....	....	....	....
	Quebec Aces	QHL	42	14	16	30	....	....	....	62	5	0	2	2	4
1956-57	Cleveland Barons	AHL	58	21	25	46	....	....	....	74	7	2	1	3	0
1957-58	Cleveland Barons	AHL	65	23	19	42	....	....	....	60	6	5	2	7	6
1958-59	**Boston Bruins**	**NHL**	**1**	**0**	**0**	**0**	**0**	**0**	**0**	**0**	**3**	**0**	**0**	**0**	**0**
	Providence Reds	AHL	59	18	21	39	....	....	....	54	....	....	....	....	....
1959-60	Providence Reds	AHL	60	30	31	61	....	....	....	52	5	1	4	5	16
1960-61	Providence Reds	AHL	63	20	43	63	....	....	....	65	....	....	....	....	....
1961-62	Providence Reds	AHL	57	14	37	51	....	....	....	57	3	1	1	2	2
1962-63	Providence Reds	AHL	50	13	17	30	....	....	....	27	6	1	6	7	16
1963-64	Hershey Bears	AHL	66	14	20	34	....	....	....	36	5	2	1	3	4
1964-65	Hershey Bears	AHL	45	14	12	26	....	....	....	44	1	0	0	0	2
	NHL Totals		**1**	**0**	**0**	**0**	**0**	**0**	**0**	**0**	**3**	**0**	**0**	**0**	**0**

Claimed by **Boston** from **Cleveland** (AHL) in Inter-League Draft, June 3, 1958.

• POPEIN, LARRY
— see page 1395

• POPIEL, POUL
— see page 1395

• PORTLAND, JACK
Jack Portland
D – L. 6′2″, 185 lbs. b: Waubaushene, Ont., 7/30/1912. Deceased.

Season	Club	League	GP	G	A	Pts	AG	AA	APts	PIM	GP	G	A	Pts	PIM
1932-33	Collingwood Combines	OHA Sr.	STATISTICS NOT AVAILABLE												
1933-34	**Montreal Canadiens**	**NHL**	**31**	**0**	**2**	**2**	**0**	**5**	**5**	**10**	**2**	**0**	**0**	**0**	**0**
1934-35	**Montreal Canadiens**	**NHL**	**5**	**0**	**0**	**0**	**0**	**0**	**0**	**2**	....	....	....	....	....
	Boston Bruins	**NHL**	**15**	**1**	**1**	**2**	**2**	**2**	**4**	**2**	....	....	....	....	....
	Boston Cubs	Can-Am	28	7	5	12	....	....	....	34	3	0	0	0	4
1935-36	**Boston Bruins**	**NHL**	**2**	**0**	**0**	**0**	**0**	**0**	**0**	**0**	....	....	....	....	....
	Boston Cubs	Can-Am	47	4	6	10	....	....	....	95	....	....	....	....	....
1936-37	**Boston Bruins**	**NHL**	**46**	**2**	**4**	**6**	**4**	**9**	**13**	**58**	**3**	**0**	**0**	**0**	**4**
1937-38	**Boston Bruins**	**NHL**	**48**	**0**	**5**	**5**	**0**	**10**	**10**	**26**	**3**	**0**	**0**	**0**	**4**
1938-39	**Boston Bruins**	**NHL**	**48**	**4**	**5**	**9**	**8**	**9**	**17**	**46**	**12**	**0**	**0**	**0**	**11**
1939-40	**Boston Bruins**	**NHL**	**28**	**0**	**5**	**5**	**0**	**10**	**10**	**16**	....	....	....	....	....
	Chicago Black Hawks	**NHL**	**16**	**1**	**4**	**5**	**2**	**8**	**10**	**20**	**2**	**0**	**0**	**0**	**2**
1940-41	**Chicago Black Hawks**	**NHL**	**5**	**0**	**0**	**0**	**0**	**0**	**0**	**4**	....	....	....	....	....
	Montreal Canadiens	**NHL**	**42**	**2**	**7**	**9**	**4**	**13**	**17**	**34**	**3**	**0**	**1**	**1**	**2**
1941-42	**Montreal Canadiens**	**NHL**	**46**	**2**	**9**	**11**	**3**	**14**	**17**	**53**	**3**	**0**	**0**	**0**	**0**
1942-43	**Montreal Canadiens**	**NHL**	**49**	**3**	**14**	**17**	**4**	**18**	**22**	**52**	**5**	**1**	**2**	**3**	**2**
1943-44			MILITARY SERVICE												
1944-45			MILITARY SERVICE												
1945-46			MILITARY SERVICE												
1946-47	Buffalo Bisons	AHL	50	2	14	16	....	....	....	25	2	0	0	0	0
1947-48	Philadelphia–Washington	AHL	57	5	15	20	....	....	....	19	....	....	....	....	....
	NHL Totals		**381**	**15**	**56**	**71**	**27**	**98**	**125**	**323**	**33**	**1**	**3**	**4**	**25**

Can-Am First All-Star Team (1936)

Traded to **Boston** by **Montreal Canadiens** for Tony Savage and $7,500, December 3, 1934. Traded to **Chicago** by **Boston** for Des Smith, January 27, 1940. Traded to **Montreal** by **Chicago** for $12,500, November 19, 1940.

• POWELL, RAY
Ray Powell
C – L. 6′, 170 lbs. b: Timmons, Ont., 11/16/1925.

Season	Club	League	GP	G	A	Pts	AG	AA	APts	PIM	GP	G	A	Pts	PIM
1943-44	Brantford Lions	OHA	21	10	21	31	....	....	....	17	3	1	2	3	2
	Pittsburgh Hornets	AHL	2	0	0	0	....	....	....	0	....	....	....	....	....
1944-45	Baltimore Blades	EHL	43	33	*62	95	....	....	....	19	9	9	9	18	2
	New York Rovers	EHL	1	0	0	0	....	....	....	0	....	....	....	....	....
	Buffalo Bisons	AHL	2	0	1	1	....	....	....	0	4	2	3	5	0
1945-46	New Haven Eagles	AHL	14	2	10	12	....	....	....	2	....	....	....	....	....
	Fort Worth Rangers	USHL	33	19	29	48	....	....	....	6	....	....	....	....	....
1946-47	Omaha–Kansas City	USHL	55	28	42	70	....	....	....	6	....	....	....	....	....
1947-48	Kansas City Pla-Mors	USHL	62	37	47	84	....	....	....	16	12	5	8	13	0
1948-49	Kansas City Pla-Mors	USHL	61	*48	58	*106	....	....	....	22	2	0	2	2	0
1949-50	Kansas City Pla-Mors	USHL	64	27	*84	*111	....	....	....	11	3	0	1	1	0
1950-51	**Chicago Black Hawks**	**NHL**	**31**	**7**	**15**	**22**	**9**	**19**	**28**	**2**	....	....	....	....	....
	Milwaukee Seagulls	USHL	35	18	19	37	....	....	....	16	....	....	....	....	....
1951-52	Providence Reds	AHL	67	35	*62	*97	....	....	....	6	15	*8	7	15	6
1952-53	Providence Reds	AHL	59	17	41	58	....	....	....	2	....	....	....	....	....
1953-54	Quebec Aces	QHL	68	22	55	77	....	....	....	10	16	3	8	11	6
1954-55	Quebec Aces	QHL	53	22	43	65	....	....	....	22	8	1	3	4	0
1955-56	Quebec Aces	QHL	59	15	33	48	....	....	....	30	6	1	0	1	8
1956-57	Victoria Cougars	WHL	34	10	9	19	....	....	....	4	3	1	2	3	0
1957-58	Kelowna Packers	OSHL	48	27	42	69	....	....	....	21	10	3	1	4	0
1958-59	Kelowna Packers	OSHL	DID NOT PLAY – INJURED												
1959-60			DID NOT PLAY – RETIRED												
1960-61	Kelowna Packers	OSHL	2	2	1	3	....	....	....	2	....	....	....	....	....
	NHL Totals		**31**	**7**	**15**	**22**	**9**	**19**	**28**	**2**	....	....	....	....	....

EHL First All-Star Team (1945) • USHL First All-Star Team (1949, 1950) • Won Herman W. Paterson Cup (USHL - MVP) (1950) • AHL First All-Star Team (1952) • Won John B. Sollenberger Trophy (Top Scorer - AHL) (1952) • Won Les Cunningham Award (MVP - AHL) (1952) • QHL Second All-Star Team (1955)

Claimed by **Toronto** from **Fort Worth** (USHL) in Inter-League Draft, June, 1946. Traded to **Detroit** by **Toronto** with Doug Baldwin for Gerry Brown, September 21, 1946. Traded to **Providence** (AHL) by **Chicago** for cash, August 30, 1951.

• PRATT, BABE
Babe (Walter) Pratt **HHOF**
D – L. 6′3″, 212 lbs. b: Stony Mountain, Man., 1/7/1916. d: 12/16/1988.

Season	Club	League	GP	G	A	Pts	AG	AA	APts	PIM	GP	G	A	Pts	PIM
1932-33	Elmwood Millionaires	Wpg-Jr.	STATISTICS NOT AVAILABLE												
1933-34	Kenora Thistles	NOHA	16	14	7	21	....	....	....	33	9	6	2	8	18
1934-35	Kenora Thistles	NOHA	18	19	*23	*42	....	....	....	18	2	0	4	4	2
	Brandon Wheat Kings	Wpg-Sr.	1	0	0	0	....	....	....	0	....	....	....	....	....
1935-36	**New York Rangers**	**NHL**	**17**	**1**	**1**	**2**	**2**	**2**	**4**	**16**	....	....	....	....	....
	Philadelphia Ramblers	Can-Am	28	7	8	15	....	....	....	48	4	0	0	0	2
1936-37	**New York Rangers**	**NHL**	**47**	**8**	**7**	**15**	**17**	**16**	**33**	**23**	**9**	**3**	**1**	**4**	**11**
1937-38	**New York Rangers**	**NHL**	**47**	**5**	**14**	**19**	**10**	**29**	**39**	**56**	**2**	**0**	**0**	**0**	**2**
1938-39	**New York Rangers**	**NHL**	**48**	**2**	**19**	**21**	**4**	**36**	**40**	**20**	**7**	**1**	**2**	**3**	**9**
1939-40	**New York Rangers**	**NHL**	**48**	**4**	**13**	**17**	**9**	**26**	**35**	**61**	**12**	**3**	**1**	**4**	**18**
1940-41	**New York Rangers**	**NHL**	**47**	**3**	**17**	**20**	**6**	**31**	**37**	**52**	**3**	**1**	**1**	**2**	**6**
1941-42	**New York Rangers**	**NHL**	**47**	**4**	**24**	**28**	**7**	**37**	**44**	**55**	**6**	**1**	**3**	**4**	**24**
1942-43	**New York Rangers**	**NHL**	**4**	**0**	**2**	**2**	**0**	**3**	**3**	**6**	....	....	....	....	....
	Toronto Maple Leafs	**NHL**	**40**	**12**	**25**	**37**	**17**	**32**	**49**	**44**	**6**	**1**	**2**	**3**	**8**
1943-44	**Toronto Maple Leafs**	**NHL**	**50**	**17**	**40**	**57**	**21**	**49**	**70**	**30**	**5**	**0**	**3**	**3**	**4**
1944-45	**Toronto Maple Leafs**	**NHL**	**50**	**18**	**23**	**41**	**25**	**37**	**62**	**39**	**13**	**2**	**4**	**6**	**8**
1945-46	**Toronto Maple Leafs**	**NHL**	**41**	**5**	**20**	**25**	**8**	**37**	**45**	**36**	....	....	....	....	....
1946-47	**Boston Bruins**	**NHL**	**31**	**4**	**4**	**8**	**5**	**6**	**11**	**25**	....	....	....	....	....
	Hershey Bears	AHL	21	5	10	15	....	....	....	23	11	3	5	8	*19
1947-48	Hershey–Cleveland	AHL	52	3	18	21	....	....	....	47	2	0	0	0	0
1948-49	New Westminster Royals	PCHL	63	18	48	66	....	....	....	64	12	1	8	9	10
1949-50	New Westminster Royals	PCHL	59	8	29	37	....	....	....	56	18	2	6	8	22
1950-51	New Westminster Royals	PCHL	65	8	15	23	....	....	....	54	7	0	0	0	4
1951-52	Tacoma Rockets	PCHL	63	7	31	38	....	....	....	20	5	0	1	1	0
1952-53	New Westminster Royals	PCHL	DID NOT PLAY – COACHING												
	NHL Totals		**517**	**83**	**209**	**292**	**131**	**341**	**472**	**463**	**63**	**12**	**17**	**29**	**90**

NHL First All-Star Team (1944) • Won Hart Trophy (1944) • NHL Second All-Star Team (1945) • PCHL Northern First All-Star Team (1949, 1950) • MVP - PCHL Northern Division (1949, 1950) • PCHL First All-Star Team (1951)

Signed as a free agent by **NY Rangers**, October 18, 1935. Traded to **Toronto** by **NY Rangers** for Hank Goldup and Red Garrett, November 27, 1942. • Suspended by NHL President Red Dutton for gambling violations, January 30, 1946. Traded to **Boston** by **Toronto** for rights to Eric Pogue and cash, June 19, 1946. Traded to **Cleveland** (AHL) by **Boston** for cash, May 15, 1947.

• PRATT, JACK
Jack Pratt
C/D – R. 6′, 190 lbs. b: Edinburgh, Scotland, 4/13/1906.

Season	Club	League	GP	G	A	Pts	AG	AA	APts	PIM	GP	G	A	Pts	PIM
1927-28	Rossland Ramblers	BCHL	STATISTICS NOT AVAILABLE												
1928-29	Portland Buckaroos	PCHL	36	5	3	8	....	....	....	98	2	0	0	0	6
1929-30	Portland Buckaroos	PCHL	34	5	3	8	....	....	....	*162	4	0	*3	*3	*10
1930-31	**Boston Bruins**	**NHL**	**32**	**2**	**0**	**2**	**5**	**0**	**5**	**36**	**4**	**0**	**0**	**0**	**0**
	Boston Cubs	Can-Am	5	1	1	2	....	....	....	8	9	1	2	3	30
1931-32	**Boston Bruins**	**NHL**	**5**	**0**	**0**	**0**	**0**	**0**	**0**	**6**	....	....	....	....	....
	Boston Cubs	Can-Am	37	12	8	20	....	....	....	*137	5	0	1	1	6
1932-33	Philadelphia Arrows	Can-Am	43	16	14	30	....	....	....	75	5	2	0	2	8
1933-34	Kimberley Dynamiters	Kootenay	DID NOT PLAY – COACHING												
1934-35	Kimberley Dynamiters	Kootenay	DID NOT PLAY – COACHING												
1935-36	Portland Buckaroos	NWHL	27	19	15	34	....	....	....	43	3	0	0	0	....
1936-37	Kimberley Dynamiters	Kootenay	DID NOT PLAY – COACHING												
1937-38	Kimberley Dynamiters	Kootenay	12	6	7	13	....	....	....	27	....	....	....	....	....
1938-39	Kimberley Dynamiters	Kootenay	DID NOT PLAY – COACHING												
1939-40	Kimberley Dynamiters	Kootenay	5	0	1	1	....	....	....	8	....	....	....	....	....
	NHL Totals		**37**	**2**	**0**	**2**	**5**	**0**	**5**	**42**	**4**	**0**	**0**	**0**	**0**

Signed as a free agent by **Boston**, November 5, 1930.

• PRENTICE, DEAN
— see page 1400

• PRENTICE, ERIC
Eric "Doc" Prentice
LW – L. 5′11″, 150 lbs. b: Schumacher, Ont., 8/22/1926.

Season	Club	League	GP	G	A	Pts	AG	AA	APts	PIM	GP	G	A	Pts	PIM
1942-43	Timmins Buffalo Ankerites	TBJHL	STATISTICS NOT AVAILABLE												
1943-44	**Toronto Maple Leafs**	**NHL**	**5**	**0**	**0**	**0**	**0**	**0**	**0**	**4**	....	....	....	....	....
	Providence–Hershey	AHL	14	3	3	6	....	....	....	14	7	2	0	2	0
1944-45	Pittsburgh Hornets	AHL	33	9	7	16	....	....	....	10	....	....	....	....	....
1945-46	Omaha Knights	USHL	3	0	2	2	....	....	....	2	....	....	....	....	....
	Hollywood Wolves	PCHL	21	6	6	12	....	....	....	19	12	4	9	13	12
1946-47	Hollywood Wolves	PCHL	60	18	22	40	....	....	....	12	7	2	3	5	6
1947-48	Fresno Falcons	PCHL	62	18	12	30	....	....	....	58	6	1	2	3	9
1948-49	Philadelphia Rockets	AHL	63	22	24	46	....	....	....	10	....	....	....	....	....
1949-50	Oakland–L.A.–Fresno	PCHL	65	20	16	36	....	....	....	22	....	....	....	....	....
	NHL Totals		**5**	**0**	**0**	**0**	**0**	**0**	**0**	**4**	....	....	....	....	....

• PRICE, JACK
Jack Price
D – L. 5′9″, 180 lbs. b: Goderich, Ont., 5/8/1932.

Season	Club	League	GP	G	A	Pts	AG	AA	APts	PIM	GP	G	A	Pts	PIM
1950-51	Galt Black Hawks	OHA	54	5	15	20	....	....	....	74	3	1	0	1	8
1951-52	Galt Black Hawks	OHA	53	7	28	35	....	....	....	102	3	0	1	1	0
	Chicago Black Hawks	**NHL**	**1**	**0**	**0**	**0**	**0**	**0**	**0**	**0**	....	....	....	....	....
1952-53	**Chicago Black Hawks**	**NHL**	**10**	**0**	**0**	**0**	**0**	**0**	**0**	**2**	**4**	**0**	**0**	**0**	**0**
	Chatham Maroons	OHA Sr.	46	15	19	34	....	....	....	98	....	....	....	....	....
1953-54	**Chicago Black Hawks**	**NHL**	**46**	**4**	**6**	**10**	**6**	**8**	**14**	**22**	....	....	....	....	....
	Ottawa Senators	QHL	17	1	3	4	....	....	....	26	....	....	....	....	....
1954-55	Pittsburgh Hornets	AHL	57	3	8	11	....	....	....	78	10	0	0	0	6
1955-56	Winnipeg Warriors	WHL	3	0	0	0	....	....	....	6	....	....	....	....	....
	Pittsburgh Hornets	AHL	61	6	12	18	....	....	....	65	4	0	0	0	10
1956-57	Hershey Bears	AHL	64	4	21	25	....	....	....	56	7	0	2	2	14
1957-58	Hershey Bears	AHL	70	2	14	16	....	....	....	46	11	1	1	2	8
1958-59	Hershey Bears	AHL	65	2	7	9	....	....	....	44	13	0	1	1	10
1959-60	Hershey Bears	AHL	71	1	11	12	....	....	....	63	....	....	....	....	....
1960-61	Sudbury Wolves	EPHL	30	4	14	18	....	....	....	20	....	....	....	....	....
	Edmonton Flyers	WHL	37	1	6	7	....	....	....	14	....	....	....	....	....
1961-62	Pittsburgh Hornets	AHL	69	1	14	15	....	....	....	64	....	....	....	....	....
1962-63	Pittsburgh Hornets	AHL	22	1	5	6	....	....	....	14	....	....	....	....	....
	Edmonton Flyers	WHL	38	1	9	10	....	....	....	20	3	0	0	0	7
	Sarnia Rams	OHA Sr.	8	1	2	3	....	....	....	30	....	....	....	....	....
1963-64	Windsor Bulldogs	IHL	7	1	1	2	....	....	....	5	....	....	....	....	....
	NHL Totals		**57**	**4**	**6**	**10**	**6**	**8**	**14**	**24**	**4**	**0**	**0**	**0**	**0**

Traded to **Detroit** (Hershey - AHL) bu **Toronto** (Pittsburgh - AHL) for cash, July 6, 1956.

• PRICE, NOEL
— see page 1401

• PRIMEAU, JOE Joe "Gentleman Joe" Primeau HHOF

C – L. 5'11", 153 lbs. b: Lindsay, Ont., 1/29/1906. d: 5/14/1989.

Season	Club	League	GP	G	A	Pts	AG	AA	APts	PIM	Playoffs GP	G	A	Pts	PIM
1923-24	St. Michael's Majors	OHA	6	1	1	2	....	....	....	....	....	....	....	....	....
1924-25	Toronto St. Mary's	OHA	8	7	3	10	....	....	....	....	....	....	....	....	....
1925-26	Toronto St. Mary's	OHA	7	*15	2	*17	....	....	....	2	2	2	*1	3	....
1926-27	Toronto Marlboros	OHA Sr.	10	11	3	14	....	....	....	4	....	....	....	....	....
1927-28	**Toronto Maple Leafs**	**NHL**	**2**	**0**	**0**	**0**	**0**	**0**	**0**	**0**	....	....	....	....	....
	Toronto Ravinas	Can-Pro	41	26	13	39	....	....	....	36	2	1	0	1	0
1928-29	**Toronto Maple Leafs**	**NHL**	**6**	**0**	**1**	**1**	**0**	**9**	**9**	**2**	....	....	....	....	....
	London Panthers	Can-Pro	35	12	10	22	....	....	....	16	....	....	....	....	....
1929-30	**Toronto Maple Leafs**	**NHL**	**43**	**5**	**21**	**26**	**10**	**69**	**79**	**22**	....	....	....	....	....
1930-31	**Toronto Maple Leafs**	**NHL**	**38**	**9**	***32**	**41**	**22**	**119**	**141**	**18**	**2**	**0**	**0**	**0**	**0**
1931-32	**Toronto Maple Leafs**	**NHL**	**46**	**13**	***37**	**50**	**28**	**106**	**134**	**25**	**7**	**0**	***6**	**6**	**2**
1932-33	**Toronto Maple Leafs**	**NHL**	**48**	**11**	**21**	**32**	**26**	**56**	**82**	**4**	**8**	**0**	**1**	**1**	**4**
1933-34	**Toronto Maple Leafs**	**NHL**	**45**	**14**	***32**	**46**	**31**	**87**	**118**	**8**	**5**	**2**	**4**	**6**	**6**
1934-35	**Toronto Maple Leafs**	**NHL**	**37**	**10**	**20**	**30**	**21**	**45**	**66**	**16**	**7**	**0**	**3**	**3**	**0**
1935-36	**Toronto Maple Leafs**	**NHL**	**45**	**4**	**13**	**17**	**10**	**31**	**41**	**10**	**9**	**3**	**4**	**7**	**0**
	NHL Totals		**310**	**66**	**177**	**243**	**148**	**522**	**670**	**105**	**38**	**5**	**18**	**23**	**12**

Won Lady Byng Trophy (1932) • NHL Second All-Star Team (1934)

Played in NHL All-Star Game (1934)

Signed as a free agent by **Toronto**, July 17, 1928.

• PRINGLE, ELLIE Ellie "Moose" Pringle

D – L. 6'2", 205 lbs. b: Toronto, Ont., 8/31/1911. Deceased.

Season	Club	League	GP	G	A	Pts	AG	AA	APts	PIM	Playoffs GP	G	A	Pts	PIM
1928-29	Newmarket Royals	OHA	STATISTICS NOT AVAILABLE												
	Toronto Marlboros	OHA	9	6	0	6	....	....	....	....	2	1	0	1	....
1929-30	Toronto Marlboros	OHA	8	0	0	0	....	....	....	22	....	....	....	....	....
	Toronto Willys-Overland	City Sr.	STATISTICS NOT AVAILABLE												
1930-31	**New York Americans**	**NHL**	**6**	**0**	**0**	**0**	**0**	**0**	**0**	**0**	....	....	....	....	....
	New Haven Eagles	Can-Am	30	3	1	4	....	....	....	66	....	....	....	....	....
1931-32	Bronx Tigers	Can-Am	38	2	3	5	....	....	....	83	2	0	0	0	0
1932-33	New Haven Eagles	Can-Am	42	5	3	8	....	....	....	103	....	....	....	....	....
1933-34	Windsor Bulldogs	IAHL	44	0	0	0	....	....	....	82	....	....	....	....	....
1934-35	London Tecumsehs	IAHL	25	3	1	4	....	....	....	58	....	....	....	....	....
	St. Paul Saints	CHL	15	2	3	5	....	....	....	36	....	....	....	....	....
1935-36	London–Rochester	IAHL	36	2	4	6	....	....	....	59	....	....	....	....	....
1936-37	Tulsa Oilers	AHA	48	4	7	11	....	....	....	72	....	....	....	....	....
1937-38	Vancouver Lions	PCHL	38	2	5	7	....	....	....	56	6	2	0	2	6
1938-39	Vancouver Lions	PCHL	43	6	9	15	....	....	....	37	2	0	0	0	4
	NHL Totals		**6**	**0**	**0**	**0**	**0**	**0**	**0**	**0**	....	....	....	....	....

Signed as a free agent by **NY Americans**, October 22, 1930.

• PRODGERS, GOLDIE Goldie (Samuel George) Prodgers

F/D – R. 5'10", 180 lbs. b: London, Ont., 10/18/1891. d: 10/25/1935.

Season	Club	League	GP	G	A	Pts	AG	AA	APts	PIM	Playoffs GP	G	A	Pts	PIM
1909-10	London Wingers	City Jr.	STATISTICS NOT AVAILABLE												
1910-11	Waterloo Professionals	OPHL	16	9	0	0	....	....		....	....	....	....	....	....
1911-12	Quebec Bulldogs	NHA	18	3	0	3	....	....	....	15	2	0	0	0	0
1912-13	Victoria Aristocrats	PCHA	15	6	0	6	....	....	....	21	3	1	0	1	0
1913-14	Quebec Bulldogs	NHA	20	2	3	5	....	....	....	11	....	....	....	....	....
1914-15	Montreal Wanderers	NHA	18	8	5	13	....	....	....	54	2	0	0	0	15
1915-16	Montreal Canadiens	NHA	24	8	3	11	....	....	....	86	4	3	0	3	13
1916-17	Toronto 228th Battalion	NHA	12	16	2	18	....	....	....	24	....	....	....	....	
1917-18			MILITARY SERVICE												
1918-19			MILITARY SERVICE												
1919-20	**Toronto St. Pats**	**NHL**	**16**	**8**	**6**	**14**	**18**	**41**	**59**	**4**	....	....	....	....	....
1920-21	**Hamilton Tigers**	**NHL**	**24**	**18**	**9**	**27**	**47**	**81**	**128**	**8**	....	....	....	....	....
1921-22	**Hamilton Tigers**	**NHL**	**24**	**15**	**6**	**21**	**42**	**38**	**80**	**4**	....	....	....	....	....
1922-23	**Hamilton Tigers**	**NHL**	**20**	**13**	**3**	**16**	**44**	**27**	**71**	**13**	....	....	....	....	....
1923-24	**Hamilton Tigers**	**NHL**	**23**	**9**	**1**	**10**	**37**	**17**	**54**	**6**	....	....	....	....	....
1924-25	**Hamilton Tigers**	**NHL**	**1**	**0**	**0**	**0**	**0**	**0**	**0**	**0**	....	....	....	....	....
1925-26			DID NOT PLAY – RETIRED												
1926-27	London Panthers	Can-Pro	10	1	0	1	....			10	....	....	....	....	....
1927-28	London Panthers	Can-Pro	DID NOT PLAY – COACHING												
	NHL Totals		**111**	**63**	**25**	**88**	**188**	**204**	**392**	**35**	....	....	....	....	....
	Other Major League Totals		123	52	13	65	....	....	....	211	11	4	0	4	28

NHL rights transferred to **Quebec** by **NHL** when Quebec franchise returned to NHL, November 25, 1919. • Suspended by **Quebec** after refusing to report to training camp, November 27, 1919. Traded to **Montreal Canadiens** by **Quebec** for Eddie Carpenter, December 21, 1919. Traded to **Toronto St. Pats** by **Montreal Canadiens** for Harry Cameron, January 14, 1920. Traded to **Hamilton** by **Toronto St. Pats** with Joe Matte for cash, November 27, 1920.

• PRONOVOST, ANDRE — see page 1404

• PRONOVOST, MARCEL — see page 1405

• PROVOST, CLAUDE — see page 1406

• PRYSTAI, METRO Metro Prystai

C – L. 5'8", 155 lbs. b: Yorkton, Sask., 11/7/1927.

Season	Club	League	GP	G	A	Pts	AG	AA	APts	PIM	Playoffs GP	G	A	Pts	PIM
1943-44	Moose Jaw Canucks	SJHL	2	1	0	1	....	....	....	0	1	0	0	0	0
	Moose Jaw Victorias	SSHL	....	....	....	....	....	....	....	....	2	0	0	0	0
1944-45	Moose Jaw Canucks	SJHL	15	13	8	21	....	....	....	6	21	15	15	30	19
1945-46	Moose Jaw Canucks	SJHL	16	25	25	*50	....	....	....	8	4	5	8	13	0
1946-47	Moose Jaw Canucks	SJHL	22	32	39	*71	....	....	....	8	6	5	*9	*14	0
1947-48	**Chicago Black Hawks**	**NHL**	**54**	**7**	**11**	**18**	**10**	**16**	**26**	**25**	....	....	....	....	....
1948-49	**Chicago Black Hawks**	**NHL**	**59**	**12**	**7**	**19**	**19**	**11**	**30**	**19**	....	....	....	....	....
1949-50	**Chicago Black Hawks**	**NHL**	**65**	**29**	**22**	**51**	**39**	**28**	**67**	**31**	....	....	....	....	....
1950-51	**Detroit Red Wings**	**NHL**	**62**	**20**	**17**	**37**	**27**	**22**	**49**	**27**	**3**	**1**	**0**	**1**	**0**
1951-52	**Detroit Red Wings**	**NHL**	**69**	**21**	**22**	**43**	**30**	**29**	**59**	**16**	**8**	**2**	***5**	***7**	**0**
1952-53	**Detroit Red Wings**	**NHL**	**70**	**16**	**34**	**50**	**25**	**48**	**73**	**12**	**6**	**4**	**4**	**8**	**2**
1953-54	**Detroit Red Wings**	**NHL**	**70**	**12**	**15**	**27**	**18**	**20**	**38**	**26**	**12**	**2**	**3**	**5**	**0**
1954-55	**Detroit Red Wings**	**NHL**	**12**	**2**	**3**	**5**	**3**	**4**	**7**	**9**	....	....	....	....	....
	Chicago Black Hawks	**NHL**	**57**	**11**	**13**	**24**	**16**	**17**	**33**	**28**	....	....	....	....	....
1955-56	**Chicago Black Hawks**	**NHL**	**8**	**1**	**3**	**4**	**1**	**4**	**5**	**8**	....	....	....	....	....
	Detroit Red Wings	**NHL**	**63**	**12**	**16**	**28**	**17**	**20**	**37**	**10**	**9**	**1**	**2**	**3**	**6**
1956-57	**Detroit Red Wings**	**NHL**	**70**	**7**	**15**	**22**	**9**	**17**	**26**	**16**	**5**	**2**	**0**	**2**	**0**
1957-58	Edmonton Flyers	WHL	21	13	14	27	....	....	....	6	....	....	....	....	....
	Detroit Red Wings	**NHL**	**15**	**1**	**1**	**2**	**1**	**1**	**2**	**4**	....	....	....	....	....
1958-59	Edmonton Flyers	WHL	4	1	0	1	....	....	....	4	....	....	....	....	....
1959-60	Omaha Knights	IHL	DID NOT PLAY – COACHING												
	NHL Totals		**674**	**151**	**179**	**330**	**215**	**237**	**452**	**231**	**43**	**12**	**14**	**26**	**8**

Played in NHL All-Star Game (1950, 1953, 1954)

Traded to **Detroit** by **Chicago** with Jim Henry, Gaye Stewart and Bob Goldham for Al Dewsbury, Harry Lumley, Jack Stewart, Don Morrison and Pete Babando, July 13, 1950. Traded to **Chicago** by **Detroit** for Lorne Davis, November 9, 1954. Traded to **Detroit** by **Chicago** for Ed Sandford, October 24, 1955.

• PUDAS, AL Al Pudas

RW/LW – R. 5'10", 160 lbs. b: Siikajoki, Finland, 2/17/1899. Deceased.

Season	Club	League	GP	G	A	Pts	AG	AA	APts	PIM	Playoffs GP	G	A	Pts	PIM
1922-23	Port Arthur Ports	MHL Sr.	16	17	8	25	....	....	....	5	2	1	0	1	0
1923-24	Port Arthur Bearcats	MHL Sr.	16	11	2	13	....	....	....	2	2	1	0	1	2
1924-25	Port Arthur Bearcats	MHL Sr.	20	3	3	6	....	....	....	....	10	11	10	21	13
1925-26	Port Arthur Bearcats	MHL Sr.	20	11	2	13	....	....	....	20	9	*7	*6	*13	18
1926-27	**Toronto Maple Leafs**	**NHL**	**4**	**0**	**0**	**0**	**0**	**0**	**0**	**0**	....	....	....	....	....
	Hamilton–Windsor	Can-Pro	27	18	2	20	....	....	....	10	2	3	0	3	0
1927-28	Stratford–London–Detroit	Can-Pro	30	6	1	7	....	....	....	4	2	0	0	0	0
	NHL Totals		**4**	**0**	**0**	**0**	**0**	**0**	**0**	**0**	....	....	....	....	....

Signed as a free agent by **Toronto St. Pats**, November 10, 1926. Traded to **Hamilton** (Can-Pro) by **Toronto** (Windsor-Can-Pro) for George Patterson, February 1, 1927.

• PULFORD, BOB — see page 1407

• PURPUR, FIDO Fido (Clifford Joseph) Purpur USHOF

RW – R. 5'6", 155 lbs. b: Grand Forks, ND, 9/26/1914.

Season	Club	League	GP	G	A	Pts	AG	AA	APts	PIM	Playoffs GP	G	A	Pts	PIM
1931-32	Grand Forks Falcons	H.S.	STATISTICS NOT AVAILABLE												
1932-33	Minneapolis Millers	CHL	37	13	3	16	....	....	....	13	7	1	1	2	6
1933-34	Minneapolis Millers	CHL	44	15	10	25	....	....	....	79	3	2	1	3	2
1934-35	**St. Louis Eagles**	**NHL**	**25**	**1**	**2**	**3**	**2**	**4**	**6**	**8**	....	....	....	....	....
	Minneapolis Millers	CHL	14	4	2	6	....	....	....	29	....	....	....	....	....
1935-36	St. Louis Flyers	AHA	47	13	5	18	....	....	....	34	7	1	*3	4	2
1936-37	St. Louis Flyers	AHA	32	7	15	22	....	....		29	6	2	3	5	2
1937-38	St. Louis Flyers	AHA	48	23	15	38	....	....	....	15	7	0	3	3	4
1938-39	St. Louis Flyers	AHA	48	35	43	78	....	....	....	34	7	3	3	6	4
1939-40	St. Louis Flyers	AHA	46	32	38	70	....	....	....	44	5	1	3	4	4
1940-41	St. Louis Flyers	AHA	46	25	16	41	....	....	....	32	9	*5	0	5	4
1941-42	**Chicago Black Hawks**	**NHL**	**8**	**0**	**0**	**0**	**0**	**0**	**0**	**0**	....	....	....	....	....
	Kansas City Americans	AHA	39	18	30	48	....	....	....	19	0	*10	6	*16	10
1942-43	**Chicago Black Hawks**	**NHL**	**50**	**13**	**16**	**29**	**18**	**20**	**38**	**14**	....	....	....	....	....
1943-44	**Chicago Black Hawks**	**NHL**	**40**	**9**	**10**	**19**	**11**	**12**	**23**	**13**	**9**	**1**	**1**	**2**	**0**
1944-45	**Chicago Black Hawks**	**NHL**	**21**	**2**	**7**	**9**	**3**	**11**	**14**	**11**	....	....	....	....	....
	Indianapolis Capitals	AHL	26	8	14	22	....	....	....	10	5	1	2	0	2
	Detroit Red Wings	**NHL**	....	....	....	....	....	....	....	....	**7**	**0**	**1**	**1**	**4**
1945-46	St. Louis Flyers	AHL	56	18	15	33	....	....	....	21	....	....	....	....	....
1946-47	St. Paul Saints	USHL	56	15	23	38	....	....	....	16	....	....	....	....	....
	NHL Totals		**144**	**25**	**35**	**60**	**34**	**47**	**81**	**46**	**16**	**1**	**2**	**3**	**4**

AHA First All-Star Team (1939, 1940)

Traded to **St. Louis** by **Minneapolis** (AHA) for Nick Wasne and $1,600, December 28, 1934. Claimed by **Toronto** from **St. Louis** in Dispersal Draft, October 15, 1935. Traded to **St. Louis** (AHA) by **Toronto** for cash, November 6, 1935. Traded to **Chicago** by **St. Louis** (AHA) for Sammy McManus and cash, May 3, 1941. Traded to **Detroit** by **Chicago** for Byron McDonald, January 5, 1945. Traded to **St. Louis** (AHL) by **Detroit** for cash, August 24, 1945.

• PUSIE, JEAN Jean Pusie

D – L. 6', 205 lbs. b: Montreal, Que., 10/15/1910. d: 4/21/1956.

Season	Club	League	GP	G	A	Pts	AG	AA	APts	PIM	GP	G	A	Pts	PIM
			REGULAR SEASON								PLAYOFFS				
1928-29	Banque Nationale	Mtl-Sr.	STATISTICS NOT AVAILABLE												
1929-30	Verdun CPR	Mtl-Sr.	STATISTICS NOT AVAILABLE												
	London Panthers	IAHL	11	1	0	1	....	....	....	2	2	0	0	0	2
1930-31	**Montreal Canadiens**	**NHL**	**6**	**0**	**0**	**0**	**0**	**0**	**0**	**0**	**3**	**0**	**0**	**0**	**0**
	Galt Terriers	OPHL	22	16	8	24	....	....	....	29	2	0	1	1	0
	Detroit Olympics	IAHL	4	0	0	0	....	....	....	0	....	....	....	....	....
1931-32	**Montreal Canadiens**	**NHL**	**1**	**0**	**0**	**0**	**0**	**0**	**0**	**0**	....	....	....	....	....
	Philadelphia Arrows	Can-Am	14	0	4	4	....	....	....	8	....	....	....	....	....
	Trois-Rivieres Renards	ECHL	14	5	2	7	....	....	....	24	....	....	....	....	....
1932-33	Quebec Castors	Can-Am	1	0	1	1	....	....	....	0	....	....	....	....	....
	Regina–Vancouver	WCHL	30	*30	*22	*52	....	....	....	31	2	0	1	1	0
1933-34	**New York Rangers**	**NHL**	**19**	**0**	**2**	**2**	**0**	**5**	**5**	**17**	....	....	....	....	....
	London Tecumsehs	IAHL	26	6	6	12	....	....	....	47	6	3	2	5	2
1934-35	**Boston Bruins**	**NHL**	**4**	**1**	**0**	**1**	**2**	**0**	**2**	**0**	**4**	**0**	**0**	**0**	**0**
	Boston Cubs	Can-Am	34	14	13	27	....	....	....	59	....	....	....	....	....
1935-36	Boston Cubs	Can-Am	16	4	5	9	....	....	....	18	....	....	....	....	....
	Montreal Canadiens	**NHL**	**31**	**0**	**2**	**2**	**0**	**5**	**5**	**11**	....	....	....	....	....
1936-37	Providence Reds	AHL	26	5	8	13	....	....	....	39	2	0	0	0	0
1937-38	Cleveland Barons	AHL	39	2	3	5	....	....	....	13	2	1	1	2	0
1938-39	St. Louis Flyers	AHA	35	18	12	30	....	....	....	60	5	2	2	4	16
1939-40	Vancouver Lions	PCHL	30	13	12	25	....	....	....	*85	....	....	....	....	....
1940-41	Seattle Olympics	PCHL	28	10	13	23	....	....	....	48	....	....	....	....	....
1941-42	St. Louis Flyers	AHA	35	9	12	21	....	....	....	19	....	....	....	....	....
1942-43	Montreal Locomotive	City Sr.	STATISTICS NOT AVAILABLE												
1943-44	Montreal Army	City Sr.	6	0	2	2	....	....	....	12	2	0	1	1	2
	NHL Totals		**61**	**1**	**4**	**5**	**2**	**10**	**12**	**28**	**7**	**0**	**0**	**0**	**0**

Signed as a free agent by **Montreal Canadiens**, February 4, 1930. Traded to **NY Rangers** by **Montreal Canadiens** for $3,000, October 10, 1933. Traded to **Boston** by **NY Rangers** for Percy Jackson, November, 1934. Traded to **Montreal Canadiens** by **Boston** with Walt Buswell and cash for Roger Jenkins, July 13, 1935. Traded to **Boston** (Can-Am) by **Montreal Canadiens** for cash, February 9, 1936. Signed as a free agent by **St. Louis** (AHA), September 24, 1938.

• QUACKENBUSH, BILL Bill (Hubert G.) Quackenbush HHOF

D – L. 5'11", 190 lbs. b: Toronto, Ont., 3/2/1922.

Season	Club	League	GP	G	A	Pts	AG	AA	APts	PIM	GP	G	A	Pts	PIM
1940-41	Toronto Native Sons	OHA	13	4	9	13	....	....	....	0	....	....	....	....	....
1941-42	Brantford Lions	OHA	23	5	29	34	....	....	....	16	7	2	4	6	8
1942-43	**Detroit Red Wings**	**NHL**	**10**	**1**	**1**	**2**	**1**	**1**	**2**	**4**	....	....	....	....	....
	Indianapolis Capitals	AHL	37	6	13	19	....	....	....	0	7	0	1	1	6
1943-44	**Detroit Red Wings**	**NHL**	**43**	**4**	**14**	**18**	**5**	**17**	**22**	**6**	**2**	**1**	**0**	**1**	**0**
	Indianapolis Capitals	AHL	1	1	0	1	....	....	....	0	....	....	....	....	....
1944-45	**Detroit Red Wings**	**NHL**	**50**	**7**	**14**	**21**	**10**	**23**	**33**	**10**	**14**	**0**	**2**	**2**	**2**
1945-46	**Detroit Red Wings**	**NHL**	**48**	**11**	**10**	**21**	**17**	**19**	**36**	**6**	**5**	**0**	**1**	**1**	**0**
1946-47	**Detroit Red Wings**	**NHL**	**44**	**5**	**17**	**22**	**7**	**24**	**31**	**6**	**5**	**0**	**0**	**0**	**2**
1947-48	**Detroit Red Wings**	**NHL**	**58**	**6**	**16**	**22**	**9**	**23**	**32**	**17**	**10**	**0**	**2**	**2**	**0**
1948-49	**Detroit Red Wings**	**NHL**	**60**	**6**	**17**	**23**	**9**	**27**	**36**	**0**	**11**	**1**	**1**	**2**	**0**
1949-50	**Boston Bruins**	**NHL**	**70**	**8**	**17**	**25**	**11**	**22**	**33**	**4**	....	....	....	....	....
1950-51	**Boston Bruins**	**NHL**	**70**	**5**	**24**	**29**	**7**	**31**	**38**	**12**	**6**	**0**	**1**	**1**	**0**
1951-52	**Boston Bruins**	**NHL**	**69**	**2**	**17**	**19**	**3**	**22**	**25**	**6**	**7**	**0**	**3**	**3**	**0**
1952-53	**Boston Bruins**	**NHL**	**69**	**2**	**16**	**18**	**3**	**22**	**25**	**6**	**11**	**0**	**4**	**4**	**4**
1953-54	**Boston Bruins**	**NHL**	**45**	**0**	**17**	**17**	**0**	**23**	**23**	**6**	**4**	**0**	**0**	**0**	**0**
1954-55	**Boston Bruins**	**NHL**	**68**	**2**	**20**	**22**	**3**	**26**	**29**	**8**	**5**	**0**	**5**	**5**	**0**
1955-56	**Boston Bruins**	**NHL**	**70**	**3**	**22**	**25**	**4**	**27**	**31**	**4**	....	....	....	....	....
	NHL Totals		**774**	**62**	**222**	**284**	**89**	**307**	**396**	**95**	**80**	**2**	**19**	**21**	**8**

NHL Second All-Star Team (1947, 1953) • NHL First All-Star Team (1948, 1949, 1951) • Won Lady Byng Trophy (1949)

Played in NHL All-Star Game (1947, 1948, 1949, 1950, 1951, 1952, 1953, 1954)

Signed as a free agent by **Detroit**, October 19, 1942. Traded to **Boston** by **Detroit** with Pete Horeck for Pete Babando, Pete Durham, Clare Martin and Jimmy Peters Sr., August 16, 1949.

• QUACKENBUSH, MAX Max Quackenbush

D – L. 6'2", 180 lbs. b: Toronto, Ont., 8/29/1928.

Season	Club	League	GP	G	A	Pts	AG	AA	APts	PIM	GP	G	A	Pts	PIM
1947-48	Windsor Spitfires	OHA	35	8	22	30	....	....	....	82	12	1	0	1	23
	Windsor Hettche	IHL	23	5	9	14	....	....	....	71	....	....	....	....	....
1948-49	Omaha Knights	USHL	66	3	14	17	....	....	....	61	4	0	1	1	0
1949-50	Indianapolis Capitals	AHL	68	6	22	28	....	....	....	34	4	0	1	1	0
1950-51	Indianapolis Capitals	AHL	23	2	4	6	....	....	....	24	....	....	....	....	....
	Boston Bruins	**NHL**	**47**	**4**	**6**	**10**	**5**	**8**	**13**	**26**	**6**	**0**	**0**	**0**	**4**
1951-52	St. Louis Flyers	AHL	50	5	15	20	....	....	....	54	....	....	....	....	....
	Chicago Black Hawks	**NHL**	**14**	**0**	**1**	**1**	**0**	**1**	**1**	**4**	....	....	....	....	....
1952-53	Calgary Stampeders	WHL	65	2	21	23	....	....	....	31	3	0	1	1	0
1953-54	Calgary Stampeders	WHL	70	11	28	39	....	....	....	48	25	5	10	15	4
1954-55	Calgary Stampeders	WHL	63	8	24	32	....	....	....	56	9	1	3	4	4
	NHL Totals		**61**	**4**	**7**	**11**	**5**	**9**	**14**	**30**	**6**	**0**	**0**	**0**	**4**

Loaned to **Boston** by **Detroit** for the remainder of the 1950-51 season for the loan of Steve Kraftcheck to Indianapolis (AHL), December 5, 1950. Traded to **Chicago** by **Detroit** for Doug McCaig, September 18, 1951.

• QUENNEVILLE, LEO Leo Quenneville

LW/C – L. 5'10", 170 lbs. b: St. Anicet, Que., 6/15/1900. Deceased.

Season	Club	League	GP	G	A	Pts	AG	AA	APts	PIM	GP	G	A	Pts	PIM
			REGULAR SEASON								PLAYOFFS				
1921-22	Chicoutimi Bluets	QPHL	9	13	0	13	....	....	....	....	1	0	0	0	....
1922-23	Chicoutimi Bluets	QPHL	10	6	0	6	....	....	....	....	1	0	0	0	....
1923-24	Trois-Rivieres Renards	ECHL	11	5	0	5	....	....	....	....	....	....	....	....	....
1924-25	Trois-Rivieres Reds	ECHL	16	14	0	14	....	....	....	....	2	0	0	0	0
1925-26	Chicoutimi Sagueneens	QPHL	STATISTICS NOT AVAILABLE												
1926-27	Quebec Castors	Can-Am	31	4	2	6	....	....	....	56	2	0	0	0	4
1927-28	Quebec Castors	Can-Am	40	10	9	19	....	....	....	58	6	2	0	2	*18
1928-29	Hamilton Tigers	IAHL	7	1	0	1	....	....	....	16	....	....	....	....	....
	Newark Bulldogs	Can-Am	40	11	6	17	....	....	....	68	....	....	....	....	....
1929-30	**New York Rangers**	**NHL**	**25**	**0**	**3**	**3**	**0**	**10**	**10**	**10**	**3**	**0**	**0**	**0**	**0**
	Springfield Indians	Can-Am	12	2	1	3	....	....	....	19	....	....	....	....	....
1930-31	London Panthers	IAHL	48	14	6	20	....	....	....	50	....	....	....	....	....
1931-32	London Tecumsehs	IAHL	45	11	17	28	....	....	....	41	6	0	0	0	4
1932-33	London Tecumsehs	IAHL	40	11	8	19	....	....	....	55	6	2	1	3	4
1933-34	Quebec Beavers	Can-Am	36	6	17	23	....	....	....	23	....	....	....	....	....
1934-35	Quebec Beavers	Can-Am	41	9	12	21	....	....	....	19	3	0	0	0	0
	NHL Totals		**25**	**0**	**3**	**3**	**0**	**10**	**10**	**10**	**3**	**0**	**0**	**0**	**0**

Claimed by **NY Rangers** from **Newark** (Can-Am) in Inter-League Draft, May 13, 1929. Traded to **London** (IAHL) by **NY Rangers** for cash October 14, 1930.

• QUILTY, JOHN John Quilty

C – L. 5'10", 175 lbs. b: Ottawa, Ont., 1/21/1921. d: 9/12/1969.

Season	Club	League	GP	G	A	Pts	AG	AA	APts	PIM	GP	G	A	Pts	PIM
1939-40	Ottawa St. Pats	City Jr.	STATISTICS NOT AVAILABLE												
1940-41	**Montreal Canadiens**	**NHL**	**48**	**18**	**16**	**34**	**36**	**29**	**65**	**31**	**3**	**0**	**2**	**2**	**0**
1941-42	**Montreal Canadiens**	**NHL**	**48**	**12**	**12**	**24**	**21**	**18**	**39**	**44**	**3**	**0**	**1**	**1**	**0**
1942-43	Toronto RCAF	OHA Sr.	9	6	9	15	....	....	....	12	....	....	....	....	....
1943-44	Vancouver RCAF	PCHL	14	12	14	26	....	....	....	8	3	1	2	3	2
1944-45			MILITARY SERVICE												
1945-46	Ottawa Senators	QSHL	2	0	0	0	....	....	....	0	3	1	0	1	0
1946-47	**Montreal Canadiens**	**NHL**	**3**	**1**	**1**	**2**	**1**	**1**	**2**	**0**	**7**	**3**	**2**	**5**	**9**
	Buffalo Bisons	AHL	51	17	17	34	....	....	....	38	2	0	0	0	0
1947-48	**Montreal Canadiens**	**NHL**	**20**	**2**	**3**	**5**	**3**	**4**	**7**	**4**	....	....	....	....	....
	Boston Bruins	**NHL**	**6**	**3**	**2**	**5**	**4**	**3**	**7**	**2**	....	....	....	....	....
1948-49	North Sydney Victorias	CBSHL	31	5	15	20	....	....	....	18	6	2	3	5	0
1949-50	Ottawa RCAF Flyers	ECSHL	27	10	12	22	....	....	....	6	5	2	4	6	2
1950-51	Ottawa RCAF Flyers	ECSHL	38	0	12	12	....	....	....	54	7	1	3	4	14
	Ottawa Senators	QSHL	....	....	....	....	....	....	....	....	3	0	0	0	4
1951-52	Ottawa Senators	QHL	3	0	0	0	....	....	....	0	....	....	....	....	....
	Renfrew Millionaires	ECSHL	40	9	27	36	....	....	....	52	3	1	1	2	10
	NHL Totals		**125**	**36**	**34**	**70**	**65**	**55**	**120**	**81**	**13**	**3**	**5**	**8**	**9**

Won Calder Trophy (1941)

Signed as a free agent by **Montreal**, October 29, 1940. Traded to **Boston** by **Montreal** with Jim Peters for Joe Carveth December 16, 1949.

• RADLEY, YIP Yip (Harry John) Radley

D – L. 6', 198 lbs. b: Ottawa, Ont., 6/27/1908. d: 8/19/1963.

Season	Club	League	GP	G	A	Pts	AG	AA	APts	PIM	GP	G	A	Pts	PIM
1926-27	Ottawa Rideaus	City Sr.	14	1	2	3	....	....	....	....	....	....	....	....	....
1927-28	Ottawa Rideaus	City Sr.	4	0	0	0	....	....	....	....	....	....	....	....	....
1928-29	Ottawa Montagnards	City Sr.	15	2	1	3	....	....	....	....	....	....	....	....	....
1929-30	Ottawa Montagnards	City Sr.	20	3	1	4	....	....	....	57	6	3	1	4	*20
1930-31	**New York Americans**	**NHL**	**1**	**0**	**0**	**0**	**0**	**0**	**0**	**0**	....	....	....	....	....
	New Haven Eagles	Can-Am	34	1	2	3	....	....	....	77	....	....	....	....	....
1931-32	New Haven Eagles	Can-Am	39	4	0	4	....	....	....	26	2	0	0	0	0
1932-33	New Haven Eagles	Can-Am	27	1	0	1	....	....	....	34	....	....	....	....	....
1933-34	Cleveland Indians	IAHL	43	4	6	10	....	....	....	92	....	....	....	....	....
1934-35	Cleveland Indians	IAHL	5	0	0	0	....	....	....	4	....	....	....	....	....
	St. Louis Flyers	AHA	40	6	6	12	....	....	....	63	6	1	1	2	*26
1935-36	Tulsa Oilers	AHA	47	5	6	11	....	....	....	*72	2	1	1	2	2
1936-37	**Montreal Maroons**	**NHL**	**17**	**0**	**1**	**1**	**0**	**2**	**2**	**13**	....	....	....	....	....
	Providence Reds	AHL	4	1	0	1	....	....	....	0	....	....	....	....	....
	New Haven Eagles	AHL	2	0	0	0	....	....	....	0	....	....	....	....	....
1937-38	Tulsa Oilers	AHA	47	0	10	10	....	....	....	68	4	0	1	1	5
1938-39	Kansas City Greyhounds	AHA	10	0	1	1	....	....	....	12	....	....	....	....	....
	Wichita Skyhawks	AHA	19	4	5	9	....	....	....	8	....	....	....	....	....
1939-40	Wichita Skyhawks	AHA	6	0	1	1	....	....	....	6	....	....	....	....	....
1940-41	Kingston Combines	OHA Sr.	DID NOT PLAY – COACHING												
1941-42	Kingston Combines	OHA Sr.	16	0	2	2	....	....	....	13	....	....	....	....	....
	NHL Totals		**18**	**0**	**1**	**1**	**0**	**2**	**2**	**13**	....	....	....	....	....

AHA Second All-Star Team (1936)

Signed as a free agent by **NY Americans**, October 22, 1930. Signed as a free agent by **Montreal Maroons**, October 16, 1936 .

Season	Club	League	GP	G	A	Pts	AG	AA	APts	PIM	GP	G	A	Pts	PIM
			REGULAR SEASON								PLAYOFFS				

• RAGLAN, CLARE   Clare "Rags" Raglan
D – L. 6'1", 193 lbs.   b: Pembroke, Ont., 9/4/1927.

Season	Club	League	GP	G	A	Pts	AG	AA	APts	PIM	GP	G	A	Pts	PIM
1944-45	Toronto Marlboros	OHA	6	0	1	1	....	....	....	16	....	....	....	....	....
1945-46	Toronto Marlboros	OHA	25	2	10	12	....	....	....	41	4	0	2	2	6
1946-47	Toronto Marlboros	OHA	20	5	4	9	....	....	....	50	2	0	2	2	0
1947-48	Quebec Aces	QSHL	45	9	11	20	....	....	....	106	10	0	1	1	16
1948-49	Quebec Aces	QSHL	63	11	24	35	....	....	....	121	3	0	2	2	4
1949-50	Indianapolis Capitals	AHL	68	4	17	21	....	....	....	61	8	0	2	2	11
1950-51	**Detroit Red Wings**	**NHL**	**33**	**3**	**1**	**4**	**4**	**1**	**5**	**14**	....	....	....	....	....
	Indianapolis Capitals	AHL	30	2	10	12	....	....	....	35	3	0	1	1	4
1951-52	**Chicago Black Hawks**	**NHL**	**35**	**0**	**5**	**5**	**0**	**6**	**6**	**28**	....	....	....	....	....
	St. Louis Flyers	AHL	30	2	12	14	....	....	....	42	....	....	....	....	....
1952-53	**Chicago Black Hawks**	**NHL**	**32**	**1**	**3**	**4**	**2**	**4**	**6**	**10**	**3**	**0**	**0**	**0**	**0**
	Edmonton Flyers	WHL	18	3	2	5	....	....	....	38	....	....	....	....	....
1953-54	Quebec Aces	QHL	63	10	12	22	....	....	....	86	21	0	3	3	23
1954-55	Buffalo Bisons	AHL	57	5	8	13	....	....	....	92	10	0	4	4	14
1955-56	Buffalo Bisons	AHL	43	2	18	20	....	....	....	48	3	0	1	1	6
1956-57	Vancouver Canucks	WHL	18	2	3	5	....	....	....	16	....	....	....	....	....
1957-58	Saskatoon–Vancouver	WHL	50	4	13	17	....	....	....	50	....	....	....	....	....
1958-59	Belleville McFarlands	EOHL	22	0	9	9	....	....	....	26	....	....	....	....	....
	Kingston CKLC's	EOHL	30	4	24	28	....	....	....	44	12	0	5	5	6
1959-60	Washington Presidents	EHL	49	3	12	15	....	....	....	41	....	....	....	....	....
1960-61	Windsor Bulldogs	OHA Sr.	8	1	4	5	....	....	....	20	....	....	....	....	....
	NHL Totals		**100**	**4**	**9**	**13**	**6**	**11**	**17**	**52**	**3**	**0**	**0**	**0**	**0**

Traded to **Chicago** by **Detroit** with George Gee, Jimmy Peters Sr., Clare Martin, Max McNab and Jim McFadden for Hugh Coflin and $75,000, August 20, 1951.

• RALEIGH, DON   Don "Bones" Raleigh
C – L. 5'11", 150 lbs.   b: Kenora, Ont., 6/27/1926.

Season	Club	League	GP	G	A	Pts	AG	AA	APts	PIM	GP	G	A	Pts	PIM
1942-43	Winnipeg Monarchs	MJHL	12	8	1	9	....	....	....	0	2	1	1	2	0
1943-44	**New York Rangers**	**NHL**	**15**	**2**	**2**	**4**	**2**	**2**	**4**	**2**	....	....	....	....	....
	Brooklyn Crescents	EHL	26	23	20	43	....	....	....	6	11	*16	9	25	4
1944-45	Winnipeg Monarchs	MJHL	5	14	9	23	....	....	....	2	7	5	7	12	10
	Winnipeg Army	City Sr.	4	3	1	4	....	....	....	0	2	1	2	3	0
1945-46	Brandon Elks	MJHL	10	*24	*24	*48	....	....	....	2	7	7	11	18	18
1946-47	University of Manitoba	WCIAU	3	8	6	14	....	....	....	2	....	....	....	....	....
	Winnipeg Flyers	City Sr.	3	4	1	5	....	....	....	0	4	3	*15	*18	0
1947-48	**New York Rangers**	**NHL**	**52**	**15**	**18**	**33**	**22**	**26**	**48**	**2**	**6**	**2**	**0**	**2**	**2**
1948-49	**New York Rangers**	**NHL**	**41**	**10**	**16**	**26**	**16**	**25**	**41**	**8**	....	....	....	....	....
1949-50	**New York Rangers**	**NHL**	**70**	**12**	**25**	**37**	**16**	**32**	**48**	**11**	**12**	**4**	**5**	**9**	**4**
1950-51	**New York Rangers**	**NHL**	**64**	**15**	**24**	**39**	**20**	**31**	**51**	**18**	....	....	....	....	....
	New York Rovers	EHL	2	0	0	0	....	....	....	0	....	....	....	....	....
1951-52	**New York Rangers**	**NHL**	**70**	**19**	**42**	**61**	**27**	**55**	**82**	**14**	....	....	....	....	....
1952-53	**New York Rangers**	**NHL**	**55**	**4**	**18**	**22**	**6**	**25**	**31**	**2**	....	....	....	....	....
1953-54	**New York Rangers**	**NHL**	**70**	**15**	**30**	**45**	**23**	**41**	**64**	**16**	....	....	....	....	....
1954-55	**New York Rangers**	**NHL**	**69**	**8**	**32**	**40**	**12**	**41**	**53**	**19**	....	....	....	....	....
1955-56	**New York Rangers**	**NHL**	**29**	**1**	**12**	**13**	**1**	**15**	**16**	**4**	....	....	....	....	....
	Providence Reds	AHL	13	4	20	24		....	....	0	....	....	....	....	....
	Saskatoon Quakers	WHL	25	17	19	36	....	....	....	2	3	1	1	2	2
1956-57	Brandon Regals	WHL	68	13	47	60	....	....	....	14	9	0	3	3	0
1957-58	Saskatoon Quakers	WHL	40	10	23	33	....	....	....	8	....	....	....	....	....
	NHL Totals		**535**	**101**	**219**	**320**	**145**	**293**	**438**	**96**	**18**	**6**	**5**	**11**	**6**

Played in NHL All-Star Game (1951, 1954)

• RAMSAY, BEATTIE   Beattie Ramsay
D – L. 5'7", 143 lbs.   b: Lumsden, Sask., 12/12/1895.   Deceased.

Season	Club	League	GP	G	A	Pts	AG	AA	APts	PIM	GP	G	A	Pts	PIM
1919-20	University of Toronto	OHA Sr.	6	3	2	5	....	....	....	....	6	4	*4	8	....
1920-21	University of Toronto	OHA Sr.	10	5	4	9	....	....	....	....	8	6	3	9	....
1921-22	University of Toronto	OHA Sr.	10	11	4	15	....	....	....	....	....	....	....	....	....
1922-23	Toronto Granites	OHA Sr.	....	....	....	....	....	....	....	....	8	3	3	6	0
1923-24	Toronto Granites	OHA Sr.	12	7	7	14	....	....	....	....	....	....	....	....	....
	Canada	Olympics	5	9	6	15	....	....	....	....	....	....	....	....	....
1924-25	Princeton University	Ivy	DID NOT PLAY – COACHING												
1925-26	Princeton University	Ivy	DID NOT PLAY – COACHING												
1926-27	Princeton University	Ivy	DID NOT PLAY – COACHING												
1927-28	**Toronto Maple Leafs**	**NHL**	**43**	**0**	**2**	**2**	**0**	**17**	**17**	**10**	....	....	....	....	....
1928-29	Yorkton Terriers	SSHL	DID NOT PLAY – COACHING												
	NHL Totals		**43**	**0**	**2**	**2**	**0**	**17**	**17**	**10**	....	....	....	....	....

Signed as a free agent by **Toronto**, November 12, 1927.

• RAMSAY, LES   Les Ramsay
LW – L. 5'9", 155 lbs.   b: Verdun, Quebec, 7/1/1920.

Season	Club	League	GP	G	A	Pts	AG	AA	APts	PIM	GP	G	A	Pts	PIM
1936-37	Verdun Maple Leafs	Mtl-Jr.	11	1	5	6	....	....	....	6	....	....	....	....	....
	Verdun Sr. Maple Leafs	Mtl-Sr.	4	1	0	1	....	....	....	0	....	....	....		
1937-38	Verdun Maple Leafs	Mtl Jr.	9	2	5	7	....	....	....	12	....	....	....		....
	Verdun Sr. Maple Leafs	Mtl-Sr.	7	3	1	4	....	....	....	2	5	0	1	1	10
1938-39	Verdun Maple Leafs	Mtl Jr.	11	2	10	12	....	....	....	31	10	6	*5	*11	10
	Verdun Maple Leafs	Mtl-Sr.	1	0	0	0	....	....	....	0	....	....	....	....	....
1939-40	Washington Eagles	EHL	61	25	52	77	....	....	....	24	3	2	1	3	0
1940-41	Montreal Sr. Canadiens	QSHL	34	16	23	39	....	....	....	30	....	....	....		....
1941-42	Montreal Sr. Canadians	QSHL	28	8	12	20	....	....	....	16	6	1	2	3	12
	Glace Bay Miners	CBSHL	10	7	2	9	....	....	....	38	....	....	....	....	....
1942-43	Ottawa Flyers	City Sr.	18	11	16	27	....	....	....	33	8	8	5	13	2
1943-44	Ottawa Commandos	QSHL	7	2	1	3	....	....	....	8	....	....	....	....	....
1944-45	**Chicago Black Hawks**	**NHL**	**11**	**2**	**2**	**4**	**3**	**3**	**6**	**2**	....	....	....	....	....
	Ottawa Commandos	QSHL	9	5	5	10	....	....	....	6		....	....	....	....
1945-46	Hull Volants	QSHL	13	2	6	8	....	....	....	8	....	....	....	....	....
	Lachine Rapides	QPHL	29	4	21	25	....	....	....	20	4	1	2	3	6
1946-47	Lachine Rapides	QPHL	50	22	41	63	....	....	....	44	11	3	4	7	6
1947-48	Moncton Hawks	MMHL	46	20	32	52	....	....	....	21	11	5	3	8	2
1948-49	Moncton Hawks	MMHL	5	2	1	3	....	....	....	2	....	....	....	....	....
	Glace Bay Miners	CBSHL	3	2	2	4	....	....	....	2	....	....	....	....	....
	Antigonish Bulldogs	CBSHL	STATISTICS NOT AVAILABLE												
1949-50	Plouefe Raftsmen	QPHL	STATISTICS NOT AVAILABLE												
1950-51	Saint John Beavers	MMHL	7	5	2	7		....	....	0	7	1	2	3	0
	NHL Totals		**11**	**2**	**2**	**4**	**3**	**3**	**6**	**2**	....	....	....	....	....

• RANDALL, KEN   Ken Randall
RW/D – R. 5'10", 180 lbs.   b: Kingston, Ont..   Deceased.

Season	Club	League	GP	G	A	Pts	AG	AA	APts	PIM	GP	G	A	Pts	PIM
1909-10	Brantford Professionals	OPHL	10	10	0	10	....	....	....	....	....	....	....	....	....
1910-11	Port Hope Professionals	EOPHL	6	*19	0	*19	....	....	....	....	2	*4	0	*4	....
1911-12	Montreal Wanderers	NHA	1	0	0	0	....	....	....	0	....	....	....	....	....
1912-13	Toronto Blueshirts	NHA	2	0	0	0	....	....	....	0	....	....	....	....	....
	Sydney Millionaires	MPHL	12	17	0	17	....	....	....	18	2	1	0	1	0
1913-14	Sydney Millionaires	MPHL	24	28	0	28	....	....	....	68	2	*5	0	*5	8
1914-15	Sydney Millionaires	MPHL	8	*11	0	*11	....	....	....	17	....	....	....	....	....
1915-16	Toronto Blueshirts	NHA	24	7	5	12	....	....	....	111	....	....	....	....	....
1916-17	Toronto Blueshirts	NHA	13	10	0	10	....	....	....	42	....	....	....	....	....
	Montreal Wanderers	NHA	5	2	0	2	....	....	....	39	....	....	....	....	....
1917-18	**Toronto Arenas**	**NHL**	**19**	**12**	**2**	**14**	**30**	**0**	**30**	**96**	**7**	**2**	**1**	**3**	***33**
1918-19	**Toronto Arenas**	**NHL**	**15**	**9**	**6**	**15**	**32**	**58**	**90**	**47**	....	....	....	....	....
1919-20	**Toronto St. Pats**	**NHL**	**22**	**10**	**8**	**18**	**23**	**55**	**78**	**42**	....	....	....	....	....
1920-21	**Toronto St. Pats**	**NHL**	**22**	**6**	**5**	**11**	**15**	**44**	**59**	**74**	**2**	**0**	**0**	**0**	**11**
1921-22	**Toronto St. Pats**	**NHL**	**24**	**10**	**6**	**16**	**27**	**38**	**65**	**32**	**6**	**2**	**0**	**2**	**23**
1922-23	**Toronto St. Pats**	**NHL**	**24**	**3**	**5**	**8**	**10**	**45**	**55**	**51**	....	....	....	....	....
1923-24	**Hamilton Tigers**	**NHL**	**24**	**7**	**1**	**8**	**29**	**17**	**46**	**18**	....	....	....	....	....
1924-25	**Hamilton Tigers**	**NHL**	**30**	**8**	**0**	**8**	**27**	**0**	**27**	**49**	....	....	....	....	....
1925-26	**New York Americans**	**NHL**	**34**	**4**	**2**	**6**	**12**	**23**	**35**	**94**	....	....	....	....	....
1926-27	**New York Americans**	**NHL**	**3**	**0**	**0**	**0**	**0**	**0**	**0**	**0**	....	....	....	....	....
	Niagara Falls–Hamilton	Can-Pro	28	7	2	9	....	....	....	56	2	0	0	0	7
1927-28	Providence Reds	Can-Am	19	0	0	0	....	....	....	6	....	....	....	....	....
1928-29	New Haven Eagles	Can-Am	DID NOT PLAY – COACHING												
1929-30	Kitchener Dutchmen	Can-Pro	DID NOT PLAY – COACHING												
1930-31	Oshawa Patricians	OPHL	2	0	0	0	....	....	....	0	7	0	0	0	4
1931-32	Amherst Ramblers	NSSHL	DID NOT PLAY – COACHING												
	NHL Totals		**217**	**69**	**35**	**104**	**205**	**280**	**485**	**503**	**15**	**4**	**1**	**5**	**67**
	Other Major League Totals		91	74	5	79	....	....	....	278	4	6	0	6	8

Rights not retained by **Montreal Wanderers** after NHA folded, November 26, 1917. Signed as a free agent by **Toronto Areans**, December 9, 1918. Traded to **Hamilton** by **Toronto St. Pats** with cash for Amos Arbour, George Carey and Bert Corbeau, December 14, 1923. Transferred to **NY Americans** after NHL club purchased **Hamilton** franchise, September 26, 1925.

• RANIERI, GEORGE   George Ranieri
LW – L. 5'8", 190 lbs.   b: Toronto, Ont., 1/14/1936.

Season	Club	League	GP	G	A	Pts	AG	AA	APts	PIM	GP	G	A	Pts	PIM
1953-54	Hamilton Tiger Cubs	OHA	6	0	1	1	....	....	....	4	....	....	....	....	....
	Barrie Flyers	OHA	48	20	18	38	....	....	....	92	....	....	....	....	....
1954-55	Barrie Flyers	OHA	49	14	28	42	....	....	....	101	....	....	....	....	....
	Edmonton Flyers	WHL	2	0	0	0	....	....	....	0	....	....	....	....	....
1955-56	Barrie Flyers	OHA	48	29	28	57	....	....	....	74	18	6	*14	20	28
	Edmonton Flyers	WHL	2	0	1	1	....	....	....	8	....	....	....	....	....
1956-57	**Boston Bruins**	**NHL**	**2**	**0**	**0**	**0**	**0**	**0**	**0**	**0**	....	....	....	....	....
	Victoria Cougars	WHL	50	7	12	19	....	....	....	64	....	....	....	....	....
	Hershey Bears	AHL	4	1	0	1	....	....	....	0	....	....	....	....	....
1957-58	Quebec Aces	QHL	5	0	1	1	....	....	....	4	....	....	....	....	....
	Hershey Bears	AHL	8	0	2	2	....	....	....	4	....	....	....	....	....
	Louisville Rebels	IHL	52	25	19	44	....	....	....	64	11	3	5	8	22
1958-59	Louisville Rebels	IHL	59	*60	64	*124	....	....	....	64	11	11	13	24	6
1959-60	Louisville Rebels	IHL	8	8	4	12	....	....	....	18	....	....	....	....	....
	New York Rovers	EHL	64	35	45	80	....	....	....	45	....	....	....	....	....
1960-61	Providence Reds	AHL	72	30	41	71	....	....	....	30	....	....	....	....	....
1961-62	Providence Reds	AHL	49	21	22	43	....	....	....	38	....	....	....	....	....
1962-63	Providence Reds	AHL	58	21	23	44	....	....	....	52	6	1	1	2	2
1963-64	Providence Reds	AHL	54	20	26	46	....	....		38	....	....	....	....	....
1964-65	Providence Reds	AHL	61	18	22	40	....	....	....	38	....	....	....	....	....
	NHL Totals		**2**	**0**	**0**	**0**	**0**	**0**	**0**	**0**	....	....	....	....	....

IHL First All-Star Team (1959) • Won George H. Wilkinson Trophy (Top Scorer - IHL) (1959)

• RATELLE, JEAN   *— see page 1411*

• RAVLICH, MATT   *— see page 1413*

• RAYMOND, ARMAND   Armand Raymond
D – L. 5'9", 185 lbs.   b: Mechanicsville, NY, 1/12/1913.   Deceased.

Season	Club	League	GP	G	A	Pts	AG	AA	APts	PIM	GP	G	A	Pts	PIM
1931-32	St. Francis Xavier	Mtl-Jr.	10	0	0	0	....	....	....	8	2	0	0	0	8
1932-33	St. Francis Xavier	Mtl-Jr.	10	1	0	1	....	....	....	15	2	0	0	0	2
1933-34	St. Francis Xavier	Mtl-Jr.	7	1	1	2	....	....	....	20	....	....	....	....	....
	St. Francis Xavier	Mtl-Sr.	13	2	0	2	....	....	....	*36	....	....	....	....	....
1934-35			DID NOT PLAY												
1935-36	Atlantic City Seagulls	EHL	21	0	4	4	....	....	....	14	8	1	1	2	6
1936-37	Montreal Sr. Canadiens	QSHL	21	3	3	6	....	....	....	30	2	0	0	0	4
1937-38	**Montreal Canadiens**	**NHL**	**11**	**0**	**1**	**1**	**0**	**2**	**2**	**10**	....	....	....	....	....
	Montreal Concordia	QSHL	21	6	7	13	....	....	....	32	1	0	0	0	2
1938-39	Montreal Concordia	QSHL	STATISTICS NOT AVAILABLE												
1939-40	**Montreal Canadiens**	**NHL**	**11**	**0**	**1**	**1**	**0**	**2**	**2**	**0**	....	....	....	....	....
	Providence Reds	AHL	22	0	4	4	....	....	....	14	....	....	....	....	....
1940-41	St. Jerome Papermakers	Mtl-Sr.	33	18	20	38	....	....	....	86	12	2	5	7	14
1941-42	Shawinigan Cataracts	Mtl-Sr	28	1	21	22	....	....	....	40	10	1	1	2	12
	NHL Totals		**22**	**0**	**2**	**2**	**0**	**4**	**4**	**10**	....	....	....	....	....

• RAYMOND, PAUL Paul Raymond

RW – R. 5'8", 150 lbs. b: Montreal, Que., 2/27/1913. d: 4/4/1995.

			REGULAR SEASON								PLAYOFFS				
Season	Club	League	GP	G	A	Pts	AG	AA	APts	PIM	GP	G	A	Pts	PIM
1930-31	Montreal Jr. Canadiens	City Jr.	4	2	1	3	....	....	....	2	....	....	....	....	....
1931-32	Montreal Sr. Canadiens	City Sr.	11	5	4	9	....	....	....	8	2	2	0	2	0
1932-33	**Montreal Canadiens**	**NHL**	**16**	**0**	**0**	**0**	**0**	**0**	**0**	**0**	....	....	....	....	....
	Providence Reds	IAHL	20	1	5	6	....	....	....	0	2	0	0	0	0
1933-34	**Montreal Canadiens**	**NHL**	**29**	**1**	**0**	**1**	**2**	**0**	**2**	**2**	**2**	**0**	**0**	**0**	**0**
	Windsor Bulldogs	IAHL	20	1	1	2	....	....	....	6	....	....	....	....	....
1934-35	**Montreal Canadiens**	**NHL**	**20**	**1**	**1**	**2**	**2**	**2**	**4**	**0**	....	....	....	....	....
	Quebec Beavers	Can-Am	30	9	12	21	....	....	....	24	3	0	0	0	4
1935-36	Springfield Indians	Can-Am	48	6	27	33	....	....	....	55	3	2	1	3	0
1936-37	Springfield Indians	AHL	41	11	15	26	....	....	....	49	5	0	2	2	0
1937-38	Springfield–New Haven	AHL	47	10	18	28	....	....	....	14	2	0	0	0	0
1938-39	**Montreal Canadiens**	**NHL**	**11**	**0**	**2**	**2**	**0**	**4**	**4**	**4**	**3**	**0**	**0**	**0**	**2**
	New Haven Eagles	AHL	51	2	5	7	....	....	....	22	....	....	....	....	....
1939-40	Montreal Royals	City Sr.	26	6	27	33	....	....	....	12	11	5	*12	17	0
1940-41	Montreal Royals	City Sr.	33	13	19	32	....	....	....	31	14	1	4	5	6
1941-42	Montreal Royals	City Sr.	38	17	18	35	....	....	....	24	....	....	....	....	....
1942-43	Montreal Royals	City Sr.	5	0	0	0	....	....	....	8	....	....	....	....	....
1943-44			MILITARY SERVICE												
1944-45			MILITARY SERVICE												
1945-46	Montreal Royals	QSHL	26	8	14	22	....	....	....	6	9	2	6	8	6
1946-47	Montreal Royals	QSHL	2	0	1	1	....	....	....	0	....	....	....	....	....
	Lachine Rapides	QPHL	26	9	15	24	....	....	....	13	9	1	1	2	2
	NHL Totals		**76**	**2**	**3**	**5**	**4**	**6**	**10**	**6**	**5**	**0**	**0**	**0**	**2**

Signed as a free agent by **Montreal Canadiens**, October 28, 1932. Traded to **New Haven** (AHL) by **Springfield** (AHL) for Max Kaminsky, December 23, 1937. Signed as a free agent by **Montreal Canadiens**, February 21, 1938.

• READ, MEL Mel "Pee Wee" Read

C – L. 5'8", 165 lbs. b: Montreal, Que., 4/10/1924.

			REGULAR SEASON								PLAYOFFS				
Season	Club	League	GP	G	A	Pts	AG	AA	APts	PIM	GP	G	A	Pts	PIM
1940-41	Verdun Maple Leafs	Mtl-Jr.	12	7	8	15	....	....	....	2	2	0	0	0	0
	Verdun Sr. Maple Leafs	Mtl-Sr.	1	0	0	0	....	....	....	0	....	....	....	....	....
1941-42	Cornwall Flyers	Mtl-Sr.	40	11	10	21	....	....	....	14	5	0	0	0	4
1942-43	Montreal Sr. Canadiens	City Sr.	22	7	7	14	....	....	....	4	....	....	....	....	....
	Montreal Navy	City Sr.	11	12	*13	*25	....	....	....	4	6	*7	3	10	4
1944-45	Montreal Royals	QSHL	12	4	3	7	....	....	....	9	3	0	1	1	0
1945-46	Dallas Texans	USHL	56	*39	53	92	....	....	....	28	....	....	....	....	....
1946-47	**New York Rangers**	**NHL**	**1**	**0**	**0**	**0**	**0**	**0**	**0**	**0**	....	....	....	....	....
	New Haven Ramblers	AHL	59	13	27	40	....	....	....	42	3	1	2	3	2
1947-48	St. Paul Saints	USHL	62	19	30	49	....	....	....	36	....	....	....	....	....
1948-49	Shawinigan Cataracts	QSHL	1	0	1	1	....	....	....	0	....	....	....	....	....
	Tacoma Rockets	PCHL	70	27	43	70	....	....	....	41	6	2	5	7	0
1949-50	Tacoma Rockets	PCHL	70	20	*67	87	....	....	....	23	5	3	3	6	0
1950-51	Tacoma Rockets	PCHL	70	22	42	64	....	....	....	18	6	1	2	3	2
1951-52	Shawinigan Cataracts	QSHL	58	7	23	30	....	....	....	8	....	....	....	....	....
	NHL Totals		**1**	**0**	**0**	**0**	**0**	**0**	**0**	**0**	....	....	....	....	....

USHL Second All-Star Team (1946) • PCHL Northern First All-Star Team (1950)

• REARDON, KEN Ken Reardon HHOF

D – L. 5'10", 180 lbs. b: Winnipeg, Man., 4/1/1921.

			REGULAR SEASON								PLAYOFFS				
Season	Club	League	GP	G	A	Pts	AG	AA	APts	PIM	GP	G	A	Pts	PIM
1937-38	Winnipeg Monarchs	City Jr.	STATISTICS NOT AVAILABLE												
1938-39	Edmonton Athletic Club	City Jr.	5	0	1	1	....	....	....	8	....	....	....	....	....
1939-40	Edmonton Athletic Club	City Jr.	STATISTICS NOT AVAILABLE												
1940-41	**Montreal Canadiens**	**NHL**	**34**	**2**	**8**	**10**	**4**	**15**	**19**	**41**	**3**	**0**	**0**	**0**	**4**
1941-42	**Montreal Canadiens**	**NHL**	**41**	**3**	**12**	**15**	**5**	**18**	**23**	**93**	**3**	**0**	**0**	**0**	**4**
1942-43	Ottawa Commandos	QSHL	26	7	16	23	....	....	....	77	23	3	9	12	*47
	Ottawa Army	City Sr.	10	10	7	17	....	....	....	15	....	....	....	....	....
	Ottawa Army	City Sr.	10	10	7	17	....	....	....	15	....	....	....	....	....
1943-44	Ottawa Commandos	QSHL	1	1	0	1	....	....	....	0	....	....	....	....	....
1944-45			MILITARY SERVICE												
1945-46	**Montreal Canadiens**	**NHL**	**43**	**5**	**4**	**9**	**8**	**7**	**15**	**45**	**9**	**1**	**1**	**2**	**4**
	Montreal Royals	QSHL	2	0	0	0	....	....	....	4	....	....	....	....	....
1946-47	**Montreal Canadiens**	**NHL**	**52**	**5**	**17**	**22**	**7**	**24**	**31**	**84**	**7**	**1**	**2**	**3**	**20**
1947-48	**Montreal Canadiens**	**NHL**	**58**	**7**	**15**	**22**	**10**	**22**	**32**	**129**	....	....	....	....	....
1948-49	**Montreal Canadiens**	**NHL**	**46**	**3**	**13**	**16**	**5**	**21**	**26**	**103**	**7**	**0**	**0**	**0**	**18**
1949-50	**Montreal Canadiens**	**NHL**	**67**	**1**	**27**	**28**	**1**	**34**	**35**	**109**	**2**	**0**	**2**	**2**	**12**
	NHL Totals		**341**	**26**	**96**	**122**	**40**	**141**	**181**	**604**	**31**	**2**	**5**	**7**	**62**

NHL Second All-Star Team (1946, 1948, 1949) • NHL First All-Star Team (1947, 1950)

Played in NHL All-Star Game (1947, 1948, 1949)

Signed as a free agent by **Montreal**, October 26, 1940.

• REARDON, TERRY Terry Reardon

C/RW – R. 5'10", 170 lbs. b: Winnipeg, Man., 4/6/1919. d: 2/14/1993.

			REGULAR SEASON								PLAYOFFS				
Season	Club	League	GP	G	A	Pts	AG	AA	APts	PIM	GP	G	A	Pts	PIM
1935-36	St. Boniface Seals	City Jr.	13	9	3	12	....	....	....	4	....	....	....	....	....
1936-37	St. Boniface Seals	City Jr.	16	*22	10	32	....	....	....	27	7	*8	2	*10	*17
1937-38	Brandon Wheat Kings	City Jr.	16	*29	*16	*45	....	....	....	20	5	5	1	6	6
1938-39	**Boston Bruins**	**NHL**	**4**	**0**	**0**	**0**	**0**	**0**	**0**	**0**	....	....	....	....	....
	Hershey Bears	AHL	50	7	20	27	....	....	....	31	5	1	0	1	2
1939-40	Hershey Bears	AHL	55	13	24	37	....	....	....	26	4	4	0	4	2
	Boston Bruins	**NHL**	....	....	....	....	....	....	....	....	**1**	**0**	**1**	**1**	**0**
1940-41	**Boston Bruins**	**NHL**	**34**	**6**	**5**	**11**	**12**	**9**	**21**	**19**	**11**	**2**	**4**	**6**	**6**
	Hershey Bears	AHL	19	3	8	11	....	....	....	10	....	....	....	....	....
1941-42	**Montreal Canadiens**	**NHL**	**33**	**17**	**17**	**34**	**29**	**26**	**55**	**14**	**3**	**2**	**2**	**4**	**2**
1942-43	**Montreal Canadiens**	**NHL**	**13**	**6**	**6**	**12**	**8**	**8**	**16**	**2**	....	....	....	....	....
	Montreal Army	QSHL	19	7	17	24	....	....	....	6	7	4	2	6	2
1943-44	Nanaimo Army	PCHL	11	6	7	13	....	....	....	12	....	....	....	....	....
1944-45			MILITARY SERVICE												
1945-46	**Boston Bruins**	**NHL**	**49**	**12**	**11**	**23**	**18**	**20**	**38**	**21**	**10**	**4**	**0**	**4**	**2**
1946-47	**Boston Bruins**	**NHL**	**60**	**6**	**14**	**20**	**8**	**20**	**28**	**17**	**5**	**0**	**3**	**3**	**2**
1947-48	Providence Reds	AHL	49	4	10	14	....	....	....	28	5	2	1	3	10
1948-49	Providence Reds	AHL	68	2	10	12	....	....	....	16	14	4	1	5	2
1949-50	Providence Reds	AHL	61	2	9	11	....	....	....	9	1	0	0	0	12
1950-51	Providence Reds	AHL	46	5	16	21	....	....	....	12	....	....	....	....	....
1951-52	Providence Reds	AHL	19	2	6	8	....	....	....	16	11	0	7	7	12
1952-53	Providence Reds	AHL	15	0	2	2	....	....	....	6	....	....	....	....	....
1953-54	Sydney Millionaires	MMHL	58	6	25	31	....	....	....	32	13	0	4	4	2
1954-55	Providence Reds	AHL	15	1	8	9	....	....	....	2	....	....	....	....	....
	NHL Totals		**193**	**47**	**53**	**100**	**75**	**83**	**158**	**73**	**30**	**8**	**10**	**18**	**12**

Rights traded to **Boston** by **NY Americans** with Tom Cooper to complete transaction that sent Joe Jerwa to Boston (January 25, 1937), October 17, 1937. Loaned to **Montreal** by **Boston** for the loan of Paul Gauthier, June 27, 1941.

• REAUME, MARC — *see page 1414*

• REAY, BILLY Billy Reay

C – L. 5'7", 155 lbs. b: Winnipeg, Man., 8/21/1918.

			REGULAR SEASON								PLAYOFFS				
Season	Club	League	GP	G	A	Pts	AG	AA	APts	PIM	GP	G	A	Pts	PIM
1936-37	St. Boniface Seals	City Jr.	15	4	4	8	....	....	....	6	7	1	0	1	2
1937-38	St. Boniface Seals	City Jr.	15	15	7	22	....	....	....	14	10	5	5	10	12
1938-39	Winnipeg Hudson's Bay	City Sr.	8	5	3	8	....	....	....	4	....	....	....	....	....
	Calgary Stampeders	City Sr.	32	11	8	19	....	....	....	44	....	....	....	....	....
1939-40	Omaha Knights	AHA	48	18	20	38	....	....	....	23	9	*6	1	7	4
1940-41	Omaha Knights	AHA	46	18	22	40	....	....	....	32	....	....	....	....	....
1941-42	Quebec Aces	QSHL	1	1	0	1	....	....	....	0	15	6	10	16	22
1942-43	Quebec Aces	QSHL	29	16	26	42	....	....	....	22	4	2	0	2	2
1943-44	**Detroit Red Wings**	**NHL**	**2**	**2**	**0**	**2**	**2**	**0**	**2**	**0**	....	....	....	....	....
	Quebec Aces	QSHL	25	15	*31	46	....	....	....	19	14	5	16	21	2
1944-45	**Detroit Red Wings**	**NHL**	**2**	**0**	**0**	**0**	**0**	**0**	**0**	**0**	....	....	....	....	....
	Quebec Aces	QSHL	20	17	29	46	....	....	....	6	7	3	1	4	4
1945-46	**Montreal Canadiens**	**NHL**	**44**	**17**	**12**	**29**	**26**	**22**	**48**	**10**	**9**	**1**	**2**	**3**	**4**
1946-47	**Montreal Canadiens**	**NHL**	**59**	**22**	**20**	**42**	**30**	**29**	**59**	**17**	**11**	**6**	**1**	**7**	**14**
1947-48	**Montreal Canadiens**	**NHL**	**60**	**6**	**14**	**20**	**9**	**20**	**29**	**24**	....	....	....	....	....
1948-49	**Montreal Canadiens**	**NHL**	**60**	**22**	**23**	**45**	**35**	**37**	**72**	**33**	**7**	**1**	**5**	**6**	**4**
1949-50	**Montreal Canadiens**	**NHL**	**68**	**19**	**26**	**45**	**26**	**33**	**59**	**48**	**4**	**0**	**1**	**1**	**0**
1950-51	**Montreal Canadiens**	**NHL**	**60**	**6**	**18**	**24**	**8**	**23**	**31**	**24**	**11**	**3**	**3**	**6**	**10**
1951-52	**Montreal Canadiens**	**NHL**	**68**	**7**	**34**	**41**	**10**	**44**	**54**	**20**	**10**	**2**	**2**	**4**	**7**
1952-53	**Montreal Canadiens**	**NHL**	**56**	**4**	**15**	**19**	**6**	**21**	**27**	**26**	**11**	**0**	**2**	**2**	**4**
1953-54	Victoria Cougars	WHL	69	10	14	24	....	....	....	30	5	0	0	0	2
1954-55	Victoria Cougars	WHL	70	3	28	31	....	....	....	43	5	1	1	2	4
	NHL Totals		**479**	**105**	**162**	**267**	**152**	**229**	**381**	**202**	**63**	**13**	**16**	**29**	**43**

Won Vimy Trophy (MVP - QSHL) (1945)

Played in NHL All-Star Game (1952)

Signed as a free agent by **Detroit**, October 2, 1939. Traded to **Montreal** by **Detroit** for Ray Getliffe and Rolly Rossignol, September 11, 1945. Detroit received Fern Gauthier (October 18, 1945) as compensation after Getliffe decided to retire.

• REDAHL, GORD Gord Redahl

RW – L. 5'11", 170 lbs. b: Kinistino, Sask., 8/28/1935.

			REGULAR SEASON								PLAYOFFS				
Season	Club	League	GP	G	A	Pts	AG	AA	APts	PIM	GP	G	A	Pts	PIM
1952-53	Flin Flon Bombers	SJHL	1	0	0	0	....	....	....	0	....	....	....	....	....
1953-54	Flin Flon Bombers	SJHL	39	27	19	46	....	....	....	10	17	8	8	16	8
	Saskatoon Quakers	WHL	1	1	0	1	....	....	....	0	....	....	....	....	....
1954-55	Flin Flon Bombers	SJHL	45	33	23	56	....	....	....	49	5	2	1	3	4
1955-56	Flin Flon Bombers	SJHL	48	39	39	78	....	....	....	62	12	9	5	14	8
	Saskatoon Quakers	WHL	1	0	0	0	....	....	....	2	....	....	....	....	....
1956-57	Winnipeg Warriors	WHL	65	14	12	26	....	....	....	19	....	....	....	....	....
1957-58	Winnipeg Warriors	WHL	57	20	27	47	....	....	....	30	7	5	3	8	4
1958-59	**Boston Bruins**	**NHL**	**18**	**0**	**1**	**1**	**0**	**1**	**1**	**2**	....	....	....	....	....
	Providence–Rochester	AHL	31	4	2	6	....	....	....	13	....	....	....	....	....
1959-60	Winnipeg Warriors	WHL	70	24	22	46	....	....	....	20	....	....	....	....	....
1960-61	Winnipeg Warriors	WHL	67	19	24	43	....	....	....	19	....	....	....	....	....
1961-62	Pittsburgh Hornets	AHL	10	3	3	6	....	....	....	6	....	....	....	....	....
	San Francisco Seals	WHL	51	16	17	33	....	....	....	10	....	....	....	....	....
1962-63	Calgary Stampeders	WHL	55	14	25	39	....	....	....	10	....	....	....	....	....
	Pittsburgh Hornets	AHL	5	1	0	1	....	....	....	2	....	....	....	....	....
1963-64	Denver Invaders	WHL	69	25	33	58	....	....	....	24	6	2	4	6	4
1964-65	Victoria Maple Leafs	WHL	70	32	29	61	....	....	....	22	12	3	4	7	6
1965-66	Victoria Maple Leafs	WHL	66	23	26	49	....	....	....	12	14	3	3	6	2
1966-67	Rochester Americans	AHL	6	0	3	3	....	....	....	0	....	....	....	....	....
	Victoria Cougars	WHL	41	9	10	19	....	....	....	12	5	0	1	1	0
1967-68	Phoenix Roadrunners	WHL	52	16	16	32	....	....	....	10	4	0	0	0	0
1968-69	Denver Spurs	WHL	65	18	17	35	....	....	....	18	....	....	....	....	....
1969-70	Denver Spurs	WHL	14	0	3	3	....	....	....	0	....	....	....	....	....
	NHL Totals		**18**	**0**	**1**	**1**	**0**	**1**	**1**	**2**	....	....	....	....	....

Claimed by **Boston** from **Winnipeg** (WHL) in Inter-League Draft, June 3, 1958. Traded to **Toronto** (Rochester - AHL) by **Boston** (Providence - AHL) for cash, November, 1958. Traded to **Pittsburgh** (AHL) by **San Francisco** (WHL) for Bob Bailey, February 27, 1962. Claimed by **Toronto** from **Denver** (WHL) in Inter-League Draft, June, 1964. Traded to **Denver** (WHL) by **Toronto** for cash, July, 1968.

• REDDING, GEORGE George "Shorty" Redding

LW/D – L. 5'7", 145 lbs. b: Peterborough, Ont., 3/6/1903. Deceased.

Season	Club	League	GP	G	A	Pts	AG	AA	APts	PIM	Playoffs GP	G	A	Pts	PIM
1921-22	Hamilton Tigers	OHA Sr.	10	1	4	5									
1922-23	Hamilton Tigers	OHA Sr.	11	0	1	1					2	0	0	0	2
1923-24	Hamilton Tigers	OHA Sr.	10	4	4	8					2	0	0	0	
1924-25	**Boston Bruins**	**NHL**	**27**	**3**	**2**	**5**	**10**	**26**	**36**	**10**					
1925-26	**Boston Bruins**	**NHL**	**8**	**0**	**0**	**0**	**0**	**0**	**0**	**0**					
1926-27	Boston Tigers	Can-Am	31	7	0	7				39					
1927-28	Boston Tigers	Can-Am	39	7	3	10				48	2	1	0	1	2
1928-29	London Panthers	Can-Pro	33	0	0	0				60					
1929-30	Minneapolis Millers	AHA	47	4	3	7				64					
1930-31	Minneapolis Millers	AHA	43	9	3	12				73					
1931-32	Buffalo Majors	AHA	13	0	2	2				8					
1932-33	Hamilton Pats	OHA Sr.	DID NOT PLAY – COACHING												
	NHL Totals		**35**	**3**	**2**	**5**	**10**	**26**	**36**	**10**					

Signed as a free agent by **Boston**, October 16, 1924. Traded to **Minneapolis** (AHA) by **London** (IAHL) for Babe Donnelly, October 24, 1929.

• REGAN, BILL Bill Regan

D – L. 6'1", 190 lbs. b: Creighton Mines, Ont., 12/11/1908. Deceased.

Season	Club	League	GP	G	A	Pts	AG	AA	APts	PIM	Playoffs GP	G	A	Pts	PIM
1925-26	St. Michael's Majors	OHA	5	2	1	3									
1926-27	St. Michael's Majors	OHA	1	0	0	0					6	4	1	5	
1927-28	St. Michael's Majors	OHA	6	12	3	15					6	2	2	4	
1928-29	St. Michael's Majors	OHA	6	3	4	7									
1929-30	**New York Rangers**	**NHL**	**10**	**0**	**0**	**0**	**0**	**0**	**0**	**4**	**4**	**0**	**0**	**0**	**0**
	Boston Tigers	Can-Am	28	6	5	11				45					
1930-31	**New York Rangers**	**NHL**	**42**	**2**	**1**	**3**	**5**	**4**	**9**	**49**	**4**	**0**	**0**	**0**	**2**
1931-32	Bronx Tigers	Can-Am	40	5	10	15				106	2	0	0	0	6
1932-33	Springfield Indians	Can-Am	13	1	2	3				30					
	New York Americans	**NHL**	**15**	**1**	**1**	**2**	**2**	**3**	**5**	**14**					
	New Haven Eagles	Can-Am	15	7	3	10				32					
1933-34	Buffalo–Cleveland	IAHL	45	9	13	22				85					
1934-35			DID NOT PLAY												
1935-36			DID NOT PLAY												
1936-37	Creighton Mines	NOHA	13	2	0	2				34	2	0	0	0	*8
	Sudbury Frood Miners	NOHA									6	1	1	2	4
	NHL Totals		**67**	**3**	**2**	**5**	**7**	**7**	**14**	**67**	**8**	**0**	**0**	**0**	**2**

Traded to **NY Rangers** by **Boston** for Harry Foster and $15,000, February 17, 1930. Loaned to **NY Americans** by **NY Rangers** for remainder of 1932-33 season, December 27, 1932.

• REGAN, LARRY Larry Regan

RW – R. 5'9", 162 lbs. b: North Bay, Ont., 8/9/1930.

Season	Club	League	GP	G	A	Pts	AG	AA	APts	PIM	Playoffs GP	G	A	Pts	PIM
1946-47	Ottawa Jr. Senators	City Jr.	24	22	18	40				2	2	0	2	2	0
	Ottawa Senators	QSHL	3	1	0	1				0	3	0	0	0	0
1947-48	Ottawa Senators	QSHL	41	17	14	31				35	5	0	2	2	0
1948-49	Toronto Marlboros	OHA	40	19	15	34				25	10	4	2	6	0
1949-50	Toronto Marlboros	OHA	48	38	36	64				22	5	1	3	4	0
1950-51	Ottawa Senators	QSHL	52	14	31	45				28	9	0	3	3	0
1951-52	Ottawa Senators	QSHL	50	11	10	21				27	7	0	0	0	8
1952-53	Shawinigan Cataracts	QSHL	52	15	27	42				21					
1953-54	Quebec Aces	QHL	70	19	32	51				14	23	7	6	13	8
1954-55	Quebec Aces	QHL	51	11	30	41				39	8	1	2	3	6
1955-56	Quebec Aces	QHL	3	3	1	4				2	7	4	4	8	4
	Pembroke Lumber Kings	OVSHL	22	5	14	19				10					
1956-57	**Boston Bruins**	**NHL**	**69**	**14**	**19**	**33**	**19**	**22**	**41**	**29**	**8**	**0**	**2**	**2**	**10**
1957-58	**Boston Bruins**	**NHL**	**59**	**11**	**28**	**39**	**14**	**31**	**45**	**22**	**12**	**3**	**8**	**11**	**6**
1958-59	**Boston Bruins**	**NHL**	**36**	**5**	**6**	**11**	**6**	**6**	**12**	**10**					
	Toronto Maple Leafs	**NHL**	**32**	**4**	**21**	**25**	**5**	**22**	**27**	**2**	**8**	**1**	**1**	**2**	**2**
1959-60	**Toronto Maple Leafs**	**NHL**	**47**	**4**	**16**	**20**	**5**	**16**	**21**	**6**	**10**	**3**	**3**	**6**	**0**
1960-61	**Toronto Maple Leafs**	**NHL**	**37**	**3**	**5**	**8**	**4**	**5**	**9**	**2**	**4**	**0**	**0**	**0**	**0**
1961-62	Pittsburgh Hornets	AHL	49	10	19	29				12					
1962-63	Innsbruck	Austria	DID NOT PLAY – COACHING												
1963-64	Innsbruck	Austria	DID NOT PLAY – COACHING												
1964-65	Etobicoke Indians	Jr. B	DID NOT PLAY – COACHING												
1965-66	Baltimore Clippers	AHL	64	16	34	50				41					
	NHL Totals		**280**	**41**	**95**	**136**	**53**	**102**	**155**	**71**	**42**	**7**	**14**	**21**	**18**

Won Calder Memorial Trophy (1957)

Claimed by **Boston** from **Quebec** (QHL) in Inter-League Draft, June 5, 1956. Claimed on waivers by **Toronto** from **Boston**, January 7, 1959.

• REIBEL, EARL Earl "Dutch" Reibel

C – R. 5'8", 160 lbs. b: Kitchener, Ont., 7/21/1930.

Season	Club	League	GP	G	A	Pts	AG	AA	APts	PIM	Playoffs GP	G	A	Pts	PIM
1948-49	Kitchener Greenshirts	Jr. B	STATISTICS NOT AVAILABLE												
1949-50	Windsor Spitfires	OHA	48	53	*76	*129				14	11	7	*14	*21	2
1950-51	Omaha Knights	USHL	32	13	25	38				6	10	0	6	6	2
1951-52	Indianapolis Capitals	AHL	68	33	34	67				8					
1952-53	Edmonton Flyers	WHL	70	34	56	*90				14	12	6	6	12	4
1953-54	**Detroit Red Wings**	**NHL**	**69**	**15**	**33**	**48**	**23**	**45**	**68**	**18**	**9**	**1**	**3**	**4**	**0**
1954-55	**Detroit Red Wings**	**NHL**	**70**	**25**	**41**	**66**	**37**	**53**	**90**	**15**	**11**	**5**	**7**	**12**	**2**
1955-56	**Detroit Red Wings**	**NHL**	**68**	**17**	**39**	**56**	**25**	**49**	**74**	**10**	**10**	**0**	**2**	**2**	**2**
1956-57	**Detroit Red Wings**	**NHL**	**70**	**13**	**23**	**36**	**18**	**27**	**45**	**6**	**5**	**0**	**2**	**2**	**0**
1957-58	**Detroit Red Wings**	**NHL**	**29**	**4**	**5**	**9**	**5**	**5**	**10**	**4**					
	Chicago Black Hawks	**NHL**	**40**	**4**	**12**	**16**	**5**	**13**	**18**	**6**					
1958-59	**Boston Bruins**	**NHL**	**63**	**6**	**8**	**14**	**8**	**8**	**16**	**16**	**4**	**0**	**0**	**0**	**0**
1959-60	Providence Reds	AHL	69	20	46	66				6	5	0	1	1	0
1960-61	Providence Reds	AHL	43	7	18	25				2					
	NHL Totals		**409**	**84**	**161**	**245**	**121**	**200**	**321**	**75**	**39**	**6**	**14**	**20**	**4**

Won Dudley "Red" Garrett Memorial Award (Top Rookie - AHL) (1952) • WHL First All-Star Team (1953) • Won Lady Byng Trophy (1956)

Played in NHL All-Star Game (1954, 1955)

Traded to **Chicago** by **Detroit** with Bill Dea, Bill Dineen and Lorne Ferguson for Hec Lalande, Nick Mickoski, Bob Bailey and Jack McIntyre, December 17, 1957. Traded to **Boston** by **Chicago** for cash, June, 1958.

• REID, DAVE Dave Reid

C – L. 6'2", 180 lbs. b: Toronto, Ont., 1/11/1934.

Season	Club	League	GP	G	A	Pts	AG	AA	APts	PIM	Playoffs GP	G	A	Pts	PIM
1951-52	Weston Dukes	Jr. B	STATISTICS NOT AVAILABLE												
	Toronto Marlboros	OHA	3	2	2	4				0					
1952-53	**Toronto Maple Leafs**	**NHL**	**2**	**0**	**0**	**0**	**0**	**0**	**0**	**0**					
	Toronto Marlboros	OHA	52	12	19	31				29	7	0	1	1	4
1953-54	Toronto Marlboros	OHA	59	22	31	53				38	15	8	11	19	4
1954-55	**Toronto Maple Leafs**	**NHL**	**1**	**0**	**0**	**0**	**0**	**0**	**0**	**0**					
	University of Toronto	OQAA	STATISTICS NOT AVAILABLE												
1955-56	**Toronto Maple Leafs**	**NHL**	**4**	**0**	**0**	**0**	**0**	**0**	**0**	**0**					
	University of Toronto	OQAA	STATISTICS NOT AVAILABLE												
1956-57	Ottawa-Hull Canadiens	QHL	15	4	1	5				2					
	Ottawa-Hull Canadiens	EOHL	12	8	5	13				6					
	NHL Totals		**7**	**0**	**0**	**0**	**0**	**0**	**0**	**0**					

• REID, GERRY Gerry Reid

C – R. 6'1", 180 lbs. b: Owen Sound, Ont., 10/13/1928.

Season	Club	League	GP	G	A	Pts	AG	AA	APts	PIM	Playoffs GP	G	A	Pts	PIM
1946-47	Owen Sound Mercuries	OHA Sr.	12	6	8	14				0	6	4	4	8	0
1947-48	Barrie Flyers	OHA	36	28	34	62				10	20	*21	14	*35	14
1948-49	Indianapolis Capitals	AHL	68	31	47	78				18	2	0	0	0	2
	Detroit Red Wings	**NHL**									**2**	**0**	**0**	**0**	**2**
1949-50	Indianapolis Capitals	AHL	62	28	31	59				10	8	3	6	9	2
1950-51	Indianapolis Capitals	AHL	69	17	51	68				4	3	1	0	1	2
1951-52	Cleveland Barons	AHL	52	15	22	37				9	5	0	0	0	0
1952-53	Owen Sound Mercuries	OHA Sr.	21	15	20	35				4	11	7	3	10	0
1953-54	Owen Sound Mercuries	OHA Sr.	48	37	34	71				8	7	6	9	15	2
1954-55	Owen Sound Mercuries	OHA Sr.	50	24	33	57				10	5	2	3	5	0
1955-56	Owen Sound Mercuries	OHA Sr.	48	23	20	43				10	6	0	1	1	2
1956-57	Owen Sound Mercuries	OHA Sr.	52	20	29	49				10					
	NHL Totals		**0**	**0**	**0**	**0**	**0**	**0**	**0**	**0**	**2**	**0**	**0**	**0**	**2**

• REID, GORD Gord Reid

D – L. 5'10", 195 lbs. b: Mount Albert, Ont., 2/19/1912.

Season	Club	League	GP	G	A	Pts	AG	AA	APts	PIM	Playoffs GP	G	A	Pts	PIM
1933-34	Port Colborne Sailors	OHA Sr.	STATISTICS NOT AVAILABLE												
1934-35	New Haven Eagles	Can-Am	47	9	5	14				76					
1935-36	New Haven Eagles	Can-Am	48	3	9	12				*102					
1936-37	**New York Americans**	**NHL**	**1**	**0**	**0**	**0**	**0**	**0**	**0**	**2**					
	New Haven Eagles	AHL	40	0	4	4				54					
1937-38	New Haven Eagles	AHL	12	0	1	1				10					
	Kansas City Greyhounds	AHA	36	3	1	4				51					
1938-39	St. Paul Saints	AHA	46	3	4	7				50	3	0	0	0	2
1939-40	St. Paul Saints	AHA	47	4	19	23				56	7	1	0	1	12
1940-41	St. Paul Saints	AHA	40	3	4	7				30	4	0	0	0	0
1941-42	St. Paul Saints	AHA	50	4	7	11				51	2	1	0	1	5
1942-43	New Haven Eagles	AHL	18	1	2	3				10					
1943-44	Providence Reds	AHL	40	2	8	10				30					
	NHL Totals		**1**	**0**	**0**	**0**	**0**	**0**	**0**	**2**					

• REID, REG Reg "Rusty" Reid

LW – L. 5'8", 138 lbs. b: Seaforth, Ont., 2/17/1899. Deceased.

Season	Club	League	GP	G	A	Pts	AG	AA	APts	PIM	Playoffs GP	G	A	Pts	PIM
1924-25	**Toronto St. Pats**	**NHL**	**28**	**2**	**0**	**2**	**7**	**0**	**7**	**2**	**2**	**0**	**0**	**0**	**0**
1925-26	**Toronto St. Pats**	**NHL**	**12**	**0**	**0**	**0**	**0**	**0**	**0**	**2**					
1926-27	Stratford–Windsor	Can-Pro	26	8	3	11				4	1	0	0	0	0
1927-28	Stratford Nationals	Can-Pro	14	0	0	0				0					
1928-29			DID NOT PLAY – RETIRED												
1929-30			DID NOT PLAY – RETIRED												
1930-31	Stratford Nationals	OPHL	5	0	0	0				0					
	NHL Totals		**40**	**2**	**0**	**2**	**7**	**0**	**7**	**4**	**2**	**0**	**0**	**0**	**0**

Signed as a free agent by **Toronto St. Pats**, November 12, 1924.

• REIGLE, ED Ed "Rags" Reigle

D – L. 5'9", 180 lbs. b: Winnipeg, Man., 6/19/1924.

Season	Club	League	GP	G	A	Pts	AG	AA	APts	PIM	Playoffs GP	G	A	Pts	PIM
1940-41	East Kildonan Juniors	MJHL	1	0	0	0				2					
1941-42	East Kildonan Juniors	MJHL	18	4	7	11				29	2	1	0	1	4
1942-43	Oshawa Generals	OHA	22	4	6	10				28	10	4	3	7	21
1943-44			MILITARY SERVICE												
1944-45	Indianapolis Capitals	AHL	28	1	5	6				24	5	1	3	4	2
1945-46	Omaha Knights	USHL	46	12	11	23				100	7	0	4	4	7
	Indianapolis Capitals	AHL	7	0	3	3				7					
1946-47	Omaha Knights	USHL	19	0	0	0				22	11	1	1	2	2
	Detroit Metal Mouldings	IHL	4	1	0	1				2					
1947-48	Omaha Knights	USHL	53	16	17	33				58	3	0	0	0	*20
1948-49	Omaha Knights	USHL	62	9	25	34				109	4	0	0	0	2
1949-50	Cleveland Barons	AHL	62	5	20	25				62	9	0	4	4	16
1950-51	**Boston Bruins**	**NHL**	**17**	**0**	**2**	**2**	**0**	**3**	**3**	**25**					
	Hershey Bears	AHL	50	6	31	37				76	3	0	0	0	6
1951-52	Cleveland Barons	AHL	64	10	35	45				119	5	0	3	3	0
1952-53	Cleveland Barons	AHL	49	3	35	38				47					
1953-54	Cleveland Barons	AHL	68	10	26	36				95	7	1	4	5	8
1954-55	Cleveland Barons	AHL	62	7	30	37				90	4	0	1	1	2
1955-56	North Bay Trappers	NOHA	51	7	18	25				66	10	0	6	6	8
1956-57	North Bay Trappers	NOHA	54	8	22	30				62	13	3	5	8	16
	NHL Totals		**17**	**0**	**2**	**2**	**0**	**3**	**3**	**25**					

AHL Second All-Star Team (1952, 1953)

Traded to **Boston** by **Cleveland** (AHL) for cash, April 17, 1950. Traded to **NY Rangers** by **Boston** with Steve Kraftcheck for $30,000, May 14, 1951. Traded to **Cleveland** (AHL) by **NY Rangers** with Jack Gordon, Fred Shero, Fern Perreault and cash for Wally Hergesheimer and Hy Buller, May 14, 1951.

• REINIKKA, OLLIE

Ollie Reinikka

C/RW – R. 5'10", 160 lbs. b: Shuswap, B.C., 8/2/1901. Deceased.

Season	Club	League	GP	G	A	Pts	AG	AA	APts	PIM	GP	G	A	Pts	PIM
			REGULAR SEASON								PLAYOFFS				
1923-24	Canmore Roses	Edm-Sr.	STATISTICS NOT AVAILABLE												
1924-25	Vancouver Maroons	WCHL	19	1	0	1	....	....	....	4	....	....	....	....	....
1925-26	Vancouver Maroons	WHL	27	10	2	12	....	....	....	8	....	....	....	....	....
1926-27	**New York Rangers**	**NHL**	**16**	**0**	**0**	**0**	**0**	**0**	**0**	**0**	....	....	....	....	....
	Springfield Indians	Can-Am	16	0	0	0	....	....	....	10	4	1	0	1	4
1927-28	Stratford Nationals	Can-Pro	42	8	3	11	....	....	....	12	5	1	0	1	2
1928-29	Hamilton Tigers	Can-Pro	19	0	3	3	....	....	....	6	....	....	....	....	....
	Seattle Seahawks	PCHL	15	2	1	3	....	....	....	2	5	1	1	2	0
1929-30	Seattle Eskimos	PCHL	35	12	3	15	....	....	....	12	....	....	....	....	....
1930-31	London Tecumsehs	IAHL	44	7	5	12	....	....	....	19	....	....	....	....	....
1931-32	London Tecumsehs	IAHL	26	2	0	2	....	....	....	2	....	....	....	....	....
1932-33			DID NOT PLAY – RETIRED												
1933-34			DID NOT PLAY – RETIRED												
1934-35	Rossland Miners	Kootenay	16	6	8	14	....	....	....	3	2	0	1	1	2
1935-36	Rossland Miners	Kootenay	4	1	2	3	....	....	....	1	2	1	3	4	0
1936-37	Rossland Miners	Kootenay	14	1	7	8	....	....	....	6	....	....	....	....	....
	NHL Totals		**16**	**0**	**0**	**0**	**0**	**0**	**0**	**0**	....	....	....	....	....
	Other Major League Totals		46	11	2	13	....	....	....	12	....	....	....	....	....

Signed as a free agent by **Vancouver** (WCHL), November 17, 1924. Traded to **NY Rangers** by **Vancouver** (WHL) for cash, October 25, 1926. Traded to **Stratford** (Can-Pro) by **NY Rangers** for cash, November 11, 1927. Traded to **Seattle** (PCHL) by **Hamilton** (Can-Pro) for cash, January 30, 1929. Traded to **London** (IAHL) by **Seattle** (PCHL) for cash, September 11, 1930.

• REISE, LEO JR.

Leo Jr. Reise

D – L. 6', 205 lbs. b: Stoney Creek, Ont., 6/7/1922.

Season	Club	League	GP	G	A	Pts	AG	AA	APts	PIM	GP	G	A	Pts	PIM
1940-41	Brantford Lions	Jr. B	STATISTICS NOT AVAILABLE												
1941-42	Guelph Biltmores	OHA	14	5	7	12	....	....	....	28	10	1	3	4	22
1942-43			MILITARY SERVICE												
1943-44	Victoria Navy	City Sr.	17	1	2	3	....	....	....	24	....	....	....	....	....
	Halifax Navy	City Sr.	....	....	....	....	....	....	....	....	4	0	0	0	2
1944-45	Winnipeg Navy	City Sr.	17	9	2	11	....	....	....	26	6	1	2	3	11
1945-46	**Chicago Black Hawks**	**NHL**	**6**	**0**	**0**	**0**	**0**	**0**	**0**	**6**	....	....	....	....	....
	Kansas City Pla-Mors	USHL	50	7	18	25	....	....	....	30	....	....	....	....	....
1946-47	**Chicago Black Hawks**	**NHL**	**17**	**0**	**0**	**0**	**0**	**0**	**0**	**18**	....	....	....	....	....
	Kansas City Pla-Mors	USHL	2	0	1	1	....	....	....	0	....	....	....	....	....
	Indianapolis Capitals	AHL	5	0	4	4	....	....	....	8	....	....	....	....	....
	Detroit Red Wings	**NHL**	**31**	**4**	**6**	**10**	**5**	**9**	**14**	**14**	**5**	**0**	**1**	**1**	**4**
1947-48	**Detroit Red Wings**	**NHL**	**58**	**5**	**4**	**9**	**7**	**6**	**13**	**30**	**10**	**2**	**1**	**3**	**12**
1948-49	**Detroit Red Wings**	**NHL**	**59**	**3**	**7**	**10**	**5**	**11**	**16**	**60**	**11**	**1**	**0**	**1**	**4**
1949-50	**Detroit Red Wings**	**NHL**	**70**	**4**	**17**	**21**	**5**	**22**	**27**	**46**	**14**	**2**	**0**	**2**	**19**
1950-51	**Detroit Red Wings**	**NHL**	**68**	**5**	**16**	**21**	**7**	**21**	**28**	**67**	**6**	**2**	**3**	**5**	**2**
1951-52	**Detroit Red Wings**	**NHL**	**54**	**0**	**11**	**11**	**0**	**14**	**14**	**34**	**6**	**1**	**0**	**1**	***27**
1952-53	**New York Rangers**	**NHL**	**61**	**4**	**15**	**19**	**6**	**21**	**27**	**53**	....	....	....	....	....
1953-54	**New York Rangers**	**NHL**	**70**	**3**	**5**	**8**	**5**	**7**	**12**	**71**	....	....	....	....	....
1954-55	Owen Sound Mercuries	OHA Sr.	8	1	1	2	....	....	....	4	5	1	1	2	6
	NHL Totals		**494**	**28**	**81**	**109**	**40**	**111**	**151**	**399**	**52**	**8**	**5**	**13**	**68**

USHL First All-Star Team (1946) • NHL Second All-Star Team (1950, 1951)

Played in NHL All-Star Game (1950, 1951, 1952, 1953)

Traded to **Detroit** by **Chicago** with Pete Horeck for Adam Brown and Ray Powell, December, 1946. Traded to **NY Rangers** by **Detroit** for Reg Sinclair and John Morrison, August 18, 1952.

• REISE, LEO SR.

Leo Sr. Reise

D – R. 5'11", 175 lbs. b: Pembroke, Ont., 6/1/1892. d: 7/8/1975.

Season	Club	League	GP	G	A	Pts	AG	AA	APts	PIM	GP	G	A	Pts	PIM
1917-18	Hamilton Tigers	OHA Sr.	8	8	0	8	....	....	....	....	....	....	....	....	....
1918-19	Hamilton Tigers	OHA Sr.	8	5	1	6	....	....	....	....	6	2	0	2	....
1919-20	Hamilton Tigers	OHA Sr.	5	8	3	11	....	....	....	....	2	0	0	0	....
1920-21	**Hamilton Tigers**	**NHL**	**6**	**2**	**0**	**2**	**5**	**0**	**5**	**8**	....	....	....	....	....
1921-22	**Hamilton Tigers**	**NHL**	**24**	**9**	***14**	**23**	**25**	**91**	**116**	**11**	....	....	....	....	....
1922-23	**Hamilton Tigers**	**NHL**	**24**	**6**	**6**	**12**	**20**	**54**	**74**	**35**	....	....	....	....	....
1923-24	**Hamilton Tigers**	**NHL**	**4**	**0**	**0**	**0**	**0**	**0**	**0**	**0**	....	....	....	....	....
	Saskatoon Crescents	WCHL	18	4	2	6	....	....	....	6	....	....	....	....	....
1924-25	Saskatoon Crescents	WCHL	28	8	3	11	....	....	....	46	2	0	0	0	0
1925-26	Saskatoon Crescents	WHL	30	2	10	12	....	....	....	32	2	0	0	0	4
1926-27	Niagara Falls Cataracts	Can-Pro	3	3	1	4	....	....	....	0	....	....	....	....	....
	New York Americans	**NHL**	**40**	**7**	**6**	**13**	**20**	**51**	**71**	**24**	....	....	....	....	....
1927-28	**New York Americans**	**NHL**	**43**	**8**	**1**	**9**	**24**	**8**	**32**	**62**	....	....	....	....	....
1928-29	**New York Americans**	**NHL**	**44**	**4**	**1**	**5**	**16**	**9**	**25**	**32**	**2**	**0**	**0**	**0**	**0**
1929-30	**New York Americans**	**NHL**	**24**	**0**	**0**	**0**	**0**	**0**	**0**	**0**	....	....	....	....	....
	New York Rangers	**NHL**	**14**	**0**	**1**	**1**	**0**	**3**	**3**	**8**	**4**	**0**	**0**	**0**	**16**
1930-31	London Tecumsehs	IAHL	8	0	0	0	....	....	....	6	....	....	....	....	....
	Pittsburgh Yellowjackets	IAHL	37	5	5	10	....	....	....	18	6	1	2	3	2
1931-32	Pittsburgh Yellowjackets	IAHL	21	0	0	0	....	....	....	19	....	....	....	....	....
	NHL Totals		**223**	**36**	**29**	**65**	**110**	**216**	**326**	**180**	**6**	**0**	**0**	**0**	**16**
	Other Major League Totals		76	14	15	29	....	....	....	84	4	0	0	0	4

Signed as a free agent by **Hamilton**, February 23, 1921. Traded to **Saskatoon** (WCHL) by **Hamilton** for cash, December 29, 1923. Signed as a free agent by **Niagara Falls** (Can-Pro), November 1, 1926. Traded to **NY Americans** by **Niagara Falls** (Can-Pro) for cash, November 22, 1926. Traded to **NY Rangers** by **NY Americans** for cash, February 6, 1930. Traded to **London** (IAHL) by **NY Rangers** for cash, October 22, 1930.

• RICHARD, HENRI

— see page 1419

• RICHARD, MAURICE

Maurice "The Rocket" Richard **HHOF**

RW – L. 5'10", 170 lbs. b: Montreal, Que., 8/4/1921.

Season	Club	League	GP	G	A	Pts	AG	AA	APts	PIM	GP	G	A	Pts	PIM
			REGULAR SEASON								PLAYOFFS				
1938-39	Verdun Maple Leafs	Mtl-Jr.	STATISTICS NOT AVAILABLE												
1939-40	Verdun Sr. Maple Leafs	Mtl-Sr.	1	0	0	0	....	....	....	0	....	....	....	....	....
1940-41	Montreal Royals	Mtl-Sr.	1	0	1	1	....	....	....	0	....	....	....	....	....
1941-42	Montreal Royals	Mtl-Sr.	31	8	9	17	....	....	....	27	6	2	1	3	6
1942-43	**Montreal Canadiens**	**NHL**	**16**	**5**	**6**	**11**	**7**	**8**	**15**	**4**	....	....	....	....	....
1943-44	**Montreal Canadiens**	**NHL**	**46**	**32**	**22**	**54**	**41**	**27**	**68**	**45**	**9**	**12**	**5**	**17**	**10**
1944-45	**Montreal Canadiens**	**NHL**	**50**	***50**	**23**	**73**	**71**	**37**	**108**	**46**	**6**	**6**	**2**	**8**	**10**
1945-46	**Montreal Canadiens**	**NHL**	**50**	**27**	**21**	**48**	**42**	**39**	**81**	**50**	**9**	***7**	**4**	**11**	**15**
1946-47	**Montreal Canadiens**	**NHL**	**60**	***45**	**26**	**71**	**62**	**37**	**99**	**69**	**10**	**6**	**5**	**11**	**44**
1947-48	**Montreal Canadiens**	**NHL**	**53**	**28**	**25**	**53**	**41**	**37**	**78**	**89**	....	....	....	....	....
1948-49	**Montreal Canadiens**	**NHL**	**59**	**20**	**18**	**38**	**32**	**29**	**61**	**110**	**7**	**2**	**1**	**3**	**14**
1949-50	**Montreal Canadiens**	**NHL**	**70**	***43**	**22**	**65**	**59**	**28**	**87**	**114**	**5**	**1**	**1**	**2**	**6**
1950-51	**Montreal Canadiens**	**NHL**	**65**	**42**	**24**	**66**	**58**	**31**	**89**	**97**	**11**	**9**	**4**	**13**	**13**
1951-52	**Montreal Canadiens**	**NHL**	**48**	**27**	**17**	**44**	**39**	**22**	**61**	**44**	**11**	**4**	**2**	**6**	**6**
1952-53	**Montreal Canadiens**	**NHL**	**70**	**28**	**33**	**61**	**43**	**47**	**90**	***112**	**12**	**7**	**1**	**8**	**2**
1953-54	**Montreal Canadiens**	**NHL**	**70**	***37**	**30**	**67**	**58**	**41**	**99**	**112**	**11**	**3**	**0**	**3**	**22**
1954-55	**Montreal Canadiens**	**NHL**	**67**	***38**	**36**	**74**	**57**	**47**	**104**	**125**	....	....	....	....	....
1955-56	**Montreal Canadiens**	**NHL**	**70**	**38**	**33**	**71**	**56**	**42**	**98**	**89**	**10**	**5**	**9**	**14**	***24**
1956-57	**Montreal Canadiens**	**NHL**	**63**	**33**	**29**	**62**	**46**	**34**	**80**	**74**	**10**	**8**	**3**	**11**	**8**
1957-58	**Montreal Canadiens**	**NHL**	**28**	**15**	**19**	**34**	**20**	**21**	**41**	**28**	**10**	**11**	**4**	**15**	**10**
1958-59	**Montreal Canadiens**	**NHL**	**42**	**17**	**21**	**38**	**22**	**22**	**44**	**27**	**4**	**0**	**0**	**0**	**2**
1959-60	**Montreal Canadiens**	**NHL**	**51**	**19**	**16**	**35**	**24**	**16**	**40**	**50**	**8**	**1**	**3**	**4**	**2**
	NHL Totals		**978**	**544**	**421**	**965**	**778**	**565**	**1343**	**1285**	**133**	**82**	**44**	**126**	**188**

NHL Second All-Star Team (1944, 1951, 1952, 1953, 1954, 1957) • NHL First All-Star Team (1945, 1946, 1947, 1948, 1949, 1950, 1955, 1956) • Won Hart Trophy (1947)

Played in NHL All-Star Game (1947, 1948, 1949, 1950, 1951, 1952, 1953, 1954, 1955, 1956, 1957, 1958, 1959)

Signed as a free agent by **Montreal**, October 29, 1942.

• RICHARDSON, DAVE

— see page 1421

• RILEY, JACK

Jack Riley

C – L. 5'11", 160 lbs. b: Berckenia, Ireland, 12/29/1910.

Season	Club	League	GP	G	A	Pts	AG	AA	APts	PIM	GP	G	A	Pts	PIM
1928-29	Calgary Canadians	City Jr.	STATISTICS NOT AVAILABLE												
1929-30	Seattle Eskimos	PCHL	5	0	0	0	....	....	....	0	....	....	....	....	....
1930-31	Chicago Shamrocks	AHA	26	6	8	14	....	....	....	16	....	....	....	....	....
	Minneapolis Millers	AHA	16	4	2	6	....	....	....	8	....	....	....	....	....
1931-32	Chicago Shamrocks	AHA	46	17	16	33	....	....	....	28	4	3	0	3	2
1932-33	**Detroit Red Wings**	**NHL**	**1**	**0**	**0**	**0**	**0**	**0**	**0**	**0**	....	....	....	....	....
	Detroit–Cleveland	IAHL	42	10	15	25	....	....	....	20	....	....	....	....	....
1933-34	**Montreal Canadiens**	**NHL**	**48**	**6**	**11**	**17**	**13**	**29**	**42**	**4**	**2**	**0**	**1**	**1**	**0**
1934-35	**Montreal Canadiens**	**NHL**	**47**	**4**	**11**	**15**	**8**	**24**	**32**	**4**	**2**	**0**	**2**	**2**	**0**
1935-36	**Boston Bruins**	**NHL**	**8**	**0**	**0**	**0**	**0**	**0**	**0**	**0**	....	....	....	....	....
	Boston Cubs	Can-Am	30	3	10	13	....	....	....	8	....	....	....	....	....
1936-37	Tulsa Oilers	AHA	48	14	17	31	....	....	....	16	....	....	....	....	....
1937-38	Tulsa Oilers	AHA	47	13	23	36	....	....	....	19	4	1	0	1	2
1938-39	Tulsa Oilers	AHA	43	16	25	41	....	....	....	14	8	2	2	4	9
1939-40	Wichita Skyhawks	AHA	44	19	18	37	....	....	....	19	....	....	....	....	....
1940-41	Vancouver Lions	PCHL	47	16	*40	56	....	....	....	14	6	2	1	3	0
1941-42	Philadelphia–Hershey	AHL	9	4	0	4	....	....	....	0	10	0	0	0	0
	Montreal Pats	QSHL	31	15	11	26	....	....	....	8	....	....	....	....	....
1942-43	Cornwall Army	QSHL	20	7	13	20	....	....	....	11	6	0	1	1	0
	Vancouver Norvans	PCHL	6	5	9	14	....	....	....	0	3	0	1	1	0
1943-44	Vancouver St. Regis	PCHL	2	0	0	0	....	....	....	0	....	....	....	....	....
1944-45	Hershey Bears	AHL	35	5	7	12	....	....	....	7	6	0	0	0	0
	NHL Totals		**104**	**10**	**22**	**32**	**21**	**53**	**74**	**8**	**4**	**0**	**3**	**3**	**0**

Traded to **Chicago** (AHA) by **Minneapolis** (AHA) for George Burland and Stan Fuller, January 8, 1931. NHL rights transferred to **Detroit** from **Chicago** (AHA) after AHA club owners purchased Detroit (NHL and IAHL) franchises, September 2, 1932. Traded to **Cleveland** (IAHL) by **Detroit** with Tony Prelesnik for Deacon Waite, December 2, 1932. Traded to **Montreal** by **Cleveland** (IAHL) for cash, June, 1933. Traded to **Boston** by **Montreal Canadiens** for Paul Haynes, September 30, 1935.

• RILEY, JIM

Jim Riley

LW – L. 5'11", 180 lbs. b: Bayfield, NB, 5/25/1897. Deceased.

Season	Club	League	GP	G	A	Pts	AG	AA	APts	PIM	GP	G	A	Pts	PIM
1915-16	Victoria Aristocrats	PCHA	12	4	1	5	....	....	....	14	....	....	....	....	....
1916-17	Seattle Metropolitans	PCHA	24	11	5	16	....	....	....	34	4	0	0	0	3
1917-18	Seattle Metropolitans	PCHA	18	4	3	7	....	....	....	15	2	1	0	1	3
1918-19			MILITARY SERVICE												
1919-20	Seattle Metropolitans	PCHA	22	11	4	15	....	....	....	49	7	1	*4	5	3
1920-21	Seattle Metropolitans	PCHA	24	23	5	28	....	....	....	20	2	0	0	0	0
1921-22	Seattle Metropolitans	PCHA	24	16	2	18	....	....	....	27	2	0	0	0	3
1922-23	Seattle Metropolitans	PCHA	30	23	4	27	....	....	....	70	....	....	....	....	....
1923-24	Seattle Metropolitans	PCHA	13	2	2	4	....	....	....	11	2	0	1	1	2
1924-25			PLAYED PROFESSIONAL BASEBALL												
1925-26			PLAYED PROFESSIONAL BASEBALL												
1926-27	**Chicago Black Hawks**	**NHL**	**3**	**0**	**0**	**0**	**0**	**0**	**0**	**0**	....	....	....	....	....
	Detroit Cougars	**NHL**	**6**	**0**	**2**	**2**	**0**	**17**	**17**	**14**	....	....	....	....	....
1927-28			PLAYED PROFESSIONAL BASEBALL												
1928-29	Los Angeles Richfields	Cal-Pro	....	2	2	4	....	....	....	....	....	....	....	....	....
	NHL Totals		**9**	**0**	**2**	**2**	**0**	**17**	**17**	**14**	....	....	....	....	....
	Other Major League Totals		167	94	26	120	....	....	....	240	19	2	5	7	14

PCHA Second All-Star Team (1920, 1921, 1922) • PCHA First All-Star Team (1923)

• Retired from Seattle (PCHA) after the 1923-24 season to concentrate on professional baseball career. Signed as a free agent by **Chicago**, January 19, 1927. Traded to **Detroit Cougars** by **Chicago** for cash, January 31, 1927. Traded to **Detroit Olympics** (Can-Pro) by **Detroit Cougars** for cash, October 11, 1927.

• RIOPELLE, RIP
Rip (Howard) Riopelle
LW – L. 5'11", 165 lbs. b: Ottawa, Ont., 1/30/1922.

Season	Club	League	GP	G	A	Pts	AG	AA	APts	PIM	PO GP	PO G	PO A	PO Pts	PO PIM
1937-38	Ottawa Lasalle	QJHL	13	7	2	9				4					
	Ottawa Lasalle	City Sr.	1	0	0	0				0					
1938-39	Ottawa St. Pats	City Sr.	STATISTICS NOT AVAILABLE												
1939-40	Ottawa St. Pats	City Sr.	STATISTICS NOT AVAILABLE												
1940-41	Ottawa Car Bombers	City Sr.	1	0	1	1				2					
1941-42	Ottawa St. Pats	City Sr.	STATISTICS NOT AVAILABLE												
1942-43	Toronto RCAF	OHA Sr.	10	14	6	20				2	13	6	7	13	2
1943-44	Arnprior RCAF	OHA Sr.	5	6	6	12				2					
1944-45			MILITARY SERVICE												
1945-46	Montreal Royals	QSHL	36	20	21	41				16	11	7	6	13	4
1946-47	Montreal Royals	QSHL	34	10	19	29				26	11	3	6	9	4
1947-48	**Montreal Canadiens**	**NHL**	**55**	**5**	**2**	**7**	**7**	**3**	**10**	**12**					
1948-49	**Montreal Canadiens**	**NHL**	**48**	**10**	**6**	**16**	**16**	**9**	**25**	**34**	**7**	**1**	**1**	**2**	**2**
1949-50	**Montreal Canadiens**	**NHL**	**66**	**12**	**8**	**20**	**16**	**10**	**26**	**27**	**1**	**0**	**0**	**0**	**0**
1950-51	Ottawa Senators	QSHL	DID NOT PLAY – INJURED												
1951-52	Ottawa Senators	QSHL	54	18	28	46				18	7	1	4	5	0
1952-53	Ottawa Senators	QSHL	60	20	31	51				20	11	3	7	10	4
1953-54	Ottawa Senators	QHL	72	31	*60	*91				46	22	3	9	12	4
1954-55	Ottawa Senators	QHL	20	4	4	8				12					
	NHL Totals		**169**	**27**	**16**	**43**	**39**	**22**	**61**	**73**	**8**	**1**	**1**	**2**	**2**

QHL Second All-Star Team (1953) • QHL First All-Star Team (1954) • Won President's Cup (Scoring Champion - QHL) (1954)

Traded to **Ottawa** (QSHL) by **Montreal** for cash, October 4, 1951.

• RIPLEY, VIC
Vic Ripley
LW – L. 5'8", 170 lbs. b: Elgin, Ont., 5/30/1906. Deceased.

Season	Club	League	GP	G	A	Pts	AG	AA	APts	PIM	PO GP	PO G	PO A	PO Pts	PO PIM
1922-23	Calgary Canadians	City Jr.	13	15	8	23									
1923-24	Calgary Canadians	City Jr.	STATISTICS NOT AVAILABLE												
1924-25	Calgary Canadians	City Jr.	STATISTICS NOT AVAILABLE												
1925-26	Minneapolis Millers	CHL	35	6	2	8				16	3	1	0	1	2
1926-27	Minneapolis Millers	AHA	34	7	1	8				30	6	0	0	0	2
1927-28	Kitchener Millionaires	Can-Pro	39	26	*14	*40				69	5	1	1	2	12
1928-29	**Chicago Black Hawks**	**NHL**	**34**	**11**	**2**	**13**	**44**	**18**	**62**	**31**					
1929-30	**Chicago Black Hawks**	**NHL**	**40**	**8**	**8**	**16**	**16**	**26**	**42**	**33**	**2**	**0**	**0**	**0**	**2**
1930-31	**Chicago Black Hawks**	**NHL**	**37**	**8**	**4**	**12**	**19**	**14**	**33**	**9**	**9**	**2**	**1**	**3**	**4**
1931-32	**Chicago Black Hawks**	**NHL**	**46**	**12**	**6**	**18**	**26**	**17**	**43**	**47**	**2**	**0**	**0**	**0**	**0**
1932-33	**Chicago Black Hawks**	**NHL**	**15**	**2**	**4**	**6**	**5**	**11**	**16**	**6**					
	Boston Bruins	**NHL**	**23**	**2**	**5**	**7**	**5**	**13**	**18**	**21**	**5**	**1**	**0**	**1**	**0**
1933-34	**Boston Bruins**	**NHL**	**14**	**2**	**1**	**3**	**4**	**3**	**7**	**6**					
	New York Rangers	**NHL**	**34**	**5**	**12**	**17**	**11**	**32**	**43**	**10**	**2**	**1**	**0**	**1**	**4**
1934-35	**New York Rangers**	**NHL**	**4**	**0**	**2**	**2**	**0**	**4**	**4**	**0**					
	St. Louis Eagles	**NHL**	**31**	**1**	**5**	**6**	**2**	**11**	**13**	**10**					
1935-36	Cleveland Falcons	IAHL	48	14	32	46				51	2	0	0	0	0
1936-37	Cleveland–New Haven	AHL	13	0	2	2				6					
1937-38	Spokane Clippers	PCHL	42	19	16	35				19					
1938-39	Spokane Clippers	PCHL	44	20	22	42				22					
1939-40	Seattle Seahawks	PCHL	36	11	15	26				24					
1940-41	Portland Buckaroos	PCHL	47	11	20	31				37					
	NHL Totals		**278**	**51**	**49**	**100**	**132**	**149**	**281**	**173**	**20**	**4**	**1**	**5**	**10**

Traded to **Calgary** (PrHL) by **Minneapolis** (AHA) for cash, June, 1927. Traded to **Kitchener** (IAHL) by **Calgary** (PrHL) for cash, October 16, 1927. Claimed by **Chicago** from **Kitchener** (IAHL) in Inter-League Draft, May 14, 1928. Traded to **Boston** by **Chicago** for Billy Burch, January 17, 1933. Traded to **NY Rangers** by **Boston** with Roy Burmeister for Babe Siebert, December 18, 1933. Traded to **St. Louis** by **NY Rangers** for cash, November 29, 1934.

• RITCHIE, DAVE
Dave Ritchie
D – R. 5'7", 180 lbs. b: Montreal, Que. Deceased.

Season	Club	League	GP	G	A	Pts	AG	AA	APts	PIM	PO GP	PO G	PO A	PO Pts	PO PIM
1914-15	Quebec Bulldogs	NHA	14	2	1	3				0					
1915-16	Quebec Bulldogs	NHA	23	9	4	13				38					
1916-17	Quebec Bulldogs	NHA	19	17	8	27				17					
1917-18	**Montreal Wanderers**	**NHL**	**4**	**5**	**2**	**7**	**12**	**0**	**12**	**3**					
	Ottawa Senators	**NHL**	**13**	**4**	**6**	**10**	**10**	**0**	**10**	**18**					
1918-19	**Toronto Arenas**	**NHL**	**5**	**0**	**0**	**0**	**0**	**0**	**0**	**9**					
1919-20	**Quebec Bulldogs**	**NHL**	**23**	**6**	**3**	**9**	**13**	**20**	**33**	**18**					
1920-21	**Montreal Canadiens**	**NHL**	**5**	**0**	**0**	**0**	**0**	**0**	**0**	**0**					
1921-22			DID NOT PLAY – REFEREE												
1922-23			DID NOT PLAY – REFEREE												
1923-24			DID NOT PLAY – REFEREE												
1924-25	**Montreal Canadiens**	**NHL**	**5**	**0**	**0**	**0**	**0**	**0**	**0**	**0**	**1**	**0**	**0**	**0**	**0**
1925-26	**Montreal Canadiens**	**NHL**	**2**	**0**	**0**	**0**	**0**	**0**	**0**	**0**					
	NHL Totals		**57**	**15**	**11**	**26**	**35**	**20**	**55**	**48**	**1**	**0**	**0**	**0**	**0**
	Other Major League Totals		56	28	13	43				55					

Signed as a free agent by **Quebec**, November, 1914. Claimed by **Montreal Wanderers** from **Quebec** in Dispersal Draft, November 26, 1917. Claimed by **Ottawa** from **Montreal Wanderers** in Dispersal Draft, January 4, 1918. Signed as a free agent by **Toronto Arenas**, January 17, 1919. Transferred to **Quebec** by **Toronto Arenas** when Quebec franchise returned to NHL, November 25, 1919. Transferred to **Hamilton** after **Quebec** franchise relocated, November 2, 1920. Traded to **Montreal Canadiens** by **Hamilton** with Harry Mummery and Jack McDonald for Jack Coughlin and the loan of Bill Coutu for the 1920-21 season, November 29, 1920. Signed as a free agent by **Montreal Canadiens**, January 28, 1925. Signed as a free agent by **Montreal Canadiens**, January 13, 1926.

• RITSON, ALEX
Alex Ritson
C – L. 5'11", 172 lbs. b: Peace River, Alta., 3/7/1922.

Season	Club	League	GP	G	A	Pts	AG	AA	APts	PIM	PO GP	PO G	PO A	PO Pts	PO PIM
1940-41	Regina Generals	SJHL	19	9	12	21				14	4	1	5	6	2
1941-42	Tulsa Oilers	AHA	50	14	13	27				12	2	0	0	0	0
1942-43	Washington–Providence	AHL	52	14	30	44				19	2	0	0	0	0
1943-44	Indianapolis Capitals	AHL	53	22	21	43				13	5	0	1	1	0
1944-45	**New York Rangers**	**NHL**	**1**	**0**	**0**	**0**	**0**	**0**	**0**	**0**					
	Hershey Bears	AHL	42	13	29	42				13	11	5	3	8	4
1945-46	New Haven Eagles	AHL	25	4	6	10				4					
	Omaha Knights	USHL	3	0	0	0				5					
	Fort Worth Rangers	USHL	7	0	4	4				0					
1946-47	Fort Worth Rangers	USHL	60	21	26	47				37	9	1	1	2	0
1947-48	Fort Worth Rangers	USHL	66	22	40	62				42	4	0	1	1	0
1948-49	Tulsa Oilers	USHL	66	16	43	59				73	7	1	1	2	12
1949-50	Cincinnati Mohawks	AHL	6	0	0	0				7					
	Louisville Blades	USHL	45	10	18	28				18					
	Seattle Ironmen	PCHL	16	1	4	5				11	4	2	0	2	0
1950-51	Seattle Ironmen	PCHL	3	0	0	0				0					
	Vernon Canadians	OSHL	47	33	36	69				44	10	4	2	6	4
1951-52	Vernon Canadians	OSHL	48	24	25	49				47					
	NHL Totals		**1**	**0**	**0**	**0**	**0**	**0**	**0**	**0**					

Claimed by **NY Rangers** from **Indianapolis** (AHL) in Inter-League Draft, May 12, 1944.

• RITTINGER, ALAN
Alan Rittinger
RW/LW – R. 5'9", 155 lbs. b: Regina, Sask., 1/28/1925.

Season	Club	League	GP	G	A	Pts	AG	AA	APts	PIM	PO GP	PO G	PO A	PO Pts	PO PIM
1942-43	Regina Abbotts	SJHL	10	1	4	5				17	4	1	1	2	0
1943-44	**Boston Bruins**	**NHL**	**19**	**3**	**7**	**10**	**4**	**8**	**12**	**0**					
	Boston Olympics	EHL	31	18	25	43				16	8	3	4	7	10
1944-45	Boston Olympics	EHL	48	29	39	68				100	12	7	12	19	19
1945-46	New Haven Eagles	AHL	14	0	7	7				12					
	Fort Worth Rangers	USHL	41	12	25	37				32					
1946-47	Seattle Ironmen	PCHL	60	24	26	50				73	10	2	4	6	17
1947-48	Oakland Oaks	PCHL	53	17	29	46				72					
1948-49	Vancouver Canucks	PCHL	10	4	0	4				8					
1949-50	Kerrisdale Monarchs	Van-Sr.	34	23	19	42				68	4	1	1	2	4
1950-51	Kerrisdale Monarchs	Van-Sr.	42	13	17	30				58	5	1	2	3	4
1951-52	Vancouver Wheelers	City Sr.	21	20	14	34				38	6	4	3	7	8
	NHL Totals		**19**	**3**	**7**	**10**	**4**	**8**	**12**	**0**					

• RIVERS, GUS
Gus (AKA Desrivieres) Rivers
RW – R. 5'11", 180 lbs. b: Winnipeg, Man., 11/19/1909. d: 10/15/1985.

Season	Club	League	GP	G	A	Pts	AG	AA	APts	PIM	PO GP	PO G	PO A	PO Pts	PO PIM
1927-28	Winnipeg Elmwoods	City Jr.	5	2	1	3				6	2	2	1	3	0
	Winnipeg Eatons	City Sr.	6	1	2	3				8	2	1	1	2	4
1928-29	University of Manitoba	City Sr.	5	6	2	8				4	1	0	0	0	0
	Winnipeg CPR	City Sr.	9	7	5	12				8	3	0	*2	2	2
1929-30	**Montreal Canadiens**	**NHL**	**19**	**1**	**0**	**1**	**2**	**0**	**2**	**2**	**6**	**1**	**0**	**1**	**2**
	Winnipeg Winnipegs	MHL Sr.	6	1	4	5				12					
1930-31	**Montreal Canadiens**	**NHL**	**44**	**2**	**5**	**7**	**5**	**18**	**23**	**6**	**10**	**1**	**0**	**1**	**0**
1931-32	**Montreal Canadiens**	**NHL**	**25**	**1**	**0**	**1**	**2**	**0**	**2**	**4**					
	Providence Reds	Can-Am	19	11	12	23				10	5	1	*2	3	2
1932-33	Providence Reds	Can-Am	43	11	18	29				25	2	1	1	2	0
1933-34	Providence Reds	Can-Am	35	11	8	19				17	3	0	0	0	0
1934-35	Providence Reds	Can-Am	45	18	23	41				8	6	1	1	2	7
1935-36	Providence Reds	Can-Am	45	13	17	30				25	7	*3	3	*6	2
1936-37	Providence Reds	Can-Am	43	8	14	22				17	3	2	1	3	0
	NHL Totals		**88**	**4**	**5**	**9**	**9**	**18**	**27**	**12**	**16**	**2**	**0**	**2**	**2**

Signed as a free agent by **Montreal Canadiens**, January 22, 1930.

• RIVERS, WAYNE
— see page 1425

• ROACH, MICKEY
Mickey Roach
C – L. 5'6", 158 lbs. b: Boston, MA, 5/1/1895. d: 4/1/1977.

Season	Club	League	GP	G	A	Pts	AG	AA	APts	PIM	PO GP	PO G	PO A	PO Pts	PO PIM
1914-15	Boston Arenas	AAHA	10	*14	0	*14					7	4	0	4	
1915-16	Boston Arenas	USAHA	6	11	0	11									
1916-17	New York Crescents	USAHA	6	5	0	5					6	4	0	4	
1917-18	New York Wanderers	USAHA	10	12	0	12									
1918-19	Hamilton Tigers	OHA Sr.	8	17	*12	*29					6	5	*4	9	
1919-20	**Toronto St. Pats**	**NHL**	**21**	**11**	**2**	**13**	**25**	**13**	**38**	**4**					
1920-21	**Toronto St. Pats**	**NHL**	**9**	**1**	**1**	**2**	**2**	**9**	**11**	**2**					
	Hamilton Tigers	**NHL**	**14**	**9**	**8**	**17**	**23**	**72**	**95**	**0**					
1921-22	**Hamilton Tigers**	**NHL**	**24**	**14**	**6**	**20**	**39**	**38**	**77**	**7**					
1922-23	**Hamilton Tigers**	**NHL**	**23**	**17**	**8**	**25**	**58**	**73**	**131**	**8**					
1923-24	**Hamilton Tigers**	**NHL**	**21**	**5**	**3**	**8**	**20**	**53**	**73**	**0**					
1924-25	**Hamilton Tigers**	**NHL**	**30**	**6**	**4**	**10**	**21**	**53**	**74**	**4**					
1925-26	**New York Americans**	**NHL**	**25**	**3**	**0**	**3**	**9**	**0**	**9**	**4**					
1926-27	**New York Americans**	**NHL**	**44**	**11**	**0**	**11**	**32**	**0**	**32**	**14**					
1927-28	Niagara Falls Cataracts	Can-Pro	41	12	6	18				23					
1928-29	Windsor Bulldogs	Can-Pro	42	8	9	17				0	7	1	0	1	2
1929-30	Buffalo Bisons	IAHL	10	0	0	0				0					
1930-31	Buffalo Bisons	IAHL	DID NOT PLAY – COACHING												
	NHL Totals		**211**	**77**	**32**	**109**	**229**	**311**	**540**	**43**					

Signed as a free agent by **Toronto St. Pats**, December 16, 1919. Traded to **Hamilton** by **Toronto** for cash, January 21, 1921. Transferred to **NY Americans** after NHL club purchased **Hamilton** franchise, September 26, 1925.

● ROBERT, CLAUDE Claude Robert

LW – L. 5′11″, 175 lbs. b: Montreal, Que., 8/10/1928.

			REGULAR SEASON								PLAYOFFS				
Season	Club	League	GP	G	A	Pts	AG	AA	APts	PIM	GP	G	A	Pts	PIM
1947-48	Montreal Nationale	QJHL	32	21	22	43	....	....	....	41	20	8	17	25	18
1948-49	Montreal Royals	QSHL	44	14	7	21	....	....	....	28	....	....	....	....	....
1949-50	Chicoutimi Sagueneens	QSHL	60	31	25	56	....	....	....	79	5	1	6	7	2
1950-51	**Montreal Canadiens**	**NHL**	**23**	**1**	**0**	**1**	**1**	**0**	**1**	**9**	....	....	....	....	....
	Cincinnati Mohawks	AHL	26	5	5	10	....	....	....	28	....	....	....	....	....
1951-52	Quebec Aces	QSHL	60	22	27	49	....	....	....	53	20	8	7	15	34
1952-53	New Westminster Royals	WHL	29	8	11	19	....	....	....	37	7	0	4	4	0
	Quebec Aces	QSHL	29	3	12	15	....	....	....	35	....	....	....	....	....
1953-54	Ottawa Senators	QHL	19	3	6	9	....	....	....	20	....	....	....	....	....
	Charlottetown Islanders	MMHL	38	23	32	55	....	....	....	34	7	2	0	2	4
1954-55	North Bay Trappers	NOHA	16	4	9	13	....	....	....	7	....	....	....	....	....
	Fort Wayne–Toledo	IHL	19	3	5	8	....	....	....	12	....	....	....	....	....
	NHL Totals		**23**	**1**	**0**	**1**	**1**	**0**	**1**	**9**	....	....	....	....	....

● ROBERTS, DOUG — *see page 1427*

● ROBERTS, JIMMY — *see page 1428*

● ROBERTSON, FRED Fred Robertson

D – L. 5′10″, 198 lbs. b: Carlisle, England, 10/22/1911. d: 9/20/1997.

Season	Club	League	GP	G	A	Pts	AG	AA	APts	PIM	GP	G	A	Pts	PIM
1929-30	Sudbury K of C	City Sr.	5	3	0	3	....	....	....	0	....	....	....	....	....
	Toronto Canoe Club	OHA	4	2	0	2	....	....	....	20	....	....	....	....	....
1930-31	Toronto Marlboros	OHA Sr.	8	0	0	0	....	....	....	14	3	0	0	0	4
1931-32	**Toronto Maple Leafs**	**NHL**	**8**	**0**	**0**	**0**	**0**	**0**	**0**	**23**	**7**	**0**	**0**	**0**	**0**
	Toronto Marlboros	OHA Sr.	20	7	6	13	....	....	....	*58	1	0	1	1	2
1932-33	Syracuse Stars	IAHL	42	3	4	7	....	....	....	*109	5	1	1	2	6
1933-34	**Toronto Maple Leafs**	**NHL**	**2**	**0**	**0**	**0**	**0**	**0**	**0**	**0**	....	....	....	....	....
	Detroit Red Wings	**NHL**	**24**	**1**	**0**	**1**	**2**	**0**	**2**	**12**	....	....	....	....	....
	Detroit Olympics	IAHL	19	0	0	0	....	....	....	34	6	1	4	5	18
1934-35	Syracuse–Cleveland	IAHL	45	3	4	7	....	....	....	42	2	0	0	0	2
1935-36	Cleveland Falcons	IAHL	48	5	5	10	....	....	....	82	2	0	0	0	8
1936-37	Cleveland Falcons	AHL	35	0	7	7	....	....	....	28	....	....	....	....	....
1937-38	Cleveland Falcons	AHL	48	3	4	7	....	....	....	74	2	0	0	0	8
1938-39	Cleveland Falcons	AHL	51	0	1	1	....	....	....	45	9	0	2	2	8
1939-40	Cleveland Barons	AHL	45	5	3	8	....	....	....	38	....	....	....	....	....
1940-41	Cleveland Barons	AHL	56	7	8	15	....	....	....	45	7	1	0	1	6
1941-42	Cleveland Barons	AHL	48	5	8	13	....	....	....	22	5	0	1	1	2
1942-43	Cleveland Barons	AHL	56	2	9	11	....	....	....	33	4	0	1	1	22
1943-44	Cleveland–Pittsburgh	AHL	37	4	6	10	....	....	....	14	....	....	....	....	....
1944-45	Pittsburgh–Hershey	AHL	50	3	20	23	....	....	....	26	11	0	3	3	4
1945-46	Hershey–St. Louis	AHL	30	2	7	9	....	....	....	10	....	....	....	....	....
	NHL Totals		**34**	**1**	**0**	**1**	**2**	**0**	**2**	**35**	**7**	**0**	**0**	**0**	**0**

AHL First All-Star Team (1940) • AHL Second All-Star Team (1941, 1942)

Traded to **Detroit** by **Toronto** for $6,500, November 13, 1933.

● ROBERTSON, GEORGE George "Robbie" Robertson

LW/C – L. 6′1″, 172 lbs. b: Winnipeg, Man., 5/11/1928.

Season	Club	League	GP	G	A	Pts	AG	AA	APts	PIM	GP	G	A	Pts	PIM
1944-45	Winnipeg Monarchs	MJHL	7	7	6	13	....	....	....	6	16	4	10	14	20
1945-46	Winnipeg Monarchs	MJHL	9	8	2	10	....	....	....	2	7	5	5	10	12
1946-47	Stratford Kroehlers	OHA	30	20	27	47	....	....	....	20	2	1	3	4	0
1947-48	**Montreal Canadiens**	**NHL**	**1**	**0**	**0**	**0**	**0**	**0**	**0**	**0**	....	....	....	....	....
	Montreal Royals	QSHL	47	11	27	38	....	....	....	18	3	0	0	0	0
1948-49	**Montreal Canadiens**	**NHL**	**30**	**2**	**5**	**7**	**3**	**8**	**11**	**6**	....	....	....	....	....
	Buffalo–Washington	AHL	24	4	16	20	....	....	....	2	....	....	....	....	....
1949-50	Cincinnati Mohawks	AHL	26	3	5	8	....	....	....	0	....	....	....	....	....
	Victoria Cougars	PCHL	24	1	11	12	....	....	....	6	....	....	....	....	....
1950-51	Springfield Indians	AHL	5	1	3	4	....	....	....	0	....	....	....	....	....
	Sydney Millionaires	MMHL	26	12	20	32	....	....	....	25	17	4	9	13	13
1951-52	Sydney Millionaires	MMHL	86	26	44	70	....	....	....	56	....	....	....	....	....
1952-53	Sydney Millionaires	MMHL	74	18	48	66	....	....	....	24	6	1	2	3	0
1953-54	Sydney Millionaires	MMHL	70	32	48	80	....	....	....	30	14	4	2	6	2
1954-55	Saskatoon Quakers	WHL	35	4	15	19	....	....	....	8	....	....	....	....	....
	Grand Rapids Rockets	IHL	23	7	8	15	....	....	....	4	4	0	0	0	2
1955-56	Soo Greyhounds	NOHA	60	12	34	46	....	....	....	14	5	1	4	5	0
	NHL Totals		**31**	**2**	**5**	**7**	**3**	**8**	**11**	**6**	....	....	....	....	....

● ROBINSON, DOUG — *see page 1430*

● ROBINSON, EARL Earl Robinson

RW/C – R. 5′10″, 160 lbs. b: Montreal, Que., 3/11/1907. Deceased.

Season	Club	League	GP	G	A	Pts	AG	AA	APts	PIM	GP	G	A	Pts	PIM
1926-27	Montreal Victorias	City Sr.	5	3	0	3	....	....	....	2	....	....	....	....	....
1927-28	Philadelphia Arrows	Can-Am	34	18	7	25	....	....	....	21	....	....	....	....	....
1928-29	**Montreal Maroons**	**NHL**	**38**	**2**	**1**	**3**	**8**	**9**	**17**	**2**	....	....	....	....	....
1929-30	**Montreal Maroons**	**NHL**	**31**	**1**	**2**	**3**	**2**	**6**	**8**	**10**	**4**	**0**	**0**	**0**	**0**
	Windsor Bulldogs	IAHL	5	3	2	5	....	....	....	0	....	....	....	....	....
1930-31	Windsor Bulldogs	IAHL	48	*44	19	*63	....	....	....	18	6	*6	4	*10	0
1931-32	**Montreal Maroons**	**NHL**	**26**	**0**	**3**	**3**	**0**	**8**	**8**	**2**	....	....	....	....	....
	Windsor Bulldogs	IAHL	21	10	4	14	....	....	....	8	6	2	3	5	4
1932-33	**Montreal Maroons**	**NHL**	**44**	**15**	**9**	**24**	**35**	**24**	**59**	**6**	**2**	**0**	**0**	**0**	**0**
1933-34	**Montreal Maroons**	**NHL**	**47**	**12**	**16**	**28**	**27**	**43**	**70**	**14**	**4**	**2**	**0**	**2**	**0**
1934-35	**Montreal Maroons**	**NHL**	**48**	**17**	**18**	**35**	**36**	**40**	**76**	**23**	**7**	**2**	**2**	**4**	**0**
1935-36	**Montreal Maroons**	**NHL**	**39**	**6**	**14**	**20**	**15**	**34**	**49**	**27**	**3**	**0**	**0**	**0**	**0**
1936-37	**Montreal Maroons**	**NHL**	**47**	**16**	**18**	**34**	**35**	**42**	**77**	**19**	**5**	**1**	**2**	**3**	**0**
1937-38	**Montreal Maroons**	**NHL**	**39**	**4**	**7**	**11**	**8**	**14**	**22**	**13**	....	....	....	....	....
1938-39	**Chicago Black Hawks**	**NHL**	**47**	**9**	**6**	**15**	**19**	**11**	**30**	**13**	....	....	....	....	....
1939-40	**Montreal Canadiens**	**NHL**	**11**	**1**	**4**	**5**	**2**	**8**	**10**	**4**	....	....	....	....	....
	New Haven Eagles	AHL	25	11	14	25	....	....	....	2	3	2	2	4	0
1940-41	New Haven Eagles	AHL	56	16	19	35	....	....	....	19	2	0	0	0	0
1941-42	Providence Reds	AHL	1	0	0	0	....	....	....	0	....	....	....	....	....
	New Haven Eagles	AHL	48	13	20	33	....	....	....	2	2	0	0	0	2
1942-43	Research Colonels	Tor-Sr.	10	13	16	29	....	....	....	6	....	....	....	....	....
	NHL Totals		**417**	**83**	**98**	**181**	**187**	**239**	**426**	**133**	**25**	**5**	**4**	**9**	**0**

Played in NHL All-Star Game (1937, 1939)

Traded to **Chicago** by **Montreal Maroons** with Russ Blinco and Baldy Northcott for $30,000, September 15, 1938. Traded to **Montreal Canadiens** by **Chicago** for cash, October 11, 1939.

● ROCHE, DES Des (Michael Patrick) Roche

RW – R. 5′7″, 165 lbs. b: Kemptville, Ont., 2/1/1909. Deceased.

Season	Club	League	GP	G	A	Pts	AG	AA	APts	PIM	GP	G	A	Pts	PIM
1927-28	Montreal St. Anthony's	City Sr.	13	7	0	7	....	....	....	....	....	....	....	....	....
1928-29	Montreal Bell Telephone	City Sr.	....	5	4	9	....	....	....	20	....	....	....	....	....
	Montreal Martin	City Sr.	....	7	0	7	....	....	....	....	....	....	....	....	....
1929-30	Montreal AAA	City Sr.	10	6	0	6	....	....	....	8	2	1	0	1	2
	Montreal Bell Telephone	City Sr.	STATISTICS NOT AVAILABLE												
1930-31	**Montreal Maroons**	**NHL**	**19**	**0**	**1**	**1**	**0**	**4**	**4**	**6**	....	....	....	....	....
	Windsor Bulldogs	IAHL	26	10	2	12	....	....	....	16	6	1	0	1	2
1931-32	Windsor Bulldogs	IAHL	42	11	12	23	....	....	....	42	6	2	0	2	6
1932-33	**Montreal Maroons**	**NHL**	**5**	**0**	**0**	**0**	**0**	**0**	**0**	**0**	....	....	....	....	....
	Windsor Bulldogs	IAHL	20	7	4	11	....	....	....	32	....	....	....	....	....
	Ottawa Senators	**NHL**	**16**	**3**	**6**	**9**	**7**	**16**	**23**	**6**	....	....	....	....	....
1933-34	**Ottawa Senators**	**NHL**	**46**	**14**	**10**	**24**	**31**	**27**	**58**	**22**	....	....	....	....	....
1934-35	**St. Louis Eagles**	**NHL**	**7**	**0**	**0**	**0**	**0**	**0**	**0**	**0**	....	....	....	....	....
	Montreal Canadiens	**NHL**	**5**	**0**	**1**	**1**	**0**	**2**	**2**	**0**	....	....	....	....	....
	Detroit Red Wings	**NHL**	**15**	**3**	**0**	**3**	**6**	**0**	**6**	**10**	....	....	....	....	....
	Buffalo–Detroit	IAHL	8	1	4	5	....	....	....	8	5	*6	2	*8	4
1935-36	Pittsburgh–Cleveland	IAHL	44	10	12	22	....	....	....	36	2	0	0	0	0
1936-37	St. Louis Flyers	AHA	4	3	0	3	....	....	....	2	....	....	....	....	....
1937-38	Tulsa Oilers	AHA	32	12	9	21	....	....	....	27	....	....	....	....	....
1938-39	Spokane Clippers	PCHL	45	14	11	25	....	....	....	33	....	....	....	....	....
	NHL Totals		**113**	**20**	**18**	**38**	**44**	**49**	**93**	**44**	....	....	....	....	....

Signed as a free agent by **Montreal Maroons**, September 2, 1930. Traded to **Ottawa** by **Montreal Maroons** for Wally Kilrea, February 3, 1933. Transferred to **St. Louis** after **Ottawa** franchise relocated, September 22, 1934. Traded to **Boston** by **St. Louis** with Max Kaminsky for Joe Lamb, December 4, 1934. Traded to **Montreal Canadiens** by **Boston** for cash, December 8, 1934. Traded to **Buffalo** (IAHL) by **Montreal Canadiens** for cash, December 26, 1934. Traded to **Detroit** by **Buffalo** (IAHL) for cash, January 1, 1935. Traded to **Pittsburgh** (IAHL) by **Detroit** for cash, October 17, 1935.

● ROCHE, EARL Earl Roche

LW – L. 5′11″, 175 lbs. b: Prescott, Ont., 2/22/1910. d: 1966.

Season	Club	League	GP	G	A	Pts	AG	AA	APts	PIM	GP	G	A	Pts	PIM
1928-29	Montreal Bell Telephone	City Sr.	....	*10	4	*14	....	....	....	24	....	....	....	....	....
	Montreal Martins	City Sr.	....	2	0	2	....	....	....	2	....	....	....	....	....
1929-30	Montreal AAA	City Sr.	10	6	0	6	....	....	....	18	2	*1	*1	*2	6
1930-31	**Montreal Maroons**	**NHL**	**42**	**2**	**0**	**2**	**5**	**0**	**5**	**18**	**2**	**0**	**0**	**0**	**0**
1931-32	Windsor Bulldogs	IAHL	48	22	18	40	....	....	....	51	6	0	1	1	2
1932-33	**Montreal Maroons**	**NHL**	**5**	**0**	**0**	**0**	**0**	**0**	**0**	**0**	....	....	....	....	....
	Windsor Bulldogs	IAHL	17	6	8	14	....	....	....	23	....	....	....	....	....
	Boston Bruins	**NHL**	**3**	**0**	**0**	**0**	**0**	**0**	**0**	**0**	....	....	....	....	....
	Ottawa Senators	**NHL**	**20**	**4**	**5**	**9**	**9**	**13**	**22**	**6**	....	....	....	....	....
1933-34	**Ottawa Senators**	**NHL**	**45**	**13**	**16**	**29**	**29**	**43**	**72**	**22**	....	....	....	....	....
	Detroit Olympics	IAHL	5	0	0	0	....	....	....	2	....	....	....	....	....
1934-35	**St. Louis Eagles**	**NHL**	**19**	**3**	**3**	**6**	**6**	**7**	**13**	**2**	....	....	....	....	....
	Detroit Red Wings	**NHL**	**13**	**3**	**3**	**6**	**6**	**7**	**13**	**0**	....	....	....	....	....
	Detroit–Buffalo	IAHL	8	3	2	5	....	....	....	6	5	1	*4	5	0
1935-36	Pittsburgh–Cleveland	IAHL	47	21	19	40	....	....	....	56	2	0	0	0	0
1936-37	Cleveland Barons	AHL	44	11	17	28	....	....	....	48	....	....	....	....	....
1937-38	Cleveland Barons	AHL	46	4	9	13	....	....	....	12	1	0	2	2	2
1938-39	Cleveland–Hershey	AHL	51	4	13	17	....	....	....	14	5	0	3	3	0
	Providence Reds	AHL	1	0	0	0	....	....	....	0	....	....	....	....	....
1939-40	New Haven Eagles	AHL	54	13	28	41	....	....	....	14	3	0	3	3	0
1940-41	New Haven Eagles	AHL	51	18	17	35	....	....	....	22	2	0	0	0	2
1941-42	New Haven Eagles	AHL	56	9	20	29	....	....	....	19	2	0	0	0	2
	NHL Totals		**147**	**25**	**27**	**52**	**55**	**70**	**125**	**48**	**2**	**0**	**0**	**0**	**0**

Signed as a free agent by **Montreal Maroons**, September 2, 1930. Signed as a free agent by **Boston**, January 14, 1933. Traded to **Ottawa** by **Boston** to complete transaction that sent Alex Smith to Boston, January 25, 1933. Transferred to **St. Louis** after **Ottawa** franchise relocated, September 22, 1934. Traded to **Buffalo** (IAHL) by **St. Louis** for cash, December 20, 1934. Traded to **Detroit** by **Buffalo** (IAHL) for cash, January 1, 1935.

● ROCHE, ERNEST Ernest Roche

D – L. 6′1″, 170 lbs. b: Montreal, Que., 2/4/1930.

Season	Club	League	GP	G	A	Pts	AG	AA	APts	PIM	GP	G	A	Pts	PIM
1946-47	Montreal Jr. Canadiens	QJHL	27	3	9	12	....	....	....	52	16	3	15	18	30
1947-48	Montreal Jr. Canadiens	QJHL	32	9	10	19	....	....	....	68	5	0	0	0	6
1948-49	Montreal Jr. Canadiens	QJHL	48	11	12	23	....	....	....	73	4	1	1	2	2
1948-49	Montreal Jr. Canadiens	QJHL	48	11	12	23	....	....	....	73	4	1	1	2	2
1949-50	Montreal Jr. Canadiens	QJHL	36	12	12	24	....	....	....	81	28	6	23	29	56
1950-51	**Montreal Canadiens**	**NHL**	**4**	**0**	**0**	**0**	**0**	**0**	**0**	**2**	....	....	....	....	....
	Cincinnati Mohawks	AHL	60	3	10	13	....	....	....	21	....	....	....	....	....
1951-52	Buffalo Bisons	AHL	4	0	1	1	....	....	....	2	....	....	....	....	....
	Victoria Cougars	PCHL	64	6	17	23	....	....	....	60	10	0	1	1	4
1952-53	Victoria Cougars	WHL	65	10	25	35	....	....	....	69	....	....	....	....	....
1953-54	Montreal Royals	QHL	51	1	15	16	....	....	....	48	9	2	1	3	4
	Victoria Cougars	WHL	5	0	0	0	....	....	....	4	....	....	....	....	....
1954-55	Montreal Royals	QHL	56	11	11	22	....	....	....	52	14	1	4	5	14
1955-56	Springfield Indians	AHL	22	3	5	8	....	....	....	10	....	....	....	....	....
	Shawinigan Cataracts	QHL	24	2	8	10	....	....	....	10	11	0	1	1	4
1956-57	Montreal Royals	QHL	64	4	21	25	....	....	....	66	4	0	0	0	0
1956-57	Hull-Ottawa Canadiens	EOHL	1	0	0	0	....	....	....	0	....	....	....	....	....
1957-58	Montreal Royals	QHL	53	5	15	20	....	....	....	40	7	1	1	2	2
1958-59	Montreal Royals	QHL	51	1	8	9	....	....	....	16	3	0	0	0	0
1959-60	Sudbury Wolves	EPHL	62	4	29	33	....	....	....	38	14	2	3	5	22
1960-61	Sudbury Wolves	EPHL	5	0	2	2	....	....	....	2	....	....	....	....	....
	Windsor Maple Leafs	NSSHL	....	4	6	10	....	....	....	6	....	....	....	....	....
	Milwaukee Falcons	IHL	10	2	0	2	....	....	....	4	....	....	....	....	....
	NHL Totals		**4**	**0**	**0**	**0**	**0**	**0**	**0**	**2**	....	....	....	....	....

Claimed by **Springfield** (AHL) from **Montreal** in Reverse Draft, June 1, 1955.

• ROCHEFORT, DAVE
Dave Rochefort
C – L. 6′, 180 lbs. b: Red Deer, Alta., 7/22/1946.

Season	Club	League	GP	G	A	Pts	AG	AA	APts	PIM	GP	G	A	Pts	PIM
			REGULAR SEASON								PLAYOFFS				
1963-64	Edmonton Oil Kings	AJHL	6	3	5	8	....	....	....	21	....	....	....	....	....
1964-65	Edmonton Oil Kings	AJHL	STATISTICS NOT AVAILABLE												
1965-66	Edmonton Oil Kings	ASHL	24	6	10	16	....	....	....	34	....	....	....	....	....
1966-67	**Detroit Red Wings**	**NHL**	**1**	**0**	**0**	**0**	**0**	**0**	**0**	**0**	....	....	....	....	....
	Memphis Wings	CHL	32	5	8	13	....	....	....	10	....	....	....	....	....
	Pittsburgh Hornets	AHL	1	0	0	0	....	....	....	0	....	....	....	....	....
1967-68	Fort Worth Wings	CHL	65	15	18	33	....	....	....	55	12	2	0	2	16
1968-69	Baltimore Clippers	AHL	46	2	7	9	....	....	....	22	....	....	....	....	....
1969-70	Oklahoma City Blazers	CHL	3	0	1	1	....	....	....	2	....	....	....	....	....
	Salt Lake Golden Eagles	WHL	59	7	16	23	....	....	....	40	....	....	....	....	....
1970-71	Edmonton Oil Kings	ASHL	STATISTICS NOT AVAILABLE												
1971-72	Edmonton Oil Kings	ASHL	....	29	23	43	....	....	....	43	....	....	....	....	....
	NHL Totals		**1**	**0**	**0**	**0**	**0**	**0**	**0**	**0**	....	....	....	....	....

• ROCHEFORT, LEON
— see page 1432

• ROCKBURN, HARVEY
Harvey "Hard Rock" Rockburn
D – L. 5′10″, 180 lbs. b: Ottawa, Ont., 8/20/1908. d: 6/9/1977.

Season	Club	League	GP	G	A	Pts	AG	AA	APts	PIM	GP	G	A	Pts	PIM
1925-26	Ottawa Gunners	City Sr.	15	3	1	4	....	....	....	....	6	0	0	0	0
1926-27	Ottawa Shamrocks	City Sr.	2	1	1	2	....	....	....	....	....	....	....	....	....
	Berlin Mountaineers	NEHL	27	6	4	10	....	....	....	24	....	....	....	....	....
1927-28	Detroit Olympics	Can-Pro	36	2	1	3	....	....	....	82	2	0	0	0	8
1928-29	Detroit Olympics	Can-Pro	37	2	1	3	....	....	....	*176	7	1	0	1	*42
1929-30	**Detroit Cougars**	**NHL**	**36**	**4**	**0**	**4**	**8**	**0**	**8**	**97**	....	....	....	....	....
1930-31	**Detroit Falcons**	**NHL**	**42**	**0**	**1**	**1**	**0**	**4**	**4**	***118**	....	....	....	....	....
1931-32	Detroit Olympics	IAHL	46	6	3	9	....	....	....	*149	6	1	0	1	20
1932-33	**Ottawa Senators**	**NHL**	**16**	**0**	**1**	**1**	**0**	**3**	**3**	**39**	....	....	....	....	....
	Windsor Bulldogs	IAHL	18	1	0	1	....	....	....	36	....	....	....	....	....
	Providence Reds	Can-Am	4	0	0	0	....	....	....	20	....	....	....	....	....
1933-34	London Panthers	IAHL	41	6	11	17	....	....	....	*113	4	0	0	0	12
1934-35	Windsor Bulldogs	IAHL	40	4	2	6	....	....	....	*114	....	....	....	....	....
1935-36	Cleveland–Rochester	IAHL	33	0	1	1	....	....	....	83	....	....	....	....	....
1936-37	Kansas City Greyhounds	AHA	48	5	3	8	....	....	....	73	2	0	0	0	4
1937-38	St. Paul Saints	AHA	32	2	5	7	....	....	....	46	....	....	....	....	....
	Portland Buckaroos	PCHL	6	0	0	0	....	....	....	16	....	....	....	....	....
1938-39			REINSTATED AS AN AMATEUR												
1939-40	Ottawa Lasalle	City Sr.	15	0	5	5	....	....	....	36	4	2	1	3	9
	NHL Totals		**94**	**4**	**2**	**6**	**8**	**7**	**15**	**254**	....	....	....	....	....

AHA Second All-Star Team (1937)

Signed as a free agent by **Stratford** (Can-Pro), October 24, 1927. Traded to **Detroit Cougars** by **Stratford** (Can-Pro) for cash, October 31, 1927. Signed as a free agent by **Ottawa**, February 2, 1933.

• RODDEN, EDDIE
Eddie Rodden
C – R. 5′7″, 150 lbs. b: Mattawa, Ont., 3/22/1901. Deceased.

Season	Club	League	GP	G	A	Pts	AG	AA	APts	PIM	GP	G	A	Pts	PIM
1921-22	Toronto Aura Lee	OHA Sr.	10	9	6	15	....	....	....	....	2	0	1	1	....
1922-23	Toronto Granites	OHA Sr.	7	3	1	4	....	....	....	....	4	4	1	5	....
1923-24	Eveleth Rangers	USAHA	21	9	0	9	....	....	....	....	....	....	....	....	....
1924-25	Eveleth Arrowheads	USAHA	39	1	0	1	....	....	....	....	3	0	0	0	....
1925-26	Eveleth Rangers	USAHA	36	7	9	16	....	....	....	42	....	....	....	....	....
1926-27	Minneapolis Millers	AHA	19	6	3	9	....	....	....	8	....	....	....	....	....
	Chicago Black Hawks	**NHL**	**19**	**3**	**3**	**6**	**9**	**25**	**34**	**0**	**2**	**0**	**1**	**1**	**0**
1927-28	**Chicago Black Hawks**	**NHL**	**9**	**0**	**2**	**2**	**0**	**17**	**17**	**6**	....	....	....	....	....
	Toronto Maple Leafs	**NHL**	**25**	**3**	**6**	**9**	**9**	**51**	**60**	**36**	....	....	....	....	....
1928-29	**Boston Bruins**	**NHL**	**20**	**0**	**0**	**0**	**0**	**0**	**0**	**10**	....	....	....	....	....
	Windsor Bulldogs	Can-Pro	19	6	5	11	....	....	....	14	3	1	0	1	20
1929-30	London Panthers	IAHL	42	13	*30	43	....	....	....	50	2	1	0	1	2
1930-31	**New York Rangers**	**NHL**	**24**	**0**	**3**	**3**	**0**	**11**	**11**	**8**	....	....	....	....	....
	Pittsburgh Yellowjackets	IAHL	29	7	7	14	....	....	....	21	6	0	1	1	6
1931-32	Pittsburgh Yellowjackets	IAHL	42	5	13	18	....	....	....	43	....	....	....	....	....
1932-33	Quebec Beavers	Can-Am	11	3	3	0	....	....	....	12	....				
	Windsor Bulldogs	IAHL	21	2	4	6	....	....	....	10	6	0	0	0	2
1933-34	Tulsa Oilers	AHA	13	2	6	8	....	....	....	10	4	1	1	2	0
	NHL Totals		**97**	**6**	**14**	**20**	**18**	**104**	**122**	**60**	**2**	**0**	**1**	**1**	**0**

Signed as a free agent by **Minneapolis** (AHA), October 21, 1926. Traded to **Chicago** by **Minneapolis** (AHA) for Ken Doraty, January 27, 1927. Traded to **Toronto** by **Chicago** to complete three team transaction that sent Bert McCaffrey to Pittsburgh and Ty Arbour to Chicago, November 7, 1927. Traded to **Boston** by **Toronto** for cash, June 20, 1928. Traded to **London** (IAHL) by **Boston** for cash, October 16, 1929. Traded to **NY Rangers** by **London** (IAHL) for $8,500, September 11, 1930. Traded to **Pittsburgh** (IAHL) by **NY Rangers** for cash, January 3, 1931.

• ROLFE, DALE
— see page 1434

• ROMNES, DOC
Doc (Elwyn) Romnes **USHOF**
LW/C – L. 5′11″, 156 lbs. b: White Bear, MN, 1/1/1909. Deceased.

Season	Club	League	GP	G	A	Pts	AG	AA	APts	PIM	GP	G	A	Pts	PIM
			REGULAR SEASON								PLAYOFFS				
1927-28	St. Paul Saints	AHA	40	2	3	5	....	....	....	16	....	....	....	....	....
1928-29	St. Paul Saints	AHA	39	7	3	10	....	....	....	22	8	2	0	2	6
1929-30	St. Paul Saints	AHA	36	15	4	19	....	....	....	26	....	....	....	....	....
1930-31	**Chicago Black Hawks**	**NHL**	**30**	**5**	**7**	**12**	**12**	**25**	**37**	**8**	**9**	**1**	**1**	**2**	**2**
	London Tecumsehs	IAHL	13	5	5	10	....	....	....	14	....	....	....	....	....
1931-32	**Chicago Black Hawks**	**NHL**	**18**	**1**	**0**	**1**	**2**	**0**	**2**	**6**	**2**	**0**	**0**	**0**	**0**
	Pittsburgh Yellowjackets	IAHL	31	11	2	13	....	....	....	6	....	....	....	....	....
1932-33	**Chicago Black Hawks**	**NHL**	**47**	**10**	**12**	**22**	**23**	**32**	**55**	**2**	....	....	....	....	....
1933-34	**Chicago Black Hawks**	**NHL**	**47**	**8**	**21**	**29**	**18**	**57**	**75**	**6**	**8**	**2**	***7**	**9**	**0**
1934-35	**Chicago Black Hawks**	**NHL**	**35**	**10**	**14**	**24**	**21**	**31**	**52**	**8**	**2**	**0**	**0**	**0**	**0**
1935-36	**Chicago Black Hawks**	**NHL**	**48**	**13**	**25**	**38**	**32**	**61**	**93**	**6**	**2**	**1**	**2**	**3**	**0**
1936-37	**Chicago Black Hawks**	**NHL**	**28**	**4**	**14**	**18**	**9**	**33**	**42**	**2**	....	....	....	....	....
1937-38	**Chicago Black Hawks**	**NHL**	**44**	**10**	**22**	**32**	**21**	**46**	**67**	**4**	**12**	**2**	**4**	**6**	**2**
1938-39	**Chicago Black Hawks**	**NHL**	**12**	**0**	**4**	**4**	**0**	**7**	**7**	**0**	....	....	....	....	....
	Toronto Maple Leafs	**NHL**	**36**	**7**	**16**	**23**	**15**	**30**	**45**	**0**	**10**	**1**	**4**	**5**	**0**
1939-40	**New York Americans**	**NHL**	**15**	**0**	**1**	**1**	**0**	**2**	**2**	**0**	....	....	....	....	....
	Omaha Knights	AHA	14	12	19	31	....	....	....	6	9	3	4	7	0
	NHL Totals		**360**	**68**	**136**	**204**	**153**	**324**	**477**	**42**	**45**	**7**	**18**	**25**	**4**

Won Lady Byng Trophy (1936)

Traded to **Chicago** by **St. Paul** (AHA) for cash, October 28, 1930. Traded to **Toronto** by **Chicago** for Bill Thoms, December 8, 1938. Traded to **NY Americans** by **Toronto** with Buzz Boll, Harvey Jackson, Murray Armstrong and Jim Fowler for Sweeny Schriner, May 15, 1939. Traded to **Omaha** (AHA) by **NY Americans** for cash, February 7, 1940.

• RONAN, SKENE
Skene (Erskine) Ronan
D/C – L. 5′6″, 150 lbs. b: Ottawa, Ont.. Deceased.

Season	Club	League	GP	G	A	Pts	AG	AA	APts	PIM	GP	G	A	Pts	PIM
1907-08	Ottawa Primrose	City Sr.	5	*11	0	*11	....	....	....	....	....	....	....	....	....
1908-09	Toronto Professionals	OPHL	7	4	0	4	....	....	....	4	....	....	....	....	....
	Pittsburgh Bankers	WPHL	8	5	0	5	....	....	....	....	....	....	....	....	....
	Haileybury Silver Kings	TPHL	5	6	0	6	....	....	....	7	2	1	0	1	6
1909-10	Haileybury Silver Kings	NHA	11	3	0	3	....	....	....	21	....	....	....	....	....
1910-11	Renfrew Creamery Kings	NHA	5	3	0	3	....	....	....	9	....	....	....	....	....
1911-12	Ottawa Senators	NHA	18	*35	0	*35	....	....	....	5	....	....	....	....	....
1912-13	Ottawa Senators	NHA	20	18	0	18	....	....	....	39	....	....	....	....	....
1913-14	Ottawa Senators	NHA	19	18	5	23	....	....	....	65	....	....	....	....	....
1914-15	Toronto Shamrocks	NHA	18	21	4	25	....	....	....	55	....	....	....	....	....
1915-16	Toronto Blue Shirts	NHA	9	0	3	3	....	....	....	8	....	....	....	....	....
	Montreal Canadiens	NHA	8	6	4	10	....	....	....	14	2	1	0	1	0
1916-17	Ottawa Munitions	City Sr.	DID NOT PLAY – COACHING												
1917-18	Ottawa Munitions	City Sr.	DID NOT PLAY – COACHING												
1918-19	**Ottawa Senators**	**NHL**	**10**	**0**	**0**	**0**	**0**	**0**	**0**	**9**	....	....	....	....	....
	NHL Totals		**10**	**0**	**0**	**0**	**0**	**0**	**0**	**9**	....	....	....	....	....
	Other Major League Totals		115	108	16	124	....	....	....	220	2	1	0	1	0

Traded to **Ottawa** by **Montreal Canadiens** for rights to Harry Hyland, December 9, 1918. Released by **Ottawa**, January 26, 1919. Re-signed as a free agent by **Ottawa**, February 17, 1919.

• RONSON, LEN
— see page 1435

• RONTY, PAUL
Paul Ronty
C – L. 6′, 160 lbs. b: Toronto, Ont., 6/12/1928.

Season	Club	League	GP	G	A	Pts	AG	AA	APts	PIM	GP	G	A	Pts	PIM
1945-46	Boston Olympics	EHL	49	19	25	44	....	....	....	14	12	6	11	17	2
1946-47	Hershey Bears	AHL	64	19	40	59	....	....	....	12	11	0	2	2	2
1947-48	**Boston Bruins**	**NHL**	**24**	**3**	**11**	**14**	**4**	**16**	**20**	**0**	**5**	**0**	**4**	**4**	**0**
	Hershey Bears	AHL	31	15	24	39	....	....	....	2	....	....	....	....	....
1948-49	**Boston Bruins**	**NHL**	**60**	**20**	**29**	**49**	**32**	**46**	**78**	**11**	**5**	**1**	**2**	**3**	**2**
1949-50	**Boston Bruins**	**NHL**	**70**	**23**	**36**	**59**	**31**	**46**	**77**	**8**	....	....	....	....	....
1950-51	**Boston Bruins**	**NHL**	**70**	**10**	**22**	**32**	**13**	**20**	**41**	**20**	**6**	**0**	**1**	**1**	**2**
1951-52	**New York Rangers**	**NHL**	**65**	**12**	**31**	**43**	**17**	**40**	**57**	**16**	....	....	....	....	....
1952-53	**New York Rangers**	**NHL**	**70**	**16**	**38**	**54**	**25**	**54**	**79**	**20**	....	....	....	....	....
1953-54	**New York Rangers**	**NHL**	**70**	**13**	**33**	**46**	**20**	**45**	**65**	**18**	....	....	....	....	....
1954-55	**New York Rangers**	**NHL**	**55**	**4**	**11**	**15**	**6**	**14**	**20**	**0**	....	....	....	....	....
	Montreal Canadiens	**NHL**	**4**	**0**	**0**	**0**	**0**	**0**	**0**	**2**	**5**	**0**	**0**	**0**	**2**
	NHL Totals		**488**	**101**	**211**	**312**	**148**	**289**	**437**	**103**	**21**	**1**	**7**	**8**	**6**

Played in NHL All-Star Game (1949, 1950, 1953, 1954)

Traded to **NY Rangers** by **Boston** for Gus Kyle, cash and the rights to Pentti Lund, September 20, 1951. Claimed on waivers by **Montreal** from **NY Rangers**, February 20, 1955.

• ROSS, ART
Art Ross **HHOF**
D – L. 5′11″, 190 lbs. b: Naughton, Ont., 1/13/1886. d: 8/5/1964.

Season	Club	League	GP	G	A	Pts	AG	AA	APts	PIM	GP	G	A	Pts	PIM
1904-05	Montreal Merchants	CAHL	8	10	0	10	....	....	....	....	....	....	....	....	....
1905-06	Brandon Kings	MHL Sr.	7	6	0	6	....	....	....	....	....	....	....	....	....
1906-07	Brandon Kings	MHL Sr.	9	5	0	5	....	....	....	....	2	0	0	0	0
	Kenora Thistles	MHL Sr.	....	....	....	....	....	....	....		2	0	0	0	0
1907-08	Montreal Wanderers	ECAHA	10	8	0	8	....	....	....	27	5	3	0	3	23
	Pembroke Lumber Kings	Ott-Sr.	1	5	0	5	....	....	....	....	....	....	....	....	....
1908-09	Montreal Wanderers	ECHA	9	2	0	2	....	....	....	30	2	0	0	0	....
	Montreal Wanderers	NYSHL	2	2	0	2	....	....	....	3	....	....	....	....	....
	Cobalt Silver Kings	TPHL	....	....	....	....	....	....	....	....	2	1	0	1	0
1909-10	Haileybury Silver Kings	NHA	12	6	0	6	....	....	....	25	....	....	....	....	....
	All-Montreal	CHA	4	4	0	4	....	....	....	3	....	....	....	....	....
1910-11	Montreal Wanderers	NHA	11	4	0	4	....	....	....	24	....	....	....	....	....
1911-12	Montreal Wanderers	NHA	18	16	0	16	....	....	....	35		....	....	....	....
1912-13	Montreal Wanderers	NHA	19	11	0	11	....	....	....	58	....	....	....	....	....
1913-14	Montreal Wanderers	NHA	18	4	5	9	....	....	....	74	....	....	....	....	....
1914-15	Ottawa Senators	NHA	16	3	1	4	....	....	....	55	5	2	0	2	0
1915-16	Ottawa Senators	NHA	21	8	8	16	....	....	....	69	....	....	....	....	....
1916-17	Montreal Wanderers	NHA	16	6	3	9	....	....	....	63	....	....	....	....	....
1917-18	**Montreal Wanderers**	**NHL**	**3**	**1**	**0**	**1**	**2**	**0**	**2**	**12**	....	....	....	....	....
	NHL Totals		**3**	**1**	**0**	**1**	**2**	**0**	**2**	**12**	....	....	....	....	....
	Other Major League Totals		163	77	17	94	....	....	....	463	16	5	0	5	23

Won Lester Patrick Trophy (1984)

Rights retained by **Montreal Wanderers** after NHA folded, November 26, 1917

• ROSS, JIM   Jim Ross

D – R. 6'3", 185 lbs.   b: Edinburgh, Scotland, 5/20/1926.

Season	Club	League	GP	G	A	Pts	AG	AA	APts	PIM	Playoffs GP	G	A	Pts	PIM
1945-46	Toronto de Lasalle	City Jr.	STATISTICS NOT AVAILABLE												
1946-47	Perth Panthers	Britain	60	26	22	48	....	....	....	64	....	....	....	....	....
1947-48	Detroit Metal Moldings	IHL	30	7	13	20	....	....	....	35	3	0	1	1	6
1948-49	Detroit Jerry Lynch	IHL	31	9	20	29	....	....	....	38	2	0	1	1	0
1949-50	Sydney Millionaires	CBSHL	72	14	31	45	....	....	....	81	14	7	4	11	14
1950-51	Quebec Aces	QSHL	50	6	21	27	....	....	....	62	19	1	4	5	16
1951-52	**New York Rangers**	**NHL**	**51**	**2**	**9**	**11**	**3**	**12**	**15**	**25**	....	....	....	....	....
	Cincinnati Mohawks	AHL	7	0	3	3	....	....	....	4	....	....	....	....	....
1952-53	**New York Rangers**	**NHL**	**11**	**0**	**2**	**2**	**0**	**3**	**3**	**4**	....	....	....	....	....
	Saskatoon Quakers	WHL	42	3	10	13	....	....	....	40	13	1	7	8	12
1953-54	Saskatoon Quakers	WHL	57	5	17	22	....	....	....	38	6	2	1	3	2
1954-55	Saskatoon Quakers	WHL	65	6	11	17	....	....	....	31	....	....	....	....	....
	NHL Totals		**62**	**2**	**11**	**13**	**3**	**15**	**18**	**29**	....	....	....	....	....

IHL Northern Division First All-Star Team (1949) • WHL First All-Star Team (1954)

• ROSSIGNOL, ROLAND   Roland "Roly" Rossignol

RW – R. 5'9", 168 lbs.   b: Edmundston, N.B., 10/18/1921.

Season	Club	League	GP	G	A	Pts	AG	AA	APts	PIM	Playoffs GP	G	A	Pts	PIM
1936-37	Edmundston High School	H.S.	1	0	0	0	....	....	....	0	3	1	0	1	2
1937-38	Edmundston Fraser Pulp	NNBSL	8	7	2	9	....	....	....	6	2	1	0	1	6
1938-39	Edmundston Fraser Pulp	NNBSL	5	5	8	13	....	....	....	2	2	2	0	2	....
	Edmunston Eskimos	City Sr.	3	1	1	2	....	....	....	....	4	1	2	3	2
	Edmundston High Scool	H.S.	....	....	....	....	....	....	....	....	1	1	1	2	0
1939-40	Verdun Maple Leafs	Mtl-Jr.	12	2	5	7	....	....	....	10	4	1	2	3	11
1940-41	Verdun Maple Leafs	Mtl-Sr.	1	0	0	0	....	....	....	0	....	....	....	....	....
	Washington Eagles	EHL	65	23	23	46	....	....	....	44	2	0	0	0	0
1941-42	Quebec Aces	QCHL	32	12	10	22	....	....	....	30	13	1	2	3	2
1942-43	Quebec Aces	QCHL	34	16	16	32	....	....	....	18	4	1	1	2	4
1943-44	**Detroit Red Wings**	**NHL**	**1**	**0**	**1**	**1**	**0**	**1**	**1**	**0**	....	....	....	....	....
	Quebec Aces	QSHL	25	22	18	40	....	....	....	20	15	13	13	26	2
1944-45	**Montreal Canadiens**	**NHL**	**5**	**2**	**2**	**4**	**3**	**3**	**6**	**2**	**1**	**0**	**0**	**0**	**2**
	Pittsburgh Hornets	AHL	38	19	24	43	....	....	....	29	....	....	....	....	....
1945-46	**Detroit Red Wings**	**NHL**	**8**	**1**	**2**	**3**	**2**	**4**	**6**	**4**	....	....	....	....	....
	Indianapolis Capitals	AHL	48	26	21	47	....	....	....	25	5	1	1	2	4
1946-47	St. Louis–Providence	AHL	58	17	19	36	....	....	....	25	....	....	....	....	....
1947-48	Providence Reds	AHL	6	2	2	4	....	....	....	2	....	....	....	....	....
1948-49			DID NOT PLAY – INJURED												
1949-50	Quebec Aces	QSHL	42	12	23	35	....	....	....	17	9	1	1	2	....
1950-51	Jonquiere Aces	QPHL	STATISTICS NOT AVAILABLE												
1951-52			DID NOT PLAY												
1952-53	Mont Joli Castors	SLSHL	58	42	59	101	....	....	....	75	....	....	....	....	....
1953-54	Riviere-du-Loop 3 L's	SLSHL	8	2	5	7	....	....	....	4	....	....	....	....	....
	Dalhousie Rangers	NNBSL	....	25	24	49	....	....	....	41	....	....	....	....	....
1954-55	Dalhousie Rangers	NNBSL	....	*43	*62	*105	....	....	....	28	....	....	....	....	....
1955-56	Bathurst Papermakers	NNBSL	....	40	42	82	....	....	....	24	....	....	....	....	....
1956-57	Bathurst Papermakers	NNBSL	....	21	42	63	....	....	....	34	....	....	....	....	....
1957-58	Bathurst Papermakers	NNBSL	....	12	53	65	....	....	....	37	....	....	....	....	....
1958-59	Bathurst Papermakers	NNBSL	....	13	23	36	....	....	....	30	....	....	....	....	....
1959-60	Bathurst Papermakers	NNBSL	DID NOT PLAY – COACHING												
1960-61	Bathurst Papermakers	NNBSL	DID NOT PLAY – COACHING												
1961-62	Bathurst Papermakers	NNBSL	....	17	27	44	....	....	....	16	....	....	....	....	....
1962-63	Bathurst Papermakers	NNBSL	....	6	12	18	....	....	....	14	....	....	....	....	....
	NHL Totals		**14**	**3**	**5**	**8**	**5**	**8**	**13**	**6**	**1**	**0**	**0**	**0**	**2**

Loaned to **Detroit** by **Montreal** as an emergency injury replacement, March 11, 1944. Traded to **Detroit** by **Montreal** with Ray Getliffe for Billy Reay, September 11, 1945. Getliffe decided to retire and Detroit was awarded the rights to Fern Gauthier as compensation, October 19, 1945.

• ROTHSCHILD, SAM   Sam Rothschild

LW – L. 5'6", 145 lbs.   b: Sudbury, Ont., 10/16/1899.   d: 4/15/1987.

Season	Club	League	GP	G	A	Pts	AG	AA	APts	PIM	Playoffs GP	G	A	Pts	PIM
1916-17	Montreal Harmonia	Inter-Sr.	9	*16	0	*16	....	....	....	....	....	....	....	....	....
1917-18	McGill University Redmen	Mtl-Sr.	STATISTICS NOT AVAILABLE												
1918-19	Montreal Stars	City Sr.	5	2	3	5	....	....	....	6	....	....	....	....	....
1919-20	Sudbury Jr. Wolves	NOHA	STATISTICS NOT AVAILABLE												
1920-21	Sudbury Wolves	NOHA	9	10	2	12	....	....	....	0	....	....	....	....	....
1921-22	Sudbury Wolves	NOHA	6	5	5	10	....	....	....	3	....	....	....	....	....
1922-23	Sudbury Wolves	NOHA	7	6	4	10	....	....	....	22	2	1	0	1	2
1923-24	Sudbury Wolves	NOHA	STATISTICS NOT AVAILABLE												
1924-25	**Montreal Maroons**	**NHL**	**27**	**5**	**4**	**9**	**17**	**53**	**70**	**4**	....	....	....	....	....
1925-26	**Montreal Maroons**	**NHL**	**33**	**2**	**1**	**3**	**6**	**11**	**17**	**8**	**8**	**0**	**0**	**0**	**0**
1926-27	**Montreal Maroons**	**NHL**	**22**	**1**	**1**	**2**	**3**	**8**	**11**	**8**	**2**	**0**	**0**	**0**	**0**
1927-28	**New York Americans**	**NHL**	**5**	**0**	**0**	**0**	**0**	**0**	**0**	**4**	....	....	....	....	....
	Pittsburgh Pirates	**NHL**	**12**	**0**	**0**	**0**	**0**	**0**	**0**	**0**	....	....	....	....	....
	NHL Totals		**99**	**8**	**6**	**14**	**26**	**72**	**98**	**24**	**10**	**0**	**0**	**0**	**0**

Signed as a free agent by **Montreal Maroons**, October 20, 1924. Signed as a free agent by **NY Americans**, January 5, 1928. Traded to **Pittsburgh** by **NY Americans** for cash, December 25, 1927. • Suspended by Pittsburgh for breaking training rules, January, 1928.

• ROULSTON, ROLLY   Rolly "Orville" Roulston

LW/D – L. 6'1", 195 lbs.   b: Toronto, Ont., 4/12/1911.   d: 4/24/1983.

Season	Club	League	GP	G	A	Pts	AG	AA	APts	PIM	Playoffs GP	G	A	Pts	PIM
1928-29	Toronto Canoe Club	OHA	1	0	0	0	....	....	....	....	....	....	....	....	....
1929-30	Toronto Canoe Club	OHA	9	3	0	3	....	....	....	10	....	....	....	....	....
1930-31	Portland Buckaroos	PCHL	34	3	0	3	....	....	....	68	....	....	....	....	....
1931-32	Cleveland Indians	IAHL	36	0	3	3	....	....	....	34	....	....	....	....	....
1932-33	Cleveland Indians	IAHL	10	0	0	0	....	....	....	2	....	....	....	....	....
	Hershey B'ars	EHL	10	10	1	11	....	....	....	4	2	1	0	1	0
1933-34	Tulsa Oilers	AHA	47	20	12	32	....	....	....	36	4	0	0	0	2
	Wichita Vikings	AHA	1	0	0	0	....	....	....	6	4	0	0	0	2
1934-35	Detroit Olympics	IAHL	40	3	2	5	....	....	....	23	5	0	1	1	2
	Windsor Bulldogs	IAHL	2	0	0	0	....	....	....	0	....	....	....	....	....
1935-36	**Detroit Red Wings**	**NHL**	**1**	**0**	**0**	**0**	**0**	**0**	**0**	**0**	....	....	....	....	....
	Detroit Olympics	IAHL	44	9	8	17	....	....	....	40	6	2	1	3	6
1936-37	**Detroit Red Wings**	**NHL**	**21**	**0**	**5**	**5**	**0**	**12**	**12**	**10**	....	....	....	....	....
	Pittsburgh Hornets	AHL	8	3	1	4	....	....	....	10	....	....	....	....	....
1937-38	**Detroit Red Wings**	**NHL**	**2**	**0**	**1**	**1**	**0**	**2**	**2**	**0**	....	....	....	....	....
	Pittsburgh Hornets	AHL	48	4	5	9	....	....	....	31	2	0	1	1	0
1938-39	Hershey Bears	AHL	52	3	14	17	....	....	....	75	5	2	0	2	4
1939-40	Hershey Bears	AHL	45	7	12	19	....	....	....	22	6	1	0	1	4
1940-41	Hershey Bears	AHL	50	4	9	13	....	....	....	20	10	0	0	0	4
1941-42	Philadelphia Rockets	AHL	39	6	9	15	....	....	....	16	....	....	....	....	....
	Pittsburgh Hornets	AHL	1	0	0	0	....	....	....	0	....	....	....	....	....
	NHL Totals		**24**	**0**	**6**	**6**	**0**	**14**	**14**	**10**	....	....	....	....	....

EHL First All-Star Team (1933)

Traded to **Detroit** by **Tulsa** (AHA) for cash, September, 1933. Traded to **Hershey** (IAHL) by **Detroit** for cash, June 23, 1938.

• ROUSSEAU, BOBBY   *— see page 1437*

• ROUSSEAU, GUY   Guy Rousseau

LW – L. 5'6", 140 lbs.   b: Montreal, Que., 12/21/1934.

Season	Club	League	GP	G	A	Pts	AG	AA	APts	PIM	Playoffs GP	G	A	Pts	PIM
1950-51	Verdun LaSalle	Mtl-Jr.	41	6	21	27	....	....	....	21	3	0	1	1	0
1951-52	St. Jerome Eagles	Mtl-Jr.	50	33	*66	99	....	....	....	28	....	....	....	....	....
1952-53	Quebec Citadelle	QJHL	46	43	*52	*95	....	....	....	12	7	4	5	9	8
1953-54	Quebec Frontenacs	QJHL	51	42	47	89	....	....	....	21	8	*11	10	*21	4
1954-55	Quebec Citadelle	QJHL	40	22	33	55	....	....	....	42	18	*11	*18	*29	12
	Montreal Canadiens	**NHL**	**2**	**0**	**1**	**1**	**0**	**1**	**1**	**0**	....	....	....	....	....
1955-56	Montreal Royals	QHL	61	11	27	38	....	....	....	36	13	1	6	7	4
1956-57	**Montreal Canadiens**	**NHL**	**2**	**0**	**0**	**0**	**0**	**0**	**0**	**0**	....	....	....	....	....
	Montreal Royals	QHL	66	15	27	42	....	....	....	46	4	0	1	1	4
1957-58	Chicoutimi Sagueneens	QHL	63	29	41	70	....	....	....	30	6	0	2	2	0
1958-59	Rochester Americans	AHL	65	20	20	40	....	....	....	22	3	2	1	3	4
1959-60	Rochester Americans	AHL	42	15	16	31	....	....	....	16	11	7	4	11	2
1960-61	Rochester Americans	AHL	71	26	41	67	....	....	....	30	....	....	....	....	....
1961-62	Quebec Aces	AHL	63	19	21	40	....	....	....	26	....	....	....	....	....
1962-63	Quebec Aces	AHL	47	7	21	28	....	....	....	0	....	....	....	....	....
1963-64	Cleveland Barons	AHL	70	18	16	34	....	....	....	11	9	6	3	9	4
1964-65	Quebec Aces	AHL	41	10	18	28	....	....	....	10	5	1	0	1	0
1965-66	Sherbrooke Saints	QSHL	40	8	10	18	....	....	....	10	....	....	....	....	....
	NHL Totals		**4**	**0**	**1**	**1**	**0**	**1**	**1**	**0**	....	....	....	....	....

QHL First All-Star Team (1958)

Traded to **Chicoutimi** (QHL) by **Montreal** with Jack LeClair and Jacques Deslauriers for Stan Smrke, October, 1957.

• ROUSSEAU, ROLAND   Roland Rousseau

D – L. 5'8", 160 lbs.   b: Montreal, Que., 12/1/1929.

Season	Club	League	GP	G	A	Pts	AG	AA	APts	PIM	Playoffs GP	G	A	Pts	PIM
1947-48	Verdun Maple Leafs	Mtl-Jr.	32	3	7	10	....	....	....	20	4	0	0	0	2
1948-49	Montreal Jr. Royals	QJHL	47	5	8	13	....	....	....	73	25	3	5	8	48
	Montreal Royals	QSHL	....	....	....	....	....	....	....	....	2	0	0	0	0
1949-50	Montreal Jr. Royals	QJHL	1	1	1	2	....	....	....	8	....	....	....	....	....
	Laval Nationale	Mtl-Jr.	34	9	16	25	....	....	....	81	7	2	3	5	10
	Montreal Royals	QSHL	2	0	0	0	....	....	....	6	5	0	0	0	2
1950-51	Montreal Royals	QSHL	56	4	13	17	....	....	....	53	7	2	0	2	6
1951-52	Montreal Royals	QSHL	54	2	22	24	....	....	....	86	7	0	2	2	2
	Cincinnati Mohawks	AHL	....	....	....	....	....	....	....	....	3	0	0	0	2
1952-53	**Montreal Canadiens**	**NHL**	**2**	**0**	**0**	**0**	**0**	**0**	**0**	**0**	....	....	....	....	....
	Montreal Royals	QSHL	49	4	15	19	....	....	....	48	16	1	2	3	14
1953-54	Buffalo Bisons	AHL	66	5	10	15	....	....	....	64	3	2	0	2	2
1954-55	Montreal Royals	QHL	59	3	11	14	....	....	....	78	10	0	1	1	4
1955-56	Montreal Royals	QHL	63	5	9	14	....	....	....	58	13	1	2	3	8
1956-57	Chicoutimi Sagueneens	QHL	65	1	16	17	....	....	....	74	10	2	1	3	2
1957-58	Chicoutimi Sagueneens	QHL	60	1	11	12	....	....	....	87	6	0	0	0	0
	NHL Totals		**2**	**0**	**0**	**0**	**0**	**0**	**0**	**0**	....	....	....	....	....

• ROWE, BOBBY
Bobby "Stubby" Rowe
RW/D – L. 5'6", 160 lbs. b: Heathcote, Ont.. Deceased.

			REGULAR SEASON								PLAYOFFS				
Season	Club	League	GP	G	A	Pts	AG	AA	APts	PIM	GP	G	A	Pts	PIM
1907-08	Renfrew Creamery Kings	Ott-Sr.	....	....	....	....	....	....	....	....	2	*9	0	*9	....
1908-09	Haileybury Silver Kings	TPHL	1	0	0	0	....	....	....	0	....	....	....	....	....
	Renfrew Creamery Kings	Ott-Sr.	STATISTICS NOT AVAILABLE												
1909-10	Renfrew Millionaires	NHA	8	11	0	11	....	....	....	38	....	....	....	....	....
1910-11	Renfrew Millionaires	NHA	16	11	0	11	....	....	....	*82	....	....	....	....	....
1911-12	Victoria Aristocrats	PCHA	16	10	0	10	....	....	....	*62	....	....	....	....	....
1912-13	Victoria Aristocrats	PCHA	15	8	7	15	....	....	....	34	2	1	0	1	0
1913-14	Victoria Aristocrats	PCHA	12	8	7	15	....	....	....	11	3	0	0	0	0
1914-15	Victoria Aristocrats	PCHA	12	6	1	7	....	....	....	13	....	....	....	....	....
1915-16	Seattle Metropolitans	PCHA	17	3	5	8	....	....	....	25	....	....	....	....	....
1916-17	Seattle Metropolitans	PCHA	25	9	12	21	....	....	....	45	4	0	2	2	0
1917-18	Seattle Metropolitans	PCHA	17	3	2	5	....	....	....	28	....	....	....	....	....
1918-19	Seattle Metropolitans	PCHA	20	5	6	11	....	....	....	19	7	1	1	2	6
1919-20	Seattle Metropolitans	PCHA	22	2	4	6	....	....	....	16	7	2	1	3	*19
1920-21	Seattle Metropolitans	PCHA	24	0	2	2	....	....	....	29	2	0	1	1	0
1921-22	Seattle Metropolitans	PCHA	23	2	1	3	....	....	....	34	2	0	0	0	*6
1922-23	Seattle Metropolitans	PCHA	30	7	2	9	....	....	....	*71	....	....	....	....	....
1923-24	Seattle Metropolitans	PCHA	24	10	2	12	....	....	....	30	2	0	0	0	*8
1924-25	**Boston Bruins**	**NHL**	**4**	**1**	**0**	**1**	**3**	**0**	**3**	**0**	....	....	....	....	....
1925-26	Portland Rosebuds	WHL	2	0	0	0	....	....	....	0	....	....	....	....	....
	NHL Totals		**4**	**1**	**0**	**1**	**3**	**0**	**3**	**0**	....	....	....	....	....
	Other Major League Totals		283	95	51	146	....	....	....	537	29	4	5	9	39

PCHA Second All-Star Team (1917, 1920) • PCHA First All-Star Team (1918, 1919, 1923)

Signed as a free agent by **Victoria** (PCHA), November, 1911. Traded to **Boston** by **Seattle** (WCHL) for cash, November 2, 1924. Signed as a free agent by **Portland** (WHL), January 26, 1926.

• ROWE, RON
Ron Rowe
C/LW – L. 5'8", 170 lbs. b: Toronto, Ont., 11/30/1923.

Season	Club	League	GP	G	A	Pts	AG	AA	APts	PIM	GP	G	A	Pts	PIM
1942-43	Toronto Marlboros	OHA	20	26	21	47	....	....	....	40	3	4	4	8	16
1943-44	Montreal Jr. Royals	City Jr.	8	6	4	10	....	....	....	19	4	3	4	7	0
	Montreal Navy	City Sr.	8	7	6	13	....	....	....	26	4	3	2	5	*19
	Montreal Canada Car	City Sr.	2	1	2	3	....	....	....	0	....	....	....	....	....
1944-45	St. John's Navy	Nfld.	STATISTICS NOT AVAILABLE												
1945-46	Halifax Navy	City Sr.	9	*15	7	22	....	....	....	25	12	*22	11	*33	*42
1946-47	Boston Olympics	EHL	56	41	40	81	....	....	....	78	7	4	2	6	*26
1947-48	**New York Rangers**	**NHL**	**5**	**1**	**0**	**1**	**1**	**0**	**1**	**0**	....	....	....	....	....
	St. Paul Saints	USHL	3	0	1	1	....	....	....	0	....	....	....	....	....
	New York Rovers	EHL	14	9	6	15	....	....	....	28	....	....	....	....	....
	New York Rovers	QSHL	28	17	17	34	....	....	....	49	2	2	0	2	4
1948-49	Tacoma Rockets	PCHL	70	30	37	67	....	....	....	105	1	1	0	1	0
1949-50	Tacoma Rockets	PCHL	68	47	44	*91	....	....	....	64	5	4	1	5	14
1950-51	Tacoma Rockets	PCHL	70	33	34	67	....	....		105	6	2	1	3	12
1951-52	Vancouver Canucks	PCHL	12	1	3	4	....	....	....	22	....	....	....	....	....
	Moncton Hawks	MMHL	58	31	31	62	....	....	....	12	....	....	....	....	....
	Sydney Millionaires	MMHL	5	0	0	0	....	....	....	0	....	....	....	....	....
1952-53	Sydney Millionaires	MMHL	70	33	39	72	....	....	....	71	8	2	3	5	10
1953-54	North Bay Trappers	NOHA	15	7	6	13	....	....	....	0	....	....	....	....	....
	Soo Greyhounds	NOHA	4	0	1	1	....	....	....	0	....	....	....	....	....
	Pembroke Lumber Kings	NOHA	27	11	9	20	....	....	....	0	4	1	0	1	0
1954-55	Pembroke Lumber Kings	NOHA	15	6	2	8	....	....	....	10	2	0	0	0	0
1955-56	Pembroke Lumber Kings	NOHA	51	16	26	42	....	....		6	....	....	....	....	....
1956-57	Pembroke Lumber Kings	EOHL	40	7	11	18	....	....	....	18	....	....	....	....	....
	NHL Totals		**5**	**1**	**0**	**1**	**1**	**0**	**1**	**0**	....	....	....	....	....

• ROZZINI, GINO
Gino "Rosy" Rozzini
C – L. 5'8", 150 lbs. b: Shawinigan Falls, Que., 10/24/1918.

Season	Club	League	GP	G	A	Pts	AG	AA	APts	PIM	GP	G	A	Pts	PIM
1936-37	Creighton Mines	NOHA	17	5	7	12	....	....	....	18	2	0	2	2	4
1937-38	Creighton Eagles	NOHA	15	8	5	13	....	....	....	22	4	0	0	0	8
1938-39	Creighton Eagles	NOHA	12	5	1	6	....	....	....	6	6	2	*3	5	6
1939-40	Sudbury Open Pit Miners	NOHA	16	10	2	12	....	....	....	24	....	....	....	....	....
1940-41	St. Catharines Saints	OHA Sr.	31	15	13	28	....	....	....	67	12	7	5	12	8
1941-42	Quebec Aces	QCHL	40	14	28	42	....	....	....	34	14	5	5	10	12
1942-43	Quebec Aces	QCHL	34	12	21	33	....	....	....	41	4	1	2	3	0
1943-44	Quebec Aces	QSHL	13	6	5	11	....	....	....	10	15	12	9	21	16
1944-45	**Boston Bruins**	**NHL**	**31**	**5**	**10**	**15**	**7**	**16**	**23**	**20**	**6**	**1**	**2**	**3**	**6**
	Boston Olympics	EHL	10	19	11	30	....	....	....	14	....	....	....	....	....
1945-46	Hershey Bears	AHL	56	31	40	71	....	....	....	63	3	0	2	2	4
1946-47	Tulsa Oilers	USHL	13	3	5	8	....	....	....	6	....	....	....	....	....
	Hershey Bears	AHL	37	5	10	15	....	....	....	14	11	3	2	5	0
1947-48	St. Paul Saints	USHL	65	22	60	82	....	....	....	79	....	....	....	....	....
1948-49	New Haven Ramblers	AHL	58	16	33	49	....	....	....	45	....	....	....	....	....
1949-50	St. Paul Saints	USHL	68	27	40	67	....	....	....	59	3	0	2	2	0
1950-51	Tacoma Rockets	PCHL	70	10	27	37	....	....	....	67	4	1	1	2	0
1951-52	Vancouver Canucks	PCHL	8	0	1	1	....	....	....	6	....	....	....	....	....
	Spokane Flyers	WIHL	52	23	41	64	....	....	....	100	4	1	2	3	5
1952-53	Spokane Flyers	WIHL	57	34	54	88	....	....	....	77	9	1	3	4	0
1953-54	Spokane Flyers	WIHL	58	22	45	67	....	....	....	73	5	3	5	8	16
1954-55	Spokane Flyers	WIHL	24	9	12	21	....	....	....	31	....	....	....	....	....
1955-56	Spokane Flyers	WIHL	45	25	46	71	....	....	....	32	9	2	8	10	15
1956-57			DID NOT PLAY												
1957-58	Rossland Warriors	WIHL	DID NOT PLAY – COACHING												
1958-59	Rossland Warriors	WIHL	2	0	2	2	....	....	....	6	....	....	....	....	....
	NHL Totals		**31**	**5**	**10**	**15**	**7**	**16**	**23**	**20**	**6**	**1**	**2**	**3**	**6**

Signed as a free agent by **Boston**, November 2, 1944.

• RUELLE, BERNIE
Bernie Ruelle
LW – L. 5'9", 165 lbs. b: Houghton, MI, 11/23/1920.

Season	Club	League	GP	G	A	Pts	AG	AA	APts	PIM	GP	G	A	Pts	PIM
1939-40	Detroit Pontiacs	MOHL	34	5	8	13	....	....	....	14	....	....	....	....	....
1940-41	Detroit Holzbaugh	MOHL	25	6	6	12	....	....	....	11	5	4	2	6	8
1941-42	Toledo–Detroit	MOHL	28	16	14	30	....	....	....	6	7	3	2	5	4
1942-43			DID NOT PLAY												
1943-44	**Detroit Red Wings**	**NHL**	**2**	**1**	**0**	**1**	**1**	**0**	**1**	**0**	....	....	....	....	....
	Indianapolis Capitals	AHL	48	8	15	23	....	....	....	9	5	1	0	1	2
1944-45			MILITARY SERVICE												
1945-46			MILITARY SERVICE												
1946-47	Tacoma–Fresno	PCHL	44	14	9	23	....	....	....	20	2	0	0	0	0
	NHL Totals		**2**	**1**	**0**	**1**	**1**	**0**	**1**	**0**	....	....	....	....	....

• RUNGE, PAUL
Paul Runge
C/LW – L. 5'11", 167 lbs. b: Edmonton, Alta., 9/10/1908. d: 4/27/1972.

			REGULAR SEASON								PLAYOFFS				
Season	Club	League	GP	G	A	Pts	AG	AA	APts	PIM	GP	G	A	Pts	PIM
1927-28	Edmonton Superiors	City Sr.	STATISTICS NOT AVAILABLE												
1928-29	Portland–Victoria	PCHL	32	4	0	4	....	....	....	0	....	....	....	....	....
1929-30	Victoria Cubs	PCHL	36	5	5	10	....	....	....	35	....	....	....	....	....
1930-31	**Boston Bruins**	**NHL**	**1**	**0**	**0**	**0**	**0**	**0**	**0**	**0**	....	....	....	....	....
	Boston Cubs	Can-Am	39	9	11	20	....	....	....	35	9	*7	2	*9	17
1931-32	**Boston Bruins**	**NHL**	**14**	**0**	**1**	**1**	**0**	**3**	**3**	**8**	....	....	....	....	....
	Boston Cubs	Can-Am	29	11	11	22	....	....	....	29	....	....	....	....	....
1932-33	Philadelphia Arrows	Can-Am	44	21	*27	*48	....	....	....	38	5	2	1	3	2
1933-34	**Montreal Maroons**	**NHL**	**4**	**0**	**0**	**0**	**0**	**0**	**0**	**0**	....	....	....	....	....
	Windsor Bulldogs	IAHL	25	7	12	19	....	....	....	10	....	....	....	....	....
	Quebec Beavers	Can-Am	8	1	3	4	....	....	....	2	....	....	....	....	....
1934-35	**Montreal Canadiens**	**NHL**	**3**	**0**	**0**	**0**	**0**	**0**	**0**	**2**	....	....	....	....	....
	Quebec Beavers	Can-Am	48	25	33	*58	....	....	....	28	3	0	1	1	0
1935-36	**Montreal Canadiens**	**NHL**	**12**	**0**	**2**	**2**	**0**	**5**	**5**	**4**	....	....	....	....	....
	Boston Bruins	**NHL**	**33**	**8**	**2**	**10**	**20**	**5**	**25**	**14**	**2**	**0**	**0**	**0**	**2**
1936-37	**Montreal Canadiens**	**NHL**	**4**	**1**	**0**	**1**	**2**	**0**	**2**	**2**	....	....	....	....	....
	Montreal Maroons	**NHL**	**30**	**4**	**10**	**14**	**9**	**23**	**32**	**6**	**5**	**0**	**0**	**0**	**4**
	New Haven Eagles	AHL	8	0	3	3	....	....	....	5	....	....	....	....	....
1937-38	**Montreal Maroons**	**NHL**	**39**	**5**	**7**	**12**	**10**	**14**	**24**	**21**	....	....	....	....	....
1938-39	Cleveland Barons	AHL	54	7	28	35	....	....	....	26	8	1	4	5	4
1939-40	Cleveland Barons	AHL	48	7	15	22	....	....	....	7	....	....	....	....	....
1940-41	Buffalo Bisons	AHL	20	3	6	9	....	....	....	9	....	....	....	....	....
	Minneapolis Millers	AHA	29	12	14	26	....	....	....	4	3	0	2	2	0
1941-42	Dallas Texans	AHA	46	16	41	57	....	....	....	29	....	....	....	....	....
	NHL Totals		**140**	**18**	**22**	**40**	**41**	**50**	**91**	**57**	**7**	**0**	**0**	**0**	**6**

Signed as a free agent by **Boston**, November 5, 1930. Traded to **Philadelphia** (Can-Am) by **Boston** for cash, September, 1932. Traded to **Montreal Maroons** by **Philadelphia** (Can-Am) for cash, November 25, 1933. Traded to **Montreal Canadiens** by **Montreal Maroons** for Stan McCabe, December 6, 1933. Traded to **Boston** by **Montreal Canadiens** for cash, December 24, 1935. Traded to **Montreal Canadiens** by **Boston** for cash, April, 1936. Traded to **Montreal Maroons** by **Montreal Canadiens** for Bill MacKenzie, December 3, 1936. Traded to **Cleveland** (AHL) by **Montreal Maroons** for cash, October 3, 1938.

• RUPP, DUANE
— see page 1441

• RUSSELL, CHURCH
Church Russell
LW/C – L. 5'11", 175 lbs. b: Winnipeg, Man., 3/16/1923. Deceased.

Season	Club	League	GP	G	A	Pts	AG	AA	APts	PIM	GP	G	A	Pts	PIM
1941-42	Winnipeg Rangers	MJHL	18	6	11	17	....	....	....	0	....	....	....	....	....
1942-43	Winnipeg Rangers	MJHL	12	*23	*13	*36	....	....	....	0	6	*16	4	*20	2
1943-44	Victoria Navy	PCHL	15	4	6	10	....	....	....	4	....	....	....	....	....
1944-45	St. Louis Flyers	AHL	47	8	7	15	....	....	....	7	....	....	....	....	....
1945-46	**New York Rangers**	**NHL**	**17**	**0**	**5**	**5**	**0**	**9**	**9**	**2**	....	....	....	....	....
	New York Rovers	EHL	38	27	*43	70	....	....	....	4	....	....	....	....	....
1946-47	**New York Rangers**	**NHL**	**54**	**20**	**8**	**28**	**27**	**11**	**38**	**8**	....	....	....	....	....
1947-48	**New York Rangers**	**NHL**	**19**	**0**	**3**	**3**	**0**	**4**	**4**	**2**	....	....	....	....	....
	Cleveland Barons	AHL	40	13	18	31	....	....	....	8	9	3	5	8	0
	New York Rovers	QSHL	2	0	0	0	....	....	....	0	....	....	....	....	....
1948-49	Cleveland Barons	AHL	56	17	22	39	....	....	....	10	5	1	1	2	2
1949-50	Pittsburgh Hornets	AHL	67	7	22	29	....	....	....	15	....	....	....	....	....
1950-51	Vancouver Canucks	PCHL	58	12	21	33	....	....	....	8	....	....	....	....	....
1951-52	Winnipeg Maroons	City Sr.	6	5	4	9	....	....	....	2	....	....	....	....	....
1952-53			DID NOT PLAY												
1953-54	Brandon Regals	MHL Sr.	DID NOT PLAY – COACHING												
1954-55	Brandon Regals	MHL Sr.	8	5	4	9	....	....	....	2	....	....	....	....	....
	NHL Totals		**90**	**20**	**16**	**36**	**27**	**24**	**51**	**12**	....	....	....	....	....

EHL First All-Star Team (1946)

Traded to **Cleveland** (AHL) by **NY Rangers** for George Johnston, September, 1947.

• SABOURIN, BOB
Bob Sabourin
LW – L. 5'9", 177 lbs. b: Sudbury, Ont., 3/17/1933.

Season	Club	League	GP	G	A	Pts	AG	AA	APts	PIM	GP	G	A	Pts	PIM
1948-49	St. Michael's Majors	OHA	10	2	2	4	....	....	....	0	....	....	....	....	....
1949-50	St. Michael's Majors	OHA	47	21	11	32	....	....	....	38	5	3	0	3	2
1950-51	St. Michael's Majors	OHA	54	25	18	43	....	....	....	54	....	....	....	....	....
1951-52	St. Michael's Majors	OHA	51	31	23	54	....	....	....	26	8	2	4	6	4
	Toronto Maple Leafs	**NHL**	**1**	**0**	**0**	**0**	**0**	**0**	**0**	**2**	....	....	....	....	....
1952-53	Pittsburgh Hornets	AHL	51	22	20	42	....	....	....	19	10	*6	0	6	14
1953-54	Ottawa Senators	QHL	4	2	5	7	....	....	....	2	....	....	....	....	....
	Pittsburgh Hornets	AHL	64	16	30	46	....	....	....	29	5	3	1	4	6
1954-55	Pittsburgh Hornets	AHL	49	8	19	27	....	....	....	14	3	0	0	0	2
1955-56	Pittsburgh Hornets	AHL	47	6	16	22	....	....	....	39	3	0	0	0	0
1956-57	Springfield Indians	AHL	59	11	29	40	....	....	....	21	....	....	....	....	....
1957-58	Quebec Aces	QHL	64	28	32	60	....	....	....	8	13	5	1	6	12
1958-59	Trois-Rivieres Lions	QHL	59	25	25	50	....	....	....	12	8	1	2	3	5
1959-60	Trois-Rivieres Lions	EPHL	66	22	31	53	....	....	....	24	4	1	0	1	14
1960-61	Kitchener Dutchemen	EPHL	70	20	30	50	....	....	....	24	7	1	1	2	2
1961-62	North Bay Trappers	EPHL	67	12	24	36	....	....		16	....	....	....	....	....
1962-63	Sudbury Wolves	EPHL	1	0	0	0	....	....	....	0	....	....	....	....	....
	Calgary–Seattle	WHL	61	17	23	40	....	....	....	14	17	8	8	16	6
1963-64	Seattle Totems	WHL	68	13	19	32	....	....	....	15	....	....	....	....	....
1964-65	Seattle Totems	WHL	57	11	10	21	....	....	....	12	7	1	0	1	4
1965-66	Long Island Ducks	EHL	72	31	43	74	....	....	....	40	12	3	7	10	22
1966-67	Jacksonville Rockets	EHL	71	16	30	46	....	....	....	38	....	....	....	....	....
1967-68	Jacksonville Rockets	EHL	55	13	22	35	....	....	....	10	....	....	....	....	....
	NHL Totals		**1**	**0**	**0**	**0**	**0**	**0**	**0**	**2**	....	....	....	....	....

EHL North Second All-Star Team (1966)

Loaned to **Toronto** by **St. Michael's** (OHA) as an emergency injury replacement, March 13, 1952. Traded to **Springfield** (AHL) by **Toronto** with Bob Bailey for $15,000, May, 1956.

• ST. LAURENT, DOLLARD
Dollard St. Laurent
D – L. 5'11", 175 lbs. b: Verdun, Que., 5/12/1929.

Season	Club	League	GP	G	A	Pts	AG	AA	APts	PIM	GP	G	A	Pts	PIM
			REGULAR SEASON								PLAYOFFS				
1947-48	Montreal Jr. Canadiens	QJHL	15	3	10	13	....	....	....	12	....	....	....	....	....
1948-49	Montreal Jr. Canadiens	QJHL	44	15	27	42	....	....	....	77	4	0	4	4	8
1949-50	Montreal Royals	QSHL	45	7	15	22	....	....	....	66	....	....	....	....	....
1950-51	**Montreal Canadiens**	**NHL**	**3**	**0**	**0**	**0**	**0**	**0**	**0**	**0**	....	....	....	....	....
	Montreal Royals	QSHL	57	12	30	42	....	....	....	69	7	3	2	5	14
1951-52	**Montreal Canadiens**	**NHL**	**40**	**3**	**10**	**13**	**4**	**13**	**17**	**30**	**9**	**0**	**3**	**3**	**6**
	Montreal Royals	QSHL	27	10	16	26	....	....	....	22	....	....	....	....	....
1952-53	**Montreal Canadiens**	**NHL**	**54**	**2**	**6**	**8**	**3**	**8**	**11**	**34**	**12**	**0**	**3**	**3**	**4**
1953-54	**Montreal Canadiens**	**NHL**	**53**	**3**	**12**	**15**	**5**	**16**	**21**	**43**	**10**	**1**	**2**	**3**	**8**
1954-55	**Montreal Canadiens**	**NHL**	**58**	**3**	**14**	**17**	**4**	**18**	**22**	**24**	**12**	**0**	**5**	**5**	**12**
1955-56	**Montreal Canadiens**	**NHL**	**46**	**4**	**9**	**13**	**6**	**11**	**17**	**58**	**4**	**0**	**0**	**0**	**2**
1956-57	**Montreal Canadiens**	**NHL**	**64**	**1**	**11**	**12**	**1**	**13**	**14**	**49**	**7**	**0**	**1**	**1**	**13**
1957-58	**Montreal Canadiens**	**NHL**	**65**	**3**	**20**	**23**	**4**	**22**	**26**	**68**	**5**	**0**	**0**	**0**	**10**
1958-59	**Chicago Black Hawks**	**NHL**	**70**	**4**	**8**	**12**	**5**	**8**	**13**	**28**	**6**	**0**	**1**	**1**	**2**
1959-60	**Chicago Black Hawks**	**NHL**	**68**	**4**	**13**	**17**	**5**	**13**	**18**	**60**	**4**	**0**	**1**	**1**	**0**
1960-61	**Chicago Black Hawks**	**NHL**	**67**	**2**	**17**	**19**	**2**	**17**	**19**	**58**	**11**	**1**	**2**	**3**	**12**
1961-62	**Chicago Black Hawks**	**NHL**	**64**	**0**	**13**	**13**	**0**	**13**	**13**	**44**	**12**	**0**	**4**	**4**	**18**
1962-63	Quebec Aces	AHL	54	3	14	17	....	....	....	34	....	....	....	....	....
	NHL Totals		**652**	**29**	**133**	**162**	**39**	**152**	**191**	**496**	**92**	**2**	**22**	**24**	**87**

Played in NHL All-Star Game (1953, 1956, 1957, 1958, 1961)

Traded to **Chicago** by **Montreal** for cash and future considerations (Norm Johnson, February 20, 1959), June, 1958. Traded to **Quebec** (AHL) by **Chicago** for cash, September 6, 1962.

• SAMIS, PHIL
Phil Samis
D – R. 5'9", 180 lbs. b: Edmonton, Alta., 12/28/1927.

Season	Club	League	GP	G	A	Pts	AG	AA	APts	PIM	GP	G	A	Pts	PIM
1943-44	Edmonton Maple Leafs	Jr. B	STATISTICS NOT AVAILABLE												
1944-45	St. Michael's College	Tor-Jr.	....	....	....	....	....	....	....	....	2	0	0	0	2
	St. Michael's Majors	OHA	3	0	1	1	....	....	....	2	....	....	....	....	....
1945-46	Oshawa Generals	OHA	27	11	9	20	....	....	....	*83	12	1	3	4	18
1946-47	Oshawa Generals	OHA	27	5	20	25	....	....	....	120	5	0	0	0	20
1947-48	Pittsburgh Hornets	AHL	68	4	10	14	....	....	....	*181	2	0	2	2	2
	Toronto Maple Leafs	**NHL**	....	....	....	....	....	....	....	....	**5**	**0**	**1**	**1**	**2**
1948-49	Pittsburgh Hornets	AHL	60	3	7	10	....	....	....	91	....	....	....	....	....
1949-50	**Toronto Maple Leafs**	**NHL**	**2**	**0**	**0**	**0**	**0**	**0**	**0**	**0**	....	....	....	....	....
	Pittsburgh Hornets	AHL	66	2	11	13	....	....	....	139	....	....	....	....	....
1950-51	Cleveland Barons	AHL	64	3	14	17	....	....	....	105	11	2	3	5	*21
1951-52	Cleveland Barons	AHL	60	11	14	25	....	....	....	117	5	1	1	2	13
1952-53	Cleveland Barons	AHL	1	0	0	0	....	....	....	0	....	....	....	....	....
	Montreal Royals	QSHL	56	4	11	15	....	....	....	76	15	0	1	1	15
	NHL Totals		**2**	**0**	**0**	**0**	**0**	**0**	**0**	**0**	**5**	**0**	**1**	**1**	**2**

• SANDERSON, DEREK
— see page 1450

• SANDFORD, ED
Ed "Sandy" Sandford
LW – R. 6'1", 180 lbs. b: New Toronto, Ont., 8/20/1928.

Season	Club	League	GP	G	A	Pts	AG	AA	APts	PIM	GP	G	A	Pts	PIM
1945-46	St. Michael's Majors	OHA	26	10	9	19	....	....	....	28	11	5	5	10	12
1946-47	St. Michael's Majors	OHA	27	30	*37	67	....	....	....	38	9	*12	12	*24	31
1947-48	**Boston Bruins**	**NHL**	**59**	**10**	**15**	**25**	**15**	**22**	**37**	**25**	**5**	**1**	**0**	**1**	**0**
1948-49	**Boston Bruins**	**NHL**	**56**	**16**	**20**	**36**	**25**	**32**	**57**	**57**	**5**	**1**	**3**	**4**	**2**
1949-50	**Boston Bruins**	**NHL**	**19**	**1**	**4**	**5**	**1**	**5**	**6**	**6**	....	....	....	....	....
1950-51	**Boston Bruins**	**NHL**	**51**	**10**	**13**	**23**	**13**	**17**	**30**	**33**	**6**	**0**	**1**	**1**	**4**
1951-52	**Boston Bruins**	**NHL**	**65**	**13**	**12**	**25**	**18**	**15**	**33**	**54**	**7**	**2**	**2**	**4**	**0**
	Boston Olympics	EHL	2	1	0	1	....	....	....	0	....	....	....	....	....
1952-53	**Boston Bruins**	**NHL**	**61**	**14**	**21**	**35**	**21**	**29**	**50**	**44**	**11**	**8**	**3**	**11**	**11**
1953-54	**Boston Bruins**	**NHL**	**70**	**16**	**31**	**47**	**24**	**42**	**66**	**42**	**3**	**0**	**1**	**1**	**4**
1954-55	**Boston Bruins**	**NHL**	**60**	**14**	**20**	**34**	**20**	**26**	**46**	**38**	**5**	**1**	**1**	**2**	**6**
1955-56	**Detroit Red Wings**	**NHL**	**4**	**0**	**0**	**0**	**0**	**0**	**0**	**0**	....	....	....	....	....
	Chicago Black Hawks	**NHL**	**57**	**12**	**9**	**21**	**17**	**11**	**28**	**56**	....	....	....	....	....
	NHL Totals		**502**	**106**	**145**	**251**	**154**	**199**	**353**	**355**	**42**	**13**	**11**	**24**	**27**

NHL Second All-Star Team (1954)

Played in NHL All-Star Game (1951, 1952, 1953, 1954, 1955)

Traded to **Detroit** by **Boston** with Gilles Boisvert, Real Chevrefils, Warren Godfrey and Norm Corcoran for Marcel Bonin, Vic Stasiuk, Terry Sawchuk and Lorne Davis, June 4, 1955. Traded to **Chicago** by **Detroit** for Metro Prystai, October 24, 1955.

• SANDS, CHARLIE
Charlie Sands
C/RW – R. 5'9", 160 lbs. b: Fort William, Ont., 5/23/1911. Deceased.

Season	Club	League	GP	G	A	Pts	AG	AA	APts	PIM	GP	G	A	Pts	PIM
1929-30	Fort William Forts	TBSHL	14	1	1	2	....	....	....	0	....	....	....	....	....
1930-31	Port Arthur Ports	TBSHL	22	10	1	11	....	....	....	25	2	0	0	0	0
1931-32	Port Arthur Ports	TBSHL	17	6	3	9	....	....	....	10	2	1	0	1	9
1932-33	**Toronto Maple Leafs**	**NHL**	**3**	**0**	**3**	**3**	**0**	**8**	**8**	**0**	**9**	**2**	**2**	**4**	**2**
	Syracuse Stars	IAHL	37	10	5	15	....	....	....	10	1	0	0	0	4
1933-34	**Toronto Maple Leafs**	**NHL**	**45**	**8**	**8**	**16**	**18**	**21**	**39**	**2**	**5**	**1**	**0**	**1**	**0**
1934-35	**Boston Bruins**	**NHL**	**41**	**15**	**12**	**27**	**32**	**27**	**59**	**0**	**4**	**0**	**0**	**0**	**0**
1935-36	**Boston Bruins**	**NHL**	**40**	**6**	**4**	**10**	**15**	**10**	**25**	**8**	**2**	**0**	**0**	**0**	**0**
	Boston Cubs	Can-Am	5	1	3	4	....	....	....	0	....	....	....	....	....
1936-37	**Boston Bruins**	**NHL**	**47**	**18**	**5**	**23**	**39**	**12**	**51**	**6**	**3**	**1**	**2**	**3**	**0**
1937-38	**Boston Bruins**	**NHL**	**46**	**17**	**12**	**29**	**36**	**25**	**61**	**12**	**3**	**1**	**1**	**2**	**0**
1938-39	**Boston Bruins**	**NHL**	**37**	**7**	**5**	**12**	**15**	**9**	**24**	**10**	**1**	**0**	**0**	**0**	**0**
	Hershey Bears	AHL	4	3	1	4	....	....	....	0	....	....	....	....	....
1939-40	**Montreal Canadiens**	**NHL**	**47**	**9**	**20**	**29**	**19**	**40**	**59**	**10**	....	....	....	....	....
1940-41	**Montreal Canadiens**	**NHL**	**43**	**5**	**13**	**18**	**10**	**24**	**34**	**4**	**2**	**1**	**0**	**1**	**0**
1941-42	**Montreal Canadiens**	**NHL**	**38**	**11**	**16**	**27**	**19**	**24**	**43**	**6**	**3**	**0**	**1**	**1**	**2**
1942-43	**Montreal Canadiens**	**NHL**	**31**	**3**	**9**	**12**	**4**	**11**	**15**	**0**	**2**	**0**	**0**	**0**	**0**
	Washington Lions	AHL	1	0	1	1	....	....	....	0	....	....	....	....	....
1943-44	**New York Rangers**	**NHL**	**9**	**0**	**2**	**2**	**0**	**2**	**2**	**0**	....	....	....	....	....
1944-45	Pasadena Panthers	PCHL	STATISTICS NOT AVAILABLE												
1945-46	Los Angeles Monarchs	PCHL	11	3	3	6	....	....	....	0	....	....	....	....	....
	NHL Totals		**427**	**99**	**109**	**208**	**207**	**213**	**420**	**58**	**34**	**6**	**6**	**12**	**4**

Played in NHL All-Star Game (1934)

Traded to **Boston** by **Toronto** for cash, May 12, 1934. Traded to **Montreal** by **Boston** for Herb Cain, November 1, 1939. Loaned to **NY Rangers** by **Montreal** with John Mahaffy, Dutch Hiller, Fern Gauthier and future considerations (Tony Demers, December, 1943) for loan of Phil Watson, October 27, 1943.

• SASKAMOOSE, FRED
Fred "Chief Running Deer" Saskamoose
C – R. 5'8", 165 lbs. b: Sandy Lake Reserve, Sask., 12/25/1933.

Season	Club	League	GP	G	A	Pts	AG	AA	APts	PIM	GP	G	A	Pts	PIM
1950-51	Moose Jaw Canucks	WCJHL	18	7	7	14	....	....	....	9	....	....	....	....	....
1951-52	Moose Jaw Canucks	WCJHL	42	19	22	41	....	....	....	59	....	....	....	....	....
1952-53	Moose Jaw Canucks	WCJHL	36	18	17	35	....	....	....	40	9	7	5	12	4
1953-54	Moose Jaw Canucks	WCJHL	34	31	26	57	....	....	....	56	5	4	2	6	8
	Chicago Black Hawks	**NHL**	**11**	**0**	**0**	**0**	**0**	**0**	**0**	**6**	....	....	....	....	....
1954-55	Moose Jaw Canucks	WCJHL	1	0	0	0	....	....	....	0	....	....	....	....	....
	New Westminster Royals	WHL	21	3	8	11	....	....	....	6	....	....	....	....	....
	Chicoutimi Sagueneens	QHL	22	4	4	8	....	....	....	2	6	2	1	3	2
1955-56	Calgary Stampeders	WHL	2	0	0	0	....	....	....	2	....	....	....	....	....
1956-57	Kamloops Chiefs	OSHL	23	7	10	17	....	....	....	36	....	....	....	....	....
1957-58	Kamloops Chiefs	OSHL	51	26	27	53	....	....	....	63	15	7	6	13	34
1958-59			DID NOT PLAY												
1959-60	Kamloops Chiefs	OSHL	20	10	20	30	....	....	....	42	5	0	0	0	0
	NHL Totals		**11**	**0**	**0**	**0**	**0**	**0**	**0**	**6**	....	....	....	....	....

• SATHER, GLEN
— see page 1452

• SAUNDERS, TED
Ted "Bud" Saunders
RW – R. 5'8", 165 lbs. b: Ottawa, Ont., 8/29/1911.

Season	Club	League	GP	G	A	Pts	AG	AA	APts	PIM	GP	G	A	Pts	PIM
1928-29	Ottawa New Edinburghs	City Sr.	15	3	1	4	....	....	....	....	2	1	0	1	0
1929-30	Iroquois Falls Eskimos	NOHA	STATISTICS NOT AVAILABLE												
1930-31	Springfield Indians	Can-Am	38	19	4	23	....	....	....	28	7	3	2	5	6
1931-32	Springfield Indians	Can-Am	30	5	3	8	....	....	....	20	....	....	....	....	....
	Cleveland Indians	IAHL	6	0	0	0	....	....	....	2	....	....	....	....	....
1932-33	Boston Cubs	Can-Am	47	*29	10	39	....	....	....	82	7	*5	2	*7	18
1933-34	**Ottawa Senators**	**NHL**	**18**	**1**	**3**	**4**	**2**	**8**	**10**	**4**	....	....	....	....	....
	Detroit Olympics	IAHL	21	1	4	5	....	....	....	14	6	0	0	0	4
1934-35	Philadelphia Arrows	Can-Am	48	*28	20	48	....	....	....	35	....	....	....	....	....
1935-36	Springfield Indians	Can-Am	48	19	22	41	....	....	....	36	3	0	0	0	0
1936-37	Springfield Indians	AHL	43	17	13	30	....	....	....	32	5	1	0	1	2
1937-38	Springfield Indians	AHL	45	8	21	29	....	....	....	41	....	....	....	....	....
1938-39	Springfield Indians	AHL	53	10	19	29	....	....	....	33	3	0	1	1	2
1939-40	St. Paul Saints	AHA	46	23	25	48	....	....	....	51	7	*6	4	*10	4
1940-41	St. Paul Saints	AHA	46	18	15	33	....	....	....	14	4	2	1	3	0
1941-42	Cornwall–Ottawa	QSHL	40	*31	25	*56	....	....	....	20	8	2	2	4	4
1942-43	Ottawa Commandos	QSHL	28	10	13	23	....	....	....	15	....	....	....	....	....
	Ottawa Army Medics	City Sr.	9	10	8	18	....	....	....	2	....	....	....	....	....
1943-44	Truro Bearcats	NSSHL	10	*17	6	23	....	....	....	0	....	....	....	....	....
	NHL Totals		**18**	**1**	**3**	**4**	**2**	**8**	**10**	**4**	....	....	....	....	....

Can-Am Second All-Star Team (1936)

Traded to **Ottawa** by **Boston** with Perk Galbraith and Bud Cook for Bob Gracie, October 4, 1933. Traded to **Detroit** (IAHL) by **Ottawa** for cash, December 8, 1933.

• SAVAGE, TONY
Tony (Gordon) Savage
D – L. 6', 175 lbs. b: Calgary, Alta., 7/18/1906. d: 2/28/1974.

Season	Club	League	GP	G	A	Pts	AG	AA	APts	PIM	GP	G	A	Pts	PIM
1925-26	Calgary Canadiens	City Jr.	STATISTICS NOT AVAILABLE												
1926-27	Calgary Tigers	PrHL	29	1	2	3	....	....	....	27	2	0	0	0	0
1927-28	London–Kitchener	Can-Pro	32	0	0	0	....	....	....	2	....	....	....	....	....
1928-29	Kitchener Dutchmen	Can-Pro	37	8	1	9	....	....	....	33	3	0	0	0	4
1929-30	Seattle Eskimos	PCHL	35	7	1	8	....	....	....	28	....	....	....	....	....
1930-31	Seattle Eskimos	PCHL	33	11	5	16	....	....	....	83	4	*2	0	2	10
1931-32	Syracuse Stars	IAHL	48	8	13	21	....	....	....	58	....	....	....	....	....
1932-33	Syracuse Stars	IAHL	35	9	6	15	....	....	....	75	6	1	2	3	8
1933-34	Calgary Tigers	NWHL	29	9	12	21	....	....	....	48	5	3	1	4	4
1934-35	**Montreal Canadiens**	**NHL**	**41**	**1**	**5**	**6**	**2**	**11**	**13**	**4**	**2**	**0**	**0**	**0**	**0**
	Boston Bruins	**NHL**	**8**	**0**	**0**	**0**	**0**	**0**	**0**	**2**	....	....	....	....	....
1935-36	Calgary Tigers	NWHL	34	22	17	39	....	....	....	45	....	....	....	....	....
1936-37			REINSTATED AS AN AMATEUR												
1937-38	Olds Elks	ASHL	25	13	9	22	....	....	....	25	3	0	1	1	6
1938-39	Saskatoon Quakers	City Sr.	7	1	2	3	....	....	....	2	....	....	....	....	....
1939-40	Lethbridge Maple Leafs	ASHL	5	0	2	2	....	....	....	2	....	....	....	....	....
	NHL Totals		**49**	**1**	**5**	**6**	**2**	**11**	**13**	**6**	**2**	**0**	**0**	**0**	**0**

Traded to **Montreal Canadiens** by **Calgary** (NWHL) for cash, October, 1934. Traded to **Boston** by **Montreal Canadiens** for Tom Filmore and cash, November 5, 1934. Traded to **Montreal Canadiens** by **Boston** with $7,500 for Jack Portland, December 3, 1934.

• SAVARD, SERGE
— see page 1455

• SCHAEFFER, BUTCH
Butch (Paul) Schaeffer
D – R. 5'10", 190 lbs. b: Hinkley, MN, 11/7/1911.

Season	Club	League	GP	G	A	Pts	AG	AA	APts	PIM	GP	G	A	Pts	PIM
1934-35	Chicago Baby Ruth	City Sr.	2	0	0	0	....	....	....	0					
1935-36	Chicago Baby Ruth	City Sr.	STATISTICS NOT AVAILABLE												
1936-37	**Chicago Black Hawks**	**NHL**	**5**	**0**	**0**	**0**	**0**	**0**	**0**	**6**	....	....	....	....	....
1937-38	Eveleth Rangers	USHL	STATISTICS NOT AVAILABLE												
1938-39	Eveleth Rangers	USHL	27	0	6	6	....	....	....	25	5	0	0	0	8
	NHL Totals		**5**	**0**	**0**	**0**	**0**	**0**	**0**	**6**	....	....	....	....	....

• SCHERZA, CHUCK
Chuck (Charles) Scherza
LW/C – L. 5'10", 190 lbs. b: Brandon, Man., 2/15/1923.

Season	Club	League	GP	G	A	Pts	AG	AA	APts	PIM	PO GP	PO G	PO A	PO Pts	PO PIM
1941-42	Regina Abbotts	SJHL	12	7	*7	14	....	....	....	8	5	1	2	3	6
1942-43	Oshawa Generals	OHA	21	8	5	13	....	....	....	26	10	7	6	13	6
1943-44	**Boston Bruins**	**NHL**	**9**	**1**	**1**	**2**	**1**	**1**	**2**	**6**	....	....	....	....	....
	New York Rangers	**NHL**	**5**	**3**	**2**	**5**	**4**	**2**	**6**	**11**	....	....	....	....	....
1944-45	**New York Rangers**	**NHL**	**22**	**2**	**3**	**5**	**3**	**5**	**8**	**18**	....	....	....	....	....
	Hershey Bears	AHL	27	6	3	9	....	....	....	29	11	1	6	7	8
1945-46	Providence Reds	AHL	61	15	27	42	....	....	....	81	2	0	0	0	0
1946-47	Providence Reds	AHL	64	21	36	57	....	....	....	78	....	....	....	....	....
1947-48	Providence Reds	AHL	68	18	65	83	....	....	....	72	5	1	0	1	2
1948-49	Providence Reds	AHL	68	14	13	27	....	....	....	54	14	0	4	4	7
1949-50	Providence Reds	AHL	63	6	10	16	....	....	....	41	4	0	0	0	0
1950-51	Providence Reds	AHL	69	13	26	39	....	....	....	33	....	....	....	....	....
1951-52	Providence Reds	AHL	68	11	9	20	....	....	....	32	15	1	2	3	2
1952-53	Providence Reds	AHL	59	9	37	46	....	....	....	40	....	....	....	....	....
1953-54	Providence Reds	AHL	67	18	47	65	....	....	....	50	....	....	....	....	....
1954-55	Providence Reds	AHL	62	14	27	41	....	....	....	58	....	....	....	....	....
1955-56	Trois-Rivieres Lions	QHL	49	14	23	37	....	....	....	42	....	....	....	....	....
1956-57	North Bay Trappers	NOHA	47	13	33	46	....	....	....	64	13	1	*12	13	14
1957-58	North Bay Trappers	NOHA	6	1	4	5	....	....	....	6	....	....	....	....	....
1958-59	North Bay Trappers	NOHA	12	1	4	5	....	....	....	8	....	....	....	....	....
	NHL Totals		**36**	**6**	**6**	**12**	**8**	**8**	**16**	**35**	....	....	....	....	....

Traded to **NY Rangers** by **Boston** for cash, November, 1943.

• SCHINKEL, KEN
— see page 1456

• SCHMIDT, CLARENCE
Clarence Schmidt
RW – R. 5'11", 165 lbs. b: Williams, MN, 9/17/1925.

Season	Club	League	GP	G	A	Pts	AG	AA	APts	PIM	PO GP	PO G	PO A	PO Pts	PO PIM
1942-43	Boston Olympics	EHL	36	25	12	37	....	....	....	22	9	4	1	5	5
1943-44	**Boston Bruins**	**NHL**	**7**	**1**	**0**	**1**	**1**	**0**	**1**	**2**	....	....	....	....	....
	Boston Olympics	EHL	13	7	6	13	....	....	....	14	8	6	3	9	5
1944-45	Warroad Lakers	MHL Sr.	STATISTICS NOT AVAILABLE												
	NHL Totals		**7**	**1**	**0**	**1**	**1**	**0**	**1**	**2**	....	....	....	....	....

• SCHMIDT, JACKIE
Jackie Schmidt
LW – L. 5'10", 155 lbs. b: Odessa, Sask., 11/11/1924.

Season	Club	League	GP	G	A	Pts	AG	AA	APts	PIM	PO GP	PO G	PO A	PO Pts	PO PIM
1941-42	Regina Abbotts	SJHL	11	10	3	13	....	....	....	4	5	2	0	2	6
1942-43	**Boston Bruins**	**NHL**	**45**	**6**	**7**	**13**	**8**	**9**	**17**	**6**	**5**	**0**	**0**	**0**	**0**
	Providence Reds	AHL	4	1	3	4	....	....	....	6	....	....	....	....	....
1943-44	Toronto RCAF	City Sr.	4	0	0	0	....	....	....	0	....	....	....	....	....
	Toronto CIL	City Sr.	....	9	16	25	....	....	....	4	7	7	5	12	4
	Halifax Navy	City Sr.	....	....	....	....	....	....	....	....	4	0	0	0	2
1944-45	Dartmouth RCAF	City Sr.	7	5	4	9	....	....	....	4	....	....	....	....	....
1945-46			MILITARY SERVICE												
1946-47	New West.–Portland	PCHL	61	13	20	33	....	....	....	23	14	0	0	0	4
1947-48	Valleyfield Braves	QSHL	40	23	14	37	....	....	....	15	6	2	3	5	2
1948-49	Valleyfield Braves	QSHL	63	28	41	69	....	....	....	32	4	0	0	0	0
1949-50	Valleyfield Braves	QSHL	57	33	22	55	....	....	....	28	5	1	3	4	....
1950-51	Valleyfield Braves	QSHL	56	27	40	67	....	....	....	37	16	11	6	17	0
1951-52	Valleyfield Braves	QSHL	37	12	17	29	....	....	....	8	5	1	0	1	4
1952-53	Valleyfield Braves	QSHL	51	9	17	26	....	....	....	27	4	1	0	1	0
1953-54	Pembroke Lumber Kings	NOHA	58	15	39	54	....	....	....	16	4	1	0	1	0
1954-55	Pembroke Lumber Kings	NOHA	14	2	4	6	....	....	....	2	....	....	....	....	....
	Amherst Ramblers	NSSHL	43	22	36	58	....	....	....	7	8	1	3	4	2
1955-56	Amherst Ramblers	NSSHL	50	28	76	104	....			39	15	9	10	*19	4
1956-57	Mirimachi Beavers	NSSHL	12	6	13	19	....	....	....	17	....	....	....	....	....
	NHL Totals		**45**	**6**	**7**	**13**	**8**	**9**	**17**	**6**	**5**	**0**	**0**	**0**	**0**

• SCHMIDT, JOSEPH
Joseph Schmidt
D – R. 5'10", 157 lbs. b: Odessa, Sask., 11/5/1926.

Season	Club	League	GP	G	A	Pts	AG	AA	APts	PIM	PO GP	PO G	PO A	PO Pts	PO PIM
1942-43	Regina Abbotts	SJHL	1	0	0	0	....	....	....	2	....	....	....	....	....
1943-44	Regina Abbotts	SJHL	2	0	0	0	....	....	....	0	....	....	....	....	....
	Boston Bruins	**NHL**	**2**	**0**	**0**	**0**	**0**	**0**	**0**	**0**	....	....	....	....	....
	Boston Olympics	EHL	32	12	22	34	....	....	....	8	9	1	2	3	2
1944-45	Saskatoon Falcons	SJHL	7	0	0	0	....	....	....	10	2	0	0	0	9
	Boston Olympics	EHL	48	31	36	67	....	....	....	16	12	14	4	18	7
1945-46	Boston Olympics	EHL	11	1	2	3	....	....	....	2	....	....	....	....	....
	Seattle Ironmen	PCHL	17	0	0	0	....	....	....	20	....	....	....	....	....
	Fort Worth Rangers	USHL	26	1	1	2	....	....	....	26	....	....	....	....	....
1946-47	Houston–Fort Worth	USHL	35	1	3	4	....	....	....	28	....	....	....	....	....
1947-48	Fort Worth Rangers	USHL	55	17	11	28	....	....	....	55	5	0	2	2	0
1948-49	Fort Worth Rangers	USHL	8	4	2	6	....	....	....	17	....	....	....	....	....
	Springfield Indians	AHL	50	7	18	25	....	....	....	61	3	1	1	2	0
1949-50	Kerrisdale Monarchs	Van-Sr.	STATISTICS NOT AVAILABLE												
1950-51	Vancouver Canucks	PCHL	11	1	2	3	....	....	....	12	....	....	....	....	....
	Kerrisdale Monarchs	Van-Sr.	34	11	26	37	....	....	....	69	5	5	3	8	2
1951-52	Vancouver Wheelers	City Sr	32	18	14	32	....	....	....	26	....	....	....	....	....
	NHL Totals		**2**	**0**	**0**	**0**	**0**	**0**	**0**	**0**	....	....	....	....	....

• SCHMIDT, MILT
Milt Schmidt **HHOF**
C/D – L. 6', 185 lbs. b: Kitchener, Ont., 3/5/1918.

Season	Club	League	GP	G	A	Pts	AG	AA	APts	PIM	PO GP	PO G	PO A	PO Pts	PO PIM
1933-34	Kitchener Empires	OHA	7	2	4	6	....	....	....	2	4	2	*3	5	0
1934-35	Kitchener Greenshirts	OHA	17	*20	6	26	....	....	....	14	3	2	2	4	0
1935-36	Kitchener Greenshirts	OHA	5	4	3	7	....	....	....	2	4	4	1	*5	11
1936-37	**Boston Bruins**	**NHL**	**26**	**2**	**8**	**10**	**4**	**19**	**23**	**15**	**3**	**0**	**0**	**0**	**0**
	Providence Reds	AHL	23	8	1	9	....	....	....	12	....	....	....	....	....
1937-38	**Boston Bruins**	**NHL**	**44**	**13**	**14**	**27**	**27**	**29**	**56**	**15**	**3**	**0**	**0**	**0**	**0**
1938-39	**Boston Bruins**	**NHL**	**41**	**15**	**17**	**32**	**32**	**32**	**64**	**13**	**12**	**3**	**3**	**6**	**2**
1939-40	**Boston Bruins**	**NHL**	**48**	**22**	***30**	***52**	**48**	**61**	**109**	**37**	**6**	**0**	**0**	**0**	**0**
1940-41	**Boston Bruins**	**NHL**	**45**	**13**	**25**	**38**	**26**	**46**	**72**	**23**	**11**	**5**	**6**	**11**	**9**
1941-42	**Boston Bruins**	**NHL**	**36**	**14**	**21**	**35**	**24**	**32**	**56**	**34**	....	....	....	....	....
	Ottawa RCAF	City Sr.	....	....	....	....	....	....	....	....	19	10	24	34	*29
1942-43			MILITARY SERVICE												
1943-44			MILITARY SERVICE												
1944-45			MILITARY SERVICE												
1945-46	**Boston Bruins**	**NHL**	**48**	**13**	**18**	**31**	**20**	**34**	**54**	**21**	**10**	**3**	**5**	**8**	**2**
1946-47	**Boston Bruins**	**NHL**	**59**	**27**	**35**	**62**	**37**	**51**	**88**	**40**	**5**	**3**	**1**	**4**	**4**
1947-48	**Boston Bruins**	**NHL**	**33**	**9**	**17**	**26**	**13**	**25**	**38**	**28**	**5**	**2**	**5**	**7**	**2**
1948-49	**Boston Bruins**	**NHL**	**44**	**10**	**22**	**32**	**16**	**35**	**51**	**25**	**4**	**0**	**2**	**2**	**8**
1949-50	**Boston Bruins**	**NHL**	**68**	**19**	**22**	**41**	**26**	**28**	**54**	**41**	....	....	....	....	....
1950-51	**Boston Bruins**	**NHL**	**62**	**22**	**39**	**61**	**30**	**51**	**81**	**33**	**6**	**0**	**1**	**1**	**7**
1951-52	**Boston Bruins**	**NHL**	**69**	**21**	**29**	**50**	**30**	**38**	**68**	**57**	**7**	**2**	**1**	**3**	**0**
1952-53	**Boston Bruins**	**NHL**	**68**	**11**	**23**	**34**	**17**	**32**	**49**	**30**	**10**	**5**	**1**	**6**	**6**
1953-54	**Boston Bruins**	**NHL**	**62**	**14**	**18**	**32**	**21**	**24**	**45**	**28**	**4**	**1**	**0**	**1**	**20**
1954-55	**Boston Bruins**	**NHL**	**23**	**4**	**8**	**12**	**6**	**10**	**16**	**26**	....	....	....	....	....
1955-56	**Boston Bruins**	**NHL**	DID NOT PLAY – COACHING												
	NHL Totals		**776**	**229**	**346**	**575**	**377**	**547**	**924**	**466**	**86**	**24**	**25**	**49**	**60**

NHL First All-Star Team (1940, 1947, 1951) • NHL Scoring Leader (1940) • Won Hart Trophy (1951) • NHL Second All-Star Team (1952) • Won Lester Patrick Trophy (1996)

Played in NHL All-Star Game (1947, 1948, 1951, 1952)

Signed as a free agent by **Boston**, October 9, 1935.

• SCHNARR, WERNER
Werner Schnarr
C – L. 5'7", 145 lbs. b: Kitchener, Ont., 3/23/1903. Deceased.

Season	Club	League	GP	G	A	Pts	AG	AA	APts	PIM	PO GP	PO G	PO A	PO Pts	PO PIM
1921-22	Quaker City Seniors	USAHA	STATISTICS NOT AVAILABLE												
1922-23	Kitchener Union Jacks	OHA	....	....	....	....	....	....	....	....	8	*14	*5	*19	....
1923-24	Kitchener Greenshirts	OHA Sr.	1	0	0	0	....	....	....	0	....	....	....	....	....
	Kitchener Twin City	OHA Sr.	10	10	5	15	....	....	....	....	....	....	....	....	....
1924-25	**Boston Bruins**	**NHL**	**24**	**0**	**0**	**0**	**0**	**0**	**0**	**0**	....	....	....	....	....
1925-26	**Boston Bruins**	**NHL**	**1**	**0**	**0**	**0**	**0**	**0**	**0**	**0**	....	....	....	....	....
1926-27	London–Stratford	Can-Pro	3	0	0	0	....	....	....	0	....	....	....	....	....
1927-28			STATISTICS NOT AVAILABLE												
1928-29	Kitchener Dutchmen	Can-Pro	2	0	0	0	....	....	....	0	....	....	....	....	....
1929-30	Guelph Maple Leafs	Can-Pro	27	17	*19	36	....	....	....	16	4	3	*5	8	8
1930-31	Kitchener Silverwoods	OPHL	30	13	7	20	....	....	....	29	4	2	2	4	0
	NHL Totals		**25**	**0**	**0**	**0**	**0**	**0**	**0**	**0**	....	....	....	....	....

Signed as a free agent by **Boston**, October 29, 1924.

• SCHOCK, RON
— see page 1458

• SCHRINER, SWEENEY
Sweeney (David) Schriner **HHOF**
LW – L. 6', 185 lbs. b: Sarator, Russia, 11/30/1911. d: 7/4/1990.

Season	Club	League	GP	G	A	Pts	AG	AA	APts	PIM	PO GP	PO G	PO A	PO Pts	PO PIM
1930-31	Calgary Canadians	AJHL	2	*2	0	2	....	....	....	0	....	....	....	....	....
1931-32	Calgary Bronks	ASHL	18	*19	3	*22	....	....	....	32	3	1	*2	*3	0
1932-33	Calgary Bronks	ASHL	15	*22	4	*26	....	....	....	8	5	*3	1	*4	6
1933-34	Syracuse Stars	IAHL	44	17	11	28	....	....	....	28	4	0	0	0	0
1934-35	**New York Americans**	**NHL**	**48**	**18**	**22**	**40**	**38**	**49**	**87**	**6**	....	....	....	....	....
1935-36	**New York Americans**	**NHL**	**48**	**19**	**26**	***45**	**47**	**64**	**111**	**8**	**5**	**3**	**1**	**4**	**2**
1936-37	**New York Americans**	**NHL**	**48**	**21**	**25**	***46**	**46**	**59**	**105**	**17**	....	....	....	....	....
1937-38	**New York Americans**	**NHL**	**48**	**21**	**17**	**38**	**45**	**35**	**80**	**22**	**6**	**1**	**0**	**1**	**0**
1938-39	**New York Americans**	**NHL**	**48**	**13**	**31**	**44**	**27**	**59**	**86**	**20**	**2**	**0**	**0**	**0**	**30**
1939-40	**Toronto Maple Leafs**	**NHL**	**39**	**11**	**15**	**26**	**24**	**30**	**54**	**10**	**9**	**1**	**3**	**4**	**4**
1940-41	**Toronto Maple Leafs**	**NHL**	**48**	**24**	**14**	**38**	**49**	**26**	**75**	**0**	**7**	**2**	**1**	**3**	**4**
1941-42	**Toronto Maple Leafs**	**NHL**	**47**	**20**	**16**	**36**	**34**	**24**	**58**	**21**	**13**	**6**	**3**	**9**	**10**
1942-43	**Toronto Maple Leafs**	**NHL**	**37**	**19**	**17**	**36**	**27**	**22**	**49**	**13**	**4**	**2**	**2**	**4**	**0**
1943-44	Calgary Combines	WCSHL	10	9	9	18	....	....	....	14	3	3	2	5	4
	Vancouver St. Regis	PCHL	....	....	....	....	....	....	....	....	3	6	3	9	0
1944-45	**Toronto Maple Leafs**	**NHL**	**26**	**22**	**15**	**37**	**31**	**24**	**55**	**10**	**13**	**3**	**1**	**4**	**4**
1945-46	**Toronto Maple Leafs**	**NHL**	**47**	**13**	**6**	**19**	**20**	**11**	**31**	**15**	....	....	....	....	....
1946-47	Lethbridge Maple Leafs	WCSHL	DID NOT PLAY – COACHING												
1947-48	Regina Capitals	WCSHL	DID NOT PLAY – COACHING												
1948-49	Regina Capitals	WCSHL	36	26	27	53	....	....	....	30	8	*10	2	12	0
	NHL Totals		**484**	**201**	**204**	**405**	**388**	**403**	**791**	**148**	**59**	**18**	**11**	**29**	**54**

NHL Rookie of the Year (1935) • NHL First All-Star Team (1936, 1941) • NHL Scoring Leader (1936, 1937) • NHL Second All-Star Team (1937)

Played in NHL All-Star Game (1937)

Traded to **Toronto** by **NY Americans** for Busher Jackson, Buzz Boll, Doc Romnes, Jim Fowler and Murray Armstrong, May 15, 1939.

• SCLISIZZI, ENIO Enio Sclisizzi

LW – L. 5'10", 170 lbs. b: Milton, Ont., 8/1/1925.

Season	Club	League	GP	G	A	Pts	AG	AA	APts	PIM	GP	G	A	Pts	PIM
			REGULAR SEASON								PLAYOFFS				
1944-45	Cornwallis Navy	City Sr.	STATISTICS NOT AVAILABLE												
1945-46	Stratford Indians	OHA Sr.	14	6	5	11	....	....	....	2	5	5	4	9	4
1946-47	Indianapolis Capitals	AHL	60	20	14	34	....	....	....	45	....	....	....	....	....
	Detroit Red Wings	**NHL**	....	....	....	....	....	....	....	....	**1**	**0**	**0**	**0**	**0**
1947-48	**Detroit Red Wings**	**NHL**	**4**	**1**	**0**	**1**	**1**	**0**	**1**	**0**	**6**	**0**	**0**	**0**	**4**
	Indianapolis Capitals	AHL	61	29	38	67	....	....	....	58	....	....	....	....	....
1948-49	**Detroit Red Wings**	**NHL**	**50**	**9**	**8**	**17**	**14**	**13**	**27**	**24**	**6**	**0**	**0**	**0**	**2**
	Indianapolis Capitals	AHL	12	3	7	10	....	....	....	6	....	....	....	....	....
1949-50	**Detroit Red Wings**	**NHL**	**4**	**0**	**0**	**0**	**0**	**0**	**0**	**2**	....	....	....	....	....
	Indianapolis Capitals	AHL	62	19	26	45	....	....	....	47	8	1	4	5	7
1950-51	Indianapolis Capitals	AHL	64	30	36	66	....	....	....	43	3	2	0	2	0
1951-52	**Detroit Red Wings**	**NHL**	**9**	**2**	**1**	**3**	**3**	**1**	**4**	**0**	....	....	....	....	....
	Indianapolis Capitals	AHL	55	24	34	58	....	....	....	35	....	....	....	....	....
1952-53	**Chicago Black Hawks**	**NHL**	**14**	**0**	**2**	**2**	**0**	**3**	**3**	**0**	....	....	....	....	....
	St. Louis Flyers	AHL	10	4	4	8	....	....	....	2	....	....	....	....	....
	Calgary Stampeders	WHL	16	12	11	23	....	....	....	12	5	5	2	7	4
1953-54	Edmonton Flyers	WHL	70	28	36	64	....	....	....	46	13	6	4	10	8
1954-55	Edmonton Flyers	WHL	59	29	24	53	....	....	....	50	9	0	5	5	12
1955-56	Buffalo Bisons	AHL	60	18	28	46	....	....	....	56	5	1	3	4	2
1956-57	Calgary Stampeders	WHL	67	26	24	50	....	....	....	42	3	2	0	2	2
1957-58	Calgary Stampeders	WHL	68	22	15	37	....	....	....	19	14	5	3	8	16
1958-59	Victoria Cougars	WHL	60	12	29	41	....	....	....	22	3	1	1	2	2
	NHL Totals		**81**	**12**	**11**	**23**	**18**	**17**	**35**	**26**	**13**	**0**	**0**	**0**	**6**

AHL First All-Star Team (1952) • WHL First All-Star Team (1954)

Traded to **Chicago** by **Detroit** with Fred Glover for cash, August 14, 1952. Traded to **Victoria** (WHL) by **Calgary** (WHL) with George Ford and Murray Wilkie for Ed Dorohoy, August, 1958.

• SCOTT, GANTON Ganton Scott

RW – R. 5'9", 165 lbs. b: Toronto, Ont., 3/23/1903. Deceased.

Season	Club	League	GP	G	A	Pts	AG	AA	APts	PIM	GP	G	A	Pts	PIM
1921-22	Toronto Aura Lee	OHA	6	*11	1	*12	....	....	....	....	....	....	....	....	....
1922-23	**Toronto St. Pats**	**NHL**	**17**	**0**	**0**	**0**	**0**	**0**	**0**	**0**	....	....	....	....	....
1923-24	**Toronto St. Pats**	**NHL**	**4**	**0**	**0**	**0**	**0**	**0**	**0**	**0**	....	....	....	....	....
	Hamilton Tigers	**NHL**	**4**	**0**	**0**	**0**	**0**	**0**	**0**	**0**	....	....	....	....	....
1924-25	**Montreal Maroons**	**NHL**	**28**	**1**	**1**	**2**	**3**	**13**	**16**	**0**	....	....	....	....	....
1925-26	Edmonton Eskimos	WHL	7	0	1	1	....	....	....	0	....	....	....	....	....
	Saskatoon Crescents	WHL	6	0	1	1	....	....	....	2	....	....	....	....	....
	Palais-de-Glace	Cal-Pro	STATISTICS NOT AVAILABLE												
1926-27	Los Angeles Richfields	Cal-Pro	STATISTICS NOT AVAILABLE												
1927-28	Los Angeles Richfields	Cal-Pro	STATISTICS NOT AVAILABLE												
1928-29	San Francisco Tigers	Cal-Pro	....	*31	6	*37	....	....	....	32	....	....	....	....	....
1929-30	San Francisco Tigers	Cal-Pro	....	12	6	18	....	....	....	....	....	....	....	....	....
1930-31	San Francisco Hawks	Cal-Pro	....	11	10	21	....	....	....	29	....	....	....	....	....
1931-32	Oakland Shieks	Cal-Pro	....	15	5	20	....	....	....	....	....	....	....	....	....
	NHL Totals		**53**	**1**	**1**	**2**	**3**	**13**	**16**	**0**	....	....	....	....	....
	Other Major League Totals		13	0	2	2	....	....	....	2	....	....	....	....	....

Signed as a free agent by **Toronto St. Pats**, October 9, 1922. Traded to **Hamilton** by **Toronto St. Pats** for cash, January 16, 1924. Signed as a free agent by **Montreal Maroons**, October 31, 1924. Signed as a free agent by **Edmonton** (WHL), December 29, 1925. Traded to **Saskatoon** (WHL) by **Edmonton** (WHL) for cash, January 25, 1926.

• SCOTT, LAURIE Laurie Scott

LW/C – L. 5'6", 155 lbs. b: South River, Ont., 6/19/1900. d: 2/15/1977.

Season	Club	League	GP	G	A	Pts	AG	AA	APts	PIM	GP	G	A	Pts	PIM
1922-23	Saskatoon Sheiks	WCHL	21	7	6	13	....	....	....	6	....	....	....	....	....
1923-24	Saskatoon Crescents	WCHL	30	20	5	25	....	....	....	8	....	....	....	....	....
1924-25	Saskatoon Crescents	WCHL	26	12	6	18	....	....	....	41	2	0	0	0	2
1925-26	Saskatoon Crescents	WHL	29	11	4	15	....	....	....	32	2	1	0	1	2
1926-27	**New York Americans**	**NHL**	**39**	**6**	**2**	**8**	**17**	**17**	**34**	**22**	....	....	....	....	....
1927-28	**New York Rangers**	**NHL**	**23**	**0**	**1**	**1**	**0**	**8**	**8**	**6**	....	....	....	....	....
	Springfield Indians	Can-Am	17	3	3	6	....	....	....	8	4	0	0	0	2
1928-29	Springfield Indians	Can-Am	40	9	1	10	....	....	....	42	....	....	....	....	....
1929-30	Duluth Hornets	AHA	48	19	13	32	....	....	....	46	4	3	1	4	4
1930-31	Duluth Hornets	AHA	48	29	11	40	....	....	....	51	4	1	1	2	4
1931-32	Duluth Hornets	AHA	48	12	9	21	....	....	....	47	8	3	0	3	7
1932-33	Eveleth Rangers	CHL	38	10	9	19	....	....	....	23	3	0	0	0	5
1933-34	Oklahoma City Warriors	AHA	37	9	10	19	....	....	....	7	....	....	....	....	....
1934-35	St. Louis Flyers	AHA	41	17	22	39	....	....	....	8	3	2	*4	6	0
	NHL Totals		**62**	**6**	**3**	**9**	**17**	**25**	**42**	**28**	....	....	....	....	....
	Other Major League Totals		106	50	21	71	....	....	....	87	4	1	0	1	4

Signed as a free agent by **Saskatoon** (WCHL), December 21, 1922. Traded to **Toronto St. Pats** by **Saskatoon** with Corb Denneny and Leo Bourgeault for cash, October 18, 1926. • Ruled to be property of **Toronto St. Pats** by NHL President Frank Calder after **NY Americans** claimed his rights, November 4, 1926. Traded to **NY Americans** by **Toronto** for Jesse Spring, November 15, 1926. Traded to **NY Rangers** by **NY Americans** for cash, October 14, 1927. Traded to **Duluth** (AHA) by **NY Rangers** for cash, October 18, 1929.

• SEIBERT, EARL Earl Seibert HHOF

D – R. 6'2", 198 lbs. b: Kitchener, Ont., 12/7/1911. d: 5/12/1990.

Season	Club	League	GP	G	A	Pts	AG	AA	APts	PIM	GP	G	A	Pts	PIM
			REGULAR SEASON								PLAYOFFS				
1927-28	Kitchener Jr. Greenshirts	OHA	STATISTICS NOT AVAILABLE												
	Kitchener Greenshirts	OHA Sr.	1	0	0	0	....	....	....	2	....	....	....	....	....
1928-29	Kitchener Jr. Greenshirts	OHA	STATISTICS NOT AVAILABLE												
1929-30	Springfield Indians	Can-Am	40	4	1	5	....	....	....	84	....	....	....	....	....
1930-31	Springfield Indians	Can-Am	38	16	11	27	....	....	....	96	4	2	0	2	16
1931-32	**New York Rangers**	**NHL**	**46**	**4**	**6**	**10**	**8**	**17**	**25**	**88**	**7**	**1**	**2**	**3**	**14**
1932-33	**New York Rangers**	**NHL**	**45**	**2**	**3**	**5**	**5**	**8**	**13**	**92**	**8**	**1**	**0**	**1**	**14**
1933-34	**New York Rangers**	**NHL**	**48**	**13**	**10**	**23**	**29**	**27**	**56**	**66**	**2**	**0**	**0**	**0**	**4**
1934-35	**New York Rangers**	**NHL**	**48**	**6**	**19**	**25**	**13**	**42**	**55**	**86**	**4**	**0**	**0**	**0**	**6**
1935-36	**New York Rangers**	**NHL**	**17**	**2**	**3**	**5**	**5**	**7**	**12**	**6**	....	....	....	....	....
	Chicago Black Hawks	**NHL**	**15**	**3**	**6**	**9**	**7**	**14**	**21**	**19**	**2**	**2**	**0**	**2**	**0**
1936-37	**Chicago Black Hawks**	**NHL**	**43**	**9**	**6**	**15**	**19**	**14**	**33**	**46**	....	....	....	....	....
1937-38	**Chicago Black Hawks**	**NHL**	**48**	**8**	**13**	**21**	**17**	**27**	**44**	**38**	**10**	**5**	**2**	**7**	**12**
1938-39	**Chicago Black Hawks**	**NHL**	**48**	**4**	**11**	**15**	**8**	**20**	**28**	**57**	....	....	....	....	....
1939-40	**Chicago Black Hawks**	**NHL**	**36**	**3**	**7**	**10**	**6**	**14**	**20**	**35**	**2**	**0**	**1**	**1**	**8**
1940-41	**Chicago Black Hawks**	**NHL**	**46**	**3**	**17**	**20**	**6**	**31**	**37**	**52**	**5**	**0**	**0**	**0**	**12**
1941-42	**Chicago Black Hawks**	**NHL**	**46**	**7**	**14**	**21**	**12**	**21**	**33**	**52**	**3**	**0**	**0**	**0**	**0**
1942-43	**Chicago Black Hawks**	**NHL**	**44**	**5**	**27**	**32**	**7**	**34**	**41**	**48**	....	....	....	....	....
1943-44	**Chicago Black Hawks**	**NHL**	**50**	**8**	**25**	**33**	**10**	**30**	**40**	**20**	**9**	**0**	**2**	**2**	**2**
1944-45	**Chicago Black Hawks**	**NHL**	**22**	**7**	**8**	**15**	**10**	**13**	**23**	**13**	....	....	....	....	....
	Detroit Red Wings	**NHL**	**25**	**5**	**9**	**14**	**7**	**14**	**21**	**10**	**14**	**2**	**1**	**3**	**4**
1945-46	**Detroit Red Wings**	**NHL**	**18**	**0**	**3**	**3**	**0**	**6**	**6**	**18**	....	....	....	....	....
	Indianapolis Capitals	AHL	24	2	9	11	....	....	....	19	5	0	0	0	0
1946-47	Springfield Indians	AHL	DID NOT PLAY – COACHING												
	NHL Totals		**645**	**89**	**187**	**276**	**169**	**339**	**508**	**746**	**66**	**11**	**8**	**19**	**76**

NHL First All-Star Team (1935, 1942, 1943, 1944) • NHL Second All-Star Team (1936, 1937, 1938, 1939, 1940, 1941)

Played in NHL All-Star Game (1939)

Traded to **NY Rangers** by **Springfield** (Can-Am) for cash, May 9, 1931. Traded to **Chicago** by **NY Rangers** for Art Coulter, January 15, 1926. Traded to **Detroit** by **Chicago** for Cully Simon, Don Grosso and Byron McDonald, January 2, 1945.

• SEILING, ROD — see page 1462

• SELBY, BRIT — see page 1463

• SENICK, GEORGE George Senick

LW – L. 5'11", 195 lbs. b: Saskatoon, Sask., 9/16/1929.

Season	Club	League	GP	G	A	Pts	AG	AA	APts	PIM	GP	G	A	Pts	PIM
1946-47	Saskatoon Jr. Quakers	SJHL	23	21	28	49	....	....	....	66	2	0	0	0	0
1947-48	Omaha Knights	USHL	62	20	23	43	....	....	....	81	3	0	0	0	0
1948-49	Seattle Ironmen	PCHL	55	26	16	42	....	....	....	*166	....	....	....	....	....
	Houston Huskies	USHL	5	0	0	0	....	....	....	0	....	....	....	....	....
1949-50	Seattle Ironmen	PCHL	70	31	31	62	....	....	....	145	4	2	1	3	6
1950-51	Seattle Ironmen	PCHL	16	6	4	10	....	....	....	28	....	....	....	....	....
	Saskatoon Quakers	SSHL	15	13	13	26	....	....	....	45	11	*11	9	*20	10
1951-52	Saskatoon Quakers	PCHL	67	26	23	49	....	....	....	98	13	*11	10	*21	*24
1952-53	**New York Rangers**	**NHL**	**13**	**2**	**3**	**5**	**3**	**4**	**7**	**8**	....	....	....	....	....
	Saskatoon Quakers	WHL	48	27	46	73	....	....	....	61	13	5	9	14	14
1953-54	Saskatoon Quakers	WHL	43	21	21	42	....	....	....	51	6	3	2	5	19
1954-55	Saskatoon–Vancouver	WHL	34	10	11	21	....	....	....	20	....	....	....	....	....
	Spokane Flyers	WIHL	11	7	10	17	....	....	....	19	4	3	2	5	4
1955-56	Brandon Regals	WHL	66	34	37	71	....	....	....	71	....	....	....	....	....
1956-57	Seattle Americans	WHL	50	26	26	52	....	....	....	40	....	....	....	....	....
1957-58	Sudbury Wolves	NOHA	50	26	32	58	....	....	....	59	7	2	4	6	18
1958-59	Sudbury Wolves	NOHA	30	11	15	26	....	....	....	74	1	0	0	0	0
1959-60	Saskatoon Quakers	SSHL	20	*26	22	48	....	....	....	54	7	*14	*13	*27	12
1960-61	Saskatoon Quakers	SSHL	DID NOT PLAY – COACHING												
1961-62	Saskatoon Quakers	SSHL	29	30	*54	*84	....	....	....	60	8	6	*17	*23	20
1962-63	Saskatoon Quakers	SSHL	28	*44	38	82	....	....	....	47	11	5	*21	*26	*23
1963-64			DID NOT PLAY – RETIRED												
1964-65	Saskatoon Quakers	SSHL	5	3	10	13	....	....	....	4	....	....	....	....	....
1965-66	Saskatoon Quakers	SSHL	30	27	32	59	....	....	....	40	12	8	*15	*23	13
	NHL Totals		**13**	**2**	**3**	**5**	**3**	**4**	**7**	**8**	....	....	....	....	....

WHL First All-Star Team (1953)

• SHACK, EDDIE — see page 1467

• SHACK, JOE Joe Shack

LW – L. 5'10", 170 lbs. b: Winnipeg, Man., 12/8/1915. d: 5/5/1987.

Season	Club	League	GP	G	A	Pts	AG	AA	APts	PIM	GP	G	A	Pts	PIM
1933-34	Winnipeg Elmwoods	MJHL	11	14	2	16	....	....	....	0	2	0	1	1	2
1934-35	Winnipeg Elmwoods	MJHL	10	6	7	13	....	....	....	16	4	2	1	3	6
1935-36	Winnipeg Winnipegs	MHL Sr.	10	6	3	9	....	....	....	15	3	0	1	1	2
1936-37	Harringay Greyhounds	Britain	....	18	9	27	....	....	....	12	....	....	....	....	....
1937-38	Harringay Greyhounds	Britain	....	14	18	32	....	....	....	....	....	....	....	....	....
1938-39	Harringay Greyhounds	Britain	....	33	*27	*60	....	....	....	....	....	....	....	....	....
1939-40	Ottawa Senators	QSHL	28	10	17	27	....	....	....	16	....	....	....	....	....
1940-41	Ottawa Senators	QSHL	35	21	21	42	....	....	....	22	8	3	1	4	8
1941-42	New Haven Eagles	AHL	56	16	29	45	....	....	....	12	2	0	0	0	0
1942-43	**New York Rangers**	**NHL**	**20**	**5**	**9**	**14**	**7**	**11**	**18**	**6**	....	....	....	....	....
1943-44	Ottawa Commandos	QSHL	19	7	16	23	....	....	....	11	3	0	4	4	0
	Montreal Vics	City Sr.	12	10	10	20	....	....	....	14	....	....	....	....	....
1944-45	**New York Rangers**	**NHL**	**50**	**4**	**18**	**22**	**5**	**29**	**34**	**14**	....	....	....	....	....
1945-46	St. Paul Saints	USHL	51	28	31	59	....	....	....	37	6	0	1	1	4
1946-47	St. Paul Saints	USHL	55	25	30	55	....	....	....	29	....	....	....	....	....
1947-48	St. Paul Saints	USHL	62	12	31	43	....	....	....	19	....	....	....	....	....
1948-49	Harringay Racers	Britain	28	28	*41	*69	....	....	....	34	....	....	....	....	....
1949-50	Harringay Racers	Britain	57	30	52	82	....	....	....	62	....	....	....	....	....
1950-51	Harringay Racers	Britain	44	36	40	76	....	....	....	62	....	....	....	....	....
1951-52	Harringay Racers	Britain	59	41	51	92	....	....	....	62	....	....	....	....	....
1952-53	Harringay Racers	Britain	60	57	56	113	....	....	....	86	....	....	....	....	....
1953-54	Harringay Racers	Britain	24	16	14	30	....	....	....	47	....	....	....	....	....
1954-55	Dunferline Vikings	Britain	5	4	0	4	....	....	....	0	....	....	....	....	....
1955-56	Sweden	Nat-Tm.	DID NOT PLAY – COACHING												
	NHL Totals		**70**	**9**	**27**	**36**	**12**	**40**	**52**	**20**	....	....	....	....	....

Traded to **NY Rangers** by **New Haven** (AHL) for cash after New Haven (AHL) franchise folded, January 18, 1943.

• SHANNON, CHUCK Chuck "Specs" Shannon

D – L. 5'11", 192 lbs. b: Campbellford, Ont., 3/22/1916.

Season	Club	League	GP	G	A	Pts	AG	AA	APts	PIM	GP	G	A	Pts	PIM
			REGULAR SEASON								PLAYOFFS				
1932-33	Niagara Falls Cataracts	OHA	6	6	2	8	....	....	....	6	5	1	*2	3	0
1933-34	Sudbury Wolves	City Sr.	8	*9	*6	*15	....	....	....	12	2	3	1	4	0
1934-35	Sudbury Wolves	City Sr.	10	*19	5	*24	....	....	....	10	5	*5	*4	*9	4
1935-36	Syracuse Stars	IAHL	46	10	14	24	....	....	....	16	3	0	0	0	0
1936-37	Syracuse Stars	AHL	48	6	19	25	....	....	....	40	9	2	2	4	0
1937-38	Syracuse Stars	AHL	43	8	19	27	....	....	....	33	8	0	4	4	4
1938-39	Syracuse Stars	AHL	19	0	9	9	....	....	....	12	3	0	1	1	0
	Springfield Indians	AHL	1	0	0	0	....	....	....	0	....	....	....	....	....
1939-40	**New York Americans**	**NHL**	**4**	**0**	**0**	**0**	**0**	**0**	**0**	**2**	....	....	....	....	....
	Kansas City Greyhounds	AHA	24	5	7	12	....	....	....	8	....	....	....	....	....
	Springfield Indians	AHL	19	2	4	6	....	....	....	17	....	....	....	....	....
1940-41	Buffalo Bisons	AHL	53	10	24	34	....	....	....	42	....	....	....	....	....
1941-42	Buffalo Bisons	AHL	55	6	13	19	....	....	....	32	....	....	....	....	....
1942-43	Pittsburgh Hornets	AHL	50	8	12	20	....	....	....	36	2	0	2	2	4
1943-44	Pittsburgh Hornets	AHL	42	3	12	15	....	....	....	4	....	....	....	....	....
	Providence Reds	AHL	1	0	0	0	....	....	....	0	....	....	....	....	....
1944-45	Pittsburgh Hornets	AHL	23	1	4	5	....	....	....	10	....	....	....	....	....
1945-46	Toronto Staffords	OHA Sr.	16	4	9	13	....	....	....	20	10	0	2	2	8
1946-47	Owen Sound Mohawks	OHA Sr.	22	3	10	13	....	....	....	12	9	2	1	3	14
1947-48	Hamilton Pats	OHA Sr.	13	1	5	6	....	....	....	2	2	0	1	1	2
	NHL Totals		**4**	**0**	**0**	**0**	**0**	**0**	**0**	**2**	....	....	....	....	....

AHL First All-Star Team (1938)

Traded to **NY Americans** by **Toronto** for cash, October 13, 1939. • Rights returned to **Toronto** when **NY Americans** failed to complete the transaction, July 1, 1940. Traded to **Buffalo** (AHL) by **Toronto** for cash, October 20, 1940.

• SHANNON, GERRY Gerry "River" Shannon

LW – L. 5'11", 170 lbs. b: Campbellford, Ont., 10/25/1910. d: 5/6/1983.

Season	Club	League	GP	G	A	Pts	AG	AA	APts	PIM	GP	G	A	Pts	PIM
1926-27	Niagara Falls Cataracts	OHA	....	....	....	....	....	....	....	....	4	*2	0*	....	....
1927-28	Niagara Falls Cataracts	OHA	STATISTICS NOT AVAILABLE												
1928-29	Oakville Lions	OHA	12	2	0	2	....	....	....	....	....	....	....	....	....
1929-30	Niagara Falls Cataracts	OHA	4	7	*4	11	....	....	....	0	2	2	1	3	0
1930-31	Port Colborne Sailors	OHA Sr.	10	3	3	6	....	....	....	15	5	1	2	3	8
1931-32	Port Colborne Sailors	OHA Sr.	20	6	3	9	....	....	....	38	4	0	0	0	4
1932-33	Niagara Falls Cataracts	OHA Sr.	22	16	12	*28	....	....	....	16	5	1	*3	4	10
1933-34	**Ottawa Senators**	**NHL**	**48**	**11**	**15**	**26**	**24**	**40**	**64**	**26**	....	....	....	....	....
1934-35	**St. Louis Eagles**	**NHL**	**25**	**2**	**2**	**4**	**4**	**4**	**8**	**11**	....	....	....	....	....
	Boston Bruins	**NHL**	**17**	**1**	**1**	**2**	**2**	**2**	**4**	**4**	**4**	**0**	**0**	**0**	**2**
	Boston Cubs	Can-Am	7	4	2	6	....	....	....	2	....	....	....	....	....
1935-36	**Boston Bruins**	**NHL**	**23**	**0**	**1**	**1**	**0**	**2**	**2**	**6**	....	....	....	....	....
	Boston Cubs	Can-Am	22	11	6	17	....	....	....	24	....	....	....	....	....
1936-37	**Montreal Maroons**	**NHL**	**31**	**9**	**7**	**16**	**19**	**16**	**35**	**13**	**5**	**0**	**1**	**1**	**0**
	Providence Reds	AHL	6	1	3	4	....	....	....	7	....	....	....	....	....
1937-38	**Montreal Maroons**	**NHL**	**36**	**0**	**3**	**3**	**0**	**6**	**6**	**20**	....	....	....	....	....
	Springfield Indians	AHL	8	1	2	3	....	....	....	0	....	....	....	....	....
1938-39	Hershey Bears	AHL	31	9	2	11	....	....	....	4	5	1	1	2	8
1939-40	Hershey Bears	AHL	52	13	18	31	....	....	....	8	6	1	2	3	2
1940-41	Buffalo Bisons	AHL	....	10	24	34	....	....	....	42	....	....	....	....	....
	NHL Totals		**180**	**23**	**29**	**52**	**49**	**70**	**119**	**80**	**9**	**0**	**1**	**1**	**2**

Signed as a free agent by **Ottawa**, May 10, 1933. Transferred to **St. Louis** after **Ottawa** franchise relocated, September 22, 1934. Traded to **Boston** by **St. Louis** for Frank Jerwa, January 10, 1935. Traded to **Montreal Maroons** by **Boston** for cash, December 4, 1936 Traded to **Cleveland** (AHL) by **Montreal Maroons** for cash, October 6, 1938. Traded to **Hershey** (AHL) by **Cleveland** (AHL) for cash, October 11, 1938.

• SHAY, NORMAN Norman Shay

D/RW – L. 5'9", 158 lbs. b: Huntsville, Ont., 2/3/1899. Deceased.

Season	Club	League	GP	G	A	Pts	AG	AA	APts	PIM	GP	G	A	Pts	PIM
1921-22	Boston Westminsters	USAHA	....	....			....	....	....	....	4	1	0	1	....
1922-23	New Haven Westminsters	USAHA	....	7	0	7	....	....	....	....	....	....	....	....	....
1923-24	New Haven Bears	USAHA	12	6	0	6	....	....	....	....	....	....	....	....	....
1924-25	**Boston Bruins**	**NHL**	**18**	**1**	**1**	**2**	**3**	**13**	**16**	**14**	....	....	....	....	....
1925-26	**Boston Bruins**	**NHL**	**13**	**1**	**0**	**1**	**3**	**0**	**3**	**2**	....	....	....	....	....
	Toronto St.Pats	**NHL**	**22**	**3**	**1**	**4**	**9**	**11**	**20**	**18**	....	....	....	....	....
1926-27	New Haven Eagles	Can-Am	22	4	2	6	....	....	....	48	4	0	0	0	2
1927-28	Philadelphia Arrows	Can-Am	7	1	0	1	....	....	....	14	....	....	....	....	....
1928-29	Philadelphia Arrows	Can-Am	3	0	0	0	....	....	....	0	....	....	....	....	....
1929-30	New Haven Eagles	Can-Am	40	6	3	9	....	....	....	59	....	....	....	....	....
	NHL Totals		**53**	**5**	**2**	**7**	**15**	**24**	**39**	**34**	....	....	....	....	....

Signed as a free agent by **Boston**, January 9, 1925. Traded to **Toronto St. Pats** by **Boston** for cash, January 14, 1926. Claimed on waivers by **New Haven** (Can-Am) from **Toronto St. Pats**, October 18, 1926.

• SHEA, PAT Pat (Francis) Shea

D – L. 5'10", 100 lbs. b: Potlatch, ID, 10/29/1912. Deceased.

Season	Club	League	GP	G	A	Pts	AG	AA	APts	PIM	GP	G	A	Pts	PIM
1930-31	White Bear Mines	NWHL	STATISTICS NOT AVAILABLE												
1931-32	**Chicago Black Hawks**	**NHL**	**10**	**0**	**1**	**1**	**0**	**3**	**3**	**0**	....	....	....	....	....
	Pittsburgh Yellowjackets	IAHL	3	0	0	0	....	....	....	0	....	....	....	....	....
1932-33	Tulsa Oilers	AHA	39	8	8	16	....	....	....	37	4	0	1	1	*10
1933-34	Minneapolis Millers	CHL	40	5	7	12	....	....	....	88	3	*3	0	3	4
1934-35	Minneapolis Millers	CHL	46	6	13	19	....	....	....	38	5	0	0	0	4
1935-36	Kansas City Greyhounds	AHA	41	10	9	19	....	....	....	33	....	....	....	....	....
	Rochester Cardinals	IAHL	8	0	2	2	....	....	....	6	....	....	....	....	....
1936-37	Kansas City Greyhounds	AHA	40	2	6	8	....	....	....	26	3	0	0	0	11
1937-38	Kansas City Greyhounds	AHA	46	11	12	23	....	....	....	*73	....	....	....	....	....
1938-39	Kansas City Greyhounds	AHA	48	13	14	27	....	....	....	58	....	....	....	....	....
1939-40	Minneapolis Millers	AHA	48	12	13	25	....	....	....	57	3	2	0	2	5
1940-41	Minneapolis Millers	AHA	45	7	8	15	....	....	....	25	3	0	0	0	0
1941-42	Minneapolis Millers	AHA	46	2	11	13	....	....	....	38	....	....	....	....	....
	NHL Totals		**10**	**0**	**1**	**1**	**0**	**3**	**3**	**0**	....	....	....	....	....

AHA Second All-Star Team (1940)

Signed as a free agent by **Chicago**, October 14, 1931.

• SHEPPARD, FRANK Frank Sheppard

C/LW – L. 5'6", 157 lbs. b: Montreal, Que., 10/19/1907. Deceased.

Season	Club	League	GP	G	A	Pts	AG	AA	APts	PIM	GP	G	A	Pts	PIM
1925-26	Winnipeg Maroons	USAHA	29	3	3	6	....	....	....	16	....	....	....	....	....
1926-27	Detroit Millionaires	MOHL	STATISTICS NOT AVAILABLE												
1927-28	**Detroit Cougars**	**NHL**	**8**	**1**	**1**	**2**	**3**	**8**	**11**	**0**	....	....	....	....	....
	St. Paul Saints	AHA	33	12	4	16	....	....	....	32	....	....	....	....	....
1928-29	Tulsa Oilers	AHA	40	21	10	31	....	....	....	31	4	2	0	2	2
	St. Paul Saints	AHA	2	0	0	0	....	....	....	0	....	....	....	....	....
1929-30	Tulsa Oilers	AHA	43	11	6	17	....	....	....	41	7	1	1	2	2
1930-31	Tulsa Oilers	AHA	48	21	11	32	....	....	....	54	4	1	1	2	8
1931-32	Tulsa Oilers	AHA	41	8	4	12	....	....	....	50	....	....	....	....	....
1932-33	Regina—Vancouver	NWHL	27	19	13	32	....	....	....	23	2	1	0	1	2
1933-34	Edmonton Eskimos	NWHL	7	1	2	3	....	....	....	2	....	....	....	....	....
1934-35	Calgary–Edmonton	NWHL	14	1	4	5	....	....	....	14	....	....	....	....	....
1935-36	Vancouver Lions	NWHL	39	10	7	17	....	....	....	50	7	3	3	6	5
1936-37	Vancouver Lions	NWHL	7	2	1	3	....	....	....	4	....	....	....	....	....
	NHL Totals		**8**	**1**	**1**	**2**	**3**	**8**	**11**	**0**	....	....	....	....	....

Signed as a free agent by **Detroit Cougars**, September 9, 1927.

• SHEPPARD, JOHNNY Johnny "Jake" Sheppard

LW – L. 5'7", 165 lbs. b: Montreal, Que., 7/23/1903. Deceased.

Season	Club	League	GP	G	A	Pts	AG	AA	APts	PIM	GP	G	A	Pts	PIM
1921-22	Selkirk Fishermen	MHL Sr.	11	10	2	12	....	....	....	19	....	....	....	....	....
1922-23	Edmonton Eskimos	WCHL	21	1	1	2	....	....	....	6	2	0	0	0	0
1923-24	Edmonton Eskimos	WCHL	25	6	2	8	....	....	....	14	....	....	....	....	....
1924-25	Edmonton Eskimos	WCHL	28	14	4	18	....	....	....	26	....	....	....	....	....
1925-26	Edmonton Eskimos	WHL	23	7	7	14	....	....	....	16	2	1	0	1	4
1926-27	**Detroit Cougars**	**NHL**	**43**	**13**	**8**	**21**	**38**	**69**	**107**	**60**	....	....	....	....	....
	Detroit Greyhounds	AHA	2	0	0	0	....	....	....	0	....	....	....	....	....
1927-28	**Detroit Cougars**	**NHL**	**44**	**10**	**10**	**20**	**31**	**85**	**116**	**40**	....	....	....	....	....
1928-29	**New York Americans**	**NHL**	**43**	**5**	**4**	**9**	**20**	**37**	**57**	**38**	**2**	**0**	**0**	**0**	**0**
1929-30	**New York Americans**	**NHL**	**43**	**14**	**15**	**29**	**28**	**49**	**77**	**32**	....	....	....	....	....
1930-31	**New York Americans**	**NHL**	**42**	**5**	**8**	**13**	**12**	**29**	**41**	**16**	....	....	....	....	....
1931-32	**New York Americans**	**NHL**	**5**	**1**	**0**	**1**	**2**	**0**	**2**	**2**	....	....	....	....	....
	Bronx Tigers	Can-Am	33	17	11	28	....	....	....	27	2	1	0	1	2
1932-33	**New York Americans**	**NHL**	**46**	**17**	**9**	**26**	**40**	**24**	**64**	**32**	....	....	....	....	....
1933-34	**Boston Bruins**	**NHL**	**4**	**0**	**0**	**0**	**0**	**0**	**0**	**0**	....	....	....	....	....
	Chicago Black Hawks	**NHL**	**38**	**3**	**4**	**7**	**7**	**11**	**18**	**4**	**8**	**0**	**0**	**0**	**0**
1934-35	Seattle Seahawks	NWHL	36	6	17	23	....	....	....	38	5	2	2	4	0
1935-36	Seattle Seahawks	NWHL	39	13	10	23	....	....	....	29	4	2	*4	6	2
	NHL Totals		**308**	**68**	**58**	**126**	**178**	**304**	**482**	**224**	**10**	**0**	**0**	**0**	**0**
	Other Major League Totals		97	28	14	42	....	....	....	62	4	1	0	1	4

Signed as a free agent by **Edmonton** (WCHL), November 23, 1922. Traded to **Detroit Cougars** by **Edmonton** for cash, October 5, 1926. Traded to **NY Americans** by **Detroit Cougars** for Ebbie Goodfellow and $12,500, October 14, 1928. Traded to **Boston** by **NY Americans** with Lloyd Gross and George Patterson for Bob Gracie and Art Chapman, September 8, 1933. Signed as a free agent by **Chicago** after securing release from **Boston**, November 24, 1933.

• SHERF, JOHN John Sherf

LW – L. 5'11", 178 lbs. b: Calumet, MI, 4/8/1913. Deceased.

Season	Club	League	GP	G	A	Pts	AG	AA	APts	PIM	GP	G	A	Pts	PIM
1934-35	University of Michigan	MOHL	STATISTICS NOT AVAILABLE												
1935-36	**Detroit Red Wings**	**NHL**	**1**	**0**	**0**	**0**	**0**	**0**	**0**	**0**	....	....	....	....	....
	Detroit Olympics	IAHL	39	10	7	17	....	....	....	38	6	1	2	3	7
1936-37	**Detroit Red Wings**	**NHL**	**1**	**0**	**0**	**0**	**0**	**0**	**0**	**0**	**5**	**0**	**1**	**1**	**2**
	Pittsburgh Hornets	AHL	45	7	11	18	....	....	....	36	4	1	0	1	2
1937-38	**Detroit Red Wings**	**NHL**	**6**	**0**	**0**	**0**	**0**	**0**	**0**	**2**	....	....	....	....	....
	Philadelphia Ramblers	AHL	38	7	15	22	....	....	....	8	5	1	1	2	6
1938-39	**Detroit Red Wings**	**NHL**	**3**	**0**	**0**	**0**	**0**	**0**	**0**	**0**	**3**	**0**	**0**	**0**	**0**
1938-39	Pittsburgh Hornets	AHL	53	18	22	40	....	....	....	26	....	....	....	....	....
	Cleveland Falcons	AHL	1	0	0	0	....	....	....	0	....	....	....	....	....
1939-40	Pittsburgh Hornets	AHL	55	20	15	35			....	38	9	1	4	5	2
1940-41	Pittsburgh Hornets	AHL	54	21	14	35	....	....	....	31	6	1	3	4	2
1941-42	Pittsburgh Hornets	AHL	56	19	37	56	....	....	....	10	....	....	....	....	....
1942-43			MILITARY SERVICE												
1943-44	**Detroit Red Wings**	**NHL**	**8**	**0**	**0**	**0**	**0**	**0**	**0**	**6**	....	....	....	....	....
	NHL Totals		**19**	**0**	**0**	**0**	**0**	**0**	**0**	**8**	**8**	**0**	**1**	**1**	**2**

Signed as a free agent by **Detroit**, October 15, 1935. Loaned to **Philadelphia** (AHL) by **Detroit** for remainder of 1937-38 season with cash for Ed Wares, January 17, 1938.

• SHERO, FRED Fred "The Fog" Shero

D – L. 5'10", 175 lbs. b: Winnipeg, Man., 10/23/1925. Deceased.

Season	Club	League	GP	G	A	Pts	AG	AA	APts	PIM	GP	G	A	Pts	PIM
1942-43	St. James Monarchs	MJHL	16	3	3	6	....	....	....	2	4	1	1	2	2
1943-44	New York Rovers	EHL	15	5	7	12	....	....	....	6	....	....	....	....	....
	Brooklyn Crescents	EHL	29	11	14	25	....	....	....	7	10	2	5	7	8
1944-45	Port Arthur Navy	TBSHL	1	0	0	0	....	....	....	2	....	....	....	....	....
	Winnipeg Rangers	MJHL	2	0	5	5	....	....	....	0	3	1	1	2	8
	Winnipeg Navy	City Sr.	15	5	8	13	....	....	....	16	6	2	2	4	4
1945-46	New York Rovers	EHL	30	10	15	25	....	....	....	20	12	2	5	7	8
1946-47	New Haven Ramblers	AHL	3	0	0	0	....	....	....	6	....	....	....	....	....
	New York Rovers	EHL	46	9	22	31	....	....	....	44	9	1	3	4	25
1947-48	St. Paul Saints	USHL	40	9	14	23	....	....	....	20	....	....	....	....	....
	New York Rangers	**NHL**	**19**	**1**	**0**	**1**	**1**	**0**	**1**	**2**	**6**	**0**	**1**	**1**	**6**
1948-49	**New York Rangers**	**NHL**	**59**	**3**	**6**	**9**	**5**	**9**	**14**	**64**	....	....	....	....	....
1949-50	**New York Rangers**	**NHL**	**67**	**2**	**8**	**10**	**3**	**10**	**13**	**71**	**7**	**0**	**1**	**1**	**2**
	New Haven Ramblers	AHL	2	1	0	1	....	....	....	0	....	....	....	....	....
1950-51	Cincinnati Mohawks	AHL	65	5	17	22	....	....	....	94	....	....	....	....	....
1951-52	Cleveland Barons	AHL	15	2	2	4	....	....	....	10	3	0	1	1	2
	Seattle Ironmen	PCHL	43	1	16	17	....	....	....	46	....	....	....	....	....
1952-53	Cleveland Barons	AHL	64	4	14	18	....	....	....	54	9	2	1	3	16
1953-54	Cleveland Barons	AHL	69	21	32	53	....	....	....	95	9	2	3	5	16
1954-55	Cleveland Barons	AHL	37	8	14	22	....	....	....	54	....	....	....	....	....
1955-56	Winnipeg Warriors	WHL	59	8	24	32	....	....	....	90	6	0	2	2	8
1956-57	Winnipeg Warriors	WHL	66	8	24	32	....	....	....	52	....	....	....	....	....
1957-58	Shawinigan Cataracts	QHL	48	1	5	6	....	....	....	50	4	0	1	1	10
1958-59	Moose Jaw Canucks	SJHL	DID NOT PLAY – COACHING												
	NHL Totals		**145**	**6**	**14**	**20**	**9**	**19**	**28**	**137**	**13**	**0**	**2**	**2**	**8**

EHL First All-Star Team (1947) • AHL Second All-Star Team (1954) • Won Jack Adams Award (1974) • Won Lester Patrick Trophy (1980)

Traded to **Cleveland** (AHL) by **NY Rangers** with Ed Reigle, Jack Gordon, Fern Perreault and cash for Hy Buller and Wally Hergesheimer, May 14, 1951.

• SHERRITT, GORDON Gordon "Moose" Sherritt
D – L. 6'1", 195 lbs. b: Oakville, Man., 4/8/1922.

Season	Club	League	GP	G	A	Pts	AG	AA	APts	PIM	GP	G	A	Pts	PIM
			REGULAR SEASON								PLAYOFFS				
1937-38	Portage Terriers	MJHL	10	1	0	1	....	....	....	12	....	....	....	....	....
1938-39	Portage Terriers	MJHL	16	1	0	1	....	....	....	16	2	0	0	0	0
1939-40	Harringay Greyhounds	Britain	....	10	4	14	....	....	....	....	....	....	....	....	....
1940-41	Edmonton Flyers	ASHL	21	0	0	0	....	....	....	29	....	....	....	....	....
1941-42	Moose Jaw Maple Leafs	SSHL	32	0	8	8	....	....	....	46	9	0	2	2	18
1942-43	New Haven–Indianapolis	AHL	53	2	13	15	....	....	....	63	7	0	1	1	8
1943-44	**Detroit Red Wings**	**NHL**	**8**	**0**	**0**	**0**	**0**	**0**	**0**	**12**	....	....	....	....	....
	Indianapolis Capitals	AHL	43	2	12	14	....	....	....	*165	5	1	2	3	*18
1944-45	Indianapolis Capitals	AHL	51	3	11	14	....	....	....	86	5	0	1	1	2
1945-46	Cleveland Barons	AHL	18	0	9	9	....	....	....	50	....	....	....	....	....
	Minneapolis Millers	USHL	18	1	5	6	....	....	....	24	....	....	....	....	....
1946-47	Minneapolis Millers	USHL	48	2	13	15	....	....	....	96	3	0	0	0	0
1947-48	Minneapolis Millers	USHL	61	1	12	13	....	....	....	76	10	1	3	4	10
1948-49	Minneapolis Millers	USHL	64	3	35	38	....	....	....	63	....	....	....	....	....
	NHL Totals		**8**	**0**	**0**	**0**	**0**	**0**	**0**	**12**	....	....	....	....	....

Traded to **Cleveland** (AHL) by **Detroit** for cash, October 4, 1945.

• SHEWCHUCK, JACK Jack Shewchuck
D – L. 6'1", 190 lbs. b: Brantford, Ont., 6/19/1917. d: 5/15/1989.

Season	Club	League	GP	G	A	Pts	AG	AA	APts	PIM	GP	G	A	Pts	PIM
1935-36	Sudbury Wolves	NOHA	10	2	0	2	....	....	....	22	....	....	....	....	....
	Copper Cliff Jr. Redmen	NOHA	4	6	4	10	....	....	....	6	....	....	....	....	....
1936-37	Copper Cliff Jr. Redmen	NOHA	14	1	3	4	....	....	....	22	....	....	....	....	....
1937-38	Providence Reds	AHL	42	4	3	7	....	....	....	69	7	0	0	0	6
1938-39	**Boston Bruins**	**NHL**	**3**	**0**	**0**	**0**	**0**	**0**	**0**	**2**	....	....	....	....	....
	Providence Reds	AHL	46	8	17	25	....	....	....	72	5	1	1	2	8
1939-40	**Boston Bruins**	**NHL**	**47**	**2**	**4**	**6**	**4**	**8**	**12**	**55**	**6**	**0**	**0**	**0**	**0**
1940-41	**Boston Bruins**	**NHL**	**20**	**2**	**2**	**4**	**4**	**4**	**8**	**8**	....	....	....	....	....
	Hershey Bears	AHL	31	1	5	6	....	....	....	22	9	0	0	0	2
1941-42	**Boston Bruins**	**NHL**	**22**	**2**	**0**	**2**	**3**	**0**	**3**	**14**	**5**	**0**	**1**	**1**	**7**
	Hershey Bears	AHL	34	1	9	10	....	....	....	28	....	....	....	....	....
1942-43	**Boston Bruins**	**NHL**	**48**	**2**	**6**	**8**	**3**	**8**	**11**	**50**	**9**	**0**	**0**	**0**	**12**
1943-44			MILITARY SERVICE												
1944-45	**Boston Bruins**	**NHL**	**47**	**1**	**7**	**8**	**1**	**11**	**12**	**31**	....	....	....	....	....
1945-46	Hershey Bears	AHL	55	3	15	18	....	....	....	89	3	0	1	1	2
1946-47	St. Louis Flyers	AHL	51	1	9	10	....	....	....	34	....	....	....	....	....
1947-48	St. Louis Flyers	AHL	65	1	12	13	....	....	....	58	....	....	....	....	....
1948-49	Kitchener Dutchmen	OHA Sr.	35	3	11	14	....	....	....	43	12	0	0	0	20
1949-50	Kitchener Dutchmen	OHA Sr.	41	7	7	14	....	....	....	69	13	1	2	3	26
1950-51	Kitchener Dutchmen	OHA Sr.	3	0	0	0	....	....	....	8	....	....	....	....	....
1951-52	Brantford Redmen	OHA Sr.	10	0	1	1	....	....	....	0	....	....	....	....	....
	NHL Totals		**187**	**9**	**19**	**28**	**15**	**31**	**46**	**160**	**20**	**0**	**1**	**1**	**19**

Signed as a free agent by **Boston**, October 26, 1937.

• SHIBICKY, ALEX Alex Shibicky
RW – R. 6', 180 lbs. b: Winnipeg, Man., 5/19/1914.

Season	Club	League	GP	G	A	Pts	AG	AA	APts	PIM	GP	G	A	Pts	PIM
1932-33	Winnipeg Columbus Club	City Jr.	11	3	0	3	....	....	....	18	3	1	0	1	0
1933-34	Selkirk Jr. Fishermen	MHL Jr.	12	11	4	15	....	....	....	19	5	6	3	9	0
	Selkirk Fishermen	MHL Sr.	1	0	0	0	....	....	....	0	....	....	....	....	....
	Brooklyn Crescents	EHL	21	16	9	25	....	....	....	31	8	*8	1	9	4
1935-36	**New York Rangers**	**NHL**	**18**	**4**	**2**	**6**	**10**	**5**	**15**	**6**	....	....	....	....	....
	Philadelphia Ramblers	Can-Am	28	16	6	22	....	....	....	13	....	....	....	....	....
1936-37	**New York Rangers**	**NHL**	**47**	**14**	**8**	**22**	**30**	**19**	**49**	**30**	**9**	**1**	**4**	**5**	**0**
1937-38	**New York Rangers**	**NHL**	**48**	**17**	**18**	**35**	**36**	**37**	**73**	**26**	**3**	**2**	**0**	**2**	**2**
1938-39	**New York Rangers**	**NHL**	**48**	**24**	**9**	**33**	**51**	**17**	**68**	**24**	**7**	**3**	**1**	**4**	**2**
1939-40	**New York Rangers**	**NHL**	**44**	**11**	**21**	**32**	**24**	**42**	**66**	**33**	**11**	**2**	**5**	**7**	**4**
1940-41	**New York Rangers**	**NHL**	**41**	**10**	**14**	**24**	**20**	**26**	**46**	**14**	**3**	**1**	**0**	**1**	**2**
1941-42	**New York Rangers**	**NHL**	**45**	**20**	**14**	**34**	**34**	**21**	**55**	**16**	**6**	**3**	**2**	**5**	**2**
1942-43	Ottawa Engineers	QSHL	9	9	13	22	....	....	....	6	....	....	....	....	....
	Ottawa Commandos	QSHL	18	15	7	22	....	....	....	25	22	18	18	36	14
1943-44	Ottawa Commandos	QSHL	10	6	6	12	....	....	....	6	....	....	....	....	....
1944-45	Ottawa Engineers	City Sr.	4	3	5	8	....	....	....	0	5	8	3	11	4
1945-46	**New York Rangers**	**NHL**	**33**	**10**	**5**	**15**	**15**	**9**	**24**	**12**	....	....	....	....	....
	Providence Reds	AHL	18	7	12	19	....	....	....	4	1	0	0	0	0
1946-47	New Haven Ramblers	AHL	53	20	12	32	....	....	....	28	3	0	2	2	0
1947-48	New Westminster Royals	PCHL	DID NOT PLAY – COACHING												
	NHL Totals		**324**	**110**	**91**	**201**	**220**	**176**	**396**	**161**	**39**	**12**	**12**	**24**	**12**

EHL First All-Star Team (1935)

Signed as a free agent by **NY Rangers**, October 18, 1934.

• SHIELDS, AL Al Shields
D – R. 6', 188 lbs. b: Ottawa, Ont., 5/10/1907. d: 9/24/1975.

Season	Club	League	GP	G	A	Pts	AG	AA	APts	PIM	GP	G	A	Pts	PIM
			REGULAR SEASON								PLAYOFFS				
1927-28	Ottawa Montagnards	City Sr.	15	6	0	6	....	....	....	....	6	0	0	0	0
	New Haven Eagles	Can-Am	5	0	0	0	....	....	....	0	....	....	....	....	....
	Ottawa Senators	**NHL**	**7**	**0**	**1**	**1**	**0**	**8**	**8**	**2**	**2**	**0**	**0**	**0**	**0**
1928-29	**Ottawa Senators**	**NHL**	**42**	**0**	**1**	**1**	**0**	**9**	**9**	**10**	....	....	....	....	....
	St. Louis Flyers	AHA	6	1	1	2	....	....	....	2	....	....	....	....	....
1929-30	**Ottawa Senators**	**NHL**	**44**	**6**	**3**	**9**	**12**	**10**	**22**	**32**	**2**	**0**	**0**	**0**	**0**
1930-31	**Philadelphia Quakers**	**NHL**	**43**	**7**	**3**	**10**	**17**	**11**	**28**	**98**	....	....	....	....	....
1931-32	**New York Americans**	**NHL**	**48**	**4**	**1**	**5**	**8**	**3**	**11**	**45**	....	....	....	....	....
1932-33	**Ottawa Senators**	**NHL**	**48**	**7**	**4**	**11**	**16**	**11**	**27**	**119**	....	....	....	....	....
1933-34	**Ottawa Senators**	**NHL**	**47**	**4**	**7**	**11**	**9**	**19**	**28**	**44**	....	....	....	....	....
1934-35	**Montreal Maroons**	**NHL**	**42**	**4**	**8**	**12**	**8**	**18**	**26**	**45**	**7**	**0**	**1**	**1**	**6**
1935-36	**Montreal Maroons**	**NHL**	**45**	**2**	**7**	**9**	**5**	**17**	**22**	**81**	**3**	**0**	**0**	**0**	**6**
1936-37	**New York Americans**	**NHL**	**27**	**3**	**0**	**3**	**6**	**0**	**6**	**79**	....	....	....	....	....
	Boston Bruins	**NHL**	**18**	**0**	**4**	**4**	**0**	**9**	**9**	**15**	**3**	**0**	**0**	**0**	**2**
1937-38	**Montreal Maroons**	**NHL**	**48**	**5**	**7**	**12**	**10**	**14**	**24**	**67**	....	....	....	....	....
1938-39	New Haven Eagles	AHL	25	2	2	4	....	....	....	17	....	....	....	....	....
1939-40	New Haven Eagles	AHL	45	5	9	14	....	....	....	26	3	0	2	2	2
1940-41	New Haven Eagles	AHL	51	9	16	25	....	....	....	59	2	0	0	0	2
	Buffalo Bisons	AHL	3	0	0	0	....	....	....	0	2	0	0	0	2
1941-42	Washington Lions	AHL	51	3	10	13	....	....	....	24	2	0	0	0	0
1942-43	Arnprior RCAF	Ott-Sr.	8	4	6	10	....	....	....	16	2	0	1	1	4
1943-44	Arnprior RCAF	Ott-Sr.	5	1	3	4	....	....	....	6	....	....	....	....	....
	NHL Totals		**459**	**42**	**46**	**88**	**91**	**129**	**220**	**637**	**17**	**0**	**1**	**1**	**14**

Played in NHL All-Star Game (1934)

Signed as a free agent by **Ottawa**, March 3, 1928. Traded to **Philadelphia** by **Ottawa** with Syd Howe and Wally Kilrea for $35,000, November 6, 1930. Claimed by **NY Americans** from **Ottawa** for 1931-32 season in Dispersal Draft, September 26, 1931. Traded to **Montreal Maroons** by **Ottawa** for Irv Frew and future considerations (Normie Smith and Vern Ayres, October 22, 1934), September 20, 1934. Loaned to **NY Americans** by **Montreal Maroons** for cash, September 15, 1936. Loaned to **Boston** by **NY Americans** with the rights to Terry Reardon and Tom Cooper for Joe Jerwa with Montreal Maroons holding rights of recall, January 25, 1937. Returned to **Montreal Maroons** July 1,1937.

• SHILL, BILL Bill Shill
RW – R. 6'1", 175 lbs. b: Toronto, Ont., 3/6/1923.

Season	Club	League	GP	G	A	Pts	AG	AA	APts	PIM	GP	G	A	Pts	PIM
1940-41	Toronto Young Rangers	OHA	12	7	5	12	....	....	....	10	5	3	0	3	4
1941-42	Toronto Young Rangers	OHA	16	23	11	34	....	....	....	36	6	8	2	10	8
1942-43	**Boston Bruins**	**NHL**	**7**	**4**	**1**	**5**	**6**	**1**	**7**	**4**	....	....	....	....	....
	Toronto Navy	OHA Sr.	6	6	6	12	....	....	....	11	7	3	3	6	2
1943-44			MILITARY SERVICE												
1944-45	Cornwallis Navy	NSSHL	13	7	6	13	....	....	....	2	3	4	1	5	0
1945-46	**Boston Bruins**	**NHL**	**45**	**15**	**12**	**27**	**23**	**22**	**45**	**12**	**7**	**1**	**2**	**3**	**2**
1946-47	**Boston Bruins**	**NHL**	**27**	**2**	**0**	**2**	**3**	**0**	**3**	**2**	....	....	....	....	....
	Hershey–Buffalo	AHL	20	1	3	4	....	....	....	2	....	....	....	....	....
1947-48	Dallas Texans	USHL	66	16	21	37	....	....	....	30	....	....	....	....	....
1948-49	Seattle–Vancouver	PCHL	63	43	26	69	....	....	....	38	3	0	2	2	0
1949-50	Vancouver Canucks	PCHL	69	34	42	76	....	....	....	20	12	7	6	13	2
1950-51	Vancouver Canucks	PCHL	70	36	21	57	....	....	....	33	....	....	....	....	....
1951-52	Vancouver Canucks	PCHL	17	5	3	8	....	....	....	9	....	....	....	....	....
	Ottawa Senators	QSHL	3	0	1	1	....	....	....	0	....	....	....	....	....
	Brantford Redmen	OHA Sr.	31	25	25	50	....	....	....	16	7	2	5	7	6
1952-53	Brantford Redmen	OHA Sr.	46	36	27	63	....	....	....	44	5	2	3	5	4
1953-54	Toronto Lyndhursts	City Sr.	DID NOT PLAY – COACHING												
	Canada	WEC-A	7	6	3	9	....	....	....	2	....	....	....	....	....
	NHL Totals		**79**	**21**	**13**	**34**	**32**	**23**	**55**	**18**	**7**	**1**	**2**	**3**	**2**

PCHL First All-Star Team (1951) • WEC-A First All-Star Team (1954)

• SHILL, JACK Jack Shill
C – L. 5'9", 175 lbs. b: Toronto, Ont., 1/12/1913. d: 10/25/1976.

Season	Club	League	GP	G	A	Pts	AG	AA	APts	PIM	GP	G	A	Pts	PIM
1929-30	Toronto Marlboros	OHA	1	0	0	0	....	....	....	0	....	....	....	....	....
1930-31	Toronto Marlboros	OHA	8	5	3	8	....	....	....	19	2	1	1	2	6
1931-32	Toronto Marlboros	OHA	10	12	4	*16	....	....	....	*31	4	1	0	1	2
	Toronto Marlboros	OHA Sr.	....	....	....	....	....	....	....	....	1	0	0	0	0
1932-33	Toronto Marlboros	OHA	3	3	1	4	....	....	....	6	....	....	....	....	....
	Toronto Marlboros	OHA Sr.	11	5	1	6	....	....	....	18	2	0	0	0	8
1933-34	**Toronto Maple Leafs**	**NHL**	**7**	**0**	**1**	**1**	**0**	**3**	**3**	**0**	**2**	**0**	**0**	**0**	**0**
	Toronto Marlboros	OHA Sr.	22	15	10	25	....	....	....	34	2	1	0	1	2
1934-35	**Boston Bruins**	**NHL**	**45**	**4**	**4**	**8**	**8**	**9**	**17**	**22**	**2**	**0**	**0**	**0**	**0**
	Boston Cubs	Can-Am	6	2	2	4	....	....	....	4	....	....	....	....	....
1935-36	**Toronto Maple Leafs**	**NHL**	**3**	**0**	**1**	**1**	**0**	**2**	**2**	**0**	**9**	**0**	**3**	**3**	**8**
	Syracuse Stars	IAHL	46	20	20	40	....	....	....	82	1	0	0	0	0
1936-37	**Toronto Maple Leafs**	**NHL**	**32**	**4**	**4**	**8**	**9**	**9**	**18**	**26**	**2**	**0**	**0**	**0**	**0**
1937-38	**New York Americans**	**NHL**	**22**	**1**	**3**	**4**	**2**	**6**	**8**	**10**	....	....	....	....	....
	Chicago Black Hawks	**NHL**	**23**	**4**	**3**	**7**	**8**	**6**	**14**	**8**	**10**	**1**	**3**	**4**	**15**
1938-39	**Chicago Black Hawks**	**NHL**	**28**	**2**	**4**	**6**	**4**	**7**	**11**	**4**	....	....	....	....	....
1939-40	Providence Reds	AHL	50	14	26	40	....	....	....	51	8	3	7	10	2
1940-41	Providence Reds	AHL	41	16	22	38	....	....	....	20	3	1	0	1	9
1941-42	Providence Reds	AHL	55	18	28	46	....	....	....	17	....	....	....	....	....
1942-43	Research Colonels	Tor-Sr.	2	0	0	0	....	....	....	0	....	....	....	....	....
	NHL Totals		**160**	**15**	**20**	**35**	**31**	**42**	**73**	**70**	**25**	**1**	**6**	**7**	**23**

IAHL First All-Star Team (1936)

Loaned to **Boston** by **Toronto** for 1934-35 season for cash, May 12, 1934. Traded to **NY Americans** by **Toronto** for rights to Wally Stanowski, October 7, 1937. Traded to **Chicago** by **NY Americans** for cash, January 26, 1938. Traded to **Providence** (IAHL) by **Chicago** for cash, October 24, 1939. Traded to **Buffalo** (AHL) by **Chicago** (Providence - AHL) with cash for Jacques Toupin, October 29, 1942.

• SHORE, EDDIE — Eddie "The Edmonton Express" Shore — HHOF

D – R. 5'11", 190 lbs. b: Fort Qu'Appelle, Sask., 11/25/1902. d: 3/16/1985.

Season	Club	League	GP	G	A	Pts	AG	AA	APts	PIM	GP	G	A	Pts	PIM
1923-24	Melville Millionaires	SSHL	....	....	....	....	....	....	....	....	11	*10	8	*18	0
1924-25	Regina Caps	WCHL	24	6	0	6	....	....	....	75	....	....	....	....	....
1925-26	Edmonton Eskimos	WHL	30	12	2	14	....	....	....	86	2	0	0	0	6
1926-27	**Boston Bruins**	**NHL**	**40**	**12**	**6**	**18**	**35**	**51**	**86**	**130**	**8**	**1**	**1**	**2**	***40**
1927-28	**Boston Bruins**	**NHL**	**43**	**11**	**6**	**17**	**34**	**51**	**85**	***165**	**2**	**0**	**0**	**0**	**8**
1928-29	**Boston Bruins**	**NHL**	**39**	**12**	**7**	**19**	**48**	**65**	**113**	**96**	**5**	**1**	**1**	**2**	***28**
1929-30	**Boston Bruins**	**NHL**	**42**	**12**	**19**	**31**	**24**	**62**	**86**	**105**	**6**	**1**	**0**	**1**	***26**
1930-31	**Boston Bruins**	**NHL**	**44**	**15**	**16**	**31**	**37**	**58**	**95**	**105**	**5**	**2**	**1**	**3**	**24**
1931-32	**Boston Bruins**	**NHL**	**45**	**9**	**13**	**22**	**19**	**36**	**55**	**80**	....	....	....	....	....
1932-33	**Boston Bruins**	**NHL**	**48**	**8**	**27**	**35**	**19**	**72**	**91**	**102**	**5**	**0**	**1**	**1**	**14**
1933-34	**Boston Bruins**	**NHL**	**30**	**2**	**10**	**12**	**4**	**27**	**31**	**57**	....	....	....	....	....
1934-35	**Boston Bruins**	**NHL**	**48**	**7**	**26**	**33**	**15**	**58**	**73**	**32**	**4**	**0**	**1**	**1**	**2**
1935-36	**Boston Bruins**	**NHL**	**45**	**3**	**16**	**19**	**7**	**39**	**46**	**61**	**2**	**1**	**1**	**2**	**12**
1936-37	**Boston Bruins**	**NHL**	**20**	**3**	**1**	**4**	**6**	**2**	**8**	**12**	....	....	....	....	....
1937-38	**Boston Bruins**	**NHL**	**48**	**3**	**14**	**17**	**6**	**29**	**35**	**42**	**3**	**0**	**1**	**1**	**6**
1938-39	**Boston Bruins**	**NHL**	**44**	**4**	**14**	**18**	**8**	**26**	**34**	**47**	**12**	**0**	**4**	**4**	**19**
1939-40	**Boston Bruins**	**NHL**	**4**	**2**	**1**	**3**	**4**	**2**	**6**	**4**	....	....	....	....	....
	New York Americans	**NHL**	**10**	**2**	**3**	**5**	**4**	**6**	**10**	**9**	**3**	**0**	**2**	**2**	**2**
	Springfield Indians	AHL	15	1	14	15	....	....	....	18	2	0	1	1	0
1940-41	Springfield Indians	AHL	56	4	13	17	....	....	....	66	3	0	0	0	2
1941-42	Springfield Indians	AHL	35	5	12	17	....	....	....	61	5	0	3	3	6
1942-43			DID NOT PLAY												
1943-44	Buffalo Bisons	AHL	1	0	0	0	....	....	....	0	....	....	....	....	....
	NHL Totals		**550**	**105**	**179**	**284**	**270**	**584**	**854**	**1047**	**55**	**6**	**13**	**19**	**181**
	Other Major League Totals		54	18	2	20	....	....	....	161	2	0	0	0	6

WHL First All-Star Team (1926) • NHL First All-Star Team (1931, 1932, 1933, 1935, 1936, 1938, 1939) • Won Hart Trophy (1933, 1935, 1936, 1938) • NHL Second All-Star Team (1934) • Won Lester Patrick Trophy (1970)

Played in NHL All-Star Game (1934, 1937, 1939)

Signed as a free agent by **Regina** (WCHL), December 2, 1924. Transferred to **Portland** (WCHL) after **Regina** franchise relocated, September 1, 1925. Traded to **Edmonton** (WHL) by **Portland** (WHL) with Art Gagne for Joe McCormick and Bob Trapp, October 7, 1925. Traded to **Boston** by **Edmonton** (WHL) for cash, August 20, 1926. Traded to **NY Americans** by **Boston** for Ed Wiseman and $5000, January 24, 1940.

• SHORE, HAMBY — Hamby (Hamilton) Shore

D/LW – L. 6', 175 lbs. b: Ottawa, Ont., 2/12/1886. d: 10/14/1918.

Season	Club	League	GP	G	A	Pts	AG	AA	APts	PIM	GP	G	A	Pts	PIM
1904-05	Ottawa Senators	FAHL	3	6	0	6	....	....	....	....	....	....	....	....	....
1905-06	Winnipeg Seniors	MHL Sr.	STATISTICS NOT AVAILABLE												
1906-07	Pembroke Lumber Kings	Ott-Sr.	1	0	0	0	....	....	....	0	....	....	....	....	....
	Ottawa Senators	ECAHA	10	15	0	15	....	....	....	....	....	....	....	....	....
1907-08	Winnipeg Maple Leafs	MHL-Pro	15	27	0	27	....	....	....	....	2	2	0	2	0
	Strathcona Seniors	MHL-Pro	14	23	0	23	....	....	....	....	....	....	....	....	....
1908-09			DID NOT PLAY												
1909-10	Ottawa Senators	CHA	2	2	0	2	....	....	....	....	....	....	....	....	....
	Ottawa Senators	NHA	12	6	0	6	....	....	....	44	4	3	0	3	6
1910-11	Ottawa Senators	NHA	16	7	0	7	....	....	....	53	2	0	0	0	6
1911-12	Ottawa Senators	NHA	18	8	0	8	....	....	....	35	....	....	....	....	....
1912-13	Ottawa Senators	NHA	19	15	0	15	....	....	....	66	....	....	....	....	....
1913-14	Ottawa Senators	NHA	13	6	3	9	....	....	....	46	....	....	....	....	....
1914-15	Ottawa Senators	NHA	20	5	1	6	....	....	....	53	5	0	0	0	0
1915-16	Ottawa Senators	NHA	19	2	1	3	....	....	....	83	....	....	....	....	....
1916-17	Ottawa Senators	NHA	19	11	3	14	....	....	....	80	2	0	0	0	6
1917-18	**Ottawa Senators**	**NHL**	**20**	**3**	**8**	**11**	**7**	**0**	**7**	**51**	....	....			
	NHL Totals		**20**	**3**	**8**	**11**	**7**	**0**	**7**	**51**	....	....	....	....	....
	Other Major League Totals		148	77	8	85	....	....	....	469	13	3	0	3	18

• Missed entire 1908-09 season due to ilness. Signed as a free agent by **Ottawa** (NHA), November, 1909. Rights retained by **Ottawa** after NHA folded, November 26, 1917.

• SIEBERT, BABE — Babe (Albert) Siebert — HHOF

LW/D – L. 5'10", 182 lbs. b: Plattsville, Ont., 1/14/1904. d: 8/25/1939.

Season	Club	League	GP	G	A	Pts	AG	AA	APts	PIM	GP	G	A	Pts	PIM
1922-23	Kitchener Greenshirts	OHA	....	....	....	....	....	....	....	....	8	6	4	10	....
1923-24	Kitchener Twin City	OHA Sr.	10	9	4	13	....	....	....	....	....	....	....	....	....
1924-25	Niagara Falls Cataracts	OHA Sr.	20	9	2	11	....	....	....	26	10	*7	0	*7	3
1925-26	**Montreal Maroons**	**NHL**	**35**	**16**	**8**	**24**	**50**	**94**	**144**	**108**	**8**	**2**	**2**	**4**	**6**
1926-27	**Montreal Maroons**	**NHL**	**42**	**5**	**3**	**8**	**14**	**25**	**39**	**116**	**2**	**1**	**0**	**1**	**2**
1927-28	**Montreal Maroons**	**NHL**	**39**	**8**	**9**	**17**	**24**	**77**	**101**	**109**	**9**	**2**	**0**	**2**	**26**
1928-29	**Montreal Maroons**	**NHL**	**40**	**3**	**5**	**8**	**12**	**46**	**58**	**52**	....	....	....	....	....
1929-30	**Montreal Maroons**	**NHL**	**39**	**14**	**19**	**33**	**28**	**62**	**90**	**94**	**3**	**0**	**0**	**0**	**0**
1930-31	**Montreal Maroons**	**NHL**	**43**	**16**	**12**	**28**	**39**	**44**	**83**	**76**	**2**	**0**	**0**	**0**	**6**
1931-32	**Montreal Maroons**	**NHL**	**48**	**21**	**18**	**39**	**45**	**50**	**95**	**64**	**4**	**0**	**1**	**1**	**4**
1932-33	**New York Rangers**	**NHL**	**43**	**9**	**10**	**19**	**21**	**26**	**47**	**38**	**8**	**1**	**0**	**1**	**12**
1933-34	**New York Rangers**	**NHL**	**13**	**0**	**1**	**1**	**0**	**3**	**3**	**18**	....	....	....	....	....
	Boston Bruins	**NHL**	**32**	**5**	**6**	**11**	**11**	**16**	**27**	**31**	....	....	....	....	....
1934-35	**Boston Bruins**	**NHL**	**48**	**6**	**18**	**24**	**13**	**40**	**53**	**80**	**4**	**0**	**0**	**0**	**6**
1935-36	**Boston Bruins**	**NHL**	**45**	**12**	**9**	**21**	**30**	**22**	**52**	**66**	**2**	**0**	**1**	**1**	**0**
1936-37	**Montreal Canadiens**	**NHL**	**44**	**8**	**20**	**28**	**17**	**47**	**64**	**38**	**5**	**1**	**2**	**3**	**2**
1937-38	**Montreal Canadiens**	**NHL**	**37**	**8**	**11**	**19**	**17**	**23**	**40**	**56**	**3**	**1**	**1**	**2**	**0**
1938-39	**Montreal Canadiens**	**NHL**	**44**	**9**	**7**	**16**	**19**	**13**	**32**	**36**	**3**	**0**	**0**	**0**	**0**
	NHL Totals		**592**	**140**	**156**	**296**	**340**	**588**	**928**	**982**	**53**	**8**	**7**	**15**	**64**

NHL First All-Star Team (1936, 1937, 1938) • Won Hart Trophy (1937)

Played In NHL All-Star Game (1937)

Signed as a free agent by **Montreal Maroons**, March 16, 1925. Traded to **NY Rangers** by **Montreal Maroons** for cash, July 2, 1933. Traded to **Boston** by **NY Rangers** for Vic Ripley and Roy Burmeister, December 18, 1933. Traded to **Montreal Canadiens** by **Boston** with Roger Jenkins for Leroy Goldsworthy, Sammy McManus and $10,000, September 10, 1936.

• SIMON, CULLY — Cully (Cullen) Simon

D – L. 5'10", 190 lbs. b: Brockville, Ont., 5/8/1918. d: 8/2/1980.

Season	Club	League	GP	G	A	Pts	AG	AA	APts	PIM	GP	G	A	Pts	PIM
1937-38	Pembroke Lumber Kings	Ott-Jr.	7	5	5	10	....	....	....	14	2	2	2	4	*8
1938-39	Valleyfield Braves	QPHL	3	0	0	0	....	....	....	2	....	....	....	....	....
1939-40	Verdun Bulldogs	QPHL	41	3	7	10	....	....	....	44	2	0	0	0	2
1940-41	Cornwall Flyers	QSHL	36	2	10	12	....	....	....	53	4	0	0	0	9
1941-42	Omaha Knights	AHA	38	0	5	5	....	....	....	49	8	0	1	1	20
1942-43	**Detroit Red Wings**	**NHL**	**34**	**1**	**1**	**2**	**1**	**1**	**2**	**34**	**9**	**0**	**1**	**1**	**4**
	Indianapolis Capitals	AHL	17	1	4	5	....	....	....	8	....	....	....	....	....
1943-44	**Detroit Red Wings**	**NHL**	**46**	**3**	**7**	**10**	**4**	**8**	**12**	**52**	**5**	**0**	**0**	**0**	**2**
1944-45	**Detroit Red Wings**	**NHL**	**21**	**0**	**2**	**2**	**0**	**3**	**3**	**26**	....	....	....	....	....
	Chicago Black Hawks	**NHL**	**29**	**0**	**1**	**1**	**0**	**2**	**2**	**9**	....	....	....	....	....
1945-46	Pembroke Lumber Kings	Ott-Sr.	DID NOT PLAY – COACHING												
1946-47	Pembroke Lumber Kings	Ott-Sr.	24	4	8	12	....	....	....	18	8	0	4	4	20
1947-48	Pembroke Lumber Kings	Ott-Sr.	14	4	3	7	....	....	....	28	5	1	1	2	9
1948-49	Pembroke Lumber Kings	Ott-Sr.	9	1	2	3	....	....	....	8	13	4	7	11	28
1949-50	Pembroke Lumber Kings	ECSHL	34	5	16	21	....	....	....	47	4	0	1	1	9
1950-51	Pembroke Lumber Kings	ECSHL	31	1	12	13	....	....	....	40	8	0	4	4	10
1951-52	Pembroke Lumber Kings	ECSHL	36	2	16	18	....	....	....	46	22	3	8	11	47
	NHL Totals		**130**	**4**	**11**	**15**	**5**	**14**	**19**	**121**	**14**	**0**	**1**	**1**	**6**

Traded to **Chicago** by **Detroit** with Don Grosso and Byron McDonald for Earl Seibert, January 2, 1945.

• SIMON, THAIN — Thain Simon

D – L. 6', 200 lbs. b: Brockville, Ont., 4/24/1922.

Season	Club	League	GP	G	A	Pts	AG	AA	APts	PIM	GP	G	A	Pts	PIM
1941-42	Brantford Lions	OHA	23	15	8	23	....	....	....	21	7	1	6	7	10
1942-43	Ottawa RCAF	City Sr.	16	1	4	5	....	....	....	4	17	0	2	2	22
1943-44			MILITARY SERVICE												
1944-45			MILITARY SERVICE												
1945-46	Pembroke Lumber Kings	Ott-Sr.	7	1	1	2	....	....	....	4	12	0	5	5	17
1946-47	**Detroit Red Wings**	**NHL**	**3**	**0**	**0**	**0**	**0**	**0**	**0**	**0**	....	....	....	....	....
	Indianapolis Capitals	AHL	46	2	4	6	....	....	....	14	....	....	....	....	....
1947-48	Omaha Knights	USHL	33	1	3	4	....	....	....	21	....	....	....	....	....
	Indianapolis Capitals	AHL	9	1	0	1	....	....	....	4	....	....	....	....	....
1948-49	St. Louis Flyers	AHL	65	4	6	10	....	....	....	14	7	0	1	1	4
1949-50	Pembroke Lumber Kings	ECSHL	34	3	11	14	....	....	....	28	3	0	1	1	4
1950-51	Pembroke Lumber Kings	ECSHL	32	3	8	11	....	....	....	26	8	2	4	6	2
1951-52	Pembroke Lumber Kings	ECSHL	40	4	15	19	....	....	....	24	24	0	6	6	18
1952-53	Pembroke Lumber Kings	Ott-Jr.	DID NOT PLAY – COACHING												
	NHL Totals		**3**	**0**	**0**	**0**	**0**	**0**	**0**	**0**	....	....	....	....	....

Traded to **St. Louis** (AHL) by **Detroit** with Red Almas, Lloyd Doran, Barry Sullivan and Tony Licari for Joe Lund and Hec Highton, September 9, 1948.

• SIMPSON, CLIFF — Cliff Simpson

C – R. 5'11", 175 lbs. b: Toronto, Ont., 4/4/1923. d: 5/30/1987.

Season	Club	League	GP	G	A	Pts	AG	AA	APts	PIM	GP	G	A	Pts	PIM
1939-40	Toronto Young Rangers	OHA	20	12	5	17	....	....	....	8	2	0	0	0	0
1940-41	Toronto Young Rangers	OHA	13	11	8	19	....	....	....	17	5	2	3	5	2
1941-42	Brantford Lions	OHA	23	39	26	65	....	....	....	26	7	5	14	19	22
1942-43	Indianapolis Capitals	AHL	10	0	11	11	....			13	....	....	....	....	....
	Toronto Army Daggers	OHA Sr.	7	12	4	16	....	....	....	12	4	6	3	9	14
1943-44			MILITARY SERVICE												
1944-45	Barriefield Bears	City Sr.	....	*28	8	36	....	....	....	4	....	....	....	....	....
1945-46	Indianapolis Capitals	AHL	52	21	15	36	....	....	....	10	5	2	4	6	0
1946-47	**Detroit Red Wings**	**NHL**	**6**	**0**	**1**	**1**	**0**	**1**	**1**	**0**	**1**	**0**	**0**	**0**	**0**
	Indianapolis Capitals	AHL	54	42	36	78			....	28	....	....	....	....	....
1947-48	Indianapolis Capitals	AHL	00	40	63	110				31	....	....	....	....	....
	Detroit Red Wings	**NHL**	....	....	....	....	....	....	....	....	**1**	**0**	**0**	**0**	**2**
1948-49	Indianapolis Capitals	AHL	52	25	21	46	....	....	....	12	2	2	0	2	0
1949-50	St. Louis Flyers	AHL	56	31	52	83	....	....	....	8	2	0	0	0	0
1950-51	St. Louis Flyers	AHL	65	40	34	74	....	....	....	8	....	....	....	....	....
1951-52	St. Louis Flyers	AHL	47	26	26	52		....	....	6	....	....	....	....	....
	NHL Totals		**6**	**0**	**1**	**1**	**0**	**1**	**1**	**0**	**2**	**0**	**0**	**0**	**2**

AHL Second All-Star Team (1947) • AHL First All-Star Team (1948)

• SIMPSON, JOE — Joe "Bullet Joe" Simpson — HHOF

D – R. 5'10", 175 lbs. b: Selkirk, Man., 8/13/1893. d: 12/25/1973.

Season	Club	League	GP	G	A	Pts	AG	AA	APts	PIM	GP	G	A	Pts	PIM
1912-13	Winnipeg Strathconas	MHL Sr.	....	....	....	....	....	....	....	....	2	0	0	0	0
1913-14	Selkirk Fishermen	Wpg-Jr.	STATISTICS NOT AVAILABLE												
1914-15	Winnipeg Victorias	MHL Sr.	8	8	2	10	....	....	....	16	....	....	....	....	....
1915-16	Winnipeg 61st Battalion	MHL Sr.	8	9	2	11	....	....	....	24	4	3	2	5	4
1916-17			MILITARY SERVICE												
1917-18			MILITARY SERVICE												
1918-19	Selkirk Fishermen	MHL Sr.	4	0	0	0	....	....	....	0	....	....	....	....	....
1919-20	Selkirk Fishermen	MHL Sr.	10	19	4	23	....	....	....	6	....	....	....	....	....
1920-21	Edmonton Eskimos	Big 4	15	2	6	8	....	....	....	21	....	....	....	....	....
1921-22	Edmonton Eskimos	WCHL	25	21	12	33	....	....	....	15	2	1	0	1	2
1922-23	Edmonton Eskimos	WCHL	30	15	14	29	....	....	....	6	4	0	1	1	0
1923-24	Edmonton Eskimos	WCHL	30	10	4	14	....	....	....	6	....	....	....	....	....
1924-25	Edmonton Eskimos	WCHL	28	11	12	23	....	....	....	16	....	....	....	....	....
1925-26	**New York Americans**	**NHL**	**32**	**2**	**2**	**4**	**6**	**23**	**29**	**2**	....	....	....	....	....
1926-27	**New York Americans**	**NHL**	**43**	**4**	**2**	**6**	**12**	**17**	**29**	**39**	....	....	....	....	....
1927-28	**New York Americans**	**NHL**	**24**	**2**	**0**	**2**	**6**	**0**	**6**	**32**	....	....	....	....	....
1928-29	**New York Americans**	**NHL**	**43**	**3**	**2**	**5**	**12**	**18**	**30**	**29**	**2**	**0**	**0**	**0**	**0**
1929-30	**New York Americans**	**NHL**	**44**	**8**	**13**	**21**	**16**	**42**	**58**	**41**	....	....	....	....	....
1930-31	**New York Americans**	**NHL**	**42**	**2**	**0**	**2**	**5**	**0**	**5**	**13**	....	....	....	....	....
1931-32	New Haven Eagles	Can-Am	DID NOT PLAY – COACHING												
	NHL Totals		**228**	**21**	**19**	**40**	**57**	**100**	**157**	**156**	**2**	**0**	**0**	**0**	**0**
	Other Major League Totals		113	57	42	99	....	....	....	43	6	1	1	2	2

WCHL First All-Star Team (1922, 1923, 1924, 1925)

Signed as a free agent by **Edmonton** (WCHL), November 4, 1921. Traded to **NY Americans** by **Edmonton** (WHL) for $10,000, September 18, 1925.

• SINCLAIR, REG Reg Sinclair
RW/C – R. 6', 165 lbs. b: Lachine, Que., 3/6/1925.

Season	Club	League	GP	G	A	Pts	AG	AA	APts	PIM	PO GP	PO G	PO A	PO Pts	PO PIM
1944-45	McGill University	Mtl-Sr.	12	12	5	17				14					
1945-46	McGill University	Mtl-Sr.	9	9	3	12				10	3	3	2	5	4
1946-47	McGill University	Mtl-Sr.	6	0	1	1									
1947-48	McGill University	Mtl-Sr.	12	11	6	17				28					
1948-49	McGill University	Mtl-Sr.	12	*21	14	*35				17					
1949-50	Sherbrooke Saints	QSHL	56	15	31	46				94	22	*15	15	*30	34
1950-51	**New York Rangers**	**NHL**	**70**	**18**	**21**	**39**	**24**	**27**	**51**	**70**					
1951-52	**New York Rangers**	**NHL**	**69**	**20**	**10**	**30**	**28**	**13**	**41**	**33**					
1952-53	**Detroit Red Wings**	**NHL**	**69**	**11**	**12**	**23**	**17**	**17**	**34**	**36**	**3**	**1**	**0**	**1**	**0**
	NHL Totals		**208**	**49**	**43**	**92**	**69**	**57**	**126**	**139**	**3**	**1**	**0**	**1**	**0**

Played in NHL All-Star Game (1951, 1952)

Signed as a free agent by **NY Rangers**, October 3, 1950. Traded to **Detroit** by **NY Rangers** with Johnny Morrison for Leo Reise Jr., August 18, 1952.

• SINGBUSH, ALEX Alex Singbush
D – L. 5'11", 180 lbs. b: Portage la Prairie, 1/31/1914. d: 3/8/1969.

Season	Club	League	GP	G	A	Pts	AG	AA	APts	PIM	PO GP	PO G	PO A	PO Pts	PO PIM
1932-33	Winnipeg K of C	City Jr.	6	0	0	0				2	2	0	0	0	0
1933-34	Portage Terriers	MHL Jr.	14	5	7	12				*48	2	0	0	0	4
1934-35	Sudbury Refinery ORC	NOHA	6	1	1	2				18					
1935-36	Sudbury Refinery ORC	NOHA	9	3	4	7				26					
1936-37	Sudbury Refinery ORC	NOHA	17	4	6	10				*64					
1937-38	New Haven Eagles	AHL	43	4	3	7				44	2	0	0	0	0
1938-39	New Haven–Philadelphia	AHL	56	2	1	3				85	9	0	1	1	6
1939-40	New Haven Eagles	AHL	54	12	14	26				76	3	0	0	0	2
1940-41	**Montreal Canadiens**	**NHL**	**32**	**0**	**5**	**5**	**0**	**9**	**9**	**15**	**3**	**0**	**0**	**0**	**4**
	New Haven Eagles	AHL	8	0	2	2				2					
1941-42	Washington Lions	AHL	55	6	7	13				50	2	0	0	0	4
1942-43	Washington–Providence	AHL	54	7	11	18				63	2	0	0	0	0
1943-44	Sudbury Open Pit Miners	City Sr.	8	1	0	1				6					
1944-45	Sudbury Open Pit Miners	City Sr.	8	0	4	4				2	7	0	0	0	10
1945-46	Providence Reds	AHL	1	0	0	0				0					
	Hull Volants	QSHL	5	0	0	0				4					
	NHL Totals		**32**	**0**	**5**	**5**	**0**	**9**	**9**	**15**	**3**	**0**	**0**	**0**	**4**

Traded to **Washington** (AHL) by **Montreal** for cash, October 9, 1941.

• SKILTON, RAYMIE Raymie Skilton
D – R. 5'10", 190 lbs. b: Cambridge, MA, 9/26/1889. d: 7/1/1961.

Season	Club	League	GP	G	A	Pts	AG	AA	APts	PIM	PO GP	PO G	PO A	PO Pts	PO PIM
1912-13	Sherbrooke Saints	IPAHU	STATISTICS NOT AVAILABLE												
1913-14	Boston Irish Americans	AAHL	7	8	0	8									
1914-15	Boston Arenas	AAHL	5	9	0	9					6	7	0	7	
1915-16	Boston AAA	AAHL	7	2	0	2					3	2	0	2	
1916-17	Boston Arenas	AAHL	8	4	0	4									
1917-18	**Montreal Wanderers**	**NHL**	**1**	**0**	**0**	**0**	**0**	**0**	**0**	**0**					
	Boston Navy Yard	AAHL	11	11	0	11									
1918-19			MILITARY SERVICE												
1919-20			DID NOT PLAY – RETIRED												
1920-21	Boston Shoe Traders	USAHA	3	2	0	2									
1921-22	Boston Shoe Traders	USAHA	STATISTICS NOT AVAILABLE												
1922-23	Boston Vics	USAHA	3	1	0	1									
	NHL Totals		**1**	**0**	**0**	**0**	**0**	**0**	**0**	**0**					

Signed as a free agent by **Montreal Wanderers**, December 21, 1917.

• SKINNER, ALF Alf "Dutch" Skinner
RW – R. 5'10", 180 lbs. b: Toronto, Ont., 1/26/1896. d: 4/11/1961.

Season	Club	League	GP	G	A	Pts	AG	AA	APts	PIM	PO GP	PO G	PO A	PO Pts	PO PIM
1912-13	Parkdale Canoe Club	OHA	STATISTICS NOT AVAILABLE												
1913-14	Toronto Rowing Club	OHA Sr.	6	4	0	4				0					
1914-15	Toronto Shamrocks	NHA	16	5	2	7				68					
1915-16	Toronto Blueshirts	NHA	23	7	4	11				66					
1916-17	Toronto Blueshirts	NHA	14	5	2	7				49					
	Montreal Wanderers	NHA	6	5	1	6				26					
1917-18	**Toronto Arenas**	**NHL**	**20**	**13**	**5**	**18**	**33**	**0**	**33**	**34**	**7**	**8**	**3**	**11**	**27**
1918-19	**Toronto Arenas**	**NHL**	**16**	**12**	**5**	**17**	**43**	**48**	**91**	**26**					
1919-20	Vancouver Millionaires	PCHL	22	15	2	17				28	2	1	0	1	0
1920-21	Vancouver Millionaires	PCHL	24	20	4	24				22	5	7	1	8	18
1921-22	Vancouver Millionaires	PCHL	24	11	2	13				21	9	1	0	1	13
1922-23	Vancouver Maroons	PCHL	23	13	2	15				28	6	1	1	2	6
1923-24	Vancouver Maroons	PCHA	29	5	2	7				38	7	0	0	0	2
1924-25	**Boston Bruins**	**NHL**	**9**	**0**	**0**	**0**	**0**	**0**	**0**	**6**					
	Montreal Maroons	**NHL**	**18**	**1**	**1**	**2**	**3**	**13**	**16**	**22**					
1925-26	**Pittsburgh Pirates**	**NHL**	**7**	**0**	**0**	**0**	**0**	**0**	**0**	**2**					
1926-27	Duluth Hornets	AHA	23	2	3	5				40					
1927-28	Kitchener Millionaires	Can-Pro	18	4	0	4				42					
1928-29	Kitchener Dutchmen	Can-Pro	39	14	5	19				63	3	0	0	0	10
1929-30	Guelph Maple Leafs	Can-Am	DID NOT PLAY – COACHING												
	NHL Totals		**70**	**26**	**11**	**37**	**79**	**61**	**140**	**90**	**7**	**8**	**3**	**11**	**27**
	Other Major League Totals		88	27	11	38				247	7	0	0	0	2

PCHA Second All-Star Team (1920, 1921, 1922, 1923)

Signed as a free agent by **Toronto Shamrocks**, November, 1914. Signed as a free agent by **Toronto Blueshirts**, November, 1915. Signed as a free agent by **Toronto Arenas**, November 5, 1917. Traded to **Vancouver** (PCHA) by **Toronto Arenas** for cash, December 7, 1919. Traded to **Boston** by **Vancouver** (PCHA) for cash, November 2, 1924. Traded to **Montreal Maroons** by **Boston** for Bernie Morris and Bob Benson, January 3, 1925. Signed as a free agent by **Pittsburgh**, November 10, 1925. Signed as a free agent by **Duluth** (AHA), November 10, 1926.

• SKOV, GLEN Glen Skov
C/LW – L. 6'2", 180 lbs. b: Wheatley, Ont., 1/26/1931.

Season	Club	League	GP	G	A	Pts	AG	AA	APts	PIM	PO GP	PO G	PO A	PO Pts	PO PIM
1946-47	Windsor Spitfires	OHA	2	0	0	0				0					
1947-48	Detroit Hettche	IHL	18	4	4	8				8	8	5	3	8	6
1948-49	Windsor Spitfires	OHA	35	16	12	28				42	4	0	0	0	2
	Windsor Ryancretes	IHL	11	2	7	9				4	3	0	6	6	0
1949-50	Windsor Spitfires	OHA	47	51	51	102				23	8	7	2	9	0
	Detroit Red Wings	**NHL**	**2**	**0**	**0**	**0**	**0**	**0**	**0**	**0**					
1950-51	**Detroit Red Wings**	**NHL**	**19**	**7**	**6**	**13**	**9**	**8**	**17**	**13**	**6**	**0**	**0**	**0**	**0**
	Omaha Knights	USHL	45	26	33	59				55					
1951-52	**Detroit Red Wings**	**NHL**	**70**	**12**	**14**	**26**	**17**	**18**	**35**	**48**	**8**	**1**	**4**	**5**	**16**
1952-53	**Detroit Red Wings**	**NHL**	**70**	**12**	**15**	**27**	**18**	**21**	**39**	**54**	**6**	**1**	**0**	**1**	**2**
1953-54	**Detroit Red Wings**	**NHL**	**70**	**17**	**10**	**27**	**26**	**14**	**40**	**95**	**12**	**1**	**2**	**3**	**16**
1954-55	**Detroit Red Wings**	**NHL**	**70**	**14**	**16**	**30**	**20**	**20**	**40**	**53**	**11**	**2**	**0**	**2**	**8**
1955-56	**Chicago Black Hawks**	**NHL**	**70**	**7**	**20**	**27**	**10**	**25**	**35**	**26**					
1956-57	**Chicago Black Hawks**	**NHL**	**67**	**14**	**28**	**42**	**19**	**33**	**52**	**69**					
1957-58	**Chicago Black Hawks**	**NHL**	**70**	**17**	**18**	**35**	**22**	**20**	**42**	**35**					
1958-59	**Chicago Black Hawks**	**NHL**	**70**	**3**	**5**	**8**	**4**	**5**	**9**	**4**	**6**	**2**	**1**	**3**	**4**
1959-60	**Chicago Black Hawks**	**NHL**	**69**	**3**	**4**	**7**	**4**	**4**	**8**	**16**	**4**	**0**	**0**	**0**	**2**
1960-61	**Montreal Canadiens**	**NHL**	**3**	**0**	**0**	**0**	**0**	**0**	**0**	**0**					
	Hull-Ottawa Canadians	EPHL	67	16	26	42				24	14	2	6	8	2
	NHL Totals		**650**	**106**	**136**	**242**	**149**	**168**	**317**	**413**	**53**	**7**	**7**	**14**	**48**

Played in NHL All-Star Game (1954)

Traded to **Chicago** by **Detroit** with Tony Leswick, John Wilson and Ben Woit for Dave Creighton, Gord Hollingworth, John McCormack and Jerry Toppazzini, May 28, 1955. Traded to **Montreal** by **Chicago** with Terry Gray, the rights to Danny Lewicki, Bob Bailey and Lorne Ferguson for Ab McDonald, Reggie Fleming, Bob Courcy and Cec Hoekstra, June 7, 1960.

• SLEAVER, JOHN John Sleaver
C – R. 6'1", 180 lbs. b: Copper Cliff, Ont., 8/18/1934.

Season	Club	League	GP	G	A	Pts	AG	AA	APts	PIM	PO GP	PO G	PO A	PO Pts	PO PIM
1950-51	Galt Black Hawks	OHA	46	9	14	23				23	3	0	1	1	4
1951-52	Galt Black Hawks	OHA	54	22	35	57				53	3	0	3	3	4
1952-53	Galt Black Hawks	OHA	56	20	36	56				96	10	3	7	10	6
1953-54	Galt Black Hawks	OHA	58	23	37	60				67					
	Chicago Black Hawks	**NHL**	**1**	**0**	**0**	**0**	**0**	**0**	**0**	**2**					
1954-55	Galt Black Hawks	OHA	49	14	20	34				36	4	3	0	3	4
1955-56	Windsor Bulldogs	OHA Sr.	48	13	17	30				27					
	Buffalo Bisons	AHL	2	1	1	2				2					
1956-57	**Chicago Black Hawks**	**NHL**	**12**	**1**	**0**	**1**	**1**	**0**	**1**	**4**					
	Buffalo Bisons	AHL	29	7	9	16				2					
	Windsor Bulldogs	OHA Sr.	21	7	15	22				43					
1957-58	Quebec Aces	QHL	59	17	19	36				56	13	3	5	8	23
	Buffalo Bisons	AHL	1	0	0	0				0					
1958-59	Trois-Rivieres Lions	QHL	61	10	14	24				42	8	0	4	4	12
1959-60	Sudbury Wolves	EPHL	70	20	35	55				42	14	2	6	8	12
1960-61	Sudbury Wolves	EPHL	60	17	34	51				34					
	Vancouver Canucks	WHL	3	0	0	0				2					
1961-62	North Bay Trappers	EPHL	70	24	34	58				59					
1962-63	Springfield Indians	AHL	38	6	16	22				8					
1963-64	Denver Invaders	WHL	69	23	46	69				59	5	1	5	6	4
1964-65	Victoria Maple Leafs	WHL	70	14	49	63				39	12	3	6	9	16
1965-66	Victoria Maple Leafs	WHL	72	19	49	68				47	14	1	6	7	10
1966-67	Providence Reds	AHL	72	13	42	55				24					
1967-68	Providence Reds	AHL	72	15	35	50				42	8	0	3	3	6
1968-69	Providence Reds	AHL	73	7	18	25				29	9	2	5	7	0
1969-70	Columbus Checkers	IHL	72	12	49	61				71					
	NHL Totals		**13**	**1**	**0**	**1**	**1**	**0**	**1**	**6**					

NHL rights transferred to **Toronto** after NHL club purchased **Denver** (WHL) franchise and relocated team to Victoria, June, 1964. Claimed by **Providence** (AHL) from **Toronto** in Reverse Draft, June, 1966.

• SLOAN, TOD Tod (Aloysius Martin) "Slinker" Sloan
C/RW – R. 5'10", 152 lbs. b: Pontiac, Que., 11/30/1927.

Season	Club	League	GP	G	A	Pts	AG	AA	APts	PIM	PO GP	PO G	PO A	PO Pts	PO PIM
1944-45	St. Michael's Majors	OHA	19	21	16	37				14	23	27	14	41	32
1945-46	St. Michael's Majors	OHA	25	*43	*32	*75				49	11	16	6	22	16
1946-47	Pittsburgh Hornets	AHL	64	15	24	39				31	12	2	2	4	0
1947-48	**Toronto Maple Leafs**	**NHL**	**1**	**0**	**0**	**0**	**0**	**0**	**0**	**0**					
	Pittsburgh Hornets	AHL	61	20	24	44				18	2	1	0	1	2
1948-49	**Toronto Maple Leafs**	**NHL**	**29**	**3**	**4**	**7**	**5**	**6**	**11**	**0**					
	Pittsburgh Hornets	AHL	35	18	16	34				23					
1949-50	Cleveland Barons	AHL	62	37	29	66				28	9	*10	4	*14	7
1950-51	**Toronto Maple Leafs**	**NHL**	**70**	**31**	**25**	**56**	**42**	**32**	**74**	**105**	**11**	**4**	**5**	**9**	**18**
1951-52	**Toronto Maple Leafs**	**NHL**	**68**	**25**	**23**	**48**	**36**	**30**	**66**	**89**	**4**	**0**	**0**	**0**	**10**
1952-53	**Toronto Maple Leafs**	**NHL**	**70**	**15**	**10**	**25**	**23**	**14**	**37**	**76**					
1953-54	**Toronto Maple Leafs**	**NHL**	**67**	**11**	**32**	**43**	**17**	**44**	**61**	**100**	**5**	**1**	**1**	**2**	**4**
1954-55	**Toronto Maple Leafs**	**NHL**	**63**	**13**	**15**	**28**	**19**	**19**	**38**	**89**	**4**	**0**	**0**	**0**	**2**
1955-56	**Toronto Maple Leafs**	**NHL**	**70**	**37**	**29**	**66**	**55**	**36**	**91**	**100**	**2**	**0**	**0**	**0**	**5**
1956-57	**Toronto Maple Leafs**	**NHL**	**52**	**14**	**21**	**35**	**19**	**24**	**43**	**33**					
1957-58	**Toronto Maple Leafs**	**NHL**	**59**	**13**	**25**	**38**	**17**	**27**	**44**	**58**					
1958-59	**Chicago Black Hawks**	**NHL**	**59**	**27**	**35**	**62**	**34**	**37**	**71**	**79**	**6**	**3**	**5**	**8**	**0**
1959-60	**Chicago Black Hawks**	**NHL**	**70**	**20**	**20**	**40**	**25**	**20**	**45**	**54**	**3**	**0**	**0**	**0**	**0**
1960-61	**Chicago Black Hawks**	**NHL**	**67**	**11**	**23**	**34**	**13**	**23**	**36**	**48**	**12**	**1**	**1**	**2**	**8**
1961-62	Galt Terriers	OHA Sr.	9	11	4	15				8					
	Canada	WEC-A	6	6	4	10				4					
	NHL Totals		**745**	**220**	**262**	**482**	**305**	**312**	**617**	**831**	**47**	**9**	**12**	**21**	**47**

NHL Second All-Star Team (1956)

Played in NHL All-Star Game (1951, 1952, 1956)

Traded to **Chicago** by **Toronto** for cash, June 6, 1958.

• SLOBODIAN, PETER
Peter Slobodian
D – L. 6'1", 185 lbs. b. Dauphin, Man., 4/24/1918. d: 11/17/1986.

Season	Club	League	GP	G	A	Pts	AG	AA	APts	PIM	GP	G	A	Pts	PIM
			REGULAR SEASON								PLAYOFFS				
1936-37	Brandon Wheat Kings	MHL Jr.	14	0	0	0	....	....	....	20	4	2	0	2	10
1937-38	Brandon Wheat Kings	MHL Jr.	14	3	6	9	....	....	....	22	5	0	3	3	14
1938-39	Regina Aces	RCHL	30	5	5	10	....	....	....	*74	....	....	....	....	....
1939-40	Regina Aces	RCHL	18	4	10	14	....	....	....	48	9	3	1	4	26
1940-41	**New York Americans**	**NHL**	**41**	**3**	**2**	**5**	**6**	**4**	**10**	**54**	....	....	....	....	....
1941-42	Lethbridge Maple Leafs	ASHL	30	4	14	18	....	....	....	*149	9	4	0	4	*32
1942-43	Lethbridge Bombers	ASHL	20	8	6	14	....	....	....	*83	2	0	1	1	6
1943-44	Calgary Combines	ASHL	9	2	0	2	....	....	....	15	....	....	....	....	....
1944-45	Calgary RCAF	City Sr.	11	2	2	4	....	....	....	*48	....	....	....	....	....
1945-46	Calgary Stampeders	WCSHL	....	....	....	....	....	....	....	....	18	0	1	1	*30
1946-47	Hershey Bears	AHL	52	4	15	19	....	....	....	99	11	1	2	3	16
1947-48	Hershey Bears	AHL	54	2	8	10	....	....	....	105	2	0	1	1	6
1948-49	Lethbridge Maple Leafs	WCSHL	35	1	16	17	....	....	....	74	3	0	2	2	4
1949-50	Lethbridge Native Sons	AJHL	DID NOT PLAY – COACHING												
	NHL Totals		**41**	**3**	**2**	**5**	**6**	**4**	**10**	**54**	....	....	....	....	....

Signed as a free agent by **NY Americans**, October 11, 1940.

• SLOWINSKI, EDDIE
Eddie Slowinski
RW – R. 5'11", 195 lbs. b: Winnipeg, Man., 11/18/1922.

Season	Club	League	GP	G	A	Pts	AG	AA	APts	PIM	GP	G	A	Pts	PIM
1940-41	Winnipeg Monarchs	MJHL	....	....	....	....	....	....	....	....	3	2	0	2	2
1941-42	Winnipeg Monarchs	MJHL	18	18	20	38	....	....	....	40	1	0	1	1	4
1942-43	Ottawa Army	City Sr.	4	6	5	11	....	....	....	0	....	....	....	....	....
	Ottawa Commandos	QSHL	27	17	12	29	....	....	....	8	15	4	2	6	16
1943-44	Red Deer Rangers	ASHL	16	6	9	15	....	....	....	0	5	3	0	3	9
1944-45	Calgary Navy	City Sr.	16	16	11	27	....	....	....	10	....	....	....	....	....
	Winnipeg Navy	City Sr.	....	....	....	....	....	....	....	....	4	0	0	0	0
1945-46	Ottawa Senators	QSHL	30	26	29	55	....	....	....	10	9	3	6	9	4
1946-47	Ottawa Senators	QSHL	40	*26	18	44	....	....	....	18	10	3	1	4	4
1947-48	**New York Rangers**	**NHL**	**38**	**6**	**5**	**11**	**9**	**7**	**16**	**2**	**4**	**0**	**0**	**0**	**0**
	New Haven Ramblers	AHL	18	9	9	18	....	....	....	2	....	....	....	....	....
1948-49	**New York Rangers**	**NHL**	**20**	**1**	**1**	**2**	**2**	**2**	**4**	**2**	....	....	....	....	....
	New Haven Ramblers	AHL	5	2	2	4	....	....	....	0	....	....	....	....	....
	St. Paul Saints	USHL	16	5	12	17	....	....	....	0	7	5	6	11	2
1949-50	**New York Rangers**	**NHL**	**63**	**14**	**23**	**37**	**19**	**29**	**48**	**12**	**12**	**2**	***6**	**8**	**6**
1950-51	**New York Rangers**	**NHL**	**69**	**14**	**18**	**32**	**19**	**23**	**42**	**15**	....	....	....	....	....
1951-52	**New York Rangers**	**NHL**	**64**	**21**	**22**	**43**	**30**	**29**	**59**	**18**	....	....	....	....	....
1952-53	**New York Rangers**	**NHL**	**37**	**2**	**5**	**7**	**3**	**7**	**10**	**14**	....	....	....	....	....
1953-54	Buffalo Bisons	AHL	67	38	41	79	....	....	....	16	3	1	0	1	2
1954-55	Buffalo Bisons	AHL	59	22	35	57	....	....	....	37	10	5	5	10	4
1955-56	Buffalo Bisons	AHL	63	23	26	49	....	....	....	24	5	1	0	1	2
1956-57	Springfield Indians	AHL	59	18	24	42	....	....	....	10	....	....	....	....	....
1957-58	Providence Reds	AHL	3	0	0	0	....	....	....	2	....	....	....	....	....
	NHL Totals		**291**	**58**	**74**	**132**	**82**	**97**	**179**	**63**	**16**	**2**	**6**	**8**	**6**

AHL First All-Star Team (1954)

Traded to **Montreal** by **NY Rangers** with Pete Babando for Ivan Irwin, August 8, 1953. Traded to **Buffalo** (AHL) by **Montreal** with Gaye Stewart and Pete Babando for Jack LeClair and cash, August 17, 1953.

• SLY, DARRYL
— *see page 1483*

• SMART, ALEX
Alex Smart
LW – L. 5'10", 150 lbs. b: Brandon, Man., 5/29/1918.

Season	Club	League	GP	G	A	Pts	AG	AA	APts	PIM	GP	G	A	Pts	PIM
1935-36	Portage Terriers	MHL Jr.	16	10	4	14	....	....	....	4	6	*9	*6	*15	2
1936-37	Portage Terriers	MHL Jr.	16	15	4	19	....	....	....	10	4	0	2	2	6
1937-38	Toronto Marlboros	OHA	12	12	11	23	....	....	....	10	6	4	8	12	9
1938-39	Verdun Maple Leafs	Mtl-Sr.	22	6	9	15	....	....	....	18	2	1	1	2	4
1939-40	Verdun Maple Leafs	Mtl-Sr.	21	0	0	17	....	....		13	8	7	1	8	9
1940-41	Montreal Sr. Canadiens	Mtl-Sr.	33	7	15	22	....	....	....	21	....	....	....	....	....
1941-42	Montreal Sr. Canadiens	Mtl-Sr.	36	15	6	21		....	....	40	6	4	4	8	4
1942-43	**Montreal Canadiens**	**NHL**	**8**	**5**	**2**	**7**	**7**	**3**	**10**	**0**	....	....	....	....	....
	Montreal Sr. Canadiens	QSHL	23	12	11	23	....	....	....	8	....	....	....	....	....
1943-44	Montreal Royals	QSHL	20	9	14	23	....	....	....	9	5	4	3	7	2
	Montreal Vickers	City Sr.	10	8	13	21	....	....	....	12	....	....	....	....	....
1944-45	Montreal Royals	QSHL	24	19	19	38	....	....	....	12	7	2	3	5	2
1945-46	Montreal Royals	QSHL	37	16	24	40	....	....	....	33	11	5	5	10	6
1946-47	Ottawa Senators	QSHL	38	14	21	35	....	....	....	26	9	1	6	7	4
1947-48	Ottawa Senators	QSHL	47	28	38	66	....	....	....	11	22	6	15	21	8
1948-49	Ottawa Senators	QSHL	40	14	27	41	....	....	....	29	25	4	4	8	8
1949-50	Ottawa Senators	QSHL	28	8	12	20	....	....	....	28	7	0	3	3	12
1950-51	Eastview St. Charles	Ott-Jr.	DID NOT PLAY – COACHING												
	NHL Totals		**8**	**5**	**2**	**7**	**7**	**3**	**10**	**0**	....	....	....	....	....

Signed as a free agent by **Montreal**, February 1, 1943.

• SMILLIE, DON
Don Smillie
LW – L. 6', 185 lbs. b. Toronto, Ont., 9/13/1910.

Season	Club	League	GP	G	A	Pts	AG	AA	APts	PIM	GP	G	A	Pts	PIM
1928-29	Toronto Young Rangers	OHA	12	10	0	10	....	....	....	....	9	6	1	7	....
	University of Toronto	OHA Sr.	9	6	0	6	....	....	....	10	3	1	0	1	0
1930-31	University of Toronto	OHA Sr.	10	1	2	3	....	....	....	16	....			....	....
1931-32	University of Toronto	OHA Sr.	12	4	3	7	....	....	....	18	....	....	....	....	....
1932-33	University of Toronto	OHA Sr.	11	5	3	8	....	....	....	16	....	....	....	....	....
1933-34	**Boston Bruins**	**NHL**	**12**	**2**	**2**	**4**	**4**	**5**	**9**	**4**	....	....	....	....	....
	Boston Cubs	Can-Am	15	1	2	3	....	....	....	11	....	....	....	....	....
	Toronto Nationals	OHA Sr.	11	3	1	4	....	....	....	14	....	....	....	....	....
1934-35	Boston Cubs	Can-Am	6	0	1	1	....	....	....	4	....	....	....	....	....
	Syracuse–Windsor	IAHL	33	8	4	12	....	....	....	10	....	....	....	....	....
1935-36	Windsor–London	IAHL	46	8	11	19	....	....	....	35	8	1	0	1	7
	St. Louis Flyers	AHA	3	0	0	0	....	....	....	0	....	....	....	....	....
	NHL Totals		**12**	**2**	**2**	**4**	**4**	**5**	**9**	**4**	....	....	....	....	....

• SMITH, ALEX
Alex "Boots" Smith
D – L. 5'11", 176 lbs. b: Liverpool, England, 4/2/1902. d: 11/29/1963.

Season	Club	League	GP	G	A	Pts	AG	AA	APts	PIM	GP	G	A	Pts	PIM
			REGULAR SEASON								PLAYOFFS				
1922-23	Ottawa Gunners	City Sr.	3	1	0	1	....	....	....	0	....	....	....	....	....
1923-24	Ottawa Collegiate	H.S.	STATISTICS NOT AVAILABLE												
1924-25	**Ottawa Senators**	**NHL**	**7**	**0**	**0**	**0**	**0**	**0**	**0**	**2**	....	....	....	....	....
	Ottawa Rideaus	City Sr.	11	7	1	8	....	....	....	....	3	0	0	0	0
1925-26	**Ottawa Senators**	**NHL**	**36**	**0**	**0**	**0**	**0**	**0**	**0**	**36**	**2**	**0**	**0**	**0**	**14**
1926-27	**Ottawa Senators**	**NHL**	**42**	**4**	**1**	**5**	**12**	**8**	**20**	**58**	**6**	**0**	**0**	**0**	**8**
1927-28	**Ottawa Senators**	**NHL**	**44**	**9**	**4**	**13**	**28**	**34**	**62**	**90**	**2**	**0**	**0**	**0**	**4**
1928-29	**Ottawa Senators**	**NHL**	**44**	**1**	**7**	**8**	**4**	**65**	**69**	**96**	....	....	....	....	....
1929-30	**Ottawa Senators**	**NHL**	**43**	**2**	**6**	**8**	**4**	**19**	**23**	**91**	**2**	**0**	**0**	**0**	**4**
1930-31	**Ottawa Senators**	**NHL**	**37**	**5**	**6**	**11**	**12**	**22**	**34**	**73**	....	....	....	....	....
1931-32	**Detroit Falcons**	**NHL**	**48**	**6**	**8**	**14**	**13**	**22**	**35**	**47**	**2**	**0**	**0**	**0**	**4**
1932-33	**Ottawa Senators**	**NHL**	**34**	**2**	**0**	**2**	**5**	**0**	**5**	**42**	....	....	....	....	....
	Boston Bruins	**NHL**	**15**	**5**	**4**	**9**	**12**	**11**	**23**	**30**	**5**	**0**	**2**	**2**	**6**
1933-34	**Boston Bruins**	**NHL**	**45**	**4**	**6**	**10**	**9**	**16**	**25**	**32**	....	....	....	....	....
1934-35	**New York Americans**	**NHL**	**48**	**3**	**8**	**11**	**6**	**18**	**24**	**46**	....	....	....	....	....
1935-36	Ottawa RCAF	City Sr.	DID NOT PLAY – COACHING												
	NHL Totals		**443**	**41**	**50**	**91**	**105**	**215**	**320**	**643**	**19**	**0**	**2**	**2**	**40**

Signed as a free agent by **Ottawa**, February 10, 1925. Claimed by **Detroit Falcons** from **Ottawa** for 1931-32 season in Dispersal Draft, September 26, 1931. Traded to **Boston** by **Ottawa** for future considerations (Earl Roche), January 25, 1933. Traded to **NY Americans** by **Boston** for cash, October 18, 1934.

• SMITH, ART
Art Smith
D – L. 5'10", 200 lbs. b: Toronto, Ont., 11/29/1906. d: 5/16/1962.

Season	Club	League	GP	G	A	Pts	AG	AA	APts	PIM	GP	G	A	Pts	PIM
1923-24	Oakwood Collegiate	OHA	STATISTICS NOT AVAILABLE												
1924-25	Toronto Canoe Club	OHA	8	5	4	9	....	....	....	....	2	*2	0	2	....
	Toronto Canoe Club	OHA Sr.	2	1	0	1	....	....	....	....	....	....	....	....	....
1925-26	Toronto Canoe Club	OHA	8	5	1	6	....	....	....	....	....	....	....	....	....
1926-27	Toronto Canoe Club	OHA Sr.	10	8	3	11	....	....	....	4	....	....	....	....	....
	Toronto Maple Leafs	**NHL**	**15**	**5**	**3**	**8**	**15**	**25**	**40**	**22**	....	....	....	....	....
	Toronto Falcons	Can-Pro	29	11	1	12	....	....	....	46	....	....	....	....	....
1928-29	**Toronto Maple Leafs**	**NHL**	**43**	**5**	**0**	**5**	**20**	**0**	**20**	**91**	**4**	**1**	**1**	**2**	**8**
1929-30	**Toronto Maple Leafs**	**NHL**	**43**	**3**	**3**	**6**	**6**	**10**	**16**	**75**	....	....	....	....	....
1930-31	**Ottawa Senators**	**NHL**	**43**	**2**	**4**	**6**	**5**	**14**	**19**	**61**	....	....	....	....	....
1931-32	Boston Cubs	Can-Am	1	0	0	0	....	....	....	0	....	....	....	....	....
	Chicago Shamrocks	AHA	14	0	1	1	....	....	....	20	....	....	....	....	....
	NHL Totals		**144**	**15**	**10**	**25**	**46**	**49**	**95**	**249**	**4**	**1**	**1**	**2**	**8**

Traded to **Ottawa** by **Toronto** with Eric Pettinger and $35,000 for King Clancy, October 10, 1930.

• SMITH, BRIAN S.
Brian S. Smith
LW – L. 6', 180 lbs. b: Creighton Mine, Ont., 12/6/1937.

Season	Club	League	GP	G	A	Pts	AG	AA	APts	PIM	GP	G	A	Pts	PIM
1954-55	Hamilton Tiger Cubs	OHA	33	7	3	10	....	....	....	14	3	0	1	1	7
1955-56	Hamilton Tiger Cubs	OHA	41	20	17	37	....	....	....	24	....	....	....	....	....
1956-57	Hamilton Tiger Cubs	OHA	52	27	23	50	....	....	....	32	4	1	0	1	0
1957-58	Hamilton Tiger Cubs	OHA	50	24	17	41	....	....	....	65	13	6	2	8	29
	Detroit Red Wings	**NHL**	**4**	**0**	**1**	**1**	**0**	**1**	**1**	**0**		....	....	....	....
1958-59	Edmonton Flyers	WHL	20	4	4	8	....	....	....	12	....	....	....	....	....
1959-60	**Detroit Red Wings**	**NHL**	**31**	**2**	**5**	**7**	**2**	**5**	**7**	**2**	**5**	**0**	**0**	**0**	**0**
	Hershey Bears	AHL	34	13	9	22	....	....	....	29	....	....	....	....	....
1960-61	**Detroit Red Wings**	**NHL**	**26**	**0**	**2**	**2**	**0**	**2**	**2**	**10**	....	....	....	....	....
	Edmonton Flyers	WHL	11	5	3	8	....	....	....	2	....	....	....	....	....
	Hershey Bears	AHL	31	6	14	20	....	....	....	17	8	1	0	1	2
1961-62	Buffalo Bisons	AHL	58	10	18	28	....	....	....	14	11	1	0	1	0
1962-63	Buffalo Bisons	AHL	65	15	21	36	....	....		16	13	2	3	5	9
1963-64	Buffalo Bisons	AHL	58	6	3	9	....	....	....	13	....	....	....	....	....
1964-65	Los Angeles Blades	WHL	69	35	28	63	....	....	....	38	....	....	....	....	
1965-66	Los Angeles Blades	WHL	71	19	20	39	....	....	....	16	....	....	....	....	....
1966-67	Buffalo Bisons	AHL	60	15	17	32	....			30	....	....	....	....	....
1967-68	Phoenix Roadrunners	WHL	52	11	12	23	....	....	....	5	....	....	....	....	....
1968-69	Jacksonville Rockets	EHL	21	7	8	15	....	....	....	0	....	....	....	....	....
	NHL Totals		**61**	**2**	**8**	**10**	**2**	**8**	**10**	**12**	**5**	**0**	**0**	**0**	**0**

WHL Second All-Star Team (1965)

Traded to **Chicago** by **Detroit** with Gerry Melnyk for Ed Litzenberger, June 13, 1961. Traded to **Phoenix** (WHL) by **Portland** (WHL) with Rick Charron and Tom McVie for Andy Hebenton, September, 1967.

• SMITH, CARL
Carl "Winky" Smith
RW – L. 5'5", 150 lbs. b: Cache Bay, Ont., 9/18/1917. d: 1/9/1967.

Season	Club	League	GP	G	A	Pts	AG	AA	APts	PIM	GP	G	A	Pts	PIM
1934-35	St. Michael's Majors	Tor-Jr.	12	9	2	11	....	....	....	8	3	3	1	4	4
1935-36	Oshawa Chevvies	Tor-Sr.	13	4	4	8	....	....	....	12	....	....	....	....	....
1936-37	Oshawa G-Men	Tor-Sr.	9	3	1	4	....	....	....	12	....	....	....	....	....
1937-38	Oshawa G-Men	OHA Sr.	16	14	10	24	....	....	....	16	2	0	0	0	4
1938-39	Oshawa G-Men	OHA Sr.	18	12	18	30	....	....	....	37	7	1	4	5	6
1939-40	Detroit Holzbaugh	MOHL	31	16	16	32	....	....	....	14	12	3	4	7	28
1940-41	St. Louis Flyers	AHA	48	21	19	40	....	....	....	18	9	2	3	5	6
1941-42	St. Louis Flyers	AHA	50	11	17	28	....	....	....	43	2	1	1	2	0
1942-43	New Haven–Buffalo	AHL	52	14	23	37	....	....	....	21	9	2	7	9	0
1943-44	**Detroit Red Wings**	**NHL**	**7**	**1**	**1**	**2**	**1**	**1**	**2**	**2**	....	....	....	....	....
	Indianapolis Capitals	AHL	45	20	26	46	....	....	....	20	5	1	4	5	2
1944-45	St. Louis Flyers	AHL	58	10	26	36	....	....	....	23	....	....	....	....	....
1945-46	Indianapolis Capitals	AHL	5	0	2	2	....	....	....	2	....	....	....	....	....
	Omaha Knights	USHL	54	29	38	67	....	....	....	33	7	3	1	4	7
1946-47	Omaha Knights	USHL	56	15	21	36	....	....	....	20	11	8	7	15	0
1947-48	Omaha Knights	USHL	38	19	34	53	....	....	....	2	3	1	0	1	0
1948-49	Omaha Knights	USHL	61	11	33	44	....	....	....	36	4	0	0	0	0
	NHL Totals		**7**	**1**	**1**	**2**	**1**	**1**	**2**	**2**	....	....	....	....	....

USHL First All-Star Team (1946)

• SMITH, CLINT Clint "Snuffy" Smith HHOF

C – L. 5'8", 165 lbs. b: Assiniboia, Sask., 12/12/1913.

			REGULAR SEASON								PLAYOFFS				
Season	Club	League	GP	G	A	Pts	AG	AA	APts	PIM	GP	G	A	Pts	PIM
1930-31	Saskatoon Wesleys	SJHL	1	0	0	0	....	....	....	0	....	....	....	....	....
1931-32	Saskatoon Wesleys	SJHL	4	*5	1	*6	....	....	....	0	....	....	....	....	....
	Saskatoon Crescents	SSHL	18	*19	3	22	....	....	....	0	4	*6	0	*6	4
1932-33	Springfield Indians	Can-Am	12	0	0	0	....	....	....	0	....	....	....	....	....
	Saskatoon Quakers	NWHL	27	7	6	13	....	....	....	8	....	....	....	....	....
1933-34	Vancouver Lions	NWHL	34	*25	14	39	....	....	....	8	7	5	*4	*9	2
1934-35	Vancouver Lions	NWHL	32	22	*22	*44	....	....	....	2	8	3	*5	8	4
1935-36	Vancouver Lions	NWHL	40	21	*32	*53	....	....	....	10	7	2	*4	6	2
1936-37	**New York Rangers**	**NHL**	**2**	**1**	**0**	**1**	**2**	**0**	**2**	**0**	....	....	....	....	....
	Philadelphia Ramblers	AHL	47	25	29	54	....	....	....	15	6	*4	3	7	0
1937-38	**New York Rangers**	**NHL**	**48**	**14**	**23**	**37**	**30**	**48**	**78**	**0**	**3**	**2**	**0**	**2**	**0**
1938-39	**New York Rangers**	**NHL**	**48**	**21**	**20**	**41**	**45**	**37**	**82**	**2**	**7**	**1**	**2**	**3**	**0**
1939-40	**New York Rangers**	**NHL**	**41**	**8**	**16**	**24**	**17**	**32**	**49**	**2**	**11**	**1**	**3**	**4**	**2**
1940-41	**New York Rangers**	**NHL**	**48**	**14**	**11**	**25**	**28**	**20**	**48**	**0**	**3**	**0**	**0**	**0**	**0**
1941-42	**New York Rangers**	**NHL**	**47**	**10**	**24**	**34**	**17**	**37**	**54**	**4**	**5**	**0**	**0**	**0**	**0**
1942-43	**New York Rangers**	**NHL**	**47**	**12**	**21**	**33**	**17**	**27**	**44**	**4**	....	....	....	....	....
1943-44	**Chicago Black Hawks**	**NHL**	**50**	**23**	***49**	**72**	**29**	**60**	**89**	**4**	**9**	**4**	**8**	**12**	**0**
1944-45	**Chicago Black Hawks**	**NHL**	**50**	**23**	**31**	**54**	**32**	**51**	**83**	**0**	....	....	....	....	....
1945-46	**Chicago Black Hawks**	**NHL**	**50**	**26**	**24**	**50**	**40**	**45**	**85**	**2**	**4**	**2**	**1**	**3**	**0**
1946-47	**Chicago Black Hawks**	**NHL**	**52**	**9**	**17**	**26**	**12**	**24**	**36**	**6**	....	....	....	....	....
1947-48	Tulsa Oilers	USHL	64	38	33	71	....	....	....	10	2	0	1	1	0
1948-49	St. Paul Saints	USHL	2	2	0	2	....	....	....	2	....	....	....	....	....
1949-50	St. Paul Saints	USHL	21	7	15	22	....	....	....	2	2	0	0	0	2
1950-51	St. Paul Saints	USHL	23	3	9	12	....	....	....	0	....	....	....	....	....
1951-52	Cincinnati Mohawks	AHL	2	0	0	0	....	....	....	2	....	....	....	....	....
	NHL Totals		**483**	**161**	**236**	**397**	**269**	**381**	**650**	**24**	**42**	**10**	**14**	**24**	**2**

Won Lady Byng Trophy (1939, 1944) • Won Herman W. Paterson Cup (USHL - MVP) (1948)

Signed as a free agent by **NY Rangers**, October 13, 1932. Signed as a free agent by **Chicago**, September, 1943.

• SMITH, DALLAS — *see page 1486*

• SMITH, DES Des Smith

D – L. 6', 185 lbs. b: Ottawa, Ont., 2/22/1914.

			REGULAR SEASON								PLAYOFFS				
Season	Club	League	GP	G	A	Pts	AG	AA	APts	PIM	GP	G	A	Pts	PIM
1930-31	Ottawa St. Malachys	City Jr.	13	1	0	1	....	....	....	32	....	....	....	....	....
1931-32	Ottawa Jr. Montagnards	City Jr.	12	2	4	6	....	....	....	18	2	0	0	0	11
	Ottawa Montagnards	City Sr.	1	0	0	0	....	....	....	0	....	....	....	....	....
1932-33	Ottawa Jr. Montagnards	City Jr.	15	3	5	8	....	....	....	25	2	0	0	0	4
	Ottawa Montagnards	City Sr.	1	0	0	0	....	....	....	0	1	0	0	0	0
1933-34	Ottawa Montagnards	City Sr.	21	6	5	11	....	....	....	37	3	0	1	1	4
1934-35	Charlottetown Abegweits	MSHL	19	0	2	2	....	....	....	54	....	....	....	....	....
	Saint John St. Peters	NBSHL	14	6	15	21	....	....	....	*19	12	4	1	5	*21
1935-36	Wembley Lions	Britain	....	9	6	15	....	....	....	46	....	....	....	....	....
1936-37	Wembley Lions	Britain	....	8	8	16	....	....	....	40	....	....	....	....	....
1937-38	**Montreal Maroons**	**NHL**	**40**	**3**	**1**	**4**	**6**	**2**	**8**	**47**	....	....	....	....	....
1938-39	**Montreal Canadiens**	**NHL**	**16**	**3**	**3**	**6**	**6**	**6**	**12**	**8**	**3**	**0**	**0**	**0**	**4**
	New Haven Eagles	AHL	34	4	9	13	....	....	....	34	....	....	....	....	....
1939-40	**Chicago Black Hawks**	**NHL**	**24**	**1**	**4**	**5**	**2**	**8**	**10**	**27**	....	....	....	....	....
	Boston Bruins	**NHL**	**20**	**2**	**2**	**4**	**4**	**4**	**8**	**23**	**6**	**0**	**0**	**0**	**0**
1940-41	**Boston Bruins**	**NHL**	**48**	**6**	**8**	**14**	**12**	**15**	**27**	**61**	**11**	**0**	**2**	**2**	**12**
1941-42	**Boston Bruins**	**NHL**	**48**	**7**	**7**	**14**	**12**	**11**	**23**	**70**	**5**	**1**	**2**	**3**	**2**
1942-43	Ottawa Army	City Sr.	DID NOT PLAY – COACHING												
1943-44	Ottawa Army	City Sr.	DID NOT PLAY – COACHING												
1944-45	Montreal Army	City Sr.	10	6	2	8	....	....	....	10	3	0	1	1	4
1945-46	Shawinigan Cataracts	QSHL	14	0	3	3	....	....	....	12	....	....	....	....	....
	Springfield Indians	AHL	2	1	0	1	....	....	....	0	....	....	....	....	....
	NHL Totals		**196**	**22**	**25**	**47**	**42**	**46**	**88**	**236**	**25**	**1**	**4**	**5**	**18**

Signed as a free agent by **Montreal Maroons**, October 7, 1937. Traded to **Montreal Canadiens** by **Montreal Maroons** for cash, September 14, 1938. Traded to **Chicago** by **Montreal Canadiens** for cash, May 15, 1939. Traded to **Boston** by **Chicago** for Jack Portland, January 27, 1940.

• SMITH, DON Don Smith

LW/C – L. 5'7", 160 lbs. b: Cornwall, Ont.. Deceased.

			REGULAR SEASON								PLAYOFFS				
Season	Club	League	GP	G	A	Pts	AG	AA	APts	PIM	GP	G	A	Pts	PIM
1904-05	Cornwall Seniors	City Sr.	7	4	0	4	....	....	....	....	....	....	....	....	....
1905-06	Cornwall Hockey Club	City Sr.	5	2	0	2	....	....	....	....	....	....	....	....	....
1906-07	Cornwall Hockey Club	City Sr.	9	*16	0	*16	....	....	....	....	....	....	....	....	....
1907-08	Portage la Prairie	MHL Sr.	14	19	0	19	....	....	....	....	....	....	....	....	....
1908-09	St. Kitts Professionals	OPHL	6	10	0	10	....	....	....	12	....	....	....	....	....
	Toronto Torontos	OPHL	8	11	0	11	....	....	....	15	....	....	....	....	....
1909-10	Montreal Shamrocks	CHA	3	7	0	7	....	....	....	3	....	....	....	....	....
	Montreal Shamrocks	NHA	12	14	0	14	....	....	....	*58	....	....	....	....	....
1910-11	Renfrew Creamery Kings	NHA	16	26	0	26	....	....	....	49	....	....	....	....	....
1911-12	Victoria Aristocrats	PCHL	16	19	0	19	....	....	....	22	....	....	....	....	....
1912-13	Montreal Canadiens	NHA	20	19	0	19	....	....	....	52	....	....	....	....	....
1913-14	Montreal Canadiens	NHA	20	18	10	28	....	....	....	18	2	1	0	1	7
1914-15	Montreal Canadiens	NHA	11	2	5	7	....	....	....	18	....	....	....	....	....
	Montreal Wanderers	NHA	8	4	3	7	....	....	....	21	2	1	0	1	12
1915-16	Montreal Wanderers	NHA	23	14	2	16	....	....	....	56	....	....	....	....	....
1916-17			MILITARY SERVICE												
1917-18			MILITARY SERVICE												
1918-19			MILITARY SERVICE												
1919-20	**Montreal Canadiens**	**NHL**	**12**	**1**	**0**	**1**	**2**	**0**	**2**	**6**	....	....	....	....	....
	NHL Totals		**12**	**1**	**0**	**1**	**2**	**0**	**2**	**6**	....	....	....	....	....
	Other Major League Totals		141	144	20	164	....	....	....	302	4	2	0	2	19

Traded to **Montreal Wanderers** by **Montreal Canadiens** for cash, February 2, 1915. Rights not retained by **Montreal Wanderers** after NHA folded, November 26, 1917. Signed as a free agent by **Montreal Canadiens**, November, 1919.

• SMITH, DON A. Don A. Smith

LW/C – L. 5'10", 165 lbs. b: Regina, Sask., 5/4/1929.

			REGULAR SEASON								PLAYOFFS				
Season	Club	League	GP	G	A	Pts	AG	AA	APts	PIM	GP	G	A	Pts	PIM
1947-48	Medicine Hat Tigers	AJHL	12	4	3	7	....	....	....	2	....	....	....	....	....
1948-49	Medicine Hat Tigers	AJHL	17	5	8	13	....	....	....	8	....	....	....	....	....
1949-50	**New York Rangers**	**NHL**	**11**	**1**	**1**	**2**	**1**	**1**	**2**	**0**	**1**	**0**	**0**	**0**	**0**
	New York Rovers	EHL	32	15	9	24	....	....	....	2	....	....	....	....	....
1950-51	St. Paul Saints	USHL	59	18	19	37	....	....	....	34	4	1	1	2	2
1951-52	Cincinnati Mohawks	AHL	7	2	1	3	....	....	....	0	....	....	....	....	....
	Vancouver Canucks	PCHL	35	11	16	27	....	....	....	47	....	....	....	....	....
1952-53	Vancouver Canucks	WHL	66	13	15	28	....	....	....	29	9	2	2	4	18
	Fort Wayne Komets	IHL	7	1	0	1	....	....	....	2	....	....	....	....	....
1953-54	Vancouver Canucks	WHL	19	1	1	2	....	....	....	6	....	....	....	....	....
	Cincinnati Mohawks	IHL	53	27	31	58	....	....	....	110	11	3	1	4	20
1954-55	Cincinnati Mohawks	IHL	60	14	13	27	....	....	....	99	10	3	5	8	8
1955-56	Cincinnati Mohawks	IHL	59	37	44	81	....	....	....	45	8	*7	3	*10	2
1956-57	Cincinnati Mohawks	IHL	60	32	32	64	....	....	....	64	7	*5	3	8	6
1957-58	Cincinnati Mohawks	IHL	59	28	49	77	....	....	....	76	4	1	1	2	2
1958-59	Indianapolis Chiefs	IHL	30	21	19	40	....	....	....	26	....	....	....	....	....
1959-60	Regina Caps	SSHL	21	18	18	36	....	....	....	38	9	7	7	14	8
1960-61	Regina Caps	SSHL	STATISTICS NOT AVAILABLE												
1961-62	Saskatoon Quakers	SSHL	29	23	33	56	....	....	....	4	8	*9	5	14	2
1962-63	Saskatoon Quakers	SSHL	25	19	30	49	....	....	....	8	11	7	10	17	4
1963-64	Saskatoon Quakers	SSHL	40	20	31	51	....	....	....	51	11	7	10	17	16
1964-65			DID NOT PLAY												
1965-66	Yorkton Terriers	WCSHL	30	7	12	19	....	....	....	25	5	1	1	2	2
1966-67	Yorkton Terriers	WCSHL	13	3	1	4	....	....	....	0	....	....	....	....	....
	Saskatoon Quakers	SSHL	34	6	13	19	....	....	....	59	4	0	1	1	4
1967-68	Saskatoon Quakers	SSHL	....	2	10	12	....	....	....	40	....	0	0	0	10
	NHL Totals		**11**	**1**	**1**	**2**	**1**	**1**	**2**	**0**	**1**	**0**	**0**	**0**	**0**

• SMITH, FLOYD — *see page 1487*

• SMITH, GLEN Glen Smith

RW – R. 5'8", 155 lbs. b: Lucky Lake, Sask., 3/19/1931.

			REGULAR SEASON								PLAYOFFS				
Season	Club	League	GP	G	A	Pts	AG	AA	APts	PIM	GP	G	A	Pts	PIM
1948-49	Moose Jaw Canucks	WCJHL	26	7	1	8	....	....	....	10	9	4	2	6	11
1949-50	Moose Jaw Canucks	WCJHL	33	20	22	42	....	....	....	28	4	1	0	1	0
1950-51	**Chicago Black Hawks**	**NHL**	**2**	**0**	**0**	**0**	**0**	**0**	**0**	**0**	....	....	....	....	....
	Milwaukee Seagulls	USHL	64	10	14	24	....	....	....	31	....	....	....	....	....
1951-52	Nelson Maple Leafs	WIHL	42	16	15	31	....	....	....	19	9	4	3	7	2
1952-53	Nelson Maple Leafs	WIHL	39	13	8	21	....	....	....	10	5	2	0	2	2
1953-54	Moose Jaw Millionaires	SSHL	39	25	37	62	....	....	....	15	7	1	4	5	2
1954-55	Fort Wayne Komets	IHL	24	4	6	10	....	....	....	4	....	....	....	....	....
	NHL Totals		**2**	**0**	**0**	**0**	**0**	**0**	**0**	**0**	....	....	....	....	....

• SMITH, GLENN GRAFTON Glenn Grafton "George" Smith

D – L. 5'8", 180 lbs. b: Meaford, Ont., 1895. Deceased.

			REGULAR SEASON								PLAYOFFS				
Season	Club	League	GP	G	A	Pts	AG	AA	APts	PIM	GP	G	A	Pts	PIM
1913-14	Woodstock Athletics	OHA	STATISTICS NOT AVAILABLE												
1914-15			MILITARY SERVICE												
1915-16	Toronto Riversides	OHA Sr.	7	5	0	5	....	....	....	....	6	5	0	5	0
1916-17	Toronto Riversides	OHA Sr.	8	4	0	4	....	....	....	....	2	0	0	0	4
1917-18	Toronto Crescents	OHA Sr.	9	10	0	10	....	....	....	....	....	....	....	....	....
1918-19	Toronto Dentals	OHA Sr.	7	8	1	9	....	....	....	....	1	0	0	0	....
1919-20	Toronto Dentals	OHA Sr.	DID NOT PLAY – SUSPENDED												
1920-21	Toronto St. Francis	OHA Sr.	1	0	0	0	....	....	....	0	....	....	....	....	....
1921-22	**Toronto St. Pats**	**NHL**	**9**	**0**	**0**	**0**	**0**	**0**	**0**	**0**	....	....	....	....	....
	NHL Totals		**9**	**0**	**0**	**0**	**0**	**0**	**0**	**0**	....	....	....	....	....

Signed as a free agent by **Toronto St. Pats**, December 16, 1921.

• SMITH, HOOLEY Hooley (Reginald) Smith HHOF

C/RW – R. 5'10", 155 lbs. b: Toronto, Ont., 1/7/1903. d: 8/24/1963.

			REGULAR SEASON								PLAYOFFS				
Season	Club	League	GP	G	A	Pts	AG	AA	APts	PIM	GP	G	A	Pts	PIM
1920-21	Parkdale Canoe Club	OHA	3	3	0	3	....	....	....	....	....	....	....	....	....
1921-22	Toronto Granites	OHA Sr.	5	1	0	1	....	....	....	....	1	0	0	0	....
1922-23	Toronto Granites	OHA Sr.	8	3	3	6	....	....	....	....	8	2	*6	8	14
1923-24	Toronto Granites	OHA Sr.	15	10	*14	24	....	....	....	....	5	17	*16	33	....
	Canada	Olympics	5	17	*16	33	....	....	....	4	....	....	....	....	....
1924-25	**Ottawa Senators**	**NHL**	**30**	**10**	**3**	**13**	**35**	**40**	**75**	**81**	....	....	....	....	....
1925-26	**Ottawa Senators**	**NHL**	**28**	**16**	**9**	**25**	**50**	**106**	**156**	**53**	**2**	**0**	**0**	**0**	**14**
1926-27	**Ottawa Senators**	**NHL**	**43**	**9**	**6**	**15**	**26**	**51**	**77**	**125**	**6**	**1**	**0**	**1**	**16**
1927-28	**Montreal Maroons**	**NHL**	**34**	**14**	**5**	**19**	**43**	**42**	**85**	**72**	**9**	**2**	**1**	**3**	**23**
1928-29	**Montreal Maroons**	**NHL**	**41**	**10**	**9**	**19**	**40**	**83**	**123**	**120**	....	....	....	....	....
1929-30	**Montreal Maroons**	**NHL**	**42**	**21**	**9**	**30**	**42**	**29**	**71**	**83**	**4**	**1**	**1**	**2**	**14**
1930-31	**Montreal Maroons**	**NHL**	**39**	**12**	**14**	**26**	**29**	**51**	**80**	**68**	....	....	....	....	....
1931-32	**Montreal Maroons**	**NHL**	**43**	**11**	**33**	**44**	**23**	**94**	**117**	**49**	**4**	**2**	**1**	**3**	**2**
1932-33	**Montreal Maroons**	**NHL**	**48**	**20**	**21**	**41**	**47**	**56**	**103**	**66**	**2**	**2**	**0**	**2**	**2**
1933-34	**Montreal Maroons**	**NHL**	**47**	**18**	**19**	**37**	**40**	**51**	**91**	**58**	**4**	**0**	**1**	**1**	**6**
1934-35	**Montreal Maroons**	**NHL**	**46**	**5**	**22**	**27**	**11**	**49**	**60**	**41**	**6**	**0**	**0**	**0**	**14**
1935-36	**Montreal Maroons**	**NHL**	**47**	**19**	**19**	**38**	**47**	**46**	**93**	**75**	**3**	**0**	**0**	**0**	**2**
1936-37	**Boston Bruins**	**NHL**	**44**	**8**	**10**	**18**	**17**	**23**	**40**	**36**	**3**	**0**	**0**	**0**	**0**
1937-38	**New York Americans**	**NHL**	**47**	**10**	**10**	**20**	**21**	**21**	**42**	**23**	**6**	**0**	**3**	**3**	**0**
1938-39	**New York Americans**	**NHL**	**48**	**8**	**11**	**19**	**17**	**20**	**37**	**18**	**2**	**0**	**0**	**0**	**14**
1939-40	**New York Americans**	**NHL**	**47**	**7**	**8**	**15**	**15**	**16**	**31**	**41**	**3**	**3**	**1**	**4**	**2**
1940-41	**New York Americans**	**NHL**	**41**	**2**	**7**	**9**	**4**	**13**	**17**	**4**	....	....	....	....	....
	NHL Totals		**715**	**200**	**215**	**415**	**507**	**791**	**1298**	**1013**	**54**	**11**	**8**	**19**	**109**

NHL Second All-Star Team (1932) • NHL First All-Star Team (1936)

Played in NHL All-Star Game (1934)

Signed as a free agent by **Ottawa**, October 31, 1924. Traded to **Montreal Maroons** by **Ottawa** for Harry Broadbent and cash, October 7, 1927. Traded to **Boston** by **Montreal Maroons** for cash and future considerations (Gerry Shannon, December 4, 1936), October 26, 1936. Traded to **NY Americans** by **Boston** for cash, November, 5, 1937.

• SMITH, KENNY
Kenny Smith
LW – L. 5'7", 150 lbs. b: Moose Jaw, Sask., 5/8/1924.

Season	Club	League	GP	G	A	Pts	AG	AA	APts	PIM	GP	G	A	Pts	PIM
			REGULAR SEASON								PLAYOFFS				
1940-41	Regina Pats	SJHL	15	13	7	20	....	....	....	2	4	*4	1	5	0
1941-42	Oshawa Generals	OHA	24	17	14	31	....	....	....	0	12	12	6	18	10
1942-43	Oshawa Generals	OHA	22	33	21	54	....	....	....	2	10	*15	15	*30	2
1943-44	Oshawa Generals	OHA	26	*53	26	*79	....	....	....	2	10	6	7	13	0
1944-45	**Boston Bruins**	**NHL**	49	20	14	34	28	23	51	2	7	3	4	7	0
1945-46	**Boston Bruins**	**NHL**	23	2	6	8	3	11	14	0	8	0	4	4	0
	Hershey Bears	AHL	27	10	13	23	....	....	....	8	....	....	....	....	....
1946-47	**Boston Bruins**	**NHL**	60	14	7	21	19	10	29	4	5	3	0	3	2
1947-48	**Boston Bruins**	**NHL**	60	11	12	23	16	17	33	14	5	2	3	5	0
1948-49	**Boston Bruins**	**NHL**	59	20	20	40	32	32	64	6	5	0	2	2	4
1949-50	**Boston Bruins**	**NHL**	66	10	31	41	13	40	53	12	....	....	....	....	....
1950-51	**Boston Bruins**	**NHL**	14	1	3	4	1	4	5	11	....	....	....	....	....
	Pittsburgh Hornets	AHL	55	8	23	31	....	....	....	33	13	2	7	9	4
1951-52	Providence Reds	AHL	59	20	36	55	....	....	....	26	15	3	1	4	8
1952-53	Providence Reds	AHL	25	4	7	11	....	....	....	13	....	....	....	....	....
1953-54	Providence Reds	AHL	23	3	9	12	....	....	....	12	....	....	....	....	....
	Sydney Millionaires	MMHL	6	0	0	0	....	....	....	0	....	....	....	....	....
1954-55	Hershey Bears	AHL	50	12	16	28	....	....	....	16	....	....	....	....	....
1955-56	Hershey Bears	AHL	64	16	35	51	....	....	....	22	....	....	....	....	....
1956-57	Hershey Bears	AHL	17	0	2	2	....	....	....	4	....	....	....	....	....
	NHL Totals		331	78	93	171	112	137	249	49	30	8	13	21	6

Traded to **Toronto** by **Boston** with Fern Flaman and Phil Maloney for Leo Boivin, Bill Ezinicki and Vic Lynn, November 15, 1950. Traded to **Providence** (AHL) by **Toronto** for cash, November 10, 1951.

• SMITH, NAKINA
Nakina (Dalton) Smith
C – L. 5'10", 150 lbs. b: Cache Bay, Ont., 7/26/1915.

Season	Club	League	GP	G	A	Pts	AG	AA	APts	PIM	GP	G	A	Pts	PIM
1931-32	Sudbury Jr. Wolves	City Jr.	3	*5	2	*7	....	....	....	4	....	....	....	....	....
	Sudbury Wolves	City Sr.	9	7	2	9	....	....	....	6	....	....	....	....	....
1932-33	Sudbury Jr. Wolves	City Jr.	7	4	1	5	....	....	....	16	2	0	1	1	2
1933-34	Toronto Torontos	OHA Sr.	5	4	3	7	....	....	....	7	2	0	0	0	0
1934-35	Oshawa Chevies	Tor-Sr.	15	8	*19	*27	....	....	....	2	....	....	....	....	....
1935-36	London–Rochester	IAHL	46	5	11	16	....	....	....	8	....	....	....	....	....
1936-37	New Haven Eagles	AHL	46	4	17	21	....	....	....	10	....	....	....	....	....
1937-38	Minneapolis Millers	AHA	48	15	25	40	....	....	....	30	7	1	2	3	0
1938-39	Minneapolis Millers	AHA	48	30	*52	82	....	....	....	10	4	1	0	1	0
1939-40	Minneapolis Millers	AHA	45	32	36	68	....	....	....	12	3	0	2	2	2
1940-41	St. Louis Flyers	AHA	46	6	21	27	....	....	....	8	9	3	5	*8	10
1941-42	St. Louis Flyers	AHA	50	19	39	58	....	....	....	27	3	0	1	1	0
1942-43	Washington–New Haven	AHL	55	14	26	40	....	....	....	28	....	....	....	....	....
	Philadelphia Falcons	EHL	....	....	....	....	....	....	....	....	9	8	9	17	2
1943-44	**Detroit Red Wings**	**NHL**	10	1	2	3	1	2	3	0	....	....	....	....	....
	Indianapolis Capitals	AHL	34	11	23	34	....	....	....	11	5	0	1	1	0
1944-45	St. Louis Flyers	AHL	60	11	31	42	....	....	....	22	....	....	....	....	....
1945-46	Dallas Texans	USHL	25	5	13	18	....	....	....	2	....	....	....	....	....
	Minneapolis Millers	USHL	27	11	13	24	....	....	....	4	....	....	....	....	....
	Buffalo Bisons	AHL	3	0	3	3	....	....	....	0	....	....	....	....	....
1946-47	St. Paul Saints	USHL	60	14	32	46	....	....	....	6	....	....	....	....	....
1947-48	St. Paul Saints	USHL	53	9	13	22	....	....	....	2	....	....	....	....	....
1948-49	Los Angeles Monarchs	PCHL	63	34	28	62	....	....	....	34	7	0	4	4	10
1949-50	Los Angeles Monarchs	PCHL	1	0	1	1	....	....	....	0	....	....	....	....	....
	NHL Totals		10	1	2	3	1	2	3	0	....	....	....	....	....

AHA First All-Star Team (1939) • AHA Second All-Star Team (1940) • PCHL Southern Second All-Star Team (1949)

• SMITH, RODGER
Rodger Smith
D – L. 6', 175 lbs. b: Ottawa, Ont., 7/26/1896. d: 1/31/1935.

Season	Club	League	GP	G	A	Pts	AG	AA	APts	PIM	GP	G	A	Pts	PIM
1919-20	Ottawa War Vets	City Sr.	7	3	0	3	....	....	....	22			....	....	....
1920-21	Ottawa Gunners	City Sr.	13	6	0	6	....	....	....	....	6	1	3	4	*9
1921-22	Ottawa Gunners	City Sr.	10	6	3	9	....	....	....	9	6	6	5	11	15
1922-23	Ottawa Gunners	City Sr.	17	*19	*10	*29	....	....	....	21	....	....	....	....	....
1923-24	Pittsburgh Yellowjackets	USAHA	20	9	2	11	....	....		....	12	4	1	5	12
1924-25	Pittsburgh Yellowjackets	USAHA	34	8	0	8	....	....	....	....	8	1	0	1	....
1925-26	**Pittsburgh Pirates**	**NHL**	36	9	1	10	28	11	39	22	2	1	0	1	0
1926-27	**Pittsburgh Pirates**	**NHL**	36	4	0	4	12	0	12	6	....	....	....	....	....
1927-28	**Pittsburgh Pirates**	**NHL**	43	1	0	1	3	0	3	30	2	2	0	2	0
1928-29	**Pittsburgh Pirates**	**NHL**	44	4	2	6	16	18	34	49	....	....	....	....	....
1929-30	**Pittsburgh Pirates**	**NHL**	42	2	1	3	4	3	7	65	....	....	....	....	....
1930-31	**Philadelphia Quakers**	**NHL**	9	0	0	0	0	0	0	0	....	....	....	....	....
	Pittsburgh Yellowjackets	IAHL	26	1	0	1	....	....	....	2	6	0	0	0	4
	Niagara Falls Cataracts	Can-Pro	12	0	0	0	....	....	....	0	....	....	....	....	....
1931-32	Chicoutimi Carabins	ECHL	23	6	10	16	....	....	....	36	3	0	0	0	2
	NHL Totals		210	20	4	24	63	32	95	172	4	3	0	3	0

Signed as a free agent by **Pittsburgh**, September 26, 1925. Transferred to **Philadelphia** after **Pittsburgh** franchise relocated, October 18, 1930. Traded to **Pittsburgh** (IAHL) by **Philadelphia**, December 16, 1930.

• SMITH, SID
Sid Smith
LW – L. 5'10", 173 lbs. b: Toronto, Ont., 7/11/1925.

Season	Club	League	GP	G	A	Pts	AG	AA	APts	PIM	GP	G	A	Pts	PIM
			REGULAR SEASON								PLAYOFFS				
1944-45	Oshawa Generals	OHA	20	10	7	17	....	....	....	18	3	0	1	1	0
1945-46	Toronto Staffords	OHA Sr.	13	9	12	21	....	....	....	2	10	6	7	13	0
1946-47	**Toronto Maple Leafs**	**NHL**	14	2	1	3	3	1	4	0	....	....	....	....	....
	Quebec Aces	QSHL	15	12	5	17	....	....	....	6	....	....	....	....	....
	Pittsburgh Hornets	AHL	23	12	5	17	....	....	....	4	....	....	....	....	....
1947-48	**Toronto Maple Leafs**	**NHL**	31	7	10	17	10	15	25	10	2	0	0	0	0
	Pittsburgh Hornets	AHL	30	23	17	40	....	....	....	11	....	....	....	....	....
1948-49	**Toronto Maple Leafs**	**NHL**	1	0	0	0	0	0	0	0	6	5	2	7	0
	Pittsburgh Hornets	AHL	68	*55	57	*112	....	....	....	4	....	....	....	....	....
1949-50	**Toronto Maple Leafs**	**NHL**	68	22	23	45	30	29	59	6	7	0	3	3	2
1950-51	**Toronto Maple Leafs**	**NHL**	70	30	21	51	41	27	68	10	11	7	3	10	0
1951-52	**Toronto Maple Leafs**	**NHL**	70	27	30	57	39	39	78	6	4	0	0	0	0
1952-53	**Toronto Maple Leafs**	**NHL**	70	20	19	39	31	27	58	6	....	....	....	....	....
1953-54	**Toronto Maple Leafs**	**NHL**	70	22	16	38	34	22	56	28	5	1	1	2	0
1954-55	**Toronto Maple Leafs**	**NHL**	70	33	21	54	49	27	76	14	4	3	1	4	0
1955-56	**Toronto Maple Leafs**	**NHL**	55	4	17	21	6	21	27	8	5	1	0	1	0
1956-57	**Toronto Maple Leafs**	**NHL**	70	17	24	41	23	28	51	4	....	....	....	....	....
1957-58	**Toronto Maple Leafs**	**NHL**	12	2	1	3	3	1	4	2	....	....	....	....	....
	Whitby Dunlops	OHA Sr.	28	24	19	43	....	....	....	4	....	....	....	....	....
	Canada	WEC-A	7	9	5	14	....	....	....	2	....	....	....	....	....
1958-59	Whitby Dunlops	OHA Sr.	51	*35	35	70	....	....	....	20	10	*7	4	11	2
	NHL Totals		601	186	183	369	269	237	506	94	44	17	10	27	2

AHL First All-Star Team (1949) • Won John B. Sollenberger Trophy (Top Scorer - AHL) (1949) • NHL Second All-Star Team (1951, 1952) • Won Lady Byng Trophy (1952, 1955) • NHL First All-Star Team (1955)

Played in NHL All-Star Game (1949, 1950, 1951, 1952, 1953, 1954, 1955)

• SMITH, STAN
Stan Smith
C – L. 5'10", 165 lbs. b: Coal Creek, B.C., 8/13/1917.

Season	Club	League	GP	G	A	Pts	AG	AA	APts	PIM	GP	G	A	Pts	PIM
1936-37	Trail Tigers	Koot-Jr.	STATISTICS NOT AVAILABLE												
	Trail Smoke Eaters	Kootenay	2	0	2	2	....	....	....	0	....	....	....	....	....
1937-38	Rossland Miners	Kootenay	23	19	17	36	....	....	....	14	....	....	....	....	....
1938-39	New York Rovers	EHL	53	23	27	50	....	....	....	12	....	....	....	....	....
1939-40	**New York Rangers**	**NHL**	1	0	0	0	0	0	0	0	....	....	....	....	....
	Philadelphia Rockets	AHL	53	11	22	33	....	....	....	9	....	....	....	....	....
1940-41	**New York Rangers**	**NHL**	8	2	1	3	4	2	6	0	....	....	....	....	....
	Philadelphia Rockets	AHL	49	18	22	40	....	....	....	2	....	....	....	....	....
1941-42	Cleveland Barons	AHL	21	9	6	15	....	....	....	0	5	1	2	3	0
1942-43	Calgary Army	ASHL	8	1	3	4	....	....	....	0	2	0	3	3	0
1943-44	Nanaimo Clippers	City Sr.	....	....	....	....	....	....	....	....	2	0	2	2	0
1944-45			MILITARY SERVICE												
1945-46			MILITARY SERVICE												
1946-47	Minneapolis Millers	USHL	42	15	27	42	....	....	....	0	2	0	0	0	0
1947-48	Minneapolis Millers	USHL	51	17	25	42	....	....	....	2	10	3	5	8	0
1948-49	Minneapolis Millers	USHL	64	18	32	50	....	....	....	0	....	....	....	....	....
1949-50	Minneapolis Millers	USHL	32	1	10	11	....	....	....	2	....	....	....	....	....
	San Francisco Shamrocks	PCHL	31	2	14	16	....	....	....	2	4	0	0	0	0
	NHL Totals		9	2	1	3	4	2	6	0					....

Signed as a free agent by **NY Rangers**, October 23, 1939. Traded to **Cleveland** by **NY Rangers** for cash, September 9, 1941.

• SMITH, STU
Stu Smith
LW – L. 5'8", 165 lbs. b: Basswood, Man., 9/25/1918.

Season	Club	League	GP	G	A	Pts	AG	AA	APts	PIM	GP	G	A	Pts	PIM
1932-33	Kenora Thistles	MHL Jr.	10	*12	1	*13	....	....	....	4	7	3	1	4	6
1933-34	Kenora Thistles	MHL Jr.	16	*22	6	*28	....	....	....	10	9	*11	1	*12	12
1934-35	Kenora Canadians	MHL Sr.	11	9	4	13	....	....	....	5	....	....	....	....	....
1935-36	Kenora Thistles	MHL Sr.	12	*11	2	13	....	....	....	5	....	....	....	....	....
1936-37	Sudbury Creighton Mines	NOHA	14	*13	5	18	....	....	....	20	2	*2	0	2	0
1937-38	Sudbury Creighton Mines	NOHA	6	5	2	7			....	2	5	*3	0	3	8
1938-39	Kirkland Lake Blue Devils	NOHA	7	13	8	21	....	....	....	2	8	*10	2	12	4
1939-40	Kirkland Lake Blue Devils	NOHA	15	9	8	17	....	....	....	8	20	6	9	15	12
1940-41	**Montreal Canadiens**	**NHL**	3	2	1	3	4	2	6	2	1	0	0	0	0
	Quebec Royal Rifles	QSHL	35	*33	26	*59	....	....	....	37	4	0	0	0	4
1941-42	**Montreal Canadiens**	**NHL**	1	0	1	1	0	2	2	0	....	....	....	....	....
	Washington Eagles	EHL	55	22	28	50	....	....	....	2	2	0	0	0	0
1942-43	Ottawa Canadiens	QSHL	10	11	14	25	....	....	....	6	8	6	7	13	2
1943-44	Ottawa Commandos	QSHL	25	10	17	27	....	....	....	2	3	1	1	2	2
	Hull Volants	QSHL	....	....	....	....	....	....	....	....	4	3	3	6	0
1944-45	Ottawa Commandos	QSHL	24	20	25	45	....	....	....	11	2	2	0	2	2
1945-46	Ottawa Senators	QSHL	36	29	35	64	....	....	....	10	7	7	2	9	9
1946-47	Ottawa Senators	QSHL	34	20	27	47	....	....	....	14	8	2	1	3	2
1947-48	Ottawa Senators	QSHL	45	21	42	63	....	....	....	6	12	5	7	12	8
1948-49	Ottawa Senators	QSHL	40	12	18	30	....	....	....	2	11	5	5	10	0
1949-50	Ottawa Senators	QSHL	53	27	22	49	....	....	....	6	5	2	2	4	0
1950-51	Smith Falls Rideaus	ECSHL	17	25	11	36	....	....	....	....	21	*22	16	38	8
1951-52	Smith Falls Rideaus	ECSHL	43	38	46	84	....	....	....	6	8	2	3	5	0
1952-53	Smith Falls Rideaus	ECSHL	47	38	38	*76	....	....	....	12	23	13	16	29	6
1953-54	Smith Falls Rideaus	ECSHL	19	19	23	42	....	....	....	6	13	0	5	5	12
	NHL Totals		4	2	2	4	4	4	8	2	1	0	0	0	0

• SMITH, TOMMY
Tommy Smith HHOF
C – L. 5'6", 150 lbs. b: Ottawa, Ont., 9/27/1886. d: 8/1/1966.

Season	Club	League	GP	G	A	Pts	AG	AA	APts	PIM	GP	G	A	Pts	PIM
1905-06	Ottawa Vics	FAHL	8	*12	0	*12	....	....	....	....	....	....	....	....	....
	Ottawa Senators	ECAHA	3	6	0	6	....	....	....	12	1	0	0	0	9
1906-07	Pittsburgh Hockey Club	IHL	23	31	13	44	....	....	....	47	....	....	....	....	....
1907-08	Pittsburgh Lyceum	WPHL	16	*33	0	*33	....	....	....	....	1	2	0	2	....
1908-09	Pittsburgh Lyceum	WPHL	6	13	0	13	....	....	....	....	....	....	....	....	....
	Brantford Redmen	OPHL	13	*40	0	*40	....	....	....	30	....	....	....	....	....
	Haileybury Silver Kings	City Sr.	1	3	0	3	....	....	....	2	2	*3	0	*3	0
1909-10	Brantford Redmen	OPHL	1	1	0	1	....	....	....	....	....	....	....	....	....
	Cobalt Silver Kings	NHA	10	24	0	24	....	....	....	....	....	....	....	....	....
1910-11	Galt Professionals	OPHL	18	22	0	22	....	....	....	....	3	*7	0	*7	0
1911-12	Moncton Victorias	MPHL	18	53	0	53	....	....	....	*48	2	2	0	2	3
1912-13	Quebec Bulldogs	NHA	18	39	0	39	....	....	....	30	2	4	0	4	0
1913-14	Quebec Bulldogs	NHA	20	*39	6	*45	....	....	....	35	....	....	....	....	....
1914-15	Toronto Shamrocks	NHA	10	*17	2	*19	....	....	....	14	....	....	....	....	....
	Quebec Bulldogs	NHA	9	*23	2	*25	....	....	....	29	....	....	....	....	....
1915-16	Quebec Bulldogs	NHA	22	16	3	19	....	....	....	30	....	....	....	....	....
1916-17	Montreal Canadiens	NHA	15	9	3	12	....	....	....	32	6	4	0	4	....
1917-18	Mechanical Transport	Mtl-Sr.	DID NOT PLAY – COACHING												
1918-19	Glace Bay Miners	CBSHL	DID NOT PLAY – COACHING												
1919-20	**Quebec Bulldogs**	**NHL**	**10**	**0**	**1**	**1**	**0**	**7**	**7**	**11**	....	....	....	....	....
	NHL Totals		**10**	**0**	**1**	**1**	**0**	**7**	**7**	**11**	....	....	....	....	....
	Other Major League Totals		177	314	29	343	....	....	....	295	13	17	0	17	3

Traded to **Montreal Canadiens** (NHA) by **Quebec** (NHA) for cash, January 4, 1917. Rights retained by **Montreal Canadiens** after NHA folded, November 26, 1917. Traded to **Ottawa** by **Montreal Canadiens** for cash, November 28, 1918. Transferred to **Quebec** by **Ottawa** when Quebec franchise returned to NHL, November 25, 1919.

• SMITH, WAYNE
Wayne Smith
D – L. 6', 195 lbs. b: Kamsack, Sask., 2/12/1943.

Season	Club	League	GP	G	A	Pts	AG	AA	APts	PIM	GP	G	A	Pts	PIM
1959-60	Saskatoon Quakers	SJHL	1	0	1	1	....	....	....	0	....	....	....	....	....
1960-61	Saskatoon Quakers	SJHL	60	12	19	31	....	....	....	79	....	....	....	....	....
1961-62	University of Denver	WCHA	DID NOT PLAY – FRESHMAN												
1962-63	University of Denver	WCHA	6	8	3	11				24	....	....	....	....	....
1963-64	University of Denver	WCHA	31	6	5	11				85	....	....	....	....	....
1964-65	University of Denver	WCHA	STATISTICS NOT AVAILABLE												
1965-66	University of Denver	WCHA	32	8	17	25	....	....	....	72	....	....	....	....	....
1966-67	**Chicago Black Hawks**	**NHL**	**2**	**1**	**1**	**2**	**1**	**1**	**2**	**2**	**1**	**0**	**0**	**0**	**0**
	St. Louis Braves	CHL	70	4	9	13	....	....	....	50	....	....	....	....	....
1967-68	Portland Buckaroos	WHL	68	2	14	16	....	....	....	52	12	0	0	0	0
1968-69	San Diego Gulls	WHL	1	0	0	0	....	....	....	0	....	....	....	....	....
	NHL Totals		**2**	**1**	**1**	**2**	**1**	**1**	**2**	**2**	**1**	**0**	**0**	**0**	**0**

WCHA Second All-Star Team (1964) • NCAA Championship All-Tournament Team (1964, 1966) • WCHA First All-Star Team (1965, 1966) • NCAA West First All-American Team (1965, 1966)

Signed as a free agent by **Chicago**, June 15, 1966.

• SMRKE, STAN
Stan Smrke
LW – L. 5'11", 180 lbs. b: Belgrade, Yugoslavia, 9/2/1928. d: 4/14/1977.

Season	Club	League	GP	G	A	Pts	AG	AA	APts	PIM	GP	G	A	Pts	PIM
1945-46	Copper Cliff Jr. Redmen	NOHA	3	4	0	4	....	....	....	0	....	....	....	....	....
1946-47	Toronto Young Rangers	OHA	5	0	0	0	....	....	....	0	....	....	....	....	....
1947-48	Atlantic City–Baltimore	EHL	28	9	16	25	....	....	....	14	....	....	....	....	....
1948-49	Chicoutimi Volants	QPHL	36	27	18	45	....	....	....	....	....	....	....	....	....
1949-50	Chicoutimi Sagueneens	QSHL	58	24	26	50	....	....	....	64	5	5	0	5	5
1950-51	Chicoutimi Sagueneens	QSHL	54	16	36	52	....	....	....	48	6	0	2	2	2
1951-52	Chicoutimi Sagueneens	QSHL	40	10	13	23	....	....	....	25	18	5	6	11	15
1952-53	Chicoutimi Sagueneens	QSHL	59	35	46	81	....	....	....	28	20	5	8	13	13
1953-54	Chicoutimi Sagueneens	QHL	62	11	32	43	....	....	....	24	7	0	2	2	0
1954-55	Chicoutimi Sagueneens	QHL	60	25	36	61	....	....	....	34	7	2	2	4	2
1955-56	Chicoutimi Sagueneens	QHL	45	26	32	58	....	....	....	20	5	1	3	4	7
1956-57	**Montreal Canadiens**	**NHL**	**4**	**0**	**0**	**0**	**0**	**0**	**0**	**0**	....	....	....	....	....
	Chicoutimi Sagueneens	QHL	33	20	18	38	....	....	....	22	....	....	....	....	....
1957-58	**Montreal Canadiens**	**NHL**	**5**	**0**	**3**	**3**	**0**	**3**	**3**	**0**	....	....	....	....	....
	Rochester Americans	AHL	63	20	19	39	....	....	....	32	....	....	....	....	....
1958-59	Chicoutimi Sagueneens	QHL	57	36	32	68	....	....	....	40	....	....	....	....	....
1959-60	Rochester Americans	AHL	67	*40	36	76	....	....	....	18	11	*7	6	13	2
1960-61	Rochester Americans	AHL	21	10	12	22	....	....	....	6	....	....	....	....	....
1961-62	Rochester Americans	AHL	40	7	19	26	....	....	....	14	2	0	0	0	0
1962-63	Rochester Americans	AHL	71	22	25	47	....	....	....	16	2	1	0	1	0
1963-64	Rochester Americans	AHL	59	23	19	42	....	....	....	26	2	0	0	0	0
1964-65	Rochester Americans	AHL	71	33	59	92	....	....	....	28	10	5	4	9	4
1965-66	Rochester Americans	AHL	50	11	20	31	....	....	....	8	8	0	1	1	0
1966-67	Rochester Americans	AHL	71	31	30	61	....	....	....	24	13	2	7	9	2
	NHL Totals		**9**	**0**	**3**	**3**	**0**	**3**	**3**	**0**	....	....	....	....	....

QSHL First All-Star Team (1953) • QHL Second All-Star Team (1956, 1959) • AHL First All-Star Team (1960)

Played in NHL All-Star Game (1957)

Traded to **Montreal** by **Chicoutimi** (QHL) for Jack LeClair, Jacques DesLauriers and Guy Rousseau, October, 1957. • Scored only NHL goal in 1957 All-Star Game, October 5, 1957. Traded to **Toronto** by **Montreal** for Al MacNeil, June 7, 1960.

• SMYLIE, ROD
Rod "Doctor" Smylie
RW/LW – R. 5'10", 170 lbs. b: Toronto, Ont., 9/28/1895. Deceased.

Season	Club	League	GP	G	A	Pts	AG	AA	APts	PIM	GP	G	A	Pts	PIM
1916-17	Toronto Dentals	OHA Sr.	7	7	0	7	....	....	....	....	7	5	2	7	4
1917-18	Toronto Dentals	OHA Sr.	8	13	0	13	....	....	....	....	2	0	0	0	0
1918-19	Toronto Dentals	OHA Sr.	7	8	5	13	....	....	....	....	2	1	1	2	0
1919-20	Toronto Dentals	OHA Sr.	5	8	3	11	....	....	....	0	....	....	....	....	....
1920-21	**Toronto St. Pats**	**NHL**	**23**	**2**	**1**	**3**	**5**	**9**	**14**	**2**	**2**	**0**	**0**	**0**	**0**
1921-22	**Toronto St. Pats**	**NHL**	**20**	**0**	**0**	**0**	**0**	**0**	**0**	**2**	**6**	**1**	***3**	**4**	**2**
1922-23	**Toronto St. Pats**	**NHL**	**2**	**0**	**0**	**0**	**0**	**0**	**0**	**0**	....	....	....	....	....
1923-24	**Ottawa Senators**	**NHL**	**14**	**1**	**1**	**2**	**4**	**17**	**21**	**6**	....	....	....	....	....
1924-25	**Toronto St. Pats**	**NHL**	**11**	**0**	**0**	**0**	**0**	**0**	**0**	**0**	**1**	**0**	**0**	**0**	**0**
1925-26	**Toronto St.Pats**	**NHL**	**5**	**0**	**0**	**0**	**0**	**0**	**0**	**0**	....	....	....	....	....
	NHL Totals		**75**	**3**	**2**	**5**	**9**	**26**	**35**	**10**	**9**	**1**	**3**	**4**	**2**

Signed as a free agent by **Toronto St. Pats**, December 15, 1920. Signed as a free agent by **Ottawa**, January 2, 1924. Signed as a free agent by **Toronto St. Pats**, January 27, 1925.

• SOLINGER, BOB
Bob "Solly" Solinger
RW/LW – L. 5'9", 170 lbs. b: Star City, Sask., 12/23/1925.

Season	Club	League	GP	G	A	Pts	AG	AA	APts	PIM	GP	G	A	Pts	PIM
1944-45	Prince Albert Hawks	SJHL	12	14	3	17	....	....	....	6	5	7	5	*12	6
1945-46	Cleveland Barons	AHL	1	0	0	0	....	....	....	0	....	....	....	....	....
	Philadelphia Falcons	EHL	44	10	9	19	....	....	....	50	12	5	3	8	11
1946-47	Minneapolis Millers	USHL	2	0	0	0	....	....	....	0	....	....	....	....	....
	Edmonton Flyers	WCSHL	38	11	16	27	....	....	....	*72	4	4	3	7	10
1947-48	Cleveland Barons	AHL	67	40	29	69	....	....	....	41	9	*7	6	*13	0
1948-49	Cleveland Barons	AHL	68	16	31	47	....	....	....	29	5	3	3	6	4
1949-50	Pittsburgh Hornets	AHL	44	10	17	27	....	....	....	34	....	....	....	....	....
1950-51	Pittsburgh Hornets	AHL	69	22	32	54	....	....	....	34	13	10	6	*16	4
1951-52	**Toronto Maple Leafs**	**NHL**	**24**	**5**	**3**	**8**	**7**	**4**	**11**	**4**	....	....	....	....	....
	Pittsburgh Hornets	AHL	44	23	20	43	....	....	....	24	11	3	6	9	4
1952-53	**Toronto Maple Leafs**	**NHL**	**18**	**1**	**1**	**2**	**2**	**1**	**3**	**2**	....	....	....	....	....
	Pittsburgh Hornets	AHL	42	26	30	56	....	....	....	51	10	4	5	9	24
1953-54	**Toronto Maple Leafs**	**NHL**	**39**	**3**	**2**	**5**	**5**	**3**	**8**	**2**	....	....	....	....	....
	Pittsburgh Hornets	AHL	22	10	19	29	....	....	....	4	5	1	1	2	12
1954-55	**Toronto Maple Leafs**	**NHL**	**17**	**1**	**5**	**6**	**1**	**6**	**7**	**11**	....	....	....	....	....
	Pittsburgh Hornets	AHL	46	12	24	36	....	....	....	36	10	6	7	13	6
1955-56	Pittsburgh Hornets	AHL	63	27	46	73	....	....	....	74	4	0	3	3	0
1956-57	Hershey Bears	AHL	61	19	30	49	....	....	....	16	7	1	1	2	11
1957-58	Hershey Bears	AHL	66	16	32	48	....	....	....	28	11	1	8	9	4
1958-59	Hershey Bears	AHL	69	12	24	36	....	....	....	46	12	3	7	10	23
1959-60	**Detroit Red Wings**	**NHL**	**1**	**0**	**0**	**0**	**0**	**0**	**0**	**0**	....	....	....	....	....
	Hershey Bears	AHL	45	8	15	23	....	....	....	18	....	....	....	....	....
	Edmonton Flyers	WHL	21	10	9	19	....	....	....	14	4	0	1	1	0
1960-61	Edmonton Flyers	WHL	67	23	19	42	....	....	....	10	....	....	....	....	....
1961-62	San Francisco Seals	WHL	70	30	55	85	....	....	....	4	2	1	0	1	0
1962-63	Los Angeles Blades	WHL	67	33	43	76	....	....	....	28	3	2	1	3	2
1963-64	Los Angeles Blades	WHL	59	13	20	33	....	....	....	25	6	2	2	4	0
1964-65	Red Deer Rustlers	ASHL	STATISTICS NOT AVAILABLE												
1965-66	Lacombe Rockets	ASHL	30	12	10	22	....	....	....	59	....	....	....	....	....
1966-67	Edmonton Nuggets	ASHL	25	7	17	24	....	....	....	26	8	4	3	7	10
1967-68	Edmonton Nuggets	ASHL	....	2	4	6	....	....	....	6	....	3	6	9	6
1968-69	Edmonton Monarchs	ASHL	....	8	25	33	....	....	....	36	....	0	7	7	2
	NHL Totals		**99**	**10**	**11**	**21**	**15**	**14**	**29**	**19**	....	....	....	....	....

Won Dudley "Red" Garrett Memorial Award (Top Rookie - AHL) (1948) • AHL Second All-Star Team (1953) • WHL Second All-Star Team (1962, 1963)

Traded to **Toronto** by **Cleveland** (AHL) for Ray Ceresino, Harry Taylor and the loan of Tod Sloan, September 6, 1949. Traded to **Detroit** (Hershey - AHL) by **Toronto** for cash, July 6, 1956. Traded to **San Francisco** (WHL) by **Detroit** for cash, July, 1962. Traded to **LA Blades** (WHL) by **San Francisco** (WHL) for Danny Belisle, July, 1962.

• SOMERS, ART
Art Somers
C – L. 5'5", 167 lbs. b: Winnipeg, Man., 1/19/1902. Deceased.

Season	Club	League	GP	G	A	Pts	AG	AA	APts	PIM	GP	G	A	Pts	PIM
1922-23	Winnipeg Falcons	MHL Sr.	16	10	6	16	....	....	....	33	2	0	0	0	2
1923-24	Winnipeg Falcons	MHL Sr.	12	10	6	16	....	....	....	14	....	....	....	....	....
1924-25	Fort William Forts	MHL Sr.	20	5	2	7	....	....	....	41	....	....	....	....	....
1925-26	Winnipeg Maroons	CHL	36	*21	5	26	....	....	....	61	5	1	1	2	12
1926-27	Winnipeg Maroons	CHL	32	11	10	21	....	....	....	73	3	0	1	1	7
1927-28	Winnipeg Maroons	CHL	40	8	6	14	....	....	....	71	....	....	....	....	....
1928-29	Vancouver Lions	PCHL	35	*23	7	*30	....	....	....	66	3	*3	0	3	2
1929-30	**Chicago Black Hawks**	**NHL**	**44**	**11**	**13**	**24**	**22**	**42**	**64**	**74**	**2**	**0**	**0**	**0**	**2**
1930-31	**Chicago Black Hawks**	**NHL**	**33**	**3**	**6**	**9**	**7**	**22**	**29**	**33**	**9**	**0**	**0**	**0**	**0**
1931-32	**New York Rangers**	**NHL**	**48**	**11**	**15**	**26**	**23**	**42**	**65**	**45**	**7**	**0**	**1**	**1**	**8**
1932-33	**New York Rangers**	**NHL**	**48**	**7**	**15**	**22**	**16**	**40**	**56**	**28**	**8**	**1**	***4**	**5**	**8**
1933-34	**New York Rangers**	**NHL**	**8**	**1**	**2**	**3**	**2**	**5**	**7**	**5**	**2**	**0**	**0**	**0**	**0**
	Windsor Bulldogs	IAHL	7	2	2	4	....	....	....	5	....	....	....	....	....
1934-35	**New York Rangers**	**NHL**	**41**	**0**	**5**	**5**	**0**	**11**	**11**	**4**	**2**	**0**	**0**	**0**	**2**
1935-36	Prince Albert Mintos	AJHL	DID NOT PLAY – COACHING												
	NHL Totals		**222**	**33**	**56**	**89**	**70**	**162**	**232**	**189**	**30**	**1**	**5**	**6**	**20**

Traded to **NY Rangers** by **Chicago** with Vic Desjardins for Paul Thompson, October 15, 1931.

• SONMOR, GLEN
Glen Sonmor
LW – L. 5'11", 165 lbs. b: Moose Jaw, Sask., 4/22/1929.

Season	Club	League	GP	G	A	Pts	AG	AA	APts	PIM	GP	G	A	Pts	PIM
1945-46	Hamilton Lloyds	Jr. B	1	0	1	1	....	....	....	0	....	....	....	....	....
1946-47			STATISTICS NOT AVAILABLE												
1947-48	Guelph Biltmores	OHA	36	21	15	36	....	....	....	20	....	....	....	....	....
1948-49	Brandon Wheat Kings	WCJHL	30	18	*30	48	....	....	....	40	25	10	*14	24	44
1949-50	Minneapolis Millers	USHL	55	17	43	60	....	....	....	25	7	2	4	6	7
1950-51	Cleveland Barons	AHL	65	14	35	49	....	....	....	47	11	3	4	7	14
1951-52	St. Louis Flyers	AHL	67	24	30	54	....	....	....	32	....	....	....	....	....
1952-53	Cleveland Barons	AHL	64	25	26	51	....	....	....	62	11	0	2	2	18
1953-54	**New York Rangers**	**NHL**	**15**	**2**	**0**	**2**	**3**	**0**	**3**	**17**	....	....	....	....	....
	Cleveland Barons	AHL	31	13	12	25	....	....	....	45	....	....	....	....	....
1954-55	**New York Rangers**	**NHL**	**13**	**0**	**0**	**0**	**0**	**0**	**0**	**4**	....	....	....	....	....
	Cleveland Barons	AHL	36	11	21	32	....	....	....	34	....	....	....	....	....
1955-56			DID NOT PLAY – INJURED												
1956-57	Ohio State University	CCHA	DID NOT PLAY – COACHING												
	NHL Totals		**28**	**2**	**0**	**2**	**3**	**0**	**3**	**21**	....	....	....	....	....

• Suffered career-ending eye injury in game vs. Pittsburgh (AHL) February 27, 1955.

• SORRELL, JOHN John "Long John" Sorrell
LW – L. 5'11", 155 lbs. b: Chesterville, Ont., 1/16/1906. d: 11/30/1984.

			REGULAR SEASON								PLAYOFFS				
Season	Club	League	GP	G	A	Pts	AG	AA	APts	PIM	GP	G	A	Pts	PIM
1927-28	Quebec Beavers	Can-Am	40	7	3	10	....	....	....	27	6	1	0	1	2
1928-29	Windsor Bulldogs	Can-Pro	42	16	7	23	....	....	....	36	8	1	1	2	6
1929-30	London Panthers	IAHL	42	*31	13	44	....	....	....	26	2	0	0	0	0
1930-31	**Detroit Falcons**	**NHL**	**39**	**9**	**7**	**16**	**22**	**25**	**47**	**10**	....	....	....	....	....
1931-32	**Detroit Falcons**	**NHL**	**48**	**8**	**5**	**13**	**17**	**14**	**31**	**22**	**2**	**1**	**0**	**1**	**0**
1932-33	**Detroit Red Wings**	**NHL**	**47**	**14**	**10**	**24**	**33**	**26**	**59**	**11**	**4**	**2**	**2**	**4**	**4**
1933-34	**Detroit Red Wings**	**NHL**	**47**	**21**	**10**	**31**	**47**	**27**	**74**	**8**	**8**	**0**	**2**	**2**	**0**
1934-35	**Detroit Red Wings**	**NHL**	**47**	**20**	**16**	**36**	**43**	**36**	**79**	**12**	....	....	....	....	....
	Detroit Olympics	IAHL	1	1	2	3	....	....	....	0	....	....	....	....	....
1935-36	**Detroit Red Wings**	**NHL**	**48**	**13**	**15**	**28**	**32**	**36**	**68**	**8**	**7**	**3**	**4**	**7**	**0**
1936-37	**Detroit Red Wings**	**NHL**	**48**	**8**	**16**	**24**	**17**	**38**	**55**	**4**	**10**	**2**	**4**	**6**	**2**
1937-38	**Detroit Red Wings**	**NHL**	**23**	**3**	**7**	**10**	**6**	**14**	**20**	**0**	....	....	....	....	....
	New York Americans	**NHL**	**17**	**8**	**2**	**10**	**17**	**4**	**21**	**9**	**6**	**4**	**0**	**4**	**2**
1938-39	**New York Americans**	**NHL**	**48**	**13**	**9**	**22**	**27**	**17**	**44**	**10**	**2**	**0**	**0**	**0**	**0**
1939-40	**New York Americans**	**NHL**	**48**	**8**	**16**	**24**	**17**	**32**	**49**	**4**	**3**	**0**	**3**	**3**	**2**
1940-41	**New York Americans**	**NHL**	**30**	**2**	**6**	**8**	**4**	**11**	**15**	**2**	....	....	....	....	....
	Springfield–Hershey	AHL	20	1	7	8	....	....	....	16	10	1	2	3	10
1941-42	Hershey Bears	AHL	53	23	14	37	....	....	....	2	10	0	4	4	0
1942-43	Hershey Bears	AHL	49	24	28	52	....	....	....	8	6	4	2	6	0
1943-44	Indianapolis Capitals	AHL	51	16	22	38	....	....	....	6	5	4	4	8	2
1944-45	Indianapolis Capitals	AHL	56	21	21	42	....	....	....	8	5	2	0	2	2
1945-46	Indianapolis Capitols	AHL	DID NOT PLAY – COACHING												
	NHL Totals		**490**	**127**	**119**	**246**	**282**	**280**	**562**	**100**	**42**	**12**	**15**	**27**	**10**

Traded to **London** (IAHL) by **Montreal Canadiens** for cash, November 5, 1929. Traded to **Detroit Falcons** by **London** (IAHL) for Herb Stuart, February 8, 1930. Traded to **NY Americans** by **Detroit** for Hap Emms, February 13, 1938.

• SPARROW, EMORY Emory "Spunk" Sparrow
RW/C – L. 5'11", 180 lbs. b: Hartney, Man., 9/15/1898. d: 2/2/1965.

			REGULAR SEASON								PLAYOFFS				
Season	Club	League	GP	G	A	Pts	AG	AA	APts	PIM	GP	G	A	Pts	PIM
1915-16	Winnipeg 61st Battalion	MHL Sr.	7	4	4	8	....	....	....	20	....	....	....	....	....
1916-17			MILITARY SERVICE												
1917-18	Winnipeg Somme	MHL Sr.	8	14	7	21	....	....	....	22	....	....	....	....	....
1918-19	Winnipeg Argonauts	MHL Sr.	9	22	*10	*32	....	....	....	6	....	....	....	....	....
1919-20	Moose Jaw Canucks	SSHL	10	11	1	12	....	....	....	30	2	1	0	1	3
1920-21	Moose Jaw Canucks	SSHL	13	15	6	21	....	....	....	*56	4	3	0	3	6
1921-22	Regina Capitals	WCHL	14	10	2	12	....	....	....	6	4	0	0	0	7
1922-23	Regina Capitals	WCHL	23	6	4	10	....	....	....	33	....	....	....	....	....
1923-24	Edmonton Eskimos	WCHL	23	11	6	17	....	....	....	34	....	....	....	....	....
1924-25	Calgary Tigers	WCHL	16	7	8	15	....	....	....	48	2	0	0	0	2
	Boston Bruins	**NHL**	**6**	**0**	**0**	**0**	**0**	**0**	**0**	**4**	....	....	....	....	....
1925-26	Calgary Tigers	WHL	11	3	2	5	....	....	....	34	....	....	....	....	....
	Edmonton Eskimos	WHL	17	11	2	13	....	....	....	32	2	0	0	0	6
1926-27	Calgary Tigers	PHL	32	26	*25	51	....	....	....	58	2	2	0	2	2
1927-28	Minneapolis Millers	AHA	5	1	1	2	....	....	....	8	....	....	....	....	....
	Regina Capitals	PHL	16	9	7	16	....	....	....	14	....	....	....	....	....
1928-29	Philadelphia Arrows	Can-Am	23	2	2	4	....	....	....	22	....	....	....	....	....
	NHL Totals		**6**	**0**	**0**	**0**	**0**	**0**	**0**	**4**	....	....	....	....	....
	Other Major League Totals		104	48	24	72	....	....	....	187	8	0	0	0	15

Signed as a free agent by **Regina** (WCHL), December 27, 1921. Traded to **Edmonton** (WCHL) by **Regina** (WCHL) with $1500 for Art Gagne, October 3, 1923. Traded to **Calgary** (WCHL) by **Edmonton** (WCHL) for cash, August 28, 1924. Loaned to **Boston** by **Calgary** (WCHL), December 8, 1924. Traded to **Edmonton** (WHL) by **Calgary** (WHL) for cash, January 19, 1926. Traded to **Detroit Cougars** by **Edmonton** (WHL) for cash, October 5, 1926.

• SPENCE, GORDON Gordon (Edmund) Spence
LW – L. 5'7", 150 lbs. b: Haileybury, Ont., 7/25/1897. Deceased.

			REGULAR SEASON								PLAYOFFS				
Season	Club	League	GP	G	A	Pts	AG	AA	APts	PIM	GP	G	A	Pts	PIM
1916-17	Toronto 228th	NHA	1	0	0	0					....	....	....	....	....
1917-18			MILITARY SERVICE												
1918-19	New Liskeard Seniors	Sr. NOHA	STATISTICS NOT AVAILABLE												
1919-20	Haileybury Rexalls	Sr. NOHA	STATISTICS NOT AVAILABLE												
1920-21	New Liskeard Seniors	Sr. NOHA	STATISTICS NOT AVAILABLE												
1921-22	New Liskeard Seniors	Sr. NOHA	STATISTICS NOT AVAILABLE												
1922-23			DID NOT PLAY												
1923-24			DID NOT PLAY												
1924-25	New Liskeard Senios	NOHA	STATISTICS NOT AVAILABLE												
1925-26	**Toronto St. Pats**	**NHL**	**3**	**0**	**0**	**0**	**0**	**0**	**0**	**0**	....	....	....	....	....
1926-27	South Porcupine Porkies	Sr. NOHA	STATISTICS NOT AVAILABLE												
	NHL Totals		**3**	**0**	**0**	**0**	**0**	**0**	**0**	**0**	....	....	....	....	....

Signed as a free agent by **Toronto St. Pats**, December 31, 1925.

• SPENCER, IRV — *see page 1495*

• SPEYER, CHRIS Chris "Duke" Speyer
D – L. 5'10", 170 lbs. b: Toronto, Ont., 2/6/1907. Deceased.

			REGULAR SEASON								PLAYOFFS				
Season	Club	League	GP	G	A	Pts	AG	AA	APts	PIM	GP	G	A	Pts	PIM
1921-22	Toronto Granites	OHA	5	0	1	1	....	....	....	....	....	....	....	....	....
1922-23	Toronto Aura Lee	OHA Sr.	12	1	0	1	....	....	....	....	....	....	....	....	....
1923-24	**Toronto St. Pats**	**NHL**	**3**	**0**	**0**	**0**	**0**	**0**	**0**	**0**	....	....	....	....	....
	Toronto Aura Lee	OHA Sr.	6	3	1	4	....	....	....	....	....	....	....	....	....
1924-25	**Toronto St. Pats**	**NHL**	**2**	**0**	**0**	**0**	**0**	**0**	**0**	**0**	....	....	....	....	....
1925-26	Toronto Aura Lee	OHA Sr.	STATISTICS NOT AVAILABLE												
1926-27	Niagara Falls–London	Can-Pro	24	3	0	3	....	....	....	24	4	0	0	0	0
1927-28	Niagara Falls Cataracts	Can-Pro	38	3	5	8	....	....	....	46	....	....	....	....	....
1928-29	New Haven Eagles	Can-Am	39	3	2	5	....	....	....	38	2	0	0	0	6
1929-30	New Haven Eagles	Can-Am	40	8	8	16	....	....	....	87	....	....	....	....	....
1930-31	New Haven Eagles	Can-Am	40	8	10	18	....	....	....	83	....	....	....	....	....
1931-32	New Haven Eagles	Can-Am	38	6	13	19	....	....	....	53	2	1	1	2	2
1932-33	New Haven Eagles	Can-Am	48	13	13	26	....	....	....	50	....	....	....	....	....
1933-34	**New York Americans**	**NHL**	**9**	**0**	**0**	**0**	**0**	**0**	**0**	**0**	....	....	....	....	....
	Syracuse Stars	IAHL	4	0	0	0	....	....	....	0	....	....	....	....	....
	New Haven Eagles	Can-Am	20	2	3	5	....	....	....	10	....	....	....	....	....
1934-35	Providence Reds	Can-Am	47	7	3	10	....	....	....	21	6	0	1	1	0
1935-36	Springfield Indians	Can-Am	48	8	12	20	....	....	....	18	2	0	1	1	2
	NHL Totals		**14**	**0**	**0**	**0**	**0**	**0**	**0**	**0**	....	....	....	....	....

Can-Am Second All-Star Team (1930)

Signed as a free agent by **Toronto St. Pats**, February 23, 1924. Signed as a free agent by **NY Americans**, November 1, 1933.

• SPRING, JESSE Jesse Spring
D – L. 6', 185 lbs. b: Alba, PA, 1/18/1901. d: 3/25/1942.

			REGULAR SEASON								PLAYOFFS				
Season	Club	League	GP	G	A	Pts	AG	AA	APts	PIM	GP	G	A	Pts	PIM
1922-23	Toronto Clarkes	City Sr.	STATISTICS NOT AVAILABLE												
1923-24	**Hamilton Tigers**	**NHL**	**20**	**3**	**2**	**5**	**12**	**35**	**47**	**8**	....	....	....	....	....
1924-25	**Hamilton Tigers**	**NHL**	**29**	**2**	**0**	**2**	**7**	**0**	**7**	**11**	....	....	....	....	....
1925-26	**Pittsburgh Pirates**	**NHL**	**32**	**5**	**0**	**5**	**15**	**0**	**15**	**23**	**2**	**0**	**2**	**2**	**2**
1926-27	**Toronto Maple Leafs**	**NHL**	**2**	**0**	**0**	**0**	**0**	**0**	**0**	**0**	....	....	....	....	....
	Niagara Falls Cataracts	Can-Pro	10	0	0	0	....	....	....	14	....	....	....	....	....
1927-28	Niagara Falls Cataracts	Can-Pro	39	1	3	4	....	....	....	57	....	....	....	....	....
1928-29	**New York Americans**	**NHL**	**23**	**0**	**0**	**0**	**0**	**0**	**0**	**0**	....	....	....	....	....
	New Haven Eagles	Can-Am	1	0	0	0	....	....	....	0	....	....	....	....	....
	Pittsburgh Pirates	**NHL**	**5**	**0**	**0**	**0**	**0**	**0**	**0**	**2**	....	....	....	....	....
1929-30	**New York Americans**	**NHL**	**29**	**0**	**0**	**0**	**0**	**0**	**0**	**0**	....	....	....	....	....
	Pittsburgh Pirates	**NHL**	**22**	**1**	**0**	**1**	**2**	**0**	**2**	**18**	....	....	....	....	....
1930-31	Detroit Olympics	IAHL	28	2	3	5	....	....	....	22	....	....	....	....	....
1931-32	Cleveland Indians	IAHL	30	3	1	4	....	....	....	22	....	....	....	....	....
1932-33	Oshawa Blue Imps	OHA	DID NOT PLAY – COACHING												
	NHL Totals		**162**	**11**	**2**	**13**	**36**	**35**	**71**	**62**	**2**	**0**	**2**	**2**	**2**

Signed as a free agent by **Hamilton**, December 18, 1923. Transferred to **NY Americans** after NHL club purchased **Hamilton** franchise, September 26, 1925. Loaned to **Pittsburgh** by **NY Americans** for 1925-26 season, November 25, 1925. Traded to **Toronto** by **NY Americans** for Laurie Scott, November 15, 1926. Traded to **NY Americans** for cash, January, 1927. Traded to **Pittsburgh** by **NY Americans** with Edmond Bouchard for Tex White, February 15, 1929. Signed as a free agent by **Detroit Falcons**, November 6, 1930.

• STACKHOUSE, TED Ted Stackhouse
D – R. 6'1", 200 lbs. b: Wolfville, N.S.. d: 11/24/1975.

			REGULAR SEASON								PLAYOFFS				
Season	Club	League	GP	G	A	Pts	AG	AA	APts	PIM	GP	G	A	Pts	PIM
1920-21	Wolfville Seniors	NSSHL	1	0	1	1	....	....	....	0	....	....	....	....	....
1921-22	**Toronto St. Pats**	**NHL**	**13**	**0**	**0**	**0**	**0**	**0**	**0**	**2**	**5**	**0**	**0**	**0**	**0**
1922-23	Amherst Ramblers	NSSHL	1	0	0	0	....	....	....	0	....	....	....	....	....
	Sydney Millionaires	CBSHL	2	0	2	2	....	....	....	2	....	....	....	....	....
1923-24			REINSTATED AS AN AMATEUR												
1924-25			DID NOT PLAY – REFEREE												
1925-26	Manchester New England	NEHL	STATISTICS NOT AVAILABLE												
1926-27	Nashua Nationals	NEHL	26	9	3	12	....	....	....	9	4	1	1	2	2
	Providence Reds	Can-Am	5	0	0	0	....	....	....	2	....	....	....	....	....
1927-28	Nashua Nationals	NEHL	20	4	3	7	....	....	....	10	4	1	1	2	2
	NHL Totals		**13**	**0**	**0**	**0**	**0**	**0**	**0**	**2**	**5**	**0**	**0**	**0**	**0**

Signed as a free agent by **Toronto St. Pats**, December 23, 1921. Signed as a free agent by **Toronto St. Pats**, January 25, 1922.

• STAHAN, BUTCH Butch (Francis Ralph) Stahan
D – L. 6'1", 195 lbs. b: Minnedosa, Man., 10/29/1918. Deceased.

			REGULAR SEASON								PLAYOFFS				
Season	Club	League	GP	G	A	Pts	AG	AA	APts	PIM	GP	G	A	Pts	PIM
1934-35	Portage Terriers	MJHL	16	2	3	5	....	....	....	18	....	....	....	....	....
1935-36	Portage Terriers	MJHL	16	6	5	11	....	....	....	17	6	1	1	2	4
1936-37	Portage Terriers	MJHL	6	0	0	0	....	....	....	2	....	....	....	....	....
	Flin Flon Bombers	SSHL	18	6	4	10	....	....	....	43	6	0	0	0	*8
1937-38	Brandon Wheat Kings	MJHL	16	1	6	7	....	....	....	16	5	0	0	0	0
	Flin Flon Bombers	SSHL	24	0	1	1	....	....	....	0	0	2	0	2	10
1938-39	Creighton Eagles	NOHA	7	3	0	3	....	....	....	*27	1	0	0	0	2
1939-40	Kirkland Lakes Blue Devils	NOHA	13	2	2	4	....	....	....	32	5	1	1	2	4
1940-41	Quebec Aces	QSHL	36	6	12	18	....	....	....	60	4	0	1	1	22
1941-42	Quebec Aces	QSHL	....	....	....	....	....	....	....	....	8	1	4	5	*18
1942-43	Quebec Aces	QSHL	34	12	23	35	....	....	....	83	4	3	1	4	8
1943-44	Quebec Aces	QSHL	25	7	21	28	....	....	....	74	15	7	7	14	*44
1944-45	Montreal Royals	QSHL	19	7	11	18	....	....	....	72	4	0	1	1	14
	Montreal Canadiens	**NHL**	....	....	....	....	....	....	....	....	**3**	**0**	**1**	**1**	**2**
1945-46	Montreal Royals	QSHL	39	9	15	24	....	....	....	76	11	3	2	5	34
1946-47	Ottawa Senators	QSHL	40	10	26	36	....	....	....	116	9	2	8	10	30
1947-48	Ottawa Senators	QSHL	41	12	21	33	....	....	....	44	25	2	11	13	*67
1948-49	Ottawa Senators	QSHL	62	9	34	43	....	....	....	92	11	0	3	3	14
1949-50	Ottawa Senators	QSHL	60	9	18	27	....	....	....	116	7	0	4	4	16
1950-51	Ottawa Senators	QSHL	56	2	22	24	....	....	....	106	11	2	3	5	18
1951-52	Ottawa Senators	QSHL	59	10	16	26	....	....	....	76	7	2	0	2	4
1952-53	Ottawa Senators	QSHL	56	3	13	16	....	....	....	118	9	0	2	2	14
1953-54	Ottawa Senators	QHL	34	0	5	5	....	....	....	56	2	0	0	0	4
	Pembroke Lumber Kings	Ott-Sr.	11	1	1	2	....	....	....	24	....	....	....	....	....
1954-55	Ottawa Senators	QHL	8	0	1	1	....	....	....	23	....	....	....	....	....
	Toledo Mercurys	IHL	30	0	13	13	....	....	....	63	2	0	1	1	4
1955-56	Toledo-Marion Mercurys	IHL	59	4	29	32	....	....	....	198	9	2	3	5	12
1956-57	Toledo Mercurys	IHL	60	7	22	29	....	....	....	96	5	1	2	3	4
	NHL Totals		**0**	**0**	**0**	**0**	**0**	**0**	**0**	**0**	**3**	**0**	**1**	**1**	**2**

Traded to **Buffalo** (AHL) by **Montreal** for Tom Rockey, October 8, 1946.

• STALEY, AL Al "Rod" Staley
C – R. 6'1", 175 lbs. b: Regina, Sask., 9/21/1928

			REGULAR SEASON								PLAYOFFS				
Season	Club	League	GP	G	A	Pts	AG	AA	APts	PIM	GP	G	A	Pts	PIM
1944-45	Regina Commandos	SJHL	17	3	3	6	....	....	....	4	9	4	0	4	6
1945-46	Regina Commandos	SJHL	17	12	12	24	....	....	....	10	9	2	4	6	10
1946-47	Regina Pats	SJHL	23	22	27	49	....	....	....	21	6	*9	4	13	6
1947-48	Regina Pats	SJHL	28	37	30	67	....	....	....	43	5	3	*7	10	14
1948-49	**New York Rangers**	**NHL**	**1**	**0**	**1**	**1**	**0**	**2**	**2**	**0**	....	....	....	....	....
	New Haven Ramblers	AHL	2	0	0	0	....	....	....	0	....	....	....	....	....
	New York Rovers	EHL	51	17	21	38	....	....	....	15	....	....	....	....	....
1949-50	Regina–Saskatoon	WCSHL	25	8	4	12	....	....	....	6	5	2	1	3	8
1950-51	Saskatoon Quakers	WCSHL	59	28	29	57	....	....	....	46	4	0	3	3	0
1951-52	Trail Smoke Eaters	WIHL	43	20	24	44	....	....	....	61	3	1	3	4	0
1952-53	Moose Jaw Millers	SSHL	30	23	27	50	....	....	....	57	10	6	4	10	4
	NHL Totals		**1**	**0**	**1**	**1**	**0**	**2**	**2**	**0**	....	....	....	....	....

• STANFIELD, FRED — *see page 1498*

• STANFIELD, JACK Jack Stanfield
LW – L. 5′11″, 176 lbs. b: Toronto, Ont., 5/30/1942.

			REGULAR SEASON								PLAYOFFS				
Season	Club	League	GP	G	A	Pts	AG	AA	APts	PIM	GP	G	A	Pts	PIM
1960-61	Dixie Beehives	Jr. B	STATISTICS NOT AVAILABLE												
1961-62	St. Catharines Teepees	OHA	42	8	11	19	....	....	....	12	6	1	0	1	0
1962-63	Philadelphia Ramblers	EHL	68	33	34	67	....	....	....	38	3	0	0	0	4
1963-64	St. Louis Braves	CHL	63	23	33	56	....	....	....	39	6	1	1	2	0
1964-65	Buffalo Bisons	AHL	72	19	20	39	....	....	....	34	9	2	5	7	4
1965-66	Buffalo Bisons	AHL	59	13	11	24	....	....	....	42	....	....	....	....	....
	Chicago Black Hawks	**NHL**	....	....	....	....	....	....	....	....	**1**	**0**	**0**	**0**	**0**
1966-67	Los Angeles Blades	WHL	47	12	10	22	....	....	....	29	....	....	....	....	....
1967-68	Dallas Black Hawks	CHL	67	20	21	41	....	....	....	31	2	0	0	0	0
1968-69	San Diego Gulls	WHL	68	14	13	27	....	....	....	18	7	1	1	2	0
1969-70	Rochester Americans	AHL	66	21	21	42	....	....	....	19	....	....	....	....	....
1970-71	Rochester Americans	AHL	48	11	9	20	....	....	....	35	....	....	....	....	....
1971-72	Rochester Americans	AHL	62	11	16	27	....	....	....	74	....	....	....	....	....
1972-73	Houston Aeros	WHA	71	8	12	20	....	....	....	8	9	1	0	1	0
1973-74	Houston Aeros	WHA	41	1	3	4	....	....	....	2	7	0	0	0	2
	Macon Whoopees	SHL	3	6	1	7	....	....	....	4	....	....	....	....	....
	NHL Totals		**0**	**0**	**0**	**0**	**0**	**0**	**0**	**0**	**1**	**0**	**0**	**0**	**0**
	Other Major League Totals		112	9	15	24	....	....	....	10	16	1	0	1	2

Claimed by **Vancouver** (WHL) from **Chicago** in Reverse Draft, June, 1969. Selected by **Dayton-Houston** (WHA) in 1972 WHA General Player Draft, February 12, 1972.

• STANKIEWICZ, ED Ed Stankiewicz
C – R. 5′9″, 165 lbs. b: Kitchener, Ont., 12/1/1929.

			REGULAR SEASON								PLAYOFFS				
Season	Club	League	GP	G	A	Pts	AG	AA	APts	PIM	GP	G	A	Pts	PIM
1949-50	Windsor Spitfires	OHA	47	54	48	102	....	....	....	48	11	6	11	17	23
1950-51	Toronto Marlboros	OHA Sr.	32	7	17	24	....	....	....	42	3	0	0	0	6
1951-52	St. Louis Flyers	AHL	2	2	2	4	....	....	....	0	....	....	....	....	....
	Kitchener Dutchmen	OHA Sr.	48	41	46	87	....	....	....	34	5	1	3	4	11
1952-53	St. Louis Flyers	AHL	61	13	25	38	....	....	....	48	....	....	....	....	....
1953-54	**Detroit Red Wings**	**NHL**	**1**	**0**	**0**	**0**	**0**	**0**	**0**	**2**	....	....	....	....	....
	Sherbrooke Saints	QHL	71	31	30	61	....	....	....	67	5	1	1	2	2
1954-55	Edmonton Flyers	WHL	59	27	45	72	....	....	....	96	9	1	5	6	*28
1955-56	**Detroit Red Wings**	**NHL**	**5**	**0**	**0**	**0**	**0**	**0**	**0**	**0**	....	....	....	....	....
	Edmonton Flyers	WHL	54	33	30	63	....	....	....	54	3	2	0	2	4
1956-57	Edmonton Flyers	WHL	16	2	8	10	....	....	....	26	....	....	....	....	....
1957-58	Hershey Bears	AHL	65	13	19	32	....	....	....	56	11	3	1	4	18
1958-59	Hershey Bears	AHL	59	16	17	33	....	....	....	88	13	*5	2	7	34
1959-60	Seattle–Spokane	WHL	69	19	27	46	....	....	....	56	....	....	....	....	....
1960-61	Spokane–Seattle	WHL	66	19	20	39	....	....	....	73	11	1	2	3	21
1961-62	Sudbury Wolves	EPHL	69	31	24	55	....	....	....	86	5	3	0	3	8
1962-63	Los Angeles Blades	WHL	56	9	15	24	....	....	....	82	....	....	....	....	....
1963-64	Long Island Ducks	EHL	67	34	34	68	....	....	....	94	5	1	1	2	23
1964-65	Long Island Ducks	EHL	71	48	47	95	....	....	....	84	15	2	4	6	18
	NHL Totals		**6**	**0**	**0**	**0**	**0**	**0**	**0**	**2**	....	....	....	....	....

EHL Second All-Star Team (1964) • EHL North Second All-Star Team (1965)

Traded to **Spokane** (WHL) by **Seattle** (WHL) for Jim Powers, November, 1959. Traded to **LA Blades** (WHL) by **Detroit** for cash, July, 1962.

• STANLEY, ALLAN — *see page 1498*

• STANLEY, BARNEY Barney (Russell) Stanley HHOF
RW – L. 6′, 175 lbs. b: Paisley, Ont., 1/1/1893. d: 5/16/1971.

			REGULAR SEASON								PLAYOFFS				
Season	Club	League	GP	G	A	Pts	AG	AA	APts	PIM	GP	G	A	Pts	PIM
1914-15	Vancouver Millionaires	PCHA	5	7	1	8	....	....	....	0	3	6	0	6	0
	Edmonton Albertas	ASHL	STATISTICS NOT AVAILABLE												
1915-16	Vancouver Millionaires	PCHA	14	6	6	12	....	....	....	9	....	....	....	....	....
1916-17	Vancouver Millionaires	PCHA	23	28	*18	46	....	....	....	9	....	....	....	....	....
1917-18	Vancouver Millionaires	PCHA	18	11	6	17	....	....	....	9	6	3	0	3	9
1918-19	Vancouver Millionaires	PCHA	20	10	6	16	....	....	....	19	2	0	0	0	0
1919-20	Edmonton Eskimos	Big 4	12	10	12	22	....	....	....	20	2	0	1	1	*5
1920-21	Calgary Canadians	Big 4	15	11	*10	21	....	....	....	5	....	....	....	....	....
1921-22	Calgary Tigers	WCHL	24	26	5	31	....	....	....	17	....	....	....	....	....
1922-23	Regina Capitals	WCHL	29	14	7	21	....	....	....	10	2	1	0	1	2
1923-24	Regina Capitals	WCHL	30	15	11	26	....	....	....	27	2	1	0	1	2
1924-25	Edmonton Eskimos	WCHL	25	12	5	17	....	....	....	36	....	....	....	....	....
1925-26	Edmonton Eskimos	WHL	29	14	8	22	....	....	....	47	2	1	0	1	0
1926-27	Winnipeg Maroons	AHA	35	8	8	16	....	....	....	78	3	0	0	0	2
1927-28	**Chicago Black Hawks**	**NHL**	**1**	**0**	**0**	**0**	**0**	**0**	**0**	**0**	....	....	....	....	....
1928-29	Minneapolis Millers	AHA	40	8	5	13	....	....	....	34	4	1	0	1	2
1929-30	Edmonton Poolers	AJHL	DID NOT PLAY – COACHING												
	NHL Totals		**1**	**0**	**0**	**0**	**0**	**0**	**0**	**0**	....	....	....	....	....
	Other Major League Totals		217	143	73	216	....	....	....	183	17	12	0	12	13

PCHA Second All-Star Team (1918) • WCHL First All-Star Team (1922, 1923)

Signed as a free agent by **Vancouver** (PCHA), February, 1915. Reinstated as an amateur, November 23, 1919. Signed as a free agent by **Calgary** (WCHL), November 30, 1921. Traded to **Regina** (WCHL) by **Calgary** (WCHL) for cash, November 13, 1922. Signed as a free agent by **Edmonton** (WCHL), November 7, 1924. Signed as a free agent by **Chicago** as Manager/Coach, September, 1927.

• STANOWSKI, WALLY Wally "The Whirling Dervish" Stanowski
D – L. 5′11″, 180 lbs. b: Winnipeg, Man., 4/28/1919.

			REGULAR SEASON								PLAYOFFS				
Season	Club	League	GP	G	A	Pts	AG	AA	APts	PIM	GP	G	A	Pts	PIM
1936-37	St. Boniface Seals	MHL Jr.	15	7	6	13	....	....	....	4	7	3	1	4	4
1937-38	St. Boniface Seals	MHL Jr.	15	8	13	21	....	....	....	7	10	4	*7	11	6
	Canadian Airways	Wpg-Sr.	6	4	3	7	....	....	....	0	....	....	....	....	....
1938-39	Syracuse Stars	AHL	54	1	16	17	....	....	....	8	3	0	2	2	0
1939-40	**Toronto Maple Leafs**	**NHL**	**27**	**2**	**7**	**9**	**4**	**14**	**18**	**11**	**10**	**1**	**0**	**1**	**2**
	Providence Reds	AHL	8	0	3	3	....	....	....	6	....	....	....	....	....
1940-41	**Toronto Maple Leafs**	**NHL**	**47**	**7**	**14**	**21**	**14**	**26**	**40**	**35**	**7**	**0**	**3**	**3**	**2**
1941-42	**Toronto Maple Leafs**	**NHL**	**24**	**1**	**7**	**8**	**2**	**11**	**13**	**10**	**13**	**2**	**8**	**10**	**2**
1942-43	Winnipeg RCAF	City Sr.	13	5	12	17	....	....	....	20	17	8	6	14	20
1943-44	Winnipeg RCAF	City Sr.	9	1	3	4	....	....	....	12	....	....	....	....	....
1944-45	Winnipeg RCAF	City Sr.	3	1	1	2	....	....	....	8	....	....	....	....	....
	Toronto Maple Leafs	**NHL**	**34**	**2**	**9**	**11**	**3**	**14**	**17**	**16**	**13**	**0**	**1**	**1**	**5**
1945-46	**Toronto Maple Leafs**	**NHL**	**45**	**3**	**10**	**13**	**5**	**19**	**24**	**10**	....	....	....	....	....
1946-47	**Toronto Maple Leafs**	**NHL**	**51**	**3**	**16**	**19**	**4**	**23**	**27**	**12**	**8**	**0**	**0**	**0**	**0**
1947-48	**Toronto Maple Leafs**	**NHL**	**54**	**2**	**11**	**13**	**3**	**16**	**19**	**12**	**9**	**0**	**2**	**2**	**2**
1948-49	**New York Rangers**	**NHL**	**60**	**1**	**8**	**9**	**2**	**13**	**15**	**16**	....	....	....	....	....
1949-50	**New York Rangers**	**NHL**	**37**	**1**	**1**	**2**	**1**	**1**	**2**	**10**	....	....	....	....	....
1950-51	**New York Rangers**	**NHL**	**49**	**1**	**5**	**6**	**1**	**6**	**7**	**28**	....	....	....	....	....
	Cincinnati Mohawks	AHL	7	0	0	0	....	....	....	2	....	....	....	....	....
1951-52	Cincinnati Mohawks	AHL	33	0	11	11	....	....	....	42	....	....	....	....	....
	NHL Totals		**428**	**23**	**88**	**111**	**39**	**143**	**182**	**160**	**60**	**3**	**14**	**17**	**13**

NHL First All-Star Team (1941)

Played in NHL All-Star Game (1947)

Traded to **NY Rangers** by **Toronto** with Elwyn Morris for Cal Gardner, Bill Juzda, Rene Trudell and the rights to Frank Mathers, June, 1948.

• STAPLETON, PAT — *see page 1500*

• STARR, HAROLD Harold "Twinkie" Starr
D – L. 5′11″, 176 lbs. b: Ottawa, Ont., 7/6/1906.

			REGULAR SEASON								PLAYOFFS				
Season	Club	League	GP	G	A	Pts	AG	AA	APts	PIM	GP	G	A	Pts	PIM
1925-26	Ottawa Shamrocks	City Sr.	2	1	0	1	....	....	....	0	....	....	....	....	....
1926-27	Ottawa Shamrocks	City Sr.	15	3	2	5	....	....	....	....	....	....	....	....	....
1927-28	Ottawa Shamrocks	City Sr.	STATISTICS NOT AVAILABLE												
1928-29	Ottawa Shamrocks	City Sr.	11	1	1	2	....	....	....	....	5	*4	0	*4	10
1929-30	**Ottawa Senators**	**NHL**	**28**	**2**	**1**	**3**	**4**	**3**	**7**	**12**	**2**	**1**	**0**	**1**	**0**
	London Panthers	IAHL	13	2	2	4	....	....	....	22	....	....	....	....	....
1930-31	**Ottawa Senators**	**NHL**	**35**	**2**	**1**	**3**	**5**	**4**	**9**	**48**	....	....	....	....	....
1931-32	**Montreal Maroons**	**NHL**	**47**	**1**	**2**	**3**	**2**	**6**	**8**	**47**	**4**	**0**	**0**	**0**	**0**
1932-33	**Ottawa Senators**	**NHL**	**31**	**0**	**0**	**0**	**0**	**0**	**0**	**30**	....	....	....	....	....
	Montreal Canadiens	**NHL**	**15**	**0**	**0**	**0**	**0**	**0**	**0**	**6**	**2**	**0**	**0**	**0**	**2**
1933-34	**Montreal Maroons**	**NHL**	....	....	....	....	....	....	....	....	**3**	**0**	**0**	**0**	**0**
	Windsor Bulldogs	IAHL	41	5	2	7	....	....	....	40	....	....	....	....	....
1934-35	**New York Rangers**	**NHL**	**33**	**1**	**1**	**2**	**2**	**2**	**4**	**31**	**4**	**0**	**0**	**0**	**2**
	Windsor Bulldogs	IAHL	15	0	0	0	....	....	....	12	....	....	....	....	....
1935-36	**New York Rangers**	**NHL**	**16**	**0**	**0**	**0**	**0**	**0**	**0**	**12**	....	....	....	....	....
	Cleveland Falcons	IAHL	16	1	1	2	....	....	....	19	2	0	0	0	0
1936-37			REINSTATED AS AN AMATEUR												
1937-38	Ottawa Senators	QSHL	22	1	2	3	....	....	....	12	5	0	0	0	0
1938-39	Ottawa LaSalle	City Sr.	16	3	0	3	....	....	....	12	5	1	2	3	10
	NHL Totals		**205**	**6**	**5**	**11**	**13**	**15**	**28**	**186**	**15**	**1**	**0**	**1**	**4**

Claimed by **Montreal Maroons** from **Ottawa** for 1931-32 season in Dispersal Draft, September 26, 1931. Traded to **Montreal Canadiens** by **Ottawa** with Leo Bourgeault for Marty Burke and future considerations (Nick Wasnie, March 23, 1933), January 14, 1933. Claimed on waivers by **Montreal Maroons** from **Montreal Canadiens**, December 5, 1933. Traded to **NY Rangers** by **Montreal Maroons** for cash, December 23, 1934.

• STARR, WILF Wilf "Twinkie" Starr
C – L. 5′11″, 190 lbs. b: St. Boniface, Man., 7/22/1909.

			REGULAR SEASON								PLAYOFFS				
Season	Club	League	GP	G	A	Pts	AG	AA	APts	PIM	GP	G	A	Pts	PIM
1927-28	Winnipeg Columbus Club	City Jr.	3	2	2	4	....	....	....	....	2	2	0	2	2
	Winnipeg CPR	City Sr.	3	2	0	2	....	....	....	8	....	....	....	....	....
1928-29	Winnipeg CPR	City Sr.	7	6	1	7	....	....	....	14	3	0	0	0	0
	University of Manitoba	City Sr.	6	6	4	10	....	....	....	12	2	0	0	0	2
1929-30	Winnipeg Winnipegs	City Sr.	12	7	*5	*12	....	....	....	10	2	0	0	0	0
1930-31	Springfield Indians	Can-Am	25	8	4	12	....	....	....	35	7	0	0	0	16
1931-32	Springfield Indians	Can-Am	38	19	11	30	....	....	....	38	....	....	....	....	....
1932-33	**New York Americans**	**NHL**	**26**	**4**	**3**	**7**	**9**	**8**	**17**	**8**	....	....	....	....	....
	Springfield Indians	Can-Am	8	1	0	1	....	....	....	4	....	....	....	....	....
1933-34	**Detroit Red Wings**	**NHL**	**28**	**2**	**2**	**4**	**4**	**5**	**9**	**17**	**7**	**0**	**2**	**2**	**2**
	Detroit Olympics	IAHL	19	8	2	10	....	....	....	22	....	....	....	....	....
1934-35	**Detroit Red Wings**	**NHL**	**24**	**1**	**1**	**2**	**2**	**2**	**4**	**0**	....	....	....	....	....
	Windsor–Detroit	IAHL	19	8	9	17	....	....	....	21	....	....	....	....	....
1935-36	**Detroit Red Wings**	**NHL**	**9**	**1**	**0**	**1**	**2**	**0**	**2**	**0**	....	....	....	....	....
	Detroit Olympics	IAHL	24	5	13	18	....	....	....	38	6	*6	*6	*12	*22
1936-37	Pittsburgh Hornets	AHL	44	5	21	26	....	....	....	87	5	0	2	2	10
1937-38	Providence Reds	AHL	31	5	13	18	....	....	....	28	7	3	4	7	4
1938-39	Providence Reds	AHL	50	16	33	49	....	....	....	61	5	0	3	3	*15
1939-40	Providence Reds	AHL	53	15	26	41	....	....	....	71	8	2	5	7	2
	NHL Totals		**87**	**8**	**6**	**14**	**17**	**15**	**32**	**25**	**7**	**0**	**2**	**2**	**2**

Signed as a free agent by **NY Rangers**, October 29, 1930. Traded to **NY Americans** by **NY Rangers** for cash, October 26, 1933. Traded to **Detroit** by **NY Americans** for cash, September, 1933.

• STASIUK, VIC

Vic "Yogi" Stasiuk
LW – L. 6', 185 lbs. b: Lethbridge, Alta., 5/23/1929.

Season	Club	League	GP	G	A	Pts	AG	AA	APts	PIM	PO GP	PO G	PO A	PO Pts	PO PIM
1946-47	Lethbridge Maple Leafs	AJHL	9	0	6	6	....	....	....	11	1	1	1	2	0
1947-48	Wetaskiwin Canadians	Edm-Jr.	STATISTICS NOT AVAILABLE												
1948-49	Kansas City Pla-Mors	USHL	66	7	13	20	....	....	....	52	2	0	0	0	0
1949-50	Chicago Black Hawks	NHL	17	1	1	2	1	1	2	2	....	....	....	....	....
	Kansas City Pla-Mors	USHL	39	10	13	23	....	....	....	27	....	....	....	....	....
1950-51	Chicago Black Hawks	NHL	20	5	3	8	7	4	11	6	....	....	....	....	....
	Detroit Red Wings	NHL	50	3	10	13	4	13	17	12	....	....	....	....	....
1951-52	Detroit Red Wings	NHL	58	5	9	14	7	12	19	19	7	0	2	2	0
	Indianapolis Capitals	AHL	8	7	1	8	....	....	....	6	....	....	....	....	....
1952-53	Detroit Red Wings	NHL	3	0	0	0	0	0	0	0	....	....	....	....	....
	Edmonton Flyers	WHL	48	37	43	80	....	....	....	71	....	....	....	....	....
1953-54	Detroit Red Wings	NHL	42	5	2	7	8	3	11	4	....	....	....	....	....
	Edmonton Flyers	WHL	21	6	12	18	....	....	....	37	13	2	6	8	23
1954-55	Detroit Red Wings	NHL	59	8	11	19	12	14	26	67	11	5	3	8	6
	Edmonton Flyers	WHL	11	7	6	13	....	....	....	32	....	....	....	....	....
1955-56	Boston Bruins	NHL	59	19	18	37	28	22	50	118	....	....	....	....	....
1956-57	Boston Bruins	NHL	64	24	16	40	33	19	52	69	10	2	1	3	2
1957-58	Boston Bruins	NHL	70	21	35	56	28	38	66	55	12	0	5	5	13
1958-59	Boston Bruins	NHL	70	27	33	60	34	35	69	63	7	4	2	6	11
1959-60	Boston Bruins	NHL	69	29	39	68	36	40	76	121	....	....	....	....	....
1960-61	Boston Bruins	NHL	46	5	25	30	6	25	31	35	....	....	....	....	....
	Detroit Red Wings	NHL	23	10	13	23	12	13	25	16	11	2	5	7	4
1961-62	Detroit Red Wings	NHL	59	15	28	43	18	28	46	45	....	....	....	....	....
1962-63	Detroit Red Wings	NHL	36	6	11	17	7	11	18	37	11	3	0	3	4
	Pittsburgh Hornets	AHL	22	9	20	29	....	....	....	24	....	....	....	....	....
1963-64	Pittsburgh Hornets	AHL	42	10	10	20	....	....	....	32	5	0	0	0	4
1964-65	Pittsburgh Hornets	AHL	63	14	21	35	....	....	....	58	3	0	0	0	0
1965-66	Memphis Wings	CHL	25	9	3	12	....	....	....	14	....	....	....	....	....
	NHL Totals		**745**	**183**	**254**	**437**	**241**	**278**	**519**	**669**	**69**	**16**	**18**	**34**	**40**

WHL First All-Star Team (1953)

Played in NHL All-Star Game (1960)

Traded to **Detroit** by **Chicago** with Bert Olmstead for Steve Black and Lee Fogolin, December 10, 1950. Traded to **Boston** by **Detroit** with Marcel Bonin, Lorne Davis and Terry Sawchuk for Gilles Boisvert, Real Chevrefils, Norm Corcoran, Warren Godfrey and Ed Sandford, June 3, 1955. Traded to **Detroit** by **Boston** with Leo Labine for Gary Aldcorn, Murray Oliver and Tom McCarthy, January, 1961.

• STEELE, FRANK

Frank Steele
RW/D – R. 5'11", 170 lbs. b: Niagara Falls, Ont., 3/19/1905. Deceased.

Season	Club	League	GP	G	A	Pts	AG	AA	APts	PIM	PO GP	PO G	PO A	PO Pts	PO PIM
1926-27	Hamilton Tigers	Can-Pro	5	0	0	0	....	....	....	0	....	....	....	....	....
1927-28	Calumet Miners	NMHL	....	....	....	....	....	....	....	....	....	....	....	....	....
1928-29	Niagara Falls Cataracts	Can-Pro	40	7	2	9	....	....	....	47	....	....	....	....	....
1929-30	Detroit Olympics	IAHL	42	15	3	18	....	....	....	47	3	0	0	0	2
1930-31	Detroit Falcons	NHL	1	0	0	0	0	0	0	0	....	....	....	....	....
	Detroit Olympics	IAHL	40	10	6	16	....	....	....	34	....	....	....	....	....
1931-32	Detroit Olympics	IAHL	48	7	6	13	....	....	....	44	6	0	0	0	4
1932-33	Detroit Olympics	IAHL	16	3	0	3	....	....	....	12	....	....	....	....	....
	Kansas City Greyhounds	AHA	7	0	0	0	....	....	....	4	....	....	....	....	....
	Wichita Blue Jays	AHA	24	0	8	8	....	....	....	17	....	....	....	....	....
1933-34	Windsor Bulldogs	IAHL	44	10	13	23	....	....	....	39	....	....	....	....	....
1934-35	Windsor Bulldogs	IAHL	43	11	9	20	....	....	....	12	....	....	....	....	....
1935-36	Windsor Bulldogs	IAHL	45	9	4	13	....	....	....	30	7	0	1	1	12
1936-37			REINSTATED AS AN AMATEUR												
1937-38	Detroit Holzbaugh	MOHL	4	1	0	1	....	....	....	4	....	....	....	....	....
	Detroit Pontiacs	MOHL	20	3	4	7	....	....	....	21	2	0	0	0	5
1938-39	Detroit Pontiacs	MOHL	37	2	5	7	....	....	....	18	7	1	1	2	8
1939-40	Detroit Pontiacs	MOHL	29	1	2	3	....	....	....	13	....	....	....	....	....
	NHL Totals		**1**	**0**	**0**	**0**	**0**	**0**	**0**	**0**	....	....	....	....	....

Signed as a free agent by **Hamilton** (Can-Pro), November 2, 1926. Signed as a free agent by **Detroit Cougars**, August 30, 1929.

• STEMKOWSKI, PETE

— *see page 1502*

• STEPHENS, PHIL

Phil Stephens
C/D – R. 5'11", 165 lbs. b: St. Lambert, Ont., 2/15/1893. d: 4/8/1968.

Season	Club	League	GP	G	A	Pts	AG	AA	APts	PIM	PO GP	PO G	PO A	PO Pts	PO PIM
1914-15	Montreal Wanderers	NHA	15	0	1	1	....	....	....	6	2	0	0	0	....
1915-16	Montreal Wanderers	NHA	22	2	2	4	....	....	....	33	....	....	....	....	....
1916-17	Montreal Wanderers	NHA	15	4	1	5	....	....	....	35	....	....	....	....	....
1917-18	Montreal Wanderers	NHL	4	1	0	1	2	0	2	3	....	....	....	....	....
1918-19			MILITARY SERVICE												
1919-20			DID NOT PLAY												
1920-21			DID NOT PLAY												
1921-22	Montreal Canadiens	NHL	4	0	0	0	0	0	0	0	....	....	....	....	....
1922-23	Saskatoon Sheiks	WCHL	15	0	0	0	....	....	....	3	....	....	....	....	....
1923-24	Saskatoon Crescents	WCHL	26	6	2	8	....	....	....	14	....	....	....	....	....
1924-25	Saskatoon Crescents	WCHL	25	2	0	2	....	....	....	30	....	....	....	....	....
1925-26	Boston Bruins	NHL	17	0	0	0	0	0	0	0	....	....	....	....	....
1926-27	Springfield Indians	Can-Am	6	0	1	1	....	....	....	0	....	....	....	....	....
	Saskatoon Sheiks	PHL	23	8	2	10	....	....	....	11	4	1	1	2	6
1927-28	Saskatoon Sheiks	PHL	28	3	1	4	....	....	....	8	....	....	....	....	....
1928-29	Oakland Shieks	Cal-Pro	....	6	2	8	....	....	....	....	....	....	....	....	....
1929-30	Oakland Sheiks	Cal-Pro	STATISTICS NOT AVAILABLE												
1930-31	Oakland Sheiks	Cal-Pro	....	12	4	16	....	....	....	....	4	0	1	1	....
1931-32	Oakland Sheiks	Cal-Pro	....	1	0	1	....	....	....	....	....	....	....	....	....
	NHL Totals		**25**	**1**	**0**	**1**	**2**	**0**	**2**	**3**	....	....	....	....	....
	Other Major League Totals		118	14	6	20	....	....	....	121	2	0	0	0	0

Rights retained by **Montreal Wanderers** after NHA folded, November 26, 1917. Signed as a free agent by **Montreal Canadiens**, December 6, 1921. Claimed on waivers by **Saskatoon** (WCHL) from **Montreal Canadiens**, November 13, 1922. Signed as a free agent by **Boston**, November 14, 1925.

• STERNER, ULF

Ulf Sterner
LW – L. 6'2", 187 lbs. b: Deje, Sweden, 2/11/1941.

Season	Club	League	GP	G	A	Pts	AG	AA	APts	PIM	PO GP	PO G	PO A	PO Pts	PO PIM
1956-57	Forshaga IF	Sweden	7	3	0	3	....	....	....	....	....	....	....	....	....
1957-58	Forshaga IF	Sweden	14	2	0	2	....	....	....	....	....	....	....	....	....
1958-59	Forshaga IF	Sweden	11	7	8	15	....	....	....	....	....	....	....	....	....
1959-60	Forshaga IF	Sweden	14	17	6	23	....	....	....	14	....	....	....	....	....
1959-60	Sweden	Olympics	5	0	1	1	....	....	....	0	....	....	....	....	....
1960-61	Forshaga IF	Sweden	13	14	8	22	....	....	....	2	....	....	....	....	....
	Sweden	WEC-A	7	5	0	5	....	....	....	2	....	....	....	....	....
1961-62	Vastra Frolunda	Sweden	13	12	9	21	....	....	....	26	7	6	4	10	5
	Sweden	WEC-A	7	9	7	16	....	....	....	2	....	....	....	....	....
1962-63	Vastra Frolunda	Sweden	14	14	6	20	....	....	....	6	7	7	4	11	0
	Sweden	WEC-A	7	7	2	9	....	....	....	2	....	....	....	....	....
1963-64	Vastra Frolunda	Sweden	12	10	2	12	....	....	....	6	7	1	4	5	10
	Sweden	Olympics	7	6	5	11	....	....	....	0	....	....	....	....	....
1964-65	New York Rangers	NHL	4	0	0	0	0	0	0	0	....	....	....	....	....
	St. Paul Rangers	CHL	16	12	9	21	....	....	....	2	....	....	....	....	....
	Baltimore Clippers	AHL	52	18	26	44	....	....	....	12	5	1	0	1	2
1965-66	Rogle	Sweden	15	32	11	43	....	....	....	....	6	12	3	15	....
	Sweden	WEC-A	7	4	1	5	....	....	....	0	....	....	....	....	....
1966-67	Rogle	Sweden	19	4	11	15	....	....	....	11	....	....	....	....	....
	Sweden	WEC-A	7	2	3	5	....	....	....	7	....	....	....	....	....
1967-68	Frajestad	Sweden	21	16	8	24	....	....	....	19	....	....	....	....	....
1968-69	Vastra Frolunda	Sweden	19	19	20	39	....	....	....	10	7	5	7	12	2
	Sweden	WEC-A	10	5	9	14	....	....	....	8	....	....	....	....	....
1969-70	Farjestad BK Karlstad	Sweden	17	14	22	36	....	....	....	....	5	3	4	7	2
	Sweden	WEC-A	10	1	7	8	....	....	....	7	....	....	....	....	....
1970-71	Farjestad BK Karlstad	Sweden	6	4	7	11	....	....	....	13	14	10	3	13	14
	Sweden	WEC-A	10	2	2	4	....	....	....	2	....	....	....	....	....
1971-72	Farjestad BK Karlstad	Sweden	14	10	15	*25	....	....	....	28	14	5	6	11	24
1972-73	Farjestad BK Karlstad	Sweden	14	7	*15	22	....	....	....	23	14	10	2	12	29
	Sweden	WEC-A	9	5	2	7	....	....	....	6	....	....	....	....	....
	NHL Totals		**4**	**0**	**0**	**0**	**0**	**0**	**0**	**0**	....	....	....	....	....

WEC-A All-Star Team (1962, 1969) • Swedish Player of the Year (1963) • Named Best Forward at WEC-A (1969)

Signed as a free agent by **NY Rangers**, October 1, 1964.

• STEWART, GAYE

Gaye "Box Car" Stewart
LW – L. 5'11", 175 lbs. b: Fort William, Ont., 6/28/1923.

Season	Club	League	GP	G	A	Pts	AG	AA	APts	PIM	PO GP	PO G	PO A	PO Pts	PO PIM
1939-40	Port Arthur Juniors	TBJHL	16	*17	6	23	....	....	....	18	5	*8	2	*10	4
1940-41	Toronto Marlboros	OHA	16	*31	13	*44	....	....	....	16	12	13	7	20	10
1941-42	Toronto Marlboros	OHA	8	10	3	13	....	....	....	18	....	....	....	....	....
	Toronto Marlboros	OHA Sr.	13	13	8	21	....	....	....	2	6	3	4	7	4
	Hershey Bears	AHL	5	4	2	6	....	....	....	0	10	4	5	9	0
	Toronto Maple Leafs	NHL	....	....	....	....	....	....	....	....	1	0	0	0	0
1942-43	Toronto Maple Leafs	NHL	48	24	23	47	34	29	63	20	4	0	2	2	4
1943-44	Montreal Royals	QSHL	10	4	7	11	....	....	....	8	4	6	2	8	0
	Montreal Navy	City Sr.	6	5	7	12	....	....	....	2	5	*7	4	11	4
1944-45	Cornwallis Navy	City Sr.	11	9	7	16	....	....	....	12	3	3	4	*7	2
1945-46	Toronto Maple Leafs	NHL	50	*37	15	52	58	28	86	8	....	....	....	....	....
1946-47	Toronto Maple Leafs	NHL	60	19	14	33	20	20	40	16	11	2	5	7	8
	Valleyfield Braves	QSHL	1	1	0	1	....	....	....	0	....	....	....	....	....
1947-48	Toronto Maple Leafs	NHL	7	1	0	1	1	0	1	0	....	....	....	....	....
	Chicago Black Hawks	NHL	54	26	29	55	38	43	81	83	....	....	....	....	....
1948-49	Chicago Black Hawks	NHL	54	20	18	38	32	29	61	57	....	....	....	....	....
1949-50	Chicago Black Hawks	NHL	70	24	19	43	32	24	56	43	....	....	....	....	....
1950-51	Detroit Red Wings	NHL	67	18	13	31	24	17	41	18	6	0	2	2	4
1951-52	New York Rangers	NHL	69	15	25	40	21	33	54	22	....	....	....	....	....
1952-53	New York Rangers	NHL	18	1	1	2	2	1	3	8	....	....	....	....	....
	Montreal Canadiens	NHL	5	0	2	2	0	3	3	0	....	....	....	....	....
	Quebec Aces	QSHL	29	13	20	33	....	....	....	28	22	*16	12	28	8
1953-54	Buffalo Bisons	AHL	70	42	53	95	....	....	....	38	3	0	2	2	4
	Montreal Canadiens	NHL	....	....	....	....	....	....	....	....	3	0	0	0	0
1954-55	Buffalo Bisons	AHL	60	17	19	36	....	....	....	36	....	....	....	....	....
	NHL Totals		**502**	**185**	**159**	**344**	**268**	**227**	**495**	**274**	**25**	**2**	**9**	**11**	**16**

Won Calder Trophy (1943) • NHL First All-Star Team (1946) • NHL Second All-Star Team (1948) • AHL First All-Star Team (1954)

Played in NHL All-Star Game (1947, 1948, 1950, 1951)

Traded to **Chicago** by **Toronto** with Bud Poile, Bob Goldham, Gus Bodnar and Ernie Dickens for Max Bentley and Cy Thomas, November 3, 1947. Traded to **Detroit** by **Chicago** with Metro Prystai, Bob Goldham and Jim Henry for Harry Lumley, Jack Stewart, Al Dewsbury, Pete Babando and Don Morrison, July 13, 1950. Traded to **NY Rangers** by **Detroit** for Tony Leswick, June 8, 1951. Claimed on waivers by **Montreal** from **NY Rangers**, December 1, 1952. Traded to **Buffalo** (AHL) by **Montreal** with Eddie Slowinski and Pete Babando for Jackie LeClair and cash, August 17, 1954.

			REGULAR SEASON								PLAYOFFS				
Season	Club	League	GP	G	A	Pts	AG	AA	APts	PIM	GP	G	A	Pts	PIM

• STEWART, JACK Jack "Black Jack" Stewart HHOF

D – L. 5'10", 190 lbs. b: Pilot Mound, Man., 5/6/1917. d: 5/25/1983.

Season	Club	League	GP	G	A	Pts	AG	AA	APts	PIM	GP	G	A	Pts	PIM
1935-36	Portage Terriers	MHL Jr.	16	0	0	0	....	....	....	6	6	0	1	1	4
1936-37	Portage Terriers	MHL Jr.	16	4	1	5	....	....	....	20	4	1	1	2	2
1937-38	Pittsburgh Hornets	AHL	48	0	1	1	....	....	....	16	2	0	0	0	0
1938-39	Pittsburgh Hornets	AHL	21	0	0	0	....	....	....	20	....	....	....	....	....
	Detroit Red Wings	**NHL**	**32**	**0**	**1**	**1**	**0**	**2**	**2**	**18**	....	....	....	....	....
1939-40	**Detroit Red Wings**	**NHL**	**48**	**1**	**0**	**1**	**2**	**0**	**2**	**40**	**5**	**0**	**0**	**0**	**4**
1940-41	**Detroit Red Wings**	**NHL**	**47**	**2**	**6**	**8**	**4**	**11**	**15**	**56**	**9**	**1**	**2**	**3**	**8**
1941-42	**Detroit Red Wings**	**NHL**	**44**	**4**	**7**	**11**	**7**	**11**	**18**	**93**	**12**	**0**	**1**	**1**	**12**
1942-43	**Detroit Red Wings**	**NHL**	**44**	**2**	**9**	**11**	**3**	**11**	**14**	**68**	**10**	**1**	**2**	**3**	***35**
1943-44	Montreal RCAF	QSHL	7	3	5	8	....	....	....	18	....	....	....	....	....
1944-45	Winnipeg RCAF	City Sr.	2	0	1	1	....	....	....	2	....	....	....	....	....
1945-46	**Detroit Red Wings**	**NHL**	**47**	**4**	**11**	**15**	**6**	**20**	**26**	***73**	**5**	**0**	**0**	**0**	**14**
1946-47	**Detroit Red Wings**	**NHL**	**55**	**5**	**9**	**14**	**7**	**13**	**20**	**83**	**5**	**0**	**1**	**1**	**12**
1947-48	**Detroit Red Wings**	**NHL**	**60**	**5**	**14**	**19**	**7**	**20**	**27**	**91**	**9**	**1**	**3**	**4**	**6**
1948-49	**Detroit Red Wings**	**NHL**	**60**	**4**	**11**	**15**	**6**	**17**	**23**	**96**	**11**	**1**	**1**	**2**	***32**
1949-50	**Detroit Red Wings**	**NHL**	**65**	**3**	**11**	**14**	**4**	**14**	**18**	**86**	**14**	**1**	**4**	**5**	**20**
1950-51	**Chicago Black Hawks**	**NHL**	**26**	**0**	**2**	**2**	**0**	**3**	**3**	**49**	....	....	....	....	....
1951-52	**Chicago Black Hawks**	**NHL**	**37**	**1**	**3**	**4**	**1**	**4**	**5**	**12**	....	....	....	....	....
1952-53	Chatham Maroons	OHA Sr.	45	2	27	29	....	....	....	*134	....	....	....	....	....
1953-54	Chatham Maroons	OHA Sr.	21	0	8	8	....	....	....	35	6	0	0	0	8
	NHL Totals		**565**	**31**	**84**	**115**	**47**	**126**	**173**	**765**	**80**	**5**	**14**	**19**	**143**

NHL First All-Star Team (1943, 1948, 1949) • NHL Second All-Star Team (1946, 1947)

Played in NHL All-Star Game (1947, 1948, 1949, 1950)

Signed as a free agent by **Detroit**, October 27, 1937. Traded to **Chicago** by **Detroit** with Harry Lumley, Al Dewsbury, Pete Babando and Don Morrison for Metro Prystai, Bob Goldham, Gaye Stewart and Jim Henry, July 13, 1950.

• STEWART, KEN Ken Stewart

D – L. 6', 175 lbs. b: Port Arthur, Ont., 3/29/1913. Deceased.

Season	Club	League	GP	G	A	Pts	AG	AA	APts	PIM	GP	G	A	Pts	PIM
1937-38	Lethbridge Maple Leafs	Kootenay	24	13	*26	39	....	....	....	2	2	2	2	4	2
1938-39	Lethbridge Maple Leafs	Cgy-Sr.	31	17	18	35	....	....	....	20	9	7	2	9	4
1939-40	Lethbridge Maple Leafs	Cgy-Sr.	30	16	12	28	....	....	....	4	2	2	0	2	2
1940-41	Lethbridge Maple Leafs	Cgy-Sr.	30	28	16	44	....	....	....	2	15	2	8	10	8
1941-42	**Chicago Black Hawks**	**NHL**	**6**	**1**	**1**	**2**	**2**	**2**	**4**	**2**	....	....	....	....	....
	Kansas City Americans	AHA	41	17	25	42	....	....	....	6	5	6	2	8	0
1942-43	Calgary Army	City Sr.	23	13	15	28	....	....	....	16	10	1	4	5	8
1943-44	Calgary Army	City Sr.	15	5	2	7	....	....	....	6	2	1	1	2	0
1944-45	Calgary Army	City Sr.	15	8	7	15	....	....	....	0	....	....	....	....	....
1945-46	Regina Caps	WCSHL	23	15	16	31	....	....	....	16	....	....	....	....	....
1946-47	Los Angeles Ramblers	Calif-Sr.	48	26	35	61	....	....	....	14	....	....	....	....	....
1947-48	Calgary Stampeders	WCSHL	47	14	22	36	....	....	....	20	11	1	2	3	4
1948-49			DID NOT PLAY												
1949-50	Kelowna Packers	Kootenay	19	10	10	20	....	....	....	14	....	....	....	....	....
1950-51	Kamloops Elks	Kootenay	52	24	31	55	....	....	....	11	5	3	1	4	4
	NHL Totals		**6**	**1**	**1**	**2**	**2**	**2**	**4**	**2**	....	....	....	....	....

• STEWART, NELS Nels "Old Poison" Stewart HHOF

C – L. 6'1", 195 lbs. b: Montreal, Que., 12/29/1902. d: 8/21/1957.

Season	Club	League	GP	G	A	Pts	AG	AA	APts	PIM	GP	G	A	Pts	PIM
1919-20	Parkdale Canoe Club	OHA Sr.	8	18	2	20	....	....	....	....	1	1	0	1	....
1920-21	Cleveland Indians	USAHA	10	*23	0	*23	....	....	....	....	8	*6	0	*6	....
1921-22	Cleveland Indians	USAHA	12	13	0	13	....	....	....	....	....	....	....	....	....
1922-23	Cleveland Indians	USAHA	20	*22	0	*22	....	....	....	....	....	....	....	....	....
1923-24	Cleveland Indians	USAHA	20	*21	*8	*29	....	....	....	....	8	*5	2	*7	....
1924-25	Cleveland Indians	USAHA	40	*21	0	*21	....	....	....	....	8	*6	3	*9	24
1925-26	**Montreal Maroons**	**NHL**	**36**	***34**	**8**	***42**	**110**	**94**	**204**	**119**	**8**	***6**	***3**	***9**	**24**
1926-27	**Montreal Maroons**	**NHL**	**43**	**17**	**4**	**21**	**50**	**34**	**84**	***133**	**2**	**0**	**0**	**0**	**4**
1927-28	**Montreal Maroons**	**NHL**	**41**	**27**	**7**	**34**	**84**	**59**	**143**	**104**	**9**	**2**	**2**	**4**	**13**
1928-29	**Montreal Maroons**	**NHL**	**44**	**21**	**8**	**29**	**86**	**74**	**160**	**74**	....	....	....	....	....
1929-30	**Montreal Maroons**	**NHL**	**44**	**39**	**16**	**55**	**78**	**52**	**130**	**81**	**4**	**1**	**1**	**2**	**2**
1930-31	**Montreal Maroons**	**NHL**	**42**	**25**	**14**	**39**	**62**	**51**	**113**	**75**	**2**	**1**	**0**	**1**	**6**
1931-32	**Montreal Maroons**	**NHL**	**38**	**22**	**11**	**33**	**47**	**31**	**78**	**61**	**4**	**0**	**1**	**1**	**2**
1932-33	**Boston Bruins**	**NHL**	**47**	**18**	**18**	**36**	**42**	**48**	**90**	**62**	**5**	**2**	**0**	**2**	**4**
1933-34	**Boston Bruins**	**NHL**	**48**	**22**	**17**	**39**	**49**	**46**	**95**	**68**	....	....	....	....	....
1934-35	**Boston Bruins**	**NHL**	**47**	**21**	**18**	**39**	**45**	**40**	**85**	**45**	**4**	**0**	**1**	**1**	**0**
1935-36	**New York Americans**	**NHL**	**48**	**14**	**15**	**29**	**35**	**36**	**71**	**16**	**5**	**1**	**2**	**3**	**4**
1936-37	**Boston Bruins**	**NHL**	**11**	***3**	**2**	**5**	**6**	**5**	**11**	**6**	....	....	....	....	....
	New York Americans	**NHL**	**32**	***20**	**10**	**30**	**44**	**23**	**67**	**31**	....	....	....	....	....
1937-38	**New York Americans**	**NHL**	**48**	**19**	**17**	**36**	**40**	**35**	**75**	**29**	**6**	**2**	**3**	**5**	**2**
1938-39	**New York Americans**	**NHL**	**46**	**16**	**19**	**35**	**34**	**36**	**70**	**43**	**2**	**0**	**0**	**0**	**0**
1939-40	**New York Americans**	**NHL**	**35**	**6**	**7**	**13**	**13**	**14**	**27**	**6**	**3**	**0**	**0**	**0**	**0**
	NHL Totals		**650**	**324**	**191**	**515**	**825**	**678**	**1503**	**953**	**54**	**15**	**13**	**28**	**61**

NHL Scoring Leader (1926) • Won Hart Trophy (1926, 1930)

Played in NHL All-Star Game (1934)

Signed as a free agent by **Montreal Maroons**, June 25, 1925. Traded to **Boston** by **Montreal Maroons** for cash, October 17, 1932. Traded to **NY Americans** by **Boston** with Joe Jerwa for cash, September 28, 1935. Rights returned to **Boston** by **NY Americans** after NY Americans were unable to complete purchase agreement, May 27, 1936. Traded to **NY Americans** by **Boston** for cash, December 19, 1936.

• STEWART, RON — *see page 1507*

• STODDARD, JACK Jack Stoddard

RW – R. 6'3", 185 lbs. b: Stony Creek, Ont., 9/26/1926.

Season	Club	League	GP	G	A	Pts	AG	AA	APts	PIM	GP	G	A	Pts	PIM
1943-44	Stratford–Hamilton	OHA	18	5	4	9	....	....	....	2	....	....	....	....	....
1944-45	Hamilton Pats	OHA Sr.	4	4	1	5	....	....	....	0	....	....	....	....	....
1945-46	Hamilton Lloyds	OHA	16	4	7	11	....	....	....	17	....	....	....	....	....
1946-47	Baltimore Clippers	EHL	53	22	19	41	....	....	....	22	9	*8	3	11	2
1947-48	Providence Reds	AHL	45	6	7	13	....	....	....	4	5	1	1	2	0
	Quebec Aces	QSHL	10	5	1	6	....	....	....	16	....	....	....	....	....
1948-49	Providence Reds	AHL	61	25	28	53	....	....	....	36	14	4	4	8	6
1949-50	Providence Reds	AHL	69	32	29	61	....	....	....	31	4	1	2	3	2
1950-51	Providence Reds	AHL	70	37	27	64	....	....	....	24	....	....	....	....	....
1951-52	**New York Rangers**	**NHL**	**20**	**4**	**2**	**6**	**6**	**3**	**9**	**2**	....	....	....	....	....
	Providence Reds	AHL	35	20	28	48	....	....	....	16	....	....	....	....	....
1952-53	**New York Rangers**	**NHL**	**60**	**12**	**13**	**25**	**18**	**18**	**36**	**29**	....	....	....	....	....
1953-54	Cleveland Barons	AHL	66	23	34	57	....	....	....	43	5	0	0	0	0
1954-55	Providence Reds	AHL	58	13	16	29	....	....	....	15	....	....	....	....	....
1955-56	Trois-Rivieres Lions	QHL	27	5	13	18	....	....	....	19	....	....	....	....	....
	Owen Sound Mercurys	OHA Sr.	6	4	3	7	....	....	....	4	6	2	2	4	6
1956-57	Owen Sound Mercurys	OHA Sr.	52	15	28	43	....	....	....	56	....	....	....	....	....
1957-58	Kitchener Dutchmen	NOHA	32	10	16	26	....	....	....	22	....	....	....	....	....
1958-59			DID NOT PLAY – RETIRED												
1959-60	Chatham Maroons	OHA Sr.	1	0	0	0	....	....	....	0	8	4	1	5	2
1960-61	Woodstock Athletics	OHA Sr.	....	14	17	31	....	....	....	22	....	....	....	....	....
1961-62	Woodstock Athletics	OHA Sr.	1	0	2	2	....	....	....	0	....	....	....	....	....
	NHL Totals		**80**	**16**	**15**	**31**	**24**	**21**	**45**	**31**	....	....	....	....	....

Traded to **NY Rangers** by **Providence** (AHL) for Pat Egan, Zellio Toppazzini and Jean-Paul Denis, December, 1951.

• STRAIN, NEIL Neil Strain

LW/C – L. 5'9", 165 lbs. b: Kenora, Ont., 2/24/1926. d: 1975.

Season	Club	League	GP	G	A	Pts	AG	AA	APts	PIM	GP	G	A	Pts	PIM
1945-46	Portage Terriers	MJHL	10	12	10	22	....	....	....	0	....	....	....	....	....
1946-47	Valleyfield Braves	QSHL	38	13	21	34	....	....	....	18	....	....	....	....	....
1947-48	San Francisco Shamrocks	PCHL	66	21	22	43	....	....	....	36	4	6	1	7	6
1948-49	San Francisco Shamrocks	PCHL	67	29	24	53	....	....	....	42	....	....	....	....	....
1949-50	Cleveland Barons	AHL	4	2	3	5	....	....	....	0	....	....	....	....	....
	Minneapolis Millers	USHL	37	12	13	25	....	....	....	6	7	2	2	4	2
1950-51	Denver Falcons	USHL	39	10	21	31	....	....	....	10	....	....	....	....	....
1951-52	Saskatoon Quakers	PCHL	69	33	40	73	....	....	....	26	13	5	7	12	0
1952-53	**New York Rangers**	**NHL**	**52**	**11**	**13**	**24**	**17**	**18**	**35**	**12**	....	....	....	....	....
	Saskatoon Quakers	WHL	19	9	9	18	....	....	....	0	....	....	....	....	....
1953-54	Edmonton Flyers	WHL	8	1	1	2	....	....	....	0	....	....	....	....	....
	NHL Totals		**52**	**11**	**13**	**24**	**17**	**18**	**35**	**12**	....	....	....	....	....

Traded to **NY Rangers** (Denver-USHL) by **Cleveland** (AHL) with Bill Richardson, Bob Jackson and Joe McArthur for Wally Hergeishimer, September 5, 1950.

• STRATE, GORD Gord Strate

D – L. 6'1", 190 lbs. b: Edmonton, Alta., 5/28/1935.

Season	Club	League	GP	G	A	Pts	AG	AA	APts	PIM	GP	G	A	Pts	PIM
1952-53	Edmonton Oil Kings	WCJHL	31	3	3	6	....	....	....	32	13	0	1	1	6
1953-54	Edmonton Oil Kings	WCJHL	33	1	7	8	....	....	....	41	10	3	3	6	12
1954-55	Edmonton Oil Kings	WCJHL	40	6	12	18	....	....	....	55	3	0	0	0	2
	Edmonton Flyers	WHL	2	1	0	1	....	....	....	0	....	....	....	....	....
1955-56	Brandon Regals	WHL	60	0	6	6	....	....	....	64	....	....	....	....	....
1956-57	**Detroit Red Wings**	**NHL**	**5**	**0**	**0**	**0**	**0**	**0**	**0**	**4**	....	....	....	....	....
	Edmonton Flyers	WHL	64	0	15	15	....	....	....	33	8	0	0	0	0
1957-58	**Detroit Red Wings**	**NHL**	**45**	**0**	**0**	**0**	**0**	**0**	**0**	**24**	....	....	....	....	....
	Cleveland Barons	AHL	15	0	1	1	....	....	....	4	7	0	1	1	2
1958-59	**Detroit Red Wings**	**NHL**	**11**	**0**	**0**	**0**	**0**	**0**	**0**	**6**	....	....	....	....	....
	Hershey Bears	AHL	53	0	2	2	....	....	....	40	13	0	0	0	5
1959-60	Edmonton Flyers	WHL	69	1	8	9	....	....	....	47	4	1	0	1	0
1960-61	Sudbury Wolves	EPHL	14	0	3	3	....	....	....	10	....	....	....	....	....
	Edmonton Flyers	WHL	57	1	7	8	....	....	....	40	....	....	....	....	....
1961-62	Sudbury Wolves	EPHL	70	2	17	19	....	....	....	83	5	0	0	0	4
	NHL Totals		**61**	**0**	**0**	**0**	**0**	**0**	**0**	**34**	....	....	....	....	....

WHL Prairie Division Second All-Star Team (1957)

• STRATTON, ART — *see page 1510*

• STROBEL, ART Art Strobel

LW – L. 5'6", 160 lbs. b: Regina, Sask., 11/28/1922.

Season	Club	League	GP	G	A	Pts	AG	AA	APts	PIM	GP	G	A	Pts	PIM
1941-42	Regina Abbotts	SJHL	7	0	0	0	....	....	....	0	....	....	....	....	....
1942-43	Regina Commandos	SJHL	13	4	5	9	....	....	....	2	6	2	*3	5	4
	Yorkton Terriers	SSHL	1	0	0	0	....	....	....	0	....	....	....	....	....
1943-44	**New York Rangers**	**NHL**	**7**	**0**	**0**	**0**	**0**	**0**	**0**	**0**	....	....	....	....	....
	New York Rovers	EHL	30	12	18	30	....	....	....	2	9	6	7	13	10
1944-45	Hershey Bears	AHL	56	11	15	26	....	....	....	8	11	5	0	5	4
1945-46	Hershey Bears	AHL	4	0	3	3	....	....	....	0	....	....	....	....	....
	Minneapolis Millers	USHL	43	6	8	14	....	....	....	6	....	....	....	....	....
1946-47	Minneapolis Millers	USHL	59	17	17	34	....	....	....	27	3	0	0	0	4
1947-48	Minneapolis Millers	USHL	59	19	23	42	....	....	....	15	10	0	2	2	2
1948-49	Minneapolis Millers	USHL	61	14	29	43	....	....	....	13	....	....	....	....	....
1949-50	Portland Buckaroos	PCHL	71	20	23	43	....	....	....	28	....	....	....	....	....
1950-51			DID NOT PLAY – RETIRED												
1951-52			DID NOT PLAY – RETIRED												
1952-53	Rochester Mustangs	USHL	32	32	30	62	....	....	....	6	....	....	....	....	....
	NHL Totals		**7**	**0**	**0**	**0**	**0**	**0**	**0**	**0**	....	....	....	....	....

• STUART, BILLY Billy "Red" Stuart

D – L. 5'11", 190 lbs. b: Sackville, N.B., 2/1/1900. d: 3/7/1978.

			REGULAR SEASON								PLAYOFFS				
Season	**Club**	**League**	**GP**	**G**	**A**	**Pts**	**AG**	**AA**	**APts**	**PIM**	**GP**	**G**	**A**	**Pts**	**PIM**
1916-17	Amherst Ramblers	NSSHL	4	6	0	6	....	....	....	....	4	*7	0	*7	....
1917-18	Amherst Victorias	NSSHL	7	8	2	10	....	....	....	....	5	4	*3	7	....
1918-19	Springhill Miners	NSSHL	STATISTICS NOT AVAILABLE												
1919-20	Amherst Ramblers	NSSHL	6	*21	3	*24	....	....	....	18	13	*30	8	*38	*35
1920-21	Amherst Ramblers	NSSHL	1	0	0	0	....	....	....	0	....	....	....	....	....
	Toronto St. Pats	**NHL**	**19**	**2**	**1**	**3**	**5**	**9**	**14**	**4**	**2**	**0**	**0**	**0**	**0**
1921-22	**Toronto St. Pats**	**NHL**	**24**	**3**	**7**	**10**	**8**	**44**	**52**	**16**	**7**	**1**	**3**	**4**	**6**
1922-23	**Toronto St. Pats**	**NHL**	**23**	**7**	**3**	**10**	**23**	**27**	**50**	**16**	....	....	....	....	....
1923-24	**Toronto St.Pats**	**NHL**	**24**	**4**	**3**	**7**	**16**	**53**	**69**	**16**	....	....	....	....	....
1924-25	**Toronto St. Pats**	**NHL**	**5**	**0**	**0**	**0**	**0**	**0**	**0**	**0**	....	....	....	....	....
	Boston Bruins	**NHL**	**24**	**5**	**2**	**7**	**17**	**26**	**43**	**32**	....	....	....	....	....
1925-26	**Boston Bruins**	**NHL**	**33**	**6**	**1**	**7**	**18**	**11**	**29**	**41**	....	....	....	....	....
1926-27	**Boston Bruins**	**NHL**	**43**	**3**	**1**	**4**	**9**	**8**	**17**	**20**	**8**	**0**	**0**	**0**	**6**
1927-28	Minneapolis Millers	AHA	39	5	2	7	....	....	....	80	7	1	0	1	12
1928-29	Minneapolis Millers	AHA	39	17	6	23	....	....	....	87	4	0	*2	2	6
1929-30	Minneapolis Millers	AHA	48	12	8	20	....	....	....	70	....	....	....	....	....
1930-31	Seattle Eskimos	PCHL	34	5	8	13	....	....	....	20	4	0	1	1	*14
1931-32	Duluth Hornets	AHA	48	15	2	17	....	....	....	56	8	0	1	1	10
1932-33	Minneapolis Millers	CHL	39	3	1	4	....	....	....	37	7	1	1	2	6
1933-34	Halifax Wolverines	NSSHL	DID NOT PLAY – COACHING												
	NHL Totals		**195**	**30**	**18**	**48**	**96**	**178**	**274**	**145**	**17**	**1**	**3**	**4**	**12**

Signed as a free agent by **Toronto St. Pats**, January 5, 1920. Traded to **Boston** by **Toronto St. Pats** for cash, December 14, 1924. Traded to **Minneapolis** (AHA) by **Boston** with cash and future considerations for Nobby Clark and Dutch Gainor, October 24, 1927. Traded to **Seattle** (PCHL) by **Minneapolis** (AHA) for cash, July 25, 1930.

• SULLIVAN, BARRY Barry "Big Ben" Sullivan

RW – R. 6', 185 lbs. b: Preston, Ont., 9/21/1927.

			REGULAR SEASON								PLAYOFFS				
Season	**Club**	**League**	**GP**	**G**	**A**	**Pts**	**AG**	**AA**	**APts**	**PIM**	**GP**	**G**	**A**	**Pts**	**PIM**
1943-44	Stratford–Galt	OHA	21	19	12	31	....	....	....	2	2	0	1	1	2
1944-45	Oshawa Generals	OHA	20	21	14	35	....	....	....	19	3	2	4	6	0
1945-46	Omaha Knights	USHL	40	11	14	25	....	....	....	15	....	....	....	....	....
1946-47	Omaha Knights	USHL	38	21	21	42	....	....	....	12	11	7	9	16	8
	Indianapolis Capitals	AHL	19	0	1	1	....	....	....	2	....	....	....	....	....
1947-48	**Detroit Red Wings**	**NHL**	**1**	**0**	**0**	**0**	**0**	**0**	**0**	**0**	....	....	....	....	....
	Indianapolis Capitals	AHL	68	22	26	48	....	....	....	14	....	....	....	....	....
1948-49	St. Louis Flyers	AHL	63	32	38	70	....	....	....	21	7	3	3	6	0
1949-50	St. Louis Flyers	AHL	69	19	38	57	....	....	....	20	2	0	0	0	0
1950-51	St. Louis–Providence	AHL	53	16	29	45	....	....	....	8	....	....	....	....	....
1951-52	Providence Reds	AHL	61	25	47	72	....	....	....	12	14	6	*12	*18	8
1952-53	Providence Reds	AHL	61	23	37	60	....	....	....	31	....	....	....	....	....
	NHL Totals		**1**	**0**	**0**	**0**	**0**	**0**	**0**	**0**	....	....	....	....	....

AHL Second All-Star Team (1952)

Traded to **St. Louis** (AHL) by **Detroit** with Red Almas, Lloyd Doran, Tony Licari and Thain Simon for Joe Lund and Hec Highton, September 9, 1948.

• SULLIVAN, FRANK Frank "Sully" Sullivan

D – R. 5'11", 178 lbs. b: Toronto, Ont., 6/16/1929.

			REGULAR SEASON								PLAYOFFS				
Season	**Club**	**League**	**GP**	**G**	**A**	**Pts**	**AG**	**AA**	**APts**	**PIM**	**GP**	**G**	**A**	**Pts**	**PIM**
1946-47	Toronto Marlboros	OHA	2	2	0	2	....	....	....	0	....	....	....	....	....
1947-48	Oshawa Generals	OHA	33	8	18	26	....	....	....	60	6	1	4	5	16
1948-49	Oshawa Generals	OHA	44	14	22	36	....	....	....	112	2	1	3	4	2
1949-50	**Toronto Maple Leafs**	**NHL**	**1**	**0**	**0**	**0**	**0**	**0**	**0**	**0**	....	....	....	....	....
	Toronto Marlboros	OHA Sr.	41	4	6	10	....	....		38	14	0	*10	*16	14
1950-51	St. Michael's Monarchs	OHA Sr.	33	4	9	13	....	....	....	54	18	1	*15	16	40
1951-52	Pittsburgh Hornets	AHL	61	10	16	26	....	....	....	76	11	0	9	9	4
1952-53	**Toronto Maple Leafs**	**NHL**	**5**	**0**	**0**	**0**	**0**	**0**	**0**	**2**	....	....	....	....	....
	Pittsburgh Hornets	AHL	51	11	16	27	....	....	....	88	10	0	2	2	4
1953-54	Pittsburgh Hornets	AHL	62	6	36	42	....	....	....	56	5	1	1	2	10
1954-55	**Chicago Black Hawks**	**NHL**	**1**	**0**	**0**	**0**	**0**	**0**	**0**	**0**	....	....	....	....	....
	Buffalo Bisons	AHL	64	11	33	44	....	....	....	34	10	2	6	8	6
1955-56	**Chicago Black Hawks**	**NHL**	**1**	**0**	**0**	**0**	**0**	**0**	**0**	**0**	....	....	....	....	....
	Buffalo Bisons	AHL	55	6	40	46	....	....	....	40	5	1	1	2	4
1956-57	Buffalo Bisons	AHL	56	4	41	45	....	....	....	46	....	....	....	....	....
1957-58	Buffalo Bisons	AHL	65	2	36	38	....	....	....	34	....	....	....	....	....
1958-59	Springfield Indians	AHL	69	9	28	37	....	....	....	48	....	....	....	....	....
	NHL Totals		**8**	**0**	**0**	**0**	**0**	**0**	**0**	**2**	....	....	....	....	....

AHL Second All-Star Team (1955, 1957) • AHL First All-Star Team (1956)

Traded to **Chicago** (Buffalo - AHL) by **Toronto** with George Blair and Jackie LeClair for Brian Cullen, May 4, 1954.

• SULLIVAN, RED Red (George) Sullivan

C – L. 5'11", 155 lbs. b: Peterborough, Ont., 12/24/1929.

			REGULAR SEASON								PLAYOFFS				
Season	**Club**	**League**	**GP**	**G**	**A**	**Pts**	**AG**	**AA**	**APts**	**PIM**	**GP**	**G**	**A**	**Pts**	**PIM**
1947-48	St. Catharines Teepees	OHA	26	10	12	22	....	....	....	34	3	2	3	5	0
1948-49	St. Catharines Teepees	OHA	46	32	*48	80	....	....	....	53	5	6	4	10	6
1949-50	St. Catharines Teepees	OHA	13	14	15	29	....	....	....	19	....	....	....	....	....
	Boston Bruins	**NHL**	**3**	**0**	**1**	**1**	**0**	**1**	**1**	**0**	....	....	....	....	....
	Hershey Bears	AHL	51	10	30	40	....	....	....	36	....	....	....	....	....
1950-51	Hershey Bears	AHL	70	28	56	84	....	....	....	36	6	1	2	3	0
	Boston Bruins	**NHL**	....	....	....	....	....	....	....	....	**2**	**0**	**0**	**0**	**2**
1951-52	**Boston Bruins**	**NHL**	**67**	**12**	**12**	**24**	**17**	**15**	**32**	**24**	**7**	**0**	**0**	**0**	**0**
1952-53	**Boston Bruins**	**NHL**	**32**	**3**	**8**	**11**	**5**	**11**	**16**	**8**	**3**	**0**	**0**	**0**	**0**
	Hershey Bears	AHL	36	10	40	50	....	....	....	18	....	....	....	....	....
1953-54	Hershey Bears	AHL	69	30	*89	*119	....	....	....	54	11	2	7	9	4
1954-55	**Chicago Black Hawks**	**NHL**	**70**	**19**	**42**	**61**	**28**	**55**	**83**	**51**	....	....	....	....	....
1955-56	**Chicago Black Hawks**	**NHL**	**63**	**14**	**26**	**40**	**20**	**33**	**53**	**58**	....	....	....	....	....
1956-57	**New York Rangers**	**NHL**	**42**	**6**	**17**	**23**	**8**	**20**	**28**	**36**	**5**	**1**	**2**	**3**	**4**
1957-58	**New York Rangers**	**NHL**	**70**	**11**	**35**	**46**	**14**	**38**	**52**	**61**	**1**	**0**	**0**	**0**	**0**
1958-59	**New York Rangers**	**NHL**	**70**	**21**	**42**	**63**	**27**	**45**	**72**	**56**	....	....	....	....	....
1959-60	**New York Rangers**	**NHL**	**70**	**12**	**25**	**37**	**15**	**26**	**41**	**81**	....	....	....	....	....
1960-61	**New York Rangers**	**NHL**	**70**	**9**	**31**	**40**	**11**	**32**	**43**	**66**	....	....	....	....	....
1961-62	Kitchener Beavers	EPHL	61	16	46	62	....	....	....	81	7	1	6	7	4
1962-63	Baltimore Clippers	AHL	31	14	22	36	....	....	....	25	....	....	....	....	....
1963-64	**New York Rangers**	**NHL**	DID NOT PLAY – COACHING												
	NHL Totals		**557**	**107**	**239**	**346**	**145**	**276**	**421**	**441**	**18**	**1**	**2**	**3**	**6**

AHL First All-Star Team (1954) • Won John B. Sollenberger Trophy (Top Scorer - AHL) (1954) • Won Les Cunningham Award (MVP - AHL) (1954)

Played in NHL All-Star Game (1955, 1956, 1958, 1959, 1960)

Traded to **Chicago** by **Boston** for cash, September 10, 1954. Traded to **NY Rangers** by **Chicago** for Wally Hergesheimer, June 19, 1956.

• SUMMERHILL, BILL Bill Summerhill

RW – R. 5'9", 170 lbs. b: Toronto, Ont., 7/9/1915. d: 10/29/1978.

			REGULAR SEASON								PLAYOFFS				
Season	**Club**	**League**	**GP**	**G**	**A**	**Pts**	**AG**	**AA**	**APts**	**PIM**	**GP**	**G**	**A**	**Pts**	**PIM**
1937-38	Verdun Maple Leafs	QSHL	22	16	*20	*36	....	....	....	20	8	*8	1	9	18
	Montreal Canadiens	**NHL**	....	....	....	....	....	....	....	....	**1**	**0**	**0**	**0**	**0**
1938-39	**Montreal Canadiens**	**NHL**	**43**	**6**	**10**	**16**	**13**	**19**	**32**	**28**	**2**	**0**	**0**	**0**	**2**
	New Haven Eagles	AHL	6	1	2	3	....	....	....	0	....	....	....	....	....
1939-40	**Montreal Canadiens**	**NHL**	**13**	**3**	**2**	**5**	**6**	**4**	**10**	**24**	....	....	....	....	....
	New Haven Eagles	AHL	27	14	27	41	....	....	....	16	3	1	1	2	2
1940-41	Cleveland Barons	AHL	49	14	13	27	....	....	....	48	8	2	2	4	8
1941-42	**Brooklyn Americans**	**NHL**	**16**	**5**	**5**	**10**	**9**	**8**	**17**	**18**	....	....	....	....	....
	Springfield Indians	AHL	36	21	28	49	....	....	....	42	5	5	1	6	2
1942-43	Buffalo Bisons	AHL	56	41	27	68	....	....	....	64	9	*5	9	*14	2
1943-44			MILITARY SERVICE												
1944-45			MILITARY SERVICE												
1945-46	New Haven Eagles	AHL	21	5	1	12	....	....	....	16	....	....	....	....	....
	Fort Worth Rangers	USHL	13	4	3	7	....	....	....	8	....	....	....	....	....
1946-47	Springfield Indians	AHL	61	26	30	56	....	....	....	37	2	1	1	2	0
1947-48	Springfield Indians	AHL	67	27	47	74	....	....	....	22	....	....	....	....	....
1948-49	Springfield Indians	AHL	65	30	36	66	....	....	....	36	3	3	4	7	2
1949-50	Springfield Indians	AHL	25	10	15	25	....	....	....	18		....	....	....	....
1950-51	New Haven Ramblers	AHL	27	12	11	23	....	....	....	16	....	....	....	....	....
	Portland Eagles	PCHL	40	15	16	31	....	....	....	10	6	1	0	1	4
	NHL Totals		**72**	**14**	**17**	**31**	**28**	**31**	**59**	**70**	**3**	**0**	**0**	**0**	**2**

AHL Second All-Star Team (1943)

Traded to **Cleveland** (AHL) by **Montreal Canadiens** with Bill MacKenzie for Jim O'Neil, May 17, 1940. Traded to **Brooklyn Americans** by **Cleveland** for cash, October 6, 1941.

• SUOMI, AL Al Suomi

LW – L. 5'10", 170 lbs. b: Eveleth, MN, 10/20/1913. Deceased.

			REGULAR SEASON								PLAYOFFS				
Season	**Club**	**League**	**GP**	**G**	**A**	**Pts**	**AG**	**AA**	**APts**	**PIM**	**GP**	**G**	**A**	**Pts**	**PIM**
1934-35	Chicago Baby Ruth	City Sr.	2	2	0	2		....	....	....	....	....	....	....	....
1935-36	Detroit Tool Shop	MOHL	17	8	5	13	....	....	....	6	4	0	1	1	0
1936-37	**Chicago Black Hawks**	**NHL**	**5**	**0**	**0**	**0**	**0**	**0**	**0**	**0**	....	....	....	....	....
	Virginia Americans	TBSHL	20	8	4	12	....	....	....	12	....	....	....	....	....
	Detroit Pontiacs	MOHL	20	2	0	2	....	....	....	14	....	....	....	....	....
	NHL Totals		**5**	**0**	**0**	**0**	**0**	**0**	**0**	**0**	....	....	....	....	....

• SUTHERLAND, BILL *— see page 1516*

• SUTHERLAND, MAX Max Sutherland

LW – L. 5'10", 165 lbs. b: Grenfell, Sask., 2/8/1907. Deceased.

			REGULAR SEASON								PLAYOFFS				
Season	**Club**	**League**	**GP**	**G**	**A**	**Pts**	**AG**	**AA**	**APts**	**PIM**	**GP**	**G**	**A**	**Pts**	**PIM**
1921-22	Moose Jaw Monarchs	City Jr.	1	0	0	0	....	....	....	0	....	....	....	....	....
1922-23	Moose Jaw Maple Leafs	City Sr.	10	5	0	5	....	....	....	4	....	....	....	....	....
1923-24	Moose Jaw Canucks	City Jr.	6	2	4	6	....	....	....	3	....	....	....	....	....
	Pense Wanderers	City Sr.	2	1	2	3	....	....	....	0	....	....	....	....	....
1924-25	Moose Jaw Maple Leafs	City Sr.	8	6	0	6	....	....	....	14	....	....	....	....	....
1925-26	Moose Jaw Millers	City Sr.	18	13	5	18	....	....	....	12	....	....	....	....	....
1926-27	Moose Jaw Maroons	PrHL	32	17	7	24	....	....	....	38	....	....	....	....	....
1927-28	Moose Jaw Maroons	PrHL	28	13	5	18	....	....	....	*53	....	....	....	....	....
1928-29	Seattle Eskimos	PCHL	30	5	1	6	....	....	....	80	5	0	0	0	*12
1929-30	Seattle Eskimos	PCHL	36	10	3	13	....	....	....	102	....	....	....	....	....
1930-31	Seattle Eskimos	PCHL	34	9	2	11	....	....	....	96	4	1	0	1	2
1931-32	**Boston Bruins**	**NHL**	**2**	**0**	**0**	**0**	**0**	**0**	**0**	**0**	....	....	....	....	....
	Boston Cubs	Can-Am	35	7	7	14	....	....	....	51	5	0	1	1	8
1932-33	Calgary Tigers	WCHL	30	10	4	14	....	....	....	51	6	2	0	2	11
1933-34	Calgary Tigers	NWHL	28	14	4	18	....	....	....	50	5	2	0	2	4
1934-35	Calgary Tigers	NWHL	18	5	3	8	....	....	....	4	....	....	....	....	....
1935-36			DID NOT PLAY												
1936-37	Olds Elks	Edm-Sr.	DID NOT PLAY – COACHING												
1937-38	Olds Elks	Edm-Sr.	25	12	10	22	....	....	....	31	3	1	0	1	6
1938-39	Olds Elks	Edm-Sr.	13	7	6	13	....	....	....	30	....	....	....	....	....
	NHL Totals		**2**	**0**	**0**	**0**	**0**	**0**	**0**	**0**	....	....	....	....	....

Traded to **Boston** by **Seattle** (PCHL) for cash, October 21, 1931.

Season	Club	League	REGULAR SEASON								PLAYOFFS				
			GP	G	A	Pts	AG	AA	APts	PIM	GP	G	A	Pts	PIM

• SWEENEY, BILL
Bill Sweeney
C – L. 5'10", 165 lbs. b: Guelph, Ont., 1/30/1937. d: 1991.

1953-54	Guelph Biltmores	OHA	14	4	3	7	....	....	....	0	3	0	1	1	2
1954-55	Guelph Biltmores	OHA	47	18	37	55	....	....	....	25	6	5	5	10	7
1955-56	Guelph Biltmores	OHA	48	29	38	67	....	....	....	16	3	0	1	1	2
1956-57	Guelph Biltmores	OHA	52	49	*57	*106	....	....	....	20	10	*19	7	*26	11
1957-58	Providence Reds	AHL	70	31	46	77	....	....	....	24	5	1	1	2	2
1958-59	Buffalo Bisons	AHL	70	31	44	75	....	....	....	12	11	4	5	9	4
1959-60	**New York Rangers**	**NHL**	**4**	**1**	**0**	**1**	**1**	**0**	**1**	**0**	....	....	....	....	....
	Springfield Indians	AHL	67	37	59	96	....	....	....	14	10	*7	7	*14	0
1960-61	Springfield Indians	AHL	70	40	*68	*108	....	....	....	26	8	4	5	9	2
1961-62	Springfield Indians	AHL	70	40	61	*101	....	....	....	14	11	5	5	*10	0
1962-63	Springfield Indians	AHL	69	38	65	*103	....	....	....	16	....	....	....	....	....
1963-64	Springfield Indians	AHL	72	25	48	73	....	....	....	18	....	....	....	....	....
1964-65	Springfield Indians	AHL	51	13	31	44	....	....	....	26	....	....	....	....	....
1965-66	Springfield Indians	AHL	72	22	37	59	....	....	....	10	6	2	3	5	0
1966-67	Springfield Indians	AHL	65	16	50	66	....	....	....	12	....	....	....	....	....
1967-68	Vancouver Canucks	WHL	15	3	5	8	....	....	....	2	....	....	....	....	....
	Springfield Kings	AHL	9	1	1	2	....	....	....	0	....	....	....	....	....
	Memphis South Stars	CHL	1	0	0	0	....	....	....	0	....	....	....	....	....
1968-69	Rochester Americans	AHL	10	0	0	0	....	....	....	2	....	....	....	....	....
1969-70	Oakville Oaks	OHA Sr.	11	2	10	12	....	....	....	0	....	....	....	....	....
	NHL Totals		**4**	**1**	**0**	**1**	**1**	**0**	**1**	**0**	....	....	....	....	....

Won Dudley "Red" Garrett Memorial Award (Top Rookie - AHL) (1958) • AHL First All-Star Team (1960, 1962) • AHL Second All-Star Team (1961) • Won John B. Sollenberger Trophy (Top Scorer - AHL) (1961, 1962, 1963)

Traded to **Vancouver** (WHL) by **NY Rangers** for cash, September, 1967.

• TALBOT, JEAN-GUY
— see page 1523

• TATCHELL, SPENCE
Spence Tatchell
D – L. 5'11", 175 lbs. b: Lloydminster, Sask., 7/16/1924.

1941-42	Winnipeg Rangers	City Jr.	1	0	0	0	....	....	....	2	....	....	....	....	....
1942-43	Winnipeg Monarchs	City Jr.	7	9	2	11	....	....	....	8	....	....	....	....	....
	New York Rangers	**NHL**	**1**	**0**	**0**	**0**	**0**	**0**	**0**	**0**	....	....	....	....	....
	New York Rovers	EHL	43	3	10	13	....	....	....	27	9	0	2	2	4
1943-44	Cornwallis Navy	City Sr.	5	4	6	10	....	....	....	....	10	1	8	9	9
1944-45			MILITARY SERVICE												
1945-46	Nelson Maple Leafs	Kootenay	20	6	2	8	....	....	....	10	8	2	2	4	9
1946-47	Nelson Maple Leafs	Kootenay	34	16	14	30	....	....	....	8	7	2	1	3	0
1947-48	Nelson Maple Leafs	Kootenay	35	7	13	20	....	....	....	6	3	0	1	1	2
1948-49	Nelson Maple Leafs	Kootenay	42	9	13	22	....	....	....	6	5	2	3	5	0
1949-50	Nelson Maple Leafs	Kootenay	1	0	0	0	....	....	....	0	....	....	....	....	....
	Kimberley Dynamiters	Kootenay	33	15	18	33	....	....	....	9	5	2	4	6	2
1950-51	Kimberley Dynamiters	Kootenay	32	10	20	30	....	....	....	8	7	1	2	3	....
1951-52	Kimberley Dynamiters	Kootenay	35	15	18	33	....	....	....	8	2	1	1	2	0
1952-53	Kimberley Dynamiters	Kootenay	30	6	12	18	....	....	....	6	4	0	2	2	0
1953-54	Kimberley Dynamiters	WIHL	18	1	9	10	....	....	....	8	....	....	....	....	....
	NHL Totals		**1**	**0**	**0**	**0**	**0**	**0**	**0**	**0**	....	....	....	....	....

• TAYLOR, BILLY
Billy "Billy the Kid" Taylor
C – R. 5'9", 150 lbs. b: Winnipeg, Man., 5/3/1919. d: 6/12/1990.

1936-37	Toronto British Consols	City Jr.	12	12	14	*26	....	....	....	20	6	7	3	*10	0
1937-38	Oshawa Generals	OHA	12	19	7	26	....	....	....	27	7	*8	*9	*17	10
1938-39	Oshawa Generals	OHA	14	*22	*31	*53	....	....	....	37	16	*18	*24	*42	22
	Oshawa Sr. Generals	OHA	....	....	....	....	....	....	....	....	1	0	0	0	0
1939-40	**Toronto Maple Leafs**	**NHL**	**29**	**4**	**6**	**10**	**9**	**12**	**21**	**9**	**2**	**1**	**0**	**1**	**0**
	Pittsburgh Hornets	AHL	17	14	14	28	....	....	....	11	9	*7	5	*12	4
1940-41	**Toronto Maple Leafs**	**NHL**	**47**	**9**	**26**	**35**	**18**	**48**	**66**	**15**	**7**	**0**	**3**	**3**	**5**
1941-42	**Toronto Maple Leafs**	**NHL**	**48**	**12**	**26**	**38**	**21**	**40**	**61**	**20**	**13**	**2**	***8**	**10**	**4**
1942-43	**Toronto Maple Leafs**	**NHL**	**50**	**18**	**42**	**60**	**26**	**54**	**80**	**2**	**6**	**2**	**2**	**4**	**0**
1943-44	Simcoe Army	OHA Sr.	MILITARY SERVICE												
1944-45	Newmarket Army	Tor-Sr.	10	12	13	25	....	....	....	6	....	....	....	....	....
1945-46	**Toronto Maple Leafs**	**NHL**	**48**	**23**	**18**	**41**	**36**	**34**	**70**	**14**	....	....	....	....	....
1946-47	**Detroit Red Wings**	**NHL**	**60**	**17**	**46**	**63**	**23**	**67**	**90**	**35**	**5**	**1**	**5**	**6**	**4**
1947-48	**Boston Bruins**	**NHL**	**39**	**4**	**16**	**20**	**6**	**23**	**29**	**25**	....	....	....	....	....
	New York Rangers	**NHL**	**2**	**0**	**0**	**0**	**0**	**0**	**0**	**0**	....	....	....	....	....
1948-49			DID NOT PLAY – SUSPENDED												
	NHL Totals		**323**	**87**	**180**	**267**	**139**	**278**	**417**	**120**	**33**	**6**	**18**	**24**	**13**

Traded to **Detroit** by **Toronto** for Harry Watson, September 21, 1946. Traded to **Boston** by **Detroit** for Bep Guidolin, October 15, 1947. Traded to **NY Rangers** by **Boston** with future considerations (Pentti Lund and Ray Manson) for Grant Warwick, February 6, 1948.
• Suspended for life by NHL president Clarence Campbell for gambling infractions, March 9, 1948.

• TAYLOR, BILLY JR.
Billy Jr. Taylor
C – L. 6'1", 175 lbs. b: Winnipeg, Man., 10/14/1942. Deceased.

1960-61	Guelph Royals	OHA	48	12	19	31	....	....	....	89	14	7	5	12	*77
1961-62	Guelph Royals	OHA	38	20	26	46	....	....	....	81	....	....	....	....	....
	Kitchener Beavers	EPHL	2	0	0	0	....	....	....	0	....	....	....	....	....
1962-63	Guelph Royals	OHA	49	32	31	63	....	....	....	61	....	....	....	....	....
	Sudbury Wolves	EPHL	4	0	1	1	....	....	....	4	4	0	0	0	0
1963-64	St. Paul Rangers	CHL	69	30	29	59	....	....	....	87	11	4	4	8	10
1964-65	**New York Rangers**	**NHL**	**2**	**0**	**0**	**0**	**0**	**0**	**0**	**0**	....	....	....	....	....
	Baltimore Clippers	AHL	5	1	1	2	....	....	....	4	....	....	....	....	....
	St. Paul–St. Louis	CHL	43	17	24	41	....	....	....	65	....	....	....	....	....
1965-66	St. Louis Braves	CHL	68	13	21	34	....	....	....	72	5	1	1	2	2
1966-67	Buffalo Bisons	AHL	63	9	26	35	....	....	....	38	....	....	....	....	....
1967-68	Memphis South Stars	CHL	30	2	7	9	....	....	....	34	1	0	0	0	2
	NHL Totals		**2**	**0**	**0**	**0**	**0**	**0**	**0**	**0**	....	....	....	....	....

Traded to **Chicago** by **NY Rangers** with Camille Henry, Don Johns and Wally Chevrier for Doug Robinson, Wayne Hillman and John Brenneman, February 4, 1967. Claimed by **Minnesota** from **Chicago** in Intra-League Draft, June, 1967.

Season	Club	League	REGULAR SEASON								PLAYOFFS				
			GP	G	A	Pts	AG	AA	APts	PIM	GP	G	A	Pts	PIM

• TAYLOR, BOB
Bob Taylor
RW – R. 6'1", 190 lbs. b: Newton, MA, 8/12/1904. d: 12/12/1993.

1924-25	Boston Hockey Club	USAHA	5	2	0	2	....	....	....	4	....	....	....	....	....
1925-26	Boston Hockey Club	USAHA	4	2	0	2	....	....	....	....	....	....	....	....	....
	Boston AA	USAHA	....	....	....	....	....	....	....	....	2	0	0	0	0
1926-27	Boston Tigers	Can-Am	32	11	1	12	....	....	....	24	....	....	....	....	....
1927-28	Boston Tigers	Can-Am	40	8	2	10	....	....	....	30	2	0	0	0	2
1928-29	Boston Tigers	Can-Am	37	12	4	16	....	....	....	56	4	2	0	2	6
1929-30	**Boston Bruins**	**NHL**	**8**	**0**	**0**	**0**	**0**	**0**	**0**	**6**	....	....	....	....	....
	Philadelphia Arrows	Can-Am	34	11	3	14	....	....	....	46	2	0	0	0	8
1930-31	Boston Cubs	Can-Am	40	8	3	11	....	....	....	40	9	1	2	3	10
1931-32	Boston Cubs	Can-Am	1	0	0	0	....	....	....	2	....	....	....	....	....
	Providence Reds	Can-Am	37	6	5	11	....	....	....	20	5	1	*2	3	0
1932-33	Providence Reds	Can-Am	45	10	4	14	....	....	....	12	2	0	0	0	0
1933-34	Providence Reds	Can-Am	39	3	7	10	....	....	....	0	3	2	1	3	0
1934-35	Providence Reds	Can-Am	38	2	5	7	....	....	....	0	2	0	0	0	0
1935-36	Providence Reds	Can-Am	2	0	0	0	....	....	....	4	....	....	....	....	....
	NHL Totals		**8**	**0**	**0**	**0**	**0**	**0**	**0**	**6**	....	....	....	....	....

Claimed by **Boston** from **Boston Tigers** (Can-Am) in Inter-League Draft, May 13, 1929.

• TAYLOR, HARRY
Harry Taylor
C – R. 5'8", 165 lbs. b: St. James, Man., 3/28/1926.

1943-44	St. James Monarchs	MHL Jr.	10	10	5	15	....	....	....	4	6	*12	4	*16	0
1944-45	St. James Monarchs	MHL Jr.	DID NOT PLAY – INJURED												
1945-46	Winnipeg Monarchs	MHL Jr.	8	5	10	15	....	....	....	4	7	3	6	9	4
1946-47	**Toronto Maple Leafs**	**NHL**	**9**	**0**	**2**	**2**	**0**	**3**	**3**	**0**	....	....	....	....	....
	Tulsa Oilers	USHL	5	2	6	8	....	....	....	2	....	....	....	....	....
	Pittsburgh Hornets	AHL	38	4	10	14	....	....	....	18	12	1	0	1	8
1947-48	Providence Reds	AHL	54	24	39	63	....	....	....	44	5	1	0	1	4
1948-49	**Toronto Maple Leafs**	**NHL**	**42**	**4**	**7**	**11**	**6**	**11**	**17**	**30**	**1**	**0**	**0**	**0**	**0**
	Pittsburgh Hornets	AHL	16	2	8	10	....	....	....	15	....	....	....	....	....
1949-50	Cleveland Barons	AHL	57	27	27	54	....	....	....	39	9	1	3	4	10
1950-51	Cleveland Barons	AHL	61	9	31	40	....	....	....	15	10	4	5	9	4
1951-52	**Chicago Black Hawks**	**NHL**	**15**	**1**	**1**	**2**	**1**	**1**	**2**	**0**	....	....	....	....	....
	St. Louis Flyers	AHL	46	19	22	41	....	....	....	30	....	....	....	....	....
1952-53	St. Louis Flyers	AHL	39	14	14	28	....	....	....	16	....	....	....	....	....
1953-54	Buffalo Bisons	AHL	70	10	31	41	....	....	....	24	2	0	1	1	0
1954-55	Buffalo Bisons	AHL	1	0	0	0	....	....	....	0	....	....	....	....	....
	Ottawa Senators	QHL	12	0	4	4	....	....	....	4	....	....	....	....	....
	Soo Greyhounds	NOHA	24	5	9	14	....	....	....	18	14	3	3	6	4
1955-56	Soo Greyhounds	NOHA	48	12	21	33	....	....	....	28	5	3	1	4	0
	NHL Totals		**66**	**5**	**10**	**15**	**7**	**15**	**22**	**30**	**1**	**0**	**0**	**0**	**0**

Signed as a free agent by **Toronto**, May 1, 1946. Traded to **Cleveland** (AHL) by **Toronto** with Ray Ceresino and the loan of Tod Sloan for Bob Solinger, September 6, 1949. Traded to **Sault Ste. Marie** (NOHA) by **Buffalo** (AHL) for cash, December, 1954.

• TAYLOR, RALPH
Ralph "Bouncer" Taylor
D – R. 5'9", 180 lbs. b: Toronto, Ont., 10/2/1905. d: 7/3/1976.

1923-24	Toronto Canoe Club	OHA	5	3	2	5	....	....	....	8	....	....	....	....	....
1924-25	Toronto Canoe Club	OHA	8	9	2	11	....	....	....	0	2	0	2	2	....
1925-26	Toronto Canoe Club	OHA	8	2	2	4	....	....	....	....	....	....	....	....	....
1926-27	Chicago Cardinals	AHA	29	4	1	5	....	....	....	57	....	....	....	....	....
1927-28	**Chicago Black Hawks**	**NHL**	**22**	**1**	**1**	**2**	**3**	**8**	**11**	**39**	....	....	....	....	....
	Moose Jaw Maroons	PHL	16	7	2	9	....	....	....	20	....	....	....	....	....
1928-29	**Chicago Black Hawks**	**NHL**	**38**	**0**	**0**	**0**	**0**	**0**	**0**	**56**	....	....	....	....	....
	St. Louis Flyers	AHA	8	2	0	2	....	....	....	14	....	....	....	....	....
1929-30	**Chicago Black Hawks**	**NHL**	**17**	**1**	**0**	**1**	**2**	**0**	**2**	**42**	....	....	....	....	....
	New York Rangers	**NHL**	**22**	**2**	**0**	**2**	**4**	**0**	**4**	**32**	**4**	**0**	**0**	**0**	**10**
1930-31	Chicago Shamrocks	AHA	34	6	6	12	....	....	....	68	....	....	....	....	....
1931-32	Chicago Shamrocks	AHA	48	4	2	6	....	....	....	81	4	0	0	0	8
1932-33	Detroit Olympics	IAHL	35	3	4	7	....	....	....	62	....	....	....	....	....
1933-34	Tulsa Oilers	AHA	2	2	1	3	....	....	....	2	....	....	....	....	....
	Kansas City Greyhounds	AHA	46	4	6	10	....	....	....	47	3	2	1	3	10
1934-35	Kansas City Greyhounds	AHA	44	6	1	7	....	....	....	59	2	0	0	0	2
1935-36	Kansas City Greyhounds	AHA	48	6	8	14	....	....	....	44	....	....	....	....	....
1936-37	Kansas City Greyhounds	AHA	42	5	3	8	....	....	....	30	3	0	0	0	7
	Tulsa Oilers	AHA	1	0	0	0	....	....	....	0	....	....	....	....	....
1937-38	Kansas City Greyhounds	AHA	6	1	0	1	....	....	....	6	....	....	....	....	....
	St. Louis Flyers	AHA	21	0	1	1	....	....	....	14	7	0	0	0	6
1938-39	St. Louis Flyers	AHA	38	0	1	1	....	....	....	27	7	1	2	3	10
	NHL Totals		**99**	**4**	**1**	**5**	**9**	**8**	**17**	**169**	**4**	**0**	**0**	**0**	**10**

Signed as a free agent by **Chicago** (AHA), October 29, 1926. Claimed on waivers by **NY Rangers** from **Chicago**, January 8, 1930. Traded to **Chicago Shamrocks** (AHA) by **NY Rangers** for $7500, October 27, 1930. NHL rights transferred to **Detroit** from **Chicago Shamrocks** (AHA) after AHA club owners purchased Detroit (NHL and IAHL) franchises, September 2, 1932.

• TAYLOR, TED
— see page 1526

• TEAL, SKIP
Skip (Allan) Teal
C – L. 5'8", 155 lbs. b: Ridgeway, Ont., 7/17/1933.

1949-50	St. Catharines Teepees	OHA	....	....	....	....	....	....	....	....	3	1	2	3	0
1950-51	St. Catharines Teepees	OHA	51	37	28	65	....	....	....	87	8	1	3	4	4
1951-52	Barrie Flyers	OHA	14	4	9	13	....	....	....	56	....	....	....	....	....
1952-53	Barrie Flyers	OHA	36	26	24	50	....	....	....	48	14	12	6	18	15
1953-54	Hershey Bears	AHL	66	16	21	37	....	....	....	38	11	3	4	7	16
1954-55	**Boston Bruins**	**NHL**	**1**	**0**	**0**	**0**	**0**	**0**	**0**	**0**	....	....	....	....	....
	Hershey Bears	AHL	58	14	29	43	....	....	....	87	....	....	....	....	....
1955-56	Victoria Cougars	WHL	67	22	21	43	....	....	....	34	8	1	1	2	2
1956-57	Quebec Aces	QHL	66	23	41	64	....	....	....	48	10	2	6	8	0
1957-58	Quebec Aces	QHL	60	16	56	72	....	....	....	19	13	6	*14	20	4
	Springfield Indians	AHL	4	0	1	1	....	....	....	0	....	....	....	....	....
1958-59	Quebec Aces	QHL	62	24	38	62	....	....	....	42	....	....	....	....	....
1959-60	Kingston Frontenacs	EPHL	70	27	43	70	....	....	....	30	....	....	....	....	....
1960-61	Clinton Comets	EHL	63	46	66	112	....	....	....	32	4	1	1	2	0
1961-62	Clinton Comets	EHL	59	34	66	100	....	....	....	26	6	2	3	5	2
1962-63	Clinton Comets	EHL	51	35	58	91	....	....	....	12	13	10	8	18	10
	NHL Totals		**1**	**0**	**0**	**0**	**0**	**0**	**0**	**0**	....	....	....	....	....

EHL Second All-Star Team (1961, 1962, 1963)

TESSIER, ORVAL
Orval Tessier
C – L. 5'8", 160 lbs. b: Cornwall, Ont., 6/30/1933.

Season	Club	League	GP	G	A	Pts	AG	AA	APts	PIM	Playoffs GP	G	A	Pts	PIM
1951-52	Kitchener Greenshirts	OHA	52	*62	25	87	....	....	....	18	4	3	1	4	8
1952-53	Kitchener–Barrie	OHA	55	54	40	94	....	....	....	19	15	7	13	20	12
1953-54	Montreal Royals	QHL	60	21	18	39	....	....	....	13	9	2	1	3	6
1954-55	Montreal Canadiens	NHL	4	0	0	0	0	0	0	0	....	....	....	....	....
	Montreal Royals	QHL	60	*36	30	66	....	....	....	8	12	4	7	11	0
1955-56	Boston Bruins	NHL	23	2	3	5	3	4	7	6	....	....	....	....	....
	Hershey Bears	AHL	2	0	1	1	....	....	....	0	....	....	....	....	....
	Quebec Aces	QHL	28	5	10	15	....	....	....	4	7	1	2	3	2
1956-57	Quebec Aces	QHL	68	*43	38	*81	....	....	....	24	10	7	5	12	0
1957-58	Springfield Indians	AHL	12	5	3	8	....	....	....	2	....	....	....	....	....
1958-59	Trois-Rivieres Lions	QHL	62	27	39	66	....	....	....	4	8	2	3	5	9
1959-60	Kingston Frontenacs	EPHL	70	*59	*67	*126	....	....	....	10	....	....	....	....	....
1960-61	Boston Bruins	NHL	32	3	4	7	4	4	8	0	....	....	....	....	....
	Kingston Frontenacs	EPHL	34	22	21	43	....	....	....	6	5	4	2	6	0
1961-62	Kingston Frontenacs	EPHL	66	54	60	*114	....	....	....	12	11	5	9	14	0
1962-63	Portland Buckaroos	WHL	36	15	21	36	....	....	....	9	7	0	0	0	0
1963-64	Portland Buckaroos	WHL	66	14	34	48	....	....	....	4	5	1	2	3	0
1964-65	Clinton Comets	EHL	66	60	58	118	....	....	....	8	11	2	7	9	0
	NHL Totals		59	5	7	12	7	8	15	6	....	....	....	....	....

QHL First All-Star Team (1955, 1957) • Won President's Cup (Scoring Champion - QHL) (1957) • QHL Second All-Star Team (1959) • EHL North Second All-Star Team (1965) • Won Jack Adams Award (1983)

Claimed by **Boston** from **Montreal** in Intra-League Draft, June 1, 1955. Traded to **Montreal** by **Boston** (Portland-WHL) for cash, August, 1964.

THIBEAULT, LORRAN
Lorran "Larry Half-n-Half" Thibeault
LW – L. 5'7", 180 lbs. b: Chrletone, Ont., 10/2/1918.

Season	Club	League	GP	G	A	Pts	AG	AA	APts	PIM	Playoffs GP	G	A	Pts	PIM
1936-37	Cornwall Flyers	Ott-Sr.	23	3	4	7	....	....	....	10	6	0	0	0	0
1937-38	Hull Volants	Ott-Sr.	20	10	4	14	....	....	....	6	9	2	2	4	5
1938-39	Hull Volants	Ott-Sr.	9	15	2	17	....	....	....	14	....	....	....	....	....
	Springfield Indians	AHL	8	0	1	1	....	....	....	7	3	0	0	0	0
1939-40	Springfield Indians	AHL	29	11	14	25	....	....	....	6	3	0	0	0	2
1940-41	Springfield Indians	AHL	54	14	18	32	....	....	....	32	3	1	0	1	2
1941-42	Cornwall Flyers	QSHL	36	17	18	35	....	....	....	45	5	1	4	5	6
1942-43	Cornwall Flyers	QSHL	33	21	27	*48	....	....	....	22	6	1	2	3	2
1943-44	Buffalo Bisons	AHL	51	18	45	63	....	....	....	46	9	7	10	17	14
1944-45	Detroit Red Wings	NHL	4	0	2	2	0	3	3	2	....	....	....	....	....
	Indianapolis Capitals	AHL	31	2	12	14	....	....	....	20	2	0	0	0	2
1945-46	Montreal Canadiens	NHL	1	0	0	0	0	0	0	0	....	....	....	....	....
	Buffalo Bisons	AHL	6	2	3	5	....	....	....	4	....	....	....	....	....
	Hull Volants	QSHL	25	9	18	27			....	48	....	....	....	....	....
1946-47	Victoriaville Tigers	QPHL	35	21	41	62	....	....	....	40	5	2	3	5	2
1947-48	Houston Huskies	USHL	46	12	17	29	....	....	....	28	4	0	0	0	0
1948-49	Houston Huskies	USHL	22	7	6	13	....	....	....	14	....	....	....	....	....
	San Diego Skyhawks	PCHL	15	6	4	10	....	....	....	18	....	....	....	....	....
1949-50	Victoria Cougars	AHL	66	20	28	48	....	....	....	46	....	....	....	....	....
1950-51	Buckingham Beavers	ECSHL	DID NOT PLAY – COACHING												
1951-52	Buckingham Beavers	ECSHL	24	10	16	26	....	....	....	24	....	....	....	....	....
	Thurso Lumber Kings	Mtl-Sr.	10	3	3	6	....	....	....	15	6	1	1	2	4
1952-53	Thurso Lumber Kings	Mtl-Sr.	DID NOT PLAY – COACHING												
1953-54	Edmonton Flyers	WHL	61	4	8	12	....	....	....	16	13	2	1	3	2
1954-55			DID NOT PLAY												
1955-56	New Westminster Royals	WHL	8	1	2	3	....	....	....	14	....	....	....	....	....
	Quebec Aces	QHL	28	1	5	6	....	....	....	6	....	....	....	....	....
	NHL Totals		5	0	2	2	0	3	3	2	....	....	....	....	....

Signed as a free agent by **Detroit**, October 21, 1944. Traded to **Buffalo** (AHL) by **Detroit** for cash, October 17, 1945. Traded to **Montreal** by **Buffalo** (AHL) for cash and the loan of Wilf Field, Ken Mosdell and Frank Eddolls, October 28, 1945.

THOMAS, CY
Cy Thomas
LW/RW – L. 5'11", 185 lbs. b: Dowlais, Wales, 8/5/1926.

Season	Club	League	GP	G	A	Pts	AG	AA	APts	PIM	Playoffs GP	G	A	Pts	PIM
1945-46	Edmonton Canadians	AJHL	STATISTICS NOT AVAILABLE												
1946-47	Edmonton Flyers	WCSHL	30	12	7	19	....	....	....	18	4	0	3	3	7
1947-48	Chicago Black Hawks	NHL	6	1	0	1	1	0	1	8	....	....	....	....	....
	Toronto Maple Leafs	NHL	8	1	2	3	1	3	4	4	....	....	....	....	....
	Pittsburgh Hornets	AHL	29	2	4	6	....	....	....	14	2	0	0	0	0
	Spokane Flyers	Kootenay	18	9	19	28	....	....	....	28	....	....	....	....	....
1948-49	University of Alberta	Edm-Sr.	8	8	8	16	....	....	....	16	....	....	....	....	....
1949-50	Saskatoon Quakers	WCSHL	50	30	24	54	....	....	....	90	5	1	1	2	6
1950-51	Halifax St. Mary's	MMHL	60	29	29	58	....	....	....	103	12	6	5	11	25
1951-52	Calgary Stampeders	PCHL	69	24	43	67	....	....	....	83	....	....	....	....	....
	NHL Totals		14	2	2	4	2	3	5	12	....	....	....	....	....

Traded to **Toronto** by **Chicago** with Max Bentley for Bob Goldham, Ernie Dickens, Bud Poile, Gus Bodnar and Gaye Stewart, November 2, 1947.

THOMPSON, CLIFF
Cliff Thompson
D – L. 5'11", 185 lbs. b: Winchester, MA, 12/9/1918.

Season	Club	League	GP	G	A	Pts	AG	AA	APts	PIM	Playoffs GP	G	A	Pts	PIM
1938-39	Boston Olympics	EHL	4	3	1	4	....	....	....	2	....	....	....	....	....
1939-40	Boston Olympics	EHL	35	16	14	30	....	....	....	33	5	0	2	2	4
1940-41	Boston Olympics	EHL	65	12	18	30	....	....	....	80	4	0	4	4	4
1941-42	Boston Bruins	NHL	3	0	0	0	0	0	0	2	....	....	....	....	....
	Hershey Bears	EHL	20	3	5	8	....	....	....	2	....	....	....	....	....
	St. Paul Saints	AHA	28	5	6	11	....	....	....	22	2	1	0	1	0
	Boston Olympics	EHL	....	....	....	....	....	....	....	....	1	0	1	1	0
1942-43			MILITARY SERVICE												
1943-44			MILITARY SERVICE												
1944-45			MILITARY SERVICE												
1945-46	Boston Olympics	EHL	43	7	13	20	....	....	....	18	12	2	4	6	0
1946-47	Boston Olympics	EHL	53	11	19	30	....	....	....	51	9	2	6	8	6
1947-48	Boston Olympics	EHL	19	5	16	21	....	....	....	22	....	....	....	....	....
	Boston Olympics	QSHL	48	10	20	30	....	....	....	57	....	....	....	....	....
1948-49	Boston Bruins	NHL	10	0	1	1	0	2	2	0	....	....	....	....	....
	Hershey Bears	AHL	9	0	0	0	....	....	....	2	....	....	....	....	....
	Boston Olympics	QSHL	26	4	18	22	....	....	....	35	....	....	....	....	....
1949-50	Boston Olympics	EHL	26	7	14	21	....	....	....	57	3	2	1	3	0
	NHL Totals		13	0	1	1	0	2	2	2	....	....	....	....	....

EHL Second All-Star Team (1947, 1948)

THOMPSON, KENNETH
Kenneth Thompson
LW/C – L. 5'10", 160 lbs. b: Oakengates, England, 5/29/1881. Deceased.

Season	Club	League	GP	G	A	Pts	AG	AA	APts	PIM	Playoffs GP	G	A	Pts	PIM
1914-15	Montreal All-Montreal	City Sr.	11	14	0	14	....	....	....	9	....	....	....	....	....
1915-16	Laval University	Mtl-Sr.	10	8	0	8	....	....	....	6	1	0	0	0	0
1916-17	Montreal Wanderers	NHA	15	1	0	1	....	....	....	8	....	....	....	....	....
1917-18	Montreal Wanderers	NHL	1	0	0	0	0	0	0	0	....	....	....	....	....
	NHL Totals		1	0	0	0	0	0	0	0	....	....	....	....	....
	Other Major League Totals		15	1	0	1	....	....	....	8	....	....	....	....	....

Rights retained by **Montreal Wanderers** after NHA folded, November 26, 1917.

THOMPSON, PAUL
Paul Thompson
LW – L. 5'11", 180 lbs. b: Calgary, Alta., 11/2/1906. Deceased.

Season	Club	League	GP	G	A	Pts	AG	AA	APts	PIM	Playoffs GP	G	A	Pts	PIM
1925-26	Calgary Canadians	City Jr.	STATISTICS NOT AVAILABLE												
1926-27	New York Rangers	NHL	43	7	3	10	20	25	45	12	2	0	0	0	0
1927-28	New York Rangers	NHL	42	4	4	8	12	34	46	22	8	0	0	0	30
1928-29	New York Rangers	NHL	44	10	7	17	40	65	105	38	6	0	*2	2	6
1929-30	New York Rangers	NHL	44	7	12	19	14	39	53	36	4	0	0	0	2
1930-31	New York Rangers	NHL	44	7	7	14	17	25	42	36	4	3	0	3	2
1931-32	Chicago Black Hawks	NHL	48	8	14	22	17	39	56	34	2	0	0	0	2
1932-33	Chicago Black Hawks	NHL	48	13	20	33	31	53	84	27	....	....	....	....	....
1933-34	Chicago Black Hawks	NHL	48	20	16	36	45	43	88	17	8	4	3	7	6
1934-35	Chicago Black Hawks	NHL	48	16	23	39	34	52	86	20	2	0	0	0	0
1935-36	Chicago Black Hawks	NHL	45	17	23	40	42	56	98	19	2	0	3	3	0
1936-37	Chicago Black Hawks	NHL	47	17	18	35	37	42	79	28	....	....	....	....	....
1937-38	Chicago Black Hawks	NHL	48	22	22	44	47	46	93	14	10	4	3	7	6
1938-39	Chicago Black Hawks	NHL	33	5	10	15	10	19	29	33	....	....	....	....	....
1939-40	Chicago Black Hawks	NHL	DID NOT PLAY – COACHING												
	NHL Totals		582	153	179	332	366	538	904	336	48	11	11	22	54

NHL Second All-Star Team (1936)

Signed as a free agent by **NY Rangers**, October 12, 1926. Traded to **Chicago** by **NY Rangers** for Art Somers and Vic Desjardins, October 15, 1931.

THOMPSON, RHYS
Rhys "Tommy" Thompson
D – L. 6'1", 195 lbs. b: Toronto, Ont., 8/9/1918. Deceased.

Season	Club	League	GP	G	A	Pts	AG	AA	APts	PIM	Playoffs GP	G	A	Pts	PIM
1935-36	Toronto Young Rangers	City Jr.	9	3	2	5	....	....	....	20	2	0	0	0	2
1936-37	Toronto Young Rangers	City Jr.	11	1	2	3	....	....	....	13	3	0	0	0	2
1937-38	Toronto Young Rangers	OHA	9	5	2	7	....	....	....	13	3	2	1	3	8
1938-39			DID NOT PLAY												
1939-40	Montreal Canadiens	NHL	7	0	0	0	0	0	0	16	....	....	....	....	....
	New Haven Eagles	AHL	18	0	1	1	....	....	....	10	....	....	....	....	....
1940-41	Springfield Indians	AHL	51	3	7	10	....	....	....	30	....	....	....	....	....
1941-42	Springfield Indians	AHL	56	1	16	17	....	....	....	57	3	0	0	0	0
1942-43	Toronto Maple Leafs	NHL	18	0	2	2	0	3	3	22	....	....	....	....	....
	Providence Reds	AHL	23	2	12	14	....	....	....	48	2	0	0	0	0
1943-44	Kingston Frontenacs	Ott-Sr.	2	0	0	0	....	....	....	4	....	....	....	....	....
	Petawawa Grenades	Ott-Sr.	5	1	6	7	....	....	....	17	....	....	....	....	....
1944-45			MILITARY SERVICE												
1945-46	Toronto Staffords	OHA Sr.	14	2	2	4	....	....	....	19	10	2	0	2	8
	NHL Totals		25	0	2	2	0	3	3	38	....	....	....	....	....

Traded to **NY Americans** (Springfield - AHL) by **Montreal** for cash, October, 1940. Rights transferred to **Toronto** from **Brooklyn** in Special Dispersal Draw, September 11, 1942.

THOMS, BILL
Bill Thoms
C – L. 5'9", 170 lbs. b: Newmarket, Ont., 3/5/1910. d: 12/26/1964.

Season	Club	League	GP	G	A	Pts	AG	AA	APts	PIM	Playoffs GP	G	A	Pts	PIM
1929-30	West Toronto Nationals	OHA	7	7	*13	20	....	....	....	6	15	14	*9	*23	14
1930-31	Toronto Marlboros	OHA Sr.	10	*11	2	*13	....	....	....	4	3	0	0	0	2
1931-32	Toronto Marlboros	OHA Sr.	20	*16	6	*22	....	....	....	26	2	1	0	1	0
	Syracuse Stars	IAHL	12	2	4	6	....	....	....	2	....	....	....	....	....
1932-33	Toronto Maple Leafs	NHL	29	3	9	12	7	24	31	15	9	1	1	2	4
	Syracuse Stars	IAHL	20	7	7	14	....	....	....	18	....	....	....	....	....
	Toronto Marlboros	OHA Sr.	1	0	0	0	....	....	....	0	....	....	....	....	....
1933-34	Toronto Maple Leafs	NHL	47	8	18	26	18	48	66	24	5	0	2	2	0
1934-35	Toronto Maple Leafs	NHL	47	9	13	22	19	29	48	15	7	2	0	2	0
1935-36	Toronto Maple Leafs	NHL	48	*23	15	38	58	36	94	29	9	3	*5	8	0
1936-37	Toronto Maple Leafs	NHL	48	10	9	19	22	21	43	14	2	0	0	0	0
1937-38	Toronto Maple Leafs	NHL	48	14	24	38	30	50	80	14	7	0	1	1	0
1938-39	Toronto Maple Leafs	NHL	12	1	4	5	2	7	9	4	....	....	....	....	....
	Chicago Black Hawks	NHL	36	6	11	17	13	20	33	16	....	....	....	....	....
1939-40	Chicago Black Hawks	NHL	47	9	13	22	19	26	45	2	1	0	0	0	0
1940-41	Chicago Black Hawks	NHL	47	13	19	32	26	35	61	4	....	....	....	....	....
1941-42	Chicago Black Hawks	NHL	47	15	30	45	26	46	72	4	3	0	1	1	0
1942-43	Chicago Black Hawks	NHL	47	15	28	43	21	36	57	3	....	....	....	....	....
1943-44	Chicago Black Hawks	NHL	7	3	5	8	4	6	10	2	....	....	....	....	....
1944-45	Chicago Black Hawks	NHL	21	2	6	8	3	10	13	8	....	....	....	....	....
	Boston Bruins	NHL	17	4	2	6	5	3	8	0	1	0	0	0	2
	NHL Totals		548	135	206	341	273	397	670	154	44	6	10	16	6

NHL Second All-Star Team (1936)

Played in NHL All-Star Game (1934)

Traded to **Toronto** by **Syracuse** (IAHL) for Harold Darraugh, January 3, 1933. Traded to **Chicago** by **Toronto** for Doc Romnes, December 8, 1938. Traded to **Boston** by **Chicago** for cash, January 14, 1945.

• THOMSON, BILL — Bill Thomson
C/RW – R. 5'9", 162 lbs. b: Troon, Scotland, 3/23/1914.

Season	Club	League	GP	G	A	Pts	AG	AA	APts	PIM	Playoffs GP	G	A	Pts	PIM
1930-31	Kenora Thistles	NOHA	12	7	8	*15	....	....	....	2	3	0	0	0	0
1931-32	Port Arthur Ports	TBSHL	17	4	*7	11	....	....	....	6	2	1	0	1	0
1932-33	Port Arthur Ports	TBSHL	19	7	3	10	....	....	....	4	5	1	0	1	6
1933-34	Port Arthur Ports	TBSHL	13	8	4	12	....	....	....	20	4	1	0	1	0
1934-35	Port Arthur Ports	TBSHL	14	5	2	7	....	....	....	8	4	2	1	3	0
1935-36	Port Arthur Bearcats	TBSHL	8	7	0	7	....	....	....	2	....	....	....	....	....
	Canada	Nat-Tm.	11	*7	3	*10	....	....	....	4	....	....	....	....	....
	Canada	Olympics	8	7	0	7	....	....	....	2	....	....	....	....	....
1936-37	Port Arthur Bearcats	TBSHL	31	34	15	49	....	....	....	31	3	2	0	2	2
1937-38	Syracuse Stars	AHL	47	7	9	16	....	....	....	17	8	0	0	0	0
1938-39	**Detroit Red Wings**	**NHL**	**4**	**0**	**0**	**0**	**0**	**0**	**0**	**0**	....	....	....	....	....
	Syracuse–Pittsburgh	AHL	49	9	17	26	....	....	....	12	....	....	....	....	....
1939-40	Indianapolis Capitals	AHL	38	10	26	36	....	....	....	12	5	0	4	4	2
	Syracuse Stars	AHL	2	0	0	0	....	....	....	0	....	....	....	....	....
1940-41	Indianapolis Capitals	AHL	44	5	15	20	....	....	....	23	....	....	....	....	....
	Pittsburgh Hornets	AHL	1	0	0	0	....	....	....	0	....	....	....	....	....
1941-42	Omaha Knights	AHA	50	26	27	53	....	....	....	11	8	6	*7	13	0
1942-43	Indianapolis Capitals	AHL	55	23	22	45	....	....	....	4	7	4	2	6	10
1943-44	**Detroit Red Wings**	**NHL**	**5**	**2**	**2**	**4**	**2**	**2**	**4**	**0**	**2**	**0**	**0**	**0**	**0**
	Indianapolis Capitals	AHL	45	20	38	58	....	....	....	6	5	2	4	6	0
1944-45	Indianapolis Capitals	AHL	32	9	19	28	....	....	....	17	5	1	3	4	0
1945-46	St. Louis–Hershey	AHL	51	7	23	30	....	....	....	6	3	0	3	3	2
1946-47	Hershey Bears	AHL	13	2	5	7	....	....	....	0	....	....	....	....	....
	Minneapolis Millers	USHL	26	8	13	21	....	....	....	12	3	0	1	1	0
1947-48	Tulsa Oilers	USHL	56	10	24	34	....	....	....	0	1	1	0	1	0
1948-49	Dallas Texans	USHL	11	4	3	7	....	....	....	0	....	....	....	....	....
	Seattle Ironmen	PCHL	9	0	7	7	....	....	....	0	....	....	....	....	....
	NHL Totals		**9**	**2**	**2**	**4**	**2**	**2**	**4**	**0**	**2**	**0**	**0**	**0**	**0**

Signed as a free agent by **Toronto**, October 13, 1937. Traded to **Detroit** by **Toronto** with $10,000 for Bucko McDonald, December 19, 1938. Traded to **St. Louis** (AHL) by **Indianapolis** (AHL) for cash with Detroit holding rights of recall, January, 1946.

• THOMSON, JIMMY — Jimmy "Jeems" Thomson
D – R. 5'11", 175 lbs. b: Winnipeg, Man., 2/23/1927. Deceased.

Season	Club	League	GP	G	A	Pts	AG	AA	APts	PIM	Playoffs GP	G	A	Pts	PIM
1943-44	St. Michael's Majors	OHA	22	2	2	4	....	....	....	40	12	2	2	4	20
1944-45	St. Michael's Majors	OHA	18	13	12	25	....	....	....	*52	23	11	6	17	44
1945-46	**Toronto Maple Leafs**	**NHL**	**5**	**0**	**1**	**1**	**0**	**2**	**2**	**4**	....	....	....	....	....
	Pittsburgh Hornets	AHL	28	2	5	7	....	....	....	16	6	0	2	2	2
1946-47	**Toronto Maple Leafs**	**NHL**	**60**	**2**	**14**	**16**	**3**	**20**	**23**	**97**	**11**	**0**	**1**	**1**	**22**
1947-48	**Toronto Maple Leafs**	**NHL**	**59**	**0**	**29**	**29**	**0**	**43**	**43**	**82**	**9**	**1**	**1**	**2**	**9**
1948-49	**Toronto Maple Leafs**	**NHL**	**60**	**4**	**16**	**20**	**6**	**25**	**31**	**56**	**9**	**1**	**5**	**6**	**10**
1949-50	**Toronto Maple Leafs**	**NHL**	**70**	**0**	**13**	**13**	**0**	**16**	**16**	**76**	**7**	**0**	**2**	**2**	**7**
1950-51	**Toronto Maple Leafs**	**NHL**	**69**	**3**	**33**	**36**	**4**	**43**	**47**	**76**	**11**	**0**	**1**	**1**	***34**
1951-52	**Toronto Maple Leafs**	**NHL**	**70**	**0**	**25**	**25**	**0**	**33**	**33**	**86**	**4**	**0**	**0**	**0**	**25**
1952-53	**Toronto Maple Leafs**	**NHL**	**69**	**0**	**22**	**22**	**0**	**31**	**31**	**73**	....	....	....	....	....
1953-54	**Toronto Maple Leafs**	**NHL**	**61**	**2**	**24**	**26**	**3**	**33**	**36**	**86**	**3**	**0**	**0**	**0**	**2**
1954-55	**Toronto Maple Leafs**	**NHL**	**70**	**4**	**12**	**16**	**6**	**15**	**21**	**63**	**4**	**0**	**0**	**0**	**16**
1955-56	**Toronto Maple Leafs**	**NHL**	**62**	**0**	**7**	**7**	**0**	**9**	**9**	**96**	**5**	**0**	**3**	**3**	**10**
1956-57	**Toronto Maple Leafs**	**NHL**	**62**	**0**	**12**	**12**	**0**	**14**	**14**	**50**	....	....	....	....	....
1957-58	**Chicago Black Hawks**	**NHL**	**70**	**4**	**7**	**11**	**5**	**8**	**13**	**75**	....	....	....	....	....
	NHL Totals		**787**	**19**	**215**	**234**	**27**	**292**	**319**	**920**	**63**	**2**	**13**	**15**	**135**

NHL Second All-Star Team (1951, 1952)

Played in NHL All-Star Game (1947, 1948, 1949, 1950, 1951, 1952, 1953)

Traded to **Chicago** by **Toronto** for cash, August, 1957. Traded to **Toronto** by **Chicago** for cash, July, 1958.

• THORSTEINSON, JOE — Joe "Stony" Thorsteinson
RW – R. 5'9", 157 lbs. b: Winnipeg, Man., 3/19/1905. d: 8/24/1948.

Season	Club	League	GP	G	A	Pts	AG	AA	APts	PIM	Playoffs GP	G	A	Pts	PIM
1922-23	Selkirk Fisherman	MHL Sr.	14	3	7	10	....	....	....	10	....	....	....	....	....
1923-24	Selkirk Fisherman	MHL Sr.	2	0	1	1	....	....	....	0	....	....	....	....	....
1924-25	Coleman Tigers	ASHL	STATISTICS NOT AVAILABLE												
1925-26	Winnipeg Maroons	AHA	21	4	1	5	....	....	....	22	5	1	1	2	0
1926-27	Winnipeg Maroons	AHA	26	4	1	5	....	....	....	53	3	1	0	1	2
	Moose Jaw Maroons	PrHL	16	3	0	3	....	....	....	4	....	....	....	....	....
1927-28	Regina Capitals	PrHL	26	7	3	10	....	....	....	26	....	....	....	....	....
1928-29	Duluth Hornets	AHA	39	8	4	12	....	....	....	32	....	....	....	....	....
1929-30	St. Paul Saints	AHA	48	9	6	15	....	....	....	44	....	....	....	....	....
1930-31	Buffalo Majors	AHA	42	20	14	34	....	....	....	38	....	....	....	....	....
1931-32	Bufalo Majors	AHA	9	1	0	1	....	....	....	6	....	....	....	....	....
	Duluth Hornets	AHA	37	5	4	9	....	....	....	26	4	0	0	0	2
1932-33	**New York Americans**	**NHL**	**4**	**0**	**0**	**0**	**0**	**0**	**0**	**0**	....	....	....	....	....
	Edmonton Eskimos	WCHL	5	2	0	2	....	....	....	4	....	....	....	....	....
	New Haven Eagles	Can-Am	3	0	0	0	....	....	....	2	....	....	....	....	....
1933-34	Wichita Vikings	AHA	2	2	1	3	....	....	....	4	....	....	....	....	....
	St. Louis Flyers	AHA	14	0	0	0	....	....	....	2	....	....	....	....	....
	Tulsa Oilers	AHA	9	1	3	4	....	....	....	23	....	....	....	....	....
1934-35	Minneapolis Millers	CHL	28	2	5	7	....	....	....	21	5	1	2	3	2
	NHL Totals		**4**	**0**	**0**	**0**	**0**	**0**	**0**	**0**	....	....	....	....	....

• THURIER, FRED — Fred Thurier
C – R. 5'11", 160 lbs. b: Granby, Que., 1/11/1916. Deceased.

Season	Club	League	GP	G	A	Pts	AG	AA	APts	PIM	Playoffs GP	G	A	Pts	PIM
1936-37	Montreal Sr. Canadiens	Mtl-Sr.	22	12	6	18	....	....	....	20	2	0	0	0	4
1937-38	Springfield Indians	AHL	46	10	9	19	....	....	....	18	....	....	....	....	....
1938-39	Springfield Indians	AHL	36	11	8	19	....	....	....	21	3	0	0	0	0
1939-40	Springfield Indians	AHL	54	28	32	60	....	....	....	27	3	2	1	3	12
1940-41	**New York Americans**	**NHL**	**3**	**2**	**1**	**3**	**4**	**2**	**6**	**0**	....	....	....	....	....
	Springfield Indians	AHL	41	*29	31	60	....	....	....	36	3	0	1	1	0
1941-42	**Brooklyn Americans**	**NHL**	**27**	**7**	**7**	**14**	**12**	**11**	**23**	**4**	....	....	....	....	....
	Springfield Indians	AHL	22	20	24	44	....	....	....	6	5	2	5	7	2
1942-43	Buffalo Bisons	AHL	7	6	9	15	....	....	....	2	....	....	....	....	....
	Montreal Army	QSHL	13	8	5	13	....	....	....	6	7	3	2	5	6
	Montreal Army	City Sr.	2	4	1	5	....	....	....	0	....	....	....	....	....
1943-44	Montreal Army	City Sr.	1	0	0	0	....	....	....	0	....	....	....	....	....
	Buffalo Bisons	AHL	39	33	40	73	....	....	....	43	9	*8	10	*18	14
1944-45	**New York Rangers**	**NHL**	**50**	**16**	**19**	**35**	**22**	**31**	**53**	**14**	....	....	....	....	....
1945-46	Cleveland Barons	AHL	47	21	32	53	....	....	....	18	12	*9	7	*16	6
1946-47	Cleveland Barons	AHL	63	18	33	51	....	....	....	58	4	0	0	0	0
1947-48	Cleveland Barons	AHL	68	36	38	74	....	....	....	38	9	5	8	*13	4
1948-49	Cleveland Barons	AHL	51	26	31	57	....	....	....	47	5	2	7	9	2
1949-50	Cleveland Barons	AHL	57	30	52	82	....	....	....	22	4	2	0	2	0
1950-51	Cleveland Barons	AHL	64	32	63	95	....	....	....	19	10	1	12	12	0
1951-52	Cleveland Barons	AHL	47	19	23	42	....	....	....	12	4	1	2	3	4
	NHL Totals		**80**	**25**	**27**	**52**	**38**	**44**	**82**	**18**	....	....	....	....	....

AHL First All-Star Team (1941) • AHL Second All-Star Team (1942, 1951)

Traded to **NY Americans** by **Springfield** (AHL) for cash, October 10, 1940. Rights transferred to **NY Rangers** from **Brooklyn** in Special Dispersal Draw, October 9, 1944.

• TIMGREN, RAY — Ray "Golden Boy" Timgren
LW – L. 5'9", 150 lbs. b: Windsor, Ont., 9/29/1928.

Season	Club	League	GP	G	A	Pts	AG	AA	APts	PIM	Playoffs GP	G	A	Pts	PIM
1946-47	Toronto Marlboros	OHA	20	20	7	27	....	....	....	6	2	2	3	5	0
1947-48	Toronto Marlboros	OHA	30	20	20	40	....	....	....	33	....	....	....	....	....
	Toronto Marlboros	OHA Sr.	3	1	0	1	....	....	....	0	5	1	1	2	2
1948-49	**Toronto Maple Leafs**	**NHL**	**36**	**3**	**12**	**15**	**5**	**19**	**24**	**9**	**9**	**3**	**3**	**6**	**2**
	Toronto Marlboros	OHA Sr.	26	6	22	28	....	....	....	27	....	....	....	....	....
1949-50	**Toronto Maple Leafs**	**NHL**	**68**	**7**	**18**	**25**	**9**	**23**	**32**	**22**	**6**	**0**	**4**	**4**	**2**
1950-51	**Toronto Maple Leafs**	**NHL**	**70**	**1**	**9**	**10**	**1**	**12**	**13**	**20**	**11**	**0**	**1**	**1**	**2**
1951-52	**Toronto Maple Leafs**	**NHL**	**50**	**2**	**4**	**6**	**3**	**5**	**8**	**11**	**4**	**0**	**1**	**1**	**0**
	Pittsburgh Hornets	AHL	19	13	5	18	....	....	....	11	....	....	....	....	....
1952-53	**Toronto Maple Leafs**	**NHL**	**12**	**0**	**0**	**0**	**0**	**0**	**0**	**4**	....	....	....	....	....
	Pittsburgh Hornets	AHL	50	16	12	28	....	....	....	23	10	2	0	2	0
1953-54	Pittsburgh Hornets	AHL	70	22	30	52	....	....	....	27	5	1	1	2	2
1954-55	**Toronto Maple Leafs**	**NHL**	**1**	**0**	**0**	**0**	**0**	**0**	**0**	**2**	....	....	....	....	....
	Chicago Black Hawks	**NHL**	**14**	**1**	**1**	**2**	**1**	**1**	**2**	**2**	....	....	....	....	....
	Pittsburgh Hornets	AHL	45	12	13	25	....	....	....	24	10	3	4	7	2
1955-56	Pittsburgh Hornets	AHL	8	0	4	4	....	....	....	13	....	....	....	....	....
	NHL Totals		**251**	**14**	**44**	**58**	**19**	**60**	**79**	**70**	**30**	**3**	**9**	**12**	**6**

Played in NHL All-Star Game (1949)

Traded to **Chicago** by **Toronto** for Jack Price, October 4, 1954. Loaned to **Toronto** (Pittsburgh - AHL) by **Chicago**, November 16, 1954.

• TOMSON, JACK — Jack Tomson
D – R. 6'1", 175 lbs. b: Uxbridge, England, 1/31/1918.

Season	Club	League	GP	G	A	Pts	AG	AA	APts	PIM	Playoffs GP	G	A	Pts	PIM
1934-35	Regina Wares	RCJHL	6	3	2	5	....	....	....	0	....	....	....	....	....
1935-36	Regina Christies	RCJHL	3	4	0	4	....	....	....	4	....	....	....	....	....
	Regina Aces	RCJHL	3	1	1	2	....	....	....	6	6	2	2	4	0
1936-37	Regina Aces	RCJHL	5	6	0	6	....	....	....	0	2	0	0	0	0
1937-38	Regina Aces	RCHL	24	15	8	23	....	....	....	23	3	1	0	1	0
1938-39	Seattle Seahawks	PCHL	7	0	0	0	....	....	....	0	....	....	....	....	....
	Philadelphia Ramblers	AHL	45	2	9	11	....	....	....	36	7	0	0	0	6
	New York Americans	**NHL**	....	....	....	....	....	....	....	....	**2**	**0**	**0**	**0**	**0**
1939-40	**New York Americans**	**NHL**	**12**	**1**	**1**	**2**	**2**	**2**	**4**	**0**	....	....	....	....	....
	Kansas City Greyhounds	AHA	11	0	2	2	....	....	....	6	....	....	....	....	....
	Springfield Indians	AHL	22	2	3	5	....	....	....	2	2	0	0	0	2
1940-41	**New York Americans**	**NHL**	**3**	**0**	**0**	**0**	**0**	**0**	**0**	**0**	....	....	....	....	....
	Seattle Olympics	PCHL	40	16	15	31	....	....	....	55	2	0	0	0	2
1941-42	Regina Rangers	RCHL	27	6	12	18	....	....	....	41	3	0	0	0	2
1942-43	Victoria Navy	City Sr	18	8	10	18	....	....	....	41	6	6	5	*11	11
1943-44	Victoria Navy	PCHL	16	5	4	9	....	....	....	22	....	....	....	....	....
1944-45			MILITARY SERVICE												
1945-46	New Westminster Royals	PCHL	53	16	22	38	....	....	....	65	....	....	....	....	....
1946-47	New Westminster Royals	PCHL	57	28	21	49	....	....	....	98	4	0	1	1	0
1947-48	New Westminster Royals	PCHL	54	14	23	37	....	....	....	84	4	1	1	2	0
1948-49	Seattle Ironmen	PCHL	69	12	20	32	....	....	....	31	....	....	....	....	....
1949-50	Kerrisdale Monarchs	Kootenay	24	5	8	13	....	....	....	25	3	0	0	0	2
	NHL Totals		**15**	**1**	**1**	**2**	**2**	**2**	**4**	**0**	**2**	**0**	**0**	**0**	**0**

Signed as a free agent by **NY Americans**, October 24, 1938.

• TOPPAZZINI, JERRY

Jerry "Topper" Toppazzini
RW – R. 6', 180 lbs. b: Copper Cliff, Ont., 7/29/1931.

			REGULAR SEASON								PLAYOFFS				
Season	Club	League	GP	G	A	Pts	AG	AA	APts	PIM	GP	G	A	Pts	PIM
1947-48	Copper Cliff Redmen	NOHA	9	4	1	5	....	....	....	0	3	2	1	3	0
1948-49	St. Catharines Teepees	OHA	45	24	20	44	....	....	....	37	5	2	2	4	4
1949-50	Barrie Flyers	OHA	36	15	17	32	....	....	....	60	9	1	4	5	4
1950-51	Barrie Flyers	OHA	54	40	50	90	....	....	....	116	12	7	9	16	15
1951-52	Hershey Bears	AHL	54	20	25	45	....	....	....	26	5	0	1	1	4
1952-53	**Boston Bruins**	**NHL**	**69**	**10**	**13**	**23**	**15**	**18**	**33**	**36**	**11**	**0**	**3**	**3**	**9**
1953-54	**Boston Bruins**	**NHL**	**37**	**0**	**5**	**5**	**0**	**7**	**7**	**24**	....	....	....	....	....
	Hershey Bears	AHL	16	5	10	15	....	....	....	23	....	....	....	....	....
	Chicago Black Hawks	**NHL**	**14**	**5**	**3**	**8**	**8**	**4**	**12**	**18**	....	....	....	....	....
1954-55	**Chicago Black Hawks**	**NHL**	**70**	**9**	**18**	**27**	**13**	**23**	**36**	**59**	....	....	....	....	....
1955-56	**Detroit Red Wings**	**NHL**	**40**	**1**	**7**	**8**	**1**	**9**	**10**	**31**	....	....	....	....	....
	Boston Bruins	**NHL**	**28**	**7**	**7**	**14**	**10**	**9**	**19**	**22**	....	....	....	....	....
1956-57	**Boston Bruins**	**NHL**	**55**	**15**	**23**	**38**	**20**	**27**	**47**	**26**	**10**	**0**	**1**	**1**	**2**
1957-58	**Boston Bruins**	**NHL**	**64**	**25**	**24**	**49**	**33**	**26**	**59**	**51**	**12**	**9**	**3**	**12**	**2**
1958-59	**Boston Bruins**	**NHL**	**70**	**21**	**23**	**44**	**27**	**24**	**51**	**61**	**7**	**4**	**2**	**6**	**0**
1959-60	**Boston Bruins**	**NHL**	**69**	**12**	**33**	**45**	**15**	**34**	**49**	**26**	....	....	....	....	....
1960-61	**Boston Bruins**	**NHL**	**67**	**15**	**35**	**50**	**18**	**36**	**54**	**35**	....	....	....	....	....
1961-62	**Boston Bruins**	**NHL**	**70**	**19**	**31**	**50**	**23**	**31**	**54**	**26**	....	....	....	....	....
1962-63	**Boston Bruins**	**NHL**	**65**	**17**	**18**	**35**	**21**	**19**	**40**	**6**	....	....	....	....	....
1963-64	**Boston Bruins**	**NHL**	**65**	**7**	**4**	**11**	**9**	**4**	**13**	**15**	....	....	....	....	....
1964-65	Pittsburgh Hornets	AHL	65	16	31	47	....	....	....	32	4	2	6	8	0
1965-66	Los Angeles Blades	WHL	47	6	17	23	....	....	....	8	....	....	....	....	....
1966-67	Los Angeles Blades	WHL	59	19	37	56	....	....	....	22	....	....	....	....	....
1967-68	Port Huron Flags	IHL	37	11	26	37	....	....	....	25	....	....	....	....	....
	NHL Totals		**783**	**163**	**244**	**407**	**213**	**271**	**484**	**436**	**40**	**13**	**9**	**22**	**13**

Played in NHL All-Star Game (1955, 1958, 1959)

Traded to **Chicago** by **Boston** for Gus Bodnar, February 16, 1954. Traded to **Detroit** by **Chicago** with Dave Creighton, Gord Hollingworth and John McCormack for Tony Leswick, Glen Skov, John Wilson and Benny Woit, May 28, 1955. Traded to **Boston** by **Detroit** with Real Chevrefils for Murray Costello and Lorne Ferguson, January 17, 1956. Traded to **Chicago** by **Boston** with Matt Ravlich for Murray Balfour and Mike Draper, June 9, 1964. Traded to **Detroit** (Pittsburgh - AHL) by **Chicago** for Hank Ciesla, October 10, 1964. Claimed by **LA Blades** (WHL) from **Detroit** in Reverse Draft, June, 1965.

• TOPPAZZINI, ZELLIO

Zellio Toppazzini
RW – R. 5'11", 180 lbs. b: Copper Cliff, Ont., 1/5/1930.

Season	Club	League	GP	G	A	Pts	AG	AA	APts	PIM	GP	G	A	Pts	PIM
1946-47	Copper Cliff Redmen	NOHA	9	10	3	13	....	....	....	6	5	4	4	8	5
1947-48	St. Catharines Teepees	OHA	33	27	18	45	....	....	....	53	3	4	4	8	2
1948-49	**Boston Bruins**	**NHL**	**5**	**1**	**1**	**2**	**2**	**2**	**4**	**0**	**2**	**0**	**0**	**0**	**0**
	Hershey Bears	AHL	49	9	14	23	....	....	....	15	....	....	....	....	....
1949-50	**Boston Bruins**	**NHL**	**36**	**5**	**5**	**10**	**7**	**6**	**13**	**18**	....	....	....	....	....
	Hershey Bears	AHL	34	16	9	25	....	....	....	6	....	....	....	....	....
1950-51	**Boston Bruins**	**NHL**	**4**	**0**	**1**	**1**	**0**	**1**	**1**	**0**	....	....	....	....	....
	Hershey Bears	AHL	12	6	5	11	....	....	....	2	....	....	....	....	....
	New York Rangers	**NHL**	**55**	**14**	**14**	**28**	**19**	**18**	**37**	**27**	....	....	....	....	....
1951-52	**New York Rangers**	**NHL**	**16**	**1**	**1**	**2**	**1**	**1**	**2**	**4**	....	....	....	....	....
	Cincinnati–Providence	AHL	40	22	29	51	....	....	....	6	11	3	7	10	2
1952-53	Providence Reds	AHL	64	35	32	67	....	....	....	23	....	....	....	....	....
1953-54	Providence Reds	AHL	70	33	43	76	....	....	....	18	....	....	....	....	....
1954-55	Providence Reds	AHL	62	21	*53	74	....	....	....	12	....	....	....	....	....
1955-56	Providence Reds	AHL	64	42	*71	*113	....	....	....	44	9	7	*13	*20	2
1956-57	**Chicago Black Hawks**	**NHL**	**7**	**0**	**0**	**0**	**0**	**0**	**0**	**0**	....	....	....	....	....
	Providence Reds	AHL	44	13	40	53	....	....	....	16	5	0	1	1	4
1957-58	Providence Reds	AHL	70	27	42	69	....	....	....	14	5	1	1	2	0
1958-59	Providence Reds	AHL	67	17	38	55	....	....	....	14	....	....	....	....	....
1959-60			DID NOT PLAY – RETIRED												
1960-61	Providence Reds	AHL	68	31	34	65	....	....	....	2	....	....	....	....	....
1961-62	Providence Reds	AHL	66	21	36	57	....	....	....	2	3	1	2	3	0
1962-63	Providence Reds	AHL	61	16	24	40	....	....	....	10	6	4	4	8	0
1963-64	Providence Reds	AHL	14	1	6	7	....	....	....	0	1	0	0	0	0
1964-65	Providence College	Ivy	DID NOT PLAY – COACHING												
	NHL Totals		**123**	**21**	**22**	**43**	**29**	**28**	**57**	**49**	**2**	**0**	**0**	**0**	**0**

AHL Second All-Star Team (1955) • AHL First All-Star Team (1956) • Won John B. Sollenberger Trophy (Top Scorer - AHL) (1956)

Traded to **NY Rangers** by **Boston** with Ed Harrison for Dunc Fisher, November 16, 1950. Traded to **Providence** (AHL) by **NY Rangers** with Pat Egan and Jean-Paul Denis for Jack Stoddard, December, 1951. Claimed by **Chicago** from **Providence** (AHL) in Inter-League Draft, June 5, 1956.

• TOUHEY, BILL

Bill Touhey
LW – L. 5'9", 155 lbs. b: Ottawa, Ont., 3/23/1906.

Season	Club	League	GP	G	A	Pts	AG	AA	APts	PIM	GP	G	A	Pts	PIM
1924-25	Ottawa Gunners	City Sr.	16	*15	3	*18	....	....	....	....	....	....	....	....	....
1925-26	Ottawa Montagnards	City Sr.	15	7	*5	12	....	....	....	....	5	1	0	1	....
1926-27	Stratford Nationals	Can-Pro	30	19	*10	*29	....	....	....	18	2	0	0	0	6
1927-28	**Montreal Maroons**	**NHL**	**29**	**2**	**0**	**2**	**6**	**0**	**6**	**2**	....	....	....	....	....
	Stratford Nationals	Can-Pro	11	2	3	5	....	....	....	15	5	*4	1	5	4
1928-29	**Ottawa Senators**	**NHL**	**44**	**9**	**3**	**12**	**36**	**27**	**63**	**28**	....	....	....	....	....
1929-30	**Ottawa Senators**	**NHL**	**44**	**10**	**3**	**13**	**20**	**10**	**30**	**24**	**2**	**1**	**0**	**1**	**0**
1930-31	**Ottawa Senators**	**NHL**	**44**	**15**	**15**	**30**	**37**	**55**	**92**	**8**	....	....	....	....	....
1931-32	**Boston Bruins**	**NHL**	**26**	**5**	**4**	**9**	**11**	**11**	**22**	**12**	....	....	....	....	....
	Boston Cubs	Can-Am	5	1	0	1	....	....	....	2	....	....	....	....	....
	Philadelphia Arrows	Can-Am	11	1	5	6	....	....	....	4	....	....	....	....	....
1932-33	**Ottawa Senators**	**NHL**	**47**	**12**	**7**	**19**	**28**	**18**	**46**	**12**	....	....	....	....	....
1933-34	**Ottawa Senators**	**NHL**	**46**	**12**	**8**	**20**	**27**	**21**	**48**	**21**	....	....	....	....	....
1934-35	Syracuse–Windsor	IAHL	38	5	16	21	....	....	....	2	....	....	....	....	....
1935-36	Buffalo Bisons	IAHL	40	15	15	30	....	....	....	8	5	0	0	0	0
1936-37			DID NOT PLAY												
1937-38	Ottawa Senators	City Sr.	21	8	12	20	....	....	....	2	2	1	1	2	0
1938-39	Ottawa Senators	City Sr.	22	11	11	22	....	....	....	6	6	2	4	6	2
1939-40	Ottawa Senators	City Sr.	30	9	18	27	....	....	....	4	....	....	....	....	....
	NHL Totals		**280**	**65**	**40**	**105**	**165**	**142**	**307**	**107**	**2**	**1**	**0**	**1**	**0**

Signed as a free agent by **Montreal Maroons**, November 2, 1927. Traded to **Stratford** (Can-Pro) by **Montreal Maroons** for Fred Brown with Montreal holding rights of recall, February 14, 1928. Traded to **Ottawa** by **Montreal Maroons** for cash, October 25, 1928. Claimed by **Boston** from **Ottawa** for 1931-32 season in Dispersal Draft, September 26, 1931. Transferred to **St. Louis** after **Ottawa** franchise relocated, May 14, 1934.

• TOUPIN, JACQUES

Jacques Toupin
RW – R. 5'7", 155 lbs. b: Trois Rivieres, Que., 11/10/1910. d: 2/17/1987.

			REGULAR SEASON								PLAYOFFS				
Season	Club	League	GP	G	A	Pts	AG	AA	APts	PIM	GP	G	A	Pts	PIM
1928-29	Trois-Rivieres Renards	ECHA	21	9	1	10	....	....	....	12	....	....	....	....	....
1929-30	Trois-Rivieres Renards	ECHA	9	4	3	7	....	....	....	12	....	....	....	....	....
1930-31	Trois-Rivieres Renards	ECHA	18	9	*13	*22	....	....	....	15	2	0	0	0	2
1931-32	Quebec Castors	ECHA	24	13	8	21	....	....	....	12	3	3	*6	*9	0
1932-33	Quebec Castors	Can-Am	48	13	23	36	....	....	....	24	....	....	....	....	....
1933-34	Quebec Castors	Can-Am	40	12	14	26	....	....	....	14	....	....	....	....	....
1934-35	London Tecumsehs	IAHL	15	2	8	10	....	....	....	0	5	2	2	4	2
	Quebec Beavers	Can-Am	27	5	10	15	....	....	....	0	....	....	....	....	....
1935-36	Springfield Indians	Can-Am	47	18	15	33	....	....	....	20	3	1	2	3	2
1936-37	Springfield Indians	AHL	43	14	23	37	....	....	....	6	5	0	1	1	4
1937-38	Springfield Indians	AHL	48	11	19	30	....	....	....	24	....	....	....	....	....
1938-39	Springfield Indians	AHL	53	8	31	39	....	....	....	16	3	0	0	0	0
1939-40	Springfield Indians	AHL	49	16	*34	50	....	....	....	12	....	....	....	....	....
1940-41	Buffalo Bisons	AHL	48	21	22	43	....	....	....	15	....	....	....	....	....
1941-42	Buffalo Bisons	AHL	56	15	36	51	....	....	....	34	....	....	....	....	....
1942-43	Providence Reds	AHL	53	22	39	61	....	....	....	8	2	0	2	2	0
1943-44	Providence Reds	AHL	25	16	26	42	....	....	....	14	....	....	....	....	....
	Chicago Black Hawks	**NHL**	**8**	**1**	**2**	**3**	**1**	**2**	**3**	**0**	**4**	**0**	**0**	**0**	**0**
1944-45	Shawinigan Cataracts	QPHL	22	23	25	48	....	....	....	6	6	5	4	9	0
	Valleyfield Braves	QPHL	....	....	....	....	....	....	....	....	8	4	3	7	2
1945-46	Shawinigan Cataracts	QSHL	24	13	12	25	....	....	....	22	4	0	0	0	10
	NHL Totals		**8**	**1**	**2**	**3**	**1**	**2**	**3**	**0**	**4**	**0**	**0**	**0**	**0**

Traded to **Chicago** by **Providence** (AHL) for cash, February 28, 1944.

• TOWNSEND, ART

Art "Bull" Townsend
D – L. 5'10", 185 lbs. b: Souris, Man., 10/9/1905. d: 5/7/1971.

Season	Club	League	GP	G	A	Pts	AG	AA	APts	PIM	GP	G	A	Pts	PIM
1924-25	Brandon Wheat Kings	MHL Sr.	20	7	2	9	....	....	....	....	....	....	....	....	....
1925-26	Portland Rosebuds	WHL	29	4	2	6	....	....	....	48	....	....	....	....	....
1926-27	**Chicago Black Hawks**	**NHL**	**5**	**0**	**0**	**0**	**0**	**0**	**0**	**0**	....	....	....	....	....
	Springfield Indians	Can-Am	24	7	1	8	....	....	....	40	6	0	0	0	6
1927-28	Winnipeg Maroons	AHA	38	5	4	9	....	....	....	93	....	....	....	....	....
1928-29	Tulsa Oilers	AHA	20	1	1	2	....	....	....	39	....	....	....	....	....
1929-30	Seattle Eskimos	PCHL	28	3	1	4	....	....	....	118	....	....	....	....	....
1930-31	San Francisco Tigers	Cal-Pro	....	1	5	6	....	....	....	....	....	....	....	....	....
1931-32	London Tecumseh's	IAHL	6	0	0	0	....	....	....	4	....	....	....	....	....
	Trois-Rivieres Renards	ECHA	23	5	3	8	....	....	....	38	....	....	....	....	....
1932-33	Regina—Edmonton	WCHL	25	4	4	8	....	....	....	37	8	1	2	3	8
1933-34	Edmonton Eskimos	NWHL	34	10	9	19	....	....	....	*102	2	0	1	1	4
1934-35	Edmonton–Portland	NWHL	29	4	8	12	....	....	....	53	....	....	....	....	....
1935-36	Edmonton Eskimos	NWHL	40	5	6	11	....	....	....	*84	....	....	....	....	....
1936-37	University of Alberta	Edm-Sr.	DID NOT PLAY – COACHING												
1937-38	Edmonton Superiors	City Sr.	20	7	5	12	....	....	....	49	....	....	....	....	....
1938-39	Edmonton Superiors	City Sr.	10	1	1	2	....	....	....	10	....	....	....	....	....
	NHL Totals		**5**	**0**	**0**	**0**	**0**	**0**	**0**	**0**	....	....	....	....	....
	Other Major League Totals		29	4	2	6	....	....	....	48	....	....	....	....	....

Signed as a free agent by **Regina** (WCHL), March 9, 1925. Transferred to **Portland** (WHL) after **Regina** franchise relocated, September 1, 1925. NHL rights transferred to **Chicago** after NHL club purchased **Portland** (WHL) franchise, May 16, 1926.

• TRAINOR, WES

Wes "Bucko" Trainor
C/LW – R. 5'8", 180 lbs. b: Charlottetown, P.E.I., 9/11/1922. Deceased.

Season	Club	League	GP	G	A	Pts	AG	AA	APts	PIM	GP	G	A	Pts	PIM
1938-39	Charlottetown Jr. Royals	PEI Jr.	9	6	*18	24	....	....	....	2	10	9	12	21	28
1939-40	Charlottetown Army	PEI Sr.	5	7	6	13	....	....	....	8	....	....	....	....	....
	Charlottetown Jr. Royals	PEI Jr.	....	....	....	....	....	....	....	....	10	8	5	13	6
1940-41	Petawawa Grenadiers	Ott-Sr.	18	18	17	35	....	....	....	15	9	8	*12	*20	*14
1941-42			MILITARY SERVICE												
1942-43			MILITARY SERVICE												
1943-44			MILITARY SERVICE												
1944-45			MILITARY SERVICE												
1945-46	Drummondville Intreads	QPHL	31	18	24	42	....	....	....	27	....	....	....	....	....
1946-47	Moncton Hawks	MSHL	37	20	*45	65	....	....	....	42	9	4	*11	15	8
1947-48	St. Paul Saints	USHL	35	7	8	15	....	....	....	22	....	....	....	....	....
1948-49	**New York Rangers**	**NHL**	**17**	**1**	**2**	**3**	**2**	**3**	**5**	**6**	....	....	....	....	....
	St. Paul Saints	USHL	49	19	49	68	....	....	....	43	....	....	....	....	....
1949-50	New Haven Ramblers	AHL	44	6	16	22	....	....	....	21	....	....	....	....	....
	St. Paul Saints	USHL	14	3	6	9	....	....	....	11	3	1	0	1	0
1950-51	Charlottetown Islanders	MMHL	72	25	*73	98	....	....	....	81	18	6	12	18	8
1951-52	Charlottetown Islanders	MMHL	76	13	43	56	....	....		47	4	0	1	1	2
1952-53	Grand Falls Cataracts	Nfld.	DID NOT PLAY – COACHING												
1953-54	Charlottetown Islanders	MMHL	65	18	47	65	....	....	....	36	7	0	3	3	9
	NHL Totals		**17**	**1**	**2**	**3**	**2**	**3**	**5**	**6**	....	....	....	....	....

Signed as a free agent by **NY Rangers**, September, 1947.

• TRAPP, BOB — Bob Trapp

D – L. 5'10", 170 lbs. b: Pembroke, Ont., 12/16/1899. d: 11/20/1979.

Season	Club	League	GP	G	A	Pts	AG	AA	APts	PIM	GP	G	A	Pts	PIM
			REGULAR SEASON								PLAYOFFS				
1914-15	Toronto R&AA	OHA Sr.	STATISTICS NOT AVAILABLE												
1915-16	Toronto R&AA	OHA Sr.	8	4	0	4	....	....	....	....	....	....	....	....	....
1916-17			MILITARY SERVICE												
1917-18			MILITARY SERVICE												
1918-19	Toronto Veterans	OHA Sr.	3	2	1	3	....	....	....	0	....	....	....	....	....
1919-20	Edmonton Eskimos	Big 4	12	2	2	4	....	....	....	6	2	0	0	0	0
1920-21	Edmonton Dominions	Big 4	16	6	1	7	....	....	....	2	....	....	....	....	....
1921-22	Edmonton Eskimos	WCHL	24	5	4	9	....	....	....	5	2	1	0	1	0
1922-23	Edmonton Eskimos	WCHL	26	5	5	10	....	....	....	14	4	0	1	1	2
1923-24	Edmonton Eskimos	WCHL	30	5	4	9	....	....	....	20	....	....	....	....	....
1924-25	Edmonton Eskimos	WCHL	27	8	11	19	....	....	....	33	....	....	....	....	....
1925-26	Portland Rosebuds	WHL	30	4	12	16	....	....	....	55	....	....	....	....	....
1926-27	**Chicago Black Hawks**	**NHL**	**44**	**4**	**2**	**6**	**12**	**17**	**29**	**92**	**2**	**0**	**0**	**0**	**4**
1927-28	**Chicago Black Hawks**	**NHL**	**38**	**0**	**2**	**2**	**0**	**17**	**17**	**37**	....	....	....	....	....
1928-29	Tulsa Oilers	AHA	40	8	6	14	....	....	....	30	4	1	0	1	14
1929-30	Tulsa Oilers	AHA	23	1	3	4	....	....	....	10	....	....	....	....	....
1930-31	Tulsa Oilers	AHA	45	8	13	21	....	....	....	54	4	0	0	0	2
1931-32	Tulsa Oilers	AHA	25	4	3	7	....	....	....	30	....	....	....	....	....
	Providence Reds	Can-Am	14	2	2	4	....	....	....	12	5	0	*2	2	6
1932-33	Providence Reds	Can-Am	44	3	11	14	....	....	....	50	2	1	0	1	0
1933-34	Providence Reds	Can-Am	17	0	1	1	....	....	....	2	....	....	....	....	....
	NHL Totals		**82**	**4**	**4**	**8**	**12**	**34**	**46**	**129**	**2**	**0**	**0**	**0**	**4**
	Other Major League Totals		137	27	36	63	....	....	....	127	6	1	1	2	2

WCHL Second All-Star Team (1922) • WCHL First All-Star Team (1923) • WHL First All-Star Team (1926)

Signed as a free agent by **Edmonton** (WCHL), December 5, 1921. Traded to **Portland** (WHL) by **Edmonton** (WHL) with Joe McCormick for Eddie Shore and Art Gagne, October 7, 1925. NHL rights transferred to **Chicago** after NHL club purchased **Portland** (WHL) franchise, May 16, 1926.

• TRAUB, PERCY — Percy "Puss" Traub

D – L. 5'9", 175 lbs. b: Elmwood, Ont., 8/23/1896. d: 12/5/1948.

Season	Club	League	GP	G	A	Pts	AG	AA	APts	PIM	GP	G	A	Pts	PIM
1915-16	Regina Victorias	RCHL	9	1	0	1	....	....	....	11	....	....	....	....	....
1916-17	Regina 217 Battalion	RCHL	7	2	3	5	....	....	....	19	....	....	....	....	....
1917-18	Regina Depot	RCHL	6	0	1	1	....	....	....	23	....	....	....	....	....
1918-19			MILITARY SERVICE												
1919-20	Regina Victorias	RCHL	12	2	2	4	....	....	....	20	2	1	0	1	0
1920-21	Regina Victorias	RCHL	15	4	4	8	....	....	....	22	4	0	2	2	2
1921-22	Regina Capitals	WCHL	25	8	2	10	....	....	....	32	4	0	1	1	0
1922-23	Regina Capitals	WCHL	26	3	5	8	....	....	....	27	2	0	0	0	*4
1923-24	Regina Capitals	WCHL	27	2	4	6	....	....	....	48	2	0	0	0	4
1924-25	Regina Capitals	WCHL	26	4	5	9	....	....	....	61	....	....	....	....	....
1925-26	Portland Rosebuds	WHL	28	1	3	4	....	....	....	66	....	....	....	....	....
1926-27	**Chicago Black Hawks**	**NHL**	**42**	**0**	**2**	**2**	**0**	**17**	**17**	**93**	**2**	**0**	**0**	**0**	**6**
1927-28	**Detroit Cougars**	**NHL**	**44**	**3**	**1**	**4**	**9**	**8**	**17**	**78**	....	....	....	....	....
1928-29	**Detroit Cougars**	**NHL**	**44**	**0**	**0**	**0**	**0**	**0**	**0**	**46**	**2**	**0**	**0**	**0**	**0**
1929-30			DID NOT PLAY – REFEREE												
1930-31	Regina Vics	RCHL	DID NOT PLAY – COACHING												
	NHL Totals		**130**	**3**	**3**	**6**	**9**	**25**	**34**	**217**	**4**	**0**	**0**	**0**	**6**
	Other Major League Totals		132	18	19	37	....	....	....	234	8	0	1	1	8

WCHL Second All-Star Team (1922) • WCHL First All-Star Team (1924)

Signed as a free agent by **Regina** (WCHL), November 23, 1921. Transferred to **Portland** (WHL) after **Regina** (WHL) franchise relocated, September 1, 1925. NHL rights transferred to **Chicago** after NHL club purchased **Portland** (WHL) franchise, May 16, 1926. Traded to **Detroit** by **Chicago** for $7,500, September, 1927.

• TREMBLAY, GILLES — *see page 1540*

• TREMBLAY, J.C. — *see page 1540*

• TREMBLAY, MARCEL — Marcel Tremblay

RW – R. 5'11", 165 lbs. b: St. Boniface, Man., 7/4/1915.

Season	Club	League	GP	G	A	Pts	AG	AA	APts	PIM	GP	G	A	Pts	PIM
1932-33	Winnipeg Monarchs	City Jr.	10	8	1	9	....	....	....	2	....	....	....	....	....
1933-34	Winnipeg Monarchs	City Jr.	14	6	4	10	....	....	....	2	3	1	1	2	4
1934-35			DID NOT PLAY												
1935-36			DID NOT PLAY												
1936-37	Flin Flon Bombers	SSHL	16	11	5	16	....	....	....	14	6	*5	2	7	2
1937-38	Flin Flon Bombers	SSHL	19	*19	10	29	....	....	....	22	....	....	....	....	....
1938-39	**Montreal Canadiens**	**NHL**	**10**	**0**	**2**	**2**	**0**	**4**	**4**	**0**	....	....	....	....	....
	New Haven Eagles	AHL	26	6	12	18	....	....	....	6	....	....	....	....	....
1939-40	New Haven Eagles	AHL	51	23	24	47	....	....	....	23	3	2	0	2	0
1940-41	New Haven Eagles	AHL	48	11	18	29	....	....	....	24	2	0	0	0	0
1941-42	New Haven Eagles	AHL	20	7	5	12	....	....	....	18	....	....	....	....	....
1942-43			MILITARY SERVICE												
1943-44			MILITARY SERVICE												
1944-45	Montreal Army	City Sr.	2	0	0	0	....	....	....	0	....	....	....	....	....
	NHL Totals		**10**	**0**	**2**	**2**	**0**	**4**	**4**	**0**	....	....	....	....	....

• TREMBLAY, NILS — Nils Tremblay

C – R. 5'9", 170 lbs. b: Matane, Que., 7/26/1923. Deceased.

Season	Club	League	GP	G	A	Pts	AG	AA	APts	PIM	GP	G	A	Pts	PIM
1941-42	Quebec Aces	QCHL	1	0	0	0	....	....	....	0	....	....	....	....	....
1942-43	Quebec Aces	QCHL	17	8	6	14	....	....	....	8	....	....	....	....	....
1943-44	Quebec Aces	QSHL	25	19	28	*47	....	....	....	15	15	15	15	30	14
1944-45	**Montreal Canadiens**	**NHL**	**1**	**0**	**1**	**1**	**0**	**2**	**2**	**0**	**2**	**0**	**0**	**0**	**0**
	Hull–Quebec	QSHL	21	23	31	*54	....	....	....	37	7	4	5	9	2
1945-46	**Montreal Canadiens**	**NHL**	**2**	**0**	**0**	**0**	**0**	**0**	**0**	**0**	....	....	....	....	....
	Quebec Aces	QSHL	32	19	20	39	....	....	....	51	6	3	5	8	18
1946-47	Quebec Aces	QSHL	37	25	35	60	....	....	....	43	4	3	5	8	10
1947-48	Quebec Aces	QSHL	2	0	2	2	....	....	....	2	....	....	....	....	....
	Seattle Ironmen	PCHL	3	0	2	2	....	....	....	10	....	....	....	....	....
1948-49	Ottawa Senators	QSHL	60	35	*71	106	....	....	....	51	23	14	16	30	10
1949-50	Ottawa Senators	QSHL	59	15	38	53	....	....	....	69	7	4	4	8	4
1950-51	Ottawa Senators	QSHL	52	21	29	50	....	....	....	22	11	2	2	4	4
1951-52	Sherbrooke Saints	QSHL	47	9	28	37	....	....	....	21	9	2	3	5	0
1952-53	Sherbrooke Saints	QSHL	46	13	18	31	....	....	....	21	7	0	5	5	2
1953-54	Riviere-du-Loup Raiders	QPHL	57	15	33	48	....	....	....	8	....	....	....	....	....
	NHL Totals		**3**	**0**	**1**	**1**	**0**	**2**	**2**	**0**	**2**	**0**	**0**	**0**	**0**

• TROTTIER, DAVE — Dave Trottier

LW – L. 5'10", 170 lbs. b: Pembroke, Ont., 6/25/1906. d: 1956.

Season	Club	League	GP	G	A	Pts	AG	AA	APts	PIM	GP	G	A	Pts	PIM
			REGULAR SEASON								PLAYOFFS				
1923-24	St. Michael's Majors	OHA	6	*13	2	15	....	....	....	....	....	....	....	....	....
1924-25	St. Michael's Majors	OHA	6	7	*7	14	....	....	....	....	1	1	1	2	0
1925-26	Toronto Varsity Grads	OHA Sr.	STATISTICS NOT AVAILABLE												
1926-27	Toronto Varsity Grads	OHA Sr.	11	23	*8	31	....	....	....	7	14	10	*7	17	*34
1927-28	Toronto Varsity Grads	OHA Sr.	12	*33	*10	*43	....	....	....	....	....	....	....	....	....
	Canada	Olympics	3	*12	*3	*15	....	....	....	....	....	....	....	....	....
1928-29	**Montreal Maroons**	**NHL**	**37**	**2**	**4**	**6**	**8**	**37**	**45**	**69**	....	....	....	....	....
	Montreal Victorias	City Sr.	2	0	0	0	....	....	....	0	....	....	....	....	....
1929-30	**Montreal Maroons**	**NHL**	**41**	**17**	**10**	**27**	**34**	**32**	**66**	**73**	**4**	**0**	**2**	**2**	**8**
1930-31	**Montreal Maroons**	**NHL**	**43**	**9**	**8**	**17**	**22**	**29**	**51**	**58**	**2**	**0**	**0**	**0**	**6**
1931-32	**Montreal Maroons**	**NHL**	**48**	**26**	**18**	**44**	**56**	**50**	**106**	**94**	**4**	**1**	**0**	**1**	**0**
1932-33	**Montreal Maroons**	**NHL**	**48**	**16**	**15**	**31**	**38**	**40**	**78**	**38**	**2**	**0**	**0**	**0**	**6**
1933-34	**Montreal Maroons**	**NHL**	**48**	**9**	**17**	**26**	**20**	**46**	**66**	**47**	**4**	**0**	**0**	**0**	**6**
1934-35	**Montreal Maroons**	**NHL**	**34**	**10**	**9**	**19**	**21**	**20**	**41**	**22**	**7**	**2**	**1**	**3**	**4**
1935-36	**Montreal Maroons**	**NHL**	**46**	**10**	**10**	**20**	**25**	**24**	**49**	**25**	**3**	**0**	**0**	**0**	**4**
1936-37	**Montreal Maroons**	**NHL**	**43**	**12**	**11**	**23**	**26**	**26**	**52**	**33**	**5**	**1**	**0**	**1**	**5**
1937-38	**Montreal Maroons**	**NHL**	**47**	**9**	**10**	**19**	**19**	**21**	**40**	**42**	....	....	....	....	....
1938-39	**Detroit Red Wings**	**NHL**	**11**	**1**	**1**	**2**	**2**	**2**	**4**	**16**	....	....	....	....	....
	Pittsburgh Hornets	AHL	10	5	3	8	....	....	....	6	....	....	....	....	....
	NHL Totals		**446**	**121**	**113**	**234**	**271**	**327**	**598**	**517**	**31**	**4**	**3**	**7**	**39**

Played in NHL All-Star Game (1937)

Rights traded to **Montreal Maroons** by **Toronto Granites** (OHA Sr.) for $10,000, September, 1928. Traded to **Detroit** by **Montreal Maroons** for cash, December 13, 1938.

• TRUDEL, LOUIS — Louis Trudel

LW – L. 5'11", 167 lbs. b: Salem, MA, 7/21/1912. d: 3/19/1972.

Season	Club	League	GP	G	A	Pts	AG	AA	APts	PIM	GP	G	A	Pts	PIM
1929-30	Edmonton Poolers	City Jr.	10	1	1	2	....	....	....	....	....	....	....	....	....
1930-31	Edmonton Poolers	City Jr.	STATISTICS NOT AVAILABLE												
1931-32	Edmonton Poolers	City Jr.	10	10	1	11	....	....	....	....	....	....	....	....	....
1932-33	Tulsa Oilers	AHA	31	10	6	16	....	....	....	19	4	1	0	1	4
1933-34	**Chicago Black Hawks**	**NHL**	**31**	**1**	**3**	**4**	**2**	**8**	**10**	**13**	**7**	**0**	**0**	**0**	**0**
	Syracuse Stars	IAHL	5	0	0	0	....	....	....	2	....	....	....	....	....
1934-35	**Chicago Black Hawks**	**NHL**	**47**	**11**	**11**	**22**	**23**	**24**	**47**	**28**	**2**	**0**	**0**	**0**	**0**
1935-36	**Chicago Black Hawks**	**NHL**	**47**	**3**	**4**	**7**	**7**	**10**	**17**	**27**	**2**	**0**	**0**	**0**	**2**
1936-37	**Chicago Black Hawks**	**NHL**	**45**	**6**	**12**	**18**	**13**	**28**	**41**	**11**	....	....	....	....	....
1937-38	**Chicago Black Hawks**	**NHL**	**42**	**6**	**16**	**22**	**13**	**33**	**46**	**15**	**10**	**0**	**3**	**3**	**2**
1938-39	**Montreal Canadiens**	**NHL**	**31**	**8**	**13**	**21**	**17**	**24**	**41**	**2**	**3**	**1**	**0**	**1**	**0**
1939-40	**Montreal Canadiens**	**NHL**	**47**	**12**	**7**	**19**	**26**	**14**	**40**	**24**	....	....	....	....	....
1940-41	**Montreal Canadiens**	**NHL**	**16**	**2**	**3**	**5**	**4**	**5**	**9**	**2**	....	....	....	....	....
1941-42	Washington Lions	AHL	54	*37	29	66	....	....	....	11	2	1	0	1	0
1942-43	Washington–Cleveland	AHL	55	29	34	63	....	....	....	7	4	0	1	1	2
1943-44	Cleveland Barons	AHL	52	29	47	76	....	....	....	13	11	4	2	6	2
1944-45	Cleveland Barons	AHL	60	*45	48	93	....	....	....	25	12	8	5	13	6
1945-46	Cleveland Barons	AHL	61	33	46	79	....	....	....	24	12	7	4	11	8
1946-47	Cleveland Barons	AHL	50	20	29	49	....	....	....	12	....	....	....	....	....
1947-48	Cleveland Barons	AHL	13	1	6	7	....	....	....	6	....	....	....	....	....
1948-49	Montreal Royals	QSHL	2	0	0	0	....	....	....	0	3	0	0	0	0
1949-50	Cleveland Knights	EHL	DID NOT PLAY – COACHING												
1950-51	Grand Rapids Rockets	IHL	19	10	25	35	....	....	....	10	3	0	0	0	0
1951-52	Grand Rapids Rockets	IHL	17	2	10	12	....	....	....	20	13	2	3	5	12
1952-53			DID NOT PLAY – RETIRED												
1953-54	Milwaukee Chiefs	IHL	11	1	6	7	....	....	....	4	....	....	....	....	....
	NHL Totals		**306**	**49**	**69**	**118**	**105**	**146**	**251**	**122**	**24**	**1**	**3**	**4**	**4**

AHL Second All-Star Team (1942, 1945, 1946) • AHL First All-Star Team (1945)

Played in NHL All-Star Game (1939)

Traded to **Montreal Canadiens** by **Chicago** for Joffre Desilets, August 26, 1938. Traded to **Washington** (AHL) by **Montreal** for cash, October 9, 1941.

• TRUDELL, RENE — Rene Trudell

RW – R. 5'9", 165 lbs. b: Mariapolis, Man., 1/31/1919. d: 3/19/1972.

Season	Club	League	GP	G	A	Pts	AG	AA	APts	PIM	GP	G	A	Pts	PIM
1935-36	Kildonen Juniors	MHL Jr.	2	0	0	0	....	....	....	3	....	....	....	....	....
1936-37	Winnipeg Canadians	MHL Jr.	15	17	7	24	....	....	....	20	....	....	....	....	....
1937-38	Portage Terriers	MHL Jr.	21	14	14	28	....	....	....	20	....	....	....	....	....
	Hudson's Bay Seniors	MHL Sr.	5	0	1	1	....	....	....	0	4	0	0	0	4
1938-39	Portage Terriers	MHL Jr.	18	12	11	23	....	....	....	40	3	1	0	1	6
1939-40	Harringay Racers	Britain	....	34	22	56	....	....	....	....	....	....	....	....	....
1940-41	Toledo Babcocks	USHL	22	8	21	29	....	....	....	46	2	2	0	2	4
1941-42	Yorkton Terriers	SSHL	30	11	28	39	....	....	....	62	....	....	....	....	....
1942-43	Winnipeg RCAF	City Sr.	13	6	12	18	....	....	....	26	17	5	*14	*19	*36
1943-44	Winnipeg RCAF	City Sr.	9	5	0	5	....	....	....	20	....	....	....	....	....
1944-45	Winnipeg RCAF–Army	City Sr.	10	12	3	15	....	....	....	6	2	0	0	0	6
1945-46	**New York Rangers**	**NHL**	**16**	**3**	**5**	**8**	**5**	**9**	**14**	**4**	....	....	....	....	....
	New York Rovers	EHL	40	29	32	61	....	....	....	44	....	....	....	....	....
1946-47	**New York Rangers**	**NHL**	**59**	**8**	**16**	**24**	**11**	**23**	**34**	**38**	....	....	....	....	....
1947-48	**New York Rangers**	**NHL**	**54**	**13**	**7**	**20**	**19**	**10**	**29**	**30**	**5**	**0**	**0**	**0**	**2**
1948-49	Pittsburgh–Springfield	AHL	60	18	31	49	....	....	....	34	3	3	3	6	0
	NHL Totals		**129**	**24**	**28**	**52**	**35**	**42**	**77**	**72**	**5**	**0**	**0**	**0**	**2**

EHL First All-Star Team (1946)

Traded to **Toronto** by **NY Rangers** with Cal Gardner, Bill Juzda and the rights to Frank Mathers for Wally Stanowski and Elwyn Morris, June, 1948. Traded to **Springfield** (AHL) by **Toronto** (Pittsburgh - AHL) for $5000 and future considerations, November 17, 1948.

• TUDIN, CONNIE Connie Tudin

C – L. 5'11", 170 lbs. b: Ottawa, Ont., 9/21/1917. Deceased.

Season	Club	League	GP	G	A	Pts	AG	AA	APts	PIM	GP	G	A	Pts	PIM
1936-37	Ottawa Rideaus	City Jr.	15	*31	*15	*46	....	....	....	4	8	*16	*12	*28	12
1937-38	Arnprior Greenshirts	Ott-Sr.	16	18	*17	*35	....	....	....	12	7	2	*10	*12	2
1938-39	Harringay Racers	Britain	....	11	11	22	....	....	....	....	....	....	....	....	....
1939-40	Lachine Rapides	QPHL	41	27	12	39	....	....	....	76	9	5	4	9	10
1940-41	Montreal Sr. Canadiens	Mtl-Sr.	31	11	9	20	....	....	....	52	....	....	....	....	....
	New Haven Eagles	AHL	10	2	7	9	....	....	....	2	2	1	0	1	0
1941-42	**Montreal Canadiens**	**NHL**	**4**	**0**	**1**	**1**	**0**	**2**	**2**	**4**	....	....	....	....	....
	Washington Lions	AHL	42	9	12	21	....	....	....	20	2	0	0	0	0
1942-43	Ottawa RCAF	City Sr.	17	15	14	29	....	....	....	19	15	5	5	10	19
1943-44	Arnprior RCAF	Ott-Sr.	7	9	12	21	....	....	....	10	....	....	....	....	....
1944-45	Rockcliffe RCAF	Ott-Sr.	12	16	21	37	....	....	....	7	3	7	2	9	4
	Ottawa Commandos	QSHL	1	1	0	1	....	....	....	0	....	....	....	....	....
1945-46	Ottawa–Hull	QSHL	25	9	22	31	....	....	....	2	....	....	....	....	....
	Arnprior Rams	Ott-Sr.	4	0	2	2	....	....	....	4	....	....	....	....	....
	Ottawa RCAF	City Sr.	10	9	8	17	....	....	....	....	4	2	2	4	....
1946-47	Ottawa Senators	QSHL	4	0	0	0	....	....	....	0	....	....	....	....	....
	Ottawa Senators	QSHL	18	19	15	34	....	....	....	22	9	7	7	14	12
1947-48	Ottawa Senators	QSHL	43	24	30	54	....	....	....	18	26	*16	17	*33	16
1948-49	Ottawa Senators	QSHL	57	22	36	58	....	....	....	19	12	2	4	6	4
1949-50	Ottawa Senators	QSHL	41	10	14	24	....	....	....	52	7	0	1	1	4
1950-51	Ottawa Senators	QSHL	55	4	18	22	....	....	....	59	11	2	3	5	10
1951-52	Smith Falls Rideaus	ECSHL	43	11	33	44	....	....	....	63	5	2	2	4	0
1952-53	Smith Falls Rideaus	ECSHL	45	16	27	43	....	....	....	22	24	*10	8	18	15
1953-54	Brockville Magadonas	Ott-Sr.	....	18	39	57	....	....	....	18	....	....	....	....	....
	NHL Totals		**4**	**0**	**1**	**1**	**0**	**2**	**2**	**4**	....	....	....	....	....

• TURLICK, GORD Gord Turlick

LW/C – L. 6'1", 170 lbs. b: Miskel, B.C., 9/17/1939.

Season	Club	League	GP	G	A	Pts	AG	AA	APts	PIM	GP	G	A	Pts	PIM
1957-58	Melville Millionaires	SJHL	16	1	2	3	....	....	....	6	....	....	....	....	....
1958-59	Melville–Prince Albert	SJHL	39	7	9	16	....	....	....	37	5	0	1	1	4
1959-60	Prince Albert Raiders	SJHL	58	*65	36	101	....	....	....	50	7	4	2	6	2
	Boston Bruins	**NHL**	**2**	**0**	**0**	**0**	**0**	**0**	**0**	**2**	....	....	....	....	....
1960-61	Sudbury Wolves	EPHL	5	0	0	0	....	....	....	4	....	....	....	....	....
	New York Rovers–Clinton	EHL	52	10	14	24	....	....	....	15	....	....	....	....	....
1961-62	Indianapolis Chiefs	IHL	4	1	0	0	....	....	....	0	....	....	....	....	....
	Kimberley Dynamiters	WIHL	24	12	7	19	....	....	....	4	....	....	....	....	....
1962-63	Kimberley Dynamiters	WIHL	DID NOT PLAY – INJURED												
1963-64	Spokane Jets	WIHL	50	25	35	60	....	....	....	18	....	....	....	....	....
1964-65	Spokane Jets	WIHL	43	20	16	36	....	....	....	27	....	....	....	....	....
1965-66	Spokane Jets	WIHL	50	27	37	61	....	....	....	36	....	....	....	....	....
1966-67	Spokane Jets	WIHL	48	19	34	53	....	....	....	29	....	....	....	....	....
1967-68	Spokane Jets	WIHL	43	18	27	45	....	....	....	24	....	....	....	....	....
1968-69	Spokane Jets	WIHL	38	11	13	24	....	....	....	27	....	....	....	....	....
1969-70	Spokane Jets	WIHL	50	22	26	48	....	....	....	36	....	....	....	....	....
1970-71	Spokane Jets	WIHL	50	19	25	44	....	....	....	20	....	....	....	....	....
1971-72	Spokane Jets	WIHL	36	8	17	25	....	....	....	9	19	1	0	1	....
	NHL Totals		**2**	**0**	**0**	**0**	**0**	**0**	**0**	**2**	....	....	....	....	....

• TURNER, BOB Bob Turner

D – L. 6', 170 lbs. b: Regina, Sask., 1/31/1934.

Season	Club	League	GP	G	A	Pts	AG	AA	APts	PIM	GP	G	A	Pts	PIM
1951-52	Regina Pats	WCJHL	31	2	10	12	....	....	....	40	6	0	1	1	4
1952-53	Regina Pats	WCJHL	33	10	4	14	....	....	....	90	7	0	2	2	16
	Regina Capitals	SSHL	....	....	....	....	....	....	....	....	2	0	1	1	0
1953-54	Regina Pats	WCJHL	38	15	14	29	....	....	....	55	16	1	5	6	48
1954-55	Shawinigan Cataracts	QHL	61	4	14	18	....	....	....	98	13	0	2	2	4
1955-56	**Montreal Canadiens**	**NHL**	**33**	**1**	**4**	**5**	**1**	**5**	**6**	**35**	**10**	**0**	**1**	**1**	**10**
	Shawinigan Cataracts	QHL	37	6	12	18	....	....	....	55	....	....	....	....	....
1956-57	**Montreal Canadiens**	**NHL**	**58**	**1**	**4**	**5**	**1**	**5**	**6**	**48**	**6**	**0**	**1**	**1**	**0**
	Rochester Americans	AHL	8	0	2	2	....	....	....	4	....	....	....	....	....
1957-58	**Montreal Canadiens**	**NHL**	**66**	**0**	**3**	**3**	**0**	**3**	**3**	**30**	**10**	**0**	**0**	**0**	**2**
1958-59	**Montreal Canadiens**	**NHL**	**68**	**4**	**24**	**28**	**5**	**26**	**31**	**66**	**11**	**0**	**2**	**2**	**20**
1959-60	**Montreal Canadiens**	**NHL**	**54**	**0**	**9**	**9**	**0**	**9**	**9**	**40**	**8**	**0**	**0**	**0**	**0**
1960-61	**Montreal Canadiens**	**NHL**	**60**	**2**	**2**	**4**	**2**	**2**	**4**	**16**	**5**	**0**	**0**	**0**	**0**
1961-62	**Chicago Black Hawks**	**NHL**	**69**	**8**	**2**	**10**	**10**	**2**	**12**	**52**	**12**	**1**	**0**	**1**	**6**
1962-63	**Chicago Black Hawks**	**NHL**	**70**	**3**	**3**	**6**	**4**	**3**	**7**	**20**	**6**	**0**	**0**	**0**	**6**
1963-64	Buffalo Bisons	AHL	68	6	15	21	....	....	....	84	....	....	....	....	....
	NHL Totals		**478**	**19**	**51**	**70**	**23**	**55**	**78**	**307**	**68**	**1**	**4**	**5**	**44**

Played in NHL All-Star Game (1956, 1957, 1958, 1959, 1960, 1961)

Traded to **Chicago** by **Montreal** for Fred Hilts, June, 1961.

• TUSTIN, NORMAN Norman Tustin

LW – L. 5'11", 175 lbs. b: Regina, Sask., 1/3/1919.

Season	Club	League	GP	G	A	Pts	AG	AA	APts	PIM	GP	G	A	Pts	PIM
1938-39	Owen Sound Greys	OHA	STATISTICS NOT AVAILABLE												
1939-40	Atlantic City Seagulls	EHL	61	31	16	47	....	....	....	23	3	*6	1	*7	2
1940-41	Minneapolis Millers	AHA	48	*29	21	50	....	....	....	12	3	1	2	3	0
1941-42	**New York Rangers**	**NHL**	**18**	**2**	**4**	**6**	**3**	**6**	**9**	**0**	....	....	....	....	....
	New Haven Eagles	AHL	31	19	11	30	....	....	....	2	2	0	0	0	0
1942-43	Toronto RCAF	OHA Sr.	6	4	5	9	....	....	....	5	3	2	0	2	2
1943-44	Toronto RCAF	OHA Sr.	15	7	9	16	....	....	....	12	....	....	....	....	....
1944-45			MILITARY SERVICE												
1945-46			MILITARY SERVICE												
1946-47	New Haven Ramblers	AHL	64	18	18	36	....	....	....	8	3	0	1	1	0
1947-48	Hershey–St. Louis	AHL	63	18	27	45	....	....	....	4	....	....	....	....	....
1948-49	St. Louis Flyers	AHL	28	5	13	18	....	....	....	2	....	....	....	....	....
1949-50	St. Louis Flyers	AHL	30	7	5	12	....	....	....	6	....	....	....	....	....
	Kansas City Mohawks	USHL	21	10	11	21	....	....	....	9	3	0	0	0	0
1950-51			REINSTATED AS AN AMATEUR												
1951-52	Sarnia Sailors	OHA Sr.	5	3	2	5	....	....	....	2	....	....	....	....	....
	NHL Totals		**18**	**2**	**4**	**6**	**3**	**6**	**9**	**0**	....	....	....	....	....

AHA First All-Star Team (1941)

• TUTEN, AUT Aut (Audley) Tuten

D – L. 5'10", 180 lbs. b: Enterprize, AL, 1/14/1915.

Season	Club	League	GP	G	A	Pts	AG	AA	APts	PIM	GP	G	A	Pts	PIM
1933-34	Regina Pats	RCJHL	2	0	2	2	....	....	....	2	4	0	1	1	*8
1934-35	Hershey B'ars	EHL	21	3	6	9	....	....	....	35	9	3	1	4	*16
1935-36	Hershey B'ars	EHL	40	9	5	14	....	....	....	64	8	3	2	5	*20
1936-37	Hershey B'ars	EHL	46	7	8	15	....	....	....	*82	4	0	1	1	6
1937-38	Hershey B'ars	EHL	43	6	9	15	....	....	....	62	....	....	....	....	....
1938-39	Baltimore Orioles	EHL	53	13	9	22	....	....	....	*109	....	....	....	....	....
1939-40	Kansas City Greyhounds	AHA	48	10	15	25	....	....	....	104	....	....	....	....	....
1940-41	Kansas City Americans	AHA	47	11	16	27	....	....	....	75	8	1	1	2	12
1941-42	**Chicago Black Hawks**	**NHL**	**5**	**1**	**1**	**2**	**2**	**2**	**4**	**10**	....	....	....	....	....
	Kansas City Americans	AHA	45	13	17	30	....	....	....	72	6	2	4	6	19
1942-43	**Chicago Black Hawks**	**NHL**	**34**	**3**	**7**	**10**	**4**	**9**	**13**	**38**	....	....	....	....	....
1943-44			MILITARY SERVICE												
1944-45			MILITARY SERVICE												
1945-46			MILITARY SERVICE												
1946-47	Kansas City Americans	AHA	10	2	3	5	....	....	....	4	....	....	....	....	....
	Oakland Oaks	PCHL	45	23	22	45	....	....	....	41	....	....	....	....	....
1947-48			DID NOT PLAY – REFEREE												
1948-49	Los Angeles–San Diego	PCHL	24	2	5	7	....	....	....	33	....	....	....	....	....
	NHL Totals		**39**	**4**	**8**	**12**	**6**	**11**	**17**	**48**	....	....	....	....	....

EHL Second All-Star Team (1937, 1938) • EHL First All-Star Team (1939) • AHA Second All-Star Team (1940, 1942) • AHA First All-Star Team (1941)

• ULLMAN, NORM — see page 1548

• VADNAIS, CAROL — see page 1549

• VAIL, MELVILLE Melville "Sparky" Vail

D/LW – L. 6', 185 lbs. b: Meaford, Ont., 7/5/1906. Deceased.

Season	Club	League	GP	G	A	Pts	AG	AA	APts	PIM	GP	G	A	Pts	PIM
1925-26	North Bay Trappers	NOHA	STATISTICS NOT AVAILABLE												
1926-27	Springfield Indians	Can-Am	31	17	6	23	....	....	....	73	6	1	0	1	16
1927-28	Springfield Indians	Can-Am	39	18	4	22	....	....	....	92	4	1	1	2	14
1928-29	**New York Rangers**	**NHL**	**18**	**3**	**0**	**3**	**12**	**0**	**12**	**16**	**6**	**0**	**0**	**0**	**2**
	Springfield Indians	Can-Am	22	7	3	10	....	....	....	42	....	....	....	....	....
1929-30	**New York Rangers**	**NHL**	**32**	**1**	**1**	**2**	**2**	**3**	**5**	**2**	**4**	**0**	**0**	**0**	**0**
	Springfield Indians	Can-Am	9	1	2	3	....	....	....	30	....	....	....	....	....
1930-31	Providence Reds	Can-Am	38	12	21	33	....	....	....	44	....	....	....	....	....
1931-32	Providence Reds	Can-Am	36	7	18	25	....	....	....	40	1	0	0	0	2
1932-33	Providence Reds	Can-Am	41	6	12	18	....	....	....	20	2	0	0	0	0
1933-34	Syracuse—Detroit	IAHL	42	4	8	12	....	....	....	53	....	....	....	....	....
1934-35	Cleveland Falcons	IAHL	43	8	24	32	....	....	....	47	2	0	0	0	0
1935-36	Pittsburgh Yellowjackets	IAHL	45	5	12	17	....	....	....	52	....	....	....	....	....
1936-1938			DID NOT PLAY												
1938-39	Toronto Red Indians	City Sr.	....	1	3	4	....	....	....	....	....	....	....	....	....
1939-40	Toronto Red Indians	City Sr.	....	3	*25	28	....	....	....	....	....	....	....	....	....
	NHL Totals		**50**	**4**	**1**	**5**	**14**	**3**	**17**	**18**	**10**	**0**	**0**	**0**	**2**

Signed as a free agent by **NY Rangers**, September 2, 1926. Traded to **Providence** (Can-Am) by **NY Rangers** for cash, October 27, 1930. Traded to **Detroit** (IAHL) by **Providence** (Can-Am) for Frank Peters, October 30, 1933. Traded to **Syracuse** (IAHL) by **Windsor** (IAHL) for Andy Bellemer, December, 1934.

• VAN IMPE, ED — see page 1552

• VASKO, ELMER — see page 1554

• VOKES, ED Ed Vokes

LW – L. 5'9", 160 lbs. b: Quill Lake, Sask., 1904. Deceased.

Season	Club	League	GP	G	A	Pts	AG	AA	APts	PIM	GP	G	A	Pts	PIM
1928-29	Oakland Shieks	Cal-Pro	10	0	0	0	....	....	....	....	....	....	....	....	....
1929-30	Oakland Shieks	Cal-Pro	....	25	8	33	....	....	....	20	....	....	....	....	....
1930-31	**Chicago Black Hawks**	**NHL**	**5**	**0**	**0**	**0**	**0**	**0**	**0**	**0**	....	....	....	....	....
	London Tecumsehs	IAHL	12	0	0	0	....	....	....	0	....	....	....	....	....
	Niagara Falls Cataracts	Can-Pro	2	0	0	0	....	....	....	4	....	....	....	....	....
1931-32	San Francisco Rangers	Cal-Pro	....	29	9	38	....	....	....	....	....	....	....	....	....
1932-33	San Francisco Rangers	Cal-Pro	STATISTICS NOT AVAILABLE												
	NHL Totals		**5**	**0**	**0**	**0**	**0**	**0**	**0**	**0**	....	....	....	....	....

Traded to **Chicago** by **Oakland** (Cal-Pro) for cash, December 15, 1930. Traded to **Pittsburgh** (IAHL) by **Chicago** for cash, February 12, 1931. Loaned to **Niagara Falls** (Can-Pro) by **Pittsburgh** 13, 1931.

• VOSS, CARL Carl Voss HHOF

C – L. 5'9", 168 lbs. b: Chelsea, MA, 1/6/1907. d: 9/13/1973.

Season	Club	League	GP	G	A	Pts	AG	AA	APts	PIM	Playoffs GP	G	A	Pts	PIM
1925-26	Kingston Frontenacs	OHA Sr.	STATISTICS NOT AVAILABLE												
1926-27	**Toronto Maple Leafs**	**NHL**	**12**	**0**	**0**	**0**	**0**	**0**	**0**	**0**	....	....	....	....	....
	Toronto Marlboros	OHA	4	0	0	0	....	....	....	....	2	0	1	1	....
	Toronto Marlboros	OHA Sr.	2	0	0	0	....	....	....	0	....	....	....	....	....
1927-28	Toronto Falcons	Can-Pro	23	3	4	7	....	....	....	15	2	0	0	0	2
1928-29	**Toronto Maple Leafs**	**NHL**	**2**	**0**	**0**	**0**	**0**	**0**	**0**	**0**	....	....	....	....	....
	London Panthers	Can-Pro	42	11	9	20	....	....	....	44	....	....	....	....	....
1929-30	Buffalo Bisons	IAHL	42	14	8	22	....	....	....	22	7	3	0	3	6
1930-31	Buffalo Bisons	IAHL	47	16	10	26	....	....	....	46	6	3	3	6	8
1931-32	Buffalo Bisons	IAHL	46	18	23	*41	....	....	....	53	6	1	*5	*6	7
1932-33	**New York Rangers**	**NHL**	**10**	**2**	**1**	**3**	**5**	**3**	**8**	**4**	....	....	....	....	....
	Detroit Red Wings	**NHL**	**38**	**6**	**14**	**20**	**14**	**37**	**51**	**6**	**4**	**1**	**1**	**2**	**0**
1933-34	**Detroit Red Wings**	**NHL**	**8**	**0**	**2**	**2**	**0**	**5**	**5**	**2**	....	....	....	....	....
	Ottawa Senators	**NHL**	**40**	**7**	**16**	**23**	**15**	**43**	**58**	**10**	....	....	....	....	....
1934-35	**St. Louis Eagles**	**NHL**	**48**	**13**	**18**	**31**	**28**	**40**	**68**	**14**	....	....	....	....	....
1935-36	**New York Americans**	**NHL**	**46**	**3**	**9**	**12**	**7**	**22**	**29**	**10**	**5**	**0**	**0**	**0**	**0**
1936-37	**Montreal Maroons**	**NHL**	**20**	**0**	**2**	**2**	**0**	**5**	**5**	**4**	**5**	**1**	**0**	**1**	**0**
1937-38	**Montreal Maroons**	**NHL**	**3**	**0**	**0**	**0**	**0**	**0**	**0**	**0**	....	....	....	....	....
	Chicago Black Hawks	**NHL**	**34**	**3**	**8**	**11**	**6**	**16**	**22**	**0**	**10**	**3**	**2**	**5**	**0**
	NHL Totals		**261**	**34**	**70**	**104**	**75**	**171**	**246**	**50**	**24**	**5**	**3**	**8**	**0**

NHL Rookie of the Year (1933)

Signed as a free agent by **Toronto**, February 16, 1927. Traded to **Buffalo** (IAHL) by **Toronto** with Wes King for Gord Brydson, November 13, 1929. Traded to **NY Rangers** by **Buffalo** (IAHL) for Lorne Carr and $15,000, October 4, 1932. Traded to **Detroit** by **NY Rangers** for cash, December 11, 1932. Traded to **Ottawa** by **Detroit** with cash for Ralph Weiland, November 26, 1933. Transferred to **St. Louis** after **Ottawa** franchise relocated, September 22, 1934. Claimed by **Detroit** from **St. Louis** in Dispersal Draft, October 15, 1935. Traded to **NY Americans** by **Detroit** for Pete Kelly, October 16, 1935. Traded to **Montreal Maroons** by **NY Americans** for Joe Lamb and $10,000, September 6, 1936. Signed as a free agent by **Chicago**, December 6, 1937.

• WAITE, FRANK Frank "Deacon" Waite

C – L. 5'11", 150 lbs. b: Fort Qu'Appelle, Sask., 4/9/1905. d: 7/18/1989.

Season	Club	League	GP	G	A	Pts	AG	AA	APts	PIM	Playoffs GP	G	A	Pts	PIM
1923-24	Brandon Wheat Kings	MHL Sr.	11	3	2	5	....	....	....	3	4	0	1	1	6
1924-25	Trail Smoke Eaters	Kootenay	STATISTICS NOT AVAILABLE												
1925-26	Vancouver Maroons	WHL	28	0	1	1	....	....	....	4	....	....	....	....	....
1926-27	Springfield Indians	Can-Am	25	7	4	11	....	....	....	24	6	1	1	2	4
1927-28	Springfield Indians	Can-Am	39	7	*15	22	....	....	....	36	4	1	1	2	6
1928-29	Boston Tigers	Can-Am	39	12	10	22	....	....	....	42	4	2	0	2	12
1929-30	Boston Tigers	Can-Am	40	23	*34	*57	....	....	....	57	5	2	3	5	6
1930-31	**New York Rangers**	**NHL**	**17**	**1**	**3**	**4**	**2**	**11**	**13**	**4**	....	....	....	....	....
	Springfield Indians	Can-Am	25	5	*25	30	....	....	....	28	6	0	1	1	0
1931-32	Syracuse Stars	IAHL	43	7	*26	33	....	....	....	33	....	....	....	....	....
1932-33	Detroit–Cleveland	IAHL	42	6	12	18	....	....	....	12	....	....	....	....	....
1933-34	London Panthers	IAHL	11	1	3	4	....	....	....	6	....	....	....	....	....
	Philadelphia Arrows	Can-Am	31	11	19	30	....	....	....	15	2	0	1	1	10
	NHL Totals		**17**	**1**	**3**	**4**	**2**	**11**	**13**	**4**	....	....	....	....	....
	Other Major League Totals		28	0	1	1	....	....	....	4	....	....	....	....	....

Signed as a free agent by **Vancouver** (WHL), September, 1925. Signed as a free agent by **NY Rangers**, September 2, 1926. Traded to **Boston** by **NY Rangers** for cash, September, 1928. Traded to **Springfield** (Can-Am) by **Boston** for cash, September, 1930. Traded to **NY Rangers** by **Springfield** (Can-Am) for cash, November 4, 1930. Traded to **Syracuse** (IAHL) by **NY Rangers** for cash, October 21, 1931. Signed as a free agent by **Cleveland** (IAHL), November 5, 1932. Traded to **Detroit** by **Cleveland** (IAHL) for Jack Riley and Tony Prelesnik, December 2, 1932. Traded to **Chicago** (London-IAHL) by **Detroit** with Leroy Goldsworthy for Gene Carrigan, October 20, 1933.

• WALKER, JACK Jack (John) Walker HHOF

F – L. 5'8", 153 lbs. b: Silver Mountain, Ont., 11/29/1888. d: 2/16/1950.

Season	Club	League	GP	G	A	Pts	AG	AA	APts	PIM	Playoffs GP	G	A	Pts	PIM
1911-12	Port Arthur Lake Cities	NOHA	11	13	0	13	....	....	....	....	....	....	....	....	....
1912-13	Toronto Blueshirts	NHA	1	0	0	0	....	....	....	0	....	....	....	....	....
	Moncton Victorias	MPHL	15	21	0	21	....	....	....	9	....	....	....	....	....
1913-14	Toronto Blueshirts	NHA	20	20	*16	36	....	....	....	17	5	4	0	4	2
1914-15	Toronto Blueshirts	NHA	19	12	7	19	....	....	....	11	....	....	....	....	....
1915-16	Seattle Metropolitans	PCHA	18	13	6	19	....	....	....	6	....	....	....	....	....
1916-17	Seattle Metropolitans	PCHA	24	11	15	26	....	....	....	3	4	1	3	4	0
1917-18	Seattle Metropolitans	PCHA	1	0	0	0	....	....	....	0	....	....	....	....	....
1918-19	Seattle Metropolitans	PCHA	20	9	6	15	....	....	....	9	7	3	2	5	*12
1919-20	Seattle Metropolitans	PCHA	22	4	8	12	....	....	....	3	7	2	3	5	0
1920-21	Seattle Metropolitans	PCHA	23	6	4	10	....	....	....	6	2	0	0	0	0
1921-22	Seattle Metropolitans	PCHA	20	8	4	12	....	....	....	0	2	0	0	0	0
1922-23	Seattle Metropolitans	PCHA	29	13	10	23	....	....	....	4	....	....	....	....	....
1923-24	Seattle Metropolitans	PCHA	29	18	5	23	....	....	....	0	2	0	0	0	0
1924-25	Victoria Cougars	WCHL	28	7	7	*14	....	....	....	6	8	*8	2	10	0
1925-26	Victoria Cougars	WCHL	30	9	8	17	....	....	....	16	8	0	0	0	2
1926-27	**Detroit Cougars**	**NHL**	**37**	**3**	**4**	**7**	**9**	**34**	**43**	**6**	....	....	....	....	....
1927-28	**Detroit Cougars**	**NHL**	**43**	**2**	**4**	**6**	**6**	**34**	**40**	**12**	....	....	....	....	....
1928-29	Seattle Eskimos	NWHL	34	5	8	13	....	....	....	4	5	0	*2	2	2
1929-30	Seattle Eskimos	NWHL	26	6	*11	17	....	....	....	2	....	....	....	....	....
1930-31	Seattle Eskimos	PCHL	34	2	*13	15	....	....	....	8	4	0	*3	*3	0
1931-32	Hollywood Stars	Cal-Pro	....	5	13	18	....	....	....	....	....	....	....	....	....
1932-33	Oakland Sheiks	Cal-Pro	DID NOT PLAY – COACHING												
	NHL Totals		**80**	**5**	**8**	**13**	**15**	**68**	**83**	**18**	....	....	....	....	....
	Other Major League Totals		269	142	88	230	....	....	....	74	37	18	10	28	14

PCHA Second All-Star Team (1917, 1919, 1920) • PCHA First All-Star Team (1921, 1922, 1924)

Signed as a free agent by **Seattle** (PCHA), December, 1915. Signed as a free agent by **Victoria** (WCHL), November 10, 1924. Traded to **Detroit Cougars** by **Victoria** (WHL) for cash, May 15, 1926.

• WALL, BOB — *see page 1563*

• WALTON, BOBBY Bobby Walton

C/RW – R. 5'9", 165 lbs. b: Ottawa, Ont., 8/5/1917.

Season	Club	League	GP	G	A	Pts	AG	AA	APts	PIM	Playoffs GP	G	A	Pts	PIM
1929-30	Ottawa Canoe Club	City Jr.	11	7	3	10	....	....	....	6	....	....	....	....	....
1930-31	Ottawa Rideaus	City Jr.	16	*14	5	19	....	....	....	20	2	0	1	1	4
	Ottawa Rideaus	City Sr.	....	....	....	....	....	....	....	....	2	0	0	0	2
1931-32	Ottawa New Edinburghs	City Sr.	26	6	4	10	....	....	....	77	2	0	0	0	0
1932-33	Ottawa New Edinburghs	City Sr.	14	6	5	11	....	....	....	12	....	....	....	....	....
1933-34	Ottawa Montagnards	City Sr.	21	*17	*13	*30	....	....	....	12	3	0	0	0	2
1934-35	Wembley Lions	Britain	STATISTICS NOT AVAILABLE												
1935-36	Wembley Lions	Britain	....	17	9	26	....	....	....	15	....	....	....	....	....
1936-37	Wembley Lions	Britain	....	27	17	44	....	....	....	22	....	....	....	....	....
1937-38	Kirkland Lake Blue Devils	NOHA	10	8	8	16	....	....	....	10	2	0	1	1	*6
1938-39	Kirkland Lake Blue Devils	NOHA	10	7	9	16	....	....	....	22	3	0	1	1	0
1939-40	Kirkland Lake Blue Devils	NOHA	15	6	10	16	....	....	....	8	20	9	13	22	0
1940-41	Niagara Falls Brights	OHA Sr.	24	15	11	26	....	....	....	10	3	0	1	1	0
	Sydney Millionaires	CBSHL	1	2	5	7	....	....	....	2	21	*18	*21	*39	8
1941-42	Montreal Royals	QSHL	29	6	17	23	....	....	....	22	2	0	0	0	0
1942-43	Sudbury Open Pit Miners	NOHA	5	6	4	10	....	....	....	4	....	....	....	....	....
1943-44	**Montreal Canadiens**	**NHL**	**4**	**0**	**0**	**0**	**0**	**0**	**0**	**0**	....	....	....	....	....
	Buffalo Bisons	AHL	32	7	14	21	....	....	....	6	9	0	0	0	0
1944-45	Pittsburgh Hornets	AHL	58	37	58	*95	....	....	....	27	....	....	....	....	....
1945-46	Pittsburgh Hornets	AHL	47	25	26	51	....	....	....	22	6	1	5	6	4
1946-47	Cleveland Barons	AHL	62	20	28	48	....	....	....	22	4	0	1	1	0
1947-48	Washington Lions	AHL	66	20	23	43	....	....	....	8	....	....	....	....	....
	NHL Totals		**4**	**0**	**0**	**0**	**0**	**0**	**0**	**0**	....	....	....	....	....

AHL First All-Star Team (1945)

• WALTON, MIKE — *see page 1564*

• WARD, DON Don Ward

D – L. 6'2", 200 lbs. b: Sarnia, Ont., 10/19/1935.

Season	Club	League	GP	G	A	Pts	AG	AA	APts	PIM	Playoffs GP	G	A	Pts	PIM
1955-56	Sarnia Legionnaires	Jr. B	STATISTICS NOT AVAILABLE												
1956-57	Windsor Bulldogs	OHA Sr.	21	3	6	9	....	....	....	24	....	....	....	....	....
	Buffalo Bisons	AHL	31	3	6	9	....	....	....	48	....	....	....	....	....
1957-58	**Chicago Black Hawks**	**NHL**	**3**	**0**	**0**	**0**	**0**	**0**	**0**	**0**	....	....	....	....	....
	Buffalo Bisons	AHL	54	1	11	12	....	....	....	65	....	....	....	....	....
1958-59	Calgary Stampeders	WHL	64	4	18	22	....	....	....	131	8	1	4	5	8
1959-60	**Boston Bruins**	**NHL**	**31**	**0**	**1**	**1**	**0**	**1**	**1**	**16**	....	....	....	....	....
	Providence Reds	AHL	27	2	3	5	....	....	....	54	5	0	0	0	0
1960-61	Winnipeg Warriors	WHL	70	5	12	17	....	....	....	95	....	....	....	....	....
1961-62	Seattle Totems	WHL	70	7	23	30	....	....	....	91	2	0	0	0	4
1962-63	Seattle Totems	WHL	69	3	18	21	....	....	....	131	17	1	2	3	10
1963-64	Seattle Totems	WHL	70	5	25	30	....	....	....	122	....	....	....	....	....
1964-65	Seattle Totems	WHL	70	3	8	11	....	....	....	140	7	1	1	2	10
1965-66	Seattle Totems	WHL	56	5	8	13	....	....	....	84	....	....	....	....	....
1966-67	Seattle Totems	WHL	44	0	5	5	....	....	....	48	6	0	1	1	2
1967-68	Seattle Totems	WHL	70	2	12	14	....	....	....	107	9	1	2	3	14
1968-69	Seattle Totems	WHL	73	3	15	18	....	....	....	129	4	0	1	1	4
1969-70	Seattle Totems	WHL	72	3	17	20	....	....	....	96	6	0	2	2	20
1970-71	Seattle Totems	WHL	56	0	11	11	....	....	....	80	....	....	....	....	....
1971-72	Seattle Totems	WHL	41	1	8	9	....	....	....	82	....	....	....	....	....
1972-73	Greensboro Generals	EHL	13	0	1	1	....	....	....	30	7	1	2	3	24
	NHL Totals		**34**	**0**	**1**	**1**	**0**	**1**	**1**	**16**	....	....	....	....	....

Claimed by **Boston** from **Calgary** (WHL) in Inter-League Draft, June 9, 1959. Claimed by **Portland** (WHL) from **Boston** in Reverse Draft, June, 1961. Traded to **Seattle** (WHL) by **Portland** (WHL) for Tom McVie, August, 1961.

• WARD, JIMMY Jimmy Ward

RW – R. 5'11", 167 lbs. b: Fort William, Ont., 9/1/1906. d: 11/15/1990.

Season	Club	League	GP	G	A	Pts	AG	AA	APts	PIM	Playoffs GP	G	A	Pts	PIM
1925-26	Kenora Thistles	TBSHL	16	10	3	13	....	....	....	16	....	....	....	....	....
1926-27	Fort William Forts	TBSHL	20	18	5	23	....	....	....	20	2	0	0	0	0
1927-28	**Montreal Maroons**	**NHL**	**42**	**10**	**2**	**12**	**31**	**17**	**48**	**44**	**9**	**1**	**1**	**2**	**6**
1928-29	**Montreal Maroons**	**NHL**	**43**	**14**	**8**	**22**	**57**	**74**	**131**	**46**	....	....	....	....	....
1929-30	**Montreal Maroons**	**NHL**	**44**	**10**	**7**	**17**	**20**	**23**	**43**	**54**	**4**	**0**	**1**	**1**	**12**
1930-31	**Montreal Maroons**	**NHL**	**41**	**14**	**8**	**22**	**34**	**29**	**63**	**52**	**2**	**0**	**0**	**0**	**2**
1931-32	**Montreal Maroons**	**NHL**	**48**	**19**	**19**	**38**	**41**	**53**	**94**	**39**	**4**	**2**	**1**	**3**	**0**
1932-33	**Montreal Maroons**	**NHL**	**48**	**16**	**17**	**33**	**38**	**45**	**83**	**52**	**2**	**0**	**0**	**0**	**0**
1933-34	**Montreal Maroons**	**NHL**	**48**	**14**	**9**	**23**	**31**	**24**	**55**	**46**	**4**	**0**	**0**	**0**	**0**
1934-35	**Montreal Maroons**	**NHL**	**41**	**9**	**6**	**15**	**19**	**13**	**32**	**24**	**7**	**1**	**1**	**2**	**0**
1935-36	**Montreal Maroons**	**NHL**	**48**	**12**	**19**	**31**	**30**	**46**	**76**	**30**	**3**	**0**	**0**	**0**	**6**
1936-37	**Montreal Maroons**	**NHL**	**40**	**14**	**14**	**28**	**30**	**33**	**63**	**34**	....	....	....	....	....
1937-38	**Montreal Maroons**	**NHL**	**48**	**11**	**15**	**26**	**23**	**31**	**54**	**34**	....	....	....	....	....
1938-39	**Montreal Canadiens**	**NHL**	**36**	**4**	**3**	**7**	**8**	**6**	**14**	**0**	**1**	**0**	**0**	**0**	**0**
1939-40	New Haven Eagles	IAHL	49	5	14	19	....	....	....	28	....	....	....	....	....
	NHL Totals		**527**	**147**	**127**	**274**	**362**	**394**	**756**	**455**	**36**	**4**	**4**	**8**	**26**

Played in NHL All-Star Game (1934, 1937)

Signed as a free agent by **Montreal Maroons**, August 26, 1927. Traded to **Montreal Canadiens** by **Montreal Maroons** for cash, September 14, 1938.

• WARES, EDDIE
Eddie Wares
D/RW – R. 5'11", 182 lbs. b: Calgary, Alta., 3/19/1915.

Season	Club	League	GP	G	A	Pts	AG	AA	APts	PIM	GP	G	A	Pts	PIM
			REGULAR SEASON								PLAYOFFS				
1931-32	Calgary Shamrocks	City Jr.	1	0	0	0	....	....	....	0	....	....	....	....	....
1932-33	Calgary Jimmies	City Jr.	STATISTICS NOT AVAILABLE												
1933-34	Calgary Jimmies	City Jr.	3	5	2	7	....	....	....	4	....	....	....	....	....
1934-35	Calgary Bronks	City Sr.	12	13	4	17	....	....	....	6	2	1	0	1	0
1935-36	Philadelphia Arrows	Can-Am	48	7	6	13	....	....	....	29	3	1	0	1	2
1936-37	**New York Rangers**	**NHL**	**2**	**2**	**0**	**2**	**4**	**0**	**4**	**0**	....	....	....	....	....
	Philadelphia Ramblers	AHL	47	10	23	33	....	....	....	30	6	1	1	2	8
1937-38	**Detroit Red Wings**	**NHL**	**21**	**9**	**7**	**16**	**19**	**14**	**33**	**2**	....	....	....	....	....
	Philadelphia Ramblers	AHL	25	12	14	26	....	....	....	4	....	....	....	....	....
1938-39	**Detroit Red Wings**	**NHL**	**28**	**8**	**8**	**16**	**17**	**15**	**32**	**10**	**6**	**1**	**0**	**1**	**8**
1939-40	**Detroit Red Wings**	**NHL**	**33**	**2**	**6**	**8**	**4**	**12**	**16**	**19**	**5**	**0**	**0**	**0**	**0**
	Indianapolis Capitals	AHL	1	0	0	0	....	....	....	0	....	....	....	....	....
1940-41	**Detroit Red Wings**	**NHL**	**42**	**10**	**16**	**26**	**20**	**29**	**49**	**34**	**9**	**0**	**0**	**0**	**0**
	Indianapolis Capitals	AHL	1	0	0	0	....	....	....	0	....	....	....	....	....
1941-42	**Detroit Red Wings**	**NHL**	**43**	**9**	**29**	**38**	**15**	**44**	**59**	**31**	**12**	**1**	**3**	**4**	**22**
1942-43	**Detroit Red Wings**	**NHL**	**47**	**12**	**18**	**30**	**17**	**23**	**40**	**10**	**10**	**3**	**3**	**6**	**4**
1943-44	Calgary Combines	City Sr.	16	4	4	8	....	....	....	18	2	2	2	4	6
1944-45	Calgary Navy	City Sr.	2	0	0	0	....	....	....	4	....	....	....	....	....
	Halifax Navy	City Sr.	....	....	....	....	....	....	....	....	3	2	0	2	4
1945-46	**Chicago Black Hawks**	**NHL**	**45**	**4**	**11**	**15**	**6**	**20**	**26**	**34**	**3**	**0**	**1**	**1**	**0**
1946-47	**Chicago Black Hawks**	**NHL**	**60**	**4**	**7**	**11**	**5**	**10**	**15**	**21**	....	....	....	....	....
1947-48	Cleveland Barons	AHL	66	6	22	28	....	....	....	20	9	0	1	1	2
1948-49	Cleveland Barons	AHL	44	1	17	18	....	....	....	10	....	....	....	....	....
	Kansas City Pla-Mors	USHL	20	4	6	10	....	....	....	0	2	0	0	0	0
1949-50	Victoria Cougars	PCHL	42	5	11	16	....	....	....	6	....	....	....	....	....
1950-51	Nelson Maple Leafs	WIHL	34	6	12	18	....	....	....	66	4	0	0	0	6
1951-52	Nelson Maple Leafs	WIHL	26	6	7	13	....	....	....	12	8	0	3	3	0
1952-53	Nelson Maple Leafs	WIHL	6	1	6	7	....	....	....	20	....	....	....	....	....
	NHL Totals		**321**	**60**	**102**	**162**	**107**	**167**	**274**	**161**	**45**	**5**	**7**	**12**	**34**

Signed as a free agent by **Montreal Maroons**, September 30, 1935. Traded to **NY Rangers** by **Montreal Maroons** for rights to George Brown, October 30, 1935. Traded to **Detroit** by **NY Rangers** for the loan of John Sherf and cash, January 17, 1938. Traded to **Chicago** by **Detroit** for cash, October 11, 1945.

• WARWICK, BILL
Bill Warwick
LW – L. 5'7", 155 lbs. b: Regina, Sask., 11/17/1924.

Season	Club	League	GP	G	A	Pts	AG	AA	APts	PIM	GP	G	A	Pts	PIM
1941-42	Regina Abbotts	RCJHL	10	1	3	4	....	....	....	8	5	4	1	5	2
1942-43	**New York Rangers**	**NHL**	**1**	**0**	**1**	**1**	**0**	**1**	**1**	**4**	....	....	....	....	....
	New York Rovers	EHL	43	26	29	55	....	....	....	47	10	9	4	13	6
1943-44	**New York Rangers**	**NHL**	**13**	**3**	**2**	**5**	**4**	**2**	**6**	**12**	....	....	....	....	....
	Brooklyn Crescents	EHL	2	0	1	1	....	....	....	0	....	....	....	....	....
	New York Rovers	EHL	27	14	14	28	....	....	....	34	11	7	9	16	12
1944-45	Hershey Bears	AHL	40	10	7	17	....	....	....	26	6	0	0	0	0
	New York Rovers	EHL	1	2	1	3	....	....	....	2	....	....	....	....	....
1945-46	Providence Reds	AHL	42	14	13	27	....	....	....	34	2	0	0	0	2
1946-47	Providence–Philadelphia	AHL	64	25	27	52	....	....	....	42	....	....	....	....	....
1947-48	Springfield Indians	AHL	3	0	0	0	....	....	....	2	....	....	....	....	....
	Fort Worth Rangers	USHL	46	23	15	38	....	....	....	41	4	1	1	2	2
1948-49	Springfield Indians	AHL	14	3	4	7	....	....	....	10	....	....	....	....	....
	Fort Worth Rangers	USHL	52	32	27	59	....	....	....	30	2	1	0	1	15
1949-50	Minneapolis Millers	USHL	70	35	46	81	....	....	....	47	7	3	0	3	4
	Cleveland Barons	AHL	....	....	....	....	....	....	....	....	2	0	3	3	2
1950-51	Denver Falcons	USHL	40	13	23	36	....	....	....	20	....	....	....	....	....
1951-52	Ottawa Senators	QSHL	28	0	3	3	....	....	....	30	....	....	....	....	....
	Halifax St. Mary's	MMHL	39	17	24	41	....	....	....	18	9	3	2	5	20
1952-53	Penticton Vees	OSHL	38	21	34	55	....	....	....	82	11	3	*11	14	*35
1953-54	Penticton Vees	OSHL	58	*50	45	*95	....	....	....	127	10	8	6	14	28
1954-55	Penticton Vees	OSHL	54	*36	37	*73	....	....	....	*168	....	....	....	....	....
	Canada	WEC-A	8	14	8	*22	....	....	....	12	....	....	....	....	....
1955-56	Penticton Vees	OSHL	49	32	44	76	....	....	....	210	....	....	....	....	....
1956-57	Trail Smoke Eaters	WIHL	45	27	34	61	....	....	....	*166	9	2	5	7	*44
1957-58	Kamloops Chiefs	OSHL	47	17	28	45	....	....	....	*148	8	2	5	7	10
	NHL Totals		**14**	**3**	**3**	**6**	**4**	**3**	**7**	**16**	....	....	....	....	....

EHL Second All-Star Team (1943) • Named Best Forward at WEC-A (1955)

• WARWICK, GRANT
Grant "Nobby" Warwick
RW – R. 5'6", 155 lbs. b: Regina, Sask., 10/11/1921.

Season	Club	League	GP	G	A	Pts	AG	AA	APts	PIM	GP	G	A	Pts	PIM
1938-39	Regina Abbotts	RCJHL	4	0	0	0	....	....	....	2	....	....	....	....	....
1939-40	Regina Abbotts	RCJHL	11	0	0	0	....	....	....	0	2	2	*4	*6	11
1940-41	Regina Rangers	RCHL	31	14	18	32	....	....	....	16	8	5	1	6	2
1941-42	**New York Rangers**	**NHL**	**44**	**16**	**17**	**33**	**27**	**26**	**53**	**36**	**6**	**0**	**1**	**1**	**2**
1942-43	**New York Rangers**	**NHL**	**50**	**17**	**18**	**35**	**24**	**23**	**47**	**31**	....	....	....	....	....
1943-44	**New York Rangers**	**NHL**	**18**	**8**	**9**	**17**	**10**	**11**	**21**	**14**	....	....	....	....	....
1944-45	**New York Rangers**	**NHL**	**42**	**20**	**22**	**42**	**28**	**36**	**64**	**25**	....	....	....	....	....
1945-46	**New York Rangers**	**NHL**	**45**	**19**	**18**	**37**	**29**	**34**	**63**	**19**	....	....	....	....	....
1946-47	**New York Rangers**	**NHL**	**54**	**20**	**20**	**40**	**27**	**29**	**56**	**24**	....	....	....	....	....
1947-48	**New York Rangers**	**NHL**	**40**	**17**	**12**	**29**	**25**	**17**	**42**	**30**	....	....	....	....	....
	Boston Bruins	**NHL**	**18**	**6**	**5**	**11**	**9**	**7**	**16**	**8**	**5**	**0**	**3**	**3**	**4**
1948-49	**Boston Bruins**	**NHL**	**58**	**22**	**15**	**37**	**35**	**24**	**59**	**14**	**5**	**2**	**0**	**2**	**0**
1949-50	**Montreal Canadiens**	**NHL**	**26**	**2**	**6**	**8**	**3**	**8**	**11**	**19**	....	....	....	....	....
	Buffalo Bisons	AHL	37	19	28	47	....	....	....	33	3	2	0	2	0
1950-51	Buffalo Bisons	AHL	65	34	65	99	....	....	....	43	4	2	1	3	2
1951-52	Buffalo Bisons	AHL	55	24	41	65	....	....	....	35	3	0	0	0	2
	Halifax St. Mary's	MMHL	....	....	....	....	....	....	....	....	5	1	0	1	2
1952-53	Penticton Vees	OSHL	31	19	27	46	....	....	....	49	11	7	8	15	15
1953-54	Penticton Vees	OSHL	54	36	43	79	....	....	....	79	10	*11	7	*18	8
1954-55	Penticton Vees	OSHL	38	22	34	56	....	....	....	62	....	....	....	....	....
	Canada	WEC-A	8	6	*11	17	....	....	....	5	....	....	....	....	....
1955-56	Penticton Vees	OSHL	54	*54	59	*113	....	....	....	44	....	....	....	....	....
1956-57	Trail Smoke Eaters	WIHL	43	18	30	48	....	....	....	70	8	5	5	10	8
1957-58	Kamloops Chiefs	OSHL	49	9	31	40	....	....	....	45	15	1	*13	14	14
	NHL Totals		**395**	**147**	**142**	**289**	**217**	**215**	**432**	**220**	**16**	**2**	**4**	**6**	**6**

Won Calder Trophy (1942)

Played in NHL All-Star Game (1947)

Claimed by **NY Rangers** from **Cleveland** (AHL) in Inter-League Draft, June 27, 1941. Traded to **Boston** by **NY Rangers** for Billy Taylor, Pentti Lund and Ray Manson, February 6, 1948. Traded to **Montreal** by **Boston** for cash, October 10, 1949.

• WASNIE, NICK
Nick Wasnie
RW – R. 5'11", 174 lbs. b: Winnipeg, Man., 1/1/1904. d: 5/26/1991.

Season	Club	League	GP	G	A	Pts	AG	AA	APts	PIM	GP	G	A	Pts	PIM
			REGULAR SEASON								PLAYOFFS				
1925-26	Winnipeg Maroons	City Sr.	31	7	1	8	....	....	....	35	5	1	0	1	0
1926-27	Winnipeg Maroons	AHA	21	7	3	10	....	....	....	33	....	....	....	....	....
1927-28	**Chicago Black Hawks**	**NHL**	**14**	**1**	**0**	**1**	**3**	**0**	**3**	**22**	....	....	....	....	....
	Quebec Beavers	Can-Am	22	8	3	11	....	....	....	32	6	*3	0	*3	*18
1928-29	Newark Bulldogs	Can-Am	40	14	6	20	....	....	....	76	....	....	....	....	....
1929-30	**Montreal Canadiens**	**NHL**	**44**	**12**	**11**	**23**	**24**	**36**	**60**	**64**	**6**	**2**	**2**	**4**	**12**
1930-31	**Montreal Canadiens**	**NHL**	**44**	**9**	**2**	**11**	**22**	**7**	**29**	**26**	**4**	**4**	**1**	**5**	**8**
1931-32	**Montreal Canadiens**	**NHL**	**48**	**10**	**2**	**12**	**21**	**6**	**27**	**16**	**4**	**0**	**0**	**0**	**0**
1932-33	**New York Americans**	**NHL**	**48**	**11**	**12**	**23**	**26**	**32**	**58**	**36**	....	....	....	....	....
1933-34	**Ottawa Senators**	**NHL**	**37**	**11**	**6**	**17**	**24**	**16**	**40**	**10**	....	....	....	....	....
1934-35	**St. Louis Eagles**	**NHL**	**13**	**3**	**1**	**4**	**6**	**2**	**8**	**2**	....	....	....	....	....
	Minneapolis Millers	CHL	33	16	19	35	....	....	....	32	5	2	3	5	4
1935-36	Pittsburgh–Rochester	IAHL	42	17	25	42	....	....	....	60	....	....	....	....	....
1936-37	Kansas City Greyhounds	AHA	46	18	19	37	....	....	....	52	3	0	1	1	0
1937-38	Kansas City Greyhounds	AHA	45	9	12	21	....	....	....	14	....	....	....	....	....
1938-39	Kansas City Greyhounds	AHA	48	34	27	61	....	....	....	19	....	....	....	....	....
1939-40	Kansas City Greyhounds	AHA	48	18	21	39	....	....	....	36	....	....	....	....	....
	NHL Totals		**248**	**57**	**34**	**91**	**126**	**99**	**225**	**176**	**14**	**6**	**3**	**9**	**20**

AHA First All-Star Team (1937)

Signed as a free agent by **Chicago**, October 12, 1927. Traded to **Saskatoon** (PrHL) by **Chicago** with Corb Denneny for Cally McCalmon and Earl Miller, January 11, 1928. Signed as a free agent by **Montreal Canadiens**, November 10, 1929. Loaned to **NY Americans** by **Montreal Canadiens** for 1932-33 season, October, 1932. Traded to **Ottawa** by **Montreal Canadiens** for cash to complete transaction that sent Marty Burke to Montreal Canadiens (February 6, 1933), March 23, 1933. Transferred to **St. Louis** after **Ottawa** franchise relocated, 1934. Traded to **Minneapolis** (AHA) by **St. Louis** with $1,600 for Fido Purpur, December 28, 1934.

• WATSON, BRYAN
— see page 1568

• WATSON, HARRY
Harry "Whipper" Watson **HHOF**
LW – L. 6'1", 207 lbs. b: Saskatoon, Sask., 5/6/1923. d: 11/8/1957.

Season	Club	League	GP	G	A	Pts	AG	AA	APts	PIM	GP	G	A	Pts	PIM
1939-40	Saskatoon Chiefs	City Jr.	STATISTICS NOT AVAILABLE												
	Saskatoon Dodgers	City Jr.	....	....	....	....	....	....	....	....	2	*6	2	8	2
1940-41	Saskatoon Quakers	City Jr.	6	10	8	18	....	....	....	4	14	10	5	15	2
1941-42	**Brooklyn Americans**	**NHL**	**47**	**10**	**8**	**18**	**17**	**12**	**29**	**6**	....	....	....	....	....
1942-43	**Detroit Red Wings**	**NHL**	**50**	**13**	**18**	**31**	**18**	**23**	**41**	**10**	**7**	**0**	**0**	**0**	**0**
1943-44	Montreal RCAF	QSHL	7	7	4	11	....	....	....	4	....	....	....	....	....
	Saskatoon Quakers	SSHL	2	6	2	8	....	....	....	2	....	....	....	....	....
1944-45	Winnipeg RCAF	City Sr.	1	2	0	2	....	....	....	0	4	7	0	7	2
1945-46	**Detroit Red Wings**	**NHL**	**44**	**14**	**10**	**24**	**21**	**19**	**40**	**4**	**5**	**2**	**0**	**2**	**0**
1946-47	**Toronto Maple Leafs**	**NHL**	**44**	**19**	**15**	**34**	**26**	**21**	**47**	**10**	**11**	**3**	**2**	**5**	**6**
1947-48	**Toronto Maple Leafs**	**NHL**	**57**	**21**	**20**	**41**	**31**	**29**	**60**	**16**	**9**	**5**	**2**	**7**	**9**
1948-49	**Toronto Maple Leafs**	**NHL**	**60**	**26**	**19**	**45**	**41**	**30**	**71**	**0**	**9**	**4**	**2**	**6**	**2**
1949-50	**Toronto Maple Leafs**	**NHL**	**60**	**19**	**16**	**35**	**26**	**20**	**46**	**11**	**7**	**0**	**0**	**0**	**2**
1950-51	**Toronto Maple Leafs**	**NHL**	**68**	**18**	**19**	**37**	**24**	**24**	**48**	**18**	**5**	**1**	**2**	**3**	**4**
1951-52	**Toronto Maple Leafs**	**NHL**	**70**	**22**	**17**	**39**	**31**	**22**	**53**	**18**	**4**	**1**	**0**	**1**	**2**
1952-53	**Toronto Maple Leafs**	**NHL**	**63**	**16**	**8**	**24**	**25**	**11**	**36**	**8**	....	....	....	....	....
1953-54	**Toronto Maple Leafs**	**NHL**	**70**	**21**	**7**	**28**	**32**	**9**	**41**	**30**	**5**	**0**	**1**	**1**	**2**
1954-55	**Toronto Maple Leafs**	**NHL**	**8**	**1**	**1**	**2**	**1**	**1**	**2**	**0**	....	....	....	....	....
	Chicago Black Hawks	**NHL**	**43**	**14**	**16**	**30**	**20**	**20**	**40**	**4**	....	....	....	....	....
1955-56	**Chicago Black Hawks**	**NHL**	**55**	**11**	**14**	**25**	**16**	**17**	**33**	**6**	....	....	....	....	....
1956-57	**Chicago Black Hawks**	**NHL**	**70**	**11**	**19**	**30**	**15**	**22**	**37**	**9**	....	....	....	....	....
1957-58	Buffalo Bisons	AHL	52	8	15	23	....	....	....	10	....	....	....	....	....
1958-59	St. Catharines Teepees	OHA	DID NOT PLAY – COACHING												
	NHL Totals		**809**	**236**	**207**	**443**	**344**	**280**	**624**	**150**	**62**	**16**	**9**	**25**	**27**

Played in NHL All-Star Game (1947, 1948, 1949, 1951, 1952, 1953, 1955)

Signed as a free agent by **NY Americans**, October 10, 1941. Rights transferred to **Detroit** from **Brooklyn** in Special Dispersal Draw, October 9, 1942. Traded to **Toronto** by **Detroit** for Billy Taylor, September 21, 1946. Traded to **Chicago** by **Toronto** for cash, August, 1957.

• WATSON, JIM A.
— see page 1568

• WATSON, JOE
— see page 1569

• WATSON, PHIL
Phil Watson
RW/C – R. 5'11", 165 lbs. b: Montreal, Que., 4/24/1914. Deceased.

Season	Club	League	GP	G	A	Pts	AG	AA	APts	PIM	GP	G	A	Pts	PIM
1932-33	St. Francis Xavier	Mtl-Jr.	11	10	5	15	....	....	....	16	2	0	0	0	0
1933-34	St. Francis Xavier	Mtl-Sr.	16	7	6	13	....	....	....	14	....	....	....	....	....
1934-35	Montreal Royals	City Sr.	19	7	7	14	....	....	....	24	7	1	2	3	4
1935-36	**New York Rangers**	**NHL**	**24**	**0**	**2**	**2**	**0**	**5**	**5**	**24**	....	....	....	....	....
	Philadelphia Arrows	Can-Am	22	9	5	14	....	....	....	32	....	....	....	....	....
1936-37	**New York Rangers**	**NHL**	**48**	**11**	**17**	**28**	**24**	**40**	**64**	**22**	**9**	**0**	**2**	**2**	**9**
1937-38	**New York Rangers**	**NHL**	**48**	**7**	**25**	**32**	**15**	**52**	**67**	**52**	**3**	**0**	**2**	**2**	**0**
1938-39	**New York Rangers**	**NHL**	**48**	**15**	**22**	**37**	**32**	**41**	**73**	**42**	**7**	**1**	**1**	**2**	**7**
1939-40	**New York Rangers**	**NHL**	**48**	**7**	**28**	**35**	**15**	**57**	**72**	**42**	**3**	**3**	**6**	**9**	**16**
1940-41	**New York Rangers**	**NHL**	**40**	**11**	**25**	**36**	**22**	**46**	**68**	**49**	**3**	**0**	**2**	**2**	**9**
1941-42	**New York Rangers**	**NHL**	**48**	**15**	***37**	**52**	**26**	**57**	**83**	**58**	**6**	**1**	**4**	**5**	**8**
1942-43	**New York Rangers**	**NHL**	**46**	**14**	**28**	**42**	**20**	**36**	**56**	**44**	....	....	....	....	....
1943-44	**Montreal Canadiens**	**NHL**	**44**	**17**	**32**	**49**	**21**	**39**	**60**	**61**	**9**	**3**	**5**	**8**	**16**
1944-45	**New York Rangers**	**NHL**	**45**	**11**	**8**	**19**	**15**	**13**	**28**	**24**	....	....	....	....	....
1945-46	**New York Rangers**	**NHL**	**49**	**12**	**14**	**26**	**18**	**26**	**44**	**43**	....	....	....	....	....
1946-47	**New York Rangers**	**NHL**	**48**	**6**	**12**	**18**	**8**	**17**	**25**	**17**	....	....	....	....	....
1947-48	**New York Rangers**	**NHL**	**54**	**18**	**15**	**33**	**26**	**22**	**48**	**54**	**5**	**2**	**3**	**5**	**2**
1948-49	New York Rovers	EHL	DID NOT PLAY – COACHING												
	NHL Totals		**590**	**144**	**265**	**409**	**242**	**451**	**693**	**532**	**45**	**10**	**25**	**35**	**67**

NHL Second All-Star Team (1942)

Signed as a free agent by **NY Rangers** for $4,500, October 27, 1935. Loaned to **NY Rangers** by **Montreal** for 1943-44 season for loan of Charlie Sands, Fern Gauthier, Dutch Hiller, John Mahaffy and future considerations (Tony Demers, December, 1943), November, 1943.

• WEBSTER, AUBREY Aubrey Webster
RW – R. 5'9", 168 lbs. b: Kenora, Ont., 9/25/1912. Deceased.

Season	Club	League	REGULAR SEASON								PLAYOFFS				
			GP	G	A	Pts	AG	AA	APts	PIM	GP	G	A	Pts	PIM
1930-31	Weyburn Beavers	SSHL	12	9	2	11	....	....	....	8	....	....	....	....	....
	Philadelphia Quakers	**NHL**	**1**	**0**	**0**	**0**	**0**	**0**	**0**	**0**	....	....	....	....	....
1931-32	Fredericton Capitals	NBSHL	23	15	6	21	....	....	....	6	7	7	1	8	2
1932-33	Moncton Hawks	NBSHL	18	2	2	4	....	....	....	7	9	2	1	3	8
1933-34	Moncton Hawks	MSHL	36	22	9	31	....	....	....	22	13	10	1	11	4
1934-35	**Montreal Maroons**	**NHL**	**4**	**0**	**0**	**0**	**0**	**0**	**0**	**0**	....	....	....	....	....
	Windsor Bulldogs	IAHL	37	11	16	27	....	....	....	6	....	....	....	....	....
1935-36	Windsor Bulldogs	IAHL	48	13	14	27	....	....	....	15	8	1	1	2	2
1936-37	Spokane Clippers	PCHL	40	9	7	16	....	....	....	32	6	0	2	2	2
1937-38	Spokane C;ippers	PCHL	42	11	22	33	....	....	....	49	....	....	....	....	....
1938-39	Portland Buckaroos	PCHL	40	19	16	35	....	....	....	25	5	1	3	4	14
1939-40	Portland Buckaroos	PCHL	22	9	5	14	....	....	....	10	....	....	....	....	....
	Wichita Skyhawks	AHA	20	3	7	10	....	....	....	2	....	....	....	....	....
1940-41	Spokane Bombers	PCHL	32	9	19	28	....	....	....	14	....	....	....	....	....
1941-42			MILITARY SERVICE												
1942-43			MILITARY SERVICE												
1943-44			MILITARY SERVICE												
1944-45			MILITARY SERVICE												
1945-46	Portland Eagles	PCHL	57	9	21	30	....	....	....	44	8	2	3	5	2
	NHL Totals		**5**	**0**	**0**	**0**	**0**	**0**	**0**	**0**	....	....	....	....	....

Signed as a free agent by **Montreal Maroons**, August, 1934. Traded to **Windsor** (IAHL) by **Montreal Maroons** for cash, December 26, 1934.

• WEBSTER, DON Don Webster
LW – L. 5'8", 180 lbs. b: Toronto, Ont., 7/3/1924. Deceased.

Season	Club	League	GP	G	A	Pts	AG	AA	APts	PIM	GP	G	A	Pts	PIM
1941-42	Toronto Marlboros	OHA	18	6	6	12	....	....	....	47	2	0	2	2	6
1942-43	Providence Reds	AHL	48	11	19	30	....	....	....	67	2	0	0	0	2
1943-44	**Toronto Maple Leafs**	**NHL**	**27**	**7**	**6**	**13**	**9**	**7**	**16**	**28**	**5**	**0**	**0**	**0**	**12**
1944-45	Buffalo–Hershey	AHL	44	5	14	19	....	....	....	51	....	....	....	....	....
1945-46	Hershey Bears	AHL	5	1	3	4	....	....	....	4	....	....	....	....	....
	Fort Worth Rangers	USHL	4	0	0	0	....	....	....	2	....	....	....	....	....
	Shawinigan Cataracts	QSHL	9	2	2	4	....	....	....	8	....	....	....	....	....
	Washington Lions	EAHL	27	5	7	12	....	....	....	49	11	4	2	6	4
1946-47	San Diego Skyhawks	PCHL	60	9	19	28	....	....	....	114	2	0	0	0	2
1947-48	Springfield Indians	AHL	17	1	2	3	....	....	....	24	....	....	....	....	....
	Tulsa Oilers	USHL	46	9	19	28	....	....	....	80	2	1	0	1	4
1948-49	Tulsa Oilers	USHL	52	7	11	18	....	....	....	*137	7	0	3	3	4
1949-50	Los Angeles	PCHL	57	1	13	14	....	....	....	*187	17	3	2	5	52
1950-51	Victoria Cougars	PCHL	64	2	18	20	....	....	....	145	12	0	0	0	*41
1951-52			DID NOT PLAY												
1952-53	Victoria Cougars	WHL	66	0	15	15	....	....	....	123	....	....	....	....	....
	NHL Totals		**27**	**7**	**6**	**13**	**9**	**7**	**16**	**28**	**5**	**0**	**0**	**0**	**12**

Traded to **Providence** (AHL) by **Toronto** with George Boothman for Bill Ezinicki, October 13, 1944.

• WEBSTER, JOHN John "Chick" Webster
C – L. 5'11", 160 lbs. b: Toronto, Ont., 11/3/1920.

Season	Club	League	GP	G	A	Pts	AG	AA	APts	PIM	GP	G	A	Pts	PIM
1937-38	Toronto Native Sons	OHA	12	3	6	9	....	....	....	0	....	....	....	....	....
1938-39	Toronto Native Sons	OHA	14	6	4	10	....	....	....	8	8	4	3	7	8
1939-40	Toronto Native Sons	OHA	11	3	6	9	....	....	....	21	....	....	....	....	....
1940-41	Baltimore Orioles	EHL	62	24	37	61	....	....	....	21	....	....	....	....	....
1941-42	St. Catharines Saints	OHA Sr.	12	1	7	8	....	....	....	26	....	....	....	....	....
1942-43	Petawawa Grenades	Ott-Sr.	3	5	1	6	....	....	....	6	10	10	7	17	21
1943-44			MILITARY SERVICE												
1944-45			MILITARY SERVICE												
1945-46	Baltimore Orioles	EHL	15	7	9	16	....	....	....	5	12	11	9	*20	2
1946-47	New York Rovers	EHL	13	7	11	18	....	....	....	36	....	....	....	....	....
	New Haven Ramblers	AHL	47	9	15	24	....	....	....	26	....	....	....	....	....
1947-48	New Haven Ramblers	AHL	65	22	37	59	....	....	....	12	4	1	1	2	0
1948-49	New Haven Ramblers	AHL	65	16	33	49	....	....	....	24	....	....	....	....	....
1949-50	**New York Rangers**	**NHL**	**14**	**0**	**0**	**0**	**0**	**0**	**0**	**4**	....	....	....	....	....
	New Haven Ramblers	AHL	38	9	17	26	....	....	....	16	....	....	....	....	....
1950-51	Tacoma Rockets	PCHL	63	20	28	48	....	....	....	36	6	1	1	2	2
1951-52	Cincinnati Mohawks	AHL	49	6	12	18	....	....	....	15	7	3	2	5	0
1952-53	Syracuse Warriors	AHL	13	2	2	4	....	....	....	0	....	....	....	....	....
	Vancouver Canucks	WHL	5	0	0	0	....	....	....	0	....	....	....	....	....
	Soo Greyhounds	NOHA	12	1	7	8	....	....	....	4	2	0	1	1	0
	NHL Totals		**14**	**0**	**0**	**0**	**0**	**0**	**0**	**4**	....	....	....	....	....

• WEILAND, COONEY Cooney (Ralph) Weiland HHOF
C – L. 5'7", 150 lbs. b: Seaforth (Edmondville), Ont., 11/5/1904. d: 7/3/1985.

Season	Club	League	GP	G	A	Pts	AG	AA	APts	PIM	GP	G	A	Pts	PIM
1923-24	Owen Sound Grays	City Jr.	9	*33	*5	*38	....	....	....	....	15	*37	9	*46	....
1924-25	Minneapolis Rockets	USAHA	35	8	0	8	....	....	....	....	....	....	....	....	....
1925-26	Minneapolis Millers	CHL	26	10	4	14	....	....	....	20	3	1	1	2	0
1926-27	Minneapolis Millers	AHA	36	21	2	23	....	....	....	30	6	*4	1	*5	0
1927-28	Minneapolis Millers	AHA	40	*21	5	26	....	....	....	34	8	2	*2	*4	0
1928-29	**Boston Bruins**	**NHL**	**42**	**11**	**7**	**18**	**44**	**65**	**109**	**16**	**5**	**2**	**0**	**2**	**2**
1929-30	**Boston Bruins**	**NHL**	**44**	***43**	**30**	***73**	**87**	**99**	**186**	**27**	**6**	**1**	***5**	***6**	**2**
1930-31	**Boston Bruins**	**NHL**	**44**	**25**	**13**	**38**	**62**	**47**	**109**	**14**	**5**	***6**	**3**	***9**	**2**
1931-32	**Boston Bruins**	**NHL**	**46**	**14**	**12**	**26**	**30**	**33**	**63**	**20**	....	....	....	....	....
1932-33	**Ottawa Senators**	**NHL**	**48**	**16**	**11**	**27**	**38**	**29**	**67**	**4**	....	....	....	....	....
1933-34	**Ottawa Senators**	**NHL**	**9**	**2**	**0**	**2**	**4**	**0**	**4**	**4**	....	....	....	....	....
	Detroit Red Wings	**NHL**	**39**	**11**	**19**	**30**	**24**	**51**	**75**	**6**	**9**	**2**	**2**	**4**	**4**
1934-35	**Detroit Red Wings**	**NHL**	**48**	**13**	**25**	**38**	**28**	**56**	**84**	**10**	....	....	....	....	....
1935-36	**Boston Bruins**	**NHL**	**48**	**14**	**13**	**27**	**35**	**31**	**66**	**15**	**2**	**1**	**0**	**1**	**2**
1936-37	**Boston Bruins**	**NHL**	**48**	**6**	**9**	**15**	**13**	**21**	**34**	**6**	**3**	**0**	**0**	**0**	**0**
1937-38	**Boston Bruins**	**NHL**	**48**	**11**	**12**	**23**	**23**	**25**	**48**	**16**	**3**	**0**	**0**	**0**	**0**
1938-39	**Boston Bruins**	**NHL**	**45**	**7**	**9**	**16**	**15**	**17**	**32**	**9**	**12**	**0**	**0**	**0**	**0**
1939-40	**Boston Bruins**	**NHL**	DID NOT PLAY – COACHING												
	NHL Totals		**509**	**173**	**160**	**333**	**403**	**474**	**877**	**147**	**45**	**12**	**10**	**22**	**12**

NHL Scoring Leader (1930) • NHL Second All-Star Team (1935) • Won Lester Patrick Trophy (1972)

Traded to **Boston** by **Minneapolis** (AHA) for cash, December 23, 1927. Traded to **Ottawa** by **Boston** for Joe Lamb and $7,000, July 25, 1932. Traded to **Detroit** by **Ottawa** for Carl Voss and cash, November 26, 1933. Traded to **Boston** by **Detroit** with Walt Buswell for Marty Barry and Art Giroux, June 30, 1935.

• WELLINGTON, ALEX Alex "Duke" Wellington
RW – R. b: Port Arthur, Ont.. Deceased.

Season	Club	League	REGULAR SEASON								PLAYOFFS				
			GP	G	A	Pts	AG	AA	APts	PIM	GP	G	A	Pts	PIM
1910-11	Port Arthur Lake Cities	NOHL	....	....	....	....	....	....	....	....	3	7	0	7	3
1911-12	Port Arthur Lake Cities	NOHL	STATISTICS NOT AVAILABLE												
1912-13	Halifax Cresents	MPHL	6	0	0	0	....	....	....	0	....	....	....	....	....
1913-14	Port Arthur Ports	TBSHL	STATISTICS NOT AVAILABLE												
1914-15	Cleveland Indians	USAHA	STATISTICS NOT AVAILABLE												
1915-16	Pittsburgh Duquesene	USAHA	STATISTICS NOT AVAILABLE												
1916-17	New York Irish Americans	NYHL	STATISTICS NOT AVAILABLE												
1917-18	New York Wanderers	NYHL	8	1	0	1	....	....	....	....	....	....	....	....	....
1918-19			DID NOT PLAY – SUSPENDED												
1919-20	**Quebec Bulldogs**	**NHL**	**1**	**0**	**0**	**0**	**0**	**0**	**0**	**0**	....	....	....	....	....
	NY New Rochelle	USAHA	STATISTICS NOT AVAILABLE												
	NHL Totals		**1**	**0**	**0**	**0**	**0**	**0**	**0**	**0**	....	....	....	....	....
	Other Major League Totals		6	0	0	0	....	....	....	0	....	....	....	....	....

Signed as a free agent by **Quebec**, January 9, 1920.

• WENTWORTH, CY Cy (Marvin) Wentworth
D – R. 5'10", 170 lbs. b: Grimsby, Ont., 1/24/1905. Deceased.

Season	Club	League	GP	G	A	Pts	AG	AA	APts	PIM	GP	G	A	Pts	PIM
1925-26	Windsor Hornets	OHA Sr.	20	6	5	11	....	....	....	9	....	....	....	....	....
1926-27	Chicago Cardinals	AHA	34	8	4	12	....	....	....	40	....	....	....	....	....
1927-28	**Chicago Black Hawks**	**NHL**	**43**	**5**	**5**	**10**	**15**	**42**	**57**	**31**	....	....	....	....	....
1928-29	**Chicago Black Hawks**	**NHL**	**44**	**2**	**1**	**3**	**8**	**9**	**17**	**44**	....	....	....	....	....
1929-30	**Chicago Black Hawks**	**NHL**	**37**	**3**	**4**	**7**	**6**	**13**	**19**	**28**	....	....	....	....	....
1930-31	**Chicago Black Hawks**	**NHL**	**44**	**4**	**4**	**8**	**10**	**14**	**24**	**12**	**9**	**1**	**1**	**2**	**14**
1931-32	**Chicago Black Hawks**	**NHL**	**48**	**3**	**10**	**13**	**6**	**28**	**34**	**30**	**2**	**0**	**0**	**0**	**0**
1932-33	**Montreal Maroons**	**NHL**	**47**	**4**	**10**	**14**	**9**	**26**	**35**	**48**	**2**	**0**	**1**	**1**	**0**
1933-34	**Montreal Maroons**	**NHL**	**48**	**2**	**5**	**7**	**4**	**13**	**17**	**31**	**4**	**0**	**2**	**2**	**2**
1934-35	**Montreal Maroons**	**NHL**	**48**	**4**	**9**	**13**	**8**	**20**	**28**	**28**	**7**	**3**	**2**	***5**	**0**
1935-36	**Montreal Maroons**	**NHL**	**48**	**4**	**5**	**9**	**10**	**12**	**22**	**24**	**3**	**0**	**0**	**0**	**0**
1936-37	**Montreal Maroons**	**NHL**	**43**	**3**	**4**	**7**	**6**	**9**	**15**	**29**	**5**	**1**	**0**	**1**	**0**
1937-38	**Montreal Maroons**	**NHL**	**48**	**4**	**5**	**9**	**8**	**10**	**18**	**32**	....	....	....	....	....
1938-39	**Montreal Canadiens**	**NHL**	**45**	**0**	**3**	**3**	**0**	**6**	**6**	**12**	**3**	**0**	**0**	**0**	**4**
1939-40	**Montreal Canadiens**	**NHL**	**32**	**1**	**3**	**4**	**2**	**6**	**8**	**6**	....	....	....	....	....
	NHL Totals		**575**	**39**	**68**	**107**	**92**	**208**	**300**	**355**	**35**	**5**	**6**	**11**	**20**

NHL Second All-Star Team (1935)

Played in NHL All-Star Game (1937, 1939)

Traded to **Chicago** by **Windsor** (Can-Pro) for cash, December, 20, 1926. Traded to **Montreal Maroons** by **Chicago** for $10,000, October 24, 1932. Traded to **Montreal Canadiens** by **Montreal Maroons** for cash, September 14, 1938.

• WESTFALL, ED — *see page 1572*

• WHARRAM, KENNY — *see page 1573*

• WHARTON, LEN Len Wharton
D – L. 6', 170 lbs. b: Winnipeg, Man., 12/13/1927.

Season	Club	League	GP	G	A	Pts	AG	AA	APts	PIM	GP	G	A	Pts	PIM
1944-45	**New York Rangers**	**NHL**	**1**	**0**	**0**	**0**	**0**	**0**	**0**	**0**	....	....	....	....	....
	New York Rovers	EHL	39	9	12	21	....	....	....	8	12	0	2	2	18
1945-46	New York Rovers	EHL	36	3	9	12	....	....	....	26	9	0	0	0	2
1946-47	Stratford Kroehlers	OHA	18	7	5	12	....	....	....	38	....	....	....	....	....
1947-48	San Diego Skyhawks	PCHL	47	11	15	26	....	....	....	18	....	....	....	....	....
1948-49	Louisville Blades	IHL	28	4	14	18	....	....	....	102	6	0	0	0	*23
1949-50	Toledo Buckeyes	EHL	45	2	11	13	....	....	....	*151	7	1	1	2	20
1950-51	Toledo Mercurys	IHL	53	6	19	25	....	....	....	*186	21	1	8	9	28
1951-52	Toledo Mercurys	IHL	44	2	15	17	....	....	....	*148	10	1	3	4	10
1952-53	Fort Wayne Komets	IHL	59	5	24	29	....	....	....	77	....	....	....	....	....
1953-54	Fort Wayne Komets	IHL	52	1	10	11	....	....	....	84	2	0	1	1	16
	NHL Totals		**1**	**0**	**0**	**0**	**0**	**0**	**0**	**0**	....	....	....	....	....

• WHITE, MOE Moe (Leonard) White
LW/C – L. 5'11", 178 lbs. b: Verdun, Que., 7/28/1919.

Season	Club	League	GP	G	A	Pts	AG	AA	APts	PIM	GP	G	A	Pts	PIM
1935-36	Verdun Maple Leafs	Mtl-Jr.	9	1	3	4	....	....	....	0	2	0	2	2	0
1936-37	Montreal Victorias	City Jr.	11	2	5	7	....	....	....	19	2	2	1	3	2
1937-38	Montreal Victorias	City Sr.	19	7	5	12	....	....	....	19	6	6	2	8	16
1938-39	Montreal Victorias	City Sr.	22	9	10	19	....	....	....	19	....	....	....	....	....
1939-40	Verdun Maple Leafs	City Sr.	30	14	14	28	....	....	....	20	8	3	3	6	10
1940-41	Glace Bay Miners	CBSHL	11	4	5	9	....	....	....	14	....	....	....	....	....
1941-42	Glace Bay Miners	CBSHL	40	31	31	62	....	....	....	44	7	5	4	9	6
1942-43	Montreal Army	QSHL	33	13	20	33	....	....	....	16	7	1	2	3	16
	Montreal Army	OHA Sr.	6	6	7	13	....	....	....	2	5	6	4	10	0
1943-44	Kingston Army	OHA Sr.	13	7	8	15	....	....	....	6	....	....	....	....	....
	Montreal Army	City Sr.	1	0	0	0	....	....	....	0	....	....	....	....	....
1944-45			MILITARY SERVICE												
1945-46	**Montreal Canadiens**	**NHL**	**4**	**0**	**1**	**1**	**0**	**2**	**2**	**2**	....	....	....	....	....
	Montreal Royals	QSHL	1	1	0	1	....	....	....	2	....	....	....	....	....
	Buffalo Bisons	AHL	11	2	2	4	....	....	....	2	....	....	....	....	....
1946-47	Houston Huskies	USHL	60	28	34	62	....	....	....	27	....	....	....	....	....
1947-48	Valleyfield Braves	QSHL	46	23	29	52	....	....	....	37	6	0	2	2	10
1948-49	Glace Bay Miners	CBSHL	57	6	*44	50	....	....	....	111	12	1	3	4	*33
1949-50	Glace Bay Miners	CBSHL	70	18	27	45	....	....	....	33	10	0	9	9	2
	NHL Totals		**4**	**0**	**1**	**1**	**0**	**2**	**2**	**2**	....	....	....	....	....

QHL Second All-Star Team (1953)

Traded to **Buffalo** (AHL) by **Montreal** with Jack Adams for Murdo MacKay with Montreal holding rights of recall, January 14, 1946. Traded to **Buffalo** (AHL) by **Montreal** for cash, October 8, 1946.

• WHITE, SHERMAN Sherman "Shermie" White
C – L. 5'10", 165 lbs. b: Cape Tormentine, N.B., 5/12/1923. Deceased.

Season	Club	League	GP	G	A	Pts	AG	AA	APts	PIM	GP	G	A	Pts	PIM
1938-39	Amherst St. Pats	NSJHL	9	*11	*5	*16	....	....	....	18	7	*17	*6	*23	*8
1939-40	Amherst Ramblers	NSSHL	7	*17	5	*22	....	....	....	4	5	*8	1	9	0
1940-41	Amherst Ramblers	NSSHL	4	12	2	14	....	....	....	0	....	....	....	....	....
1941-42	Amherst Ramblers	NSSHL	7	*14	5	19	....	....	....	0	....	....	....	....	....
1942-43	Amherst All-Stars	NSSHL	5	*14	*7	*21	....	....	....	0	2	*3	4	*7	0
	Amherst Busymen	NSSHL	5	*9	*8	*17	....	....	....	6	1	*4	1	*5	0
1943-44	Amherst Victoria Bombers	NSSHL	1	2	0	2	....	....	....	5	1	1	1	2	2
	Saint John Beavers	NBSHL	....	....	....	....	....	....	....	....	1	0	1	1	0
	Moncton #5 Providers	MIHL	1	1	0	1	....	....	....	0	3	3	3	6	0
1944-45	Moncton #5 Providers	MIHL	8	10	5	15	....	....	....	0	2	4	1	5	0
	Dartmouth RCAF	NSSHL	3	0	1	1	....	....	....	0	3	0	0	0	4
1945-46	Dartmouth RCAF	NSSHL	8	8	8	16	....	....	....	0	5	4	5	9	0
	Amherst Ramblers	NSSHL	3	6	3	9	....	....	....	0	....	....	....	....	....
	Moncton Maroons	NBSHL	3	4	7	11	....	....	....	0	3	0	3	3	0
1946-47	**New York Rangers**	**NHL**	**1**	**0**	**0**	**0**	**0**	**0**	**0**	**0**	....	....	....	....	....
	New York Rovers	EHL	19	13	9	22	....	....	....	2	....	....	....	....	....
	New Haven Ramblers	AHL	36	8	8	16	....	....	....	8	3	2	0	0	0
1947-48	New Haven Ramblers	AHL	58	9	30	39	....	....	....	10	4	0	2	2	2
1948-49	New Haven Ramblers	AHL	68	26	32	58	....	....	....	13	....	....	....	....	....
1949-50	**New York Rangers**	**NHL**	**3**	**0**	**2**	**2**	**0**	**3**	**3**	**0**	....	....	....	....	....
	New Haven Ramblers	AHL	70	17	35	52	....	....	....	6	....	....	....	....	....
1950-51	St. Louis Flyers	AHL	66	11	42	53	....	....	....	6	....	....	....	....	....
1951-52	Chicoutimi Sagueneens	QSHL	59	23	32	55	....	....	....	8	18	2	9	11	0
1952-53	Chicoutimi Sagueneens	QSHL	58	26	*57	83	....	....	....	6	20	3	*16	19	4
1953-54	Chicoutimi Sagueneens	QHL	51	10	36	46	....	....	....	4	3	1	1	2	0
1954-55	Amherst Ramblers	MSHL	40	20	46	66	....	....	....	2	8	2	4	6	2
1955-56	Amherst Ramblers	MSHL	....	42	*78	*120	....	....	....	2	14	10	9	*19	2
	Saint John Beavers	MSHL	....	....	....	....	....	....	....	....	2	0	2	2	0
1956-57	Bathurst Papermakers	City Sr.	....	20	38	58	....	....	....	7	....	....	....	....	....
1957-58	Bishop's Falls Flyers	Nfld.	11	20	15	35	....	....	....	0	....	....	....	....	....
1958-59	Glace Bay Miners	CBSHL	....	23	*54	*77	....	....	....	8	....	....	....	....	....
1959-60	Glace Bay Miners	CBSHL	STATISTICS NOT AVAILABLE												
1960-61	Amherst Ramblers	NSSHL	....	18	*55	*73	....	....	....	0	....	....	....	....	....
1961-62	Amherst Ramblers	NSSHL	....	14	27	41	....	....	....	0	9	6	9	15	0
1962-63	Amherst–Moncton	NSSHL	....	21	50	71	....	....	....	6	26	7	10	17	8
1963-64	Moncton Hawks	NSSHL	....	9	15	24	....	....	....	2	4	0	1	1	0
	NHL Totals		**4**	**0**	**2**	**2**	**0**	**3**	**3**	**0**	....	....	....	....	....

Won Vimy Trophy (MVP - QHL) (1953)

• WHITE, TEX Tex (Wilfred) White
RW – R. 5'11", 155 lbs. b: Hillbrough, Ont., 6/26/1900. d: 12/2/1949.

Season	Club	League	GP	G	A	Pts	AG	AA	APts	PIM	GP	G	A	Pts	PIM
1923-24	Pittsburgh Yellowjackets	USAHA	20	11	0	11	....	....	....	....	13	1	1	2	....
1924-25	Pittsburgh Yellowjackets	USAHA	39	7	0	7	....	....	....	....	8	1	0	1	....
1925-26	**Pittsburgh Pirates**	**NHL**	**35**	**7**	**1**	**8**	**22**	**11**	**33**	**22**	....	....	....	....	....
1926-27	**Pittsburgh Pirates**	**NHL**	**43**	**5**	**4**	**9**	**14**	**34**	**48**	**21**	....	....	....	....	....
1927-28	**Pittsburgh Pirates**	**NHL**	**44**	**5**	**1**	**6**	**15**	**8**	**23**	**54**	**2**	**0**	**0**	**0**	**2**
1928-29	**Pittsburgh Pirates**	**NHL**	**30**	**3**	**4**	**7**	**12**	**37**	**49**	**18**	....	....	....	....	....
	New York Americans	**NHL**	**13**	**2**	**1**	**3**	**8**	**9**	**17**	**8**	**2**	**0**	**0**	**0**	**2**
1929-30	**Pittsburgh Pirates**	**NHL**	**29**	**8**	**1**	**9**	**16**	**3**	**19**	**16**	....	....	....	....	....
	New Haven Eagles	Can-Am	12	2	0	2	....	....	....	6	....	....	....	....	....
1930-31	**Philadelphia Quakers**	**NHL**	**9**	**3**	**0**	**3**	**7**	**0**	**7**	**2**	....	....	....	....	....
	Pittsburgh Yellowjackets	IAHL	35	9	7	16	....	....	....	12	6	1	0	1	6
1931-32	Pittsburgh Yellowjackets	IAHL	24	1	1	2	....	....	....	22	....	....	....	....	....
	NHL Totals		**203**	**33**	**12**	**45**	**94**	**102**	**196**	**141**	**4**	**0**	**0**	**0**	**4**

Signed as a free agent by **Pittsburgh**, September 26, 1925. Loaned to **NY Americans** by **Pittsburgh** for Edmond Bouchard and Jesse Spring, February 15, 1929. Transferred to **Philadelphia** after **Pittsburgh** franchise relocated, September 27, 1930. Traded to **Pittsburgh** (IAHL) by **Philadelphia** for cash, December 16, 1930.

• WHITELAW, BOB Bob Whitelaw
D – L. 5'11", 185 lbs. b: Motherwell, Scotland, 10/5/1916.

Season	Club	League	GP	G	A	Pts	AG	AA	APts	PIM	GP	G	A	Pts	PIM
1935-36	Winnipeg Rangers	City Jr.	12	4	4	8	....	....	....	10	2	3	0	3	6
1936-37	Harringay Greyhounds	Britain	....	5	3	8	....	....	....	10	....	....	....	....	....
1937-38	Harringay Racers	Britain	....	11	6	17	....	....	....	....	....	....	....	....	....
1938-39	Pittsburgh Hornets	AHL	50	1	7	8	....	....	....	23	....	....	....	....	....
1939-40	Indianapolis Capitals	AHL	56	6	7	13	....	....	....	22	5	0	0	0	0
1940-41	**Detroit Red Wings**	**NHL**	**23**	**0**	**2**	**2**	**0**	**4**	**4**	**2**	**8**	**0**	**0**	**0**	**0**
	Indianapolis Capitals	AHL	24	1	4	5	....	....	....	8	....	....	....	....	....
1941-42	**Detroit Red Wings**	**NHL**	**9**	**0**	**0**	**0**	**0**	**0**	**0**	**0**	....	....	....	....	....
	Indianapolis Capitals	AHL	28	1	3	4	....	....	....	13	....	....	....	....	....
1942-43	Providence Reds	AHL	55	7	15	22	....	....	....	27	2	0	0	0	0
1943-44			MILITARY SERVICE												
1944-45	Winnipeg RCAF	City Sr.	11	1	2	3	....	....	....	6	....	....	....	....	....
1945-46	Wembley Lions	Britain	STATISTICS NOT AVAILABLE												
1946-47	Providence Reds	AHL	60	2	6	8	....	....	....	7	....	....	....	....	....
1947-48	Winnipeg Nationals	City Sr.	7	1	1	2	....	....	....	0	....	....	....	....	....
	NHL Totals		**32**	**0**	**2**	**2**	**0**	**4**	**4**	**2**	**8**	**0**	**0**	**0**	**0**

Signed as a free agent by **Detroit**, October 13, 1939.

• WIEBE, ART Art Wiebe
D – L. 5'10", 180 lbs b: Rosthern, Sask., 9/28/1912. d: 6/6/1971.

Season	Club	League	GP	G	A	Pts	AG	AA	APts	PIM	GP	G	A	Pts	PIM
1931-32	Edmonton Poolers	City Jr.	....	2	2	4	....	....	....	....	....	....	....	....	....
1932-33	**Chicago Black Hawks**	**NHL**	**4**	**0**	**0**	**0**	**0**	**0**	**0**	**0**	....	....	....	....	....
	St. Paul-Tulsa	AHA	16	0	0	0	....	....	....	10	....	....	....	....	....
1933-34	Kansas City Greyhounds	AHA	15	1	1	2	....	....	....	9	4	0	0	0	0
1934-35	**Chicago Black Hawks**	**NHL**	**42**	**2**	**1**	**3**	**4**	**2**	**6**	**27**	**2**	**0**	**0**	**0**	**2**
1935-36	**Chicago Black Hawks**	**NHL**	**46**	**1**	**0**	**1**	**2**	**0**	**2**	**25**	**2**	**0**	**0**	**0**	**0**
1936-37	**Chicago Black Hawks**	**NHL**	**43**	**0**	**2**	**2**	**0**	**5**	**5**	**6**	....	....	....	....	....
1937-38	**Chicago Black Hawks**	**NHL**	**43**	**0**	**3**	**3**	**0**	**6**	**6**	**24**	**10**	**0**	**1**	**1**	**2**
1938-39	**Chicago Black Hawks**	**NHL**	**47**	**1**	**2**	**3**	**2**	**4**	**6**	**24**	....	....	....	....	....
1939-40	**Chicago Black Hawks**	**NHL**	**47**	**2**	**2**	**4**	**4**	**4**	**8**	**20**	**2**	**1**	**0**	**1**	**2**
1940-41	**Chicago Black Hawks**	**NHL**	**45**	**3**	**2**	**5**	**6**	**4**	**10**	**28**	**4**	**0**	**0**	**0**	**0**
1941-42	**Chicago Black Hawks**	**NHL**	**43**	**2**	**4**	**6**	**3**	**6**	**9**	**20**	**3**	**0**	**0**	**0**	**0**
1942-43	**Chicago Black Hawks**	**NHL**	**33**	**1**	**7**	**8**	**1**	**9**	**10**	**25**	....	....	....	....	....
1943-44	**Chicago Black Hawks**	**NHL**	**21**	**2**	**4**	**6**	**2**	**5**	**7**	**2**	**8**	**0**	**2**	**2**	**4**
	NHL Totals		**414**	**14**	**27**	**41**	**24**	**45**	**69**	**201**	**31**	**1**	**3**	**4**	**10**

Traded to **Chicago** by **St. Paul** (AHA) for Helge Bostrum, December, 1932.

• WILCOX, ARCHIE Archie Wilcox
RW/D – L. 5'11", 195 lbs. b: Montreal, Que., 5/9/1904. d: 1993.

Season	Club	League	GP	G	A	Pts	AG	AA	APts	PIM	GP	G	A	Pts	PIM
1925-26	Montreal Victorias	City Sr.	10	0	0	0	....	....	....	14	3	0	0	0	2
1926-27	Providence Reds	Can-Am	21	4	3	7	....	....	....	22	....	....	....	....	....
	Stratford Nationals	Can-Pro	6	0	0	0	....	....	....	6	....	....	....	....	....
1927-28	Providence Reds	Can-Am	38	12	2	14	....	....	....	50	....	....	....	....	....
1928-29	Providence Reds	Can-Am	40	2	1	3	....	....	....	52	6	0	*2	2	14
1929-30	**Montreal Maroons**	**NHL**	**42**	**3**	**5**	**8**	**6**	**16**	**22**	**38**	**4**	**1**	**0**	**1**	**2**
1930-31	**Montreal Maroons**	**NHL**	**39**	**2**	**2**	**4**	**5**	**7**	**12**	**42**	**2**	**0**	**0**	**0**	**2**
1931-32	**Montreal Maroons**	**NHL**	**48**	**3**	**3**	**6**	**6**	**8**	**14**	**37**	**4**	**0**	**0**	**0**	**4**
1932-33	**Montreal Maroons**	**NHL**	**47**	**0**	**3**	**3**	**0**	**8**	**8**	**37**	**2**	**0**	**0**	**0**	**0**
1933-34	**Montreal Maroons**	**NHL**	**10**	**0**	**0**	**0**	**0**	**0**	**0**	**2**	....	....	....	....	....
	Boston Bruins	**NHL**	**14**	**0**	**1**	**1**	**0**	**3**	**3**	**2**	....	....	....	....	....
	Quebec Beavers	Can-Am	15	1	2	3	....	....	....	13	....	....	....	....	....
1934-35	**St. Louis Eagles**	**NHL**	**8**	**0**	**0**	**0**	**0**	**0**	**0**	**0**	....	....	....	....	....
	Boston Cubs	Can-Am	4	0	2	2	....	....	....	6	....	....	....	....	....
	Syracuse Stars	IAHL	15	0	5	5	....	....	....	8	2	0	0	0	0
	NHL Totals		**208**	**8**	**14**	**22**	**17**	**42**	**59**	**158**	**12**	**1**	**0**	**1**	**8**

Signed as a free agent by **Detroit Cougars**, October 26, 1927. Traded to **Montreal Maroons** by **Detroit Cougars** for cash, August 23, 1929. Claimed on waivers by **Boston** from **Montreal Maroons**, January 29, 1934. Traded to **St. Louis** by **Boston** for Burr Williams, December 2, 1934. Traded to **Syracuse** (IAHL) by **St. Louis** for cash, January 4, 1934.

• WILDER, ARCH Arch Wilder
LW – L. 5'9", 155 lbs. b: Melville, Sask., 4/30/1917.

Season	Club	League	GP	G	A	Pts	AG	AA	APts	PIM	GP	G	A	Pts	PIM
1935-36	Weyburn Beavers	SSHL	2	1	1	2	....	....	....	0	....	....	....	....	....
1936-37	Saskatoon Wesleys	City Jr.	STATISTICS NOT AVAILABLE												
1937-38	Detroit Pontiacs	MOHL	28	5	11	16	....	....	....	9	3	0	1	1	0
1938-39	Detroit Pontiac McLeans	MOHL	27	14	17	31	....	....	....	6	7	3	*6	9	6
1939-40	Indianapolis Capitols	AHL	56	12	12	24	....	....	....	16	5	2	0	2	2
1940-41	**Detroit Red Wings**	**NHL**	**18**	**0**	**2**	**2**	**0**	**4**	**4**	**2**	....	....	....	....	....
	Indianapolis Capitols	AHL	9	1	3	4	....	....	....	0	....	....	....	....	....
	Omaha Knights	AHA	24	1	4	5	....	....	....	4	....	....	....	....	....
1941-42	Saskatoon Quakers	SSHL	31	8	16	24	....	....	....	4	9	4	1	5	2
1942-43			MILITARY SERVICE												
1943-44			MILITARY SERVICE												
1944-45	Calgary RCAF	City Sr.	16	13	8	21	....	....	....	2	3	0	*3	3	0
1945-46	Calgary Stampeders	WCSHL	34	17	21	38	....	....	....	20	16	6	2	8	14
1946-47	Calgary Stampeders	WCSHL	40	13	12	25	....	....	....	14	7	3	4	7	0
1947-48	Calgary Stampeders	WCSHL	46	10	16	26	....	....	....	10	11	2	5	7	4
1948-49	Calgary Stampeders	WCSHL	45	6	14	20	....	....	....	10	4	0	0	0	2
1949-50	Calgary Stampeders	WCSHL	42	4	10	14	....	....	....	12	10	1	2	3	2
1950-51	Calgary Stampeders	WCSHL	30	6	13	19	....	....	....	21	6	0	2	2	0
	NHL Totals		**18**	**0**	**2**	**2**	**0**	**4**	**4**	**2**	....	....	....	....	....

• WILKINS, BARRY
— *see page 1578*

• WILKINSON, JOHN John Wilkinson
D – L. 5'11", 195 lbs. b: Ottawa, Ont., 7/9/1911. Deceased.

Season	Club	League	GP	G	A	Pts	AG	AA	APts	PIM	GP	G	A	Pts	PIM
1929-30	Ottawa Rideaus	City Jr.	12	2	0	2	....	....	....	21	8	2	0	2	*22
1930-31	Ottawa Rideaus	City Jr.	16	3	3	6	....	....	....	28	2	0	0	0	4
1931-32	Ottawa New Edinburghs	City Sr.	26	2	3	5	....	....	....	61	2	0	0	0	8
1932-33	Ottawa New Edinburghs	City Sr.	20	4	2	6	....	....	....	33	3	0	0	0	4
1933-34	Ottawa New Edinburghs	City Sr.	13	2	2	4	....	....	....	15	10	3	1	4	*24
1934-35	Ottawa Senators	City Sr.	19	5	0	5	....	....	....	42	8	0	0	0	14
1935-36	Wembley Canadians	Britain	....	6	4	10	....	....	....	18	....	....	....	....	....
1936-37	Wembley Monarchs	Britain	....	17	9	26	....	....	....	60	....	....	....	....	....
1937-38	Ottawa Senators	QSHL	17	5	5	10	....	....	....	39	3	0	0	0	5
1938-39	Ottawa Senators	QSHL	21	6	7	13	....	....	....	*56	6	0	0	0	10
1939-40	Ottawa Senators	QSHL	21	1	4	5	....	....	....	38	....	....	....	....	....
1940-41	Ottawa Senators	QSHL	33	8	13	21	....	....	....	45	8	2	2	4	2
1941-42	Montreal Pats	QSHL	21	2	2	4	....	....	....	18	....	....	....	....	....
	Halifax Navy	City Sr.	2	0	1	1	....	....	....	2	5	1	1	2	0
1942-43	Hull Volants	Ott-Sr.	14	2	4	6	....	....	....	11	4	0	1	1	4
	Halifax Navy	City Sr.	1	0	0	0	....	....	....	0	....	....	....	....	....
1943-44	**Boston Bruins**	**NHL**	**9**	**0**	**0**	**0**	**0**	**0**	**0**	**6**	....	....	....	....	....
	Ottawa Commandos	QSHL	7	1	1	2	....	....	....	6	3	0	0	0	0
	NHL Totals		**9**	**0**	**0**	**0**	**0**	**0**	**0**	**6**	....	....	....	....	....

• WILLIAMS, BURR

Burr (Burton) Williams
D – R. 5'10", 183 lbs. b: Okemah, OK, 8/30/1909. d: 2/12/1981.

			REGULAR SEASON								PLAYOFFS				
Season	Club	League	GP	G	A	Pts	AG	AA	APts	PIM	GP	G	A	Pts	PIM
1927-28	Duluth Hornets	AHA	36	7	3	10	....	....	....	61	5	1	0	1	12
1928-29	Duluth Hornets	AHA	26	5	2	7	....	....	....	44	....	....	....	....	....
1929-30	Tulsa Oilers	AHA	48	9	7	16	....	....	....	77	9	2	*2	*4	*21
1930-31	Tulsa Oilers	AHA	48	16	*16	32	....	....	....	107	4	0	0	0	13
1931-32	St. Louis Flyers	AHA	42	10	3	13	....	....	....	72	....	....	....	....	....
	Tulsa Oilers	AHA	8	1	2	3	....	....	....	14	....	....	....	....	....
1932-33	Duluth Hornets	AHA	18	8	6	14	....	....	....	30	....	....	....	....	....
	Detroit Olympics	AHL	14	3	1	4	....	....	....	20	....	....	....	....	....
1933-34	**Detroit Red Wings**	**NHL**	**1**	**0**	**1**	**1**	**0**	**3**	**3**	**12**	**2**	**0**	**0**	**0**	**8**
	Detroit Olympics	AHL	35	5	4	9	....	....	....	50	....	....	....	....	....
1934-35	**St. Louis Eagles**	**NHL**	**9**	**0**	**0**	**0**	**0**	**0**	**0**	**6**	....	....	....	....	....
	Boston Bruins	**NHL**	**7**	**0**	**0**	**0**	**0**	**0**	**0**	**6**	....	....	....	....	....
	Detroit Olympics	IAHL	26	5	8	13	....	....	....	36	5	0	0	0	*8
1935-36	Detroit Olympics	IAHL	47	7	9	16	....	....	....	53	6	1	1	2	14
1936-37	**Detroit Red Wings**	**NHL**	**2**	**0**	**0**	**0**	**0**	**0**	**0**	**4**	....	....	....	....	....
	Pittsburgh Hornets	AHL	47	3	10	13	....	....	....	78	5	1	1	2	6
1937-38	New Haven Eagles	AHL	2	0	0	0	....	....	....	0	....	....	....	....	....
	Pittsburgh Hornets	AHL	3	0	0	0	....	....	....	2	....	....	....	....	....
	Tulsa Oilers	AHA	33	6	4	10	....	....	....	42	4	0	0	0	8
1938-39	Tulsa Oilers	AHA	48	5	8	13	....	....	....	71	8	0	2	2	*20
1939-40	Tulsa Oilers	AHA	46	8	13	21	....	....	....	39	....	....	....	....	....
1940-41	St. Louis Flyers	AHA	7	0	0	0	....	....	....	12	....	....	....	....	....
	Kansas City Americans	AHA	4	0	0	0	....	....	....	0	....	....	....	....	....
	Omaha Knights	AHA	19	0	1	1	....	....	....	4	....	....	....	....	....
	Minneapolis Millers	AHA	10	4	2	6	....	....	....	4	....	....	....	....	....
	NHL Totals		**19**	**0**	**1**	**1**	**0**	**3**	**3**	**28**	**2**	**0**	**0**	**0**	**8**

IAHL Second All-Star Team (1936)

Claimed by **Toronto** from **Tulsa** (AHA) in Inter-League Draft, April 15, 1930. Traded to **Tulsa** (AHA) by **Toronto** for cash, September, 1930. Traded to **St. Louis** (AHA) by **Tulsa** (AHA) for cash, December, 1931. Claimed by **Chicago** from **St. Louis** (AHA) in Inter-League Draft, September 2, 1932. Traded to **Duluth** (AHA) by **Chicago** for cash, October, 1932. Traded to **Detroit** by **Duluth** (AHA) for cash, January 29, 1933. Traded to **St. Louis** by **Detroit** for Normie Smith, October 21, 1934. Traded to **Boston** by **St. Louis** for Archie Wilcox, December 2, 1934. Traded to **Detroit** by **Boston** for cash, December 31, 1934.

• WILLIAMS, TOMMY

— see page 1580

• WILLSON, DON

Don Willson
C – L. 5'8", 157 lbs. b: Chatham, Ont., 1/1/1914.

			REGULAR SEASON								PLAYOFFS				
Season	Club	League	GP	G	A	Pts	AG	AA	APts	PIM	GP	G	A	Pts	PIM
1931-32	Newmarket Redmen	OHA	7	6	0	6	....	....	....	2	6	*11	1	*12	2
1932-33	Newmarket Redmen	OHA	17	*15	5	*20	....	....	....	....	19	7	2	9	10
1933-34	St. Michael's Majors	OHA	8	9	9	18	....	....	....	0	3	1	1	2	0
1934-35	Oshawa Chevies	Tor-Sr.	15	10	6	16	....	....	....	8	....	....	....	....	....
1935-36	Earls Court Rangers	Britain	....	22	*16	38	....	....	....	10	....	....	....	....	....
1936-37	Earls Court Rangers	Britain	....	37	*28	65	....	....	....	16	....	....	....	....	....
1937-38	**Montreal Canadiens**	**NHL**	**18**	**2**	**7**	**9**	**4**	**14**	**18**	**0**	**3**	**0**	**0**	**0**	**0**
	Verdun Maple Leafs	QSHL	14	9	13	22	....	....	....	2	....	....	....	....	....
1938-39	**Montreal Canadiens**	**NHL**	**4**	**0**	**0**	**0**	**0**	**0**	**0**	**0**	....	....	....	....	....
	New Haven Eagles	AHL	42	10	10	20	....	....	....	2	....	....	....	....	....
1939-40	New Haven Eagles	AHL	54	12	32	44	....	....	....	6	3	0	3	3	....
1940-41	New Haven Eagles	AHL	49	11	19	30	....	....	....	6	....	....	....	....	....
1941-42	New Haven Eagles	AHL	53	16	24	40	....	....	....	10	2	0	1	1	0
1942-43	Toronto RCAF	OHA Sr.	9	7	9	16	....	....	....	2	2	1	0	1	2
1943-44			MILITARY SERVICE												
1944-45			MILITARY SERVICE												
1945-46	Toronto Staffords	OHA Sr.	16	18	9	27	....	....	....	4	10	6	10	16	0
1946-47	Toronto Staffords	OHA Sr.	24	2	5	7	....	....	....	20	5	1	2	3	2
1947-48	Toronto Marlboros	OHA Sr.	11	0	2	2	....	....	....	5	....	....	....	....	....
	NHL Totals		**22**	**2**	**7**	**9**	**4**	**14**	**18**	**0**	**3**	**0**	**0**	**0**	**0**

• WILSON, BOB

Bob Wilson
D – L. 5'9", 165 lbs. b: Sudbury, Ont., 2/18/1934.

			REGULAR SEASON								PLAYOFFS				
Season	Club	League	GP	G	A	Pts	AG	AA	APts	PIM	GP	G	A	Pts	PIM
1952-53	Galt Black Hawks	OHA	49	2	10	12	....	....	....	*165	11	1	2	3	24
1953-54	Galt Black Hawks	OHA	55	5	17	22	....	....	....	127	....	....	....	....	....
	Chicago Black Hawks	**NHL**	**1**	**0**	**0**	**0**	**0**	**0**	**0**	**0**	....	....	....	....	....
1954-55	Belleville TPT's	EOSHL	STATISTICS NOT AVAILABLE												
1955-56	Belleville TPT's	EOSHL	34	4	15	19	....	....	....	88	....	....	....	....	....
1956-57	Buffalo Bisons	AHL	1	0	0	0	....	....	....	0	....	....	....	....	....
	Huntington Hornets	IHL	44	3	10	13	....	....	....	72	....	....	....	....	....
	Windsor Bulldogs	OHA Sr.	9	0	3	3	....	....	....	16	12	0	4	4	45
1957-58	Buffalo Bisons	AHL	4	0	0	0	....	....	....	26	....	....	....	....	....
	Windsor Bulldogs	OHA Sr.	31	2	4	6	....	....	....	53	....	....	....	....	....
1958-59	Buffalo Bisons	AHL	6	0	2	2	....	....	....	10	....	....	....	....	....
	Trois-Rivieres Lions	QHL	54	1	7	8	....	....	....	170	8	0	3	3	*21
1959-60	Soo Thunderbirds	EPHL	40	3	14	17	....	....	....	60	....	....	....	....	....
	Calgary Stampeders	WHL	21	0	4	4	....	....	....	41	....	....	....	....	....
	Buffalo Bisons	AHL	4	0	1	1	....	....	....	6	....	....	....	....	....
1960-61	Soo Thunderbirds	EPHL	33	3	9	12	....	....	....	131	....	....	....	....	....
	Buffalo Bisons	AHL	40	0	5	5	....	....	....	53	4	0	1	1	33
1961-62	Soo Thunderbirds	EPHL	55	3	15	18	....	....	....	120	....	....	....	....	....
	Buffalo Bisons	AHL	....	....	....	....	....	....	....	....	2	0	0	0	0
1962-63	Buffalo Bisons	AHL	60	0	6	6	....	....	....	95	9	0	2	2	15
1963-64	Buffalo Bisons	AHL	63	1	9	10	....	....	....	123	....	....	....	....	....
1964-65	St. Louis Braves	CHL	13	1	3	4	....	....	....	27	....	....	....	....	....
	Buffalo Bisons	AHL	46	0	10	10	....	....	....	86	9	0	0	0	0
1965-66	Los Angeles Blades	WHL	68	0	7	7	....	....	....	102	....	....	....	....	....
1966-67	Baltimore Clippers	AHL	34	0	1	1	....	....	....	36	1	0	0	0	0
1967-68	Baltimore Clippers	AHL	39	1	5	6	....	....	....	59	....	....	....	....	....
1968-69			DID NOT PLAY												
1969-70	Belleville Mohawks	OHA Sr.	7	0	2	2	....	....	....	16	....	....	....	....	....
	NHL Totals		**1**	**0**	**0**	**0**	**0**	**0**	**0**	**0**	....	....	....	....	....

Claimed by **Baltimore** (AHL) from **Chicago** in Reverse Draft, June, 1966.

• WILSON, CULLY

Cully (Carol) Wilson
RW – R. 5'8", 180 lbs. b: Winnipeg, Man.. Deceased.

			REGULAR SEASON								PLAYOFFS				
Season	Club	League	GP	G	A	Pts	AG	AA	APts	PIM	GP	G	A	Pts	PIM
1910-11	Winnipeg Falcons	MHL Sr.	4	4	0	4	....	....	....	....	....	....	....	....	....
	Kenora Thistles	MHL Sr.	2	0	0	0	....	....	....	....	....	....	....	....	....
	Winnipeg Monarchs	MHL Sr.	1	2	0	2	....	....	....	....	....	....	....	....	....
1911-12	Winnipeg Falcons	MHL Sr.	STATISTICS NOT AVAILABLE												
1912-13	Toronto Blueshirts	NHA	19	12	0	12	....	....	....	45	....	....	....	....	....
1913-14	Toronto Blueshirts	NHA	20	9	4	13	....	....	....	33	2	0	0	0	2
1914-15	Toronto Blueshirts	NHA	20	22	5	27	....	....	....	*138	....	....	....	....	....
1915-16	Toronto Blueshirts	NHA	3	0	0	0	....	....	....	0	....	....	....	....	....
	Seattle Metropolitans	PCHA	18	12	5	17	....	....	....	57	....	....	....	....	....
1916-17	Seattle Metropolitans	PCHA	15	13	7	20	....	....	....	58	4	1	2	3	6
1917-18	Seattle Metropolitans	PCHA	17	8	6	14	....	....	....	46	2	0	0	0	3
1918-19	Seattle Metropolitans	PCHA	18	11	5	16	....	....	....	*37	7	2	4	6	6
1919-20	**Toronto St. Pats**	**NHL**	**23**	**20**	**6**	**26**	**46**	**41**	**87**	**86**	....	....	....	....	....
1920-21	**Toronto St. Pats**	**NHL**	**8**	**2**	**1**	**3**	**5**	**9**	**14**	**16**	....	....	....	....	....
	Montreal Canadiens	**NHL**	**9**	**6**	**1**	**7**	**15**	**9**	**24**	**30**	....	....	....	....	....
1921-22	**Hamilton Tigers**	**NHL**	**23**	**7**	**9**	**16**	**19**	**57**	**76**	**20**	....	....	....	....	....
1922-23	**Hamilton Tigers**	**NHL**	**23**	**16**	**3**	**19**	**55**	**27**	**82**	**46**	....	....	....	....	....
1923-24	Calgary Tigers	WCHL	30	16	7	23	....	....	....	37	7	*4	0	4	6
1924-25	Calgary Tigers	WCHL	28	14	6	20	....	....	....	20	2	1	0	1	6
1925-26	Calgary Tigers	WHL	30	11	4	15	....	....	....	63	....	....	....	....	....
1926-27	**Chicago Black Hawks**	**NHL**	**39**	**8**	**4**	**12**	**23**	**34**	**57**	**40**	**2**	**1**	**0**	**1**	**6**
1927-28	St. Paul Saints	AHA	38	10	2	12	....	....	....	64	....	....	....	....	....
1928-29	St. Paul Saints	AHA	40	10	5	15	....	....	....	40	8	2	*2	4	14
1929-30	St. Paul Saints	AHA	48	7	6	13	....	....	....	57	....	....	....	....	....
1930-31	San Francisco Tigers	Cal-Pro	....	10	2	12	....	....	....	....	....	....	....	....	....
	Duluth Hornets	AHA	24	10	6	16	....	....	....	24	4	0	0	0	2
1931-32	Kansas City Pla-Mors	AHA	34	1	2	3	....	....	....	28	4	0	0	0	2
	NHL Totals		**125**	**59**	**24**	**83**	**163**	**177**	**340**	**238**	**2**	**1**	**0**	**1**	**6**
	Other Major League Totals		218	128	49	177	....	....	....	534	24	8	6	14	29

PCHA First All-Star Team (1919)

Signed as a free agent by **Seattle** (PCHA), December, 1915. Signed as a free agent by **Toronto St. Pats**, November 27, 1919. Loaned to **Montreal Canadiens** by **Toronto St. Pats**, January 21, 1921. • Suspended for remainder of 1921-22 season by **Toronto St. Pats** for refusing to report to NHL club after being recalled from Montreal Canadiens, February 11, 1921. Traded to **Hamilton** by **Toronto St. Pats** for Eddie Carpenter, November 9, 1921. Traded to **Calgary** (WCHL) by **Hamilton** for cash, November 22, 1923. Traded to **Chicago** by **Calgary** (WHL) for cash, October 25, 1926. Traded to **St. Paul** (AHA) by **Chicago**, September, 1927. Transferred to **Buffalo** (AHA) after **St. Paul** (AHA) franchise relocated, October 5, 1930. Signed as a free agent by **San Francisco** (Cal-Pro), October, 1930. Traded to **Duluth** (AHA) by **San Francisco** (Cal-Pro) for cash, February 7, 1931.

• WILSON, GORD

Gord Wilson
LW – L. 6', 175 lbs. b: Port Arthur, Ont., 8/13/1932.

			REGULAR SEASON								PLAYOFFS				
Season	Club	League	GP	G	A	Pts	AG	AA	APts	PIM	GP	G	A	Pts	PIM
1951-52	Port Arthur Bruins	NOHA	STATISTICS NOT AVAILABLE												
1952-53	Hershey Bears	AHL	7	3	2	5	....	....	....	0	....	....	....	....	....
1953-54	Hershey Bears	AHL	4	1	0	1	....	....	....	0	....	....	....	....	....
1954-55	Hershey Bears	AHL	63	27	25	52	....	....	....	12	....	....	....	....	....
	Boston Bruins	**NHL**	....	....	....	....	....	....	....	....	**2**	**0**	**0**	**0**	**0**
1955-56	Hershey Bears	AHL	55	27	38	65	....	....	....	8	....	....	....	....	....
1956-57	Quebec Aces	QHL	5	1	1	2	....	....	....	2	....	....	....	....	....
	Victoria Cougars	WHL	14	0	1	1	....	....	....	0	....	....	....	....	....
1957-58	Victoria Cougars	WHL	65	26	38	64	....	....	....	4	....	....	....	....	....
1958-59	Victoria Cougars	WHL	40	12	15	27	....	....	....	0	3	0	1	1	2
1959-60	Victoria Cougars	WHL	43	5	7	12	....	....	....	0	....	....	....	....	....
	Quebec Aces	AHL	15	1	0	1	....	....	....	2	....	....	....	....	....
	NHL Totals		**0**	**0**	**0**	**0**	**0**	**0**	**0**	**0**	**2**	**0**	**0**	**0**	**0**

• WILSON, HUB

Hub Wilson
LW – L. 5'10", 180 lbs. b: Ottawa, Ont., 5/13/1909.

			REGULAR SEASON								PLAYOFFS				
Season	Club	League	GP	G	A	Pts	AG	AA	APts	PIM	GP	G	A	Pts	PIM
1930-31	Montreal CPR	City Sr.	STATISTICS NOT AVAILABLE												
	Montreal AAA	City Sr.	11	3	1	4	....	....	....	10	2	2	0	2	2
1931-32	**New York Americans**	**NHL**	**2**	**0**	**0**	**0**	**0**	**0**	**0**	**0**	....	....	....	....	....
	New Haven Eagles	Can-Am	37	6	2	8	....	....	....	20	2	0	0	0	0
1932-33	New Haven–Philadelphia	Can-Am	43	13	12	25	....	....	....	44	5	0	0	0	0
1933-34	Quebec Beavers	Can-Am	40	13	10	23	....	....	....	15	....	....	....	....	....
1934-35	Quebec Beavers	Can-Am	47	13	16	29	....	....	....	23	3	0	0	0	0
1935-36	Springfield Indians	Can-Am	38	17	17	34	....	....	....	30	3	1	1	2	0
1936-37	Springfield Indians	AHL	47	10	11	21	....	....	....	23	5	1	0	1	2
1937-38	Springfield Indians	AHL	42	12	8	20	....	....	....	24	....	....	....	....	....
1938-39	Springfield–Providence	AHL	53	10	16	26	....	....	....	12	5	3	0	3	0
1939-40	Providence Reds	AHL	53	15	14	29	....	....	....	20	8	3	3	6	8
1940-41	Providence Reds	AHL	45	14	10	24	....	....	....	14	4	2	0	2	2
1941-42	Philadelphia Rockets	AHL	1	0	0	0	....	....	....	0	....	....	....	....	....
	Pittsburgh Hornets	AHL	48	7	10	17	....	....	....	2	....	....	....	....	....
	NHL Totals		**2**	**0**	**0**	**0**	**0**	**0**	**0**	**0**	....	....	....	....	....

• WILSON, JERRY

Jerry Wilson
C – L. 6'2", 200 lbs. b: Edmonton, Alta., 4/10/1937.

			REGULAR SEASON								PLAYOFFS				
Season	Club	League	GP	G	A	Pts	AG	AA	APts	PIM	GP	G	A	Pts	PIM
1951-52	Winnipeg Canadians	City Jr.	....	12	7	19	....	....	....	19	....	....	....	....	....
1952-53	Winnipeg Canadians	City Jr.	STATISTICS NOT AVAILABLE												
1953-54	St. Boniface Canadiens	MJHL	31	12	16	28	....	....	....	50	18	8	11	19	23
1954-55	St. Boniface Canadiens	MJHL	31	35	32	67	....	....	....	59	....	....	....	....	....
1955-56	Montreal Jr. Canadiens	QJHL	DID NOT PLAY – INJURED												
1956-57	**Montreal Canadiens**	**NHL**	**3**	**0**	**0**	**0**	**0**	**0**	**0**	**2**	....	....	....	....	....
	Hull-Ottawa Canadiens	Ott-Jr.	24	9	19	28	....	....	....	47	....	....	....	....	....
	Hull-Ottawa Canadiens	EOHL	14	10	8	18	....	....	....	13	....	....	....	....	....
	Hull-Ottawa Canadiens	QHL	12	5	5	10	....	....	....	8	....	....	....	....	....
1957-58			DID NOT PLAY – INJURED												
1958-59			DID NOT PLAY – INJURED												
1959-60	Minneapolis Millers	IHL	2	0	3	3	....	....	....	2	....	....	....	....	....
	NHL Totals		**3**	**0**	**0**	**0**	**0**	**0**	**0**	**2**	....	....	....	....	....

• Missed entire 1954-55, 1957-58 and 1958-59 seasons with knee injuries. Traded to **Toronto** by **Montreal** for cash, August, 1958.

• WILSON, JOHNNY Johnny "Iron Man" Wilson
LW – L. 5'11", 168 lbs. b: Kincardine, Ont., 6/14/1929.

Season	Club	League	GP	G	A	Pts	AG	AA	APts	PIM	GP	G	A	Pts	PIM
			REGULAR SEASON								PLAYOFFS				
1947-48	Windsor Spitfires	OHA	34	23	28	51	....	....	....	15	12	4	6	10	11
	Detroit Hettche	IHL	25	21	13	34	....	....	....	19	....	....	....	....	....
1948-49	Windsor Spitfires	OHA	25	30	20	50	....	....	....	24	4	1	0	1	2
	Detroit Hettche	IHL	4	5	4	9	....	....	....	0	13	*16	7	*23	16
1949-50	Omaha Knights	USHL	70	41	39	80	....	....	....	46	7	2	5	7	4
	Detroit Red Wings	**NHL**	**1**	**0**	**0**	**0**	**0**	**0**	**0**	**0**	**8**	**0**	**1**	**1**	**0**
1950-51	Indianapolis Capitals	AHL	70	34	21	55	....	....	....	48	3	1	0	1	4
	Detroit Red Wings	**NHL**	....	....	....	....	....	....	....	....	**1**	**0**	**0**	**0**	**0**
1951-52	**Detroit Red Wings**	**NHL**	**28**	**4**	**5**	**9**	**6**	**6**	**12**	**18**	**8**	**4**	**1**	**5**	**5**
	Indianapolis Capitals	AHL	42	25	14	39	....	....	....	16	....	....	....	....	....
1952-53	**Detroit Red Wings**	**NHL**	**70**	**23**	**19**	**42**	**36**	**27**	**63**	**22**	**6**	**2**	**5**	**7**	**0**
1953-54	**Detroit Red Wings**	**NHL**	**70**	**17**	**17**	**34**	**26**	**23**	**49**	**22**	**12**	**3**	**0**	**3**	**0**
1954-55	**Detroit Red Wings**	**NHL**	**70**	**12**	**15**	**27**	**17**	**19**	**36**	**14**	**11**	**0**	**1**	**1**	**0**
1955-56	**Chicago Black Hawks**	**NHL**	**70**	**24**	**9**	**33**	**35**	**11**	**46**	**12**	....	....	....	....	....
1956-57	**Chicago Black Hawks**	**NHL**	**70**	**18**	**30**	**48**	**25**	**35**	**60**	**24**	....	....	....	....	....
1957-58	**Detroit Red Wings**	**NHL**	**70**	**12**	**27**	**39**	**16**	**29**	**45**	**14**	**4**	**2**	**1**	**3**	**0**
1958-59	**Detroit Red Wings**	**NHL**	**70**	**11**	**17**	**28**	**14**	**18**	**32**	**18**	....	....	....	....	....
1959-60	**Toronto Maple Leafs**	**NHL**	**70**	**15**	**16**	**31**	**19**	**16**	**35**	**8**	**10**	**1**	**2**	**3**	**2**
1960-61	**Toronto Maple Leafs**	**NHL**	**3**	**0**	**1**	**1**	**0**	**1**	**1**	**0**	....	....	....	....	....
	Rochester Americans	AHL	2	2	2	4	....	....	....	0	....	....	....	....	....
	New York Rangers	**NHL**	**56**	**14**	**12**	**26**	**17**	**12**	**29**	**24**	....	....	....	....	....
1961-62	**New York Rangers**	**NHL**	**40**	**11**	**3**	**14**	**13**	**3**	**16**	**14**	**6**	**2**	**2**	**4**	**4**
	NHL Totals		**688**	**161**	**171**	**332**	**224**	**200**	**424**	**190**	**66**	**14**	**13**	**27**	**11**

USHL Second All-Star Team (1950)

Played in NHL All-Star Game (1954, 1956)

Traded to **Chicago** by **Detroit** with Tony Leswick, Glen Skov and Benny Woit for Dave Creighton, Gord Hollingworth, John McCormack and Jerry Toppazzini, May 28, 1955. Traded to **Detroit** by **Chicago** with Forbes Kennedy, Bill Preston and Hank Bassen for Ted Lindsay and Glenn Hall, July, 1957. Traded to **Toronto** by **Detroit** with Frank Roggeveen for Gary Aldcorn and Barry Cullen, June 9, 1959. Traded to **NY Rangers** by **Toronto** with Pat Hannigan for Eddie Shack, November, 1960.

• WILSON, LARRY Larry Wilson
C – L. 5'11", 160 lbs. b: Kincardine, Ont., 10/23/1930. d: 8/16/1979.

Season	Club	League	GP	G	A	Pts	AG	AA	APts	PIM	GP	G	A	Pts	PIM
1947-48	Windsor Hettche	IHL	25	13	29	42	....	....	....	6	....	....	....	....	....
	Windsor Spitfires	OHA	12	4	13	17	....	....	....	2	12	3	3	6	9
1948-49	Windsor Spitfires	OHA	45	23	27	60	....	....	....	22	4	1	1	2	2
	Detroit Hettche	IHL	9	10	7	17	....	....	....	6	13	4	*17	21	20
1949-50	Omaha Knights	USHL	70	22	57	79	....	....	....	51	7	2	6	8	10
	Detroit Red Wings	**NHL**	**1**	**0**	**0**	**0**	**0**	**0**	**0**	**2**	**4**	**0**	**0**	**0**	**0**
1950-51	Indianapolis Capitals	AHL	53	12	23	35	....	....	....	14	3	0	1	1	0
1951-52	**Detroit Red Wings**	**NHL**	**5**	**0**	**0**	**0**	**0**	**0**	**0**	**4**	....	....	....	....	....
	Indianapolis Capitals	AHL	62	19	40	59	....	....	....	30	....	....	....	....	....
1952-53	**Detroit Red Wings**	**NHL**	**15**	**0**	**4**	**4**	**0**	**6**	**6**	**6**	....	....	....	....	....
	Edmonton Flyers	WHL	49	17	29	46	....	....	....	24	14	6	7	13	4
1953-54	**Chicago Black Hawks**	**NHL**	**66**	**9**	**33**	**42**	**14**	**45**	**59**	**22**	....	....	....	....	....
1954-55	**Chicago Black Hawks**	**NHL**	**63**	**12**	**11**	**23**	**17**	**14**	**31**	**39**	....	....	....	....	....
1955-56	**Chicago Black Hawks**	**NHL**	**2**	**0**	**0**	**0**	**0**	**0**	**0**	**2**	....	....	....	....	....
	Buffalo Bisons	AHL	62	39	39	78	....	....	....	74	5	0	2	2	4
1956-57	Buffalo Bisons	AHL	64	22	45	67	....	....	....	71	....	....	....	....	....
1957-58	Buffalo Bisons	AHL	70	26	53	79	....	....	....	48	....	....	....	....	....
1958-59	Buffalo Bisons	AHL	66	24	39	63	....	....	....	26	11	0	5	5	7
1959-60	Buffalo Bisons	AHL	64	33	45	78	....	....	....	10					
1960-61	Buffalo Bisons	AHL	72	30	54	84	....	....	....	62	4	0	2	2	0
1961-62	Buffalo Bisons	AHL	68	9	25	34	....	....	....	28	10	3	0	3	4
1962-63	Buffalo Bisons	AHL	72	10	20	45	....	....	....	30	13	1	3	4	0
1963-64	Buffalo Bisons	AHL	71	17	26	43	....	....	....	38	....	....	....	....	....
1964-65	Buffalo Bisons	AHL	31	0	7	7	....	....	....	12	....	....	....	....	....
1965-66	Buffalo Bisons	AHL	38	13	12	25	....	....	....	8	....	....	....	....	....
1966-67	Buffalo Bisons	AHL	65	28	37	65	....	....	....	60	....	....	....	....	....
1967-68	Buffalo Bisons	AHL	41	10	18	28	....	....	....	24	....	....	....	....	....
1968-69	Dayton Gems	IHL	50	19	42	61	....	....	....	36	....	....	....	....	....
1969-70	Dayton Gems	IHL	68	20	43	63	....	....	....	54	13	2	4	6	0
	NHL Totals		**152**	**21**	**48**	**69**	**31**	**65**	**96**	**75**	**4**	**0**	**0**	**0**	**0**

AHL Second All-Star Team (1956, 1960)

Traded to **Chicago** by **Detroit** for cash, August, 1953. Traded to **Buffalo** (AHI) by **Chicago** for cash, August, 1957.

• WILSON, WALLY Wally Wilson
C – R. 5'11", 165 lbs. b: Berwick, N.S., 5/25/1921.

Season	Club	League	GP	G	A	Pts	AG	AA	APts	PIM	GP	G	A	Pts	PIM
1939-40	Oshawa Generals	OHA	11	10	9	19	....	....	....	0	7	2	3	5	2
1940-41	Oshawa Generals	OHA	16	15	7	22	....	....	....	27	17	14	*22	*36	13
1941-42	Hershey Bears	AHL	48	16	20	36	....	....	....	8	10	4	1	5	2
1942-43	Toronto RCAF	OHA Sr.	10	13	12	25	....	....	....	10	13	5	*20	*25	20
1943-44	Toronto RCAF	OHA Sr.	11	6	5	11	....	....	....	2	....	....	....	....	....
1944-45	Quebec Aces	QSHL	3	5	0	5	....	....	....	4	3	1	5	6	0
1945-46	Pittsburgh Hornets	AHL	57	34	41	75	....	....	....	32	5	4	6	10	2
1946-47	Pittsburgh Hornets	AHL	51	21	30	51	....	....	....	38	12	5	5	10	8
1947-48	**Boston Bruins**	**NHL**	**53**	**11**	**8**	**19**	**16**	**12**	**28**	**18**	**1**	**0**	**0**	**0**	**0**
	NHL Totals		**53**	**11**	**8**	**19**	**16**	**12**	**28**	**18**	**1**	**0**	**0**	**0**	**0**

Claimed by **Toronto** from **Hershey** (AHL) in Inter-League Draft, June 14, 1945. Traded to **Boston** by **Toronto** for cash, August 17, 1947.

• WISEMAN, EDDIE Eddie Wiseman
RW – R. 5'7", 160 lbs. b: Newcastle, N.B., 12/28/1912. d: 5/6/1977.

Season	Club	League	GP	G	A	Pts	AG	AA	APts	PIM	GP	G	A	Pts	PIM
			REGULAR SEASON								PLAYOFFS				
1928-29	Regina Argos	City Jr.	5	1	1	2	....	....	....	2	....	....	....	....	....
1929-30	Regina Pats	City Jr.	3	1	0	1	....	....	....	4	....	....	....	....	....
1930-31	Chicago Shamrocks	AHA	44	8	11	19	....	....	....	16	....	....	....	....	....
1931-32	Chicago Shamrocks	AHA	44	17	17	*34	....	....	....	26	4	2	2	4	0
1932-33	**Detroit Red Wings**	**NHL**	**43**	**8**	**8**	**16**	**19**	**21**	**40**	**16**	**2**	**0**	**0**	**0**	**0**
1933-34	**Detroit Red Wings**	**NHL**	**48**	**5**	**9**	**14**	**11**	**24**	**35**	**13**	**7**	**0**	**1**	**1**	**4**
	Detroit Olympics	IAHL	1	1	0	1	....	....	....	0	....	....	....	....	....
1934-35	**Detroit Red Wings**	**NHL**	**39**	**11**	**13**	**24**	**23**	**29**	**52**	**14**	....	....	....	....	....
	Detroit Olympics	IAHL	12	3	3	6	....	....	....	8	....	....	....	....	....
1935-36	**Detroit Red Wings**	**NHL**	**1**	**0**	**0**	**0**	**0**	**0**	**0**	**0**	....	....	....	....	....
	Detroit Olympics	IAHL	3	2	1	3	....	....	....	10	....	....	....	....	....
	New York Americans	**NHL**	**44**	**12**	**16**	**28**	**30**	**39**	**69**	**15**	**4**	**2**	**1**	**3**	**0**
1936-37	**New York Americans**	**NHL**	**44**	**14**	**19**	**33**	**30**	**45**	**75**	**12**	....	....	....	....	....
1937-38	**New York Americans**	**NHL**	**48**	**18**	**14**	**32**	**38**	**29**	**67**	**32**	**6**	**0**	**4**	**4**	**10**
1938-39	**New York Americans**	**NHL**	**47**	**12**	**21**	**33**	**25**	**39**	**64**	**8**	**2**	**0**	**0**	**0**	**0**
1939-40	**New York Americans**	**NHL**	**31**	**5**	**13**	**18**	**11**	**26**	**37**	**8**	....	....	....	....	....
	Boston Bruins	**NHL**	**18**	**2**	**6**	**8**	**4**	**12**	**16**	**0**	**6**	**2**	**1**	**3**	**2**
1940-41	**Boston Bruins**	**NHL**	**48**	**16**	**24**	**40**	**32**	**44**	**76**	**10**	**11**	**6**	**2**	**8**	**0**
1941-42	**Boston Bruins**	**NHL**	**45**	**12**	**22**	**34**	**21**	**33**	**54**	**8**	**5**	**0**	**1**	**1**	**0**
1942-43	Saskatoon RCAF	SSHL	15	8	10	18	....	....	....	11	1	1	1	2	0
1943-44			MILITARY SERVICE												
1944-45	Montreal Royals	QSHL	1	1	0	1	....	....	....	0	1	0	0	0	0
1945-46	Moose Jaw Canucks	SJHL	DID NOT PLAY – COACHING												
	NHL Totals		**456**	**115**	**165**	**280**	**244**	**341**	**585**	**136**	**43**	**10**	**10**	**20**	**16**

Signed as a free agent by **Chicago** (AHA), October 29, 1930. NHL rights transferred to **Detroit** from **Chicago Shamrocks** (AHA) after AHA club owners purchased Detroit (NHL and IAHL) franchises, September 2, 1932. Traded to **NY Americans** by **Detroit** for Fred Hergert and $7500, November 22, 1935. Traded to **Boston** by **NY Americans** with $500 for Eddie Shore, January 25, 1940.

• WITIUK, STEVE Steve Witiuk
RW – R. 5'7", 165 lbs. b: Winnipeg, Man., 1/8/1929.

Season	Club	League	GP	G	A	Pts	AG	AA	APts	PIM	GP	G	A	Pts	PIM
1946-47	Winnipeg Rangers	MJHL	16	5	6	11	....	....	....	4	2	0	1	1	2
1947-48	Winnipeg Black Hawks	MJHL	22	12	5	17	....	....	....	10	....	....	....	....	....
1948-49	Winnipeg Black Hawks	MJHL	28	16	20	36	....	....	....	49	....	....	....	....	....
1949-50	Regina Caps	WCSHL	8	0	1	1	....	....	....	0	....	....	....	....	....
	Kamloops Elks	OSHL	33	20	7	27	....	....	....	45	7	6	6	12	6
1950-51	Edmonton Flyers	WCSHL	48	22	23	45	....	....	....	71	8	2	2	4	10
1951-52	**Chicago Black Hawks**	**NHL**	**33**	**3**	**8**	**11**	**4**	**10**	**14**	**14**	....	....	....	....	....
	St. Louis Flyers	AHL	14	5	2	7	....	....	....	11	....	....	....	....	....
1952-53	Calgary Stampeders	WHL	60	21	20	41	....	....	....	66	1	0	0	0	0
1953-54	Calgary Stampeders	WHL	69	19	36	55	....	....	....	52	18	3	6	9	20
1954-55	Calgary Stampeders	WHL	60	26	37	63	....	....	....	61	9	5	2	7	14
1955-56	Calgary Stampeders	WHL	66	30	34	64	....	....	....	76	8	5	6	11	12
1956-57	Calgary Stampeders	WHL	47	17	18	35	....	....	....	55	....	....	....	....	....
1957-58	Calgary–Winnipeg	WHL	65	27	46	73	....	....	....	43	7	0	2	2	2
1958-59	Winnipeg Warriors	WHL	62	12	33	45	....	....	....	43	6	1	4	5	2
1959-60	Winnipeg Warriors	WHL	62	20	27	47	....	....	....	40	....	....	....	....	....
1960-61	Spokane Spokes	WHL	67	28	24	52	....	....	....	79	4	0	1	1	4
1961-62	Spokane Comets	WHL	64	26	40	66	....	....	....	49	16	4	9	13	34
1962-63	Spokane Comets	WHL	66	21	33	54	....	....	....	96	....	....	....	....	....
1963-64	Denver Invaders	WHL	70	25	28	53	....	....	....	62	4	0	0	0	10
1964-65	Victoria Maple Leafs	WHL	56	11	21	32	....	....	....	37	11	2	2	4	16
1965-66	Victoria Maple Leafs	WHL	72	6	16	22	....	....	....	47	3	0	0	0	0
1966-67	Victoria Maple Leafs	WHL	60	5	10	15	....	....	....	34	....	....	....	....	....
1967-68	Spokane Jets	WHL	41	20	34	54	....	....	....	37	....	....	....		
	NHL Totals		**33**	**3**	**8**	**11**	**4**	**10**	**14**	**14**			....	....	....

Signed as a free agent by **Chicago**, October 1, 1951. Traded to **Toronto** (Winnipeg-WHL) by **Chicago** (Calgary-WHL) for George Ford and Murray Wilkie, January, 1958.

• WOIT, BENNY Benny (Benedict) Woit
RW/D – R. 5'11", 195 lbs. b: Fort William, Ont., 1///1928.

Season	Club	League	GP	G	A	Pts	AG	AA	APts	PIM	GP	G	A	Pts	PIM
1944-45	Port Arthur Flyers	TBJHL	11	3	6	9	....	....	....	6	3	0	0	0	4
1945-46	Port Arthur Flyers	TBJHL	4	1	1	2	....	....	....	8	5	0	2	2	2
1946-47	St. Michael's Majors	OHA	27	5	16	21	....	....	....	42	9	0	1	1	16
1947-48	Port Arthur Bruins	TBJHL	8	3	11	14	....	....	....	21	22	9	7	16	*67
1948-49	Indianapolis Capitals	AHL	68	3	12	15	....	....	....	30	2	0	1	1	0
1949-50	Indianapolis Capitals	AHL	70	7	17	24	....	....	....	29	8	2	0	2	4
1950-51	Indianapolis Capitals	AHL	69	8	22	30	....	....	....	40	3	0	0	0	0
	Detroit Red Wings	**NHL**	**2**	**0**	**0**	**0**	**0**	**0**	**0**	**2**	**4**	**0**	**0**	**0**	**2**
1951-52	**Detroit Red Wings**	**NHL**	**58**	**3**	**8**	**11**	**4**	**10**	**14**	**20**	**8**	**1**	**1**	**2**	**2**
1952-53	**Detroit Red Wings**	**NHL**	**70**	**1**	**5**	**6**	**2**	**7**	**9**	**40**	**6**	**1**	**3**	**4**	**0**
1953-54	**Detroit Red Wings**	**NHL**	**70**	**0**	**2**	**2**	**0**	**3**	**3**	**38**	**12**	**0**	**1**	**1**	**8**
1954-55	**Detroit Red Wings**	**NHL**	**62**	**2**	**3**	**5**	**3**	**4**	**7**	**22**	**11**	**0**	**1**	**1**	**6**
1955-56	**Chicago Black Hawks**	**NHL**	**63**	**1**	**8**	**9**	**1**	**10**	**11**	**46**	....	....	....	....	....
1956-57	**Chicago Black Hawks**	**NHL**	**9**	**0**	**0**	**0**	**0**	**0**	**0**	**2**	....	....	....	....	....
	Rochester Americans	AHL	47	4	12	16	....	....		54	8	1	1	2	6
1957-58	Rochester Americans	AHL	52	2	7	9	....	....	....	40	....	....	....	....	....
1958-59	Spokane Comets	WHL	61	5	9	14	....	....	....	54	4	0	3	3	4
1959-60	Providence Reds	AHL	30	1	2	3	....	....	....	16	5	1	1	2	0
1960-61	Providence Reds	AHL	58	2	10	12	....	....	....	26	....	....	....	....	....
1961-62	Kingston Frontenacs	EPHL	5	0	1	1	....	....	....	6	1	0	0	0	6
	Clinton Comets	EHL	51	8	23	31	....	....	....	51	6	1	2	3	4
1962-63	Clinton Comets	EHL	63	8	15	23	....	....	....	57	13	3	6	9	12
1963-64	Clinton Comets	EHL	69	12	35	47	....	....	....	78	15	5	7	12	31
1964-65	Clinton Comets	EHL	71	4	36	40	....	....		68	11	0	4	4	4
1965-66	New Jersey Devils	EHL	38	3	19	22	....	....	....	60	....	....	....	....	....
1966-67	Westfort Hurricanes	TBJHL	DID NOT PLAY – COACHING												
	NHL Totals		**334**	**7**	**26**	**33**	**10**	**34**	**44**	**170**	**41**	**2**	**6**	**8**	**18**

EHL First All-Star Team (1962, 1963) • FHL Second All-Star Team (1964) • EHL North First All-Star Team (1965)

Played in NHL All-Star Game (1954)

Traded to **Chicago** by **Detroit** with Tony Leswick, Glen Skov and John Wilson for Dave Creighton, Gord Hollingworth, John McCormack and Jerry Toppazzini, May 28, 1955. Claimed on waivers by **Montreal** from **Chicago**, November, 1956.

• WOJCIECHOWSKI, STEVEN
Steven (AKA Wochy) Wojciechowski
RW – R. 5'8", 158 lbs. b: Fort William, Ont., 12/25/1922.

			REGULAR SEASON								PLAYOFFS				
Season	Club	League	GP	G	A	Pts	AG	AA	APts	PIM	GP	G	A	Pts	PIM
1938-39	Fort William Maroons	TBJHL	18	14	*11	*25	....	....	....	20	5	4	0	4	7
1939-40	Port Arthur Bruins	TBJHL	16	16	9	*25	....	....	....	2	....	....	....	....	....
	Port Arthur Bearcats	TBSHL	1	0	0	0	....	....	....	0	....	....	....	....	....
1940-41	Port Arthur Bruins	TBJHL	16	16	*21	37	....	....	....	29	6	*8	4	12	4
1941-42	Port Arthur Bearcats	TBSHL	1	1	1	2	....	....	....	0	17	10	7	17	17
	Port Arthur Bruins	TBJHL	18	22	*41	63	....	....	....	55	3	4	5	9	13
1942-43	St. Catharines Saints	OHA Sr.	17	21	15	36	....	....	....	7	3	1	1	2	0
1943-44	Winnipeg Army	City Sr.	10	8	8	16	....	....	....	2	....	....	....	....	....
1944-45	**Detroit Red Wings**	**NHL**	**49**	**19**	**20**	**39**	**26**	**32**	**58**	**17**	**6**	**0**	**1**	**1**	**0**
1945-46	Indianapolis Capitals	AHL	30	14	20	34	....	....	....	14	....	....	....	....	....
	Omaha Knights	USHL	17	4	10	14	....	....	....	4	7	1	2	3	2
1946-47	**Detroit Red Wings**	**NHL**	**5**	**0**	**0**	**0**	**0**	**0**	**0**	**0**	....	....	....	....	....
	Indianapolis Capitals	AHL	56	21	24	45	....	....	....	4	....	....	....	....	....
1947-48	Philadelphia Rockets	AHL	68	37	29	66	....	....	....	27	....	....	....	....	....
1948-49	Philadelphia Rockets	AHL	68	29	28	57	....	....	....	37	....	....	....	....	....
1949-50	Cleveland Barons	AHL	47	21	23	44	....	....	....	12	6	3	3	6	4
1950-51	Cleveland Barons	AHL	58	26	30	56	....	....	....	24	....	....	....	....	....
1951-52	Cleveland Barons	AHL	68	*37	41	78	....	....	....	42	5	2	0	2	2
1952-53	Cleveland Barons	AHL	64	37	31	68	....	....	....	16	10	1	4	5	2
1953-54	Buffalo Bisons	AHL	70	26	32	58	....	....	....	18	3	0	1	1	2
1954-55	Buffalo Bisons	AHL	17	5	4	9	....	....	....	2	....	....	....	....	....
	Soo Greyhounds	NOHA	23	10	7	17	....	....	....	13	....	....	....	....	....
	NHL Totals		**54**	**19**	**20**	**39**	**26**	**32**	**58**	**17**	**6**	**0**	**1**	**1**	**0**

AHL First All-Star Team (1952)

Traded to **Cleveland** (AHL) by **Detroit** for cash, June 15, 1947. Traded to **Philadelphia** (AHL) by **Cleveland** (AHL) for cash, August, 1947.

• WOOD, ROBERT
Robert Wood
D – L. 6'1", 185 lbs. b: Lethbridge, Alta., 7/9/1930.

Season	Club	League	GP	G	A	Pts	AG	AA	APts	PIM	GP	G	A	Pts	PIM
1946-47	Lethbridge Native Sons	AJHL	1	0	1	1	....	....	....	8	....	....	....	....	....
1947-48	Lethbridge Native Sons	AJHL	22	5	9	14	....	....	....	26	6	0	0	0	2
1948-49	Lethbridge Native Sons	WCJHL	25	1	7	8	....	....	....	48	6	0	3	3	14
1949-50	Lethbridge Native Sons	WCJHL	37	3	24	27	....	....	....	56	....	....	....	....	....
1950-51	**New York Rangers**	**NHL**	**1**	**0**	**0**	**0**	**0**	**0**	**0**	**0**	....	....	....	....	....
	New York Rovers	EHL	53	3	4	7	....	....	....	77	5	0	0	0	14
	NHL Totals		**1**	**0**	**0**	**0**	**0**	**0**	**0**	**0**	....	....	....	....	....

• WOYTOWICH, BOB *— see page 1587*

• WYCHERLEY, RALPH
Ralph "Bus" Wycherley
LW – L. 6', 185 lbs. b: Saskatoon, Sask., 2/26/1920.

Season	Club	League	GP	G	A	Pts	AG	AA	APts	PIM	GP	G	A	Pts	PIM
1938-39	Brandon Elks	City Jr.	15	*25	11	*36	....	....	....	15	13	*14	5	19	10
1939-40	Brandon Elks	City Jr.	24	24	12	36	....	....	....	14	3	0	1	1	2
1940-41	**New York Americans**	**NHL**	**26**	**4**	**5**	**9**	**8**	**9**	**17**	**4**	....	....	....	....	....
	Springfield Indians	AHL	13	5	4	9	....	....	....	7	....	....	....	....	....
1941-42	**Brooklyn Americans**	**NHL**	**2**	**0**	**2**	**2**	**0**	**3**	**3**	**2**	....	....	....	....	....
	Springfield–Philadelphia	AHL	38	14	17	31	....	....	....	12	3	0	1	1	0
1942-43	Toronto RCAF	OHA Sr.	7	4	2	6	....	....	....	2	10	12	8	*20	12
1943-44	Toronto RCAF	OHA Sr.	9	6	1	7	....	....	....	2	....	....	....	....	....
	Toronto Fuels	City Sr.	8	13	7	20	....	....	....	7	6	8	8	16	4
1944-45			MILITARY SERVICE												
1945-46			MILITARY SERVICE												
1946-47	Hershey Bears	AHL	4	0	0	0	....	....	....	0	....	....	....	....	....
	Tulsa Oilers	USHL	51	32	22	54	....	....	....	6	5	2	1	3	0
1947-48	Minneapolis Millers	USHL	61	40	38	78	....	....	....	4	10	3	7	10	0
1948-49	Cleveland Barons	AHL	39	16	18	34	....	....	....	8	4	0	0	0	0
1949-50	Kansas City Mohawks	USHL	63	30	32	62	....	....	....	5	3	0	0	0	0
1950-51	Toronto Marlboros	OHA Sr.	30	14	18	32	....	....	....	8	3	1	0	1	2
	NHL Totals		**28**	**4**	**7**	**11**	**8**	**12**	**20**	**6**	....	....	....	....	....

USHL First All-Star Team (1947, 1948)

Signed as a free agent by **NY Americans**, October 11, 1940.

• WYLIE, WILLIAM
William "Wiggie" Wylie
C – L. 5'7", 145 lbs. b: Galt, Ont., 7/15/1928. d: 11/24/1983.

Season	Club	League	GP	G	A	Pts	AG	AA	APts	PIM	GP	G	A	Pts	PIM
1946-47	Galt Red Wings	OHA	24	11	23	34	....	....	....	16	8	3	6	9	0
1947-48	Galt Rockets	OHA	28	26	27	53	....	....	....	10	8	6	10	16	6
1948-49	Quebec Aces	QSHL	55	18	33	51	....	....	....	22	1	0	0	0	2
1949-50	Quebec Aces	QSHL	55	15	24	39	....	....	....	14	12	3	*12	15	6
1950-51	**New York Rangers**	**NHL**	**1**	**0**	**0**	**0**	**0**	**0**	**0**	**0**	....	....	....	....	....
	New York Rovers	EHL	48	23	35	58	....	....	....	10	6	1	5	6	0
	St. Paul Saints	USHL	2	1	1	2	....	....	....	0	....	....	....	....	....
1951-52	Cincinnati Mohawks	AHL	68	21	32	53	....	....	....	10	7	2	3	5	0
1952-53	Vancouver Canucks	WHL	48	9	19	28	....	....	....	4	....	....	....	....	....
1953-54	Vancouver Canucks	WHL	54	13	26	39	....	....	....	6	13	1	6	7	0
1954-55	Vancouver Canucks	WHL	56	9	35	44	....	....	....	4	5	1	2	3	2
1955-56	Vancouver Canucks	WHL	49	13	31	44	....	....	....	14	....	....	....	....	....
1956-57	Vancouver Canucks	WHL	68	18	52	70	....	....	....	16	....	....	....	....	....
1957-58	Kitchener Dutchmen	NOHA	50	18	45	63	....	....	....	8	14	6	*14	*20	0
1958-59	Kitchener Dutchmen	NOHA	54	20	55	75	....	....	....	4	11	5	*9	14	0
1959-60	Kitchener Dutchmen	OHA Sr.	20	5	13	18	....	....	....	0	8	0	6	6	0
1960-61	Galt Terriers	OHA Sr.	PLAYED EXHIBITION SEASON ONLY												
1961-62	Galt Terriers	OHA Sr.	19	13	18	31	....	....	....	2	....	....	....	....	....
1962-63	Galt Terriers	OHA Sr.	9	3	4	7	....	....	....	0	....	....	....	....	....
	NHL Totals		**1**	**0**	**0**	**0**	**0**	**0**	**0**	**0**	....	....	....	....	....

EHL Second All-Star Team (1951)

• YACKEL, KEN
Ken Yackel **USHOF**
RW – R. 5'11", 195 lbs. b: St. Paul, MN, 3/5/1932. Deceased.

Season	Club	League	GP	G	A	Pts	AG	AA	APts	PIM	GP	G	A	Pts	PIM
1951-52	University of Minnesota	WIAA	DID NOT PLAY – FRESHMAN												
	United States	Olympics	8	6	0	6	....	....	....	2	....	....	....	....	....
1952-53	University of Minnesota	WCHA	27	10	16	26	....	....	....	40	....	....	....	....	....
1953-54	University of Minnesota	WCHA	27	11	17	28	....	....	....	62	....	....	....	....	....
1954-55	University of Minnesota	WCHA	28	18	18	36	....	....	....	51	....	....	....	....	....
1955-56	University of Minnesota	WCHA	30	31	27	58	....	....	....	102	....	....	....	....	....
	Cleveland Barons	AHL	3	0	1	1	....	....	....	6	....	....	....	....	....
1956-57	Edina High School	H.S.	DID NOT PLAY – COACHING												
1957-58	Saskatoon–St. Paul	WHL	21	12	8	20	....	....	....	30	....	....	....	....	....
1958-59	**Boston Bruins**	**NHL**	**6**	**0**	**0**	**0**	**0**	**0**	**0**	**2**	**2**	**0**	**0**	**0**	**2**
	Providence Reds	AHL	66	16	33	49	....	....	....	83	....	....	....	....	....
1959-60	Providence Reds	AHL	57	14	21	35	....	....	....	68	5	2	1	3	16
1960-61	Minneapolis Millers	IHL	72	40	74	*114	....	....	....	102	8	5	2	7	8
1961-62	Minneapolis Millers	IHL	66	50	48	98	....	....	....	103	5	1	3	4	13
1962-63	Minneapolis Millers	IHL	70	40	60	100	....	....	....	70	12	7	11	18	12
1963-64	Muskegon Zephyrs	IHL	1	0	0	0	....	....	....	0	....	....	....	....	....
	NHL Totals		**6**	**0**	**0**	**0**	**0**	**0**	**0**	**2**	**2**	**0**	**0**	**0**	**2**

WCHA First All-Star Team (1954, 1955, 1956) • NCAA West First All-American Team (1954) • NCAA Championship All-Tournament Team (1954) • IHL First All-Star Team (1961, 1962) • Won Leo P. Lamoureux Memorial Trophy (Top Scorer - IHL) (1961) • IHL Second All-Star Team (1963)

Traded to **Boston** by **NY Rangers** (Saskatoon-WHL) for cash, September 30, 1958.

• YOUNG, DOUG
Doug "The Gleichen Cowboy" Young
D – R. 5'10", 190 lbs. b: Medicine Hat, Alta., 10/1/1908. d: 5/15/1990.

Season	Club	League	GP	G	A	Pts	AG	AA	APts	PIM	GP	G	A	Pts	PIM
1927-28	Kitchener Millionaires	Can-Pro	8	1	1	2	....	....	....	10	5	0	1	1	12
1928-29	Toronto Millionaires	Can-Pro	41	7	3	10	....	....	....	75	2	0	0	0	8
1929-30	Cleveland Indians	IAHL	41	13	5	18	....	....	....	68	6	2	0	2	2
1930-31	Cleveland Indians	IAHL	47	16	6	22	....	....	....	46	6	3	1	4	8
1931-32	**Detroit Falcons**	**NHL**	**47**	**10**	**2**	**12**	**21**	**6**	**27**	**45**	**2**	**0**	**0**	**0**	**2**
1932-33	**Detroit Red Wings**	**NHL**	**48**	**5**	**6**	**11**	**12**	**16**	**28**	**59**	**4**	**1**	**1**	**2**	**0**
1933-34	**Detroit Red Wings**	**NHL**	**47**	**4**	**0**	**4**	**9**	**0**	**9**	**36**	**9**	**0**	**0**	**0**	**10**
1934-35	**Detroit Red Wings**	**NHL**	**48**	**4**	**6**	**10**	**8**	**13**	**21**	**37**	....	....	....	....	....
	Detroit Olympics	IAHL	1	0	0	0	....	....	....	0	....	....	....	....	....
1935-36	**Detroit Red Wings**	**NHL**	**47**	**5**	**12**	**17**	**12**	**29**	**41**	**54**	**7**	**0**	**2**	**2**	**0**
1936-37	**Detroit Red Wings**	**NHL**	**11**	**0**	**0**	**0**	**0**	**0**	**0**	**6**	....	....	....	....	....
1937-38	**Detroit Red Wings**	**NHL**	**48**	**3**	**5**	**8**	**6**	**10**	**16**	**24**	....	....	....	....	....
1938-39	**Detroit Red Wings**	**NHL**	**42**	**1**	**5**	**6**	**2**	**9**	**11**	**16**	**6**	**0**	**2**	**2**	**4**
1939-40	**Montreal Canadiens**	**NHL**	**47**	**3**	**9**	**12**	**6**	**18**	**24**	**22**	....	....	....	....	....
1940-41	**Montreal Canadiens**	**NHL**	**3**	**0**	**0**	**0**	**0**	**0**	**0**	**4**	....	....	....	....	....
	Providence Reds	AHL	42	9	13	22	....	....	....	22	4	0	1	1	7
	NHL Totals		**388**	**35**	**45**	**80**	**76**	**101**	**177**	**303**	**28**	**1**	**5**	**6**	**16**

AHL First All-Star Team (1941)

Played in NHL All-Star Game (1939)

Signed as a free agent by **Kitchener** (Can-Pro), February 5, 1928. Claimed by **Philadelphia** (Can-Am) from **Cleveland** (IAHL) in Inter-League Draft, May 9, 1931. Claimed by **NY Americans** from **Philadelphia** in Dispersal Draft, September 17, 1931. Traded to **Detroit** by **NY Americans** for Ron Martin, October 18, 1931. Signed as a free agent by **Montreal**, October 30, 1939.

• YOUNG, HOWIE *— see page 1592*

• ZEIDEL, LARRY *— see page 1596*

• ZENIUK, ED
Ed Zeniuk
D – L. 5'11", 180 lbs. b: Landis, Sask., 3/8/1933.

Season	Club	League	GP	G	A	Pts	AG	AA	APts	PIM	GP	G	A	Pts	PIM
1951-52	Edmonton Oil Kings	WCJHL	43	5	16	21	....	....	....	110	9	1	4	5	*32
1952-53	Edmonton Oil Kings	WCJHL	30	3	8	11	....	....	....	104	11	0	1	1	22
1953-54	Edmonton–Seattle	WHL	58	4	11	15	....	....	....	69	4	0	0	0	2
1954-55	**Detroit Red Wings**	**NHL**	**2**	**0**	**0**	**0**	**0**	**0**	**0**	**0**	....	....	....	....	....
	Edmonton Flyers	WHL	57	2	7	9	....	....	....	88	9	0	0	0	6
1955-56	New Westminster Royals	WHL	14	1	3	4	....	....	....	31	....	....	....	....	....
	Quebec Aces	QHL	26	0	4	4	....	....	....	54	6	0	0	0	10
	NHL Totals		**2**	**0**	**0**	**0**	**0**	**0**	**0**	**0**	....	....	....	....	....

• ZOBOROSKY, MARTY
Marty "Buster" Zoborosky
D – R. 5'10", 180 lbs. b: Moose Jaw, Sask..

Season	Club	League	GP	G	A	Pts	AG	AA	APts	PIM	GP	G	A	Pts	PIM
1934-35	Moose Jaw Canucks	City Jr.	6	4	0	4	....	....	....	9	1	0	0	0	2
1935-36	Moose Jaw Canucks	City Jr.	3	0	0	0	....	....	....	8	....	....	....	....	....
	Moose Jaw Hardware	City Jr.	6	1	0	1	....	....	....	*12	4	0	1	1	8
1936-37	Prince Albert Mintos	City Sr.	20	0	1	1	....	....	....	28	2	0	0	0	4
1937-1941			STATISTICS NOT AVAILABLE												
1941-42	Kimberley Dynamiters	Kootenay	27	1	1	2	....	....	....	24	2	0	0	0	2
1942-43	Vancouver RCAF	PCHL	11	2	1	3	....	....	....	*32	9	1	2	3	*40
1943-44	Vancouver St. Regis	City Sr.	7	1	0	1	....	....	....	6	....	....	....	....	....
1944-45	**Chicago Black Hawks**	**NHL**	**1**	**0**	**0**	**0**	**0**	**0**	**0**	**2**	....	....	....	....	....
	Providence Reds	AHL	1	0	0	0	....	....	....	0	....	....	....	....	....
	NHL Totals		**1**	**0**	**0**	**0**	**0**	**0**	**0**	**2**	....	....	....	....	....

• Played under the name Marty Edwards from 1937 to 1941.

• ZUNICH, RUDY
Rudy (Rudolph) Zunich
D – L. 5'9", 170 lbs. b: Calumet, MI, 11/24/1910.

Season	Club	League	GP	G	A	Pts	AG	AA	APts	PIM	GP	G	A	Pts	PIM
1934-35	Detroit Holzbaugh	MOHL	27	18	8	26	....	....	....	*49	6	1	0	1	10
1935-36	Detroit Holzbaugh	MOHL	19	4	6	10	....	....	....	16	4	0	1	1	0
1936-37	Detroit Holzbaugh	MOHL	24	13	11	24	....	....	....	30	7	1	2	3	6
1937-38	Detroit Holzbaugh	MOHL	27	8	8	16	....	....	....	43	6	4	1	5	0
1938-39	Detroit Holzbaugh	MOHL	20	4	4	8	....	....	....	6	2	1	1	2	0
1939-40	Detroit Holzbaugh	MOHL	33	14	16	30	....	....	....	32	12	4	4	8	12
1940-41	Detroit Holzbaugh	MOHL	25	9	13	22	....	....	....	29	7	4	1	5	2
1941-42	Detroit Parisclean	MOHL	24	11	26	37	....	....	....	16	7	3	3	6	0
1942-43			MILITARY SERVICE												
1943-44	**Detroit Red Wings**	**NHL**	**2**	**0**	**0**	**0**	**0**	**0**	**0**	**2**	....	....	....	....	....
	NHL Totals		**2**	**0**	**0**	**0**	**0**	**0**	**0**	**2**	....	....	....	....	....

Signed as a free agent by **Detroit** to three-game tryout contract, October 31, 1943.

CHAPTER 72

Using the Modern Player Register

James Duplacey

THE MODERN PLAYER REGISTER begins on page 824. It contains the complete statistical history of every player whose NHL career began in 1967–68 or later plus the complete statistical history of every player who played both in the NHL before and after the start of the 1967–68 season. The 1967–68 season marks the beginning of the modern era because it is in this era that additional statistics such as power play goals and shots on goal were tabulated.

Here are notes on the various statistical categories used in the Modern Player Register:

Biographical – This field contains the player's name, given names (if that name is different than the name by which he is commonly known. For example, Butch Goring's given names are Robert Thomas and Tim Horton's given names were Miles Gilbert), nicknames, position (**C** – center, **RW** – right wing, **LW** – left wing, **F** – forward, **D** – defense), shooting side (**R** – right, **L**– left), height in feet and inches, weight in pounds, date of birth (month/day/year), place of birth (city/town and province/state for North America, city/town and country for all others) and date of death. If only the birth year is known, it is included. If the death date is not known, the date is represented by "Deceased." If any other biographical information is not known, the appropriate field is left blank.

If a player was selected in the NHL's Amateur Draft (1964 to 1978) or Entry Draft (1979 to 1998), that information is also found here. For those players who re-entered the Draft, the second team that selected the player is represented here. Details of his first selection can be found in his notes section. Draft information for those players selected in the WHA Amateur and Professional Drafts and who played in both the NHL and WHA can be found in his notes section. If the player is a member of the Hockey Hall of Fame (**HHOF**) and/or the United States Hockey Hall of Fame (**USHOF**), it is noted here.

Season – From 1917–18 to date, the hockey season started in the fall and ended the following spring and is represented as, for example, 1997–98. For players who retired or did not play for three or more seasons but later returned to the game, those years are represented as two four-digit dates, for example, as 1994–1998.

Club – This field gives information as to which team or teams the player performed with during the season. If statistics for a particular team or season could not be located, the club name has been included with an added note of explanation.

League – This field contains the league name or abbreviated league name for each team line. If a player was with his country's national team, "Nat-Team" is listed in the league column. If a player was with a team that played an exhibition season only, the league field has been left blank, but a note of explanation has been included in his trade notes located at the end of his data panel. In total, over 100 leagues from around the world were researched for the *Total Hockey* project. A full list of the leagues found in *Total Hockey* and their abbreviations can be found on page 1,878.

GP – Games Played – Games in which a player appears on the ice during a game. Players who are dressed but do not step on the ice during play are not credited with a game played.

G – Goals scored – A goal is credited to the last player from the scoring team to touch the puck before it completely crosses the goal line. A player may not direct the puck into the net with a skate or deflect a puck into the net with his stick above the height of the crossbar of the goal frame.

A – Assists – An assist is awarded to any player, or players, taking part in the play immediately preceding the goal. No more than two assists can be awarded for each goal.

Pts – Points – Any player credited with a goal or an assist receives one point.

AG – Adjusted goals – *(See page 626)*

AA - Adjusted assists – *(See page 626)*

APts - Adjusted points – *(See page 626)*

PIM – Penalties in minutes – Number of minutes a player is penalized during the season. A player is penalized two minutes for each minor penalty, five minutes for each major penalty and 10 minutes for each misconduct, game misconduct and gross misconduct penalty.

PP – Power play goals – Goals scored while the opposition has fewer players on the ice than the scoring team due to players being penalized.

SH – Shorthanded goals – goals scored while the opposition has more players on the ice than the scoring team due to players being penalized..

GW – Game-winning goals – Goal scored that gives the winning team one more goal than the total number of goals the losing team eventually scores. For example, the fourth goal scored in a 6–3 victory is considered the winning goal, regardless of when it was scored.

S – Shots on goal – Shots taken on net by an individual player that either enter the net or would do so if not for intervention by an opposing player, usually the goaltender. A long clearing shot taken from behind center ice is not considered a shot on goal, unless it is directed at an empty net. Shots off the posts or crossbar are not counted as shots on goals.

% – Shooting percentage – Percentage of shots taken by an individual player that result in goals. The percentage is calculated by dividing the number of goals by shots. The resulting figure is expressed as a percentage to one decimal place.

TGF – Total Goals For – Total number of goals scored by a player's team while he is on the ice.

PGF – Power-play Goals For – Total number of power-play goals scored by a player's team while he is on the ice.

TGA – Total Goals Against – Total number of goals scored against a player's team while he is on the ice.

PGA – Total number of power play goals scored against a player's team while he is on the ice.

+/– – Plus/minus rating – Total number of goals scored by a player's team while he is on the ice (at even strength or short handed) less the total number of goals allowed by a player's team while he is on the ice (at even strength or on the power play). Calculated as follows:

$$(TGF – PGF) – (TGA – PGA)$$

NHL Totals – NHL statistics with the exception of +/- are totaled here.

Other Major League Totals – This field includes the total of all the other major leagues in which a player has performed. *(See Chapter 68, page 642)* To be categorized as major a league must fall into one of the following three categories: it must have been professional, challenged for the Stanley Cup and/or competed with other major leagues to sign the top hockey talent of the day. Under these criteria, only the World Hockey Association (1972-1979) qualifies in the years covered by the Modern Player Register.

Award and All-Star Notes – (located beneath a players' total lines) This field contains details of all-star selections and major trophies and awards won for the NHL, the minor leagues, Canadian major junior hockey and the NCAA and CIAU. Also included are IIHF World Championship and IIHF World Junior Championship awards and all-star selections as well as appearances in the NHL All-Star Game.

Trade Notes – This field contains details on NHL trades, drafts (Waiver, Reverse, Intra-League, Inter-League, Expansion and Dispersal) and free agent signings. WHA trade notes, draft information and free agent signings are included for every player who played in both the WHA and the NHL. Special notes concerning injuries and other oddities and curiosities are indicated by a bullet (•)

CHAPTER 73
Modern Player Register
Career Records for Players Appearing in the NHL in 1967–68 or Later

			REGULAR SEASON																		PLAYOFFS							
Season	Club	League	GP	G	A	Pts	AG	AA	APts	PIM	PP	SH	GW	S	%	TGF	PGF	TGA	PGA	+/–	GP	G	A	Pts	PIM	PP	SH	GW

● AALTO, ANTTI Antti Aalto C – L. 6'2", 190 lbs. b: Lappeenranta, Finland, 3/4/1975. Anaheim's 6th choice, 134th overall, in 1993 Entry Draft.

Season	Club	League	GP	G	A	Pts	AG	AA	APts	PIM	PP	SH	GW	S	%	TGF	PGF	TGA	PGA	+/–	GP	G	A	Pts	PIM	PP	SH	GW
1991-92	SaiPa Lapeenranta	Finland 2	20	6	6	12	....	....	....	20											....	....	....	....	....			
1992-93	SaiPa Lapeenranta	Finland 2	23	6	8	14	....	....	....	14											....	....	....	....	....			
	TPS Turku	Finland	1	0	0	0	....	....	....	0											....	....	....	....	....			
1993-94	TPS Turku	Finland	33	5	9	14	....	....	....	16											10	1	1	2	4			
	Finland	WJC-A	7	0	2	2	....	....	....	8											....	....	....	....	....			
1994-95	TPS Turku	Finland	44	11	7	18	....	....	....	18											5	0	1	1	2			
	Finland	WJC-A	7	2	3	5	....	....	....	18											....	....	....	....	....			
1995-96	TPS Turku	Finland	40	15	16	31	....	....	....	22											11	3	5	8	14			
	Kiekko-67	Finland 2	2	0	2	2	....	....	....	2											....	....	....	....	....			
1996-97	TPS Turku	Finland	44	15	19	34	....	....	....	60											11	5	6	11	31			
	Finland	WC-A	5	2	0	2	....	....	....	0											....	....	....	....	....			
1997-98	**Anaheim Mighty Ducks**	**NHL**	**3**	**0**	**0**	**0**	0	0	0	0	0	0	0	1	0.0	0	0	1	0	–1	....	....	....	....	....			
	Cincinnati Mighty Ducks	AHL	29	4	9	13	....	....	....	30											....	....	....	....	....			
	NHL Totals		**3**	**0**	**0**	**0**	**0**	**0**	**0**	**0**	**0**	**0**	**0**	**1**	**0.0**	**0**	**0**	**1**	**0**		....	....	....	....	....			

● ABGRALL, DENNIS Dennis Abgrall RW – R. 6'1", 180 lbs. b: Moosomin, Sask., 4/24/1953. Los Angeles' 3rd choice, 70th overall, in 1973 Amateur Draft.

Season	Club	League	GP	G	A	Pts	AG	AA	APts	PIM	PP	SH	GW	S	%	TGF	PGF	TGA	PGA	+/–	GP	G	A	Pts	PIM	PP	SH	GW
1970-71	Saskatoon Blades	WCJHL	64	31	43	74	....	....	....	28											5	4	2	6	8			
1971-72	Saskatoon Blades	WCJHL	64	29	38	67	....	....	....	58											2	2	0	2	0			
1972-73	Saskatoon Blades	WCJHL	68	30	39	69	....	....	....	36											16	7	6	13	12			
1973-74	Portland Buckaroos	WHL	78	27	41	68	....	....	....	37											10	2	*7	9	8			
1974-75	Springfield Indians	AHL	75	25	40	65	....	....	....	17											17	9	11	20	8			
1975-76	**Los Angeles Kings**	**NHL**	**13**	**0**	**2**	**2**	0	2	2	4	0	0	0	9	0.0	3	2	8	0	–7	....	....	....	....	....			
	Fort Worth Texans	CHL	64	21	36	57	....	....	....	34											....	....	....	....	....			
1976-77	Cincinnati Stingers	WHA	80	23	39	62	....	....	....	22											4	2	0	2	5			
1977-78	Cincinnati Stingers	WHA	65	13	11	24	....	....	....	13											....	....	....	....	....			
1978-79	Binghamton Whalers	AHL	6	0	0	0	....	....	....	0											....	....	....	....	....			
	Erie Blades	NEHL	56	30	49	79	....	....	....	8											....	....	....	....	....			
1979-80			DID NOT PLAY																									
1980-81			DID NOT PLAY																									
1981-82	Liege	Neth.	23	46	32	78	....	....	....	16											....	....	....	....	....			
	NHL Totals		**13**	**0**	**2**	**2**	**0**	**2**	**2**	**4**	**0**	**0**	**0**	**9**	**0.0**	**3**	**2**	**8**	**0**		....	....	....	....	....			
	Other Major League Totals		145	36	50	86				35											4	2	0	2	5			

Selected by **LA Blades** (WHA) in 1972 WHA General Player Draft, February 12, 1972. WHA rights transferred to **Cincinnati** (WHA) after **Michigan-Baltimore** (WHA) franchise folded, June, 1975.

● ABRAHAMSSON, THOMMY Thommy Abrahamsson D – L. 6'2", 185 lbs. b: Umea, Sweden, 4/12/1947.

Season	Club	League	GP	G	A	Pts	AG	AA	APts	PIM	PP	SH	GW	S	%	TGF	PGF	TGA	PGA	+/–	GP	G	A	Pts	PIM	PP	SH	GW
1969-70	Leksands IF	Sweden	14	3	4	7	....	....	....	18											14	5	4	9	15			
	Sweden	WEC-A	10	3	1	4	....	....	....	8											....	....	....	....	....			
1970-71	Leksands IF	Sweden	14	7	4	11	....	....	....	4											14	5	1	6	25			
	Sweden	WEC-A	9	2	1	3	....	....	....	10											....	....	....	....	....			
1971-72	Leksands IF	Sweden	25	5	14	19	....	....	....	28											....	....	....	....	....			
	Sweden	Olympics	6	1	1	2	....	....	....	2											....	....	....	....	....			
	Sweden	WEC-A	10	0	1	1	....	....	....	14											....	....	....	....	....			
1972-73	Leksands IF	Sweden	14	7	3	10	....	....	....	20											14	7	3	10	8			
	Sweden	WEC-A	2	1	1	2	....	....	....	0											....	....	....	....	....			
1973-74	Leksands IF	Sweden			STATISTICS NOT AVAILABLE																	....	....	....	....	....			
	Sweden	WEC-A	10	0	3	3	....	....	....	6											....	....	....	....	....			
1974-75	New England Whalers	WHA	76	8	22	30	....	....	....	46											6	0	0	0	0			
1975-76	New England Whalers	WHA	63	14	21	35	....	....	....	47											17	2	4	6	15			
1976-77	New England Whalers	WHA	64	6	24	30	....	....	....	33											5	0	3	3	0			
1977-78	Leksands IF	Sweden	28	17	5	22	....	....	....	56											....	....	....	....	....			
1978-79	Leksands IF	Sweden	24	6	3	9	....	....	....	55											4	0	1	1	8			
1979-80	Leksands IF	Sweden	26	9	6	15	....	....	....	35											....	....	....	....	....			
1980-81	**Hartford Whalers**	**NHL**	**32**	**6**	**11**	**17**	5	8	13	16	4	0	1	66	9.1	46	17	34	1	–4	....	....	....	....	....			
	Binghamton Whalers	AHL	2	0	0	0	....	....	....	2											....	....	....	....	....			
1981-82	Timra	Sweden	28	10	4	14	....	....	....	44											....	....	....	....	....			
	NHL Totals		**32**	**6**	**11**	**17**	**5**	**8**	**13**	**16**	**4**	**0**	**1**	**66**	**9.1**	**46**	**17**	**34**	**1**		....	....	....	....	....			
	Other Major League Totals		203	28	67	95				126											28	2	7	9	15			

Swedish Player of the Year (1973)

Signed as a free agent by **New England** (WHA), August, 1974. Signed as a free agent by **Hartford**, May 23, 1980.

● ACOMB, DOUG Doug Acomb C – L. 5'11", 165 lbs. b: Toronto, Ont., 5/15/1949.

Season	Club	League	GP	G	A	Pts	AG	AA	APts	PIM	PP	SH	GW	S	%	TGF	PGF	TGA	PGA	+/–	GP	G	A	Pts	PIM	PP	SH	GW
1965-66	York Steel	Jr. B	....	26	32	58	....	....	....	....											4	0	0	0	4			
	Toronto Marlboros	OHA																				....	....	....	....	....			
1966-67	Toronto Marlboros	OHA	43	20	18	38	....	....	....	41											17	11	10	21	22			
1967-68	Toronto Marlboros	OHA	52	22	44	66	....	....	....	51											5	2	3	5	4			
	Toronto Marlboros	OHA Sr.	1	2	1	3	....	....	....	0											....	....	....	....	....			
1968-69	Toronto Marlboros	OHA	54	*55	38	93	....	....	....	71											6	2	1	3	6			
1969-70	**Toronto Maple Leafs**	**NHL**	**2**	**0**	**1**	**1**	0	1	1	0	0	0	0	0	0.0	1	0	0	0	+1	....	....	....	....	....			
	Tulsa Oilers	CHL	52	17	22	39	....	....	....	34											5	0	2	2	4			
	Buffalo Bisons	AHL	....	....	....	....	....	....	....	....											2	0	0	0	0			
1970-71	Phoenix Roadrunners	WHL	69	9	16	25	....	....	....	15											10	1	3	4	4			
1971-72	Barrie Flyers	OHA Sr.	39	*37	41	*78	....	....	....	53											....	....	....	....	....			
1972-73	Barrie Flyers	OHA Sr.	40	34	39	73	....	....	....	34											....	....	....	....	....			
1973-74	Barrie Flyers	OHA Sr.	35	22	33	55	....	....	....	22											....	....	....	....	....			
1974-75	Barrie Flyers	OHA Sr.	44	33	42	75	....	....	....	34											....	....	....	....	....			
	Port Huron Flags	IHL	6	3	5	8	....	....	....	2											5	2	7	9	4			
	NHL Totals		**2**	**0**	**1**	**1**	**0**	**1**	**1**	**0**	**0**	**0**	**0**	**0**	**0.0**	**1**	**0**	**0**	**0**		....	....	....	....	....			

● ACTON, KEITH

Keith Acton C – L. 5'8", 170 lbs. b: Stouffville, Ont., 4/15/1958. Montreal's 9th choice, 103rd overall, in 1978 Amateur Draft.

Season	Club	League	GP	G	A	Pts	AG	AA	APts	PIM	PP	SH	GW	S	%	TGF	PGF	TGA	PGA	+/–	GP	G	A	Pts	PIM	PP	SH	GW
			REGULAR SEASON																		PLAYOFFS							
1974-75	Wexford Raiders	MJHL	43	23	29	52				46																		
1975-76	Peterborough Petes	OHA	35	9	17	26				30																		
1976-77	Peterborough Petes	OHA	65	52	69	121				93											4	1	4	5	6			
1977-78	Peterborough Petes	OHA	68	42	86	128				52											21	10	8	18	16			
1978-79	Nova Scotia Voyageurs	AHL	79	15	26	41				22											10	4	2	6	4			
1979-80	**Montreal Canadiens**	**NHL**	**2**	**0**	**1**	**1**	**0**	**1**	**1**	**0**	**0**	**0**	**0**	**1**	**0.0**	**1**	**0**	**1**	**0**	**0**								
	Nova Scotia Voyageurs	AHL	75	45	53	98				38											6	1	2	3	8			
1980-81	**Montreal Canadiens**	**NHL**	**61**	**15**	**24**	**39**	**12**	**17**	**29**	**74**	**3**	**0**	**2**	**101**	**14.9**	**50**	**8**	**38**	**1**	**+5**	**2**	**0**	**0**	**0**	**6**	**0**	**0**	**0**
1981-82	**Montreal Canadiens**	**NHL**	**78**	**36**	**52**	**88**	**29**	**34**	**63**	**88**	**10**	**0**	**5**	**218**	**16.5**	**128**	**35**	**51**	**6**	**+48**	**5**	**0**	**4**	**4**	**16**	**0**	**0**	**0**
1982-83	**Montreal Canadiens**	**NHL**	**78**	**24**	**26**	**50**	**20**	**18**	**38**	**63**	**1**	**0**	**3**	**154**	**15.6**	**64**	**4**	**74**	**8**	**–6**	**3**	**0**	**0**	**0**	**0**	**0**	**0**	**0**
1983-84	**Montreal Canadiens**	**NHL**	**9**	**3**	**7**	**10**	**2**	**5**	**7**	**4**	**2**	**0**	**0**	**14**	**21.4**	**13**	**7**	**12**	**1**	**–5**								
	Minnesota North Stars	**NHL**	**62**	**17**	**38**	**55**	**14**	**26**	**40**	**60**	**4**	**2**	**5**	**151**	**11.3**	**73**	**18**	**72**	**19**	**+2**	**15**	**4**	**7**	**11**	**12**	**1**	**0**	**1**
1984-85	**Minnesota North Stars**	**NHL**	**78**	**20**	**38**	**58**	**16**	**26**	**42**	**90**	**4**	**0**	**3**	**167**	**12.0**	**81**	**23**	**86**	**25**	**–3**	**9**	**4**	**4**	**8**	**6**	**1**	**0**	**2**
1985-86	**Minnesota North Stars**	**NHL**	**79**	**26**	**32**	**58**	**21**	**21**	**42**	**100**	**5**	**2**	**2**	**169**	**15.4**	**76**	**16**	**112**	**41**	**–11**	**5**	**0**	**3**	**3**	**6**	**0**	**0**	**0**
	Canada	WEC-A	10	3	0	3				2																		
1986-87	**Minnesota North Stars**	**NHL**	**78**	**16**	**29**	**45**	**14**	**21**	**35**	**56**	**1**	**1**	**3**	**126**	**12.7**	**61**	**8**	**107**	**39**	**–15**								
1987-88	**Minnesota North Stars**	**NHL**	**46**	**8**	**11**	**19**	**7**	**8**	**15**	**74**	**0**	**1**	**0**	**49**	**16.3**	**28**	**2**	**73**	**38**	**–9**								
	Edmonton Oilers	**NHL**	**26**	**3**	**6**	**9**	**3**	**4**	**7**	**21**	**1**	**0**	**1**	**26**	**11.5**	**10**	**2**	**24**	**6**	**–10**	**7**	**2**	**0**	**2**	**16**	**0**	**0**	**2**
1988-89	**Edmonton Oilers**	**NHL**	**46**	**11**	**15**	**26**	**9**	**11**	**20**	**47**	**0**	**1**	**1**	**74**	**14.9**	**35**	**1**	**40**	**15**	**+9**								
	Philadelphia Flyers	**NHL**	**25**	**3**	**10**	**13**	**3**	**7**	**10**	**64**	**0**	**1**	**0**	**38**	**7.9**	**21**	**0**	**27**	**7**	**+1**	**16**	**2**	**3**	**5**	**18**	**0**	**0**	**0**
1989-90	**Philadelphia Flyers**	**NHL**	**69**	**13**	**14**	**27**	**11**	**10**	**21**	**80**	**0**	**2**	**0**	**94**	**13.8**	**41**	**0**	**65**	**22**	**–2**								
	Canada	WEC-A	10	2	0	2				0																		
1990-91	**Philadelphia Flyers**	**NHL**	**76**	**14**	**23**	**37**	**13**	**17**	**30**	**131**	**2**	**1**	**1**	**120**	**11.7**	**52**	**8**	**75**	**22**	**–9**								
1991-92	**Philadelphia Flyers**	**NHL**	**50**	**7**	**10**	**17**	**6**	**7**	**13**	**98**	**0**	**0**	**3**	**79**	**8.9**	**28**	**2**	**42**	**12**	**–4**								
	Canada	WC-A	6	1	0	1				2																		
1992-93	**Philadelphia Flyers**	**NHL**	**83**	**8**	**15**	**23**	**7**	**10**	**17**	**51**	**0**	**0**	**0**	**74**	**10.8**	**29**	**0**	**91**	**52**	**–10**								
1993-94	**Washington Capitals**	**NHL**	**6**	**0**	**0**	**0**	**0**	**0**	**0**	**21**	**0**	**0**	**0**	**2**	**0.0**	**0**	**0**	**4**	**0**	**–4**								
	New York Islanders	**NHL**	**71**	**2**	**7**	**9**	**2**	**5**	**7**	**50**	**0**	**0**	**0**	**33**	**6.1**	**10**	**0**	**35**	**24**	**–1**	**4**	**0**	**0**	**0**	**8**	**0**	**0**	**0**
1994-95	Hershey Bears	AHL	12	5	7	12				58																		
	NHL Totals		**1023**	**226**	**358**	**584**	**189**	**248**	**437**	**1172**	**33**	**11**	**29**	**1690**	**13.4**	**801**	**134**	**1029**	**338**		**66**	**12**	**21**	**33**	**88**	**2**	**0**	**5**

AHL Second All-Star Team (1980)

Played in NHL All-Star Game (1982)

Traded to **Minnesota** by **Montreal** with Mark Napier and Toronto's 3rd round choice (previously acquired, Minnesota selected Ken Hodge Jr.) in 1984 Entry Draft for Bobby Smith, October 28, 1983. Traded to **Edmonton** by **Minnesota** for Moe Mantha, January 22, 1988. Traded to **Philadelphia** by **Edmonton** with Edmonton's 5th round choice (Dimitri Yushkevich) in 1991 Entry Draft for Dave Brown, February 7, 1989. Traded to **Winnipeg** by **Philadelphia** with Pete Peeters for future considerations, September 28, 1989. Traded to **Philadelphia** by **Winnipeg** with Pete Peeters for Toronto's 5th round choice (previously acquired, Winnipeg selected Juha Ylonen) in 1991 Entry Draft and the cancellation of future considerations owed Philadelphia from the Shawn Cronin trade, October 3, 1989. Signed as a free agent by **Washington**, July 27, 1993. Claimed on waivers by **NY Islanders** from **Washington**, October 22, 1993.

● ADAM, RUSS

Russ Adam C – L. 5'10", 185 lbs. b: Windsor, Ont., 5/5/1961. Toronto's 7th choice, 137th overall, in 1980 Entry Draft.

Season	Club	League	GP	G	A	Pts	AG	AA	APts	PIM	PP	SH	GW	S	%	TGF	PGF	TGA	PGA	+/–	GP	G	A	Pts	PIM	PP	SH	GW
1977-78	Windsor Royals	Jr. B	35	26	44	70																						
	Windsor Spitfires	OHA	3	1	2	3				0																		
1978-79	Kitchener Rangers	OHA	62	20	17	37				39											9	4	3	7	31			
1979-80	Kitchener Rangers	OHA	54	37	34	71				143																		
1980-81	Kitchener Rangers	OHA	64	37	50	87				215											10	0	2	2	17			
1981-82	New Brunswick Hawks	AHL	52	11	21	32				50											12	3	5	8	32			
1982-83	**Toronto Maple Leafs**	**NHL**	**8**	**1**	**2**	**3**	**1**	**1**	**2**	**11**	**0**	**0**	**0**	**4**	**25.0**	**3**	**0**	**7**	**1**	**–3**								
	St. Catharines Saints	AHL	64	19	17	36				119																		
1983-84	St. Catharines Saints	AHL	70	32	24	56				76											7	0	1	1	10			
1984-85	Fort Wayne Komets	IHL	60	28	46	74				56																		
1985-86	Fort Wayne Komets	IHL	48	24	37	61				36											14	7	*13	20	9			
1986-87	St. John's Capitals	Nfld.	DID NOT PLAY – COACHING																									
1987-88	St. John's Capitals	Nfld.	47	47	55	102				90																		
1988-89	Kaufbeuren	Germany	36	8	6	14				8																		
	NHL Totals		**8**	**1**	**2**	**3**	**1**	**1**	**2**	**11**	**0**	**0**	**0**	**4**	**25.0**	**3**	**0**	**7**	**1**									

● ADAMS, GREG A.

Greg A. Adams LW – L. 6'3", 195 lbs. b: Nelson, B.C., 8/1/1963.

Season	Club	League	GP	G	A	Pts	AG	AA	APts	PIM	PP	SH	GW	S	%	TGF	PGF	TGA	PGA	+/–	GP	G	A	Pts	PIM	PP	SH	GW
1981-82	Kelowna Packers	BCJHL	45	31	42	73				24																		
1982-83	Northern Arizona University	NCAA	29	14	21	35				19																		
1983-84	Northern Arizona University	NCAA	26	44	29	73				24																		
1984-85	**New Jersey Devils**	**NHL**	**36**	**12**	**9**	**21**	**10**	**6**	**16**	**14**	**5**	**0**	**0**	**63**	**19.0**	**27**	**7**	**34**	**0**	**–14**								
	Maine Mariners	AHL	41	15	20	35				12											11	3	4	7	0			
1985-86	**New Jersey Devils**	**NHL**	**78**	**35**	**42**	**77**	**28**	**28**	**56**	**30**	**10**	**0**	**2**	**202**	**17.3**	**98**	**28**	**78**	**1**	**–7**								
	Canada	WEC-A	1	1	0	1				0																		
1986-87	**New Jersey Devils**	**NHL**	**72**	**20**	**27**	**47**	**17**	**20**	**37**	**19**	**6**	**0**	**1**	**143**	**14.0**	**75**	**25**	**66**	**0**	**–16**								
1987-88	**Vancouver Canucks**	**NHL**	**80**	**36**	**40**	**76**	**31**	**28**	**59**	**30**	**12**	**0**	**3**	**227**	**15.9**	**110**	**43**	**100**	**9**	**–24**								
1988-89	**Vancouver Canucks**	**NHL**	**61**	**19**	**14**	**33**	**16**	**10**	**26**	**24**											**7**	**2**	**3**	**5**	**2**			
1989-90	**Vancouver Canucks**	**NHL**	**65**	**30**	**20**	**50**	**26**	**14**	**40**	**18**	**13**	**0**	**1**	**181**	**16.6**	**64**	**23**	**50**	**1**	**–8**								
	Canada	WEC-A	10	8	1	9				10																		
1990-91	**Vancouver Canucks**	**NHL**	**55**	**21**	**24**	**45**	**19**	**18**	**37**	**10**	**5**	**1**	**2**	**148**	**14.2**	**65**	**21**	**53**	**4**	**–5**	**5**	**0**	**0**	**0**	**2**	**0**	**0**	**0**
1991-92	**Vancouver Canucks**	**NHL**	**76**	**30**	**27**	**57**	**27**	**20**	**47**	**26**	**13**	**1**	**5**	**184**	**16.3**	**92**	**37**	**61**	**14**	**+8**	**6**	**0**	**2**	**2**	**4**	**0**	**0**	**0**
1992-93	**Vancouver Canucks**	**NHL**	**53**	**25**	**31**	**56**	**21**	**21**	**42**	**14**	**6**	**1**	**3**	**124**	**20.2**	**79**	**22**	**44**	**18**	**+31**	**12**	**7**	**6**	**13**	**6**	**5**	**0**	**1**
1993-94	**Vancouver Canucks**	**NHL**	**68**	**13**	**24**	**37**	**12**	**19**	**31**	**20**	**5**	**1**	**2**	**139**	**9.4**	**60**	**18**	**51**	**8**	**–1**	**23**	**6**	**8**	**14**	**2**	**2**	**0**	**2**
1994-95	**Vancouver Canucks**	**NHL**	**31**	**5**	**10**	**15**	**9**	**15**	**24**	**12**	**2**	**2**	**0**	**56**	**8.9**	**27**	**5**	**30**	**9**	**+1**								
	Dallas Stars	**NHL**	**12**	**3**	**3**	**6**	**5**	**4**	**9**	**4**	**1**	**0**	**0**	**16**	**18.8**	**11**	**5**	**10**	**0**	**–4**	**5**	**2**	**0**	**2**	**0**	**0**	**0**	**0**
1995-96	**Dallas Stars**	**NHL**	**66**	**22**	**21**	**43**	**22**	**17**	**39**	**33**	**11**	**1**	**1**	**140**	**15.7**	**62**	**31**	**70**	**18**	**–21**								
1996-97	**Dallas Stars**	**NHL**	**50**	**21**	**15**	**36**	**22**	**13**	**35**	**2**	**5**	**0**	**4**	**113**	**18.6**	**58**	**16**	**16**	**1**	**+27**	**3**	**0**	**1**	**1**	**0**	**0**	**0**	**0**
1997-98	**Dallas Stars**	**NHL**	**49**	**14**	**18**	**32**	**16**	**10**	**34**	**20**	**7**	**0**	**1**	**75**	**18.7**	**55**	**21**	**23**	**0**	**+11**	**12**	**2**	**2**	**4**	**0**	**0**	**0**	**2**
	NHL Totals		**852**	**306**	**325**	**631**	**281**	**251**	**532**	**276**	**101**	**7**	**25**	**1811**	**16.9**	**883**	**302**	**688**	**83**		**73**	**19**	**22**	**41**	**16**	**7**	**0**	**5**

Played in NHL All-Star Game (1988)

Signed as a free agent by **New Jersey**, June 25, 1984. Traded to **Vancouver** by **New Jersey** with Kirk McLean for Patrik Sundstrom and Vancouver's 4th round choice (Matt Ruchty) in 1988 Entry Draft, September 10, 1987. Traded to **Dallas** by **Vancouver** with Dan Kesa and Vancouver's 5th round choice (later traded to LA Kings — LA Kings selected Jason Morgan) in 1995 Entry Draft for Russ Courtnall, April 7, 1995.

● ADAMS, GREG C.

Greg C. Adams LW – L. 6'1", 190 lbs. b: Duncan, B.C., 5/31/1960.

Season	Club	League	GP	G	A	Pts	AG	AA	APts	PIM	PP	SH	GW	S	%	TGF	PGF	TGA	PGA	+/–	GP	G	A	Pts	PIM	PP	SH	GW
1977-78	Nanaimo Clippers	BCJHL	62	53	60	113				150																		
1978-79	Victoria Cougars	WHL	71	23	31	54				151											14	5	0	5	59			
1979-80	Victoria Cougars	WHL	71	62	48	110				212											16	9	11	20	71			
1980-81	**Philadelphia Flyers**	**NHL**	**6**	**3**	**0**	**3**	**2**	**0**	**2**	**8**	**0**	**0**	**0**	**6**	**50.0**	**4**	**0**	**4**	**0**	**0**								
	Maine Mariners	AHL	71	19	20	39				158											2	2	3	5	89			
1981-82	**Philadelphia Flyers**	**NHL**	**33**	**4**	**15**	**19**	**3**	**10**	**13**	**105**	**0**	**0**	**0**	**29**	**13.8**	**25**	**3**	**15**	**0**	**+7**								
	Maine Mariners	AHL	45	16	21	37				241											4	0	3	3	28			
1982-83	**Hartford Whalers**	**NHL**	**79**	**10**	**13**	**23**	**8**	**9**	**17**	**216**	**1**	**0**	**1**	**114**	**8.8**	**42**	**6**	**82**	**0**	**–46**								
1983-84	**Washington Capitals**	**NHL**	**57**	**2**	**6**	**8**	**2**	**4**	**6**	**133**	**0**	**0**	**0**	**37**	**5.4**	**21**	**1**	**19**	**0**	**+1**	**1**	**0**	**0**	**0**	**0**	**0**	**0**	**0**
1984-85	**Washington Capitals**	**NHL**	**51**	**6**	**12**	**18**	**5**	**8**	**13**	**72**	**0**	**0**	**1**	**62**	**9.7**	**29**	**1**	**20**	**0**	**+8**	**5**	**0**	**0**	**0**	**9**	**0**	**0**	**0**
	Binghamton Whalers	AHL	28	9	16	25				58																		
1985-86	**Washington Capitals**	**NHL**	**78**	**18**	**38**	**56**	**14**	**25**	**39**	**152**	**3**	**0**	**2**	**149**	**12.1**	**68**	**21**	**55**	**2**	**+24**	**9**	**1**	**3**	**4**	**27**	**0**	**0**	**0**
1986-87	**Washington Capitals**	**NHL**	**67**	**14**	**30**	**44**	**12**	**22**	**34**	**184**	**2**	**0**	**0**	**92**	**15.2**	**70**	**17**	**45**	**1**	**+9**	**7**	**1**	**3**	**4**	**38**	**1**	**0**	**0**
1987-88	**Washington Capitals**	**NHL**	**78**	**15**	**12**	**27**	**13**	**9**	**22**	**153**	**3**	**0**	**0**	**109**	**13.8**	**50**	**17**	**36**	**0**	**–3**	**14**	**0**	**5**	**5**	**58**	**0**	**0**	**0**

			REGULAR SEASON																		PLAYOFFS							
Season	Club	League	GP	G	A	Pts	AG	AA	APts	PIM	PP	SH	GW	S	%	TGF	PGF	TGA	PGA	+/–	GP	G	A	Pts	PIM	PP	SH	GW
1988-89	**Edmonton Oilers**	**NHL**	**49**	**4**	**5**	**9**	**3**	**4**	**7**	**82**	**0**	**0**	**1**	**49**	**8.2**	**26**	**0**	**25**	**0**	**+1**								
	Vancouver Canucks	**NHL**	**12**	**4**	**2**	**6**	**3**	**1**	**4**	**35**											**7**	**0**	**0**	**0**	**21**			
1989-90	**Quebec Nordiques**	**NHL**	**7**	**1**	**3**	**4**	**1**	**2**	**3**	**17**	**0**	**0**	**0**	**8**	**12.5**	**9**	**5**	**6**	**0**	**–2**								
	Detroit Red Wings	**NHL**	**28**	**3**	**7**	**10**	**3**	**5**	**8**	**16**	**0**	**0**	**0**	**19**	**15.8**	**15**	**0**	**15**	**0**	**0**								
	NHL Totals		**545**	**84**	**143**	**227**	**69**	**99**	**168**	**1173**	**9**	**0**	**5**	**674**	**12.5**	**389**	**71**	**322**	**3**		**43**	**2**	**11**	**13**	**153**	**1**	**0**	**0**

WHL All-Star Team (1980)

Signed as a free agent by **Philadelphia**, September 28, 1979. Traded to **Hartford** by **Philadelphia** with Ken Linseman and Philadelphia's 1st (David Jensen) and 3rd (Leif Karlsson) round choices in 1982 Entry Draft for Mark Howe and Hartford's 3rd round choice (Derrick Smith) in 1982 Entry Draft, August 19, 1982. Traded to **Washington** by **Hartford** for Torrie Robertson, October 3, 1983. Traded to **Edmonton** by **Washington** for the rights to Geoff Courtnall, July 22, 1988. Traded to **Vancouver** by **Edmonton** with Doug Smith for John Leblanc and Vancouver's 5th round choice (Peter White) in 1989 Entry Draft, March 7, 1989.

• ADAMS, KEVYN

Kevyn Adams C – R. 6'1", 182 lbs. b: Washington, D.C., 10/8/1974. Boston's 1st choice, 25th overall, in 1993 Entry Draft.

Season	Club	League	GP	G	A	Pts	AG	AA	APts	PIM	PP	SH	GW	S	%	TGF	PGF	TGA	PGA	+/–	GP	G	A	Pts	PIM	PP	SH	GW
1992-93	University of Miami-Ohio	CCHA	40	17	15	32				18																		
1993-94	University of Miami-Ohio	CCHA	36	15	28	43				24																		
1994-95	University of Miami-Ohio	CCHA	38	20	29	49				30																		
1995-96	University of Miami-Ohio	CCHA	36	17	30	47				30																		
1996-97	Grand Rapids Griffins	IHL	82	22	25	47				47											5	1	1	2	4			
1997-98	**Toronto Maple Leafs**	**NHL**	**5**	**0**	**0**	**0**	**0**	**0**	**0**	**7**	**0**	**0**	**0**	**3**	**0.0**	**0**	**0**	**1**	**1**	**0**								
	St. John's Maple Leafs	AHL	59	17	20	37				99											4	0	0	0	4			
	NHL Totals		**5**	**0**	**0**	**0**	**0**	**0**	**0**	**7**	**0**	**0**	**0**	**3**	**0.0**	**0**	**0**	**1**	**1**									

CCHA Second All-Star Team (1995)

Signed as a free agent by **Toronto**, August 7, 1997.

• ADDUONO, RICK

Rick Adduono C. 5'11", 182 lbs. b: Thunder Bay, Ont., 1/25/1955. Boston's 3rd choice, 60th overall, in 1975 Amateur Draft.

Season	Club	League	GP	G	A	Pts	AG	AA	APts	PIM	PP	SH	GW	S	%	TGF	PGF	TGA	PGA	+/–	GP	G	A	Pts	PIM	PP	SH	GW
1972-73	St. Catharines Black Hawks	OHA	55	45	64	109				58																		
1973-74	St. Catharines Black Hawks	OHA	70	51	*84	*135				24																		
1974-75	St. Catharines Black Hawks	OHA	55	27	39	66				31																		
1975-76	**Boston Bruins**	**NHL**	**1**	**0**	**0**	**0**	**0**	**0**	**0**	**0**	**0**	**0**	**0**	**0**	**0.0**	**0**	**0**	**1**	**0**	**–1**								
	Rochester Americans	AHL	68	11	23	34				24											7	2	1	3	7			
	Binghamton Dusters	NAHL	2	2	0	2				0																		
1976-77	Rochester Americans	AHL	77	29	45	74				38											8	3	1	4	2			
1977-78	Rochester Americans	AHL	76	38	60	*98				34											6	1	2	3	6			
1978-79	Birmingham Bulls	WHA	80	20	33	53				67																		
1979-80	**Atlanta Flames**	**NHL**	**3**	**0**	**0**	**0**	**0**	**0**	**0**	**2**	**0**	**0**	**0**	**1**	**0.0**	**0**	**0**	**1**	**0**	**–1**								
	Birmingham Bulls	CHL	78	35	39	74				76											4	1	0	1	0			
1980-81	Klagenfurter	Austria	7	4	5	9				4																		
	New Haven Nighthawks	AHL	51	6	12	18				57											4	0	1	1	6			
1981-82	Fredericton Express	AHL	5	1	1	2				2																		
	NHL Totals		**4**	**0**	**0**	**0**	**0**	**0**	**0**	**2**	**0**	**0**	**0**	**1**	**0.0**	**0**	**0**	**2**	**0**									
	Other Major League Totals		80	20	33	53				67																		

AHL Second All-Star Team (1978) • Won John B. Sollenberger Trophy (Top Scorer - AHL) (1978)

Selected by **San Diego** (WHA) in 1975 WHA Amateur Draft, May, 1975. Signed as a free agent by **Birmingham** (WHA) after **San Diego** franchise folded, July, 1978. Signed as a free agent by **Atlanta**, October 9, 1979.

• AFFLECK, BRUCE

Bruce Affleck D – L. 6', 205 lbs. b: Salmon Arm, B.C., 5/5/1954. California's 3rd choice, 21st overall, in 1974 Amateur Draft.

Season	Club	League	GP	G	A	Pts	AG	AA	APts	PIM	PP	SH	GW	S	%	TGF	PGF	TGA	PGA	+/–	GP	G	A	Pts	PIM	PP	SH	GW
1970-71	Penticton Panthers	BCJHL	60	23	46	69				49																		
1971-72	Penticton Panthers	BCJHL	57	31	69	100				91																		
1972-73	University of Denver	WCHA	39	6	19	25				30																		
1973-74	University of Denver	WCHA	38	8	23	31				42																		
1974-75	Salt Lake Golden Eagles	CHL	35	0	14	14				28																		
	St. Louis Blues	**NHL**	**13**	**0**	**2**	**2**	**0**	**2**	**2**	**4**	**0**	**0**	**0**	**3**	**0.0**	**13**	**0**	**6**	**0**	**+7**	**1**	**0**	**0**	**0**	**0**	**0**	**0**	**0**
	Springfield Indians	AHL	8	1	3	4				12																		
1975-76	**St. Louis Blues**	**NHL**	**80**	**4**	**26**	**30**	**4**	**20**	**24**	**20**	**3**	**0**	**1**	**100**	**4.0**	**92**	**17**	**112**	**40**	**+3**	**3**	**0**	**0**	**0**	**0**	**0**	**0**	**0**
1976-77	**St. Louis Blues**	**NHL**	**80**	**5**	**20**	**25**	**5**	**16**	**21**	**24**	**1**	**0**	**0**	**133**	**3.8**	**86**	**8**	**110**	**10**	**–22**	**4**	**0**	**0**	**0**	**0**	**0**	**0**	**0**
1977-78	**St. Louis Blues**	**NHL**	**75**	**4**	**14**	**18**	**4**	**11**	**15**	**26**	**0**	**0**	**1**	**95**	**4.2**	**54**	**6**	**122**	**18**	**–56**								
1978-79	**St. Louis Blues**	**NHL**	**26**	**1**	**3**	**4**	**1**	**2**	**3**	**12**	**0**	**0**	**0**	**34**	**2.9**	**15**	**2**	**28**	**2**	**–13**								
	Salt Lake Golden Eagles	CHL	48	8	31	39				30											10	0	4	4	2			
1979-80	**Vancouver Canucks**	**NHL**	**5**	**0**	**1**	**1**	**0**	**1**	**1**	**0**	**0**	**0**	**0**	**3**	**0.0**	**2**	**0**	**3**	**1**	**0**								
	Dallas Black Hawks	CHL	72	10	53	63				39																		
1980-81	Indianapolis Checkers	CHL	77	8	50	58				41											5	2	6	8	2			
1981-82	Indianapolis Checkers	CHL	16	5	17	22				4											13	1	17	18	16			
1982-83	Indianapolis Checkers	CHL	8	2	12	14				0											13	0	18	18	2			
1983-84	**New York Islanders**	**NHL**	**1**	**0**	**0**	**0**	**0**	**0**	**0**	**0**	**0**	**0**	**0**	**2**	**0.0**	**0**	**0**	**1**	**0**	**–1**								
	Indianapolis Checkers	CHL	54	13	40	53				18											2	0	0	0	0			
	NHL Totals		**280**	**14**	**66**	**80**	**14**	**52**	**66**	**86**	**4**	**0**	**2**	**370**	**3.8**	**262**	**33**	**382**	**71**		**8**	**0**	**0**	**0**	**0**	**0**	**0**	**0**

WCHA First All-Star Team (1973) • NCAA Championship All-Tournament Team (1973) • WCHA Second All-Star Team (1974) • CHL First All-Star Team (1980, 1981, 1984) • Won Bobby Orr Trophy (CHL's Top Defenseman) (1980, 1981, 1984) • Shared Tommy Ivan Trophy (CHL's MVP) with John Vanbiesbrouck (1984)

Traded to **St. Louis** by **California** for Frank Spring, January 9, 1975. Traded to **Vancouver** by **St. Louis** with Gord Buynak for cash, November 6, 1979. Traded to **St. Louis** by **Vancouver** with Gord Buynak for cash, February 28, 1980. Signed as a free agent by **NY Islanders**, September 22, 1980.

• AGNEW, JIM

Jim Agnew D – L. 6'1", 190 lbs. b: Hartney, Man., 3/21/1966. Vancouver's 10th choice, 157th overall, in 1984 Entry Draft.

Season	Club	League	GP	G	A	Pts	AG	AA	APts	PIM	PP	SH	GW	S	%	TGF	PGF	TGA	PGA	+/–	GP	G	A	Pts	PIM	PP	SH	GW
1982-83	Brandon Wheat Kings	WHL	14	1	1	2				9																		
1983-84	Brandon Wheat Kings	WHL	71	6	17	23				107											12	0	1	1	39			
1984-85	Brandon Wheat Kings	WHL	19	3	15	18				82																		
	Portland Winter Hawks	WHL	44	5	24	29				223											6	0	2	2	44			
1985-86	Portland Winter Hawks	WHL	70	6	30	36				286											9	0	1	1	48			
1986-87	**Vancouver Canucks**	**NHL**	**4**	**0**	**0**	**0**	**0**	**0**	**0**	**0**	**0**	**0**	**0**	**1**	**0.0**	**0**	**0**	**0**	**0**	**0**								
	Fredericton Express	AHL	67	0	5	5				261																		
1987-88	**Vancouver Canucks**	**NHL**	**10**	**0**	**1**	**1**	**0**	**1**	**1**	**16**	**0**	**0**	**0**	**4**	**0.0**	**6**	**0**	**7**	**2**	**+1**								
	Fredericton Express	AHL	63	2	8	10				188											14	0	2	2	43			
1988-89	Milwaukee Admirals	IHL	47	2	10	12				181											11	0	2	2	34			
1989-90	**Vancouver Canucks**	**NHL**	**7**	**0**	**0**	**0**	**0**	**0**	**0**	**36**	**0**	**0**	**0**	**3**	**0.0**	**3**	**0**	**4**	**0**	**–1**								
	Milwaukee Admirals	IHL	51	4	10	14				238																		
1990-91	**Vancouver Canucks**	**NHL**	**20**	**0**	**0**	**0**	**0**	**0**	**0**	**81**	**0**	**0**	**0**	**12**	**0.0**	**5**	**0**	**16**	**0**	**–11**								
	Milwaukee Admirals	IHL	3	0	0	0				33																		
1991-92	**Vancouver Canucks**	**NHL**	**24**	**0**	**0**	**0**	**0**	**0**	**0**	**56**	**0**	**0**	**0**	**9**	**0.0**	**3**	**0**	**8**	**4**	**–1**	**4**	**0**	**0**	**0**	**6**	**0**	**0**	**0**
1992-93	**Hartford Whalers**	**NHL**	**16**	**0**	**0**	**0**	**0**	**0**	**0**	**68**	**0**	**0**	**0**	**3**	**0.0**	**14**	**0**	**13**	**2**	**+3**								
	Springfield Indians	AHL	1	0	1	1				2																		
	NHL Totals		**81**	**0**	**1**	**1**	**0**	**1**	**1**	**257**	**0**	**0**	**0**	**32**	**0.0**	**31**	**0**	**48**	**8**		**4**	**0**	**0**	**0**	**6**	**0**	**0**	**0**

WHL West First All-Star Team (1986) • IHL Second All-Star Team (1990)

Signed as a free agent by **Hartford**, July 8, 1992.

• AHERN, FRED

Fred Ahern RW – R. 6', 180 lbs. b: Boston, MA, 2/12/1952.

Season	Club	League	GP	G	A	Pts	AG	AA	APts	PIM	PP	SH	GW	S	%	TGF	PGF	TGA	PGA	+/–	GP	G	A	Pts	PIM	PP	SH	GW
1972-73	Bowdoin College	NCAA	21	13	21	34																						
1973-74	Bowdoin College	NCAA	21	18	20	38																						
1974-75	**California Golden Seals**	**NHL**	**3**	**2**	**1**	**3**	**2**	**1**	**3**	**0**	**1**	**0**	**1**	**10**	**20.0**	**3**	**2**	**2**	**0**	**–1**								
	Salt Lake Golden Eagles	CHL	64	26	26	52				101											9	5	3	8	11			

Season	Club	League	GP	G	A	Pts	AG	AA	APts	PIM	PP	SH	GW	S	%	TGF	PGF	TGA	PGA	+/-	GP	G	A	Pts	PIM	PP	SH	GW
			REGULAR SEASON																		PLAYOFFS							
1975-76	**California Golden Seals**	**NHL**	**44**	**17**	**8**	**25**	**16**	**6**	**22**	**43**	**3**	**0**	**4**	**88**	**19.3**	**38**	**9**	**32**	**1**	**–2**								
	Salt Lake City Golden Eagles	CHL	30	12	14	26				57																		
1976-77	United States	C Cup	5	2	0	2				0																		
	Cleveland Barons	**NHL**	**25**	**4**	**4**	**8**	**4**	**3**	**7**	**20**	**2**	**0**	**0**	**45**	**8.9**	**9**	**4**	**17**	**0**	**–12**								
1977-78	**Cleveland Barons**	**NHL**	**36**	**3**	**4**	**7**	**3**	**3**	**6**	**48**	**0**	**0**	**1**	**37**	**8.1**	**10**	**1**	**26**	**1**	**–16**								
	Colorado Rockies	**NHL**	**38**	**5**	**13**	**18**	**5**	**11**	**16**	**19**	**1**	**0**	**0**	**66**	**7.6**	**24**	**4**	**36**	**0**	**–16**	**2**	**0**	**1**	**1**	**2**	**0**	**0**	**0**
1978-79	Binghamton Whalers	AHL	75	25	32	57				56											5	1	4	5	4			
1979-80	Adirondack Red Wings	AHL	38	4	6	10				34											5	0	1	1	2			
	Oklahoma City Stars	CHL	25	4	9	13				45																		
1980-81	Baltimore Clippers	EHL	7	3	1	4				0																		
1981-82	Cape Cod Buccaneers	ACHL	38	9	27	36				38																		
	NHL Totals		**146**	**31**	**30**	**61**	**30**	**24**	**54**	**130**	**7**	**0**	**6**	**246**	**12.6**	**84**	**20**	**113**	**2**		**2**	**0**	**1**	**1**	**2**	**0**	**0**	**0**

Signed as a free agent by **California**, September , 1974. Transferred to **Cleveland** after **California** franchise relocated, August 26, 1976. Traded to **Colorado** by **Cleveland** with Ralph Klassen for Rick Jodzio and Chuck Arnason, January 9, 1978. Traded to **Cleveland** by **Colorado** for cash, May 11, 1978. Placed on **Minnesota** reserve list after **Cleveland-Minnesota** Dispersal Draft, June 15, 1979.

● AHOLA, PETER

Peter Ahola D – L. 6'3", 205 lbs. b: Espoo, Finland, 5/14/1968.

Season	Club	League	GP	G	A	Pts	AG	AA	APts	PIM	PP	SH	GW	S	%	TGF	PGF	TGA	PGA	+/-	GP	G	A	Pts	PIM	PP	SH	GW
1989-90	Boston University	H.E.	43	3	20	23				65																		
1990-91	Boston University	H.E.	39	12	24	36				88																		
1991-92	**Los Angeles Kings**	**NHL**	**71**	**7**	**12**	**19**	**6**	**9**	**15**	**101**	**0**	**0**	**0**	**74**	**9.5**	**66**	**3**	**76**	**25**	**+12**	**6**	**0**	**0**	**0**	**2**	**0**	**0**	**0**
	Phoenix Roadrunners	IHL	7	3	3	6				34																		
1992-93	**Los Angeles Kings**	**NHL**	**8**	**1**	**1**	**2**	**1**	**1**	**2**	**6**	**0**	**0**	**0**	**3**	**33.3**	**5**	**0**	**7**	**0**	**–2**								
	Pittsburgh Penguins	**NHL**	**22**	**0**	**1**	**1**	**0**	**1**	**1**	**14**	**0**	**0**	**0**	**5**	**0.0**	**8**	**0**	**13**	**3**	**–2**								
	Cleveland Lumberjacks	IHL	9	1	0	1				4																		
	San Jose Sharks	**NHL**	**20**	**2**	**3**	**5**	**2**	**2**	**4**	**16**	**0**	**0**	**0**	**32**	**6.3**	**19**	**6**	**26**	**7**	**–8**								
1993-94	**Calgary Flames**	**NHL**	**2**	**0**	**0**	**0**	**0**	**0**	**0**	**0**	**0**	**0**	**0**	**1**	**0.0**	**0**	**0**	**0**	**0**	**0**								
	Saint John Flames	AHL	66	9	19	28				59											6	1	2	3	12			
1994-95	Kiekko-Espoo	Finland	50	12	21	33				96											4	5	1	6	10			
1995-96	Durham Wasps	Britain	32	11	27	38				117																		
	HIFK Helsinki	Finland	34	7	7	14				58											3	1	0	1	2			
1996-97	HIFK Helsinki	Finland	34	7	7	14				58											3	1	0	1	2			
1997-98	TPS Turku	EuroHL	6	0	0	0				8																		
	TPS Turku	Finland	46	6	17	23				36											4	0	0	0	6			
	NHL Totals		**123**	**10**	**17**	**27**	**9**	**13**	**22**	**137**	**0**	**0**	**0**	**115**	**8.7**	**98**	**9**	**122**	**35**		**6**	**0**	**0**	**0**	**2**	**0**	**0**	**0**

Signed as a free agent by **LA Kings**, April 5, 1991. Traded to **Pittsburgh** by **LA Kings** for Jeff Chychrun, November 6, 1992. Traded to **San Jose** by **Pittsburgh** for future considerations, February 26, 1993. Traded to **Tampa Bay** by **San Jose** for Dave Capuano, June 19, 1993. Traded to **Calgary** by **Tampa Bay** for cash, October 5, 1993.

● AHRENS, CHRIS

Chris Ahrens D – R. 6', 185 lbs. b: San Bernadino, CA, 7/31/1952. Minnesota's 4th choice, 76th overall, in 1972 Amateur Draft.

Season	Club	League	GP	G	A	Pts	AG	AA	APts	PIM	PP	SH	GW	S	%	TGF	PGF	TGA	PGA	+/-	GP	G	A	Pts	PIM	PP	SH	GW
1969-70	Kitchener Greenshirts	Jr. B	38	10	19	29				134																		
	Kitchener Rangers	OHA	4	1	0	1				0																		
1970-71	Kitchener Rangers	OHA	54	7	14	21				203																		
1971-72	Kitchener Rangers	OHA	40	3	22	25				64																		
1972-73	Cleveland-Jacksonville Barons	AHL	76	2	17	19				*248																		
	Minnesota North Stars	**NHL**																			**1**	**0**	**0**	**0**	**0**			
1973-74	**Minnesota North Stars**	**NHL**	**3**	**0**	**1**	**1**	**0**	**1**	**1**	**0**	**0**	**0**	**0**	**4**	**0.0**	**1**	**0**	**0**	**0**	**+1**								
	New Haven Nighthawks	AHL	73	4	20	24				177											10	1	0	1	*45			
1974-75	**Minnesota North Stars**	**NHL**	**44**	**0**	**2**	**2**	**0**	**2**	**2**	**77**	**0**	**0**	**0**	**20**	**0.0**	**8**	**1**	**41**	**7**	**–27**								
	New Haven Nighthawks	AHL	20	1	10	11				132											16	2	5	7	*106			
1975-76	**Minnesota North Stars**	**NHL**	**2**	**0**	**0**	**0**	**0**	**0**	**0**	**2**	**0**	**0**	**0**	**1**	**0.0**	**0**	**0**	**1**	**0**	**–1**								
	New Haven Nighthawks	AHL	70	2	8	10				121											3	0	0	0	12			
1976-77	**Minnesota North Stars**	**NHL**	**2**	**0**	**0**	**0**	**0**	**0**	**0**	**5**	**0**	**0**	**0**	**1**	**0.0**	**1**	**0**	**0**	**0**	**+1**								
	Rhode Island Reds	AHL	42	1	7	8				82																		
	New Haven Nighthawks	AHL	29	1	6	7				82																		
1977-78	**Minnesota North Stars**	**NHL**	**1**	**0**	**0**	**0**	**0**	**0**	**0**	**0**	**0**	**0**	**0**	**0**	**0.0**	**1**	**0**	**1**	**0**	**0**								
	Fort Worth Texans	CHL	50	1	10	11				137																		
	Edmonton Oilers	WHA	4	0	0	0				15																		
	NHL Totals		**52**	**0**	**3**	**3**	**0**	**3**	**3**	**84**	**0**	**0**	**0**	**26**	**0.0**	**11**	**1**	**43**	**7**		**1**	**0**	**0**	**0**	**0**	**0**	**0**	**0**
	Other Major League Totals		4	0	0	0				15																		

Selected by **NY Raiders** (WHA) in 1972 WHA General Player Draft, February 12, 1972. Traded to **Edmonton** (WHA) by **Minnesota** with Pierre Jarry for future considerations, March, 1978.

● AITKEN, BRAD

Brad Aitken LW – L. 6'2", 200 lbs. b: Scarborough, Ont., 10/30/1967. Pittsburgh's 3rd choice, 46th overall, in 1986 Entry Draft.

Season	Club	League	GP	G	A	Pts	AG	AA	APts	PIM	PP	SH	GW	S	%	TGF	PGF	TGA	PGA	+/-	GP	G	A	Pts	PIM	PP	SH	GW
1984-85	Peterborough Petes	OHL	63	18	26	44				36											13	1	2	3	0			
1985-86	Peterborough Petes	OHL	48	9	28	37				77																		
	Sault Ste. Marie Greyhounds	OHL	20	8	19	27				11																		
1986-87	Sault Ste. Marie Greyhounds	OHL	52	27	38	65				86											4	1	2	3	5			
1987-88	**Pittsburgh Penguins**	**NHL**	**5**	**1**	**1**	**2**	**1**	**1**	**2**	**0**	**0**	**0**	**0**	**4**	**25.0**	**2**	**0**	**1**	**0**	**+1**								
	Muskegon Lumberjacks	IHL	74	32	31	63				128											1	0	0	0	0			
1988-89	Muskegon Lumberjacks	IHL	74	35	30	65				139											13	5	5	10	75			
1989-90	Muskegon Lumberjacks	IHL	46	10	23	33				172																		
	Phoenix Roadrunners	IHL	8	2	1	3				18																		
	Fort Wayne Komets	IHL	13	5	2	7				0											5	2	1	3	12			
1990-91	**Pittsburgh Penguins**	**NHL**	**6**	**0**	**1**	**1**	**0**	**1**	**1**	**25**	**0**	**0**	**0**	**3**	**0.0**	**1**	**0**	**3**	**0**	**–2**								
	Muskegon Lumberjacks	IHL	44	14	17	31				143																		
	Kansas City Blades	IHL	6	4	6	10				2																		
	Edmonton Oilers	**NHL**	**3**	**0**	**1**	**1**	**0**	**1**	**1**	**0**	**0**	**0**	**0**	**0**	**0.0**	**1**	**0**	**2**	**0**	**–1**								
	Cape Breton Oilers	AHL	6	2	3	5				17											3	0	2	2	6			
1991-92	St. John's Maple Leafs	AHL	59	12	27	30				169																		
1992-93	St. John's Maple Leafs	AHL	4	0	1	1				2																		
	Raleigh IceCaps	ECHL	25	11	12	23				129											10	1	9	10	12			
	NHL Totals		**14**	**1**	**3**	**4**	**1**	**3**	**4**	**25**	**0**	**0**	**0**	**7**	**14.3**	**4**	**0**	**6**	**0**									

Traded to **Edmonton** by **Pittsburgh** for Kim Issel, March 5, 1991. Signed as a free agent by **Toronto**, July 30, 1991.

● AIVAZOFF, MICAH

Micah Aivazoff C – L. 6', 195 lbs. b: Powell River, B.C., 5/4/1969. Los Angeles' 6th choice, 109th overall, in 1988 Entry Draft.

Season	Club	League	GP	G	A	Pts	AG	AA	APts	PIM	PP	SH	GW	S	%	TGF	PGF	TGA	PGA	+/-	GP	G	A	Pts	PIM	PP	SH	GW
1986-87	Victoria Cougars	WHL	72	18	39	57				112											5	1	0	1	2			
1987-88	Victoria Cougars	WHL	69	26	57	83				79											8	3	4	7	14			
1988-89	Victoria Cougars	WHL	70	35	65	100				136											8	5	7	12	2			
1989-90	New Haven Nighthawks	AHL	77	20	39	59				71																		
1990-91	New Haven Nighthawks	AHL	79	11	29	40				84																		
1991-92	Adirondack Red Wings	AHL	61	9	20	29				50											19	2	8	10	25			
1992-93	Adirondack Red Wings	AHL	79	32	53	85				100											11	8	6	14	10			
1993-94	**Detroit Red Wings**	**NHL**	**59**	**4**	**4**	**8**	**4**	**3**	**7**	**38**	**0**	**0**	**0**	**52**	**7.7**	**16**	**1**	**20**	**4**	**–1**								
1994-95	**Edmonton Oilers**	**NHL**	**21**	**0**	**1**	**1**	**0**	**1**	**1**	**2**	**0**	**0**	**0**	**6**	**0.0**	**2**	**0**	**4**	**0**	**–2**								
1995-96	**New York Islanders**	**NHL**	**12**	**0**	**1**	**1**	**0**	**1**	**1**	**6**	**0**	**0**	**0**	**8**	**0.0**	**2**	**1**	**8**	**1**	**–6**								
	Utah Grizzlies	IHL	59	14	21	35				58											22	3	5	8	33			
1996-97	Binghamton Rangers	AHL	75	12	36	48				70											4	1	1	2	0			
1997-98	San Antonio Dragons	IHL	54	13	33	46				33																		
	NHL Totals		**92**	**4**	**6**	**10**	**4**	**5**	**9**	**46**	**0**	**0**	**0**	**66**	**6.1**	**20**	**2**	**32**	**5**									

Signed as a free agent by **Detroit**, March 18, 1993. Claimed by **Pittsburgh** from **Detroit** in Waiver Draft, January 18, 1995. Claimed by **Edmonton** from **Pittsburgh** in Waiver Draft, January 18, 1995. Signed as a free agent by **NY Islanders**, August 23, 1995. Signed as a free agent by **NY Rangers**, August 23, 1996.

• ALBELIN, TOMMY

Tommy Albelin D – L. 6'1", 190 lbs. b: Stockholm, Sweden, 5/21/1964. Quebec's 7th choice, 158th overall, in 1983 Entry Draft.

			REGULAR SEASON																		PLAYOFFS							
Season	Club	League	GP	G	A	Pts	AG	AA	APts	PIM	PP	SH	GW	S	%	TGF	PGF	TGA	PGA	+/–	GP	G	A	Pts	PIM	PP	SH	GW
1982-83	Djurgardens IF Stockholm	Sweden	19	2	5	7				4											6	1	0	1	2			
	Sweden	WJC-A	7	0	3	3																						
1983-84	Djurgardens IF Stockholm	Sweden	30	9	5	14				26											4	0	1	1	2			
	Sweden	WJC-A	7	1	3	4				10																		
1984-85	Djurgardens IF Stockholm	Sweden	32	9	8	17				22											8	2	1	3	4			
	Sweden	WEC-A	10	1	0	1				10																		
1985-86	Djurgardens IF Stockholm	Sweden	35	4	8	12				26																		
	Sweden	WEC-A	10	3	0	3				12																		
1986-87	Djurgardens IF Stockholm	Sweden	33	7	5	12				49											2	0	0	0	0			
	Sweden	WEC-A	10	1	5	6				12																		
1987-88	Sweden	C Cup	6	2	2	4				2																		
	Quebec Nordiques	**NHL**	**60**	**3**	**23**	**26**	**3**	**16**	**19**	**47**	**0**	**0**	**0**	**98**	**3.1**	**66**	**26**	**59**	**12**	**–7**								
1988-89	**Quebec Nordiques**	**NHL**	**14**	**2**	**4**	**6**	**2**	**3**	**5**	**27**	**1**	**0**	**1**	**16**	**12.5**	**16**	**5**	**17**	**0**	**–6**								
	Halifax Citadels	AHL	8	2	5	7				4																		
	New Jersey Devils	**NHL**	**46**	**7**	**24**	**31**	**6**	**17**	**23**	**40**	**1**	**1**	**1**	**82**	**8.5**	**83**	**23**	**50**	**8**	**+18**								
	Sweden	WEC-A	7	0	2	2				8																		
1989-90	**New Jersey Devils**	**NHL**	**68**	**6**	**23**	**29**	**5**	**16**	**21**	**63**	**4**	**0**	**0**	**125**	**4.8**	**86**	**23**	**74**	**10**	**–1**								
1990-91	**New Jersey Devils**	**NHL**	**47**	**2**	**12**	**14**	**2**	**9**	**11**	**44**	**1**	**0**	**0**	**66**	**3.0**	**47**	**14**	**36**	**4**	**+1**	**3**	**0**	**1**	**1**	**2**	**0**	**0**	**0**
	Utica Devils	AHL	14	4	2	6				10																		
1991-92	Sweden	C Cup	6	0	0	0				6																		
	New Jersey Devils	**NHL**	**19**	**0**	**4**	**4**	**0**	**3**	**3**	**4**	**0**	**0**	**0**	**18**	**0.0**	**19**	**0**	**15**	**3**	**+7**	**1**	**1**	**1**	**2**	**0**	**0**	**0**	**0**
	Utica Devils	AHL	11	4	6	10				4																		
1992-93	**New Jersey Devils**	**NHL**	**36**	**1**	**5**	**6**	**1**	**3**	**4**	**14**	**1**	**0**	**1**	**33**	**3.0**	**33**	**7**	**35**	**9**	**0**	**5**	**2**	**0**	**2**	**0**	**1**	**0**	**1**
1993-94	**New Jersey Devils**	**NHL**	**62**	**2**	**17**	**19**	**2**	**13**	**15**	**36**	**1**	**0**	**1**	**62**	**3.2**	**61**	**13**	**50**	**22**	**+20**	**20**	**2**	**5**	**7**	**14**	**1**	**0**	**1**
	Albany River Rats	AHL	4	0	2	2				17																		
1994-95	**New Jersey Devils**	**NHL**	**48**	**5**	**10**	**15**	**9**	**15**	**24**	**20**	**2**	**0**	**0**	**60**	**8.3**	**43**	**4**	**39**	**9**	**+9**	**20**	**1**	**7**	**8**	**2**	**0**	**0**	**0**
1995-96	**New Jersey Devils**	**NHL**	**53**	**1**	**12**	**13**	**1**	**10**	**11**	**14**	**0**	**0**	**0**	**90**	**1.1**	**37**	**12**	**31**	**6**	**0**								
	Calgary Flames	**NHL**	**20**	**0**	**1**	**1**	**0**	**1**	**1**	**4**	**0**	**0**	**0**	**31**	**0.0**	**13**	**2**	**17**	**7**	**+1**	**4**	**0**	**0**	**0**	**0**	**0**	**0**	**0**
1996-97	Sweden	W Cup	4	1	0	1				2																		
	Calgary Flames	**NHL**	**72**	**4**	**11**	**15**	**4**	**10**	**14**	**14**	**2**	**0**	**0**	**103**	**3.9**	**69**	**21**	**75**	**19**	**–8**								
	Sweden	WC-A	11	1	3	4				2																		
1997-98	**Calgary Flames**	**NHL**	**69**	**2**	**17**	**19**	**2**	**17**	**19**	**32**	**1**	**0**	**2**	**88**	**2.3**	**67**	**11**	**82**	**35**	**+9**								
	Sweden	Olympics	3	0	0	0				4																		
	NHL Totals		**614**	**35**	**163**	**198**	**37**	**133**	**170**	**359**	**14**	**1**	**6**	**872**	**4.0**	**640**	**161**	**580**	**144**		**53**	**6**	**14**	**20**	**18**	**2**	**0**	**2**

Swedish World All-Star Team (1987, 1997)

Traded to **New Jersey** by **Quebec** for New Jersey's 4th round choice (Niclas Andersson) in 1989 Entry Draft, December 12, 1988. Traded to **Calgary** by **New Jersey** with Cale Hulse and Jocelyn Lemieux for Phil Housley and Dan Keczmer, February 26, 1996.

• ALEXANDER, CLAIRE

Claire "The Milkman" Alexander D – R. 6'1", 175 lbs. b: Collingwood, Ont., 6/16/1945.

Season	Club	League	GP	G	A	Pts	AG	AA	APts	PIM	PP	SH	GW	S	%	TGF	PGF	TGA	PGA	+/–	GP	G	A	Pts	PIM	PP	SH	GW
1965-66	Kitchener Rangers	OHA	45	2	15	17				26											15	0	0	0	0			
1966-67	Johnstown–Knoxville	EHL	67	17	20	37				39																		
1967-68	Collingwood Kings	OHA Sr.	40	17	32	49				36																		
1968-69	Collingwood Kings	OHA Sr.	39	30	32	62				16																		
1969-70	Orillia Terriers	OHA Sr.	27	23	5	28				24																		
1970-71	Orillia Terriers	OHA Sr	37	26	35	51				48																		
1971-72	Orillia Terriers	OHA Sr.	38	13	28	41				42																		
1972-73	Orillia Terriers	OHA Sr	38	17	29	46				40																		
	Tulsa Oilers	CHL	5	5	1	6				9																		
1973-74	Oklahoma City Blazers	CHL	72	23	37	60				34											9	3	4	7	2			
1974-75	**Toronto Maple Leafs**	**NHL**	**42**	**7**	**11**	**18**	**6**	**9**	**15**	**12**	**4**	**0**	**1**	**90**	**7.8**	**54**	**13**	**32**	**2**	**+11**	**7**	**0**	**0**	**0**	**0**	**0**	**0**	**0**
	Oklahoma City Blazers	CHL	33	8	17	25				14																		
1975-76	**Toronto Maple Leafs**	**NHL**	**33**	**2**	**6**	**8**	**2**	**5**	**7**	**6**	**0**	**0**	**0**	**46**	**4.3**	**23**	**7**	**18**	**2**	**0**	**9**	**2**	**4**	**6**	**4**	**1**	**0**	**0**
	Oklahoma City Blazers	CHL	43	25	31	56				22																		
1976-77	**Toronto Maple Leafs**	**NHL**	**48**	**1**	**12**	**13**	**1**	**10**	**11**	**12**	**0**	**0**	**0**	**61**	**1.6**	**31**	**5**	**32**	**2**	**–4**								
1977-78	**Vancouver Canucks**	**NHL**	**32**	**8**	**18**	**26**	**8**	**15**	**23**	**6**	**4**	**0**	**0**	**105**	**7.6**	**53**	**21**	**47**	**8**	**–7**								
	Tulsa Oilers	CHL	46	14	42	56				22																		
1978-79	Edmonton Oilers	WHA	54	8	23	31				16																		
	Dallas Black Hawks	CHL	7	1	2	3				0											6	1	2	3	4			
1979-80	Bad Nauheim	Germany	44	32	18	50				96																		
1980-81	Bad Nauheim	Germany	38	16	18	34				48											5	4	1	5	27			
	NHL Totals		**155**	**18**	**47**	**65**	**17**	**39**	**56**	**36**	**8**	**0**	**1**	**302**	**6.0**	**161**	**46**	**129**	**14**		**16**	**2**	**4**	**6**	**4**	**1**	**0**	**0**
	Other Major League Totals		54	8	23	31				16																		

CHL First All-Star Team (1974) • Won Ken McKenzie Trophy (CHL's Rookie of the Year) (1974) • Named CHL's Top Defenseman (1974) • CHL Second All-Star Team (1978)

Signed to five-game tryout by **Tulsa Oilers** (CHL), January, 1973. Signed as a free agent by **Toronto**, September, 1974. Traded to **Vancouver** by **Toronto** for cash, January 29, 1978. Signed as a free agent by **Edmonton** (WHA), June, 1978.

• ALFREDSSON, DANIEL

Daniel Alfredsson RW – R. 5'11", 200 lbs. b: Goteborg, Sweden, 12/11/1972. Ottawa's 5th choice, 133rd overall, in 1994 Entry Draft.

Season	Club	League	GP	G	A	Pts	AG	AA	APts	PIM	PP	SH	GW	S	%	TGF	PGF	TGA	PGA	+/–	GP	G	A	Pts	PIM	PP	SH	GW
1991-92	Molndal	Sweden 2	32	12	8	20				43																		
1992-93	Vastra Frolunda	Sweden	20	1	5	6				8																		
1993-94	Vastra Frolunda	Sweden	39	20	10	30				18											4	1	1	2				
1994-95	Vastra Frolunda	Sweden	22	7	11	18				22																		
	Sweden	WC-A	8	3	1	4				4																		
1995-96	**Ottawa Senators**	**NHL**	**82**	**26**	**35**	**61**	**26**	**29**	**55**	**28**	**8**	**2**	**3**	**212**	**12.3**	**89**	**38**	**82**	**13**	**–18**								
	Sweden	WC-A	6	1	2	3				4																		
1996-97	Sweden	W Cup	4	0	0	0				2																		
	Ottawa Senators	**NHL**	**76**	**24**	**47**	**71**	**26**	**42**	**68**	**30**	**11**	**1**	**1**	**247**	**9.7**	**97**	**37**	**67**	**12**	**+5**	**7**	**5**	**2**	**7**	**6**	**3**	**0**	**2**
1997-98	**Ottawa Senators**	**NHL**	**55**	**17**	**28**	**45**	**20**	**27**	**47**	**18**	**7**	**0**	**7**	**149**	**11.4**	**59**	**24**	**33**	**5**	**+7**	**11**	**7**	**2**	**9**	**20**	**2**	**1**	**1**
	Sweden	Olympics	4	2	3	5				2																		
	NHL Totals		**213**	**67**	**110**	**177**	**72**	**98**	**170**	**76**	**26**	**3**	**11**	**608**	**11.0**	**245**	**99**	**182**	**30**		**18**	**12**	**4**	**16**	**26**	**5**	**1**	**3**

NHL All-Rookie Team (1996) • Won Calder Memorial Trophy (1996)

Played in NHL All-Star Game (1996, 1997, 1998)

• ALLAN, JEFF

Jeff Allan D – L. 6' 1", 194 lbs. b: Hull, Quebec, 5/17/1957. Cleveland's 7th choice, 95th overall, in 1977 Amateur Draft.

Season	Club	League	GP	G	A	Pts	AG	AA	APts	PIM	PP	SH	GW	S	%	TGF	PGF	TGA	PGA	+/–	GP	G	A	Pts	PIM	PP	SH	GW
1974-75	Cornwall Royals	QMJHL	71	10	30	40				86																		
1975-76	Cornwall Royals	QMJHL	17	5	8	13				40																		
	Peterborough Petes	OHA	43	1	8	9				47																		
1976-77	Hull Festivals	QMJHL	68	15	33	48				76																		
1977-78	**Cleveland Barons**	**NHL**	**4**	**0**	**0**	**0**	**0**	**0**	**0**	**2**	**0**	**0**	**0**	**5**	**0.0**	**3**	**0**	**3**	**0**	**0**								
	Cincinnati Stingers	WHA	2	0	0	0				0																		
	Hampton Gulls	AHL	8	0	0	0				0																		
	Phoenix Roadrunners	CHL	6	0	0	0				2																		
	Toledo Goaldiggers	IHL	44	7	20	27				89											17	2	2	4	20			
1978-79	Toledo Goaldiggers	IHL	3	0	0	0				11																		
	Los Angeles Blades	PHL	19	6	5	11				100																		
	NHL Totals		**4**	**0**	**0**	**0**	**0**	**0**	**0**	**2**	**0**	**0**	**0**	**5**	**0.0**	**3**	**0**	**3**	**0**									
	Other Major League Totals		2	0	0	0				0																		

Selected by **Cincinnati** (WHA) in 1977 WHA Amateur Draft, May, 1977.

● ALLEN, CHRIS

Chris Allen D – R. 6'2", 193 lbs. b: Chatham, Ont., 5/8/1978 Florida's 2nd choice, 60th overall, in 1996 Entry Draft.

			REGULAR SEASON																		PLAYOFFS							
Season	Club	League	GP	G	A	Pts	AG	AA	APts	PIM	PP	SH	GW	S	%	TGF	PGF	TGA	PGA	+/-	GP	G	A	Pts	PIM	PP	SH	GW
1994-95	Kingston Frontenacs	OHL	43	3	5	8				15											2	0	0	0	0			
1995-96	Kingston Frontenacs	OHL	55	21	18	39				58											6	0	2	2	8			
1996-97	Kingston Frontenacs	OHL	61	14	29	43				81											5	1	2	3	4			
	Carolina Monarchs	AHL	9	0	0	0				2																		
1997-98	Kingston Frontenacs	OHL	66	38	57	95				91											10	4	2	6	6			
	Florida Panthers	**NHL**	**1**	**0**	**0**	**0**	**0**	**0**	**0**	**2**	**0**	**0**	**0**	**1**	**0.0**	**1**	**0**	**1**	**0**	**0**								
	NHL Totals		**1**	**0**	**0**	**0**	**0**	**0**	**0**	**2**	**0**	**0**	**0**	**1**	**0.0**	**1**	**0**	**1**	**0**									

OHL First All-Star Team (1998) • Canadian Major Junior First All-Star Team (1998)

● ALLEN, PETER

Peter Allen D – R. 6'2", 195 lbs. b: Calgary, Alta., 3/6/1970. Boston's 1st choice, 24th overall, in 1991 Supplemental Draft.

Season	Club	League	GP	G	A	Pts	AG	AA	APts	PIM	PP	SH	GW	S	%	TGF	PGF	TGA	PGA	+/-	GP	G	A	Pts	PIM	PP	SH	GW
1989-90	Yale University	ECAC	26	2	4	6				16																		
1990-91	Yale University	ECAC	17	0	6	6				14																		
1991-92	Yale University	ECAC	26	5	13	18				26																		
1992-93	Yale University	ECAC	30	3	15	18				32																		
1993-94	Richmond Renegades	ECHL	52	2	16	18				62																		
	P.E.I. Senators	AHL	6	0	1	1				6																		
1994-95	Canada	Nat-Team	52	5	15	20				36																		
	Canada	WC-A	7	0	0	0				4																		
1995-96	**Pittsburgh Penguins**	**NHL**	**8**	**0**	**0**	**0**	**0**	**0**	**0**	**8**	**0**	**0**	**0**	**2**	**0.0**	**4**	**0**	**2**	**0**	**+2**								
	Cleveland Lumberjacks	IHL	65	3	45	48				55											3	0	0	0	2			
1996-97	Cleveland Lumberjacks	IHL	81	14	31	45				75											14	0	6	6	24			
1997-98	Kentucky Thoroughblades	AHL	72	0	18	18				73											3	0	1	1	4			
	NHL Totals		**8**	**0**	**0**	**0**	**0**	**0**	**0**	**8**	**0**	**0**	**0**	**2**	**0.0**	**4**	**0**	**2**	**0**									

Signed as a free agent by **Pittsburgh**, August 10, 1995. Signed as a free agent by **San Jose**, August 19, 1997.

● ALLEY, STEVE

Steve Alley LW – L. 6', 185 lbs. b: Anoka, MN, 12/29/1953. Chicago's 10th choice, 141st overall, in 1973 Amateur Draft.

Season	Club	League	GP	G	A	Pts	AG	AA	APts	PIM	PP	SH	GW	S	%	TGF	PGF	TGA	PGA	+/-	GP	G	A	Pts	PIM	PP	SH	GW
1972-73	University of Wisconsin	WCHA	40	8	15	23				12																		
1973-74	University of Wisconsin	WCHA	36	12	19	31				16																		
1974-75	University of Wisconsin	WCHA	38	23	25	48				84																		
	United States	WEC-A	9	1	1	2				2																		
1975-76	United States	Nat-Team	64	29	33	62				67																		
	United States	Olympics	6	1	1	2				4																		
1976-77	University of Wisconsin	WCHA	45	32	31	63				50																		
1977-78	Birmingham Bulls	WHA	27	8	12	20				11											5	1	0	1	5			
	Hampton Gulls	AHL	30	6	3	9				27																		
	Springfield Indians	AHL	1	0	0	0				0																		
	United States	WEC-A	3	0	0	0				0																		
1978-79	Birmingham Bulls	WHA	78	17	24	41				36																		
1979-80	**Hartford Whalers**	**NHL**	**7**	**1**	**1**	**2**	**1**	**1**	**2**	**0**	**0**	**0**	**0**	**5**	**20.0**	**2**	**0**	**6**	**0**	**–4**	**3**	**0**	**1**	**1**	**0**	**0**	**0**	**0**
	Springfield Indians	AHL	59	25	28	53				46																		
	Cincinnati Stingers	CHL	10	3	6	9				12																		
1980-81	**Hartford Whalers**	**NHL**	**8**	**2**	**2**	**4**	**2**	**1**	**3**	**11**	**0**	**0**	**0**	**10**	**20.0**	**8**	**0**	**7**	**0**	**+1**								
	Binghamton Whalers	AHL	69	26	32	58				34											6	3	1	4	9			
	NHL Totals		**15**	**3**	**3**	**6**	**3**	**2**	**5**	**11**	**0**	**0**	**0**	**15**	**20.0**	**10**	**0**	**13**	**0**		**3**	**0**	**1**	**1**	**0**	**0**	**0**	**0**
	Other Major League Totals		105	25	36	61				47											5	1	0	1	5			

Selected by **New England** (WHA) in 1973 WHA Amateur Draft, June, 1973. WHA rights traded to **Birmingham** (WHA) by **New England** (WHA) for future considerations, July, 1977. Claimed by **Hartford** from **Birmingham** (WHA) in 1979 WHA Dispersal Draft, June 9, 1979.

● ALLISON, DAVE

Dave Allison D – R. 6'1", 200 lbs. b: Fort Frances, Ont., 4/14/1959.

Season	Club	League	GP	G	A	Pts	AG	AA	APts	PIM	PP	SH	GW	S	%	TGF	PGF	TGA	PGA	+/-	GP	G	A	Pts	PIM	PP	SH	GW
1976-77	Cornwall Royals	QMJHL	63	2	11	13				180											12	0	4	4	60			
1977-78	Cornwall Royals	QMJHL	60	9	29	38				302											5	2	3	5	32			
1978-79	Cornwall Royals	QMJHL	66	7	31	38				407											7	1	6	7	34			
1979-80	Nova Scotia Voyageurs	AHL	49	1	12	13				119											4	0	0	0	46			
1980-81	Nova Scotia Voyageurs	AHL	70	5	12	17				298											6	0	0	0	15			
1981-82	Nova Scotia Voyageurs	AHL	78	8	25	33				*332											9	0	3	3	*84			
1982-83	Nova Scotia Voyageurs	AHL	70	3	22	25				180											7	0	2	2	24			
1983-84	**Montreal Canadiens**	**NHL**	**3**	**0**	**0**	**0**	**0**	**0**	**0**	**12**	**0**	**0**	**0**	**2**	**0.0**	**1**	**0**	**3**	**0**	**–2**								
	Nova Scotia Voyageurs	AHL	53	2	18	20				155											6	0	3	3	25			
1984-85	Sherbrooke Canadiens	AHL	4	0	1	1				19																		
	Nova Scotia Voyageurs	AHL	68	4	18	22				175											6	0	2	2	10			
1985-86	Muskegon Lumberjacks	IHL	66	7	30	37				247											14	2	9	11	46			
1986-87	Muskegon Lumberjacks	IHL	67	11	35	46				337											15	4	3	7	20			
1987-88	Newmarket Saints	AHL	48	1	9	10				166																		
1988-89	Halifax Citadels	AHL	12	1	2	3				29																		
	Indianapolis Ice	IHL	34	0	7	7				105																		
	NHL Totals		**3**	**0**	**0**	**0**	**0**	**0**	**0**	**12**	**0**	**0**	**0**	**2**	**0.0**	**1**	**0**	**3**	**0**									

Signed as a free agent by **Montreal**, October 4, 1979. Traded to **Toronto** by **NY Rangers** for Walt Poddubny, August 18, 1986.

● ALLISON, JAMIE

Jamie Allison D – L. 6'1", 190 lbs. b: Lindsay, Ont., 5/13/1975. Calgary's 2nd choice, 44th overall, in 1993 Entry Draft.

Season	Club	League	GP	G	A	Pts	AG	AA	APts	PIM	PP	SH	GW	S	%	TGF	PGF	TGA	PGA	+/-	GP	G	A	Pts	PIM	PP	SH	GW
1991-92	Windsor Spitfires	OHL	59	4	8	12				70											4	1	1	2	2			
1992-93	Detroit Jr. Red Wings	OHL	61	0	13	13				64											15	2	5	7	23			
1993-94	Detroit Jr. Red Wings	OHL	40	2	22	24				69											17	2	9	11	35			
1994-95	Detroit Jr. Red Wings	OHL	50	1	14	15				119											18	2	7	9	35			
	Calgary Flames	**NHL**	**1**	**0**	**0**	**0**	**0**	**0**	**0**	**0**	**0**	**0**	**0**	**0**	**0.0**	**0**	**0**	**0**	**0**	**0**								
1995-96	Saint John Flames	AHL	71	3	16	19				223											14	0	2	2	16			
1996-97	**Calgary Flames**	**NHL**	**20**	**0**	**0**	**0**	**0**	**0**	**0**	**35**	**0**	**0**	**0**	**8**	**0.0**	**6**	**0**	**16**	**6**	**–4**								
	Saint John Flames	AHL	46	3	6	9				139											5	0	1	1	4			
1997-98	**Calgary Flames**	**NHL**	**43**	**3**	**8**	**11**	**4**	**8**	**12**	**104**	**0**	**0**	**1**	**27**	**11.1**	**28**	**0**	**29**	**4**	**+3**								
	Saint John Flames	AHL	16	0	5	5				49																		
	NHL Totals		**64**	**3**	**8**	**11**	**4**	**8**	**12**	**139**	**0**	**0**	**1**	**35**	**8.6**	**34**	**0**	**45**	**10**									

● ALLISON, JASON

Jason Allison C – R. 6'3", 205 lbs. b: North York, Ont., 5/29/1975. Washington's 2nd choice, 17th overall, in 1993 Entry Draft.

Season	Club	League	GP	G	A	Pts	AG	AA	APts	PIM	PP	SH	GW	S	%	TGF	PGF	TGA	PGA	+/-	GP	G	A	Pts	PIM	PP	SH	GW
1991-92	London Knights	OHL	65	11	19	30				15											7	0	0	0	0			
1992-93	London Knights	OHL	66	42	76	118				50											12	7	13	20	8			
1993-94	London Knights	OHL	56	55	87	*142				68											5	2	13	15	13			
	Canada	WJC-A	7	3	6	9				2																		
	Washington Capitals	**NHL**	**2**	**0**	**1**	**1**	**0**	**1**	**1**	**0**	**0**	**0**	**0**	**5**	**0.0**	**3**	**1**	**1**	**0**	**+1**								
	Portland Pirates	AHL																			6	2	1	3	0			
1994-95	London Knights	OHL	15	15	21	36				43																		
	Canada	WJC-A	7	3	12	15				6																		
	Washington Capitals	**NHL**	**12**	**2**	**1**	**3**	**4**	**1**	**5**	**6**	**2**	**0**	**0**	**9**	**22.2**	**5**	**4**	**4**	**0**	**–3**								
	Portland Pirates	AHL	8	5	4	9				2											7	3	8	11	2			
1995-96	**Washington Capitals**	**NHL**	**19**	**0**	**3**	**3**	**0**	**2**	**2**	**2**	**0**	**0**	**0**	**18**	**0.0**	**7**	**2**	**8**	**0**	**–3**								
	Portland Pirates	AHL	57	28	41	69				42											6	1	6	7	9			

			REGULAR SEASON																		PLAYOFFS							
Season	Club	League	GP	G	A	Pts	AG	AA	APts	PIM	PP	SH	GW	S	%	TGF	PGF	TGA	PGA	+/–	GP	G	A	Pts	PIM	PP	SH	GW
1996-97	**Washington Capitals**	**NHL**	**53**	**5**	**17**	**22**	**5**	**15**	**20**	**25**	**1**	**0**	**1**	**71**	**7.0**	**32**	**10**	**25**	**0**	**–3**	....	....	....	....	....	....	....	....
	Boston Bruins	**NHL**	**19**	**3**	**9**	**12**	**3**	**8**	**11**	**9**	**1**	**0**	**0**	**28**	**10.7**	**17**	**6**	**14**	**0**	**–3**	....	....	....	....	....	....	....	....
1997-98	**Boston Bruins**	**NHL**	**81**	**33**	**50**	**83**	**39**	**49**	**88**	**60**	**5**	**0**	**8**	**158**	**20.9**	**113**	**40**	**44**	**4**	**+33**	**6**	**2**	**6**	**8**	**4**	**1**	**0**	**0**
	NHL Totals		**186**	**43**	**81**	**124**	**51**	**76**	**127**	**102**	**9**	**0**	**9**	**289**	**14.9**	**177**	**63**	**96**	**4**		**6**	**2**	**6**	**8**	**4**	**1**	**0**	**0**

OHL First All-Star Team (1994) • Canadian Major Junior First All-Star Team (1994) • Canadian Major Junior Player of the Year (1994) • WJC-A All-Star Team (1995)

Traded to **Boston** by **Washington** with Jim Carey, Anson Carter and Washington's 3rd round choice (Lee Goren) in 1997 Entry Draft for Bill Ranford, Adam Oates and Rick Tocchet, March 1, 1997.

• ALLISON, MIKE

Mike "Red Dog" Allison LW – R. 6', 200 lbs. b: Fort Frances, Ont., 3/28/1961. NY Rangers' 2nd choice, 35th overall, in 1980 Entry Draft.

Season	Club	League	GP	G	A	Pts	AG	AA	APts	PIM	PP	SH	GW	S	%	TGF	PGF	TGA	PGA	+/–	GP	G	A	Pts	PIM	PP	SH	GW
1977-78	New Westminster Bruins	WCJHL	5	0	1	1	....	....	....	2	....	....	....	....	....	....	....	....	....	....	....	....	....	....	....	....	....	....
	Kenora Thistles	MJHL	47	30	36	66	....	....	....	70	....	....	....	....	....	....	....	....	....	....	....	....	....	....	....	....	....	....
1978-79	Sudbury Wolves	OHA	59	24	32	56	....	....	....	41	....	....	....	....	....	....	....	....	....	....	10	4	2	6	18	....	....	....
1979-80	Sudbury Wolves	OHA	67	24	71	95	....	....	....	74	....	....	....	....	....	....	....	....	....	....	9	8	6	14	6	....	....	....
1980-81	**New York Rangers**	**NHL**	**75**	**26**	**38**	**64**	**21**	**27**	**48**	**83**	**4**	**0**	**2**	**122**	**21.3**	**96**	**23**	**67**	**6**	**+12**	**14**	**3**	**1**	**4**	**20**	**1**	**0**	**2**
1981-82	**New York Rangers**	**NHL**	**48**	**7**	**15**	**22**	**6**	**10**	**16**	**74**	**0**	**0**	**0**	**62**	**11.3**	**32**	**2**	**34**	**1**	**–3**	**10**	**1**	**3**	**4**	**18**	**0**	**0**	**0**
	Springfield Indians	AHL	2	0	0	0	....	....	....	0	....	....	....	....	....	....	....	....	....	....	....	....	....	....	....	....	....	....
1982-83	**New York Rangers**	**NHL**	**39**	**11**	**9**	**20**	**9**	**6**	**15**	**37**	**1**	**0**	**0**	**45**	**24.4**	**30**	**5**	**18**	**1**	**+8**	**8**	**0**	**5**	**5**	**10**	**0**	**0**	**0**
	Tulsa Oilers	CHL	6	2	2	4	....	....	....	2	....	....	....	....	....	....	....	....	....	....	....	....	....	....	....	....	....	....
1983-84	**New York Rangers**	**NHL**	**45**	**8**	**12**	**20**	**6**	**8**	**14**	**64**	**0**	**0**	**2**	**52**	**15.4**	**31**	**0**	**34**	**8**	**+5**	**5**	**0**	**1**	**1**	**6**	**0**	**0**	**0**
1984-85	**New York Rangers**	**NHL**	**31**	**9**	**15**	**24**	**7**	**10**	**17**	**17**	**2**	**0**	**1**	**46**	**19.6**	**33**	**7**	**32**	**6**	**0**	....	....	....	....	....	....	....	....
1985-86	**New York Rangers**	**NHL**	**28**	**2**	**13**	**15**	**2**	**9**	**11**	**22**	**0**	**0**	**0**	**26**	**7.7**	**18**	**0**	**15**	**1**	**+4**	**16**	**0**	**2**	**2**	**38**	**0**	**0**	**0**
	New Haven Nighthawks	AHL	9	6	6	12	....	....	....	4	....	....	....	....	....	....	....	....	....	....	....	....	....	....	....	....	....	....
1986-87	**Toronto Maple Leafs**	**NHL**	**71**	**7**	**16**	**23**	**6**	**12**	**18**	**66**	**1**	**3**	**2**	**48**	**14.6**	**41**	**3**	**70**	**33**	**+1**	**13**	**3**	**5**	**8**	**15**	**1**	**0**	**2**
1987-88	**Toronto Maple Leafs**	**NHL**	**15**	**0**	**3**	**3**	**0**	**2**	**2**	**10**	**0**	**0**	**0**	**7**	**0.0**	**4**	**0**	**4**	**0**	**0**	....	....	....	....	....	....	....	....
	Los Angeles Kings	**NHL**	**37**	**16**	**12**	**28**	**14**	**9**	**23**	**57**	**5**	**1**	**2**	**54**	**29.6**	**45**	**15**	**38**	**11**	**+3**	**5**	**0**	**0**	**0**	**16**	**0**	**0**	**0**
1988-89	**Los Angeles Kings**	**NHL**	**55**	**14**	**22**	**36**	**12**	**15**	**27**	**122**	**6**	**0**	**2**	**71**	**19.7**	**58**	**15**	**40**	**4**	**+7**	**7**	**1**	**0**	**1**	**10**	**0**	**0**	**0**
1989-90	**Los Angeles Kings**	**NHL**	**55**	**2**	**11**	**13**	**2**	**8**	**10**	**78**	**0**	**0**	**1**	**25**	**8.0**	**29**	**2**	**44**	**11**	**–6**	**4**	**1**	**0**	**1**	**2**	**0**	**1**	**0**
	New Haven Nighthawks	AHL	5	2	2	4	....	....	....	14	....	....	....	....	....	....	....	....	....	....	....	....	....	....	....	....	....	....
	NHL Totals		**499**	**102**	**166**	**268**	**85**	**116**	**201**	**630**	**19**	**4**	**12**	**558**	**18.3**	**417**	**72**	**396**	**82**		**82**	**9**	**17**	**26**	**135**	**2**	**1**	**4**

Traded to **Toronto** by **NY Rangers** for Walt Poddubny, August 18, 1986. Traded to **LA Kings** by **Toronto** for Sean McKenna, December 14, 1987.

• ALLISON, RAY

Ray Allison RW – R. 5'10", 195 lbs. b: Cranbrook, B.C., 3/4/1959. Hartford's 1st choice, 18th overall, in 1979 Entry Draft.

Season	Club	League	GP	G	A	Pts	AG	AA	APts	PIM	PP	SH	GW	S	%	TGF	PGF	TGA	PGA	+/–	GP	G	A	Pts	PIM	PP	SH	GW
1974-75	Brandon Wheat Kings	WCJHL	2	0	0	0	....	....	....	0	....	....	....	....	....	....	....	....	....	....	....	....	....	....	....	....	....	....
1975-76	Brandon Travellers	MJHL	31	22	21	43	....	....	....	158	....	....	....	....	....	....	....	....	....	....	....	....	....	....	....	....	....	....
	Brandon Wheat Kings	WCJHL	36	9	17	26	....	....	....	50	....	....	....	....	....	....	....	....	....	....	5	2	1	3	0	....	....	....
1976-77	Brandon Wheat Kings	WCJHL	71	45	92	137	....	....	....	198	....	....	....	....	....	....	....	....	....	....	14	9	11	20	37	....	....	....
1977-78	Brandon Wheat Kings	WCJHL	71	74	86	160	....	....	....	254	....	....	....	....	....	....	....	....	....	....	8	7	8	15	35	....	....	....
1978-79	Brandon Wheat Kings	WHL	62	60	93	153	....	....	....	191	....	....	....	....	....	....	....	....	....	....	22	18	19	37	28	....	....	....
	Canada	WJC-A	5	0	5	5	....	....	....	4	....	....	....	....	....	....	....	....	....	....	....	....	....	....	....	....	....	....
1979-80	**Hartford Whalers**	**NHL**	**64**	**16**	**12**	**28**	**14**	**9**	**23**	**13**	**0**	**0**	**2**	**79**	**20.3**	**40**	**0**	**43**	**0**	**–3**	**2**	**0**	**1**	**1**	**0**	**0**	**0**	**0**
	Springfield Indians	AHL	13	6	9	15	....	....	....	18	....	....	....	....	....	....	....	....	....	....	....	....	....	....	....	....	....	....
1980-81	**Hartford Whalers**	**NHL**	**6**	**1**	**0**	**1**	**1**	**0**	**1**	**0**	**0**	**0**	**0**	**6**	**16.7**	**2**	**0**	**3**	**0**	**–1**	....	....	....	....	....	....	....	....
	Binghamton Whalers	AHL	74	31	39	70	....	....	....	81	....	....	....	....	....	....	....	....	....	....	1	0	1	1	0	....	....	....
1981-82	**Philadelphia Flyers**	**NHL**	**51**	**17**	**37**	**54**	**13**	**24**	**37**	**104**	**5**	**0**	**2**	**131**	**13.0**	**78**	**25**	**41**	**1**	**+13**	**3**	**2**	**0**	**2**	**2**	**2**	**0**	**0**
	Maine Mariners	AHL	26	15	13	28	....	....	....	75	....	....	....	....	....	....	....	....	....	....	....	....	....	....	....	....	....	....
1982-83	**Philadelphia Flyers**	**NHL**	**67**	**21**	**30**	**51**	**17**	**21**	**38**	**57**	**4**	**0**	**1**	**148**	**14.2**	**87**	**18**	**45**	**6**	**+30**	**3**	**0**	**1**	**1**	**12**	**0**	**0**	**0**
1983-84	**Philadelphia Flyers**	**NHL**	**37**	**8**	**13**	**21**	**6**	**9**	**15**	**47**	**0**	**0**	**0**	**73**	**11.0**	**37**	**7**	**20**	**1**	**+11**	**3**	**0**	**1**	**1**	**4**	**0**	**0**	**0**
1984-85	**Philadelphia Flyers**	**NHL**	**11**	**1**	**1**	**2**	**1**	**1**	**2**	**2**	**0**	**0**	**0**	**16**	**6.3**	**4**	**0**	**1**	**0**	**+3**	**1**	**0**	**0**	**0**	**2**	**0**	**0**	**0**
	Hershey Bears	AHL	49	17	22	39	....	....	....	61	....	....	....	....	....	....	....	....	....	....	....	....	....	....	....	....	....	....
1985-86	Hershey Bears	AHL	77	32	46	78	....	....	....	131	....	....	....	....	....	....	....	....	....	....	18	4	6	10	28	....	....	....
1986-87	**Philadelphia Flyers**	**NHL**	**2**	**0**	**0**	**0**	**0**	**0**	**0**	**0**	**0**	**0**	**0**	**1**	**0.0**	**0**	**0**	**3**	**1**	**–2**	....	....	....	....	....	....	....	....
	Hershey Bears	AHL	78	29	55	84	....	....	....	57	....	....	....	....	....	....	....	....	....	....	5	3	1	4	12	....	....	....
1987-88	EHC Olten	Switz.	....	35	26	61	....	....	....	....	....	....	....	....	....	....	....	....	....	....	5	*6	3	*9	....	....	....	....
	Hershey Bears	AHL	....	....	....	....	....	....	....	....	....	....	....	....	....	....	....	....	....	....	9	2	9	11	17	....	....	....
1988-89	EHC Olten	Switz.	....	23	16	39	....	....	....	....	....	....	....	....	....	....	....	....	....	....	2	2	0	2	2	....	....	....
	Hershey Bears	AHL	15	6	11	17	....	....	....	18	....	....	....	....	....	....	....	....	....	....	12	4	7	11	6	....	....	....
1989-90	Hershey Bears	AHL	70	25	30	55	....	....	....	66	....	....	....	....	....	....	....	....	....	....	....	....	....	....	....	....	....	....
	NHL Totals		**238**	**64**	**93**	**157**	**52**	**64**	**116**	**223**	**9**	**0**	**5**	**454**	**14.1**	**248**	**50**	**156**	**9**		**12**	**2**	**3**	**5**	**20**	**2**	**0**	**0**

WHL All-Star Team (1979) • Memorial Cup All-Star Team (1979)

Traded to **Philadelphia** by **Hartford** with Fred Arthur and Hartford's 1st (Ron Sutter) and 3rd (Miroslav Dvorak) round choices in 1982 Entry Draft for Rick MacLeish, Blake Wesley, Don Gillen and Philadelphia's 1st (Paul Lawless), 2nd (Mark Patterson) and 3rd (Kevin Dineen) round choices in 1982 Entry Draft, July 3, 1981.

• AMADIO, DAVE

Dave Amadio D – R. 6'1", 207 lbs. b: Glace Bay, N.S., 4/23/1939. d: 4/1/1981.

Season	Club	League	GP	G	A	Pts	AG	AA	APts	PIM	PP	SH	GW	S	%	TGF	PGF	TGA	PGA	+/–	GP	G	A	Pts	PIM	PP	SH	GW
1956-57	Hamilton Tiger Cubs	OHA	44	10	9	19	....	....	....	117	....	....	....	....	....	....	....	....	....	....	4	0	1	1	2	....	....	....
1957-58	Hamilton Tiger Cubs	OHA	52	13	21	34	....	....	....	122	....	....	....	....	....	....	....	....	....	....	15	2	5	7	56	....	....	....
	Detroit Red Wings	**NHL**	**2**	**0**	**0**	**0**	**0**	**0**	**0**	**2**	....	....	....	....	....	....	....	....	....	....	....	....	....	....	....	....	....	....
	Hershey Bears	AHL	....	....	....	....	....	....	....	....	....	....	....	....	....	....	....	....	....	....	1	0	0	0	0	....	....	....
1958-59	Edmonton Flyers	WHL	58	7	7	14	....	....	....	110	....	....	....	....	....	....	....	....	....	....	3	0	1	1	2	....	....	....
1959-60	Edmonton Flyers	WHL	13	1	4	5	....	....	....	35	....	....	....	....	....	....	....	....	....	....	....	....	....	....	....	....	....	....
	Sudbury Wolves	EPHL	50	13	17	30	....	....	....	139	....	....	....	....	....	....	....	....	....	....	14	3	7	10	14	....	....	....
1960-61	Sudbury Wolves	EPHL	25	2	14	16	....	....	....	50	....	....	....	....	....	....	....	....	....	....	....	....	....	....	....	....	....	....
1961-62	Sudbury Wolves	EPHL	9	0	5	5	....	....	....	15	....	....	....	....	....	....	....	....	....	....	....	....	....	....	....	....	....	....
	Springfield Indians	AHL	58	4	11	15	....	....	....	56	....	....	....	....	....	....	....	....	....	....	11	0	1	1	19	....	....	....
1962-63	Springfield Indians	AHL	71	8	19	27	....	....	....	95	....	....	....	....	....	....	....	....	....	....	....	....	....	....	....	....	....	....
1963-64	Springfield Indians	AHL	72	11	24	35	....	....	....	120	....	....	....	....	....	....	....	....	....	....	....	....	....	....	....	....	....	....
1964-65	Springfield Indians	AHL	72	10	24	34	....	....	....	100	....	....	....	....	....	....	....	....	....	....	....	....	....	....	....	....	....	....
1965-66	Springfield Indians	AHL	72	9	11	20	....	....	....	124	....	....	....	....	....	....	....	....	....	....	6	0	3	3	6	....	....	....
1966-67	Springfield Indians	AHL	66	11	29	40	....	....	....	89	....	....	....	....	....	....	....	....	....	....	....	....	....	....	....	....	....	....
1967-68	**Los Angeles Kings**	**NHL**	**58**	**4**	**6**	**10**	**5**	**6**	**11**	**101**	**0**	**0**	**0**	**92**	**4.3**	**59**	**10**	**77**	**18**	**–10**	**7**	**0**	**2**	**2**	**8**	**0**	**0**	**0**
	Springfield Kings	AHL	17	2	6	8	....	....	....	25	....	....	....	....	....	....	....	....	....	....	....	....	....	....	....	....	....	....
1968-69	**Los Angeles Kings**	**NHL**	**65**	**1**	**5**	**6**	**1**	**5**	**6**	**60**	**1**	**0**	**1**	**72**	**1.4**	**43**	**6**	**67**	**9**	**–21**	**9**	**1**	**0**	**1**	**10**	**0**	**0**	**0**
1969-70	Springfield Kings	AHL	40	4	15	19	....	....	....	78	....	....	....	....	....	....	....	....	....	....	13	1	1	2	10	....	....	....
1970-71	Kansas City Blues	CHL	30	2	13	15	....	....	....	45	....	....	....	....	....	....	....	....	....	....	....	....	....	....	....	....	....	....
	Denver Spurs	WHL	35	0	6	6	....	....	....	42	....	....	....	....	....	....	....	....	....	....	....	....	....	....	....	....	....	....
1971-72	Salt Lake Golden Eagles	WHL	68	6	22	28	....	....	....	93	....	....	....	....	....	....	....	....	....	....	....	....	....	....	....	....	....	....
1972-73	Salt Lake Golden Eagles	WHL	72	6	33	39	....	....	....	129	....	....	....	....	....	....	....	....	....	....	9	3	2	5	16	....	....	....
1973-74	Seattle Totems	WHL	70	6	13	19	....	....	....	60	....	....	....	....	....	....	....	....	....	....	....	....	....	....	....	....	....	....
	NHL Totals		**125**	**5**	**11**	**16**	**6**	**11**	**17**	**163**	**1**	**0**	**1**	**164**	**3.0**	**102**	**16**	**144**	**27**		**16**	**1**	**2**	**3**	**18**	**0**	**0**	**0**

Traded to **Springfield** (AHL) by **Detroit** for cash, June, 1961. NHL rights transferred to **LA Kings** after NHL club purchased **Springfield** (AHL) franchise, May, 1967.

• AMBROZIAK, PETER

Peter Ambroziak LW – L. 6', 206 lbs. b: Toronto, Ont., 9/15/1971. Buffalo's 4th choice, 72nd overall, in 1991 Entry Draft.

Season	Club	League	GP	G	A	Pts	AG	AA	APts	PIM	PP	SH	GW	S	%	TGF	PGF	TGA	PGA	+/–	GP	G	A	Pts	PIM	PP	SH	GW
1988-89	Ottawa 67's	OHL	50	8	15	23	....	....	....	11	....	....	....	....	....	....	....	....	....	....	12	1	2	3	2	....	....	....
1989-90	Ottawa 67's	OHL	60	13	19	32	....	....	....	37	....	....	....	....	....	....	....	....	....	....	4	0	0	0	2	....	....	....
1990-91	Ottawa 67's	OHL	62	30	32	62	....	....	....	56	....	....	....	....	....	....	....	....	....	....	17	15	9	24	24	....	....	....
1991-92	Ottawa 67's	OHL	49	32	49	81	....	....	....	50	....	....	....	....	....	....	....	....	....	....	11	3	7	10	33	....	....	....
	Rochester Americans	AHL	2	0	1	1	....	....	....	0	....	....	....	....	....	....	....	....	....	....	....	....	....	....	....	....	....	....
1992-93	Rochester Americans	AHL	50	8	10	18	....	....	....	37	....	....	....	....	....	....	....	....	....	....	12	4	3	7	16	....	....	....
1993-94	Rochester Americans	AHL	22	3	4	7	....	....	....	53	....	....	....	....	....	....	....	....	....	....	....	....	....	....	....	....	....	....
1994-95	**Buffalo Sabres**	**NHL**	**12**	**0**	**1**	**1**	**0**	**1**	**1**	**0**	**0**	**0**	**0**	**3**	**0.0**	**1**	**0**	**3**	**1**	**–1**	....	....	....	....	....	....	....	....
	Rochester Americans	AHL	46	14	11	25	....	....	....	35	....	....	....	....	....	....	....	....	....	....	4	0	0	0	6	....	....	....

Season	Club	League	GP	G	A	Pts	AG	AA	APts	PIM	PP	SH	GW	S	%	TGF	PGF	TGA	PGA	+/–	GP	G	A	Pts	PIM	PP	SH	GW
			REGULAR SEASON																		PLAYOFFS							
1995-96	Albany River Rats	AHL	8	2	1	3				25																		
	Cornwall Aces	AHL	50	9	15	24				42											8	1	1	2	4			
1996-97	Fort Wayne Komets	IHL	57	15	5	20				28																		
1997-98	Hershey Bears	AHL	63	7	11	18				61											5	0	1	1	6			
	NHL Totals		**12**	**0**	**1**	**1**	**0**	**1**	**1**	**0**	**0**	**0**	**0**	**3**	**0.0**	**1**	**0**	**3**	**1**									

• AMODEO, MIKE

Mike Amodeo D – L. 5'10", 190 lbs. b: Toronto, Ont., 6/22/1952. California's 7th choice, 102nd overall, in 1972 Amateur Draft.

Season	Club	League	GP	G	A	Pts	AG	AA	APts	PIM	PP	SH	GW	S	%	TGF	PGF	TGA	PGA	+/–	GP	G	A	Pts	PIM	PP	SH	GW
1969-70	Toronto Marlboros	OHA	54	5	11	16				161																		
1970-71	Toronto Marlboros	OHA	11	0	3	3				31																		
	Niagara Falls Flyers	OHA	3	0	0	0				2																		
	Oshawa Generals	OHA	24	0	12	12				65																		
1971-72	Oshawa Generals	OHA	63	6	34	40				130																		
1972-73	Ottawa Nationals	WHA	61	1	14	15				77											5	0	1	1	10			
1973-74	Toronto Toros	WHA	77	0	11	11				82											12	0	2	2	26			
1974-75	Toronto Toros	WHA	64	1	13	14				50											3	0	1	1	4			
1975-76	Toronto Toros	WHA	31	4	8	12				35																		
	Rochester Americans	AHL	10	0	2	2				4											4	0	1	1	0			
1976-77	Orebro	Sweden	34	5	3	8				38																		
1977-78	Orebro	Sweden	34	2	6	8				44																		
	Winnipeg Jets	WHA	3	1	1	2				0											7	1	3	4	19			
1978-79	Orebro	Sweden	1	0	1	1				0																		
	Winnipeg Jets	WHA	64	4	18	22				29																		
1979-80	**Winnipeg Jets**	**NHL**	**19**	**0**	**0**	**0**	**0**	**0**	**0**	**2**	**0**	**0**	**0**	**14**	**0.0**	**6**	**0**	**21**	**0**	**–15**								
	Tulsa Oilers	CHL	20	3	6	9				32																		
1980-81			DID NOT PLAY																									
1981-82	HC Merano	Italy	31	20	21	41				14																		
	Italy	WEC-A	7	0	0	0				2																		
	NHL Totals		**19**	**0**	**0**	**0**	**0**	**0**	**0**	**2**	**0**	**0**	**0**	**14**	**0.0**	**6**	**0**	**21**	**0**									
	Other Major League Totals		300	11	65	76				273											27	1	7	8	59			

Selected by **Ontario-Ottawa** (WHA) in 1972 WHA General Player Draft, February 12, 1972. Transferred to **Toronto** (WHA) after **Ottawa** (WHA) franchise relocated, May, 1973. Signed as a free agent by **Winnipeg** (WHA), March, 1978. Rights retained by **Winnipeg** prior to Expansion Draft, June 9, 1979.

• AMONTE, TONY

Tony Amonte RW – L. 6', 195 lbs. b: Hingham, MA, 8/2/1970. NY Rangers' 3rd choice, 68th overall, in 1988 Entry Draft.

Season	Club	League	GP	G	A	Pts	AG	AA	APts	PIM	PP	SH	GW	S	%	TGF	PGF	TGA	PGA	+/–	GP	G	A	Pts	PIM	PP	SH	GW
1988-89	Thayer Academy	H.S.	25	36	38	73																						
	United States	WJC-A	7	1	3	4				2																		
1989-90	Boston University	H.E.	41	25	33	58				52																		
	United States	WJC-A	7	5	2	7				4																		
1990-91	Boston University	H.E.	38	31	37	68				82																		
	United States	WEC-A	10	2	5	7				4																		
	New York Rangers	**NHL**																			**2**	**0**	**2**	**2**	**2**			
1991-92	**New York Rangers**	**NHL**	**79**	**35**	**34**	**69**	**32**	**26**	**58**	**55**	**9**	**0**	**4**	**234**	**15.0**	**100**	**28**	**60**	**0**	**+12**	**13**	**3**	**6**	**9**	**2**	**2**	**0**	**0**
1992-93	**New York Rangers**	**NHL**	**83**	**33**	**43**	**76**	**28**	**29**	**57**	**49**	**13**	**0**	**4**	**270**	**12.2**	**112**	**43**	**71**	**2**	**0**								
	United States	WC-A	6	1	2	3				8																		
1993-94	**New York Rangers**	**NHL**	**72**	**16**	**22**	**38**	**15**	**17**	**32**	**31**	**3**	**0**	**4**	**179**	**8.9**	**67**	**22**	**46**	**6**	**+5**								
	Chicago Blackhawks	**NHL**	**7**	**1**	**3**	**4**	**1**	**2**	**3**	**6**	**1**	**0**	**0**	**16**	**6.3**	**7**	**4**	**8**	**0**	**–5**	**6**	**4**	**2**	**6**	**4**	**1**	**0**	**1**
1994-95	Fasso	Italy	14	22	16	38				10																		
	Chicago Blackhawks	**NHL**	**40**	**15**	**20**	**35**	**27**	**29**	**56**	**41**	**6**	**1**	**3**	**105**	**14.3**	**50**	**17**	**34**	**8**	**+7**	**16**	**3**	**3**	**6**	**10**	**0**	**0**	**0**
1995-96	**Chicago Blackhawks**	**NHL**	**81**	**31**	**32**	**63**	**31**	**26**	**57**	**62**	**5**	**4**	**5**	**216**	**14.4**	**91**	**31**	**70**	**20**	**+10**	**7**	**2**	**4**	**6**	**6**	**1**	**0**	**0**
1996-97	United States	W Cup	7	2	4	6				6																		
	Chicago Blackhawks	**NHL**	**81**	**41**	**36**	**77**	**44**	**32**	**76**	**64**	**9**	**2**	**4**	**266**	**15.4**	**96**	**23**	**56**	**18**	**+35**	**6**	**4**	**2**	**6**	**8**	**0**	**0**	**0**
1997-98	**Chicago Blackhawks**	**NHL**	**82**	**31**	**42**	**73**	**36**	**41**	**77**	**66**	**7**	**3**	**5**	**296**	**10.5**	**102**	**30**	**75**	**24**	**+21**								
	United States	Olympics	4	0	1	1				4																		
	NHL Totals		**533**	**203**	**232**	**435**	**214**	**202**	**416**	**374**	**53**	**10**	**29**	**1582**	**12.8**	**625**	**198**	**420**	**78**		**50**	**16**	**19**	**35**	**32**	**4**	**0**	**1**

Hockey East Second All-Star Team (1991) • NCAA Championship All-Tournament Team (1991) • NHL/Upper Deck All-Rookie Team (1992)

Played in NHL All-Star Game (1997, 1998)

Traded to **Chicago** by **NY Rangers** with the rights to Matt Oates for Stephane Matteau and Brian Noonan, March 21, 1994.

• ANDERSON, EARL

Earl Anderson RW – R. 6'1", 185 lbs. b: Roseau, MN, 2/24/1951. Detroit's 5th choice, 58th overall, in 1971 Amateur Draft.

Season	Club	League	GP	G	A	Pts	AG	AA	APts	PIM	PP	SH	GW	S	%	TGF	PGF	TGA	PGA	+/–	GP	G	A	Pts	PIM	PP	SH	GW
1970-71	University of North Dakota	WCHA	32	12	17	29				22																		
1971-72	University of North Dakota	WCHA	36	23	22	45				24																		
1972-73	University of North Dakota	WCHA	36	17	30	47				12																		
	United States	Nat-Team	7	8	4	12																						
	United States	WEC-B		8	2	10																						
1973-74	London Red Wings	Britain	70	62	48	110				41																		
1974-75	**Detroit Red Wings**	**NHL**	**45**	**7**	**3**	**10**	**6**	**2**	**8**	**12**	**1**	**0**	**1**	**61**	**11.5**	**19**	**1**	**29**	**0**	**–11**								
	Virginia Wings	AHL	4	0	3	3				2																		
	Boston Bruins	**NHL**	**19**	**2**	**4**	**6**	**2**	**3**	**5**	**4**	**0**	**0**	**1**	**24**	**8.3**	**7**	**0**	**2**	**0**	**+5**	**3**	**0**	**1**	**1**	**0**	**0**	**0**	**0**
1975-76	**Boston Bruins**	**NHL**	**5**	**0**	**1**	**1**	**0**	**1**	**1**	**2**	**0**	**0**	**0**	**5**	**0.0**	**1**	**1**	**5**	**3**	**–2**								
1976-77	**Boston Bruins**	**NHL**	**40**	**10**	**11**	**21**	**10**	**9**	**19**	**4**	**1**	**0**	**3**	**65**	**15.4**	**35**	**3**	**30**	**2**	**+4**	**2**	**0**	**0**	**0**	**0**	**0**	**0**	**0**
	Rochester Americans	AHL	32	19	14	33				16																		
1977-78	Rochester Americans	AHL	72	26	40	66				22											6	1	2	3	2			
	NHL Totals		**109**	**19**	**19**	**38**	**18**	**15**	**33**	**22**	**2**	**0**	**5**	**155**	**12.3**	**62**	**5**	**66**	**5**		**5**	**0**	**1**	**1**	**0**	**0**	**0**	**0**

Traded to **Boston** by **Detroit** with Hank Nowak for Walt McKechnie and Boston's 3rd round choice (Claire Hamilton) in 1975 Amateur Draft, February 18, 1975.

• ANDERSON, GLENN

Glenn Anderson RW – L. 6'1", 190 lbs. b: Vancouver, B.C., 10/2/1960. Edmonton's 3rd choice, 69th overall, in 1979 Entry Draft.

Season	Club	League	GP	G	A	Pts	AG	AA	APts	PIM	PP	SH	GW	S	%	TGF	PGF	TGA	PGA	+/–	GP	G	A	Pts	PIM	PP	SH	GW
1977-78	Bellingham Blazers	BCJHL	64	62	69	131				46																		
1978-79	University of Denver	WCHA	40	26	29	55				58																		
1979-80	Seattle Breakers	WHL	7	5	5	10				4											2	0	1	1	0			
	Canada	Nat-Team	49	21	21	42				46																		
	Canada	Olympics	6	2	2	4				4																		
1980-81	**Edmonton Oilers**	**NHL**	**58**	**30**	**23**	**53**	**25**	**16**	**41**	**24**	**10**	**3**	**5**	**160**	**18.8**	**77**	**16**	**70**	**13**	**+4**	**9**	**5**	**7**	**12**	**12**	**3**	**0**	**0**
1981-82	**Edmonton Oilers**	**NHL**	**80**	**38**	**67**	**105**	**30**	**44**	**74**	**71**	**9**	**0**	**8**	**252**	**15.1**	**177**	**52**	**88**	**9**	**+46**	**5**	**2**	**5**	**7**	**8**	**0**	**0**	**1**
1982-83	**Edmonton Oilers**	**NHL**	**72**	**48**	**56**	**104**	**40**	**39**	**79**	**70**	**11**	**0**	**10**	**243**	**19.8**	**153**	**51**	**61**	**0**	**+41**	**16**	**10**	**10**	**20**	**32**	**1**	**0**	**2**
1983-84	**Edmonton Oilers**	**NHL**	**80**	**54**	**45**	**99**	**44**	**31**	**75**	**65**	**11**	**4**	**11**	**277**	**19.5**	**153**	**46**	**73**	**7**	**+41**	**19**	**6**	**11**	**17**	**33**	**1**	**0**	**1**
1984-85	Canada	C Cup	8	1	4	5				16																		
	Edmonton Oilers	**NHL**	**80**	**42**	**39**	**81**	**34**	**26**	**60**	**69**	**12**	**1**	**6**	**258**	**16.3**	**125**	**41**	**67**	**7**	**+24**	**18**	**10**	**16**	**26**	**38**	**2**	**0**	**1**
1985-86	**Edmonton Oilers**	**NHL**	**72**	**54**	**48**	**102**	**43**	**32**	**75**	**90**	**18**	**2**	**9**	**243**	**22.2**	**147**	**43**	**79**	**13**	**+38**	**10**	**8**	**3**	**11**	**14**	**1**	**0**	**2**
1986-87	**Edmonton Oilers**	**NHL**	**80**	**35**	**38**	**73**	**30**	**28**	**58**	**65**	**7**	**1**	**5**	**188**	**18.6**	**127**	**37**	**67**	**4**	**+27**	**21**	**14**	**13**	**27**	**59**	**4**	**0**	**2**
	NHL All-Stars	RV'87	2	1	0	1				2																		
1987-88	Canada	C Cup	7	2	1	3				4																		
	Edmonton Oilers	**NHL**	**80**	**38**	**50**	**88**	**33**	**36**	**69**	**58**	**16**	**1**	**3**	**255**	**14.9**	**137**	**55**	**95**	**18**	**+5**	**19**	**9**	**16**	**25**	**49**	**4**	**0**	**1**
1988-89	**Edmonton Oilers**	**NHL**	**79**	**16**	**48**	**64**	**14**	**34**	**48**	**93**	**7**	**0**	**3**	**212**	**7.5**	**99**	**38**	**82**	**5**	**–16**	**7**	**1**	**2**	**3**	**8**	**1**	**0**	**0**
	Canada	WEC-A	6	2	2	4				4																		
1989-90	**Edmonton Oilers**	**NHL**	**73**	**34**	**38**	**72**	**29**	**27**	**56**	**107**	**17**	**1**	**7**	**204**	**16.7**	**105**	**42**	**75**	**11**	**–1**	**22**	**10**	**12**	**22**	**20**	**2**	**0**	**2**
1990-91	**Edmonton Oilers**	**NHL**	**74**	**24**	**31**	**55**	**22**	**23**	**45**	**59**	**8**	**0**	**4**	**193**	**12.4**	**84**	**31**	**73**	**13**	**–7**	**18**	**6**	**7**	**13**	**41**	**3**	**0**	**0**
1991-92	**Toronto Maple Leafs**	**NHL**	**72**	**24**	**33**	**57**	**22**	**25**	**47**	**100**	**5**	**0**	**4**	**188**	**12.8**	**76**	**23**	**88**	**22**	**–13**								
	Canada	WC-A	6	2	1	3				16																		
1992-93	**Toronto Maple Leafs**	**NHL**	**76**	**22**	**43**	**65**	**18**	**29**	**47**	**117**	**11**	**0**	**3**	**161**	**13.7**	**101**	**46**	**37**	**1**	**+19**	**21**	**7**	**11**	**18**	**31**	**0**	**0**	**2**
1993-94	**Toronto Maple Leafs**	**NHL**	**73**	**17**	**18**	**35**	**16**	**14**	**30**	**50**	**5**	**0**	**3**	**127**	**13.4**	**60**	**22**	**44**	**0**	**–6**								
	New York Rangers	**NHL**	**12**	**4**	**2**	**6**	**4**	**2**	**6**	**12**	**2**	**0**	**0**	**22**	**18.2**	**11**	**4**	**6**	**0**	**+1**	**23**	**3**	**3**	**6**	**42**	**0**	**1**	**2**

			REGULAR SEASON																			PLAYOFFS							
Season	Club	League	GP	G	A	Pts	AG	AA	APts	PIM	PP	SH	GW	S	%	TGF	PGF	TGA	PGA	+/-		GP	G	A	Pts	PIM	PP	SH	GW
1994-95	Augsburg Panthers	Germany	5	6	2	8	...	...	...	10	...												...							
	Lukko Raumo	Finland	4	1	1	2	...	...	...	0	...												...							
	Canada	Nat-Team	26	11	8	19	...	...	...	40	...												...							
	St. Louis Blues	**NHL**	36	12	14	26	21	21	42	37	0	0	3	54	22.2	34	4	25	4	+9		6	1	1	2	*49	0	0	0
1995-96	Canada	Nat-Team	11	4	4	8	...	...	...	39	...												...							
	Augsburg Panthers	Germany	9	5	3	8	...	...	...	48	...												...							
	Edmonton Oilers	**NHL**	17	4	6	10	4	5	9	27	0	0	1	36	11.1	14	1	13	0	0									
	St. Louis Blues	**NHL**	15	2	2	4	2	2	4	6	2	0	0	35	5.7	7	4	18	4	-11		11	1	4	5	6	0	0	1
1996-97	HC La Chaux-de-Fonds	Switz.	23	14	15	29	...	...	...	103	...												...							
	NHL Totals		**1129**	**498**	**601**	**1099**	**431**	**434**	**865**	**1120**	**151**	**13**	**85**	**3108**	**16.0**	**1687**	**556**	**1061**	**131**			**225**	**93**	**121**	**214**	**442**	**22**	**1**	**17**

Played in NHL All-Star Game (1984, 1985, 1986, 1988).
Traded to **Toronto** by **Edmonton** with Grant Fuhr and Craig Berube for Vincent Damphousse, Peter Ing, Scott Thornton, Luke Richardson, future considerations and cash, September 19, 1991.
Traded to **NY Rangers** by **Toronto** with the rights to Scott Malone and Toronto's 4th round choice (Alexander Korobolin) in 1994 Entry Draft for Mike Gartner, March 21, 1994. Signed as a free agent by **St. Louis**, February 13, 1995. Signed as a free agent by **Vancouver**, January 22, 1996. Claimed on waivers by **Edmonton** from **Vancouver**, January 25, 1996. Claimed on waivers by **St. Louis** from **Edmonton**, March 12, 1996.

● **ANDERSON, JIM**   Jim Anderson   LW – L. 5'10", 165 lbs.   b: Pembroke, Ont., 12/1/1930.

Season	Club	League	GP	G	A	Pts	AG	AA	APts	PIM	PP	SH	GW	S	%	TGF	PGF	TGA	PGA	+/-		GP	G	A	Pts	PIM	PP	SH	GW
1949-50	Windsor Spitfires	OHA	3	0	0	0				2												9	1	4	5	0			
	Detroit Hettche	IHL	31	18	14	32				12																			
1950-51	Windsor Spitfires	OHA	53	21	22	43				35												7	2	2	4	6			
1951-52	Glace Bay Miners	MMHL	88	*51	33	84				14												4	3	0	3	2			
1952-53	Shawinigan Cataracts	QSHL	22	7	4	11				8																			
	Edmonton Flyers	WHL	44	11	11	22				8												15	*12	3	15	0			
1953-54	Edmonton Flyers	WHL	66	23	21	44				22												13	6	2	8	2			
1954-55	Springfield Indians	AHL	63	39	32	71				40												4	0	0	0	0			
1955-56	Springfield Indians	AHL	61	28	23	51				44																			
1956-57	Springfield Indians	AHL	64	30	25	55				32																			
1957-58	Trois-Rivieres Lions	QHL	34	14	18	32				2																			
	Buffalo–Springfield	AHL	25	4	4	8				16																			
1958-59	Springfield Indians	AHL	69	27	36	63				16																			
1959-60	Springfield Indians	AHL	56	16	21	37				10												4	1	0	1	0			
1960-61	Springfield Indians	AHL	72	*43	38	81				18												8	*5	0	5	0			
1961-62	Springfield Indians	AHL	70	38	41	79				24												11	*7	1	8	2			
1962-63	Springfield Indians	AHL	70	35	26	61				6																			
1963-64	Springfield Indians	AHL	72	*40	32	72				14																			
1964-65	Springfield Indians	AHL	72	40	29	69				14																			
1965-66	Springfield Indians	AHL	69	27	20	47				12												6	1	1	2	0			
1966-67	Springfield Indians	AHL	63	25	29	54				4																			
1967-68	**Los Angeles Kings**	**NHL**	7	1	2	3	1	2	3	2	0	0	0	20	5.0	4	0	6	0	-2									
	Springfield Kings	AHL	62	22	24	46				26												4	0	1	1	2			
1968-69	Springfield Kings	AHL	54	12	15	27				10																			
1969-70	Springfield Kings	AHL	1	0	0	0				0																			
	NHL Totals		**7**	**1**	**2**	**3**	**1**	**2**	**3**	**2**	**0**	**0**	**0**	**20**	**5.0**	**4**	**0**	**6**	**0**										

Won Dudley "Red" Garrett Memorial Award (Top Rookie - AHL) (1955) • AHL Second All-Star Team (1961, 1964)
NHL rights transferred to **LA Kings** after NHL club purchased **Springfield** (AHL) franchise, May, 1967.

● **ANDERSON, JOHN**   John Anderson   RW – L. 5'11", 200 lbs.   b: Toronto, Ont., 3/28/1957.   Toronto's 1st choice, 11th overall, in 1977 Amateur Draft.

Season	Club	League	GP	G	A	Pts	AG	AA	APts	PIM	PP	SH	GW	S	%	TGF	PGF	TGA	PGA	+/-		GP	G	A	Pts	PIM	PP	SH	GW
1973-74	Toronto Marlboros	OHA	38	22	22	44				6																			
1974-75	Toronto Marlboros	OHA	70	49	64	113				31												22	16	14	30	14			
1975-76	Toronto Marlboros	OHA	39	26	25	51				19												10	7	4	11	7			
1976-77	Toronto Marlboros	OHA	64	57	62	119				42												6	3	5	8	0			
	Canada	WJC-A	7	10	5	15				6																			
1977-78	**Toronto Maple Leafs**	**NHL**	17	1	2	3	1	2	3	2	0	0	0	14	7.1	6	0	5	0	+1		2	0	0	0	0	0	0	0
	Dallas Black Hawks	CHL	55	22	23	45				6												13	*11	8	*19	2			
1978-79	**Toronto Maple Leafs**	**NHL**	71	15	11	26	14	8	22	10	0	0	2	123	12.2	48	4	43	1	+2		6	0	2	2	0	0	0	0
1979-80	**Toronto Maple Leafs**	**NHL**	74	25	28	53	23	21	44	22	3	0	5	207	12.1	76	12	59	0	+5		3	1	1	2	0	0	0	0
1980-81	**Toronto Maple Leafs**	**NHL**	75	17	26	43	14	18	32	31	2	0	1	142	12.0	64	10	65	0	-11		2	0	0	0	0	0	0	0
1981-82	**Toronto Maple Leafs**	**NHL**	69	31	26	57	25	17	42	30	7	0	3	191	16.2	94	16	82	12	+8									
1982-83	**Toronto Maple Leafs**	**NHL**	80	31	49	80	25	34	59	24	9	0	6	199	15.6	127	46	93	6	-6		4	2	4	6	0	1	0	0
	Canada	WEC-A	6	2	2	4				6																			
1983-84	**Toronto Maple Leafs**	**NHL**	73	37	31	68	30	21	51	22	14	0	5	192	19.3	108	48	72	0	-12									
1984-85	**Toronto Maple Leafs**	**NHL**	75	32	31	63	26	21	47	27	14	1	5	194	16.5	99	38	88	7	-20									
	Canada	WEC-A	9	5	2	7				18																			
1985-86	**Quebec Nordiques**	**NHL**	65	21	28	49	17	19	36	26	8	3	5	190	11.1	97	52	59	13	-1									
	Hartford Whalers	**NHL**	14	8	17	25	6	11	17	2	1	0	1	50	16.0	33	7	9	1	+18		10	5	8	13	0	3	0	0
1986-87	**Hartford Whalers**	**NHL**	76	31	44	75	27	32	59	19	7	0	5	223	13.9	111	45	57	2	+11		6	1	2	3	0	1	0	0
1987-88	**Hartford Whalers**	**NHL**	63	17	32	49	15	23	38	20	9	0	3	149	11.4	75	46	40	6	-5									
1988-89	**Hartford Whalers**	**NHL**	62	16	24	40	14	17	31	28	1	0	0	132	12.1	71	19	41	4	+15		4	0	1	1	2	0	0	0
1989-90	Binghamton Whalers	AHL	3	1	1	2				0																			
	Milano Devils	Italy	9	7	9	16				18																			
1990-91	Fort Wayne Komets	IHL	63	40	43	83				24												1	3	0	3	0			
1991-92	New Haven Nighthawks	AHL	68	41	54	95				24												4	0	4	4	0			
1992-93	San Diego Gulls	IHL	65	34	46	80				18												11	5	6	11	4			
1993-94	San Diego Gulls	IHL	72	24	24	48				32												4	1	1	2	8			
	NHL Totals		**814**	**282**	**349**	**631**	**237**	**244**	**481**	**263**	**75**	**4**	**41**	**2006**	**14.1**	**1009**	**343**	**713**	**52**			**37**	**9**	**18**	**27**	**2**	**5**	**0**	**0**

Memorial Cup All-Star Team (1975) • OHA First All-Star Team (1977) • CHL Second All-Star Team (1978) • AHL First All-Star Team (1992) • Won Fred T. Hunt Memorial Trophy (Sportsmanship - AHL) (1992) • Won Les Cunningham Award (MVP - AHL) (1992)
Traded to **Quebec** by **Toronto** for Brad Maxwell, August 21, 1985. Traded to **Hartford** by **Quebec** for Risto Siltanen, March 8, 1986.

● **ANDERSON, MURRAY**   Murray Anderson   D – L. 5'10", 175 lbs.   b: The Pas, Man., 8/28/1949.   Montreal's 4th choice, 44th overall, in 1969 Amateur Draft.

Season	Club	League	GP	G	A	Pts	AG	AA	APts	PIM	PP	SH	GW	S	%	TGF	PGF	TGA	PGA	+/-		GP	G	A	Pts	PIM	PP	SH	GW
1967-68	Flin Flon Bombers	WCJHL	55	5	14	19				87												15	1	2	3	19			
1968-69	Flin Flon Bombers	WCJHL	53	17	30	47				120												18	0	6	6	0			
1969-70	Flin Flon Bombers	WCJHL	50	5	23	28				150												17	2	11	13	20			
1970-71	Rochester–Montreal	AHL	52	0	5	5				48																			
1971-72	Nova Scotia Voyageurs	AHL	64	11	6	17				35												15	2	3	5	2			
1972-73	Nova Scotia Voyageurs	AHL	71	1	24	25				52												13	1	2	3	22			
1973-74	New Haven Nighthawks	AHL	76	9	34	43				79												10	0	3	3	6			
1974-75	**Washington Capitals**	**NHL**	40	0	1	1	0	1	1	68	0	0	0	24	0.0	13	2	70	19	-40									
	Richmond Robins	AHL	35	3	9	12				56												7	1	2	3	4			
1975-76	Springfield Indians	AHL	75	3	21	24				62																			
1976-77	Tulsa Oilers	CHL	3	0	0	0				4																			
	NHL Totals		**40**	**0**	**1**	**1**	**0**	**1**	**1**	**68**	**0**	**0**	**0**	**24**	**0.0**	**13**	**2**	**70**	**19**										

WCJHL All-Star Team (1970)
Traded to **Minnesota** by **Montreal** with Tony Featherstone, May 29, 1973. Claimed by **Washington** from **Minnesota** in Expansion Draft, June 12, 1974.

● **ANDERSON, PERRY**   Perry Anderson   LW – L. 6'1", 225 lbs.   b: Barrie, Ont., 10/14/1961.   St. Louis' 5th choice, 117th overall, in 1980 Entry Draft.

Season	Club	League	GP	G	A	Pts	AG	AA	APts	PIM	PP	SH	GW	S	%	TGF	PGF	TGA	PGA	+/-		GP	G	A	Pts	PIM	PP	SH	GW
1978-79	Kingston Canadians	OHA	61	6	13	19				85												5	2	1	3	6			
1979-80	Kingston Canadians	OHA	63	17	16	33				52												3	0	0	0	6			
1980-81	Kingston Canadians	OHA	38	9	13	22				118																			
	Brantford Alexanders	OHA	31	8	27	35				43												6	4	2	6	15			

			REGULAR SEASON																		PLAYOFFS							
Season	Club	League	GP	G	A	Pts	AG	AA	APts	PIM	PP	SH	GW	S	%	TGF	PGF	TGA	PGA	+/-	GP	G	A	Pts	PIM	PP	SH	GW
1981-82	**St. Louis Blues**	**NHL**	**5**	**1**	**2**	**3**	**1**	**1**	**2**	**0**	**0**	**0**	**0**	**9**	**11.1**	**4**	**0**	**3**	**0**	**+1**	**10**	**2**	**0**	**2**	**4**	**1**	**0**	**0**
	Salt Lake Golden Eagles	CHL	71	32	32	64	...	...	...	117	...	...	...	...	...	...	...	...	...	...	2	1	0	1	2	...	...	...
1982-83	**St. Louis Blues**	**NHL**	**18**	**5**	**2**	**7**	**4**	**1**	**5**	**14**	**0**	**0**	**0**	**27**	**18.5**	**9**	**1**	**15**	**1**	**–6**	...	...	...	...	...	...	...	...
	Salt Lake Golden Eagles	CHL	57	23	19	42	...	...	...	140	...	...	...	...	...	...	...	...	...	...	...	...	...	...	...	...	...	...
1983-84	**St. Louis Blues**	**NHL**	**50**	**7**	**5**	**12**	**6**	**3**	**9**	**195**	**0**	**0**	**1**	**49**	**14.3**	**22**	**0**	**36**	**1**	**–13**	**9**	**0**	**0**	**0**	**27**	**0**	**0**	**0**
	Montana Magic	CHL	8	7	3	10	...	...	...	34	...	...	...	...	...	...	...	...	...	...	...	...	...	...	...	...	...	...
1984-85	**St. Louis Blues**	**NHL**	**71**	**9**	**9**	**18**	**7**	**6**	**13**	**146**	**0**	**0**	**1**	**86**	**10.5**	**30**	**0**	**28**	**0**	**+2**	**3**	**0**	**0**	**0**	**7**	**0**	**0**	**0**
1985-86	**New Jersey Devils**	**NHL**	**51**	**7**	**12**	**19**	**6**	**8**	**14**	**91**	**1**	**0**	**1**	**61**	**11.5**	**25**	**2**	**31**	**1**	**–7**	...	...	...	...	...	...	...	...
1986-87	**New Jersey Devils**	**NHL**	**57**	**10**	**9**	**19**	**9**	**6**	**15**	**107**	**2**	**0**	**1**	**46**	**21.7**	**33**	**8**	**38**	**0**	**–13**	...	...	...	...	...	...	...	...
	Maine Mariners	AHL	9	5	4	9	...	...	...	42	...	...	...	...	...	...	...	...	...	...	...	...	...	...	...	...	...	...
1987-88	**New Jersey Devils**	**NHL**	**60**	**4**	**6**	**10**	**3**	**4**	**7**	**222**	**1**	**0**	**0**	**40**	**10.0**	**22**	**5**	**26**	**1**	**–8**	**10**	**0**	**0**	**0**	**113**	**0**	**0**	**0**
1988-89	**New Jersey Devils**	**NHL**	**39**	**3**	**6**	**9**	**3**	**4**	**7**	**128**	**0**	**0**	**0**	**36**	**8.3**	**15**	**0**	**10**	**0**	**+5**	...	...	...	...	...	...	...	...
1989-90	Utica Devils	AHL	71	13	17	30		...	...	128	...	...	...	...	...	...	...	...	...	...	5	0	0	0	24	...	...	...
1990-91	**New Jersey Devils**	**NHL**	**1**	**0**	**0**	**0**	**0**	**0**	**0**	**5**	**0**	**0**	**0**	**1**	**0.0**	**0**	**0**	**0**	**0**	**0**	**4**	**0**	**1**	**1**	**10**	**0**	**0**	**0**
	Utica Devils	AHL	68	19	14	33	...	...	...	245	...	...	...	...	...	...	...	...	...	...	...	...	...	...	...	...	...	...
1991-92	**San Jose Sharks**	**NHL**	**48**	**4**	**8**	**12**	**4**	**6**	**10**	**143**	**0**	**0**	**0**	**57**	**7.0**	**16**	**0**	**33**	**0**	**–17**	...	...	...	...	...	...	...	...
1992-93	San Diego Gulls	IHL	51	8	13	21	...	...	...	217	...	...	...	...	...	...	...	...	...	...	5	0	0	0	14	...	...	...
1993-94	Salt Lake Golden Eagles	IHL	2	0	0	0	...	...	...	21	...	...	...	...	...	...	...	...	...	...	...	...	...	...	...	...	...	...
	NHL Totals		**400**	**50**	**59**	**109**	**43**	**39**	**82**	**1051**	**4**	**0**	**4**	**412**	**12.1**	**176**	**16**	**220**	**4**		**36**	**2**	**1**	**3**	**161**	**1**	**0**	**0**

CHL Second All-Star Team (1982)

Traded to **New Jersey** by **St. Louis** for Rick Meagher and New Jersey's 12th round choice (Bill Butler) in 1986 Entry Draft, August 29, 1985. Signed as a free agent by **San Jose**, July 8, 1991.

• ANDERSON, RON C.

Ron C. "Goings" Anderson RW – R. 6', 170 lbs b: Red Deer, Alta., 7/29/1945.

Season	Club	League	GP	G	A	Pts	AG	AA	APts	PIM	PP	SH	GW	S	%	TGF	PGF	TGA	PGA	+/-	GP	G	A	Pts	PIM	PP	SH	GW
1963-64	Edmonton Oil Kings	SJHL	14	6	5	11	...	...	...	4	...	...	...	...	...	...	...	...	...	...	...	...	...	...	...	...	...	...
1964-65	Edmonton Oil Kings	AJHL	STATISTICS NOT AVAILABLE																									
1965-66	Edmonton Oil Kings	ASHL	...	15	19	34	...	...	...	51	...	...	...	...	...	...	...	...	...	...	...	...	...	...	...	...	...	...
	Hamilton Red Wings	OHA	6	1	0	1	...	...	...	2	...	...	...	...	...	...	...	...	...	...	...	...	...	...	...	...	...	...
	Memphis Wings	CHL	3	1	3	4	...	...	...	4	...	...	...	...	...	...	...	...	...	...	...	...	...	...	...	...	...	...
1966-67	Memphis Wings	CHL	67	12	22	34	...	...	...	51	...	...	...	...	...	...	...	...	...	...	7	2	2	4	2	...	...	...
1967-68	**Detroit Red Wings**	**NHL**	**18**	**2**	**0**	**2**	**2**	**0**	**2**	**13**	**0**	**0**	**0**	**21**	**9.5**	**6**	**0**	**10**	**0**	**–4**	...	...	...	...	...	...	...	...
	Fort Worth Wings	CHL	39	21	19	40	...	...	...	46	...	...	...	...	...	...	...	...	...	...	...	...	...	...	...	...	...	...
1968-69	**Detroit Red Wings**	**NHL**	**7**	**0**	**0**	**0**	**0**	**0**	**0**	**8**	**0**	**0**	**0**	**4**	**0.0**	**1**	**0**	**4**	**0**	**–3**	...	...	...	...	...	...	...	...
	Los Angeles Kings	**NHL**	**56**	**3**	**5**	**8**	**3**	**5**	**8**	**26**	**0**	**0**	**0**	**68**	**4.4**	**14**	**1**	**38**	**16**	**–9**	**4**	**0**	**0**	**0**	**2**	**0**	**0**	**0**
1969-70	**St. Louis Blues**	**NHL**	**59**	**9**	**9**	**18**	**10**	**9**	**19**	**36**	**0**	**0**	**0**	**197**	**4.6**	**33**	**3**	**19**	**0**	**+11**	**1**	**0**	**0**	**0**	**2**	**0**	**0**	**0**
	Buffalo Bisons	AHL	9	8	3	11	...	...	...	16	...	...	...	...	...	...	...	...	...	...	...	...	...	...	...	...	...	...
1970-71	**Buffalo Sabres**	**NHL**	**74**	**14**	**12**	**26**	**15**	**11**	**26**	**44**	**0**	**1**	**3**	**139**	**10.1**	**38**	**1**	**70**	**22**	**–11**	...	...	...	...	...	...	...	...
1971-72	**Buffalo Sabres**	**NHL**	**37**	**0**	**4**	**4**	**0**	**4**	**4**	**19**	**0**	**0**	**0**	**35**	**0.0**	**10**	**0**	**22**	**2**	**–10**	...	...	...	...	...	...	...	...
	Salt Lake Golden Eagles	WHL	26	7	10	17	...	...	...	8	...	...	...	...	...	...	...	...	...	...	...	...	...	...	...	...	...	...
1972-73	Alberta Oilers	WHA	73	14	15	29	...	...	...	43	...	...	...	...	...	...	...	...	...	...	...	...	...	...	...	...	...	...
1973-74	Edmonton Oilers	WHA	19	5	2	7	...	...	...	6	...	...	...	...	...	...	...	...	...	...	1	0	0	0	0	...	...	...
	Winston-Salem Polar Bears	SHL	49	28	31	59	...	...	...	33	...	...	...	...	...	...	...	...	...	...	...	...	...	...	...	...	...	...
1974-75	Mohawk Valley Comets	NAHL	64	18	34	52	...	...	...	21	...	...	...	...	...	...	...	...	...	...	...	...	...	...	...	...	...	...
1975-76	Winston-Salem Polar Bears	SHL	27	0	7	7	...	...	...	14	...	...	...	...	...	...	...	...	...	...	...	...	...	...	...	...	...	...
	Tidewater Sharks	SHL	41	1	14	15	...	...	...	49	...	...	...	...	...	...	...	...	...	...	...	...	...	...	...	...	...	...
1976-77	Winston-Salem Polar Twins	SHL	24	1	6	7	...	...	...	10	...	...	...	...	...	...	...	...	...	...	...	...	...	...	...	...	...	...
	NHL Totals		**251**	**28**	**30**	**58**	**30**	**29**	**59**	**146**	**0**	**1**	**3**	**464**	**6.0**	**102**	**5**	**163**	**40**		**5**	**0**	**0**	**0**	**4**	**0**	**0**	**0**
	Other Major League Totals		92	19	17	36	...	...	...	49	...	...	...	...	...	...	...	...	...	...	1	0	0	0	0	...	...	...

SHL Second All-Star Team (1974) • SHL First All-Star Team (1970)

Traded to **LA Kings** by **Detroit** for Poul Popeil, November 12, 1968. Claimed by **St. Louis** from **LA Kings** in Intra-League Draft, June 11, 1969. Traded to **Buffalo** by **St. Louis** for Craig Cameron, October 2, 1970. Selected by **Alberta** (WHA) in 1972 WHA General Player Draft, February 12, 1972. Claimed by **San Diego** (WHL) from **Buffalo** (Salt Lake-WHL) in Reverse Draft, June, 1972.

• ANDERSON, RON H.

Ron H. Anderson RW – R. 5'10", 165 lbs. b: Moncton, N.B., 1/21/1950.

Season	Club	League	GP	G	A	Pts	AG	AA	APts	PIM	PP	SH	GW	S	%	TGF	PGF	TGA	PGA	+/-	GP	G	A	Pts	PIM	PP	SH	GW
1963-64	Moncton Rovers	Midget	...	*17	10	*27	...	...	...	7	...	...	...	...	...	...	...	...	...	...	...	...	...	...	...	...	...	...
1964-65	Moncton Aces	Midget		15	7	22	...	...	...	4	...	...	...	...	...	...	...	...	...	...	...	...	...	...	...	...	...	...
1965-66	Moncton Beavers	Juvenile	...	*20	21	*41	...	...	...	10	...	...	...	...	...	...	...	...	...	...	...	...	...	...	...	...	...	...
1966-67	Moncton Seals	NBJHL		26	*34	*60	...	...		...	...	...	...	...	...	...	...	...	...	...	...	...	...	...	...	...	...	...
	Moncton Seals	NBSHL	...	15	20	35	...	...	...	34	...	...	...	...	...	...	...	...	...	...	...	*17	21	*38	0	...	...	...
1967-68	Moncton Hawks	NBSHL	30	17	23	40	...	...	...	2	...	...	...	...	...	...	...	...	...	...	6	2	3	5	12	...	...	...
	Moncton Seals	NBJHL	...	...	...	...	...	...	...	...	...	...	...	...	...	...	...	...	...	...	6	2	3	5	12	...	...	...
	Fredericton Jr. Red Wings	NBJHL	...	...	...	...	...	...	...	...	...	...	...	...	...	...	...	...	...	...	6	*6	4	10	2	...	...	...
	Halifax Jr. Canadians	NSJHL	...	...			...	...	...	...	...	...	...	...	...	...	...	...	...	...	4	0	2	2	6	...	...	...
	Fredericton Red Wings	NBSHL	...		...	...		...	...	...	...	...	...	...	...	...	...	...	...	...	6	3	5	8	2	...	...	...
1968-69	Moncton Alpines	NBSHL	20	*30	36	*66	...	...	...	34	...	...	...	...	...	...	...	...	...	...	...	...	...	...	...	...	...	...
1969-70	Boston University	ECAC	DID NOT PLAY – FRESHMAN																									
1970-71	Boston University	ECAC	31	20	21	41	...	...	...	17	...	...	...	...	...	...	...	...	...	...	...	...	...	...	...	...	...	...
1971-72	Boston University	ECAC	31	19	27	46	...	...	...	26	...	...	...	...	...	...	...	...	...	...	...	...	...	...	...	...	...	...
1972-73	Boston Braves	AHL	73	41	29	70	...	...	...	53	...	...	...	...	...	...	...	...	...	...	...	...	...	...	...	...	...	...
1973-74	Boston Braves	AHL	75	24	31	55	...	...	...	28	...	...	...	...	...	...	...	...	...	...	...	...	...	...	...	...	...	...
1974-75	**Washington Capitals**	**NHL**	**28**	**9**	**7**	**16**	**8**	**5**	**13**	**8**	**4**	**0**	**0**	**43**	**20.9**	**23**	**9**	**34**	**0**	**–20**	...	...	...	...	...	...	...	...
	Richmond Robins	AHL	38	20	19	39	...	...	...	19	...	...	...	...	...	...	...	...	...	...	...	...	...	...	...	...	...	...
1975-76	Richmond Robins	AHL	20	2	3	5	...	...	...	6	...	...	...	...	...	...	...	...	...	...	...	...	...	...	...	...	...	...
	New Haven Nighthawks	AHL	17	1	3	4	...	...	...	8	...	...	...	...	...	...	...	...	...	...	3	0	0	0	0	...	...	...
1976-77	Veicherung	Austria	24	26	14	40	...	...	...	...	...	...	...	...	...	...	...	...	...	...	...	...	...	...	...	...	...	...
	NHL Totals		**28**	**9**	**7**	**16**	**8**	**5**	**13**	**8**	**4**	**0**	**0**	**43**	**20.9**	**23**	**9**	**34**	**0**		...	...	...	...	...	...	...	...

AHL Second All-Star Team (1973) • Won Dudley "Red" Garrett Memorial Award (Top Rookie - AHL) (1973)

Signed as a free agent by **Boston**, June, 1972. Claimed by **Washington** from **Boston** in Expansion Draft, June 12, 1974. Traded to **New Haven** (AHL) by **Washington** with Bob Gryp for Rich Nantais and Alain Langlois, February 23, 1976.

• ANDERSON, RUSS

Russ Anderson D L. 6'3", 210 lbs. b: Minneapolis, MN, 2/12/1955. Pittsburgh's 2nd choice, 31st overall, in 1975 Amateur Draft.

Season	Club	League	GP	G	A	Pts	AG	AA	APts	PIM	PP	SH	GW	S	%	TGF	PGF	TGA	PGA	+/-	GP	G	A	Pts	PIM	PP	SH	GW
1974-75	University of Minnesota	WCHA	30	2	7	9	...	...	...	56	...	...	...	...	...	...	...	...	...	...	...	...	...	...	...	...	...	...
1975-76	University of Minnesota	WCHA	28	0	5	5	...	...	...	81	...	...	...	...	...	...	...	...	...	...	...	...	...	...	...	...	...	...
1976-77	**Pittsburgh Penguins**	**NHL**	**66**	**2**	**11**	**13**	**2**	**9**	**11**	**81**	**0**	**0**	**1**	**45**	**4.4**	**63**	**6**	**62**	**10**	**+5**	**3**	**0**	**1**	**1**	**14**	**0**	**0**	**0**
	Hershey Bears	AHL	11	0	4	4	...	...	...	35	...	...	...	...	...	...	...	...	...	...	...	...	...	...	...	...	...	...
	United States	WEC-A	10	0	0	0	...	...	...	16	...	...	...	...	...	...	...	...	...	...	...	...	...	...	...	...	...	...
1977-78	**Pittsburgh Penguins**	**NHL**	**74**	**2**	**16**	**18**	**2**	**13**	**15**	**150**	**0**	**0**	**1**	**51**	**3.9**	**67**	**2**	**81**	**11**	**–5**	...	...	...	...	...	...	...	...
1978-79	**Pittsburgh Penguins**	**NHL**	**72**	**3**	**13**	**16**	**3**	**10**	**13**	**93**	**0**	**0**	**0**	**48**	**6.3**	**52**	**0**	**64**	**13**	**+1**	**2**	**0**	**0**	**0**	**0**	**0**	**0**	**0**
1979-80	**Pittsburgh Penguins**	**NHL**	**76**	**5**	**22**	**27**	**5**	**17**	**22**	**150**	**0**	**0**	**0**	**78**	**6.4**	**93**	**3**	**107**	**28**	**+11**	**5**	**0**	**2**	**2**	**14**	**0**	**0**	**0**
1980-81	**Pittsburgh Penguins**	**NHL**	**34**	**3**	**14**	**17**	**2**	**10**	**12**	**112**	**1**	**0**	**1**	**38**	**7.9**	**46**	**7**	**44**	**17**	**+12**	...	...	...	...	...	...	...	...
1981-82	**Pittsburgh Penguins**	**NHL**	**31**	**0**	**1**	**1**	**0**	**1**	**1**	**98**	**0**	**0**	**0**	**13**	**0.0**	**11**	**0**	**18**	**3**	**–4**	...	...	...	...	...	...	...	...
	Hartford Whalers	**NHL**	**25**	**1**	**3**	**4**	**1**	**2**	**3**	**85**	**0**	**0**	**1**	**24**	**4.2**	**20**	**0**	**46**	**9**	**–17**	...	...	...	...	...	...	...	...
1982-83	**Hartford Whalers**	**NHL**	**57**	**0**	**6**	**6**	**0**	**4**	**4**	**171**	**0**	**0**	**0**	**18**	**0.0**	**35**	**0**	**77**	**9**	**–33**	...	...	...	...	...	...	...	...
1983-84	**Los Angeles Kings**	**NHL**	**70**	**5**	**12**	**17**	**4**	**8**	**12**	**126**	**0**	**0**	**1**	**47**	**10.6**	**60**	**2**	**110**	**22**	**–30**	...	...	...	...	...	...	...	...
1984-85	**Los Angeles Kings**	**NHL**	**14**	**1**	**1**	**2**	**1**	**1**	**2**	**20**	**0**	**0**	**0**	**11**	**9.1**	**9**	**0**	**12**	**1**	**–2**	...	...	...	...	...	...	...	...
	New Haven Nighthawks	AHL	0	0	2	2	...	...	...	2	...	...	...	...	...	...	...	...	...	...	...	...	...	...	...	...	...	...
	NHL Totals		**519**	**22**	**99**	**121**	**20**	**75**	**95**	**1086**	**1**	**0**	**5**	**373**	**5.9**	**456**	**20**	**621**	**123**		**10**	**0**	**3**	**3**	**28**	**0**	**0**	**0**

Traded to **Hartford** by **Pittsburgh** with Pittsburgh 8th round choice (Chris Duperron) in 1983 Entry Draft for Rick MacLeish, December 29, 1991. Signed as a free agent by **LA Kings**, September 2, 1983.

• ANDERSON, SHAWN

Shawn Anderson D – L. 6'1", 200 lbs. b: Montreal, Que., 2/7/1968. Buffalo's 1st choice, 5th overall, in 1986 Entry Draft.

			REGULAR SEASON																		PLAYOFFS							
Season	Club	League	GP	G	A	Pts	AG	AA	APts	PIM	PP	SH	GW	S	%	TGF	PGF	TGA	PGA	+/–	GP	G	A	Pts	PIM	PP	SH	GW
1984-85	Lac St-Louis	Midget	42	23	42	65				10																		
1985-86	University of Maine	H.E	16	5	8	13				22																		
	Canada	Nat-Team	33	2	6	8				16																		
1986-87	**Buffalo Sabres**	**NHL**	**41**	**2**	**11**	**13**	**2**	**8**	**10**	**23**	**0**	**0**	**0**	**26**	**7.7**	**30**	**5**	**29**	**4**	**0**								
	Rochester Americans	AHL	15	2	5	7				11																		
1987-88	**Buffalo Sabres**	**NHL**	**23**	**1**	**2**	**3**	**1**	**1**	**2**	**17**	**1**	**0**	**0**	**29**	**3.4**	**25**	**8**	**25**	**5**	**–3**								
	Rochester Americans	AHL	22	5	16	21				19											6	0	0	0	0			
1988-89	**Buffalo Sabres**	**NHL**	**33**	**2**	**10**	**12**	**2**	**7**	**9**	**18**	**2**	**0**	**0**	**26**	**7.7**	**31**	**5**	**31**	**8**	**+3**	**5**	**0**	**1**	**1**	**4**	**0**	**0**	**0**
	Rochester Americans	AHL	31	5	14	19				24																		
1989-90	**Buffalo Sabres**	**NHL**	**16**	**1**	**3**	**4**	**1**	**2**	**3**	**8**	**0**	**0**	**0**	**16**	**6.3**	**17**	**4**	**11**	**0**	**+2**								
	Rochester Americans	AHL	39	2	16	18				41											9	1	0	1	4			
1990-91	**Quebec Nordiques**	**NHL**	**31**	**3**	**10**	**13**	**3**	**8**	**11**	**21**	**2**	**0**	**0**	**44**	**6.8**	**31**	**7**	**22**	**0**	**+2**								
	Halifax Citadels	AHL	4	0	1	1				2																		
1991-92	Weiswasser	Germany	38	7	15	22				83																		
1992-93	**Washington Capitals**	**NHL**	**60**	**2**	**6**	**8**	**2**	**4**	**6**	**18**	**1**	**0**	**0**	**42**	**4.8**	**22**	**5**	**19**	**0**	**–2**	**6**	**0**	**0**	**0**	**0**	**0**	**0**	**0**
	Baltimore Skipjacks	AHL	10	1	5	6				8																		
1993-94	**Washington Capitals**	**NHL**	**50**	**0**	**9**	**9**	**0**	**7**	**7**	**12**	**0**	**0**	**0**	**31**	**0.0**	**21**	**2**	**23**	**3**	**–1**	**8**	**1**	**0**	**1**	**12**	**0**	**0**	**0**
1994-95	**Philadelphia Flyers**	**NHL**	**1**	**0**	**0**	**0**	**0**	**0**	**0**	**0**	**0**	**0**	**0**	**0**	**0.0**	**1**	**0**	**1**	**0**	**0**								
	Hershey Bears	AHL	31	9	21	30				18											6	2	3	5	19			
1995-96	Milwaukee Admirals	IHL	79	22	39	61				68											5	0	7	7	0			
1996-97	Wedemark Scorpions	Germany	8	1	0	1				4																		
	Utah Grizzlies	IHL	31	2	12	14				21																		
	Manitoba Moose	IHL	17	2	7	9				5																		
1997-98	ECR Revier Lowen	Germany	32	5	14	19				45																		
	NHL Totals		**255**	**11**	**51**	**62**	**11**	**37**	**48**	**117**	**6**	**0**	**0**	**214**	**5.1**	**178**	**36**	**161**	**20**		**19**	**1**	**1**	**2**	**16**	**0**	**0**	**0**

Traded to **Washington** by **Buffalo** for Bill Houlder, September 30, 1990. Claimed by **Quebec** from **Washington** in NHL Waiver Draft, October 1, 1990. Traded to **Winnipeg** by **Quebec** for Sergei Kharin, October 22, 1991. Traded to **Washington** by **Winnipeg** for future considerations, October 23, 1991. Signed as a free agent by **Philadelphia**, August 16, 1994.

• ANDERSSON, ERIK

Erik Andersson C – L. 6'3", 210 lbs. b: Stockholm, Sweden, 8/19/1971. Calgary's 6th choice, 70th overall, in 1997 Entry Draft.

			REGULAR SEASON																		PLAYOFFS							
Season	Club	League	GP	G	A	Pts	AG	AA	APts	PIM	PP	SH	GW	S	%	TGF	PGF	TGA	PGA	+/–	GP	G	A	Pts	PIM	PP	SH	GW
1989-90	Danderyd	Sweden 2	30	14	5	19				16																		
1990-91	AIK Solna	Sweden	32	1	1	2				10																		
	Sweden	WJC-A	7	2	1	3				4																		
1991-92	AIK Solna	Sweden	3	0	0	0				0																		
1992-93			DID NOT PLAY																									
1993-94	University of Denver	WCHA	38	10	20	30				26																		
1994-95	University of Denver	WCHA	42	12	19	31				42																		
1995-96	University of Denver	WCHA	39	12	35	47				40																		
1996-97	University of Denver	WCHA	39	17	17	34				42																		
1997-98	**Calgary Flames**	**NHL**	**12**	**2**	**1**	**3**	**2**	**1**	**3**	**8**	**0**	**0**	**0**	**11**	**18.2**	**4**	**0**	**9**	**1**	**–4**								
	NHL Totals		**12**	**2**	**1**	**3**	**2**	**1**	**3**	**8**	**0**	**0**	**0**	**11**	**18.2**	**4**	**0**	**9**	**1**									

• Re-enetered NHL draft. Originally Los Angeles' 5th choice, 112th overall, in 1990 Entry Draft.

• ANDERSSON, KENT-ERIK

Kent-Erik Andersson RW. 6'2", 185 lbs. b: Orebro, Sweden, 5/24/1951.

			REGULAR SEASON																		PLAYOFFS							
Season	Club	League	GP	G	A	Pts	AG	AA	APts	PIM	PP	SH	GW	S	%	TGF	PGF	TGA	PGA	+/–	GP	G	A	Pts	PIM	PP	SH	GW
1971-72	Farjestads BK Karlstad	Sweden	22	9	6	15				2																		
1972-73	Farjestads BK Karlstad	Sweden	STATISTICS NOT AVAILABLE																									
1973-74	Farjestads BK Karlstad	Sweden	STATISTICS NOT AVAILABLE																									
1974-75	Farjestads BK Karlstad	Sweden	27	18	11	29				2																		
1975-76	Farjestads BK Karlstad	Sweden	26	8	5	13				6												0	2	2	2			
1976-77	Farjestads BK Karlstad	Sweden	33	17	17	34				30											5	2	1	3	4			
	Sweden	WEC-A	10	4	1	5				0																		
1977-78	**Minnesota North Stars**	**NHL**	**73**	**15**	**18**	**33**	**14**	**15**	**29**	**4**	**3**	**0**	**1**	**121**	**12.4**	**48**	**12**	**71**	**18**	**–17**								
	Sweden	WEC-A	10	5	1	6				12																		
1978-79	**Minnesota North Stars**	**NHL**	**41**	**9**	**4**	**13**	**8**	**3**	**11**	**4**	**2**	**2**	**4**	**59**	**15.3**	**20**	**4**	**30**	**8**	**–6**								
1979-80	**Minnesota North Stars**	**NHL**	**61**	**9**	**10**	**19**	**8**	**8**	**16**	**8**	**1**	**0**	**3**	**87**	**10.3**	**37**	**2**	**45**	**7**	**–3**	**13**	**2**	**4**	**6**	**2**	**0**	**0**	**1**
	Oklahoma City Stars	CHL	3	0	2	2				2																		
1980-81	**Minnesota North Stars**	**NHL**	**77**	**17**	**24**	**41**	**14**	**17**	**31**	**22**	**1**	**4**	**2**	**127**	**13.4**	**56**	**3**	**63**	**18**	**+8**	**19**	**2**	**4**	**6**	**2**	**0**	**0**	**0**
1981-82	Sweden	C Cup	5	0	1	1				0																		
	Minnesota North Stars	**NHL**	**70**	**9**	**12**	**21**	**7**	**8**	**15**	**18**	**0**	**0**	**2**	**78**	**11.5**	**35**	**1**	**57**	**18**	**–5**	**4**	**0**	**2**	**2**	**0**	**0**	**0**	**0**
1982-83	**New York Rangers**	**NHL**	**71**	**8**	**20**	**28**	**7**	**14**	**21**	**14**	**0**	**0**	**1**	**91**	**8.8**	**46**	**5**	**53**	**18**	**+6**	**9**	**0**	**0**	**0**	**0**	**0**	**0**	**0**
1983-84	**New York Rangers**	**NHL**	**63**	**5**	**15**	**20**	**4**	**10**	**14**	**8**	**0**	**0**	**1**	**70**	**7.1**	**36**	**1**	**43**	**13**	**+5**	**5**	**0**	**1**	**1**	**0**	**0**	**0**	**0**
1984-85	Farjestads BK Karlstad	Sweden	32	8	12	20				10											3	2	0	2	2			
1985-86	Farjestads BK Karlstad	Sweden	25	6	7	13				12											8	*5	6	*11	2			
	NHL Totals		**456**	**72**	**103**	**175**	**62**	**75**	**137**	**78**	**7**	**6**	**14**	**633**	**11.4**	**278**	**28**	**362**	**100**		**50**	**4**	**11**	**15**	**4**	**0**	**0**	**1**

Swedish Player of the Year (1977)

Signed as a free agent by **Minnesota**, June 15, 1977. Traded to **Hartford** by **Minnesota** with Mark Johnson for Jordy Douglas and Hartford's 5th round choice (Jim Poner) in 1984 Entry Draft, October 1, 1982. Traded to **NY Rangers** by **Hartford** for Ed Hospodar, October 1, 1982.

• ANDERSSON, MIKAEL

Mikael Andersson LW – L. 5'11", 181 lbs. b: Malmo, Sweden, 5/10/1966. Buffalo's 1st choice, 18th overall, in 1984 Entry Draft.

			REGULAR SEASON																		PLAYOFFS							
Season	Club	League	GP	G	A	Pts	AG	AA	APts	PIM	PP	SH	GW	S	%	TGF	PGF	TGA	PGA	+/–	GP	G	A	Pts	PIM	PP	SH	GW
1982-83	Vastra Frolunda	Sweden	1	1	0	1				0																		
1983-84	Vastra Frolunda	Sweden	18	0	3	3				6																		
	Sweden	WJC-A	7	1	2	3				8																		
1984-85	Vastra Frolunda	Sweden 2	30	16	11	27				18											6	3	2	5	2			
	Sweden	WJC-A	6	2	3	5				0																		
1985-86	**Buffalo Sabres**	**NHL**	**32**	**1**	**9**	**10**	**1**	**6**	**7**	**4**	**0**	**0**	**0**	**13**	**7.7**	**20**	**4**	**16**	**0**	**0**								
	Sweden	WJC-A	7	4	3	7				10																		
	Rochester Americans	AHL	20	10	4	14				6																		
1986-87	**Buffalo Sabres**	**NHL**	**16**	**0**	**3**	**3**	**0**	**2**	**2**	**0**	**0**	**0**	**0**	**6**	**0.0**	**8**	**1**	**15**	**6**	**–2**								
	Rochester Americans	AHL	42	6	20	26				14											9	1	2	3	2			
1987-88	**Buffalo Sabres**	**NHL**	**37**	**3**	**20**	**23**	**3**	**14**	**17**	**10**	**0**	**1**	**1**	**34**	**8.8**	**33**	**3**	**35**	**12**	**+7**	**1**	**1**	**0**	**1**	**0**	**0**	**0**	**0**
	Rochester Americans	AHL	35	12	24	36				16																		
1988-89	**Buffalo Sabres**	**NHL**	**14**	**0**	**1**	**1**	**0**	**1**	**1**	**4**	**0**	**0**	**0**	**12**	**0.0**	**6**	**0**	**9**	**2**	**–1**								
	Rochester Americans	AHL	56	18	33	51				12																		
1989-90	**Hartford Whalers**	**NHL**	**50**	**13**	**24**	**37**	**11**	**17**	**28**	**6**	**1**	**2**	**2**	**86**	**15.1**	**45**	**11**	**48**	**14**	**0**	**5**	**0**	**3**	**3**	**2**	**0**	**0**	**0**
1990-91	**Hartford Whalers**	**NHL**	**41**	**4**	**7**	**11**	**4**	**5**	**9**	**8**	**0**	**0**	**0**	**57**	**7.0**	**19**	**2**	**28**	**11**	**0**								
	Springfield Indians	AHL	26	7	22	29				10											18	*10	8	18	12			
1991-92	Sweden	C Cup	6	0	1	1				2																		
	Hartford Whalers	**NHL**	**74**	**18**	**29**	**47**	**16**	**22**	**38**	**14**	**1**	**3**	**1**	**149**	**12.1**	**65**	**8**	**69**	**30**	**+18**	**7**	**0**	**2**	**2**	**6**	**0**	**0**	**0**
	Sweden	WC-A	5	1	1	2				0																		
1992-93	**Tampa Bay Lightning**	**NHL**	**77**	**16**	**11**	**27**	**13**	**8**	**21**	**14**	**3**	**2**	**4**	**169**	**9.5**	**43**	**6**	**76**	**25**	**–14**								
	Sweden	WC-A	8	2	2	4				2																		
1993-94	**Tampa Bay Lightning**	**NHL**	**76**	**13**	**12**	**25**	**12**	**9**	**21**	**23**	**1**	**1**	**2**	**136**	**9.6**	**43**	**2**	**45**	**12**	**+8**								
	Sweden	WC-A	8	2	0	2				0																		
1994-95	Vastra Frolunda	Sweden	7	1	0	1				31																		
	Tampa Bay Lightning	**NHL**	**36**	**4**	**7**	**11**	**7**	**10**	**17**	**4**	**0**	**0**	**0**	**36**	**11.1**	**18**	**1**	**27**	**7**	**–3**								
1995-96	**Tampa Bay Lightning**	**NHL**	**64**	**8**	**11**	**19**	**8**	**9**	**17**	**2**	**0**	**0**	**1**	**104**	**7.7**	**27**	**0**	**51**	**24**	**0**	**6**	**1**	**1**	**2**	**0**	**0**	**0**	**0**

			REGULAR SEASON																		PLAYOFFS							
Season	Club	League	GP	G	A	Pts	AG	AA	APts	PIM	PP	SH	GW	S	%	TGF	PGF	TGA	PGA	+/-	GP	G	A	Pts	PIM	PP	SH	GW
1996-97	Sweden	W Cup	4	0	1	1				2																		
	Tampa Bay Lightning	**NHL**	**70**	**5**	**14**	**19**	**5**	**12**	**17**	**8**	**0**	**3**	**1**	**102**	**4.9**	**28**	**0**	**51**	**24**	**+1**								
1997-98	**Tampa Bay Lightning**	**NHL**	**72**	**6**	**11**	**17**	**7**	**11**	**18**	**29**	**0**	**1**	**1**	**105**	**5.7**	**22**	**0**	**49**	**23**	**–4**								
	Sweden	Olympics	4	1	1	2				0																		
	NHL Totals		**659**	**91**	**159**	**250**	**87**	**126**	**213**	**126**	**6**	**13**	**13**	**1009**	**9.0**	**377**	**38**	**519**	**190**		**19**	**2**	**6**	**8**	**8**	**0**	**0**	**0**

Claimed by **Hartford** from **Buffalo** in NHL Waiver Draft, October 2, 1989. Signed as a free agent by **Tampa Bay**, June 29, 1992.

• ANDERSSON, NIKLAS

Niklas Andersson LW – L. 5'9", 175 lbs. b: Kungalv, Sweden, 5/20/1971. Quebec's 1st choice, 68th overall, in 1989 Entry Draft.

Season	Club	League	GP	G	A	Pts	AG	AA	APts	PIM	PP	SH	GW	S	%	TGF	PGF	TGA	PGA	+/-	GP	G	A	Pts	PIM	PP	SH	GW
1987-88	Vastra Frolunda	Sweden 2	15	5	5	10				6											8	6	4	10	4			
1988-89	Vastra Frolunda	Sweden 2	30	13	24	37				24																		
	Sweden	WJC-A	7	2	0	2				0																		
1989-90	Vastra Frolunda	Sweden	38	10	21	31				14																		
	Sweden	WJC-A	7	3	3	6				6																		
1990-91	Vastra Frolunda	Sweden	22	6	10	16				16																		
	Sweden	WJC-A	7	5	3	8				8																		
1991-92	Sweden	C Cup	6	0	1	1				0																		
	Halifax Citadels	AHL	57	8	26	34				41																		
1992-93	**Quebec Nordiques**	**NHL**	**3**	**0**	**1**	**1**	**0**	**1**	**1**	**2**	**0**	**0**	**0**	**4**	**0.0**	**3**	**0**	**3**	**0**	**0**								
	Halifax Citadels	AHL	76	32	50	82				42																		
1993-94	Cornwall Aces	AHL	42	18	34	52				8																		
1994-95	Denver Grizzlies	IHL	66	22	39	61				28											15	8	13	21	10			
1995-96	**New York Islanders**	**NHL**	**47**	**14**	**12**	**26**	**14**	**10**	**24**	**12**	**3**	**2**	**1**	**89**	**15.7**	**35**	**7**	**40**	**9**	**–3**								
	Utah Grizzlies	IHL	30	13	22	35				25																		
	Sweden	WC-A	6	1	1	2				8																		
1996-97	Sweden	W Cup	1	0	0	0				0																		
	New York Islanders	**NHL**	**74**	**12**	**31**	**43**	**13**	**27**	**40**	**57**	**1**	**1**	**1**	**122**	**9.8**	**61**	**15**	**52**	**10**	**+4**								
	Sweden	WC-A	11	0	2	2				8																		
1997-98	**San Jose Sharks**	**NHL**	**5**	**0**	**0**	**0**	**0**	**0**	**0**	**2**	**0**	**0**	**0**	**6**	**0.0**	**0**	**0**	**1**	**0**	**–1**								
	Kentucky Thoroughblades	AHL	37	10	28	38				54																		
	Utah Grizzlies	IHL	21	6	20	26				24											4	3	1	4	4			
	NHL Totals		**129**	**26**	**44**	**70**	**27**	**38**	**65**	**73**	**4**	**3**	**2**	**221**	**11.8**	**99**	**22**	**96**	**19**									

Signed as a free agent by **NY Islanders**, July 15, 1994. Signed as a free agent by **San Jose**, September 17, 1997.

• ANDERSSON, PETER

Peter Andersson D – R. 6'2", 200 lbs. b: Ferdertalwe, Sweden, 3/2/1962. Washington's 8th choice, 173rd overall, in 1980 Entry Draft.

Season	Club	League	GP	G	A	Pts	AG	AA	APts	PIM	PP	SH	GW	S	%	TGF	PGF	TGA	PGA	+/-	GP	G	A	Pts	PIM	PP	SH	GW
1980-81	IF Bjorkloven	Sweden	31	1	2	3				16																		
1981-82	IF Bjorkloven	Sweden	33	7	7	14				36											7	1	1	2	8			
	Sweden	WJC-A	7	3	6	9				12																		
	Sweden	WEC-A	10	2	1	3				2																		
1982-83	Sweden	Nat-Team	25	3	1	4				18																		
	IF Bjorkloven	Sweden	34	8	16	24				30											3	0	0	0	4			
	Sweden	WEC-A	10	1	1	2				8																		
1983-84	**Washington Capitals**	**NHL**	**42**	**3**	**7**	**10**	**2**	**5**	**7**	**20**	**2**	**0**	**0**	**49**	**6.1**	**43**	**15**	**17**	**1**	**+12**	**3**	**0**	**1**	**1**	**2**	**0**	**0**	**0**
1984-85	Sweden	C Cup	8	1	1	2				4																		
	Washington Capitals	**NHL**	**57**	**0**	**10**	**10**	**0**	**7**	**7**	**21**	**0**	**0**	**0**	**58**	**0.0**	**51**	**14**	**36**	**4**	**+5**	**2**	**0**	**0**	**0**	**0**	**0**	**0**	**0**
	Binghamton Whalers	AHL	13	2	3	5				6																		
1985-86	**Washington Capitals**	**NHL**	**61**	**6**	**16**	**22**	**5**	**11**	**16**	**36**	**3**	**0**	**3**	**83**	**7.2**	**66**	**31**	**48**	**5**	**–8**								
	Quebec Nordiques	**NHL**	**12**	**1**	**8**	**9**	**1**	**5**	**6**	**4**	**1**	**0**	**0**	**16**	**6.3**	**26**	**8**	**10**	**0**	**+8**	**2**	**0**	**1**	**1**	**0**	**0**	**0**	**0**
1986-87	IF Bjorkloven	Sweden	30	6	10	16				30											6	2	1	3	4			
	Sweden	WEC-A	10	0	5	5				8																		
1987-88	Sweden	C Cup	5	1	1	2				2																		
	IF Bjorkloven	Sweden	40	6	12	18				40											8	1	5	6	2			
	Sweden	Olympics	8	2	2	4				4																		
1988-89	IF Bjorkloven	Sweden	22	2	9	11				10																		
	Sweden	WEC-A	8	0	1	1				4																		
1989-90	EV Zug	Switz.2	36	10	4	14															2	0	0	0	0			
	Sweden	WEC-A	10	0	2	2				6																		
1990-91	IF Bjorkloven	Sweden2	STATISTICS NOT AVAILABLE																									
	Sweden	WEC-A	10	1	0	1				4																		
1991-92	Sweden	C Cup	6	0	0	0				2																		
	IF Bjorkloven	Sweden	35	9	20	29				30											3	0	0	0	4			
	Sweden	Olympics	8	1	2	3				4																		
	NHL Totals		**172**	**10**	**41**	**51**	**8**	**28**	**36**	**81**	**6**	**0**	**3**	**206**	**4.9**	**186**	**68**	**111**	**10**		**7**	**0**	**2**	**2**	**2**	**0**	**0**	**0**

EJC-A All Star Team (1980) • Swedish World All-Star Team (1982, 1983, 1992)

Traded to **Quebec** by **Washington** for Quebec's 3rd round choice (Shawn Simpson) in 1986 Entry Draft, March 10, 1986.

• ANDERSSON, PETER

Peter Andersson D – L. 6', 196 lbs. b: Orebro, Sweden, 8/29/1965. NY Rangers' 5th choice, 75th overall, in 1983 Entry Draft.

Season	Club	League	GP	G	A	Pts	AG	AA	APts	PIM	PP	SH	GW	S	%	TGF	PGF	TGA	PGA	+/-	GP	G	A	Pts	PIM	PP	SH	GW
1981-82	Orebro	Sweden2	31	8	5	13				30											2	0	0	0	0			
1982-83	Orebro	Sweden2	25	10	10	20				16											2	1	2	3	2			
	Sweden	WJC-A	7	3	0	3																						
1983-84	Farjestads BK Karlstad	Sweden	36	4	7	11				22																		
	Sweden	WJC-A	7	0	1	1				4																		
1984-85	Farjestads BK Karlstad	Sweden	35	5	12	17				24																		
	Sweden	WJC-A	7	4	10	14				20																		
1985-86	Farjestads BK Karlstad	Sweden	34	6	10	16				18																		
1986-87	Farjestads BK Karlstad	Sweden	32	9	8	17				32																		
1987-88	Farjestads BK Karlstad	Sweden	38	14	20	34				44											8	2	2	4	4			
1988-89	Farjestads BK Karlstad	Sweden	33	6	17	23				44																		
1989-90	Malmo IF	Sweden	33	15	25	40				32																		
1990-91	Malmo IF	Sweden	34	9	17	26				26																		
1991-92	Malmo IF	Sweden	40	12	20	32				80																		
	Sweden	Olympics	8	0	1	1				4																		
1992-93	**New York Rangers**	**NHL**	**31**	**4**	**11**	**15**	**3**	**8**	**11**	**18**	**3**	**0**	**1**	**68**	**5.9**	**35**	**15**	**18**	**2**	**+4**								
	Binghamton Rangers	AHL	27	11	22	33				16																		
	Sweden	WC-A	7	1	6	7				8																		
1993-94	**New York Rangers**	**NHL**	**8**	**1**	**1**	**2**	**1**	**1**	**2**	**2**	**0**	**1**	**1**	**10**	**10.0**	**2**	**1**	**4**	**0**	**–3**								
	Florida Panthers	**NHL**	**8**	**1**	**1**	**2**	**1**	**1**	**2**	**0**	**0**	**0**	**0**	**11**	**9.1**	**7**	**2**	**10**	**0**	**–5**								
	Sweden	WC-A	8	0	1	1				6																		
1994-95	Malmo IF	Sweden	27	1	9	10				18											9	5	0	5	16			
1995-96	Malmo IF	Sweden	27	7	15	22				14																		
	Dusseldorfer EG	Germany	5	1	4	5				6											13	4	6	10	8			
1996-97	HC Bolzano	Italy	6	0	5	5				8																		
	Dusseldorfer EG	Germany	45	11	20	31				54											4	1	1	2	0			
1997-98	HC Lugano	Switz.	36	11	16	27				26											7	1	5	6	0			
	NHL Totals		**47**	**6**	**13**	**19**	**5**	**10**	**15**	**20**	**3**	**1**	**2**	**89**	**6.7**	**44**	**18**	**32**	**2**									

Traded to **Florida** by **NY Rangers** for Florida's 9th round choice (Vitali Yeremeyev) in 1994 Entry Draft, March 21, 1994.

• ANDRASCIK, STEVE

Steve Andrascik RW – R. 5'11", 200 lbs. b: Sherridon, Man., 11/6/1948. Detroit's 1st choice, 11th overall, in 1968 Amateur Draft.

Season	Club	League	GP	G	A	Pts	AG	AA	APts	PIM	PP	SH	GW	S	%	TGF	PGF	TGA	PGA	+/-	GP	G	A	Pts	PIM	PP	SH	GW
1967-68	Flin Flon Bombers	WCJHL	60	30	26	56				88											15	4	3	7	11			
1968-69	Flin Flon Bombers	WCJHL	50	32	36	68				142											18	7	8	15				
1969-70	Fort Worth Wings	CHL	69	8	7	15				80											7	0	1	1	5			

			REGULAR SEASON																		PLAYOFFS							
Season	Club	League	GP	G	A	Pts	AG	AA	APts	PIM	PP	SH	GW	S	%	TGF	PGF	TGA	PGA	+/–	GP	G	A	Pts	PIM	PP	SH	GW
1970-71	Fort Worth Wings	CHL	8	2	1	3	....	....	....	23	....	....	....	....	....	....	....	....	....	....	....	....	....	....	....	....	....	....
	Omaha Knights	CHL	65	23	14	37	....	....	....	81	....	....	....	....	....	....	....	....	....	....	11	2	0	2	24	....	....	....
1971-72	Providence Reds	AHL	74	14	10	24	....	....	....	104	....	....	....	....	....	....	....	....	....	....	5	2	0	2	8	....	....	....
	New York Rangers	**NHL**	....	....	....	....	....	....	....	....	....	....	....	....	....	....	....	....	....	....	**1**	**0**	**0**	**0**	**0**	....	....	....
1972-73	Providence Reds	AHL	41	8	9	17	....	....	....	44	....	....	....	....	....	....	....	....	....	....	4	0	3	3	9	....	....	....
1973-74	Hershey Bears	AHL	70	23	43	66	....	....	....	36	....	....	....	....	....	....	....	....	....	....	14	3	7	10	44	....	....	....
1974-75	Indianapolis Racers	WHA	20	2	4	6	....	....	....	16	....	....	....	....	....	....	....	....	....	....	....	....	....	....	....	....	....	....
	Greensboro Generals	SHL	3	1	0	1	....	....	....	0	....	....	....	....	....	....	....	....	....	....	....	....	....	....	....	....	....	....
	Michigan–Baltimore	WHA	57	4	7	11	....	....	....	42	....	....	....	....	....	....	....	....	....	....	....	....	....	....	....	....	....	....
1975-76	Cincinnati Stingers	WHA	20	3	2	5	....	....	....	21	....	....	....	....	....	....	....	....	....	....	....	....	....	....	....	....	....	....
	Hampton Gulls	SHL	32	16	15	31	....	....	....	26	....	....	....	....	....	....	....	....	....	....	9	*6	5	11	24	....	....	....
1976-77	Hershey Bears	AHL	79	16	23	39	....	....	....	59	....	....	....	....	....	....	....	....	....	....	6	1	1	2	11	....	....	....
1977-78	Hershey Bears	AHL	79	4	9	13	....	....	....	21	....	....	....	....	....	....	....	....	....	....	....	....	....	....	....	....	....	....
	NHL Totals		**0**	**0**	**0**	**0**	**0**	**0**	**0**	**0**	**0**	**0**	**0**	**0**	**0.0**	**0**	**0**	**0**	**0**		**1**	**0**	**0**	**0**	**0**	**0**	**0**	**0**
	Other Major League Totals		97	9	13	22	....	....	....	79	....	....	....	....	....	....	....	....	....	....	....	....	....	....	....	....	....	....

Traded to **NY Rangers** by **Detroit** for Don Luce, November 2, 1970. Selected by **Alberta** (WHA) in 1972 WHA General Player Draft, February 12, 1972. Traded to **Pittsburgh** by **NY Rangers** to complete transaction that sent Sheldon Kannegiesser to NY Rangers (May 16, 1973), March 2, 1973. WHA rights traded to **Cincinnati** (WHA) by **Edmonton** (WHA) for future considerations, July, 1974. Loaned to **Indianapolis** (WHA) by **Cincinnati** (WHA) for 1974-75 season, July, 1974. Traded to **Michigan** (WHA) by **Indianapolis** (WHA) with Steve Richardson for Jacques Lucas and Brian McDonald, November, 1974.

● ANDREA, PAUL

Paul Andrea RW – L. 5'10", 174 lbs. b: North Sydney, N.S., 7/31/1941.

1958-59	Guelph Biltmores	OHA	23	5	0	5	....	....	....	2	....	....	....	....	....	....	....	....	....	....	9	1	2	3	5	....	....	....
1959-60	Guelph Biltmores	OHA	48	11	20	31	....	....	....	21	....	....	....	....	....	....	....	....	....	....	5	0	2	2	0	....	....	....
1960-61	Guelph Royals	OHA	48	29	33	62	....	....	....	30	....	....	....	....	....	....	....	....	....	....	14	3	11	14	20	....	....	....
	Kitchener-Waterloo Beavers	EPHL	2	0	0	0	....	....	....	0	....	....	....	....	....	....	....	....	....	....	....	....	....	....	....	....	....	....
1961-62	Kitchener-Waterloo Beavers	EPHL	16	4	0	4	....	....	....	8	....	....	....	....	....	....	....	....	....	....	7	2	2	4	2	....	....	....
	Vancouver Canucks	WHL	24	4	1	5	....	....	....	0	....	....	....	....	....	....	....	....	....	....	....	....	....	....	....	....	....	....
1962-63	Sudbury Wolves	EPHL	28	9	10	19	....	....	....	8	....	....	....	....	....	....	....	....	....	....	8	2	1	3	4	....	....	....
1963-64	St. Paul Rangers	CHL	71	27	30	57	....	....	....	12	....	....	....	....	....	....	....	....	....	....	11	2	2	4	2	....	....	....
1964-65	St. Paul Rangers	CHL	65	25	39	64	....	....	....	8	....	....	....	....	....	....	....	....	....	....	11	3	4	7	0	....	....	....
1965-66	**New York Rangers**	**NHL**	**4**	**1**	**1**	**2**	**1**	**1**	**2**	**0**	....	....	....	....	....	....	....	....	....	....	....	....	....	....	....	....	....	....
	Minnesota Rangers	CHL	64	*37	43	80	....	....	....	12	....	....	....	....	....	....	....	....	....	....	7	1	3	4	2	....	....	....
1966-67	Omaha Knights	CHL	69	*37	46	83	....	....	....	22	....	....	....	....	....	....	....	....	....	....	12	6	7	13	2	....	....	....
1967-68	**Pittsburgh Penguins**	**NHL**	**65**	**11**	**21**	**32**	**14**	**22**	**36**	**2**	**5**	**0**	**1**	**92**	**12.0**	**45**	**19**	**29**	**1**	**–2**	....	....	....	....	....	....	....	....
1968-69	**Pittsburgh Penguins**	**NHL**	**25**	**7**	**6**	**13**	**8**	**6**	**14**	**2**	**5**	**0**	**1**	**45**	**15.6**	**16**	**12**	**14**	**0**	**–10**	....	....	....	....	....	....	....	....
	Amarillo Wranglers	CHL	47	23	29	52	....	....	....	22	....	....	....	....	....	....	....	....	....	....	....	....	....	....	....	....	....	....
1969-70	Vancouver Canucks	WHL	72	44	47	91	....	....	....	13	....	....	....	....	....	....	....	....	....	....	11	5	7	12	6	....	....	....
1970-71	**California Golden Seals**	**NHL**	**9**	**1**	**0**	**1**	**1**	**0**	**1**	**2**	**1**	**0**	**0**	**14**	**7.1**	**1**	**1**	**6**	**0**	**–6**	....	....	....	....	....	....	....	....
	Buffalo Sabres	**NHL**	**47**	**11**	**21**	**32**	**11**	**18**	**29**	**4**	**2**	**0**	**3**	**99**	**11.1**	**55**	**31**	**40**	**0**	**–16**	....	....	....	....	....	....	....	....
1971-72	Cincinnati Swords	AHL	69	14	58	72	....	....	....	18	....	....	....	....	....	....	....	....	....	....	10	5	6	11	6	....	....	....
1972-73	Cleveland Crusaders	WHA	66	21	30	51	....	....	....	12	....	....	....	....	....	....	....	....	....	....	9	2	8	10	2	....	....	....
1973-74	Cleveland Crusaders	WHA	69	15	18	33	....	....	....	14	....	....	....	....	....	....	....	....	....	....	5	1	0	1	0	....	....	....
	Jacksonville Barons	AHL	8	1	3	4	....	....	....	2	....	....	....	....	....	....	....	....	....	....	....	....	....	....	....	....	....	....
1974-75	Tulsa Oilers	CHL	9	5	1	6	....	....	....	0	....	....	....	....	....	....	....	....	....	....	....	....	....	....	....	....	....	....
	Cape Cod Codders	NAHL	33	8	32	40	....	....	....	28	....	....	....	....	....	....	....	....	....	....	....	....	....	....	....	....	....	....
	NHL Totals		**150**	**31**	**49**	**80**	**35**	**47**	**82**	**10**	**13**	**0**	**5**	**250**	**12.4**	**117**	**63**	**89**	**1**		....	....	....	....	....	....	....	....
	Other Major League Totals		135	36	48	84	....	....	....	26	....	....	....	....	....	....	....	....	....	....	14	3	8	11	2	....	....	....

CHL First All-Star Team (1966) • WHL Second All-Star Team (1970)

Traded to **Pittsburgh** by **NY Rangers** with George Konik, Dunc McCallum and Frank Francis for Larry Jeffrey, June 6, 1967. Claimed by **Oakland** from **Vancouver** (WHL) in Intra-League Draft, June 9, 1970. Claimed on waivers by **Buffalo** from **California**, November 4, 1970. Traded to **Vancouver** (WHL) by **Pittsburgh** with John Arbour and the loan of Andy Bathgate for the 1969-70 season for Bryan Hextall Jr., May 20, 1969. Selected by **Dayton-Houston** (WHA) in 1972 WHA General Player Draft, February 12, 1972. WHA rights traded to **Cleveland** (WHA) by **Houston** (WHA) for future considerations, June, 1972.

● ANDREYCHUK, DAVE

Dave Andreychuk LW – R. 6'4", 220 lbs. b: Hamilton, Ont., 9/29/1963. Buffalo's 3rd choice, 16th overall, in 1982 Entry Draft.

1980-81	Oshawa Generals	OHA	67	22	22	44	....	....	....	80	....	....	....	....	....	....	....	....	....	....	10	3	2	5	20	....	....	....
1981-82	Oshawa Generals	OHL	67	57	43	100	....	....	....	71	....	....	....	....	....	....	....	....	....	....	3	1	4	5	16	....	....	....
1982-83	Oshawa Generals	OHL	14	8	24	32	....	....	....	6	....	....	....	....	....	....	....	....	....	....	....	....	....	....	....	....	....	....
	Canada	WJC-A	7	6	5	11	....	....	....	14	....	....	....	....	....	....	....	....	....	....	....	....	....	....	....	....	....	....
	Buffalo Sabres	**NHL**	**43**	**14**	**23**	**37**	**11**	**16**	**27**	**16**	**3**	**0**	**1**	**66**	**21.2**	**55**	**24**	**25**	**0**	**+6**	**4**	**1**	**0**	**1**	**4**	**0**	**0**	**0**
1983-84	**Buffalo Sabres**	**NHL**	**78**	**38**	**42**	**80**	**31**	**28**	**59**	**42**	**10**	**0**	**7**	**178**	**21.3**	**110**	**36**	**55**	**1**	**+20**	**2**	**0**	**1**	**1**	**2**	**0**	**0**	**0**
1984-85	**Buffalo Sabres**	**NHL**	**64**	**31**	**30**	**61**	**25**	**20**	**45**	**54**	**14**	**0**	**2**	**153**	**20.3**	**89**	**43**	**50**	**0**	**–4**	**5**	**4**	**2**	**6**	**4**	**0**	**0**	**2**
1985-86	**Buffalo Sabres**	**NHL**	**80**	**36**	**51**	**87**	**29**	**34**	**63**	**61**	**12**	**0**	**3**	**225**	**16.0**	**126**	**45**	**80**	**2**	**+3**	....	....	....	....	....	....	....	....
	Canada	WEC-A	10	3	2	5	....	....	....	18	....	....	....	....	....	....	....	....	....	....	....	....	....	....	....	....	....	....
1986-87	**Buffalo Sabres**	**NHL**	**77**	**25**	**48**	**73**	**22**	**35**	**57**	**46**	**13**	**0**	**2**	**255**	**9.8**	**111**	**41**	**69**	**1**	**+2**	....	....	....	....	....	....	....	....
1987-88	**Buffalo Sabres**	**NHL**	**80**	**30**	**48**	**78**	**26**	**34**	**60**	**112**	**15**	**0**	**5**	**253**	**11.9**	**112**	**47**	**66**	**2**	**+1**	**6**	**2**	**4**	**6**	**0**	**1**	**0**	**0**
1988-89	**Buffalo Sabres**	**NHL**	**56**	**28**	**24**	**52**	**24**	**17**	**41**	**40**	**7**	**0**	**3**	**145**	**19.3**	**76**	**28**	**48**	**0**	**0**	**5**	**0**	**3**	**3**	**0**	**0**	**0**	**0**
1989-90	**Buffalo Sabres**	**NHL**	**73**	**40**	**42**	**82**	**35**	**30**	**65**	**42**	**18**	**0**	**3**	**206**	**19.4**	**131**	**62**	**63**	**0**	**+6**	**6**	**2**	**5**	**7**	**2**	**1**	**0**	**0**
1990-91	**Buffalo Sabres**	**NHL**	**80**	**36**	**33**	**69**	**33**	**25**	**58**	**32**	**13**	**0**	**4**	**234**	**15.4**	**122**	**50**	**61**	**0**	**+11**	**6**	**2**	**2**	**4**	**8**	**1**	**0**	**0**
1991-92	**Buffalo Sabres**	**NHL**	**80**	**41**	**50**	**91**	**38**	**38**	**76**	**71**	**28**	**0**	**2**	**337**	**12.2**	**155**	**86**	**79**	**1**	**–9**	**7**	**1**	**3**	**4**	**12**	**0**	**0**	**0**
1992-93	**Buffalo Sabres**	**NHL**	**52**	**29**	**32**	**61**	**24**	**22**	**46**	**48**	**20**	**0**	**2**	**171**	**17.0**	**92**	**54**	**46**	**0**	**–8**	....	....	....	....	....	....	....	....
	Toronto Maple Leafs	**NHL**	**31**	**25**	**13**	**38**	**21**	**9**	**30**	**8**	**12**	**0**	**2**	**139**	**18.0**	**54**	**28**	**14**	**0**	**+12**	**21**	**12**	**7**	**19**	**35**	**4**	**0**	**3**
1993-94	**Toronto Maple Leafs**	**NHL**	**83**	**53**	**46**	**99**	**50**	**36**	**86**	**98**	**21**	**5**	**8**	**333**	**15.9**	**148**	**69**	**77**	**20**	**+22**	**18**	**5**	**5**	**10**	**16**	**3**	**1**	**0**
1994-95	**Toronto Maple Leafs**	**NHL**	**48**	**22**	**16**	**38**	**39**	**24**	**63**	**34**	**8**	**0**	**2**	**168**	**13.1**	**61**	**25**	**44**	**1**	**–7**	**7**	**3**	**2**	**5**	**25**	**2**	**0**	**0**
1995-96	**Toronto Maple Leafs**	**NHL**	**61**	**20**	**24**	**44**	**20**	**20**	**40**	**54**	**12**	**2**	**3**	**200**	**10.0**	**71**	**40**	**46**	**4**	**–11**	....	....	....	....	....	....	....	....
	New Jersey Devils	**NHL**	**15**	**8**	**5**	**13**	**8**	**4**	**12**	**10**	**2**	**0**	**0**	**41**	**19.5**	**13**	**2**	**9**	**0**	**+2**	....	....	....	....	....	....	....	....
1996-97	**New Jersey Devils**	**NHL**	**82**	**27**	**34**	**61**	**29**	**30**	**59**	**48**	**4**	**1**	**2**	**233**	**11.6**	**83**	**16**	**30**	**1**	**+38**	**1**	**0**	**0**	**0**	**0**	**0**	**0**	**0**
1997-98	**New Jersey Devils**	**NHL**	**75**	**14**	**34**	**48**	**16**	**33**	**49**	**26**	**4**	**0**	**2**	**180**	**7.8**	**78**	**27**	**46**	**14**	**+19**	**6**	**1**	**0**	**1**	**4**	**1**	**0**	**0**
	NHL Totals		**1158**	**517**	**595**	**1112**	**481**	**455**	**936**	**842**	**216**	**8**	**53**	**3517**	**14.7**	**1687**	**723**	**908**	**47**		**94**	**33**	**34**	**67**	**112**	**13**	**1**	**5**

Played in NHL All-Star Game (1990, 1994)

Traded to **Toronto** by **Buffalo** with Daren Puppa and Buffalo's 1st round choice (Kenny Jonsson) in 1993 Entry Draft for Grant Fuhr and Toronto's 5th round choice (Kevin Popp) in 1995 Entry Draft, February 2, 1993. Traded to **New Jersey** by **Toronto** for New Jersey's 2nd round choice (Marek Posmyk) in 1996 Entry Draft and a conditional choice in 1998 or 1999 Entry Draft, March 13, 1996.

● ANDRIJEVSKI, ALEXANDER

Alexander Andrijevski RW – R. 6'5", 211 lbs. b: Moscow, USSR, 8/10/1968. Chicago's 13th choice, 220th overall, in 1991 Entry Draft.

1989-90	Dynamo Minsk	USSR	47	16	12	28	....	....	....	32	....	....	....	....	....	....	....	....	....	....	....	....	....	....	....	....	....	....
1990-91	Moscow Dynamo	USSR	44	9	8	17	....	....	....	28	....	....	....	....	....	....	....	....	....	....	....	....	....	....	....	....	....	....
1991-92	Moscow Dynamo	CIS	31	9	8	17	....	....	....	14	....	....	....	....	....	....	....	....	....	....	....	....	....	....	....	....	....	....
1992-93	**Chicago Blackhawks**	**NHL**	**1**	**0**	**0**	**0**	**0**	**0**	**0**	**0**	**0**	**0**	**0**	**0**	**0.0**	**0**	**0**	**0**	**0**	**0**	....	....	....	....	....	....	....	....
	Indianapolis Ice	IHL	66	26	25	51	....	....	....	59	....	....	....	....	....	....	....	....	....	....	4	2	3	5	10	....	....	....
1993-94	Indianapolis Ice	IHL	4	0	1	1	....	....	....	2	....	....	....	....	....	....	....	....	....	....	....	....	....	....	....	....	....	....
	Kalamazoo Wings	IHL	57	6	22	28	....	....	....	58	....	....	....	....	....	....	....	....	....	....	1	0	0	0	2	....	....	....
1994-95	HPK Hameenlina	Finland	17	8	9	17	....	....	....	18	....	....	....	....	....	....	....	....	....	....	....	....	....	....	....	....	....	....
	Tivali Minsk	CIS	4	1	1	2	....	....	....	4	....	....	....	....	....	....	....	....	....	....	....	....	....	....	....	....	....	....
1995-96	HPK Hameenlina	Finland	43	18	15	33	....	....	....	75	....	....	....	....	....	....	....	....	....	....	9	7	1	8	4	....	....	....
1996-97	HPK Hameenlina	Finland	42	17	28	45	....	....	....	26	....	....	....	....	....	....	....	....	....	....	10	2	4	6	2	....	....	....
1997-98	HPK Hameenlina	Finland	25	7	9	16	....	....	....	22	....	....	....	....	....	....	....	....	....	....	....	....	....	....	....	....	....	....
	NHL Totals		**1**	**0**	**0**	**0**	**0**	**0**	**0**	**0**	**0**	**0**	**0**	**0**	**0.0**	**0**	**0**	**0**	**0**		....	....	....	....	....	....	....	....

● ANDRUFF, RON

Ron Andruff C – R. 6', 185 lbs. b: Port Alberni, B.C., 7/10/1953. Montreal's 4th choice, 32nd overall, in 1973 Amateur Draft.

			REGULAR SEASON																			PLAYOFFS							
Season	Club	League	GP	G	A	Pts	AG	AA	APts	PIM	PP	SH	GW	S	%	TGF	PGF	TGA	PGA	+/–	GP	G	A	Pts	PIM	PP	SH	GW
1971-72	Flin Flon Bombers	WCJHL	63	20	32	52				44											7	0	3	3	17			
1972-73	Flin Flon Bombers	WCJHL	66	43	48	91				114											8	2	4	6	15			
1973-74	Nova Scotia Voyageurs	AHL	72	11	27	38				93											6	4	0	4	0			
1974-75	**Montreal Canadiens**	**NHL**	**5**	**0**	**0**	**0**	**0**	**0**	**0**	**2**	**0**	**0**	**0**	**1**	**0.0**	**1**	**1**	**1**	**0**	**–1**								
	Nova Scotia Voyageurs	AHL	65	30	31	61				50											6	4	1	5	18			
1975-76	**Montreal Canadiens**	**NHL**	**1**	**0**	**0**	**0**	**0**	**0**	**0**	**0**	**0**	**0**	**0**	**0**	**0.0**	**0**	**0**	**0**	**0**	**0**								
	Nova Scotia Voyageurs	AHL	74	*42	46	88				58											9	5	8	13	9			
1976-77	**Colorado Rockies**	**NHL**	**66**	**4**	**18**	**22**	**4**	**15**	**19**	**21**	**0**	**0**	**0**	**106**	**3.8**	**34**	**5**	**52**	**5**	**–18**								
1977-78	**Colorado Rockies**	**NHL**	**78**	**15**	**18**	**33**	**14**	**15**	**29**	**31**	**0**	**0**	**1**	**133**	**11.3**	**43**	**6**	**55**	**2**	**–16**	**2**	**0**	**0**	**0**	**0**	**0**	**0**	**0**
1978-79	**Colorado Rockies**	**NHL**	**3**	**0**	**0**	**0**	**0**	**0**	**0**	**0**	**0**	**0**	**0**	**4**	**0.0**	**0**	**0**	**4**	**0**	**–4**								
	Philadelphia Firebirds	AHL	35	16	16	32				8																		
	New Haven Nighthawks	AHL	33	9	23	32				10											10	6	11	*17	0			
1979-80	Mannheimer ERC	Germany	47	44	40	81				117																		
1980-81	Mannheimer ERC	Germany	44	35	43	78				110											10	8	7	15	16			
1981-82	Dusseldorfer SG	Germany	4	1	3	4				6																		
	NHL Totals		**153**	**19**	**36**	**55**	**18**	**30**	**48**	**54**	**0**	**0**	**1**	**244**	**7.8**	**78**	**12**	**112**	**7**		**2**	**0**	**0**	**0**	**0**	**0**	**0**	**0**

AHL First All-Star Team (1976) • Won Les Cunningham Award (MVP - AHL) (1976)

Traded to **Colorado** by **Montreal** with Sean Shanahan for cash, September 13, 1976.

● ANDRUSAK, GREG

Greg Andrusak D – R. 6'1", 190 lbs. b: Cranbrook, B.C., 11/14/1969. Pittsburgh's 5th choice, 88th overall, in 1988 Entry Draft.

Season	Club	League	GP	G	A	Pts	AG	AA	APts	PIM	PP	SH	GW	S	%	TGF	PGF	TGA	PGA	+/–	GP	G	A	Pts	PIM	PP	SH	GW
1987-88	University of Minnesota-Duluth	WCHA	37	4	5	9				42																		
1988-89	University of Minnesota-Duluth	WCHA	35	4	8	12				74																		
	Canada	Nat-Team	2	0	0	0				0																		
1989-90	University of Minnesota-Duluth	WCHA	35	5	29	34				74																		
1990-91	Canada	Nat-Team	53	4	11	15				34																		
1991-92	University of Minnesota-Duluth	WCHA	36	7	27	34				125																		
1992-93	Cleveland Lumberjacks	IHL	55	3	22	25				78											2	0	0	0	2			
	Muskegon Fury	ColHL	2	0	3	3				7																		
1993-94	**Pittsburgh Penguins**	**NHL**	**3**	**0**	**0**	**0**	**0**	**0**	**0**	**2**	**0**	**0**	**0**	**4**	**0.0**	**1**	**0**	**2**	**0**	**–1**								
	Cleveland Lumberjacks	IHL	69	13	26	39				109																		
1994-95	**Pittsburgh Penguins**	**NHL**	**7**	**0**	**4**	**4**	**0**	**6**	**6**	**6**	**0**	**0**	**0**	**7**	**0.0**	**5**	**3**	**4**	**1**	**–1**								
	Cleveland Lumberjacks	IHL	8	0	8	8				14																		
	Detroit Vipers	IHL	37	5	26	31				50																		
	Canada	WC-A	7	0	0	0				12																		
1995-96	**Pittsburgh Penguins**	**NHL**	**2**	**0**	**0**	**0**	**0**	**0**	**0**	**0**	**0**	**0**	**0**	**1**	**0.0**	**1**	**0**	**2**	**0**	**–1**								
	Detroit Vipers	IHL	58	6	30	36				128																		
	Minnesota Moose	IHL	5	0	4	4				8																		
1996-97	EHC Eisbaren Berlin	Germany	45	5	17	22				170											8	1	1	2	20			
1997-98	EHC Eisbaren Berlin	Germany	34	3	7	10				65											9	0	1	1	8			
	NHL Totals		**12**	**0**	**4**	**4**	**0**	**6**	**6**	**8**	**0**	**0**	**0**	**12**	**0.0**	**7**	**3**	**8**	**1**									

WCHA First All-Star Team (1992)

● ANGOTTI, LOU

Lou Angotti C/RW – R. 5'9", 170 lbs. b: Toronto, Ont., 1/16/1938.

Season	Club	League	GP	G	A	Pts	AG	AA	APts	PIM	PP	SH	GW	S	%	TGF	PGF	TGA	PGA	+/–	GP	G	A	Pts	PIM	PP	SH	GW
1955-56	St. Michael's Majors	OHA	48	6	6	12				29											8	4	0	4	20			
1956-57	St. Michael's Majors	OHA	52	12	19	31				28											4	1	2	3	4			
1957-58	St. Michael's Majors	OHA	52	23	19	42				72											9	7	8	15	10			
1958-59	Michigan Tech Huskies	WCHA	DID NOT PLAY – FRESHMAN																									
1959-60	Michigan Tech Huskies	WCHA	30	18	21	39				30																		
1960-61	Michigan Tech Huskies	WCHA	28	25	17	42				52																		
1961-62	Michigan Tech Huskies	WCHA	31	28	23	51				50																		
1962-63	Kitchener-Waterloo Tigers	OHA Sr	16	19	7	26				26																		
	Rochester Americans	AHL	39	16	15	31				19											1	0	0	0	0			
1963-64	Rochester Americans	AHL	60	15	30	45				28											2	1	1	2	0			
1964-65	**New York Rangers**	**NHL**	**70**	**9**	**8**	**17**	**11**	**9**	**20**	**20**																		
1965-66	**New York Rangers**	**NHL**	**21**	**2**	**2**	**4**	**2**	**2**	**4**	**2**																		
	St. Louis Braves	CHL	8	10	8	18				4																		
	Chicago Black Hawks	**NHL**	**30**	**4**	**10**	**14**	**5**	**10**	**15**	**12**											**6**	**0**	**0**	**0**	**2**			
1966-67	**Chicago Black Hawks**	**NHL**	**63**	**6**	**12**	**18**	**7**	**12**	**19**	**21**											**6**	**2**	**1**	**3**	**2**			
1967-68	**Philadelphia Flyers**	**NHL**	**70**	**12**	**37**	**49**	**15**	**39**	**54**	**35**	**2**	**0**	**1**	**146**	**8.2**	**57**	**12**	**47**	**6**	**+4**	**7**	**0**	**0**	**0**	**2**	**0**	**0**	**0**
1968-69	**Pittsburgh Penguins**	**NHL**	**71**	**17**	**20**	**37**	**19**	**19**	**38**	**36**	**3**	**0**	**3**	**122**	**13.8**	**43**	**8**	**57**	**1**	**–21**								
1969-70	**Chicago Black Hawks**	**NHL**	**70**	**12**	**26**	**38**	**14**	**26**	**40**	**25**	**5**	**0**	**2**	**97**	**12.4**	**53**	**16**	**37**	**2**	**+2**	**8**	**0**	**0**	**0**	**0**	**0**	**0**	**0**
1970-71	**Chicago Black Hawks**	**NHL**	**65**	**9**	**16**	**25**	**9**	**14**	**23**	**19**	**1**	**1**	**2**	**83**	**10.8**	**32**	**2**	**35**	**22**	**+17**	**16**	**3**	**3**	**6**	**9**	**0**	**0**	**1**
1971-72	**Chicago Black Hawks**	**NHL**	**65**	**5**	**10**	**15**	**5**	**9**	**14**	**23**	**0**	**0**	**0**	**58**	**8.6**	**20**	**2**	**31**	**13**	**0**	**6**	**0**	**0**	**0**	**0**	**0**	**0**	**0**
1972-73	**Chicago Black Hawks**	**NHL**	**77**	**15**	**22**	**37**	**15**	**18**	**33**	**26**	**4**	**1**	**4**	**91**	**16.5**	**41**	**8**	**59**	**23**	**–3**	**16**	**3**	**4**	**7**	**2**	**0**	**0**	**2**
1973-74	**St. Louis Blues**	**NHL**	**51**	**12**	**23**	**35**	**12**	**20**	**32**	**9**	**1**	**0**	**5**	**84**	**14.3**	**42**	**6**	**40**	**1**	**–3**								
1974-75	Chicago Cougars	WHA	26	2	5	7				9																		
	NHL Totals		**653**	**103**	**186**	**289**	**114**	**178**	**292**	**228**	**16**	**2**	**16**	**682**	**15.1**	**288**	**54**	**306**	**68**		**65**	**8**	**8**	**16**	**17**	**0**	**0**	**3**
	Other Major League Totals		26	2	5	7				9																		

NCAA Championship All-Tournament Team (1960, 1962) • NCAA Championship Tournament MVP (1960, 1962) • WCHA Second All-Star Team (1961) • WCHA First All-Star Team (1962) • NCAA West First All-American Team (1962)

Traded to **NY Rangers** by **Toronto** (Rochester - AHL) with Ed Lawson for Duane Rupp and Ed Ehrenverth, June, 1964. Traded to **Chicago** by **NY Rangers** for cash, January 7, 1966. Claimed by **Philadelphia** from **Chicago** in Expansion Draft, June 6, 1967. Traded to **St. Louis** by **Philadelphia** with Ian Campbell for Darryl Edestrand and Gerry Melynk, June 11, 1968. Traded to **Pittsburgh** by **St. Louis** for Ab McDonald, June 11, 1968. Traded to **St. Louis** by **Pittsburgh** with Pittsburgh's 1st round choice (Gene Carr) in 1971 Amateur Draft for Ron Schock and Craig Cameron, June 6, 1969. Selected by **NY Raiders** (WHA) in 1972 WHA General Player Draft, February 12, 1972. Claimed by **St. Louis** from **Chicago** in Intra-League Draft, June 12, 1973. WHA rights traded to **Indianapolis** (WHA) by **San Diego** (WHA) for cash, July, 1974. WHA rights traded to **Chicago** (WHA) by **Indianapolis** (WHA) for future considerations, January, 1975.

● ANHOLT, DARREL

Darrel Anholt D – L. 6'2", 230 lbs. b: Hardisty, Alta., 11/23/1962. Chicago's 3rd choice, 54th overall, in 1981 Entry Draft.

Season	Club	League	GP	G	A	Pts	AG	AA	APts	PIM	PP	SH	GW	S	%	TGF	PGF	TGA	PGA	+/–	GP	G	A	Pts	PIM	PP	SH	GW
1979-80	Red Deer Rustlers	AJHL	50	2	14	16				147																		
1980-81	Calgary Wranglers	WHL	72	5	23	28				286											22	1	7	8	55			
1981-82	Calgary Wranglers	WHL	64	10	29	39				294											9	1	4	5	16			
1982-83	Springfield Indians	AHL	80	2	18	20				109																		
1983-84	**Chicago Black Hawks**	**NHL**	**1**	**0**	**0**	**0**	**0**	**0**	**0**	**0**	**0**	**0**	**0**	**0**	**0.0**	**2**	**0**	**0**	**0**	**+2**								
	Springfield Indians	AHL	80	13	21	34				142											4	0	1	1	2			
1984-85	Milwaukee Admirals	IHL	82	5	22	27				125																		
	NHL Totals		**1**	**0**	**0**	**0**	**0**	**0**	**0**	**0**	**0**	**0**	**0**	**0**	**0.0**	**2**	**0**	**0**	**0**									

● ANTONOVICH, MIKE

Mike Antonovich C – L. 5'8", 165 lbs. b: Calumet, MN, 10/18/1951. Minnesota's 8th choice, 113th overall, in 1971 Amateur Draft.

Season	Club	League	GP	G	A	Pts	AG	AA	APts	PIM	PP	SH	GW	S	%	TGF	PGF	TGA	PGA	+/–	GP	G	A	Pts	PIM	PP	SH	GW
1969-70	University of Minnesota	WCHA	32	23	20	43				60											2	1	0	1	0			
1970-71	University of Minnesota	WCHA	32	14	16	30				20																		
1971-72	University of Minnesota	WCHA	13	8	2	10				19																		
1972-73	Minnesota Fighting Saints	WHA	75	20	19	39				44											5	2	0	2	0			
1973-74	Minnesota Fighting Saints	WHA	68	21	29	50				4											11	1	4	5	4			
1974-75	Minnesota Fighting Saints	WHA	66	24	26	50				6											12	1	4	5	2			
1975-76	Minnesota Fighting Saints	WHA	57	25	21	46				18																		
	Minnesota North Stars	**NHL**	**12**	**0**	**2**	**2**	**0**	**2**	**2**	**8**	**0**	**0**	**0**	**22**	**0.0**	**4**	**1**	**7**	**0**	**–4**								
	United States	WEC-A	10	1	3	4				14																		

			REGULAR SEASON																		PLAYOFFS							
Season	Club	League	GP	G	A	Pts	AG	AA	APts	PIM	PP	SH	GW	S	%	TGF	PGF	TGA	PGA	+/–	GP	G	A	Pts	PIM	PP	SH	GW
1976-77	Minnesota Fighting Saints	WHA	42	27	21	48				28																		
	Edmonton Oilers	WHA	7	1	1	2				0																		
	New England Whalers	WHA	26	12	9	21				10											5	2	2	4	4			
	United States	WEC-A	DID NOT PLAY																									
1977-78	New England Whalers	WHA	75	32	35	67				32											14	*10	7	*17	4			
1978-79	Springfield Indians	AHL	7	2	3	5				2																		
	New England Whalers	WHA	69	20	27	47				35											10	5	3	8	14			
1979-80	Hartford Whalers	NHL	5	0	1	1	0	1	1	2	0	0	0	4	0.0	1	0	1	0	0								
	Springfield Indians	AHL	24	14	6	20				35																		
1980-81	Tulsa Oilers	CHL	60	28	32	60				36											8	1	2	3	2			
1981-82	Minnesota North Stars	NHL	2	0	0	0	0	0	0	0	0	0	0	0	0.0	0	0	1	0	–1								
	Nashville South Stars	CHL	80	29	77	106				76											3	0	1	1	2			
	United States	WEC-A	7	0	0	0				6																		
1982-83	New Jersey Devils	NHL	30	7	7	14	6	5	11	11	2	0	0	47	14.9	19	5	21	0	–7								
	Wichita Wind	CHL	10	8	12	20				0																		
1983-84	New Jersey Devils	NHL	38	3	5	8	2	3	5	16	0	0	0	47	6.4	20	6	29	0	–15								
	Maine Mariners	AHL	25	17	13	30				8											17	4	8	12	8			
	NHL Totals		87	10	15	25	8	11	19	37	2	0	0	120	8.3	44	12	59	0									
	Other Major League Totals		485	182	188	370				177											57	21	20	41	28			

CHL Second All-Star Team (1982)

Selected by **Minnesota** (WHA) in 1972 WHA General Player Draft, February 12, 1972. Signed as a free agent by **Minnesota** after **Minnesota** (WHA) franchise folded, March 10, 1976. Signed as a free agent by **Minnesota** (WHA), after being released by **Minnesota** (NHL), September, 1976. Traded to **Edmonton** (WHA) by **Minnesota** (WHA) with Jean-Louis Levasseur, Bill Butters, Dave Keon, Jack Carlson, Steve Carlson and John McKenzie for cash, January, 1977. Traded to **New England** (WHA) by **Edmonton** (WHA) with Bill Butters for Brett Callighen and Ron Busniuk, February, 1977. Signed as a free agent by **Hartford**, October 17,1979 Signed as a free agent by **Minnesota**, November 25, 1981. Signed as a free agent by **New Jersey**, October 1, 1982.

● ANTOSKI, SHAWN

Shawn "Moose" Antoski LW – L. 6'4", 235 lbs. b: Brantford, Ont., 3/25/1970. Vancouver's 2nd choice, 18th overall, in 1990 Entry Draft.

1987-88	North Bay Centennials	OHL	52	3	4	7				163																		
1988-89	North Bay Centennials	OHL	57	6	21	27				201											9	5	3	8	24			
1989-90	North Bay Centennials	OHL	59	25	31	56				201											5	1	2	3	17			
1990-91	Vancouver Canucks	NHL	2	0	0	0	0	0	0	0	0	0	0	2	0.0	0	0	2	0	–2								
	Milwaukee Admirals	IHL	62	17	7	24				330											5	1	2	3	10			
1991-92	Vancouver Canucks	NHL	4	0	0	0	0	0	0	29	0	0	0	6	0.0	0	0	1	0	–1								
	Milwaukee Admirals	IHL	52	17	16	33				346											5	2	0	2	20			
1992-93	Vancouver Canucks	NHL	2	0	0	0	0	0	0	0	0	0	0	0	0.0	0	0	0	0	0								
	Hamilton Canucks	AHL	41	3	4	7				172																		
1993-94	Vancouver Canucks	NHL	55	1	2	3	1	2	3	190	0	0	1	25	4.0	9	1	19	0	–11	16	0	1	1	36	0	0	0
1994-95	Vancouver Canucks	NHL	7	0	0	0	0	0	0	46	0	0	0	4	0.0	0	0	4	0	–4								
	Philadelphia Flyers	NHL	25	0	0	0	0	0	0	61	0	0	0	12	0.0	4	0	4	0	0	13	0	1	1	10	0	0	0
1995-96	Philadelphia Flyers	NHL	64	1	3	4	1	2	3	204	0	0	0	34	2.9	10	1	13	0	–4	7	1	1	2	28	0	0	1
1996-97	Pittsburgh Penguins	NHL	13	0	0	0	0	0	0	49	0	0	0	3	0.0	3	0	3	0	0								
	Anaheim Mighty Ducks	NHL	2	0	0	0	0	0	0	2	0	0	0	0	0.0	1	0	0	0	+1								
1997-98	Anaheim Mighty Ducks	NHL	9	1	0	1	1	0	1	18	0	0	0	6	16.7	2	0	1	0	+1								
	NHL Totals		183	3	5	8	3	4	7	599	0	0	1	92	3.3	29	2	47	0		36	1	3	4	74	0	0	1

Traded to **Philadelphia** by **Vancouver** for Josef Beranek, February 15, 1995. Signed as a free agent by **Pittsburgh**, July 31, 1996. Traded to **Anaheim** by **Pittsburgh** with Dmitri Mironov for Alex Hicks and Fredrik Olausson, November 19, 1996.

● APPS JR., SYL

Syl Apps Jr. C – R. 6', 185 lbs. b: Toronto, Ont., 8/1/1947. NY Rangers' 4th choice, 21st overall, in 1964 Amateur Draft. HHOF

1967-68	Kingston Aces	OHA Sr.	35	16	22	38				28																		
1968-69	Kingston Aces	OHA Sr.	27	14	22	36				17																		
	Buffalo Bisons	AHL	2	1	2	3				4																		
1969-70	Omaha Rangers	CHL	68	16	38	54				43											12	*10	9	*19	4			
	Buffalo Bisons	AHL																			7	2	3	5	6			
1970-71	New York Rangers	NHL	31	1	2	3	1	2	3	11	0	0	0	25	4.0	7	2	5	0	0								
	Omaha Rangers	CHL	11	0	5	5				4																		
	Pittsburgh Penguins	NHL	31	9	16	25	9	14	23	21	4	0	1	75	12.0	34	12	21	2	+3								
1971-72	Pittsburgh Penguins	NHL	72	15	44	59	16	40	56	78	3	1	1	164	9.1	80	19	55	12	+18	4	1	0	1	2	0	0	0
1972-73	Pittsburgh Penguins	NHL	77	29	56	85	29	47	76	18	6	2	4	186	15.6	106	23	77	19	+25								
1973-74	Pittsburgh Penguins	NHL	75	24	61	85	25	53	78	37	7	4	2	177	13.6	123	38	77	13	+21								
1974-75	Pittsburgh Penguins	NHL	79	24	55	79	22	43	65	43	4	1	6	181	13.3	110	29	92	19	+8	9	2	3	5	9	1	0	1
1975-76	Pittsburgh Penguins	NHL	80	32	67	99	30	53	83	24	7	1	4	210	15.2	150	55	94	16	+17	3	0	1	1	0	0	0	0
1976-77	Pittsburgh Penguins	NHL	72	18	43	61	17	35	52	20	3	2	2	164	11.0	80	22	70	14	+2	3	1	0	1	12	1	0	0
1977-78	Pittsburgh Penguins	NHL	9	0	7	7	0	6	6	0	0	0	0	11	0.0	8	2	9	3	0								
	Los Angeles Kings	NHL	70	19	26	45	18	21	39	18	4	0	1	131	14.5	58	13	56	0	–11	2	0	1	1	0	0	0	0
1978-79	Los Angeles Kings	NHL	80	7	30	37	6	23	29	29	0	0	1	128	5.5	49	10	65	1	–25	2	1	0	1	0	1	0	0
1979-80	Los Angeles Kings	NHL	51	5	16	21	5	12	17	12	1	0	0	53	9.4	26	4	39	0	–17								
	NHL Totals		727	183	423	606	178	349	527	311	39	11	22	1505	12.2	831	229	660	99		23	5	5	10	23	3	0	1

Played in NHL All-Star Game (1975)

Traded to **Pittsburgh** by **NY Rangers** with Sheldon Kannegiesser for Glen Sather, January 26, 1971. Traded to **LA Kings** by **Pittsburgh** with Hartland Monahan for Dave Schultz, Gene Carr and L.A. Kings' 4th round choice (Shane Pearsall) in 1978 Amateur Draft, November 2, 1977.

● ARBOUR, AL

Al "Butch" Arbour D – L. 6', 180 lbs. b: Sudbury, Ont., 11/1/1932. HHOF

1949-50	Windsor Spitfires	OHA	3	0	0	0				0											1	0	0	0	0			
	Detroit Hettche	IHL	33	14	8	22				10											3	0	0	0	0			
1950-51	Windsor Spitfires	OHA	31	5	4	9				27																		
1951-52	Windsor Spitfires	OHA	55	7	12	19				86																		
1952-53	Windsor Spitfires	OHA	56	5	7	12				92																		
	Washington Lions	EHL	4	0	2	2				0																		
	Edmonton Flyers	WHL	8	0	1	1				2											15	0	5	5	10			
1953-54	Detroit Red Wings	NHL	36	0	1	1	0	1	1	18																		
	Sherbrooke Saints	QHL	19	1	3	4				24											2	0	0	0	2			
1954-55	Edmonton Flyers	WHL	41	3	9	12				39																		
	Quebec Aces	QHL	20	4	5	9				55											4	0	0	0	2			
1955-56	Edmonton Flyers	WHL	70	5	14	19				109											3	0	0	0	4			
	Detroit Red Wings	NHL																			4	0	1	1	0			
1956-57	Detroit Red Wings	NHL	44	1	6	7	1	7	8	38											5	0	0	0	6			
	Edmonton Flyers	WHL	24	2	3	5				24																		
1957-58	Detroit Red Wings	NHL	69	1	6	7	1	6	7	104											4	0	1	1	4			
1958-59	Chicago Black Hawks	NHL	70	2	10	12	3	11	14	86											6	1	2	3	26			
1959-60	Chicago Black Hawks	NHL	57	1	5	6	1	5	6	66											4	0	0	0	4			
1960-61	Chicago Black Hawks	NHL	53	3	2	5	4	2	6	40											7	0	0	0	2			
1961-62	Toronto Maple Leafs	NHL	52	1	5	6	1	5	6	68											8	0	0	0	6			
1962-63	Toronto Maple Leafs	NHL	4	1	0	1	1	0	1	4																		
	Rochester Americans	AHL	63	6	21	27				97											2	0	2	2	2			
1963-64	Toronto Maple Leafs	NHL	6	0	1	1	0	1	1	0											1	0	0	0	0			
	Rochester Americans	AHL	60	3	19	22				62											2	1	0	1	0			
1964-65	Rochester Americans	AHL	71	1	16	17				88											10	0	1	1	16			
	Toronto Maple Leafs	NHL																			1	0	0	0	2			
1965-66	Toronto Maple Leafs	NHL	4	0	1	1	0	1	1	2																		
	Rochester Americans	AHL	59	2	11	13				86											12	0	2	2	8			
1966-67	Rochester Americans	AHL	71	3	19	22				48											13	0	1	1	16			
1967-68	St. Louis Blues	NHL	74	1	10	11	1	10	11	50	1	0	0	39	2.6	58	1	90	27	–6	14	0	3	3	10	0	0	0

			REGULAR SEASON																		PLAYOFFS							
Season	Club	League	GP	G	A	Pts	AG	AA	APts	PIM	PP	SH	GW	S	%	TGF	PGF	TGA	PGA	+/–	GP	G	A	Pts	PIM	PP	SH	GW
1968-69	St. Louis Blues	NHL	67	1	6	7	1	6	7	50	0	0	1	25	4.0	54	0	62	28	+20	12	0	0	0	10	0	0	0
1969-70	St. Louis Blues	NHL	68	0	3	3	0	3	3	85	0	0	0	30	0.0	54	1	73	27	+7	14	0	1	1	16	0	0	0
1970-71	St. Louis Blues	NHL	22	0	2	2	0	2	2	6	0	0	0	3	0.0	14	0	13	5	+6	6	0	0	0	6	0	0	0
	NHL Totals		626	12	58	70	14	60	74	617	1	0	1	97	12.4	180	2	238	87		86	1	8	9	92	0	0	0

QHL Second All-Star Team (1955) • AHL First All-Star Team (1963, 1964, 1965, 1966) • Won Eddie Shore Award (Outstanding Defenseman - AHL) (1965) • Won Jack Adams Award (1979) • Won Lester Patrick Trophy (1992)

Played in NHL All-Star Game (1969)

Claimed by **Chicago** from **Detroit** in Intra-League Draft, June, 1958. Claimed by **Toronto** from **Chicago** in Intra-League Draft, June, 1961. Claimed by **St. Louis** from **Toronto** in 1967 Expansion draft, June 6, 1967.

• ARBOUR, JOHN

John Arbour D – L. 5'11", 195 lbs. b: Niagara Falls, Ont., 9/28/1945.

1962-63	Niagara Falls Flyers	OHA	47	1	5	6	....	....	....	27	....	....	....	....	....	....	....	....	....	....	24	1	1	2	12	....	....	....
1963-64	Niagara Falls Flyers	OHA	56	12	6	18	....	....	....	94	....	....	....	....	....	....	....	....	....	....	4	0	1	1	12	....	....	....
1964-65	Niagara Falls Flyers	OHA	56	0	0	0	....	....	....	138	....	....	....	....	....	....	....	....	....	....	11	0	6	6	40	....	....	....
1965-66	Niagara Falls Flyers	OHA	47	13	31	44	....	....	....	196	....	....	....	....	....	....	....	....	....	....	6	2	4	6	14	....	....	....
	Boston Bruins	**NHL**	**2**	**0**	**0**	**0**	**0**	**0**	**0**	**0**	....	....	....	....	....	....	....	....	....	....	....	....	....	....	....	....	....	....
	Oklahoma City Blazers	CHL	3	0	0	0	....	....	....	0	....	....	....	....	....	....	....	....	....	....	3	0	0	0	0	....	....	....
1966-67	Oklahoma City Blazers	CHL	67	3	21	24	....	....	....	140	....	....	....	....	....	....	....	....	....	....	9	0	1	1	11	....	....	....
1967-68	**Boston Bruins**	**NHL**	**4**	**0**	**1**	**1**	**0**	**1**	**1**	**11**	**0**	**0**	**0**	**3**	**0.0**	**1**	**0**	**0**	**0**	**+1**	....	....	....	....	....	....	....	....
	Oklahoma City Blazers	CHL	62	2	15	17	....	....	....	224	....	....	....	....	....	....	....	....	....	....	7	1	0	1	42	....	....	....
1968-69	**Pittsburgh Penguins**	**NHL**	**17**	**0**	**2**	**2**	**0**	**2**	**2**	**35**	**0**	**0**	**0**	**19**	**0.0**	**6**	**0**	**21**	**1**	**–14**	....	....	....	....	....	....	....	....
	Baltimore Clippers	AHL	59	4	17	21	....	....	....	157	....	....	....	....	....	....	....	....	....	....	4	0	0	0	15	....	....	....
1969-70	Vancouver Canucks	WHL	72	7	28	35	....	....	....	*251	....	....	....	....	....	....	....	....	....	....	11	2	3	5	*42	....	....	....
1970-71	**Vancouver Canucks**	**NHL**	**13**	**0**	**0**	**0**	**0**	**0**	**0**	**12**	**0**	**0**	**0**	**9**	**0.0**	**3**	**0**	**10**	**3**	**–4**	....	....	....	....	....	....	....	....
	St. Louis Blues	**NHL**	**53**	**1**	**6**	**7**	**1**	**5**	**6**	**81**	**0**	**0**	**0**	**57**	**1.8**	**31**	**0**	**35**	**5**	**+1**	**5**	**0**	**0**	**0**	**0**	**0**	**0**	**0**
1971-72	**St. Louis Blues**	**NHL**	**17**	**0**	**0**	**0**	**0**	**0**	**0**	**10**	**0**	**0**	**0**	**14**	**0.0**	**6**	**1**	**10**	**1**	**–4**	....	....	....	....	....	....	....	....
	Denver Spurs	WHL	20	4	12	16	....	....	....	73	....	....	....	....	....	....	....	....	....	....	....	....	....	....	....	....	....	....
1972-73	Minnesota Fighting Saints	WHA	76	6	27	33	....	....	....	188	....	....	....	....	....	....	....	....	....	....	5	0	1	1	12	....	....	....
1973-74	Minnesota Fighting Saints	WHA	77	6	43	49	....	....	....	192	....	....	....	....	....	....	....	....	....	....	11	3	6	9	27	....	....	....
1974-75	Minnesota Fighting Saints	WHA	71	11	43	54	....	....	....	67	....	....	....	....	....	....	....	....	....	....	12	0	6	6	23	....	....	....
1975-76	Denver-Ottawa	WHA	34	2	13	15	....	....	....	49	....	....	....	....	....	....	....	....	....	....	....	....	....	....	....	....	....	....
	Minnesota Fighting Saints	WHA	7	0	4	4	....	....	....	14	....	....	....	....	....	....	....	....	....	....	....	....	....	....	....	....	....	....
1976-77	Minnesota Fighting Saints	WHA	33	3	19	22	....	....	....	22	....	....	....	....	....	....	....	....	....	....	....	....	....	....	....	....	....	....
	Calgary Cowboys	WHA	37	1	15	16	....	....	....	38	....	....	....	....	....	....	....	....	....	....	....	....	....	....	....	....	....	....
	NHL Totals		106	1	9	10	1	8	9	149	0	0	0	102	1.0	47	1	76	10		5	0	0	0	0	0	0	0
	Other Major League Totals		335	29	164	193	....	....	....	570	....	....	....	....	....	....	....	....	....	....	28	3	13	16	62	....	....	....

CHL Second All-Star Team (1968)

Traded to **Pittsburgh** by **Boston** with Jean Pronovost for cash, May 21, 1968. Traded to **Vancouver** (WHL) by **Pittsburgh** with Paul Andrea and the loan of Andy Bathgate for the 1969-70 season for Bryan Hextall Jr., May 20, 1969. Traded to **St. Louis** by **Vancouver** for cash, December 3, 1970. Selected by **Minnesota** (WHA) in 1972 WHA General Player Draft, February 12, 1972. Traded to **Denver** (WHA) by **Minnesota** (WHA) for future considerations, October, 1975. Signed as a free agent by **Minnesota** (WHA) after **Denver-Ottawa** (WHA) franchise folded, January 17, 1976. Traded to **Calgary** (WHA) by **Minnesota** (WHA) with Butch Deadmarsh and Danny Gruen for cash, January, 1977.

• ARCHAMBAULT, MICHEL

Michel Archambault LW – L. 5'8", 160 lbs. b: St. Myacenthe, Que., 9/27/1950. Chicago's 2nd choice, 28th overall, in 1970 Amateur Draft.

1969-70	Drummondville Rangers	QJHL	55	69	82	151	....	....	....	167	....	....	....	....	....	....	....	....	....	....	6	6	8	14	17	....	....	....
1970-71	Dallas Black Hawks	CHL	61	17	17	34	....	....	....	56	....	....	....	....	....	....	....	....	....	....	10	5	2	7	10	....	....	....
1971-72	Dallas Black Hawks	CHL	65	31	26	57	....	....	....	115	....	....	....	....	....	....	....	....	....	....	12	6	6	12	14	....	....	....
1972-73	Quebec Nordiques	WHA	57	12	25	37	....	....	....	36	....	....	....	....	....	....	....	....	....	....	....	....	....	....	....	....	....	....
1973-74	Maine Nordiques	NAHL	72	43	65	108	....	....	....	83	....	....	....	....	....	....	....	....	....	....	8	1	7	8	0	....	....	....
1974-75	Dallas Black Hawks	CHL	70	26	40	66	....	....	....	49	....	....	....	....	....	....	....	....	....	....	8	4	2	6	8	....	....	....
1975-76	Dallas Black Hawks	CHL	76	26	47	73	....	....	....	41	....	....	....	....	....	....	....	....	....	....	10	2	2	4	2	....	....	....
1976-77	**Chicago Black Hawks**	**NHL**	**3**	**0**	**0**	**0**	**0**	**0**	**0**	**0**	**0**	**0**	**0**	**1**	**0.0**	**0**	**0**	**3**	**0**	**–3**	....	....	....	....	....	....	....	....
	Dallas Black Hawks	CHL	72	28	45	73	....	....	....	60	....	....	....	....	....	....	....	....	....	....	5	0	3	3	0	....	....	....
	NHL Totals		3	0	0	0	0	0	0	0	0	0	0	1	0.0	0	0	3	0		....	....	....	....	....	....	....	....
	Other Major League Totals		57	12	25	37	....	....	....	36	....	....	....	....	....	....	....	....	....	....	....	....	....	....	....	....	....	....

QJHL Second All-Star Team (1970) • CHL First All-Star Team (1975, 1977)

Selected by **Quebec** (WHA) in 1972 WHA General Player Draft, February 12, 1972.

• ARCHIBALD, DAVE

Dave Archibald C/LW – L. 6'1", 210 lbs. b: Chilliwack, B.C., 4/14/1969. Minnesota's 1st choice, 6th overall, in 1987 Entry Draft.

1984-85	Portland Winter Hawks	WHL	47	7	11	18	....	....	....	10	....	....	....	....	....	....	....	....	....	....	3	0	2	2	0	....	....	....
1985-86	Portland Winter Hawks	WHL	70	29	35	64	....	....	....	56	....	....	....	....	....	....	....	....	....	....	15	6	7	13	11	....	....	....
1986-87	Portland Winter Hawks	WHL	65	50	57	107	....	....	....	40	....	....	....	....	....	....	....	....	....	....	20	10	18	28	11	....	....	....
1987-88	**Minnesota North Stars**	**NHL**	**78**	**13**	**20**	**33**	**11**	**14**	**25**	**26**	**3**	**0**	**2**	**96**	**13.5**	**47**	**17**	**47**	**0**	**–17**	....	....	....	....	....	....	....	....
1988-89	**Minnesota North Stars**	**NHL**	**72**	**14**	**19**	**33**	**12**	**13**	**25**	**14**	**7**	**0**	**2**	**105**	**13.3**	**60**	**30**	**43**	**2**	**–11**	**5**	**0**	**1**	**1**	**0**	**0**	**0**	**0**
1989-90	**Minnesota North Stars**	**NHL**	**12**	**1**	**5**	**6**	**1**	**4**	**5**	**6**	**1**	**0**	**1**	**26**	**3.8**	**13**	**6**	**6**	**0**	**+1**	....	....	....	....	....	....	....	....
	New York Rangers	**NHL**	**19**	**2**	**3**	**5**	**2**	**2**	**4**	**6**	**1**	**0**	**0**	**30**	**6.7**	**10**	**4**	**6**	**0**	**0**	....	....	....	....	....	....	....	....
	Flint Spirits	IHL	41	14	38	52	....	....	....	16	....	....	....	....	....	....	....	....	....	....	4	3	2	5	0	....	....	....
1990-91	Canada	Nat-Team	29	19	12	31	....	....	....	20	....	....	....	....	....	....	....	....	....	....	....	....	....	....	....	....	....	....
	Canada	WEC-A	10	0	1	1	....	....	....	8	....	....	....	....	....	....	....	....	....	....	....	....	....	....	....	....	....	....
1991-92	Canada	Nat-Team	58	20	43	63	....	....	....	64	....	....	....	....	....	....	....	....	....	....	....	....	....	....	....	....	....	....
	Canada	Olympics	8	7	1	8	....	....	....	18	....	....	....	....	....	....	....	....	....	....	....	....	....	....	....	....	....	....
	HC Bolzano	Italy	5	4	3	7	....	....	....	16	....	....	....	....	....	....	....	....	....	....	7	8	5	13	7	....	....	....
1992-93	Binghamton Rangers	AHL	8	6	3	9	....	....	....	10	....	....	....	....	....	....	....	....	....	....	....	....	....	....	....	....	....	....
	Ottawa Senators	**NHL**	**44**	**9**	**6**	**15**	**7**	**4**	**11**	**32**	**6**	**0**	**0**	**93**	**9.7**	**26**	**12**	**52**	**22**	**–16**	....	....	....	....	....	....	....	....
1993-94	**Ottawa Senators**	**NHL**	**33**	**10**	**8**	**18**	**9**	**6**	**15**	**14**	**2**	**0**	**1**	**65**	**15.4**	**34**	**12**	**54**	**25**	**–7**	....	....	....	....	....	....	....	....
1994-95	**Ottawa Senators**	**NHL**	**14**	**2**	**2**	**4**	**4**	**3**	**7**	**19**	**0**	**0**	**1**	**27**	**7.4**	**8**	**1**	**17**	**3**	**–7**	....	....	....	....	....	....	....	....
1995-96	**Ottawa Senators**	**NHL**	**44**	**6**	**4**	**10**	**6**	**3**	**9**	**18**	**0**	**0**	**1**	**56**	**10.7**	**12**	**3**	**41**	**18**	**–14**	....	....	....	....	....	....	....	....
	Utah Grizzlies	IHL	19	1	4	5	....	....	....	10	....	....	....	....	....	....	....	....	....	....	....	....	....	....	....	....	....	....
1996-97	**New York Islanders**	**NHL**	**7**	**0**	**0**	**0**	**0**	**0**	**0**	**4**	**0**	**0**	**0**	**4**	**0.0**	**0**	**0**	**7**	**3**	**–4**	....	....	....	....	....	....	....	....
	Frankfurt Lions	Germany	34	10	19	29	....	....	....	48	....	....	....	....	....	....	....	....	....	....	9	4	2	6	16	....	....	....
1997-98	San Antonio Dragons	IHL	55	11	21	32	....	....	....	10	....	....	....	....	....	....	....	....	....	....	....	....	....	....	....	....	....	....
	NHL Totals		323	57	67	124	52	49	101	139	20	0	8	502	11.4	210	85	273	73		5	0	1	1	0	0	0	0

Traded to **NY Rangers** by **Minnesota** for Jayson More, November 1, 1989. Traded to **Ottawa** by **NY Rangers** for Ottawa's 5th round choice (later traded to LA Kings — LA Kings selected Frederick Beaubien) in 1993 Entry Draft, November 5, 1992. Signed as a free agent by **NY Islanders**, October 10, 1996.

• ARCHIBALD, JIM

Jim Archibald RW – R. 5'11", 175 lbs. b: Craik, Sask., 6/6/1961. Minnesota's 11th choice, 139th overall, in 1981 Entry Draft.

1980-81	Moose Jaw Canucks	SJHL	52	46	42	88	....	....	....	308	....	....	....	....	....	....	....	....	....	....	....	....	....	....	....	....	....	....
1981-82	University of North Dakota	WCHA	41	10	16	26	....	....	....	96	....	....	....	....	....	....	....	....	....	....	....	....	....	....	....	....	....	....
1982-83	University of North Dakota	WCHA	33	7	14	21	....	....	....	91	....	....	....	....	....	....	....	....	....	....	....	....	....	....	....	....	....	....
1983-84	University of North Dakota	WCHA	44	21	15	30	....	....	....	156	....	....	....	....	....	....	....	....	....	....	....	....	....	....	....	....	....	....
1984-85	University of North Dakota	WCHA	41	37	24	61	....	....	....	197	....	....	....	....	....	....	....	....	....	....	....	....	....	....	....	....	....	....
	Springfield Indians	AHL	8	1	0	1	....	....	....	5	....	....	....	....	....	....	....	....	....	....	....	....	....	....	....	....	....	....
	Minnesota North Stars	**NHL**	**4**	**1**	**2**	**3**	**1**	**1**	**2**	**11**	**0**	**0**	**0**	**12**	**8.3**	**6**	**0**	**6**	**0**	**0**	....	....	....	....	....	....	....	....
1985-86	**Minnesota North Stars**	**NHL**	**11**	**0**	**0**	**0**	**0**	**0**	**0**	**32**	**0**	**0**	**0**	**7**	**0.0**	**1**	**1**	**3**	**0**	**–3**	....	....	....	....	....	....	....	....
	Springfield Indians	AHL	12	1	7	8	....	....	....	34	....	....	....	....	....	....	....	....	....	....	....	....	....	....	....	....	....	....
1986-87	**Minnesota North Stars**	**NHL**	**1**	**0**	**0**	**0**	**0**	**0**	**0**	**2**	**0**	**0**	**0**	**1**	**0.0**	**0**	**0**	**1**	**0**	**–1**	....	....	....	....	....	....	....	....
	Springfield Indians	AHL	66	10	17	27	....	....	....	303	....	....	....	....	....	....	....	....	....	....	....	....	....	....	....	....	....	....
1987-88	Kalamazoo Wings	IHL	12	0	1	1	....	....	....	73	....	....	....	....	....	....	....	....	....	....	....	....	....	....	....	....	....	....
	NHL Totals		16	1	2	3	1	1	2	45	0	0	0	20	5.0	7	1	10	0		....	....	....	....	....	....	....	....

WCHA First All-Star Team (1985)

● ARESHENKOFF, RONALD

Ronald Areshenkoff C – L. 6', 175 lbs. b: Grand Forks, B.C., 6/13/1957. Buffalo's 2nd choice, 32nd overall, in 1977 Amateur Draft.

			REGULAR SEASON																		PLAYOFFS							
Season	Club	League	GP	G	A	Pts	AG	AA	APts	PIM	PP	SH	GW	S	%	TGF	PGF	TGA	PGA	+/–	GP	G	A	Pts	PIM	PP	SH	GW
1974-75	Vernon Vikings	BCHL	65	36	50	86				40																		
1975-76	Medicine Hat Tigers	WCJHL	71	25	35	60				77											3	1	2	3	0			
1976-77	Medicine Hat Tigers	WCJHL	60	51	42	93				57											4	1	0	1	0			
1977-78	Hershey Bears	AHL	38	9	14	23				38																		
1978-79			DID NOT PLAY																									
1979-80	**Edmonton Oilers**	**NHL**	**4**	**0**	**0**	**0**	**0**	**0**	**0**	**0**	**0**	**0**	**0**	**3**	**0.0**	**0**	**0**	**4**	**0**	**–4**								
	Houston Apollos	CHL	55	14	24	38				72											2	0	0	0	0			
	NHL Totals		**4**	**0**	**0**	**0**	**0**	**0**	**0**	**0**	**0**	**0**	**0**	**3**	**0.0**	**0**	**0**	**4**	**0**									

Claimed by **Edmonton** from **Buffalo** in Expansion Draft, June 13, 1979. Traded to **Philadelphia** by **Edmonton** with Edmonton's 10th round choice (Bob O'Brien) in 1980 Entry Draft for Barry Dean, June 11, 1980.

● ARMSTRONG, BILL H.

Bill H. Armstrong C – L. 6'2", 195 lbs. b: London, Ont., 6/25/1966.

Season	Club	League	GP	G	A	Pts	AG	AA	APts	PIM	PP	SH	GW	S	%	TGF	PGF	TGA	PGA	+/–	GP	G	A	Pts	PIM	PP	SH	GW
1986-87	University of Western Michigan	CCHA	43	13	20	33				86																		
1987-88	University of Western Michigan	CCHA	41	22	17	39				88																		
1988-89	University of Western Michigan	CCHA	40	23	19	42				97																		
1989-90	Hershey Bears	AHL	58	10	6	16				99																		
1990-91	**Philadelphia Flyers**	**NHL**	**1**	**0**	**1**	**1**	**0**	**1**	**1**	**0**	**0**	**0**	**0**	**1**	**0.0**	**1**	**0**	**0**	**0**	**+1**								
	Hershey Bears	AHL	70	36	27	63				150											6	2	8	10	19			
1991-92	Hershey Bears	AHL	64	26	22	48				186											6	2	2	4	6			
1992-93	Cincinnati Cyclones	IHL	42	14	11	25				99																		
	Utica Devils	AHL	32	18	21	39				60																		
1993-94	Albany River Rats	AHL	74	32	50	82				188																		
1994-95	Albany River Rats	AHL	76	32	47	79				115											13	6	5	11	20			
1995-96	Albany River Rats	AHL	10	3	4	7				22																		
	Indianapolis Ice	IHL	12	4	5	9				13																		
	Detroit Vipers	IHL	54	34	25	59				66											12	6	2	8	15			
1996-97	Grand Rapids Griffins	IHL	35	1	8	9				39																		
	Orlando Solar Bears	IHL	34	4	25	29				55											10	3	6	9	29			
1997-98	Orlando Solar Bears	IHL	62	19	18	37				106																		
	Kansas City Blades	IHL	9	1	4	5				24											5	0	2	2	11			
	NHL Totals		**1**	**0**	**1**	**1**	**0**	**1**	**1**	**0**	**0**	**0**	**0**	**1**	**0.0**	**1**	**0**	**0**	**0**									

Signed as a free agent by **Philadelphia**, May 16, 1989. Signed as a free agent by **New Jersey**, March 21, 1993.

● ARMSTRONG, DEREK

Derek Armstrong C – R. 5'11", 188 lbs. b: Ottawa, Ont., 4/23/1973. NY Islanders' 5th choice, 128th overall, in 1992 Entry Draft.

Season	Club	League	GP	G	A	Pts	AG	AA	APts	PIM	PP	SH	GW	S	%	TGF	PGF	TGA	PGA	+/–	GP	G	A	Pts	PIM	PP	SH	GW
1990-91	Hawkesbury Hawks	OJHL	54	27	45	75				49																		
	Sudbury Wolves	OHL	2	0	2	2				0																		
1991-92	Sudbury Wolves	OHL	66	31	54	85				22											9	2	2	4	2			
1992-93	Sudbury Wolves	OHL	66	44	62	106				56											14	9	10	19	26			
1993-94	**New York Islanders**	**NHL**	**1**	**0**	**0**	**0**	**0**	**0**	**0**	**0**	**0**	**0**	**0**	**2**	**0.0**	**0**	**0**	**0**	**0**	**0**								
	Salt Lake Golden Eagles	IHL	76	23	35	58				61																		
1994-95	Denver Grizzlies	IHL	59	13	18	31				65											6	0	2	2	0			
1995-96	**New York Islanders**	**NHL**	**19**	**1**	**3**	**4**	**1**	**2**	**3**	**14**	**0**	**0**	**0**	**23**	**4.3**	**5**	**1**	**12**	**2**	**–6**								
	Worcester IceCats	AHL	51	11	15	26				33											4	2	1	3	0			
1996-97	**New York Islanders**	**NHL**	**50**	**6**	**7**	**13**	**6**	**6**	**12**	**33**	**0**	**0**	**2**	**36**	**16.7**	**16**	**1**	**25**	**2**	**–8**								
	Utah Grizzlies	IHL	17	4	8	12				10											6	0	4	4	4			
1997-98	**Ottawa Senators**	**NHL**	**9**	**2**	**0**	**2**	**2**	**0**	**2**	**9**	**0**	**0**	**1**	**8**	**25.0**	**4**	**0**	**3**	**0**	**+1**								
	Detroit Vipers	IHL	10	0	1	1				2																		
	Hartford Wolf Pack	AHL	54	16	30	46				40											15	2	6	8	22			
	NHL Totals		**79**	**9**	**10**	**19**	**9**	**8**	**17**	**56**	**0**	**0**	**3**	**69**	**13.0**	**25**	**2**	**40**	**4**									

Signed as a free agent by **Ottawa**, July 28, 1997. Signed as a free agent by **NY Rangers**, July 20, 1998.

● ARMSTRONG, GEORGE

George Armstrong C/RW – R. 6'1", 184 lbs. b: Skead, Ontario, 7/6/1930. HHOF

Season	Club	League	GP	G	A	Pts	AG	AA	APts	PIM	PP	SH	GW	S	%	TGF	PGF	TGA	PGA	+/–	GP	G	A	Pts	PIM	PP	SH	GW
1946-47	Copper Cliff Redmen	NOHA	9	6	5	11				4											5	0	1	1	*10			
1947-48	Stratford Kroehlers	OHA	36	33	*40	*73				33											2	1	0	1	6			
1948-49	Toronto Marlboros	OHA	39	29	33	62				89											10	*7	*10	*17	2			
	Toronto Marlboros	OHA Sr	3	0	0	0				2											10	2	5	7	6			
1949-50	Toronto Marlboros	OHA	45	64	51	115				74											5	5	2	7	6			
	Toronto Maple Leafs	**NHL**	**2**	**0**	**0**	**0**	**0**	**0**	**0**	**0**																		
1950-51	Pittsburgh Hornets	AHL	71	15	33	48				49											13	4	9	13	6			
1951-52	**Toronto Maple Leafs**	**NHL**	**20**	**3**	**3**	**6**	**4**	**4**	**8**	**30**											**4**	**0**	**0**	**0**	**2**			
	Pittsburgh Hornets	AHL	50	30	29	59				62																		
1952-53	**Toronto Maple Leafs**	**NHL**	**52**	**14**	**11**	**25**	**21**	**15**	**36**	**54**																		
1953-54	**Toronto Maple Leafs**	**NHL**	**63**	**17**	**15**	**32**	**26**	**20**	**46**	**60**											**5**	**1**	**0**	**1**	**2**			
1954-55	**Toronto Maple Leafs**	**NHL**	**66**	**10**	**18**	**28**	**14**	**23**	**37**	**80**											**4**	**1**	**0**	**1**	**4**			
1955-56	**Toronto Maple Leafs**	**NHL**	**67**	**16**	**32**	**48**	**23**	**40**	**63**	**97**											**5**	**4**	**2**	**6**	**0**			
1956-57	**Toronto Maple Leafs**	**NHL**	**54**	**18**	**26**	**44**	**25**	**30**	**55**	**37**																		
1957-58	**Toronto Maple Leafs**	**NHL**	**59**	**17**	**25**	**42**	**22**	**27**	**49**	**93**																		
1958-59	**Toronto Maple Leafs**	**NHL**	**59**	**20**	**16**	**36**	**25**	**17**	**42**	**37**											**12**	**0**	**4**	**4**	**10**			
1959-60	**Toronto Maple Leafs**	**NHL**	**70**	**23**	**28**	**51**	**29**	**29**	**58**	**60**											**10**	**1**	**4**	**5**	**4**			
1960-61	**Toronto Maple Leafs**	**NHL**	**47**	**14**	**19**	**33**	**17**	**19**	**36**	**21**											**5**	**1**	**1**	**2**	**0**			
1961-62	**Toronto Maple Leafs**	**NHL**	**70**	**21**	**32**	**53**	**26**	**32**	**58**	**27**											**12**	**7**	**5**	**12**	**2**			
1962-63	**Toronto Maple Leafs**	**NHL**	**70**	**19**	**24**	**43**	**23**	**25**	**48**	**27**											**10**	**3**	**6**	**9**	**4**			
1963-64	**Toronto Maple Leafs**	**NHL**	**66**	**20**	**17**	**37**	**27**	**19**	**46**	**14**											**14**	**5**	**8**	**13**	**10**			
1964-65	**Toronto Maple Leafs**	**NHL**	**59**	**15**	**22**	**37**	**19**	**24**	**43**	**14**											**6**	**1**	**0**	**1**	**4**			
1965-66	**Toronto Maple Leafs**	**NHL**	**70**	**16**	**35**	**51**	**19**	**35**	**54**	**12**											**4**	**0**	**1**	**1**	**4**			
1966-67	**Toronto Maple Leafs**	**NHL**	**70**	**9**	**24**	**33**	**11**	**25**	**36**	**26**											**9**	**2**	**1**	**3**	**6**			
1967-68	**Toronto Maple Leafs**	**NHL**	**62**	**13**	**21**	**34**	**16**	**22**	**38**	**4**	**2**	**0**	**2**	**125**	**10.4**	**56**	**10**	**49**	**11**	**+8**								
1968-69	**Toronto Maple Leafs**	**NHL**	**53**	**11**	**16**	**27**	**12**	**15**	**27**	**10**	**1**	**1**	**1**	**103**	**10.7**	**36**	**10**	**56**	**21**	**–9**	**4**	**0**	**0**	**0**	**0**	**0**	**0**	**0**
1969-70	**Toronto Maple Leafs**	**NHL**	**49**	**13**	**15**	**28**	**15**	**15**	**30**	**12**	**2**	**0**	**3**	**93**	**14.0**	**37**	**4**	**39**	**15**	**+9**								
1970-71	**Toronto Maple Leafs**	**NHL**	**59**	**7**	**18**	**25**	**7**	**16**	**23**	**6**	**0**	**0**	**1**	**93**	**7.5**	**41**	**9**	**42**	**17**	**+7**	**6**	**0**	**2**	**2**	**0**	**0**	**0**	**0**
	NHL Totals		**1187**	**296**	**417**	**713**	**381**	**452**	**833**	**721**	**5**	**1**	**7**	**414**	**71.5**	**170**	**33**	**186**	**64**		**110**	**26**	**34**	**60**	**52**	**0**	**0**	**0**

Played in NHL All-Star Game (1956, 1957, 1959, 1962, 1963, 1964, 1968)

● ARMSTRONG, TIM

Tim Armstrong C – R. 5'11", 170 lbs. b: Toronto, Ont., 5/12/1967. Toronto's 11th choice, 211th overall, in 1985 Entry Draft.

Season	Club	League	GP	G	A	Pts	AG	AA	APts	PIM	PP	SH	GW	S	%	TGF	PGF	TGA	PGA	+/–	GP	G	A	Pts	PIM	PP	SH	GW
1983-84	Markham Waxers	Tier II	42	24	41	65				41																		
1984-85	Toronto Marlboros	OHL	63	17	45	62				28											5	5	2	7	0			
1985-86	Toronto Marlboros	OHL	64	35	69	104				36											4	1	3	4	9			
1986-87	Toronto Marlboros	OHL	66	29	55	84				61																		
	Newmarket Saints	AHL	5	3	0	3				2																		
1987-88	Newmarket Saints	AHL	78	19	40	59				26																		
1988-89	**Toronto Maple Leafs**	**NHL**	**11**	**1**	**0**	**1**	**1**	**0**	**1**	**6**	**0**	**0**	**0**	**5**	**20.0**	**2**	**0**	**6**	**2**	**–2**								
	Newmarket Saints	AHL	37	16	24	40				38																		
1989-90	Newmarket Saints	AHL	63	25	37	62				24																		
1990-91	VEU Feldkirch	Austria	5	0	2	2				0																		
	Binghamton Rangers	AHL	56	24	32	56				37											10	1	6	7	6			
	NHL Totals		**11**	**1**	**0**	**1**	**1**	**0**	**1**	**6**	**0**	**0**	**0**	**5**	**20.0**	**2**	**0**	**6**	**2**									

• ARNASON, CHUCK

Chuck Arnason RW – R. 5'10", 183 lbs. b: Ashburn, Man., 7/15/1951. Montreal's 2nd choice, 7th overall, in 1971 Amateur Draft.

Season	Club	League	GP	G	A	Pts	AG	AA	APts	PIM	PP	SH	GW	S	%	TGF	PGF	TGA	PGA	+/-	Playoffs GP	G	A	Pts	PIM	PP	SH	GW
1969-70	Flin Flon Bombers	WCJHL	60	34	27	61				91											17	14	18	*32	38			
1970-71	Flin Flon Bombers	WCJHL	66	*79	84	*163				153											17	15	*22	*37	30			
1971-72	**Montreal Canadiens**	**NHL**	**17**	**3**	**0**	**3**	**3**	**0**	**3**	**4**	**0**	**0**	**0**	**12**	**25.0**	**7**	**1**	**7**	**0**	**–1**								
	Nova Scotia Voyageurs	AHL	58	30	24	54				33											15	7	6	13	6			
1972-73	**Montreal Canadiens**	**NHL**	**19**	**1**	**1**	**2**	**1**	**1**	**2**	**2**	**1**	**0**	**0**	**18**	**5.6**	**6**	**2**	**5**	**0**	**–1**								
	Nova Scotia Voyageurs	AHL	38	18	20	38				4											13	5	10	15	16			
1973-74	**Atlanta Flames**	**NHL**	**33**	**7**	**6**	**13**	**7**	**5**	**12**	**13**	**0**	**0**	**1**	**62**	**11.3**	**21**	**3**	**17**	**0**	**+1**								
	Pittsburgh Penguins	**NHL**	**41**	**13**	**5**	**18**	**13**	**4**	**17**	**4**	**0**	**0**	**2**	**121**	**10.7**	**27**	**4**	**27**	**2**	**–2**								
1974-75	**Pittsburgh Penguins**	**NHL**	**78**	**26**	**32**	**58**	**24**	**25**	**49**	**32**	**7**	**0**	**3**	**214**	**12.1**	**85**	**17**	**68**	**0**	**0**	**9**	**2**	**4**	**6**	**4**	**1**	**0**	**0**
1975-76	**Pittsburgh Penguins**	**NHL**	**30**	**7**	**3**	**10**	**7**	**2**	**9**	**14**	**0**	**0**	**2**	**69**	**10.1**	**18**	**1**	**21**	**0**	**–4**								
	Kansas City Scouts	**NHL**	**39**	**14**	**10**	**24**	**13**	**8**	**21**	**21**	**5**	**0**	**0**	**122**	**11.5**	**32**	**14**	**55**	**2**	**–35**								
1976-77	**Colorado Rockies**	**NHL**	**61**	**13**	**10**	**23**	**12**	**8**	**20**	**10**	**3**	**0**	**1**	**152**	**8.6**	**35**	**9**	**49**	**0**	**–23**								
1977-78	**Colorado Rockies**	**NHL**	**29**	**4**	**8**	**12**	**4**	**7**	**11**	**10**	**2**	**0**	**0**	**50**	**8.0**	**22**	**7**	**18**	**0**	**–3**								
	Phoenix Roadrunners	CHL	6	3	3	6				4																		
	Cleveland Barons	**NHL**	**40**	**21**	**13**	**34**	**20**	**11**	**31**	**8**	**5**	**0**	**2**	**110**	**19.1**	**41**	**5**	**38**	**0**	**–2**								
1978-79	**Minnesota North Stars**	**NHL**	**1**	**0**	**0**	**0**	**0**	**0**	**0**	**0**	**0**	**0**	**0**	**0**	**0.0**	**0**	**0**	**1**	**1**	**0**								
	Oklahoma City Stars	CHL	60	24	22	46				42																		
	Washington Capitals	**NHL**	**13**	**0**	**2**	**2**	**0**	**2**	**2**	**4**	**0**	**0**	**0**	**17**	**0.0**	**5**	**2**	**4**	**0**	**–1**								
1979-80	Dallas Black Hawks	CHL	68	15	17	32				28																		
	NHL Totals		**401**	**109**	**90**	**199**	**104**	**73**	**177**	**122**	**23**	**0**	**11**	**947**	**11.5**	**299**	**65**	**310**	**5**		**9**	**2**	**4**	**6**	**4**	**1**	**0**	**0**

WCJHL All-Star Team (1971)

Traded to **Atlanta** by **Montreal** for Atlanta's 1st round choice (Rick Chartraw) in 1974 Amateur Draft, May 29, 1973. Traded to **Pittsburgh** by **Atlanta** with Bob Paradise for Al McDonough, January 4, 1974. Traded to **Kansas City** by **Pittsburgh** with Steve Durbano and Pittsburgh's 1st round choice (Paul Gardner) in 1976 Amateur Draft for Simon Nolet, Ed Gilbert and Kansas City's 1st round choice (Blair Chapman) in 1976 Amateur Draft, January 9, 1976. Transferred to **Colorado** after **Kansas City** franchise relocated, July 15, 1976. Traded to **Cleveland** by **Colorado** with Rick Jodzio for Ralph Klassen and Fred Ahearn, January 9, 1978. Placed on **Minnesota** Reserve List after **Minnesota-Cleveland** Dispersal Draft, June 15, 1978. Traded to **Washington** by **Minnesota** for future considerations, March 12, 1979. Traded to **Minnesota** by **Washington** for cash, April 24, 1979. Traded to **Vancouver** by **Minnesota** for cash, July 19, 1979.

• ARNIEL, SCOTT

Scott Arniel LW – L. 6'1", 188 lbs. b: Kingston, Ont., 9/17/1962. Winnipeg's 2nd choice, 22nd overall, in 1981 Entry Draft.

Season	Club	League	GP	G	A	Pts	AG	AA	APts	PIM	PP	SH	GW	S	%	TGF	PGF	TGA	PGA	+/-	Playoffs GP	G	A	Pts	PIM	PP	SH	GW
1979-80	Cornwall Royals	QMJHL	61	22	28	50				51																		
1980-81	Cornwall Royals	QMJHL	68	52	71	123				102											19	14	19	33	24			
	Canada	WJC-A	5	3	1	4				4																		
1981-82	Cornwall Royals	OHL	24	18	26	44				43																		
	Canada	WJC-A	7	5	6	11				4																		
	Winnipeg Jets	**NHL**	**17**	**1**	**8**	**9**	**1**	**5**	**6**	**14**	**1**	**0**	**0**	**18**	**5.6**	**11**	**2**	**7**	**0**	**+2**	**3**	**0**	**0**	**0**	**0**	**0**	**0**	**0**
1982-83	**Winnipeg Jets**	**NHL**	**75**	**13**	**5**	**18**	**11**	**3**	**14**	**46**	**1**	**2**	**0**	**92**	**14.1**	**28**	**2**	**55**	**13**	**–16**	**2**	**0**	**0**	**0**	**0**	**0**	**0**	**0**
1983-84	**Winnipeg Jets**	**NHL**	**80**	**21**	**35**	**56**	**17**	**24**	**41**	**68**	**6**	**0**	**2**	**140**	**15.0**	**89**	**27**	**73**	**1**	**–10**	**2**	**0**	**0**	**0**	**5**	**0**	**0**	**0**
1984-85	**Winnipeg Jets**	**NHL**	**79**	**22**	**22**	**44**	**18**	**15**	**33**	**81**	**3**	**0**	**3**	**142**	**15.5**	**74**	**8**	**59**	**0**	**+7**	**8**	**1**	**2**	**3**	**9**	**0**	**0**	**1**
1985-86	**Winnipeg Jets**	**NHL**	**80**	**18**	**25**	**43**	**14**	**17**	**31**	**40**	**3**	**0**	**0**	**125**	**14.4**	**72**	**9**	**73**	**2**	**–8**	**3**	**0**	**0**	**0**	**12**	**0**	**0**	**0**
1986-87	**Buffalo Sabres**	**NHL**	**63**	**11**	**14**	**25**	**10**	**10**	**20**	**59**	**0**	**0**	**3**	**90**	**12.2**	**40**	**2**	**65**	**26**	**–1**								
1987-88	**Buffalo Sabres**	**NHL**	**73**	**17**	**23**	**40**	**15**	**16**	**31**	**61**	**0**	**3**	**2**	**111**	**15.3**	**51**	**1**	**82**	**40**	**+8**	**6**	**0**	**1**	**1**	**5**	**0**	**0**	**0**
1988-89	**Buffalo Sabres**	**NHL**	**80**	**18**	**23**	**41**	**15**	**16**	**31**	**46**	**0**	**2**	**3**	**122**	**14.8**	**67**	**4**	**91**	**38**	**+10**	**5**	**1**	**0**	**1**	**4**	**0**	**1**	**0**
1989-90	**Buffalo Sabres**	**NHL**	**79**	**18**	**14**	**32**	**16**	**10**	**26**	**77**	**1**	**1**	**4**	**123**	**14.6**	**55**	**1**	**73**	**23**	**+4**	**5**	**1**	**0**	**1**	**4**	**0**	**0**	**0**
1990-91	**Winnipeg Jets**	**NHL**	**75**	**5**	**17**	**22**	**5**	**13**	**18**	**87**	**0**	**0**	**1**	**91**	**5.5**	**40**	**1**	**67**	**16**	**–12**								
1991-92	**Boston Bruins**	**NHL**	**29**	**5**	**3**	**8**	**5**	**2**	**7**	**20**	**0**	**0**	**1**	**34**	**14.7**	**14**	**0**	**16**	**7**	**+5**								
	Maine Mariners	AHL	14	4	4	8				8																		
	New Haven Nighthawks	AHL	11	3	3	6				10																		
1992-93	San Diego Gulls	IHL	79	35	48	83				116											14	6	5	11	16			
1993-94	San Diego Gulls	IHL	79	34	43	77				121											7	6	3	9	24			
1994-95	Houston Aeros	IHL	72	37	40	77				102											4	1	0	1	10			
1995-96	Houston Aeros	IHL	64	18	28	46				94																		
	Utah Grizzlies	IHL	14	3	3	6				29											22	10	7	17	28			
1996-97	Manitoba Moose	IHL	73	23	27	50				67																		
1997-98	Manitoba Moose	IHL	79	28	42	70				84											3	1	0	1	10			
	NHL Totals		**730**	**149**	**189**	**338**	**127**	**131**	**258**	**599**	**15**	**8**	**19**	**1088**	**13.7**	**541**	**57**	**661**	**166**		**34**	**3**	**3**	**6**	**39**	**0**	**1**	**1**

Traded to **Buffalo** by **Winnipeg** for Gilles Hamel, June 21, 1986. Traded to **Winnipeg** by **Buffalo** with Phil Housley, Jeff Parker and Buffalo's 1st round choice (Keith Tkachuk) in 1990 Entry Draft for Dale Hawerchuk, Winnipeg's 1st round choice (Brad May) in 1990 Entry Draft and future considerations, June 16, 1990. Traded to **Boston** by **Winnipeg** for future considerations, November 22, 1991.

• ARNOTT, JASON

Jason Arnott C – R. 6'3", 220 lbs. b: Collingwood, Ont., 10/11/1974. Edmonton's 1st choice, 7th overall, in 1993 Entry Draft.

Season	Club	League	GP	G	A	Pts	AG	AA	APts	PIM	PP	SH	GW	S	%	TGF	PGF	TGA	PGA	+/-	Playoffs GP	G	A	Pts	PIM	PP	SH	GW
1990-91	Lindsay Muskies	OJHL	42	17	44	61				10																		
1991-92	Oshawa Generals	OHL	57	9	15	24				12																		
1992-93	Oshawa Generals	OHL	56	41	57	98				74											13	9	9	18	20			
1993-94	**Edmonton Oilers**	**NHL**	**78**	**33**	**35**	**68**	**31**	**27**	**58**	**104**	**10**	**0**	**4**	**194**	**17.0**	**93**	**36**	**61**	**5**	**+1**								
	Canada	WC-A	8	0	6	6				10																		
1994-95	**Edmonton Oilers**	**NHL**	**42**	**15**	**22**	**37**	**27**	**32**	**59**	**128**	**7**	**0**	**1**	**156**	**9.6**	**55**	**27**	**44**	**2**	**–14**								
1995-96	**Edmonton Oilers**	**NHL**	**64**	**28**	**31**	**59**	**28**	**25**	**53**	**87**	**8**	**0**	**5**	**244**	**11.5**	**89**	**39**	**60**	**4**	**–6**								
1996-97	**Edmonton Oilers**	**NHL**	**67**	**19**	**38**	**57**	**20**	**34**	**54**	**92**	**10**	**1**	**2**	**248**	**7.7**	**91**	**47**	**76**	**11**	**–21**	**12**	**3**	**6**	**9**	**18**	**1**	**0**	**0**
1997-98	**Edmonton Oilers**	**NHL**	**35**	**5**	**13**	**18**	**6**	**13**	**19**	**78**	**1**	**0**	**0**	**100**	**5.0**	**26**	**13**	**32**	**3**	**–16**								
	New Jersey Devils	**NHL**	**35**	**5**	**10**	**15**	**6**	**10**	**16**	**21**	**3**	**0**	**2**	**99**	**5.1**	**28**	**16**	**20**	**0**	**–8**	**5**	**0**	**2**	**2**	**0**	**0**	**0**	**0**
	NHL Totals		**321**	**105**	**149**	**254**	**118**	**141**	**259**	**510**	**39**	**1**	**14**	**1041**	**10.1**	**382**	**178**	**293**	**25**		**17**	**3**	**8**	**11**	**18**	**1**	**0**	**0**

NHL/Upper Deck All-Rookie Team (1994)

Played in NHL All-Star Game (1997)

Traded to **New Jersey** by **Edmonton** with Bryan Muir for Valeri Zelepukin and Bill Guerin, January 4, 1998.

• ARTHUR, FRED

Fred Arthur D – L. 6'5", 210 lbs. b: Toronto, Ont., 3/6/1961. Hartford's 1st choice, 8th overall, in 1980 Entry Draft.

Season	Club	League	GP	G	A	Pts	AG	AA	APts	PIM	PP	SH	GW	S	%	TGF	PGF	TGA	PGA	+/-	Playoffs GP	G	A	Pts	PIM	PP	SH	GW
1977-78	Cornwall Royals	QMJHL	68	2	20	22				86																		
1978-79	Cornwall Royals	QMJHL	72	6	64	70				227																		
1979-80	Cornwall Royals	QMJHL	67	5	70	75				105											18	2	12	14	44			
1980-81	Cornwall Royals	QMJHL	36	3	22	25				134											19	1	11	12	45			
	Canada	WJC-A	5	0	2	2				10																		
	Hartford Whalers	**NHL**	**3**	**0**	**0**	**0**	**0**	**0**	**0**	**0**	**0**	**0**	**0**	**3**	**0.0**	**1**	**0**	**6**	**0**	**–5**								
1981-82	**Philadelphia Flyers**	**NHL**	**74**	**1**	**7**	**8**	**1**	**5**	**6**	**47**	**0**	**0**	**0**	**33**	**3.0**	**62**	**1**	**112**	**43**	**–8**	**4**	**0**	**0**	**0**	**2**	**0**	**0**	**0**
1982-83	**Philadelphia Flyers**	**NHL**	**3**	**0**	**1**	**1**	**0**	**1**	**1**	**2**	**0**	**0**	**0**	**1**	**0.0**	**2**	**0**	**3**	**0**	**–1**								
	NHL Totals		**80**	**1**	**8**	**9**	**1**	**6**	**7**	**49**	**0**	**0**	**0**	**37**	**2.7**	**65**	**1**	**121**	**43**		**4**	**0**	**0**	**0**	**2**	**0**	**0**	**0**

QMJHL First All-Star Team (1980) • Memorial Cup All-Star Team (1981)

Traded to **Philadelphia** by **Hartford** with Ray Allison and Hartford's 1st (Ron Sutter), and 3rd (Miroslav Dvorak) choices in 1982 Entry Draft for Rick MacLeish, Blake Wesley, Don Gillen and Philadelphia's 1st (Paul Lawless) 2nd (Mark Patterson) and 3rd choices in 1982 Entry Draft, July 3, 1981.

● ARVEDSON, MAGNUS

Magnus Arvedson C – L. 6'2", 198 lbs. b: Karlstad, Swe., 11/25/1971. Ottawa's 4th choice, 119th overall, in 1997 Entry Draft.

			REGULAR SEASON																		PLAYOFFS							
Season	Club	League	GP	G	A	Pts	AG	AA	APts	PIM	PP	SH	GW	S	%	TGF	PGF	TGA	PGA	+/-	GP	G	A	Pts	PIM	PP	SH	GW
1991-92	Orebro	Sweden 2	32	12	21	33				30											7	4	4	8	4			
1992-93	Orebro	Sweden 2	36	11	18	29				34											6	2	1	3	0			
1993-94	Farjestads BK Karlstad	Sweden	16	1	7	8				10																		
1994-95	Farjestads BK Karlstad	Sweden	36	1	6	7				45											4	0	0	0	6			
1995-96	Farjestads BK Karlstad	Sweden	40	10	14	24				40											8	0	3	3	10			
1996-97	Farjestads BK Karlstad	Sweden	48	13	11	24				36											14	4	7	11	8			
	Sweden	WC-A	10	2	1	3				6																		
1997-98	**Ottawa Senators**	**NHL**	**61**	**11**	**15**	**26**	**13**	**15**	**28**	**36**	**0**	**1**	**0**	**90**	**12.2**	**36**	**2**	**38**	**6**	**+2**	**11**	**0**	**1**	**1**	**6**	**0**	**0**	**0**
	NHL Totals		**61**	**11**	**15**	**26**	**13**	**15**	**28**	**36**	**0**	**1**	**0**	**90**	**12.2**	**36**	**2**	**38**	**6**		**11**	**0**	**1**	**1**	**6**	**0**	**0**	**0**

● ASHBEE, BARRY

Barry Ashbee D – R. 5'10", 180 lbs. b: Weston, Ont., 7/28/1939. d: 5/12/1977.

Season	Club	League	GP	G	A	Pts	AG	AA	APts	PIM	PP	SH	GW	S	%	TGF	PGF	TGA	PGA	+/-	GP	G	A	Pts	PIM	PP	SH	GW
1956-57	Barrie Flyers	OHA	34	0	4	4				23											3	0	0	0	0			
1957-58	Lakeshore Bruins	Jr. B	STATISTICS NOT AVAILABLE																									
1958-59	Barrie Flyers	OHA	53	8	22	30				108											6	0	3	3	12			
1959-60	Kingston Frontenacs	EPHL	62	2	11	13				72																		
1960-61	Kingston Frontenacs	EPHL	64	4	11	15				75											5	0	0	0	14			
1961-62	North Bay–Kingston	EPHL	35	2	7	9				87																		
1962-63	Hershey Bears	AHL	72	0	17	17				94											15	0	2	2	34			
1963-64	Hershey Bears	AHL	72	3	6	9				142											6	0	0	0	12			
1964-65	Hershey Bears	AHL	66	3	13	16				114											14	0	0	0	22			
1965-66	**Boston Bruins**	**NHL**	**14**	**0**	**3**	**3**	**0**	**3**	**3**	**14**																		
	Hershey Bears	AHL	36	1	10	11				100											3	0	0	0	6			
1966-67			DID NOT PLAY – INJURED																									
1967-68	Hershey Bears	AHL	65	5	15	20				86											5	0	1	1	4			
1968-69	Hershey Bears	AHL	71	5	29	34				130											11	2	5	7	14			
1969-70	Hershey Bears	AHL	72	5	25	30				80											7	0	1	1	24			
1970-71	**Philadelphia Flyers**	**NHL**	**64**	**4**	**23**	**27**	**4**	**20**	**24**	**44**	**2**	**0**	**1**	**99**	**4.0**	**84**	**26**	**70**	**15**	**+3**								
1971-72	**Philadelphia Flyers**	**NHL**	**73**	**6**	**14**	**20**	**6**	**13**	**19**	**75**	**2**	**0**	**1**	**104**	**5.8**	**80**	**12**	**87**	**21**	**+2**								
1972-73	**Philadelphia Flyers**	**NHL**	**64**	**1**	**17**	**18**	**1**	**14**	**15**	**106**	**0**	**1**	**0**	**61**	**1.6**	**69**	**3**	**92**	**24**	**–2**	**11**	**0**	**4**	**4**	**20**	**0**	**0**	**0**
1973-74	**Philadelphia Flyers**	**NHL**	**69**	**4**	**13**	**17**	**4**	**11**	**15**	**52**	**0**	**0**	**0**	**70**	**5.7**	**87**	**8**	**51**	**24**	**+52**	**6**	**0**	**0**	**0**	**2**	**0**	**0**	**0**
	NHL Totals		**284**	**15**	**70**	**85**	**15**	**61**	**76**	**291**	**4**	**1**	**2**	**334**	**4.5**	**320**	**49**	**300**	**84**		**17**	**0**	**4**	**4**	**22**	**0**	**0**	**0**

NHL Second All-Star Team (1974)

Traded to **Hershey** (AHL) by **Boston** with Ed Chadwick for Bob Perreault, June, 1962. Traded to **Philadelphia** by **Hershey** (AHL) for cash, May 22, 1970. • Suffered career-ending eye injury in game vs. NY Rangers, April 23, 1974.

● ASHBY, DON

Don "Ants" Ashby C – L. 6'1", 185 lbs. b: Kamloops, B.C., 3/8/1955. d: 5/30/1981. Toronto's 1st choice, 6th overall, in 1975 Amateur Draft.

Season	Club	League	GP	G	A	Pts	AG	AA	APts	PIM	PP	SH	GW	S	%	TGF	PGF	TGA	PGA	+/-	GP	G	A	Pts	PIM	PP	SH	GW
1972-73	Kamloops Rockets	BCJHL	STATISTICS NOT AVAILABLE																									
	Calgary Centennials	WCJHL	36	10	12	22				0											6	0	1	1	0			
1973-74	Calgary Centennials	WCJHL	68	30	38	68				52											14	6	7	13	0			
1974-75	Calgary Centennials	WCJHL	70	52	68	120				71																		
1975-76	**Toronto Maple Leafs**	**NHL**	**50**	**6**	**15**	**21**	**6**	**12**	**18**	**10**	**1**	**0**	**0**	**63**	**9.5**	**31**	**1**	**29**	**4**	**+5**								
	Oklahoma City Blazers	CHL	26	9	14	23				36											4	0	1	1	2			
1976-77	**Toronto Maple Leafs**	**NHL**	**76**	**19**	**23**	**42**	**18**	**19**	**37**	**24**	**3**	**0**	**4**	**118**	**16.1**	**58**	**10**	**69**	**7**	**–14**	**9**	**1**	**0**	**1**	**4**	**0**	**0**	**0**
	Dallas Black Hawks	CHL	3	1	0	1				0																		
1977-78	**Toronto Maple Leafs**	**NHL**	**12**	**1**	**2**	**3**	**1**	**2**	**3**	**0**	**0**	**0**	**0**	**8**	**12.5**	**4**	**1**	**7**	**0**	**–4**								
	Dallas Black Hawks	CHL	48	14	28	42				15											13	9	9	18	5			
1978-79	**Toronto Maple Leafs**	**NHL**	**3**	**0**	**0**	**0**	**0**	**0**	**0**	**0**	**0**	**0**	**0**	**2**	**0.0**	**0**	**0**	**3**	**0**	**–3**								
	New Brunswick Hawks	AHL	13	2	5	7				9																		
	Colorado Rockies	**NHL**	**12**	**2**	**3**	**5**	**2**	**2**	**4**	**0**	**2**	**0**	**0**	**24**	**8.3**	**9**	**5**	**7**	**0**	**–3**								
1979-80	**Colorado Rockies**	**NHL**	**11**	**0**	**1**	**1**	**0**	**1**	**1**	**4**	**0**	**0**	**0**	**10**	**0.0**	**4**	**0**	**9**	**3**	**–2**								
	Fort Worth Texans	CHL	45	27	27	54				18																		
	Edmonton Oilers	**NHL**	**18**	**10**	**9**	**19**	**9**	**7**	**16**	**0**	**3**	**0**	**1**	**31**	**32.3**	**28**	**6**	**22**	**1**	**+1**	**3**	**0**	**0**	**0**	**0**	**0**	**0**	**0**
1980-81	**Edmonton Oilers**	**NHL**	**6**	**2**	**3**	**5**	**2**	**2**	**4**	**2**	**1**	**0**	**1**	**13**	**15.4**	**6**	**2**	**5**	**0**	**–1**								
	Wichita Wind	CHL	70	36	60	96				46											18	9	16	25	6			
	NHL Totals		**188**	**40**	**56**	**96**	**38**	**45**	**83**	**40**	**10**	**0**	**6**	**269**	**14.9**	**140**	**25**	**151**	**15**		**12**	**1**	**0**	**1**	**4**	**0**	**0**	**0**

CHL First All-Star Team (1981)

Traded to **Colorado** by **Toronto** with Trevor Johansen for Paul Gardner, March 13, 1979. Traded to **Edmonton** by **Colorado** for Bobby Schmautz, February 25, 1980. • Died of injuries suffered in automobile accident following CHL finals, May 30, 1981.

● ASHTON, BRENT

Brent Ashton LW – L. 6'1", 210 lbs. b: Saskatoon, Sask., 5/18/1960. Vancouver's 5th choice, 26th overall, in 1979 Entry Draft.

Season	Club	League	GP	G	A	Pts	AG	AA	APts	PIM	PP	SH	GW	S	%	TGF	PGF	TGA	PGA	+/-	GP	G	A	Pts	PIM	PP	SH	GW
1975-76	Saskatoon Blades	WCJHL	11	3	4	7				11											18	1	1	2	5			
1976-77	Saskatoon Blades	WCJHL	54	26	25	51				84											6	1	2	3	15			
1977-78	Saskatoon Blades	WCJHL	46	38	26	64				47																		
1978-79	Saskatoon Blades	WHL	62	64	55	119				80											11	14	4	18	5			
1979-80	**Vancouver Canucks**	**NHL**	**47**	**5**	**14**	**19**	**5**	**11**	**16**	**11**	**0**	**0**	**0**	**69**	**7.2**	**36**	**5**	**27**	**0**	**+4**	**4**	**1**	**0**	**1**	**6**	**0**	**0**	**0**
1980-81	**Vancouver Canucks**	**NHL**	**77**	**18**	**11**	**29**	**15**	**8**	**23**	**57**	**0**	**0**	**0**	**111**	**16.2**	**46**	**2**	**56**	**2**	**–10**	**3**	**0**	**0**	**0**	**0**	**0**	**0**	**0**
1981-82	**Colorado Rockies**	**NHL**	**80**	**24**	**36**	**60**	**19**	**24**	**43**	**26**	**3**	**0**	**4**	**182**	**13.2**	**89**	**25**	**106**	**11**	**–31**								
1982-83	**New Jersey Devils**	**NHL**	**76**	**14**	**19**	**33**	**11**	**13**	**24**	**47**	**4**	**0**	**1**	**113**	**12.4**	**52**	**10**	**68**	**3**	**–23**								
1983-84	**Minnesota North Stars**	**NHL**	**68**	**7**	**10**	**17**	**6**	**7**	**13**	**54**	**0**	**0**	**0**	**82**	**8.5**	**27**	**0**	**44**	**4**	**–13**	**12**	**1**	**2**	**3**	**22**	**0**	**0**	**0**
1984-85	**Minnesota North Stars**	**NHL**	**29**	**4**	**7**	**11**	**3**	**5**	**8**	**15**	**0**	**0**	**0**	**30**	**13.3**	**15**	**0**	**27**	**13**	**+1**								
	Quebec Nordiques	**NHL**	**49**	**27**	**24**	**51**	**22**	**16**	**38**	**38**	**6**	**1**	**2**	**122**	**22.1**	**61**	**14**	**39**	**10**	**+18**	**18**	**6**	**4**	**10**	**13**	**1**	**1**	**1**
1985-86	**Quebec Nordiques**	**NHL**	**77**	**26**	**32**	**58**	**21**	**21**	**42**	**64**	**5**	**2**	**5**	**207**	**12.6**	**80**	**14**	**69**	**10**	**+7**	**3**	**2**	**1**	**3**	**9**	**0**	**1**	**0**
1986-87	**Quebec Nordiques**	**NHL**	**46**	**25**	**19**	**44**	**22**	**14**	**36**	**17**	**12**	**2**	**1**	**98**	**25.5**	**55**	**26**	**46**	**5**	**–12**								
	Detroit Red Wings	**NHL**	**35**	**15**	**16**	**31**	**13**	**12**	**25**	**22**	**3**	**1**	**3**	**86**	**17.4**	**41**	**16**	**35**	**7**	**–3**	**16**	**4**	**9**	**13**	**6**	**2**	**0**	**0**
1987-88	**Detroit Red Wings**	**NHL**	**73**	**26**	**27**	**53**	**22**	**19**	**41**	**50**	**7**	**2**	**3**	**161**	**16.1**	**81**	**23**	**57**	**9**	**+10**	**16**	**7**	**5**	**12**	**10**	**2**	**1**	**0**
1988-89	**Winnipeg Jets**	**NHL**	**75**	**31**	**37**	**68**	**26**	**26**	**52**	**36**	**7**	**1**	**1**	**180**	**17.2**	**109**	**29**	**102**	**17**	**–5**								
	Canada	WEC-A	10	3	3	6				2																		
1989-90	**Winnipeg Jets**	**NHL**	**79**	**22**	**34**	**56**	**19**	**24**	**43**	**37**	**3**	**0**	**5**	**167**	**13.2**	**80**	**12**	**77**	**13**	**+4**	**7**	**3**	**1**	**4**	**2**	**2**	**0**	**1**
1990-91	**Winnipeg Jets**	**NHL**	**61**	**12**	**24**	**36**	**11**	**18**	**29**	**58**	**1**	**0**	**2**	**107**	**11.2**	**50**	**11**	**59**	**10**	**–10**								
1991-92	**Winnipeg Jets**	**NHL**	**7**	**1**	**0**	**1**	**1**	**0**	**1**	**4**	**0**	**0**	**0**	**6**	**16.7**	**4**	**1**	**9**	**3**	**–3**								
	Boston Bruins	**NHL**	**61**	**17**	**22**	**39**	**16**	**17**	**33**	**47**	**6**	**1**	**1**	**124**	**13.7**	**66**	**19**	**58**	**7**	**–4**								
1992-93	**Boston Bruins**	**NHL**	**26**	**2**	**2**	**4**	**2**	**1**	**3**	**11**	**0**	**0**	**0**	**26**	**7.7**	**8**	**0**	**13**	**5**	**0**								
	Providence Bruins	AHL	11	4	8	12				10																		
	Calgary Flames	**NHL**	**32**	**8**	**11**	**19**	**7**	**8**	**15**	**41**	**0**	**2**	**1**	**58**	**13.8**	**32**	**4**	**23**	**6**	**+11**	**6**	**0**	**3**	**3**	**2**	**0**	**0**	**0**
1993-94	Las Vegas Thunder	IHL	16	4	10	14				29																		
	NHL Totals		**998**	**284**	**345**	**629**	**241**	**244**	**485**	**635**	**57**	**12**	**29**	**1929**	**14.7**	**932**	**211**	**915**	**135**		**85**	**24**	**25**	**49**	**70**	**7**	**3**	**2**

Rights traded to **Winnipeg** by **Vancouver** with Vancouver's 4th round choice (Tom Martin) in 1982 Entry Draft as compensation for Vancouver's signing of free agent Ivan Hlinka, July 15, 1981. Traded to **Colorado** by **Winnipeg** with Winnipeg's 3rd round choice (Dave Kasper) in 1982 Entry Draft for Lucien DeBlois, July 15, 1981. Transferred to **New Jersey** after **Colorado** franchise relocated, June 30, 1982. Traded to **Minnesota** by **New Jersey** for Dave Lewis, October 3, 1983. Traded to **Quebec** by **Minnesota** with Brad Maxwell for Tony McKegney and Bo Berglund, December 14, 1984. Traded to **Detroit** by **Quebec** with Gilbert Delorme and Mark Kumpel for Basil McRae, John Ogrodnick and Doug Shedden, January 17, 1987. Traded to **Winnipeg** by **Detroit** for Paul MacLean, June 13, 1988. Traded to **Boston** by **Winnipeg** for Petri Skriko, October 29, 1991. Traded to **Calgary** by **Boston** for C.J. Young, February 1, 1993.

● ASTLEY, MARK

Mark Astley D – L. 5'11", 185 lbs. b: Calgary, Alta., 3/30/1969. Buffalo's 9th choice, 194th overall, in 1989 Entry Draft.

Season	Club	League	GP	G	A	Pts	AG	AA	APts	PIM	PP	SH	GW	S	%	TGF	PGF	TGA	PGA	+/-	GP	G	A	Pts	PIM	PP	SH	GW
1987-88	Calgary Canucks	AJHL	52	25	37	52				106																		
1988-89	Lake Superior State	CCHA	42	3	12	15				26																		
1989-90	Lake Superior State	CCHA	43	7	25	32				29																		
1990-91	Lake Superior State	CCHA	45	19	27	46				50																		
1991-92	Lake Superior State	CCHA	39	11	36	47				65																		
	Canada	Nat-Team	11	2	2	4				6																		

Season	Club	League	GP	G	A	Pts	AG	AA	APts	PIM	PP	SH	GW	S	%	TGF	PGF	TGA	PGA	+/–	GP	G	A	Pts	PIM	PP	SH	GW
			REGULAR SEASON																		PLAYOFFS							
1992-93	HC Lugano	Switz.	30	10	12	22				57																		
	Canada	Nat-Team	22	4	14	18				14																		
1993-94	Ambri-Piotta	Switz.	23	5	9	14				17																		
	Canada	Nat-Team	13	4	8	12				6																		
	Canada	Olympics	8	0	1	1				4																		
	Buffalo Sabres	**NHL**	**1**	**0**	**0**	**0**	**0**	**0**	**0**	**0**	**0**	**0**	**0**	**2**	**0.0**	**0**	**0**	**1**	**0**	**–1**								
1994-95	**Buffalo Sabres**	**NHL**	**14**	**2**	**1**	**3**	**4**	**1**	**5**	**12**	**0**	**0**	**0**	**21**	**9.5**	**7**	**2**	**8**	**1**	**–2**	**2**	**0**	**0**	**0**	**0**	**0**	**0**	**0**
	Rochester Americans	AHL	46	5	24	29				49											3	0	2	2	2			
1995-96	**Buffalo Sabres**	**NHL**	**60**	**2**	**18**	**20**	**2**	**15**	**17**	**80**	**0**	**0**	**0**	**80**	**2.5**	**58**	**17**	**57**	**4**	**–12**								
1996-97	Phoenix Roadrunners	IHL	52	6	11	17				43																		
1997-98	HC Lugano	Switz.	19	1	5	6				19											4	0	1	1	0			
	NHL Totals		**75**	**4**	**19**	**23**	**6**	**16**	**22**	**92**	**0**	**0**	**0**	**103**	**3.9**	**65**	**19**	**66**	**5**		**2**	**0**	**0**	**0**	**0**	**0**	**0**	**0**

CCHA Second All-Star Team (1991) • CCHA First All-Star Team (1992) • NCAA West First All-American Team (1992) • NCAA All-Tournament Team (1992)

Signed as a free agent by **LA Kings**, September 6, 1996.

• ATCHEYNUM, BLAIR

Blair Atcheynum RW – R. 6′2″, 210 lbs. b: Estevan, Sask., 4/20/1969. Hartford's 2nd choice, 52nd overall, in 1989 Entry Draft.

Season	Club	League	GP	G	A	Pts	AG	AA	APts	PIM	PP	SH	GW	S	%	TGF	PGF	TGA	PGA	+/–	GP	G	A	Pts	PIM	PP	SH	GW
1985-86	Saskatoon Blades	WHL	19	1	4	5				22																		
	North Battleford Stars	SJHL	33	16	14	30				41											6	2	0	2	6			
1986-87	Saskatoon Blades	WHL	21	0	4	4				4																		
	Swift Current Broncos	WHL	5	2	1	3				0																		
	Moose Jaw Warriors	WHL	12	3	0	3				2																		
1987-88	Moose Jaw Warriors	WHL	60	32	16	48				52																		
1988-89	Moose Jaw Warriors	WHL	71	70	68	138				70											7	2	5	7	13			
1989-90	Binghamton Whalers	AHL	78	20	21	41				45																		
1990-91	Springfield Indians	AHL	72	25	27	52				42											13	0	6	6	6			
1991-92	Springfield Indians	AHL	62	16	21	37				64											6	1	1	2	2			
1992-93	**Ottawa Senators**	**NHL**	**4**	**0**	**1**	**1**	**0**	**1**	**1**	**0**	**0**	**0**	**0**	**2**	**0.0**	**1**	**0**	**4**	**0**	**–3**								
	New Haven Nighthawks	AHL	51	16	18	34				47																		
1993-94	Columbus Chill	ECHL	16	15	12	27				10																		
	Portland Pirates	AHL	2	0	0	0				0																		
	Springfield Indians	AHL	40	18	22	40				13											6	0	2	2	0			
1994-95	Minnesota Moose	IHL	17	4	6	10				7																		
	Worcester IceCats	AHL	55	17	29	46				26																		
1995-96	Cape Breton Oilers	AHL	79	30	42	72				65																		
1996-97	Hershey Bears	AHL	77	42	45	87				57											13	6	11	17	6			
1997-98	**St. Louis Blues**	**NHL**	**61**	**11**	**15**	**26**	**13**	**15**	**28**	**10**	**0**	**1**	**3**	**103**	**10.7**	**36**	**0**	**46**	**15**	**+5**	**10**	**0**	**0**	**0**	**2**	**0**	**0**	**0**
	NHL Totals		**65**	**11**	**16**	**27**	**13**	**16**	**29**	**10**	**0**	**1**	**3**	**105**	**10.5**	**37**	**0**	**50**	**15**		**10**	**0**	**0**	**0**	**2**	**0**	**0**	**0**

WHL First All-Star Team (1989) • AHL First All-Star Team (1997)

Claimed by **Ottawa** from **Hartford** in Expansion Draft, June 18, 1992. Signed as a free agent by **St. Louis**, September 15, 1997. Claimed by **Nashville** from **St. Louis** in Expansion Draft, June 26, 1998.

• ATKINSON, STEVE

Steve Atkinson RW – R. 5′11″, 170 lbs. b: Toronto, Ont., 10/16/1948. Detroit's 1st choice, 6th overall, in 1966 Amateur Draft.

Season	Club	League	GP	G	A	Pts	AG	AA	APts	PIM	PP	SH	GW	S	%	TGF	PGF	TGA	PGA	+/–	GP	G	A	Pts	PIM	PP	SH	GW
1964-65	Niagara Falls Flyers	OHA	15	1	0	1				0																		
1965-66	Niagara Falls Flyers	OHA	39	8	7	15				12											6	5	2	7	2			
1966-67	Niagara Falls Flyers	OHA	44	31	35	66				42											10	6	5	11	4			
1967-68	Niagara Falls Flyers	OHA	50	37	36	73				61											19	14	10	24	15			
1968-69	**Boston Bruins**	**NHL**	**1**	**0**	**0**	**0**	**0**	**0**	**0**	**0**	**0**	**0**	**0**	**0**	**0.0**	**0**	**0**	**1**	**0**	**–1**								
	Oklahoma City Blazers	CHL	65	40	40	80				62											12	4	0	4	13			
1969-70	Oklahoma City Blazers	CHL	63	29	23	52				63																		
1970-71	**Buffalo Sabres**	**NHL**	**57**	**20**	**18**	**38**	**21**	**16**	**37**	**12**	**0**	**1**	**2**	**126**	**15.9**	**55**	**8**	**48**	**2**	**+1**								
1971-72	**Buffalo Sabres**	**NHL**	**67**	**14**	**10**	**24**	**15**	**9**	**24**	**26**	**3**	**0**	**0**	**122**	**11.5**	**41**	**9**	**54**	**0**	**–22**								
1972-73	**Buffalo Sabres**	**NHL**	**61**	**9**	**9**	**18**	**9**	**8**	**17**	**36**	**2**	**0**	**1**	**96**	**9.4**	**34**	**6**	**33**	**0**	**–5**	**1**	**0**	**0**	**0**	**0**	**0**	**0**	**0**
1973-74	**Buffalo Sabres**	**NHL**	**70**	**6**	**10**	**16**	**6**	**9**	**15**	**22**	**0**	**0**	**1**	**109**	**5.5**	**31**	**1**	**29**	**0**	**+1**								
1974-75	**Washington Capitals**	**NHL**	**46**	**11**	**4**	**15**	**10**	**3**	**13**	**8**	**3**	**2**	**0**	**92**	**12.0**	**26**	**8**	**60**	**16**	**–26**								
	Richmond Robins	AHL	22	11	18	29				6											7	1	4	5	15			
1975-76	Toronto Toros	WHA	52	2	6	8				22																		
	Buffalo Norsemen	NAHL	37	30	31	61				38																		
1976-77	Brantford Alexanders	OHA Sr.	11	9	13	22				8																		
	Erie Blades	NAHL	28	18	20	38				19																		
1977-78	Brantford Alexanders	OHA Sr.	33	15	20	43				4																		
	NHL Totals		**302**	**60**	**51**	**111**	**61**	**45**	**106**	**104**	**8**	**3**	**4**	**545**	**11.0**	**187**	**32**	**225**	**18**		**1**	**0**	**0**	**0**	**0**	**0**	**0**	**0**
	Other Major League Totals		52	2	6	8				22																		

CHL First All-Star Team (1969) • Won Ken McKenzie Trophy (CHL's Rookie of the Year) (1969)

Traded to **Boston** by **Detroit** to complete transaction that sent Leo Boivin to Detroit (February 18, 1966), June 6, 1966. Traded to **Hershey** (AHL) by **Boston** for cash, June 9, 1970. Claimed by **St. Louis** from **Hershey** (AHL) in Inter-League Draft, June 9, 1970. Claimed on waivers by **Buffalo by St. Louis**, November 1, 1970. Selected by **Dayton-Houston** (WHA) in 1972 WHA General Player Draft, February 12, 1972. Claimed by **Washington** from **Buffalo** in Expansion Draft, June 12, 1974. WHA rights traded to **Toronto** (WHA) by **Houston** (WHA) for cash, September, 1975.

• ATTWELL, BOB

Bob Attwell RW – R. 6′, 192 lbs. b: Spokane, WA, 12/26/1959. Colorado's 4th choice, 106th overall, in 1979 Entry Draft.

Season	Club	League	GP	G	A	Pts	AG	AA	APts	PIM	PP	SH	GW	S	%	TGF	PGF	TGA	PGA	+/–	GP	G	A	Pts	PIM	PP	SH	GW
1977-78	Peterborough Petes	OHA	68	23	43	66				32											21	6	12	18	4			
1978-79	Peterborough Petes	OHA	68	32	61	93				39											19	8	8	16	8			
1979-80	**Colorado Rockies**	**NHL**	**7**	**1**	**1**	**2**	**1**	**1**	**2**	**0**	**0**	**0**	**0**	**2**	**50.0**	**3**	**0**	**8**	**0**	**–5**								
	Fort Worth Texans	CHL	74	26	35	61				18											15	4	5	9	4			
1980-81	**Colorado Rockies**	**NHL**	**15**	**0**	**4**	**4**	**0**	**3**	**3**	**0**	**0**	**0**	**0**	**11**	**0.0**	**9**	**0**	**10**	**2**	**+1**								
	Fort Worth Texans	CHL	60	13	18	31				30											5	1	2	3	0			
1981-82	Fort Worth Texans	CHL	79	31	36	67				66																		
1982-83	Moncton Alpines	AHL	74	14	19	33				31																		
1983-84	Fort Wayne Komets	IHL	70	25	35	60				22											6	1	1	2	0			
1984-85	Bad Tolz	Germany	36	42	18	60				54											18	12	11	23	20			
1985-86	Preussen-Berlin	Germany																			18	16	12	28	20			
1986-87	Preussen-Berlin	Germany	STATISTICS NOT AVAILABLE																									
1987-88	Preussen-Berlin	Germany	23	8	5	13				6																		
	NHL Totals		**22**	**1**	**5**	**6**	**1**	**4**	**5**	**0**	**0**	**0**	**0**	**13**	**7.7**	**12**	**0**	**18**	**2**									

Signed as a free agent by **Edmonton**, October 25, 1982.

• ATTWELL, RON

Ron Attwell RW – R. 6′, 185 lbs. b: Humber Summit, Ont., 2/9/1936.

Season	Club	League	GP	G	A	Pts	AG	AA	APts	PIM	PP	SH	GW	S	%	TGF	PGF	TGA	PGA	+/–	GP	G	A	Pts	PIM	PP	SH	GW
1952-53	Montreal Jr. Canadiens	QJHL	9	3	2	5				6											3	0	1	1	4			
1953-54	Montreal Jr. Canadiens	QJHL	50	15	27	42				17											8	1	0	1	4			
	Montreal Royals	QHL	1	0	0	0				0																		
1954-55	Montreal Jr. Canadiens	QJHL	30	14	27	41				35											5	2	5	7	8			
	Providence Reds	AHL	2	0	1	1				2																		
1955-56	Providence Reds	AHL	44	7	14	21				23											1	0	0	0	2			
1956-57	Trois-Rivieres Lions	QHL	67	15	21	36				27											4	0	1	1	2			
1957-58	Shawinigan Cataracts	QHL	54	12	27	39				29											14	*9	8	17	6			
	Rochester Americans	AHL	6	1	0	1				2																		
1958-59	Spokane Comets	WHL	34	7	10	17				4											4	1	1	2	4			
	Chicoutimi Sagueneens	QHL	25	5	16	21				4																		
1959-60	Spokane Comets	WHL	70	20	34	54				41																		
1960-61	Cleveland Barons	AHL	66	23	35	58				37											4	2	1	3	0			
1961-62	Cleveland Barons	AHL	70	28	55	83				43											6	2	2	4	4			
1962-63	Quebec Aces	AHL	69	14	28	42				26																		

Season	Club	League	REGULAR SEASON																		PLAYOFFS							
			GP	G	A	Pts	AG	AA	APts	PIM	PP	SH	GW	S	%	TGF	PGF	TGA	PGA	+/–	GP	G	A	Pts	PIM	PP	SH	GW
1963-64	Cleveland Barons	AHL	72	*30	38	68				32											9	1	5	6	2			
1964-65	Cleveland Barons	AHL	72	14	49	63				43																		
1965-66	Cleveland Barons	AHL	68	23	25	48				64											4	1	0	1	2			
1966-67	Cleveland Barons	AHL	70	24	37	61				46											5	1	4	5	10			
1967-68	**St. Louis Blues**	**NHL**	**18**	**1**	**7**	**8**	**1**	**7**	**8**	**6**	**1**	**0**	**0**	**31**	**3.2**	**9**	**4**	**14**	**0**	**–9**								
	New York Rangers	**NHL**	**4**	**0**	**0**	**0**	**0**	**0**	**0**	**2**	**0**	**0**	**0**	**0**	**0.0**	**0**	**0**	**0**	**0**	**0**								
	Buffalo Bisons	AHL	35	7	11	18				4											5	1	2	3	4			
1968-69	Buffalo Bisons	AHL	74	19	41	60				59											4	1	1	2	2			
1969-70	Buffalo Bisons	AHL	71	9	39	48				28											7	2	0	2	2			
	Omaha Knights	CHL																			1	0	0	0	0			
	NHL Totals		**22**	**1**	**7**	**8**	**1**	**7**	**8**	**8**	**1**	**0**	**0**	**31**	**3.2**	**9**	**4**	**14**	**0**									

Traded to **Montreal** by **Cleveland** (AHL) for cash, June 14, 1967. Traded to **St. Louis** by **Montreal** with Pat Quinn for cash, June 14, 1967. Traded to **NY Rangers** by **St. Louis** with Ron Stewart for Red Berenson and Barclay Plager, November 29, 1967.

• AUBIN, NORM

Norm Aubin C – L. 6′, 185 lbs. b: St. Leonard, Que., 7/26/1960. Toronto's 2nd choice, 51st overall, in 1979 Entry Draft.

Season	Club	League	GP	G	A	Pts	AG	AA	APts	PIM	PP	SH	GW	S	%	TGF	PGF	TGA	PGA	+/–	GP	G	A	Pts	PIM	PP	SH	GW
1976-77	Sorel Eperviers	QMJHL	50	25	26	51				32																		
1977-78	Verdun Eperviers	QMJHL	71	62	73	135				107																		
1978-79	Verdun Eperviers	QMJHL	70	*80	69	149				84											11	14	11	25	8			
1979-80	Sorel Eperviers	QMJHL	21	*41	29	70				28																		
	Sherbrooke Castors	QMJHL	42	*50	60	110				38											14	15	16	31	24			
1980-81	New Brunswick Hawks	AHL	79	43	46	89				99											13	5	6	11	34			
1981-82	**Toronto Maple Leafs**	**NHL**	**43**	**14**	**12**	**26**	**11**	**8**	**19**	**22**	**3**	**0**	**1**	**62**	**22.6**	**41**	**9**	**49**	**1**	**–16**								
	Cincinnati Tigers	CHL	31	15	17	32				36																		
1982-83	**Toronto Maple Leafs**	**NHL**	**26**	**4**	**1**	**5**	**3**	**1**	**4**	**8**	**2**	**0**	**1**	**18**	**22.2**	**8**	**3**	**15**	**1**	**–9**	**1**	**0**	**0**	**0**	**0**	**0**	**0**	**0**
	St. Catharines Saints	AHL	49	31	26	57				40																		
1983-84	St. Catharines Saints	AHL	80	47	47	94				63											7	5	3	8	8			
1984-85	Nova Scotia Voyageurs	AHL	48	23	26	49				26											6	2	5	7	8			
	NHL Totals		**69**	**18**	**13**	**31**	**14**	**9**	**23**	**30**	**5**	**0**	**2**	**80**	**22.5**	**49**	**12**	**64**	**2**		**1**	**0**	**0**	**0**	**0**	**0**	**0**	**0**

QMJHL First All-Star Team (1979)

Signed as a free agent by **Edmonton**, December, 1984.

• AUBRY, PIERRE

Pierre Aubry LW – L. 5′10″, 170 lbs. b: Cap-de-la-Madeleine, Que., 4/15/1960.

Season	Club	League	GP	G	A	Pts	AG	AA	APts	PIM	PP	SH	GW	S	%	TGF	PGF	TGA	PGA	+/–	GP	G	A	Pts	PIM	PP	SH	GW
1977-78	Quebec Remparts	QMJHL	32	18	19	37				19																		
	Trois-Rivieres Draveurs	QMJHL	41	20	25	45				34																		
1978-79	Quebec Remparts	QMJHL	7	2	3	5				5																		
	Trois-Rivieres Draveurs	QMJHL	67	53	45	98				97											13	2	5	7	10			
1979-80	Trois-Rivieres Draveurs	QMJHL	72	85	62	147				118											7	5	3	8	14			
1980-81	**Quebec Nordiques**	**NHL**	**1**	**0**	**0**	**0**	**0**	**0**	**0**	**0**	**0**	**0**	**0**	**0**	**0.0**	**0**	**0**	**0**	**0**	**0**								
	Rochester Americans	AHL	7	0	1	1				4																		
	Erie Blades	EHL	71	*66	*68	*134				99											8	7	8	15	4			
1981-82	**Quebec Nordiques**	**NHL**	**62**	**10**	**13**	**23**	**8**	**9**	**17**	**27**	**0**	**1**	**1**	**62**	**16.1**	**34**	**2**	**57**	**16**	**–9**	**15**	**1**	**1**	**2**	**30**	**0**	**0**	**1**
	Fredericton Express	AHL	11	6	5	11				10																		
1982-83	**Quebec Nordiques**	**NHL**	**77**	**7**	**9**	**16**	**6**	**6**	**12**	**48**	**0**	**0**	**1**	**63**	**11.1**	**26**	**0**	**65**	**33**	**–6**	**2**	**0**	**0**	**0**	**0**	**0**	**0**	**0**
1983-84	**Quebec Nordiques**	**NHL**	**23**	**1**	**1**	**2**	**1**	**1**	**2**	**17**	**0**	**0**	**0**	**9**	**11.1**	**2**	**0**	**7**	**2**	**–3**								
	Fredericton Express	AHL	12	4	5	9				4																		
	Detroit Red Wings	**NHL**	**14**	**4**	**1**	**5**	**3**	**1**	**4**	**8**	**0**	**0**	**0**	**13**	**30.8**	**6**	**0**	**7**	**0**	**–1**	**3**	**0**	**0**	**0**	**2**	**0**	**0**	**0**
1984-85	**Detroit Red Wings**	**NHL**	**25**	**2**	**2**	**4**	**2**	**1**	**3**	**33**	**0**	**0**	**0**	**21**	**9.5**	**5**	**0**	**6**	**0**	**–1**								
	Adirondack Red Wings	AHL	29	13	10	23				74																		
1985-86	Adirondack Red Wings	AHL	66	28	31	59				124											16	*11	4	15	20			
1986-87	Adirondack Red Wings	AHL	17	3	7	10				23											9	1	3	4	32			
	NHL Totals		**202**	**24**	**26**	**50**	**20**	**18**	**38**	**133**	**0**	**1**	**2**	**168**	**14.3**	**73**	**2**	**142**	**51**		**20**	**1**	**1**	**2**	**32**	**0**	**0**	**1**

QMJHL Second All-Star Team (1980)

Signed as a free agent by **Quebec**, October 10, 1980. Traded to **Detroit** by **Quebec** for cash, February 29, 1984.

• AUCOIN, ADRIAN

Adrian Aucoin D – R. 6′1″, 194 lbs. b: Ottawa, Ont., 7/3/1973. Vancouver's 7th choice, 117th overall, in 1992 Entry Draft.

Season	Club	League	GP	G	A	Pts	AG	AA	APts	PIM	PP	SH	GW	S	%	TGF	PGF	TGA	PGA	+/–	GP	G	A	Pts	PIM	PP	SH	GW
1990-91	Nepean Raiders	OJHL	56	17	33	50				125																		
1991-92	Boston University	H.E.	32	2	10	12				60																		
1992-93	Canada	Nat-Team	42	8	10	18				71																		
	Canada	WJC-A	7	0	1	1				8																		
1993-94	Canada	Nat-Team	59	5	12	17				80																		
	Canada	Olympics	4	0	0	0				2																		
	Hamilton Canucks	AHL	13	1	2	3				19											4	0	2	2	6			
1994-95	**Vancouver Canucks**	**NHL**	**1**	**1**	**0**	**1**	**2**	**0**	**2**	**0**	**0**	**0**	**0**	**2**	**50.0**	**1**	**0**	**0**	**0**	**+1**	**4**	**1**	**0**	**1**	**0**	**1**	**0**	**0**
	Syracuse Crunch	AHL	71	13	18	31				52																		
1995-96	**Vancouver Canucks**	**NHL**	**49**	**4**	**14**	**18**	**4**	**11**	**15**	**34**	**2**	**0**	**0**	**85**	**4.7**	**56**	**15**	**37**	**4**	**+8**	**6**	**0**	**0**	**0**	**2**	**0**	**0**	**0**
	Syracuse Crunch	AHL	29	5	13	18				47																		
1996-97	**Vancouver Canucks**	**NHL**	**70**	**5**	**16**	**21**	**5**	**14**	**19**	**63**	**1**	**0**	**0**	**116**	**4.3**	**72**	**9**	**74**	**11**	**0**								
1997-98	**Vancouver Canucks**	**NHL**	**35**	**3**	**3**	**6**	**4**	**3**	**7**	**21**	**1**	**0**	**1**	**44**	**6.8**	**17**	**6**	**21**	**6**	**–4**								
	NHL Totals		**155**	**13**	**33**	**46**	**15**	**28**	**43**	**118**	**4**	**0**	**1**	**247**	**5.3**	**146**	**30**	**132**	**21**		**10**	**1**	**0**	**1**	**2**	**1**	**0**	**0**

• AUDETTE, DONALD

Donald Audette RW – R. 5′8″, 184 lbs. b: Laval, Que., 9/23/1969. Buffalo's 8th choice, 183rd overall, in 1989 Entry Draft.

Season	Club	League	GP	G	A	Pts	AG	AA	APts	PIM	PP	SH	GW	S	%	TGF	PGF	TGA	PGA	+/–	GP	G	A	Pts	PIM	PP	SH	GW
1986-87	Laval Titan	QMJHL	66	17	22	39				36											14	2	6	8	10			
1987-88	Laval Titan	QMJHL	63	48	61	109				56											14	7	12	19	20			
1988-89	Laval Titan	QMJHL	70	76	85	161				123											17	17	12	29	43			
1989-90	Rochester Americans	AHL	70	42	46	88				78											15	9	8	17	29			
	Buffalo Sabres	**NHL**																			**2**	**0**	**0**	**0**	**0**			
1990-91	**Buffalo Sabres**	**NHL**	**8**	**4**	**3**	**7**	**4**	**2**	**6**	**4**	**2**	**0**	**1**	**17**	**23.5**	**8**	**2**	**7**	**0**	**–1**								
	Rochester Americans	AHL	5	4	0	4				2																		
1991-92	**Buffalo Sabres**	**NHL**	**63**	**31**	**17**	**48**	**28**	**13**	**41**	**75**	**5**	**0**	**6**	**153**	**20.3**	**69**	**20**	**50**	**0**	**–1**								
1992-93	**Buffalo Sabres**	**NHL**	**44**	**12**	**7**	**19**	**10**	**5**	**15**	**51**	**2**	**0**	**0**	**92**	**13.0**	**30**	**4**	**34**	**0**	**–8**	**8**	**2**	**2**	**4**	**6**	**0**	**0**	**0**
	Rochester Americans	AHL	6	8	4	12				10																		
1993-94	**Buffalo Sabres**	**NHL**	**77**	**29**	**30**	**59**	**27**	**23**	**50**	**41**	**16**	**1**	**4**	**207**	**14.0**	**78**	**35**	**41**	**0**	**+2**	**7**	**0**	**1**	**1**	**6**	**0**	**0**	**0**
1994-95	**Buffalo Sabres**	**NHL**	**46**	**24**	**13**	**37**	**43**	**19**	**62**	**27**	**13**	**0**	**7**	**124**	**19.4**	**52**	**30**	**25**	**0**	**–3**	**5**	**1**	**1**	**2**	**4**	**1**	**0**	**0**
1995-96	**Buffalo Sabres**	**NHL**	**23**	**12**	**13**	**25**	**12**	**11**	**23**	**18**	**8**	**0**	**1**	**92**	**13.0**	**33**	**20**	**13**	**0**	**0**								
1996-97	**Buffalo Sabres**	**NHL**	**73**	**28**	**22**	**50**	**30**	**19**	**49**	**48**	**8**	**0**	**5**	**182**	**15.4**	**65**	**20**	**51**	**0**	**–6**	**11**	**4**	**5**	**9**	**6**	**0**	**0**	**0**
1997-98	**Buffalo Sabres**	**NHL**	**75**	**24**	**20**	**44**	**28**	**19**	**47**	**59**	**10**	**0**	**5**	**198**	**12.1**	**68**	**26**	**33**	**1**	**+10**	**15**	**5**	**8**	**13**	**10**	**3**	**0**	**2**
	NHL Totals		**409**	**164**	**125**	**289**	**182**	**111**	**293**	**323**	**64**	**1**	**29**	**1065**	**15.4**	**403**	**157**	**254**	**1**		**48**	**12**	**17**	**29**	**32**	**4**	**0**	**2**

QMJHL First All-Star Team (1989) • AHL First All-Star Team (1990) • Won Dudley "Red" Garret Memorial Trophy (Top Rookie - AHL) (1990)

• AUGE, LES

Les Auge D – L. 6′1″, 190 lbs. b: St. Paul, MN, 5/16/1953.

Season	Club	League	GP	G	A	Pts	AG	AA	APts	PIM	PP	SH	GW	S	%	TGF	PGF	TGA	PGA	+/–	GP	G	A	Pts	PIM	PP	SH	GW
1971-72	University of Minnesota	WCHA	22	2	14	16				8																		
1972-73	University of Minnesota	WCHA	28	3	20	23				28																		
1973-74	University of Minnesota	WCHA	28	7	25	32				36																		
1974-75	University of Minnesota	WCHA	38	6	20	26				52																		
1975-76	Rochester Americans	AHL	10	0	3	3				6																		
	Dayton Gems	IHL	65	11	29	40				59											15	1	6	7	10			
1976-77	Dayton Gems	IHL	29	3	8	11				34																		
	Rochester Americans	AHL	10	0	3	3				0																		
1977-78	Hershey Bears	AHL	2	0	0	0				0																		
	Port Huron Flags	IHL	78	3	37	40				104											17	2	13	15	20			

Season	Club	League	GP	G	A	Pts	AG	AA	APts	PIM	PP	SH	GW	S	%	TGF	PGF	TGA	PGA	+/-	Playoffs GP	G	A	Pts	PIM	PP	SH	GW
1978-79	Oklahoma City Stars	CHL	70	4	14	18				42																		
	United States	WEC-A	8	1	0	1				4																		
1979-80	United States	Nat-Team	29	0	14	14				14																		
	Hershey Bears	AHL	4	0	0	0				0																		
	Fort Worth Texans	CHL	50	6	24	30				26											15	1	3	4	2			
1980-81	**Colorado Rockies**	**NHL**	**6**	**0**	**3**	**3**	**0**	**2**	**2**	**4**	**0**	**0**	**0**	**3**	**0.0**	**7**	**1**	**9**	**0**	**–3**								
	Fort Worth Texans	CHL	70	6	17	23				56											5	0	3	3	4			
1981-82	Fort Worth Texans	CHL	20	0	8	8				26																		
	NHL Totals		**6**	**0**	**3**	**3**	**0**	**2**	**2**	**4**	**0**	**0**	**0**	**3**	**0.0**	**7**	**1**	**9**	**0**									

NCAA Championship All-Tournament Team (1974) • WCHA Second All-Star Team (1975) • NCAA West First All-American Team (1975)

Signed as a free agent by **Colorado**, July 15, 1979.

• AUGUSTA, PATRIK

Patrik Augusta RW – L. 5'10", 170 lbs. b: Jihlava, Czech., 11/13/1969. Toronto's 8th choice, 149th overall, in 1992 Entry Draft.

Season	Club	League	GP	G	A	Pts	AG	AA	APts	PIM	PP	SH	GW	S	%	TGF	PGF	TGA	PGA	+/-	Playoffs GP	G	A	Pts	PIM	PP	SH	GW
1988-89	Dukla Jihlava	Czech.	15	3	1	4				4																		
1989-90	Dukla Jihlava	Czech.	46	12	12	24																						
1990-91	Dukla Jihlava	Czech.	51	20	23	43																						
1991-92	Dukla Jihlava	Czech.	42	16	16	32				26																		
	Czechoslovakia	Olympics	8	3	2	5				0																		
	Czechoslovakia	WC-A	5	2	2	4				4																		
1992-93	St. John's Maple Leafs	AHL	75	32	45	77				74											8	3	3	6	23			
1993-94	**Toronto Maple Leafs**	**NHL**	**2**	**0**	**0**	**0**	**0**	**0**	**0**	**0**	**0**	**0**	**0**	**3**	**0.0**	**0**	**0**	**0**	**0**	**0**								
	St. John's Maple Leafs	AHL	77	*53	43	96				105											11	4	8	12	4			
1994-95	St. John's Maple Leafs	AHL	71	37	32	69				98											4	2	0	2	7			
1995-96	Los Angeles Ice Dogs	IHL	79	34	51	85				83																		
1996-97	Long Beach Ice Dogs	IHL	82	45	42	87				96											18	4	4	8	33			
1997-98	Long Beach Ice Dogs	IHL	82	41	40	81				84											17	11	7	18	20			
	NHL Totals		**2**	**0**	**0**	**0**	**0**	**0**	**0**	**0**	**0**	**0**	**0**	**3**	**0.0**	**0**	**0**	**0**	**0**									

AHL Second All-Star Team (1994) • IHL Second All-Star Team (1997)

• AWREY, DON

Don Awrey C – L. 6', 175 lbs. b: Kitchener, Ont., 7/18/1943.

Season	Club	League	GP	G	A	Pts	AG	AA	APts	PIM	PP	SH	GW	S	%	TGF	PGF	TGA	PGA	+/-	Playoffs GP	G	A	Pts	PIM	PP	SH	GW
1960-61	Niagara Falls Flyers	OHA	3	0	0	0				11																		
1961-62	Niagara Falls Flyers	OHA	41	6	12	18				90											10	0	3	3	15			
1962-63	Niagara Falls Flyers	OHA	50	7	23	30				111											25	8	17	25	*87			
1963-64	**Boston Bruins**	**NHL**	**16**	**1**	**0**	**1**	**1**	**0**	**1**	**4**																		
	Minneapolis Bruins	CHL	54	4	15	19				136											5	0	0	0	9			
1964-65	**Boston Bruins**	**NHL**	**47**	**2**	**3**	**5**	**3**	**3**	**6**	**41**																		
	Hershey Bears	AHL	23	2	4	6				38											15	0	1	1	29			
1965-66	**Boston Bruins**	**NHL**	**70**	**4**	**3**	**7**	**5**	**3**	**8**	**74**																		
1966-67	**Boston Bruins**	**NHL**	**4**	**1**	**0**	**1**	**1**	**0**	**1**	**6**																		
	Hershey Bears	AHL	63	1	13	14				153											5	0	0	0	19			
1967-68	**Boston Bruins**	**NHL**	**74**	**3**	**12**	**15**	**4**	**13**	**17**	**150**	**0**	**0**	**0**	**92**	**3.3**	**95**	**2**	**104**	**29**	**+18**	**4**	**0**	**1**	**1**	**4**	**0**	**0**	**0**
1968-69	**Boston Bruins**	**NHL**	**73**	**0**	**13**	**13**	**0**	**12**	**12**	**149**	**0**	**0**	**0**	**72**	**0.0**	**104**	**3**	**98**	**22**	**+25**	**10**	**0**	**1**	**1**	**28**	**0**	**0**	**0**
1969-70	**Boston Bruins**	**NHL**	**73**	**3**	**10**	**13**	**3**	**10**	**13**	**120**	**0**	**0**	**0**	**96**	**3.1**	**85**	**0**	**100**	**42**	**+27**	**14**	**0**	**5**	**5**	**32**	**0**	**0**	**0**
1970-71	**Boston Bruins**	**NHL**	**74**	**4**	**21**	**25**	**4**	**18**	**22**	**141**	**0**	**0**	**1**	**108**	**3.7**	**116**	**2**	**87**	**13**	**+40**	**7**	**0**	**0**	**0**	**17**	**0**	**0**	**0**
1971-72	**Boston Bruins**	**NHL**	**34**	**1**	**8**	**9**	**1**	**7**	**8**	**52**	**0**	**0**	**0**	**53**	**1.9**	**57**	**2**	**44**	**9**	**+20**	**15**	**0**	**4**	**4**	**45**	**0**	**0**	**0**
	Boston Braves	AHL	3	0	1	1				2																		
1972-73	Canada	Summit	2	0	0	0				0																		
	Boston Bruins	**NHL**	**70**	**2**	**17**	**19**	**2**	**14**	**16**	**90**	**0**	**0**	**0**	**110**	**1.8**	**120**	**0**	**104**	**13**	**+29**	**4**	**0**	**0**	**0**	**6**	**0**	**0**	**0**
1973-74	**St. Louis Blues**	**NHL**	**75**	**5**	**16**	**21**	**5**	**14**	**19**	**51**	**1**	**0**	**0**	**94**	**5.3**	**85**	**7**	**114**	**29**	**–7**								
1974-75	**St. Louis Blues**	**NHL**	**20**	**0**	**8**	**8**	**0**	**6**	**6**	**4**	**0**	**0**	**0**	**17**	**0.0**	**20**	**1**	**41**	**14**	**–8**								
	Montreal Canadiens	**NHL**	**56**	**1**	**11**	**12**	**1**	**9**	**10**	**58**	**0**	**0**	**0**	**40**	**2.5**	**63**	**2**	**67**	**27**	**+21**	**11**	**0**	**6**	**6**	**12**	**0**	**0**	**0**
1975-76	**Montreal Canadiens**	**NHL**	**72**	**0**	**12**	**12**	**0**	**9**	**9**	**29**	**0**	**0**	**0**	**60**	**0.0**	**73**	**2**	**57**	**16**	**+30**								
1976-77	**Pittsburgh Penguins**	**NHL**	**79**	**1**	**12**	**13**	**1**	**10**	**11**	**40**	**0**	**0**	**0**	**45**	**2.2**	**77**	**0**	**103**	**24**	**–2**	**3**	**0**	**1**	**1**	**0**	**0**	**0**	**0**
1977-78	**New York Rangers**	**NHL**	**78**	**2**	**8**	**10**	**2**	**7**	**9**	**38**	**0**	**0**	**1**	**40**	**5.0**	**68**	**2**	**95**	**15**	**–14**	**3**	**0**	**0**	**0**	**6**	**0**	**0**	**0**
1978-79	New Haven Nighthawks	AHL	6	2	1	3				6																		
	Colorado Rockies	**NHL**	**56**	**1**	**4**	**5**	**1**	**3**	**4**	**18**	**0**	**0**	**0**	**40**	**2.5**	**31**	**0**	**79**	**15**	**–33**								
	NHL Totals		**979**	**31**	**158**	**189**	**34**	**138**	**172**	**1065**	**1**	**0**	**2**	**867**	**3.6**	**994**	**23**	**1093**	**268**		**71**	**0**	**18**	**18**	**150**	**0**	**0**	**0**

Played in NHL All-Star Game (1974)

Traded to **St. Louis** by **Boston** for Jake Rathwell and St. Louis' 2nd round choice (Mark Howe) in 1974 Amateur Draft, October 5, 1974. Traded to **Montreal** by **St. Louis** for Chuck Lefley, November 28, 1974. Traded to **Pittsburgh** by **Montreal** for Pittsburgh's 3rd round choice (Richard David) in 1978 Amateur Draft, August 11, 1976. Rights traded to **Washington** by **Pittsburgh** for Bob Paradise, October 1, 1977. Signed as a free agent by **NY Rangers**, October 4, 1977. Traded to **Colorado** by **NY Rangers** for cash, November, 1978

• AXELSSON, PER-JOHAN

Per-Johan Axelsson LW – L. 6'1", 174 lbs. b: Kungalv, Sweden, 2/26/1975. Boston's 7th choice, 177th overall, in 1995 Entry Draft.

Season	Club	League	GP	G	A	Pts	AG	AA	APts	PIM	PP	SH	GW	S	%	TGF	PGF	TGA	PGA	+/-	Playoffs GP	G	A	Pts	PIM	PP	SH	GW
1993-94	Vastra Frolunda	Sweden	11	0	0	0				4											4	0	0	0	0			
1994-95	Vastra Frolunda	Sweden	8	2	1	3				6																		
	Sweden	WJC-A	7	2	3	5				2																		
1995-96	Vastra Frolunda	Sweden	36	15	5	20				10											13	3	0	3	10			
1996-97	Vastra Frolunda	Sweden	50	19	15	34				34											3	0	2	2	0			
1997-98	**Boston Bruins**	**NHL**	**82**	**8**	**19**	**27**	**9**	**19**	**28**	**38**	**2**	**0**	**1**	**144**	**5.6**	**43**	**5**	**74**	**22**	**–14**	**6**	**1**	**0**	**1**	**0**	**0**	**0**	**0**
	NHL Totals		**82**	**8**	**19**	**27**	**9**	**19**	**28**	**38**	**2**	**0**	**1**	**144**	**5.6**	**43**	**5**	**74**	**22**		**6**	**1**	**0**	**1**	**0**	**0**	**0**	**0**

• BABCOCK, BOBBY

Bobby Babcock D – L. 6'1", 222 lbs. b: Agincourt, Ont., 8/3/1968. Washington's 11th choice, 208th overall, in 1986 Entry Draft.

Season	Club	League	GP	G	A	Pts	AG	AA	APts	PIM	PP	SH	GW	S	%	TGF	PGF	TGA	PGA	+/-	Playoffs GP	G	A	Pts	PIM	PP	SH	GW
1984-85	St. Michael's Buzzers	Jr. B	40	8	30	38				140																		
1985-86	Sault Ste. Marie Greyhounds	OHL	50	1	7	8				188																		
1986-87	Sault Ste. Marie Greyhounds	OHL	62	7	8	15				243											4	0	0	0	11			
1987-88	Sault Ste. Marie Greyhounds	OHL	8	0	2	2				30																		
	Cornwall Royals	OHL	42	0	16	16				120																		
1988-89	Cornwall Royals	OHL	42	0	9	9				163											18	1	3	4	29			
1989-90	Baltimore Skipjacks	AHL	67	0	4	4				249											7	0	0	0	23			
1990-91	**Washington Capitals**	**NHL**	**1**	**0**	**0**	**0**	**0**	**0**	**0**	**0**	**0**	**0**	**0**	**0**	**0.0**	**0**	**0**	**0**	**0**	**0**								
	Baltimore Skipjacks	AHL	38	0	3	3				112																		
1991-92	Baltimore Skipjacks	AHL	26	0	2	2				55																		
1992-93	**Washington Capitals**	**NHL**	**1**	**0**	**0**	**0**	**0**	**0**	**0**	**2**	**0**	**0**	**0**	**0**	**0.0**	**0**	**0**	**0**	**0**	**0**								
	Baltimore Skipjacks	AHL	26	0	2	2				93																		
	Hampton Roads Admirals	ECHL	26	3	13	16				96											1	0	0	0	10			
1993-94	Binghamton Rangers	AHL	20	1	6	7				67																		
	NHL Totals		**2**	**0**	**0**	**0**	**0**	**0**	**0**	**2**	**0**	**0**	**0**	**0**	**0.0**	**0**	**0**	**0**	**0**									

• BABE, WARREN

Warren Babe LW – L. 6'2", 190 lbs. b: Medicine Hat, Alta., 9/7/1968. Minnesota's 1st choice, 12th overall, in 1986 Entry Draft.

Season	Club	League	GP	G	A	Pts	AG	AA	APts	PIM	PP	SH	GW	S	%	TGF	PGF	TGA	PGA	+/-	Playoffs GP	G	A	Pts	PIM	PP	SH	GW
1984-85	Lethbridge Broncos	WHL	70	7	14	21				117																		
1985-86	Lethbridge Broncos	WHL	63	33	24	57				125																		
1986-87	Swift Current Broncos	WHL	52	28	45	73				109																		
1987-88	Kamloops Blazers	WHL	32	17	19	36				73											18	5	12	17	42			
	Canada	WJC-A	7	0	2	2				10																		
	Minnesota North Stars	**NHL**	**6**	**0**	**1**	**1**	**0**	**1**	**1**	**4**	**0**	**0**	**0**	**2**	**0.0**	**2**	**0**	**3**	**0**	**–1**								
	Kalamazoo Wings	IHL	6	0	0	0				7																		
1988-89	**Minnesota North Stars**	**NHL**	**14**	**2**	**3**	**5**	**2**	**2**	**4**	**19**	**0**	**0**	**0**	**15**	**13.3**	**7**	**0**	**4**	**0**	**+3**	**2**	**0**	**0**	**0**	**0**	**0**	**0**	**0**
	Kalamazoo Wings	IHL	62	18	24	42				102											6	1	4	5	24			

Season	Club	League	REGULAR SEASON																		PLAYOFFS							
			GP	G	A	Pts	AG	AA	APts	PIM	PP	SH	GW	S	%	TGF	PGF	TGA	PGA	+/–	GP	G	A	Pts	PIM	PP	SH	GW
1989-90			DID NOT PLAY – INJURED																									
1990-91	**Minnesota North Stars**	NHL	1	0	1	1	0	1	1	0	0	0	0	0	0.0	1	0	0	0	+1								
	Kalamazoo Wings	IHL	49	15	17	32				52																		
	NHL Totals		21	2	5	7	2	4	6	23	0	0	0	17	11.8	10	0	7	0		2	0	0	0	0	0	0	0

• Sat out entire 1989-90 season after suffering the 14th concussion of his career during 1990 IHL playoffs.

● BABIN, MITCH

Mitch Babin C – L. 6'2", 195 lbs. b: Kapuskasing, Ont., 11/1/1954. St. Louis' 10th choice, 180th overall, in 1974 Amateur Draft.

1971-72	Kenora Muskies	MJHL	46	22	22	44				89																		
1972-73	North Bay Trappers	OJHL	43	35	37	72				101																		
1973-74	North Bay Trappers	OJHL	43	29	51	80				60																		
1974-75	Denver Spurs	CHL	70	30	43	73				48											2	0	2	2	4			
1975-76	**St. Louis Blues**	NHL	8	0	0	0	0	0	0	0	0	0	0	2	0.0	1	1	2	0	–2								
	Providence Reds	AHL	54	8	9	17				14											2	0	0	0	0			
1976-77	Kansas City Blues	CHL	75	26	25	51				59											10	*4	4	8	6			
1977-78	Salt Lake Golden Eagles	CHL	17	2	4	6				6																		
	Veu Ca	Austria	....	29	18	47				....																		
	NHL Totals		8	0	0	0	0	0	0	0	0	0	0	2	0.0	1	1	2	0									

● BABY, JOHN

John Baby D – R. 6', 195 lbs. b: Sudbury, Ont., 5/18/1957. Cleveland's 5th choice, 59th overall, in 1977 Amateur Draft.

1973-74	North Bay Trappers	OPHL	36	8	21	29				109																		
1974-75	Kitchener Rangers	OHA	70	13	26	39				112																		
1975-76	Sudbury Wolves	OHA	61	16	34	50				155																		
	Kitchener Rangers	OHA	3	0	0	0				0																		
1976-77	Sudbury Wolves	OHA	61	32	61	93				118																		
1977-78	**Cleveland Barons**	NHL	24	2	7	9	2	6	8	26	0	0	0	42	4.8	23	6	28	1	–10								
	Phoenix Roadrunners	CHL	16	3	3	6				25																		
	Binghamton Whalers	AHL	25	3	1	4				16																		
1978-79	**Minnesota North Stars**	NHL	2	0	1	1	0	1	1	0	0	0	0	6	0.0	1	0	4	1	–2								
	Oklahoma City Stars	CHL	76	18	22	40				114																		
1979-80	Syracuse Firebirds	AHL	73	3	24	27				73																		
1980-81	Binghamton Whalers	AHL	66	9	25	34				80											2	0	0	0	2			
1981-82			DID NOT PLAY																									
1982-83			DID NOT PLAY																									
1983-84	Kalamazoo Wings	IHL	46	2	14	16				35											3	0	0	0	4			
	NHL Totals		26	2	8	10	2	7	9	26	0	0	0	48	4.2	24	6	32	2									

OHA Second All-Star Team (1977)

Placed on **Minnesota** Reserve List after **Cleveland-Minnesota** Dispersal Draft, June 15, 1979. Claimed by **Quebec** from **Minnesota** in Expansion Draft, June 13, 1980.

● BABYCH, DAVE

Dave Babych D – L. 6'2", 215 lbs. b: Edmonton, Alta., 5/23/1961. Winnipeg's 1st choice, 2nd overall, in 1980 Entry Draft.

1977-78	Portland Winter Hawks	WCJHL	6	1	3	4				4																		
1978-79	Portland Winter Hawks	WHL	67	20	59	79				63											25	7	22	29	22			
1979-80	Portland Winter Hawks	WHL	50	22	60	82				71											8	1	10	11	2			
1980-81	**Winnipeg Jets**	NHL	69	6	38	44	5	27	32	90	3	0	0	209	2.9	125	47	169	30	–61								
	Canada	WEC-A	7	0	2	2				8																		
1981-82	**Winnipeg Jets**	NHL	79	19	49	68	15	32	47	92	11	0	2	262	7.3	188	70	151	22	–11	4	1	2	3	29	1	0	0
1982-83	**Winnipeg Jets**	NHL	79	13	61	74	11	42	53	56	7	0	1	253	5.1	184	70	146	22	–10	3	0	0	0	0	0	0	0
1983-84	**Winnipeg Jets**	NHL	66	18	39	57	14	26	40	62	10	0	4	233	7.7	156	56	167	36	–31	3	1	1	2	0	1	0	0
1984-85	**Winnipeg Jets**	NHL	78	13	49	62	11	33	44	78	6	0	1	239	5.4	159	54	142	21	–16	8	2	7	9	6	2	0	0
1985-86	**Winnipeg Jets**	NHL	19	4	12	16	3	8	11	14	2	0	0	53	7.5	37	13	35	10	–1								
	Hartford Whalers	NHL	62	10	43	53	8	29	37	36	7	1	2	152	6.6	132	52	109	31	+2	8	1	3	4	14	0	0	0
1986-87	**Hartford Whalers**	NHL	66	8	33	41	7	24	31	44	7	0	1	157	5.1	98	53	78	15	–18	6	1	1	2	14	1	0	0
1987-88	**Hartford Whalers**	NHL	71	14	36	50	12	26	38	54	10	0	2	233	6.0	108	68	67	2	–25	6	3	2	5	2	0	0	0
1988-89	**Hartford Whalers**	NHL	70	6	41	47	5	29	34	54	4	0	2	172	3.5	115	47	80	7	–5	4	1	5	6	2	0	0	0
	Canada	WEC-A	10	2	0	2				4																		
1989-90	**Hartford Whalers**	NHL	72	6	37	43	5	26	31	62	4	0	1	164	3.7	123	61	91	13	–16	7	1	2	3	0	0	0	0
1990-91	**Hartford Whalers**	NHL	8	0	6	6	0	5	5	4	0	0	0	15	0.0	13	9	8	0	–4								
1991-92	**Vancouver Canucks**	NHL	75	5	24	29	5	18	23	63	4	0	1	148	3.4	85	29	75	17	–2	13	2	6	8	10	1	0	1
1992-93	**Vancouver Canucks**	NHL	43	3	16	19	2	11	13	44	3	0	0	78	3.8	63	22	52	17	+6	12	2	5	7	6	1	0	0
1993-94	**Vancouver Canucks**	NHL	73	4	28	32	4	22	26	52	0	0	2	96	4.2	78	18	76	16	0	24	3	5	8	12	0	0	1
1994-95	**Vancouver Canucks**	NHL	40	3	11	14	5	16	21	18	1	0	0	58	5.2	42	12	58	15	–13	11	2	2	4	14	1	1	0
1995-96	**Vancouver Canucks**	NHL	53	3	21	24	3	17	20	38	3	0	0	69	4.3	65	15	72	17	–5								
1996-97	**Vancouver Canucks**	NHL	78	5	22	27	5	19	24	38	2	0	1	105	4.8	75	7	87	17	–2								
1997-98	**Vancouver Canucks**	NHL	47	0	9	9	0	9	9	37	0	0	0	40	0.0	35	2	61	17	–11								
	Philadelphia Flyers	NHL	6	0	0	0	0	0	0	12	0	0	0	6	0.0	5	1	2	0	+2	5	1	0	1	4	1	0	0
	NHL Totals		1154	140	575	715	120	419	539	948	84	1	20	2742	5.1	1886	706	1726	325		114	21	41	62	113	9	1	2

WHL First All-Star Team (1980)

Played in NHL All-Star Game (1983, 1984)

Traded to **Hartford** by **Winnipeg** for Ray Neufeld, November 21, 1985. Claimed by **Minnesota** from **Hartford** in Expansion Draft, May 30, 1991. Traded to **Vancouver** by **Minnesota** for Tom Kurvers, June 22, 1991. Traded to **Philadelphia** by **Vancouver** with Philadelphia's 5th round choice (previously acquired, Philadelphia selected Garrett Prosofsky) in 1998 Entry Draft for Philadelphia's 3rd round choice (Justin Morrison) in 1998 Entry Draft, March 24, 1998.

● BABYCH, WAYNE

Wayne Babych RW – R. 5'11", 191 lbs. b: Edmonton, Alta., 6/6/1958. St. Louis' 1st choice, 3rd overall, in 1978 Amateur Draft.

1973-74	Edmonton Mets	AJHL	56	20	18	38				68																		
	Edmonton Oil Kings	WCJHL	1	0	1	1				0											3	0	0	0	0			
1974-75	Edmonton Oil Kings	WCJHL	68	19	17	36				157																		
1975-76	Edmonton Oil Kings	WCJHL	61	32	46	78				98											5	2	1	3	23			
1976-77	Portland Winter Hawks	WCJHL	71	50	62	112				76											10	2	6	8	10			
1977-78	Portland Winter Hawks	WCJHL	68	50	71	121				218											8	4	4	8	19			
1978-79	**St. Louis Blues**	NHL	67	27	36	63	25	28	53	75	11	0	0	196	13.8	101	34	80	2	–11								
	Canada	WEC-A	7	1	2	3				0																		
1979-80	**St. Louis Blues**	NHL	59	26	35	61	24	27	51	49	7	0	3	159	16.4	81	22	48	0	+11	3	1	2	3	2	0	0	0
1980-81	**St. Louis Blues**	NHL	78	54	42	96	45	29	74	93	14	0	7	306	17.6	142	45	83	0	+14	11	2	0	2	8	1	0	0
1981-82	**St. Louis Blues**	NHL	51	19	25	44	15	17	32	51	4	0	3	142	13.4	57	16	53	0	–12	7	3	2	5	8	0	0	1
1982-83	**St. Louis Blues**	NHL	71	16	23	39	13	16	29	62	5	0	2	148	10.8	64	23	65	0	–24								
1983-84	**St. Louis Blues**	NHL	70	13	29	42	10	20	30	52	3	0	0	115	11.3	63	13	50	1	+1	10	1	4	5	4	0	0	0
1984-85	**Pittsburgh Penguins**	NHL	65	20	34	54	16	23	39	35	3	0	3	131	15.3	81	16	72	0	–7								
1985-86	**Pittsburgh Penguins**	NHL	2	0	0	0	0	0	0	0	0	0	0	0	0.0	0	0	1	0	–1								
	Quebec Nordiques	NHL	15	6	5	11	5	3	8	18	1	0	0	32	18.8	13	3	10	0	0								
	Hartford Whalers	NHL	37	11	17	28	9	11	20	59	2	0	2	63	17.5	39	12	21	0	+6	10	0	1	1	2	0	0	0
1986-87	**Hartford Whalers**	NHL	4	0	0	0	0	0	0	4	0	0	0	2	0.0	0	0	5	0	–5								
	Binghamton Whalers	AHL	6	2	5	7				6																		
	NHL Totals		519	192	246	438	162	174	336	498	50	0	20	1294	14.8	641	184	488	3		41	7	9	16	24	1	0	1

WCJHL All-Star Team (1977, 1978)

Played in NHL All-Star Game (1981)

Claimed by **Pittsburgh** from **St. Louis** in Waiver Draft, October 9, 1984. Traded to **Quebec** by **Pittsburgh** for future considerations, October 20, 1985. Traded to **Hartford** by **Quebec** for Greg Malone, January 17, 1986.

Season	Club	League	REGULAR SEASON GP	G	A	Pts	AG	AA	APts	PIM	PP	SH	GW	S	%	TGF	PGF	TGA	PGA	+/–	PLAYOFFS GP	G	A	Pts	PIM	PP	SH	GW

● BACA, JERGUS

Jergus Baca D – L. 6'2", 211 lbs. b: Liptovsky Mikulas, Czech., 1/4/1965. Hartford's 6th choice, 141st overall, in 1990 Entry Draft.

Season	Club	League	GP	G	A	Pts	AG	AA	APts	PIM	PP	SH	GW	S	%	TGF	PGF	TGA	PGA	+/–	GP	G	A	Pts	PIM	PP	SH	GW
1987-88	VSZ Kosice	Czech.	40	5	5	10	....	....	....	32	....	....	....	....	....	....	....	....	....	....	....	....	....	....	....	....	....	....
1988-89	VSZ Kosice	Czech.	42	3	10	13	....	....	....	46	....	....	....	....	....	....	....	....	....	....	....	....	....	....	....	....	....	....
	Czechoslovakia	WEC-A	10	1	1	2	....	....	....	14	....	....	....	....	....	....	....	....	....	....	....	....	....	....	....	....	....	....
1989-90	VSZ Kosice	Czech.	47	9	16	25	....	....	....	....	....	....	....	....	....	....	....	....	....	....	....	....	....	....	....	....	....	....
	Czechoslovakia	WEC-A	8	0	0	0	....	....	....	16	....	....	....	....	....	....	....	....	....	....	....	....	....	....	....	....	....	....
1990-91	**Hartford Whalers**	**NHL**	**9**	**0**	**2**	**2**	**0**	**2**	**2**	**14**	**0**	**0**	**0**	**15**	**0.0**	**5**	**4**	**4**	**0**	**–3**	....	....	....	....	....	....	....	....
	Springfield Indians	AHL	57	6	23	29	....	....	....	89	....	....	....	....	....	....	....	....	....	....	18	3	13	16	18	....	....	....
1991-92	Czechoslovakia	C Cup	5	0	3	3	....	....	....	4	....	....	....	....	....	....	....	....	....	....	....	....	....	....	....	....	....	....
	Hartford Whalers	**NHL**	**1**	**0**	**0**	**0**	**0**	**0**	**0**	**0**	**0**	**0**	**0**	**1**	**0.0**	**0**	**0**	**1**	**0**	**–1**	....	....	....	....	....	....	....	....
	Springfield Indians	AHL	64	6	20	26	....	....	....	88	....	....	....	....	....	....	....	....	....	....	11	0	6	6	20	....	....	....
1992-93	Milwaukee Admirals	IHL	73	9	29	38	....	....	....	108	....	....	....	....	....	....	....	....	....	....	6	0	3	3	2	....	....	....
1993-94	Milwaukee Admirals	IHL	67	6	29	35	....	....	....	119	....	....	....	....	....	....	....	....	....	....	3	1	1	2	4	....	....	....
	Slovakia	Olympics	8	1	2	3	....	....	....	10	....	....	....	....	....	....	....	....	....	....	....	....	....	....	....	....	....	....
1994-95	Leksands IF	Sweden	38	2	5	7	....	....	....	50	....	....	....	....	....	....	....	....	....	....	4	1	1	2	6	....	....	....
1995-96	Milwaukee Admirals	IHL	74	3	12	15	....	....	....	130	....	....	....	....	....	....	....	....	....	....	5	1	3	4	8	....	....	....
1996-97	Slovakia	W Cup	3	1	0	1	....	....	....	6	....	....	....	....	....	....	....	....	....	....	....	....	....	....	....	....	....	....
	HC Olomouc	Czech.	52	4	9	13	....	....	....	109	....	....	....	....	....	....	....	....	....	....	....	....	....	....	....	....	....	....
	HC Kosice	Slovakia	....	....	....	....	....	....	....	....	....	....	....	....	....	....	....	....	....	....	7	2	2	4	....	....	....	....
	Slovakia	WC-A	8	0	2	2	....	....	....	4	....	....	....	....	....	....	....	....	....	....	....	....	....	....	....	....	....	....
1997-98	HC Kosice	Slovakia	33	6	12	18	....	....	....	12	....	....	....	....	....	....	....	....	....	....	11	4	3	7	4	....	....	....
	Slovakia	WC-A	6	0	0	0	....	....	....	4	....	....	....	....	....	....	....	....	....	....	....	....	....	....	....	....	....	....
	NHL Totals		**10**	**0**	**2**	**2**	**0**	**2**	**2**	**14**	**0**	**0**	**0**	**16**	**0.0**	**5**	**4**	**5**	**0**		....	....	....	....	....	....	....	....

Czechoslovakian Rookie of the Year (1988) • Czechoslovakian First All-Star Team (1989, 1990)

● BACKMAN, MIKE

Mike Backman RW – R. 5'10", 175 lbs. b: Halifax, N.S., 1/2/1955.

Season	Club	League	GP	G	A	Pts	AG	AA	APts	PIM	PP	SH	GW	S	%	TGF	PGF	TGA	PGA	+/–	GP	G	A	Pts	PIM	PP	SH	GW
1974-75	Montreal Jr. Canadiens	QMJHL	38	13	20	33	....	....	....	85	....	....	....	....	....	....	....	....	....	....	....	....	....	....	....	....	....	....
	St. Mary's University	AUAA	6	0	8	8	....	....	....	8	....	....	....	....	....	....	....	....	....	....	....	....	....	....	....	....	....	....
1975-76	St. Mary's University	AUAA	19	13	10	23	....	....	....	49	....	....	....	....	....	....	....	....	....	....	....	....	....	....	....	....	....	....
1976-77	St. Mary's University	AUAA	19	13	15	28	....	....	....	59	....	....	....	....	....	....	....	....	....	....	....	....	....	....	....	....	....	....
1977-78	St. Mary's University	AUAA	17	7	12	19	....	....	....	47	....	....	....	....	....	....	....	....	....	....	....	....	....	....	....	....	....	....
1978-79	New Haven Nighthawks	AHL	6	2	1	3	....	....	....	0	....	....	....	....	....	....	....	....	....	....	6	3	1	4	15	....	....	....
	Toledo Goaldiggers	IHL	66	25	38	63	....	....	....	171	....	....	....	....	....	....	....	....	....	....	6	4	2	6	17	....	....	....
1979-80	New Haven Nighthawks	AHL	74	18	28	46	....	....	....	156	....	....	....	....	....	....	....	....	....	....	10	6	8	14	14	....	....	....
1980-81	New Haven Nighthawks	AHL	62	27	27	54	....	....	....	224	....	....	....	....	....	....	....	....	....	....	4	1	0	1	14	....	....	....
1981-82	**New York Rangers**	**NHL**	**3**	**0**	**2**	**2**	**0**	**1**	**1**	**4**	**0**	**0**	**0**	**1**	**0.0**	**8**	**0**	**1**	**0**	**+7**	**1**	**0**	**0**	**0**	**2**	**0**	**0**	**0**
	Springfield Indians	AHL	74	24	27	51	....	....	....	147	....	....	....	....	....	....	....	....	....	....	....	....	....	....	....	....	....	....
1982-83	**New York Rangers**	**NHL**	**7**	**1**	**3**	**4**	**1**	**2**	**3**	**6**	**0**	**0**	**0**	**9**	**11.1**	**6**	**0**	**11**	**0**	**–5**	**9**	**2**	**2**	**4**	**0**	**0**	**0**	**1**
	Tulsa Oilers	CHL	71	29	47	76	....	....	....	170	....	....	....	....	....	....	....	....	....	....	....	....	....	....	....	....	....	....
1983-84	**New York Rangers**	**NHL**	**8**	**0**	**1**	**1**	**0**	**1**	**1**	**8**	**0**	**0**	**0**	**6**	**0.0**	**1**	**0**	**2**	**0**	**–1**	....	....	....	....	....	....	....	....
	Tulsa Oilers	CHL	50	12	28	40	....	....	....	103	....	....	....	....	....	....	....	....	....	....	9	4	2	6	22	....	....	....
1984-85	New Haven Nighthawks	AHL	72	10	36	46	....	....	....	120	....	....	....	....	....	....	....	....	....	....	....	....	....	....	....	....	....	....
1985-86	New Haven Nighthawks	AHL	4	0	0	0	....	....	....	4	....	....	....	....	....	....	....	....	....	....	....	....	....	....	....	....	....	....
	NHL Totals		**18**	**1**	**6**	**7**	**1**	**4**	**5**	**18**	**0**	**0**	**0**	**16**	**6.3**	**15**	**0**	**14**	**0**		**10**	**2**	**2**	**4**	**2**	**0**	**0**	**1**

CHL First All-Star Team (1983)

Signed as a free agent by **NY Rangers**, October 11, 1979.

● BACKSTROM, RALPH

Ralph Backstrom C – L. 5'10", 165 lbs. b: Kirkland Lake, Ont., 9/18/1937.

Season	Club	League	GP	G	A	Pts	AG	AA	APts	PIM	PP	SH	GW	S	%	TGF	PGF	TGA	PGA	+/–	GP	G	A	Pts	PIM	PP	SH	GW
1954-55	Montreal Jr. Canadiens	QJHL	21	7	6	13	....	....	....	2	....	....	....	....	....	....	....	....	....	....	5	2	1	3	4	....	....	....
1955-56	Montreal Jr. Canadiens	QJHL	18	10	8	18	....	....	....	4	....	....	....	....	....	....	....	....	....	....	....	....	....	....	....	....	....	....
1956-57	Hull-Ottawa Jr. Canadiens	Ott-Jr.	18	10	8	18	....	....	....	4	....	....	....	....	....	....	....	....	....	....	....	....	....	....	....	....	....	....
	Montreal Canadiens	**NHL**	**3**	**0**	**0**	**0**	**0**	**0**	**0**	**0**	....	....	....	....	....	....	....	....	....	....	....	....	....	....	....	....	....	....
	Hull-Ottawa Jr. Canadiens	EOHL	18	7	10	17	....	....	....	4	....	....	....	....	....	....	....	....	....	....	....	....	....	....	....	....	....	....
1957-58	Hull-Ottawa Jr. Canadiens	Ott-Jr.	26	24	27	51	....	....	....	64	....	....	....	....	....	....	....	....	....	....	....	....	....	....	....	....	....	....
	Hull-Ottawa Jr. Canadiens	EOHL	33	21	25	46	....	....	....	13	....	....	....	....	....	....	....	....	....	....	....	....	....	....	....	....	....	....
	Montreal Royals	QHL	1	0	1	1	....	....	....	0	....	....	....	....	....	....	....	....	....	....	....	....	....	....	....	....	....	....
	Rochester Americans	AHL	2	0	0	0	....	....	....	0	....	....	....	....	....	....	....	....	....	....	....	....	....	....	....	....	....	....
	Montreal Canadiens	**NHL**	**2**	**0**	**1**	**1**	**0**	**1**	**1**	**0**	....	....	....	....	....	....	....	....	....	....	....	....	....	....	....	....	....	....
1958-59	**Montreal Canadiens**	**NHL**	**64**	**18**	**22**	**40**	**23**	**23**	**46**	**19**	....	....	....	....	....	....	....	....	....	....	**11**	**3**	**5**	**8**	**12**	....	....	....
1959-60	**Montreal Canadiens**	**NHL**	**64**	**13**	**15**	**28**	**16**	**15**	**31**	**24**	....	....	....	....	....	....	....	....	....	....	**7**	**0**	**3**	**3**	**2**	....	....	....
1960-61	**Montreal Canadiens**	**NHL**	**69**	**12**	**20**	**32**	**15**	**20**	**35**	**44**	....	....	....	....	....	....	....	....	....	....	**5**	**0**	**0**	**0**	**4**	....	....	....
1961-62	**Montreal Canadiens**	**NHL**	**66**	**27**	**38**	**65**	**33**	**39**	**72**	**29**	....	....	....	....	....	....	....	....	....	....	**5**	**0**	**1**	**1**	**6**	....	....	....
1962-63	**Montreal Canadiens**	**NHL**	**70**	**23**	**12**	**35**	**28**	**12**	**40**	**51**	....	....	....	....	....	....	....	....	....	....	**5**	**0**	**0**	**0**	**2**	....	....	....
1963-64	**Montreal Canadiens**	**NHL**	**70**	**8**	**21**	**29**	**10**	**23**	**33**	**41**	....	....	....	....	....	....	....	....	....	....	**7**	**2**	**1**	**3**	**8**	....	....	....
1964-65	**Montreal Canadiens**	**NHL**	**70**	**25**	**30**	**55**	**32**	**33**	**65**	**41**	....	....	....	....	....	....	....	....	....	....	**13**	**2**	**3**	**5**	**10**	....	....	....
1965-66	**Montreal Canadiens**	**NHL**	**67**	**22**	**20**	**42**	**27**	**20**	**47**	**10**	....	....	....	....	....	....	....	....	....	....	**10**	**3**	**4**	**7**	**4**	....	....	....
1966-67	**Montreal Canadiens**	**NHL**	**69**	**14**	**27**	**41**	**17**	**28**	**45**	**39**	....	....	....	....	....	....	....	....	....	....	**10**	**5**	**2**	**7**	**6**	....	....	....
1967-68	**Montreal Canadiens**	**NHL**	**70**	**20**	**25**	**45**	**25**	**26**	**51**	**14**	**3**	**0**	**5**	**198**	**10.1**	**55**	**12**	**39**	**0**	**+4**	**13**	**4**	**3**	**7**	**4**	**0**	**0**	**2**
1968-69	**Montreal Canadiens**	**NHL**	**72**	**13**	**28**	**41**	**15**	**26**	**41**	**16**	**2**	**0**	**3**	**180**	**7.2**	**56**	**5**	**31**	**0**	**+20**	**14**	**3**	**4**	**7**	**10**	**0**	**1**	**1**
1969-70	**Montreal Canadiens**	**NHL**	**72**	**19**	**24**	**43**	**22**	**24**	**46**	**20**	**1**	**0**	**2**	**187**	**10.2**	**57**	**9**	**44**	**0**	**+4**	....	....	....	....	....	....	....	....
1970-71	**Montreal Canadiens**	**NHL**	**16**	**1**	**4**	**5**	**1**	**4**	**5**	**0**	**0**	**0**	**0**	**18**	**5.6**	**9**	**0**	**10**	**1**	**0**	....	....	....	....	....	....	....	....
	Los Angeles Kings	**NHL**	**33**	**14**	**13**	**27**	**15**	**11**	**26**	**8**	**2**	**1**	**1**	**108**	**13.0**	**37**	**10**	**46**	**12**	**–7**	....	....	....	....	....	....	....	....
1971-72	**Los Angeles Kings**	**NHL**	**76**	**23**	**29**	**52**	**25**	**26**	**51**	**22**	**7**	**1**	**4**	**181**	**12.7**	**64**	**15**	**95**	**24**	**–22**	....	....	....	....	....	....	....	....
1972-73	**Los Angeles Kings**	**NHL**	**63**	**20**	**29**	**49**	**20**	**24**	**44**	**6**	**1**	**1**	**6**	**132**	**15.2**	**70**	**10**	**79**	**7**	**–12**	....	....	....	....	....	....	....	....
	Chicago Black Hawks	**NHL**	**16**	**6**	**3**	**9**	**6**	**2**	**8**	**2**	**0**	**1**	**0**	**36**	**16.7**	**11**	**1**	**12**	**2**	**0**	**16**	**5**	**6**	**11**	**0**	**0**	**1**	**0**
1973-74	Chicago Cougars	WHA	78	33	50	83	....	....	....	26	....	....	....	....	....	....	....	....	....	....	18	5	*14	19	4	....	....	....
1974-75	Canada	Summit	8	4	4	8	....	....	....	10	....	....	....	....	....	....	....	....	....	....	....	....	....	....	....	....	....	....
	Chicago Cougars	WHA	70	15	24	39	....	....	....	28	....	....	....	....	....	....	....	....	....	....	....	....	....	....	....	....	....	....
1975-76	Denver-Ottawa	WHA	41	21	29	50	....	....	....	14	....	....	....	....	....	....	....	....	....	....	....	....	....	....	....	....	....	....
	New England Whalers	WHA	38	14	19	33	....	....	....	6	....	....	....	....	....	....	....	....	....	....	17	5	4	9	8	....	....	....
1976-77	New England Whalers	WHA	77	17	31	48	....	....	....	30	....	....	....	....	....	....	....	....	....	....	3	0	0	0	0	....	....	....
	NHL Totals		**1032**	**278**	**361**	**639**	**330**	**357**	**687**	**386**	**16**	**4**	**21**	**1040**	**26.7**	**359**	**62**	**356**	**46**		**116**	**27**	**32**	**59**	**68**	**0**	**2**	**3**
	Other Major League Totals		304	100	153	253	....	....	....	104	....	....	....	....	....	....	....	....	....	....	38	10	18	28	12	....	....	....

Won Calder Memorial Trophy (1959) • Won Paul Daneau Trophy (WHA Most Gentlemanly Player) (1974)

Played in NHL All-Star Game (1958, 1959, 1960, 1962, 1965, 1967)

Traded to **LA Kings** by **Montreal** for Gord Labossiere and Ray Fortin, January 26, 1971. Selected by **New England** (WHA) in 1972 WHA General Player Draft, February 12, 1972. Traded to **Chicago** by **LA Kings** for Dan Maloney, February 26, 1973. WHA rights traded to **LA Sharks** (WHA) by **New England** (WHA) for cash, June, 1973. Traded to **Chicago** (WHA) by **LA Sharks** (WHA) for cash, July, 1973. Selected by **Denver** (WHA) from **Chicago** (WHA) in WHA Expansion Draft, May, 1975. Traded to **New England** (WHA) by **Denver-Ottawa** (WHA) with Don Borgeson for cash, January 20, 1976.

● BAILEY, GARNET

Garnet "Ace" Bailey LW – L. 5'11", 192 lbs. b: Lloydminster, Sask., 6/13/1948. Boston's 3rd choice, 13th overall, in 1966 Amateur Draft.

Season	Club	League	GP	G	A	Pts	AG	AA	APts	PIM	PP	SH	GW	S	%	TGF	PGF	TGA	PGA	+/–	GP	G	A	Pts	PIM	PP	SH	GW
1965-66	Edmonton Oil Kings	AJHL	....	14	18	32	....	....	....	27	....	....	....	....	....	....	....	....	....	....	....	....	....	....	....	....	....	....
1966-67	Edmonton Oil Kings	WCJHL	56	47	46	93	....	....	....	177	....	....	....	....	....	....	....	....	....	....	9	7	6	13	16	....	....	....
1967-68	Oklahoma City Blazers	CHL	34	8	13	21	....	....	....	67	....	....	....	....	....	....	....	....	....	....	7	0	5	5	36	....	....	....
1968-69	**Boston Bruins**	**NHL**	**8**	**3**	**3**	**6**	**3**	**3**	**6**	**10**	**0**	**0**	**0**	**13**	**23.1**	**7**	**0**	**2**	**0**	**+5**	**1**	**0**	**0**	**0**	**2**	**0**	**0**	**0**
	Hershey Bears	AHL	60	24	32	56	....	....	....	104	....	....	....	....	....	....	....	....	....	....	9	4	*10	14	10	....	....	....
1969-70	**Boston Bruins**	**NHL**	**58**	**11**	**11**	**22**	**13**	**11**	**24**	**82**	**2**	**0**	**2**	**78**	**14.1**	**35**	**1**	**18**	**1**	**+17**	....	....	....	....	....	....	....	....
1970-71	**Boston Bruins**	**NHL**	**36**	**0**	**6**	**6**	**0**	**5**	**5**	**44**	**0**	**0**	**0**	**33**	**0.0**	**11**	**0**	**7**	**0**	**+4**	**1**	**0**	**0**	**0**	**10**	**0**	**0**	**0**
	Oklahoma City Blazers	CHL	11	3	8	11	....	....	....	28	....	....	....	....	....	....	....	....	....	....	....	....	....	....	....	....	....	....
1971-72	**Boston Bruins**	**NHL**	**73**	**9**	**13**	**22**	**10**	**12**	**22**	**64**	**0**	**0**	**0**	**64**	**14.1**	**39**	**1**	**27**	**0**	**+11**	**13**	**2**	**4**	**6**	**16**	**0**	**0**	**1**

			REGULAR SEASON																		PLAYOFFS							
Season	Club	League	GP	G	A	Pts	AG	AA	APts	PIM	PP	SH	GW	S	%	TGF	PGF	TGA	PGA	+/-	GP	G	A	Pts	PIM	PP	SH	GW
1972-73	**Boston Bruins**	**NHL**	57	8	13	21	8	11	19	89	0	3	1	76	10.5	31	1	35	12	+7								
	Detroit Red Wings	**NHL**	13	2	11	13	2	9	11	16	0	0	0	19	10.5	16	0	14	0	+2								
1973-74	**Detroit Red Wings**	**NHL**	45	9	14	23	9	12	21	33	3	0	2	70	12.9	37	14	36	1	–12								
	St. Louis Blues	**NHL**	22	7	3	10	7	3	10	20	0	0	0	43	16.3	21	5	23	6	–1								
1974-75	**St. Louis Blues**	**NHL**	49	15	26	41	14	20	34	113	4	0	1	102	14.7	57	15	47	1	–4								
	Washington Capitals	**NHL**	22	4	13	17	4	10	14	8	1	0	0	46	8.7	23	9	44	1	–29								
1975-76	**Washington Capitals**	**NHL**	67	13	19	32	12	15	27	75	2	0	2	131	9.9	59	21	84	4	–42								
1976-77	**Washington Capitals**	**NHL**	78	19	27	46	18	22	40	51	2	0	2	154	12.3	74	15	94	14	–21								
1977-78	**Washington Capitals**	**NHL**	40	7	12	19	7	10	17	28	0	0	2	58	12.1	33	5	44	4	–12								
1978-79	Edmonton Oilers	WHA	38	5	4	9				22											2	0	0	0	4			
1979-80	Houston Apollos	CHL	7	1	0	1				0																		
1980-81	Wichita Wind	CHL	1	0	0	0				2																		
	NHL Totals		568	107	171	278	107	143	250	633	14	3	12	887	12.1	443	87	475	44		15	2	4	6	28	0	0	1
	Other Major League Totals		38	5	4	9				22											2	0	0	0	4			

Selected by **Alberta** (WHA) in 1972 WHA General Player Draft, February 12, 1972. Traded to **Detroit** by **Boston** with future considerations (Murray Wing, June 4, 1974) for Gary Doak, March 1, 1973. Traded to **St. Louis** by **Detroit** with Ted Harris and Bill Collins for Chris Evans, Bryan Watson and Jean Hamel, February 14, 1974. Traded to **Washington** by **St. Louis** with Stan Gilbertson for Denis Dupere, February 10, 1975.

• BAILEY, REID

Reid Bailey D – L. 6'2", 200 lbs. b: Toronto, Ont., 5/28/1956.

1975-76	Sault Ste. Marie Greyhounds	OHA	9	0	2	2				47																		
	Kitchener Rangers	OHA	24	0	15	15				80																		
	Cornwall Royals	OHA	26	1	8	9				32											10	0	1	1	2			
1976-77	Port Huron Flags	IHL	72	3	14	17				148																		
1977-78	Port Huron Flags	IHL	72	3	28	31				162											17	0	7	7	58			
1978-79	Maine Mariners	AHL	56	6	8	14				127											6	0	0	0	10			
1979-80	Maine Mariners	AHL	75	0	12	12				155											12	1	1	2	22			
1980-81	**Philadelphia Flyers**	**NHL**	17	1	3	4	1	2	3	55	0	0	0	16	6.3	16	0	14	6	+8	12	0	2	2	23	0	0	0
	Maine Mariners	AHL	59	6	29	35				155																		
1981-82	**Philadelphia Flyers**	**NHL**	10	0	0	0	0	0	0	23	0	0	0	7	0.0	5	0	15	5	–5	2	0	0	0	0	0	0	0
	Maine Mariners	AHL	54	4	26	30				55											2	0	1	1	2			
1982-83	Moncton Alpines	AHL	21	0	9	9				22																		
	Toronto Maple Leafs	**NHL**	1	0	0	0	0	0	0	2	0	0	0	0	0.0	1	0	4	1	–2	2	0	0	0	2	0	0	0
	St. Catharines Saints	AHL	34	0	14	14				62																		
1983-84	St. Catharines Saints	AHL	25	0	8	8				73																		
	Hartford Whalers	**NHL**	12	0	0	0	0	0	0	25	0	0	0	8	0.0	4	0	8	2	–2								
	Binghamton Whalers	AHL	33	2	11	13				95																		
	NHL Totals		40	1	3	4	1	2	3	105	0	0	0	31	3.2	26	0	41	14		16	0	2	2	25	0	0	0

Signed as a free agent by **Philadelphia**, November 20, 1978. Signed as free agent by **Edmonton**, October 27, 1982. Traded to **Toronto** by **Edmonton** for Serge Boisvert, January 15, 1983. Signed as a free agent by **Hartford**, December 9, 1983.

• BAILLARGEON, JOEL

Joel Baillargeon LW – L. 6'1", 205 lbs. b: Quebec City, Que., 10/6/1964. Winnipeg's 7th choice, 113th overall, in 1983 Entry Draft.

1981-82	Trois-Rivieres Draveurs	QMJHL	26	1	3	4				47											22	1	1	2	58			
1982-83	Trois-Rivieres Draveurs	QMJHL	29	4	5	9				197																		
	Hull Olympiques	QMJHL	25	15	7	22				76											7	0	1	1	16			
1983-84	Chicoutimi Sagueneens	QMJHL	60	48	35	83				184																		
	Sherbrooke Jets	AHL	8	0	0	0				26																		
1984-85	Granby Bisons	QMJHL	32	25	24	49				160																		
1985-86	Sherbrooke Canadiens	AHL	56	6	12	18				115																		
1986-87	**Winnipeg Jets**	**NHL**	11	0	1	1	0	1	1	15	0	0	0	1	0.0	2	0	5	0	–3								
	Sherbrooke Canadiens	AHL	44	9	18	27				137											6	2	2	4	27			
	Fort Wayne Komets	IHL	4	1	1	2				37																		
1987-88	**Winnipeg Jets**	**NHL**	4	0	1	1	0	1	1	12	0	0	0	3	0.0	1	0	1	0	0								
	Moncton Hawks	AHL	48	8	14	22				133																		
1988-89	**Quebec Nordiques**	**NHL**	5	0	0	0	0	0	0	4	0	0	0	2	0.0	2	0	5	0	–3								
	Halifax Citadels	AHL	53	11	19	30				122											4	1	0	1	26			
1989-90	Halifax Citadels	AHL	21	0	3	3				39																		
	NHL Totals		20	0	2	2	0	2	2	31	0	0	0	6	0.0	5	0	11	0									

Traded to **Quebec** by **Winnipeg** for future considerations, July 29, 1988.

• BAIRD, KEN

Ken Baird D – L. 6', 190 lbs. b: Flin Flon, Man., 2/1/1951. California's 1st choice, 15th overall, in 1971 Amateur Draft.

1969-70	Estevan Bruins	WCJHL	1	0	0	0				0																		
	Flin Flon Bombers	WCJHL	47	2	5	7				126																		
1970-71	Flin Flon Bombers	WCJHL	66	35	40	75				211																		
1971-72	**California Golden Seals**	**NHL**	10	0	2	2	0	2	2	15	0	0	0	6	0.0	9	0	19	0	–10								
	Oklahoma City Blazers	CHL	59	5	11	16				196											6	0	2	2	29			
1972-73	Alberta Oilers	WHA	75	14	15	29				112																		
1973-74	Edmonton Oilers	WHA	68	17	19	36				115											5	1	1	2	7			
1974-75	Edmonton Oilers	WHA	77	30	28	58				151																		
1975-76	Edmonton Oilers	WHA	48	13	24	37				87											4	3	1	4	16			
1976-77	Edmonton Oilers	WHA	2	1	2	3				0																		
	Calgary Cowboys	WHA	7	0	0	0				2																		
1977-78	Edmonton Oilers	WHA	6	2	4	6				2																		
	Winnipeg Jets	WHA	49	14	7	21				21											7	0	4	4	7			
1978-79			DID NOT PLAY																									
1979-80	Duisburg	Germany	47	32	28	60				141																		
1980-81	Duisburg	Germany	39	31	40	71				108											6	2	6	8	23			
	NHL Totals		10	0	2	2	0	2	2	15	0	0	0	6	0.0	9	0	19	0									
	Other Major League Totals		332	91	99	190				490											16	4	6	10	30			

Selected by **Alberta** (WHA) in 1972 WHA General Player Draft, February 12, 1972. Signed as a free agent by **Calgary** (WHA), November, 1976. Signed as a free agent by **Edmonton** (WHA) after **Calgary** (WHA) franchise folded, May 31, 1977. Signed as a free agent by **Winnipeg** (WHA) after being released by **Edmonton** (WHA), December, 1977.

• BAKER, BILL

Bill Baker D – L. 6'1", 195 lbs. b: Grand Rapids, MN, 11/29/1956. Montreal's 8th choice, 54th overall, in 1976 Amateur Draft.

1975-76	University of Minnesota	WCHA	44	8	15	23				28																		
1976-77	University of Minnesota	WCHA	28	0	8	8				42																		
1977-78	University of Minnesota	WCHA	38	10	23	33				24																		
1978-79	University of Minnesota	WCHA	44	12	42	54				38																		
	United States	WEC-A	7	2	1	3				2																		
1979-80	United States	Nat-Team	60	5	25	30				74																		
	United States	Olympics	7	1	0	1				4																		
	Nova Scotia Voyageurs	AHL	12	4	8	12				5											1	0	1	1	0			
1980-81	**Montreal Canadiens**	**NHL**	11	0	0	0	0	0	0	32	0	0	0	8	0.0	6	0	8	1	–1								
	Nova Scotia Voyageurs	AHL	18	5	12	17				42																		
	Colorado Rockies	**NHL**	13	0	3	3	0	2	2	12	0	0	0	17	0.0	12	2	17	7	0								
	United States	WEC-A	7	0	1	1				8																		

			REGULAR SEASON																		PLAYOFFS							
Season	Club	League	GP	G	A	Pts	AG	AA	APts	PIM	PP	SH	GW	S	%	TGF	PGF	TGA	PGA	+/-	GP	G	A	Pts	PIM	PP	SH	GW
1981-82	United States	C Cup	1	0	0	0				0																		
	Colorado Rockies	**NHL**	**14**	**0**	**3**	**3**	**0**	**2**	**2**	**17**	**0**	**0**	**0**	**11**	**0.0**	**7**	**1**	**25**	**6**	**–13**								
	Fort Worth Texans	CHL	10	3	12	15				20																		
	St. Louis Blues	**NHL**	**35**	**3**	**5**	**8**	**2**	**3**	**5**	**50**	**1**	**0**	**0**	**44**	**6.8**	**43**	**6**	**51**	**6**	**–8**	**4**	**0**	**0**	**0**	**0**	**0**	**0**	**0**
1982-83	**New York Rangers**	**NHL**	**70**	**4**	**14**	**18**	**3**	**10**	**13**	**64**	**1**	**0**	**2**	**63**	**6.3**	**54**	**5**	**71**	**14**	**–8**	**2**	**0**	**0**	**0**	**0**	**0**	**0**	**0**
1983-84	Tulsa Oilers	CHL	59	11	22	33				47																		
	NHL Totals		**143**	**7**	**25**	**32**	**5**	**17**	**22**	**175**	**2**	**0**	**2**	**143**	**4.9**	**122**	**14**	**172**	**34**		**6**	**0**	**0**	**0**	**0**	**0**	**0**	**0**

WCHA First All-Star Team (1979) • NCAA West First All-American Team (1979)

Traded to **Colorado** by **Montreal** for Colorado's 3rd round choice (Daniel Letendre) in 1983 Entry Draft, March 10, 1981. Traded to **St. Louis** by **Colorado** for Joe Micheletti and Dick Lamby, December 4, 1981. Claimed by **NY Rangers** from **St. Louis** in Waiver Draft, October 4, 1982.

• BAKER, JAMIE

Jamie Baker C – L. 6', 195 lbs. b: Ottawa, Ont., 8/31/1966. Quebec's 2nd choice, 8th overall, in 1988 Supplemental Draft.

Season	Club	League	GP	G	A	Pts	AG	AA	APts	PIM	PP	SH	GW	S	%	TGF	PGF	TGA	PGA	+/-	GP	G	A	Pts	PIM	PP	SH	GW
1985-86	St. Lawrence University	ECAC	31	9	16	25				52																		
1986-87	St. Lawrence University	ECAC	32	8	24	32				59																		
1987-88	St. Lawrence University	ECAC	34	26	24	50				38																		
1988-89	St. Lawrence University	ECAC	13	11	16	27				16																		
1989-90	**Quebec Nordiques**	**NHL**	**1**	**0**	**0**	**0**	**0**	**0**	**0**	**0**	**0**	**0**	**0**	**0**	**0.0**	**0**	**0**	**1**	**0**	**–1**								
	Halifax Citadels	AHL	74	17	43	60				47											6	0	0	0	7			
1990-91	**Quebec Nordiques**	**NHL**	**18**	**2**	**0**	**2**	**2**	**0**	**2**	**8**	**0**	**1**	**0**	**18**	**11.1**	**6**	**0**	**15**	**5**	**–4**								
	Halifax Citadels	AHL	50	14	22	36				85																		
1991-92	**Quebec Nordiques**	**NHL**	**52**	**7**	**10**	**17**	**6**	**7**	**13**	**32**	**3**	**0**	**1**	**77**	**9.1**	**28**	**9**	**33**	**9**	**–5**								
	Halifax Citadels	AHL	9	5	0	5				12																		
1992-93	**Ottawa Senators**	**NHL**	**76**	**19**	**29**	**48**	**16**	**20**	**36**	**54**	**10**	**0**	**2**	**160**	**11.9**	**79**	**38**	**73**	**12**	**–20**								
1993-94	**San Jose Sharks**	**NHL**	**65**	**12**	**5**	**17**	**11**	**4**	**15**	**38**	**0**	**0**	**2**	**68**	**17.6**	**31**	**1**	**55**	**27**	**+2**	**14**	**3**	**2**	**5**	**30**	**0**	**0**	**1**
1994-95	**San Jose Sharks**	**NHL**	**43**	**7**	**4**	**11**	**12**	**6**	**18**	**22**	**0**	**1**	**0**	**60**	**11.7**	**16**	**0**	**39**	**16**	**–7**	**11**	**2**	**2**	**4**	**12**	**0**	**0**	**1**
1995-96	**San Jose Sharks**	**NHL**	**77**	**16**	**17**	**33**	**16**	**14**	**30**	**79**	**2**	**6**	**0**	**117**	**13.7**	**51**	**5**	**106**	**41**	**–19**								
1996-97	**Toronto Maple Leafs**	**NHL**	**58**	**8**	**8**	**16**	**8**	**7**	**15**	**28**	**1**	**0**	**3**	**69**	**11.6**	**34**	**4**	**45**	**17**	**+2**								
1997-98	**Toronto Maple Leafs**	**NHL**	**13**	**0**	**5**	**5**	**0**	**5**	**5**	**10**	**0**	**0**	**0**	**16**	**0.0**	**8**	**0**	**11**	**4**	**+1**								
	Chicago Wolves	IHL	53	11	34	45				80											22	4	5	9	42			
	NHL Totals		**403**	**71**	**78**	**149**	**71**	**63**	**134**	**271**	**16**	**8**	**8**	**585**	**12.1**	**253**	**57**	**378**	**131**		**25**	**5**	**4**	**9**	**42**	**0**	**0**	**2**

Signed as a free agent by **Ottawa**, September 2, 1992. Signed as a free agent by **San Jose**, September 11, 1993. Traded to **Toronto** by **San Jose** with San Jose's 5th round choice (Peter Cava) in 1996 Entry Draft for Todd Gill, June 14, 1996.

• BAKOVIC, PETER

Peter Bakovic RW – R. 6'2", 200 lbs. b: Thunder Bay, Ont., 1/31/1965.

Season	Club	League	GP	G	A	Pts	AG	AA	APts	PIM	PP	SH	GW	S	%	TGF	PGF	TGA	PGA	+/-	GP	G	A	Pts	PIM	PP	SH	GW
1982-83	Thunder Bay Flyers	Jr. B	40	30	29	59				159																		
1983-84	Kitchener Rangers	OHL	28	2	6	8				87																		
	Windsor Spitfires	OHL	35	10	25	35				74											3	0	2	2	14			
1984-85	Windsor Spitfires	OHL	58	26	48	74				*259											3	0	0	0	12			
1985-86	Moncton Golden Flames	AHL	80	18	36	54				349											10	2	2	4	30			
1986-87	Moncton Golden Flames	AHL	77	17	34	51				280											6	3	3	6	54			
1987-88	**Vancouver Canucks**	**NHL**	**10**	**2**	**0**	**2**	**2**	**0**	**2**	**48**	**0**	**0**	**0**	**7**	**28.6**	**4**	**0**	**5**	**0**	**–1**								
	Salt Lake Golden Eagles	IHL	39	16	27	43				221																		
1988-89	Milwaukee Admirals	IHL	40	16	14	30				211											11	4	4	8	46			
1989-90	Milwaukee Admirals	IHL	56	19	30	49				230											6	4	1	5	52			
1990-91	Milwaukee Admirals	IHL	69	17	45	62				220											6	0	4	4	16			
	NHL Totals		**10**	**2**	**0**	**2**	**2**	**0**	**2**	**48**	**0**	**0**	**0**	**7**	**28.6**	**4**	**0**	**5**	**0**									

Signed as a free agent by **Calgary**, October 10, 1985. Traded to **Vancouver** by **Calgary** with Brian Bradley for Craig Coxe, March 6, 1988.

• BALDERIS, HELMUT

Helmut Balderis RW – R. 5'11", 190 lbs. b: Riga, Latvia, 6/30/1952. Minnesota's 13th choice, 238th overall, in 1989 Entry Draft.

Season	Club	League	GP	G	A	Pts	AG	AA	APts	PIM	PP	SH	GW	S	%	TGF	PGF	TGA	PGA	+/-	GP	G	A	Pts	PIM	PP	SH	GW
1973-74	Dynamo Riga	USSR	24	9	6	15				13																		
1974-75	Dynamo Riga	USSR	36	34	14	48				20																		
1975-76	Dynamo Riga	USSR	38	31	14	45				18																		
	Soviet Union	WEC-A	10	3	7	10				6																		
1976-77	Soviet Union	C Cup	5	2	3	5				6																		
	Dynamo Riga	USSR	35	40	23	*63				57																		
	Soviet Union	WEC-A	9	8	7	15				4																		
1977-78	CSKA Moscow	USSR	36	17	17	*34				30																		
	Soviet Union	WEC-A	10	9	2	11				8																		
1978-79	CSKA Moscow	USSR	41	24	24	48				53																		
	USSR	Chal Cup	3	1	1	2				0																		
	Soviet Union	WEC-A	8	4	5	9				9																		
1979-80	CSKA Moscow	USSR	42	26	35	61				21																		
	CSKA Moscow	SuperS	5	5	2	7				2																		
	Soviet Union	Olympics	7	5	4	9				5																		
1980-81	Dynamo Riga	USSR	44	26	24	50				28																		
1981-82	Dynamo Riga	USSR	41	24	19	43				48											9	*15	5	*20	2			
1982-83	Dynamo Riga	USSR	40	32	31	*63				39																		
	Soviet Union	WEC-A	10	4	5	9				22																		
1983-84	Dynamo Riga	USSR	39	24	15	39				18																		
1984-85	Dynamo Riga	USSR	39	31	20	51				52																		
1985-1989			DID NOT PLAY – RETIRED																									
1989-90	**Minnesota North Stars**	**NHL**	**26**	**3**	**6**	**9**	**3**	**4**	**7**	**2**	**2**	**0**	**0**	**30**	**10.0**	**15**	**5**	**10**	**0**	**0**								
	NHL Totals		**26**	**3**	**6**	**9**	**3**	**4**	**7**	**2**	**2**	**0**	**0**	**30**	**10.0**	**15**	**5**	**10**	**0**									

USSR First All-Star Team (1977) • Won Izvestia Trophy (USSR Top Scorer) (1977, 1983) • USSR Player of the Year (1977) • WEC-A All-Star Team (1977) • Named Best Forward at WEC-A (1977)

• BALL, TERRY

Terry Ball D – R. 5'9", 160 lbs. b: Selkirk, Man., 11/29/1944.

Season	Club	League	GP	G	A	Pts	AG	AA	APts	PIM	PP	SH	GW	S	%	TGF	PGF	TGA	PGA	+/-	GP	G	A	Pts	PIM	PP	SH	GW
1961-62	Winnipeg Rangers	MJHL	39	2	2	4				65											3	0	1	1	5			
1962-63	Winnipeg Rangers	MJHL	39	8	23	31				104																		
	Brandon Wheat Kings	MJHL																			5	0	0	0	12			
1963-64	Winnipeg Rangers	MJHL	29	6	16	22				110											4	0	2	2	11			
	Brandon Wheat Kings	MJHL																			3	1	0	1	0			
	Vancouver Canucks	WHL	8	0	2	2				4																		
1964-65	Kitchener Rangers	OHA	55	6	47	53				153																		
	St. Paul Rangers	CHL																			1	0	0	0	0			
1965-66	Minnesota Rangers	CHL	DID NOT PLAY – INJURED																									
1966-67	Omaha Knights	CHL	70	5	15	20				78											5	1	0	1	2			
1967-68	**Philadelphia Flyers**	**NHL**	**1**	**0**	**0**	**0**	**0**	**0**	**0**	**0**	**0**	**0**	**0**	**0**	**0.0**	**0**	**0**	**1**	**0**	**–1**								
	Quebec Aces	AHL	72	3	39	42				99											15	1	7	8	22			
1968-69	Quebec Aces	AHL	74	14	45	59				72											15	8	8	*16	8			
1969-70	**Philadelphia Flyers**	**NHL**	**61**	**7**	**18**	**25**	**8**	**18**	**26**	**20**	**3**	**1**	**0**	**98**	**7.1**	**63**	**37**	**36**	**3**	**–7**								
	Quebec Aces	AHL	10	3	5	8				8																		
1970-71	Amarillo Wranglers	CHL	41	5	30	35				24																		
	Buffalo Sabres	**NHL**	**2**	**0**	**0**	**0**	**0**	**0**	**0**	**0**	**0**	**0**	**0**	**2**	**0.0**	**1**	**0**	**1**	**0**	**0**								
	Salt Lake Golden Eagles	WHL	22	2	12	14				20																		
1971-72	**Buffalo Sabres**	**NHL**	**10**	**0**	**1**	**1**	**0**	**1**	**1**	**6**	**0**	**0**	**0**	**8**	**0.0**	**10**	**4**	**13**	**0**	**–7**								
	Cincinnati Swords	AHL	68	17	39	56				62											10	3	8	11	2			
1972-73	Minnesota Fighting Saints	WHA	76	6	34	40				66											5	1	2	3	4			
1973-74	Minnesota Fighting Saints	WHA	71	8	28	36				34											11	1	2	3	6			
1974-75	Minnesota Fighting Saints	WHA	76	8	37	45				36											12	3	4	7	4			
1975-76	Cleveland Crusaders	WHA	23	2	15	17				18																		
	Cincinnati Stingers	WHA	36	3	14	17				12																		

			REGULAR SEASON																		PLAYOFFS							
Season	Club	League	GP	G	A	Pts	AG	AA	APts	PIM	PP	SH	GW	S	%	TGF	PGF	TGA	PGA	+/–	GP	G	A	Pts	PIM	PP	SH	GW
1976-77	Birmingham Bulls	WHA	23	1	6	7				8																		
	Oklahoma City Blazers	CHL	15	0	4	4				4																		
1977-78	HIFK Helsinki	Finland	33	1	4	5				44																		
	NHL Totals		**74**	**7**	**19**	**26**	**8**	**19**	**27**	**26**	**3**	**1**	**0**	**108**	**6.5**	**74**	**41**	**51**	**3**									
	Other Major League Totals		305	28	134	162				174											28	5	8	13	14			

AHL First All-Star Team (1972)

Claimed by **Philadelphia** from **NY Rangers** in Expansion Draft, June 6, 1967. Traded to **Pittsburgh** by **Philadelphia** for George Swarbrick, June 11, 1970. Traded to **Buffalo** by **Pittsburgh** for Jean-Guy Legace, January 24, 1971. Selected by **Minnesota** (WHA) in 1972 WHA General Player Draft, February 12, 1972. Claimed by **Cleveland** (WHA) from **Minnesota** (WHA) in WHA Intra-League Draft, June, 1975. Traded to **Cincinnati** (WHA) by **Cleveland** (WHA) for future considerations, January, 1976. Claimed on waivers by **Birmingham** (WHA) from **Cincinnati** (WHA), October, 1976.

• BALON, DAVE

Dave Balon LW – L. 5'10", 180 lbs. b: Wakaw, Sask., 8/2/1938.

Season	Club	League	GP	G	A	Pts	AG	AA	APts	PIM	PP	SH	GW	S	%	TGF	PGF	TGA	PGA	+/–	GP	G	A	Pts	PIM	PP	SH	GW
1955-56	Prince Albert Mintos	SJHL	14	5	5	10				14											12	3	2	5	14			
1956-57	Prince Albert Mintos	SJHL	40	29	30	59				112											13	6	5	11	13			
1957-58	Prince Albert Mintos	SJHL	51	35	44	79				113											6	3	1	4	12			
	Vancouver Canucks	WHL	4	0	2	2				8																		
1958-59	Saskatoon Quakers	WHL	57	12	25	37				80																		
1959-60	**New York Rangers**	**NHL**	**3**	**0**	**0**	**0**	**0**	**0**	**0**	**0**																		
	Vancouver Canucks	WHL	3	1	1	2				2																		
	Trois-Rivieres Lions	EPHL	61	28	42	70				104											7	2	2	4	19			
1960-61	**New York Rangers**	**NHL**	**13**	**1**	**2**	**3**	**1**	**2**	**3**	**8**																		
	Kitchener-Waterloo Beavers	EPHL	55	15	26	41				77											7	1	1	2	12			
1961-62	**New York Rangers**	**NHL**	**30**	**4**	**11**	**15**	**5**	**11**	**16**	**11**											**6**	**2**	**3**	**5**	**2**			
	Kitchener-Waterloo Beavers	EPHL	37	24	19	42				87																		
1962-63	**New York Rangers**	**NHL**	**70**	**11**	**13**	**24**	**13**	**14**	**27**	**72**																		
1963-64	**Montreal Canadiens**	**NHL**	**70**	**24**	**18**	**42**	**32**	**20**	**52**	**80**											**7**	**1**	**1**	**2**	**25**			
1964-65	**Montreal Canadiens**	**NHL**	**63**	**18**	**23**	**41**	**23**	**25**	**48**	**61**											**10**	**0**	**0**	**0**	**10**			
1965-66	**Montreal Canadiens**	**NHL**	**45**	**3**	**7**	**10**	**4**	**7**	**11**	**24**											**9**	**2**	**3**	**5**	**16**			
	Houston Apollos	CHL	9	6	6	12				0																		
1966-67	**Montreal Canadiens**	**NHL**	**48**	**11**	**8**	**19**	**13**	**8**	**21**	**31**											**9**	**0**	**2**	**2**	**6**			
1967-68	**Minnesota North Stars**	**NHL**	**73**	**15**	**32**	**47**	**19**	**34**	**53**	**84**	**4**	**1**	**2**	**152**	**9.9**	**66**	**18**	**63**	**5**	**–10**	**14**	**4**	***9**	**13**	**14**	**1**	**0**	**1**
1968-69	**New York Rangers**	**NHL**	**75**	**10**	**21**	**31**	**11**	**20**	**31**	**57**	**1**	**2**	**3**	**134**	**7.5**	**45**	**8**	**38**	**6**	**+5**	**4**	**1**	**0**	**1**	**0**	**0**	**0**	**0**
1969-70	**New York Rangers**	**NHL**	**76**	**33**	**37**	**70**	**38**	**37**	**75**	**100**	**4**	**1**	**3**	**202**	**16.3**	**99**	**15**	**49**	**5**	**+40**	**6**	**1**	**1**	**2**	**32**	**0**	**1**	**0**
1970-71	**New York Rangers**	**NHL**	**78**	**36**	**24**	**60**	**38**	**21**	**59**	**34**	**9**	**0**	**7**	**176**	**20.5**	**87**	**19**	**63**	**9**	**+14**	**13**	**3**	**2**	**5**	**4**	**2**	**0**	**1**
1971-72	**New York Rangers**	**NHL**	**16**	**4**	**5**	**9**	**4**	**5**	**9**	**2**	**1**	**0**	**1**	**30**	**13.3**	**13**	**2**	**6**	**0**	**+5**								
	Vancouver Canucks	**NHL**	**59**	**19**	**19**	**38**	**20**	**17**	**37**	**21**	**6**	**0**	**3**	**103**	**18.4**	**60**	**21**	**54**	**0**	**–15**								
1972-73	**Vancouver Canucks**	**NHL**	**57**	**3**	**2**	**5**	**3**	**2**	**5**	**22**	**1**	**0**	**0**	**23**	**13.0**	**13**	**3**	**26**	**0**	**–16**								
1973-74	Quebec Nordiques	WHA	9	0	0	0				2																		
	Binghamton Dusters	AHL	7	0	1	1				0																		
	NHL Totals		**776**	**192**	**222**	**414**	**224**	**223**	**447**	**607**	**26**	**4**	**19**	**820**	**23.4**	**383**	**86**	**299**	**25**		**78**	**14**	**21**	**35**	**109**	**3**	**1**	**2**
	Other Major League Totals		9	0	0	0				2																		

Played in NHL All-Star Game (1965, 1967, 1968, 1971)

Traded to **Montreal** by **NY Rangers** with Gump Worsley, Leon Rochefort and Len Ronson for Phil Goyette, Don Marshall and Jacques Plante, June 4, 1963. Selected by **Minnesota** from **Montreal** in Expansion Draft, June 6, 1967. Traded to **NY Rangers** by **Minnesota** for Wayne Hillman, Dan Sequin and Joey Johnston, June 12, 1968. Traded to **Vancouver** by **NY Rangers** with Wayne Connelly and Ron Stewart for Gary Doak and Jim Wiste, November 16, 1971. Selected by **Quebec** (WHA) in 1972 WHA General Player Draft, February 12, 1972.

• BALTIMORE, BRYON

Bryon Baltimore D – R. 6'2", 190 lbs. b: Whitehorse, Yukon, 8/26/1952.

Season	Club	League	GP	G	A	Pts	AG	AA	APts	PIM	PP	SH	GW	S	%	TGF	PGF	TGA	PGA	+/–	GP	G	A	Pts	PIM	PP	SH	GW
1970-71	University of Alberta	CWUAA	35	8	15	23				82																		
1971-72	University of Alberta	CWUAA	34	5	23	28				78																		
1972-73	Springfield Kings	AHL	73	15	12	27				36																		
1973-74	Springfield Kings	AHL	68	4	21	25				72																		
1974-75	Chicago Cougars	WHA	77	8	12	20				110																		
1975-76	Denver-Ottawa	WHA	41	1	8	9				32																		
	Indianapolis Racers	WHA	37	1	10	11				30											7	0	1	1	4			
1976-77	Indianapolis Racers	WHA	55	0	15	15				63											9	0	0	0	5			
1977-78	Indianapolis Racers	WHA	22	1	7	8				23																		
	Cincinnati Stingers	WHA	28	2	9	11				47																		
1978-79	Indianapolis Racers	WHA	2	1	1	2				2																		
	Cincinnati Stingers	WHA	69	4	10	14				83											3	0	0	0	2			
1979-80	**Edmonton Oilers**	**NHL**	**2**	**0**	**0**	**0**	**0**	**0**	**0**	**4**	**0**	**0**	**0**	**2**	**0.0**	**6**	**0**	**2**	**0**	**+4**								
	Houston Apollos	CHL	61	1	25	26				76											6	0	1	1	11			
1980-81	Wichita Wind	CHL	46	1	10	11				66											16	0	8	8	20			
	NHL Totals		**2**	**0**	**0**	**0**	**0**	**0**	**0**	**4**	**0**	**0**	**0**	**2**	**0.0**	**6**	**0**	**2**	**0**									
	Other Major League Totals		331	18	72	90				390											19	0	1	1	11			

Signed as a free agent by **Chicago** (WHA), July, 1974. Selected by **Denver** (WHA) from **Chicago** (WHA) in WHA Expansion Draft, May, 1975. Traded to **Indianapolis** (WHA) by **Denver-Ottawa** (WHA) with Darryl Maggs, Francois Rochon and Mari Lomenda for cash, January 20, 1976. Traded to **Cincinnati** (WHA) by **Indianapolis** (WHA) with Hugh Harris for Blaine Stoughton and Gilles Marotte, January, 1978. Claimed by **Edmonton** from **Cincinnati** (WHA) in WHA Dispersal Draft, June 9, 1979.

• BANCROFT, STEVE

Steve Bancroft D – L. 6'1", 214 lbs. b: Toronto, Ont., 10/6/1970. Toronto's 3rd choice, 21st overall, in 1989 Entry Draft.

Season	Club	League	GP	G	A	Pts	AG	AA	APts	PIM	PP	SH	GW	S	%	TGF	PGF	TGA	PGA	+/–	GP	G	A	Pts	PIM	PP	SH	GW
1987-88	Belleville Bulls	OHL	56	1	8	9				42																		
1988-89	Belleville Bulls	OHL	66	7	30	37				99											5	0	2	2	10			
1989-90	Belleville Bulls	OHL	53	10	33	43				135											11	3	9	12	38			
1990-91	Newmarket Saints	AHL	9	0	3	3				22																		
	Maine Mariners	AHL	53	2	12	14				46											2	0	0	0	2			
1991-92	Maine Mariners	AHL	26	1	3	4				45																		
	Indianapolis Ice	IHL	36	8	23	31				49																		
1992-93	**Chicago Blackhawks**	**NHL**	**1**	**0**	**0**	**0**	**0**	**0**	**0**	**0**	**0**	**0**	**0**	**0**	**0.0**	**0**	**0**	**0**	**0**	**0**								
	Indianapolis Ice	IHL	53	10	35	45				138																		
	Moncton Hawks	AHL	21	3	13	16				16											5	0	0	0	16			
1993-94	Cleveland Lumberjacks	IHL	33	2	12	14				58																		
1994-95	Detroit Vipers	IHL	6	1	3	4				0																		
	Fort Wayne Komets	IHL	50	7	17	24				100																		
	St. John's Maple Leafs	AHL	4	2	0	2				2											5	0	3	3	8			
1995-96	Los Angeles Ice Dogs	IHL	15	3	10	13				22																		
	Chicago Wolves	IHL	64	9	41	50				91											9	1	7	8	22			
1996-97	Chicago Wolves	IHL	39	6	10	16				66																		
	Las Vegas Thunder	IHL	36	9	28	37				64											3	0	0	0	2			
1997-98	Las Vegas Thunder	IHL	70	15	44	59				148																		
	Saint John Flames	AHL	9	0	4	4				12											19	2	11	13	30			
	NHL Totals		**1**	**0**	**0**	**0**	**0**	**0**	**0**	**0**	**0**	**0**	**0**	**0**	**0.0**	**0**	**0**	**0**	**0**									

Traded to **Boston** by **Toronto** for Rob Cimetta, November 9, 1990. Traded to **Chicago** by **Boston** with Boston's 11th round choice (later traded to Winnipeg — Winnipeg selected Russel Hewson) in 1993 Entry Draft for Chicago's 11th round choice (Eugene Pavlov) in 1992 Entry Draft, January 9, 1992. Traded to **Winnipeg** by **Chicago** with future considerations for Troy Murray, February 21, 1993. Claimed by **Florida** from **Winnipeg** in Expansion Draft, June 24, 1993. Signed as a free agent by **Pittsburgh**, August 2, 1993.

• BANDURA, JEFF

Jeff Bandura D – R. 6'1", 195 lbs. b: White Rock, B.C., 2/4/1957. Vancouver's 2nd choice, 22nd overall, in 1977 Amateur Draft.

Season	Club	League	GP	G	A	Pts	AG	AA	APts	PIM	PP	SH	GW	S	%	TGF	PGF	TGA	PGA	+/–	GP	G	A	Pts	PIM	PP	SH	GW
1973-74	Merrit Luckies	BCJHL	40	1	14	15				35																		
1974-75	The Pas Blue Devils	AJHL	4	0	0	0				26																		
	Calgary Centennials	WCJHL	66	3	12	15				157																		
1975-76	Calgary Centennials	WCJHL	32	4	16	20				59																		
	Edmonton Oil Kings	WCJHL	35	6	21	27				64											5	0	3	3	14			
1976-77	Portland Winter Hawks	WCJHL	71	3	28	31				224											10	4	3	7	18			

			REGULAR SEASON																		PLAYOFFS							
Season	Club	League	GP	G	A	Pts	AG	AA	APts	PIM	PP	SH	GW	S	%	TGF	PGF	TGA	PGA	+/–	GP	G	A	Pts	PIM	PP	SH	GW
1977-78	Tulsa Oilers	CHL	60	2	18	20				88											7	0	1	1	14			
1978-79	Dallas Black Hawks	CHL	65	4	25	29				169											9	0	1	1	28			
1979-80	Dallas Black Hawks	CHL	80	4	26	30				114																		
1980-81	**New York Rangers**	**NHL**	**2**	**0**	**1**	**1**	**0**	**1**	**1**	**0**	**0**	**0**	**0**	**2**	**0.0**	**1**	**0**	**4**	**0**	**–3**								
	Dallas Black Hawks	CHL	11	0	2	2				15																		
	New Haven Nighthawks	AHL	55	1	14	15				131											4	0	0	0	13			
	NHL Totals		**2**	**0**	**1**	**1**	**0**	**1**	**1**	**0**	**0**	**0**	**0**	**2**	**0.0**	**1**	**0**	**4**	**0**									

CHL Second All-Star Team (1979)

Traded to **NY Rangers** by **Vancouver** with Jere Gillis for Mario Marois and Jim Mayer, November 11, 1980.

• BANHAM, FRANK

Frank Banham RW – R. 6', 190 lbs. b: Calahoo, Alta., 4/14/1975. Washington's 4th choice, 147th overall, in 1993 Entry Draft.

Season	Club	League	GP	G	A	Pts	AG	AA	APts	PIM	PP	SH	GW	S	%	TGF	PGF	TGA	PGA	+/–	GP	G	A	Pts	PIM	PP	SH	GW
1991-92	Fernie Ghostriders	RMJHL	47	45	45	90				120																		
1992-93	Saskatoon Blades	WHL	71	29	33	62				55											9	2	7	9	8			
1993-94	Saskatoon Blades	WHL	65	28	39	67				99											16	8	11	19	36			
1994-95	Saskatoon Blades	WHL	70	50	39	89				63											8	2	6	8	12			
1995-96	Saskatoon Blades	WHL	72	*83	69	152				116											4	6	0	6	2			
	Baltimore Bandits	AHL	9	1	4	5				0											7	1	1	2	2			
1996-97	**Anaheim Mighty Ducks**	**NHL**	**3**	**0**	**0**	**0**	**0**	**0**	**0**	**0**	**0**	**0**	**0**	**1**	**0.0**	**0**	**0**	**2**	**0**	**–2**								
	Baltimore Bandits	AHL	21	11	13	24				4																		
1997-98	**Anaheim Mighty Ducks**	**NHL**	**21**	**9**	**2**	**11**	**11**	**2**	**13**	**12**	**1**	**0**	**0**	**43**	**20.9**	**17**	**5**	**18**	**0**	**–6**								
	Cincinnati Mighty Ducks	AHL	35	7	8	15				39																		
	NHL Totals		**24**	**9**	**2**	**11**	**11**	**2**	**13**	**12**	**1**	**0**	**0**	**44**	**20.5**	**17**	**5**	**20**	**0**									

WHL East First All-Star Team (1996)

Signed as a free agent by **Anaheim**, January 27, 1996.

• BANKS, DARREN

Darren Banks LW – L. 6'2", 215 lbs. b: Toronto, Ont., 3/18/1966.

Season	Club	League	GP	G	A	Pts	AG	AA	APts	PIM	PP	SH	GW	S	%	TGF	PGF	TGA	PGA	+/–	GP	G	A	Pts	PIM	PP	SH	GW
1986-87	Brock University	OUAA	24	5	3	8				82																		
1987-88	Brock University	OUAA	26	10	11	21				110																		
1988-89	Brock University	OUAA	26	19	14	33				88																		
1989-90	Salt Lake Golden Eagles	IHL	6	0	0	0				11											1	0	0	0	10			
	Fort Wayne Komets	IHL	2	0	1	1				0																		
	Knoxville Cherokees	ECHL	52	25	22	47				258																		
1990-91	Salt Lake Golden Eagles	IHL	56	9	7	16				286											3	0	1	1	6			
1991-92	Salt Lake Golden Eagles	IHL	55	5	5	10				303																		
1992-93	**Boston Bruins**	**NHL**	**16**	**2**	**1**	**3**	**2**	**1**	**3**	**64**	**0**	**0**	**0**	**15**	**13.3**	**6**	**0**	**1**	**0**	**+5**								
	Providence Bruins	AHL	43	9	5	14				199											1	0	0	0	0			
1993-94	**Boston Bruins**	**NHL**	**4**	**0**	**1**	**1**	**0**	**1**	**1**	**9**	**0**	**0**	**0**	**3**	**0.0**	**1**	**0**	**1**	**0**	**0**								
	Providence Bruins	AHL	41	6	3	9				189																		
1994-95	Adirondack Red Wings	AHL	20	3	2	5				65																		
	Portland Pirates	AHL	12	1	2	3				38																		
	Las Vegas Thunder	IHL	2	0	0	0				19																		
	Detroit Falcons	ColHL	22	9	10	19				51											12	3	5	8	59			
1995-96	Detroit Falcons	ColHL	38	11	17	28				290																		
	Utica Blizzard	ColHL	6	1	2	3				22																		
	Las Vegas Thunder	IHL	5	0	2	2				10											10	0	0	0	54			
1996-97	Detroit Vipers	IHL	64	10	13	23				306											16	3	5	8	32			
1997-98	Quebec Rafales	IHL	4	0	1	1				9																		
	San Antonio Dragons	IHL	7	0	0	0				6																		
	Detroit Vipers	IHL	59	16	14	30				175											21	2	3	5	97			
	NHL Totals		**20**	**2**	**2**	**4**	**2**	**2**	**4**	**73**	**0**	**0**	**0**	**18**	**11.1**	**7**	**0**	**2**	**0**									

Signed as a free agent by **Calgary**, December 12, 1990. Signed as a free agent by **Boston**, July 16, 1992.

• BANNISTER, DREW

Drew Bannister D – R. 6'2", 200 lbs. b: Belleville, Ont., 9/4/1974. Tampa Bay's 2nd choice, 26th overall, in 1992 Entry Draft.

Season	Club	League	GP	G	A	Pts	AG	AA	APts	PIM	PP	SH	GW	S	%	TGF	PGF	TGA	PGA	+/–	GP	G	A	Pts	PIM	PP	SH	GW
1990-91	Sault Ste. Marie Greyhounds	OHL	41	2	8	10				51											4	0	0	0	0			
1991-92	Sault Ste. Marie Greyhounds	OHL	64	4	21	25				122											16	3	10	13	36			
1992-93	Sault Ste. Marie Greyhounds	OHL	59	5	28	33				114											18	2	7	9	12			
1993-94	Sault Ste. Marie Greyhounds	OHL	58	7	43	50				108											14	6	9	15	20			
	Canada	WJC-A	7	0	4	4				10																		
1994-95	Atlanta Knights	IHL	72	5	7	12				74											5	0	2	2	22			
1995-96	**Tampa Bay Lightning**	**NHL**	**13**	**0**	**1**	**1**	**0**	**1**	**1**	**4**	**0**	**0**	**0**	**10**	**0.0**	**7**	**0**	**8**	**0**	**–1**								
	Atlanta Knights	IHL	61	3	13	16				105											3	0	0	0	4			
1996-97	**Tampa Bay Lightning**	**NHL**	**64**	**4**	**13**	**17**	**4**	**11**	**15**	**44**	**1**	**0**	**0**	**57**	**7.0**	**43**	**13**	**53**	**2**	**–21**								
	Edmonton Oilers	**NHL**	**1**	**0**	**1**	**1**	**0**	**1**	**1**	**0**	**0**	**0**	**0**	**2**	**0.0**	**2**	**1**	**3**	**0**	**–2**	**12**	**0**	**0**	**0**	**30**	**0**	**0**	**0**
1997-98	**Edmonton Oilers**	**NHL**	**34**	**0**	**2**	**2**	**0**	**2**	**2**	**42**	**0**	**0**	**0**	**27**	**0.0**	**16**	**1**	**33**	**11**	**–7**								
	Anaheim Mighty Ducks	**NHL**	**27**	**0**	**6**	**6**	**0**	**6**	**6**	**47**	**0**	**0**	**0**	**23**	**0.0**	**14**	**0**	**24**	**8**	**–2**								
	NHL Totals		**139**	**4**	**23**	**27**	**4**	**21**	**25**	**137**	**1**	**0**	**0**	**119**	**3.4**	**82**	**15**	**121**	**21**		**12**	**0**	**0**	**0**	**30**	**0**	**0**	**0**

Memorial Cup All-Star Team (1993) • OHL Second All-Star Team (1994)

Traded to **Edmonton** by **Tampa Bay** with Tampa Bay's 6th round choice (Peter Sarno) in 1997 Entry Draft for Jeff Norton, March 18, 1997. Traded to **Anaheim** by **Edmonton** for Bobby Dollas, January 9, 1998.

• BARAHONA, RALPH

Ralph Barahona C – L. 5'10", 180 lbs. b: Long Beach, CA, 11/16/1965.

Season	Club	League	GP	G	A	Pts	AG	AA	APts	PIM	PP	SH	GW	S	%	TGF	PGF	TGA	PGA	+/–	GP	G	A	Pts	PIM	PP	SH	GW
1986-87	U. Wisconsin-Stevens Point	NCHA	29	21	21	42				8																		
1987-88	U. Wisconsin-Stevens Point	NCHA	31	25	26	51				16																		
1988-89	U. Wisconsin-Stevens Point	NCHA	41	33	47	80				40																		
1989-90	U. Wisconsin-Stevens Point	NCHA	35	17	26	43				20																		
1990-91	**Boston Bruins**	**NHL**	**3**	**2**	**1**	**3**	**2**	**1**	**3**	**0**	**0**	**0**	**0**	**5**	**40.0**	**3**	**1**	**0**	**0**	**+2**								
	Maine Mariners	AHL	72	24	33	57				14											2	1	1	2	0			
1991-92	**Boston Bruins**	**NHL**	**3**	**0**	**1**	**1**	**0**	**1**	**1**	**0**	**0**	**0**	**0**	**0**	**0.0**	**2**	**0**	**1**	**0**	**+1**								
	Maine Mariners	AHL	74	27	32	59				39																		
1992-93	Utica Devils	AHL	2	0	0	0				0																		
	Cincinnati Cyclones	IHL	30	8	6	14				4																		
	Fort Wayne Komets	IHL	7	0	2	2				2																		
1993-94	Raleigh IceCaps	ECHL	36	14	21	35				12																		
	Hampton Roads Admirals	ECHL	27	13	20	33				12											7	3	5	8	4			
1995-96	San Diego Gulls	WCHL	56	31	56	87																						
	NHL Totals		**6**	**2**	**2**	**4**	**2**	**2**	**4**	**0**	**0**	**0**	**0**	**5**	**40.0**	**5**	**1**	**1**	**0**									

Signed as a free agent by **Boston**, September 26, 1990.

• BARBER, BILL

Bill Barber LW – L. 6', 195 lbs. b: Callander, Ont., 7/11/1952. Philadelphia's 1st choice, 7th overall, in 1972 Amateur Draft. **HHOF**

Season	Club	League	GP	G	A	Pts	AG	AA	APts	PIM	PP	SH	GW	S	%	TGF	PGF	TGA	PGA	+/–	GP	G	A	Pts	PIM	PP	SH	GW
1969-70	Kitchener Rangers	OHA	54	37	49	86				42																		
1970-71	Kitchener Rangers	OHA	61	46	59	105				129																		
1971-72	Kitchener Rangers	OHA	62	44	63	107				89																		
1972-73	**Philadelphia Flyers**	**NHL**	**69**	**30**	**34**	**64**	**30**	**28**	**58**	**46**	**7**	**0**	**2**	**214**	**14.0**	**98**	**32**	**57**	**1**	**+10**	**11**	**3**	**2**	**5**	**22**	**0**	**0**	**0**
	Richmond Robins	AHL	11	9	5	14				4																		
1973-74	**Philadelphia Flyers**	**NHL**	**75**	**34**	**35**	**69**	**35**	**30**	**65**	**54**	**9**	**2**	**6**	**290**	**11.7**	**108**	**38**	**52**	**16**	**+34**	**17**	**3**	**6**	**9**	**18**	**0**	**0**	**1**
1974-75	**Philadelphia Flyers**	**NHL**	**79**	**34**	**37**	**71**	**32**	**29**	**61**	**66**	**8**	**5**	**4**	**276**	**12.3**	**120**	**43**	**55**	**24**	**+46**	**17**	**6**	**9**	**15**	**8**	**0**	**0**	**0**
1975-76	**Philadelphia Flyers**	**NHL**	**80**	**50**	**62**	**112**	**47**	**49**	**96**	**104**	**15**	**4**	**10**	**380**	**13.2**	**162**	**57**	**57**	**26**	**+74**	**16**	**6**	**7**	**13**	**18**	**3**	**0**	**0**
1976-77	Canada	C Cup	7	2	0	2				4																		
	Philadelphia Flyers	**NHL**	**73**	**20**	**35**	**55**	**19**	**28**	**47**	**62**	**3**	**0**	**3**	**245**	**8.2**	**91**	**27**	**51**	**19**	**+32**	**10**	**1**	**4**	**5**	**2**	**0**	**0**	**0**

			REGULAR SEASON																		PLAYOFFS							
Season	Club	League	GP	G	A	Pts	AG	AA	APts	PIM	PP	SH	GW	S	%	TGF	PGF	TGA	PGA	+/–	GP	G	A	Pts	PIM	PP	SH	GW
1977-78	**Philadelphia Flyers**	NHL	80	41	31	72	40	25	65	34	8	4	9	262	15.6	107	34	66	24	+31	12	6	3	9	2	1	0	0
1978-79	**Philadelphia Flyers**	NHL	79	34	46	80	31	35	66	22	10	6	4	258	13.2	122	50	79	26	+19	8	3	4	7	10	0	0	0
	NHL All-Stars	Chal Cup	3	0	1	1	....	....	....	0	....	....	....	....	....	....	....	....	....	....	....	....	....	....	....	....	....	....
1979-80	**Philadelphia Flyers**	NHL	79	40	32	72	36	25	61	17	7	2	7	265	15.1	119	30	85	35	+39	19	12	9	21	23	1	3	4
1980-81	**Philadelphia Flyers**	NHL	80	43	42	85	36	29	65	69	16	2	2	292	14.7	129	57	95	29	+6	12	11	5	16	0	3	1	1
1981-82	**Philadelphia Flyers**	NHL	80	45	44	89	36	29	65	85	13	4	6	350	12.9	136	64	122	54	+4	4	1	5	6	4	0	1	0
	Canada	WEC-A	10	8	1	9	....	....	....	10	....	....	....	....	....	....	....	....	....	....	....	....	....	....	....	....	....	....
1982-83	**Philadelphia Flyers**	NHL	66	27	33	60	22	23	45	28	5	2	1	215	12.6	90	25	62	14	+17	3	1	1	2	2	1	0	0
1983-84	**Philadelphia Flyers**	NHL	63	22	32	54	18	22	40	36	3	0	1	203	10.8	79	27	59	11	+4	....	....	....	....	....	....	....	....
	NHL Totals		903	420	463	883	382	352	734	623	104	31	54	3250	12.9	1361	484	840	279		129	53	55	108	109	9	5	6

NHL First All-Star Team (1976) • NHL Second All-Star Team (1979, 1981) • WEC-A All-Star Team (1982)

Played in NHL All-Star Game (1975, 1976, 1978, 1980, 1981, 1982)

• BARBER, DON

Don Barber RW/LW – L. 6′2″, 205 lbs. b: Victoria, B.C., 12/2/1964. Edmonton's 5th choice, 124th overall, in 1983 Entry Draft.

1982-83	Kelowna Buckeroos	BCJHL	35	26	31	57	....	....	....	54	....	....	....	....	....	....	....	....	....	....	....	....	....	....	....	....	....	....
1983-84	St. Albert Saints	AJHL	53	42	38	80	....	....	....	74	....	....	....	....	....	....	....	....	....	....	....	....	....	....	....	....	....	....
1984-85	Bowling Green University	CCHA	39	15	22	37	....	....	....	44	....	....	....	....	....	....	....	....	....	....	....	....	....	....	....	....	....	....
1985-86	Bowling Green University	CCHA	35	21	22	43	....	....	....	64	....	....	....	....	....	....	....	....	....	....	....	....	....	....	....	....	....	....
1986-87	Bowling Green University	CCHA	43	29	34	63	....	....	....	107	....	....	....	....	....	....	....	....	....	....	....	....	....	....	....	....	....	....
1987-88	Bowling Green University	CCHA	38	18	47	65	....	....	....	62	....	....	....	....	....	....	....	....	....	....	....	....	....	....	....	....	....	....
1988-89	**Minnesota North Stars**	NHL	23	8	5	13	7	4	11	8	3	0	2	42	19.0	19	9	9	1	+2	4	1	1	2	2	0	0	1
	Kalamazoo Wings	IHL	39	14	17	31	....	....	....	23	....	....	....	....	....	....	....	....	....	....	....	....	....	....	....	....	....	....
1989-90	**Minnesota North Stars**	NHL	44	15	19	34	13	14	27	32	4	0	2	100	15.0	58	17	38	1	+4	7	3	3	6	8	2	0	1
	Kalamazoo Wings	IHL	10	4	4	8	....	....	....	38	....	....	....	....	....	....	....	....	....	....	....	....	....	....	....	....	....	....
1990-91	Minnesota North Stars	FrTour	4	1	0	1	....	....	....	2	....	....	....	....	....	....	....	....	....	....	....	....	....	....	....	....	....	....
	Minnesota North Stars	NHL	7	0	0	0	0	0	0	4	0	0	0	10	0.0	0	0	4	1	–3	....	....	....	....	....	....	....	....
	Winnipeg Jets	NHL	16	1	2	3	1	2	3	14	0	0	0	19	5.3	6	1	8	0	–3	....	....	....	....	....	....	....	....
	Moncton Hawks	AHL	38	17	21	38	....	....	....	32	....	....	....	....	....	....	....	....	....	....	9	4	6	10	8	....	....	....
1991-92	**Winnipeg Jets**	NHL	11	0	3	3	0	2	2	4	0	0	0	6	0.0	8	5	1	0	+2	....	....	....	....	....	....	....	....
	Halifax Citadels	AHL	25	12	10	22	....	....	....	8	....	....	....	....	....	....	....	....	....	....	....	....	....	....	....	....	....	....
	Quebec Nordiques	NHL	2	0	0	0	0	0	0	0	0	0	0	1	0.0	0	0	1	0	–1	....	....	....	....	....	....	....	....
	San Jose Sharks	NHL	12	1	3	4	1	2	3	2	0	0	0	17	5.9	8	3	12	0	–7	....	....	....	....	....	....	....	....
1992-93	Kansas City Blades	IHL	9	3	1	4	....	....	....	4	....	....	....	....	....	....	....	....	....	....	....	....	....	....	....	....	....	....
	NHL Totals		115	25	32	57	22	24	46	64	7	0	4	195	12.8	99	35	73	3		11	4	4	8	10	2	0	2

Traded to **Minnesota** by **Edmonton** with Marc Habsheid amd Emanuel Viveiros for Gord Sherven and Don Biggs, December 20, 1985. Traded to **Winnipeg** by **Minnesota** for Doug Smail, November 7, 1990. Claimed on waivers by **Quebec** from **Winnipeg**, November 12, 1991. Traded to **San Jose** by **Quebec** for Murray Garbutt, March 7, 1992.

• BARLOW, BOB

Bob Barlow LW – L. 5′10″, 165 lbs. b: Hamilton, Ont., 6/17/1935.

1953-54	Barrie Flyers	OHA	29	5	7	12	....	....	....	4	....	....	....	....	....	....	....	....	....	....	....	....	....	....	....	....	....	....
1954-55	Barrie Flyers	OHA	46	33	27	60	....	....	....	41	....	....	....	....	....	....	....	....	....	....	....	....	....	....	....	....	....	....
	Cleveland Barons	AHL	3	0	0	0	....	....	....	0	....	....	....	....	....	....	....	....	....	....	....	....	....	....	....	....	....	....
1955-56	Cleveland Barons	AHL	2	1	0	1	....	....	....	0	....	....	....	....	....	....	....	....	....	....	....	....	....	....	....	....	....	....
	North Bay Trappers	NOHA	56	20	18	38	....	....	....	56	....	....	....	....	....	....	....	....	....	....	10	2	2	4	4	....	....	....
1956-57	Cleveland Barons	AHL	3	0	2	2	....	....	....	2	....	....	....	....	....	....	....	....	....	....	....	....	....	....	....	....	....	....
	North Bay Trappers	NOHA	56	21	20	41	....	....	....	27	....	....	....	....	....	....	....	....	....	....	13	7	5	12	8	....	....	....
1957-58	Cleveland Barons	AHL	6	4	0	4	....	....	....	2	....	....	....	....	....	....	....	....	....	....	7	2	2	4	4	....	....	....
	North Bay Trappers	NOHA	60	27	36	63	....	....	....	39	....	....	....	....	....	....	....	....	....	....	....	....	....	....	....	....	....	....
1958-59	Cleveland Barons	AHL	70	27	27	54	....	....	....	39	....	....	....	....	....	....	....	....	....	....	7	1	2	3	20	....	....	....
1959-60	Quebec Aces	AHL	72	28	32	60	....	....	....	50	....	....	....	....	....	....	....	....	....	....	....	....	....	....	....	....	....	....
1960-61	Quebec Aces	AHL	67	12	17	29	....	....	....	41	....	....	....	....	....	....	....	....	....	....	....	....	....	....	....	....	....	....
1961-62	Quebec Aces	AHL	61	11	12	23	....	....	....	25	....	....	....	....	....	....	....	....	....	....	....	....	....	....	....	....	....	....
1962-63	Seattle Totems	WHL	70	*47	30	77	....	....	....	17	....	....	....	....	....	....	....	....	....	....	17	8	9	17	10	....	....	....
1963-64	Seattle Totems	WHL	66	35	20	55	....	....	....	18	....	....	....	....	....	....	....	....	....	....	....	....	....	....	....	....	....	....
1964-65	Seattle Totems	WHL	70	30	17	47	....	....	....	50	....	....	....	....	....	....	....	....	....	....	7	3	2	5	10	....	....	....
1965-66	Victoria Maple Leafs	WHL	71	42	39	81	....	....	....	20	....	....	....	....	....	....	....	....	....	....	14	*10	9	19	21	....	....	....
1966-67	Victoria Maple Leafs	WHL	70	21	38	59	....	....	....	44	....	....	....	....	....	....	....	....	....	....	....	....	....	....	....	....	....	....
1967-68	Rochester Americans	AHL	72	43	52	95	....	....	....	72	....	....	....	....	....	....	....	....	....	....	11	*9	3	12	25	....	....	....
1968-69	Vancouver Canucks	WHL	74	36	48	84	....	....	....	50	....	....	....	....	....	....	....	....	....	....	8	4	6	10	11	....	....	....
1969-70	**Minnesota North Stars**	NHL	70	16	17	33	18	17	35	10	6	1	1	157	10.2	54	18	40	1	–3	6	2	2	4	6	1	0	0
1970-71	**Minnesota North Stars**	NHL	7	0	0	0	0	0	0	0	0	0	0	7	0.0	0	0	0	0	0	....	....	....	....	....	....	....	....
	Phoenix Roadrunners	WHL	44	19	26	45	....	....	....	21	....	....	....	....	....	....	....	....	....	....	10	3	3	6	26	....	....	....
1971-72	Phoenix Roadrunners	WHL	64	16	21	37	....	....	....	24	....	....	....	....	....	....	....	....	....	....	5	0	1	1	2	....	....	....
1972-73	Phoenix Roadrunners	WHL	51	26	42	68	....	....	....	41	....	....	....	....	....	....	....	....	....	....	10	4	7	11	28	....	....	....
1973-74	Phoenix Roadrunners	WHL	48	19	30	49	....	....	....	12	....	....	....	....	....	....	....	....	....	....	9	6	5	*11	6	....	....	....
1974-75	Phoenix Roadrunners	WHA	51	6	20	26	....	....	....	8	....	....	....	....	....	....	....	....	....	....	....	....	....	....	....	....	....	....
	Tulsa Oilers	CHL	25	7	12	19	....	....	....	10	....	....	....	....	....	....	....	....	....	....	2	0	1	1	2	....	....	....
1975-76	Tucson Mavericks	CHL	2	0	3	3	....	....	....	2	....	....	....	....	....	....	....	....	....	....	....	....	....	....	....	....	....	....
	NHL Totals		77	16	17	33	18	17	35	10	6	1	1	164	9.8	54	18	40	1		6	2	2	4	6	1	0	0
	Other Major League Totals		51	6	20	26	....	....	....	8	....	....	....	....	....	....	....	....	....	....	....	....	....	....	....	....	....	....

WHL Second All-Star Team (1963, 1969) • WHL First All-Star Team (1966) • AHL First All-Star Team (1968)

Traded to **Quebec** (AHL) by **Cleveland** (AHL) for cash, July, 1959. Rights transferred to **Toronto** from **Seattle** (WHL) after NHL club purchased Seattle (WHL) franschise and relocated team to Victoria (WHL), July, 1965. Traded to **Vancouver** (WHL) by **Toronto** for cash, June, 1968. Claimed by **Philadelphia** from **Vancouver** (WHL) in Inter-League Draft, June 10, 1969. Traded to **Minnesota** by **Philadelphia** for cash, June 10, 1969. Selected by **Dayton-Houston** (WHA) in 1972 WHA General Player Draft, February 12, 1972. Traded to **Phoenix** (WHL) by **Minnesota** for cash, September, 1971. WHA rights transferred to **Phoenix** (WHA) after owners of Phoenix (WHL) franchise awarded WHA expansion team, September 14, 1973.

• BARNABY, MATTHEW

Matthew Barnaby RW – L. 6′, 188 lbs. b: Ottawa, Ont., 5/4/1973. Buffalo's 5th choice, 83rd overall, in 1992 Entry Draft.

1990-91	Beauport Harfangs	QMJHL	52	9	5	14	....	....	....	262	....	....	....	....	....	....	....	....	....	....	....	....	....	....	....	....	....	....
1991-92	Beauport Harfangs	QMJHL	63	29	37	66	....	....	....	*476	....	....	....	....	....	....	....	....	....	....	....	....	....	....	....	....	....	....
1992-93	**Buffalo Sabres**	NHL	2	1	0	1	1	0	1	10	1	0	0	8	12.5	1	1	0	0	0	1	0	1	1	4	0	0	0
	Victoriaville Tigers	QMJHL	65	44	67	111	....	....	....	*448	....	....	....	....	....	....	....	....	....	....	6	2	4	6	44	....	....	....
1993-94	**Buffalo Sabres**	NHL	35	2	4	6	2	3	5	106	1	0	0	13	15.4	10	4	13	0	–7	3	0	0	0	17	0	0	0
	Rochester Americans	AHL	42	10	32	42	....	....	....	153	....	....	....	....	....	....	....	....	....	....	....	....	....	....	....	....	....	....
1994-95	**Buffalo Sabres**	NHL	23	1	1	2	2	1	3	116	0	0	0	27	3.7	5	1	7	1	–2	....	....	....	....	....	....	....	....
	Rochester Americans	AHL	56	21	29	50	....	....	....	274	....	....	....	....	....	....	....	....	....	....	....	....	....	....	....	....	....	....
1995-96	**Buffalo Sabres**	NHL	73	15	16	31	15	13	28	*335	0	0	0	131	11.5	42	0	46	2	–2	....	....	....	....	....	....	....	....
1996-97	**Buffalo Sabres**	NHL	68	19	24	43	20	21	41	249	2	0	1	121	15.7	58	8	36	2	+16	8	0	4	4	36	0	0	0
1997-98	**Buffalo Sabres**	NHL	72	5	20	25	6	19	25	289	0	0	2	96	5.2	36	4	26	2	+8	15	7	6	13	22	3	0	1
	NHL Totals		273	43	65	108	46	57	103	1105	4	0	3	396	10.9	152	18	128	7		27	7	11	18	79	3	0	1

● **BARNES, BLAIR** Blair Barnes RW – R. 5'11", 190 lbs. b: Windsor, Ont., 9/21/1960. Edmonton's 6th choice, 126th overall, in 1979 Entry Draft.

			REGULAR SEASON																		PLAYOFFS							
Season	Club	League	GP	G	A	Pts	AG	AA	APts	PIM	PP	SH	GW	S	%	TGF	PGF	TGA	PGA	+/-	GP	G	A	Pts	PIM	PP	SH	GW
1976-77	Markham Waxers	Jr B	46	32	34	66																						
1977-78	Windsor Spitfires	OHA	65	22	26	48				163																		
1978-79	Windsor Spitfires	OHA	67	42	76	118				195											7	4	5	9	6			
1979-80	Windsor Spitfires	OHA	66	63	67	130				98											16	17	12	29	26			
1980-81	Wichita Wind	CHL	30	10	14	24				49																		
1981-82	Wichita Wind	CHL	80	28	34	62				99											5	0	1	1	2			
1982-83	**Los Angeles Kings**	**NHL**	**1**	**0**	**0**	**0**	**0**	**0**	**0**	**0**	**0**	**0**	**0**	**0**	**0.0**	**0**	**0**	**0**	**0**	**0**								
	New Haven Nighthawks	AHL	72	29	34	63				80											1	0	0	0	0			
1983-84	Nova Scotia Voyageurs	AHL	80	32	32	64				91											6	4	2	6	12			
	NHL Totals		**1**	**0**	**0**	**0**	**0**	**0**	**0**	**0**	**0**	**0**	**0**	**0**	**0.0**	**0**	**0**	**0**	**0**									

Traded to **LA Kings** by **Edmonton** for Paul Mulvey, June 22, 1982.

● **BARNES, NORM** Norm Barnes D – L. 6', 190 lbs. b: Toronto, Ont., 8/24/1953. Philadelphia's 9th choice, 122nd overall, in 1973 Amateur Draft.

Season	Club	League	GP	G	A	Pts	AG	AA	APts	PIM	PP	SH	GW	S	%	TGF	PGF	TGA	PGA	+/-	GP	G	A	Pts	PIM	PP	SH	GW
1971-72	Michigan State Spartans	WCHA	33	5	16	21				68																		
1972-73	Michigan State Spartans	WCHA	34	9	26	35				74																		
1973-74	Michigan State Spartans	WCHA	37	8	56	64				107																		
1974-75	Philadelphia Firebirds	NAHL	18	4	6	10				38																		
	Richmond Robins	AHL	17	0	5	5				32																		
1975-76	Richmond Robins	AHL	67	2	7	9				74											8	0	0	0	2			
1976-77	**Philadelphia Flyers**	**NHL**	**1**	**0**	**0**	**0**	**0**	**0**	**0**	**0**	**0**	**0**	**0**	**0**	**0.0**	**0**	**0**	**0**	**0**	**0**								
	Baltimore Clippers	SHL	46	5	27	32				90																		
	Springfield Indians	AHL	2	0	0	0				0																		
	Philadelphia Firebirds	NAHL	22	3	18	21				27											4	1	1	2	7			
1977-78	Maine Mariners	AHL	50	4	8	12				62											12	1	5	6	28			
1978-79	Maine Mariners	AHL	67	9	21	30				108											10	3	3	6	19			
	Philadelphia Flyers	**NHL**																			**2**	**0**	**0**	**0**	**0**			
1979-80	**Philadelphia Flyers**	**NHL**	**59**	**4**	**21**	**25**	**4**	**16**	**20**	**59**	**0**	**0**	**1**	**73**	**5.5**	**84**	**8**	**70**	**17**	**+23**	**10**	**0**	**0**	**0**	**8**	**0**	**0**	**0**
1980-81	**Philadelphia Flyers**	**NHL**	**22**	**0**	**3**	**3**	**0**	**2**	**2**	**18**	**0**	**0**	**0**	**12**	**0.0**	**16**	**1**	**26**	**8**	**–3**								
	Hartford Whalers	**NHL**	**54**	**1**	**10**	**11**	**1**	**7**	**8**	**82**	**0**	**0**	**0**	**72**	**1.4**	**68**	**4**	**133**	**39**	**–30**								
	Canada	WEC-A	6	0	1	1				6																		
1981-82	**Hartford Whalers**	**NHL**	**20**	**1**	**4**	**5**	**1**	**3**	**4**	**19**	**0**	**0**	**0**	**25**	**4.0**	**20**	**0**	**36**	**12**	**–4**								
	Binghamton Whalers	AHL	56	4	17	21				58											15	1	4	5	16			
	NHL Totals		**156**	**6**	**38**	**44**	**6**	**28**	**34**	**178**	**0**	**0**	**1**	**182**	**3.3**	**188**	**13**	**265**	**76**		**12**	**0**	**0**	**0**	**8**	**0**	**0**	**0**

WCHA First All-Star Team (1974) • NCAA West First All-American Team (1974) • AHL First All-Star Team (1982)

Played in NHL All-Star Game (1980)

Traded to **Hartford** by **Philadelphia** with Jack McIlhargey for Hartford's 2nd round choice (later traded to Toronto — Toronto selected Peter Ihnacak) in 1982 Entry Draft, November 2, 1980.

● **BARNES, STU** Stu Barnes C – R. 5'11", 174 lbs. b: Spruce Grove, Alta., 12/25/1970. Winnipeg's 1st choice, 4th overall, in 1989 Entry Draft.

Season	Club	League	GP	G	A	Pts	AG	AA	APts	PIM	PP	SH	GW	S	%	TGF	PGF	TGA	PGA	+/-	GP	G	A	Pts	PIM	PP	SH	GW
1987-88	New Westminster Bruins	WHL	71	37	64	101				88											5	2	3	5	6			
1988-89	Tri-City Americans	WHL	70	59	82	141				117											7	6	5	11	10			
1989-90	Tri-City Americans	WHL	63	52	92	144				165											7	1	5	6	26			
	Canada	WJC-A	7	2	4	6				6																		
1990-91	Canada	Nat-Team	53	22	27	49				68																		
1991-92	**Winnipeg Jets**	**NHL**	**46**	**8**	**9**	**17**	**7**	**7**	**14**	**26**	**4**	**0**	**0**	**75**	**10.7**	**33**	**14**	**21**	**0**	**–2**								
	Moncton Hawks	AHL	30	13	19	32				10											11	3	9	12	6			
1992-93	**Winnipeg Jets**	**NHL**	**38**	**12**	**10**	**22**	**10**	**7**	**17**	**10**	**3**	**0**	**3**	**73**	**16.4**	**34**	**5**	**32**	**0**	**–3**	**6**	**1**	**3**	**4**	**2**	**0**	**0**	**0**
	Moncton Hawks	AHL	42	23	31	54				58																		
1993-94	**Winnipeg Jets**	**NHL**	**18**	**5**	**4**	**9**	**5**	**3**	**8**	**8**	**2**	**0**	**0**	**24**	**20.8**	**12**	**4**	**9**	**0**	**–1**								
	Florida Panthers	**NHL**	**59**	**18**	**20**	**38**	**17**	**15**	**32**	**30**	**6**	**1**	**3**	**148**	**12.2**	**57**	**19**	**36**	**3**	**+5**								
1994-95	**Florida Panthers**	**NHL**	**41**	**10**	**19**	**29**	**18**	**28**	**46**	**8**	**1**	**0**	**2**	**93**	**10.8**	**44**	**12**	**30**	**5**	**+7**								
1995-96	**Florida Panthers**	**NHL**	**72**	**19**	**25**	**44**	**19**	**20**	**39**	**46**	**8**	**0**	**5**	**158**	**12.0**	**67**	**32**	**53**	**6**	**–12**	**22**	**6**	**10**	**16**	**4**	**2**	**0**	**2**
1996-97	**Florida Panthers**	**NHL**	**19**	**2**	**8**	**10**	**2**	**7**	**9**	**10**	**1**	**0**	**0**	**44**	**4.5**	**15**	**8**	**11**	**1**	**–3**								
	Pittsburgh Penguins	**NHL**	**62**	**17**	**22**	**39**	**18**	**19**	**37**	**16**	**4**	**0**	**3**	**132**	**12.9**	**53**	**14**	**67**	**8**	**–20**	**5**	**0**	**1**	**1**	**0**	**0**	**0**	**0**
1997-98	**Pittsburgh Penguins**	**NHL**	**78**	**30**	**35**	**65**	**35**	**34**	**69**	**30**	**15**	**1**	**5**	**196**	**15.3**	**101**	**40**	**61**	**15**	**+15**	**6**	**3**	**3**	**6**	**2**	**0**	**0**	**1**
	NHL Totals		**433**	**121**	**152**	**273**	**131**	**140**	**271**	**184**	**44**	**2**	**21**	**943**	**12.8**	**416**	**148**	**320**	**38**		**39**	**10**	**17**	**27**	**8**	**2**	**0**	**3**

WHL West Second All-Star Team (1988, 1989)

Traded to **Florida** by **Winnipeg** with St. Louis' 6th round choice (previously acquired by Winnipeg — later traded to Edmonton — later traded to Winnipeg — Winnipeg selected Chris Kibermanis) in 1994 Entry Draft for Randy Gilhen, November 25, 1993. Traded to **Pittsburgh** by **Florida** with Jason Woolley for Chris Wells, November 19, 1996.

● **BARON, MURRAY** Murray "Bear" Baron D – L. 6'3", 215 lbs. b: Prince George, B.C., 6/1/1967. Philadelphia's 7th choice, 167th overall, in 1986 Entry Draft.

Season	Club	League	GP	G	A	Pts	AG	AA	APts	PIM	PP	SH	GW	S	%	TGF	PGF	TGA	PGA	+/-	GP	G	A	Pts	PIM	PP	SH	GW
1985-86	Vernon Lakers	BCJHL	46	12	32	44				179											7	1	2	3	13			
1986-87	University of North Dakota	WCHA	41	4	10	14				62																		
1987-88	University of North Dakota	WCHA	41	1	10	11				95																		
1988-89	University of North Dakota	WCHA	40	2	6	8				92																		
	Hershey Bears	AHL	9	0	3	3				8																		
1989-90	**Philadelphia Flyers**	**NHL**	**16**	**2**	**2**	**4**	**2**	**1**	**3**	**12**	**0**	**0**	**0**	**18**	**11.1**	**11**	**0**	**12**	**0**	**–1**								
	Hershey Bears	AHL	50	0	10	10				101																		
1990-91	**Philadelphia Flyers**	**NHL**	**67**	**8**	**8**	**16**	**7**	**6**	**13**	**74**	**3**	**0**	**1**	**86**	**9.3**	**60**	**13**	**57**	**7**	**–3**								
	Hershey Bears	AHL	6	2	3	5				0																		
1991-92	**St. Louis Blues**	**NHL**	**67**	**3**	**8**	**11**	**3**	**6**	**9**	**94**	**0**	**0**	**0**	**55**	**5.5**	**47**	**1**	**68**	**19**	**–3**	**2**	**0**	**0**	**0**	**2**	**0**	**0**	**0**
1992-93	**St. Louis Blues**	**NHL**	**53**	**2**	**2**	**4**	**2**	**1**	**3**	**59**	**0**	**0**	**1**	**42**	**4.8**	**41**	**1**	**56**	**11**	**–5**	**11**	**0**	**0**	**0**	**12**	**0**	**0**	**0**
1993-94	**St. Louis Blues**	**NHL**	**77**	**5**	**9**	**14**	**5**	**7**	**12**	**123**	**0**	**0**	**0**	**73**	**6.8**	**57**	**2**	**101**	**32**	**–14**	**4**	**0**	**0**	**0**	**10**	**0**	**0**	**0**
1994-95	**St. Louis Blues**	**NHL**	**39**	**0**	**5**	**5**	**0**	**7**	**7**	**93**	**0**	**0**	**0**	**28**	**0.0**	**38**	**0**	**52**	**23**	**+9**	**7**	**1**	**1**	**2**	**2**	**0**	**0**	**0**
1995-96	**St. Louis Blues**	**NHL**	**82**	**2**	**9**	**11**	**2**	**7**	**9**	**190**	**0**	**0**	**0**	**86**	**2.3**	**61**	**3**	**98**	**43**	**+3**	**13**	**1**	**0**	**1**	**20**	**0**	**1**	**0**
1996-97	**St. Louis Blues**	**NHL**	**11**	**0**	**2**	**2**	**0**	**2**	**2**	**11**	**0**	**0**	**0**	**7**	**0.0**	**8**	**0**	**15**	**3**	**–4**								
	Montreal Canadiens	**NHL**	**60**	**1**	**5**	**6**	**1**	**4**	**5**	**107**	**0**	**0**	**0**	**52**	**1.9**	**44**	**1**	**78**	**10**	**16**								
	Phoenix Coyotes	**NHL**	**8**	**0**	**0**	**0**	**0**	**0**	**0**	**4**	**0**	**0**	**0**	**5**	**0.0**	**7**	**0**	**8**	**1**	**0**	**1**	**0**	**0**	**0**	**0**	**0**	**0**	**0**
1997-98	**Phoenix Coyotes**	**NHL**	**45**	**1**	**5**	**6**	**1**	**5**	**6**	**106**	**0**	**0**	**0**	**23**	**4.3**	**23**	**0**	**50**	**17**	**–10**	**6**	**0**	**2**	**2**	**6**	**0**	**0**	**0**
	NHL Totals		**525**	**24**	**55**	**79**	**23**	**46**	**69**	**873**	**3**	**0**	**2**	**475**	**5.1**	**397**	**21**	**595**	**175**		**44**	**2**	**3**	**5**	**52**	**0**	**1**	**0**

Traded to **St. Louis** by **Philadelphia** with Ron Sutter for Dan Quinn and Rod Brind'Amour, September 22, 1991. Traded to **Montreal** by **St. Louis** with Shayne Corson and St. Louis' 5th round choice (Gennady Razin) in 1997 Entry Draft for Pierre Turgeon, Rory Fitzpatrick and Craig Conroy, October 29, 1996. Traded to **Phoenix** by **Montreal** with Chris Murray for Dave Manson, March 18, 1997.

● **BARON, NORMAND** Normand Baron LW – L. 6', 205 lbs. b: Verdun, Que., 12/15/1957.

Season	Club	League	GP	G	A	Pts	AG	AA	APts	PIM	PP	SH	GW	S	%	TGF	PGF	TGA	PGA	+/-	GP	G	A	Pts	PIM	PP	SH	GW
1976-77	Montreal Jr. Canadiens	QMJHL	7	1	1	2				0																		
1977-1983			DID NOT PLAY																									
1983-84	**Montreal Canadiens**	**NHL**	**4**	**0**	**0**	**0**	**0**	**0**	**0**	**12**	**0**	**0**	**0**	**2**	**0.0**	**0**	**0**	**2**	**0**	**–2**	**3**	**0**	**0**	**0**	**22**	**0**	**0**	**0**
	Nova Scotia Voyageurs	AHL	68	11	11	22				275																		
1984-85	Sherbrooke Canadiens	AHL	39	5	5	10				98											3	0	0	0	22			
	Peoria Rivermen	IHL	17	4	4	8				61																		
1985-86	**St. Louis Blues**	**NHL**	**23**	**2**	**0**	**2**	**2**	**0**	**2**	**39**	**0**	**0**	**0**	**13**	**15.4**	**5**	**0**	**12**	**0**	**–7**								
	Peoria Rivermen	IHL	17	4	4	8				61																		
	Flint Spirits	IHL	11	1	7	8				43																		
	NHL Totals		**27**	**2**	**0**	**2**	**2**	**0**	**2**	**51**	**0**	**0**	**0**	**15**	**13.3**	**5**	**0**	**14**	**0**		**3**	**0**	**0**	**0**	**22**	**0**	**0**	**0**

• Worked as a professional weight lifter from 1977 to 1983. Signed as a free agent by **Montreal**, March 15, 1984. Rights traded to **St. Louis** by **Montreal** for cash, September 30, 1985.

			REGULAR SEASON																		PLAYOFFS							
Season	Club	League	GP	G	A	Pts	AG	AA	APts	PIM	PP	SH	GW	S	%	TGF	PGF	TGA	PGA	+/–	GP	G	A	Pts	PIM	PP	SH	GW

● BARR, DAVE

Dave Barr RW – R. 6'1", 195 lbs. b: Toronto, Ont., 11/30/1960.

Season	Club	League	GP	G	A	Pts	AG	AA	APts	PIM	PP	SH	GW	S	%	TGF	PGF	TGA	PGA	+/–	GP	G	A	Pts	PIM	PP	SH	GW
1977-78	Billings Bighorns	WCJHL	2	0	1	1	....	....	....	0	....	....	....	....	....	....	....	....	....	....	....	....	....	....	....	....	....	....
1978-79	Edmonton Oil Kings	WHL	72	16	19	35	....	....	....	61	....	....	....	....	....	....	....	....	....	....	8	4	0	4	2	....	....	....
1979-80	Great Falls Americans	WHL	3	0	1	1	....	....	....	10	....	....	....	....	....	....	....	....	....	....	....	....	....	....	....	....	....	....
	Portland Winter Hawks	WHL	27	4	12	16	....	....	....	18	....	....	....	....	....	....	....	....	....	....	....	....	....	....	....	....	....	....
	Lethbridge Broncos	WHL	30	12	25	37	....	....	....	29	....	....	....	....	....	....	....	....	....	....	....	....	....	....	....	....	....	....
1980-81	Lethbridge Broncos	WHL	72	26	62	88	....	....	....	106	....	....	....	....	....	....	....	....	....	....	10	4	10	14	4	....	....	....
1981-82	**Boston Bruins**	**NHL**	**2**	**0**	**0**	**0**	**0**	**0**	**0**	**0**	**0**	**0**	**0**	**1**	**0.0**	**0**	**0**	**0**	**0**	**0**	**5**	**1**	**0**	**1**	**0**	**0**	**0**	**0**
	Erie Blades	AHL	76	18	48	66	....	....	....	29	....	....	....	....	....	....	....	....	....	....	....	....	....	....	....	....	....	....
1982-83	**Boston Bruins**	**NHL**	**10**	**1**	**1**	**2**	**1**	**1**	**2**	**7**	**0**	**0**	**0**	**11**	**9.1**	**3**	**0**	**2**	**0**	**+1**	**10**	**0**	**0**	**0**	**2**	**0**	**0**	**0**
	Baltimore Skipjacks	AHL	72	27	51	78	....	....	....	67	....	....	....	....	....	....	....	....	....	....	....	....	....	....	....	....	....	....
1983-84	**New York Rangers**	**NHL**	**6**	**0**	**0**	**0**	**0**	**0**	**0**	**2**	**0**	**0**	**0**	**9**	**0.0**	**1**	**0**	**1**	**0**	**0**	....	....	....	....	....	....	....	....
	Tulsa Oilers	CHL	50	28	37	65	....	....	....	24	....	....	....	....	....	....	....	....	....	....	....	....	....	....	....	....	....	....
	St. Louis Blues	**NHL**	**1**	**0**	**0**	**0**	**0**	**0**	**0**	**0**	**0**	**0**	**0**	**0**	**0.0**	**0**	**0**	**1**	**0**	**–1**	....	....	....	....	....	....	....	....
1984-85	**St. Louis Blues**	**NHL**	**75**	**16**	**18**	**34**	**13**	**12**	**25**	**32**	**2**	**0**	**1**	**75**	**21.3**	**48**	**7**	**40**	**4**	**+5**	**2**	**0**	**0**	**0**	**2**	**0**	**0**	**0**
1985-86	**St. Louis Blues**	**NHL**	**72**	**13**	**38**	**51**	**10**	**25**	**35**	**70**	**0**	**0**	**2**	**106**	**12.3**	**72**	**10**	**52**	**1**	**+11**	**11**	**1**	**1**	**2**	**14**	**1**	**0**	**0**
1986-87	**St. Louis Blues**	**NHL**	**2**	**0**	**0**	**0**	**0**	**0**	**0**	**0**	**0**	**0**	**0**	**3**	**0.0**	**1**	**0**	**0**	**0**	**+1**	....	....	....	....	....	....	....	....
	Hartford Whalers	**NHL**	**30**	**2**	**4**	**6**	**2**	**3**	**5**	**19**	**0**	**1**	**0**	**25**	**8.0**	**14**	**0**	**19**	**4**	**–1**	....	....	....	....	....	....	....	....
	Detroit Red Wings	**NHL**	**37**	**13**	**13**	**26**	**11**	**9**	**20**	**49**	**4**	**0**	**5**	**55**	**23.6**	**42**	**12**	**27**	**4**	**+7**	**13**	**1**	**0**	**1**	**14**	**0**	**0**	**0**
1987-88	**Detroit Red Wings**	**NHL**	**51**	**14**	**26**	**40**	**12**	**18**	**30**	**58**	**3**	**1**	**0**	**64**	**21.9**	**67**	**11**	**43**	**7**	**+20**	**16**	**5**	**7**	**12**	**22**	**2**	**0**	**0**
1988-89	**Detroit Red Wings**	**NHL**	**73**	**27**	**32**	**59**	**23**	**22**	**45**	**69**	**5**	**2**	**3**	**140**	**19.3**	**103**	**18**	**93**	**20**	**+12**	**6**	**3**	**1**	**4**	**6**	**1**	**0**	**1**
1989-90	**Detroit Red Wings**	**NHL**	**62**	**10**	**25**	**35**	**9**	**18**	**27**	**45**	**2**	**3**	**0**	**96**	**10.4**	**55**	**5**	**68**	**23**	**+5**	....	....	....	....	....	....	....	....
	Adirondack Red Wings	AHL	9	1	14	15	....	....	....	17	....	....	....	....	....	....	....	....	....	....	....	....	....	....	....	....	....	....
1990-91	**Detroit Red Wings**	**NHL**	**70**	**18**	**22**	**40**	**17**	**17**	**34**	**55**	**2**	**2**	**2**	**98**	**18.4**	**54**	**2**	**57**	**25**	**+20**	....	....	....	....	....	....	....	....
1991-92	**New Jersey Devils**	**NHL**	**41**	**6**	**12**	**18**	**5**	**9**	**14**	**32**	**0**	**1**	**0**	**49**	**12.2**	**22**	**1**	**19**	**7**	**+9**	....	....	....	....	....	....	....	....
	Utica Devils	AHL	1	0	0	0	....	....	....	7	....	....	....	....	....	....	....	....	....	....	....	....	....	....	....	....	....	....
1992-93	**New Jersey Devils**	**NHL**	**62**	**6**	**8**	**14**	**5**	**5**	**10**	**61**	**0**	**1**	**1**	**41**	**14.6**	**24**	**0**	**52**	**29**	**+1**	**5**	**1**	**0**	**1**	**6**	**0**	**0**	**0**
1993-94	**Dallas Stars**	**NHL**	**20**	**2**	**5**	**7**	**2**	**4**	**6**	**21**	**0**	**0**	**0**	**20**	**10.0**	**8**	**0**	**14**	**0**	**–6**	**3**	**0**	**1**	**1**	**4**	**0**	**0**	**0**
	Kalamazoo Wings	IHL	4	3	2	5	....	....	....	5	....	....	....	....	....	....	....	....	....	....	....	....	....	....	....	....	....	....
1994-95	Kalamazoo Wings	IHL	66	18	41	59	....	....	....	77	....	....	....	....	....	....	....	....	....	....	16	1	4	5	8	....	....	....
1995-96	Orlando Solar Bears	IHL	82	38	62	100	....	....	....	87	....	....	....	....	....	....	....	....	....	....	23	8	13	21	14	....	....	....
1996-97	Orlando Solar Bears	IHL	50	15	29	44	....	....	....	29	....	....	....	....	....	....	....	....	....	....	9	2	3	5	8	....	....	....
	NHL Totals		**614**	**128**	**204**	**332**	**110**	**143**	**253**	**520**	**18**	**11**	**14**	**793**	**16.1**	**514**	**66**	**488**	**124**		**71**	**12**	**10**	**22**	**70**	**4**	**0**	**1**

Signed as a free agent by **Boston**, September 28, 1981. Traded to **NY Rangers** by **Boston** for Dave Silk, October 5, 1983. Traded to **St. Louis** by **NY Rangers** with NY Rangers' 3rd round choice (Alan Perry) in the 1984 Entry Draft for Larry Patey and Bob Brooke, March 5, 1984. Traded to **Hartford** by **St. Louis** for Tim Bothwell, October 21, 1986. Traded to **Detroit** by **Hartford** for Randy Ladouceur, January 12, 1987. Acquired by **New Jersey** from **Detroit** with Randy McKay as compensation for Detroit's signing of free agent Troy Crowder, September 9, 1991. Signed as a free agent by **Dallas**, August 28, 1993.

● BARRAULT, DOUG

Doug Barrault RW – R. 6'2", 205 lbs. b: Golden, B.C., 4/21/1970. Minnesota's 8th choice, 155th overall, in 1990 Entry Draft.

Season	Club	League	GP	G	A	Pts	AG	AA	APts	PIM	PP	SH	GW	S	%	TGF	PGF	TGA	PGA	+/–	GP	G	A	Pts	PIM	PP	SH	GW
1988-89	Lethbridge Hurricanes	WHL	57	14	13	27	....	....	....	34	....	....	....	....	....	....	....	....	....	....	....	....	....	....	....	....	....	....
1989-90	Lethbridge Hurricanes	WHL	54	14	16	30	....	....	....	36	....	....	....	....	....	....	....	....	....	....	19	7	3	10	0	....	....	....
1990-91	Lethbridge Hurricanes	WHL	4	2	2	4	....	....	....	16	....	....	....	....	....	....	....	....	....	....	....	....	....	....	....	....	....	....
	Seattle Thunderbirds	WHL	61	42	42	84	....	....	....	69	....	....	....	....	....	....	....	....	....	....	6	5	3	8	4	....	....	....
1991-92	Kalamazoo Wings	IHL	60	5	14	19	....	....	....	26	....	....	....	....	....	....	....	....	....	....	....	....	....	....	....	....	....	....
1992-93	**Minnesota North Stars**	**NHL**	**2**	**0**	**0**	**0**	**0**	**0**	**0**	**2**	**0**	**0**	**0**	**0**	**0.0**	**0**	**0**	**1**	**0**	**–1**	....	....	....	....	....	....	....	....
	Kalamazoo Wings	IHL	78	32	34	66	....	....	....	74	....	....	....	....	....	....	....	....	....	....	....	....	....	....	....	....	....	....
1993-94	**Florida Panthers**	**NHL**	**2**	**0**	**0**	**0**	**0**	**0**	**0**	**0**	**0**	**0**	**0**	**2**	**0.0**	**0**	**0**	**2**	**0**	**–2**	....	....	....	....	....	....	....	....
	Cincinnati Cyclones	IHL	75	36	28	64	....	....	....	59	....	....	....	....	....	....	....	....	....	....	9	8	2	10	0	....	....	....
1994-95	Cincinnati Cyclones	IHL	74	20	40	60	....	....	....	57	....	....	....	....	....	....	....	....	....	....	10	2	6	8	20	....	....	....
1995-96	Atlanta Knights	IHL	19	5	9	14	....	....	....	16	....	....	....	....	....	....	....	....	....	....	....	....	....	....	....	....	....	....
	Chicago Wolves	IHL	54	12	18	30	....	....	....	39	....	....	....	....	....	....	....	....	....	....	9	2	3	5	6	....	....	....
1996-97	Chicago Wolves	IHL	16	3	5	8	....	....	....	12	....	....	....	....	....	....	....	....	....	....	....	....	....	....	....	....	....	....
1997-98	Chicago Wolves	IHL	63	9	16	25	....	....	....	26	....	....	....	....	....	....	....	....	....	....	1	0	0	0	0	....	....	....
	United States	WC-A	1	0	0	0	....	....	....	0	....	....	....	....	....	....	....	....	....	....	....	....	....	....	....	....	....	....
	NHL Totals		**4**	**0**	**0**	**0**	**0**	**0**	**0**	**2**	**0**	**0**	**0**	**2**	**0.0**	**0**	**0**	**3**	**0**		....	....	....	....	....	....	....	....

WHL West Second All-Star Team (1991)

Transferred to **Dallas** after **Minnesota** franchise relocated, June 9, 1993. Claimed by **Florida** from **Dallas** in Expansion Draft, June 24, 1993.

● BARRETT, FRED

Fred Barrett D – L. 5'11", 195 lbs. b: Ottawa, Ont., 1/26/1950. Minnesota's 2nd choice, 20th overall, in 1970 Amateur Draft.

Season	Club	League	GP	G	A	Pts	AG	AA	APts	PIM	PP	SH	GW	S	%	TGF	PGF	TGA	PGA	+/–	GP	G	A	Pts	PIM	PP	SH	GW
1966-67	Ottawa Capitals	Jr. B	STATISTICS NOT AVAILABLE																									
	Toronto Marlboros	OHA	2	0	0	0	....	....	....	2	....	....	....	....	....	....	....	....	....	....	9	0	0	0	2	....	....	....
1967-68	Toronto Marlboros	OHA	51	5	8	13	....	....	....	98	....	....	....	....	....	....	....	....	....	....	5	0	0	0	22	....	....	....
1968-69	Toronto Marlboros	OHA	52	3	17	20	....	....	....	113	....	....	....	....	....	....	....	....	....	....	6	1	2	3	15	....	....	....
1969-70	Toronto Marlboros	OHA	48	8	20	28	....	....	....	146	....	....	....	....	....	....	....	....	....	....	....	....	....	....	....	....	....	....
1970-71	**Minnesota North Stars**	**NHL**	**57**	**0**	**13**	**13**	**0**	**11**	**11**	**75**	**0**	**0**	**0**	**75**	**0.0**	**58**	**1**	**70**	**15**	**+2**	....	....	....	....	....	....	....	....
1971-72	Cleveland Barons	AHL	51	2	27	29	....	....	....	91	....	....	....	....	....	....	....	....	....	....	1	0	0	0	2	....	....	....
1972-73	**Minnesota North Stars**	**NHL**	**46**	**2**	**4**	**6**	**2**	**3**	**5**	**21**	**0**	**0**	**0**	**51**	**3.9**	**49**	**0**	**51**	**16**	**+14**	**6**	**0**	**0**	**0**	**4**	**0**	**0**	**0**
1973-74	**Minnesota North Stars**	**NHL**	**40**	**0**	**7**	**7**	**0**	**6**	**6**	**12**	**0**	**0**	**0**	**31**	**0.0**	**24**	**0**	**30**	**5**	**–1**	....	....	....	....	....	....	....	....
1974-75	**Minnesota North Stars**	**NHL**	**62**	**3**	**18**	**21**	**3**	**14**	**17**	**82**	**0**	**0**	**0**	**79**	**3.8**	**68**	**4**	**123**	**38**	**–21**	....	....	....	....	....	....	....	....
1975-76	**Minnesota North Stars**	**NHL**	**79**	**2**	**9**	**11**	**2**	**7**	**9**	**66**	**0**	**0**	**1**	**70**	**2.9**	**62**	**3**	**133**	**49**	**–25**	....	....	....	....	....	....	....	....
1976-77	**Minnesota North Stars**	**NHL**	**60**	**1**	**8**	**9**	**1**	**6**	**7**	**46**	**0**	**0**	**0**	**54**	**1.9**	**42**	**4**	**86**	**17**	**–31**	**2**	**0**	**0**	**0**	**2**	**0**	**0**	**0**
1977-78	**Minnesota North Stars**	**NHL**	**79**	**0**	**15**	**15**	**0**	**12**	**12**	**59**	**0**	**0**	**0**	**87**	**0.0**	**65**	**1**	**140**	**41**	**–35**	....	....	....	....	....	....	....	....
1978-79	**Minnesota North Stars**	**NHL**	**45**	**1**	**9**	**10**	**1**	**7**	**8**	**48**	**0**	**0**	**0**	**36**	**2.8**	**44**	**2**	**57**	**11**	**–4**	....	....	....	....	....	....	....	....
1979-80	**Minnesota North Stars**	**NHL**	**80**	**8**	**14**	**22**	**7**	**11**	**18**	**71**	**0**	**0**	**0**	**85**	**9.4**	**80**	**1**	**88**	**26**	**+17**	**14**	**0**	**0**	**0**	**22**	**0**	**0**	**0**
1980-81	**Minnesota North Stars**	**NHL**	**62**	**4**	**8**	**12**	**3**	**6**	**9**	**72**	**0**	**0**	**1**	**73**	**5.5**	**56**	**2**	**74**	**21**	**+1**	**14**	**0**	**1**	**1**	**16**	**0**	**0**	**0**
1981-82	**Minnesota North Stars**	**NHL**	**69**	**1**	**15**	**16**	**1**	**10**	**11**	**89**	**0**	**0**	**0**	**43**	**2.3**	**66**	**0**	**101**	**23**	**–12**	**4**	**0**	**1**	**1**	**16**	**0**	**0**	**0**
1982-83	**Minnesota North Stars**	**NHL**	**51**	**1**	**3**	**4**	**1**	**2**	**3**	**22**	**0**	**0**	**0**	**29**	**3.4**	**25**	**0**	**48**	**13**	**–10**	**4**	**0**	**0**	**0**	**0**	**0**	**0**	**0**
1983-84	**Los Angeles Kings**	**NHL**	**15**	**2**	**0**	**2**	**2**	**0**	**2**	**8**	**0**	**0**	**0**	**4**	**50.0**	**12**	**0**	**15**	**1**	**–2**	....	....	....	....	....	....	....	....
	NHL Totals		**745**	**25**	**123**	**148**	**23**	**95**	**118**	**671**	**0**	**0**	**2**	**717**	**3.5**	**651**	**18**	**1016**	**276**		**44**	**0**	**2**	**2**	**60**	**0**	**0**	**0**

Traded to **LA Kings** by **Minnesota** for future considerations, September 30, 1983.

● BARRETT, JOHN

John Barrett D – L. 6'1", 210 lbs. b: Ottawa, Ont., 7/1/1958. Detroit's 10th choice, 129th overall, in 1978 Amateur Draft.

Season	Club	League	GP	G	A	Pts	AG	AA	APts	PIM	PP	SH	GW	S	%	TGF	PGF	TGA	PGA	+/–	GP	G	A	Pts	PIM	PP	SH	GW
1976-77	Windsor Spitfires	OHA	63	7	17	24	....	....	....	168	....	....	....	....	....	....	....	....	....	....	9	1	1	2	12	....	....	....
1977-78	Windsor Spitfires	OHA	67	8	18	26	....	....	....	133	....	....	....	....	....	....	....	....	....	....	6	2	1	3	30	....	....	....
1978-79	Milwaukee Admirals	IHL	42	8	13	21	....	....	....	117	....	....	....	....	....	....	....	....	....	....	....	....	....	....	....	....	....	....
	Kalamazoo Wings	IHL	31	1	12	13	....	....	....	54	....	....	....	....	....	....	....	....	....	....	15	2	11	13	48	....	....	....
1979-80	Kalamazoo Wings	IHL	52	8	33	41	....	....	....	63	....	....	....	....	....	....	....	....	....	....	....	....	....	....	....	....	....	....
	Adirondack Red Wings	AHL	28	0	4	4	....	....	....	59	....	....	....	....	....	....	....	....	....	....	5	1	2	3	6	....	....	....
1980-81	**Detroit Red Wings**	**NHL**	**56**	**3**	**10**	**13**	**2**	**7**	**9**	**60**	**0**	**0**	**1**	**97**	**3.1**	**51**	**3**	**111**	**42**	**–21**	....	....	....	....	....	....	....	....
	Adirondack Red Wings	AHL	21	4	11	15	....	....	....	63	....	....	....	....	....	....	....	....	....	....	....	....	....	....	....	....	....	....
1981-82	**Detroit Red Wings**	**NHL**	**69**	**1**	**12**	**13**	**1**	**8**	**9**	**93**	**0**	**0**	**0**	**97**	**1.0**	**55**	**1**	**111**	**26**	**–31**	....	....	....	....	....	....	....	....
1982-83	**Detroit Red Wings**	**NHL**	**79**	**4**	**10**	**14**	**3**	**7**	**10**	**74**	**0**	**0**	**0**	**72**	**5.6**	**67**	**1**	**109**	**25**	**–18**	....	....	....	....	....	....	....	....
1983-84	**Detroit Red Wings**	**NHL**	**78**	**2**	**8**	**10**	**2**	**5**	**7**	**78**	**0**	**0**	**0**	**63**	**3.2**	**71**	**1**	**95**	**25**	**0**	**4**	**0**	**0**	**0**	**4**	**0**	**0**	**0**
1984-85	**Detroit Red Wings**	**NHL**	**71**	**6**	**19**	**25**	**5**	**13**	**18**	**117**	**0**	**0**	**1**	**72**	**8.3**	**63**	**1**	**106**	**29**	**–15**	**3**	**0**	**1**	**1**	**11**	**0**	**0**	**0**
1985-86	**Detroit Red Wings**	**NHL**	**65**	**2**	**12**	**14**	**2**	**8**	**10**	**125**	**0**	**0**	**0**	**60**	**3.3**	**57**	**2**	**122**	**38**	**–29**	....	....	....	....	....	....	....	....
	Washington Capitals	**NHL**	**14**	**0**	**3**	**3**	**0**	**2**	**2**	**12**	**0**	**0**	**0**	**7**	**0.0**	**10**	**0**	**7**	**0**	**+3**	**9**	**2**	**1**	**3**	**35**	**0**	**0**	**1**
1986-87	**Washington Capitals**	**NHL**	**55**	**2**	**2**	**4**	**2**	**1**	**3**	**43**	**0**	**0**	**0**	**37**	**5.4**	**25**	**2**	**47**	**8**	**–16**	....	....	....	....	....	....	....	....

			REGULAR SEASON																		PLAYOFFS							
Season	Club	League	GP	G	A	Pts	AG	AA	APts	PIM	PP	SH	GW	S	%	TGF	PGF	TGA	PGA	+/-	GP	G	A	Pts	PIM	PP	SH	GW
1987-88	Binghamton Whalers	AHL	5	0	2	2	....	....	....	6	....	....	....	....	....	....	....	....	....	....	....	....	....	....	....	....	....	....
	Minnesota North Stars	NHL	1	0	1	1	0	1	1	2	0	0	0	0	0.0	0	0	3	0	−3	....	....	....	....	....	....	....	....
	Kalamazoo Wings	IHL	2	0	1	1	....	....	....	2	....	....	....	....	....	....	....	....	....	....	....	....	....	....	....	....	....	....
	NHL Totals		488	20	77	97	17	52	69	604	0	0	2	505	4.0	399	11	711	193		16	2	2	4	50	0	0	1

Traded to **Washington** by **Detroit** with Greg Smith for Darren Veitch, March 10, 1986. Traded to **Minnesota** by **Washington** for future considerations, February 22, 1988.

• BARRIE, DOUG

Doug Barrie D – R. 5'9", 175 lbs. b: Edmonton, Alta., 10/2/1946.

Season	Club	League	GP	G	A	Pts	AG	AA	APts	PIM	PP	SH	GW	S	%	TGF	PGF	TGA	PGA	+/-	GP	G	A	Pts	PIM	PP	SH	GW
1965-66	Edmonton Oil Kings	ASHL	....	2	7	9	....	....	....	80	....	....	....	....	....	....	....	....	....	....	....	....	....	....	....	....	....	....
1966-67	Memphis Wings	CHL	11	1	5	6	....	....	....	14	....	....	....	....	....	....	....	....	....	....	....	....	....	....	....	....	....	....
	Pittsburgh Hornets	AHL	27	0	2	2	....	....	....	6	....	....	....	....	....	....	....	....	....	....	....	....	....	....	....	....	....	....
1967-68	Kansas City–Omaha–Tulsa	CHL	63	1	14	15	....	....	....	171	....	....	....	....	....	....	....	....	....	....	11	1	5	6	*55	....	....	....
1968-69	Pittsburgh Penguins	NHL	8	1	1	2	1	1	2	8	0	0	0	10	10.0	4	1	6	1	−2	....	....	....	....	....	....	....	....
	Amarillo Wranglers	CHL	66	7	29	36	....	....	....	163	....	....	....	....	....	....	....	....	....	....	....	....	....	....	....	....	....	....
1969-70	Baltimore Clippers	AHL	70	5	9	14	....	....	....	139	....	....	....	....	....	....	....	....	....	....	5	2	6	8	10	....	....	....
1970-71	Buffalo Sabres	NHL	75	4	23	27	4	20	24	168	0	0	0	128	3.1	82	7	117	23	−19	....	....	....	....	....	....	....	....
1971-72	Buffalo Sabres	NHL	27	2	5	7	2	5	7	45	0	0	1	24	8.3	17	1	44	7	−21	....	....	....	....	....	....	....	....
	Los Angeles Kings	NHL	48	3	13	16	3	12	15	47	1	0	0	69	4.3	56	11	61	6	−10	....	....	....	....	....	....	....	....
1972-73	Alberta Oilers	WHA	54	9	22	31	....	....	....	111	....	....	....	....	....	....	....	....	....	....	....	....	....	....	....	....	....	....
1973-74	Edmonton Oilers	WHA	69	4	27	31	....	....	....	214	....	....	....	....	....	....	....	....	....	....	4	1	0	1	16	....	....	....
1974-75	Edmonton Oilers	WHA	78	12	33	45	....	....	....	122	....	....	....	....	....	....	....	....	....	....	....	....	....	....	....	....	....	....
1975-76	Edmonton Oilers	WHA	79	4	21	25	....	....	....	81	....	....	....	....	....	....	....	....	....	....	4	0	1	1	15	....	....	....
1976-77	Edmonton Oilers	WHA	70	8	19	27	....	....	....	92	....	....	....	....	....	....	....	....	....	....	4	0	0	0	0	....	....	....
	NHL Totals		158	10	42	52	10	38	48	268	1	0	1	231	4.3	159	20	228	37		....	....	....	....	....	....	....	....
	Other Major League Totals		350	37	122	159	....	....	....	620	....	....	....	....	....	....	....	....	....		12	1	1	2	31	....	....	....

CHL Second All-Star Team (1969)

Traded to **Toronto** by **Detroit** for cash, March 8, 1968. Traded to **Detroit** by **Toronto** for cash, June 6, 1968. Traded to **Pittsburgh** by **Detroit** for cash, October, 1968. Claimed by **Buffalo** from **Pittsburgh** in Expansion Draft, June 10, 1970. Traded to **LA Kings** by **Buffalo** with Mike Keeler for Mike Byers and Larry Hillman, December 16, 1971. Selected by **Alberta** (WHA) in 1972 WHA General Player Draft, February 12, 1972.

• BARRIE, LEN

Len Barrie C – L. 6', 200 lbs. b: Kimberley, B.C., 6/4/1969. Edmonton's 7th choice, 124th overall, in 1988 Entry Draft.

Season	Club	League	GP	G	A	Pts	AG	AA	APts	PIM	PP	SH	GW	S	%	TGF	PGF	TGA	PGA	+/-	GP	G	A	Pts	PIM	PP	SH	GW
1985-86	Calgary Wranglers	WHL	32	3	0	3	....	....	....	18	....	....	....	....	....	....	....	....	....	....	....	....	....	....	....	....	....	....
1986-87	Calgary Wranglers	WHL	34	13	13	26	....	....	....	81	....	....	....	....	....	....	....	....	....	....	....	....	....	....	....	....	....	....
	Victoria Cougars	WHL	34	7	6	13	....	....	....	92	....	....	....	....	....	....	....	....	....	....	5	0	1	1	15	....	....	....
1987-88	Victoria Cougars	WHL	70	37	49	86	....	....	....	192	....	....	....	....	....	....	....	....	....	....	8	2	0	2	29	....	....	....
1988-89	Victoria Cougars	WHL	67	39	48	87	....	....	....	157	....	....	....	....	....	....	....	....	....	....	7	5	2	7	23	....	....	....
1989-90	Kamloops Blazers	WHL	70	*85	*100	*185	....	....	....	108	....	....	....	....	....	....	....	....	....	....	17	*14	23	*37	24	....	....	....
	Philadelphia Flyers	NHL	1	0	0	0	0	0	0	0	0	0	0	0	0.0	0	0	2	0	−2	....	....	....	....	....	....	....	....
1990-91	Hershey Bears	AHL	63	26	32	58	....	....	....	60	....	....	....	....	....	....	....	....	....	....	7	4	0	4	12	....	....	....
1991-92	Hershey Bears	AHL	75	42	43	85	....	....	....	78	....	....	....	....	....	....	....	....	....	....	3	0	2	2	32	....	....	....
1992-93	Philadelphia Flyers	NHL	8	2	2	4	2	1	3	9	0	0	0	14	14.3	5	0	3	0	+2	....	....	....	....	....	....	....	....
	Hershey Bears	AHL	61	31	45	76	....	....	....	162	....	....	....	....	....	....	....	....	....	....	....	....	....	....	....	....	....	....
1993-94	Florida Panthers	NHL	2	0	0	0	0	0	0	0	0	0	0	0	0.0	0	0	2	0	−2	....	....	....	....	....	....	....	....
	Cincinnati Cyclones	IHL	77	45	71	116	....	....	....	246	....	....	....	....	....	....	....	....	....	....	11	8	13	21	60	....	....	....
1994-95	Cleveland Lumberjacks	IHL	28	13	30	43	....	....	....	137	....	....	....	....	....	....	....	....	....	....	....	....	....	....	....	....	....	....
	Pittsburgh Penguins	NHL	48	3	11	14	5	16	21	66	0	0	1	37	8.1	19	4	21	2	−4	4	1	0	1	8	1	0	0
1995-96	Pittsburgh Penguins	NHL	5	0	0	0	0	0	0	18	0	0	0	5	0.0	0	0	1	0	−1	....	....	....	....	....	....	....	....
	Cleveland Lumberjacks	IHL	55	29	43	72	....	....	....	178	....	....	....	....	....	....	....	....	....	....	3	2	3	5	6	....	....	....
1996-97	San Antonio Dragons	IHL	57	26	40	66	....	....	....	196	....	....	....	....	....	....	....	....	....	....	9	5	5	10	20	....	....	....
1997-98	San Antonio Dragons	IHL	32	7	13	20	....	....	....	90	....	....	....	....	....	....	....	....	....	....	....	....	....	....	....	....	....	....
	Frankfurt Lions	Germany	25	11	19	30	....	....	....	32	....	....	....	....	....	....	....	....	....	....	6	2	3	5	35	....	....	....
	NHL Totals		64	5	13	18	7	17	24	93	0	0	1	56	8.9	24	4	29	2		4	1	0	1	8	1	0	0

WHL West First All-Star Team (1990) • IHL Second All-Star Team (1994)

Signed as a free agent by **Philadelphia**, February 28, 1990. Signed as a free agent by **Florida**, July 20, 1993. Signed as a free agent by **Pittsburgh**, August 15, 1994.

• BARTEL, ROBIN

Robin Bartel D – L. 6', 200 lbs. b: Drake, Sask., 5/16/1961.

Season	Club	League	GP	G	A	Pts	AG	AA	APts	PIM	PP	SH	GW	S	%	TGF	PGF	TGA	PGA	+/-	GP	G	A	Pts	PIM	PP	SH	GW
1980-81	Prince Albert Raiders	SJHL	86	22	63	85	....	....	....	....	....	....	....	....	....	....	....	....	....	....	....	....	....	....	....	....	....	....
1981-82	Prince Albert Raiders	SJHL	83	17	73	90	....	....	....	....	....	....	....	....	....	....	....	....	....	....	....	....	....	....	....	....	....	....
1982-83	University of Saskatchewan	CWUAA	24	4	14	18	....	....	....	36	....	....	....	....	....	....	....	....	....	....	....	....	....	....	....	....	....	....
1983-84	Canada	Nat-Team	51	4	6	10	....	....	....	60	....	....	....	....	....	....	....	....	....	....	....	....	....	....	....	....	....	....
	Canada	Olympics	6	0	1	1	....	....	....	4	....	....	....	....	....	....	....	....	....	....	....	....	....	....	....	....	....	....
1984-85	Moncton Golden Flames	AHL	41	4	11	15	....	....	....	54	....	....	....	....	....	....	....	....	....	....	....	....	....	....	....	....	....	....
1985-86	Calgary Flames	NHL	1	0	0	0	0	0	0	0	0	0	0	0	0.0	0	0	1	0	−1	6	0	0	0	16	0	0	0
	Moncton Golden Flames	AHL	74	4	21	25	....	....	....	100	....	....	....	....	....	....	....	....	....	....	3	0	0	0	0	....	....	....
1986-87	Vancouver Canucks	NHL	40	0	1	1	0	1	1	14	0	0	0	16	0.0	27	1	31	7	+2	....	....	....	....	....	....	....	....
	Fredericton Express	AHL	10	0	2	2	....	....	....	15	....	....	....	....	....	....	....	....	....	....	....	....	....	....	....	....	....	....
1987-88	Fredericton Express	AHL	37	1	10	11	....	....	....	54	....	....	....	....	....	....	....	....	....	....	3	0	0	0	9	....	....	....
1988-89	Moncton Hawks	AHL	23	0	4	4	....	....	....	19	....	....	....	....	....	....	....	....	....	....	10	0	1	1	18	....	....	....
	Milwaukee Admirals	IHL	26	1	5	6	....	....	....	59	....	....	....	....	....	....	....	....	....	....	....	....	....	....	....	....	....	....
1989-90	Canada	Nat-Team	23	1	1	2	....	....	....	10	....	....	....	....	....	....	....	....	....	....	....	....	....	....	....	....	....	....
	Medway Bears	Britain	16	8	19	27	....	....	....	32	....	....	....	....	....	....	....	....	....	....	....	....	....	....	....	....	....	....
	NHL Totals		41	0	1	1	0	1	1	14	0	0	0	16	0.0	27	1	32	7		6	0	0	0	16	0	0	0

Signed as a free agent by **Calgary**, July 1, 1985. Signed as a free agent by **Vancouver**, June 27, 1986.

• BASSEN, BOB

Bob Bassen C – L. 5'10", 185 lbs. b: Calgary, Alta., 5/6/1965.

Season	Club	League	GP	G	A	Pts	AG	AA	APts	PIM	PP	SH	GW	S	%	TGF	PGF	TGA	PGA	+/-	GP	G	A	Pts	PIM	PP	SH	GW
1982-83	Medicine Hat Tigers	WHL	4	3	2	5	....	....	....	0	....	....	....	....	....	....	....	....	....	....	3	0	0	0	4	....	....	....
1983-84	Medicine Hat Tigers	WHL	72	29	29	58	....	....	....	93	....	....	....	....	....	....	....	....	....	....	14	5	11	16	12	....	....	....
1984-85	Medicine Hat Tigers	WHL	65	32	50	02	....	....	....	143	....	....	....	....	....	....	....	....	....	....	10	2	8	10	39	....	....	....
	Canada	WJC-A	7	2	0	2	....	....	....	8	....	....	....	....	....	....	....	....	....	....	....	....	....	....	....	....	....	....
1985-86	New York Islanders	NHL	11	2	1	3	2	1	3	6	0	0	0	5	40.0	3	0	5	2	0	3	0	1	1	0	0	0	0
	Springfield Indians	AHL	54	13	21	34	....	....	....	111	....	....	....	....	....	....	....	....	....	....	....	....	....	....	....	....	....	....
1986-87	New York Islanders	NHL	77	7	10	17	6	7	13	89	0	0	1	59	11.9	23	0	54	14	−17	14	1	2	3	21	0	0	0
1987-88	New York Islanders	NHL	77	6	16	22	5	11	16	99	1	0	2	65	9.2	41	3	49	19	+8	6	0	1	1	23	0	0	0
1988-89	New York Islanders	NHL	19	1	4	5	1	3	4	21	0	0	0	14	7.1	8	1	13	6	0	....	....	....	....	....	....	....	....
	Chicago Blackhawks	NHL	49	4	12	16	3	8	11	62	0	0	1	37	10.8	22	0	34	17	+5	10	1	1	2	34	0	0	0
1989-90	Chicago Blackhawks	NHL	6	1	1	2	1	1	2	8	0	0	0	7	14.3	2	0	1	0	+1	1	0	0	0	2	0	0	0
	Indianapolis Ice	IHL	73	22	32	54	....	....	....	179	....	....	....	....	....	....	....	....	....	....	12	3	8	11	33	....	....	....
1990-91	St. Louis Blues	NHL	79	16	18	34	15	14	29	183	0	2	1	117	13.7	56	1	65	27	+17	13	1	3	4	24	0	0	0
1991-92	St. Louis Blues	NHL	79	7	25	32	6	19	25	167	0	0	1	101	6.9	53	2	57	18	+12	6	0	2	2	4	0	0	0
	Canada	WC-A	3	1	1	2	....	....	....	0	....	....	....	....	....	....	....	....	....	....	....	....	....	....	....	....	....	....
1992-93	St. Louis Blues	NHL	53	9	10	19	7	7	14	63	0	1	0	61	14.8	34	1	54	21	0	11	0	0	0	10	0	0	0
1993-94	St. Louis Blues	NHL	46	2	7	9	2	5	7	44	0	1	0	73	2.7	18	0	50	18	−14	....	....	....	....	....	....	....	....
	Quebec Nordiques	NHL	37	11	8	19	10	6	16	55	1	0	0	56	19.6	28	4	41	14	−3	....	....	....	....	....	....	....	....
1994-95	Quebec Nordiques	NHL	47	12	15	27	21	22	43	33	0	1	1	66	18.2	37	0	33	10	+14	5	2	4	6	0	0	0	0

			REGULAR SEASON																		PLAYOFFS							
Season	**Club**	**League**	**GP**	**G**	**A**	**Pts**	**AG**	**AA**	**APts**	**PIM**	**PP**	**SH**	**GW**	**S**	**%**	**TGF**	**PGF**	**TGA**	**PGA**	**+/–**	**GP**	**G**	**A**	**Pts**	**PIM**	**PP**	**SH**	**GW**
1995-96	**Dallas Stars**	**NHL**	**13**	**0**	**1**	**1**	**0**	**1**	**1**	**15**	**0**	**0**	**0**	**9**	**0.0**	**3**	**0**	**12**	**3**	**–6**	....	....	....	....	....	....	....	....
	Michigan K-Wings	IHL	1	0	0	0	....	....	....	4	....	....	....	....	....	....	....	....	....	....	....	....	....	....	....	....	....	....
1996-97	**Dallas Stars**	**NHL**	**46**	**5**	**7**	**12**	**5**	**6**	**11**	**41**	**0**	**0**	**2**	**50**	**10.0**	**22**	**0**	**19**	**2**	**+5**	**7**	**3**	**1**	**4**	**4**	**0**	**0**	**0**
1997-98	**Dallas Stars**	**NHL**	**58**	**3**	**4**	**7**	**4**	**4**	**8**	**57**	**0**	**0**	**1**	**40**	**7.5**	**10**	**0**	**19**	**5**	**–4**	**17**	**1**	**0**	**1**	**12**	**0**	**0**	**0**
	NHL Totals		**697**	**86**	**139**	**225**	**88**	**115**	**203**	**943**	**2**	**5**	**10**	**760**	**11.3**	**360**	**12**	**506**	**176**		**93**	**9**	**15**	**24**	**134**	**0**	**0**	**0**

WHL First All-Star Team (1985) • IHL First All-Star Team (1990)

Signed as a free agent by **NY Islanders**, October 19, 1984. Traded to **Chicago** by **NY Islanders** with Steve Konroyd for Marc Bergevin and Gary Nylund, November 25, 1988. Claimed by **St. Louis** from **Chicago** in NHL Waiver Draft, October 1, 1990. Traded to **Quebec** by **St. Louis** with Garth Butcher and Ron Sutter for Steve Duchesne and Denis Chasse, January 23, 1994. Signed as a free agent by **Dallas**, August 10, 1995. Traded to **Calgary** by **Dallas** for Aaron Gavey, July 14, 1998.

• BATES, SHAWN

Shawn Bates C – R. 5'11", 205 lbs. b: Melrose, MA, 4/3/1975. Boston's 4th choice, 103rd overall, in 1993 Entry Draft.

Season	Club	League	GP	G	A	Pts	AG	AA	APts	PIM	PP	SH	GW	S	%	TGF	PGF	TGA	PGA	+/–	GP	G	A	Pts	PIM	PP	SH	GW
1992-93	Medford-Mass High School	H.S.	25	49	46	95	....	....	....	20	....	....	....	....	....	....	....	....	....	....	....	....	....	....	....	....	....	....
1993-94	Boston University	H.E.	41	10	19	29	....	....	....	24	....	....	....	....	....	....	....	....	....	....	....	....	....	....	....	....	....	....
1994-95	Boston University	H.E.	38	18	12	30	....	....	....	48	....	....	....	....	....	....	....	....	....	....	....	....	....	....	....	....	....	....
	United States	WJC-A	7	5	1	6	....	....	....	2	....	....	....	....	....	....	....	....	....	....	....	....	....	....	....	....	....	....
1995-96	Boston University	H.E.	40	28	22	50	....	....	....	54	....	....	....	....	....	....	....	....	....	....	....	....	....	....	....	....	....	....
1996-97	Boston University	H.E.	41	17	18	35	....	....	....	64	....	....	....	....	....	....	....	....	....	....	....	....	....	....	....	....	....	....
1997-98	**Boston Bruins**	**NHL**	**13**	**2**	**0**	**2**	**2**	**0**	**2**	**2**	**0**	**0**	**0**	**12**	**16.7**	**3**	**1**	**6**	**1**	**–3**	....	....	....	....	....	....	....	....
	Providence Bruins	AHL	50	15	19	34	....	....	....	22	....	....	....	....	....	....	....	....	....	....	....	....	....	....	....	....	....	....
	NHL Totals		**13**	**2**	**0**	**2**	**2**	**0**	**2**	**2**	**0**	**0**	**0**	**12**	**16.7**	**3**	**1**	**6**	**1**		....	....	....	....	....	....	....	....

NCAA Championship All-Tournament Team (1995)

• BATHE, FRANK

Frank Bathe D – L. 6'1", 185 lbs. b: Oshawa, Ont., 9/27/1954.

Season	Club	League	GP	G	A	Pts	AG	AA	APts	PIM	PP	SH	GW	S	%	TGF	PGF	TGA	PGA	+/–	GP	G	A	Pts	PIM	PP	SH	GW
1972-73	Windsor Spitfires	SOJHL	59	10	25	35	....	....	....	232	....	....	....	....	....	....	....	....	....	....	....	....	....	....	....	....	....	....
1973-74	Windsor Spitfires	SOJHL	58	19	34	53	....	....	....	306	....	....	....	....	....	....	....	....	....	....	....	....	....	....	....	....	....	....
1974-75	**Detroit Red Wings**	**NHL**	**19**	**0**	**3**	**3**	**0**	**2**	**2**	**31**	**0**	**0**	**0**	**7**	**0.0**	**12**	**1**	**16**	**0**	**–5**	....	....	....	....	....	....	....	....
	Virginia Wings	AHL	50	7	11	18	....	....	....	146	....	....	....	....	....	....	....	....	....	....	....	....	....	....	....	....	....	....
1975-76	**Detroit Red Wings**	**NHL**	**7**	**0**	**1**	**1**	**0**	**1**	**1**	**9**	**0**	**0**	**0**	**6**	**0.0**	**2**	**0**	**7**	**4**	**–1**	....	....	....	....	....	....	....	....
	New Haven Nighthawks	AHL	7	0	1	1	....	....	....	24	....	....	....	....	....	....	....	....	....	....	....	....	....	....	....	....	....	....
	Kalamazoo Wings	IHL	14	0	5	5	....	....	....	46	....	....	....	....	....	....	....	....	....	....	....	....	....	....	....	....	....	....
	Port Huron Flags	IHL	43	2	3	5	....	....	....	148	....	....	....	....	....	....	....	....	....	....	15	0	4	4	54	....	....	....
1976-77	Port Huron Flags	IHL	71	7	30	37	....	....	....	250	....	....	....	....	....	....	....	....	....	....	....	....	....	....	....	....	....	....
1977-78	**Philadelphia Flyers**	**NHL**	**1**	**0**	**0**	**0**	**0**	**0**	**0**	**0**	**0**	**0**	**0**	**0**	**0.0**	**0**	**0**	**0**	**0**	**0**	....	....	....	....	....	....	....	....
	Maine Mariners	AHL	78	4	11	15	....	....	....	159	....	....	....	....	....	....	....	....	....	....	12	1	1	2	24	....	....	....
1978-79	**Philadelphia Flyers**	**NHL**	**21**	**1**	**3**	**4**	**1**	**2**	**3**	**76**	**0**	**0**	**0**	**10**	**10.0**	**15**	**0**	**12**	**6**	**+9**	**6**	**1**	**0**	**1**	**12**	**0**	**0**	**0**
	Maine Mariners	AHL	26	3	3	6	....	....	....	106	....	....	....	....	....	....	....	....	....	....	....	....	....	....	....	....	....	....
1979-80	**Philadelphia Flyers**	**NHL**	**47**	**0**	**7**	**7**	**0**	**5**	**5**	**111**	**0**	**0**	**0**	**34**	**0.0**	**45**	**0**	**47**	**9**	**+7**	**1**	**0**	**0**	**0**	**0**	**0**	**0**	**0**
1980-81	**Philadelphia Flyers**	**NHL**	**44**	**0**	**3**	**3**	**0**	**2**	**2**	**175**	**0**	**0**	**0**	**35**	**0.0**	**20**	**1**	**42**	**20**	**–3**	**12**	**0**	**3**	**3**	**16**	**0**	**0**	**0**
1981-82	**Philadelphia Flyers**	**NHL**	**28**	**1**	**3**	**4**	**1**	**2**	**3**	**68**	**0**	**0**	**0**	**36**	**2.8**	**31**	**1**	**33**	**14**	**+11**	**4**	**0**	**0**	**0**	**2**	**0**	**0**	**0**
1982-83	**Philadelphia Flyers**	**NHL**	**57**	**1**	**8**	**9**	**1**	**6**	**7**	**72**	**0**	**0**	**0**	**60**	**1.7**	**37**	**0**	**49**	**16**	**+4**	**3**	**0**	**0**	**0**	**12**	**0**	**0**	**0**
1983-84	Maine Mariners	AHL	4	1	0	1	....	....	....	2	....	....	....	....	....	....	....	....	....	....	....	....	....	....	....	....	....	....
	Philadelphia Flyers	**NHL**	....	....	....	....	....	....	....	....	....	....	....	....	....	....	....	....	....	....	**1**	**0**	**0**	**0**	**0**	....	....	....
	NHL Totals		**224**	**3**	**28**	**31**	**3**	**20**	**23**	**542**	**0**	**0**	**0**	**188**	**1.6**	**162**	**3**	**206**	**69**		**27**	**1**	**3**	**4**	**42**	**0**	**0**	**0**

Signed as a free agent by **Detroit**, October 10, 1974. Signed as a free agent by **Philadelphia**, October 7, 1977.

• BATHGATE, ANDY

Andy Bathgate C – R. 5'8", 140 lbs. b: Winnipeg, Man., 8/28/1932. **HHOF**

Season	Club	League	GP	G	A	Pts	AG	AA	APts	PIM	PP	SH	GW	S	%	TGF	PGF	TGA	PGA	+/–	GP	G	A	Pts	PIM	PP	SH	GW
1948-49	Winnipeg Rangers	MJHL	1	0	0	0	....	....	....	0	....	....	....	....	....	....	....	....	....	....	....	....	....	....	....	....	....	....
1949-50	Guelph Biltmores	OHA	41	21	25	46	....	....	....	28	....	....	....	....	....	....	....	....	....	....	26	16	14	*30	20	....	....	....
1950-51	Guelph Biltmores	OHA	52	33	57	90	....	....	....	66	....	....	....	....	....	....	....	....	....	....	5	6	1	7	9	....	....	....
1951-52	Guelph Biltmores	OHA	34	27	50	77	....	....	....	20	....	....	....	....	....	....	....	....	....	....	23	14	22	36	39	....	....	....
1952-53	Guelph Biltmores	OHA	2	2	1	3	....	....	....	0	....	....	....	....	....	....	....	....	....	....	....	....	....	....	....	....	....	....
	New York Rangers	**NHL**	**18**	**0**	**1**	**1**	**0**	**1**	**1**	**6**	....	....	....	....	....	....	....	....	....	....	....	....	....	....	....	....	....	....
	Vancouver Canucks	WHL	37	13	13	26	....	....	....	29	....	....	....	....	....	....	....	....	....	....	9	11	4	15	2	....	....	....
1953-54	**New York Rangers**	**NHL**	**20**	**2**	**2**	**4**	**3**	**3**	**6**	**18**	....	....	....	....	....	....	....	....	....	....	....	....	....	....	....	....	....	....
	Vancouver Canucks	WHL	17	12	10	22	....	....	....	6	....	....	....	....	....	....	....	....	....	....	....	....	....	....	....	....	....	....
	Cleveland Barons	AHL	36	13	19	32	....	....	....	44	....	....	....	....	....	....	....	....	....	....	9	3	5	8	8	....	....	....
1954-55	**New York Rangers**	**NHL**	**70**	**20**	**20**	**40**	**29**	**26**	**55**	**37**	....	....	....	....	....	....	....	....	....	....	....	....	....	....	....	....	....	....
1955-56	**New York Rangers**	**NHL**	**70**	**19**	**47**	**66**	**28**	**60**	**88**	**59**	....	....	....	....	....	....	....	....	....	....	**5**	**1**	**2**	**3**	**2**	....	....	....
1956-57	**New York Rangers**	**NHL**	**70**	**27**	**50**	**77**	**37**	**59**	**96**	**60**	....	....	....	....	....	....	....	....	....	....	**5**	**2**	**0**	**2**	**27**	....	....	....
1957-58	**New York Rangers**	**NHL**	**65**	**30**	**48**	**78**	**40**	**53**	**93**	**42**	....	....	....	....	....	....	....	....	....	....	**6**	**5**	**3**	**8**	**6**	....	....	....
1958-59	**New York Rangers**	**NHL**	**70**	**40**	**48**	**88**	**52**	**52**	**104**	**48**	....	....	....	....	....	....	....	....	....	....	....	....	....	....	....	....	....	....
1959-60	**New York Rangers**	**NHL**	**70**	**26**	**48**	**74**	**33**	**50**	**83**	**28**	....	....	....	....	....	....	....	....	....	....	....	....	....	....	....	....	....	....
1960-61	**New York Rangers**	**NHL**	**70**	**29**	**48**	**77**	**36**	**49**	**85**	**22**	....	....	....	....	....	....	....	....	....	....	....	....	....	....	....	....	....	....
1961-62	**New York Rangers**	**NHL**	**70**	**28**	***56**	***84**	**34**	**57**	**91**	**44**	....	....	....	....	....	....	....	....	....	....	**6**	**1**	**2**	**3**	**4**	....	....	....
1962-63	**New York Rangers**	**NHL**	**70**	**35**	**46**	**81**	**44**	**49**	**93**	**54**	....	....	....	....	....	....	....	....	....	....	....	....	....	....	....	....	....	....
1963-64	**New York Rangers**	**NHL**	**56**	**16**	***43**	**59**	**21**	**48**	**69**	**26**	....	....	....	....	....	....	....	....	....	....	....	....	....	....	....	....	....	....
	Toronto Maple Leafs	**NHL**	**15**	**3**	***15**	**18**	**4**	**17**	**21**	**8**	....	....	....	....	....	....	....	....	....	....	**14**	**5**	**4**	**9**	**25**	....	....	....
1964-65	**Toronto Maple Leafs**	**NHL**	**55**	**16**	**29**	**45**	**20**	**31**	**51**	**34**	....	....	....	....	....	....	....	....	....	....	**6**	**1**	**0**	**1**	**6**	....	....	....
1965-66	**Detroit Red Wings**	**NHL**	**70**	**15**	**32**	**47**	**18**	**32**	**50**	**25**	....	....	....	....	....	....	....	....	....	....	**12**	***6**	**3**	**9**	**6**	....	....	....
1966-67	**Detroit Red Wings**	**NHL**	**60**	**8**	**23**	**31**	**10**	**24**	**34**	**24**	....	....	....	....	....	....	....	....	....	....	....	....	....	....	....	....	....	....
	Pittsburgh Hornets	AHL	6	4	6	10	....	....	....	7	....	....	....	....	....	....	....	....	....	....	....	....	....	....	....	....	....	....
1967-68	**Pittsburgh Penguins**	**NHL**	**74**	**20**	**39**	**59**	**25**	**41**	**66**	**55**	**2**	**0**	**4**	**293**	**6.8**	**86**	**28**	**69**	**0**	**–11**	....	....	....	....	....	....	....	....
1968-69	Vancouver Canucks	WHL	71	37	36	73	....	....	....	44	....	....	....	....	....	....	....	....	....	....	8	3	5	8	5	....	....	....
1969-70	Vancouver Canucks	WHL	72	40	68	108	....	....	....	66	....	....	....	....	....	....	....	....	....	....	16	7	5	12	8	....	....	....
1970-71	**Pittsburgh Penguins**	**NHL**	**76**	**15**	**29**	**44**	**16**	**26**	**42**	**34**	**7**	**0**	**3**	**209**	**7.2**	**68**	**31**	**48**	**0**	**–11**	....	....	....	....	....	....	....	....
1971-72	Ambri-Piotta	Switz.	DID NOT PLAY – COACHING																									
1972-73	Ambri-Piotta	Switz.	DID NOT PLAY – COACHING																									
1973-74	Ambri-Piotta	Switz.	DID NOT PLAY – COACHING																									
1974-75	Vancouver Blazers	WHA	11	1	6	7	....	....	....	2	....	....	....	....	....	....	....	....	....	....	....	....	....	....	....	....	....	....
	NHL Totals		**1069**	**349**	**624**	**973**	**450**	**678**	**1128**	**624**	**9**	**0**	**7**	**502**	**69.5**	**154**	**59**	**117**	**0**		**54**	**21**	**14**	**35**	**76**	**0**	**0**	**0**
	Other Major League Totals		11	1	6	7	....	....	....	2	....	....	....	....	....	....	....	....	....		....	....	....	....	....	....	....	....

NHL Second All-Star Team (1958, 1963) • NHL First All-Star Team (1959, 1962) • Won Hart Trophy (1959) • WHL First All-Star Team (1970) • Won Leader Cup (WHL - MVP) (1970)

Played in NHL All-Star Game (1957, 1958, 1959, 1960, 1961, 1962, 1963, 1964)

Traded to **NY Rangers** by **Cleveland** (AHL) with Vic Howe for Glen Sonmor and Eric Pogue, August, 1954. Traded to **Toronto** by **NY Rangers** with Don McKenny for Dick Duff, Bob Nevin, Arnie Brown, Bill Collins and Rod Seiling, February 22, 1964. Traded to **Detroit** by **Toronto** with Billy Harris and Gary Jarrett for Marcel Pronovost, Ed Joyal, Larry Jeffrey, Lowell McDonald and Aut Erickson, May 20, 1965. Claimed by **Pittsburgh** from **Detroit** in Expansion Draft, June 6, 1967. Loaned to **Vancouver** (WHL) by **Pittsburgh** for 1968-69 season for future considerations, October, 1968. Loaned to **Vancouver** (WHL) by **Pittsburgh** for 1969-70 season to complete transaction that sent Paul Andrea and John Arbour to Pittsburgh, May 20, 1969. Selected by **Miami-Philadelphia** (WHA) in 1972 WHA General Player Draft, February 12, 1972. Transferred to **Vancouver** (WHA) after **Philadelphia** (WHA) franchise relocated, May, 1973.

• BATTAGLIA, JON

Jon "Bates" Battaglia LW – L. 6'2", 185 lbs. b: Chicago, IL, 12/13/1975. Anaheim's 6th choice, 132nd overall, in 1994 Entry Draft.

Season	Club	League	GP	G	A	Pts	AG	AA	APts	PIM	PP	SH	GW	S	%	TGF	PGF	TGA	PGA	+/–	GP	G	A	Pts	PIM	PP	SH	GW
1993-94	Caledon Canadians	Jr. B	47	35	39	74	....	....	....	212	....	....	....	....	....	....	....	....	....	....	....	....	....	....	....	....	....	....
1994-95	Lake Superior State	CCHA	38	6	14	20	....	....	....	34	....	....	....	....	....	....	....	....	....	....	....	....	....	....	....	....	....	....
1995-96	Lake Superior State	CCHA	40	13	22	35	....	....	....	48	....	....	....	....	....	....	....	....	....	....	....	....	....	....	....	....	....	....
1996-97	Lake Superior State	CCHA	38	12	27	39	....	....	....	80	....	....	....	....	....	....	....	....	....	....	....	....	....	....	....	....	....	....
1997-98	**Carolina Hurricanes**	**NHL**	**33**	**2**	**4**	**6**	**2**	**4**	**6**	**10**	**0**	**0**	**1**	**21**	**9.5**	**8**	**0**	**11**	**2**	**–1**	....	....	....	....	....	....	....	....
	Beast of New Haven	AHL	48	15	21	36	....	....	....	48	....	....	....	....	....	....	....	....	....	....	1	0	0	0	0	....	....	....
	United States	WC-A	6	1	1	2	....	....	....	6	....	....	....	....	....	....	....	....	....	....	....	....	....	....	....	....	....	....
	NHL Totals		**33**	**2**	**4**	**6**	**2**	**4**	**6**	**10**	**0**	**0**	**1**	**21**	**9.5**	**8**	**0**	**11**	**2**		....	....	....	....	....	....	....	....

Traded to **Hartford** by **Anaheim** with Anaheim's 4th round choice in 1998 Entry Draft for Mark Janssens, March 18, 1997.

● **BATTERS, JEFF**   Jeff Batters   D – R. 6'2", 215 lbs.   b: Victoria, B.C., 10/23/1970.   d: 8/23/1996.   St. Louis' 7th choice, 135th overall, in 1989 Entry Draft.

			REGULAR SEASON																		PLAYOFFS							
Season	Club	League	GP	G	A	Pts	AG	AA	APts	PIM	PP	SH	GW	S	%	TGF	PGF	TGA	PGA	+/-	GP	G	A	Pts	PIM	PP	SH	GW
1988-89	University of Alaska-Anchorage	NCAA II	33	8	14	22				123																		
1989-90	University of Alaska-Anchorage	NCAA II	34	6	9	15				102																		
1990-91	University of Alaska-Anchorage	NCAA II	39	16	14	30				90																		
1991-92	University of Alaska-Anchorage	NCAA II	33	6	16	22				84																		
1992-93	Peoria Rivermen	IHL	74	5	18	23				113											4	0	0	0	10			
1993-94	**St. Louis Blues**	**NHL**	**6**	**0**	**0**	**0**	**0**	**0**	**0**	**7**	**0**	**0**	**0**	**1**	**0.0**	**2**	**0**	**1**	**0**	**+1**								
	Peoria Rivermen	IHL	59	3	9	12				175											6	0	0	0	18			
1994-95	Peoria Rivermen	IHL	42	0	11	11				128											5	0	1	1	18			
	St. Louis Blues	**NHL**	**10**	**0**	**0**	**0**	**0**	**0**	**0**	**21**	**0**	**0**	**0**	**3**	**0.0**	**5**	**0**	**12**	**2**	**–5**								
1995-96	Kansas City Blades	IHL	77	5	29	34				223											5	0	1	1	12			
	Canada	WC-A	2	0	0	0				0																		
	NHL Totals		**16**	**0**	**0**	**0**	**0**	**0**	**0**	**28**	**0**	**0**	**0**	**4**	**0.0**	**7**	**0**	**13**	**2**									

Signed as a free agent by **San Jose**, September 27, 1995.

● **BATYRSHIN, RUSLAN**   Ruslan Batyrshin   D – L. 6'1", 185 lbs.   b: Moscow, USSR, 2/19/1975.   Winnipeg's 4th choice, 79th overall, in 1993 Entry Draft.

Season	Club	League	GP	G	A	Pts	AG	AA	APts	PIM	PP	SH	GW	S	%	TGF	PGF	TGA	PGA	+/-	GP	G	A	Pts	PIM	PP	SH	GW
1991-92	Moscow Dynamo 2	CIS 3	40	0	2	2				52																		
1992-93	Moscow Dynamo 2	CIS 2	STATISTICS NOT AVAILABLE																									
1993-94	Moscow Dynamo	CIS	10	0	0	0				10											3	0	0	0	22			
1994-95	Moscow Dynamo	CIS	36	2	2	4				65											12	1	1	2	6			
	Russia	WJC-A	7	1	4	5				10																		
1995-96	**Los Angeles Kings**	**NHL**	**2**	**0**	**0**	**0**	**0**	**0**	**0**	**6**	**0**	**0**	**0**	**0**	**0.0**	**0**	**0**	**0**	**0**	**0**								
	Phoenix Roadrunners	IHL	71	1	9	10				144											2	0	0	0	2			
1996-97	Phoenix Roadrunners	IHL	59	3	4	7				123																		
1997-98	Springfield Falcons	AHL	47	0	6	6				130																		
	Grand Rapids Griffins	IHL	22	0	2	2				54																		
	NHL Totals		**2**	**0**	**0**	**0**	**0**	**0**	**0**	**6**	**0**	**0**	**0**	**0**	**0.0**	**0**	**0**	**0**	**0**									

Rights traded to **LA Kings** by **Winnipeg** with Winnipeg's 2nd round choice (Marian Cisar) in 1996 Entry Draft for Brent Thompson and future considerations, August 8, 1994.

● **BAUMGARTNER, KEN**   Ken "Bomber" Baumgartner   LW – L. 6'1", 205 lbs.   b: Flin Flon, Man., 3/11/1966.   Buffalo's 12th choice, 245th overall, in 1985 Entry Draft.

Season	Club	League	GP	G	A	Pts	AG	AA	APts	PIM	PP	SH	GW	S	%	TGF	PGF	TGA	PGA	+/-	GP	G	A	Pts	PIM	PP	SH	GW
1983-84	Prince Albert Raiders	WHL	57	1	6	7				203											4	0	0	0	23			
1984-85	Prince Albert Raiders	WHL	60	3	9	12				252											13	1	3	4	89			
1985-86	Prince Albert Raiders	WHL	70	4	23	27				277											20	3	9	12	112			
1986-87	New Haven Nighthawks	AHL	13	0	3	3				99											6	0	0	0	60			
1987-88	**Los Angeles Kings**	**NHL**	**30**	**2**	**3**	**5**	**2**	**2**	**4**	**189**	**0**	**0**	**0**	**17**	**11.8**	**24**	**0**	**19**	**0**	**+5**	**5**	**0**	**1**	**1**	**28**	**0**	**0**	**0**
	New Haven Nighthawks	AHL	48	1	5	6				181																		
1988-89	**Los Angeles Kings**	**NHL**	**49**	**1**	**3**	**4**	**1**	**2**	**3**	**288**	**0**	**0**	**0**	**15**	**6.7**	**27**	**0**	**41**	**5**	**–9**	**5**	**0**	**0**	**0**	**8**	**0**	**0**	**0**
	New Haven Nighthawks	AHL	10	1	3	4				26																		
1989-90	**Los Angeles Kings**	**NHL**	**12**	**1**	**0**	**1**	**1**	**0**	**1**	**28**	**0**	**0**	**0**	**7**	**14.3**	**1**	**0**	**13**	**2**	**–10**								
	New York Islanders	**NHL**	**53**	**0**	**5**	**5**	**0**	**4**	**4**	**194**	**0**	**0**	**0**	**41**	**0.0**	**40**	**0**	**34**	**0**	**+6**	**4**	**0**	**0**	**0**	**27**	**0**	**0**	**0**
1990-91	**New York Islanders**	**NHL**	**78**	**1**	**6**	**7**	**1**	**5**	**6**	**282**	**0**	**0**	**0**	**41**	**2.4**	**28**	**0**	**43**	**1**	**–14**								
1991-92	**New York Islanders**	**NHL**	**44**	**0**	**1**	**1**	**0**	**1**	**1**	**202**	**0**	**0**	**0**	**11**	**0.0**	**9**	**0**	**20**	**1**	**–10**								
	Toronto Maple Leafs	**NHL**	**11**	**0**	**0**	**0**	**0**	**0**	**0**	**23**	**0**	**0**	**0**	**5**	**0.0**	**3**	**0**	**2**	**0**	**+1**								
1992-93	**Toronto Maple Leafs**	**NHL**	**63**	**1**	**0**	**1**	**1**	**0**	**1**	**155**	**0**	**0**	**0**	**23**	**4.3**	**2**	**0**	**14**	**1**	**–11**	**7**	**1**	**0**	**1**	**0**	**0**	**0**	**0**
1993-94	**Toronto Maple Leafs**	**NHL**	**64**	**4**	**4**	**8**	**4**	**3**	**7**	**185**	**0**	**0**	**0**	**34**	**11.8**	**13**	**0**	**19**	**0**	**–6**	**10**	**0**	**0**	**0**	**18**	**0**	**0**	**0**
1994-95	**Toronto Maple Leafs**	**NHL**	**2**	**0**	**0**	**0**	**0**	**0**	**0**	**5**	**0**	**0**	**0**	**1**	**0.0**	**0**	**0**	**0**	**0**	**0**								
1995-96	**Toronto Maple Leafs**	**NHL**	**60**	**2**	**3**	**5**	**2**	**2**	**4**	**152**	**0**	**0**	**1**	**27**	**7.4**	**8**	**0**	**13**	**0**	**–5**								
	Anaheim Mighty Ducks	**NHL**	**12**	**0**	**1**	**1**	**0**	**1**	**1**	**41**	**0**	**0**	**0**	**5**	**0.0**	**2**	**0**	**2**	**0**	**0**								
1996-97	**Anaheim Mighty Ducks**	**NHL**	**67**	**0**	**11**	**11**	**0**	**10**	**10**	**182**	**0**	**0**	**0**	**20**	**0.0**	**16**	**0**	**16**	**0**	**0**	**11**	**0**	**1**	**1**	**11**	**0**	**0**	**0**
1997-98	**Boston Bruins**	**NHL**	**82**	**0**	**1**	**1**	**0**	**1**	**1**	**199**	**0**	**0**	**0**	**28**	**0.0**	**3**	**0**	**17**	**0**	**–14**	**6**	**0**	**0**	**0**	**14**	**0**	**0**	**0**
	NHL Totals		**627**	**12**	**38**	**50**	**12**	**31**	**43**	**2125**	**0**	**0**	**1**	**275**	**4.4**	**176**	**0**	**253**	**10**		**48**	**1**	**2**	**3**	**106**	**0**	**0**	**0**

Traded to **LA Kings** by **Buffalo** with Sean McKenna and Larry Playfair for Brian Engblom and Doug Smith, January 29, 1986. Traded to **NY Islanders** by **LA Kings** with Hubie McDonough for Mikko Makela, November 29, 1989. Traded to **Toronto** by **NY Islanders** with Dave McLlwain for Daniel Marois and Claude Loiselle, March 10, 1992. Traded to **Anaheim** by **Toronto** for Winnipeg's 4th round choice (previously acquired by Anaheim — later traded to Montreal — Montreal selected Kim Staal) in 1996 Entry Draft, March 20, 1996. Signed as a free agent by **Boston**, July 14, 1997.

● **BAUMGARTNER, MIKE**   Mike Baumgartner   D – L. 6'2", 195 lbs.   b: Roseau, MN, 1/30/1949.   Chicago's 5th choice, 60th overall, in 1969 Amateur Draft.

Season	Club	League	GP	G	A	Pts	AG	AA	APts	PIM	PP	SH	GW	S	%	TGF	PGF	TGA	PGA	+/-	GP	G	A	Pts	PIM	PP	SH	GW
1967-68	University of North Dakota	WCHA	DID NOT PLAY – FRESHMAN																									
1968-69	University of North Dakota	WCHA	29	2	5	7				12																		
1969-70	University of North Dakota	WCHA	30	9	5	14				12																		
1970-71	University of North Dakota	WCHA	33	6	13	19				29																		
1971-72	Dallas Black Hawks	CHL	72	3	22	25				66											12	1	2	3	0			
1972-73	Dallas Black Hawks	CHL	72	10	37	47				75											4	0	2	2	4			
1973-74	Omaha Knights	CHL	70	7	36	43				28											5	0	1	1	6			
1974-75	**Kansas City Scouts**	**NHL**	**17**	**0**	**0**	**0**	**0**	**0**	**0**	**0**	**0**	**0**	**0**	**12**	**0.0**	**6**	**0**	**18**	**3**	**–9**								
1975-76	Springfield Indians	AHL	1	0	0	0				2																		
	NHL Totals		**17**	**0**	**0**	**0**	**0**	**0**	**0**	**0**	**0**	**0**	**0**	**12**	**0.0**	**6**	**0**	**18**	**3**									

Traded to **Atlanta** by **Chicago** for Lynn Powis, August 30, 1973. Traded to **Montreal** by **Atlanta** for cash, May 27, 1974. Traded to **Kansas City** by **Montreal** for cash, August 22, 1974.

● **BAUMGARTNER, NOLAN**   Nolan Baumgartner   D – R. 6'1", 200 lbs.   b: Calgary, Alta., 3/23/1976.   Washington's 1st choice, 10th overall, in 1994 Entry Draft.

Season	Club	League	GP	G	A	Pts	AG	AA	APts	PIM	PP	SH	GW	S	%	TGF	PGF	TGA	PGA	+/-	GP	G	A	Pts	PIM	PP	SH	GW
1992-93	Kamloops Blazers	WHL	43	0	5	5				30											11	1	1	2	0			
1993-94	Kamloops Blazers	WHL	69	13	42	55				109											19	3	14	17	33			
1994-95	Kamloops Blazers	WHL	62	8	36	44				71											21	4	13	17	16			
	Canada	WJC-A	7	0	1	1				4																		
1995-96	Kamloops Blazers	WHL	28	13	15	28				45											16	1	9	10	26			
	Canada	WJC-A	6	1	1	2				22																		
	Washington Capitals	**NHL**	**1**	**0**	**0**	**0**	**0**	**0**	**0**	**0**	**0**	**0**	**0**	**0**	**0.0**	**0**	**0**	**1**	**0**	**–1**	**1**	**0**	**0**	**0**	**10**	**0**	**0**	**0**
1996-97	Portland Pirates	AHL	8	2	2	4				4																		
1997-98	**Washington Capitals**	**NHL**	**4**	**0**	**1**	**1**	**0**	**1**	**1**	**0**	**0**	**0**	**0**	**4**	**0.0**	**4**	**2**	**3**	**1**	**0**								
	Portland Pirates	AHL	70	2	24	26				70											10	1	4	5	10			
	NHL Totals		**5**	**0**	**1**	**1**	**0**	**1**	**1**	**0**	**0**	**0**	**0**	**4**	**0.0**	**4**	**2**	**4**	**1**		**1**	**0**	**0**	**0**	**10**	**0**	**0**	**0**

Memorial Cup All-Star Team (1994, 1995) • WHL West First All-Star Team (1995, 1996) • Canadian Major Junior First All-Star Team (1995) • Canadian Major Junior Defenseman of the Year (1995) • WJC-A All-Star Team (1996)

● **BAUN, BOB**   Bob "Boomer" Baun   D – R. 5'9", 175 lbs.   b: Lanigan, Sask., 9/9/1936.

Season	Club	League	GP	G	A	Pts	AG	AA	APts	PIM	PP	SH	GW	S	%	TGF	PGF	TGA	PGA	+/-	GP	G	A	Pts	PIM	PP	SH	GW
1952-53	Toronto Marlboros	OHA	16	1	1	2				12											7	0	2	2	6			
1953-54	Toronto Marlboros	OHA	59	2	15	17				63											15	3	0	3	10			
1954-55	Toronto Marlboros	OHA	47	3	6	9				99											13	0	1	1	31			
1955-56	Toronto Marlboros	OHA	48	5	14	19				93											11	3	2	5	38			
1956-57	**Toronto Maple Leafs**	**NHL**	**20**	**0**	**5**	**5**	**0**	**6**	**6**	**37**																		
	Rochester Americans	AHL	46	2	13	15				117																		
1957-58	**Toronto Maple Leafs**	**NHL**	**67**	**1**	**9**	**10**	**1**	**10**	**11**	**91**																		
1958-59	**Toronto Maple Leafs**	**NHL**	**51**	**1**	**8**	**9**	**1**	**8**	**9**	**87**											**12**	**0**	**0**	**0**	**24**			
1959-60	**Toronto Maple Leafs**	**NHL**	**61**	**8**	**9**	**17**	**10**	**9**	**19**	**59**											**10**	**1**	**0**	**1**	**17**			
1960-61	**Toronto Maple Leafs**	**NHL**	**70**	**1**	**14**	**15**	**1**	**14**	**15**	**70**											**3**	**0**	**0**	**0**	**8**			
1961-62	**Toronto Maple Leafs**	**NHL**	**65**	**4**	**11**	**15**	**5**	**11**	**16**	**94**											**12**	**0**	**3**	**3**	**19**			
1962-63	**Toronto Maple Leafs**	**NHL**	**48**	**4**	**8**	**12**	**5**	**8**	**13**	**65**											**10**	**0**	**3**	**3**	**6**			
1963-64	**Toronto Maple Leafs**	**NHL**	**52**	**4**	**14**	**18**	**5**	**15**	**20**	**113**											**14**	**2**	**3**	**5**	***42**			
1964-65	**Toronto Maple Leafs**	**NHL**	**70**	**0**	**18**	**18**	**0**	**19**	**19**	**160**											**6**	**0**	**1**	**1**	**14**			

			REGULAR SEASON																		PLAYOFFS							
Season	**Club**	**League**	**GP**	**G**	**A**	**Pts**	**AG**	**AA**	**APts**	**PIM**	**PP**	**SH**	**GW**	**S**	**%**	**TGF**	**PGF**	**TGA**	**PGA**	**+/–**	**GP**	**G**	**A**	**Pts**	**PIM**	**PP**	**SH**	**GW**
1965-66	**Toronto Maple Leafs**	**NHL**	**44**	**0**	**6**	**6**	**0**	**6**	**6**	**68**	....	....	....	....	....	....	....	....	....	....	**4**	**0**	**1**	**1**	**8**	....	....	....
1966-67	**Toronto Maple Leafs**	**NHL**	**54**	**2**	**8**	**10**	**2**	**8**	**10**	**83**	....	....	....	....	....	....	....	....	....	....	**10**	**0**	**0**	**0**	**4**	....	....	....
1967-68	**Oakland Seals**	**NHL**	**67**	**3**	**10**	**13**	**4**	**10**	**14**	**81**	**0**	**0**	**0**	**80**	**3.8**	**56**	**7**	**83**	**16**	**–18**	....	....	....	....	....	....	....	....
1968-69	**Detroit Red Wings**	**NHL**	**76**	**4**	**16**	**20**	**4**	**15**	**19**	**121**	**0**	**0**	**0**	**117**	**3.4**	**103**	**1**	**125**	**47**	**+24**	....	....	....	....	....	....	....	....
1969-70	**Detroit Red Wings**	**NHL**	**71**	**1**	**18**	**19**	**1**	**18**	**19**	**112**	**0**	**0**	**0**	**112**	**0.9**	**84**	**3**	**110**	**36**	**+7**	**4**	**0**	**0**	**0**	**6**	**0**	**0**	**0**
1970-71	**Detroit Red Wings**	**NHL**	**11**	**0**	**3**	**3**	**0**	**3**	**3**	**24**	**0**	**0**	**0**	**16**	**0.0**	**10**	**0**	**16**	**4**	**–2**	....	....	....	....	....	....	....	....
	Toronto Maple Leafs	**NHL**	**58**	**1**	**17**	**18**	**1**	**15**	**16**	**123**	**0**	**0**	**0**	**104**	**1.0**	**76**	**8**	**66**	**15**	**+17**	**6**	**0**	**1**	**1**	**19**	**0**	**0**	**0**
1971-72	**Toronto Maple Leafs**	**NHL**	**74**	**2**	**12**	**14**	**2**	**11**	**13**	**101**	**0**	**0**	**0**	**158**	**1.3**	**68**	**9**	**82**	**31**	**+8**	**5**	**0**	**0**	**0**	**4**	**0**	**0**	**0**
1972-73	**Toronto Maple Leafs**	**NHL**	**5**	**1**	**1**	**2**	**1**	**1**	**2**	**4**	**0**	**0**	**0**	**5**	**20.0**	**4**	**0**	**10**	**1**	**–5**	....	....	....	....	....	....	....	....
	NHL Totals		**964**	**37**	**187**	**224**	**43**	**187**	**230**	**1493**	**0**	**0**	**0**	**592**	**6.3**	**401**	**28**	**492**	**150**		**96**	**3**	**12**	**15**	**171**	**0**	**0**	**0**

Played in NHL All-Star Game (1962, 1963, 1964, 1965, 1968)

Claimed by **Oakland** from **Toronto** in Expansion Draft, June 6, 1967. Traded to **Detroit** by **Oakland** with Ron Harris for Gary Jarrett, Doug Roberts, Howie Young and Chris Worthy, May 27, 1968. Claimed on waivers by **Buffalo** from **Detroit**, November 3, 1970. Traded to **St. Louis** by **Buffalo** for Larry Keenan and Jean-Guy Talbot, November 4, 1970. Traded to **Toronto** by **St. Louis** for Brit Selby, November 13, 1970.

• BAUTIN, SERGEI

Sergei Bautin D – L. 6'3", 200 lbs. b: Rogachev, USSR, 3/11/1967. Winnipeg's 1st choice, 17th overall, in 1992 Entry Draft.

Season	Club	League	GP	G	A	Pts	AG	AA	APts	PIM	PP	SH	GW	S	%	TGF	PGF	TGA	PGA	+/–	GP	G	A	Pts	PIM	PP	SH	GW
1990-91	Moscow Dynamo	USSR	33	2	0	2	....	....	....	28	....	....	....	....	....	....	....	....	....	....	....	....	....	....	....	....	....	....
	Moscow Dynamo	SuperS	4	0	0	0	....	....	....	5	....	....	....	....	....	....	....	....	....	....	....	....	....	....	....	....	....	....
1991-92	Moscow Dynamo	CIS	32	1	2	3	....	....	....	88	....	....	....	....	....	....	....	....	....	....	5	0	1	1	....	....	....	....
	Russia	Olympics	8	0	0	0	....	....	....	6	....	....	....	....	....	....	....	....	....	....	....	....	....	....	....	....	....	....
	Russia	WC-A	6	1	1	2	....	....	....	8	....	....	....	....	....	....	....	....	....	....	....	....	....	....	....	....	....	....
1992-93	**Winnipeg Jets**	**NHL**	**71**	**5**	**18**	**23**	**4**	**12**	**16**	**96**	**0**	**0**	**0**	**82**	**6.1**	**65**	**2**	**97**	**32**	**–2**	**6**	**0**	**0**	**0**	**2**	**0**	**0**	**0**
1993-94	**Winnipeg Jets**	**NHL**	**59**	**0**	**7**	**7**	**0**	**5**	**5**	**78**	**0**	**0**	**0**	**39**	**0.0**	**45**	**4**	**80**	**26**	**–13**	....	....	....	....	....	....	....	....
	Detroit Red Wings	**NHL**	**1**	**0**	**0**	**0**	**0**	**0**	**0**	**0**	**0**	**0**	**0**	**0**	**0.0**	**1**	**0**	**0**	**0**	**+1**	....	....	....	....	....	....	....	....
	Adirondack Red Wings	AHL	9	1	5	6	....	....	....	6	....	....	....	....	....	....	....	....	....	....	....	....	....	....	....	....	....	....
1994-95	Adirondack Red Wings	AHL	32	0	10	10	....	....	....	57	....	....	....	....	....	....	....	....	....	....	1	0	0	0	4	....	....	....
1995-96	**San Jose Sharks**	**NHL**	**1**	**0**	**0**	**0**	**0**	**0**	**0**	**2**	**0**	**0**	**0**	**0**	**0.0**	**1**	**0**	**2**	**0**	**–1**	....	....	....	....	....	....	....	....
	Kansas City Blades	IHL	60	0	14	14	....	....	....	113	....	....	....	....	....	....	....	....	....	....	3	0	0	0	6	....	....	....
1996-97	Lulea HF	Sweden	36	1	0	1	....	....	....	*153	....	....	....	....	....	....	....	....	....	....	8	1	2	3	31	....	....	....
	Russia	WC-A	9	0	2	2	....	....	....	14	....	....	....	....	....	....	....	....	....	....	....	....	....	....	....	....	....	....
1997-98	Lulea HF	EuroHL	6	0	1	1	....	....	....	29	....	....	....	....	....	....	....	....	....	....	....	....	....	....	....	....	....	....
	Lulea HF	Sweden	43	3	5	8	....	....	....	21	....	....	....	....	....	....	....	....	....	....	2	0	0	0	4	....	....	....
	NHL Totals		**132**	**5**	**25**	**30**	**4**	**17**	**21**	**176**	**0**	**0**	**0**	**121**	**4.1**	**112**	**6**	**179**	**58**		**6**	**0**	**0**	**0**	**2**	**0**	**0**	**0**

Traded to **Detroit** by **Winnipeg** with Bob Essensa for Tim Cheveldae and Dallas Drake, March 8, 1994. Signed as a free agent by **San Jose**, October 12, 1995.

• BAWA, ROBIN

Robin Bawa RW – R. 6'2", 214 lbs. b: Chemainus, B.C., 3/26/1966.

Season	Club	League	GP	G	A	Pts	AG	AA	APts	PIM	PP	SH	GW	S	%	TGF	PGF	TGA	PGA	+/–	GP	G	A	Pts	PIM	PP	SH	GW
1982-83	Kamloops Blazers	WHL	66	10	24	34	....	....	....	17	....	....	....	....	....	....	....	....	....	....	7	1	2	3	0	....	....	....
1983-84	Kamloops Blazers	WHL	64	16	28	44	....	....	....	40	....	....	....	....	....	....	....	....	....	....	13	4	2	6	4	....	....	....
1984-85	Kamloops Blazers	WHL	52	6	19	25	....	....	....	45	....	....	....	....	....	....	....	....	....	....	15	4	9	13	14	....	....	....
1985-86	Kamloops Blazers	WHL	63	29	43	72	....	....	....	78	....	....	....	....	....	....	....	....	....	....	16	5	13	18	4	....	....	....
1986-87	Kamloops Blazers	WHL	62	57	56	113	....	....	....	91	....	....	....	....	....	....	....	....	....	....	13	6	7	13	22	....	....	....
1987-88	Fort Wayne Komets	IHL	55	12	27	39	....	....	....	239	....	....	....	....	....	....	....	....	....	....	6	1	3	4	24	....	....	....
1988-89	Baltimore Skipjacks	AHL	75	23	24	47	....	....	....	205	....	....	....	....	....	....	....	....	....	....	....	....	....	....	....	....	....	....
1989-90	**Washington Capitals**	**NHL**	**5**	**1**	**0**	**1**	**1**	**0**	**1**	**6**	**0**	**0**	**0**	**1**	**100.0**	**1**	**0**	**4**	**0**	**–3**	....	....	....	....	....	....	....	....
	Baltimore Skipjacks	AHL	61	7	18	25	....	....	....	189	....	....	....	....	....	....	....	....	....	....	11	1	2	3	49	....	....	....
1990-91	Fort Wayne Komets	IHL	72	21	26	47	....	....	....	381	....	....	....	....	....	....	....	....	....	....	18	4	4	8	87	....	....	....
1991-92	**Vancouver Canucks**	**NHL**	**2**	**0**	**0**	**0**	**0**	**0**	**0**	**0**	**0**	**0**	**0**	**1**	**0.0**	**1**	**1**	**0**	**0**	**0**	**1**	**0**	**0**	**0**	**0**	**0**	**0**	**0**
	Milwaukee Admirals	IHL	70	27	14	41	....	....	....	238	....	....	....	....	....	....	....	....	....	....	5	2	2	4	8	....	....	....
1992-93	Hamilton Canucks	AHL	23	3	4	7	....	....	....	58	....	....	....	....	....	....	....	....	....	....	....	....	....	....	....	....	....	....
	San Jose Sharks	**NHL**	**42**	**5**	**0**	**5**	**4**	**0**	**4**	**47**	**0**	**0**	**1**	**25**	**20.0**	**9**	**0**	**38**	**4**	**–25**	....	....	....	....	....	....	....	....
	Kansas City Blades	IHL	5	2	0	2	....	....	....	20	....	....	....	....	....	....	....	....	....	....	....	....	....	....	....	....	....	....
1993-94	**Anaheim Mighty Ducks**	**NHL**	**12**	**0**	**1**	**1**	**0**	**1**	**1**	**7**	**0**	**0**	**0**	**1**	**0.0**	**1**	**0**	**4**	**0**	**–3**	....	....	....	....	....	....	....	....
	San Diego Gulls	IHL	25	6	15	21	....	....	....	54	....	....	....	....	....	....	....	....	....	....	6	0	0	0	52	....	....	....
1994-95	Kalamazoo Wings	IHL	71	22	12	34	....	....	....	184	....	....	....	....	....	....	....	....	....	....	....	....	....	....	....	....	....	....
	Milwaukee Admirals	IHL	4	1	1	2	....	....	....	19	....	....	....	....	....	....	....	....	....	....	15	1	5	6	48	....	....	....
1995-96	San Francisco Spiders	IHL	77	23	25	48	....	....	....	234	....	....	....	....	....	....	....	....	....	....	4	0	2	2	4	....	....	....
1996-97	Fort Wayne Komets	IHL	54	10	23	33	....	....	....	181	....	....	....	....	....	....	....	....	....	....	....	....	....	....	....	....	....	....
1997-98	Fort Wayne Komets	IHL	58	12	15	27	....	....	....	125	....	....	....	....	....	....	....	....	....	....	....	....	....	....	....	....	....	....
	NHL Totals		**61**	**6**	**1**	**7**	**5**	**1**	**6**	**60**	**0**	**0**	**1**	**28**	**21.4**	**12**	**1**	**46**	**4**		**1**	**0**	**0**	**0**	**0**	**0**	**0**	**0**

WHL West All-Star Team (1987)

Signed as a free agent by **Washington**, May 22, 1987. Traded to **Vancouver** by **Washington** for cash, July 31, 1991. Traded to **San Jose** by **Vancouver** for Rick Lessard, December 15, 1992. Claimed by **Anaheim** from **San Jose** in Expansion Draft, June 24, 1993. Signed as a free agent by **Dallas**, July 22, 1994.

• BAXTER, PAUL

Paul Baxter D – R. 5'11", 200 lbs. b: Winnipeg, Man., 10/28/1955. Pittsburgh's 3rd choice, 49th overall, in 1975 Amateur Draft.

Season	Club	League	GP	G	A	Pts	AG	AA	APts	PIM	PP	SH	GW	S	%	TGF	PGF	TGA	PGA	+/–	GP	G	A	Pts	PIM	PP	SH	GW
1972-73	Winnipeg Monarchs	MJHL	44	9	22	31	....	....	....	359	....	....	....	....	....	....	....	....	....	....	....	....	....	....	....	....	....	....
1973-74	Winnipeg Clubs	WCJHL	63	10	30	40	....	....	....	384	....	....	....	....	....	....	....	....	....	....	....	....	....	....	....	....	....	....
1974-75	Cape Cod Codders	NAHL	2	1	0	1	....	....	....	2	....	....	....	....	....	....	....	....	....	....	....	....	....	....	....	....	....	....
	Cleveland Crusaders	WHA	5	0	0	0	....	....	....	37	....	....	....	....	....	....	....	....	....	....	....	....	....	....	....	....	....	....
1975-76	Syracuse Blazers	NAHL	3	1	2	3	....	....	....	9	....	....	....	....	....	....	....	....	....	....	....	....	....	....	....	....	....	....
	Cleveland Crusaders	WHA	67	3	7	10	....	....	....	201	....	....	....	....	....	....	....	....	....	....	3	0	0	0	10	....	....	....
1976-77	Maine Nordiques	NAHL	6	1	4	5	....	....	....	52	....	....	....	....	....	....	....	....	....	....	....	....	....	....	....	....	....	....
	Quebec Nordiques	WHA	66	6	17	23	....	....	....	244	....	....	....	....	....	....	....	....	....	....	12	2	2	4	35	....	....	....
1977-78	Quebec Nordiques	WHA	76	6	29	35	....	....	....	240	....	....	....	....	....	....	....	....	....	....	11	4	7	11	42	....	....	....
1978-79	Quebec Nordiques	WHA	76	10	36	46	....	....	....	240	....	....	....	....	....	....	....	....	....	....	4	0	2	2	7	....	....	....
1979-80	**Quebec Nordiques**	**NHL**	**61**	**7**	**13**	**20**	**6**	**10**	**16**	**145**	**4**	**0**	**1**	**90**	**7.8**	**67**	**22**	**81**	**9**	**–27**	....	....	....	....	....	....	....	....
1980-81	**Pittsburgh Penguins**	**NHL**	**51**	**5**	**14**	**19**	**4**	**10**	**14**	**204**	**1**	**0**	**0**	**62**	**8.1**	**51**	**5**	**79**	**22**	**–11**	**5**	**0**	**1**	**1**	**28**	**0**	**0**	**0**
1981-82	**Pittsburgh Penguins**	**NHL**	**76**	**9**	**34**	**43**	**7**	**22**	**29**	***409**	**4**	**0**	**2**	**177**	**5.1**	**114**	**30**	**129**	**36**	**–9**	**5**	**0**	**0**	**0**	**14**	**0**	**0**	**0**
1982-83	**Pittsburgh Penguins**	**NHL**	**75**	**11**	**21**	**32**	**9**	**14**	**23**	**238**	**5**	**0**	**0**	**159**	**6.9**	**94**	**28**	**147**	**32**	**–49**	....	....	....	....	....	....	....	....
1983-84	**Calgary Flames**	**NHL**	**74**	**7**	**20**	**27**	**6**	**14**	**20**	**182**	**1**	**0**	**1**	**87**	**8.0**	**80**	**2**	**85**	**6**	**–1**	**11**	**0**	**2**	**2**	**37**	**0**	**0**	**0**
1984-85	**Calgary Flames**	**NHL**	**70**	**5**	**14**	**19**	**4**	**9**	**13**	**126**	**0**	**0**	**1**	**83**	**6.0**	**96**	**1**	**73**	**17**	**+39**	**4**	**0**	**1**	**1**	**18**	**0**	**0**	**0**
1985-86	**Calgary Flames**	**NHL**	**47**	**4**	**3**	**7**	**3**	**2**	**5**	**194**	**0**	**1**	**0**	**41**	**9.8**	**47**	**0**	**54**	**12**	**+5**	**13**	**0**	**1**	**1**	**55**	**0**	**0**	**0**
1986-87	**Calgary Flames**	**NHL**	**18**	**0**	**2**	**2**	**0**	**1**	**1**	**66**	**0**	**0**	**0**	**13**	**0.0**	**8**	**0**	**13**	**0**	**–5**	**2**	**0**	**0**	**0**	**10**	**0**	**0**	**0**
1987-88	Salt Lake Golden Eagles	IHL	DID NOT PLAY – COACHING																									
	NHL Totals		**472**	**48**	**121**	**169**	**39**	**82**	**121**	**1564**	**15**	**1**	**5**	**712**	**6.7**	**557**	**88**	**661**	**134**		**40**	**0**	**5**	**5**	**162**	**0**	**0**	**0**
	Other Major League Totals		290	25	89	114	....	....	....	962	....	....	....	....	....	....	....	....	....		30	6	11	17	94	....	....	....

Selected by **Cleveland** (WHA) in 1974 WHA Amateur Draft, June, 1974. Signed as a free agent by **Quebec** (WHA) after **Cleveland** (WHA) franchise folded, June, 1976. Reclaimed by **Pittsburgh** from **Quebec** prior to Expansion Draft, June 9, 1979. Claimed as a priority selection by **Quebec** prior to Expansion Draft, June 9, 1979. Signed as a free agent by **Pittsburgh** from **Quebec**, August 7, 1980. Signed as a free agent by **Calgary**, September 29, 1983.

			REGULAR SEASON																		PLAYOFFS							
Season	Club	League	GP	G	A	Pts	AG	AA	APts	PIM	PP	SH	GW	S	%	TGF	PGF	TGA	PGA	+/-	GP	G	A	Pts	PIM	PP	SH	GW

• BEADLE, SANDY

Sandy Beadle LW – L. 6'2", 185 lbs. b: Regina, Sask., 7/12/1960. Winnipeg's 9th choice, 149th overall, in 1980 Entry Draft.

Season	Club	League	GP	G	A	Pts	AG	AA	APts	PIM	PP	SH	GW	S	%	TGF	PGF	TGA	PGA	+/-	GP	G	A	Pts	PIM	PP	SH	GW
1978-79	Regina Blues	SJHL	52	41	57	98	....	....	....	25	....	....	....	....	....	....	....	....	....	....	....	....	....	....	....	....	....	....
	Regina Pats	WHL	2	1	1	2	....	....	....	0	....	....	....	....	....	....	....	....	....	....	....	....	....	....	....	....	....	....
1979-80	Northeastern University	ECAC	23	11	16	27	....	....	....	6	....	....	....	....	....	....	....	....	....	....	....	....	....	....	....	....	....	....
1980-81	Northeastern University	ECAC	26	29	30	59	....	....	....	26	....	....	....	....	....	....	....	....	....	....	....	....	....	....	....	....	....	....
	Winnipeg Jets	**NHL**	**6**	**1**	**0**	**1**	**1**	**0**	**1**	**2**	**0**	**0**	**0**	**7**	**14.3**	**2**	**0**	**4**	**0**	**–2**	....	....	....	....	....	....	....	....
	Tulsa Oilers	CHL	....	....	....	....	....	....	....	....	....	....	....	....	....	....	....	....	....	....	6	0	1	1	2	....	....	....
1981-82	Tulsa Oilers	CHL	54	12	21	33	....	....	....	34	....	....	....	....	....	....	....	....	....	....	3	0	0	0	7	....	....	....
1982-83	Sherbrooke Jets	AHL	9	2	3	5	....	....	....	0	....	....	....	....	....	....	....	....	....	....	....	....	....	....	....	....	....	....
	Fort Wayne Komets	IHL	13	3	10	13	....	....	....	11	....	....	....	....	....	....	....	....	....	....	....	....	....	....	....	....	....	....
1983-84	Sherbrooke Jets	AHL	70	2	5	7	....	....	....	8	....	....	....	....	....	....	....	....	....	....	....	....	....	....	....	....	....	....
	NHL Totals		**6**	**1**	**0**	**1**	**1**	**0**	**1**	**2**	**0**	**0**	**0**	**7**	**14.3**	**2**	**0**	**4**	**0**		....	....	....	....	....	....	....	....

ECAC First All-Star Team (1981) • NCAA East First All-American Team (1981)

• BEATON, FRANK

Frank (Seldom) Beaton LW – L. 5'10", 200 lbs. b: Antigonish, N.S., 4/28/1953.

Season	Club	League	GP	G	A	Pts	AG	AA	APts	PIM	PP	SH	GW	S	%	TGF	PGF	TGA	PGA	+/-	GP	G	A	Pts	PIM	PP	SH	GW
1971-72	Sarnia Steeplejacks	OJHL	49	5	10	15	....	....	....	226	....	....	....	....	....	....	....	....	....	....	....	....	....	....	....	....	....	....
1972-73	Windsor Spitfires	OJHL	16	3	10	13	....	....	....	91	....	....	....	....	....	....	....	....	....	....	....	....	....	....	....	....	....	....
1973-74	Flint Generals	IHL	66	8	14	22	....	....	....	90	....	....	....	....	....	....	....	....	....	....	7	2	2	4	18	....	....	....
1974-75	Flint Generals	IHL	65	4	17	21	....	....	....	175	....	....	....	....	....	....	....	....	....	....	5	0	0	0	13	....	....	....
1975-76	Cincinnati Stingers	WHA	29	2	3	5	....	....	....	61	....	....	....	....	....	....	....	....	....	....	....	....	....	....	....	....	....	....
	Hampton Gulls	SHL	45	17	14	31	....	....	....	*276	....	....	....	....	....	....	....	....	....	....	1	1	1	2	0	....	....	....
1976-77	Hampton Gulls	SHL	7	2	3	5	....	....	....	14	....	....	....	....	....	....	....	....	....	....	....	....	....	....	....	....	....	....
	Edmonton Oilers	WHA	68	4	9	13	....	....	....	*274	....	....	....	....	....	....	....	....	....	....	5	0	2	2	21	....	....	....
1977-78	Hampton Gulls	AHL	6	0	2	2	....	....	....	33	....	....	....	....	....	....	....	....	....	....	....	....	....	....	....	....	....	....
	Birmingham Bulls	WHA	56	6	9	15	....	....	....	279	....	....	....	....	....	....	....	....	....	....	5	2	0	2	10	....	....	....
1978-79	**New York Rangers**	**NHL**	**2**	**0**	**0**	**0**	**0**	**0**	**0**	**0**	**0**	**0**	**0**	**0**	**0.0**	**0**	**0**	**1**	**0**	**–1**	....	....	....	....	....	....	....	....
	New Haven Nighthawks	AHL	74	6	23	29	....	....	....	319	....	....	....	....	....	....	....	....	....	....	10	2	0	2	40	....	....	....
1979-80	**New York Rangers**	**NHL**	**23**	**1**	**1**	**2**	**1**	**1**	**2**	**43**	**0**	**0**	**0**	**19**	**5.3**	**9**	**0**	**14**	**0**	**–5**	....	....	....	....	....	....	....	....
	New Haven Nighthawks	AHL	40	10	14	24	....	....	....	106	....	....	....	....	....	....	....	....	....	....	10	1	4	5	52	....	....	....
1980-81	New Haven Nighthawks	AHL	15	1	1	2	....	....	....	20	....	....	....	....	....	....	....	....	....	....	....	....	....	....	....	....	....	....
	Birmingham Bulls	CHL	41	8	5	13	....	....	....	143	....	....	....	....	....	....	....	....	....	....	....	....	....	....	....	....	....	....
1981-82	Indianapolis Checkers	CHL	77	13	28	41	....	....	....	270	....	....	....	....	....	....	....	....	....	....	13	3	6	9	36	....	....	....
1982-83	Birmingham South Stars	CHL	69	15	19	34	....	....	....	188	....	....	....	....	....	....	....	....	....	....	10	4	2	6	18	....	....	....
	NHL Totals		**25**	**1**	**1**	**2**	**1**	**1**	**2**	**43**	**0**	**0**	**0**	**19**	**5.3**	**9**	**0**	**15**	**0**		....	....	....	....	....	....	....	....
	Other Major League Totals		153	12	21	33	....	....	....	614	....	....	....	....	....	....	....	....	....		10	2	2	4	31	....	....	....

Signed as a free agent by **Cincinnati** (WHA), August, 1975. Traded to **Edmonton** (WHA) by **Cincinnati** (WHA) for cash, October, 1976. Signed as a free agent by **Birmingham** (WHA), November, 1977. Signed as a free agent by **NY Rangers**, July 28, 1978. Traded to **Calgary** by **NY Rangers** for rights to Dale Lewis, November 18, 1980. Signed as a free agent by **NY Islanders**, August 25, 1981. Traded to **Minnesota** by **NY Islanders** for future considerations, September 27, 1982.

• BEAUDIN, NORM

Norm Beaudin RW – R. 5'8", 165 lbs. b: Montmartre, Sask., 11/28/1941.

Season	Club	League	GP	G	A	Pts	AG	AA	APts	PIM	PP	SH	GW	S	%	TGF	PGF	TGA	PGA	+/-	GP	G	A	Pts	PIM	PP	SH	GW
1959-60	Regina Pats	SJHL	58	24	29	53	....	....	....	18	....	....	....	....	....	....	....	....	....	....	13	7	2	9	4	....	....	....
1960-61	Regina Pats	SJHL	60	38	42	80	....	....	....	25	....	....	....	....	....	....	....	....	....	....	10	9	10	19	6	....	....	....
1961-62	Regina Pats	SJHL	52	*57	31	88	....	....	....	28	....	....	....	....	....	....	....	....	....	....	....	....	....	....	....	....	....	....
	Spokane Comets	WHL	....	....	....	....	....	....	....	....	....	....	....	....	....	....	....	....	....	....	4	1	3	4	0	....	....	....
1962-63	Hull-Ottawa Canadiens	EPHL	72	19	22	41	....	....	....	16	....	....	....	....	....	....	....	....	....	....	3	1	0	1	2	....	....	....
1963-64	Cincinnati Wings	CHL	54	19	30	49	....	....	....	14	....	....	....	....	....	....	....	....	....	....	....	....	....	....	....	....	....	....
	Pittsburgh Hornets	AHL	16	6	9	15	....	....	....	4	....	....	....	....	....	....	....	....	....	....	5	1	3	4	4	....	....	....
1964-65	Memphis Wings	CHL	53	41	24	65	....	....	....	28	....	....	....	....	....	....	....	....	....	....	....	....	....	....	....	....	....	....
	Pittsburgh Hornets	AHL	13	4	2	0	....	....	....	2	....	....	....	....	....	....	....	....	....	....	2	1	0	1	0	....	....	....
1965-66	Pittsburgh Hornets	AHL	70	29	29	58	....	....	....	35	....	....	....	....	....	....	....	....	....	....	3	1	1	2	0	....	....	
1966-67	Memphis Wings	CHL	65	*39	37	76	....	....	....	32	....	....	....	....	....	....	....	....	....	....	7	4	3	7	0	....	....	....
1967-68	**St. Louis Blues**	**NHL**	**13**	**1**	**1**	**2**	**1**	**1**	**2**	**4**	**1**	**0**	**0**	**9**	**11.1**	**4**	**4**	**4**	**0**	**–4**	....	....	....	....	....	....	....	....
	Kansas City Blues	CHL	59	22	23	45	....	....	....	26	....	....	....	....	....	....	....	....	....	....	7	5	7	12	5	....	....	....
1968-69	Buffalo Bisons	AHL	74	32	39	71	....	....	....	10	....	....	....	....	....	....	....	....	....	....	6	1	3	4	7	....	....	....
1969-70	Cleveland Barons	AHL	70	37	44	81	....	....	....	10	....	....	....	....	....	....	....	....	....	....	....	....	....	....	....	....	....	....
1970-71	**Minnesota North Stars**	**NHL**	**12**	**0**	**1**	**1**	**0**	**1**	**1**	**0**	**0**	**0**	**0**	**16**	**0.0**	**3**	**1**	**5**	**0**	**–3**	....	....	....	....	....	....	....	....
	Cleveland Barons	AHL	59	27	48	75	....	....	....	39	....	....	....	....	....	....	....	....	....	....	8	2	2	4	4	....	....	....
1971-72	Cleveland Barons	AHL	75	33	33	66	....	....	....	16	....	....	....	....	....	....	....	....	....	....	5	2	1	3	4	....	....	....
1972-73	Winnipeg Jets	WHA	78	38	65	103	....	....	....	15	....	....	....	....	....	....	....	....	....	....	14	*13	15	*28	2	....	....	....
1973-74	Winnipeg Jets	WHA	74	27	28	55	....	....	....	8	....	....	....	....	....	....	....	....	....	....	4	3	1	4	2	....	....	....
1974-75	Winnipeg Jets	WHA	79	16	31	47	....	....	....	8	....	....	....	....	....	....	....	....	....	....	....	....	....	....	....	....	....	....
1975-76	Winnipeg Jets	WHA	80	16	31	47	....	....	....	38	....	....	....	....	....	....	....	....	....	....	13	2	3	5	10	....		....
	NHL Totals		**25**	**1**	**2**	**3**	**1**	**2**	**3**	**4**	**1**	**0**	**0**	**25**	**4.0**	**7**	**5**	**9**	**0**		....	....	....	....	....	....	....	....
	Other Major League Totals		311	97	155	252	....	....	....	69	....	....	....	....	....	....	....	....	....		31	18	19	37	14	....	....	....

AHL Second All-Star Team (1970)

Claimed by **Detroit** from **Hull-Ottawa** (EPHL) In Inter-League Draft, June 4, 1963. Claimed by **St. Louis** from **Detroit** in Expansion Draft, June 6, 1967. Traded to **Montreal** by **St. Louis** with Bob Schmautz for Ernie Wakely, June 27, 1969. Traded to **Minnesota** by **Montreal** for cash, June, 1970. Selected by **Winnipeg** (WHA) in 1972 WHA General Player Draft, February 12, 1972.

• BEAUDOIN, SERGE

Serge Beaudoin D – L. 6'2", 215 lbs. b: Montreal, Que., 11/30/1952. Philadelphia's 7th choice, 103rd overall, in 1972 Amateur Draft.

Season	Club	League	GP	G	A	Pts	AG	AA	APts	PIM	PP	SH	GW	S	%	TGF	PGF	TGA	PGA	+/-	GP	G	A	Pts	PIM	PP	SH	GW
1969-70	Laval Saints	QJHL	38	2	15	17	....	....	....	178	....	....	....	....	....	....	....	....	....	....	....	....	....	....	....	....	....	....
1970-71	Trois-Rivieres Ducs	QJHL	56	8	33	41	....	....	....	191	....	....	....	....	....	....	....	....	....	....	11	0	7	7	41	....	....	....
1971-72	Trois-Rivieres Ducs	QMJHL	61	17	50	67	....	....	....	244	....	....	....	....	....	....	....	....	....	....	5	0	1	1	59	....	....	....
1972-73	Roanoke Valley Rebels	EHL	76	10	43	53	....	....	....	221	....	....	....	....	....	....	....	....	....	....	16	1	10	11	43	....	....	....
1973-74	Vancouver Blazers	WHA	26	1	11	12	....	....	....	37	....	....	....	....	....	....	....	....	....	....	....	....	....	....	....	....	....	....
	Roanoke Valley Rebels	SHL	37	8	20	28	....	....	....	179	....	....	....	....	....	....	....	....	....	....	....	....	....	....	....	....	....	....
1974-75	Tulsa Oilers	CHL	37	6	31	37	....	....	....	139	....	....	....	....	....	....	....	....	....	....	2	0	0	0	8	....	....	....
	Vancouver Blazers	WHA	4	0	0	0	....	....	....	2	....	....	....	....	....	....	....	....	....	....	....	....	....	....	....	....	....	....
1975-76	Phoenix Roadrunners	WHA	76	0	21	21	....	....	....	102	....	....	....	....	....	....	....	....	....	....	5	1	0	1	10	....	....	....
1976-77	Phoenix Roadrunners	WHA	77	6	24	30	....	....	....	136	....	....	....	....	....	....	....	....	....	....	....	....	....	....	....	....	....	....
1977-78	Cincinnati Stingers	WHA	13	0	1	1	....	....	....	10	....	....	....	....	....	....	....	....	....	....	....	....	....	....	....	....	....	....
	Birmingham Bulls	WHA	64	8	25	33	....	....	....	105	....	....	....	....	....	....	....	....	....	....	5	1	0	1	46	....	....	....
1978-79	Binghamton Whalers	AHL	3	1	1	2	....	....	....	0	....	....	....	....	....	....	....	....	....	....	....	....	....	....	....	....	....	....
	Birmingham Bulls	WHA	72	5	21	26	....	....	....	127	....	....	....	....	....	....	....	....	....	....	....	....	....	....	....	....	....	....
1979-80	**Atlanta Flames**	**NHL**	**3**	**0**	**0**	**0**	**0**	**0**	**0**	**0**	**0**	**0**	**0**	**1**	**0.0**	**0**	**0**	**1**	**0**	**–1**	....	....	....	....	....	....	....	....
	Birmingham Bulls	CHL	76	6	26	32	....	....	....	135	....	....	....	....	....	....	....	....	....	....	3	0	1	1	6	....	....	....
1980-81	Birmingham Bulls	CHL	7	0	3	3	....	....	....	12	....	....	....	....	....	....	....	....	....	....	....	....	....	....	....	....	....	....
	NHL Totals		**3**	**0**	**0**	**0**	**0**	**0**	**0**	**0**	**0**	**0**	**0**	**1**	**0.0**	**0**	**0**	**1**	**0**		....	....	....	....	....	....		
	Other Major League Totals		332	20	103	123	....	....	....	519	....	....	....	....	....	....	....	....	....		10	2	0	2	56	....	....	....

SHL Second All-Star Team (1974)

Selected by **Miami-Philadelphia** (WHA) in 1972 WHA General Player Draft, February 12, 1972. Transferred to **Vancouver** (WHA) when **Philadelphia** (WHA) franchise relocated, May, 1973. Traded to **Phoenix** (WHA) by **Vancouver** (WHA) with Pete McNamee and John Migneault for Hugh Harris, November, 1974. Signed as a free agent by **Cincinnati** (WHA) after **Phoenix** (WHA) franchise folded, September, 1977. Traded to **Birmingham** (WHA) by **Cincinnati** (WHA) for cash, November 5, 1977. Signed as a free agent by **Atlanta**, August 15, 1979.

• BEAUDOIN, YVES

Yves Beaudoin D – R. 5'11", 180 lbs. b: Pointe-aux-Trembles, Que., 1/7/1965. Washington's 6th choice, 203rd overall, in 1983 Entry Draft.

Season	Club	League	GP	G	A	Pts	AG	AA	APts	PIM	PP	SH	GW	S	%	TGF	PGF	TGA	PGA	+/-	GP	G	A	Pts	PIM	PP	SH	GW
1981-82	Hull Olympiques	QMJHL	50	2	18	20	....	....	....	39	....	....	....	....	....	....	....	....	....	....	....	....	....	....	....	....	....	....
1982-83	Hull Olympiques	QMJHL	6	1	2	3	....	....	....	9	....	....	....	....	....	....	....	....	....	....	....	....	....	....	....	....	....	....
	Shawinigan Cataracts	QMJHL	56	11	23	34	....	....	....	51	....	....	....	....	....	....	....	....	....	....	10	2	2	4	18	....	....	....
1983-84	Shawinigan Cataracts	QMJHL	68	14	43	57	....	....	....	93	....	....	....	....	....	....	....	....	....	....	6	1	6	7	2	....	....	....
1984-85	Shawinigan Cataracts	QMJHL	58	20	38	58	....	....	....	78	....	....	....	....	....	....	....	....	....	....	9	4	3	7	31	....	....	....
	Canada	WJC-A	7	0	3	3	....	....	....	4	....	....	....	....	....	....	....	....	....	....	....	....	....	....	....	....	....	....

			REGULAR SEASON																		PLAYOFFS							
Season	**Club**	**League**	**GP**	**G**	**A**	**Pts**	**AG**	**AA**	**APts**	**PIM**	**PP**	**SH**	**GW**	**S**	**%**	**TGF**	**PGF**	**TGA**	**PGA**	**+/–**	**GP**	**G**	**A**	**Pts**	**PIM**	**PP**	**SH**	**GW**
1985-86	**Washington Capitals**	**NHL**	**4**	**0**	**0**	**0**	**0**	**0**	**0**	**0**	**0**	**0**	**0**	**7**	**0.0**	**0**	**0**	**4**	**0**	**–4**								
	Binghamton Whalers	AHL	48	5	12	17				36											6	1	2	3	0			
1986-87	**Washington Capitals**	**NHL**	**6**	**0**	**0**	**0**	**0**	**0**	**0**	**5**	**0**	**0**	**0**	**4**	**0.0**	**1**	**0**	**5**	**0**	**–4**								
	Binghamton Whalers	AHL	63	11	25	36				35											11	0	1	1	6			
1987-88	**Washington Capitals**	**NHL**	**1**	**0**	**0**	**0**	**0**	**0**	**0**	**0**	**0**	**0**	**0**	**0**	**0.0**	**0**	**0**	**1**	**0**	**–1**								
	Binghamton Whalers	AHL	64	11	39	50				56											4	0	2	2	6			
1988-89	Innsbruck	Austria	46	9	26	35																						
1989-90	Nottingham Panthers	Britain	22	18	25	43				34																		
	NHL Totals		**11**	**0**	**0**	**0**	**0**	**0**	**0**	**5**	**0**	**0**	**0**	**11**	**0.0**	**1**	**0**	**10**	**0**									

QMJHL First All-Star Team (1985) • Memorial Cup All-Star Team (1985)

• BEAUFAIT, MARK

Mark Beaufait C – R. 5′9″, 170 lbs. b: Livonia, MI, 5/13/1970. San Jose's 2nd choice, 7th overall, in 1991 Supplemental Draft.

Season	Club	League	GP	G	A	Pts	AG	AA	APts	PIM	PP	SH	GW	S	%	TGF	PGF	TGA	PGA	+/–	GP	G	A	Pts	PIM	PP	SH	GW
1988-89	Northern Michigan University	WCHA	11	2	1	3				2																		
1989-90	Northern Michigan University	WCHA	34	10	14	24				12																		
1990-91	Northern Michigan University	WCHA	47	19	30	49				18																		
1991-92	Northern Michigan University	WCHA	39	31	44	75				43																		
1992-93	**San Jose Sharks**	**NHL**	**5**	**1**	**0**	**1**	**1**	**0**	**1**	**0**	**0**	**0**	**0**	**3**	**33.3**	**1**	**0**	**3**	**1**	**–1**								
	Kansas City Blades	IHL	66	19	40	59				22											9	1	1	2	8			
1993-94	United States	Nat-Team	51	22	29	51				36																		
	United States	Olympics	8	1	4	5				2																		
	Kansas City Blades	IHL	21	12	9	21				18																		
1994-95	San Diego Gulls	IHL	68	24	39	63				22											5	2	2	4	2			
1995-96	Orlando Solar Bears	IHL	77	30	79	109				87											22	9	*19	*28	22			
1996-97	Orlando Solar Bears	IHL	80	26	65	91				63											10	5	8	13	18			
1997-98	Orlando Solar Bears	IHL	76	24	61	85				56											17	6	16	22	10			
	NHL Totals		**5**	**1**	**0**	**1**	**1**	**0**	**1**	**0**	**0**	**0**	**0**	**3**	**33.3**	**1**	**0**	**3**	**1**									

IHL Second All-Star Team (1997)

• BECK, BARRY

Barry "Bubba" Beck D – L. 6′3″, 216 lbs. b: Vancouver, B.C., 6/3/1957. Colorado's 1st choice, 2nd overall, in 1977 Amateur Draft.

Season	Club	League	GP	G	A	Pts	AG	AA	APts	PIM	PP	SH	GW	S	%	TGF	PGF	TGA	PGA	+/–	GP	G	A	Pts	PIM	PP	SH	GW
1973-74	Langley Lancers	BCJHL	63	8	28	36				329																		
	Kamloops Blazers	WCJHL	1	0	0	0				0																		
1974-75	New Westminster Bruins	WCJHL	58	9	33	42				162											18	4	9	13	52			
	Kamloops Blazers	WCJHL	1	0	0	0				0																		
1975-76	New Westminster Bruins	WCJHL	68	19	80	99				325											17	3	9	12	58			
1976-77	New Westminster Bruins	WCJHL	61	16	46	62				167											12	4	6	10	39			
1977-78	**Colorado Rockies**	**NHL**	**75**	**22**	**38**	**60**	**21**	**31**	**52**	**89**	**6**	**0**	**4**	**271**	**8.1**	**133**	**42**	**133**	**28**	**–14**	**2**	**0**	**1**	**1**	**0**	**0**	**0**	**0**
1978-79	**Colorado Rockies**	**NHL**	**63**	**14**	**28**	**42**	**13**	**21**	**34**	**91**	**5**	**0**	**0**	**217**	**6.5**	**102**	**36**	**124**	**28**	**–30**								
	NHL All-Stars	Chal Cup	3	0	1	1				2																		
1979-80	**Colorado Rockies**	**NHL**	**10**	**1**	**5**	**6**	**1**	**4**	**5**	**8**	**0**	**0**	**0**	**20**	**5.0**	**11**	**3**	**16**	**6**	**–2**								
	New York Rangers	**NHL**	**61**	**14**	**45**	**59**	**13**	**35**	**48**	**98**	**5**	**0**	**4**	**150**	**9.3**	**124**	**46**	**80**	**18**	**+16**	**9**	**1**	**4**	**5**	**6**	**1**	**0**	**0**
1980-81	**New York Rangers**	**NHL**	**75**	**11**	**23**	**34**	**9**	**16**	**25**	**231**	**6**	**1**	**0**	**182**	**6.0**	**114**	**30**	**111**	**36**	**+9**	**14**	**5**	**8**	**13**	**32**	**1**	**1**	**0**
1981-82	Canada	C Cup	7	0	0	0				2																		
	New York Rangers	**NHL**	**60**	**9**	**29**	**38**	**7**	**19**	**26**	**111**	**5**	**0**	**0**	**160**	**5.6**	**125**	**40**	**99**	**33**	**+19**	**10**	**1**	**5**	**6**	**14**	**1**	**0**	**0**
1982-83	**New York Rangers**	**NHL**	**66**	**12**	**22**	**34**	**10**	**15**	**25**	**112**	**4**	**0**	**1**	**162**	**7.4**	**120**	**22**	**116**	**40**	**+22**	**9**	**2**	**4**	**6**	**8**	**0**	**0**	**0**
1983-84	**New York Rangers**	**NHL**	**72**	**9**	**27**	**36**	**7**	**18**	**25**	**134**	**2**	**1**	**0**	**159**	**5.7**	**103**	**10**	**132**	**51**	**+12**	**4**	**1**	**0**	**1**	**6**	**0**	**0**	**0**
1984-85	**New York Rangers**	**NHL**	**56**	**7**	**19**	**26**	**6**	**13**	**19**	**65**	**2**	**2**	**0**	**70**	**10.0**	**90**	**18**	**110**	**27**	**–11**	**3**	**0**	**1**	**1**	**11**	**0**	**0**	**0**
1985-86	**New York Rangers**	**NHL**	**25**	**4**	**8**	**12**	**3**	**5**	**8**	**24**	**3**	**0**	**1**	**53**	**7.5**	**39**	**15**	**30**	**13**	**+7**								
1986-1989			DID NOT PLAY – RETIRED																									
1989-90	**Los Angeles Kings**	**NHL**	**52**	**1**	**7**	**8**	**1**	**5**	**6**	**53**	**0**	**0**	**0**	**36**	**2.8**	**49**	**2**	**70**	**26**	**+3**								
	NHL Totals		**615**	**104**	**251**	**355**	**91**	**182**	**273**	**1016**	**38**	**4**	**10**	**1480**	**7.0**	**1010**	**264**	**1021**	**306**		**51**	**10**	**23**	**33**	**77**	**3**	**1**	**0**

WCJHL First All-Star Team (1976, 1977) • Memorial Cup All-Star Team (1976, 1977) • Won Stafford Smythe Memorial Trophy (Memorial Cup Tournament MVP) (1977)

Played in NHL All-Star Game (1978, 1979, 1980, 1981, 1982)

Traded to **NY Rangers** by **Colorado** for Pat Hickey, Lucien Deblois, Mike McEwen, Dean Turner and Bobby Crawford, November 2, 1979. Traded to **LA Kings** by **NY Rangers** for cash and future considerations, September 1, 1988.

• BEDDOES, CLAYTON

Clayton Beddoes C – L. 5′11″, 190 lbs. b: Bentley, Alta., 11/10/1970.

Season	Club	League	GP	G	A	Pts	AG	AA	APts	PIM	PP	SH	GW	S	%	TGF	PGF	TGA	PGA	+/–	GP	G	A	Pts	PIM	PP	SH	GW
1990-91	Lake Superior State	CCHA	45	14	28	42				26																		
1991-92	Lake Superior State	CCHA	38	14	26	40				24																		
1992-93	Lake Superior State	CCHA	43	18	40	58				30																		
1993-94	Lake Superior State	CCHA	44	23	31	54				56																		
1994-95	Providence Bruins	AHL	65	16	20	36				39											13	3	1	4	18			
1995-96	**Boston Bruins**	**NHL**	**39**	**1**	**6**	**7**	**1**	**5**	**6**	**44**	**0**	**0**	**0**	**18**	**5.6**	**9**	**0**	**19**	**5**	**–5**								
	Providence Bruins	AHL	32	10	15	25				24											4	2	3	5	0			
1996-97	**Boston Bruins**	**NHL**	**21**	**1**	**2**	**3**	**1**	**2**	**3**	**13**	**0**	**0**	**0**	**11**	**9.1**	**5**	**0**	**7**	**1**	**–1**								
	Providence Bruins	AHL	36	11	23	34				60											7	2	0	2	4			
1997-98	Detroit Vipers	IHL	65	22	24	46				63											22	5	10	15	16			
	NHL Totals		**60**	**2**	**8**	**10**	**2**	**7**	**9**	**57**	**0**	**0**	**0**	**29**	**6.9**	**14**	**0**	**26**	**6**									

CCHA Second All-Star Team (1994) • NCAA West Second All-American Team (1994) • NCAA Championship All-Tournament Team (1994)

Signed as a free agent by **Boston**, June 2, 1994. Signed as a free agent by **Ottawa**, July 28, 1997.

• BEDNARSKI, JOHN

John Bednarski D – L. 5′10″, 195 lbs. b: Thunder Bay, Ont., 7/4/1952.

Season	Club	League	GP	G	A	Pts	AG	AA	APts	PIM	PP	SH	GW	S	%	TGF	PGF	TGA	PGA	+/–	GP	G	A	Pts	PIM	PP	SH	GW
1970-71	West Kildonan North Stars	MJHL	46	10	27	37				*229																		
	Winnipeg Jets	WCJHL	3	0	0	0				2																		
1971-72	Winnipeg Jets	WCJHL	65	4	17	21				212																		
1972-73	Rochester Americans	AHL	72	14	24	38				205											6	1	8	9	16			
1973-74	Providence Reds	AHL	76	15	46	61				*222											15	3	11	14	35			
1974-75	**New York Rangers**	**NHL**	**35**	**1**	**10**	**11**	**1**	**8**	**9**	**37**	**0**	**0**	**0**	**45**	**2.2**	**32**	**2**	**35**	**4**	**–1**	**1**	**0**	**0**	**0**	**17**	**0**	**0**	**0**
	Providence Reds	AHL	25	6	5	11				66											1	0	0	0	6			
1975-76	**New York Rangers**	**NHL**	**59**	**1**	**8**	**9**	**1**	**6**	**7**	**77**	**0**	**0**	**0**	**62**	**1.6**	**41**	**1**	**62**	**7**	**–15**								
1976-77	**New York Rangers**	**NHL**	**5**	**0**	**0**	**0**	**0**	**0**	**0**	**0**	**0**	**0**	**0**	**3**	**0.0**	**1**	**0**	**5**	**1**	**–3**								
	New Haven Nighthawks	AHL	74	10	48	58				110											6	2	6	8	4			
1977-78	New Haven Nighthawks	AHL	64	12	40	52				98											15	0	6	6	21			
1978-79	New Haven Nighthawks	AHL	77	13	41	54				146											10	2	5	7	28			
1979-80	**Edmonton Oilers**	**NHL**	**1**	**0**	**0**	**0**	**0**	**0**	**0**	**0**	**0**	**0**	**0**	**2**	**0.0**	**0**	**0**	**0**	**0**	**0**								
	Cincinnati Stingers	CHL	28	6	18	24				53																		
	Adirondack Red Wings	AHL	46	11	33	44				54											5	0	4	4	16			
1980-81	Rochester Americans	AHL	76	3	18	21				156																		
1981-82	Erie Blades	AHL	66	10	30	40				59																		
	NHL Totals		**100**	**2**	**18**	**20**	**2**	**14**	**16**	**114**	**0**	**0**	**0**	**112**	**1.8**	**74**	**3**	**102**	**12**		**1**	**0**	**0**	**0**	**17**	**0**	**0**	**0**

AHL Second All-Star Team (1974, 1978) • AHL First All-Star Team (1977, 1979)

Signed as a free agent by **NY Rangers**, September, 1972. Signed as a free agent by **Edmonton**, July 15, 1979. Signed as a free agent by **Buffalo**, June 26, 1980.

• BEERS, BOB

Bob Beers D – R. 6′2″, 200 lbs. b: Pittsburgh, PA, 5/20/1967. Boston's 10th choice, 210th overall, in 1985 Entry Draft.

Season	Club	League	GP	G	A	Pts	AG	AA	APts	PIM	PP	SH	GW	S	%	TGF	PGF	TGA	PGA	+/–	GP	G	A	Pts	PIM	PP	SH	GW
1984-85	Buffalo Jr. Sabres	NYJHL	47	11	39	50				96																		
1985-86	Northern Arizona University	NCAA	28	11	39	50				96																		
1986-87	University of Maine	H.E.	28	0	13	13				46																		
1987-88	University of Maine	H.E.	41	3	11	14				72																		
1988-89	University of Maine	H.E.	44	10	27	37				53																		

			REGULAR SEASON																		PLAYOFFS							
Season	Club	League	GP	G	A	Pts	AG	AA	APts	PIM	PP	SH	GW	S	%	TGF	PGF	TGA	PGA	+/-	GP	G	A	Pts	PIM	PP	SH	GW
1989-90	**Boston Bruins**	**NHL**	**3**	**0**	**1**	**1**	**0**	**1**	**1**	**6**	**0**	**0**	**0**	**0**	**0.0**	**4**	**1**	**2**	**1**	**+2**	**14**	**1**	**1**	**2**	**18**	**0**	**0**	**0**
	Maine Mariners	AHL	74	7	36	43	....	....	....	63	....	....	....	....	....	....	....	....	....	....	....	....	....	....	....	....	....	....
1990-91	**Boston Bruins**	**NHL**	**16**	**0**	**1**	**1**	**0**	**1**	**1**	**10**	**0**	**0**	**0**	**9**	**0.0**	**7**	**1**	**15**	**1**	**–8**	**6**	**0**	**0**	**0**	**4**	**0**	**0**	**0**
	Maine Mariners	AHL	36	2	16	18	....	....	....	21	....	....	....	....	....	....	....	....	....	....	....	....	....	....	....	....	....	....
1991-92	**Boston Bruins**	**NHL**	**31**	**0**	**5**	**5**	**0**	**4**	**4**	**29**	**0**	**0**	**0**	**25**	**0.0**	**14**	**2**	**27**	**2**	**–13**	**1**	**0**	**0**	**0**	**0**	**0**	**0**	**0**
	Maine Mariners	AHL	33	6	23	29	....	....	....	24	....	....	....	....	....	....	....	....	....	....	....	....	....	....	....	....	....	....
1992-93	Providence Bruins	AHL	6	1	2	3	....	....	....	10	....	....	....	....	....	....	....	....	....	....	....	....	....	....	....	....	....	....
	Tampa Bay Lightning	**NHL**	**64**	**12**	**24**	**36**	**10**	**16**	**26**	**70**	**7**	**0**	**0**	**138**	**8.7**	**87**	**38**	**106**	**32**	**–25**	....	....	....	....	....	....	....	....
	Atlanta Knights	IHL	1	0	0	0	....	....	....	0	....	....	....	....	....	....	....	....	....	....	....	....	....	....	....	....	....	....
	United States	WC-A	6	1	2	3	....	....	....	2	....	....	....	....	....	....	....	....	....	....	....	....	....	....	....	....	....	....
1993-94	**Tampa Bay Lightning**	**NHL**	**16**	**1**	**5**	**6**	**1**	**4**	**5**	**12**	**1**	**0**	**0**	**35**	**2.9**	**13**	**7**	**20**	**3**	**–11**	....	....	....	....	....	....	....	....
	Edmonton Oilers	**NHL**	**66**	**10**	**27**	**37**	**9**	**21**	**30**	**74**	**5**	**0**	**0**	**152**	**6.6**	**85**	**29**	**92**	**25**	**–11**	....	....	....	....	....	....	....	....
	United States	WC-A	8	2	0	2	....	....	....	4	....	....	....	....	....	....	....	....	....	....	....	....	....	....	....	....	....	....
1994-95	**New York Islanders**	**NHL**	**22**	**2**	**7**	**9**	**4**	**10**	**14**	**6**	**1**	**0**	**0**	**38**	**5.3**	**22**	**4**	**37**	**11**	**–8**	....	....	....	....	....	....	....	....
1995-96	**New York Islanders**	**NHL**	**13**	**0**	**5**	**5**	**0**	**4**	**4**	**10**	**0**	**0**	**0**	**9**	**0.0**	**16**	**7**	**14**	**3**	**–2**	....	....	....	....	....	....	....	....
	Utah Grizzlies	IHL	65	6	36	42	....	....	....	54	....	....	....	....	....	....	....	....	....	....	22	1	12	13	16	....	....	....
1996-97	**Boston Bruins**	**NHL**	**27**	**3**	**4**	**7**	**3**	**4**	**7**	**8**	**1**	**0**	**0**	**49**	**6.1**	**21**	**2**	**22**	**3**	**0**	....	....	....	....	....	....	....	....
	Providence Bruins	AHL	45	10	12	22	....	....	....	18	....	....	....	....	....	....	....	....	....	....	....	....	....	....	....	....	....	....
	United States	WC-A	8	1	0	1	....	....	....	8	....	....	....	....	....	....	....	....	....	....	....	....	....	....	....	....	....	....
	NHL Totals		**258**	**28**	**79**	**107**	**27**	**65**	**92**	**225**	**15**	**0**	**0**	**455**	**6.2**	**269**	**91**	**335**	**81**		**21**	**1**	**1**	**2**	**22**	**0**	**0**	**0**

WCHA First All-Star Team (1982)

Hockey East Second All-Star Team (1989) • NCAA East Second All-American Team (1989)

Traded to **Tampa Bay** by **Boston** for Stephane Richer, October 28, 1992. Traded to **Edmonton** by **Tampa Bay** for Chris Joseph, November 11, 1993. Signed as a free agent by **NY Islanders**, August 29, 1994. Signed as a free agent by **Boston**, August 5, 1996.

• BEERS, EDDY

Eddy Beers LW – L. 6'2", 195 lbs. b: Merritt, B.C., 10/12/1959.

Season	Club	League	GP	G	A	Pts	AG	AA	APts	PIM	PP	SH	GW	S	%	TGF	PGF	TGA	PGA	+/-	GP	G	A	Pts	PIM	PP	SH	GW
1978-79	University of Denver	WCHA	17	7	5	12	....	....	....	23	....	....	....	....	....	....	....	....	....	....	....	....	....	....	....	....	....	....
1979-80	University of Denver	WCHA	36	13	20	33	....	....	....	24	....	....	....	....	....	....	....	....	....	....	....	....	....	....	....	....	....	....
1980-81	University of Denver	WCHA	39	24	15	39	....	....	....	63	....	....	....	....	....	....	....	....	....	....	....	....	....	....	....	....	....	....
1981-82	University of Denver	WCHA	42	50	34	84	....	....	....	59	....	....	....	....	....	....	....	....	....	....	....	....	....	....	....	....	....	....
	Calgary Flames	**NHL**	**5**	**1**	**1**	**2**	**1**	**1**	**2**	**21**	**0**	**0**	**0**	**7**	**14.3**	**3**	**0**	**3**	**0**	**0**	....	....	....	....	....	....	....	....
1982-83	**Calgary Flames**	**NHL**	**41**	**11**	**15**	**26**	**9**	**10**	**19**	**21**	**2**	**0**	**2**	**72**	**15.3**	**43**	**5**	**27**	**0**	**+11**	**8**	**1**	**1**	**2**	**27**	**0**	**0**	**1**
	Colorado Flames	CHL	29	12	17	29	....	....	....	52	....	....	....	....	....	....	....	....	....	....	....	....	....	....	....	....	....	....
1983-84	**Calgary Flames**	**NHL**	**73**	**36**	**39**	**75**	**29**	**26**	**55**	**88**	**16**	**0**	**4**	**189**	**19.0**	**122**	**48**	**67**	**0**	**+7**	**11**	**2**	**5**	**7**	**12**	**0**	**0**	**0**
1984-85	**Calgary Flames**	**NHL**	**74**	**28**	**40**	**68**	**23**	**27**	**50**	**94**	**13**	**0**	**0**	**171**	**16.4**	**104**	**38**	**59**	**0**	**+7**	**3**	**1**	**0**	**1**	**0**	**1**	**0**	**0**
1985-86	**Calgary Flames**	**NHL**	**33**	**11**	**10**	**21**	**9**	**7**	**16**	**8**	**4**	**0**	**1**	**83**	**13.3**	**42**	**22**	**23**	**0**	**–3**	....	....	....	....	....	....	....	....
	St. Louis Blues	**NHL**	**24**	**7**	**11**	**18**	**6**	**7**	**13**	**24**	**4**	**0**	**0**	**53**	**13.2**	**25**	**8**	**20**	**0**	**–3**	**19**	**3**	**4**	**7**	**8**	**2**	**0**	**1**
	NHL Totals		**250**	**94**	**116**	**210**	**77**	**78**	**155**	**256**	**39**	**0**	**7**	**575**	**16.3**	**339**	**121**	**199**	**0**		**41**	**7**	**10**	**17**	**47**	**3**	**0**	**2**

Signed as a free agent by **Calgary**, April 1, 1982. Traded to **St. Louis** by **Calgary** with Charlie Bourgeois and Gino Cavallini for Joe Mullen, Terry Johnson and Rik Wilson, February 1, 1986.

• BEGIN, STEVE

Steve Begin C – L. 5'11", 180 lbs. b: Trois-Rivieres, Que., 6/14/1978. Calgary's 3rd choice, 40th overall, in 1996 Entry Draft.

Season	Club	League	GP	G	A	Pts	AG	AA	APts	PIM	PP	SH	GW	S	%	TGF	PGF	TGA	PGA	+/-	GP	G	A	Pts	PIM	PP	SH	GW
1995-96	Val d'Or Foreurs	QMJHL	64	13	23	36	....	....	....	218	....	....	....	....	....	....	....	....	....	....	13	1	3	4	33	....	....	....
1996-97	Val d'Or Foreurs	QMJHL	58	13	33	46	....	....	....	229	....	....	....	....	....	....	....	....	....	....	10	0	3	3	8	....	....	....
	Saint John Flames	AHL	....	....	....	....	....	....	....	....	....	....	....	....	....	....	....	....	....	....	4	0	2	2	6	....	....	....
1997-98	Val d'Or Foreurs	QMJHL	35	18	17	35	....	....	....	73	....	....	....	....	....	....	....	....	....	....	15	2	12	14	34	....	....	....
	Canada	WJC-A	7	0	0	0	....	....	....	10	....	....	....	....	....	....	....	....	....	....	....	....	....	....	....	....	....	....
	Calgary Flames	**NHL**	**5**	**0**	**0**	**0**	**0**	**0**	**0**	**23**	**0**	**0**	**0**	**2**	**0.0**	**0**	**0**	**2**	**2**	**0**	....	....	....	....	....	....	....	....
	NHL Totals		**5**	**0**	**0**	**0**	**0**	**0**	**0**	**23**	**0**	**0**	**0**	**2**	**0.0**	**0**	**0**	**2**	**2**		....	....	....	....	....	....	....	....

• BELAK, WADE

Wade Belak D – R. 6'4", 213 lbs. b: Saskatoon, Sask., 7/3/1976. Quebec's 1st choice, 12th overall, in 1994 Entry Draft.

Season	Club	League	GP	G	A	Pts	AG	AA	APts	PIM	PP	SH	GW	S	%	TGF	PGF	TGA	PGA	+/-	GP	G	A	Pts	PIM	PP	SH	GW
1992-93	North Battleford North Stars	SJHL	50	5	15	20	....	....	....	146	....	....	....	....	....	....	....	....	....	....	....	....	....	....	....	....	....	....
	Saskatoon Blades	WHL	7	0	0	0	....	....	....	23	....	....	....	....	....	....	....	....	....	....	7	0	0	0	0	....	....	....
1993-94	Saskatoon Blades	WHL	69	4	13	17	....	....	....	226	....	....	....	....	....	....	....	....	....	....	16	2	2	4	43	....	....	....
1994-95	Saskatoon Blades	WHL	72	4	14	18	....	....	....	290	....	....	....	....	....	....	....	....	....	....	9	0	0	0	36	....	....	....
	Cornwall Aces	AHL	....	....	....	....	....	....	....	....	....	....	....	....	....	....	....	....	....	....	11	1	2	3	40	....	....	....
1995-96	Saskatoon Blades	WHL	63	3	15	18	....	....	....	207	....	....	....	....	....	....	....	....	....	....	4	0	0	0	9	....	....	....
	Cornwall Aces	AHL	5	0	0	0	....	....	....	18	....	....	....	....	....	....	....	....	....	....	2	0	0	0	2	....	....	....
1996-97	**Colorado Avalanche**	**NHL**	**5**	**0**	**0**	**0**	**0**	**0**	**0**	**11**	**0**	**0**	**0**	**1**	**0.0**	**0**	**0**	**1**	**0**	**–1**	....	....	....	....	....	....	....	....
	Hershey Bears	AHL	65	1	7	8	....	....	....	320	....	....	....	....	....	....	....	....	....	....	16	0	1	1	61	....	....	....
1997-98	**Colorado Avalanche**	**NHL**	**8**	**1**	**1**	**2**	**1**	**1**	**2**	**27**	**0**	**0**	**1**	**2**	**50.0**	**2**	**0**	**5**	**0**	**–3**	....	....	....	....	....	....	....	....
	Hershey Bears	AHL	11	0	0	0	....	....	....	30	....	....	....	....	....	....	....	....	....	....	....	....	....	....	....	....	....	....
	NHL Totals		**13**	**1**	**1**	**2**	**1**	**1**	**2**	**38**	**0**	**0**	**1**	**3**	**33.3**	**2**	**0**	**6**	**0**		....	....	....	....	....	....	....	....

Rights transferred to **Colorado** after **Quebec** franchise relocated, June 21, 1995.

• BELANGER, ALAIN

Alain (Bam-Bam) Belanger RW – R. 6'1", 190 lbs. b: St. Janvier, Que., 1/18/1956. Toronto's 2nd choice, 48th overall, in 1976 Amateur Draft.

Season	Club	League	GP	G	A	Pts	AG	AA	APts	PIM	PP	SH	GW	S	%	TGF	PGF	TGA	PGA	+/-	GP	G	A	Pts	PIM	PP	SH	GW
1973-74	Drummondville Rangers	QMJHL	28	1	2	3	....	....	....	104	....	....	....	....	....	....	....	....	....	....	....	....	....	....	....	....	....	....
1974-75	Sherbrooke Beavers	QMJHL	51	17	19	36	....	....	....	342	....	....	....	....	....	....	....	....	....	....	....	....	....	....	....	....	....	....
1975-76	Sherbrooke Beavers	QMJHL	65	26	25	51	....	....	....	274	....	....	....	....	....	....	....	....	....	....	....	....	....	....	....	....	....	....
1976-77	Dallas Black Hawks	CHL	30	16	10	26	....	....	....	149	....	....	....	....	....	....	....	....	....	....	....	....	....	....	....	....	....	....
1977-78	**Toronto Maple Leafs**	**NHL**	**9**	**0**	**1**	**1**	**0**	**1**	**1**	**6**	**0**	**0**	**0**	**2**	**0.0**	**2**	**0**	**2**	**0**	**0**	....	....	....	....	....	....	....	....
	Dallas Black Hawks	CHL	61	7	16	23	....	....	....	*262	....	....	....	....	....	....	....	....	....	....	12	1	4	5	44	....	....	....
1978-79	New Brunswick Hawks	AHL	57	8	12	20	....	....	....	197	....	....	....	....	....	....	....	....	....	....	5	1	0	1	2	....	....	....
1979-80	New Brunswick Hawks	AHL	49	4	16	20	....	....	....	120	....	....	....	....	....	....	....	....	....	....	....	....	....	....	....	....	....	....
1980-81			DID NOT PLAY																									
1981-82			DID NOT PLAY																									
1982-83	Sherbrooke Jets	AHL	21	0	0	0		....	....	79	....	....	....	....	....	....	....	....	....	....	....	....	....	....	....	....	....	....
	NHL Totals		**9**	**0**	**1**	**1**	**0**	**1**	**1**	**6**	**0**	**0**	**0**	**2**	**0.0**	**2**	**0**	**2**	**0**		....	....	....	....	....	....	....	....

• BELANGER, JESSE

Jesse Belanger C – R. 6'1", 190 lbs. b: St. Georges de Beauce, Que., 6/15/1969.

Season	Club	League	GP	G	A	Pts	AG	AA	APts	PIM	PP	SH	GW	S	%	TGF	PGF	TGA	PGA	+/-	GP	G	A	Pts	PIM	PP	SH	GW
1987-88	Granby Bisons	QMJHL	69	33	43	76	....	....	....	10	....	....	....	....	....	....	....	....	....	....	5	3	3	6	0	....	....	....
1988-89	Granby Bisons	QMJHL	67	40	63	103	....	....	....	26	....	....	....	....	....	....	....	....	....	....	4	0	5	5	0	....	....	....
1989-90	Granby Bisons	QMJHL	67	53	54	107	....	....	....	53	....	....	....	....	....	....	....	....	....	....	....	....	....	....	....	....	....	....
1990-91	Fredericton Canadiens	AHL	75	40	58	98	....	....	....	30	....	....	....	....	....	....	....	....	....	....	6	2	4	6	0	....	....	....
1991-92	**Montreal Canadiens**	**NHL**	**4**	**0**	**0**	**0**	**0**	**0**	**0**	**0**	**0**	**0**	**0**	**4**	**0.0**	**2**	**0**	**3**	**0**	**–1**	....	....	....	....	....	....	....	....
	Fredericton Canadiens	AHL	65	30	41	71	....	....	....	26	....	....	....	....	....	....	....	....	....	....	7	3	3	6	2	....	....	....
1992-93	**Montreal Canadiens**	**NHL**	**19**	**4**	**2**	**6**	**3**	**1**	**4**	**4**	**0**	**0**	**0**	**24**	**16.7**	**8**	**0**	**13**	**6**	**+1**	**9**	**0**	**1**	**1**	**0**	**0**	**0**	**0**
	Fredericton Canadiens	AHL	39	19	32	51	....	....	....	24	....	....	....	....	....	....	....	....	....	....	....	....	....	....	....	....	....	....
1993-94	**Florida Panthers**	**NHL**	**70**	**17**	**33**	**50**	**16**	**25**	**41**	**16**	**11**	**0**	**3**	**104**	**16.3**	**69**	**34**	**42**	**3**	**–4**	....	....	....	....	....	....	....	....
1994-95	**Florida Panthers**	**NHL**	**47**	**15**	**14**	**29**	**27**	**21**	**48**	**18**	**6**	**0**	**3**	**89**	**16.9**	**38**	**18**	**25**	**0**	**–5**	....	....	....	....	....	....	....	....
1995-96	**Florida Panthers**	**NHL**	**63**	**17**	**21**	**38**	**17**	**17**	**34**	**10**	**7**	**0**	**1**	**140**	**12.1**	**65**	**41**	**30**	**1**	**–5**	....	....	....	....	....	....	....	....
	Vancouver Canucks	**NHL**	**9**	**3**	**0**	**3**	**3**	**0**	**3**	**4**	**1**	**0**	**1**	**11**	**27.3**	**3**	**1**	**2**	**0**	**0**	**3**	**0**	**2**	**2**	**2**	**0**	**0**	**0**
1996-97	**Edmonton Oilers**	**NHL**	**6**	**0**	**0**	**0**	**0**	**0**	**0**	**0**	**0**	**0**	**0**	**8**	**0.0**	**1**	**1**	**4**	**1**	**–3**	....	....	....	....	....	....	....	....
	Hamilton Bulldogs	AHL	6	4	3	7	....	....	....	0	....	....	....	....	....	....	....	....	....	....	....	....	....	....	....	....	....	....
	Quebec Rafales	IHL	47	34	28	62	....	....	....	18	....	....	....	....	....	....	....	....	....	....	9	3	5	8	13	....	....	....
1997-98	SC Herisau	Switz.	5	4	3	7	....	....	....	4	....	....	....	....	....	....	....	....	....	....	....	....	....	....	....	....	....	....
	Las Vegas Thunder	IHL	54	32	36	68	....	....	....	20	....	....	....	....	....	....	....	....	....	....	4	0	1	1	0	....	....	....
	NHL Totals		**218**	**56**	**70**	**126**	**66**	**64**	**130**	**52**	**25**	**0**	**8**	**380**	**14.7**	**186**	**95**	**119**	**11**		**12**	**0**	**3**	**3**	**2**	**0**	**0**	**0**

Signed as a free agent by **Montreal**, October 3, 1990. Claimed by **Florida** from **Montreal** in Expansion Draft, June 24, 1993. Traded to **Vancouver** by **Florida** for Vancouver's 3rd round choice (Oleg Kvasha) in 1996 Entry Draft and future considerations, March 20, 1996. Signed as a free agent by **Edmonton**, September 16, 1996.

● BELANGER, KEN

Ken Belanger LW – L. 6'4", 225 lbs. b: Sault Ste. Marie, Ont., 5/14/1974. Hartford's 7th choice, 153rd overall, in 1992 Entry Draft.

Season	Club	League	GP	G	A	Pts	AG	AA	APts	PIM	PP	SH	GW	S	%	TGF	PGF	TGA	PGA	+/–	Playoffs GP	G	A	Pts	PIM	PP	SH	GW
1991-92	Ottawa 67's	OHL	51	4	4	8				174											11	0	0	0	24			
1992-93	Ottawa 67's	OHL	34	6	12	18				139																		
	Guelph Platers	OHL	29	10	14	24				86											5	2	1	3	14			
1993-94	Guelph Platers	OHL	55	11	22	33				185											9	2	3	5	30			
1994-95	St. John's Maple Leafs	AHL	47	5	5	10				246											4	0	0	0	30			
	Toronto Maple Leafs	**NHL**	**3**	**0**	**0**	**0**	**0**	**0**	**0**	**9**	**0**	**0**	**0**	**1**	**0.0**	**0**	**0**	**0**	**0**	**0**								
1995-96	St. John's Maple Leafs	AHL	40	16	14	30				222																		
	New York Islanders	**NHL**	**7**	**0**	**0**	**0**	**0**	**0**	**0**	**27**	**0**	**0**	**0**	**0**	**0.0**	**0**	**0**	**2**	**0**	**–2**								
1996-97	**New York Islanders**	**NHL**	**18**	**0**	**2**	**2**	**0**	**2**	**2**	**102**	**0**	**0**	**0**	**5**	**0.0**	**3**	**0**	**4**	**0**	**–1**								
	Kentucky Thoroughblades	AHL	38	10	12	22				164											4	0	1	1	27			
1997-98	**New York Islanders**	**NHL**	**37**	**3**	**1**	**4**	**4**	**1**	**5**	**101**	**0**	**0**	**1**	**10**	**30.0**	**6**	**0**	**5**	**0**	**+1**								
	NHL Totals		**65**	**3**	**3**	**6**	**4**	**3**	**7**	**239**	**0**	**0**	**1**	**16**	**18.8**	**9**	**0**	**11**	**0**									

Traded to **Toronto** by **Hartford** for Toronto's 9th round choice (Matt Ball) in 1994 Entry Draft, March 18, 1994. Traded to **NY Islanders** by **Toronto** with Damian Rhodes for future considerations, January 23, 1996.

● BELANGER, ROGER

Roger Belanger C – R. 6', 190 lbs. b: St. Catharines, Ont., 12/1/1965. Pittsburgh's 3rd choice, 16th overall, in 1984 Entry Draft.

Season	Club	League	GP	G	A	Pts	AG	AA	APts	PIM	PP	SH	GW	S	%	TGF	PGF	TGA	PGA	+/–	Playoffs GP	G	A	Pts	PIM	PP	SH	GW
1981-82	London Nationals	Midget	25	20	21	41																						
1982-83	London Knights	OHL	68	17	14	31				53											1	0	0	0	5			
1983-84	Kingston Canadians	OHL	67	44	46	90				66																		
1984-85	Hamilton Steelhawks	OHL	3	3	3	6				0											17	3	10	13	47			
	Pittsburgh Penguins	**NHL**	**44**	**3**	**5**	**8**	**2**	**3**	**5**	**32**	**0**	**0**	**0**	**65**	**4.6**	**17**	**2**	**28**	**0**	**–13**								
1985-86	Baltimore Skipjacks	AHL	69	17	21	38				61																		
1986-87	Baltimore Skipjacks	AHL	32	9	11	20				14																		
	Muskegon Lumberjacks	IHL	5	1	2	3				0																		
1987-88	New Haven Nighthawks	AHL	2	0	0	0				0																		
	Muskegon Lumberjacks	IHL	5	1	3	4				6																		
	NHL Totals		**44**	**3**	**5**	**8**	**2**	**3**	**5**	**32**	**0**	**0**	**0**	**65**	**4.6**	**17**	**2**	**28**	**0**									

● BELIVEAU, JEAN

Jean "Le Gros Bill" Beliveau C – L. 6'3", 205 lbs. b: Trois Rivieres, Que., 8/31/1931. **HHOF**

Season	Club	League	GP	G	A	Pts	AG	AA	APts	PIM	PP	SH	GW	S	%	TGF	PGF	TGA	PGA	+/–	Playoffs GP	G	A	Pts	PIM	PP	SH	GW
1946-47	Victoriaville Panthers	Inter-Sr.	....	47	21	68																						
1947-48	Victoriaville Tigers	QJHL	42	46	21	67																						
1948-49	Victoriaville Tigers	QJHL	42	*48	27	75				54											4	4	2	6	2			
1949-50	Quebec Citadelle	QJHL	35	36	44	80				47											14	*22	9	*31	15			
1950-51	Quebec Citadelle	QJHL	46	*61	63	*124				120											22	*23	*31	*54	*76			
	Quebec Aces	QSHL	1	2	1	3				0																		
	Montreal Canadiens	**NHL**	**2**	**1**	**1**	**2**	**1**	**1**	**2**	**0**																		
1951-52	Quebec Aces	QSHL	59	*45	38	*83				88											15	14	10	24	14			
1952-53	**Montreal Canadiens**	**NHL**	**3**	**5**	**0**	**5**	**8**	**0**	**8**	**0**																		
	Quebec Aces	QSHL	57	*50	39	*89				59											19	14	15	*29	*25			
1953-54	**Montreal Canadiens**	**NHL**	**44**	**13**	**21**	**34**	**20**	**29**	**49**	**22**											**10**	**2**	***8**	**10**	**4**			
1954-55	**Montreal Canadiens**	**NHL**	**70**	**37**	**36**	**73**	**55**	**47**	**102**	**58**											**12**	**6**	**7**	**13**	**18**			
1955-56	**Montreal Canadiens**	**NHL**	**70**	***47**	**41**	***88**	**70**	**52**	**122**	**143**											**10**	***12**	**7**	**19**	***22**			
1956-57	**Montreal Canadiens**	**NHL**	**69**	**33**	**51**	**84**	**46**	**60**	**106**	**105**											**10**	**6**	**6**	**12**	**15**			
1957-58	**Montreal Canadiens**	**NHL**	**55**	**27**	**32**	**59**	**36**	**35**	**71**	**93**											**10**	**4**	**8**	**12**	**10**			
1958-59	**Montreal Canadiens**	**NHL**	**64**	***45**	**46**	**91**	**58**	**49**	**107**	**67**											**3**	**1**	**4**	**5**	**4**			
1959-60	**Montreal Canadiens**	**NHL**	**60**	**34**	**40**	**74**	**43**	**41**	**84**	**57**											**8**	**5**	**2**	**7**	**6**			
1960-61	**Montreal Canadiens**	**NHL**	**69**	**32**	***58**	**90**	**40**	**60**	**100**	**57**											**6**	**0**	**5**	**5**	**0**			
1961-62	**Montreal Canadiens**	**NHL**	**43**	**18**	**23**	**41**	**22**	**23**	**45**	**36**											**6**	**2**	**1**	**3**	**4**			
1962-63	**Montreal Canadiens**	**NHL**	**69**	**18**	**49**	**67**	**22**	**52**	**74**	**68**											**5**	**2**	**1**	**3**	**2**			
1963-64	**Montreal Canadiens**	**NHL**	**68**	**28**	**50**	**78**	**37**	**56**	**93**	**42**											**5**	**2**	**0**	**2**	**18**			
1964-65	**Montreal Canadiens**	**NHL**	**58**	**20**	**23**	**43**	**26**	**25**	**51**	**76**											**13**	**8**	**8**	**16**	**34**			
1965-66	**Montreal Canadiens**	**NHL**	**67**	**29**	***48**	**77**	**35**	**49**	**84**	**50**											**10**	**5**	**5**	**10**	**6**			
1966-67	**Montreal Canadiens**	**NHL**	**53**	**12**	**26**	**38**	**15**	**27**	**42**	**22**											**10**	**6**	**5**	**11**	***26**			
1967-68	**Montreal Canadiens**	**NHL**	**59**	**31**	**37**	**68**	**39**	**39**	**78**	**28**	**9**	**0**	**3**	**206**	**15.0**	**86**	**27**	**32**	**0**	**+27**	**10**	**7**	**4**	**11**	**6**	**3**	**0**	**1**
1968-69	**Montreal Canadiens**	**NHL**	**69**	**33**	**49**	**82**	**37**	**46**	**83**	**55**	**7**	**0**	**5**	**235**	**14.0**	**102**	**28**	**59**	**0**	**+15**	**14**	**5**	***10**	**15**	**8**	**1**	**1**	**0**
1969-70	**Montreal Canadiens**	**NHL**	**63**	**19**	**30**	**49**	**22**	**30**	**52**	**10**	**3**	**0**	**1**	**169**	**11.2**	**61**	**28**	**32**	**0**	**+1**								
1970-71	**Montreal Canadiens**	**NHL**	**70**	**25**	**51**	**76**	**26**	**45**	**71**	**40**	**7**	**0**	**4**	**172**	**14.5**	**101**	**37**	**40**	**0**	**+24**	**20**	**6**	***16**	**22**	**28**	**2**	**0**	**0**
	NHL Totals		**1125**	**507**	**712**	**1219**	**658**	**766**	**1424**	**1029**	**26**	**0**	**13**	**782**	**64.8**	**350**	**120**	**163**	**0**		**162**	**79**	**97**	**176**	**211**	**6**	**1**	**1**

QHL First All-Star Team (1953) • Won President's Cup (Scoring Champion - QHL) (1953) • NHL First All-Star Team (1955, 1956, 1957, 1959, 1960, 1961) • Won Art Ross Trophy (1956) • Won Hart Trophy (1956, 1964) • NHL Second All-Star Team (1958, 1964, 1966, 1969) • Won Conn Smythe Trophy (1965)

Played in NHL All-Star Game (1953, 1954, 1955, 1956, 1957, 1958, 1959, 1960, 1963, 1964, 1965, 1968, 1969)

● BELL, BRUCE

Bruce Bell D – L. 6'1", 190 lbs. b: Toronto, Ont., 2/15/1965. Quebec's 2nd choice, 53rd overall, in 1983 Entry Draft.

Season	Club	League	GP	G	A	Pts	AG	AA	APts	PIM	PP	SH	GW	S	%	TGF	PGF	TGA	PGA	+/–	Playoffs GP	G	A	Pts	PIM	PP	SH	GW
1981-82	Sault Ste. Marie Greyhounds	OHL	67	11	18	29				63											12	0	2	2	24			
1982-83	Sault Ste. Marie Greyhounds	OHL	5	0	2	2				2																		
	Windsor Spitfires	OHL	61	10	35	45				39											3	0	4	4	0			
1983-84	Brantford Alexanders	OHL	63	7	41	48				55											6	0	3	3	16			
1984-85	**Quebec Nordiques**	**NHL**	**75**	**6**	**31**	**37**	**5**	**21**	**26**	**44**	**2**	**0**	**1**	**116**	**5.2**	**110**	**23**	**60**	**5**	**+32**	**16**	**2**	**2**	**4**	**21**	**1**	**0**	**0**
1985-86	**St. Louis Blues**	**NHL**	**75**	**2**	**18**	**20**	**2**	**12**	**14**	**43**	**2**	**0**	**0**	**96**	**2.1**	**99**	**33**	**67**	**3**	**+2**	**14**	**0**	**2**	**2**	**13**	**0**	**0**	**0**
1986-87	**St. Louis Blues**	**NHL**	**45**	**3**	**13**	**16**	**3**	**9**	**12**	**18**	**1**	**0**	**0**	**50**	**6.0**	**48**	**12**	**33**	**0**	**+3**	**4**	**1**	**1**	**2**	**7**	**0**	**0**	**0**
1987-88	**New York Rangers**	**NHL**	**13**	**1**	**2**	**3**	**1**	**1**	**2**	**8**	**0**	**0**	**1**	**12**	**8.3**	**14**	**6**	**19**	**1**	**–10**								
	Colorado Rangers	IHL	65	11	34	45				107											4	2	3	5	0			
1988-89	Halifax Citadels	AHL	12	0	6	6				0											2	0	1	1	2			
	Adirondack Red Wings	AHL	9	1	4	5				4																		
1989-90	**Edmonton Oilers**	**NHL**	**1**	**0**	**0**	**0**	**0**	**0**	**0**	**0**	**0**	**0**	**0**	**1**	**0.0**	**1**	**0**	**1**	**0**	**0**								
	Cape Breton Oilers	AHL	52	8	26	34				64											6	3	4	7	2			
1990-91	Cape Breton Oilers	AHL	14	2	5	7				7																		
	Kalamazoo Wings	IHL	48	5	21	26				32											3	0	0	0	8			
1991-92	St. John's Maple Leafs	AHL	45	5	16	21				70											10	4	7	11	8			
1992-93	Milwaukee Admirals	IHL	70	10	28	38				120											6	0	2	2	6			
1993-94	Brantford Smoke	ColHL	51	10	38	48				22																		
	Binghamton Rangers	AHL	13	1	5	6				16																		
1994-95	Fort Worth Fire	CHL	48	12	50	62				77																		
1995-96	Durham Wasps	Britain	17	5	12	17				30																		
	Humberside Hawks	Britain	11	3	5	8				76																		
1996-97	VSV Villach	Austria	48	6	34	40				115																		
1997-98	Reno Renegades	WCHL	24	4	11	15				14																		
	Phoenix Mustangs	WCHL	9	1	2	3				8																		
	Houston Aeros	IHL	2	0	0	0				2																		
	Chicago Wolves	IHL	8	0	0	0				16																		
	NHL Totals		**209**	**12**	**64**	**76**	**11**	**43**	**54**	**113**	**5**	**0**	**2**	**275**	**4.4**	**272**	**74**	**180**	**9**		**34**	**3**	**5**	**8**	**41**	**1**	**0**	**0**

NHL All-Rookie Team (1985) • CHL Second All-Star Team (1995)

Traded to **St. Louis** by **Quebec** for Gilbert Delorme, October 2, 1985. Traded to **NY Rangers** by **St. Louis** with future considerations for Tony Mckegney and Rob Whistle, May 28, 1987. Traded to **Quebec** by **NY Rangers** with Jari Gronstad, Walt Poddubny and the NY Rangers' 4th round choice (Eric Dubois) in 1989 Entry Draft for Jason Lafrieniere and Normand Rochefort, August 1, 1988. Claimed on waivers by **Detroit** from **Quebec**, December 20, 1988. Signed as a free agent by **Edmonton**, February 1, 1990. Traded to **Minnesota** by **Edmonton** for Kari Takko, November, 22, 1990.

			REGULAR SEASON																					PLAYOFFS							
Season	Club	League	GP	G	A	Pts	AG	AA	APts	PIM	PP	SH	GW	S	%	TGF	PGF	TGA	PGA	+/−		GP	G	A	Pts	PIM	PP	SH	GW

● BELLAND, NEIL   Neil Belland   D – L. 5'11", 180 lbs.   b: Parry Sound, Ont., 4/3/1961.

1977-78	North Bay Trappers	OHA	49	25	35	60	....	....	....	24																			
1978-79	Kingston Canadians	OHA	64	8	41	49	....	....	....	14																			
1979-80	Kingston Canadians	OHA	54	7	44	51	....	....	....	44												3	0	0	0	12			
1980-81	Kingston Canadians	OHA	53	28	54	82	....	....	....	54												14	5	6	11	23			
1981-82	**Vancouver Canucks**	**NHL**	**28**	**3**	**6**	**9**	2	4	6	16	1	0	0	33	9.1	27	9	19	0	−1		17	1	7	8	16	1	0	0
	Dallas Black Hawks	CHL	27	2	20	22	....	....	....	18												....	....	....	....	....			
1982-83	**Vancouver Canucks**	**NHL**	**14**	**2**	**4**	**6**	2	3	5	4	0	0	0	13	15.4	13	5	12	0	−4		....	....	....	....	....			
	Fredericton Express	AHL	46	4	17	21	....	....	....	12												7	1	2	3	8			
1983-84	**Vancouver Canucks**	**NHL**	**44**	**7**	**13**	**20**	6	9	15	24	2	0	0	84	8.3	51	17	53	11	−8		4	1	2	3	7	0	0	1
	Fredericton Express	AHL	17	3	15	18	....	....	....	2												....	....	....	....	....			
1984-85	**Vancouver Canucks**	**NHL**	**13**	**0**	**6**	**6**	0	4	4	6	0	0	0	22	0.0	14	5	14	1	−4		....	....	....	....	....			
	Fredericton Express	AHL	57	7	34	41	....	....	....	31												6	0	2	2	4			
1985-86	**Vancouver Canucks**	**NHL**	**7**	**1**	**2**	**3**	1	1	2	4	1	0	1	10	10.0	8	6	4	0	−2		....	....	....	....	....			
	Fredericton Express	AHL	36	6	18	24	....	....	....	10												6	1	6	7	2			
1986-87	**Pittsburgh Penguins**	**NHL**	**3**	**0**	**1**	**1**	0	1	1	0	0	0	0	4	0.0	1	1	0	0	0		....	....	....	....	....			
	Baltimore Skipjacks	AHL	61	6	18	24	....	....	....	12												....	....	....	....	....			
1987-88	Lukko	Finland	44	8	14	22	....	....	....	36												....	....	....	....	....			
	Hershey Bears	AHL	....	....	....	....	....	....	....	....												1	0	0	0	0			
1988-89	Innsbruck	Austria	46	17	39	56	....	....	....	....												....	....	....	....	....			
1989-90	Innsbruck	Austria	34	15	38	53	....	....	....	51												....	....	....	....	....			
1990-91	Canada	Nat-Team	9	0	4	4	....	....	....	10												....	....	....	....	....			
	Innsbruck	Austria	17	5	7	12	....	....	....	....												....	....	....	....	....			
1991-92	EC Graz	Austria	28	11	1	22	....	....	....	....												....	....	....	....	....			
1992-93	EC Graz	Austria	1	0	0	0	....	....	....	....												....	....	....	....	....			
1993-94	EC Graz	Austria	57	8	29	37	....	....	....	....												....	....	....	....	....			
	NHL Totals		**109**	**13**	**32**	**45**	11	22	33	54	4	0	1	166	7.8	114	43	102	12			21	2	9	11	23	1	0	1

AHL Second All-Star Team (1985)

Signed as a free agent by **Vancouver**, October 1, 1980. Signed as a free agent by **Pittsburgh**, September 29, 1986.

● BELLOWS, BRIAN   Brian Bellows   LW – R. 5'11", 210 lbs.   b: St. Catharines, Ont., 9/1/1964.   Minnesota's 1st choice, 2nd overall, in 1982 Entry Draft.

1980-81	Kitchener Rangers	OHA	66	49	67	116	....	....	....	23												16	14	13	27	13			
1981-82	Kitchener Rangers	OHL	47	45	52	97	....	....	....	23												15	16	13	29	11			
1982-83	**Minnesota North Stars**	**NHL**	**78**	**35**	**30**	**65**	29	21	50	27	15	1	3	184	19.0	99	44	74	7	−12		9	5	4	9	18	2	0	0
1983-84	**Minnesota North Stars**	**NHL**	**78**	**41**	**42**	**83**	33	28	61	66	14	5	5	236	17.4	115	41	104	28	−2		16	2	12	14	6	0	1	0
1984-85	Canada	C Cup	5	0	1	1	....	....	....	0												....	....	....	....	....			
	Minnesota North Stars	**NHL**	**78**	**26**	**36**	**62**	21	24	45	72	8	1	3	211	12.3	92	39	87	16	−18		9	2	4	6	9	0	1	0
1985-86	**Minnesota North Stars**	**NHL**	**77**	**31**	**48**	**79**	25	32	57	46	11	2	2	256	12.1	112	36	78	18	+16		5	5	0	5	16	3	0	0
1986-87	**Minnesota North Stars**	**NHL**	**65**	**26**	**27**	**53**	23	20	43	34	8	1	2	200	13.0	78	30	84	23	−13		....	....	....	....	....			
	Canada	WEC-A	10	1	3	4	....	....	....	8												....	....	....	....	....			
1987-88	**Minnesota North Stars**	**NHL**	**77**	**40**	**41**	**81**	34	29	63	81	21	1	4	283	14.1	111	49	88	18	−8		....	....	....	....	....			
1988-89	**Minnesota North Stars**	**NHL**	**60**	**23**	**27**	**50**	20	19	39	55	7	0	4	196	11.7	75	40	55	6	−14		5	2	3	5	8	2	0	0
	Canada	WEC-A	10	8	6	14	....	....	....	2												....	....	....	....	....			
1989-90	**Minnesota North Stars**	**NHL**	**80**	**55**	**44**	**99**	48	31	79	72	21	1	9	300	18.3	143	58	93	12	−3		7	4	3	7	10	3	0	1
	Canada	WEC-A	8	3	6	9	....	....	....	8												....	....	....	....	....			
1990-91	Minnesota North Stars	FrTour	4	1	2	3	....	....	....	22												....	....	....	....	....			
	Minnesota North Stars	**NHL**	**80**	**35**	**40**	**75**	32	30	62	43	17	0	4	296	11.8	111	56	71	3	−13		23	10	19	29	30	6	0	1
1991-92	**Minnesota North Stars**	**NHL**	**80**	**30**	**45**	**75**	27	34	61	41	12	1	4	255	11.8	100	48	89	17	−20		7	4	4	8	14	2	0	1
1992-93	**Montreal Canadiens**	**NHL**	**82**	**40**	**48**	**88**	33	33	66	44	16	0	5	260	15.4	127	55	71	3	+4		18	6	9	15	18	2	0	0
1993-94	**Montreal Canadiens**	**NHL**	**77**	**33**	**38**	**71**	31	29	60	36	13	0	2	251	13.1	110	49	53	1	+9		6	1	2	3	2	0	0	0
1994-95	**Montreal Canadiens**	**NHL**	**41**	**8**	**8**	**16**	14	12	26	8	1	0	1	110	7.3	34	9	32	0	−7		....	....	....	....	....			
1995-96	**Tampa Bay Lightning**	**NHL**	**79**	**23**	**26**	**49**	23	21	44	39	13	0	4	190	12.1	77	46	46	1	−14		6	2	0	2	4	0	0	1
1996-97	**Tampa Bay Lightning**	**NHL**	**7**	**1**	**2**	**3**	1	2	3	0	0	0	0	17	5.9	5	1	8	0	−4		....	....	....	....	....			
	Anaheim Mighty Ducks	**NHL**	**62**	**15**	**13**	**28**	16	11	27	22	8	0	1	151	9.9	44	19	37	1	−11		11	2	4	6	2	1	0	0
1997-98	Berlin Capitals	Germany	31	15	17	32	....	....	....	18												....	....	....	....	....			
	Washington Capitals	**NHL**	**11**	**6**	**3**	**9**	7	3	10	6	5	0	2	26	23.1	9	5	7	0	−3		21	6	7	13	6	2	0	1
	NHL Totals		**1112**	**468**	**518**	**986**	417	379	796	692	190	13	55	3422	13.7	1442	625	1077	147			143	51	71	122	143	23	2	5

OHL First All-Star Team (1982) • Won George Parsons Trophy (Memorial Cup Tournament Most Sportsmanlike Player) (1982) • Named Best Forward at WEC-A (1989) • NHL Second All-Star Team (1990)

Played in NHL All-Star Game (1984, 1988, 1992)

Traded to **Montreal** by **Minnesota** for Russ Courtnall, August 31, 1992. Traded to **Tampa Bay** by **Montreal** for Marc Bureau, June 30, 1995. Traded to **Anaheim** by **Tampa Bay** for Anaheim's 6th round choice (Andrei Skopintsev) in 1997 Entry Draft, November 19, 1996. Signed as a free agent by **Washington**, March 21, 1998.

● BENDA, JAN   Jan Benda   C – R, 6'2", 208 lbs.   b: Roof, Belgium, 3/28/1972.

1990-91	Oshawa Generals	OHL	51	4	11	15	....	....	....	64											....	16	2	4	6	19	....		
1991-92	Oshawa Generals	OHL	61	12	23	35	....	....	....	68												7	1	1	2	12			
1992-93	Freiburg	Germany	41	6	11	17	....	....	....	49												9	3	3	6	12			
1993-94	Munchen	Germany	43	16	11	27	....	....	....	67												10	3	2	5	21			
1994-95	Binghamton Rangers	AHL	4	0	0	0	....	....	....	0												....	....	....	....	....			
	Richmond Renegades	ECHL	62	21	39	60	....	....	....	187												17	8	5	13	50			
1995-96	Slavia Praha	Czech.	28	8	11	19	....	....	....	....												7	1	5	6	....			
1996-97	Sparta Praha	Czech.	49	7	21	28	....	....	....	61												10	1	1	2	12			
1997-98	**Washington Capitals**	**NHL**	**9**	**0**	**3**	**3**	0	3	3	6												8	0	7	7	6			
	Portland Pirates	AHL	62	25	29	54	....	....	....	90												....	....	....	....	....			
	NHL Totals		**9**	**0**	**3**	**3**	0	3	3	6	0	0	0	0	0.0	0	0	0	0			....	....	....	....	....			

Signed as a free agent by **Washington**, October 1, 1997.

● BENNETT, ADAM   Adam Bennett   D – R, 6'4", 206 lbs.   b: Georgetown, Ont., 3/30/1971.   Chicago's 1st choice, 6th overall, in 1989 Entry Draft.

1986-87	Georgetown Raiders	Jr. B	1	0	0	0	....	....	....	0												....	....	....	....	....			
1987-88	Georgetown Raiders	Jr. B	32	9	31	40	....	....	....	63												....	....	....	....	....			
1988-89	Sudbury Wolves	OHL	66	7	22	29	....	....	....	133												....	....	....	....	....			
1989-90	Sudbury Wolves	OHL	65	18	43	61	....	....	....	116												7	1	2	3	23			
1990-91	Sudbury Wolves	OHL	54	21	29	50	....	....	....	123												5	1	2	3	11			
	Indianapolis Ice	IHL	3	0	1	1	....	....	....	12												2	0	0	0	0			
1991-92	**Chicago Blackhawks**	**NHL**	**5**	**0**	**0**	**0**	0	0	0	12	0	0	0	6	0.0	2	0	2	1	+1		....	....	....	....	....			
	Indianapolis Ice	IHL	59	4	10	14	....	....	....	89												....	....	....	....	....			
1992-93	**Chicago Blackhawks**	**NHL**	**16**	**0**	**2**	**2**	0	1	1	8	0	0	0	15	0.0	6	2	9	3	−2		2	0	0	0	0			
	Indianapolis Ice	IHL	39	8	16	24	....	....	....	69												....	....	....	....	....			
1993-94	**Edmonton Oilers**	**NHL**	**48**	**3**	**6**	**9**	3	5	8	49	1	0	0	57	5.3	36	7	42	5	−8		....	....	....	....	....			
	Cape Breton Oilers	AHL	7	2	5	7	....	....	....	7												....	....	....	....	....			
1994-95	Cape Breton Oilers	AHL	10	0	3	3	....	....	....	6												....	....	....	....	....			
1995-96	Richmond Renegades	ECHL	5	0	1	1	....	....	....	6												....	....	....	....	....			
	NHL Totals		**69**	**3**	**8**	**11**	3	6	9	69	1	0	0	78	3.8	44	9	53	9			....	....	....	....	....			

OHL Second All-Star Team (1991)

Traded to **Edmonton** by **Chicago** for Kevin Todd, October 7, 1993.

• BENNETT, BILL
Bill Bennett LW – L. 6'5", 235 lbs. b: Warwick, RI, 5/31/1953.

			REGULAR SEASON																		PLAYOFFS							
Season	Club	League	GP	G	A	Pts	AG	AA	APts	PIM	PP	SH	GW	S	%	TGF	PGF	TGA	PGA	+/–	GP	G	A	Pts	PIM	PP	SH	GW
1975-76	Central Wisconsin Flyers	USHL	STATISTICS NOT AVAILABLE																									
1976-77	Columbus Owls	IHL	70	27	30	57	....	....	....	131	....	....	....	....	....	....	....	....	....	....	7	1	2	3	2	....	....	....
	Rochester Americans	AHL	....	....	....	....	....	....	....	....	....	....	....	....	....	....	....	....	....	....	4	1	1	2	12	....	....	....
1977-78	Rochester Americans	AHL	67	11	19	30	....	....	....	107	....	....	....	....	....	....	....	....	....	....	6	0	4	4	14	....	....	....
1978-79	**Boston Bruins**	**NHL**	**7**	**1**	**4**	**5**	**1**	**3**	**4**	**2**	**0**	**0**	**0**	**4**	**25.0**	**6**	**0**	**2**	**0**	**+4**	....	....	....	....	....	....	....	....
	Rochester Americans	AHL	72	33	38	71	....	....	....	89	....	....	....	....	....	....	....	....	....	....	....	....	....	....	....	....	....	....
1979-80	**Hartford Whalers**	**NHL**	**24**	**3**	**3**	**6**	**3**	**2**	**5**	**63**	**2**	**0**	**0**	**15**	**20.0**	**10**	**2**	**7**	**0**	**+1**	....	....	....	....	....	....	....	....
	Springfield Indians	AHL	35	20	16	36	....	....	....	25	....	....	....	....	....	....	....	....	....	....	....	....	....	....	....	....	....	....
1980-81	Wichita Wind	CHL	28	6	4	10	....	....	....	39	....	....	....	....	....	....	....	....	....	....	9	2	1	3	68	....	....	....
1981-82	Hershey Bears	AHL	10	0	2	2	....	....	....	36	....	....	....	....	....	....	....	....	....	....	....	....	....	....	....	....	....	....
	Fort Wayne Komets	IHL	11	1	4	5	....	....	....	2	....	....	....	....	....	....	....	....	....	....	....	....	....	....	....	....	....	....
	NHL Totals		**31**	**4**	**7**	**11**	**4**	**5**	**9**	**65**	**2**	**0**	**0**	**19**	**21.1**	**16**	**2**	**9**	**0**		....	....	....	....	....	....	....	....

Signed as a free agent by **Boston**, October, 1976. Claimed by **Hartford** from **Boston** in Expansion Draft, June 13, 1979.

• BENNETT, CURT
Curt Bennett LW – L. 6'3", 195 lbs. b: Regina, Sask., 3/27/1948. St. Louis' 2nd choice, 16th overall, in 1968 Amateur Draft.

Season	Club	League	GP	G	A	Pts	AG	AA	APts	PIM	PP	SH	GW	S	%	TGF	PGF	TGA	PGA	+/–	GP	G	A	Pts	PIM	PP	SH	GW
1967-68	Brown University	ECAC	....	15	28	43	....	....	....	34	....	....	....	....	....	....	....	....	....	....	....	....	....	....	....	....	....	....
1968-69	Brown University	ECAC	....	9	20	29	....	....	....	36	....	....	....	....	....	....	....	....	....	....	....	....	....	....	....	....	....	....
1969-70	Brown University	ECAC	....	26	37	63	....	....	....	22	....	....	....	....	....	....	....	....	....	....	....	....	....	....	....	....	....	....
1970-71	**St. Louis Blues**	**NHL**	**4**	**2**	**0**	**2**	**2**	**0**	**2**	**0**	**0**	**0**	**1**	**4**	**50.0**	**3**	**0**	**3**	**0**	**0**	**2**	**0**	**0**	**0**	**0**	**0**	**0**	**0**
	Kansas City Blues	CHL	63	19	23	42	....	....	....	63	....	....	....	....	....	....	....	....	....	....	....	....	....	....	....	....	....	....
1971-72	**St. Louis Blues**	**NHL**	**31**	**3**	**5**	**8**	**3**	**5**	**8**	**30**	**0**	**0**	**0**	**32**	**9.4**	**12**	**0**	**16**	**0**	**–4**	**10**	**0**	**0**	**0**	**12**	**0**	**0**	**0**
	Denver Spurs	WHL	32	13	19	32	....	....	....	52	....	....	....	....	....	....	....	....	....	....	....	....	....	....	....	....	....	....
1972-73	**New York Rangers**	**NHL**	**16**	**0**	**1**	**1**	**0**	**1**	**1**	**11**	**0**	**0**	**0**	**13**	**0.0**	**6**	**0**	**8**	**0**	**–2**	....	....	....	....	....	....	....	....
	Atlanta Flames	**NHL**	**52**	**18**	**17**	**35**	**18**	**14**	**32**	**9**	**1**	**0**	**2**	**135**	**13.3**	**44**	**7**	**58**	**8**	**–13**	....	....	....	....	....	....	....	....
1973-74	**Atlanta Flames**	**NHL**	**71**	**17**	**24**	**41**	**17**	**21**	**38**	**34**	**1**	**0**	**1**	**136**	**12.5**	**56**	**5**	**48**	**0**	**+3**	**4**	**0**	**1**	**1**	**34**	**0**	**0**	**0**
1974-75	**Atlanta Flames**	**NHL**	**80**	**31**	**33**	**64**	**29**	**26**	**55**	**40**	**6**	**0**	**6**	**210**	**14.8**	**95**	**21**	**69**	**5**	**+10**	....	....	....	....	....	....	....	....
1975-76	**Atlanta Flames**	**NHL**	**80**	**34**	**31**	**65**	**32**	**24**	**56**	**61**	**8**	**0**	**8**	**221**	**15.4**	**91**	**27**	**74**	**11**	**+1**	**2**	**0**	**0**	**0**	**4**	**0**	**0**	**0**
1976-77	United States	C Cup	5	0	3	3	....	....	....	0	....	....	....	....	....	....	....	....	....	....	....	....	....	....	....	....	....	....
	Atlanta Flames	**NHL**	**76**	**22**	**25**	**47**	**21**	**20**	**41**	**36**	**5**	**1**	**5**	**183**	**12.0**	**74**	**15**	**84**	**11**	**–14**	**3**	**1**	**0**	**1**	**7**	**0**	**0**	**0**
1977-78	**Atlanta Flames**	**NHL**	**25**	**3**	**7**	**10**	**3**	**6**	**9**	**10**	**0**	**0**	**0**	**44**	**6.8**	**17**	**0**	**23**	**2**	**–4**	....	....	....	....	....	....	....	....
	St. Louis Blues	**NHL**	**50**	**7**	**17**	**24**	**7**	**14**	**21**	**54**	**1**	**0**	**1**	**92**	**7.6**	**34**	**6**	**53**	**3**	**–22**	....	....	....	....	....	....	....	....
	United States	WEC-A	10	3	0	3	....	....	....	0	....	....	....	....	....	....	....	....	....	....	....	....	....	....	....	....	....	....
1978-79	**St. Louis Blues**	**NHL**	**74**	**14**	**19**	**33**	**13**	**14**	**27**	**62**	**1**	**0**	**1**	**141**	**9.9**	**44**	**1**	**88**	**22**	**–23**	....	....	....	....	....	....	....	....
	United States	WEC-A	8	0	1	1	....	....	....	2	....	....	....	....	....	....	....	....	....	....	....	....	....	....	....	....	....	....
1979-80	**Atlanta Flames**	**NHL**	**21**	**1**	**3**	**4**	**1**	**2**	**3**	**0**	**0**	**0**	**0**	**21**	**4.8**	**6**	**0**	**15**	**3**	**–6**	....	....	....	....	....	....	....	....
	Birmingham Bulls	CHL	7	3	0	3	....	....	....	14	....	....	....	....	....	....	....	....	....	....	....	....	....	....	....	....	....	....
1980-81	Furukawa Denko	Japan	20	10	10	20	....	....	....	....	....	....	....	....	....	....	....	....	....	....	....	....	....	....	....	....	....	....
1981-82	Furukawa Denko	Japan	20	11	19	30	....	....	....	....	....	....	....	....	....	....	....	....	....	....	....	....	....	....	....	....	....	....
	NHL Totals		**580**	**152**	**182**	**334**	**146**	**147**	**293**	**347**	**23**	**1**	**25**	**1232**	**12.3**	**482**	**82**	**539**	**65**		**21**	**1**	**1**	**2**	**57**	**0**	**0**	**0**

ECAC Second All-Star Team (1969) • ECAC First All-Star Team (1970) • NCAA East First All-American Team (1970)

Played in NHL All-Star Game (1975, 1976)

Traded to **NY Rangers** by **St. Louis** with Peter McDuffe to complete earlier transaction that sent Steve Durbano to St. Louis (May 24, 1972), June 7, 1972. Traded to **Atlanta** by **NY Rangers** for Ron Harris, November 28, 1972. Traded to **St. Louis** by **Atlanta** with Phil Myre and Barry Gibbs for Yves Belanger, Dick Redmond, Bob McMillan and St. Louis' 2nd round choice (Mike Perovich) in 1979 Amateur Draft, December 12, 1977. Traded to **Atlanta** by **St. Louis** for Bobby Simpson, May 24, 1979.

• BENNETT, HARVEY
Harvey Bennett C – L. 6'4", 215 lbs. b: Cranston, RI, 8/9/1952.

Season	Club	League	GP	G	A	Pts	AG	AA	APts	PIM	PP	SH	GW	S	%	TGF	PGF	TGA	PGA	+/–	GP	G	A	Pts	PIM	PP	SH	GW
1972-73	Boston College	ECAC	27	3	7	10	....	....	....	21	....	....	....	....	....	....	....	....	....	....	....	....	....	....	....	....	....	....
1973-74	Des Moines Capitols	IHL	74	31	50	81	....	....	....	93	....	....	....	....	....	....	....	....	....	....	10	3	6	9	17	....	....	....
1974-75	**Pittsburgh Penguins**	**NHL**	**7**	**0**	**0**	**0**	**0**	**0**	**0**	**0**	**0**	**0**	**0**	**2**	**0.0**	**0**	**0**	**2**	**0**	**–2**	....	....	....	....	....	....	....	....
	Hershey Bears	AHL	61	17	19	36	....	....	....	99	....	....	....	....	....	....	....	....	....	....	12	5	3	8	37	....	....	....
1975-76	**Pittsburgh Penguins**	**NHL**	**25**	**3**	**3**	**6**	**3**	**2**	**5**	**53**	**1**	**0**	**1**	**20**	**15.0**	**16**	**1**	**11**	**0**	**+4**	....	....	....	....	....	....	....	....
	Washington Capitals	**NHL**	**49**	**12**	**10**	**22**	**11**	**8**	**19**	**39**	**1**	**0**	**1**	**72**	**16.7**	**43**	**7**	**63**	**0**	**–27**	....	....	....	....	....	....	....	....
1976-77	United States	C Cup	4	0	2	2	....	....	....	2	....	....	....	....	....	....	....	....	....	....	....	....	....	....	....	....	....	....
	Washington Capitals	**NHL**	**18**	**2**	**6**	**8**	**2**	**5**	**7**	**34**	**0**	**0**	**0**	**22**	**9.1**	**15**	**2**	**23**	**1**	**–9**	....	....	....	....	....	....	....	....
	Philadelphia Flyers	**NHL**	**51**	**12**	**8**	**20**	**11**	**6**	**17**	**60**	**0**	**0**	**2**	**53**	**22.6**	**30**	**4**	**35**	**0**	**–9**	**4**	**0**	**0**	**0**	**2**	**0**	**0**	**0**
1977-78	**Philadelphia Flyers**	**NHL**	**2**	**1**	**0**	**1**	**1**	**0**	**1**	**7**	**0**	**0**	**0**	**2**	**50.0**	**1**	**0**	**0**	**0**	**+1**	....	....	....	....	....	....	....	....
	Minnesota North Stars	**NHL**	**64**	**11**	**10**	**21**	**11**	**8**	**19**	**91**	**1**	**0**	**0**	**67**	**16.4**	**27**	**5**	**54**	**0**	**–32**	....	....	....	....	....	....	....	....
	United States	WEC-A	8	3	0	3	....	....	....	19	....	....	....	....	....	....	....	....	....	....	....	....	....	....	....	....	....	....
1978-79	**St. Louis Blues**	**NHL**	**52**	**3**	**9**	**12**	**3**	**7**	**10**	**63**	**0**	**0**	**0**	**44**	**6.8**	**18**	**0**	**41**	**5**	**–18**	....	....	....	....	....	....	....	....
	Salt Lake Golden Eagles	CHL	1	0	0	0	....	....	....	0	....	....	....	....	....	....	....	....	....	....	....	....	....	....	....	....	....	....
1979-80	Birmingham Bulls	CHL	69	15	22	37	....	....	....	96	....	....	....	....	....	....	....	....	....	....	4	0	2	2	2	....	....	....
1980-81	Furukawa Denko	Japan	STATISTICS NOT AVAILABLE																									
1981-82	Furukawa Denko	Japan	STATISTICS NOT AVAILABLE																									
	NHL Totals		**268**	**44**	**46**	**90**	**42**	**36**	**78**	**347**	**3**	**0**	**4**	**282**	**15.6**	**150**	**19**	**229**	**6**		**4**	**0**	**0**	**0**	**2**	**0**	**0**	**0**

Signed as a free agent by **Pittsburgh**, June 25, 1974. Traded to **Washington** by **Pittsburgh** for Stan Gilbertson, December 16, 1975. Traded to **Philadelphia** by **Washington** for cash, November 24, 1976. Traded to **Minnesota** by **Philadelphia** for Blake Dunlop and Minnesota's 3rd round choice (Gord Salt) in 1978 Amateur Draft, October 28, 1977. Traded to **St. Louis** by **Minnesota** for St. Louis' 2nd round choice (Jali Wahlsten) in 1981 Amateur-Entry Draft, August 28, 1978.

• BENNETT, RICK
Rick Bennett LW – L. 6'4", 215 lbs. b: Springfield, MA, 7/24/1967. Minnesota's 4th choice, 54th overall, in 1986 Entry Draft.

Season	Club	League	GP	G	A	Pts	AG	AA	APts	PIM	PP	SH	GW	S	%	TGF	PGF	TGA	PGA	+/–	GP	G	A	Pts	PIM	PP	SH	GW
1985-86	Wilbraham Monson Academy	H.S.	20	30	69	99	....	....	....	25	....	....	....	....	....	....	....	....	....	....	....	....	....	....	....	....	....	....
1986-87	Providence College	H.E.	32	15	12	27	....	....	....	34	....	....	....	....	....	....	....	....	....	....	....	....	....	....	....	....	....	....
1987-88	Providence College	H.E.	33	9	16	25	....	....	....	70	....	....	....	....	....	....	....	....	....	....	....	....	....	....	....	....	....	....
1988-89	Providence College	H.E.	32	14	32	46	....	....	....	74	....	....	....	....	....	....	....	....	....	....	....	....	....	....	....	....	....	....
1989-90	Providence College	H.E.	31	12	24	36	....	....	....	74	....	....	....	....	....	....	....	....	....	....	....	....	....	....	....	....	....	....
	New York Rangers	**NHL**	**6**	**1**	**0**	**1**	**1**	**0**	**1**	**5**	**0**	**0**	**0**	**6**	**16.7**	**1**	**0**	**6**	**1**	**–4**	....	....	....	....	....	....	....	....
1990-91	**New York Rangers**	**NHL**	**6**	**0**	**0**	**0**	**0**	**0**	**0**	**6**	**0**	**0**	**0**	**3**	**0.0**	**2**	**0**	**4**	**0**	**–2**	....	....	....	....	....	....	....	....
	Binghamton Rangers	AHL	71	27	32	59	....	....	....	206	....	....	....	....	....	....	....	....	....	....	10	2	1	3	27	....	....	....
1991-92	**New York Rangers**	**NHL**	**3**	**0**	**1**	**1**	**0**	**1**	**1**	**2**	**0**	**0**	**0**	**2**	**0.0**	**1**	**0**	**1**	**0**	**0**	....	....	....	....	....	....	....	....
	Binghamton Rangers	AHL	69	19	23	42	....	....	....	112	....	....	....	....	....	....	....	....	....	....	11	0	1	1	23	....	....	....
1992-93	Binghamton Rangers	AHL	76	15	22	37	....	....	....	114	....	....	....	....	....	....	....	....	....	....	10	0	0	0	30	....	....	....
1993-94	Springfield Indians	AHL	67	9	19	28	....	....	....	82	....	....	....	....	....	....	....	....	....	....	6	1	0	1	31	....	....	....
1994-95	Springfield Falcons	AHL	34	3	5	8	....	....	....	74	....	....	....	....	....	....	....	....	....	....	....	....	....	....	....	....	....	....
	Hershey Bears	AHL	30	3	4	7	....	....	....	40	....	....	....	....	....	....	....	....	....	....	3	2	1	3	14	....	....	....
1995-96	Jacksonville Lizard Kings	ECHL	67	28	34	62	....	....	....	182	....	....	....	....	....	....	....	....	....	....	18	5	10	15	30	....	....	....
	Cincinnati Cyclones	IHL	4	0	1	1	....	....	....	0	....	....	....	....	....	....	....	....	....	....	1	0	0	0	2	....	....	....
1996-97	Jacksonville Lizard Kings	ECHL	64	23	33	56	....	....	....	120	....	....	....	....	....	....	....	....	....	....	....	....	....	....	....	....	....	....
	Albany River Rats	AHL	4	0	0	0	....	....	....	0	....	....	....	....	....	....	....	....	....	....	....	....	....	....	....	....	....	....
1997-98	Pee Dee Pride	ECHL	68	12	30	42	....	....	....	137	....	....	....	....	....	....	....	....	....	....	8	3	2	5	14	....	....	....
	NHL Totals		**15**	**1**	**1**	**2**	**1**	**1**	**2**	**13**	**0**	**0**	**0**	**11**	**9.1**	**4**	**0**	**11**	**1**		....	....	....	....	....	....	....	....

Hockey East Second All-Star Team (1990)

Rights traded to **NY Rangers** by **Minnesota** with Brian Lawton and Igor Liba for Paul Jerrard, Mark Tinordi, Bret Barnett, Mike Sullivan and LA Kings' 3rd round choice (previously acquired, Minnesota selected Murray Garbutt) in the 1989 Entry Draft, October 11, 1988.

• BENNING, BRIAN
Brian Benning D – L. 6', 195 lbs. b: Edmonton, Alta., 6/10/1966. St. Louis' 1st choice, 26th overall, in 1984 Entry Draft.

Season	Club	League	GP	G	A	Pts	AG	AA	APts	PIM	PP	SH	GW	S	%	TGF	PGF	TGA	PGA	+/–	GP	G	A	Pts	PIM	PP	SH	GW
1983-84	Portland Winter Hawks	WHL	38	6	41	47	....	....	....	108	....	....	....	....	....	....	....	....	....	....	....	....	....	....	....	....	....	....
1984-85	Kamloops Blazers	WHL	17	3	18	21	....	....	....	26	....	....	....	....	....	....	....	....	....	....	....	....	....	....	....	....	....	....
	St. Louis Blues	**NHL**	**4**	**0**	**2**	**2**	**0**	**1**	**1**	**0**	**0**	**0**	**0**	**1**	**0.0**	**2**	**2**	**6**	**0**	**–6**	....	....	....	....	....	....	....	....
1985-86	Canada	Nat-Team	60	6	13	19	....	....	....	43	....	....	....	....	....	....	....	....	....	....	....	....	....	....	....	....	....	....
	St. Louis Blues	**NHL**	....	....	....	....	....	....	....	....	**0**	**0**	**0**	**0**	**0.0**	**0**	**0**	**0**	**0**	**0**	**6**	**1**	**2**	**3**	**13**	**1**	**0**	**0**

			REGULAR SEASON																		PLAYOFFS							
Season	Club	League	GP	G	A	Pts	AG	AA	APts	PIM	PP	SH	GW	S	%	TGF	PGF	TGA	PGA	+/-	GP	G	A	Pts	PIM	PP	SH	GW
1986-87	**St. Louis Blues**	**NHL**	**78**	**13**	**36**	**49**	**11**	**26**	**37**	**110**	**7**	**0**	**2**	**144**	**9.0**	**143**	**57**	**114**	**30**	**+2**	**6**	**0**	**4**	**4**	**9**	**0**	**0**	**0**
1987-88	**St. Louis Blues**	**NHL**	**77**	**8**	**29**	**37**	**7**	**21**	**28**	**107**	**5**	**0**	**5**	**130**	**6.2**	**126**	**51**	**105**	**25**	**–5**	**10**	**1**	**6**	**7**	**25**	**1**	**0**	**0**
1988-89	**St. Louis Blues**	**NHL**	**66**	**8**	**26**	**34**	**7**	**18**	**25**	**102**	**3**	**0**	**0**	**91**	**8.8**	**94**	**44**	**76**	**3**	**–23**	**7**	**1**	**1**	**2**	**11**	**1**	**0**	**0**
1989-90	**St. Louis Blues**	**NHL**	**7**	**1**	**1**	**2**	**1**	**1**	**2**	**2**	**0**	**0**	**0**	**8**	**12.5**	**8**	**3**	**8**	**0**	**–3**	....	....	....	....	....	....	....	....
	Los Angeles Kings	**NHL**	**48**	**5**	**18**	**23**	**4**	**13**	**17**	**104**	**3**	**0**	**0**	**114**	**4.4**	**78**	**21**	**62**	**6**	**+1**	**7**	**0**	**2**	**2**	**10**	**0**	**0**	**0**
1990-91	**Los Angeles Kings**	**NHL**	**61**	**7**	**24**	**31**	**6**	**18**	**24**	**127**	**2**	**0**	**1**	**120**	**5.8**	**82**	**26**	**46**	**2**	**+12**	**12**	**0**	**5**	**5**	**6**	**0**	**0**	**0**
1991-92	**Los Angeles Kings**	**NHL**	**53**	**2**	**30**	**32**	**2**	**23**	**25**	**99**	**0**	**0**	**0**	**102**	**2.0**	**83**	**29**	**58**	**8**	**+4**	....	....	....	....	....	....	....	....
	Philadelphia Flyers	**NHL**	**22**	**2**	**12**	**14**	**2**	**9**	**11**	**35**	**2**	**0**	**0**	**50**	**4.0**	**27**	**12**	**31**	**7**	**–9**	....	....	....	....	....	....	....	....
1992-93	**Philadelphia Flyers**	**NHL**	**37**	**9**	**17**	**26**	**7**	**12**	**19**	**93**	**6**	**0**	**0**	**87**	**10.3**	**64**	**23**	**52**	**11**	**0**	....	....	....	....	....	....	....	....
	Edmonton Oilers	**NHL**	**18**	**1**	**7**	**8**	**1**	**5**	**6**	**59**	**0**	**0**	**0**	**28**	**3.6**	**19**	**4**	**22**	**6**	**–1**	....	....	....	....	....	....	....	....
	Canada	WC-A	8	1	2	3	....	....	....	0	....	....	....	....	....	....	....	....	....	....	....	....	....	....	....	....	....	....
1993-94	**Florida Panthers**	**NHL**	**73**	**6**	**24**	**30**	**6**	**19**	**25**	**107**	**2**	**0**	**0**	**112**	**5.4**	**81**	**27**	**76**	**15**	**–7**	....	....	....	....	....	....	....	....
1994-95	**Florida Panthers**	**NHL**	**24**	**1**	**7**	**8**	**2**	**10**	**12**	**18**	**1**	**0**	**0**	**26**	**3.8**	**20**	**5**	**25**	**4**	**–6**	....	....	....	....	....	....	....	....
	NHL Totals		**568**	**63**	**233**	**296**	**56**	**176**	**232**	**963**	**31**	**0**	**8**	**1013**	**6.2**	**827**	**304**	**681**	**117**		**48**	**3**	**20**	**23**	**74**	**3**	**0**	**0**

NHL All-Rookie Team (1987)

Traded to **LA Kings** by **St. Louis** for LA Kings' 3rd round choice (Kyle Reeves) in 1991 Entry Draft, November 10, 1989. Traded to **Pittsburgh** by **LA Kings** with Jeff Chychrun and LA Kings' 1st round choice (later traded to Philadelphia — Philadelphia selected Jason Bowen) in 1992 Entry Draft for Paul Coffey, February 19, 1992. Traded to **Philadelphia** by **Pittsburgh** with Mark Recchi and LA Kings' 1st round choice (previously acquired, Philadelphia selected Jason Bowen) in 1992 Entry Draft for Rick Tocchet, Kjell Samuelsson, Ken Wregget and Philadelphia's 3rd round choice (Dave Roche) in 1993 Entry Draft, February 19, 1992. Traded to **Edmonton** by **Philadelphia** for Greg Hawgood and Josef Beranek, January 16, 1993. Signed as a free agent by **Florida**, July 13, 1993.

• BENNING, JIM

Jim Benning D – L. 6', 180 lbs. b: Edmonton, Alta., 4/29/1963. Toronto's 1st choice, 6th overall, in 1981 Entry Draft.

Season	Club	League	GP	G	A	Pts	AG	AA	APts	PIM	PP	SH	GW	S	%	TGF	PGF	TGA	PGA	+/-	GP	G	A	Pts	PIM	PP	SH	GW
1978-79	Fort Saskatchewan Traders	AJHL	45	14	57	71	....	....	....	10	....	....	....	....	....	....	....	....	....	....	....	....	....	....	....	....	....	....
1979-80	Portland Winter Hawks	WHL	71	11	60	71	....	....	....	42	....	....	....	....	....	....	....	....	....	....	8	3	9	12	6	....	....	....
1980-81	Portland Winter Hawks	WHL	72	28	*111	139	....	....	....	61	....	....	....	....	....	....	....	....	....	....	9	1	5	6	16	....	....	....
1981-82	**Toronto Maple Leafs**	**NHL**	**74**	**7**	**24**	**31**	**6**	**16**	**22**	**46**	**2**	**0**	**0**	**90**	**7.8**	**82**	**25**	**91**	**7**	**–27**	....	....	....	....	....	....	....	....
1982-83	**Toronto Maple Leafs**	**NHL**	**74**	**5**	**17**	**22**	**4**	**12**	**16**	**47**	**3**	**0**	**0**	**68**	**7.4**	**78**	**29**	**58**	**1**	**–8**	**4**	**1**	**1**	**2**	**2**	**0**	**0**	**0**
1983-84	**Toronto Maple Leafs**	**NHL**	**79**	**12**	**39**	**51**	**10**	**26**	**36**	**66**	**6**	**0**	**1**	**136**	**8.8**	**139**	**54**	**109**	**20**	**–4**	....	....	....	....	....	....	....	....
1984-85	**Toronto Maple Leafs**	**NHL**	**80**	**9**	**35**	**44**	**7**	**24**	**31**	**55**	**6**	**0**	**2**	**160**	**5.6**	**110**	**52**	**101**	**4**	**–39**	....	....	....	....	....	....	....	....
1985-86	**Toronto Maple Leafs**	**NHL**	**52**	**4**	**21**	**25**	**3**	**14**	**17**	**71**	**2**	**0**	**0**	**76**	**5.3**	**78**	**23**	**64**	**5**	**–4**	....	....	....	....	....	....	....	....
1986-87	**Toronto Maple Leafs**	**NHL**	**5**	**0**	**0**	**0**	**0**	**0**	**0**	**4**	**0**	**0**	**0**	**3**	**0.0**	**5**	**2**	**3**	**0**	**0**	....	....	....	....	....	....	....	....
	Newmarket Saints	AHL	10	1	5	6	....	....	....	0	....	....	....	....	....	....	....	....	....	....	....	....	....	....	....	....	....	....
	Vancouver Canucks	**NHL**	**54**	**2**	**11**	**13**	**2**	**8**	**10**	**40**	**0**	**0**	**1**	**60**	**3.3**	**57**	**11**	**40**	**3**	**+9**	....	....	....	....	....	....	....	....
1987-88	**Vancouver Canucks**	**NHL**	**77**	**7**	**26**	**33**	**6**	**18**	**24**	**58**	**1**	**1**	**1**	**102**	**6.9**	**97**	**29**	**92**	**24**	**0**	....	....	....	....	....	....	....	....
1988-89	**Vancouver Canucks**	**NHL**	**65**	**3**	**9**	**12**	**3**	**6**	**9**	**48**	**1**	**0**	**0**	**55**	**5.5**	**45**	**10**	**43**	**4**	**–4**	**3**	**0**	**0**	**0**	**0**	**0**	**0**	**0**
1989-90	**Vancouver Canucks**	**NHL**	**45**	**3**	**9**	**12**	**3**	**6**	**9**	**26**	**0**	**1**	**0**	**49**	**6.1**	**42**	**6**	**41**	**9**	**+4**	....	....	....	....	....	....	....	....
1990-91	Milwaukee Admirals	IHL	66	1	31	32	....	....	....	75	....	....	....	....	....	....	....	....	....	....	6	0	0	0	0	....	....	....
1991-92	Varese	Italy	18	0	12	12	....	....	....	14	....	....	....	....	....	....	....	....	....	....	7	0	2	2	50	....	....	....
	NHL Totals		**605**	**52**	**191**	**243**	**44**	**130**	**174**	**461**	**21**	**2**	**5**	**799**	**6.5**	**733**	**241**	**642**	**77**		**7**	**1**	**1**	**2**	**2**	**0**	**0**	**0**

WHL First All-Star Team (1981)

Traded to **Vancouver** by **Toronto** with Dan Hodgson for Rick Lanz, December 12, 1986.

• BENYSEK, LADISLAV

Ladislav Benysek D – L. 6'2", 190 lbs. b: Olomouc, Czech., 3/24/1975. Edmonton's 16th choice, 266th overall, in 1994 Entry Draft.

Season	Club	League	GP	G	A	Pts	AG	AA	APts	PIM	PP	SH	GW	S	%	TGF	PGF	TGA	PGA	+/-	GP	G	A	Pts	PIM	PP	SH	GW
1993-94	HC Olomouc	Czech. Jr.	STATISTICS NOT AVAILABLE																									
1994-95	Cape Breton Oilers	AHL	58	2	7	9	....	....	....	54	....	....	....	....	....	....	....	....	....	....	....	....	....	....	....	....	....	....
1995-96	HC Olomouc	Czech.	33	1	4	5	....	....	....	....	....	....	....	....	....	....	....	....	....	....	4	0	0	0	....	....	....	....
1996-97	Sparta Praha	Czech.	36	5	5	10	....	....	....	28	....	....	....	....	....	....	....	....	....	....	5	0	1	1	2	....	....	....
1997-98	**Edmonton Oilers**	**NHL**	**2**	**0**	**0**	**0**	**0**	**0**	**0**	**0**	....	....	....	....	....	....	....	....	....	....	....	....	....	....	....	....	....	....
	Hamilton Bulldogs	AHL	53	2	14	16	....	....	....	29	....	....	....	....	....	....	....	....	....	....	9	1	1	2	2	....	....	....
	NHL Totals		**2**	**0**	**0**	**0**	**0**	**0**	**0**	**0**	**0**	**0**	**0**	**0**	**0.0**	**0**	**0**	**0**	**0**		....	....	....	....	....	....	....	....

• BERALDO, PAUL

Paul Beraldo RW – R. 5'11", 175 lbs. b: Hamilton, Ont., 10/5/1967. Boston's 6th choice, 139th overall, in 1986 Entry Draft.

Season	Club	League	GP	G	A	Pts	AG	AA	APts	PIM	PP	SH	GW	S	%	TGF	PGF	TGA	PGA	+/-	GP	G	A	Pts	PIM	PP	SH	GW
1984-85	Grimsby Lions	Jr. B	25	9	4	13	....	....	....	24	....	....	....	....	....	....	....	....	....	....	....	....	....	....	....	....	....	....
1985-86	Sault Ste. Marie Greyhounds	OHL	61	15	13	28	....	....	....	48	....	....	....	....	....	....	....	....	....	....	....	....	....	....	....	....	....	....
1986-87	Sault Ste. Marie Greyhounds	OHL	63	39	51	90	....	....	....	117	....	....	....	....	....	....	....	....	....	....	4	3	2	5	6	....	....	....
1987-88	**Boston Bruins**	**NHL**	**3**	**0**	**0**	**0**	**0**	**0**	**0**	**0**	**0**	**0**	**0**	**1**	**0.0**	**1**	**0**	**4**	**0**	**–3**	....	....	....	....	....	....	....	....
	Maine Mariners	AHL	62	22	15	37	....	....	....	112	....	....	....	....	....	....	....	....	....	....	2	0	0	0	19	....	....	....
1988-89	**Boston Bruins**	**NHL**	**7**	**0**	**0**	**0**	**0**	**0**	**0**	**4**	**0**	**0**	**0**	**1**	**0.0**	**0**	**0**	**2**	**0**	**–2**	....	....	....	....	....	....	....	....
	Maine Mariners	AHL	73	25	28	53	....	....	....	134	....	....	....	....	....	....	....	....	....	....	....	....	....	....	....	....	....	....
1989-90	Canada	Nat-Team	9	2	8	10	....	....	....	20	....	....	....	....	....	....	....	....	....	....	....	....	....	....	....	....	....	....
	Maine Mariners	AHL	51	14	27	41	....	....	....	31	....	....	....	....	....	....	....	....	....	....	....	....	....	....	....	....	....	....
1990-91	Milano Devils	Italy	34	34	27	61	....	....	....	77	....	....	....	....	....	....	....	....	....	....	10	12	12	24	13	....	....	....
1991-92	Milano Devils	Italy	16	23	13	36	....	....	....	24	....	....	....	....	....	....	....	....	....	....	12	10	5	15	11	....	....	....
1992-93	Milano Devils	Italy	27	24	14	38	....	....	....	23	....	....	....	....	....	....	....	....	....	....	....	....	....	....	....	....	....	....
1993-94	Preussen Berlin	Germany	12	6	10	16	....	....	....	14	....	....	....	....	....	....	....	....	....	....	....	....	....	....	....	....	....	....
	Milano Devils	Italy	3	2	0	2	....	....	....	10	....	....	....	....	....	....	....	....	....	....	....	....	....	....	....	....	....	....
	Italy	WC-A	6	2	1	3	....	....	....	6	....	....	....	....	....	....	....	....	....	....	....	....	....	....	....	....	....	....
1994-95	Milano Devils	Italy	1	0	0	0	....	....	....	0	....	....	....	....	....	....	....	....	....	....	....	....	....	....	....	....	....	....
1995-96	Ratingen Lions	Germany	16	14	7	21	....	....	....	56	....	....	....	....	....	....	....	....	....	....	....	....	....	....	....	....	....	....
1996-97	Mannheim Eagles	Germany	50	23	25	48	....	....	....	71	....	....	....	....	....	....	....	....	....	....	9	3	2	5	22	....	....	....
1997-98	Kassel Huskies	Germany	18	8	8	16	....	....	....	18	....	....	....	....	....	....	....	....	....	....	....	....	....	....	....	....	....	....
	Star Bulls Rosenheim	Germany	43	5	5	10	....	....	....	12	....	....	....	....	....	....	....	....	....	....	....	....	....	....	....	....	....	....
	NHL Totals		**10**	**0**	**0**	**0**	**0**	**0**	**0**	**4**	**0**	**0**	**0**	**2**	**0.0**	**1**	**0**	**6**	**0**		....	....	....	....	....	....	....	....

• BERANEK, JOSEF

Josef Beranek LW – L. 6'2", 190 lbs. b: Litvinov, Czechoslovakia, 10/25/1969. Edmonton's 3rd choice, 78th overall, in 1989 Entry Draft.

Season	Club	League	GP	G	A	Pts	AG	AA	APts	PIM	PP	SH	GW	S	%	TGF	PGF	TGA	PGA	+/-	GP	G	A	Pts	PIM	PP	SH	GW
1987-88	CHZ Litvinov	Czech.	14	7	4	11	....	....	....	12	....	....	....	....	....	....	....	....	....	....	....	....	....	....	....	....	....	....
1988-89	CHZ Litvinov	Czech.	32	18	10	28	....	....	....	47	....	....	....	....	....	....	....	....	....	....	....	....	....	....	....	....	....	....
	Czechoslovakia	WJC-A	7	4	9	13	....	....	....	6	....	....	....	....	....	....	....	....	....	....	....	....	....	....	....	....	....	....
1989-90	Dukla Trencin	Czech.	49	19	23	42	....	....	....	....	....	....	....	....	....	....	....	....	....	....	....	....	....	....	....	....	....	....
1990-91	CHZ Litvinov	Czech.	58	29	31	60	....	....	....	98	....	....	....	....	....	....	....	....	....	....	....	....	....	....	....	....	....	....
	Czechoslovakia	WEC-A	8	2	2	4	....	....	....	6	....	....	....	....	....	....	....	....	....	....	....	....	....	....	....	....	....	....
1991-92	Czechoslovakia	C Cup	5	1	1	2	....	....	....	4	....	....	....	....	....	....	....	....	....	....	....	....	....	....	....	....	....	....
	Edmonton Oilers	**NHL**	**58**	**12**	**16**	**28**	**11**	**12**	**23**	**18**	**0**	**0**	**1**	**79**	**15.2**	**34**	**4**	**32**	**0**	**–2**	**12**	**2**	**1**	**3**	**0**	**1**	**0**	**1**
1992-93	**Edmonton Oilers**	**NHL**	**26**	**2**	**6**	**8**	**2**	**4**	**6**	**28**	**0**	**0**	**0**	**44**	**4.5**	**11**	**2**	**21**	**5**	**–7**	....	....	....	....	....	....	....	....
	Cape Breton Oilers	AHL	6	1	2	3	....	....	....	8	....	....	....	....	....	....	....	....	....	....	....	....	....	....	....	....	....	....
	Philadelphia Flyers	**NHL**	**40**	**13**	**12**	**25**	**11**	**8**	**19**	**50**	**1**	**0**	**0**	**86**	**15.1**	**36**	**5**	**32**	**0**	**–1**	....	....	....	....	....	....	....	....
	Czech Republic	WC-A	8	3	3	6	....	....	....	22	....	....	....	....	....	....	....	....	....	....	....	....	....	....	....	....	....	....
1993-94	**Philadelphia Flyers**	**NHL**	**80**	**28**	**21**	**49**	**26**	**16**	**42**	**85**	**6**	**0**	**2**	**182**	**15.4**	**62**	**13**	**51**	**0**	**–2**	....	....	....	....	....	....	....	....
	Czech Republic	WC-A	6	1	2	3	....	....	....	0	....	....	....	....	....	....	....	....	....	....	....	....	....	....	....	....	....	....
1994-95	Petra Vsetin	Czech.	16	7	7	14	....	....	....	26	....	....	....	....	....	....	....	....	....	....	....	....	....	....	....	....	....	....
	Philadelphia Flyers	**NHL**	**14**	**5**	**5**	**10**	**9**	**7**	**16**	**2**	**1**	**0**	**0**	**39**	**12.8**	**13**	**4**	**6**	**0**	**+3**	....	....	....	....	....	....	....	....
	Vancouver Canucks	**NHL**	**37**	**8**	**13**	**21**	**14**	**19**	**33**	**28**	**2**	**0**	**0**	**95**	**8.4**	**31**	**10**	**31**	**0**	**–10**	**11**	**1**	**1**	**2**	**12**	**0**	**0**	**0**
1995-96	**Vancouver Canucks**	**NHL**	**61**	**6**	**14**	**20**	**6**	**11**	**17**	**60**	**0**	**0**	**1**	**131**	**4.6**	**29**	**3**	**55**	**18**	**–11**	**3**	**2**	**1**	**3**	**0**	**0**	**0**	**0**
1996-97	Czech Republic	W Cup	3	0	0	0	....	....	....	4	....	....	....	....	....	....	....	....	....	....	....	....	....	....	....	....	....	....
	Petra Vsetin	Czech.	39	19	24	43	....	....	....	115	....	....	....	....	....	....	....	....	....	....	3	3	2	5	4	....	....	....
	Pittsburgh Penguins	**NHL**	**8**	**3**	**1**	**4**	**3**	**1**	**4**	**4**	**1**	**0**	**0**	**15**	**20.0**	**5**	**1**	**7**	**2**	**–1**	**5**	**0**	**0**	**0**	**2**	**0**	**0**	**0**

			REGULAR SEASON																		PLAYOFFS							
Season	**Club**	**League**	**GP**	**G**	**A**	**Pts**	**AG**	**AA**	**APts**	**PIM**	**PP**	**SH**	**GW**	**S**	**%**	**TGF**	**PGF**	**TGA**	**PGA**	**+/–**	**GP**	**G**	**A**	**Pts**	**PIM**	**PP**	**SH**	**GW**
1997-98	Petra Vsetin	EuroHL	8	5	4	9	....	....	....	10	....	....	....	....	....	....	....	....	....	....	....	....	....	....	....	....	....	....
	Petra Vsetin	Czech.	45	24	27	51	....	....	....	92	....	....	....	....	....	....	....	....	....	....	10	2	8	10	14	....	....	....
	Czech Republic	Olympics	6	1	0	1	....	....	....	4	....	....	....	....	....	....	....	....	....	....	....	....	....	....	....	....	....	....
	Czech Republic	WC-A	9	0	3	3	....	....	....	12	....	....	....	....	....	....	....	....	....	....	....	....	....	....	....	....	....	....
	NHL Totals		**324**	**77**	**88**	**165**	**82**	**78**	**160**	**275**	**11**	**0**	**4**	**671**	**11.5**	**221**	**42**	**235**	**25**		**31**	**5**	**3**	**8**	**14**	**1**	**0**	**1**

Traded to **Philadelphia** by **Edmonton** with Greg Hawgood for Brian Benning, January 16, 1993. Traded to **Vancouver** by **Philadelphia** for Shawn Antoski, February 15, 1995. Traded to **Pittsburgh** by **Vancouver** for future considerations, March 18, 1997. Traded to **Edmonton** by **Pittsburgh** for Bobby Dollas and Tony Hrkac, June 16, 1998.

• BERARD, BRYAN

Bryan Berard D – L. 6'1", 190 lbs. b: Woonsocket, RI, 3/5/1977. Ottawa's 1st choice, 1st overall, in 1995 Entry Draft.

Season	Club	League	GP	G	A	Pts	AG	AA	APts	PIM	PP	SH	GW	S	%	TGF	PGF	TGA	PGA	+/–	GP	G	A	Pts	PIM	PP	SH	GW
1993-94	Mount St. Charles	H.S.	32	11	36	47	....	....	....	97	....	....	....	....	....	....	....	....	....	....	....	....	....	....	....	....	....	....
1994-95	Detroit Whalers	OHL	58	20	55	75	....	....	....	97	....	....	....	....	....	....	....	....	....	....	21	4	20	24	38	....	....	....
	United States	WJC-A	7	0	1	1	....	....	....	36	....	....	....	....	....	....	....	....	....	....	....	....	....	....	....	....	....	....
1995-96	Detroit Whalers	OHL	56	31	58	89	....	....	....	116	....	....	....	....	....	....	....	....	....	....	17	7	18	25	41	....	....	....
	United States	WJC-A	6	1	4	5	....	....	....	20	....	....	....	....	....	....	....	....	....	....	....	....	....	....	....	....	....	....
1996-97	**New York Islanders**	**NHL**	**82**	**8**	**40**	**48**	**8**	**35**	**43**	**86**	**3**	**0**	**1**	**172**	**4.7**	**105**	**33**	**73**	**2**	**+1**	....	....	....	....	....	....	....	....
	United States	WC-A	1	1	0	1	....	....	....	0	....	....	....	....	....	....	....	....	....	....	....	....	....	....	....	....	....	....
1997-98	**New York Islanders**	**NHL**	**75**	**14**	**32**	**46**	**16**	**31**	**47**	**59**	**8**	**1**	**2**	**192**	**7.3**	**97**	**45**	**92**	**8**	**–32**	....	....	....	....	....	....	....	....
	United States	Olympics	2	0	0	0	....	....	....	0	....	....	....	....	....	....	....	....	....	....	....	....	....	....	....	....	....	....
	NHL Totals		**157**	**22**	**72**	**94**	**24**	**66**	**90**	**145**	**11**	**1**	**3**	**364**	**6.0**	**202**	**78**	**165**	**10**		....	....	....	....	....	....	....	....

OHL First All-Star Team (1995, 1996) • Canadian Major Junior First All-Star Team (1995, 1996) • Canadian Major Junior Rookie of the Year (1995) • Canadian Major Junior Defenseman of the Year (1996) • NHL All-Rookie Team (1997) • Won Calder Memorial Trophy (1997)

Traded to **NY Islanders** by **Ottawa** with Don Beaupre and Martin Straka for Damian Rhodes and Wade Redden, January 23, 1996.

• BEREHOWSKY, DRAKE

Drake Berehowsky D – R. 6'1", 211 lbs. b: Toronto, Ont., 1/3/1972. Toronto's 1st choice, 10th overall, in 1990 Entry Draft.

Season	Club	League	GP	G	A	Pts	AG	AA	APts	PIM	PP	SH	GW	S	%	TGF	PGF	TGA	PGA	+/–	GP	G	A	Pts	PIM	PP	SH	GW
1988-89	Kingston Frontenacs	OHL	63	7	39	46	....	....	....	85	....	....	....	....	....	....	....	....	....	....	....	....	....	....	....	....	....	....
	Canada	Nat-Team	1	0	0	0	....	....	....	0	....	....	....	....	....	....	....	....	....	....	....	....	....	....	....	....	....	....
1989-90	Kingston Frontenacs	OHL	9	3	11	14	....	....	....	28	....	....	....	....	....	....	....	....	....	....	....	....	....	....	....	....	....	....
1990-91	Kingston Frontenacs	OHL	13	5	13	18	....	....	....	38	....	....	....	....	....	....	....	....	....	....	....	....	....	....	....	....	....	....
	North Bay Centennials	OHL	26	7	23	30	....	....	....	51	....	....	....	....	....	....	....	....	....	....	10	2	7	9	21	....	....	....
	Toronto Maple Leafs	**NHL**	**8**	**0**	**1**	**1**	**0**	**1**	**1**	**25**	**0**	**0**	**0**	**4**	**0.0**	**2**	**1**	**8**	**1**	**–6**	....	....	....	....	....	....	....	....
1991-92	North Bay Centennials	OHL	62	19	63	82	....	....	....	147	....	....	....	....	....	....	....	....	....	....	21	7	24	31	22	....	....	....
	Toronto Maple Leafs	**NHL**	**1**	**0**	**0**	**0**	**0**	**0**	**0**	**0**	**0**	**0**	**0**	**0**	**0.0**	**0**	**0**	**0**	**0**	**0**	....	....	....	....	....	....	....	....
	St. John's Maple Leafs	AHL	....	....	....	....	....	....	....	....	....	....	....	....	....	....	....	....	....	....	6	0	5	5	21	....	....	....
1992-93	**Toronto Maple Leafs**	**NHL**	**41**	**4**	**15**	**19**	**3**	**10**	**13**	**61**	**1**	**0**	**1**	**41**	**9.8**	**35**	**17**	**17**	**0**	**+1**	....	....	....	....	....	....	....	....
	St. John's Maple Leafs	AHL	28	10	17	27	....	....	....	38	....	....	....	....	....	....	....	....	....	....	....	....	....	....	....	....	....	....
1993-94	**Toronto Maple Leafs**	**NHL**	**49**	**2**	**8**	**10**	**2**	**6**	**8**	**63**	**2**	**0**	**2**	**29**	**6.9**	**29**	**17**	**15**	**0**	**–3**	....	....	....	....	....	....	....	....
	St. John's Maple Leafs	AHL	18	3	12	15	....	....	....	40	....	....	....	....	....	....	....	....	....	....	....	....	....	....	....	....	....	....
1994-95	**Toronto Maple Leafs**	**NHL**	**25**	**0**	**2**	**2**	**0**	**3**	**3**	**15**	**0**	**0**	**0**	**12**	**0.0**	**10**	**2**	**18**	**0**	**–10**	....	....	....	....	....	....	....	....
	Pittsburgh Penguins	**NHL**	**4**	**0**	**0**	**0**	**0**	**0**	**0**	**13**	**0**	**0**	**0**	**2**	**0.0**	**3**	**0**	**2**	**0**	**+1**	**1**	**0**	**0**	**0**	**0**	**0**	**0**	**0**
1995-96	**Pittsburgh Penguins**	**NHL**	**1**	**0**	**0**	**0**	**0**	**0**	**0**	**0**	**0**	**0**	**0**	**0**	**0.0**	**1**	**0**	**0**	**0**	**+1**	....	....	....	....	....	....	....	....
	Cleveland Lumberjacks	IHL	74	6	28	34	....	....	....	141	....	....	....	....	....	....	....	....	....	....	3	0	3	3	6	....	....	....
1996-97	Carolina Monarchs	AHL	49	2	15	17	....	....	....	55	....	....	....	....	....	....	....	....	....	....	....	....	....	....	....	....	....	....
	San Antonio Dragons	IHL	16	3	4	7	....	....	....	36	....	....	....	....	....	....	....	....	....	....	....	....	....	....	....	....	....	....
1997-98	**Edmonton Oilers**	**NHL**	**67**	**1**	**6**	**7**	**1**	**6**	**7**	**169**	**1**	**0**	**1**	**58**	**1.7**	**39**	**8**	**33**	**3**	**+1**	**12**	**1**	**2**	**3**	**14**	**0**	**0**	**1**
	Hamilton Bulldogs	AHL	8	2	0	2	....	....	....	21	....	....	....	....	....	....	....	....	....	....	....	....	....	....	....	....	....	....
	NHL Totals		**196**	**7**	**32**	**39**	**6**	**26**	**32**	**346**	**4**	**0**	**4**	**146**	**4.8**	**119**	**45**	**93**	**4**		**13**	**1**	**2**	**3**	**14**	**0**	**0**	**1**

Canadian Major Junior Defenseman of the Year (1992) • OHL First All-Star Team (1992)

Traded to **Pittsburgh** by **Toronto** for Grant Jennings, April 7, 1995. Signed as a free agent by **Edmonton**, September 30, 1997.

• BERENSON, RED

Red (Gordon) "The Red Baron" Berenson C – L. 6', 185 lbs. b: Regina, Sask., 12/8/1939.

Season	Club	League	GP	G	A	Pts	AG	AA	APts	PIM	PP	SH	GW	S	%	TGF	PGF	TGA	PGA	+/–	GP	G	A	Pts	PIM	PP	SH	GW
1956-57	Regina Pats	SJHL	51	21	23	44	....	....	....	86	....	....	....	....	....	....	....	....	....	....	7	4	2	6	4	....	....	....
1957-58	Regina Pats	SJHL	51	46	*49	95	....	....	....	92	....	....	....	....	....	....	....	....	....	....	12	7	3	10	*42	....	....	....
1958-59	Belleville McFarlands	EOHL	1	2	1	3	....	....	....	2	....	....	....	....	....	....	....	....	....	....	....	....	....	....	....	....	....	....
	Canada	WEC-A	8	9	4	13	....	....	....	....	....	....	....	....	....	....	....	....	....	....	....	....	....	....	....	....	....	....
1959-60	University of Michigan	CCHA	....	12	7	19	....	....	....	12	....	....	....	....	....	....	....	....	....	....	....	....	....	....	....	....	....	....
1960-61	University of Michigan	CCHA	....	24	25	49	....	....	....	....	....	....	....	....	....	....	....	....	....	....	....	....	....	....	....	....	....	....
1961-62	University of Michigan	CCHA	....	*43	29	72	....	....	....	40	....	....	....	....	....	....	....	....	....	....	....	....	....	....	....	....	....	....
	Montreal Canadiens	**NHL**	**4**	**1**	**2**	**3**	**1**	**2**	**3**	**4**	....	....	....	....	....	....	....	....	....	....	**5**	**2**	**0**	**2**	**0**	....	....	....
1962-63	**Montreal Canadiens**	**NHL**	**37**	**2**	**6**	**8**	**2**	**6**	**8**	**15**	....	....	....	....	....	....	....	....	....	....	**5**	**0**	**0**	**0**	**0**	....	....	....
	Hull-Ottawa Canadiens	EPHL	30	23	25	48	....	....	....	28	....	....	....	....	....	....	....	....	....	....	....	....	....	....	....	....	....	....
1963-64	**Montreal Canadiens**	**NHL**	**69**	**7**	**9**	**16**	**9**	**10**	**19**	**12**	....	....	....	....	....	....	....	....	....	....	**7**	**0**	**0**	**0**	**4**	....	....	....
1964-65	**Montreal Canadiens**	**NHL**	**3**	**1**	**2**	**3**	**1**	**2**	**3**	**0**	....	....	....	....	....	....	....	....	....	....	**9**	**0**	**1**	**1**	**2**	....	....	....
	Quebec Aces	AHL	65	22	34	56	....	....	....	16	....	....	....	....	....	....	....	....	....	....	5	1	2	3	8	....	....	....
1965-66	**Montreal Canadiens**	**NHL**	**23**	**3**	**4**	**7**	**4**	**4**	**8**	**12**	....	....	....	....	....	....	....	....	....	....	....	....	....	....	....	....	....	....
	Quebec Aces	AHL	34	17	36	53	....	....	....	14	....	....	....	....	....	....	....	....	....	....	6	1	5	6	2	....	....	....
1966-67	**New York Rangers**	**NHL**	**30**	**0**	**5**	**5**	**0**	**5**	**5**	**2**	....	....	....	....	....	....	....	....	....	....	**4**	**0**	**1**	**1**	**2**	....	....	....
1967-68	**New York Rangers**	**NHL**	**19**	**2**	**1**	**3**	**2**	**1**	**3**	**2**	**0**	**0**	**0**	**25**	**8.0**	**3**	**0**	**8**	**4**	**–1**	....	....	....	....	....	....	....	....
	St. Louis Blues	**NHL**	**55**	**22**	**29**	**51**	**27**	**30**	**57**	**22**	**7**	**0**	**7**	**219**	**10.0**	**69**	**21**	**71**	**15**	**–8**	**18**	**5**	**2**	**7**	**9**	**1**	**1**	**0**
1968-69	**St. Louis Blues**	**NHL**	**76**	**35**	**47**	**82**	**40**	**44**	**84**	**43**	**7**	**1**	**6**	**288**	**12.2**	**106**	**30**	**62**	**12**	**+26**	**12**	**7**	**3**	**10**	**20**	**2**	**1**	**0**
1969-70	**St. Louis Blues**	**NHL**	**67**	**33**	**39**	**72**	**38**	**39**	**77**	**38**	**16**	**0**	**8**	**282**	**11.7**	**105**	**61**	**56**	**9**	**–3**	**16**	**7**	**5**	**12**	**8**	**3**	**1**	**1**
1970-71	**St. Louis Blues**	**NHL**	**45**	**16**	**26**	**42**	**17**	**23**	**40**	**12**	**6**	**1**	**1**	**174**	**9.2**	**56**	**27**	**47**	**11**	**–7**	....	....	....	....	....	....	....	....
	Detroit Red Wings	**NHL**	**24**	**5**	**12**	**17**	**5**	**11**	**16**	**4**	**1**	**0**	**1**	**51**	**9.8**	**24**	**11**	**26**	**6**	**–7**	....	....	....	....	....	....	....	....
1971-72	**Detroit Red Wings**	**NHL**	**78**	**28**	**41**	**69**	**30**	**37**	**67**	**16**	**5**	**2**	**2**	**218**	**12.8**	**101**	**37**	**95**	**23**	**–8**	....	....	....	....	....	....	....	....
1972-73	Canada	Summit	2	0	1	1	....	....	....	0	....	....	....	....	....	....	....	....	....	....	....	....	....	....	....	....	....	....
	Detroit Red Wings	**NHL**	**78**	**13**	**30**	**43**	**13**	**25**	**38**	**8**	**5**	**0**	**1**	**180**	**7.2**	**68**	**19**	**68**	**5**	**–14**	....	....	....	....	....	....	....	....
1973-74	**Detroit Red Wings**	**NHL**	**76**	**24**	**42**	**66**	**25**	**36**	**61**	**28**	**6**	**1**	**2**	**179**	**13.4**	**98**	**36**	**106**	**22**	**–22**	....	....	....	....	....	....	....	....
1974-75	**Detroit Red Wings**	**NHL**	**27**	**3**	**3**	**6**	**3**	**2**	**5**	**8**	**1**	**0**	**0**	**40**	**7.5**	**9**	**5**	**31**	**17**	**–10**	....	....	....	....	....	....	....	....
	St. Louis Blues	**NHL**	**44**	**12**	**19**	**31**	**11**	**15**	**26**	**12**	**4**	**1**	**1**	**111**	**10.8**	**45**	**13**	**53**	**14**	**–7**	**2**	**1**	**0**	**1**	**0**	**1**	**0**	**0**
1975-76	**St. Louis Blues**	**NHL**	**72**	**20**	**27**	**47**	**19**	**21**	**40**	**47**	**9**	**2**	**1**	**171**	**11.7**	**72**	**40**	**80**	**37**	**–11**	**3**	**1**	**2**	**3**	**0**	**0**	**0**	**0**
1976-77	**St. Louis Blues**	**NHL**	**80**	**21**	**28**	**49**	**20**	**23**	**43**	**8**	**4**	**0**	**3**	**178**	**11.8**	**75**	**26**	**97**	**20**	**–28**	**4**	**0**	**0**	**0**	**4**	**0**	**0**	**0**
1977-78	**St. Louis Blues**	**NHL**	**80**	**13**	**25**	**38**	**13**	**20**	**33**	**12**	**0**	**1**	**2**	**140**	**9.3**	**54**	**17**	**89**	**32**	**–20**	....	....	....	....	....	....	....	....
	NHL Totals		**987**	**261**	**397**	**658**	**280**	**356**	**636**	**305**	**71**	**9**	**35**	**2256**	**11.6**	**885**	**343**	**889**	**227**		**85**	**23**	**14**	**37**	**49**	**7**	**3**	**1**

WCHA First All-Star Team (1961, 1962) • NCAA West First All-American Team (1961, 1962) • NCAA Championship All-Tournament Team (1962) • Won Jack Adams Award (1981)

Played in NHL All-Star Game (1965, 1969, 1970, 1971, 1972, 1974)

Traded to **NY Rangers** by **Montreal** for Ted Taylor and Garry Peters, June 13, 1966. Traded to **St. Louis** by **NY Rangers** with Barclay Plager for Ron Stewart and Ron Attwell, November 29, 1967. Traded to **Detroit** by **St. Louis** with Tim Ecclestone for Garry Unger and Wayne Connelly, February 6, 1971. Traded to **St. Louis** by **Detroit** for Phil Roberto and St. Louis' 3rd round choice (Blair Davidson) in 1975 Amateur Draft, December 30, 1974.

• BEREZAN, PERRY

Perry Berezan C – R. 6'2", 190 lbs. b: Edmonton, Alta., 12/5/1964. Calgary's 3rd choice, 56th overall, in 1983 Entry Draft.

Season	Club	League	GP	G	A	Pts	AG	AA	APts	PIM	PP	SH	GW	S	%	TGF	PGF	TGA	PGA	+/–	GP	G	A	Pts	PIM	PP	SH	GW
1981-82	St. Albert Saints	AJHL	47	16	36	52	....	....	....	47	....	....	....	....	....	....	....	....	....	....	....	....	....	....	....	....	....	....
1982-83	St. Albert Saints	AJHL	57	37	40	77	....	....	....	110	....	....	....	....	....	....	....	....	....	....	....	....	....	....	....	....	....	....
1983-84	University of North Dakota	WCHA	44	28	24	52	....	....	....	29	....	....	....	....	....	....	....	....	....	....	....	....	....	....	....	....	....	....
1984-85	University of North Dakota	WCHA	42	23	35	58	....	....	....	32	....	....	....	....	....	....	....	....	....	....	....	....	....	....	....	....	....	....
	Calgary Flames	**NHL**	**9**	**3**	**2**	**5**	**2**	**1**	**3**	**4**	**0**	**0**	**1**	**13**	**23.1**	**7**	**0**	**2**	**0**	**+5**	**2**	**1**	**0**	**1**	**4**	**1**	**0**	**0**
1985-86	**Calgary Flames**	**NHL**	**55**	**12**	**21**	**33**	**10**	**14**	**24**	**39**	**0**	**2**	**3**	**117**	**10.3**	**55**	**0**	**64**	**28**	**+19**	**8**	**1**	**1**	**2**	**6**	**0**	**0**	**1**
1986-87	**Calgary Flames**	**NHL**	**24**	**5**	**3**	**8**	**4**	**2**	**6**	**24**	**0**	**1**	**0**	**31**	**16.1**	**14**	**0**	**20**	**10**	**+4**	**2**	**0**	**2**	**2**	**7**	**0**	**0**	**0**
1987-88	**Calgary Flames**	**NHL**	**29**	**7**	**12**	**19**	**6**	**9**	**15**	**66**	**0**	**2**	**1**	**69**	**10.1**	**28**	**1**	**34**	**18**	**+11**	**8**	**0**	**2**	**2**	**13**	**0**	**0**	**0**
1988-89	**Calgary Flames**	**NHL**	**35**	**4**	**4**	**8**	**3**	**3**	**6**	**23**	**0**	**1**	**0**	**49**	**8.2**	**16**	**0**	**19**	**8**	**+5**	....	....	....	....	....	....	....	....
	Minnesota North Stars	**NHL**	**16**	**1**	**4**	**5**	**1**	**3**	**4**	**4**	**0**	**0**	**0**	**16**	**6.3**	**8**	**0**	**12**	**5**	**+1**	**5**	**1**	**2**	**3**	**4**	**0**	**0**	**0**
1989-90	**Minnesota North Stars**	**NHL**	**64**	**3**	**12**	**15**	**3**	**9**	**12**	**31**	**0**	**0**	**0**	**75**	**4.0**	**20**	**0**	**50**	**26**	**–4**	**5**	**1**	**0**	**1**	**0**	**0**	**0**	**0**

			REGULAR SEASON																		PLAYOFFS							
Season	Club	League	GP	G	A	Pts	AG	AA	APts	PIM	PP	SH	GW	S	%	TGF	PGF	TGA	PGA	+/–	GP	G	A	Pts	PIM	PP	SH	GW
1990-91	Minnesota North Stars	FrTour	3	0	1	1				6																		
	Minnesota North Stars	**NHL**	**52**	**11**	**6**	**17**	**10**	**5**	**15**	**30**	**1**	**3**	**1**	**73**	**15.1**	**24**	**3**	**40**	**17**	**–2**	**1**	**0**	**0**	**0**	**0**	**0**	**0**	**0**
	Kalamazoo Wings	IHL	2	0	0	0				2																		
1991-92	**San Jose Sharks**	**NHL**	**66**	**12**	**7**	**19**	**11**	**5**	**16**	**30**	**4**	**1**	**2**	**112**	**10.7**	**43**	**9**	**91**	**31**	**–26**								
1992-93	**San Jose Sharks**	**NHL**	**28**	**3**	**4**	**7**	**2**	**3**	**5**	**28**	**1**	**1**	**0**	**37**	**8.1**	**10**	**1**	**39**	**12**	**–18**								
	Kansas City Blades	IHL	9	4	4	8				31																		
	NHL Totals		**378**	**61**	**75**	**136**	**52**	**54**	**106**	**279**	**6**	**11**	**8**	**592**	**10.3**	**225**	**14**	**371**	**155**		**31**	**4**	**7**	**11**	**34**	**1**	**0**	**1**

Traded to **Minnesota** by **Calgary** with Shane Churla for Brian MacLellan and Minnesota's 4th round choice (Robert Reichel) in 1989 Entry Draft, March 4, 1989. Signed as a free agent by **San Jose**, October 10, 1991.

• BEREZIN, SERGEI

Sergei Berezin RW – R. 5'10", 187 lbs. b: Voskresensk, USSR, 11/5/1971. Toronto's 8th choice, 256th overall, in 1994 Entry Draft.

Season	Club	League	GP	G	A	Pts	AG	AA	APts	PIM	PP	SH	GW	S	%	TGF	PGF	TGA	PGA	+/–	GP	G	A	Pts	PIM	PP	SH	GW
1990-91	Khimik Voskresensk	FrTour	1	0	0	0				0																		
	Khimik Voskresensk	USSR	30	6	2	8				4																		
1991-92	Khimik Voskresensk	CIS	36	7	5	12				10																		
1992-93	Khimik Voskresensk	CIS	38	9	3	12				12											2	1	0	1	0			
1993-94	Khimik Voskresensk	CIS	40	31	10	41				16											3	2	0	2	2			
	Russia	Olympics	8	3	2	5				2																		
	Russia	WC-A	6	2	1	3				2																		
1994-95	Kolner Haie	Germany	43	38	19	57				8											18	17	8	25	14			
	Russia	WC-A	6	7	1	8				4																		
1995-96	Kolner Haie	Germany	45	49	31	80				8											14	13	9	22	10			
	Russia	WC-A	8	4	5	9				2																		
1996-97	Russia	W Cup	2	1	0	1				0																		
	Toronto Maple Leafs	**NHL**	**73**	**25**	**16**	**41**	**27**	**14**	**41**	**2**	**7**	**0**	**2**	**177**	**14.1**	**64**	**20**	**47**	**0**	**–3**								
1997-98	**Toronto Maple Leafs**	**NHL**	**68**	**16**	**15**	**31**	**19**	**15**	**34**	**10**	**3**	**0**	**3**	**167**	**9.6**	**47**	**11**	**40**	**1**	**–3**								
	Russia	WC-A	6	6	2	8				2																		
	NHL Totals		**141**	**41**	**31**	**72**	**46**	**29**	**75**	**12**	**10**	**0**	**5**	**344**	**11.9**	**111**	**31**	**87**	**1**									

NHL All-Rookie Team (1997)

• BERG, AKI-PETTERI

Aki-Petteri Berg D – L. 6'3", 198 lbs. b: Turku, Finland, 2/28/1977. Los Angeles' 1st choice, 3rd overall, in 1995 Entry Draft.

Season	Club	League	GP	G	A	Pts	AG	AA	APts	PIM	PP	SH	GW	S	%	TGF	PGF	TGA	PGA	+/–	GP	G	A	Pts	PIM	PP	SH	GW
1993-94	TPS Turku	Finland	6	0	6	6				4																		
1994-95	Kiekko-67	Finland 2	28	3	9	12				34																		
	TPS Turku	Finland	5	0	0	0				4																		
1995-96	**Los Angeles Kings**	**NHL**	**51**	**0**	**7**	**7**	**0**	**6**	**6**	**29**	**0**	**0**	**0**	**56**	**0.0**	**34**	**3**	**50**	**6**	**–13**								
	Phoenix Roadrunners	IHL	20	0	3	3				18											2	0	0	0	4			
1996-97	**Los Angeles Kings**	**NHL**	**41**	**2**	**6**	**8**	**2**	**5**	**7**	**24**	**2**	**0**	**0**	**65**	**3.1**	**35**	**11**	**41**	**8**	**–9**								
	Finland	WJC-A	6	0	2	2				8																		
	Phoenix Roadrunners	IHL	23	1	3	4				21																		
1997-98	**Los Angeles Kings**	**NHL**	**72**	**0**	**8**	**8**	**0**	**8**	**8**	**61**	**0**	**0**	**0**	**58**	**0.0**	**42**	**4**	**49**	**14**	**+3**	**4**	**0**	**3**	**3**	**0**	**0**	**0**	**0**
	Finland	Olympics	6	0	0	0				6																		
	NHL Totals		**164**	**2**	**21**	**23**	**2**	**19**	**21**	**114**	**2**	**0**	**0**	**179**	**1.1**	**111**	**18**	**140**	**28**		**4**	**0**	**3**	**3**	**0**	**0**	**0**	**0**

EJC-A All-Star Team (1995)

• BERG, BILL

Bill Berg LW – L. 6'1", 205 lbs. b: St. Catharines, Ont., 10/21/1967. NY Islanders' 3rd choice, 59th overall, in 1986 Entry Draft.

Season	Club	League	GP	G	A	Pts	AG	AA	APts	PIM	PP	SH	GW	S	%	TGF	PGF	TGA	PGA	+/–	GP	G	A	Pts	PIM	PP	SH	GW
1985-86	Toronto Marlboros	OHL	64	3	35	38				143											4	0	0	0	19			
	Springfield Indians	AHL	4	1	1	2				4																		
1986-87	Toronto Marlboros	OHL	57	3	15	18				138																		
1987-88	Springfield Indians	AHL	76	6	26	32				148																		
	Peoria Rivermen	IHL	5	0	1	1				8											7	0	3	3	31			
1988-89	**New York Islanders**	**NHL**	**7**	**1**	**2**	**3**	**1**	**1**	**2**	**10**	**1**	**0**	**0**	**10**	**10.0**	**11**	**7**	**7**	**1**	**–2**								
	Springfield Indians	AHL	69	17	32	49				122																		
1989-90	Springfield Indians	AHL	74	12	42	54				74											15	5	12	17	35			
1990-91	**New York Islanders**	**NHL**	**78**	**9**	**14**	**23**	**8**	**11**	**19**	**67**	**0**	**0**	**0**	**95**	**9.5**	**41**	**1**	**62**	**19**	**–3**								
1991-92	**New York Islanders**	**NHL**	**47**	**5**	**9**	**14**	**5**	**7**	**12**	**28**	**1**	**0**	**1**	**60**	**8.3**	**21**	**3**	**49**	**13**	**–18**								
	Capital District Islanders	AHL	3	0	2	2				16																		
1992-93	**New York Islanders**	**NHL**	**22**	**6**	**3**	**9**	**5**	**2**	**7**	**49**	**0**	**2**	**0**	**30**	**20.0**	**14**	**0**	**19**	**9**	**+4**								
	Toronto Maple Leafs	**NHL**	**58**	**7**	**8**	**15**	**6**	**5**	**11**	**54**	**0**	**1**	**2**	**83**	**8.4**	**29**	**0**	**40**	**10**	**–1**	**21**	**1**	**1**	**2**	**18**	**0**	**0**	**0**
1993-94	**Toronto Maple Leafs**	**NHL**	**83**	**8**	**11**	**19**	**7**	**8**	**15**	**93**	**0**	**0**	**1**	**99**	**8.1**	**31**	**0**	**58**	**24**	**–3**	**18**	**1**	**2**	**3**	**10**	**0**	**0**	**0**
1994-95	**Toronto Maple Leafs**	**NHL**	**32**	**5**	**1**	**6**	**9**	**1**	**10**	**26**	**0**	**0**	**2**	**57**	**8.8**	**7**	**0**	**21**	**3**	**–11**	**7**	**0**	**1**	**1**	**4**	**0**	**0**	**0**
1995-96	**Toronto Maple Leafs**	**NHL**	**23**	**1**	**1**	**2**	**1**	**1**	**2**	**33**	**0**	**0**	**0**	**33**	**3.0**	**6**	**0**	**18**	**6**	**–6**								
	New York Rangers	**NHL**	**18**	**2**	**1**	**3**	**2**	**1**	**3**	**8**	**0**	**1**	**0**	**27**	**7.4**	**7**	**0**	**15**	**8**	**0**	**10**	**1**	**0**	**1**	**0**	**0**	**0**	**0**
1996-97	**New York Rangers**	**NHL**	**67**	**8**	**6**	**14**	**8**	**5**	**13**	**37**	**0**	**2**	**3**	**84**	**9.5**	**23**	**0**	**29**	**8**	**+2**	**3**	**0**	**0**	**0**	**2**	**0**	**0**	**0**
1997-98	**New York Rangers**	**NHL**	**67**	**1**	**9**	**10**	**1**	**9**	**10**	**55**	**0**	**0**	**0**	**74**	**1.4**	**15**	**1**	**47**	**18**	**–15**								
	NHL Totals		**502**	**53**	**65**	**118**	**53**	**51**	**104**	**460**	**2**	**6**	**9**	**652**	**8.1**	**205**	**12**	**365**	**119**		**59**	**3**	**4**	**7**	**34**	**0**	**0**	**0**

Claimed on waivers by **Toronto** from **NY Islanders**, December 3, 1992. Traded to **NY Rangers** by **Toronto** for Nick Kypreos, February 29, 1996.

• BERGEN, TODD

Todd Bergen C – L. 6'3", 185 lbs. b: Prince Albert, Sask., 7/11/1963. Philadelphia's 5th choice, 98th overall, in 1982 Entry Draft.

Season	Club	League	GP	G	A	Pts	AG	AA	APts	PIM	PP	SH	GW	S	%	TGF	PGF	TGA	PGA	+/–	GP	G	A	Pts	PIM	PP	SH	GW
1981-82	Prince Albert Raiders	SJHL	59	30	62	92				35																		
1982-83	Prince Albert Raiders	WHL	70	34	47	81				17																		
1983-84	Prince Albert Raiders	WHL	43	57	39	96				15											5	2	5	7	4			
	Springfield Indians	AHL	1	0	0	0				0																		
1984-85	**Philadelphia Flyers**	**NHL**	**14**	**11**	**5**	**16**	**9**	**3**	**12**	**4**	**3**	**0**	**3**	**38**	**28.9**	**20**	**6**	**5**	**0**	**+9**	**17**	**4**	**9**	**13**	**8**	**2**	**0**	**1**
	Hershey Bears	AHL	38	20	19	39				2																		
1985-86			DID NOT PLAY – SUSPENDED																									
1986-87	Springfield Indians	AHL	27	12	11	23				14																		
	NHL Totals		**14**	**11**	**5**	**16**	**9**	**3**	**12**	**4**	**3**	**0**	**3**	**38**	**28.9**	**20**	**6**	**5**	**0**		**17**	**4**	**9**	**13**	**8**	**2**	**0**	**1**

• Suspended by **Philadelphia** for refusing to report to training camp, September, 1985. Traded to **Minnesota** by **Philadelphia** with Ed Hospodar for Dave Richter and Bo Berglund, November 29, 1985.

• BERGER, MIKE

Mike Berger D – R. 6', 195 lbs. b: Edmonton, Alta., 6/2/1967. Minnesota's 2nd choice, 69th overall, in 1985 Entry Draft.

Season	Club	League	GP	G	A	Pts	AG	AA	APts	PIM	PP	SH	GW	S	%	TGF	PGF	TGA	PGA	+/–	GP	G	A	Pts	PIM	PP	SH	GW
1982-83	Lethbridge Broncos	WHL	1	0	0	0				0																		
1983-84	Lethbridge Broncos	WHL	41	2	9	11				60											5	0	1	1	7			
1984-85	Lethbridge Broncos	WHL	58	9	31	40				85											4	0	3	3	9			
1985-86	Lethbridge Broncos	WHL	21	2	9	11				39																		
	Spokane Chiefs	WHL	36	7	31	38				36											9	1	5	6	14			
1986-87	Spokane Chiefs	WHL	65	26	49	75				80											2	0	0	0	2			
	Indianapolis Checkers	IHL	4	0	3	3				4											6	0	1	1	13			
1987-88	**Minnesota North Stars**	**NHL**	**29**	**3**	**1**	**4**	**3**	**1**	**4**	**65**	**3**	**0**	**0**	**41**	**7.3**	**11**	**7**	**30**	**7**	**–19**								
	Kalamazoo Wings	IHL	36	5	10	15				94											6	2	0	2	8			
1988-89	**Minnesota North Stars**	**NHL**	**1**	**0**	**0**	**0**	**0**	**0**	**0**	**2**	**0**	**0**	**0**	**0**	**0.0**	**0**	**0**	**1**	**0**	**–1**								
	Kalamazoo Wings	IHL	67	9	16	25				96											6	0	2	2	8			
1989-90	Phoenix Roadrunners	IHL	51	5	12	17				75																		
	Binghamton Whalers	AHL	10	0	4	4				10																		
1990-91	Kansas City Blades	IHL	46	7	14	21				43																		
	Knoxville Cherokees	ECHL	7	1	7	8				31																		
1991-92	Thunder Bay Thunder Hawks	ColHL	54	17	27	44				127																		

			REGULAR SEASON																		PLAYOFFS							
Season	Club	League	GP	G	A	Pts	AG	AA	APts	PIM	PP	SH	GW	S	%	TGF	PGF	TGA	PGA	+/–	GP	G	A	Pts	PIM	PP	SH	GW
1992-93	Tulsa Oilers	CHL	47	16	26	42	....	....	....	116	....	....	....	....	....	....	....	....	....	....	7	2	3	5	4	....	....	....
	Thunder Bay Thunder Hawks	ColHL	8	3	5	8	....	....	....	20	....	....	....	....	....	....	....	....	....	....	....	....	....	....	....	....	....	....
1993-94	Tulsa Oilers	CHL	58	15	19	34	....	....	....	134	....	....	....	....	....	....	....	....	....	....	11	7	4	11	22	....	....	....
	NHL Totals		**30**	**3**	**1**	**4**	**3**	**1**	**4**	**67**	**3**	**0**	**0**	**41**	**7.3**	**11**	**7**	**31**	**7**		....	....	....	....	....	....	....	....

WHL West Second All-Star Team (1986, 1987) • CHL Second All-Star Team (1993)

Traded to **Hartford** by **Minnesota** for Kevin Sullivan, October 7, 1989.

• BERGERON, MICHEL

Michel Bergeron RW – R. 5'10", 170 lbs. b: Chicoutimi, Que., 11/11/1954. Detroit's 4th choice, 63rd overall, in 1974 Amateur Draft.

1971-72	Sorel Black Hawks	QMJHL	24	23	21	44	....	....	....	11	....	....	....	....	....	....	....	....	....	....	4	0	1	1	29	....	....	....
1972-73	Sorel Black Hawks	QMJHL	63	40	62	102	....	....	....	54	....	....	....	....	....	....	....	....	....	....	....	....	....	....	....	....	....	....
1973-74	Sorel Balck Hawks	QMJHL	70	62	81	143	....	....	....	120	....	....	....	....	....	....	....	....	....	....	....	....	....	....	....	....	....	....
1974-75	**Detroit Red Wings**	**NHL**	**25**	**10**	**7**	**17**	**9**	**5**	**14**	**10**	**1**	**0**	**0**	**51**	**19.6**	**23**	**1**	**17**	**0**	**+5**	....	....	....	....	....	....	....	....
	Virginia Wings	AHL	49	9	13	22	....	....	....	14	....	....	....	....	....	....	....	....	....	....	....	....	....	....	....	....	....	....
1975-76	**Detroit Red Wings**	**NHL**	**72**	**32**	**27**	**59**	**30**	**21**	**51**	**48**	**12**	**0**	**4**	**190**	**16.8**	**73**	**24**	**47**	**0**	**+2**	....	....	....	....	....	....	....	....
1976-77	**Detroit Red Wings**	**NHL**	**74**	**21**	**12**	**33**	**20**	**10**	**30**	**98**	**3**	**0**	**5**	**197**	**10.7**	**48**	**10**	**80**	**2**	**–40**	....	....	....	....	....	....	....	....
	Kansas City Blues	CHL	4	3	5	8	....	....	....	4	....	....	....	....	....	....	....	....	....	....	....	....	....	....	....	....	....	....
1977-78	**Detroit Red Wings**	**NHL**	**3**	**1**	**0**	**1**	**1**	**0**	**1**	**0**	**0**	**0**	**0**	**6**	**16.7**	**1**	**0**	**3**	**0**	**–2**	....	....	....	....	....	....	....	....
	New York Islanders	**NHL**	**25**	**9**	**6**	**15**	**9**	**5**	**14**	**2**	**0**	**0**	**2**	**40**	**22.5**	**22**	**0**	**6**	**0**	**+16**	....	....	....	....	....	....	....	....
	Fort Worth Texans	CHL	9	2	1	3	....	....	....	4	....	....	....	....	....	....	....	....	....	....	....	....	....	....	....	....	....	....
1978-79	**Washington Capitals**	**NHL**	**30**	**7**	**6**	**13**	**6**	**5**	**11**	**7**	**1**	**0**	**1**	**53**	**13.2**	**16**	**2**	**32**	**0**	**–18**	....	....	....	....	....	....	....	....
	Milwaukee Admirals	IHL	15	3	5	8	....	....	....	2	....	....	....	....	....	....	....	....	....	....	8	7	4	11	2	....	....	....
1979-80	Nova Scotia Voyageurs	AHL	33	11	20	31	....	....	....	30	....	....	....	....	....	....	....	....	....	....	....	....	....	....	....	....	....	....
	Milwaukee Admirals	IHL	34	25	37	62	....	....	....	34	....	....	....	....	....	....	....	....	....	....	2	0	1	1	20	....	....	....
1980-81	Milwaukee Admirals	IHL	71	30	49	79	....	....	....	22	....	....	....	....	....	....	....	....	....	....	7	2	4	6	11	....	....	....
1981-82	Milwaukee Admirals	IHL	22	8	15	23	....	....	....	4	....	....	....	....	....	....	....	....	....	....	....	....	....	....	....	....	....	....
	Kalamazoo Wings	IHL	22	5	9	14	....	....	....	13	....	....	....	....	....	....	....	....	....	....	....	....	....	....	....	....	....	....
	NHL Totals		**229**	**80**	**58**	**138**	**75**	**46**	**121**	**165**	**17**	**0**	**12**	**537**	**14.9**	**183**	**37**	**185**	**2**		....	....	....	....	....	....	....	....

Traded to **NY Islanders** by **Detroit** for Andre St. Laurent, October 20, 1977. Traded to **Washington** by **NY Islanders** for Washington's 2nd round choice (Tomas Jonsson) in 1979 Amateur Draft, October 19, 1978.

• BERGERON, YVES

Yves Bergeron RW – R. 5'9", 165 lbs. b: Malartic, Que., 1/11/1952. Pittsburgh's 8th choice, 120th overall, in 1972 Amateur Draft.

1969-70	Shawinigan Bruins	QJHL	52	36	43	79	....	....	....	131	....	....	....	....	....	....	....	....	....	....	5	0	5	5	2	....	....	....
1970-71	Shawinigan Bruins	QJHL	62	35	54	89	....	....	....	87	....	....	....	....	....	....	....	....	....	....	15	3	14	17	6	....	....	....
1971-72	Shawinigan Bruins	QMJHL	57	31	60	91	....	....	....	54	....	....	....	....	....	....	....	....	....	....	9	1	3	4	15	....	....	....
1972-73	Quebec Nordiques	WHA	65	14	19	33	....	....	....	32	....	....	....	....	....	....	....	....	....	....	....	....	....	....	....	....	....	....
1973-74	Maine Nordiques	NAHL	73	27	52	79	....	....	....	54	....	....	....	....	....	....	....	....	....	....	8	2	1	3	11	....	....	....
1974-75	**Pittsburgh Penguins**	**NHL**	**2**	**0**	**0**	**0**	**0**	**0**	**0**	**0**	**0**	**0**	**0**	**0**	**0.0**	**0**	**0**	**3**	**0**	**–3**	....	....	....	....	....	....	....	....
	Hershey Bears	AHL	67	31	28	59	....	....	....	116	....	....	....	....	....	....	....	....	....	....	12	4	9	13	46	....	....	....
1975-76	Hershey Bears	AHL	67	26	23	49	....	....	....	87	....	....	....	....	....	....	....	....	....	....	10	2	4	6	14	....	....	....
1976-77	**Pittsburgh Penguins**	**NHL**	**1**	**0**	**0**	**0**	**0**	**0**	**0**	**0**	**0**	**0**	**0**	**2**	**0.0**	**0**	**0**	**0**	**0**	**0**	....	....	....	....	....	....	....	....
	Hershey Bears	AHL	72	23	27	50	....	....	....	90	....	....	....	....	....	....	....	....	....	....	6	1	1	2	0	....	....	....
1977-78			DID NOT PLAY																									
1978-79	Bathurst Alpines	NNBSL	....	....	....	....	....	....	....	....	....	....	....	....	....	....	....	....	....	....	4	1	3	4	51	....	....	....
1979-80	Bathurst Alpines	NNBSL	....	....	....	....	....	....	....	....	....	....	....	....	....	....	....	....	....	....	5	1	2	3	30	....	....	....
1980-81	Bathurst Alpines	NNBSL	....	....	....	....	....	....	....	....	....	....	....	....	....	....	....	....	....	....	8	1	2	3	19	....	....	....
1981-82	Bathurst Alpines	NNBSL	....	....	....	....	....	....	....	....	....	....	....	....	....	....	....	....	....	....	11	4	8	12	24	....	....	....
1982-83	Bathurst Alpines	NNBSL	26	14	15	29	....	....	....	92	....	....	....	....	....	....	....	....	....	....	7	2	3	5	10	....	....	....
1983-84	Bathurst Alpines	NNBSL	19	6	6	12	....	....	....	40	....	....	....	....	....	....	....	....	....	....	5	3	1	4	6	....	....	....
1984-85	Bathurst Alpines	NNBSL	....	....	....	....	....	....	....	....	....	....	....	....	....	....	....	....	....	....	4	0	2	2	4	....	....	....
	NHL Totals		**3**	**0**	**0**	**0**	**0**	**0**	**0**	**0**	**0**	**0**	**0**	**2**	**0.0**	**0**	**0**	**3**	**0**		....	....	....	....	....	....	....	....
	Other Major League Totals		65	14	19	33	....	....	....	32	....	....	....	....	....	....	....	....	....		....	....	....	....	....	....	....	....

QJHL Second All-Star Team (1971)

Selected by **Quebec** (WHA) in 1972 WHA General Players Draft, February 12, 1972. • Served as playing/coach with **Bathurst Alpines** (NNBSL) from 1978-1985.

• BERGEVIN, MARC

Marc Bergevin D – L. 6'1", 197 lbs. b: Montreal, Que., 8/11/1965. Chicago's 3rd choice, 60th overall, in 1983 Entry Draft.

1982-83	Chicoutimi Sagueneens	QMJHL	64	3	27	30	....	....	....	113	....	....	....	....	....	....	....	....	....	....	....	....	....	....	....	....	....	....
1983-84	Chicoutimi Sagueneens	QMJHL	70	10	35	45	....	....	....	125	....	....	....	....	....	....	....	....	....	....	....	....	....	....	....	....	....	....
	Springfield Indians	AHL	7	0	1	1	....	....	....	2	....	....	....	....	....	....	....	....	....	....	....	....	....	....	....	....	....	....
1984-85	**Chicago Black Hawks**	**NHL**	**60**	**0**	**6**	**6**	**0**	**4**	**4**	**54**	**0**	**0**	**0**	**41**	**0.0**	**36**	**0**	**46**	**1**	**–9**	**6**	**0**	**3**	**3**	**2**	**0**	**0**	**0**
	Springfield Indians	AHL	....	....	....	....	....	....	....	....	....	....	....	....	....	....	....	....	....	....	4	0	0	0	0	....	....	....
1985-86	**Chicago Black Hawks**	**NHL**	**71**	**7**	**7**	**14**	**6**	**5**	**11**	**60**	**0**	**0**	**1**	**50**	**14.0**	**47**	**0**	**49**	**2**	**0**	**3**	**0**	**0**	**0**	**0**	**0**	**0**	**0**
1986-87	**Chicago Blackhawks**	**NHL**	**66**	**4**	**10**	**14**	**3**	**7**	**10**	**66**	**0**	**0**	**0**	**56**	**7.1**	**48**	**0**	**53**	**9**	**+4**	**3**	**1**	**0**	**1**	**2**	**0**	**0**	**0**
1987-88	**Chicago Blackhawks**	**NHL**	**58**	**1**	**6**	**7**	**1**	**4**	**5**	**85**	**0**	**0**	**0**	**51**	**2.0**	**32**	**2**	**67**	**18**	**–19**	....	....	....	....	....	....	....	....
	Saginaw Hawks	IHL	10	2	7	9	....	....	....	20	....	....	....	....	....	....	....	....	....	....	....	....	....	....	....	....	....	....
1988-89	**Chicago Blackhawks**	**NHL**	**11**	**0**	**0**	**0**	**0**	**0**	**0**	**18**	**0**	**0**	**0**	**9**	**0.0**	**7**	**0**	**15**	**5**	**–3**	....	....	....	....	....	....	....	....
	New York Islanders	**NHL**	**58**	**2**	**13**	**15**	**2**	**9**	**11**	**62**	**1**	**0**	**0**	**56**	**3.6**	**55**	**3**	**77**	**27**	**+2**	....	....	....	....	....	....	....	....
1989-90	**New York Islanders**	**NHL**	**18**	**0**	**4**	**4**	**0**	**3**	**3**	**30**	**0**	**0**	**0**	**12**	**0.0**	**14**	**2**	**24**	**4**	**–8**	....	....	....	....	....	....	....	....
	Springfield Indians	AHL	47	7	16	23	....	....	....	66	....	....	....	....	....	....	....	....	....	....	17	2	11	13	16	....	....	....
1990-91	Capital District Islanders	AHL	7	0	5	5	....	....	....	6	....	....	....	....	....	....	....	....	....	....	....	....	....	....	....	....	....	....
	Hartford Whalers	**NHL**	**4**	**0**	**0**	**0**	**0**	**0**	**0**	**4**	**0**	**0**	**0**	**2**	**0.0**	**0**	**0**	**3**	**0**	**–3**	....	....	....	....	....	....	....	....
	Springfield Indians	AHL	58	4	23	27	....	....	....	85	....	....	....	....	....	....	....	....	....	....	18	0	7	7	26	....	....	....
1991-92	**Hartford Whalers**	**NHL**	**75**	**7**	**17**	**24**	**6**	**13**	**19**	**64**	**4**	**1**	**1**	**96**	**7.3**	**73**	**26**	**91**	**31**	**–13**	**5**	**0**	**0**	**0**	**2**	**0**	**0**	**0**
1992-93	**Tampa Bay Lightning**	**NHL**	**78**	**2**	**12**	**14**	**2**	**8**	**10**	**66**	**0**	**0**	**0**	**69**	**2.9**	**50**	**1**	**107**	**42**	**–16**	....	....	....	....	....	....	....	....
1993-94	**Tampa Bay Lightning**	**NHL**	**83**	**1**	**15**	**16**	**1**	**12**	**13**	**87**	**0**	**0**	**1**	**76**	**1.3**	**56**	**4**	**95**	**38**	**–5**	....	....	....	....	....	....	....	....
	Canada	WC-A	8	0	0	0	....	....	....	2	....	....	....	....	....	....	....	....	....	....	....	....	....	....	....	....	....	....
1994-95	**Tampa Bay Lightning**	**NHL**	**44**	**2**	**4**	**6**	**4**	**6**	**10**	**51**	**0**	**1**	**0**	**32**	**6.3**	**35**	**1**	**62**	**22**	**–6**	....	....	....	....	....	....	....	....
1995-96	**Detroit Red Wings**	**NHL**	**70**	**1**	**9**	**10**	**1**	**7**	**8**	**33**	**0**	**0**	**0**	**26**	**3.8**	**53**	**1**	**56**	**11**	**+7**	**17**	**1**	**0**	**1**	**14**	**1**	**0**	**0**
1996-97	**St. Louis Blues**	**NHL**	**82**	**0**	**4**	**4**	**0**	**4**	**4**	**53**	**0**	**0**	**0**	**30**	**0.0**	**46**	**1**	**72**	**18**	**–9**	**6**	**1**	**0**	**1**	**8**	**0**	**0**	**0**
1997-98	**St. Louis Blues**	**NHL**	**81**	**3**	**7**	**10**	**4**	**7**	**11**	**90**	**0**	**0**	**0**	**40**	**7.5**	**58**	**0**	**86**	**26**	**–2**	**10**	**0**	**1**	**1**	**8**	**0**	**0**	**0**
	NHL Totals		**859**	**30**	**114**	**144**	**30**	**89**	**119**	**823**	**5**	**2**	**3**	**646**	**4.6**	**610**	**41**	**903**	**254**		**50**	**3**	**4**	**7**	**36**	**1**	**0**	**0**

Traded to **NY Islanders** by **Chicago** with Gary Nylund for Steve Konroyd and Bob Bassen, November 25, 1988. Traded to **Hartford** by **NY Islanders** for Hartford's 5th round choice (Ryan Duthie) in 1992 Entry Draft, October 30, 1990. Signed as a free agent by **Tampa Bay**, July 9, 1992. Traded to **Detroit** by **Tampa Bay** with Ben Hankinson for Shawn Burr and Detroit's 3rd round choice (later traded to Boston — Boston selected Jason Doyle) in 1996 Entry Draft, August 17, 1995. Signed as a free agent by **St. Louis**, July 31, 1996.

• BERGKVIST, STEFAN

Stefan Bergkvist D – L. 6'2", 224 lbs. b: Leksand, Sweden, 3/10/1975. Pittsburgh's 1st choice, 26th overall, in 1993 Entry Draft.

1992-93	Leksands IF	Sweden	15	0	0	0	....	....	....	6	....	....	....	....	....	....	....	....	....	....	....	....	....	....	....	....	....	....
1993-94	Leksands IF	Sweden	6	0	0	0	....	....	....	0	....	....	....	....	....	....	....	....	....	....	....	....	....	....	....	....	....	....
1994-95	London Knights	OHL	64	3	17	20	....	....	....	93	....	....	....	....	....	....	....	....	....	....	4	0	0	0	5	....	....	....
1995-96	**Pittsburgh Penguins**	**NHL**	**2**	**0**	**0**	**0**	**0**	**0**	**0**	**2**	**0**	**0**	**0**	**4**	**0.0**	**1**	**0**	**1**	**0**	**0**	**4**	**0**	**0**	**0**	**2**	**0**	**0**	**0**
	Cleveland Lumberjacks	IHL	61	2	8	10	....	....	....	58	....	....	....	....	....	....	....	....	....	....	3	0	0	0	14	....	....	....
1996-97	**Pittsburgh Penguins**	**NHL**	**5**	**0**	**0**	**0**	**0**	**0**	**0**	**7**	**0**	**0**	**0**	**0**	**0.0**	**1**	**0**	**2**	**0**	**–1**	....	....	....	....	....	....	....	....
	Cleveland Lumberjacks	IHL	33	0	1	1	....	....	....	54	....	....	....	....	....	....	....	....	....	....	4	0	0	0	0	....	....	....
1997-98	Cleveland Lumberjacks	IHL	71	3	6	9	....	....	....	129	....	....	....	....	....	....	....	....	....	....	10	0	2	2	24	....	....	....
	NHL Totals		**7**	**0**	**0**	**0**	**0**	**0**	**0**	**9**	**0**	**0**	**0**	**4**	**0.0**	**2**	**0**	**3**	**0**		**4**	**0**	**0**	**0**	**2**	**0**	**0**	**0**

• BERGLAND, TIM

Tim Bergland RW – R. 6'3", 194 lbs. b: Crookston, MN, 1/11/1965. Washington's 1st choice, 77th overall, in 1983 Entry Draft.

1982-83	Lincoln High School	H.S.	20	26	22	48	....	....	....	....	....	....	....	....	....	....	....	....	....	....	....	....	....	....	....	....	....	....
1983-84	University of Minnesota	WCHA	24	4	11	15	....	....	....	4	....	....	....	....	....	....	....	....	....	....	....	....	....	....	....	....	....	....
1984-85	University of Minnesota	WCHA	34	5	9	14	....	....	....	8	....	....	....	....	....	....	....	....	....	....	....	....	....	....	....	....	....	....
1985-86	University of Minnesota	WCHA	48	11	16	27	....	....	....	26	....	....	....	....	....	....	....	....	....	....	....	....	....	....	....	....	....	....

Season	Club	League	GP	G	A	Pts	AG	AA	APts	PIM	PP	SH	GW	S	%	TGF	PGF	TGA	PGA	+/-	GP	G	A	Pts	PIM	PP	SH	GW
			REGULAR SEASON																		PLAYOFFS							
1986-87	University of Minnesota	WCHA	49	18	17	35	....	....	....	48	....	....	....	....	....	....	....	....	....	....	....	....	....	....	....	....	....	....
1987-88	Fort Wayne Komets	IHL	13	2	1	3	....	....	....	9	....	....	....	....	....	....	....	....	....	....	....	....	....	....	....	....	....	....
	Binghamton Whalers	AHL	63	21	26	47	....	....	....	31	....	....	....	....	....	....	....	....	....	....	4	0	0	0	0	....	....	....
1988-89	Baltimore Skipjacks	AHL	78	24	29	53	....	....	....	39	....	....	....	....	....	....	....	....	....	....	....	....	....	....	....	....	....	....
1989-90	Washington Capitals	FrTour	1	1	0	1	....	....	....	0	....	....	....	....	....	....	....	....	....	....	....	....	....	....	....	....	....	....
	Washington Capitals	**NHL**	**32**	**2**	**5**	**7**	**2**	**4**	**6**	**31**	**0**	**0**	**0**	**20**	**10.0**	**10**	**0**	**14**	**6**	**+2**	**15**	**1**	**1**	**2**	**10**	**0**	**0**	**0**
	Baltimore Skipjacks	AHL	47	12	19	31	....	....	....	55	....	....	....	....	....	....	....	....	....	....	....	....	....	....	....	....	....	....
1990-91	**Washington Capitals**	**NHL**	**47**	**5**	**9**	**14**	**5**	**7**	**12**	**21**	**0**	**0**	**0**	**41**	**12.2**	**15**	**0**	**18**	**2**	**–1**	**11**	**1**	**1**	**2**	**12**	**0**	**0**	**0**
	Baltmore Skipjacks	AHL	15	8	9	17	....	....	....	16	....	....	....	....	....	....	....	....	....	....	....	....	....	....	....	....	....	....
1991-92	**Washington Capitals**	**NHL**	**22**	**1**	**4**	**5**	**1**	**3**	**4**	**2**	**0**	**0**	**0**	**18**	**5.6**	**9**	**0**	**15**	**3**	**–3**	....	....	....	....	....	....	....	....
	Baltimore Skipjacks	AHL	11	6	10	16	....	....	....	5	....	....	....	....	....	....	....	....	....	....	....	....	....	....	....	....	....	....
1992-93	**Tampa Bay Lightning**	**NHL**	**27**	**3**	**3**	**6**	**2**	**2**	**4**	**11**	**0**	**0**	**0**	**44**	**6.8**	**12**	**2**	**19**	**4**	**–5**	....	....	....	....	....	....	....	....
	Atlanta Knights	IHL	49	18	21	39	....	....	....	26	....	....	....	....	....	....	....	....	....	....	9	3	3	6	10	....	....	....
1993-94	**Tampa Bay Lightning**	**NHL**	**51**	**6**	**5**	**11**	**6**	**4**	**10**	**6**	**0**	**0**	**0**	**61**	**9.8**	**21**	**0**	**46**	**11**	**–14**	....	....	....	....	....	....	....	....
	Atlanta Knights	IHL	19	6	7	13	....	....	....	6	....	....	....	....	....	....	....	....	....	....	....	....	....	....	....	....	....	....
	Washington Capitals	**NHL**	**3**	**0**	**0**	**0**	**0**	**0**	**0**	**4**	**0**	**0**	**0**	**4**	**0.0**	**0**	**0**	**1**	**0**	**–1**	....	....	....	....	....	....	....	....
1994-95	Chicago Wolves	IHL	81	12	21	33	....	....	....	70	....	....	....	....	....	....	....	....	....	....	3	1	2	3	4	....	....	....
	United States	WC-A	5	2	1	3	....	....	....	2	....	....	....	....	....	....	....	....	....	....	....	....	....	....	....	....	....	....
1995-96	Chicago Wolves	IHL	81	9	19	28	....	....	....	45	....	....	....	....	....	....	....	....	....	....	9	0	1	1	4	....	....	....
	NHL Totals		**182**	**17**	**26**	**43**	**16**	**20**	**36**	**75**	**0**	**0**	**0**	**188**	**9.0**	**67**	**2**	**113**	**26**		**26**	**2**	**2**	**4**	**22**	**0**	**0**	**0**

Claimed by **Tampa Bay** from **Washington** in Expansion Draft, June 18, 1992. Claimed on waivers by **Washington** from **Tampa Bay**, March 19, 1984. Signed as a free agent by **Chicago** (IHL), Septmeber 30, 1994.

• BERGLOFF, BOB

Bob Bergloff D – R. 6'1", 185 lbs. b: Dickinson, ND, 7/26/1958. Minnesota's 6th choice, 87th overall, in 1978 Amateur Draft.

Season	Club	League	GP	G	A	Pts	AG	AA	APts	PIM	PP	SH	GW	S	%	TGF	PGF	TGA	PGA	+/-	GP	G	A	Pts	PIM	PP	SH	GW
1979-80	University of Minnesota	WCHA	40	9	22	31	....	....	....	54	....	....	....	....	....	....	....	....	....	....	....	....	....	....	....	....	....	....
1980-81	University of Minnesota	WCHA	45	2	16	18	....	....	....	89	....	....	....	....	....	....	....	....	....	....	....	....	....	....	....	....	....	....
1981-82	Nashville South Stars	CHL	74	2	20	22	....	....	....	111	....	....	....	....	....	....	....	....	....	....	3	0	0	0	7	....	....	....
	Toledo Goaldiggers	IHL	3	1	1	2	....	....	....	11	....	....	....	....	....	....	....	....	....	....	....	....	....	....	....	....	....	....
1982-83	**Minnesota North Stars**	**NHL**	**2**	**0**	**0**	**0**	**0**	**0**	**0**	**5**	**0**	**0**	**0**	**1**	**0.0**	**0**	**0**	**1**	**0**	**–1**	....	....	....	....	....	....	....	....
	Birmingham South Stars	CHL	78	6	20	26	....	....	....	156	....	....	....	....	....	....	....	....	....	....	13	0	4	4	10	....	....	....
1983-84	Salt Lake Golden Eagles	CHL	44	4	17	21	....	....	....	78	....	....	....	....	....	....	....	....	....	....	2	0	0	0	4	....	....	....
1984-85	Salt Lake Golden Eagles	IHL	9	0	4	4	....	....	....	15	....	....	....	....	....	....	....	....	....	....	....	....	....	....	....	....	....	....
1985-86	New Haven Nighthawks	AHL	7	0	1	1	....	....	....	7	....	....	....	....	....	....	....	....	....	....	4	0	2	2	2	....	....	....
1986-87			DID NOT PLAY																									
1987-88	Dundee Tigers	Britain	36	14	44	58	....	....	....	103	....	....	....	....	....	....	....	....	....	....	....	....	....	....	....	....	....	....
	NHL Totals		**2**	**0**	**0**	**0**	**0**	**0**	**0**	**5**	**0**	**0**	**0**	**1**	**0.0**	**0**	**0**	**1**	**0**		....	....	....	....	....	....	....	....

• BERGLUND, BO

Bo Berglund RW – L. 5'10", 175 lbs. b: Sjalevad, Sweden, 4/6/1955. Quebec's 8th choice, 242nd overall, in 1983 Entry Draft.

Season	Club	League	GP	G	A	Pts	AG	AA	APts	PIM	PP	SH	GW	S	%	TGF	PGF	TGA	PGA	+/-	GP	G	A	Pts	PIM	PP	SH	GW
1973-74	Sweden	WJC-A	5	1	4	5	....	....	....	0	....	....	....	....	....	....	....	....	....	....	....	....	....	....	....	....	....	....
1974-75	MoDo AIK	Sweden	26	15	17	32	....	....	....	16	....	....	....	....	....	....	....	....	....	....	....	....	....	....	....	....	....	....
	Sweden	WJC-A	....	0	1	1	....	....	....	....	....	....	....	....	....	....	....	....	....	....	....	....	....	....	....	....	....	....
1975-76	MoDo AIK	Sweden	35	16	19	35	....	....	....	43	....	....	....	....	....	....	....	....	....	....	....	....	....	....	....	....	....	....
1976-77	MoDo AIK	Sweden	33	17	21	38	....	....	....	30	....	....	....	....	....	....	....	....	....	....	4	3	2	5	0	....	....	....
1977-78	Djurgarden IF Stockholm	Sweden	15	7	5	12	....	....	....	6	....	....	....	....	....	....	....	....	....	....	....	....	....	....	....	....	....	....
1978-79	Djurgarden IF Stockholm	Sweden	36	23	13	36	....	....	....	46	....	....	....	....	....	....	....	....	....	....	6	2	3	5	4	....	....	....
1979-80	Djurgarden IF Stockholm	Sweden	36	20	17	37	....	....	....	50	....	....	....	....	....	....	....	....	....	....	....	....	....	....	....	....	....	....
	Sweden	Olympics	7	1	3	4	....	....	....	4	....	....	....	....	....	....	....	....	....	....	....	....	....	....	....	....	....	....
1980-81	Djurgarden IF Stockholm	Sweden	31	13	9	22	....	....	....	64	....	....	....	....	....	....	....	....	....	....	....	....	....	....	....	....	....	....
1981-82	Djurgarden IF Stockholm	Sweden	34	16	36	42	....	....	....	58	....	....	....	....	....	....	....	....	....	....	....	....	....	....	....	....	....	....
1982-83	Djurgarden IF Stockholm	Sweden	32	19	13	32	....	....	....	00	....	....	....	....	....	....	....	....	....	....	8	5	1	6	8	....	....	....
1983-84	**Quebec Nordiques**	**NHL**	**75**	**16**	**27**	**43**	**13**	**18**	**31**	**20**	**1**	**0**	**1**	**83**	**19.3**	**64**	**17**	**41**	**0**	**+6**	**7**	**2**	**0**	**2**	**4**	**0**	**0**	**1**
1984-85	**Quebec Nordiques**	**NHL**	**12**	**4**	**1**	**5**	**3**	**1**	**4**	**6**	**0**	**0**	**1**	**15**	**26.7**	**6**	**1**	**3**	**0**	**+2**	....	....	....	....	....	....	....	....
	Minnesota North Stars	**NHL**	**33**	**6**	**9**	**15**	**5**	**6**	**11**	**8**	**1**	**0**	**1**	**38**	**15.8**	**20**	**2**	**21**	**0**	**–3**	**2**	**0**	**0**	**0**	**2**	**0**	**0**	**0**
	Springfield Indians	AHL	3	1	2	3	....	....	....	0	....	....	....	....	....	....	....	....	....	....	....	....	....	....	....	....	....	....
1985-86	**Minnesota North Stars**	**NHL**	**3**	**2**	**0**	**2**	**2**	**0**	**2**	**2**	**1**	**0**	**0**	**6**	**33.3**	**2**	**0**	**2**	**0**	**0**	....	....	....	....	....	....	....	....
	Springfield Indians	AHL	3	0	1	1	....	....	....	2	....	....	....	....	....	....	....	....	....	....	....	....	....	....	....	....	....	....
	Philadelphia Flyers	**NHL**	**7**	**0**	**2**	**2**	**0**	**1**	**1**	**4**	**0**	**0**	**0**	**5**	**0.0**	**2**	**0**	**2**	**0**	**0**	....	....	....	....	....	....	....	....
	Hershey Bears	AHL	43	17	28	45	....	....	....	40	....	....	....	....	....	....	....	....	....	....	18	7	10	17	17	....	....	....
1986-87			DID NOT PLAY																									
1987-88	AIK Solna	Sweden	39	25	31	*56	....	....	....	44	....	....	....	....	....	....	....	....	....	....	5	3	4	7	4	....	....	....
	Sweden	Olympics	8	4	4	8	....	....	....	4	....	....	....	....	....	....	....	....	....	....	....	....	....	....	....	....	....	....
1988-89	AIK Solna	Sweden	33	11	17	28	....	....	....	42	....	....	....	....	....	....	....	....	....	....	1	0	0	0	0	....	....	....
	Sweden	WEC-A	9	4	0	4	....	....	....	4	....	....	....	....	....	....	....	....	....	....	....	....	....	....	....	....	....	....
1989-90	AIK Solna	Sweden	24	5	11	16	....	....	....	20	....	....	....	....	....	....	....	....	....	....	....	....	....	....	....	....	....	....
	NHL Totals		**130**	**28**	**39**	**67**	**23**	**26**	**49**	**40**	**3**	**0**	**3**	**147**	**19.0**	**94**	**20**	**69**	**0**		**9**	**2**	**0**	**2**	**6**	**0**	**0**	**1**

Swedish World All-Star Team (1988) • Swedish Player of the Year (1988)

Traded to **Minnesota** by **Quebec** with Tony McKegney for Brad Maxwell and Brent Ashton, December 14, 1984 Traded to **Philadelphia** by **Minnesota** with Dave Ritcher for Todd Bergen and Ed Hospodar, November 29, 1985.

• BERGMAN, GARY

Gary Bergman D – L. 5'11", 188 lbs. b: Kenora, Ont., 10/7/1938.

Season	Club	League	GP	G	A	Pts	AG	AA	APts	PIM	PP	SH	GW	S	%	TGF	PGF	TGA	PGA	+/-	GP	G	A	Pts	PIM	PP	SH	GW
1957-58	Winnipeg Braves	MJHL	30	4	2	6	....	....	....	73	....	....	....	....	....	....	....	....	....	....	5	1	2	3	14	....	....	....
	Winnipeg Warriors	WHL	2	0	0	0	....	....	....	0	....	....	....	....	....	....	....	....	....	....	....	....	....	....	....	....	....	....
1958-59	Winnipeg Braves	MJHL	29	15	15	30	....	....	....	114	....	....	....	....	....	....	....	....	....	....	24	4	*20	24	46	....	....	....
1959-60	Winnipeg Warriors	WHL	58	1	9	10	....	....	....	147	....	....	....	....	....	....	....	....	....	....	....	....	....	....	....	....	....	....
1960-61	Buffalo Bisons	AHL	67	5	14	19	....	....	....	104	....	....	....	....	....	....	....	....	....	....	4	0	0	0	12	....	....	....
1961-62	Cleveland Barons	AHL	68	10	30	40	....	....	....	164	....	....	....	....	....	....	....	....	....	....	6	1	2	3	14	....	....	....
1962-63	Quebec–Cleveland	AHL	55	5	21	26	....	....	....	141	....	....	....	....	....	....	....	....	....	....	7	1	5	6	10	....	....	....
1963-64	Springfield Indians	AHL	60	13	24	37	....	....	....	106	....	....	....	....	....	....	....	....	....	....	....	....	....	....	....	....	....	....
1964-65	**Detroit Red Wings**	**NHL**	**58**	**4**	**7**	**11**	**5**	**8**	**13**	**85**	....	....	....	....	....	....	....	....	....	....	**5**	**0**	**1**	**1**	**4**	....	....	....
1965-66	**Detroit Red Wings**	**NHL**	**61**	**3**	**16**	**19**	**4**	**16**	**20**	**96**	....	....	....	....	....	....	....	....	....	....	**12**	**0**	**3**	**3**	**14**	....	....	....
	Memphis Wings	CHL	5	2	3	5	....	....	....	4	....	....	....	....	....	....	....	....	....	....	....	....	....	....	....	....	....	....
1966-67	**Detroit Red Wings**	**NHL**	**70**	**5**	**30**	**35**	**6**	**31**	**37**	**129**	....	....	....	....	....	....	....	....	....	....	....	....	....	....	....	....	....	....
1967-68	**Detroit Red Wings**	**NHL**	**74**	**13**	**28**	**41**	**16**	**29**	**45**	**109**	**5**	**2**	**3**	**165**	**7.9**	**124**	**22**	**141**	**38**	**–1**	....	....	....	....	....	....	....	....
1968-69	**Detroit Red Wings**	**NHL**	**76**	**7**	**30**	**37**	**8**	**28**	**36**	**80**	**2**	**0**	**2**	**191**	**3.7**	**126**	**12**	**98**	**29**	**+45**	....	....	....	....	....	....	....	....
1969-70	**Detroit Red Wings**	**NHL**	**69**	**6**	**17**	**23**	**7**	**17**	**24**	**122**	**1**	**0**	**1**	**146**	**4.1**	**84**	**14**	**94**	**28**	**+4**	**4**	**0**	**1**	**1**	**2**	**0**	**0**	**0**
1970-71	**Detroit Red Wings**	**NHL**	**68**	**8**	**25**	**33**	**8**	**22**	**30**	**149**	**0**	**1**	**0**	**168**	**4.8**	**85**	**18**	**128**	**33**	**–28**	....	....	....	....	....	....	....	....
1971-72	**Detroit Red Wings**	**NHL**	**75**	**6**	**31**	**37**	**6**	**28**	**34**	**138**	**1**	**0**	**0**	**141**	**4.3**	**133**	**35**	**111**	**20**	**+7**	....	....	....	....	....	....	....	....
1972-73	Canada	Summit	8	0	3	3	....	....	....	13	....	....	....	....	....	....	....	....	....	....	....	....	....	....	....	....	....	....
	Detroit Red Wings	**NHL**	**68**	**3**	**28**	**31**	**3**	**23**	**26**	**71**	**0**	**0**	**0**	**174**	**1.7**	**127**	**30**	**105**	**18**	**+10**	....	....	....	....	....	....	....	....
1973-74	**Detroit Red Wings**	**NHL**	**11**	**0**	**6**	**6**	**0**	**5**	**5**	**18**	**0**	**0**	**0**	**10**	**0.0**	**14**	**1**	**24**	**5**	**–6**	....	....	....	....	....	....	....	....
	Minnesota North Stars	**NHL**	**57**	**3**	**23**	**26**	**3**	**20**	**23**	**66**	**1**	**0**	**1**	**87**	**3.4**	**66**	**8**	**79**	**9**	**–12**	....	....	....	....	....	....	....	....
1974-75	**Detroit Red Wings**	**NHL**	**76**	**5**	**25**	**30**	**5**	**20**	**25**	**104**	**2**	**1**	**0**	**100**	**5.0**	**95**	**27**	**119**	**26**	**–25**	....	....	....	....	....	....	....	....
1975-76	**Kansas City Scouts**	**NHL**	**75**	**5**	**33**	**38**	**5**	**26**	**31**	**82**	**1**	**0**	**1**	**125**	**4.0**	**85**	**27**	**143**	**33**	**–52**	....	....	....	....	....	....	....	....
	NHL Totals		**838**	**68**	**299**	**367**	**76**	**273**	**349**	**1249**	**13**	**4**	**8**	**1307**	**5.2**	**939**	**194**	**1042**	**239**		**21**	**0**	**5**	**5**	**20**	**0**	**0**	**0**

Played in NHL All-Star Game (1973)

Claimed by **Chicago** (Buffalo - AHL) from **Winnipeg** (WHL) in Inter-League Draft, June, 1960. Traded to **Quebec** (AHL) by **Montreal** for cash, July, 1962. Traded to **Montreal** (Cleveland - AHL) by **Buffalo** (AHL) for cash, October, 1961. Traded to **Cleveland** (AHL) by **Quebec** (AHL) for Terry Gray, November 1, 1962. Loaned to **Springfield** (AHL) by **Montreal** with Brian D. Smith, Wayne Boddy, Fred Hilts, Lorne O'Donnell and John Rodger for Terry Gray, Bruce Cline, Wayne Larkin, John Chasczewski and Ted Harris, June, 1963. Claimed by **Detroit** from **Montreal** in Intra-League Draft, June 10, 1964. Traded to **Minnesota** by **Detroit** for Ted Harris, November 7, 1973. Traded to **Detroit** by **Minnesota** for Detroit's 3rd round choice (Alex Pirus) in 1975 Amateur Draft, October 1, 1974. Traded to **Kansas City** by **Detroit** with Bill McKenzie for Peter McDuffe and Glen Burdon, August 22, 1975.

Season	Club	League	GP	G	A	Pts	AG	AA	APts	PIM	PP	SH	GW	S	%	TGF	PGF	TGA	PGA	+/–	GP	G	A	Pts	PIM	PP	SH	GW
			REGULAR SEASON																		PLAYOFFS							

• BERGMAN, THOMMIE
Thommie Bergman D – L. 6′2″, 200 lbs. b: Munkfors, Sweden, 12/10/1947.

Season	Club	League	GP	G	A	Pts	AG	AA	APts	PIM	PP	SH	GW	S	%	TGF	PGF	TGA	PGA	+/–	GP	G	A	Pts	PIM	PP	SH	GW
1969-70	Sodertalje	Sweden	14	5	4	9	....	....	....	2	....	....	....	....	....	....	....	....	....	....	14	4	2	6	12	....	....	....
1970-71	Sodertalje	Sweden	12	8	2	10	....	....	....	18	....	....	....	....	....	....	....	....	....	....	14	3	6	9	14	....	....	....
	Sweden	WEC-A	10	1	0	1	....	....	....	4	....	....	....	....	....	....	....	....	....	....	....	....	....	....	....	....	....	....
1971-72	Vastra Frolunda	Sweden	26	9	9	18	....	....	....	36	....	....	....	....	....	....	....	....	....	....	8	2	4	6	8	....	....	....
	Sweden	Olympics	5	1	1	2	....	....	....	10	....	....	....	....	....	....	....	....	....	....	....	....	....	....	....	....	....	....
	Sweden	WEC-A	8	2	4	6	....	....	....	8	....	....	....	....	....	....	....	....	....	....	....	....	....	....	....	....	....	....
1972-73	**Detroit Red Wings**	**NHL**	**75**	**9**	**12**	**21**	**9**	**10**	**19**	**70**	**1**	**0**	**2**	**165**	**5.5**	**102**	**17**	**92**	**13**	**+6**	....	....	....	....	....	....	....	....
1973-74	**Detroit Red Wings**	**NHL**	**43**	**0**	**3**	**3**	**0**	**3**	**3**	**21**	**0**	**0**	**0**	**49**	**0.0**	**24**	**1**	**45**	**7**	**–15**	....	....	....	....	....	....	....	....
	Virginia Wings	AHL	8	0	3	3	....	....	....	9	....	....	....	....	....	....	....	....	....	....	....	....	....	....	....	....	....	....
1974-75	**Detroit Red Wings**	**NHL**	**18**	**0**	**1**	**1**	**0**	**1**	**1**	**27**	**0**	**0**	**0**	**20**	**0.0**	**4**	**0**	**15**	**4**	**–7**	....	....	....	....	....	....	....	....
	Winnipeg Jets	WHA	49	4	15	19	....	....	....	70	....	....	....	....	....	....	....	....	....	....	....	....	....	....	....	....	....	....
1975-76	Winnipeg Jets	WHA	81	11	30	41	....	....	....	111	....	....	....	....	....	....	....	....	....	....	13	3	10	13	8	....	....	....
1976-77	Sweden	C Cup	3	0	2	2	....	....	....	6	....	....	....	....	....	....	....	....	....	....	....	....	....	....	....	....	....	....
	Winnipeg Jets	WHA	42	2	24	26	....	....	....	37	....	....	....	....	....	....	....	....	....	....	....	....	....	....	....	....	....	....
1977-78	Winnipeg Jets	WHA	62	5	28	33	....	....	....	43	....	....	....	....	....	....	....	....	....	....	....	....	....	....	....	....	....	....
	Detroit Red Wings	**NHL**	**14**	**1**	**6**	**7**	**1**	**5**	**6**	**16**	**0**	**0**	**0**	**18**	**5.6**	**17**	**1**	**21**	**6**	**+1**	**7**	**0**	**2**	**2**	**2**	**0**	**0**	**0**
1978-79	**Detroit Red Wings**	**NHL**	**68**	**10**	**17**	**27**	**9**	**13**	**22**	**64**	**3**	**1**	**1**	**88**	**11.4**	**72**	**12**	**114**	**29**	**–25**	....	....	....	....	....	....	....	....
1979-80	**Detroit Red Wings**	**NHL**	**28**	**1**	**5**	**6**	**1**	**4**	**5**	**45**	**0**	**0**	**0**	**39**	**2.6**	**29**	**3**	**31**	**9**	**+4**	....	....	....	....	....	....	....	....
	Adirondack Red Wings	AHL	15	0	2	2	....	....	....	7	....	....	....	....	....	....	....	....	....	....	....	....	....	....	....	....	....	....
1980-81	Vastra Frolunda	Sweden	33	9	8	17	....	....	....	*101	....	....	....	....	....	....	....	....	....	....	2	0	0	0	4	....	....	....
	NHL Totals		**246**	**21**	**44**	**65**	**20**	**36**	**56**	**243**	**4**	**1**	**3**	**379**	**5.5**	**248**	**34**	**318**	**68**		**7**	**0**	**2**	**2**	**2**	**0**	**0**	**0**
	Other Major League Totals		234	22	97	119	....	....	....	261	....	....	....	....	....	....	....	....	....	....	13	3	10	13	8	....	....	....

Signed as a free agent by **Detroit**, March, 1972. Traded to **Winnipeg** (WHA) by **Detroit** for cash, December, 1974. Signed as a free agent by **Detroit**, March 16, 1978.

• BERGQVIST, JONAS
Jonas Bergqvist RW – L. 6′, 185 lbs. b: Hassleholm, Sweden, 9/26/1962. Calgary's 6th choice, 126th overall, in 1988 Entry Draft.

Season	Club	League	GP	G	A	Pts	AG	AA	APts	PIM	PP	SH	GW	S	%	TGF	PGF	TGA	PGA	+/–	GP	G	A	Pts	PIM	PP	SH	GW
1981-82	Leksands IF	Sweden	33	6	7	13	....	....	....	10	....	....	....	....	....	....	....	....	....	....	....	....	....	....	....	....	....	....
	Sweden	WJC-A	7	4	5	9	....	....	....	9	....	....	....	....	....	....	....	....	....	....	....	....	....	....	....	....	....	....
1982-83	Leksands IF	Sweden	35	8	11	19	....	....	....	20	....	....	....	....	....	....	....	....	....	....	....	....	....	....	....	....	....	....
1983-84	Leksands IF	Sweden	29	11	11	22	....	....	....	16	....	....	....	....	....	....	....	....	....	....	....	....	....	....	....	....	....	....
1984-85	Leksands IF	Sweden	35	11	11	22	....	....	....	26	....	....	....	....	....	....	....	....	....	....	....	....	....	....	....	....	....	....
1985-86	Leksands IF	Sweden	36	16	21	37	....	....	....	16	....	....	....	....	....	....	....	....	....	....	....	....	....	....	....	....	....	....
	Sweden	WEC-A	10	4	3	7	....	....	....	12	....	....	....	....	....	....	....	....	....	....	....	....	....	....	....	....	....	....
1986-87	Leksands IF	Sweden	36	9	11	20	....	....	....	26	....	....	....	....	....	....	....	....	....	....	....	....	....	....	....	....	....	....
	Sweden	WEC-A	9	1	3	4	....	....	....	4	....	....	....	....	....	....	....	....	....	....	....	....	....	....	....	....	....	....
1987-88	Sweden	C Cup	6	2	0	2	....	....	....	4	....	....	....	....	....	....	....	....	....	....	....	....	....	....	....	....	....	....
	Leksands IF	Sweden	37	19	12	31	....	....	....	32	....	....	....	....	....	....	....	....	....	....	3	0	0	0	0	....	....	....
	Sweden	Olympics	8	3	0	3	....	....	....	4	....	....	....	....	....	....	....	....	....	....	....	....	....	....	....	....	....	....
1988-89	Leksands IF	Sweden	27	15	20	35	....	....	....	18	....	....	....	....	....	....	....	....	....	....	10	4	3	7	2	....	....	....
	Sweden	WEC-A	10	3	2	5	....	....	....	4	....	....	....	....	....	....	....	....	....	....	....	....	....	....	....	....	....	....
1989-90	Calgary Flames	FrTour	DID NOT PLAY																									
	Calgary Flames	**NHL**	**22**	**2**	**5**	**7**	**2**	**4**	**6**	**10**	**0**	**0**	**0**	**30**	**6.7**	**15**	**0**	**6**	**1**	**+10**	....	....	....	....	....	....	....	....
	Salt Lake Golden Eagles	IHL	13	6	10	16	....	....	....	4	....	....	....	....	....	....	....	....	....	....	....	....	....	....	....	....	....	....
1990-91	Mannheim Berlin	Germany	36	16	23	39	....	....	....	22	....	....	....	....	....	....	....	....	....	....	....	....	....	....	....	....	....	....
	Sweden	WEC-A	9	4	2	6	....	....	....	8	....	....	....	....	....	....	....	....	....	....	....	....	....	....	....	....	....	....
1991-92	Sweden	C Cup	6	0	1	1	....	....	....	0	....	....	....	....	....	....	....	....	....	....	....	....	....	....	....	....	....	....
	Leksands IF	Sweden	22	11	10	21	....	....	....	4	....	....	....	....	....	....	....	....	....	....	....	....	....	....	....	....	....	....
1992-93	Leksands IF	Sweden	39	15	23	38	....	....	....	40	....	....	....	....	....	....	....	....	....	....	2	0	0	0	0	....	....	....
	Sweden	WC-A	8	3	1	4	....	....	....	14	....	....	....	....	....	....	....	....	....	....	....	....	....	....	....	....	....	....
1993-94	Leksands IF	Sweden	35	12	23	35	....	....	....	29	....	....	....	....	....	....	....	....	....	....	....	....	....	....	....	....	....	....
	Sweden	Olympics	8	1	3	4	....	....	....	4	....	....	....	....	....	....	....	....	....	....	....	....	....	....	....	....	....	....
	Sweden	WC-A	8	3	5	8	....	....	....	4	....	....	....	....	....	....	....	....	....	....	....	....	....	....	....	....	....	....
1994-95	Leksands IF	Sweden	33	17	12	29	....	....	....	16	....	....	....	....	....	....	....	....	....	....	4	0	0	0	4	....	....	....
	Sweden	WC-A	5	1	0	1	....	....	....	0	....	....	....	....	....	....	....	....	....	....	....	....	....	....	....	....	....	....
1995-96	Leksands IF	Sweden	37	16	14	30	....	....	....	30	....	....	....	....	....	....	....	....	....	....	5	2	1	3	0	....	....	....
	Sweden	WC-A	6	4	0	4	....	....	....	0	....	....	....	....	....	....	....	....	....	....	....	....	....	....	....	....	....	....
1996-97	Sweden	W Cup	4	1	0	1	....	....	....	2	....	....	....	....	....	....	....	....	....	....	....	....	....	....	....	....	....	....
	Leksands IF	Sweden	38	13	16	29	....	....	....	22	....	....	....	....	....	....	....	....	....	....	9	4	2	6	12	....	....	....
1997-98	Leksands IF	Sweden	31	14	19	33	....	....	....	18	....	....	....	....	....	....	....	....	....	....	3	0	1	1	8	....	....	....
	Sweden	WC-A	10	2	0	2	....	....	....	6	....	....	....	....	....	....	....	....	....	....	....	....	....	....	....	....	....	....
	NHL Totals		**22**	**2**	**5**	**7**	**2**	**4**	**6**	**10**	**0**	**0**	**0**	**30**	**6.7**	**15**	**0**	**6**	**1**		....	....	....	....	....	....	....	....

Swedish World All-Star Team (1989, 1996) • Swedish Player of the Year (1996)

• BERNIER, SERGE
Serge Bernier RW – R. 6′1″, 190 lbs. b: Padoue, Que., 4/29/1947. Philadelphia's 1st choice, 5th overall, in 1967 Amateur Draft.

Season	Club	League	GP	G	A	Pts	AG	AA	APts	PIM	PP	SH	GW	S	%	TGF	PGF	TGA	PGA	+/–	GP	G	A	Pts	PIM	PP	SH	GW
1966-67	Sorel Eperviers	QJHL	STATISTICS NOT AVAILABLE																									
1967-68	Quebec Aces	AHL	33	7	11	18	....	....	....	56	....	....	....	....	....	....	....	....	....	....	6	6	4	10	6	....	....	....
1968-69	**Philadelphia Flyers**	**NHL**	**1**	**0**	**0**	**0**	**0**	**0**	**0**	**2**	**0**	**0**	**0**	**3**	**0.0**	**0**	**0**	**0**	**0**	**0**	....	....	....	....	....	....	....	....
	Quebec Aces	AHL	70	27	32	59	....	....	....	118	....	....	....	....	....	....	....	....	....	....	12	1	6	7	2	....	....	....
1969-70	**Philadelphia Flyers**	**NHL**	**1**	**0**	**1**	**1**	**0**	**1**	**1**	**0**	**0**	**0**	**0**	**2**	**0.0**	**1**	**0**	**2**	**0**	**–1**	....	....	....	....	....	....	....	....
	Quebec Aces	AHL	70	22	48	70	....	....	....	88	....	....	....	....	....	....	....	....	....	....	5	2	3	5	36	....	....	....
1970-71	**Philadelphia Flyers**	**NHL**	**77**	**23**	**28**	**51**	**24**	**25**	**49**	**77**	**2**	**0**	**1**	**205**	**11.2**	**67**	**11**	**65**	**2**	**–7**	**4**	**1**	**1**	**2**	**0**	**1**	**0**	**0**
1971-72	**Philadelphia Flyers**	**NHL**	**44**	**12**	**11**	**23**	**13**	**10**	**23**	**51**	**5**	**0**	**3**	**120**	**10.0**	**32**	**13**	**39**	**0**	**–20**	....	....	....	....	....	....	....	....
	Los Angeles Kings	**NHL**	**26**	**11**	**11**	**22**	**12**	**10**	**22**	**12**	**1**	**0**	**1**	**97**	**11.3**	**33**	**10**	**20**	**0**	**+3**	....	....	....	....	....	....	....	....
1972-73	**Los Angeles Kings**	**NHL**	**75**	**22**	**46**	**68**	**22**	**39**	**61**	**43**	**6**	**0**	**3**	**255**	**8.6**	**104**	**46**	**78**	**0**	**–20**	....	....	....	....	....	....	....	....
1973-74	Quebec Nordiques	WHA	74	37	49	86	....	....	....	107	....	....	....	....	....	....	....	....	....	....	....	....	....	....	....	....	....	....
1974-75	Canada	Summit	8	1	2	3	....	....	....	2	....	....	....	....	....	....	....	....	....	....	....	....	....	....	....	....	....	....
	Quebec Nordiques	WHA	76	54	68	122	....	....	....	75	....	....	....	....	....	....	....	....	....	....	16	8	8	16	6	....	....	....
1975-76	Quebec Nordiques	WHA	70	34	68	102	....	....	....	91	....	....	....	....	....	....	....	....	....	....	5	2	6	8	6	....	....	....
1976-77	Quebec Nordiques	WHA	74	43	53	96	....	....	....	94	....	....	....	....	....	....	....	....	....	....	17	*14	*22	*36	10	....	....	....
1977-78	Quebec Nordiques	WHA	58	26	52	78	....	....	....	48	....	....	....	....	....	....	....	....	....	....	11	4	10	14	17	....	....	....
1978-79	Quebec Nordiques	WHA	65	36	46	82	....	....	....	71	....	....	....	....	....	....	....	....	....	....	1	0	0	0	2	....	....	....
1979-80	**Quebec Nordiques**	**NHL**	**32**	**8**	**14**	**22**	**7**	**11**	**18**	**31**	**3**	**0**	**3**	**76**	**10.5**	**38**	**17**	**33**	**7**	**–5**	....	....	....	....	....	....	....	....
1980-81	**Quebec Nordiques**	**NHL**	**46**	**2**	**8**	**10**	**2**	**6**	**8**	**18**	**1**	**0**	**0**	**35**	**5.7**	**21**	**11**	**23**	**5**	**–8**	**1**	**0**	**0**	**0**	**0**	**0**	**0**	**0**
	NHL Totals		**302**	**78**	**119**	**197**	**80**	**102**	**182**	**234**	**18**	**0**	**11**	**793**	**9.8**	**296**	**108**	**260**	**14**		**5**	**1**	**1**	**2**	**0**	**1**	**0**	**0**
	Other Major League Totals		417	230	336	566	....	....	....	486	....	....	....	....	....	....	....	....	....		50	28	46	74	41	....	....	....

WHA Second All-Star Team (1975) • Won WHA Playoff MVP Trophy (1977)

Traded to **LA Kings** by **Philadelphia** with Bill Lesuk and Jim Johnson for Bill Flett, Jean Potvin and Ross Lonsberry, January 28, 1972. Selected by **Ontario-Ottawa** (WHA) in 1972 WHA General Player Draft, February 12, 1972. WHA rights traded to **Quebec** (WHA) by **Ottawa** (WHA) for future considerations, June, 1973. Rights retained by **Quebec** prior to Expansion Draft, June 9, 1979.

• BERRY, BOB
Bob Berry LW – L. 6′, 185 lbs. b: Montreal, Que., 11/29/1943.

Season	Club	League	GP	G	A	Pts	AG	AA	APts	PIM	PP	SH	GW	S	%	TGF	PGF	TGA	PGA	+/–	GP	G	A	Pts	PIM	PP	SH	GW
1963-64	Verdun Maple Leafs	QJHL	25	38	27	65	....	....	....	93	....	....	....	....	....	....	....	....	....	....	....	....	....	....	....	....	....	....
	Peterborough Petes	OHA	11	4	3	7	....	....	....	36	....	....	....	....	....	....	....	....	....	....	2	0	0	0	4	....	....	....
1964-65	George Williams College	OQAA	17	13	27	40	....	....	....	....	....	....	....	....	....	....	....	....	....	....	....	....	....	....	....	....	....	....
1965-66	George Williams College	OQAA	27	36	48	84	....	....	....	....	....	....	....	....	....	....	....	....	....	....	....	....	....	....	....	....	....	....
1966-67	George Williams College	OQAA	31	48	41	89	....	....	....	....	....	....	....	....	....	....	....	....	....	....	....	....	....	....	....	....	....	....
	Canada	Nat-Team	....	1	1	2	....	....	....	0	....	....	....	....	....	....	....	....	....	....	....	....	....	....	....	....	....	....
1967-68	Hull Nationals	QSHL	39	32	24	56	....	....	....	80	....	....	....	....	....	....	....	....	....	....	....	....	....	....	....	....	....	....
1968-69	**Montreal Canadiens**	**NHL**	**2**	**0**	**0**	**0**	**0**	**0**	**0**	**0**	**0**	**0**	**0**	**0**	**0.0**	**0**	**0**	**0**	**0**	**0**	....	....	....	....	....	....	....	....
	Cleveland Barons	AHL	68	24	29	53	....	....	....	104	....	....	....	....	....	....	....	....	....	....	5	0	3	3	10	....	....	....
1969-70	Montreal Voyageurs	AHL	71	18	41	59	....	....	....	104	....	....	....	....	....	....	....	....	....	....	8	1	0	1	11	....	....	....
1970-71	**Los Angeles Kings**	**NHL**	**77**	**25**	**38**	**63**	**26**	**34**	**60**	**52**	**4**	**0**	**2**	**149**	**16.8**	**87**	**16**	**77**	**1**	**–5**	....	....	....	....	....	....	....	....

Season	Club	League	GP	G	A	Pts	AG	AA	APts	PIM	PP	SH	GW	S	%	TGF	PGF	TGA	PGA	+/–	GP	G	A	Pts	PIM	PP	SH	GW
			REGULAR SEASON																		PLAYOFFS							
1971-72	**Los Angeles Kings**	**NHL**	**78**	**17**	**22**	**39**	**18**	**20**	**38**	**44**	**3**	**0**	**3**	**102**	**16.7**	**59**	**10**	**72**	**0**	**–23**								
1972-73	**Los Angeles Kings**	**NHL**	**78**	**36**	**28**	**64**	**36**	**23**	**59**	**75**	**14**	**0**	**2**	**176**	**20.5**	**94**	**33**	**74**	**0**	**–13**								
1973-74	**Los Angeles Kings**	**NHL**	**77**	**23**	**33**	**56**	**23**	**29**	**52**	**56**	**8**	**0**	**1**	**122**	**18.9**	**85**	**22**	**63**	**0**	**0**	**5**	**0**	**0**	**0**	**0**	**0**	**0**	**0**
1974-75	**Los Angeles Kings**	**NHL**	**80**	**25**	**23**	**48**	**23**	**18**	**41**	**60**	**7**	**0**	**7**	**136**	**18.4**	**75**	**18**	**38**	**2**	**+21**	**3**	**1**	**2**	**3**	**2**	**0**	**0**	**0**
1975-76	**Los Angeles Kings**	**NHL**	**80**	**20**	**22**	**42**	**19**	**17**	**36**	**37**	**3**	**0**	**3**	**156**	**12.8**	**78**	**14**	**62**	**0**	**+2**	**9**	**1**	**1**	**2**	**0**	**0**	**0**	**1**
1976-77	**Los Angeles Kings**	**NHL**	**69**	**13**	**25**	**38**	**12**	**20**	**32**	**20**	**2**	**0**	**1**	**85**	**15.3**	**58**	**8**	**39**	**1**	**+12**	**9**	**0**	**3**	**3**	**4**	**0**	**0**	**0**
	Fort Worth Texans	CHL	7	4	4	8				0																		
1977-78	Springfield Indians	AHL	74	26	27	53				56											4	0	0	0	0			
	NHL Totals		**541**	**159**	**191**	**350**	**157**	**161**	**318**	**344**	**41**	**0**	**19**	**926**	**17.2**	**536**	**121**	**425**	**4**		**26**	**2**	**6**	**8**	**6**	**0**	**0**	**1**

Played in NHL All-Star Game (1973, 1974)

Traded to **LA Kings** by **Montreal** for cash, October 8, 1972.

• BERRY, BRAD

Brad Berry D – L. 6'2", 190 lbs. b: Bashaw, Alta., 4/1/1965. Winnipeg's 3rd choice, 29th overall, in 1983 Entry Draft.

Season	Club	League	GP	G	A	Pts	AG	AA	APts	PIM	PP	SH	GW	S	%	TGF	PGF	TGA	PGA	+/–	GP	G	A	Pts	PIM	PP	SH	GW
1982-83	St. Albert Saints	AJHL	55	9	33	42				97																		
1983-84	University of North Dakota	WCHA	32	2	7	9				8																		
1984-85	University of North Dakota	WCHA	40	4	26	30				26																		
	Canada	WJC-A	7	0	1	1				2																		
1985-86	University of North Dakota	WCHA	40	6	29	35				26																		
	Winnipeg Jets	**NHL**	**13**	**1**	**0**	**1**	**1**	**0**	**1**	**10**	**0**	**0**	**0**	**16**	**6.3**	**14**	**0**	**15**	**2**	**+1**	**3**	**0**	**0**	**0**	**0**	**0**	**0**	**0**
1986-87	**Winnipeg Jets**	**NHL**	**52**	**2**	**8**	**10**	**2**	**6**	**8**	**60**	**0**	**0**	**0**	**39**	**5.1**	**42**	**0**	**46**	**10**	**+6**	**7**	**0**	**1**	**1**	**14**	**0**	**0**	**0**
1987-88	**Winnipeg Jets**	**NHL**	**48**	**0**	**6**	**6**	**0**	**4**	**4**	**75**	**0**	**0**	**0**	**31**	**0.0**	**35**	**0**	**59**	**13**	**–11**								
	Moncton Hawks	AHL	10	1	3	4				14																		
1988-89	**Winnipeg Jets**	**NHL**	**38**	**0**	**9**	**9**	**0**	**6**	**6**	**45**	**0**	**0**	**0**	**21**	**0.0**	**21**	**0**	**33**	**4**	**–8**								
	Moncton Hawks	AHL	38	3	16	19				39																		
1989-90	**Winnipeg Jets**	**NHL**	**12**	**1**	**2**	**3**	**1**	**1**	**2**	**6**	**0**	**0**	**0**	**7**	**14.3**	**11**	**1**	**12**	**0**	**–2**	**1**	**0**	**0**	**0**	**0**	**0**	**0**	**0**
	Moncton Hawks	AHL	38	1	9	10				58																		
1990-91	Brynas IF Gavle	Sweden	38	3	1	4				38																		
	Canada	Nat-Team	4	0	1	1				0																		
1991-92	**Minnesota North Stars**	**NHL**	**7**	**0**	**0**	**0**	**0**	**0**	**0**	**6**	**0**	**0**	**0**	**2**	**0.0**	**2**	**0**	**3**	**0**	**–1**	**2**	**0**	**0**	**0**	**2**	**0**	**0**	**0**
	Kalamazoo Wings	IHL	65	5	18	23				90											5	2	0	2	6			
1992-93	**Minnesota North Stars**	**NHL**	**63**	**0**	**3**	**3**	**0**	**2**	**2**	**109**	**0**	**0**	**0**	**49**	**0.0**	**40**	**0**	**59**	**21**	**+2**								
1993-94	**Dallas Stars**	**NHL**	**8**	**0**	**0**	**0**	**0**	**0**	**0**	**12**	**0**	**0**	**0**	**4**	**0.0**	**2**	**0**	**4**	**0**	**–2**								
	Kalamazoo Wings	IHL	45	3	19	22				91											1	0	0	0	0			
1994-95	Kalamazoo Wings	IHL	65	4	11	15				146											1	0	0	0	0			
1995-96	Michigan K-Wings	IHL	80	4	13	17				73											10	0	5	5	12			
1996-97	Michigan K-Wings	IHL	77	4	7	11				68											4	0	0	0	4			
1997-98	Michigan K-Wings	IHL	67	3	8	11				60																		
	NHL Totals		**241**	**4**	**28**	**32**	**4**	**19**	**23**	**323**	**0**	**0**	**0**	**169**	**2.4**	**167**	**1**	**231**	**50**		**13**	**0**	**1**	**1**	**16**	**0**	**0**	**0**

Signed as a free agent by **Minnesota**, October 4, 1991. Transferred to **Dallas** after **Minnesota** franchise relocated, June 9, 1993.

• BERRY, DOUG

Doug Berry C – L. 6'1", 190 lbs. b: New Westminster, B.C., 6/3/1957. Colorado's 2nd choice, 38th overall, in 1977 Amateur Draft.

Season	Club	League	GP	G	A	Pts	AG	AA	APts	PIM	PP	SH	GW	S	%	TGF	PGF	TGA	PGA	+/–	GP	G	A	Pts	PIM	PP	SH	GW
1974-75	Kelowna Wings	BCJHL		37	*103	140																						
1975-76	University of Denver	WCHA	39	12	28	40				32																		
1976-77	University of Denver	WCHA	40	17	41	58				42																		
1977-78	University of Denver	WCHA	32	25	39	64				34																		
1978-79	Edmonton Oilers	WHA	29	6	3	9				4																		
	Dallas Black Hawks	CHL	44	19	34	53				15											9	0	7	7	0			
1979-80	**Colorado Rockies**	**NHL**	**75**	**7**	**23**	**30**	**6**	**18**	**24**	**16**	**0**	**1**	**1**	**66**	**10.6**	**46**	**10**	**60**	**1**	**–23**								
1980-81	**Colorado Rockies**	**NHL**	**46**	**3**	**10**	**13**	**2**	**7**	**9**	**9**	**0**	**1**	**0**	**44**	**6.8**	**27**	**3**	**48**	**9**	**–15**								
	Fort Worth Texans	CHL	23	8	7	15				2											5	1	3	4	4			
1981-82	Wichita Wind	CHL	10	4	5	9				2											7	0	4	4	0			
	Mannheim Eagles	Germany	44	19	37	56				30																		
1982-83	Mannheim Eagles	Germany	36	19	34	53				36																		
1983-84	Mannheim Eagles	Germany	47	26	47	73				36																		
1984-85	Geneva	Switz.	26	24	18	42				14																		
1985-86	Kolner Haie	Germany	46	31	31	62				10																		
1986-87	Kolner Haie	Germany	42	19	50	69				38											9	8	12	20				
1987-88	Kolner Haie	Germany	46	22	40	62				30																		
1988-89	Kolner Haie	Germany	29	9	23	32				23											9	1	4	5	6			
1989-90	Kolner Haie	Germany	44	18	31	49				30																		
1990-91	Kolner Haie	Germany	58	16	48	64				45																		
1991-92	Kolner Haie	Germany	32	13	25	38				18																		
	NHL Totals		**121**	**10**	**33**	**43**	**8**	**25**	**33**	**25**	**0**	**2**	**1**	**110**	**9.1**	**73**	**13**	**108**	**10**									
	Other Major League Totals		29	6	3	9				4																		

WCHA First All-Star Team (1978) • NCAA West First All-American Team (1978)

Selected by **Calgary** (WHA) in 1977 WHA Amateur Draft, May, 1977. Signed as a free agent by **Edmonton** (WHA) after **Calgary** (WHA) franchise folded, July, 1978. Reclaimed by **Colorado** from **Edmonton** (WHA) prior to Expansion Draft, June 9, 1979.

• BERRY, FRED

Fred Berry C – L. 5'9", 175 lbs. b: Edmonton, Alta., 3/26/1956. Detroit's 3rd choice, 40th overall, in 1976 Amateur Draft.

Season	Club	League	GP	G	A	Pts	AG	AA	APts	PIM	PP	SH	GW	S	%	TGF	PGF	TGA	PGA	+/–	GP	G	A	Pts	PIM	PP	SH	GW
1973-74	Merritt Luckies	BCHL	60	*60	*76	*136				91																		
1974-75	Victoria Cougars	WCJHL	1	0	1	1				0																		
	New Westminster Bruins	WCJHL	69	32	43	75				120											18	12	12	24	38			
1975-76	New Westminster Bruins	WCJHL	72	59	87	146				164											17	6	15	21	45			
1976-77	**Detroit Red Wings**	**NHL**	**3**	**0**	**0**	**0**	**0**	**0**	**0**	**0**	**0**	**0**	**0**	**4**	**0.0**	**0**	**0**	**3**	**0**	**–3**								
	Kalamazoo Wings	IHL	66	17	42	59				146											10	9	8	17	12			
1977-78	Kansas City Red Wings	CHL	65	11	14	25				79																		
1978-79	Kalamazoo Wings	IHL	19	7	11	18				43																		
	Toledo Goaldiggers	IHL	49	27	43	70				91																		
1979-80	Toledo Goaldiggers	IHL	33	11	29	40				33																		
	Milwaukee Admirals	IHL	26	9	22	31				29											2	1	1	2	5			
	Hampton Aces	EHL	6	3	4	7				4																		
1980-81	Milwaukee Admirals	IHL	72	35	71	106				73											7	5	7	12	45			
1981-82	Milwaukee Admirals	IHL	76	47	65	112				114											5	4	4	8	65			
1982-83	Milwaukee Admirals	IHL	71	47	74	121				57											10	3	5	8	0			
1983-84	Milwaukee Admirals	IHL	82	38	58	96				50											4	3	1	4	2			
1984-85			DID NOT PLAY – INJURED																									
1985-86	Milwaukee Admirals	IHL	81	31	58	89				51											5	3	2	5	2			
1986-87	Milwaukee Admirals	IHL	57	18	31	49				50																		
	NHL Totals		**3**	**0**	**0**	**0**	**0**	**0**	**0**	**0**	**0**	**0**	**0**	**4**	**0.0**	**0**	**0**	**3**	**0**									

IHL Second All-Star Team (1982)

Traded to **Toledo** (IHL) by **Kalamazoo** (IHL) with Al Strongman and Dean Williams for Pete Crawford and Randy Mohns, December, 1978.

• BERRY, KEN

Ken Berry LW – L. 5'9", 175 lbs. b: Burnaby, B.C., 6/21/1960. Vancouver's 5th choice, 112th overall, in 1980 Entry Draft.

Season	Club	League	GP	G	A	Pts	AG	AA	APts	PIM	PP	SH	GW	S	%	TGF	PGF	TGA	PGA	+/–	GP	G	A	Pts	PIM	PP	SH	GW
1976-77	B.C. Wrigley's	Midget																			5	*10	3	13				
1977-78	Bellingham Bulls	BCJHL		55	70	125																						
	New Westminster Bruins	WCJHL	5	0	0	0				0											6	3	4	7	2			
1978-79	University of Denver	WCHA	39	17	20	37				52																		
1979-80	Canada	Nat-Team	57	19	20	39				48																		
	Canada	Olympics	6	4	1	5				8																		

			REGULAR SEASON																		PLAYOFFS							
Season	Club	League	GP	G	A	Pts	AG	AA	APts	PIM	PP	SH	GW	S	%	TGF	PGF	TGA	PGA	+/–	GP	G	A	Pts	PIM	PP	SH	GW
1980-81	University of Denver	WCHA	40	22	34	56				74																		
	Wichita Wind	CHL	9	7	6	13				13											17	2	4	6	28			
1981-82	**Edmonton Oilers**	**NHL**	15	2	3	5	2	2	4	9	0	0	0	9	22.2	5	1	11	1	–6								
	Wichita Wind	CHL	58	28	29	57				70																		
1982-83	Moncton Alpines	AHL	76	24	26	50				80																		
1983-84	**Edmonton Oilers**	**NHL**	13	2	3	5	2	2	4	10	0	1	0	18	11.1	12	0	6	0	+6								
	Moncton Alpines	AHL	53	18	20	38				75																		
1984-85	Nova Scotia Voyageurs	AHL	71	30	27	57				40											6	2	2	4	2			
1985-86	Bayreuth	Germany	33	27	25	52				88																		
	Canada	Nat-Team	8	1	2	3				20																		
1986-87	Canada	Nat-Team	52	17	27	44				60																		
1987-88	Canada	Nat-Team	59	18	15	33				47																		
	Canada	Olympics	8	2	4	6				4																		
	Vancouver Canucks	**NHL**	14	2	3	5	2	2	4	6	1	0	0	26	7.7	9	1	11	2	–1								
1988-89	**Vancouver Canucks**	**NHL**	13	2	1	3	2	1	3	5	0	0	0	10	20.0	7	1	7	3	+2								
	Milwaukee Admirals	IHL	5	4	4	8				2																		
1989-90	EC Munich	Germany	36	24	33	57				70											3	2	0	2	2			
1990-91	EC Munich	Germany	47	27	18	45				76																		
1991-92	EC Munich	Germany	39	17	15	32				71																		
1992-93	EC Munich	Germany	29	4	5	9				58																		
	NHL Totals		55	8	10	18	8	7	15	30	1	1	0	63	12.7	33	3	35	6									

Traded to **Edmonton** by **Vancouver** with Gary Lariviere for Blair MacDonald and Lars-Gunnar Petersson, March 10, 1981. Signed as a free agent by **Vancouver**, March 2, 1988.

• BERTUZZI, TODD

Todd Bertuzzi C – L. 6'3", 224 lbs. b: Sudbury, Ont., 2/2/1975. NY Islanders' 1st choice, 23rd overall, in 1993 Entry Draft.

1991-92	Guelph Storm	OHL	47	7	14	21				145																		
1992-93	Guelph Storm	OHL	59	27	32	59				164											5	2	2	4	6			
1993-94	Guelph Storm	OHL	61	28	54	82				165											9	2	6	8	30			
1994-95	Guelph Storm	OHL	62	54	65	119				58											14	*15	18	33	41			
1995-96	**New York Islanders**	**NHL**	76	18	21	39	18	17	35	83	4	0	2	127	14.2	69	23	60	0	–14								
1996-97	**New York Islanders**	**NHL**	64	10	13	23	11	11	22	68	3	0	1	79	12.7	43	10	36	0	–3								
	Utah Grizzlies	IHL	13	5	5	10				16																		
1997-98	**New York Islanders**	**NHL**	52	7	11	18	8	11	19	58	1	0	1	63	11.1	22	5	36	0	–19								
	Vancouver Canucks	**NHL**	22	6	9	15	7	9	16	63	1	1	1	39	15.4	22	4	19	3	+2								
	Canada	WC-A	6	1	2	3				16																		
	NHL Totals		214	41	54	95	44	48	92	272	9	1	5	308	13.3	156	42	151	3									

OHL Second All-Star team (1995)

Traded to **Vancouver** by **NY Islanders** with Bryan McCabe and NY Islanders' 3rd round choice (Jarkko Ruutu) in 1998 Entry Draft for Trevor Linden, February 6, 1998.

• BERUBE, CRAIG

Craig Berube LW – L. 6'1", 205 lbs. b: Calahoo, Alta., 12/17/1965.

1982-83	Kamloops Blazers	WHL	4	0	0	0				0																		
1983-84	New Westminster Royals	WHL	70	11	20	31				104											8	1	2	3	5			
1984-85	New Westminster Royals	WHL	70	25	44	69				191											10	3	2	5	4			
1985-86	Kamloops Blazers	WHL	32	17	14	31				119																		
	Medicine Hat Tigers	WHL	34	14	16	30				95											25	7	8	15	102			
1986-87	**Philadelphia Flyers**	**NHL**	7	0	0	0	0	0	0	57	0	0	0	4	0.0	2	0	0	0	+2	5	0	0	0	17			
	Hershey Bears	AHL	63	7	17	24				325																		
1987-88	**Philadelphia Flyers**	**NHL**	27	3	2	5	3	1	4	108	0	0	2	13	23.1	7	0	7	1	+1								
	Hershey Bears	AHL	31	5	9	14				119																		
1988-89	**Philadelphia Flyers**	**NHL**	53	1	1	2	1	1	2	199	0	0	0	31	3.2	6	0	21	0	–15	16	0	0	0	56	0	0	0
	Hershey Bears	AHL	7	0	2	2				19																		
1989-90	**Philadelphia Flyers**	**NHL**	74	4	14	18	3	10	13	291	0	0	0	52	7.7	28	0	35	0	–7								
1990-91	**Philadelphia Flyers**	**NHL**	74	8	9	17	7	7	14	293	0	0	0	46	17.4	25	1	30	0	–6								
1991-92	**Toronto Maple Leafs**	**NHL**	40	5	7	12	5	5	10	109	1	0	1	42	11.9	21	3	20	0	–2								
	Calgary Flames	**NHL**	36	1	4	5	1	3	4	155	0	0	0	27	3.7	16	0	19	0	–3								
1992-93	**Calgary Flames**	**NHL**	77	4	8	12	3	5	8	209	0	0	2	58	6.9	27	0	33	0	–6	6	0	1	1	21	0	0	0
1993-94	**Washington Capitals**	**NHL**	84	7	7	14	7	5	12	305	0	0	0	48	14.6	23	2	25	0	–4	8	0	0	0	21	0	0	0
1994-95	**Washington Capitals**	**NHL**	43	2	4	6	4	6	10	173	0	0	0	22	9.1	7	0	12	0	–5	7	0	0	0	29	0	0	0
1995-96	**Washington Capitals**	**NHL**	50	2	10	12	2	8	10	151	1	0	1	28	7.1	17	2	15	1	+1	2	0	0	0	19	0	0	0
1996-97	**Washington Capitals**	**NHL**	80	4	3	7	4	3	7	218	0	0	1	55	7.3	10	1	20	0	–11								
1997-98	**Washington Capitals**	**NHL**	74	6	9	15	7	9	16	189	0	0	0	68	8.8	20	0	23	0	–3	21	1	0	1	21	0	0	1
	NHL Totals		719	47	78	125	47	63	110	2457	2	0	7	494	9.5	209	9	260	2		65	1	1	2	184	0	0	1

Signed as a free agent by **Philadelphia**, March 19, 1986. Traded to **Edmonton** by **Philadelphia** with Craig Fisher and Scott Mellanby for Dave Brown, Corey Foster and Jari Kurri, May 30, 1991. Traded to **Toronto** by **Edmonton** with Grant Fuhr and Glenn Anderson for Vincent Damphousse, Peter Ing, Scott Thornton, Luke Richardson, future considerations and cash, September 19, 1991. Traded to **Calgary** by **Toronto** with Alexander Godynyuk, Gary Leeman, Michel Petit and Jeff Reese for Doug Gilmour, Jamie Macoun, Ric Nattress, Rick Wamsley and Kent Manderville, January 2, 1992. Traded to **Washington** by **Calgary** for Washington's 5th round choice (Darryl Lafrance) in 1993 Entry Draft, June 26, 1993.

• BETHEL, JOHN

John Bethel LW – L. 5'11", 185 lbs. b: Montreal, Que., 1/15/1957. NY Rangers' 7th choice, 98th overall, in 1977 Amateur Draft.

1976-77	Boston University	ECAC	33	14	12	26				30																		
1977-78	Boston University	ECAC	30	25	38	63				53																		
1978-79	Boston University	ECAC	19	5	10	15				28																		
1979-80	**Winnipeg Jets**	**NHL**	17	0	2	2	0	2	2	4	0	0	0	12	0.0	4	1	6	0	–3								
	Tulsa Oilers	CHL	45	17	11	28				50																		
1980-81	Tulsa Oilers	CHL	58	23	35	58				51																		
1981-82	Tulsa Oilers	CHL	74	19	51	70				83											3	0	0	0	2			
1982-83	Sherbrooke Jets	AHL	63	28	39	67				53																		
	NHL Totals		17	0	2	2	0	2	2	4	0	0	0	12	0.0	4	1	6	0									

Signed as a free agent by **Winnipeg**, September, 1979.

• BETS, MAXIM

Maxim Bets LW – L. 6'1", 185 lbs. b: Chelyabinsk, USSR, 1/31/1974. St. Louis' 1st choice, 37th overall, in 1993 Entry Draft.

1991-92	Traktor Chelyabinsk	CIS	25	1	1	2				8																		
1992-93	Spokane Chiefs	WHL	54	49	57	106				130											9	5	6	11	20			
1993-94	Spokane Chiefs	WHL	63	46	70	116				111											3	1	1	2	12			
	Russia	WJC-A	7	0	0	0				8																		
	Anaheim Mighty Ducks	**NHL**	3	0	0	0	0	0	0	0	0	0	0	1	0.0	0	0	3	0	–3								
	San Diego Gulls	IHL																			9	0	2	2	0			
1994-95	San Diego Gulls	IHL	36	2	6	8				31																		
	Worcester IceCats	AHL	9	1	1	2				6																		
1995-96	Baltimore Bandits	AHL	34	5	5	10				18																		
	Raleigh IceCaps	ECHL	9	0	4	4				6											4	0	0	0	0			
1996-97	CSKA Moscow	Russia	16	3	2	5				12																		
1997-98	Traktor Chelyabinsk	CIS	35	12	9	21				16																		
	NHL Totals		3	0	0	0	0	0	0	0	0	0	0	1	0.0	0	0	3	0									

Traded to **Anaheim** by **St. Louis** with St. Louis' 6th round choice (later returned to St. Louis — St. Louis selected Denis Hamel) in 1995 Entry Draft for Alexei Kasatonov, March 21, 1994.

• BEUKEBOOM, JEFF

Jeff Beukeboom D – R. 6'5", 230 lbs. b: Ajax, Ont., 3/28/1965. Edmonton's 1st choice, 19th overall, in 1983 Entry Draft.

1982-83	Sault Ste. Marie Greyhounds	OHL	70	0	25	25				143											16	1	4	5	46			
1983-84	Sault Ste. Marie Greyhounds	OHL	61	6	30	36				178											16	1	7	8	43			
1984-85	Sault Ste. Marie Greyhounds	OHL	37	4	20	24				85											16	4	6	10	47			
	Canada	WJC-A	3	1	0	1				4																		

			REGULAR SEASON																		PLAYOFFS							
Season	Club	League	GP	G	A	Pts	AG	AA	APts	PIM	PP	SH	GW	S	%	TGF	PGF	TGA	PGA	+/–	GP	G	A	Pts	PIM	PP	SH	GW
1985-86	Nova Scotia Oilers	AHL	77	9	20	29	....	....	....	175	....	....	....	....	....	....	....	....	....	....	....	....	....	....	....	....	....	....
	Edmonton Oilers	**NHL**	....	....	....	....	....	....	....	....	....	....	....	....	....	....	....	....	....	....	**1**	**0**	**0**	**0**	**4**	....	....	....
1986-87	**Edmonton Oilers**	**NHL**	**44**	**3**	**8**	**11**	**3**	**6**	**9**	**124**	**1**	**0**	**1**	**24**	**12.5**	**49**	**1**	**44**	**3**	**+7**	....	....	....	....	....	....	....	....
	Nova Scotia Oilers	AHL	14	1	7	8	....	....	....	35	....	....	....	....	....	....	....	....	....	....	....	....	....	....	....	....	....	....
1987-88	**Edmonton Oilers**	**NHL**	**73**	**5**	**20**	**25**	**4**	**14**	**18**	**201**	**1**	**0**	**1**	**76**	**6.6**	**94**	**16**	**73**	**22**	**+27**	**7**	**0**	**0**	**0**	**16**	**0**	**0**	**0**
1988-89	**Edmonton Oilers**	**NHL**	**36**	**0**	**5**	**5**	**0**	**4**	**4**	**94**	**0**	**0**	**0**	**26**	**0.0**	**28**	**2**	**35**	**11**	**+2**	**1**	**0**	**0**	**0**	**2**	**0**	**0**	**0**
	Cape Breton Oilers	AHL	8	0	4	4	....	....	....	36	....	....	....	....	....	....	....	....	....	....	....	....	....	....	....	....	....	....
1989-90	**Edmonton Oilers**	**NHL**	**46**	**1**	**12**	**13**	**1**	**9**	**10**	**86**	**0**	**0**	**0**	**36**	**2.8**	**43**	**6**	**46**	**14**	**+5**	**2**	**0**	**0**	**0**	**0**	**0**	**0**	**0**
1990-91	**Edmonton Oilers**	**NHL**	**67**	**3**	**7**	**10**	**3**	**5**	**8**	**150**	**0**	**0**	**0**	**48**	**6.3**	**65**	**4**	**82**	**27**	**+6**	**18**	**1**	**3**	**4**	**28**	**0**	**0**	**0**
1991-92	**Edmonton Oilers**	**NHL**	**18**	**0**	**5**	**5**	**0**	**4**	**4**	**78**	**0**	**0**	**0**	**7**	**0.0**	**17**	**0**	**23**	**10**	**+4**	....	....	....	....	....	....	....	....
	New York Rangers	**NHL**	**56**	**1**	**10**	**11**	**1**	**7**	**8**	**122**	**0**	**0**	**0**	**41**	**2.4**	**73**	**0**	**74**	**20**	**+19**	**13**	**2**	**3**	**5**	**47**	**0**	**0**	**0**
1992-93	**New York Rangers**	**NHL**	**82**	**2**	**17**	**19**	**2**	**12**	**14**	**153**	**0**	**0**	**0**	**54**	**3.7**	**91**	**2**	**112**	**32**	**+9**	....	....	....	....	....	....	....	....
1993-94	**New York Rangers**	**NHL**	**68**	**8**	**8**	**16**	**7**	**6**	**13**	**170**	**1**	**0**	**0**	**58**	**13.8**	**63**	**1**	**75**	**31**	**+18**	**22**	**0**	**6**	**6**	**50**	**0**	**0**	**0**
1994-95	**New York Rangers**	**NHL**	**44**	**1**	**3**	**4**	**2**	**4**	**6**	**70**	**0**	**0**	**0**	**29**	**3.4**	**34**	**0**	**49**	**18**	**+3**	**9**	**0**	**0**	**0**	**10**	**0**	**0**	**0**
1995-96	**New York Rangers**	**NHL**	**82**	**3**	**11**	**14**	**3**	**9**	**12**	**220**	**0**	**0**	**1**	**65**	**4.6**	**67**	**1**	**87**	**40**	**+19**	**11**	**0**	**3**	**3**	**6**	**0**	**0**	**0**
1996-97	**New York Rangers**	**NHL**	**80**	**3**	**9**	**12**	**3**	**8**	**11**	**167**	**0**	**0**	**0**	**55**	**5.5**	**80**	**4**	**82**	**28**	**+22**	**15**	**0**	**1**	**1**	**34**	**0**	**0**	**0**
1997-98	**New York Rangers**	**NHL**	**63**	**0**	**5**	**5**	**0**	**5**	**5**	**195**	**0**	**0**	**0**	**23**	**0.0**	**30**	**1**	**71**	**17**	**–25**	....	....	....	....	....	....	....	....
	NHL Totals		**759**	**30**	**120**	**150**	**29**	**93**	**122**	**1830**	**3**	**0**	**3**	**542**	**5.5**	**734**	**38**	**853**	**273**		**99**	**3**	**16**	**19**	**197**	**0**	**0**	**0**

OHL First All-Star Team (1985)

Traded to **NY Rangers** by **Edmonton** for David Shaw, November 12, 1991.

• BEVERLEY, NICK

Nick Beverley D – R. 6′2″, 185 lbs. b: Toronto, Ont., 4/21/1947.

Season	Club	League	GP	G	A	Pts	AG	AA	APts	PIM	PP	SH	GW	S	%	TGF	PGF	TGA	PGA	+/–	GP	G	A	Pts	PIM	PP	SH	GW
1963-64	Oshawa Generals	OHA	3	0	1	1	....	....	....	4	....	....	....	....	....	....	....	....	....	....	6	0	0	0	0	....	....	....
1964-65	Oshawa Generals	OHA	56	0	10	10	....	....	....	42	....	....	....	....	....	....	....	....	....	....	6	0	1	1	19	....	....	....
1965-66	Oshawa Generals	OHA	47	0	10	10	....	....	....	41	....	....	....	....	....	....	....	....	....	....	17	1	4	5	18	....	....	....
1966-67	Oshawa Generals	OHA	48	8	14	22	....	....	....	57	....	....	....	....	....	....	....	....	....	....	....	....	....	....	....	....	....	....
	Boston Bruins	**NHL**	**2**	**0**	**0**	**0**	**0**	**0**	**0**	**0**	....	....	....	....	....	....	....	....	....	....	....	....	....	....	....	....	....	....
1967-68	Oklahoma City Blazers	CHL	70	7	20	27	....	....	....	60	....	....	....	....	....	....	....	....	....	....	4	0	0	0	17	....	....	....
1968-69	Oklahoma City Blazers	CHL	62	3	22	25	....	....	....	32	....	....	....	....	....	....	....	....	....	....	12	0	4	4	4	....	....	....
1969-70	**Boston Bruins**	**NHL**	**2**	**0**	**0**	**0**	**0**	**0**	**0**	**2**	**0**	**0**	**0**	**0**	**0.0**	**0**	**0**	**0**	**0**	**0**	....	....	....	....	....	....	....	....
	Oklahoma City Blazers	CHL	58	6	24	30	....	....	....	26	....	....	....	....	....	....	....	....	....	....	....	....	....	....	....	....	....	....
1970-71	Hershey Bears	AHL	70	3	23	26	....	....	....	46	....	....	....	....	....	....	....	....	....	....	4	0	0	0	2	....	....	....
1971-72	**Boston Bruins**	**NHL**	**1**	**0**	**0**	**0**	**0**	**0**	**0**	**0**	**0**	**0**	**0**	**0**	**0.0**	**0**	**0**	**0**	**0**	**0**	....	....	....	....	....	....	....	....
	Boston Braves	AHL	73	9	31	40	....	....	....	36	....	....	....	....	....	....	....	....	....	....	9	0	5	5	2	....	....	....
1972-73	**Boston Bruins**	**NHL**	**76**	**1**	**10**	**11**	**1**	**8**	**9**	**26**	**0**	**0**	**0**	**57**	**1.8**	**55**	**0**	**58**	**10**	**+7**	**4**	**0**	**0**	**0**	**0**	**0**	**0**	**0**
1973-74	**Boston Bruins**	**NHL**	**1**	**0**	**0**	**0**	**0**	**0**	**0**	**0**	**0**	**0**	**0**	**0**	**0.0**	**0**	**0**	**1**	**0**	**–1**	....	....	....	....	....	....	....	....
	Pittsburgh Penguins	**NHL**	**67**	**2**	**14**	**16**	**2**	**12**	**14**	**21**	**0**	**0**	**1**	**74**	**2.7**	**69**	**3**	**98**	**16**	**–16**	....	....	....	....	....	....	....	....
1974-75	**New York Rangers**	**NHL**	**67**	**3**	**15**	**18**	**3**	**12**	**15**	**19**	**0**	**0**	**0**	**79**	**3.8**	**66**	**2**	**64**	**13**	**+13**	**3**	**0**	**1**	**1**	**0**	**0**	**0**	**0**
1975-76	**New York Rangers**	**NHL**	**63**	**1**	**8**	**9**	**1**	**6**	**7**	**46**	**0**	**0**	**0**	**75**	**1.3**	**56**	**0**	**87**	**22**	**–9**	....	....	....	....	....	....	....	....
1976-77	**New York Rangers**	**NHL**	**9**	**0**	**0**	**0**	**0**	**0**	**0**	**2**	**0**	**0**	**0**	**1**	**0.0**	**5**	**0**	**10**	**5**	**0**	....	....	....	....	....	....	....	....
	Minnesota North Stars	**NHL**	**52**	**2**	**17**	**19**	**2**	**14**	**16**	**6**	**0**	**0**	**0**	**59**	**3.4**	**62**	**2**	**77**	**17**	**0**	....	....	....	....	....	....	....	....
1977-78	**Minnesota North Stars**	**NHL**	**57**	**7**	**14**	**21**	**7**	**11**	**18**	**18**	**0**	**0**	**1**	**87**	**8.0**	**52**	**5**	**69**	**21**	**–1**	....	....	....	....	....	....	....	....
1978-79	**Los Angeles Kings**	**NHL**	**7**	**0**	**3**	**3**	**0**	**2**	**2**	**0**	**0**	**0**	**0**	**2**	**0.0**	**7**	**2**	**4**	**1**	**+2**	....	....	....	....	....	....	....	....
	Colorado Rockies	**NHL**	**52**	**2**	**4**	**6**	**2**	**3**	**5**	**6**	**0**	**1**	**0**	**42**	**4.8**	**28**	**2**	**53**	**11**	**–16**	....	....	....	....	....	....	....	....
1979-80	**Colorado Rockies**	**NHL**	**46**	**0**	**9**	**9**	**0**	**7**	**7**	**10**	**0**	**0**	**0**	**23**	**0.0**	**43**	**0**	**68**	**21**	**–4**	....	....	....	....	....	....	....	....
	Fort Worth Texans	CHL	12	0	6	6	....	....	....	4	....	....	....	....	....	....	....	....	....	....	....	....	....	....	....	....	....	....
	NHL Totals		**502**	**18**	**94**	**112**	**18**	**75**	**93**	**156**	**0**	**1**	**2**	**499**	**3.6**	**443**	**16**	**589**	**137**		**7**	**0**	**1**	**1**	**0**	**0**	**0**	**0**

Traded to **Pittsburgh** by **Boston** for Darryl Edestrand, October 25, 1973. Traded to **NY Rangers** by **Pittsburgh** for Vic Hadfield, May 27, 1974. Traded to **Minnesota** by **NY Rangers** with Bill Fairbairn for Bill Goldsworthy, November 11, 1976. Claimed on waivers by **LA Kings** from **Minnesota**, September 5, 1978. Traded to **Colorado** by **LA Kings** for Colorado's 4th round choice (Dave Ross) in 1982 Entry Draft, November 18, 1979. Claimed by **Hartford** from **Colorado** in Expansion Draft, June 13, 1979. Signed as a free agent by **Colorado**, September 15, 1979.

• BIALOWAS, DWIGHT

Dwight Bialowas D – R. 6′, 185 lbs. b: Regina, Sask., 9/8/1952. Atlanta's 2nd choice, 18th overall, in 1972 Amateur Draft.

Season	Club	League	GP	G	A	Pts	AG	AA	APts	PIM	PP	SH	GW	S	%	TGF	PGF	TGA	PGA	+/–	GP	G	A	Pts	PIM	PP	SH	GW
1969-70	Regina Pats	SJHL		5	18	23	....	....	....	18	....	....	....	....	....	....	....	....	....	....	....	....	....	....	....	....	....	....
1970-71	Regina Pats	WCJHL	63	12	20	41		....	....	40		....	....	....	....	....	....	....	....	....	....	....	....	....	....	....	....	....
1971-72	Regina Pats	WCJHL	61	12	39	51	....	....	....	45	....	....	....	....		....	....	....	....		....	....	....	....	....	....	....	....
1972-73	Omaha Knights	CHL	70	11	24	35	....	....	....	58	....	....	....	....	....	....	....	....	....	....	11	0	6	6	10	....	....	....
1973-74	**Atlanta Flames**	**NHL**	**11**	**0**	**0**	**0**	**0**	**0**	**0**	**2**	**0**	**0**	**0**	**3**	**0.0**	**2**	**0**	**8**	**0**	**–6**	....	....	....	....	....	....	....	....
	Omaha Knights	CHL	30	6	12	18	....	....	....	22	....	....	....	....	....	....	....	....	....	....	....	....	....	....	....	....	....	....
	Nova Scotia Voyageurs	AHL	4	1	0	1	....	....	....	4	....	....	....	....	....	....	....	....	....	....	6	0	1	1	4	....	....	
1974-75	**Atlanta Flames**	**NHL**	**37**	**3**	**9**	**12**	**3**	**7**	**10**	**20**	**2**	**0**	**0**	**42**	**7.1**	**30**	**9**	**25**	**7**	**+3**	....	....	....	....	....	....	....	....
	Minnesota North Stars	**NHL**	**40**	**2**	**10**	**12**	**2**	**8**	**10**	**2**	**1**	**0**	**0**	**62**	**3.2**	**41**	**6**	**50**	**10**	**–5**	....	....	....	....	....	....	....	....
1975-76	**Minnesota North Stars**	**NHL**	**58**	**5**	**18**	**23**	**5**	**14**	**19**	**22**	**5**	**0**	**1**	**87**	**5.7**	**64**	**20**	**56**	**3**	**–9**	....	....	....	....	....	....	....	....
	New Haven Nighthawks	AHL	17	1	6	7	....	....	....	15	....	....	....	....	....	....	....	....	....	....	....	....	....	....	....	....	....	....
1976-77	**Minnesota North Stars**	**NHL**	**18**	**1**	**9**	**10**	**1**	**7**	**8**	**0**	**1**	**0**	**0**	**21**	**4.8**	**18**	**12**	**9**	**0**	**–3**	....	....	....	....	....	....	....	....
	New Haven Nighthawks	AHL	39	4	20	24	....	....	....	25	....		....	....	....		....	....	....	....	6	0	1	1	0	....	....	....
1977-78	Fort Worth Texans	CHL	62	6	21	27	....	....	....	24	....	....	....	....	....	....	....	....	....	....	3	0	0	0	2	....	....	....
	NHL Totals		**164**	**11**	**46**	**57**	**11**	**36**	**47**	**46**	**9**	**0**	**1**	**215**	**5.1**	**155**	**47**	**148**	**20**		....	....	....	....	....	....	....	....

Traded to **Minnesota** by **Atlanta** with Dean Talafous for Barry Gibbs, January 3, 1975.

• BIALOWAS, FRANK

Frank "The Animal" Bialowas LW – L. 5′11″, 220 lbs. b: Winnipeg, Man., 9/25/1970.

Season	Club	League	GP	G	A	Pts	AG	AA	APts	PIM	PP	SH	GW	S	%	TGF	PGF	TGA	PGA	+/–	GP	G	A	Pts	PIM	PP	SH	GW
1991-92	Roanoke Valley Rebels	ECHL	23	4	2	6	....	....	....	150	....	....	....	....	....	....	....	....	....	....	3	0	0	0	4	....	....	....
1992-93	Richmond Renegades	ECHL	60	3	18	21	....	....	....	261	....	....	....	....	....	....	....	....	....	....	1	0	0	0	2	....	....	....
	St. John's Maple Leafs	AHL	7	1	0	1	....	....	....	28	....	....	....	....	....	....	....	....	....	....	1	0	0	0	0	....	....	....
1993-94	**Toronto Maple Leafs**	**NHL**	**3**	**0**	**0**	**0**	**0**	**0**	**0**	**12**	**0**	**0**	**0**	**1**	**0.0**	**0**	**0**	**0**	**0**	**0**	....	....	....	....	....	....	....	....
	St. John's Maple Leafs	AHL	69	2	8	10	....	....	....	352	....	....	....	....	....	....	....	....	....	....	7	0	3	3	25	....	....	....
1994-95	St. John's Maple Leafs	AHL	51	2	3	5	....	....	....	277	....	....	....	....	....	....	....	....	....	....	4	0	0	0	12	....	....	....
1995-96	Portland Pirates	AHL	65	4	3	7	....	....	....	211	....	....	....	....	....	....	....	....	....	....	7	0	0	0	42	....	....	....
1996-97	Philadelphia Phantoms	AHL	67	7	6	13	....	....	....	254	....	....	....	....	....	....	....	....	....	....	6	0	2	2	41	....	....	....
1997-98	Philadelphia Phantoms	AHL	65	5	7	12	....	....	....	259	....	....	....	....	....	....	....	....	....	....	19	0	0	0	26	....		....
	NHL Totals		**3**	**0**	**0**	**0**	**0**	**0**	**0**	**12**	**0**	**0**	**0**	**1**	**0.0**	**0**	**0**	**0**	**0**		....	....	....	....	....	....	....	....

Signed as a free agent by **Toronto**, March 20, 1994. Signed as a free agent by **Washington**, September 8, 1995. Traded to **Philadelphia** by **Washington** for future considerations, July 18, 1996.

• BIANCHIN, WAYNE

Wayne Bianchin LW – L. 5′10″, 180 lbs. b: Nanaimo, B.C., 9/6/1953. Pittsburgh's 2nd choice, 23rd overall, in 1973 Amateur Draft.

Season	Club	League	GP	G	A	Pts	AG	AA	APts	PIM	PP	SH	GW	S	%	TGF	PGF	TGA	PGA	+/–	GP	G	A	Pts	PIM	PP	SH	GW
1970-71	Kamloops Rockets	BCJHL	57	30	42	72	....	....	....	....	....	....	....	....	....	....	....	....	....	....	....	....	....	....	....	....	....	....
1971-72	Calgary Centennials	WCJHL	7	1	5	6	....	....	....	7	....	....	....	....	....	....	....	....	....	....	....	....	....	....	....	....	....	....
	Victoria Cougars	WCJHL	22	7	3	10	....	....	....	57	....	....	....	....	....	....	....	....	....	....	....	....	....	....	....	....	....	....
	Flin Flon Bombers	WCJHL	27	7	3	10	....	....	....	8	....	....	....	....	....	....	....	....	....	....	27	12	15	27	8	....	....	....
1972-73	Flin Flon Bombers	WCJHL	68	60	54	114	....	....	....	90	....	....	....	....	....	....	....	....	....	....	9	5	7	12	28	....	....	....
1973-74	**Pittsburgh Penguins**	**NHL**	**69**	**12**	**13**	**25**	**12**	**11**	**23**	**38**	**1**	**0**	**1**	**118**	**10.2**	**35**	**4**	**47**	**1**	**–15**	....	....	....	....	....	....	....	....
	Hershey Bears	AHL	4	1	2	3	....	....	....	2	....	....	....	....	....	....	....	....	....	....	....	....	....	....	....	....	....	....
1974-75	**Pittsburgh Penguins**	**NHL**	**2**	**0**	**0**	**0**	**0**	**0**	**0**	**0**	**0**	**0**	**0**	**0**	**0.0**	**0**	**0**	**1**	**0**	**–1**	....	....	....	....	....	....	....	....
	Hershey Bears	AHL	3	0	1	1	....	....	....	0	....	....	....	....	....	....	....	....	....	....	....	....	....	....	....	....	....	....
	Syracuse Eagles	AHL	12	5	4	9	....	....	....	26	....	....	....	....	....	....	....	....	....	....	....	....	....	....	....	....	....	....
	Johnstown Jets	NAHL	8	8	2	10	....	....	....	4	....	....	....	....	....	....	....	....	....	....	....	....	....	....	....	....	....	....
1975-76	**Pittsburgh Penguins**	**NHL**	**14**	**1**	**5**	**6**	**1**	**4**	**5**	**4**	**0**	**0**	**1**	**26**	**3.8**	**9**	**0**	**13**	**0**	**–4**	....	....	....	....	....	....	....	....
	Hershey Bears	AHL	54	22	24	46	....	....	....	17	....	....	....	....	....	....	....	....	....	....	6	1	3	4	4	....	....	....
1976-77	**Pittsburgh Penguins**	**NHL**	**79**	**28**	**6**	**34**	**27**	**5**	**32**	**28**	**4**	**0**	**3**	**130**	**21.5**	**56**	**10**	**48**	**1**	**–1**	**3**	**0**	**1**	**1**	**6**	**0**	**0**	**0**
1977-78	**Pittsburgh Penguins**	**NHL**	**61**	**20**	**13**	**33**	**19**	**11**	**30**	**40**	**3**	**1**	**2**	**95**	**21.1**	**50**	**10**	**55**	**1**	**–14**	....		....	....	....	....	....	....
1978-79	**Pittsburgh Penguins**	**NHL**	**40**	**7**	**4**	**11**	**6**	**3**	**9**	**20**	**1**	**0**	**3**	**57**	**12.3**	**24**	**5**	**21**	**0**	**–2**	....	....	....	....	....	....	....	....

			REGULAR SEASON																		PLAYOFFS							
Season	Club	League	GP	G	A	Pts	AG	AA	APts	PIM	PP	SH	GW	S	%	TGF	PGF	TGA	PGA	+/–	GP	G	A	Pts	PIM	PP	SH	GW
1979-80	**Edmonton Oilers**	**NHL**	**11**	**0**	**0**	**0**	**0**	**0**	**0**	**7**	**0**	**0**	**0**	**7**	**0.0**	**0**	**0**	**4**	**0**	**–4**	....	....	....	....	....	....	....	....
	Houston Apollos	CHL	57	20	19	39	....	....	....	20	....	....	....	....	....	....	....	....	....	....	6	2	5	7	4	....	....	....
1980-81	Asiago HC	Italy	....	34	24	58	....	....	....	29	....	....	....	....	....	....	....	....	....	....	14	6	9	15	6	....	....	....
	Italy	WEC-B	7	3	9	12	....	....	....	2	....	....	....	....	....	....	....	....	....	....	....	....	....	....	....	....	....	....
	NHL Totals		**276**	**68**	**41**	**109**	**65**	**34**	**99**	**137**	**9**	**1**	**10**	**433**	**15.7**	**174**	**29**	**189**	**3**		**3**	**0**	**1**	**1**	**6**	**0**	**0**	**0**

WEC-B All-Star Team (1981)

Claimed by **Edmonton** from **Pittsburgh** in Expansion Draft, June 13, 1979.

• BICANEK, RADIM

Radim Bicanek D – L. 6′1″, 195 lbs. b: Uherske Hradiste, Czech., 1/18/1975. Ottawa's 2nd choice, 27th overall, in 1993 Entry Draft.

Season	Club	League	GP	G	A	Pts	AG	AA	APts	PIM	PP	SH	GW	S	%	TGF	PGF	TGA	PGA	+/–	GP	G	A	Pts	PIM	PP	SH	GW
1992-93	Dukla Jihlava	Czech.	43	2	3	5	....	....	....	....	....	....	....	....	....	....	....	....	....	....	....	....	....	....	....	....	....	....
	Czech Republic	WJC-A	7	1	0	1	....	....	....	0	....	....	....	....	....	....	....	....	....	....	....	....	....	....	....	....	....	....
1993-94	Belleville Bulls	OHL	63	16	27	43	....	....	....	49	....	....	....	....	....	....	....	....	....	....	12	2	8	10	21	....	....	....
1994-95	Belleville Bulls	OHL	49	13	26	39	....	....	....	61	....	....	....	....	....	....	....	....	....	....	16	6	5	11	30	....	....	....
	Ottawa Senators	**NHL**	**6**	**0**	**0**	**0**	**0**	**0**	**0**	**0**	**0**	**0**	**0**	**6**	**0.0**	**3**	**0**	**0**	**0**	**+3**	....	....	....	....	....	....	....	....
	P.E.I. Senators	AHL	....	....	....	....	....	....	....	....	....	....	....	....	....	....	....	....	....	....	3	0	1	1	0	....	....	....
1995-96	P.E.I. Senators	AHL	74	7	19	26	....	....	....	87	....	....	....	....	....	....	....	....	....	....	5	0	2	2	6	....	....	....
1996-97	**Ottawa Senators**	**NHL**	**21**	**0**	**1**	**1**	**0**	**1**	**1**	**8**	**0**	**0**	**0**	**27**	**0.0**	**11**	**1**	**17**	**3**	**–4**	**7**	**0**	**0**	**0**	**8**	**0**	**0**	**0**
	Worcester IceCats	AHL	44	1	15	16	....	....	....	22	....	....	....	....	....	....	....	....	....	....	....	....	....	....	....	....	....	....
1997-98	**Ottawa Senators**	**NHL**	**1**	**0**	**0**	**0**	**0**	**0**	**0**	**0**	**0**	**0**	**0**	**0**	**0.0**	**0**	**0**	**0**	**0**	**0**	....	....	....	....	....	....	....	....
	Detroit Vipers	IHL	9	1	3	4	....	....	....	16	....	....	....	....	....	....	....	....	....	....	....	....	....	....	....	....	....	....
	Manitoba Moose	IHL	42	1	7	8	....	....	....	52	....	....	....	....	....	....	....	....	....	....	....	....	....	....	....	....	....	....
	NHL Totals		**28**	**0**	**1**	**1**	**0**	**1**	**1**	**8**	**0**	**0**	**0**	**33**	**0.0**	**14**	**1**	**17**	**3**		**7**	**0**	**0**	**0**	**8**	**0**	**0**	**0**

EJC-A All-Star Team (1993)

• BIDNER, TODD

Todd Bidner LW – L. 6′2″, 205 lbs. b: Petrolia, Ont., 7/5/1961. Washington's 5th choice, 110th overall, in 1980 Entry Draft.

Season	Club	League	GP	G	A	Pts	AG	AA	APts	PIM	PP	SH	GW	S	%	TGF	PGF	TGA	PGA	+/–	GP	G	A	Pts	PIM	PP	SH	GW
1977-78	Petrolia Jets	Jr. B	44	10	33	43	....	....	....	50	....	....	....	....	....	....	....	....	....	....	....	....	....	....	....	....	....	....
1978-79	Toronto Marlboros	OHA	64	10	12	22	....	....	....	64	....	....	....	....	....	....	....	....	....	....	....	....	....	....	....	....	....	....
1979-80	Toronto Marlboros	OHA	68	22	26	48	....	....	....	69	....	....	....	....	....	....	....	....	....	....	4	0	0	0	2	....	....	....
1980-81	Toronto Marlboros	OHA	67	34	43	77	....	....	....	124	....	....	....	....	....	....	....	....	....	....	5	2	4	6	6	....	....	....
	Hershey Bears	AHL	1	0	0	0	....	....	....	0	....	....	....	....	....	....	....	....	....	....	....	....	....	....	....	....	....	....
1981-82	**Washington Capitals**	**NHL**	**12**	**2**	**1**	**3**	**2**	**1**	**3**	**7**	**0**	**0**	**1**	**5**	**40.0**	**5**	**0**	**7**	**2**	**0**	....	....	....	....	....	....	....	....
	Hershey Bears	AHL	30	6	12	18	....	....	....	28	....	....	....	....	....	....	....	....	....	....	....	....	....	....	....	....	....	....
	Wichita Wind	CHL	15	2	9	11	....	....	....	17	....	....	....	....	....	....	....	....	....	....	7	1	2	3	9	....	....	....
1982-83	Moncton Alpines	AHL	59	15	12	27	....	....	....	64	....	....	....	....	....	....	....	....	....	....	....	....	....	....	....	....	....	....
1983-84	Moncton Alpines	AHL	60	17	16	33	....	....	....	75	....	....	....	....	....	....	....	....	....	....	....	....	....	....	....	....	....	....
1984-85	Nova Scotia Voyageurs	AHL	4	2	2	4	....	....	....	4	....	....	....	....	....	....	....	....	....	....	....	....	....	....	....	....	....	....
	Adirondack Red Wings	AHL	74	22	35	57	....	....	....	61	....	....	....	....	....	....	....	....	....	....	....	....	....	....	....	....	....	....
1985-86	Fife Flyers	Britain	31	71	52	123	....	....	....	116	....	....	....	....	....	....	....	....	....	....	5	7	10	17	10	....	....	....
1986-87	Peterborough Pirates	Britain	29	79	112	191	....	....	....	95	....	....	....	....	....	....	....	....	....	....	8	21	18	39	30	....	....	....
1987-88	Peterborough Pirates	Britain	30	50	52	102	....	....	....	86	....	....	....	....	....	....	....	....	....	....	....	....	....	....	....	....	....	....
1988-89	Peterborough Pirates	Britain	33	76	67	143	....	....	....	70	....	....	....	....	....	....	....	....	....	....	....	....	....	....	....	....	....	....
1989-90	Peterborough Pirates	Britain	13	21	17	38	....	....	....	16	....	....	....	....	....	....	....	....	....	....	....	....	....	....	....	....	....	....
	Telford Tigers	Britain	13	23	42	65	....	....	....	32	....	....	....	....	....	....	....	....	....	....	....	....	....	....	....	....	....	....
1990-91	Nottingham Panthers	Britain	20	20	28	48	....	....	....	67	....	....	....	....	....	....	....	....	....	....	6	4	4	8	10	....	....	....
	Telford Tigers	Britain	16	25	24	49	....	....	....	42	....	....	....	....	....	....	....	....	....	....	....	....	....	....	....	....	....	....
1991-92	Bracknell Bees	Britain	19	20	20	49	....	....	....	70	....	....	....	....	....	....	....	....	....	....	....	....	....	....	....	....	....	....
	Humberside Seahawks	Britain	17	21	21	42	....	....	....	50	....	....	....	....	....	....	....	....	....	....	4	4	3	7	12	....	....	....
1992-93	Humberside Seahawks	Britain	13	15	18	33	....	....	....	26	....	....	....	....	....	....	....	....	....	....	....	....	....	....	....	....	....	....
	Telford Tigers	Britain	15	22	26	48	....	....	....	92	....	....	....	....	....	....	....	....	....	....	....	....	....	....	....	....	....	....
1993-94	Teeside Bombers	Britain	36	49	31	80	....	....	....	108	....	....	....	....	....	....	....	....	....	....	....	....	....	....	....	....	....	....
1994-95	Durham Wasps	Britain	30	30	27	57	....	....	....	141	....	....	....	....	....	....	....	....	....	....	....	....	....	....	....	....	....	....
1995-96	Durham Wasps	Britain	21	9	12	21	....	....	....	72	....	....	....	....	....	....	....	....	....	....	....	....	....	....	....	....	....	....
	Humberside Hawks	Britain	4	4	4	8	....	....	....	4	....	....	....	....	....	....	....	....	....	....	....	....	....	....	....	....	....	....
1996-97	Guildford Flames	Britain	5	2	3	5	....	....	....	2	....	....	....	....	....	....	....	....	....	....	....	....	....	....	....	....	....	....
	Blackburn Hawks	Britain	8	14	17	31	....	....	....	6	....	....	....	....	....	....	....	....	....	....	10	9	17	26	22	....	....	....
	NHL Totals		**12**	**2**	**1**	**3**	**2**	**1**	**3**	**7**	**0**	**0**	**1**	**5**	**40.0**	**5**	**0**	**7**	**2**		....	....	....	....	....	....	....	....

Traded to **Edmonton** by **Washington** for Doug Hicks, March 9, 1982. Traded to **Detroit** by **Edmonton** for Rejean Cloutier, October 17, 1984.

• BIGGS, DON

Don Biggs C – R. 5′8″, 185 lbs. b: Mississauga, Ont., 4/7/1965. Minnesota's 9th choice, 162nd overall, in 1983 Entry Draft.

Season	Club	League	GP	G	A	Pts	AG	AA	APts	PIM	PP	SH	GW	S	%	TGF	PGF	TGA	PGA	+/–	GP	G	A	Pts	PIM	PP	SH	GW
1981-82	Missisaugua Reps	Midget	54	49	67	116	....	....	....	125	....	....	....	....	....	....	....	....	....	....	....	....	....	....	....	....	....	....
1982-83	Oshawa Generals	OHL	70	22	53	75	....	....	....	145	....	....	....	....	....	....	....	....	....	....	16	3	6	9	17	....	....	....
1983-84	Oshawa Generals	OHL	58	31	60	91	....	....	....	149	....	....	....	....	....	....	....	....	....	....	7	4	4	8	18	....	....	....
1984-85	Oshawa Generals	OHL	60	48	69	117	....	....	....	105	....	....	....	....	....	....	....	....	....	....	5	3	4	7	6	....	....	....
	Minnesota North Stars	**NHL**	**1**	**0**	**0**	**0**	**0**	**0**	**0**	**0**	**0**	**0**	**0**	**0**	**0.0**	**0**	**0**	**0**	**0**	**0**	....	....	....	....	....	....	....	....
	Springfield Indians	AHL	6	0	3	3	....	....	....	0	....	....	....	....	....	....	....	....	....	....	2	1	0	1	0	....	....	....
1985-86	Springfield Indians	AHL	28	15	16	31	....	....	....	46	....	....	....	....	....	....	....	....	....	....	....	....	....	....	....	....	....	....
	Nova Scotia Oilers	AHL	47	6	23	29	....	....	....	36	....	....	....	....	....	....	....	....	....	....	....	....	....	....	....	....	....	....
1986-87	Nova Scotia Oilers	AHL	80	22	25	47	....	....	....	165	....	....	....	....	....	....	....	....	....	....	5	1	2	3	4	....	....	....
1987-88	Hershey Bears	AHL	77	38	41	79	....	....	....	151	....	....	....	....	....	....	....	....	....	....	12	5	11	16	22	....	....	....
1988-89	Hershey Bears	AHL	76	36	67	103	....	....	....	158	....	....	....	....	....	....	....	....	....	....	11	5	9	14	30	....	....	....
1989-90	**Philadelphia Flyers**	**NHL**	**11**	**2**	**0**	**2**	**2**	**0**	**2**	**8**	**1**	**0**	**0**	**14**	**14.3**	**2**	**1**	**5**	**0**	**–4**	....	....	....	....	....	....	....	....
	Hershey Bears	AHL	66	39	53	92	....	....	....	125	....	....	....	....	....	....	....	....	....	....	....	....	....	....	....	....	....	....
1990-91	Rochester Americans	AHL	65	31	57	88	....	....	....	115	....	....	....	....	....	....	....	....	....	....	15	9	14	23	14	....	....	....
1991-92	Binghampton	AHL	74	32	50	82	....	....	....	122	....	....	....	....	....	....	....	....	....	....	11	3	7	10	8	....	....	....
1992-93	Binghamton Rangers	AHL	78	54	84	138	....	....	....	112	....	....	....	....	....	....	....	....	....	....	14	3	9	12	32	....	....	....
1993-94	Cincinnati Cyclones	IHL	80	30	59	89	....	....	....	128	....	....	....	....	....	....	....	....	....	....	11	8	9	17	29	....	....	....
1994-95	Cincinnati Cyclones	IHL	77	27	49	76	....	....	....	152	....	....	....	....	....	....	....	....	....	....	10	1	9	10	29	....	....	....
1995-96	Cincinnati Cyclones	IHL	82	27	57	84	....	....	....	160	....	....	....	....	....	....	....	....	....	....	17	9	10	19	24	....	....	....
1996-97	Cincinnati Cyclones	IHL	82	25	41	66	....	....	....	128	....	....	....	....	....	....	....	....	....	....	3	1	2	3	19	....	....	....
1997-98	Cincinnati Cyclones	IHL	82	25	52	77	....	....	....	88	....	....	....	....	....	....	....	....	....	....	9	5	4	9	27	....	....	....
	NHL Totals		**12**	**2**	**0**	**2**	**2**	**0**	**2**	**8**	**1**	**0**	**0**	**14**	**14.3**	**2**	**1**	**5**	**0**		....	....	....	....	....	....	....	....

Traded to **Edmonton** by **Minnesota** with Gord Sherven for Marc Habsheid, Don Barber and Emanuel Viveiros, December 20, 1985. Signed as a free agent by **Philadelphia**, July 17, 1987. Traded to **NY Rangers** by **Philadelphia** for future considerations, August 8, 1991.

• BIGNELL, LARRY

Larry Bignell D – L. 6′, 175 lbs. b: Edmonton, Alta., 1/7/1950. Pittsburgh's 3rd choice, 35th overall, in 1970 Amateur Draft.

Season	Club	League	GP	G	A	Pts	AG	AA	APts	PIM	PP	SH	GW	S	%	TGF	PGF	TGA	PGA	+/–	GP	G	A	Pts	PIM	PP	SH	GW
1969-70	Edmonton Oil Kings	WCJHL	58	5	22	27	....	....	....	91	....	....	....	....	....	....	....	....	....	....	....	....	....	....	....	....	....	....
1970-71	Amarillo Wranglers	CHL	63	3	16	19	....	....	....	64	....	....	....	....	....	....	....	....	....	....	....	....	....	....	....	....	....	....
1971-72	Hershey Bears	AHL	58	4	10	14	....	....	....	59	....	....	....	....	....	....	....	....	....	....	3	0	0	0	4	....	....	....
1972-73	Hershey Bears	AHL	65	6	15	21	....	....	....	94	....	....	....	....	....	....	....	....	....	....	7	1	1	2	16	....	....	....
1973-74	**Pittsburgh Penguins**	**NHL**	**20**	**0**	**3**	**3**	**0**	**3**	**3**	**2**	**0**	**0**	**0**	**13**	**0.0**	**17**	**2**	**23**	**5**	**–3**	....	....	....	....	....	....	....	....
	Hershey Bears	AHL	17	2	2	4	....	....	....	40	....	....	....	....	....	....	....	....	....	....	....	....	....	....	....	....	....	....
	Richmond Robins	AHL	35	7	10	17	....	....	....	103	....	....	....	....	....	....	....	....	....	....	5	4	3	7	6	....	....	....
1974-75	Baltimore Clippers	AHL	44	8	18	26	....	....	....	139	....	....	....	....	....	....	....	....	....	....	....	....	....	....	....	....	....	....
	Hershey Bears	AHL	30	0	8	8	....	....	....	67	....	....	....	....	....	....	....	....	....	....	8	2	5	7	27	....	....	....
	Pittsburgh Penguins	**NHL**	....	....	....	....	....	....	....	....	....	....	....	....	....	....	....	....	....	....	**3**	**0**	**0**	**0**	**2**	....	....	....

			REGULAR SEASON																		PLAYOFFS							
Season	Club	League	GP	G	A	Pts	AG	AA	APts	PIM	PP	SH	GW	S	%	TGF	PGF	TGA	PGA	+/-	GP	G	A	Pts	PIM	PP	SH	GW
1975-76	Hershey Bears	AHL	29	1	9	10				85											10	0	1	1	29			
	Denver-Ottawa	WHA	41	5	5	10				43																		
1976-77	Hershey Bears	AHL	72	7	19	26				135											6	0	1	1	11			
	NHL Totals		**20**	**0**	**3**	**3**	**0**	**3**	**3**	**2**	**0**	**0**	**0**	**13**	**0.0**	**17**	**2**	**23**	**5**		**3**	**0**	**0**	**0**	**2**	**0**	**0**	**0**
	Other Major League Totals		41	5	5	10				43																		

Selected by **Vancouver** (WHA) in 1973 WHA Professional Player Draft, June, 1973. WHA rights traded to **Denver** (WHA) by **Calgary** (WHA) for cash, July, 1975. Signed as a free agent by **Hershey** (AHL) after **Denver-Ottawa** (WHA) franchise folded, January 17, 1976.

• BILODEAU, GILLES

Gilles Bilodeau LW – L. 6'1", 220 lbs. b: St. Prime, Que., 7/31/1955.

Season	Club	League	GP	G	A	Pts	AG	AA	APts	PIM	PP	SH	GW	S	%	TGF	PGF	TGA	PGA	+/-	GP	G	A	Pts	PIM	PP	SH	GW
1974-75	Sorel Eperviers	QMJHL	66	6	9	15				377																		
1975-76	Toronto Toros	WHA	14	0	1	1				38																		
	Beauce Jaros	NAHL	58	8	17	25				*451											5	0	1	1	46			
1976-77	Birmingham Bulls	WHA	34	2	6	8				133																		
	Charlotte Checkers	SHL	28	3	6	9				*242																		
1977-78	Birmingham Bulls	WHA	59	2	2	4				258											3	0	0	0	27			
	Binghamton Whalers	AHL	4	1	2	3				7																		
1978-79	Quebec Nordiques	WHA	36	3	6	9				141											3	0	0	0	25			
	Binghamton Whalers	AHL	30	2	1	3				114																		
1979-80	**Quebec Nordiques**	**NHL**	**9**	**0**	**1**	**1**	**0**	**1**	**1**	**25**	**0**	**0**	**0**	**1**	**0.0**	**1**	**0**	**2**	**0**	**–1**								
	Syracuse Firebirds	AHL	61	1	6	7				131											3	0	1	1	25			
1980-81	Richmond Rifles	EHL	39	6	6	12				207											8	0	2	2	30			
	NHL Totals		**9**	**0**	**1**	**1**	**0**	**1**	**1**	**25**	**0**	**0**	**0**	**1**	**0.0**	**1**	**0**	**2**	**0**									
	Other Major League Totals		143	7	15	22				570											6	0	0	0	52			

Selected by **Toronto** (WHA) in 1975 WHA Amateur Draft, May, 1975. Transferred to **Birmingham** (WHA) after **Toronto** (WHA) franchise relocated, June 30, 1976. Signed as a free agent by **Quebec** (WHA), September 29, 1978. Rights retained by **Quebec** prior to Expansion Draft, June 9, 1979.

• BISSETT, TOM

Tom Bissett C – L. 6', 180 lbs. b: Seattle, WA, 3/13/1966. Detroit's 11th choice, 211th overall, in 1986 Entry Draft.

Season	Club	League	GP	G	A	Pts	AG	AA	APts	PIM	PP	SH	GW	S	%	TGF	PGF	TGA	PGA	+/-	GP	G	A	Pts	PIM	PP	SH	GW
1985-86	Michigan Tech Huskies	WCHA	40	12	21	33				18																		
1986-87	Michigan Tech Huskies	WCHA	40	16	19	35				12																		
1987-88	Michigan Tech Huskies	WCHA	41	18	26	44				20																		
1988-89	Michigan Tech Huskies	WCHA	42	19	28	47				16																		
	Adirondack Red Wings	AHL	5	0	1	1				0																		
1989-90	Adirondack Red Wings	AHL	16	11	4	15				4																		
	Hampton Roads Admirals	ECHL	5	7	7	14				2																		
1990-91	**Detroit Red Wings**	**NHL**	**5**	**0**	**0**	**0**	**0**	**0**	**0**	**0**	**0**	**0**	**0**	**2**	**0.0**	**1**	**0**	**5**	**0**	**–4**								
	Adirondack Red Wings	AHL	73	44	38	82				12											2	0	0	0	0			
1991-92	Brynas IF Gavle	Sweden	40	25	15	40				32																		
	United States	WC-A	6	1	0	1				0																		
1992-93	Brynas IF Gavle	Sweden	40	21	11	32				20											10	*7	1	8	8			
1993-94	Rapperswil-Jona	Switz. B	36	24	24	48																						
1994-95	Rapperswil-Jona	Switz.	33	12	15	27				18																		
1995-96	Kaufbeuren Eagles	Germany	1	0	1	1				0																		
	Houston Aeros	IHL	3	0	0	0				0																		
1996-97	HIFK Helsinki	Finland	50	14	9	23				26																		
	NHL Totals		**5**	**0**	**0**	**0**	**0**	**0**	**0**	**0**	**0**	**0**	**0**	**2**	**0.0**	**1**	**0**	**5**	**0**									

• BJUGSTAD, SCOTT

Scott Bjugstad RW – L. 6'1", 185 lbs. b: St. Paul, MN, 6/2/1961. Minnesota's 13th choice, 181st overall, in 1981 Entry Draft.

Season	Club	League	GP	G	A	Pts	AG	AA	APts	PIM	PP	SH	GW	S	%	TGF	PGF	TGA	PGA	+/-	GP	G	A	Pts	PIM	PP	SH	GW
1979-80	University of Minnesota	WCHA	18	2	2	4				2																		
1980-81	University of Minnesota	WCHA	35	12	23	25				34																		
1981-82	University of Minnesota	WCHA	36	29	14	43				24																		
1982-83	University of Minnesota	WCHA	26	21	35	56				12																		
1983-84	United States	Nat-Team	54	31	20	51				28																		
	United States	Olympics	6	3	1	4				6																		
	Minnesota North Stars	**NHL**	**5**	**0**	**0**	**0**	**0**	**0**	**0**	**2**	**0**	**0**	**0**	**5**	**0.0**	**0**	**0**	**1**	**0**	**–1**								
	Salt Lake Golden Eagles	CHL	15	10	8	18				6											5	3	4	7	0			
1984-85	**Minnesota North Stars**	**NHL**	**72**	**11**	**4**	**15**	**9**	**3**	**12**	**32**	**1**	**0**	**1**	**108**	**10.2**	**22**	**3**	**72**	**32**	**–21**								
	Springfield Indians	AHL	5	2	3	5				2																		
1985-86	**Minnesota North Stars**	**NHL**	**80**	**43**	**33**	**76**	**35**	**22**	**57**	**24**	**14**	**2**	**6**	**217**	**19.8**	**109**	**40**	**89**	**25**	**+5**	**5**	**0**	**1**	**1**	**0**	**0**	**0**	**0**
1986-87	**Minnesota North Stars**	**NHL**	**39**	**4**	**9**	**13**	**3**	**6**	**9**	**43**	**0**	**0**	**0**	**58**	**6.9**	**20**	**7**	**27**	**8**	**6**								
	Springfield Indians	AHL	11	4	6	10				7																		
1987-88	**Minnesota North Stars**	**NHL**	**33**	**10**	**12**	**22**	**9**	**9**	**18**	**15**	**3**	**0**	**3**	**72**	**13.9**	**36**	**11**	**23**	**0**	**+2**								
1988-89	Kalamazoo Wings	IHL	4	5	0	5				4																		
	Pittsburgh Penguins	**NHL**	**24**	**3**	**0**	**3**	**3**	**0**	**3**	**4**	**0**	**0**	**1**	**21**	**14.3**	**4**	**0**	**16**	**0**	**–12**								
1989-90	**Los Angeles Kings**	**NHL**	**11**	**1**	**2**	**3**	**1**	**1**	**2**	**2**	**0**	**0**	**1**	**10**	**10.0**	**0**	**0**	**4**	**0**	**+2**	**2**	**0**	**0**	**0**	**2**	**0**	**0**	**0**
	New Haven Nighthawks	AHL	47	45	21	66				40																		
1990-91	**Los Angeles Kings**	**NHL**	**31**	**2**	**4**	**6**	**2**	**3**	**5**	**12**	**0**	**0**	**1**	**39**	**5.1**	**12**	**1**	**21**	**5**	**–5**	**2**	**0**	**0**	**0**	**0**	**0**	**0**	**0**
	Phoenix Roadrunners	IHL	3	7	2	9				2																		
1991-92	**Los Angeles Kings**	**NHL**	**22**	**2**	**4**	**6**	**2**	**3**	**5**	**10**	**0**	**0**	**0**	**25**	**8.0**	**9**	**0**	**11**	**1**	**–1**								
	Phoenix Roadrunners	IHL	28	14	14	28				12																		
1992-93	Phoenix Roadrunners	IHL	7	5	4	9				4																		
	Houston Aeros	IHL	3	0	0	0				0																		
	NHL Totals		**317**	**76**	**68**	**144**	**64**	**47**	**111**	**144**	**18**	**2**	**13**	**555**	**13.7**	**218**	**62**	**264**	**71**		**9**	**0**	**1**	**1**	**2**	**0**	**0**	**0**

WCHA First All-Star Team (1983)

Traded to **Pittsburgh** by **Minnesota** with Gord Dineen for Ville Siren and Steve Gotaas, December 17, 1988. Signed as a free agent by **LA Kings**, August 24, 1989.

• BLACK, JAMES

James Black C – L. 6', 202 lbs. b: Regina, Sask., 8/15/1969 Hartford's 4th choice, 94th overall, in 1989 Entry Draft.

Season	Club	League	GP	G	A	Pts	AG	AA	APts	PIM	PP	SH	GW	S	%	TGF	PGF	TGA	PGA	+/-	GP	G	A	Pts	PIM	PP	SH	GW
1987-88	Portland Winter Hawks	WHL	72	30	50	80				50																		
1988-89	Portland Winter Hawks	WHL	71	45	51	96				57											19	13	6	19	28			
1989-90	**Hartford Whalers**	**NHL**	**1**	**0**	**0**	**0**	**0**	**0**	**0**	**0**	**0**	**0**	**0**	**0**	**0.0**	**0**	**0**	**0**	**0**	**0**								
	Binghamton Whalers	AHL	80	37	35	72				34																		
1990-91	**Hartford Whalers**	**NHL**	**1**	**0**	**0**	**0**	**0**	**0**	**0**	**0**	**0**	**0**	**0**	**0**	**0.0**	**0**	**0**	**0**	**0**	**0**								
	Springfield Indians	AHL	79	35	61	96				34											18	9	9	18	6			
1991-92	**Hartford Whalers**	**NHL**	**30**	**4**	**6**	**10**	**4**	**4**	**8**	**10**	**1**	**0**	**1**	**54**	**7.4**	**16**	**6**	**27**	**13**	**–4**								
	Springfield Indians	AHL	47	15	25	40				33											10	3	2	5	18			
1992-93	**Minnesota North Stars**	**NHL**	**10**	**2**	**1**	**3**	**2**	**1**	**3**	**4**	**0**	**0**	**0**	**10**	**20.0**	**4**	**0**	**4**	**0**	**0**								
	Kalamazoo Wings	IHL	63	25	45	70				40																		
1993-94	**Dallas Stars**	**NHL**	**13**	**2**	**3**	**5**	**2**	**2**	**4**	**2**	**2**	**0**	**0**	**16**	**12.5**	**6**	**2**	**8**	**0**	**–4**								
	Buffalo Sabres	**NHL**	**2**	**0**	**0**	**0**	**0**	**0**	**0**	**0**	**2**	**0**	**0**	**2**	**0.0**	**0**	**0**	**0**	**0**	**0**								
	Rochester Americans	AHL	45	19	32	51				28											4	2	3	5	0			
1994-95	Las Vegas Thunder	IHL	78	29	44	73				54											10	1	6	7	4			
1995-96	**Chicago Blackhawks**	**NHL**	**13**	**3**	**3**	**6**	**3**	**2**	**5**	**16**	**0**	**0**	**1**	**23**	**13.0**	**7**	**0**	**6**	**0**	**+1**	**8**	**1**	**0**	**1**	**2**	**0**	**0**	**0**
	Indianapolis Ice	IHL	67	32	50	82				56																		
1996-97	**Chicago Blackhawks**	**NHL**	**64**	**12**	**11**	**23**	**13**	**10**	**23**	**20**	**0**	**0**	**3**	**122**	**9.8**	**32**	**1**	**33**	**8**	**+6**	**5**	**1**	**1**	**2**	**2**	**0**	**0**	**0**
1997-98	**Chicago Blackhawks**	**NHL**	**52**	**10**	**5**	**15**	**12**	**5**	**17**	**8**	**2**	**1**	**3**	**90**	**11.1**	**18**	**4**	**31**	**9**	**–8**								
	NHL Totals		**186**	**33**	**29**	**62**	**36**	**24**	**60**	**60**	**7**	**1**	**8**	**317**	**10.4**	**83**	**13**	**109**	**30**		**13**	**2**	**1**	**3**	**4**	**0**	**0**	**0**

Traded to **Minnesota** by **Hartford** for Mark Janssens, September 3, 1992. Transferred to **Dallas** after **Minnesota** franchise relocated, June 9, 1993. Traded to **Buffalo** by **Dallas** with Dallas' 7th round choice (Steve Webb) in 1994 Entry Draft for Gord Donnelly, December 15, 1993. Signed as a free agent by **Chicago**, September 18, 1995

• BLACKBURN, BOB

Bob Blackburn D – L. 5'11", 198 lbs. b: Rouyn, Que., 2/1/1938.

Season	Club	League	GP	G	A	Pts	AG	AA	APts	PIM	PP	SH	GW	S	%	TGF	PGF	TGA	PGA	+/-	GP	G	A	Pts	PIM	PP	SH	GW
			REGULAR SEASON																		PLAYOFFS							
1956-57	Barrie Flyers	OHA	21	0	0	0	....	....	....	7	....	....	....	....	....	....	....	....	....	....	1	0	0	0	0	....	....	....
1957-58	Barrie Flyers	OHA	51	13	26	39	....	....	....	171	....	....	....	....	....	....	....	....	....	....	4	3	0	3	23	....	....	....
1958-59	Quebec Aces	QHL	29	1	1	2	....	....	....	36	....	....	....	....	....	....	....	....	....	....	....	....	....	....	....	....	....	....
	Washington Presidents	EHL	21	1	10	11	....	....	....	44	....	....	....	....	....	....	....	....	....	....	....	....	....	....	....	....	....	....
1959-60	Kingston Frontenacs	EPHL	27	0	7	7	....	....	....	41	....	....	....	....	....	....	....	....	....	....	....	....	....	....	....	....	....	....
	Providence Reds	AHL	37	0	2	2	....	....	....	8	....	....	....	....	....	....	....	....	....	....	....	....	....	....	....	....	....	....
1960-61	Providence Reds	AHL	50	1	5	6	....	....	....	53	....	....	....	....	....	....	....	....	....	....	....	....	....	....	....	....	....	....
1961-62	Providence Reds	AHL	64	1	11	12	....	....	....	157	....	....	....	....	....	....	....	....	....	....	3	0	1	1	2	....	....	....
1962-63	Providence Reds	AHL	47	2	7	9	....	....	....	56	....	....	....	....	....	....	....	....	....	....	6	0	0	0	4	....	....	....
1963-64	Providence Reds	AHL	70	2	20	22	....	....	....	175	....	....	....	....	....	....	....	....	....	....	3	0	2	2	4	....	....	....
1964-65	Providence Reds	AHL	67	1	17	18	....	....	....	162	....	....	....	....	....	....	....	....	....	....	....	....	....	....	....	....	....	....
1965-66	Providence Reds	AHL	27	0	4	4	....	....	....	52	....	....	....	....	....	....	....	....	....	....	....	....	....	....	....	....	....	....
	Vancouver Canucks	WHL	28	1	5	6	....	....	....	44	....	....	....	....	....	....	....	....	....	....	7	0	0	0	12	....	....	....
1966-67	Vancouver Canucks	WHL	69	2	11	13	....	....	....	120	....	....	....	....	....	....	....	....	....	....	8	0	4	4	16	....	....	....
1967-68	Buffalo Bisons	AHL	69	2	15	17	....	....	....	116	....	....	....	....	....	....	....	....	....	....	5	1	1	2	14	....	....	....
1968-69	**New York Rangers**	**NHL**	**11**	**0**	**0**	**0**	**0**	**0**	**0**	**0**	**0**	**0**	**0**	**6**	**0.0**	**5**	**0**	**2**	**1**	**+4**	....	....	....	....	....	....	....	....
	Buffalo Bisons	AHL	58	3	15	18	....	....	....	73	....	....	....	....	....	....	....	....	....	....	6	0	1	1	14	....	....	....
1969-70	Baltimore Clippers	AHL	6	0	0	0	....	....	....	0	....	....	....	....	....	....	....	....	....	....	....	....	....	....	....	....	....	....
	Pittsburgh Penguins	**NHL**	**60**	**4**	**7**	**11**	**5**	**7**	**12**	**51**	**0**	**0**	**1**	**49**	**8.2**	**38**	**2**	**69**	**19**	**–14**	**6**	**0**	**0**	**0**	**4**	**0**	**0**	**0**
1970-71	**Pittsburgh Penguins**	**NHL**	**64**	**4**	**5**	**9**	**4**	**4**	**8**	**54**	**0**	**0**	**1**	**87**	**4.6**	**56**	**0**	**68**	**12**	**0**	....	....	....	....	....	....	....	....
1971-72	Rochester Americans	AHL	64	7	11	18	....	....	....	72	....	....	....	....	....	....	....	....	....	....	....	....	....	....	....	....	....	....
	NHL Totals		**135**	**8**	**12**	**20**	**9**	**11**	**20**	**105**	**0**	**0**	**2**	**142**	**5.6**	**99**	**2**	**139**	**32**		**6**	**0**	**0**	**0**	**4**	**0**	**0**	**0**

AHL First All-Star Team (1969) • Won Eddie Shore Award (Outstanding Defenseman - AHL) (1969)

Traded to **Vancouver** (WHL) by **Providence** (AHL) for Wayne Moloin and Ron Hutchinson, February 3, 1966 Claimed by **Buffalo** (AHL) from **NY Rangers** in Reverse Draft, June 6, 1967. Traded to **NY Rangers** by **Buffalo** (AHL) for cash, August, 1968. Claimed by **Pittsburgh** from **NY Rangers** in Intra-League Draft, June 11, 1969. Traded to **Vancouver** by **Pittsburgh** for cash, October 3, 1971.

• BLACKBURN, DON

Don Blackburn LW – L. 6', 190 lbs. b: Kirkland Lake, Ont., 5/14/1938.

Season	Club	League	GP	G	A	Pts	AG	AA	APts	PIM	PP	SH	GW	S	%	TGF	PGF	TGA	PGA	+/-	GP	G	A	Pts	PIM	PP	SH	GW
1956-57	Hamilton Tiger Cubs	OHA	52	9	8	17	....	....	....	17	....	....	....	....	....	....	....	....	....	....	4	0	2	2	0	....	....	....
1957-58	Hamilton Tiger Cubs	OHA	52	15	18	33	....	....	....	37	....	....	....	....	....	....	....	....	....	....	15	4	3	7	16	....	....	....
1958-59	Victoria Cougars	WHL	50	15	16	31	....	....	....	14	....	....	....	....	....	....	....	....	....	....	....	....	....	....	....	....	....	....
1959-60	Victoria Cougars	WHL	41	8	7	15	....	....	....	8	....	....	....	....	....	....	....	....	....	....	11	1	1	2	2	....	....	....
	Providence Reds	AHL	16	1	1	2	....	....	....	8	....	....	....	....	....	....	....	....	....	....	....	....	....	....	....	....	....	....
1960-61	Kingston Frontenacs	EPHL	59	14	31	45	....	....	....	27	....	....	....	....	....	....	....	....	....	....	5	1	0	1	0	....	....	....
1961-62	Kingston Frontenacs	EPHL	51	13	24	37	....	....	....	30	....	....	....	....	....	....	....	....	....	....	11	2	12	14	5	....	....	....
1962-63	**Boston Bruins**	**NHL**	**6**	**0**	**5**	**5**	**0**	**5**	**5**	**4**	....	....	....	....	....	....	....	....	....	....	....	....	....	....	....	....	....	....
	Kingston Frontenacs	EPHL	67	42	54	96	....	....	....	22	....	....	....	....	....	....	....	....	....	....	5	4	4	8	0	....	....	....
1963-64	Quebec Aces	AHL	63	19	19	38	....	....	....	39	....	....	....	....	....	....	....	....	....	....	9	1	1	2	9	....	....	....
1964-65	Quebec Aces	AHL	70	19	42	61	....	....	....	34	....	....	....	....	....	....	....	....	....	....	5	0	2	2	0	....	....	....
1965-66	Quebec Aces	AHL	72	36	42	78	....	....	....	51	....	....	....	....	....	....	....	....	....	....	6	1	4	5	4	....	....	....
1966-67	Rochester Americans	AHL	70	20	37	57	....	....	....	24	....	....	....	....	....	....	....	....	....	....	13	3	3	6	10	....	....	....
1967-68	**Philadelphia Flyers**	**NHL**	**67**	**9**	**20**	**29**	**11**	**21**	**32**	**23**	**1**	**0**	**2**	**157**	**5.7**	**43**	**8**	**37**	**0**	**–2**	**7**	**3**	**0**	**3**	**8**	**1**	**0**	**1**
1968-69	**Philadelphia Flyers**	**NHL**	**48**	**7**	**9**	**16**	**8**	**8**	**16**	**36**	**0**	**0**	**2**	**94**	**7.4**	**20**	**0**	**33**	**0**	**–13**	**4**	**0**	**0**	**0**	**2**	**0**	**0**	**0**
	Baltimore Clippers	AHL	12	6	13	19	....	....	....	10	....	....	....	....	....	....	....	....	....	....	....	....	....	....	....	....	....	....
1969-70	**New York Rangers**	**NHL**	**3**	**0**	**0**	**0**	**0**	**0**	**0**	**0**	**0**	**0**	**0**	**1**	**0.0**	**0**	**0**	**0**	**0**	**0**	**1**	**0**	**0**	**0**	**0**	**0**	**0**	**0**
	Buffalo Bisons	AHL	68	27	44	71	....	....	....	40	....	....	....	....	....	....	....	....	....	....	13	5	7	12	6	....	....	....
1970-71	**New York Rangers**	**NHL**	**1**	**0**	**0**	**0**	**0**	**0**	**0**	**0**	**0**	**0**	**0**	**0**	**0.0**	**0**	**0**	**0**	**0**	**0**	....	....	....	....	....	....	....	....
	Rochester Americans	AHL	62	25	44	69	....	....	....	22	....	....	....	....	....	....	....	....	....	....	....	....	....	....	....	....	....	....
1971-72	Providence Reds	AHL	76	34	65	99	....	....	....	12	....	....	....	....	....	....	....	....	....	....	5	1	3	4	2	....	....	....
1972-73	**New York Islanders**	**NHL**	**56**	**7**	**10**	**17**	**7**	**8**	**15**	**20**	**1**	**0**	**1**	**65**	**10.8**	**29**	**4**	**58**	**0**	**–33**	....	....	....	....	....	....	....	....
	Minnesota North Stars	**NHL**	**4**	**0**	**0**	**0**	**0**	**0**	**0**	**4**	**0**	**0**	**0**	**0**	**0.0**	**0**	**0**	**0**	**0**	**0**	....	....	....	....	....	....	....	....
1973-74	New England Whalers	WHA	75	20	39	59	....	....	....	18	....	....	....	....	....	....	....	....	....	....	7	2	4	6	4	....	....	....
1974-75	New England Whalers	WHA	50	18	32	50	....	....	....	16	....	....	....	....	....	....	....	....	....	....	5	1	2	3	2	....	....	....
	Cape Cod Codders	NAHL	2	2	2	4	....	....	....	0	....	....	....	....	....	....	....	....	....	....	....	....	....	....	....	....	....	....
1975-76	New England Whalers	WHA	21	2	3	5	....	....	....	6	....	....	....	....	....	....	....	....	....	....	....	....	....	....	....	....	....	....
	Cape Cod Codders	NAHL	8	4	4	8	....	....	....	0	....	....	....	....	....	....	....	....	....	....	....	....	....	....	....	....	....	....
	NHL Totals		**185**	**23**	**44**	**67**	**26**	**42**	**68**	**87**	**2**	**0**	**5**	**317**	**7.3**	**92**	**12**	**128**	**0**		**12**	**3**	**0**	**3**	**10**	**1**	**0**	**1**
	Other Major League Totals		146	40	74	114	....	....	....	40	....	....	....	....	....	....	....	....	....	....	12	3	6	9	6	....	....	....

AHL Second All-Star Team (1970, 1972) • AHL First All-Star Team (1971) • Won John B. Sollenberger Trophy (Top Scorer - AHL) (1972)

Claimed by **Montreal** (Quebec - AHL) from **Boston** in Inter-League Draft, June, 1963. Claimed by **Toronto** from **Montreal** in Intra-League Draft, June 15, 1966. Claimed by **Philadelphia** from **Toronto** in Expansion Draft, June 6, 1967. Traded to **NY Rangers** by **Philadelphia** with Leon Rochefort for Reg Fleming, June 6, 1969. Selected by **NY Raiders** (WHA) in 1972 WHA General Player Draft, February 12, 1972. Claimed by **NY Islanders** from **NY Rangers** in Intra-League Draft, June 6, 1972. Traded to **Minnesota** by **NY Islanders** for cash, March 1, 1973. WHA rights traded to **New England** (WHA) by **NY Raiders** (WHA) for future considerations, September, 1973.

• BLADON, TOM

Tom "Bomber" Bladon D – R. 6'1", 195 lbs. b: Edmonton, Alta., 12/29/1952. Philadelphia's 2nd choice, 23rd overall, in 1972 Amateur Draft.

Season	Club	League	GP	G	A	Pts	AG	AA	APts	PIM	PP	SH	GW	S	%	TGF	PGF	TGA	PGA	+/-	GP	G	A	Pts	PIM	PP	SH	GW
1969-70	Edmonton Maple Leafs	AJHL	46	12	17	29	....	....	....	115	....	....	....	....	....	....	....	....	....	....	....	....	....	....	....	....	....	....
1970-71	Edmonton Oil Kings	WCJHL	66	13	25	38	....	....	....	124	....	....	....	....	....	....	....	....	....	....	....	....	....	....	....	....	....	....
1971-72	Edmonton Oil Kings	WCJHL	65	11	44	55	....	....	....	90	....	....	....	....	....	....	....	....	....	....	....	....	....	....	....	....	....	....
1972-73	**Philadelphia Flyers**	**NHL**	**78**	**11**	**31**	**42**	**11**	**26**	**37**	**26**	**7**	**0**	**0**	**151**	**7.3**	**116**	**48**	**64**	**5**	**+9**	**11**	**0**	**4**	**4**	**2**	**0**	**0**	**0**
1973-74	**Philadelphia Flyers**	**NHL**	**70**	**12**	**22**	**34**	**12**	**19**	**31**	**37**	**6**	**0**	**2**	**159**	**7.5**	**97**	**35**	**45**	**7**	**+24**	**16**	**4**	**6**	**10**	**25**	**3**	**0**	**1**
1974-75	**Philadelphia Flyers**	**NHL**	**76**	**9**	**20**	**29**	**8**	**16**	**24**	**54**	**5**	**0**	**3**	**174**	**5.2**	**108**	**35**	**42**	**11**	**+42**	**13**	**1**	**3**	**4**	**12**	**1**	**0**	**0**
1975-76	**Philadelphia Flyers**	**NHL**	**80**	**14**	**23**	**37**	**13**	**18**	**31**	**68**	**5**	**0**	**2**	**182**	**7.7**	**124**	**30**	**70**	**21**	**+45**	**16**	**2**	**6**	**8**	**14**	**1**	**0**	**0**
1976-77	**Philadelphia Flyers**	**NHL**	**80**	**10**	**43**	**53**	**10**	**35**	**45**	**39**	**2**	**0**	**2**	**158**	**6.3**	**118**	**22**	**95**	**33**	**+34**	**10**	**1**	**3**	**4**	**4**	**0**	**0**	**0**
1977-78	**Philadelphia Flyers**	**NHL**	**79**	**11**	**24**	**35**	**11**	**20**	**31**	**57**	**1**	**1**	**1**	**153**	**7.2**	**92**	**13**	**73**	**26**	**+32**	**12**	**0**	**2**	**2**	**11**	**0**	**0**	**0**
1978-79	**Pittsburgh Penguins**	**NHL**	**78**	**4**	**23**	**27**	**4**	**18**	**22**	**64**	**1**	**0**	**0**	**135**	**3.0**	**105**	**23**	**124**	**25**	**–17**	**7**	**0**	**4**	**4**	**2**	**0**	**0**	**0**
1979-80	**Pittsburgh Penguins**	**NHL**	**57**	**2**	**6**	**8**	**2**	**5**	**7**	**35**	**1**	**0**	**1**	**69**	**2.9**	**48**	**11**	**79**	**17**	**–25**	**1**	**0**	**1**	**1**	**0**	**0**	**0**	**0**
1980-81	**Edmonton Oilers**	**NHL**	**1**	**0**	**0**	**0**	**0**	**0**	**0**	**0**	**0**	**0**	**0**	**0**	**0.0**	**0**	**0**	**1**	**0**	**–1**	....	....	....	....	....	....	....	....
	Winnipeg Jets	**NHL**	**9**	**0**	**5**	**5**	**0**	**3**	**3**	**10**	**0**	**0**	**0**	**13**	**0.0**	**12**	**5**	**19**	**2**	**–10**	....	....	....	....	....	....	....	....
	Detroit Red Wings	**NHL**	**2**	**0**	**0**	**0**	**0**	**0**	**0**	**2**	**0**	**0**	**0**	**1**	**0.0**	**2**	**0**	**2**	**0**	**0**	....	....	....	....	....	....	....	....
	Adirondack Red Wings	AHL	41	3	15	18	....	....	....	28	....	....	....	....	....	....	....	....	....	....	18	3	3	6	16	....	....	....
	NHL Totals		**610**	**73**	**197**	**270**	**71**	**160**	**231**	**392**	**28**	**1**	**9**	**1195**	**6.1**	**822**	**222**	**614**	**147**		**86**	**8**	**29**	**37**	**70**	**5**	**0**	**1**

WCJHL Second All-Star Team (1972)

Played in NHL All-Star Game (1977, 1978)

Traded to **Pittsburgh** by **Philadelphia** with Ross Lonsberry and Orest Kindrachuk for Pittsburgh's 1st round choice (Behn Wilson) in 1978 Amateur Draft, June 14, 1978. Signed as a free agent by **Edmonton**, July 10, 1980. Signed as a free agent by **Winnipeg**, December 13, 1980. Signed as a free agent by **Detroit**, January 14, 1981.

• BLAISDELL, MIKE

Mike "Wally" Blaisdell RW – R. 6'1", 196 lbs. b: Moose Jaw, Sask., 1/18/1960. Detroit's 1st choice, 11th overall, in 1980 Entry Draft.

Season	Club	League	GP	G	A	Pts	AG	AA	APts	PIM	PP	SH	GW	S	%	TGF	PGF	TGA	PGA	+/-	GP	G	A	Pts	PIM	PP	SH	GW
1977-78	Regina Blues	SJHL	60	70	46	116	....	....	....	43	....	....	....	....	....	....	....	....	....	....	....	....	....	....	....	....	....	....
	Regina Pats	WCJHL	6	5	5	10	....	....	....	2	....	....	....	....	....	....	....	....	....	....	13	4	7	11	0	....	....	....
1978-79	University of Wisconsin	WCHA	20	7	1	8	....	....	....	4	....	....	....	....	....	....	....	....	....	....	....	....	....	....	....	....	....	....
1979-80	Regina Pats	WHL	63	71	38	109	....	....	....	62	....	....	....	....	....	....	....	....	....	....	18	*16	9	25	26	....	....	....
1980-81	**Detroit Red Wings**	**NHL**	**32**	**3**	**6**	**9**	**2**	**4**	**6**	**10**	**0**	**0**	**0**	**45**	**6.7**	**18**	**3**	**22**	**0**	**–7**	....	....	....	....	....	....	....	....
	Adirondack Red Wings	AHL	41	10	4	14	....	....	....	8	....	....	....	....	....	....	....	....	....	....	12	2	2	4	5	....	....	....
1981-82	**Detroit Red Wings**	**NHL**	**80**	**23**	**32**	**55**	**18**	**21**	**39**	**48**	**5**	**0**	**3**	**165**	**13.9**	**75**	**9**	**83**	**2**	**–15**	....	....	....	....	....	....	....	....
1982-83	**Detroit Red Wings**	**NHL**	**80**	**18**	**23**	**41**	**15**	**16**	**31**	**22**	**0**	**0**	**2**	**171**	**10.5**	**72**	**7**	**72**	**1**	**–6**	....	....	....	....	....	....	....	....
1983-84	**New York Rangers**	**NHL**	**36**	**5**	**6**	**11**	**4**	**4**	**8**	**31**	**0**	**0**	**1**	**63**	**7.9**	**22**	**1**	**21**	**0**	**0**	....	....	....	....	....	....	....	....
	Tulsa Oilers	CHL	32	10	8	18	....	....	....	23	....	....	....	....	....	....	....	....	....	....	9	6	6	12	6	....	....	....
1984-85	**New York Rangers**	**NHL**	**12**	**1**	**0**	**1**	**1**	**0**	**1**	**11**	**0**	**0**	**0**	**20**	**5.0**	**3**	**1**	**6**	**0**	**–4**	....	....	....	....	....	....	....	....
	New Haven Nighthawks	AHL	64	21	23	44	....	....	....	41	....	....	....	....	....	....	....	....	....	....	....	....	....	....	....	....	....	....
1985-86	**Pittsburgh Penguins**	**NHL**	**66**	**15**	**14**	**29**	**12**	**9**	**21**	**36**	**0**	**0**	**0**	**125**	**12.0**	**51**	**3**	**33**	**0**	**+15**	....	....	....	....	....	....	....	....

			REGULAR SEASON																		PLAYOFFS							
Season	Club	League	GP	G	A	Pts	AG	AA	APts	PIM	PP	SH	GW	S	%	TGF	PGF	TGA	PGA	+/–	GP	G	A	Pts	PIM	PP	SH	GW
1986-87	**Pittsburgh Penguins**	**NHL**	**10**	**1**	**1**	**2**	**1**	**1**	**2**	**2**	**0**	**0**	**0**	**12**	**8.3**	**4**	**0**	**2**	**0**	**+2**								
	Baltimore Skipjacks	AHL	43	12	12	24				47																		
1987-88	**Toronto Maple Leafs**	**NHL**	**18**	**3**	**2**	**5**	**3**	**1**	**4**	**2**	**0**	**0**	**1**	**32**	**9.4**	**8**	**0**	**13**	**0**	**–5**	**6**	**1**	**2**	**3**	**10**	**0**	**0**	**0**
	Newmarket Saints	AHL	57	25	28	53				30																		
1988-89	**Toronto Maple Leafs**	**NHL**	**9**	**1**	**0**	**1**	**1**	**0**	**1**	**4**	**0**	**0**	**0**	**8**	**12.5**	**2**	**1**	**6**	**0**	**–5**								
	Newmarket Saints	AHL	40	16	7	23				48																		
1989-90	Canada	Nat-Team	50	12	18	30				40																		
1990-91	Albany Choppers	IHL	6	2	0	2				0																		
	Durham Wasps	Britain	18	36	35	71				114																		
1991-92	Durham Wasps	Britain	36	74	52	126				86											8	11	13	24	22			
1992-93	Durham Wasps	Britain	13	24	18	41				46																		
1993-94	Nottingham Panthers	Britain	DID NOT PLAY – COACHING																									
1994-95	Nottingham Panthers	Britain	11	7	10	17				60																		
1995-96	Nottingham Panthers	Britain	33	26	33	59				77											8	1	6	7	4			
1996-97	Nottingham Panthers	Britain	7	2	2	4				6																		
	NHL Totals		**343**	**70**	**84**	**154**	**57**	**56**	**113**	**166**	**5**	**0**	**7**	**641**	**10.9**	**255**	**25**	**258**	**3**		**6**	**1**	**2**	**3**	**10**	**0**	**0**	**0**

Traded to **NY Rangers** by **Detroit** with Willie Huber and Mark Osborne for Don Duguay, Eddie Mio and Eddie Johnstone, June 13, 1983. Claimed by **Pittsburgh** from **NY Rangers** in Waiver Draft, October 7, 1985. Signed as a free agent by **Toronto**, July 10, 1987.

• BLAKE, ROB

Rob Blake D – R. 6'3", 215 lbs. b: Simcoe, Ont., 12/10/1969. Los Angeles' 4th choice, 70th overall, in 1988 Entry Draft.

Season	Club	League	GP	G	A	Pts	AG	AA	APts	PIM	PP	SH	GW	S	%	TGF	PGF	TGA	PGA	+/–	GP	G	A	Pts	PIM	PP	SH	GW
1986-87	Stratford Cullitons	OJHL	31	11	20	31				115																		
1987-88	Bowling Green University	CCHA	43	5	8	13				88																		
1988-89	Bowling Green University	CCHA	46	11	21	32				140																		
1989-90	Bowling Green University	CCHA	42	23	36	59				140																		
	Los Angeles Kings	**NHL**	**4**	**0**	**0**	**0**	**0**	**0**	**0**	**4**	**0**	**0**	**0**	**3**	**0.0**	**4**	**1**	**6**	**3**	**0**	**8**	**1**	**3**	**4**	**4**	**1**	**0**	**0**
1990-91	**Los Angeles Kings**	**NHL**	**75**	**12**	**34**	**46**	**11**	**26**	**37**	**125**	**9**	**0**	**2**	**150**	**8.0**	**110**	**46**	**84**	**23**	**+3**	**12**	**1**	**4**	**5**	**26**	**1**	**0**	**0**
	Canada	WEC-A	2	0	2	2				0																		
1991-92	**Los Angeles Kings**	**NHL**	**57**	**7**	**13**	**20**	**6**	**10**	**16**	**102**	**5**	**0**	**0**	**131**	**5.3**	**96**	**35**	**81**	**15**	**–5**	**6**	**2**	**1**	**3**	**12**	**0**	**0**	**0**
1992-93	**Los Angeles Kings**	**NHL**	**76**	**16**	**43**	**59**	**13**	**29**	**42**	**152**	**10**	**0**	**4**	**243**	**6.6**	**145**	**56**	**103**	**32**	**+18**	**23**	**4**	**6**	**10**	**46**	**1**	**1**	**0**
1993-94	**Los Angeles Kings**	**NHL**	**84**	**20**	**48**	**68**	**19**	**37**	**56**	**137**	**7**	**0**	**6**	**304**	**6.6**	**157**	**67**	**141**	**44**	**–7**								
	Canada	WC-A	8	0	2	2				6																		
1994-95	**Los Angeles Kings**	**NHL**	**24**	**4**	**7**	**11**	**7**	**10**	**17**	**38**	**4**	**0**	**1**	**76**	**5.3**	**23**	**12**	**38**	**11**	**–16**								
1995-96	**Los Angeles Kings**	**NHL**	**6**	**1**	**2**	**3**	**1**	**2**	**3**	**8**	**0**	**0**	**0**	**13**	**7.7**	**11**	**7**	**7**	**3**	**0**								
1996-97	Canada	W Cup	4	0	1	1				0																		
	Los Angeles Kings	**NHL**	**62**	**8**	**23**	**31**	**8**	**20**	**28**	**82**	**4**	**0**	**1**	**169**	**4.7**	**69**	**20**	**97**	**20**	**–28**								
	Canada	WC-A	11	2	2	4				22																		
1997-98	**Los Angeles Kings**	**NHL**	**81**	**23**	**27**	**50**	**27**	**26**	**53**	**94**	**11**	**0**	**4**	**261**	**8.8**	**113**	**41**	**111**	**36**	**–3**	**4**	**0**	**0**	**0**	**6**	**0**	**0**	**0**
	Canada	Olympics	6	1	1	2				2																		
	Canada	WC-A	5	1	0	1				6																		
	NHL Totals		**469**	**91**	**197**	**288**	**92**	**160**	**252**	**742**	**50**	**0**	**18**	**1350**	**6.7**	**728**	**285**	**668**	**187**		**53**	**8**	**14**	**22**	**94**	**3**	**1**	**0**

CCHA Second All-Star Team (1989) • CCHA First All-Star Team (1990) • NCAA West First All-American Team (1990) • NHL/Upper Deck All-Rookie Team (1991) • WC-A All-Star Team (1997) • Named Best Defenseman at WC-A (1997) • Named Best Defenseman at Olympic Games (1998) • NHL First All-Star Team (1998) • Won James Norris Memorial Trophy (1998)

Played in NHL All-Star Game (1994)

• BLIGHT, RICK

Rick Blight RW – R. 6'2", 195 lbs. b: Portage La Prairie, Man., 10/17/1955. Vancouver's 1st choice, 10th overall, in 1975 Amateur Draft.

Season	Club	League	GP	G	A	Pts	AG	AA	APts	PIM	PP	SH	GW	S	%	TGF	PGF	TGA	PGA	+/–	GP	G	A	Pts	PIM	PP	SH	GW
1970-71	Portage Terriers	MJHL	47	20	19	39				33																		
1971-72	Portage Terriers	MJHL	45	32	35	67				73																		
	Brandon Wheat Kings	WCJHL	1	1	0	1				0																		
1972-73	Brandon Wheat Kings	WCJHL	68	31	62	93				70																		
1973-74	Brandon Wheat Kings	WCJHL	67	49	81	130				122																		
1974-75	Brandon Wheat Kings	WCJHL	65	60	52	112				65																		
	Canada	WJC-A	....	2	2	4				....																		
1975-76	**Vancouver Canucks**	**NHL**	**74**	**25**	**31**	**56**	**23**	**24**	**47**	**29**	**10**	**0**	**3**	**212**	**11.8**	**79**	**27**	**57**	**1**	**–4**	**2**	**0**	**1**	**1**	**0**	**0**	**0**	**0**
1976-77	**Vancouver Canucks**	**NHL**	**78**	**28**	**40**	**68**	**27**	**32**	**59**	**32**	**11**	**0**	**5**	**197**	**14.2**	**102**	**41**	**62**	**1**	**0**								
1977-78	**Vancouver Canucks**	**NHL**	**80**	**25**	**38**	**63**	**24**	**31**	**55**	**33**	**11**	**0**	**2**	**238**	**10.5**	**93**	**41**	**84**	**0**	**–32**								
1978-79	**Vancouver Canucks**	**NHL**	**56**	**5**	**10**	**15**	**5**	**8**	**13**	**16**	**1**	**0**	**1**	**91**	**5.5**	**26**	**9**	**45**	**0**	**–28**	**3**	**0**	**4**	**4**	**2**	**0**	**0**	**0**
	Dallas Black Hawks	CHL	15	8	7	15				7																		
1979-80	**Vancouver Canucks**	**NHL**	**33**	**12**	**6**	**18**	**11**	**5**	**16**	**54**	**1**	**0**	**0**	**82**	**14.6**	**28**	**5**	**16**	**0**	**+7**								
1980-81	**Vancouver Canucks**	**NHL**	**3**	**1**	**0**	**1**	**1**	**0**	**1**	**4**	**0**	**0**	**0**	**9**	**11.1**	**1**	**0**	**2**	**0**	**–1**								
	Dallas Black Hawks	CHL	71	46	49	95				122											6	0	3	3	9			
1981-82	Cincinnati Tigers	CHL	37	16	23	39				21																		
	Wichita Wind	CHL	16	18	14	32				18											7	3	0	3	6			
1982-83	Moncton Alpines	AHL	19	8	7	15				6																		
	Los Angeles Kings	**NHL**	**2**	**0**	**0**	**0**	**0**	**0**	**0**	**2**	**0**	**0**	**0**	**2**	**0.0**	**2**	**1**	**5**	**1**	**–3**								
	New Haven Nighthawks	AHL	47	17	24	41				8											7	0	1	1	0			
	NHL Totals		**326**	**96**	**125**	**221**	**91**	**100**	**191**	**170**	**34**	**0**	**11**	**831**	**11.6**	**331**	**124**	**271**	**3**		**5**	**0**	**5**	**5**	**2**	**0**	**0**	**0**

CHL Second All-Star Team (1981)

Signed as a free agent by **Toronto**, August 31, 1981. Signed as a free agent by **Edmonton**, October 25, 1982. Traded to **LA Kings** by **Edmonton** for Alan Hangsleben, December 7, 1982.

• BLOCK, KEN

Ken Block D – L. 5'10", 191 lbs. b: Steinbach, Man., 3/18/1944.

Season	Club	League	GP	G	A	Pts	AG	AA	APts	PIM	PP	SH	GW	S	%	TGF	PGF	TGA	PGA	+/–	GP	G	A	Pts	PIM	PP	SH	GW
1962-63	Flin Flon Bombers	SJHL	54	5	12	17				22											6	2	5	7	4			
1963-64	Flin Flon Bombers	MJHL	62	14	43	57				59											2	1	3	4	0			
1964-65	New York Rovers	EHL	70	5	31	36				51																		
	Baltimore Clippers	AHL	5	0	2	2				2											5	1	0	1	2			
1965-66	Baltimore Clippers	AHL	37	2	8	10				6																		
	Minnesota Rangers	CHL	30	0	6	6				0																		
1966-67	Omaha Knights	CHL	10	0	4	4				6																		
	Vancouver Canucks	WHL	62	8	22	30				18											8	1	3	4	0			
1967-68	Memphis South Stars	CHL	18	5	5	10				24																		
	Vancouver Canucks	WHL	17	2	6	8				4																		
	Rochester Americans	AHL	24	1	1	2				0																		
1968-69	Vancouver Canucks	WHL	22	1	2	3				6																		
	Rochester Americans	AHL	45	4	15	19				10																		
1969-70	Rochester Americans	AHL	69	9	35	44				51																		
1970-71	**Vancouver Canucks**	**NHL**	**1**	**0**	**0**	**0**	**0**	**0**	**0**	**0**	**0**	**0**	**0**	**0**	**0.0**	**0**	**0**	**1**	**0**	**–1**								
	Rochester Americans	AHL	71	5	33	38				38																		
1971-72	Rochester Americans	AHL	71	4	29	33				69																		
1972-73	New York Raiders	WHA	78	5	53	58				43																		
1973-74	New York-New Jersey	WHA	74	3	43	46				22																		
1974-75	San Diego Mariners	WHA	36	1	11	12				12																		
	Indianapolis Racers	WHA	37	0	17	17				18																		
1975-76	Indianapolis Racers	WHA	79	1	25	26				28											7	0	4	4	2			
1976-77	Indianapolis Racers	WHA	52	3	10	13				25											9	0	2	2	6			
1977-78	Indianapolis Racers	WHA	77	1	25	26				34																		
1978-79	Indianapolis Racers	WHA	22	2	3	5				10																		
	NHL Totals		**1**	**0**	**0**	**0**	**0**	**0**	**0**	**0**	**0**	**0**	**0**	**0**	**0.0**	**0**	**0**	**1**	**0**									
	Other Major League Totals		433	14	184	198				182											16	0	6	6	8			

Claimed by **LA Kings** from **NY Rangers** in Expansion Draft, June 6, 1967. Traded to **Toronto** by **LA Kings** for rights to Red Kelly, June 8, 1967. NHL rights transferred to **Vancouver** when owners of **Vancouver** (WHL) club awarded NHL expansion franchise, May 20, 1970. Selected by **NY Raiders** (WHA) in 1972 WHA General Player Draft, February 13, 1972. Transferred to **San Diego** (WHA) after **New York-New Jersey** (WHA) franchise relocated, April 30, 1974. Traded to **Indianapolis** (WHA) by **San Diego** (WHA) for Jim Hargreaves, January , 1975.

• BLOEMBERG, JEFF

Jeff Bloemberg D – R. 6'2", 205 lbs. b: Listowel, Ont., 1/31/1968. NY Rangers' 5th choice, 93rd overall, in 1986 Entry Draft.

			REGULAR SEASON																		PLAYOFFS							
Season	Club	League	GP	G	A	Pts	AG	AA	APts	PIM	PP	SH	GW	S	%	TGF	PGF	TGA	PGA	+/–	GP	G	A	Pts	PIM	PP	SH	GW
1984-85	Listowel Cyclones	OJHL	31	7	14	21	....	....	....	....	....	....	....	....	....	....	....	....	....	....	....	....	....	....	....	....	....	....
1985-86	North Bay Centennials	OHL	60	2	11	13	....	....	....	76	....	....	....	....	....	....	....	....	....	....	8	1	2	3	9	....	....	....
1986-87	North Bay Centennials	OHL	60	5	13	18	....	....	....	91	....	....	....	....	....	....	....	....	....	....	21	1	6	7	13	....	....	....
1987-88	North Bay Centennials	OHL	46	9	26	35	....	....	....	60	....	....	....	....	....	....	....	....	....	....	4	1	4	5	2	....	....	....
	Colorado Rangers	IHL	5	0	0	0	....	....	....	0	....	....	....	....	....	....	....	....	....	....	11	1	0	1	8	....	....	....
1988-89	**New York Rangers**	**NHL**	**9**	**0**	**0**	**0**	**0**	**0**	**0**	**0**	**0**	**0**	**0**	**9**	**0.0**	**6**	**0**	**6**	**2**	**+2**	....	....	....	....	....	....	....	....
	Denver Rangers	IHL	64	7	22	29	....	....	....	55	....	....	....	....	....	....	....	....	....	....	1	0	0	0	0	....	....	....
1989-90	**New York Rangers**	**NHL**	**28**	**3**	**3**	**6**	**3**	**2**	**5**	**25**	**2**	**0**	**1**	**20**	**15.0**	**21**	**8**	**33**	**12**	**–8**	**7**	**0**	**3**	**3**	**5**	**0**	**0**	**0**
	Flint Spirits	IHL	41	7	14	21	....	....	....	24	....	....	....	....	....	....	....	....	....	....	....	....	....	....	....	....	....	....
1990-91	**New York Rangers**	**NHL**	**3**	**0**	**2**	**2**	**0**	**2**	**2**	**0**	**0**	**0**	**0**	**4**	**0.0**	**5**	**2**	**0**	**0**	**+3**	....	....	....	....	....	....	....	....
	Binghamton Rangers	AHL	77	16	46	62	....	....	....	28	....	....	....	....	....	....	....	....	....	....	10	0	6	6	10	....	....	....
1991-92	**New York Rangers**	**NHL**	**3**	**0**	**1**	**1**	**0**	**1**	**1**	**0**	**0**	**0**	**0**	**5**	**0.0**	**2**	**0**	**1**	**0**	**+1**	....	....	....	....	....	....	....	....
	Binghamton Rangers	AHL	66	6	41	47	....	....	....	22	....	....	....	....	....	....	....	....	....	....	11	1	10	11	10	....	....	....
1992-93	Cape Breton Oilers	AHL	76	6	45	51	....	....	....	34	....	....	....	....	....	....	....	....	....	....	16	5	10	15	10	....	....	....
1993-94	Springfield Indians	AHL	78	8	28	36	....	....	....	36	....	....	....	....	....	....	....	....	....	....	6	0	3	3	8	....	....	....
1994-95	Adirondack Red Wings	AHL	44	5	19	24	....	....	....	10	....	....	....	....	....	....	....	....	....	....	4	0	0	0	0	....	....	....
1995-96	Adirondack Red Wings	AHL	72	10	28	38	....	....	....	32	....	....	....	....	....	....	....	....	....	....	3	0	1	1	4	....	....	....
1996-97	Adirondack Red Wings	AHL	69	5	31	36	....	....	....	24	....	....	....	....	....	....	....	....	....	....	4	0	3	3	2	....	....	....
1997-98	Berlin Capitals	Germany	27	3	7	10	....	....	....	16	....	....	....	....	....	....	....	....	....	....	....	....	....	....	....	....	....	....
	NHL Totals		**43**	**3**	**6**	**9**	**3**	**5**	**8**	**25**	**2**	**0**	**1**	**38**	**7.9**	**34**	**10**	**40**	**14**		**7**	**0**	**3**	**3**	**5**	**0**	**0**	**0**

AHL Second All-Star Team (1991)

Claimed by **Tampa Bay** from **NY Rangers** in Expansion Draft, June 18, 1992. Traded to **Edmonton** by **Tampa Bay** for future considerations, September 25, 1992. Signed as a free agent by **Hartford**, August 9, 1993. Signed as a free agent by **Detroit**, May 9, 1995.

• BLOMQVIST, TIMO

Timo Blomqvist D – R. 6', 200 lbs. b: Helsinki, Finland, 1/23/1961. Washington's 4th choice, 89th overall, in 1980 Entry Draft.

1977-78	Jokerit Helsinki	Finland	22	1	0	1	....	....	....	2	....	....	....	....	....	....	....	....	....	....	....	....	....	....	....	....	....	....
1978-79	Jokerit Helsinki	Finland	36	4	2	6	....	....	....	35	....	....	....	....	....	....	....	....	....	....	....	....	....	....	....	....	....	....
	Finland	WJC-A	6	1	1	2	....	....	....	34	....	....	....	....	....	....	....	....	....	....	....	....	....	....	....	....	....	....
1979-80	Jokerit Helsinki	Finland	32	3	1	4	....	....	....	52	....	....	....	....	....	....	....	....	....	....	....	....	....	....	....	....	....	....
	Finland	WJC-A	5	2	0	2	....	....	....	2	....	....	....	....	....	....	....	....	....	....	....	....	....	....	....	....	....	....
1980-81	Kiekkoreipas	Finland	30	6	7	13	....	....	....	14	....	....	....	....	....	....	....	....	....	....	....	....	....	....	....	....	....	....
	Finland	WJC-A	5	1	3	4	....	....	....	14	....	....	....	....	....	....	....	....	....	....	....	....	....	....	....	....	....	....
1981-82	**Washington Capitals**	**NHL**	**44**	**1**	**11**	**12**	**1**	**7**	**8**	**62**	**0**	**0**	**0**	**53**	**1.9**	**36**	**9**	**50**	**6**	**–17**	....	....	....	....	....	....	....	....
	Hershey Bears	AHL	13	0	8	8	....	....	....	14	....	....	....	....	....	....	....	....	....	....	....	....	....	....	....	....	....	....
1982-83	**Washington Capitals**	**NHL**	**61**	**1**	**17**	**18**	**1**	**12**	**13**	**67**	**1**	**0**	**1**	**70**	**1.4**	**85**	**13**	**68**	**11**	**+15**	**3**	**0**	**0**	**0**	**16**	**0**	**0**	**0**
	Hershey Bears	AHL	8	2	7	9	....	....	....	16	....	....	....	....	....	....	....	....	....	....	....	....	....	....	....	....	....	....
1983-84	**Washington Capitals**	**NHL**	**65**	**1**	**19**	**20**	**1**	**13**	**14**	**84**	**0**	**0**	**0**	**69**	**1.4**	**63**	**4**	**51**	**9**	**+17**	**8**	**0**	**0**	**0**	**8**	**0**	**0**	**0**
1984-85	**Washington Capitals**	**NHL**	**53**	**1**	**4**	**5**	**1**	**3**	**4**	**51**	**0**	**0**	**0**	**59**	**1.7**	**42**	**0**	**39**	**8**	**+11**	**2**	**0**	**0**	**0**	**0**	**0**	**0**	**0**
	Finland	WEC-A	9	0	3	3	....	....	....	6	....	....	....	....	....	....	....	....	....	....	....	....	....	....	....	....	....	....
1985-86	Binghamton Whalers	AHL	71	6	18	24	....	....	....	76	....	....	....	....	....	....	....	....	....	....	6	0	4	4	6	....	....	....
1986-87	**New Jersey Devils**	**NHL**	**20**	**0**	**2**	**2**	**0**	**1**	**1**	**29**	**0**	**0**	**0**	**16**	**0.0**	**19**	**3**	**27**	**8**	**–3**	....	....	....	....	....	....	....	....
1987-88	Finland	C Cup	4	0	0	0	....	....	....	0	....	....	....	....	....	....	....	....	....	....	....	....	....	....	....	....	....	....
	MoDo	Sweden	36	6	10	16	....	....	....	64	....	....	....	....	....	....	....	....	....	....	4	0	2	2	10	....	....	....
	Finland	Olympics	8	1	1	2	....	....	....	10	....	....	....	....	....	....	....	....	....	....	....	....	....	....	....	....	....	....
1988-89	MoDo	Sweden	39	4	8	12	....	....	....	92	....	....	....	....	....	....	....	....	....	....	....	....	....	....	....	....	....	....
	Finland	WEC-A	7	0	1	1	....	....	....	8	....	....	....	....	....	....	....	....	....	....	....	....	....	....	....	....	....	....
1989-90	MoDo	Sweden	14	2	3	5	....	....	....	36	....	....	....	....	....	....	....	....	....	....	....	....	....	....	....	....	....	....
1990-91	Malmo IF	Sweden	40	5	3	8	....	....	....	59	....	....	....	....	....	....	....	....	....	....	2	0	0	0	2	....	....	....
1991-92	Malmo IF	Sweden	39	5	8	13	....	....	....	36	....	....	....	....	....	....	....	....	....	....	10	0	2	2	8	....	....	....
	Finland	Olympics	8	0	1	1	....	....	....	8	....	....	....	....	....	....	....	....	....	....	....	....	....	....	....	....	....	....
1992-93	Malmo IF	Sweden	35	2	4	6	....	....	....	46	....	....	....	....	....	....	....	....	....	....	6	0	0	0	4	....	....	....
1993-94	Sparta Sarpsborg	Norway	30	3	12	15	....	....	....	63	....	....	....	....	....	....	....	....	....	....	2	0	0	0	6	....	....	....
1994-95	Kiekko-Espoo	Finland	34	6	4	10	....	....	....	46	....	....	....	....	....	....	....	....	....	....	4	0	1	1	6	....	....	....
1995-96	Kiekko-Espoo	Finland	48	4	4	8	....	....	....	68	....	....	....	....	....	....	....	....	....	....	....	....	....	....	....	....	....	....
1996-97	WEV Wien	Austria	37	2	7	9	....	....	....	84	....	....	....	....	....	....	....	....	....	....	....	....	....	....	....	....	....	....
	NHL Totals		**243**	**4**	**53**	**57**	**4**	**36**	**40**	**293**	**1**	**0**	**1**	**267**	**1.5**	**245**	**29**	**235**	**42**		**13**	**0**	**0**	**0**	**24**	**0**	**0**	**0**

EJC-A All-Star Team (1978, 1979) • Named Best Defenseman at EJC-A (1979)

Signed as a free agent by **New Jersey**, July 2, 1986.

• BLOMSTEN, ARTO

Arto Blomsten D – L. 6'3", 210 lbs. b: Vaasa, Finland, 3/16/1965. Winnipeg's 11th choice, 239th overall, in 1986 Entry Draft.

1983-84	Djurgarden IF Stockholm	Sweden	3	0	0	0	....	....	....	4	....	....	....	....	....	....	....	....	....	....	....	....	....	....	....	....	....	....
1984-85	Djurgarden IF Stockholm	Sweden	19	3	1	4	....	....	....	22	....	....	....	....	....	....	....	....	....	....	8	0	0	0	8	....	....	....
	Sweden	WJC-A	6	0	0	0	....	....	....	6	....	....	....	....	....	....	....	....	....	....	....	....	....	....	....	....	....	....
1985-86	Djurgarden IF Stockholm	Sweden	8	0	3	3	....	....	....	6	....	....	....	....	....	....	....	....	....	....	....	....	....	....	....	....	....	....
1986-87	Djurgarden IF Stockholm	Sweden	29	2	4	6	....	....	....	28	....	....	....	....	....	....	....	....	....	....	....	....	....	....	....	....	....	....
1987-88	Djurgarden IF Stockholm	Sweden	39	12	6	18	....	....	....	36	....	....	....	....	....	....	....	....	....	....	2	1	0	1	0	....	....	....
1988-89	Djurgarden IF Stockholm	Sweden	40	10	9	19	....	....	....	38	....	....	....	....	....	....	....	....	....	....	....	....	....	....	....	....	....	....
1989-90	Djurgarden IF Stockholm	Sweden	36	5	21	26	....	....	....	28	....	....	....	....	....	....	....	....	....	....	8	0	1	1	6	....	....	....
1990-91	Djurgarden IF Stockholm	Sweden	38	2	9	11	....	....	....	38	....	....	....	....	....	....	....	....	....	....	7	2	1	3	12	....	....	....
1991-92	Djurgarden IF Stockholm	Sweden	39	6	8	14	....	....	....	34	....	....	....	....	....	....	....	....	....	....	10	2	0	2	8	....	....	....
	Sweden	WC-A	8	4	0	4	....	....	....	6	....	....	....	....	....	....	....	....	....	....	....	....	....	....	....	....	....	....
1992-93	Djurgarden IF Stockholm	Sweden	40	4	16	20	....	....	....	52	....	....	....	....	....	....	....	....	....	....	....	....	....	....	....	....	....	....
	Sweden	WC-A	8	0	0	0	....	....	....	16	....	....	....	....	....	....	....	....	....	....	....	....	....	....	....	....	....	....
1993-94	**Winnipeg Jets**	**NHL**	**18**	**0**	**2**	**2**	**0**	**2**	**2**	**6**	**0**	**0**	**0**	**15**	**0.0**	**6**	**1**	**15**	**4**	**–6**	....	....	....	....	....	....	....	....
	Moncton Hawks	AHL	44	6	27	33	....	....	....	25	....	....	....	....	....	....	....	....	....	....	20	4	10	14	8	....	....	....
1994-95	**Winnipeg Jets**	**NHL**	**1**	**0**	**0**	**0**	**0**	**0**	**0**	**2**	**0**	**0**	**0**	**0**	**0.0**	**0**	**0**	**0**	**0**	**0**	....	....	....	....	....	....	....	....
	Springfield Falcons	AHL	27	3	16	19	....	....	....	20	....	....	....	....	....	....	....	....	....	....	....	....	....	....	....	....	....	....
	Los Angeles Kings	**NHL**	**4**	**0**	**1**	**1**	**0**	**1**	**1**	**0**	**0**	**0**	**0**	**1**	**0.0**	**3**	**0**	**2**	**1**	**+2**	....	....	....	....	....	....	....	....
	Phoenix Roadrunners	IHL	2	1	2	3	....	....	....	0	....	....	....	....	....	....	....	....	....	....	8	3	6	9	6	....	....	....
1995-96	**Los Angeles Kings**	**NHL**	**2**	**0**	**1**	**1**	**0**	**1**	**1**	**0**	**0**	**0**	**0**	**1**	**0.0**	**2**	**0**	**2**	**1**	**+1**	....	....	....	....	....	....	....	....
	Phoenix Roadrunners	IHL	47	4	15	19	....	....	....	10	....	....	....	....	....	....	....	....	....	....	4	0	4	4	2	....	....	....
1996-97	Vastra Frolunda	Sweden	41	4	10	14	....	....	....	45	....	....	....	....	....	....	....	....	....	....	3	0	0	0	0	....	....	....
1997-98	Vastra Frolunda	Sweden	24	3	1	4	....	....	....	18	....	....	....	....	....	....	....	....	....	....	7	0	0	0	10	....	....	....
	NHL Totals		**25**	**0**	**4**	**4**	**0**	**4**	**4**	**8**	**0**	**0**	**0**	**17**	**0.0**	**11**	**1**	**19**	**6**		....	....	....	....	....	....	....	....

Traded to **LA Kings** by **Winnipeg** for LA Kings' 8th round choice (Frederik Loven) in 1995 Entry Draft, March 27, 1995.

• BLOOM, MIKE

Mike Bloom LW – L. 6'3", 206 lbs. b: Ottawa, Ont., 4/12/1952. Boston's 1st choice, 16th overall, in 1972 Amateur Draft.

1969-70	St. Catharines Black Hawks	OHA	42	20	14	34	....	....	....	94	....	....	....	....	....	....	....	....	....	....	....	....	....	....	....	....	....	....
1970-71	St. Catharines Black Hawks	OHA	58	20	33	53	....	....	....	117	....	....	....	....	....	....	....	....	....	....	....	....	....	....	....	....	....	....
1971-72	St. Catharines Black Hawks	OHA	50	25	40	65	....	....	....	116	....	....	....	....	....	....	....	....	....	....	....	....	....	....	....	....	....	....
1972-73	Boston Braves	AHL	32	4	5	9	....	....	....	41	....	....	....	....	....	....	....	....	....	....	....	....	....	....	....	....	....	....
	San Diego Gulls	WHL	39	14	15	29	....	....	....	54	....	....	....	....	....	....	....	....	....	....	6	2	1	3	19	....	....	....
1973-74	San Diego Gulls	WHL	76	25	44	69	....	....	....	108	....	....	....	....	....	....	....	....	....	....	4	1	3	4	7	....	....	....
1974-75	**Washington Capitals**	**NHL**	**67**	**7**	**19**	**26**	**6**	**15**	**21**	**84**	**0**	**0**	**0**	**88**	**8.0**	**39**	**7**	**86**	**0**	**–54**	....	....	....	....	....	....	....	....
	Detroit Red Wings	**NHL**	**13**	**4**	**8**	**12**	**4**	**6**	**10**	**10**	**1**	**0**	**1**	**20**	**20.0**	**19**	**1**	**17**	**1**	**+2**	....	....	....	....	....	....	....	....
1975-76	**Detroit Red Wings**	**NHL**	**76**	**13**	**17**	**30**	**12**	**13**	**25**	**99**	**1**	**0**	**1**	**130**	**10.0**	**39**	**5**	**58**	**5**	**–19**	....	....	....	....	....	....	....	....
1976-77	**Detroit Red Wings**	**NHL**	**45**	**6**	**3**	**9**	**6**	**2**	**8**	**22**	**0**	**0**	**0**	**40**	**15.0**	**13**	**0**	**23**	**0**	**–10**	....	....	....	....	....	....	....	....
	Rhode Island Reds	AHL	12	8	2	10	....	....	....	12	....	....	....	....	....	....	....	....	....	....	....	....	....	....	....	....	....	....
	Kansas City Blues	CHL	21	14	13	27	....	....	....	33	....	....	....	....	....	....	....	....	....	....	10	2	5	7	14	....	....	....

Season	Club	League	REGULAR SEASON																	PLAYOFFS							
			GP	G	A	Pts	AG	AA	APts	PIM	PP	SH	GW	S	%	TGF	PGF	TGA	PGA	+/-	GP	G	A	Pts	PIM	PP	SH	GW
1977-78	Kansas City Red Wings	CHL	76	23	54	77	....	....	....	155	....	....	....	....	....	....	....	....	....	....	....	....	....	....	....	....	....	....
1978-79	San Diego Hawks	PHL	52	25	27	52	....	....	....	60	....	....	....	....	....	....	....	....	....	....	....	....	....	....	....	....	....	....
1979-80	Rheem Racers	Neth.	14	4	9	13	....	....	....	....	....	....	....	....	....	....	....	....	....	....	....	....	....	....	....	....	....	....
	NHL Totals		**201**	**30**	**47**	**77**	**28**	**36**	**64**	**215**	**2**	**0**	**2**	**278**	**10.8**	**110**	**13**	**184**	**6**		....	....	....	....	....	....	....	....

Claimed by **Washington** from **Boston** in Expansion Draft, June 12, 1974. Traded to **Detroit** by **Washington** for Blair Stewart, March 9, 1975.

• BLOUIN, SYLVAIN

Sylvain Blouin LW – L. 6'2", 207 lbs. b: Montreal, Que., 5/21/1974. NY Rangers' 5th choice, 104th overall, in 1994 Entry Draft.

Season	Club	League	GP	G	A	Pts	AG	AA	APts	PIM	PP	SH	GW	S	%	TGF	PGF	TGA	PGA	+/-	GP	G	A	Pts	PIM	PP	SH	GW
1991-92	Laval Titan	QMJHL	28	0	0	0	....	....	....	23	....	....	....	....	....	....	....	....	....	....	9	0	0	0	35	....	....	....
1992-93	Laval Titan	QMJHL	68	0	10	10	....	....	....	373	....	....	....	....	....	....	....	....	....	....	13	1	0	1	*66	....	....	....
1993-94	Laval Titan	QMJHL	62	18	22	40	....	....	....	*492	....	....	....	....	....	....	....	....	....	....	21	4	13	17	*177	....	....	....
1994-95	Chicago Wolves	IHL	1	0	0	0	....	....	....	2	....	....	....	....	....	....	....	....	....	....	....	....	....	....	....	....	....	....
	Charlotte Checkers	ECHL	50	5	7	12	....	....	....	280	....	....	....	....	....	....	....	....	....	....	3	0	0	0	6	....	....	....
	Binghamton Rangers	AHL	10	1	0	1	....	....	....	46	....	....	....	....	....	....	....	....	....	....	2	0	0	0	24	....	....	....
1995-96	Binghamton Rangers	AHL	71	5	8	13	....	....	....	*352	....	....	....	....	....	....	....	....	....	....	4	0	3	3	4	....	....	....
1996-97	**New York Rangers**	**NHL**	**6**	**0**	**0**	**0**	**0**	**0**	**0**	**18**	**0**	**0**	**0**	**1**	**0.0**	**0**	**0**	**1**	**0**	**–1**	....	....	....	....	....	....	....	....
	Binghamton Rangers	AHL	62	13	17	30	....	....	....	301	....	....	....	....	....	....	....	....	....	....	4	2	1	3	16	....	....	....
1997-98	**New York Rangers**	**NHL**	**1**	**0**	**0**	**0**	**0**	**0**	**0**	**5**	**0**	**0**	**0**	**0**	**0.0**	**0**	**0**	**0**	**0**	**0**	....	....	....	....	....	....	....	....
	Hartford Wolf Pack	AHL	53	8	9	17	....	....	....	286	....	....	....	....	....	....	....	....	....	....	9	0	1	1	63	....	....	....
	NHL Totals		**7**	**0**	**0**	**0**	**0**	**0**	**0**	**23**	**0**	**0**	**0**	**1**	**0.0**	**0**	**0**	**1**	**0**		....	....	....	....	....	....	....	....

Traded to **Montreal** by **NY Rangers** with NY Rangers' 6th round choice in 1999 Entry Draft for Peter Popovic, June 30, 1998.

• BLUM, JOHN

John Blum D – R. 6'3", 205 lbs. b: Detroit, MI, 10/8/1959.

Season	Club	League	GP	G	A	Pts	AG	AA	APts	PIM	PP	SH	GW	S	%	TGF	PGF	TGA	PGA	+/-	GP	G	A	Pts	PIM	PP	SH	GW
1977-78	University of Michigan	WCHA	7	0	0	0	....	....	....	4	....	....	....	....	....	....	....	....	....	....	....	....	....	....	....	....	....	....
1978-79	University of Michigan	WCHA	35	1	11	12	....	....	....	87	....	....	....	....	....	....	....	....	....	....	....	....	....	....	....	....	....	....
1979-80	University of Michigan	WCHA	37	9	41	50	....	....	....	79	....	....	....	....	....	....	....	....	....	....	....	....	....	....	....	....	....	....
1980-81	University of Michigan	WCHA	38	9	43	52	....	....	....	93	....	....	....	....	....	....	....	....	....	....	....	....	....	....	....	....	....	....
1981-82	Wichita Wind	CHL	78	8	33	41	....	....	....	247	....	....	....	....	....	....	....	....	....	....	7	0	3	3	24	....	....	....
1982-83	**Edmonton Oilers**	**NHL**	**5**	**0**	**3**	**3**	**0**	**2**	**2**	**24**	**0**	**0**	**0**	**0**	**0.0**	**5**	**0**	**3**	**0**	**+2**	....	....	....	....	....	....	....	....
	Moncton Alpines	AHL	76	10	30	40	....	....	....	219	....	....	....	....	....	....	....	....	....	....	....	....	....	....	....	....	....	....
1983-84	**Edmonton Oilers**	**NHL**	**4**	**0**	**1**	**1**	**0**	**1**	**1**	**2**	**0**	**0**	**0**	**3**	**0.0**	**2**	**0**	**2**	**0**	**0**	....	....	....	....	....	....	....	....
	Moncton Alpines	AHL	57	3	22	25	....	....	....	202	....	....	....	....	....	....	....	....	....	....	....	....	....	....	....	....	....	....
	Boston Bruins	**NHL**	**12**	**1**	**1**	**2**	**1**	**1**	**2**	**30**	**0**	**0**	**1**	**9**	**11.1**	**16**	**1**	**11**	**1**	**+5**	**3**	**0**	**0**	**0**	**4**	**0**	**0**	**0**
1984-85	**Boston Bruins**	**NHL**	**75**	**3**	**13**	**16**	**2**	**9**	**11**	**263**	**0**	**0**	**0**	**36**	**8.3**	**56**	**0**	**69**	**13**	**0**	**5**	**0**	**0**	**0**	**13**	**0**	**0**	**0**
1985-86	**Boston Bruins**	**NHL**	**61**	**1**	**7**	**8**	**1**	**5**	**6**	**80**	**0**	**0**	**0**	**34**	**2.9**	**45**	**0**	**65**	**28**	**+8**	**3**	**0**	**0**	**0**	**6**	**0**	**0**	**0**
	Moncton Golden Flames	AHL	12	1	5	6	....	....	....	37	....	....	....	....	....	....	....	....	....	....	....	....	....	....	....	....	....	....
1986-87	**Washington Capitals**	**NHL**	**66**	**2**	**8**	**10**	**2**	**6**	**8**	**133**	**0**	**0**	**0**	**32**	**6.3**	**25**	**0**	**34**	**10**	**+1**	**6**	**0**	**1**	**1**	**4**	**0**	**0**	**0**
1987-88	**Boston Bruins**	**NHL**	**19**	**0**	**1**	**1**	**0**	**1**	**1**	**70**	**0**	**0**	**0**	**6**	**0.0**	**10**	**0**	**17**	**2**	**–5**	**3**	**0**	**1**	**1**	**0**	**0**	**0**	**0**
	Maine Mariners	AHL	43	5	18	23	....	....	....	136	....	....	....	....	....	....	....	....	....	....	8	0	6	6	35	....	....	....
1988-89	**Detroit Red Wings**	**NHL**	**6**	**0**	**0**	**0**	**0**	**0**	**0**	**8**	**0**	**0**	**0**	**3**	**0.0**	**2**	**0**	**5**	**1**	**–2**	....	....	....	....	....	....	....	....
	Adirondack Red Wings	AHL	56	1	19	20	....	....	....	168	....	....	....	....	....	....	....	....	....	....	12	0	1	1	18	....	....	....
1989-90	**Boston Bruins**	**NHL**	**2**	**0**	**0**	**0**	**0**	**0**	**0**	**0**	**0**	**0**	**0**	**0**	**0.0**	**0**	**0**	**2**	**1**	**–1**	....	....	....	....	....	....	....	....
	Maine Mariners	AHL	77	1	20	21	....	....	....	134	....	....	....	....	....	....	....	....	....	....	....	....	....	....	....	....	....	....
1990-91	Maine Mariners	AHL	57	4	8	12	....	....	....	75	....	....	....	....	....	....	....	....	....	....	1	0	0	0	2	....	....	....
1991-92	Capital District Islanders	AHL	51	0	6	6	....	....	....	76	....	....	....	....	....	....	....	....	....	....	1	0	0	0	2	....	....	....
1992-93	Daytona Beach Sun Devils	SunHL	12	0	2	2	....	....	....	67	....	....	....	....	....	....	....	....	....	....	....	....	....	....	....	....	....	....
1993-94			STATISTICS NOT AVAILABLE																									
1994-95	Detroit Falcons	ColHL	71	1	14	15	....	....	....	98	....	....	....	....	....	....	....	....	....	....	12	0	2	2	20	....	....	....
	NHL Totals		**250**	**7**	**34**	**41**	**6**	**25**	**31**	**610**	**0**	**0**	**1**	**123**	**5.7**	**161**	**1**	**208**	**56**		**20**	**0**	**2**	**2**	**27**	**0**	**0**	**0**

WCHA Second All-Star Team (1981)

Signed as a free agent by **Edmonton**, May 5, 1981. Traded to **Boston** by **Edmonton** for Larry Melynk, March 6, 1984. Claimed by **Washington** from **Boston** in Waiver Draft, October 6, 1986. Traded to **Boston** by **Washington** for Boston's 7th round choice (Brad Schlegal) in 1988 Entry Draft, June 1, 1987. Signed as a free agent by **Detroit**, August 12, 1988. Signed as a free agent by **Boston**, July 6, 1989.

• BODAK, BOB

Bob Bodak LW – L. 6'2", 200 lbs. b: Thunder Bay, Ont., 5/28/1961.

Season	Club	League	GP	G	A	Pts	AG	AA	APts	PIM	PP	SH	GW	S	%	TGF	PGF	TGA	PGA	+/-	GP	G	A	Pts	PIM	PP	SH	GW
1983-84	Lakehead University	GPAC	22	23	24	47	....	....	....	18	....	....	....	....	....	....	....	....	....	....	....	....	....	....	....	....	....	....
1984-85	Springfield Indians	AHL	79	20	25	45	....	....	....	52	....	....	....	....	....	....	....	....	....	....	4	1	0	1	2	....	....	....
1985-86	Springfield Indians	AHL	4	0	0	0	....	....	....	4	....	....	....	....	....	....	....	....	....	....	....	....	....	....	....	....	....	....
	Moncton Golden Flames	AHL	58	27	15	42	....	....	....	114	....	....	....	....	....	....	....	....	....	....	10	3	3	6	0	....	....	....
1986-87	Moncton Golden Flames	AHL	48	11	20	31	....	....	....	75	....	....	....	....	....	....	....	....	....	....	6	1	1	2	18	....	....	....
1987-88	**Calgary Flames**	**NHL**	**3**	**0**	**0**	**0**	**0**	**0**	**0**	**22**	**0**	**0**	**0**	**0**	**0.0**	**0**	**0**	**2**	**0**	**–2**	....	....	....	....	....	....	....	....
	Salt Lake Golden Eagles	IHL	44	12	10	22	....	....	....	117	....	....	....	....	....	....	....	....	....	....	18	1	3	4	74	....	....	....
1988-89	Salt Lake Golden Eagles	IHL	4	0	0	0	....	....	....	2	....	....	....	....	....	....	....	....	....	....	....	....	....	....	....	....	....	....
	Binghamton Whalers	AHL	44	15	25	40	....	....	....	135	....	....	....	....	....	....	....	....	....	....	....	....	....	....	....	....	....	....
1989-90	**Hartford Whalers**	**NHL**	**1**	**0**	**0**	**0**	**0**	**0**	**0**	**7**	**0**	**0**	**0**	**1**	**0.0**	**0**	**0**	**0**	**0**	**0**	....	....	....	....	....	....	....	....
	Binghamton Whalers	AHL	79	32	25	57	....	....	....	59	....	....	....	....	....	....	....	....	....	....	....	....	....	....	....	....	....	....
1990-91	Binghamton Rangers	AHL	27	2	11	13	....	....	....	36	....	....	....	....	....	....	....	....	....	....	....	....	....	....	....	....	....	....
	San Diego Gulls	IHL	17	1	5	6	....	....	....	18	....	....	....	....	....	....	....	....	....	....	....	....	....	....	....	....	....	....
	Albany Choppers	IHL	5	1	1	2	....	....	....	13	....	....	....	....	....	....	....	....	....	....	....	....	....	....	....	....	....	....
1991-92	Erie Panthers	ECHL	28	9	11	20	....	....	....	48	....	....	....	....	....	....	....	....	....	....	....	....	....	....	....	....	....	....
	NHL Totals		**4**	**0**	**0**	**0**	**0**	**0**	**0**	**29**	**0**	**0**	**0**	**1**	**0.0**	**0**	**0**	**2**	**0**		....	....	....	....	....	....	....	....

Signed as a free agent by **Calgary**, January 28, 1986. Signed as a free agent by **Hartford**, May 10, 1989.

• BODDY, GREGG

Gregg Boddy D – L. 6'2", 200 lbs. b: Ponoka, Alta., 3/19/1949. Los Angeles' 2nd choice, 27th overall, in 1969 Amateur Draft.

Season	Club	League	GP	G	A	Pts	AG	AA	APts	PIM	PP	SH	GW	S	%	TGF	PGF	TGA	PGA	+/-	GP	G	A	Pts	PIM	PP	SH	GW
1966-67	Edmonton Oil Kings	WCJHL	55	1	5	6	....	....	....	42	....	....	....	....	....	....	....	....	....	....	9	0	1	1	12	....	....	....
1967-68	Edmonton Oil Kings	WCJHL	59	3	14	17	....	....	....	101	....	....	....	....	....	....	....	....	....	....	....	....	....	....	....	....	....	....
1968-69	Edmonton Oil Kings	WCJHL	59	1	21	22	....	....	....	119	....	....	....	....	....	....	....	....	....	....	....	....	....	....	....	....	....	....
1969-70	Springfield Kings	AHL	68	2	9	11	....	....	....	70	....	....	....	....	....	....	....	....	....	....	14	0	3	3	14	....	....	....
1970-71	Montreal Voyageurs	AHL	63	0	17	17	....	....	....	108	....	....	....	....	....	....	....	....	....	....	3	0	0	0	0	....	....	....
1971-72	**Vancouver Canucks**	**NHL**	**40**	**2**	**5**	**7**	**2**	**5**	**7**	**45**	**0**	**0**	**1**	**29**	**6.9**	**28**	**0**	**35**	**9**	**+2**	....	....	....	....	....	....	....	....
	Rochester Americans	AHL	28	2	6	8	....	....	....	77	....	....	....	....	....	....	....	....	....	....	....	....	....	....	....	....	....	....
1972-73	**Vancouver Canucks**	**NHL**	**74**	**3**	**11**	**14**	**3**	**9**	**12**	**70**	**1**	**0**	**0**	**54**	**5.6**	**44**	**4**	**87**	**12**	**–35**	....	....	....	....	....	....	....	....
1973-74	**Vancouver Canucks**	**NHL**	**53**	**2**	**10**	**12**	**2**	**9**	**11**	**59**	**0**	**0**	**1**	**52**	**3.8**	**34**	**3**	**48**	**13**	**–4**	....	....	....	....	....	....	....	....
	Seattle Totems	WHL	4	0	1	1	....	....	....	0	....	....	....	....	....	....	....	....	....	....	....	....	....	....	....	....	....	....
1974-75	**Vancouver Canucks**	**NHL**	**72**	**11**	**12**	**23**	**10**	**9**	**19**	**56**	**2**	**1**	**1**	**83**	**13.3**	**50**	**7**	**63**	**15**	**–5**	**3**	**0**	**0**	**0**	**0**	**0**	**0**	**0**
1975-76	**Vancouver Canucks**	**NHL**	**34**	**5**	**6**	**11**	**5**	**5**	**10**	**33**	**0**	**0**	**1**	**28**	**17.9**	**17**	**2**	**17**	**0**	**–2**	....	....	....	....	....	....	....	....
	Tulsa Oilers	CHL	24	0	9	9	....	....	....	29	....	....	....	....	....	....	....	....	....	....	9	0	2	2	19	....	....	....
1976-77	San Diego Mariners	WHA	18	1	2	3	....	....	....	19	....	....	....	....	....	....	....	....	....	....	....	....	....	....	....	....	....	....
	Edmonton Oilers	WHA	46	1	17	18	....	....	....	41	....	....	....	....	....	....	....	....	....	....	4	1	2	3	14	....	....	....
	NHL Totals		**273**	**23**	**44**	**67**	**22**	**37**	**59**	**263**	**3**	**1**	**4**	**246**	**9.3**	**173**	**16**	**250**	**49**		**3**	**0**	**0**	**0**	**0**	**0**	**0**	**0**
	Other Major League Totals		64	2	19	21	....	....	....	60	....	....	....	....	....	....	....	....	....	....	4	1	2	3	14	....	....	....

Traded to **Montreal** by **LA Kings** with Leon Rochefort and Wayne Thomas for Larry Mickey, Lucien Grenier and Jack Norris, May 22, 1970. Traded to **Vancouver** by **Montreal** for cash and Vancouver's 3rd round choice (Jim Cahoon) in 1971 Amateur Draft, May 25, 1971. Selected by **New England** (WHA) in 1972 WHA General Player Draft, February 12, 1972. WHA rights traded to **San Diego** (WHA) by **New England** (WHA) for cash, September, 1976. Traded to **Edmonton** (WHA) by **San Diego** (WHA) for Larry Hornung, November, 1976.

• BODGER, DOUG

Doug Bodger D – L. 6'2", 210 lbs. b: Chemainus, B.C., 6/18/1966. Pittsburgh's 2nd choice, 9th overall, in 1984 Entry Draft.

Season	Club	League	GP	G	A	Pts	AG	AA	APts	PIM	PP	SH	GW	S	%	TGF	PGF	TGA	PGA	+/-	GP	G	A	Pts	PIM	PP	SH	GW
1982-83	Kamloops Blazers	WHL	72	26	66	92	....	....	....	98	....	....	....	....	....	....	....	....	....	....	7	0	5	5	2	....	....	....
1983-84	Kamloops Blazers	WHL	70	21	77	98	....	....	....	90	....	....	....	....	....	....	....	....	....	....	17	2	15	17	12	....	....	....
1984-85	**Pittsburgh Penguins**	**NHL**	**65**	**5**	**26**	**31**	**4**	**18**	**22**	**67**	**3**	**0**	**1**	**119**	**4.2**	**93**	**23**	**115**	**21**	**–24**	....	....	....	....	....	....	....	....
1985-86	**Pittsburgh Penguins**	**NHL**	**79**	**4**	**33**	**37**	**3**	**22**	**25**	**63**	**1**	**0**	**1**	**140**	**2.9**	**120**	**45**	**108**	**36**	**+3**	....	....	....	....	....	....	....	....

			REGULAR SEASON																		PLAYOFFS							
Season	Club	League	GP	G	A	Pts	AG	AA	APts	PIM	PP	SH	GW	S	%	TGF	PGF	TGA	PGA	+/–	GP	G	A	Pts	PIM	PP	SH	GW
1986-87	**Pittsburgh Penguins**	**NHL**	76	11	38	49	10	28	38	52	5	0	1	176	6.3	118	43	95	26	+6	....	....	....	....	....	....	....	....
	Canada	WEC-A	10	1	1	2	....	....	....	4	....	....	....	....	....	....	....	....	....	....	....	....	....	....	....	....	....	....
1987-88	**Pittsburgh Penguins**	**NHL**	69	14	31	45	12	22	34	103	13	0	1	184	7.6	120	69	108	53	–4	....	....	....	....	....	....	....	....
1988-89	**Pittsburgh Penguins**	**NHL**	10	1	4	5	1	3	4	7	0	0	0	22	4.5	17	8	3	0	+6	....	....	....	....	....	....	....	....
	Buffalo Sabres	**NHL**	61	7	40	47	6	28	34	52	6	0	1	134	5.2	111	47	77	22	+9	5	1	1	2	11	1	0	0
1989-90	**Buffalo Sabres**	**NHL**	71	12	36	48	10	26	36	64	8	0	1	167	7.2	120	56	86	22	0	6	1	5	6	6	0	0	0
1990-91	**Buffalo Sabres**	**NHL**	58	5	23	28	5	17	22	54	2	0	0	139	3.6	92	34	84	18	–8	4	0	1	1	0	0	0	0
1991-92	**Buffalo Sabres**	**NHL**	73	11	35	46	10	26	36	108	4	0	1	180	6.1	142	71	101	31	+1	7	2	1	3	2	2	0	1
1992-93	**Buffalo Sabres**	**NHL**	81	9	45	54	7	31	38	87	6	0	0	154	5.8	158	64	122	42	+14	8	2	3	5	0	2	0	0
1993-94	**Buffalo Sabres**	**NHL**	75	7	32	39	7	25	32	76	5	1	1	144	4.9	110	50	80	28	+8	7	0	3	3	6	0	0	0
1994-95	**Buffalo Sabres**	**NHL**	44	3	17	20	5	25	30	47	2	0	0	87	3.4	50	30	38	15	–3	5	0	4	4	0	0	0	0
1995-96	**Buffalo Sabres**	**NHL**	16	0	5	5	0	4	4	18	0	0	0	27	0.0	16	9	23	10	–6	....	....	....	....	....	....	....	....
	San Jose Sharks	**NHL**	57	4	19	23	4	15	19	50	3	0	0	94	4.3	68	27	85	26	–18	....	....	....	....	....	....	....	....
	Canada	WC-A	8	0	3	3	....	....	....	0	....	....	....	....	....	....	....	....	....	....	....	....	....	....	....	....	....	....
1996-97	**San Jose Sharks**	**NHL**	81	1	15	16	1	13	14	64	0	0	1	96	1.0	66	18	94	32	–14	....	....	....	....	....	....	....	....
1997-98	**San Jose Sharks**	**NHL**	28	4	6	10	5	6	11	32	0	0	1	41	9.8	29	9	33	13	0	....	....	....	....	....	....	....	....
	New Jersey Devils	**NHL**	49	5	5	10	6	5	11	25	3	0	0	55	9.1	31	9	25	2	–1	5	0	0	0	0	0	0	0
	NHL Totals		993	103	410	513	96	314	410	969	61	1	10	1959	5.3	1461	612	1277	397		47	6	18	24	25	5	0	1

WHL Second All-Star Team (1983)

Traded to **Buffalo** by **Pittsburgh** wih Darrin Shannon for Tom Barrasso and Buffalo's 3rd round choice (Joe Dziedzic) in 1990 Entry Draft, November 12, 1988. Traded to **San Jose** by **Buffalo** for an optional 1st round choice in 1996 Entry Draft, Philadelphia's 4th round choice (previously acquired, Buffalo selected Mike Martone) in 1996 Entry Draft, Vaclav Varada and Martin Spanhel, November 16, 1995. Traded to **New Jersey** by **San Jose** with Dody Wood for John MacLean and Ken Sutton, December 7, 1997. Traded to **Los Angeles** by **New Jersey** for Boston's 4th round choice (previously acquired, New Jersey selected Pierre Dagenais) in 1998 Entry Draft, June 18, 1998.

• BOEHM, RON

Ron Boehm LW – L. 5′8″, 160 lbs. b: Saskatoon, Sask., 8/14/1943.

1962-63	Estevan Bruins	SJHL	54	15	31	45	....	....	....	42	....	....	....	....	....	....	....	....	....	....	11	2	5	7	4	....	....	....
1963-64	Estevan Bruins	SJHL	62	36	57	93	....	....	....	80	....	....	....	....	....	....	....	....	....	....	11	7	11	18	18	....	....	....
1964-65	Minneapolis Bruins	CHL	49	12	19	31	....	....	....	42	....	....	....	....	....	....	....	....	....	....	4	0	1	1	2	....	....	....
1965-66	Minnesota Rangers	CHL	70	8	20	28	....	....	....	37	....	....	....	....	....	....	....	....	....	....	7	0	5	5	4	....	....	....
1966-67	Vancouver Canucks	WHL	71	18	24	42	....	....	....	49	....	....	....	....	....	....	....	....	....	....	8	2	0	2	2	....	....	....
1967-68	**Oakland Seals**	**NHL**	16	2	1	3	2	1	3	10	1	0	0	18	11.1	6	1	14	4	–5	....	....	....	....	....	....	....	....
	Vancouver Canucks	WHL	43	5	11	16	....	....	....	34	....	....	....	....	....	....	....	....	....	....	....	....	....	....	....	....	....	....
1968-69	Omaha Knights	CHL	67	12	16	28	....	....	....	41	....	....	....	....	....	....	....	....	....	....	7	3	1	4	7	....	....	....
1969-70	Omaha Knights	CHL	65	18	25	43	....	....	....	55	....	....	....	....	....	....	....	....	....	....	7	1	4	5	2	....	....	....
1970-71	Seattle Totems	WHL	72	10	26	36	....	....	....	39	....	....	....	....	....	....	....	....	....	....	....	....	....	....	....	....	....	....
1971-72	Boston Braves	AHL	74	18	37	55	....	....	....	61	....	....	....	....	....	....	....	....	....	....	9	2	3	5	4	....	....	....
1972-73	Boston Braves	AHL	28	6	16	22	....	....	....	28	....	....	....	....	....	....	....	....	....	....	4	1	0	1	4	....	....	....
1973-74	Boston Braves	AHL	76	18	23	41	....	....	....	60	....	....	....	....	....	....	....	....	....	....	....	....	....	....	....	....	....	....
1974-75	Binghamton Dusters	NAHL	39	9	23	32	....	....	....	61	....	....	....	....	....	....	....	....	....	....	15	3	4	7	4	....	....	....
	NHL Totals		16	2	1	3	2	1	3	10	1	0	0	18	11.1	6	1	14	4		....	....	....	....	....	....	....	....

Won WHL Rookie of the Year Award (1967)

Claimed by **Vancouver** (WHL) from **Boston** in Inter-League Draft, June 9, 1965. Claimed by **Oakland** from **NY Rangers** in Expansion Draft, June 8, 1967. Traded to **NY Rangers** by **Oakland** for cash, September 13, 1968. Claimed by **Cleveland** (AHL) from **NY Rangers** in Reverse Draft, June, 1971. Traded to **Boston** by **Cleveland** (AHL) for cash, June, 1971.

• BOH, RICK

Rick Boh C – R. 5′10″, 185 lbs. b: Kamloops, B.C., 5/18/1964. Minnesota's 2nd choice, 9th overall, in 1987 Supplemental Draft.

1983-84	Colorado College	WCHA	27	1	5	6	....	....	....	12	....	....	....	....	....	....	....	....	....	....	....	....	....	....	....	....	....	....
1984-85	Colorado College	WCHA	38	10	18	28	....	....	....	24	....	....	....	....	....	....	....	....	....	....	....	....	....	....	....	....	....	....
1985-86	Colorado College	WCHA	40	30	29	59	....	....	....	14	....	....	....	....	....	....	....	....	....	....	....	....	....	....	....	....	....	....
1986-87	Colorado College	WCHA	38	22	42	64	....	....	....	37	....	....	....	....	....	....	....	....	....	....	....	....	....	....	....	....	....	....
	Canada	Nat-Team	10	3	3	6	....	....	....	0	....	....	....	....	....	....	....	....	....	....	....	....	....	....	....	....	....	....
1987-88	**Minnesota North Stars**	**NHL**	8	2	1	3	2	1	3	4	0	0	0	8	25.0	5	0	4	0	+1	....	....	....	....	....	....	....	....
	Kalamazoo Wings	IHL	75	26	41	67	....	....	....	45	....	....	....	....	....	....	....	....	....	....	7	2	1	3	5	....	....	....
1988-89	HC Fiemme	Italy	31	29	37	66	....	....	....	34	....	....	....	....	....	....	....	....	....	....	....	....	....	....	....	....	....	....
	NHL Totals		8	2	1	3	2	1	3	4	0	0	0	8	25.0	5	0	4	0		....	....	....	....	....	....	....	....

WCHA Second All-Star Team (1987)

• BOHONOS, LONNY

Lonny Bohonos RW – R. 5′11″, 190 lbs. b: Winnipeg, Man., 5/20/1973.

1991-92	Moose Jaw Canucks	WHL	8	1	1	2	....	....	....	0	....	....	....	....	....	....	....	....	....	....	....	....	....	....	....	....	....	....
1992-93	Seattle Breakers	WHL	46	13	13	26	....	....	....	27	....	....	....	....	....	....	....	....	....	....	....	....	....	....	....	....	....	....
	Portland Winter Hawks	WHL	27	20	17	37	....	....	....	16	....	....	....	....	....	....	....	....	....	....	15	8	13	21	19	....	....	....
1993-94	Portland Winter Hawks	WHL	70	*62	*90	*152	....	....	....	80	....	....	....	....	....	....	....	....	....	....	10	8	11	19	13	....	....	....
1994-95	Syracuse Crunch	AHL	67	30	45	75	....	....	....	71	....	....	....	....	....	....	....	....	....	....	....	....	....	....	....	....	....	....
1995-96	**Vancouver Canucks**	**NHL**	3	0	1	1	0	1	1	0	0	0	0	3	0.0	1	0	0	0	+1	....	....	....	....	....	....	....	....
	Syracuse Crunch	AHL	74	40	39	79	....	....	....	82	....	....	....	....	....	....	....	....	....	....	16	14	8	22	16	....	....	....
1996-97	**Vancouver Canucks**	**NHL**	36	11	11	22	12	10	22	10	2	0	1	67	16.4	28	9	22	0	–3	....	....	....	....	....	....	....	....
	Syracuse Crunch	AHL	41	22	30	52	....	....	....	28	....	....	....	....	....	....	....	....	....	....	3	2	2	4	4	....	....	....
1997-98	**Vancouver Canucks**	**NHL**	31	2	1	3	2	1	3	4	0	0	0	37	5.4	3	0	12	0	–9	....	....	....	....	....	....	....	....
	Syracuse Crunch	AHL	17	12	12	24	....	....	....	8	....	....	....	....	....	....	....	....	....	....	....	....	....	....	....	....	....	....
	Toronto Maple Leafs	**NHL**	6	3	3	6	4	3	7	4	0	0	0	13	23.1	7	1	5	0	+1	....	....	....	....	....	....	....	....
	St. John's Maple Leafs	AHL	11	7	9	16	....	....	....	10	....	....	....	....	....	....	....	....	....	....	2	1	1	2	2	....	....	....
	NHL Totals		76	16	16	32	18	15	33	18	2	0	1	120	13.3	39	10	39	0		....	....	....	....	....	....	....	....

WHL West First All-Star Team (1994) • Canadian Major Junior First All-Star Team (1994)

Signed as a free agent by **Vancouver**, May 31, 1994. Traded to **Toronto** by **Vancouver** for Brandon Convery, March 7, 1998.

• BOILEAU, PATRICK

Patrick Boileau D – R. 6′, 190 lbs. b: Montreal, Que., 2/22/1975. Washington's 3rd choice, 69th overall, in 1993 Entry Draft.

1992-93	Laval Titan	QMJHL	69	4	19	23	....	....	....	73	....	....	....	....	....	....	....	....	....	....	13	1	2	3	10	....	....	....
1993-94	Laval Titan	QMJHL	64	13	57	70	....	....	....	56	....	....	....	....	....	....	....	....	....	....	21	1	7	8	24	....	....	....
1994-95	Laval Titan	QMJHL	38	8	25	33	....	....	....	46	....	....	....	....	....	....	....	....	....	....	20	4	16	20	24	....	....	....
1995-96	Portland Pirates	AHL	78	10	28	38	....	....	....	41	....	....	....	....	....	....	....	....	....	....	19	1	3	4	12	....	....	....
1996-97	**Washington Capitals**	**NHL**	1	0	0	0	0	0	0	0	0	0	0	0	0.0	0	0	0	0	0	....	....	....	....	....	....	....	....
	Portland Pirates	AHL	67	16	28	44	....	....	....	63	....	....	....	....	....	....	....	....	....	....	5	1	1	2	4	....	....	....
1997-98	Portland Pirates	AHL	47	6	21	27	....	....	....	53	....	....	....	....	....	....	....	....	....	....	10	0	1	1	8	....	....	....
	NHL Totals		1	0	0	0	0	0	0	0	0	0	0	0	0.0	0	0	0	0		....	....	....	....	....	....	....	....

• BOIMISTRUCK, FRED

Fred Boimistruck D – R. 5′11″, 190 lbs. b: Sudbury, Ont., 1/14/1962. Toronto's 3rd choice, 43rd overall, in 1980 Entry Draft.

1979-80	Cornwall Royals	QMJHL	70	12	34	46	....	....	....	99	....	....	....	....	....	....	....	....	....	....	11	0	8	8	6	....	....	....
1980-81	Cornwall Royals	QMJHL	68	22	48	70	....	....	....	158	....	....	....	....	....	....	....	....	....	....	18	4	11	15	61	....	....	....
	Canada	WJC-A	5	3	0	3	....	....	....	8	....	....	....	....	....	....	....	....	....	....	....	....	....	....	....	....	....	....
1981-82	**Toronto Maple Leafs**	**NHL**	57	2	11	13	2	7	9	32	0	0	1	48	4.2	67	1	70	13	+9	....	....	....	....	....	....	....	....
1982-83	**Toronto Maple Leafs**	**NHL**	26	2	3	5	2	2	4	13	0	0	0	26	7.7	28	3	35	7	–3	....	....	....	....	....	....	....	....
	St. Catharines Saints	AHL	50	6	23	29	....	....	....	32	....	....	....	....	....	....	....	....	....	....	....	....	....	....	....	....	....	....
1983-84	St. Catharines Saints	AHL	80	2	28	30	....	....	....	68	....	....	....	....	....	....	....	....	....	....	7	1	0	1	19	....	....	....
1984-85	Fort Wayne Komets	IHL	2	0	1	1	....	....	....	5	....	....	....	....	....	....	....	....	....	....	....	....	....	....	....	....	....	....
	HC Langnau	Switz.	6	1	2	3	....	....	....	....	....	....	....	....	....	....	....	....	....	....	....	....	....	....	....	....	....	....
	NHL Totals		83	4	14	18	4	9	13	45	0	0	1	74	5.4	95	4	105	20		....	....	....	....	....	....	....	....

QMJHL First All-Star Team (1981)

• BOISVERT, SERGE
Serge Boisvert RW – R. 5'9", 172 lbs. b: Drummondville, Que., 6/1/1959.

			REGULAR SEASON																		PLAYOFFS							
Season	Club	League	GP	G	A	Pts	AG	AA	APts	PIM	PP	SH	GW	S	%	TGF	PGF	TGA	PGA	+/-	GP	G	A	Pts	PIM	PP	SH	GW
1977-78	Sherbrooke Castors	QMJHL	55	17	33	50	....	....	....	19	....	....	....	....	....	....	....	....	....	....	10	2	2	4	2	....	....	....
1978-79	Sherbrooke Castors	QMJHL	72	50	72	122	....	....	....	45	....	....	....	....	....	....	....	....	....	....	12	11	17	28	2	....	....	....
1979-80	Sherbrooke Castors	QMJHL	70	52	72	124	....	....	....	47	....	....	....	....	....	....	....	....	....	....	15	14	18	32	4	....	....	....
1980-81	New Brunswick Hawks	AHL	60	19	27	46	....	....	....	31	....	....	....	....	....	....	....	....	....	....	5	0	0	0	2	....	....	....
1981-82	Yukisirushi	Japan	30	29	20	49	....	....	....	....	....	....	....	....	....	....	....	....	....	....	....	....	....	....	....	....	....	....
1982-83	**Toronto Maple Leafs**	**NHL**	**17**	**0**	**2**	**2**	**0**	**1**	**1**	**4**	**0**	**0**	**0**	**18**	**0.0**	**4**	**0**	**14**	**0**	**–10**	....	....	....	....	....	....	....	....
	St. Catharines Saints	AHL	19	10	9	19	....	....	....	2	....	....	....	....	....	....	....	....	....	....	....	....	....	....	....	....	....	....
	Moncton Alpines	AHL	29	6	12	18	....	....	....	7	....	....	....	....	....	....	....	....	....	....	....	....	....	....	....	....	....	....
1983-84	Moncton Alpines	AHL	66	15	13	28	....	....	....	34	....	....	....	....	....	....	....	....	....	....	....	....	....	....	....	....	....	....
1984-85	**Montreal Canadiens**	**NHL**	**14**	**2**	**2**	**4**	**2**	**1**	**3**	**0**	**0**	**0**	**0**	**18**	**11.1**	**7**	**1**	**9**	**0**	**–3**	**12**	**3**	**5**	**8**	**2**	**1**	**0**	**0**
	Sherbrooke Canadiens	AHL	63	38	41	79	....	....	....	8	....	....	....	....	....	....	....	....	....	....	10	1	9	10	12	....	....	....
1985-86	**Montreal Canadiens**	**NHL**	**9**	**2**	**2**	**4**	**2**	**1**	**3**	**2**	**0**	**0**	**0**	**18**	**11.1**	**5**	**0**	**7**	**3**	**+1**	**8**	**0**	**1**	**1**	**0**	**0**	**0**	**0**
	Sherbrooke Canadiens	AHL	69	40	48	88	....	....	....	18	....	....	....	....	....	....	....	....	....	....	....	....	....	....	....	....	....	....
1986-87	**Montreal Canadiens**	**NHL**	**1**	**0**	**0**	**0**	**0**	**0**	**0**	**0**	**0**	**0**	**0**	**0**	**0.0**	**0**	**0**	**0**	**0**	**0**	....	....	....	....	....	....	....	....
	Sherbrooke Canadiens	AHL	78	27	54	81	....	....	....	29	....	....	....	....	....	....	....	....	....	....	15	8	10	18	15	....	....	....
1987-88	**Montreal Canadiens**	**NHL**	**5**	**1**	**1**	**2**	**1**	**1**	**2**	**2**	**0**	**0**	**0**	**5**	**20.0**	**3**	**0**	**3**	**0**	**0**	**3**	**0**	**1**	**1**	**2**	**0**	**0**	**0**
	Canada	Nat-Team	63	22	26	48	....	....	....	34	....	....	....	....	....	....	....	....	....	....	....	....	....	....	....	....	....	....
	Canada	Olympics	8	7	2	9	....	....	....	2	....	....	....	....	....	....	....	....	....	....	....	....	....	....	....	....	....	....
1988-89	HC Davos	Switz.	36	20	14	34	....	....	....	....	....	....	....	....	....	....	....	....	....	....	....	6	7	13	....	....	....	....
1989-90	Canada	Nat-Team	5	1	0	1	....	....	....	0	....	....	....	....	....	....	....	....	....	....	....	....	....	....	....	....	....	....
	Vastra Frolunda	Sweden	39	18	14	32	....	....	....	24	....	....	....	....	....	....	....	....	....	....	....	....	....	....	....	....	....	....
1990-91	Vastra Frolunda	Sweden	22	4	4	8	....	....	....	10	....	....	....	....	....	....	....	....	....	....	....	....	....	....	....	....	....	....
1991-92	Vastra Frolunda	Sweden	40	12	16	28	....	....	....	30	....	....	....	....	....	....	....	....	....	....	....	....	....	....	....	....	....	....
1992-93	Vastra Frolunda	Sweden	20	6	6	12	....	....	....	44	....	....	....	....	....	....	....	....	....	....	....	....	....	....	....	....	....	....
1993-94	Vastra Frolunda	Sweden	36	6	9	15	....	....	....	26	....	....	....	....	....	....	....	....	....	....	4	1	1	2	....	....	....	....
1994-95	Spektrum Flyers Oslo	Neth.	27	15	17	32	....	....	....	24	....	....	....	....	....	....	....	....	....	....	....	....	....	....	....	....	....	....
1995-96	Spektrum Flyers Oslo	Neth.	28	25	23	48	....	....	....	....	....	....	....	....	....	....	....	....	....	....	....	....	....	....	....	....	....	....
	NHL Totals		**46**	**5**	**7**	**12**	**5**	**4**	**9**	**8**	**0**	**0**	**0**	**59**	**8.5**	**19**	**1**	**33**	**3**		**23**	**3**	**7**	**10**	**4**	**1**	**0**	**0**

AHL Second All-Star Team (1986, 1987)

Signed as a free agent by **Toronto**, October 9, 1980. Traded to **Edmonton** by **Toronto** for Reid Bailey, January 15, 1983. Signed as a free agent by **Montreal**, February 8, 1985.

• BOIVIN, CLAUDE
Claude Boivin LW – L. 6'2", 200 lbs. b: Ste. Foy, Que., 3/1/1970. Philadelphia's 1st choice, 14th overall, in 1988 Entry Draft.

Season	Club	League	GP	G	A	Pts	AG	AA	APts	PIM	PP	SH	GW	S	%	TGF	PGF	TGA	PGA	+/-	GP	G	A	Pts	PIM	PP	SH	GW
1987-88	Drummondville Voltigeurs	QMJHL	63	23	26	49	....	....	....	233	....	....	....	....	....	....	....	....	....	....	17	5	3	8	74	....	....	....
1988-89	Drummondville Voltigeurs	QMJHL	63	20	36	56	....	....	....	218	....	....	....	....	....	....	....	....	....	....	4	0	2	2	27	....	....	....
1989-90	Laval Titan	QMJHL	59	24	51	75	....	....	....	309	....	....	....	....	....	....	....	....	....	....	13	7	13	20	59	....	....	....
1990-91	Hershey Bears	AHL	65	13	32	45	....	....	....	159	....	....	....	....	....	....	....	....	....	....	7	1	5	6	28	....	....	....
1991-92	**Philadelphia Flyers**	**NHL**	**58**	**5**	**13**	**18**	**5**	**10**	**15**	**187**	**0**	**0**	**0**	**46**	**10.9**	**26**	**0**	**28**	**0**	**–2**	....	....	....	....	....	....	....	....
	Hershey Bears	AHL	20	4	5	9	....	....	....	96	....	....	....	....	....	....	....	....	....	....	....	....	....	....	....	....	....	....
1992-93	**Philadelphia Flyers**	**NHL**	**30**	**5**	**4**	**9**	**4**	**3**	**7**	**76**	**0**	**0**	**1**	**21**	**23.8**	**13**	**0**	**18**	**0**	**–5**	....	....	....	....	....	....	....	....
1993-94	**Philadelphia Flyers**	**NHL**	**26**	**1**	**1**	**2**	**1**	**1**	**2**	**57**	**0**	**0**	**0**	**11**	**9.1**	**3**	**1**	**14**	**1**	**–11**	....	....	....	....	....	....	....	....
	Hershey Bears	AHL	4	1	6	7	....	....	....	6	....	....	....	....	....	....	....	....	....	....	....	....	....	....	....	....	....	....
	Ottawa Senators	**NHL**	**15**	**1**	**0**	**1**	**1**	**0**	**1**	**38**	**0**	**0**	**0**	**6**	**16.7**	**2**	**0**	**8**	**0**	**–6**	....	....	....	....	....	....	....	....
1994-95	**Ottawa Senators**	**NHL**	**3**	**0**	**1**	**1**	**0**	**1**	**1**	**6**	**0**	**0**	**0**	**0**	**0.0**	**1**	**0**	**2**	**0**	**–1**	....	....	....	....	....	....	....	....
	P.E.I. Senators	AHL	22	10	9	19	....	....	....	89	....	....	....	....	....	....	....	....	....	....	9	1	2	3	32	....	....	....
	NHL Totals		**132**	**12**	**19**	**31**	**11**	**15**	**26**	**364**	**0**	**0**	**1**	**84**	**14.3**	**45**	**1**	**70**	**1**		....	....	....	....	....	....	....	....

Traded to **Ottawa** by **Philadelphia** with Kirk Daubenspeck for Mark Lamb, March 5, 1994.

• BOIVIN, LEO
Leo Boivin D – L. 5'8", 183 lbs. b: Prescott, Ont., 8/2/1932. **HHOF**

Season	Club	League	GP	G	A	Pts	AG	AA	APts	PIM	PP	SH	GW	S	%	TGF	PGF	TGA	PGA	+/-	GP	G	A	Pts	PIM	PP	SH	GW
1948-49	Inkerman Rockets	Jr. B	STATISTICS NOT AVAILABLE																									
1949-50	Port Arthur Bruins	TBJHL	18	4	4	8	....	....	....	32	....	....	....	....	....	....	....	....	....	....	5	0	3	3	10	....	....	....
1950-51	Port Arthur Bruins	TBJHL	20	16	11	27	....	....	....	37	....	....	....	....	....	....	....	....	....	....	13	3	6	9	28	....	....	....
1951-52	**Toronto Maple Leafs**	**NHL**	**2**	**0**	**1**	**1**	**0**	**1**	**1**	**0**	....	....	....	....	....	....	....	....	....	....	....	....	....	....	....	....	....	....
	Pittsburgh Hornets	AHL	30	2	3	5	....	....	....	32	....	....	....	....	....	....	....	....	....	....	10	0	1	1	16	....	....	....
1952-53	**Toronto Maple Leafs**	**NHL**	**70**	**2**	**13**	**15**	**3**	**18**	**21**	**97**	....	....	....	....	....	....	....	....	....	....	....	....	....	....	....	....	....	....
1953-54	**Toronto Maple Leafs**	**NHL**	**58**	**1**	**6**	**7**	**2**	**8**	**10**	**81**	....	....	....	....	....	....	....	....	....	....	**5**	**0**	**0**	**0**	**2**	....	....	....
1954-55	**Toronto Maple Leafs**	**NHL**	**7**	**0**	**0**	**0**	**0**	**0**	**0**	**8**	....	....	....	....	....	....	....	....	....	....	....	....	....	....	....	....	....	....
	Boston Bruins	**NHL**	**59**	**6**	**11**	**17**	**9**	**14**	**23**	**105**	....	....	....	....	....	....	....	....	....	....	**5**	**0**	**1**	**1**	**4**	....	....	....
1955-56	**Boston Bruins**	**NHL**	**68**	**4**	**16**	**20**	**6**	**20**	**26**	**80**	....	....	....	....	....	....	....	....	....	....	....	....	....	....	....	....	....	....
1956-57	**Boston Bruins**	**NHL**	**55**	**2**	**8**	**10**	**3**	**9**	**12**	**55**	....	....	....	....	....	....	....	....	....	....	**10**	**2**	**3**	**5**	**12**	....	....	....
1957-58	**Boston Bruins**	**NHL**	**33**	**0**	**4**	**4**	**0**	**4**	**4**	**54**	....	....	....	....	....	....	....	....	....	....	**12**	**0**	**3**	**3**	**21**	....	....	....
1958-59	**Boston Bruins**	**NHL**	**70**	**5**	**16**	**21**	**6**	**17**	**23**	**94**	....	....	....	....	....	....	....	....	....	....	**7**	**1**	**2**	**3**	**4**	....	....	....
1959-60	**Boston Bruins**	**NHL**	**70**	**4**	**21**	**25**	**5**	**21**	**26**	**66**	....	....	....	....	....	....	....	....	....	....	....	....	....	....	....	....	....	....
1960-61	**Boston Bruins**	**NHL**	**57**	**6**	**17**	**23**	**7**	**17**	**24**	**50**	....	....	....	....	....	....	....	....	....	....	....	....	....	....	....	....	....	....
1961-62	**Boston Bruins**	**NHL**	**65**	**5**	**18**	**23**	**6**	**18**	**24**	**70**	....	....	....	....	....	....	....	....	....	....	....	....	....	....	....	....	....	....
1962-63	**Boston Bruins**	**NHL**	**62**	**2**	**24**	**26**	**2**	**25**	**27**	**48**	....	....	....	....	....	....	....	....	....	....	....	....	....	....	....	....	....	....
1963-64	**Boston Bruins**	**NHL**	**65**	**10**	**14**	**24**	**13**	**15**	**28**	**42**	....	....	....	....	....	....	....	....	....	....	....	....	....	....	....	....	....	....
1964-65	**Boston Bruins**	**NHL**	**67**	**3**	**10**	**13**	**4**	**11**	**15**	**68**	....	....	....	....	....	....	....	....	....	....	....	....	....	....	....	....	....	....
1965-66	**Boston Bruins**	**NHL**	**46**	**0**	**5**	**5**	**0**	**5**	**5**	**34**	....	....	....	....	....	....	....	....	....	....	....	....	....	....	....	....	....	....
	Detroit Red Wings	**NHL**	**16**	**0**	**5**	**5**	**0**	**5**	**5**	**16**	....	....	....	....	....	....	....	....	....	....	**12**	**0**	**1**	**1**	**16**	....	....	....
1966-67	**Detroit Red Wings**	**NHL**	**69**	**4**	**17**	**21**	**5**	**17**	**22**	**78**	....	....	....	....	....	....	....	....	....	....	....	....	....	....	....	....	....	....
1967-68	**Pittsburgh Penguins**	**NHL**	**73**	**9**	**13**	**22**	**11**	**14**	**25**	**74**	**4**	**0**	**1**	**163**	**5.5**	**99**	**14**	**117**	**17**	**–15**	....	....	....	....	....	....	....	....
1968-69	**Pittsburgh Penguins**	**NHL**	**41**	**5**	**13**	**18**	**6**	**12**	**18**	**26**	**2**	**0**	**1**	**74**	**6.8**	**51**	**15**	**47**	**5**	**–6**	....	....	....	....	....	....	....	....
	Minnesota North Stars	**NHL**	**28**	**1**	**6**	**7**	**1**	**6**	**7**	**16**	**1**	**0**	**0**	**64**	**1.6**	**29**	**5**	**48**	**5**	**–19**	....	....	....	....	....	....	....	....
1969-70	**Minnesota North Stars**	**NHL**	**69**	**3**	**12**	**15**	**3**	**12**	**15**	**30**	**0**	**0**	**0**	**95**	**3.2**	**70**	**1**	**111**	**40**	**–2**	**3**	**0**	**0**	**0**	**0**	**0**	**0**	**0**
	NHL Totals		**1150**	**72**	**250**	**322**	**92**	**269**	**361**	**1192**	**7**	**0**	**2**	**396**	**18.2**	**249**	**35**	**323**	**67**		**54**	**3**	**10**	**13**	**59**	**0**	**0**	**0**

Played in NHL All-Star Game (1961, 1962, 1964)

Traded to **Toronto** by **Boston** with Fern Flaman, Ken Smith and Phil Maloney for Bill Ezinicki and Vic Lynn, November 16, 1950. Traded to **Boston** by **Toronto** for Joe Klukay, November 9, 1954. Traded to **Detroit** by **Boston** for Gary Doak, Bill Lesuk and future considerations (Steve Atkinson, June, 1966), February 18, 1966. Claimed by **Pittsburgh** from **Detroit** in Expansion Draft, June 6, 1967. Traded to **Minnesota** by **Pittsburgh** for Duane Rupp, January 24, 1969.

• BOLAND, MIKE A.
Mike A. Boland RW – R. 5'10", 183 lbs. b. Montreal, Que., 12/16/1949.

Season	Club	League	GP	G	A	Pts	AG	AA	APts	PIM	PP	SH	GW	S	%	TGF	PGF	TGA	PGA	+/-	GP	G	A	Pts	PIM	PP	SH	GW
1969-70	University of Toronto	OQAA	STATISTICS NOT AVAILABLE																									
1970-71	Springfield Kings	AHL	34	7	5	12	....	....	....	33	....	....	....	....	....	....	....	....	....	....	12	2	6	8	4	....	....	....
1971-72	Springfield Kings	AHL	48	4	20	24	....	....	....	47	....	....	....	....	....	....	....	....	....	....	5	1	0	1	2	....	....	....
1972-73	Ottawa Nationals	WHA	41	1	15	16	....	....	....	44	....	....	....	....	....	....	....	....	....	....	1	0	0	0	12	....	....	....
1973-74	Richmond Robins	AHL	38	10	19	29	....	....	....	49	....	....	....	....	....	....	....	....	....	....	5	3	1	4	8	....	....	....
1974-75	**Philadelphia Flyers**	**NHL**	**2**	**0**	**0**	**0**	**0**	**0**	**0**	**0**	**0**	**0**	**0**	**0**	**0.0**	**0**	**0**	**0**	**0**	**0**	....	....	....	....	....	....	....	....
	Richmond Robins	AHL	5	0	1	1	....	....	....	21	....	....	....	....	....	....	....	....	....	....	....	....	....	....	....	....	....	....
	Philadelphia Firebirds	NAHL	59	31	55	86	....	....	....	49	....	....	....	....	....	....	....	....	....	....	3	2	1	3	0	....	....	....
1975-76	Philadelphia Firebirds	NAHL	13	4	8	12	....	....	....	9	....	....	....	....	....	....	....	....	....	....	....	....	....	....	....	....	....	....
	Cape Cod Codders	NAHL	35	13	23	36	....	....	....	24	....	....	....	....	....	....	....	....	....	....	....	....	....	....	....	....	....	....
1976-77	HIFK Helsinki	Finland	....	....	....	....	....	....	....	....	....	....	....	....	....	....	....	....	....	....	4	0	0	0	0	....	....	....
1977-78	HIFK Helsinki	Finland	DID NOT PLAY – COACHING																									
1978-79	Philadelphia Firebirds	AHL	3	0	0	0	....	....	....	0	....	....	....	....	....	....	....	....	....	....	....	....	....	....	....	....	....	....
	NHL Totals		**2**	**0**	**0**	**0**	**0**	**0**	**0**	**0**	**0**	**0**	**0**	**0**	**0.0**	**0**	**0**	**0**	**0**		....	....	....	....	....	....	....	....
	Other Major League Totals		41	1	15	16	....	....	....	44	....	....	....	....	....	....	....	....	....		1	0	0	0	12	....	....	....

NAHL Second All-Star Team (1975)

Selected by **Ontario-Ottawa** (WHA) in 1972 WHA General Player Draft, February 13, 1972. Signed as a free agent by **Philadelphia**, September, 1973.

Season	Club	League	GP	G	A	Pts	AG	AA	APts	PIM	PP	SH	GW	S	%	TGF	PGF	TGA	PGA	+/–	GP	G	A	Pts	PIM	PP	SH	GW
			REGULAR SEASON																		PLAYOFFS							

• BOLAND, MIKE J.

Mike J. Boland D – R. 6', 190 lbs. b: London, Ont., 10/29/1954. Kansas City's 7th choice, 110th overall, in 1974 Amateur Draft.

Season	Club	League	GP	G	A	Pts	AG	AA	APts	PIM	PP	SH	GW	S	%	TGF	PGF	TGA	PGA	+/–	GP	G	A	Pts	PIM	PP	SH	GW
1972-73	Sault Ste. Marie Greyhounds	OHA	55	4	15	19	....	....	....	139	....	....	....	....	....	....	....	....	....	....	....	....	....	....	....	....	....	....
1973-74	Sault Ste. Marie Greyhounds	OHA	67	11	39	50	....	....	....	200	....	....	....	....	....	....	....	....	....	....	....	....	....	....	....	....	....	....
1974-75	**Kansas City Scouts**	**NHL**	**1**	**0**	**0**	**0**	**0**	**0**	**0**	**0**	**0**	**0**	**0**	**0**	**0.0**	**0**	**0**	**0**	**0**	**0**	....	....	....	....	....	....	....	....
	Port Huron Flags	IHL	71	2	12	14	....	....	....	172	....	....	....	....	....	....	....	....	....	....	5	2	1	3	14	....	....	....
1975-76	Port Huron Flags	IHL	75	8	16	24	....	....	....	208	....	....	....	....	....	....	....	....	....	....	15	0	6	6	51	....	....	....
1976-77	Port Huron Flags	IHL	66	7	37	44	....	....	....	306	....	....	....	....	....	....	....	....	....	....	....	....	....	....	....	....	....	....
1977-78	Port Huron Flags	IHL	2	0	0	0	....	....	....	4	....	....	....	....	....	....	....	....	....	....	....	....	....	....	....	....	....	....
	Fort Wayne Komets	IHL	74	7	39	46	....	....	....	228	....	....	....	....	....	....	....	....	....	....	11	3	3	6	40	....	....	....
1978-79	**Buffalo Sabres**	**NHL**	**22**	**1**	**2**	**3**	**1**	**2**	**3**	**29**	**0**	**0**	**0**	**17**	**5.9**	**21**	**0**	**16**	**1**	**+6**	**3**	**1**	**0**	**1**	**2**	**0**	**0**	**0**
	Hershey Bears	AHL	46	3	17	20	....	....	....	86	....	....	....	....	....	....	....	....	....	....	....	....	....	....	....	....	....	....
1979-80	Rochester Americans	AHL	80	4	28	32	....	....	....	178	....	....	....	....	....	....	....	....	....	....	4	1	1	2	6	....	....	....
1980-81	Rochester Americans	AHL	5	0	1	1	....	....	....	8	....	....	....	....	....	....	....	....	....	....	....	....	....	....	....	....	....	....
	Salt Lake Golden Eagles	CHL	69	5	21	26	....	....	....	188	....	....	....	....	....	....	....	....	....	....	17	2	1	3	*70	....	....	....
1981-82	Salt Lake Golden Eagles	CHL	64	1	13	14	....	....	....	161	....	....	....	....	....	....	....	....	....	....	10	1	2	3	45	....	....	....
1982-83	Fort Wayne Komets	IHL	1	0	0	0	....	....	....	0	....	....	....	....	....	....	....	....	....	....	....	....	....	....	....	....	....	....
	Hershey Bears	AHL	57	0	11	11	....	....	....	68	....	....	....	....	....	....	....	....	....	....	5	0	0	0	6	....	....	....
1983-84	Fort Wayne Komets	IHL	81	8	49	57	....	....	....	161	....	....	....	....	....	....	....	....	....	....	6	0	3	3	35	....	....	....
	NHL Totals		**23**	**1**	**2**	**3**	**1**	**2**	**3**	**29**	**0**	**0**	**0**	**17**	**5.9**	**21**	**0**	**16**	**1**		**3**	**1**	**0**	**1**	**2**	**0**	**0**	**0**

Signed as a free agent by **Buffalo**, January 5, 1979.

• BOLDIREV, IVAN

Ivan "Ike" Boldirev C – L. 6', 190 lbs. b: Zranjanin, Yugoslavia, 8/15/1949. Boston's 3rd choice, 11th overall, in 1969 Amateur Draft.

Season	Club	League	GP	G	A	Pts	AG	AA	APts	PIM	PP	SH	GW	S	%	TGF	PGF	TGA	PGA	+/–	GP	G	A	Pts	PIM	PP	SH	GW
1966-67	Sault Ste. Marie Greyhounds	NOHA	40	26	42	68	....	....	....	35	....	....	....	....	....	....	....	....	....	....	....	....	....	....	....	....	....	....
1967-68	Oshawa Generals	OHA	50	18	26	44	....	....	....	76	....	....	....	....	....	....	....	....	....	....	....	....	....	....	....	....	....	....
1968-69	Oshawa Generals	OHA	54	25	34	59	....	....	....	101	....	....	....	....	....	....	....	....	....	....	....	....	....	....	....	....	....	....
1969-70	Oklahoma City Blazers	CHL	65	18	49	67	....	....	....	114	....	....	....	....	....	....	....	....	....	....	....	....	....	....	....	....	....	....
1970-71	**Boston Bruins**	**NHL**	**2**	**0**	**0**	**0**	**0**	**0**	**0**	**0**	**0**	**0**	**0**	**1**	**0.0**	**0**	**0**	**0**	**0**	**0**	....	....	....	....	....	....	....	....
	Oklahoma City Blazers	CHL	68	19	52	71	....	....	....	98	....	....	....	....	....	....	....	....	....	....	5	1	4	5	9	....	....	....
1971-72	**Boston Bruins**	**NHL**	**11**	**0**	**2**	**2**	**0**	**2**	**2**	**6**	**0**	**0**	**0**	**2**	**0.0**	**3**	**0**	**1**	**0**	**+2**	....	....	....	....	....	....	....	....
	California Golden Seals	**NHL**	**57**	**16**	**23**	**39**	**17**	**21**	**38**	**54**	**4**	**2**	**2**	**109**	**14.7**	**55**	**21**	**66**	**18**	**–14**	....	....	....	....	....	....	....	....
1972-73	**California Golden Seals**	**NHL**	**56**	**11**	**23**	**34**	**11**	**19**	**30**	**58**	**3**	**0**	**3**	**157**	**7.0**	**46**	**11**	**66**	**8**	**–23**	....	....	....	....	....	....	....	....
1973-74	**California Golden Seals**	**NHL**	**78**	**25**	**31**	**56**	**26**	**27**	**53**	**22**	**2**	**0**	**2**	**220**	**11.4**	**77**	**18**	**115**	**5**	**–51**	....	....	....	....	....	....	....	....
1974-75	**Chicago Black Hawks**	**NHL**	**80**	**24**	**43**	**67**	**22**	**34**	**56**	**54**	**6**	**0**	**1**	**195**	**12.3**	**87**	**15**	**75**	**0**	**–3**	**8**	**4**	**2**	**6**	**2**	**1**	**0**	**1**
1975-76	**Chicago Black Hawks**	**NHL**	**78**	**28**	**34**	**62**	**26**	**27**	**53**	**33**	**5**	**0**	**4**	**178**	**15.7**	**76**	**18**	**82**	**1**	**–23**	**4**	**0**	**1**	**1**	**0**	**0**	**0**	**0**
1976-77	**Chicago Black Hawks**	**NHL**	**80**	**24**	**38**	**62**	**23**	**31**	**54**	**40**	**4**	**0**	**4**	**164**	**14.6**	**72**	**17**	**73**	**3**	**–15**	**2**	**0**	**1**	**1**	**0**	**0**	**0**	**0**
1977-78	**Chicago Black Hawks**	**NHL**	**80**	**35**	**45**	**80**	**34**	**37**	**71**	**34**	**10**	**0**	**2**	**242**	**14.5**	**95**	**33**	**65**	**0**	**–3**	**4**	**0**	**2**	**2**	**2**	**0**	**0**	**0**
1978-79	**Chicago Black Hawks**	**NHL**	**66**	**29**	**35**	**64**	**26**	**27**	**53**	**25**	**10**	**0**	**4**	**192**	**15.1**	**91**	**24**	**60**	**0**	**+7**	....	....	....	....	....	....	....	....
	Atlanta Flames	**NHL**	**13**	**6**	**8**	**14**	**5**	**6**	**11**	**6**	**4**	**0**	**0**	**33**	**18.2**	**23**	**11**	**11**	**0**	**+1**	**2**	**0**	**2**	**2**	**2**	**0**	**0**	**0**
1979-80	**Atlanta Flames**	**NHL**	**52**	**16**	**24**	**40**	**14**	**18**	**32**	**20**	**1**	**0**	**2**	**121**	**13.2**	**65**	**13**	**53**	**0**	**–1**	....	....	....	....	....	....	....	....
	Vancouver Canucks	**NHL**	**27**	**16**	**11**	**27**	**14**	**8**	**22**	**14**	**5**	**0**	**3**	**82**	**19.5**	**38**	**13**	**28**	**2**	**–1**	**4**	**0**	**2**	**2**	**0**	**0**	**0**	**0**
1980-81	**Vancouver Canucks**	**NHL**	**72**	**26**	**33**	**59**	**21**	**23**	**44**	**34**	**9**	**0**	**3**	**195**	**13.3**	**92**	**31**	**75**	**2**	**–12**	**1**	**1**	**1**	**2**	**0**	**0**	**0**	**0**
1981-82	**Vancouver Canucks**	**NHL**	**78**	**33**	**40**	**73**	**26**	**26**	**52**	**45**	**10**	**0**	**4**	**202**	**16.3**	**89**	**32**	**77**	**3**	**–17**	**17**	**8**	**3**	**11**	**4**	**3**	**0**	**1**
1982-83	**Vancouver Canucks**	**NHL**	**39**	**5**	**20**	**25**	**4**	**14**	**18**	**12**	**3**	**0**	**1**	**74**	**6.8**	**42**	**14**	**37**	**0**	**–9**	....	....	....	....	....	....	....	....
	Detroit Red Wings	**NHL**	**33**	**13**	**17**	**30**	**11**	**12**	**23**	**14**	**3**	**1**	**0**	**62**	**21.0**	**39**	**7**	**46**	**8**	**–6**	....	....	....	....	....	....	....	....
1983-84	**Detroit Red Wings**	**NHL**	**75**	**35**	**48**	**83**	**28**	**33**	**61**	**20**	**12**	**0**	**4**	**185**	**18.9**	**114**	**43**	**71**	**3**	**+3**	**4**	**0**	**5**	**5**	**4**	**0**	**0**	**0**
1984-85	**Detroit Red Wings**	**NHL**	**75**	**19**	**30**	**49**	**16**	**20**	**36**	**16**	**11**	**0**	**3**	**104**	**18.3**	**77**	**35**	**67**	**0**	**–25**	**2**	**0**	**1**	**1**	**0**	**0**	**0**	**0**
	NHL Totals		**1052**	**361**	**505**	**866**	**324**	**385**	**709**	**507**	**102**	**3**	**42**	**2518**	**14.3**	**1181**	**356**	**1068**	**53**		**48**	**13**	**20**	**33**	**14**	**4**	**0**	**2**

CHL Second All-Star Team (1971)

Played in NHL All-Star Game (1978)

Traded to **California** by **Boston** for Richard Leduc and Chris Oddleifson, November 17, 1971. Traded to **Chicago** by **California** for Len Frig and Mike Christie, May 24, 1974. Traded to **Atlanta** by **Chicago** with Phil Russell and Darcy Rota for Tom Lysiak, Pat Ribble, Greg Fox, Harold Phillipoff and Miles Zaharko, March 1, 1979. Traded to **Vancouver** by **Atlanta** with Darcy Rota for Don Lever and Brad Smith, February 8, 1980. Traded to **Detroit** by **Vancouver** for Mark Kirton, January 17, 1983.

• BOLDUC, DANNY

Danny Bolduc LW – L. 5'9", 180 lbs. b: Waterville, ME, 4/6/1953.

Season	Club	League	GP	G	A	Pts	AG	AA	APts	PIM	PP	SH	GW	S	%	TGF	PGF	TGA	PGA	+/–	GP	G	A	Pts	PIM	PP	SH	GW
1972-73	Harvard University	ECAC	13	15	17	32	....	....	....	17	....	....	....	....	....	....	....	....	....	....	....	....	....	....	....	....	....	....
1973-74	Harvard University	ECAC	29	15	9	24	....	....	....	24	....	....	....	....	....	....	....	....	....	....	....	....	....	....	....	....	....	....
1974-75	Harvard University	ECAC	29	13	11	24	....	....	....	18	....	....	....	....	....	....	....	....	....	....	....	....	....	....	....	....	....	....
1975-76	United States	Nat-Team	60	41	31	72	....	....	....	54	....	....	....	....	....	....	....	....	....	....	....	....	....	....	....	....	....	....
	New England Whalers	WHA	14	2	5	7	....	....	....	14	....	....	....	....	....	....	....	....	....	....	16	1	6	7	4	....	....	....
1976-77	New England Whalers	WHA	33	8	3	11	....	....	....	15	....	....	....	....	....	....	....	....	....	....	....	....	....	....	....	....	....	....
	Rhode Island Reds	AHL	44	11	22	33	....	....	....	23	....	....	....	....	....	....	....	....	....	....	....	....	....	....	....	....	....	....
1977-78	New England Whalers	WHA	41	5	5	10	....	....	....	22	....	....	....	....	....	....	....	....	....	....	14	2	4	6	4	....	....	....
	Springfield Indians	AHL	35	14	9	23	....	....	....	35	....	....	....	....	....	....	....	....	....	....	....	....	....	....	....	....	....	....
1978-79	**Detroit Red Wings**	**NHL**	**56**	**16**	**13**	**29**	**15**	**10**	**25**	**14**	**3**	**0**	**4**	**81**	**19.8**	**36**	**7**	**38**	**0**	**–9**	....	....	....	....	....	....	....	....
	Kansas City Red Wings	CHL	23	21	11	32	....	....	....	11	....	....	....	....	....	....	....	....	....	....	....	....	....	....	....	....	....	....
1979-80	**Detroit Red Wings**	**NHL**	**44**	**6**	**5**	**11**	**5**	**4**	**9**	**19**	**2**	**0**	**0**	**52**	**11.5**	**16**	**2**	**28**	**0**	**–14**	....	....	....	....	....	....	....	....
	Adirondack Red Wings	AHL	13	1	3	4	....	....	....	4	....	....	....	....	....	....	....	....	....	....	5	0	0	0	0	....	....	....
1980-81	Adirondack Red Wings	AHL	77	23	25	48	....	....	....	58	....	....	....	....	....	....	....	....	....	....	18	4	6	10	36	....	....	....
1981-82	Nova Scotia Voyageurs	AHL	74	39	40	79	....	....	....	60	....	....	....	....	....	....	....	....	....	....	5	2	0	2	0	....	....	....
1982-83	Colorado Flames	CHL	79	27	45	72	....	....	....	39	....	....	....	....	....	....	....	....	....	....	6	2	3	5	2	....	....	....
1983-84	**Calgary Flames**	**NHL**	**2**	**0**	**1**	**1**	**0**	**1**	**1**	**0**	**0**	**0**	**0**	**4**	**0.0**	**2**	**0**	**1**	**0**	**+1**	**1**	**0**	**0**	**0**	**0**	**0**	**0**	**0**
	Colorado Flames	CHL	60	37	17	54	....	....	....	34	....	....	....	....	....	....	....	....	....	....	6	2	1	3	4	....	....	....
1984-85	Moncton Golden Flames	AHL	45	7	8	15	....	....	....	22	....	....	....	....	....	....	....	....	....	....	....	....	....	....	....	....	....	....
	NHL Totals		**102**	**22**	**19**	**41**	**20**	**15**	**35**	**33**	**5**	**0**	**4**	**137**	**16.1**	**54**	**9**	**67**	**0**		**1**	**0**	**0**	**0**	**0**	**0**	**0**	**0**
	Other Major League Totals		88	15	13	28	....	....	....	51	....	....	....	....	....	....	....	....	....	....	30	3	10	13	8	....	....	....

CHL Second All-Star Team (1983)

Signed as a free agent by **New England** (WHA), March, 1976. Signed as a free agent by **Detroit**, August 24, 1978. Signed as a free agent by **Montreal**, March 9, 1982. Signed as a free agent by **Calgary**, September 1, 1982.

• BOLDUC, MICHEL

Michel Bolduc D – L. 6'2", 190 lbs. b: Angegardien, Que., 3/13/1961. Quebec's 6th choice, 150th overall, in 1980 Entry Draft.

Season	Club	League	GP	G	A	Pts	AG	AA	APts	PIM	PP	SH	GW	S	%	TGF	PGF	TGA	PGA	+/–	GP	G	A	Pts	PIM	PP	SH	GW
1977-78	Hull Festivals	QMJHL	60	1	5	6	....	....	....	36	....	....	....	....	....	....	....	....	....	....	....	....	....	....	....	....	....	....
1978-79	Hull Olympiques	QMJHL	6	0	1	1	....	....	....	5	....	....	....	....	....	....	....	....	....	....	....	....	....	....	....	....	....	....
	Chicoutimi Sagueneens	QMJHL	66	1	23	24	....	....	....	142	....	....	....	....	....	....	....	....	....	....	....	....	....	....	....	....	....	....
1979-80	Chicoutimi Sagueneens	QMJHL	65	3	29	32	....	....	....	219	....	....	....	....	....	....	....	....	....	....	12	1	3	4	44	....	....	....
1980-81	Chicoutimi Sagueneens	QMJHL	67	11	35	46	....	....	....	244	....	....	....	....	....	....	....	....	....	....	12	0	4	4	34	....	....	....
1981-82	**Quebec Nordiques**	**NHL**	**3**	**0**	**0**	**0**	**0**	**0**	**0**	**0**	**0**	**0**	**0**	**1**	**0.0**	**0**	**0**	**0**	**0**	**0**	....	....	....	....	....	....	....	....
	Fredericton Express	AHL	69	4	9	13	....	....	....	130	....	....	....	....	....	....	....	....	....	....	....	....	....	....	....	....	....	....
1982-83	**Quebec Nordiques**	**NHL**	**7**	**0**	**0**	**0**	**0**	**0**	**0**	**6**	**0**	**0**	**0**	**4**	**0.0**	**6**	**0**	**5**	**1**	**+2**	....	....	....	....	....	....	....	....
	Fredericton Express	AHL	68	4	18	22	....	....	....	165	....	....	....	....	....	....	....	....	....	....	11	1	1	2	50	....	....	....
1983-84	Fredericton Express	AHL	70	2	15	17	....	....	....	96	....	....	....	....	....	....	....	....	....	....	7	0	1	1	19	....	....	....
1984-85	Fredericton Express	AHL	29	0	9	9	....	....	....	74	....	....	....	....	....	....	....	....	....	....	....	....	....	....	....	....	....	....
	Maine Mariners	AHL	31	1	7	8	....	....	....	86	....	....	....	....	....	....	....	....	....	....	11	1	1	2	23	....	....	....
1985-86	Maine Mariners	AHL	66	1	6	7	....	....	....	29	....	....	....	....	....	....	....	....	....	....	5	0	1	1	6	....	....	....
1986-87	Riviere-du-Loop 3 L's	QSHL	29	2	19	21	....	....	....	105	....	....	....	....	....	....	....	....	....	....	....	1	3	4	6	....	....	....
	NHL Totals		**10**	**0**	**0**	**0**	**0**	**0**	**0**	**6**	**0**	**0**	**0**	**5**	**0.0**	**6**	**0**	**5**	**1**		....	....	....	....	....	....	....	....

Claimed on waivers by **New Jersey** from **Quebec**, January 25, 1985.

• BOLONCHUK, LARRY

Larry Bolonchuk D – L. 5'10", 190 lbs. b: Winnipeg, Man., 2/26/1952. Vancouver's 5th choice, 67th overall, in 1972 Amateur Draft.

			REGULAR SEASON																		PLAYOFFS							
Season	Club	League	GP	G	A	Pts	AG	AA	APts	PIM	PP	SH	GW	S	%	IGF	PGF	TGA	PGA	+/-	GP	G	A	Pts	PIM	PP	SH	GW
1970-71	Winnipeg Jets	WCJHL	66	4	31	35	....	....	....	140	....	....	....	....	....	....	....	....	....	....	....	....	....	....	....	....	....	....
1971-72	Winnipeg Jets	WCJHL	67	7	32	39	....	....	....	175	....	....	....	....	....	....	....	....	....	....	....	....	....	....	....	....	....	....
1972-73	**Vancouver Canucks**	**NHL**	**15**	**0**	**0**	**0**	**0**	**0**	**0**	**6**	**0**	**0**	**0**	**11**	**0.0**	**9**	**0**	**24**	**4**	**–11**	....	....	....	....	....	....	....	....
	Seattle Totems	WHL	59	2	9	11	....	....	....	97	....	....	....	....	....	....	....	....	....	....	....	....	....	....	....	....	....	....
1973-74	Des Moines Capitols	IHL	71	6	27	33	....	....	....	166	....	....	....	....	....	....	....	....	....	....	10	2	4	6	*42	....	....	....
	Seattle Totems	WHL	3	0	2	2	....	....	....	4	....	....	....	....	....	....	....	....	....	....	....	....	....	....	....	....	....	....
1974-75	Dayton Gems	IHL	58	9	21	30	....	....	....	139	....	....	....	....	....	....	....	....	....	....	14	0	13	13	31	....	....	....
1975-76	**Washington Capitals**	**NHL**	**1**	**0**	**1**	**1**	**0**	**1**	**1**	**0**	**0**	**0**	**0**	**1**	**0.0**	**1**	**0**	**2**	**0**	**–1**	....	....	....	....	....	....	....	....
	Dayton Gems	IHL	77	4	39	43	....	....	....	174	....	....	....	....	....	....	....	....	....	....	15	0	11	11	59	....	....	....
1976-77	**Washington Capitals**	**NHL**	**9**	**0**	**0**	**0**	**0**	**0**	**0**	**12**	**0**	**0**	**0**	**3**	**0.0**	**2**	**0**	**17**	**3**	**–12**	....	....	....	....	....	....	....	....
	Dayton Gems	IHL	71	2	21	23	....	....	....	124	....	....	....	....	....	....	....	....	....	....	4	0	2	2	6	....	....	....
1977-78	**Washington Capitals**	**NHL**	**49**	**3**	**8**	**11**	**3**	**7**	**10**	**79**	**0**	**0**	**0**	**41**	**7.3**	**30**	**0**	**66**	**17**	**–19**	....	....	....	....	....	....	....	....
	Hampton Gulls	AHL	14	1	1	2	....	....	....	38	....	....	....	....	....	....	....	....	....	....	....	....	....	....	....	....	....	....
	Hershey Bears	AHL	19	0	7	7	....	....	....	12	....	....	....	....	....	....	....	....	....	....	....	....	....	....	....	....	....	....
1978-79	Binghamton Dusters	AHL	75	2	28	30	....	....	....	108	....	....	....	....	....	....	....	....	....	....	10	0	1	1	18	....	....	....
1979-80	Cincinnati Stingers	CHL	1	0	0	0	....	....	....	4	....	....	....	....	....	....	....	....	....	....	....	....	....	....	....	....	....	....
	Dayton Gems	IHL	73	7	32	39	....	....	....	139	....	....	....	....	....	....	....	....	....	....	....	....	....	....	....	....	....	....
	NHL Totals		**74**	**3**	**9**	**12**	**3**	**8**	**11**	**97**	**0**	**0**	**0**	**56**	**5.4**	**42**	**0**	**109**	**24**		....	....	....	....	....	....	....	....

IHL Second All-Star Team (1977)

Claimed by **Washington** from **Vancouver** in Expansion Draft, June 12, 1974.

• BOMBARDIR, BRAD

Brad Bombardir D – L. 6'2", 190 lbs. b: Powell River, B.C., 5/5/1972. New Jersey's 5th choice, 56th overall, in 1990 Entry Draft.

Season	Club	League	GP	G	A	Pts	AG	AA	APts	PIM	PP	SH	GW	S	%	IGF	PGF	TGA	PGA	+/-	GP	G	A	Pts	PIM	PP	SH	GW
1989-90	Powell River Paper Kings	BCJHL	60	10	35	45	....	....	....	93	....	....	....	....	....	....	....	....	....	....	....	....	....	....	....	....	....	....
1990-91	University of North Dakota	WCHA	33	3	6	9	....	....	....	18	....	....	....	....	....	....	....	....	....	....	....	....	....	....	....	....	....	....
1991-92	University of North Dakota	WCHA	35	3	14	17	....	....	....	54	....	....	....	....	....	....	....	....	....	....	....	....	....	....	....	....	....	....
	Canada	WJC-A	7	0	3	3	....	....	....	4	....	....	....	....	....	....	....	....	....	....	....	....	....	....	....	....	....	....
1992-93	University of North Dakota	WCHA	38	8	15	23	....	....	....	34	....	....	....	....	....	....	....	....	....	....	....	....	....	....	....	....	....	....
1993-94	University of North Dakota	WCHA	38	5	17	22	....	....	....	38	....	....	....	....	....	....	....	....	....	....	....	....	....	....	....	....	....	....
1994-95	Albany River Rats	AHL	77	5	22	27	....	....	....	22	....	....	....	....	....	....	....	....	....	....	14	0	3	3	6	....	....	....
1995-96	Albany River Rats	AHL	80	6	25	31	....	....	....	63	....	....	....	....	....	....	....	....	....	....	3	0	1	1	4	....	....	....
1996-97	Albany River Rats	AHL	32	0	8	8	....	....	....	6	....	....	....	....	....	....	....	....	....	....	16	1	3	4	8	....	....	....
1997-98	**New Jersey Devils**	**NHL**	**43**	**1**	**5**	**6**	**1**	**5**	**6**	**8**	**0**	**0**	**0**	**16**	**6.3**	**29**	**0**	**19**	**1**	**+11**	....	....	....	....	....	....	....	....
	Albany River Rats	AHL	5	0	0	0	....	....	....	0	....	....	....	....	....	....	....	....	....	....	....	....	....	....	....	....	....	....
	NHL Totals		**43**	**1**	**5**	**6**	**1**	**5**	**6**	**8**	**0**	**0**	**0**	**16**	**6.3**	**29**	**0**	**19**	**1**		....	....	....	....	....	....	....	....

AHL Second All-Star Team (1996)

• BONAR, DAN

Dan Bonar C – R. 5'9", 175 lbs. b: Brandon, Man., 9/23/1956.

Season	Club	League	GP	G	A	Pts	AG	AA	APts	PIM	PP	SH	GW	S	%	IGF	PGF	TGA	PGA	+/-	GP	G	A	Pts	PIM	PP	SH	GW
1973-74	Portage Terriers	MJHL	48	39	41	80	....	....	....	81	....	....	....	....	....	....	....	....	....	....	....	....	....	....	....	....	....	....
1974-75	Brandon Wheat Kings	WHL	70	43	41	84	....	....	....	62	....	....	....	....	....	....	....	....	....	....	5	2	4	6	10	....	....	....
1975-76	Brandon Wheat Kings	WHL	69	44	59	103	....	....	....	49	....	....	....	....	....	....	....	....	....	....	5	2	3	5	0	....	....	....
1976-77	Brandon Wheat Kings	WCJHL	72	75	50	125	....	....	....	70	....	....	....	....	....	....	....	....	....	....	16	6	14	20	44	....	....	....
1977-78	Fort Wayne Komets	IHL	79	47	61	108	....	....	....	43	....	....	....	....	....	....	....	....	....	....	11	6	9	15	6	....	....	....
1978-79	Springfield Indians	AHL	80	33	39	72	....	....	....	30	....	....	....	....	....	....	....	....	....	....	....	....	....	....	....	....	....	....
1979-80	Binghamton Whalers	AHL	64	29	32	61	....	....	....	91	....	....	....	....	....	....	....	....	....	....	....	....	....	....	....	....	....	....
1980-81	**Los Angeles Kings**	**NHL**	**71**	**11**	**15**	**26**	**9**	**10**	**19**	**57**	**3**	**1**	**3**	**64**	**17.2**	**41**	**6**	**69**	**34**	**0**	**4**	**1**	**1**	**2**	**11**	**0**	**1**	**0**
1981-82	**Los Angeles Kings**	**NHL**	**79**	**13**	**23**	**36**	**10**	**15**	**25**	**111**	**1**	**0**	**0**	**123**	**10.6**	**48**	**1**	**92**	**41**	**–4**	**10**	**2**	**3**	**5**	**11**	**0**	**0**	**0**
1982-83	**Los Angeles Kings**	**NHL**	**20**	**1**	**1**	**2**	**1**	**1**	**2**	**40**	**0**	**0**	**0**	**16**	**6.3**	**2**	**0**	**18**	**9**	**–7**	....	....	....	....	....	....	....	....
	New Haven Nighthawks	AHL	22	10	13	23	....	....	....	29	....	....	....	....	....	....	....	....	....	....	11	1	7	8	13	....	....	....
1983-84	New Haven Nighthawks	AHL	35	9	14	23	....	....	....	27	....	....	....	....	....	....	....	....	....	....	....	....	....	....	....	....	....	....
	Nova Scotia Voyageurs	AHL	44	13	23	36	....	....	....	75	....	....	....	....	....	....	....	....	....	....	12	4	7	11	38	....	....	....
1984-85	Adirondack Red Wings	AHL	31	3	13	16	....	....	....	43	....	....	....	....	....	....	....	....	....	....	....	....	....	....	....	....	....	....
	NHL Totals		**170**	**25**	**39**	**64**	**20**	**26**	**46**	**208**	**4**	**1**	**3**	**203**	**12.3**	**91**	**7**	**179**	**84**		**14**	**3**	**4**	**7**	**22**	**0**	**1**	**0**

IHL First All-Star Team (1978) • Won Garry F. Longman Memorial Trophy (Top Rookie - IHL) (1978) • Won James Gatschene Memorial Trophy (MVP - IHL) (1978)

Signed as a free agent by **LA Kings**, August 7, 1978. Traded to **Montreal** by **LA Kings** for cash, December 20, 1983.

• BONDRA, PETER

Peter Bondra RW – L. 6'1", 200 lbs. b: Luck, USSR, 2/7/1968. Washington's 9th choice, 156th overall, in 1990 Entry Draft.

Season	Club	League	GP	G	A	Pts	AG	AA	APts	PIM	PP	SH	GW	S	%	IGF	PGF	TGA	PGA	+/-	GP	G	A	Pts	PIM	PP	SH	GW
1986-87	VSZ Kosice	Czech.	32	4	5	9	....	....	....	24	....	....	....	....	....	....	....	....	....	....	....	....	....	....	....	....	....	....
1987-88	VSZ Kosice	Czech.	45	27	11	38	....	....	....	20	....	....	....	....	....	....	....	....	....	....	....	....	....	....	....	....	....	....
1988-89	VSZ Kosice	Czech.	40	30	10	40	....	....	....	20	....	....	....	....	....	....	....	....	....	....	....	....	....	....	....	....	....	....
1989-90	VSZ Kosice	Czech.	49	36	19	55	....	....	....	....	....	....	....	....	....	....	....	....	....	....	....	....	....	....	....	....	....	....
1990-91	**Washington Capitals**	**NHL**	**54**	**12**	**16**	**28**	**11**	**12**	**23**	**47**	**4**	**0**	**1**	**95**	**12.6**	**36**	**6**	**40**	**0**	**–10**	**4**	**0**	**1**	**1**	**2**	**0**	**0**	**0**
1991-92	**Washington Capitals**	**NHL**	**71**	**28**	**28**	**56**	**26**	**21**	**47**	**42**	**4**	**0**	**3**	**158**	**17.7**	**73**	**13**	**47**	**3**	**+16**	**7**	**6**	**2**	**8**	**4**	**1**	**0**	**0**
1992-93	**Washington Capitals**	**NHL**	**83**	**37**	**48**	**85**	**31**	**33**	**64**	**70**	**10**	**0**	**7**	**239**	**15.5**	**116**	**35**	**75**	**2**	**+8**	**6**	**0**	**6**	**6**	**0**	**0**	**0**	**0**
1993-94	**Washington Capitals**	**NHL**	**69**	**24**	**19**	**43**	**22**	**15**	**37**	**40**	**4**	**0**	**2**	**200**	**12.0**	**69**	**12**	**36**	**1**	**+22**	**9**	**2**	**4**	**6**	**4**	**0**	**0**	**1**
1994-95	VSZ Kosice	Slovakia	2	1	0	1	....	....	....	0	....	....	....	....	....	....	....	....	....	....	....	....	....	....	....	....	....	....
	Washington Capitals	**NHL**	**47**	***34**	**9**	**43**	**61**	**13**	**74**	**24**	**12**	**6**	**3**	**177**	**19.2**	**60**	**28**	**33**	**10**	**+9**	**7**	**5**	**3**	**8**	**10**	**2**	**0**	**1**
1995-96	Detroit Vipers	IHL	7	8	1	9	....	....	....	0	....	....	....	....	....	....	....	....	....	....	....	....	....	....	....	....	....	....
	Washington Capitals	**NHL**	**67**	**52**	**28**	**80**	**51**	**23**	**74**	**40**	**11**	**4**	**7**	**322**	**16.1**	**102**	**32**	**60**	**8**	**+18**	**6**	**3**	**2**	**5**	**8**	**2**	**0**	**1**
1996-97	Slovakia	W Cup	3	3	0	3	....	....	....	2	....	....	....	....	....	....	....	....	....	....	....	....	....	....	....	....	....	....
	Washington Capitals	**NHL**	**77**	**46**	**31**	**77**	**49**	**27**	**76**	**72**	**10**	**4**	**3**	**314**	**14.6**	**99**	**30**	**65**	**3**	**+7**	....	....	....	....	....	....	....	....
1997-98	**Washington Capitals**	**NHL**	**76**	**52**	**26**	**78**	**61**	**25**	**86**	**44**	**11**	**5**	**13**	**284**	**18.3**	**103**	**34**	**64**	**9**	**+14**	**17**	**7**	**5**	**12**	**12**	**3**	**0**	**2**
	NHL Totals		**544**	**285**	**205**	**490**	**312**	**169**	**481**	**379**	**66**	**19**	**39**	**1789**	**15.9**	**658**	**190**	**420**	**36**		**56**	**23**	**23**	**46**	**40**	**8**	**0**	**5**

Played in NHL All-Star Game (1993, 1996, 1997, 1998)

• BONK, RADEK

Radek Bonk C – L. 6'3", 205 lbs. b: Krnov, Czech., 1/9/1976. Ottawa's 1st choice, 3rd overall, in 1994 Entry Draft.

Season	Club	League	GP	G	A	Pts	AG	AA	APts	PIM	PP	SH	GW	S	%	IGF	PGF	TGA	PGA	+/-	GP	G	A	Pts	PIM	PP	SH	GW
1992-93	ZPS Zlin	Czech.	30	5	5	10	....	....	....	10	....	....	....	....	....	....	....	....	....	....	....	....	....	....	....	....	....	....
1993-94	Las Vegas Thunder	IHL	76	42	45	87	....	....	....	208	....	....	....	....	....	....	....	....	....	....	5	1	2	3	10	....	....	....
1994-95	Las Vegas Thunder	IHL	33	7	13	20	....	....	....	62	....	....	....	....	....	....	....	....	....	....	....	....	....	....	....	....	....	....
	Ottawa Senators	**NHL**	**42**	**3**	**8**	**11**	**5**	**12**	**17**	**28**	**1**	**0**	**0**	**40**	**7.5**	**15**	**6**	**14**	**0**	**–5**	....	....	....	....	....	....	....	....
	P.E.I. Senators	AHL	....	....	....	....	....	....	....	....	....	....	....	....	....	....	....	....	....	....	1	0	0	0	0	....	....	....
1995-96	**Ottawa Senators**	**NHL**	**76**	**16**	**19**	**35**	**16**	**15**	**31**	**36**	**5**	**0**	**1**	**161**	**9.9**	**59**	**19**	**63**	**18**	**–5**	....	....	....	....	....	....	....	....
	Czech Republic	WC-A	8	2	2	4	....	....	....	14	....	....	....	....	....	....	....	....	....	....	....	....	....	....	....	....	....	....
1996-97	Czech Republic	W Cup	3	1	0	1	....	....	....	0	....	....	....	....	....	....	....	....	....	....	....	....	....	....	....	....	....	....
	Ottawa Senators	**NHL**	**53**	**5**	**13**	**18**	**5**	**11**	**16**	**14**	**0**	**1**	**0**	**82**	**6.1**	**34**	**2**	**45**	**9**	**–4**	**7**	**0**	**1**	**1**	**4**	**0**	**0**	**0**
1997-98	**Ottawa Senators**	**NHL**	**65**	**7**	**9**	**16**	**8**	**9**	**17**	**16**	**1**	**0**	**0**	**93**	**7.5**	**27**	**7**	**35**	**2**	**–13**	**5**	**0**	**0**	**0**	**2**	**0**	**0**	**0**
	NHL Totals		**236**	**31**	**49**	**80**	**34**	**47**	**81**	**94**	**7**	**1**	**1**	**376**	**8.2**	**135**	**34**	**157**	**29**		**12**	**0**	**1**	**1**	**6**	**0**	**0**	**0**

Won Garry F. Longman Memorial Trophy (Top Rookie - IHL) (1994)

• BONSIGNORE, JASON

Jason Bonsignore C – R. 6'4", 220 lbs. b: Rochester, NY, 4/15/1976. Edmonton's 1st choice, 4th overall, in 1994 Entry Draft.

Season	Club	League	GP	G	A	Pts	AG	AA	APts	PIM	PP	SH	GW	S	%	IGF	PGF	TGA	PGA	+/-	GP	G	A	Pts	PIM	PP	SH	GW
1992-93	Newmarket Royals	OHL	66	22	20	42	....	....	....	6	....	....	....	....	....	....	....	....	....	....	7	0	3	3	0	....	....	....
1993-94	Newmarket Royals	OHL	17	7	17	24	....	....	....	22	....	....	....	....	....	....	....	....	....	....	....	....	....	....	....	....	....	....
	United States	Nat-Team	5	0	2	2	....	....	....	0	....	....	....	....	....	....	....	....	....	....	....	....	....	....	....	....	....	....
	United States	WJC-A	7	0	0	0	....	....	....	26	....	....	....	....	....	....	....	....	....	....	....	....	....	....	....	....	....	....
	Niagara Falls Thunder	OHL	41	15	47	62	....	....	....	41	....	....	....	....	....	....	....	....	....	....	....	....	....	....	....	....	....	....
1994-95	Niagara Falls Thunder	OHL	26	12	21	33	....	....	....	51	....	....	....	....	....	....	....	....	....	....	....	....	....	....	....	....	....	....
	United States	WJC-A	7	2	2	4	....	....	....	6	....	....	....	....	....	....	....	....	....	....	....	....	....	....	....	....	....	....
	Sudbury Wolves	OHL	23	15	14	29	....	....	....	45	....	....	....	....	....	....	....	....	....	....	17	13	10	23	12	....	....	....
	Edmonton Oilers	**NHL**	**1**	**1**	**0**	**1**	**2**	**0**	**2**	**0**	**0**	**0**	**0**	**3**	**33.3**	**2**	**1**	**2**	**0**	**–1**	....	....	....	....	....	....	....	....

Season	Club	League	GP	G	A	Pts	AG	AA	APts	PIM	PP	SH	GW	S	%	TGF	PGF	TGA	PGA	+/–	GP	G	A	Pts	PIM	PP	SH	GW
							REGULAR SEASON														PLAYOFFS							
1995-96	Sudbury Wolves	OHL	18	10	16	26	....	....	....	37	....	....	....	....	....	....	....	....	....	....	....	....	....	....	....	....	....	....
	Edmonton Oilers	**NHL**	**20**	**0**	**2**	**2**	**0**	**2**	**2**	**4**	**0**	**0**	**0**	**13**	**0.0**	**5**	**1**	**11**	**1**	**–6**	....	....	....	....	....	....	....	....
	Cape Breton Oilers	AHL	12	1	4	5	....	....	....	12	....	....	....	....	....	....	....	....	....	....	....	....	....	....	....	....	....	....
1996-97	Hamilton Bulldogs	AHL	78	21	33	54	....	....	....	78	....	....	....	....	....	....	....	....	....	....	7	0	0	0	4	....	....	....
1997-98	Hamilton Bulldogs	AHL	8	0	2	2	....	....	....	14	....	....	....	....	....	....	....	....	....	....	....	....	....	....	....	....	....	....
	San Antonio Dragons	IHL	22	3	8	11	....	....	....	34	....	....	....	....	....	....	....	....	....	....	....	....	....	....	....	....	....	....
	Tampa Bay Lightning	**NHL**	**35**	**2**	**8**	**10**	**2**	**8**	**10**	**22**	**0**	**0**	**0**	**29**	**6.9**	**12**	**2**	**22**	**1**	**–11**	....	....	....	....	....	....	....	....
	Cleveland Lumberjacks	IHL	6	4	0	4	....	....	....	32	....	....	....	....	....	....	....	....	....	....	8	1	1	2	20	....	....	....
	NHL Totals		**56**	**3**	**10**	**13**	**4**	**10**	**14**	**26**	**0**	**0**	**0**	**45**	**6.7**	**19**	**4**	**35**	**2**		....	....	....	....	....	....	....	....

Traded to **Tampa Bay** by **Edmonton** with Bryan Marchment and Steve Kelly for Roman Hamrlik and Paul Comrie, December 30, 1997.

• BONVIE, DENNIS

Dennis Bonvie RW/D – R. 5'11", 205 lbs. b: Antigonish, N.S., 7/23/1973.

Season	Club	League	GP	G	A	Pts	AG	AA	APts	PIM	PP	SH	GW	S	%	TGF	PGF	TGA	PGA	+/–	GP	G	A	Pts	PIM	PP	SH	GW
1991-92	Kitchener Rangers	OHL	7	1	1	2	....	....	....	23	....	....	....	....	....	....	....	....	....	....	....	....	....	....	....	....	....	....
	North Bay Centennials	OHL	49	0	12	12	....	....	....	261	....	....	....	....	....	....	....	....	....	....	21	0	1	1	91	....	....	....
1992-93	North Bay Centennials	OHL	64	3	21	24	....	....	....	*316	....	....	....	....	....	....	....	....	....	....	5	0	0	0	34	....	....	....
1993-94	Cape Breton Oilers	AHL	63	1	10	11	....	....	....	278	....	....	....	....	....	....	....	....	....	....	4	0	0	0	11	....	....	....
1994-95	**Edmonton Oilers**	**NHL**	**2**	**0**	**0**	**0**	**0**	**0**	**0**	**0**	**0**	**0**	**0**	**0**	**0.0**	**0**	**0**	**0**	**0**	**0**	....	....	....	....	....	....	....	....
	Cape Breton Oilers	AHL	74	5	15	20	....	....	....	422	....	....	....	....	....	....	....	....	....	....	....	....	....	....	....	....	....	....
1995-96	**Edmonton Oilers**	**NHL**	**8**	**0**	**0**	**0**	**0**	**0**	**0**	**47**	**0**	**0**	**0**	**0**	**0.0**	**0**	**0**	**3**	**0**	**–3**	....	....	....	....	....	....	....	....
	Cape Breton Oilers	AHL	38	13	14	27	....	....	....	269	....	....	....	....	....	....	....	....	....	....	....	....	....	....	....	....	....	....
1996-97	Hamilton Bulldogs	AHL	73	9	20	29	....	....	....	*522	....	....	....	....	....	....	....	....	....	....	22	3	11	14	*91	....	....	....
1997-98	**Edmonton Oilers**	**NHL**	**4**	**0**	**0**	**0**	**0**	**0**	**0**	**27**	**0**	**0**	**0**	**0**	**0.0**	**0**	**0**	**0**	**0**	**0**	....	....	....	....	....	....	....	....
	Hamilton Bulldogs	AHL	57	11	19	30	....	....	....	295	....	....	....	....	....	....	....	....	....	....	9	0	5	5	18	....	....	....
	NHL Totals		**14**	**0**	**0**	**0**	**0**	**0**	**0**	**74**	**0**	**0**	**0**	**0**	**0.0**	**0**	**0**	**3**	**0**		....	....	....	....	....	....	....	....

Signed as a free agent by **Edmonton**, August 25, 1994.

• BOO, JIM

Jim Boo D – R. 6'1", 200 lbs. b: Rolla, MO, 11/12/1954.

Season	Club	League	GP	G	A	Pts	AG	AA	APts	PIM	PP	SH	GW	S	%	TGF	PGF	TGA	PGA	+/–	GP	G	A	Pts	PIM	PP	SH	GW
1975-76	University of Minnesota	WCHA	19	0	1	1	....	....	....	21	....	....	....	....	....	....	....	....	....	....	....	....	....	....	....	....	....	....
1976-77	University of Minnesota	WCHA	37	2	10	12	....	....	....	66	....	....	....	....	....	....	....	....	....	....	....	....	....	....	....	....	....	....
1977-78	University of Minnesota	WCHA	37	4	17	21	....	....	....	63	....	....	....	....	....	....	....	....	....	....	....	....	....	....	....	....	....	....
	Minnesota North Stars	**NHL**	**6**	**0**	**0**	**0**	**0**	**0**	**0**	**22**	**0**	**0**	**0**	**2**	**0.0**	**0**	**0**	**6**	**0**	**–6**	....	....	....	....	....	....	....	....
	Fort Worth Texans	CHL	9	0	2	2	....	....	....	17	....	....	....	....	....	....	....	....	....	....	9	0	1	1	23	....	....	....
1978-79	Oklahoma City Stars	CHL	71	2	19	21	....	....	....	170	....	....	....	....	....	....	....	....	....	....	....	....	....	....	....	....	....	....
1979-80	Oklahoma City Stars	CHL	54	3	14	17	....	....	....	24	....	....	....	....	....	....	....	....	....	....	....	....	....	....	....	....	....	....
	NHL Totals		**6**	**0**	**0**	**0**	**0**	**0**	**0**	**22**	**0**	**0**	**0**	**2**	**0.0**	**0**	**0**	**6**	**0**		....	....	....	....	....	....	....	....

Signed as a free agent by **Minnesota**, July 1, 1978.

• BORDELEAU, CHRISTIAN

Christian Bordeleau C – L. 5'8", 172 lbs. b: Noranda, Que., 9/23/1947.

Season	Club	League	GP	G	A	Pts	AG	AA	APts	PIM	PP	SH	GW	S	%	TGF	PGF	TGA	PGA	+/–	GP	G	A	Pts	PIM	PP	SH	GW
1962-63	Noranda Copper Kings	NOHA	....	42	36	*78	....	....	....	....	....	....	....	....	....	....	....	....	....	....	....	....	....	....	....	....	....	....
1963-64	Montreal Jr. Canadiens	OHA	49	16	18	34	....	....	....	10	....	....	....	....	....	....	....	....	....	....	17	3	2	5	2	....	....	....
1964-65	Montreal Jr. Canadiens	OHA	50	28	28	56	....	....	....	46	....	....	....	....	....	....	....	....	....	....	7	6	2	8	8	....	....	....
1965-66	Montreal Jr. Canadiens	OHA	43	15	48	63	....	....	....	57	....	....	....	....	....	....	....	....	....	....	10	9	5	14	13	....	....	....
1966-67	Montreal Jr. Canadiens	OHA	33	8	19	27	....	....	....	30	....	....	....	....	....	....	....	....	....	....	....	....	....	....	....	....	....	....
1967-68	Houston Apollos	CHL	68	23	28	51	....	....	....	22	....	....	....	....	....	....	....	....	....	....	....	....	....	....	....	....	....	....
1968-69	**Montreal Canadiens**	**NHL**	**13**	**1**	**3**	**4**	**1**	**3**	**4**	**4**	**0**	**0**	**0**	**14**	**7.1**	**4**	**0**	**4**	**1**	**+1**	**6**	**1**	**0**	**1**	**0**	**0**	**0**	**1**
	Houston Apollos	CHL	54	21	36	57	....	....	....	33	....	....	....	....	....	....	....	....	....	....	....	....	....	....	....	....	....	....
1969-70	**Montreal Canadiens**	**NHL**	**48**	**2**	**13**	**15**	**2**	**13**	**15**	**18**	**0**	**0**	**0**	**51**	**3.9**	**23**	**0**	**29**	**8**	**+2**	....	....	....	....	....	....	....	....
1970-71	**St. Louis Blues**	**NHL**	**78**	**21**	**32**	**53**	**22**	**28**	**50**	**48**	**3**	**2**	**7**	**187**	**11.2**	**71**	**16**	**52**	**11**	**+14**	**5**	**0**	**1**	**1**	**17**	**0**	**0**	**0**
1971-72	**St. Louis Blues**	**NHL**	**41**	**8**	**9**	**17**	**8**	**8**	**16**	**6**	**1**	**0**	**1**	**123**	**6.5**	**27**	**7**	**47**	**14**	**–13**	....	....	....	....	....	....	....	....
	Chicago Black Hawks	**NHL**	**25**	**6**	**8**	**14**	**6**	**7**	**13**	**6**	**1**	**0**	**1**	**35**	**17.1**	**18**	**2**	**11**	**0**	**+5**	**8**	**3**	**6**	**9**	**0**	**0**	**0**	**1**
1972-73	Winnipeg Jets	WHA	78	47	54	101	....	....	....	12	....	....	....	....	....	....	....	....	....	....	12	5	8	13	4	....	....	....
1973-74	Winnipeg Jets	WHA	75	26	49	75	....	....	....	22	....	....	....	....	....	....	....	....	....	....	3	3	2	5	0	....	....	....
1974-75	Winnipeg Jets	WHA	18	8	8	16	....	....	....	0	....	....	....	....	....	....	....	....	....	....	....	....	....	....	....	....	....	....
	Quebec Nordiques	WHA	53	15	33	48	....	....	....	24	....	....	....	....	....	....	....	....	....	....	15	2	*13	15	2	....	....	....
1975-76	Quebec Nordiques	WHA	74	37	72	109	....	....	....	42	....	....	....	....	....	....	....	....	....	....	5	1	1	2	4	....	....	....
1976-77	Quebec Nordiques	WHA	72	32	75	107	....	....	....	34	....	....	....	....	....	....	....	....	....	....	8	4	5	9	0	....	....	....
1977-78	Quebec Nordiques	WHA	26	9	22	31	....	....	....	28	....	....	....	....	....	....	....	....	....	....	10	1	5	6	6	....	....	....
1978-79	Quebec Nordiques	WHA	16	5	12	17	....	....	....	0	....	....	....	....	....	....	....	....	....	....	....	....	....	....	....	....	....	....
1979-80	Salt Lake Golden Eagles	CHL	11	3	6	9	....	....	....	4	....	....	....	....	....	....	....	....	....	....	....	....	....	....	....	....	....	....
	NHL Totals		**205**	**38**	**65**	**103**	**39**	**59**	**98**	**82**	**5**	**2**	**9**	**410**	**9.3**	**143**	**25**	**143**	**34**		**19**	**4**	**7**	**11**	**17**	**0**	**0**	**2**
	Other Major League Totals		412	179	325	504				162											53	16	34	50	16	....	....	....

Traded to **St. Louis** by **Montreal** for cash, May 22, 1970. Traded to **Chicago** by **St. Louis** for Danny O'Shea, February 8, 1972. Selected by **LA Sharks** (WHA) in 1972 WHA General Player Draft, February 12, 1972. WHA rights traded to **Winnipeg** (WHA) by **LA Sharks** (WHA) for cash, August 25, 1972. Traded to **St. Louis** by **Chicago** for cash, September 15, 1972. Traded to **Quebec** (WHA) by **Winnipeg** (WHA) for Alain Beaule, December 5, 1974. Reclaimed by **St. Louis** from **Quebec** prior to Expansion Draft, June 9, 1979.

• BORDELEAU, J.P.

J.P. (Jean-Pierre) Bordeleau RW – R. 6'1", 175 lbs. b: Noranda, Que., 6/13/1949. Chicago's 1st choice, 13th overall, in 1969 Amateur Draft.

Season	Club	League	GP	G	A	Pts	AG	AA	APts	PIM	PP	SH	GW	S	%	TGF	PGF	TGA	PGA	+/–	GP	G	A	Pts	PIM	PP	SH	GW
1967-68	Montreal Jr. Canadiens	OHA	54	22	21	43	....	....	....	96	....	....	....	....	....	....	....	....	....	....	11	2	4	6	8	....	....	....
1968-69	Montreal Jr. Canadiens	OHA	51	17	36	53	....	....	....	150	....	....	....	....	....	....	....	....	....	....	14	2	11	13	8	....	....	....
1969-70	Dallas Black Hawks	CHL	62	14	15	29	....	....	....	44	....	....	....	....	....	....	....	....	....	....	....	....	....	....	....	....	....	....
	Chicago Black Hawks	**NHL**	....	....	....	....	....	....	....	....	....	....	....	....	....	....	....	....	....	....	**1**	**0**	**0**	**0**	**0**	....	....	....
1970-71	Dallas Black Hawks	CHL	35	15	15	30	....	....	....	48	....	....	....	....	....	....	....	....	....	....	6	2	0	2	4	....	....	....
1971-72	**Chicago Black Hawks**	**NHL**	**3**	**0**	**2**	**2**	**0**	**2**	**2**	**2**	**0**	**0**	**0**	**4**	**0.0**	**2**	**0**	**2**	**1**	**+1**	....	....	....	....	....	....	....	....
	Dallas Black Hawks	CHL	70	41	31	72	....	....	....	72	....	....	....	....	....	....	....	....	....	....	12	10	2	12	0	....	....	....
1972-73	**Chicago Black Hawks**	**NHL**	**73**	**15**	**15**	**30**	**15**	**13**	**28**	**6**	**0**	**1**	**2**	**113**	**13.3**	**44**	**6**	**35**	**4**	**+7**	**14**	**1**	**0**	**1**	**4**	**1**	**0**	**0**
1973-74	**Chicago Black Hawks**	**NHL**	**64**	**11**	**9**	**20**	**11**	**8**	**19**	**11**	**0**	**0**	**3**	**50**	**22.0**	**34**	**1**	**24**	**2**	**+11**	**11**	**0**	**2**	**2**	**2**	**0**	**0**	**0**
1974-75	**Chicago Black Hawks**	**NHL**	**59**	**7**	**8**	**15**	**6**	**6**	**12**	**4**	**0**	**0**	**1**	**42**	**16.7**	**18**	**1**	**26**	**4**	**–5**	**7**	**2**	**2**	**4**	**2**	**0**	**0**	**0**
1975-76	**Chicago Black Hawks**	**NHL**	**76**	**12**	**18**	**30**	**11**	**14**	**25**	**6**	**1**	**0**	**2**	**71**	**16.9**	**48**	**12**	**46**	**1**	**–9**	**4**	**0**	**0**	**0**	**0**	**0**	**0**	**0**
1976-77	**Chicago Black Hawks**	**NHL**	**60**	**15**	**14**	**29**	**14**	**11**	**25**	**20**	**2**	**0**	**1**	**84**	**17.9**	**46**	**8**	**56**	**4**	**–14**	**2**	**0**	**0**	**0**	**2**	**0**	**0**	**0**
1977-78	**Chicago Black Hawks**	**NHL**	**76**	**15**	**25**	**40**	**14**	**20**	**34**	**32**	**0**	**2**	**3**	**103**	**14.6**	**67**	**12**	**52**	**6**	**+9**	**4**	**0**	**1**	**1**	**0**	**0**	**0**	**0**
1978-79	**Chicago Black Hawks**	**NHL**	**63**	**15**	**21**	**36**	**14**	**16**	**30**	**34**	**2**	**1**	**2**	**101**	**14.9**	**51**	**12**	**54**	**8**	**–7**	**4**	**0**	**1**	**1**	**2**	**0**	**0**	**0**
1979-80	**Chicago Black Hawks**	**NHL**	**45**	**7**	**14**	**21**	**6**	**11**	**17**	**28**	**1**	**0**	**0**	**53**	**13.2**	**28**	**2**	**28**	**5**	**+3**	**1**	**0**	**0**	**0**	**0**	**0**	**0**	**0**
1980-81	New Brunswick Hawks	AHL	64	24	28	52	....	....	....	71	....	....	....	....	....	....	....	....	....	....	13	4	9	13	6	....	....	....
1981-82	New Brunswick Hawks	AHL	15	5	8	13	....	....	....	10	....	....	....	....	....	....	....	....	....	....	....	....	....	....	....	....	....	....
1982-83	Riverview Trappers	NBSHL	DID NOT PLAY – COACHING																									
1983-84	Riverview Trappers	NBSHL	2	0	3	3	....	....	....	2	....	....	....	....	....	....	....	....	....	....	....	....	....	....	....	....	....	....
	NHL Totals		**519**	**97**	**126**	**223**	**91**	**101**	**192**	**143**	**6**	**4**	**14**	**621**	**15.6**	**338**	**54**	**323**	**35**		**48**	**3**	**6**	**9**	**12**	**1**	**0**	**0**

CHL First All-Star Team (1972)

• BORDELEAU, PAULIN

Paulin Bordeleau RW – R. 5'9", 162 lbs. b: Noranda, Que., 1/29/1953. Vancouver's 3rd choice, 19th overall, in 1973 Amateur Draft.

Season	Club	League	GP	G	A	Pts	AG	AA	APts	PIM	PP	SH	GW	S	%	TGF	PGF	TGA	PGA	+/–	GP	G	A	Pts	PIM	PP	SH	GW
1969-70	Montreal Jr. Canadiens	OHA	41	18	29	47	....	....	....	48	....	....	....	....	....	....	....	....	....	....	....	....	....	....	....	....	....	....
1970-71	Toronto Marlboros	OHA	45	27	42	69	....	....	....	69	....	....	....	....	....	....	....	....	....	....	....	....	....	....	....	....	....	....
1971-72	Toronto Marlboros	OHA	34	34	33	67	....	....	....	37	....	....	....	....	....	....	....	....	....	....	....	....	....	....	....	....	....	....
1972-73	Toronto Marlboros	OHA	56	54	43	97	....	....	....	26	....	....	....	....	....	....	....	....	....	....	....	7	9	16	5	....	....	....
1973-74	**Vancouver Canucks**	**NHL**	**68**	**11**	**13**	**24**	**11**	**11**	**22**	**20**	**4**	**0**	**1**	**77**	**14.3**	**38**	**14**	**40**	**0**	**–16**	....	....	....	....	....	....	....	....
1974-75	**Vancouver Canucks**	**NHL**	**67**	**17**	**31**	**48**	**16**	**24**	**40**	**21**	**3**	**0**	**6**	**101**	**16.8**	**70**	**21**	**41**	**1**	**+9**	**5**	**2**	**1**	**3**	**0**	**1**	**0**	**0**
1975-76	**Vancouver Canucks**	**NHL**	**48**	**5**	**12**	**17**	**5**	**9**	**14**	**6**	**0**	**0**	**1**	**35**	**14.3**	**26**	**5**	**24**	**2**	**–1**	....	....	....	....	....	....	....	....
	Tulsa Oilers	CHL	14	5	9	14	....	....	....	11	....	....	....	....	....	....	....	....	....	....	....	....	....	....	....	....	....	....
1976-77	Quebec Nordiques	WHA	80	42	41	83	....	....	....	52	....	....	....	....	....	....	....	....	....	....	16	12	9	21	12	....	....	....
1977-78	Quebec Nordiques	WHA	77	42	23	65	....	....	....	29	....	....	....	....	....	....	....	....	....	....	11	4	6	10	2	....	....	....
1978-79	Quebec Nordiques	WHA	77	17	12	29	....	....	....	44	....	....	....	....	....	....	....	....	....	....	4	1	0	1	0	....	....	....

Season	Club	League	GP	G	A	Pts	AG	AA	APts	PIM	PP	SH	GW	S	%	TGF	PGF	TGA	PGA	+/-	GP	G	A	Pts	PIM	PP	SH	GW
1979-80			DID NOT PLAY																									
1980-81	HC Tours	France		26	14	40																						
1981-82	HC Megeve	France		33	20	53																						
1982-83	HC Megeve	France	STATISTICS NOT AVAILABLE																									
1983-84	HC Megeve	France	32	39	29	68																						
1984-85	HC Megeve	France	32	16	10	26																						
1985-86	HC Megeve	France	32	22	44	66																						
	France	WEC-B	7	2	1	3				4																		
1986-87	HC Mont Blanc	France		57	47	104																						
	France	WEC-B	7	9	6	15				15																		
1987-88	HC Mont Blanc	France	28	20	22	42				63																		
	France	Olympics	6	2	2	4				24																		
NHL Totals			183	33	56	89	32	44	76	47	7	0	8	213	15.5	134	40	105		3	5	2	1	3	0	1	0	0
Other Major League Totals			234	101	76	177				125											31	17	15	32	14			

Selected by **Toronto** (WHA) in 1973 WHA Amateur Draft, June, 1973. WHA rights traded to **Quebec** (WHA) by **Birmingham** (WHA) for future considerations, August, 1976.

● BORDELEAU, SEBASTIEN
Sebastien Bordeleau   C – R. 5'11", 187 lbs.   b: Vancouver, B.C., 2/15/1975.   Montreal's 3rd choice, 73rd overall, in 1993 Entry Draft.

Season	Club	League	GP	G	A	Pts	AG	AA	APts	PIM	PP	SH	GW	S	%	TGF	PGF	TGA	PGA	+/-	GP	G	A	Pts	PIM	PP	SH	GW
1991-92	Hull Olympiques	QMJHL	62	26	32	58				91											5	0	3	3	23			
1992-93	Hull Olympiques	QMJHL	60	18	39	57				95											10	3	8	11	20			
1993-94	Hull Olympiques	QMJHL	60	26	57	83				147											17	6	14	20	26			
1994-95	Hull Olympiques	QMJHL	68	52	76	128				142											18	*13	19	*32	25			
	Fredericton Canadiens	AHL																			1	0	0	0	0			
1995-96	**Montreal Canadiens**	**NHL**	4	0	0	0	0	0	0	0	0	0	0	0	0.0	0	0	1	0	-1								
	Fredericton Canadiens	AHL	43	17	29	46				68											7	0	2	2	8			
1996-97	**Montreal Canadiens**	**NHL**	28	2	9	11	2	8	10	2	0	0	0	27	7.4	13	0	23	7	-3								
	Fredericton Canadiens	AHL	33	17	21	38				50																		
1997-98	**Montreal Canadiens**	**NHL**	53	6	8	14	7	8	15	36	2	1	0	55	10.9	23	10	13	5	+5	5	0	0	0	2	0	0	0
NHL Totals			85	8	17	25	9	16	25	38	2	1	0	82	9.8	36	10	37	12		5	0	0	0	2	0	0	0

QMJHL First All-Star Team (1995)

Traded to **Nashville** by **Montreal** for future considerations, June 26, 1998.

● BOROTSIK, JACK
Jack Borotsik   C – L. 5'9", 180 lbs.   b: Brandon, Man., 11/26/1949.

Season	Club	League	GP	G	A	Pts	AG	AA	APts	PIM	PP	SH	GW	S	%	TGF	PGF	TGA	PGA	+/-	GP	G	A	Pts	PIM	PP	SH	GW
1965-66	Brandon Wheat Kings	SJHL	1	1	0	1				0											2	0	0	0	0			
1966-67	Brandon Wheat Kings	SJHL	STATISTICS NOT AVAILABLE																									
1967-68	Brandon Wheat Kings	WCJHL	60	36	49	85				37																		
1968-69	Brandon Wheat Kings	WCJHL	59	24	40	64				2																		
1969-70	Brandon University	WCIAA	20	14	10	24																						
1970-71	Dayton Gems	IHL	71	15	38	53				4											10	3	4	7	5			
1971-72	Dayton Gems	IHL	67	29	41	70				6											5	0	5	5	2			
1972-73	Denver Spurs	WHL	71	24	38	62				15											5	1	1	2	0			
1973-74	Denver Spurs	WHL	58	7	17	24				2																		
1974-75	**St. Louis Blues**	**NHL**	1	0	0	0	0	0	0	0	0	0	0	0	0.0	0	0	0	0	0								
	Denver Spurs	CHL	76	13	42	55				10											2	0	0	0	0			
1975-76	Brandon Elks	WCSHL	DID NOT PLAY – COACHING																									
1976-77	Brandon Elks	WCSHL	DID NOT PLAY – COACHING																									
1977-78	Brandon Elks	WCSHL		11	36	47				6																		
NHL Totals			1	0	0	0	0	0	0	0	0	0	0	0	0.0	0	0	0	0	0								

Signed as a free agent by **St. Louis**, October 12, 1972.

● BORSATO, LUCIANO
Luciano Borsato   C – R. 5'11", 190 lbs.   b: Richmond Hill, Ont., 1/7/1966.   Winnipeg's 7th choice, 135th overall, in 1984 Entry Draft.

Season	Club	League	GP	G	A	Pts	AG	AA	APts	PIM	PP	SH	GW	S	%	TGF	PGF	TGA	PGA	+/-	GP	G	A	Pts	PIM	PP	SH	GW
1983-84	Bramalea Blues	OJHL	37	20	36	56				59																		
1984-85	Clarkson University	ECAC	33	15	17	32				37																		
1985-86	Clarkson University	ECAC	28	14	17	31				44																		
1986-87	Clarkson University	ECAC	31	16	41	57				55																		
1987-88	Clarkson University	ECAC	33	15	29	44				38																		
	Moncton Hawks	AHL	3	1	1	2				0																		
1988-89	Moncton Hawks	AHL	6	2	5	7				4																		
	Tappara Tampere	Finland	44	31	36	67				69											7	0	3	3	4			
1989-90	Moncton Hawks	AHL	1	1	0	1				0																		
1990-91	**Winnipeg Jets**	**NHL**	1	0	1	1	0	1	1	2	0	0	0	1	0.0	1	0	1	0	0								
	Moncton Hawks	AHL	41	14	24	38				40											9	3	7	10	22			
1991-92	**Winnipeg Jets**	**NHL**	56	15	21	36	14	16	30	45	5	0	1	81	18.5	50	22	34	0	-6	1	0	0	0	0	0	0	0
	Moncton Hawks	AHL	14	2	7	9				39																		
1992-93	**Winnipeg Jets**	**NHL**	67	15	20	35	12	14	26	38	1	1	3	101	14.9	47	6	58	16	-1	6	1	0	1	4	0	1	0
1993-94	**Winnipeg Jets**	**NHL**	75	5	13	18	5	10	15	28	1	1	0	65	7.7	28	6	56	23	-11								
1994-95	**Winnipeg Jets**	**NHL**	4	0	0	0	0	0	0	0	0	0	0	2	0.0	0	0	1	0	-1								
	Springfield Falcons	AHL	22	9	11	20				14																		
	Canada	WC-A	7	3	1	4				18																		
1995-96	Kolner Haie	Germany	49	25	36	61				52											12	6	8	14	28			
1996-97	Kolner Haie	Germany	23	13	21	34				32											4	2	3	5	0			
1997-98	Kolner Haie	EuroHL	5	1	2	3				14																		
	Kolner Haie	Germany	29	12	16	27				77											3	0	1	1	27			
NHL Totals			203	35	55	90	31	41	72	113	7	2	6	250	14.0	126	34	150	39		7	1	0	1	4	0	1	0

ECAC Second All-Star Team (1988) • NCAA East Second All-American Team (1988)

● BORSCHEVSKY, NIKOLAI
Nikolai "Stick" Borschevsky   RW – L. 5'9", 180 lbs.   b: Tomsk, USSR, 1/12/1965.   Toronto's 3rd choice, 77th overall, in 1992 Entry Draft.

Season	Club	League	GP	G	A	Pts	AG	AA	APts	PIM	PP	SH	GW	S	%	TGF	PGF	TGA	PGA	+/-	GP	G	A	Pts	PIM	PP	SH	GW
1983-84	Moscow Dynamo	USSR	34	4	5	9				4																		
	Soviet Union	WJC-A	7	6	7	13				4																		
1984-85	Moscow Dynamo	USSR	34	5	9	14				6																		
1985-86	Moscow Dynamo	USSR	31	6	4	10				4																		
	Moscow Dynamo	SuperS	4	0	0	0				0																		
1986-87	Moscow Dynamo	USSR	28	1	4	5				0																		
1987-88	Moscow Dynamo	USSR	37	11	7	18				6																		
1988-89	Moscow Dynamo	USSR	43	7	8	15				18																		
1989-90	Spartak Moscow	FrTour	1	1	1	2				0																		
	Spartak Moscow	USSR	48	17	25	42				8																		
1990-91	Spartak Moscow	FrTour	1	0	2	2				0																		
	Spartak Moscow	USSR	45	19	16	35				16																		
1991-92	Spartak Moscow	CIS	40	25	14	39				16																		
	Russia	Olympics	8	7	2	9				0																		
	Russia	WC-A	6	1	3	4				2																		
1992-93	**Toronto Maple Leafs**	**NHL**	78	34	40	74	28	27	55	28	12	0	4	204	16.7	111	45	33	0	+33	16	2	7	9	0	0	0	1
1993-94	**Toronto Maple Leafs**	**NHL**	45	14	20	34	13	15	28	10	7	0	1	105	13.3	52	27	19	0	+6	15	2	2	4	4	1	0	0
1994-95	Spartak Moscow	CIS	9	5	1	6				14																		
	Toronto Maple Leafs	**NHL**	19	0	5	5	0	7	7	0	0	0	0	28	0.0	12	1	9	1	+3								
	Calgary Flames	**NHL**	8	0	5	5	0	7	7	0	0	0	0	12	0.0	12	3	2	0	+7								

			REGULAR SEASON																		PLAYOFFS							
Season	Club	League	GP	G	A	Pts	AG	AA	APts	PIM	PP	SH	GW	S	%	TGF	PGF	TGA	PGA	+/–	GP	G	A	Pts	PIM	PP	SH	GW
1995-96	**Dallas Stars**	**NHL**	**12**	**1**	**3**	**4**	**1**	**2**	**3**	**6**	**0**	**0**	**1**	**22**	**4.5**	**7**	**1**	**13**	**0**	**–7**	....	....	....	....	....	....	....	....
	Kolner Haie	Germany	8	0	4	4	....	....	....	27	....	....	....	....	....	....	....	....	....	....	8	2	2	4	4	....	....	....
1996-97	Spartak Moscow	Russia	42	15	*29	*44	....	....	....	52	....	....	....	....	....	....	....	....	....	....	....	....	....	....	....	....	....	....
1997-98	Spartak Moscow	CIS	46	10	17	27	....	....	....	30	....	....	....	....	....	....	....	....	....	....	....	....	....	....	....	....	....	....
	NHL Totals		**162**	**49**	**73**	**122**	**42**	**58**	**100**	**44**	**19**	**0**	**6**	**371**	**13.2**	**194**	**77**	**76**	**1**		**31**	**4**	**9**	**13**	**4**	**1**	**0**	**1**

EJC-A All-Star Team (1983) • WJC-A All-Star Team (1984) • Won Izvestia Trophy (Russian Top Scorer) (1997)

Traded to **Calgary** by **Toronto** for Calgary's 6th round choice (Chris Bogas) in 1996 Entry Draft, April 6, 1995. Signed as a free agent by **Dallas**, September 13, 1995.

• BOSCHMAN, LAURIE

Laurie Boschman C – L. 6′, 185 lbs. b: Major, Sask., 6/4/1960. Toronto's 1st choice, 9th overall, in 1979 Entry Draft.

1976-77	Brandon Bobcats	MJHL	47	17	40	57	....	....	....	139	....	....	....	....	....	....	....	....	....	....	....	....	....	....	....	....	....	....
	Brandon Wheat Kings	WCJHL	3	0	1	1	....	....	....	0	....	....	....	....	....	....	....	....	....	....	12	1	1	2	17	....	....	....
1977-78	Brandon Wheat Kings	WCJHL	72	42	57	99	....	....	....	227	....	....	....	....	....	....	....	....	....	....	8	2	5	7	45	....	....	....
1978-79	Brandon Wheat Kings	WHL	65	66	83	149	....	....	....	215	....	....	....	....	....	....	....	....	....	....	22	11	23	34	56	....	....	....
1979-80	**Toronto Maple Leafs**	**NHL**	**80**	**16**	**32**	**48**	**14**	**25**	**39**	**78**	**2**	**0**	**4**	**99**	**16.2**	**73**	**9**	**62**	**0**	**+2**	**3**	**1**	**1**	**2**	**18**	**1**	**0**	**0**
1980-81	**Toronto Maple Leafs**	**NHL**	**53**	**14**	**19**	**33**	**12**	**13**	**25**	**178**	**3**	**0**	**4**	**70**	**20.0**	**47**	**7**	**55**	**5**	**–10**	**3**	**0**	**0**	**0**	**7**	**0**	**0**	**0**
	New Brunswick Hawks	AHL	4	4	1	5	....	....	....	47	....	....	....	....	....	....	....	....	....	....	....	....	....	....	....	....	....	....
1981-82	**Toronto Maple Leafs**	**NHL**	**54**	**9**	**19**	**28**	**7**	**13**	**20**	**150**	**1**	**0**	**1**	**64**	**14.1**	**50**	**3**	**62**	**12**	**–3**	....	....	....	....	....	....	....	....
	Edmonton Oilers	**NHL**	**11**	**2**	**3**	**5**	**2**	**2**	**4**	**37**	**0**	**0**	**0**	**4**	**50.0**	**8**	**0**	**6**	**0**	**+2**	**3**	**0**	**1**	**1**	**4**	**0**	**0**	**0**
1982-83	**Edmonton Oilers**	**NHL**	**62**	**8**	**12**	**20**	**7**	**8**	**15**	**183**	**0**	**0**	**0**	**59**	**13.6**	**30**	**0**	**30**	**3**	**+3**	....	....	....	....	....	....	....	....
	Winnipeg Jets	**NHL**	**12**	**3**	**5**	**8**	**2**	**3**	**5**	**36**	**1**	**0**	**0**	**25**	**12.0**	**16**	**3**	**10**	**0**	**+3**	**3**	**0**	**1**	**1**	**12**	**0**	**0**	**0**
1983-84	**Winnipeg Jets**	**NHL**	**61**	**28**	**46**	**74**	**23**	**31**	**54**	**234**	**9**	**0**	**3**	**138**	**20.3**	**95**	**26**	**93**	**20**	**–4**	**3**	**0**	**1**	**1**	**5**	**0**	**0**	**0**
1984-85	**Winnipeg Jets**	**NHL**	**80**	**32**	**44**	**76**	**26**	**30**	**56**	**180**	**5**	**2**	**4**	**167**	**19.2**	**105**	**19**	**126**	**32**	**–8**	**8**	**2**	**1**	**3**	**21**	**0**	**1**	**0**
1985-86	**Winnipeg Jets**	**NHL**	**77**	**27**	**42**	**69**	**22**	**28**	**50**	**241**	**3**	**2**	**2**	**158**	**17.1**	**94**	**20**	**122**	**19**	**–29**	**3**	**0**	**1**	**1**	**6**	**0**	**0**	**0**
1986-87	**Winnipeg Jets**	**NHL**	**80**	**17**	**24**	**41**	**15**	**17**	**32**	**152**	**1**	**1**	**2**	**161**	**10.6**	**69**	**11**	**82**	**7**	**–17**	**10**	**2**	**3**	**5**	**32**	**1**	**0**	**0**
1987-88	**Winnipeg Jets**	**NHL**	**80**	**25**	**23**	**48**	**21**	**16**	**37**	**229**	**10**	**1**	**3**	**166**	**15.1**	**71**	**31**	**80**	**16**	**–24**	**5**	**1**	**3**	**4**	**9**	**0**	**0**	**0**
1988-89	**Winnipeg Jets**	**NHL**	**70**	**10**	**26**	**36**	**8**	**18**	**26**	**163**	**3**	**0**	**1**	**113**	**8.8**	**58**	**12**	**73**	**10**	**–17**	....	....	....	....	....	....	....	....
1989-90	**Winnipeg Jets**	**NHL**	**66**	**10**	**17**	**27**	**9**	**12**	**21**	**103**	**3**	**1**	**1**	**87**	**11.5**	**39**	**4**	**55**	**9**	**–11**	**2**	**0**	**0**	**0**	**2**	**0**	**0**	**0**
1990-91	**New Jersey Devils**	**NHL**	**78**	**11**	**9**	**20**	**10**	**7**	**17**	**79**	**0**	**1**	**1**	**91**	**12.1**	**37**	**1**	**67**	**30**	**–1**	**7**	**1**	**1**	**2**	**16**	**0**	**0**	**0**
1991-92	**New Jersey Devils**	**NHL**	**75**	**8**	**20**	**28**	**7**	**15**	**22**	**121**	**0**	**0**	**2**	**89**	**9.0**	**44**	**1**	**69**	**35**	**+9**	**7**	**1**	**0**	**1**	**8**	**0**	**0**	**1**
1992-93	**Ottawa Senators**	**NHL**	**70**	**9**	**7**	**16**	**7**	**5**	**12**	**101**	**0**	**1**	**1**	**84**	**10.7**	**26**	**3**	**85**	**36**	**–26**	....	....	....	....	....	....	....	....
1993-94			DID NOT PLAY – RETIRED																									
1994-95	Fife Flyers	Britain	7	9	9	18	....	....	....	6	....	....	....	....	....	....	....	....	....	....	6	5	8	13	12	....	....	....
	NHL Totals		**1009**	**229**	**348**	**577**	**192**	**243**	**435**	**2265**	**41**	**9**	**29**	**1575**	**14.5**	**862**	**150**	**1077**	**234**		**57**	**8**	**13**	**21**	**140**	**2**	**1**	**1**

WHL All-Star Team (1979) • Memorial Cup All-Star Team (1979)

Traded to **Edmonton** by **Toronto** for Walt Poddubny and Phil Drouilliard, March 9, 1982. Traded to **Winnipeg** by **Edmonton** for Willy Lidstrom, March 7, 1983. Traded to **New Jersey** by **Winnipeg** for Bob Brooke, September 6, 1990. Claimed by **Ottawa** from **New Jersey** in Expansion Draft, June 18, 1992.

• BOSSY, MIKE

Mike Bossy RW – R. 6′, 186 lbs. b: Montreal, Que., 1/22/1957. NY Islanders' 1st choice, 15th overall, in 1977 Amateur Draft. **HHOF**

1972-73	Laval National	QMJHL	4	1	2	3	....	....	....	0	....	....	....	....	....	....	....	....	....	....	....	....	....	....	....	....	....	....
1973-74	Laval National	QMJHL	68	70	48	118	....	....	....	45	....	....	....	....	....	....	....	....	....	....	11	6	16	22	2	....	....	....
1974-75	Laval National	QMJHL	67	*84	65	149	....	....	....	42	....	....	....	....	....	....	....	....	....	....	16	18	20	38	2	....	....	....
1975-76	Laval National	QMJHL	64	79	57	136	....	....	....	25	....	....	....	....	....	....	....	....	....	....	....	....	....	....	....	....	....	....
1976-77	Laval National	QMJHL	61	75	51	126	....	....	....	12	....	....	....	....	....	....	....	....	....	....	7	5	5	10	12	....	....	....
1977-78	**New York Islanders**	**NHL**	**73**	**53**	**38**	**91**	**51**	**31**	**82**	**6**	**25**	**0**	**5**	**235**	**22.6**	**130**	**57**	**42**	**0**	**+31**	**7**	**2**	**2**	**4**	**2**	**0**	**0**	**1**
1978-79	**New York Islanders**	**NHL**	**80**	***69**	**57**	**126**	**63**	**44**	**107**	**25**	**27**	**0**	**9**	**279**	**24.7**	**174**	**70**	**41**	**0**	**+63**	**10**	**6**	**2**	**8**	**2**	**2**	**0**	**1**
	NHL All-Stars	Chal Cup	3	2	2	4	....	....	....	0	....	....	....	....	....	....	....	....	....	....	....	....	....	....	....	....	....	....
1979-80	**New York Islanders**	**NHL**	**75**	**51**	**41**	**92**	**46**	**32**	**78**	**12**	**16**	**0**	**8**	**244**	**20.9**	**126**	**47**	**51**	**0**	**+28**	**16**	**10**	**13**	**23**	**8**	**6**	**0**	**1**
1980-81	**New York Islanders**	**NHL**	**79**	***68**	**51**	**119**	**56**	**36**	**92**	**32**	**28**	**2**	**10**	**315**	**21.6**	**161**	**64**	**65**	**5**	**+37**	**18**	***17**	***18**	***35**	**4**	**9**	**0**	**3**
1981-82	Canada	C Cup	7	8	3	11	....	....	....	2	....	....	....	....	....	....	....	....	....	....	....	....	....	....	....	....	....	....
	New York Islanders	**NHL**	**80**	**64**	**83**	**147**	**51**	**55**	**106**	**22**	**17**	**0**	**10**	**301**	**21.3**	**178**	**58**	**54**	**3**	**+69**	**19**	***17**	**10**	**27**	**0**	**6**	**0**	**3**
1982-83	**New York Islanders**	**NHL**	**79**	**60**	**58**	**118**	**50**	**40**	**90**	**20**	**19**	**0**	**8**	**272**	**22.1**	**141**	**48**	**66**	**0**	**+27**	**19**	***17**	**9**	**26**	**10**	**6**	**0**	**5**
1983-84	**New York Islanders**	**NHL**	**67**	**51**	**67**	**118**	**41**	**46**	**87**	**8**	**6**	**0**	**11**	**246**	**20.7**	**147**	**35**	**46**	**0**	**+66**	**21**	**8**	**10**	**18**	**4**	**2**	**0**	**3**
1984-85	Canada	C Cup	8	5	4	9	....	....	....	2	....	....	....	....	....	....	....	....	....	....	....	....	....	....	....	....	....	....
	New York Islanders	**NHL**	**76**	**58**	**59**	**117**	**48**	**40**	**88**	**38**	**14**	**4**	**7**	**285**	**20.4**	**151**	**49**	**74**	**9**	**+37**	**10**	**5**	**6**	**11**	**4**	**2**	**0**	**0**
1985-86	**New York Islanders**	**NHL**	**80**	**61**	**62**	**123**	**49**	**42**	**91**	**14**	**21**	**1**	**9**	**302**	**20.2**	**155**	**50**	**87**	**12**	**+30**	**3**	**1**	**2**	**3**	**4**	**0**	**0**	**0**
1986-87	**New York Islanders**	**NHL**	**63**	**38**	**37**	**75**	**33**	**27**	**60**	**33**	**8**	**1**	**5**	**226**	**16.8**	**105**	**53**	**62**	**3**	**–7**	**6**	**2**	**3**	**5**	**0**	**2**	**0**	**0**
	NHL Totals		**752**	**573**	**553**	**1126**	**488**	**393**	**881**	**210**	**181**	**8**	**82**	**2705**	**21.2**	**1468**	**531**	**588**	**32**		**129**	**85**	**75**	**160**	**38**	**35**	**0**	**17**

QMJHL First All-Star Team (1975) • QMJHL West First All-Star Team (1976) • QMJHL Second All-Star Team (1977) • NHL Second All-Star Team (1978, 1979, 1985) • Won Calder Memorial Trophy (1978) • NHL First All-Star Team (1981, 1982, 1983, 1984, 1986) • Canada Cup All-Star Team (1981) • Won Conn Smythe Trophy (1982) • Won Lady Byng Trophy (1983, 1984, 1986)

Played in NHL All-Star Game (1978, 1980, 1981, 1982, 1983, 1985, 1986)

• BOTELL, MARK

Mark Botell D – L. 6′4″, 220 lbs. b: Scarborough, Ont., 8/27/1961. Philadelphia's 8th choice, 168th overall, in 1980 Entry Draft.

1978-79	Niagara Falls Flyers	OHA	55	2	8	10	....	....	....	122	....	....	....	....	....	....	....	....	....	....	14	2	1	3	6	....	....	....
1979-80	Niagara Falls Flyersw	OHA	20	2	5	7	....	....	....	11	....	....	....	....	....	....	....	....	....	....	....	....	....	....	....	....	....	....
	Windsor Spitfires	OHA	2	0	0	0	....	....	....	0	....	....	....	....	....	....	....	....	....	....	....	....	....	....	....	....	....	....
	Brantford Alexanders	OHA	15	2	3	5	....	....	....	24	....	....	....	....	....	....	....	....	....	....	11	1	5	6	10	....	....	....
1980-81	Brantford Alexanders	OHA	58	11	20	31	....	....	....	143	....	....	....	....	....	....	....	....	....	....	4	0	2	2	12	....	....	....
	Maine Mariners	AHL	2	0	1	1	....	....	....	0	....	....	....	....	....	....	....	....	....	....	20	4	4	8	36	....	....	....
1981-82	**Philadelphia Flyers**	**NHL**	**32**	**4**	**10**	**14**	**3**	**7**	**10**	**31**	**0**	**0**	**1**	**50**	**8.0**	**43**	**11**	**27**	**3**	**+8**	....	....	....	....	....	....	....	....
	Maine Mariners	AHL	42	3	14	17	....	....	....	41	....	....	....	....	....	....	....	....	....	....	3	0	1	1	4	....	....	....
1982-83	Toledo Goaldiggers	IHL	24	6	14	20	....	....	....	43	....	....	....	....	....	....	....	....	....	....	....	....	....	....	....	....	....	....
	Maine Mariners	AHL	30	1	4	5	....	....	....	26	....	....	....	....	....	....	....	....	....	....	....	....	....	....	....	....	....	....
1983-84	Montana Magic	CHL	2	0	0	0	....	....	....	2	....	....	....	....	....	....	....	....	....	....	....	....	....	....	....	....	....	....
	Toledo Goaldiggers	IHL	78	16	27	43	....	....	....	164	....	....	....	....	....	....	....	....	....	....	9	2	1	3	6	....	....	....
1984-85	Peoria Rivermen	IHL	70	6	21	27	....	....	....	77	....	....	....	....	....	....	....	....	....	....	20	1	3	4	35	....	....	....
1985-86	St. Catharines Saints	AHL	11	1	3	4	....	....	....	17	....	....	....	....	....	....	....	....	....	....	12	1	3	4	8	....	....	....
	NHL Totals		**32**	**4**	**10**	**14**	**3**	**7**	**10**	**31**	**0**	**0**	**1**	**50**	**8.0**	**43**	**11**	**27**	**3**		....	....	....	....	....	....	....	....

• BOTHWELL, TIM

Tim Bothwell D – L. 6′3″, 190 lbs. b: Vancouver, B.C., 5/6/1955.

1973-74	Burlington Mohawks	Jr. B	STATISTICS NOT AVAILABLE																									
1974-75	Brown University	ECAC	9	6	9	15	....	....	....	14	....	....	....	....	....	....	....	....	....	....	....	....	....	....	....	....	....	....
1975-76	Brown University	ECAC	29	12	22	34	....	....	....	30	....	....	....	....	....	....	....	....	....	....	....	....	....	....	....	....	....	....
1976-77	Brown University	ECAC	27	7	27	34	....	....	....	40	....	....	....	....	....	....	....	....	....	....	....	....	....	....	....	....	....	....
1977-78	Brown University	ECAC	29	9	26	35	....	....	....	48	....	....	....	....	....	....	....	....	....	....	....	....	....	....	....	....	....	....
1978-79	**New York Rangers**	**NHL**	**1**	**0**	**0**	**0**	**0**	**0**	**0**	**2**	**0**	**0**	**0**	**2**	**0.0**	**0**	**0**	**2**	**1**	**–1**	....	....	....	....	....	....	....	....
	New Haven Nighthawks	AHL	66	15	33	48	....	....	....	44	....	....	....	....	....	....	....	....	....	....	10	4	6	10	8	....	....	....
1979-80	**New York Rangers**	**NHL**	**45**	**4**	**6**	**10**	**4**	**5**	**9**	**20**	**0**	**0**	**2**	**37**	**10.8**	**36**	**1**	**45**	**7**	**–3**	**9**	**0**	**0**	**0**	**8**	**0**	**0**	**0**
	New Haven Nighthawks	AHL	22	6	7	13	....	....	....	25	....	....	....	....	....	....	....	....	....	....	....	....	....	....	....	....	....	....
1980-81	**New York Rangers**	**NHL**	**3**	**0**	**1**	**1**	**0**	**1**	**1**	**0**	**0**	**0**	**0**	**0**	**0.0**	**3**	**0**	**3**	**0**	**0**	....	....	....	....	....	....	....	....
	New Haven Nighthawks	AHL	73	10	53	69	....	....	....	98	....	....	....	....	....	....	....	....	....	....	4	1	2	3	6	....	....	....
1981-82	**New York Rangers**	**NHL**	**13**	**0**	**3**	**3**	**0**	**2**	**2**	**10**	**0**	**0**	**0**	**6**	**0.0**	**9**	**1**	**13**	**0**	**–5**	....	....	....	....	....	....	....	....
	Springfield Indians	AHL	10	0	4	4	....	....	....	7	....	....	....	....	....	....	....	....	....	....	....	....	....	....	....	....	....	....
1982-83	**St. Louis Blues**	**NHL**	**61**	**4**	**11**	**15**	**3**	**8**	**11**	**34**	**0**	**1**	**1**	**62**	**6.5**	**73**	**9**	**93**	**21**	**–8**	....	....	....	....	....	....	....	....
1983-84	**St. Louis Blues**	**NHL**	**62**	**2**	**13**	**15**	**2**	**9**	**11**	**65**	**1**	**0**	**0**	**59**	**3.4**	**69**	**1**	**71**	**25**	**+22**	**11**	**0**	**2**	**2**	**14**	**0**	**0**	**0**
	Montana Magic	CHL	4	0	3	3	....	....	....	0	....	....	....	....	....	....	....	....	....	....	....	....	....	....	....	....	....	....
1984-85	**St. Louis Blues**	**NHL**	**79**	**4**	**22**	**26**	**3**	**15**	**18**	**62**	**1**	**0**	**0**	**102**	**3.9**	**113**	**9**	**112**	**35**	**+27**	**3**	**0**	**0**	**0**	**2**	**0**	**0**	**0**
1985-86	**Hartford Whalers**	**NHL**	**62**	**2**	**8**	**10**	**2**	**5**	**7**	**53**	**0**	**0**	**0**	**50**	**4.0**	**68**	**2**	**72**	**19**	**+13**	**10**	**0**	**0**	**0**	**8**	**0**	**0**	**0**
1986-87	**Hartford Whalers**	**NHL**	**4**	**1**	**0**	**1**	**1**	**0**	**1**	**0**	**0**	**0**	**0**	**3**	**33.3**	**2**	**0**	**8**	**1**	**–5**	....	....	....	....	....	....	....	....
	St. Louis Blues	**NHL**	**72**	**5**	**16**	**21**	**4**	**12**	**16**	**46**	**0**	**0**	**1**	**75**	**6.7**	**68**	**9**	**89**	**16**	**–14**	**6**	**0**	**0**	**0**	**6**	**0**	**0**	**0**

			REGULAR SEASON																		PLAYOFFS							
Season	Club	League	GP	G	A	Pts	AG	AA	APts	PIM	PP	SH	GW	S	%	TGF	PGF	TGA	PGA	+/–	GP	G	A	Pts	PIM	PP	SH	GW
1987-88	St. Louis Blues	NHL	78	6	13	19	5	9	14	76	0	0	1	88	6.8	76	0	125	55	+6	10	0	1	1	18	0	0	0
1988-89	St. Louis Blues	NHL	22	0	0	0	0	0	0	14	0	0	0	10	0.0	14	0	17	7	+4	....	....	....	....	....	....	....	....
	Peoria Rivermen	IHL	14	0	7	7	....	....	....	14	....	....	....	....	....	....	....	....	....	....	....	....	....	....	....	....	....	....
1989-90	New Haven Nighthawks	AHL	75	3	26	29	....	....	....	56	....	....	....	....	....	....	....	....	....	....	....	....	....	....	....	....	....	....
	NHL Totals		502	28	93	121	24	66	90	382	2	1	5	494	5.7	531	32	650	187		49	0	3	3	56	0	0	0

ECAC First All-Star Team (1977)

Signed as a free agent by **NY Rangers**, June 8, 1978. Claimed by **St. Louis** from **NY Rangers** in Waiver Draft, October 4, 1982. Rights traded to **Hartford** by **St. Louis** for cash, October 4, 1985. Traded to **St. Louis** by **Hartford** for Dave Barr, October 21, 1986.

• BOTTERILL, JASON

Jason Botterill LW – L. 6'3", 205 lbs. b: Edmonton, Alta., 5/19/1976. Dallas' 1st choice, 20th overall, in 1994 Entry Draft.

Season	Club	League	GP	G	A	Pts	AG	AA	APts	PIM	PP	SH	GW	S	%	TGF	PGF	TGA	PGA	+/–	GP	G	A	Pts	PIM	PP	SH	GW
1993-94	University of Michigan	CCHA	36	20	19	39	....	....	....	94	....	....	....	....	....	....	....	....	....	....	....	....	....	....	....	....	....	....
	Canada	WJC-A	7	1	0	1	....	....	....	8	....	....	....	....	....	....	....	....	....	....	....	....	....	....	....	....	....	....
1994-95	Univesity of Michigan	CCHA	34	14	14	28	....	....	....	117	....	....	....	....	....	....	....	....	....	....	....	....	....	....	....	....	....	....
	Canada	WJC-A	7	0	4	4	....	....	....	6	....	....	....	....	....	....	....	....	....	....	....	....	....	....	....	....	....	....
1995-96	University of Michigan	CCHA	37	*32	25	57	....	....	....	*143	....	....	....	....	....	....	....	....	....	....	....	....	....	....	....	....	....	....
	Canada	WJC-A	6	1	3	4	....	....	....	6	....	....	....	....	....	....	....	....	....	....	....	....	....	....	....	....	....	....
1996-97	University of Michigan	CCHA	42	*37	24	61	....	....	....	129	....	....	....	....	....	....	....	....	....	....	....	....	....	....	....	....	....	....
1997-98	Dallas Stars	NHL	4	0	0	0	0	0	0	19	0	0	0	2	0.0	0	0	1	0	–1	....	....	....	....	....	....	....	....
	Michigan K-Wings	IHL	50	11	11	22	....	....	....	82	....	....	....	....	....	....	....	....	....	....	4	0	0	0	5	....	....	....
	NHL Totals		4	0	0	0	0	0	0	19	0	0	0	2	0.0	0	0	1	0		....	....	....	....	....	....	....	....

CCHA Second All-Star Team (1996) • NCAA West Second All-American Team (1997)

• BOTTING, CAM

Cam Botting RW. 6'2", 205 lbs. b: Kingston, Ont., 3/10/1954. Atlanta's 4th choice, 64th overall, in 1974 Amateur Draft.

Season	Club	League	GP	G	A	Pts	AG	AA	APts	PIM	PP	SH	GW	S	%	TGF	PGF	TGA	PGA	+/–	GP	G	A	Pts	PIM	PP	SH	GW
1971-72	Hamilton Red Wings	OHA	27	1	6	7	....	....	....	17	....	....	....	....	....	....	....	....	....	....	....	....	....	....	....	....	....	....
1972-73	Niagara Falls Flyers	SOJHL	48	30	23	53	....	....	....	113	....	....	....	....	....	....	....	....	....	....	....	....	....	....	....	....	....	....
	Hamilton Red Wings	OHA	8	1	3	4	....	....	....	7	....	....	....	....	....	....	....	....	....	....	....	....	....	....	....	....	....	....
1973-74	Niagara Falls Flyers	SOJHL	48	40	56	96	....	....	....	210	....	....	....	....	....	....	....	....	....	....	....	....	....	....	....	....	....	....
1974-75	Omaha Knights	CHL	15	2	3	5	....	....	....	9	....	....	....	....	....	....	....	....	....	....	....	....	....	....	....	....	....	....
	Des Moines Oak Leafs	IHL	49	8	5	13	....	....	....	30	....	....	....	....	....	....	....	....	....	....	7	0	3	3	9	....	....	....
1975-76	Atlanta Flames	NHL	2	0	1	1	0	1	1	0	0	0	0	0	0.0	1	0	0	0	+1	....	....	....	....	....	....	....	....
	Tulsa Oilers	CHL	73	22	29	51	....	....	....	68	....	....	....	....	....	....	....	....	....	....	9	2	5	7	6	....	....	....
1976-77	Tulsa Oilers	CHL	74	26	23	49	....	....	....	74	....	....	....	....	....	....	....	....	....	....	9	3	1	4	0	....	....	....
1977-78	Tulsa Oilers	CHL	76	17	26	43	....	....	....	52	....	....	....	....	....	....	....	....	....	....	7	0	2	2	4	....	....	....
1979-1982			DID NOT PLAY																									
1982-83	Flint Generals	IHL	12	2	4	6	....	....	....	9	....	....	....	....	....	....	....	....	....	....	....	....	....	....	....	....	....	....
	Erie Golden Blades	ACHL	49	9	27	36	....	....	....	13	....	....	....	....	....	....	....	....	....	....	5	2	3	5	0	....	....	....
1983-84	Erie Golden Blades	ACHL	13	2	2	4	....	....	....	22	....	....	....	....	....	....	....	....	....	....	....	....	....	....	....	....	....	....
	NHL Totals		2	0	1	1	0	1	1	0	0	0	0	0	0.0	1	0	0	0		....	....	....	....	....	....	....	....

• BOUCHA, HENRY

Henry Boucha C – R. 6', 185 lbs. b: Warroad, MN, 6/1/1951. Detroit's 2nd choice, 16th overall, in 1971 Amateur Draft. **USHOF**

Season	Club	League	GP	G	A	Pts	AG	AA	APts	PIM	PP	SH	GW	S	%	TGF	PGF	TGA	PGA	+/–	GP	G	A	Pts	PIM	PP	SH	GW
1969-70	Winnipeg Jets	WCJHL	51	27	26	53	....	....	....	37	....	....	....	....	....	....	....	....	....	....	....	....	....	....	....	....	....	....
1970-71	United States	Nat-Team	STATISTICS NOT AVAILABLE																									
	United States	WEC-A	10	7	1	8	....	....	....	2	....	....	....	....	....	....	....	....	....	....	....	....	....	....	....	....	....	....
1971-72	United States	Nat-Team	STATISTICS NOT AVAILABLE																									
	United States	Olympics	6	2	4	6	....	....	....	6	....	....	....	....	....	....	....	....	....	....	....	....	....	....	....	....	....	....
	Detroit Red Wings	NHL	16	1	0	1	1	0	1	2	0	0	0	11	9.1	5	1	7	0	–3	....	....	....	....	....	....	....	....
1972-73	Detroit Red Wings	NHL	73	14	14	28	14	12	26	82	0	1	0	136	10.3	44	1	63	18	–2	....	....	....	....	....	....	....	....
	Virginia Wings	AHL	7	3	2	5	....	....	....	9	....	....	....	....	....	....	....	....	....	....	....	....	....	....	....	....	....	....
1973-74	Detroit Red Wings	NHL	70	19	12	31	19	10	29	32	2	3	5	132	14.4	51	7	92	26	–22	....	....	....	....	....	....	....	....
1974-75	Minnesota North Stars	NHL	51	15	14	29	14	11	25	23	1	0	1	129	11.6	52	13	81	30	–12	....	....	....	....	....	....	....	....
1975-76	Minnesota Fighting Saints	WHA	36	15	20	35	....	....	....	47	....	....	....	....	....	....	....	....	....	....	....	....	....	....	....	....	....	....
	Kansas City Scouts	NHL	28	4	7	11	4	5	9	14	2	0	0	42	9.5	23	8	33	5	–13	....	....	....	....	....	....	....	....
1976-77	Colorado Rockies	NHL	9	0	2	2	0	2	2	4	0	0	0	10	0.0	2	0	5	3	0	....	....	....	....	....	....	....	....
	NHL Totals		247	53	49	102	52	40	92	157	5	4	6	460	11.5	177	30	281	82		....	....	....	....	....	....	....	....
	Other Major League Totals		36	15	20	35	....	....	....	47	....	....	....	....	....	....	....	....			....	....	....	....	....	....	....	....

Selected by **Minnesota** (WHA) in 1972 WHA General Player Draft, February 12, 1972. Traded to **Minnesota** by **Detroit** for Danny Grant, August 27, 1974. Rights traded to **Kansas City** by **Minnesota** for Kansas City's 2nd round choice (Steve Christoff) in 1978 Amateur Draft, December 9, 1974. Transferred to **Colorado** after **Kansas City** franchise relocated, July 15, 1976.

• BOUCHARD, JOEL

Joel Bouchard D – L. 6', 190 lbs. b: Montreal, Que., 1/23/1974. Calgary's 7th choice, 129th overall, in 1992 Entry Draft.

Season	Club	League	GP	G	A	Pts	AG	AA	APts	PIM	PP	SH	GW	S	%	TGF	PGF	TGA	PGA	+/–	GP	G	A	Pts	PIM	PP	SH	GW
1990-91	Longueuil Chevaliers	QMJHL	53	3	19	22	....	....	....	34	....	....	....	....	....	....	....	....	....	....	8	1	0	1	11	....	....	....
1991-92	Verdun Jr. Canadiens	QMJHL	70	9	20	29	....	....	....	55	....	....	....	....	....	....	....	....	....	....	19	1	7	8	20	....	....	....
1992-93	Verdun Jr. Canadiens	QMJHL	60	10	49	59	....	....	....	126	....	....	....	....	....	....	....	....	....	....	4	0	2	2	4	....	....	....
	Canada	WJC-A	7	0	0	0	....	....	....	0	....	....	....	....	....	....	....	....	....	....	....	....	....	....	....	....	....	....
1993-94	Verdun Jr. Canadiens	QMJHL	60	15	55	70	....	....	....	62	....	....	....	....	....	....	....	....	....	....	4	1	0	1	6	....	....	....
	Canada	WJC-A	7	0	1	1	....	....	....	10	....	....	....	....	....	....	....	....	....	....	....	....	....	....	....	....	....	....
	Saint John Flames	AHL	1	0	0	0	....	....	....	0	....	....	....	....	....	....	....	....	....	....	2	0	0	0	0	....	....	....
1994-95	Calgary Flames	NHL	2	0	0	0	0	0	0	0	0	0	0	0	0.0	0	0	0	0	0	....	....	....	....	....	....	....	....
	Saint John Flames	AHL	77	6	25	31	....	....	....	63	....	....	....	....	....	....	....	....	....	....	5	1	0	1	4	....	....	....
1995-96	Calgary Flames	NHL	4	0	0	0	0	0	0	4	0	0	0	0	0.0	1	0	1	0	0	....	....	....	....	....	....	....	....
	Saint John Flames	AHL	74	8	25	33	....	....	....	104	....	....	....	....	....	....	....	....	....	....	16	1	4	5	10	....	....	....
1996-97	Calgary Flames	NHL	76	4	5	9	4	4	8	49	0	1	0	61	6.6	50	3	97	27	–23	....	....	....	....	....	....	....	....
	Canada	WC-A	11	0	1	1	....	....	....	2	....	....	....	....	....	....	....	....	....	....	....	....	....	....	....	....	....	....
1997-98	Calgary Flames	NHL	44	5	7	12	6	7	13	57	0	1	1	51	9.8	28	1	41	14	0	....	....	....	....	....	....	....	....
	Saint John Flames	AHL	3	2	1	3	....	....	....	6	....	....	....	....	....	....	....	....	....	....	....	....	....	....	....	....	....	....
	NHL Totals		126	9	12	21	10	11	21	110	0	2	1	112	8.0	79	4	139	41		....	....	....	....	....	....	....	....

QMJHL First All-Star Team (1994)

Claimed by **Nashville** from **Calgary** in Expansion Draft, June 26, 1998.

• BOUCHARD, PIERRE

Pierre Bouchard D – L. 6'2", 205 lbs. b: Montreal, Que., 2/20/1948. Montreal's 1st choice, 5th overall, in 1965 Amateur Draft.

Season	Club	League	GP	G	A	Pts	AG	AA	APts	PIM	PP	SH	GW	S	%	TGF	PGF	TGA	PGA	+/–	GP	G	A	Pts	PIM	PP	SH	GW
1965-66	Palestre National	QJHL	40	6	19	25	....	....	....	53	....	....	....	....	....	....	....	....	....	....	....	....	....	....	....	....	....	....
1966-67	Montreal Jr. Canadiens	OHA	48	4	9	13	....	....	....	105	....	....	....	....	....	....	....	....	....	....	6	0	0	0	2	....	....	....
1967-68	Montreal Jr. Canadiens	OHA	54	10	18	28	....	....	....	134	....	....	....	....	....	....	....	....	....	....	11	2	2	4	20	....	....	....
1968-69	Cleveland Barons	AHL	69	6	16	22	....	....	....	32	....	....	....	....	....	....	....	....	....	....	5	1	1	2	4	....	....	....
1969-70	Montreal Voyageurs	AHL	65	5	13	18	....	....	....	124	....	....	....	....	....	....	....	....	....	....	8	1	3	4	24	....	....	....
1970-71	Montreal Canadiens	NHL	51	0	3	3	0	3	3	50	0	0	0	33	0.0	34	0	31	0	+3	13	0	1	1	10	0	0	0
1971-72	Montreal Canadiens	NHL	60	3	5	8	3	5	8	39	0	0	0	42	7.1	39	0	30	1	+10	1	0	0	0	0	0	0	0
1972-73	Montreal Canadiens	NHL	41	0	7	7	0	6	6	69	0	0	0	31	0.0	38	0	27	0	+11	17	1	3	4	13	0	0	0
1973-74	Montreal Canadiens	NHL	60	1	14	15	1	12	13	25	0	0	0	53	1.9	60	0	60	8	+8	6	0	2	2	4	0	0	0
1974-75	Montreal Canadiens	NHL	79	3	9	12	3	7	10	65	0	0	0	67	4.5	72	0	51	3	+24	10	0	2	2	10	0	0	0
1975-76	Montreal Canadiens	NHL	66	1	11	12	1	9	10	50	0	0	1	72	1.4	54	0	44	10	+20	13	2	0	2	8	1	0	1
1976-77	Montreal Canadiens	NHL	73	4	11	15	4	9	13	52	0	1	0	73	5.5	68	0	38	3	+33	6	0	1	1	6	0	0	0
1977-78	Montreal Canadiens	NHL	59	4	6	10	4	5	9	29	0	0	1	55	7.3	42	0	17	2	+27	10	0	1	1	5	0	0	0
1978-79	Washington Capitals	NHL	1	0	0	0	0	0	0	0	0	0	0	0	0.0	1	0	0	0	+1	....	....	....	....	....	....	....	....
1979-80	Washington Capitals	NHL	54	5	9	14	5	7	12	16	0	0	0	59	8.5	64	1	87	17	–7	....	....	....	....	....	....	....	....

Season	Club	League	GP	G	A	Pts	AG	AA	APts	PIM	PP	SH	GW	S	%	TGF	PGF	TGA	PGA	+/–	GP	G	A	Pts	PIM	PP	SH	GW
1980-81	Washington Capitals	NHL	50	3	7	10	2	5	7	28	0	0	0	36	8.3	39	1	73	17	–18								
1981-82	Washington Capitals	NHL	1	0	0	0	0	0	0	10	0	0	0	1	0.0	0	0	2	0	–2								
	Hershey Bears	AHL	62	2	10	12				26											5	0	0	0	6			
	NHL Totals		595	24	82	106	23	68	91	433	0	1	2	522	4.6	511	2	460	61		76	3	10	13	56	1	0	1

Claimed by **Washington** from **Montreal** in Waiver Draft, October 9, 1978.

● BOUCHER, PHILIPPE
Philippe Boucher   D – R. 6'3", 190 lbs.   b: St. Apollinaire, Que., 3/24/1973.   Buffalo's 1st choice, 13th overall, in 1991 Entry Draft.

Season	Club	League	GP	G	A	Pts	AG	AA	APts	PIM	PP	SH	GW	S	%	TGF	PGF	TGA	PGA	+/–	GP	G	A	Pts	PIM	PP	SH	GW
1990-91	Granby Bisons	QMJHL	69	21	46	67				92																		
1991-92	Granby Bisons	QMJHL	49	22	37	59				47																		
	Laval Titans	QMJHL	16	7	11	18				36											10	5	6	11	8			
1992-93	Laval Titans	QMJHL	16	12	15	27				37											13	6	15	21	12			
	Buffalo Sabres	**NHL**	18	0	4	4	0	3	3	14	0	0	0	28	0.0	23	1	23	2	+1	3	0	1	1	2			
	Rochester Americans	AHL	5	4	3	7				8																		
1993-94	**Buffalo Sabres**	**NHL**	38	6	8	14	6	6	12	29	4	0	0	67	9.0	45	25	21	0	–1	7	1	1	2	2	1	0	
	Rochester Americans	AHL	31	10	22	32				51																		
1994-95	**Buffalo Sabres**	**NHL**	9	1	4	5	2	6	8	0	0	0	0	15	6.7	12	5	1	0	+6								
	Rochester Americans	AHL	43	14	27	41				26																		
	Los Angeles Kings	**NHL**	6	1	0	1	2	0	2	4	0	0	0	15	6.7	4	1	8	2	–3								
1995-96	**Los Angeles Kings**	**NHL**	53	7	16	23	7	13	20	31	5	0	1	145	4.8	61	24	76	13	–26								
	Phoenix Roadrunners	IHL	10	4	3	7				4																		
1996-97	**Los Angeles Kings**	**NHL**	60	7	18	25	7	16	23	25	2	0	1	159	4.4	63	14	57	8	0								
1997-98	**Los Angeles Kings**	**NHL**	45	6	10	16	7	10	17	49	1	0	0	80	7.5	42	9	35	8	+6								
	Long Beach Ice Dogs	IHL	2	0	1	1				4																		
	NHL Totals		229	28	60	88	31	54	85	152	12	0	3	509	5.5	250	79	221	33		7	1	1	2	2	1	0	0

Canadian Major Junior Rookie of the Year (1991) • QMJHL Second All-Star Team (1991, 1992)
Traded to **LA Kings** by **Buffalo** with Denis Tsygurov and Grant Fuhr for Alexei Zhitnik, Robb Stauber, Charlie Huddy and LA Kings' 5th round choice (Marian Menhart) in 1995 Entry Draft, February 14, 1995.

● BOUDREAU, BRUCE
Bruce "Gabby" Boudreau   C – L. 5'9", 170 lbs.   b: Toronto, Ont., 1/9/1955.   Toronto's 3rd choice, 42nd overall, in 1975 Amateur Draft.

Season	Club	League	GP	G	A	Pts	AG	AA	APts	PIM	PP	SH	GW	S	%	TGF	PGF	TGA	PGA	+/–	GP	G	A	Pts	PIM	PP	SH	GW
1972-73	Toronto Marlboros	OHA	61	38	49	87				22																		
1973-74	Toronto Marlboros	OHA	53	46	67	113				51																		
1974-75	Toronto Marlboros	OHA	69	*68	97	*165				52											22	12	*28	40	26			
1975-76	Minnesota Fighting Saints	WHA	30	3	6	9				4																		
	Johnstown Jets	NAHL	34	25	35	60				14																		
1976-77	**Toronto Maple Leafs**	**NHL**	15	2	5	7	2	4	6	4	0	0	0	17	11.8	8	2	4	0	+2	3	0	0	0	0	0	0	0
	Dallas Black Hawks	CHL	58	*37	34	71				40											1	1	1	2	0			
1977-78	**Toronto Maple Leafs**	**NHL**	40	11	18	29	11	15	26	12	1	0	2	71	15.5	36	5	23	0	+8								
	Dallas Black Hawks	CHL	22	13	9	22				11																		
1978-79	**Toronto Maple Leafs**	**NHL**	26	4	3	7	4	2	6	2	0	0	0	30	13.3	10	1	12	0	–3								
	New Brunswick Hawks	AHL	49	20	38	58				20											5	1	1	2	8			
1979-80	**Toronto Maple Leafs**	**NHL**	2	0	0	0	0	0	0	0	0	0	0	0	0.0	0	0	0	0	0								
	New Brunswick Hawks	AHL	75	36	54	90				47											17	6	7	13	23			
1980-81	**Toronto Maple Leafs**	**NHL**	39	10	14	24	8	10	18	18	0	0	0	47	21.3	31	1	39	2	–7	2	1	0	1	0	0	0	0
	New Brunswick Hawks	AHL	40	17	41	58				22											8	6	5	11	14			
1981-82	**Toronto Maple Leafs**	**NHL**	12	0	2	2	0	1	1	6	0	0	0	5	0.0	2	0	8	0	–6								
	Cincinnati Tigers	CHL	65	42	61	103				42											4	3	1	4	8			
1982-83	St. Catharines Saints	AHL	80	50	72	122				65																		
	Toronto Maple Leafs	**NHL**																			4	1	0	1	0			
1983-84	St. Catharines Saints	AHL	80	47	62	109				44											7	0	5	5	11			
1984-85	Baltimore Skipjacks	AHL	17	4	7	11				4											15	3	9	12	4			
1985-86	**Chicago Black Hawks**	**NHL**	7	1	0	1	1	0	1	2	0	0	0	3	33.3	1	0	0	0	+1								
	Nova Scotia Oilers	AHL	65	30	36	66				36																		
1986-87	Nova Scotia Oilers	AHL	78	35	47	82				40											5	3	3	6	4			
1987-88	Springfield Indians	AHL	80	42	*74	*116				84																		
1988-89	Springfield Indians	AHL	50	28	36	64				42																		
	Newmarket Saints	AHL	20	7	16	23				12											4	0	1	1	6			
1989-90	Phoenix Roadrunners	IHL	82	41	68	109				89																		
1990-91	Fort Wayne Komets	IHL	81	40	*80	120				111											19	11	7	18	30			
1991-92	Fort Wayne Komets	IHL	77	34	50	84				100											7	3	4	7	10			
	Adirondack Red Wings	AHL																			4	1	1	2	2			
	NHL Totals		141	28	42	70	26	32	58	46	1	0	3	173	16.2	88	9	86	2		9	2	0	2	0	0	0	0
	Other Major League Totals		30	3	6	9				4																		

OHA Second All-Star Team (1974) • CHL Second All-Star Team (1982) • AHL First All-Star Team (1988) • Won Fred T. Hunt Memorial Trophy (Sportsmanship - AHL) (1988) • Won John B. Sollenberger Trophy (Top Scorer - AHL) (1988)
Selected by **Minnesota** (WHA) in 1974 WHA Amateur Draft, June, 1974. Claimed by **Toronto** as a fill-in during Expansion Draft, June 13, 1979. Signed as a free agent by **Chicago**, October 10, 1985.

● BOUDRIAS, ANDRE
Andre Boudrias   LW – L. 5'8", 165 lbs.   b: Montreal, Que., 9/19/1943.

Season	Club	League	GP	G	A	Pts	AG	AA	APts	PIM	PP	SH	GW	S	%	TGF	PGF	TGA	PGA	+/–	GP	G	A	Pts	PIM	PP	SH	GW
1961-62	Montreal Jr. Canadiens	OHA	50	34	*63	*97				54											6	2	3	5	4			
	Hull-Ottawa Canadiens	EPHL	1	0	0	0				0																		
	North Bay Trappers	EPHL	1	0	3	3				2											1	0	0	0	0			
1962-63	Montreal Jr. Canadiens	OHA	50	12	43	55				72											10	3	4	7	18			
	Hull-Ottawa Canadiens	EPHL	3	0	1	1				0																		
1963-64	Montreal Jr. Canadiens	OHA	55	38	*97	*135				48											16	11	*26	*37	18			
	Montreal Canadiens	**NHL**	4	1	4	5	1	4	5	2																		
1964-65	**Montreal Canadiens**	**NHL**	1	0	0	0	0	0	0	2																		
	Quebec Aces	AHL	14	4	9	13				4																		
	Omaha Knights	CHL	52	15	49	64				10											6	1	3	4	2			
1965-66	Quebec Aces	AHL	1	2	0	2				0																		
	Houston Apollos	CHL	70	27	46	73				53																		
1966-67	**Montreal Canadiens**	**NHL**	2	0	1	1	0	1	1	2																		
	Houston Apollos	CHL	67	16	48	64				58											6	1	2	3	6			
1967-68	**Minnesota North Stars**	**NHL**	74	18	35	53	22	37	59	42	4	0	3	183	9.8	80	19	90	26	–3	14	3	6	9	8			
1968-69	**Minnesota North Stars**	**NHL**	53	4	9	13	4	8	12	6	1	0	0	87	4.6	16	3	69	26	–30								
	Chicago Black Hawks	**NHL**	20	4	10	14	4	9	13	4	1	0	1	40	10.0	22	2	10	1	+11								
1969-70	**St. Louis Blues**	**NHL**	50	3	14	17	3	14	17	20	1	0	0	95	3.2	9	7	20	5	+7	14	2	4	6	4			
	Kansas City Blues	CHL	19	7	16	23				16																		
1970-71	**Vancouver Canucks**	**NHL**	77	25	41	66	26	36	62	16	7	1	2	254	9.8	80	19	91	39	+15								
1971-72	**Vancouver Canucks**	**NHL**	78	27	34	61	29	31	60	26	6	0	2	224	12.1	82	27	96	7	–34								
1972-73	**Vancouver Canucks**	**NHL**	77	30	40	70	30	33	63	24	8	0	2	194	15.5	97	29	89	1	–20								
1973-74	**Vancouver Canucks**	**NHL**	78	16	59	75	16	51	67	18	3	1	1	180	8.9	96	31	90	19	–6								
1974-75	**Vancouver Canucks**	**NHL**	77	16	62	78	15	49	64	46	9	0	2	167	9.6	95	41	47	1	+8	5	1	0	1	4			

Season	Club	League	GP	G	A	Pts	AG	AA	APts	PIM	PP	SH	GW	S	%	TGF	PGF	TGA	PGA	+/–	GP	G	A	Pts	PIM	PP	SH	GW
			REGULAR SEASON																		PLAYOFFS							
1975-76	**Vancouver Canucks**	**NHL**	**71**	**7**	**31**	**38**	**7**	**24**	**31**	**10**	**2**	**0**	**0**	**69**	**10.1**	**52**	**19**	**49**	**9**	**–7**	**1**	**0**	**0**	**0**	**0**	**0**	**0**	**0**
1976-77	Quebec Nordiques	WHA	74	12	31	43				12											17	3	12	15	6			
1977-78	Quebec Nordiques	WHA	66	10	17	27				22											11	0	2	2	4			
	NHL Totals		**662**	**151**	**340**	**491**	**157**	**297**	**454**	**218**	**42**	**2**	**18**	**1493**	**10.1**	**655**	**197**	**651**	**134**		**34**	**6**	**10**	**16**	**12**	**1**	**0**	**1**
	Other Major League Totals		140	22	48	70				34											28	3	14	17	10			

Played in NHL All-Star Game (1967)

Traded to **Minnesota** by **Montreal** with Bob Charlebois and Bernard Cote for Minnesota's 1st round choice (Chuck Arnason) in 1971 Amateur Draft, June 6, 1967. Traded to **Chicago** by **Minnesota** with Mike McMahon for Tom Reid and Bill Orban, February 14, 1969. Claimed by **St. Louis** from **Chicago** in Intra-League Draft, June 11, 1969. Traded to **Vancouver** by **St. Louis** for cash, June 10, 1970. Selected by **Minnesota** (WHA) in 1972 WHA General Player Draft, February 12, 1972. WHA rights traded to **Quebec** (WHA) by **Minnesota** (WHA) for Gordie Gallant, September, 1976.

• BOUGHNER, BARRY

Barry Boughner LW – L. 5'10", 180 lbs. b: Delhi, Ont., 1/29/1948.

Season	Club	League	GP	G	A	Pts	AG	AA	APts	PIM	PP	SH	GW	S	%	TGF	PGF	TGA	PGA	+/–	GP	G	A	Pts	PIM	PP	SH	GW
1966-67	London Nationals	OHA	42	1	7	8				11											6	1	2	3	6			
1967-68	London Nationals	OHA	52	15	19	34				43											5	2	1	3	0			
1968-69	Des Moines Oak Leafs	IHL	58	19	13	32				34																		
1969-70	**Oakland Seals**	**NHL**	**4**	**0**	**0**	**0**	**0**	**0**	**0**	**2**	**0**	**0**	**0**	**5**	**0.0**	**1**	**0**	**1**	**0**	**0**								
	Providence Reds	AHL	71	9	13	22				16																		
1970-71	**California Golden Seals**	**NHL**	**16**	**0**	**0**	**0**	**0**	**0**	**0**	**9**	**0**	**0**	**0**	**7**	**0.0**	**0**	**0**	**3**	**0**	**–3**								
	Providence Reds	AHL	21	1	0	1				4																		
1971-72	Des Moines Oak Leafs	IHL	66	14	19	33				83											3	1	1	2	2			
1972-73	New Haven Nighthawks	AHL	63	9	17	26				14																		
1973-74	Albuquerque 6-Guns	CHL	62	11	14	25				19																		
1974-75	Brantford Foresters	OHA Sr.	12	3	4	7				15																		
	NHL Totals		**20**	**0**	**0**	**0**	**0**	**0**	**0**	**11**	**0**	**0**	**0**	**12**	**0.0**	**1**	**0**	**4**	**0**									

Signed as a free agent by **Port Huron** (IHL), September, 1968. Traded to **California** (Des Moines - IHL) by **Port Huron** with Ron Schwindt for Reg Bechtold and Joe Cooper, November, 1968.

• BOUGHNER, BOB

Bob Boughner D – R. 6', 206 lbs. b: Windsor, Ont., 3/8/1971. Detroit's 2nd choice, 32nd overall, in 1989 Entry Draft.

Season	Club	League	GP	G	A	Pts	AG	AA	APts	PIM	PP	SH	GW	S	%	TGF	PGF	TGA	PGA	+/–	GP	G	A	Pts	PIM	PP	SH	GW
1988-89	Sault Ste. Marie Greyhounds	OHL	64	6	15	21				182																		
1989-90	Sault Ste. Marie Greyhounds	OHL	49	7	23	30				122																		
1990-91	Sault Ste. Marie Greyhounds	OHL	64	13	33	46				156											14	2	9	11	35			
1991-92	Toledo Storm	ECHL	28	3	10	13				79											5	2	0	2	15			
	Adirondack Red Wings	AHL	1	0	0	0				7																		
1992-93	Adirondack Red Wings	AHL	69	1	16	17				190																		
1993-94	Adirondack Red Wings	AHL	72	8	14	22				292											10	1	1	2	18			
1994-95	Cincinnati Cyclones	IHL	81	2	14	16				192											10	0	0	0	18			
1995-96	Carolina Monarchs	AHL	46	2	15	17				127																		
	Buffalo Sabres	**NHL**	**31**	**0**	**1**	**1**	**0**	**1**	**1**	**104**	**0**	**0**	**0**	**14**	**0.0**	**10**	**0**	**9**	**2**	**+3**								
1996-97	**Buffalo Sabres**	**NHL**	**77**	**1**	**7**	**8**	**1**	**6**	**7**	**225**	**0**	**0**	**0**	**34**	**2.9**	**41**	**0**	**38**	**9**	**+12**	**11**	**0**	**1**	**1**	**9**	**0**	**0**	**0**
1997-98	**Buffalo Sabres**	**NHL**	**69**	**1**	**3**	**4**	**1**	**3**	**4**	**165**	**0**	**0**	**0**	**26**	**3.8**	**29**	**0**	**35**	**11**	**+5**	**14**	**0**	**4**	**4**	**15**	**0**	**0**	**0**
	NHL Totals		**177**	**2**	**11**	**13**	**2**	**10**	**12**	**494**	**0**	**0**	**0**	**74**	**2.7**	**80**	**0**	**82**	**22**		**25**	**0**	**5**	**5**	**24**	**0**	**0**	**0**

Signed as a free agent by **Florida**, July 25, 1994. Traded to **Buffalo** by **Florida** for Buffalo's 3rd round choice (Chris Allen) in 1996 Entry Draft, February 1, 1996. Claimed by **Nashville** from **Buffalo** in Expansion Draft, June 26, 1998.

• BOURBONNAIS, DAN

Dan Bourbonnais LW – L. 5'10", 185 lbs. b: Winnipeg, Man., 3/6/1962. Hartford's 5th choice, 103rd overall, in 1981 Entry Draft.

Season	Club	League	GP	G	A	Pts	AG	AA	APts	PIM	PP	SH	GW	S	%	TGF	PGF	TGA	PGA	+/–	GP	G	A	Pts	PIM	PP	SH	GW
1978-79	Pincher Creek Panthers	AJHL	60	17	41	58				36																		
	Calgary Wranglers	WHL	2	0	2	2				0																		
1979-80	Calgary Wranglers	WHL	66	14	29	43				41											6	2	2	4	0			
1980-81	Calgary Wranglers	WHL	72	41	62	103				34											22	5	10	15	28			
1981-82	Calgary Wranglers	WHL	50	27	32	59				175											9	8	4	10	17			
	Hartford Whalers	**NHL**	**24**	**3**	**9**	**12**	**2**	**6**	**8**	**11**	**0**	**0**	**0**	**30**	**10.0**	**17**	**3**	**22**	**0**	**–8**								
1982-83	Binghamton Whalers	AHL	75	31	33	64				24											5	4	0	4	0			
1983-84	**Hartford Whalers**	**NHL**	**35**	**0**	**16**	**16**	**0**	**11**	**11**	**0**	**0**	**0**	**0**	**42**	**0.0**	**23**	**4**	**19**	**3**	**+3**								
	Binghamton Whalers	AHL	30	16	32	48				40																		
1984-85	Binghamton Whalers	AHL	56	13	22	35				17																		
	NHL Totals		**59**	**3**	**25**	**28**	**2**	**17**	**19**	**11**	**0**	**0**	**0**	**72**	**4.2**	**40**	**7**	**41**	**3**									

• BOURBONNAIS, RICK

Rick Bourbonnais RW – R. 6', 186 lbs. b: Toronto, Ont., 4/20/1955. St. Louis' 3rd choice, 63rd overall, in 1975 Amateur Draft.

Season	Club	League	GP	G	A	Pts	AG	AA	APts	PIM	PP	SH	GW	S	%	TGF	PGF	TGA	PGA	+/–	GP	G	A	Pts	PIM	PP	SH	GW
1972-73	Kitchener Rangers	OHA	56	7	13	20				53																		
1973-74	Kitchener Rangers	OHA	70	30	35	65				40																		
1974-75	Kitchener–Ottawa	OHA	64	21	37	58				79																		
1975-76	**St. Louis Blues**	**NHL**	**7**	**0**	**0**	**0**	**0**	**0**	**0**	**8**	**0**	**0**	**0**	**5**	**0.0**	**1**	**0**	**2**	**0**	**–1**								
	Providence Reds	AHL	64	18	17	35				96											2	1	0	1	6			
1976-77	**St. Louis Blues**	**NHL**	**33**	**6**	**8**	**14**	**6**	**6**	**12**	**10**	**2**	**0**	**1**	**44**	**13.6**	**27**	**9**	**24**	**0**	**–6**	**4**	**0**	**1**	**1**	**0**	**0**	**0**	**0**
	Kansas City Blues	CHL	39	20	24	44				19																		
1977-78	**St. Louis Blues**	**NHL**	**31**	**3**	**7**	**10**	**3**	**6**	**9**	**11**	**1**	**0**	**0**	**56**	**5.4**	**19**	**5**	**26**	**0**	**–12**								
	Salt Lake Golden Eagles	CHL	40	18	21	39				12											6	3	2	5	2			
1978-79	Salt Lake Golden Eagles	CHL	74	15	22	37				35											4	0	0	0	2			
1979-80	Binghamton Dusters	AHL	49	8	11	19				20																		
	Salt Lake Golden Eagles	CHL	6	1	0	1				0																		
1980-81			DID NOT PLAY																									
1981-82	Chamonix	France		15	13	28																						
1982-83	SB Rosenheim	Germany	36	31	31	62				26																		
1983-84	SB Rosenheim	Germany	29	13	14	27				8																		
1984-85	Innsbruck	Austria	5	2	2	4				6																		
	Kempten	Germany	15	22	7	29				20											16	17	33	50				
	NHL Totals		**71**	**9**	**15**	**24**	**9**	**12**	**21**	**29**	**3**	**0**	**1**	**105**	**8.6**	**47**	**14**	**52**	**0**		**4**	**0**	**1**	**1**	**0**	**0**	**0**	**0**

• BOURGEOIS, CHARLIE

Charlie "Boo-Boo" Bourgeois D – R. 6'4", 220 lbs. b: Moncton, N.B., 11/19/1959.

Season	Club	League	GP	G	A	Pts	AG	AA	APts	PIM	PP	SH	GW	S	%	TGF	PGF	TGA	PGA	+/–	GP	G	A	Pts	PIM	PP	SH	GW
1978-79	University of Moncton	AUAA	18	3	3	6				8																		
1979-80	Cap Pele Fishermen	NBJHL	STATISTICS NOT AVAILABLE																									
1980-81	University of Moncton	AUAA	24	10	21	31				44											6	4	6	10				
1981-82	**Calgary Flames**	**NHL**	**54**	**2**	**13**	**15**	**2**	**9**	**11**	**112**	**0**	**0**	**0**	**33**	**6.1**	**50**	**0**	**47**	**2**	**+5**	**3**	**0**	**0**	**0**	**7**	**0**	**0**	**0**
	Oklahoma City Stars	CHL	13	2	2	4				17																		
1982-83	**Calgary Flames**	**NHL**	**15**	**2**	**3**	**5**	**2**	**2**	**4**	**21**	**0**	**0**	**0**	**11**	**18.2**	**10**	**0**	**16**	**2**	**–4**								
	Colorado Flames	CHL	51	10	18	28				128											6	2	3	5	30			
1983-84	**Calgary Flames**	**NHL**	**17**	**1**	**3**	**4**	**1**	**2**	**3**	**35**	**0**	**0**	**0**	**20**	**5.0**	**15**	**0**	**18**	**3**	**0**	**8**	**0**	**1**	**1**	**27**	**0**	**0**	**0**
	Colorado Flames	CHL	54	12	32	44				133																		
1984-85	**Calgary Flames**	**NHL**	**47**	**2**	**10**	**12**	**2**	**7**	**9**	**134**	**0**	**0**	**0**	**38**	**5.3**	**45**	**3**	**31**	**3**	**+14**	**4**	**0**	**0**	**0**	**17**	**0**	**0**	**0**
1985-86	**Calgary Flames**	**NHL**	**29**	**5**	**5**	**10**	**4**	**3**	**7**	**128**	**0**	**0**	**0**	**30**	**16.7**	**29**	**0**	**28**	**8**	**+9**								
	St. Louis Blues	**NHL**	**31**	**2**	**7**	**9**	**2**	**5**	**7**	**116**	**1**	**0**	**1**	**34**	**5.9**	**30**	**1**	**31**	**11**	**+9**	**19**	**2**	**2**	**4**	**116**	**1**	**0**	**0**
1986-87	**St. Louis Blues**	**NHL**	**66**	**2**	**12**	**14**	**2**	**9**	**11**	**164**	**0**	**0**	**1**	**54**	**3.7**	**61**	**4**	**47**	**6**	**+16**	**6**	**0**	**0**	**0**	**27**	**0**	**0**	**0**
1987-88	**St. Louis Blues**	**NHL**	**30**	**0**	**1**	**1**	**0**	**1**	**1**	**78**	**0**	**0**	**0**	**9**	**0.0**	**16**	**0**	**26**	**8**	**–2**								
	Hartford Whalers	**NHL**	**1**	**0**	**0**	**0**	**0**	**0**	**0**	**0**	**0**	**0**	**0**	**0**	**0.0**	**0**	**0**	**1**	**0**	**–1**								
1988-89	Binghamton Whalers	AHL	76	9	35	44				239																		

			REGULAR SEASON																		PLAYOFFS							
Season	Club	League	GP	G	A	Pts	AG	AA	APts	PIM	PP	SH	GW	S	%	TGF	PGF	TGA	PGA	+/–	GP	G	A	Pts	PIM	PP	SH	GW
1989-90	Paris Volants	France	DID NOT PLAY – COACHING																									
1990-91	Chamonix	France	DID NOT PLAY – COACHING																									
1991-92	Chamonix	France	DID NOT PLAY – COACHING																									
	Moncton Hawks	AHL	3	0	1	1	....	....	....	6	....	....	....	....	....	....	....	....	....	....	....	....	....	....	....	....	....	....
	NHL Totals		**290**	**16**	**54**	**70**	**15**	**38**	**53**	**788**	**1**	**0**	**2**	**229**	**7.0**	**256**	**8**	**245**	**43**		**40**	**2**	**3**	**5**	**194**	**1**	**0**	**0**

CHL First All-Star Team (1984)

Signed as a free agent by **Calgary**, April 19, 1981. Traded to **St. Louis** by **Calgary** with Eddie Beers for Joe Mullen, Terry Johnson and Rik Wilson, February 1, 1986. Traded to **Hartford** by **St. Louis** with Hartford's 3rd round choice (Blair Atcheynum) in 1989 Entry Draft (previously acquired, Hartford selected Rick Corriveau) in 1989 Entry Draft, March 8, 1988.

• BOURNE, BOB

Bob Bourne C – L. 6'3", 200 lbs. b: Kindersley, Sask., 6/21/1954. Kansas City's 3rd choice, 38th overall, in 1974 Amateur Draft.

Season	Club	League	GP	G	A	Pts	AG	AA	APts	PIM	PP	SH	GW	S	%	TGF	PGF	TGA	PGA	+/–	GP	G	A	Pts	PIM	PP	SH	GW
1971-72	Saskatoon Blades	WCJHL	63	28	32	60	....	....	....	36	....	....	....	....	....	....	....	....	....	....	....	....	....	....	....	....	....	....
1971-72	Saskatoon Blades	WCJHL	63	28	32	60	....	....	....	36	....	....	....	....	....	....	....	....	....	....	8	3	7	10	2	....	....	....
1972-73	Saskatoon Blades	WCJHL	66	40	53	93	....	....	....	74	....	....	....	....	....	....	....	....	....	....	16	7	10	17	30	....	....	....
1973-74	Saskatoon Blades	WCJHL	63	29	42	71	....	....	....	41	....	....	....	....	....	....	....	....	....	....	6	3	2	5	12	....	....	....
1974-75	**New York Islanders**	**NHL**	**77**	**16**	**23**	**39**	**15**	**18**	**33**	**12**	**2**	**0**	**2**	**127**	**12.6**	**55**	**10**	**36**	**0**	**+9**	**9**	**1**	**2**	**3**	**4**	**1**	**0**	**0**
1975-76	**New York Islanders**	**NHL**	**14**	**2**	**3**	**5**	**2**	**2**	**4**	**13**	**0**	**0**	**1**	**16**	**12.5**	**5**	**1**	**6**	**0**	**–2**	....	....	....	....	....	....	....	....
	Fort Worth Texans	CHL	62	29	44	73	....	....	....	80	....	....	....	....	....	....	....	....	....	....	....	....	....	....	....	....	....	....
1976-77	**New York Islanders**	**NHL**	**75**	**16**	**19**	**35**	**15**	**15**	**30**	**30**	**0**	**0**	**5**	**137**	**11.7**	**47**	**0**	**20**	**0**	**+27**	**8**	**2**	**0**	**2**	**4**	**0**	**0**	**0**
1977-78	**New York Islanders**	**NHL**	**80**	**30**	**33**	**63**	**29**	**27**	**56**	**31**	**2**	**0**	**8**	**178**	**16.9**	**81**	**10**	**56**	**0**	**+15**	**7**	**2**	**3**	**5**	**2**	**1**	**0**	**0**
1978-79	**New York Islanders**	**NHL**	**80**	**30**	**31**	**61**	**27**	**24**	**51**	**48**	**4**	**1**	**2**	**148**	**20.3**	**88**	**16**	**64**	**26**	**+34**	**10**	**1**	**3**	**4**	**6**	**0**	**0**	**0**
1979-80	**New York Islanders**	**NHL**	**73**	**15**	**25**	**40**	**14**	**19**	**33**	**52**	**3**	**0**	**1**	**155**	**9.7**	**67**	**22**	**75**	**35**	**+5**	**21**	**10**	**10**	**20**	**10**	**5**	**2**	**1**
1980-81	**New York Islanders**	**NHL**	**78**	**35**	**41**	**76**	**29**	**29**	**58**	**62**	**9**	**7**	**5**	**195**	**17.9**	**105**	**28**	**77**	**34**	**+34**	**14**	**4**	**6**	**10**	**19**	**1**	**1**	**1**
1981-82	**New York Islanders**	**NHL**	**76**	**27**	**26**	**53**	**21**	**17**	**38**	**77**	**5**	**2**	**2**	**173**	**15.6**	**82**	**11**	**73**	**29**	**+27**	**19**	**9**	**7**	**16**	**36**	**3**	**1**	**0**
1982-83	**New York Islanders**	**NHL**	**77**	**20**	**42**	**62**	**16**	**29**	**45**	**55**	**5**	**1**	**3**	**147**	**13.6**	**85**	**22**	**72**	**23**	**+14**	**20**	**8**	**20**	**28**	**14**	**0**	**1**	**2**
1983-84	**New York Islanders**	**NHL**	**78**	**22**	**34**	**56**	**18**	**23**	**41**	**75**	**5**	**5**	**2**	**140**	**15.7**	**82**	**16**	**83**	**29**	**+12**	**8**	**1**	**1**	**2**	**7**	**0**	**0**	**1**
1984-85	Canada	C Cup	8	0	3	3	....	....	....	0	....	....	....	....	....	....	....	....	....	....	....	....	....	....	....	....	....	....
	New York Islanders	**NHL**	**44**	**8**	**12**	**20**	**7**	**8**	**15**	**51**	**1**	**0**	**1**	**56**	**14.3**	**31**	**2**	**53**	**16**	**–8**	**10**	**0**	**2**	**2**	**6**	**0**	**0**	**0**
1985-86	**New York Islanders**	**NHL**	**62**	**17**	**15**	**32**	**14**	**10**	**24**	**36**	**2**	**0**	**5**	**100**	**17.0**	**40**	**5**	**66**	**24**	**–7**	**3**	**0**	**0**	**0**	**0**	**0**	**0**	**0**
1986-87	**Los Angeles Kings**	**NHL**	**78**	**13**	**9**	**22**	**11**	**6**	**17**	**35**	**0**	**3**	**0**	**93**	**14.0**	**32**	**0**	**100**	**55**	**–13**	**5**	**2**	**1**	**3**	**0**	**0**	**0**	**0**
1987-88	**Los Angeles Kings**	**NHL**	**72**	**7**	**11**	**18**	**6**	**8**	**14**	**28**	**1**	**0**	**1**	**75**	**9.3**	**25**	**8**	**98**	**50**	**–31**	**5**	**0**	**1**	**1**	**0**	**0**	**0**	**0**
	NHL Totals		**964**	**258**	**324**	**582**	**224**	**235**	**459**	**605**	**39**	**19**	**38**	**1740**	**14.8**	**825**	**151**	**879**	**321**		**139**	**40**	**56**	**96**	**108**	**11**	**5**	**5**

CHL Second All-Star Team (1976) • Won Bill Masterton Trophy (1988)

Played in NHL All-Star Game (1981)

Traded to **NY Islanders** by **Kansas City** for Bart Crashley and the rights to Larry Hornung, September 13, 1974. Claimed by **LA Kings** from **NY Islanders** in Waiver Draft, October 6, 1986.

• BOURQUE, PHIL

Phil Bourque LW – L. 6'1", 196 lbs. b: Chelmsford, MA, 6/8/1962.

Season	Club	League	GP	G	A	Pts	AG	AA	APts	PIM	PP	SH	GW	S	%	TGF	PGF	TGA	PGA	+/–	GP	G	A	Pts	PIM	PP	SH	GW
1980-81	Kingston Canadians	OHL	47	4	4	8	....	....	....	46	....	....	....	....	....	....	....	....	....	....	6	0	0	0	10	....	....	....
1981-82	Kingston Canadians	OHL	67	11	40	51	....	....	....	111	....	....	....	....	....	....	....	....	....	....	4	0	0	0	0	....	....	....
1982-83	Baltimore Skipjacks	AHL	65	1	15	16	....	....	....	93	....	....	....	....	....	....	....	....	....	....	....	....	....	....	....	....	....	....
1983-84	**Pittsburgh Penguins**	**NHL**	**5**	**0**	**1**	**1**	**0**	**1**	**1**	**12**	**0**	**0**	**0**	**6**	**0.0**	**2**	**0**	**4**	**0**	**–2**	....	....	....	....	....	....	....	....
	Baltimore Skipjacks	AHL	58	5	17	22	....	....	....	96	....	....	....	....	....	....	....	....	....	....	....	....	....	....	....	....	....	....
1984-85	Baltimore Skipjacks	AHL	79	6	15	21	....	....	....	164	....	....	....	....	....	....	....	....	....	....	13	2	5	7	23	....	....	....
1985-86	**Pittsburgh Penguins**	**NHL**	**4**	**0**	**0**	**0**	**0**	**0**	**0**	**2**	**0**	**0**	**0**	**0**	**0.0**	**1**	**0**	**3**	**0**	**–2**	....	....	....	....	....	....	....	....
	Baltimore Skipjacks	AHL	74	8	18	26	....	....	....	226	....	....	....	....	....	....	....	....	....	....	....	....	....	....	....	....	....	....
1986-87	**Pittsburgh Penguins**	**NHL**	**22**	**2**	**3**	**5**	**2**	**2**	**4**	**32**	**0**	**0**	**1**	**23**	**8.7**	**8**	**2**	**8**	**0**	**–2**	....	....	....	....	....	....	....	....
	Baltimore Skipjacks	AHL	49	15	16	31	....	....	....	183	....	....	....	....	....	....	....	....	....	....	....	....	....	....	....	....	....	....
1987-88	**Pittsburgh Penguins**	**NHL**	**21**	**4**	**12**	**16**	**3**	**9**	**12**	**20**	**2**	**0**	**1**	**56**	**7.1**	**39**	**19**	**19**	**2**	**+3**	....	....	....	....	....	....	....	....
	Muskegon Lumberjacks	IHL	52	16	36	52	....	....	....	66	....	....	....	....	....	....	....	....	....	....	6	1	2	3	16	....	....	....
1988-89	**Pittsburgh Penguins**	**NHL**	**80**	**17**	**26**	**43**	**14**	**18**	**32**	**97**	**5**	**2**	**3**	**153**	**11.1**	**97**	**47**	**100**	**28**	**–22**	**11**	**4**	**1**	**5**	**66**	**0**	**0**	**1**
1989-90	**Pittsburgh Penguins**	**NHL**	**76**	**22**	**17**	**39**	**19**	**12**	**31**	**108**	**2**	**1**	**3**	**110**	**20.0**	**70**	**20**	**73**	**16**	**–7**	....	....	....	....	....	....	....	....
1990-91	**Pittsburgh Penguins**	**NHL**	**78**	**20**	**14**	**34**	**18**	**11**	**29**	**106**	**1**	**4**	**0**	**122**	**16.4**	**65**	**3**	**81**	**26**	**+7**	**24**	**6**	**7**	**13**	**16**	**0**	**0**	**0**
1991-92	**Pittsburgh Penguins**	**NHL**	**58**	**10**	**16**	**26**	**9**	**12**	**21**	**58**	**0**	**1**	**3**	**51**	**19.6**	**35**	**2**	**55**	**16**	**–6**	**21**	**3**	**4**	**7**	**25**	**2**	**0**	**0**
1992-93	**New York Rangers**	**NHL**	**55**	**6**	**14**	**20**	**5**	**10**	**15**	**39**	**0**	**0**	**2**	**71**	**8.5**	**27**	**3**	**35**	**2**	**–9**	....	....	....	....	....	....	....	....
1993-94	**New York Rangers**	**NHL**	**16**	**0**	**1**	**1**	**0**	**1**	**1**	**8**	**0**	**0**	**0**	**2**	**0.0**	**1**	**0**	**3**	**0**	**–2**	....	....	....	....	....	....	....	....
	Ottawa Senators	**NHL**	**11**	**2**	**3**	**5**	**2**	**2**	**4**	**0**	**0**	**2**	**0**	**19**	**10.5**	**9**	**1**	**14**	**4**	**–2**	....	....	....	....	....	....	....	....
	United States	WC-A	8	0	1	1	....	....	....	6	....	....	....	....	....	....	....	....	....	....	....	....	....	....	....	....	....	....
1994-95	**Ottawa Senators**	**NHL**	**38**	**4**	**3**	**7**	**7**	**4**	**11**	**20**	**0**	**0**	**0**	**34**	**11.8**	**11**	**0**	**44**	**16**	**–17**	....	....	....	....	....	....	....	....
1995-96	**Ottawa Senators**	**NHL**	**13**	**1**	**1**	**2**	**1**	**1**	**2**	**14**	**0**	**0**	**0**	**12**	**8.3**	**4**	**0**	**14**	**7**	**–3**	....	....	....	....	....	....	....	....
	Detroit Vipers	IHL	36	4	13	17	....	....	....	70	....	....	....	....	....	....	....	....	....	....	10	1	3	4	10	....	....	....
1996-97	Chicago Wolves	IHL	77	7	14	21	....	....	....	50	....	....	....	....	....	....	....	....	....	....	4	0	2	2	2	....	....	....
1997-98	Star Bulls Rosenheim	Germany	40	4	7	11	....	....	....	60	....	....	....	....	....	....	....	....	....	....	....	....	....	....	....	....	....	....
	NHL Totals		**477**	**88**	**111**	**199**	**80**	**83**	**163**	**516**	**10**	**10**	**13**	**659**	**13.4**	**369**	**97**	**453**	**117**		**56**	**13**	**12**	**25**	**107**	**2**	**0**	**1**

IHL First All-Star Team (1988) • Won Governor's Trophy (Outstanding Defenseman - IHL) (1988)

Signed as a free agent by **Pittsburgh**, October 4, 1982. Signed as a free agent by **NY Rangers**, August 31, 1992. Traded to **Ottawa** by **NY Rangers** for future considerations, March 21, 1994.

• BOURQUE, RAY

Ray Bourque D – L. 5'11", 219 lbs. b: Montreal, Que., 12/28/1960. Boston's 1st choice, 8th overall, in 1979 Entry Draft.

Season	Club	League	GP	G	A	Pts	AG	AA	APts	PIM	PP	SH	GW	S	%	TGF	PGF	TGA	PGA	+/–	GP	G	A	Pts	PIM	PP	SH	GW
1976-77	Sorel Eperviers	QMJHL	69	12	36	48	....	....	....	61	....	....	....	....	....	....	....	....	....	....	....	....	....	....	....	....	....	....
1977-78	Verdun Eperviers	QMJHL	72	22	57	79	....	....	....	90	....	....	....	....	....	....	....	....	....	....	4	2	1	3	0	....	....	....
1978-79	Verdun Eperviers	QMJHL	63	22	71	93	....	....	....	44	....	....	....	....	....	....	....	....	....	....	11	3	16	19	18	....	....	....
1979-80	**Boston Bruins**	**NHL**	**80**	**17**	**48**	**65**	**15**	**37**	**52**	**73**	**3**	**2**	**1**	**185**	**9.2**	**162**	**50**	**82**	**22**	**+52**	**10**	**2**	**9**	**11**	**27**	**0**	**0**	**0**
1980-81	**Boston Bruins**	**NHL**	**67**	**27**	**29**	**56**	**22**	**20**	**42**	**96**	**9**	**1**	**6**	**207**	**13.0**	**128**	**47**	**87**	**35**	**+29**	**3**	**0**	**1**	**1**	**2**	**0**	**0**	**0**
1981-82	Canada	C Cup	7	1	4	5	....	....	....	6	....	....	....	....	....	....	....	....	....	....	....	....	....	....	....	....	....	....
	Boston Bruins	**NHL**	**65**	**17**	**49**	**66**	**13**	**32**	**45**	**51**	**4**	**0**	**2**	**211**	**8.1**	**139**	**43**	**96**	**22**	**+22**	**9**	**1**	**5**	**6**	**16**	**0**	**0**	**1**
1982-83	**Boston Bruins**	**NHL**	**65**	**22**	**51**	**73**	**18**	**35**	**53**	**20**	**7**	**0**	**5**	**205**	**10.7**	**150**	**53**	**73**	**25**	**+49**	**17**	**8**	**15**	**23**	**10**	**2**	**0**	**1**
1983-84	**Boston Bruins**	**NHL**	**78**	**31**	**65**	**96**	**25**	**44**	**69**	**57**	**12**	**1**	**5**	**340**	**9.1**	**187**	**66**	**92**	**22**	**+51**	**3**	**0**	**2**	**2**	**0**	**0**	**0**	**0**
1984-85	Canada	C Cup	8	0	4	4	....	....	....	8	....	....	....	....	....	....	....	....	....	....	....	....	....	....	....	....	....	....
	Boston Bruins	**NHL**	**73**	**20**	**66**	**86**	**16**	**45**	**61**	**53**	**10**	**1**	**1**	**333**	**6.0**	**167**	**58**	**114**	**35**	**+30**	**5**	**0**	**3**	**3**	**4**	**0**	**0**	**0**
1985-86	**Boston Bruins**	**NHL**	**74**	**19**	**58**	**77**	**15**	**39**	**54**	**68**	**11**	**0**	**3**	**289**	**6.6**	**169**	**76**	**122**	**46**	**+17**	**3**	**0**	**0**	**0**	**0**	**0**	**0**	**0**
1986-87	**Boston Bruins**	**NHL**	**78**	**23**	**72**	**95**	**20**	**52**	**72**	**36**	**6**	**1**	**3**	**334**	**6.9**	**168**	**59**	**98**	**33**	**+44**	**4**	**1**	**2**	**3**	**0**	**0**	**0**	**0**
	NHL All-Stars	RV'87	2	1	0	1	....	....	....	2	....	....	....	....	....	....	....	....	....	....	....	....	....	....	....	....	....	....
1987-88	Canada	C Cup	9	2	6	8	....	....	....	10	....	....	....	....	....	....	....	....	....	....	....	....	....	....	....	....	....	....
	Boston Bruins	**NHL**	**78**	**17**	**64**	**81**	**15**	**46**	**61**	**72**	**7**	**1**	**5**	**344**	**4.9**	**163**	**54**	**109**	**34**	**+34**	**23**	**3**	**18**	**21**	**26**	**0**	**0**	**1**
1988-89	**Boston Bruins**	**NHL**	**60**	**18**	**43**	**61**	**15**	**30**	**45**	**52**	**6**	**0**	**0**	**243**	**7.4**	**120**	**46**	**83**	**29**	**+20**	**10**	**0**	**4**	**4**	**6**	**0**	**0**	**0**
1989-90	**Boston Bruins**	**NHL**	**76**	**19**	**65**	**84**	**16**	**47**	**63**	**50**	**8**	**0**	**3**	**310**	**6.1**	**170**	**75**	**97**	**33**	**+31**	**17**	**5**	**12**	**17**	**16**	**1**	**0**	**0**
1990-91	**Boston Bruins**	**NHL**	**76**	**21**	**73**	**94**	**19**	**56**	**75**	**75**	**7**	**0**	**3**	**323**	**6.5**	**173**	**66**	**106**	**32**	**+33**	**19**	**7**	**18**	**25**	**12**	**3**	**0**	**0**
1991-92	**Boston Bruins**	**NHL**	**80**	**21**	**60**	**81**	**19**	**45**	**64**	**56**	**7**	**1**	**2**	**334**	**6.3**	**160**	**68**	**122**	**41**	**+11**	**12**	**3**	**6**	**9**	**12**	**2**	**0**	**0**
1992-93	**Boston Bruins**	**NHL**	**78**	**19**	**63**	**82**	**16**	**43**	**59**	**40**	**8**	**0**	**7**	**330**	**5.8**	**187**	**76**	**114**	**41**	**+38**	**4**	**1**	**0**	**1**	**2**	**1**	**0**	**0**
1993-94	**Boston Bruins**	**NHL**	**72**	**20**	**71**	**91**	**19**	**55**	**74**	**58**	**10**	**3**	**1**	**386**	**5.2**	**171**	**79**	**97**	**31**	**+26**	**13**	**2**	**8**	**10**	**0**	**1**	**0**	**0**
1994-95	**Boston Bruins**	**NHL**	**46**	**12**	**31**	**43**	**21**	**46**	**67**	**20**	**9**	**0**	**2**	**210**	**5.7**	**82**	**42**	**56**	**19**	**+3**	**5**	**0**	**3**	**3**	**0**	**0**	**0**	**0**
1995-96	**Boston Bruins**	**NHL**	**82**	**20**	**62**	**82**	**20**	**51**	**71**	**58**	**9**	**2**	**2**	**390**	**5.1**	**176**	**61**	**127**	**43**	**+31**	**5**	**1**	**6**	**7**	**2**	**1**	**0**	**0**
1996-97	**Boston Bruins**	**NHL**	**62**	**19**	**31**	**50**	**20**	**27**	**47**	**18**	**8**	**1**	**3**	**230**	**8.3**	**101**	**29**	**111**	**28**	**–11**	....	....	....	....	....	....	....	....
1997-98	**Boston Bruins**	**NHL**	**82**	**13**	**35**	**48**	**15**	**34**	**49**	**80**	**9**	**0**	**3**	**264**	**4.9**	**117**	**54**	**87**	**26**	**+2**	**6**	**1**	**4**	**5**	**2**	**1**	**0**	**0**
	Canada	Olympics	6	1	2	3	....	....	....	4	....	....	....	....	....	....	....	....	....	....	....	....	....	....	....	....	....	....
	NHL Totals		**1372**	**375**	**1036**	**1411**	**339**	**784**	**1123**	**1033**	**150**	**14**	**57**	**5468**	**6.9**	**2890**	**1102**	**1873**	**597**		**168**	**35**	**116**	**151**	**137**	**12**	**0**	**3**

QMJHL First All-Star Team (1978, 1979) • Won Calder Memorial Trophy (1980) • NHL First All-Star Team (1980, 1982, 1984, 1985, 1987, 1988, 1990, 1991, 1992, 1993, 1994, 1996) • NHL Second All-Star Team (1981, 1983, 1986, 1989, 1995) • Won James Norris Memorial Trophy (1987, 1988, 1990, 1991, 1994) • Canada Cup All-Star Team (1987) • Won King Clancy Memorial Trophy (1992)

Played in NHL All-Star Game (1981, 1982, 1983, 1984, 1985, 1986, 1988, 1989, 1989, 1990, 1991, 1992, 1993, 1994, 1996, 1997, 1998)

• BOUTETTE, PAT

Pat "Booter" Boutette C/RW – L. 5'8", 175 lbs. b. Windsor, Ont., 3/1/1952. Toronto's 9th choice, 139th overall, in 1972 Amateur Draft.

			REGULAR SEASON																		PLAYOFFS							
Season	Club	League	GP	G	A	Pts	AG	AA	APts	PIM	PP	SH	GW	S	%	TGF	PGF	TGA	PGA	+/–	GP	G	A	Pts	PIM	PP	SH	GW
1969-70	London Knights	OHA	53	11	17	28	....	....	....	87	....	....	....	....	....	....	....	....	....	....	....	....	....	....	....	....	....	....
1970-71	University of Minnesota	WCHA	33	18	13	31	....	....	....	86	....	....	....	....	....	....	....	....	....	....	....	....	....	....	....	....	....	....
1971-72	University of Minnesota	WCHA	34	17	20	37	....	....	....	71	....	....	....	....	....	....	....	....	....	....	....	....	....	....	....	....	....	....
1972-73	University of Minnesota	WCHA	34	18	45	63	....	....	....	91	....	....	....	....	....	....	....	....	....	....	....	....	....	....	....	....	....	....
1973-74	Oklahoma City Blazers	CHL	70	17	34	51	....	....	....	118	....	....	....	....	....	....	....	....	....	....	10	0	*7	7	35	....	....	....
1974-75	Oklahoma City Blazers	CHL	77	26	42	68	....	....	....	163	....	....	....	....	....	....	....	....	....	....	5	2	4	6	4	....	....	....
1975-76	Toronto Maple Leafs	NHL	77	10	22	32	9	17	26	140	2	0	2	92	10.9	51	9	45	2	–1	10	1	4	5	16	0	0	0
1976-77	Toronto Maple Leafs	NHL	80	18	18	36	17	15	32	107	3	0	1	104	17.3	71	4	54	0	+13	9	0	4	4	17	0	0	0
1977-78	Toronto Maple Leafs	NHL	80	17	19	36	16	15	31	120	2	0	1	130	13.1	54	5	49	0	0	13	3	3	6	40	0	0	0
1978-79	Toronto Maple Leafs	NHL	80	14	19	33	13	14	27	136	0	0	2	89	15.7	53	1	51	2	+3	6	2	2	4	22	0	0	0
1979-80	Toronto Maple Leafs	NHL	32	0	4	4	0	3	3	17	0	0	0	11	0.0	7	0	21	8	–6	....	....	....	....	....	....	....	....
	Hartford Whalers	NHL	47	13	31	44	12	24	36	75	3	0	0	72	18.1	77	16	62	18	+17	3	1	0	1	6	0	1	0
1980-81	Hartford Whalers	NHL	80	28	52	80	23	36	59	160	8	2	3	182	15.4	130	37	132	26	–13	....	....	....	....	....	....	....	....
	Canada	WEC-A	8	1	1	2	....	....	....	16	....	....	....	....	....	....	....	....	....	....	....	....	....	....	....	....	....	....
1981-82	Pittsburgh Penguins	NHL	80	23	51	74	18	34	52	230	14	1	2	140	16.4	131	72	113	31	–23	5	3	1	4	8	2	0	0
1982-83	Pittsburgh Penguins	NHL	80	27	29	56	22	20	42	152	13	1	4	142	19.0	118	65	143	57	–33	....	....	....	....	....	....	....	....
1983-84	Pittsburgh Penguins	NHL	73	14	26	40	11	18	29	142	10	0	1	107	13.1	69	33	153	59	–58	....	....	....	....	....	....	....	....
1984-85	Pittsburgh Penguins	NHL	14	1	3	4	1	2	3	24	0	1	0	11	9.1	9	3	24	13	–5	....	....	....	....	....	....	....	....
	Hartford Whalers	NHL	33	6	8	14	5	5	10	51	0	0	2	43	14.0	29	4	37	6	–6	....	....	....	....	....	....	....	....
	Binghamton Whalers	AHL	27	8	17	25	....	....	....	10	....	....	....	....	....	....	....	....	....	....	7	0	2	2	0	....	....	....
	NHL Totals		756	171	282	453	147	203	350	1354	55	5	18	1123	15.2	799	249	884	222		46	10	14	24	109	2	1	0

WCHA Second All-Star Team (1973) • NCAA West First All-American Team (1973)

Traded to **Hartford** by **Toronto** for Bob Stephenson, December 24, 1979. Traded to **Pittsburgh** by **Hartford** with Kevin McClelland as compensation for Hartford's signing of free agent Greg Malone, June 29, 1981. Traded to **Hartford** by **Pittsburgh** for the rights to Ville Siren, November 16, 1984.

• BOUTILIER, PAUL

Paul Boutilier D – L. 6', 200 lbs. b: Sydney, N.S., 5/3/1963. NY Islanders' 1st choice, 21st overall, in 1981 Entry Draft.

1980-81	Sherbrooke Beavers	QMJHL	72	10	29	39	....	....	....	95	....	....	....	....	....	....	....	....	....	....	14	3	7	10	10	....	....	....
1981-82	Sherbrooke Beavers	QMJHL	57	20	60	80	....	....	....	62	....	....	....	....	....	....	....	....	....	....	21	7	31	38	12	....	....	....
	New York Islanders	NHL	1	0	0	0	0	0	0	0	0	0	0	0	0.0	0	0	0	0	0	....	....	....	....	....	....	....	....
1982-83	St. Jean Beavers	QMJHL	22	5	14	19	....	....	....	30	....	....	....	....	....	....	....	....	....	....	....	....	....	....	....	....	....	....
	New York Islanders	NHL	29	4	5	9	3	3	6	24	3	0	1	52	7.7	25	5	25	0	–5	2	0	0	0	2	0	0	0
1983-84	New York Islanders	NHL	28	0	11	11	0	7	7	36	0	0	0	31	0.0	33	1	14	0	+18	21	1	7	8	10	0	0	1
	Indianapolis Checkers	CHL	50	6	17	23	....	....	....	56	....	....	....	....	....	....	....	....	....	....	....	....	....	....	....	....	....	....
1984-85	New York Islanders	NHL	78	12	23	35	10	16	26	90	2	1	3	137	8.8	109	20	111	22	0	10	0	2	2	16	0	0	0
1985-86	New York Islanders	NHL	77	4	30	34	3	20	23	100	0	0	0	124	3.2	94	22	107	30	–5	3	0	0	0	2	0	0	0
1986-87	Boston Bruins	NHL	52	5	9	14	4	6	10	84	1	1	0	68	7.4	60	14	58	10	–2	....	....	....	....	....	....	....	....
	Minnesota North Stars	NHL	10	2	4	6	2	3	5	8	0	0	0	21	9.5	13	2	12	2	+1	....	....	....	....	....	....	....	....
1987-88	New York Rangers	NHL	4	0	1	1	0	1	1	6	0	0	0	3	0.0	3	1	3	0	–1	....	....	....	....	....	....	....	....
	New Haven Nighthawks	AHL	9	0	3	3	....	....	....	10	....	....	....	....	....	....	....	....	....	....	....	....	....	....	....	....	....	....
	Colorado Rangers	IHL	9	2	6	8	....	....	....	4	....	....	....	....	....	....	....	....	....	....	....	....	....	....	....	....	....	....
	Winnipeg Jets	NHL	6	0	0	0	0	0	0	6	0	0	0	6	0.0	3	0	8	3	–2	5	0	0	0	15	0	0	0
	Moncton Hawks	AHL	41	9	29	38	....	....	....	40	....	....	....	....	....	....	....	....	....	....	....	....	....	....	....	....	....	....
1988-89	Winnipeg Jets	NHL	3	0	0	0	0	0	0	4	0	0	0	4	0.0	5	0	3	0	+2	....	....	....	....	....	....	....	....
	Moncton Hawks	AHL	77	6	54	60	....	....	....	101	....	....	....	....	....	....	....	....	....	....	10	2	7	9	4	....	....	....
1989-90	SC Bern	Switz.	36	12	28	40	....	....	....	....	....	....	....	....	....	....	....	....	....	....	....	....	....	....	....	....	....	....
	Maine Mariners	AHL	12	0	4	4	....	....	....	21	....	....	....	....	....	....	....	....	....	....	....	....	....	....	....	....	....	....
	NHL Totals		288	27	83	110	22	56	78	358	6	2	4	446	6.1	345	65	341	67		41	1	9	10	45	0	0	1

QMJHL First All-Star Team (1982) • Memorial Cup All-Star Team (1982) • AHL First All-Star Team (1989)

Transferred to **Boston** by **NY Islanders** as compensation for the NY Islanders' signing of free agent Brian Curran, August 6, 1987. Traded to **Minnesota** by **Boston** for Minnesota's 4th round choice (Darwin MacPherson) in 1987 Entry Draft, September 28, 1987. Traded to **NY Rangers** by **Minnesota** with Jari Gronstad for Jay Caulfield and Dave Gagner, October 8, 1987. Traded to **Winnipeg** by **NY Rangers** for future considerations, December 16, 1987.

• BOWEN, JASON

Jason Bowen LW – L. 6'4", 215 lbs. b: Port Alice, B.C., 11/9/1973. Philadelphia's 2nd choice, 15th overall, in 1992 Entry Draft.

1989-90	Tri-City Americans	WHL	61	8	5	13	....	....	....	129	....	....	....	....	....	....	....	....	....	....	7	0	3	3	4	....	....	....
1990-91	Tri-City Americans	WHL	60	7	13	20	....	....	....	252	....	....	....	....	....	....	....	....	....	....	6	2	2	4	18	....	....	....
1991-92	Tri-City Americans	WHL	19	5	3	0	....	....	....	135	....	....	....	....	....	....	....	....	....	....	5	0	1	1	42	....	....	....
1992-93	Tri-City Americans	WHL	62	10	12	22	....	....	....	219	....	....	....	....	....	....	....	....	....	....	3	1	1	2	18	....	....	....
	Philadelphia Flyers	NHL	7	1	0	1	1	0	1	2	0	0	0	3	33.3	1	0	0	0	+1	....	....	....	....	....	....	....	....
1993-94	Philadelphia Flyers	NHL	56	1	5	6	1	4	5	87	0	0	1	50	2.0	35	0	31	8	+12		....	....	....	....	....	....	....
1994-95	Philadelphia Flyers	NHL	4	0	0	0	0	0	0	0	0	0	0	2	0.0	0	0	2	0	–2	....	....	....	....	....	....	....	....
	Hershey Bears	AHL	55	5	5	10	....	....	....	116	....	....	....	....	....	....	....	....	....	....	6	0	0	0	46	....	....	....
1995-96	Philadelphia Flyers	NHL	2	0	0	0	0	0	0	2	0	0	0	2	0.0	0	0	0	0	0	....	....	....	....	....	....	....	....
	Hershey Bears	AHL	72	6	7	13	....	....	....	128	....	....	....	....	....	....	....	....	....	....	4	2	0	2	13	....	....	....
1996-97	Philadelphia Flyers	NHL	4	0	1	1	0	1	1	8	0	0	0	1	0.0	2	0	1	0	+1	....	....	....	....	....	....	....	....
	Philadelphia Phantoms	AHL	61	10	12	22	....	....	....	160	....	....	....	....	....	....	....	....	....	....	6	0	1	1	10	....	....	....
1997-98	Philadelphia Phantoms	AHL	3	0	0	0	....	....	....	19	....	....	....	....	....	....	....	....	....	....	....	....	....	....	....	....	....	....
	Edmonton Oilers	NHL	4	0	0	0	0	0	0	10	0	0	0	3	0.0	0	0	0	0	0	....	....	....	....	....	....	....	....
	Hamilton Bulldogs	AHL	51	5	14	19	....	....	....	108	....	....	....	....	....	....	....	....	....	....	7	1	1	2	22	....	....	....
	Canada	WC-A	4	0	0	0	....	....	....	0	....	....	....	....	....	....	....	....	....	....	....	....	....	....	....	....	....	....
	NHL Totals		77	2	6	8	2	5	7	109	0	0	1	61	3.3	38	0	34	8		....	....	....	....	....	....	....	....

Traded to **Edmonton** by **Philadelphia** for Brantt Myhres, October 15, 1997.

• BOWMAN, KIRK

Kirk Bowman LW – L. 5'9", 178 lbs. b: Leamington, Ont., 9/30/1952.

1970-71	Guelph GMC's	SOJHL	44	42	29	71	....	....	....	....	....	....	....	....	....	....	....	....	....	....	....	....	....	....	....	....	....	....
1971-72	Columbus Golden Seals	IHL	19	10	8	18	....	....	....	9	....	....	....	....	....	....	....	....	....	....	....	....	....	....	....	....	....	....
	Greensboro Generals	EHL	46	15	15	30	....	....	....	19	....	....	....	....	....	....	....	....	....	....	11	4	5	9	6	....	....	....
1972-73	Greensboro Generals	EHL	70	27	51	78	....	....	....	23	....	....	....	....	....	....	....	....	....	....	7	1	0	0	0	....	....	....
	Flint Generals	IHL	....	....	....	....	....	....	....	....	....	....	....	....	....	....	....	....	....	....	1	1	2	3	0	....	....	....
1973-74	Los Angeles Sharks	WHA	10	0	2	2	....	....	....	0	....	....	....	....	....	....	....	....	....	....	....	....	....	....	....	....	....	....
	Greensboro Generals	SHL	58	23	55	78	....	....	....	20	....	....	....	....	....	....	....	....	....	....	6	1	8	9	0	....	....	....
1974-75	Dallas Black Hawks	CHL	....	....	....	....	....	....	....	....	....	....	....	....	....	....	....	....	....	....	4	0	3	3	0	....	....	....
	Flint Generals	IHL	75	29	*79	108	....	....	....	62	....	....	....	....	....	....	....	....	....	....	5	2	5	7	2	....	....	....
1975-76	Dallas Black Hawks	CHL	....	....	....	....	....	....	....	....	....	....	....	....	....	....	....	....	....	....	10	3	*8	11	4	....	....	....
	Flint Generals	IHL	78	44	*63	107	....	....	....	12	....	....	....	....	....	....	....	....	....	....	4	2	3	5	5	....	....	....
1976-77	Chicago Black Hawks	NHL	55	10	13	23	10	11	21	6	2	0	2	64	15.6	36	8	45	10	–7	2	1	0	1	0	1	0	0
	Flint Generals	IHL	11	5	14	19	....	....	....	2	....	....	....	....	....	....	....	....	....	....	....	....	....	....	....	....	....	....
1977-78	Chicago Black Hawks	NHL	33	1	4	5	1	3	4	13	0	0	0	41	2.4	13	1	17	5	0	3	0	0	0	0	0	0	0
	Dallas Black Hawks	CHL	39	10	23	33	....	....	....	6	....	....	....	....	....	....	....	....	....	....	....	....	....	....	....	....	....	....
1978-79	New Brunswick Hawks	AHL	80	26	56	82	....	....	....	44	....	....	....	....	....	....	....	....	....	....	5	2	3	5	2	....	....	....
	Chicago Black Hawks	NHL	....	....	....	....	....	....	....	....	....	....	....	....	....	....	....	....	....	....	2	0	0	0	0	....	....	....
1979-80			DID NOT PLAY – RETIRED																									
1980-81			DID NOT PLAY – RETIRED																									
1981-82	Schwenninger ERC	Germany	44	35	36	71	....	....	....	33	....	....	....	....	....	....	....	....	....	....	....	....	....	....	....	....	....	....
1982-83	Schwenninger ERC	Germany	36	21	16	37	....	....	....	14	....	....	....	....	....	....	....	....	....	....	....	....	....	....	....	....	....	....
1983-84	Schwenninger ERC	Germany	45	28	33	61	....	....	....	34	....	....	....	....	....	....	....	....	....	....	....	....	....	....	....	....	....	....
1984-85	SC Bern	Switz.	36	14	5	19	....	....	....	....	....	....	....	....	....	....	....	....	....	....	....	0	3	3	....	....	....	....

			REGULAR SEASON																		PLAYOFFS							
Season	Club	League	GP	G	A	Pts	AG	AA	APts	PIM	PP	SH	GW	S	%	TGF	PGF	TGA	PGA	+/–	GP	G	A	Pts	PIM	PP	SH	GW
1985-86	SC Bern	Switz.	36	37	41	78															5	4	2	6				
1986-87	SC Bern	Switz.	36	29	41	70																						
1987-88	SC Bern	Switz.	....	11	25	36																						
	NHL Totals		**88**	**11**	**17**	**28**	**11**	**14**	**25**	**19**	**2**	**0**	**2**	**105**	**10.5**	**49**	**9**	**62**	**15**		**7**	**1**	**0**	**1**	**0**	**1**	**0**	**0**
	Other Major League Totals		10	0	2	2				0																		

IHL Second All-Star Team (1976)

Signed as a free agent by **Columbus** (IHL), September, 1971. Claimed on waivers by **Greensboro** from **Columbus**, December, 1971. Rights transferred to **LA Sharks** (WHA) after WHA club signed **Greensboro** (SHL) as a minor league affiliate, June, 1973. Signed as a free agent by **Chicago**, September, 1974.

• BOWNESS, RICK

Rick Bowness RW – R. 6'1", 185 lbs. b: Moncton, N.B., 1/25/1955. Atlanta's 2nd choice, 26th overall, in 1975 Amateur Draft.

Season	Club	League	GP	G	A	Pts	AG	AA	APts	PIM	PP	SH	GW	S	%	TGF	PGF	TGA	PGA	+/–	GP	G	A	Pts	PIM	PP	SH	GW
1972-73	Quebec Remparts	QMJHL	30	2	7	9				2																		
1973-74	St. Mary's University	AUAA	1	0	0	0				0																		
	Quebec Remparts	QMJHL	34	16	29	45				64																		
	Montreal Jr. Canadiens	QMJHL	33	9	17	26				31											9	4	4	8	4			
1974-75	Montreal Jr. Canadiens	QMJHL	71	24	76	100				130											8	5	3	8	29			
1975-76	**Atlanta Flames**	**NHL**	**5**	**0**	**0**	**0**	**0**	**0**	**0**	**0**	**0**	**0**	**0**	**6**	**0.0**	**0**	**0**	**5**	**0**	**–5**								
	Nova Scotia Voyageurs	AHL	2	0	1	1				0																		
	Tulsa Oilers	CHL	64	25	38	63				160											9	4	3	7	12			
1976-77	**Atlanta Flames**	**NHL**	**28**	**0**	**4**	**4**	**0**	**3**	**3**	**29**	**0**	**0**	**0**	**21**	**0.0**	**8**	**0**	**18**	**1**	**–9**								
	Tulsa Oilers	CHL	39	15	15	30				72											8	0	1	1	20			
1977-78	**Detroit Red Wings**	**NHL**	**61**	**8**	**11**	**19**	**8**	**9**	**17**	**76**	**2**	**0**	**2**	**46**	**17.4**	**29**	**4**	**33**	**0**	**–8**	**4**	**0**	**0**	**0**	**2**	**0**	**0**	**0**
1978-79	**St. Louis Blues**	**NHL**	**24**	**1**	**3**	**4**	**1**	**2**	**3**	**30**	**0**	**0**	**0**	**18**	**5.6**	**9**	**0**	**27**	**1**	**–17**								
	Salt Lake Golden Eagles	CHL	48	25	28	53				92											10	5	4	9	27			
1979-80	**St. Louis Blues**	**NHL**	**10**	**1**	**2**	**3**	**1**	**2**	**3**	**11**	**0**	**0**	**0**	**4**	**25.0**	**4**	**0**	**6**	**0**	**–2**								
	Salt Lake Golden Eagles	CHL	71	25	46	71				135											13	5	9	14	39			
1980-81	**Winnipeg Jets**	**NHL**	**45**	**8**	**17**	**25**	**7**	**12**	**19**	**45**	**0**	**0**	**1**	**55**	**14.5**	**32**	**2**	**65**	**0**	**–35**								
	Tulsa Oilers	CHL	35	12	20	32				82																		
1981-82	Tulsa Oilers	CHL	79	34	53	87				201											3	0	2	2	2			
	Winnipeg Jets	**NHL**																			**1**	**0**	**0**	**0**	**0**			
1982-83	Sherbrooke Jets	AHL	65	17	31	48				117																		
1983-84	Sherbrooke Jets	AHL	21	9	11	20				44																		
	NHL Totals		**173**	**18**	**37**	**55**	**17**	**28**	**45**	**191**	**2**	**0**	**3**	**150**	**12.0**	**82**	**6**	**154**	**2**		**5**	**0**	**0**	**0**	**2**	**0**	**0**	**0**

Traded to **Detroit** by **Atlanta** for cash, August 18, 1977. Traded to **St. Louis** by **Detroit** for cash, October 10, 1978. Traded to **Winnipeg** by **St. Louis** for Craig Norwich, June 19, 1980.

• BOYD, RANDY

Randy Boyd D – L. 5'11", 190 lbs. b: Coniston, Ont., 1/23/1962. Pittsburgh's 2nd choice, 51st overall, in 1980 Entry Draft.

Season	Club	League	GP	G	A	Pts	AG	AA	APts	PIM	PP	SH	GW	S	%	TGF	PGF	TGA	PGA	+/–	GP	G	A	Pts	PIM	PP	SH	GW
1979-80	Ottawa 67's	OHA	65	3	21	24				148											11	0	2	2	13			
1980-81	Ottawa 67's	OHA	64	11	43	54				225											7	2	3	5	35			
1981-82	Ottawa 67's	OHL	26	9	29	38				51																		
	Pittsburgh Penguins	**NHL**	**23**	**0**	**2**	**2**	**0**	**1**	**1**	**49**	**0**	**0**	**0**	**26**	**0.0**	**16**	**1**	**22**	**2**	**–5**	**3**	**0**	**0**	**0**	**11**	**0**	**0**	**0**
1982-83	**Pittsburgh Penguins**	**NHL**	**56**	**4**	**14**	**18**	**3**	**10**	**13**	**71**	**1**	**0**	**0**	**102**	**3.9**	**48**	**12**	**100**	**28**	**–36**								
	Baltimore Skipjacks	AHL	21	5	10	15				43																		
1983-84	**Pittsburgh Penguins**	**NHL**	**5**	**0**	**1**	**1**	**0**	**1**	**1**	**6**	**0**	**0**	**0**	**14**	**0.0**	**4**	**0**	**8**	**2**	**–2**								
	Baltimore Skipjacks	AHL	20	6	13	19				69																		
	Chicago Black Hawks	**NHL**	**23**	**0**	**4**	**4**	**0**	**3**	**3**	**16**	**0**	**0**	**0**	**21**	**0.0**	**10**	**0**	**15**	**5**	**0**								
	Springfield Indians	AHL	27	2	11	13				48											4	0	2	2	34			
1984-85	**Chicago Black Hawks**	**NHL**	**3**	**0**	**0**	**0**	**0**	**0**	**0**	**6**	**0**	**0**	**0**	**2**	**0.0**	**1**	**0**	**1**	**0**	**0**	**3**	**0**	**1**	**1**	**7**	**0**	**0**	**0**
	Milwaukee Admirals	IHL	68	18	55	73				162																		
1985-86	**New York Islanders**	**NHL**	**55**	**2**	**12**	**14**	**2**	**8**	**10**	**79**	**0**	**0**	**0**	**52**	**3.8**	**52**	**7**	**43**	**7**	**+9**	**3**	**0**	**0**	**0**	**2**	**0**	**0**	**0**
1986-87	**New York Islanders**	**NHL**	**30**	**7**	**17**	**24**	**6**	**12**	**18**	**37**	**3**	**1**	**0**	**69**	**10.1**	**50**	**22**	**30**	**2**	**0**	**4**	**0**	**1**	**1**	**6**	**0**	**0**	**0**
	Springfield Indians	AHL	48	9	30	39				96																		
1987-88	**Vancouver Canucks**	**NHL**	**60**	**7**	**16**	**23**	**6**	**11**	**17**	**64**	**2**	**0**	**1**	**85**	**8.2**	**71**	**21**	**65**	**6**	**–9**								
1988-89	**Vancouver Canucks**	**NHL**	**2**	**0**	**1**	**1**	**0**	**1**	**1**	**0**	**0**	**0**	**0**	**6**	**0.0**	**1**	**1**	**1**	**0**	**–1**								
	Milwaukee Admirals	IHL	73	24	55	79				218											9	0	6	6	26			
1989-90			DID NOT PLAY																									
1990-91			DID NOT PLAY																									
1991-92	Milwaukee Admirals	IHL	42	7	9	16				80											2	0	1	1	2			
1992-93	Milwaukee Admirals	IHL	8	1	4	5				8																		
	Wichita Thunder	CHL	22	10	26	36				92																		
1993-94	Memphis RiverKings	ECHL	DID NOT PLAY – COACHING																									
	NHL Totals		**257**	**20**	**67**	**87**	**17**	**47**	**64**	**328**	**6**	**1**	**1**	**377**	**5.3**	**253**	**64**	**285**	**52**		**13**	**0**	**2**	**2**	**26**	**0**	**0**	**0**

OHA First All-Star Team (1981) • IHL First All-Star Team (1985, 1989) • Won Governors' Trophy (Top Defenseman - IHL) (1989)

Traded to **Chicago** by **Pittsburgh** for Greg Fox, December 6, 1983. Claimed by **NY Islanders** from **Chicago** in Waiver Draft, October 7, 1985. Claimed by **Vancouver** from **NY Islanders** in Waiver Draft, October 5, 1987.

• BOYER, WALLY

Wally Boyer C – L. 5'8", 165 lbs. b: Cowan, Man., 9/27/1937.

Season	Club	League	GP	G	A	Pts	AG	AA	APts	PIM	PP	SH	GW	S	%	TGF	PGF	TGA	PGA	+/–	GP	G	A	Pts	PIM	PP	SH	GW
1955-56	Toronto Marlboros	OHA	48	14	19	33				51											11	2	2	4	4			
1956-57	Toronto Marlboros	OHA	40	17	17	34				21											8	2	6	8	19			
1957-58	Toronto Marlboros	OHA	27	11	11	22				17											12	6	*14	20	17			
1958-59	New Westminster Royals	WHL	27	5	5	10				0																		
	Hershey Bears	AHL	4	0	1	1				2																		
	Chicoutimi–Montreal	QHL	28	3	7	10				8											4	0	0	0	0			
1959-60	Sudbury Wolves	EPHL	70	23	42	65				36											11	2	4	6	4			
1960-61	Rochester Americans	AHL	70	24	33	57				31																		
1961-62	Rochester Americans	AHL	67	20	21	41				67											2	0	0	0	0			
1962-63	Springfield Indians	AHL	66	28	45	73				59																		
1963-64	Rochester Americans	AHL	52	20	19	39				55											2	1	0	1	2			
1964-65	Rochester Americans	AHL	70	20	41	61				28											10	2	4	6	4			
1965-66	**Toronto Maple Leafs**	**NHL**	**46**	**4**	**17**	**21**	**5**	**17**	**22**	**23**											**4**	**0**	**1**	**1**	**0**			
	Rochester Americans	AHL	19	3	10	13				13																		
1966-67	**Chicago Black Hawks**	**NHL**	**42**	**5**	**6**	**11**	**6**	**6**	**12**	**15**											**1**	**0**	**0**	**0**	**0**			
	Portland Buckaroos	WHL	17	7	6	13				10																		
1967-68	**Oakland Seals**	**NHL**	**74**	**13**	**20**	**33**	**16**	**21**	**37**	**44**	**1**	**0**	**0**	**142**	**9.2**	**52**	**11**	**44**	**3**	**0**								
1968-69	**Pittsburgh Penguins**	**NHL**	**62**	**10**	**19**	**29**	**11**	**18**	**29**	**17**	**2**	**0**	**0**	**127**	**7.9**	**46**	**21**	**50**	**4**	**–21**								
1969-70	**Pittsburgh Penguins**	**NHL**	**72**	**11**	**12**	**23**	**13**	**12**	**25**	**34**	**2**	**0**	**1**	**112**	**9.8**	**41**	**14**	**55**	**23**	**–5**	**10**	**1**	**2**	**3**	**0**	**0**	**1**	**0**
1970-71	**Pittsburgh Penguins**	**NHL**	**68**	**11**	**30**	**41**	**11**	**26**	**37**	**30**	**4**	**0**	**0**	**111**	**9.9**	**55**	**11**	**45**	**11**	**+10**								
1971-72	**Pittsburgh Penguins**	**NHL**	**1**	**0**	**1**	**1**	**0**	**1**	**1**	**0**	**0**	**0**	**0**	**0**	**0.0**	**1**	**0**	**2**	**0**	**–1**								
	Hershey Bears	AHL	64	18	30	48				43											3	1	0	1	2			
1972-73	Winnipeg Jets	WHA	69	6	28	34				27											14	4	2	6	4			
	NHL Totals		**365**	**54**	**105**	**159**	**62**	**101**	**163**	**163**	**9**	**0**	**1**	**492**	**11.0**	**195**	**57**	**196**	**41**		**15**	**1**	**3**	**4**	**0**	**0**	**1**	**0**
	Other Major League Totals		69	6	28	34				27											14	4	2	6	4			

Traded to **Hershey** (AHL) by **Toronto** with Mike Nykolyk and Ron Hurst for Willie Marshall, June, 1958. Toronto retains right of recall. Rights traded to **Springfield** (AHL) by **Toronto** with Jim Wilcox, Roger Cote, Bill White and Don Mattussi for Kent Douglas, June 7, 1962. Toronto retains right of recall. Claimed by **Montreal** from **Toronto** in Intra-League Draft, June 15, 1966. Claimed by **Chicago** from **Montreal** in Intra-League Draft, June 15, 1966. Claimed by **Oakland** from **Chicago** in Expansion Draft, June 6, 1967. Traded to **Montreal** by **Oakland** with Alain Caron and the rights to Lyle Bradley for Norm Ferguson, Michel Jacques, Francois Lacombe and Stan Fuller, May 21, 1968. Traded to **Pittsburgh** by **Montreal** for Al MacNeil, June 12, 1968. Selected by **Winnipeg** (WHA) in 1972 WHA General Player Draft, February 12, 1972.

• BOYER, ZAC

Zac Boyer RW – R. 6'1", 199 lbs. b: Inuvik, N.W.T., 10/25/1971. Chicago's 6th choice, 88th overall, in 1991 Entry Draft.

Season	Club	League	GP	G	A	Pts	AG	AA	APts	PIM	PP	SH	GW	S	%	TGF	PGF	TGA	PGA	+/–	GP	G	A	Pts	PIM	PP	SH	GW
1988-89	Kamloops Blazers	WHL	42	10	17	27				22											16	9	8	17	10			
1989-90	Kamloops Blazers	WHL	71	24	47	71				163											17	4	4	8	8			
1990-91	Kamloops Blazers	WHL	64	45	60	105				58											12	6	10	16	8			
1991-92	Kamloops Blazers	WHL	70	40	69	109				90											17	9	*20	*29	16			

			REGULAR SEASON																		PLAYOFFS							
Season	Club	League	GP	G	A	Pts	AG	AA	APts	PIM	PP	SH	GW	S	%	TGF	PGF	TGA	PGA	+/–	GP	G	A	Pts	PIM	PP	SH	GW
1992-93	Indianapolis Ice	IHL	59	7	14	21				26																		
1993-94	Indianapolis Ice	IHL	54	13	12	25				67																		
1994-95	**Dallas Stars**	**NHL**	**1**	**0**	**0**	**0**	**0**	**0**	**0**	**0**	**0**	**0**	**0**	**1**	**0.0**	**0**	**0**	**0**	**0**	**0**	**2**	**0**	**0**	**0**	**0**	**0**	**0**	**0**
	Kalamazoo Wings	IHL	22	9	7	16				22											15	3	9	12	8			
1995-96	**Dallas Stars**	**NHL**	**2**	**0**	**0**	**0**	**0**	**0**	**0**	**0**	**0**	**0**	**0**	**3**	**0.0**	**0**	**0**	**0**	**0**	**0**								
	Michigan K-Wings	IHL	67	24	27	51				58											10	11	6	17	0			
1996-97	Orlando Solar Bears	IHL	80	25	49	74				63											3	0	1	1	2			
	NHL Totals		**3**	**0**	**0**	**0**	**0**	**0**	**0**	**0**	**0**	**0**	**0**	**4**	**0.0**	**0**	**0**	**0**	**0**		**2**	**0**	**0**	**0**	**0**	**0**	**0**	**0**

Signed as a free agent by **Dallas**, July 25, 1994.

• BOYKO, DARREN

Darren Boyko C – R. 5'9", 169 lbs. b: Winnipeg, Man., 1/16/1964.

Season	Club	League	GP	G	A	Pts	AG	AA	APts	PIM	PP	SH	GW	S	%	TGF	PGF	TGA	PGA	+/–	GP	G	A	Pts	PIM	PP	SH	GW
1980-81	St. Boniface Canadiens	MJHL	48	48	68	*116																						
1981-82	Winnipeg Jets	WHL	65	35	37	72				14																		
1982-83	Winnipeg Jets	WHL	72	49	18	130				8											3	0	2	2	0			
1983-84	University of Toronto	OUAA	40	33	51	84				24											9	7	10	17	4			
1984-85	University of Toronto	OUAA	39	31	53	84				42											2	1	0	1	6			
1985-86	HIFK Helsinki	Finland	36	18	26	44				8											8	1	3	4	2			
1986-87	HIFK Helsinki	Finland	44	22	13	35				44																		
1987-88	HIFK Helsinki	Finland	44	14	40	54				16																		
1988-89	**Winnipeg Jets**	**NHL**	**1**	**0**	**0**	**0**	**0**	**0**	**0**	**0**	**0**	**0**	**0**	**0**	**0.0**	**0**	**0**	**1**	**0**	**–1**								
	Moncton Hawks	AHL	18	3	7	10				2											4	0	0	0	0			
	HIFK Helsinki	Finland	34	15	15	30				10											2	0	0	0	0			
1989-90	HIFK Helsinki	Finland	42	12	20	32				36											2	1	0	1	2			
1990-91	HIFK Helsinki	Finland	42	16	22	38				20											3	0	3	3	4			
1991-92	HIFK Helsinki	Finland	44	14	23	37				18																		
1992-93	HIFK Helsinki	Finland	47	15	16	31				6																		
1993-94	HIFK Helsinki	Finland	48	18	20	38				14																		
1994-95	HIFK Helsinki	Finland	48	15	20	35				24											3	0	0	0	2			
1995-96	HIFK Helsinki	Finland	47	12	20	32				30																		
1996-97	Berlin Capitals	Germany	32	4	18	22				8											4	0	2	2	2			
1996-97	Vastra Frolunda	Sweden	1	0	0	0				0																		
	Berlin Capitals	Germany	32	4	18	22				8											4	0	2	2	2			
	NHL Totals		**1**	**0**	**0**	**0**	**0**	**0**	**0**	**0**	**0**	**0**	**0**	**0**	**0.0**	**0**	**0**	**1**	**0**									

Signed as a free agent by **Winnipeg**, May 16, 1988.

• BOZEK, STEVE

Steve Bozek LW – L. 5'11", 180 lbs. b: Kelowna, B.C., 11/26/1960. Los Angeles' 5th choice, 52nd overall, in 1980 Entry Draft.

Season	Club	League	GP	G	A	Pts	AG	AA	APts	PIM	PP	SH	GW	S	%	TGF	PGF	TGA	PGA	+/–	GP	G	A	Pts	PIM	PP	SH	GW
1978-79	Northern Michigan University	CCHA	33	12	12	24				21																		
1979-80	Northern Michigan University	CCHA	41	42	47	89				32																		
1980-81	Northern Michigan University	CCHA	44	35	55	90				0																		
1981-82	**Los Angeles Kings**	**NHL**	**71**	**33**	**23**	**56**	**26**	**15**	**41**	**68**	**10**	**0**	**5**	**182**	**18.1**	**93**	**27**	**73**	**1**	**–6**	**10**	**4**	**1**	**5**	**6**	**2**	**0**	**1**
1982-83	**Los Angeles Kings**	**NHL**	**53**	**13**	**13**	**26**	**11**	**9**	**20**	**14**	**3**	**0**	**1**	**104**	**12.5**	**33**	**5**	**61**	**15**	**–18**								
1983-84	**Calgary Flames**	**NHL**	**46**	**10**	**10**	**20**	**8**	**7**	**15**	**16**	**0**	**0**	**2**	**76**	**13.2**	**28**	**0**	**44**	**0**	**–16**	**10**	**3**	**1**	**4**	**15**	**1**	**0**	**0**
1984-85	**Calgary Flames**	**NHL**	**54**	**13**	**22**	**35**	**11**	**15**	**26**	**6**	**0**	**0**	**1**	**93**	**14.0**	**48**	**1**	**46**	**10**	**+11**	**3**	**1**	**0**	**1**	**4**	**1**	**0**	**0**
1985-86	**Calgary Flames**	**NHL**	**64**	**21**	**22**	**43**	**17**	**15**	**32**	**24**	**5**	**4**	**3**	**147**	**14.3**	**77**	**16**	**61**	**24**	**+24**	**14**	**2**	**6**	**8**	**32**	**0**	**0**	**0**
1986-87	**Calgary Flames**	**NHL**	**71**	**17**	**18**	**35**	**15**	**13**	**28**	**22**	**2**	**2**	**4**	**139**	**12.2**	**47**	**5**	**71**	**32**	**+3**	**4**	**1**	**0**	**1**	**2**	**0**	**0**	**0**
1987-88	**Calgary Flames**	**NHL**	**26**	**3**	**7**	**10**	**3**	**5**	**8**	**12**	**0**	**1**	**0**	**37**	**8.1**	**14**	**0**	**24**	**7**	**–3**								
	St. Louis Blues	**NHL**	**7**	**0**	**0**	**0**	**0**	**0**	**0**	**2**	**0**	**0**	**0**	**6**	**0.0**	**1**	**0**	**6**	**3**	**–2**	**7**	**1**	**1**	**2**	**6**	**0**	**0**	**0**
1988-89	**Vancouver Canucks**	**NHL**	**71**	**17**	**18**	**35**	**14**	**13**	**27**	**64**	**0**	**2**	**2**	**138**	**12.3**	**44**	**2**	**72**	**31**	**+1**	**7**	**0**	**2**	**2**	**4**	**0**	**0**	**0**
1989-90	**Vancouver Canucks**	**NHL**	**58**	**14**	**9**	**23**	**12**	**6**	**18**	**32**	**0**	**1**	**2**	**105**	**13.3**	**35**	**0**	**64**	**26**	**–3**								
1990-91	**Vancouver Canucks**	**NHL**	**62**	**15**	**17**	**32**	**14**	**13**	**27**	**22**	**0**	**1**	**2**	**126**	**11.9**	**44**	**2**	**75**	**27**	**–6**	**3**	**0**	**0**	**0**	**0**	**0**	**0**	**0**
	Canada	WEC-A	8	1	1	2				4																		
1991-92	**San Jose Sharks**	**NHL**	**58**	**8**	**8**	**16**	**7**	**6**	**13**	**27**	**2**	**0**	**0**	**105**	**7.6**	**26**	**5**	**77**	**26**	**–30**								
1992-93	HC Bolzano	Italy	15	6	5	11				19																		
	HC Bolzano	Alpenliga	17	13	11	24				6																		
	NHL Totals		**641**	**164**	**167**	**331**	**138**	**117**	**255**	**309**	**22**	**11**	**22**	**1258**	**13.0**	**490**	**63**	**674**	**202**		**58**	**12**	**11**	**23**	**69**	**4**	**0**	**1**

CCHA First All-Star Team (1980, 1981) • NCAA West First All-American Team (1981) • NCAA Championship All-Tournament Team (1981)

Traded to **Calgary** by **LA Kings** for Carl Mokosak and Kevin LaVallee, June 20, 1983. Traded to **St. Louis** by **Calgary** with Brett Hull for Rob Ramage and Rick Wamsley, March 7, 1986. Traded to **Calgary** by **St. Louis** with Mark Hunter, Doug Gilmour and Michael Dark for Craig Coxe Mike Bullard and Tim Corkey, September 6, 1988. Traded to **Vancouver** by **Calgary** with Paul Reinhart for Vancouver's 3rd round choice (Veli-Pekka Kautonen) in 1989 Entry Draft, September 6, 1988. Signed as a free agent by **San Jose**, August 9, 1991.

• BOZON, PHILIPPE

Philippe Bozon LW – L. 5'10", 185 lbs. b: Chamonix, France, 11/30/1966.

Season	Club	League	GP	G	A	Pts	AG	AA	APts	PIM	PP	SH	GW	S	%	TGF	PGF	TGA	PGA	+/–	GP	G	A	Pts	PIM	PP	SH	GW
1984-85	St-Jean Beavers	QMJHL	67	32	50	82				82											5	0	5	5	4			
1985-86	St-Jean Beavers	QMJHL	65	59	52	111				72											10	10	6	16	16			
	Peoria Rivermen	IHL																			5	1	0	1	0			
1986-87	St-Jean Beavers	QMJHL	25	20	21	41				75											8	5	5	10	30			
	Peoria Rivermen	IHL	28	4	11	15				17																		
1987-88	HC Mont-Blanc	France	18	11	15	26				34											10	15	6	21	6			
	France	Olympics	6	3	2	5				0																		
1988-89	HC Mont Blanc	France	18	11	18	29				18											11	11	17	28	38			
	France	WEC-B	7	8	3	11				10																		
1989-90	CSG Grenoble	France	36	45	38	83				34											6	4	3	7	2			
	France	WEC-B	7	4	2	6				4																		
1990-91	CSG Grenoble	France	26	22	16	38				16											10	7	8	15	8			
	France	WEC-B	7	5	5	10				0																		
1991-92	HC Chamonix	France	10	12	8	20				20																		
	France	Olympics	7	3	2	5				4																		
	France	WC-A	3	1	1	2				4																		
	St. Louis Blues	**NHL**	**9**	**1**	**3**	**4**	**1**	**2**	**3**	**4**	**0**	**0**	**0**	**19**	**5.3**	**12**	**4**	**3**	**0**	**+5**	**6**	**1**	**0**	**1**	**27**	**0**	**0**	**0**
1992-93	**St. Louis Blues**	**NHL**	**54**	**6**	**6**	**12**	**5**	**4**	**9**	**55**	**0**	**0**	**0**	**90**	**6.7**	**22**	**0**	**26**	**1**	**–3**	**9**	**1**	**0**	**1**	**0**	**0**	**0**	**0**
	Peoria Rivermen	IHL	4	3	2	5				2																		
1993-94	**St. Louis Blues**	**NHL**	**80**	**9**	**16**	**25**	**8**	**12**	**20**	**42**	**0**	**1**	**1**	**118**	**7.6**	**43**	**1**	**60**	**22**	**+4**	**4**	**0**	**0**	**0**	**4**	**0**	**0**	**0**
	France	WC-A	3	0	0	0				2																		
1994-95	CSG Grenoble	France	21	8	20	28				38																		
	France	WC-A	6	2	3	5				0																		
	St. Louis Blues	**NHL**	**1**	**0**	**0**	**0**	**0**	**0**	**0**	**0**	**0**	**0**	**0**	**0**	**0.0**	**0**	**0**	**0**	**0**	**0**								
1995-96	HC La Chaux-de-Fonds	Switz.	29	31	28	59				48											7	8	5	13	6			
	France	WC-A	7	4	2	6				4																		
1996-97	Adler Mannheim	Germany	22	11	7	18				6											9	6	9	*15	2			
	France	WC-A	8	2	4	6				27																		
1997-98	Adler Mannheim	EuroHL	5	2	4	6				14																		
	Adler Mannheim	Germany	41	20	17	37				36											10	5	5	10	16			
	France	Olympics	4	5	2	7				4																		
	France	WC-A	3	2	1	3				2																		
	NHL Totals		**144**	**16**	**25**	**41**	**14**	**18**	**32**	**101**	**0**	**1**	**1**	**227**	**7.0**	**77**	**5**	**89**	**23**		**19**	**2**	**0**	**2**	**31**	**0**	**0**	**0**

QMJHL Second All-Star Team (1986) • WEC-B All-Star Team (1989, 1991) • Named Best Forward at WEC-B (1991)

Signed as a free agent by **St. Louis**, September 29, 1985.

Season	Club	League	REGULAR SEASON																		PLAYOFFS							
			GP	G	A	Pts	AG	AA	APts	PIM	PP	SH	GW	S	%	TGF	PGF	TGA	PGA	+/–	GP	G	A	Pts	PIM	PP	SH	GW

• BRACKENBURY, CURT
Curt Brackenbury RW – R. 5'10", 200 lbs. b: Kapuskasing, Ont., 1/31/1952.

1971-72	Kamloops Blazers	BCJHL	STATISTICS NOT AVAILABLE																									
1972-73	Jersey Devils	EHL	68	17	27	44				66																		
1973-74	Des Moines Capitols	IHL	13	1	5	6				4																		
	Long Island Cougars	NAHL	45	8	20	28				194																		
	Chicago Cougars	WHA	4	0	1	1				11																		
1974-75	Hampton Gulls	SHL	46	19	24	43				212											13	5	5	10	48			
	Minnesota Fighting Saints	WHA	7	0	0	0				22											12	0	2	2	59			
1975-76	Minnesota Fighting Saints	WHA	59	4	9	13				255																		
	Quebec Nordiques	WHA	15	4	5	9				110											5	0	0	0	18			
1976-77	Quebec Nordiques	WHA	77	16	13	29				146											17	3	5	8	51			
1977-78	Quebec Nordiques	WHA	33	4	9	13				54											10	1	1	2	31			
1978-79	Quebec Nordiques	WHA	70	13	13	26				155											4	1	1	2	2			
1979-80	**Quebec Nordiques**	**NHL**	**63**	**6**	**8**	**14**	**5**	**6**	**11**	**55**	**0**	**0**	**1**	**42**	**14.3**	**27**	**3**	**53**	**8**	**–21**								
1980-81	**Edmonton Oilers**	**NHL**	**58**	**2**	**7**	**9**	**2**	**5**	**7**	**153**	**0**	**0**	**0**	**20**	**10.0**	**19**	**1**	**25**	**4**	**–3**	**2**	**0**	**0**	**0**	**0**	**0**	**0**	**0**
1981-82	**Edmonton Oilers**	**NHL**	**14**	**0**	**2**	**2**	**0**	**1**	**1**	**12**	**0**	**0**	**0**	**2**	**0.0**	**5**	**0**	**3**	**0**	**+2**								
	Wichita Wind	CHL	47	11	27	38				99											7	0	7	7	13			
1982-83	**St. Louis Blues**	**NHL**	**6**	**1**	**0**	**1**	**1**	**0**	**1**	**6**	**0**	**0**	**0**	**2**	**50.0**	**1**	**0**	**9**	**0**	**–8**								
	Salt Lake Golden Eagles	CHL	44	4	19	23				137											5	0	1	1	2			
	NHL Totals		**141**	**9**	**17**	**26**	**8**	**12**	**20**	**226**	**0**	**0**	**1**	**66**	**13.6**	**52**	**4**	**90**	**12**		**2**	**0**	**0**	**0**	**0**	**0**	**0**	**0**
	Other Major League Totals		265	41	50	91				753											48	5	9	14	161			

Signed as a free agent by **Chicago** (WHA), October, 1973. Traded to **Minnesota** (WHA) by **Chicago** (WHA) for cash, November, 1974. Signed as a free agent by **Quebec** (WHA) after **Minnesota** (WHA) franchise folded, March, 1976. Claimed by **Edmonton** from **Quebec** in Waiver Draft, October 10, 1980. Signed as a free agent by **St. Louis**, October 1, 1982.

• BRADLEY, BRIAN
Brian Bradley C – R. 5'10", 180 lbs. b: Kitchener, Ont., 1/21/1965. Calgary's 2nd choice, 52nd overall, in 1983 Entry Draft.

1982-83	London Knights	OHL	67	37	82	119				37											3	1	0	1	0			
1983-84	London Knights	OHL	49	40	60	100				24											4	2	4	6	0			
1984-85	London Knights	OHL	32	27	49	76				22											8	5	10	15	4			
	Canada	WJC-A	7	9	5	14				2																		
1985-86	**Calgary Flames**	**NHL**	**5**	**0**	**1**	**1**	**0**	**1**	**1**	**0**	**0**	**0**	**0**	**4**	**0.0**	**1**	**0**	**5**	**1**	**–3**	**1**	**0**	**0**	**0**	**0**	**0**	**0**	**0**
	Moncton Golden Flames	AHL	59	23	42	65				40											10	6	9	15	4			
1986-87	**Calgary Flames**	**NHL**	**40**	**10**	**18**	**28**	**9**	**13**	**22**	**16**	**2**	**0**	**2**	**64**	**15.6**	**42**	**13**	**32**	**9**	**+6**								
	Moncton Golden Flames	AHL	20	12	16	28				8																		
1987-88	Canada	Nat-Team	47	18	19	37				42																		
	Canada	Olympics	7	0	4	4				0																		
	Vancouver Canucks	**NHL**	**11**	**3**	**5**	**8**	**3**	**4**	**7**	**6**	**0**	**0**	**0**	**26**	**11.5**	**12**	**5**	**15**	**5**	**–3**								
1988-89	**Vancouver Canucks**	**NHL**	**71**	**18**	**27**	**45**	**15**	**19**	**34**	**42**	**6**	**0**	**3**	**151**	**11.9**	**56**	**13**	**51**	**3**	**–5**	**7**	**3**	**4**	**7**	**10**	**1**	**0**	**0**
1989-90	**Vancouver Canucks**	**NHL**	**67**	**19**	**29**	**48**	**16**	**21**	**37**	**65**	**2**	**0**	**0**	**121**	**15.7**	**74**	**19**	**60**	**10**	**+5**								
1990-91	**Vancouver Canucks**	**NHL**	**44**	**11**	**20**	**31**	**10**	**15**	**25**	**42**	**3**	**0**	**3**	**84**	**13.1**	**47**	**11**	**39**	**1**	**–2**								
	Toronto Maple Leafs	**NHL**	**26**	**0**	**11**	**11**	**0**	**8**	**8**	**20**	**0**	**0**	**0**	**32**	**0.0**	**18**	**8**	**17**	**0**	**–7**								
1991-92	**Toronto Maple Leafs**	**NHL**	**59**	**10**	**21**	**31**	**9**	**16**	**25**	**48**	**4**	**0**	**3**	**78**	**12.8**	**48**	**23**	**30**	**2**	**–3**								
1992-93	**Tampa Bay Lightning**	**NHL**	**80**	**42**	**44**	**86**	**35**	**30**	**65**	**92**	**16**	**0**	**6**	**205**	**20.5**	**113**	**53**	**86**	**2**	**–24**								
1993-94	**Tampa Bay Lightning**	**NHL**	**78**	**24**	**40**	**64**	**22**	**31**	**53**	**56**	**6**	**0**	**2**	**180**	**13.3**	**88**	**34**	**65**	**3**	**–8**								
1994-95	**Tampa Bay Lightning**	**NHL**	**46**	**13**	**27**	**40**	**23**	**40**	**63**	**42**	**3**	**0**	**2**	**111**	**11.7**	**56**	**19**	**43**	**0**	**–6**								
1995-96	**Tampa Bay Lightning**	**NHL**	**75**	**23**	**56**	**79**	**23**	**46**	**69**	**77**	**9**	**0**	**5**	**189**	**12.2**	**103**	**53**	**63**	**2**	**–11**	**5**	**0**	**3**	**3**	**6**	**0**	**0**	**0**
1996-97	**Tampa Bay Lightning**	**NHL**	**35**	**7**	**17**	**24**	**7**	**15**	**22**	**16**	**1**	**2**	**1**	**93**	**7.5**	**41**	**13**	**29**	**3**	**+2**								
1997-98	**Tampa Bay Lightning**	**NHL**	**14**	**2**	**5**	**7**	**2**	**5**	**7**	**6**	**2**	**0**	**0**	**24**	**8.3**	**12**	**5**	**16**	**0**	**–9**								
	NHL Totals		**651**	**182**	**321**	**503**	**174**	**264**	**438**	**528**	**54**	**2**	**27**	**1362**	**13.4**	**711**	**269**	**551**	**41**		**13**	**3**	**7**	**10**	**16**	**1**	**0**	**0**

Played in NHL All-Star Game (1993, 1994)

Traded to **Vancouver** by **Calgary** with Peter Bakovic and Kevin Guy for Craig Coxe, March 6, 1988. Traded to **Toronto** by **Vancouver** for Tom Kurvers, January 12, 1991. Claimed by **Tampa Bay** from **Toronto** in Expansion Draft, June 18, 1992.

• BRADLEY, LYLE
Lyle Bradley C/RW – R. 5'9", 160 lbs. b: Lloydminster, Sask., 7/31/1943.

1960-61	Estevan Bruins	SJHL	2	0	0	0				2																		
1961-62	Etevan Bruins	SJHL	STATISTICS NOT AVAILABLE																									
1962-63	Estevan Bruins	SJHL	54	23	45	68				54											11	10	8	18	14			
1963-64	University of Denver	WCHA	DID NOT PLAY – FRESHMAN																									
1964-65	University of Denver	WCHA	12	3	7	10				16																		
1965-66	University of Denver	WCHA	32	12	34	46				43																		
1966-67	Des Moines Oak Leafs	IHL	69	28	63	91				113											7	2	3	5	8			
1967-68	Des Moines Oak Leafs	IHL	72	27	54	81				98																		
1968-69	Houston Apollos	CHL	26	1	5	6				12																		
	Quebec Aces	AHL	22	6	7	13				38											15	3	4	7	6			
1969-70	Salt Lake Golden Eagles	WHL	16	3	2	5				10																		
	Denver Spurs	WHL	24	7	11	18				25																		
1970-71	Denver Spurs	WHL	71	25	43	68				74											5	1	2	3	2			
1971-72	Portland Buckaroos	WHL	28	7	12	19				20																		
	Salt Lake Golden Eagles	WHL	40	16	24	40				25																		
1972-73	Salt Lake Golden Eagles	WHL	71	29	58	87				83											9	1	4	5	15			
1973-74	**California Golden Seals**	**NHL**	**4**	**1**	**0**	**1**	**1**	**0**	**1**	**2**	**1**	**0**	**0**	**8**	**12.5**	**3**	**2**	**3**	**0**	**–2**								
	Salt Lake Golden Eagles	WHL	76	34	*81	115				29											5	1	1	2	4			
1974-75	Salt Lake Golden Eagles	CHL	55	20	32	52				28											11	3	12	15	11			
1975-76	Salt Lake City Golden Eagles	CHL	76	17	57	74				65											5	1	3	4	2			
1976-77	**Cleveland Barons**	**NHL**	**2**	**0**	**0**	**0**	**0**	**0**	**0**	**0**	**0**	**0**	**0**	**2**	**0.0**	**1**	**0**	**1**	**0**	**0**								
	Salt Lake Golden Eagles	CHL	67	24	44	68				43																		
1977-78	Salt Lake Golden Eagles	CHL	62	16	41	57				50											6	1	2	3	2			
	NHL Totals		**6**	**1**	**0**	**1**	**1**	**0**	**1**	**2**	**1**	**0**	**0**	**10**	**10.0**	**4**	**2**	**4**	**0**									

WHL First All-Star Team (1974) • Won Leader Cup (WHL - MVP) (1974)

Rights traded to **Montreal** by **Oakland** with Alain Caron and Wally Boyer for Norm Ferguson, Stan Fuller, Michel Jacques and Francois Lacombe, May, 1968. Loaned to **Quebec** (AHL) by **Montreal**, February, 1969. Traded to **Portland** (WHL) by **Montreal** for cash, June, 1971. Traded to **California** (Salt Lake-WHL) by **Portland** (WHL) with Fred Hilts for Guyle Fielder and the loan of Jake Rathwell, January, 1972. Transferred to **Cleveland** after **California** franchise relocated, August 26, 1976.

• BRADY, NEIL
Neil Brady C – L. 6'2", 200 lbs. b: Montreal, Que., 4/12/1968. New Jersey's 1st choice, 3rd overall, in 1986 Entry Draft.

1984-85	Calgary Wranglers	Midget	37	25	50	75				75																		
	Medicine Hat Tigers	WHL	....	....	....	....				....											3	0	0	0	2			
1985-86	Medicine Hat Tigers	WHL	72	21	60	81				104											21	9	11	20	23			
1986-87	Medicine Hat Tigers	WHL	57	19	64	83				126											18	1	4	5	25			
1987-88	Medicine Hat Tigers	WHL	61	16	35	51				110											15	0	3	3	19			
1988-89	Utica Devils	AHL	75	16	21	37				56											4	0	3	3	0			
1989-90	**New Jersey Devils**	**NHL**	**19**	**1**	**4**	**5**	**1**	**3**	**4**	**13**	**0**	**0**	**0**	**10**	**10.0**	**7**	**0**	**11**	**3**	**–1**								
	Utica Devils	AHL	38	10	13	23				21											5	0	1	1	10			
1990-91	**New Jersey Devils**	**NHL**	**3**	**0**	**0**	**0**	**0**	**0**	**0**	**0**	**0**	**0**	**0**	**6**	**0.0**	**0**	**0**	**0**	**0**	**0**								
	Utica Devils	AHL	77	33	63	96				91																		
1991-92	**New Jersey Devils**	**NHL**	**7**	**1**	**0**	**1**	**1**	**0**	**1**	**4**	**0**	**0**	**0**	**3**	**33.3**	**1**	**0**	**0**	**0**	**+1**								
	Utica Devils	AHL	33	12	30	42				28																		
1992-93	**Ottawa Senators**	**NHL**	**55**	**7**	**17**	**24**	**6**	**12**	**18**	**57**	**5**	**0**	**0**	**68**	**10.3**	**37**	**19**	**45**	**2**	**–25**								
	New Haven Nighthawks	AHL	8	6	3	9				2																		
1993-94	**Dallas Stars**	**NHL**	**5**	**0**	**1**	**1**	**0**	**1**	**1**	**21**	**0**	**0**	**0**	**1**	**0.0**	**1**	**0**	**2**	**0**	**–1**								
	Kalamazoo Wings	IHL	43	10	16	26				188											5	1	1	2	10			
1994-95	Kalamazoo Wings	IHL	70	13	45	58				140											15	5	14	19	22			

			REGULAR SEASON																		PLAYOFFS							
Season	Club	League	GP	G	A	Pts	AG	AA	APts	PIM	PP	SH	GW	S	%	TGF	PGF	TGA	PGA	+/-	GP	G	A	Pts	PIM	PP	SH	GW
1995-96	Michigan K-Wings	IHL	61	14	20	34	....	....	....	127	....	....	....	....	....	....	....	....	....	....	10	1	4	5	0	....	....	....
1996-97	Michigan K-Wings	IHL	76	13	20	33	....	....	....	62	....	....	....	....	....	....	....	....	....	....	4	1	0	1	0	....	....	....
1997-98	Houston Aeros	IHL	65	9	26	35	....	....	....	56	....	....	....	....	....	....	....	....	....	....	4	2	0	2	34	....	....	....
	NHL Totals		**89**	**9**	**22**	**31**	**8**	**16**	**24**	**95**	**5**	**0**	**0**	**88**	**10.2**	**46**	**19**	**58**	**5**		....	....	....	....	....	....	....	....

Traded to **Ottawa** by **New Jersey** for future considerations, September 3, 1992. Signed as a free agent by **Dallas**, December 3, 1993.

• BRAGNALO, RICK

Rick Bragnalo C – L. 5'8", 160 lbs. b: Thunder Bay, Ont., 12/1/1951.

Season	Club	League	GP	G	A	Pts	AG	AA	APts	PIM	PP	SH	GW	S	%	TGF	PGF	TGA	PGA	+/-	GP	G	A	Pts	PIM	PP	SH	GW
1970-71	University of Denver	WCHA	36	13	16	29	....	....	....	20	....	....	....	....	....	....	....	....	....	....	....	....	....	....	....	....	....	....
1971-72	University of Denver	WCHA	38	11	7	18	....	....	....	24	....	....	....	....	....	....	....	....	....	....	....	....	....	....	....	....	....	....
1972-73	University of Denver	WCHA	34	12	21	33	....	....	....	52	....	....	....	....	....	....	....	....	....	....	....	....	....	....	....	....	....	....
1973-74	University of Denver	WCHA	29	24	22	46	....	....	....	22	....	....	....	....	....	....	....	....	....	....	....	....	....	....	....	....	....	....
1974-75	Dayton Gems	IHL	75	41	72	*113	....	....	....	50	....	....	....	....	....	....	....	....	....	....	....	....	....	....	....	....	....	....
1975-76	Dayton Gems	IHL	48	29	34	63	....	....	....	55	....	....	....	....	....	....	....	....	....	....	....	....	....	....	....	....	....	....
	Washington Capitals	**NHL**	**19**	**2**	**10**	**12**	**2**	**8**	**10**	**8**	**0**	**0**	**0**	**28**	**7.1**	**15**	**7**	**13**	**1**	**–4**	....	....	....	....	....	....	....	....
1976-77	**Washington Capitals**	**NHL**	**80**	**11**	**12**	**23**	**11**	**10**	**21**	**16**	**1**	**2**	**1**	**89**	**12.4**	**31**	**3**	**51**	**7**	**–16**	....	....	....	....	....	....	....	....
1977-78	**Washington Capitals**	**NHL**	**44**	**2**	**13**	**15**	**2**	**11**	**13**	**22**	**0**	**0**	**0**	**60**	**3.3**	**25**	**4**	**50**	**23**	**–6**	....	....	....	....	....	....	....	....
	Hershey Bears	AHL	30	11	17	28	....	....	....	15	....	....	....	....	....	....	....	....	....	....	....	....	....	....	....	....	....	....
1978-79	**Washington Capitals**	**NHL**	**2**	**0**	**0**	**0**	**0**	**0**	**0**	**0**	**0**	**0**	**0**	**0**	**0.0**	**0**	**0**	**1**	**0**	**–1**	....	....	....	....	....	....	....	....
	Hershey Bears	AHL	68	21	39	60	....	....	....	41	....	....	....	....	....	....	....	....	....	....	4	0	1	1	2	....	....	....
1979-80	Hershey Bears	AHL	1	0	0	0	....	....	....	0	....	....	....	....	....	....	....	....	....	....	....	....	....	....	....	....	....	....
	Port Huron Flags	IHL	67	22	61	83	....	....	....	26	....	....	....	....	....	....	....	....	....	....	11	3	10	13	12	....	....	....
1980-81	SG Brunico	Italy	....	29	43	72	....	....	....	24	....	....	....	....	....	....	....	....	....	....	15	6	10	16	45	....	....	....
	Italy	WEC-B	7	4	7	11	....	....	....	22	....	....	....	....	....	....	....	....	....	....	....	....	....	....	....	....	....	....
1981-82	SG Brunico	Italy	32	33	48	81	....	....	....	63	....	....	....	....	....	....	....	....	....	....	6	7	*8	15	2	....	....	....
	Italy	WEC-A	7	3	2	5	....	....	....	8	....	....	....	....	....	....	....	....	....	....	....	....	....	....	....	....	....	....
1982-83	SG Brunico	Italy	32	49	59	108	....	....	....	21	....	....	....	....	....	....	....	....	....	....	....	....	....	....	....	....	....	....
	Italy	WEC-A	10	1	2	3	....	....	....	6	....	....	....	....	....	....	....	....	....	....	....	....	....	....	....	....	....	....
1983-84	SG Brunico	Italy	26	26	42	68	....	....	....	44	....	....	....	....	....	....	....	....	....	....	7	7	8	15	20	....	....	....
1984-85	SG Brunico	Italy	18	18	27	45	....	....	....	12	....	....	....	....	....	....	....	....	....	....	6	4	8	12	4	....	....	....
	Italy	WEC-B	7	1	2	3	....	....	....	10	....	....	....	....	....	....	....	....	....	....	....	....	....	....	....	....	....	....
1985-86	SG Brunico	Italy	36	23	43	66	....	....	....	36	....	....	....	....	....	....	....	....	....	....	5	4	7	11	2	....	....	....
1986-87	SG Brunico	Italy	42	25	37	62	....	....	....	38	....	....	....	....	....	....	....	....	....	....	....	....	....	....	....	....	....	....
1987-88	SG Brunico	Italy	35	21	30	51	....	....	....	38	....	....	....	....	....	....	....	....	....	....	....	....	....	....	....	....	....	....
1988-89	SG Brunico	Italy	41	27	30	57	....	....	....	40	....	....	....	....	....	....	....	....	....	....	....	....	....	....	....	....	....	....
1989-90			DID NOT PLAY																									
1990-91	HC Milano	Italy	35	10	23	33	....	....	....	8	....	....	....	....	....	....	....	....	....	....	....	....	....	....	....	....	....	....
1991-92	HC Milano	Italy	27	5	12	17	....	....	....	2	....	....	....	....	....	....	....	....	....	....	....	....	....	....	....	....	....	....
	NHL Totals		**145**	**15**	**35**	**50**	**15**	**29**	**44**	**46**	**1**	**2**	**1**	**177**	**8.5**	**71**	**14**	**115**	**31**		....	....	....	....	....	....	....	....

IHL First All-Star Team (1975) • Won Garry F. Longman Memorial Trophy (Top Rookie - IHL) (1975) • Won Leo P. Lamoureux Memorial Trophy (Top Scorer - IHL) (1975) • WEC-B All-Star Team (1981)

Signed as a free agent by **Washington**, March 1, 1976.

• BRASAR, PER-OLOV

Per-Olov Brasar LW – L. 5'8", 172 lbs. b: Falun, Sweden, 9/30/1950.

Season	Club	League	GP	G	A	Pts	AG	AA	APts	PIM	PP	SH	GW	S	%	TGF	PGF	TGA	PGA	+/-	GP	G	A	Pts	PIM	PP	SH	GW
1969-70	Leksands IF	Sweden	13	3	3	6	....	....	....	0	....	....	....	....	....	....	....	....	....	....	14	4	4	8	2	....	....	....
1970-71	Leksands IF	Sweden 2	13	2	3	5	....	....	....	0	....	....	....	....	....	....	....	....	....	....	14	9	5	14	0	....	....	....
1971-72	Leksands IF	Sweden	28	11	7	18	....	....	....	2	....	....	....	....	....	....	....	....	....	....	....	....	....	....	....	....	....	....
1972-73	Leksands IF	Sweden	14	6	2	8	....	....	....	2	....	....	....	....	....	....	....	....	....	....	14	9	5	14	2	....	....	....
1973-74	Sweden	Nat-Team	10	4	5	9	....	....	....	0	....	....	....	....	....	....	....	....	....	....	....	....	....	....	....	....	....	....
	Sweden	WEC-A	9	4	5	9	....	....	....	0	....	....	....	....	....	....	....	....	....	....	....	....	....	....	....	....	....	....
1974-75	Leksands IF	Sweden	30	19	23	42	....	....	....	4	....	....	....	....	....	....	....	....	....	....	5	0	5	5	0	....	....	....
	Sweden	WEC-A	9	0	1	1	....	....	....	0	....	....	....	....	....	....	....	....	....	....	....	....	....	....	....	....	....	....
1975-76	Leksands IF	Sweden	34	11	12	23	....	....	....	4	....	....	....	....	....	....	....	....	....	....	....	1	4	5	6	....	....	....
	Sweden	WEC-A	10	0	0	0	....	....	....	6	....	....	....	....	....	....	....	....	....	....	....	....	....	....	....	....	....	....
1976-77	Sweden	C Cup	5	0	1	1	....	....	....	2	....	....	....	....	....	....	....	....	....	....	....	....	....	....	....	....	....	....
	Leksands IF	Sweden	30	23	18	41	....	....	....	14	....	....	....	....	....	....	....	....	....	....	5	3	2	5	0	....	....	....
	Sweden	WEC-A	10	3	8	11	....	....	....	2	....	....	....	....	....	....	....	....	....	....	....	....	....	....	....	....	....	....
1977-78	**Minnesota North Stars**	**NHL**	**77**	**20**	**37**	**57**	**19**	**30**	**49**	**6**	**7**	**2**	**2**	**170**	**11.8**	**81**	**30**	**86**	**28**	**–7**	....	....	....	....	....	....	....	....
	Sweden	WEC-A	10	1	4	5	....	....	....	18	....	....	....	....	....	....	....	....	....	....	....	....	....	....	....	....	....	....
1978-79	**Minnesota North Stars**	**NHL**	**68**	**6**	**28**	**34**	**5**	**21**	**26**	**6**	**2**	**0**	**0**	**126**	**4.8**	**60**	**20**	**68**	**14**	**–4**	....	....	....	....	....	....	....	....
1979-80	**Minnesota North Stars**	**NHL**	**22**	**1**	**14**	**15**	**1**	**11**	**12**	**0**	**0**	**0**	**1**	**38**	**2.6**	**20**	**7**	**13**	**1**	**+1**	....	....	....	....	....	....	....	....
	Vancouver Canucks	**NHL**	**48**	**9**	**10**	**19**	**8**	**8**	**16**	**7**	**1**	**0**	**0**	**101**	**8.9**	**44**	**17**	**41**	**10**	**–4**	**4**	**1**	**2**	**3**	**0**	**0**	**0**	**1**
1980-81	**Vancouver Canucks**	**NHL**	**80**	**22**	**41**	**63**	**18**	**29**	**47**	**8**	**3**	**0**	**1**	**167**	**13.2**	**103**	**31**	**81**	**21**	**+12**	**3**	**0**	**0**	**0**	**0**	**0**	**0**	**0**
1981-82	**Vancouver Canucks**	**NHL**	**53**	**6**	**12**	**18**	**5**	**8**	**13**	**6**	**0**	**0**	**1**	**90**	**6.7**	**31**	**9**	**49**	**18**	**–9**	**6**	**0**	**0**	**0**	**0**	**0**	**0**	**0**
1982-83	Leksands IF	Sweden	35	6	9	15	....	....	....	8	....	....	....	....	....	....	....	....	....	....	....	....	....	....	....	....	....	....
	NHL Totals		**348**	**64**	**142**	**206**	**56**	**107**	**163**	**33**	**13**	**2**	**5**	**692**	**9.2**	**339**	**114**	**328**	**92**		**13**	**1**	**2**	**3**	**0**	**0**	**0**	**1**

Signed as a free agent by **Minnesota**, August, 1977. Traded to **Vancouver** by **Minnesota** for Vancouver's 2nd round choice (Mike Sands) in 1981 Entry Draft, December 10, 1979.

• BRASHEAR, DONALD

Donald Brashear LW – L. 6'2", 220 lbs. b: Bedford, IN, 1/7/1972.

Season	Club	League	GP	G	A	Pts	AG	AA	APts	PIM	PP	SH	GW	S	%	TGF	PGF	TGA	PGA	+/-	GP	G	A	Pts	PIM	PP	SH	GW
1989-90	Longueuil Chevaliers	QMJHL	64	12	14	26	....	....	....	169	....	....	....	....	....	....	....	....	....	....	7	0	0	0	11	....	....	....
1990-91	Longueuil Chevaliers	QMJHL	68	12	26	38	....	....	....	195	....	....	....	....	....	....	....	....	....	....	8	0	3	3	33	....	....	....
1991-92	Verdun College Francais	QMJHL	65	18	24	42	....	....	....	283	....	....	....	....	....	....	....	....	....	....	18	4	2	6	98	....	....	....
1992-93	Fredericton Canadiens	AHL	76	11	3	14	....	....	....	261	....	....	....	....	....	....	....	....	....	....	5	0	0	0	8	....	....	....
1993-94	**Montreal Canadiens**	**NHL**	**14**	**2**	**2**	**4**	**2**	**2**	**4**	**34**	**0**	**0**	**0**	**15**	**13.3**	**4**	**0**	**5**	**1**	**0**	**2**	**0**	**0**	**0**	**0**	**0**	**0**	**0**
	Fredericton Canadiens	AHL	62	38	28	66	....	....	....	250	....	....	....	....	....	....	....	....	....	....	....	....	....	....	....	....	....	....
1994-95	Fredericton Canadiens	AHL	29	10	9	19	....	....	....	182	....	....	....	....	....	....	....	....	....	....	17	7	5	12	77	....	....	....
	Montreal Canadiens	**NHL**	**20**	**1**	**1**	**2**	**2**	**1**	**3**	**63**	**0**	**0**	**1**	**10**	**10.0**	**2**	**0**	**7**	**0**	**–5**	....	....	....	....	....	....	....	....
1995-96	**Montreal Canadiens**	**NHL**	**67**	**0**	**4**	**4**	**0**	**3**	**3**	**223**	**0**	**0**	**0**	**25**	**0.0**	**12**	**2**	**20**	**0**	**–10**	**6**	**0**	**0**	**0**	**2**	**0**	**0**	**0**
1996-97	**Montreal Canadiens**	**NHL**	**10**	**0**	**0**	**0**	**0**	**0**	**0**	**38**	**0**	**0**	**0**	**6**	**0.0**	**0**	**0**	**2**	**0**	**–2**	....	....	....	....	....	....	....	....
	Vancouver Canucks	**NHL**	**59**	**8**	**5**	**13**	**8**	**4**	**12**	**207**	**0**	**0**	**2**	**55**	**14.5**	**20**	**4**	**22**	**0**	**–6**	....	....	....	....	....	....	....	....
	United States	WC-A	8	2	3	5	....	....	....	8	....	....	....	....	....	....	....	....	....	....	....	....	....	....	....	....	....	....
1997-98	**Vancouver Canucks**	**NHL**	**77**	**9**	**9**	**18**	**11**	**9**	**20**	**372**	**0**	**0**	**1**	**64**	**14.1**	**29**	**1**	**37**	**0**	**–9**	....	....	....	....	....	....	....	....
	United States	WC-A	6	0	0	0	....	....	....	10	....	....	....	....	....	....	....	....	....	....	....	....	....	....	....	....	....	....
	NHL Totals		**247**	**20**	**21**	**41**	**23**	**19**	**42**	**937**	**0**	**0**	**4**	**175**	**11.4**	**67**	**7**	**93**	**1**		**8**	**0**	**0**	**0**	**2**	**0**	**0**	**0**

Signed as a free agent by **Montreal**, July 28, 1992. Traded to **Vancouver** by **Montreal** for Jassen Cullimore, November 13, 1996.

• BREAULT, FRANCOIS

Francois Breault RW – L. 5'11", 185 lbs. b: Acton Vale, Que., 5/11/1967.

Season	Club	League	GP	G	A	Pts	AG	AA	APts	PIM	PP	SH	GW	S	%	TGF	PGF	TGA	PGA	+/-	GP	G	A	Pts	PIM	PP	SH	GW
1984-85	Chicoutimi Sagueneens	QMJHL	68	8	6	14	....	....	....	50	....	....	....	....	....	....	....	....	....	....	14	2	1	3	40	....	....	....
1985-86	Trois-Rivieres Draveurs	QMJHL	60	15	13	28	....	....	....	73	....	....	....	....	....	....	....	....	....	....	5	0	1	1	18	....	....	....
1986-87	Granby Bisons	QMJHL	60	24	33	57	....	....	....	134	....	....	....	....	....	....	....	....	....	....	....	....	....	....	....	....	....	....
1987-88	Trois-Rivieres Draveurs	QMJHL	28	16	19	35	....	....	....	108	....	....	....	....	....	....	....	....	....	....	5	0	1	1	14	....	....	....
	Maine Mariners	AHL	11	0	1	1	....	....	....	37	....	....	....	....	....	....	....	....	....	....	....	....	....	....	....	....	....	....
1988-89	New Haven Nighthawks	AHL	68	21	24	45	....	....	....	51	....	....	....	....	....	....	....	....	....	....	....	....	....	....	....	....	....	....
1989-90	New Haven Nighthawks	AHL	37	17	21	38	....	....	....	33	....	....	....	....	....	....	....	....	....	....	....	....	....	....	....	....	....	....
1990-91	**Los Angeles Kings**	**NHL**	**17**	**1**	**4**	**5**	**1**	**3**	**4**	**6**	**0**	**0**	**0**	**12**	**8.3**	**5**	**0**	**6**	**0**	**–1**	....	....	....	....	....	....	....	....
1991-92	**Los Angeles Kings**	**NHL**	**6**	**1**	**0**	**1**	**1**	**0**	**1**	**30**	**0**	**0**	**0**	**6**	**16.7**	**1**	**0**	**1**	**0**	**0**	....	....	....	....	....	....	....	....
	Phoenix Roadrunners	IHL	54	14	19	33	....	....	....	40	....	....	....	....	....	....	....	....	....	....	....	....	....	....	....	....	....	....

			REGULAR SEASON																		PLAYOFFS							
Season	Club	League	GP	G	A	Pts	AG	AA	APts	PIM	PP	SH	GW	S	%	TGF	PGF	TGA	PGA	+/-	GP	G	A	Pts	PIM	PP	SH	GW
1992-93	**Los Angeles Kings**	**NHL**	**4**	**0**	**0**	**0**	**0**	**0**	**0**	**6**	**0**	**0**	**0**	**0**	**0.0**	**0**	**0**	**1**	**0**	**–1**	....	....	....	....	....	....	....	....
	Phoenix Roadrunners	IHL	31	5	11	16	....	....	....	26	....	....	....	....	....	....	....	....	....	....	....	....	....	....	....	....	....	....
	Utica Devils	AHL	32	8	20	28	....	....	....	56	....	....	....	....	....	....	....	....	....	....	4	2	0	2	0	....	....	....
1993-94	Durham Wasps	Britain	14	23	17	40	....	....	....	20	....	....	....	....	....	....	....	....	....	....	6	6	4	10	2	....	....	....
	NHL Totals		**27**	**2**	**4**	**6**	**2**	**3**	**5**	**42**	**0**	**0**	**0**	**18**	**11.1**	**6**	**0**	**8**	**0**		....	....	....	....	....	....	....	....

Signed as a free agent by **LA Kings**, July, 1988.

• BREITENBACH, KEN

Ken Breitenbach D – L. 6'1", 190 lbs. b: Welland, Ont., 1/9/1955. Buffalo's 2nd choice, 35th overall, in 1975 Amateur Draft.

Season	Club	League	GP	G	A	Pts	AG	AA	APts	PIM	PP	SH	GW	S	%	TGF	PGF	TGA	PGA	+/-	GP	G	A	Pts	PIM	PP	SH	GW
1971-72	Welland Sabres	Jr. B	34	6	18	24	....	....	....	44	....	....	....	....	....	....	....	....	....	....	....	....	....	....	....	....	....	....
1972-73	St. Catharines Black Hawks	OHA	37	1	8	9	....	....	....	0	....	....	....	....	....	....	....	....	....	....	....	....	....	....	....	....	....	....
1973-74	St. Catharines Black Hawks	OHA	68	4	34	38	....	....	....	46	....	....	....	....	....	....	....	....	....	....	....	....	....	....	....	....	....	....
1974-75	St. Catharines Black Hawks	OHA	65	7	30	37	....	....	....	143	....	....	....	....	....	....	....	....	....	....	....	....	....	....	....	....	....	....
1975-76	**Buffalo Sabres**	**NHL**	**7**	**0**	**0**	**0**	**0**	**0**	**0**	**6**	**0**	**0**	**0**	**0**	**0.0**	**5**	**1**	**0**	**0**	**+4**	**1**	**0**	**0**	**0**	**0**	**0**	**0**	**0**
	Hershey Bears	AHL	57	1	19	20	....	....	....	58	....	....	....	....	....	....	....	....	....	....	10	1	2	3	6	....	....	....
1976-77	**Buffalo Sabres**	**NHL**	**31**	**0**	**5**	**5**	**0**	**4**	**4**	**18**	**0**	**0**	**0**	**11**	**0.0**	**10**	**0**	**14**	**2**	**–2**	**4**	**0**	**0**	**0**	**0**	**0**	**0**	**0**
	Hershey Bears	AHL	37	3	8	11	....	....	....	29	....	....	....	....	....	....	....	....	....	....	....	....	....	....	....	....	....	....
1977-78			DID NOT PLAY – INJURED																									
1978-79	**Buffalo Sabres**	**NHL**	**30**	**1**	**8**	**9**	**1**	**6**	**7**	**25**	**0**	**0**	**0**	**41**	**2.4**	**34**	**0**	**33**	**4**	**+5**	**3**	**0**	**1**	**1**	**4**	**0**	**0**	**0**
	Hershey Bears	AHL	17	3	2	5	....	....	....	14	....	....	....	....	....	....	....	....	....	....	....	....	....	....	....	....	....	....
	NHL Totals		**68**	**1**	**13**	**14**	**1**	**10**	**11**	**49**	**0**	**0**	**0**	**52**	**1.9**	**49**	**1**	**47**	**6**		**8**	**0**	**1**	**1**	**4**	**0**	**0**	**0**

OHA Second All-Star Team (1975)

• BRENNAN, DAN

Dan Brennan LW – L. 6'3", 210 lbs. b: Dawson Creek, B.C., 10/1/1962. Los Angeles' 7th choice, 165th overall, in 1981 Entry Draft.

Season	Club	League	GP	G	A	Pts	AG	AA	APts	PIM	PP	SH	GW	S	%	TGF	PGF	TGA	PGA	+/-	GP	G	A	Pts	PIM	PP	SH	GW
1980-81	University of North Dakota	WCHA	37	3	9	12	....	....	....	66	....	....	....	....	....	....	....	....	....	....	....	....	....	....	....	....	....	....
1981-82	University of North Dakota	WCHA	42	10	17	27	....	....	....	78	....	....	....	....	....	....	....	....	....	....	....	....	....	....	....	....	....	....
1982-83	University of North Dakota	WCHA	31	9	11	20	....	....	....	60	....	....	....	....	....	....	....	....	....	....	....	....	....	....	....	....	....	....
1983-84	University of North Dakota	WCHA	45	28	37	65	....	....	....	36	....	....	....	....	....	....	....	....	....	....	....	....	....	....	....	....	....	....
	Los Angeles Kings	**NHL**	**2**	**0**	**0**	**0**	**0**	**0**	**0**	**0**	**0**	**0**	**0**	**1**	**0.0**	**0**	**0**	**1**	**0**	**–1**	....	....	....	....	....	....	....	....
1984-85	New Haven Nighthawks	AHL	80	25	33	58	....	....	....	56	....	....	....	....	....	....	....	....	....	....	....	....	....	....	....	....	....	....
1985-86	**Los Angeles Kings**	**NHL**	**6**	**0**	**1**	**1**	**0**	**1**	**1**	**9**	**0**	**0**	**0**	**6**	**0.0**	**2**	**0**	**3**	**0**	**–1**	....	....	....	....	....	....	....	....
	New Haven Nighthawks	AHL	62	8	22	30	....	....	....	76	....	....	....	....	....	....	....	....	....	....	2	0	0	0	10	....	....	....
	NHL Totals		**8**	**0**	**1**	**1**	**0**	**1**	**1**	**9**	**0**	**0**	**0**	**7**	**0.0**	**2**	**0**	**4**	**0**		....	....	....	....	....	....	....	....

WCHA First All-Star Team (1984)

• BRENNAN, RICH

Rich Brennan D – R. 6'2", 200 lbs. b: Schenectady, NY, 11/26/1972. Quebec's 3rd choice, 46th overall, in 1991 Entry Draft.

Season	Club	League	GP	G	A	Pts	AG	AA	APts	PIM	PP	SH	GW	S	%	TGF	PGF	TGA	PGA	+/-	GP	G	A	Pts	PIM	PP	SH	GW
1990-91	Tabor Academy	H.S.	34	13	37	50	....	....	....	91	....	....	....	....	....	....	....	....	....	....	....	....	....	....	....	....	....	....
1991-92	Boston University	H.E.	30	4	13	17	....	....	....	50	....	....	....	....	....	....	....	....	....	....	....	....	....	....	....	....	....	....
	United States	WJC-A	7	0	2	2	....	....	....	4	....	....	....	....	....	....	....	....	....	....	....	....	....	....	....	....	....	....
1992-93	Boston University	H.E.	40	9	11	20	....	....	....	68	....	....	....	....	....	....	....	....	....	....	....	....	....	....	....	....	....	....
1993-94	Boston University	H.E.	41	8	27	35	....	....	....	82	....	....	....	....	....	....	....	....	....	....	....	....	....	....	....	....	....	....
1994-95	Boston University	H.E.	31	5	22	27	....	....	....	56	....	....	....	....	....	....	....	....	....	....	....	....	....	....	....	....	....	....
1995-96	Brantford Smoke	ColHL	5	1	2	3	....	....	....	2	....	....	....	....	....	....	....	....	....	....	....	....	....	....	....	....	....	....
	Cornwall Aces	AHL	36	4	8	12	....	....	....	61	....	....	....	....	....	....	....	....	....	....	7	0	0	0	6	....	....	....
1996-97	**Colorado Avalanche**	**NHL**	**2**	**0**	**0**	**0**	**0**	**0**	**0**	**0**	**0**	**0**	**0**	**0**	**0.0**	**0**	**0**	**0**	**0**	**0**	....	....	....	....	....	....	....	....
	Hershey Bears	AHL	74	11	45	56	....	....	....	88	....	....	....	....	....	....	....	....	....	....	23	2	16	18	22	....	....	....
1997-98	**San Jose Sharks**	**NHL**	**11**	**1**	**2**	**3**	**1**	**2**	**3**	**2**	**1**	**0**	**0**	**24**	**4.2**	**9**	**5**	**8**	**0**	**–4**	....	....	....	....	....	....	....	....
	Kentucky Thoroughblades	AHL	42	11	17	28	....	....	....	71	....	....	....	....	....	....	....	....	....	....	....	....	....	....	....	....	....	....
	Hartford Wolf Pack	AHL	9	2	4	6	....	....	....	12	....	....	....	....	....	....	....	....	....	....	15	4	5	9	14	....	....	....
	NHL Totals		**13**	**1**	**2**	**3**	**1**	**2**	**3**	**2**	**1**	**0**	**0**	**24**	**4.2**	**9**	**5**	**8**	**0**		....	....	....	....	....	....	....	....

Hockey East First All-Star Team (1994) • NCAA East Second All-American Team (1994)

Rights transferred to **Colorado** after **Quebec** franchise relocated, June 21, 1995. Signed as a free agent by **San Jose**, July 9, 1997. Traded to **NY Rangers** by **San Jose** for Jason Muzzatti, March 24, 1998.

• BRENNEMAN, JOHN

John Brenneman LW – L. 5'10", 175 lbs. b: Fort Erie, Ont., 1/5/1943.

Season	Club	League	GP	G	A	Pts	AG	AA	APts	PIM	PP	SH	GW	S	%	TGF	PGF	TGA	PGA	+/-	GP	G	A	Pts	PIM	PP	SH	GW
1959-60	St. Catharines Teepees	OHA	48	11	18	29	....	....	....	17	....	....	....	....	....	....	....	....	....	....	17	5	3	8	8	....	....	....
1960-61	St. Catharines Teepees	OHA	48	12	13	25	....	....	....	26	....	....	....	....	....	....	....	....	....	....	6	2	4	6	2	....	....	....
1961-62	St. Catharines Teepees	OHA	49	12	30	42	....	....	....	10	....	....	....	....	....	....	....	....	....	....	6	2	4	6	4	....	....	....
1962-63	St. Catharines Teepees	OHA	48	31	27	58	....	....	....	38	....	....	....	....	....	....	....	....	....	....	....	....	....	....	....	....	....	....
	Buffalo Bisons	AHL	4	1	0	1	....	....	....	0	....	....	....	....	....	....	....	....	....	....	....	....	....	....	....	....	....	....
1963-64	St. Louis Braves	CHL	70	28	47	75	....	....	....	28	....	....	....	....	....	....	....	....	....	....	6	2	1	3	11	....	....	....
1964-65	**Chicago Black Hawks**	**NHL**	**17**	**1**	**0**	**1**	**1**	**0**	**1**	**2**	....	....	....	....	....	....	....	....	....	....	....	....	....	....	....	....	....	....
	St. Louis Braves	CHL	27	7	17	24	....	....	....	20	....	....	....	....	....	....	....	....	....	....	....	....	....	....	....	....	....	....
	New York Rangers	**NHL**	**22**	**3**	**3**	**6**	**4**	**3**	**7**	**6**	....	....	....	....	....	....	....	....	....	....	....	....	....	....	....	....	....	....
1965-66	**New York Rangers**	**NHL**	**11**	**0**	**0**	**0**	**0**	**0**	**0**	**14**	....	....	....	....	....	....	....	....	....	....	....	....	....	....	....	....	....	....
	Baltimore Clippers	AHL	33	5	8	13	....	....	....	16	....	....	....	....	....	....	....	....	....	....	....	....	....	....	....	....	....	....
	Minnesota Rangers	CHL	20	10	7	17	....	....	....	16	....	....	....	....	....	....	....	....	....	....	7	0	2	2	0	....	....	....
1966-67	**Toronto Maple Leafs**	**NHL**	**41**	**6**	**4**	**10**	**7**	**4**	**11**	**4**	....	....	....	....	....	....	....	....	....	....	....	....	....	....	....	....	....	....
	Rochester Americans	AHL	13	3	10	13	....	....	....	4	....	....	....	....	....	....	....	....	....	....	13	0	3	3	0	....	....	....
1967-68	**Detroit Red Wings**	**NHL**	**9**	**0**	**2**	**2**	**0**	**2**	**2**	**0**	**0**	**0**	**0**	**12**	**0.0**	**3**	**0**	**1**	**0**	**+2**	....	....	....	....	....	....	....	....
	Fort Worth Wings	CHL	14	5	2	7	....	....	....	10	....	....	....	....	....	....	....	....	....	....	....	....	....	....	....	....	....	....
	Oakland Seals	**NHL**	**31**	**10**	**8**	**18**	**12**	**8**	**20**	**14**	**2**	**0**	**0**	**61**	**16.4**	**27**	**7**	**31**	**2**	**–9**	....	....	....	....	....	....	....	....
	San Diego Gulls	WHL	5	2	2	4	....	....	....	4	....	....	....	....	....	....	....	....	....	....	....	....	....	....	....	....	....	....
1968-69	**Oakland Seals**	**NHL**	**21**	**1**	**2**	**3**	**1**	**2**	**3**	**6**	**0**	**0**	**0**	**16**	**6.3**	**6**	**1**	**9**	**0**	**–4**	....	....	....	....	....	....	....	....
	Cleveland Barons	AHL	49	14	13	27	....	....	....	41	....	....	....	....	....	....	....	....	....	....	5	1	0	1	0	....	....	....
1969-70			DID NOT PLAY – RETIRED																									
1970-71	Dayton Gems	IHL	50	23	18	41	....	....	....	20	....	....	....	....	....	....	....	....	....	....	10	3	4	7	4	....	....	....
1971-72			DID NOT PLAY – RETIRED																									
1972-73			DID NOT PLAY – RETIRED																									
1973-74	Cambridge Hornets	OHA Sr.	16	7	5	12	....	....	....	12	....	....	....	....	....	....	....	....	....	....	....	....	....	....	....	....	....	....
	NHL Totals		**152**	**21**	**19**	**40**	**25**	**19**	**44**	**46**	**2**	**0**	**0**	**89**	**23.6**	**36**	**8**	**41**	**2**		....	....	....	....	....	....	....	....

CHL First All-Star Team (1964)

Traded to **NY Rangers** by **Chicago** with Doug Robinson and Wayne Hillman for Camille Henry, Don Johns, Billy Taylor and Wally Chevrier, February 4, 1965. Claimed by **Toronto** from **NY Rangers** in Intra-League Draft, June 15, 1966. Claimed by **St. Louis** from **Toronto** in Expansion Draft, June 6, 1967. Traded to **Detroit** by **St. Louis** for Craig Cameron, Larry Hornung and Don Giesebrecht, October 19, 1967. Traded to **Oakland** by **Detroit** with Ted Hampson and Bert Marshall for Kent Douglas, January 9, 1968.

• BREWER, CARL

Carl Brewer D – L. 5'9", 180 lbs. b: Toronto, Ont., 10/21/1938.

Season	Club	League	GP	G	A	Pts	AG	AA	APts	PIM	PP	SH	GW	S	%	TGF	PGF	TGA	PGA	+/-	GP	G	A	Pts	PIM	PP	SH	GW
1955-56	Toronto Marlboros	OHA	10	1	3	4	....	....	....	6	....	....	....	....	....	....	....	....	....	....	11	3	5	8	10	....	....	....
1956-57	Toronto Marlboros	OHA	48	8	24	32	....	....	....	154	....	....	....	....	....	....	....	....	....	....	9	4	3	7	33	....	....	....
1957-58	Toronto Marlboros	OHA	50	10	37	47	....	....	....	212	....	....	....	....	....	....	....	....	....	....	13	3	9	12	*75	....	....	....
	Toronto Maple Leafs	**NHL**	**2**	**0**	**0**	**0**	**0**	**0**	**0**	**0**	....	....	....	....	....	....	....	....	....	....	....	....	....	....	....	....	....	....
1958-59	**Toronto Maple Leafs**	**NHL**	**69**	**3**	**21**	**24**	**4**	**22**	**26**	**125**	....	....	....	....	....	....	....	....	....	....	**12**	**0**	**6**	**6**	***40**	....	....	....
	Rochester Americans	AHL	1	0	1	1	....	....	....	2	....	....	....	....	....	....	....	....	....	....	....	....	....	....	....	....	....	....
1959-60	**Toronto Maple Leafs**	**NHL**	**67**	**4**	**19**	**23**	**5**	**19**	**24**	***150**	....	....	....	....	....	....	....	....	....	....	**10**	**2**	**3**	**5**	**16**	....	....	....
1960-61	**Toronto Maple Leafs**	**NHL**	**51**	**1**	**14**	**15**	**1**	**14**	**15**	**92**	....	....	....	....	....	....	....	....	....	....	**5**	**0**	**0**	**0**	**4**	....	....	....
1961-62	**Toronto Maple Leafs**	**NHL**	**67**	**1**	**22**	**23**	**1**	**22**	**23**	**89**	....	....	....	....	....	....	....	....	....	....	**8**	**0**	**2**	**2**	**22**	....	....	....
1962-63	**Toronto Maple Leafs**	**NHL**	**70**	**2**	**23**	**25**	**2**	**24**	**26**	**168**	....	....	....	....	....	....	....	....	....	....	**10**	**0**	**1**	**1**	**12**	....	....	....
1963-64	**Toronto Maple Leafs**	**NHL**	**57**	**4**	**9**	**13**	**5**	**10**	**15**	**114**	....	....	....	....	....	....	....	....	....	....	**12**	**0**	**1**	**1**	**30**	....	....	....
1964-65	**Toronto Maple Leafs**	**NHL**	**70**	**4**	**23**	**27**	**5**	**25**	**30**	***177**	....	....	....	....	....	....	....	....	....	....	**6**	**1**	**2**	**3**	**12**	....	....	....
1965-66			DID NOT PLAY – RETIRED																									

			REGULAR SEASON																		PLAYOFFS							
Season	Club	League	GP	G	A	Pts	AG	AA	APts	PIM	PP	SH	GW	S	%	TGF	PGF	TGA	PGA	+/–	GP	G	A	Pts	PIM	PP	SH	GW
1966-67	Canada	Nat-Team	STATISTICS NOT AVAILABLE																									
	Canada	WEC-A	7	1	6	7	....	....	....	10	....	....	....	....	....	....	....	....	....	....	....	....	....	....	....	....	....	....
1967-68	Muskegon Mohawks	IHL	63	13	55	68	....	....	....	82	....	....	....	....	....	....	....	....	....	....	9	3	9	12	4	....	....	....
1968-69	Finland	Nat Team	DID NOT PLAY – COACHING																									
1969-70	**Detroit Red Wings**	**NHL**	70	2	37	39	2	37	39	51	0	0	0	109	1.8	128	33	80	29	+44	4	0	0	0	2	0	0	0
1970-71	**St. Louis Blues**	**NHL**	19	2	9	11	2	8	10	29	0	0	0	35	5.7	31	16	21	5	–1	5	0	2	2	8	0	0	0
1971-72	**St. Louis Blues**	**NHL**	42	2	16	18	2	15	17	40	0	0	1	58	3.4	54	12	62	14	–6	....	....	....	....	....	....	....	....
1972-73			DID NOT PLAY – RETIRED																									
1973-74	Toronto Toros	WHA	77	2	23	25	....	....	....	42	....	....	....	....	....	....	....	....	....	....	12	0	4	4	11	....	....	....
1974-1979			DID NOT PLAY – RETIRED																									
1979-80	New Brunswick Hawks	AHL	3	0	0	0	....	....	....	0	....	....	....	....	....	....	....	....	....	....	....	....	....	....	....	....	....	....
	Toronto Maple Leafs	**NHL**	20	0	5	5	0	4	4	2	0	0	0	11	0.0	19	1	28	5	–5	....	....	....	....	....	....	....	....
	NHL Totals		604	25	198	223	29	200	229	1037	0	0	1	213	11.7	232	62	191	53		72	3	17	20	146	0	0	0
	Other Major League Totals		77	2	23	25	....	....	....	42	....	....	....	....	....	....	....	....	....		12	0	4	4	11	....	....	....

NHL Second All-Star Team (1962, 1965, 1970) • NHL First All-Star Team (1963) • WEC-A All-Star Team (1967) • IHL First All-Star Team (1968) • Won Governors' Trophy (Top Defenseman - IHL) (1968)

Played in NHL All-Star Game (1959, 1962, 1964)

Traded to **Detroit** by **Toronto** with Frank Mahovlich, Pete Stemkowski, Paul Henderson and Garry Unger for Floyd Smith, Paul Henderson and Norm Ullman, March 3, 1968 . Traded to **St. Louis** by **Detroit** for future considerations (Mike Lowe, Ab McDonald and Bob Wall, May 12, 1971), February 22, 1971. Selected by **LA Sharks** (WHA) in 1972 WHA General Player Draft, February 12, 1972. WHA rights traded to **Toronto** (WHA) by **LA Sharks** (WHA) for cash, October, 1973. Signed as a free agent by **Toronto**, January 2, 1980.

• BRICKLEY, ANDY

Andy Brickley LW/C – L. 5'11", 200 lbs. b: Melrose, MA, 8/9/1961. Philadelphia's 11th choice, 210th overall, in 1980 Entry Draft.

Season	Club	League	GP	G	A	Pts	AG	AA	APts	PIM	PP	SH	GW	S	%	TGF	PGF	TGA	PGA	+/–	GP	G	A	Pts	PIM	PP	SH	GW
1979-80	University of New Hampshire	ECAC	27	15	17	32	....	....	....	8	....	....	....	....	....	....	....	....	....	....	....	....	....	....	....	....	....	....
1980-81	University of New Hampshire	ECAC	31	27	25	52	....	....	....	16	....	....	....	....	....	....	....	....	....	....	....	....	....	....	....	....	....	....
	United States	WJC-A	5	1	1	2	....	....	....	4	....	....	....	....	....	....	....	....	....	....	....	....	....	....	....	....	....	....
1981-82	University of New Hampshire	ECAC	35	26	27	53	....	....	....	6	....	....	....	....	....	....	....	....	....	....	....	....	....	....	....	....	....	....
1982-83	**Philadelphia Flyers**	**NHL**	3	1	1	2	1	1	2	0	1	0	0	7	14.3	5	3	3	0	–1	....	....	....	....	....	....	....	....
	Maine Mariners	AHL	76	29	54	83	....	....	....	10	....	....	....	....	....	....	....	....	....	....	17	9	5	14	0	....	....	....
1983-84	Springfield Indians	AHL	7	1	5	6	....	....	....	2	....	....	....	....	....	....	....	....	....	....	....	....	....	....	....	....	....	....
	Pittsburgh Penguins	**NHL**	50	18	20	38	14	14	28	9	7	1	2	75	24.0	62	21	57	9	–7	....	....	....	....	....	....	....	....
	Baltimore Skipjacks	AHL	4	0	5	5	....	....	....	2	....	....	....	....	....	....	....	....	....	....	....	....	....	....	....	....	....	....
1984-85	**Pittsburgh Penguins**	**NHL**	45	7	15	22	6	10	16	10	1	0	1	58	12.1	38	7	45	0	–14	....	....	....	....	....	....	....	....
	Baltimore Skipjacks	AHL	31	13	14	27	....	....	....	8	....	....	....	....	....	....	....	....	....	....	15	*10	8	18	0	....	....	....
1985-86	Maine Mariners	AHL	60	26	34	60	....	....	....	20	....	....	....	....	....	....	....	....	....	....	5	0	4	4	0	....	....	....
1986-87	**New Jersey Devils**	**NHL**	51	11	12	23	10	9	19	8	1	3	0	55	20.0	33	3	62	17	–15	....	....	....	....	....	....	....	....
1987-88	**New Jersey Devils**	**NHL**	45	8	14	22	7	10	17	14	2	1	3	61	13.1	33	5	42	15	+1	4	0	1	1	4	0	0	0
	Utica Devils	AHL	9	5	8	13	....	....	....	4	....	....	....	....	....	....	....	....	....	....	....	....	....	....	....	....	....	....
1988-89	**Boston Bruins**	**NHL**	71	13	22	35	11	15	26	20	2	0	3	98	13.3	63	16	59	16	+4	10	0	2	2	0	0	0	0
1989-90	**Boston Bruins**	**NHL**	43	12	28	40	10	20	30	8	6	0	1	69	17.4	61	19	35	4	+11	2	0	0	0	0	0	0	0
1990-91	**Boston Bruins**	**NHL**	40	2	9	11	2	7	9	8	0	0	0	28	7.1	27	5	26	0	–4	....	....	....	....	....	....	....	....
	Maine Mariners	AHL	17	8	17	25	....	....	....	2	....	....	....	....	....	....	....	....	....	....	1	0	0	0	0	....	....	....
1991-92	**Boston Bruins**	**NHL**	23	10	17	27	9	13	22	2	5	0	1	28	35.7	38	15	18	1	+6	....	....	....	....	....	....	....	....
	Maine Mariners	AHL	14	5	15	20	....	....	....	2	....	....	....	....	....	....	....	....	....	....	....	....	....	....	....	....	....	....
	United States	WC-A	6	1	1	2	....	....	....	0	....	....	....	....	....	....	....	....	....	....	....	....	....	....	....	....	....	....
1992-93	**Winnipeg Jets**	**NHL**	12	0	2	2	0	1	1	2	0	0	0	5	0.0	4	0	6	2	0	1	1	1	2	0	0	0	0
	Moncton Hawks	AHL	38	15	36	51	....	....	....	10	....	....	....	....	....	....	....	....	....	....	5	4	2	6	0	....	....	....
1993-94	**Winnipeg Jets**	**NHL**	2	0	0	0	0	0	0	0	0	0	0	0	0.0	0	0	2	0	–2	....	....	....	....	....	....	....	....
	Moncton Hawks	AHL	53	20	39	59	....	....	....	20	....	....	....	....	....	....	....	....	....	....	19	8	*19	*27	4	....	....	....
1994-95	Denver Grizzlies	IHL	58	15	35	50	....	....	....	16	....	....	....	....	....	....	....	....	....	....	16	5	*25	*30	2	....	....	....
1995-96	Utah Grizzlies	IHL	36	12	34	46	....	....	....	24	....	....	....	....	....	....	....	....	....	....	16	6	13	19	8	....	....	....
1996-97	Utah Grizzlies	IHL	1	1	0	1	....	....	....	0	....	....	....	....	....	....	....	....	....	....	7	1	0	1	0	....	....	....
	NHL Totals		385	82	140	222	70	100	170	81	25	5	11	484	16.9	364	94	355	64		17	1	4	5	4	0	0	0

ECAC First All-Star Team (1982) • NCAA East First All-American Team (1982) • AHL Second All-Star Team (1983)

Traded to **Pittsburgh** by **Philadelphia** with Ron Flockhart, Mark Taylor and Philadelphia's 1st (Roger Belanger) and 3rd (later traded to Vancouver who selected Mike Stevens) round choices in 1984 Entry Draft for Rich Sutter and Pittsburgh's 2nd (Greg Smyth) and 3rd (David McLay) round choices in 1984 Entry Draft, October 23, 1983. Signed as a free agent by **New Jersey**, July 8, 1986. Claimed by **Boston** from **New Jersey** in Waiver Draft, October 3, 1988. Signed as a free agent by **Winnipeg**, November 11, 1992. Signed as a free agent by **NY Islanders**, July 27, 1994.

• BRIDGMAN, MEL

Mel Bridgman C – L. 6', 190 lbs. b: Trenton, Ont., 4/28/1955. Philadelphia's 1st choice, 1st overall, in 1975 Amateur Draft.

Season	Club	League	GP	G	A	Pts	AG	AA	APts	PIM	PP	SH	GW	S	%	TGF	PGF	TGA	PGA	+/–	GP	G	A	Pts	PIM	PP	SH	GW
1971-72	Victoria Cougars	WCJHL	4	0	0	0	....	....	....	0	....	....	....	....	....	....	....	....	....	....	....	....	....	....	....	....	....	....
1972-73	Nanaimo Clippers	BCJHL	49	37	50	87	....	....	....	13	....	....	....	....	....	....	....	....	....	....	....	....	....	....	....	....	....	....
	Victoria Cougars	WCJHL	4	1	1	2	....	....	....	0	....	....	....	....	....	....	....	....	....	....	....	....	....	....	....	....	....	....
1973-74	Victoria Cougars	WCJHL	62	26	39	65	....	....	....	149	....	....	....	....	....	....	....	....	....	....	....	....	....	....	....	....	....	....
1974-75	Victoria Cougars	WCJHL	66	66	91	*157	....	....	....	175	....	....	....	....	....	....	....	....	....	....	12	12	6	18	34	....	....	....
	Canada	WJC-A	5	4	1	5	....	....	....	9	....	....	....	....	....	....	....	....	....	....	....	....	....	....	....	....	....	....
1975-76	**Philadelphia Flyers**	**NHL**	80	23	27	50	21	21	42	86	5	1	2	166	13.9	64	10	34	2	+22	16	6	8	14	31	0	0	2
1976-77	**Philadelphia Flyers**	**NHL**	70	19	38	57	18	31	49	120	4	0	2	136	14.0	77	10	39	7	+35	7	1	0	1	8	0	1	0
1977-78	**Philadelphia Flyers**	**NHL**	76	16	32	48	15	26	41	203	3	1	2	154	10.4	71	11	51	17	+26	12	1	7	8	36	0	0	1
1978-79	**Philadelphia Flyers**	**NHL**	76	24	35	59	22	27	49	184	0	0	3	157	15.3	77	12	65	14	+14	8	1	2	3	17	0	0	0
1979-80	**Philadelphia Flyers**	**NHL**	74	16	31	47	14	24	38	136	2	2	2	145	11.0	60	9	61	23	+13	19	2	9	11	70	0	0	0
1980-81	**Philadelphia Flyers**	**NHL**	77	14	37	51	12	26	38	195	1	0	3	138	10.1	73	10	68	33	+28	12	2	4	6	39	0	0	0
1981-82	**Philadelphia Flyers**	**NHL**	9	7	5	12	6	3	9	47	3	0	1	22	31.8	14	4	18	8	0	....	....	....	....	....	....	....	....
	Calgary Flames	**NHL**	63	26	49	75	21	32	53	94	6	2	3	141	18.4	123	46	80	19	+16	3	2	0	2	14	0	0	0
1982-83	**Calgary Flames**	**NHL**	79	19	31	50	16	21	37	103	9	0	1	131	14.5	93	38	68	12	–1	9	3	4	7	33	2	0	0
1983-84	**New Jersey Devils**	**NHL**	79	23	38	61	19	26	45	121	9	1	0	127	18.1	93	27	130	37	–27	....	....	....	....	....	....	....	....
1984-85	**New Jersey Devils**	**NHL**	80	22	39	61	18	26	44	105	5	3	3	143	15.4	92	29	117	38	–16	....	....	....	....	....	....	....	....
1985-86	**New Jersey Devils**	**NHL**	78	23	40	63	18	27	45	80	5	1	1	136	16.9	91	25	110	43	–1	....	....	....	....	....	....	....	....
1986-87	**New Jersey Devils**	**NHL**	51	8	31	39	7	22	29	80	1	1	1	73	11.0	56	11	68	15	–8	....	....	....	....	....	....	....	....
	Detroit Red Wings	**NHL**	13	2	2	4	2	1	3	19	0	1	1	13	15.4	8	0	14	7	+1	16	5	2	7	28	0	1	1
1987-88	**Detroit Red Wings**	**NHL**	57	6	11	17	5	0	13	42	0	0	1	40	15.0	26	1	25	4	+4	16	4	1	5	12	0	0	0
	Adirondack Red Wings	AHL	2	1	2	3	....	....	....	0	....	....	....	....	....	....	....	....	....	....	....	....	....	....	....	....	....	....
1988-89	**Vancouver Canucks**	**NHL**	15	4	3	7	3	2	5	10	2	0	0	17	23.5	10	5	11	2	–4	7	1	2	3	10	1	0	0
	NHL Totals		977	252	449	701	217	323	540	1625	55	13	26	1739	14.5	1028	248	959	281		125	28	39	67	298	3	2	4

WCJHL First All-Star Team (1975)

Traded to **Calgary** by **Philadelphia** for Brad Marsh, November 11, 1981. Traded to **New Jersey** by **Calgary** with Phil Russell for Steve Tambellini and Joel Quenneville, June 21, 1983. Traded to **Detroit** by **New Jersey** for Chris Cichocki and Detroit's 3rd round choice (later traded to Buffalo — Buffalo selected Andrew McVicar) in 1987 Entry Draft, March 9, 1987. Signed as a free agent by **Vancouver**, October 4, 1988.

• BRIERE, DANIEL

Daniel Briere C – L. 5'9", 160 lbs. b: Gatineau, Que., 10/6/1977. Phoenix's 2nd choice, 24th overall, in 1996 Entry Draft.

Season	Club	League	GP	G	A	Pts	AG	AA	APts	PIM	PP	SH	GW	S	%	TGF	PGF	TGA	PGA	+/–	GP	G	A	Pts	PIM	PP	SH	GW
1994-95	Drummondville Voltigeurs	QMJHL	72	51	72	123	....	....	....	54	....	....	....	....	....	....	....	....	....	....	4	2	3	5	2	....	....	....
1995-96	Drummondville Voltigeurs	QMJHL	67	*67	*96	*163	....	....	....	84	....	....	....	....	....	....	....	....	....	....	6	6	12	18	8	....	....	....
1996-97	Drummondville Voltigeurs	QMJHL	59	52	78	130	....	....	....	94	....	....	....	....	....	....	....	....	....	....	8	7	7	14	14	....	....	....
	Canada	WJC-A	7	2	4	6	....	....	....	4	....	....	....	....	....	....	....	....	....	....	....	....	....	....	....	....	....	....
1997-98	**Phoenix Coyotes**	**NHL**	5	1	0	1	1	0	1	2	0	0	0	4	25.0	1	0	0	0	+1	....	....	....	....	....	....	....	....
	Springfield Falcons	AHL	68	36	56	92	....	....	....	42	....	....	....	....	....	....	....	....	....	....	4	1	2	3	4	....	....	....
	NHL Totals		5	1	0	1	1	0	1	2	0	0	0	4	25.0	1	0	0	0		....	....	....	....	....	....	....	....

QMJHL Second All-Star Team (1996, 1997) • AHL First All-Star Team (1998) • Won Dudley "Red" Garrett Memorial Trophy (Top Rookie - AHL) (1998)

• BRIERE, MICHEL
Michel Briere C – L. 5'10", 165 lbs. b: Shawinigan Falls, Que., 10/21/1949. d: 5/14/1971. Pittsburgh's 2nd choice, 26th overall, in 1969 Amateur Draft.

Season	Club	League	GP	G	A	Pts	AG	AA	APts	PIM	PP	SH	GW	S	%	TGF	PGF	TGA	PGA	+/–	GP	G	A	Pts	PIM	PP	SH	GW
			REGULAR SEASON																		PLAYOFFS							
1968-69	Shawinigan Bruins	QJHL	55	75	86	161	....	....	....	....	....	....	....	....	....	....	....	....	....	....	....	....	....	....	....	....	....	....
1969-70	**Pittsburgh Penguins**	**NHL**	**76**	**12**	**32**	**44**	**14**	**32**	**46**	**20**	**4**	**0**	**3**	**223**	**5.4**	**56**	**21**	**52**	**2**	**–15**	**10**	**5**	**3**	**8**	**17**	**1**	**3**	**0**
	NHL Totals		**76**	**12**	**32**	**44**	**14**	**32**	**46**	**20**	**4**	**0**	**3**	**223**	**5.4**	**56**	**21**	**52**	**2**		**10**	**5**	**3**	**8**	**17**	**1**	**3**	**0**

• Suffered career-ending injuries in automobile accident, May 15, 1970.

• BRIGLEY, TRAVIS
Travis Brigley LW – L. 6'1", 190 lbs. b: Coronation, Alta., 6/16/1977. Calgary's 2nd choice, 39th overall, in 1996 Entry Draft.

Season	Club	League	GP	G	A	Pts	AG	AA	APts	PIM	PP	SH	GW	S	%	TGF	PGF	TGA	PGA	+/–	GP	G	A	Pts	PIM	PP	SH	GW
1993-94	Lethbridge Hurricanes	WHL	1	0	0	0	....	....	....	0	....	....	....	....	....	....	....	....	....	....	....	....	....	....	....	....	....	....
1994-95	Lethbridge Hurricanes	WHL	64	14	18	32	....	....	....	14	....	....	....	....	....	....	....	....	....	....	....	....	....	....	....	....	....	....
1995-96	Lethbridge Hurricanes	WHL	69	34	43	77	....	....	....	94	....	....	....	....	....	....	....	....	....	....	4	2	3	5	8	....	....	....
1996-97	Lethbridge Hurricanes	WHL	71	43	47	90	....	....	....	56	....	....	....	....	....	....	....	....	....	....	19	9	9	18	31	....	....	....
1997-98	**Calgary Flames**	**NHL**	**2**	**0**	**0**	**0**	**0**	**0**	**0**	**2**	**0**	**0**	**0**	**1**	**0.0**	**0**	**0**	**1**	**1**	**0**	....	....	....	....	....	....	....	....
	Saint John Flames	AHL	79	17	15	32	....	....	....	28	....	....	....	....	....	....	....	....	....	....	8	0	0	0	0	....	....	....
	NHL Totals		**2**	**0**	**0**	**0**	**0**	**0**	**0**	**2**	**0**	**0**	**0**	**1**	**0.0**	**0**	**0**	**1**	**1**		....	....	....	....	....	....	....	....

• BRIMANIS, ARIS
Aris Brimanis D – R. 6'3", 210 lbs. b: Cleveland, OH, 3/14/1972. Philadelphia's 3rd choice, 86th overall, in 1991 Entry Draft.

Season	Club	League	GP	G	A	Pts	AG	AA	APts	PIM	PP	SH	GW	S	%	TGF	PGF	TGA	PGA	+/–	GP	G	A	Pts	PIM	PP	SH	GW
1990-91	Bowling Green University	CCHA	38	3	6	9	....	....	....	42	....	....	....	....	....	....	....	....	....	....	....	....	....	....	....	....	....	....
1991-92	Bowling Green University	CCHA	32	2	9	11	....	....	....	38	....	....	....	....	....	....	....	....	....	....	....	....	....	....	....	....	....	....
1992-93	Brandon Wheat Kings	WHL	71	8	50	58	....	....	....	110	....	....	....	....	....	....	....	....	....	....	4	2	1	3	7	....	....	....
1993-94	**Philadelphia Flyers**	**NHL**	**1**	**0**	**0**	**0**	**0**	**0**	**0**	**0**	**0**	**0**	**0**	**1**	**0.0**	**1**	**0**	**2**	**0**	**–1**	....	....	....	....	....	....	....	....
	Hershey Bears	AHL	75	8	15	23	....	....	....	65	....	....	....	....	....	....	....	....	....	....	11	2	3	5	12	....	....	....
1994-95	Hershey Bears	AHL	76	8	17	25	....	....	....	68	....	....	....	....	....	....	....	....	....	....	6	1	1	2	14	....	....	....
1995-96	**Philadelphia Flyers**	**NHL**	**17**	**0**	**2**	**2**	**0**	**2**	**2**	**12**	**0**	**0**	**0**	**11**	**0.0**	**7**	**0**	**10**	**2**	**–1**	....	....	....	....	....	....	....	....
	Hershey Bears	AHL	54	9	22	31	....	....	....	64	....	....	....	....	....	....	....	....	....	....	5	1	2	3	4	....	....	....
1996-97	**Philadelphia Flyers**	**NHL**	**3**	**0**	**1**	**1**	**0**	**1**	**1**	**0**	**0**	**0**	**0**	**1**	**0.0**	**3**	**0**	**3**	**0**	**0**	....	....	....	....	....	....	....	....
	Philadelphia Phantoms	AHL	65	14	18	32	....	....	....	69	....	....	....	....	....	....	....	....	....	....	10	2	2	4	13	....	....	....
1997-98	Philadelphia Phantoms	AHL	30	1	11	12	....	....	....	26	....	....	....	....	....	....	....	....	....	....	....	....	....	....	....	....	....	....
	Michigan K-Wings	IHL	35	3	9	12	....	....	....	24	....	....	....	....	....	....	....	....	....	....	4	1	0	1	4	....	....	....
	NHL Totals		**21**	**0**	**3**	**3**	**0**	**3**	**3**	**12**	**0**	**0**	**0**	**13**	**0.0**	**11**	**0**	**15**	**2**		....	....	....	....	....	....	....	....

• BRIND'AMOUR, ROD
Rod Brind'Amour C – L. 6'1", 202 lbs. b: Ottawa, Ont., 8/9/1970. St. Louis' 1st choice, 9th overall, in 1988 Entry Draft.

Season	Club	League	GP	G	A	Pts	AG	AA	APts	PIM	PP	SH	GW	S	%	TGF	PGF	TGA	PGA	+/–	GP	G	A	Pts	PIM	PP	SH	GW
1987-88	Notre Dame Hounds	SJHL	56	46	61	107	....	....	....	136	....	....	....	....	....	....	....	....	....	....	....	....	....	....	....	....	....	....
1988-89	Michigan State Spartans	CCHA	42	27	32	59	....	....	....	63	....	....	....	....	....	....	....	....	....	....	....	....	....	....	....	....	....	....
	Canada	WJC-A	7	2	3	5	....	....	....	4	....	....	....	....	....	....	....	....	....	....	....	....	....	....	....	....	....	....
	St. Louis Blues	**NHL**	....	....	....	....	....	....	....	....	....	....	....	....	....	....	....	....	....	....	**5**	**2**	**0**	**2**	**4**	....	....	....
1989-90	**St. Louis Blues**	**NHL**	**79**	**26**	**35**	**61**	**22**	**25**	**47**	**46**	**10**	**0**	**1**	**160**	**16.3**	**103**	**29**	**59**	**8**	**+23**	**12**	**5**	**8**	**13**	**6**	**1**	**0**	**0**
1990-91	**St. Louis Blues**	**NHL**	**78**	**17**	**32**	**49**	**16**	**24**	**40**	**93**	**4**	**0**	**3**	**169**	**10.1**	**97**	**32**	**65**	**2**	**+2**	**13**	**2**	**5**	**7**	**10**	**1**	**0**	**0**
1991-92	**Philadelphia Flyers**	**NHL**	**80**	**33**	**44**	**77**	**30**	**33**	**63**	**100**	**8**	**4**	**5**	**202**	**16.3**	**112**	**35**	**116**	**36**	**–3**	....	....	....	....	....	....	....	....
	Canada	WC-A	6	1	1	2	....	....	....	4	....	....	....	....	....	....	....	....	....	....	....	....	....	....	....	....	....	....
1992-93	**Philadelphia Flyers**	**NHL**	**81**	**37**	**49**	**86**	**31**	**34**	**65**	**89**	**13**	**4**	**4**	**206**	**18.0**	**123**	**45**	**121**	**35**	**–8**	....	....	....	....	....	....	....	....
	Canada	WC-A	8	3	1	4	....	....	....	6	....	....	....	....	....	....	....	....	....	....	....	....	....	....	....	....	....	....
1993-94	**Philadelphia Flyers**	**NHL**	**84**	**35**	**62**	**97**	**33**	**48**	**81**	**85**	**14**	**1**	**4**	**230**	**15.2**	**131**	**42**	**137**	**39**	**–9**	....	....	....	....	....	....	....	....
	Canada	WC-A	8	4	2	6	....	....	....	2	....	....	....	....	....	....	....	....	....	....	....	....	....	....	....	....	....	....
1994-95	**Philadelphia Flyers**	**NHL**	**48**	**12**	**27**	**39**	**21**	**40**	**61**	**33**	**4**	**1**	**2**	**86**	**14.0**	**56**	**26**	**52**	**18**	**–4**	**15**	**6**	**9**	**15**	**8**	**2**	**1**	**1**
1995-96	**Philadelphia Flyers**	**NHL**	**82**	**26**	**61**	**87**	**26**	**50**	**76**	**110**	**4**	**4**	**5**	**213**	**12.2**	**114**	**43**	**94**	**43**	**+20**	**12**	**2**	**5**	**7**	**6**	**1**	**0**	**0**
1996-97	Canada	W Cup	7	1	2	3	....	....	....	0	....	....	....	....	....	....	....	....	....	....	....	....	....	....	....	....	....	....
	Philadelphia Flyers	**NHL**	**82**	**27**	**32**	**59**	**29**	**28**	**57**	**41**	**8**	**2**	**3**	**205**	**13.2**	**93**	**21**	**100**	**30**	**+2**	**19**	***13**	**8**	**21**	**10**	**4**	**2**	**1**
1997-98	**Philadelphia Flyers**	**NHL**	**82**	**36**	**38**	**74**	**42**	**37**	**79**	**54**	**10**	**2**	**8**	**205**	**17.6**	**96**	**39**	**85**	**26**	**–2**	**5**	**2**	**2**	**4**	**7**	**0**	**0**	**0**
	Canada	Olympics	6	1	2	3	....	....	....	0	....	....	....	....	....	....	....	....	....	....	....	....	....	....	....	....	....	....
	NHL Totals		**696**	**249**	**380**	**629**	**250**	**319**	**569**	**651**	**75**	**18**	**35**	**1676**	**14.9**	**925**	**312**	**829**	**237**		**81**	**32**	**37**	**69**	**51**	**9**	**3**	**2**

NHL All-Rookie Team (1990)

Played in NHL All-Star Game (1992)

Traded to **Philadelphia** by **St. Louis** with Dan Quinn for Ron Sutter and Murray Baron, September 22, 1991.

• BRINDLEY, DOUG
Doug Brindley LW/C – L. 6'1", 175 lbs. b: Walkerton, Ont., 6/8/1949. Toronto's 2nd choice, 20th overall, in 1969 Amateur Draft.

Season	Club	League	GP	G	A	Pts	AG	AA	APts	PIM	PP	SH	GW	S	%	TGF	PGF	TGA	PGA	+/–	GP	G	A	Pts	PIM	PP	SH	GW
1967-68	Niagara Falls Flyers	OHA	54	15	28	43	....	....	....	20	....	....	....	....	....	....	....	....	....	....	19	15	7	22	18	....	....	....
1968-69	Niagara Falls Flyers	OHA	54	40	37	77	....	....	....	62	....	....	....	....	....	....	....	....	....	....	14	12	6	22	16	....	....	....
1969-70	Tulsa Oilers	CHL	65	22	25	47	....	....	....	14	....	....	....	....	....	....	....	....	....	....	6	0	6	6	0	....	....	....
	Buffalo Bisons	AHL	....	....	....	....	....	....	....	....	....	....	....	....	....	....	....	....	....	....	1	0	1	1	0	....	....	....
1970-71	**Toronto Maple Leafs**	**NHL**	**3**	**0**	**0**	**0**	**0**	**0**	**0**	**0**	**0**	**0**	**0**	**0**	**0.0**	**0**	**0**	**0**	**0**	**0**	....	....	....	....	....	....	....	....
	Tulsa Oilers	CHL	65	29	38	67	....	....	....	17	....	....	....	....	....	....	....	....	....	....	....	....	....	....	....	....	....	....
1971-72	Rochester Americans	AHL	74	20	27	47	....	....	....	12	....	....	....	....	....	....	....	....	....	....	....	....	....	....	....	....	....	....
1972-73	Cleveland Crusaders	WHA	73	15	11	26	....	....	....	6	....	....	....	....	....	....	....	....	....	....	9	0	0	0	6	....	....	....
1973-74	Cleveland Crusaders	WHA	30	13	9	22	....	....	....	13	....	....	....	....	....	....	....	....	....	....	5	0	1	1	2	....	....	....
	Jacksonville Barons	AHL	50	19	14	33	....	....	....	65	....	....	....	....	....	....	....	....	....	....	....	....	....	....	....	....	....	....
1974-75	Mohawk Valley Comets	NAHL	71	28	44	72	....	....	....	36	....	....	....	....	....	....	....	....	....	....	....	....	....	....	....	....	....	....
1975-76	Syracuse Blazers	NAHL	70	43	58	101	....	....	....	34	....	....	....	....	....	....	....	....	....	....	8	0	8	8	4	....	....	....
	NHL Totals		**3**	**0**	**0**	**0**	**0**	**0**	**0**	**0**	**0**	**0**	**0**	**0**	**0.0**	**0**	**0**	**0**	**0**		....	....	....	....	....	....	....	....
	Other Major League Totals		103	28	20	48	....	....	....	19	....	....	....	....	....	....	....	....	....	....	14	0	1	1	8	....	....	....

Traded to **Vancouver** (WHL) by **Toronto** (Rochester - AHL) For Andre Hinse, July, 1972. Selected by **Alberta** (WHA) in 1972 WHA General Player Draft, February 12, 1972. WHA rights traded to **Cleveland** (WHA) by **Alberta** (WHA) for cash, August, 1972. Traded to **Indianapolis** (WHA) by **Cleveland** (WHA) for cash, August, 1974. Claimed by **Cleveland** (WHA) from **Indianapolis** (WHA) in 1975 WHA Intra-League Draft, June, 1975.

• BRISEBOIS, PATRICE
Patrice Brisebois D – R. 6'1", 188 lbs. b: Montreal, Que., 1/27/1971. Montreal's 2nd choice, 30th overall, in 1989 Entry Draft.

Season	Club	League	GP	G	A	Pts	AG	AA	APts	PIM	PP	SH	GW	S	%	TGF	PGF	TGA	PGA	+/–	GP	G	A	Pts	PIM	PP	SH	GW
1987-88	Laval Titan	QMJHL	48	10	34	44	....	....	....	95	....	....	....	....	....	....	....	....	....	....	6	0	2	2	2	....	....	....
1988-89	Laval Titan	QMJHL	50	20	45	65	....	....	....	95	....	....	....	....	....	....	....	....	....	....	17	8	14	22	45	....	....	....
1989-90	Laval Titan	QMJHL	56	18	70	88	....	....	....	108	....	....	....	....	....	....	....	....	....	....	13	7	9	16	26	....	....	....
	Canada	WJC-A	7	2	2	4	....	....	....	6	....	....	....	....	....	....	....	....	....	....	....	....	....	....	....	....	....	....
1990-91	Drummondville Voltigeurs	QMJHL	54	17	44	61	....	....	....	72	....	....	....	....	....	....	....	....	....	....	14	6	18	24	49	....	....	....
	Canada	WJC-A	7	1	6	7	....	....	....	2	....	....	....	....	....	....	....	....	....	....	....	....	....	....	....	....	....	....
	Montreal Canadiens	**NHL**	**10**	**0**	**2**	**2**	**0**	**2**	**2**	**4**	**0**	**0**	**0**	**11**	**0.0**	**13**	**5**	**7**	**0**	**+1**	....	....	....	....	....	....	....	....
1991-92	**Montreal Canadiens**	**NHL**	**26**	**2**	**8**	**10**	**2**	**6**	**8**	**20**	**0**	**0**	**1**	**37**	**5.4**	**41**	**16**	**22**	**6**	**+9**	**11**	**2**	**4**	**6**	**6**	**1**	**0**	**1**
	Fredericton Canadiens	AHL	53	12	27	39	....	....	....	51	....	....	....	....	....	....	....	....	....	....	....	....	....	....	....	....	....	....
1992-93	**Montreal Canadiens**	**NHL**	**70**	**10**	**21**	**31**	**8**	**14**	**22**	**79**	**4**	**0**	**2**	**123**	**8.1**	**89**	**33**	**60**	**10**	**+6**	**20**	**0**	**4**	**4**	**18**	**0**	**0**	**0**
1993-94	**Montreal Canadiens**	**NHL**	**53**	**2**	**21**	**23**	**2**	**16**	**18**	**63**	**1**	**0**	**0**	**71**	**2.8**	**55**	**17**	**41**	**8**	**+5**	**7**	**0**	**4**	**4**	**6**	**0**	**0**	**0**
1994-95	**Montreal Canadiens**	**NHL**	**35**	**4**	**8**	**12**	**7**	**12**	**19**	**26**	**0**	**0**	**2**	**67**	**6.0**	**36**	**7**	**37**	**6**	**–2**	....	....	....	....	....	....	....	....
1995-96	**Montreal Canadiens**	**NHL**	**69**	**9**	**27**	**36**	**9**	**22**	**31**	**65**	**3**	**0**	**1**	**127**	**7.1**	**104**	**41**	**80**	**27**	**+10**	**6**	**1**	**2**	**3**	**6**	**0**	**0**	**0**
1996-97	**Montreal Canadiens**	**NHL**	**49**	**2**	**13**	**15**	**2**	**11**	**13**	**24**	**0**	**0**	**1**	**72**	**2.8**	**49**	**13**	**58**	**15**	**–7**	**3**	**1**	**1**	**2**	**24**	**0**	**0**	**1**
1997-98	**Montreal Canadiens**	**NHL**	**79**	**10**	**27**	**37**	**12**	**26**	**38**	**67**	**5**	**0**	**1**	**125**	**8.0**	**92**	**27**	**71**	**22**	**+16**	**10**	**1**	**0**	**1**	**0**	**0**	**0**	**0**
	NHL Totals		**391**	**39**	**127**	**166**	**42**	**109**	**151**	**348**	**13**	**0**	**8**	**633**	**6.2**	**479**	**159**	**376**	**94**		**57**	**5**	**15**	**20**	**60**	**1**	**0**	**2**

QMJHL Second All-Star Team (1990) • Canadian Major Junior Defenseman of the Year (1991) • QMJHL First All-Star Team (1991) • Memorial Cup All-Star Team (1991)

• BRITZ, GREG
Greg Britz RW – L. 6', 190 lbs. b: Buffalo, NY, 1/3/1961.

Season	Club	League	GP	G	A	Pts	AG	AA	APts	PIM	PP	SH	GW	S	%	TGF	PGF	TGA	PGA	+/–	GP	G	A	Pts	PIM	PP	SH	GW
1979-80	Harvard University	ECAC	26	8	5	13	....	....	....	17	....	....	....	....	....	....	....	....	....	....	....	....	....	....	....	....	....	....
1980-81	Harvard University	ECAC	24	3	4	7	....	....	....	10	....	....	....	....	....	....	....	....	....	....	....	....	....	....	....	....	....	....
1981-82	Harvard University	ECAC	24	11	13	24	....	....	....	12	....	....	....	....	....	....	....	....	....	....	....	....	....	....	....	....	....	....
1982-83	Harvard University	ECAC	33	16	23	39	....	....	....	25	....	....	....	....	....	....	....	....	....	....	....	....	....	....	....	....	....	....

			REGULAR SEASON																		PLAYOFFS							
Season	Club	League	GP	G	A	Pts	AG	AA	APts	PIM	PP	SH	GW	S	%	TGF	PGF	TGA	PGA	+/-	GP	G	A	Pts	PIM	PP	SH	GW
1983-84	**Toronto Maple Leafs**	**NHL**	**6**	**0**	**0**	**0**	**0**	**0**	**0**	**2**	**0**	**0**	**0**	**1**	**0.0**	**1**	**0**	**2**	**0**	**–1**	....	....	....	....	....	....	....	....
	St. Catharines Saints	AHL	44	23	16	39	....	....	....	25	....	....	....	....	....	....	....	....	....	....	7	1	0	1	0	....	....	....
1984-85	**Toronto Maple Leafs**	**NHL**	**1**	**0**	**0**	**0**	**0**	**0**	**0**	**2**	**0**	**0**	**0**	**0**	**0.0**	**0**	**0**	**0**	**0**	**0**	....	....	....	....	....	....	....	....
	St. Catharines Saints	AHL	74	15	17	32	....	....	....	31	....	....	....	....	....	....	....	....	....	....	....	....	....	....	....	....	....	....
1985-86	St. Catharines Saints	AHL	72	17	19	36	....	....	....	52	....	....	....	....	....	....	....	....	....	....	13	3	3	6	7	....	....	....
1986-87	**Hartford Whalers**	**NHL**	**1**	**0**	**0**	**0**	**0**	**0**	**0**	**0**	**0**	**0**	**0**	**0**	**0.0**	**0**	**0**	**1**	**1**	**0**	....	....	....	....	....	....	....	....
	Binghamton Whalers	AHL	74	25	16	41	....	....	....	66	....	....	....	....	....	....	....	....	....	....	13	3	3	6	6	....	....	....
	NHL Totals		**8**	**0**	**0**	**0**	**0**	**0**	**0**	**4**	**0**	**0**	**0**	**1**	**0.0**	**1**	**0**	**3**	**1**		....	....	....	....	....	....	....	....

Signed as a free agent by **Toronto**, November 2, 1983. Signed as a free agent by **Hartford**, November, 1986.

• BROCHU, STEPHANE

Stephane Brochu D – L. 6′, 185 lbs. b: Sherbrooke, Que., 8/15/1967. NY Rangers' 9th choice, 175th overall, in 1985 Entry Draft.

Season	Club	League	GP	G	A	Pts	AG	AA	APts	PIM	PP	SH	GW	S	%	TGF	PGF	TGA	PGA	+/-	GP	G	A	Pts	PIM	PP	SH	GW
1983-84	Magog Cantonniers	Midget	38	7	24	31	....	....	....	38	....	....	....	....	....	....	....	....	....	....	....	....	....	....	....	....	....	....
1984-85	Quebec Remparts	QMJHL	59	2	16	18	....	....	....	56	....	....	....	....	....	....	....	....	....	....	4	0	2	2	2	....	....	....
1985-86	St-Jean Castors	QMJHL	63	14	27	41	....	....	....	121	....	....	....	....	....	....	....	....	....	....	3	1	0	1	2	....	....	....
1986-87	St-Jean Castors	QMJHL	....	....	....	....	....	....	....	....	....	....	....	....	....	....	....	....	....	....	8	0	2	2	11	....	....	....
1987-88	St-Jean Castors	QMJHL	29	4	35	39	....	....	....	88	....	....	....	....	....	....	....	....	....	....	....	....	....	....	....	....	....	....
	Colorado Rangers	IHL	52	4	10	14	....	....	....	70	....	....	....	....	....	....	....	....	....	....	12	3	3	6	13	....	....	....
1988-89	**New York Rangers**	**NHL**	**1**	**0**	**0**	**0**	**0**	**0**	**0**	**0**	**0**	**0**	**0**	**1**	**0.0**	**1**	**0**	**0**	**0**	**+1**	....	....	....	....	....	....	....	....
	Denver Rangers	IHL	67	5	14	19	....	....	....	109	....	....	....	....	....	....	....	....	....	....	3	0	0	0	0	....	....	....
1989-90	Flint Spirits	IHL	5	0	0	0	....	....	....	2	....	....	....	....	....	....	....	....	....	....	....	....	....	....	....	....	....	....
	Fort Wayne Komets	IHL	63	9	19	28	....	....	....	98	....	....	....	....	....	....	....	....	....	....	5	0	2	2	6	....	....	....
1990-91	Fort Wayne Komets	IHL	73	14	29	43	....	....	....	49	....	....	....	....	....	....	....	....	....	....	14	1	3	4	31	....	....	....
1991-92	Kansas City Blades	IHL	3	0	0	0	....	....	....	0	....	....	....	....	....	....	....	....	....	....	....	....	....	....	....	....	....	....
	Flint Bulldogs	ColHL	53	13	27	40	....	....	....	80	....	....	....	....	....	....	....	....	....	....	....	....	....	....	....	....	....	....
1992-93	Flint Bulldogs	ColHL	44	6	28	34	....	....	....	77	....	....	....	....	....	....	....	....	....	....	6	4	8	12	22	....	....	....
1993-94	Flint Bulldogs	ColHL	54	8	32	40	....	....	....	116	....	....	....	....	....	....	....	....	....	....	10	1	4	5	2	....	....	....
1994-95	Flint Generals	ColHL	60	12	37	49	....	....	....	39	....	....	....	....	....	....	....	....	....	....	6	0	9	9	8	....	....	....
1995-96	Flint Generals	ColHL	68	4	41	45	....	....	....	68	....	....	....	....	....	....	....	....	....	....	15	5	12	17	18	....	....	....
1996-97	Detroit Vipers	IHL	1	0	0	0	....	....	....	2	....	....	....	....	....	....	....	....	....	....	....	....	....	....	....	....	....	....
	Adirondack Red Wings	AHL	18	0	8	8	....	....	....	12	....	....	....	....	....	....	....	....	....	....	....	....	....	....	....	....	....	....
	Flint Generals	ColHL	42	8	45	53	....	....	....	32	....	....	....	....	....	....	....	....	....	....	14	5	*20	*25	14	....	....	....
1997-98	Chicago Wolves	IHL	1	0	0	0	....	....	....	0	....	....	....	....	....	....	....	....	....	....	....	....	....	....	....	....	....	....
	Detroit Vipers	IHL	3	0	0	0	....	....	....	2	....	....	....	....	....	....	....	....	....	....	....	....	....	....	....	....	....	....
	Fort Wayne Komets	IHL	2	1	0	1	....	....	....	0	....	....	....	....	....	....	....	....	....	....	....	....	....	....	....	....	....	....
	Flint Generals	UHL	54	10	62	72	....	....	....	52	....	....	....	....	....	....	....	....	....	....	17	2	18	20	12	....	....	....
	NHL Totals		**1**	**0**	**0**	**0**	**0**	**0**	**0**	**0**	**0**	**0**	**0**	**1**	**0.0**	**1**	**0**	**0**	**0**		....	....	....	....	....	....	....	....

• BROOKE, BOB

Bob Brooke C – R. 5′11″, 195 lbs. b: Melrose, MA, 12/18/1960. St. Louis' 3rd choice, 75th overall, in 1980 Entry Draft.

Season	Club	League	GP	G	A	Pts	AG	AA	APts	PIM	PP	SH	GW	S	%	TGF	PGF	TGA	PGA	+/-	GP	G	A	Pts	PIM	PP	SH	GW
1979-80	Yale University	ECAC	24	7	22	29	....	....	....	38	....	....	....	....	....	....	....	....	....	....	....	....	....	....	....	....	....	....
	United States	WJC-A	5	3	2	5	....	....	....	8	....	....	....	....	....	....	....	....	....	....	....	....	....	....	....	....	....	....
1980-81	Yale University	ECAC	27	12	30	42	....	....	....	59	....	....	....	....	....	....	....	....	....	....	....	....	....	....	....	....	....	....
1981-82	Yale University	ECAC	25	12	30	42	....	....	....	60	....	....	....	....	....	....	....	....	....	....	....	....	....	....	....	....	....	....
1982-83	Yale University	ECAC	21	10	27	37	....	....	....	48	....	....	....	....	....	....	....	....	....	....	....	....	....	....	....	....	....	....
	United States	Olympics	6	1	1	2	....	....	....	10	....	....	....	....	....	....	....	....	....	....	....	....	....	....	....	....	....	....
	United States	Nat-Team	54	7	18	25	....	....	....	75	....	....	....	....	....	....	....	....	....	....	....	....	....	....	....	....	....	....
	New York Rangers	**NHL**	**9**	**1**	**2**	**3**	**1**	**1**	**2**	**4**	**0**	**0**	**0**	**10**	**10.0**	**5**	**0**	**5**	**1**	**+1**	**5**	**0**	**0**	**0**	**7**	**0**	**0**	**0**
1984-85	United States	C Cup	5	0	1	1	....	....	....	4	....	....	....	....	....	....	....	....	....	....	....	....	....	....	....	....	....	....
	New York Rangers	**NHL**	**72**	**7**	**9**	**16**	**6**	**6**	**12**	**79**	**0**	**0**	**2**	**93**	**7.5**	**35**	**1**	**66**	**14**	**–18**	**3**	**0**	**0**	**0**	**8**	**0**	**0**	**0**
	United States	WEC-A	10	0	1	1	....	....	....	14	....	....	....	....	....	....	....	....	....	....	....	....	....	....	....	....	....	....
1985-86	**New York Rangers**	**NHL**	**79**	**24**	**20**	**44**	**19**	**13**	**32**	**111**	**6**	**2**	**1**	**178**	**13.5**	**75**	**18**	**92**	**41**	**+6**	**16**	**6**	**9**	**15**	**28**	**0**	**2**	**2**
1986-87	**New York Rangers**	**NHL**	**15**	**3**	**5**	**8**	**3**	**4**	**7**	**20**	**0**	**0**	**0**	**24**	**12.5**	**17**	**6**	**22**	**8**	**–3**	....	....	....	....	....	....	....	....
	Minnesota North Stars	**NHL**	**65**	**10**	**18**	**28**	**9**	**13**	**22**	**78**	**1**	**1**	**0**	**114**	**8.8**	**45**	**6**	**75**	**30**	**–6**	....	....	....	....	....	....	....	....
	United States	WEC-A	10	2	1	3	....	....	....	10	....	....	....	....	....	....	....	....	....	....	....	....	....	....	....	....	....	....
1987-88	United States	C Cup	5	1	0	1	....	....	....	4	....	....	....	....	....	....	....	....	....	....	....	....	....	....	....	....	....	....
	Minnesota North Stars	**NHL**	**77**	**5**	**20**	**25**	**4**	**14**	**18**	**108**	**1**	**1**	**1**	**127**	**3.9**	**73**	**21**	**105**	**47**	**–6**	....	....	....	....	....	....	....	....
1988-89	**Minnesota North Stars**	**NHL**	**57**	**7**	**9**	**16**	**6**	**6**	**12**	**57**	**0**	**1**	**2**	**77**	**9.1**	**24**	**0**	**46**	**10**	**–12**	**5**	**3**	**0**	**3**	**2**	**0**	**0**	**0**
1989-90	**Minnesota North Stars**	**NHL**	**38**	**4**	**4**	**8**	**3**	**3**	**6**	**33**	**0**	**3**	**0**	**65**	**6.2**	**16**	**4**	**27**	**10**	**–5**	....	....	....	....	....	....	....	....
	New Jersey Devils	**NHL**	**35**	**8**	**10**	**18**	**7**	**7**	**14**	**30**	**0**	**0**	**1**	**44**	**18.2**	**26**	**0**	**34**	**11**	**+3**	**5**	**0**	**0**	**0**	**14**	**0**	**0**	**0**
	NHL Totals		**447**	**69**	**97**	**166**	**58**	**67**	**125**	**520**	**8**	**8**	**7**	**732**	**9.4**	**316**	**56**	**472**	**172**		**34**	**9**	**9**	**18**	**59**	**0**	**2**	**2**

ECAC First All-Star Team (1983) • NCAA East First All-American Team (1983)

Rights traded to **NY Rangers** by **St. Louis** with Larry Patey for Dave Barr, NY Rangers' 3rd round choice (Alan Perry) in 1984 Entry Draft and cash, March 5, 1984. Traded to **Minnesota** by **NY Rangers** with Minnesota's 4th round choice (previously acquired, Minnesota selected Jeffrey Stolp) in 1988 Entry Draft for Curt Giles, Tony McKegney and Minnesota's 2nd round choice (Troy Mallette) in 1988 Entry Draft, November 13, 1986. Traded to **New Jersey** by **Minnesota** for Aaron Broten, January 5, 1990. Traded to **Winnipeg** by **New Jersey** for Laurie Boschman, September 6, 1990.

• BROOKS, GORD

Gord Brooks RW – R. 5′8″, 168 lbs. b: Cobourg, Ont., 9/11/1950. St. Louis' 3rd choice, 51st overall, in 1970 Amateur Draft.

Season	Club	League	GP	G	A	Pts	AG	AA	APts	PIM	PP	SH	GW	S	%	TGF	PGF	TGA	PGA	+/-	GP	G	A	Pts	PIM	PP	SH	GW
1968-69	Hamilton Red Wings	OHA	54	9	7	16	....	....	....	47	....	....	....	....	....	....	....	....	....	....	5	1	1	2	5	....	....	....
1969-70	Hamilton Red Wings	OHA	21	6	5	11	....	....	....	32	....	....	....	....	....	....	....	....	....	....	....	....	....	....	....	....	....	....
	London Knights	OHA	31	9	23	32	....	....	....	47	....	....	....	....	....	....	....	....	....	....	....	....	....	....	....	....	....	....
1970-71	Kansas City Blues	CHL	67	16	16	32	....	....	....	44	....	....	....	....	....	....	....	....	....	....	....	....	....	....	....	....	....	....
1971-72	**St. Louis Blues**	**NHL**	**2**	**0**	**0**	**0**	**0**	**0**	**0**	**0**	**0**	**0**	**0**	**2**	**0.0**	**2**	**0**	**2**	**0**	**0**	....	....	....	....	....	....	....	....
	Kansas City Blues	CHL	62	21	18	39	....	....	....	34	....	....	....	....	....	....	....	....	....	....	....	....	....	....	....	....	....	....
1972-73	Fort Worth Wings	CHL	23	10	16	26	....	....	....	22	....	....	....	....	....	....	....	....	....	....	3	0	0	0	0	....	....	....
1973-74	**St. Louis Blues**	**NHL**	**30**	**6**	**8**	**14**	**6**	**7**	**13**	**12**	**0**	**0**	**1**	**51**	**11.8**	**18**	**1**	**18**	**1**	**0**	....	....	....	....	....	....	....	....
	Denver Spurs	WHL	41	20	20	40	....	....	....	34	....	....	....	....	....	....	....	....	....	....	....	....	....	....	....	....	....	....
1974-75	**Washington Capitals**	**NHL**	**38**	**1**	**10**	**11**	**1**	**8**	**9**	**25**	**1**	**0**	**0**	**79**	**1.3**	**15**	**5**	**33**	**4**	**–19**	....	....	....	....	....	....	....	....
	Richmond Robins	AHL	15	3	4	7	....	....	....	8	....	....	....	....	....	....	....	....	....	....	3	0	0	0	2	....	....	....
1975-76	Philadelphia Firebirds	NAHL	68	39	54	93	....	....	....	46	....	....	....	....	....	....	....	....	....	....	16	15	17	32	4	....	....	....
1976-77	Philadelphia Firebirds	NAHL	74	65	59	124	....	....	....	37	....	....	....	....	....	....	....	....	....	....	4	1	5	6	4	....	....	....
1977-78	Philadelphia Firebirds	AHL	81	42	56	98	....	....	....	40	....	....	....	....	....	....	....	....	....	....	4	0	0	0	2	....	....	....
1978-79	Philadelphia Firebirds	AHL	80	43	31	74	....	....	....	27	....	....	....	....	....	....	....	....	....	....	....	....	....	....	....	....	....	....
1979-80	Syracuse Firebirds	AHL	77	34	41	75	....	....	....	38	....	....	....	....	....	....	....	....	....	....	4	1	1	2	0	....	....	....
1980-81	Klagenfurt	Austria	13	13	13	26	....	....	....	12	....	....	....	....	....	....	....	....	....	....	....	....	....	....	....	....	....	....
	Saginaw Gears	IHL	39	17	25	42	....	....	....	4	....	....	....	....	....	....	....	....	....	....	13	8	9	17	6	....	....	....
1981-82	Saginaw Gears	IHL	82	49	64	113	....	....	....	35	....	....	....	....	....	....	....	....	....	....	14	*12	9	*21	0	....	....	....
1982-83	Saginaw Gears	IHL	21	15	9	24	....	....	....	6	....	....	....	....	....	....	....	....	....	....	....	....	....	....	....	....	....	....
1983-84	Toledo Goaldiggers	IHL	5	0	3	3	....	....	....	0	....	....	....	....	....	....	....	....	....	....	....	....	....	....	....	....	....	....
	NHL Totals		**70**	**7**	**18**	**25**	**7**	**15**	**22**	**37**	**1**	**0**	**1**	**132**	**5.3**	**35**	**6**	**53**	**5**		....	....	....	....	....	....	....	....

NAHL Second All-Star Team (1977) • AHL First All-Star Team (1978) • Won John B. Sollenberger Trophy (Top Scorer - AHL) (1978) • IHL First All-Star Team (1982)

Claimed by **Washington** from **St. Louis** in Expansion Draft, June 12, 1974.

• BROSSART, WILLIE

Willie Brossart LW – L. 6′, 190 lbs. b: Allan, Sask., 5/29/1949. Philadelphia's 3rd choice, 28th overall, in 1969 Amateur Draft.

Season	Club	League	GP	G	A	Pts	AG	AA	APts	PIM	PP	SH	GW	S	%	TGF	PGF	TGA	PGA	+/-	GP	G	A	Pts	PIM	PP	SH	GW
1967-68	Swift Current Broncos	WCJHL	59	12	34	46	....	....	....	199	....	....	....	....	....	....	....	....	....	....	....	....	....	....	....	....	....	....
1968-69	Swift Current–Estevan	WCJHL	62	8	27	35	....	....	....	94	....	....	....	....	....	....	....	....	....	....	10	1	3	4	14	....	....	....
1969-70	Quebec Aces	AHL	57	5	9	14	....	....	....	67	....	....	....	....	....	....	....	....	....	....	6	0	0	0	0	....	....	....
1970-71	**Philadelphia Flyers**	**NHL**	**1**	**0**	**0**	**0**	**0**	**0**	**0**	**0**	**0**	**0**	**0**	**3**	**0.0**	**1**	**1**	**2**	**0**	**–2**	....	....	....	....	....	....	....	....
	Quebec Aces	AHL	62	8	17	25	....	....	....	182	....	....	....	....	....	....	....	....	....	....	1	0	2	2	0	....	....	....
1971-72	**Philadelphia Flyers**	**NHL**	**42**	**0**	**4**	**4**	**0**	**4**	**4**	**12**	**0**	**0**	**0**	**42**	**0.0**	**18**	**1**	**29**	**5**	**–7**	....	....	....	....	....	....	....	....
	Richmond Robins	AHL	29	3	14	17	....	....	....	76	....	....	....	....	....	....	....	....	....	....	....	....	....	....	....	....	....	....
1972-73	**Philadelphia Flyers**	**NHL**	**4**	**0**	**1**	**1**	**0**	**1**	**1**	**0**	**0**	**0**	**0**	**6**	**0.0**	**2**	**1**	**7**	**1**	**–6**	....	....	....	....	....	....	....	....
	Richmond Robins	AHL	54	1	29	30	....	....	....	66	....	....	....	....	....	....	....	....	....	....	3	0	0	0	0	....	....	....

			REGULAR SEASON																		PLAYOFFS							
Season	Club	League	GP	G	A	Pts	AG	AA	APts	PIM	PP	SH	GW	S	%	TGF	PGF	TGA	PGA	+/–	GP	G	A	Pts	PIM	PP	SH	GW
1973-74	Toronto Maple Leafs	NHL	17	0	1	1	0	1	1	20	0	0	0	9	0.0	14	0	13	1	+2	1	0	0	0	0	0	0	0
1974-75	Toronto Maple Leafs	NHL	4	0	0	0	0	0	0	2	0	0	0	1	0.0	2	0	3	1	0	....	....	....	....	....	....	....	....
	Washington Capitals	NHL	12	1	0	1	1	0	1	14	0	0	0	12	8.3	13	3	28	4	–14	....	....	....	....	....	....	....	....
1975-76	Washington Capitals	NHL	49	0	8	8	0	6	6	40	0	0	0	36	0.0	36	3	101	19	–49	....	....	....	....	....	....	....	....
	Richmond Robins	AHL	30	2	7	9	....	....	....	22	....	....	....	....	....	....	....	....	....	....	8	0	3	3	2	....	....	....
1976-77	Richmond Wildcats	SHL	36	4	20	24	....	....	....	24	....	....	....	....	....	....	....	....	....	....	....	....	....	....	....	....	....	....
	Baltimore Clippers	SHL	8	0	4	4	....	....	....	0	....	....	....	....	....	....	....	....	....	....	....	....	....	....	....	....	....	....
	NHL Totals		129	1	14	15	1	12	13	88	0	0	0	109	0.9	86	9	183	31		1	0	0	0	0	0	0	0

Traded to **Toronto** by **Philadelphia** for cash, May 23, 1973. Traded to **Washington** by **Toronto** with Tim Ecclestone for Rod Seiling, November 2, 1974.

• BROTEN, AARON

Aaron Broten LW/C – L. 5'10", 180 lbs. b: Roseau, MN, 11/14/1960. Colorado's 3rd choice, 106th overall, in 1980 Entry Draft.

1978-79	Roseau High School	H.S.	STATISTICS NOT AVAILABLE																									
	United States	WJC-A	5	4	3	7	....	....	....	0	....	....	....	....	....	....	....	....	....	....	....	....	....	....	....	....	....	....
1979-80	University of Minnesota	WCHA	41	25	47	72	....	....	....	8	....	....	....	....	....	....	....	....	....	....	....	....	....	....	....	....	....	....
1980-81	University of Minnesota	WCHA	45	*47	*59	*106	....	....	....	24	....	....	....	....	....	....	....	....	....	....	....	....	....	....	....	....	....	....
	United States	WEC-A	8	2	2	4	....	....	....	0	....	....	....	....	....	....	....	....	....	....	....	....	....	....	....	....	....	....
	Colorado Rockies	NHL	2	0	0	0	0	0	0	0	0	0	0	1	0.0	0	0	0	0	0	....	....	....	....	....	....	....	....
1981-82	Colorado Rockies	NHL	58	15	24	39	12	16	28	6	5	1	5	67	22.4	61	21	53	2	–11	....	....	....	....	....	....	....	....
	Fort Worth Texans	CHL	19	15	21	36	....	....	....	11	....	....	....	....	....	....	....	....	....	....	....	....	....	....	....	....	....	....
	United States	WEC-A	7	2	2	4	....	....	....	8	....	....	....	....	....	....	....	....	....	....	....	....	....	....	....	....	....	....
1982-83	New Jersey Devils	NHL	73	16	39	55	13	27	40	28	5	1	1	126	12.7	87	44	83	20	–20	....	....	....	....	....	....	....	....
	Wichita Wind	CHL	4	0	4	4	....	....	....	0	....	....	....	....	....	....	....	....	....	....	....	....	....	....	....	....	....	....
1983-84	New Jersey Devils	NHL	80	13	23	36	10	16	26	36	3	0	1	102	12.7	60	19	73	4	–28	....	....	....	....	....	....	....	....
1984-85	United States	C Cup	5	0	4	4	....	....	....	2	....	....	....	....	....	....	....	....	....	....	....	....	....	....	....	....	....	....
	New Jersey Devils	NHL	80	22	35	57	18	24	42	38	10	0	2	170	12.9	75	28	68	3	–18	....	....	....	....	....	....	....	....
	United States	WEC-A	10	0	1	1	....	....	....	8	....	....	....	....	....	....	....	....	....	....	....	....	....	....	....	....	....	....
1985-86	New Jersey Devils	NHL	66	18	25	43	14	17	31	26	4	0	1	157	11.5	67	16	77	28	+2	....	....	....	....	....	....	....	....
	United States	WEC-A	10	2	6	8	....	....	....	14	....	....	....	....	....	....	....	....	....	....	....	....	....	....	....	....	....	....
1986-87	New Jersey Devils	NHL	80	26	53	79	23	38	61	36	6	0	3	179	14.5	107	40	83	21	+5	....	....	....	....	....	....	....	....
	United States	WEC-A	10	5	6	11	....	....	....	6	....	....	....	....	....	....	....	....	....	....	....	....	....	....	....	....	....	....
1987-88	United States	C Cup	5	0	2	2	....	....	....	2	....	....	....	....	....	....	....	....	....	....	....	....	....	....	....	....	....	....
	New Jersey Devils	NHL	80	26	57	83	22	41	63	80	7	2	4	180	14.4	125	49	67	11	+20	20	5	11	16	20	3	0	1
1988-89	New Jersey Devils	NHL	80	16	43	59	14	30	44	81	4	0	2	178	9.0	99	40	98	32	–7	....	....	....	....	....	....	....	....
1989-90	New Jersey Devils	NHL	42	10	8	18	9	6	15	36	1	2	0	83	12.0	24	4	46	11	–15	....	....	....	....	....	....	....	....
	Minnesota North Stars	NHL	35	9	9	18	8	6	14	22	0	0	2	65	13.8	26	4	31	1	–8	7	0	5	5	8	0	0	0
1990-91	Minnesota North Stars	FrTour	3	1	0	1	....	....	....	2	....	....	....	....	....	....	....	....	....	....	....	....	....	....	....	....	....	....
	Quebec Nordiques	NHL	20	5	4	9	5	3	8	6	1	0	0	40	12.5	13	2	30	16	–3	....	....	....	....	....	....	....	....
	Toronto Maple Leafs	NHL	27	6	4	10	5	3	8	32	0	0	1	45	13.3	16	1	10	7	+12	....	....	....	....	....	....	....	....
1991-92	Winnipeg Jets	NHL	25	4	5	9	4	4	8	14	0	0	3	29	13.8	12	1	11	2	+2	7	2	2	4	12	0	0	0
	Moncton Hawks	AHL	4	0	2	2	....	....	....	0	....	....	....	....	....	....	....	....	....	....	....	....	....	....	....	....	....	....
	NHL Totals		748	186	329	515	157	231	388	441	46	6	25	1422	13.1	772	269	730	158		34	7	18	25	40	3	0	1

WCHA First All-Star Team (1981) • NCAA Championship All-Tournament Team (1981)

Transferred to **New Jersey** after **Colorado** franchise relocated, June 30, 1982. Traded to **Minnesota** by **New Jersey** for Bob Brooke, January 5, 1990. Claimed by **Quebec** from **Minnesota** in Waiver Draft, October 1, 1990. Traded to **Toronto** by **Quebec** with Lucien DeBlois and Michel Petit for Scott Pearson and Toronto's 2nd round choices in 1991 (later traded to Washington—Washington selected Eric Lavigne) and 1992 (Toumas Gronman) Entry Drafts, November 17, 1990. Signed as a free agent by **Winnipeg**, January 21, 1992.

• BROTEN, NEAL

Neal Broten C – L. 5'9", 175 lbs. b: Roseau, MN, 11/29/1959. Minnesota's 3rd choice, 42nd overall, in 1979 Entry Draft.

1978-79	University of Minnesota	WCHA	40	21	50	71	....	....	....	18	....	....	....	....	....	....	....	....	....	....	....	....	....	....	....	....	....	....
	United States	WJC-A	5	2	4	6	....	....	....	10	....	....	....	....	....	....	....	....	....	....	....	....	....	....	....	....	....	....
1979-80	United States	Nat-Team	55	25	30	55	....	....	....	20	....	....	....	....	....	....	....	....	....	....	....	....	....	....	....	....	....	....
	United States	Olympics	7	2	1	3	....	....	....	2	....	....	....	....	....	....	....	....	....	....	....	....	....	....	....	....	....	....
1980-81	University of Minnesota	WCHA	36	17	54	71	....	....	....	56	....	....	....	....	....	....	....	....	....	....	....	....	....	....	....	....	....	....
	Minnesota North Stars	NHL	3	2	0	2	2	0	2	12	0	0	0	6	33.3	3	0	2	0	+1	19	1	7	8	9	0	0	1
1981-82	United States	C Cup	6	3	2	5	....	....	....	0	....	....	....	....	....	....	....	....	....	....	....	....	....	....	....	....	....	....
	Minnesota North Stars	NHL	73	38	60	98	30	40	70	42	7	2	4	188	20.2	123	38	91	20	+14	4	0	2	2	0	0	0	0
1982-83	Minnesota North Stars	NHL	79	32	45	77	26	31	57	43	8	2	4	165	19.4	115	37	62	8	+24	9	1	6	7	10	1	0	0
1983-84	Minnesota North Stars	NHL	76	28	61	89	23	41	64	43	8	3	5	185	15.1	132	53	90	27	+16	16	5	5	10	4	2	0	1
1984-85	United States	C Cup	6	3	1	4	....	....	....	4	....	....	....	....	....	....	....	....	....	....	....	....	....	....	....	....	....	....
	Minnesota North Stars	NHL	80	19	37	56	16	25	41	39	5	1	1	188	10.1	93	39	98	26	–18	9	2	5	7	10	0	0	0
1985-86	Minnesota North Stars	NHL	80	29	76	105	23	51	74	47	6	0	0	193	15.0	150	60	81	5	+14	5	3	2	5	2	1	0	0
1986-87	Minnesota North Stars	NHL	46	18	35	53	16	25	41	33	5	1	4	112	16.1	85	37	47	11	+12	....	....	....	....	....	....	....	....
1987-88	Minnesota North Stars	NHL	54	9	30	39	8	21	29	32	4	1	0	121	7.4	70	36	73	16	–23	....	....	....	....	....	....	....	....
1988-89	Minnesota North Stars	NHL	68	18	38	56	15	27	42	57	4	5	1	160	11.3	75	28	65	19	+1	5	2	2	4	4	1	1	0
1989-90	Minnesota North Stars	NHL	80	23	62	85	20	44	64	45	9	1	4	212	10.8	123	55	111	27	–16	7	2	2	4	18	1	0	0
	United States	WEC-A	8	1	5	6	....	....	....	4	....	....	....	....	....	....	....	....	....	....	....	....	....	....	....	....	....	....
1990-91	Minnesota North Stars	FrTour	3	0	3	3	....	....	....	2	....	....	....	....	....	....	....	....	....	....	....	....	....	....	....	....	....	....
	Minnesota North Stars	NHL	79	13	56	69	12	43	55	26	1	2	0	191	6.8	104	50	89	32	–3	23	9	13	22	6	2	1	0
1991-92	Preussen	Germany	8	3	5	8	....	....	....	2	....	....	....	....	....	....	....	....	....	....	....	....	....	....	....	....	....	....
	Minnesota North Stars	NHL	76	8	26	34	7	20	27	16	4	1	1	119	6.7	62	32	82	37	–15	7	1	5	6	2	0	0	0
1992-93	Minnesota North Stars	NHL	82	12	21	33	10	14	24	22	0	3	3	123	9.8	57	5	94	49	+7	....	....	....	....	....	....	....	....
1993-94	Dallas Stars	NHL	79	17	35	52	16	27	43	62	2	1	1	153	11.1	85	21	85	31	+10	9	2	1	3	6	0	0	1
1994-95	Dallas Stars	NHL	17	0	4	4	0	6	6	4	0	0	0	29	0.0	6	1	21	8	–8	....	....	....	....	....	....	....	....
	New Jersey Devils	NHL	30	8	20	28	14	29	43	20	2	0	3	43	18.6	34	7	26	8	+9	20	7	12	19	6	1	0	4
1995-96	New Jersey Devils	NHL	55	7	16	23	7	13	20	14	1	1	1	73	9.6	42	15	53	23	–3	....	....	....	....	....	....	....	....
1996-97	New Jersey Devils	NHL	3	0	1	1	0	1	1	0	0	0	0	3	0.0	2	1	2	0	–1	....	....	....	....	....	....	....	....
	Los Angeles Kings	NHL	19	0	4	4	0	4	4	0	0	0	0	17	0.0	10	3	18	2	–9	....	....	....	....	....	....	....	....
	Phoenix Roadrunners	IHL	11	3	3	6	....	....	....	4	....	....	....	....	....	....	....	....	....	....	....	....	....	....	....	....	....	....
	Dallas Stars	NHL	20	8	7	15	8	6	14	12	1	1	2	35	22.9	15	1	13	5	+6	2	0	1	1	0	0	0	0
	NHL Totals		1099	289	634	923	253	468	721	569	67	25	34	2316	12.5	1386	519	1203	354		135	35	63	98	77	9	2	7

WCHA First All-Star Team (1981) • NCAA West First All-American Team (1981) • Won Hobey Baker Memorial Award (Top U.S. Collegiate Player) (1981)

Played in NHL All-Star Game (1983, 1986)

Transferred to **Dallas** after **Minnesota** franchise relocated, June 9, 1993. Traded to **New Jersey** by **Dallas** for Corey Millen, February 27, 1995. Traded to **LA Kings** by **New Jersey** for future considerations, November 22, 1996. Claimed on waivers by **Dallas** from **LA Kings**, January 28, 1997.

• BROTEN, PAUL

Paul Broten RW – R. 5'11", 188 lbs. b: Roseau, MN, 10/27/1965. NY Rangers' 3rd choice, 77th overall, in 1984 Entry Draft.

1983-84	Roseau High School	H.S.	26	26	29	55	....	....	....	4	....	....	....	....	....	....	....	....	....	....	....	....	....	....	....	....	....	....
1984-85	University of Minnesota	WCHA	44	8	8	16	....	....	....	26	....	....	....	....	....	....	....	....	....	....	....	....	....	....	....	....	....	....
1985-86	University of Minnesota	WCHA	38	6	16	22	....	....	....	24	....	....	....	....	....	....	....	....	....	....	....	....	....	....	....	....	....	....
1986-87	University of Minnesota	WCHA	48	17	22	39	....	....	....	52	....	....	....	....	....	....	....	....	....	....	....	....	....	....	....	....	....	....
1987-88	University of Minnesota	WCHA	38	18	21	39	....	....	....	42	....	....	....	....	....	....	....	....	....	....	....	....	....	....	....	....	....	....
1988-89	Denver Rangers	IHL	77	28	31	59	....	....	....	133	....	....	....	....	....	....	....	....	....	....	4	0	2	2	6	....	....	....
1989-90	New York Rangers	NHL	32	5	3	8	4	2	6	26	0	0	0	43	11.6	10	0	23	9	–4	6	1	1	2	2	0	1	0
	Flint Spirits	IHL	28	17	9	26	....	....	....	55	....	....	....	....	....	....	....	....	....	....	....	....	....	....	....	....	....	....
1990-91	New York Rangers	NHL	28	4	6	10	4	5	9	18	0	0	0	34	11.8	15	0	13	5	+7	5	0	0	0	2	0	0	0
	Binghamton Rangers	AHL	8	2	2	4	....	....	....	4	....	....	....	....	....	....	....	....	....	....	....	....	....	....	....	....	....	....
1991-92	New York Rangers	NHL	74	13	15	28	12	11	23	102	0	3	1	96	13.5	46	0	52	20	+14	13	1	2	3	10	0	0	0
1992-93	New York Rangers	NHL	60	5	9	14	4	6	10	48	0	1	0	57	8.8	19	0	52	27	–6	....	....	....	....	....	....	....	....
1993-94	Dallas Stars	NHL	64	12	12	24	11	9	20	30	0	0	3	76	15.8	39	1	26	6	+18	9	1	1	2	2	0	0	0
1994-95	Dallas Stars	NHL	47	7	9	16	12	13	25	36	0	0	0	67	10.4	27	2	37	5	–7	5	1	2	3	2	0	0	0

			REGULAR SEASON																		PLAYOFFS							
Season	Club	League	GP	G	A	Pts	AG	AA	APts	PIM	PP	SH	GW	S	%	TGF	PGF	TGA	PGA	+/–	GP	G	A	Pts	PIM	PP	SH	GW
1995-96	**St. Louis Blues**	**NHL**	**17**	**0**	**1**	**1**	**0**	**1**	**1**	**4**	**0**	**0**	**0**	**11**	**0.0**	**3**	**0**	**4**	**0**	**–1**	....	....	....	....	....	....	....	....
	Worcester IceCats	AHL	50	22	21	43	....	....	....	42	....	....	....	....	....	....	....	....	....	....	3	0	0	0	0	....	....	....
1996-97	Fort Wayne Komets	IHL	59	19	28	47	....	....	....	82	....	....	....	....	....	....	....	....	....	....	....	....	....	....	....	....	....	....
1997-98	Cincinnati Cyclones	IHL	81	9	12	21	....	....	....	80	....	....	....	....	....	....	....	....	....	....	9	3	1	4	8	....	....	....
	NHL Totals		**322**	**46**	**55**	**101**	**47**	**47**	**94**	**264**	**0**	**4**	**4**	**384**	**12.0**	**159**	**3**	**207**	**72**		**38**	**4**	**6**	**10**	**18**	**0**	**1**	**0**

Claimed by **Dallas** from **NY Rangers** in Waiver Draft, October 3, 1993. Traded to **St. Louis** by **Dallas** for Guy Carbonneau, October 2, 1995.

• BROUSSEAU, PAUL

Paul Brousseau RW – R. 6'2", 203 lbs. b: Pierrefonds, Que., 9/18/1973. Quebec's 2nd choice, 28th overall, in 1992 Entry Draft.

Season	Club	League	GP	G	A	Pts	AG	AA	APts	PIM	PP	SH	GW	S	%	TGF	PGF	TGA	PGA	+/–	GP	G	A	Pts	PIM	PP	SH	GW
1989-90	Chicoutimi Sagueneens	QMJHL	57	17	24	41	....	....	....	32	....	....	....	....	....	....	....	....	....	....	7	0	3	3	0	....	....	....
1990-91	Trois-Rivières Draveurs	QMJHL	67	30	66	96	....	....	....	48	....	....	....	....	....	....	....	....	....	....	6	3	2	5	2	....	....	....
1991-92	Hull Olympiques	QMJHL	57	35	61	96	....	....	....	54	....	....	....	....	....	....	....	....	....	....	6	3	5	8	10	....	....	....
1992-93	Hull Olympiques	QMJHL	59	27	48	75	....	....	....	49	....	....	....	....	....	....	....	....	....	....	10	7	8	15	6	....	....	....
1993-94	Cornwall Aces	AHL	69	18	26	44	....	....	....	35	....	....	....	....	....	....	....	....	....	....	1	0	0	0	0	....	....	....
1994-95	Cornwall Aces	AHL	57	19	17	36	....	....	....	29	....	....	....	....	....	....	....	....	....	....	7	2	1	3	10	....	....	....
1995-96	**Colorado Avalanche**	**NHL**	**8**	**1**	**1**	**2**	**1**	**1**	**2**	**2**	**0**	**0**	**0**	**10**	**10.0**	**1**	**0**	**3**	**0**	**+1**		....	....	....	....	....	....	....
	Cornwall Aces	AHL	63	21	22	43	....	....	....	60	....	....	....	....	....	....	....	....	....	....	8	4	0	4	2	....	....	....
1996-97	**Tampa Bay Lightning**	**NHL**	**6**	**0**	**0**	**0**	**0**	**0**	**0**	**0**	**0**	**0**	**0**	**3**	**0.0**	**0**	**0**	**4**	**0**	**–4**	....	....	....	....	....	....	....	....
	Adirondack Red Wings	AHL	66	35	31	66	....	....	....	25	....	....	....	....	....	....	....	....	....	....	4	1	2	3	0	....	....	....
1997-98	**Tampa Bay Lightning**	**NHL**	**11**	**0**	**2**	**2**	**0**	**2**	**2**	**27**	**0**	**0**	**0**	**6**	**0.0**	**4**	**0**	**4**	**0**	**0**	....	....	....	....	....	....	....	....
	Adirondack Red Wings	AHL	67	45	20	65	....	....	....	18	....	....	....	....	....	....	....	....	....	....	3	1	1	2	0	....	....	....
	NHL Totals		**25**	**1**	**3**	**4**	**1**	**3**	**4**	**29**	**0**	**0**	**0**	**19**	**5.3**	**8**	**0**	**11**	**0**		....	....	....	....	....	....	....	....

Rights transferred to **Colorado** after **Quebec** franchise relocated, June 21, 1995. Signed as a free agent by **Tampa Bay**, September 10, 1996. Claimed by **Nashville** from **Tampa Bay** in Expansion Draft, June 26, 1998.

• BROWN, ARNIE

Arnie Brown D – L. 6'1", 185 lbs. b: Oshawa, Ont., 1/28/1942.

Season	Club	League	GP	G	A	Pts	AG	AA	APts	PIM	PP	SH	GW	S	%	TGF	PGF	TGA	PGA	+/–	GP	G	A	Pts	PIM	PP	SH	GW
1959-60	St. Michael's Majors	OHA	48	2	5	7	....	....	....	112	....	....	....	....	....	....	....	....	....	....	10	0	2	2	14	....	....	....
1960-61	St. Michael's Majors	OHA	47	7	11	18	....	....	....	110	....	....	....	....	....	....	....	....	....	....	20	6	9	15	60	....	....	....
1961-62	Toronto Marlboros	OHA	19	7	10	17	....	....	....	70	....	....	....	....	....	....	....	....	....	....	7	0	8	8	23	....	....	....
	Rochester Americans	AHL	3	0	3	3	....	....	....	2	....	....	....	....	....	....	....	....	....	....	....	....	....	....	....	....	....	....
	Toronto Maple Leafs	**NHL**	**2**	**0**	**0**	**0**	**0**	**0**	**0**	**0**	....	....	....	....	....	....	....	....	....	....	....	....	....	....	....	....	....	....
1962-63	Rochester Americans	AHL	71	4	24	28	....	....	....	143	....	....	....	....	....	....	....	....	....	....	2	0	0	0	6	....	....	....
1963-64	**Toronto Maple Leafs**	**NHL**	**4**	**0**	**0**	**0**	**0**	**0**	**0**	**6**	....	....	....	....	....	....	....	....	....	....	....	....	....	....	....	....	....	....
	Rochester Americans	AHL	47	4	23	27	....	....	....	119	....	....	....	....	....	....	....	....	....	....	....	....	....	....	....	....	....	....
	Baltimore Clippers	AHL	11	0	3	3	....	....	....	8	....	....	....	....	....	....	....	....	....	....	....	....	....	....	....	....	....	....
1964-65	**New York Rangers**	**NHL**	**58**	**1**	**11**	**12**	**1**	**12**	**13**	**145**	....	....	....	....	....	....	....	....	....	....	....	....	....	....	....	....	....	....
1965-66	**New York Rangers**	**NHL**	**64**	**1**	**7**	**8**	**1**	**7**	**8**	**106**	....	....	....	....	....	....	....	....	....	....	....	....	....	....	....	....	....	....
1966-67	**New York Rangers**	**NHL**	**69**	**2**	**10**	**12**	**2**	**10**	**12**	**61**	....	....	....	....	....	....	....	....	....	....	**4**	**0**	**0**	**0**	**6**	....	....	....
1967-68	**New York Rangers**	**NHL**	**74**	**1**	**25**	**26**	**1**	**26**	**27**	**83**	**0**	**0**	**0**	**116**	**0.9**	**84**	**1**	**90**	**24**	**+17**	**6**	**0**	**1**	**1**	**8**	**0**	**0**	**0**
1968-69	**New York Rangers**	**NHL**	**74**	**10**	**12**	**22**	**11**	**11**	**22**	**48**	**0**	**0**	**1**	**189**	**5.3**	**74**	**4**	**91**	**22**	**+1**	**4**	**0**	**1**	**1**	**0**	**0**	**0**	**0**
1969-70	**New York Rangers**	**NHL**	**73**	**15**	**21**	**36**	**17**	**21**	**38**	**78**	**3**	**0**	**2**	**220**	**6.8**	**118**	**18**	**91**	**19**	**+28**	**4**	**0**	**4**	**4**	**9**	**0**	**0**	**0**
1970-71	**New York Rangers**	**NHL**	**48**	**3**	**12**	**15**	**3**	**11**	**14**	**24**	**0**	**0**	**2**	**114**	**2.6**	**53**	**11**	**52**	**10**	**0**	....	....	....	....	....	....	....	....
	Detroit Red Wings	**NHL**	**27**	**2**	**6**	**8**	**2**	**5**	**7**	**30**	....	....	....	....	....	....	....	....	....	....	....	....	....	....	....	....	....	....
1971-72	**Detroit Red Wings**	**NHL**	**77**	**2**	**23**	**25**	**2**	**21**	**23**	**84**	**0**	**0**	**0**	**0**	**0.0**	**0**	**0**	**0**	**0**	**0**	....	....	....	....	....	....	....	....
1972-73	**New York Islanders**	**NHL**	**48**	**4**	**8**	**12**	**4**	**7**	**11**	**27**	**1**	**0**	**0**	**50**	**8.0**	**40**	**6**	**101**	**20**	**–47**	....	....	....	....	....	....	....	....
	Atlanta Flames	**NHL**	**15**	**1**	**0**	**1**	**1**	**0**	**1**	**17**	**0**	**0**	**0**	**13**	**7.7**	**6**	**0**	**17**	**1**	**–10**	....	....	....	....	....	....	....	....
1973-74	**Atlanta Flames**	**NHL**	**48**	**2**	**6**	**8**	**2**	**5**	**7**	**29**	**0**	**0**	**0**	**58**	**3.4**	**35**	**0**	**52**	**3**	**–14**	**4**	**0**	**0**	**0**	**0**	**0**	**0**	**0**
1974-75	Michigan-Baltimore	WHA	50	3	4	7	....	....	....	27	....	....	....	....	....	....	....	....	....	....	....	....	....	....	....	....	....	....
	Vancouver Blazers	WHA	10	0	1	1	....	....	....	13	....	....	....	....	....	....	....	....	....	....	....	....	....	....	....	....	....	....
	NHL Totals		**681**	**44**	**141**	**185**	**47**	**136**	**183**	**738**	**4**	**0**	**5**	**760**	**5.8**	**410**	**40**	**494**	**99**		**22**	**0**	**6**	**6**	**23**	**0**	**0**	**0**
	Other Major League Totals		60	3	5	8	....	....	....	40	....	....	....	....	....	....	....	....	....		....	....	....	....	....	....	....	....

Traded to **NY Rangers** by **Toronto** with Rod Seiling, Dick Duff, Bob Nevin and Bill Collins for Andy Bathgate and Don McKenney, February 22, 1964. Traded to **Detroit** by **NY Rangers** with Mike Robitaille and Tom Miller for Bruce MacGregor and Larry Brown, February 2, 1970. Selected by **Chicago** (WHA) in 1972 WHA General Player Draft, February 12, 1972. Traded to **NY Islanders** by **Detroit** with Gerry Gray for Denis Dejordy and Don McLaughlin, October 4, 1972. Traded to **Atlanta** by **NY Islanders** for Ernie Hicks and future considerations (Billy MacMillan, May 29, 1973), February 13, 1973. WHA rights traded to **Michigan** (WHA) by **Chicago** for cash, October, 1974. Signed as a free agent by **Vancouver** (WHA) after **Michigan-Baltimore** (WHA) franchise folded, March, 1975.

• BROWN, BRAD

Brad Brown D – R. 6'3", 220 lbs. b: Baie Verte, Nfld., 12/27/1975. Montreal's 1st choice, 18th overall, in 1994 Entry Draft.

Season	Club	League	GP	G	A	Pts	AG	AA	APts	PIM	PP	SH	GW	S	%	TGF	PGF	TGA	PGA	+/–	GP	G	A	Pts	PIM	PP	SH	GW
1991-92	North Bay Centennials	OHL	49	2	9	11	....	....	....	170	....	....	....	....	....	....	....				18	0	6	6	43	....	....	....
1992-93	North Bay Centennials	OHL	61	4	9	13	....	....	....	228	....	....	....	....	....	....	....	....	....	....	2	0	2	2	13	....	....	....
1993-94	North Bay Centennials	OHL	66	8	24	32	....	....	....	196	....	....	....	....	....	....	....	....	....		18	3	12	15	33	....	....	....
1994-95	North Bay Centennials	OHL	64	8	38	46	....	....	....	172	....	....	....	....	....	....	....	....	....	....	6	1	4	5	8	....	....	....
1995-96	Barrie Colts	OHL	27	3	13	16	....	....	....	82	....	....	....	....	....	....	....	....	....	....								
	Fredericton Canadiens	AHL	38	0	3	3	....	....	....	148	....	....	....	....	....	....	....	....	....	....	10	2	1	3	6	....	....	....
1996-97	**Montreal Canadiens**	**NHL**	**8**	**0**	**0**	**0**	**0**	**0**	**0**	**22**	**0**	**0**	**0**	**0**	**0.0**	**2**	**0**	**3**	**0**	**–1**	....	....	....	....	....	....	....	....
	Fredericton Canadiens	AHL	64	3	7	10	....	....	....	368	....	....	....	....	....	....	....	....	....	....	....	....	....	....	....	....	....	....
1997-98	Fredericton Canadiens	AHL	64	1	8	9	....	....	....	297	....	....	....	....	....	....	....	....	....	....	4	0	0	0	29	....	....	....
	NHL Totals		**8**	**0**	**0**	**0**	**0**	**0**	**0**	**22**	**0**	**0**	**0**	**0**	**0.0**	**2**	**0**	**3**	**0**		....	....	....	....	....	....	....	....

• BROWN, CAM

Cam Brown LW – L. 6'1", 210 lbs. b: Saskatoon, Sask., 5/15/1969.

Season	Club	League	GP	G	A	Pts	AG	AA	APts	PIM	PP	SH	GW	S	%	TGF	PGF	TGA	PGA	+/–	GP	G	A	Pts	PIM	PP	SH	GW
1987-88	Brandon Wheat Kings	WHL	69	2	13	15	....	....	....	185	....	....	....	....	....	....	....	....	....	....	4	1	1	2	15	....	....	....
1988-89	Brandon Wheat Kings	WHL	72	17	42	59	....	....	....	225	....	....	....	....	....	....	....	....	....	....	....	....	....	....	....	....	....	....
1989-90	Brandon Wheat Kings	WHL	68	34	41	75	....	....	....	182	....	....	....	....	....	....	....	....	....	....	....	....	....	....	....	....	....	....
1990-91	**Vancouver Canucks**	**NHL**	**1**	**0**	**0**	**0**	**0**	**0**	**0**	**7**	**0**	**0**	**0**	**0**	**0.0**	**0**	**0**	**0**	**0**	**0**	....	....	....	....	....	....	....	....
	Milwaukee Admirals	IHL	74	11	13	24	....	....	....	218	....	....	....	....	....	....	....	....	....	....	3	0	0	0	0	....	....	....
1991-92	Milwaukee Admirals	IHL	51	6	8	14	....	....	....	179	....	....	....	....	....	....	....	....	....	....	1	0	0	0	0	....	....	....
	Columbus Chill	ECHL	10	11	6	17	....	....	....	64	....	....	....	....	....	....	....	....	....	....	....	....	....	....	....	....	....	....
1992-93	Hamilton Canucks	AHL	1	0	0	0	....	....	....	2	....	....	....	....	....	....	....	....	....	....	....	....	....	....	....	....	....	....
	Rochester Americans	AHL	4	0	0	0	....	....	....	26	....	....	....	....	....	....	....	....	....	....	....	....	....	....	....	....	....	....
	Columbus Chill	ECHL	36	13	18	31	....	....	....	218	....	....	....	....	....	....	....	....	....	....	....	....	....	....	....	....	....	....
	Erie Panthers	ECHL	15	4	3	7	....	....	....	50	....	....	....	....	....	....	....	....	....	....	5	0	1	1	62	....	....	....
1993-94				DID NOT PLAY																								
1994-95	Erie Panthers	ECHL	60	14	28	42	....	....	....	341	....	....	....	....	....	....	....	....	....	....	....	....	....	....	....	....	....	....
	NHL Totals		**1**	**0**	**0**	**0**	**0**	**0**	**0**	**7**	**0**	**0**	**0**	**0**	**0.0**	**0**	**0**	**0**	**0**		....	....	....	....	....	....	....	....

Signed as a free agent by **Vancouver**, April 6, 1990.

• BROWN, CURTIS

Curtis Brown C – L. 6', 190 lbs. b: Unity, Sask., 2/12/1976. Buffalo's 2nd choice, 43rd overall, in 1994 Entry Draft.

Season	Club	League	GP	G	A	Pts	AG	AA	APts	PIM	PP	SH	GW	S	%	TGF	PGF	TGA	PGA	+/–	GP	G	A	Pts	PIM	PP	SH	GW
1992-93	Moose Jaw Warriors	WHL	71	13	16	29	....	....	....	30	....	....	....	....	....	....	....	....	....	....	....	....	....	....	....	....	....	....
1993-94	Moose Jaw Warriors	WHL	72	27	38	65	....	....	....	82	....	....	....	....	....	....	....	....	....	....	....	....	....	....	....	....	....	....
1994-95	Moose Jaw Wariors	WHL	70	51	53	104	....	....	....	63	....	....	....	....	....	....	....	....	....	....	10	8	7	15	20	....	....	....
	Buffalo Sabres	**NHL**	**1**	**1**	**1**	**2**	**2**	**1**	**3**	**2**	**0**	**0**	**0**	**4**	**25.0**	**3**	**0**	**1**	**0**	**+2**	....	....	....	....	....	....	....	....
1995-96	Moose Jaw Warriors	WHL	25	20	18	38	....	....	....	30	....	....	....	....	....	....	....	....	....	....	....	....	....	....	....	....	....	....
	Canada	WJC-A	5	0	1	1	....	....	....	2	....	....	....	....	....	....	....	....	....	....	....	....	....	....	....	....	....	....
	Prince Albert Raiders	WHL	19	12	21	33	....	....	....	8	....	....	....	....	....	....	....	....	....	....	18	10	15	25	18	....	....	....
	Buffalo Sabres	**NHL**	**4**	**0**	**0**	**0**	**0**	**0**	**0**	**0**	**0**	**0**	**0**	**1**	**0.0**	**0**	**0**	**0**	**0**	**0**	....	....	....	....	....	....	....	....
	Rochester Americans	AHL	....	....	....	....	....	....	....	....	....	....	....	....	....	....	....	....	....	....	12	0	1	1	2	....	....	....

			REGULAR SEASON																		PLAYOFFS							
Season	**Club**	**League**	**GP**	**G**	**A**	**Pts**	**AG**	**AA**	**APts**	**PIM**	**PP**	**SH**	**GW**	**S**	**%**	**TGF**	**PGF**	**TGA**	**PGA**	**+/–**	**GP**	**G**	**A**	**Pts**	**PIM**	**PP**	**SH**	**GW**
1996-97	**Buffalo Sabres**	**NHL**	**28**	**4**	**3**	**7**	**4**	**3**	**7**	**18**	**0**	**0**	**1**	**31**	**12.9**	**12**	**0**	**8**	**0**	**+4**	....	....	....	....	....	....	....	....
	Rochester Americans	AHL	51	22	21	43	....	....	....	30	....	....	....	....	....	....	....	....	....	....	10	4	6	10	4	....	....	....
1997-98	**Buffalo Sabres**	**NHL**	**63**	**12**	**12**	**24**	**14**	**12**	**26**	**34**	**1**	**1**	**2**	**91**	**13.2**	**41**	**8**	**29**	**7**	**+11**	**13**	**1**	**2**	**3**	**10**	**1**	**0**	**0**
	NHL Totals		**96**	**17**	**16**	**33**	**20**	**16**	**36**	**54**	**1**	**1**	**3**	**127**	**13.4**	**56**	**8**	**38**	**7**		**13**	**1**	**2**	**3**	**10**	**1**	**0**	**0**

WHL East First All-Star Team (1995) • WHL East Second All-Star Team (1996)

• BROWN, DAVID

David Brown RW – R. 6'5", 222 lbs. b: Saskatoon, Sask., 10/12/1962. Philadelphia's 7th choice, 140th overall, in 1982 Entry Draft.

Season	Club	League	GP	G	A	Pts	AG	AA	APts	PIM	PP	SH	GW	S	%	TGF	PGF	TGA	PGA	+/–	GP	G	A	Pts	PIM	PP	SH	GW
1980-81	Spokane Flyers	WHL	9	2	2	4	....	....	....	21	....	....	....	....	....	....	....	....	....	....	....	....	....	....	....	....	....	....
1981-82	Saskatoon Blades	WHL	62	11	33	44	....	....	....	344	....	....	....	....	....	....	....	....	....	....	5	1	0	1	4	....	....	....
1982-83	**Philadelphia Flyers**	**NHL**	**2**	**0**	**0**	**0**	**0**	**0**	**0**	**5**	**0**	**0**	**0**	**2**	**0.0**	**0**	**0**	**1**	**0**	**–1**	....	....	....	....	....	....	....	....
	Maine Mariners	AHL	71	8	6	14	....	....	....	*418	....	....	....	....	....	....	....	....	....	....	16	0	0	0	*107	....	....	....
1983-84	**Philadelphia Flyers**	**NHL**	**19**	**1**	**5**	**6**	**1**	**3**	**4**	**98**	**0**	**0**	**0**	**9**	**11.1**	**8**	**1**	**3**	**0**	**+4**	**2**	**0**	**0**	**0**	**12**	**0**	**0**	**0**
	Springfield Indians	AHL	59	17	14	31	....	....	....	150	....	....	....	....	....	....	....	....	....	....	....	....	....	....	....	....	....	....
1984-85	**Philadelphia Flyers**	**NHL**	**57**	**3**	**6**	**9**	**2**	**4**	**6**	**165**	**0**	**0**	**1**	**53**	**5.7**	**15**	**0**	**18**	**0**	**–3**	**11**	**0**	**0**	**0**	**59**	**0**	**0**	**0**
1985-86	**Philadelphia Flyers**	**NHL**	**76**	**10**	**7**	**17**	**8**	**5**	**13**	**277**	**0**	**0**	**1**	**73**	**13.7**	**23**	**1**	**16**	**1**	**+7**	**5**	**0**	**0**	**0**	**16**	**0**	**0**	**0**
1986-87	**Philadelphia Flyers**	**NHL**	**62**	**7**	**3**	**10**	**6**	**2**	**8**	**274**	**0**	**0**	**0**	**53**	**13.2**	**17**	**0**	**24**	**0**	**–7**	**26**	**1**	**2**	**3**	**59**	**0**	**0**	**0**
1987-88	**Philadelphia Flyers**	**NHL**	**47**	**12**	**5**	**17**	**10**	**4**	**14**	**114**	**0**	**0**	**4**	**41**	**29.3**	**26**	**0**	**16**	**0**	**+10**	**7**	**1**	**0**	**1**	**27**	**0**	**0**	**0**
1988-89	**Philadelphia Flyers**	**NHL**	**50**	**0**	**3**	**3**	**0**	**2**	**2**	**100**	**0**	**0**	**0**	**28**	**0.0**	**6**	**0**	**14**	**0**	**–8**	....	....	....	....	....	....	....	....
	Edmonton Oilers	**NHL**	**22**	**0**	**2**	**2**	**0**	**1**	**1**	**56**	**0**	**0**	**0**	**14**	**0.0**	**5**	**0**	**9**	**0**	**–4**	**7**	**0**	**0**	**0**	**6**	**0**	**0**	**0**
1989-90	**Edmonton Oilers**	**NHL**	**60**	**0**	**6**	**6**	**0**	**4**	**4**	**145**	**0**	**0**	**0**	**32**	**0.0**	**9**	**0**	**12**	**0**	**–3**	**3**	**0**	**0**	**0**	**0**	**0**	**0**	**0**
1990-91	**Edmonton Oilers**	**NHL**	**58**	**3**	**4**	**7**	**3**	**3**	**6**	**160**	**0**	**0**	**0**	**32**	**9.4**	**10**	**0**	**17**	**0**	**–7**	**16**	**0**	**1**	**1**	**30**	**0**	**0**	**0**
1991-92	**Philadelphia Flyers**	**NHL**	**70**	**4**	**2**	**6**	**4**	**1**	**5**	**81**	**0**	**0**	**0**	**50**	**8.0**	**15**	**0**	**26**	**0**	**–11**	....	....	....	....	....	....	....	....
1992-93	**Philadelphia Flyers**	**NHL**	**70**	**0**	**2**	**2**	**0**	**1**	**1**	**78**	**0**	**0**	**0**	**19**	**0.0**	**8**	**1**	**12**	**0**	**–5**	....	....	....	....	....	....	....	....
1993-94	**Philadelphia Flyers**	**NHL**	**71**	**1**	**4**	**5**	**1**	**3**	**4**	**137**	**0**	**0**	**0**	**16**	**6.3**	**10**	**1**	**21**	**0**	**–12**	....	....	....	....	....	....	....	....
1994-95	**Philadelphia Flyers**	**NHL**	**28**	**1**	**2**	**3**	**2**	**3**	**5**	**53**	**0**	**0**	**0**	**8**	**12.5**	**4**	**1**	**4**	**0**	**–1**	**3**	**0**	**0**	**0**	**0**	**0**	**0**	**0**
1995-96	**San Jose Sharks**	**NHL**	**37**	**3**	**1**	**4**	**3**	**1**	**4**	**46**	**0**	**0**	**0**	**8**	**37.5**	**8**	**0**	**4**	**0**	**+4**	....	....	....	....	....	....	....	....
	NHL Totals		**729**	**45**	**52**	**97**	**40**	**37**	**77**	**1789**	**0**	**0**	**6**	**438**	**10.3**	**164**	**5**	**197**	**1**		**80**	**2**	**3**	**5**	**209**	**0**	**0**	**0**

Traded to **Edmonton** by **Philadelphia** for Keith Acton and Edmonton's 5th round choice (Dmitri Yuskevich) in 1991 Entry Draft, February 7, 1989. Traded to **Philadelphia** by **Edmonton** with Corey Foster for Craig Fisher, Scott Mellanby and Craig Berube, May 30, 1991. Signed as a free agent by **San Jose**, August 10, 1995.

• BROWN, DOUG

Doug Brown RW – R. 5'10", 185 lbs. b: Southborough, MA, 6/12/1964.

Season	Club	League	GP	G	A	Pts	AG	AA	APts	PIM	PP	SH	GW	S	%	TGF	PGF	TGA	PGA	+/–	GP	G	A	Pts	PIM	PP	SH	GW
1982-83	Boston College	ECAC	22	9	8	17	....	....	....	0	....	....	....	....	....	....	....	....	....	....	....	....	....	....	....	....	....	....
1983-84	Boston College	ECAC	38	11	10	21	....	....	....	6	....	....	....	....	....	....	....	....	....	....	....	....	....	....	....	....	....	....
1984-85	Boston College	H.E.	45	37	31	68	....	....	....	10	....	....	....	....	....	....	....	....	....	....	....	....	....	....	....	....	....	....
1985-86	Boston College	H.E.	38	16	40	56	....	....	....	16	....	....	....	....	....	....	....	....	....	....	....	....	....	....	....	....	....	....
	United States	WEC-A	10	2	1	3	....	....	....	2	....	....	....	....	....	....	....	....	....	....	....	....	....	....	....	....	....	....
1986-87	**New Jersey Devils**	**NHL**	**4**	**0**	**1**	**1**	**0**	**1**	**1**	**0**	**0**	**0**	**0**	**10**	**0.0**	**1**	**0**	**6**	**1**	**–4**	....	....	....	....	....	....	....	....
	Maine Mariners	AHL	73	24	34	58	....	....	....	15	....	....	....	....	....	....	....	....	....	....	....	....	....	....	....	....	....	....
1987-88	**New Jersey Devils**	**NHL**	**70**	**14**	**11**	**25**	**12**	**8**	**20**	**20**	**1**	**4**	**2**	**112**	**12.5**	**46**	**4**	**63**	**28**	**+7**	**19**	**5**	**1**	**6**	**6**	**0**	**1**	**1**
	Utica Devils	AHL	2	0	2	2	....	....	....	2	....	....	....	....	....	....	....	....	....	....	....	....	....	....	....	....	....	....
1988-89	**New Jersey Devils**	**NHL**	**63**	**15**	**10**	**25**	**13**	**7**	**20**	**15**	**4**	**0**	**2**	**110**	**13.6**	**38**	**10**	**67**	**32**	**–7**	....	....	....	....	....	....	....	....
	Utica Devils	AHL	4	1	4	5	....	....	....	0	....	....	....	....	....	....	....	....	....	....	....	....	....	....	....	....	....	....
	United States	WEC-A	10	1	2	3	....	....	....	0	....	....	....	....	....	....	....	....	....	....	....	....	....	....	....	....	....	....
1989-90	**New Jersey Devils**	**NHL**	**69**	**14**	**20**	**34**	**12**	**14**	**26**	**16**	**1**	**3**	**3**	**135**	**10.4**	**48**	**5**	**56**	**20**	**+7**	**6**	**0**	**1**	**1**	**2**	**0**	**0**	**0**
1990-91	**New Jersey Devils**	**NHL**	**58**	**14**	**16**	**30**	**13**	**12**	**25**	**4**	**0**	**2**	**2**	**122**	**11.5**	**41**	**0**	**47**	**24**	**+18**	**7**	**2**	**2**	**4**	**2**	**0**	**1**	**0**
	United States	WEC-A	10	0	1	1	....	....	....	0	....	....	....	....	....	....	....	....	....	....	....	....	....	....	....	....	....	....
1991-92	United States	C Cup	8	1	2	3	....	....	....	0	....	....	....	....	....	....	....	....	....	....	....	....	....	....	....	....	....	....
	New Jersey Devils	**NHL**	**71**	**11**	**17**	**28**	**10**	**13**	**23**	**27**	**1**	**2**	**1**	**140**	**7.9**	**42**	**1**	**45**	**21**	**+17**	....	....	....	....	....	....	....	....
1992-93	**New Jersey Devils**	**NHL**	**15**	**0**	**5**	**5**	**0**	**3**	**3**	**2**	**0**	**0**	**0**	**17**	**0.0**	**6**	**0**	**10**	**7**	**+3**	....	....	....	....	....	....	....	....
	Utica Devils	AHL	25	11	17	28	....	....	....	8	....	....	....	....	....	....	....	....	....	....	....	....	....	....	....	....	....	....
1993-94	**Pittsburgh Penguins**	**NHL**	**77**	**18**	**37**	**55**	**17**	**29**	**46**	**18**	**2**	**0**	**1**	**152**	**11.8**	**71**	**4**	**61**	**13**	**+19**	**6**	**0**	**0**	**0**	**2**	**0**	**0**	**0**
1994-95	**Detroit Red Wings**	**NHL**	**45**	**9**	**12**	**21**	**16**	**18**	**34**	**16**	**1**	**1**	**2**	**69**	**13.0**	**33**	**3**	**22**	**6**	**+14**	**18**	**4**	**8**	**12**	**2**	**0**	**1**	**1**
1995-96	**Detroit Red Wings**	**NHL**	**62**	**12**	**15**	**27**	**12**	**12**	**24**	**4**	**0**	**1**	**1**	**115**	**10.4**	**41**	**4**	**37**	**11**	**+11**	**13**	**3**	**3**	**6**	**4**	**0**	**1**	**0**
1996-97	**Detroit Red Wings**	**NHL**	**49**	**6**	**7**	**13**	**6**	**6**	**12**	**8**	**1**	**0**	**0**	**69**	**8.7**	**17**	**2**	**26**	**8**	**–3**	**14**	**3**	**3**	**6**	**2**	**0**	**0**	**0**
1997-98	**Detroit Red Wings**	**NHL**	**80**	**19**	**23**	**42**	**22**	**22**	**44**	**12**	**6**	**1**	**5**	**145**	**13.1**	**63**	**19**	**36**	**9**	**+17**	**9**	**4**	**2**	**6**	**0**	**3**	**0**	**1**
	NHL Totals		**663**	**132**	**174**	**306**	**133**	**145**	**278**	**142**	**17**	**14**	**19**	**1196**	**11.0**	**447**	**52**	**476**	**180**		**92**	**21**	**20**	**41**	**20**	**3**	**4**	**3**

Hockey East Second All-Star Team (1985, 1986)

Signed as a free agent by **New Jersey**, August 6, 1986. Signed as a free agent by **Pittsburgh**, September 28, 1993. Claimed by **Detroit** from **Pittsburgh** in NHL Waiver Draft, January 18, 1995. Claimed by **Nashville** from **Detroit** in Expansion Draft, June 26, 1998. Traded to **Detroit** by **Nashville** for Petr Sykora, Detroit's 3rd round choice in 1999 Entry Draft and future considerations, July 14, 1998.

• BROWN, GREG

Greg Brown D – R. 6', 185 lbs. b: Hartford, CT, 3/7/1968. Buffalo's 2nd choice, 26th overall, in 1986 Entry Draft.

Season	Club	League	GP	G	A	Pts	AG	AA	APts	PIM	PP	SH	GW	S	%	TGF	PGF	TGA	PGA	+/–	GP	G	A	Pts	PIM	PP	SH	GW
1984-85	St. Marks High School	H.S.	24	16	24	40	....	....	....	12	....	....	....	....	....	....	....	....	....	....	....	....	....	....	....	....	....	....
1985-86	St. Marks High School	H.S.	19	22	28	50	....	....	....	30	....	....	....	....	....	....	....	....	....	....	....	....	....	....	....	....	....	....
	United States	WJC-A	7	0	2	2	....	....	....	6	....	....	....	....	....	....	....	....	....	....	....	....	....	....	....	....	....	....
1986-87	Boston College	H.E.	37	10	27	37	....	....	....	22	....	....	....	....	....	....	....	....	....	....	....	....	....	....	....	....	....	....
1987-88	United States	Nat-Team	55	6	29	35	....	....	....	22	....	....	....	....	....	....	....	....	....	....	....	....	....	....	....	....	....	....
	United States	Olympics	6	0	4	4	....	....	....	2	....	....	....	....	....	....	....	....	....	....	....	....	....	....	....	....	....	....
1988-89	Boston College	H.E.	40	9	34	43	....	....	....	24	....	....	....	....	....	....	....	....	....	....	....	....	....	....	....	....	....	....
	United States	WEC-A	10	0	1	1	....	....	....	4	....	....	....	....	....	....	....	....	....	....	....	....	....	....	....	....	....	....
1989-90	Boston College	H.E.	42	5	35	40	....	....	....	42	....	....	....	....	....	....	....	....	....	....	....	....	....	....	....	....	....	....
	United States	WEC-A	10	2	3	5	....	....	....	0	....	....	....	....	....	....	....	....	....	....	....	....	....	....	....	....	....	....
1990-91	**Buffalo Sabres**	**NHL**	**39**	**1**	**2**	**3**	**1**	**2**	**3**	**35**	**0**	**0**	**0**	**26**	**3.8**	**22**	**3**	**39**	**0**	**–20**	....	....	....	....	....	....	....	....
	Rochester Americans	AHL	31	6	17	23	....	....	....	16	....	....	....	....	....	....	....	....	....	....	14	1	4	5	8	....	....	....
1991-92	Rochester Americans	AHL	56	8	30	38	....	....	....	25	....	....	....	....	....	....	....	....	....	....	16	1	5	6	4	....	....	....
	United States	Nat-Team	8	0	0	0	....	....	....	5	....	....	....	....	....	....	....	....	....	....	....	....	....	....	....	....	....	....
	United States	Olympics	7	0	0	0	....	....	....	2	....	....	....	....	....	....	....	....	....	....	....	....	....	....	....	....	....	....
1992-93	**Buffalo Sabres**	**NHL**	**10**	**0**	**1**	**1**	**0**	**1**	**1**	**6**	**0**	**0**	**0**	**10**	**0.0**	**4**	**0**	**11**	**2**	**–5**	....	....	....	....	....	....	....	....
	Rochester Americans	AHL	61	11	38	49	....	....	....	46	....	....	....	....	....	....	....	....	....	....	16	3	8	11	14	....	....	....
1993-94	**Pittsburgh Penguins**	**NHL**	**36**	**3**	**8**	**11**	**3**	**6**	**9**	**28**	....	....	....	....	....	....	....	....	....	....	**6**	**0**	**1**	**1**	**4**	....	....	....
	San Diego Gulls	IHL	42	8	25	33	....	....	....	26	....	....	....	....	....	....	....	....	....	....	....	....	....	....	....	....	....	....
1994-95	Cleveland Lumberjacks	IHL	28	5	14	19	....	....	....	22	....	....	....	....	....	....	....	....	....	....	....	....	....	....	....	....	....	....
	Winnipeg Jets	**NHL**	**9**	**0**	**3**	**3**	**0**	**4**	**4**	**17**	**0**	**0**	**0**	**12**	**0.0**	**11**	**3**	**7**	**0**	**+1**	....	....	....	....	....	....	....	....
1995-96	Rogle BK	Sweden	22	4	7	11	....	....	....	32	....	....	....	....	....	....	....	....	....	....	....	....	....	....	....	....	....	....
1996-97	VEU Feldkirch	Austria	6	0	2	2	....	....	....	8	....	....	....	....	....	....	....	....	....	....	....	....	....	....	....	....	....	....
	EHC Kloten	Switz.	46	3	12	15	....	....	....	36	....	....	....	....	....	....	....	....	....	....	4	1	1	2	2	....	....	....
1997-98	EV Landshut	Germany	48	3	19	22	....	....	....	12	....	....	....	....	....	....	....	....	....	....	6	2	4	6	12	....	....	....
	United States	WC-A	6	0	0	0	....	....	....	0	....	....	....	....	....	....	....	....	....	....	....	....	....	....	....	....	....	....
	NHL Totals		**94**	**4**	**14**	**18**	**4**	**13**	**17**	**86**	**0**	**0**	**0**	**48**	**8.3**	**37**	**6**	**57**	**2**		**6**	**0**	**1**	**1**	**4**	**0**	**0**	**0**

Hockey East First All-Star Team (1989, 1990)

Signed as a free agent by **Pittsburgh**, September 29, 1993. Traded to **Winnipeg** by **Pittsburgh** for future considerations, April 7, 1995.

• BROWN, JEFF

Jeff Brown D – R. 6'1", 204 lbs. b: Ottawa, Ont., 4/30/1966. Quebec's 2nd choice, 36th overall, in 1984 Entry Draft.

Season	Club	League	GP	G	A	Pts	AG	AA	APts	PIM	PP	SH	GW	S	%	TGF	PGF	TGA	PGA	+/–	GP	G	A	Pts	PIM	PP	SH	GW
1982-83	Sudbury Wolves	OHL	65	9	37	46	....	....	....	39	....	....	....	....	....	....	....	....	....	....	....	....	....	....	....	....	....	....
1983-84	Sudbury Wolves	OHL	68	17	60	77	....	....	....	39	....	....	....	....	....	....	....	....	....	....	....	....	....	....	....	....	....	....
1984-85	Sudbury Wolves	OHL	56	16	48	64	....	....	....	26	....	....	....	....	....	....	....	....	....	....	....	....	....	....	....	....	....	....
1985-86	Sudbury Wolves	OHL	45	22	28	50	....	....	....	24	....	....	....	....	....	....	....	....	....	....	4	0	2	2	11	....	....	....
	Quebec Nordiques	**NHL**	**8**	**3**	**2**	**5**	**2**	**1**	**3**	**6**	**0**	**0**	**0**	**16**	**18.8**	**15**	**4**	**6**	**0**	**+5**	**1**	**0**	**0**	**0**	**0**	**0**	**0**	**0**
	Fredericton Express	AHL	....	....	....	....	....	....	....	....	....	....	....	....	....	....	....	....	....	....	1	0	1	1	0	....	....	....
1986-87	**Quebec Nordiques**	**NHL**	**44**	**7**	**22**	**29**	**6**	**16**	**22**	**16**	**3**	**0**	**0**	**99**	**7.1**	**70**	**32**	**29**	**2**	**+11**	**13**	**3**	**3**	**6**	**2**	**2**	**0**	**0**
	Fredericton Express	AHL	26	2	14	16	....	....	....	16	....	....	....	....	....	....	....	....	....	....	....	....	....	....	....	....	....	....

			REGULAR SEASON																		PLAYOFFS							
Season	Club	League	GP	G	A	Pts	AG	AA	APts	PIM	PP	SH	GW	S	%	TGF	PGF	TGA	PGA	+/–	GP	G	A	Pts	PIM	PP	SH	GW
1987-88	Quebec Nordiques	NHL	78	16	36	52	14	26	40	64	9	0	4	208	7.7	126	73	95	17	–25	....	....	....	....	....	....	....	....
1988-89	Quebec Nordiques	NHL	78	21	47	68	18	33	51	62	13	1	1	276	7.6	135	69	116	28	–22	....	....	....	....	....	....	....	....
1989-90	Quebec Nordiques	NHL	29	6	10	16	5	7	12	18	2	0	3	104	5.8	43	20	42	5	–14	....	....	....	....	....	....	....	....
	St. Louis Blues	NHL	48	10	28	38	9	20	29	37	6	1	0	180	5.6	88	44	69	13	–12	12	2	10	12	4	1	0	1
1990-91	St. Louis Blues	NHL	67	12	47	59	11	36	47	39	6	1	0	176	6.8	120	50	86	20	+4	13	3	9	12	6	0	0	0
1991-92	St. Louis Blues	NHL	80	20	39	59	18	29	47	38	10	0	2	214	9.3	135	52	97	22	+8	6	2	1	3	2	0	0	1
1992-93	St. Louis Blues	NHL	71	25	53	78	21	36	57	58	12	2	3	220	11.4	146	75	95	18	–6	11	3	8	11	6	1	0	2
1993-94	St. Louis Blues	NHL	63	13	47	60	12	36	48	46	7	0	3	196	6.6	117	60	91	21	–13	....	....	....	....	....	....	....	....
	Vancouver Canucks	NHL	11	1	5	6	1	4	5	10	0	0	0	41	2.4	14	6	8	2	+2	24	6	9	15	37	3	0	0
1994-95	Vancouver Canucks	NHL	33	8	23	31	14	34	48	16	3	0	0	111	7.2	51	30	34	11	–2	5	1	3	4	2	0	0	0
1995-96	Vancouver Canucks	NHL	28	1	16	17	1	13	14	18	0	0	0	62	1.6	47	14	35	8	+6	....	....	....	....	....	....	....	....
	Hartford Whalers	NHL	48	7	31	38	7	25	32	38	5	0	0	115	6.1	80	36	62	20	+2	....	....	....	....	....	....	....	....
1996-97	Hartford Whalers	NHL	1	0	0	0	0	0	0	0	0	0	0	0	0.0	0	0	0	0	0	....	....	....	....	....	....	....	....
1997-98	Carolina Hurricanes	NHL	32	3	10	13	4	10	14	16	3	0	0	57	5.3	39	18	30	8	–1	....	....	....	....	....	....	....	....
	Toronto Maple Leafs	NHL	19	1	8	9	1	8	9	10	1	0	0	30	3.3	21	10	12	3	+2	....	....	....	....	....	....	....	....
	Washington Capitals	NHL	9	0	6	6	0	6	6	6	0	0	0	15	0.0	13	6	4	1	+4	2	0	2	2	0	0	0	0
	NHL Totals		747	154	430	584	144	340	484	498	80	5	16	2120	7.3	1260	599	911	199		87	20	45	65	59	7	0	4

Transferred to **Carolina** after **Hartford** franchise relocated, June 25, 1997. Traded to **Toronto** by **Carolina** for a conditional draft choice, January 2, 1998. Traded to **Washington** by **Toronto** for Sylvain Cote, March 24, 1998.

• BROWN, JIM

Jim Brown D – R. 6′4″, 210 lbs. b: Phoenix, AZ, 3/1/1960. Los Angeles' 6th choice, 92nd overall, in 1979 Entry Draft.

Season	Club	League	GP	G	A	Pts	AG	AA	APts	PIM	PP	SH	GW	S	%	TGF	PGF	TGA	PGA	+/–	GP	G	A	Pts	PIM	PP	SH	GW
1978-79	University of Notre Dame	CCHA	STATISTICS NOT AVAILABLE																									
1979-80	University of Notre Dame	CCHA	36	5	13	18	....	....	....	40	....	....	....	....	....	....	....	....	....	....	....	....	....	....	....	....	....	....
1980-81	University of Notre Dame	CCHA	27	2	7	9	....	....	....	45	....	....	....	....	....	....	....	....	....	....	....	....	....	....	....	....	....	....
1981-82	University of Notre Dame	CCHA	39	8	19	27	....	....	....	101	....	....	....	....	....	....	....	....	....	....	....	....	....	....	....	....	....	....
1982-83	**Los Angeles Kings**	**NHL**	**3**	**0**	**1**	**1**	**0**	**1**	**1**	**5**	**0**	**0**	**0**	**0**	**0.0**	**2**	**0**	**4**	**0**	**–2**	....	....	....	....	....	....	....	....
	New Haven Nighthawks	AHL	75	3	12	15	....	....	....	120	....	....	....	....	....	....	....	....	....	....	12	2	4	6	8	....	....	....
1983-84	New Haven Nighthawks	AHL	39	2	4	6	....	....	....	18	....	....	....	....	....	....	....	....	....	....	....	....	....	....	....	....	....	....
	NHL Totals		3	0	1	1	0	1	1	5	0	0	0	0	0.0	2	0	4	0		....	....	....	....	....	....	....	....

• BROWN, KEITH

Keith Brown D – R. 6′1″, 196 lbs. b: Corner Brook, Nfld., 5/6/1960. Chicago's 1st choice, 7th overall, in 1979 Entry Draft.

Season	Club	League	GP	G	A	Pts	AG	AA	APts	PIM	PP	SH	GW	S	%	TGF	PGF	TGA	PGA	+/–	GP	G	A	Pts	PIM	PP	SH	GW
1976-77	Fort Saskatchewan Traders	AJHL	59	14	61	75	....	....	....	14	....	....	....	....	....	....	....	....	....	....	....	....	....	....	....	....	....	....
	Portland Winter Hawks	WCJHL	2	0	0	0	....	....	....	0	....	....	....	....	....	....	....	....	....	....	....	....	....	....	....	....	....	....
1977-78	Portland Winter Hawks	WCJHL	72	11	53	64	....	....	....	51	....	....	....	....	....	....	....	....	....	....	8	0	3	3	2	....	....	....
1978-79	Portland Winter Hawks	WHL	70	11	85	96	....	....	....	75	....	....	....	....	....	....	....	....	....	....	25	3	*30	33	21	....	....	....
	Canada	WJC-A	5	0	2	2	....	....	....	0	....	....	....	....	....	....	....	....	....	....	....	....	....	....	....	....	....	....
1979-80	**Chicago Black Hawks**	**NHL**	**76**	**2**	**18**	**20**	**2**	**14**	**16**	**27**	**0**	**0**	**2**	**105**	**1.9**	**63**	**3**	**69**	**16**	**+7**	**6**	**0**	**0**	**0**	**4**	**0**	**0**	**0**
1980-81	**Chicago Black Hawks**	**NHL**	**80**	**9**	**34**	**43**	**7**	**24**	**31**	**80**	**0**	**1**	**1**	**130**	**6.9**	**99**	**7**	**122**	**35**	**+5**	**3**	**0**	**2**	**2**	**2**	**0**	**0**	**0**
1981-82	**Chicago Black Hawks**	**NHL**	**33**	**4**	**20**	**24**	**3**	**13**	**16**	**26**	**2**	**0**	**0**	**87**	**4.6**	**66**	**16**	**58**	**12**	**+4**	**4**	**0**	**2**	**2**	**5**	**0**	**0**	**0**
1982-83	**Chicago Black Hawks**	**NHL**	**50**	**4**	**27**	**31**	**3**	**19**	**22**	**20**	**2**	**0**	**0**	**116**	**3.4**	**90**	**27**	**79**	**24**	**+8**	**7**	**0**	**0**	**0**	**11**	**0**	**0**	**0**
1983-84	**Chicago Black Hawks**	**NHL**	**74**	**10**	**25**	**35**	**8**	**17**	**25**	**94**	**3**	**0**	**0**	**148**	**6.8**	**91**	**18**	**119**	**28**	**–18**	**5**	**0**	**1**	**1**	**10**	**0**	**0**	**0**
1984-85	**Chicago Black Hawks**	**NHL**	**56**	**1**	**22**	**23**	**1**	**15**	**16**	**55**	**0**	**0**	**0**	**100**	**1.0**	**76**	**15**	**80**	**21**	**+2**	**11**	**2**	**7**	**9**	**31**	**1**	**0**	**0**
1985-86	**Chicago Black Hawks**	**NHL**	**70**	**11**	**29**	**40**	**9**	**19**	**28**	**87**	**1**	**1**	**0**	**151**	**7.3**	**112**	**37**	**103**	**22**	**–6**	**3**	**0**	**1**	**1**	**9**	**0**	**0**	**0**
1986-87	**Chicago Blackhawks**	**NHL**	**73**	**4**	**23**	**27**	**3**	**17**	**20**	**86**	**2**	**0**	**0**	**100**	**4.0**	**85**	**8**	**108**	**36**	**+5**	**4**	**0**	**1**	**1**	**6**	**0**	**0**	**0**
1987-88	**Chicago Blackhawks**	**NHL**	**24**	**3**	**6**	**9**	**3**	**4**	**7**	**45**	**0**	**0**	**1**	**39**	**7.7**	**31**	**5**	**34**	**13**	**+5**	**5**	**0**	**2**	**2**	**10**	**0**	**0**	**0**
1988-89	**Chicago Blackhawks**	**NHL**	**74**	**2**	**16**	**18**	**2**	**11**	**13**	**84**	**1**	**0**	**0**	**105**	**1.9**	**67**	**13**	**100**	**41**	**–5**	**13**	**1**	**3**	**4**	**25**	**0**	**0**	**0**
1989-90	**Chicago Blackhawks**	**NHL**	**67**	**5**	**20**	**25**	**4**	**14**	**18**	**87**	**2**	**0**	**0**	**111**	**4.5**	**98**	**16**	**88**	**32**	**+26**	**18**	**0**	**4**	**4**	**43**	**0**	**0**	**0**
1990-91	**Chicago Blackhawks**	**NHL**	**45**	**1**	**10**	**11**	**1**	**8**	**9**	**55**	**0**	**0**	**0**	**71**	**1.4**	**39**	**13**	**25**	**8**	**+9**	**6**	**1**	**0**	**1**	**8**	**0**	**0**	**0**
1991-92	**Chicago Blackhawks**	**NHL**	**57**	**6**	**10**	**16**	**5**	**7**	**12**	**69**	**2**	**1**	**1**	**105**	**5.7**	**54**	**16**	**47**	**16**	**+7**	**14**	**0**	**8**	**8**	**18**	**0**	**0**	**0**
1992-93	**Chicago Blackhawks**	**NHL**	**33**	**2**	**6**	**8**	**2**	**4**	**6**	**39**	**0**	**0**	**0**	**47**	**4.3**	**29**	**3**	**28**	**5**	**+3**	**4**	**0**	**1**	**1**	**2**	**0**	**0**	**0**
1993-94	**Florida Panthers**	**NHL**	**51**	**4**	**8**	**12**	**4**	**6**	**10**	**60**	**1**	**0**	**0**	**52**	**7.7**	**50**	**7**	**64**	**22**	**+11**	....	....	....	....	....	....	....	....
1994-95	**Florida Panthers**	**NHL**	**13**	**0**	**0**	**0**	**0**	**0**	**0**	**2**	**0**	**0**	**0**	**10**	**0.0**	**9**	**2**	**11**	**5**	**+1**	....	....	....	....	....	....	....	....
	NHL Totals		876	68	274	342	57	192	249	916	16	3	5	1477	4.6	1059	206	1125	336		103	4	32	36	184	1	0	0

WHL All-Star Team (1979)

Traded to **Florida** by **Chicago** for Darin Kimble, September 30, 1993.

• BROWN, KEVIN

Kevin Brown RW – R. 6′1″, 212 lbs. b: Birmingham, England, 5/11/1974. Los Angeles' 3rd choice, 87th overall, in 1992 Entry Draft.

Season	Club	League	GP	G	A	Pts	AG	AA	APts	PIM	PP	SH	GW	S	%	TGF	PGF	TGA	PGA	+/–	GP	G	A	Pts	PIM	PP	SH	GW
1991-92	Belleville Bulls	OHL	66	24	24	48	....	....	....	52	....	....	....	....	....	....	....	....	....	....	5	1	4	5	8	....	....	....
1992-93	Belleville Bulls	OHL	6	2	5	7	....	....	....	4	....	....	....	....	....	....	....	....	....	....	....	....	....	....	....	....	....	....
	Detroit Jr. Red Wings	OHL	56	48	86	134	....	....	....	76	....	....	....	....	....	....	....	....	....	....	15	10	18	28	18	....	....	....
1993-94	Detroit Jr. Red Wings	OHL	57	54	81	135	....	....	....	85	....	....	....	....	....	....	....	....	....	....	17	14	*26	*40	28	....	....	....
1994-95	**Los Angeles Kings**	**NHL**	**23**	**2**	**3**	**5**	**4**	**4**	**8**	**18**	**0**	**0**	**0**	**25**	**8.0**	**0**	**2**	**14**	**0**	**–7**	....	....	....	....	....	....	....	....
	Phoenix Roadrunners	IHL	48	19	31	50	....	....	....	64	....	....	....	....	....	....	....	....	....	....	....	....	....	....	....	....	....	....
1995-96	**Los Angeles Kings**	**NHL**	**7**	**1**	**0**	**1**	**1**	**0**	**1**	**4**	**0**	**0**	**0**	**9**	**11.1**	**2**	**0**	**4**	**0**	**–2**	....	....	....	....	....	....	....	....
	Phoenix Roadrunners	IHL	45	10	10	20	....	....	....	39	....	....	....	....	....	....	....	....	....	....	....	....	....	....	....	....	....	....
	P.E.I. Senators	AHL	8	3	6	9	....	....	....	2	....	....	....	....	....	....	....	....	....	....	3	1	3	4	0	....	....	....
1996-97	**Hartford Whalers**	**NHL**	**11**	**0**	**4**	**4**	**0**	**4**	**4**	**6**	**0**	**0**	**0**	**12**	**0.0**	**5**	**2**	**9**	**0**	**–6**	....	....	....	....	....	....	....	....
	Springfield Falcons	AHL	48	32	16	48	....	....	....	45	....	....	....	....	....	....	....	....	....	....	17	*11	6	17	24	....	....	....
1997-98	**Carolina Hurricanes**	**NHL**	**4**	**0**	**0**	**0**	**0**	**0**	**0**	**0**	**0**	**0**	**0**	**0**	**0.0**	**1**	**1**	**2**	**0**	**–2**	....	....	....	....	....	....	....	....
	Beast of New Haven	AHL	67	28	44	72	....	....	....	65	....	....	....	....	....	....	....	....	....	....	3	0	2	2	0	....	....	....
	NHL Totals		45	3	7	10	5	8	13	28	0	0	0	46	6.5	17	5	29	0		....	....	....	....	....	....	....	....

OHL Second All-Star Team (1993) • OHL First All-Star Team (1994) • Canadian Major Junior Second All-Star Team (1994)

Traded to **Ottawa** by **LA Kings** for Jaroslav Modry and Ottawa's 8th round choice (Stephen Valiquette) in 1996 Entry Draft, March 20, 1996. Traded to **Anaheim** by **Ottawa** for Mike Maneluk, July 1, 1996. Traded to **Hartford** by **Anaheim** for the rights to Espen Knutsen, October 1, 1996. Transferred to **Carolina** after **Hartford** franchise relocated, June 25, 1997.

• BROWN, LARRY

Larry Brown D – L. 6′2″, 210 lbs. b: Brandon, Man., 4/14/1947.

Season	Club	League	GP	G	A	Pts	AG	AA	APts	PIM	PP	SH	GW	S	%	TGF	PGF	TGA	PGA	+/–	GP	G	A	Pts	PIM	PP	SH	GW
1963-64	Brandon Wheat Kings	MJHL	....	....	....	....	....	....	....	....	....	....	....	....	....	....	....	....	....	....	2	0	0	0	0	....	....	....
1964-65	Brandon Wheat Kings	SJHL	54	2	11	13	....	....	....	12	....	....	....	....	....	....	....	....	....	....	2	0	0	0	0	....	....	....
1965-66	Brandon Wheat Kings	SJHL	59	6	18	24	....	....	....	19	....	....	....	....	....	....	....	....	....	....	11	0	4	4	0	....	....	....
1966-67	Brandon Wheat Kings	WCJHL	STATISTICS NOT AVAILABLE																									
1967-68	New Haven Blades	EHL	71	6	21	27	....	....	....	39	....	....	....	....	....	....	....	....	....	....	10	1	7	8	8	....	....	....
1968-69	Omaha Knights	CHL	69	5	14	19	....	....	....	14	....	....	....	....	....	....	....	....	....	....	7	4	1	5	6	....	....	....
1969-70	**New York Rangers**	**NHL**	**15**	**0**	**3**	**3**	**0**	**3**	**3**	**8**	**0**	**0**	**0**	**17**	**0.0**	**11**	**1**	**7**	**3**	**+6**	....	....	....	....	....	....	....	....
	Buffalo Bisons	AHL	41	2	8	10	....	....	....	46	....	....	....	....	....	....	....	....	....	....	....	....	....	....	....	....	....	....
1970-71	**Detroit Red Wings**	**NHL**	**33**	**1**	**4**	**5**	**1**	**4**	**5**	**8**	**0**	**0**	**1**	**52**	**1.9**	**18**	**2**	**40**	**9**	**–15**	....	....	....	....	....	....	....	....
	New York Rangers	**NHL**	**31**	**1**	**1**	**2**	**1**	**1**	**2**	**10**	**1**	**0**	**0**	**56**	**1.8**	**25**	**3**	**16**	**2**	**+8**	**11**	**0**	**1**	**1**	**0**	**0**	**0**	**0**
1971-72	**Philadelphia Flyers**	**NHL**	**12**	**0**	**0**	**0**	**0**	**0**	**0**	**2**	**0**	**0**	**0**	**9**	**0.0**	**4**	**0**	**12**	**5**	**–3**	....	....	....	....	....	....	....	....
	Richmond Robins	AHL	9	1	1	2	....	....	....	10	....	....	....	....	....	....	....	....	....	....	....	....	....	....	....	....	....	....
1972-73	**Los Angeles Kings**	**NHL**	**55**	**0**	**7**	**7**	**0**	**6**	**6**	**8**	**0**	**0**	**0**	**46**	**0.0**	**36**	**0**	**44**	**4**	**–4**	....	....	....	....	....	....	....	....
1973-74	**Los Angeles Kings**	**NHL**	**45**	**0**	**4**	**4**	**0**	**3**	**3**	**14**	**0**	**0**	**0**	**31**	**0.0**	**35**	**1**	**37**	**7**	**+4**	**2**	**0**	**0**	**0**	**0**	**0**	**0**	**0**
	Springfield Kings	AHL	8	0	4	4	....	....	....	6	....	....	....	....	....	....	....	....	....	....	....	....	....	....	....	....	....	....
1974-75	**Los Angeles Kings**	**NHL**	**78**	**1**	**15**	**16**	**1**	**12**	**13**	**50**	**0**	**0**	**0**	**83**	**1.2**	**87**	**1**	**79**	**24**	**+31**	**3**	**0**	**2**	**2**	**0**	**0**	**0**	**0**
1975-76	**Los Angeles Kings**	**NHL**	**74**	**2**	**5**	**7**	**2**	**4**	**6**	**33**	**0**	**0**	**0**	**49**	**4.1**	**47**	**1**	**91**	**18**	**–27**	**9**	**0**	**0**	**0**	**2**	**0**	**0**	**0**
1976-77	**Los Angeles Kings**	**NHL**	**55**	**1**	**6**	**7**	**1**	**5**	**6**	**24**	**0**	**0**	**0**	**59**	**1.7**	**39**	**2**	**68**	**14**	**–17**	**9**	**0**	**1**	**1**	**6**	**0**	**0**	**0**
	Fort Worth Texans	CHL	14	0	2	2	....	....	....	8	....	....	....	....	....	....	....	....	....	....	....	....	....	....	....	....	....	....
1977-78	**Los Angeles Kings**	**NHL**	**57**	**1**	**8**	**9**	**1**	**7**	**8**	**23**	**0**	**0**	**0**	**24**	**4.2**	**40**	**3**	**65**	**15**	**–13**	**1**	**0**	**0**	**0**	**2**	**0**	**0**	**0**

			REGULAR SEASON																		PLAYOFFS							
Season	Club	League	GP	G	A	Pts	AG	AA	APts	PIM	PP	SH	GW	S	%	TGF	PGF	TGA	PGA	+/–	GP	G	A	Pts	PIM	PP	SH	GW
1978-79	Springfield Indians	AHL	65	3	6	9	....	....	....	20	....	....	....	....	....	....	....	....	....	....	....	....	....	....	....	....	....	....
1979-80	Cincinnati Stingers	CHL	31	0	5	5	....	....	....	41	....	....	....	....	....	....	....	....	....	....	....	....	....	....	....	....	....	....
	Houston Apollos	CHL	39	1	4	5	....	....	....	14	....	....	....	....	....	....	....	....	....	....	4	1	1	2	0	....	....	....
	NHL Totals		455	7	53	60	7	45	52	180	1	0	1	426	1.6	342	14	459	101		35	0	4	4	10	0	0	0

Traded to **Detroit** by **NY Rangers** for Pete Stemkowski, October 31, 1970. Traded to **NY Rangers** by **Detroit** with Bruce MacGregor for Arnie Brown, Mike Robitaille and Tom Miller, February 2, 1971. Claimed by **Philadelphia** from **NY Rangers** in Intra-League Draft, June 8, 1971. Claimed on waivers by **LA Kings** from **Philadelphia**, January 28, 1972. Claimed by **Edmonton** from **LA Kings** in Expansion Draft, June 13, 1979.

• BROWN, ROB

Rob Brown RW – L. 5'11", 185 lbs. b: Kingston, Ont., 4/10/1968. Pittsburgh's 4th choice, 67th overall, in 1986 Entry Draft.

Season	Club	League	GP	G	A	Pts	AG	AA	APts	PIM	PP	SH	GW	S	%	TGF	PGF	TGA	PGA	+/–	GP	G	A	Pts	PIM	PP	SH	GW
1984-85	Kamloops Blazers	WHL	60	29	50	79	....	....	....	95	....	....	....	....	....	....	....	....	....	....	15	8	8	26	28	....	....	....
1985-86	Kamloops Blazers	WHL	69	58	*115	*173	....	....	....	171	....	....	....	....	....	....	....	....	....	....	16	*18	*28	*46	14	....	....	....
1986-87	Kamloops Blazers	WHL	63	*76	*136	*212	....	....	....	101	....	....	....	....	....	....	....	....	....	....	5	6	5	11	6	....	....	....
1987-88	**Pittsburgh Penguins**	**NHL**	51	24	20	44	21	14	35	56	13	0	1	80	30.0	66	28	30	0	+8	....	....	....	....	....	....	....	....
	Canada	WJC-A	7	6	2	8	....	....	....	2	....	....	....	....	....	....	....	....	....	....	....	....	....	....	....	....	....	....
1988-89	**Pittsburgh Penguins**	**NHL**	68	49	66	115	42	47	89	118	24	0	6	169	29.0	164	77	63	3	+27	11	5	3	8	22	1	0	3
1989-90	**Pittsburgh Penguins**	**NHL**	80	33	47	80	28	34	62	102	12	0	3	157	21.0	119	41	88	0	–10	....	....	....	....	....	....	....	....
1990-91	**Pittsburgh Penguins**	**NHL**	25	6	10	16	5	8	13	31	2	0	0	32	18.8	21	8	13	0	0	....	....	....	....	....	....	....	....
	Hartford Whalers	**NHL**	44	18	24	42	17	18	35	101	10	0	2	94	19.1	68	35	40	0	–7	5	1	0	1	7	1	0	1
1991-92	**Hartford Whalers**	**NHL**	42	16	15	31	15	11	26	39	13	0	2	65	24.6	42	29	27	0	–14	....	....	....	....	....	....	....	....
	Chicago Blackhawks	**NHL**	25	5	11	16	5	8	13	34	3	0	1	41	12.2	23	9	16	1	–1	8	2	4	6	4	1	0	0
1992-93	**Chicago Blackhawks**	**NHL**	15	1	6	7	1	4	5	33	0	0	0	16	6.3	11	1	4	0	+6	....	....	....	....	....	....	....	....
	Indianapolis Ice	IHL	19	14	19	33	....	....	....	32	....	....	....	....	....	....	....	....	....	....	2	0	1	1	2	....	....	....
1993-94	**Dallas Stars**	**NHL**	1	0	0	0	0	0	0	0	0	0	0	1	0.0	0	0	1	0	–1	....	....	....	....	....	....	....	....
	Kalamazoo Wings	IHL	79	42	*113	*155	....	....	....	188	....	....	....	....	....	....	....	....	....	....	5	1	3	4	6	....	....	....
1994-95	**Los Angeles Kings**	**NHL**	2	0	0	0	0	0	0	0	0	0	0	1	0.0	0	0	2	0	–2	....	....	....	....	....	....	....	....
	Phoenix Roadrunners	IHL	69	34	73	107	....	....	....	135	....	....	....	....	....	....	....	....	....	....	9	4	12	16	0	....	....	....
1995-96	Chicago Wolves	IHL	79	52	*91	*143	....	....	....	100	....	....	....	....	....	....	....	....	....	....	9	4	11	15	6	....	....	....
1996-97	Chicago Wolves	IHL	76	37	*80	*117	....	....	....	98	....	....	....	....	....	....	....	....	....	....	4	2	4	6	16	....	....	....
1997-98	**Pittsburgh Penguins**	**NHL**	82	15	25	40	18	24	42	59	4	0	4	172	8.7	62	27	36	0	–1	6	1	0	1	4	1	0	0
	NHL Totals		435	167	224	391	152	168	320	573	81	0	19	828	20.2	576	255	320	4		30	9	7	16	37	4	0	4

WHL First All-Star Team (1986, 1987) • Canadian Major Junior Player of the Year (1987) • IHL First All-Star Team (1994, 1996, 1997) • Won Leo P. Lamoureux Memorial Trophy (Top Scorer - IHL) (1994, 1996, 1997) • Won James Gatschene Memorial Trophy (MVP - IHL) (1994) • IHL Second All-Star Team (1995)

Played in NHL All-Star Game (1989)

Traded to **Hartford** by **Pittsburgh** for Scott Young, December 21, 1990. Traded to **Chicago** by **Hartford** for Steve Konroyd, January 24, 1992. Signed as a free agent by **Dallas**, August 12, 1993. Signed as a free agent by **LA Kings**, June 14, 1994.

• BROWN, SEAN

Sean Brown D – L. 6'2", 205 lbs. b: Oshawa, Ont., 11/5/1976. Boston's 3rd choice, 21st overall, in 1995 Entry Draft.

Season	Club	League	GP	G	A	Pts	AG	AA	APts	PIM	PP	SH	GW	S	%	TGF	PGF	TGA	PGA	+/–	GP	G	A	Pts	PIM	PP	SH	GW
1993-94	Belleville Bulls	OHL	28	1	2	3	....	....	....	53	....	....	....	....	....	....	....	....	....	....	8	0	0	0	17	....	....	....
1994-95	Belleville Bulls	OHL	58	2	16	18	....	....	....	200	....	....	....	....	....	....	....	....	....	....	16	4	2	6	*67	....	....	....
1995-96	Belleville Bulls	OHL	37	10	23	33	....	....	....	150	....	....	....	....	....	....	....	....	....	....	....	....	....	....	....	....	....	....
	Sarnia Sting	OHL	26	8	17	25	....	....	....	112	....	....	....	....	....	....	....	....	....	....	10	1	0	1	38	....	....	....
1996-97	**Edmonton Oilers**	**NHL**	5	0	0	0	0	0	0	4	0	0	0	2	0.0	1	1	1	0	–1	....	....	....	....	....	....	....	....
	Hamilton Bulldogs	AHL	61	1	7	8	....	....	....	238	....	....	....	....	....	....	....	....	....	....	19	1	0	1	47	....	....	....
1997-98	**Edmonton Oilers**	**NHL**	18	0	1	1	0	1	1	43	0	0	0	9	0.0	7	0	11	3	–1	....	....	....	....	....	....	....	....
	Hamilton Bulldogs	AHL	43	4	6	10	....	....	....	166	....	....	....	....	....	....	....	....	....	....	6	0	2	2	38	....	....	....
	NHL Totals		23	0	1	1	0	1	1	47	0	0	0	11	0.0	8	1	12	3		....	....	....	....	....	....	....	....

OHL Second All-Star Team (1996)

Rights traded to **Edmonton** by **Boston** with Mariusz Czerkawski and Boston's 1st round choice (Matthieu Descoteaux) in 1996 Entry Draft for Bill Ranford, January 11, 1996.

• BROWNSCHIDLE, JACK

Jack Brownschidle D – L. 6'2", 195 lbs. b: Buffalo, N.Y., 10/2/1955. St. Louis' 5th choice, 99th overall, in 1975 Amateur Draft.

Season	Club	League	GP	G	A	Pts	AG	AA	APts	PIM	PP	SH	GW	S	%	TGF	PGF	TGA	PGA	+/–	GP	G	A	Pts	PIM	PP	SH	GW
1972-73	Niagara Falls Flyers	SOJHL	32	9	19	28	....	....	....	20	....	....	....	....	....	....	....	....	....	....	....	....	....	....	....	....	....	....
1973-74	University of Notre Dame	WCHA	....	1	6	7	....	....	....	18	....	....	....	....	....	....	....	....	....	....	....	....	....	....	....	....	....	....
	United States	Nat-Team	18	2	3	5	....	....	....	....	....	....	....	....	....	....	....	....	....	....	....	....	....	....	....	....	....	....
1974-75	University of Notre Dame	WCHA	....	3	10	13	....	....	....	20	....	....	....	....	....	....	....	....	....	....	....	....	....	....	....	....	....	....
	United States	WEC-A	10	1	1	2	....	....	....	4	....	....	....	....	....	....	....	....	....	....	....	....	....	....	....	....	....	....
1975-76	University of Notre Dame	WCHA	38	12	24	36	....	....	....	24	....	....	....	....	....	....	....	....	....	....	....	....	....	....	....	....	....	....
1976-77	University of Notre Dame	WCHA	38	13	35	48	....	....	....	30	....	....	....	....	....	....	....	....	....	....	....	....	....	....	....	....	....	....
1977-78	**St. Louis Blues**	**NHL**	40	2	15	17	2	12	14	23	1	0	0	62	3.2	40	13	47	9	–11	....	....	....	....	....	....	....	....
	Salt Lake Golden Eagles	CHL	25	4	12	16	....	....	....	0	....	....	....	....	....	....	....	....	....	....	....	....	....	....	....	....	....	....
1978-79	**St. Louis Blues**	**NHL**	64	10	24	34	9	18	27	14	5	0	1	101	9.9	82	27	86	10	–21	....	....	....	....	....	....	....	....
	Salt Lake Golden Eagles	CHL	11	0	10	10	....	....	....	0	....	....	....	....	....	....	....	....	....	....	....	....	....	....	....	....	....	....
	United States	WEC-A	8	1	1	2	....	....	....	5	....	....	....	....	....	....	....	....	....	....	....	....	....	....	....	....	....	....
1979-80	**St. Louis Blues**	**NHL**	77	12	32	44	11	25	36	8	3	0	2	130	9.2	110	34	74	14	+16	3	0	0	0	0	0	0	0
1980-81	**St. Louis Blues**	**NHL**	71	5	23	28	4	16	20	12	3	1	1	96	5.2	109	43	89	28	+5	11	0	3	3	2	0	0	0
1981-82	**St. Louis Blues**	**NHL**	80	5	33	38	4	22	26	26	3	0	1	149	3.4	129	48	128	42	–5	8	0	2	2	14	0	0	0
1982-83	**St. Louis Blues**	**NHL**	72	1	22	23	1	15	16	30	1	0	0	127	0.8	99	20	105	23	–3	4	0	0	0	2	0	0	0
1983-84	**St. Louis Blues**	**NHL**	51	1	7	8	1	5	6	19	1	0	0	50	2.0	37	8	75	25	–21	....	....	....	....	....	....	....	....
	Hartford Whalers	**NHL**	13	2	2	4	2	1	3	10	0	0	1	17	11.8	8	0	13	0	–5	....	....	....	....	....	....	....	....
1984-85	**Hartford Whalers**	**NHL**	17	1	4	5	1	3	4	5	1	0	0	27	3.7	16	4	13	1	0	....	....	....	....	....	....	....	....
	Binghamton Whalers	AHL	56	4	17	21	....	....	....	8	....	....	....	....	....	....	....	....	....	....	....	....	....	....	....	....	....	....
1985-86	**Hartford Whalers**	**NHL**	9	0	0	0	0	0	0	4	0	0	0	7	0.0	2	0	11	5	–4	....	....	....	....	....	....	....	....
	Binghamton Whalers	AHL	58	5	26	31	....	....	....	18	....	....	....	....	....	....	....	....	....	....	6	0	3	3	0	....	....	....
1986-87	Rochester Americans	AHL	74	8	22	30	....	....	....	13	....	....	....	....	....	....	....	....	....	....	12	1	3	4	0	....	....	....
	NHL Totals		494	39	162	201	35	117	152	151	18	1	6	766	5.1	632	197	641	157		26	0	5	5	18	0	0	0

WCHA First All-Star Team (1976, 1977) • NCAA West First All-American Team (1976) • NCAA West First All-American Team (1977) • AHL Second All-Star Team (1986)

Claimed on waivers by **Hartford** from **St. Louis**, March 2, 1984.

• BROWNSCHIDLE, JEFF

Jeff Brownschidle D – R. 6'2", 200 lbs. b: Buffalo, NY, 3/1/1959.

Season	Club	League	GP	G	A	Pts	AG	AA	APts	PIM	PP	SH	GW	S	%	TGF	PGF	TGA	PGA	+/–	GP	G	A	Pts	PIM	PP	SH	GW
1977-78	University of Notre Dame	WCHA	35	6	10	16	....	....	....	30	....	....	....	....	....	....	....	....	....	....	....	....	....	....	....	....	....	....
1978-79	University of Notre Dame	WCHA	32	5	15	20	....	....	....	40	....	....	....	....	....	....	....	....	....	....	....	....	....	....	....	....	....	....
	United States	WJC-A	5	1	2	3	....	....	....	2	....	....	....	....	....	....	....	....	....	....	....	....	....	....	....	....	....	....
1979-80	University of Notre Dame	WCHA	39	14	37	51	....	....	....	50	....	....	....	....	....	....	....	....	....	....	....	....	....	....	....	....	....	....
1980-81	University of Notre Dame	WCHA	36	4	28	32	....	....	....	56	....	....	....	....	....	....	....	....	....	....	....	....	....	....	....	....	....	....
1981-82	**Hartford Whalers**	**NHL**	3	0	1	1	0	1	1	2	0	0	0	4	0.0	3	1	6	1	–3	....	....	....	....	....	....	....	....
	Binghamton Whalers	AHL	52	4	23	27	....	....	....	24	....	....	....	....	....	....	....	....	....	....	15	2	4	6	6	....	....	....
1982-83	**Hartford Whalers**	**NHL**	4	0	0	0	0	0	0	0	0	0	0	0	0.0	1	0	7	0	–6	....	....	....	....	....	....	....	....
	Binghamton Whalers	AHL	64	9	18	27	....	....	....	52	....	....	....	....	....	....	....	....	....	....	5	0	1	1	23	....	....	....
1983-84	Binghamton Whalers	AHL	29	2	7	9	....	....	....	50	....	....	....	....	....	....	....	....	....	....	....	....	....	....	....	....	....	....
	Salt Lake Golden Eagles	CHL	11	1	7	8	....	....	....	12	....	....	....	....	....	....	....	....	....	....	....	....	....	....	....	....	....	....
	NHL Totals		7	0	1	1	0	1	1	2	0	0	0	4	0.0	4	1	13	1		....	....	....	....	....	....	....	....

Signed as a free agent by **Hartford**, June 9, 1981.

• BRUBAKER, JEFF

Jeff Brubaker LW – L. 6'2", 207 lbs. b: Frederick, MD, 2/24/1958. Boston's 5th choice, 102nd overall, in 1978 Amateur Draft.

Season	Club	League	GP	G	A	Pts	AG	AA	APts	PIM	PP	SH	GW	S	%	TGF	PGF	TGA	PGA	+/–	GP	G	A	Pts	PIM	PP	SH	GW
1974-75	St. Paul Vulcans	USHL	57	13	14	27	....	....	....	130	....	....	....	....	....	....	....	....	....	....	....	....	....	....	....	....	....	....
1975-76	St. Paul Vulcans	USHL	47	6	34	40	....	....	....	152	....	....	....	....	....	....	....	....	....	....	....	....	....	....	....	....	....	....
1976-77	Michigan State Spartans	WCHA	18	0	3	3	....	....	....	30	....	....	....	....	....	....	....	....	....	....	....	....	....	....	....	....	....	....
	Peterborough Petes	OHA	26	0	5	5	....	....	....	143	....	....	....	....	....	....	....	....	....	....	4	0	2	2	7	....	....	....
1977-78	Peterborough Petes	OHA	68	20	24	44	....	....	....	307	....	....	....	....	....	....	....	....	....	....	21	6	5	11	52	....	....	....

			REGULAR SEASON																		PLAYOFFS							
Season	Club	League	GP	G	A	Pts	AG	AA	APts	PIM	PP	SH	GW	S	%	TGF	PGF	TGA	PGA	+/–	GP	G	A	Pts	PIM	PP	SH	GW
1978-79	New England Whalers	WHA	12	0	0	0	....	....	....	19	....	....	....	....	....	....	....	....	....	....	3	0	0	0	12	....	....	....
	Rochester Americans	AHL	57	4	10	14	....	....	....	253	....	....	....	....	....	....	....	....	....	....	....	....	....	....	....	....	....	....
1979-80	**Hartford Whalers**	**NHL**	**3**	**0**	**1**	**1**	**0**	**1**	**1**	**2**	**0**	**0**	**0**	**2**	**0.0**	**1**	**1**	**2**	**0**	**–2**	....	....	....	....	....	....	....	....
	Springfield Indians	AHL	50	12	13	25	....	....	....	165	....	....	....	....	....	....	....	....	....	....	....	....	....	....	....	....	....	....
1980-81	**Hartford Whalers**	**NHL**	**43**	**5**	**3**	**8**	**4**	**2**	**6**	**93**	**0**	**0**	**0**	**29**	**17.2**	**14**	**0**	**19**	**0**	**–5**	....	....	....	....	....	....	....	....
	Binghamton Whalers	AHL	33	18	11	29	....	....	....	138	....	....	....	....	....	....	....	....	....	....	....	....	....	....	....	....	....	....
1981-82	**Montreal Canadiens**	**NHL**	**3**	**0**	**1**	**1**	**0**	**1**	**1**	**32**	**0**	**0**	**0**	**3**	**0.0**	**1**	**0**	**0**	**0**	**+1**	**2**	**0**	**0**	**0**	**27**	**0**	**0**	**0**
	Nova Scotia Voyageurs	AHL	60	28	12	40	....	....	....	256	....	....	....	....	....	....	....	....	....	....	6	2	1	3	32	....	....	....
1982-83	Nova Scotia Voyageurs	AHL	78	31	27	58	....	....	....	183	....	....	....	....	....	....	....	....	....	....	7	1	1	2	25	....	....	....
1983-84	**Calgary Flames**	**NHL**	**4**	**0**	**0**	**0**	**0**	**0**	**0**	**19**	**0**	**0**	**0**	**2**	**0.0**	**0**	**0**	**1**	**0**	**–1**	....	....	....	....	....	....	....	....
	Colorado Flames	CHL	57	16	19	35	....	....	....	218	....	....	....	....	....	....	....	....	....	....	6	3	1	4	15	....	....	....
1984-85	**Toronto Maple Leafs**	**NHL**	**68**	**8**	**4**	**12**	**7**	**3**	**10**	**209**	**2**	**0**	**1**	**39**	**20.5**	**17**	**3**	**32**	**0**	**–18**	....	....	....	....	....	....	....	....
1985-86	**Toronto Maple Leafs**	**NHL**	**21**	**0**	**0**	**0**	**0**	**0**	**0**	**67**	**0**	**0**	**0**	**8**	**0.0**	**2**	**0**	**2**	**0**	**0**	....	....	....	....	....	....	....	....
	Edmonton Oilers	**NHL**	**4**	**1**	**0**	**1**	**1**	**0**	**1**	**12**	**0**	**0**	**0**	**4**	**25.0**	**1**	**0**	**0**	**0**	**+1**	....	....	....	....	....	....	....	....
	Nova Scotia Oilers	AHL	19	4	3	7	....	....	....	41	....	....	....	....	....	....	....	....	....	....	....	....	....	....	....	....	....	....
1986-87	Nova Scotia Oilers	AHL	47	10	16	26	....	....	....	80	....	....	....	....	....	....	....	....	....	....	....	....	....	....	....	....	....	....
	Hershey Bears	AHL	12	1	2	3	....	....	....	30	....	....	....	....	....	....	....	....	....	....	3	2	0	2	10	....	....	....
1987-88	**New York Rangers**	**NHL**	**31**	**2**	**0**	**2**	**2**	**0**	**2**	**78**	**0**	**0**	**0**	**9**	**22.2**	**4**	**0**	**4**	**0**	**0**	....	....	....	....	....	....	....	....
	Colorado Rangers	IHL	30	12	10	22	....	....	....	53	....	....	....	....	....	....	....	....	....	....	13	2	2	4	21	....	....	....
1988-89	**Detroit Red Wings**	**NHL**	**1**	**0**	**0**	**0**	**0**	**0**	**0**	**0**	**0**	**0**	**0**	**0**	**0.0**	**0**	**0**	**0**	**0**	**0**	....	....	....	....	....	....	....	....
	Adirondack Red Wings	AHL	63	3	10	13	....	....	....	137	....	....	....	....	....	....	....	....	....	....	....	....	....	....	....	....	....	....
	NHL Totals		**178**	**16**	**9**	**25**	**14**	**7**	**21**	**512**	**2**	**0**	**1**	**96**	**16.7**	**40**	**4**	**60**	**0**		**2**	**0**	**0**	**0**	**27**	**0**	**0**	**0**
	Other Major League Totals		12	0	0	0	....	....	....	19	....	....	....	....	....	....	....	....	....		3	0	0	0	12	....	....	....

Selected by **New England** (WHA) in 1978 WHA Amateur Draft, June, 1978. NHL rights retained by **Hartford** prior to Expansion Draft, June 9, 1979. Claimed by **Montreal** from **Hartford** in Waiver Draft, October 5, 1981. Claimed by **Quebec** from **Montreal** in Waivor Draft, October 3, 1983. Claimed by **Calgary** from **Quebec** in Waiver Draft, October 3, 1983. Signed as a free agent by **Edmonton**, June 21, 1984. Claimed by **Toronto** from **Edmonton** in Waiver Draft, October 9, 1984. Claimed on waivers by **Edmonton** from **Toronto**, December 5, 1985. Traded to **Philadelphia** by **Edmonton** for Dom Campedelli, March 9, 1987. Traded to **NY Rangers** by **Philadelphia** for cash, July 21, 1987. Signed as a free agent by **Detroit**, October, 1988.

• BRUCE, DAVID

David Bruce LW – R. 5′11″, 190 lbs. b: Thunder Bay, Ont., 10/7/1964. Vancouver's 2nd choice, 30th overall, in 1983 Entry Draft.

Season	Club	League	GP	G	A	Pts	AG	AA	APts	PIM	PP	SH	GW	S	%	TGF	PGF	TGA	PGA	+/–	GP	G	A	Pts	PIM	PP	SH	GW
1981-82	Thunder Bay Flyers	TBJHL	35	27	31	58	....	....	....	74	....	....	....	....	....	....	....	....	....	....	....	....	....	....	....	....	....	....
1982-83	Kitchener Rangers	OHL	67	36	35	71	....	....	....	199	....	....	....	....	....	....	....	....	....	....	12	7	9	16	27	....	....	....
1983-84	Kitchener Rangers	OHL	62	52	40	92	....	....	....	203	....	....	....	....	....	....	....	....	....	....	10	5	8	13	20	....	....	....
1984-85	Fredericton Express	AHL	56	14	11	25	....	....	....	104	....	....	....	....	....	....	....	....	....	....	5	0	0	0	37	....	....	....
1985-86	**Vancouver Canucks**	**NHL**	**12**	**0**	**1**	**1**	**0**	**1**	**1**	**14**	**0**	**0**	**0**	**17**	**0.0**	**4**	**0**	**6**	**0**	**–2**	**1**	**0**	**0**	**0**	**0**	**0**	**0**	**0**
	Fredericton Express	AHL	66	25	16	41	....	....	....	151	....	....	....	....	....	....	....	....	....	....	2	0	1	1	12	....	....	....
1986-87	**Vancouver Canucks**	**NHL**	**50**	**9**	**7**	**16**	**8**	**5**	**13**	**109**	**0**	**0**	**2**	**76**	**11.8**	**27**	**0**	**26**	**1**	**+2**	....	....	....	....	....	....	....	....
	Fredericton Express	AHL	17	7	6	13	....	....	....	73	....	....	....	....	....	....	....	....	....	....	....	....	....	....	....	....	....	....
1987-88	**Vancouver Canucks**	**NHL**	**28**	**7**	**3**	**10**	**6**	**2**	**8**	**57**	**1**	**0**	**0**	**46**	**15.2**	**16**	**6**	**17**	**1**	**–6**	....	....	....	....	....	....	....	....
	Fredericton Express	AHL	30	27	18	45	....	....	....	115	....	....	....	....	....	....	....	....	....	....	....	....	....	....	....	....	....	....
1988-89	**Vancouver Canucks**	**NHL**	**53**	**7**	**7**	**14**	**6**	**5**	**11**	**65**	**1**	**0**	**2**	**86**	**8.1**	**24**	**6**	**36**	**2**	**–16**	....	....	....	....	....	....	....	....
1989-90	Milwaukee Admirals	IHL	68	40	35	75	....	....	....	148	....	....	....	....	....	....	....	....	....	....	6	5	3	8	0	....	....	....
1990-91	**St. Louis Blues**	**NHL**	**12**	**1**	**2**	**3**	**1**	**2**	**3**	**14**	**0**	**0**	**0**	**23**	**4.3**	**7**	**1**	**5**	**0**	**+1**	**2**	**0**	**0**	**0**	**2**	**0**	**0**	**0**
	Peoria Rivermen	IHL	60	*64	52	116	....	....	....	78	....	....	....	....	....	....	....	....	....	....	18	*18	11	*29	40	....	....	....
1991-92	**San Jose Sharks**	**NHL**	**60**	**22**	**16**	**38**	**20**	**12**	**32**	**46**	**10**	**1**	**1**	**137**	**16.1**	**50**	**17**	**59**	**6**	**–20**	....	....	....	....	....	....	....	....
	Kansas City Blades	IHL	7	5	5	10	....	....	....	6	....	....	....	....	....	....	....	....	....	....	....	....	....	....	....	....	....	....
1992-93	**San Jose Sharks**	**NHL**	**17**	**2**	**3**	**5**	**2**	**2**	**4**	**33**	**2**	**0**	**0**	**36**	**5.6**	**11**	**9**	**20**	**4**	**–14**	....	....	....	....	....	....	....	....
1993-94	**San Jose Sharks**	**NHL**	**2**	**0**	**0**	**0**	**0**	**0**	**0**	**0**	**0**	**0**	**0**	**5**	**0.0**	**0**	**0**	**2**	**0**	**–2**	....	....	....	....	....	....	....	....
	Kansas City Blades	IHL	72	40	24	64	....	....	....	115	....	....	....	....	....	....	....	....	....	....	....	....	....	....	....	....	....	....
1994-95	Kansas City Blades	IHL	63	33	25	58	....	....	....	80	....	....	....	....	....	....	....	....	....	....	....	....	....	....	....	....	....	....
1995-96	Kansas City Blades	IHL	62	27	26	53	....	....	....	84	....	....	....	....	....	....	....	....	....	....	1	0	0	0	8	....	....	....
1996-97	Kansas City Blades	IHL	79	45	24	69	....	....	....	90	....	....	....	....	....	....	....	....	....	....	3	0	0	0	2	....	....	....
1997-98	Kansas City Blades	IHL	54	20	12	32	....	....	....	58	....	....	....	....	....	....	....	....	....	....	11	3	2	5	21	....	....	....
	NHL Totals		**234**	**48**	**39**	**87**	**43**	**29**	**72**	**338**	**14**	**1**	**5**	**426**	**11.3**	**139**	**39**	**171**	**14**		**3**	**0**	**0**	**0**	**2**	**0**	**0**	**0**

IHL First All-Star Team (1990, 1991) • Won James Gatschene Memorial Trophy (MVP - IHL) (1991)

Signed as a free agent by **St. Louis**, July 6, 1990. Claimed by **San Jose** from **St. Louis** in Expansion Draft, May 30, 1991.

• BRUMWELL, MURRAY

Murray Brumwell D – L. 6′2″, 190 lbs. b: Calgary, Alta., 3/31/1960.

Season	Club	League	GP	G	A	Pts	AG	AA	APts	PIM	PP	SH	GW	S	%	TGF	PGF	TGA	PGA	+/–	GP	G	A	Pts	PIM	PP	SH	GW
1977-78	Calgary Canucks	AJHL	59	4	40	44	....	....	....	79	....	....	....	....	....	....	....	....	....	....	....	....	....	....	....	....	....	....
	Calgary Wranglers	WCJHL	1	0	0	0	....	....	....	2	....	....	....	....	....	....	....	....	....	....	....	....	....	....	....	....	....	....
	Saskatoon Blades	WCJHL	1	0	2	2	....	....	....	0	....	....	....	....	....	....	....	....	....	....	....	....	....	....	....	....	....	....
1978-79	Billings Bighorns	WHL	61	11	32	43	....	....	....	62	....	....	....	....	....	....	....	....	....	....	....	....	....	....	....	....	....	....
1979-80	Billings Bighorns	WHL	67	18	54	72	....	....	....	50	....	....	....	....	....	....	....	....	....	....	....	....	....	....	....	....	....	....
1980-81	**Minnesota North Stars**	**NHL**	**1**	**0**	**0**	**0**	**0**	**0**	**0**	**0**	**0**	**0**	**0**	**0**	**0.0**	**1**	**0**	**0**	**0**	**+1**	....	....	....	....	....	....	....	....
	Oklahoma City Stars	CHL	79	12	43	55	....	....	....	79	....	....	....	....	....	....	....	....	....	....	3	0	0	0	4	....	....	....
1981-82	**Minnesota North Stars**	**NHL**	**21**	**0**	**3**	**3**	**0**	**2**	**2**	**18**	**0**	**0**	**0**	**12**	**0.0**	**19**	**1**	**23**	**5**	**0**	**2**	**0**	**0**	**0**	**2**	**0**	**0**	**0**
	Nashville South Stars	CHL	55	4	21	25	....	....	....	66	....	....	....	....	....	....	....	....	....	....	....	....	....	....	....	....	....	....
1982-83	**New Jersey Devils**	**NHL**	**59**	**5**	**14**	**19**	**4**	**10**	**14**	**34**	**1**	**0**	**0**	**61**	**8.2**	**60**	**19**	**73**	**12**	**–20**	....	....	....	....	....	....	....	....
	Wichita Wind	CHL	11	4	1	5	....	....	....	4	....	....	....	....	....	....	....	....	....	....	....	....	....	....	....	....	....	....
1983-84	**New Jersey Devils**	**NHL**	**42**	**7**	**13**	**20**	**6**	**9**	**15**	**14**	**5**	**0**	**0**	**55**	**12.7**	**48**	**15**	**48**	**10**	**–5**	....	....	....	....	....	....	....	....
	Maine Mariners	AHL	35	4	25	29	....	....	....	16	....	....	....	....	....	....	....	....	....	....	17	1	5	6	15	....	....	....
1984-85	Maine Mariners	AHL	64	8	31	39	....	....	....	12	....	....	....	....	....	....	....	....	....	....	10	4	5	9	19	....	....	....
1985-86	**New Jersey Devils**	**NHL**	**1**	**0**	**0**	**0**	**0**	**0**	**0**	**0**	**0**	**0**	**0**	**3**	**0.0**	**0**	**0**	**2**	**1**	**–1**	....	....	....	....	....	....	....	....
	Maine Mariners	AHL	66	9	28	37	....	....	....	35	....	....	....	....	....	....	....	....	....	....	5	0	3	3	2	....	....	....
1986-87	**New Jersey Devils**	**NHL**	**1**	**0**	**0**	**0**	**0**	**0**	**0**	**2**	**0**	**0**	**0**	**2**	**0.0**	**1**	**0**	**1**	**1**	**+1**	....	....	....	....	....	....	....	....
	Maine Mariners	AHL	69	10	38	48	....	....	....	30	....	....	....	....	....	....	....	....	....	....	....	....	....	....	....	....	....	....
1987-88	**New Jersey Devils**	**NHL**	**3**	**0**	**1**	**1**	**0**	**1**	**1**	**2**	**0**	**0**	**0**	**4**	**0.0**	**2**	**0**	**2**	**0**	**0**	....	....	....	....	....	....	....	....
	Utica Devils	AHL	77	13	53	66	....	....	....	44	....	....	....	....	....	....	....	....	....	....	....	....	....	....	....	....	....	....
1988-89	Utica Devils	AHL	73	5	29	34	....	....	....	29	....	....	....	....	....	....	....	....	....	....	5	0	0	0	2	....	....	....
1989-90	New Haven Nighthawks	AHL	62	7	29	36	....	....	....	24	....	....	....	....	....	....	....	....	....	....	....	....	....	....	....	....	....	....
1990-91	New Haven Nighthawks	AHL	67	8	18	26	....	....	....	27	....	....	....	....	....	....	....	....	....	....	....	....	....	....	....	....	....	....
	NHL Totals		**128**	**12**	**31**	**43**	**10**	**22**	**32**	**70**	**6**	**0**	**0**	**137**	**8.8**	**131**	**35**	**149**	**29**		**2**	**0**	**0**	**0**	**2**	**0**	**0**	**0**

AHL Second All-Star Team (1988)

Signed as a free agent by **Minnesota**, August 7, 1980. Claimed by **New Jersey** from **Minnesota** in Waiver Draft, October 4, 1982.

• BRUNET, BENOIT

Benoit Brunet LW – L. 5′11″, 195 lbs. b: Pointe-Claire, Que., 8/24/1968. Montreal's 2nd choice, 27th overall, in 1986 Entry Draft.

Season	Club	League	GP	G	A	Pts	AG	AA	APts	PIM	PP	SH	GW	S	%	TGF	PGF	TGA	PGA	+/–	GP	G	A	Pts	PIM	PP	SH	GW
1985-86	Hull Olympiques	QMJHL	71	33	37	70	....	....	....	81	....	....	....	....	....	....	....	....	....	....	....	....	....	....	....	....	....	....
1986-87	Hull Olympiques	QMJHL	60	43	67	110	....	....	....	105	....	....	....	....	....	....	....	....	....	....	6	7	5	12	8	....	....	....
1987-88	Hull Olympiques	QMJHL	62	54	89	143	....	....	....	131	....	....	....	....	....	....	....	....	....	....	10	3	10	13	11	....	....	....
1988-89	**Montreal Canadiens**	**NHL**	**2**	**0**	**1**	**1**	**0**	**1**	**1**	**0**	**0**	**0**	**0**	**1**	**0.0**	**2**	**0**	**2**	**0**	**0**	....	....	....	....	....	....	....	....
	Sherbrooke Canadiens	AHL	73	41	76	117	....	....	....	95	....	....	....	....	....	....	....	....	....	....	6	2	0	2	4	....	....	....
1989-90	Sherbrooke Canadiens	AHL	72	32	35	67	....	....	....	82	....	....	....	....	....	....	....	....	....	....	12	8	7	15	20	....	....	....
1990-91	Montreal Canadiens	FrTour	1	0	0	0	....	....	....	0	....	....	....	....	....	....	....	....	....	....	....	....	....	....	....	....	....	....
	Montreal Canadiens	**NHL**	**17**	**1**	**3**	**4**	**1**	**2**	**3**	**0**	**0**	**0**	**0**	**12**	**8.3**	**7**	**1**	**7**	**0**	**–1**	....	....	....	....	....	....	....	....
	Fredericton Canadiens	AHL	24	13	18	31	....	....	....	16	....	....	....	....	....	....	....	....	....	....	6	5	6	11	2	....	....	....
1991-92	**Montreal Canadiens**	**NHL**	**18**	**4**	**6**	**10**	**4**	**4**	**8**	**14**	**0**	**0**	**0**	**37**	**10.8**	**15**	**6**	**5**	**0**	**+4**	....	....	....	....	....	....	....	....
	Fredericton Canadiens	AHL	6	7	9	16	....	....	....	27	....	....	....	....	....	....	....	....	....	....	....	....	....	....	....	....	....	....
1992-93	**Montreal Canadiens**	**NHL**	**47**	**10**	**15**	**25**	**8**	**10**	**18**	**19**	**0**	**0**	**1**	**71**	**14.1**	**39**	**4**	**23**	**1**	**+13**	**20**	**2**	**8**	**10**	**8**	**1**	**0**	**1**
1993-94	**Montreal Canadiens**	**NHL**	**71**	**10**	**20**	**30**	**9**	**15**	**24**	**20**	**0**	**3**	**1**	**92**	**10.9**	**42**	**0**	**44**	**16**	**+14**	**7**	**1**	**4**	**5**	**16**	**0**	**0**	**0**
1994-95	**Montreal Canadiens**	**NHL**	**45**	**7**	**10**	**25**	**12**	**26**	**38**	**16**	**1**	**1**	**2**	**80**	**8.8**	**34**	**4**	**32**	**9**	**+7**	....	....	....	....	....	....	....	....

			REGULAR SEASON																		PLAYOFFS							
Season	**Club**	**League**	**GP**	**G**	**A**	**Pts**	**AG**	**AA**	**APts**	**PIM**	**PP**	**SH**	**GW**	**S**	**%**	**TGF**	**PGF**	**TGA**	**PGA**	**+/–**	**GP**	**G**	**A**	**Pts**	**PIM**	**PP**	**SH**	**GW**
1995-96	**Montreal Canadiens**	**NHL**	**26**	**7**	**8**	**15**	**7**	**7**	**14**	**17**	**3**	**1**	**4**	**48**	**14.6**	**19**	**6**	**27**	**10**	**–4**	**3**	**0**	**2**	**2**	**0**	**0**	**0**	**0**
	Fredericton Canadiens	AHL	3	2	1	3	....	....	....	6	....	....	....	....	....	....	....	....	....	....	....	....	....	....	....	....	....	....
1996-97	**Montreal Canadiens**	**NHL**	**39**	**10**	**13**	**23**	**11**	**11**	**22**	**14**	**2**	**0**	**2**	**63**	**15.9**	**36**	**5**	**36**	**11**	**+6**	**4**	**1**	**3**	**4**	**4**	**0**	**1**	**0**
1997-98	**Montreal Canadiens**	**NHL**	**68**	**12**	**20**	**32**	**14**	**19**	**33**	**61**	**1**	**2**	**2**	**87**	**13.8**	**51**	**13**	**41**	**14**	**+11**	**8**	**1**	**0**	**1**	**4**	**0**	**0**	**1**
	NHL Totals		**333**	**61**	**104**	**165**	**66**	**95**	**161**	**161**	**7**	**7**	**12**	**491**	**12.4**	**245**	**39**	**217**	**61**		**42**	**5**	**17**	**22**	**32**	**1**	**1**	**2**

QMJHL Second All-Star Team (1987) • AHL First All-Star Team (1989)

• BRUNETTE, ANDREW

Andrew Brunette LW – L. 6′, 212 lbs. b: Sudbury, Ont., 8/24/1973. Washington's 6th choice, 174th overall, in 1993 Entry Draft.

Season	Club	League	GP	G	A	Pts	AG	AA	APts	PIM	PP	SH	GW	S	%	TGF	PGF	TGA	PGA	+/–	GP	G	A	Pts	PIM	PP	SH	GW
1990-91	Owen Sound Platers	OHL	63	15	20	35	....	....	....	15	....	....	....	....	....	....	....	....	....	....	....	....	....	....	....	....	....	....
1991-92	Owen Sound Platers	OHL	66	51	47	98	....	....	....	42	....	....	....	....	....	....	....	....	....	....	5	5	0	5	8	....	....	....
1992-93	Owen Sound Platers	OHL	66	*62	*100	*162	....	....	....	91	....	....	....	....	....	....	....	....	....	....	8	8	6	14	16	....	....	....
1993-94	Portland Pirates	AHL	23	9	11	20	....	....	....	10	....	....	....	....	....	....	....	....	....	....	2	0	1	1	0	....	....	....
	Providence Bruins	AHL	3	0	0	0	....	....	....	0	....	....	....	....	....	....	....	....	....	....	....	....	....	....	....	....	....	....
	Hampton Roads Admirals	ECHL	20	12	18	30	....	....	....	32	....	....	....	....	....	....	....	....	....	....	7	7	6	13	18	....	....	....
1994-95	Portland Pirates	AHL	79	30	50	80	....	....	....	53	....	....	....	....	....	....	....	....	....	....	7	3	3	6	10	....	....	....
1995-96	**Washington Capitals**	**NHL**	**11**	**3**	**3**	**6**	**3**	**2**	**5**	**0**	**0**	**0**	**1**	**16**	**18.8**	**10**	**1**	**4**	**0**	**+5**	**6**	**1**	**3**	**4**	**0**	**0**	**0**	**0**
	Portland Pirates	AHL	69	28	66	94	....	....	....	125	....	....	....	....	....	....	....	....	....	....	20	11	18	29	15	....	....	....
1996-97	**Washington Capitals**	**NHL**	**23**	**4**	**7**	**11**	**4**	**6**	**10**	**12**	**2**	**0**	**0**	**23**	**17.4**	**15**	**7**	**11**	**0**	**–3**	....	....	....	....	....	....	....	....
	Portland Pirates	AHL	50	22	51	73	....	....	....	48	....	....	....	....	....	....	....	....	....	....	5	1	2	3	0	....	....	....
1997-98	**Washington Capitals**	**NHL**	**28**	**11**	**12**	**23**	**13**	**12**	**25**	**12**	**4**	**0**	**2**	**42**	**26.2**	**27**	**9**	**16**	**0**	**+2**	....	....	....	....	....	....	....	....
	Portland Pirates	AHL	43	21	46	67	....	....	....	64	....	....	....	....	....	....	....	....	....	....	10	1	11	12	12	....	....	....
	NHL Totals		**62**	**18**	**22**	**40**	**20**	**20**	**40**	**24**	**6**	**0**	**3**	**81**	**22.2**	**52**	**17**	**31**	**0**		**6**	**1**	**3**	**4**	**0**	**0**	**0**	**0**

OHL First All-Star Team (1993) • Canadian Major Junior Second All-Star Team (1993) • AHL Second All-Star Team (1995)

Claimed by **Nashville** from **Washington** in Expansion Draft, June 26, 1998.

• BRYDGES, PAUL

Paul Brydges C – R. 5′11″, 180 lbs. b: Guelph, Ont., 6/21/1965.

Season	Club	League	GP	G	A	Pts	AG	AA	APts	PIM	PP	SH	GW	S	%	TGF	PGF	TGA	PGA	+/–	GP	G	A	Pts	PIM	PP	SH	GW
1982-83	Guelph Platers	OHL	56	13	13	26	....	....	....	27	....	....	....	....	....	....	....	....	....	....	....	....	....	....	....	....	....	....
1983-84	Guelph Platers	OHL	68	27	23	50	....	....	....	37	....	....	....	....	....	....	....	....	....	....	....	....	....	....	....	....	....	....
1984-85	Guelph Platers	OHL	57	22	24	46	....	....	....	39	....	....	....	....	....	....	....	....	....	....	....	....	....	....	....	....	....	....
1985-86	Guelph Platers	OHL	62	17	40	57	....	....	....	88	....	....	....	....	....	....	....	....	....	....	19	10	15	25	22	....	....	....
1986-87	**Buffalo Sabres**	**NHL**	**15**	**2**	**2**	**4**	**2**	**1**	**3**	**6**	**0**	**0**	**0**	**8**	**25.0**	**9**	**0**	**9**	**4**	**+4**	....	....	....	....	....	....	....	....
	Rochester Americans	AHL	54	13	17	30	....	....	....	54	....	....	....	....	....	....	....	....	....	....	1	0	0	0	0	....	....	....
1987-88	Rochester Americans	AHL	69	15	16	31	....	....	....	86	....	....	....	....	....	....	....	....	....	....	7	1	1	2	4	....	....	....
1988-89	Rochester Americans	AHL	51	8	3	11	....	....	....	36	....	....	....	....	....	....	....	....	....	....	....	....	....	....	....	....	....	....
1989-90	New Haven Nighthawks	AHL	37	6	7	13	....	....	....	38	....	....	....	....	....	....	....	....	....	....	....	....	....	....	....	....	....	....
	NHL Totals		**15**	**2**	**2**	**4**	**2**	**1**	**3**	**6**	**0**	**0**	**0**	**8**	**25.0**	**9**	**0**	**9**	**4**		....	....	....	....	....	....	....	....

Signed as a free agent by **Buffalo**, June 11, 1986.

• BRYLIN, SERGEI

Sergei Brylin C – L. 5′10″, 190 lbs. b: Moscow, USSR, 1/13/1974. New Jersey's 2nd choice, 42nd overall, in 1992 Entry Draft.

Season	Club	League	GP	G	A	Pts	AG	AA	APts	PIM	PP	SH	GW	S	%	TGF	PGF	TGA	PGA	+/–	GP	G	A	Pts	PIM	PP	SH	GW
1991-92	CSKA Moscow	CIS	44	1	6	7	....	....	....	4	....	....	....	....	....	....	....	....	....	....	....	....	....	....	....	....	....	....
1992-93	CSKA Moscow	CIS	42	5	4	9	....	....	....	36	....	....	....	....	....	....	....	....	....	....	....	....	....	....	....	....	....	....
	Russia	WJC-A	7	3	3	6	....	....	....	6	....	....	....	....	....	....	....	....	....	....	....	....	....	....	....	....	....	....
1993-94	CSKA Moscow	CIS	39	4	6	10	....	....	....	36	....	....	....	....	....	....	....	....	....	....	3	1	0	1	2	....	....	....
	Russia	WJC-A	7	1	5	6	....	....	....	0	....	....	....	....	....	....	....	....	....	....	....	....	....	....	....	....	....	....
	Russian Penguins	IHL	13	4	5	9	....	....	....	18	....	....	....	....	....	....	....	....	....	....	....	....	....	....	....	....	....	....
1994-95	**New Jersey Devils**	**NHL**	**26**	**6**	**8**	**14**	**11**	**12**	**23**	**8**	**0**	**0**	**0**	**41**	**14.6**	**20**	**5**	**3**	**0**	**+12**	**12**	**1**	**2**	**3**	**4**	**0**	**0**	**0**
	Albany River Rats	AHL	63	19	35	54	....	....	....	78	....	....	....	....	....	....	....	....	....	....	....	....	....	....	....	....	....	....
1995-96	**New Jersey Devils**	**NHL**	**50**	**4**	**5**	**9**	**4**	**4**	**8**	**26**	**0**	**0**	**1**	**51**	**7.8**	**19**	**2**	**21**	**2**	**–2**	....	....	....	....	....	....	....	....
	Russia	WC-A	8	3	2	5	....	....	....	12	....	....	....	....	....	....	....	....	....	....	....	....	....	....	....	....	....	....
1996-97	**New Jersey Devils**	**NHL**	**29**	**2**	**2**	**4**	**2**	**2**	**4**	**20**	**0**	**0**	**0**	**34**	**5.9**	**9**	**2**	**20**	**0**	**–13**	....	....	....	....	....	....	....	....
	Albany River Rats	AHL	43	17	24	41	....	....	....	38	....	....	....	....	....	....	....	....	....	....	16	4	8	12	12	....	....	....
1997-98	**New Jersey Devils**	**NHL**	**18**	**2**	**3**	**5**	**2**	**3**	**5**	**0**	**0**	**0**	**0**	**20**	**10.0**	**5**	**0**	**1**	**0**	**+4**	....	....	....	....	....	....	....	....
	Albany River Rats	AHL	44	21	22	43	....	....	....	60	....	....	....	....	....	....	....	....	....	....	....	....	....	....	....	....	....	....
	NHL Totals		**123**	**14**	**18**	**32**	**19**	**21**	**40**	**54**	**0**	**0**	**1**	**146**	**9.6**	**53**	**9**	**45**	**2**		**12**	**1**	**2**	**3**	**4**	**0**	**0**	**0**

• BUBLA, JIRI

Jiri Bubla D – L. 5′11″, 200 lbs. b: Usti nad Labem, CSSR, 1/27/1950.

Season	Club	League	GP	G	A	Pts	AG	AA	APts	PIM	PP	SH	GW	S	%	TGF	PGF	TGA	PGA	+/–	GP	G	A	Pts	PIM	PP	SH	GW
1970-71	Czechoslovakia	WEC-A	9	1	0	1	....	....	....	2	....	....	....	....	....	....	....	....	....	....	....	....	....	....	....	....	....	....
1971-72	Czechoslovakia	WEC-A	10	0	1	1	....	....	....	8	....	....	....	....	....	....	....	....	....	....	....	....	....	....	....	....	....	....
1972-73	Czechoslovakia	WEC-A	10	1	2	3	....	....	....	6	....	....	....	....	....	....	....	....	....	....	....	....	....	....	....	....	....	....
1973-74	Czechoslovakia	WEC-A	10	1	3	4	....	....	....	2	....	....	....	....	....	....	....	....	....	....	....	....	....	....	....	....	....	....
1974-75	Czechoslovakia	WEC-A	10	1	2	3	....	....	....	6	....	....	....	....	....	....	....	....	....	....	....	....	....	....	....	....	....	....
1975-76	Czechoslovakia	Olympics	5	1	3	4	....	....	....	6	....	....	....	....	....	....	....	....	....	....	....	....	....	....	....	....	....	....
	Czechoslovakia	WEC-A	10	4	3	7	....	....	....	2	....	....	....	....	....	....	....	....	....	....	....	....	....	....	....	....	....	....
1976-77	Czechoslovakia	C Cup	7	3	2	5	....	....	....	4	....	....	....	....	....	....	....	....	....	....	....	....	....	....	....	....	....	....
	Czechoslovakia	WEC-A	10	0	4	4	....	....	....	6	....	....	....	....	....	....	....	....	....	....	....	....	....	....	....	....	....	....
1977-78	Czechoslovakia	WEC-A	9	1	2	3	....	....	....	8	....	....	....	....	....	....	....	....	....	....	....	....	....	....	....	....	....	....
1978-79	Czechoslovakia	WEC-A	8	2	2	4	....	....	....	8	....	....	....	....	....	....	....	....	....	....	....	....	....	....	....	....	....	....
1979-80	Czechoslovakia	Olympics	6	0	3	3	....	....	....	2	....	....	....	....	....	....	....	....	....	....	....	....	....	....	....	....	....	....
1980-81	Sparta Praha	Czech.	40	4	16	20	....	....	....	....	....	....	....	....	....	....	....	....	....	....	....	....	....	....	....	....	....	....
1981-82	**Vancouver Canucks**	**NHL**	**23**	**1**	**1**	**2**	**1**	**1**	**2**	**16**	**0**	**0**	**0**	**23**	**4.3**	**27**	**1**	**21**	**3**	**+8**	....	....	....	....	....	....	....	....
1982-83	**Vancouver Canucks**	**NHL**	**72**	**2**	**28**	**30**	**2**	**19**	**21**	**59**	**1**	**0**	**0**	**92**	**2.2**	**96**	**31**	**82**	**8**	**–9**	**1**	**0**	**0**	**0**	**5**	**0**	**0**	**0**
1983-84	**Vancouver Canucks**	**NHL**	**62**	**6**	**33**	**39**	**5**	**22**	**27**	**43**	**2**	**0**	**1**	**84**	**7.1**	**107**	**39**	**97**	**19**	**–10**	**2**	**0**	**0**	**0**	**0**	**0**	**0**	**0**
1984-85	**Vancouver Canucks**	**NHL**	**56**	**2**	**15**	**17**	**2**	**10**	**12**	**54**	**0**	**0**	**0**	**73**	**2.7**	**50**	**5**	**88**	**28**	**–15**	....	....	....	....	....	....	....	....
1985-86	**Vancouver Canucks**	**NHL**	**43**	**6**	**24**	**30**	**5**	**16**	**21**	**30**	**4**	**0**	**1**	**62**	**9.7**	**78**	**32**	**88**	**17**	**–25**	**3**	**0**	**0**	**0**	**2**	**0**	**0**	**0**
	NHL Totals		**256**	**17**	**101**	**118**	**15**	**68**	**83**	**202**	**7**	**0**	**2**	**334**	**5.1**	**358**	**108**	**376**	**75**		**6**	**0**	**0**	**0**	**7**	**0**	**0**	**0**

WEC-A All-Star Team (1978, 1979) • Named Best Defenseman at WEC-A (1979)

Claimed in Special Czechoslovakian Entry Draft by **Colorado**, May 28, 1981. Rights traded to **Vancouver** by **Colorado** to complete transaction that sent Brent Ashton to Winnipeg, July 15, 1981.

• BUCHANAN, RON

Ron "Senior" Buchanan C – L. 6′3″, 170 lbs. b: Montreal, Que., 11/15/1944.

Season	Club	League	GP	G	A	Pts	AG	AA	APts	PIM	PP	SH	GW	S	%	TGF	PGF	TGA	PGA	+/–	GP	G	A	Pts	PIM	PP	SH	GW
1962-63	Oshawa Generals	OHA	39	13	25	38	....	....	....	18	....	....	....	....	....	....	....	....	....	....	....	....	....	....	....	....	....	....
1963-64	Oshawa Generals	OHA	56	52	47	99	....	....	....	38	....	....	....	....	....	....	....	....	....	....	4	4	3	7	12	....	....	....
1964-65	Oshawa Generals	OHA	49	50	53	103	....	....	....	21	....	....	....	....	....	....	....	....	....	....	6	5	3	8	0	....	....	....
	Minneapolis Bruins	CHL	....	....	....	....	....	....	....	....	....	....	....	....	....	....	....	....	....	....	4	0	0	0	0	....	....	....
1965-66	Oklahoma City Blazers	CHL	70	27	16	43	....	....	....	33	....	....	....	....	....	....	....	....	....	....	9	5	5	10	0	....	....	....
1966-67	**Boston Bruins**	**NHL**	**3**	**0**	**0**	**0**	**0**	**0**	**0**	**0**	....	....	....	....	....	....	....	....	....	....	....	....	....	....	....	....	....	....
	Oklahoma City Blazers	CHL	56	34	35	69	....	....	....	23	....	....	....	....	....	....	....	....	....	....	11	5	5	10	6	....	....	....
1967-68	Oklahoma City Blazers	CHL	64	26	48	74	....	....	....	41	....	....	....	....	....	....	....	....	....	....	....	....	....	....	....	....	....	....
1968-69	Quebec Aces	AHL	11	3	1	4	....	....	....	2	....	....	....	....	....	....	....	....	....	....	....	....	....	....	....	....	....	....
	Kansas City Blues	CHL	50	16	45	61	....	....	....	16	....	....	....	....	....	....	....	....	....	....	....	....	....	....	....	....	....	....
1969-70	**St. Louis Blues**	**NHL**	**2**	**0**	**0**	**0**	**0**	**0**	**0**	**0**	**0**	**0**	**0**	**4**	**0.0**	**0**	**0**	**1**	**0**	**–1**	....	....	....	....	....	....	....	....
	Kansas City Blues	CHL	66	26	48	74	....	....	....	79	....	....	....	....	....	....	....	....	....	....	....	....	....	....	....	....	....	....
	Buffalo Bisons	AHL	....	....	....	....	....	....	....	....	....	....	....	....	....	....	....	....	....	....	1	0	0	0	0	....	....	....
1970-71	Kansas City Blues	CHL	63	23	33	56	....	....	....	31	....	....	....	....	....	....	....	....	....	....	....	....	....	....	....	....	....	....
1971-72	Denver Spurs	WHL	69	38	42	80	....	....	....	10	....	....	....	....	....	....	....	....	....	....	9	5	6	11	8	....	....	....
1972-73	Cleveland Crusaders	WHA	75	37	44	81	....	....	....	20	....	....	....	....	....	....	....	....	....	....	9	7	3	10	0	....	....	....
1973-74	Cleveland Crusaders	WHA	49	18	27	45	....	....	....	2	....	....	....	....	....	....	....	....	....	....	5	0	0	0	2	....	....	....

Season	Club	League	REGULAR SEASON GP	G	A	Pts	AG	AA	APts	PIM	PP	SH	GW	S	%	TGF	PGF	TGA	PGA	+/−	PLAYOFFS GP	G	A	Pts	PIM	PP	SH	GW
1974-75	Cleveland Crusaders	WHA	4	2	0	2	...	...	...	2											...	...	...	...	...			
	Edmonton Oilers	WHA	22	6	9	15	...	...	...	4																		
	Indianapolis Racers	WHA	32	16	15	31	...	...	...	16																		
1975-76	Indianapolis Racers	WHA	23	4	7	11	...	...	...	4																		
	NHL Totals		5	0	0	0	0	0	0	0	0	0	0	4	0.0	0	0	0	1	0	...							
	Other Major League Totals		205	83	102	185				48											14	7	3	10	2			

CHL Second All-Star Team (1968)

Claimed by **Philadelphia** from **Boston** in Intra-League Draft, June 12, 1968. Traded to **St. Louis** by **Philadelphia** for cash, May 14, 1969. Selected by **Minnesota** (WHA) in 1972 WHA General Player Draft, February 12, 1972. WHA rights traded to **Cleveland** (WHA) by **Minnesota** (WHA), July, 1972. Traded to **Edmonton** (WHA) by **Cleveland** (WHA) for Jim Harrison, October 14, 1974. Traded to **Indianapolis** (WHA) by **Edmonton** (WHA) for Murray Kennett, January, 1975.

● BUCHBERGER, KELLY
Kelly Buchberger   RW – L. 6'2", 200 lbs. b: Langenburg, Sask., 12/2/1966. Edmonton's 8th choice, 188th overall, in 1985 Entry Draft.

Season	Club	League	GP	G	A	Pts	AG	AA	APts	PIM	PP	SH	GW	S	%	TGF	PGF	TGA	PGA	+/−	GP	G	A	Pts	PIM	PP	SH	GW
1984-85	Moose Jaw Warriors	WHL	51	12	17	29	...	...	...	114																		
1985-86	Moose Jaw Warriors	WHL	72	14	22	36	...	...	...	206											13	11	4	15	37			
1986-87	Nova Scotia Oilers	AHL	70	12	20	32	...	...	...	257											5	0	1	1	23			
	Edmonton Oilers	**NHL**	...	...	...	...				...											3	0	1	1	5			
1987-88	Edmonton Oilers	NHL	19	1	0	1	1	0	1	81	0	0	0	10	10.0	4	0	5	0	−1								
	Nova Scotia Oilers	AHL	49	21	23	44	...	...	...	206											2	0	0	0	11			
1988-89	Edmonton Oilers	NHL	66	5	9	14	4	6	10	234	1	0	1	57	8.8	27	8	33	0	−14	...	...	...	...	...			
1989-90	Edmonton Oilers	NHL	55	2	6	8	2	4	6	168	0	0	2	35	5.7	12	0	20	0	−8	19	0	5	5	13	0	0	0
1990-91	Edmonton Oilers	NHL	64	3	1	4	3	1	4	160	0	0	0	54	5.6	14	0	20	0	−6	12	2	1	3	25	0	0	0
1991-92	Edmonton Oilers	NHL	79	20	24	44	18	18	36	157	0	4	3	90	22.2	52	2	74	33	+9	16	1	4	5	32	0	0	0
1992-93	Edmonton Oilers	NHL	83	12	18	30	10	12	22	133	1	2	3	92	13.0	42	4	113	48	−27								
	Canada	WC-A	8	0	2	2				6																		
1993-94	Edmonton Oilers	NHL	84	3	18	21	3	14	17	199	0	0	0	93	3.2	33	3	82	32	−20								
	Canada	WC-A	8	0	0	0				8																		
1994-95	Edmonton Oilers	NHL	48	7	17	24	12	25	37	82	2	1	5	73	9.6	37	3	67	33	0								
1995-96	Edmonton Oilers	NHL	82	11	14	25	11	11	22	184	0	2	3	119	9.2	44	3	104	43	−20								
	Canada	WC-A	4	0	0	0				6																		
1996-97	Edmonton Oilers	NHL	81	8	30	38	8	27	35	159	0	0	3	78	10.3	51	1	70	24	+4	12	5	2	7	16	0	0	1
1997-98	Edmonton Oilers	NHL	82	6	17	23	7	17	24	122	1	1	1	86	7.0	37	3	79	35	−10	12	1	2	3	25	0	0	0
	NHL Totals		743	78	154	232	79	135	214	1679	5	10	23	787	9.9	353	27	667	248		74	9	15	24	116	0	0	1

● BUCYK, JOHN
John "Chief" Bucyk   LW – L. 6', 190 lbs. b: Edmonton, Alta., 5/12/1935.   HHOF

Season	Club	League	GP	G	A	Pts	AG	AA	APts	PIM	PP	SH	GW	S	%	TGF	PGF	TGA	PGA	+/−	GP	G	A	Pts	PIM	PP	SH	GW
1951-52	Edmonton Maple Leafs	AJHL	STATISTICS NOT AVAILABLE																		1	0	0	0	0			
	Edmonton Oil Kings	WCJHL																			13	5	1	6	14			
1952-53	Edmonton Oil Kings	WCJHL	34	19	11	30	...	...	...	24											9	13	9	22	22			
1953-54	Edmonton Oil Kings	WCJHL	33	29	38	67	...	...	...	38																		
	Edmonton Flyers	WHL	2	2	0	2				2																		
1954-55	Edmonton Flyers	WHL	70	30	58	88	...	...	...	57											9	1	6	7	7			
1955-56	**Detroit Red Wings**	**NHL**	38	1	8	9	1	10	11	20											10	1	1	2	8			
	Edmonton Flyers	WHL	6	0	0	0				9																		
1956-57	**Detroit Red Wings**	**NHL**	66	10	11	21	14	13	27	41											5	0	1	1	0			
1957-58	**Boston Bruins**	**NHL**	68	21	31	52	28	34	62	57											12	0	4	4	16			
1958-59	**Boston Bruins**	**NHL**	69	24	36	60	31	39	70	36											7	2	4	6	6			
1959-60	Boston Bruins	NHL	56	16	36	52	20	37	57	26																		
1960-61	Boston Bruins	NHL	70	19	20	39	23	20	43	48																		
1961-62	Boston Bruins	NHL	67	20	40	60	24	41	65	32																		
1962-63	Boston Bruins	NHL	69	27	39	66	34	41	75	36																		
1963-64	Boston Bruins	NHL	62	18	36	54	24	40	64	36																		
1964-65	Boston Bruins	NHL	68	26	29	55	33	31	64	24																		
1965-66	Boston Bruins	NHL	63	27	30	57	33	30	63	12																		
1966-67	Boston Bruins	NHL	59	18	30	48	22	31	53	12																		
1967-68	Boston Bruins	NHL	72	30	39	69	37	41	78	8	6	1	4	172	17.4	101	29	54	0	+18	3	0	2	2	0	0	0	0
1968-69	Boston Bruins	NHL	70	24	42	66	27	40	67	18	11	0	3	192	12.5	95	36	62	0	−3	10	5	6	11	0	2	1	0
1969-70	Boston Bruins	NHL	76	31	38	69	36	38	74	13	14	0	6	190	16.3	116	61	38	2	+19	14	11	8	19	2	4	1	0
1970-71	Boston Bruins	NHL	78	51	65	116	54	58	112	8	22	0	5	225	22.7	154	70	48	0	+36	7	2	5	7	0	0	0	0
1971-72	Boston Bruins	NHL	78	32	51	83	34	47	81	4	13	0	7	174	18.4	123	65	42	0	+16	15	9	11	20	6	0	0	0
1972-73	Boston Bruins	NHL	78	40	53	93	40	44	84	12	10	0	10	168	23.8	133	53	62	0	+8	5	0	3	3	0	0	0	0
1973-74	Boston Bruins	NHL	76	31	44	75	32	30	70	8	12	0	10	139	22.3	115	47	55	0	+13	16	8	10	18	4	3	0	1
1974-75	Boston Bruins	NHL	78	29	52	81	27	41	68	10	9	0	4	167	17.4	133	63	60	1	+11	3	1	0	1	0	0	0	0
1975-76	Boston Bruins	NHL	77	36	47	83	34	37	71	20	13	0	5	151	23.8	129	56	51	0	+22	12	2	7	9	0	0	0	0
1976-77	Boston Bruins	NHL	49	20	23	43	19	19	38	12	6	0	2	98	20.4	58	21	39	0	−2	5	0	0	0	0	0	0	0
1977-78	Boston Bruins	NHL	53	5	13	18	5	11	16	4	5	0	1	47	10.6	28	15	15	0	−2								
	NHL Totals		1540	556	813	1369	602	781	1413	497	121		59	1723	32.3	1185	516	526	3		124	41	62	103	42	11	2	1

Won WHL Rookie of the Year Award (1955) ● NHL Second All-Star Team (1968) ● NHL First All-Star Team (1971) ● Won Lady Byng Trophy (1971, 1974) ● Won Lester Patrick Trophy (1977)
Played in NHL All-Star Game (1955, 1963, 1964, 1965, 1968, 1970, 1971)

Traded to **Boston** by **Detroit** for Terry Sawchuk, July 24, 1957.

● BUCYK, RANDY
Randy Bucyk   C – L. 5'11", 185 lbs. b: Edmonton, Alta., 11/9/1962.

Season	Club	League	GP	G	A	Pts	AG	AA	APts	PIM	PP	SH	GW	S	%	TGF	PGF	TGA	PGA	+/−	GP	G	A	Pts	PIM	PP	SH	GW
1980-81	Northeastern University	ECAC	31	18	17	35	...	...	...	0																		
1981-82	Northeastern University	ECAC	33	19	17	36	...	...	...	10																		
1982-83	Northeastern University	ECAC	28	16	20	36	...	...	...	16																		
1983-84	Northeastern University	ECAC	29	16	13	29	...	...	...	11																		
1984-85	Sherbrooke Canadiens	AHL	62	21	26	47	...	...	...	20											8	0	0	0	20			
1985-86	**Montreal Canadiens**	**NHL**	17	4	2	6	3	1	4	8	0	0	0	21	19.0	8	0	4	1	+5	2	0	0	0	0	0	0	0
	Sherbrooke Canadiens	AHL	43	18	33	51	...	...	...	22																		
1986-87	Sherbrooke Canadiens	AHL	70	24	39	63	...	...	...	28											17	3	11	14	2			
1987-88	**Calgary Flames**	**NHL**	2	0	0	0	0	0	0	0	0	0	0	2	0.0	1	0	2	0	−1								
	Salt Lake Golden Eagles	IHL	75	37	45	82	...	...	...	68											19	7	8	15	12			
1988-89	Salt Lake Golden Eagles	IHL	79	28	59	81	...	...	...	24											14	5	5	10	4			
	Canada	Nat-Team	4	0	0	0				2																		
1989-90	Salt Lake Golden Eagles	IHL	67	22	41	63	...	...	...	16											11	2	6	8	10			
1990-91	Salt Lake Golden Eagles	IHL	18	4	4	8	...	...	...	11																		
	NHL Totals		19	4	2	6	3	1	4	8	0	0	0	23	17.4	9	0	6	1		2	0	0	0	0	0	0	0

Signed as a free agent by **Montreal**, January 15, 1986. Signed as a free agent by **Calgary**, June 29, 1987.

• BUHR, DOUG
Doug Buhr LW – L. 6'3", 215 lbs. b: Vancouver, B.C., 6/29/1949.

			REGULAR SEASON																		PLAYOFFS							
Season	Club	League	GP	G	A	Pts	AG	AA	APts	PIM	PP	SH	GW	S	%	TGF	PGF	TGA	PGA	+/-	GP	G	A	Pts	PIM	PP	SH	GW
1971-72	University of British Columbia	WCIAA	STATISTICS NOT AVAILABLE																									
1972-73	Springfield Kings	AHL	71	10	12	22	....	....	....	152	....	....	....	....	....	....	....	....	....	....	....	....	....	....	....	....	....	....
1973-74	Springfield Kings	AHL	29	2	4	6	....	....	....	42	....	....	....	....	....	....	....	....	....	....	....	....	....	....	....	....	....	....
	Portland Buckaroos	WHL	37	1	4	5	....	....	....	117	....	....	....	....	....	....	....	....	....	....	10	1	0	1	27	....	....	....
1974-75	**Kansas City Scouts**	**NHL**	**6**	**0**	**2**	**2**	**0**	**2**	**2**	**4**	**0**	**0**	**0**	**3**	**0.0**	**2**	**0**	**2**	**0**	**0**	....	....	....	....	....	....	....	....
	Springfield Indians	AHL	44	5	6	11	....	....	....	81	....	....	....	....	....	....	....	....	....	....	....	....	....	....	....	....	....	....
	Oklahoma City Blazers	CHL	15	3	0	3	....	....	....	48	....	....	....	....	....	....	....	....	....	....	4	0	0	0	2	....	....	....
1975-76	Trail Smoke Eaters	WIHL	STATISTICS NOT AVAILABLE																									
1976-77	Trail Smoke Eaters	WIHL	....	12	13	25	....	....	....	162	....	....	....	....	....	....	....	....	....	....	....	....	....	....	....	....	....	....
1977-78	Trail Smoke Eaters	WIHL	....	11	15	26	....	....	....	76	....	....	....	....	....	....	....	....	....	....	....	....	....	....	....	....	....	....
	NHL Totals		**6**	**0**	**2**	**2**	**0**	**2**	**2**	**4**	**0**	**0**	**0**	**3**	**0.0**	**2**	**0**	**2**	**0**		....	....	....	....	....	....	....	....

Signed as a free agent by **LA Kings**, October 2, 1972. Traded to **Kansas City** by **LA Kings** for cash, February, 1975.

• BULIS, JAN
Jan Bulis C – L. 6', 194 lbs. b: Pardubice, Czech., 3/18/1978. Washington's 3rd choice, 43rd overall, in 1996 Entry Draft.

Season	Club	League	GP	G	A	Pts	AG	AA	APts	PIM	PP	SH	GW	S	%	TGF	PGF	TGA	PGA	+/-	GP	G	A	Pts	PIM	PP	SH	GW
1995-96	Barrie Colts	OHL	59	29	30	59	....	....	....	22	....	....	....	....	....	....	....	....	....	....	7	2	3	5	2	....	....	....
1996-97	Barrie Colts	OHL	64	42	61	103	....	....	....	42	....	....	....	....	....	....	....	....	....	....	9	3	7	10	10	....	....	....
1997-98	Kingston Frontenacs	OHL	2	0	1	1	....	....	....	0	....	....	....	....	....	....	....	....	....	....	12	8	10	18	12	....	....	....
	Washington Capitals	**NHL**	**48**	**5**	**11**	**16**	**6**	**11**	**17**	**18**	**0**	**0**	**0**	**37**	**13.5**	**24**	**2**	**27**	**0**	**–5**	....	....	....	....	....	....	....	....
	Portland Pirates	AHL	3	1	4	5	....	....	....	12	....	....	....	....	....	....	....	....	....	....	....	....	....	....	....	....	....	....
	NHL Totals		**48**	**5**	**11**	**16**	**6**	**11**	**17**	**18**	**0**	**0**	**0**	**37**	**13.5**	**24**	**2**	**27**	**0**		....	....	....	....	....	....	....	....

• BULLARD, MIKE
Mike Bullard C – L. 6', 195 lbs. b: Ottawa, Ont., 3/10/1961. Pittsburgh's 1st choice, 9th overall, in 1980 Entry Draft.

Season	Club	League	GP	G	A	Pts	AG	AA	APts	PIM	PP	SH	GW	S	%	TGF	PGF	TGA	PGA	+/-	GP	G	A	Pts	PIM	PP	SH	GW
1978-79	Brantford Alexanders	OHA	66	43	56	99	....	....	....	66	....	....	....	....	....	....	....	....	....	....	....	....	....	....	....	....	....	....
1979-80	Brantford Alexanders	OHA	66	66	84	150	....	....	....	86	....	....	....	....	....	....	....	....	....	....	11	10	6	16	29	....	....	....
1980-81	Brantford Alexanders	OHA	42	47	60	107	....	....	....	55	....	....	....	....	....	....	....	....	....	....	6	4	5	9	10	....	....	....
	Pittsburgh Penguins	**NHL**	**15**	**1**	**2**	**3**	**1**	**1**	**2**	**19**	**0**	**0**	**0**	**18**	**5.6**	**8**	**1**	**8**	**0**	**–1**	**4**	**3**	**3**	**6**	**0**	**1**	**0**	**1**
1981-82	**Pittsburgh Penguins**	**NHL**	**75**	**36**	**27**	**63**	**29**	**18**	**47**	**91**	**10**	**0**	**5**	**145**	**24.8**	**82**	**26**	**58**	**1**	**–1**	**5**	**1**	**1**	**2**	**4**	**0**	**0**	**0**
1982-83	**Pittsburgh Penguins**	**NHL**	**57**	**22**	**22**	**44**	**18**	**15**	**33**	**60**	**3**	**0**	**2**	**148**	**14.9**	**61**	**15**	**68**	**1**	**–21**	....	....	....	....	....	....	....	....
1983-84	**Pittsburgh Penguins**	**NHL**	**76**	**51**	**41**	**92**	**41**	**28**	**69**	**57**	**15**	**0**	**0**	**213**	**23.9**	**119**	**43**	**112**	**3**	**–33**	....	....	....	....	....	....	....	....
1984-85	**Pittsburgh Penguins**	**NHL**	**68**	**32**	**31**	**63**	**26**	**21**	**47**	**75**	**14**	**0**	**3**	**185**	**17.3**	**88**	**36**	**97**	**2**	**–43**	....	....	....	....	....	....	....	....
1985-86	**Pittsburgh Penguins**	**NHL**	**77**	**41**	**42**	**83**	**33**	**28**	**61**	**69**	**16**	**2**	**5**	**213**	**19.2**	**114**	**51**	**97**	**18**	**–16**	....	....	....	....	....	....	....	....
	Canada	WEC-A	10	2	1	3	....	....	....	2	....	....	....	....	....	....	....	....	....	....	....	....	....	....	....	....	....	....
1986-87	**Pittsburgh Penguins**	**NHL**	**14**	**2**	**10**	**12**	**2**	**7**	**9**	**17**	**0**	**0**	**0**	**49**	**4.1**	**13**	**0**	**48**	**30**	**–5**	....	....	....	....	....	....	....	....
	Calgary Flames	**NHL**	**57**	**28**	**26**	**54**	**24**	**19**	**43**	**34**	**10**	**0**	**3**	**138**	**20.3**	**75**	**21**	**47**	**3**	**+10**	**6**	**4**	**3**	**7**	**2**	**3**	**0**	**1**
1987-88	**Calgary Flames**	**NHL**	**79**	**48**	**55**	**103**	**41**	**39**	**80**	**68**	**21**	**0**	**3**	**230**	**20.9**	**153**	**71**	**57**	**0**	**+25**	**6**	**0**	**2**	**2**	**6**	**0**	**0**	**0**
1988-89	**St. Louis Blues**	**NHL**	**20**	**4**	**12**	**16**	**3**	**8**	**11**	**46**	**2**	**0**	**0**	**52**	**7.7**	**23**	**8**	**14**	**0**	**+1**	....	....	....	....	....	....	....	....
	Philadelphia Flyers	**NHL**	**54**	**23**	**26**	**49**	**20**	**18**	**38**	**60**	**8**	**0**	**3**	**137**	**16.8**	**68**	**26**	**42**	**1**	**+1**	**19**	**3**	**9**	**12**	**32**	**1**	**0**	**0**
1989-90	**Philadelphia Flyers**	**NHL**	**70**	**27**	**37**	**64**	**23**	**26**	**49**	**67**	**6**	**0**	**4**	**181**	**14.9**	**86**	**31**	**55**	**0**	**0**	....	....	....	....	....	....	....	....
1990-91	Ambri-Piotta	Switz.	36	36	33	69	....	....	....	....	....	....	....	....	....	....	....	....	....	....	5	6	4	10	....	....	....	....
1991-92	**Toronto Maple Leafs**	**NHL**	**65**	**14**	**14**	**28**	**13**	**11**	**24**	**40**	**7**	**0**	**0**	**140**	**10.0**	**51**	**30**	**40**	**0**	**–19**	....	....	....	....	....	....	....	....
1992-93	Rapperswil	Switz.2	36	51	32	83	....	....	....	39	....	....	....	....	....	....	....	....	....	....	7	6	7	13	4	....	....	....
1993-94	EV Landshut	Germany	44	*37	26	*63	....	....	....	45	....	....	....	....	....	....	....	....	....	....	....	....	....	....	....	....	....	....
1994-95	EV Landshut	Germany	38	22	43	65	....	....	....	83	....	....	....	....	....	....	....	....	....	....	18	*17	10	*27	28	....	....	....
1995-96	EV Landshut	Germany	50	29	41	70	....	....	....	56	....	....	....	....	....	....	....	....	....	....	11	6	11	17	20	....	....	....
1996-97	EV Landshut	Germany	47	19	*51	70	....	....	....	69	....	....	....	....	....	....	....	....	....	....	7	6	4	10	40	....	....	....
1997-98	EV Landshut	Germany	45	12	24	36	....	....	....	63	....	....	....	....	....	....	....	....	....	....	6	5	5	10	8	....	....	....
	NHL Totals		**727**	**329**	**345**	**674**	**274**	**239**	**513**	**703**	**112**	**2**	**28**	**1849**	**17.8**	**941**	**359**	**743**	**59**		**40**	**11**	**18**	**29**	**44**	**5**	**0**	**2**

OHA Second All-Star Team (1980)

Played in NHL All-Star Game (1984)

Traded to **Calgary** by **Pittsburgh** for Dan Quinn, November 12, 1986. Traded to **St. Louis** by **Calgary** with Craig Coxe and Tim Corkey for Mark Hunter, Doug Gilmour, Steve Bozek and Michael Dark, September 6, 1988. Traded to **Philadelphia** by **St. Louis** for Peter Zezel, November 29, 1988. Rights traded to **Toronto** by **Philadelphia** for Toronto's 3rd round choice (Vaclav Prospal) in 1993 Entry Draft, July 29, 1991.

• BULLEY, TED
Ted Bulley LW – L. 6'1", 192 lbs. b: Windsor, Ont., 3/25/1955. Chicago's 7th choice, 115th overall, in 1975 Amateur Draft.

Season	Club	League	GP	G	A	Pts	AG	AA	APts	PIM	PP	SH	GW	S	%	TGF	PGF	TGA	PGA	+/-	GP	G	A	Pts	PIM	PP	SH	GW
1972-73	Windsor Spitfires	Tier II	....	9	10	19	....	....	....	....	....	....	....	....	....	....	....	....	....	....	....	....	....	....	....	....	....	....
1973-74	Hull Festivals	QMJHL	67	28	37	65	....	....	....	116	....	....	....	....	....	....	....	....	....	....	....	....	....	....	....	....	....	....
1974-75	Hull Festivals	QMJHL	70	48	61	109	....	....	....	124	....	....	....	....	....	....	....	....	....	....	4	1	2	3	9	....	....	....
1975-76	Flint Generals	IHL	38	15	13	28	....	....	....	123	....	....	....	....	....	....	....	....	....	....	....	....	....	....	....	....	....	....
	Dallas Black Hawks	CHL	2	0	0	0	....	....	....	0	....	....	....	....	....	....	....	....	....	....	7	0	1	1	4	....	....	....
1976-77	**Chicago Black Hawks**	**NHL**	**2**	**0**	**0**	**0**	**0**	**0**	**0**	**0**	**0**	**0**	**0**	**0**	**0.0**	**0**	**0**	**2**	**0**	**–2**	....	....	....	....	....	....	....	....
	Dallas Black Hawks	CHL	2	2	2	4	....	....	....	10	....	....	....	....	....	....	....	....	....	....	....	....	....	....	....	....	....	....
1977-78	**Chicago Black Hawks**	**NHL**	**79**	**23**	**28**	**51**	**22**	**23**	**45**	**141**	**6**	**0**	**5**	**150**	**15.3**	**81**	**25**	**53**	**1**	**+4**	**4**	**1**	**1**	**2**	**2**	**0**	**0**	**0**
1978-79	**Chicago Black Hawks**	**NHL**	**75**	**27**	**23**	**50**	**25**	**18**	**43**	**153**	**1**	**0**	**8**	**105**	**25.7**	**85**	**15**	**52**	**0**	**+18**	**2**	**0**	**0**	**0**	**0**	**0**	**0**	**0**
1979-80	**Chicago Black Hawks**	**NHL**	**66**	**14**	**17**	**31**	**13**	**13**	**26**	**136**	**1**	**0**	**1**	**125**	**11.2**	**48**	**12**	**48**	**0**	**–12**	**7**	**2**	**3**	**5**	**10**	**0**	**0**	**0**
1980-81	**Chicago Black Hawks**	**NHL**	**68**	**18**	**16**	**34**	**15**	**11**	**26**	**95**	**3**	**0**	**2**	**112**	**16.1**	**60**	**9**	**33**	**0**	**+18**	....	....	....	....	....	....	....	....
1981-82	**Chicago Black Hawks**	**NHL**	**59**	**12**	**18**	**30**	**9**	**12**	**21**	**120**	**2**	**0**	**2**	**83**	**14.5**	**47**	**5**	**43**	**0**	**–1**	**15**	**2**	**1**	**3**	**12**	**0**	**0**	**1**
1982-83	**Washington Capitals**	**NHL**	**39**	**4**	**9**	**13**	**3**	**6**	**9**	**47**	**0**	**0**	**1**	**35**	**11.4**	**19**	**1**	**22**	**1**	**–3**	**1**	**0**	**0**	**0**	**0**	**0**	**0**	**0**
1983-84	**Pittsburgh Penguins**	**NHL**	**26**	**3**	**2**	**5**	**2**	**1**	**3**	**12**	**0**	**0**	**1**	**27**	**11.1**	**5**	**0**	**20**	**1**	**–14**	....	....	....	....	....	....	....	....
	Baltimore Skipjacks	AHL	49	16	19	35	....	....	....	82	....	....	....	....	....	....	....	....	....	....	10	2	5	7	2	....	....	....
1984-85	Baltimore Skipjacks	AHL	57	9	11	20	....	....	....	125	....	....	....	....	....	....	....	....	....	....	14	1	1	2	25	....	....	....
	NHL Totals		**414**	**101**	**113**	**214**	**89**	**84**	**173**	**704**	**13**	**0**	**20**	**637**	**15.9**	**345**	**67**	**273**	**3**		**29**	**5**	**5**	**10**	**24**	**0**	**0**	**1**

Traded to **Washington** by **Chicago** with Dave Hutchinson for Washington's 6th round choice (Jari Torkki) in 1983 Entry Draft and 5th round choice (Darin Sceviour) in 1984 Entry Draft, August 24, 1982. Signed as a free agent by **Pittsburgh**, September 30, 1983.

• BURAKOVSKY, ROBERT
Robert Burakovsky RW – R. 5'10", 185 lbs. b: Malmo, Sweden, 11/24/1966. NY Rangers' 11th choice, 217th overall, in 1985 Entry Draft.

Season	Club	League	GP	G	A	Pts	AG	AA	APts	PIM	PP	SH	GW	S	%	TGF	PGF	TGA	PGA	+/-	GP	G	A	Pts	PIM	PP	SH	GW
1985-86	Leksands IF	Sweden	19	4	3	7	....	....	....	4	....	....	....	....	....	....	....	....	....	....	....	....	....	....	....	....	....	....
	Sweden	WJC-A	7	1	1	2	....	....	....	0	....	....	....	....	....	....	....	....	....	....	....	....	....	....	....	....	....	....
1986-87	Leksands IF	Sweden	36	21	15	36	....	....	....	26	....	....	....	....	....	....	....	....	....	....	....	....	....	....	....	....	....	....
1987-88	Leksands IF	Sweden	36	10	11	21	....	....	....	10	....	....	....	....	....	....	....	....	....	....	1	0	0	0	2	....	....	....
1988-89	Leksands IF	Sweden	40	23	20	43	....	....	....	44	....	....	....	....	....	....	....	....	....	....	10	6	7	13	4	....	....	....
1989-90	AIK Solna	Sweden	37	27	29	*56	....	....	....	32	....	....	....	....	....	....	....	....	....	....	3	0	2	2	12	....	....	....
1990-91	AIK Solna	Sweden	30	8	15	23	....	....	....	26	....	....	....	....	....	....	....	....	....	....	....	....	....	....	....	....	....	....
1991-92	Malmo IF	Sweden	40	19	22	41	....	....	....	42	....	....	....	....	....	....	....	....	....	....	9	5	0	5	4	....	....	....
1992-93	Malmo IF	Sweden	32	8	10	18	....	....	....	40	....	....	....	....	....	....	....	....	....	....	6	4	4	8	9	....	....	....
1993-94	**Ottawa Senators**	**NHL**	**23**	**2**	**3**	**5**	**2**	**2**	**4**	**6**	**0**	**0**	**0**	**40**	**5.0**	**8**	**0**	**15**	**0**	**–7**	....	....	....	....	....	....	....	....
	P.E.I. Senators	AHL	52	29	38	67	....	....	....	28	....	....	....	....	....	....	....	....	....	....	....	....	....	....	....	....	....	....
1994-95	Klagenfurt AC	Austria	28	28	36	64	....	....	....	40	....	....	....	....	....	....	....	....	....	....	3	2	2	4	2	....	....	....
1995-96	Malmo IF	Sweden	40	23	21	44	....	....	....	34	....	....	....	....	....	....	....	....	....	....	5	2	1	3	6	....	....	....
1996-97	Malmo IF	Sweden	33	19	17	36	....	....	....	44	....	....	....	....	....	....	....	....	....	....	....	....	....	....	....	....	....	....
	Kassel Huskies	Germany	11	5	7	12	....	....	....	4	....	....	....	....	....	....	....	....	....	....	10	4	6	10	6	....	....	....
1997-98	Kassel Huskies	Germany	17	7	6	13	....	....	....	0	....	....	....	....	....	....	....	....	....	....	....	....	....	....	....	....	....	....
	Ilves Tampere	Finland	11	5	4	9	....	....	....	40	....	....	....	....	....	....	....	....	....	....	9	7	3	10	0	....	....	....
	NHL Totals		**23**	**2**	**3**	**5**	**2**	**2**	**4**	**6**	**0**	**0**	**0**	**40**	**5.0**	**8**	**0**	**15**	**0**		....	....	....	....	....	....	....	....

Rights traded to **Ottawa** by **NY Rangers** for future considerations, May 7, 1993.

			REGULAR SEASON																		PLAYOFFS							
Season	Club	League	GP	G	A	Pts	AG	AA	APts	PIM	PP	SH	GW	S	%	TGF	PGF	TGA	PGA	+/–	GP	G	A	Pts	PIM	PP	SH	GW

● **BURDON, GLEN** Glen Burdon C – L. 6'2", 178 lbs. b: Regina, Sask., 8/4/1954. Kansas City's 2nd choice, 20th overall, in 1974 Amateur Draft.

Season	Club	League	GP	G	A	Pts	AG	AA	APts	PIM	PP	SH	GW	S	%	TGF	PGF	TGA	PGA	+/–	GP	G	A	Pts	PIM	PP	SH	GW
1971-72	Regina Pats	WCJHL	60	17	36	53	....	....	....	78	....	....	....	....	....	....	....	....	....	....	....	....	....	....	....	....	....	....
1972-73	Regina Pats	WCJHL	46	21	28	49	....	....	....	13	....	....	....	....	....	....	....	....	....	....	....	....	....	....	....	....	....	....
1973-74	Regina Pats	WCJHL	68	19	56	75	....	....	....	44	....	....	....	....	....	....	....	....	....	....	....	....	....	....	....	....	....	....
1974-75	**Kansas City Scouts**	**NHL**	**11**	**0**	**2**	**2**	**0**	**2**	**2**	**0**	**0**	**0**	**0**	**2**	**0.0**	**2**	**0**	**5**	**0**	**–3**	....	....	....	....	....	....	....	....
	Baltimore Clippers	AHL	5	0	0	0	....	....	....	0	....	....	....	....	....	....	....	....	....	....	....	....	....	....	....	....	....	....
	Providence Reds	AHL	25	1	2	3	....	....	....	12	....	....	....	....	....	....	....	....	....	....	....	....	....	....	....	....	....	....
1975-76	New Haven Nighthawks	AHL	23	1	5	6	....	....	....	6	....	....	....	....	....	....	....	....	....	....	....	....	....	....	....	....	....	....
1976-77	Kansas City Blues	CHL	3	0	0	0	....	....	....	0	....	....	....	....	....	....	....	....	....	....	....	....	....	....	....	....	....	....
1977-78			DID NOT PLAY																									
1978-79	Fort Wayne Komets	IHL	5	0	2	2	....	....	....	7	....	....	....	....	....	....	....	....	....	....	....	....	....	....	....	....	....	....
	NHL Totals		**11**	**0**	**2**	**2**	**0**	**2**	**2**	**0**	**0**	**0**	**0**	**2**	**0.0**	**2**	**0**	**5**	**0**		....	....	....	....	....	....	....	....

Traded to **Detroit** by **Kansas City** with Peter McDuffe for Bill McKenzie and Gary Bergman, August 22, 1975.

● **BURE, PAVEL** Pavel (The Russian Rocket) Bure RW – L. 5'10", 189 lbs. b: Moscow, USSR, 3/31/1971. Vancouver's 4th choice, 113th overall, in 1989 Entry Draft.

Season	Club	League	GP	G	A	Pts	AG	AA	APts	PIM	PP	SH	GW	S	%	TGF	PGF	TGA	PGA	+/–	GP	G	A	Pts	PIM	PP	SH	GW
1987-88	CSKA Moscow	USSR	5	1	1	2	....	....	....	0	....	....	....	....	....	....	....	....	....	....	....	....	....	....	....	....	....	....
1988-89	CSKA Moscow	USSR	32	17	9	26	....	....	....	8	....	....	....	....	....	....	....	....	....	....	....	....	....	....	....	....	....	....
	Soviet Union	WJC-A	7	8	6	14	....	....	....	4	....	....	....	....	....	....	....	....	....	....	....	....	....	....	....	....	....	....
1989-90	CSKA Moscow	FrTour	1	0	0	0	....	....	....	0	....	....	....	....	....	....	....	....	....	....	....	....	....	....	....	....	....	....
	CSKA Moscow	USSR	46	14	10	24	....	....	....	20	....	....	....	....	....	....	....	....	....	....	....	....	....	....	....	....	....	....
	Soviet Union	WJC-A	7	7	3	10	....	....	....	10	....	....	....	....	....	....	....	....	....	....	....	....	....	....	....	....	....	....
	Soviet Union	WEC-A	10	2	4	6	....	....	....	10	....	....	....	....	....	....	....	....	....	....	....	....	....	....	....	....	....	....
1990-91	CSKA Moscow	FrTour	1	1	0	1	....	....	....	2	....	....	....	....	....	....	....	....	....	....	....	....	....	....	....	....	....	....
	CSKA Moscow	USSR	44	35	11	46	....	....	....	24	....	....	....	....	....	....	....	....	....	....	....	....	....	....	....	....	....	....
	Soviet Union	WEC-A	10	3	8	11	....	....	....	2	....	....	....	....	....	....	....	....	....	....	....	....	....	....	....	....	....	....
1991-92	**Vancouver Canucks**	**NHL**	**65**	**34**	**26**	**60**	**31**	**20**	**51**	**30**	**7**	**3**	**6**	**268**	**12.7**	**84**	**29**	**69**	**14**	**0**	**13**	**6**	**4**	**10**	**14**	**0**	**0**	**0**
1992-93	**Vancouver Canucks**	**NHL**	**83**	**60**	**50**	**110**	**50**	**34**	**84**	**69**	**13**	**7**	**9**	**407**	**14.7**	**140**	**48**	**80**	**23**	**+35**	**12**	**5**	**7**	**12**	**8**	**0**	**0**	**1**
1993-94	**Vancouver Canucks**	**NHL**	**76**	***60**	**47**	**107**	**56**	**36**	**92**	**86**	**25**	**4**	**9**	**374**	**16.0**	**131**	**55**	**85**	**10**	**+1**	**24**	***16**	**15**	**31**	**40**	**3**	**0**	**2**
1994-95	EV Landshut	Germany	1	3	0	3	....	....	....	2	....	....	....	....	....	....	....	....	....	....	....	....	....	....	....	....	....	....
	Spartak Moscow	CIS	1	2	0	2	....	....	....	2	....	....	....	....	....	....	....	....	....	....	....	....	....	....	....	....	....	....
	Vancouver Canucks	**NHL**	**44**	**20**	**23**	**43**	**36**	**34**	**70**	**47**	**6**	**2**	**2**	**198**	**10.1**	**73**	**36**	**58**	**13**	**–8**	**11**	**7**	**6**	**13**	**10**	**2**	**2**	**0**
1995-96	**Vancouver Canucks**	**NHL**	**15**	**6**	**7**	**13**	**6**	**6**	**12**	**8**	**1**	**1**	**0**	**78**	**7.7**	**20**	**8**	**19**	**5**	**–2**	....	....	....	....	....	....	....	....
1996-97	**Vancouver Canucks**	**NHL**	**63**	**23**	**32**	**55**	**24**	**28**	**52**	**40**	**4**	**1**	**2**	**265**	**8.7**	**82**	**30**	**86**	**20**	**–14**	....	....	....	....	....	....	....	....
1997-98	**Vancouver Canucks**	**NHL**	**82**	**51**	**39**	**90**	**60**	**38**	**98**	**48**	**13**	**6**	**4**	**329**	**15.5**	**118**	**40**	**107**	**34**	**+5**	....	....	....	....	....	....	....	....
	Russia	Olympics	6	9	0	9	....	....	....	2	....	....	....	....	....	....	....	....	....	....	....	....	....	....	....	....	....	....
	NHL Totals		**428**	**254**	**224**	**478**	**263**	**196**	**459**	**328**	**69**	**24**	**32**	**1919**	**13.2**	**648**	**246**	**504**	**119**		**60**	**34**	**32**	**66**	**72**	**5**	**2**	**3**

EJC-A All-Star Team (1988, 1989) • Named Best Forward at EJC-A (1989) • WJC-A All-Star Team (1989) • Named Best Forward at WJC-A (1989) • Named Soviet National League Rookie-of-the-Year (1989) • Won Calder Memorial Trophy (1992) • NHL First All-Star Team (1994) • Named Best Forward at Olympic Games (1998)

Played in NHL All-Star Game (1993, 1994, 1997, 1998)

● **BURE, VALERI** Valeri Bure RW – R. 5'10", 168 lbs. b: Moscow, USSR, 6/13/1974. Montreal's 2nd choice, 33rd overall, in 1992 Entry Draft.

Season	Club	League	GP	G	A	Pts	AG	AA	APts	PIM	PP	SH	GW	S	%	TGF	PGF	TGA	PGA	+/–	GP	G	A	Pts	PIM	PP	SH	GW
1990-91	CSKA Moscow	USSR	3	0	0	0	....	....	....	0	....	....	....	....	....	....	....	....	....	....	....	....	....	....	....	....	....	....
1991-92	Spokane Chiefs	WHL	53	27	22	49	....	....	....	78	....	....	....	....	....	....	....	....	....	....	10	11	6	17	10	....	....	....
1992-93	Spokane Chiefs	WHL	66	68	79	147	....	....	....	49	....	....	....	....	....	....	....	....	....	....	9	6	11	17	14	....	....	....
1993-94	Spokane Chiefs	WHL	59	40	62	102	....	....	....	48	....	....	....	....	....	....	....	....	....	....	3	5	3	8	2	....	....	....
	Russia	WJC-A	7	5	3	8	....	....	....	4	....	....	....	....	....	....	....	....	....	....	....	....	....	....	....	....	....	....
	Russia	WC-A	6	3	0	3	....	....	....	2	....	....	....	....	....	....	....	....	....	....	....	....	....	....	....	....	....	....
1994-95	**Montreal Canadiens**	**NHL**	**24**	**3**	**1**	**4**	**5**	**1**	**6**	**6**	**0**	**0**	**1**	**39**	**7.7**	**7**	**0**	**8**	**0**	**–1**	....	....	....	....	....	....	....	....
	Fredericton Canadiens	AHL	45	23	25	48	....	....	....	32	....	....	....	....	....	....	....	....	....	....	....	....	....	....	....	....	....	....
1995-96	**Montreal Canadiens**	**NHL**	**77**	**22**	**20**	**42**	**22**	**16**	**38**	**28**	**5**	**0**	**1**	**143**	**15.4**	**69**	**24**	**35**	**0**	**+10**	**6**	**0**	**1**	**1**	**6**	**0**	**0**	**0**
1996-97	Russia	W Cup	1	0	0	0	....	....	....	2	....	....	....	....	....	....	....	....	....	....	....	....	....	....	....	....	....	....
	Montreal Canadiens	**NHL**	**64**	**14**	**21**	**35**	**15**	**19**	**34**	**6**	**4**	**0**	**2**	**131**	**10.7**	**46**	**16**	**27**	**1**	**+4**	**5**	**0**	**1**	**1**	**2**	**0**	**0**	**0**
1997-98	**Montreal Canadiens**	**NHL**	**50**	**7**	**22**	**29**	**8**	**21**	**29**	**33**	**2**	**0**	**1**	**134**	**5.2**	**38**	**17**	**26**	**0**	**–5**	....	....	....	....	....	....	....	....
	Calgary Flames	**NHL**	**16**	**5**	**4**	**9**	**6**	**4**	**10**	**2**	**0**	**0**	**1**	**45**	**11.1**	**14**	**1**	**13**	**0**	**0**	....	....	....	....	....	....	....	....
	Russia	Olympics	6	1	0	1	....	....	....	0	....	....	....	....	....	....	....	....	....	....	....	....	....	....	....	....	....	....
	NHL Totals		**231**	**51**	**68**	**119**	**56**	**61**	**117**	**75**	**11**	**0**	**6**	**492**	**10.4**	**174**	**58**	**109**	**1**		**11**	**0**	**2**	**2**	**8**	**0**	**0**	**0**

WHL West First All-Star Team (1993) • WJC-A All-Star Team (1994) • WHL West Second All-Star Team (1994)

Transferred to **Colorado** after **Quebec** franchise relocated, June 21, 1995. Traded to **Calgary** by **Montreal** with Montreal's 4th round choice (Shaun Sutter) in 1998 Entry Draft for Jonas Hoglund and Zarley Zalapski, February 1, 1998.

● **BUREAU, MARC** Marc Bureau C – R. 6'1", 198 lbs. b: Trois-Rivières, Que., 5/19/1966.

Season	Club	League	GP	G	A	Pts	AG	AA	APts	PIM	PP	SH	GW	S	%	TGF	PGF	TGA	PGA	+/–	GP	G	A	Pts	PIM	PP	SH	GW
1983-84	Chicoutimi Sagueneens	QMJHL	56	6	16	22	....	....	....	14	....	....	....	....	....	....	....	....	....	....	....	....	....	....	....	....	....	....
1984-85	Chicoutimi Sagueneens	QMJHL	41	30	25	55	....	....	....	15	....	....	....	....	....	....	....	....	....	....	....	....	....	....	....	....	....	....
	Granby Predateurs	QMJHL	27	20	45	65	....	....	....	14	....	....	....	....	....	....	....	....	....	....	....	....	....	....	....	....	....	....
1985-86	Granby Predateurs	QMJHL	19	6	17	23	....	....	....	36	....	....	....	....	....	....	....	....	....	....	....	....	....	....	....	....	....	....
	Chicoutimi Sagueneens	QMJHL	44	30	45	75	....	....	....	33	....	....	....	....	....	....	....	....	....	....	9	3	7	10	10	....	....	....
1986-87	Longueuil Chevaliers	QMJHL	66	54	58	112	....	....	....	68	....	....	....	....	....	....	....	....	....	....	20	17	20	37	12	....	....	....
1987-88	Salt Lake Golden Eagles	IHL	69	7	20	27	....	....	....	86	....	....	....	....	....	....	....	....	....	....	7	0	3	3	8	....	....	....
1988-89	Salt Lake Golden Eagles	IHL	76	28	36	64	....	....	....	119	....	....	....	....	....	....	....	....	....	....	14	7	5	12	31	....	....	....
1989-90	**Calgary Flames**	**NHL**	**5**	**0**	**0**	**0**	**0**	**0**	**0**	**4**	**0**	**0**	**0**	**3**	**0.0**	**1**	**0**	**2**	**0**	**–1**	....	....	....	....	....	....	....	....
	Salt Lake Golden Eagles	IHL	67	43	48	91	....	....	....	173	....	....	....	....	....	....	....	....	....	....	11	4	8	12	0	....	....	....
1990-91	**Calgary Flames**	**NHL**	**5**	**0**	**0**	**0**	**0**	**0**	**0**	**2**	**0**	**0**	**0**	**4**	**0.0**	**0**	**0**	**6**	**2**	**–4**	....	....	....	....	....	....	....	....
	Salt Lake Golden Eagles	IHL	54	40	48	88	....	....	....	101	....	....	....	....	....	....	....	....	....	....	....	....	....	....	....	....	....	....
	Minnesota North Stars	**NHL**	**9**	**0**	**6**	**6**	**0**	**5**	**5**	**4**	**0**	**0**	**0**	**8**	**0.0**	**6**	**2**	**8**	**1**	**–3**	**23**	**3**	**2**	**5**	**20**	**0**	**1**	**0**
1991-92	**Minnesota North Stars**	**NHL**	**46**	**6**	**4**	**10**	**5**	**3**	**8**	**50**	**0**	**0**	**0**	**53**	**11.3**	**18**	**6**	**34**	**17**	**–5**	**5**	**0**	**0**	**0**	**14**	**0**	**0**	**0**
	Kalamazoo Wings	IHL	7	2	8	10	....	....	....	2	....	....	....	....	....	....	....	....	....	....	....	....	....	....	....	....	....	....
1992-93	**Tampa Bay Lightning**	**NHL**	**63**	**10**	**21**	**31**	**8**	**14**	**22**	**111**	**1**	**2**	**1**	**132**	**7.6**	**42**	**11**	**74**	**31**	**12**	....	....	....	....	....	....	....	....
1993-94	**Tampa Bay Lightning**	**NHL**	**75**	**8**	**7**	**15**	**7**	**5**	**12**	**30**	**0**	**1**	**1**	**110**	**7.3**	**27**	**1**	**48**	**13**	**–9**	....	....	....	....	....	....	....	....
1994-95	**Tampa Bay Lightning**	**NHL**	**48**	**2**	**12**	**14**	**4**	**18**	**22**	**30**	**0**	**1**	**0**	**72**	**2.8**	**18**	**1**	**46**	**21**	**–8**	....	....	....	....	....	....	....	....
1995-96	**Montreal Canadiens**	**NHL**	**65**	**3**	**7**	**10**	**3**	**6**	**9**	**46**	**0**	**0**	**1**	**43**	**7.0**	**16**	**1**	**36**	**19**	**–3**	**6**	**1**	**1**	**2**	**4**	**0**	**0**	**0**
1996-97	**Montreal Canadiens**	**NHL**	**43**	**6**	**9**	**15**	**6**	**8**	**14**	**16**	**1**	**1**	**2**	**56**	**10.7**	**20**	**1**	**28**	**13**	**+4**	....	....	....	....	....	....	....	....
1997-98	**Montreal Canadiens**	**NHL**	**74**	**13**	**6**	**19**	**15**	**6**	**21**	**12**	**0**	**0**	**2**	**82**	**15.9**	**27**	**0**	**48**	**21**	**0**	**10**	**1**	**2**	**3**	**6**	**0**	**0**	**0**
	NHL Totals		**433**	**48**	**72**	**120**	**48**	**65**	**113**	**305**	**2**	**5**	**7**	**563**	**8.5**	**174**	**23**	**330**	**138**		**44**	**5**	**5**	**10**	**44**	**0**	**1**	**0**

IHL Second All-Star Team (1990, 1991)

Signed as a free agent by **Calgary**, May 19, 1987. Traded to **Minnesota** by **Calgary** for Minnesota's 3rd round choice (Sandy McCarthy) in 1991 Entry Draft, March 5, 1991. Claimed on waivers by **Tampa Bay** from **Minnesota**, October 16, 1992. Traded to **Montreal** by **Tampa Bay** for Brian Bellows, June 30, 1995. Signed as a free agent by **Philadelphia, July 6, 1998.**

● **BURNS, CHARLIE** Charlie Burns C – L. 5'11", 170 lbs. b: Detroit, MI, 2/14/1936.

Season	Club	League	GP	G	A	Pts	AG	AA	APts	PIM	PP	SH	GW	S	%	TGF	PGF	TGA	PGA	+/–	GP	G	A	Pts	PIM	PP	SH	GW
1952-53	Toronto Marlboros	OHA	33	5	7	12	....	....	....	17	....	....	....	....	....	....	....	....	....	....	7	4	1	5	2	....	....	....
1953-54	Toronto Marlboros	OHA	59	17	14	31	....	....	....	45	....	....	....	....	....	....	....	....	....	....	7	2	3	5	0	....	....	....
1954-55	Toronto Marlboros	OHA	3	0	0	0	....	....	....	0	....	....	....	....	....	....	....	....	....	....	1	0	0	0	0	....	....	....
1955-56	Toronto Marlboros	OHA	20	5	8	13	....	....	....	16	....	....	....	....	....	....	....	....	....	....	11	5	4	9	12	....	....	....
1956-57	Whitby Dunlops	EOHL	40	16	25	41	....	....	....	29	....	....	....	....	....	....	....	....	....	....	5	4	6	10	2	....	....	....
1957-58	Whitby Dunlops	EOHL	31	24	28	52	....	....	....	32	....	....	....	....	....	....	....	....	....	....	....	....	....	....	....	....	....	....
	Canada	WEC-A	7	3	4	7	....	....	....	0	....	....	....	....	....	....	....	....	....	....	....	....	....	....	....	....	....	....
1958-59	**Detroit Red Wings**	**NHL**	**70**	**9**	**11**	**20**	**11**	**12**	**23**	**32**	....	....	....	....	....	....	....	....	....	....	....	....	....	....	....	....	....	....
1959-60	**Boston Bruins**	**NHL**	**62**	**10**	**17**	**27**	**12**	**17**	**29**	**46**	....	....	....	....	....	....	....	....	....	....	....	....	....	....	....	....	....	....
1960-61	**Boston Bruins**	**NHL**	**62**	**15**	**26**	**41**	**18**	**26**	**44**	**16**	....	....	....	....	....	....	....	....	....	....	....	....	....	....	....	....	....	....
	Kingston Frontenacs	EPHL	8	3	6	9	....	....	....	4	....	....	....	....	....	....	....	....	....	....	....	....	....	....	....	....	....	....
1961-62	**Boston Bruins**	**NHL**	**70**	**11**	**17**	**28**	**13**	**17**	**30**	**43**	....	....	....	....	....	....	....	....	....	....	....	....	....	....	....	....	....	....

			REGULAR SEASON																		PLAYOFFS							
Season	Club	League	GP	G	A	Pts	AG	AA	APts	PIM	PP	SH	GW	S	%	TGF	PGF	TGA	PGA	+/–	GP	G	A	Pts	PIM	PP	SH	GW
1962-63	Boston Bruins	NHL	68	12	10	22	15	10	25	13	....	....	....	....	....	....	....	....	....	....	....	....	....	....	....	....	....	....
1963-64	San Francisco Seals	WHL	68	33	36	69	....	....	....	27	....	....	....	....	....	....	....	....	....	....	11	1	3	4	2	....	....	....
1964-65	San Francisco Seals	WHL	51	27	36	63	....	....	....	19	....	....	....	....	....	....	....	....	....	....	....	....	....	....	....	....	....	....
1965-66	San Francisco Seals	WHL	40	10	35	45	....	....	....	26	....	....	....	....	....	....	....	....	....	....	7	1	5	6	0	....	....	....
1966-67	California Seals	WHL	71	22	38	60	....	....	....	29	....	....	....	....	....	....	....	....	....	....	6	0	0	0	9	....	....	....
1967-68	Oakland Seals	NHL	73	9	26	35	11	27	38	20	1	2	1	119	7.6	48	8	80	26	–14	....	....	....	....	....	....	....	....
1968-69	Pittsburgh Penguins	NHL	76	13	38	51	15	36	51	22	1	1	1	133	9.8	72	12	98	29	–9	....	....	....	....	....	....	....	....
1969-70	Minnesota North Stars	NHL	50	3	13	16	3	13	16	10	0	1	0	61	4.9	25	1	67	39	–4	6	1	0	1	2	0	0	0
1970-71	Minnesota North Stars	NHL	76	9	19	28	9	17	26	13	0	0	1	110	8.2	41	1	89	49	0	12	3	3	6	2	0	0	1
1971-72	Minnesota North Stars	NHL	77	11	14	25	12	13	25	24	0	1	2	88	12.5	31	3	61	38	+5	7	1	1	2	2	0	0	0
1972-73	Minnesota North Stars	NHL	65	4	7	11	4	6	10	13	0	1	0	41	9.8	16	2	59	42	–3	6	0	0	0	0	0	0	0
1973-74	New Haven Nighthawks	AHL	64	10	19	29	....	....	....	73	....	....	....	....	....	....	....	....	....	....	10	1	3	4	16	....	....	....
	NHL Totals		749	106	198	304	123	194	317	252	2	6	5	552	19.2	233	27	454	223		31	5	4	9	6	0	0	1

Named Best Forward at WEC-A (1958)

Claimed by **Boston** from **Detroit** in Intra-League Draft, June, 1959. NHL rights transferred to **Oakland** after owners of **San Francisco** (WHL) franchise granted NHL expansion team, April 26, 1966. Claimed by **Pittsburgh** from **Oakland** in Intra-League Draft, June 12, 1968. Claimed by **Minnesota** from **Pittsburgh** in Intra-League Draft, June 11, 1969.

• BURNS, GARY

Gary Burns LW/C – L. 6'1", 190 lbs. b: Cambridge, MA, 1/16/1955. Toronto's 15th choice, 191st overall, in 1975 Amateur Draft.

1974-75	University of New Hampshire	ECAC	31	17	15	32	....	....	....	42	....	....	....	....	....	....	....	....	....	....	....	....	....	....	....	....	....	....
1975-76	University of New Hampshire	ECAC	31	6	12	18	....	....	....	....	....	....	....	....	....	....	....	....	....	....	....	....	....	....	....	....	....	....
1976-77	University of New Hampshire	ECAC	38	9	6	15	....	....	....	24	....	....	....	....	....	....	....	....	....	....	....	....	....	....	....	....	....	....
1977-78	University of New Hampshire	ECAC	29	9	19	28	....	....	....	55	....	....	....	....	....	....	....	....	....	....	....	....	....	....	....	....	....	....
1978-79	Rochester Americans	AHL	79	16	30	46	....	....	....	99	....	....	....	....	....	....	....	....	....	....	....	....	....	....	....	....	....	....
1979-80	Binghamton Whalers	AHL	79	30	29	59	....	....	....	105	....	....	....	....	....	....	....	....	....	....	....	....	....	....	....	....	....	....
1980-81	New York Rangers	NHL	11	2	2	4	2	1	3	18	0	0	1	13	15.4	5	1	16	3	–9	1	0	0	0	2	0	0	0
	New Haven Nighthawks	AHL	69	25	29	54	....	....	....	137	....	....	....	....	....	....	....	....	....	....	4	1	0	1	2	....	....	....
1981-82	Springfield Indians	AHL	78	27	39	66	....	....	....	71	....	....	....	....	....	....	....	....	....	....	....	....	....	....	....	....	....	....
	New York Rangers	NHL	....	....	....	....	....	....	....	....	....	....	....	....	....	....	....	....	....	....	4	0	0	0	0	....	....	....
1982-83	Tulsa Oilers	CHL	80	21	33	54	....	....	....	61	....	....	....	....	....	....	....	....	....	....	....	....	....	....	....	....	....	....
1983-84	Tulsa Oilers	CHL	68	28	30	58	....	....	....	95	....	....	....	....	....	....	....	....	....	....	9	3	*9	12	2	....	....	....
1984-85	Rochester Americans	AHL	76	22	27	49	....	....	....	64	....	....	....	....	....	....	....	....	....	....	2	0	1	1	6	....	....	....
1985-86	Salt Lake Golden Eagles	IHL	78	23	35	58	....	....	....	85	....	....	....	....	....	....	....	....	....	....	4	1	0	1	6	....	....	....
	NHL Totals		11	2	2	4	2	1	3	18	0	0	1	13	15.4	5	1	16	3		5	0	0	0	2	0	0	0

Signed as a free agent by **Boston**, October 10, 1978. Signed as a free agent by **NY Rangers**, September 16, 1980.

• BURNS, ROBIN

Robin Burns LW – L. 6', 195 lbs. b: Montreal, Que., 8/27/1946.

1963-64	Notre Dame de Grace	QJHL	44	13	16	29	....	....	....	50	....	....	....	....	....	....	....	....	....	....	....	....	....	....	....	....	....	....
1964-65	Montreal Jr. Canadiens	OHA	39	1	5	6	....	....	....	66	....	....	....	....	....	....	....	....	....	....	7	2	1	3	8	....	....	....
1965-66	Montreal Jr. Canadiens	OHA	42	6	2	8	....	....	....	97	....	....	....	....	....	....	....	....	....	....	10	0	4	4	20	....	....	....
1966-67	Montreal Jr. Canadiens	OHA	46	11	12	23	....	....	....	99	....	....	....	....	....	....	....	....	....	....	4	1	2	3	6	....	....	....
1967-68	Houston Apollos	CHL	65	21	25	46	....	....	....	41	....	....	....	....	....	....	....	....	....	....	....	....	....	....	....	....	....	....
1968-69	Houston Apollos	CHL	61	12	18	30	....	....	....	63	....	....	....	....	....	....	....	....	....	....	3	0	0	0	0	....	....	....
1969-70	Montreal Voyageurs	AHL	62	13	7	20	....	....	....	33	....	....	....	....	....	....	....	....	....	....	8	0	1	1	0	....	....	....
1970-71	Pittsburgh Penguins	NHL	10	0	3	3	0	3	3	4	0	0	0	10	0.0	6	0	5	0	+1	....	....	....	....	....	....	....	....
	Amarillo Wranglers	CHL	46	16	24	40	....	....	....	49	....	....	....	....	....	....	....	....	....	....	....	....	....	....	....	....	....	....
1971-72	Pittsburgh Penguins	NHL	5	0	0	0	0	0	0	8	0	0	0	4	0.0	1	1	4	0	–4	....	....	....	....	....	....	....	....
	Hershey Bears	AHL	65	18	15	33	....	....	....	58	....	....	....	....	....	....	....	....	....	....	4	1	1	2	10	....	....	....
1972-73	Pittsburgh Penguins	NHL	26	0	2	2	0	2	2	20	0	0	0	26	0.0	3	0	9	0	–6	....	....	....	....	....	....	....	....
	Hershey Bears	AHL	39	22	25	47	....	....	....	51	....	....	....	....	....	....	....	....	....	....	....	....	....	....	....	....	....	....
1973-74	Hershey Bears	AHL	74	31	35	66	....	....	....	77	....	....	....	....	....	....	....	....	....	....	14	*10	4	14	6	....	....	....
1974-75	Kansas City Scouts	NHL	71	18	15	33	17	12	29	70	7	0	1	126	14.3	50	17	73	0	–40	....	....	....	....	....	....	....	....
1975-76	Kansas City Scouts	NHL	78	13	18	31	12	14	26	37	2	0	0	145	9.0	39	10	69	0	–40	....	....	....	....	....	....	....	....
	NHL Totals		190	31	38	69	29	31	60	139	9	0	1	311	10.0	99	28	160	0		....	....	....	....	....	....	....	....

Traded to **Pittsburgh** by **Montreal** for cash, October 2, 1970. Claimed by **Kansas City** from **Pittsburgh** in Expansion Draft, June 12, 1974.

• BURR, SHAWN

Shawn Burr LW/C – L. 6'1", 200 lbs. b: Sarnia, Ont., 7/1/1966. Detroit's 1st choice, 7th overall, in 1984 Entry Draft.

1982-83	Sarnia Steeplejacks	OJHL	52	50	85	135	....	....	....	125	....	....	....	....	....	....	....	....	....	....	....	....	....	....	....	....	....	....
1983-84	Kitchener Rangers	OHL	68	41	44	85	....	....	....	50	....	....	....	....	....	....	....	....	....	....	16	5	12	17	22	....	....	....
1984-85	Kitchener Rangers	OHL	48	24	42	66	....	....	....	50	....	....	....	....	....	....	....	....	....	....	4	3	3	6	2	....	....	....
	Detroit Red Wings	NHL	9	0	0	0	0	0	0	2	0	0	0	4	0.0	1	0	5	0	–4	....	....	....	....	....	....	....	....
	Adirondack Red Wings	AHL	4	0	0	0	....	....	....	2	....	....	....	....	....	....	....	....	....	....	....	....	....	....	....	....	....	....
1985-86	Kitchener Rangers	OHL	59	60	67	127	....	....	....	104	....	....	....	....	....	....	....	....	....	....	5	2	3	5	8	....	....	....
	Detroit Red Wings	NHL	5	1	0	1	1	0	1	4	1	0	0	6	16.7	4	2	1	0	+1	....	....	....	....	....	....	....	....
	Adirondack Red Wings	AHL	3	2	2	4	....	....	....	2	....	....	....	....	....	....	....	....	....	....	17	5	7	12	32	....	....	....
1986-87	Detroit Red Wings	NHL	80	22	25	47	19	18	37	107	1	2	1	153	14.4	61	4	81	26	+2	16	7	2	9	20	0	0	2
1987-88	Detroit Red Wings	NHL	78	17	23	40	15	16	31	97	5	3	3	124	13.7	58	8	68	25	+7	9	3	1	4	14	0	0	1
1988-89	Detroit Red Wings	NHL	79	19	27	46	16	19	35	78	1	4	2	149	12.8	59	5	71	22	+5	6	1	2	3	6	0	0	0
1989-90	Detroit Red Wings	NHL	76	24	32	56	21	23	44	82	4	3	2	173	13.9	86	18	83	29	+14	....	....	....	....	....	....	....	....
	Adirondack Red Wings	AHL	3	4	2	6	....	....	....	2	....	....	....	....	....	....	....	....	....	....	....	....	....	....	....	....	....	....
	Canada	WEC-A	10	4	1	5	....	....	....	14	....	....	....	....	....	....	....	....	....	....	....	....	....	....	....	....	....	....
1990-91	Detroit Red Wings	NHL	80	20	30	50	18	23	41	112	6	0	4	164	12.2	70	11	64	19	+14	7	0	4	4	15	0	0	0
1991-92	Detroit Red Wings	NHL	79	19	32	51	17	24	41	118	2	0	3	140	13.6	76	5	67	22	+26	11	1	5	6	10	0	0	0
1992-93	Detroit Red Wings	NHL	80	10	25	35	8	17	25	74	1	1	2	99	10.1	53	1	68	34	+18	7	2	1	3	2	0	1	0
1993-94	Detroit Red Wings	NHL	51	10	12	22	9	9	18	31	0	1	1	64	15.6	32	0	32	12	+12	7	2	0	2	6	0	0	2
1994-95	Detroit Red Wings	NHL	42	6	8	14	11	12	23	60	0	0	3	65	9.2	29	1	23	8	+13	16	0	2	2	6	0	0	0
1995-96	Tampa Bay Lightning	NHL	81	13	15	28	13	12	25	119	1	0	2	122	10.7	48	1	67	24	+4	6	0	2	2	8	0	0	0
1996-97	Tampa Bay Lightning	NHL	74	14	21	35	15	19	34	106	1	0	3	128	10.9	53	7	51	10	+5	....	....	....	....	....	....	....	....
1997-98	San Jose Sharks	NHL	42	6	6	12	7	6	13	50	0	0	0	63	9.5	16	0	18	4	+2	6	0	0	0	8	0	0	0
	NHL Totals		856	181	256	437	170	198	368	1040	23	14	26	1454	12.4	646	63	699	235		91	16	19	35	95	0	1	5

OHL Second All-Star Team (1986)

Traded to **Tampa Bay** by **Detroit** with Detroit's 3rd round choice (later traded to Boston — Boston selected Jason Doyle) in 1996 Entry Draft for Marc Bergevin and Ben Hankinson, August 17, 1995. Traded to **San Jose** by **Tampa Bay** for San Jose's 5th round choice (Mark Thompson) in 1997 Entry Draft, June 21, 1997.

• BURRIDGE, RANDY

Randy Burridge LW – L. 5'9", 188 lbs. b: Fort Erie, Ont., 1/7/1966. Boston's 7th choice, 157th overall, in 1985 Entry Draft.

1982-83	Fort Erie Meteors	OJHL	42	32	56	88	....	....	....	32	....	....	....	....	....	....	....	....	....	....	....	....	....	....	....	....	....	....
1983-84	Peterborough Petes	OHL	55	6	7	13	....	....	....	44	....	....	....	....	....	....	....	....	....	....	8	3	2	5	7	....	....	....
1984-85	Peterborough Petes	OHL	66	49	57	106	....	....	....	88	....	....	....	....	....	....	....	....	....	....	17	9	16	25	18	....	....	....
1985-86	Peterborough Petes	OHL	17	15	11	26	....	....	....	23	....	....	....	....	....	....	....	....	....	....	3	1	3	4	2	....	....	....
	Boston Bruins	NHL	52	17	25	42	14	17	31	28	1	0	2	90	18.9	58	14	34	7	+17	3	0	4	4	12	0	0	0
	Moncton Golden Flames	AHL	....	....	....	....	....	....	....	....	....	....	....	....	....	....	....	....	....	....	3	0	2	2	2	....	....	....
1986-87	Boston Bruins	NHL	23	1	4	5	1	3	4	16	0	0	1	27	3.7	12	0	23	5	–6	2	1	0	1	2	0	0	0
	Moncton Golden Flames	AHL	47	26	41	67	....	....	....	139	....	....	....	....	....	....	....	....	....	....	3	1	2	3	30	....	....	....
1987-88	Boston Bruins	NHL	79	27	28	55	23	20	43	105	5	3	3	159	17.0	85	21	92	28	0	23	2	10	12	16	0	0	0
1988-89	Boston Bruins	NHL	80	31	30	61	26	21	47	39	6	2	6	189	16.4	89	22	79	31	+19	10	5	2	7	6	1	1	0
1989-90	Boston Bruins	NHL	63	17	15	32	15	11	26	47	7	0	1	118	14.4	66	20	47	10	+9	21	4	11	15	14	0	1	0
1990-91	Boston Bruins	NHL	62	15	13	28	14	10	24	40	1	0	4	108	13.9	55	5	50	17	+17	19	0	3	3	39	0	0	0
1991-92	Washington Capitals	NHL	66	23	44	67	21	33	54	50	9	0	3	131	17.6	98	43	69	10	–4	2	0	1	1	0	0	0	0
1992-93	Washington Capitals	NHL	4	0	0	0	0	0	0	0	0	0	0	7	0.0	1	0	0	0	+1	4	1	0	1	0	0	0	0
	Baltimore Skipjacks	AHL	2	0	1	1	....	....	....	2	....	....	....	....	....	....	....	....	....	....	....	....	....	....	....	....	....	....
1993-94	Washington Capitals	NHL	78	25	17	42	23	13	36	73	8	1	5	150	16.7	78	34	52	7	–1	11	0	2	2	12	0	0	0

			REGULAR SEASON																		PLAYOFFS							
Season	Club	League	GP	G	A	Pts	AG	AA	APts	PIM	PP	SH	GW	S	%	TGF	PGF	TGA	PGA	+/–	GP	G	A	Pts	PIM	PP	SH	GW
1994-95	**Washington Capitals**	**NHL**	**2**	**0**	**0**	**0**	**0**	**0**	**0**	**2**	**0**	**0**	**0**	**2**	**0.0**	**0**	**0**	**0**	**0**	**0**	....	....	....	....	....	....	....	....
	Los Angeles Kings	**NHL**	**38**	**4**	**15**	**19**	**7**	**22**	**29**	**8**	**2**	**0**	**0**	**50**	**8.0**	**27**	**6**	**26**	**1**	**–4**	....	....	....	....	....	....	....	....
1995-96	**Buffalo Sabres**	**NHL**	**74**	**25**	**33**	**58**	**25**	**27**	**52**	**30**	**6**	**0**	**3**	**154**	**16.2**	**89**	**40**	**52**	**3**	**0**	....	....	....	....	....	....	....	....
1996-97	**Buffalo Sabres**	**NHL**	**55**	**10**	**21**	**31**	**11**	**19**	**30**	**20**	**1**	**3**	**0**	**85**	**11.8**	**48**	**11**	**28**	**8**	**+17**	**12**	**5**	**1**	**6**	**2**	**0**	**0**	**0**
1997-98	**Buffalo Sabres**	**NHL**	**30**	**4**	**6**	**10**	**5**	**6**	**11**	**0**	**1**	**0**	**1**	**40**	**10.0**	**12**	**1**	**14**	**3**	**0**	....	....	....	....	....	....	....	....
	Rochester Americans	AHL	6	0	1	1	....	....	....	19	....	....	....	....	....	....	....	....	....	....	1	0	1	1	0	....	....	....
	NHL Totals		**706**	**199**	**251**	**450**	**185**	**202**	**387**	**458**	**47**	**9**	**29**	**1310**	**15.2**	**718**	**217**	**566**	**130**		**107**	**18**	**34**	**52**	**103**	**1**	**2**	**0**

Played in NHL All-Star Game (1992)

Traded to **Washington** by **Boston** for Stephen Leach, June 21, 1991. Traded to **LA Kings** by **Washington** for Warren Rychel, February 10, 1995. Signed as a free agent by **Buffalo**, October 5, 1995.

• BURROWS, DAVE

Dave Burrows D – L. 6'1", 190 lbs. b: Toronto, Ont., 1/11/1949.

Season	Club	League	GP	G	A	Pts	AG	AA	APts	PIM	PP	SH	GW	S	%	TGF	PGF	TGA	PGA	+/–	GP	G	A	Pts	PIM	PP	SH	GW
1967-68	Dixie Beehives	OJHL	STATISTICS NOT AVAILABLE																									
	St. Catharines Black Hawks	OHA	9	0	3	3	....	....	....	4	....	....	....	....	....	....	....	....	....	....	5	0	0	0	0	....	....	....
1968-69	St. Catharines Black Hawks	OHA	54	3	16	19	....	....	....	36	....	....	....	....	....	....	....	....	....	....	18	1	4	5	12	....	....	....
1969-70	Dallas Black Hawks	CHL	69	4	9	13	....	....	....	45	....	....	....	....	....	....	....	....	....	....	....	....	....	....	....	....	....	....
	Portland Buckaroos	WHL	....	....	....	....	....	....	....	....	....	....	....	....	....	....	....	....	....	....	11	1	2	3	6	....	....	....
1970-71	Dallas Black Hawks	CHL	67	1	11	12	....	....	....	49	....	....	....	....	....	....	....	....	....	....	10	0	2	2	4	....	....	....
1971-72	**Pittsburgh Penguins**	**NHL**	**77**	**2**	**10**	**12**	**2**	**9**	**11**	**48**	**0**	**0**	**0**	**100**	**2.0**	**77**	**7**	**104**	**27**	**–7**	**4**	**0**	**0**	**0**	**4**	**0**	**0**	**0**
1972-73	**Pittsburgh Penguins**	**NHL**	**78**	**3**	**24**	**27**	**3**	**20**	**23**	**42**	**0**	**0**	**0**	**132**	**2.3**	**99**	**5**	**118**	**20**	**–4**	....	....	....	....	....	....	....	....
1973-74	**Pittsburgh Penguins**	**NHL**	**71**	**3**	**14**	**17**	**3**	**12**	**15**	**30**	**2**	**0**	**0**	**123**	**2.4**	**87**	**15**	**112**	**27**	**–13**	....	....	....	....	....	....	....	....
1974-75	**Pittsburgh Penguins**	**NHL**	**78**	**2**	**15**	**17**	**2**	**12**	**14**	**49**	**0**	**0**	**1**	**126**	**1.6**	**99**	**7**	**127**	**38**	**+3**	**9**	**1**	**1**	**2**	**12**	**0**	**0**	**1**
1975-76	**Pittsburgh Penguins**	**NHL**	**80**	**7**	**22**	**29**	**7**	**17**	**24**	**51**	**1**	**1**	**1**	**125**	**5.6**	**152**	**15**	**155**	**45**	**+27**	**3**	**0**	**0**	**0**	**0**	**0**	**0**	**0**
1976-77	**Pittsburgh Penguins**	**NHL**	**69**	**3**	**6**	**9**	**3**	**5**	**8**	**29**	**1**	**0**	**1**	**92**	**3.3**	**84**	**11**	**106**	**18**	**–15**	**3**	**0**	**2**	**2**	**0**	**0**	**0**	**0**
1977-78	**Pittsburgh Penguins**	**NHL**	**67**	**4**	**15**	**19**	**4**	**12**	**16**	**24**	**0**	**0**	**1**	**92**	**4.3**	**79**	**2**	**139**	**32**	**–30**	....	....	....	....	....	....	....	....
1978-79	**Toronto Maple Leafs**	**NHL**	**65**	**2**	**11**	**13**	**2**	**8**	**10**	**28**	**0**	**0**	**0**	**70**	**2.9**	**65**	**1**	**99**	**25**	**–10**	**6**	**0**	**1**	**1**	**7**	**0**	**0**	**0**
1979-80	**Toronto Maple Leafs**	**NHL**	**80**	**3**	**16**	**19**	**3**	**12**	**15**	**42**	**0**	**0**	**0**	**102**	**2.9**	**94**	**2**	**132**	**40**	**0**	**3**	**0**	**1**	**1**	**2**	**0**	**0**	**0**
1980-81	**Toronto Maple Leafs**	**NHL**	**6**	**0**	**0**	**0**	**0**	**0**	**0**	**2**	**0**	**0**	**0**	**3**	**0.0**	**1**	**0**	**7**	**2**	**–4**	....	....	....	....	....	....	....	....
	Pittsburgh Penguins	**NHL**	**53**	**0**	**2**	**2**	**0**	**1**	**1**	**28**	**0**	**0**	**0**	**32**	**0.0**	**37**	**0**	**72**	**22**	**–13**	**1**	**0**	**0**	**0**	**0**	**0**	**0**	**0**
	NHL Totals		**724**	**29**	**135**	**164**	**29**	**108**	**137**	**373**	**4**	**1**	**4**	**997**	**2.9**	**874**	**65**	**1171**	**296**		**29**	**1**	**5**	**6**	**25**	**0**	**0**	**1**

Played in NHL All-Star Game (1974, 1976, 1980)

Claimed by **Pittsburgh** from **Chicago** in Intra-League Draft, June 8, 1971. Traded to **Toronto** by **Pittsburgh** for Randy Carlyle and George Ferguson, June 8, 1978. Traded to **Pittsburgh** by **Toronto** with Paul Gardner for Kim Davis and Paul Marshall, November 18, 1980.

• BURT, ADAM

Adam Burt D – L. 6'2", 207 lbs. b: Detroit, MI, 1/15/1969. Hartford's 2nd choice, 39th overall, in 1987 Entry Draft.

Season	Club	League	GP	G	A	Pts	AG	AA	APts	PIM	PP	SH	GW	S	%	TGF	PGF	TGA	PGA	+/–	GP	G	A	Pts	PIM	PP	SH	GW
1985-86	North Bay Centennials	OHL	49	0	11	11	....	....	....	81	....	....	....	....	....	....	....	....	....	....	10	0	0	0	24	....	....	....
1986-87	North Bay Centennials	OHL	57	4	27	31	....	....	....	138	....	....	....	....	....	....	....	....	....	....	24	1	6	7	68	....	....	....
	United States	WJC-A	7	0	1	1	....	....	....	8	....	....	....	....	....	....	....	....	....	....	....	....	....	....	....	....	....	....
1987-88	North Bay Centennials	OHL	66	17	53	70	....	....	....	176	....	....	....	....	....	....	....	....	....	....	2	0	3	3	6	....	....	....
	Binghamton Whalers	AHL	....	....	....	....	....	....	....	....	....	....	....	....	....	....	....	....	....	....	2	1	1	2	0	....	....	....
1988-89	North Bay Centennials	OHL	23	4	11	15	....	....	....	45	....	....	....	....	....	....	....	....	....	....	12	2	12	14	12	....	....	....
	United States	WJC-A	7	1	6	7	....	....	....	2	....	....	....	....	....	....	....	....	....	....	....	....	....	....	....	....	....	....
	Hartford Whalers	**NHL**	**5**	**0**	**0**	**0**	**0**	**0**	**0**	**6**	**0**	**0**	**0**	**1**	**0.0**	**0**	**0**	**1**	**0**	**–1**	....	....	....	....	....	....	....	....
	Binghamton Whalers	AHL	5	0	2	2	....	....	....	13	....	....	....	....	....	....	....	....	....	....	....	....	....	....	....	....	....	....
1989-90	**Hartford Whalers**	**NHL**	**63**	**4**	**8**	**12**	**3**	**6**	**9**	**105**	**1**	**0**	**0**	**83**	**4.8**	**63**	**3**	**71**	**14**	**+3**	**2**	**0**	**0**	**0**	**0**	**0**	**0**	**0**
1990-91	**Hartford Whalers**	**NHL**	**42**	**2**	**7**	**9**	**2**	**5**	**7**	**63**	**1**	**0**	**1**	**43**	**4.7**	**46**	**11**	**49**	**10**	**–4**	....	....	....	....	....	....	....	....
	Springfield Indians	AHL	9	1	3	4	....	....	....	22	....	....	....	....	....	....	....	....	....	....	....	....	....	....	....	....	....	....
1991-92	**Hartford Whalers**	**NHL**	**66**	**9**	**15**	**24**	**8**	**11**	**19**	**93**	**4**	**0**	**1**	**89**	**10.1**	**66**	**20**	**79**	**17**	**–16**	**2**	**0**	**0**	**0**	**0**	**0**	**0**	**0**
1992-93	**Hartford Whalers**	**NHL**	**65**	**6**	**14**	**20**	**5**	**10**	**15**	**116**	**0**	**0**	**0**	**81**	**7.4**	**60**	**8**	**77**	**14**	**–11**	....	....	....	....	....	....	....	....
	United States	WC-A	6	2	1	3	....	....	....	6	....	....	....	....	....	....	....	....	....	....	....	....	....	....	....	....	....	....
1993-94	**Hartford Whalers**	**NHL**	**63**	**1**	**17**	**18**	**1**	**13**	**14**	**75**	**0**	**0**	**0**	**91**	**1.1**	**56**	**7**	**80**	**27**	**–4**	....	....	....	....	....	....	....	....
1994-95	**Hartford Whalers**	**NHL**	**46**	**7**	**11**	**18**	**12**	**16**	**28**	**65**	**3**	**0**	**1**	**73**	**9.6**	**54**	**14**	**53**	**13**	**0**	....	....	....	....	....	....	....	....
1995-96	**Hartford Whalers**	**NHL**	**78**	**4**	**9**	**13**	**4**	**7**	**11**	**121**	**0**	**0**	**1**	**90**	**4.4**	**57**	**7**	**77**	**23**	**–4**	....	....	....	....	....	....	....	....
1996-97	**Hartford Whalers**	**NHL**	**71**	**2**	**11**	**13**	**2**	**10**	**12**	**79**	**0**	**0**	**0**	**85**	**2.4**	**68**	**13**	**84**	**16**	**–13**	....	....	....	....	....	....	....	....
1997-98	**Carolina Hurricanes**	**NHL**	**70**	**1**	**11**	**12**	**1**	**11**	**12**	**106**	**0**	**1**	**0**	**51**	**2.0**	**48**	**1**	**75**	**22**	**–6**	....	....	....	....	....	....	....	....
	United States	WC-A	6	0	0	0	....	....	....	4	....	....	....	....	....	....	....	....	....	....	....	....	....	....	....	....	....	....
	NHL Totals		**576**	**36**	**103**	**139**	**38**	**89**	**127**	**829**	**9**	**1**	**4**	**687**	**5.2**	**518**	**84**	**646**	**156**		**4**	**0**	**0**	**0**	**0**	**0**	**0**	**0**

OHL Second All-Star Team (1988)

Transferred to **Carolina** after **Hartford** franchise relocated, June 25, 1997.

• BURTON, NELSON

Nelson Burton LW – L. 6', 205 lbs. b: Sydney, N.S., 11/6/1957. Washington's 4th choice, 57th overall, in 1977 Amateur Draft.

Season	Club	League	GP	G	A	Pts	AG	AA	APts	PIM	PP	SH	GW	S	%	TGF	PGF	TGA	PGA	+/–	GP	G	A	Pts	PIM	PP	SH	GW
1974-75	Hull Festivals	QMJHL	67	20	19	39	....	....	....	333	....	....	....	....	....	....	....	....	....	....	....	....	....	....	....	....	....	....
1975-76	Quebec Remparts	QMJHL	71	26	25	51	....	....	....	322	....	....	....	....	....	....	....	....	....	....	13	0	3	3	*90	....	....	....
1976-77	Quebec Remparts	QMJHL	67	22	28	50	....	....	....	398	....	....	....	....	....	....	....	....	....	....	9	1	5	6	70	....	....	....
1977-78	**Washington Capitals**	**NHL**	**5**	**1**	**0**	**1**	**1**	**0**	**1**	**8**	**0**	**0**	**0**	**3**	**33.3**	**1**	**0**	**4**	**0**	**–3**	....	....	....	....	....	....	....	....
	Hershey Bears	AHL	57	4	7	11	....	....	....	*323	....	....	....	....	....	....	....	....	....	....	....	....	....	....	....	....	....	....
1978-79	**Washington Capitals**	**NHL**	**3**	**0**	**0**	**0**	**0**	**0**	**0**	**13**	**0**	**0**	**0**	**0**	**0.0**	**1**	**0**	**4**	**1**	**–2**	....	....	....	....	....	....	....	....
	Hershey Bears	AHL	51	6	19	25	....	....	....	204	....	....	....	....	....	....	....	....	....	....	....	....	....	....	....	....	....	....
1979-80	Syracuse Firebirds	AHL	2	0	1	1	....	....	....	0	....	....	....	....	....	....	....	....	....	....	....	....	....	....	....	....	....	....
	Nova Scotia Voyageurs	AHL	70	3	10	13	....	....	....	190	....	....	....	....	....	....	....	....	....	....	3	0	0	0	37	....	....	....
1980-81	Erie Blades	EHL	68	20	24	44	....	....	....	*305	....	....	....	....	....	....	....	....	....	....	8	0	0	0	60	....	....	....
1981-82	Nashville South Stars	CHL	49	1	4	5	....	....	....	128	....	....	....	....	....	....	....	....	....	....	3	0	0	0	0	....	....	....
1982-83	Baltimore Skipjacks	AHL	60	3	8	11	....	....	....	71	....	....	....	....	....	....	....	....	....	....	....	....	....	....	....	....	....	....
1983-84	Erie Golden Blades	ACHL	65	10	12	22	....	....	....	156	....	....	....	....	....	....	....	....	....	....	9	0	1	1	79	....	....	....
	NHL Totals		**8**	**1**	**0**	**1**	**1**	**0**	**1**	**21**	**0**	**0**	**0**	**3**	**33.3**	**2**	**0**	**8**	**1**		....	....	....	....	....	....	....	....

Traded to **Quebec** by **Washington** for Dave Parro, June 15, 1979. Traded to **Minnesota** by **Quebec** for Danny Chicoine, June 9, 1982.

• BUSKAS, ROD

Rod Buskas D – R. 6'1", 206 lbs. b: Wetaskiwin, Alta., 1/7/1961. Pittsburgh's 5th choice, 112th overall, in 1981 Entry Draft.

Season	Club	League	GP	G	A	Pts	AG	AA	APts	PIM	PP	SH	GW	S	%	TGF	PGF	TGA	PGA	+/–	GP	G	A	Pts	PIM	PP	SH	GW
1978-79	Red Deer Rustlers	AJHL	37	13	22	35	....	....	....	63	....	....	....	....	....	....	....	....	....	....	....	....	....	....	....	....	....	....
	Billings Bighorns	WHL	1	0	0	0	....	....	....	0	....	....	....	....	....	....	....	....	....	....	....	....	....	....	....	....	....	....
	Medicine Hat Tigers	WHL	34	1	12	13	....	....	....	60	....	....	....	....	....	....	....	....	....	....	....	....	....	....	....	....	....	....
1979-80	Medicine Hat Tigers	WHL	72	7	40	47	....	....	....	284	....	....	....	....	....	....	....	....	....	....	16	1	6	7	31	....	....	....
1980-81	Medicine Hat Tigers	WHL	72	14	46	60	....	....	....	164	....	....	....	....	....	....	....	....	....	....	5	1	1	2	8	....	....	....
1981-82	Erie Blades	AHL	69	1	18	19	....	....	....	78	....	....	....	....	....	....	....	....	....	....	....	....	....	....	....	....	....	....
1982-83	**Pittsburgh Penguins**	**NHL**	**41**	**2**	**2**	**4**	**2**	**1**	**3**	**102**	**1**	**0**	**0**	**27**	**7.4**	**18**	**1**	**43**	**11**	**–15**	....	....	....	....	....	....	....	....
	Baltimore Skipjacks	AHL	31	2	8	10	....	....	....	45	....	....	....	....	....	....	....	....	....	....	....	....	....	....	....	....	....	....
1983-84	**Pittsburgh Penguins**	**NHL**	**47**	**2**	**4**	**6**	**2**	**3**	**5**	**60**	**1**	**0**	**0**	**39**	**5.1**	**30**	**4**	**57**	**13**	**–18**	....	....	....	....	....	....	....	....
	Baltimore Skipjacks	AHL	33	2	12	14	....	....	....	100	....	....	....	....	....	....	....	....	....	....	10	1	3	4	22	....	....	....
1984-85	**Pittsburgh Penguins**	**NHL**	**69**	**2**	**7**	**9**	**2**	**5**	**7**	**191**	**0**	**0**	**0**	**53**	**3.8**	**67**	**6**	**103**	**21**	**–21**	....	....	....	....	....	....	....	....
1985-86	**Pittsburgh Penguins**	**NHL**	**72**	**2**	**7**	**9**	**2**	**5**	**7**	**159**	**1**	**0**	**0**	**50**	**4.0**	**49**	**2**	**73**	**17**	**–9**	....	....	....	....	....	....	....	....
1986-87	**Pittsburgh Penguins**	**NHL**	**68**	**3**	**15**	**18**	**3**	**11**	**14**	**123**	**1**	**0**	**0**	**90**	**3.3**	**73**	**7**	**81**	**17**	**+2**	....	....	....	....	....	....	....	....
1987-88	**Pittsburgh Penguins**	**NHL**	**76**	**4**	**8**	**12**	**3**	**6**	**9**	**206**	**0**	**0**	**1**	**53**	**7.5**	**56**	**1**	**91**	**42**	**+6**	....	....	....	....	....	....	....	....
1988-89	**Pittsburgh Penguins**	**NHL**	**52**	**1**	**5**	**6**	**1**	**4**	**5**	**105**	**0**	**0**	**0**	**15**	**6.7**	**28**	**0**	**52**	**22**	**–2**	**10**	**0**	**0**	**0**	**23**	**0**	**0**	**0**
1989-90	**Vancouver Canucks**	**NHL**	**17**	**0**	**3**	**3**	**0**	**2**	**2**	**36**	**0**	**0**	**0**	**11**	**0.0**	**14**	**0**	**14**	**1**	**+1**	....	....	....	....	....	....	....	....
	Pittsburgh Penguins	**NHL**	**6**	**0**	**0**	**0**	**0**	**0**	**0**	**13**	**0**	**0**	**0**	**1**	**0.0**	**2**	**0**	**9**	**3**	**–4**	....	....	....	....	....	....	....	....
1990-91	**Los Angeles Kings**	**NHL**	**57**	**3**	**8**	**11**	**3**	**6**	**9**	**182**	**0**	**0**	**0**	**60**	**5.0**	**62**	**1**	**62**	**15**	**+14**	**2**	**0**	**2**	**2**	**22**	**0**	**0**	**0**
1991-92	**Los Angeles Kings**	**NHL**	**5**	**0**	**0**	**0**	**0**	**0**	**0**	**11**	**0**	**0**	**0**	**1**	**0.0**	**4**	**0**	**6**	**1**	**–1**	....	....	....	....	....	....	....	....
	Chicago Blackhawks	**NHL**	**42**	**0**	**4**	**4**	**0**	**3**	**3**	**80**	**0**	**0**	**0**	**22**	**0.0**	**14**	**0**	**29**	**3**	**–12**	**6**	**0**	**1**	**1**	**0**	**0**	**0**	**0**

			REGULAR SEASON																		PLAYOFFS							
Season	Club	League	GP	G	A	Pts	AG	AA	APts	PIM	PP	SH	GW	S	%	TGF	PGF	TGA	PGA	+/–	GP	G	A	Pts	PIM	PP	SH	GW
1992-93	Chicago Blackhawks	NHL	4	0	0	0	0	0	0	26	0	0	0	3	0.0	2	0	0	0	+2	....	....	....	....	....	....	....	....
	Indianapolis Ice	IHL	15	0	3	3	....	....	....	40	....	....	....	....	....	....	....	....	....	....	....	....	....	....	....	....	....	....
	Salt Lake Golden Eagles	IHL	31	0	2	2	....	....	....	52	....	....	....	....	....	....	....	....	....	....	....	....	....	....	....	....	....	....
1993-94	Las Vegas Thunder	IHL	69	2	9	11	....	....	....	131	....	....	....	....	....	....	....	....	....	....	5	0	2	2	2	....	....	....
1994-95	Las Vegas Thunder	IHL	27	2	3	5	....	....	....	53	....	....	....	....	....	....	....	....	....	....	10	1	0	1	19	....	....	....
	NHL Totals		556	19	63	82	18	46	64	1294	4	0	1	425	4.5	419	22	620	166		18	0	3	3	45	0	0	0

Traded to **Vancouver** by **Pittsburgh** for Vancouver's 6th round choice (Ian Moran) in 1990 Entry Draft, October 24, 1989. Traded to **Pittsburgh** by **Vancouver** with Barry Pederson and Tony Tanti for Dave Capuano, Andrew McBain and Dan Quinn, January 8, 1990. Claimed by **LA Kings** from **Pittsburgh** in Waiver Draft, October 1, 1990. Traded to **Chicago** by **LA Kings** for Chris Norton and future considerations, October 28, 1991.

• BUSNIUK, MIKE

Mike Busniuk D – R. 6'3", 200 lbs. b: Thunder Bay, Ont., 12/13/1951. Montreal's 10th choice, 67th overall, in 1971 Amateur Draft.

1970-71	University of Denver	WCHA	36	1	10	11	....	....	....	46	....	....	....	....	....	....	....	....	....	....	....	....	....	....	....	....	....	....
1971-72	University of Denver	WCHA	38	1	19	20	....	....	....	77	....	....	....	....	....	....	....	....	....	....	....	....	....	....	....	....	....	....
1972-73	University of Denver	WCHA	39	20	17	37	....	....	....	70	....	....	....	....	....	....	....	....	....	....	....	....	....	....	....	....	....	....
1973-74	University of Denver	WCHA	32	17	18	35	....	....	....	14	....	....	....	....	....	....	....	....	....	....	....	....	....	....	....	....	....	....
1974-75	Nova Scotia Voyageurs	AHL	69	15	17	32	....	....	....	94	....	....	....	....	....	....	....	....	....	....	6	1	0	1	2	....	....	....
1975-76	Beauce Jaros	NAHL	65	14	52	66	....	....	....	179	....	....	....	....	....	....	....	....	....	....	14	1	12	13	61	....	....	....
	Nova Scotia Voyageurs	AHL	....	....	....	....	....	....	....	....	....	....	....	....	....	....	....	....	....	....	1	0	0	0	4	....	....	....
1976-77	Nova Scotia Voyageurs	AHL	80	1	15	16	....	....	....	160	....	....	....	....	....	....	....	....	....	....	12	0	0	0	4	....	....	....
1977-78	Maine Mariners	AHL	75	5	15	20	....	....	....	72	....	....	....	....	....	....	....	....	....	....	12	0	1	1	44	....	....	....
1978-79	Maine Mariners	AHL	79	10	34	44	....	....	....	215	....	....	....	....	....	....	....	....	....	....	10	0	5	5	4	....	....	....
1979-80	Philadelphia Flyers	NHL	71	2	18	20	2	14	16	93	0	0	1	56	3.6	83	0	66	22	+39	19	2	4	6	23	0	0	0
	Maine Mariners	AHL	3	2	1	3	....	....	....	7	....	....	....	....	....	....	....	....	....	....	....	....	....	....	....	....	....	....
1980-81	Philadelphia Flyers	NHL	72	1	5	6	1	3	4	204	0	0	0	33	3.0	64	1	57	21	+27	6	0	1	1	11	0	0	0
1981-82	Maine Mariners	AHL	78	12	26	38	....	....	....	203	....	....	....	....	....	....	....	....	....	....	4	1	0	1	20	....	....	....
1982-83	Maine Mariners	AHL	11	0	5	5	....	....	....	14	....	....	....	....	....	....	....	....	....	....	17	1	5	6	52	....	....	....
1983-84	Maine Mariners	AHL	2	0	1	1	....	....	....	2	....	....	....	....	....	....	....	....	....	....	16	1	1	2	*105	....	....	....
1984-85	SG Bruneck	Italy	26	9	16	25	....	....	....	29	....	....	....	....	....	....	....	....	....	....	6	4	4	8	14	....	....	....
	NHL Totals		143	3	23	26	3	17	20	297	0	0	1	89	3.4	147	1	123	43		25	2	5	7	34	0	0	0

Signed as a free agent by **Philadelphia**, October 23, 1977.

• BUSNIUK, RON

Ron Busniuk RW – R. 5'11", 180 lbs. b: Fort William, Ont., 8/13/1948.

1965-66	Fort William Bearcats	TBJHL	....	15	27	42	....	....	....	....	....	....	....	....	....	....	....	....	....	....	....	....	....	....	....	....	....	....
1966-67	University of Minnesota-Duluth	WCHA	DID NOT PLAY – FRESHMAN																									
1967-68	University of Minnesota-Duluth	WCHA	27	10	10	20	....	....	....	....	....	....	....	....	....	....	....	....	....	....	....	....	....	....	....	....	....	....
1968-69	University of Minnesota-Duluth	WCHA	29	7	20	27	....	....	....	....	....	....	....	....	....	....	....	....	....	....	....	....	....	....	....	....	....	....
1969-70	University of Minnesota-Duluth	WCHA	40	14	32	46	....	....	....	73	....	....	....	....	....	....	....	....	....	....	....	....	....	....	....	....	....	....
1970-71	Montreal Voyageurs	AHL	59	11	9	20	....	....	....	136	....	....	....	....	....	....	....	....	....	....	3	0	1	1	10	....	....	....
1971-72	Nova Scotia Voyageurs	AHL	67	13	13	26	....	....	....	133	....	....	....	....	....	....	....	....	....	....	15	3	5	8	*74	....	....	....
1972-73	Buffalo Sabres	NHL	1	0	0	0	0	0	0	9	0	0	0	1	0.0	1	0	1	0	0	....	....	....	....	....	....	....	....
	Cincinnati Swords	AHL	71	5	34	39	....	....	....	205	....	....	....	....	....	....	....	....	....	....	15	1	7	8	39	....	....	....
1973-74	Buffalo Sabres	NHL	5	0	3	3	0	3	3	4	0	0	0	3	0.0	4	2	3	0	–1	....	....	....	....	....	....	....	....
	Cincinnati Swords	AHL	68	7	24	31	....	....	....	146	....	....	....	....	....	....	....	....	....	....	5	1	1	2	8	....	....	....
1974-75	Minnesota Fighting Saints	WHA	73	2	21	23	....	....	....	176	....	....	....	....	....	....	....	....	....	....	12	2	1	3	*63	....	....	....
1975-76	Minnesota Fighting Saints	WHA	59	2	11	13	....	....	....	150	....	....	....	....	....	....	....	....	....	....	....	....	....	....	....	....	....	....
	New England Whalers	WHA	11	0	3	3	....	....	....	55	....	....	....	....	....	....	....	....	....	....	17	0	2	2	14	....	....	....
1976-77	New England Whalers	WHA	55	1	9	10	....	....	....	141	....	....	....	....	....	....	....	....	....	....	....	....	....	....	....	....	....	....
	Edmonton Oilers	WHA	29	2	2	4	....	....	....	83	....	....	....	....	....	....	....	....	....	....	5	0	2	2	37	....	....	....
1977-78	Edmonton Oilers	WHA	59	2	18	20	....	....	....	157	....	....	....	....	....	....	....	....	....	....	5	0	0	0	18	....	....	....
	NHL Totals		6	0	3	3	0	3	3	13	0	0	0	4	0.0	5	2	4	0		....	....	....	....	....	....	....	....

AHL First All-Star Team (1974) • WCHA First All-Star Team (1970) • NCAA West First All-American Team (1970)

Traded to **Buffalo** by **Montreal** for cash, June 8, 1972. Selected by **Minnesota** (WHA) in 1973 WHA Professional Draft, June, 1973. Claimed by **Detroit** from **Buffalo** in Intra-League Draft, June 10, 1974. Signed as a free agent by **New England** (WHA) after **Minnesota** (WHA) franchise folded, March, 1976. Traded to **Edmonton** (WHA) by **New England** (WHA) with Brett Callighen for Mike Antonovich and Bill Butters, February, 1977.

• BUTCHER, GARTH

Garth Butcher D – R. 6', 204 lbs. b: Regina, Sask., 1/8/1963. Vancouver's 1st choice, 10th overall, in 1981 Entry Draft.

1979-80	Regina Capitals	SJHL	51	15	31	46	....	....	....	236	....	....	....	....	....	....	....	....	....	....	....	....	....	....	....	....	....	....
	Regina Pats	WHL	13	0	4	4	....	....	....	20	....	....	....	....	....	....	....	....	....	....	9	0	0	0	45	....	....	....
1980-81	Regina Pats	WHL	69	9	77	86	....	....	....	230	....	....	....	....	....	....	....	....	....	....	11	5	17	22	60	....	....	....
1981-82	Regina Pats	WHL	65	24	68	92	....	....	....	318	....	....	....	....	....	....	....	....	....	....	19	3	17	20	95	....	....	....
	Canada	WJC-A	7	1	3	4	....	....	....	0	....	....	....	....	....	....	....	....	....	....	....	....	....	....	....	....	....	....
	Vancouver Canucks	NHL	5	0	0	0	0	0	0	9	0	0	0	7	0.0	5	0	2	1	+4	1	0	0	0	0	0	0	0
1982-83	Kamloops Blazers	WHL	5	4	2	6	....	....	....	4	....	....	....	....	....	....	....	....	....	....	6	4	8	12	16	....	....	....
	Vancouver Canucks	NHL	55	1	13	14	1	9	10	104	0	0	0	60	1.7	50	3	58	4	–7	3	1	0	1	2	0	0	0
1983-84	Vancouver Canucks	NHL	28	2	0	2	2	0	2	34	0	0	0	33	6.1	21	0	42	9	–12	....	....	....	....	....	....	....	....
	Fredericton Express	AHL	25	4	13	17	....	....	....	43	....	....	....	....	....	....	....	....	....	....	6	0	2	2	19	....	....	....
1984-85	Vancouver Canucks	NHL	75	3	9	12	2	6	8	152	0	0	1	59	5.1	68	1	131	33	–31	....	....	....	....	....	....	....	....
	Fredericton Express	AHL	3	1	0	1	....	....	....	11	....	....	....	....	....	....	....	....	....	....	....	....	....	....	....	....	....	....
1985-86	Vancouver Canucks	NHL	70	4	7	11	3	5	8	188	0	0	0	57	7.0	42	1	87	21	–25	3	0	0	0	0	0	0	0
1986-87	Vancouver Canucks	NHL	70	5	15	20	4	11	15	207	0	0	0	95	5.3	56	2	97	31	–12	....	....	....	....	....	....	....	....
1987-88	Vancouver Canucks	NHL	80	6	17	23	5	12	17	285	1	0	0	77	7.8	66	10	95	25	–14	....	....	....	....	....	....	....	....
1988-89	Vancouver Canucks	NHL	78	0	20	20	0	14	14	227	0	0	0	101	0.0	70	3	87	24	+4	7	1	1	2	22	0	0	1
1989-90	Vancouver Canucks	NHL	80	6	14	20	5	10	15	205	1	0	1	87	6.9	71	3	114	36	–10	....	....	....	....	....	....	....	....
1990-91	Vancouver Canucks	NHL	69	6	12	18	5	9	14	257	1	0	1	70	8.6	63	6	118	43	–18	....	....	....	....	....	....	....	....
	St. Louis Blues	NHL	13	0	4	4	0	3	3	32	0	0	0	5	0.0	11	0	12	5	+4	13	2	1	3	54	0	0	0
1991-92	St. Louis Blues	NHL	68	5	15	20	5	11	16	189	0	0	0	50	10.0	70	1	83	19	+5	5	1	2	3	16	0	0	0
	Canada	WC-A	3	1	0	1	....	....	....	4	....	....	....	....	....	....	....	....	....	....	....	....	....	....	....	....	....	....
1992-93	St. Louis Blues	NHL	84	5	10	15	4	7	11	211	0	0	2	83	6.0	74	4	92	22	0	11	1	1	2	20	0	0	1
1993-94	St. Louis Blues	NHL	43	1	6	7	1	5	6	76	0	1	0	37	2.7	41	1	64	18	–6	....	....	....	....	....	....	....	....
	Quebec Nordiques	NHL	34	3	9	12	3	7	10	67	0	1	1	29	10.3	33	0	55	21	–1	....	....	....	....	....	....	....	....
1994-95	Toronto Maple Leafs	NHL	45	1	7	8	2	10	12	59	0	0	0	24	4.2	36	0	51	10	–5	7	0	0	0	8	0	0	0
	NHL Totals		897	48	158	206	42	119	161	2302	3	2	6	874	5.5	777	35	1188	322		50	6	5	11	122	0	0	2

WHL First All-Star Team (1981, 1982)

Played in NHL All-Star Game (1993)

Traded to **St. Louis** by **Vancouver** with Dan Quinn for Geoff Courtnall, Rocbert Dirk, Sergio Momesso, Cliff Ronning and St. Louis' 5th round choice (Brian Loney) in 1992 Entry Draft, Marchy 5, 1991. Traded to **Quebec** by **St. Louis** with Ron Sutter and Bob Bassen for Steve Duchesne and Denis Chase, January 23, 1994. Traded to **Toronto** by **Quebec** with Mats Sundin, Todd Warriner and Philadelphia's 1st round choice (previously acquired by Quebec — later traded to Washington — Washington selected Nolan Baumgartner) in 1994 Entry Draft for Wendel Clark, Sylvain Lefebvre, Landon Wilson and Toronto's 1st round choice (Jeffrey Kealty) in 1994 Entry Draft, June 28, 1994.

• BUTENSCHON, SVEN

Sven Butenschon D – L. 6'5", 201 lbs. b: Itzehoe, West Germany, 3/22/1976. Pittsburgh's 3rd choice, 57th overall, in 1994 Entry Draft.

1993-94	Brandon Wheat Kings	WHL	70	3	19	22	....	....	....	51	....	....	....	....	....	....	....	....	....	....	4	0	0	0	6	....	....	....
1994-95	Brandon Wheat Kings	WHl	21	1	5	6	....	....	....	44	....	....	....	....	....	....	....	....	....	....	18	1	2	3	11	....	....	....
1995-96	Brandon Wheat Kings	WHL	70	4	37	41	....	....	....	99	....	....	....	....	....	....	....	....	....	....	19	1	12	13	18	....	....	....
1996-97	Cleveland Lumberjacks	IHL	75	3	12	15	....	....	....	68	....	....	....	....	....	....	....	....	....	....	10	0	1	1	4	....	....	....
1997-98	Pittsburgh Penguins	NHL	8	0	0	0	0	0	0	6	0	0	0	4	0.0	5	1	6	1	–1	....	....	....	....	....	....	....	....
	Syracuse Crunch	AHL	65	14	23	37	....	....	....	66	....	....	....	....	....	....	....	....	....	....	5	1	2	3	0	....	....	....
	NHL Totals		8	0	0	0	0	0	0	6	0	0	0	4	0.0	5	1	6	1		....	....	....	....	....	....	....	....

			REGULAR SEASON																		PLAYOFFS							
Season	Club	League	GP	G	A	Pts	AG	AA	APts	PIM	PP	SH	GW	S	%	TGF	PGF	TGA	PGA	+/–	GP	G	A	Pts	PIM	PP	SH	GW

• BUTLER, JERRY

Jerry "Bugsy" Butler RW – R. 6', 180 lbs. b: Sarnia, Ont., 2/27/1951. NY Rangers' 5th choice, 55th overall, in 1971 Amateur Draft.

Season	Club	League	GP	G	A	Pts	AG	AA	APts	PIM	PP	SH	GW	S	%	TGF	PGF	TGA	PGA	+/–	GP	G	A	Pts	PIM	PP	SH	GW
1969-70	Sarnia Bees	Jr. B	STATISTICS NOT AVAILABLE																									
1970-71	Hamilton Red Wings	OHA	59	6	20	26	....	....	....	131	....	....	....	....	....	....	....	....	....	....	....	....	....	....	....	....	....	....
1971-72	Omaha Knights	CHL	72	19	18	37	....	....	....	173	....	....	....	....	....	....	....	....	....	....	....	....	....	....	....	....	....	....
1972-73	**New York Rangers**	**NHL**	**8**	**1**	**0**	**1**	**1**	**0**	**1**	**4**	**0**	**0**	**0**	**11**	**9.1**	**2**	**0**	**1**	**0**	**+1**	....	....	....	....	....	....	....	....
	Providence Reds	AHL	64	29	30	59	....	....	....	97	....	....	....	....	....	....	....	....	....	....	4	1	2	3	11	....	....	....
1973-74	**New York Rangers**	**NHL**	**26**	**6**	**10**	**16**	**6**	**9**	**15**	**24**	**1**	**0**	**1**	**60**	**10.0**	**28**	**3**	**21**	**3**	**+7**	**12**	**0**	**2**	**2**	**25**	**0**	**0**	**0**
	Providence Reds	AHL	48	20	22	42	....	....	....	114	....	....	....	....	....	....	....	....	....	....	....	....	....	....	....	....	....	....
1974-75	**New York Rangers**	**NHL**	**78**	**17**	**16**	**33**	**16**	**13**	**29**	**102**	**1**	**2**	**1**	**157**	**10.8**	**52**	**6**	**65**	**14**	**–5**	**3**	**1**	**0**	**1**	**16**	**0**	**0**	**0**
1975-76	**St. Louis Blues**	**NHL**	**66**	**17**	**24**	**41**	**16**	**19**	**35**	**75**	**1**	**0**	**3**	**154**	**11.0**	**56**	**9**	**56**	**9**	**0**	**3**	**0**	**0**	**0**	**0**	**0**	**0**	**0**
1976-77	**St. Louis Blues**	**NHL**	**80**	**12**	**20**	**32**	**11**	**16**	**27**	**65**	**0**	**0**	**0**	**152**	**7.9**	**50**	**2**	**98**	**19**	**–31**	**4**	**0**	**0**	**0**	**14**	**0**	**0**	**0**
1977-78	**St. Louis Blues**	**NHL**	**9**	**0**	**2**	**2**	**0**	**2**	**2**	**5**	**0**	**0**	**0**	**15**	**0.0**	**5**	**1**	**10**	**0**	**–6**	....	....	....	....	....	....	....	....
	Toronto Maple Leafs	**NHL**	**73**	**9**	**7**	**16**	**9**	**6**	**15**	**49**	**1**	**1**	**1**	**99**	**9.1**	**34**	**2**	**67**	**25**	**–10**	**13**	**1**	**1**	**2**	**18**	**0**	**0**	**0**
1978-79	**Toronto Maple Leafs**	**NHL**	**76**	**8**	**7**	**15**	**7**	**5**	**12**	**52**	**0**	**2**	**2**	**77**	**10.4**	**30**	**0**	**66**	**34**	**–2**	**6**	**0**	**0**	**0**	**4**	**0**	**0**	**0**
1979-80	**Toronto Maple Leafs**	**NHL**	**55**	**7**	**8**	**15**	**6**	**6**	**12**	**29**	**0**	**0**	**1**	**60**	**11.7**	**24**	**1**	**53**	**27**	**–3**	....	....	....	....	....	....	....	....
	Vancouver Canucks	**NHL**	**23**	**4**	**4**	**8**	**4**	**3**	**7**	**21**	**1**	**0**	**1**	**24**	**16.7**	**11**	**1**	**23**	**8**	**–5**	**4**	**0**	**0**	**0**	**2**	**0**	**0**	**0**
1980-81	**Vancouver Canucks**	**NHL**	**80**	**12**	**15**	**27**	**10**	**10**	**20**	**60**	**0**	**2**	**2**	**99**	**12.1**	**42**	**0**	**83**	**43**	**+2**	**3**	**1**	**0**	**1**	**0**	**0**	**0**	**0**
1981-82	**Vancouver Canucks**	**NHL**	**25**	**3**	**1**	**4**	**2**	**1**	**3**	**15**	**0**	**0**	**0**	**21**	**14.3**	**10**	**0**	**29**	**14**	**–5**	....	....	....	....	....	....	....	....
	Dallas Black Hawks	CHL	47	6	24	30	....	....	....	30	....	....	....	....	....	....	....	....	....	....	16	4	5	9	36	....	....	....
1982-83	**Winnipeg Jets**	**NHL**	**42**	**3**	**6**	**9**	**2**	**4**	**6**	**14**	**0**	**1**	**1**	**24**	**12.5**	**13**	**1**	**29**	**12**	**–5**	....	....	....	....	....	....	....	....
	NHL Totals		**641**	**99**	**120**	**219**	**90**	**94**	**184**	**515**	**5**	**8**	**13**	**953**	**10.4**	**357**	**26**	**601**	**208**		**48**	**3**	**3**	**6**	**79**	**0**	**0**	**0**

Traded to **St. Louis** by **NY Rangers** with Ted Irvine and Bert Wilson for Bill Collins and John Davidson, June 18, 1975. Traded to **Toronto** by **St. Louis** for Inge Hammarstrom, November 1, 1977. Traded to **Vancouver** by **Toronto** with Tiger Williams for Bill Derlago and Rick Vaive, February 18, 1980. Signed as a free agent by **Winnipeg**, October 8, 1982.

• BUTSAYEV, VIACHESLAV

Viacheslav Butsayev C – L. 6'2", 200 lbs. b: Togliatti, USSR, 6/13/1970. Philadelphia's 10th choice, 109th overall, in 1990 Entry Draft.

Season	Club	League	GP	G	A	Pts	AG	AA	APts	PIM	PP	SH	GW	S	%	TGF	PGF	TGA	PGA	+/–	GP	G	A	Pts	PIM	PP	SH	GW
1989-90	CSKA Moscow	USSR	48	14	4	18	....	....	....	30	....	....	....	....	....	....	....	....	....	....	....	....	....	....	....	....	....	....
1990-91	CSKA Moscow	USSR	46	14	9	23	....	....	....	32	....	....	....	....	....	....	....	....	....	....	....	....	....	....	....	....	....	....
	Soviet Union	WEC-A	10	4	1	5	....	....	....	10	....	....	....	....	....	....	....	....	....	....	....	....	....	....	....	....	....	....
1991-92	CSKA Moscow	CIS	36	12	13	25	....	....	....	26	....	....	....	....	....	....	....	....	....	....	....	....	....	....	....	....	....	....
	Russia	Olympics	8	1	1	2	....	....	....	4	....	....	....	....	....	....	....	....	....	....	....	....	....	....	....	....	....	....
	Russia	WC-A	6	0	1	1	....	....	....	10	....	....	....	....	....	....	....	....	....	....	....	....	....	....	....	....	....	....
1992-93	CSKA Moscow	CIS	5	3	4	7	....	....	....	6	....	....	....	....	....	....	....	....	....	....	....	....	....	....	....	....	....	....
	Philadelphia Flyers	**NHL**	**52**	**2**	**14**	**16**	**2**	**10**	**12**	**61**	**0**	**0**	**0**	**58**	**3.4**	**34**	**3**	**28**	**0**	**+3**	....	....	....	....	....	....	....	....
	Hershey Bears	AHL	24	8	10	18	....	....	....	51	....	....	....	....	....	....	....	....	....	....	....	....	....	....	....	....	....	....
	Russia	WC-A	8	1	2	3	....	....	....	8	....	....	....	....	....	....	....	....	....	....	....	....	....	....	....	....	....	....
1993-94	**Philadelphia Flyers**	**NHL**	**47**	**12**	**9**	**21**	**11**	**7**	**18**	**58**	**0**	**0**	**3**	**79**	**15.2**	**30**	**5**	**25**	**2**	**+2**	....	....	....	....	....	....	....	....
	San Jose Sharks	**NHL**	**12**	**0**	**2**	**2**	**0**	**2**	**2**	**10**	**2**	**0**	**0**	**6**	**0.0**	**2**	**1**	**3**	**0**	**–2**	....	....	....	....	....	....	....	....
1994-95	Togliatti	CIS	9	2	6	8	....	....	....	6	....	....	....	....	....	....	....	....	....	....	....	....	....	....	....	....	....	....
	San Jose Sharks	**NHL**	**6**	**2**	**0**	**2**	**4**	**0**	**4**	**0**	**0**	**0**	**0**	**6**	**33.3**	**2**	**0**	**4**	**0**	**–2**	....	....	....	....	....	....	....	....
	Kansas City Blades	IHL	13	3	4	7	....	....	....	12	....	....	....	....	....	....	....	....	....	....	3	0	0	0	2	....	....	....
1995-96	**Anaheim Mighty Ducks**	**NHL**	**7**	**1**	**0**	**1**	**1**	**0**	**1**	**0**	**0**	**0**	**0**	**9**	**11.1**	**1**	**0**	**5**	**0**	**–4**	....	....	....	....	....	....	....	....
	Baltimore Bandits	AHL	62	23	42	65	....	....	....	70	....	....	....	....	....	....	....	....	....	....	12	4	8	12	28	....	....	....
1996-97	Farjestad BK Karlstad	Sweden	40	6	7	13	....	....	....	108	....	....	....	....	....	....	....	....	....	....	8	3	4	7	41	....	....	....
	Russia	WC-A	9	2	2	4	....	....	....	8	....	....	....	....	....	....	....	....	....	....	....	....	....	....	....	....	....	....
1997-98	Fort Wayne Komets	IHL	76	36	51	87	....	....	....	128	....	....	....	....	....	....	....	....	....	....	4	2	2	4	4	....	....	....
	NHL Totals		**124**	**17**	**25**	**42**	**18**	**19**	**37**	**129**	**2**	**0**	**3**	**158**	**10.8**	**69**	**9**	**65**	**2**		....	....	....	....	....	....	....	....

IHL Second All-Star Team (1998)

Traded to **San Jose** by **Philadelphia** for Rob Zettler, February 1, 1994. Signed as a free agent by **Anaheim**, October 19, 1995.

• BUTTERS, BILL

Bill Butters D – R. 5'10", 185 lbs. b: St. Paul, MN, 1/10/1951.

Season	Club	League	GP	G	A	Pts	AG	AA	APts	PIM	PP	SH	GW	S	%	TGF	PGF	TGA	PGA	+/–	GP	G	A	Pts	PIM	PP	SH	GW
1970-71	University of Minnesota	WCHA	27	0	1	1	....	....	....	52	....	....	....	....	....	....	....	....	....	....	....	....	....	....	....	....	....	....
1971-72	University of Minnesota	WCHA	29	1	9	10	....	....	....	100	....	....	....	....	....	....	....	....	....	....	....	....	....	....	....	....	....	....
1972-73	University of Minnesota	WCHA	33	3	6	9	....	....	....	110	....	....	....	....	....	....	....	....	....	....	....	....	....	....	....	....	....	....
1973-74	Oklahoma City Blazers	CHL	71	7	18	25	....	....	....	174	....	....	....	....	....	....	....	....	....	....	10	2	4	6	37	....	....	....
1974-75	Oklahoma City Blazers	CHL	32	5	9	14	....	....	....	192	....	....	....	....	....	....	....	....	....	....	....	....	....	....	....	....	....	....
	Minnesota Fighting Saints	WHA	24	2	2	4	....	....	....	58	....	....	....	....	....	....	....	....	....	....	12	1	0	1	21	....	....	....
1975-76	Minnesota Fighting Saints	WHA	59	0	15	15	....	....	....	170	....	....	....	....	....	....	....	....	....	....	....	....	....	....	....	....	....	....
	Houston Aeros	WHA	14	0	4	4	....	....	....	18	....	....	....	....	....	....	....	....	....	....	17	0	3	3	51	....	....	....
1976-77	Minnesota Fighting Saints	WHA	42	0	7	7	....	....	....	133	....	....	....	....	....	....	....	....	....	....	....	....	....	....	....	....	....	....
	Edmonton Oilers	WHA	7	0	2	2	....	....	....	17	....	....	....	....	....	....	....	....	....	....	....	....	....	....	....	....	....	....
	New England Whalers	WHA	26	1	8	9	....	....	....	66	....	....	....	....	....	....	....	....	....	....	5	0	1	1	15	....	....	....
1977-78	New England Whalers	WHA	45	1	13	14	....	....	....	69	....	....	....	....	....	....	....	....	....	....	....	....	....	....	....	....	....	....
	Minnesota North Stars	**NHL**	**23**	**1**	**0**	**1**	**1**	**0**	**1**	**30**	**0**	**0**	**0**	**18**	**5.6**	**19**	**0**	**31**	**9**	**–3**	....	....	....	....	....	....	....	....
1978-79	**Minnesota North Stars**	**NHL**	**49**	**0**	**4**	**4**	**0**	**3**	**3**	**47**	**0**	**0**	**0**	**17**	**0.0**	**22**	**0**	**46**	**12**	**–12**	....	....	....	....	....	....	....	....
	Oklahoma City Stars	CHL	14	1	2	3	....	....	....	31	....	....	....	....	....	....	....	....	....	....	....	....	....	....	....	....	....	....
1979-80	Oklahoma City Stars	CHL	73	3	8	11	....	....	....	134	....	....	....	....	....	....	....	....	....	....	....	....	....	....	....	....	....	....
	NHL Totals		**72**	**1**	**4**	**5**	**1**	**3**	**4**	**77**	**0**	**0**	**0**	**35**	**2.9**	**41**	**0**	**77**	**21**		....	....	....	....	....	....	....	....
	Other Major League Totals		217	4	51	55	....	....	....	530	....	....	....	....	....	....	....	....	....	....	34	1	4	5	87	....	....	....

Signed as a free agent by **Toronto**, September 27, 1973. Rights traded to **Minnesota** (WHA) by **Toronto** for cash, February, 1975. Signed as a free agent by **Toronto** (WHA) after **Minnesota** (WHA) franchise folded, February 27, 1976. Traded to **Houston** (WHA) by **Toronto** (WHA) for Paul Crowley and future considerations, February 27, 1976. Claimed by **Birmingham** (WHA) from **Houston** (WHA) in 1976 WHA Intra-League Draft, June, 1976. Traded to **Minnesota** (WHA) by **Birmingham** (WHA) for cash, September, 1976. Traded to **Edmonton** (WHA) by **Minnesota** (WHA) with Mike Antonovich, Jean-Louis Levasseur, Dave Keon, Jack Carlson, Steve Carlson and John McKenzie for cash, January, 1977. Traded to **New England** (WHA) by **Edmonton** (WHA) with Mike Antonovich for Brett Callighen and Ron Busniuk, February, 1977. Signed as a free agent by **Minnesota** after clearing WHA waivers, February 16, 1978.

• BUYNAK, GORDON

Gordon Buynak D – L. 6'1", 180 lbs. b: Detroit, MI, 3/19/1954. St. Louis' 2nd choice, 43rd overall, in 1974 Amateur Draft.

Season	Club	League	GP	G	A	Pts	AG	AA	APts	PIM	PP	SH	GW	S	%	TGF	PGF	TGA	PGA	+/–	GP	G	A	Pts	PIM	PP	SH	GW
1971-72	Detroit Jr. Red Wings	SOJHL	53	2	17	19	....	....	....	132	....	....	....	....	....	....	....	....	....	....	....	....	....	....	....	....	....	....
1972-73	Detroit Jr. Red Wings	SOJHL	57	10	14	24	....	....	....	150	....	....	....	....	....	....	....	....	....	....	....	....	....	....	....	....	....	....
1973-74	Kingston Canadians	OHA	70	9	35	44	....	....	....	187	....	....	....	....	....	....	....	....	....	....	....	....	....	....	....	....	....	....
1974-75	**St. Louis Blues**	**NHL**	**4**	**0**	**0**	**0**	**0**	**0**	**0**	**2**	**0**	**0**	**0**	**3**	**0.0**	**3**	**0**	**5**	**5**	**+3**	....	....	....	....	....	....	....	....
	Denver Spurs	CHL	56	1	16	17	....	....	....	102	....	....	....	....	....	....	....	....	....	....	2	0	1	1	2	....	....	....
1975-76	Providence Reds	AHL	70	3	14	17	....	....	....	79	....	....	....	....	....	....	....	....	....	....	3	0	0	0	4	....	....	....
1976-77	Kansas City Blues	CHL	43	0	11	11	....	....	....	34	....	....	....	....	....	....	....	....	....	....	....	....	....	....	....	....	....	....
	Salt Lake Golden Eagles	CHL	20	2	6	8	....	....	....	10	....	....	....	....	....	....	....	....	....	....	....	....	....	....	....	....	....	....
1977-78	Salt Lake Golden Eagles	CHL	65	1	9	10	....	....	....	76	....	....	....	....	....	....	....	....	....	....	6	0	0	0	8	....	....	....
1978-79	Tulsa Oilers	CHL	72	4	12	16	....	....	....	88	....	....	....	....	....	....	....	....	....	....	....	....	....	....	....	....	....	....
1979-80	Dallas Black Hawks	CHL	42	2	6	8	....	....	....	33	....	....	....	....	....	....	....	....	....	....	....	....	....	....	....	....	....	....
	Salt Lake Golden Eagles	CHL	16	0	4	4	....	....	....	25	....	....	....	....	....	....	....	....	....	....	6	0	1	1	0	....	....	....
	NHL Totals		**4**	**0**	**0**	**0**	**0**	**0**	**0**	**2**	**0**	**0**	**0**	**3**	**0.0**	**3**	**0**	**5**	**5**		....	....	....	....	....	....	....	....

Traded to **Vancouver** by **St. Louis** with Bruce Affleck for cash, November 6, 1979. Traded to **St. Louis** by **Vancouver** with Bruce Affleck for cash, February 28, 1980.

● BUZEK, PETR Petr Buzek D – L. 6', 205 lbs. b: Jihlava, Czech., 4/26/1977. Dallas' 3rd choice, 63rd overall, in 1995 Entry Draft.

			REGULAR SEASON																		PLAYOFFS							
Season	Club	League	GP	G	A	Pts	AG	AA	APts	PIM	PP	SH	GW	S	%	TGF	PGF	TGA	PGA	+/–	GP	G	A	Pts	PIM	PP	SH	GW
1993-94	Dukla Jihlava	Czech.	3	0	0	0	....	....	....	....	....	....	....	....	....	....	....	....	....	....	....	....	....	....	....	....	....	....
1994-95	Dukla Jihlava	Czech.	43	2	5	7	....	....	....	47	....	....	....	....	....	....	....	....	....	....	2	0	0	0	2	....	....	....
1994-95	Czech Republic	WJC-A	7	2	2	4	....	....	....	10	....	....	....	....	....	....	....	....	....	....	....	....	....	....	....	....	....	....
1995-96			DID NOT PLAY – INJURED																									
1996-97	Michigan K-Wings	IHL	67	4	6	10	....	....	....	48	....	....	....	....	....	....	....	....	....	....	....	....	....	....	....	....	....	....
1997-98	**Dallas Stars**	**NHL**	**2**	**0**	**0**	**0**	**0**	**0**	**0**	**2**	**0**	**0**	**0**	**0**	**0.0**	**1**	**0**	**0**	**0**	**+1**	....	....	....	....	....	....	....	....
	Michigan K-Wings	IHL	60	10	15	25	....	....	....	58	....	....	....	....	....	....	....	....	....	....	2	0	1	1	17	....	....	....
	NHL Totals		**2**	**0**	**0**	**0**	**0**	**0**	**0**	**2**	**0**	**0**	**0**	**0**	**0.0**	**1**	**0**	**0**	**0**		....	....	....	....	....	....	....	....

EJC-A All-Star Team (1995)

● BYAKIN, ILJA Ilja Byakin D – L. 5'9", 185 lbs. b: Sverdlovsk, USSR, 2/2/1963. Edmonton's 11th choice, 267th overall, in 1993 Entry Draft.

Season	Club	League	GP	G	A	Pts	AG	AA	APts	PIM	PP	SH	GW	S	%	TGF	PGF	TGA	PGA	+/–	GP	G	A	Pts	PIM	PP	SH	GW
1983-84	Spartak Moscow	USSR	44	9	12	21	....	....	....	26	....	....	....	....	....	....	....	....	....	....	....	....	....	....	....	....	....	....
1984-85	Spartak Moscow	USSR	46	7	11	18	....	....	....	56	....	....	....	....	....	....	....	....	....	....	....	....	....	....	....	....	....	....
1985-86	Spartak Moscow	USSR	34	8	7	15	....	....	....	41	....	....	....	....	....	....	....	....	....	....	....	....	....	....	....	....	....	....
1986-87			DID NOT PLAY																									
1987-88	Sverdlovsk	USSR	30	10	10	20	....	....	....	37	....	....	....	....	....	....	....	....	....	....	....	....	....	....	....	....	....	....
	Soviet Union	Olympics	8	1	4	5	....	....	....	4	....	....	....	....	....	....	....	....	....	....	....	....	....	....	....	....	....	....
1988-89	Sverdlovsk	USSR	40	11	9	20	....	....	....	53	....	....	....	....	....	....	....	....	....	....	....	....	....	....	....	....	....	....
	Soviet Union	WEC-A	9	0	2	2	....	....	....	4	....	....	....	....	....	....	....	....	....	....	....	....	....	....	....	....	....	....
1989-90	Sverdlovsk	USSR	27	14	7	21	....	....	....	20	....	....	....	....	....	....	....	....	....	....	....	....	....	....	....	....	....	....
	Soviet Union	WEC-A	10	0	3	3	....	....	....	8	....	....	....	....	....	....	....	....	....	....	....	....	....	....	....	....	....	....
1990-91	CSKA Moscow	USSR	29	4	7	11	....	....	....	20	....	....	....	....	....	....	....	....	....	....	....	....	....	....	....	....	....	....
	Soviet Union	WEC-A	10	2	1	3	....	....	....	4	....	....	....	....	....	....	....	....	....	....	....	....	....	....	....	....	....	....
1991-92	Rapperswil	Switz.2	36	27	40	67	....	....	....	36	....	....	....	....	....	....	....	....	....	....	....	....	....	....	....	....	....	....
	Russia	WC-A	6	3	1	4	....	....	....	2	....	....	....	....	....	....	....	....	....	....	....	....	....	....	....	....	....	....
1992-93	Landshut	Germany	44	12	19	31	....	....	....	43	....	....	....	....	....	....	....	....	....	....	6	5	6	11	6	....	....	....
	Russia	WC-A	8	3	4	7	....	....	....	6	....	....	....	....	....	....	....	....	....	....	....	....	....	....	....	....	....	....
1993-94	**Edmonton Oilers**	**NHL**	**44**	**8**	**20**	**28**	**7**	**15**	**22**	**30**	**6**	**0**	**3**	**51**	**15.7**	**52**	**21**	**36**	**2**	**–3**	....	....	....	....	....	....	....	....
	Cape Breton Oilers	AHL	12	2	9	11	....	....	....	8	....	....	....	....	....	....	....	....	....	....	....	....	....	....	....	....	....	....
	Russia	WC-A	6	2	3	5	....	....	....	2	....	....	....	....	....	....	....	....	....	....	....	....	....	....	....	....	....	....
1994-95	Yekaterinburg	CIS	4	3	2	5	....	....	....	14	....	....	....	....	....	....	....	....	....	....	....	....	....	....	....	....	....	....
	San Jose Sharks	**NHL**	**13**	**0**	**5**	**5**	**0**	**7**	**7**	**14**	**0**	**0**	**0**	**19**	**0.0**	**13**	**7**	**16**	**1**	**–9**	....	....	....	....	....	....	....	....
	Kansas City Blades	IHL	1	0	2	2	....	....	....	0	....	....	....	....	....	....	....	....	....	....	16	4	10	14	43	....	....	....
1995-96	Malmo IF	Sweden	36	10	15	25	....	....	....	52	....	....	....	....	....	....	....	....	....	....	3	1	0	1	19	....	....	....
1996-97	Malmo IF	Sweden	47	11	14	25	....	....	....	78	....	....	....	....	....	....	....	....	....	....	4	0	1	1	0	....	....	....
1997-98	San Antonio Dragons	IHL	6	0	1	1	....	....	....	10	....	....	....	....	....	....	....	....	....	....	....	....	....	....	....	....	....	....
	Las Vegas Thunder	IHL	52	3	7	10	....	....	....	40	....	....	....	....	....	....	....	....	....	....	....	....	....	....	....	....	....	....
	NHL Totals		**57**	**8**	**25**	**33**	**7**	**22**	**29**	**44**	**6**	**0**	**3**	**70**	**11.4**	**65**	**28**	**52**	**3**		....	....	....	....	....	....	....	....

Signed as a free agent by **San Jose**, September 18, 1994.

● BYCE, JOHN John Byce C – L. 6'1", 180 lbs. b: Madison, WI, 8/9/1967. Boston's 11th choice, 220th overall, in 1985 Entry Draft.

Season	Club	League	GP	G	A	Pts	AG	AA	APts	PIM	PP	SH	GW	S	%	TGF	PGF	TGA	PGA	+/–	GP	G	A	Pts	PIM	PP	SH	GW
1984-85	Madison High School	H.S.	24	39	47	86	....	....	....	32	....	....	....	....	....	....	....	....	....	....	....	....	....	....	....	....	....	....
1985-86			DID NOT PLAY																									
1986-87	University of Wisconsin	WCHA	40	1	4	5	....	....	....	12	....	....	....	....	....	....	....	....	....	....	....	....	....	....	....	....	....	....
1987-88	University of Wisconsin	WCHA	41	22	12	34	....	....	....	18	....	....	....	....	....	....	....	....	....	....	....	....	....	....	....	....	....	....
1988-89	University of Wisconsin	WCHA	42	27	28	55	....	....	....	16	....	....	....	....	....	....	....	....	....	....	....	....	....	....	....	....	....	....
1989-90	University of Wisconsin	WCHA	46	27	44	71	....	....	....	20	....	....	....	....	....	....	....	....	....	....	....	....	....	....	....	....	....	....
	Boston Bruins	**NHL**	....	....	....	....	....	....	....	....	....	....	....	....	....	....	....	....	....	....	**8**	**2**	**0**	**2**	**2**	....	....	....
1990-91	**Boston Bruins**	**NHL**	**18**	**1**	**3**	**4**	**1**	**2**	**3**	**6**	**0**	**0**	**0**	**13**	**7.7**	**6**	**1**	**4**	**0**	**+1**	....	....	....	....	....	....	....	....
	Maine Mariners	AHL	53	19	29	48	....	....	....	20	....	....	....	....	....	....	....	....	....	....	....	....	....	....	....	....	....	....
1991-92	**Boston Bruins**	**NHL**	**3**	**1**	**0**	**1**	**1**	**0**	**1**	**0**	**1**	**0**	**0**	**2**	**50.0**	**2**	**1**	**2**	**0**	**–1**	....	....	....	....	....	....	....	....
	Maine Mariners	AHL	55	29	21	50	....	....	....	41	....	....	....	....	....	....	....	....	....	....	....	....	....	....	....	....	....	....
	Baltimore Skipjacks	AHL	20	9	5	14	....	....	....	4	....	....	....	....	....	....	....	....	....	....	....	....	....	....	....	....	....	....
	United States	WC-A	6	0	2	2	....	....	....	2	....	....	....	....	....	....	....	....	....	....	....	....	....	....	....	....	....	....
1992-93	Baltimore Skipjacks	AHL	62	35	44	79	....	....	....	26	....	....	....	....	....	....	....	....	....	....	7	4	5	9	4	....	....	....
1993-94	HV 71 Jonkoping	Sweden	33	8	4	12	....	....	....	8	....	....	....	....	....	....	....	....	....	....	....	....	....	....	....	....	....	....
	Milwaukee Admirals	IHL	28	7	4	11	....	....	....	10	....	....	....	....	....	....	....	....	....	....	3	2	1	3	0	....	....	....
1994-95	Portland Pirates	AHL	6	1	1	2	....	....	....	2	....	....	....	....	....	....	....	....	....	....	....	....	....	....	....	....	....	....
	San Diego Gulls	IHL	5	2	3	5	....	....	....	2	....	....	....	....	....	....	....	....	....	....	....	....	....	....	....	....	....	....
	Milwaukee Admirals	IHL	30	9	11	20	....	....	....	10	....	....	....	....	....	....	....	....	....	....	15	4	5	9	4	....	....	....
1995-96	Los Angeles Ice Dogs	IHL	80	29	29	58	....	....	....	14	....	....	....	....	....	....	....	....	....	....	14	4	7	11	0	....	....	....
1996-97	Long Beach Ice Dogs	IHL	80	29	29	58	....	....	....	14	....	....	....	....	....	....	....	....	....	....	14	4	7	11	0	....	....	....
1997-98	Long Beach Ice Dogs	IHL	17	9	8	17	....	....	....	10	....	....	....	....	....	....	....	....	....	....	12	4	1	5	4	....	....	....
	NHL Totals		**21**	**2**	**3**	**5**	**2**	**2**	**4**	**6**	**1**	**0**	**0**	**15**	**13.3**	**8**	**2**	**6**	**0**		**8**	**2**	**0**	**2**	**2**	**0**	**0**	**0**

WCHA Second All-Star Team (1989, 1990) • NCAA All-Tournament Team (1990)

Traded to **Washington** by **Boston** with Dennis Smith for Brent Hughes and future considerations, February 24, 1992.

● BYERS, JERRY Jerry Byers LW – L. 5'11", 170 lbs. b: Kentville, N.S., 3/29/1952. Minnesota's 1st choice, 12th overall, in 1972 Amateur Draft.

Season	Club	League	GP	G	A	Pts	AG	AA	APts	PIM	PP	SH	GW	S	%	TGF	PGF	TGA	PGA	+/–	GP	G	A	Pts	PIM	PP	SH	GW
1969-70	Kitchener Greenshirts	Jr. B	20	19	11	30	....	....	....	20	....	....	....	....	....	....	....	....	....	....	....	....	....	....	....	....	....	....
	Kitchener Rangers	OHA	36	18	24	42	....	....	....	8	....	....	....	....	....	....	....	....	....	....	....	....	....	....	....	....	....	....
1970-71	Kitchener Rangers	OHA	62	41	39	80	....	....	....	46	....	....	....	....	....	....	....	....	....	....	....	....	....	....	....	....	....	....
1971-72	Kitchener Rangers	OHA	60	41	60	101	....	....	....	49	....	....	....	....	....	....	....	....	....	....	....	....	....	....	....	....	....	....
1972-73	**Minnesota North Stars**	**NHL**	**14**	**0**	**2**	**2**	**0**	**2**	**2**	**6**	**0**	**0**	**0**	**17**	**0.0**	**3**	**1**	**4**	**0**	**–2**	....	....	....	....	....	....	....	....
	Jacksonville Barons	AHL	59	20	17	37	....	....	....	12	....	....	....	....	....	....	....	....	....	....	....	....	....	....	....	....	....	....
1973-74	**Minnesota North Stars**	**NHL**	**10**	**0**	**0**	**0**	**0**	**0**	**0**	**0**	**0**	**0**	**0**	**11**	**0.0**	**1**	**1**	**5**	**0**	**–5**	....	....	....	....	....	....	....	....
	New Haven Nighthawks	AHL	62	31	47	78	....	....	....	37	....	....	....	....	....	....	....	....	....	....	10	4	6	10	4	....	....	....
1974-75	**Atlanta Flames**	**NHL**	**12**	**1**	**1**	**2**	**1**	**1**	**2**	**9**	**0**	**0**	**0**	**10**	**10.0**	**2**	**0**	**6**	**0**	**–4**	....	....	....	....	....	....	....	....
	Omaha Knights	CHL	58	21	31	52	....	....	....	29	....	....	....	....	....	....	....	....	....	....	6	9	2	11	2	....	....	....
1975-76	Providence Reds	AHL	74	27	34	61	....	....	....	28	....	....	....	....	....	....	....	....	....	....	3	0	2	2	2	....	....	....
1976-77	New Haven Nighthawks	AHL	77	31	34	65	....	....	....	18	....	....	....	....	....	....	....	....	....	....	6	1	3	4	0	....	....	....
1977-78	**New York Rangers**	**NHL**	**7**	**2**	**1**	**3**	**2**	**1**	**3**	**0**	**0**	**0**	**1**	**7**	**28.6**	**5**	**0**	**6**	**0**	**–1**	....	....	....	....	....	....	....	....
	New Haven Nighthawks	AHL	74	32	31	63	....	....	....	13	....	....	....	....	....	....	....	....	....	....	15	7	3	10	4	....	....	....
1978-79	Nova Scotia Voyageurs	AHL	78	33	42	75	....	....	....	28	....	....	....	....	....	....	....	....	....	....	10	0	5	5	4	....	....	....
1979-80	Nova Scotia Voyageurs	AHL	74	23	36	59	....	....	....	16	....	....	....	....	....	....	....	....	....	....	6	1	2	3	2	....	....	....
1980-81	Salzburg	Austria	23	20	15	35	....	....	....	27	....	....	....	....	....	....	....	....	....	....	....	....	....	....	....	....	....	....
	NHL Totals		**43**	**3**	**4**	**7**	**3**	**4**	**7**	**15**	**0**	**0**	**1**	**45**	**6.7**	**11**	**2**	**21**	**0**		....	....	....	....	....	....	....	....

AHL Second All-Star Team (1974, 1979)

Traded to **Atlanta** by **Minnesota** with Buster Harvey for John Flesch and Don Martineau, May 27, 1974. Traded to **NY Rangers** by **Atlanta** for Curt Ridley, September 9, 1975.

● BYERS, LYNDON Lyndon Byers RW – R. 6'1", 200 lbs. b: Nipawin, Sask., 2/29/1964. Boston's 3rd choice, 39th overall, in 1982 Entry Draft.

Season	Club	League	GP	G	A	Pts	AG	AA	APts	PIM	PP	SH	GW	S	%	TGF	PGF	TGA	PGA	+/–	GP	G	A	Pts	PIM	PP	SH	GW
1980-81	Notre Dame Hounds	SJHL	37	35	42	77	....	....	....	106	....	....	....	....	....	....	....	....	....	....	....	....	....	....	....	....	....	....
1981-82	Regina Pats	WHL	57	18	25	43	....	....	....	169	....	....	....	....	....	....	....	....	....	....	20	5	6	11	48	....	....	....
1982-83	Regina Pats	WHL	70	32	38	70	....	....	....	153	....	....	....	....	....	....	....	....	....	....	5	1	1	2	16	....	....	....
1983-84	Regina Pats	WHL	58	32	57	89	....	....	....	154	....	....	....	....	....	....	....	....	....	....	23	17	18	35	78	....	....	....
	Canada	WJC-A	6	1	1	2	....	....	....	4	....	....	....	....	....	....	....	....	....	....	....	....	....	....	....	....	....	....
	Boston Bruins	**NHL**	**10**	**2**	**4**	**6**	**2**	**3**	**5**	**32**	**0**	**0**	**0**	**11**	**18.2**	**8**	**0**	**5**	**0**	**+3**	....	....	....	....	....	....	....	....
1984-85	**Boston Bruins**	**NHL**	**33**	**3**	**8**	**11**	**2**	**5**	**7**	**41**	**0**	**0**	**0**	**25**	**12.0**	**18**	**1**	**17**	**0**	**0**	....	....	....	....	....	....	....	....
	Hershey Bears	AHL	27	4	6	10	....	....	....	55	....	....	....	....	....	....	....	....	....	....	....	....	....	....	....	....	....	....

			REGULAR SEASON																		PLAYOFFS							
Season	Club	League	GP	G	A	Pts	AG	AA	APts	PIM	PP	SH	GW	S	%	TGF	PGF	TGA	PGA	+/–	GP	G	A	Pts	PIM	PP	SH	GW
1985-86	**Boston Bruins**	**NHL**	**5**	**0**	**2**	**2**	**0**	**1**	**1**	**9**	**0**	**0**	**0**	**1**	**0.0**	**3**	**0**	**2**	**0**	**+1**	....	....	....	....	....	....	....	....
	Moncton Golden Flames	AHL	14	2	4	6	....	....	....	26	....	....	....	....	....	....	....	....	....	....	....	....	....	....	....	....	....	....
	Milwaukee Admirals	IHL	8	0	2	2	....	....	....	22	....	....	....	....	....	....	....	....	....	....	....	....	....	....	....	....	....	....
1986-87	**Boston Bruins**	**NHL**	**18**	**2**	**3**	**5**	**2**	**2**	**4**	**53**	**0**	**0**	**0**	**14**	**14.3**	**5**	**0**	**6**	**0**	**–1**	**1**	**0**	**0**	**0**	**0**	**0**	**0**	**0**
	Moncton Golden Flames	AHL	27	5	5	10	....	....	....	63	....	....	....	....	....	....	....	....	....	....	....	....	....	....	....	....	....	....
1987-88	**Boston Bruins**	**NHL**	**53**	**10**	**14**	**24**	**9**	**10**	**19**	**236**	**0**	**0**	**2**	**69**	**14.5**	**39**	**2**	**27**	**0**	**+10**	**11**	**1**	**2**	**3**	**62**	**0**	**0**	**0**
	Maine Mariners	AHL	2	0	1	1	....	....	....	18	....	....	....	....	....	....	....	....	....	....	....	....	....	....	....	....	....	....
1988-89	**Boston Bruins**	**NHL**	**49**	**0**	**4**	**4**	**0**	**3**	**3**	**218**	**0**	**0**	**0**	**25**	**0.0**	**9**	**0**	**18**	**1**	**–8**	**2**	**0**	**0**	**0**	**0**	**0**	**0**	**0**
	Maine Mariners	AHL	4	1	3	4	....	....	....	2	....	....	....	....	....	....	....	....	....	....	....	....	....	....	....	....	....	....
1989-90	**Boston Bruins**	**NHL**	**43**	**4**	**4**	**8**	**3**	**3**	**6**	**159**	**0**	**0**	**0**	**43**	**9.3**	**10**	**0**	**10**	**0**	**0**	**17**	**1**	**0**	**1**	**12**	**0**	**0**	**0**
1990-91	**Boston Bruins**	**NHL**	**19**	**2**	**2**	**4**	**2**	**2**	**4**	**82**	**0**	**0**	**0**	**20**	**10.0**	**6**	**0**	**8**	**0**	**–2**	**1**	**0**	**0**	**0**	**10**	**0**	**0**	**0**
1991-92	**Boston Bruins**	**NHL**	**31**	**1**	**1**	**2**	**1**	**1**	**2**	**129**	**0**	**0**	**0**	**12**	**8.3**	**4**	**0**	**9**	**0**	**–5**	**5**	**0**	**0**	**0**	**12**	**0**	**0**	**0**
	Maine Mariners	AHL	11	5	4	9	....	....	....	47	....	....	....	....	....	....	....	....	....	....	....	....	....	....	....	....	....	....
1992-93	**San Jose Sharks**	**NHL**	**18**	**4**	**1**	**5**	**3**	**1**	**4**	**122**	**0**	**0**	**0**	**18**	**22.2**	**6**	**0**	**8**	**0**	**–2**	....	....	....	....	....	....	....	....
	Kansas City Blades	IHL	4	1	1	2	....	....	....	22	....	....	....	....	....	....	....	....	....	....	....	....	....	....	....	....	....	....
	San Diego Gulls	IHL	9	0	3	3	....	....	....	35	....	....	....	....	....	....	....	....	....	....	....	....	....	....	....	....	....	....
1993-94	Las Vegas Thunder	IHL	31	3	5	8	....	....	....	176	....	....	....	....	....	....	....	....	....	....	1	0	0	0	4	....	....	....
1994-95	Minnesota Moose	IHL	7	1	0	1	....	....	....	16	....	....	....	....	....	....	....	....	....	....	....	....	....	....	....	....	....	....
	NHL Totals		**279**	**28**	**43**	**71**	**24**	**31**	**55**	**1081**	**0**	**0**	**2**	**238**	**11.8**	**108**	**3**	**110**	**1**		**37**	**2**	**2**	**4**	**96**	**0**	**0**	**0**

Signed as a free agent by **San Jose**, November 7, 1992.

• BYERS, MIKE

Mike Byers RW – R. 5'10", 185 lbs. b: Toronto, Ont., 9/11/1946.

Season	Club	League	GP	G	A	Pts	AG	AA	APts	PIM	PP	SH	GW	S	%	TGF	PGF	TGA	PGA	+/–	GP	G	A	Pts	PIM	PP	SH	GW
1962-63	Toronto Marlboros	OHA	2	4	1	5	....	....	....	0	....	....	....	....	....	....	....	....	....	....	9	3	5	8	6	....	....	....
1963-64	Toronto Marlboros	OHA	2	0	0	0	....	....	....	0	....	....	....	....	....	....	....	....	....	....	....	....	....	....	....	....	....	....
1964-65	Toronto Marlboros	OHA	56	22	18	40	....	....	....	37	....	....	....	....	....	....	....	....	....	....	19	1	4	5	8	....	....	....
1965-66	Toronto Marlboros	OHA	47	21	21	42	....	....	....	45	....	....	....	....	....	....	....	....	....	....	14	4	2	6	4	....	....	....
1966-67	Toronto Marlboros	OHA	41	25	19	44	....	....	....	20	....	....	....	....	....	....	....	....	....	....	17	3	3	6	15	....	....	....
1967-68	**Toronto Maple Leafs**	**NHL**	**10**	**2**	**2**	**4**	**2**	**2**	**4**	**0**	**1**	**0**	**0**	**16**	**12.5**	**5**	**1**	**2**	**0**	**+2**	....	....	....	....	....	....	....	....
	Tulsa Oilers	CHL	27	14	5	19	....	....	....	32	....	....	....	....	....	....	....	....	....	....	11	1	3	4	2	....	....	....
	Rochester Americans	AHL	31	7	8	15	....	....	....	0	....	....	....	....	....	....	....	....	....	....	....	....	....	....	....	....	....	....
1968-69	**Toronto Maple Leafs**	**NHL**	**5**	**0**	**0**	**0**	**0**	**0**	**0**	**2**	**0**	**0**	**0**	**8**	**0.0**	**1**	**0**	**1**	**0**	**0**	....	....	....	....	....	....	....	....
	Tulsa Oilers	CHL	51	17	17	34	....	....	....	6	....	....	....	....	....	....	....	....	....	....	....	....	....	....	....	....	....	....
	Philadelphia Flyers	**NHL**	**5**	**0**	**2**	**2**	**0**	**2**	**2**	**0**	**0**	**0**	**0**	**8**	**0.0**	**2**	**2**	**1**	**0**	**–1**	**4**	**0**	**1**	**1**	**0**	**0**	**0**	**0**
1969-70	Quebec Aces	AHL	62	15	23	38	....	....	....	11	....	....	....	....	....	....	....	....	....	....	6	1	0	1	0	....	....	....
1970-71	**Los Angeles Kings**	**NHL**	**72**	**27**	**18**	**45**	**28**	**16**	**44**	**14**	**4**	**0**	**5**	**179**	**15.1**	**73**	**12**	**68**	**2**	**–5**	....	....	....	....	....	....	....	....
1971-72	**Los Angeles Kings**	**NHL**	**28**	**4**	**5**	**9**	**4**	**5**	**9**	**11**	**0**	**0**	**1**	**48**	**8.3**	**20**	**4**	**30**	**1**	**–13**	....	....	....	....	....	....	....	....
	Buffalo Sabres	**NHL**	**46**	**9**	**7**	**16**	**10**	**6**	**16**	**12**	**3**	**0**	**1**	**69**	**13.0**	**43**	**13**	**51**	**1**	**–20**	....	....	....	....	....	....	....	....
1972-73	Los Angeles Sharks	WHA	56	19	17	36	....	....	....	20	....	....	....	....	....	....	....	....	....	....	....	....	....	....	....	....	....	....
	New England Whalers	WHA	19	6	4	10	....	....	....	4	....	....	....	....	....	....	....	....	....	....	12	6	5	11	6	....	....	....
1973-74	New England Whalers	WHA	78	29	21	50	....	....	....	6	....	....	....	....	....	....	....	....	....	....	7	2	4	6	12	....	....	....
1974-75	New England Whalers	WHA	72	22	26	48	....	....	....	10	....	....	....	....	....	....	....	....	....	....	6	2	2	4	2	....	....	....
1975-76	New England Whalers	WHA	21	4	3	7	....	....	....	0	....	....	....	....	....	....	....	....	....	....	....	....	....	....	....	....	....	....
	Cincinnati Stingers	WHA	20	3	3	6	....	....	....	0	....	....	....	....	....	....	....	....	....	....	....	....	....	....	....	....	....	....
1976-77	Rochester Americans	AHL	66	25	29	54	....	....	....	10	....	....	....	....	....	....	....	....	....	....	8	2	4	6	0	....	....	....
	NHL Totals		**166**	**42**	**34**	**76**	**44**	**31**	**75**	**39**	**8**	**0**	**7**	**328**	**12.8**	**144**	**32**	**153**	**4**		**4**	**0**	**1**	**1**	**0**	**0**	**0**	**0**
	Other Major League Totals		266	83	74	157	....	....	....	40	....	....	....	....	....	....	....	....	....	....	25	10	11	21	20	....	....	....

Traded to **Philadelphia** by **Toronto** with Bill Sutherland and Gerry Meehan for Brit Selby and Forbes Kennedy, March 2, 1969. Traded to **LA Kings** by **Philadelphia** for Brent Hughes, May 21, 1970. Traded to **Buffalo** by **LA Kings** with Larry Hillman for Doug Barrie and Mike Keeler, December16, 1971. Selected by **LA Sharks** (WHA) in 1972 WHA General Player Draft, February 12, 1972. Traded to **New England** (WHA) by **LA Sharks** (WHA) for Mike Hyndman, February, 1973. Signed as a free agent by **Cincinnati** (WHA) following release by **New England** (WHA), February, 1976.

• BYLSMA, DAN

Dan "Disco" Bylsma LW – L. 6'2", 215 lbs. b: Grand Haven, MI, 9/19/1970. Winnipeg's 7th choice, 109th overall, in 1989 Entry Draft.

Season	Club	League	GP	G	A	Pts	AG	AA	APts	PIM	PP	SH	GW	S	%	TGF	PGF	TGA	PGA	+/–	GP	G	A	Pts	PIM	PP	SH	GW
1988-89	Bowling Green University	CCHA	32	3	7	10	....	....	....	10	....	....	....	....	....	....	....	....	....	....	....	....	....	....	....	....	....	....
1989-90	Bowling Green University	CCHA	44	13	17	30	....	....	....	30	....	....	....	....	....	....	....	....	....	....	....	....	....	....	....	....	....	....
1990-91	Bowling Green University	CCHA	40	9	12	21	....	....	....	48	....	....	....	....	....	....	....	....	....	....	....	....	....	....	....	....	....	....
1991-92	Bowling Green University	CCHA	34	11	14	25	....	....	....	24	....	....	....	....	....	....	....	....	....	....	....	....	....	....	....	....	....	....
1992-93	Greensboro Monarchs	ECHL	60	25	35	60	....	....	....	66	....	....	....	....	....	....	....	....	....	....	1	0	1	1	10	....	....	....
	Rochester Americans	AHL	2	0	1	1	....	....	....	0	....	....	....	....	....	....	....	....	....	....	....	....	....	....	....	....	....	....
1993-94	Greensboro Monarchs	ECHL	25	14	16	30	....	....	....	52	....	....	....	....	....	....	....	....	....	....	....	....	....	....	....	....	....	....
	Albany River Rats	AHL	3	0	1	1	....	....	....	2	....	....	....	....	....	....	....	....	....	....	....	....	....	....	....	....	....	....
	Moncton Hawks	AHL	50	12	16	28	....	....	....	25	....	....	....	....	....	....	....	....	....	....	21	3	4	7	31	....	....	....
1994-95	Phoenix Roadrunners	IHL	81	19	23	42	....	....	....	41	....	....	....	....	....	....	....	....	....	....	9	4	4	8	4	....	....	....
1995-96	**Los Angeles Kings**	**NHL**	**4**	**0**	**0**	**0**	**0**	**0**	**0**	**0**	**0**	**0**	**0**	**6**	**0.0**	**2**	**0**	**4**	**2**	**0**	....	....	....	....	....	....	....	....
	Phoenix Roadrunners	IHL	78	22	20	42	....	....	....	48	....	....	....	....	....	....	....	....	....	....	4	1	0	1	2	....	....	....
1996-97	**Los Angeles Kings**	**NHL**	**79**	**3**	**6**	**9**	**3**	**5**	**8**	**32**	**0**	**0**	**0**	**86**	**3.5**	**16**	**1**	**55**	**25**	**–15**	....	....	....	....	....	....	....	....
1997-98	**Los Angeles Kings**	**NHL**	**65**	**3**	**9**	**12**	**4**	**9**	**13**	**33**	**0**	**0**	**0**	**57**	**5.3**	**23**	**0**	**28**	**14**	**+9**	**2**	**0**	**0**	**0**	**0**	**0**	**0**	**0**
	Long Beach Ice Dogs	IHL	8	2	3	5	....	....	....	0	....	....	....	....	....	....	....	....	....	....	....	....	....	....	....	....	....	....
	NHL Totals		**148**	**6**	**15**	**21**	**7**	**14**	**21**	**65**	**0**	**0**	**0**	**149**	**4.0**	**41**	**1**	**87**	**41**		**2**	**0**	**0**	**0**	**0**	**0**	**0**	**0**

Signed as a free agent by **LA Kings**, July 7, 1994.

• BYRAM, SHAWN

Shawn Byram LW – L. 6'2", 204 lbs. b: Neepawa, Man., 9/12/1968. NY Islanders' 4th choice, 80th overall, in 1986 Entry Draft.

Season	Club	League	GP	G	A	Pts	AG	AA	APts	PIM	PP	SH	GW	S	%	TGF	PGF	TGA	PGA	+/–	GP	G	A	Pts	PIM	PP	SH	GW
1984-85	Regina Pats	WHL	4	0	1	1	....	....	....	0	....	....	....	....	....	....	....	....	....	....	1	0	0	0	0	....	....	....
1985-86	Regina Pats	WHL	46	7	6	13	....	....	....	45	....	....	....	....	....	....	....	....	....	....	9	0	1	1	11	....	....	....
1986-87	Regina Pats	WHL	12	3	3	6	....	....	....	25	....	....	....	....	....	....	....	....	....	....	....	....	....	....	....	....	....	....
	Prince Albert Raiders	WHL	55	16	18	34	....	....	....	122	....	....	....	....	....	....	....	....	....	....	7	1	1	2	10	....	....	....
1987-88	Prince Albert Raiders	WHL	61	23	28	51	....	....	....	178	....	....	....	....	....	....	....	....	....	....	10	5	2	7	27	....	....	....
1988-89	Springfield Indians	AHL	45	5	11	16	....	....	....	195	....	....	....	....	....	....	....	....	....	....	....	....	....	....	....	....	....	....
	Indianapolis Ice	IHL	1	0	0	0	....	....	....	2	....	....	....	....	....	....	....	....	....	....	....	....	....	....	....	....	....	....
1989-90	Springfield Indians	AHL	31	4	4	8	....	....	....	30	....	....	....	....	....	....	....	....	....	....	....	....	....	....	....	....	....	....
	Johnstown Chiefs	ECHL	8	5	5	10	....	....	....	35	....	....	....	....	....	....	....	....	....	....	....	....	....	....	....	....	....	....
1990-91	**New York Islanders**	**NHL**	**4**	**0**	**0**	**0**	**0**	**0**	**0**	**14**	**0**	**0**	**0**	**2**	**0.0**	**2**	**1**	**3**	**0**	**–2**	....	....	....	....	....	....	....	....
	Capital District Islanders	AHL	62	28	35	63	....	....	....	162	....	....	....	....	....	....	....	....	....	....	....	....	....	....	....	....	....	....
1991-92	**Chicago Blackhawks**	**NHL**	**1**	**0**	**0**	**0**	**0**	**0**	**0**	**0**	**0**	**0**	**0**	**1**	**0.0**	**1**	**0**	**1**	**0**	**0**	....	....	....	....	....	....	....	....
	Indianapolis Ice	IHL	69	18	21	39	....	....	....	154	....	....	....	....	....	....	....	....	....	....	....	....	....	....	....	....	....	....
1992-93	Indianapolis Ice	IHL	41	2	13	15	....	....	....	123	....	....	....	....	....	....	....	....	....	....	5	1	2	3	8	....	....	....
1993-94	Indianapolis Ice	IHL	77	23	24	47	....	....	....	170	....	....	....	....	....	....	....	....	....	....	....	....	....	....	....	....	....	....
1994-95	Fassa	Italy	15	15	16	31	....	....	....	43	....	....	....	....	....	....	....	....	....	....	....	....	....	....	....	....	....	....
	Bracknell Bees	Britain	24	24	24	48	....	....	....	97	....	....	....	....	....	....	....	....	....	....	....	....	....	....	....	....	....	....
1995-96	Manchester Storm	Britain	42	70	120	190	....	....	....	135	....	....	....	....	....	....	....	....	....	....	....	....	....	....	....	....	....	....
1996-97	Manchester Storm	Britain	23	8	12	20	....	....	....	38	....	....	....	....	....	....	....	....	....	....	....	....	....	....	....	....	....	....
	WEV Wien	Austria	6	1	13	14	....	....	....	2	....	....	....	....	....	....	....	....	....	....	....	....	....	....	....	....	....	....
	Fresno Fighting Falcons	WCHL	6	3	5	8	....	....	....	13	....	....	....	....	....	....	....	....	....	....	5	2	5	7	67	....	....	....
1997-98	Ayr Scottish Eagles	Britain	45	18	31	49	....	....	....	101	....	....	....	....	....	....	....	....	....	....	9	5	3	8	4	....	....	....
	NHL Totals		**5**	**0**	**0**	**0**	**0**	**0**	**0**	**14**	**0**	**0**	**0**	**3**	**0.0**	**3**	**1**	**4**	**0**		....	....	....	....	....	....	....	....

Signed as a free agent by **Chicago**, August 15, 1991.

• CAFFERY, TERRY

Terry Caffery C – R. 5'9", 165 lbs. b: Toronto, Ont., 4/1/1949. Chicago's 1st choice, 3rd overall, in 1966 Amateur Draft.

Season	Club	League	GP	G	A	Pts	AG	AA	APts	PIM	PP	SH	GW	S	%	TGF	PGF	TGA	PGA	+/–	GP	G	A	Pts	PIM	PP	SH	GW
1965-66	Toronto Marlboros	OHA	43	14	25	39	....	....	....	36	....	....	....	....	....	....	....	....	....	....	13	3	6	9	18	....	....	....
1966-67	Toronto Marlboros	OHA	39	16	29	45	....	....	....	29	....	....	....	....	....	....	....	....	....	....	17	10	15	25	10	....	....	....
1967-68	Toronto Marlboros	OHA	48	36	47	83	....	....	....	64	....	....	....	....	....	....	....	....	....	....	2	0	0	0	0	....	....	....

Season	Club	League	REGULAR SEASON																		PLAYOFFS							
			GP	G	A	Pts	AG	AA	APts	PIM	PP	SH	GW	S	%	TGF	PGF	TGA	PGA	+/–	GP	G	A	Pts	PIM	PP	SH	GW
1968-69	Ottawa Nationals	OHA Sr.	5	4	8	12	....	....	....	0	....	....	....	....	....	....	....	....	....	....	....	....	....	....	....	....	....	....
	Canada	WEC-A	10	4	4	8	....	....	....	8	....	....	....	....	....	....	....	....	....	....	....	....	....	....	....	....	....	....
1969-70	**Chicago Black Hawks**	**NHL**	**6**	**0**	**0**	**0**	**0**	**0**	**0**	**0**	**0**	**0**	**0**	**2**	**0.0**	**1**	**1**	**0**	**0**	**0**	....	....	....	....	....	....	....	....
	Dallas Black Hawks	CHL	42	12	28	48	....	....	....	4	....	....	....	....	....	....	....	....	....	....	....	....	....	....	....	....	....	....
1970-71	**Minnesota North Stars**	**NHL**	**8**	**0**	**0**	**0**	**0**	**0**	**0**	**0**	**0**	**0**	**0**	**1**	**0.0**	**0**	**0**	**2**	**0**	**–2**	**1**	**0**	**0**	**0**	**0**	**0**	**0**	**0**
	Dallas Black Hawks	CHL	40	13	34	47	....	....	....	22	....	....	....	....	....	....	....	....	....	....	....	....	....	....	....	....	....	....
1971-72	Cleveland Barons	AHL	65	29	59	88	....	....	....	18	....	....	....	....	....	....	....	....	....	....	6	1	3	4	0	....	....	....
1972-73	New England Whalers	WHA	74	39	61	100	....	....	....	14	....	....	....	....	....	....	....	....	....	....	8	3	7	10	0	....	....	....
1973-74			DID NOT PLAY – INJURED																									
1974-75	New England Whalers	WHA	67	15	37	52	....	....	....	12	....	....	....	....	....	....	....	....	....	....	....	....	....	....	....	....	....	....
1975-76	New England Whalers	WHA	4	0	0	0	....	....	....	0	....	....	....	....	....	....	....	....	....	....	....	....	....	....	....	....	....	....
	Calgary Cowboys	WHA	21	5	13	18	....	....	....	4	....	....	....	....	....	....	....	....	....	....	....	....	....	....	....	....	....	....
	NHL Totals		**14**	**0**	**0**	**0**	**0**	**0**	**0**	**0**	**0**	**0**	**0**	**3**	**0.0**	**1**	**1**	**2**	**0**		**1**	**0**	**0**	**0**	**0**	**0**	**0**	**0**
	Other Major League Totals		166	59	111	170	....	....	....	30	....	....	....	....	....	....	....	....	....		8	3	7	10	0	....	....	....

OHA Second All-Star Team (1968) • Won Dudley "Red" Garrett Memorial Award (Top Rookie - AHL) (1972) • Won Lou Kaplan Trophy (WHA Rookie of the Year) (1973)

Traded to **Minnesota** by **Chicago** with Doug Mohns for Danny O'Shea, February 23, 1971. Selected by **Miami-Philadelphia** (WHA) in 1972 WHA General Player Draft, February 12, 1972. WHA rights traded to **New England** (WHA) by **Philadelphia** (WHA) for future considerations, June, 1972. • Missed entire 1973-74 season after undergoing off-season knee surgery. Traded to **Calgary** (WHA) by **New England** (WHA) for future considerations, October 25, 1975.

• CAHAN, LARRY

Larry "Hank" Cahan D – R. 6'2", 222 lbs. b: Fort William, Ont., 12/25/1933. d: 6/25/1992.

Season	Club	League	GP	G	A	Pts	AG	AA	APts	PIM	PP	SH	GW	S	%	TGF	PGF	TGA	PGA	+/–	GP	G	A	Pts	PIM	PP	SH	GW
1951-52	Fort William Hurricanes	TBJHL	29	6	17	23	....	....	....	82	....	....	....	....	....	....	....	....	....	....	21	3	7	10	57	....	....	....
1952-53	Fort William Hurricanes	TBJHL	30	12	17	29	....	....	....	98	....	....	....	....	....	....	....	....	....	....	4	1	2	3	10	....	....	....
1953-54	Pittsburgh Hornets	AHL	70	1	25	26	....	....	....	*179	....	....	....	....	....	....	....	....	....	....	5	1	0	1	2	....	....	....
1954-55	**Toronto Maple Leafs**	**NHL**	**59**	**0**	**6**	**6**	**0**	**8**	**8**	**64**	....	....	....	....	....	....	....	....	....	....	**4**	**0**	**0**	**0**	**0**	....	....	....
1955-56	**Toronto Maple Leafs**	**NHL**	**21**	**0**	**2**	**2**	**0**	**2**	**2**	**46**	....	....	....	....	....	....	....	....	....	....	....	....	....	....	....	....	....	....
	Pittsburgh Hornets	AHL	39	6	9	15	....	....	....	160	....	....	....	....	....	....	....	....	....	....	4	0	1	1	12	....	....	....
1956-57	**New York Rangers**	**NHL**	**61**	**5**	**4**	**9**	**7**	**5**	**12**	**65**	....	....	....	....	....	....	....	....	....	....	**3**	**0**	**0**	**0**	**2**	....	....	....
1957-58	**New York Rangers**	**NHL**	**34**	**1**	**1**	**2**	**1**	**1**	**2**	**20**	....	....	....	....	....	....	....	....	....	....	**5**	**0**	**0**	**0**	**4**	....	....	....
1958-59	**New York Rangers**	**NHL**	**16**	**1**	**0**	**1**	**1**	**0**	**1**	**8**	....	....	....	....	....	....	....	....	....	....	....	....	....	....	....	....	....	....
	Vancouver Canucks	WHL	9	2	6	8	....	....	....	22	....	....	....	....	....	....	....	....	....	....	9	1	2	3	18	....	....	....
	Springfield Indians	AHL	33	3	11	14	....	....	....	75	....	....	....	....	....	....	....	....	....	....	....	....	....	....	....	....	....	....
	Buffalo Bisons	AHL	....	....	....	....	....	....	....	....	....	....	....	....	....	....	....	....	....	....	3	0	0	0	0	....	....	....
1959-60	Vancouver Canucks	WHL	70	11	22	33	....	....	....	116	....	....	....	....	....	....	....	....	....	....	11	0	4	4	*19	....	....	....
1960-61	Vancouver Canucks	WHL	70	13	15	28	....	....	....	81	....	....	....	....	....	....	....	....	....	....	9	2	2	4	12	....	....	....
1961-62	**New York Rangers**	**NHL**	**57**	**2**	**7**	**9**	**2**	**7**	**9**	**85**	....	....	....	....	....	....	....	....	....	....	**6**	**0**	**0**	**0**	**10**	....	....	....
1962-63	**New York Rangers**	**NHL**	**56**	**6**	**14**	**20**	**7**	**15**	**22**	**47**	....	....	....	....	....	....	....	....	....	....	....	....	....	....	....	....	....	....
1963-64	**New York Rangers**	**NHL**	**53**	**4**	**8**	**12**	**5**	**9**	**14**	**80**	....	....	....	....	....	....	....	....	....	....	....	....	....	....	....	....	....	....
	Baltimore Clippers	AHL	12	2	8	10	....	....	....	16	....	....	....	....	....	....	....	....	....	....	....	....	....	....	....	....	....	....
1964-65	**New York Rangers**	**NHL**	**26**	**0**	**5**	**5**	**0**	**5**	**5**	**32**	....	....	....	....	....	....	....	....	....	....	....	....	....	....	....	....	....	....
	Baltimore Clippers	AHL	16	1	6	7	....	....	....	34	....	....	....	....	....	....	....	....	....	....	....	....	....	....	....	....	....	....
	Vancouver Canucks	WHL	26	2	15	17	....	....	....	67	....	....	....	....	....	....	....	....	....	....	5	0	3	3	28	....	....	....
1965-66	Vancouver Canucks	WHL	72	14	34	48	....	....	....	156	....	....	....	....	....	....	....	....	....	....	7	4	12	16	4	....	....	....
1966-67	Vancouver Canucks	WHL	72	18	36	54	....	....	....	88	....	....	....	....	....	....	....	....	....	....	8	1	4	5	6	....	....	....
1967-68	**Oakland Seals**	**NHL**	**74**	**9**	**15**	**24**	**11**	**16**	**27**	**80**	**5**	**0**	**1**	**161**	**5.6**	**80**	**21**	**112**	**24**	**–29**	....	....	....	....	....	....	....	....
1968-69	**Los Angeles Kings**	**NHL**	**72**	**3**	**11**	**14**	**3**	**10**	**13**	**76**	**0**	**0**	**1**	**129**	**2.3**	**59**	**5**	**94**	**20**	**–20**	**11**	**1**	**1**	**2**	**22**	**0**	**1**	**0**
1969-70	**Los Angeles Kings**	**NHL**	**70**	**4**	**8**	**12**	**5**	**8**	**13**	**52**	**2**	**0**	**0**	**95**	**4.2**	**56**	**3**	**123**	**45**	**–25**	....	....	....	....	....	....	....	....
1970-71	**Los Angeles Kings**	**NHL**	**67**	**3**	**11**	**14**	**3**	**10**	**13**	**45**	**1**	**0**	**0**	**113**	**2.7**	**60**	**4**	**103**	**18**	**–29**	....	....	....	....	....	....	....	....
1971-72	Seattle Totems	WHL	50	4	12	16	....	....	....	44	....	....	....	....	....	....	....	....	....	....	....	....	....	....	....	....	....	....
1972-73	Chicago Cougars	WHA	75	1	10	11	....	....	....	44	....	....	....	....	....	....	....	....	....	....	....	....	....	....	....	....	....	....
1973-74	Chicago Cougars	WHA	3	0	0	0	....	....	....	2	....	....	....	....	....	....	....	....	....	....	....	....	....	....	....	....	....	....
	NHL Totals		**666**	**38**	**92**	**130**	**45**	**96**	**141**	**700**	**8**	**0**	**2**	**498**	**7.6**	**255**	**33**	**432**	**107**		**29**	**1**	**1**	**2**	**38**	**0**	**1**	**0**
	Other Major League Totals		78	1	10	11	....	....	....	46	....	....	....	....	....	....	....	....	....		....	....	....	....	....	....	....	....

WHL Second All-Star Team (1960, 1966) • WHL First All-Star Team (1961, 1967) • Won Hal Laycoe Cup (WHL Top Defenseman) (1967)

Claimed by **NY Rangers** from **Toronto** in Intra-League Draft, June 6, 1956. Claimed by **Oakland** from **NY Rangers** in Expansion Draft, June 6, 1967. Claimed by **Montreal** from **Oakland** in Intra-League Draft, June 12, 1968. Traded to **LA Kings** by **Montreal** for Brian D. Smith and Yves Locas, July 1, 1968. Selected by **LA Sharks** (WHA) in 1972 WHA General Player Draft, February 12, 1972. WHA rights traded to **Chicago** (WHA) by **LA Sharks** (WHA) with Bob Liddongton and Bobby Whitlock for Bill Young and future considerations, June, 1972.

• CAIRNS, DON

Don Cairns LW – L. 6'1", 195 lbs. b: Calgary, Alta., 10/8/1955. Kansas City's 2nd choice, 20th overall, in 1975 Amateur Draft.

Season	Club	League	GP	G	A	Pts	AG	AA	APts	PIM	PP	SH	GW	S	%	TGF	PGF	TGA	PGA	+/–	GP	G	A	Pts	PIM	PP	SH	GW
1973-74	Calgary Wranglers	AJHL	54	30	31	61	....	....	....	180	....	....	....	....	....	....	....	....	....	....	....	....	....	....	....	....	....	....
1974-75	Victoria Cougars	WCJHL	68	32	37	69	....	....	....	214	....	....	....	....	....	....	....	....	....	....	....	....	....	....	....	....	....	....
1975-76	**Kansas City Scouts**	**NHL**	**7**	**0**	**0**	**0**	**0**	**0**	**0**	**0**	**0**	**0**	**0**	**2**	**0.0**	**0**	**0**	**1**	**0**	**–1**	....	....	....	....	....	....	....	....
	Springfield Indians	AHL	15	4	2	6	....	....	....	13	....	....	....	....	....	....	....	....	....	....	....	....	....	....	....	....	....	....
	Port Huron Flags	IHL	18	6	8	14	....	....	....	13	....	....	....	....	....	....	....	....	....	....	15	3	8	11	19	....	....	....
1976-77	**Colorado Rockies**	**NHL**	**2**	**0**	**1**	**1**	**0**	**1**	**1**	**2**	**0**	**0**	**0**	**3**	**0.0**	**1**	**0**	**0**	**0**	**+1**	....	....	....	....	....	....	....	....
	Flint Generals	IHL	10	3	5	8	....	....	....	13	....	....	....	....	....	....	....	....	....	....	....	....	....	....	....	....	....	....
	Oklahoma City Blazers	CHL	21	1	2	3	....	....	....	34	....	....	....	....	....	....	....	....	....	....	....	....	....	....	....	....	....	....
1977-78	Phoenix Roadrunners	CHL	9	1	3	4	....	....	....	2	....	....	....	....	....	....	....	....	....	....	....	....	....	....	....	....	....	....
	NHL Totals		**9**	**0**	**1**	**1**	**0**	**1**	**1**	**2**	**0**	**0**	**0**	**5**	**0.0**	**1**	**0**	**1**	**0**		....	....	....	....	....	....	....	....

Transferred to **Colorado** after **Kansas City** franchise relocated, July 15, 1976.

• CAIRNS, ERIC

Eric Cairns D – L. 6'5", 230 lbs. b: Oakville, Ont., 6/27/1974. NY Rangers' 3rd choice, 72nd overall, in 1992 Entry Draft.

Season	Club	League	GP	G	A	Pts	AG	AA	APts	PIM	PP	SH	GW	S	%	TGF	PGF	TGA	PGA	+/–	GP	G	A	Pts	PIM	PP	SH	GW
1990-91	Burlington Cougars	OJHL	37	5	16	21	....	....	....	120	....	....	....	....	....	....	....	....	....	....	....	....	....	....	....	....	....	....
1991-92	Detroit Ambassadors	OHL	64	1	11	12	....	....	....	232	....	....	....	....	....	....	....	....	....	....	7	0	0	0	31	....	....	....
1992-93	Detroit Jr. Red Wings	OHL	64	3	13	16	....	....	....	194	....	....	....	....	....	....	....	....	....	....	15	0	3	3	24	....	....	....
1993-94	Detroit Jr. Red Wings	OHL	59	7	35	42	....	....	....	204	....	....	....	....	....	....	....	....	....	....	17	0	4	4	46	....	....	....
1994-95	Birmingham Bulls	ECHL	11	1	3	4	....	....	....	49	....	....	....	....	....	....	....	....	....	....	....	....	....	....	....	....	....	....
	Binghamton Rangers	AHL	27	0	3	3	....	....	....	134	....	....	....	....	....	....	....	....	....	....	9	1	1	2	28	....	....	....
1995-96	Binghamton Rangers	AHL	46	1	13	14	....	....	....	192	....	....	....	....	....	....	....	....	....	....	4	0	0	0	37	....	....	....
	Charlotte Checkers	ECHL	6	0	1	1	....	....	....	34	....	....	....	....	....	....	....	....	....	....	....	....	....	....	....	....	....	....
1996-97	**New York Rangers**	**NHL**	**40**	**0**	**1**	**1**	**0**	**1**	**1**	**147**	**0**	**0**	**0**	**17**	**0.0**	**9**	**1**	**15**	**0**	**–7**	**3**	**0**	**0**	**0**	**0**	**0**	**0**	**0**
	Binghamton Rangers	AHL	10	1	1	2	....	....	....	96	....	....	....	....	....	....	....	....	....	....	....	....	....	....	....	....	....	....
1997-98	**New York Rangers**	**NHL**	**39**	**0**	**3**	**3**	**0**	**3**	**3**	**92**	**0**	**0**	**0**	**17**	**0.0**	**13**	**0**	**18**	**2**	**–3**	....	....	....	....	....	....	....	....
	Hartford Wolf Pack	AHL	7	1	2	3	....	....	....	43	....	....	....	....	....	....	....	....	....	....	....	....	....	....	....	....	....	....
	NHL Totals		**79**	**0**	**4**	**4**	**0**	**4**	**4**	**239**	**0**	**0**	**0**	**34**	**0.0**	**22**	**1**	**33**	**2**		**3**	**0**	**0**	**0**	**0**	**0**	**0**	**0**

• CALDER, ERIC

Eric Calder D – R. 6'1", 180 lbs. b: Kitchener, Ont., 7/26/1963. Washington's 2nd choice, 45th overall, in 1981 Entry Draft.

Season	Club	League	GP	G	A	Pts	AG	AA	APts	PIM	PP	SH	GW	S	%	TGF	PGF	TGA	PGA	+/–	GP	G	A	Pts	PIM	PP	SH	GW
1979-80	Waterloo Black Hawks	OJHL	42	13	36	49	....	....	....	33	....	....	....	....	....	....	....	....	....	....	....	....	....	....	....	....	....	....
1980-81	Cornwall Royals	QMJHL	66	9	34	43	....	....	....	39	....	....	....	....	....	....	....	....	....	....	14	0	6	6	25	....	....	....
	Canada	WJC-A	5	1	0	1	....	....	....	4	....	....	....	....	....	....	....	....	....	....	....	....	....	....	....	....	....	....
1981-82	Cornwall Royals	OHL	65	12	36	48	....	....	....	95	....	....	....	....	....	....	....	....	....	....	....	....	....	....	....	....	....	....
	Washington Capitals	**NHL**	**1**	**0**	**0**	**0**	**0**	**0**	**0**	**0**	**0**	**0**	**0**	**0**	**0.0**	**0**	**0**	**0**	**0**	**0**	....	....	....	....	....	....	....	....
1982-83	Cornwall Royals	OHL	66	5	30	35	....	....	....	72	....	....	....	....	....	....	....	....	....	....	8	0	5	5	6	....	....	....
	Washington Capitals	**NHL**	**1**	**0**	**0**	**0**	**0**	**0**	**0**	**0**	**0**	**0**	**0**	**0**	**0.0**	**0**	**0**	**0**	**0**	**0**	....	....	....	....	....	....	....	....
1983-84	Fort Wayne Komets	IHL	3	0	2	2	....	....	....	0	....	....	....	....	....	....	....	....	....	....	....	....	....	....	....	....	....	....
	Hershey Bears	AHL	68	2	6	8	....	....	....	50	....	....	....	....	....	....	....	....	....	....	....	....	....	....	....	....	....	....
	NHL Totals		**2**	**0**	**0**	**0**	**0**	**0**	**0**	**0**	**0**	**0**	**0**	**0**	**0.0**	**0**	**0**	**0**	**0**		....	....	....	....	....	....	....	....

• CALLANDER, DREW
Drew Callander C/RW – R. 6'2", 185 lbs. b: Regina, Sask., 8/17/1956. Philadelphia's 2nd choice, 35th overall, in 1976 Amateur Draft.

			REGULAR SEASON																		PLAYOFFS							
Season	Club	League	GP	G	A	Pts	AG	AA	APts	PIM	PP	SH	GW	S	%	TGF	PGF	TGA	PGA	+/–	GP	G	A	Pts	PIM	PP	SH	GW
1973-74	Regina Pats	WCJHL	68	9	7	16				7																		
1974-75	Regina Pats	WCJHL	51	17	15	32				36																		
1975-76	Regina Pats	WCJHL	72	49	56	105				64																		
1975-76	Regina Pats	WCJHL	72	49	56	105				64																		
1976-77	**Philadelphia Flyers**	**NHL**	**2**	**1**	**0**	**1**	**1**	**0**	**1**	**0**	**0**	**0**	**0**	**1**	**100.0**	**1**	**0**	**0**	**0**	**+1**								
	Springfield Indians	AHL	59	18	22	40				41																		
1977-78	**Philadelphia Flyers**	**NHL**	**1**	**0**	**0**	**0**	**0**	**0**	**0**	**0**	**0**	**0**	**0**	**0**	**0.0**	**0**	**0**	**0**	**0**	**0**								
	Maine Mariners	AHL	78	40	42	82				72											12	6	4	10	30			
1978-79	**Philadelphia Flyers**	**NHL**	**15**	**2**	**1**	**3**	**2**	**1**	**3**	**5**	**0**	**0**	**0**	**22**	**9.1**	**7**	**1**	**7**	**0**	**–1**								
	Maine Mariners	AHL	9	1	4	5				9																		
	Vancouver Canucks	**NHL**	**17**	**2**	**0**	**2**	**2**	**0**	**2**	**2**	**0**	**0**	**0**	**19**	**10.5**	**3**	**0**	**12**	**0**	**–9**								
	Dallas Black Hawks	CHL	26	12	10	22				23											9	4	6	10	12			
1979-80	**Vancouver Canucks**	**NHL**	**4**	**1**	**1**	**2**	**1**	**1**	**2**	**0**	**0**	**0**	**0**	**3**	**33.3**	**2**	**0**	**4**	**0**	**–2**								
	Dallas Black Hawks	CHL	33	15	10	25				20																		
1980-81	Dallas Black Hawks	CHL	77	43	29	72				51											6	0	2	2	2			
1981-82	Dallas Black Hawks	CHL	80	40	47	87				79											16	8	15	23	34			
1982-83	Duisburg	Germany	40	55	58	113																						
1983-84	Kolner Haie	Germany	42	19	7	26				44																		
1984-85	Kolner Haie	Germany	38	16	20	36				36											7	3	8	11	10			
1985-86	Bayreuth	Germany	36	12	17	29				22											17	15	13	28	31			
1986-87	Muskegon Lumberjacks	IHL	80	34	52	86				92											10	5	5	10	0			
	NHL Totals		**39**	**6**	**2**	**8**	**6**	**2**	**8**	**7**	**0**	**0**	**0**	**45**	**13.3**	**13**	**1**	**23**	**0**									

Traded to **Vancouver** by **Philadelphia** with Kevin McCarthy for Dennis Ververgaert, December 29, 1978.

• CALLANDER, JOHN
John "Jock" Callander RW – R. 6'1", 188 lbs. b: Regina, Sask., 4/23/1961.

Season	Club	League	GP	G	A	Pts	AG	AA	APts	PIM	PP	SH	GW	S	%	TGF	PGF	TGA	PGA	+/–	GP	G	A	Pts	PIM	PP	SH	GW
1978-79	Regina Blues	SJHL	42	44	42	86				24																		
	Regina Pats	WHL	19	3	2	5				0																		
1979-80	Regina Pats	WHL	39	9	11	20				25											18	8	5	13	0			
1980-81	Regina Pats	WHL	72	67	86	153				37											11	6	7	13	14			
1981-82	Regina Pats	WHL	71	79	111	*190				59											20	13	*26	39	37			
1982-83	Salt Lake Golden Eagles	CHL	68	20	27	47				26											6	0	1	1	9			
1983-84	Montana Magic	CHL	72	27	32	59				69																		
	Toledo Goaldiggers	IHL	2	0	0	0				0																		
1984-85	Muskegon Mohawks	IHL	82	39	68	107				86											17	8	*13	*21	33			
1985-86	Muskegon Lumberjacks	IHL	82	39	72	111				121											14	*12	11	*23	12			
1986-87	Muskegon Lumberjacks	IHL	82	54	82	*136				110											15	13	7	20	23			
1987-88	**Pittsburgh Penguins**	**NHL**	**41**	**11**	**16**	**27**	**9**	**11**	**20**	**45**	**4**	**0**	**1**	**59**	**18.6**	**57**	**29**	**42**	**1**	**–13**								
	Muskegon Lumberjacks	IHL	31	20	36	56				49											6	2	3	5	25			
1988-89	**Pittsburgh Penguins**	**NHL**	**30**	**6**	**5**	**11**	**5**	**4**	**9**	**20**	**2**	**0**	**0**	**35**	**17.1**	**24**	**8**	**19**	**0**	**–3**	**10**	**2**	**5**	**7**	**10**	**0**	**0**	**0**
	Muskegon Lumberjacks	IHL	48	25	39	64				40											7	5	5	10	30			
1989-90	**Pittsburgh Penguins**	**NHL**	**30**	**4**	**7**	**11**	**3**	**5**	**8**	**49**	**0**	**0**	**1**	**22**	**18.2**	**20**	**1**	**19**	**0**	**0**								
	Muskegon Lumberjacks	IHL	46	29	49	78				118											15	6	*14	20	54			
1990-91	Muskegon Lumberjacks	IHL	30	14	20	34				102																		
1991-92	Muskegon Lumberjacks	IHL	81	42	70	112				160											10	4	10	14	13			
	Pittsburgh Penguins	**NHL**																			**12**	**1**	**3**	**4**	**2**			
1992-93	**Tampa Bay Lightning**	**NHL**	**8**	**1**	**1**	**2**	**1**	**1**	**2**	**2**	**0**	**0**	**0**	**12**	**8.3**	**2**	**0**	**7**	**0**	**–5**								
	Atlanta Knights	IHL	69	34	50	84				172											9	*7	5	12	25			
1993-94	Cleveland Lumberjacks	IHL	81	31	70	101				126																		
1994-95	Cleveland Lumberjacks	IHL	61	24	36	60				90											4	2	2	4	6			
1995-96	Cleveland Lumberjacks	IHL	81	42	53	95				150											3	1	0	1	8			
1996-97	Cleveland Lumberjacks	IHL	61	20	34	54				56											14	7	6	13	10			
1997-98	Cleveland Lumberjacks	IHL	72	20	33	53				105											10	5	6	11	6			
	NHL Totals		**109**	**22**	**29**	**51**	**18**	**21**	**39**	**116**	**6**	**0**	**2**	**128**	**17.2**	**103**	**38**	**87**	**1**		**22**	**3**	**8**	**11**	**12**	**0**	**0**	**0**

IHL First All-Star Team (1987, 1992) • Won Leo P. Lamoureux Memorial Trophy (Top Scorer - IHL) (Tied with Jeff Pyle) (1987) • Won James Gatschene Memorial Trophy (MVP - IHL) (Tied with Jeff Pyle) (1987)

Signed as a free agent by **St. Louis**, September 28, 1981. Signed as a free agent by **Pittsburgh**, July 31, 1887. Signed as a free agent by **Tampa Bay**, July 29, 1992.

• CALLIGHEN, BRETT
Brett "Key" Callighen C – L. 5'11", 182 lbs. b: Toronto, Ont., 5/15/1953.

Season	Club	League	GP	G	A	Pts	AG	AA	APts	PIM	PP	SH	GW	S	%	TGF	PGF	TGA	PGA	+/–	GP	G	A	Pts	PIM	PP	SH	GW
1973-74	Centennial College	OCAA	STATISTICS NOT AVAILABLE																									
1974-75	Dallas Black Hawks	CHL	5	0	1	1				2																		
	Flint Generals	IHL	50	6	20	26				80																		
	Kalamazoo Wings	IHL	21	3	11	14				40																		
1975-76	Kalamazoo Wings	IHL	72	25	33	58				104											6	2	2	4	21			
1976-77	New England Whalers	WHA	33	6	10	16				41																		
	Rhode Island Reds	AHL	22	4	8	12				32																		
	Edmonton Oilers	WHA	29	9	16	25				48											5	4	1	5	7			
1977-78	Edmonton Oilers	WHA	80	20	30	50				112											5	0	2	2	16			
1978-79	Edmonton Oilers	WHA	71	31	39	70				79											13	5	10	15	15			
1979-80	**Edmonton Oilers**	**NHL**	**59**	**23**	**35**	**58**	**21**	**27**	**48**	**72**	**7**	**0**	**0**	**159**	**14.5**	**94**	**34**	**66**	**5**	**–1**	**3**	**0**	**2**	**2**	**0**	**0**	**0**	**0**
1980-81	**Edmonton Oilers**	**NHL**	**55**	**25**	**35**	**60**	**21**	**24**	**45**	**32**	**6**	**0**	**1**	**127**	**19.7**	**96**	**25**	**61**	**3**	**+13**	**9**	**4**	**4**	**8**	**6**	**1**	**0**	**1**
1981-82	**Edmonton Oilers**	**NHL**	**46**	**8**	**19**	**27**	**6**	**13**	**19**	**28**	**3**	**0**	**1**	**87**	**9.2**	**54**	**9**	**30**	**1**	**+16**	**2**	**0**	**0**	**0**	**2**	**0**	**0**	**0**
	NHL Totals		**160**	**56**	**89**	**145**	**48**	**64**	**112**	**132**	**16**	**0**	**2**	**373**	**15.0**	**244**	**68**	**157**	**9**		**14**	**4**	**6**	**10**	**8**	**1**	**0**	**1**
	Other Major League Totals		213	66	95	161				280											23	9	13	22	38			

Signed as a free agent by **New England** (WHA), October, 1976. Traded to **Edmonton** (WHA) by **New England** (WHA) with Ron Busniuk for Mike Antonovich and Bill Butters, February, 1977. Traded to **New England** (WHA) by **Edmonton** (WHA) for future considerations, June, 1977. Traded to **Edmonton** (WHA) by **New England** (WHA) with Dave Dryden and future considerations for Jean-Louis Levasseur, September, 1977. NHL rights retained by **Edmonton** prior to Expansion Draft, June 9, 1979.

• CALOUN, JAN
Jan Caloun RW – R. 5'10", 190 lbs. b: Usti-Nad-Labem, Czoch., 12/20/1972. San Jose's 4th choice, 75th overall, in 1992 Entry Draft.

Season	Club	League	GP	G	A	Pts	AG	AA	APts	PIM	PP	SH	GW	S	%	TGF	PGF	TGA	PGA	+/–	GP	G	A	Pts	PIM	PP	SH	GW
1990-91	Chemopetrol Litvinov	Czech.	50	28	19	47				12																		
1991-92	Chemopetrol Litvinov	Czech.	46	39	13	52				24																		
	Czechoslovakia	WJC-A	7	8	1	9				20																		
1992-93	Chemopetrol Litvinov	Czech.	47	45	22	67																						
	Czech Republic	WC-A	8	0	2	2				8																		
1993-94	Chemopetrol Litvinov	Czech.	38	25	17	42															4	2	2	4				
1994-95	Kansas City Blades	IHL	76	34	39	73				50											21	13	10	23	18			
1995-96	**San Jose Sharks**	**NHL**	**11**	**8**	**3**	**11**	**8**	**2**	**10**	**0**	**2**	**0**	**0**	**20**	**40.0**	**13**	**3**	**6**	**0**	**+4**								
	Kansas City Blades	IHL	61	38	30	68				58											5	0	1	1	6			
1996-97	**San Jose Sharks**	**NHL**	**2**	**0**	**0**	**0**	**0**	**0**	**0**	**0**	**0**	**0**	**0**	**3**	**0.0**	**0**	**0**	**2**	**0**	**–2**								
	Kentucky Thoroughblades	AHL	66	43	43	86				68											4	0	1	1	4			
1997-98	HIFK Helsinki	Finland	41	22	26	48				8											9	6	11	17	6			
	Czech Republic	Olympics	3	0	0	0				6																		
	NHL Totals		**13**	**8**	**3**	**11**	**8**	**2**	**10**	**0**	**2**	**0**	**0**	**23**	**34.8**	**13**	**3**	**8**	**0**									

AHL Second All-Star Team (1997)

• CAMAZZOLA, JAMES

James Camazzola LW – L. 5'11", 190 lbs. b: Vancouver, B.C., 1/5/1964. Chicago's 10th choice, 196th overall, in 1982 Entry Draft.

			REGULAR SEASON																		PLAYOFFS							
Season	Club	League	GP	G	A	Pts	AG	AA	APts	PIM	PP	SH	GW	S	%	TGF	PGF	TGA	PGA	+/–	GP	G	A	Pts	PIM	PP	SH	GW
1981-82	Penticton Knights	BCJHL	STATISTICS NOT AVAILABLE																									
1982-83	Kamloops Jr. Oilers	WHL	66	57	58	115				54																		
1983-84	Seattle Breakers	WHL	3	1	1	2				0																		
	Kamloops Jr. Oilers	WHL	29	26	24	50				25											17	12	19	31	44			
	Chicago Black Hawks	**NHL**	**1**	**0**	**0**	**0**	**0**	**0**	**0**	**0**	**0**	**0**	**0**	**1**	**0.0**	**0**	**0**	**0**	**0**	**0**								
1984-85	New Westminster Bruins	WHL	25	19	29	48				25											11	10	12	22	4			
1985-86	Nova Scotia Oilers	AHL	3	0	0	0				0																		
	Saginaw Generals	IHL	42	16	22	38				10											8	0	3	3	15			
1986-87	**Chicago Blackhawks**	**NHL**	**2**	**0**	**0**	**0**	**0**	**0**	**0**	**0**	**0**	**0**	**0**	**2**	**0.0**	**0**	**0**	**0**	**0**	**0**								
	Nova Scotia Oilers	AHL	48	13	18	31				31											3	0	0	0	0			
1987-88	Maine Mariners	AHL	62	13	23	36				80											10	1	7	8	8			
1988-89	HC Asiago	Italy	44	14	37	51				58																		
1989-90	HC Asiago	Italy	40	13	54	67				18																		
1990-91	HC Asiago	Italy	29	13	21	34				51																		
1991-92	HC Asiago	Italy	27	12	19	31				11																		
1992-93	HC Asiago	Italy	19	5	12	17				2																		
1993-94	Courmaosta	Italy	24	19	15	29				10																		
1994-95	Courmostra	Italy	34	21	21	42				49																		
	NHL Totals		**3**	**0**	**0**	**0**	**0**	**0**	**0**	**0**	**0**	**0**	**0**	**3**	**0.0**	**0**	**0**	**0**	**0**									

Memorial Cup All-Star Team (1984)

• CAMAZZOLA, TONY

Tony Camazzola D – L. 6'2", 210 lbs. b: Vancouver, B.C., 9/11/1962. Washington's 9th choice, 194th overall, in 1980 Entry Draft.

Season	Club	League	GP	G	A	Pts	AG	AA	APts	PIM	PP	SH	GW	S	%	TGF	PGF	TGA	PGA	+/–	GP	G	A	Pts	PIM	PP	SH	GW
1979-80	Brandon Wheat Kings	WHL	7	0	2	2				21											7	0	0	0	2			
1980-81	Brandon Wheat Kings	WHL	69	4	20	24				144											5	0	1	1	10			
1981-82	Brandon Wheat Kings	WHL	64	6	23	29				210											4	1	1	2	26			
	Washington Capitals	**NHL**	**3**	**0**	**0**	**0**	**0**	**0**	**0**	**4**	**0**	**0**	**0**	**0**	**0.0**	**0**	**0**	**0**	**0**	**0**								
1982-83	Hershey Bears	AHL	52	3	8	11				106																		
1983-84	Hershey Bears	AHL	63	6	10	16				138																		
1984-85	Fort Wayne Komets	IHL	15	0	3	3				56																		
	Toledo Goaldiggers	IHL	28	2	8	10				84											6	0	1	1	9			
1985-86	Fort Wayne Komets	IHL	54	5	7	12				144											14	6	0	6	7			
1986-87	Fort Wayne Komets	IHL	74	21	16	37				137											11	4	1	5	44			
1987-88	Fort Wayne Komets	IHL	46	10	6	16				140											5	2	0	2	19			
1988-89	Fort Wayne Komets	IHL	12	2	3	5				26																		
1989-90	Fort Wayne Komets	IHL	2	0	0	0				15																		
	NHL Totals		**3**	**0**	**0**	**0**	**0**	**0**	**0**	**4**	**0**	**0**	**0**	**0**	**0.0**	**0**	**0**	**0**	**0**									

• CAMERON, AL

Al Cameron D – L. 6'1", 205 lbs. b: Edmonton, Alta., 10/21/1955. Detroit's 3rd choice, 37th overall, in 1975 Amateur Draft.

Season	Club	League	GP	G	A	Pts	AG	AA	APts	PIM	PP	SH	GW	S	%	TGF	PGF	TGA	PGA	+/–	GP	G	A	Pts	PIM	PP	SH	GW
1972-73	Chilliwack Bruins	BCJHL	STATISTICS NOT AVAILABLE																									
	New Westminster Bruins	WCJHL	1	0	0	0				0																		
1973-74	New Westminster Bruins	WCJHL	67	4	17	21				90											11	0	2	2	24			
1974-75	New Westminster Bruins	WCJHL	69	10	26	36				184											16	2	3	5	54			
1975-76	**Detroit Red Wings**	**NHL**	**38**	**2**	**8**	**10**	**2**	**6**	**8**	**49**	**1**	**0**	**0**	**59**	**3.4**	**34**	**4**	**51**	**14**	**–7**								
	Kalamazoo Wings	IHL	43	3	17	20				71																		
1976-77	**Detroit Red Wings**	**NHL**	**80**	**3**	**13**	**16**	**3**	**11**	**14**	**112**	**1**	**0**	**0**	**139**	**2.2**	**62**	**16**	**121**	**32**	**–43**								
1977-78	**Detroit Red Wings**	**NHL**	**63**	**2**	**7**	**9**	**2**	**6**	**8**	**94**	**1**	**0**	**0**	**71**	**2.8**	**35**	**3**	**44**	**0**	**–12**	**7**	**0**	**1**	**1**	**2**	**0**	**0**	**0**
	Kansas City Red Wings	CHL	6	1	6	7				4																		
1978-79	**Detroit Red Wings**	**NHL**	**9**	**0**	**3**	**3**	**0**	**2**	**2**	**8**	**0**	**0**	**0**	**7**	**0.0**	**8**	**0**	**7**	**0**	**+1**								
	Kansas City Red Wings	CHL	64	5	25	30				89											4	0	1	1	2			
1979-80	**Winnipeg Jets**	**NHL**	**63**	**3**	**11**	**14**	**3**	**8**	**11**	**72**	**0**	**0**	**0**	**79**	**3.8**	**59**	**5**	**106**	**26**	**–26**								
	Tulsa Oilers	CHL	15	1	2	3				20																		
1980-81	**Winnipeg Jets**	**NHL**	**29**	**1**	**2**	**3**	**1**	**1**	**2**	**21**	**0**	**0**	**0**	**16**	**6.3**	**19**	**1**	**46**	**9**	**–19**								
	Tulsa Oilers	CHL	42	6	26	32				38											3	0	0	0	2			
	NHL Totals		**282**	**11**	**44**	**55**	**11**	**34**	**45**	**356**	**3**	**0**	**0**	**371**	**3.0**	**217**	**29**	**375**	**81**		**7**	**0**	**1**	**1**	**2**	**0**	**0**	**0**

Claimed by **Winnipeg** from **Detroit** in Expansion Draft, June 13, 1979.

• CAMERON, CRAIG

Craig Cameron RW – R. 6', 200 lbs. b: Edmonton, Alta., 7/19/1945.

Season	Club	League	GP	G	A	Pts	AG	AA	APts	PIM	PP	SH	GW	S	%	TGF	PGF	TGA	PGA	+/–	GP	G	A	Pts	PIM	PP	SH	GW
1965-66	Edmonton Oil Kings	ASHL	....	17	15	32				19																		
1966-67	**Detroit Red Wings**	**NHL**	**1**	**0**	**0**	**0**	**0**	**0**	**0**	**0**																		
	Memphis Wings	CHL	1	0	0	0				2																		
	Pittsburgh Hornets	AHL	50	9	11	20				12																		
1967-68	**St. Louis Blues**	**NHL**	**32**	**7**	**2**	**9**	**9**	**2**	**11**	**8**	**0**	**0**	**1**	**43**	**16.3**	**15**	**2**	**11**	**0**	**+2**	**14**	**1**	**0**	**1**	**11**	**0**	**0**	**0**
	Kansas City Blues	CHL	32	12	12	24				27																		
1968-69	**St. Louis Blues**	**NHL**	**72**	**11**	**5**	**16**	**12**	**5**	**17**	**40**	**2**	**0**	**1**	**123**	**8.9**	**33**	**3**	**40**	**2**	**–8**	**2**	**0**	**0**	**0**	**0**	**0**	**0**	**0**
1969-70	Baltimore Clippers	AHL	67	10	18	28				40											5	2	2	4	0			
1970-71	**St. Louis Blues**	**NHL**	**78**	**14**	**6**	**20**	**15**	**5**	**20**	**32**	**0**	**1**	**2**	**86**	**16.3**	**33**	**0**	**47**	**3**	**–11**	**6**	**2**	**0**	**2**	**4**	**0**	**0**	**0**
1971-72	**Minnesota North Stars**	**NHL**	**64**	**2**	**1**	**3**	**2**	**1**	**3**	**11**	**0**	**0**	**0**	**32**	**6.3**	**6**	**0**	**13**	**6**	**–1**	**5**	**0**	**1**	**1**	**2**	**0**	**0**	**0**
1972-73	**New York Islanders**	**NHL**	**72**	**19**	**14**	**33**	**19**	**12**	**31**	**27**	**2**	**0**	**2**	**144**	**13.2**	**43**	**4**	**97**	**20**	**–38**								
1973-74	**New York Islanders**	**NHL**	**78**	**15**	**14**	**29**	**15**	**12**	**27**	**28**	**2**	**0**	**2**	**121**	**12.4**	**50**	**8**	**82**	**25**	**–15**								
1974-75	**New York Islanders**	**NHL**	**37**	**1**	**6**	**7**	**1**	**5**	**6**	**4**	**0**	**0**	**0**	**52**	**1.9**	**0**	**0**	**0**	**0**	**0**								
	Minnesota North Stars	**NHL**	**40**	**10**	**7**	**17**	**9**	**5**	**14**	**12**	**1**	**0**	**1**	**65**	**15.4**	**26**	**3**	**33**	**15**	**+5**								
1975-76	**Minnesota North Stars**	**NHL**	**78**	**8**	**10**	**18**	**7**	**8**	**15**	**34**	**1**	**0**	**0**	**73**	**11.0**	**30**	**3**	**96**	**42**	**–27**								
1976-77	New Haven Nighthawks	AHL	79	14	26	40				33											6	0	0	0	2			
	NHL Totals		**552**	**87**	**65**	**152**	**89**	**55**	**144**	**196**	**8**	**1**	**9**	**739**	**11.8**	**236**	**23**	**419**	**113**		**27**	**3**	**1**	**4**	**17**	**0**	**0**	**0**

Traded to **St. Louis** by **Detroit** with Larry Hornung and Don Giesebrecht for John Brenneman, October 9, 1967. Traded to **Pittsburgh** (Baltimore - AHL) by **St. Louis** with Ron Schock for Lou Angotti and Pittsburgh's 1st round choice (Gene Carr) in 1971 Amateur Draft, June 6, 1969. Claimed by **LA Kings** from **Pittsburgh** in Intra-League Draft, June 9, 1970. Claimed by **Buffalo** from **in Expansion Draft**, June 10, 1970. Traded to **St. Louis** by **Buffalo** for Ron Anderson, October 2, 1970. Claimed on waivers by **Minnesota** from **St. Louis**, October 1, 1971. Claimed by **NY Islanders** from **Minnesota** in Expansion Draft, June 6, 1972. Traded to **Minnesota** by **NY Islanders** for Jude Drouin, January 7, 1972.

• CAMERON, DAVE

Dave Cameron C – L. 6', 185 lbs. b: Charlottetown, P.E.I., 7/29/1958. NY Islanders' 7th choice, 135th overall, in 1978 Amateur Draft.

Season	Club	League	GP	G	A	Pts	AG	AA	APts	PIM	PP	SH	GW	S	%	TGF	PGF	TGA	PGA	+/–	GP	G	A	Pts	PIM	PP	SH	GW
1976-77	University of P.E.I.	AUAA	20	7	10	17				12																		
1977-78	University of P.E.I.	AUAA	16	13	*30	43				26																		
1978-79	University of P.E.I.	AUAA	13	7	22	29				39																		
1979-80	Fort Wayne Komets	IHL	6	3	6	9				9																		
	Indianapolis Checkers	CHL	70	15	21	36				101											7	0	0	0	16			
1980-81	Indianapolis Checkers	CHL	78	40	30	70				156											5	2	3	5	4			
1981-82	**Colorado Rockies**	**NHL**	**66**	**11**	**12**	**23**	**9**	**8**	**17**	**103**	**0**	**1**	**0**	**65**	**16.9**	**38**	**5**	**63**	**16**	**–14**								
	Fort Worth Texans	CHL	2	0	0	0				0																		
1982-83	**New Jersey Devils**	**NHL**	**35**	**5**	**4**	**9**	**4**	**3**	**7**	**50**	**1**	**0**	**0**	**29**	**17.2**	**16**	**3**	**28**	**7**	**–8**								
	Wichita Wind	CHL	25	6	9	15				40																		
1983-84	**New Jersey Devils**	**NHL**	**67**	**9**	**12**	**21**	**7**	**8**	**15**	**85**	**2**	**0**	**0**	**79**	**11.4**	**37**	**7**	**69**	**28**	**–11**								
1984-85	Maine Mariners	AHL	12	0	1	1				32																		
	Moncton Golden Flames	AHL	37	8	16	24				82																		
1985-86	Charlottetown Islanders	PEI Sr.	15	9	16	25				54																		
1986-87	Charlottetown Islanders	PEI Sr.	11	5	17	22				69																		
1987-88	Summerside Caps	PEI Jr.	DID NOT PLAY – COACHING																									

			REGULAR SEASON																		PLAYOFFS							
Season	Club	League	GP	G	A	Pts	AG	AA	APts	PIM	PP	SH	GW	S	%	TGF	PGF	TGA	PGA	+/–	GP	G	A	Pts	PIM	PP	SH	GW
1988-89	Summerside Caps	PEI Jr.	DID NOT PLAY – COACHING																									
1989-90	Fredericton Alpines	MBSHL	14	0	8	8				30											6	1	6	7				
1990-91	Charlottetown Islanders	PEI Sr.	25	23	21	44				69																		
	NHL Totals		**168**	**25**	**28**	**53**	**20**	**19**	**39**	**238**	**3**	**1**	**0**	**173**	**14.5**	**91**	**15**	**160**	**51**									

CHL Second All-Star Team (1981)

Traded to **Colorado** by **NY Islanders** with Bob Lorimer for Colorado's 1st round choice (Pat Lafontaine) in 1983 Entry Draft, October 1, 1981. Transferred to **New Jersey** after **Colorado** franchise relocated, June 30, 1982.

• CAMPBELL, BRYAN

Bryan Campbell   C – L. 6', 175 lbs.   b: Sudbury, Ont., 3/27/1944.

Season	Club	League	GP	G	A	Pts	AG	AA	APts	PIM	PP	SH	GW	S	%	TGF	PGF	TGA	PGA	+/–	GP	G	A	Pts	PIM	PP	SH	GW
1961-62	Hamilton Red Wings	OHA	23	5	3	8				0											9	0	0	0	0			
1962-63	Hamilton Red Wings	OHA	49	21	40	61				19											5	2	2	4	2			
1963-64	Hamilton Red Wings	OHA	39	13	25	38				32																		
	Cincinnati Wings	CHL	6	1	3	4				2																		
1964-65	Memphis Wings	CHL	69	23	39	62				54																		
1965-66	Memphis Wings	CHL	56	24	31	55				32																		
1966-67	Omaha Knights	CHL	65	26	42	68				46											12	1	9	10	4			
1967-68	**Los Angeles Kings**	**NHL**	**44**	**6**	**15**	**21**	**7**	**16**	**23**	**16**	**0**	**0**	**1**	**55**	**10.9**	**26**	**4**	**23**	**3**	**+2**								
1968-69	**Los Angeles Kings**	**NHL**	**18**	**2**	**1**	**3**	**2**	**1**	**3**	**4**	**0**	**0**	**0**	**37**	**5.4**	**5**	**2**	**10**	**0**	**–7**	**6**	**2**	**1**	**3**	**0**	**0**	**0**	**1**
	Springfield Kings	AHL	53	27	28	55				24																		
1969-70	**Los Angeles Kings**	**NHL**	**31**	**4**	**4**	**8**	**5**	**4**	**9**	**4**	**0**	**0**	**0**	**54**	**7.4**	**10**	**2**	**28**	**5**	**–15**								
	Springfield Kings	AHL	15	7	14	21				2																		
	Chicago Black Hawks	**NHL**	**14**	**1**	**1**	**2**	**1**	**1**	**2**	**2**	**0**	**0**	**0**	**7**	**14.3**	**2**	**0**	**0**	**0**	**+2**	**8**	**1**	**2**	**3**	**0**	**1**	**0**	**0**
1970-71	**Chicago Black Hawks**	**NHL**	**78**	**17**	**37**	**54**	**18**	**33**	**51**	**26**	**3**	**0**	**1**	**155**	**11.0**	**74**	**12**	**36**	**0**	**+26**	**4**	**0**	**1**	**1**	**0**	**0**	**0**	**0**
1971-72	**Chicago Black Hawks**	**NHL**	**75**	**5**	**13**	**18**	**5**	**12**	**17**	**22**	**0**	**0**	**1**	**87**	**5.7**	**28**	**0**	**27**	**1**	**+2**	**4**	**0**	**0**	**0**	**2**	**0**	**0**	**0**
1972-73	Philadelphia Blazers	WHA	75	25	48	73				85											3	0	1	1	8			
1973-74	Vancouver Blazers	WHA	76	27	62	89				50																		
1974-75	Vancouver Blazers	WHA	78	29	34	63				24																		
1975-76	Cincinnati Stingers	WHA	77	22	50	72				24																		
1976-77	Indianapolis Racers	WHA	8	1	4	5				6																		
	Edmonton Oilers	WHA	66	12	42	54				18											5	3	1	4	0			
1977-78	Edmonton Oilers	WHA	53	7	13	20				12																		
	NHL Totals		**260**	**35**	**71**	**106**	**38**	**67**	**105**	**74**	**3**	**0**	**3**	**395**	**8.9**	**145**	**20**	**124**	**9**		**22**	**3**	**4**	**7**	**2**	**1**	**0**	**1**
	Other Major League Totals		433	123	253	376				219											8	3	2	5	8			

Claimed by **NY Rangers** from **Detroit** in Intra-League Draft, June 15, 1966. Claimed by **LA Kings** from **NY Rangers** in Expansion Draft, June 6, 1967. Traded to **Chicago** by **LA Kings** with Bill White and Gerry Desjardins for Gilles Marotte, Jim Stanfield and Denis DeJordy, February 20, 1970. Selected by **Chicago** (WHA) in 1972 WHA General Player Draft, February 12, 1972. WHA rights traded to **Philadelphia** (WHA) by **Chicago** (WHA) for cash, May, 1972. Traded to **Cincinnati** (WHA) by **Calgary** (WHA) for cash, September, 1975. Traded to **Indianapolis** (WHA) by **Cincinnati** (WHA) for future considerations, August 2, 1976. Traded to **Edmonton** (WHA) by **Indianapolis** (WHA) for Gene Peacosh, November, 1976.

• CAMPBELL, COLIN

Colin "Colie" Campbell   D – L. 5'9", 190 lbs.   b: London, Ont., 1/28/1953.   Pittsburgh's 3rd choice, 27th overall, in 1973 Amateur Draft.

Season	Club	League	GP	G	A	Pts	AG	AA	APts	PIM	PP	SH	GW	S	%	TGF	PGF	TGA	PGA	+/–	GP	G	A	Pts	PIM	PP	SH	GW
1970-71	Peterborough Petes	OHA	59	5	18	23				160																		
1971-72	Peterborough Petes	OHA	50	2	23	25				158																		
1972-73	Peterborough Petes	OHA	60	7	40	47				189																		
1973-74	Vancouver Blazers	WHA	78	3	20	23				191																		
1974-75	**Pittsburgh Penguins**	**NHL**	**59**	**4**	**15**	**19**	**4**	**12**	**16**	**172**	**0**	**1**	**0**	**84**	**4.8**	**78**	**2**	**62**	**14**	**+28**	**9**	**1**	**3**	**4**	**21**	**0**	**1**	**1**
	Hershey Bears	AHL	15	1	3	4				55																		
1975-76	**Pittsburgh Penguins**	**NHL**	**64**	**7**	**10**	**17**	**7**	**8**	**15**	**105**	**1**	**0**	**2**	**64**	**10.9**	**60**	**2**	**77**	**15**	**–4**	**3**	**0**	**0**	**0**	**0**	**0**	**0**	**0**
1976-77	**Colorado Rockies**	**NHL**	**54**	**3**	**8**	**11**	**3**	**6**	**9**	**67**	**0**	**0**	**0**	**87**	**3.4**	**34**	**3**	**63**	**10**	**–22**								
1977-78	**Pittsburgh Penguins**	**NHL**	**55**	**1**	**9**	**10**	**1**	**7**	**8**	**103**	**1**	**0**	**1**	**54**	**1.9**	**33**	**5**	**57**	**10**	**–19**								
1978-79	**Pittsburgh Penguins**	**NHL**	**65**	**2**	**18**	**20**	**2**	**14**	**16**	**137**	**0**	**0**	**1**	**52**	**3.8**	**58**	**1**	**52**	**9**	**+14**	**7**	**1**	**4**	**5**	**30**	**0**	**0**	**0**
1979-80	**Edmonton Oilers**	**NHL**	**72**	**2**	**11**	**13**	**2**	**8**	**10**	**196**	**0**	**0**	**0**	**80**	**2.5**	**61**	**1**	**97**	**19**	**–18**	**3**	**0**	**0**	**0**	**11**	**0**	**0**	**0**
1980-81	**Vancouver Canucks**	**NHL**	**42**	**1**	**8**	**9**	**1**	**6**	**7**	**75**	**0**	**0**	**0**	**37**	**2.7**	**39**	**0**	**34**	**5**	**+10**	**3**	**0**	**1**	**1**	**9**	**0**	**0**	**0**
1981-82	**Vancouver Canucks**	**NHL**	**47**	**0**	**8**	**8**	**0**	**5**	**5**	**131**	**0**	**0**	**0**	**35**	**0.0**	**45**	**2**	**56**	**17**	**+4**	**16**	**2**	**2**	**4**	**89**	**0**	**0**	**1**
1982-83	**Detroit Red Wings**	**NHL**	**53**	**1**	**7**	**8**	**1**	**5**	**6**	**74**	**0**	**0**	**0**	**30**	**3.3**	**38**	**1**	**49**	**14**	**+2**								
1983-84	**Detroit Red Wings**	**NHL**	**68**	**3**	**4**	**7**	**2**	**3**	**5**	**108**	**0**	**0**	**1**	**48**	**6.3**	**50**	**0**	**69**	**19**	**0**	**4**	**0**	**0**	**0**	**21**	**0**	**0**	**0**
1984-85	**Detroit Red Wings**	**NHL**	**57**	**1**	**5**	**6**	**1**	**3**	**4**	**124**	**0**	**0**	**0**	**36**	**2.8**	**49**	**0**	**88**	**25**	**–14**								
	NHL Totals		**636**	**25**	**103**	**128**	**24**	**77**	**101**	**1292**	**2**	**1**	**5**	**607**	**4.1**	**545**	**17**	**704**	**157**		**45**	**4**	**10**	**14**	**181**	**0**	**1**	**2**
	Other Major League Totals		78	3	20	23				191																		

Selected by **Vancouver** (WHA) in 1973 WHA Amateur Draft, June, 1973. Loaned to **Colorado** by **Pittsburgh** for 1976-77 season as compensation in transaction that sent Denis Herron to Pittsburgh for Simon Nolet and Michel Plasse, September 1, 1976. Claimed by **Edmonton** from **Pittsburgh** in Expansion Draft, June 13, 1979. Claimed by **Vancouver** from **Edmonton** in Waiver Draft, October 10, 1980. Signed as a free agent by **Detroit**, June 26, 1982.

• CAMPBELL, JIM

Jim Campbell   C – R. 6'2", 185 lbs.   b: Worcester, MA, 4/3/1973.   Montreal's 2nd choice, 28th overall, in 1991 Entry Draft.

Season	Club	League	GP	G	A	Pts	AG	AA	APts	PIM	PP	SH	GW	S	%	TGF	PGF	TGA	PGA	+/–	GP	G	A	Pts	PIM	PP	SH	GW
1990-91	Northwood-Mass School	H.S.	26	36	47	83				36																		
1991-92	Hull Olympiques	QMJHL	64	41	44	85				51											6	7	3	10	8			
	United States	WJC-A	7	2	4	6				4																		
1992-93	Hull Olympiques	QMJHL	50	42	29	71				66											8	11	4	15	43			
	United States	WJC-A	7	5	2	7				2																		
1993-94	United States	Nat-Team	56	24	33	57				59																		
	United States	Olympics	8	0	0	0				6																		
	Fredericton Canadiens	AHL	19	6	17	23				6																		
1994-95	Fredericton Canadiens	AHL	77	27	24	51				103											12	0	7	7	8			
1995-96	Fredericton Canadiens	AHL	44	28	23	51				24																		
	Anaheim Mighty Ducks	**NHL**	**16**	**2**	**3**	**5**	**2**	**2**	**4**	**36**	**1**	**0**	**0**	**25**	**8.0**	**6**	**2**	**4**	**0**	**0**								
	Baltimore Bandits	AHL	16	13	7	20				8											12	7	5	12	10			
1996-97	**St. Louis Blues**	**NHL**	**68**	**23**	**20**	**43**	**24**	**18**	**42**	**68**	**5**	**0**	**6**	**169**	**13.6**	**61**	**16**	**50**	**8**	**+3**	**4**	**1**	**0**	**1**	**6**	**1**	**0**	**0**
	United States	WC-A	4	0	0	0				2																		
1997-98	**St. Louis Blues**	**NHL**	**76**	**22**	**19**	**41**	**26**	**19**	**45**	**55**	**7**	**0**	**6**	**147**	**15.0**	**72**	**28**	**45**	**1**	**0**	**10**	**7**	**3**	**10**	**12**	**4**	**0**	**2**
	NHL Totals		**160**	**47**	**42**	**89**	**52**	**39**	**91**	**159**	**13**	**0**	**12**	**341**	**13.8**	**139**	**46**	**99**	**9**		**14**	**8**	**3**	**11**	**18**	**5**	**0**	**2**

NHL All-Rookie Team (1997)

Traded to **Anaheim** by **Montreal** for Robert Dirk, January 21, 1996. Signed as a free agent by **St. Louis**, July 11, 1996.

• CAMPBELL, SCOTT

Scott Campbell   D – L. 6'3", 205 lbs.   b: Toronto, Ont., 6/22/1957.   St. Louis' 1st choice, 9th overall, in 1977 Amateur Draft.

Season	Club	League	GP	G	A	Pts	AG	AA	APts	PIM	PP	SH	GW	S	%	TGF	PGF	TGA	PGA	+/–	GP	G	A	Pts	PIM	PP	SH	GW
1974-75	London Knights	OHA	68	4	15	19				52																		
1975-76	London Knights	OHA	62	6	25	31				66																		
1976-77	London Knights	OHA	60	23	44	67				86																		
1977-78	Houston Aeros	WHA	75	8	29	37				116											6	1	1	2	8			
1978-79	Winnipeg Jets	WHA	74	3	15	18				248											10	0	2	2	25			
1979-80	**Winnipeg Jets**	**NHL**	**63**	**3**	**17**	**20**	**3**	**13**	**16**	**136**	**0**	**0**	**2**	**92**	**3.3**	**61**	**14**	**109**	**23**	**–39**								
1980-81	**Winnipeg Jets**	**NHL**	**14**	**1**	**4**	**5**	**1**	**3**	**4**	**55**	**0**	**0**	**0**	**12**	**8.3**	**14**	**0**	**20**	**9**	**+3**								
	Tulsa Oilers	CHL	3	0	0	0				9																		
1981-82	**St. Louis Blues**	**NHL**	**3**	**0**	**0**	**0**	**0**	**0**	**0**	**52**	**0**	**0**	**0**	**4**	**0.0**	**1**	**0**	**2**	**0**	**–1**								
	Salt Lake Golden Eagles	CHL	3	0	1	1				31																		
	NHL Totals		**80**	**4**	**21**	**25**	**4**	**16**	**20**	**243**	**0**	**0**	**2**	**108**	**3.7**	**76**	**14**	**131**	**32**									
	Other Major League Totals		149	11	44	55				364											16	1	3	4	33			

Selected by **Houston** (WHA) in 1977 WHA Amateur Draft, June, 1977. Signed as a free agent by **Winnipeg** (WHA) after **Houston** (WHA) franchise folded, July, 1978. Reclaimed by **St. Louis** from **Winnipeg** prior to Expansion Draft, June 9, 1979. Claimed as a priority selection by **Winnipeg**, June 9, 1979. Traded to **St. Louis** by **Winnipeg** with John Markell for Bryan Maxwell, Ed Staniowski and Paul MacLean, July 3, 1981.

• CAMPBELL, WADE
Wade Campbell D – R. 6'4", 220 lbs. b: Peace River, Alta., 1/2/1961.

			REGULAR SEASON																		PLAYOFFS							
Season	Club	League	GP	G	A	Pts	AG	AA	APts	PIM	PP	SH	GW	S	%	TGF	PGF	TGA	PGA	+/–	GP	G	A	Pts	PIM	PP	SH	GW
1980-81	University of Alberta	CWUAA	42	8	26	34	....	....	....	85	....	....	....	....	....	....	....	....	....	....	....	....	....	....	....	....	....	....
1981-82	University of Alberta	CWUAA	42	8	26	34	....	....	....	85	....	....	....	....	....	....	....	....	....	....	....	....	....	....	....	....	....	....
1982-83	Winnipeg Jets	NHL	42	1	2	3	1	1	2	50	0	0	0	36	2.8	27	0	40	1	–12	....	....	....	....	....	....	....	....
	Sherbrooke Jets	AHL	18	4	2	6	....	....	....	23	....	....	....	....	....	....	....	....	....	....	....	....	....	....	....	....	....	....
1983-84	Winnipeg Jets	NHL	79	7	14	21	6	9	15	147	0	0	0	89	7.9	87	3	123	37	–2	3	0	0	0	7	0	0	0
1984-85	Winnipeg Jets	NHL	40	1	6	7	1	4	5	21	0	1	0	28	3.6	26	0	31	6	+1	3	0	0	0	2	0	0	0
	Sherbrooke Canadiens	AHL	28	2	6	8	....	....	....	70	....	....	....	....	....	....	....	....	....	....	....	....	....	....	....	....	....	....
1985-86	Winnipeg Jets	NHL	24	0	1	1	0	1	1	27	0	0	0	13	0.0	9	0	31	10	–12	....	....	....	....	....	....	....	....
	Sherbrooke Canadiens	AHL	9	0	2	2	....	....	....	26	....	....	....	....	....	....	....	....	....	....	....	....	....	....	....	....	....	....
	Boston Bruins	NHL	8	0	0	0	0	0	0	15	0	0	0	0	0.0	1	0	2	2	+1	....	....	....	....	....	....	....	....
	Moncton Golden Flames	AHL	17	2	2	4	....	....	....	21	....	....	....	....	....	....	....	....	....	....	10	0	0	0	16	....	....	....
1986-87	Boston Bruins	NHL	14	0	3	3	0	2	2	24	0	0	0	20	0.0	14	0	16	1	–1	4	0	0	0	11	0	0	0
	Moncton Golden Flames	AHL	64	12	23	35	....	....	....	34	....	....	....	....	....	....	....	....	....	....	....	....	....	....	....	....	....	....
1987-88	Boston Bruins	NHL	6	0	1	1	0	1	1	21	0	0	0	3	0.0	3	0	3	1	+1	....	....	....	....	....	....	....	....
	Maine Mariners	AHL	69	11	29	40	....	....	....	118	....	....	....	....	....	....	....	....	....	....	10	2	4	6	29	....	....	....
1988-89	Bordeaux	France	30	8	12	20	....	....	....	79	....	....	....	....	....	....	....	....	....	....	....	....	....	....	....	....	....	....
1989-90	Bordeaux	France	STATISTICS NOT AVAILABLE																									
1990-91	Cape Breton Oilers	AHL	66	8	13	21	....	....	....	54	....	....	....	....	....	....	....	....	....	....	4	1	1	2	4	....	....	....
	NHL Totals		213	9	27	36	8	18	26	305	0	1	0	189	4.8	167	3	246	58		10	0	0	0	20	0	0	0

Signed as a free agent by **Winnipeg**, October 5, 1982. Traded to **Boston** by **Winnipeg** for Bill Derlago, January 31, 1986.

• CAMPEDELLI, DOM
Dom Campedelli D – R. 6'1", 185 lbs. b: Cohasset, MA, 4/3/1964. Toronto's 10th choice, 129th overall, in 1982 Entry Draft.

Season	Club	League	GP	G	A	Pts	AG	AA	APts	PIM	PP	SH	GW	S	%	TGF	PGF	TGA	PGA	+/–	GP	G	A	Pts	PIM	PP	SH	GW
1982-83	Boston College	ECAC	26	1	10	11	....	....	....	26	....	....	....	....	....	....	....	....	....	....	....	....	....	....	....	....	....	....
1983-84	Boston College	ECAC	37	10	19	29	....	....	....	24	....	....	....	....	....	....	....	....	....	....	....	....	....	....	....	....	....	....
1984-85	Boston College	H.E.	44	5	44	49	....	....	....	74	....	....	....	....	....	....	....	....	....	....	....	....	....	....	....	....	....	....
1985-86	Montreal Canadiens	NHL	2	0	0	0	0	0	0	0	0	0	0	1	0.0	0	0	2	0	–2	....	....	....	....	....	....	....	....
	Sherbrooke Canadiens	AHL	38	4	10	14	....	....	....	27	....	....	....	....	....	....	....	....	....	....	....	....	....	....	....	....	....	....
1986-87	Sherbrooke Canadiens	AHL	7	3	2	5	....	....	....	2	....	....	....	....	....	....	....	....	....	....	....	....	....	....	....	....	....	....
	Hershey Bears	AHL	45	7	15	22	....	....	....	70	....	....	....	....	....	....	....	....	....	....	....	....	....	....	....	....	....	....
	Nova Scotia Oilers	AHL	12	0	4	4	....	....	....	7	....	....	....	....	....	....	....	....	....	....	5	0	0	0	17	....	....	....
1987-88	Nova Scotia Oilers	AHL	70	5	17	22	....	....	....	117	....	....	....	....	....	....	....	....	....	....	3	1	1	2	2	....	....	....
	NHL Totals		2	0	0	0	0	0	0	0	0	0	0	1	0.0	0	0	2	0		....	....	....	....	....	....	....	....

Traded to **Montreal** by **Toronto** for Montreal's 2nd round choice (Darryl Shannon) in 1986 Entry Draft and Toronto's 4th round choice (previously acquired, Toronto selected Kent Hulst), September 18, 1985. Traded to **Philadelphia** by **Montreal** for Andre Villeneuve, October 30, 1986. Traded to **Edmonton** by **Philadelphia** for Jeff Brubaker, March 9, 1987.

• CAPUANO, DAVE
Dave Capuano LW – L. 6'2", 190 lbs. b: Warwick, RI, 7/27/1968. Pittsburgh's 2nd choice, 25th overall, in 1986 Entry Draft.

Season	Club	League	GP	G	A	Pts	AG	AA	APts	PIM	PP	SH	GW	S	%	TGF	PGF	TGA	PGA	+/–	GP	G	A	Pts	PIM	PP	SH	GW
1985-86	Mount St. Charles	H.S.	22	39	48	87	....	....	....	20	....	....	....	....	....	....	....	....	....	....	....	....	....	....	....	....	....	....
1986-87	University of Maine	H.E.	38	18	41	59	....	....	....	14	....	....	....	....	....	....	....	....	....	....	....	....	....	....	....	....	....	....
	United States	WJC-A	7	1	1	2	....	....	....	2	....	....	....	....	....	....	....	....	....	....	....	....	....	....	....	....	....	....
1987-88	University of Maine	H.E.	42	*34	*51	*85	....	....	....	51	....	....	....	....	....	....	....	....	....	....	....	....	....	....	....	....	....	....
1988-89	University of Maine	H.E.	41	37	30	67	....	....	....	38	....	....	....	....	....	....	....	....	....	....	....	....	....	....	....	....	....	....
1989-90	Pittsburgh Penguins	NHL	6	0	0	0	0	0	0	2	0	0	0	1	0.0	1	0	1	0	0	....	....	....	....	....	....	....	....
	Muskegon Lumberjacks	IHL	27	15	15	30	....	....	....	22	....	....	....	....	....	....	....	....	....	....	....	....	....	....	....	....	....	....
	Vancouver Canucks	NHL	27	3	5	8	3	4	7	10	0	0	1	25	12.0	10	1	16	0	–7	....	....	....	....	....	....	....	....
	Milwaukee Admirals	IHL	2	0	4	4	....	....	....	0	....	....	....	....	....	....	....	....	....	....	6	1	5	6	0	....	....	....
1990-91	Vancouver Canucks	NHL	61	13	31	44	12	23	35	42	5	0	1	77	16.9	56	17	38	0	+1	6	1	1	2	5	0	0	0
1991-92	Milwaukee Admirals	IHL	9	2	6	8	....	....	....	8	....	....	....	....	....	....	....	....	....	....	....	....	....	....	....	....	....	....
1992-93	Hamilton Canucks	AHL	4	0	1	1	....	....	....	0	....	....	....	....	....	....	....	....	....	....	....	....	....	....	....	....	....	....
	Tampa Bay Lightning	NHL	6	1	1	2	1	1	2	2	1	0	0	10	10.0	3	3	4	0	–4	....	....	....	....	....	....	....	....
	Atlanta Knights	IHL	58	19	40	59	....	....	....	50	....	....	....	....	....	....	....	....	....	....	8	2	2	4	9	....	....	....
1993-94	San Jose Sharks	NHL	4	0	1	1	0	1	1	0	0	0	0	5	0.0	2	2	5	0	–5	....	....	....	....	....	....	....	....
	Providence Bruins	AHL	51	24	29	53	....	....	....	64	....	....	....	....	....	....	....	....	....	....	....	....	....	....	....	....	....	....
	NHL Totals		104	17	38	55	16	29	45	56	6	0	2	118	14.4	72	23	64	0		6	1	1	2	5	0	0	0

Hockey East First All-Star Team (1988, 1989) • NCAA Championship All-Tournament Team (1988)

Traded to **Vancouver** by **Pittsburgh** with Andrew McBain and Dan Quinn for Rod Buskas, Barry Pederson and Tony Tanti, January 8, 1990. Traded to **Tampa Bay** by **Vancouver** with Vancouver 4th round choice (later traded to New Jersey — traded to Calgary — Calgary selected Ryan Duthie) in 1994 Entry Draft, for Anatoli Semenov, November 3, 1992. Traded to **San Jose** by **Tampa Bay** for Peter Ahola, June 19, 1993. Traded to **Boston** by **San Jose** for cash, November 5, 1993.

• CAPUANO, JACK
Jack Capuano D – L. 6'2", 210 lbs. b: Cranston, RI, 7/7/1966. Toronto's 4th choice, 88th overall, in 1984 Entry Draft.

Season	Club	League	GP	G	A	Pts	AG	AA	APts	PIM	PP	SH	GW	S	%	TGF	PGF	TGA	PGA	+/–	GP	G	A	Pts	PIM	PP	SH	GW
1983-84	Kent Prep School	H.S.	21	10	8	18	....	....	....	....	....	....	....	....	....	....	....	....	....	....	....	....	....	....	....	....	....	....
1984-85	University of Maine	H.E.	DID NOT PLAY – FRESHMAN																									
1985-86	University of Maine	H.E.	39	9	18	27	....	....	....	51	....	....	....	....	....	....	....	....	....	....	....	....	....	....	....	....	....	....
1986-87	University of Maine	H.E.	42	10	34	44	....	....	....	20	....	....	....	....	....	....	....	....	....	....	....	....	....	....	....	....	....	....
1987-88	University of Maine	H.E.	43	13	37	50	....	....	....	87	....	....	....	....	....	....	....	....	....	....	....	....	....	....	....	....	....	....
1988-89	Newmarket Saints	AHL	74	5	16	21	....	....	....	52	....	....	....	....	....	....	....	....	....	....	1	0	0	0	0	....	....	....
1989-90	Toronto Maple Leafs	NHL	1	0	0	0	0	0	0	0	0	0	0	1	0.0	0	0	1	0	–1	....	....	....	....	....	....	....	....
	Newmarket Saints	AHL	8	0	2	2	....	....	....	7	....	....	....	....	....	....	....	....	....	....	....	....	....	....	....	....	....	....
	Springfield Indians	AHL	14	0	4	4	....	....	....	8	....	....	....	....	....	....	....	....	....	....	....	....	....	....	....	....	....	....
	Milwaukee Admirals	IHL	17	3	10	13	....	....	....	60	....	....	....	....	....	....	....	....	....	....	6	0	1	1	12	....	....	....
1990-91	Vancouver Canucks	NHL	3	0	0	0	0	0	0	0	0	0	0	4	0.0	1	0	1	0	0	....	....	....	....	....	....	....	....
	Milwaukee Admirals	IHL	80	20	30	50	....	....	....	76	....	....	....	....	....	....	....	....	....	....	6	0	1	1	2	....	....	....
1991-92	Boston Bruins	NHL	2	0	0	0	0	0	0	0	0	0	0	1	0.0	1	0	2	0	–1	....	....	....	....	....	....	....	....
	Maine Mariners	AHL	74	14	26	40	....	....	....	35	....	....	....	....	....	....	....	....	....	....	....	....	....	....	....	....	....	....
	NHL Totals		6	0	0	0	0	0	0	0	0	0	0	6	0.0	2	0	4	0		....	....	....	....	....	....	....	....

Hockey East Second All-Star Team (1987) • Hockey East First All-Star Team (1988) • IHL Second All-Star Team (1991)

Traded to **NY Islanders** by **Toronto** with Paul Gagne and Derek Laxdal for Mike Stevens and Gilles Thibaudeau, December 20, 1989. Traded to **Vancouver** by **NY Islanders** for Jeff Rohlicek, March 6, 1990. Signed as a free agent by **Boston**, August 1, 1991.

• CARBONNEAU, GUY
Guy Carbonneau C – R. 5'11", 186 lbs. b: Sept-Iles, Que., 3/18/1960. Montreal's 4th choice, 44th overall, in 1979 Entry Draft.

Season	Club	League	GP	G	A	Pts	AG	AA	APts	PIM	PP	SH	GW	S	%	TGF	PGF	TGA	PGA	+/–	GP	G	A	Pts	PIM	PP	SH	GW
1976-77	Chicoutimi Sagueneens	QMJHL	59	9	20	29	....	....	....	8	....	....	....	....	....	....	....	....	....	....	4	1	0	1	0	....	....	....
1977-78	Chicoutimi Sagueneens	QMJHL	70	28	55	83	....	....	....	60	....	....	....	....	....	....	....	....	....	....	....	....	....	....	....	....	....	....
1978-79	Chicoutimi Sagueneens	QMJHL	72	62	79	141	....	....	....	47	....	....	....	....	....	....	....	....	....	....	4	2	1	3	4	....	....	....
1979-80	Chicoutimi Sagueneens	QMJHL	72	72	110	182	....	....	....	66	....	....	....	....	....	....	....	....	....	....	12	9	15	24	28	....	....	....
	Nova Scotia Voyageurs	AHL	....	....	....	....	....	....	....	....	....	....	....	....	....	....	....	....	....	....	2	1	1	2	2	....	....	....
1980-81	Montreal Canadiens	NHL	2	0	1	1	0	1	1	0	0	0	0	1	0.0	1	1	0	0	0	....	....	....	....	....	....	....	....
	Nova Scotia Voyageurs	AHL	78	35	53	88	....	....	....	87	....	....	....	....	....	....	....	....	....	....	6	1	3	4	9	....	....	....
1981-82	Nova Scotia Voyageurs	AHL	77	27	67	94	....	....	....	124	....	....	....	....	....	....	....	....	....	....	9	2	7	9	8	....	....	....
1982-83	Montreal Canadiens	NHL	77	18	29	47	15	20	35	68	0	5	2	109	16.5	69	4	78	31	+18	3	0	0	0	2	0	0	0
1983-84	Montreal Canadiens	NHL	78	24	30	54	19	20	39	75	3	7	2	166	14.5	72	13	83	29	+5	15	4	3	7	12	0	0	1
1984-85	Montreal Canadiens	NHL	79	23	34	57	19	23	42	43	0	4	2	163	14.1	83	2	86	33	+28	12	4	3	7	8	0	1	1
1985-86	Montreal Canadiens	NHL	80	20	36	56	16	24	40	57	1	2	3	147	13.6	84	5	109	48	+18	20	7	5	12	35	0	2	1
1986-87	Montreal Canadiens	NHL	79	18	27	45	16	20	36	68	0	0	2	120	15.0	61	1	78	27	+9	17	3	8	11	20	0	0	0
1987-88	Montreal Canadiens	NHL	80	17	21	38	15	15	30	61	0	3	1	109	15.6	47	0	71	38	+14	11	0	4	4	2	0	0	0
1988-89	Montreal Canadiens	NHL	79	26	30	56	22	21	43	44	1	2	10	142	18.3	72	5	61	31	+37	21	4	5	9	10	0	1	0
1989-90	Montreal Canadiens	NHL	68	19	36	55	16	26	42	37	1	1	3	125	15.2	74	5	79	31	+21	11	2	3	5	6	0	0	0
1990-91	Montreal Canadiens	FrTour	3	0	0	0	....	....	....	2	....	....	....	....	....	....	....	....	....	....	....	....	....	....	....	....	....	....
	Montreal Canadiens	NHL	78	20	24	44	18	18	36	63	4	1	3	131	15.3	72	10	95	32	–1	13	1	5	6	10	0	0	1
1991-92	Montreal Canadiens	NHL	72	18	21	39	16	16	32	39	1	1	4	120	15.0	50	1	68	21	+2	11	1	1	2	6	0	0	0
1992-93	Montreal Canadiens	NHL	61	4	13	17	3	9	12	20	0	1	0	73	5.5	24	0	68	35	–9	20	3	3	6	10	0	1	2

Season	Club	League	REGULAR SEASON																		PLAYOFFS							
			GP	G	A	Pts	AG	AA	APts	PIM	PP	SH	GW	S	%	TGF	PGF	TGA	PGA	+/-	GP	G	A	Pts	PIM	PP	SH	GW
1993-94	**Montreal Canadiens**	**NHL**	**79**	**14**	**24**	**38**	**13**	**19**	**32**	**48**	**0**	**0**	**1**	**120**	**11.7**	**57**	**4**	**67**	**30**	**+16**	**7**	**1**	**3**	**4**	**4**	**0**	**0**	**0**
1994-95	**St. Louis Blues**	**NHL**	**42**	**5**	**11**	**16**	**9**	**16**	**25**	**16**	**1**	**0**	**1**	**33**	**15.2**	**28**	**1**	**24**	**8**	**+11**	**7**	**1**	**2**	**3**	**6**	**0**	**0**	**0**
1995-96	**Dallas Stars**	**NHL**	**71**	**8**	**15**	**23**	**8**	**12**	**20**	**38**	**0**	**2**	**1**	**54**	**14.8**	**32**	**0**	**63**	**29**	**–2**	....	....	....	....	....	....	....	....
1996-97	**Dallas Stars**	**NHL**	**73**	**5**	**16**	**21**	**5**	**14**	**19**	**36**	**0**	**1**	**0**	**99**	**5.1**	**35**	**0**	**45**	**19**	**+9**	**7**	**0**	**1**	**1**	**6**	**0**	**0**	**0**
1997-98	**Dallas Stars**	**NHL**	**77**	**7**	**17**	**24**	**8**	**17**	**25**	**40**	**0**	**1**	**1**	**81**	**8.6**	**38**	**1**	**54**	**20**	**+3**	**16**	**3**	**1**	**4**	**6**	**0**	**0**	**0**
	NHL Totals		**1175**	**246**	**385**	**631**	**218**	**291**	**509**	**753**	**12**	**31**	**36**	**1793**	**13.7**	**899**	**53**	**1129**	**462**		**191**	**34**	**47**	**81**	**143**	**0**	**5**	**6**

QMJHL Second All-Star Team (1980) • Won Frank J. Selke Trophy (1988, 1989, 1992)

Traded to **St. Louis** by **Montreal** for Jim Montgomery, August 19, 1994. Traded to **Dallas** by **St. Louis** for Paul Broten, October 2, 1995.

• CARDIN, CLAUDE

Claude Cardin LW – L. 5′10″, 178 lbs. b: Sorel, Que., 2/17/1941.

Season	Club	League	GP	G	A	Pts	AG	AA	APts	PIM	PP	SH	GW	S	%	TGF	PGF	TGA	PGA	+/-	GP	G	A	Pts	PIM	PP	SH	GW
1963-64	Quebec Aces	AHL	3	0	0	0	....	....	....	4	....	....	....	....	....	....	....	....	....	....	....	....	....	....	....	....	....	....
	Omaha Knights	CHL	....	....	....	....	....	....	....	....	....	....	....	....	....	....	....	....	....	....	4	0	0	0	0	....	....	....
1964-65	Sherbrooke Castors	QSHL	STATISTICS NOT AVAILABLE																									
1965-66	Sherbrooke Castors	QSHL	STATISTICS NOT AVAILABLE																									
1966-67	Sherbrooke Castors	QSHL	30	9	32	41	....	....	....	12	....	....	....	....	....	....	....	....	....	....	....	....	....	....	....	....	....	....
1967-68	**St. Louis Blues**	**NHL**	**1**	**0**	**0**	**0**	**0**	**0**	**0**	**0**	**0**	**0**	**0**	**1**	**0.0**	**0**	**0**	**1**	**0**	**–1**	....	....	....	....	....	....	....	....
	Kansas City Blues	CHL	63	17	35	52	....	....	....	193	....	....	....	....	....	....	....	....	....	....	6	3	5	8	23	....	....	....
1968-69	Portland Buckaroos	WHL	5	0	3	3	....	....	....	0	....	....	....	....	....	....	....	....	....	....	....	....	....	....	....	....	....	....
	Kansas City Blues	CHL	58	10	34	44	....	....	....	153	....	....	....	....	....	....	....	....	....	....	4	1	1	2	4	....	....	....
1969-70	St. Hyacinthe Saints	QSHL	STATISTICS NOT AVAILABLE																									
	Kansas City Blues	CHL	3	1	2	3	....	....	....	5	....	....	....	....	....	....	....	....	....	....	....	....	....	....	....	....	....	....
1970-71	Syracuse–Long Island–Jersey	EHL	16	3	9	12	....	....	....	12	....	....	....	....	....	....	....	....	....	....	....	....	....	....	....	....	....	....
	Des Moines Oak Leafs	IHL	29	10	17	27	....	....	....	20	....	....	....	....	....	....	....	....	....	....	14	3	10	13	34	....	....	....
	NHL Totals		**1**	**0**	**0**	**0**	**0**	**0**	**0**	**0**	**0**	**0**	**0**	**1**	**0.0**	**0**	**0**	**1**	**0**		....	....	....	....	....	....	....	....

Traded to **St. Louis** by **Montreal** for cash, June 21, 1967.

• CARDWELL, STEVE

Steve Cardwell LW – L. 5′11″, 190 lbs. b: Toronto, Ont., 8/13/1950. Pittsburgh's 5th choice, 63rd overall, in 1970 Amateur Draft.

Season	Club	League	GP	G	A	Pts	AG	AA	APts	PIM	PP	SH	GW	S	%	TGF	PGF	TGA	PGA	+/-	GP	G	A	Pts	PIM	PP	SH	GW
1968-69	Oshawa Generals	OHA	50	11	11	22	....	....	....	54	....	....	....	....	....	....	....	....	....	....	....	....	....	....	....	....	....	....
1969-70	Oshawa Generals	OHA	46	14	19	33	....	....	....	77	....	....	....	....	....	....	....	....	....	....	....	....	....	....	....	....	....	....
1970-71	**Pittsburgh Penguins**	**NHL**	**5**	**0**	**1**	**1**	**0**	**1**	**1**	**15**	**0**	**0**	**0**	**2**	**0.0**	**1**	**0**	**5**	**0**	**–4**	....	....	....	....	....	....	....	....
	Amarillo Wranglers	CHL	63	16	34	50	....	....	....	166	....	....	....	....	....	....	....	....	....	....	....	....	....	....	....	....	....	....
1971-72	**Pittsburgh Penguins**	**NHL**	**28**	**7**	**8**	**15**	**7**	**7**	**14**	**18**	**2**	**0**	**1**	**47**	**14.9**	**23**	**5**	**18**	**0**	**0**	**4**	**0**	**0**	**0**	**2**	**0**	**0**	**0**
	Hershey Bears	AHL	46	17	26	43	....	....	....	32	....	....	....	....	....	....	....	....	....	....	....	....	....	....	....	....	....	....
1972-73	**Pittsburgh Penguins**	**NHL**	**20**	**2**	**2**	**4**	**2**	**2**	**4**	**2**	**0**	**0**	**0**	**21**	**9.5**	**4**	**0**	**6**	**0**	**–2**	....	....	....	....	....	....	....	....
	Hershey Bears	AHL	30	16	23	39	....	....	....	20	....	....	....	....	....	....	....	....	....	....	7	5	2	7	22	....	....	....
1973-74	Minnesota Fighting Saints	WHA	77	23	23	46	....	....	....	100	....	....	....	....	....	....	....	....	....	....	10	0	0	0	20	....	....	....
1974-75	Cleveland Crusaders	WHA	75	9	13	22	....	....	....	127	....	....	....	....	....	....	....	....	....	....	5	0	1	1	14	....	....	....
1975-76	Hershey Bears	AHL	72	22	33	55	....	....	....	165	....	....	....	....	....	....	....	....	....	....	9	0	2	2	11	....	....	....
1976-77			DID NOT PLAY																									
1977-78	Whitby Warriors	OHA Sr.	15	12	8	20	....	....	....	62	....	....	....	....	....	....	....	....	....	....	....	....	....	....	....	....	....	....
	San Francisco Shamrocks	PHL	33	21	28	49	....	....	....	92	....	....	....	....	....	....	....	....	....	....	....	....	....	....	....	....	....	....
1978-79	Tucson Rustlers	PHL	22	3	10	13	....	....	....	51	....	....	....	....	....	....	....	....	....	....	....	....	....	....	....	....	....	....
	NHL Totals		**53**	**9**	**11**	**20**	**9**	**10**	**19**	**35**	**2**	**0**	**1**	**70**	**12.9**	**28**	**5**	**29**	**0**		**4**	**0**	**0**	**0**	**2**	**0**	**0**	**0**
	Other Major League Totals		152	32	36	68	....	....	....	227	....	....	....	....	....	....	....	....	....		15	0	1	1	34	....	....	....

Selected by **Ontario-Ottawa** (WHA) in 1972 WHA General Player Draft, February 12, 1972. WHA rights traded to **Minnesota** (WHA) by **Ottawa** (WHA) for cash, July, 1973. Selected by **Indianapolis** (WHA) from **Minnesota** (WHA) in 1974 WHA Expansion Draft, June, 1975. Traded to **Cleveland** (WHA) by **Indianapolis** (WHA) for future considerations, August, 1975.

• CARKNER, TERRY

Terry Carkner D – L. 6′3″, 210 lbs. b: Smiths Falls, Ont., 3/7/1966. NY Rangers' 1st choice, 14th overall, in 1984 Entry Draft.

Season	Club	League	GP	G	A	Pts	AG	AA	APts	PIM	PP	SH	GW	S	%	TGF	PGF	TGA	PGA	+/-	GP	G	A	Pts	PIM	PP	SH	GW
1983-84	Peterborough Petes	OHL	58	4	19	23	....	....	....	77	....	....	....	....	....	....	....	....	....	....	8	0	6	6	13	....	....	....
1984-85	Peterborough Petes	OHL	64	14	47	61	....	....	....	125	....	....	....	....	....	....	....	....	....	....	17	2	10	12	11	....	....	....
1985-86	Peterborough Petes	OHL	54	12	32	44	....	....	....	106	....	....	....	....	....	....	....	....	....	....	16	1	7	8	17	....	....	....
	Canada	WJC-A	7	0	4	4	....	....	....	0	....	....	....	....	....	....	....	....	....	....	....	....	....	....	....	....	....	....
1986-87	**New York Rangers**	**NHL**	**52**	**2**	**13**	**15**	**2**	**9**	**11**	**118**	**0**	**0**	**0**	**33**	**6.1**	**52**	**8**	**51**	**6**	**–1**	**1**	**0**	**0**	**0**	**0**	**0**	**0**	**0**
	New Haven Nighthawks	AHL	12	2	6	8	....	....	....	56	....	....	....	....	....	....	....	....	....	....	3	1	0	1	0	....	....	....
1987-88	**Quebec Nordiques**	**NHL**	**63**	**3**	**24**	**27**	**3**	**17**	**20**	**159**	**2**	**0**	**1**	**54**	**5.6**	**58**	**36**	**47**	**17**	**–8**	....	....	....	....	....	....	....	....
1988-89	**Philadelphia Flyers**	**NHL**	**78**	**11**	**32**	**43**	**9**	**22**	**31**	**149**	**2**	**1**	**1**	**84**	**13.1**	**96**	**28**	**107**	**33**	**–6**	**19**	**1**	**5**	**6**	**28**	**0**	**1**	**0**
1989-90	**Philadelphia Flyers**	**NHL**	**63**	**4**	**18**	**22**	**3**	**13**	**16**	**169**	**1**	**0**	**1**	**60**	**6.7**	**62**	**11**	**90**	**31**	**–8**	....	....	....	....	....	....	....	....
1990-91	**Philadelphia Flyers**	**NHL**	**79**	**7**	**25**	**32**	**6**	**19**	**25**	**204**	**6**	**0**	**1**	**97**	**7.2**	**98**	**34**	**128**	**47**	**–15**	....	....	....	....	....	....	....	....
1991-92	**Philadelphia Flyers**	**NHL**	**73**	**4**	**12**	**16**	**4**	**9**	**13**	**195**	**0**	**1**	**0**	**70**	**5.7**	**60**	**7**	**102**	**35**	**–14**	....	....	....	....	....	....	....	....
1992-93	**Philadelphia Flyers**	**NHL**	**83**	**3**	**16**	**19**	**2**	**11**	**13**	**150**	**0**	**0**	**0**	**45**	**6.7**	**91**	**7**	**113**	**47**	**+18**	....	....	....	....	....	....	....	....
	Canada	WC-A	8	0	0	0	....	....	....	0	....	....	....	....	....	....	....	....	....	....	....	....	....	....	....	....	....	....
1993-94	**Detroit Red Wings**	**NHL**	**68**	**1**	**6**	**7**	**1**	**5**	**6**	**130**	**0**	**0**	**0**	**32**	**3.1**	**60**	**2**	**65**	**20**	**+13**	**7**	**0**	**0**	**0**	**4**	**0**	**0**	**0**
1994-95	**Detroit Red Wings**	**NHL**	**20**	**1**	**2**	**3**	**2**	**3**	**5**	**21**	**0**	**0**	**0**	**9**	**11.1**	**16**	**0**	**9**	**0**	**+7**	....	....	....	....	....	....	....	....
1995-96	**Florida Panthers**	**NHL**	**73**	**3**	**10**	**13**	**3**	**8**	**11**	**80**	**1**	**0**	**0**	**42**	**7.1**	**67**	**3**	**83**	**29**	**+10**	**22**	**0**	**4**	**4**	**10**	**0**	**0**	**0**
1996-97	**Florida Panthers**	**NHL**	**70**	**0**	**14**	**14**	**0**	**12**	**12**	**96**	**0**	**0**	**0**	**38**	**0.0**	**47**	**2**	**74**	**25**	**–4**	**5**	**0**	**0**	**0**	**6**	**0**	**0**	**0**
1997-98	**Florida Panthers**	**NHL**	**74**	**1**	**7**	**8**	**1**	**7**	**8**	**63**	**0**	**0**	**1**	**34**	**2.9**	**48**	**1**	**74**	**33**	**+6**	....	....	....	....	....	....	....	....
	NHL Totals		**796**	**40**	**179**	**219**	**36**	**135**	**171**	**1534**	**12**	**2**	**5**	**598**	**6.7**	**755**	**139**	**941**	**323**		**54**	**1**	**9**	**10**	**48**	**0**	**1**	**0**

OHL Second All-Star Team (1985) • OHL First All-Star Team (1986)

Traded to **Quebec** by **NY Rangers** with Jeff Jackson for John Ogrodnick and David Shaw, September 30, 1987. Traded to **Philadelphia** by **Quebec** for Greg Smyth and Philadelphia's 3rd round choice (John Tanner) in the 1989 Entry Draft, July 25, 1988. Traded to **Detroit** by **Philadelphia** for Yves Racine and Detroit's 4th round choice (Sebastien Vallee) in 1994 Entry Draft, October 5, 1993. Signed as a free agent by **Florida**, August 8, 1995.

• CARLETON, WAYNE

Wayne "Swoop" Carleton LW – L. 6′3″, 212 lbs. b: Sudbury, Ont., 8/4/1946.

Season	Club	League	GP	G	A	Pts	AG	AA	APts	PIM	PP	SH	GW	S	%	TGF	PGF	TGA	PGA	+/-	GP	G	A	Pts	PIM	PP	SH	GW
1961-62	Unionville Seaforths	Tor-Jr.	15	9	3	12	....	....	....	....	....	....	....	....	....	....	....	....	....	....	....	....	....	....	....	....	....	....
	Toronto Marlboros	OHA	16	5	8	13	....	....	....	5	....	....	....	....	....	....	....	....	....	....	12	2	4	6	4	....	....	....
1962-63	Toronto Marlboros	OHA	38	27	24	51	....	....	....	11	....	....	....	....	....	....	....	....	....	....	11	6	4	10	21	....	....	....
1963-64	Toronto Marlboros	OHA	54	42	22	64	....	....	....	26	....	....	....	....	....	....	....	....	....	....	5	3	2	5	0	....	....	....
1964-65	Toronto Marlboros	OHA	15	13	10	23	....	....	....	12	....	....	....	....	....	....	....	....	....	....	14	5	6	11	17	....	....	....
1965-66	Toronto Marlboros	OHA	16	9	5	14	....	....	....	24	....	....	....	....	....	....	....	....	....	....	14	9	6	15	28	....	....	....
	Toronto Maple Leafs	**NHL**	**2**	**0**	**1**	**1**	**0**	**1**	**1**	**0**	....	....	....	....	....	....	....	....	....	....	....	....	....	....	....	....	....	....
	Tulsa Oilers	CHL		....	....	....	....	....	....	....	....	....	....	....	....	....	....	....	....	....	6	3	4	7	0	....	....	....
1966-67	**Toronto Maple Leafs**	**NHL**	**5**	**1**	**0**	**1**	**1**	**0**	**1**	**14**	....	....	....	....	....	....	....	....	....	....	....	....	....	....	....	....	....	....
	Tulsa Oilers	CHL	52	17	15	32	....	....	....	48	....	....	....	....	....	....	....	....	....	....	....	....	....	....	....	....	....	....
	Rochester Americans	AHL	13	5	5	10	....	....	....	8	....	....	....	....	....	....	....	....	....	....	13	5	2	7	*31	....	....	....
1967-68	**Toronto Maple Leafs**	**NHL**	**65**	**8**	**11**	**19**	**10**	**11**	**21**	**34**	**0**	**0**	**1**	**140**	**5.7**	**36**	**4**	**27**	**0**	**+5**	....	....	....	....	....	....	....	....
1968-69	**Toronto Maple Leafs**	**NHL**	**12**	**1**	**3**	**4**	**1**	**3**	**4**	**6**	**0**	**0**	**0**	**24**	**4.2**	**5**	**1**	**12**	**0**	**–8**	....	....	....	....	....	....	....	....
	Rochester Americans	AHL	13	5	3	8	....	....	....	0	....	....	....	....	....	....	....	....	....	....	....	....	....	....	....	....	....	....
	Phoenix Roadrunners	WHL	32	16	13	29	....	....	....	18	....	....	....	....	....	....	....	....	....	....	....	....	....	....	....	....	....	....
1969-70	**Toronto Maple Leafs**	**NHL**	**7**	**0**	**1**	**1**	**0**	**1**	**1**	**6**	**0**	**0**	**0**	**6**	**0.0**	**3**	**0**	**2**	**0**	**+1**	....	....	....	....	....	....	....	....
	Phoenix Roadrunners	WHL	6	1	3	4	....	....	....	0	....	....	....	....	....	....	....	....	....	....	....	....	....	....	....	....	....	....
	Boston Bruins	**NHL**	**42**	**6**	**19**	**25**	**7**	**19**	**26**	**23**	**0**	**0**	**1**	**80**	**7.5**	**35**	**6**	**23**	**0**	**+6**	**14**	**2**	**4**	**6**	**14**	**0**	**0**	**0**
1970-71	**Boston Bruins**	**NHL**	**69**	**22**	**24**	**46**	**23**	**21**	**44**	**44**	**0**	**0**	**5**	**164**	**13.4**	**67**	**1**	**32**	**1**	**+35**	**4**	**0**	**0**	**0**	**0**	**0**	**0**	**0**
1971-72	**California Golden Seals**	**NHL**	**76**	**17**	**14**	**31**	**18**	**13**	**31**	**45**	**4**	**0**	**0**	**188**	**9.0**	**57**	**11**	**81**	**12**	**–23**	....	....	....	....	....	....	....	....
1972-73	Ottawa Nationals	WHA	75	42	49	91	....	....	....	42	....	....	....	....	....	....	....	....	....	....	3	3	3	6	4	....	....	....
1973-74	Toronto Toros	WHA	78	37	55	92	....	....	....	31	....	....	....	....	....	....	....	....	....	....	12	2	12	14	4	....	....	....
1974-75	New England Whalers	WHA	73	35	39	74	....	....	....	50	....	....	....	....	....	....	....	....	....	....	6	2	5	7	14	....	....	....
1975-76	New England Whalers	WHA	35	12	21	33	....	....	....	6	....	....	....	....	....	....	....	....	....	....	....	....	....	....	....	....	....	....
	Edmonton Oilers	WHA	26	5	16	21	....	....	....	6	....	....	....	....	....	....	....	....	....	....	4	1	1	2	2	....	....	....

			REGULAR SEASON																		PLAYOFFS							
Season	Club	League	GP	G	A	Pts	AG	AA	APts	PIM	PP	SH	GW	S	%	TGF	PGF	TGA	PGA	+/–	GP	G	A	Pts	PIM	PP	SH	GW
1976-77	Birmingham Bulls	WHA	3	1	0	1	....	....	....	0	....	....	....	....	....	....	....	....	....	....	....	....	....	....	....	....	....	....
1976-77	Barrie Flyers	OHA Sr.	20	7	20	27	....	....	....	6	....	....	....	....	....	....	....	....	....	....	....	....	....	....	....	....	....	....
1977-78	Barrie Flyers	OHA Sr.	35	21	23	44	....	....	....	27	....	....	....	....	....	....	....	....	....	....	....	....	....	....	....	....	....	....
	NHL Totals		**278**	**55**	**73**	**128**	**60**	**69**	**129**	**172**	**4**	**0**	**7**	**602**	**9.1**	**203**	**23**	**177**	**13**		**18**	**2**	**4**	**6**	**14**	**0**	**0**	**0**
	Other Major League Totals		290	132	180	312	....	....	....	135	....	....	....	....	....	....	....	....	....		25	8	21	29	24	....	....	....

WHA Second All-Star Team (1974)

Played in NHL All-Star Game (1968)

Traded to **Boston** by **Toronto** for Jim Harrison, December 10, 1969. Claimed by **California** from **Boston** in Intra-League Draft, June 8, 1971. Selected by **Ontario-Ottawa** (WHA) in 1972 WHA General Player Draft, February 12, 1972. Transferred to **Toronto** (WHA) after **Ottawa** (WHA) franchise relocated, May, 1973. Traded to **New England** (WHA) by **Toronto** (WHA) for future considerations (Jim Dorey, December, 1974), September, 1974. Traded to **Edmonton** (WHA) by **New England** (WHA) for Mike Rogers and future considerations, January, 1976. Signed as a free agent by **Birmingham** (WHA), January, 1977.

• CARLIN, BRIAN

Brian Carlin LW – L. 5'10", 175 lbs. b: Calgary, Alta., 6/13/1950. Los Angeles' 5th choice, 86th overall, in 1970 Amateur Draft.

Season	Club	League	GP	G	A	Pts	AG	AA	APts	PIM	PP	SH	GW	S	%	TGF	PGF	TGA	PGA	+/–	GP	G	A	Pts	PIM	PP	SH	GW
1967-68	Calgary Centennials	WCJHL	57	11	16	27	....	....	....	47	....	....	....	....	....	....	....	....	....	....	....	....	....	....	....	....	....	....
1968-69	Calgary Centennials	WCJHL	56	15	14	29	....	....	....	40	....	....	....	....	....	....	....	....	....	....	....	....	....	....	....	....	....	....
1969-70	Calgary Centennials	WCJHL	48	16	24	40	....	....	....	33	....	....	....	....	....	....	....	....	....	....	....	....	....	....	....	....	....	....
1970-71	Medicine Hat Tigers	WCJHL	65	44	56	100	....	....	....	46	....	....	....	....	....	....	....	....	....	....	....	....	....	....	....	....	....	....
1971-72	**Los Angeles Kings**	**NHL**	**5**	**1**	**0**	**1**	**1**	**0**	**1**	**0**	**0**	**0**	**0**	**3**	**33.3**	**1**	**0**	**1**	**0**	**0**								
	Springfield Kings	AHL	67	35	31	66	....	....	....	6	....	....	....	....	....	....	....	....	....	....	5	0	0	0	2	....	....	....
1972-73	Alberta Oilers	WHA	65	12	22	34	....	....	....	6	....	....	....	....	....	....	....	....	....	....	....	....	....	....	....	....	....	....
1973-74	Edmonton Oilers	WHA	5	1	0	1	....	....	....	0	....	....	....	....	....	....	....	....	....	....	....	....	....	....	....	....	....	....
	Winston-Salem Polar Bears	SHL	66	36	42	78	....	....	....	29	....	....	....	....	....	....	....	....	....	....	7	2	1	3	2	....	....	....
1974-75	Calgary Trojans	ASHL	STATISTICS NOT AVAILABLE																									
1975-76	Calgary Trojans	ASHL	STATISTICS NOT AVAILABLE																									
1976-77	Calgary Trojans	ASHL	20	18	20	38	....	....	....	10	....	....	....	....	....	....	....	....	....	....	....	....	....	....	....	....	....	....
	NHL Totals		**5**	**1**	**0**	**1**	**1**	**0**	**1**	**0**	**0**	**0**	**0**	**3**	**33.3**	**1**	**0**	**1**	**0**		....	....	....	....	....	....	....	....
	Other Major League Totals		70	13	22	35	....	....	....	6	....	....	....	....	....	....	....	....	....		....	....	....	....	....	....	....	....

SHL Second All-Star Team (1974)

Selected by **Alberta** (WHA) in 1972 WHA General Player Draft, February 12, 1972.

• CARLSON, JACK

Jack "The Big Bopper" Carlson LW – L. 6'3", 205 lbs. b: Virginia, MN, 8/23/1954. Detroit's 7th choice, 117th overall, in 1974 Amateur Draft.

Season	Club	League	GP	G	A	Pts	AG	AA	APts	PIM	PP	SH	GW	S	%	TGF	PGF	TGA	PGA	+/–	GP	G	A	Pts	PIM	PP	SH	GW
1972-73	Minnesota Rangers	CAJHL	DID NOT PLAY																									
1973-74	Marquette Rangers	USHL	42	42	29	71	....	....	....	159	....	....	....	....	....	....	....	....	....	....	....	....	....	....	....	....	....	....
1974-75	Minnesota Fighting Saints	WHA	32	5	5	10	....	....	....	85	....	....	....	....	....	....	....	....	....	....	10	1	2	3	41	....	....	....
	Johnstown Jets	NAHL	50	27	22	49	....	....	....	248	....	....	....	....	....	....	....	....	....	....	....	....	....	....	....	....	....	....
1975-76	Minnesota Fighting Saints	WHA	58	8	10	18	....	....	....	189	....	....	....	....	....	....	....	....	....	....	....	....	....	....	....	....	....	....
	Edmonton Oilers	WHA	10	1	1	2	....	....	....	31	....	....	....	....	....	....	....	....	....	....	4	0	0	0	4	....	....	....
1976-77	Minnesota Fighting Saints	WHA	36	4	3	7	....	....	....	55	....	....	....	....	....	....	....	....	....	....	....	....	....	....	....	....	....	....
	New England Whalers	WHA	35	7	5	12	....	....	....	81	....	....	....	....	....	....	....	....	....	....	5	1	1	2	9	....	....	....
1977-78	New England Whalers	WHA	67	9	20	29	....	....	....	192	....	....	....	....	....	....	....	....	....	....	9	1	1	2	14	....	....	....
1978-79	New England Whalers	WHA	34	2	7	9	....	....	....	61	....	....	....	....	....	....	....	....	....	....	....	....	....	....	....	....	....	....
	Minnesota North Stars	**NHL**	**16**	**3**	**0**	**3**	**3**	**0**	**3**	**40**	**0**	**0**	**0**	**18**	**16.7**	**9**	**0**	**7**	**0**	**+2**	....	....	....	....	....	....	....	....
1979-80			DID NOT PLAY – INJURED																									
1980-81	**Minnesota North Stars**	**NHL**	**43**	**7**	**2**	**9**	**6**	**1**	**7**	**108**	**0**	**0**	**0**	**24**	**29.2**	**18**	**0**	**23**	**0**	**–5**	**15**	**1**	**2**	**3**	**50**	**0**	**0**	**0**
1981-82	**Minnesota North Stars**	**NHL**	**57**	**8**	**4**	**12**	**6**	**3**	**9**	**103**	**1**	**0**	**1**	**39**	**20.5**	**15**	**1**	**19**	**0**	**–5**	**1**	**0**	**0**	**0**	**15**	**0**	**0**	**0**
1982-83	**St. Louis Blues**	**NHL**	**54**	**6**	**1**	**7**	**5**	**1**	**6**	**58**	**0**	**0**	**1**	**43**	**14.0**	**14**	**1**	**16**	**0**	**–3**	**4**	**0**	**0**	**0**	**5**	**0**	**0**	**0**
1983-84	**St. Louis Blues**	**NHL**	**58**	**6**	**8**	**14**	**5**	**5**	**10**	**95**	**0**	**0**	**0**	**35**	**17.1**	**21**	**1**	**14**	**3**	**+9**	**5**	**0**	**0**	**0**	**2**	**0**	**0**	**0**
1984-85			DID NOT PLAY – RETIRED																									
1985-86			DID NOT PLAY – RETIRED																									
1986-87	**Minnesota North Stars**	**NHL**	**8**	**0**	**0**	**0**	**0**	**0**	**0**	**13**	**0**	**0**	**0**	**1**	**0.0**	**1**	**0**	**1**	**0**	**0**	....	....	....	....	....	....	....	....
	NHL Totals		**236**	**30**	**15**	**45**	**25**	**10**	**35**	**417**	**1**	**0**	**2**	**160**	**18.8**	**78**	**3**	**80**	**3**		**25**	**1**	**2**	**3**	**72**	**0**	**0**	**0**
	Other Major League Totals		272	36	51	87	....	....	....	694	....	....	....	....	....	....	....	....	....		28	3	4	7	68	....	....	....

Selected by **Minnesota** (WHA) in 1974 WHA Amateur Draft, June, 1974. Signed as a free agent by **Edmonton** (WHA) after **Minnesota** (WHA) franchise folded, March, 1976. Claimed by **Florida-Minnesota** (WHA) from **Edmonton** in 1976 WHA Intra-League Draft, June, 1976. Traded to **Edmonton** (WHA) by **Minnesota** (WHA) with Mike Antonovich, Bill Butters, Dave Keon, Jean-Louis Levasseur, Steve Carlson and John McKenzie for cash, January, 1977. Traded to **New England** (WHA) by **Edmonton** (WHA) with Dave Keon, Steve Carlson, Dave Dryden and John McKenzie for future considerations (Dave Debol, June, 1977), Dan Arndt and cash, January, 1977. Rights traded to **Minnesota** by **Detroit** for future considerations, July 27, 1978. Traded to **Minnesota** by **New England** (WHA) for future considerations, February 1, 1979. • Missed entire 1979-80 season after under going off-season back surgery. Claimed by **St. Louis** from **Minnesota** in Waiver Draft, October 4, 1982. Signed as a free agent by **Minnesota**, November, 1986.

• CARLSON, KENT

Kent Carlson D – L. 6'3", 200 lbs. b: Concord, NH, 1/11/1962. Montreal's 3rd choice, 32nd overall, in 1982 Entry Draft.

Season	Club	League	GP	G	A	Pts	AG	AA	APts	PIM	PP	SH	GW	S	%	TGF	PGF	TGA	PGA	+/–	GP	G	A	Pts	PIM	PP	SH	GW
1981-82	St. Lawrence University	ECAC	28	8	14	22	....	....	....	24	....	....	....	....	....	....	....	....	....	....	....	....	....	....	....	....	....	....
1982-83	St. Lawrence University	ECAC	35	10	23	33	....	....	....	56	....	....	....	....	....	....	....	....	....	....	....	....	....	....	....	....	....	....
1983-84	**Montreal Canadiens**	**NHL**	**65**	**3**	**7**	**10**	**2**	**5**	**7**	**73**	**0**	**0**	**2**	**41**	**7.3**	**33**	**4**	**44**	**0**	**–15**	....	....	....	....	....	....	....	....
1984-85	**Montreal Canadiens**	**NHL**	**18**	**1**	**1**	**2**	**1**	**1**	**2**	**33**	**0**	**0**	**0**	**5**	**20.0**	**5**	**0**	**4**	**0**	**+1**	....	....	....	....	....	....	....	....
	Sherbrooke Canadiens	AHL	13	1	4	5	....	....	....	7	....	....	....	....	....	....	....	....	....	....	2	1	1	2	0	....	....	....
1985-86	**Montreal Canadiens**	**NHL**	**2**	**0**	**0**	**0**	**0**	**0**	**0**	**0**	**0**	**0**	**0**	**0**	**0.0**	**0**	**0**	**0**	**0**	**0**	....	....	....	....	....	....	....	....
	Sherbrooke Canadiens	AHL	35	11	15	26	....	....	....	79	....	....	....	....	....	....	....	....	....	....	....	....	....	....	....	....	....	....
	St. Louis Blues	**NHL**	**26**	**2**	**3**	**5**	**2**	**2**	**4**	**42**	**0**	**0**	**0**	**14**	**14.3**	**6**	**0**	**4**	**0**	**+2**	**5**	**0**	**0**	**0**	**11**	**0**	**0**	**0**
1986-87			DID NOT PLAY – INJURED																									
1987-88	Peoria Rivermen	IHL	52	5	16	21	....	....	....	88	....	....	....	....	....	....	....	....	....	....	....	....	....	....	....	....	....	....
	St. Louis Blues	**NHL**	....	....	....	....	....	....	....	....	....	....	....	....	....	....	....	....	....	....	**3**	**0**	**0**	**0**	**2**	....	....	....
1988-89	**Washington Capitals**	**NHL**	**2**	**1**	**0**	**1**	**1**	**0**	**1**	**0**	**0**	**0**	**0**	**1**	**100.0**	**2**	**0**	**0**	**0**	**+2**	....	....	....	....	....	....	....	....
	Baltimore Skipjacks	AHL	28	2	8	10	....	....	....	69	....	....	....	....	....	....	....	....	....	....	....	....	....	....	....	....	....	....
	NHL Totals		**113**	**7**	**11**	**18**	**6**	**8**	**14**	**148**	**0**	**0**	**2**	**61**	**11.5**	**46**	**4**	**52**	**0**		**8**	**0**	**0**	**0**	**13**	**0**	**0**	**0**

ECAC Second All-Star Team (1983)

Traded to **St. Louis** by **Montreal** for Graham Herring and St. Louis' 5th round choice (Eric Aubertin) in 1986 Entry Draft, January 31, 1986. • Missed entire 1986-87 season after undergoing off-season spinal fusion surgery. Traded to **Winnipeg** by **St. Louis** with St. Louis' 12th round choice (Sergei Kharin) in 1989 Entry Draft and 4th round choice (Scott Levins) in 1990 Entry Draft for Peter Douris, September 29, 1988. Traded to **Washington** by **Winnipeg** for future considerations, January 23, 1989.

• CARLSON, STEVE

Steve Carlson C – L. 6'3", 180 lbs. b: Virginia, MN, 8/26/1955. Detroit's 10th choice, 131st overall, in 1975 Amateur Draft.

Season	Club	League	GP	G	A	Pts	AG	AA	APts	PIM	PP	SH	GW	S	%	TGF	PGF	TGA	PGA	+/–	GP	G	A	Pts	PIM	PP	SH	GW
1973-74	Marquette Rangers	USHL	42	34	45	79	....	....	....	77	....	....	....	....	....	....	....	....	....	....	....	....	....	....	....	....	....	....
1974-75	Johnstown Jets	NAHL	70	30	58	88	....	....	....	84	....	....	....	....	....	....	....	....	....	....	12	6	4	10	....	....	....	....
1975-76	Johnstown Jets	NAHL	40	22	24	46	....	....	....	55	....	....	....	....	....	....	....	....	....	....	9	4	5	9	6	....	....	....
	Minnesota Fighting Saints	WHA	10	0	1	1	....	....	....	23	....	....	....	....	....	....	....	....	....	....	....	....	....	....	....	....	....	....
1976-77	Minnesota Fighting Saints	WHA	21	5	8	13	....	....	....	8	....	....	....	....	....	....	....	....	....	....	....	....	....	....	....	....	....	....
	New England Whalers	WHA	31	4	9	13	....	....	....	40	....	....	....	....	....	....	....	....	....	....	5	0	0	0	9	....	....	....
1977-78	Springfield Indians	AHL	37	21	15	36	....	....	....	48	....	....	....	....	....	....	....	....	....	....	....	....	....	....	....	....	....	....
	New England Whalers	WHA	38	6	7	13	....	....	....	11	....	....	....	....	....	....	....	....	....	....	13	2	7	9	2	....	....	....
1978-79	Edmonton Oilers	WHA	73	18	22	40	....	....	....	50	....	....	....	....	....	....	....	....	....	....	11	1	1	2	12	....	....	....
1979-80	**Los Angeles Kings**	**NHL**	**52**	**9**	**12**	**21**	**8**	**9**	**17**	**23**	**1**	**0**	**1**	**45**	**20.0**	**33**	**6**	**59**	**25**	**–7**	**4**	**1**	**1**	**2**	**7**	**0**	**0**	**0**
1980-81	Houston Apollos	CHL	27	13	21	34	....	....	....	29	....	....	....	....	....	....	....	....	....	....	....	....	....	....	....	....	....	....
	Springfield Indians	AHL	32	10	14	24	....	....	....	44	....	....	....	....	....	....	....	....	....	....	7	2	2	4	39	....	....	....
1981-82	Nashville South Stars	CHL	59	23	39	62	....	....	....	63	....	....	....	....	....	....	....	....	....	....	....	....	....	....	....	....	....	....
1982-83	Birmingham South Stars	CHL	69	25	42	67	....	....	....	73	....	....	....	....	....	....	....	....	....	....	9	1	4	5	4	....	....	....
1983-84	Baltimore Skipjacks	AHL	63	9	30	39	....	....	....	70	....	....	....	....	....	....	....	....	....	....	10	7	3	10	8	....	....	....

			REGULAR SEASON																		PLAYOFFS							
Season	Club	League	GP	G	A	Pts	AG	AA	APts	PIM	PP	SH	GW	S	%	TGF	PGF	TGA	PGA	+/–	GP	G	A	Pts	PIM	PP	SH	GW
1984-85	Baltimore Skipjacks	AHL	76	18	29	47	....	....	....	69	....	....	....	....	....	....	....	....	....	....	15	2	6	8	4	....	....	....
1985-86	Baltimore Skipjacks	AHL	66	9	27	36	....	....	....	56	....	....	....	....	....	....	....	....	....	....	....	....	....	....	....	....	....	....
1986-87	Baltimore Skipjacks	AHL	67	12	13	25	....	....	....	32	....	....	....	....	....	....	....	....	....	....	....	....	....	....	....	....	....	....
	NHL Totals		**52**	**9**	**12**	**21**	**8**	**9**	**17**	**23**	**1**	**0**	**1**	**45**	**20.0**	**33**	**6**	**59**	**25**		**4**	**1**	**1**	**2**	**7**	**0**	**0**	**0**
	Other Major League Totals		173	33	47	80	....	....	....	132	....	....	....	....	....	....	....	....	....		29	3	8	11	23	....	....	....

Selected by **Minnesota** (WHA) in 1974 WHA Amateur Draft, June, 1974. Signed as a free agent by **New England** (WHA) after **Minnesota** (WHA) franchise folded, May, 1976. Claimed by **Florida-Minnesota** (WHA) from **New England** (WHA) in 1976 WHA Intra-League Draft, June, 1976. Traded to **Edmonton** (WHA) by **Minnesota** (WHA) with Mike Antonovich, Bill Butters, Dave Keon, Jack Carlson, Jean-Louis Levasseur and John McKenzie fror cash, January, 1977. Traded to **New England** (WHA) by **Edmonton** (WHA) with Dave Keon, Jack Carlson, Dave Dryden and John McKenzie for future considerations (Dave Debol), Dan Arndt and cash, January, 1977. Claimed on waivers by **Edmonton** (WHA) from **New England** (WHA), May, 1978. NHL rights traded to **Detroit** by **LA Kings** for NHL rights to Steve Short, December 6, 1978. Reclaimed by **LA Kings** from **Edmonton** prior to Expansion Draft, June 9, 1979. Signed as a free agent by **Minnesota**, August 9, 1982. Signed as a free agent by **Pittsburgh**, August 15, 1983.

• CARLSSON, ANDERS

Anders Carlsson C – L. 5′11″, 185 lbs. b: Gavle, Sweden, 11/25/1960. New Jersey's 5th choice, 66th overall, in 1986 Entry Draft.

Season	Club	League	GP	G	A	Pts	AG	AA	APts	PIM	PP	SH	GW	S	%	TGF	PGF	TGA	PGA	+/–	GP	G	A	Pts	PIM	PP	SH	GW
1978-79	Brynas IF Gavle	Sweden	1	0	0	0	....	....	....	2	....	....	....	....	....	....	....	....	....	....	....	....	....	....	....	....	....	....
1979-80	Brynas IF Gavle	Sweden	17	0	1	1	....	....	....	6	....	....	....	....	....	....	....	....	....	....	1	0	0	0	0	....	....	....
1980-81	Byrnas IF Gavle	Sweden	36	8	8	16	....	....	....	36	....	....	....	....	....	....	....	....	....	....	....	....	....	....	....	....	....	....
1981-82	Brynas IF Gavle	Sweden	35	5	5	10	....	....	....	22	....	....	....	....	....	....	....	....	....	....	....	....	....	....	....	....	....	....
1982-83	Brynas IF Gavle	Sweden	35	18	13	31	....	....	....	26	....	....	....	....	....	....	....	....	....	....	....	....	....	....	....	....	....	....
1983-84	Brynas IF Gavle	Sweden	35	8	26	34	....	....	....	34	....	....	....	....	....	....	....	....	....	....	....	....	....	....	....	....	....	....
1984-85	Sodertalje	Sweden	36	20	14	34	....	....	....	18	....	....	....	....	....	....	....	....	....	....	8	0	3	3	18	....	....	....
1985-86	Sodertalje	Sweden	36	12	26	38	....	....	....	20	....	....	....	....	....	....	....	....	....	....	7	2	4	6	0	....	....	....
	Sweden	WEC-A	10	6	6	12	....	....	....	12	....	....	....	....	....	....	....	....	....	....	....	....	....	....	....	....	....	....
1986-87	**New Jersey Devils**	**NHL**	**48**	**2**	**18**	**20**	**2**	**13**	**15**	**14**	**0**	**0**	**0**	**35**	**5.7**	**32**	**6**	**38**	**1**	**–11**	....	....	....	....	....	....	....	....
	Maine Mariners	AHL	6	0	6	6	....	....	....	2	....	....	....	....	....	....	....	....	....	....	....	....	....	....	....	....	....	....
	Sweden	WEC-A	10	4	3	7	....	....	....	6	....	....	....	....	....	....	....	....	....	....	....	....	....	....	....	....	....	....
1987-88	Sweden	C Cup	6	1	0	1	....	....	....	0	....	....	....	....	....	....	....	....	....	....	....	....	....	....	....	....	....	....
	New Jersey Devils	**NHL**	**9**	**1**	**0**	**1**	**1**	**0**	**1**	**0**	**0**	**0**	**0**	**6**	**16.7**	**2**	**0**	**8**	**1**	**–5**	**3**	**1**	**0**	**1**	**2**	**0**	**0**	**1**
	Utica Devils	AHL	33	12	22	34	....	....	....	16	....	....	....	....	....	....	....	....	....	....	....	....	....	....	....	....	....	....
1988-89	**New Jersey Devils**	**NHL**	**47**	**4**	**8**	**12**	**3**	**6**	**9**	**20**	**0**	**0**	**0**	**42**	**9.5**	**20**	**3**	**33**	**19**	**+3**	....	....	....	....	....	....	....	....
	Utica Devils	AHL	7	2	4	6	....	....	....	4	....	....	....	....	....	....	....	....	....	....	....	....	....	....	....	....	....	....
	Sweden	WEC-A	10	2	3	5	....	....	....	8	....	....	....	....	....	....	....	....	....	....	....	....	....	....	....	....	....	....
1989-90	Brynas IF Gavle	Sweden	40	12	*31	43	....	....	....	29	....	....	....	....	....	....	....	....	....	....	2	0	2	2	0	....	....	....
	Sweden	WEC-A	8	1	0	1	....	....	....	2	....	....	....	....	....	....	....	....	....	....	....	....	....	....	....	....	....	....
1990-91	Brynas IF Gavle	Sweden	34	11	24	35	....	....	....	22	....	....	....	....	....	....	....	....	....	....	2	1	1	2	2	....	....	....
	Sweden	WEC-A	6	1	1	2	....	....	....	6	....	....	....	....	....	....	....	....	....	....	....	....	....	....	....	....	....	....
1991-92	Byrnas IF Gavle	Sweden	DID NOT PLAY – INJURED																		....	....	....	....	....	....	....	....
1992-93	Brynas IF Gavle	Sweden	40	13	18	31	....	....	....	28	....	....	....	....	....	....	....	....	....	....	10	3	2	5	6	....	....	....
1993-94	Brynas IF Gavle	Sweden	36	6	11	17	....	....	....	47	....	....	....	....	....	....	....	....	....	....	7	2	2	4	4	....	....	....
1994-95	Vastaras IK	Sweden	39	16	22	38	....	....	....	40	....	....	....	....	....	....	....	....	....	....	4	1	3	4	4	....	....	....
1995-96	Leksands IF	Sweden	36	8	18	26	....	....	....	26	....	....	....	....	....	....	....	....	....	....	5	2	1	3	4	....	....	....
1996-97	Leksands IF	Sweden	50	12	27	39	....	....	....	52	....	....	....	....	....	....	....	....	....	....	9	1	8	0	12	....	....	....
	Sweden	WC-A	11	1	1	2	....	....	....	6	....	....	....	....	....	....	....	....	....	....	....	....	....	....	....	....	....	....
1997-98	Leksands IF	EuroHL	6	1	6	7	....	....	....	8	....	....	....	....	....	....	....	....	....	....	....	....	....	....	....	....	....	....
	Leksands IF	Sweden	41	11	20	31	....	....	....	28	....	....	....	....	....	....	....	....	....	....	2	0	0	0	0	....	....	....
	NHL Totals		**104**	**7**	**26**	**33**	**6**	**19**	**25**	**34**	**0**	**0**	**0**	**83**	**8.4**	**54**	**9**	**79**	**21**		**3**	**1**	**0**	**1**	**2**	**0**	**0**	**1**

Swedish World All-Star Team (1986)

• CARLYLE, RANDY

Randy Carlyle D – L. 5′10″, 200 lbs. b: Sudbury, Ont., 4/19/1956. Toronto's 1st choice, 30th overall, in 1976 Amateur Draft.

Season	Club	League	GP	G	A	Pts	AG	AA	APts	PIM	PP	SH	GW	S	%	TGF	PGF	TGA	PGA	+/–	GP	G	A	Pts	PIM	PP	SH	GW
1973-74	Sudbury Wolves	OHA	12	0	8	8	....	....	....	21	....	....	....	....	....	....	....	....	....	....	....	....	....	....	....	....	....	....
1974-75	Sudbury Wolves	OHA	67	17	47	64	....	....	....	118	....	....	....	....	....	....	....	....	....	....	15	3	6	9	21	....	....	....
1975-76	Sudbury Wolves	OHA	60	15	64	79	....	....	....	126	....	....	....	....	....	....	....	....	....	....	17	6	13	19	50	....	....	....
1976-77	**Toronto Maple Leafs**	**NHL**	**45**	**0**	**5**	**5**	**0**	**4**	**4**	**51**	**0**	**0**	**0**	**30**	**0.0**	**23**	**0**	**45**	**3**	**–19**	**9**	**0**	**1**	**1**	**20**	**0**	**0**	**0**
	Dallas Black Hawks	CHL	26	2	7	9	....	....	....	63	....	....	....	....	....	....	....	....	....	....	....	....	....	....	....	....	....	....
1977-78	**Toronto Maple Leafs**	**NHL**	**49**	**2**	**11**	**13**	**2**	**9**	**11**	**31**	**0**	**0**	**0**	**54**	**3.7**	**37**	**4**	**39**	**10**	**+4**	**7**	**0**	**1**	**1**	**8**	**0**	**0**	**0**
	Dallas Black Hawks	CHL	21	3	14	17	....	....	....	31	....	....	....	....	....	....	....	....	....	....	....	....	....	....	....	....	....	....
1978-79	**Pittsburgh Penguins**	**NHL**	**70**	**13**	**34**	**47**	**12**	**26**	**38**	**78**	**3**	**1**	**3**	**200**	**6.5**	**110**	**32**	**99**	**19**	**+4**	**7**	**0**	**0**	**0**	**12**	**0**	**0**	**0**
1979-80	**Pittsburgh Penguins**	**NHL**	**67**	**8**	**28**	**36**	**7**	**21**	**28**	**45**	**3**	**0**	**1**	**123**	**6.5**	**89**	**28**	**99**	**15**	**–23**	**5**	**1**	**0**	**1**	**4**	**0**	**0**	**0**
1980-81	**Pittsburgh Penguins**	**NHL**	**76**	**16**	**67**	**83**	**13**	**47**	**60**	**136**	**7**	**1**	**1**	**242**	**6.6**	**177**	**75**	**167**	**49**	**–16**	**5**	**4**	**5**	**9**	**9**	**0**	**1**	**0**
1981-82	**Pittsburgh Penguins**	**NHL**	**73**	**11**	**64**	**75**	**9**	**42**	**51**	**131**	**7**	**1**	**0**	**193**	**5.7**	**167**	**78**	**154**	**49**	**–16**	**5**	**1**	**3**	**4**	**16**	**0**	**0**	**0**
1982-83	**Pittsburgh Penguins**	**NHL**	**61**	**15**	**41**	**56**	**12**	**28**	**40**	**110**	**8**	**1**	**0**	**177**	**8.5**	**112**	**47**	**131**	**40**	**–26**	....	....	....	....	....	....	....	....
1983-84	**Pittsburgh Penguins**	**NHL**	**50**	**3**	**23**	**26**	**2**	**16**	**18**	**82**	**0**	**0**	**1**	**107**	**2.8**	**68**	**30**	**91**	**28**	**–25**	....	....	....	....	....	....	....	....
	Winnipeg Jets	**NHL**	**5**	**0**	**3**	**3**	**0**	**2**	**2**	**2**	**0**	**0**	**0**	**5**	**0.0**	**10**	**3**	**4**	**1**	**+4**	**3**	**0**	**2**	**2**	**4**	**0**	**0**	**0**
1984-85	**Winnipeg Jets**	**NHL**	**71**	**13**	**38**	**51**	**11**	**26**	**37**	**98**	**6**	**0**	**2**	**135**	**9.6**	**155**	**45**	**128**	**41**	**+23**	**8**	**1**	**5**	**6**	**13**	**1**	**0**	**0**
1985-86	**Winnipeg Jets**	**NHL**	**68**	**16**	**33**	**49**	**13**	**22**	**35**	**93**	**3**	**0**	**2**	**152**	**10.5**	**123**	**37**	**128**	**30**	**–12**	....	....	....	....	....	....	....	....
1986-87	**Winnipeg Jets**	**NHL**	**71**	**16**	**26**	**42**	**14**	**19**	**33**	**93**	**5**	**0**	**4**	**172**	**9.3**	**106**	**27**	**100**	**15**	**–6**	**10**	**1**	**5**	**6**	**18**	**0**	**0**	**0**
1987-88	**Winnipeg Jets**	**NHL**	**78**	**15**	**44**	**59**	**13**	**31**	**44**	**210**	**8**	**0**	**1**	**165**	**9.1**	**134**	**75**	**103**	**24**	**–20**	**5**	**0**	**2**	**2**	**10**	**0**	**0**	**0**
1988-89	**Winnipeg Jets**	**NHL**	**78**	**6**	**38**	**44**	**5**	**27**	**32**	**78**	**2**	**0**	**2**	**124**	**4.8**	**108**	**38**	**108**	**19**	**–19**	....	....	....	....	....	....	....	....
	Canada	WEC-A	9	1	4	5	....	....	....	4	....	....	....	....	....	....	....	....	....	....	....	....	....	....	....	....	....	....
1989-90	**Winnipeg Jets**	**NHL**	**53**	**3**	**15**	**18**	**3**	**11**	**14**	**50**	**2**	**0**	**0**	**92**	**3.3**	**71**	**11**	**63**	**11**	**+8**	....	....	....	....	....	....	....	....
1990-91	**Winnipeg Jets**	**NHL**	**52**	**9**	**19**	**28**	**8**	**14**	**22**	**44**	**2**	**0**	**1**	**89**	**10.1**	**66**	**14**	**59**	**13**	**+6**	....	....	....	....	....	....	....	....
1991-92	**Winnipeg Jets**	**NHL**	**66**	**1**	**9**	**10**	**1**	**7**	**8**	**54**	**0**	**0**	**0**	**84**	**1.2**	**49**	**4**	**68**	**27**	**+4**	**5**	**1**	**0**	**1**	**6**	**0**	**0**	**0**
1992-93	**Winnipeg Jets**	**NHL**	**22**	**1**	**1**	**2**	**1**	**1**	**2**	**14**	**0**	**0**	**0**	**21**	**4.8**	**10**	**0**	**23**	**7**	**–8**	....	....	....	....	....	....	....	....
	NHL Totals		**1055**	**148**	**499**	**647**	**128**	**353**	**479**	**1400**	**56**	**4**	**18**	**2173**	**6.8**	**1621**	**548**	**1609**	**401**		**69**	**9**	**24**	**33**	**120**	**1**	**1**	**0**

OHA Second All-Star Team (1976) • NHL First All-Star Team (1981) • Won James Norris Trophy (1981)

Played in NHL All-Star Game (1981, 1982, 1985, 1993)

Traded to **Pittsburgh** by **Toronto** with George Ferguson for Dave Burrows, June 14, 1978. Traded to **Winnipeg** by **Pittsburgh** for Winnipeg's 1st round choice (Doug Bodger) in 1984 Entry Draft and future considerations (Moe Mantha, May 1, 1984), March 5, 1984.

• CARNBACK, PATRIK

Patrik Carnback C – L. 6′, 187 lbs. b: Goteborg, Sweden, 2/1/1968. Montreal's 7th choice, 125th overall, in 1988 Entry Draft.

Season	Club	League	GP	G	A	Pts	AG	AA	APts	PIM	PP	SH	GW	S	%	TGF	PGF	TGA	PGA	+/–	GP	G	A	Pts	PIM	PP	SH	GW
1986-87	Vastra Frolunda	Sweden 2	28	3	1	4	....	....	....	4	....	....	....	....	....	....	....	....	....	....	....	....	....	....	....	....	....	....
1987-88	Vastra Frolunda	Sweden 2	33	16	19	35	....	....	....	24	....	....	....	....	....	....	....	....	....	....	11	4	5	9	8	....	....	....
1988-89	Vastra Frolunda	Sweden 2	53	39	36	75	....	....	....	52	....	....	....	....	....	....	....	....	....	....	....	....	....	....	....	....	....	....
1989-90	Vastra Frolunda	Sweden	40	26	27	53	....	....	....	34	....	....	....	....	....	....	....	....	....	....	....	....	....	....	....	....	....	....
1990-91	Vastra Frolunda	Sweden	22	10	9	19	....	....	....	46	....	....	....	....	....	....	....	....	....	....	28	15	24	39	24	....	....	....
1991-92	Vastra Frolunda	Sweden	33	17	22	39	....	....	....	32	....	....	....	....	....	....	....	....	....	....	3	1	5	6	20	....	....	....
	Sweden	Olympics	7	1	1	2	....	....	....	2	....	....	....	....	....	....	....	....	....	....	....	....	....	....	....	....	....	....
	Sweden	WC-A	8	2	2	4	....	....	....	16	....	....	....	....	....	....	....	....	....	....	....	....	....	....	....	....	....	....
1992-93	**Montreal Canadiens**	**NHL**	**6**	**0**	**0**	**0**	**0**	**0**	**0**	**2**	**0**	**0**	**0**	**4**	**0.0**	**0**	**0**	**4**	**0**	**–4**	....	....	....	....	....	....	....	....
	Fredericton Canadiens	AHL	45	20	37	57	....	....	....	45	....	....	....	....	....	....	....	....	....	....	5	0	3	3	14	....	....	....
1993-94	**Anaheim Mighty Ducks**	**NHL**	**73**	**12**	**11**	**23**	**11**	**8**	**19**	**54**	**3**	**0**	**2**	**81**	**14.8**	**30**	**4**	**37**	**3**	**–8**	....	....	....	....	....	....	....	....
	Sweden	WC-A	8	1	0	1	....	....	....	8	....	....	....	....	....	....	....	....	....	....	....	....	....	....	....	....	....	....
1994-95	Vastra Frolunda	Sweden	14	2	6	8	....	....	....	20	....	....	....	....	....	....	....	....	....	....	....	....	....	....	....	....	....	....
	Anaheim Mighty Ducks	**NHL**	**41**	**6**	**15**	**21**	**11**	**22**	**33**	**32**	**0**	**0**	**0**	**58**	**10.3**	**24**	**2**	**32**	**2**	**–8**	....	....	....	....	....	....	....	....
1995-96	**Anaheim Mighty Ducks**	**NHL**	**34**	**6**	**12**	**18**	**6**	**10**	**16**	**34**	**1**	**0**	**0**	**54**	**11.1**	**30**	**10**	**17**	**0**	**+3**	....	....	....	....	....	....	....	....
	Kolner Haie	Germany	5	1	6	7	....	....	....	2	....	....	....	....	....	....	....	....	....	....	14	8	8	16	33	....	....	....
1996-97	Kolner Haie	Germany	45	20	41	61	....	....	....	72	....	....	....	....	....	....	....	....	....	....	4	1	1	2	2	....	....	....
1997-98	Vastra Frolunda	Sweden	44	8	17	25	....	....	....	38	....	....	....	....	....	....	....	....	....	....	6	3	3	6	6	....	....	....
	NHL Totals		**154**	**24**	**38**	**62**	**28**	**40**	**68**	**122**	**4**	**0**	**2**	**197**	**12.2**	**84**	**16**	**90**	**5**		....	....	....	....	....	....	....	....

Swedish Rookie of the Year (1990)

Traded to **Anaheim** by **Montreal** with Todd Ewen for Anaheim's 3rd round choice (Chris Murray) in 1994 Entry Draft, August 10, 1993.

			REGULAR SEASON																		PLAYOFFS							
Season	Club	League	GP	G	A	Pts	AG	AA	APts	PIM	PP	SH	GW	S	%	TGF	PGF	TGA	PGA	+/–	GP	G	A	Pts	PIM	PP	SH	GW

• CARNEY, KEITH

Keith Carney D – L. 6'2", 205 lbs. b: Providence, RI, 2/3/1970. Buffalo's 3rd choice, 76th overall, in 1988 Entry Draft.

Season	Club	League	GP	G	A	Pts	AG	AA	APts	PIM	PP	SH	GW	S	%	TGF	PGF	TGA	PGA	+/–	GP	G	A	Pts	PIM	PP	SH	GW
1987-88	Mount St. Charles	H.S.	23	12	43	55	....	....	....	....	....	....	....	....	....	....	....	....	....	....	....	....	....	....	....	....	....	....
1988-89	University of Maine	H.E.	40	4	22	26	....	....	....	24	....	....	....	....	....	....	....	....	....	....	....	....	....	....	....	....	....	....
1989-90	University of Maine	H.E.	41	3	41	44	....	....	....	43	....	....	....	....	....	....	....	....	....	....	....	....	....	....	....	....	....	....
	United States	WJC-A	7	0	3	3	....	....	....	2	....	....	....	....	....	....	....	....	....	....	....	....	....	....	....	....	....	....
1990-91	University of Maine	H.E.	40	7	49	56	....	....	....	38	....	....	....	....	....	....	....	....	....	....	....	....	....	....	....	....	....	....
1991-92	United States	Nat-Team	49	2	17	19	....	....	....	16	....	....	....	....	....	....	....	....	....	....	....	....	....	....	....	....	....	....
	Buffalo Sabres	**NHL**	**14**	**1**	**2**	**3**	**1**	**1**	**2**	**18**	**1**	**0**	**0**	**17**	**5.9**	**16**	**5**	**15**	**1**	**–3**	**7**	**0**	**3**	**3**	**0**	**0**	**0**	**0**
	Rochester Americans	AHL	24	1	10	11	....	....	....	2	....	....	....	....	....	....	....	....	....	....	2	0	2	2	0	....	....	....
1992-93	**Buffalo Sabres**	**NHL**	**30**	**2**	**4**	**6**	**2**	**3**	**5**	**55**	**0**	**0**	**1**	**26**	**7.7**	**26**	**5**	**24**	**6**	**+3**	**8**	**0**	**3**	**3**	**6**	**0**	**0**	**0**
	Rochester Americans	AHL	41	5	21	26	....	....	....	32	....	....	....	....	....	....	....	....	....	....	....	....	....	....	....	....	....	....
1993-94	**Buffalo Sabres**	**NHL**	**7**	**1**	**3**	**4**	**1**	**2**	**3**	**4**	**0**	**0**	**0**	**6**	**16.7**	**7**	**2**	**7**	**1**	**–1**	....	....	....	....	....	....	....	....
	Chicago Blackhawks	**NHL**	**30**	**3**	**5**	**8**	**3**	**4**	**7**	**35**	**0**	**0**	**0**	**31**	**9.7**	**34**	**2**	**26**	**9**	**+15**	**6**	**0**	**1**	**1**	**4**	**0**	**0**	**0**
	Indianapolis Ice	IHL	28	0	14	14	....	....	....	20	....	....	....	....	....	....	....	....	....	....	....	....	....	....	....	....	....	....
1994-95	**Chicago Blackhawks**	**NHL**	**18**	**1**	**0**	**1**	**2**	**0**	**2**	**11**	**0**	**0**	**1**	**14**	**7.1**	**8**	**1**	**9**	**1**	**–1**	**4**	**0**	**1**	**1**	**0**	**0**	**0**	**0**
1995-96	**Chicago Blackhawks**	**NHL**	**82**	**5**	**14**	**19**	**5**	**11**	**16**	**94**	**1**	**0**	**1**	**69**	**7.2**	**77**	**3**	**63**	**20**	**+31**	**10**	**0**	**3**	**3**	**4**	**0**	**0**	**0**
1996-97	**Chicago Blackhawks**	**NHL**	**81**	**3**	**15**	**18**	**3**	**13**	**16**	**62**	**0**	**0**	**1**	**77**	**3.9**	**75**	**4**	**80**	**35**	**+26**	**6**	**1**	**1**	**2**	**2**	**0**	**0**	**0**
1997-98	**Chicago Blackhawks**	**NHL**	**60**	**2**	**13**	**15**	**2**	**13**	**15**	**73**	**0**	**1**	**0**	**53**	**3.8**	**40**	**0**	**69**	**22**	**–7**	....	....	....	....	....	....	....	....
	United States	Olympics	4	0	0	0	....	....	....	2	....	....	....	....	....	....	....	....	....	....	....	....	....	....	....	....	....	....
	Phoenix Coyotes	**NHL**	**20**	**1**	**6**	**7**	**1**	**6**	**7**	**18**	**1**	**0**	**0**	**18**	**5.6**	**24**	**4**	**26**	**11**	**+5**	**6**	**0**	**0**	**0**	**4**	**0**	**0**	**0**
	NHL Totals		**342**	**19**	**62**	**81**	**20**	**53**	**73**	**370**	**3**	**1**	**4**	**311**	**6.1**	**307**	**26**	**319**	**106**		**47**	**1**	**12**	**13**	**20**	**0**	**0**	**0**

Hockey East Second All-Star Team (1990) • NCAA East Second All-American Team (1990) • Hockey East First All-Star Team (1991) • NCAA East First All-American Team (1991)

Traded to **Chicago** by **Buffalo** with Buffalo's 6th round choice (Marc Magliarditi) in 1995 Entry Draft for Craig Muni and Chicago's 5th round choice (Daniel Bienvenue) in 1995 Entry Draft, October 26, 1993. Traded to **Phoenix** by **Chicago** with Jim Cummins for Chad Kilger and Jayson More, March 4, 1998.

• CARON, ALAIN

Alain "Boom-Boom" Caron RW – R. 5'9", 182 lbs. b: Dolbeau, Que., 4/27/1938. Deceased.

Season	Club	League	GP	G	A	Pts	AG	AA	APts	PIM	PP	SH	GW	S	%	TGF	PGF	TGA	PGA	+/–	GP	G	A	Pts	PIM	PP	SH	GW
1956-57	Dolbeau Dragons	QJHL	45	69	48	117	....	....	....	118	....	....	....	....	....	....	....	....	....	....	....	....	....	....	....	....	....	....
1957-58	Chicoutimi Sagueneens	QHL	61	8	9	17	....	....	....	26	....	....	....	....	....	....	....	....	....	....	6	0	0	0	0	....	....	....
1958-59	Chicoutimi Sagueneens	QHL	56	15	18	33	....	....	....	67	....	....	....	....	....	....	....	....	....	....	....	....	....	....	....	....	....	....
1959-60	Sault Ste. Marie Thunderbirds	EPHL	25	10	4	14	....	....	....	4	....	....	....	....	....	....	....	....	....	....	....	....	....	....	....	....	....	....
	Quebec Aces	AHL	38	9	4	13	....	....	....	16	....	....	....	....	....	....	....	....	....	....	....	....	....	....	....	....	....	....
1960-61	Quebec Aces	AHL	9	5	1	6	....	....	....	2	....	....	....	....	....	....	....	....	....	....	....	....	....	....	....	....	....	....
	Sault Ste. Marie Thunderbirds	EPHL	35	11	6	17	....	....	....	16	....	....	....	....	....	....	....	....	....	....	....	....	....	....	....	....	....	....
1961-62	Amherst Ramblers	NSSHL	30	*76	46	*122	....	....	....	29	....	....	....	....	....	....	....	....	....	....	9	8	7	15	4	....	....	....
	Quebec Aces	AHL	1	0	0	0	....	....	....	0	....	....	....	....	....	....	....	....	....	....	....	....	....	....	....	....	....	....
1962-63	St. Louis Braves	EPHL	54	*61	36	97	....	....	....	22	....	....	....	....	....	....	....	....	....	....	....	....	....	....	....	....	....	....
	Charlotte Checkers	EHL	13	10	5	15	....	....	....	7	....	....	....	....	....	....	....	....	....	....	....	....	....	....	....	....	....	....
1963-64	St. Louis Braves	CHL	71	*77	48	*125	....	....	....	22	....	....	....	....	....	....	....	....	....	....	6	6	2	8	6	....	....	....
1964-65	St. Louis Braves	CHL	60	46	19	65	....	....	....	31	....	....	....	....	....	....	....	....	....	....	....	....	....	....	....	....	....	....
	Buffalo Bisons	AHL	....	....	....	....	....	....	....	....	....	....	....	....	....	....	....	....	....	....	5	0	0	0	2	....	....	....
1965-66	Buffalo Bisons	AHL	72	47	29	76	....	....	....	28	....	....	....	....	....	....	....	....	....	....	....	....	....	....	....	....	....	....
1966-67	Portland Buckaroos	WHL	71	35	25	60	....	....	....	24	....	....	....	....	....	....	....	....	....	....	4	0	0	0	2	....	....	....
1967-68	**Oakland Seals**	**NHL**	**58**	**9**	**13**	**22**	**11**	**14**	**25**	**18**	**3**	**0**	**0**	**121**	**7.4**	**34**	**18**	**38**	**0**	**–22**	....	....	....	....	....	....	....	....
	Buffalo Bisons	AHL	6	8	2	10	....	....	....	2	....	....	....	....	....	....	....	....	....	....	....	....	....	....	....	....	....	....
1968-69	**Montreal Canadiens**	**NHL**	**2**	**0**	**0**	**0**	**0**	**0**	**0**	**0**	**0**	**0**	**0**	**0**	**0.0**	**0**	**0**	**0**	**0**	**0**	....	....	....	....	....	....	....	....
	Houston Apollos	CHL	68	38	27	65	....	....	....	37	....	....	....	....	....	....	....	....	....	....	3	0	0	0	0	....	....	....
1969-70	Montreal Voyageurs	AHL	71	35	30	65	....	....	....	32	....	....	....	....	....	....	....	....	....	....	8	2	0	2	6	....	....	....
1970-71	San Diego Gulls	WHL	70	33	15	48	....	....	....	12	....	....	....	....	....	....	....	....	....	....	6	1	1	2	4	....	....	....
1971-72	Oklahoma City Blazers	CHL	67	22	20	42	....	....	....	28	....	....	....	....	....	....	....	....	....	....	6	1	0	1	0	....	....	....
1972-73	Quebec Nordiques	WHA	68	36	27	63	....	....	....	14	....	....	....	....	....	....	....	....	....	....	....	....	....	....	....	....	....	....
1973-74	Quebec Nordiques	WHA	59	31	15	46	....	....	....	10	....	....	....	....	....	....	....	....	....	....	....	....	....	....	....	....	....	....
1974-75	Quebec Nordiques	WHA	21	7	3	10	....	....	....	2	....	....	....	....	....	....	....	....	....	....	....	....	....	....	....	....	....	....
	Michigan–Baltimore	WHA	47	8	5	13	....	....	....	4	....	....	....	....	....	....	....	....	....	....	....	....	....	....	....	....	....	....
	Syracuse Blazers	NAHL	1	1	0	1	....	....	....	0	....	....	....	....	....	....	....	....	....	....	....	....	....	....	....	....	....	....
1975-76	Beauce Jaros	NAHL	73	*78	59	137	....	....	....	26	....	....	....	....	....	....	....	....	....	....	14	*21	13	34	12	....	....	....
	NHL Totals		**60**	**9**	**13**	**22**	**11**	**14**	**25**	**18**	**3**	**0**	**0**	**121**	**7.4**	**34**	**18**	**38**	**0**		....	....	....	....	....	....	....	....
	Other Major League Totals		195	82	50	132	....	....	....	30	....	....	....	....	....	....	....	....	....		....	....	....	....	....	....	....	....

NAHL Second All-Star Team (1976)

Traded to **Quebec** (AHL) by **Chicoutimi** (QHL) for cash, November, 1959. Claimed by **Oakland** from **Chicago** in Expansion Draft, June 6, 1967. Traded to **Montreal** by **Oakland** with Wally Boyer and Oakland's 1st round (Jim Pritchard) in 1968 and 1st round choice (Ray Martynuik) in 1970 Amateur Drafts for Norm Ferguson and Stan Fuller, May 21, 1968. Claimed by **Philadelphia** (San Diego-WHL) from **Montreal** in Reverse Draft, June, 1970. Traded to **Boston** by **San Diego** (WHL) for cash, August, 1971. Signed as a free agent by **Quebec** (WHA), August, 1972. Traded to **Michigan-Baltimore** (WHA) by **Quebec** (WHA) with Michel Rouleau and Pierre Guite for Marc Tardif and Steve Sutherland, December, 1974. Claimed by **Quebec** (WHA) from **Michigan-Baltimore** (WHA) in 1975 WHA Dispersal Draft, June, 1975.

• CARPENTER, BOB

Bob Carpenter C – L. 6', 200 lbs. b: Beverly, MA, 7/13/1963. Washington's 1st choice, 3rd overall, in 1981 Entry Draft.

Season	Club	League	GP	G	A	Pts	AG	AA	APts	PIM	PP	SH	GW	S	%	TGF	PGF	TGA	PGA	+/–	GP	G	A	Pts	PIM	PP	SH	GW
1980-81	St. John's Prep School	H.S.	18	14	24	38	....	....	....	....	....	....	....	....	....	....	....	....	....	....	....	....	....	....	....	....	....	....
	United States	WJC-A	5	5	4	9	....	....	....	6	....	....	....	....	....	....	....	....	....	....	....	....	....	....	....	....	....	....
1981-82	**Washington Capitals**	**NHL**	**80**	**32**	**35**	**67**	**25**	**23**	**48**	**69**	**7**	**1**	**3**	**263**	**12.2**	**105**	**28**	**102**	**2**	**–23**	....	....	....	....	....	....	....	....
1982-83	**Washington Capitals**	**NHL**	**80**	**32**	**37**	**69**	**26**	**26**	**52**	**64**	**14**	**0**	**4**	**197**	**16.2**	**110**	**44**	**68**	**2**	**0**	**4**	**1**	**0**	**1**	**2**	**0**	**0**	**0**
1983-84	**Washington Capitals**	**NHL**	**80**	**28**	**40**	**68**	**23**	**27**	**50**	**51**	**8**	**0**	**5**	**228**	**12.3**	**93**	**31**	**63**	**1**	**0**	**8**	**2**	**1**	**3**	**25**	**1**	**0**	**0**
1984-85	United States	C Cup	6	1	4	5	....	....	....	4	....	....	....	....	....	....	....	....	....	....	....	....	....	....	....	....	....	....
	Washington Capitals	**NHL**	**80**	**53**	**42**	**95**	**43**	**28**	**71**	**87**	**12**	**0**	**7**	**260**	**20.4**	**139**	**51**	**76**	**8**	**+20**	**5**	**1**	**4**	**5**	**8**	**0**	**0**	**0**
1985-86	**Washington Capitals**	**NHL**	**80**	**27**	**29**	**56**	**22**	**19**	**41**	**105**	**7**	**0**	**3**	**205**	**13.2**	**94**	**28**	**92**	**14**	**–12**	**9**	**5**	**4**	**9**	**12**	**2**	**0**	**1**
1986-87	**Washington Capitals**	**NHL**	**22**	**5**	**7**	**12**	**4**	**5**	**9**	**21**	**4**	**0**	**0**	**47**	**10.6**	**23**	**10**	**28**	**8**	**–7**	....	....	....	....	....	....	....	....
	New York Rangers	**NHL**	**28**	**2**	**8**	**10**	**2**	**6**	**8**	**20**	**1**	**0**	**0**	**41**	**4.9**	**16**	**4**	**26**	**2**	**–12**	....	....	....	....	....	....	....	....
	Los Angeles Kings	**NHL**	**10**	**2**	**3**	**5**	**2**	**2**	**4**	**6**	**0**	**0**	**0**	**23**	**8.7**	**11**	**0**	**24**	**5**	**–8**	**5**	**1**	**2**	**3**	**2**	**0**	**0**	**0**
	United States	WEC-A	10	2	2	4	....	....	....	8	....	....	....	....	....	....	....	....	....	....	....	....	....	....	....	....	....	....
1987-88	United States	C Cup	5	1	2	3	....	....	....	4	....	....	....	....	....	....	....	....	....	....	....	....	....	....	....	....	....	....
	Los Angeles Kings	**NHL**	**71**	**19**	**33**	**52**	**16**	**23**	**39**	**84**	**10**	**0**	**2**	**176**	**10.8**	**82**	**28**	**107**	**32**	**–21**	**5**	**1**	**1**	**2**	**0**	**0**	**0**	**0**
1988-89	**Los Angeles Kings**	**NHL**	**39**	**11**	**15**	**26**	**9**	**11**	**20**	**16**	**3**	**0**	**1**	**91**	**12.1**	**48**	**13**	**35**	**3**	**+3**	....	....	....	....	....	....	....	....
	Boston Bruins	**NHL**	**18**	**5**	**9**	**14**	**4**	**6**	**10**	**10**	**1**	**0**	**2**	**46**	**10.9**	**16**	**3**	**9**	**0**	**+4**	**8**	**1**	**1**	**2**	**4**	**1**	**0**	**1**
1989-90	**Boston Bruins**	**NHL**	**80**	**25**	**31**	**56**	**22**	**22**	**44**	**97**	**5**	**0**	**5**	**220**	**11.4**	**90**	**32**	**80**	**19**	**–3**	**21**	**4**	**6**	**10**	**39**	**2**	**0**	**1**
1990-91	**Boston Bruins**	**NHL**	**29**	**8**	**8**	**16**	**7**	**6**	**13**	**22**	**2**	**0**	**0**	**54**	**14.8**	**28**	**10**	**30**	**14**	**+2**	**1**	**0**	**1**	**1**	**2**	**0**	**0**	**0**
1991-92	**Boston Bruins**	**NHL**	**60**	**25**	**23**	**48**	**23**	**17**	**40**	**46**	**6**	**1**	**6**	**171**	**14.6**	**72**	**21**	**69**	**15**	**–3**	**8**	**0**	**1**	**1**	**6**	**0**	**0**	**0**
1992-93	**Washington Capitals**	**NHL**	**68**	**11**	**17**	**28**	**9**	**12**	**21**	**65**	**2**	**0**	**0**	**141**	**7.8**	**51**	**10**	**66**	**9**	**–16**	**6**	**1**	**4**	**5**	**6**	**0**	**0**	**0**
1993-94	**New Jersey Devils**	**NHL**	**76**	**10**	**23**	**33**	**9**	**18**	**27**	**51**	**0**	**2**	**1**	**125**	**8.0**	**50**	**2**	**76**	**35**	**+7**	**20**	**1**	**7**	**8**	**20**	**0**	**0**	**0**
1994-95	**New Jersey Devils**	**NHL**	**41**	**5**	**11**	**16**	**9**	**16**	**25**	**19**	**0**	**0**	**0**	**69**	**7.2**	**26**	**0**	**40**	**13**	**–1**	**17**	**1**	**4**	**5**	**6**	**1**	**0**	**0**
1995-96	**New Jersey Devils**	**NHL**	**52**	**5**	**5**	**10**	**5**	**4**	**9**	**14**	**0**	**1**	**0**	**63**	**7.9**	**21**	**0**	**45**	**14**	**–10**	....	....	....	....	....	....	....	....
1996-97	**New Jersey Devils**	**NHL**	**62**	**4**	**15**	**19**	**4**	**13**	**17**	**14**	**0**	**1**	**0**	**76**	**5.3**	**30**	**0**	**44**	**20**	**+6**	**10**	**1**	**2**	**3**	**2**	**0**	**0**	**0**
1997-98	**New Jersey Devils**	**NHL**	**66**	**9**	**9**	**18**	**11**	**9**	**20**	**22**	**0**	**1**	**1**	**81**	**11.1**	**30**	**1**	**49**	**16**	**–4**	**6**	**1**	**0**	**1**	**0**	**0**	**0**	**0**
	NHL Totals		**1122**	**318**	**400**	**718**	**275**	**293**	**568**	**883**	**82**	**7**	**40**	**2577**	**12.3**	**1135**	**316**	**1129**	**232**		**133**	**21**	**38**	**59**	**134**	**7**	**0**	**3**

Played in NHL All-Star Game (1985)

Traded to **NY Rangers** by **Washington** with Washington's 2nd round choice (Jason Prosofsky) in 1989 Entry Draft for Bob Crawford, Kelly Miller and Mike Ridley, January 1, 1987. Traded to **LA Kings** by **NY Rangers** with Tom Laidlaw for Jeff Crossman, Marcel Dionne and LA Kings' 3rd round choice (later traded to Minnesota — Minnesota selected Murray Garbutt) in 1989 Entry Draft. Traded to **Boston** by **LA Kings** for Steve Kasper, January 23, 1989. Signed as a free agent by **Washington**, June 30, 1992. Signed as a free agent by **New Jersey**, September 30, 1993.

• CARR, GENE

Gene Carr C – L. 5'11", 185 lbs. b: Nanaimo, B.C., 9/17/1951. St. Louis' 1st choice, 4th overall, in 1971 Amateur Draft.

Season	Club	League	GP	G	A	Pts	AG	AA	APts	PIM	PP	SH	GW	S	%	TGF	PGF	TGA	PGA	+/–	GP	G	A	Pts	PIM	PP	SH	GW
1969-70	Flin Flon Bombers	WCJHL	60	22	51	73	....	....	....	118	....	....	....	....	....	....	....	....	....	....	6	6	5	11	4	....	....	....
1970-71	Flin Flon Bombers	WCJHL	62	36	68	104	....	....	....	150	....	....	....	....	....	....	....	....	....	....	17	12	18	30	42	....	....	....
1971-72	**St. Louis Blues**	**NHL**	**15**	**3**	**2**	**5**	**3**	**2**	**5**	**9**	**0**	**0**	**0**	**29**	**10.3**	**8**	**2**	**6**	**0**	**0**	....	....	....	....	....	....	....	....
	New York Rangers	**NHL**	**59**	**8**	**8**	**16**	**8**	**7**	**15**	**25**	**1**	**0**	**3**	**74**	**10.8**	**37**	**3**	**18**	**0**	**+16**	**16**	**1**	**3**	**4**	**21**	**0**	**0**	**0**

Season	Club	League	REGULAR SEASON																		PLAYOFFS							
			GP	G	A	Pts	AG	AA	APts	PIM	PP	SH	GW	S	%	TGF	PGF	TGA	PGA	+/–	GP	G	A	Pts	PIM	PP	SH	GW
1972-73	**New York Rangers**	**NHL**	**50**	**9**	**10**	**19**	**9**	**8**	**17**	**50**	**1**	**0**	**1**	**65**	**13.8**	**32**	**5**	**31**	**0**	**–4**	**1**	**0**	**1**	**1**	**0**	**0**	**0**	**0**
1973-74	**New York Rangers**	**NHL**	**29**	**1**	**5**	**6**	**1**	**4**	**5**	**15**	**1**	**0**	**0**	**23**	**4.3**	**10**	**2**	**16**	**0**	**–8**	....	....	....	....	....	....	....	....
	Providence Reds	AHL	10	4	10	14	....	....	....	18	....	....	....	....	....	....	....	....	....	....	....	....	....	....	....	....	....	....
	Los Angeles Kings	**NHL**	**21**	**6**	**11**	**17**	**6**	**9**	**15**	**36**	**0**	**1**	**1**	**37**	**16.2**	**19**	**4**	**14**	**1**	**+2**	**5**	**2**	**1**	**3**	**14**	**1**	**0**	**0**
1974-75	**Los Angeles Kings**	**NHL**	**80**	**7**	**32**	**39**	**6**	**25**	**31**	**103**	**2**	**0**	**2**	**157**	**4.5**	**65**	**6**	**41**	**1**	**+19**	**3**	**1**	**2**	**3**	**29**	**0**	**0**	**0**
1975-76	**Los Angeles Kings**	**NHL**	**38**	**8**	**11**	**19**	**7**	**9**	**16**	**16**	**0**	**0**	**1**	**61**	**13.1**	**27**	**5**	**23**	**0**	**–1**	....	....	....	....	....	....	....	....
1976-77	**Los Angeles Kings**	**NHL**	**68**	**15**	**12**	**27**	**14**	**10**	**24**	**25**	**0**	**1**	**2**	**99**	**15.2**	**34**	**3**	**36**	**10**	**+5**	**9**	**1**	**1**	**2**	**2**	**0**	**0**	**0**
1977-78	**Los Angeles Kings**	**NHL**	**5**	**2**	**0**	**2**	**2**	**0**	**2**	**4**	**0**	**0**	**0**	**8**	**25.0**	**3**	**0**	**3**	**0**	**0**	....	....	....	....	....	....	....	....
	Pittsburgh Penguins	**NHL**	**70**	**17**	**37**	**54**	**16**	**30**	**46**	**76**	**4**	**0**	**2**	**145**	**11.7**	**81**	**37**	**61**	**2**	**–15**	....	....	....	....	....	....	....	....
1978-79	**Atlanta Flames**	**NHL**	**30**	**3**	**8**	**11**	**3**	**6**	**9**	**6**	**0**	**0**	**0**	**35**	**8.6**	**15**	**3**	**16**	**0**	**–4**	**1**	**0**	**0**	**0**	**0**	**0**	**0**	**0**
	Tulsa Oilers	CHL	22	4	8	12	....	....	....	35	....	....	....	....	....	....	....	....	....	....	....	....	....	....	....	....	....	....
	NHL Totals		**465**	**79**	**136**	**215**	**75**	**110**	**185**	**365**	**9**	**2**	**12**	**733**	**10.8**	**331**	**70**	**265**	**14**		**35**	**5**	**8**	**13**	**66**	**1**	**0**	**0**

WCJHL All-Star Team (1971)

Traded to **NY Rangers** by **St. Louis** with Jim Lorentz and Wayne Connelly for Jack Egars, Andre Dupont and Mike Murphy, November 15, 1971. Traded to **LA Kings** by **NY Rangers** for LA Kings' 1st round choice (Ron Duguay) in 1977 Amateur Draft, February 15, 1974. Traded to **Pittsburgh** by **LA Kings** with Dave Schultz and LA Kings' 4th round choice (Shane Pearsall) in 1978 Amateur Draft for Syl Apps and Hartland Monahan, November 2, 1977. Signed as a free agent by **Atlanta**, June 6, 1978.

• CARRIERE, LARRY

Larry Carriere D – L. 6'1", 190 lbs. b: Montreal, Que., 1/30/1952. Buffalo's 2nd choice, 25th overall, in 1972 Amateur Draft.

Season	Club	League	GP	G	A	Pts	AG	AA	APts	PIM	PP	SH	GW	S	%	TGF	PGF	TGA	PGA	+/–	PO GP	PO G	PO A	PO Pts	PO PIM	PO PP	PO SH	PO GW
1969-70	Loyola University	OQAA	32	10	34	44	....	....	....	....	....	....	....	....	....	....	....	....	....	....	....	....	....	....	....	....	....	....
1970-71	Loyola University	QUAA	27	8	24	32	....	....	....	72	....	....	....	....	....	....	....	....	....	....	....	....	....	....	....	....	....	....
1971-72	Loyola University	QUAA	32	20	29	49	....	....	....	69	....	....	....	....	....	....	....	....	....	....	....	....	....	....	....	....	....	....
1972-73	**Buffalo Sabres**	**NHL**	**40**	**2**	**8**	**10**	**2**	**7**	**9**	**52**	**1**	**0**	**0**	**34**	**5.9**	**26**	**5**	**25**	**3**	**–1**	**6**	**0**	**1**	**1**	**8**	**0**	**0**	**0**
	Cincinnati Swords	AHL	30	7	11	18	....	....	....	54	....	....	....	....	....	....	....	....	....	....	....	....	....	....	....	....	....	....
1973-74	**Buffalo Sabres**	**NHL**	**78**	**6**	**24**	**30**	**6**	**21**	**27**	**103**	**3**	**0**	**0**	**113**	**5.3**	**108**	**20**	**101**	**16**	**+3**	....	....	....	....	....	....	....	....
1974-75	**Buffalo Sabres**	**NHL**	**80**	**1**	**11**	**12**	**1**	**9**	**10**	**111**	**0**	**0**	**0**	**84**	**1.2**	**67**	**2**	**75**	**22**	**+12**	**17**	**0**	**2**	**2**	**32**	**0**	**0**	**0**
1975-76	**Atlanta Flames**	**NHL**	**75**	**4**	**15**	**19**	**4**	**12**	**16**	**96**	**1**	**1**	**0**	**126**	**3.2**	**77**	**2**	**95**	**25**	**+5**	**2**	**0**	**0**	**0**	**2**	**0**	**0**	**0**
1976-77	**Atlanta Flames**	**NHL**	**25**	**2**	**3**	**5**	**2**	**2**	**4**	**16**	**0**	**0**	**1**	**28**	**7.1**	**25**	**1**	**25**	**4**	**+3**	....	....	....	....	....	....	....	....
	Vancouver Canucks	**NHL**	**49**	**1**	**9**	**10**	**1**	**7**	**8**	**55**	**0**	**1**	**0**	**65**	**1.5**	**43**	**1**	**63**	**10**	**–11**	....	....	....	....	....	....	....	....
1977-78	**Vancouver Canucks**	**NHL**	**7**	**0**	**3**	**3**	**0**	**2**	**2**	**11**	**0**	**0**	**0**	**10**	**0.0**	**5**	**0**	**7**	**2**	**0**	....	....	....	....	....	....	....	....
	Los Angeles Kings	**NHL**	**2**	**0**	**0**	**0**	**0**	**0**	**0**	**0**	**0**	**0**	**0**	**0**	**0.0**	**0**	**0**	**0**	**0**	**0**	....	....	....	....	....	....	....	....
	Springfield Indians	AHL	40	2	14	16	....	....	....	33	....	....	....	....	....	....	....	....	....	....	....	....	....	....	....	....	....	....
	Buffalo Sabres	**NHL**	**9**	**0**	**0**	**0**	**0**	**0**	**0**	**18**	**0**	**0**	**0**	**4**	**0.0**	**2**	**1**	**2**	**0**	**–1**	....	....	....	....	....	....	....	....
	Tulsa Oilers	CHL	6	0	1	1	....	....	....	12	....	....	....	....	....	....	....	....	....	....	....	....	....	....	....	....	....	....
1978-79			DID NOT PLAY																									
1979-80	**Toronto Maple Leafs**	**NHL**	**2**	**0**	**1**	**1**	**0**	**1**	**1**	**0**	**0**	**0**	**0**	**1**	**0.0**	**2**	**0**	**3**	**0**	**–1**	**2**	**0**	**0**	**0**	**0**	**0**	**0**	**0**
	NHL Totals		**367**	**16**	**74**	**90**	**16**	**61**	**77**	**462**	**5**	**2**	**1**	**465**	**3.4**	**355**	**32**	**396**	**82**		**27**	**0**	**3**	**3**	**42**	**0**	**0**	**0**

Traded to **Atlanta** by **Buffalo** with Buffalo's 1st round choice (later traded to Washington — Washington selected Greg Carroll) in 1976 Amateur Draft, October 1, 1975. Traded to **Vancouver** by **Atlanta** with Hilliard Graves for John Gould and LA Kings' 2nd round choice (previously acquired, Atlanta selected Brian Hill) in 1977 Amateur Draft, December 2, 1976. Signed as a free agent by **Buffalo**, March 12, 1978. Signed as a free agent by **Toronto**, April 5, 1980.

• CARROLL, BILLY

Billy Carroll C – L. 5'10", 190 lbs. b: Toronto, Ont., 1/19/1959. NY Islanders' 3rd choice, 38th overall, in 1979 Entry Draft.

Season	Club	League	GP	G	A	Pts	AG	AA	APts	PIM	PP	SH	GW	S	%	TGF	PGF	TGA	PGA	+/–	PO GP	PO G	PO A	PO Pts	PO PIM	PO PP	PO SH	PO GW
1976-77	London Knights	OHA	64	18	31	49	....	....	....	37	....	....	....	....	....	....	....	....	....	....	....	....	....	....	....	....	....	....
1977-78	London Knights	OHA	68	46	46	73	....	....	....	42	....	....	....	....	....	....	....	....	....	....	11	3	6	9	6	....	....	....
1978-79	London Knights	OHA	63	35	50	85	....	....	....	38	....	....	....	....	....	....	....	....	....	....	7	1	5	6	14	....	....	....
1979-80	Indianapolis Checkers	CHL	49	9	17	26	....	....	....	19	....	....	....	....	....	....	....	....	....	....	7	0	1	1	0	....	....	....
1980-81	**New York Islanders**	**NHL**	**18**	**4**	**4**	**8**	**3**	**3**	**6**	**6**	**0**	**0**	**1**	**25**	**16.0**	**13**	**1**	**17**	**8**	**+3**	**18**	**3**	**9**	**12**	**4**	**0**	**1**	**1**
	Indianapolis Checkers	CHL	50	27	37	64	....	....	....	67	....	....	....	....	....	....	....	....	....	....	....	....	....	....	....	....	....	....
1981-82	**New York Islanders**	**NHL**	**72**	**9**	**20**	**29**	**7**	**13**	**20**	**32**	**0**	**3**	**1**	**42**	**21.4**	**39**	**0**	**50**	**23**	**+12**	**19**	**2**	**2**	**4**	**8**	**0**	**2**	**0**
1982-83	**New York Islanders**	**NHL**	**71**	**1**	**11**	**12**	**1**	**8**	**9**	**24**	**0**	**1**	**0**	**52**	**1.9**	**25**	**1**	**39**	**18**	**+3**	**20**	**1**	**1**	**2**	**2**	**0**	**1**	**0**
1983-84	**New York Islanders**	**NHL**	**39**	**5**	**2**	**7**	**4**	**1**	**5**	**12**	**0**	**0**	**2**	**39**	**12.8**	**11**	**0**	**31**	**19**	**–1**	**5**	**0**	**0**	**0**	**0**	**0**	**0**	**0**
1984-85	**Edmonton Oilers**	**NHL**	**65**	**8**	**9**	**17**	**7**	**6**	**13**	**22**	**0**	**0**	**1**	**44**	**18.2**	**24**	**0**	**30**	**6**	**0**	**9**	**0**	**0**	**0**	**4**	**0**	**0**	**0**
1985-86	**Edmonton Oilers**	**NHL**	**5**	**0**	**2**	**2**	**0**	**1**	**1**	**0**	**0**	**0**	**0**	**0**	**0.0**	**2**	**0**	**2**	**2**	**+2**	....	....	....	....	....	....	....	....
	Nova Scotia Oilers	AHL	26	7	18	25	....	....	....	15	....	....	....	....	....	....	....	....	....	....	....	....	....	....	....	....	....	....
	Detroit Red Wings	**NHL**	**21**	**2**	**4**	**6**	**2**	**3**	**5**	**11**	**0**	**0**	**0**	**13**	**15.4**	**6**	**0**	**27**	**13**	**–8**	....	....	....	....	....	....	....	....
1986-87	**Detroit Red Wings**	**NHL**	**31**	**1**	**2**	**3**	**1**	**1**	**2**	**6**	**0**	**0**	**1**	**12**	**8.3**	**6**	**0**	**24**	**9**	**–9**	....	....	....	....	....	....	....	....
	NHL Totals		**322**	**30**	**54**	**84**	**25**	**36**	**61**	**113**	**0**	**4**	**6**	**227**	**13.2**	**126**	**2**	**220**	**98**		**71**	**6**	**12**	**18**	**18**	**0**	**4**	**1**

OHA Second All-Star Team (1979)

Claimed by **Edmonton** from **NY Islanders** in Waiver Draft, October 9, 1984. Traded to **Detroit** by **Edmonton** for Bruce Eakin, December 28, 1985.

• CARROLL, GREG

Greg Carroll C – L. 6', 185 lbs. b: Gimley, Man., 11/10/1956. Washington's 2nd choice, 15th overall, in 1976 Amateur Draft.

Season	Club	League	GP	G	A	Pts	AG	AA	APts	PIM	PP	SH	GW	S	%	TGF	PGF	TGA	PGA	+/–	PO GP	PO G	PO A	PO Pts	PO PIM	PO PP	PO SH	PO GW
1974-75	Medicine Hat Tigers	WCJHL	70	22	37	59	....	....	....	77	....	....	....	....	....	....	....	....	....	....	....	....	....	....	....	....	....	....
1975-76	Medicine Hat Tigers	WCJHL	71	60	111	171	....	....	....	118	....	....	....	....	....	....	....	....	....	....	9	4	11	15	2	....	....	....
1976-77	Cincinnati Stingers	WHA	77	15	39	54	....	....	....	53	....	....	....	....	....	....	....	....	....	....	4	1	2	3	0	....	....	....
1977-78	New England Whalers	WHA	48	9	14	23	....	....	....	27	....	....	....	....	....	....	....	....	....	....	....	....	....	....	....	....	....	....
	Cincinnati Stingers	WHA	26	6	13	19	....	....	....	36	....	....	....	....	....	....	....	....	....	....	....	....	....	....	....	....	....	....
1978-79	**Washington Capitals**	**NHL**	**24**	**5**	**6**	**11**	**5**	**5**	**10**	**12**	**0**	**0**	**0**	**29**	**17.2**	**16**	**0**	**25**	**7**	**–2**	....	....	....	....	....	....	....	....
	Detroit Red Wings	**NHL**	**36**	**2**	**9**	**11**	**2**	**7**	**9**	**8**	**1**	**0**	**0**	**16**	**12.5**	**19**	**6**	**19**	**0**	**–6**	....	....	....	....	....	....	....	....
1979-80	**Hartford Whalers**	**NHL**	**71**	**13**	**19**	**32**	**12**	**15**	**27**	**24**	**0**	**1**	**2**	**86**	**15.3**	**48**	**1**	**79**	**27**	**–5**	....	....	....	....	....	....	....	....
	Springfield Indians	AHL	6	2	2	4	....	....	....	2	....	....	....	....	....	....	....	....	....	....	....	....	....	....	....	....	....	....
	NHL Totals		**131**	**20**	**34**	**54**	**19**	**27**	**46**	**44**	**1**	**1**	**2**	**130**	**15.4**	**83**	**7**	**123**	**34**		....	....	....	....	....	....	....	....
	Other Major League Totals		151	30	66	96	....	....	....	116	....	....	....	....	....	....	....	....	....	....	4	1	2	3	0	....	....	....

Selected by **Cincinnati** (WHA) in 1976 WHA Amateur Draft, June, 1976. Traded to **New England** (WHA) by **Cincinnati** (WHA) with Bryan Maxwell for the rights to Mike Liut and future considerations, May, 1977. Traded to **Cincinnati** (WHA) by **New England** (WHA) for Ron Plumb, February, 1978. Signed as a free agent by **Washington** after being released by **Cincinnati** (WHA), September 21, 1978. Claimed on waivers by **Detroit** from **Washington**, January 6, 1979. Signed by **Hartford** as a free agent, October 30, 1979.

• CARRUTHERS, DWIGHT

Dwight (Gordon) Carruthers D – R. 5'10", 186 lbs. b: Lashburn, Sask., 11/7/1944.

Season	Club	League	GP	G	A	Pts	AG	AA	APts	PIM	PP	SH	GW	S	%	TGF	PGF	TGA	PGA	+/–	PO GP	PO G	PO A	PO Pts	PO PIM	PO PP	PO SH	PO GW
1962-63	Weyburn Red Wings	SJHL	54	5	15	20	....	....	....	78	....	....	....	....	....	....	....	....	....	....	13	1	2	3	15	....	....	....
1963-64	Weyburn Red Wings	SJHL	61	6	26	32	....	....	....	46	....	....	....	....	....	....	....	....	....	....	8	1	7	8	6	....	....	....
1964-65	Weyburn Red Wings	SJHL	40	9	33	42	....	....	....	103	....	....	....	....	....	....	....	....	....	....	15	4	11	15	20	....	....	....
1965-66	**Detroit Red Wings**	**NHL**	**1**	**0**	**0**	**0**	**0**	**0**	**0**	**0**	....	....	....	....	....	....	....	....	....	....	....	....	....	....	....	....	....	....
	Memphis Wings	CHL	4	0	1	1	....	....	....	2	....	....	....	....	....	....	....	....	....	....	....	....	....	....	....	....	....	....
	Johnstown Jets	EHL	69	7	22	29	....	....	....	132	....	....	....	....	....	....	....	....	....	....	3	0	3	3	6	....	....	....
1966-67	San Diego Gulls	WHL	29	2	3	5	....	....	....	10	....	....	....	....	....	....	....	....	....	....	....	....	....	....	....	....	....	....
1967-68	**Philadelphia Flyers**	**NHL**	**1**	**0**	**0**	**0**	**0**	**0**	**0**	**0**	**0**	**0**	**0**	**0**	**0.0**	**0**	**0**	**0**	**0**	**0**	....	....	....	....	....	....	....	....
	Seattle Totems	WHL	70	9	16	25	....	....	....	34	....	....	....	....	....	....	....	....	....	....	9	2	4	6	8	....	....	....
1968-69	Amarillo Wranglers	CHL	62	10	19	29	....	....	....	42	....	....	....	....	....	....	....	....	....	....	....	....	....	....	....	....	....	....
	Seattle Totems	WHL	1	0	1	1	....	....	....	0	....	....	....	....	....	....	....	....	....	....	4	0	0	0	2	....	....	....
1969-70	Seattle–Phoenix	WHL	56	2	8	10	....	....	....	24	....	....	....	....	....	....	....	....	....	....	....	....	....	....	....	....	....	....
1971-72	Spokane Flyers	WIHL	STATISTICS NOT AVAILABLE																									
1972-73	Spokane Flyers	WIHL	STATISTICS NOT AVAILABLE																									
1973-74	Spokane Flyers	WIHL	STATISTICS NOT AVAILABLE																									
1974-75	Spokane Flyers	WIHL	48	12	37	49	....	....	....	60	....	....	....	....	....	....	....	....	....	....	....	....	....	....	....	....	....	....
1975-76	Spokane Flyers	WIHL	33	4	20	24	....	....	....	46	....	....	....	....	....	....	....	....	....	....	....	....	....	....	....	....	....	....
	NHL Totals		**2**	**0**	**0**	**0**	**0**	**0**	**0**	**0**	**0**	**0**	**0**	**0**	**0.0**	**0**	**0**	**0**	**0**		....	....	....	....	....	....	....	....

Claimed by **Philadelphia** from **Detroit** in Expansion Draft, June 6, 1967.

			REGULAR SEASON																		PLAYOFFS							
Season	Club	League	GP	G	A	Pts	AG	AA	APts	PIM	PP	SH	GW	S	%	TGF	PGF	TGA	PGA	+/–	GP	G	A	Pts	PIM	PP	SH	GW

● CARSON, JIMMY Jimmy Carson C – R. 6'1", 200 lbs. b: Southfield, MI, 7/20/1968. Los Angeles' 1st choice, 2nd overall, in 1986 Entry Draft.

Season	Club	League	GP	G	A	Pts	AG	AA	APts	PIM	PP	SH	GW	S	%	TGF	PGF	TGA	PGA	+/–	GP	G	A	Pts	PIM	PP	SH	GW
1984-85	Verdun Jr. Canadiens	QMJHL	68	44	72	116	....	....	....	12	....	....	....	....	....	....	....	....	....	....	14	9	17	26	12	....	....	....
1985-86	Verdun Jr. Canadiens	QMJHL	69	70	83	153	....	....	....	46	....	....	....	....	....	....	....	....	....	....	5	2	6	8	0	....	....	....
1986-87	**Los Angeles Kings**	**NHL**	**80**	**37**	**42**	**79**	**32**	**30**	**62**	**22**	**18**	**0**	**2**	**215**	**17.2**	**105**	**48**	**64**	**2**	**–5**	**5**	**1**	**2**	**3**	**6**	**0**	**0**	**0**
	United States	WEC-A	10	2	3	5	....	....	....	4	....	....	....	....	....	....	....	....	....	....	....	....	....	....	....	....	....	....
1987-88	**Los Angeles Kings**	**NHL**	**80**	**55**	**52**	**107**	**47**	**37**	**84**	**45**	**22**	**0**	**7**	**264**	**20.8**	**141**	**68**	**94**	**2**	**–19**	**5**	**5**	**3**	**8**	**4**	**1**	**0**	**0**
1988-89	**Edmonton Oilers**	**NHL**	**80**	**49**	**51**	**100**	**42**	**36**	**78**	**36**	**19**	**0**	**5**	**240**	**20.4**	**128**	**49**	**77**	**1**	**+3**	**7**	**2**	**1**	**3**	**6**	**1**	**0**	**1**
1989-90	**Edmonton Oilers**	**NHL**	**4**	**1**	**2**	**3**	**1**	**1**	**2**	**0**	**1**	**0**	**0**	**11**	**9.1**	**4**	**3**	**3**	**0**	**–2**	....	....	....	....	....	....	....	....
	Detroit Red Wings	**NHL**	**44**	**20**	**16**	**36**	**17**	**11**	**28**	**8**	**10**	**0**	**1**	**127**	**15.7**	**55**	**24**	**37**	**0**	**–6**	....	....	....	....	....	....	....	....
1990-91	**Detroit Red Wings**	**NHL**	**64**	**21**	**25**	**46**	**19**	**19**	**38**	**28**	**5**	**1**	**4**	**175**	**12.0**	**67**	**21**	**44**	**1**	**+3**	**7**	**2**	**1**	**3**	**4**	**0**	**0**	**1**
1991-92	**Detroit Red Wings**	**NHL**	**80**	**34**	**35**	**69**	**31**	**26**	**57**	**30**	**11**	**0**	**3**	**150**	**22.7**	**93**	**26**	**50**	**0**	**+17**	**11**	**2**	**3**	**5**	**0**	**0**	**0**	**0**
1992-93	**Detroit Red Wings**	**NHL**	**52**	**25**	**26**	**51**	**21**	**18**	**39**	**18**	**13**	**0**	**4**	**108**	**23.1**	**72**	**40**	**32**	**0**	**0**	....	....	....	....	....	....	....	....
	Los Angeles Kings	**NHL**	**34**	**12**	**10**	**22**	**10**	**7**	**17**	**14**	**4**	**0**	**1**	**81**	**14.8**	**33**	**9**	**26**	**0**	**–2**	**18**	**5**	**4**	**9**	**2**	**2**	**0**	**0**
1993-94	**Los Angeles Kings**	**NHL**	**25**	**4**	**7**	**11**	**4**	**5**	**9**	**2**	**1**	**0**	**0**	**47**	**8.5**	**16**	**2**	**16**	**0**	**–2**	....	....	....	....	....	....	....	....
	Vancouver Canucks	**NHL**	**34**	**7**	**10**	**17**	**7**	**8**	**15**	**22**	**2**	**0**	**1**	**82**	**8.5**	**27**	**11**	**30**	**1**	**–13**	**2**	**0**	**1**	**1**	**0**	**0**	**0**	**0**
1994-95	**Hartford Whalers**	**NHL**	**38**	**9**	**10**	**19**	**16**	**15**	**31**	**29**	**4**	**0**	**3**	**58**	**15.5**	**27**	**8**	**14**	**0**	**+5**	....	....	....	....	....	....	....	....
1995-96	**Hartford Whalers**	**NHL**	**11**	**1**	**0**	**1**	**1**	**0**	**1**	**0**	**0**	**0**	**0**	**9**	**11.1**	**2**	**0**	**1**	**0**	**+1**	....	....	....	....	....	....	....	....
	Lausanne	Switz.	13	3	4	7	....	....	....	14	....	....	....	....	....	....	....	....	....	....	....	....	....	....	....	....	....	....
1996-97	Detroit Vipers	IHL	18	7	16	23	....	....	....	4	....	....	....	....	....	....	....	....	....	....	13	4	6	10	12	....	....	....
1997-98	Detroit Vipers	IHL	49	10	28	38	....	....	....	34	....	....	....	....	....	....	....	....	....	....	9	3	4	7	6	....	....	....
	NHL Totals		**626**	**275**	**286**	**561**	**248**	**213**	**461**	**254**	**110**	**1**	**31**	**1567**	**17.5**	**770**	**309**	**488**	**7**		**55**	**17**	**15**	**32**	**22**	**4**	**0**	**2**

QMJHL Second All-Star Team (1986) • Named to NHL All-Rookie Team (1987)

Played in NHL All-Star Game (1989)

Traded to **Edmonton** by **LA Kings** with Martin Gelinas, LA Kings' 1st round choices in 1989 (later traded to New Jersey — New Jersey selected Jason Miller), 1991 (Martin Rucinsky) and 1993 (Nick Stajduhar) Entry Drafts and cash for Wayne Gretzky, Mike Krushelnyski and Marty McSorley, August 9, 1988. Traded to **Detroit** by **Edmonton** with Kevin McClelland and Edmonton's 5th round choice (later traded to Montreal — Montreal selected Brad Layzell) in 1991 Entry Draft for Petr Klima, Joe Murphy, Adam Graves and Jeff Sharples, November 2, 1989. Traded to **LA Kings** by **Detroit** with Marc Potvin and Gary Shuchuk for Paul Coffey, Sylvain Couturier and Jim Hiller, January 29, 1993. Traded to **Vancouver** by **LA Kings** for Dixon Ward, January 8, 1994. Signed as a free agent by **Hartford**, July 15, 1994.

● CARSON, LINDSAY Lindsay Carson C – L. 6'2", 195 lbs. b: Oxbow, Sask., 11/21/1960. Philadelphia's 4th choice, 56th overall, in 1979 Entry Draft.

Season	Club	League	GP	G	A	Pts	AG	AA	APts	PIM	PP	SH	GW	S	%	TGF	PGF	TGA	PGA	+/–	GP	G	A	Pts	PIM	PP	SH	GW
1977-78	Saskatoon Blades	WCJHL	62	23	55	78	....	....	....	124	....	....	....	....	....	....	....	....	....	....	....	....	....	....	....	....	....	....
1978-79	Saskatoon Blades	WHL	37	21	29	50	....	....	....	56	....	....	....	....	....	....	....	....	....	....	....	....	....	....	....	....	....	....
	Billings Bighorns	WHL	30	13	22	35	....	....	....	50	....	....	....	....	....	....	....	....	....	....	8	4	7	11	2	....	....	....
1979-80	Billings Bighorns	WHL	70	42	66	108	....	....	....	101	....	....	....	....	....	....	....	....	....	....	....	....	....	....	....	....	....	....
1980-81	Saginaw Gears	IHL	79	11	25	36	....	....	....	84	....	....	....	....	....	....	....	....	....	....	20	4	12	16	45	....	....	....
1981-82	**Philadelphia Flyers**	**NHL**	**18**	**0**	**1**	**1**	**0**	**1**	**1**	**32**	**0**	**0**	**0**	**24**	**0.0**	**1**	**0**	**18**	**2**	**–15**	....	....	....	....	....	....	....	....
	Maine Mariners	AHL	54	20	31	51	....	....	....	92	....	....	....	....	....	....	....	....	....	....	4	0	0	0	12	....	....	....
1982-83	**Philadelphia Flyers**	**NHL**	**78**	**18**	**19**	**37**	**15**	**13**	**28**	**67**	**0**	**0**	**2**	**150**	**12.0**	**54**	**1**	**34**	**1**	**+20**	**1**	**0**	**0**	**0**	**0**	**0**	**0**	**0**
1983-84	**Philadelphia Flyers**	**NHL**	**16**	**1**	**3**	**4**	**1**	**2**	**3**	**10**	**0**	**0**	**1**	**16**	**6.3**	**6**	**0**	**13**	**0**	**–7**	**1**	**0**	**0**	**0**	**5**	**0**	**0**	**0**
	Springfield Indians	AHL	5	2	4	6	....	....	....	5	....	....	....	....	....	....	....	....	....	....	....	....	....	....	....	....	....	....
1984-85	**Philadelphia Flyers**	**NHL**	**77**	**20**	**19**	**39**	**16**	**13**	**29**	**123**	**1**	**0**	**1**	**120**	**16.7**	**52**	**2**	**55**	**5**	**0**	**17**	**0**	**3**	**3**	**24**	**0**	**0**	**0**
1985-86	**Philadelphia Flyers**	**NHL**	**50**	**9**	**12**	**21**	**7**	**8**	**15**	**84**	**0**	**0**	**0**	**59**	**15.3**	**27**	**0**	**17**	**0**	**+10**	**1**	**0**	**0**	**0**	**5**	**0**	**0**	**0**
1986-87	**Philadelphia Flyers**	**NHL**	**71**	**11**	**15**	**26**	**10**	**11**	**21**	**141**	**0**	**1**	**2**	**100**	**11.0**	**45**	**2**	**50**	**5**	**–2**	**24**	**3**	**5**	**8**	**22**	**0**	**0**	**0**
1987-88	**Philadelphia Flyers**	**NHL**	**36**	**2**	**7**	**9**	**2**	**5**	**7**	**37**	**0**	**0**	**0**	**34**	**5.9**	**10**	**2**	**14**	**2**	**–4**	....	....	....	....	....	....	....	....
	Hartford Whalers	**NHL**	**27**	**5**	**4**	**9**	**4**	**3**	**7**	**30**	**1**	**1**	**1**	**39**	**12.8**	**19**	**2**	**17**	**0**	**0**	**5**	**1**	**2**	**3**	**0**	**0**	**0**	**0**
1988-89	Binghamton Whalers	AHL	24	4	10	14	....	....	....	35	....	....	....	....	....	....	....	....	....	....	....	....	....	....	....	....	....	....
	NHL Totals		**373**	**66**	**80**	**146**	**55**	**56**	**111**	**524**	**2**	**2**	**7**	**542**	**12.2**	**214**	**9**	**218**	**15**		**49**	**4**	**10**	**14**	**56**	**0**	**0**	**0**

Traded to **Hartford** by **Philadelphia** for Paul Lawless, January 22, 1988.

● CARTER, ANSON Anson Carter C – R. 6'1", 175 lbs. b: Toronto, Ont., 6/6/1974. Quebec's 11th choice, 220th overall, in 1992 Entry Draft.

Season	Club	League	GP	G	A	Pts	AG	AA	APts	PIM	PP	SH	GW	S	%	TGF	PGF	TGA	PGA	+/–	GP	G	A	Pts	PIM	PP	SH	GW
1991-92	Wexford Raiders	MJHL	42	18	22	40	....	....	....	24	....	....	....	....	....	....	....	....	....	....	....	....	....	....	....	....	....	....
1992-93	Michigan State Spartans	CCHA	34	15	7	22	....	....	....	20	....	....	....	....	....	....	....	....	....	....	....	....	....	....	....	....	....	....
1993-94	Michigan State Spartans	CCHA	39	30	24	54	....	....	....	36	....	....	....	....	....	....	....	....	....	....	....	....	....	....	....	....	....	....
	Canada	WJC-A	7	3	2	5	....	....	....	0	....	....	....	....	....	....	....	....	....	....	....	....	....	....	....	....	....	....
1994-95	Michigan State Spartans	CCHA	39	34	17	51	....	....	....	40	....	....	....	....	....	....	....	....	....	....	....	....	....	....	....	....	....	....
1995-96	Michigan State Spartans	CCHA	42	23	20	43	....	....	....	36	....	....	....	....	....	....	....	....	....	....	....	....	....	....	....	....	....	....
1996-97	**Washington Capitals**	**NHL**	**19**	**3**	**2**	**5**	**3**	**2**	**5**	**7**	**1**	**0**	**1**	**28**	**10.7**	**7**	**1**	**6**	**0**	**0**	....	....	....	....	....	....	....	....
	Portland Pirates	AHL	27	19	19	38	....	....	....	11	....	....	....	....	....	....	....	....	....	....	....	....	....	....	....	....	....	....
	Boston Bruins	**NHL**	**19**	**8**	**5**	**13**	**8**	**4**	**12**	**2**	**1**	**1**	**1**	**51**	**15.7**	**17**	**5**	**24**	**5**	**–7**	....	....	....	....	....	....	....	....
	Canada	WC-A	11	4	2	6	....	....	....	4	....	....	....	....	....	....	....	....	....	....	....	....	....	....	....	....	....	....
1997-98	**Boston Bruins**	**NHL**	**78**	**16**	**27**	**43**	**19**	**26**	**45**	**31**	**6**	**0**	**4**	**179**	**8.9**	**66**	**20**	**41**	**2**	**+7**	**6**	**1**	**1**	**2**	**0**	**0**	**0**	**0**
	NHL Totals		**116**	**27**	**34**	**61**	**30**	**32**	**62**	**40**	**8**	**1**	**6**	**258**	**10.5**	**90**	**26**	**71**	**7**		**6**	**1**	**1**	**2**	**0**	**0**	**0**	**0**

CCHA First All-Star Team (1994, 1995) • NCAA West Second All-American Team (1995) • CCHA Second All-Star Team (1996)

Rights transferred to **Colorado** after **Quebec** franchise relocated, June 21, 1995. Traded to **Washington** by **Colorado** for Washington's 4th round choice (Ben Storey) in 1996 Entry Draft, April 3, 1996. Traded to **Boston** by **Washington** with Jim Carey, Jason Allison and Washington's 3rd round choice (Lee Goren) in 1997 Entry Draft for Bill Ranford, Adam Oates and Rick Tocchet, March 1, 1997.

● CARTER, JOHN John Carter LW – L. 5'10", 181 lbs. b: Winchester, MA, 5/3/1963.

Season	Club	League	GP	G	A	Pts	AG	AA	APts	PIM	PP	SH	GW	S	%	TGF	PGF	TGA	PGA	+/–	GP	G	A	Pts	PIM	PP	SH	GW
1982-83	RPI Engineers	ECAC	29	16	22	38	....	....	....	33	....	....	....	....	....	....	....	....	....	....	....	....	....	....	....	....	....	....
1983-84	RPI Engineers	ECAC	38	35	39	74	....	....	....	52	....	....	....	....	....	....	....	....	....	....	....	....	....	....	....	....	....	....
1984-85	RPI Engineers	ECAC	37	43	29	72	....	....	....	52	....	....	....	....	....	....	....	....	....	....	....	....	....	....	....	....	....	....
1985-86	RPI Engineers	ECAC	27	23	18	41	....	....	....	68	....	....	....	....	....	....	....	....	....	....	....	....	....	....	....	....	....	....
	United States	WEC-A	9	1	2	3	....	....	....	14	....	....	....	....	....	....	....	....	....	....	....	....	....	....	....	....	....	....
	Boston Bruins	**NHL**	**3**	**0**	**0**	**0**	**0**	**0**	**0**	**0**	**0**	**0**	**0**	**2**	**0.0**	**0**	**0**	**0**	**0**	**0**	....	....	....	....	....	....	....	....
1986-87	**Boston Bruins**	**NHL**	**8**	**0**	**1**	**1**	**0**	**1**	**1**	**0**	**0**	**0**	**0**	**12**	**0.0**	**4**	**0**	**1**	**0**	**+3**	....	....	....	....	....	....	....	....
	Moncton Golden Flames	AHL	58	25	30	55	....	....	....	60	....	....	....	....	....	....	....	....	....	....	6	2	3	5	5	....	....	....
1987-88	**Boston Bruins**	**NHL**	**4**	**0**	**1**	**1**	**0**	**1**	**1**	**2**	**0**	**0**	**0**	**8**	**0.0**	**3**	**0**	**0**	**0**	**+3**	....	....	....	....	....	....	....	....
	Maine Mariners	AHL	76	38	38	76	....	....	....	145	....	....	....	....	....	....	....	....	....	....	10	4	4	8	44	....	....	....
1988-89	**Boston Bruins**	**NHL**	**44**	**12**	**10**	**22**	**10**	**7**	**17**	**24**	**4**	**1**	**0**	**96**	**12.5**	**45**	**16**	**31**	**1**	**–1**	**10**	**1**	**2**	**3**	**6**	**0**	**0**	**0**
	Maine Mariners	AHL	24	13	6	19	....	....	....	12	....	....	....	....	....	....	....	....	....	....	....	....	....	....	....	....	....	....
1989-90	**Boston Bruins**	**NHL**	**76**	**17**	**22**	**39**	**15**	**16**	**31**	**26**	**2**	**1**	**1**	**142**	**12.0**	**58**	**7**	**50**	**16**	**+17**	**21**	**6**	**3**	**9**	**45**	**0**	**1**	**0**
	Maine Mariners	AHL	2	2	2	4	....	....	....	2	....	....	....	....	....	....	....	....	....	....	....	....	....	....	....	....	....	....
1990-91	**Boston Bruins**	**NHL**	**50**	**4**	**7**	**11**	**4**	**5**	**9**	**68**	**1**	**1**	**2**	**61**	**6.6**	**27**	**1**	**45**	**6**	**–13**	....	....	....	....	....	....	....	....
	Maine Mariners	AHL	16	5	9	14	....	....	....	16	....	....	....	....	....	....	....	....	....	....	1	0	0	0	10	....	....	....
1991-92	**San Jose Sharks**	**NHL**	**4**	**0**	**0**	**0**	**0**	**0**	**0**	**0**	**0**	**0**	**0**	**5**	**0.0**	**0**	**0**	**6**	**4**	**–2**	....	....	....	....	....	....	....	....
	Kansas City Blades	IHL	42	11	15	26	....	....	....	116	....	....	....	....	....	....	....	....	....	....	15	6	9	15	18	....	....	....
1992-93	**San Jose Sharks**	**NHL**	**55**	**7**	**9**	**16**	**6**	**6**	**12**	**81**	**0**	**1**	**0**	**110**	**6.4**	**25**	**2**	**77**	**29**	**–25**	....	....	....	....	....	....	....	....
	Kansas City Blades	IHL	9	4	2	6	....	....	....	14	....	....	....	....	....	....	....	....	....	....	....	....	....	....	....	....	....	....
1993-94	Providence Bruins	AHL	47	11	5	16	....	....	....	82	....	....	....	....	....	....	....	....	....	....	....	....	....	....	....	....	....	....
1994-95	Worcester IceCats	AHL	64	18	9	27	....	....	....	96	....	....	....	....	....	....	....	....	....	....	....	....	....	....	....	....	....	....
	NHL Totals		**244**	**40**	**50**	**90**	**35**	**36**	**71**	**201**	**7**	**4**	**3**	**436**	**9.2**	**162**	**26**	**210**	**56**		**31**	**7**	**5**	**12**	**51**	**0**	**1**	**0**

ECAC Second All-Star Team (1984) • ECAC First All-Star Team (1985)

Signed as a free agent by **Boston**, May 3, 1988. Signed as a free agent by **San Jose**, August 22, 1991.

● CARTER, RON Ron Carter RW – L. 6'1", 205 lbs. b: Montreal, Que., 3/14/1958. Montreal's 4th choice, 36th overall, in 1978 Amateur Draft.

Season	Club	League	GP	G	A	Pts	AG	AA	APts	PIM	PP	SH	GW	S	%	TGF	PGF	TGA	PGA	+/–	GP	G	A	Pts	PIM	PP	SH	GW
1975-76	Sherbrooke Beavers	QMJHL	65	34	36	70	....	....	....	12	....	....	....	....	....	....	....	....	....	....	....	....	....	....	....	....	....	....
1976-77	Sherbrooke Beavers	QMJHL	72	77	50	127	....	....	....	18	....	....	....	....	....	....	....	....	....	....	....	....	....	....	....	....	....	....
1977-78	Sherbrooke Beavers	QMJHL	71	*88	86	*174	....	....	....	28	....	....	....	....	....	....	....	....	....	....	....	....	....	....	....	....	....	....

Season	Club	League	GP	G	A	Pts	AG	AA	APts	PIM	PP	SH	GW	S	%	TGF	PGF	TGA	PGA	+/-	GP	G	A	Pts	PIM	PP	SH	GW
			REGULAR SEASON																		PLAYOFFS							
1978-79	Springfield Indians	AHL	1	0	0	0	....	....	....	0	....	....	....	....	....	....	....	....	....	....	....	....	....	....	....	....	....	....
	Dallas Black Hawks	CHL	54	22	16	38	....	....	....	8	....	....	....	....	....	....	....	....	....	....	7	2	2	4	5	....	....	....
1979-80	**Edmonton Oilers**	**NHL**	**2**	**0**	**0**	**0**	**0**	**0**	**0**	**0**	**0**	**0**	**0**	**0**	**0.0**	**0**	**0**	**0**	**0**	**0**	....	....	....	....	....	....	....	....
	Houston Apollos	CHL	76	40	30	70	....	....	....	17	....	....	....	....	....	....	....	....	....	....	4	2	1	3	0	....	....	....
1980-81	Rochester Americans	AHL	38	31	19	50	....	....	....	8	....	....	....	....	....	....	....	....	....	....	....	....	....	....	....	....	....	....
	Erie Blades	EHL	38	23	21	44	....	....	....	6	....	....	....	....	....	....	....	....	....	....	....	....	....	....	....	....	....	....
1981-82	Rochester Americans	AHL	12	6	4	10	....	....	....	0	....	....	....	....	....	....	....	....	....	....	....	....	....	....	....	....	....	....
	Flint Generals	IHL	49	29	23	52	....	....	....	2	....	....	....	....	....	....	....	....	....	....	4	0	0	0	5	....	....	....
1982-83	Nashville South Stars	ACHL	58	47	49	96	....	....	....	21	....	....	....	....	....	....	....	....	....	....	....	....	....	....	....	....	....	....
1983-84	Virginia Lancers	ACHL	62	51	59	110	....	....	....	20	....	....	....	....	....	....	....	....	....	....	4	1	2	3	10	....	....	....
1984-85	Virginia Lancers	ACHL	57	56	48	104	....	....	....	10	....	....	....	....	....	....	....	....	....	....	4	1	2	3	2	....	....	....
1985-86	Virginia Lancers	ACHL	20	14	13	27	....	....	....	2	....	....	....	....	....	....	....	....	....	....	....	....	....	....	....	....	....	....
	Mohawk Valley Comets	ACHL	32	34	18	52	....	....	....	4	....	....	....	....	....	....	....	....	....	....	6	2	5	7	0	....	....	....
	NHL Totals		**2**	**0**	**0**	**0**	**0**	**0**	**0**	**0**	**0**	**0**	**0**	**0**	**0.0**	**0**	**0**	**0**	**0**		....	....	....	....	....	....	....	....

QMJHL First All-Star Team (1978)

Signed as an underage free agent by **Edmonton** (WHA), July, 1978. NHL rights retained by **Edmonton** prior to Expansion Draft, June 9, 1979.

• CASHMAN, WAYNE

Wayne Cashman   RW – R. 6'1", 208 lbs.   b: Kingston, Ont., 6/24/1945.

Season	Club	League	GP	G	A	Pts	AG	AA	APts	PIM	PP	SH	GW	S	%	TGF	PGF	TGA	PGA	+/-	GP	G	A	Pts	PIM	PP	SH	GW
1962-63	Oshawa Generals	OHA	1	0	1	1	....	....	....	0	....	....	....	....	....	....	....	....	....	....	....	....	....	....	....	....	....	....
1963-64	Oshawa Generals	OHA	27	9	12	21	....	....	....	37	....	....	....	....	....	....	....	....	....	....	6	2	2	4	15	....	....	....
1964-65	Oshawa Generals	OHA	55	27	46	73	....	....	....	104	....	....	....	....	....	....	....	....	....	....	6	3	2	5	11	....	....	....
	Boston Bruins	**NHL**	**1**	**0**	**0**	**0**	**0**	**0**	**0**	**0**	....	....	....	....	....	....	....	....	....	....	....	....	....	....	....	....	....	....
1965-66	Oshawa Generals	OHA	48	26	44	70	....	....	....	98	....	....	....	....	....	....	....	....	....	....	17	*15	20	*35	21	....	....	....
1966-67	Oklahoma City Blazers	CHL	70	20	36	56	....	....	....	98	....	....	....	....	....	....	....	....	....	....	11	3	4	7	4	....	....	....
1967-68	**Boston Bruins**	**NHL**	**12**	**0**	**4**	**4**	**0**	**4**	**4**	**2**	**0**	**0**	**0**	**12**	**0.0**	**4**	**1**	**8**	**0**	**–5**	**1**	**0**	**0**	**0**	**0**	**0**	**0**	**0**
	Oklahoma City Blazers	CHL	42	21	30	51	....	....	....	66	....	....	....	....	....	....	....	....	....	....	....	....	....	....	....	....	....	....
1968-69	**Boston Bruins**	**NHL**	**51**	**8**	**23**	**31**	**9**	**22**	**31**	**49**	**1**	**0**	**1**	**66**	**12.1**	**49**	**7**	**23**	**0**	**+19**	**6**	**0**	**1**	**1**	**0**	**0**	**0**	**0**
	Hershey Bears	AHL	21	6	9	15	....	....	....	30	....	....	....	....	....	....	....	....	....	....	....	....	....	....	....	....	....	....
1969-70	**Boston Bruins**	**NHL**	**70**	**9**	**26**	**35**	**10**	**26**	**36**	**79**	**0**	**0**	**1**	**104**	**8.7**	**56**	**7**	**34**	**7**	**+22**	**14**	**5**	**4**	**9**	**50**	**0**	**2**	**0**
1970-71	**Boston Bruins**	**NHL**	**77**	**21**	**58**	**79**	**22**	**51**	**73**	**100**	**4**	**0**	**3**	**175**	**12.0**	**134**	**20**	**56**	**1**	**+59**	**7**	**3**	**2**	**5**	**15**	**0**	**0**	**1**
1971-72	**Boston Bruins**	**NHL**	**74**	**23**	**29**	**52**	**25**	**26**	**51**	**103**	**1**	**0**	**3**	**150**	**15.3**	**98**	**7**	**51**	**2**	**+42**	**15**	**4**	**7**	**11**	**42**	**1**	**0**	**0**
1972-73	Canada	Summit	2	0	2	2	....	....	....	14	....	....	....	....	....	....	....	....	....	....	....	....	....	....	....	....	....	....
	Boston Bruins	**NHL**	**76**	**29**	**39**	**68**	**29**	**33**	**62**	**100**	**6**	**0**	**3**	**169**	**17.2**	**98**	**16**	**77**	**0**	**+5**	**5**	**1**	**1**	**2**	**4**	**0**	**0**	**0**
1973-74	**Boston Bruins**	**NHL**	**78**	**30**	**59**	**89**	**31**	**51**	**82**	**111**	**5**	**2**	**2**	**156**	**19.2**	**138**	**21**	**72**	**4**	**+49**	**16**	**5**	**9**	**14**	**46**	**1**	**0**	**1**
1974-75	**Boston Bruins**	**NHL**	**42**	**11**	**22**	**33**	**10**	**17**	**27**	**24**	**2**	**0**	**3**	**75**	**14.7**	**57**	**16**	**34**	**0**	**+7**	**1**	**0**	**2**	**2**	**0**	**0**	**0**	**0**
1975-76	**Boston Bruins**	**NHL**	**80**	**28**	**43**	**71**	**26**	**34**	**60**	**87**	**9**	**0**	**6**	**169**	**16.6**	**111**	**22**	**61**	**2**	**+30**	**11**	**1**	**5**	**6**	**16**	**0**	**0**	**0**
1976-77	**Boston Bruins**	**NHL**	**65**	**15**	**37**	**52**	**14**	**30**	**44**	**76**	**3**	**0**	**3**	**105**	**14.3**	**77**	**21**	**52**	**0**	**+4**	**14**	**1**	**8**	**9**	**18**	**0**	**0**	**0**
1977-78	**Boston Bruins**	**NHL**	**76**	**24**	**38**	**62**	**23**	**31**	**54**	**69**	**1**	**0**	**2**	**134**	**17.9**	**93**	**9**	**51**	**1**	**+34**	**15**	**4**	**6**	**10**	**13**	**3**	**0**	**2**
1978-79	**Boston Bruins**	**NHL**	**75**	**27**	**40**	**67**	**25**	**31**	**56**	**63**	**10**	**0**	**4**	**133**	**20.3**	**110**	**30**	**55**	**0**	**+18**	**10**	**4**	**6**	**9**	**8**	**1**	**0**	**1**
1979-80	**Boston Bruins**	**NHL**	**44**	**11**	**21**	**32**	**10**	**16**	**26**	**19**	**3**	**1**	**2**	**60**	**18.3**	**52**	**25**	**32**	**2**	**–3**	**10**	**3**	**3**	**6**	**32**	**1**	**0**	**0**
1980-81	**Boston Bruins**	**NHL**	**77**	**25**	**35**	**60**	**21**	**24**	**45**	**80**	**7**	**0**	**2**	**111**	**22.5**	**100**	**30**	**55**	**2**	**+17**	**3**	**0**	**1**	**1**	**0**	**0**	**0**	**0**
1981-82	**Boston Bruins**	**NHL**	**64**	**12**	**31**	**43**	**9**	**20**	**29**	**59**	**3**	**0**	**1**	**90**	**13.3**	**64**	**18**	**63**	**0**	**–17**	**9**	**0**	**2**	**2**	**6**	**0**	**0**	**0**
1982-83	**Boston Bruins**	**NHL**	**65**	**4**	**11**	**15**	**3**	**8**	**11**	**20**	**1**	**0**	**1**	**36**	**11.1**	**38**	**12**	**24**	**0**	**+2**	**8**	**0**	**1**	**1**	**0**	**0**	**0**	**0**
	NHL Totals		**1027**	**277**	**516**	**793**	**267**	**424**	**691**	**1041**	**56**	**3**	**37**	**1745**	**15.9**	**1285**	**277**	**748**	**21**		**145**	**31**	**57**	**88**	**250**	**7**	**2**	**5**

NHL Second All-Star Team (1974)

Played in NHL All-Star Game (1974)

• CASSELMAN, MIKE

Mike Casselman   C – L. 5'11", 190 lbs.   b: Morrisburg, Ont., 8/23/1968.   Detroit's 1st choice, 3rd overall, in 1990 Supplemental Draft.

Season	Club	League	GP	G	A	Pts	AG	AA	APts	PIM	PP	SH	GW	S	%	TGF	PGF	TGA	PGA	+/-	GP	G	A	Pts	PIM	PP	SH	GW
1987-88	Clarkson University	ECAC	24	4	1	5	....	....	....	....	....	....	....	....	....	....	....	....	....	....	....	....	....	....	....	....	....	....
1988-89	Clarkson University	ECAC	31	3	14	17	....	....	....	....	....	....	....	....	....	....	....	....	....	....	....	....	....	....	....	....	....	....
1989-90	Clarkson University	ECAC	34	22	21	43	....	....	....	69	....	....	....	....	....	....	....	....	....	....	....	....	....	....	....	....	....	....
1990-91	Clarkson University	ECAC	40	19	35	54	....	....	....	44	....	....	....	....	....	....	....	....	....	....	....	....	....	....	....	....	....	....
1991-92	Toledo Storm	ECHL	61	39	60	99	....	....	....	83	....	....	....	....	....	....	....	....	....	....	5	0	1	1	6	....	....	....
	Adirondack Red Wings	AHL	1	0	0	0	....	....	....	0	....	....	....	....	....	....	....	....	....	....	....	....	....	....	....	....	....	....
1992-93	Adirondack Red Wings	AHL	60	12	19	31	....	....	....	27	....	....	....	....	....	....	....	....	....	....	8	3	3	6	0	....	....	....
	Toledo Storm	ECHL	3	0	1	1	....	....	....	2	....	....	....	....	....	....	....	....	....	....	....	....	....	....	....	....	....	....
1993-94	Adirondack Red Wings	AHL	77	17	38	55	....	....	....	34	....	....	....	....	....	....	....	....	....	....	12	2	4	6	10	....	....	....
1994-95	Adirondack Red Wings	AHL	60	17	43	60	....	....	....	42	....	....	....	....	....	....	....	....	....	....	4	0	0	0	2	....	....	....
1995-96	**Florida Panthers**	**NHL**	**3**	**0**	**0**	**0**	**0**	**0**	**0**	**0**	**0**	**0**	**0**	**2**	**0.0**	**0**	**0**	**1**	**0**	**–1**	....	....	....	....	....	....	....	....
	Carolina Monarchs	AHL	70	34	68	102	....	....	....	46	....	....	....	....	....	....	....	....	....	....	....	....	....	....	....	....	....	....
1996-97	Cincinnati Cyclones	IHL	68	30	34	64	....	....	....	54	....	....	....	....	....	....	....	....	....	....	3	1	0	1	2	....	....	....
1997-98	Cincinnati Cyclones	IHL	55	19	28	47	....	....	....	44	....	....	....	....	....	....	....	....	....	....	....	....	....	....	....	....	....	....
	Rochester Americans	AHL	25	8	7	15	....	....	....	14	....	....	....	....	....	....	....	....	....	....	4	1	1	2	2	....	....	....
	NHL Totals		**3**	**0**	**0**	**0**	**0**	**0**	**0**	**0**	**0**	**0**	**0**	**2**	**0.0**	**0**	**0**	**1**	**0**		....	....	....	....	....	....	....	....

ECHL Second All-Star Team (1992)

Signed as a free agent by **Florida**, October 31, 1995. Signed as a free agent by **San Jose**, September 24, 1997.

• CASSELS, ANDREW

Andrew Cassels   C – L. 5'11", 177 lbs.   b: Bramalea, Ont., 7/23/1969.   Montreal's 1st choice, 17th overall, in 1987 Entry Draft.

Season	Club	League	GP	G	A	Pts	AG	AA	APts	PIM	PP	SH	GW	S	%	TGF	PGF	TGA	PGA	+/-	GP	G	A	Pts	PIM	PP	SH	GW
1986-87	Ottawa 67's	OHL	66	26	66	92	....	....	....	28	....	....	....	....	....	....	....	....	....	....	11	5	9	14	7	....	....	....
1987-88	Ottawa 67's	OHL	61	48	*103	*151	....	....	....	39	....	....	....	....	....	....	....	....	....	....	16	8	*24	*32	13	....	....	....
1988-89	Ottawa 67's	OHL	56	37	97	134	....	....	....	66	....	....	....	....	....	....	....	....	....	....	12	5	10	15	10	....	....	....
	Canada	WJC-A	7	2	5	7	....	....	....	2	....	....	....	....	....	....	....	....	....	....	....	....	....	....	....	....	....	....
1989-90	**Montreal Canadiens**	**NHL**	**6**	**2**	**0**	**2**	**2**	**0**	**2**	**2**	**0**	**0**	**1**	**5**	**40.0**	**3**	**0**	**2**	**0**	**+1**	....	....	....	....	....	....	....	....
	Sherbrooke Canadiens	AHL	55	22	45	67	....	....	....	25	....	....	....	....	....	....	....	....	....	....	12	2	11	13	6	....	....	....
1990-91	Montreal Canadiens	FrTour	1	0	1	1	....	....	....	0	....	....	....	....	....	....	....	....	....	....	....	....	....	....	....	....	....	....
	Montreal Canadiens	**NHL**	**54**	**6**	**19**	**25**	**5**	**14**	**19**	**20**	**1**	**0**	**3**	**55**	**10.9**	**39**	**10**	**28**	**1**	**+2**	**8**	**0**	**2**	**2**	**2**	**0**	**0**	**0**
1991-92	**Hartford Whalers**	**NHL**	**67**	**11**	**30**	**41**	**10**	**23**	**33**	**18**	**2**	**2**	**3**	**99**	**11.1**	**58**	**18**	**56**	**19**	**+3**	**7**	**2**	**4**	**6**	**6**	**1**	**0**	**0**
1992-93	**Hartford Whalers**	**NHL**	**84**	**21**	**64**	**85**	**17**	**44**	**61**	**62**	**8**	**3**	**1**	**134**	**15.7**	**117**	**53**	**128**	**53**	**–11**	....	....	....	....	....	....	....	....
1993-94	**Hartford Whalers**	**NHL**	**79**	**16**	**42**	**58**	**15**	**32**	**47**	**37**	**8**	**1**	**3**	**126**	**12.7**	**88**	**39**	**105**	**35**	**–21**	....	....	....	....	....	....	....	....
1994-95	**Hartford Whalers**	**NHL**	**46**	**7**	**30**	**37**	**12**	**44**	**56**	**18**	**1**	**0**	**1**	**74**	**9.5**	**51**	**16**	**52**	**14**	**–3**	....	....	....	....	....	....	....	....
1995-96	**Hartford Whalers**	**NHL**	**81**	**20**	**43**	**63**	**20**	**35**	**55**	**39**	**6**	**0**	**1**	**135**	**14.8**	**101**	**39**	**87**	**33**	**+8**	....	....	....	....	....	....	....	....
	Canada	WC-A	6	1	0	1	....	....	....	0	....	....	....	....	....	....	....	....	....	....	....	....	....	....	....	....	....	....
1996-97	**Hartford Whalers**	**NHL**	**81**	**22**	**44**	**66**	**23**	**39**	**62**	**46**	**8**	**0**	**2**	**142**	**15.5**	**88**	**33**	**89**	**18**	**–16**	....	....	....	....	....	....	....	....
1997-98	**Calgary Flames**	**NHL**	**81**	**17**	**27**	**44**	**20**	**26**	**46**	**32**	**6**	**1**	**2**	**138**	**12.3**	**62**	**18**	**65**	**14**	**–7**	....	....	....	....	....	....	....	....
	NHL Totals		**579**	**122**	**299**	**421**	**124**	**257**	**381**	**274**	**40**	**7**	**17**	**908**	**13.4**	**607**	**226**	**612**	**187**		**15**	**2**	**6**	**8**	**8**	**1**	**0**	**0**

OHL First All-Star Team (1988,1989)

Traded to **Hartford** by **Montreal** for Hartford's 2nd round choice (Valeri Bure) in 1992 Entry Draft, September 17, 1991. Traded to **Calgary** by **Carolina** with Jean-Sebastien Giguere for Gary Roberts and Trevor Kidd, August 25, 1997.

• CASSIDY, BRUCE

Bruce Cassidy   D – L. 5'11", 176 lbs.   b: Ottawa, Ont., 5/20/1965.   Chicago's 1st choice, 18th overall, in 1983 Entry Draft.

Season	Club	League	GP	G	A	Pts	AG	AA	APts	PIM	PP	SH	GW	S	%	TGF	PGF	TGA	PGA	+/-	GP	G	A	Pts	PIM	PP	SH	GW
1981-82	Hawkesbury Hawks	OJHL	37	13	30	43	....	....	....	32	....	....	....	....	....	....	....	....	....	....	....	....	....	....	....	....	....	....
1982-83	Ottawa 67's	OHL	70	25	86	111	....	....	....	33	....	....	....	....	....	....	....	....	....	....	9	3	9	12	10	....	....	....
1983-84	Ottawa 67's	OHL	67	27	68	95	....	....	....	58	....	....	....	....	....	....	....	....	....	....	13	6	16	22	6	....	....	....
	Canada	WJC-A	7	0	0	0	....	....	....	6	....	....	....	....	....	....	....	....	....	....	....	....	....	....	....	....	....	....
	Chicago Black Hawks	**NHL**	**1**	**0**	**0**	**0**	**0**	**0**	**0**	**0**	**0**	**0**	**0**	**1**	**0.0**	**0**	**0**	**0**	**0**	**0**	....	....	....	....	....	....	....	....
1984-85	Ottawa 67's	OHL	28	13	27	40	....	....	....	15	....	....	....	....	....	....	....	....	....	....	....	....	....	....	....	....	....	....
1985-86	**Chicago Black Hawks**	**NHL**	**1**	**0**	**0**	**0**	**0**	**0**	**0**	**0**	**0**	**0**	**0**	**2**	**0.0**	**0**	**0**	**0**	**0**	**0**	....	....	....	....	....	....	....	....
	Nova Scotia Oilers	AHL	4	0	0	0	....	....	....	0	....	....	....	....	....	....	....	....	....	....	....	....	....	....	....	....	....	....

			REGULAR SEASON																		PLAYOFFS							
Season	**Club**	**League**	**GP**	**G**	**A**	**Pts**	**AG**	**AA**	**APts**	**PIM**	**PP**	**SH**	**GW**	**S**	**%**	**TGF**	**PGF**	**TGA**	**PGA**	**+/–**	**GP**	**G**	**A**	**Pts**	**PIM**	**PP**	**SH**	**GW**
1986-87	**Chicago Blackhawks**	**NHL**	**2**	**0**	**0**	**0**	**0**	**0**	**0**	**0**	**0**	**0**	**0**	**0**	**0.0**	**2**	**1**	**2**	**0**	**–1**	....	....	....	....	....	....	....	....
	Nova Scotia Oilers	AHL	19	2	8	10	....	....	....	4	....	....	....	....	....	....	....	....	....	....	....	....	....	....	....	....	....	....
	Canada	Nat-Team	12	3	6	9	....	....	....	4	....	....	....	....	....	....	....	....	....	....	....	....	....	....	....	....	....	....
	Saginaw Generals	IHL	10	2	13	15	....	....	....	6	....	....	....	....	....	....	....	....	....	....	2	1	1	2	0	....	....	....
1987-88	**Chicago Blackhawks**	**NHL**	**21**	**3**	**10**	**13**	**3**	**7**	**10**	**6**	**2**	**0**	**0**	**46**	**6.5**	**28**	**14**	**18**	**1**	**–3**	....	....	....	....	....	....	....	....
	Saginaw Hawks	IHL	60	9	37	46	....	....	....	59	....	....	....	....	....	....	....	....	....	....	10	2	3	5	19	....	....	....
1988-89	**Chicago Blackhawks**	**NHL**	**9**	**0**	**2**	**2**	**0**	**1**	**1**	**4**	**0**	**0**	**0**	**12**	**0.0**	**3**	**2**	**7**	**1**	**–5**	**1**	**0**	**0**	**0**	**0**	**0**	**0**	**0**
	Saginaw Hawks	IHL	72	16	64	80	....	....	....	80	....	....	....	....	....	....	....	....	....	....	6	0	2	2	6	....	....	....
1989-90	**Chicago Blackhawks**	**NHL**	**2**	**1**	**1**	**2**	**1**	**1**	**2**	**0**	**1**	**0**	**0**	**3**	**33.3**	**3**	**1**	**3**	**0**	**–1**	....	....	....	....	....	....	....	....
	Indianapolis Ice	IHL	75	11	46	57	....	....	....	56	....	....	....	....	....	....	....	....	....	....	14	1	10	11	20	....	....	....
1990-91	HC Alleghe	Italy	36	23	52	75	....	....	....	20	....	....	....	....	....	....	....	....	....	....	10	7	8	15	2	....	....	....
1991-92	HC Alleghe	Italy	27	14	29	43	....	....	....	12	....	....	....	....	....	....	....	....	....	....	....	....	....	....	....	....	....	....
1992-93	HC Alleghe	Italy	25	12	30	42	....	....	....	10	....	....	....	....	....	....	....	....	....	....	8	5	9	14	....	....	....	....
1993-94	ESV Kaufbeuren	Germany	33	8	9	17	....	....	....	12	....	....	....	....	....	....	....	....	....	....	4	1	2	3	....	....	....	....
1994-95	Indianapolis Ice	IHL	29	2	13	15	....	....	....	16	....	....	....	....	....	....	....	....	....	....	....	....	....	....	....	....	....	....
1995-96	Indianapolis Ice	IHL	56	5	16	21	....	....	....	46	....	....	....	....	....	....	....	....	....	....	5	1	0	1	4	....	....	....
1996-97	Indianapolis Ice	IHL	10	0	4	4	....	....	....	11	....	....	....	....	....	....	....	....	....	....	....	....	....	....	....	....	....	....
	NHL Totals		**36**	**4**	**13**	**17**	**4**	**9**	**13**	**10**	**3**	**0**	**0**	**64**	**6.3**	**36**	**18**	**30**	**2**		**1**	**0**	**0**	**0**	**0**	**0**	**0**	**0**

OHL Second All-Star Team (1984) • Memorial Cup All-Star Team (1984) • IHL First All-Star Team (1989, 1990)

Signed as a free agent by **Chicago**, July 28, 1994.

• CASSIDY, TOM

Tom Cassidy C – L. 5′11″, 180 lbs. b: Blind River, Ont., 3/15/1952. California's 1st choice, 22nd overall, in 1972 Amateur Draft.

Season	Club	League	GP	G	A	Pts	AG	AA	APts	PIM	PP	SH	GW	S	%	TGF	PGF	TGA	PGA	+/–	GP	G	A	Pts	PIM	PP	SH	GW
1969-70	Kitchener Rangers	OHA	24	5	2	7	....	....	....	14	....	....	....	....	....	....	....	....	....	....	....	....	....	....	....	....	....	....
1970-71	Kitchener Rangers	OHA	62	42	62	104	....	....	....	94	....	....	....	....	....	....	....	....	....	....	....	....	....	....	....	....	....	....
1971-72	Kitchener Rangers	OHA	55	32	44	76	....	....	....	109	....	....	....	....	....	....	....	....	....	....	....	....	....	....	....	....	....	....
1972-73	Baltimore Clippers	AHL	73	21	32	53	....	....	....	86	....	....	....	....	....	....	....	....	....	....	....	....	....	....	....	....	....	....
1973-74	Springfield Kings	AHL	15	3	8	11	....	....	....	14	....	....	....	....	....	....	....	....	....	....	....	....	....	....	....	....	....	....
	Salt Lake Golden Eagles	WHL	31	12	11	23	....	....	....	4	....	....	....	....	....	....	....	....	....	....	....	....	....	....	....	....	....	....
1974-75	Springfield Indians	AHL	72	32	59	91	....	....	....	201	....	....	....	....	....	....	....	....	....	....	17	4	11	15	8	....	....	....
1975-76	Oklahoma City Blazers	CHL	76	35	50	85	....	....	....	124	....	....	....	....	....	....	....	....	....	....	4	1	2	3	4	....	....	....
1976-77	Columbus Owls	IHL	75	47	61	108	....	....	....	172	....	....	....	....	....	....	....	....	....	....	7	1	5	6	2	....	....	....
1977-78	**Pittsburgh Penguins**	**NHL**	**26**	**3**	**4**	**7**	**3**	**3**	**6**	**15**	**0**	**0**	**0**	**16**	**18.8**	**10**	**0**	**20**	**6**	**–4**	....	....	....	....	....	....	....	....
	Binghamton Whalers	AHL	40	7	7	14	....	....	....	19	....	....	....	....	....	....	....	....	....	....	....	....	....	....	....	....	....	....
1978-79	Rochester Americans	AHL	51	11	35	46	....	....	....	55	....	....	....	....	....	....	....	....	....	....	....	....	....	....	....	....	....	....
	Oklahoma City Stars	CHL	19	2	5	7	....	....	....	23	....	....	....	....	....	....	....	....	....	....	....	....	....	....	....	....	....	....
	NHL Totals		**26**	**3**	**4**	**7**	**3**	**3**	**6**	**15**	**0**	**0**	**0**	**16**	**18.8**	**10**	**0**	**20**	**6**		....	....	....	....	....	....	....	....

Traded to **LA Kings** by **California** for cash, March 12, 1974. Signed as a free agent by **Boston**, October 30, 1976. Signed as a free agent by **Pittsburgh**, October 11, 1977.

• CASSOLATO, TONY

Tony Cassolato RW – R. 5′11″, 180 lbs. b: Guelph, Ont., 5/7/1956.

Season	Club	League	GP	G	A	Pts	AG	AA	APts	PIM	PP	SH	GW	S	%	TGF	PGF	TGA	PGA	+/–	GP	G	A	Pts	PIM	PP	SH	GW
1973-74	Peterborough Petes	OHA	68	11	32	43	....	....	....	47	....	....	....	....	....	....	....	....	....	....	....	....	....	....	....	....	....	....
	Canada	WJC-A	3	0	0	0	....	....	....	0	....	....	....	....	....	....	....	....	....	....	....	....	....	....	....	....	....	....
1974-75	Peterborough Petes	OHA	70	43	41	84	....	....	....	52	....	....	....	....	....	....	....	....	....	....	11	3	5	8	15	....	....	....
1975-76	Peterborough Petes	OHA	60	26	39	65	....	....	....	59	....	....	....	....	....	....	....	....	....	....	....	....	....	....	....	....	....	....
1976-77	San Diego Mariners	WHA	43	13	12	25	....	....	....	26	....	....	....	....	....	....	....	....	....	....	3	0	0	0	4	....	....	....
	Charlotte Checkers	SHL	19	9	10	19	....	....	....	18	....	....	....	....	....	....	....	....	....	....	16	6	*16	*22	6	....	....	....
1977-78	Birmingham Bulls	WHA	77	18	25	43	....	....	....	59	....	....	....	....	....	....	....	....	....	....	4	0	0	0	4	....	....	....
1978-79	Birmingham Bulls	WHA	64	13	7	20	....	....	....	62	....	....	....	....	....	....	....	....	....	....	....	....	....	....	....	....	....	....
	Binghamton Whalers	AHL	6	1	1	2	....	....	....	0	....	....	....	....	....	....	....	....	....	....	....	....	....	....	....	....	....	....
1979-80	**Washington Capitals**	**NHL**	**9**	**0**	**2**	**2**	**0**	**2**	**2**	**0**	**0**	**0**	**0**	**6**	**0.0**	**3**	**0**	**1**	**0**	**+2**	....	....	....	....	....	....	....	....
	Hershey Bears	AHL	73	21	33	54	....	....	....	45	....	....	....	....	....	....	....	....	....	....	16	6	16	22	6	....	....	....
1980-81	**Washington Capitals**	**NHL**	**2**	**0**	**0**	**0**	**0**	**0**	**0**	**0**	**0**	**0**	**0**	**1**	**0.0**	**0**	**0**	**0**	**0**	**0**	....	....	....	....	....	....	....	....
	Hershey Bears	AHL	74	*48	46	95	....	....	....	23	....	....	....	....	....	....	....	....	....	....	10	7	7	14	2	....	....	....
1981-82	**Washington Capitals**	**NHL**	**12**	**1**	**4**	**5**	**1**	**3**	**4**	**4**	**0**	**0**	**0**	**15**	**6.7**	**7**	**2**	**4**	**0**	**+1**	....	....	....	....	....	....	....	....
	Hershey Bears	AHL	54	29	37	66	....	....	....	56	....	....	....	....	....	....	....	....	....	....	5	3	5	8	2	....	....	....
1982-83	Hershey Bears	AHL	75	53	38	91	....	....	....	22	....	....	....	....	....	....	....	....	....	....	5	0	3	3	0	....	....	....
1983-84	Riessersee	Germany	46	26	21	47	....	....	....	39	....	....	....	....	....	....	....	....	....	....	....	....	....	....	....	....	....	....
1984-85	SG Brunico	Italy	26	29	30	59	....	....	....	37	....	....	....	....	....	....	....	....	....	....	6	6	4	10	6	....	....	....
	NHL Totals		**23**	**1**	**6**	**7**	**1**	**5**	**6**	**4**	**0**	**0**	**0**	**22**	**4.5**	**10**	**2**	**5**	**0**		....	....	....	....	....	....	....	....
	Other Major League Totals		184	44	44	88	....	....	....	147	....	....	....	....	....	....	....	....	....		7	0	0	0	8	....	....	....

AHL Second All-Star Team (1981, 1983) • Won Fred T. Hunt Memorial Trophy (Sportsmanship - AHL) (1981)

Signed as a free agent by **San Diego** (WHA), October, 1976. Signed as a free agent by **Birmingham** (WHA) after **San Diego** (WHA) franchise folded, September, 1977. Signed as a free agent by **Washington**, August 12, 1979.

• CAUFIELD, JAY

Jay Caufield RW – R. 6′4″, 237 lbs. b: Philadelphia, PA, 7/17/1960.

Season	Club	League	GP	G	A	Pts	AG	AA	APts	PIM	PP	SH	GW	S	%	TGF	PGF	TGA	PGA	+/–	GP	G	A	Pts	PIM	PP	SH	GW
1984-85	University of North Dakota	WCHA	1	0	0	0	....	....	....	0	....	....	....	....	....	....	....	....	....	....	....	....	....	....	....	....	....	....
1985-86	Toledo Goaldiggers	IHL	30	5	4	9	....	....	....	54	....	....	....	....	....	....	....	....	....	....	....	....	....	....	....	....	....	....
	New Haven Nighthawks	AHL	40	2	3	5	....	....	....	40	....	....	....	....	....	....	....	....	....	....	1	0	0	0	0	....	....	....
1986-87	**New York Rangers**	**NHL**	**13**	**2**	**1**	**3**	**2**	**1**	**3**	**45**	**0**	**0**	**0**	**8**	**25.0**	**5**	**0**	**7**	**0**	**–2**	**3**	**0**	**0**	**0**	**12**	**0**	**0**	**0**
	Flint Spirits	IHL	12	4	3	7	....	....	....	59	....	....	....	....	....	....	....	....	....	....	....	....	....	....	....	....	....	....
	New Haven Nighthawks	AHL	13	0	0	0	....	....	....	43	....	....	....	....	....	....	....	....	....	....	....	....	....	....	....	....	....	....
1987-88	**Minnesota North Stars**	**NHL**	**1**	**0**	**0**	**0**	**0**	**0**	**0**	**0**	**0**	**0**	**0**	**0**	**0.0**	**0**	**0**	**0**	**0**	**0**	....	....	....	....	....	....	....	....
	Kalamazoo Wings	IHL	65	5	10	15	....	....	....	273	....	....	....	....	....	....	....	....	....	....	6	0	1	1	47	....	....	....
1988-89	**Pittsburgh Penguins**	**NHL**	**58**	**1**	**4**	**5**	**1**	**3**	**4**	**285**	**0**	**0**	**0**	**10**	**10.0**	**12**	**0**	**17**	**1**	**–4**	**9**	**0**	**0**	**0**	**28**	**0**	**0**	**0**
1989-90	**Pittsburgh Penguins**	**NHL**	**37**	**1**	**2**	**3**	**1**	**1**	**2**	**123**	**0**	**0**	**0**	**6**	**16.7**	**4**	**0**	**4**	**0**	**0**	....	....	....	....	....	....	....	....
1990-91	**Pittsburgh Penguins**	**NHL**	**23**	**1**	**1**	**2**	**1**	**1**	**2**	**71**	**0**	**0**	**1**	**5**	**20.0**	**4**	**0**	**6**	**0**	**–2**	....	....	....	....	....	....	....	....
	Muskegon Lumberjacks	IHL	3	1	0	1	....	....	....	18	....	....	....	....	....	....	....	....	....	....	....	....	....	....	....	....	....	....
1991-92	**Pittsburgh Penguins**	**NHL**	**50**	**0**	**0**	**0**	**0**	**0**	**0**	**175**	**0**	**0**	**0**	**16**	**0.0**	**1**	**0**	**7**	**0**	**–6**	**5**	**0**	**0**	**0**	**2**	**0**	**0**	**0**
1992-93	**Pittsburgh Penguins**	**NHL**	**26**	**0**	**0**	**0**	**0**	**0**	**0**	**60**	**0**	**0**	**0**	**6**	**0.0**	**0**	**0**	**1**	**0**	**–1**	....	....	....	....	....	....	....	....
1993-94	Kalamazoo Wings	IHL	45	2	3	5	....	....	....	176	....	....	....	....	....	....	....	....	....	....	4	0	0	0	18	....	....	....
	NHL Totals		**208**	**5**	**8**	**13**	**5**	**6**	**11**	**759**	**0**	**0**	**1**	**51**	**9.8**	**26**	**0**	**42**	**1**		**17**	**0**	**0**	**0**	**42**	**0**	**0**	**0**

• Played football at University of North Dakota, 1982-1986. Signed as a free agent by **NY Rangers**, October 8, 1985. Traded to **Minnesota** by **NY Rangers** with Dave Gagner for Jari Gronstad and Paul Boutilier, October 8, 1987. Claimed by **Pittsburgh** from **Minnesota** in Waiver Draft, October 3, 1988.

• CAVALLINI, GINO

Gino Cavallini LW – L. 6′1″, 215 lbs. b: Toronto, Ont., 11/24/1962.

Season	Club	League	GP	G	A	Pts	AG	AA	APts	PIM	PP	SH	GW	S	%	TGF	PGF	TGA	PGA	+/–	GP	G	A	Pts	PIM	PP	SH	GW
1981-82	St. Michael's Buzzers	Jr. B	33	22	33	55	....	....	....	50	....	....	....	....	....	....	....	....	....	....	....	....	....	....	....	....	....	....
1982-83	Bowling Green University	CCHA	40	8	16	24	....	....	....	52	....	....	....	....	....	....	....	....	....	....	....	....	....	....	....	....	....	....
1983-84	Bowling Green University	CCHA	43	25	23	48	....	....	....	16	....	....	....	....	....	....	....	....	....	....	....	....	....	....	....	....	....	....
1984-85	**Calgary Flames**	**NHL**	**27**	**6**	**10**	**16**	**5**	**7**	**12**	**14**	**1**	**0**	**0**	**44**	**13.6**	**29**	**6**	**12**	**0**	**+11**	**3**	**0**	**0**	**0**	**4**	**0**	**0**	**0**
	Moncton Golden Flames	AHL	51	29	19	48	....	....	....	28	....	....	....	....	....	....	....	....	....	....	....	....	....	....	....	....	....	....
1985-86	**Calgary Flames**	**NHL**	**27**	**7**	**7**	**14**	**6**	**5**	**11**	**26**	**4**	**0**	**0**	**51**	**13.7**	**27**	**16**	**18**	**0**	**–7**	....	....	....	....	....	....	....	....
	Moncton Golden Flames	AHL	4	3	2	5	....	....	....	7	....	....	....	....	....	....	....	....	....	....	....	....	....	....	....	....	....	....
	St. Louis Blues	**NHL**	**30**	**6**	**5**	**11**	**5**	**3**	**8**	**36**	**1**	**0**	**0**	**44**	**13.6**	**16**	**2**	**16**	**0**	**–2**	**17**	**4**	**5**	**9**	**10**	**0**	**0**	**2**
1986-87	**St. Louis Blues**	**NHL**	**80**	**18**	**26**	**44**	**16**	**19**	**35**	**54**	**4**	**0**	**2**	**161**	**11.2**	**68**	**9**	**55**	**0**	**+4**	**6**	**3**	**1**	**4**	**2**	**1**	**0**	**1**
1987-88	**St. Louis Blues**	**NHL**	**64**	**15**	**17**	**32**	**13**	**12**	**25**	**62**	**2**	**1**	**3**	**131**	**11.5**	**47**	**5**	**59**	**13**	**–4**	**10**	**5**	**5**	**10**	**19**	**2**	**0**	**0**
1988-89	**St. Louis Blues**	**NHL**	**74**	**20**	**23**	**43**	**17**	**16**	**33**	**79**	**1**	**0**	**4**	**153**	**13.1**	**65**	**9**	**56**	**2**	**+2**	**9**	**0**	**2**	**2**	**17**	**0**	**0**	**0**
1989-90	**St. Louis Blues**	**NHL**	**80**	**15**	**15**	**30**	**13**	**11**	**24**	**77**	**1**	**0**	**4**	**134**	**11.2**	**46**	**5**	**49**	**0**	**–8**	**12**	**1**	**3**	**4**	**12**	**0**	**0**	**1**
1990-91	**St. Louis Blues**	**NHL**	**78**	**8**	**27**	**35**	**7**	**20**	**27**	**81**	**3**	**0**	**2**	**131**	**6.1**	**58**	**12**	**43**	**1**	**+4**	**13**	**1**	**3**	**4**	**2**	**0**	**0**	**0**
1991-92	**St. Louis Blues**	**NHL**	**48**	**9**	**7**	**16**	**8**	**5**	**13**	**40**	**0**	**0**	**2**	**72**	**12.5**	**30**	**2**	**36**	**0**	**–8**	....	....	....	....	....	....	....	....
	Quebec Nordiques	**NHL**	**18**	**1**	**7**	**8**	**1**	**5**	**6**	**4**	**0**	**0**	**0**	**39**	**2.6**	**21**	**10**	**12**	**0**	**–1**	....	....	....	....	....	....	....	....
1992-93	**Quebec Nordiques**	**NHL**	**67**	**9**	**15**	**24**	**7**	**10**	**17**	**34**	**0**	**0**	**0**	**71**	**12.7**	**38**	**1**	**27**	**0**	**+10**	**4**	**0**	**0**	**0**	**0**	**0**	**0**	**0**
1993-94	Milwaukee Admirals	IHL	78	43	35	78	....	....	....	64	....	....	....	....	....	....	....	....	....	....	4	3	4	7	6	....	....	....

			REGULAR SEASON																		PLAYOFFS							
Season	**Club**	**League**	**GP**	**G**	**A**	**Pts**	**AG**	**AA**	**APts**	**PIM**	**PP**	**SH**	**GW**	**S**	**%**	**TGF**	**PGF**	**TGA**	**PGA**	**+/–**	**GP**	**G**	**A**	**Pts**	**PIM**	**PP**	**SH**	**GW**
1994-95	Milwaukee Admirals	IHL	80	53	35	88	....	....	....	54	....	....	....	....	....	....	....	....	....	....	15	7	2	9	10	....	....	....
1995-96	Milwaukee Admirals	IHL	82	43	39	82	....	....	....	20	....	....	....	....	....	....	....	....	....	....	5	3	1	4	2	....	....	....
1996-97	EV Landshut	Germany	48	25	29	54	....	....	....	32	....	....	....	....	....	....	....	....	....	....	7	3	2	5	4	....	....	....
	HC Bolzano	Italy	3	2	1	3	....	....	....	0	....	....	....	....	....	....	....	....	....	....	....	....	....	....	....	....	....	....
1997-98	EV Landshut	Germany	48	12	18	30	....	....	....	30	....	....	....	....	....	....	....	....	....	....	6	1	5	6	25	....	....	....
	NHL Totals		**593**	**114**	**159**	**273**	**98**	**113**	**211**	**507**	**17**	**1**	**17**	**1031**	**11.1**	**445**	**77**	**383**	**16**		**74**	**14**	**19**	**33**	**66**	**3**	**0**	**4**

IHL Second All-Star Team (1995)

Signed as a free agent by **Calgary**, May 16, 1984. Traded to **St. Louis** by **Calgary** with Eddy Beers and Charlie Bourgeois for Joe Mullen, Terry Johnson and Rik Wilson, February 1, 1986. Claimed on waivers by **Quebec** from **St Louis**, February 27, 1992.

• CAVALLINI, PAUL

Paul Cavallini D – L. 6'1", 202 lbs. b: Toronto, Ont., 10/13/1965. Washington's 9th choice, 205th overall, in 1984 Entry Draft.

Season	Club	League	GP	G	A	Pts	AG	AA	APts	PIM	PP	SH	GW	S	%	TGF	PGF	TGA	PGA	+/–	GP	G	A	Pts	PIM	PP	SH	GW
1983-84	Henry Carr Crusaders	H.S.	54	20	41	61	....	....	....	190	....	....	....	....	....	....	....	....	....	....	....	....	....	....	....	....	....	....
1984-85	Providence College	H.E.	37	4	10	14	....	....	....	52	....	....	....	....	....	....	....	....	....	....	....	....	....	....	....	....	....	....
1985-86	Canada	Nat-Team	52	1	11	12	....	....	....	95	....	....	....	....	....	....	....	....	....	....	....	....	....	....	....	....	....	....
	Binghamton Whalers	AHL	15	3	4	7	....	....	....	20	....	....	....	....	....	....	....	....	....	....	6	0	2	2	56	....	....	....
1986-87	**Washington Capitals**	**NHL**	**6**	**0**	**2**	**2**	**0**	**1**	**1**	**8**	**0**	**0**	**0**	**6**	**0.0**	**4**	**1**	**7**	**0**	**–4**	....	....	....	....	....	....	....	....
	Binghamton Whalers	AHL	66	12	24	36	....	....	....	188	....	....	....	....	....	....	....	....	....	....	13	2	7	9	35	....	....	....
1987-88	**Washington Capitals**	**NHL**	**24**	**2**	**3**	**5**	**2**	**2**	**4**	**66**	**0**	**0**	**1**	**18**	**11.1**	**12**	**0**	**15**	**3**	**0**	....	....	....	....	....	....	....	....
	St. Louis Blues	**NHL**	**48**	**4**	**7**	**11**	**3**	**5**	**8**	**86**	**1**	**0**	**0**	**53**	**7.5**	**48**	**8**	**47**	**14**	**+7**	**10**	**1**	**6**	**7**	**26**	**0**	**1**	**0**
1988-89	**St. Louis Blues**	**NHL**	**65**	**4**	**20**	**24**	**3**	**14**	**17**	**128**	**0**	**0**	**0**	**93**	**4.3**	**83**	**12**	**78**	**32**	**+25**	**10**	**2**	**2**	**4**	**14**	**0**	**0**	**0**
1989-90	**St. Louis Blues**	**NHL**	**80**	**8**	**39**	**47**	**7**	**28**	**35**	**106**	**2**	**1**	**0**	**135**	**5.9**	**134**	**26**	**112**	**42**	**+38**	**12**	**2**	**3**	**5**	**20**	**0**	**0**	**0**
1990-91	**St. Louis Blues**	**NHL**	**67**	**10**	**25**	**35**	**9**	**19**	**28**	**89**	**3**	**0**	**0**	**116**	**8.6**	**92**	**13**	**72**	**12**	**+19**	**13**	**2**	**3**	**5**	**20**	**1**	**0**	**0**
1991-92	**St. Louis Blues**	**NHL**	**66**	**10**	**25**	**35**	**9**	**19**	**28**	**95**	**3**	**1**	**2**	**164**	**6.1**	**93**	**19**	**86**	**19**	**+7**	**4**	**0**	**1**	**1**	**6**	**0**	**0**	**0**
1992-93	**St. Louis Blues**	**NHL**	**11**	**1**	**4**	**5**	**1**	**3**	**4**	**10**	**1**	**0**	**0**	**22**	**4.5**	**13**	**3**	**12**	**5**	**+3**	....	....	....	....	....	....	....	....
	Washington Capitals	**NHL**	**71**	**5**	**8**	**13**	**4**	**5**	**9**	**46**	**0**	**0**	**0**	**77**	**6.5**	**53**	**1**	**57**	**8**	**+3**	**6**	**0**	**2**	**2**	**18**	**0**	**0**	**0**
1993-94	**Dallas Stars**	**NHL**	**74**	**11**	**33**	**44**	**10**	**25**	**35**	**82**	**6**	**0**	**3**	**145**	**7.6**	**95**	**32**	**55**	**5**	**+13**	**9**	**1**	**8**	**9**	**4**	**1**	**0**	**1**
1994-95	**Dallas Stars**	**NHL**	**44**	**1**	**11**	**12**	**2**	**16**	**18**	**28**	**0**	**0**	**0**	**69**	**1.4**	**43**	**14**	**27**	**6**	**+8**	**5**	**0**	**2**	**2**	**6**	**0**	**0**	**0**
1995-96	**Dallas Stars**	**NHL**	**8**	**0**	**0**	**0**	**0**	**0**	**0**	**6**	**0**	**0**	**0**	**5**	**0.0**	**4**	**3**	**4**	**0**	**–3**	....	....	....	....	....	....	....	....
	NHL Totals		**564**	**56**	**177**	**233**	**50**	**137**	**187**	**750**	**16**	**2**	**6**	**903**	**6.2**	**674**	**132**	**572**	**146**		**69**	**8**	**27**	**35**	**114**	**2**	**1**	**1**

Won Alka-Seltzer Plus Award (1990)

Played in NHL All-Star Game (1990)

Traded to **St. Louis** by **Washington** for Montreal's 2nd round choice (previously acquired, Washington selected Wade Bartley) in 1988 Entry Draft, December 11, 1987. Traded to **Washington** by **St. Louis** for Kevin Miller, November 2, 1992. Traded to **Dallas** by **Washington** for future considerations (Enrico Ciccone, June 25, 1993), June 20, 1993.

• CERNIK, FRANTISEK

Frantisek "Frank" Cernik LW/RW – R. 5'10", 189 lbs. b: Novy Jicin, Czech., 6/3/1953.

Season	Club	League	GP	G	A	Pts	AG	AA	APts	PIM	PP	SH	GW	S	%	TGF	PGF	TGA	PGA	+/–	GP	G	A	Pts	PIM	PP	SH	GW
1975-76	Czechoslovakia	WEC-A	9	3	3	6	....	....	....	2	....	....	....	....	....	....	....	....	....	....	....	....	....	....	....	....	....	....
1976-77	Czechoslovakia	C Cup	7	0	1	1	....	....	....	4	....	....	....	....	....	....	....	....	....	....	....	....	....	....	....	....	....	....
	Dukla	Czech.	....	30	13	43	....	....	....	....	....	....	....	....	....	....	....	....	....	....	....	....	....	....	....	....	....	....
1977-78	Dukla	Czech. 2	STATISTICS NOT AVAILABLE																									
	Czechoslovakia	WEC-A	8	7	0	7	....	....	....	2	....	....	....	....	....	....	....	....	....	....	....	....	....	....	....	....	....	....
1978-79	Vitovice	Czech.	....	24	15	39	....	....	....	....	....	....	....	....	....	....	....	....	....	....	....	....	....	....	....	....	....	....
1979-80	Vitkovice	Czech.	42	16	12	28	....	....	....	....	....	....	....	....	....	....	....	....	....	....	....	....	....	....	....	....	....	....
1980-81	Vitkovice	Czech.	43	25	26	51	....	....	....	....	....	....	....	....	....	....	....	....	....	....	....	....	....	....	....	....	....	....
	Czechoslovakia	WEC-A	8	2	0	2	....	....	....	4	....	....	....	....	....	....	....	....	....	....	....	....	....	....	....	....	....	....
1981-82	Czechoslovakia	C Cup	6	0	0	0	....	....	....	0	....	....	....	....	....	....	....	....	....	....	....	....	....	....	....	....	....	....
	Vitkovice	Czech.	41	28	23	51	....	....	....	50	....	....	....	....	....	....	....	....	....	....	10	1	5	6	4	....	....	....
	Czechoslovakia	WEC-A	10	1	5	6	....	....	....	4	....	....	....	....	....	....	....	....	....	....	....	....	....	....	....	....	....	....
1982-83	Vitkovice	Czech.	44	33	27	60	....	....	....	....	....	....	....	....	....	....	....	....	....	....	....	....	....	....	....	....	....	....
	Czechoslovakia	WEC-A	10	1	3	4	....	....	....	8	....	....	....	....	....	....	....	....	....	....	....	....	....	....	....	....	....	....
1983-84	Vitkovice	Czech.	44	25	23	48	....	....	....	....	....	....	....	....	....	....	....	....	....	....	....	....	....	....	....	....	....	....
	Czechoslovakia	Olympics	7	3	0	3	....	....	....	4	....	....	....	....	....	....	....	....	....	....	....	....	....	....	....	....	....	....
1984-85	**Detroit Red Wings**	**NHL**	**49**	**5**	**4**	**9**	**4**	**3**	**7**	**13**	**0**	**0**	**0**	**50**	**10.0**	**15**	**1**	**21**	**0**	**–7**	....	....	....	....	....	....	....	....
1985-86	EV Kaufbeuren	Germany	40	23	44	67	....	....	....	21	....	....	....	....	....	....	....	....	....	....	....	....	....	....	....	....	....	....
1986-87	VEU Feldkirch	Austria	39	23	37	60	....	....	....	23	....	....	....	....	....	....	....	....	....	....	....	....	....	....	....	....	....	....
1987-88	EC Graz	Austria B	30	*64	40	*104	....	....	....	....	....	....	....	....	....	....	....	....	....	....	....	....	....	....	....	....	....	....
	NHL Totals		**49**	**5**	**4**	**9**	**4**	**3**	**7**	**13**	**0**	**0**	**0**	**50**	**10.0**	**15**	**1**	**21**	**0**		....	....	....	....	....	....	....	....

Signed as a free agent by **Quebec**, September 17, 1979. Signed as a free agent by **Detroit**, July 5, 1983.

• CHABOT, JOHN

John Chabot C – L. 6'2", 200 lbs. b: Summerside, P.E.I., 5/18/1962. Montreal's 3rd choice, 40th overall, in 1980 Entry Draft.

Season	Club	League	GP	G	A	Pts	AG	AA	APts	PIM	PP	SH	GW	S	%	TGF	PGF	TGA	PGA	+/–	GP	G	A	Pts	PIM	PP	SH	GW
1979-80	Hull Olympiques	QMJHL	68	26	57	83	....	....	....	28	....	....	....	....	....	....	....	....	....	....	4	1	2	3	0	....	....	....
1980-81	Hull Olympiques	QMJHL	70	27	62	89	....	....	....	24	....	....	....	....	....	....	....	....	....	....	....	....	....	....	....	....	....	....
	Nova Scotia Voyageurs	AHL	1	0	0	0	....	....	....	0	....	....	....	....	....	....	....	....	....	....	2	0	0	0	0	....	....	....
1981-82	Sherbrooke Beavers	QMJHL	62	34	*109	143	....	....	....	42	....	....	....	....	....	....	....	....	....	....	19	6	26	32	6	....	....	....
1982-83	Nova Scotia Voyageurs	AHL	76	16	73	89	....	....	....	19	....	....	....	....	....	....	....	....	....	....	7	1	3	4	0	....	....	....
1983-84	**Montreal Canadiens**	**NHL**	**56**	**18**	**25**	**43**	**14**	**17**	**31**	**13**	**4**	**1**	**2**	**69**	**26.1**	**53**	**12**	**52**	**9**	**–2**	**11**	**1**	**4**	**5**	**0**	**0**	**0**	**1**
1984-85	**Montreal Canadiens**	**NHL**	**10**	**1**	**6**	**7**	**1**	**4**	**5**	**2**	**0**	**0**	**0**	**8**	**12.5**	**11**	**5**	**3**	**0**	**+3**	....	....	....	....	....	....	....	....
	Pittsburgh Penguins	**NHL**	**67**	**8**	**45**	**53**	**7**	**30**	**37**	**12**	**2**	**1**	**2**	**105**	**7.6**	**74**	**23**	**120**	**32**	**–37**	....	....	....	....	....	....	....	....
1985-86	**Pittsburgh Penguins**	**NHL**	**77**	**14**	**31**	**45**	**11**	**21**	**32**	**6**	**1**	**2**	**3**	**89**	**15.7**	**57**	**2**	**102**	**40**	**–1**	....	....	....	....	....	....	....	....
1986-87	**Pittsburgh Penguins**	**NHL**	**72**	**14**	**22**	**36**	**12**	**16**	**28**	**8**	**0**	**0**	**1**	**90**	**15.6**	**58**	**4**	**96**	**34**	**–7**	....	....	....	....	....	....	....	....
1987-88	**Detroit Red Wings**	**NHL**	**78**	**13**	**44**	**57**	**11**	**31**	**42**	**10**	**0**	**2**	**0**	**83**	**15.7**	**73**	**8**	**94**	**41**	**+12**	**16**	**4**	**15**	**19**	**2**	**1**	**0**	**0**
1988-89	**Detroit Red Wings**	**NHL**	**52**	**2**	**10**	**12**	**2**	**7**	**9**	**6**	**0**	**2**	**0**	**49**	**4.1**	**16**	**1**	**61**	**28**	**–18**	**6**	**1**	**1**	**2**	**0**	**0**	**0**	**1**
	Adirondack Red Wings	AHL	8	3	12	15	....	....	....	0	....	....	....	....	....	....	....	....	....	....	....	....	....	....	....	....	....	....
1989-90	**Detroit Red Wings**	**NHL**	**69**	**9**	**40**	**49**	**8**	**29**	**37**	**24**	**0**	**2**	**0**	**91**	**9.9**	**64**	**17**	**88**	**46**	**+5**	....	....	....	....	....	....	....	....
1990-91	**Detroit Red Wings**	**NHL**	**27**	**5**	**5**	**10**	**5**	**4**	**9**	**4**	**2**	**0**	**1**	**26**	**19.2**	**23**	**8**	**15**	**6**	**+6**	....	....	....	....	....	....	....	....
	Adirondack Red Wings	AHL	27	11	30	41	....	....	....	4	....	....	....	....	....	....	....	....	....	....	2	0	1	1	0	....	....	....
1991-92	Milano Devils	Italy	18	10	36	46	....	....	....	4	....	....	....	....	....	....	....	....	....	....	12	3	13	16	2	....	....	....
	Canada	Nat-Team	8	1	3	4	....	....	....	0	....	....	....	....	....	....	....	....	....	....	....	....	....	....	....	....	....	....
1992-93	Preussen Berlin	Germany	20	10	17	27	....	....	....	14	....	....	....	....	....	....	....	....	....	....	....	....	....	....	....	....	....	....
1993-94	Preussen Berlin	Germany	32	9	29	38	....	....	....	27	....	....	....	....	....	....	....	....	....	....	....	....	....	....	....	....	....	....
1994-95	Preussen Berlin	Germany	43	20	*48	*68	....	....	....	48	....	....	....	....	....	....	....	....	....	....	12	5	7	12	14	....	....	....
	Canada	Nat-Team	3	1	2	3	....	....	....	0	....	....	....	....	....	....	....	....	....	....	....	....	....	....	....	....	....	....
1995-96	Preussen Berlin	Germany	50	16	65	81	....	....	....	20	....	....	....	....	....	....	....	....	....	....	11	5	*14	19	14	....	....	....
1996-97	Berlin Capitals	Germany	45	12	34	46	....	....	....	43	....	....	....	....	....	....	....	....	....	....	4	2	1	3	0	....	....	....
	EV Zug	Switz.	....	....	....	....	....	....	....	....	....	....	....	....	....	....	....	....	....	....	2	0	1	1	0	....	....	....
1997-98	Frankfurt Lions	Germany	47	12	46	58	....	....	....	72	....	....	....	....	....	....	....	....	....	....	7	0	5	5	2	....	....	....
	NHL Totals		**508**	**84**	**228**	**312**	**71**	**159**	**230**	**85**	**9**	**10**	**9**	**610**	**13.8**	**429**	**80**	**630**	**242**		**33**	**6**	**20**	**26**	**2**	**1**	**0**	**2**

QMJHL First All-Star Team (1982) • Memorial Cup All-Star Team (1982)

Traded to **Pittsburgh** by **Montreal** for Ron Flockhart, November 9, 1984. Signed as a free agent by **Detroit**, June 25, 1987.

• CHALUPA, MILAN

Milan Chalupa D – R. 5'10", 183 lbs. b: Oudolen, Czech., 7/4/1953. Detroit's 3rd choice, 49th overall, in 1984 Entry Draft.

Season	Club	League	GP	G	A	Pts	AG	AA	APts	PIM	PP	SH	GW	S	%	TGF	PGF	TGA	PGA	+/–	GP	G	A	Pts	PIM	PP	SH	GW
1975-76	Czechoslovakia	Olympics	5	0	1	1	....	....	....	4	....	....	....	....	....	....	....	....	....	....	....	....	....	....	....	....	....	....
	Czechoslovakia	WEC-A	9	1	4	5	....	....	....	2	....	....	....	....	....	....	....	....	....	....	....	....	....	....	....	....	....	....
1976-77	Czechoslovakia	C Cup	7	1	1	2	....	....	....	10	....	....	....	....	....	....	....	....	....	....	....	....	....	....	....	....	....	....
	Czechoslovakia	WEC-A	10	1	0	1	....	....	....	2	....	....	....	....	....	....	....	....	....	....	....	....	....	....	....	....	....	....
1977-78	Czechoslovakia	WEC-A	3	1	0	1	....	....	....	0	....	....	....	....	....	....	....	....	....	....	....	....	....	....	....	....	....	....
1978-79	Czechoslovakia	WEC-A	8	1	2	3	....	....	....	10	....	....	....	....	....	....	....	....	....	....	....	....	....	....	....	....	....	....
1979-80	Dukla Jihlava	Czech.	43	8	6	14	....	....	....	....	....	....	....	....	....	....	....	....	....	....	6	0	3	3	8	....	....	....
	Czechoslovakia	Olympics	6	0	3	3	....	....	....	8	....	....	....	....	....	....	....	....	....	....	....	....	....	....	....	....	....	....
1980-81	Dukla Jihlava	Czech.	41	2	15	17	....	....	....	....	....	....	....	....	....	....	....	....	....	....	5	0	1	1	4	....	....	....
	Czechoslovakia	WEC-A	5	0	1	1	....	....	....	5	....	....	....	....	....	....	....	....	....	....	....	....	....	....	....	....	....	....

			REGULAR SEASON																		PLAYOFFS							
Season	Club	League	GP	G	A	Pts	AG	AA	APts	PIM	PP	SH	GW	S	%	TGF	PGF	TGA	PGA	+/–	GP	G	A	Pts	PIM	PP	SH	GW
1981-82	Czechoslovakia	C Cup	6	0	2	2	....	....	....	4	....	....	....	....	....	....	....	....	....	....	....	....	....	....	....	....	....	....
	Dukla Jihlava	Czech.	41	4	8	12	....	....	....	30	....	....	....	....	....	....	....	....	....	....	....	....	....	....	....	....	....	....
	Czechoslovakia	WEC-A	10	0	1	1	....	....	....	2	....	....	....	....	....	....	....	....	....	....	....	....	....	....	....	....	....	....
1982-83	Dukla Jihlava	Czech.	38	9	16	25	....	....	....	....	....	....	....	....	....	....	....	....	....	....	....	....	....	....	....	....	....	....
	Czechoslovakia	WEC-A	8	2	1	3	....	....	....	2	....	....	....	....	....	....	....	....	....	....	....	....	....	....	....	....	....	....
1983-84	Dukla Jihlava	Czech.	39	3	11	14	....	....	....	....	....	....	....	....	....	....	....	....	....	....	....	....	....	....	....	....	....	....
	Czechoslovakia	Olympics	7	2	1	3	....	....	....	6	....	....	....	....	....	....	....	....	....	....	....	....	....	....	....	....	....	....
1984-85	**Detroit Red Wings**	**NHL**	**14**	**0**	**5**	**5**	**0**	**3**	**3**	**6**	**0**	**0**	**0**	**10**	**0.0**	**15**	**0**	**11**	**0**	**+4**	....	....	....	....	....	....	....	....
	Adirondack Red Wings	AHL	1	0	0	0	....	....	....	2	....	....	....	....	....	....	....	....	....	....	....	....	....	....	....	....	....	....
1985-86	EHC Freiburg	Germany	STATISTICS NOT AVAILABLE																									
1986-87	EHC Freiburg	Germany	STATISTICS NOT AVAILABLE																									
1987-88	EHC Freiburg	Germany	STATISTICS NOT AVAILABLE																									
1988-89	EHC Freiburg	Germany	33	6	23	29	....	....	....	24	....	....	....	....	....	....	....	....	....	....	....	....	....	....	....	....	....	....
1989-90	EHC Freiburg	Germany	41	2	25	27	....	....	....	30	....	....	....	....	....	....	....	....	....	....	....	....	....	....	....	....	....	....
1990-91	EHC Freiburg	Germany	10	0	1	1	....	....	....	10	....	....	....	....	....	....	....	....	....	....	....	....	....	....	....	....	....	....
	NHL Totals		**14**	**0**	**5**	**5**	**0**	**3**	**3**	**6**	**0**	**0**	**0**	**10**	**0.0**	**15**	**0**	**11**	**0**		....	....	....	....	....	....	....	....

• CHAMBERS, SHAWN

Shawn Chambers D – L. 6'2", 200 lbs. b: Sterling Hts., MI, 10/11/1966. Minnesota's 1st choice, 4th overall, in 1987 Supplemental Draft.

Season	Club	League	GP	G	A	Pts	AG	AA	APts	PIM	PP	SH	GW	S	%	TGF	PGF	TGA	PGA	+/–	GP	G	A	Pts	PIM	PP	SH	GW
1985-86	University of Alaska-Fairbanks	G-North	25	15	21	36	....	....	....	34	....	....	....	....	....	....	....	....	....	....	....	....	....	....	....	....	....	....
1986-87	University of Alaska-Fairbanks	G-North	28	11	19	30	....	....	....	....	....	....	....	....	....	....	....	....	....	....	....	....	....	....	....	....	....	....
	Seattle Thunderbirds	WHL	28	8	25	33	....	....	....	58	....	....	....	....	....	....	....	....	....	....	....	....	....	....	....	....	....	....
	Fort Wayne Komets	IHL	12	2	6	8	....	....	....	0	....	....	....	....	....	....	....	....	....	....	10	1	4	5	5	....	....	....
1987-88	**Minnesota North Stars**	**NHL**	**19**	**1**	**7**	**8**	**1**	**5**	**6**	**21**	**1**	**0**	**0**	**28**	**3.6**	**12**	**5**	**15**	**2**	**–6**	....	....	....	....	....	....	....	....
	Kalamazoo Wings	IHL	19	1	6	7	....	....	....	22	....	....	....	....	....	....	....	....	....	....	....	....	....	....	....	....	....	....
1988-89	**Minnesota North Stars**	**NHL**	**72**	**5**	**19**	**24**	**4**	**13**	**17**	**80**	**1**	**2**	**0**	**131**	**3.8**	**82**	**23**	**89**	**26**	**–4**	**3**	**0**	**2**	**2**	**0**	**0**	**0**	**0**
1989-90	**Minnesota North Stars**	**NHL**	**78**	**8**	**18**	**26**	**7**	**13**	**20**	**81**	**0**	**1**	**2**	**116**	**6.9**	**83**	**15**	**114**	**44**	**–2**	**7**	**2**	**1**	**3**	**10**	**1**	**0**	**0**
1990-91	Minnesota Northy Stars	FrTour	1	0	1	1	....	....	....	4	....	....	....	....	....	....	....	....	....	....	....	....	....	....	....	....	....	....
	Minnesota North Stars	**NHL**	**29**	**1**	**3**	**4**	**1**	**2**	**3**	**24**	**0**	**0**	**0**	**55**	**1.8**	**27**	**3**	**26**	**4**	**+2**	**23**	**0**	**7**	**7**	**16**	**0**	**0**	**0**
	Kalamazoo Wings	IHL	3	1	1	2	....	....	....	0	....	....	....	....	....	....	....	....	....	....	....	....	....	....	....	....	....	....
1991-92	**Washington Capitals**	**NHL**	**2**	**0**	**0**	**0**	**0**	**0**	**0**	**2**	**0**	**0**	**0**	**1**	**0.0**	**1**	**0**	**4**	**0**	**–3**	....	....	....	....	....	....	....	....
	Baltimore Skipjacks	AHL	5	2	3	5	....	....	....	9	....	....	....	....	....	....	....	....	....	....	....	....	....	....	....	....	....	....
1992-93	**Tampa Bay Lightning**	**NHL**	**55**	**10**	**29**	**39**	**8**	**20**	**28**	**36**	**5**	**0**	**1**	**152**	**6.6**	**76**	**35**	**90**	**28**	**–21**	....	....	....	....	....	....	....	....
	Atlanta Knights	IHL	6	0	2	2	....	....	....	18	....	....	....	....	....	....	....	....	....	....	....	....	....	....	....	....	....	....
1993-94	**Tampa Bay Lightning**	**NHL**	**66**	**11**	**23**	**34**	**10**	**18**	**28**	**23**	**6**	**1**	**1**	**142**	**7.7**	**86**	**38**	**69**	**15**	**–6**	....	....	....	....	....	....	....	....
	United States	WC-A	8	0	3	3	....	....	....	4	....	....	....	....	....	....	....	....	....	....	....	....	....	....	....	....	....	....
1994-95	**Tampa Bay Lightning**	**NHL**	**24**	**2**	**12**	**14**	**4**	**18**	**22**	**6**	**1**	**0**	**0**	**44**	**4.5**	**29**	**8**	**23**	**2**	**0**	....	....	....	....	....	....	....	....
	New Jersey Devils	**NHL**	**21**	**2**	**5**	**7**	**4**	**7**	**11**	**6**	**1**	**0**	**0**	**23**	**8.7**	**16**	**4**	**13**	**3**	**+2**	**20**	**4**	**5**	**9**	**2**	**2**	**0**	**0**
1995-96	**New Jersey Devils**	**NHL**	**64**	**2**	**21**	**23**	**2**	**17**	**19**	**18**	**2**	**0**	**1**	**112**	**1.8**	**59**	**22**	**58**	**22**	**+1**	....	....	....	....	....	....	....	....
1996-97	United States	W Cup	1	0	0	0	....	....	....	0	....	....	....	....	....	....	....	....	....	....	....	....	....	....	....	....	....	....
	New Jersey Devils	**NHL**	**73**	**4**	**17**	**21**	**4**	**15**	**19**	**19**	**1**	**0**	**0**	**114**	**3.5**	**72**	**10**	**54**	**9**	**+17**	**10**	**1**	**6**	**7**	**6**	**1**	**0**	**0**
1997-98	**Dallas Stars**	**NHL**	**57**	**2**	**22**	**24**	**2**	**21**	**23**	**26**	**1**	**1**	**0**	**73**	**2.7**	**60**	**19**	**36**	**6**	**+11**	**14**	**0**	**3**	**3**	**20**	**0**	**0**	**0**
	NHL Totals		**560**	**48**	**176**	**224**	**47**	**149**	**196**	**342**	**19**	**5**	**5**	**991**	**4.8**	**603**	**182**	**591**	**161**		**77**	**7**	**24**	**31**	**54**	**4**	**0**	**0**

Traded to **Washington** by **Minnesota** for Steve Maltais and Trent Klatt, June 21, 1991. Claimed by **Tampa Bay** from **Washington** in Expansion Draft, June 18, 1992. Traded to **New Jersey** by **Tampa Bay** with Danton Cole for Alexander Semak and Ben Hankinson, March 14, 1995. Signed as a free agent by **Dallas**, July 17, 1997.

• CHAPDELAINE, RENE

Rene Chapdelaine D – R. 6'1", 195 lbs. b: Weyburn, Sask., 9/27/1966. Los Angeles' 7th choice, 149th overall, in 1986 Entry Draft.

Season	Club	League	GP	G	A	Pts	AG	AA	APts	PIM	PP	SH	GW	S	%	TGF	PGF	TGA	PGA	+/–	GP	G	A	Pts	PIM	PP	SH	GW
1984-85	Weyburn Red Wings	SJHL	61	3	17	20	....	....	....	....	....	....	....	....	....	....	....	....	....	....	....	....	....	....	....	....	....	....
1985-86	Lake Superior State	CCHA	32	1	4	5	....	....	....	47	....	....	....	....	....	....	....	....	....	....	....	....	....	....	....	....	....	....
1986-87	Lake Superior State	CCHA	28	1	5	6	....	....	....	51	....	....	....	....	....	....	....	....	....	....	....	....	....	....	....	....	....	....
1987-88	Lake Superior State	CCHA	35	1	9	10	....	....	....	44	....	....	....	....	....	....	....	....	....	....	....	....	....	....	....	....	....	....
1988-89	Lake Superior State	CCHA	46	4	9	13	....	....	....	62	....	....	....	....	....	....	....	....	....	....	....	....	....	....	....	....	....	....
1989-90	New Haven Nighthawks	AHL	41	0	1	1	....	....	....	35	....	....	....	....	....	....	....	....	....	....	....	....	....	....	....	....	....	....
1990-91	**Los Angeles Kings**	**NHL**	**3**	**0**	**1**	**1**	**0**	**1**	**1**	**10**	**0**	**0**	**0**	**1**	**0.0**	**3**	**0**	**3**	**1**	**+1**	....	....	....	....	....	....	....	....
	New Haven Nighthawks	AHL	65	3	11	14	....	....	....	49	....	....	....	....	....	....	....	....	....	....	....	....	....	....	....	....	....	....
	Phoenix Roadrunners	IHL	17	0	2	2	....	....	....	10	....	....	....	....	....	....	....	....	....	....	11	0	0	0	8	....	....	....
1991-92	**Los Angeles Kings**	**NHL**	**16**	**0**	**1**	**1**	**0**	**1**	**1**	**10**	**0**	**0**	**0**	**6**	**0.0**	**9**	**0**	**12**	**3**	**0**	....	....	....	....	....	....	....	....
	Phoenix Roadrunners	IHL	62	4	22	26	....	....	....	87	....	....	....	....	....	....	....	....	....	....	....	....	....	....	....	....	....	....
	New Haven Nighthawks	AHL	....	....	....	....	....	....	....	....	....	....	....	....	....	....	....	....	....	....	4	0	2	2	0	....	....	....
1992-93	**Los Angeles Kings**	**NHL**	**13**	**0**	**0**	**0**	**0**	**0**	**0**	**12**	**0**	**0**	**0**	**5**	**0.0**	**4**	**0**	**12**	**2**	**–6**	....	....	....	....	....	....	....	....
	Phoenix Roadrunners	IHL	44	1	17	18	....	....	....	54	....	....	....	....	....	....	....	....	....	....	....	....	....	....	....	....	....	....
	San Diego Gulls	IHL	9	1	1	2	....	....	....	8	....	....	....	....	....	....	....	....	....	....	14	0	1	1	27	....	....	....
1993-94	Peoria Rivermen	IHL	80	8	9	17	....	....	....	100	....	....	....	....	....	....	....	....	....	....	6	1	3	4	10	....	....	....
1994-95	Peoria Rivermen	IHL	45	3	2	5	....	....	....	62	....	....	....	....	....	....	....	....	....	....	9	0	2	2	12	....	....	....
1995-96	Peoria Rivermen	IHL	70	2	10	12	....	....	....	135	....	....	....	....	....	....	....	....	....	....	12	1	0	1	8	....	....	....
1996-97	San Antonio Dragons	IHL	69	7	11	18	....	....	....	125	....	....	....	....	....	....	....	....	....	....	9	2	3	5	10	....	....	....
1997-98	San Antonio Dragons	IHL	73	2	11	13	....	....	....	128	....	....	....	....	....	....	....	....	....	....	....	....	....	....	....	....	....	....
	NHL Totals		**32**	**0**	**2**	**2**	**0**	**2**	**2**	**32**	**0**	**0**	**0**	**12**	**0.0**	**16**	**0**	**27**	**6**		....	....	....	....	....	....	....	....

• CHAPMAN, BLAIR

Blair Chapman RW – R. 6'1", 190 lbs. b: Lloydminster, Sask., 6/13/1956. Pittsburgh's 1st choice, 2nd overall, in 1976 Amateur Draft.

Season	Club	League	GP	G	A	Pts	AG	AA	APts	PIM	PP	SH	GW	S	%	TGF	PGF	TGA	PGA	+/–	GP	G	A	Pts	PIM	PP	SH	GW
1974-75	Saskatoon Blades	WCJHL	65	41	44	85	....	....	....	92	....	....	....	....	....	....	....	....	....	....	....	....	....	....	....	....	....	....
1975-76	Saskatoon Blades	WCJHL	69	71	86	157	....	....	....	67	....	....	....	....	....	....	....	....	....	....	....	....	....	....	....	....	....	....
1976-77	**Pittsburgh Penguins**	**NHL**	**80**	**14**	**23**	**37**	**13**	**19**	**32**	**16**	**1**	**0**	**3**	**152**	**9.2**	**65**	**12**	**66**	**1**	**–12**	**3**	**1**	**1**	**2**	**7**	**0**	**0**	**0**
1977-78	**Pittsburgh Penguins**	**NHL**	**75**	**24**	**20**	**44**	**23**	**16**	**39**	**37**	**4**	**0**	**2**	**180**	**13.3**	**68**	**12**	**78**	**11**	**–11**	....	....	....	....	....	....	....	....
1978-79	**Pittsburgh Penguins**	**NHL**	**71**	**10**	**8**	**18**	**9**	**6**	**15**	**18**	**1**	**0**	**0**	**96**	**10.4**	**35**	**4**	**45**	**2**	**–12**	**7**	**1**	**0**	**1**	**2**	**0**	**0**	**0**
1979-80	**Pittsburgh Penguins**	**NHL**	**1**	**0**	**0**	**0**	**0**	**0**	**0**	**0**	**0**	**0**	**0**	**1**	**0.0**	**0**	**0**	**0**	**0**	**0**	....	....	....	....	....	....	....	....
	St. Louis Blues	**NHL**	**63**	**25**	**26**	**51**	**23**	**20**	**43**	**28**	**7**	**0**	**6**	**124**	**20.2**	**86**	**25**	**67**	**1**	**–5**	**3**	**0**	**0**	**0**	**0**	**0**	**0**	**0**
1980-81	**St. Louis Blues**	**NHL**	**55**	**20**	**26**	**46**	**16**	**18**	**34**	**41**	**5**	**0**	**3**	**114**	**17.5**	**67**	**24**	**40**	**0**	**+3**	**9**	**2**	**5**	**7**	**6**	**0**	**0**	**0**
1981-82	**St. Louis Blues**	**NHL**	**18**	**6**	**11**	**17**	**5**	**7**	**12**	**8**	**2**	**0**	**0**	**28**	**21.4**	**25**	**10**	**15**	**1**	**+1**	**3**	**0**	**0**	**0**	**0**	**0**	**0**	**0**
	Salt Lake Golden Eagles	CHL	1	1	0	1	....	....	....	0	....	....	....	....	....	....	....	....	....	....	....	....	....	....	....	....	....	....
1982-83	**St. Louis Blues**	**NHL**	**39**	**7**	**11**	**18**	**6**	**8**	**14**	**10**	**3**	**0**	**1**	**46**	**15.2**	**33**	**9**	**32**	**0**	**–8**	....	....	....	....	....	....	....	....
	Salt Lake Golden Eagles	CHL	22	17	6	23	....	....	....	20	....	....	....	....	....	....	....	....	....	....	6	4	3	7	0	....	....	....
	NHL Totals		**402**	**106**	**125**	**231**	**95**	**94**	**189**	**158**	**23**	**0**	**15**	**741**	**14.3**	**379**	**96**	**343**	**16**		**25**	**4**	**6**	**10**	**15**	**0**	**0**	**0**

Traded to **St. Louis** by **Pittsburgh** for Bob Stewart, November 13, 1979.

• CHAPMAN, BRIAN

Brian Chapman D – L. 6', 195 lbs. b: Brockville, Ont., 2/10/1968. Hartford's 3rd choice, 74th overall, in 1986 Entry Draft.

Season	Club	League	GP	G	A	Pts	AG	AA	APts	PIM	PP	SH	GW	S	%	TGF	PGF	TGA	PGA	+/–	GP	G	A	Pts	PIM	PP	SH	GW
1984-85	Brockville Braves	OJHL	50	11	32	43	....	....	....	145	....	....	....	....	....	....	....	....	....	....	....	....	....	....	....	....	....	....
1985-86	Belleville Bulls	OHL	66	6	31	37	....	....	....	168	....	....	....	....	....	....	....	....	....	....	24	2	6	8	54	....	....	....
1986-87	Belleville Bulls	OHL	54	4	32	36	....	....	....	142	....	....	....	....	....	....	....	....	....	....	6	1	1	2	10	....	....	....
	Binghamton Whalers	AHL	....	....	....	....	....	....	....	....	....	....	....	....	....	....	....	....	....	....	1	0	0	0	0	....	....	....
1987-88	Belleville Bulls	OHL	63	11	57	68	....	....	....	180	....	....	....	....	....	....	....	....	....	....	6	1	4	5	13	....	....	....
1988-89	Binghamton Whalers	AHL	71	5	25	30	....	....	....	216	....	....	....	....	....	....	....	....	....	....	....	....	....	....	....	....	....	....
1989-90	Binghamton Whalers	AHL	68	2	15	17	....	....	....	180	....	....	....	....	....	....	....	....	....	....	....	....	....	....	....	....	....	....
1990-91	**Hartford Whalers**	**NHL**	**3**	**0**	**0**	**0**	**0**	**0**	**0**	**29**	**0**	**0**	**0**	**0**	**0.0**	**1**	**0**	**2**	**1**	**0**	....	....	....	....	....	....	....	....
	Springfield Indians	AHL	60	4	23	27	....	....	....	200	....	....	....	....	....	....	....	....	....	....	18	1	4	5	62	....	....	....
1991-92	Springfield Indians	AHL	73	3	26	29	....	....	....	245	....	....	....	....	....	....	....	....	....	....	10	2	2	4	25	....	....	....
1992-93	Springfield Indians	AHL	72	17	34	51	....	....	....	212	....	....	....	....	....	....	....	....	....	....	15	2	5	7	43	....	....	....
1993-94	Phoenix Roadrunners	IHL	78	6	35	41	....	....	....	280	....	....	....	....	....	....	....	....	....	....	....	....	....	....	....	....	....	....
1994-95	Phoenix Roadrunners	IHL	60	2	23	25	....	....	....	181	....	....	....	....	....	....	....	....	....	....	9	1	5	6	31	....	....	....
1995-96	Phoenix Roadrunners	IHL	66	8	11	19	....	....	....	187	....	....	....	....	....	....	....	....	....	....	4	0	1	1	14	....	....	....

Season	Club	League	GP	G	A	Pts	AG	AA	APts	PIM	PP	SH	GW	S	%	TGF	PGF	TGA	PGA	+/-	GP	G	A	Pts	PIM	PP	SH	GW
			REGULAR SEASON																		PLAYOFFS							
1996-97	Phoenix Roadrunners	IHL	69	9	16	25				109																		
	Long Beach Ice Dogs	IHL	14	1	7	8				67											13	0	3	3	18			
1997-98	Long Beach Ice Dogs	IHL	6	0	1	1				15																		
	Manitoba Moose	IHL	77	3	25	28				159											3	0	0	0	10			
	NHL Totals		**3**	**0**	**0**	**0**	**0**	**0**	**0**	**29**	**0**	**0**	**0**	**0**	**0.0**	**1**	**0**	**2**	**1**									

Signed as a free agent by **LA Kings**, July 15, 1993.

• CHARA, ZDENO

Zdeno Chara D – L. 6'8", 231 lbs. b: Trencin, Czech., 3/18/1977. NY Islanders' 3rd choice, 56th overall, in 1996 Entry Draft.

Season	Club	League	GP	G	A	Pts	AG	AA	APts	PIM	PP	SH	GW	S	%	TGF	PGF	TGA	PGA	+/-	GP	G	A	Pts	PIM	PP	SH	GW
1994-95	Dukla Trencin	Slov-Jr.	2	0	0	0				0																		
	Dukla Trencin	Slov-Jr.	30	22	22	44				113																		
1995-96	Dukla Trencin	Slov-Jr.	22	1	13	14				80																		
	Piestany	Slovakia	10	1	3	4				10																		
	Sparta Praha	Czech.	15	1	2	3				42																		
	Sparta Praha	Czech.	1	0	0	0				0																		
1996-97	Prince George Cougars	WHL	49	3	19	22				120											15	1	7	8	45			
1997-98	**New York Islanders**	**NHL**	**25**	**0**	**1**	**1**	**0**	**1**	**1**	**50**	**0**	**0**	**0**	**10**	**0.0**	**10**	**0**	**12**	**3**	**+1**								
	Kentucky Thoroughblades	AHL	48	4	9	13				125											1	0	0	0	4			
	NHL Totals		**25**	**0**	**1**	**1**	**0**	**1**	**1**	**50**	**0**	**0**	**0**	**10**	**0.0**	**10**	**0**	**12**	**3**									

• CHARBONNEAU, JOSE

Jose Charbonneau RW – R. 6', 195 lbs. b: Ferme-Neuve, Que., 11/21/1966. Montreal's 1st choice, 12th overall, in 1985 Entry Draft.

Season	Club	League	GP	G	A	Pts	AG	AA	APts	PIM	PP	SH	GW	S	%	TGF	PGF	TGA	PGA	+/-	GP	G	A	Pts	PIM	PP	SH	GW
1983-84	Drummondville Voltigeurs	QMJHL	65	31	59	90				110																		
1984-85	Drummondville Voltigeurs	QMJHL	46	34	40	74				91											12	5	10	15	20			
1985-86	Drummondville Voltigeurs	QMJHL	57	44	45	89				158											23	16	20	36	40			
1986-87	Sherbrooke Canadiens	AHL	72	14	27	41				94											16	5	12	17	17			
1987-88	**Montreal Canadiens**	**NHL**	**16**	**0**	**2**	**2**	**0**	**1**	**1**	**6**	**0**	**0**	**0**	**22**	**0.0**	**6**	**0**	**5**	**0**	**+1**	**8**	**0**	**0**	**0**	**4**	**0**	**0**	**0**
	Sherbrooke Canadiens	AHL	55	30	35	65				108																		
1988-89	**Montreal Canadiens**	**NHL**	**9**	**1**	**3**	**4**	**1**	**2**	**3**	**6**	**0**	**0**	**0**	**15**	**6.7**	**11**	**7**	**6**	**1**	**–1**								
	Sherbrooke Canadiens	AHL	33	13	15	28				95																		
	Vancouver Canucks	**NHL**	**13**	**0**	**1**	**1**	**0**	**1**	**1**	**6**	**0**	**0**	**0**	**16**	**0.0**	**3**	**0**	**6**	**0**	**–3**								
	Milwaukee Admirals	IHL	13	8	5	13				46											10	3	2	5	23			
1989-90	Milwaukee Admirals	IHL	65	23	38	61				137											5	0	1	1	8			
1990-91	Canada	Nat-Team	56	22	29	51				54																		
1991-92			DID NOT PLAY																									
1992-93	Canada	Nat-Team	1	0	0	0				0																		
1993-94	**Vancouver Canucks**	**NHL**	**30**	**7**	**7**	**14**	**7**	**5**	**12**	**49**	**1**	**0**	**0**	**28**	**25.0**	**19**	**4**	**18**	**0**	**–3**	**3**	**1**	**0**	**1**	**4**	**0**	**0**	**0**
	Hamilton Canucks	AHL	7	3	2	5				8																		
1994-95	**Vancouver Canucks**	**NHL**	**3**	**1**	**0**	**1**	**2**	**0**	**2**	**0**	**0**	**0**	**0**	**2**	**50.0**	**3**	**0**	**3**	**0**	**0**								
	Las Vegas Thunder	IHL	27	8	12	20				102											9	1	1	2	71			
1995-96	EV Landshut	Germany	47	32	24	56				102											11	10	6	16	28			
1996-97	EV Landshut	Germany	13	5	4	9				41																		
	Wedemark Scorpions	Germany	30	10	21	31				97											5	1	0	1	27			
1997-98	Frankfurt Lions	Germany	40	13	16	29				156											7	4	1	5	18			
	NHL Totals		**71**	**9**	**13**	**22**	**10**	**9**	**19**	**67**	**1**	**0**	**0**	**83**	**10.8**	**42**	**11**	**38**	**1**		**11**	**1**	**0**	**1**	**8**	**0**	**0**	**0**

Traded to **Vancouver** by **Montreal** for Dan Woodley, January 25, 1989. Signed as a free agent by **Vancouver**, October 3, 1993.

• CHARBONNEAU, STEPHANE

Stephane Charbonneau RW – R. 6'2", 195 lbs. b: Ste-Adele, Que., 6/27/1970.

Season	Club	League	GP	G	A	Pts	AG	AA	APts	PIM	PP	SH	GW	S	%	TGF	PGF	TGA	PGA	+/-	GP	G	A	Pts	PIM	PP	SH	GW
1989-90	Shawinigan Cataractes	QMJHL	62	37	58	95				154																		
1990-91	Shawinigan Cataractes	QMJHL	6	4	3	7				2																		
	Chicoutimi Sagueneens	QMJHL	66	37	30	67				109											17	*13	9	22	43			
1991-92	**Quebec Nordiques**	**NHL**	**2**	**0**	**0**	**0**	**0**	**0**	**0**	**0**	**0**	**0**	**0**	**4**	**0.0**	**0**	**0**	**3**	**1**	**–2**								
	Halifax Citadels	AHL	64	22	25	47				183																		
1992-93	Halifax Citadels	AHL	56	18	20	38				125																		
1993-94	Erie Panthers	ECHL	23	22	8	30				130																		
	Phoenix Roadrunners	IHL	32	7	6	13				43																		
1994-95	Cornwall Aces	AHL	1	0	1	1				0																		
	Portland Pirates	AHL	7	3	5	8				0																		
	Erie Panthers	ECHL	64	50	41	91				129																		
1995-96	Portland Pirates	AHL	23	5	3	8				23											1	0	0	0	0			
	Flint Generals	ColHL	1	1	0	1				0																		
1996-97	Portland Pirates	AHL	9	1	0	1				2																		
	Baton Rouge Kingfish	ECHL	43	19	24	43				63																		
	Mississippi Sea Wolves	ECHL	13	8	6	14				14											3	2	0	2	18			
	NHL Totals		**2**	**0**	**0**	**0**	**0**	**0**	**0**	**0**	**0**	**0**	**0**	**4**	**0.0**	**0**	**0**	**3**	**1**									

ECHL Second All-Star Team (1995)

Signed as a free agent by **Quebec**, April 25, 1991.

• CHARLEBOIS, BOB

Bob Charlebois LW – L. 6', 175 lbs. b: Cornwall, Ont., 5/27/1944.

Season	Club	League	GP	G	A	Pts	AG	AA	APts	PIM	PP	SH	GW	S	%	TGF	PGF	TGA	PGA	+/-	GP	G	A	Pts	PIM	PP	SH	GW
1960-61	St. Jerome Alouettes	QJHL	35	41	46	87																						
1961-62	Montreal Jr. Canadiens	OHA	46	9	9	18				28											6	2	1	3	6			
1962-63	Montreal Jr. Canadiens	OHA	50	23	15	38				78											10	5	5	10	20			
1963-64	Montreal Jr. Canadiens	OHA	53	35	43	78				50											17	10	12	22	14			
1964-65	Omaha Knights	CHL	70	24	34	58				43											6	4	3	7	2			
1965-66	Houston Apollos	CHL	70	23	26	49				32																		
1966-67	Houston Apollos	CHL	67	27	34	61				38											6	0	1	1	2			
1967-68	**Minnesota North Stars**	**NHL**	**7**	**1**	**0**	**1**	**1**	**0**	**1**	**0**	**1**	**0**	**0**	**8**	**12.5**	**1**	**1**	**4**	**1**	**–3**								
	Memphis South Stars	CHL	47	25	24	49				16																		
	Phoenix Roadrunners	WHL	15	2	8	10				4											4	1	2	3	0			
1968-69	Phoenix Roadrunners	WHL	74	31	30	61				12																		
1969-70	Phoenix Roadrunners	WHL	73	24	34	58				12																		
1970-71	Phoenix Roadrunners	WHL	62	15	25	40				20											7	2	3	5	0			
1971-72	Tulsa Oilers	CHL	6	0	0	0				4																		
1972-73	Ottawa Nationals	WHA	78	24	40	64				28											5	1	1	2	4			
1973-74	New England Whalers	WHA	74	4	7	11				6											7	0	0	0	4			
1974-75	New England Whalers	WHA	8	1	0	1				0											4	1	0	1	0			
	Cape Cod Codders	NAHL	45	24	57	81				54																		
1975-76	New England Whalers	WHA	28	3	3	6				0																		
	Cape Cod Codders	NAHL	25	12	20	32				26																		
	Binghamton Dusters	NAHL	5	0	5	5				0																		
	NHL Totals		**7**	**1**	**0**	**1**	**1**	**0**	**1**	**0**	**1**	**0**	**0**	**8**	**12.5**	**1**	**1**	**4**	**1**									
	Other Major League Totals		188	32	50	82				34											16	2	1	3	8			

Traded to **Minnesota** by **Montreal** with Andre Boudrias and Bernard Cote for Minnesota's 1st round choice (Chuck Arnason) in 1971 Amateur Draft, June 6, 1967. Traded to **Phoenix** (WHL) by **Minnesota** with Leo Thiffault to complete earlier transaction that sent Walt Mckechnie to Minnesota (February, 1968), June, 1968. Signed as a free agent by **Ottawa** (WHA), August, 1972. Traded to **New England** (WHA) by **Ottawa** (WHA) for Brit Selby, September, 1973.

• CHARLESWORTH, TODD

Todd Charlesworth D – L. 6'1", 190 lbs. b: Calgary, Alta., 3/22/1965. Pittsburgh's 2nd choice, 22nd overall, in 1983 Entry Draft.

Season	Club	League	GP	G	A	Pts	AG	AA	APts	PIM	PP	SH	GW	S	%	TGF	PGF	TGA	PGA	+/-	GP	G	A	Pts	PIM	PP	SH	GW
1981-82	Gloucester Rangers	OJHL	50	13	24	37				67																		
1982-83	Oshawa Generals	OHL	70	6	23	29				55											17	0	4	4	20			
1983-84	Oshawa Generals	OHL	57	11	35	46				54											7	0	4	4	4			
	Pittsburgh Penguins	**NHL**	**10**	**0**	**0**	**0**	**0**	**0**	**0**	**8**	**0**	**0**	**0**	**6**	**0.0**	**6**	**0**	**14**	**1**	**–7**								
1984-85	**Pittsburgh Penguins**	**NHL**	**67**	**1**	**8**	**9**	**1**	**5**	**6**	**31**	**0**	**0**	**1**	**68**	**1.5**	**58**	**2**	**96**	**17**	**–23**								

			REGULAR SEASON																		PLAYOFFS							
Season	Club	League	GP	G	A	Pts	AG	AA	APts	PIM	PP	SH	GW	S	%	TGF	PGF	TGA	PGA	+/-	GP	G	A	Pts	PIM	PP	SH	GW
1985-86	**Pittsburgh Penguins**	**NHL**	**2**	**0**	**1**	**1**	**0**	**1**	**1**	**0**	**0**	**0**	**0**	**1**	**0.0**	**0**	**0**	**1**	**0**	**-1**	....	....	....	....	....	....	....	....
	Baltimore Skipjacks	AHL	19	1	3	4	....	....	....	10	....	....	....	....	....	....	....	....	....	....	....	....	....	....	....	....	....	....
	Muskegon Lumberjacks	IHL	51	9	27	36	....	....	....	78	....	....	....	....	....	....	....	....	....	....	14	3	8	11	14	....	....	....
1986-87	**Pittsburgh Penguins**	**NHL**	**1**	**0**	**0**	**0**	**0**	**0**	**0**	**0**	**0**	**0**	**0**	**0**	**0.0**	**1**	**0**	**1**	**0**	**0**	....	....	....	....	....	....	....	....
	Baltimore Skipjacks	AHL	75	5	21	26	....	....	....	64	....	....	....	....	....	....	....	....	....	....	....	....	....	....	....	....	....	....
1987-88	**Pittsburgh Penguins**	**NHL**	**6**	**2**	**0**	**2**	**2**	**0**	**2**	**2**	**0**	**0**	**0**	**4**	**50.0**	**3**	**0**	**3**	**0**	**0**	....	....	....	....	....	....	....	....
	Muskegon Lumberjacks	IHL	64	9	31	40	....	....	....	49	....	....	....	....	....	....	....	....	....	....	5	0	0	0	18	....	....	....
1988-89	Muskegon Lumberjacks	IHL	74	10	53	63	....	....	....	85	....	....	....	....	....	....	....	....	....	....	14	2	13	15	8	....	....	....
1989-90	**New York Rangers**	**NHL**	**7**	**0**	**0**	**0**	**0**	**0**	**0**	**6**	**0**	**0**	**0**	**4**	**0.0**	**1**	**0**	**6**	**2**	**-3**	....	....	....	....	....	....	....	....
	Flint Spirits	IHL	26	3	6	9	....	....	....	12	....	....	....	....	....	....	....	....	....	....	....	....	....	....	....	....	....	....
	Cape Breton Oilers	AHL	32	0	9	9	....	....	....	13	....	....	....	....	....	....	....	....	....	....	....	....	....	....	....	....	....	....
1990-91	Binghamton Rangers	AHL	11	0	3	3	....	....	....	2	....	....	....	....	....	....	....	....	....	....	....	....	....	....	....	....	....	....
	Muskegon Lumberjacks	IHL	62	5	32	37	....	....	....	46	....	....	....	....	....	....	....	....	....	....	5	1	3	4	2	....	....	....
1991-92			DID NOT PLAY – RETIRED																									
1992-93	Muskegon Fury	ColHL	45	9	37	46	....	....	....	22	....	....	....	....	....	....	....	....	....	....	7	1	3	4	4	....	....	....
1993-94	Muskegon Fury	ColHL	37	8	30	38	....	....	....	33	....	....	....	....	....	....	....	....	....	....	3	0	1	1	0	....	....	....
1994-95	Muskegon Fury	ColHL	62	21	49	70	....	....	....	60	....	....	....	....	....	....	....	....	....	....	17	1	14	15	12	....	....	....
	NHL Totals		**93**	**3**	**9**	**12**	**3**	**6**	**9**	**47**	**0**	**0**	**1**	**83**	**3.6**	**69**	**2**	**121**	**20**		....	....	....	....	....	....	....	....

IHL Second All-Star Team (1989) • ColHL First All-Star Team (1995)

Signed as a free agent by **Edmonton**, June 21, 1989. Traded to **NY Rangers** by **Edmonton** for future considerations, January 18, 1990.

• CHARRON, ERIC

Eric Charron D – L. 6'3", 192 lbs. b: Verdun, Que., 1/14/1970. Montreal's 1st choice, 20th overall, in 1988 Entry Draft.

Season	Club	League	GP	G	A	Pts	AG	AA	APts	PIM	PP	SH	GW	S	%	TGF	PGF	TGA	PGA	+/-	GP	G	A	Pts	PIM	PP	SH	GW
1987-88	Trois-Rivières Draveurs	QMJHL	67	3	13	16	....	....	....	135	....	....	....	....	....	....	....	....	....	....	....	....	....	....	....	....	....	....
1988-89	Trois-Rivières Draveurs	QMJHL	38	2	16	18	....	....	....	111	....	....	....	....	....	....	....	....	....	....	....	....	....	....	....	....	....	....
	Verdun Jr. Canadiens	QMJHL	28	2	15	17	....	....	....	66	....	....	....	....	....	....	....	....	....	....	....	....	....	....	....	....	....	....
	Sherbrooke Canadiens	AHL	1	0	0	0	....	....	....	0	....	....	....	....	....	....	....	....	....	....	....	....	....	....	....	....	....	....
1989-90	St-Hyacinthe Lasers	QMJHL	68	13	38	51	....	....	....	152	....	....	....	....	....	....	....	....	....	....	11	3	4	7	67	....	....	....
	Sherbrooke Canadiens	AHL	....	....	....	....	....	....	....	....	....	....	....	....	....	....	....	....	....	....	2	0	0	0	0	....	....	....
1990-91	Fredericton Canadiens	AHL	71	1	11	12	....	....	....	108	....	....	....	....	....	....	....	....	....	....	2	1	0	1	29	....	....	....
1991-92	Fredericton Canadiens	AHL	59	2	11	13	....	....	....	98	....	....	....	....	....	....	....	....	....	....	6	1	0	1	4	....	....	....
1992-93	**Montreal Canadiens**	**NHL**	**3**	**0**	**0**	**0**	**0**	**0**	**0**	**2**	**0**	**0**	**0**	**0**	**0.0**	**0**	**0**	**0**	**0**	**0**	....	....	....	....	....	....	....	....
	Fredericton Canadiens	AHL	54	3	13	16	....	....	....	93	....	....	....	....	....	....	....	....	....	....	....	....	....	....	....	....	....	....
	Atlanta Knights	IHL	11	0	2	2	....	....	....	12	....	....	....	....	....	....	....	....	....	....	3	0	1	1	6	....	....	....
1993-94	**Tampa Bay Lightning**	**NHL**	**4**	**0**	**0**	**0**	**0**	**0**	**0**	**2**	**0**	**0**	**0**	**1**	**0.0**	**2**	**0**	**2**	**0**	**0**	....	....	....	....	....	....	....	....
	Atlanta Knights	IHL	66	5	18	23	....	....	....	144	....	....	....	....	....	....	....	....	....	....	14	1	4	5	28	....	....	....
1994-95	**Tampa Bay Lightning**	**NHL**	**45**	**1**	**4**	**5**	**2**	**6**	**8**	**26**	**0**	**0**	**0**	**33**	**3.0**	**26**	**1**	**33**	**9**	**+1**	....	....	....	....	....	....	....	....
1995-96	**Tampa Bay Lightning**	**NHL**	**14**	**0**	**0**	**0**	**0**	**0**	**0**	**18**	**0**	**0**	**0**	**11**	**0.0**	**6**	**0**	**19**	**7**	**-6**	....	....	....	....	....	....	....	....
	Washington Capitals	**NHL**	**4**	**0**	**1**	**1**	**0**	**1**	**1**	**4**	**0**	**0**	**0**	**2**	**0.0**	**4**	**0**	**2**	**1**	**+3**	**6**	**0**	**0**	**0**	**8**	**0**	**0**	**0**
	Portland Pirates	AHL	45	0	8	8	....	....	....	88	....	....	....	....	....	....	....	....	....	....	20	1	1	2	33	....	....	....
1996-97	**Washington Capitals**	**NHL**	**25**	**1**	**1**	**2**	**1**	**1**	**2**	**20**	**0**	**0**	**0**	**11**	**9.1**	**8**	**0**	**9**	**2**	**+1**	....	....	....	....	....	....	....	....
	Portland Pirates	AHL	29	6	8	14	....	....	....	55	....	....	....	....	....	....	....	....	....	....	5	0	3	3	0	....	....	....
1997-98	**Calgary Flames**	**NHL**	**2**	**0**	**0**	**0**	**0**	**0**	**0**	**4**	**0**	**0**	**0**	**1**	**0.0**	**1**	**0**	**1**	**0**	**0**	....	....	....	....	....	....	....	....
	Saint John Flames	AHL	56	8	20	28	....	....	....	136	....	....	....	....	....	....	....	....	....	....	20	1	7	8	55	....	....	....
	NHL Totals		**97**	**2**	**6**	**8**	**3**	**8**	**11**	**76**	**0**	**0**	**0**	**59**	**3.4**	**47**	**1**	**66**	**19**		**6**	**0**	**0**	**0**	**8**	**0**	**0**	**0**

Traded to **Tampa Bay** by **Montreal** with Alain Cote and future considerations (Donald Dufresne, June 18, 1993) for Rob Ramage, March 20, 1993. Traded to **Washington** by **Tampa Bay** for Washington's 7th round choice (Eero Somervuori) in 1997 Entry Draft, November 16, 1995. Traded to **Calgary** by **Washington** for Calgary's 7th round choice (Nathan Forster) in 1998 Entry Draft, September 4, 1997.

• CHARRON, GUY

Guy Charron C – L. 5'10", 170 lbs. b: Verdun, Que., 1/24/1949.

Season	Club	League	GP	G	A	Pts	AG	AA	APts	PIM	PP	SH	GW	S	%	TGF	PGF	TGA	PGA	+/-	GP	G	A	Pts	PIM	PP	SH	GW
1967-68	Verdun Jr. Maple Leafs	QJHL	42	29	36	65	....	....	....	....	....	....	....	....	....	....	....	....	....	....	....	....	....	....	....	....	....	....
1968-69	Montreal Jr. Canadiens	OHA	50	27	27	54	....	....	....	12	....	....	....	....	....	....	....	....	....	....	14	11	15	26	6	....	....	....
1969-70	**Montreal Canadiens**	**NHL**	**5**	**0**	**0**	**0**	**0**	**0**	**0**	**0**	**0**	**0**	**0**	**2**	**0.0**	**0**	**0**	**2**	**0**	**-2**	....	....	....	....	....	....	....	....
	Montreal Voyageurs	AHL	65	37	45	82	....	....	....	20	....	....	....	....	....	....	....	....	....	....	8	*8	4	12	2	....	....	....
1970-71	**Montreal Canadiens**	**NHL**	**15**	**2**	**2**	**4**	**2**	**2**	**4**	**2**	**0**	**0**	**0**	**13**	**15.4**	**6**	**0**	**8**	**0**	**-2**	....	....	....	....	....	....	....	....
	Montreal Voyageurs	AHL	23	5	13	18	....	....	....	6	....	....	....	....	....	....	....	....	....	....	....	....	....	....	....	....	....	....
	Detroit Red Wings	**NHL**	**24**	**8**	**4**	**12**	**8**	**4**	**12**	**4**	**2**	**0**	**1**	**55**	**14.5**	**17**	**2**	**15**	**0**	**0**	....	....	....	....	....	....	....	....
1971-72	**Detroit Red Wings**	**NHL**	**64**	**9**	**16**	**25**	**10**	**15**	**25**	**14**	**0**	**0**	**1**	**119**	**7.6**	**36**	**5**	**39**	**0**	**-8**	....	....	....	....	....	....	....	....
1972-73	**Detroit Red Wings**	**NHL**	**75**	**18**	**18**	**36**	**18**	**15**	**33**	**23**	**0**	**0**	**2**	**117**	**15.4**	**56**	**5**	**43**	**1**	**+9**	....	....	....	....	....	....	....	....
1973-74	**Detroit Red Wings**	**NHL**	**76**	**25**	**30**	**55**	**26**	**26**	**52**	**10**	**6**	**0**	**2**	**205**	**12.2**	**80**	**25**	**88**	**2**	**-31**	....	....	....	....	....	....	....	....
1974-75	**Detroit Red Wings**	**NHL**	**26**	**1**	**10**	**11**	**1**	**8**	**9**	**6**	**0**	**0**	**1**	**27**	**3.7**	**16**	**11**	**14**	**0**	**-9**	....	....	....	....	....	....	....	....
	Kansas City Scouts	**NHL**	**51**	**13**	**29**	**42**	**12**	**23**	**35**	**21**	**4**	**0**	**0**	**157**	**8.3**	**53**	**27**	**73**	**6**	**-41**	....	....	....	....	....	....	....	....
1975-76	**Kansas City Scouts**	**NHL**	**78**	**27**	**44**	**71**	**25**	**35**	**60**	**12**	**9**	**0**	**4**	**226**	**11.9**	**89**	**30**	**134**	**24**	**-51**	....	....	....	....	....	....	....	....
1976-77	**Washington Capitals**	**NHL**	**80**	**36**	**46**	**82**	**35**	**37**	**72**	**10**	**6**	**1**	**4**	**261**	**13.8**	**105**	**34**	**106**	**7**	**-28**	....	....	....	....	....	....	....	....
	Canada	WEC-A	1	0	0	0	....	....	....	0	....	....	....	....	....	....	....	....	....	....	....	....	....	....	....	....	....	....
1977-78	**Washington Capitals**	**NHL**	**80**	**38**	**35**	**73**	**37**	**29**	**66**	**12**	**4**	**0**	**3**	**260**	**14.6**	**105**	**30**	**102**	**2**	**-25**	....	....	....	....	....	....	....	....
	Canada	WEC-A	9	0	1	1	....	....	....	0	....	....	....	....	....	....	....	....	....	....	....	....	....	....	....	....	....	....
1978-79	**Washington Capitals**	**NHL**	**80**	**28**	**42**	**70**	**25**	**32**	**57**	**24**	**9**	**0**	**4**	**225**	**12.4**	**104**	**32**	**92**	**6**	**-14**	....	....	....	....	....	....	....	....
	Canada	WEC-A	6	1	3	4	....	....	....	2	....	....	....	....	....	....	....	....	....	....	....	....	....	....	....	....	....	....
1979-80	**Washington Capitals**	**NHL**	**33**	**11**	**20**	**31**	**10**	**15**	**25**	**6**	**5**	**0**	**1**	**80**	**13.8**	**37**	**11**	**31**	**3**	**-2**	....	....	....	....	....	....	....	....
1980-81	**Washington Capitals**	**NHL**	**47**	**5**	**13**	**18**	**4**	**9**	**13**	**2**	**2**	**1**	**0**	**62**	**8.1**	**26**	**11**	**43**	**24**	**-4**	....	....	....	....	....	....	....	....
1981-82	Arosa	Switz.	STATISTICS NOT AVAILABLE																									
1982-83	New Haven Nighthawks	AHL	2	1	2	3	....	....	....	14	....	....	....	....	....	....	....	....	....	....	12	2	5	7	4	....	....	....
1983-84	Quebec Remparts	QMJHL	DID NOT PLAY – COACHING																									
	NHL Totals		**734**	**221**	**309**	**530**	**213**	**250**	**463**	**146**	**47**	**2**	**23**	**1809**	**12.2**	**730**	**223**	**790**	**75**		....	....	....	....	....	....	....	....

Played in NHL All-Star Game (1977)

Traded to **Detroit** by **Montreal** with Mickey Redmond and Bill Collins for Frank Mahovlich, January 13, 1971. Traded to **Kansas City** by **Detroit** with Claude Houde for Bart Crashley, Ted Snell and Larry Giroux, December 14, 1974. Signed as a free agent by **Washington**, September 1, 1976.

• CHARTIER, DAVE

Dave Chartier C – R. 5'9", 170 lbs. b: St. Lazare, Man., 2/15/1961. Los Angeles' 9th choice, 174th overall, in 1982 Entry Draft.

Season	Club	League	GP	G	A	Pts	AG	AA	APts	PIM	PP	SH	GW	S	%	TGF	PGF	TGA	PGA	+/-	GP	G	A	Pts	PIM	PP	SH	GW
1977-78	Brandon Bobcats	SJHL	47	30	22	52	....	....	....	98	....	....	....	....	....	....	....	....	....	....	....	....	....	....	....	....	....	....
	Brandon Wheat Kings	WCJHL	2	1	0	1	....	....	....	0	....	....	....	....	....	....	....	....	....	....	....	....	....	....	....	....	....	....
1978-79	Brandon Wheat Kings	WHL	48	14	12	26	....	....	....	83	....	....	....	....	....	....	....	....	....	....	....	....	....	....	....	....	....	....
1979-80	Brandon Wheat Kings	WHL	69	39	29	68	....	....	....	285	....	....	....	....	....	....	....	....	....	....	....	....	....	....	....	....	....	....
1980-81	Brandon Wheat Kings	WHL	69	64	60	124	....	....	....	295	....	....	....	....	....	....	....	....	....	....	....	....	....	....	....	....	....	....
	Winnipeg Jets	**NHL**	**1**	**0**	**0**	**0**	**0**	**0**	**0**	**0**	**0**	**0**	**0**	**0**	**0.0**	**0**	**0**	**0**	**0**	**0**	....	....	....	....	....	....	....	....
	Tulsa Oilers	CHL	1	1	0	1	....	....	....	4	....	....	....	....	....	....	....	....	....	....	8	1	2	3	9	....	....	....
1981-82	Tulsa Oilers	CHL	74	18	17	35	....	....	....	126	....	....	....	....	....	....	....	....	....	....	3	0	1	1	2	....	....	....
1982-83	Sherbrooke Jets	AHL	48	9	10	19	....	....	....	87	....	....	....	....	....	....	....	....	....	....	....	....	....	....	....	....	....	....
1983-84	Sherbrooke Jets	AHL	43	13	14	27	....	....	....	59	....	....	....	....	....	....	....	....	....	....	....	....	....	....	....	....	....	....
1984-85	Fort Wayne Komets	IHL	4	1	2	3	....	....	....	9	....	....	....	....	....	....	....	....	....	....	....	....	....	....	....	....	....	....
	NHL Totals		**1**	**0**	**0**	**0**	**0**	**0**	**0**	**0**	**0**	**0**	**0**	**0**	**0.0**	**0**	**0**	**0**	**0**		....	....	....	....	....	....	....	....

• CHARTRAW, RICK

Rick Chartraw D/RW – R. 6'2", 210 lbs. b: Caracas, Venezuala, 7/13/1954. Montreal's 3rd choice, 10th overall, in 1974 Amateur Draft.

Season	Club	League	GP	G	A	Pts	AG	AA	APts	PIM	PP	SH	GW	S	%	TGF	PGF	TGA	PGA	+/-	GP	G	A	Pts	PIM	PP	SH	GW
1972-73	Kitchener Rangers	OHA	59	10	22	32	....	....	....	101	....	....	....	....	....	....	....	....	....	....	....	....	....	....	....	....	....	....
1973-74	Kitchener Rangers	OHA	70	17	44	61	....	....	....	150	....	....	....	....	....	....	....	....	....	....	....	....	....	....	....	....	....	....
1974-75	**Montreal Canadiens**	**NHL**	**12**	**0**	**0**	**0**	**0**	**0**	**0**	**6**	**0**	**0**	**0**	**7**	**0.0**	**7**	**1**	**10**	**0**	**-4**	....	....	....	....	....	....	....	....
	Nova Scotia Voyageurs	AHL	58	7	20	27	....	....	....	148	....	....	....	....	....	....	....	....	....	....	6	1	2	3	4	....	....	....
1975-76	**Montreal Canadiens**	**NHL**	**16**	**1**	**3**	**4**	**1**	**2**	**3**	**25**	**0**	**0**	**0**	**22**	**4.5**	**17**	**0**	**5**	**0**	**+12**	**2**	**0**	**0**	**0**	**0**	**0**	**0**	**0**
	Nova Scotia Voyageurs	AHL	33	12	24	36	....	....	....	49	....	....	....	....	....	....	....	....	....	....	....	....	....	....	....	....	....	....
1976-77	United States	C Cup	5	0	0	0	....	....	....	8	....	....	....	....	....	....	....	....	....	....	....	....	....	....	....	....	....	....
	Montreal Canadiens	**NHL**	**43**	**3**	**4**	**7**	**3**	**3**	**6**	**59**	**0**	**0**	**1**	**42**	**7.1**	**37**	**0**	**10**	**0**	**+27**	**13**	**2**	**1**	**3**	**17**	**0**	**0**	**0**

			REGULAR SEASON																		PLAYOFFS							
Season	Club	League	GP	G	A	Pts	AG	AA	APts	PIM	PP	SH	GW	S	%	TGF	PGF	TGA	PGA	+/–	GP	G	A	Pts	PIM	PP	SH	GW
1977-78	**Montreal Canadiens**	**NHL**	68	4	12	16	4	10	14	64	0	0	1	75	5.3	43	0	28	1	+16	10	1	0	1	10	0	0	1
1978-79	**Montreal Canadiens**	**NHL**	62	5	11	16	5	8	13	29	0	0	1	81	6.2	49	1	35	1	+14	16	2	1	3	24	0	0	0
1979-80	**Montreal Canadiens**	**NHL**	66	5	7	12	5	5	10	35	0	0	0	65	7.7	33	0	27	0	+6	10	2	2	4	0	0	0	0
1980-81	**Montreal Canadiens**	**NHL**	14	0	0	0	0	0	0	4	0	0	0	10	0.0	3	0	8	0	–5	....	....	....	....	....	....	....	....
	Los Angeles Kings	**NHL**	21	1	6	7	1	4	5	28	0	0	1	32	3.1	27	6	22	2	+1	4	0	1	1	4	0	0	0
1981-82	**Los Angeles Kings**	**NHL**	33	2	8	10	2	5	7	56	1	0	0	32	6.3	33	2	61	19	–11	10	0	2	2	17	0	0	0
	New Haven Nighthawks	AHL	33	3	9	12	....	....	....	39	....	....	....	....	....	....	....	....	....	....	....	....	....	....	....	....	....	....
1982-83	**Los Angeles Kings**	**NHL**	31	3	5	8	2	3	5	31	0	0	0	32	9.4	29	0	57	14	–14	....	....	....	....	....	....	....	....
	New York Rangers	**NHL**	26	2	2	4	2	1	3	37	0	0	0	21	9.5	14	0	22	10	+2	9	0	2	2	6	0	0	0
1983-84	**New York Rangers**	**NHL**	4	0	0	0	0	0	0	4	0	0	0	0	0.0	0	0	3	0	–3	....	....	....	....	....	....	....	....
	Tulsa Oilers	CHL	28	1	4	5	....	....	....	25	....	....	....	....	....	....	....	....	....	....	....	....	....	....	....	....	....	....
	Edmonton Oilers	**NHL**	24	2	6	8	2	4	6	21	0	0	0	23	8.7	27	0	25	3	+5	1	0	0	0	2	0	0	0
	NHL Totals		**420**	**28**	**64**	**92**	**27**	**45**	**72**	**399**	**1**	**0**	**4**	**442**	**6.3**	**319**	**10**	**313**	**50**		**75**	**7**	**9**	**16**	**80**	**0**	**0**	**1**

OHA First All-Star Team (1974) • AHL First All-Star Team (1975)

Traded to **LA Kings** by **Montreal** for LA Kings' 2nd round choice (Claude Lemieux) in 1983 Entry Draft, February 17, 1981. Claimed on waivers by **NY Rangers** from **LA Kings**, January 13, 1983. Traded to **Edmonton** by **NY Rangers** for Edmonton's 9th round choice (Heinz Ehlers) in 1984 Entry Draft, January 20, 1984.

• CHASE, KELLY

Kelly Chase RW – R. 5'11", 193 lbs. b: Porcupine Plain, Sask., 10/25/1967.

1985-86	Saskatoon Blades	WHL	57	7	18	25	....	....	....	172	....	....	....	....	....	....	....	....	....	....	10	3	4	7	37	....	....	....
1986-87	Saskatoon Blades	WHL	68	17	29	46	....	....	....	285	....	....	....	....	....	....	....	....	....	....	11	2	8	10	37	....	....	....
1987-88	Saskatoon Blades	WHL	70	21	34	55	....	....	....	*343	....	....	....	....	....	....	....	....	....	....	9	3	5	8	32	....	....	....
1988-89	Peoria Rivermen	IHL	38	14	7	21	....	....	....	278	....	....	....	....	....	....	....	....	....	....	....	....	....	....	....	....	....	....
1989-90	**St. Louis Blues**	**NHL**	43	1	3	4	1	2	3	244	0	0	0	9	11.1	7	0	8	0	–1	9	1	0	1	46	0	0	0
	Peoria Rivermen	IHL	10	1	2	3	....	....	....	76	....	....	....	....	....	....	....	....	....	....	....	....	....	....	....	....	....	....
1990-91	**St. Louis Blues**	**NHL**	2	1	0	1	1	0	1	15	0	0	1	1	100.0	1	0	0	0	+1	6	0	0	0	18	0	0	0
	Peoria Rivermen	IHL	61	20	34	54	....	....	....	406	....	....	....	....	....	....	....	....	....	....	10	4	3	7	61	....	....	....
1991-92	**St. Louis Blues**	**NHL**	46	1	2	3	1	1	2	264	0	0	0	29	3.4	6	0	12	0	–6	1	0	0	0	7	0	0	0
1992-93	**St. Louis Blues**	**NHL**	49	2	5	7	2	3	5	204	0	0	0	28	7.1	9	0	18	0	–9	....	....	....	....	....	....	....	....
1993-94	**St. Louis Blues**	**NHL**	68	2	5	7	2	4	6	278	0	0	0	57	3.5	15	0	20	0	–5	4	0	1	1	6	0	0	0
1994-95	**Hartford Whalers**	**NHL**	28	0	4	4	0	6	6	141	0	0	0	15	0.0	6	0	5	0	+1	....	....	....	....	....	....	....	....
1995-96	**Hartford Whalers**	**NHL**	55	2	4	6	2	3	5	230	0	0	1	19	10.5	6	0	10	0	–4	....	....	....	....	....	....	....	....
1996-97	**Hartford Whalers**	**NHL**	28	1	2	3	1	2	3	122	0	0	0	5	20.0	6	0	4	0	+2	....	....	....	....	....	....	....	....
	Toronto Maple Leafs	**NHL**	2	0	0	0	0	0	0	27	0	0	0	1	0.0	0	0	0	0	0	....	....	....	....	....	....	....	....
1997-98	**St. Louis Blues**	**NHL**	67	4	3	7	5	3	8	231	0	0	1	29	13.8	16	0	6	0	+10	7	0	0	0	23	0	0	0
	NHL Totals		**388**	**14**	**28**	**42**	**15**	**24**	**39**	**1756**	**0**	**0**	**3**	**193**	**7.3**	**72**	**0**	**83**	**0**		**27**	**1**	**1**	**2**	**100**	**0**	**0**	**0**

Won King Clancy Memorial Trophy (1998)

Signed as a free agent by **St. Louis**, February 23, 1988. Claimed by **Hartford** from **St. Louis** in NHL Waiver Draft, January 18, 1995. Traded to **Toronto** by **Hartford** for Toronto's 8th round choice in 1998 Entry Draft, March 18, 1997. Traded to **St. Louis** by **Toronto** for future considerations, September 30, 1997.

• CHASSE, DENIS

Denis Chasse RW – R. 6'2", 200 lbs. b: Montreal, Que., 2/7/1970.

1987-88	St-Jean Lynx	QMJHL	13	0	1	1	....	....	....	2	....	....	....	....	....	....	....	....	....	....	1	0	0	0	0	....	....	....
1988-89	Verdun Jr. Canadiens	QMJHL	38	12	12	24	....	....	....	61	....	....	....	....	....	....	....	....	....	....	....	....	....	....	....	....	....	....
	Drummondville Voltigeurs	QMJHL	30	15	16	31	....	....	....	77	....	....	....	....	....	....	....	....	....	....	3	0	2	2	28	....	....	....
1989-90	Drummondville Voltigeurs	QMJHL	34	14	29	43	....	....	....	85	....	....	....	....	....	....	....	....	....	....	....	....	....	....	....	....	....	....
	Chicoutimi Sagueneens	QMJHL	33	19	27	46	....	....	....	105	....	....	....	....	....	....	....	....	....	....	7	7	4	11	50	....	....	....
1990-91	Drummondville Voltigeurs	QMJHL	62	47	54	101	....	....	....	246	....	....	....	....	....	....	....	....	....	....	13	9	11	20	56	....	....	....
1991-92	Halifax Citadels	AHL	73	26	35	61	....	....	....	254	....	....	....	....	....	....	....	....	....	....	....	....	....	....	....	....	....	....
1992-93	Halifax Citadels	AHL	75	35	41	76	....	....	....	242	....	....	....	....	....	....	....	....	....	....	....	....	....	....	....	....	....	....
1993-94	Cornwall Aces	AHL	48	27	39	66	....	....	....	104	....	....	....	....	....	....	....	....	....	....	....	....	....	....	....	....	....	....
	St. Louis Blues	**NHL**	3	0	1	1	0	1	1	15	0	0	0	5	0.0	2	0	1	0	+1	....	....	....	....	....	....	....	....
1994-95	**St. Louis Blues**	**NHL**	47	7	9	16	12	13	25	133	1	0	0	48	14.6	32	4	16	0	+12	7	1	7	8	23	0	0	0
1995-96	**St. Louis Blues**	**NHL**	42	3	0	3	3	0	3	108	1	0	1	25	12.0	6	1	14	0	–9	....	....	....	....	....	....	....	....
	Worcester IceCats	AHL	3	0	0	0	....	....	....	6	....	....	....	....	....	....	....	....	....	....	....	....	....	....	....	....	....	....
	Washington Capitals	**NHL**	3	0	0	0	0	0	0	5	0	0	0	3	0.0	1	0	2	0	–1	....	....	....	....	....	....	....	....
	Winnipeg Jets	**NHL**	15	0	0	0	0	0	0	12	0	0	0	3	0.0	2	0	6	0	–4	....	....	....	....	....	....	....	....
1996-97	**Ottawa Senators**	**NHL**	22	1	4	5	1	4	5	19	0	0	0	12	8.3	6	0	3	0	+3	....	....	....	....	....	....	....	....
	Detroit Vipers	IHL	9	2	1	3	....	....	....	33	....	....	....	....	....	....	....	....	....	....	....	....	....	....	....	....	....	....
	Indianapolis Ice	IHL	3	0	0	0	....	....	....	10	....	....	....	....	....	....	....	....	....	....	4	1	1	2	23	....	....	....
1997-98	Adler Mannheim	EuroHL	3	0	1	1	....	....	....	12	....	....	....	....	....	....	....	....	....	....	....	....	....	....	....	....	....	....
	Adler Mannheim	Germany	15	2	5	7	....	....	....	72	....	....	....	....	....	....	....	....	....	....	....	....	....	....	....	....	....	....
	Augsburg Panthers	Germany	29	6	6	12	....	....	....	97	....	....	....	....	....	....	....	....	....	....	....	....	....	....	....	....	....	....
	NHL Totals		**132**	**11**	**14**	**25**	**16**	**18**	**34**	**292**	**2**	**0**	**1**	**96**	**11.5**	**49**	**5**	**42**	**0**		**7**	**1**	**7**	**8**	**23**	**0**	**0**	**0**

Signed as a free agent by **Quebec**, May 14, 1991. Traded to **St. Louis** by **Quebec** with Steve Duchesne for Garth Butcher, Ron Sutter and Bob Bassen, January 23, 1994. Traded to **Washington** by **St. Louis** for Rob Pearson, January 29, 1996. Traded to **Winnipeg** by **Washington** for Stewart Malgunas, February 15, 1996. Signed as a free agent by **Ottawa**, September 5, 1996. Traded to **Chicago** by **Ottawa** with the rights to Kevin Bolibruck and Ottawa's 6th round choice in 1998 Entry Draft for Mike Prokopec, March 18, 1997.

• CHEBATURKIN, VLADIMIR

Vladimir Chebaturkin D – L. 6'2", 213 lbs. b: Tyumen, USSR, 4/23/1975. NY Islanders' 3rd choice, 66th overall, in 1993 Entry Draft.

1993-94	Kristall Elektrostal	CIS 2	42	4	4	8	....	....	....	38	....	....	....	....	....	....	....	....	....	....	....	....	....	....	....	....	....	....
1994-95	Kristall Elektrostal	CIS	52	2	6	8	....	....	....	90	....	....	....	....	....	....	....	....	....	....	....	....	....	....	....	....	....	....
	Russia	WJC-A	7	0	2	2	....	....	....	2	....	....	....	....	....	....	....	....	....	....	....	....	....	....	....	....	....	....
1995-96	Kristall Elektrostal	CIS	44	1	6	7	....	....	....	30	....	....	....	....	....	....	....	....	....	....	1	0	0	0	0	....	....	....
1996-97	Utah Grizzlies	IHL	68	0	4	4	....	....	....	34	....	....	....	....	....	....	....	....	....	....	....	....	....	....	....	....	....	....
1997-98	**New York Islanders**	**NHL**	2	0	2	2	0	2	2	0	0	0	0	0	0.0	3	1	3	0	–1	....	....	....	....	....	....	....	....
	Kentucky Thoroughblades	AHL	54	6	8	14	....	....	....	52	....	....	....	....	....	....	....	....	....	....	2	0	0	0	4	....	....	....
	NHL Totals		**2**	**0**	**2**	**2**	**0**	**2**	**2**	**0**	**0**	**0**	**0**	**0**	**0.0**	**3**	**1**	**3**	**0**		....	....	....	....	....	....	....	....

• CHELIOS, CHRIS

Chris Chelios D – R. 6'1", 190 lbs. b: Chicago, IL, 1/25/1962. Montreal's 5th choice, 40th overall, in 1981 Entry Draft.

1980-81	Moose Jaw Canucks	SJHL	54	23	64	87	....	....	....	175	....	....	....	....	....	....	....	....	....	....	....	....	....	....	....	....	....	....
1981-82	University of Wisconsin	WCHA	43	6	43	49	....	....	....	50	....	....	....	....	....	....	....	....	....	....	....	....	....	....	....	....	....	....
	United States	WJC-A	7	1	2	3	....	....	....	10	....	....	....	....	....	....	....	....	....	....	....	....	....	....	....	....	....	....
1982-83	University of Wisconsin	WCHA	26	9	17	26	....	....	....	50	....	....	....	....	....	....	....	....	....	....	....	....	....	....	....	....	....	....
1983-84	United States	Nat-Team	60	14	35	49	....	....	....	58	....	....	....	....	....	....	....	....	....	....	....	....	....	....	....	....	....	....
	United States	Olympics	6	0	3	3	....	....	....	8	....	....	....	....	....	....	....	....	....	....	....	....	....	....	....	....	....	....
	Montreal Canadiens	**NHL**	12	0	2	2	0	1	1	12	0	0	0	23	0.0	8	0	16	3	–5	15	1	9	10	17	1	0	0
1984-85	United States	C Cup	6	0	2	2	....	....	....	2	....	....	....	....	....	....	....	....	....	....	....	....	....	....	....	....	....	....
	Montreal Canadiens	**NHL**	74	9	55	64	7	37	44	87	2	1	0	199	4.5	139	43	106	21	+11	9	2	8	10	17	2	0	0
1985-86	**Montreal Canadiens**	**NHL**	41	8	26	34	6	17	23	67	2	0	0	101	7.9	83	37	55	13	+4	20	2	9	11	49	1	0	0
1986-87	**Montreal Canadiens**	**NHL**	71	11	33	44	10	24	34	124	6	0	2	141	7.8	102	35	97	25	–5	17	4	9	13	38	2	1	0
	NHL All-Stars	RV'87	2	0	0	0	....	....	....	0	....	....	....	....	....	....	....	....	....	....	....	....	....	....	....	....	....	....
1987-88	United States	C Cup	5	0	2	2	....	....	....	2	....	....	....	....	....	....	....	....	....	....	....	....	....	....	....	....	....	....
	Montreal Canadiens	**NHL**	71	20	41	61	17	29	46	172	10	1	5	199	10.1	125	38	105	32	+14	11	3	1	4	29	1	0	0
1988-89	**Montreal Canadiens**	**NHL**	80	15	58	73	13	41	54	185	8	0	6	206	7.3	167	62	106	36	+35	21	4	15	19	28	1	0	2
1989-90	**Montreal Canadiens**	**NHL**	53	9	22	31	8	16	24	136	1	2	1	123	7.3	82	19	74	31	+20	5	0	1	1	8	0	0	0
1990-91	**Chicago Blackhawks**	**NHL**	77	12	52	64	11	39	50	192	5	2	2	187	6.4	143	63	97	40	+23	6	1	7	8	46	1	0	0
1991-92	United States	C Cup	8	1	3	4	....	....	....	4	....	....	....	....	....	....	....	....	....	....	....	....	....	....	....	....	....	....
	Chicago Blackhawks	**NHL**	80	9	47	56	8	35	43	245	2	2	2	239	3.8	138	55	91	32	+24	18	6	15	21	37	3	0	1
1992-93	**Chicago Blackhawks**	**NHL**	84	15	58	73	12	40	52	282	8	0	2	290	5.2	165	81	115	45	+14	4	0	2	2	14	0	0	0
1993-94	**Chicago Blackhawks**	**NHL**	76	16	44	60	15	34	49	212	7	1	2	219	7.3	136	61	102	39	+12	6	1	1	2	8	1	0	0
	United States	WC-A	DID NOT PLAY																									
1994-95	Biel	Switz.	3	0	3	3	....	....	....	4	....	....	....	....	....	....	....	....	....	....	....	....	....	....	....	....	....	....
	Chicago Blackhawks	**NHL**	48	5	33	38	9	49	58	72	3	1	0	166	3.0	94	40	59	22	+17	16	4	7	11	12	0	1	3

			REGULAR SEASON																		PLAYOFFS							
Season	Club	League	GP	G	A	Pts	AG	AA	APts	PIM	PP	SH	GW	S	%	TGF	PGF	TGA	PGA	+/–	GP	G	A	Pts	PIM	PP	SH	GW
1995-96	**Chicago Blackhawks**	**NHL**	**81**	**14**	**58**	**72**	**14**	**47**	**61**	**140**	**7**	**0**	**3**	**219**	**6.4**	**151**	**54**	**115**	**43**	**+25**	**9**	**0**	**3**	**3**	**8**	**0**	**0**	**0**
1996-97	United States	W Cup	7	0	4	4	....	....	....	10	....	....	....	....	....	....	....	....	....	....	....	....	....	....	....	....	....	....
	Chicago Blackhawks	**NHL**	**72**	**10**	**38**	**48**	**11**	**34**	**45**	**112**	**2**	**0**	**2**	**194**	**5.2**	**111**	**34**	**93**	**32**	**+16**	**6**	**0**	**1**	**1**	**8**	**0**	**0**	**0**
1997-98	**Chicago Blackhawks**	**NHL**	**81**	**3**	**39**	**42**	**4**	**38**	**42**	**151**	**1**	**0**	**0**	**205**	**1.5**	**105**	**38**	**112**	**38**	**–7**	....	....	....	....	....	....	....	....
	United States	Olympics	4	2	0	2	....	....	....	2	....	....	....	....	....	....	....	....	....	....	....	....	....	....	....	....	....	....
	NHL Totals		**1001**	**156**	**606**	**762**	**145**	**481**	**626**	**2189**	**64**	**10**	**27**	**2711**	**5.8**	**1749**	**660**	**1343**	**452**		**163**	**28**	**88**	**116**	**319**	**13**	**2**	**6**

WCHA Second All-Star Team (1983) • NCAA Championship All-Tournament Team (1983) • NHL All-Rookie Team (1985) • NHL First All-Star Team (1989, 1993, 1995, 1996) • Won James Norris Memorial Trophy (1989, 1993, 1996) • NHL Second All-Star Team (1991, 1997) • Canada Cup All-Star Team (1991) • World Cup All-Star Team (1996)

Played in NHL All-Star Game (1985, 1990, 1991, 1992, 1993, 1994, 1996, 1997, 1998)

Traded to **Chicago** by **Montreal** with Montreal's 2nd round choice (Michael Pomichter) in 1991 Entry Draft for Denis Savard, June 29, 1990.

• CHERNOFF, MIKE

Mike Chernoff LW – L. 5'10", 175 lbs. b: Yorkton, Sask., 5/13/1946.

Season	Club	League	GP	G	A	Pts	AG	AA	APts	PIM	PP	SH	GW	S	%	TGF	PGF	TGA	PGA	+/–	GP	G	A	Pts	PIM	PP	SH	GW
1963-64	Moose Jaw Canucks	SJHL	59	7	11	18	....	....	....	154	....	....	....	....	....	....	....	....	....	....	5	0	1	1	6	....	....	....
1964-65	Moose Jaw Canucks	SJHL	47	23	30	53	....	....	....	125	....	....	....	....	....	....	....	....	....	....	....	....	....	....	....	....	....	....
1965-66	Moose Jaw Canucks	SJHL	59	45	36	81	....	....	....	95	....	....	....	....	....	....	....	....	....	....	1	0	1	1	0	....	....	....
1966-67	St. Louis Braves	CHL	70	14	16	30	....	....	....	55	....	....	....	....	....	....	....	....	....	....	....	....	....	....	....	....	....	....
1967-68	Dallas Black Hawks	CHL	31	8	7	15	....	....	....	41	....	....	....	....	....	....	....	....	....	....	....	....	....	....	....	....	....	....
1968-69	**Minnesota North Stars**	**NHL**	**1**	**0**	**0**	**0**	**0**	**0**	**0**	**0**	**0**	**0**	**0**	**0**	**0.0**	**0**	**0**	**0**	**0**	**0**	....	....	....	....	....	....	....	....
	Memphis South Stars	CHL	68	20	31	51	....	....	....	48	....	....	....	....	....	....	....	....	....	....	....	....	....	....	....	....	....	....
1969-70	Iowa Stars	CHL	69	36	39	75	....	....	....	29	....	....	....	....	....	....	....	....	....	....	11	7	4	11	6	....	....	....
1970-71	Cleveland Barons	AHL	72	31	23	54	....	....	....	37	....	....	....	....	....	....	....	....	....	....	8	3	1	4	2	....	....	....
1971-72	Cleveland Barons	AHL	71	8	13	21	....	....	....	30	....	....	....	....	....	....	....	....	....	....	6	0	0	0	0	....	....	....
1972-73	Jacksonville Barons	AHL	76	35	33	68	....	....	....	37	....	....	....	....	....	....	....	....	....	....	....	....	....	....	....	....	....	....
1973-74	Vancouver Blazers	WHA	36	11	10	21	....	....	....	4	....	....	....	....	....	....	....	....	....	....	....	....	....	....	....	....	....	....
	Roanoke Valley Rebels	SHL	4	2	4	6	....	....	....	7	....	....	....	....	....	....	....	....	....	....	....	....	....	....	....	....	....	....
1974-75	Vancouver Blazers	WHA	3	0	0	0	....	....	....	0	....	....	....	....	....	....	....	....	....	....	....	....	....	....	....	....	....	....
	Tulsa Oilers	CHL	20	7	12	19	....	....	....	25	....	....	....	....	....	....	....	....	....	....	....	....	....	....	....	....	....	....
	Johnstown Jets	NAHL	41	9	19	28	....	....	....	32	....	....	....	....	....	....	....	....	....	....	14	8	6	14	0	....	....	....
	NHL Totals		**1**	**0**	**0**	**0**	**0**	**0**	**0**	**0**	**0**	**0**	**0**	**0**	**0.0**	**0**	**0**	**0**	**0**		....	....	....	....	....	....	....	....
	Other Major League Totals		39	11	10	21	....	....	....	4	....	....	....	....	....	....	....	....	....	....	....	....	....	....	....	....	....	....

Signed as a free agent by **Minnesota**, October, 1968. Selected by **Winnipeg** (WHA) in 1972 WHA General Player Draft, February 12, 1972. WHA rights traded to **Vancouver** (WHA) by **Winnipeg** (WHA) for cash, July, 1973.

• CHERNOMAZ, RICH

Rich Chernomaz RW – R. 5'8", 185 lbs. b: Selkirk, Man., 9/1/1963. Colorado's 2nd choice, 26th overall, in 1981 Entry Draft.

Season	Club	League	GP	G	A	Pts	AG	AA	APts	PIM	PP	SH	GW	S	%	TGF	PGF	TGA	PGA	+/–	GP	G	A	Pts	PIM	PP	SH	GW
1979-80	Saskatoon Northmen	SJHL	51	33	37	70	....	....	....	75	....	....	....	....	....	....	....	....	....	....	....	....	....	....	....	....	....	....
	Saskatoon Blades	WHL	25	9	10	19	....	....	....	33	....	....	....	....	....	....	....	....	....	....	....	....	....	....	....	....	....	....
1980-81	Victoria Cougars	WHL	72	49	64	113	....	....	....	92	....	....	....	....	....	....	....	....	....	....	15	11	15	26	38	....	....	....
1981-82	Victoria Cougars	WHL	49	36	62	98	....	....	....	69	....	....	....	....	....	....	....	....	....	....	4	1	2	3	13	....	....	....
	Colorado Rockies	**NHL**	**2**	**0**	**0**	**0**	**0**	**0**	**0**	**0**	**0**	**0**	**0**	**2**	**0.0**	**0**	**0**	**2**	**0**	**–2**	....	....	....	....	....	....	....	....
1982-83	Victoria Cougars	WHL	64	71	53	124	....	....	....	113	....	....	....	....	....	....	....	....	....	....	12	10	5	15	18	....	....	....
1983-84	**New Jersey Devils**	**NHL**	**7**	**2**	**1**	**3**	**2**	**1**	**3**	**2**	**0**	**0**	**0**	**7**	**28.6**	**3**	**0**	**6**	**0**	**–3**	....	....	....	....	....	....	....	....
	Maine Mariners	AHL	69	17	29	46	....	....	....	39	....	....	....	....	....	....	....	....	....	....	2	0	1	1	0	....	....	....
1984-85	**New Jersey Devils**	**NHL**	**3**	**0**	**2**	**2**	**0**	**1**	**1**	**2**	**0**	**0**	**0**	**2**	**0.0**	**2**	**0**	**0**	**0**	**+2**	....	....	....	....	....	....	....	....
	Maine Mariners	AHL	64	17	34	51	....	....	....	64	....	....	....	....	....	....	....	....	....	....	10	2	2	4	4	....	....	....
1985-86	Maine Mariners	AHL	78	21	28	49	....	....	....	82	....	....	....	....	....	....	....	....	....	....	5	0	0	0	2	....	....	....
1986-87	**New Jersey Devils**	**NHL**	**25**	**6**	**4**	**10**	**5**	**3**	**8**	**8**	**2**	**0**	**0**	**44**	**13.6**	**15**	**4**	**23**	**1**	**–11**	....	....	....	....	....	....	....	....
	Maine Mariners	AHL	58	35	27	62	....	....	....	65	....	....	....	....	....	....	....	....	....	....	....	....	....	....	....	....	....	....
1987-88	**Calgary Flames**	**NHL**	**2**	**1**	**0**	**1**	**1**	**0**	**1**	**0**	**0**	**0**	**0**	**5**	**20.0**	**3**	**0**	**2**	**0**	**+1**	....	....	....	....	....	....	....	....
	Salt Lake Golden Eagles	IHL	73	48	47	95	....	....	....	122	....	....	....	....	....	....	....	....	....	....	18	4	14	18	30	....	....	....
1988-89	**Calgary Flames**	**NHL**	**1**	**0**	**0**	**0**	**0**	**0**	**0**	**0**	**0**	**0**	**0**	**2**	**0.0**	**0**	**0**	**1**	**0**	**–1**	....	....	....	....	....	....	....	....
	Salt Lake Golden Eagles	IHL	81	33	68	101	....	....	....	122	....	....	....	....	....	....	....	....	....	....	14	7	5	12	47	....	....	....
1989-90	Salt Lake Golden Eagles	IHL	65	39	35	74	....	....	....	170	....	....	....	....	....	....	....	....	....	....	11	6	6	12	32	....	....	....
1990-91	Salt Lake Golden Eagles	IHL	81	39	58	97	....	....	....	213	....	....	....	....	....	....	....	....	....	....	4	3	1	4	8	....	....	....
1991-92	**Calgary Flames**	**NHL**	**11**	**0**	**0**	**0**	**0**	**0**	**0**	**6**	**0**	**0**	**0**	**21**	**0.0**	**4**	**4**	**11**	**2**	**–9**	....	....	....	....	....	....	....	....
	Salt Lake Golden Eagles	IHL	66	20	40	60	....	....	....	201	....	....	....	....	....	....	....	....	....	....	5	1	2	3	10	....	....	....
1992-93	Salt Lake Golden Eagles	IHL	76	26	48	74	....	....	....	172	....	....	....	....	....	....	....	....	....	....	....	....	....	....	....	....	....	....
1993-94	St. John's Maple Leafs	AHL	78	45	65	110	....	....	....	199	....	....	....	....	....	....	....	....	....	....	11	5	11	16	18	....	....	....
1994-95	St. John's Maple Leafs	AHL	77	24	45	69	....	....	....	235	....	....	....	....	....	....	....	....	....	....	5	1	1	2	8	....	....	....
	Canada	WC-A	8	0	3	3	....	....	....	10	....	....	....	....	....	....	....	....	....	....	....	....	....	....	....	....	....	....
1995-96	Schwenningen Wild Wings	Germany	49	24	43	67	....	....	....	105	....	....	....	....	....	....	....	....	....	....	2	1	1	2	24	....	....	....
1996-97	Schwenningen Wild Wings	Germany	47	25	39	64	....	....	....	126	....	....	....	....	....	....	....	....	....	....	5	3	5	8	8	....	....	....
1997-98	Schwenningen Wild Wings	Germany	51	12	37	49	....	....	....	156	....	....	....	....	....	....	....	....	....	....	....	....	....	....	....	....	....	....
	NHL Totals		**51**	**9**	**7**	**16**	**8**	**5**	**13**	**18**	**2**	**0**	**0**	**83**	**10.8**	**27**	**8**	**45**	**3**		....	....	....	....	....	....	....	....

WHL First All-Star Team (1983) • IHL Second All-Star Team (1988) • AHL First All-Star Team (1994) • Won Les Cunningham Award (MVP - AHL) (1994)

Transferred to **New Jersey** after **Colorado** franchise relocated, June 30, 1982. Signed as a free agent by **Calgary**, August 4, 1987. Signed as a free agent by **Toronto**, August 3, 1993.

• CHERRY, DICK

Dick Cherry D – L. 6', 195 lbs. b: Kingston, Ont., 3/28/1937.

Season	Club	League	GP	G	A	Pts	AG	AA	APts	PIM	PP	SH	GW	S	%	TGF	PGF	TGA	PGA	+/–	GP	G	A	Pts	PIM	PP	SH	GW
1955-56	Barrie Flyers	OHA	48	18	32	50	....	....	....	69	....	....	....	....	....	....	....	....	....	....	18	1	3	4	19	....	....	....
1956-57	Barrie Flyers	OHA	52	15	30	45	....	....	....	42	....	....	....	....	....	....	....	....	....	....	3	1	0	1	6	....	....	....
	Boston Bruins	**NHL**	**6**	**0**	**0**	**0**	**0**	**0**	**0**	**4**	....	....	....	....	....	....	....	....	....	....	....	....	....	....	....	....	....	....
1957-58	Quebec Aces	QHL	47	3	15	18	....	....	....	27	....	....	....	....	....	....	....	....	....	....	....	....	....	....	....	....	....	....
	Springfield Indians	AHL	12	0	0	0	....	....	....	6	....	....	....	....	....	....	....	....	....	....	6	0	0	0	0	....	....	....
1958-59	Providence Reds	AHL	65	2	9	11	....	....	....	66	....	....	....	....	....	....	....	....	....	....	....	....	....	....	....	....	....	....
1959-60	Providence Reds	AHL	71	5	13	18	....	....	....	52	....	....	....	....	....	....	....	....	....	....	5	0	0	0	4	....	....	....
1960-61	Providence Reds	AHL	68	2	20	22	....	....	....	66	....	....	....	....	....	....	....	....	....	....	....	....	....	....	....	....	....	....
1961-62	Kingston Frontenacs	EPHL	43	11	24	35	....	....	....	29	....	....	....	....	....	....	....	....	....	....	10	4	3	7	9	....	....	....
1962-63	Kingston Frontenacs	EPHL	53	28	32	60	....	....	....	10	....	....	....	....	....	....	....	....	....	....	5	*6	3	9	0	....	....	....
1963-64			DID NOT PLAY																									
1964-65			DID NOT PLAY																									
1965-66	Kingston Aces	OHA Sr.	25	20	27	47	....	....	....	27	....	....	....	....	....	....	....	....	....	....	....	....	....	....	....	....	....	....
1966-67	Oklahoma City Blazers	CHL	69	8	25	33	....	....	....	86	....	....	....	....	....	....	....	....	....	....	11	1	4	5	13	....	....	....
1967-68			DID NOT PLAY																									
1968-69	**Philadelphia Flyers**	**NHL**	**71**	**9**	**6**	**15**	**10**	**6**	**16**	**18**	**1**	**1**	**2**	**91**	**9.9**	**23**	**2**	**51**	**19**	**–11**	**4**	**1**	**0**	**1**	**4**	**0**	**0**	**0**
1969-70	**Philadelphia Flyers**	**NHL**	**68**	**3**	**4**	**7**	**3**	**4**	**7**	**23**	**0**	**0**	**1**	**99**	**3.0**	**22**	**3**	**61**	**18**	**–24**	....	....	....	....	....	....	....	....
1970-71	Oklahoma City Blazers	CHL	64	14	50	64	....	....	....	44	....	....	....	....	....	....	....	....	....	....	5	0	6	6	4	....	....	....
1971-72	Kingston Aces	OHA Sr.	21	3	14	17	....	....	....	27	....	....	....	....	....	....	....	....	....	....	....	....	....	....	....	....	....	....
1972-73	Kingston Aces	OHA Sr.	41	10	33	43	....	....	....	14	....	....	....	....	....	....	....	....	....	....	....	....	....	....	....	....	....	....
1973-74			DID NOT PLAY – RETIRED																									
1974-75	Napanee Comets	OHA Sr.	39	18	41	59	....	....	....	14	....	....	....	....	....	....	....	....	....	....	....	....	....	....	....	....	....	....
	NHL Totals		**145**	**12**	**10**	**22**	**13**	**10**	**23**	**45**	**1**	**1**	**3**	**190**	**6.3**	**45**	**5**	**112**	**37**		**4**	**1**	**0**	**1**	**4**	**0**	**0**	**0**

• Retired to teach high-school in Kingston, 1963-1965. Claimed by **Philadelphia** from **Boston** in Expansion Draft, June 6, 1967. Claimed by **Boston** from **Philadelphia** in Intra-League Draft, June 9, 1970.

• CHERVYAKOV, DENIS

Denis Chervyakov D – L. 6', 185 lbs. b: Leningrad, USSR, 4/20/1970. Boston's 9th choice, 256th overall, in 1992 Entry Draft.

Season	Club	League	GP	G	A	Pts	AG	AA	APts	PIM	PP	SH	GW	S	%	TGF	PGF	TGA	PGA	+/–	GP	G	A	Pts	PIM	PP	SH	GW
1990-91	SKA-Torpedo Yaroslavl	FrTour	1	0	0	0	....	....	....	2	....	....	....	....	....	....	....	....	....	....	....	....	....	....	....	....	....	....
	Leningrad	USSR	28	2	1	3	....	....	....	40	....	....	....	....	....	....	....	....	....	....	....	....	....	....	....	....	....	....
1991-92	Riga	CIS	14	0	1	1	....	....	....	12	....	....	....	....	....	....	....	....	....	....	....	....	....	....	....	....	....	....
1992-93	**Boston Bruins**	**NHL**	**2**	**0**	**0**	**0**	**0**	**0**	**0**	**2**	**0**	**0**	**0**	**2**	**0.0**	**1**	**0**	**2**	**0**	**–1**	....	....	....	....	....	....	....	....
	Providence Bruins	AHL	48	4	12	16	....	....	....	99	....	....	....	....	....	....	....	....	....	....	....	....	....	....	....	....	....	....
	Atlanta Knights	IHL	1	0	0	0	....	....	....	0	....	....	....	....	....	....	....	....	....	....	....	....	....	....	....	....	....	....

			REGULAR SEASON																		PLAYOFFS							
Season	Club	League	GP	G	A	Pts	AG	AA	APts	PIM	PP	SH	GW	S	%	TGF	PGF	TGA	PGA	+/–	GP	G	A	Pts	PIM	PP	SH	GW
1993-94	Providence Bruins	AHL	58	2	16	18				128																		
1994-95	Providence Bruins	AHL	65	1	18	19				130											10	0	2	2	14			
1995-96	Providence Bruins	AHL	64	3	7	10				58											4	1	0	1	21			
1996-97	Kentucky Thoroughblades	AHL	52	2	11	13				78																		
1997-98	Assat Pori	Finland	2	0	0	0				2																		
	Lukko Rauma	Finland	24	0	0	0				14																		
	Tappara Tampere	Finland	14	0	2	2				14											4	0	0	0	0			
	NHL Totals		**2**	**0**	**0**	**0**	**0**	**0**	**0**	**2**	**0**	**0**	**0**	**2**	**0.0**	**1**	**0**	**2**	**0**									

Signed as a free agent by **NY Islanders**, September 12, 1996.

• CHIASSON, STEVE

Steve Chiasson D – L. 6'1", 205 lbs. b: Barrie, Ont., 4/14/1967. Detroit's 3rd choice, 50th overall, in 1985 Entry Draft.

Season	Club	League	GP	G	A	Pts	AG	AA	APts	PIM	PP	SH	GW	S	%	TGF	PGF	TGA	PGA	+/–	GP	G	A	Pts	PIM	PP	SH	GW
1984-85	Guelph Platers	OHL	61	8	22	30				139																		
1985-86	Guelph Platers	OHL	54	12	30	42				126											18	10	10	20	37			
1986-87	**Detroit Red Wings**	**NHL**	**45**	**1**	**4**	**5**	**1**	**3**	**4**	**73**	**0**	**0**	**0**	**44**	**2.3**	**31**	**10**	**32**	**4**	**–7**	**2**	**0**	**0**	**0**	**19**	**0**	**0**	**0**
	Canada	WJC-A	6	2	2	4				21																		
1987-88	**Detroit Red Wings**	**NHL**	**29**	**2**	**9**	**11**	**2**	**6**	**8**	**57**	**0**	**0**	**0**	**45**	**4.4**	**38**	**5**	**31**	**13**	**+15**	**9**	**2**	**2**	**4**	**31**	**1**	**0**	**0**
	Adirondack Red Wings	AHL	23	6	11	17				58																		
1988-89	**Detroit Red Wings**	**NHL**	**65**	**12**	**35**	**47**	**10**	**25**	**35**	**149**	**5**	**2**	**0**	**187**	**6.4**	**115**	**36**	**112**	**27**	**–6**	**5**	**2**	**1**	**3**	**6**	**1**	**0**	**0**
1989-90	**Detroit Red Wings**	**NHL**	**67**	**14**	**28**	**42**	**12**	**20**	**32**	**114**	**4**	**0**	**2**	**190**	**7.4**	**106**	**33**	**112**	**23**	**–16**								
1990-91	**Detroit Red Wings**	**NHL**	**42**	**3**	**17**	**20**	**3**	**13**	**16**	**80**	**1**	**0**	**1**	**101**	**3.0**	**55**	**16**	**50**	**11**	**0**	**5**	**3**	**1**	**4**	**19**	**1**	**0**	**0**
1991-92	**Detroit Red Wings**	**NHL**	**62**	**10**	**24**	**34**	**9**	**18**	**27**	**136**	**5**	**0**	**2**	**143**	**7.0**	**104**	**33**	**78**	**29**	**+22**	**11**	**1**	**5**	**6**	**12**	**1**	**0**	**0**
1992-93	**Detroit Red Wings**	**NHL**	**79**	**12**	**50**	**62**	**10**	**34**	**44**	**155**	**6**	**0**	**1**	**227**	**5.3**	**159**	**61**	**130**	**46**	**+14**	**7**	**2**	**2**	**4**	**19**	**1**	**0**	**1**
1993-94	**Detroit Red Wings**	**NHL**	**82**	**13**	**33**	**46**	**12**	**25**	**37**	**122**	**4**	**1**	**2**	**238**	**5.5**	**121**	**35**	**104**	**35**	**+17**	**7**	**2**	**3**	**5**	**2**	**2**	**0**	**1**
1994-95	**Calgary Flames**	**NHL**	**45**	**2**	**23**	**25**	**4**	**34**	**38**	**39**	**1**	**0**	**0**	**110**	**1.8**	**69**	**23**	**48**	**12**	**+10**	**7**	**1**	**2**	**3**	**9**	**1**	**0**	**0**
1995-96	**Calgary Flames**	**NHL**	**76**	**8**	**25**	**33**	**8**	**20**	**28**	**62**	**5**	**0**	**2**	**175**	**4.6**	**92**	**27**	**101**	**39**	**+3**	**4**	**2**	**1**	**3**	**0**	**0**	**0**	**0**
1996-97	**Calgary Flames**	**NHL**	**47**	**5**	**11**	**16**	**5**	**10**	**15**	**32**	**1**	**2**	**1**	**112**	**4.5**	**50**	**19**	**49**	**7**	**–11**								
	Hartford Whalers	**NHL**	**18**	**3**	**11**	**14**	**3**	**10**	**13**	**7**	**3**	**0**	**0**	**56**	**5.4**	**26**	**14**	**27**	**5**	**–10**								
	Canada	WC-A	11	0	3	3				8																		
1997-98	**Carolina Hurricanes**	**NHL**	**66**	**7**	**27**	**34**	**8**	**26**	**34**	**65**	**6**	**0**	**0**	**173**	**4.0**	**75**	**29**	**65**	**17**	**–2**								
	NHL Totals		**723**	**92**	**297**	**389**	**87**	**244**	**331**	**1091**	**41**	**5**	**11**	**1801**	**5.1**	**1041**	**341**	**939**	**268**		**57**	**15**	**17**	**32**	**117**	**8**	**0**	**2**

Won Stafford Smythe Memorial Trophy (Memorial Cup Tournament MVP) (1986)

Played in NHL All-Star Game (1993)

Traded to **Calgary** by **Detroit** for Mike Vernon, June 29, 1994. Traded to **Hartford** by **Calgary** with Colorado's 3rd round choice (previously acquired, Hartford/Carolina selected Francis Lessard) in 1997 Entry Draft for Hnat Domenichelli, Glen Featherstone, New Jersey's 2nd round choice (previously acquired, Calgary selected Dimitri Kokorev) in 1997 Entry Draft and Vancouver's 3rd round choice (previously acquired, Calgary selected Paul Manning) in 1998 Entry Draft, March 5, 1997. Transferred to **Carolina** after **Hartford** franchise relocated, June 25, 1997.

• CHIBIREV, IGOR

Igor Chibirev C – L. 6', 180 lbs. b: Kiev, USSR, 4/19/1968. Hartford's 8th choice, 266th overall, in 1993 Entry Draft.

Season	Club	League	GP	G	A	Pts	AG	AA	APts	PIM	PP	SH	GW	S	%	TGF	PGF	TGA	PGA	+/–	GP	G	A	Pts	PIM	PP	SH	GW
1987-88	CSKA Moscow	USSR	29	5	1	6				8																		
	Soviet Union	WJC-A	7	4	3	7				0																		
1988-89	CSKA Moscow	USSR	34	7	9	16				16																		
	CSKA Moscow	SuperS	2	0	0	0				0																		
1989-90	CSKA Moscow	FrTour	1	1	0	1				0																		
	CSKA Moscow	USSR	46	8	2	10				12																		
	CSKA Moscow	SuperS	5	1	1	2				0																		
1990-91	CSKA Moscow	FrTour	1	0	1	1				0																		
	CSKA Moscow	USSR	40	10	9	19				4																		
	CSKA Moscow	SuperS	7	0	1	1				15																		
1991-92	CSKA Moscow	CIS	38	21	17	38				46																		
1992-93	Fort Wayne Komets	IHL	60	33	36	69				2											12	*7	13	20	2			
1993-94	**Hartford Whalers**	**NHL**	**37**	**4**	**11**	**15**	**4**	**8**	**12**	**2**	**0**	**0**	**1**	**30**	**13.3**	**18**	**3**	**10**	**2**	**+7**								
	Springfield Indians	AHL	36	28	23	51				4																		
1994-95	**Hartford Whalers**	**NHL**	**8**	**3**	**1**	**4**	**5**	**1**	**6**	**0**	**0**	**0**	**0**	**9**	**33.3**	**5**	**1**	**3**	**0**	**+1**								
	Fort Wayne Komets	IHL	56	34	28	62				10																		
1995-96	Ambri-Piotta	Switz.	36	*37	33	*70				12											6	5	6	11	4			
1996-97	Klagenfurter	Austria	8	2	5	7				2																		
1996-97	Ambri-Piotta	Switz.	29	15	26	41				2																		
1997-98	Ambri-Piotta	Switz.	40	35	41	76				24											13	9	14	23	8			
	NHL Totals		**45**	**7**	**12**	**19**	**9**	**9**	**18**	**2**	**0**	**0**	**1**	**39**	**17.9**	**23**	**4**	**13**	**2**									

• CHICOINE, DAN

Dan Chicoine RW – R. 5'11", 192 lbs. b: Sherbrooke, Que., 11/30/1957. Cleveland's 2nd choice, 23rd overall, in 1977 Amateur Draft.

Season	Club	League	GP	G	A	Pts	AG	AA	APts	PIM	PP	SH	GW	S	%	TGF	PGF	TGA	PGA	+/–	GP	G	A	Pts	PIM	PP	SH	GW
1973-74	Sherbrooke Castors	QMJHL	64	8	18	26				43																		
1974-75	Sherbrooke Castors	QMJHL	56	15	37	52				41																		
1975-76	Sherbrooke Castors	QMJHL	67	44	47	91				76																		
1976-77	Sherbrooke Castors	QMJHL	67	46	44	90				118																		
1977-78	**Cleveland Barons**	**NHL**	**6**	**0**	**0**	**0**	**0**	**0**	**0**	**0**	**0**	**0**	**0**	**5**	**0.0**	**2**	**0**	**4**	**0**	**–2**								
	Phoenix Roadrunners	CHL	17	2	7	9				24																		
	New Haven Nighthawks	AHL	41	5	11	16				33											14	1	3	4	16			
1978-79	**Minnesota North Stars**	**NHL**	**1**	**0**	**0**	**0**	**0**	**0**	**0**	**0**	**0**	**0**	**0**	**0**	**0.0**	**0**	**0**	**0**	**0**	**0**								
	Oklahoma City Stars	CHL	60	26	22	48				53																		
1979-80	**Minnesota North Stars**	**NHL**	**24**	**1**	**2**	**3**	**1**	**2**	**3**	**12**	**0**	**0**	**0**	**25**	**4.0**	**8**	**0**	**18**	**0**	**–10**	**1**	**0**	**0**	**0**	**0**	**0**	**0**	**0**
	Oklahoma City Stars	CHL	26	2	12	14				21																		
1980-81	Oklahoma City Stars	CHL	31	5	12	17				31											3	1	0	1	4			
1981-82			DID NOT PLAY																									
1982-83	Sherbrooke Jets	AHL	21	2	4	6				26																		
	NHL Totals		**31**	**1**	**2**	**3**	**1**	**2**	**3**	**12**	**0**	**0**	**0**	**30**	**3.3**	**10**	**0**	**22**	**0**		**1**	**0**	**0**	**0**	**0**	**0**	**0**	**0**

Placed on **Minnesota** Reserve List after **Cleveland-Minnesota** Dispersal Draft, June 15, 1978. Claimed by **Minnesota** as a fill-in during Expansion Draft, June 13, 1979. Traded to **Quebec** by **Minnesota** for Nelson Burton, June 9, 1981.

• CHINNICK, RICK

Rick Chinnick RW – L. 5'11", 180 lbs. b: Chatham, Ont., 8/15/1953. Minnesota's 6th choice, 41st overall, in 1973 Amateur Draft.

Season	Club	League	GP	G	A	Pts	AG	AA	APts	PIM	PP	SH	GW	S	%	TGF	PGF	TGA	PGA	+/–	GP	G	A	Pts	PIM	PP	SH	GW
1971-72	Peterborough Petes	OHA	63	21	30	51				25																		
1972-73	Peterborough Petes	OHA	63	42	44	86				31																		
1973-74	**Minnesota North Stars**	**NHL**	**1**	**0**	**1**	**1**	**0**	**1**	**1**	**0**	**0**	**0**	**0**	**1**	**0.0**	**1**	**0**	**1**	**0**	**0**								
	New Haven Nighthawks	AHL	76	18	15	33				12											10	2	3	5	2			
1974-75	**Minnesota North Stars**	**NHL**	**3**	**0**	**1**	**1**	**0**	**1**	**1**	**0**	**0**	**0**	**0**	**6**	**0.0**	**1**	**0**	**1**	**0**	**0**								
	New Haven Nighthawks	AHL	58	20	17	37				19											16	10	7	17	4			
1975-76	New Haven Nighthawks	AHL	75	21	40	61				8											3	0	1	1	0			
1976-77	Saginaw Gears	IHL	78	37	33	70				24											19	9	14	23	0			
1977-78	Saginaw Gears	IHL	77	30	45	75				18											5	1	5	6	0			
1978-79			DID NOT PLAY – RETIRED																									
1979-80			DID NOT PLAY – RETIRED																									
1980-81	Chatham Maroons	OHA Sr.		25	32	57																						
	NHL Totals		**4**	**0**	**2**	**2**	**0**	**2**	**2**	**0**	**0**	**0**	**0**	**7**	**0.0**	**2**	**0**	**2**	**0**									

Traded to **Detroit** by **Minnesota** for Bryan Hextall Jr., November 21, 1975.

• CHIPPERFIELD, RON

Ron "Magnificent 7" Chipperfield C – R. 5'11", 186 lbs. b: Brandon, Man., 3/28/1954. California's 2nd choice, 17th overall, in 1974 Amateur Draft.

Season	Club	League	GP	G	A	Pts	AG	AA	APts	PIM	PP	SH	GW	S	%	TGF	PGF	TGA	PGA	+/–	GP	G	A	Pts	PIM	PP	SH	GW
1969-70	Dauphin Kings	MJHL	34	*39	40	79				18																		
1970-71	Brandon Wheat Kings	WCJHL	64	40	43	83				62																		
1971-72	Brandon Wheat Kings	WCJHL	63	59	53	112				63																		
1972-73	Brandon Wheat Kings	WCJHL	59	72	41	113				82																		
1973-74	Brandon Wheat Kings	WCJHL	66	*90	72	*162				82																		

			REGULAR SEASON																		PLAYOFFS							
Season	Club	League	GP	G	A	Pts	AG	AA	APts	PIM	PP	SH	GW	S	%	TGF	PGF	TGA	PGA	+/–	GP	G	A	Pts	PIM	PP	SH	GW
1974-75	Vancouver Blazers	WHA	78	19	20	39	....	....	....	30	....	....	....	....	....	....	....	....	....	....	....	....	....	....	....	....	....	....
1975-76	Calgary Cowboys	WHA	75	42	41	83	....	....	....	32	....	....	....	....	....	....	....	....	....	....	10	5	4	9	6	....	....	....
1976-77	Calgary Cowboys	WHA	81	27	27	54	....	....	....	32	....	....	....	....	....	....	....	....	....	....	....	....	....	....	....	....	....	....
1977-78	Edmonton Oilers	WHA	80	33	52	85	....	....	....	48	....	....	....	....	....	....	....	....	....	....	5	1	1	2	0	....	....	....
1978-79	Edmonton Oilers	WHA	55	32	37	69	....	....	....	47	....	....	....	....	....	....	....	....	....	....	13	9	10	19	8	....	....	....
1979-80	**Edmonton Oilers**	**NHL**	67	18	19	37	16	15	31	24	2	1	1	129	14.0	51	9	65	8	–15	....	....	....	....	....	....	....	....
	Quebec Nordiques	**NHL**	12	4	4	8	4	3	7	8	0	0	1	26	15.4	14	4	20	1	–9	....	....	....	....	....	....	....	....
1980-81	**Quebec Nordiques**	**NHL**	4	0	1	1	0	1	1	2	0	0	0	0	0.0	1	0	2	0	–1	....	....	....	....	....	....	....	....
	Rochester Americans	AHL	6	3	2	5	....	....	....	6	....	....	....	....	....	....	....	....	....	....	....	....	....	....	....	....	....	....
1981-82	HC Bolzano	Italy	30	*78	50	*128	....	....	....	40	....	....	....	....	....	....	....	....	....	....	6	*10	*8	*18	10	....	....	....
1982-83	HC Bolzano	Italy	32	78	58	136	....	....	....	54	....	....	....	....	....	....	....	....	....	....	....	....	....	....	....	....	....	....
1983-84	HC Bolzano	Italy	22	19	24	43	....	....	....	14	....	....	....	....	....	....	....	....	....	....	....	....	....	....	....	....	....	....
	NHL Totals		83	22	24	46	20	19	39	34	2	1	2	155	14.2	66	13	87	9		....	....	....	....	....	....	....	....
	Other Major League Totals		369	153	177	330	....	....	....	189	....	....	....	....	....	....	....	....	....		28	15	15	30	14	....	....	....

WCJHL First All-Star Team (1974)

Selected by **Vancouver** (WHA) in 1974 WHA Amateur Draft, June 1974. NHL rights traded to **Philadelphia** by **California** for George Pesut, December 11, 1974. Transferred to **Calgary** (WHA) after **Vancouver** (WHA) franchise relocated, May 7, 1975. Signed as a free agent by **Edmonton** (WHA) after **Calgary** (WHA) franchise folded, May 31, 1977 Rights retained by **Edmonton** prior to Expansion Draft, June 9,1979. Traded to **Quebec** by **Edmonton** for Ron Low, March 11, 1980.

• CHISHOLM, COLIN

Colin Chisholm D – R. 6′3″, 200 lbs. b: Edmonton, Alta., 2/25/1963. Buffalo's 4th choice, 60th overall, in 1981 Entry Draft.

Season	Club	League	GP	G	A	Pts	AG	AA	APts	PIM	PP	SH	GW	S	%	TGF	PGF	TGA	PGA	+/–	GP	G	A	Pts	PIM	PP	SH	GW
1980-81	Calgary Wranglers	WHL	70	0	18	18	....	....	....	156	....	....	....	....	....	....	....	....	....	....	22	2	3	5	34	....	....	....
1981-82	Calgary Wranglers	WHL	70	1	15	16	....	....	....	150	....	....	....	....	....	....	....	....	....	....	9	0	3	3	24	....	....	....
1982-83	University of Alberta	CWUAA	17	1	7	8	....	....	....	38	....	....	....	....	....	....	....	....	....	....	11	1	1	2	27	....	....	....
1983-84	University of Alberta	CWUAA	24	2	17	19	....	....	....	12	....	....	....	....	....	....	....	....	....	....	10	....	....	....	70	....	....	....
1984-85	University of Alberta	CWUAA	24	3	31	34	....	....	....	100	....	....	....	....	....	....	....	....	....	....	16	0	0	0	24	....	....	....
1985-86	University of Alberta	CWUAA	46	6	23	29	....	....	....	97	....	....	....	....	....	....	....	....	....	....	....	....	....	....	....	....	....	....
1986-87	**Minnesota North Stars**	**NHL**	1	0	0	0	0	0	0	0	0	0	0	0	0.0	0	0	0	0	0	....	....	....	....	....	....	....	....
	Springfield Indians	AHL	75	1	11	12	....	....	....	141	....	....	....	....	....	....	....	....	....	....	....	....	....	....	....	....	....	....
1987-88	Kalamazoo Wings	IHL	44	1	3	4	....	....	....	59	....	....	....	....	....	....	....	....	....	....	....	....	....	....	....	....	....	....
	NHL Totals		1	0	0	0	0	0	0	0	0	0	0	0	0.0	0	0	0	0		....	....	....	....	....	....	....	....

Signed as a free agent by **Minnesota**, June 11, 1986

• CHORNEY, MARC

Marc Chorney D – L. 6′, 200 lbs. b: Sudbury, Ont., 11/8/1959. Pittsburgh's 5th choice, 115th overall, in 1979 Entry Draft.

Season	Club	League	GP	G	A	Pts	AG	AA	APts	PIM	PP	SH	GW	S	%	TGF	PGF	TGA	PGA	+/–	GP	G	A	Pts	PIM	PP	SH	GW
1977-78	University of North Dakota	WCHA	38	1	8	9	....	....	....	54	....	....	....	....	....	....	....	....	....	....	....	....	....	....	....	....	....	....
1978-79	University of North Dakota	WCHA	31	5	11	16	....	....	....	70	....	....	....	....	....	....	....	....	....	....	....	....	....	....	....	....	....	....
1979-80	University of North Dakota	WCHA	39	7	38	45	....	....	....	54	....	....	....	....	....	....	....	....	....	....	....	....	....	....	....	....	....	....
1980-81	University of North Dakota	WCHA	35	8	34	42	....	....	....	72	....	....	....	....	....	....	....	....	....	....	....	....	....	....	....	....	....	....
	Pittsburgh Penguins	**NHL**	8	1	6	7	1	4	5	14	0	0	0	3	33.3	10	1	9	1	+1	2	0	1	1	2	0	0	0
1981-82	**Pittsburgh Penguins**	**NHL**	60	1	6	7	1	4	5	63	0	0	1	37	2.7	36	1	62	16	–11	5	0	0	0	0	0	0	0
	Erie Blades	AHL	6	1	3	4	....	....	....	4	....	....	....	....	....	....	....	....	....	....	....	....	....	....	....	....	....	....
1982-83	**Pittsburgh Penguins**	**NHL**	67	3	5	8	2	3	5	66	0	0	0	66	4.5	42	2	116	46	–30	....	....	....	....	....	....	....	....
1983-84	**Pittsburgh Penguins**	**NHL**	4	0	1	1	0	1	1	8	0	0	0	5	0.0	3	1	10	4	–4	....	....	....	....	....	....	....	....
	Los Angeles Kings	**NHL**	71	3	9	12	2	6	8	58	0	0	0	57	5.3	52	2	86	12	–24	....	....	....	....	....	....	....	....
1984-85	Binghamton Whalers	AHL	48	4	25	29	....	....	....	38	....	....	....	....	....	....	....	....	....	....	7	0	4	4	9	....	....	....
	NHL Totals		210	8	27	35	6	18	24	209	0	0	1	168	4.8	143	7	283	79		7	0	1	1	2	0	0	0

NCAA Championship All-Tournament Team (1980) • WCHA First All-Star Team (1981) • NCAA West First All-American Team (1981)

Traded to **LA Kings** by **Pittsburgh** for LA Kings' 6th round choice (Stuart Marston) in 1985 Entry Draft, October 15, 1983. Signed as a free agent by **Washington**, July 11, 1984.

• CHORSKE, TOM

Tom Chorske RW – R. 6′1″, 205 lbs. b: Minneapolis, MN, 9/18/1966. Montreal's 2nd choice, 16th overall, in 1985 Entry Draft.

Season	Club	League	GP	G	A	Pts	AG	AA	APts	PIM	PP	SH	GW	S	%	TGF	PGF	TGA	PGA	+/–	GP	G	A	Pts	PIM	PP	SH	GW
1983-84	Minnesota Southwest High	H.S.	23	44	26	70	....	....	....	....	....	....	....	....	....	....	....	....	....	....	....	....	....	....	....	....	....	....
1985-86	University of Minnesota	WCHA	39	6	4	10	....	....	....	16	....	....	....	....	....	....	....	....	....	....	....	....	....	....	....	....	....	....
	United States	WJC-A	7	1	0	1	....	....	....	2	....	....	....	....	....	....	....	....	....	....	....	....	....	....	....	....	....	....
1986-87	University of Minnesota	WCHA	47	20	22	42	....	....	....	20	....	....	....	....	....	....	....	....	....	....	....	....	....	....	....	....	....	....
1987-88	United States	Nat-Team	36	9	16	25	....	....	....	24	....	....	....	....	....	....	....	....	....	....	....	....	....	....	....	....	....	....
1988-89	University of Minnesota	WCHA	37	25	24	49	....	....	....	28	....	....	....	....	....	....	....	....	....	....	....	....	....	....	....	....	....	....
	United States	WEC-A	9	2	1	3	....	....	....	6	....	....	....	....	....	....	....	....	....	....	....	....	....	....	....	....	....	....
1989-90	**Montreal Canadiens**	**NHL**	14	3	1	4	3	1	4	2	0	0	0	19	15.8	6	1	3	0	+2	....	....	....	....	....	....	....	....
	Sherbrooke Canadiens	AHL	59	22	24	46	....	....	....	54	....	....	....	....	....	....	....	....	....	....	12	4	4	8	8	....	....	....
1990-91	Montreal Canadiens	FrTour	2	0	1	1	....	....	....	0	....	....	....	....	....	....	....	....	....	....	....	....	....	....	....	....	....	....
	Montreal Canadiens	**NHL**	57	9	11	20	8	8	16	32	3	0	1	82	11.0	34	14	28	0	–8	....	....	....	....	....	....	....	....
1991-92	**New Jersey Devils**	**NHL**	76	19	17	36	17	13	30	32	0	3	2	143	13.3	53	0	70	25	+8	7	0	3	3	4	0	0	0
1992-93	**New Jersey Devils**	**NHL**	50	7	12	19	6	8	14	25	0	0	1	63	11.1	30	0	41	10	–1	1	0	0	0	0	0	0	0
	Utica Devils	AHL	6	1	4	5	....	....	....	2	....	....	....	....	....	....	....	....	....	....	....	....	....	....	....	....	....	....
1993-94	**New Jersey Devils**	**NHL**	76	21	20	41	20	15	35	32	1	1	4	131	16.0	55	1	58	18	+14	20	4	3	7	0	0	0	1
1994-95	Milano Devils	Italy	7	11	5	16	....	....	....	6	....	....	....	....	....	....	....	....	....	....	....	....	....	....	....	....	....	....
	New Jersey Devils	**NHL**	42	10	8	18	18	12	30	16	0	0	2	59	16.9	27	0	42	11	–4	17	1	5	6	4	0	0	0
1995-96	**Ottawa Senators**	**NHL**	72	15	14	29	15	11	26	21	0	2	1	118	12.7	44	3	87	37	–9	....	....	....	....	....	....	....	....
	United States	WC-A	8	1	2	3	....	....	....	16	....	....	....	....	....	....	....	....	....	....	....	....	....	....	....	....	....	....
1996-97	**Ottawa Senators**	**NHL**	68	18	8	26	19	7	26	16	1	1	1	116	15.5	39	3	47	10	–1	5	0	1	1	2	0	0	0
1997-98	**New York Islanders**	**NHL**	82	12	23	35	14	22	36	39	1	4	2	132	9.1	57	11	58	19	+7	....	....	....	....	....	....	....	....
	United States	WC-A	6	1	1	2	....	....	....	0	....	....	....	....	....	....	....	....	....	....	....	....	....	....	....	....	....	....
	NHL Totals		537	114	114	228	120	97	217	215	6	11	14	863	13.2	345	33	434	130		50	5	12	17	10	0	0	1

WCHA First All-Star Team (1989)

Traded to **New Jersey** by **Montreal** with Stephane Richer for Kirk Muller and Roland Melanson, September 20, 1991. Claimed on waivers by **Ottawa** from **New Jersey**, October 5, 1995. Claimed by **NY Islanders** from **Ottawa** in NHL Waiver Draft, September 28, 1997.

• CHOUINARD, GUY

Guy Chouinard C – R. 5′11″, 182 lbs. b: Quebec City, Que., 10/20/1956. Atlanta's 1st choice, 28th overall, in 1974 Amateur Draft.

Season	Club	League	GP	G	A	Pts	AG	AA	APts	PIM	PP	SH	GW	S	%	TGF	PGF	TGA	PGA	+/–	GP	G	A	Pts	PIM	PP	SH	GW
1971-72	Quebec Remparts	QMJHL	58	29	41	70	....	....	....	6	....	....	....	....	....	....	....	....	....	....	....	....	....	....	....	....	....	....
1972-73	Quebec Remparts	QMJHL	59	43	*86	129	....	....	....	11	....	....	....	....	....	....	....	....	....	....	15	18	14	32	2	....	....	....
1973-74	Quebec Remparts	QMJHL	62	75	85	160	....	....	....	22	....	....	....	....	....	....	....	....	....	....	16	15	16	31	5	....	....	....
1974-75	**Atlanta Flames**	**NHL**	5	0	0	0	0	0	0	2	0	0	0	5	0.0	0	0	2	0	–2	....	....	....	....	....	....	....	....
	Omaha Knights	CHL	70	28	40	68	....	....	....	6	....	....	....	....	....	....	....	....	....	....	6	1	6	7	0	....	....	....
1975-76	**Atlanta Flames**	**NHL**	4	0	2	2	0	2	2	2	0	0	0	8	0.0	4	1	1	0	+2	2	0	0	0	0	0	0	0
	Nova Scotia Voyageurs	AHL	70	40	40	80	....	....	....	14	....	....	....	....	....	....	....	....	....	....	9	6	*9	*15	0	....	....	....
1976-77	**Atlanta Flames**	**NHL**	80	17	33	50	16	27	43	8	3	0	0	167	10.2	65	27	50	0	–12	3	2	0	2	0	1	0	0
1977-78	**Atlanta Flames**	**NHL**	73	28	30	58	27	24	51	8	11	0	1	146	19.2	78	32	38	0	+8	2	1	0	1	0	0	0	0
1978-79	**Atlanta Flames**	**NHL**	80	50	57	107	46	44	90	14	11	0	5	229	21.8	148	51	75	1	+23	2	1	2	3	0	1	0	0
1979-80	**Atlanta Flames**	**NHL**	76	31	46	77	28	35	63	22	9	0	1	208	14.9	103	35	64	1	+5	4	1	3	4	4	1	0	0
1980-81	**Calgary Flames**	**NHL**	52	31	52	83	26	36	62	24	10	0	1	141	22.0	109	50	41	0	+18	16	3	14	17	4	0	0	0
1981-82	**Calgary Flames**	**NHL**	64	23	57	80	18	38	56	12	13	0	4	182	12.6	113	53	65	0	–5	3	0	1	1	0	0	0	0
1982-83	**Calgary Flames**	**NHL**	80	13	59	72	11	41	52	18	7	0	2	158	8.2	105	60	69	0	–24	9	1	6	7	4	0	0	0
1983-84	**St. Louis Blues**	**NHL**	64	12	34	46	10	23	33	10	4	0	2	117	10.3	69	34	50	0	–15	5	0	2	2	0	0	0	0
1984-85	Peoria Rivermen	IHL	9	2	5	7	....	....	....	0	....	....	....	....	....	....	....	....	....	....	....	....	....	....	....	....	....	....
	NHL Totals		578	205	370	575	182	270	452	120	68	0	16	1361	15.1	794	343	455	2		46	9	28	37	12	3	0	0

Won George Parsons Trophy (Memorial Cup Tournament Most Sportsmanlike Player) (1974) • Won Ken McKenzie Trophy (CHL's Rookie of the Year) (1975) • AHL Second All-Star Team (1976)

Transferred to **Calgary** after **Atlanta** franchise relocated, June 24, 1980. Traded to **St. Louis** by **Calgary** for future considerations, September 6, 1983.

● CHRISTIAN, DAVE

Dave Christian RW – R. 5'11", 175 lbs. b: Warroad, MN, 5/12/1959. Winnipeg's 2nd choice, 40th overall, in 1979 Entry Draft.

Season	Club	League	GP	G	A	Pts	AG	AA	APts	PIM	PP	SH	GW	S	%	TGF	PGF	TGA	PGA	+/–	GP	G	A	Pts	PIM	PP	SH	GW
			REGULAR SEASON																		PLAYOFFS							
1977-78	University of North Dakota	WCHA	38	8	16	24	....	....	....	14	....	....	....	....	....	....	....	....	....	....	....	....	....	....	....	....	....	....
1978-79	University of North Dakota	WCHA	40	22	24	46	....	....	....	22	....	....	....	....	....	....	....	....	....	....	....	....	....	....	....	....	....	....
1979-80	United States	Nat-Team	59	10	20	30	....	....	....	26	....	....	....	....	....	....	....	....	....	....	....	....	....	....	....	....	....	....
	United States	Olympics	7	0	8	8	....	....	....	6	....	....	....	....	....	....	....	....	....	....	....	....	....	....	....	....	....	....
	Winnipeg Jets	**NHL**	**15**	**8**	**10**	**18**	**7**	**8**	**15**	**2**	**3**	**0**	**0**	**34**	**23.5**	**25**	**13**	**19**	**2**	**–5**	....	....	....	....	....	....	....	....
1980-81	**Winnipeg Jets**	**NHL**	**80**	**28**	**43**	**71**	**23**	**30**	**53**	**22**	**9**	**1**	**0**	**185**	**15.1**	**110**	**45**	**148**	**29**	**–54**	....	....	....	....	....	....	....	....
	United States	WEC-A	8	8	3	11	....	....	....	6	....	....	....	....	....	....	....	....	....	....	....	....	....	....	....	....	....	....
1981-82	United States	C Cup	6	1	0	1	....	....	....	4	....	....	....	....	....	....	....	....	....	....	....	....	....	....	....	....	....	....
	Winnipeg Jets	**NHL**	**80**	**25**	**51**	**76**	**20**	**34**	**54**	**28**	**6**	**1**	**3**	**218**	**11.5**	**133**	**63**	**131**	**20**	**–41**	**4**	**0**	**1**	**1**	**2**	**0**	**0**	**0**
1982-83	**Winnipeg Jets**	**NHL**	**55**	**18**	**26**	**44**	**15**	**18**	**33**	**23**	**4**	**0**	**2**	**131**	**13.7**	**84**	**37**	**63**	**11**	**–5**	**3**	**0**	**0**	**0**	**0**	**0**	**0**	**0**
1983-84	**Washington Capitals**	**NHL**	**80**	**29**	**52**	**81**	**23**	**35**	**58**	**28**	**9**	**0**	**6**	**164**	**17.7**	**121**	**38**	**58**	**1**	**+26**	**8**	**5**	**4**	**9**	**5**	**1**	**0**	**0**
1984-85	United States	C Cup	6	2	1	3	....	....	....	2	....	....	....	....	....	....	....	....	....	....	....	....	....	....	....	....	....	....
	Washington Capitals	**NHL**	**80**	**26**	**43**	**69**	**21**	**29**	**50**	**14**	**5**	**0**	**2**	**152**	**17.1**	**99**	**24**	**63**	**8**	**+20**	**5**	**1**	**1**	**2**	**0**	**0**	**0**	**0**
1985-86	**Washington Capitals**	**NHL**	**80**	**41**	**42**	**83**	**33**	**28**	**61**	**15**	**18**	**2**	**4**	**218**	**18.8**	**119**	**52**	**92**	**28**	**+3**	**9**	**4**	**4**	**8**	**0**	**1**	**0**	**0**
1986-87	**Washington Capitals**	**NHL**	**76**	**23**	**27**	**50**	**20**	**20**	**40**	**8**	**5**	**0**	**2**	**152**	**15.1**	**88**	**26**	**79**	**12**	**–5**	**7**	**1**	**3**	**4**	**6**	**0**	**0**	**1**
1987-88	**Washington Capitals**	**NHL**	**80**	**37**	**21**	**58**	**32**	**15**	**47**	**26**	**14**	**0**	**5**	**187**	**19.8**	**90**	**40**	**73**	**9**	**–14**	**14**	**5**	**6**	**11**	**6**	**1**	**0**	**0**
1988-89	**Washington Capitals**	**NHL**	**80**	**34**	**31**	**65**	**29**	**22**	**51**	**12**	**16**	**1**	**1**	**177**	**19.2**	**107**	**47**	**78**	**20**	**+2**	**6**	**1**	**1**	**2**	**0**	**1**	**0**	**0**
	United States	WEC-A	6	4	3	7	....	....	....	2	....	....	....	....	....	....	....	....	....	....	....	....	....	....	....	....	....	....
1989-90	Washington Capitals	FrTour	4	1	2	3	....	....	....	0	....	....	....	....	....	....	....	....	....	....	....	....	....	....	....	....	....	....
	Washington Capitals	**NHL**	**28**	**3**	**8**	**11**	**3**	**6**	**9**	**4**	**0**	**0**	**1**	**54**	**5.6**	**24**	**7**	**37**	**8**	**–12**	....	....	....	....	....	....	....	....
	Boston Bruins	**NHL**	**50**	**12**	**17**	**29**	**10**	**12**	**22**	**8**	**2**	**0**	**3**	**99**	**12.1**	**51**	**12**	**36**	**1**	**+4**	**21**	**4**	**1**	**5**	**4**	**1**	**0**	**0**
1990-91	**Boston Bruins**	**NHL**	**78**	**32**	**21**	**53**	**29**	**16**	**45**	**41**	**9**	**0**	**2**	**173**	**18.5**	**87**	**26**	**70**	**17**	**+8**	**19**	**8**	**4**	**12**	**4**	**0**	**0**	**2**
1991-92	United States	C Cup	7	1	1	2	....	....	....	0	....	....	....	....	....	....	....	....	....	....	....	....	....	....	....	....	....	....
	St. Louis Blues	**NHL**	**78**	**20**	**24**	**44**	**18**	**18**	**36**	**41**	**1**	**3**	**3**	**142**	**14.1**	**73**	**17**	**66**	**12**	**+2**	**4**	**3**	**0**	**3**	**0**	**0**	**0**	**0**
1992-93	**Chicago Blackhawks**	**NHL**	**60**	**4**	**14**	**18**	**3**	**10**	**13**	**12**	**1**	**0**	**1**	**75**	**5.3**	**31**	**10**	**20**	**5**	**+6**	**1**	**0**	**0**	**0**	**0**	**0**	**0**	**0**
1993-94	**Chicago Blackhawks**	**NHL**	**9**	**0**	**3**	**3**	**0**	**2**	**2**	**0**	**0**	**0**	**0**	**6**	**0.0**	**4**	**1**	**4**	**1**	**0**	**1**	**0**	**0**	**0**	**0**	**0**	**0**	**0**
	Indianapolis Ice	IHL	40	8	18	26	....	....	....	6	....	....	....	....	....	....	....	....	....	....	....	....	....	....	....	....	....	....
1994-95	Minnesota Moose	IHL	81	38	42	80	....	....	....	16	....	....	....	....	....	....	....	....	....	....	3	0	1	1	0	....	....	....
1995-96	Minnesota Moose	IHL	69	21	25	46	....	....	....	8	....	....	....	....	....	....	....	....	....	....	....	....	....	....	....	....	....	....
	NHL Totals		**1009**	**340**	**433**	**773**	**286**	**303**	**589**	**284**	**102**	**8**	**35**	**2167**	**15.7**	**1246**	**458**	**1037**	**184**		**102**	**32**	**25**	**57**	**27**	**5**	**0**	**3**

Played in NHL All-Star Game (1991)

Traded to **Washington** by **Winnipeg** for Washington's 1st round choice (Bobby Dollas) in 1983 Entry Draft, June 8, 1993. Traded to **Boston** by **Washington** for Bob Joyce, December 13, 1989. Transferred to **St. Louis** by **Boston** with Boston's 3rd round choice (Vitali Prokhorov) and 7th round choice (Lance Burns) in 1992 Entry Draft as compensation for Boston's signing of free agents Glen Featherstone and Dave Thomilson, July 30, 1991. Claimed by **Chicago** from **St. Louis** in Waiver Draft, October 4, 1992.

● CHRISTIAN, JEFF

Jeff Christian LW – L. 6'2", 210 lbs. b: Burlington, Ont., 7/30/1970. New Jersey's 2nd choice, 23rd overall, in 1988 Entry Draft.

Season	Club	League	GP	G	A	Pts	AG	AA	APts	PIM	PP	SH	GW	S	%	TGF	PGF	TGA	PGA	+/–	GP	G	A	Pts	PIM	PP	SH	GW
1987-88	London Knights	OHL	64	15	29	44	....	....	....	154	....	....	....	....	....	....	....	....	....	....	9	1	5	6	27	....	....	....
1988-89	London Knights	OHL	60	27	30	57	....	....	....	221	....	....	....	....	....	....	....	....	....	....	20	3	4	7	56	....	....	....
1989-90	London Knights	OHL	18	14	7	21	....	....	....	64	....	....	....	....	....	....	....	....	....	....	....	....	....	....	....	....	....	....
	Owen Sound Platers	OHL	37	19	26	45				145	....	....	....	....	....	....	....	....	....	....	10	6	7	13	43	....	....	....
1990-91	Utica Devils	AHL	80	24	42	66	....	....	....	165	....	....	....	....	....	....	....	....	....	....	....	....	....	....	....	....	....	....
1991-92	**New Jersey Devils**	**NHL**	**2**	**0**	**0**	**0**	**0**	**0**	**0**	**2**	**0**	**0**	**0**	**1**	**0.0**	**0**	**0**	**0**	**0**	**0**	....	....	....	....	....	....	....	....
	Utica Devils	AHL	76	27	24	51	....	....	....	198	....	....	....	....	....	....	....	....	....	....	4	0	0	0	16	....	....	....
1992-93	Utica Devils	AHL	22	4	6	10	....	....	....	39	....	....	....	....	....	....	....	....	....	....	....	....	....	....	....	....	....	....
	Hamilton Canucks	AHL	11	2	5	7	....	....	....	35	....	....	....	....	....	....	....	....	....	....	....	....	....	....	....	....	....	....
	Cincinnati Cyclones	IHL	36	5	12	17	....	....	....	113	....	....	....	....	....	....	....	....	....	....	....	....	....	....	....	....	....	....
1993-94	Albany River Rats	AHL	76	34	43	77	....	....	....	227	....	....	....	....	....	....	....	....	....	....	5	1	2	3	19	....	....	....
1994-95	**Pittsburgh Penguins**	**NHL**	**1**	**0**	**0**	**0**	**0**	**0**	**0**	**0**	**0**	**0**	**0**	**2**	**0.0**	**0**	**0**	**0**	**0**	**0**	....	....	....	....	....	....	....	....
	Cleveland Lumberjacks	IHL	56	13	24	37	....	....	....	126	....	....	....	....	....	....	....	....	....	....	2	0	1	1	8	....	....	....
1995-96	**Pittsburgh Penguins**	**NHL**	**3**	**0**	**0**	**0**	**0**	**0**	**0**	**2**	**0**	**0**	**0**	**0**	**0.0**	**0**	**0**	**0**	**0**	**0**	....	....	....	....	....	....	....	....
	Cleveland Lumberjacks	IHL	66	23	32	55	....	....	....	131	....	....	....	....	....	....	....	....	....	....	3	0	1	1	8	....	....	....
1996-97	**Pittsburgh Penguins**	**NHL**	**11**	**2**	**2**	**4**	**2**	**2**	**4**	**13**	**0**	**0**	**0**	**18**	**11.1**	**5**	**0**	**0**	**0**	**–3**	....	....	....	....	....	....	....	....
	Cleveland Lumberjacks	IHL	60	40	40	80	....	....	....	262	....	....	....	....	....	....	....	....	....	....	12	6	8	14	44	....	....	....
1997-98	**Phoenix Coyotes**	**NHL**	**1**	**0**	**0**	**0**	**0**	**0**	**0**	**0**	**0**	**0**	**0**	**0**	**0.0**	**0**	**0**	**1**	**0**	**–1**	....	....	....	....	....	....	....	....
	Las Vegas Thunder	IHL	30	12	15	27	....	....	....	90	....	....	....	....	....	....	....	....	....	....	4	2	2	4	20	....	....	....
	NHL Totals		**18**	**2**	**2**	**4**	**2**	**2**	**4**	**17**	**0**	**0**	**0**	**21**	**9.5**	**5**	**0**	**9**	**0**		....	....	....	....	....	....	....	....

Signed as a free agent by **Pittsburgh**, August 2, 1994. Signed as a free agent by **Phoenix**, July 28, 1997.

● CHRISTIE, MIKE

Mike Christie D – L. 6', 190 lbs. b: Big Spring, TX, 12/20/1949.

Season	Club	League	GP	G	A	Pts	AG	AA	APts	PIM	PP	SH	GW	S	%	TGF	PGF	TGA	PGA	+/–	GP	G	A	Pts	PIM	PP	SH	GW
1969-70	University of Denver	WCHA	31	2	16	18	....	....	....	38	....	....	....	....	....	....	....	....	....	....	....	....	....	....	....	....	....	....
1970-71	University of Denver	WCHA	36	8	25	33	....	....	....	57	....	....	....	....	....	....	....	....	....	....	....	....	....	....	....	....	....	....
1971-72	University of Denver	WCHA	DID NOT PLAY – INJURED																									
1972-73	Dallas Black Hawks	CHL	32	5	11	16	....	....	....	51	....	....	....	....	....	....	....	....	....	....	....	....	....	....	....	....	....	....
1973-74	Dallas Black Hawks	CHL	71	5	37	42	....	....	....	110	....	....	....	....	....	....	....	....	....	....	10	1	2	3	23	....	....	....
1974-75	**California Golden Seals**	**NHL**	**34**	**0**	**14**	**14**	**0**	**11**	**11**	**76**	**0**	**0**	**0**	**30**	**0.0**	**43**	**6**	**67**	**17**	**–13**	....	....	....	....	....	....	....	....
1975-76	**California Golden Seals**	**NHL**	**78**	**3**	**18**	**21**	**3**	**14**	**17**	**152**	**0**	**0**	**0**	**63**	**4.8**	**83**	**2**	**112**	**13**	**–18**	....	....	....	....	....	....	....	....
1976-77	United States	C Cup	4	0	0	0	....	....	....	2	....	....	....	....	....	....	....	....	....	....	....	....	....	....	....	....	....	....
	Cleveland Barons	**NHL**	**79**	**6**	**27**	**33**	**6**	**22**	**28**	**79**	**0**	**0**	**2**	**61**	**9.8**	**90**	**3**	**101**	**24**	**+18**	....	....	....	....	....	....	....	....
1977-78	**Cleveland Barons**	**NHL**	**34**	**1**	**6**	**7**	**1**	**5**	**6**	**49**	**0**	**0**	**0**	**14**	**7.1**	**30**	**0**	**47**	**3**	**–14**	....	....	....	....	....	....	....	....
	Colorado Rockies	**NHL**	**35**	**2**	**8**	**10**	**2**	**7**	**9**	**28**	**0**	**0**	**0**	**36**	**5.6**	**44**	**5**	**55**	**10**	**–6**	**2**	**0**	**0**	**0**	**0**	**0**	**0**	**0**
1978-79	**Colorado Rockies**	**NHL**	**68**	**1**	**10**	**11**	**1**	**8**	**9**	**88**	**0**	**0**	**0**	**50**	**2.0**	**48**	**6**	**102**	**16**	**–44**	....	....	....	....	....	....	....	....
1979-80	**Colorado Rockies**	**NHL**	**74**	**1**	**17**	**18**	**1**	**13**	**14**	**78**	**0**	**0**	**0**	**50**	**2.0**	**62**	**2**	**120**	**30**	**–30**	....	....	....	....	....	....	....	....
1980-81	**Colorado Rockies**	**NHL**	**1**	**0**	**0**	**0**	**0**	**0**	**0**	**0**	**0**	**0**	**0**	**1**	**0.0**	**1**	**0**	**1**	**1**	**+1**	....	....	....	....	....	....	....	....
	Tulsa Oilers	CHL	20	1	0	1	....	....	....	27	....	....	....	....	....	....	....	....	....	....	....	....	....	....	....	....	....	....
	Vancouver Canucks	**NHL**	**9**	**1**	**1**	**2**	**1**	**1**	**2**	**0**	**0**	**0**	**0**	**5**	**20.0**	**10**	**0**	**1**	**0**	**+9**	....	....	....	....	....	....	....	....
	Dallas Black Hawks	CHL	40	2	20	22	....	....	....	95	....	....	....	....	....	....	....	....	....	....	6	0	3	3	10	....	....	....
	NHL Totals		**412**	**15**	**101**	**116**	**15**	**81**	**96**	**550**	**0**	**0**	**2**	**310**	**4.8**	**419**	**24**	**606**	**114**		**2**	**0**	**0**	**0**	**0**	**0**	**0**	**0**

WCHA First All-Star Team (1971) • NCAA West First All-American Team (1971)

Signed as a free agent by **Chicago**, September, 1972. Traded to **California** by **Chicago** with Len Frig for Ivan Boldirev, May 24, 1974. Transferred to **Cleveland** after **California** franchise relocated, August 26, 1976. Traded to **Colorado** by **Cleveland** for Dennis O'Brien, January 12, 1978. Traded to **Vancouver** by **Colorado** for cash, December 8, 1980

● CHRISTOFF, STEVE

Steve Christoff C – R. 6'1", 180 lbs. b: Richfield, MN, 1/23/1958. Minnesota's 3rd choice, 24th overall, in 1978 Amateur Draft.

Season	Club	League	GP	G	A	Pts	AG	AA	APts	PIM	PP	SH	GW	S	%	TGF	PGF	TGA	PGA	+/–	GP	G	A	Pts	PIM	PP	SH	GW
1976-77	University of Minnesota	WCHA	38	7	9	16	....	....	....	20	....	....	....	....	....	....	....	....	....	....	....	....	....	....	....	....	....	....
1977-78	University of Minnesota	WCHA	38	32	34	66	....	....	....	18	....	....	....	....	....	....	....	....	....	....	....	....	....	....	....	....	....	....
1978-79	University of Minnesota	WCHA	43	38	39	77	....	....	....	50	....	....	....	....	....	....	....	....	....	....	....	....	....	....	....	....	....	....
	United States	WEC-A	8	3	2	5	....	....	....	4	....	....	....	....	....	....	....	....	....	....	....	....	....	....	....	....	....	....
1979-80	United States	Nat-Team	57	35	26	61			....	22	....	....	....	....	....	....	....	....	....	....	....	....	....	....	....	....	....	....
	United States	Olympics	7	2	1	3			....	6	....	....	....	....	....	....	....	....	....	....	....	....	....	....	....	....	....	....
	Minnesota North Stars	**NHL**	**20**	**8**	**7**	**15**	**7**	**5**	**12**	**19**	**0**	**0**	**1**	**34**	**23.5**	**22**	**5**	**14**	**0**	**+3**	**14**	**8**	**4**	**12**	**7**	**2**	**0**	**0**
1980-81	**Minnesota North Stars**	**NHL**	**56**	**26**	**13**	**39**	**21**	**9**	**30**	**58**	**9**	**0**	**2**	**132**	**19.7**	**63**	**20**	**56**	**4**	**–9**	**18**	**8**	**8**	**16**	**16**	**5**	**0**	**1**
	Oklahoma City Stars	CHL	3	1	0	1	....	....	....	0	....	....	....	....	....	....	....	....	....	....	....	....	....	....	....	....	....	....

			REGULAR SEASON																		PLAYOFFS							
Season	Club	League	GP	G	A	Pts	AG	AA	APts	PIM	PP	SH	GW	S	%	TGF	PGF	TGA	PGA	+/–	GP	G	A	Pts	PIM	PP	SH	GW
1981-82	United States	C Cup	6	1	5	6	....	....	....	4	....	....	....	....	....	....	....	....	....	....	....	....	....	....	....	....	....	....
	Minnesota North Stars	**NHL**	**69**	**26**	**29**	**55**	**21**	**19**	**40**	**14**	**4**	**0**	**1**	**178**	**14.6**	**79**	**12**	**58**	**0**	**+9**	**2**	**0**	**0**	**0**	**2**	**0**	**0**	**0**
1982-83	**Calgary Flames**	**NHL**	**45**	**9**	**8**	**17**	**7**	**6**	**13**	**4**	**0**	**0**	**2**	**52**	**17.3**	**31**	**1**	**33**	**0**	**–3**	**1**	**0**	**0**	**0**	**0**	**0**	**0**	**0**
1983-84	**Los Angeles Kings**	**NHL**	**58**	**8**	**7**	**15**	**6**	**5**	**11**	**13**	**0**	**0**	**1**	**74**	**10.8**	**24**	**3**	**40**	**0**	**–19**	....	....	....	....	....	....	....	....
	NHL Totals		**248**	**77**	**64**	**141**	**62**	**44**	**106**	**108**	**13**	**0**	**7**	**470**	**16.4**	**219**	**41**	**201**	**4**		**35**	**16**	**12**	**28**	**25**	**7**	**0**	**1**

WCHA Second All-Star Team (1978) • NCAA Championship All-Tournament Team (1979)

Traded to **Calgary** by **Minnesota** with Bill Nyrop and Minnesota's 2nd round choice (Dave Reierson) in 1982 Entry Draft for Willi Plett and Calgary's 4th round choice (Dusan Pasek) in 1982 Entry Draft, June 7, 1982. Traded to **Minnesota** by **Calgary** with Calgary's 2nd round choice (Frantisek Musil) in 1983 Entry Draft for Mike Eaves and Keith Hanson, June 6, 1983. Traded to **LA Kings** by **Minnesota** with Minnesota's 5th round choice (Petr Prajsler) in 1985 Entry Draft for Dave Lewis and future considerations, October 3, 1983.

• CHURCH, BRAD

Brad Church LW – L. 6'1", 210 lbs. b: Dauphin, Man., 11/14/1976. Washington's 1st choice, 17th overall, in 1995 Entry Draft.

Season	Club	League	GP	G	A	Pts	AG	AA	APts	PIM	PP	SH	GW	S	%	TGF	PGF	TGA	PGA	+/–	GP	G	A	Pts	PIM	PP	SH	GW
1993-94	Prince Albert Raiders	WHL	71	33	20	53	....	....	....	197	....	....	....	....	....	....	....	....	....	....	....	....	....	....	....	....	....	....
1994-95	Prince Albert Raiders	WHL	62	26	24	50	....	....	....	184	....	....	....	....	....	....	....	....	....	....	15	6	9	15	32	....	....	....
1995-96	Prince Albert Raiders	WHL	69	42	46	88	....	....	....	123	....	....	....	....	....	....	....	....	....	....	18	15	*20	*35	74	....	....	....
1996-97	Portland Pirates	AHL	50	4	8	12	....	....	....	92	....	....	....	....	....	....	....	....	....	....	1	0	0	0	0	....	....	....
1997-98	**Washington Capitals**	**NHL**	**2**	**0**	**0**	**0**	**0**	**0**	**0**	**0**	**0**	**0**	**0**	**4**	**0.0**	**0**	**0**	**0**	**0**	**0**	....	....	....	....	....	....	....	....
	Portland Pirates	AHL	59	6	5	11	....	....	....	98	....	....	....	....	....	....	....	....	....	....	9	2	4	6	14	....	....	....
	NHL Totals		**2**	**0**	**0**	**0**	**0**	**0**	**0**	**0**	**0**	**0**	**0**	**4**	**0.0**	**0**	**0**	**0**	**0**		....	....	....	....	....	....	....	....

• CHURLA, SHANE

Shane Churla RW – R. 6'1", 200 lbs. b: Fernie, B.C., 6/24/1965. Hartford's 4th choice, 110th overall, in 1985 Entry Draft.

Season	Club	League	GP	G	A	Pts	AG	AA	APts	PIM	PP	SH	GW	S	%	TGF	PGF	TGA	PGA	+/–	GP	G	A	Pts	PIM	PP	SH	GW
1983-84	Medicine Hat Tigers	WHL	48	3	7	10	....	....	....	115	....	....	....	....	....	....	....	....	....	....	14	1	5	6	41	....	....	....
1984-85	Medicine Hat Tigers	WHL	70	14	20	34	....	....	....	370	....	....	....	....	....	....	....	....	....	....	9	1	0	1	55	....	....	....
1985-86	Binghamton Whalers	AHL	52	4	10	14	....	....	....	306	....	....	....	....	....	....	....	....	....	....	3	0	0	0	22	....	....	....
1986-87	**Hartford Whalers**	**NHL**	**20**	**0**	**1**	**1**	**0**	**1**	**1**	**78**	**0**	**0**	**0**	**2**	**0.0**	**3**	**0**	**4**	**0**	**–1**	**2**	**0**	**0**	**0**	**42**	**0**	**0**	**0**
	Binghamton Whalers	AHL	24	1	5	6	....	....	....	249	....	....	....	....	....	....	....	....	....	....	....	....	....	....	....	....	....	....
1987-88	**Hartford Whalers**	**NHL**	**2**	**0**	**0**	**0**	**0**	**0**	**0**	**14**	**0**	**0**	**0**	**0**	**0.0**	**0**	**0**	**1**	**0**	**–1**	....	....	....	....	....	....	....	....
	Binghamton Whalers	AHL	25	5	8	13	....	....	....	168	....	....	....	....	....	....	....	....	....	....	....	....	....	....	....	....	....	....
	Calgary Flames	**NHL**	**29**	**1**	**5**	**6**	**1**	**4**	**5**	**132**	**0**	**0**	**0**	**15**	**6.7**	**16**	**0**	**14**	**0**	**+2**	**7**	**0**	**1**	**1**	**17**	**0**	**0**	**0**
1988-89	**Calgary Flames**	**NHL**	**5**	**0**	**0**	**0**	**0**	**0**	**0**	**25**	**0**	**0**	**0**	**2**	**0.0**	**0**	**0**	**3**	**0**	**–3**	....	....	....	....	....	....	....	....
	Salt Lake Golden Eagles	IHL	32	3	13	16	....	....	....	278	....	....	....	....	....	....	....	....	....	....	....	....	....	....	....	....	....	....
	Minnesota North Stars	**NHL**	**13**	**1**	**0**	**1**	**1**	**0**	**1**	**54**	**0**	**0**	**0**	**6**	**16.7**	**1**	**0**	**1**	**0**	**0**	....	....	....	....	....	....	....	....
1989-90	**Minnesota North Stars**	**NHL**	**53**	**2**	**3**	**5**	**2**	**2**	**4**	**292**	**0**	**0**	**1**	**40**	**5.0**	**13**	**1**	**16**	**0**	**–4**	**7**	**0**	**0**	**0**	**44**	**0**	**0**	**0**
1990-91	Minnesota North Stars	FrTour	3	0	0	0	....	....	....	4	....	....	....	....	....	....	....	....	....	....	....	....	....	....	....	....	....	....
	Minnesota North Stars	**NHL**	**40**	**2**	**2**	**4**	**2**	**2**	**4**	**286**	**0**	**0**	**0**	**32**	**6.3**	**12**	**0**	**11**	**0**	**+1**	**22**	**2**	**1**	**3**	**90**	**0**	**0**	**1**
1991-92	**Minnesota North Stars**	**NHL**	**57**	**4**	**1**	**5**	**4**	**1**	**5**	**278**	**0**	**0**	**0**	**42**	**9.5**	**12**	**0**	**24**	**0**	**–12**	....	....	....	....	....	....	....	....
1992-93	**Minnesota North Stars**	**NHL**	**73**	**5**	**16**	**21**	**4**	**11**	**15**	**286**	**1**	**0**	**1**	**61**	**8.2**	**40**	**16**	**32**	**0**	**–8**	....	....	....	....	....	....	....	....
1993-94	**Dallas Stars**	**NHL**	**69**	**6**	**7**	**13**	**6**	**5**	**11**	**333**	**3**	**0**	**0**	**62**	**9.7**	**24**	**7**	**26**	**1**	**–8**	**9**	**1**	**3**	**4**	**35**	**1**	**0**	**0**
1994-95	**Dallas Stars**	**NHL**	**27**	**1**	**3**	**4**	**2**	**4**	**6**	**186**	**0**	**0**	**1**	**22**	**4.5**	**7**	**0**	**7**	**0**	**0**	**5**	**0**	**0**	**0**	**20**	**0**	**0**	**0**
1995-96	**Dallas Stars**	**NHL**	**34**	**3**	**4**	**7**	**3**	**3**	**6**	**168**	**0**	**0**	**0**	**18**	**16.7**	**15**	**3**	**8**	**0**	**+4**	....	....	....	....	....	....	....	....
	Los Angeles Kings	**NHL**	**11**	**1**	**2**	**3**	**1**	**2**	**3**	**37**	**0**	**0**	**0**	**9**	**11.1**	**5**	**1**	**13**	**0**	**–9**	....	....	....	....	....	....	....	....
	New York Rangers	**NHL**	**10**	**0**	**0**	**0**	**0**	**0**	**0**	**26**	**0**	**0**	**0**	**5**	**0.0**	**0**	**0**	**3**	**0**	**–3**	**11**	**2**	**2**	**4**	**14**	**0**	**0**	**0**
1996-97	**New York Rangers**	**NHL**	**45**	**0**	**1**	**1**	**0**	**1**	**1**	**106**	**0**	**0**	**0**	**19**	**0.0**	**4**	**0**	**14**	**0**	**–10**	**15**	**0**	**0**	**0**	**20**	**0**	**0**	**0**
	NHL Totals		**488**	**26**	**45**	**71**	**26**	**36**	**62**	**2301**	**4**	**0**	**3**	**335**	**7.8**	**152**	**28**	**177**	**1**		**78**	**5**	**7**	**12**	**282**	**1**	**0**	**1**

Traded to **Calgary** by **Hartford** with Dana Murzyn for Neil Sheehy, Carey Wilson, and the rights to Lane MacDonald, January 3, 1988. Traded to **Minnesota** by **Calgary** with Perry Berezan for Brian MacLellan and Minnesota's 4th round choice (Robert Reichel) in 1989 Entry Draft, March 4, 1989. Claimed by **San Jose** from **Minnesota** in Dispersal Draft, May 30, 1991. Traded to **Minnesota** by **San Jose** for Kelly Kisio, June 3, 1991. Transferred to **Dallas** after **Minnesota** franchise relocated, June 9, 1993. Traded to **LA Kings** by **Dallas** with Doug Zmolek for Darryl Sydor and LA Kings' 5th round choice (Ryan Christie) in 1996 Entry Draft, February 17, 1996. Traded to **NY Rangers** by **LA Kings** with Marty McSorley and Jari Kurri for Ray Ferraro, Ian Laperriere, Mattias Norstrom, Nathan Lafayette and NY Rangers' 4th round choice (Sean Blanchard) in 1997 Entry Draft, March 14, 1996.

• CHYCHRUN, JEFF

Jeff Chychrun D – R. 6'4", 215 lbs. b: LaSalle, Que., 5/3/1966. Philadelphia's 3rd choice, 37th overall, in 1984 Entry Draft.

Season	Club	League	GP	G	A	Pts	AG	AA	APts	PIM	PP	SH	GW	S	%	TGF	PGF	TGA	PGA	+/–	GP	G	A	Pts	PIM	PP	SH	GW
1983-84	Kingston Canadians	OHL	63	1	13	14	....	....	....	137	....	....	....	....	....	....	....	....	....	....	....	....	....	....	....	....	....	....
1984-85	Kingston Canadians	OHL	58	4	10	14	....	....	....	206	....	....	....	....	....	....	....	....	....	....	....	....	....	....	....	....	....	....
1985-86	Kingston Canadians	OHL	61	4	21	25	....	....	....	127	....	....	....	....	....	....	....	....	....	....	10	2	1	3	17	....	....	....
	Hershey Bears	AHL	....	....	....	....	....	....	....	....	....	....	....	....	....	....	....	....	....	....	4	0	1	1	9	....	....	....
	Kalamazoo Wings	IHL	....	....	....	....	....	....	....	....	....	....	....	....	....	....	....	....	....	....	3	1	0	1	0	....	....	....
1986-87	**Philadelphia Flyers**	**NHL**	**1**	**0**	**0**	**0**	**0**	**0**	**0**	**4**	**0**	**0**	**0**	**1**	**0.0**	**0**	**0**	**0**	**0**	**0**	....	....	....	....	....	....	....	....
	Hershey Bears	AHL	74	1	17	18	....	....	....	239	....	....	....	....	....	....	....	....	....	....	4	0	0	0	10	....	....	....
1987-88	**Philadelphia Flyers**	**NHL**	**3**	**0**	**0**	**0**	**0**	**0**	**0**	**4**	**0**	**0**	**0**	**1**	**0.0**	**0**	**0**	**3**	**2**	**–1**	....	....	....	....	....	....	....	....
	Hershey Bears	AHL	55	0	5	5	....	....	....	210	....	....	....	....	....	....	....	....	....	....	12	0	2	2	44	....	....	....
1988-89	**Philadelphia Flyers**	**NHL**	**80**	**1**	**4**	**5**	**1**	**3**	**4**	**245**	**0**	**0**	**1**	**53**	**1.9**	**58**	**2**	**70**	**25**	**+11**	**19**	**0**	**2**	**2**	**65**	**0**	**0**	**0**
1989-90	**Philadelphia Flyers**	**NHL**	**79**	**2**	**7**	**9**	**2**	**5**	**7**	**250**	**0**	**0**	**1**	**52**	**3.8**	**51**	**1**	**76**	**14**	**–12**	....	....	....	....	....	....	....	....
1990-91	**Philadelphia Flyers**	**NHL**	**36**	**0**	**6**	**6**	**0**	**5**	**5**	**105**	**0**	**0**	**0**	**25**	**0.0**	**20**	**0**	**21**	**2**	**+1**	....	....	....	....	....	....	....	....
1991-92	**Los Angeles Kings**	**NHL**	**26**	**0**	**3**	**3**	**0**	**2**	**2**	**76**	**0**	**0**	**0**	**22**	**0.0**	**17**	**0**	**25**	**4**	**–4**	....	....	....	....	....	....	....	....
	Phoenix Roadrunners	IHL	3	0	0	0	....	....	....	6	....	....	....	....	....	....	....	....	....	....	....	....	....	....	....	....	....	....
	Pittsburgh Penguins	**NHL**	**17**	**0**	**1**	**1**	**0**	**1**	**1**	**35**	**0**	**0**	**0**	**4**	**0.0**	**5**	**0**	**13**	**0**	**–8**	....	....	....	....	....	....	....	....
1992-93	**Pittsburgh Penguins**	**NHL**	**1**	**0**	**0**	**0**	**0**	**0**	**0**	**2**	**0**	**0**	**0**	**0**	**0.0**	**1**	**0**	**0**	**0**	**+1**	....	....	....	....	....	....	....	....
	Los Angeles Kings	**NHL**	**17**	**0**	**1**	**1**	**0**	**1**	**1**	**23**	**0**	**0**	**0**	**3**	**0.0**	**3**	**0**	**6**	**0**	**–3**	....	....	....	....	....	....	....	....
	Phoenix Roadrunners	IHL	11	2	0	2	....	....	....	44	....	....	....	....	....	....	....	....	....	....	....	....	....	....	....	....	....	....
1993-94	**Edmonton Oilers**	**NHL**	**2**	**0**	**0**	**0**	**0**	**0**	**0**	**0**	**0**	**0**	**0**	**2**	**0.0**	**1**	**0**	**1**	**1**	**+1**	....	....	....	....	....	....	....	....
	Cape Breton Oilers	AHL	41	2	16	18	....	....	....	111	....	....	....	....	....	....	....	....	....	....	....	....	....	....	....	....	....	....
	NHL Totals		**262**	**3**	**22**	**25**	**3**	**17**	**20**	**744**	**0**	**0**	**2**	**163**	**1.8**	**156**	**3**	**215**	**48**		**19**	**0**	**2**	**2**	**65**	**0**	**0**	**0**

Traded to **LA Kings** by **Philadelphia** with Jari Kurri for Steve Duchesne, Steve Kasper and LA Kings' 4th round choice (Aris Brimanis) in 1991 Entry Draft, May 30, 1991. Traded to **Pittsburgh** by **LA Kings** with Brian Benning and LA Kings' 1st round choice (later traded to Philadelphia — Philadelphia selected Jason Bowen) in 1992 Entry Draft for Paul Coffey, February 19, 1992. Traded to **LA Kings** by **Pittsburgh** for Peter Ahola, November 6, 1992. Traded to **Edmonton** by **LA Kings** for future considerations, November 2, 1993. Signed as a free agent by **Hartford**, May 27, 1994.

• CHYNOWETH, DEAN

Dean Chynoweth D – R. 6'1", 191 lbs. b: Calgary, Alta., 10/30/1968. NY Islanders' 1st choice, 13th overall, in 1987 Entry Draft.

Season	Club	League	GP	G	A	Pts	AG	AA	APts	PIM	PP	SH	GW	S	%	TGF	PGF	TGA	PGA	+/–	GP	G	A	Pts	PIM	PP	SH	GW
1985-86	Medicine Hat Tigers	WHL	69	3	12	15	....	....	....	208	....	....	....	....	....	....	....	....	....	....	17	3	2	5	52	....	....	....
1986-87	Medicine Hat Tigers	WHL	67	3	18	21	....	....	....	285	....	....	....	....	....	....	....	....	....	....	13	4	2	6	28	....	....	....
1987-88	Medicine Hat Tigers	WHL	64	1	21	22	....	....	....	274	....	....	....	....	....	....	....	....	....	....	16	0	6	6	*87	....	....	....
1988-89	**New York Islanders**	**NHL**	**6**	**0**	**0**	**0**	**0**	**0**	**0**	**48**	**0**	**0**	**0**	**0**	**0.0**	**0**	**0**	**7**	**3**	**–4**	....	....	....	....	....	....	....	....
1989-90	**New York Islanders**	**NHL**	**20**	**0**	**2**	**2**	**0**	**1**	**1**	**39**	**0**	**0**	**0**	**8**	**0.0**	**10**	**0**	**16**	**6**	**0**	....	....	....	....	....	....	....	....
	Springfield Indians	AHL	40	0	7	7	....	....	....	98	....	....	....	....	....	....	....	....	....	....	17	0	4	4	36	....	....	....
1990-91	**New York Islanders**	**NHL**	**25**	**1**	**1**	**2**	**1**	**1**	**2**	**59**	**0**	**0**	**0**	**14**	**7.1**	**12**	**0**	**19**	**1**	**–6**	....	....	....	....	....	....	....	....
	Capital District Islanders	AHL	44	1	5	6	....	....	....	176	....	....	....	....	....	....	....	....	....	....	....	....	....	....	....	....	....	....
1991-92	**New York Islanders**	**NHL**	**11**	**1**	**0**	**1**	**1**	**0**	**1**	**23**	**0**	**0**	**0**	**6**	**16.7**	**4**	**0**	**9**	**2**	**–3**	....	....	....	....	....	....	....	....
	Capital District Islanders	AHL	43	4	6	10	....	....	....	164	....	....	....	....	....	....	....	....	....	....	6	1	1	2	39	....	....	....
1992-93	Capital District Islanders	AHL	52	3	10	13	....	....	....	197	....	....	....	....	....	....	....	....	....	....	4	0	1	1	9	....	....	....
1993-94	**New York Islanders**	**NHL**	**39**	**0**	**4**	**4**	**0**	**3**	**3**	**122**	**0**	**0**	**0**	**26**	**0.0**	**26**	**0**	**37**	**14**	**+3**	**2**	**0**	**0**	**0**	**2**	**0**	**0**	**0**
	Salt Lake Golden Eagles	IHL	5	0	1	1	....	....	....	33	....	....	....	....	....	....	....	....	....	....	....	....	....	....	....	....	....	....
1994-95	**New York Islanders**	**NHL**	**32**	**0**	**2**	**2**	**0**	**3**	**3**	**77**	**0**	**0**	**0**	**22**	**0.0**	**23**	**0**	**23**	**9**	**+9**	....	....	....	....	....	....	....	....
1995-96	**New York Islanders**	**NHL**	**14**	**0**	**1**	**1**	**0**	**1**	**1**	**40**	**0**	**0**	**0**	**6**	**0.0**	**4**	**0**	**9**	**1**	**–4**	....	....	....	....	....	....	....	....
	Boston Bruins	**NHL**	**35**	**2**	**5**	**7**	**2**	**4**	**6**	**88**	**0**	**0**	**0**	**32**	**6.3**	**19**	**0**	**24**	**4**	**–1**	**4**	**0**	**0**	**0**	**24**	**0**	**0**	**0**
1996-97	**Boston Bruins**	**NHL**	**57**	**0**	**3**	**3**	**0**	**3**	**3**	**171**	**0**	**0**	**0**	**30**	**0.0**	**27**	**0**	**46**	**7**	**–12**	....	....	....	....	....	....	....	....
	Providence Bruins	AHL	2	0	0	0	....	....	....	13	....	....	....	....	....	....	....	....	....	....	....	....	....	....	....	....	....	....
1997-98	**Boston Bruins**	**NHL**	**2**	**0**	**0**	**0**	**0**	**0**	**0**	**0**	**0**	**0**	**0**	**1**	**0.0**	**0**	**0**	**4**	**0**	**–4**	....	....	....	....	....	....	....	....
	Providence Bruins	AHL	28	2	2	4	....	....	....	123	....	....	....	....	....	....	....	....	....	....	....	....	....	....	....	....	....	....
	Quebec Rafales	IHL	15	2	2	4	....	....	....	39	....	....	....	....	....	....	....	....	....	....	....	....	....	....	....	....	....	....
	NHL Totals		**241**	**4**	**18**	**22**	**4**	**16**	**20**	**667**	**0**	**0**	**0**	**145**	**2.8**	**125**	**0**	**194**	**47**		**6**	**0**	**0**	**0**	**26**	**0**	**0**	**0**

Traded to **Boston** by **NY Islanders** for Boston's 5th round choice (Petr Sachl) in 1996 Entry Draft, December 9, 1995.

• CHYZOWSKI, DAVE

Dave Chyzowski LW – L. 6'1", 190 lbs. b: Edmonton, Alta., 7/11/1971. NY Islanders' 1st choice, 2nd overall, in 1989 Entry Draft.

			REGULAR SEASON																		PLAYOFFS							
Season	Club	League	GP	G	A	Pts	AG	AA	APts	PIM	PP	SH	GW	S	%	TGF	PGF	TGA	PGA	+/–	GP	G	A	Pts	PIM	PP	SH	GW
1987-88	Kamloops Blazers	WHL	66	16	17	33	....	....	....	117	....	....	....	....	....	....	....	....	....	....	18	2	4	6	26	....	....	....
1988-89	Kamloops Blazers	WHL	68	56	48	104	....	....	....	139	....	....	....	....	....	....	....	....	....	....	16	15	13	28	32	....	....	....
1989-90	Kamloops Blazers	WHL	4	5	2	7	....	....	....	17	....	....	....	....	....	....	....	....	....	....	17	11	6	17	46	....	....	....
	Canada	WJC-A	7	9	4	13	....	....	....	2	....	....	....	....	....	....	....	....	....	....	....	....	....	....	....	....	....	....
	New York Islanders	**NHL**	**34**	**8**	**6**	**14**	**7**	**4**	**11**	**45**	**3**	**0**	**1**	**59**	**13.6**	**20**	**7**	**17**	**0**	**–4**	....	....	....	....	....	....	....	....
	Springfield Indians	AHL	4	0	0	0	....	....	....	7	....	....	....	....	....	....	....	....	....	....	....	....	....	....	....	....	....	....
1990-91	**New York Islanders**	**NHL**	**56**	**5**	**9**	**14**	**5**	**7**	**12**	**61**	**0**	**0**	**0**	**66**	**7.6**	**22**	**2**	**39**	**0**	**–19**	....	....	....	....	....	....	....	....
	Capital District Islanders	AHL	7	3	6	9	....	....	....	22	....	....	....	....	....	....	....	....	....	....	....	....	....	....	....	....	....	....
1991-92	**New York Islanders**	**NHL**	**12**	**1**	**1**	**2**	**1**	**1**	**2**	**17**	**0**	**0**	**0**	**18**	**5.6**	**5**	**3**	**6**	**0**	**–4**	....	....	....	....	....	....	....	....
	Capital District Islanders	AHL	55	15	18	33	....	....	....	121	....	....	....	....	....	....	....	....	....	....	6	1	1	2	23	....	....	....
1992-93	Capital District Islanders	AHL	66	15	21	36	....	....	....	177	....	....	....	....	....	....	....	....	....	....	3	2	0	2	0	....	....	....
1993-94	**New York Islanders**	**NHL**	**3**	**1**	**0**	**1**	**1**	**0**	**1**	**4**	**0**	**0**	**0**	**4**	**25.0**	**1**	**0**	**2**	**0**	**–1**	**2**	**0**	**0**	**0**	**0**	**0**	**0**	**0**
	Salt Lake Golden Eagles	IHL	66	27	13	40	....	....	....	151	....	....	....	....	....	....	....	....	....	....	....	....	....	....	....	....	....	....
1994-95	**New York Islanders**	**NHL**	**13**	**0**	**0**	**0**	**0**	**0**	**0**	**11**	**0**	**0**	**0**	**11**	**0.0**	**2**	**0**	**4**	**0**	**–2**	....	....	....	....	....	....	....	....
	Kalamazoo Wings	IHL	4	0	4	4	....	....	....	8	....	....	....	....	....	....	....	....	....	....	16	9	5	14	27	....	....	....
1995-96	Adirondack Red Wings	AHL	80	44	39	83	....	....	....	160	....	....	....	....	....	....	....	....	....	....	3	0	0	0	6	....	....	....
1996-97	**Chicago Blackhawks**	**NHL**	**8**	**0**	**0**	**0**	**0**	**0**	**0**	**6**	**0**	**0**	**0**	**6**	**0.0**	**1**	**0**	**0**	**0**	**+1**	....	....	....	....	....	....	....	....
	Indianapolis Ice	IHL	76	34	40	74	....	....	....	261	....	....	....	....	....	....	....	....	....	....	4	0	2	2	38	....	....	....
1997-98	Orlando Solar Bears	IHL	17	9	7	16	....	....	....	32	....	....	....	....	....	....	....	....	....	....	....	....	....	....	....	....	....	....
	San Antonio Dragons	IHL	10	1	5	6	....	....	....	39	....	....	....	....	....	....	....	....	....	....	....	....	....	....	....	....	....	....
	Kansas City Blades	IHL	38	19	14	33	....	....	....	88	....	....	....	....	....	....	....	....	....	....	11	5	4	9	11	....	....	....
	NHL Totals		**126**	**15**	**16**	**31**	**14**	**12**	**26**	**144**	**3**	**0**	**1**	**164**	**9.1**	**51**	**12**	**68**	**0**		**2**	**0**	**0**	**0**	**0**	**0**	**0**	**0**

WHL West All-Star Team (1989) • WJC-A All-Star Team (1990)

Signed as a free agent by **Detroit**, August 29, 1995. Signed as a free agent by **Chicago**, September 26, 1996.

• CIAVAGLIA, PETER

Peter Ciavaglia C – L. 5'10", 173 lbs. b: Albany, NY, 7/15/1969. Calgary's 8th choice, 145th overall, in 1987 Entry Draft.

Season	Club	League	GP	G	A	Pts	AG	AA	APts	PIM	PP	SH	GW	S	%	TGF	PGF	TGA	PGA	+/–	GP	G	A	Pts	PIM	PP	SH	GW
1986-87	Nicholos–Wheatfield	NYJHL	....	53	84	137	....	....	....	....	....	....	....	....	....	....	....	....	....	....	....	....	....	....	....	....	....	....
1987-88	Harvard University	ECAC	30	10	23	33	....	....	....	16	....	....	....	....	....	....	....	....	....	....	....	....	....	....	....	....	....	....
1988-89	Harvard University	ECAC	34	15	48	63	....	....	....	36	....	....	....	....	....	....	....	....	....	....	....	....	....	....	....	....	....	....
	United States	WJC-A	7	1	4	5	....	....	....	0	....	....	....	....	....	....	....	....	....	....	....	....	....	....	....	....	....	....
1989-90	Harvard University	ECAC	28	17	18	35	....	....	....	22	....	....	....	....	....	....	....	....	....	....	....	....	....	....	....	....	....	....
1990-91	Harvard University	ECAC	27	24	*38	*62	....	....	....	2	....	....	....	....	....	....	....	....	....	....	....	....	....	....	....	....	....	....
1991-92	**Buffalo Sabres**	**NHL**	**2**	**0**	**0**	**0**	**0**	**0**	**0**	**0**	**0**	**0**	**0**	**1**	**0.0**	**1**	**0**	**0**	**0**	**+1**	....	....	....	....	....	....	....	....
	Rochester Americans	AHL	77	37	61	98	....	....	....	16	....	....	....	....	....	....	....	....	....	....	6	2	5	7	6	....	....	....
1992-93	**Buffalo Sabres**	**NHL**	**3**	**0**	**0**	**0**	**0**	**0**	**0**	**0**	**0**	**0**	**0**	**2**	**0.0**	**1**	**0**	**1**	**0**	**0**	....	....	....	....	....	....	....	....
	Rochester Americans	AHL	64	35	67	102	....	....	....	32	....	....	....	....	....	....	....	....	....	....	17	9	16	25	12	....	....	....
1993-94	United States	Nat-Team	18	2	9	11	....	....	....	6	....	....	....	....	....	....	....	....	....	....	....	....	....	....	....	....	....	....
	Leksands IF	Sweden	39	14	18	32	....	....	....	34	....	....	....	....	....	....	....	....	....	....	4	1	2	3	0	....	....	....
	United States	Olympics	8	2	4	6	....	....	....	0	....	....	....	....	....	....	....	....	....	....	....	....	....	....	....	....	....	....
	United States	WC-A	7	1	0	1	....	....	....	2	....	....	....	....	....	....	....	....	....	....	....	....	....	....	....	....	....	....
1994-95	Detroit Vipers	IHL	73	22	59	81	....	....	....	83	....	....	....	....	....	....	....	....	....	....	5	1	1	2	6	....	....	....
1995-96	Detroit Vipers	IHL	75	22	56	78	....	....	....	38	....	....	....	....	....	....	....	....	....	....	12	6	11	17	12	....	....	....
1996-97	Detroit Vipers	IHL	72	21	51	72	....	....	....	54	....	....	....	....	....	....	....	....	....	....	21	*14	19	*33	32	....	....	....
1997-98	Detroit Vipers	IHL	35	11	30	41	....	....	....	10	....	....	....	....	....	....	....	....	....	....	23	8	11	19	12	....	....	....
	NHL Totals		**5**	**0**	**0**	**0**	**0**	**0**	**0**	**0**	**0**	**0**	**0**	**3**	**0.0**	**2**	**0**	**1**	**0**		....	....	....	....	....	....	....	....

ECAC Second All-Star Team (1989, 1991) • NCAA East Second All-American Team (1991) • Won "Bud" Poile Trophy (Playoff MVP - IHL) (1997)

Signed as a free agent by **Buffalo**, August 30, 1991.

• CICCARELLI, DINO

Dino Ciccarelli RW – R. 5'10", 185 lbs. b: Sarnia, Ont., 2/8/1960.

Season	Club	League	GP	G	A	Pts	AG	AA	APts	PIM	PP	SH	GW	S	%	TGF	PGF	TGA	PGA	+/–	GP	G	A	Pts	PIM	PP	SH	GW
1977-78	London Knights	OHA	68	72	70	142	....	....	....	49	....	....	....	....	....	....	....	....	....	....	9	6	10	16	6	....	....	....
1978-79	London Knights	OHA	30	8	11	19	....	....	....	35	....	....	....	....	....	....	....	....	....	....	7	3	5	8	0	....	....	....
1979-80	London Knights	OHA	62	50	53	103	....	....	....	72	....	....	....	....	....	....	....	....	....	....	5	2	6	8	15	....	....	....
	Canada	WJC-A	5	5	1	6	....	....	....	2	....	....	....	....	....	....	....	....	....	....	....	....	....	....	....	....	....	....
1980-81	**Minnesota North Stars**	**NHL**	**32**	**18**	**12**	**30**	**15**	**8**	**23**	**29**	**8**	**0**	**0**	**126**	**14.3**	**45**	**15**	**28**	**0**	**+2**	**19**	**14**	**7**	**21**	**25**	**5**	**0**	**3**
	Oklahoma City Stars	CHL	48	32	35	67	....	....	....	16	....	....	....	....	....	....	....	....	....	....	....	....	....	....	....	....	....	....
1981-82	**Minnesota North Stars**	**NHL**	**76**	**55**	**51**	**106**	**44**	**34**	**78**	**138**	**20**	**0**	**4**	**289**	**19.0**	**145**	**54**	**77**	**0**	**+14**	**4**	**3**	**1**	**4**	**2**	**2**	**0**	**1**
1981-82	Canada	WEC-A	9	2	1	3	....	....	....	0	....	....	....	....	....	....	....	....	....	....	....	....	....	....	....	....	....	....
1982-83	**Minnesota North Stars**	**NHL**	**77**	**37**	**38**	**75**	**30**	**26**	**56**	**94**	**14**	**0**	**4**	**210**	**17.6**	**111**	**38**	**57**	**0**	**+16**	**9**	**4**	**6**	**10**	**11**	**1**	**0**	**2**
1983-84	**Minnesota North Stars**	**NHL**	**79**	**38**	**33**	**71**	**31**	**22**	**53**	**58**	**16**	**0**	**2**	**211**	**18.0**	**111**	**46**	**66**	**2**	**+1**	**16**	**4**	**5**	**9**	**27**	**1**	**0**	**1**
1984-85	**Minnesota North Stars**	**NHL**	**51**	**15**	**17**	**32**	**12**	**11**	**23**	**41**	**6**	**0**	**0**	**133**	**11.3**	**51**	**14**	**48**	**1**	**–10**	**9**	**3**	**3**	**6**	**8**	**1**	**0**	**0**
1985-86	**Minnesota North Stars**	**NHL**	**75**	**44**	**45**	**89**	**35**	**30**	**65**	**51**	**19**	**0**	**5**	**262**	**16.8**	**122**	**46**	**64**	**0**	**+12**	**5**	**0**	**1**	**1**	**6**	**0**	**0**	**0**
1986-87	**Minnesota North Stars**	**NHL**	**80**	**52**	**51**	**103**	**45**	**37**	**82**	**88**	**22**	**0**	**5**	**255**	**20.4**	**143**	**55**	**78**	**0**	**+10**	....	....	....	....	....	....	....	....
	Canada	WEC-A	10	4	2	6	....	....	....	2	....	....	....	....	....	....	....	....	....	....	....	....	....	....	....	....	....	....
1987-88	**Minnesota North Stars**	**NHL**	**67**	**41**	**45**	**86**	**35**	**32**	**67**	**79**	**13**	**1**	**2**	**262**	**15.6**	**107**	**48**	**109**	**21**	**–29**	....	....	....	....	....	....	....	....
1988-89	**Minnesota North Stars**	**NHL**	**65**	**32**	**27**	**59**	**27**	**19**	**46**	**64**	**13**	**0**	**5**	**208**	**15.4**	**82**	**34**	**64**	**0**	**–16**	....	....	....	....	....	....	....	....
	Washington Capitals	**NHL**	**11**	**12**	**3**	**15**	**10**	**2**	**12**	**12**	**3**	**0**	**3**	**39**	**30.8**	**20**	**8**	**2**	**0**	**+10**	**6**	**3**	**3**	**6**	**12**	**3**	**0**	**0**
1989-90	Washington Capitals	FrTour	3	3	0	3	....	....	....	2	....	....	....	....	....	....	....	....	....	....	....	....	....	....	....	....	....	....
	Washington Capitals	**NHL**	**80**	**41**	**38**	**79**	**35**	**27**	**62**	**122**	**10**	**0**	**6**	**267**	**15.4**	**120**	**38**	**88**	**1**	**–5**	**8**	**8**	**3**	**11**	**6**	**1**	**0**	**1**
1990-91	**Washington Capitals**	**NHL**	**54**	**21**	**18**	**39**	**19**	**14**	**33**	**66**	**2**	**0**	**2**	**186**	**11.3**	**60**	**15**	**62**	**0**	**–17**	**11**	**5**	**4**	**9**	**22**	**3**	**0**	**2**
1991-92	**Washington Capitals**	**NHL**	**78**	**38**	**38**	**76**	**35**	**29**	**64**	**78**	**13**	**0**	**7**	**279**	**13.6**	**109**	**37**	**82**	**0**	**–10**	**7**	**5**	**4**	**9**	**14**	**1**	**0**	**0**
1992-93	**Detroit Red Wings**	**NHL**	**82**	**41**	**56**	**97**	**34**	**38**	**72**	**81**	**21**	**0**	**8**	**200**	**20.5**	**143**	**67**	**64**	**0**	**+12**	**7**	**4**	**2**	**6**	**16**	**3**	**0**	**0**
1993-94	**Detroit Red Wings**	**NHL**	**66**	**28**	**29**	**57**	**26**	**22**	**48**	**73**	**12**	**0**	**1**	**153**	**18.3**	**107**	**42**	**56**	**1**	**+10**	**7**	**5**	**2**	**7**	**14**	**1**	**0**	**0**
1994-95	**Detroit Red Wings**	**NHL**	**42**	**16**	**27**	**43**	**28**	**40**	**68**	**39**	**6**	**0**	**3**	**106**	**15.1**	**63**	**26**	**25**	**0**	**+12**	**16**	**9**	**2**	**11**	**22**	**6**	**0**	**2**
1995-96	**Detroit Red Wings**	**NHL**	**64**	**22**	**21**	**43**	**22**	**17**	**39**	**99**	**13**	**0**	**5**	**107**	**20.6**	**78**	**37**	**27**	**0**	**+14**	**17**	**6**	**2**	**8**	**26**	**6**	**0**	**1**
1996-97	**Tampa Bay Lightning**	**NHL**	**77**	**35**	**25**	**60**	**37**	**22**	**59**	**116**	**12**	**0**	**6**	**229**	**15.3**	**92**	**32**	**72**	**1**	**–11**	....	....	....	....	....	....	....	....
1997-98	**Tampa Bay Lightning**	**NHL**	**34**	**11**	**6**	**17**	**13**	**6**	**19**	**42**	**3**	**0**	**3**	**104**	**10.6**	**22**	**9**	**27**	**0**	**–14**	....	....	....	....	....	....	....	....
	Florida Panthers	**NHL**	**28**	**5**	**11**	**16**	**6**	**11**	**17**	**28**	**2**	**0**	**1**	**57**	**8.8**	**29**	**13**	**18**	**0**	**–2**	....	....	....	....	....	....	....	....
	NHL Totals		**1210**	**608**	**591**	**1193**	**539**	**447**	**986**	**1398**	**227**	**1**	**72**	**3683**	**16.3**	**1760**	**674**	**1114**	**27**		**141**	**73**	**45**	**118**	**211**	**34**	**0**	**13**

OHA Second All-Star Team (1978)

Played in NHL All-Star Game (1982, 1983, 1989, 1997)

Signed as a free agent by **Minnesota**, September 28, 1979. Traded to **Washington** by **Minnesota** with Bob Rouse for Mike Gartner and Larry Murphy, March 7, 1989. Traded to **Detroit** by **Washington** for Kevin Miller, June 20, 1992. Traded to **Tampa Bay** by **Detroit** for future considerations, August 27, 1996. Traded to **Florida** by **Tampa Bay** with Jeff Norton for Mark Fitzpatrick and Jody Hull, January 15, 1998.

• CICCONE, ENRICO

Enrico Ciccone D – L. 6'5", 220 lbs. b: Montreal, Que., 4/10/1970. Minnesota's 5th choice, 92nd overall, in 1990 Entry Draft.

Season	Club	League	GP	G	A	Pts	AG	AA	APts	PIM	PP	SH	GW	S	%	TGF	PGF	TGA	PGA	+/–	GP	G	A	Pts	PIM	PP	SH	GW
1987-88	Shawinigan Cataractes	QMJHL	61	2	12	14	....	....	....	324	....	....	....	....	....	....	....	....	....	....	....	....	....	....	....	....	....	....
1988-89	Shawinigan Cataractes	QMJHL	34	7	11	18	....	....	....	132	....	....	....	....	....	....	....	....	....	....	....	....	....	....	....	....	....	....
	Trois-Rivières Draveurs	QMJHL	24	0	7	7	....	....	....	153	....	....	....	....	....	....	....	....	....	....	....	....	....	....	....	....	....	....
1989-90	Trois-Rivières Draveurs	QMJHL	40	4	24	28	....	....	....	227	....	....	....	....	....	....	....	....	....	....	3	0	0	0	15	....	....	....
1990-91	Kalamazoo Wings	IHL	57	4	9	13	....	....	....	384	....	....	....	....	....	....	....	....	....	....	4	0	1	1	32	....	....	....
1991-92	**Minnesota North Stars**	**NHL**	**11**	**0**	**0**	**0**	**0**	**0**	**0**	**48**	**0**	**0**	**0**	**2**	**0.0**	**2**	**0**	**4**	**0**	**–2**	....	....	....	....	....	....	....	....
	Kalamazoo Wings	IHL	53	4	16	20	....	....	....	406	....	....	....	....	....	....	....	....	....	....	10	0	1	1	58	....	....	....
1992-93	**Minnesota North Stars**	**NHL**	**31**	**0**	**1**	**1**	**0**	**1**	**1**	**115**	**0**	**0**	**0**	**13**	**0.0**	**10**	**0**	**11**	**3**	**+2**	....	....	....	....	....	....	....	....
	Kalamazoo Wings	IHL	13	1	3	4	....	....	....	50	....	....	....	....	....	....	....	....	....	....	....	....	....	....	....	....	....	....
	Hamilton Canucks	AHL	6	1	3	4	....	....	....	44	....	....	....	....	....	....	....	....	....	....	....	....	....	....	....	....	....	....
1993-94	**Washington Capitals**	**NHL**	**46**	**1**	**1**	**2**	**1**	**1**	**2**	**174**	**0**	**0**	**0**	**23**	**4.3**	**10**	**0**	**13**	**1**	**–2**	....	....	....	....	....	....	....	....
	Portland Pirates	AHL	6	0	0	0	....	....	....	27	....	....	....	....	....	....	....	....	....	....	....	....	....	....	....	....	....	....
	Tampa Bay Lightning	**NHL**	**11**	**0**	**1**	**1**	**0**	**1**	**1**	**52**	**0**	**0**	**0**	**10**	**0.0**	**4**	**0**	**7**	**1**	**–2**	....	....	....	....	....	....	....	....
1994-95	**Tampa Bay Lightning**	**NHL**	**41**	**2**	**4**	**6**	**4**	**6**	**10**	***225**	**0**	**0**	**0**	**43**	**4.7**	**25**	**0**	**23**	**1**	**+3**	....	....	....	....	....	....	....	....

			REGULAR SEASON																		PLAYOFFS							
Season	Club	League	GP	G	A	Pts	AG	AA	APts	PIM	PP	SH	GW	S	%	TGF	PGF	TGA	PGA	+/–	GP	G	A	Pts	PIM	PP	SH	GW
1995-96	**Tampa Bay Lightning**	**NHL**	**55**	**2**	**3**	**5**	**2**	**2**	**4**	**258**	**0**	**0**	**0**	**48**	**4.2**	**27**	**1**	**47**	**17**	**–4**	....	....	....	....	....	....	....	....
	Chicago Blackhawks	**NHL**	**11**	**0**	**1**	**1**	**0**	**1**	**1**	**48**	**0**	**0**	**0**	**12**	**0.0**	**6**	**0**	**2**	**1**	**+5**	**9**	**1**	**0**	**1**	**30**	**0**	**0**	**0**
1996-97	**Chicago Blackhawks**	**NHL**	**67**	**2**	**2**	**4**	**2**	**2**	**4**	**233**	**0**	**0**	**1**	**65**	**3.1**	**28**	**0**	**33**	**4**	**–1**	**4**	**0**	**0**	**0**	**18**	**0**	**0**	**0**
1997-98	**Carolina Hurricanes**	**NHL**	**14**	**0**	**3**	**3**	**0**	**3**	**3**	**83**	**0**	**0**	**0**	**8**	**0.0**	**5**	**0**	**3**	**1**	**+3**	....	....	....	....	....	....	....	....
	Vancouver Canucks	**NHL**	**13**	**0**	**1**	**1**	**0**	**1**	**1**	**47**	**0**	**0**	**0**	**7**	**0.0**	**9**	**1**	**15**	**5**	**–2**	....	....	....	....	....	....	....	....
	Tampa Bay Lightning	**NHL**	**12**	**0**	**0**	**0**	**0**	**0**	**0**	**45**	**0**	**0**	**0**	**7**	**0.0**	**3**	**0**	**7**	**1**	**–3**	....	....	....	....	....	....	....	....
	NHL Totals		**312**	**7**	**17**	**24**	**9**	**18**	**27**	**1328**	**0**	**0**	**1**	**238**	**2.9**	**129**	**2**	**165**	**35**		**13**	**1**	**0**	**1**	**48**	**0**	**0**	**0**

Traded to **Washington** by **Dallas** to complete transaction that sent Paul Cavallini to Dallas (June 20, 1993), June 25, 1993. Traded to **Tampa Bay** by **Washington** with Washington's 3rd round choice (later traded to Anaheim — Anaheim selected Craig Reichert) in 1994 Entry Draft and the return of future draft choices transferred in the Pat Elynuik trade for Joe Reekie, March 21, 1994. Traded to **Chicago** by **Tampa Bay** with Tampa Bay's 2nd round choice (Jeff Paul) in 1996 Entry Draft for Patrick Poulin, Igor Ulanov and Chicago's 2nd round choice (later traded to New Jersey — New Jersey selected Pierre Dagenais) in 1996 Entry Draft, March 20, 1996. Traded to **Carolina** by **Chicago** for Ryan Risidore and Carolina's 5th round choice in 1998 Entry Draft, July 25, 1997. Traded to **Vancouver** by **Carolina** with Sean Burke and Geoff Sanderson for Kirk McLean and Martin Gelinas, January 3, 1998. Traded to **Tampa Bay** by **Vancouver** for Jamie Huscroft, March 14, 1998.

• CICHOCKI, CHRIS

Chris Cichocki RW – R. 5'11", 185 lbs. b: Detroit, MI, 9/17/1963.

1982-83	Michigan Tech Huskies	CCHA	36	12	10	22	....	....	....	10	....	....	....	....	....	....	....	....	....	....	....	....	....	....	....	....	....	....
1983-84	Michigan Tech Huskies	CCHA	40	25	20	45	....	....	....	36	....	....	....	....	....	....	....	....	....	....	....	....	....	....	....	....	....	....
1984-85	Michigan Tech Huskies	CCHA	40	30	24	54	....	....	....	14	....	....	....	....	....	....	....	....	....	....	....	....	....	....	....	....	....	....
1985-86	**Detroit Red Wings**	**NHL**	**59**	**10**	**11**	**21**	**8**	**7**	**15**	**21**	**1**	**1**	**0**	**76**	**13.2**	**32**	**4**	**43**	**7**	**–8**	....	....	....	....	....	....	....	....
	Adirondack Red Wings	AHL	9	4	4	8	....	....	....	6	....	....	....	....	....	....	....	....	....	....	....	....	....	....	....	....	....	....
1986-87	**Detroit Red Wings**	**NHL**	**2**	**0**	**0**	**0**	**0**	**0**	**0**	**2**	**0**	**0**	**0**	**0**	**0.0**	**1**	**0**	**3**	**0**	**–2**	....	....	....	....	....	....	....	....
	Adirondack Red Wings	AHL	55	31	34	65	....	....	....	27	....	....	....	....	....	....	....	....	....	....	....	....	....	....	....	....	....	....
	Maine Mariners	AHL	7	2	2	4	....	....	....	0	....	....	....	....	....	....	....	....	....	....	....	....	....	....	....	....	....	....
1987-88	**New Jersey Devils**	**NHL**	**5**	**1**	**0**	**1**	**1**	**0**	**1**	**2**	**0**	**0**	**0**	**2**	**50.0**	**3**	**0**	**2**	**0**	**+1**	....	....	....	....	....	....	....	....
	Utica Devils	AHL	69	36	30	66	....	....	....	66	....	....	....	....	....	....	....	....	....	....	....	....	....	....	....	....	....	....
1988-89	**New Jersey Devils**	**NHL**	**2**	**0**	**1**	**1**	**0**	**1**	**1**	**2**	**0**	**0**	**0**	**2**	**0.0**	**1**	**0**	**1**	**0**	**0**	....	....	....	....	....	....	....	....
	Utica Devils	AHL	59	32	31	63	....	....	....	50	....	....	....	....	....	....	....	....	....	....	5	0	1	1	2	....	....	....
1989-90	Utica Devils	AHL	11	3	1	4	....	....	....	10	....	....	....	....	....	....	....	....	....	....	....	....	....	....	....	....	....	....
	Binghamton Whalers	AHL	60	21	26	47	....	....	....	22	....	....	....	....	....	....	....	....	....	....	....	....	....	....	....	....	....	....
1990-91	Binghamton Rangers	AHL	80	35	30	65	....	....	....	70	....	....	....	....	....	....	....	....	....	....	9	0	4	4	2	....	....	....
1991-92	Binghamton Rangers	AHL	75	28	29	57	....	....	....	132	....	....	....	....	....	....	....	....	....	....	6	5	4	9	4	....	....	....
1992-93	Binghamton Rangers	AHL	65	23	29	52	....	....	....	78	....	....	....	....	....	....	....	....	....	....	9	3	2	5	25	....	....	....
1993-94	Cincinnati Cyclones	IHL	69	22	20	42	....	....	....	101	....	....	....	....	....	....	....	....	....	....	11	2	2	4	12	....	....	....
1994-95	Cincinnati Cyclones	IHL	75	22	30	52	....	....	....	50	....	....	....	....	....	....	....	....	....	....	8	0	3	3	6	....	....	....
1995-96	Cincinnati Cyclones	IHL	57	4	7	11	....	....	....	30	....	....	....	....	....	....	....	....	....	....	14	0	1	1	10	....	....	....
	NHL Totals		**68**	**11**	**12**	**23**	**9**	**8**	**17**	**27**	**1**	**1**	**0**	**80**	**13.8**	**37**	**4**	**49**	**7**		....	....	....	....	....	....	....	....

Signed as a free agent by **Detroit**, June 28, 1985. Traded to **New Jersey** by **Detroit** with Detroit's 3rd round choice (later traded to Buffalo — Buffalo selected Andrew McVicar) in 1987 Entry Draft for Mel Bridgman, March 9, 1987.

• CIERNIK, IVAN

Ivan Ciernik LW – L. 6'1", 198 lbs. b: Levice, Czech., 10/30/1977. Ottawa's 6th choice, 216th overall, in 1996 Entry Draft.

1994-95	MHC Nitra	Slov-Jr.	30	22	15	37	....	....	....	36	....	....	....	....	....	....	....	....	....	....	....	....	....	....	....	....	....	....
	MHC Nitra	Slovakia	7	1	0	1	....	....	....	2	....	....	....	....	....	....	....	....	....	....	....	....	....	....	....	....	....	....
1995-96	MHC Nitra	Slovakia	35	9	7	16	....	....	....	36	....	....	....	....	....	....	....	....	....	....	8	3	3	6	....	....	....	....
	Slovakia	WJC-A	6	2	0	2	....	....	....	2	....	....	....	....	....	....	....	....	....	....	....	....	....	....	....	....	....	....
1996-97	MHC Nitra	Slovakia	41	11	19	30	....	....	....	....	....	....	....	....	....	....	....	....	....	....	....	....	....	....	....	....	....	....
	Slovakia	WJC-A	6	1	2	3	....	....	....	18	....	....	....	....	....	....	....	....	....	....	....	....	....	....	....	....	....	....
1997-98	**Ottawa Senators**	**NHL**	**2**	**0**	**0**	**0**	**0**	**0**	**0**	**0**	**0**	**0**	**0**	**0**	**0.0**	**0**	**0**	**0**	**0**	**0**	....	....	....	....	....	....	....	....
	Worcester IceCats	AHL	53	9	12	21	....	....	....	38	....	....	....	....	....	....	....	....	....	....	1	0	0	0	2	....	....	....
	NHL Totals		**2**	**0**	**0**	**0**	**0**	**0**	**0**	**0**	**0**	**0**	**0**	**0**	**0.0**	**0**	**0**	**0**	**0**		....	....	....	....	....	....	....	....

• CIERNY, JOZEF

Jozef Cierny LW – L. 6'2", 185 lbs. b: Zvolen, Czech., 5/13/1974. Buffalo's 2nd choice, 35th overall, in 1992 Entry Draft.

1991-92	ZTK Zvolen	Czech.2	26	10	3	13	....	....	....	8	....	....	....	....	....	....	....	....	....	....	....	....	....	....	....	....	....	....
1992-93	Rochester Americans	AHL	54	27	27	54	....	....	....	36	....	....	....	....	....	....	....	....	....	....	....	....	....	....	....	....	....	....
1993-94	**Edmonton Oilers**	**NHL**	**1**	**0**	**0**	**0**	**0**	**0**	**0**	**0**	**0**	**0**	**0**	**0**	**0.0**	**0**	**0**	**1**	**0**	**–1**	....	....	....	....	....	....	....	....
	Cape Breton Oilers	AHL	73	30	27	57	....	....	....	88	....	....	....	....	....	....	....	....	....	....	4	1	1	2	4	....	....	....
1994-95	Cape Breton Oilers	AHL	73	28	24	52	....	....	....	58	....	....	....	....	....	....	....	....	....	....	....	....	....	....	....	....	....	....
1995-96	Detroit Vipers	IHL	20	2	5	7	....	....	....	16	....	....	....	....	....	....	....	....	....	....	....	....	....	....	....	....	....	....
	Los Angeles Ice Dogs	IHL	43	23	16	39	....	....	....	36	....	....	....	....	....	....	....	....	....	....	....	....	....	....	....	....	....	....
1996-97	Long Beach Ice Dogs	IHL	68	27	27	54	....	....	....	106	....	....	....	....	....	....	....	....	....	....	16	8	5	13	7	....	....	....
1997-98	Nurnberg Ice Tigers	Germany	45	20	22	42	....	....	....	61	....	....	....	....	....	....	....	....	....	....	....	....	....	....	....	....	....	....
	NHL Totals		**1**	**0**	**0**	**0**	**0**	**0**	**0**	**0**	**0**	**0**	**0**	**0**	**0.0**	**0**	**0**	**1**	**0**		....	....	....	....	....	....	....	....

Traded to **Edmonton** by **Buffalo** with Buffalo's 4th round choice (Jussi Tarvainen) in 1994 Entry Draft for Craig Simpson, September 1, 1993.

• CIGER, ZDENO

Zdeno Ciger LW – L. 6'1", 190 lbs. b: Martin, Czech., 10/19/1969. New Jersey's 3rd choice, 54th overall, in 1988 Entry Draft.

1987-88	Dukla Trencin	Czech.	8	3	4	7	....	....	....	2	....	....	....	....	....	....	....	....	....	....	....	....	....	....	....	....	....	....
1988-89	Dukla Trencin	Czech.	43	18	13	31	....	....	....	18	....	....	....	....	....	....	....	....	....	....	....	....	....	....	....	....	....	....
	Czechoslovakia	WEC-A	10	2	5	7	....	....	....	8	....	....	....	....	....	....	....	....	....	....	....	....	....	....	....	....	....	....
1989-90	Dukla Trencin	Czech.	53	18	28	46	....	....	....	....	....	....	....	....	....	....	....	....	....	....	....	....	....	....	....	....	....	....
1989-90	Czechoslovakia	WEC-A	10	5	1	6	....	....	....	4	....	....	....	....	....	....	....	....	....	....	....	....	....	....	....	....	....	....
1990-91	**New Jersey Devils**	**NHL**	**45**	**8**	**17**	**25**	**7**	**13**	**20**	**8**	**2**	**0**	**1**	**82**	**9.8**	**32**	**8**	**21**	**0**	**+3**	**6**	**0**	**2**	**2**	**4**	**0**	**0**	**0**
	Utica Devils	AHL	8	5	4	9	....	....	....	2	....	....	....	....	....	....	....	....	....	....	....	....	....	....	....	....	....	....
1991-92	Czechoslovakia	C Cup	5	0	0	0	....	....	....	2	....	....	....	....	....	....	....	....	....	....	....	....	....	....	....	....	....	....
	New Jersey Devils	**NHL**	**20**	**6**	**5**	**11**	**5**	**4**	**9**	**10**	**1**	**0**	**0**	**33**	**18.2**	**18**	**5**	**15**	**0**	**–2**	**7**	**2**	**4**	**6**	**0**	**0**	**0**	**1**
1992-93	**New Jersey Devils**	**NHL**	**27**	**4**	**8**	**12**	**3**	**5**	**8**	**2**	**2**	**0**	**1**	**39**	**10.3**	**18**	**6**	**28**	**8**	**–8**	....	....	....	....	....	....	....	....
	Edmonton Oilers	**NHL**	**37**	**9**	**15**	**24**	**7**	**10**	**17**	**6**	**0**	**0**	**1**	**67**	**13.4**	**34**	**12**	**32**	**5**	**–5**	....	....	....	....	....	....	....	....
1993-94	**Edmonton Oilers**	**NHL**	**84**	**22**	**35**	**57**	**21**	**27**	**48**	**8**	**8**	**0**	**1**	**158**	**13.9**	**79**	**28**	**67**	**5**	**–11**	....	....	....	....	....	....	....	....
1994-95	Dukla Trencin	Slovakia	34	23	25	48	....	....	....	8	....	....	....	....	....	....	....	....	....	....	9	2	9	11	2	....	....	....
	Slovakia	WC-B	7	7	4	11	....	....	....	4	....	....	....	....	....	....	....	....	....	....	....	....	....	....	....	....	....	....
	Edmonton Oilers	**NHL**	**5**	**2**	**2**	**4**	**4**	**3**	**7**	**0**	**1**	**0**	**1**	**10**	**20.0**	**6**	**3**	**4**	**0**	**–1**	....	....	....	....	....	....	....	....
1995-96	**Edmonton Oilers**	**NHL**	**78**	**31**	**39**	**70**	**31**	**32**	**63**	**41**	**12**	**0**	**3**	**184**	**16.8**	**107**	**49**	**73**	**0**	**–15**	....	....	....	....	....	....	....	....
	Slovakia	WC-A	5	1	1	2	....	....	....	2	....	....	....	....	....	....	....	....	....	....	....	....	....	....	....	....	....	....
1996-97	Slovakia	W Cup	3	1	0	1	....	....	....	2	....	....	....	....	....	....	....	....	....	....	....	....	....	....	....	....	....	....
	Bratislava	Slovakia	44	26	27	53	....	....	....	....	....	....	....	....	....	....	....	....	....	....	2	1	3	4	....	....	....	....
	Slovakia	WC-A	8	4	1	5	....	....	....	12	....	....	....	....	....	....	....	....	....	....	....	....	....	....	....	....	....	....
1997-98	Slovan	EuroHL	8	1	5	6	....	....	....	6	....	....	....	....	....	....	....	....	....	....	....	....	....	....	....	....	....	....
	Slovan	Slovakia	36	14	31	45	....	....	....	2	....	....	....	....	....	....	....	....	....	....	11	6	10	16	4	....	....	....
	Slovakia	Olympics	4	1	1	2	....	....	....	4	....	....	....	....	....	....	....	....	....	....	....	....	....	....	....	....	....	....
	Slovakia	WC-A	6	0	1	1	....	....	....	2	....	....	....	....	....	....	....	....	....	....	....	....	....	....	....	....	....	....
	NHL Totals		**296**	**82**	**121**	**203**	**78**	**94**	**172**	**75**	**26**	**0**	**8**	**573**	**14.3**	**294**	**111**	**240**	**18**		**13**	**2**	**6**	**8**	**4**	**0**	**0**	**1**

Czechoslovakian Rookie of the Year (1989)

Traded to **Edmonton** by **New Jersey** with Kevin Todd for Bernie Nicholls, January 13, 1993.

• CIMELLARO, TONY

Tony Cimellaro C – L. 5'11", 180 lbs. b: Kingston, Ont., 6/14/1971.

1988-89	North Bay Trappers	OHL	11	2	1	3	....	....	....	7	....	....	....	....	....	....	....	....	....	....	....	....	....	....	....	....	....	....
	Kingston Frontenacs	OHL	47	6	7	13	....	....	....	12	....	....	....	....	....	....	....	....	....	....	....	....	....	....	....	....	....	....
1989-90	Kingston Frontenacs	OHL	62	8	31	39	....	....	....	26	....	....	....	....	....	....	....	....	....	....	7	1	4	5	2	....	....	....
1990-91	Kingston Frontenacs	OHL	64	26	25	51	....	....	....	42	....	....	....	....	....	....	....	....	....	....	....	....	....	....	....	....	....	....
1991-92	Belleville Bulls	OHL	48	39	44	83	....	....	....	51	....	....	....	....	....	....	....	....	....	....	5	6	4	10	10	....	....	....
1992-93	**Ottawa Senators**	**NHL**	**2**	**0**	**0**	**0**	**0**	**0**	**0**	**0**	**0**	**0**	**0**	**4**	**0.0**	**1**	**1**	**2**	**0**	**–2**	....	....	....	....	....	....	....	....
	New Haven Nighthawks	AHL	76	18	16	34	....	....	....	73	....	....	....	....	....	....	....	....	....	....	....	....	....	....	....	....	....	....

			REGULAR SEASON																		PLAYOFFS							
Season	Club	League	GP	G	A	Pts	AG	AA	APts	PIM	PP	SH	GW	S	%	TGF	PGF	TGA	PGA	+/–	GP	G	A	Pts	PIM	PP	SH	GW
1993-94	P.E.I. Senators	AHL	19	1	0	1	....	....	....	30	....	....	....	....	....	....	....	....	....	....	....	....	....	....	....	....	....	....
	Asiago HC	Italy	16	16	11	27	....	....	....	13	....	....	....	....	....	....	....	....	....	....	....	....	....	....	....	....	....	....
1994-95	Durham Wasps	Britain	4	2	5	7	....	....	....	10	....	....	....	....	....	....	....	....	....	....	....	....	....	....	....	....	....	....
	Blackburn Hawks	Britain	24	40	33	73	....	....	....	76	....	....	....	....	....	....	....	....	....	....	....	....	....	....	....	....	....	....
1995-96	Vojens	Denamrk	40	38	27	65	....	....	....	87	....	....	....	....	....	....	....	....	....	....	....	....	....	....	....	....	....	....
1996-97	Ratinger Lowen	Germany	46	4	9	13	....	....	....	42	....	....	....	....	....	....	....	....	....	....	7	1	1	2	22	....	....	....
	NHL Totals		**2**	**0**	**0**	**0**	**0**	**0**	**0**	**0**	**0**	**0**	**0**	**4**	**0.0**	**1**	**1**	**2**	**0**		....	....	....	....	....	....	....	....

Signed as a free agent by **Ottawa**, July 30, 1992.

• CIMETTA, ROBERT

Robert Cimetta LW/RW – L. 6′, 190 lbs. b: Toronto, Ont., 2/15/1970. Boston's 1st choice, 18th overall, in 1988 Entry Draft.

Season	Club	League	GP	G	A	Pts	AG	AA	APts	PIM	PP	SH	GW	S	%	TGF	PGF	TGA	PGA	+/–	GP	G	A	Pts	PIM	PP	SH	GW
1986-87	Toronto Marlboros	OHL	66	21	35	56	....	....	....	65	....	....	....	....	....	....	....	....	....	....	....	....	....	....	....	....	....	....
1987-88	Toronto Marlboros	OHL	64	34	42	76	....	....	....	90	....	....	....	....	....	....	....	....	....	....	4	2	2	4	7	....	....	....
1988-89	Toronto Marlboros	OHL	58	*55	47	102	....	....	....	89	....	....	....	....	....	....	....	....	....	....	6	3	3	6	0	....	....	....
	Canada	WJC-A	7	7	4	11	....	....	....	4	....	....	....	....	....	....	....	....	....	....	....	....	....	....	....	....	....	....
	Boston Bruins	**NHL**	**7**	**2**	**0**	**2**	**2**	**0**	**2**	**0**	**0**	**0**	**1**	**4**	**50.0**	**2**	**0**	**6**	**0**	**–4**	**1**	**0**	**0**	**0**	**15**	**0**	**0**	**0**
1989-90	**Boston Bruins**	**NHL**	**47**	**8**	**9**	**17**	**7**	**6**	**13**	**33**	**0**	**0**	**0**	**28**	**28.6**	**28**	**5**	**19**	**0**	**+4**	....	....	....	....	....	....	....	....
	Maine Mariners	AHL	9	3	2	5	....	....	....	13	....	....	....	....	....	....	....	....	....	....	....	....	....	....	....	....	....	....
1990-91	**Toronto Maple Leafs**	**NHL**	**25**	**2**	**4**	**6**	**2**	**3**	**5**	**21**	**2**	**0**	**1**	**18**	**11.1**	**11**	**2**	**14**	**0**	**–5**	....	....	....	....	....	....	....	....
	Newmarket Saints	AHL	29	16	18	34	....	....	....	24	....	....	....	....	....	....	....	....	....	....	....	....	....	....	....	....	....	....
1991-92	**Toronto Maple Leafs**	**NHL**	**24**	**4**	**3**	**7**	**4**	**2**	**6**	**12**	**0**	**0**	**0**	**31**	**12.9**	**14**	**3**	**8**	**2**	**+5**	....	....	....	....	....	....	....	....
	St. John's Maple Leafs	AHL	19	4	13	17	....	....	....	23	....	....	....	....	....	....	....	....	....	....	10	3	7	10	24	....	....	....
1992-93	St. John's Maple Leafs	AHL	76	28	57	85	....	....	....	125	....	....	....	....	....	....	....	....	....	....	9	2	10	12	32	....	....	....
1993-94	Indianapolis Ice	IHL	79	26	54	80	....	....	....	178	....	....	....	....	....	....	....	....	....	....	....	....	....	....	....	....	....	....
1994-95	Mannheim Eagles	Germany	39	29	31	60	....	....	....	*126	....	....	....	....	....	....	....	....	....	....	9	6	6	12	32	....	....	....
1995-96	Mannheim Eagles	Germany	50	21	42	63	....	....	....	76	....	....	....	....	....	....	....	....	....	....	1	0	1	1	25	....	....	....
1996-97	Berlin Capitals	Germany	8	4	5	9	....	....	....	16	....	....	....	....	....	....	....	....	....	....	....	....	....	....	....	....	....	....
	Mannheim Eagles	Germany	36	18	21	39	....	....	....	40	....	....	....	....	....	....	....	....	....	....	9	5	9	14	10	....	....	....
1997-98	Mannheim Eagles	Germany	41	12	20	32	....	....	....	82	....	....	....	....	....	....	....	....	....	....	6	2	3	5	18	....	....	....
	NHL Totals		**103**	**16**	**16**	**32**	**15**	**11**	**26**	**66**	**2**	**0**	**2**	**81**	**19.8**	**55**	**10**	**47**	**2**		**1**	**0**	**0**	**0**	**15**	**0**	**0**	**0**

OHL First All-Star Team (1989)

Traded to **Toronto** by **Boston** for Steve Bancroft, November 9, 1990.

• CIRELLA, JOE

Joe Cirella D – R. 6′3″, 210 lbs. b: Hamilton, Ont., 5/9/1963. Colorado's 1st choice, 5th overall, in 1981 Entry Draft.

Season	Club	League	GP	G	A	Pts	AG	AA	APts	PIM	PP	SH	GW	S	%	TGF	PGF	TGA	PGA	+/–	GP	G	A	Pts	PIM	PP	SH	GW
1980-81	Oshawa Generals	OHA	56	5	31	36	....	....	....	220	....	....	....	....	....	....	....	....	....	....	11	0	2	2	41	....	....	....
1981-82	Oshawa Generals	OHL	3	0	1	1	....	....	....	0	....	....	....	....	....	....	....	....	....	....	11	7	10	17	32	....	....	....
	Colorado Rockies	**NHL**	**65**	**7**	**12**	**19**	**6**	**8**	**14**	**52**	**2**	**0**	**1**	**71**	**9.9**	**57**	**10**	**90**	**7**	**–36**	....	....	....	....	....	....	....	....
1982-83	Oshawa Generals	OHL	56	13	55	68	....	....	....	110	....	....	....	....	....	....	....	....	....	....	17	4	16	20	37	....	....	....
	Canada	WJC-A	7	0	0	0	....	....	....	6	....	....	....	....	....	....	....	....	....	....	....	....	....	....	....	....	....	....
	New Jersey Devils	**NHL**	**2**	**0**	**1**	**1**	**0**	**1**	**1**	**4**	**0**	**0**	**0**	**3**	**0.0**	**2**	**2**	**2**	**0**	**–2**	....	....	....	....	....	....	....	....
1983-84	**New Jersey Devils**	**NHL**	**79**	**11**	**33**	**44**	**9**	**22**	**31**	**137**	**6**	**0**	**0**	**156**	**7.1**	**101**	**37**	**125**	**18**	**–43**	....	....	....	....	....	....	....	....
1984-85	**New Jersey Devils**	**NHL**	**66**	**6**	**18**	**24**	**5**	**12**	**17**	**141**	**2**	**0**	**0**	**97**	**6.2**	**72**	**23**	**111**	**17**	**–45**	....	....	....	....	....	....	....	....
1985-86	**New Jersey Devils**	**NHL**	**66**	**6**	**23**	**29**	**5**	**15**	**20**	**147**	**2**	**0**	**0**	**89**	**6.7**	**97**	**25**	**116**	**32**	**–12**	....	....	....	....	....	....	....	....
1986-87	**New Jersey Devils**	**NHL**	**65**	**9**	**22**	**31**	**8**	**16**	**24**	**111**	**6**	**0**	**0**	**115**	**7.8**	**102**	**36**	**122**	**36**	**–20**	....	....	....	....	....	....	....	....
1987-88	**New Jersey Devils**	**NHL**	**80**	**8**	**31**	**39**	**7**	**22**	**29**	**191**	**2**	**0**	**2**	**135**	**5.9**	**111**	**32**	**124**	**60**	**+15**	**19**	**0**	**7**	**7**	**49**	**0**	**0**	**0**
1988-89	**New Jersey Devils**	**NHL**	**80**	**3**	**19**	**22**	**3**	**13**	**16**	**155**	**0**	**1**	**1**	**84**	**3.6**	**61**	**5**	**142**	**72**	**–14**	....	....	....	....	....	....	....	....
1989-90	**Quebec Nordiques**	**NHL**	**56**	**4**	**14**	**18**	**3**	**10**	**13**	**67**	**1**	**0**	**0**	**76**	**5.3**	**53**	**7**	**94**	**21**	**–27**	....	....	....	....	....	....	....	....
1990-91	**Quebec Nordiques**	**NHL**	**39**	**2**	**10**	**12**	**2**	**8**	**10**	**59**	**0**	**0**	**0**	**60**	**3.3**	**41**	**13**	**80**	**24**	**–28**	....	....	....	....	....	....	....	....
	New York Rangers	**NHL**	**19**	**1**	**0**	**1**	**1**	**0**	**1**	**52**	**0**	**0**	**0**	**22**	**4.5**	**14**	**2**	**15**	**4**	**+1**	**6**	**0**	**2**	**2**	**26**	**0**	**0**	**0**
1991-92	**New York Rangers**	**NHL**	**67**	**3**	**12**	**15**	**3**	**9**	**12**	**121**	**1**	**0**	**0**	**58**	**5.2**	**57**	**6**	**61**	**21**	**+11**	**13**	**0**	**4**	**4**	**23**	**0**	**0**	**0**
1992-93	**New York Rangers**	**NHL**	**55**	**3**	**6**	**9**	**2**	**4**	**6**	**85**	**0**	**1**	**0**	**37**	**8.1**	**46**	**2**	**57**	**14**	**+1**	....	....	....	....	....	....	....	....
1993-94	**Florida Panthers**	**NHL**	**63**	**1**	**9**	**10**	**1**	**7**	**8**	**99**	**0**	**0**	**0**	**63**	**1.6**	**54**	**3**	**76**	**33**	**+8**	....	....	....	....	....	....	....	....
1994-95	**Florida Panthers**	**NHL**	**20**	**0**	**1**	**1**	**0**	**1**	**1**	**21**	**0**	**0**	**0**	**13**	**0.0**	**9**	**2**	**20**	**6**	**–7**	....	....	....	....	....	....	....	....
1995-96	**Ottawa Senators**	**NHL**	**6**	**0**	**0**	**0**	**0**	**0**	**0**	**4**	**0**	**0**	**0**	**3**	**0.0**	**2**	**0**	**7**	**2**	**–3**	....	....	....	....	....	....	....	....
	Milwaukee Admirals	IHL	40	1	8	9	....	....	....	65	....	....	....	....	....	....	....	....	....	....	5	0	1	1	20	....	....	....
1996-97	Kolner Haie	Germany	49	2	7	9	....	....	....	164	....	....	....	....	....	....	....	....	....	....	4	0	0	0	8	....	....	....
	NHL Totals		**828**	**64**	**211**	**275**	**55**	**148**	**203**	**1446**	**22**	**2**	**4**	**1082**	**5.9**	**879**	**205**	**1242**	**367**		**38**	**0**	**13**	**13**	**98**	**0**	**0**	**0**

OHL First All-Star Team (1983) • Memorial Cup All-Star Team (1983)

Played in NHL All-Star Game (1984)

Transferred to **New Jersey** after **Colorado** franchise relocated, June 30, 1982. Traded to **Quebec** by **New Jersey** with Claude Loiselle and New Jersey's 8th round choice (Alexander Karpotsev) in 1990 Entry Draft for Walt Poddubny and Quebec's 4th round choice (Mike Bodnarchuk) in 1990 Entry Draft, June 17, 1989. Traded to **NY Rangers** by **Quebec** for Aaron Miller and NY Rangers' 5th round choice (Bill Lindsay) in 1991 Entry Draft, January 17, 1991. Claimed by **Florida** from **NY Rangers** in Expansion Draft, June 24, 1993. Signed as a free agent by **Ottawa**, October 10, 1995.

• CIRONE, JASON

Jason Cirone C – L. 5′9″, 185 lbs. b: Toronto, Ont., 2/21/1971. Winnipeg's 3rd choice, 46th overall, in 1989 Entry Draft.

Season	Club	League	GP	G	A	Pts	AG	AA	APts	PIM	PP	SH	GW	S	%	TGF	PGF	TGA	PGA	+/–	GP	G	A	Pts	PIM	PP	SH	GW
1987-88	Cornwall Royals	OHL	53	12	11	23	....	....	....	41	....	....	....	....	....	....	....	....	....	....	11	1	2	3	4	....	....	....
1988-89	Cornwall Royals	OHL	64	39	44	83	....	....	....	67	....	....	....	....	....	....	....	....	....	....	17	19	8	27	14	....	....	....
1989-90	Cornwall Royals	OHL	32	22	41	63	....	....	....	56	....	....	....	....	....	....	....	....	....	....	6	4	2	6	14	....	....	....
1990-91	Cornwall Royals	OHL	40	31	29	60	....	....	....	66	....	....	....	....	....	....	....	....	....	....	....	....	....	....	....	....	....	....
	Windsor Spitfires	OHL	23	27	23	50	....	....	....	31	....	....	....	....	....	....	....	....	....	....	11	9	8	17	14	....	....	....
1991-92	**Winnipeg Jets**	**NHL**	**3**	**0**	**0**	**0**	**0**	**0**	**0**	**2**	**0**	**0**	**0**	**1**	**0.0**	**1**	**0**	**1**	**0**	**0**	....	....	....	....	....	....	....	....
	Moncton Hawks	AHL	64	32	27	59	....	....	....	124	....	....	....	....	....	....	....	....	....	....	10	1	1	2	8	....	....	....
1992-93	Asiago HC	Alpenliga	25	24	14	38	....	....	....	36	....	....	....	....	....	....	....	....	....	....	....	....	....	....	....	....	....	....
	Asiago HC	Italy	16	6	5	11	....	....	....	18	....	....	....	....	....	....	....	....	....	....	2	1	5	6	10	....	....	....
1993-94	Cincinnati Cyclones	IHL	26	4	2	6	....	....	....	61	....	....	....	....	....	....	....	....	....	....	....	....	....	....	....	....	....	....
	Birmingham Bulls	ECHL	11	3	3	6	....	....	....	45	....	....	....	....	....	....	....	....	....	....	10	8	8	16	*67	....	....	....
1994-95	Cincinnati Cyclones	IHL	74	22	15	37	....	....	....	170	....	....	....	....	....	....	....	....	....	....	9	1	1	2	14	....	....	....
1995-96	Rochester Americans	AHL	24	4	5	9	....	....	....	34	....	....	....	....	....	....	....	....	....	....	....	....	....	....	....	....	....	....
	Los Angeles Ice Dogs	IHL	26	8	10	18	....	....	....	47	....	....	....	....	....	....	....	....	....	....	....	....	....	....	....	....	....	....
1996-97	Long Beach Ice Dogs	IHL	11	4	3	7	....	....	....	14	....	....	....	....	....	....	....	....	....	....	....	....	....	....	....	....	....	....
	Kansas City Blades	IHL	70	18	38	56	....	....	....	88	....	....	....	....	....	....	....	....	....	....	3	0	3	3	2	....	....	....
1997-98	Kansas City Blades	IHL	82	22	30	52	....	....	....	166	....	....	....	....	....	....	....	....	....	....	11	3	3	6	20	....	....	....
	NHL Totals		**3**	**0**	**0**	**0**	**0**	**0**	**0**	**2**	**0**	**0**	**0**	**1**	**0.0**	**1**	**0**	**1**	**0**		....	....	....	....	....	....	....	....

Traded to **Florida** by **Winnipeg** for Dave Tomlinson, August 3, 1993.

• CLACKSON, KIM

Kim Clackson D – R. 5'11", 195 lbs. b: Saskatoon, Sask., 2/13/1955. Pittsburgh's 5th choice, 85th overall, in 1975 Amateur Draft.

			REGULAR SEASON																		PLAYOFFS							
Season	Club	League	GP	G	A	Pts	AG	AA	APts	PIM	PP	SH	GW	S	%	TGF	PGF	TGA	PGA	+/–	GP	G	A	Pts	PIM	PP	SH	GW
1972-73	Victoria Cougars	WCJHL	64	1	1	2	....	....	....	235	....	....	....	....	....	....	....	....	....	....	....	....	....	....	....	....	....	....
1973-74	Victoria Cougars	WCJHL	1	0	0	0	....	....	....	0	....	....	....	....	....	....	....	....	....	....	....	....	....	....	....	....	....	....
	Flin Flon Bombers	WCJHL	47	2	6	8	....	....	....	263	....	....	....	....	....	....	....	....	....	....	....	....	....	....	....	....	....	....
1974-75	Victoria Cougars	WCJHL	58	7	26	33	....	....	....	359	....	....	....	....	....	....	....	....	....	....	....	....	....	....	....	....	....	....
1975-76	Indianapolis Racers	WHA	77	1	12	13	....	....	....	351	....	....	....	....	....	....	....	....	....	....	6	0	0	0	25	....	....	....
1976-77	Indianapolis Racers	WHA	71	3	8	11	....	....	....	168	....	....	....	....	....	....	....	....	....	....	9	0	1	1	24	....	....	....
1977-78	Winnipeg Jets	WHA	52	2	7	9	....	....	....	203	....	....	....	....	....	....	....	....	....	....	9	0	1	1	63	....	....	....
1978-79	Winnipeg Jets	WHA	71	0	12	12	....	....	....	210	....	....	....	....	....	....	....	....	....	....	9	0	5	5	28	....	....	....
1979-80	**Pittsburgh Penguins**	**NHL**	**45**	**0**	**3**	**3**	**0**	**2**	**2**	**166**	**0**	**0**	**0**	**12**	**0.0**	**13**	**1**	**20**	**0**	**–8**	**3**	**0**	**0**	**0**	**37**	**0**	**0**	**0**
1980-81	**Quebec Nordiques**	**NHL**	**61**	**0**	**5**	**5**	**0**	**3**	**3**	**204**	**0**	**0**	**0**	**20**	**0.0**	**28**	**0**	**32**	**1**	**–3**	**5**	**0**	**0**	**0**	**33**	**0**	**0**	**0**
	NHL Totals		**106**	**0**	**8**	**8**	**0**	**5**	**5**	**370**	**0**	**0**	**0**	**32**	**0.0**	**41**	**1**	**52**	**1**		**8**	**0**	**0**	**0**	**70**	**0**	**0**	**0**
	Other Major League Totals		271	6	39	45				932	....	....	....	....	....	....	....	....	....	....	33	0	7	7	140	....	....	....

Selected by **Minnesota** (WHA) in 1975 WHA Amateur Draft, June, 1975. Signed as a free agent by **Indianapolis** (WHA) after **Minnesota** (WHA) franchise folded, February 27, 1976. Signed as a free agent by **Winnipeg** (WHA), August, 1977. Claimed by **Pittsburgh** as a fill-in during Expansion Draft, June 13, 1979. Transferred to **Quebec** by **Pittsburgh** as compensation for Pittsburgh's signing of free agent Paul Baxter, August 7, 1980.

• CLANCY, TERRY

Terry Clancy RW – L. 5'11", 195 lbs. b: Ottawa, Ont., 4/2/1943.

Season	Club	League	GP	G	A	Pts	AG	AA	APts	PIM	PP	SH	GW	S	%	TGF	PGF	TGA	PGA	+/–	GP	G	A	Pts	PIM	PP	SH	GW
1960-61	St. Michael's Majors	OHA	38	2	3	5	....	....	....	30	....	....	....	....	....	....	....	....	....	....	20	2	3	5	16	....	....	....
1961-62	St. Michael's Majors	Tor-Jr.	32	4	14	18	....	....	....	16	....	....	....	....	....	....	....	....	....	....	12	6	3	9	20	....	....	....
1962-63	Montreal Jr. Canadiens	OHA	27	6	7	13	....	....	....	29	....	....	....	....	....	....	....	....	....	....	10	1	6	7	10	....	....	....
1963-64	Canada	Nat-Team	STATISTICS NOT AVAILABLE																									
	Canada	Olympics	7	1	1	2	....	....	....	2	....	....	....	....	....	....	....	....	....	....	....	....	....	....	....	....	....	....
	Rochester Americans	AHL	3	0	0	0	....	....	....	0	....	....	....	....	....	....	....	....	....	....	....	....	....	....	....	....	....	....
1964-65	Rochester Americans	AHL	30	1	5	6	....	....	....	6	....	....	....	....	....	....	....	....	....	....	....	....	....	....	....	....	....	....
	Tulsa Oilers	CHL	33	10	10	20	....	....	....	18	....	....	....	....	....	....	....	....	....	....	12	4	1	5	14	....	....	....
1965-66	Tulsa Oilers	CHL	70	15	18	33	....	....	....	74	....	....	....	....	....	....	....	....	....	....	11	3	5	8	5	....	....	....
1966-67	Rochester Americans	AHL	72	14	24	38	....	....	....	51	....	....	....	....	....	....	....	....	....	....	10	0	2	2	4	....	....	....
1967-68	**Oakland Seals**	**NHL**	**7**	**0**	**0**	**0**	**0**	**0**	**0**	**2**	**0**	**0**	**0**	**4**	**0.0**	**2**	**0**	**6**	**0**	**–4**	....	....	....	....	....	....	....	....
	Vancouver Canucks	WHL	46	6	9	15	....	....	....	10	....	....	....	....	....	....	....	....	....	....	....	....	....	....	....	....	....	....
	Buffalo Bisons	AHL	14	4	1	5	....	....	....	4	....	....	....	....	....	....	....	....	....	....	....	....	....	....	....	....	....	....
1968-69	**Toronto Maple Leafs**	**NHL**	**2**	**0**	**0**	**0**	**0**	**0**	**0**	**0**	**0**	**0**	**0**	**3**	**0.0**	**0**	**0**	**1**	**0**	**–1**	....	....	....	....	....	....	....	....
	Tulsa Oilers	CHL	47	5	13	18	....	....	....	24	....	....	....	....	....	....	....	....	....	....	5	1	0	1	2	....	....	....
1969-70	**Toronto Maple Leafs**	**NHL**	**52**	**6**	**5**	**11**	**7**	**5**	**12**	**31**	**0**	**0**	**1**	**77**	**7.8**	**19**	**0**	**19**	**4**	**+4**	....	....	....	....	....	....	....	....
1970-71	Phoenix Roadrunners	WHL	18	2	1	3	....	....	....	9	....	....	....	....	....	....	....	....	....	....	....	....	....	....	....	....	....	....
	Montreal Voyageurs	AHL	33	5	3	8	....	....	....	6	....	....	....	....	....	....	....	....	....	....	3	0	0	0	0	....	....	....
1971-72			DID NOT PLAY																									
1972-73	**Toronto Maple Leafs**	**NHL**	**32**	**0**	**1**	**1**	**0**	**1**	**1**	**6**	**0**	**0**	**0**	**12**	**0.0**	**8**	**0**	**29**	**11**	**–10**	....	....	....	....	....	....	....	....
1973-74	Albuquerque 6-Guns	CHL	19	4	0	4	....	....	....	21	....	....	....	....	....	....	....	....	....	....	....	....	....	....	....	....	....	....
	London Lions	Britain	35	6	13	19	....	....	....	22	....	....	....	....	....	....	....	....	....	....	....	....	....	....	....	....	....	....
1974-75	Virginia Wings	AHL	9	0	0	0	....	....	....	0	....	....	....	....	....	....	....	....	....	....	....	....	....	....	....	....	....	....
	NHL Totals		**93**	**6**	**6**	**12**	**7**	**6**	**13**	**39**	**0**	**0**	**1**	**96**	**6.3**	**29**	**0**	**55**	**15**		....	....	....	....	....	....	....	....

Signed as a free agent by **Toronto**, October, 1964. Claimed by **Oakland** from **Toronto** in Expansion Draft, June 6, 1967. Traded to **Toronto** by **Oakland** for cash, May 14, 1968. Traded to **Montreal Canadiens** by **Toronto** for cash, December 23, 1970. Traded to **Toronto** by **Montreal Canadiens** for cash, August 30, 1971. Traded to **Detroit** by **Toronto** for cash, October 17, 1973.

• CLARK, BRETT

Brett Clark D – L. 6', 175 lbs. b: Moosomin, Sask., 12/23/1976. Montreal's 7th choice, 154th overall, in 1996 Entry Draft.

Season	Club	League	GP	G	A	Pts	AG	AA	APts	PIM	PP	SH	GW	S	%	TGF	PGF	TGA	PGA	+/–	GP	G	A	Pts	PIM	PP	SH	GW
1995-96	University of Maine	H.E.	39	7	31	38	....	....	....	22	....	....	....	....	....	....	....	....	....	....	....	....	....	....	....	....	....	....
1996-97	Canada	Nat-Team	57	6	21	27	....	....	....	52	....	....	....	....	....	....	....	....	....	....	....	....	....	....	....	....	....	....
1997-98	**Montreal Canadiens**	**NHL**	**41**	**1**	**0**	**1**	**1**	**0**	**1**	**20**	**0**	**0**	**0**	**26**	**3.8**	**10**	**0**	**15**	**2**	**–3**	....	....	....	....	....	....	....	....
	Fredericton Canadiens	AHL	20	0	6	6	....	....	....	6	....	....	....	....	....	....	....	....	....	....	4	0	1	1	17	....	....	....
	NHL Totals		**41**	**1**	**0**	**1**	**1**	**0**	**1**	**20**	**0**	**0**	**0**	**26**	**3.8**	**10**	**0**	**15**	**2**		....	....	....	....	....	....	....	....

• CLARK, DAN

Dan Clark D – L. 6'1", 195 lbs. b: Toronto, Ont., 11/3/1957. NY Rangers' 8th choice, 110th overall, in 1978 Amateur Draft.

Season	Club	League	GP	G	A	Pts	AG	AA	APts	PIM	PP	SH	GW	S	%	TGF	PGF	TGA	PGA	+/–	GP	G	A	Pts	PIM	PP	SH	GW
1974-75	Langley Lords	BCJHL	50	11	22	33	....	....	....	127	....	....	....	....	....	....	....	....	....	....	....	....	....	....	....	....	....	....
1975-76	Kamloops Chiefs	WCJHL	71	0	26	26	....	....	....	109	....	....	....	....	....	....	....	....	....	....	12	2	2	4	25	....	....	....
1976-77	Kamloops Chiefs	WCHL	61	4	27	31	....	....	....	189	....	....	....	....	....	....	....	....	....	....	....	....	....	....	....	....	....	....
1977-78	Maine Mariners	AHL	6	0	1	1	....	....	....	6	....	....	....	....	....	....	....	....	....	....	....	....	....	....	....	....	....	....
	Milwaukee Admirals	IHL	67	7	18	25	....	....	....	245	....	....	....	....	....	....	....	....	....	....	5	0	0	0	4	....	....	....
1978-79	**New York Rangers**	**NHL**	**4**	**0**	**1**	**1**	**0**	**1**	**1**	**6**	**0**	**0**	**0**	**4**	**0.0**	**2**	**0**	**2**	**1**	**+1**	....	....	....	....	....	....	....	....
	New Haven Nighthawks	AHL	71	8	20	28	....	....	....	167	....	....	....	....	....	....	....	....	....	....	10	0	3	3	27	....	....	....
1979-80	New Haven Nighthawks	AHL	75	0	24	24	....	....	....	247	....	....	....	....	....	....	....	....	....	....	10	1	4	5	21	....	....	....
1980-81	New Haven Nighthawks	AHL	54	2	16	18	....	....	....	163	....	....	....	....	....	....	....	....	....	....	4	0	0	0	8	....	....	....
1981-82	Hershey Bears	AHL	19	0	6	6	....	....	....	58	....	....	....	....	....	....	....	....	....	....	....	....	....	....	....	....	....	....
	Springfield Indians	AHL	10	0	3	3	....	....	....	26	....	....	....	....	....	....	....	....	....	....	....	....	....	....	....	....	....	....
	NHL Totals		**4**	**0**	**1**	**1**	**0**	**1**	**1**	**6**	**0**	**0**	**0**	**4**	**0.0**	**2**	**0**	**2**	**1**		....	....	....	....	....	....	....	....

• Re-entered NHL draft. Originally Philadelphia's 6th choice, 89th overall, in 1977 Amateur Draft.

• CLARK, DEAN

Dean Clark D – L. 6'1", 180 lbs. b: Edmonton, Alta., 1/10/1964. Edmonton's 8th choice, 167th overall, in 1982 Entry Draft.

Season	Club	League	GP	G	A	Pts	AG	AA	APts	PIM	PP	SH	GW	S	%	TGF	PGF	TGA	PGA	+/–	GP	G	A	Pts	PIM	PP	SH	GW
1981-82	St. Albert Saints	SJHL	59	21	32	53	....	....	....	146	....	....	....	....	....	....	....	....	....	....	....	....	....	....	....	....	....	....
1982-83	Kamloops Junior Oilers	WHL	39	17	24	41	....	....	....	63	....	....	....	....	....	....	....	....	....	....	7	2	6	8	12	....	....	....
1983-84	Kamloops Junior Oilers	WHL	54	18	28	46	....	....	....	64	....	....	....	....	....	....	....	....	....	....	13	0	3	3	12	....	....	....
	Edmonton Oilers	**NHL**	**1**	**0**	**0**	**0**	**0**	**0**	**0**	**0**	**0**	**0**	**0**	**0**	**0.0**	**0**	**0**	**0**	**0**	**0**	....	....	....	....	....	....	....	....
1984-85	Kamloops Junior Oilers	WHL	36	15	36	51	....	....	....	33	....	....	....	....	....	....	....	....	....	....	....	....	....	....	....	....	....	....
1985-86			DID NOT PLAY																									
1986-87	University of Alberta	CWUAA	40	10	23	33	....	....	....	55	....	....	....	....	....	....	....	....	....	....	....	....	....	....	....	....	....	....
	NHL Totals		**1**	**0**	**0**	**0**	**0**	**0**	**0**	**0**	**0**	**0**	**0**	**0**	**0.0**	**0**	**0**	**0**	**0**		....	....	....	....	....	....	....	....

Originally NY Rangers' 8th choice, 110th overall, in 1978 Amateur Draft.

• CLARK, GORDIE

Gordie Clark RW – R. 5'10", 180 lbs. b: Glasgow, Scotland, 5/31/1952. Boston's 7th choice, 112th overall, in 1972 Amateur Draft.

Season	Club	League	GP	G	A	Pts	AG	AA	APts	PIM	PP	SH	GW	S	%	TGF	PGF	TGA	PGA	+/–	GP	G	A	Pts	PIM	PP	SH	GW
1968-69	Saint John Schooners	NBJHL	28	*38	31	69	....	....	....	57	....	....	....	....	....	....	....	....	....	....	17	*22	18	*40	9	....	....	....
1969-70			DID NOT PLAY																									
1970-71	University of New Hampshire	ECAC	DID NOT PLAY – FRESHMAN																									
1971-72	University of New Hampshire	ECAC	30	27	30	57	....	....	....	....	....	....	....	....	....	....	....	....	....	....	....	....	....	....	....	....	....	....
1972-73	University of New Hampshire	ECAC	29	24	28	52	....	....	....	52	....	....	....	....	....	....	....	....	....	....	....	....	....	....	....	....	....	....
1973-74	University of New Hampshire	ECAC	31	25	28	53	....	....	....	20	....	....	....	....	....	....	....	....	....	....	....	....	....	....	....	....	....	....
1974-75	**Boston Bruins**	**NHL**	**1**	**0**	**0**	**0**	**0**	**0**	**0**	**0**	**0**	**0**	**0**	**1**	**0.0**	**0**	**0**	**0**	**0**	**0**	....	....	....	....	....	....	....	....
	Rochester Americans	AHL	65	22	42	64	....	....	....	34	....	....	....	....	....	....	....	....	....	....	12	7	5	12	6	....	....	....
1975-76	**Boston Bruins**	**NHL**	**7**	**0**	**1**	**1**	**0**	**1**	**1**	**0**	**0**	**0**	**0**	**3**	**0.0**	**2**	**0**	**7**	**0**	**–5**	**1**	**0**	**0**	**0**	**0**	**0**	**0**	**0**
	Rochester Americans	AHL	72	30	49	79	....	....	....	7	....	....	....	....	....	....	....	....	....	....	7	2	3	5	5	....	....	....
1976-77	Rochester Americans	AHL	58	34	38	72	....	....	....	50	....	....	....	....	....	....	....	....	....	....	12	7	9	16	4	....	....	....
1977-78	Rochester Americans	AHL	75	37	51	88	....	....	....	18	....	....	....	....	....	....	....	....	....	....	6	2	0	2	0	....	....	....
1978-79	Cincinnati Stingers	WHA	21	3	3	6	....	....	....	2	....	....	....	....	....	....	....	....	....	....	....	....	....	....	....	....	....	....
	Springfield Indians	AHL	33	12	15	27	....	....	....	8	....	....	....	....	....	....	....	....	....	....	....	....	....	....	....	....	....	....
	Maine Mariners	AHL	13	7	11	18	....	....	....	2	....	....	....	....	....	....	....	....	....	....	10	6	9	15	2	....	....	....
1979-80	Maine Mariners	AHL	79	*47	43	90	....	....	....	64	....	....	....	....	....	....	....	....	....	....	12	5	4	9	7	....	....	....
1980-81	Maine Mariners	AHL	59	25	29	54	....	....	....	32	....	....	....	....	....	....	....	....	....	....	15	6	9	15	4	....	....	....

			REGULAR SEASON																		PLAYOFFS							
Season	Club	League	GP	G	A	Pts	AG	AA	APts	PIM	PP	SH	GW	S	%	TGF	PGF	TGA	PGA	+/–	GP	G	A	Pts	PIM	PP	SH	GW
1981-82	Maine Mariners	AHL	80	50	51	101	....	....	....	34	....	....	....	....	....	....	....	....	....	....	4	5	0	5	5	....	....	....
1982-83	Riessersee	Germany	35	40	19	59	....	....	....	46	....	....	....	....	....	....	....	....	....	....	6	4	2	6	5	....	....	....
	Maine Mariners	AHL	6	3	3	6	....	....	....	2	....	....	....	....	....	....	....	....	....	....	16	2	9	11	2	....	....	....
	NHL Totals		**8**	**0**	**1**	**1**	**0**	**1**	**1**	**0**	**0**	**0**	**0**	**4**	**0.0**	**2**	**0**	**7**	**0**		**1**	**0**	**0**	**0**	**0**	**0**	**0**	**0**
	Other Major League Totals		21	3	3	6	....	....	....	2	....	....	....	....	....	....	....	....	....		....	....	....	....	....	....	....	....

ECAC First All-Star Team (1972, 1973, 1974) • NCAA East First All-American Team (1973, 1974) • AHL Second All-Star Team (1976, 1977) • AHL First All-Star Team (1980, 1982)

Signed as a free agent by **Cincinnati** (WHA), August, 1978.

• CLARK, WENDEL

Wendel Clark LW – L. 5'11", 194 lbs. b: Kelvington, Sask., 10/25/1966. Toronto's 1st choice, 1st overall, in 1985 Entry Draft.

Season	Club	League	GP	G	A	Pts	AG	AA	APts	PIM	PP	SH	GW	S	%	TGF	PGF	TGA	PGA	+/–	GP	G	A	Pts	PIM	PP	SH	GW
1983-84	Saskatoon Blades	WHL	72	23	45	68	....	....	....	225	....	....	....	....	....	....	....	....	....	....	....	....	....	....	....	....	....	....
1984-85	Saskatoon Blades	WHL	64	32	55	87	....	....	....	253	....	....	....	....	....	....	....	....	....	....	3	3	3	6	7	....	....	....
	Canada	WJC-A	7	3	2	5	....	....	....	10	....	....	....	....	....	....	....	....	....	....	....	....	....	....	....	....	....	....
1985-86	**Toronto Maple Leafs**	**NHL**	**66**	**34**	**11**	**45**	**27**	**7**	**34**	**227**	**4**	**0**	**3**	**164**	**20.7**	**62**	**12**	**78**	**1**	**–27**	**10**	**5**	**1**	**6**	**47**	**1**	**0**	**1**
1986-87	**Toronto Maple Leafs**	**NHL**	**80**	**37**	**23**	**60**	**32**	**17**	**49**	**271**	**15**	**0**	**1**	**246**	**15.0**	**101**	**33**	**94**	**3**	**–23**	**13**	**6**	**5**	**11**	**38**	**3**	**0**	**1**
1987-88	**Toronto Maple Leafs**	**NHL**	**28**	**12**	**11**	**23**	**10**	**8**	**18**	**80**	**4**	**0**	**1**	**93**	**12.9**	**34**	**11**	**36**	**0**	**–13**	....	....	....	....	....	....	....	....
1988-89	**Toronto Maple Leafs**	**NHL**	**15**	**7**	**4**	**11**	**6**	**3**	**9**	**66**	**3**	**0**	**1**	**30**	**23.3**	**15**	**5**	**13**	**0**	**–3**	....	....	....	....	....	....	....	....
1989-90	**Toronto Maple Leafs**	**NHL**	**38**	**18**	**8**	**26**	**16**	**6**	**22**	**116**	**7**	**0**	**2**	**85**	**21.2**	**42**	**14**	**26**	**0**	**+2**	**5**	**1**	**1**	**2**	**19**	**0**	**0**	**0**
1990-91	**Toronto Maple Leafs**	**NHL**	**63**	**18**	**16**	**34**	**17**	**12**	**29**	**152**	**4**	**0**	**2**	**181**	**9.9**	**68**	**18**	**58**	**3**	**–5**	....	....	....	....	....	....	....	....
1991-92	**Toronto Maple Leafs**	**NHL**	**43**	**19**	**21**	**40**	**17**	**16**	**33**	**123**	**7**	**0**	**4**	**158**	**12.0**	**57**	**24**	**48**	**1**	**–14**	....	....	....	....	....	....	....	....
1992-93	**Toronto Maple Leafs**	**NHL**	**66**	**17**	**22**	**39**	**14**	**15**	**29**	**193**	**2**	**0**	**5**	**146**	**11.6**	**60**	**14**	**44**	**0**	**+2**	**21**	**10**	**10**	**20**	**51**	**2**	**0**	**1**
1993-94	**Toronto Maple Leafs**	**NHL**	**64**	**46**	**30**	**76**	**43**	**23**	**66**	**115**	**21**	**0**	**8**	**275**	**16.7**	**104**	**42**	**52**	**0**	**+10**	**18**	**9**	**7**	**16**	**24**	**2**	**0**	**1**
1994-95	**Quebec Nordiques**	**NHL**	**37**	**12**	**18**	**30**	**21**	**26**	**47**	**45**	**5**	**0**	**0**	**95**	**12.6**	**42**	**15**	**29**	**1**	**–1**	**6**	**1**	**2**	**3**	**6**	**0**	**0**	**0**
1995-96	**New York Islanders**	**NHL**	**58**	**24**	**19**	**43**	**24**	**15**	**39**	**60**	**6**	**0**	**2**	**192**	**12.5**	**72**	**29**	**57**	**2**	**–12**	....	....	....	....	....	....	....	....
	Toronto Maple Leafs	**NHL**	**13**	**8**	**7**	**15**	**8**	**6**	**14**	**16**	**2**	**0**	**1**	**45**	**17.8**	**27**	**12**	**8**	**0**	**+7**	**6**	**2**	**2**	**4**	**2**	**1**	**0**	**0**
1996-97	**Toronto Maple Leafs**	**NHL**	**65**	**30**	**19**	**49**	**32**	**17**	**49**	**75**	**6**	**0**	**6**	**212**	**14.2**	**66**	**16**	**52**	**0**	**–2**	....	....	....	....	....	....	....	....
1997-98	**Toronto Maple Leafs**	**NHL**	**47**	**12**	**7**	**19**	**14**	**7**	**21**	**80**	**4**	**0**	**3**	**140**	**8.6**	**31**	**13**	**39**	**0**	**–21**	....	....	....	....	....	....	....	....
	NHL Totals		**683**	**294**	**216**	**510**	**281**	**178**	**459**	**1619**	**90**	**0**	**39**	**2062**	**14.3**	**781**	**258**	**634**	**11**		**79**	**34**	**28**	**62**	**187**	**9**	**0**	**4**

WHL East First All-Star Team (1985) • NHL All-Rookie Team (1986)

Played in NHL All-Star Game (1986)

Traded to **Quebec** by **Toronto** with Sylvain Lefebvre, Landon Wilson and Toronto's 1st round choice (Jeffrey Kealty) in 1994 Entry Draft for Mats Sundin, Garth Butcher, Todd Warriner and Philadelphia's 1st round choice (previously acquired by Quebec — later traded to Washington — Washington selected Nolan Baumgartner) in 1994 Entry Draft, June 28, 1994. Transferred to **Colorado** after **Quebec** franchise relocated, June 21, 1995. Traded to **NY Islanders** by **Colorado** for Claude Lemieux, October 3, 1995. Traded to **Toronto** by **NY Islanders** with Mathieu Schneider and D.J. Smith for Darby Hendrickson, Sean Haggerty, Kenny Jonsson and Toronto's 1st round choice (Roberto Luongo) in 1997 Entry Draft, March 13, 1996. Signed as a free agent by **Tampa Bay**, July 16, 1998.

• CLARKE, BOBBY

Bobby Clarke C – R. 5'10", 185 lbs. b: Flin Flon, Man., 8/13/1949. Philadelphia's 2nd choice, 17th overall, in 1969 Amateur Draft. **HHOF**

Season	Club	League	GP	G	A	Pts	AG	AA	APts	PIM	PP	SH	GW	S	%	TGF	PGF	TGA	PGA	+/–	GP	G	A	Pts	PIM	PP	SH	GW
1966-67	Flin Flon Bombers	SJHL	4	4	3	7	....	....	....	0	....	....	....	....	....	....	....	....	....	....	....	....	....	....	....	....	....	....
1967-68	Flin Flon Bombers	WCJHL	59	51	*117	*168	....	....	....	148	....	....	....	....	....	....	....	....	....	....	15	4	10	14	2	....	....	....
1968-69	Flin Flon Bombers	WCJHL	58	51	*86	*137	....	....	....	123	....	....	....	....	....	....	....	....	....	....	18	9	*16	*25	....	....	....	....
1969-70	**Philadelphia Flyers**	**NHL**	**76**	**15**	**31**	**46**	**17**	**31**	**48**	**68**	**5**	**1**	**0**	**214**	**7.0**	**60**	**24**	**60**	**24**	**+1**	....	....	....	....	....	....	....	....
1970-71	**Philadelphia Flyers**	**NHL**	**77**	**27**	**36**	**63**	**28**	**32**	**60**	**78**	**10**	**1**	**5**	**185**	**14.6**	**78**	**20**	**70**	**21**	**+9**	**4**	**0**	**0**	**0**	**2**	**0**	**0**	**0**
1971-72	**Philadelphia Flyers**	**NHL**	**78**	**35**	**46**	**81**	**37**	**42**	**79**	**87**	**11**	**1**	**3**	**225**	**15.6**	**105**	**32**	**69**	**18**	**+22**	....	....	....	....	....	....	....	....
1972-73	Canada	Summit	8	2	4	6	....	....	....	18	....	....	....	....	....	....	....	....	....	....	....	....	....	....	....	....	....	....
	Philadelphia Flyers	**NHL**	**78**	**37**	**67**	**104**	**37**	**56**	**93**	**80**	**10**	**2**	**4**	**231**	**16.0**	**141**	**50**	**93**	**34**	**+32**	**11**	**2**	**6**	**8**	**6**	**2**	**0**	**1**
1973-74	**Philadelphia Flyers**	**NHL**	**77**	**35**	**52**	**87**	**36**	**45**	**81**	**113**	**10**	**5**	**5**	**221**	**15.8**	**108**	**37**	**63**	**27**	**+35**	**17**	**5**	**11**	**16**	**42**	**1**	**0**	**2**
1974-75	**Philadelphia Flyers**	**NHL**	**80**	**27**	***89**	**116**	**25**	**71**	**96**	**125**	**10**	**3**	**4**	**193**	**14.0**	**150**	**52**	**52**	**33**	**+79**	**17**	**4**	***12**	**16**	**16**	**2**	**1**	**2**
1975-76	**Philadelphia Flyers**	**NHL**	**76**	**30**	***89**	**119**	**28**	**70**	**98**	**136**	**10**	**4**	**2**	**194**	**15.5**	**164**	**59**	**52**	**30**	**+83**	**16**	**2**	***14**	**16**	**28**	**1**	**0**	**0**
1976-77	Canada	C Cup	6	1	2	3	....	....	....	0	....	....	....	....	....	....	....	....	....	....	....	....	....	....	....	....	....	....
	Philadelphia Flyers	**NHL**	**76**	**27**	**63**	**90**	**26**	**51**	**77**	**71**	**6**	**6**	**3**	**158**	**17.1**	**123**	**38**	**70**	**24**	**+39**	**10**	**5**	**5**	**10**	**8**	**2**	**0**	**0**
1977-78	**Philadelphia Flyers**	**NHL**	**71**	**21**	**68**	**89**	**20**	**56**	**76**	**83**	**5**	**2**	**1**	**131**	**16.0**	**115**	**35**	**51**	**18**	**+47**	**12**	**4**	**7**	**11**	**8**	**1**	**0**	**0**
1978-79	**Philadelphia Flyers**	**NHL**	**80**	**16**	**57**	**73**	**15**	**44**	**59**	**68**	**5**	**1**	**1**	**143**	**11.2**	**105**	**40**	**83**	**30**	**+12**	**8**	**2**	**4**	**6**	**8**	**1**	**0**	**0**
	NHL All-Stars	Chal Cup	3	0	1	1	....	....	....	0	....	....	....	....	....	....	....	....	....	....	....	....	....	....	....	....	....	....
1979-80	**Philadelphia Flyers**	**NHL**	**76**	**12**	**57**	**69**	**11**	**44**	**55**	**65**	**1**	**2**	**2**	**139**	**8.6**	**104**	**18**	**77**	**33**	**+42**	**19**	**8**	**12**	**20**	**16**	**3**	**0**	**2**
1980-81	**Philadelphia Flyers**	**NHL**	**80**	**19**	**46**	**65**	**16**	**32**	**48**	**140**	**5**	**1**	**2**	**150**	**12.7**	**102**	**40**	**73**	**28**	**+17**	**12**	**3**	**3**	**6**	**6**	**0**	**1**	**0**
1981-82	**Philadelphia Flyers**	**NHL**	**62**	**17**	**46**	**63**	**13**	**30**	**43**	**154**	**2**	**1**	**3**	**110**	**15.5**	**93**	**25**	**68**	**28**	**+28**	**4**	**4**	**2**	**6**	**4**	**1**	**1**	**0**
	Canada	WEC-A	9	0	1	1	....	....	....	6	....	....	....	....	....	....	....	....	....	....	....	....	....	....	....	....	....	....
1982-83	**Philadelphia Flyers**	**NHL**	**80**	**23**	**62**	**85**	**19**	**43**	**62**	**115**	**6**	**1**	**2**	**164**	**14.0**	**108**	**25**	**64**	**18**	**+37**	**3**	**1**	**0**	**1**	**2**	**0**	**0**	**0**
1983-84	**Philadelphia Flyers**	**NHL**	**73**	**17**	**43**	**60**	**14**	**29**	**43**	**70**	**3**	**1**	**1**	**129**	**13.2**	**83**	**18**	**68**	**26**	**+23**	**3**	**2**	**1**	**3**	**6**	**0**	**0**	**0**
	NHL Totals		**1144**	**358**	**852**	**1210**	**342**	**676**	**1018**	**1453**	**99**	**32**	**38**	**2587**	**13.8**	**1648**	**513**	**1021**	**392**		**136**	**42**	**77**	**119**	**152**	**14**	**3**	**7**

WCJHL All-Star Team (1968, 1969) • Won Bill Masterton Trophy (1972) • NHL Second All-Star Team (1973, 1974) • Won Lester B. Pearson Award (1973) • Won Hart Trophy (1973, 1975, 1976) • NHL First All-Star Team (1975, 1976) • NHL Plus/Minus Leader (1976) • Won Lester Patrick Trophy (1980) • Won Frank J. Selke Trophy (1983)

Played in NHL All-Star Game (1970, 1971, 1972, 1973, 1974, 1975, 1977, 1978)

• CLEARY, DANIEL

Daniel Cleary LW – L. 6', 203 lbs. b: Carbonear, Nfld., 12/18/1978. Chicago's 1st choice, 13th overall, in 1997 Entry Draft.

Season	Club	League	GP	G	A	Pts	AG	AA	APts	PIM	PP	SH	GW	S	%	TGF	PGF	TGA	PGA	+/–	GP	G	A	Pts	PIM	PP	SH	GW
1994-95	Belleville Bulls	OHL	62	26	55	81	....	....	....	62	....	....	....	....	....	....	....	....	....	....	16	7	10	17	23	....	....	....
1995-96	Belleville Bulls	OHL	64	53	62	115	....	....	....	74	....	....	....	....	....	....	....	....	....	....	14	10	17	27	40	....	....	....
1996-97	Belleville Bulls	OHL	64	32	48	80	....	....	....	88	....	....	....	....	....	....	....	....	....	....	6	3	4	7	6	....	....	....
1997-98	Belleville Bulls	OHL	30	16	31	47	....	....	....	14	....	....	....	....	....	....	....	....	....	....	10	6	17	23	10	....	....	....
	Chicago Blackhawks	**NHL**	**6**	**0**	**0**	**0**	**0**	**0**	**0**	**0**	**0**	**0**	**0**	**4**	**0.0**	**0**	**0**	**2**	**0**	**–2**	....	....	....	....	....	....	....	....
	Indianapolis Ice	IHL	4	2	1	3	....	....	....	6	....	....	....	....	....	....	....	....	....	....	....	....	....	....	....	....	....	....
	NHL Totals		**6**	**0**	**0**	**0**	**0**	**0**	**0**	**0**	**0**	**0**	**0**	**4**	**0.0**	**0**	**0**	**2**	**0**		....	....	....	....	....	....	....	....

OHL First All-Star Team (1996, 1997)

• CLEMENT, BILL

Bill Clement C – L. 6'1", 194 lbs. b: Thurso, Que., 12/20/1950. Philadelphia's 1st choice, 18th overall, in 1970 Amateur Draft.

Season	Club	League	GP	G	A	Pts	AG	AA	APts	PIM	PP	SH	GW	S	%	TGF	PGF	TGA	PGA	+/–	GP	G	A	Pts	PIM	PP	SH	GW
1967-68	Ottawa 67's	OHA	36	6	19	25	....	....	....	41	....	....	....	....	....	....	....	....	....	....	....	....	....	....	....	....	....	....
1968-69	Ottawa 67's	OHA	53	18	28	46	....	....	....	101	....	....	....	....	....	....	....	....	....	....	7	1	4	5	6	....	....	....
1969-70	Ottawa 67's	OHA	54	19	36	55	....	....	....	62	....	....	....	....	....	....	....	....	....	....	....	....	....	....	....	....	....	....
1970-71	Quebec Aces	AHL	69	19	39	58	....	....	....	88	....	....	....	....	....	....	....	....	....	....	1	0	0	0	0	....	....	....
1971-72	**Philadelphia Flyers**	**NHL**	**49**	**9**	**14**	**23**	**10**	**13**	**23**	**39**	**0**	**0**	**1**	**94**	**9.6**	**30**	**4**	**50**	**10**	**–14**	....	....	....	....	....	....	....	....
	Richmond Robins	AHL	26	8	9	17	....	....	....	20	....	....	....	....	....	....	....	....	....	....	....	....	....	....	....	....	....	....
1972-73	**Philadelphia Flyers**	**NHL**	**73**	**14**	**14**	**28**	**14**	**12**	**26**	**51**	**0**	**1**	**3**	**132**	**10.6**	**38**	**0**	**57**	**8**	**–11**	**2**	**0**	**0**	**0**	**0**	**0**	**0**	**0**
1973-74	**Philadelphia Flyers**	**NHL**	**39**	**9**	**8**	**17**	**9**	**7**	**16**	**34**	**0**	**2**	**2**	**54**	**16.7**	**24**	**1**	**12**	**4**	**+15**	**4**	**1**	**0**	**1**	**4**	**0**	**0**	**0**
1974-75	**Philadelphia Flyers**	**NHL**	**68**	**21**	**16**	**37**	**19**	**13**	**32**	**42**	**1**	**0**	**2**	**140**	**15.0**	**44**	**4**	**31**	**12**	**+21**	**12**	**1**	**0**	**1**	**8**	**0**	**0**	**0**
1975-76	**Washington Capitals**	**NHL**	**46**	**10**	**17**	**27**	**9**	**13**	**22**	**20**	**2**	**0**	**0**	**95**	**10.5**	**44**	**12**	**74**	**12**	**–30**	....	....	....	....	....	....	....	....
	Atlanta Flames	**NHL**	**31**	**13**	**14**	**27**	**12**	**11**	**23**	**29**	**2**	**1**	**3**	**71**	**18.3**	**39**	**5**	**36**	**5**	**+3**	**2**	**0**	**1**	**1**	**0**	**0**	**0**	**0**
1976-77	**Atlanta Flames**	**NHL**	**67**	**17**	**26**	**43**	**16**	**21**	**37**	**27**	**2**	**5**	**1**	**114**	**14.9**	**61**	**9**	**77**	**21**	**–4**	**3**	**1**	**1**	**2**	**0**	**0**	**1**	**0**
1977-78	**Atlanta Flames**	**NHL**	**70**	**20**	**30**	**50**	**19**	**24**	**43**	**34**	**1**	**3**	**4**	**105**	**19.0**	**70**	**12**	**74**	**34**	**+18**	**2**	**0**	**0**	**0**	**2**	**0**	**0**	**0**
1978-79	**Atlanta Flames**	**NHL**	**65**	**12**	**23**	**35**	**11**	**18**	**29**	**14**	**0**	**0**	**1**	**86**	**14.0**	**47**	**5**	**84**	**37**	**–5**	**2**	**0**	**0**	**0**	**0**	**0**	**0**	**0**
1979-80	**Atlanta Flames**	**NHL**	**64**	**7**	**14**	**21**	**6**	**11**	**17**	**32**	**0**	**2**	**2**	**51**	**13.7**	**20**	**1**	**53**	**29**	**+3**	**4**	**0**	**0**	**0**	**4**	**0**	**0**	**0**
1980-81	**Calgary Flames**	**NHL**	**78**	**12**	**20**	**32**	**10**	**14**	**24**	**33**	**1**	**2**	**2**	**94**	**12.8**	**41**	**3**	**104**	**50**	**–16**	**16**	**2**	**1**	**3**	**6**	**0**	**0**	**0**
1981-82	**Calgary Flames**	**NHL**	**69**	**4**	**12**	**16**	**3**	**8**	**11**	**28**	**0**	**0**	**0**	**56**	**7.1**	**25**	**0**	**59**	**32**	**–2**	**3**	**0**	**0**	**0**	**2**	**0**	**0**	**0**
	NHL Totals		**719**	**148**	**208**	**356**	**138**	**165**	**303**	**383**	**9**	**16**	**21**	**1092**	**13.6**	**491**	**56**	**711**	**254**		**50**	**5**	**3**	**8**	**26**	**0**	**1**	**0**

Played in NHL All-Star Game (1976, 1978)

Traded to **Washington** by **Philadelphia** with Don MacLean and Washington's 1st round choice (Alex Forsythe) in 1975 Amateur Draft for Washington's 1st round choice (Mel Bridgman) in 1975 Amateur Draft, June 4, 1975. Traded to **Atlanta** by **Washington** for Gerry Meehan, Jean Lemieux and Buffalo's 1st round choice (acquired previously, Atlanta selected Gregg Carroll), January 22, 1976. Transferred to **Calgary** after **Atlanta** franchise relocated, June 24, 1980.

• CLIPPINGDALE, STEVE

Steve Clippingdale LW – L. 6'2", 195 lbs. b: Vancouver, B.C., 4/29/1956. Los Angeles' 1st choice, 21st overall, in 1976 Amateur Draft.

Season	Club	League	GP	G	A	Pts	AG	AA	APts	PIM	PP	SH	GW	S	%	TGF	PGF	TGA	PGA	+/–	Playoffs GP	G	A	Pts	PIM	PP	SH	GW
1973-74	University of Wisconsin	WCHA	4	1	3	4	....	....	....	0	....	....	....	....	....	....	....	....	....	....	....	....	....	....	....	....	....	....
1974-75	New Westminster Bruins	WCJHL	62	26	19	45	....	....	....	27	....	....	....	....	....	....	....	....	....	....	17	4	1	5	11	....	....	....
1975-76	New Westminster Bruins	WCJHL	72	51	66	117	....	....	....	80	....	....	....	....	....	....	....	....	....	....	17	15	14	29	12	....	....	....
1976-77	**Los Angeles Kings**	**NHL**	**16**	**1**	**2**	**3**	**1**	**2**	**3**	**9**	**0**	**0**	**0**	**11**	**9.1**	**5**	**0**	**2**	**0**	**+3**	**1**	**0**	**0**	**0**	**0**	**0**	**0**	**0**
	Fort Worth Texans	CHL	54	24	17	41	....	....	....	49	....	....	....	....	....	....	....	....	....	....	....	....	....	....	....	....	....	....
1977-78	Springfield Indians	AHL	74	33	21	54	....	....	....	59	....	....	....	....	....	....	....	....	....	....	4	1	2	3	5	....	....	....
1978-79	Dallas Black Hawks	CHL	64	27	38	65	....	....	....	99	....	....	....	....	....	....	....	....	....	....	1	0	0	0	0	....	....	....
1979-80	**Washington Capitals**	**NHL**	**3**	**0**	**0**	**0**	**0**	**0**	**0**	**0**	**0**	**0**	**0**	**1**	**0.0**	**0**	**0**	**0**	**0**	**0**	....	....	....	....	....	....	....	....
	Hershey Bears	AHL	47	19	14	33	....	....	....	47	....	....	....	....	....	....	....	....	....	....	5	2	0	2	4	....	....	....
	NHL Totals		**19**	**1**	**2**	**3**	**1**	**2**	**3**	**9**	**0**	**0**	**0**	**12**	**8.3**	**5**	**0**	**2**	**0**		**1**	**0**	**0**	**0**	**0**	**0**	**0**	**0**

Traded to **Washington** by **LA Kings** for Mike Marson, June 11, 1979

• CLOUTIER, REAL

Real "Buddy" Cloutier RW – L. 5'10", 185 lbs. b: St. Emile, Que., 7/30/1956. Chicago's 1st choice, 9th overall, in 1976 Amateur Draft.

Season	Club	League	GP	G	A	Pts	AG	AA	APts	PIM	PP	SH	GW	S	%	TGF	PGF	TGA	PGA	+/–	Playoffs GP	G	A	Pts	PIM	PP	SH	GW
1972-73	Quebec Remparts	QMJHL	57	39	60	99	....	....	....	15	....	....	....	....	....	....	....	....	....	....	15	8	13	21	14	....	....	....
1973-74	Quebec Remparts	QMJHL	69	93	123	216	....	....	....	40	....	....	....	....	....	....	....	....	....	....	16	26	24	50	28	....	....	....
1974-75	Quebec Nordiques	WHA	63	26	27	53	....	....	....	36	....	....	....	....	....	....	....	....	....	....	12	4	3	7	2	....	....	....
1975-76	Quebec Nordiques	WHA	80	60	54	114	....	....	....	27	....	....	....	....	....	....	....	....	....	....	5	4	5	9	0	....	....	....
1976-77	Quebec Nordiques	WHA	76	66	75	*141	....	....	....	39	....	....	....	....	....	....	....	....	....	....	17	*14	13	27	10	....	....	....
1977-78	Quebec Nordiques	WHA	73	56	73	129	....	....	....	19	....	....	....	....	....	....	....	....	....	....	10	9	7	16	15	....	....	....
1978-79	Quebec Nordiques	WHA	77	*75	54	*129	....	....	....	48	....	....	....	....	....	....	....	....	....	....	4	2	2	4	4	....	....	....
1979-80	**Quebec Nordiques**	**NHL**	**67**	**42**	**47**	**89**	**38**	**36**	**74**	**12**	**13**	**0**	**3**	**254**	**16.5**	**124**	**49**	**82**	**1**	**–6**	....	....	....	....	....	....	....	....
1980-81	**Quebec Nordiques**	**NHL**	**34**	**15**	**16**	**31**	**12**	**11**	**23**	**18**	**2**	**0**	**2**	**89**	**16.9**	**45**	**21**	**23**	**1**	**+2**	**3**	**0**	**0**	**0**	**10**	**0**	**0**	**0**
1981-82	**Quebec Nordiques**	**NHL**	**67**	**37**	**60**	**97**	**29**	**40**	**69**	**34**	**8**	**0**	**5**	**214**	**17.3**	**130**	**50**	**55**	**1**	**+26**	**16**	**7**	**5**	**12**	**10**	**1**	**0**	**1**
1982-83	**Quebec Nordiques**	**NHL**	**68**	**28**	**39**	**67**	**23**	**27**	**50**	**30**	**5**	**0**	**3**	**185**	**15.1**	**94**	**32**	**66**	**0**	**–4**	**4**	**0**	**0**	**0**	**0**	**0**	**0**	**0**
1983-84	**Buffalo Sabres**	**NHL**	**77**	**24**	**36**	**60**	**19**	**24**	**43**	**25**	**9**	**0**	**6**	**169**	**14.2**	**96**	**41**	**56**	**0**	**–1**	**2**	**0**	**0**	**0**	**0**	**0**	**0**	**0**
1984-85	**Buffalo Sabres**	**NHL**	**4**	**0**	**0**	**0**	**0**	**0**	**0**	**0**	**0**	**0**	**0**	**6**	**0.0**	**0**	**0**	**2**	**0**	**–2**	....	....	....	....	....	....	....	....
	Flint Generals	IHL	40	11	25	36	....	....	....	6	....	....	....	....	....	....	....	....	....	....	....	....	....	....	....	....	....	....
	Rochester Americans	AHL	12	4	3	7	....	....	....	0	....	....	....	....	....	....	....	....	....	....	....	....	....	....	....	....	....	....
	NHL Totals		**317**	**146**	**198**	**344**	**121**	**138**	**259**	**119**	**37**	**0**	**19**	**917**	**15.9**	**489**	**193**	**284**	**3**		**25**	**7**	**5**	**12**	**20**	**1**	**0**	**1**
	Other Major League Totals		369	283	283	566	....	....	....	169	....	....	....	....	....	....	....	....	....	....	48	33	30	63	31	....	....	....

QMJHL Second All-Star Team (1974) • WHA Second All-Star Team (1976, 1977, 1978) • Won W. D. (Bill) Hunter Trophy (WHA Scoring Leader) (1977, 1979) • WHA First All-Star Team (1979)
Played in NHL All-Star Game (1980)

Selected by **Quebec** (WHA) in 1974 WHA Amateur Draft, June, 1974. Rights retained by **Quebec** prior to Expansion Draft, June 9, 1979. Traded to **Buffalo** by **Quebec** with Quebec's 1st round choice (Adam Creighton) in 1983 Entry Draft for Tony McKegney, Andre Savard, Jean Sauve and Buffalo's 3rd round choice (Liro Jarvi) in 1983 Entry Draft, June 8, 1983.

• CLOUTIER, REJEAN

Rejean Cloutier D – L. 6', 185 lbs. b: Windsor, Que., 2/15/1960.

Season	Club	League	GP	G	A	Pts	AG	AA	APts	PIM	PP	SH	GW	S	%	TGF	PGF	TGA	PGA	+/–	Playoffs GP	G	A	Pts	PIM	PP	SH	GW
1977-78	Sherbrooke Castors	QMJHL	23	8	11	19	....	....	....	59	....	....	....	....	....	....	....	....	....	....	....	....	....	....	....	....	....	....
1978-79	Sherbrooke Castors	QMJHL	70	6	31	37	....	....	....	93	....	....	....	....	....	....	....	....	....	....	12	2	11	13	13	....	....	....
1979-80	Sherbrooke Castors	QMJHL	65	11	57	68	....	....	....	163	....	....	....	....	....	....	....	....	....	....	15	3	11	14	44	....	....	....
	Detroit Red Wings	**NHL**	**3**	**0**	**1**	**1**	**0**	**1**	**1**	**0**	**0**	**0**	**0**	**1**	**0.0**	**3**	**0**	**1**	**0**	**+2**	....	....	....	....	....	....	....	....
1980-81	Adirondack Red Wings	AHL	76	7	30	37	....	....	....	193	....	....	....	....	....	....	....	....	....	....	15	1	2	3	27	....	....	....
1981-82	**Detroit Red Wings**	**NHL**	**2**	**0**	**1**	**1**	**0**	**1**	**1**	**2**	....	....	....	....	....	....	....	....	....	....	....	....	....	....	....	....	....	....
	Adirondack Red Wings	AHL	64	11	27	38	....	....	....	140	....	....	....	....	....	....	....	....	....	....	5	0	2	2	6	....	....	....
1982-83	Adirondack Red Wings	AHL	80	13	44	57	....	....	....	137	....	....	....	....	....	....	....	....	....	....	6	2	3	5	15	....	....	....
1983-84	Adirondack Red Wings	AHL	77	9	30	39	....	....	....	208	....	....	....	....	....	....	....	....	....	....	7	2	4	6	9	....	....	....
1984-85	Adirondack Red Wings	AHL	3	0	0	0	....	....	....	2	....	....	....	....	....	....	....	....	....	....	....	....	....	....	....	....	....	....
	Nova Scotia Voyageurs	AHL	72	8	19	27	....	....	....	152	....	....	....	....	....	....	....	....	....	....	6	1	1	2	14	....	....	....
1985-86	Sherbrooke Canadiens	AHL	67	7	23	30	....	....	....	142	....	....	....	....	....	....	....	....	....	....	....	....	....	....	....	....	....	....
	Saginaw Generals	IHL	2	0	0	0	....	....	....	4	....	....	....	....	....	....	....	....	....	....	....	....	....	....	....	....	....	....
1986-87	Sherbrooke Canadiens	AHL	76	7	37	44	....	....	....	182	....	....	....	....	....	....	....	....	....	....	17	3	9	12	59	....	....	....
1988-89	HC Grenoble	France	40	10	16	26	....	....	....	114	....	....	....	....	....	....	....	....	....	....	....	....	....	....	....	....	....	....
	NHL Totals		**5**	**0**	**2**	**2**	**0**	**2**	**2**	**2**	**0**	**0**	**0**	**1**	**0.0**	**3**	**0**	**1**	**0**		....	....	....	....	....	....	....	....

AHL Second All-Star Team (1983)

Signed as a free agent by **Detroit**, October 30, 1979. Traded to **Edmonton** by **Detroit** for Todd Bidner, October 17, 1986.

• CLOUTIER, ROLAND

Roland Cloutier C – L. 5'8", 157 lbs. b: Rouyn, Que., 10/6/1957. Detroit's 13th choice, 178th overall, in 1977 Amateur Draft.

Season	Club	League	GP	G	A	Pts	AG	AA	APts	PIM	PP	SH	GW	S	%	TGF	PGF	TGA	PGA	+/–	Playoffs GP	G	A	Pts	PIM	PP	SH	GW
1975-76	Trois-Rivieres Draveurs	QMJHL	67	21	34	55	....	....	....	18	....	....	....	....	....	....	....	....	....	....	....	....	....	....	....	....	....	....
1976-77	Trois-Rivieres Draveurs	QMJHL	72	63	68	131	....	....	....	43	....	....	....	....	....	....	....	....	....	....	....	....	....	....	....	....	....	....
1977-78	**Detroit Red Wings**	**NHL**	**1**	**0**	**0**	**0**	**0**	**0**	**0**	**0**	**0**	**0**	**0**	**1**	**0.0**	**0**	**0**	**2**	**0**	**–2**	....	....	....	....	....	....	....	....
	Kansas City Red Wings	CHL	70	18	38	56	....	....	....	13	....	....	....	....	....	....	....	....	....	....	....	....	....	....	....	....	....	....
1978-79	**Detroit Red Wings**	**NHL**	**19**	**6**	**6**	**12**	**5**	**5**	**10**	**2**	**1**	**0**	**1**	**40**	**15.0**	**16**	**5**	**11**	**0**	**0**	....	....	....	....	....	....	....	....
	Kansas City Red Wings	CHL	59	32	29	61	....	....	....	21	....	....	....	....	....	....	....	....	....	....	4	0	0	0	12	....	....	....
1979-80	**Quebec Nordiques**	**NHL**	**14**	**2**	**3**	**5**	**2**	**2**	**4**	**0**	**0**	**0**	**0**	**19**	**10.5**	**10**	**0**	**10**	**1**	**+1**	....	....	....	....	....	....	....	....
	Syracuse Firebirds	AHL	64	19	37	56	....	....	....	16	....	....	....	....	....	....	....	....	....	....	4	1	2	3	7	....	....	....
1980-81	Nova Scotia Voyageurs	AHL	60	18	21	39	....	....	....	41	....	....	....	....	....	....	....	....	....	....	6	1	1	2	0	....	....	....
1981-82	ASG Tours	France	30	27	*28	*55	....	....	....	....	....	....	....	....	....	....	....	....	....	....	....	....	....	....	....	....	....	....
1982-83	ASG Tours	France	32	32	28	60	....	....	....	....	....	....	....	....	....	....	....	....	....	....	....	....	....	....	....	....	....	....
1983-84	HC Gap	France	32	47	33	80	....	....	....	....	....	....	....	....	....	....	....	....	....	....	....	....	....	....	....	....	....	....
1984-85	HC Gap	France	31	37	31	68	....	....	....	....	....	....	....	....	....	....	....	....	....	....	....	....	....	....	....	....	....	....
1985-86	HC Gap	France	32	41	28	69	....	....	....	....	....	....	....	....	....	....	....	....	....	....	....	....	....	....	....	....	....	....
1986-87	HC Gap	France	33	57	30	87	....	....	....	....	....	....	....	....	....	....	....	....	....	....	....	....	....	....	....	....	....	....
1987-88	HC Gap	France	33	25	18	43	....	....	....	19	....	....	....	....	....	....	....	....	....	....	....	....	....	....	....	....	....	....
	NHL Totals		**34**	**8**	**9**	**17**	**7**	**7**	**14**	**2**	**1**	**0**	**1**	**60**	**13.3**	**26**	**5**	**23**	**1**		....	....	....	....	....	....	....	....

Claimed by **Quebec** from **Detroit** in Expansion Draft, June 13, 1979.

• COALTER, GARY

Gary Coalter RW – R. 5'10", 185 lbs. b: Toronto, Ont., 7/8/1950. NY Rangers' 5th choice, 67th overall, in 1970 Amateur Draft.

Season	Club	League	GP	G	A	Pts	AG	AA	APts	PIM	PP	SH	GW	S	%	TGF	PGF	TGA	PGA	+/–	Playoffs GP	G	A	Pts	PIM	PP	SH	GW
1967-68	Hamilton Red Wings	OHA	53	8	13	21	....	....	....	57	....	....	....	....	....	....	....	....	....	....	11	1	3	4	7	....	....	....
1968-69	Hamilton Red Wings	OHA	52	18	23	41	....	....	....	144	....	....	....	....	....	....	....	....	....	....	5	0	1	1	6	....	....	....
1969-70	Hamilton Red Wings	OHA	54	22	26	48	....	....	....	79	....	....	....	....	....	....	....	....	....	....	....	....	....	....	....	....	....	....
1970-71	Omaha Knights	CHL	68	15	24	39	....	....	....	88	....	....	....	....	....	....	....	....	....	....	11	4	3	7	29	....	....	....
1971-72	Omaha Knights	CHL	72	15	31	46	....	....	....	105	....	....	....	....	....	....	....	....	....	....	....	....	....	....	....	....	....	....
1972-73	Providence Reds	AHL	45	10	13	23	....	....	....	67	....	....	....	....	....	....	....	....	....	....	....	....	....	....	....	....	....	....
	Omaha Knights	CHL	25	5	8	13	....	....	....	30	....	....	....	....	....	....	....	....	....	....	11	4	3	7	8	....	....	....
1973-74	**California Golden Seals**	**NHL**	**4**	**0**	**0**	**0**	**0**	**0**	**0**	**0**	**0**	**0**	**0**	**6**	**0.0**	**0**	**0**	**4**	**0**	**–4**	....	....	....	....	....	....	....	....
	Salt Lake Golden Eagles	WHL	71	38	31	69	....	....	....	45	....	....	....	....	....	....	....	....	....	....	5	0	0	0	11	....	....	....
1974-75	**Kansas City Scouts**	**NHL**	**30**	**2**	**4**	**6**	**2**	**3**	**5**	**2**	**0**	**0**	**1**	**20**	**10.0**	**8**	**1**	**15**	**0**	**–8**	....	....	....	....	....	....	....	....
	Baltimore Clippers	AHL	22	8	4	12	....	....	....	28	....	....	....	....	....	....	....	....	....	....	....	....	....	....	....	....	....	....
1975-76	Springfield Indians	AHL	55	15	17	32	....	....	....	47	....	....	....	....	....	....	....	....	....	....	....	....	....	....	....	....	....	....
1976-77	Maine Nordiques	NAHL	74	31	54	85	....	....	....	71	....	....	....	....	....	....	....	....	....	....	12	3	7	10	0	....	....	....
1977-78	Philadelphia Firebirds	AHL	73	25	34	59	....	....	....	22	....	....	....	....	....	....	....	....	....	....	4	1	1	2	0	....	....	....
1978-79	Philadelphia Firebirds	AHL	63	16	10	26	....	....	....	30	....	....	....	....	....	....	....	....	....	....	....	....	....	....	....	....	....	....
	NHL Totals		**34**	**2**	**4**	**6**	**2**	**3**	**5**	**2**	**0**	**0**	**1**	**26**	**7.7**	**8**	**1**	**19**	**0**		....	....	....	....	....	....	....	....

Traded to **California** by **NY Rangers** for cash, May 11, 1973. Claimed by **Kansas City** from **California** in Expansion Draft, June 12, 1974.

			REGULAR SEASON																		PLAYOFFS							
Season	**Club**	**League**	**GP**	**G**	**A**	**Pts**	**AG**	**AA**	**APts**	**PIM**	**PP**	**SH**	**GW**	**S**	**%**	**TGF**	**PGF**	**TGA**	**PGA**	**+/–**	**GP**	**G**	**A**	**Pts**	**PIM**	**PP**	**SH**	**GW**

• COATES, STEVE

Steve Coates RW – R. 5'9", 172 lbs. b: Toronto, Ont., 7/2/1950.

Season	Club	League	GP	G	A	Pts	AG	AA	APts	PIM	PP	SH	GW	S	%	TGF	PGF	TGA	PGA	+/–	GP	G	A	Pts	PIM	PP	SH	GW
1969-70	Michigan Tech Huskies	WCHA	3	0	0	0	....	....	....	4	....	....	....	....	....	....	....	....	....	....	....	....	....	....	....	....	....	....
1970-71	Michigan Tech Huskies	WCHA	33	7	9	16	....	....	....	46	....	....	....	....	....	....	....	....	....	....	....	....	....	....	....	....	....	....
1971-72	Michigan Tech Huskies	WCHA	30	7	9	16	....	....	....	36	....	....	....	....	....	....	....	....	....	....	....	....	....	....	....	....	....	....
1972-73	Michigan Tech Huskies	WCHA	34	11	11	22	....	....	....	28	....	....	....	....	....	....	....	....	....	....	....	....	....	....	....	....	....	....
	Calumet Cooper Islanders	USHL	4	5	6	11	....	....	....	7	....	....	....	....	....	....	....	....	....	....	....	....	....	....	....	....	....	....
1973-74	Des Moines Capitols	IHL	72	31	39	70	....	....	....	167	....	....	....	....	....	....	....	....	....	....	10	6	3	9	35	....	....	....
1974-75	Richmond Robins	AHL	50	7	7	14	....	....	....	168	....	....	....	....	....	....	....	....	....	....	7	3	0	3	7	....	....	....
1975-76	Richmond Robins	AHL	69	25	19	44	....	....	....	141	....	....	....	....	....	....	....	....	....	....	....	....	....	....	....	....	....	....
1976-77	**Detroit Red Wings**	**NHL**	**5**	**1**	**0**	**1**	**1**	**0**	**1**	**24**	**0**	**0**	**0**	**5**	**20.0**	**1**	**0**	**2**	**0**	**–1**	....	....	....	....	....	....	....	....
	Springfield Indians	AHL	57	17	23	40	....	....	....	122	....	....	....	....	....	....	....	....	....	....	....	....	....	....	....	....	....	....
1977-78	Kansas City Red Wings	CHL	63	14	20	34	....	....	....	83	....	....	....	....	....	....	....	....	....	....	....	....	....	....	....	....	....	....
	Maine Mariners	AHL	15	3	2	5	....	....	....	11	....	....	....	....	....	....	....	....	....	....	6	0	2	2	8	....	....	....
1978-79	Philadelphia Firebirds	AHL	74	15	25	40	....	....	....	107	....	....	....	....	....	....	....	....	....	....	....	....	....	....	....	....	....	....
1979-80	Syracuse Firebirds	AHL	67	10	23	33	....	....	....	95	....	....	....	....	....	....	....	....	....	....	....	....	....	....	....	....	....	....
	NHL Totals		**5**	**1**	**0**	**1**	**1**	**0**	**1**	**24**	**0**	**0**	**0**	**5**	**20.0**	**1**	**0**	**2**	**0**		....	....	....	....	....	....	....	....

Signed as a free agent by **Philadelphia**, June, 1973. Traded to **Detroit** by **Philadelphia** with Terry Murray, Bob Ritchie and Dave Kelly for Rick Lapointe and Mike Korney, February 17, 1977.

• COCHRANE, GLEN

Glen Cochrane D – L. 6'2", 205 lbs. b: Cranbrook, B.C., 1/29/1958. Philadelphia's 6th choice, 50th overall, in 1978 Amateur Draft.

Season	Club	League	GP	G	A	Pts	AG	AA	APts	PIM	PP	SH	GW	S	%	TGF	PGF	TGA	PGA	+/–	GP	G	A	Pts	PIM	PP	SH	GW
1974-75	La Pass Red Devils	AJHL	16	1	4	5	....	....	....	61	....	....	....	....	....	....	....	....	....	....	....	....	....	....	....	....	....	....
1975-76	La Pass Red Devils	AJHL	60	17	42	59	....	....	....	210	....	....	....	....	....	....	....	....	....	....	....	....	....	....	....	....	....	....
	Calgary Centennials	WCJHL	3	0	0	0	....	....	....	0	....	....	....	....	....	....	....	....	....	....	....	....	....	....	....	....	....	....
1976-77	Calgary Centennials	WCJHL	35	1	5	6	....	....	....	105	....	....	....	....	....	....	....	....	....	....	....	....	....	....	....	....	....	....
	Victoria Cougars	WCJHL	36	1	7	8	....	....	....	60	....	....	....	....	....	....	....	....	....	....	4	0	0	0	31	....	....	....
1977-78	Victoria Cougars	WCJHL	72	7	40	47	....	....	....	311	....	....	....	....	....	....	....	....	....	....	13	1	5	6	51	....	....	....
1978-79	**Philadelphia Flyers**	**NHL**	**1**	**0**	**0**	**0**	**0**	**0**	**0**	**0**	**0**	**0**	**0**	**0**	**0.0**	**0**	**0**	**2**	**0**	**–2**	....	....	....	....	....	....	....	....
	Maine Mariners	AHL	76	1	22	23	....	....	....	320	....	....	....	....	....	....	....	....	....	....	10	3	4	7	24	....	....	....
1979-80	Maine Mariners	AHL	77	1	11	12	....	....	....	269	....	....	....	....	....	....	....	....	....	....	8	2	0	2	83	....	....	....
1980-81	**Philadelphia Flyers**	**NHL**	**31**	**1**	**8**	**9**	**1**	**6**	**7**	**219**	**0**	**0**	**1**	**25**	**4.0**	**25**	**2**	**26**	**6**	**+3**	**6**	**1**	**1**	**2**	**18**	**0**	**0**	**0**
	Maine Mariners	AHL	38	4	13	17	....	....	....	201	....	....	....	....	....	....	....	....	....	....	....	....	....	....	....	....	....	....
1981-82	**Philadelphia Flyers**	**NHL**	**63**	**6**	**12**	**18**	**5**	**8**	**13**	**329**	**0**	**1**	**0**	**67**	**9.0**	**68**	**1**	**63**	**15**	**+19**	**2**	**0**	**0**	**0**	**2**	**0**	**0**	**0**
1982-83	**Philadelphia Flyers**	**NHL**	**77**	**2**	**22**	**24**	**2**	**15**	**17**	**237**	**0**	**0**	**1**	**94**	**2.1**	**99**	**1**	**63**	**7**	**+42**	**3**	**0**	**0**	**0**	**4**	**0**	**0**	**0**
1983-84	**Philadelphia Flyers**	**NHL**	**67**	**7**	**16**	**23**	**6**	**11**	**17**	**225**	**0**	**0**	**3**	**69**	**10.1**	**65**	**1**	**58**	**10**	**+16**	....	....	....	....	....	....	....	....
1984-85	**Philadelphia Flyers**	**NHL**	**18**	**0**	**3**	**3**	**0**	**2**	**2**	**100**	**0**	**0**	**0**	**7**	**0.0**	**3**	**0**	**8**	**1**	**–4**	....	....	....	....	....	....	....	....
	Hershey Bears	AHL	9	0	8	8	....	....	....	35	....	....	....	....	....	....	....	....	....	....	....	....	....	....	....	....	....	....
1985-86	**Vancouver Canucks**	**NHL**	**49**	**0**	**3**	**3**	**0**	**2**	**2**	**125**	**0**	**0**	**0**	**24**	**0.0**	**15**	**0**	**28**	**8**	**–5**	**2**	**0**	**0**	**0**	**5**	**0**	**0**	**0**
1986-87	**Vancouver Canucks**	**NHL**	**14**	**0**	**0**	**0**	**0**	**0**	**0**	**52**	**0**	**0**	**0**	**2**	**0.0**	**3**	**0**	**3**	**0**	**0**	....	....	....	....	....	....	....	....
1987-88	**Chicago Blackhawks**	**NHL**	**73**	**1**	**8**	**9**	**1**	**6**	**7**	**204**	**0**	**0**	**0**	**21**	**4.8**	**20**	**0**	**29**	**2**	**–7**	**5**	**0**	**0**	**0**	**2**	**0**	**0**	**0**
1988-89	**Chicago Blackhawks**	**NHL**	**6**	**0**	**0**	**0**	**0**	**0**	**0**	**13**	**0**	**0**	**0**	**1**	**0.0**	**0**	**0**	**4**	**3**	**–1**	....	....	....	....	....	....	....	....
	Edmonton Oilers	**NHL**	**12**	**0**	**0**	**0**	**0**	**0**	**0**	**52**	**0**	**0**	**0**	**3**	**0.0**	**2**	**1**	**3**	**0**	**–2**	....	....	....	....	....	....	....	....
	NHL Totals		**411**	**17**	**72**	**89**	**15**	**50**	**65**	**1550**	**0**	**1**	**5**	**313**	**5.4**	**300**	**8**	**287**	**52**		**18**	**1**	**1**	**2**	**31**	**0**	**0**	**0**

Traded to **Vancouver** by **Philadelphia** for Vancouver's 2nd round choice (Kent Hawley) in 1986 Entry Draft, March 12, 1985. Claimed by **Chicago** from **Vancouver** in Waiver Draft, October 5, 1987. Claimed on waivers by **Edmonton** from **Chicago**, November 7, 1988.

• COFFEY, PAUL

Paul Coffey D – L. 6', 190 lbs. b: Weston, Ont., 6/1/1961. Edmonton's 1st choice, 6th overall, in 1980 1980 Draft.

Season	Club	League	GP	G	A	Pts	AG	AA	APts	PIM	PP	SH	GW	S	%	TGF	PGF	TGA	PGA	+/–	GP	G	A	Pts	PIM	PP	SH	GW
1978-79	Sault Ste. Marie Greyhounds	OHA	68	17	72	89	....	....	....	103	....	....	....	....	....	....	....	....	....	....	....	....	....	....	....	....	....	....
1979-80	Sault Ste. Marie Greyhounds	OHA	23	10	21	31	....	....	....	63	....	....	....	....	....	....	....	....	....	....	....	....	....	....	....	....	....	....
	Kitchener Rangers	OHA	52	19	52	71	....	....	....	130	....	....	....	....	....	....	....	....	....	....	....	....	....	....	....	....	....	....
1980-81	**Edmonton Oilers**	**NHL**	**74**	**9**	**23**	**32**	**7**	**16**	**23**	**130**	**2**	**0**	**0**	**113**	**8.0**	**97**	**21**	**78**	**6**	**+4**	**9**	**4**	**3**	**7**	**22**	**1**	**0**	**0**
1981-82	**Edmonton Oilers**	**NHL**	**80**	**29**	**60**	**89**	**23**	**40**	**63**	**106**	**13**	**0**	**1**	**234**	**12.4**	**203**	**64**	**120**	**16**	**+35**	**5**	**1**	**1**	**2**	**6**	**1**	**0**	**0**
1982-83	**Edmonton Oilers**	**NHL**	**80**	**29**	**67**	**96**	**24**	**46**	**70**	**87**	**9**	**1**	**2**	**259**	**11.2**	**219**	**69**	**117**	**19**	**+52**	**16**	**7**	**7**	**14**	**14**	**2**	**2**	**0**
1983-84	**Edmonton Oilers**	**NHL**	**80**	**40**	**86**	**126**	**32**	**59**	**91**	**104**	**14**	**1**	**4**	**258**	**15.5**	**230**	**71**	**128**	**21**	**+52**	**19**	**8**	**14**	**22**	**21**	**2**	**0**	**1**
1984-85	Canada	C Cup	8	3	8	11	....	....	....	4	....	....	....	....	....	....	....	....	....	....	....	....	....	....	....	....	....	....
	Edmonton Oilers	**NHL**	**80**	**37**	**84**	**121**	**30**	**57**	**87**	**97**	**12**	**2**	**6**	**284**	**13.0**	**212**	**61**	**121**	**25**	**+55**	**18**	**12**	**25**	**37**	**44**	**3**	**1**	**4**
1985-86	**Edmonton Oilers**	**NHL**	**79**	**48**	**90**	**138**	**39**	**61**	**100**	**120**	**9**	**9**	**3**	**307**	**15.6**	**247**	**68**	**162**	**44**	**+61**	**10**	**1**	**9**	**10**	**30**	**1**	**0**	**0**
1986-87	**Edmonton Oilers**	**NHL**	**59**	**17**	**50**	**67**	**15**	**36**	**51**	**49**	**10**	**2**	**3**	**165**	**10.3**	**130**	**46**	**96**	**24**	**+12**	**17**	**3**	**8**	**11**	**30**	**1**	**0**	**1**
1987-88	Canada	C Cup	9	2	4	6	....	....	....	0	....	....	....	....	....	....	....	....	....	....	....	....	....	....	....	....	....	....
	Pittsburgh Penguins	**NHL**	**46**	**15**	**52**	**67**	**13**	**37**	**50**	**93**	**6**	**2**	**2**	**193**	**7.8**	**125**	**67**	**84**	**25**	**–1**	....	....	....	....	....	....	....	....
1988-89	**Pittsburgh Penguins**	**NHL**	**75**	**30**	**83**	**113**	**25**	**59**	**84**	**195**	**11**	**0**	**2**	**342**	**8.8**	**209**	**102**	**144**	**27**	**–10**	**11**	**2**	**13**	**15**	**31**	**2**	**0**	**1**
1989-90	**Pittsburgh Penguins**	**NHL**	**80**	**29**	**74**	**103**	**25**	**53**	**78**	**95**	**10**	**0**	**3**	**324**	**9.0**	**195**	**80**	**168**	**28**	**–25**	....	....	....	....	....	....	....	....
	Canada	WEC A	10	1	6	7	....	....	....	10	....	....	....	....	....	....	....	....	....	....	....	....	....	....	....	....	....	....
1990-91	**Pittsburgh Penguins**	**NHL**	**76**	**24**	**69**	**93**	**22**	**52**	**74**	**128**	**8**	**0**	**3**	**240**	**10.0**	**174**	**78**	**125**	**11**	**–18**	**12**	**2**	**9**	**11**	**6**	**0**	**0**	**0**
1991-92	Canada	C Cup	8	1	6	7	....	....	....	8	....	....	....	....	....	....	....	....	....	....	....	....	....	....	....	....	....	....
	Pittsburgh Penguins	**NHL**	**54**	**10**	**54**	**64**	**9**	**41**	**50**	**62**	**5**	**0**	**1**	**207**	**4.8**	**120**	**45**	**91**	**20**	**+4**	....	....	....	....	....	....	....	....
	Los Angeles Kings	**NHL**	**10**	**1**	**4**	**5**	**1**	**3**	**4**	**25**	**0**	**0**	**0**	**25**	**4.0**	**11**	**5**	**11**	**2**	**–3**	**6**	**4**	**3**	**7**	**2**	**3**	**0**	**0**
1992-93	**Los Angeles Kings**	**NHL**	**50**	**8**	**49**	**57**	**7**	**34**	**41**	**50**	**2**	**0**	**0**	**182**	**4.4**	**118**	**53**	**79**	**23**	**+9**	....	....	....	....	....	....	....	....
	Detroit Red Wings	**NHL**	**30**	**4**	**26**	**30**	**3**	**18**	**21**	**27**	**3**	**0**	**0**	**72**	**5.6**	**67**	**32**	**30**	**2**	**+7**	**7**	**2**	**9**	**11**	**2**	**0**	**0**	**0**
1993-94	**Detroit Red Wings**	**NHL**	**80**	**14**	**63**	**77**	**13**	**49**	**62**	**106**	**5**	**0**	**3**	**278**	**5.0**	**169**	**57**	**105**	**21**	**+28**	**7**	**1**	**6**	**7**	**8**	**0**	**0**	**0**
1994-95	**Detroit Red Wings**	**NHL**	**45**	**14**	**44**	**58**	**25**	**65**	**90**	**72**	**4**	**1**	**2**	**181**	**7.7**	**108**	**47**	**54**	**11**	**+18**	**18**	**6**	**12**	**18**	**10**	**2**	**1**	**0**
1995-96	**Detroit Red Wings**	**NHL**	**76**	**14**	**60**	**74**	**14**	**49**	**63**	**90**	**3**	**1**	**3**	**234**	**6.0**	**133**	**58**	**68**	**12**	**+19**	**17**	**5**	**9**	**14**	**30**	**3**	**2**	**1**
1996-97	**Hartford Whalers**	**NHL**	**20**	**3**	**5**	**8**	**3**	**4**	**7**	**18**	**1**	**0**	**1**	**39**	**7.7**	**23**	**7**	**20**	**4**	**0**	....	....	....	....	....	....	....	....
1996-97	Canada	W Cup	8	0	7	7	....	....	....	12	....	....	....	....	....	....	....	....	....	....	....	....	....	....	....	....	....	....
	Philadelphia Flyers	**NHL**	**37**	**6**	**20**	**26**	**6**	**18**	**24**	**20**	**0**	**1**	**1**	**71**	**8.5**	**59**	**15**	**44**	**11**	**+11**	**17**	**1**	**8**	**9**	**6**	**0**	**0**	**0**
1997-98	**Philadelphia Flyers**	**NHL**	**57**	**2**	**27**	**29**	**2**	**26**	**28**	**30**	**1**	**0**	**1**	**107**	**1.9**	**74**	**33**	**40**	**2**	**+3**	....	....	....	....	....	....	....	....
	NHL Totals		**1268**	**383**	**1090**	**1473**	**338**	**823**	**1161**	**1704**	**128**	**20**	**41**	**4115**	**9.3**	**2923**	**1079**	**1885**	**354**		**189**	**59**	**136**	**195**	**262**	**21**	**6**	**8**

OHA Second All-Star Team (1980) • NHL Second All-Star Team (1982, 1983, 1984, 1990) • Canada Cup All-Star Team (1984) • Won James Norris Memorial Trophy (1985, 1986, 1995) • NHL First All-Star Team (1985, 1986, 1989, 1995)

Played in NHL All-Star Game (1982, 1983, 1984, 1985, 1986, 1988, 1989, 1990, 1991, 1992, 1993, 1994, 1996, 1997)

Traded to **Pittsburgh** by **Edmonton** with Dave Hunter and Wayne Van Dorp for Craig Simpson, Dave Hannan, Moe Mantha and Chris Joseph, November 24, 1987. Traded to **LA Kings** by **Pittsburgh** for Brian Benning, Jeff Chychrun and LA Kings' 1st round choice (later traded to Philadelphia — Philadelphia selected Jason Bowen) in 1992 Entry Draft, February 19, 1992. Traded to **Detroit** by **LA Kings** with Sylvain Couturier and Jim Hiller for Jimmy Carson, Marc Potvin and Gary Shuchuk, January 29, 1993. Traded to **Hartford** by **Detroit** with Keith Primeau and Detroit's 1st round choice (Nikos Tselios) in 1997 Entry Draft for Brendan Shanahan and Brian Glynn, October 9, 1996. Traded to **Philadelphia** by **Hartford** with Hartford's/Carolina's 3rd round choice (Kris Mallette) in 1997 Entry Draft for Kevin Haller, Philadelphia's 1st round choice (later traded to San Jose — San Jose selected Scott Hannan) in 1997 Entry Draft and Hartford's 7th round choice (previously acquired, Carolina selected Andrew Merrick) in 1997 Entry Draft, December 15, 1996. Traded to **Chicago** by **Philadelphia** for NY Islanders' 5th round choice (previously acquired, Philadelphia selected Francis Belanger) in 1998 Entry Draft, June 27, 1998.

• COLE, DANTON

Danton Cole C/RW – R. 5'11", 185 lbs. b: Pontiac, MI, 1/10/1967. Winnipeg's 6th choice, 123rd overall, in 1985 Entry Draft.

Season	Club	League	GP	G	A	Pts	AG	AA	APts	PIM	PP	SH	GW	S	%	TGF	PGF	TGA	PGA	+/–	GP	G	A	Pts	PIM	PP	SH	GW
1985-86	Michigan State Spartans	CCHA	43	11	10	21	....	....	....	22	....	....	....	....	....	....	....	....	....	....	....	....	....	....	....	....	....	....
1986-87	Michigan State Spartans	CCHA	44	9	15	24	....	....	....	16	....	....	....	....	....	....	....	....	....	....	....	....	....	....	....	....	....	....
1987-88	Michigan State Spartans	CCHA	46	20	36	56	....	....	....	38	....	....	....	....	....	....	....	....	....	....	....	....	....	....	....	....	....	....
1988-89	Michigan State Spartans	CCHA	47	29	33	62	....	....	....	46	....	....	....	....	....	....	....	....	....	....	....	....	....	....	....	....	....	....
1989-90	**Winnipeg Jets**	**NHL**	**2**	**1**	**1**	**2**	**1**	**1**	**2**	**0**	**0**	**0**	**0**	**2**	**50.0**	**2**	**0**	**4**	**1**	**–1**	....	....	....	....	....	....	....	....
	Moncton Hawks	AHL	80	31	42	73	....	....	....	18	....	....	....	....	....	....	....	....	....	....	....	....	....	....	....	....	....	....
	United States	WEC-A	10	2	1	3	....	....	....	6	....	....	....	....	....	....	....	....	....	....	....	....	....	....	....	....	....	....
1990-91	**Winnipeg Jets**	**NHL**	**66**	**13**	**11**	**24**	**12**	**8**	**20**	**24**	**1**	**1**	**1**	**109**	**11.9**	**38**	**6**	**60**	**14**	**–14**	....	....	....	....	....	....	....	....
	Moncton Hawks	AHL	3	1	1	2	....	....	....	0	....	....	....	....	....	....	....	....	....	....	....	....	....	....	....	....	....	....
	United States	WEC A	10	6	4	10	....	....	....	14	....	....	....	....	....	....	....	....	....	....	....	....	....	....	....	....	....	....
1991-92	**Winnipeg Jets**	**NHL**	**52**	**7**	**5**	**12**	**6**	**4**	**10**	**32**	**1**	**2**	**0**	**65**	**10.8**	**19**	**2**	**46**	**14**	**–15**	....	....	....	....	....	....	....	....

			REGULAR SEASON																		PLAYOFFS							
Season	Club	League	GP	G	A	Pts	AG	AA	APts	PIM	PP	SH	GW	S	%	TGF	PGF	TGA	PGA	+/–	GP	G	A	Pts	PIM	PP	SH	GW
1992-93	**Tampa Bay Lightning**	**NHL**	**67**	**12**	**15**	**27**	**10**	**10**	**20**	**23**	**0**	**1**	**1**	**100**	**12.0**	**41**	**3**	**75**	**35**	**–2**	....	....	....	....	....	....	....	....
	Atlanta Knights	IHL	1	1	0	1	....	....	....	2	....	....	....	....	....	....	....	....	....	....	....	....	....	....	....	....	....	....
1993-94	**Tampa Bay Lightning**	**NHL**	**81**	**20**	**23**	**43**	**19**	**18**	**37**	**32**	**8**	**1**	**4**	**149**	**13.4**	**65**	**21**	**64**	**27**	**+7**	....	....	....	....	....	....	....	....
	United States	WC-A	5	1	1	2	....	....	....	2	....	....	....	....	....	....	....	....	....	....	....	....	....	....	....	....	....	....
1994-95	**Tampa Bay Lightning**	**NHL**	**26**	**3**	**3**	**6**	**5**	**4**	**9**	**6**	**1**	**0**	**0**	**56**	**5.4**	**17**	**3**	**21**	**6**	**–1**	....	....	....	....	....	....	....	....
	New Jersey Devils	**NHL**	**12**	**1**	**2**	**3**	**2**	**3**	**5**	**8**	**0**	**0**	**0**	**20**	**5.0**	**6**	**0**	**6**	**0**	**0**	**1**	**0**	**0**	**0**	**0**	**0**	**0**	**0**
1995-96	**New York Islanders**	**NHL**	**10**	**1**	**0**	**1**	**1**	**0**	**1**	**0**	**0**	**0**	**0**	**5**	**20.0**	**1**	**0**	**2**	**1**	**0**	....	....	....	....	....	....	....	....
	Utah Grizzlies	IHL	34	28	15	43	....	....	....	22	....	....	....	....	....	....	....	....	....	....	....	....	....	....	....	....	....	....
	Chicago Blackhawks	**NHL**	**2**	**0**	**0**	**0**	**0**	**0**	**0**	**0**	**0**	**0**	**0**	**1**	**0.0**	**0**	**0**	**0**	**0**	**0**	....	....	....	....	....	....	....	....
	Indianapolis Ice	IHL	32	9	13	22	....	....	....	20	....	....	....	....	....	....	....	....	....	....	5	1	5	6	8	....	....	....
1996-97	Krefeld Pinguine	Germany	28	7	12	19	....	....	....	14	....	....	....	....	....	....	....	....	....	....	....	....	....	....	....	....	....	....
	Grand Rapids Griffins	IHL	35	8	18	26	....	....	....	24	....	....	....	....	....	....	....	....	....	....	5	3	1	4	2	....	....	....
1997-98	Grand Rapids Griffins	IHL	81	13	13	26	....	....	....	36	....	....	....	....	....	....	....	....	....	....	3	1	1	2	0	....	....	....
	NHL Totals		**318**	**58**	**60**	**118**	**56**	**48**	**104**	**125**	**11**	**5**	**6**	**507**	**11.4**	**189**	**35**	**278**	**98**		**1**	**0**	**0**	**0**	**0**	**0**	**0**	**0**

Traded to **Tampa Bay** by **Winnipeg** for future considerations, June 19, 1992. Traded to **New Jersey** by **Tampa Bay** with Shawn Chambers for Alexander Semak and Ben Hankinson, March 14, 1995. Signed as a free agent by **NY Islanders**, August 26, 1995. Traded to **Chicago** by **NY Islanders** for Bob Halkidis, February 2, 1996.

• COLLEY, TOM

Tom Colley C – L. 5'9", 162 lbs. b: Toronto, Ont., 8/21/1953. Minnesota's 4th choice, 57th overall, in 1973 Amateur Draft.

Season	Club	League	GP	G	A	Pts	AG	AA	APts	PIM	PP	SH	GW	S	%	TGF	PGF	TGA	PGA	+/–	GP	G	A	Pts	PIM	PP	SH	GW
1971-72	Niagara Falls Flyers	OHA	63	23	22	45	....	....	....	53	....	....	....	....	....	....	....	....	....	....	....	....	....	....	....	....	....	....
1972-73	Sudbury Wolves	OHA	67	36	81	117	....	....	....	84	....	....	....	....	....	....	....	....	....	....	....	....	....	....	....	....	....	....
1973-74	New Haven Nighthawks	AHL	66	9	18	27	....	....	....	28	....	....	....	....	....	....	....	....	....	....	10	2	2	4	4	....	....	....
1974-75	**Minnesota North Stars**	**NHL**	**1**	**0**	**0**	**0**	**0**	**0**	**0**	**2**	**0**	**0**	**0**	**0**	**0.0**	**0**	**0**	**3**	**0**	**–3**	....	....	....	....	....	....	....	....
	New Haven Nighthawks	AHL	76	29	47	76	....	....	....	51	....	....	....	....	....	....	....	....	....	....	16	6	12	18	8	....	....	....
1975-76	New Haven Nighthawks	AHL	76	38	31	69	....	....	....	35	....	....	....	....	....	....	....	....	....	....	3	0	1	1	0	....	....	....
1976-77	New Haven Nighthawks	AHL	80	37	56	93	....	....	....	36	....	....	....	....	....	....	....	....	....	....	6	2	2	4	0	....	....	....
1977-78	New Haven Nighthawks	AHL	80	32	54	86	....	....	....	17	....	....	....	....	....	....	....	....	....	....	15	2	6	8	2	....	....	....
1978-79	New Haven Nighthawks	AHL	77	36	32	68	....	....	....	24	....	....	....	....	....	....	....	....	....	....	10	3	9	12	2	....	....	....
1979-80	New Haven Nighthawks	AHL	79	23	43	66	....	....	....	43	....	....	....	....	....	....	....	....	....	....	7	0	4	4	4	....	....	....
1980-81	Binghamton Whalers	AHL	74	17	33	50	....	....	....	31	....	....	....	....	....	....	....	....	....	....	6	4	3	7	2	....	....	....
1981-82	Collingwood Royals	OHA Sr.	....	21	42	63	....	....	....	....	....	....	....	....	....	....	....	....	....	....	....	....	....	....	....	....	....	....
	NHL Totals		**1**	**0**	**0**	**0**	**0**	**0**	**0**	**2**	**0**	**0**	**0**	**0**	**0.0**	**0**	**0**	**3**	**0**		....	....	....	....	....	....	....	....

• COLLINS, BILL

Bill Collins RW – R. 6'1", 178 lbs. b: Ottawa, Ont., 7/13/1943.

Season	Club	League	GP	G	A	Pts	AG	AA	APts	PIM	PP	SH	GW	S	%	TGF	PGF	TGA	PGA	+/–	GP	G	A	Pts	PIM	PP	SH	GW
1960-61	Toronto Marlboros	OHA	37	4	9	13	....	....	....	46	....	....	....	....	....	....	....	....	....	....	....	....	....	....	....	....	....	....
1961-62	Whitby Mohawks	Jr. A	27	16	24	40	....	....	....	78	....	....	....	....	....	....	....	....	....	....	2	1	2	3	18	....	....	....
1962-63	Whitby Mohawks	Jr. A	22	22	22	44	....	....	....	32	....	....	....	....	....	....	....	....	....	....	4	7	4	11	18	....	....	....
	Sudbury Wolves	EPHL	....	....	....	....	....	....	....	....	....	....	....	....	....	....	....	....	....	....	6	1	1	2	2	....	....	....
1963-64	Denver Invaders	WHL	58	17	15	32	....	....	....	54	....	....	....	....	....	....	....	....	....	....	....	....	....	....	....	....	....	....
	Baltimore Clippers	AHL	11	0	1	1	....	....	....	0	....	....	....	....	....	....	....	....	....	....	....	....	....	....	....	....	....	....
1964-65	Baltimore Clippers	AHL	6	0	0	0	....	....	....	0	....	....	....	....	....	....	....	....	....	....	....	....	....	....	....	....	....	....
	St. Paul Rangers	CHL	58	12	29	41	....	....	....	47	....	....	....	....	....	....	....	....	....	....	11	5	2	7	24	....	....	....
1965-66	Minnesota Rangers	CHL	56	18	29	47	....	....	....	55	....	....	....	....	....	....	....	....	....	....	7	0	5	5	4	....	....	....
1966-67	Baltimore Clippers	AHL	69	20	18	38	....	....	....	50	....	....	....	....	....	....	....	....	....	....	6	1	1	2	12	....	....	....
1967-68	**Minnesota North Stars**	**NHL**	**71**	**9**	**11**	**20**	**11**	**11**	**22**	**41**	**0**	**0**	**1**	**114**	**7.9**	**35**	**5**	**60**	**14**	**–16**	**10**	**2**	**4**	**6**	**4**	**0**	**0**	**1**
1968-69	**Minnesota North Stars**	**NHL**	**75**	**9**	**10**	**19**	**10**	**9**	**19**	**24**	**0**	**1**	**1**	**123**	**7.3**	**30**	**0**	**91**	**35**	**–26**	....	....	....	....	....	....	....	....
1969-70	**Minnesota North Stars**	**NHL**	**74**	**29**	**9**	**38**	**34**	**9**	**43**	**48**	**2**	**6**	**2**	**186**	**15.6**	**49**	**3**	**89**	**47**	**+4**	**6**	**0**	**1**	**1**	**8**	**0**	**0**	**0**
1970-71	**Montreal Canadiens**	**NHL**	**40**	**6**	**2**	**8**	**6**	**2**	**8**	**39**	**0**	**0**	**1**	**57**	**10.5**	**15**	**0**	**36**	**22**	**+1**	....	....	....	....	....	....	....	....
	Detroit Red Wings	**NHL**	**36**	**5**	**16**	**21**	**5**	**14**	**19**	**10**	**1**	**0**	**0**	**105**	**4.8**	**30**	**8**	**38**	**15**	**–1**	....	....	....	....	....	....	....	....
1971-72	**Detroit Red Wings**	**NHL**	**71**	**15**	**25**	**40**	**16**	**23**	**39**	**38**	**2**	**0**	**2**	**157**	**9.6**	**68**	**10**	**68**	**13**	**+3**	....	....	....	....	....	....	....	....
1972-73	**Detroit Red Wings**	**NHL**	**78**	**21**	**21**	**42**	**21**	**18**	**39**	**44**	**1**	**1**	**6**	**186**	**11.3**	**61**	**2**	**83**	**23**	**–1**	....	....	....	....	....	....	....	....
1973-74	**Detroit Red Wings**	**NHL**	**54**	**13**	**15**	**28**	**13**	**13**	**26**	**37**	**2**	**3**	**0**	**134**	**9.7**	**46**	**5**	**72**	**11**	**–20**	....	....	....	....	....	....	....	....
	St. Louis Blues	**NHL**	**12**	**2**	**2**	**4**	**2**	**2**	**4**	**14**	**0**	**0**	**0**	**21**	**9.5**	**6**	**1**	**21**	**6**	**–10**	....	....	....	....	....	....	....	....
1974-75	**St. Louis Blues**	**NHL**	**70**	**22**	**15**	**37**	**20**	**12**	**32**	**34**	**2**	**2**	**2**	**142**	**15.5**	**56**	**7**	**82**	**37**	**+4**	**2**	**1**	**0**	**1**	**0**	**0**	**0**	**0**
1975-76	**New York Rangers**	**NHL**	**50**	**4**	**4**	**8**	**4**	**3**	**7**	**38**	**0**	**1**	**0**	**47**	**8.5**	**14**	**1**	**39**	**7**	**–19**	....	....	....	....	....	....	....	....
1976-77	**Philadelphia Flyers**	**NHL**	**9**	**1**	**1**	**2**	**1**	**1**	**2**	**4**	**0**	**0**	**1**	**5**	**20.0**	**3**	**0**	**4**	**0**	**–1**	....	....	....	....	....	....	....	....
	Washington Capitals	**NHL**	**54**	**11**	**14**	**25**	**11**	**11**	**22**	**26**	**0**	**2**	**1**	**87**	**12.6**	**36**	**0**	**66**	**23**	**–7**	....	....	....	....	....	....	....	....
1977-78	**Washington Capitals**	**NHL**	**74**	**10**	**9**	**19**	**10**	**7**	**17**	**18**	**0**	**1**	**1**	**104**	**9.6**	**30**	**0**	**93**	**31**	**–32**	....	....	....	....	....	....	....	....
	NHL Totals		**768**	**157**	**154**	**311**	**164**	**135**	**299**	**415**	**10**	**17**	**18**	**1468**	**10.7**	**479**	**42**	**842**	**284**		**18**	**3**	**5**	**8**	**12**	**0**	**0**	**1**

Claimed by **Minnesota** from **NY Rangers** in Expansion Draft, June 6, 1967. Traded to **Montreal** by **NY Rangers** for Jude Drouin, June 10, 1970. Traded to **Detroit** by **Montreal** with Mickey Redmond and Guy Charron for Frank Mahovlich, January 13, 1971. Traded to **St. Louis** by **Detroit** with Ted Harris and Garnet Bailey for Chris Evans, Bryan Watson and Jean Hamel, February 14, 1974. Traded to **NY Rangers** by **St. Louis** with John Davidson for Ted Irvine, Bert Wilson and Jerry Butler, June 18, 1975. Signed as a free agent by **Philadelphia**, October 20, 1976. Traded to **Washington** by **Philadelphia** for cash, December 4, 1976.

• COLLYARD, BOB

Bob Collyard C – L. 5'9", 170 lbs. b: Hitting, MN, 10/16/1949. St. Louis' 7th choice, 73rd overall, in 1969 Amateur Draft.

Season	Club	League	GP	G	A	Pts	AG	AA	APts	PIM	PP	SH	GW	S	%	TGF	PGF	TGA	PGA	+/–	GP	G	A	Pts	PIM	PP	SH	GW
1968-69	Colorado College	WCHA	25	31	17	48	....	....	....	46	....	....	....	....	....	....	....	....	....	....	....	....	....	....	....	....	....	....
1969-70	Colorado College	WCHA	30	18	39	57	....	....	....	36	....	....	....	....	....	....	....	....	....	....	....	....	....	....	....	....	....	....
1970-71	Colorado College	WCHA	15	10	20	30	....	....	....	6	....	....	....	....	....	....	....	....	....	....	....	....	....	....	....	....	....	....
	Kansas City Blues	CHL	2	0	0	0	....	....	....	0	....	....	....	....	....	....	....	....	....	....	....	....	....	....	....	....	....	....
1971-72	Kansas City Blues	CHL	59	13	22	35	....	....	....	14	....	....	....	....	....	....	....	....	....	....	....	....	....	....	....	....	....	....
1972-73	Fort Worth Wings	CHL	67	17	*50	67	....	....	....	53	....	....	....	....	....	....	....	....	....	....	4	2	3	5	2	....	....	....
1973-74	**St. Louis Blues**	**NHL**	**10**	**1**	**3**	**4**	**1**	**3**	**4**	**4**	**0**	**0**	**0**	**12**	**8.3**	**5**	**0**	**4**	**0**	**+1**	....	....	....	....	....	....	....	....
	Denver Spurs	WHL	65	27	47	74	....	....	....	22	....	....	....	....	....	....	....	....	....	....	....	....	....	....	....	....	....	....
1974-75	Philadelphia Firebirds	NAHL	72	42	61	103	....	....	....	78	....	....	....	....	....	....	....	....	....	....	4	3	3	6	12	....	....	....
1975-76	Philadelphia Firebirds	NAHL	73	45	84	129	....	....	....	82	....	....	....	....	....	....	....	....	....	....	16	12	*25	*37	10	....	....	....
1976-77	Philadelphia Firebirds	NAHL	71	31	85	116	....	....	....	76	....	....	....	....	....	....	....	....	....	....	4	3	2	5	7	....	....	....
1977-78	Philadelphia Firebirds	AHL	79	28	62	90	....	....	....	42	....	....	....	....	....	....	....	....	....	....	4	0	1	1	0	....	....	....
	United States	WEC-A	10	1	5	6	....	....	....	2	....	....	....	....	....	....	....	....	....	....	....	....	....	....	....	....	....	....
1978-79	Philadelphia Firebirds	AHL	69	21	35	56	....	....	....	32	....	....	....	....	....	....	....	....	....	....	....	....	....	....	....	....	....	....
	United States	WEC-A	8	2	0	2	....	....	....	8	....	....	....	....	....	....	....	....	....	....	....	....	....	....	....	....	....	....
1979-80	Bad Nauheim	Germany	37	19	34	53	....	....	....	58	....	....	....	....	....	....	....	....	....	....	....	....	....	....	....	....	....	....
1980-81	Bad Nauheim	Germany	44	29	25	54	....	....	....	23	....	....	....	....	....	....	....	....	....	....	5	2	2	4	28	....	....	....
1981-82	Milwaukee Admirals	IHL	77	24	46	70	....	....	....	32	....	....	....	....	....	....	....	....	....	....	5	2	2	4	9	....	....	....
1982-83	Milwaukee Admirals	IHL	10	0	4	4	....	....	....	0	....	....	....	....	....	....	....	....	....	....	....	....	....	....	....	....	....	....
	Kalamazoo Wings	IHL	5	0	6	6	....	....	....	0	....	....	....	....	....	....	....	....	....	....	....	....	....	....	....	....	....	....
	NHL Totals		**10**	**1**	**3**	**4**	**1**	**3**	**4**	**4**	**0**	**0**	**0**	**12**	**8.3**	**5**	**0**	**4**	**0**		....	....	....	....	....	....	....	....

WCHA Second All-Star Team (1969) • NCAA West First All-American Team (1969, 1970) • WCHA First All-Star Team (1970, 1971) • CHL Second All-Star Team (1973) • NAHL Second All-Star Team (1975, 1976, 1977)

Claimed by **Washington** from **St. Louis** in Expansion Draft, June 12, 1974.

• COLMAN, MICHAEL

Michael Colman D – R. 6'3", 225 lbs. b: Stoneham, MA, 8/4/1968. d: 4/5/1995.

Season	Club	League	GP	G	A	Pts	AG	AA	APts	PIM	PP	SH	GW	S	%	TGF	PGF	TGA	PGA	+/–	GP	G	A	Pts	PIM	PP	SH	GW
1987-88	Humboldt Broncos	SJHL	55	3	7	10	....	....	....	188	....	....	....	....	....	....	....	....	....	....	....	....	....	....	....	....	....	....
1988-89	Humboldt Broncos	SJHL	64	3	17	20	....	....	....	161	....	....	....	....	....	....	....	....	....	....	....	....	....	....	....	....	....	....
1989-90	Ferris State Bulldogs	CCHA	23	0	4	4	....	....	....	62	....	....	....	....	....	....	....	....	....	....	....	....	....	....	....	....	....	....
1990-91	Kansas City Blades	IHL	66	1	6	7	....	....	....	115	....	....	....	....	....	....	....	....	....	....	....	....	....	....	....	....	....	....
1991-92	**San Jose Sharks**	**NHL**	**15**	**0**	**1**	**1**	**0**	**1**	**1**	**32**	**0**	**0**	**0**	**7**	**0.0**	**7**	**0**	**16**	**1**	**–8**	....	....	....	....	....	....	....	....
	Kansas City Blades	IHL	59	0	4	4	....	....	....	130	....	....	....	....	....	....	....	....	....	....	3	0	0	0	4	....	....	....
1992-93	Kansas City Blades	IHL	80	1	5	6	....	....	....	191	....	....	....	....	....	....	....	....	....	....	12	1	0	1	34	....	....	....
1993-94	Kansas City Blades	IHL	77	4	7	11	....	....	....	215	....	....	....	....	....	....	....	....	....	....	....	....	....	....	....	....	....	....
	NHL Totals		**15**	**0**	**1**	**1**	**0**	**1**	**1**	**32**	**0**	**0**	**0**	**7**	**0.0**	**7**	**0**	**16**	**1**		....	....	....	....	....	....	....	....

Signed as a free agent by **San Jose**, September 3, 1991. • Died of injuries sustained in an automobile accident, April 5, 1994.

• COMEAU, REY
Rey Comeau C – L. 5'8", 190 lbs. b: Montreal, Que., 10/25/1948.

			REGULAR SEASON																		PLAYOFFS							
Season	Club	League	GP	G	A	Pts	AG	AA	APts	PIM	PP	SH	GW	S	%	TGF	PGF	TGA	PGA	+/–	GP	G	A	Pts	PIM	PP	SH	GW
1965-66	West Island Flyers	QJHL	37	*40	32	72	....	....	....	37	....	....	....	....	....	....	....	....	....	....	....	....	....	....	....	....	....	....
1966-67	Verdun Maple Leafs	QJHL	STATISTICS NOT AVAILABLE																									
1967-68	Verdun Maple Leafs	QJHL	36	29	50	79	....	....	....	....	....	....	....	....	....	....	....	....	....	....	....	....	....	....	....	....	....	....
1968-69	Houston Apollos	CHL	1	0	0	0	....	....	....	0	....	....	....	....	....	....	....	....	....	....	....	....	....	....	....	....	....	....
	Cleveland Barons	AHL	71	17	23	40	....	....	....	26	....	....	....	....	....	....	....	....	....	....	4	1	0	1	0	....	....	....
1969-70	Cleveland Barons	AHL	71	27	38	65	....	....	....	26	....	....	....	....	....	....	....	....	....	....	....	....	....	....	....	....	....	....
1970-71	Cleveland Barons	AHL	41	17	25	42	....	....	....	30	....	....	....	....	....	....	....	....	....	....	....	....	....	....	....	....	....	....
	Montreal Voyageurs	AHL	29	9	14	23	....	....	....	34	....	....	....	....	....	....	....	....	....	....	3	1	2	3	4	....	....	....
1971-72	**Montreal Canadiens**	**NHL**	**4**	**0**	**0**	**0**	**0**	**0**	**0**	**0**	**0**	**0**	**0**	**2**	**0.0**	**0**	**0**	**0**	**0**	**0**	....	....	....	....	....	....	....	....
	Nova Scotia Voyageurs	AHL	68	23	41	64	....	....	....	63	....	....	....	....	....	....	....	....	....	....	15	6	14	20	10	....	....	....
1972-73	**Atlanta Flames**	**NHL**	**77**	**21**	**21**	**42**	**21**	**18**	**39**	**19**	**3**	**0**	**2**	**146**	**14.4**	**55**	**11**	**63**	**19**	**0**	....	....	....	....	....	....	....	....
1973-74	**Atlanta Flames**	**NHL**	**78**	**11**	**23**	**34**	**11**	**20**	**31**	**16**	**0**	**1**	**4**	**130**	**8.5**	**44**	**3**	**94**	**38**	**–15**	**4**	**2**	**1**	**3**	**6**	**1**	**0**	**0**
1974-75	**Atlanta Flames**	**NHL**	**75**	**14**	**20**	**34**	**13**	**16**	**29**	**40**	**2**	**0**	**3**	**116**	**12.1**	**45**	**6**	**34**	**4**	**+9**	....	....	....	....	....	....	....	....
1975-76	**Atlanta Flames**	**NHL**	**79**	**17**	**22**	**39**	**16**	**17**	**33**	**42**	**1**	**0**	**2**	**124**	**13.7**	**46**	**3**	**39**	**5**	**+9**	....	....	....	....	....	....	....	....
1976-77	**Atlanta Flames**	**NHL**	**80**	**15**	**18**	**33**	**14**	**15**	**29**	**16**	**2**	**1**	**4**	**133**	**11.3**	**48**	**3**	**50**	**12**	**+7**	**3**	**0**	**0**	**0**	**2**	**0**	**0**	**0**
1977-78	**Atlanta Flames**	**NHL**	**79**	**10**	**22**	**32**	**10**	**18**	**28**	**20**	**0**	**1**	**1**	**114**	**8.8**	**42**	**2**	**51**	**11**	**0**	**2**	**0**	**0**	**0**	**0**	**0**	**0**	**0**
1978-79	**Colorado Rockies**	**NHL**	**70**	**8**	**10**	**18**	**7**	**8**	**15**	**16**	**1**	**2**	**0**	**85**	**9.4**	**25**	**1**	**77**	**33**	**–20**	....	....	....	....	....	....	....	....
1979-80	**Colorado Rockies**	**NHL**	**22**	**2**	**5**	**7**	**2**	**4**	**6**	**6**	**0**	**0**	**0**	**21**	**9.5**	**13**	**2**	**17**	**6**	**0**	....	....	....	....	....	....	....	....
	Fort Worth Texans	CHL	57	14	35	49	....	....	....	16	....	....	....	....	....	....	....	....	....	....	....	....	....	....	....	....	....	....
1980-81	Fort Worth Texans	CHL	77	19	16	35	....	....	....	40	....	....	....	....	....	....	....	....	....	....	5	2	3	5	4	....	....	....
	NHL Totals		**564**	**98**	**141**	**239**	**94**	**116**	**210**	**175**	**9**	**5**	**16**	**871**	**11.3**	**318**	**31**	**425**	**128**		**9**	**2**	**1**	**3**	**8**	**1**	**0**	**0**

Claimed by **Vancouver** from **Montreal** in Intra-League Draft, June 8, 1971. Traded to **Montreal** by **Vancouver** for cash, September 14, 1971. Traded to **Atlanta** by **Montreal** for cash, June 16, 1972. Signed as a free agent by **Colorado**, June 23, 1978.

• CONACHER, BRIAN
Brian Conacher LW – L. 6'3", 197 lbs. b: Toronto, Ont., 8/31/1941.

			REGULAR SEASON																		PLAYOFFS							
Season	Club	League	GP	G	A	Pts	AG	AA	APts	PIM	PP	SH	GW	S	%	TGF	PGF	TGA	PGA	+/–	GP	G	A	Pts	PIM	PP	SH	GW
1958-59	Toronto Marlboros	OHA	6	0	1	1	....	....	....	0	....	....	....	....	....	....	....	....	....	....	3	0	2	2	0	....	....	....
1959-60	Toronto Marlboros	OHA	42	17	17	34	....	....	....	2	....	....	....	....	....	....	....	....	....	....	3	0	0	0	2	....	....	....
1960-61	Toronto Marlboros	OHA	14	2	5	7	....	....	....	7	....	....	....	....	....	....	....	....	....	....	....	....	....	....	....	....	....	....
1961-62	Toronto Marlboros	OHA	25	12	27	39	....	....	....	4	....	....	....	....	....	....	....	....	....	....	12	7	8	15	18	....	....	....
	Rochester Americans	AHL	3	0	0	0	....	....	....	2	....	....	....	....	....	....	....	....	....	....	....	....	....	....	....	....	....	....
	Toronto Maple Leafs	**NHL**	**1**	**0**	**0**	**0**	**0**	**0**	**0**	**0**	....	....	....	....	....	....	....	....	....	....	....	....	....	....	....	....	....	....
1962-63	University of Western Ontario	OUAA	STATISTICS NOT AVAILABLE																									
1963-64	Canada	Nat-Team	STATISTICS NOT AVAILABLE																									
	Canada	Olympics	7	7	1	8	....	....	....	6	....	....	....	....	....	....	....	....	....	....	....	....	....	....	....	....	....	....
1964-65	Canada	Nat-Team	STATISTICS NOT AVAILABLE																									
	Canada	WEC-A	7	1	3	4	....	....	....	6	....	....	....	....	....	....	....	....	....	....	....	....	....	....	....	....	....	....
1965-66	**Toronto Maple Leafs**	**NHL**	**2**	**0**	**0**	**0**	**0**	**0**	**0**	**2**	....	....	....	....	....	....	....	....	....	....	....	....	....	....	....	....	....	....
	Rochester Americans	AHL	69	14	16	30	....	....	....	66	....	....	....	....	....	....	....	....	....	....	12	6	0	6	18	....	....	....
1966-67	**Toronto Maple Leafs**	**NHL**	**66**	**14**	**13**	**27**	**17**	**13**	**30**	**47**	....	....	....	....	....	....	....	....	....	....	**12**	**3**	**2**	**5**	**21**	....	....	....
1967-68	**Toronto Maple Leafs**	**NHL**	**64**	**11**	**14**	**25**	**14**	**15**	**29**	**31**	**0**	**1**	**1**	**88**	**12.5**	**35**	**2**	**34**	**8**	**+7**	....	....	....	....	....	....	....	....
	Rochester Americans	AHL	5	2	2	4	....	....	....	6	....	....	....	....	....	....	....	....	....	....	....	....	....	....	....	....	....	....
1968-69	Canada	Nat-Team	STATISTICS NOT AVAILABLE																									
1969-70	Canada	Nat-Team	STATISTICS NOT AVAILABLE																									
1970-71	Canada	Nat-Team	STATISTICS NOT AVAILABLE																									
1971-72	**Detroit Red Wings**	**NHL**	**22**	**3**	**1**	**4**	**3**	**1**	**4**	**4**	**0**	**1**	**0**	**21**	**14.3**	**4**	**0**	**14**	**7**	**–3**	....	....	....	....	....	....	....	....
	Fort Worth Wings	CHL	40	13	13	26	....	....	....	4	....	....	....	....	....	....	....	....	....	....	7	3	2	5	4	....	....	....
1972-73	Ottawa Nationals	WHA	69	8	19	27	....	....	....	32	....	....	....	....	....	....	....	....	....	....	5	1	3	4	4	....	....	....
	NHL Totals		**155**	**28**	**28**	**56**	**34**	**29**	**63**	**84**	**0**	**2**	**1**	**109**	**25.7**	**39**	**2**	**48**	**15**		**12**	**3**	**2**	**5**	**21**	**0**	**0**	**0**
	Other Major League Totals		69	8	19	27	....	....	....	32	....	....	....	....	....	....	....	....	....		5	1	3	4	4	....	....	....

Played in NHL All-Star Game (1968)

Claimed by **Detroit** from **Toronto** in Intra-League Draft, June 11, 1968. Traded to **Minnesota** by **Detroit** with Danny Lawson for Wayne Connelly, February 15, 1969. Traded to **Toronto** by **Minnesota** with Terry O'Malley for Murray Oliver, May 20, 1970. Signed as a free agent by **Ottawa** (WHA), October, 1972.

• CONACHER, PAT
Pat Conacher LW – L. 5'8", 190 lbs. b: Edmonton, Alta., 5/1/1959. NY Rangers' 3rd choice, 76th overall, in 1979 Entry Draft.

			REGULAR SEASON																		PLAYOFFS							
Season	Club	League	GP	G	A	Pts	AG	AA	APts	PIM	PP	SH	GW	S	%	TGF	PGF	TGA	PGA	+/–	GP	G	A	Pts	PIM	PP	SH	GW
1977-78	Billings Bighorns	WCJHL	72	31	44	75	....	....	....	105	....	....	....	....	....	....	....	....	....	....	20	15	14	29	22	....	....	....
1978-79	Billings Bighorns	WHL	39	25	37	62	....	....	....	50	....	....	....	....	....	....	....	....	....	....	....	....	....	....	....	....	....	....
	Saskatoon Blades	WHL	33	15	32	47	....	....	....	37	....	....	....	....	....	....	....	....	....	....	....	....	....	....	....	....	....	....
1979-80	**New York Rangers**	**NHL**	**17**	**0**	**5**	**5**	**0**	**4**	**4**	**4**	**0**	**0**	**0**	**15**	**0.0**	**6**	**0**	**16**	**0**	**–10**	**3**	**0**	**1**	**1**	**2**	**0**	**0**	**0**
	New Haven Nighthawks	AHL	53	11	14	25	....	....	....	43	....	....	....	....	....	....	....	....	....	....	7	1	1	2	4	....	....	....
			DID NOT PLAY																									
1981-82	Springfield Indians	AHL	77	23	22	45	....	....	....	38	....	....	....	....	....	....	....	....	....	....	....	....	....	....	....	....	....	....
1982-83	**New York Rangers**	**NHL**	**5**	**0**	**1**	**1**	**0**	**1**	**1**	**4**	**0**	**0**	**0**	**5**	**0.0**	**1**	**0**	**1**	**0**	**0**	....	....	....	....	....	....	....	....
	Tulsa Oilers	CHL	63	29	28	57	....	....	....	44	....	....	....	....	....	....	....	....	....	....	....	....	....	....	....	....	....	....
1983-84	**Edmonton Oilers**	**NHL**	**45**	**2**	**8**	**10**	**2**	**5**	**7**	**31**	**0**	**0**	**0**	**18**	**11.1**	**17**	**0**	**23**	**4**	**–2**	**3**	**1**	**0**	**1**	**2**	**0**	**0**	**0**
	Moncton Alpines	AHL	28	7	16	23	....	....	....	30	....	....	....	....	....	....	....	....	....	....	....	....	....	....	....	....	....	....
1984-85	Nova Scotia Voyageurs	AHL	68	20	45	65	....	....	....	44	....	....	....	....	....	....	....	....	....	....	6	3	2	5	0	....	....	....
1985-86	**New Jersey Devils**	**NHL**	**2**	**0**	**2**	**2**	**0**	**1**	**1**	**2**	**0**	**0**	**0**	**3**	**0.0**	**2**	**0**	**2**	**0**	**0**	....	....	....	....	....	....	....	....
	Maine Mariners	AHL	69	15	30	45	....	....	....	83	....	....	....	....	....	....	....	....	....	....	5	1	1	2	11	....	....	....
1986-87	Maine Mariners	AHL	56	12	14	26	....	....	....	47	....	....	....	....	....	....	....	....	....	....	....	....	....	....	....	....	....	....
1987-88	**New Jersey Devils**	**NHL**	**24**	**2**	**5**	**7**	**2**	**4**	**6**	**12**	**0**	**0**	**0**	**22**	**9.1**	**18**	**1**	**18**	**9**	**+8**	**17**	**2**	**2**	**4**	**14**	**0**	**1**	**1**
	Utica Devils	AHL	47	14	33	47	....	....	....	32	....	....	....	....	....	....	....	....	....	....	....	....	....	....	....	....	....	....
1988-89	**New Jersey Devils**	**NHL**	**55**	**7**	**5**	**12**	**6**	**4**	**10**	**14**	**0**	**1**	**1**	**59**	**11.9**	**23**	**1**	**49**	**20**	**–7**	....	....	....	....	....	....	....	....
1989-90	**New Jersey Devils**	**NHL**	**19**	**3**	**3**	**6**	**3**	**2**	**5**	**4**	**0**	**0**	**0**	**18**	**16.7**	**11**	**0**	**14**	**5**	**+2**	**5**	**1**	**0**	**1**	**10**	**0**	**0**	**0**
	Utica Devils	AHL	57	13	36	49	....	....	....	53	....	....	....	....	....	....	....	....	....	....	....	....	....	....	....	....	....	....
1990-91	**New Jersey Devils**	**NHL**	**49**	**5**	**11**	**16**	**5**	**8**	**13**	**27**	**0**	**0**	**0**	**45**	**11.1**	**28**	**0**	**37**	**18**	**+9**	**7**	**0**	**2**	**2**	**2**	**0**	**0**	**0**
	Utica Devils	AHL	4	0	1	1	....	....	....	6	....	....	....	....	....	....	....	....	....	....	....	....	....	....	....	....	....	....
1991-92	**New Jersey Devils**	**NHL**	**44**	**7**	**3**	**10**	**6**	**2**	**8**	**16**	**0**	**1**	**1**	**38**	**18.4**	**15**	**0**	**35**	**20**	**0**	**7**	**1**	**1**	**2**	**4**	**0**	**1**	**0**
1992-93	**Los Angeles Kings**	**NHL**	**81**	**9**	**8**	**17**	**7**	**5**	**12**	**20**	**0**	**2**	**1**	**65**	**13.8**	**36**	**3**	**96**	**47**	**–16**	**24**	**6**	**4**	**10**	**6**	**0**	**0**	**0**
1993-94	**Los Angeles Kings**	**NHL**	**77**	**15**	**13**	**28**	**14**	**10**	**24**	**71**	**0**	**3**	**1**	**98**	**15.3**	**44**	**3**	**76**	**35**	**0**	....	....	....	....	....	....	....	....
1994-95	**Los Angeles Kings**	**NHL**	**48**	**7**	**9**	**16**	**12**	**13**	**25**	**12**	**0**	**1**	**0**	**64**	**10.9**	**27**	**0**	**56**	**20**	**–9**	....	....	....	....	....	....	....	....
1995-96	**Los Angeles Kings**	**NHL**	**35**	**5**	**2**	**7**	**5**	**2**	**7**	**18**	**0**	**1**	**2**	**35**	**14.3**	**12**	**0**	**27**	**7**	**–8**	....	....	....	....	....	....	....	....
	Calgary Flames	**NHL**	**7**	**0**	**0**	**0**	**0**	**0**	**0**	**0**	**0**	**0**	**0**	**1**	**0.0**	**2**	**0**	**5**	**2**	**–1**	....	....	....	....	....	....	....	....
	New York Islanders	**NHL**	**13**	**1**	**1**	**2**	**1**	**1**	**2**	**0**	**0**	**0**	**0**	**9**	**11.1**	**4**	**0**	**11**	**3**	**–4**	....	....	....	....	....	....	....	....
	NHL Totals		**521**	**63**	**76**	**139**	**63**	**62**	**125**	**235**	**0**	**9**	**6**	**495**	**12.7**	**246**	**8**	**466**	**190**		**66**	**11**	**10**	**21**	**40**	**0**	**2**	**1**

Signed as a free agent by **Edmonton**, October 4, 1983. Signed as a free agent by **New Jersey**, April 14, 1985. Traded to **LA Kings** by **New Jersey** for future considerations, September 3, 1992. Traded to **Calgary** by **LA Kings** for Craig Ferguson, February 10, 1996. Traded to **NY Islanders** by **Calgary** with Calgary's 6th round choice (later returned to Calgary — Calgary selected Ilja Demidov) in 1997 Entry Draft for Bob Sweeney, March 20, 1996.

• CONN, ROB
Rob Conn LW/RW – R. 6'2", 200 lbs. b: Calgary, Alta., 9/3/1968.

			REGULAR SEASON																		PLAYOFFS							
Season	Club	League	GP	G	A	Pts	AG	AA	APts	PIM	PP	SH	GW	S	%	TGF	PGF	TGA	PGA	+/–	GP	G	A	Pts	PIM	PP	SH	GW
1988-89	University of Alaska-Anchorage	G-North	33	21	17	38	....	....	....	46	....	....	....	....	....	....	....	....	....	....	....	....	....	....	....	....	....	....
1989-90	University of Alaska-Anchorage	G-North	34	27	21	48	....	....	....	46	....	....	....	....	....	....	....	....	....	....	....	....	....	....	....	....	....	....
1990-91	University of Alaska-Anchorage	G-North	43	28	32	60	....	....	....	53	....	....	....	....	....	....	....	....	....	....	....	....	....	....	....	....	....	....
1991-92	**Chicago Blackhawks**	**NHL**	**2**	**0**	**0**	**0**	**0**	**0**	**0**	**2**	**0**	**0**	**0**	**3**	**0.0**	**1**	**0**	**0**	**0**	**+1**	....	....	....	....	....	....	....	....
	Indianapolis Ice	IHL	72	19	16	35	....	....	....	100	....	....	....	....	....	....	....	....	....	....	....	....	....	....	....	....	....	....
1992-93	Indianapolis Ice	IHL	75	13	14	27	....	....	....	81	....	....	....	....	....	....	....	....	....	....	5	0	1	1	6	....	....	....
1993-94	Indianapolis Ice	IHL	51	16	11	27	....	....	....	46	....	....	....	....	....	....	....	....	....	....	....	....	....	....	....	....	....	....
1994-95	Indianapolis Ice	IHL	10	4	4	8	....	....	....	11	....	....	....	....	....	....	....	....	....	....	....	....	....	....	....	....	....	....
	Albany River Rats	AHL	68	35	32	67	....	....	....	76	....	....	....	....	....	....	....	....	....	....	14	4	6	10	16	....	....	....

			REGULAR SEASON																		PLAYOFFS							
Season	Club	League	GP	G	A	Pts	AG	AA	APts	PIM	PP	SH	GW	S	%	TGF	PGF	TGA	PGA	+/–	GP	G	A	Pts	PIM	PP	SH	GW
1995-96	**Buffalo Sabres**	**NHL**	**28**	**2**	**5**	**7**	**2**	**4**	**6**	**18**	**0**	**0**	**0**	**36**	**5.6**	**8**	**0**	**17**	**0**	**–9**	....	....	....	....	....	....	....	....
	Rochester Americans	AHL	36	22	15	37	....	....	....	40	....	....	....	....	....	....	....	....	....	....	19	7	6	13	10	....	....	....
1996-97	Indianapolis Ice	IHL	72	25	32	57	....	....	....	81	....	....	....	....	....	....	....	....	....	....	4	0	0	0	8	....	....	....
	NHL Totals		**30**	**2**	**5**	**7**	**2**	**4**	**6**	**20**	**0**	**0**	**0**	**39**	**5.1**	**9**	**0**	**17**	**0**		....	....	....	....	....	....	....	....

Signed as a free agent by **Chicago**, July 31, 1991. Traded to **New Jersey** by **Chicago** for Dean Malkoc, January 30, 1995. Claimed by **Buffalo** from **New Jersey** in NHL Waiver Draft, October 2, 1995. Signed as a free agent by **Chicago**, September 26, 1996.

• CONNELLY, WAYNE

Wayne Connelly C – R. 5'10", 170 lbs. b: Rouyn, Que., 12/16/1939.

Season	Club	League	GP	G	A	Pts	AG	AA	APts	PIM	PP	SH	GW	S	%	TGF	PGF	TGA	PGA	+/–	GP	G	A	Pts	PIM	PP	SH	GW
1955-56	Kitchener Canucks	OHA	9	0	1	1	....	....	....	2	....	....	....	....	....	....	....	....	....	....	8	0	0	0	0	....	....	....
1956-57	Peterborough Petes	OHA	52	19	7	26	....	....	....	83	....	....	....	....	....	....	....	....	....	....	....	....	....	....	....	....	....	....
1957-58	Peterborough Petes	OHA	52	18	19	37	....	....	....	32	....	....	....	....	....	....	....	....	....	....	5	0	1	1	6	....	....	....
1958-59	Peterborough Petes	OHA	54	36	54	90	....	....	....	46	....	....	....	....	....	....	....	....	....	....	19	6	*13	*19	38	....	....	....
1959-60	Peterborough Petes	OHA	47	*48	34	82	....	....	....	47	....	....	....	....	....	....	....	....	....	....	12	10	9	19	4	....	....	....
	Montreal Royals	EPHL	....	....	....	....	....	....	....	....	....	....	....	....	....	....	....	....	....	....	8	6	4	10	4	....	....	....
1960-61	**Montreal Canadiens**	**NHL**	**3**	**0**	**0**	**0**	**0**	**0**	**0**	**0**	....	....	....	....	....	....	....	....	....	....	....	....	....	....	....	....	....	....
	Montreal Royals	EPHL	64	28	21	49	....	....	....	36	....	....	....	....	....	....	....	....	....	....	....	....	....	....	....	....	....	....
1961-62	**Boston Bruins**	**NHL**	**61**	**8**	**12**	**20**	**10**	**12**	**22**	**34**	....	....	....	....	....	....	....	....	....	....	....	....	....	....	....	....	....	....
	Hull-Ottawa Canadiens	EPHL	7	2	3	5	....	....	....	4	....	....	....	....	....	....	....	....	....	....	....	....	....	....	....	....	....	....
1962-63	**Boston Bruins**	**NHL**	**18**	**2**	**6**	**8**	**2**	**6**	**8**	**2**	....	....	....	....	....	....	....	....	....	....	....	....	....	....	....	....	....	....
	Kingston Frontenacs	EPHL	34	10	24	34	....	....	....	19	....	....	....	....	....	....	....	....	....	....	5	1	4	5	2	....	....	....
1963-64	**Boston Bruins**	**NHL**	**26**	**2**	**3**	**5**	**3**	**3**	**6**	**12**	....	....	....	....	....	....	....	....	....	....	....	....	....	....	....	....	....	....
	San Francisco Seals	WHL	33	12	18	30	....	....	....	10	....	....	....	....	....	....	....	....	....	....	11	2	3	5	8	....	....	....
1964-65	San Francisco Seals	WHL	70	36	36	72	....	....	....	51	....	....	....	....	....	....	....	....	....	....	....	....	....	....	....	....	....	....
1965-66	San Francisco Seals	WHL	72	45	41	86	....	....	....	14	....	....	....	....	....	....	....	....	....	....	7	4	4	8	2	....	....	....
1966-67	**Boston Bruins**	**NHL**	**64**	**13**	**17**	**30**	**16**	**17**	**33**	**12**	....	....	....	....	....	....	....	....	....	....	....	....	....	....	....	....	....	....
1967-68	**Minnesota North Stars**	**NHL**	**74**	**35**	**21**	**56**	**44**	**22**	**66**	**40**	**14**	**0**	**8**	**258**	**13.6**	**82**	**40**	**75**	**1**	**–32**	**14**	***8**	**3**	**11**	**2**	**3**	**0**	**0**
1968-69	**Minnesota North Stars**	**NHL**	**55**	**14**	**16**	**30**	**16**	**15**	**31**	**11**	**4**	**0**	**1**	**193**	**7.3**	**55**	**22**	**58**	**0**	**–25**	....	....	....	....	....	....	....	....
	Detroit Red Wings	**NHL**	**19**	**4**	**9**	**13**	**4**	**8**	**12**	**0**	**1**	**0**	**0**	**58**	**6.9**	**22**	**10**	**20**	**1**	**–7**	....	....	....	....	....	....	....	....
1969-70	**Detroit Red Wings**	**NHL**	**76**	**23**	**36**	**59**	**27**	**36**	**63**	**10**	**5**	**0**	**5**	**242**	**9.5**	**114**	**42**	**56**	**11**	**+27**	**4**	**1**	**3**	**4**	**2**	**1**	**0**	**0**
1970-71	**Detroit Red Wings**	**NHL**	**51**	**8**	**13**	**21**	**8**	**11**	**19**	**12**	**1**	**0**	**2**	**115**	**7.0**	**39**	**13**	**52**	**3**	**–23**	....	....	....	....	....	....	....	....
	St. Louis Blues	**NHL**	**28**	**5**	**16**	**21**	**5**	**14**	**19**	**9**	**3**	**0**	**0**	**102**	**4.9**	**35**	**19**	**22**	**0**	**–6**	**6**	**2**	**1**	**3**	**0**	**1**	**0**	**1**
1971-72	**St. Louis Blues**	**NHL**	**15**	**5**	**5**	**10**	**5**	**5**	**10**	**2**	**2**	**0**	**0**	**48**	**10.4**	**15**	**7**	**14**	**0**	**–6**	....	....	....	....	....	....	....	....
	Vancouver Canucks	**NHL**	**53**	**14**	**20**	**34**	**15**	**18**	**33**	**12**	**6**	**0**	**3**	**151**	**9.3**	**52**	**23**	**47**	**3**	**–15**	....	....	....	....	....	....	....	....
1972-73	Minnesota Fighting Saints	WHA	78	40	30	70	....	....	....	16	....	....	....	....	....	....	....	....	....	....	5	1	3	4	0	....	....	....
1973-74	Minnesota Fighting Saints	WHA	78	42	53	95	....	....	....	16	....	....	....	....	....	....	....	....	....	....	11	6	7	13	4	....	....	....
1974-75	Minnesota Fighting Saints	WHA	76	38	33	71	....	....	....	16	....	....	....	....	....	....	....	....	....	....	12	8	4	12	10	....	....	....
1975-76	Minnesota Fighting Saints	WHA	59	24	23	47	....	....	....	19	....	....	....	....	....	....	....	....	....	....	....	....	....	....	....	....	....	....
	Cleveland Crusaders	WHA	12	5	2	7	....	....	....	4	....	....	....	....	....	....	....	....	....	....	3	1	0	1	2	....	....	....
1976-77	Calgary Cowboys	WHA	25	5	6	11	....	....	....	4	....	....	....	....	....	....	....	....	....	....	....	....	....	....	....	....	....	....
	Edmonton Oilers	WHA	38	13	15	28	....	....	....	18	....	....	....	....	....	....	....	....	....	....	5	0	1	1	0	....	....	....
	NHL Totals		**543**	**133**	**174**	**307**	**155**	**167**	**322**	**156**	**36**	**0**	**19**	**1167**	**11.4**	**414**	**176**	**344**	**19**		**24**	**11**	**7**	**18**	**4**	**5**	**0**	**1**
	Other Major League Totals		366	167	162	329	....	....	....	93	....	....	....	....	....	....	....	....	....	....	36	16	15	31	16	....	....	....

WHL Second All-Star Team (1965, 1966)

Traded to **Boston** by **Montreal** for cash, June 10, 1961. Claimed by **Minnesota** from **Boston** in Expansion Draft, June 6, 1967. Traded to **Detroit** by **Minnesota** for Danny Lawson and Brian Conacher, February 15, 1969. Traded to **St. Louis** by **Detroit** with Garry Unger for Red Berenson and Tim Ecclestone, February 6, 1971. Traded to **NY Rangers** by **St. Louis** with Gene Carr and Jim Lorentz for Andre Dupont, Jack Egers and Mike Murphy, November 15, 1971. Traded to **Vancouver** by **NY Rangers** with Dave Balon and Ron Stewart for Gary Doak and Jim Wiste, November 16, 1971. Selected by **Minnesota** (WHA) in 1972 WHA General Player Draft, February 12, 1972. Signed as a free agent by **Cleveland** (WHA) after **Minnesota** (WHA) franchise folded, March, 1976. Traded to **New England** (WHA) by **Cleveland** (WHA) for Fred O'Donnell and Bob McManama, June, 1976. Traded to **Calgary** (WHA) by **New England** (WHA) for cash, October, 1976. Traded to **Edmonton** (WHA) by **Calgary** (WHA) with Claude St. Sauveur for cash, January, 1977.

• CONNOR, CAM

Cam Connor RW – L. 6'2", 200 lbs. b: Winnipeg, Man., 8/10/1954. Montreal's 1st choice, 5th overall, in 1974 Amateur Draft.

Season	Club	League	GP	G	A	Pts	AG	AA	APts	PIM	PP	SH	GW	S	%	TGF	PGF	TGA	PGA	+/–	GP	G	A	Pts	PIM	PP	SH	GW
1971-72	St. Boniface Canadians	MJHL	32	4	10	14	....	....	....	97	....	....	....	....	....	....	....	....	....	....	....	....	....	....	....	....	....	....
	Winnipeg Jets	WCJHL	5	0	4	4	....	....	....	4	....	....	....	....	....	....	....	....	....	....	....	....	....	....	....	....	....	....
1972-73	St. Boniface Canadians	MJHL	STATISTICS NOT AVAILABLE																									
1973-74	Flin Flon Bombers	WCJHL	65	47	44	91	....	....	....	376	....	....	....	....	....	....	....	....	....	....	....	....	....	....	....	....	....	....
1974-75	Phoenix Roadrunners	WHA	57	9	19	28	....	....	....	168	....	....	....	....	....	....	....	....	....	....	5	0	0	0	2	....	....	....
1975-76	Phoenix Roadrunners	WHA	73	18	21	39	....	....	....	295	....	....	....	....	....	....	....	....	....	....	5	1	0	1	21	....	....	....
1976-77	Houston Aeros	WHA	76	35	32	67	....	....	....	224	....	....	....	....	....	....	....	....	....	....	11	3	4	7	47	....	....	....
1977-78	Houston Aeros	WHA	68	21	16	37	....	....	....	217	....	....	....	....	....	....	....	....	....	....	2	1	0	1	22	....	....	....
1978-79	**Montreal Canadiens**	**NHL**	**23**	**1**	**3**	**4**	**1**	**2**	**3**	**39**	**0**	**0**	**0**	**12**	**8.3**	**7**	**0**	**5**	**0**	**+2**	**8**	**1**	**0**	**1**	**0**	**0**	**0**	**1**
1979-80	**Edmonton Oilers**	**NHL**	**38**	**7**	**13**	**20**	**6**	**10**	**16**	**136**	**0**	**0**	**0**	**44**	**15.9**	**28**	**2**	**24**	**0**	**+2**	....	....	....	....	....	....	....	....
	Houston Apollos	CHL	5	1	1	2	....	....	....	20	....	....	....	....	....	....	....	....	....	....	....	....	....	....	....	....	....	....
	New York Rangers	**NHL**	**12**	**0**	**3**	**3**	**0**	**2**	**2**	**37**	**0**	**0**	**0**	**10**	**0.0**	**8**	**0**	**5**	**0**	**+3**	**2**	**0**	**0**	**0**	**2**	**0**	**0**	**0**
1980-81	**New York Rangers**	**NHL**	**15**	**1**	**3**	**4**	**1**	**2**	**3**	**44**	**0**	**0**	**0**	**16**	**6.3**	**11**	**0**	**5**	**0**	**+6**	....	....	....	....	....	....	....	....
	New Haven Nighthawks	AHL	61	33	28	61	....	....	....	243	....	....	....	....	....	....	....	....	....	....	4	0	2	2	4	....	....	....
1981-82	Springfield Indians	AHL	78	17	34	51	....	....	....	195	....	....	....	....	....	....	....	....	....	....	....	....	....	....	....	....	....	....
	New York Rangers	**NHL**	....	....	....	....	....	....	....	....	**0**	**0**	**0**	**0**	**0.0**	**0**	**0**	**0**	**0**	**0**	**10**	**4**	**0**	**4**	**4**	**1**	**0**	**1**
1982-83	**New York Rangers**	**NHL**	**1**	**0**	**0**	**0**	**0**	**0**	**0**	**0**	**0**	**0**	**0**	**0**	**0.0**	**0**	**0**	**0**	**0**	**0**	....	....	....	....	....	....	....	....
	Tulsa Oilers	CHL	3	2	2	4	....	....	....	0	....	....	....	....	....	....	....	....	....	....	....	....	....	....	....	....	....	....
1983-84	Tulsa Oilers	CHL	64	18	32	50	....	....	....	218	....	....	....	....	....	....	....	....	....	....	6	1	1	2	34	....	....	....
	NHL Totals		**89**	**9**	**22**	**31**	**8**	**16**	**24**	**256**	**0**	**0**	**0**	**82**	**11.0**	**54**	**2**	**39**	**0**		**20**	**5**	**0**	**5**	**6**	**1**	**0**	**2**
	Other Major League Totals		274	83	88	171	....	....	....	904	....	....	....	....	....	....	....	....	....	....	23	5	4	9	92	....	....	....

Selected by **Phoenix** (WHA) in 1974 WHA Amateur Draft, June, 1974. Traded to **Houston** (WHA) by **Phoenix** (WHA) for Bob Liddington, October, 1976. Claimed by **Edmonton** from **Montreal** in Expansion Draft, June 13, 1979. Traded to **NY Rangers** by **Edmonton** with Edmonton's 3rd round choice (Peter Sundstrum) for Don Murdoch, March 11, 1980.

• CONROY, AL

Al Conroy C – R. 5'8", 170 lbs. b: Calgary, Alta., 1/17/1966.

Season	Club	League	GP	G	A	Pts	AG	AA	APts	PIM	PP	SH	GW	S	%	TGF	PGF	TGA	PGA	+/–	GP	G	A	Pts	PIM	PP	SH	GW
1982-83	Medicine Hat Tigers	WHL	68	38	57	95	....	....	....	203	....	....	....	....	....	....	....	....	....	....	5	4	3	7	16	....	....	....
1983-84	Medicine Hat Tigers	WHL	69	38	74	112	....	....	....	89	....	....	....	....	....	....	....	....	....	....	14	10	13	23	39	....	....	....
1984-85	Medicine Hat Tigers	WHL	68	41	97	138	....	....	....	150	....	....	....	....	....	....	....	....	....	....	10	1	9	10	20	....	....	....
1985-86	Medicine Hat Tigers	WHL	61	41	60	101	....	....	....	141	....	....	....	....	....	....	....	....	....	....	25	11	20	31	54	....	....	....
	Canada	WJC-A	7	4	4	8	....	....	....	6	....	....	....	....	....	....	....	....	....	....	....	....	....	....	....	....	....	....
1986-87	Rapperswill	Switz.	36	30	32	62	....	....	....	0	....	....	....	....	....	....	....	....	....	....	....	....	....	....	....	....	....	....
	Rochester Americans	AHL	13	4	4	8	....	....	....	40	....	....	....	....	....	....	....	....	....	....	13	1	3	4	50	....	....	....
1987-88	Varese	Italy	36	25	39	64	....	....	....	....	....	....	....	....	....	....	....	....	....	....	....	....	....	....	....	....	....	....
	Adirondack Red Wings	AHL	13	5	8	13	....	....	....	20	....	....	....	....	....	....	....	....	....	....	11	1	3	4	41	....	....	....
1988-89	Dortmund	Germany	46	53	78	131	....	....	....	....	....	....	....	....	....	....	....	....	....	....	....	....	....	....	....	....	....	....
1989-90	Adirondack Red Wings	AHL	77	23	33	56	....	....	....	147	....	....	....	....	....	....	....	....	....	....	5	0	0	0	20	....	....	....
1990-91	Adirondack Red Wings	AHL	80	26	39	65	....	....	....	172	....	....	....	....	....	....	....	....	....	....	2	1	1	2	0	....	....	....
1991-92	**Philadelphia Flyers**	**NHL**	**31**	**2**	**9**	**11**	**2**	**7**	**9**	**74**	**0**	**0**	**0**	**25**	**8.0**	**19**	**1**	**17**	**0**	**+1**	....	....	....	....	....	....	....	....
	Hershey Bears	AHL	47	17	28	45	....	....	....	90	....	....	....	....	....	....	....	....	....	....	6	4	2	6	12	....	....	....
1992-93	**Philadelphia Flyers**	**NHL**	**21**	**3**	**2**	**5**	**2**	**1**	**3**	**17**	**0**	**0**	**1**	**24**	**12.5**	**9**	**0**	**10**	**0**	**–1**	....	....	....	....	....	....	....	....
	Hershey Bears	AHL	60	28	32	60	....	....	....	130	....	....	....	....	....	....	....	....	....	....	....	....	....	....	....	....	....	....
1993-94	**Philadelphia Flyers**	**NHL**	**62**	**4**	**3**	**7**	**4**	**2**	**6**	**65**	**0**	**1**	**0**	**40**	**10.0**	**14**	**0**	**48**	**22**	**–12**	....	....	....	....	....	....	....	....
1994-95	Detroit Vipers	IHL	71	18	40	58	....	....	....	151	....	....	....	....	....	....	....	....	....	....	....	....	....	....	....	....	....	....
	Houston Aeros	IHL	9	3	4	7	....	....	....	17	....	....	....	....	....	....	....	....	....	....	4	1	2	3	8	....	....	....
1995-96	Houston Aeros	IHL	82	24	38	62	....	....	....	134	....	....	....	....	....	....	....	....	....	....	....	....	....	....	....	....	....	....
1996-97	Houston Aeros	IHL	70	15	32	47	....	....	....	171	....	....	....	....	....	....	....	....	....	....	13	4	10	14	26	....	....	....
1997-98	Kushiro Cranes	Japan	40	21	41	62	....	....	....	66	....	....	....	....	....	....	....	....	....	....	....	....	....	....	....	....	....	....
	NHL Totals		**114**	**9**	**14**	**23**	**8**	**10**	**18**	**156**	**0**	**1**	**1**	**89**	**10.1**	**42**	**1**	**75**	**22**		....	....	....	....	....	....	....	....

Signed as a free agent by **Detroit**, August 16, 1989. Signed as a free agent by **Philadelphia**, August 21, 1991.

• CONROY, CRAIG
Craig Conroy C – R. 6'2", 198 lbs. b: Potsdam, NY, 9/4/1971. Montreal's 7th choice, 123rd overall, in 1990 Entry Draft.

			REGULAR SEASON																		PLAYOFFS							
Season	Club	League	GP	G	A	Pts	AG	AA	APts	PIM	PP	SH	GW	S	%	TGF	PGF	TGA	PGA	+/–	GP	G	A	Pts	PIM	PP	SH	GW
1989-90	Northwood Prep School	H.S.	31	33	43	76	....	....	....	....	....	....	....	....	....	....	....	....	....	....	....	....	....	....	....	....	....	....
1990-91	Clarkson University	ECAC	40	8	21	29	....	....	....	24	....	....	....	....	....	....	....	....	....	....	....	....	....	....	....	....	....	....
1991-92	Clarkson University	ECAC	31	19	17	36	....	....	....	36	....	....	....	....	....	....	....	....	....	....	....	....	....	....	....	....	....	....
1992-93	Clarkson University	ECAC	35	10	23	33	....	....	....	26	....	....	....	....	....	....	....	....	....	....	....	....	....	....	....	....	....	....
1993-94	Clarkson University	ECAC	34	26	*40	*66	....	....	....	46	....	....	....	....	....	....	....	....	....	....	....	....	....	....	....	....	....	....
1994-95	**Montreal Canadiens**	**NHL**	**6**	**1**	**0**	**1**	**2**	**0**	**2**	**0**	**0**	**0**	**0**	**4**	**25.0**	**1**	**0**	**2**	**0**	**–1**	....	....	....	....	....	....	....	....
	Fredericton Canadiens	AHL	55	26	18	44	....	....	....	29	....	....	....	....	....	....	....	....	....	....	11	7	3	10	6	....	....	....
1995-96	**Montreal Canadiens**	**NHL**	**7**	**0**	**0**	**0**	**0**	**0**	**0**	**2**	**0**	**0**	**0**	**1**	**0.0**	**0**	**0**	**4**	**0**	**–4**	....	....	....	....	....	....	....	....
	Fredericton Canadiens	AHL	67	31	38	69	....	....	....	65	....	....	....	....	....	....	....	....	....	....	10	5	7	12	6	....	....	....
1996-97	Fredericton Canadiens	AHL	9	10	6	16	....	....	....	10	....	....	....	....	....	....	....	....	....	....	....	....	....	....	....	....	....	....
	St. Louis Blues	**NHL**	**61**	**6**	**11**	**17**	**6**	**10**	**16**	**43**	**0**	**0**	**1**	**74**	**8.1**	**23**	**1**	**39**	**17**	**0**	**6**	**0**	**0**	**0**	**8**	**0**	**0**	**0**
	Worcester IceCats	AHL	5	5	6	11	....	....	....	2	....	....	....	....	....	....	....	....	....	....	....	....	....	....	....	....	....	....
1997-98	**St. Louis Blues**	**NHL**	**81**	**14**	**29**	**43**	**16**	**28**	**44**	**46**	**0**	**3**	**1**	**118**	**11.9**	**54**	**1**	**56**	**23**	**+20**	**10**	**1**	**2**	**3**	**8**	**0**	**0**	**1**
	NHL Totals		**155**	**21**	**40**	**61**	**24**	**38**	**62**	**91**	**0**	**3**	**2**	**197**	**10.7**	**78**	**2**	**101**	**40**		**16**	**1**	**2**	**3**	**16**	**0**	**0**	**1**

ECAC First All-Star Team (1994) • NCAA East First All-American Team (1994) • NCAA Final Four All-Tournament Team (1994)

Traded to **St. Louis** by **Montreal** with Pierre Turgeon and Rory Fitzpatrick for Murray Baron, Shayne Corson and St. Louis' 5th round choice (Gennady Razin) in 1997 Entry Draft, October 29, 1996.

• CONTINI, JOE
Joe Contini C – L. 5'10", 178 lbs. b: Galt, Ont., 1/29/1957. Colorado's 7th choice, 126th overall, in 1977 Amateur Draft.

			REGULAR SEASON																		PLAYOFFS							
Season	Club	League	GP	G	A	Pts	AG	AA	APts	PIM	PP	SH	GW	S	%	TGF	PGF	TGA	PGA	+/–	GP	G	A	Pts	PIM	PP	SH	GW
1974-75	Hamilton Red Wings	OHA	68	27	63	90	....	....	....	152	....	....	....	....	....	....	....	....	....	....	....	....	....	....	....	....	....	....
1975-76	Hamilton Fincups	OHA	54	28	52	80	....	....	....	105	....	....	....	....	....	....	....	....	....	....	....	....	....	....	....	....	....	....
1976-77	St. Catharines Fincups	OHL	28	17	29	46	....	....	....	61	....	....	....	....	....	....	....	....	....	....	....	....	....	....	....	....	....	....
	Canada	WJC-A	7	4	5	9	....	....	....	32	....	....	....	....	....	....	....	....	....	....	....	....	....	....	....	....	....	....
1977-78	**Colorado Rockies**	**NHL**	**37**	**12**	**9**	**21**	**12**	**7**	**19**	**28**	**3**	**0**	**0**	**49**	**24.5**	**29**	**8**	**23**	**0**	**–2**	**2**	**0**	**0**	**0**	**0**	**0**	**0**	**0**
	Phoenix Roadrunners	CHL	2	0	0	0	....	....	....	2	....	....	....	....	....	....	....	....	....	....	....	....	....	....	....	....	....	....
	Flint Generals	IHL	31	17	28	45	....	....	....	25	....	....	....	....	....	....	....	....	....	....	....	....	....	....	....	....	....	....
1978-79	**Colorado Rockies**	**NHL**	**30**	**5**	**12**	**17**	**5**	**9**	**14**	**6**	**2**	**0**	**1**	**26**	**19.2**	**27**	**14**	**32**	**0**	**–19**	....	....	....	....	....	....	....	....
	Philadelphia Firebirds	AHL	36	8	9	17	....	....	....	45	....	....	....	....	....	....	....	....	....	....	....	....	....	....	....	....	....	....
1979-80	Fort Worth Texans	CHL	8	1	2	3	....	....	....	13	....	....	....	....	....	....	....	....	....	....	....	....	....	....	....	....	....	....
	Oklahoma City Stars	CHL	58	19	43	62	....	....	....	56	....	....	....	....	....	....	....	....	....	....	....	....	....	....	....	....	....	....
1980-81	**Minnesota North Stars**	**NHL**	**1**	**0**	**0**	**0**	**0**	**0**	**0**	**0**	**0**	**0**	**0**	**0**	**0.0**	**0**	**0**	**0**	**0**	**0**	....	....	....	....	....	....	....	....
	Oklahoma City Stars	CHL	77	32	63	95	....	....	....	28	....	....	....	....	....	....	....	....	....	....	3	0	1	1	2	....	....	....
1981-82	Hershey Bears	AHL	56	20	37	57	....	....	....	68	....	....	....	....	....	....	....	....	....	....	5	1	5	6	6	....	....	....
	Muskegon Mohawks	IHL	17	9	7	16	....	....	....	4	....	....	....	....	....	....	....	....	....	....	....	....	....	....	....	....	....	....
	NHL Totals		**68**	**17**	**21**	**38**	**17**	**16**	**33**	**34**	**5**	**0**	**1**	**75**	**22.7**	**56**	**22**	**55**	**0**		**2**	**0**	**0**	**0**	**0**	**0**	**0**	**0**

Claimed by **Colorado** as a fill-in during Expansion Draft, June 13, 1979. Signed as a free agent by **Minnesota**, February 1, 1980.

• CONVERY, BRANDON
Brandon Convery C – R. 6'1", 182 lbs. b: Kingston, Ont., 2/4/1974. Toronto's 1st choice, 8th overall, in 1992 Entry Draft.

			REGULAR SEASON																		PLAYOFFS							
Season	Club	League	GP	G	A	Pts	AG	AA	APts	PIM	PP	SH	GW	S	%	TGF	PGF	TGA	PGA	+/–	GP	G	A	Pts	PIM	PP	SH	GW
1990-91	Sudbury Wolves	OHL	56	26	22	48	....	....	....	18	....	....	....	....	....	....	....	....	....	....	5	1	1	2	2	....	....	....
1991-92	Sudbury Wolves	OHL	44	40	26	66	....	....	....	44	....	....	....	....	....	....	....	....	....	....	5	3	2	5	4	....	....	....
1992-93	Sudbury Wolves	OHL	7	7	9	16	....	....	....	6	....	....	....	....	....	....	....	....	....	....	....	....	....	....	....	....	....	....
	Niagara Falls Thunder	OHL	51	38	39	77	....	....	....	24	....	....	....	....	....	....	....	....	....	....	4	1	3	4	4	....	....	....
	St. John's Maple Leafs	AHL	3	0	0	0	....	....	....	0	....	....	....	....	....	....	....	....	....	....	5	0	1	1	0	....	....	....
1993-94	Niagara Falls Thunder	OHL	29	24	29	53	....	....	....	30	....	....	....	....	....	....	....	....	....	....	....	....	....	....	....	....	....	....
	Canada	WJC-A	7	1	0	1	....	....	....	2	....	....	....	....	....	....	....	....	....	....	....	....	....	....	....	....	....	....
	Belleville Bulls	OHL	23	16	19	35	....	....	....	22	....	....	....	....	....	....	....	....	....	....	12	4	10	14	13	....	....	....
	St. John's Maple Leafs	AHL	....	....	....	....	....	....	....	....	....	....	....	....	....	....	....	....	....	....	1	0	0	0	0	....	....	....
1994-95	St. John's Maple Leafs	AHL	76	34	37	71	....	....	....	43	....	....	....	....	....	....	....	....	....	....	5	2	2	4	4	....	....	....
	Canada	WC-A	8	0	1	1	....	....	....	0	....	....	....	....	....	....	....	....	....	....	....	....	....	....	....	....	....	....
1995-96	**Toronto Maple Leafs**	**NHL**	**11**	**5**	**2**	**7**	**5**	**2**	**7**	**4**	**3**	**0**	**1**	**16**	**31.3**	**7**	**3**	**11**	**0**	**–7**	**5**	**0**	**0**	**0**	**2**	**0**	**0**	**0**
	St. John's Maple Leafs	AHL	57	[illegible]	[illegible]	15	....	....	....	28	....	....	....	....														
1996-97	**Toronto Maple Leafs**	**NHL**	**39**	**2**	**8**	**10**	**2**	**7**	**9**	**20**	**0**	**0**	**0**	**41**	**4.9**	**13**	**3**	**25**	**6**	**–9**	....	....	....	....	....	....	....	....
	St. John's Maple Leafs	AHL	25	14	14	28	....	....	....	15	....	....	....	....	....	....	....	....	....	....	....	....	....	....	....	....	....	....
1997-98	St. John's Maple Leafs	AHL	49	27	36	63	....	....	....	35	....	....	....	....	....	....	....	....	....	....	....	....	....	....	....	....	....	....
	Vancouver Canucks	**NHL**	**7**	**0**	**2**	**2**	**0**	**2**	**2**	**0**	**0**	**0**	**0**	**2**	**0.0**	**4**	**3**	**1**	**0**	**0**	....	....	....	....	....	....	....	....
	Syracuse Crunch	AHL	2	1	2	3	....	....	....	5	....	....	....	....	....	....	....	....	....	....	....	....	....	....	....	....	....	....
	NHL Totals		**57**	**7**	**12**	**19**	**7**	**11**	**18**	**24**	**3**	**0**	**1**	**59**	**11.9**	**24**	**9**	**37**	**6**		**5**	**0**	**0**	**0**	**2**	**0**	**0**	**0**

Traded to **Vancouver** by **Toronto** for Lonny Bohonos, March 7, 1998.

• COOK, BOB
Bob "Cookie" Cook RW – R. 6', 190 lbs. b: Sudbury, Ont., 1/6/1946. Deceased.

			REGULAR SEASON																		PLAYOFFS							
Season	Club	League	GP	G	A	Pts	AG	AA	APts	PIM	PP	SH	GW	S	%	TGF	PGF	TGA	PGA	+/–	GP	G	A	Pts	PIM	PP	SH	GW
1965-66	London Nationals	OHA	14	2	10	12	....	....	....	14	....	....	....	....	....	....	....	....	....	....	....	....	....	....	....	....	....	....
	Kitchener Rangers	OHA	31	10	7	17	....	....	....	72	....	....	....	....	....	....	....	....	....	....	19	9	5	14	51	....	....	....
1966-67	Vancouver Canucks	WHL	55	7	7	14	....	....	....	31	....	....	....	....	....	....	....	....	....	....	5	0	0	0	11	....	....	....
1967-68	Vancouver Canucks	WHL	1	0	0	0	....	....	....	0	....	....	....	....	....	....	....	....	....	....	....	....	....	....	....	....	....	....
	Rochester Americans	AHL	61	22	16	38	....	....	....	95	....	....	....	....	....	....	....	....	....	....	1	0	0	0	0	....	....	....
1968-69	Rochester Americans	AHL	59	4	6	10	....	....	....	24	....	....	....	....	....	....	....	....	....	....	....	....	....	....	....	....	....	....
	Tulsa Oilers	CHL	12	6	7	13	....	....	....	14	....	....	....	....	....	....	....	....	....	....	6	0	2	2	8	....	....	....
1969-70	Rochester Americans	AHL	71	26	18	44	....	....	....	78	....	....	....	....	....	....	....	....	....	....	....	....	....	....	....	....	....	....
1970-71	**Vancouver Canucks**	**NHL**	**2**	**0**	**0**	**0**	**0**	**0**	**0**	**0**	**0**	**0**	**0**	**2**	**0.0**	**0**	**0**	**0**	**0**	**0**	....	....	....	....	....	....	....	....
	Rochester Americans	AHL	68	22	19	41	....	....	....	66	....	....	....	....	....	....	....	....	....	....	....	....	....	....	....	....	....	....
1971-72	Fort Worth Wings	CHL	15	4	4	8	....	....	....	24	....	....	....	....	....	....	....	....	....	....	....	....	....	....	....	....	....	....
	Seattle Totems	WHL	15	3	3	6	....	....	....	27	....	....	....	....	....	....	....	....	....	....	....	....	....	....	....	....	....	....
	Tidewater Wings	AHL	35	9	8	17	....	....	....	40	....	....	....	....	....	....	....	....	....	....	....	....	....	....	....	....	....	....
1972-73	**Detroit Red Wings**	**NHL**	**13**	**3**	**1**	**4**	**3**	**1**	**4**	**4**	**1**	**0**	**0**	**23**	**13.0**	**4**	**1**	**14**	**0**	**–11**	....	....	....	....	....	....	....	....
	Virginia Wings	AHL	23	17	9	26	....	....	....	70	....	....	....	....	....	....	....	....	....	....	....	....	....	....	....	....	....	....
	New York Islanders	**NHL**	**33**	**8**	**6**	**14**	**8**	**5**	**13**	**14**	**1**	**0**	**0**	**83**	**9.6**	**22**	**2**	**20**	**0**	**–9**	....	....	....	....	....	....	....	....
1973-74	**New York Islanders**	**NHL**	**22**	**2**	**1**	**3**	**2**	**1**	**3**	**4**	**0**	**0**	**0**	**20**	**10.0**	**7**	**1**	**3**	**0**	**+3**	....	....	....	....	....	....	....	....
	Baltimore Clippers	AHL	52	19	19	38	....	....	....	35	....	....	....	....	....	....	....	....	....	....	9	5	5	10	10	....	....	....
1974-75	**Minnesota North Stars**	**NHL**	**2**	**0**	**1**	**1**	**0**	**1**	**1**	**0**	**0**	**0**	**0**	**9**	**0.0**	**1**	**0**	**2**	**0**	**–1**	....	....	....	....	....	....	....	....
	Fort Worth Texans	CHL	22	3	6	9	....	....	....	37	....	....	....	....	....	....	....	....	....	....	....	....	....	....	....	....	....	....
	New Haven Nighthawks	AHL	50	15	26	41	....	....	....	43	....	....	....	....	....	....	....	....	....	....	16	7	5	12	14	....	....	....
	NHL Totals		**72**	**13**	**9**	**22**	**13**	**8**	**21**	**22**	**2**	**0**	**0**	**137**	**9.5**	**34**	**4**	**48**	**0**		....	....	....	....	....	....	....	....

NHL rights transferred to **Vancouver** after owners of **Rochester** (AHL) franchise granted NHL expansion team, May 22, 1970. Traded to **Detroit** by **Vancouver** for cash, November 21, 1971. Traded to **NY Islanders** by **Detroit** with Ralph Stewart for Ken Murray and Brian Lavender, January 17, 1973. Traded to **Minnesota** by **NY Islanders** for cash, January 5, 1975.

• COOPER, DAVID
David Cooper D – L. 6'2", 204 lbs. b: Ottawa, Ont., 11/2/1973. Buffalo's 1st choice, 11th overall, in 1992 Entry Draft.

			REGULAR SEASON																		PLAYOFFS							
Season	Club	League	GP	G	A	Pts	AG	AA	APts	PIM	PP	SH	GW	S	%	TGF	PGF	TGA	PGA	+/–	GP	G	A	Pts	PIM	PP	SH	GW
1989-90	Medicine Hat Tigers	WHL	61	4	11	15	....	....	....	65	....	....	....	....	....	....	....	....	....	....	3	0	2	2	2	....	....	....
1990-91	Medicine Hat Tigers	WHL	64	12	31	43	....	....	....	66	....	....	....	....	....	....	....	....	....	....	11	1	3	4	23	....	....	....
1991-92	Medicine Hat Tigers	WHL	72	17	47	64	....	....	....	176	....	....	....	....	....	....	....	....	....	....	4	1	4	5	8	....	....	....
1992-93	Medicine Hat Tigers	WHL	63	15	50	65	....	....	....	88	....	....	....	....	....	....	....	....	....	....	10	2	2	4	32	....	....	....
	Rochester Americans	AHL	....	....	....	....	....	....	....	....	....	....	....	....	....	....	....	....	....	....	2	0	0	0	2	....	....	....
1993-94	Rochester Americans	AHL	68	10	25	35	....	....	....	82	....	....	....	....	....	....	....	....	....	....	4	1	1	2	2	....	....	....
1994-95	Rochester Americans	AHL	21	2	4	6	....	....	....	48	....	....	....	....	....	....	....	....	....	....	....	....	....	....	....	....	....	....
	South Carolina Stingrays	ECHL	[illegible]	[illegible]	10	28	....	....	....	[illegible]	....	....	....	....	....	....					9	3	8	11	24			
1995-96	Rochester Americans	AHL	67	9	18	27	....	....	....	79	....	....	....	....	....	....	....	....	....	....	8	0	1	1	12	....	....	....

Season	Club	League	GP	G	A	Pts	AG	AA	APts	PIM	PP	SH	GW	S	%	TGF	PGF	TGA	PGA	+/–	GP	G	A	Pts	PIM	PP	SH	GW
			REGULAR SEASON																		PLAYOFFS							
1996-97	**Toronto Maple Leafs**	**NHL**	**19**	**3**	**3**	**6**	**3**	**3**	**6**	**16**	**2**	**0**	**0**	**23**	**13.0**	**14**	**6**	**12**	**1**	**–3**	....	....	....	....	....	....	....	....
	St. John's Maple Leafs	AHL	44	16	19	35	....	....	....	65	....	....	....	....	....	....	....	....	....	....	....	....	....	....	....	....	....	....
1997-98	**Toronto Maple Leafs**	**NHL**	**9**	**0**	**4**	**4**	**0**	**4**	**4**	**8**	**0**	**0**	**0**	**13**	**0.0**	**5**	**1**	**2**	**0**	**+2**	....	....	....	....	....	....	....	....
	St. John's Maple Leafs	AHL	60	19	23	42	....	....	....	117	....	....	....	....	....	....	....	....	....	....	4	0	1	1	6	....	....	....
	NHL Totals		**28**	**3**	**7**	**10**	**3**	**7**	**10**	**24**	**2**	**0**	**0**	**36**	**8.3**	**19**	**7**	**14**	**1**		....	....	....	....	....	....	....	....

WHL East First All-Star Team (1992) • AHL Second All-Star Team (1998)

Signed as a free agent by **Toronto**, September 26, 1996. Traded to **Calgary** by **Toronto** for Ladislav Kohn, July 2, 1998.

• COOPER, ED

Ed Cooper LW – L. 5'10", 188 lbs. b: Loon Lake, Sask., 8/28/1960. Colorado's 4th choice, 85th overall, in 1980 Entry Draft.

Season	Club	League	GP	G	A	Pts	AG	AA	APts	PIM	PP	SH	GW	S	%	TGF	PGF	TGA	PGA	+/–	GP	G	A	Pts	PIM	PP	SH	GW
1977-78	Estevan Bruins	SJHL	49	30	37	67	....	....	....	137	....	....	....	....	....	....	....	....	....	....	....	....	....	....	....	....	....	....
	New Westminster Bruins	WCJHL	1	0	0	0	....	....	....	0	....	....	....	....	....	....	....	....	....	....	....	....	....	....	....	....	....	....
1978-79	Portland Winter Hawks	WHL	66	8	17	25	....	....	....	61	....	....	....	....	....	....	....	....	....	....	25	6	4	10	15	....	....	....
1979-80	Portland Winter Hawks	WHL	44	35	43	78	....	....	....	76	....	....	....	....	....	....	....	....	....	....	8	5	2	7	21	....	....	....
1980-81	**Colorado Rockies**	**NHL**	**47**	**7**	**7**	**14**	**6**	**5**	**11**	**46**	**1**	**0**	**2**	**52**	**13.5**	**26**	**1**	**34**	**3**	**–6**	....	....	....	....	....	....	....	....
	Fort Worth Texans	CHL	26	6	9	15	....	....	....	21	....	....	....	....	....	....	....	....	....	....	....	....	....	....	....	....	....	....
1981-82	**Colorado Rockies**	**NHL**	**2**	**1**	**0**	**1**	**1**	**0**	**1**	**0**	**0**	**0**	**0**	**1**	**100.0**	**2**	**0**	**2**	**0**	**0**	....	....	....	....	....	....	....	....
	Fort Worth Texans	CHL	47	12	25	37	....	....	....	26	....	....	....	....	....	....	....	....	....	....	....	....	....	....	....	....	....	....
	Wichita Wind	CHL	4	1	4	5	....	....	....	0	....	....	....	....	....	....	....	....	....	....	6	1	1	2	0	....	....	....
1982-83			DID NOT PLAY																									
1983-84	Muskegon Mohawks	IHL	5	1	3	4	....	....	....	0	....	....	....	....	....	....	....	....	....	....	....	....	....	....	....	....	....	....
1984-85	Nelson Maple Leafs	WIHL	10	7	9	16	....	....	....	4	....	....	....	....	....	....	....	....	....	....	....	....	....	....	....	....	....	....
	NHL Totals		**49**	**8**	**7**	**15**	**7**	**5**	**12**	**46**	**1**	**0**	**2**	**53**	**15.1**	**28**	**1**	**36**	**3**		....	....	....	....	....	....	....	....

Traded to **Edmonton** by **Colorado** for Stan Weir, March 9, 1982.

• CORBET, RENE

Rene Corbet LW – L. 6', 187 lbs. b: Victoriaville, Que., 6/25/1973. Quebec's 2nd choice, 24th overall, in 1991 Entry Draft.

Season	Club	League	GP	G	A	Pts	AG	AA	APts	PIM	PP	SH	GW	S	%	TGF	PGF	TGA	PGA	+/–	GP	G	A	Pts	PIM	PP	SH	GW
1990-91	Drummondville Voltigeurs	QMJHL	45	25	40	65	....	....	....	34	....	....	....	....	....	....	....	....	....	....	14	11	6	17	15	....	....	....
1991-92	Drummondville Voltigeurs	QMJHL	56	46	50	96	....	....	....	90	....	....	....	....	....	....	....	....	....	....	4	1	2	3	17	....	....	....
1992-93	Drummondville Voltigeurs	QMJHL	63	*79	69	*148	....	....	....	143	....	....	....	....	....	....	....	....	....	....	10	7	13	20	16	....	....	....
1993-94	**Quebec Nordiques**	**NHL**	**9**	**1**	**1**	**2**	**1**	**1**	**2**	**0**	**0**	**0**	**0**	**14**	**7.1**	**6**	**1**	**4**	**0**	**+1**	....	....	....	....	....	....	....	....
	Cornwall Aces	AHL	68	37	40	77	....	....	....	56	....	....	....	....	....	....	....	....	....	....	13	7	2	9	18	....	....	....
1994-95	**Quebec Nordiques**	**NHL**	**8**	**0**	**3**	**3**	**0**	**4**	**4**	**2**	**0**	**0**	**0**	**4**	**0.0**	**4**	**0**	**1**	**0**	**+3**	**2**	**0**	**1**	**1**	**0**	**0**	**0**	**0**
	Cornwall Aces	AHL	65	33	24	57	....	....	....	79	....	....	....	....	....	....	....	....	....	....	12	2	8	10	27	....	....	....
1995-96	**Colorado Avalanche**	**NHL**	**33**	**3**	**6**	**9**	**3**	**5**	**8**	**33**	**0**	**0**	**0**	**35**	**8.6**	**15**	**0**	**6**	**1**	**+10**	**8**	**3**	**2**	**5**	**2**	**1**	**0**	**1**
	Cornwall Aces	AHL	9	5	6	11	....	....	....	10	....	....	....	....	....	....	....	....	....	....	....	....	....	....	....	....	....	....
1996-97	**Colorado Avalanche**	**NHL**	**76**	**12**	**15**	**27**	**13**	**13**	**26**	**67**	**1**	**0**	**3**	**128**	**9.4**	**41**	**6**	**27**	**6**	**+14**	**17**	**2**	**2**	**4**	**27**	**0**	**0**	**0**
1997-98	**Colorado Avalanche**	**NHL**	**68**	**16**	**12**	**28**	**19**	**12**	**31**	**133**	**4**	**0**	**4**	**117**	**13.7**	**41**	**13**	**21**	**1**	**+8**	**2**	**0**	**0**	**0**	**2**	**0**	**0**	**0**
	NHL Totals		**194**	**32**	**37**	**69**	**36**	**35**	**71**	**235**	**5**	**0**	**7**	**298**	**10.7**	**107**	**20**	**59**	**8**		**29**	**5**	**5**	**10**	**31**	**1**	**0**	**1**

QMJHL First All-Star Team (1993) • Canadian Major Junior First All-Star Team (1993) • Won Dudley "Red" Garrett Memorial Trophy (Top Rookie - AHL) (1994)

Transferred to **Colorado** after **Quebec** franchise relocated, June 21, 1995.

• CORBETT, MICHAEL

Michael Corbett RW/D – L. 6'2", 195 lbs. b: Toronto, Ont., 10/4/1942.

Season	Club	League	GP	G	A	Pts	AG	AA	APts	PIM	PP	SH	GW	S	%	TGF	PGF	TGA	PGA	+/–	GP	G	A	Pts	PIM	PP	SH	GW
1960-61	St. Michael's Majors	OHA	2	0	1	1	....	....	....	0	....	....	....	....	....	....	....	....	....	....	1	0	0	0	0	....	....	....
1961-62	St. Michael's Majors	Tor-Jr.	31	19	33	52	....	....	....	44	....	....	....	....	....	....	....	....	....	....	11	7	6	13	37	....	....	....
1962-63	Neil McNeil Maroons	OHA	37	*44	50	94	....	....	....	76	....	....	....	....	....	....	....	....	....	....	16	10	14	24	40	....	....	....
	Sudbury Wolves	EPHL	5	1	4	5	....	....	....	0	....	....	....	....	....	....	....	....	....	....	....	....	....	....	....	....	....	....
1963-64	Rochester Americans	AHL	50	5	10	15	....	....	....	18	....	....	....	....	....	....	....	....	....	....	....	....	....	....	....	....	....	....
	Denver Invaders	WHL	6	1	0	1	....	....	....	29	....	....	....	....	....	....	....	....	....	....	5	0	3	3	8	....	....	....
1964-65	Tulsa Oilers	CHL	55	4	18	22	....	....	....	63	....	....	....	....	....	....	....	....	....	....	9	0	1	1	10	....	....	....
1965-66	Minnesota Rangers	CHL	4	0	2	2	....	....	....	2	....	....	....	....	....	....	....	....	....	....	....	....	....	....	....	....	....	....
	Baltimore Clippers	AHL	35	4	5	9	....	....	....	50	....	....	....	....	....	....	....	....	....	....	....	....	....	....	....	....	....	....
1966-67	Providence Reds	AHL	5	0	1	1	....	....	....	14	....	....	....	....	....	....	....	....	....	....	....	....	....	....	....	....	....	....
	Springfield Indians	AHL	5	0	0	0	....	....	....	12	....	....	....	....	....	....	....	....	....	....	....	....	....	....	....	....	....	....
1967-68	Vancouver Canucks	WHL	70	17	21	38	....	....	....	83	....	....	....	....	....	....	....	....	....	....	....	....	....	....	....	....	....	....
	Los Angeles Kings	**NHL**	....	....	....	....	....	....	....	....	....	....	....	....	....	....	....	....	....	....	**2**	**0**	**1**	**1**	**2**	....	....	....
1968-69	Springfield Kings	AHL	25	3	4	7	....	....	....	54	....	....	....	....	....	....	....	....	....	....	....	....	....	....	....	....	....	....
	Dayton Gems	IHL	34	3	13	16	....	....	....	61	....	....	....	....	....	....	....	....	....	....	9	2	6	8	4	....	....	....
1969-70	Galt Hornets	OHA Sr.	28	3	17	20	....	....	....	69	....	....	....	....	....	....	....	....	....	....	....	....	....	....	....	....	....	....
1970-71			DID NOT PLAY																									
1971-72	Orillia Terriers	OHA Sr.	16	3	14	17	....	....	....	32	....	....	....	....	....	....	....	....	....	....	....	....	....	....	....	....	....	....
	Oakville Oaks	OHA Sr.	18	5	12	17	....	....	....	68	....	....	....	....	....	....	....	....	....	....	....	....	....	....	....	....	....	....
1972-73	Brantford Alexanders	OHA Sr.	28	6	14	20	....	....	....	30	....	....	....	....	....	....	....	....	....	....	....	....	....	....	....	....	....	....
1973-74	Brantford Alexanders	OHA Sr.	34	6	22	28	....	....	....	39	....	....	....	....	....	....	....	....	....	....	....	....	....	....	....	....	....	....
	NHL Totals		**0**	**0**	**0**	**0**	**0**	**0**	**0**	**0**	**0**	**0**	**0**	**0**	**0.0**	**0**	**0**	**0**	**0**		**2**	**0**	**1**	**1**	**2**	**0**	**0**	**0**

Claimed by **Baltimore** (AHL) from **Toronto** in Reverse Draft, June 9, 1965. Traded to **Providence** (AHL) by **Baltimore** (AHL) with Ed Lawson and Ken Stephenson for Aldo Guidolin, Willie Marshall, Jim Bartlett and Ian Anderson, June, 1966. Claimed on waivers by **Springfield** (AHL) from **Providence** (AHL), December, 1966. NHL rights transferred to **LA Kings** after NHL club purchased **Springfield** (AHL) franchise, May, 1967. Loaned to **Vancouver** (WHL) by **LA Kings** (Springfield - AHL), October, 1967.

• CORKUM, BOB

Bob Corkum C – R. 6'2", 210 lbs. b: Salisbury, MA, 12/18/1967. Buffalo's 3rd choice, 47th overall, in 1986 Entry Draft.

Season	Club	League	GP	G	A	Pts	AG	AA	APts	PIM	PP	SH	GW	S	%	TGF	PGF	TGA	PGA	+/–	GP	G	A	Pts	PIM	PP	SH	GW
1985-86	University of Maine	H.E.	39	7	26	33	....	....	....	53	....	....	....	....	....	....	....	....	....	....	....	....	....	....	....	....	....	....
1986-87	University of Maine	H.E.	35	18	11	29	....	....	....	24	....	....	....	....	....	....	....	....	....	....	....	....	....	....	....	....	....	....
	United States	WJC-A	7	4	0	4	....	....	....	6	....	....	....	....	....	....	....	....	....	....	....	....	....	....	....	....	....	....
1987-88	University of Maine	H.E.	40	14	18	32	....	....	....	64	....	....	....	....	....	....	....	....	....	....	....	....	....	....	....	....	....	....
1988-89	University of Maine	H.E.	45	17	31	48	....	....	....	64	....	....	....	....	....	....	....	....	....	....	....	....	....	....	....	....	....	....
1989-90	**Buffalo Sabres**	**NHL**	**8**	**2**	**0**	**2**	**2**	**0**	**2**	**4**	**0**	**0**	**1**	**6**	**33.3**	**5**	**1**	**2**	**0**	**+2**	**5**	**1**	**0**	**1**	**4**	**0**	**0**	**0**
	Rochester Americans	AHL	43	8	11	19	....	....	....	45	....	....	....	....	....	....	....	....	....	....	12	2	5	7	16	....	....	....
1990-91	Rochester Americans	AHL	69	13	21	34	....	....	....	77	....	....	....	....	....	....	....	....	....	....	15	4	4	8	4	....	....	....
1991-92	**Buffalo Sabres**	**NHL**	**20**	**2**	**4**	**6**	**2**	**3**	**5**	**21**	**0**	**0**	**0**	**23**	**8.7**	**9**	**0**	**24**	**6**	**–9**	**4**	**1**	**0**	**1**	**0**	**1**	**0**	**0**
	Rochester Americans	AHL	52	16	12	28	....	....	....	47	....	....	....	....	....	....	....	....	....	....	8	0	6	6	8	....	....	....
1992-93	**Buffalo Sabres**	**NHL**	**68**	**6**	**4**	**10**	**5**	**3**	**8**	**38**	**0**	**1**	**1**	**69**	**8.7**	**17**	**0**	**46**	**26**	**–3**	**5**	**0**	**0**	**0**	**2**	**0**	**0**	**0**
1993-94	**Anaheim Mighty Ducks**	**NHL**	**76**	**23**	**28**	**51**	**21**	**22**	**43**	**18**	**3**	**3**	**0**	**180**	**12.8**	**68**	**12**	**87**	**35**	**+4**	....	....	....	....	....	....	....	....
1994-95	**Anaheim Mighty Ducks**	**NHL**	**44**	**10**	**9**	**19**	**18**	**13**	**31**	**25**	**0**	**0**	**1**	**100**	**10.0**	**28**	**4**	**48**	**17**	**–7**	....	....	....	....	....	....	....	....
1995-96	**Anaheim Mighty Ducks**	**NHL**	**48**	**5**	**7**	**12**	**5**	**6**	**11**	**26**	**0**	**0**	**1**	**88**	**5.7**	**20**	**0**	**45**	**25**	**0**	....	....	....	....	....	....	....	....
	Philadelphia Flyers	**NHL**	**28**	**4**	**3**	**7**	**4**	**2**	**6**	**8**	**0**	**0**	**2**	**38**	**10.5**	**14**	**2**	**10**	**1**	**+3**	**12**	**1**	**2**	**3**	**6**	**0**	**0**	**0**
1996-97	**Phoenix Coyotes**	**NHL**	**80**	**9**	**11**	**20**	**10**	**10**	**20**	**40**	**0**	**1**	**3**	**119**	**7.6**	**38**	**2**	**61**	**18**	**–7**	**7**	**2**	**2**	**4**	**4**	**0**	**0**	**1**
1997-98	**Phoenix Coyotes**	**NHL**	**76**	**12**	**9**	**21**	**14**	**9**	**23**	**28**	**0**	**5**	**0**	**105**	**11.4**	**31**	**0**	**71**	**33**	**–7**	**6**	**1**	**0**	**1**	**4**	**0**	**0**	**0**
	NHL Totals		**448**	**73**	**75**	**148**	**81**	**68**	**149**	**208**	**3**	**10**	**9**	**728**	**10.0**	**230**	**21**	**394**	**161**		**39**	**6**	**4**	**10**	**20**	**1**	**0**	**1**

Claimed by **Anaheim** from **Buffalo** in Expansion Draft, June 24, 1993. Traded to **Philadelphia** by **Anaheim** for Chris Herperger and Winnipeg's 7th round choice (previously acquired, Anaheim selected Tony Monahan) in 1997 Entry Draft, February 6, 1996. Claimed by **Phoenix** from **Philadelphia** in Waiver Draft, September 30, 1996.

• CORNFORTH, MARK

mark Cornforth D – L. 6'1", 193 lbs. b: Montreal, Que., 11/13/1972.

Season	Club	League	GP	G	A	Pts	AG	AA	APts	PIM	PP	SH	GW	S	%	TGF	PGF	TGA	PGA	+/–	GP	G	A	Pts	PIM	PP	SH	GW
1991-92	Merrimack College	H.E.	23	1	9	10	....	....	....	40	....	....	....	....	....	....	....	....	....	....	....	....	....	....	....	....	....	....
1992-93	Merrimack College	H.E.	36	3	18	21	....	....	....	75	....	....	....	....	....	....	....	....	....	....	....	....	....	....	....	....	....	....
1993-94	Merrimack College	H.E.	37	5	13	18	....	....	....	58	....	....	....	....	....	....	....	....	....	....	....	....	....	....	....	....	....	....
1994-95	Merrimack College	H.E.	30	8	20	28	....	....	....	93	....	....	....	....	....	....	....	....	....	....	....	....	....	....	....	....	....	....
	Syracuse Crunch	AHL	2	0	1	1	....	....	....	2	....	....	....	....	....	....	....	....	....	....	....	....	....	....	....	....	....	....
1995-96	**Boston Bruins**	**NHL**	**6**	**0**	**0**	**0**	**0**	**0**	**0**	**4**	**0**	**0**	**0**	**1**	**0.0**	**7**	**0**	**4**	**1**	**+4**	....	....	....	....	....	....	....	....
	Providence Bruins	AHL	65	5	10	15	....	....	....	117	....	....	....	....	....	....	....	....	....	....	4	0	0	0	4	....	....	....

Season	Club	League	GP	G	A	Pts	AG	AA	APts	PIM	PP	SH	GW	S	%	TGF	PGF	TGA	PGA	+/–	GP	G	A	Pts	PIM	PP	SH	GW
			REGULAR SEASON																		PLAYOFFS							
1996-97	Providence Bruins	AHL	61	8	12	20	....	....	....	47	....	....	....	....	....	....	....	....	....	....	....	....	....	....	....	....	....	....
	Cleveland Lumberjacks	IHL	13	1	4	5	....	....	....	25	....	....	....	....	....	....	....	....	....	....	14	1	3	4	29	....	....	....
1997-98	Cleveland Lumberjacks	IHL	68	5	15	20	....	....	....	146	....	....	....	....	....	....	....	....	....	....	....	....	....	....	....	....	....	....
	Grand Rapids Griffins	IHL	8	1	2	3	....	....	....	20	....	....	....	....	....	....	....	....	....	....	3	0	0	0	17	....	....	....
	NHL Totals		**6**	**0**	**0**	**0**	**0**	**0**	**0**	**4**	**0**	**0**	**0**	**1**	**0.0**	**7**	**0**	**4**	**1**		....	....	....	....	....	....	....	....

Signed as a free agent by **Boston**, October 6, 1995.

• CORRIGAN, MIKE

Mike Corrigan LW – L. 5'10", 175 lbs. b: Ottawa, Ont., 1/11/1946. Detroit's 3rd choice, 88th overall, in 1980 Entry Draft.

Season	Club	League	GP	G	A	Pts	AG	AA	APts	PIM	PP	SH	GW	S	%	TGF	PGF	TGA	PGA	+/–	GP	G	A	Pts	PIM	PP	SH	GW
1962-63	Neil McNeil Maroons	OHA	31	15	15	30	....	....	....	22	....	....	....	....	....	....	....	....	....	....	16	1	3	4	15	....	....	....
1963-64	London Panthers	Jr. B	STATISTICS NOT AVAILABLE																									
1964-65	Toronto Marlboros	OHA	56	30	67	97	....	....	....	76	....	....	....	....	....	....	....	....	....	....	19	9	9	18	13	....	....	....
1965-66	Toronto Marlboros	OHA	41	25	36	61	....	....	....	70	....	....	....	....	....	....	....	....	....	....	14	10	4	14	22	....	....	....
	Rochester Americans	AHL	3	1	0	1	....	....	....	4	....	....	....	....	....	....	....	....	....	....	....	....	....	....	....	....	....	....
	Victoria Maple Leafs	WHL	....	....	....	....	....	....	....	....	....	....	....	....	....	....	....	....	....	....	6	0	0	0	0	....	....	....
	Tulsa Oilers	CHL	....	....	....	....	....	....	....	....	....	....	....	....	....	....	....	....	....	....	8	1	5	6	5	....	....	....
1966-67	Rochester Americans	AHL	49	11	21	32	....	....	....	34	....	....	....	....	....	....	....	....	....	....	....	....	....	....	....	....	....	....
	Tulsa Oilers	CHL	15	4	3	7	....	....	....	6	....	....	....	....	....	....	....	....	....	....	....	....	....	....	....	....	....	....
1967-68	**Los Angeles Kings**	**NHL**	**5**	**0**	**0**	**0**	**0**	**0**	**0**	**2**	**0**	**0**	**0**	**5**	**0.0**	**1**	**0**	**7**	**4**	**–2**	....	....	....	....	....	....	....	....
	Springfield Kings	AHL	58	24	30	54	....	....	....	57	....	....	....	....	....	....	....	....	....	....	4	1	2	3	13	....	....	....
1968-69	Springfield Kings	AHL	66	17	16	33	....	....	....	85	....	....	....	....	....	....	....	....	....	....	....	....	....	....	....	....	....	....
1969-70	**Los Angeles Kings**	**NHL**	**36**	**6**	**4**	**10**	**7**	**4**	**11**	**30**	**2**	**0**	**1**	**67**	**9.0**	**17**	**4**	**35**	**5**	**–17**	....	....	....	....	....	....	....	....
	Springfield Kings	AHL	37	19	23	42	....	....	....	49	....	....	....	....	....	....	....	....	....	....	14	7	7	14	51	....	....	....
1970-71	**Vancouver Canucks**	**NHL**	**76**	**21**	**28**	**49**	**22**	**25**	**47**	**103**	**5**	**0**	**1**	**164**	**12.8**	**68**	**21**	**72**	**5**	**–20**	....	....	....	....	....	....	....	....
1971-72	**Vancouver Canucks**	**NHL**	**19**	**3**	**4**	**7**	**3**	**4**	**7**	**25**	**1**	**0**	**0**	**42**	**7.1**	**14**	**4**	**18**	**0**	**–8**	....	....	....	....	....	....	....	....
	Los Angeles Kings	**NHL**	**56**	**12**	**22**	**34**	**13**	**20**	**33**	**95**	**3**	**0**	**1**	**102**	**11.8**	**53**	**9**	**51**	**0**	**–7**	....	....	....	....	....	....	....	....
1972-73	**Los Angeles Kings**	**NHL**	**78**	**37**	**30**	**67**	**37**	**25**	**62**	**146**	**14**	**0**	**6**	**180**	**20.6**	**94**	**34**	**77**	**0**	**–17**	....	....	....	....	....	....	....	....
1973-74	**Los Angeles Kings**	**NHL**	**75**	**16**	**26**	**42**	**16**	**22**	**38**	**119**	**4**	**0**	**1**	**131**	**12.2**	**65**	**15**	**61**	**1**	**–10**	**3**	**0**	**1**	**1**	**4**	**0**	**0**	**0**
1974-75	**Los Angeles Kings**	**NHL**	**80**	**13**	**21**	**34**	**12**	**17**	**29**	**61**	**2**	**1**	**2**	**100**	**13.0**	**54**	**19**	**39**	**13**	**+9**	**3**	**0**	**0**	**0**	**4**	**0**	**0**	**0**
1975-76	**Los Angeles Kings**	**NHL**	**71**	**22**	**21**	**43**	**20**	**16**	**36**	**71**	**9**	**0**	**4**	**135**	**16.3**	**70**	**25**	**53**	**6**	**–2**	**9**	**2**	**2**	**4**	**12**	**0**	**0**	**0**
1976-77	**Pittsburgh Penguins**	**NHL**	**73**	**14**	**27**	**41**	**13**	**22**	**35**	**36**	**2**	**0**	**1**	**124**	**11.3**	**66**	**16**	**64**	**1**	**–13**	**2**	**0**	**0**	**0**	**0**	**0**	**0**	**0**
	Fort Worth Texans	CHL	2	1	3	4	....	....	....	2	....	....	....	....	....	....	....	....	....	....	....	....	....	....	....	....	....	....
1977-78	**Pittsburgh Penguins**	**NHL**	**25**	**8**	**12**	**20**	**8**	**10**	**18**	**10**	**0**	**0**	**0**	**36**	**22.2**	**28**	**7**	**29**	**1**	**–7**	....	....	....	....	....	....	....	....
	NHL Totals		**594**	**152**	**195**	**347**	**151**	**165**	**316**	**698**	**42**	**1**	**17**	**1086**	**14.0**	**530**	**154**	**506**	**36**		**17**	**2**	**3**	**5**	**20**	**0**	**0**	**0**

Claimed by **LA Kings** from **Toronto** in Expansion Draft, June 6, 1967. Claimed by **Vancouver** from **LA Kings** in Expansion Draft, June 10, 1970. Claimed on waivers by **LA Kings** from **Vancouver**, November 22, 1971. Traded to **Pittsburgh** by **LA Kings** for Pittsburgh's 5th round choice (Julian Baretta) in 1977 Amateur Draft, October 18, 1976.

• CORRIVEAU, YVON

Yvon Corriveau LW – L. 6'1", 195 lbs. b: Welland, Ont., 2/8/1967. Washington's 1st choice, 19th overall, in 1985 Entry Draft.

Season	Club	League	GP	G	A	Pts	AG	AA	APts	PIM	PP	SH	GW	S	%	TGF	PGF	TGA	PGA	+/–	GP	G	A	Pts	PIM	PP	SH	GW
1983-84	Welland Cougars	OJHL	36	16	21	37	....	....	....	51	....	....	....	....	....	....	....	....	....	....	....	....	....	....	....	....	....	....
1984-85	Toronto Marlboros	OHL	59	23	28	51	....	....	....	65	....	....	....	....	....	....	....	....	....	....	3	0	0	0	5	....	....	....
1985-86	Toronto Marlboros	OHL	59	54	36	90	....	....	....	75	....	....	....	....	....	....	....	....	....	....	4	1	1	2	0	....	....	....
	Washington Capitals	**NHL**	**2**	**0**	**0**	**0**	**0**	**0**	**0**	**0**	**0**	**0**	**0**	**3**	**0.0**	**1**	**0**	**2**	**0**	**–1**	**4**	**0**	**3**	**3**	**2**	**0**	**0**	**0**
1986-87	Toronto Marlboros	OHL	23	14	19	33	....	....	....	23	....	....	....	....	....	....	....	....	....	....	....	....	....	....	....	....	....	....
	Washington Capitals	**NHL**	**17**	**1**	**1**	**2**	**1**	**1**	**2**	**24**	**0**	**0**	**0**	**7**	**14.3**	**4**	**0**	**8**	**0**	**–4**	....	....	....	....	....	....	....	....
	Canada	WJC-A	6	2	1	3	....	....	....	4	....	....	....	....	....	....	....	....	....	....	....	....	....	....	....	....	....	....
	Binghamton Whalers	AHL	7	0	0	0	....	....	....	2	....	....	....	....	....	....	....	....	....	....	8	0	1	1	0	....	....	....
1987-88	**Washington Capitals**	**NHL**	**44**	**10**	**9**	**19**	**9**	**6**	**15**	**84**	**0**	**0**	**1**	**52**	**19.2**	**29**	**0**	**12**	**0**	**+17**	**13**	**1**	**2**	**3**	**30**	**0**	**0**	**0**
	Binghamton Whalers	AHL	35	15	14	29	....	....	....	64	....	....	....	....	....	....	....	....	....	....	....	....	....	....	....	....	....	....
1988-89	**Washington Capitals**	**NHL**	**33**	**3**	**2**	**5**	**3**	**1**	**4**	**62**	**0**	**0**	**0**	**29**	**7.7**	**12**	**0**	**12**	**0**	**0**	**1**	**0**	**0**	**0**	**0**	**0**	**0**	**0**
	Baltimore Skipjacks	AHL	33	16	23	39	....	....	....	65	....	....	....	....	....	....	....	....	....	....	....	....	....	....	....	....	....	....
1989-90	Washington Capitals	FrTour	3	1	2	3	....	....	....	4	....	....	....	....	....	....	....	....	....	....	....	....	....	....	....	....	....	....
	Washington Capitals	**NHL**	**50**	**9**	**6**	**15**	**8**	**4**	**12**	**50**	**1**	**0**	**1**	**76**	**11.8**	**25**	**3**	**23**	**0**	**–1**	....	....	....	....	....	....	....	....
	Hartford Whalers	**NHL**	**13**	**4**	**1**	**5**	**3**	**1**	**4**	**22**	**0**	**0**	**0**	**14**	**28.6**	**7**	**0**	**5**	**1**	**+3**	**4**	**1**	**0**	**1**	**0**	**0**	**0**	**0**
1990-91	**Hartford Whalers**	**NHL**	**23**	**1**	**1**	**2**	**1**	**1**	**2**	**18**	**0**	**0**	**0**	**21**	**4.8**	**4**	**0**	**12**	**0**	**–8**	....	....	....	....	....	....	....	....
	Springfield Indians	AHL	44	17	25	42	....	....	....	10	....	....	....	....	....	....	....	....	....	....	18	*10	6	16	31	....	....	....
1991-92	**Hartford Whalers**	**NHL**	**38**	**12**	**8**	**20**	**11**	**6**	**17**	**36**	**3**	**0**	**0**	**69**	**17.4**	**33**	**7**	**26**	**5**	**+5**	**7**	**3**	**2**	**5**	**18**	**2**	**0**	**1**
	Springfield Indians	AHL	39	26	15	41	....	....	....	40	....	....	....	....	....	....	....	....	....	....	....	....	....	....	....	....	....	....
1992-93	**San Jose Sharks**	**NHL**	**20**	**3**	**7**	**10**	**2**	**5**	**7**	**0**	**1**	**0**	**0**	**32**	**9.4**	**11**	**1**	**17**	**0**	**–7**	....	....	....	....	....	....	....	....
	Hartford Whalers	**NHL**	**37**	**5**	**5**	**10**	**4**	**3**	**7**	**14**	**1**	**0**	**1**	**45**	**11.1**	**17**	**3**	**28**	**1**	**–13**	....	....	....	....	....	....	....	....
1993-94	**Hartford Whalers**	**NHL**	**3**	**0**	**0**	**0**	**0**	**0**	**0**	**0**	**0**	**0**	**0**	**0**	**0.0**	**0**	**0**	**0**	**0**	**0**	....	....	....	....	....	....	....	....
	Springfield Indians	AHL	71	42	39	81	....	....	....	53	....	....	....	....	....	....	....	....	....	....	6	7	3	10	20	....	....	....
1994-95	Minnesota Moose	IHL	62	18	24	42	....	....	....	26	....	....	....	....	....	....	....	....	....	....	3	1	1	2	0	....	....	....
1995-96	Minnesota Moose	IHL	60	21	22	43	....	....	....	40	....	....	....	....	....	....	....	....	....	....	....	....	....	....	....	....	....	....
	Detroit Vipers	IHL	14	5	6	11	....	....	....	12	....	....	....	....	....	....	....	....	....	....	4	0	1	1	6	....	....	....
1996-97	Detroit Vipers	IHL	52	9	9	18	....	....	....	85	....	....	....	....	....	....	....	....	....	....	21	2	1	3	34	....	....	....
1997-98	EHC Eisbaren Berlin	Germany	47	12	14	26	....	....	....	58	....	....	....	....	....	....	....	....	....	....	9	1	0	1	30	....	....	....
	NHL Totals		**280**	**48**	**40**	**88**	**42**	**28**	**70**	**310**	**6**	**0**	**3**	**358**	**13.4**	**143**	**14**	**145**	**7**		**29**	**5**	**7**	**12**	**50**	**2**	**0**	**1**

Traded to **Hartford** by **Washington** for Mike Liut, March 6, 1990. Traded to **Washington** by **Hartford** to complete June 15, 1992 deal in which Mark Hunter and future considerations were traded to Washington for Nick Kypreos, August 20, 1992. Claimed by **San Jose** from **Washington** in Waiver Draft, October 4, 1992. Traded to **Hartford** by **San Jose** to complete October 9, 1992 trade in which Michel Picard was traded to San Jose for future considerations, January 21, 1993.

• CORSON, SHAYNE

Shayne Corson LW – L. 6'1", 200 lbs. b: Barrie, Ont., 8/13/1966. Montreal's 2nd choice, 8th overall, in 1984 Entry Draft.

Season	Club	League	GP	G	A	Pts	AG	AA	APts	PIM	PP	SH	GW	S	%	TGF	PGF	TGA	PGA	+/–	GP	G	A	Pts	PIM	PP	SH	GW
1983-84	Brantford Alexanders	OHL	66	25	46	71	....	....	....	165	....	....	....	....	....	....	....	....	....	....	6	4	1	5	26	....	....	....
1984-85	Hamilton Steelhawks	OHL	54	27	63	90	....	....	....	154	....	....	....	....	....	....	....	....	....	....	11	3	7	10	19	....	....	....
	Canada	WJC-A	7	2	3	5	....	....	....	2	....	....	....	....	....	....	....	....	....	....	....	....	....	....	....	....	....	....
1985-86	Hamilton Steelhawks	OHL	47	41	57	98	....	....	....	153	....	....	....	....	....	....	....	....	....	....	....	....	....	....	....	....	....	....
	Canada	WJC-A	7	7	7	14	....	....	....	6	....	....	....	....	....	....	....	....	....	....	....	....	....	....	....	....	....	....
	Montreal Canadiens	**NHL**	**3**	**0**	**0**	**0**	**0**	**0**	**0**	**2**	**0**	**0**	**0**	**1**	**0.0**	**0**	**0**	**4**	**1**	**–3**	....	....	....	....	....	....	....	....
1986-87	**Montreal Canadiens**	**NHL**	**55**	**12**	**11**	**23**	**10**	**8**	**18**	**144**	**0**	**1**	**3**	**69**	**17.4**	**42**	**3**	**41**	**12**	**+10**	**17**	**6**	**5**	**11**	**30**	**1**	**1**	**1**
1987-88	**Montreal Canadiens**	**NHL**	**71**	**12**	**27**	**39**	**10**	**10**	**20**	**152**	**2**	**0**	**2**	**90**	**13.3**	**75**	**10**	**47**	**4**	**+22**	**3**	**1**	**0**	**1**	**12**	**0**	**0**	**0**
1988-89	**Montreal Canadiens**	**NHL**	**80**	**26**	**24**	**50**	**22**	**17**	**39**	**193**	**10**	**0**	**3**	**133**	**19.5**	**84**	**35**	**56**	**6**	**–1**	**21**	**4**	**5**	**9**	**65**	**2**	**0**	**2**
1989-90	**Montreal Canadiens**	**NHL**	**76**	**31**	**44**	**75**	**27**	**31**	**58**	**144**	**7**	**0**	**6**	**192**	**16.1**	**124**	**39**	**54**	**2**	**+33**	**11**	**2**	**8**	**10**	**20**	**0**	**0**	**0**
1990-91	Montreal Canadiens	FrTour	4	2	2	4	....	....	....	31	....	....	....	....	....	....	....	....	....	....	....	....	....	....	....	....	....	....
	Montreal Canadiens	**NHL**	**71**	**23**	**24**	**47**	**21**	**18**	**39**	**138**	**7**	**0**	**2**	**164**	**14.0**	**78**	**21**	**54**	**6**	**+9**	**13**	**9**	**6**	**15**	**36**	**4**	**1**	**3**
1991-92	Canada	C Cup	8	0	5	5	....	....	....	12	....	....	....	....	....	....	....	....	....	....	....	....	....	....	....	....	....	....
	Montreal Canadiens	**NHL**	**64**	**17**	**36**	**53**	**16**	**27**	**43**	**118**	**3**	**0**	**2**	**165**	**10.3**	**89**	**28**	**58**	**12**	**+15**	**10**	**2**	**5**	**7**	**15**	**0**	**0**	**0**
1992-93	**Edmonton Oilers**	**NHL**	**80**	**16**	**31**	**47**	**13**	**21**	**34**	**209**	**9**	**2**	**1**	**164**	**9.8**	**84**	**40**	**91**	**28**	**–19**	....	....	....	....	....	....	....	....
	Canada	WC-A	8	3	7	10	....	....	....	6	....	....	....	....	....	....	....	....	....	....	....	....	....	....	....	....	....	....
1993-94	**Edmonton Oilers**	**NHL**	**64**	**25**	**29**	**54**	**23**	**22**	**45**	**118**	**11**	**0**	**3**	**171**	**14.6**	**88**	**35**	**86**	**25**	**–8**	....	....	....	....	....	....	....	....
	Canada	WC-A	7	3	0	3	....	....	....	4	....	....	....	....	....	....	....	....	....	....	....	....	....	....	....	....	....	....
1994-95	**Edmonton Oilers**	**NHL**	**48**	**12**	**24**	**36**	**21**	**35**	**56**	**86**	**2**	**0**	**1**	**131**	**9.2**	**59**	**26**	**59**	**9**	**–17**	....	....	....	....	....	....	....	....
1995-96	**St. Louis Blues**	**NHL**	**77**	**18**	**28**	**46**	**18**	**23**	**41**	**192**	**13**	**0**	**0**	**150**	**12.0**	**99**	**41**	**90**	**35**	**+3**	**13**	**8**	**6**	**14**	**22**	**6**	**1**	**1**
1996-97	**St. Louis Blues**	**NHL**	**11**	**2**	**1**	**3**	**2**	**1**	**3**	**24**	**1**	**0**	**0**	**19**	**10.5**	**11**	**5**	**13**	**3**	**–4**	....	....	....	....	....	....	....	....
	Montreal Canadiens	**NHL**	**47**	**6**	**15**	**21**	**6**	**13**	**19**	**80**	**2**	**0**	**2**	**96**	**6.3**	**42**	**13**	**46**	**12**	**–5**	**5**	**1**	**0**	**1**	**4**	**0**	**1**	**0**
1997-98	**Montreal Canadiens**	**NHL**	**62**	**21**	**34**	**55**	**25**	**33**	**58**	**108**	**14**	**1**	**1**	**142**	**14.8**	**75**	**33**	**55**	**15**	**+2**	**10**	**3**	**6**	**9**	**26**	**1**	**0**	**1**
	Canada	Olympics	6	1	1	2	....	....	....	2	....	....	....	....	....	....	....	....	....	....	....	....	....	....	....	....	....	....
	NHL Totals		**809**	**221**	**328**	**549**	**214**	**268**	**482**	**1708**	**81**	**4**	**26**	**1687**	**13.1**	**950**	**329**	**754**	**170**		**103**	**36**	**41**	**77**	**230**	**14**	**4**	**8**

WJC-A All-Star Team (1986)

Played in NHL All-Star Game (1990, 1994, 1998)

Traded to **Edmonton** by **Montreal** with Brent Gilchrist and Vladimir Vujtek for Vincent Damphousse and Edmonton's 4th round choice (Adam Wiesel) in 1993 Entry Draft, August 27, 1992. Signed as a free agent by **St. Louis**, July 28, 1995. Traded to **Montreal** by **St. Louis** with Murray Baron and St. Louis' 5th round choice (Gennady Razin) in 1997 Entry Draft for Pierre Turgeon, Rory Fitzpatrick and Craig Conroy, October 29, 1996.

			REGULAR SEASON																		PLAYOFFS							
Season	Club	League	GP	G	A	Pts	AG	AA	APts	PIM	PP	SH	GW	S	%	TGF	PGF	TGA	PGA	+/–	GP	G	A	Pts	PIM	PP	SH	GW

• CORY, ROSS
Ross Cory D – L. 6'2", 195 lbs. b: Calgary, Alta., 2/4/1957.

Season	Club	League	GP	G	A	Pts	AG	AA	APts	PIM	PP	SH	GW	S	%	TGF	PGF	TGA	PGA	+/–	GP	G	A	Pts	PIM	PP	SH	GW
1976-77	University of British Columbia	CWUAA	33	7	20	27	....	....	....	54	....	....	....	....	....	....	....	....	....	....	....	....	....	....	....	....	....	....
1977-78	University of British Columbia	CWUAA	39	6	39	45	....	....	....	69	....	....	....	....	....	....	....	....	....	....	....	....	....	....	....	....	....	....
1978-79	University of British Columbia	CWUAA	29	4	20	24	....	....	....	83	....	....	....	....	....	....	....	....	....	....	....	....	....	....	....	....	....	....
1979-80	**Winnipeg Jets**	**NHL**	**46**	**2**	**9**	**11**	**2**	**7**	**9**	**32**	**1**	**0**	**0**	**47**	**4.3**	**35**	**12**	**46**	**7**	**–16**	....	....	....	....	....	....	....	....
	Tulsa Oilers	CHL	22	3	16	19	....	....	....	40	....	....	....	....	....	....	....	....	....	....	....	....	....	....	....	....	....	....
1980-81	**Winnipeg Jets**	**NHL**	**5**	**0**	**1**	**1**	**0**	**1**	**1**	**9**	**0**	**0**	**0**	**1**	**0.0**	**1**	**0**	**9**	**0**	**–8**	....	....	....	....	....	....	....	....
	Tulsa Oilers	CHL	71	10	46	56	....	....	....	94	....	....	....	....	....	....	....	....	....	....	8	1	6	7	6	....	....	....
1981-82	Tulsa Oilers	CHL	79	6	41	47	....	....	....	105	....	....	....	....	....	....	....	....	....	....	3	0	0	0	0	....	....	....
1982-83	Iserlohn	Germany	36	6	19	25	....	....	....	38	....	....	....	....	....	....	....	....	....	....	....	....	....	....	....	....	....	....
	NHL Totals		**51**	**2**	**10**	**12**	**2**	**8**	**10**	**41**	**1**	**0**	**0**	**48**	**4.2**	**36**	**12**	**55**	**7**		....	....	....	....	....	....	....	....

CHL Second All-Star Team (1981, 1982)

Signed as a free agent by **Winnipeg**, October 1, 1979.

• COSSETE, JACQUES
Jacques Cossete RW – R. 5'9", 185 lbs. b: Rouyn, Que., 6/20/1954. Pittsburgh's 2nd choice, 27th overall, in 1974 Amateur Draft.

Season	Club	League	GP	G	A	Pts	AG	AA	APts	PIM	PP	SH	GW	S	%	TGF	PGF	TGA	PGA	+/–	GP	G	A	Pts	PIM	PP	SH	GW
1971-72	Montreal Jr. Canadiens	QMJHL	57	27	23	50	....	....	....	121	....	....	....	....	....	....	....	....	....	....	....	....	....	....	....	....	....	....
1972-73	Sorel Black Hawks	QMJHL	64	61	66	127	....	....	....	194	....	....	....	....	....	....	....	....	....	....	....	....	....	....	....	....	....	....
1973-74	Sorel Black Hawks	QMJHL	68	97	117	214	....	....	....	217	....	....	....	....	....	....	....	....	....	....	....	....	....	....	....	....	....	....
1974-75	Hershey Bears	AHL	62	15	17	32	....	....	....	92	....	....	....	....	....	....	....	....	....	....	5	1	1	2	0	....	....	....
1975-76	**Pittsburgh Penguins**	**NHL**	**7**	**0**	**2**	**2**	**0**	**2**	**2**	**9**	**0**	**0**	**0**	**6**	**0.0**	**4**	**0**	**6**	**0**	**–2**	....	....	....	....	....	....	....	....
	Hershey Bears	AHL	59	18	20	38	....	....	....	117	....	....	....	....	....	....	....	....	....	....	10	7	2	9	13	....	....	....
1976-77	Hershey Bears	AHL	71	38	29	67	....	....	....	49	....	....	....	....	....	....	....	....	....	....	6	3	2	5	4	....	....	....
1977-78	**Pittsburgh Penguins**	**NHL**	**19**	**1**	**2**	**3**	**1**	**2**	**3**	**4**	**1**	**0**	**0**	**17**	**5.9**	**6**	**2**	**9**	**0**	**–5**	....	....	....	....	....	....	....	....
	Binghamton Whalers	AHL	57	39	28	67	....	....	....	69	....	....	....	....	....	....	....	....	....	....	....	....	....	....	....	....	....	....
1978-79	**Pittsburgh Penguins**	**NHL**	**38**	**7**	**2**	**9**	**6**	**2**	**8**	**16**	**1**	**0**	**1**	**35**	**20.0**	**19**	**3**	**17**	**0**	**–1**	**3**	**0**	**1**	**1**	**4**	**0**	**0**	**0**
1979-80	Syracuse Firebirds	AHL	78	25	23	48	....	....	....	87	....	....	....	....	....	....	....	....	....	....	4	1	0	1	2	....	....	....
	NHL Totals		**64**	**8**	**6**	**14**	**7**	**6**	**13**	**29**	**2**	**0**	**1**	**58**	**13.8**	**29**	**5**	**32**	**0**		**3**	**0**	**1**	**1**	**4**	**0**	**0**	**0**

QMJHL First All-Star Team (1973, 1974)

• COSTELLO, RICH
Rich Costello C – R. 6', 175 lbs. b: Farmington, MA, 6/27/1963. Philadelphia's 2nd choice, 37th overall, in 1981 Entry Draft.

Season	Club	League	GP	G	A	Pts	AG	AA	APts	PIM	PP	SH	GW	S	%	TGF	PGF	TGA	PGA	+/–	GP	G	A	Pts	PIM	PP	SH	GW
1979-80	Natick High School	H.S.	18	26	32	58	....	....	....	....	....	....	....	....	....	....	....	....	....	....	....	....	....	....	....	....	....	....
1980-81	Natick High School	H.S.	18	30	36	66	....	....	....	....	....	....	....	....	....	....	....	....	....	....	....	....	....	....	....	....	....	....
1981-82	Providence College	ECAC	32	11	16	27	....	....	....	39	....	....	....	....	....	....	....	....	....	....	....	....	....	....	....	....	....	....
1982-83	Providence College	ECAC	43	19	26	45	....	....	....	60	....	....	....	....	....	....	....	....	....	....	....	....	....	....	....	....	....	....
1983-84	United States	Nat-Team	38	7	19	26	....	....	....	31	....	....	....	....	....	....	....	....	....	....	....	....	....	....	....	....	....	....
	Toronto Maple Leafs	**NHL**	**10**	**2**	**1**	**3**	**2**	**1**	**3**	**2**	**1**	**0**	**0**	**7**	**28.6**	**4**	**1**	**8**	**0**	**–5**	....	....	....	....	....	....	....	....
	St. Catharines Saints	AHL	20	0	0	0	....	....	....	12	....	....	....	....	....	....	....	....	....	....	4	1	0	1	0	....	....	....
1984-85	St. Catharines Saints	AHL	80	8	6	14	....	....	....	45	....	....	....	....	....	....	....	....	....	....	....	....	....	....	....	....	....	....
1985-86	**Toronto Maple Leafs**	**NHL**	**2**	**0**	**1**	**1**	**0**	**1**	**1**	**0**	**0**	**0**	**0**	**2**	**0.0**	**1**	**0**	**1**	**0**	**0**	....	....	....	....	....	....	....	....
	St. Catharines Saints	AHL	76	18	22	40	....	....	....	87	....	....	....	....	....	....	....	....	....	....	13	3	6	9	30	....	....	....
1986-87	Newmarket Saints	AHL	48	6	11	17	....	....	....	53	....	....	....	....	....	....	....	....	....	....	....	....	....	....	....	....	....	....
1987-88	Utica Devils	AHL	3	1	1	2	....	....	....	2	....	....	....	....	....	....	....	....	....	....	....	....	....	....	....	....	....	....
1988-89	Schwenninger ERC	Germany	11	6	8	14	....	....	....	14	....	....	....	....	....	....	....	....	....	....	....	....	....	....	....	....	....	....
1989-90	Schwenninger ERC	Germany	STATISTICS NOT AVAILABLE																									
1990-91	Albany Choppers	IHL	9	1	3	4	....	....	....	14	....	....	....	....	....	....	....	....	....	....	....	....	....	....	....	....	....	....
	NHL Totals		**12**	**2**	**2**	**4**	**2**	**2**	**4**	**2**	**1**	**0**	**0**	**9**	**22.2**	**5**	**1**	**9**	**0**		....	....	....	....	....	....	....	....

Rights traded to **Toronto** by **Philadelphia** with Philadelphia's 2nd round choice (Peter Ihnacak) in 1982 Entry Draft and Ken Strong for Darryl Sittler, January 20, 1982.

• COTE, ALAIN
Alain Cote LW – L. 5'10", 203 lbs. b: Matau, Que., 5/3/1957. Montreal's 4th choice, 43rd overall, in 1977 Amateur Draft.

Season	Club	League	GP	G	A	Pts	AG	AA	APts	PIM	PP	SH	GW	S	%	TGF	PGF	TGA	PGA	+/–	GP	G	A	Pts	PIM	PP	SH	GW
1974-75	Chicoutimi Sagueneens	QMJHL	57	15	29	44	....	....	....	43	....	....	....	....	....	....	....	....	....	....	....	....	....	....	....	....	....	....
1975-76	Chicoutimi Sagueneens	QMJHL	72	35	49	84	....	....	....	93	....	....	....	....	....	....	....	....	....	....	5	3	3	6	2	....	....	....
1976-77	Chicoutimi Sagueneens	QMJHL	56	42	45	87	....	....	....	86	....	....	....	....	....	....	....	....	....	....	8	1	5	6	14	....	....	....
1977-78	Quebec Nordiques	WHA	27	3	5	8	....	....	....	8	....	....	....	....	....	....	....	....	....	....	11	1	2	3	0	....	....	....
	Hampton Gulls	AHL	36	15	17	32	....	....	....	38	....	....	....	....	....	....	....	....	....	....	....	....	....	....	....	....	....	....
1978-79	Quebec Nordiques	WHA	79	14	13	27	....	....	....	23	....	....	....	....	....	....	....	....	....	....	4	0	0	0	2	....	....	....
1979-80	**Quebec Nordiques**	**NHL**	**41**	**5**	**11**	**16**	**5**	**8**	**13**	**13**	**0**	**0**	**1**	**58**	**8.6**	**20**	**2**	**26**	**0**	**–8**	....	....	....	....	....	....	....	....
	Syracuse Firebirds	AHL	6	0	5	5	....	....	....	9	....	....	....	....	....	....	....	....	....	....	....	....	....	....	....	....	....	....
1980-81	**Quebec Nordiques**	**NHL**	**51**	**8**	**18**	**26**	**7**	**13**	**20**	**64**	**1**	**2**	**2**	**65**	**12.3**	**36**	**2**	**39**	**14**	**+9**	**4**	**0**	**0**	**0**	**6**	**0**	**0**	**0**
	Rochester Americans	AHL	23	1	6	7	....	....	....	14	....	....	....	....	....	....	....	....	....	....	....	....	....	....	....	....	....	....
1981-82	**Quebec Nordiques**	**NHL**	**79**	**15**	**16**	**31**	**12**	**11**	**23**	**82**	**0**	**0**	**1**	**95**	**15.8**	**50**	**1**	**86**	**26**	**–11**	**16**	**1**	**2**	**3**	**8**	**0**	**0**	**0**
1982-83	**Quebec Nordiques**	**NHL**	**79**	**12**	**28**	**40**	**10**	**19**	**29**	**45**	**0**	**0**	**0**	**88**	**13.6**	**50**	**0**	**79**	**28**	**–1**	**4**	**0**	**3**	**3**	**0**	**0**	**0**	**0**
1983-84	**Quebec Nordiques**	**NHL**	**77**	**19**	**24**	**43**	**15**	**16**	**31**	**41**	**0**	**1**	**1**	**116**	**16.4**	**65**	**0**	**69**	**25**	**+21**	**9**	**0**	**2**	**2**	**17**	**0**	**0**	**0**
1984-85	**Quebec Nordiques**	**NHL**	**80**	**13**	**22**	**35**	**11**	**15**	**26**	**31**	**1**	**1**	**0**	**127**	**10.2**	**60**	**1**	**70**	**23**	**+12**	**18**	**5**	**5**	**10**	**11**	**0**	**0**	**1**
1985-86	**Quebec Nordiques**	**NHL**	**78**	**13**	**21**	**34**	**10**	**14**	**24**	**29**	**0**	**3**	**2**	**119**	**10.9**	**60**	**1**	**90**	**28**	**–3**	**3**	**1**	**0**	**1**	**0**	**0**	**0**	**0**
1986-87	**Quebec Nordiques**	**NHL**	**80**	**12**	**24**	**36**	**10**	**17**	**27**	**38**	**0**	**2**	**1**	**137**	**8.8**	**64**	**0**	**93**	**25**	**–4**	**13**	**2**	**3**	**5**	**2**	**0**	**0**	**0**
1987-88	**Quebec Nordiques**	**NHL**	**76**	**4**	**18**	**22**	**3**	**13**	**16**	**26**	**0**	**0**	**0**	**84**	**4.8**	**36**	**2**	**60**	**29**	**+3**	....	....	....	....	....	....	....	....
1988-89	**Quebec Nordiques**	**NHL**	**55**	**2**	**8**	**10**	**2**	**6**	**8**	**14**	**0**	**1**	**0**	**31**	**6.5**	**20**	**0**	**34**	**13**	**–1**	....	....	....	....	....	....	....	....
	NHL Totals		**696**	**103**	**190**	**293**	**85**	**132**	**217**	**383**	**2**	**10**	**8**	**920**	**11.2**	**461**	**9**	**646**	**211**		**67**	**9**	**15**	**24**	**44**	**0**	**0**	**1**
	Other Major League Totals		106	17	18	35	....	....	....	31	....	....	....	....	....	....	....	....	....		15	1	2	3	2	....	....	....

Selected by **Quebec** (WHA) in 1977 WHA Amateur Draft, June, 1977. Reclaimed by **Montreal** from **Quebec** prior to Expansion Draft, June 9, 1979. Claimed by **Quebec** from **Montreal** in Expansion Draft, June 13, 1979.

• COTE, ALAIN G.
Alain G. Cote D – R. 6', 207 lbs. b: Montmagny, Que., 4/14/1967. Boston's 6th choice, 31st overall, in 1985 Entry Draft.

Season	Club	League	GP	G	A	Pts	AG	AA	APts	PIM	PP	SH	GW	S	%	TGF	PGF	TGA	PGA	+/–	GP	G	A	Pts	PIM	PP	SH	GW
1983-84	Quebec Remparts	QMJHL	60	3	17	20	....	....	....	40	....	....	....	....	....	....	....	....	....	....	5	1	3	4	8	....	....	....
1984-85	Quebec Remparts	QMJHL	68	9	25	34	....	....	....	173	....	....	....	....	....	....	....	....	....	....	4	0	1	1	12	....	....	....
1985-86	Granby Bisons	QMJHL	22	4	12	16	....	....	....	48	....	....	....	....	....	....	....	....	....	....	....	....	....	....	....	....	....	....
	Canada	WJC-A	7	1	4	5	....	....	....	6	....	....	....	....	....	....	....	....	....	....	....	....	....	....	....	....	....	....
	Boston Bruins	**NHL**	**32**	**0**	**6**	**6**	**0**	**4**	**4**	**14**	**0**	**0**	**0**	**15**	**0.0**	**25**	**0**	**25**	**5**	**+5**	....	....	....	....	....	....	....	....
1986-87	Granby Bisons	QMJHL	43	7	24	31	....	....	....	185	....	....	....	....	....	....	....	....	....	....	4	0	3	3	2	....	....	....
	Boston Bruins	**NHL**	**3**	**0**	**0**	**0**	**0**	**0**	**0**	**0**	**0**	**0**	**0**	**1**	**0.0**	**2**	**0**	**3**	**0**	**–1**	....	....	....	....	....	....	....	....
1987-88	**Boston Bruins**	**NHL**	**2**	**0**	**0**	**0**	**0**	**0**	**0**	**0**	**0**	**0**	**0**	**1**	**0.0**	**0**	**0**	**1**	**0**	**–1**	....	....	....	....	....	....	....	....
	Maine Mariners	AHL	69	9	34	43	....	....	....	108	....	....	....	....	....	....	....	....	....	....	9	2	4	6	19	....	....	....
1988-89	**Boston Bruins**	**NHL**	**31**	**2**	**3**	**5**	**2**	**2**	**4**	**51**	**0**	**0**	**0**	**45**	**4.4**	**18**	**0**	**34**	**7**	**–9**	....	....	....	....	....	....	....	....
	Maine Mariners	AHL	37	5	16	21	....	....	....	111	....	....	....	....	....	....	....	....	....	....	....	....	....	....	....	....	....	....
1989-90	**Washington Capitals**	**NHL**	**2**	**0**	**0**	**0**	**0**	**0**	**0**	**7**	**0**	**0**	**0**	**2**	**0.0**	**0**	**0**	**3**	**1**	**–2**	....	....	....	....	....	....	....	....
	Baltimore Skipjacks	AHL	57	5	19	24	....	....	....	161	....	....	....	....	....	....	....	....	....	....	3	0	0	0	9	....	....	....
1990-91	**Montreal Canadiens**	**NHL**	**28**	**0**	**6**	**6**	**0**	**5**	**5**	**26**	**0**	**0**	**0**	**24**	**0.0**	**35**	**1**	**35**	**9**	**+8**	**11**	**0**	**2**	**2**	**26**	**0**	**0**	**0**
	Fredericton Canadiens	AHL	49	8	19	27	....	....	....	110	....	....	....	....	....	....	....	....	....	....	....	....	....	....	....	....	....	....
1991-92	**Montreal Canadiens**	**NHL**	**13**	**0**	**3**	**3**	**0**	**2**	**2**	**22**	**0**	**0**	**0**	**6**	**0.0**	**10**	**0**	**7**	**4**	**+7**	....	....	....	....	....	....	....	....
	Fredericton Canadiens	AHL	20	1	10	11	....	....	....	24	....	....	....	....	....	....	....	....	....	....	7	0	1	1	4	....	....	....
1992-93	Fredericton Canadiens	AHL	61	10	17	27	....	....	....	83	....	....	....	....	....	....	....	....	....	....	....	....	....	....	....	....	....	....
	Tampa Bay Lightning	**NHL**	**2**	**0**	**0**	**0**	**0**	**0**	**0**	**0**	**0**	**0**	**0**	**1**	**0.0**	**0**	**0**	**1**	**0**	**–1**	....	....	....	....	....	....	....	....
	Atlanta Knights	IHL	8	1	0	1	....	....	....	0	....	....	....	....	....	....	....	....	....	....	1	0	0	0	0	....	....	....
1993-94	**Quebec Nordiques**	**NHL**	**6**	**0**	**0**	**0**	**0**	**0**	**0**	**4**	**0**	**0**	**0**	**4**	**0.0**	**3**	**0**	**5**	**0**	**–2**	....	....	....	....	....	....	....	....
	Cornwall Aces	AHL	67	10	34	44	....	....	....	80	....	....	....	....	....	....	....	....	....	....	13	0	2	2	10	....	....	....
1994-95	Hertz Olympia	Slovenia	55	15	25	40	....	....	....	....	....	....	....	....	....	....	....	....	....	....	....	....	....	....	....	....	....	....

			REGULAR SEASON																		PLAYOFFS							
Season	Club	League	GP	G	A	Pts	AG	AA	APts	PIM	PP	SH	GW	S	%	TGF	PGF	TGA	PGA	+/–	GP	G	A	Pts	PIM	PP	SH	GW
1995-96	San Francisco Spiders	IHL	80	5	26	31	....	....	....	133	....	....	....	....	....	....	....	....	....	....	4	0	0	0	10	....	....	....
1996-97	Quebec Rafales	IHL	76	8	17	25	....	....	....	102	....	....	....	....	....	....	....	....	....	....	9	0	2	2	30	....	....	....
1997-98	Sapporo Snow Brand	Japan	37	15	19	34	....	....	....	115	....	....	....	....	....	....	....	....	....	....	....	....	....	....	....	....	....	....
	NHL Totals		**119**	**2**	**18**	**20**	**2**	**13**	**15**	**124**	**0**	**0**	**0**	**99**	**2.0**	**93**	**1**	**114**	**26**		**11**	**0**	**2**	**2**	**26**	**0**	**0**	**0**

WJC-A All-Star Team (1986)

Traded to **Washington** by **Boston** for Bob Gould, September 28, 1989. Traded to **Montreal** by **Washington** for Marc Deschamps, June 22, 1990. Traded to **Tampa Bay** by **Montreal** with Eric Charron and future considerations (Donald Dufresne, June 18, 1993) for Rob Ramage, March 20, 1993. Signed as a free agent by **Quebec**, July 2, 1993.

• COTE, PATRICK

Patrick Cote LW – L. 6'3", 199 lbs. b. Lasalle, Que., 1/24/1975. Dallas' 2nd choice, 37th overall, in 1995 Entry Draft.

Season	Club	League	GP	G	A	Pts	AG	AA	APts	PIM	PP	SH	GW	S	%	TGF	PGF	TGA	PGA	+/–	GP	G	A	Pts	PIM	PP	SH	GW
1993-94	Beauport Harfangs	QMJHL	48	2	4	6	....	....	....	230	....	....	....	....	....	....	....	....	....	....	12	1	0	1	61	....	....	....
1994-95	Beauport Harfangs	QMJHL	56	20	20	40	....	....	....	314	....	....	....	....	....	....	....	....	....	....	17	8	8	16	115	....	....	....
1995-96	**Dallas Stars**	**NHL**	**2**	**0**	**0**	**0**	**0**	**0**	**0**	**5**	**0**	**0**	**0**	**0**	**0.0**	**0**	**0**	**2**	**0**	**–2**	....	....	....	....	....	....	....	....
	Michigan K-Wings	IHL	57	4	6	10	....	....	....	239	....	....	....	....	....	....	....	....	....	....	3	0	0	0	2	....	....	....
1996-97	**Dallas Stars**	**NHL**	**3**	**0**	**0**	**0**	**0**	**0**	**0**	**27**	**0**	**0**	**0**	**1**	**0.0**	**0**	**0**	**0**	**0**	**0**	....	....	....	....	....	....	....	....
	Michigan K-Wings	IHL	58	14	10	24	....	....	....	237	....	....	....	....	....	....	....	....	....	....	4	2	0	2	6	....	....	....
1997-98	**Dallas Stars**	**NHL**	**3**	**0**	**0**	**0**	**0**	**0**	**0**	**15**	**0**	**0**	**0**	**3**	**0.0**	**0**	**0**	**1**	**0**	**–1**	....	....	....	....	....	....	....	....
	Michigan K-Wings	IHL	4	2	0	2	....	....	....	4	....	....	....	....	....	....	....	....	....	....	....	....	....	....	....	....	....	....
	NHL Totals		**8**	**0**	**0**	**0**	**0**	**0**	**0**	**47**	**0**	**0**	**0**	**4**	**0.0**	**0**	**0**	**3**	**0**		....	....	....	....	....	....	....	....

Claimed by **Nashville** from **Dallas** in Expansion Draft, June 26, 1998.

• COTE, RAY

Ray Cote C – R. 5'11", 170 lbs. b: Pincher Creek, Alta., 5/31/1961.

Season	Club	League	GP	G	A	Pts	AG	AA	APts	PIM	PP	SH	GW	S	%	TGF	PGF	TGA	PGA	+/–	GP	G	A	Pts	PIM	PP	SH	GW
1977-78	Pincher Creek Panthers	AJHL	59	13	34	47	....	....	....	12	....	....	....	....	....	....	....	....	....	....	....	....	....	....	....	....	....	....
1978-79	Calgary Chinooks	AJHL	53	17	30	47	....	....	....	35	....	....	....	....	....	....	....	....	....	....	....	....	....	....	....	....	....	....
	Calgary Wranglers	WHL	7	2	1	3	....	....	....	0	....	....	....	....	....	....	....	....	....	....	....	....	....	....	....	....	....	....
1979-80	Calgary Wranglers	WHL	72	33	34	67	....	....	....	43	....	....	....	....	....	....	....	....	....	....	....	....	....	....	....	....	....	....
1980-81	Calgary Wranglers	WHL	70	36	52	88	....	....	....	73	....	....	....	....	....	....	....	....	....	....	22	10	13	23	11	....	....	....
1981-82	Wichita Wind	CHL	80	20	34	54	....	....	....	83	....	....	....	....	....	....	....	....	....	....	7	3	2	5	2	....	....	....
1982-83	Moncton Alpines	AHL	80	28	63	91	....	....	....	35	....	....	....	....	....	....	....	....	....	....	....	....	....	....	....	....	....	....
	Edmonton Oilers	**NHL**	....	....	....	....	....	....	....	....	....	....	....	....	....	....	....	....	....	....	**14**	**3**	**2**	**5**	**0**	....	....	....
1983-84	**Edmonton Oilers**	**NHL**	**13**	**0**	**0**	**0**	**0**	**0**	**0**	**2**	**0**	**0**	**0**	**12**	**0.0**	**1**	**0**	**6**	**0**	**–5**	....	....	....	....	....	....	....	....
	Moncton Alpines	AHL	66	26	36	62	....	....	....	99	....	....	....	....	....	....	....	....	....	....	....	....	....	....	....	....	....	....
1984-85	**Edmonton Oilers**	**NHL**	**2**	**0**	**0**	**0**	**0**	**0**	**0**	**2**	**0**	**0**	**0**	**1**	**0.0**	**0**	**0**	**0**	**0**	**0**	....	....	....	....	....	....	....	....
	Nova Scotia Voyageurs	AHL	79	36	43	79	....	....	....	63	....	....	....	....	....	....	....	....	....	....	6	2	3	5	0	....	....	....
1985-86	Nova Scotia Oilers	AHL	20	7	3	10	....	....	....	17	....	....	....	....	....	....	....	....	....	....	....	....	....	....	....	....	....	....
	Canada	Nat-Team	8	1	3	4	....	....	....	6	....	....	....	....	....	....	....	....	....	....	....	....	....	....	....	....	....	....
	Schwenniger ERC	Germany	18	12	11	23	....	....	....	14	....	....	....	....	....	....	....	....	....	....	....	....	....	....	....	....	....	....
1986-87	Canada	Nat-Team	68	20	30	50	....	....	....	34	....	....	....	....	....	....	....	....	....	....	....	....	....	....	....	....	....	....
	Adirondack Red Wings	AHL	....	....	....	....	....	....	....	....	....	....	....	....	....	....	....	....	....	....	9	2	6	8	2	....	....	....
1987-88	WEV Wiener	Austria	21	12	9	21	....	....	....	10	....	....	....	....	....	....	....	....	....	....	....	....	....	....	....	....	....	....
1988-89	WEV Wiener	Austria	40	18	31	51	....	....	....	....	....	....	....	....	....	....	....	....	....	....	....	....	....	....	....	....	....	....
	Canada	Nat-Team	8	2	2	4	....	....	....	4	....	....	....	....	....	....	....	....	....	....	....	....	....	....	....	....	....	....
1989-90			STATISTICS NOT AVAILABLE																									
1990-91	Canada	Nat-Team	18	4	7	11	....	....	....	6	....	....	....	....	....	....	....	....	....	....	....	....	....	....	....	....	....	....
1991-92	Adler Mannheim	Germany	11	3	8	11	....	....	....	0	....	....	....	....	....	....	....	....	....	....	....	....	....	....	....	....	....	....
	NHL Totals		**15**	**0**	**0**	**0**	**0**	**0**	**0**	**4**	**0**	**0**	**0**	**13**	**0.0**	**1**	**0**	**6**	**0**		**14**	**3**	**2**	**5**	**0**	**0**	**0**	**0**

Signed as a free agent by **Edmonton**, October 6, 1981.

• COTE, SYLVAIN

Sylvain Cote D – R. 6', 190 lbs. b: Quebec City, Que., 1/19/1966. Hartford's 1st choice, 11th overall, in 1984 Entry Draft.

Season	Club	League	GP	G	A	Pts	AG	AA	APts	PIM	PP	SH	GW	S	%	TGF	PGF	TGA	PGA	+/–	GP	G	A	Pts	PIM	PP	SH	GW
1982-83	Quebec Remparts	QMJHL	66	10	24	34	....	....	....	50	....	....	....	....	....	....	....	....	....	....	....	....	....	....	....	....	....	....
1983-84	Quebec Remparts	QMJHL	66	15	50	65	....	....	....	89	....	....	....	....	....	....	....	....	....	....	5	1	1	2	0	....	....	....
	Canada	WJC-A	7	0	2	2	....	....	....	13	....	....	....	....	....	....	....	....	....	....	....	....	....	....	....	....	....	....
1984-85	**Hartford Whalers**	**NHL**	**67**	**3**	**9**	**12**	**2**	**6**	**8**	**17**	**1**	**0**	**1**	**90**	**3.3**	**44**	**11**	**64**	**1**	**–30**	....	....	....	....	....	....	....	....
1985-86	Hull Olympiques	QMJHL	26	10	33	43	....	....	....	14	....	....	....	....	....	....	....	....	....	....	13	6	*28	34	22	....	....	....
	Canada	WJC-A	7	1	4	5	....	....	....	4	....	....	....	....	....	....	....	....	....	....	....	....	....	....	....	....	....	....
	Hartford Whalers	**NHL**	**2**	**0**	**0**	**0**	**0**	**0**	**0**	**0**	**0**	**0**	**0**	**0**	**0.0**	**1**	**0**	**0**	**0**	**+1**	....	....	....	....	....	....	....	....
	Binghamton Whalers	AHL	12	2	4	6	....	....	....	0	....	....	....	....	....	....	....	....	....	....	....	....	....	....	....	....	....	....
1986-87	**Hartford Whalers**	**NHL**	**67**	**3**	**7**	**10**	**2**	**6**	**8**	**20**	**0**	**0**	**0**	**100**	**2.0**	**52**	**0**	**56**	**15**	**+11**	**2**	**0**	**2**	**2**	**2**	**0**	**0**	**0**
1987-88	**Hartford Whalers**	**NHL**	**67**	**7**	**21**	**28**	**6**	**15**	**21**	**30**	**0**	**1**	**0**	**142**	**4.9**	**65**	**11**	**77**	**15**	**–8**	**6**	**1**	**1**	**2**	**4**	**1**	**0**	**0**
1988-89	**Hartford Whalers**	**NHL**	**78**	**8**	**9**	**17**	**7**	**6**	**13**	**49**	**1**	**0**	**0**	**130**	**6.2**	**74**	**5**	**98**	**22**	**–7**	**3**	**0**	**1**	**1**	**4**	**0**	**0**	**0**
1989-90	**Hartford Whalers**	**NHL**	**28**	**4**	**2**	**6**	**3**	**1**	**4**	**14**	**1**	**0**	**1**	**50**	**8.0**	**24**	**1**	**32**	**11**	**+2**	**5**	**0**	**0**	**0**	**2**	**0**	**0**	**0**
1990-91	**Hartford Whalers**	**NHL**	**73**	**7**	**12**	**19**	**6**	**9**	**15**	**17**	**1**	**0**	**0**	**154**	**4.5**	**69**	**14**	**111**	**39**	**–17**	**6**	**0**	**2**	**2**	**2**	**0**	**0**	**0**
1991-92	**Washington Capitals**	**NHL**	**78**	**11**	**29**	**40**	**10**	**22**	**32**	**31**	**6**	**0**	**2**	**151**	**7.3**	**110**	**38**	**74**	**9**	**+7**	**7**	**1**	**2**	**3**	**4**	**0**	**0**	**0**
1992-93	**Washington Capitals**	**NHL**	**77**	**21**	**29**	**50**	**17**	**20**	**37**	**34**	**8**	**2**	**3**	**206**	**10.2**	**126**	**37**	**72**	**11**	**+28**	**6**	**1**	**1**	**2**	**4**	**0**	**0**	**0**
1993-94	**Washington Capitals**	**NHL**	**84**	**16**	**35**	**51**	**15**	**27**	**42**	**66**	**3**	**2**	**2**	**212**	**7.5**	**139**	**35**	**100**	**26**	**+30**	**9**	**1**	**8**	**9**	**6**	**0**	**0**	**0**
1994-95	**Washington Capitals**	**NHL**	**47**	**5**	**14**	**19**	**9**	**21**	**30**	**53**	**1**	**0**	**2**	**124**	**4.0**	**58**	**20**	**51**	**15**	**+2**	**7**	**1**	**3**	**4**	**2**	**0**	**0**	**0**
1995-96	**Washington Capitals**	**NHL**	**81**	**5**	**33**	**38**	**5**	**27**	**32**	**40**	**3**	**0**	**2**	**212**	**2.4**	**94**	**32**	**81**	**24**	**+5**	**6**	**2**	**0**	**2**	**12**	**1**	**0**	**0**
1996-97	Canada	W Cup	2	0	1	1	....	....	....	0	....	....	....	....	....	....	....	....	....	....	....	....	....	....	....	....	....	....
	Washington Capitals	**NHL**	**57**	**6**	**18**	**24**	**6**	**16**	**22**	**28**	**2**	**0**	**0**	**131**	**4.6**	**71**	**19**	**56**	**15**	**+11**	....	....	....	....	....	....	....	....
1997-98	**Washington Capitals**	**NHL**	**59**	**1**	**15**	**16**	**1**	**15**	**16**	**36**	**0**	**0**	**0**	**83**	**1.2**	**43**	**6**	**51**	**9**	**–5**	....	....	....	....	....	....	....	....
	Toronto Maple Leafs	**NHL**	**12**	**3**	**6**	**9**	**4**	**6**	**10**	**6**	**1**	**0**	**1**	**20**	**15.0**	**16**	**6**	**11**	**3**	**+2**	....	....	....	....	....	....	....	....
	NHL Totals		**877**	**99**	**240**	**339**	**93**	**197**	**290**	**441**	**28**	**5**	**14**	**1805**	**5.5**	**986**	**235**	**934**	**215**		**57**	**7**	**20**	**27**	**42**	**2**	**0**	**0**

QMJHL Second All-Star Team (1984) • QMJHL First All-Star Team (1986)

Traded to **Washington** by **Hartford** for Washington's 2nd round choice (Andrei Nikolishin) in 1992 Entry Draft, September 8, 1991. Traded to **Toronto** by **Washington** for Jeff Brown, March 24, 1998.

• COULIS, TIM

Tim Coulis LW – L. 6', 200 lbs. b: Kenora, Ont., 2/24/1958. Washington's 2nd choice, 18th overall, in 1978 Amateur Draft.

Season	Club	League	GP	G	A	Pts	AG	AA	APts	PIM	PP	SH	GW	S	%	TGF	PGF	TGA	PGA	+/–	GP	G	A	Pts	PIM	PP	SH	GW
1976-77	Sault Ste. Marie Greyhounds	OHA	27	13	20	33	....	....	....	114	....	....	....	....	....	....	....	....	....	....	....	....	....	....	....	....	....	....
	St. Catharines Fincups	OHA	28	10	22	32	....	....	....	136	....	....	....	....	....	....	....	....	....	....	14	4	5	9	20	....	....	....
1977-78	Hamilton Fincups	OHA	46	27	25	52	....	....	....	203	....	....	....	....	....	....	....	....	....	....	11	6	3	9	64	....	....	....
1978-79			DID NOT PLAY – INJURED																									
1979-80	**Washington Capitals**	**NHL**	**19**	**1**	**2**	**3**	**1**	**2**	**3**	**27**	**0**	**0**	**0**	**12**	**8.3**	**5**	**0**	**14**	**3**	**–6**	....	....	....	....	....	....	....	....
	Hershey Bears	AHL	47	6	12	18	....	....	....	138	....	....	....	....	....	....	....	....	....	....	....	....	....	....	....	....	....	....
1980-81	Dallas Black Hawks	CHL	63	16	15	31	....	....	....	149	....	....	....	....	....	....	....	....	....	....	6	2	1	3	24	....	....	....
1981-82	Dallas Black Hawks	CHL	68	20	32	52	....	....	....	209	....	....	....	....	....	....	....	....	....	....	9	5	1	6	92	....	....	....
1982-83			DID NOT PLAY – SUSPENDED																									
1983-84	**Minnesota North Stars**	**NHL**	**2**	**0**	**0**	**0**	**0**	**0**	**0**	**4**	**0**	**0**	**0**	**0**	**0.0**	**0**	**0**	**1**	**0**	**–1**	....	....	....	....	....	....	....	....
	Salt Lake Golden Eagles	CHL	63	25	35	60	....	....	....	225	....	....	....	....	....	....	....	....	....	....	4	1	2	3	35	....	....	....
1984-85	**Minnesota North Stars**	**NHL**	**7**	**1**	**1**	**2**	**1**	**1**	**2**	**34**	**0**	**0**	**0**	**10**	**10.0**	**3**	**0**	**4**	**0**	**–1**	**3**	**1**	**0**	**1**	**2**	**0**	**0**	**1**
	Springfield Indians	AHL	52	13	17	30	....	....	....	86	....	....	....	....	....	....	....	....	....	....	....	....	....	....	....	....	....	....
1985-86	**Minnesota North Stars**	**NHL**	**19**	**2**	**2**	**4**	**2**	**1**	**3**	**73**	**0**	**0**	**0**	**13**	**15.4**	**6**	**0**	**11**	**0**	**–5**	....	....	....	....	....	....	....	....
	Springfield Indians	AHL	13	5	7	12	....	....	....	42	....	....	....	....	....	....	....	....	....	....	....	....	....	....	....	....	....	....
1986-87	Springfield Indians	AHL	38	12	19	31	....	....	....	212	....	....	....	....	....	....	....	....	....	....	....	....	....	....	....	....	....	....
1987-88	Kalamazoo Wings	IHL	18	2	6	8	....	....	....	23	....	....	....	....	....	....	....	....	....	....	....	....	....	....	....	....	....	....
	NHL Totals		**47**	**4**	**5**	**9**	**4**	**4**	**8**	**138**	**0**	**0**	**0**	**35**	**11.4**	**14**	**0**	**30**	**3**		**3**	**1**	**0**	**1**	**2**	**0**	**0**	**1**

Traded to **Toronto** by **Washington** with Robert Picard and Washington's 2nd round choice (Bob McGill) in 1980 Entry Draft for Mike Palmateer and Toronto's 3rd round choice (Torrie Robertson), June 11, 1980. Signed as a free agent by **Vancouver**, October 13, 1981. • Suspended for entire 1982-83 season after assaulting referee Bob Hall, April 24, 1982. Signed as a free agent by **Minnesota**, July 2, 1983.

• COULTER, NEAL

Neal Coulter RW – R. 6'2", 190 lbs. b: London, Ont., 1/2/1963. NY Islanders' 4th choice, 63rd overall, in 1981 Entry Draft.

			REGULAR SEASON																			PLAYOFFS							
Season	Club	League	GP	G	A	Pts	AG	AA	APts	PIM	PP	SH	GW	S	%	TGF	PGF	TGA	PGA	+/–	GP	G	A	Pts	PIM	PP	SH	GW
1979-80	Oakridge Midgets	Midget	60	35	30	65	....	....	....	150	....	....	....	....	....	....	....	....	....	....	....	....	....	....	....	....	....	....
1980-81	Toronto Marlboros	OHA	19	4	3	7	....	....	....	22	....	....	....	....	....	....	....	....	....	....	5	0	3	3	0	....	....	....
1981-82	Toronto Marlboros	OHL	62	14	16	30	....	....	....	79	....	....	....	....	....	....	....	....	....	....	....	....	....	....	....	....	....	....
1982-83	Toronto Marlboros	OHL	59	13	37	50	....	....	....	60	....	....	....	....	....	....	....	....	....	....	4	2	1	3	2	....	....	....
	Indianapolis Checkers	CHL	3	0	1	1	....	....	....	0	....	....	....	....	....	....	....	....	....	....	....	....	....	....	....	....	....	....
1983-84	Toledo Goaldiggers	IHL	5	1	3	4	....	....	....	0	....	....	....	....	....	....	....	....	....	....	....	....	....	....	....	....	....	....
	Indianapolis Checkers	CHL	58	7	10	17	....	....	....	25	....	....	....	....	....	....	....	....	....	....	4	2	0	2	0	....	....	....
1984-85	Springfield Indians	AHL	2	1	0	1	....	....	....	0	....	....	....	....	....	....	....	....	....	....	....	....	....	....	....	....	....	....
	Indianapolis Checkers	IHL	82	31	26	57	....	....	....	95	....	....	....	....	....	....	....	....	....	....	7	3	1	4	9	....	....	....
1985-86	**New York Islanders**	**NHL**	**16**	**3**	**4**	**7**	**2**	**3**	**5**	**4**	**0**	**0**	**0**	**17**	**17.6**	**9**	**0**	**13**	**3**	**–1**	....	....	....	....	....	....	....	....
	Springfield Indians	AHL	60	17	9	26	....	....	....	92	....	....	....	....	....	....	....	....	....	....	....	....	....	....	....	....	....	....
1986-87	**New York Islanders**	**NHL**	**9**	**2**	**1**	**3**	**2**	**1**	**3**	**7**	**0**	**0**	**0**	**5**	**40.0**	**4**	**0**	**9**	**3**	**–2**	....	....	....	....	....	....	....	....
	Springfield Indians	AHL	47	12	13	25	....	....	....	63	....	....	....	....	....	....	....	....	....	....	....	....	....	....	....	....	....	....
1987-88	**New York Islanders**	**NHL**	**1**	**0**	**0**	**0**	**0**	**0**	**0**	**0**	**0**	**0**	**0**	**0**	**0.0**	**0**	**0**	**1**	**0**	**–1**	....	....	....	....	....	....	....	....
	Springfield Indians	AHL	27	11	4	15	....	....	....	33	....	....	....	....	....	....	....	....	....	....	....	....	....	....	....	....	....	....
	NHL Totals		**26**	**5**	**5**	**10**	**4**	**4**	**8**	**11**	**0**	**0**	**0**	**22**	**22.7**	**13**	**0**	**23**	**6**		....	....	....	....	....	....	....	....

• COURNOYER, YVAN

Yvan "The Roadrunner" Cournoyer RW – L. 5'7", 178 lbs. b: Drummondville, Que., 11/22/1943. **HHOF**

			REGULAR SEASON																			PLAYOFFS							
Season	Club	League	GP	G	A	Pts	AG	AA	APts	PIM	PP	SH	GW	S	%	TGF	PGF	TGA	PGA	+/–	GP	G	A	Pts	PIM	PP	SH	GW
1961-62	Montreal Jr. Canadiens	OHA	35	15	16	31	....	....	....	8	....	....	....	....	....	....	....	....	....	....	6	4	4	8	0	....	....	....
1962-63	Montreal Jr. Canadiens	OHA	36	37	27	64	....	....	....	24	....	....	....	....	....	....	....	....	....	....	10	3	4	7	6	....	....	....
1963-64	Montreal Jr. Canadiens	OHA	53	*63	48	111	....	....	....	30	....	....	....	....	....	....	....	....	....	....	17	*19	8	27	15	....	....	....
	Montreal Canadiens	**NHL**	**5**	**4**	**0**	**4**	**5**	**0**	**5**	**0**	....	....	....	....	....	....	....	....	....	....	....	....	....	....	....	....	....	....
1964-65	**Montreal Canadiens**	**NHL**	**55**	**7**	**10**	**17**	**9**	**11**	**20**	**10**	....	....	....	....	....	....	....	....	....	....	**12**	**3**	**1**	**4**	**0**	....	....	....
	Quebec Aces	AHL	7	2	1	3	....	....	....	0	....	....	....	....	....	....	....	....	....	....	....	....	....	....	....	....	....	....
1965-66	**Montreal Canadiens**	**NHL**	**65**	**18**	**11**	**29**	**22**	**11**	**33**	**8**	....	....	....	....	....	....	....	....	....	....	**10**	**2**	**3**	**5**	**2**	....	....	....
1966-67	**Montreal Canadiens**	**NHL**	**69**	**25**	**15**	**40**	**31**	**15**	**46**	**14**	....	....	....	....	....	....	....	....	....	....	**10**	**2**	**3**	**5**	**6**	....	....	....
1967-68	**Montreal Canadiens**	**NHL**	**64**	**28**	**32**	**60**	**35**	**34**	**69**	**23**	**7**	**1**	**4**	**222**	**12.6**	**85**	**33**	**33**	**0**	**+19**	**13**	**6**	**8**	**14**	**4**	**3**	**0**	**1**
1968-69	**Montreal Canadiens**	**NHL**	**76**	**43**	**44**	**87**	**49**	**42**	**91**	**31**	**14**	**0**	**8**	**245**	**17.6**	**120**	**37**	**64**	**0**	**+19**	**14**	**4**	**7**	**11**	**5**	**0**	**2**	**2**
1969-70	**Montreal Canadiens**	**NHL**	**72**	**27**	**36**	**63**	**31**	**36**	**67**	**23**	**10**	**0**	**4**	**233**	**11.6**	**87**	**39**	**47**	**0**	**+1**	....	....	....	....	....	....	....	....
1970-71	**Montreal Canadiens**	**NHL**	**65**	**37**	**36**	**73**	**39**	**32**	**71**	**21**	**18**	**0**	**5**	**197**	**18.8**	**110**	**47**	**43**	**0**	**+20**	**20**	**10**	**12**	**22**	**6**	**2**	**0**	**1**
1971-72	**Montreal Canadiens**	**NHL**	**73**	**47**	**36**	**83**	**50**	**33**	**83**	**15**	**18**	**0**	**5**	**208**	**22.6**	**128**	**51**	**54**	**0**	**+23**	**6**	**2**	**1**	**3**	**2**	**0**	**0**	**0**
1972-73	Canada	Summit	8	3	2	5	....	....	....	2	....	....	....	....	....	....	....	....	....	....	....	....	....	....	....	....	....	....
	Montreal Canadiens	**NHL**	**67**	**40**	**39**	**79**	**40**	**33**	**73**	**18**	**6**	**0**	**4**	**194**	**20.6**	**117**	**25**	**42**	**0**	**+50**	**17**	***15**	**10**	***25**	**2**	**3**	**0**	**3**
1973-74	**Montreal Canadiens**	**NHL**	**67**	**40**	**33**	**73**	**41**	**29**	**70**	**18**	**10**	**0**	**9**	**187**	**21.4**	**107**	**31**	**60**	**0**	**+16**	**6**	**5**	**2**	**7**	**2**	**0**	**0**	**2**
1974-75	**Montreal Canadiens**	**NHL**	**76**	**29**	**45**	**74**	**27**	**35**	**62**	**32**	**11**	**0**	**2**	**176**	**16.5**	**116**	**48**	**52**	**0**	**+16**	**11**	**5**	**6**	**11**	**4**	**2**	**0**	**0**
1975-76	**Montreal Canadiens**	**NHL**	**71**	**32**	**36**	**68**	**30**	**28**	**58**	**20**	**8**	**0**	**12**	**163**	**19.6**	**103**	**38**	**28**	**0**	**+37**	**13**	**3**	**6**	**9**	**4**	**2**	**0**	**1**
1976-77	**Montreal Canadiens**	**NHL**	**60**	**25**	**28**	**53**	**24**	**23**	**47**	**8**	**6**	**0**	**2**	**122**	**20.5**	**70**	**14**	**29**	**0**	**+27**	....	....	....	....	....	....	....	....
1977-78	**Montreal Canadiens**	**NHL**	**68**	**24**	**29**	**53**	**23**	**24**	**47**	**12**	**4**	**0**	**6**	**125**	**19.2**	**75**	**16**	**20**	**0**	**+39**	**15**	**7**	**4**	**11**	**10**	**0**	**0**	**2**
1978-79	**Montreal Canadiens**	**NHL**	**15**	**2**	**5**	**7**	**2**	**4**	**6**	**2**	**0**	**0**	**0**	**23**	**8.7**	**11**	**3**	**3**	**0**	**+5**	....	....	....	....	....	....	....	....
	NHL Totals		**968**	**428**	**435**	**863**	**458**	**390**	**848**	**255**	**112**	**1**	**61**	**2095**	**20.4**	**1129**	**382**	**475**	**0**		**147**	**64**	**63**	**127**	**47**	**12**	**2**	**12**

NHL Second All-Star Team (1969, 1971, 1972, 1973) • Won Conn Smythe Trophy (1973)
Played in NHL All-Star Game (1967, 1971, 1972, 1973, 1974, 1978)

• COURTEAU, YVES

Yves Courteau RW – L. 6', 195 lbs. b: Montreal, Que., 4/25/1964. Detroit's 2nd choice, 23rd overall, in 1982 Entry Draft.

			REGULAR SEASON																			PLAYOFFS							
Season	Club	League	GP	G	A	Pts	AG	AA	APts	PIM	PP	SH	GW	S	%	TGF	PGF	TGA	PGA	+/–	GP	G	A	Pts	PIM	PP	SH	GW
1980-81	Laval Voisins	QMJHL	7	24	39	63	....	....	....	80	....	....	....	....	....	....	....	....	....	....	....	....	....	....	....	....	....	....
1981-82	Laval Voisins	QMJHL	64	30	38	68	....	....	....	15	....	....	....	....	....	....	....	....	....	....	18	14	13	27	28	....	....	....
1982-83	Laval Voisins	QMJHL	68	44	78	122	....	....	....	52	....	....	....	....	....	....	....	....	....	....	12	4	11	15	0	....	....	....
1983-84	Laval Titan	QMJHL	62	45	75	120	....	....	....	52	....	....	....	....	....	....	....	....	....	....	14	11	16	27	6	....	....	....
	Canada	WJC-A	7	0	1	1	....	....	....	0	....	....	....	....	....	....	....	....	....	....	....	....	....	....	....	....	....	....
1984-85	**Calgary Flames**	**NHL**	**14**	**1**	**4**	**5**	**1**	**3**	**4**	**4**	**0**	**0**	**1**	**18**	**5.6**	**9**	**0**	**7**	**0**	**+2**	....	....	....	....	....	....	....	....
	Moncton Golden Flames	AHL	59	19	21	40	....	....	....	32	....	....	....	....	....	....	....	....	....	....	....	....	....	....	....	....	....	....
1985-86	**Calgary Flames**	**NHL**	**4**	**1**	**1**	**2**	**1**	**1**	**2**	**0**	**0**	**0**	**0**	**7**	**14.3**	**2**	**0**	**3**	**2**	**+1**	**1**	**0**	**0**	**0**	**0**	**0**	**0**	**0**
	Moncton Golden Flames	AHL	70	26	22	48	....	....	....	19	....	....	....	....	....	....	....	....	....	....	10	4	2	6	5	....	....	....
1986-87	**Hartford Whalers**	**NHL**	**4**	**0**	**0**	**0**	**0**	**0**	**0**	**0**	**0**	**0**	**0**	**4**	**0.0**	**1**	**0**	**7**	**0**	**–6**	....	....	....	....	....	....	....	....
	Binghamton Whalers	AHL	57	15	28	43	....	....	....	8	....	....	....	....	....	....	....	....	....	....	7	1	4	5	12	....	....	....
1987-88	Binghamton Whalers	AHL	25	15	22	37	....	....	....	22	....	....	....	....	....	....	....	....	....	....	4	2	0	2	0	....	....	....
	NHL Totals		**22**	**2**	**5**	**7**	**2**	**4**	**6**	**4**	**0**	**0**	**1**	**29**	**6.9**	**12**	**0**	**17**	**2**		**1**	**0**	**0**	**0**	**0**	**0**	**0**	**0**

Rights traded to **Calgary** by **Detroit** for Bobby Francis, December 2, 1982. Traded to **Hartford** by **Calgary** for Mark Paterson, October 7, 1986.

• COURTENAY, ED

Ed Courtenay RW – R. 6'4", 215 lbs. b: Verdun, Que., 2/2/1968.

			REGULAR SEASON																			PLAYOFFS							
Season	Club	League	GP	G	A	Pts	AG	AA	APts	PIM	PP	SH	GW	S	%	TGF	PGF	TGA	PGA	+/–	GP	G	A	Pts	PIM	PP	SH	GW
1986-87	Laval Titan	QMJHL	48	15	20	35	....	....	....	12	....	....	....	....	....	....	....	....	....	....	1	0	0	0	0	....	....	....
1987-88	Granby Bisons	QMJHL	54	37	34	71	....	....	....	19	....	....	....	....	....	....	....	....	....	....	5	1	1	2	2	....	....	....
1988-89	Granby Bisons	QMJHL	68	59	55	114	....	....	....	68	....	....	....	....	....	....	....	....	....	....	4	1	1	2	22	....	....	....
	Kalamazoo Wings	IHL	1	0	0	0	....	....	....	0	....	....	....	....	....	....	....	....	....	....	1	0	0	0	2	....	....	....
1989-90	Kalamazoo Wings	IHL	57	25	28	53	....	....	....	16	....	....	....	....	....	....	....	....	....	....	3	0	0	0	0	....	....	....
1990-91	Kalamazoo Wings	IHL	76	35	36	71	....	....	....	37	....	....	....	....	....	....	....	....	....	....	8	2	3	5	12	....	....	....
1991-92	**San Jose Sharks**	**NHL**	**5**	**0**	**0**	**0**	**0**	**0**	**0**	**0**	**0**	**0**	**0**	**7**	**0.0**	**1**	**0**	**7**	**0**	**–6**	....	....	....	....	....	....	....	....
	Kansas City Blades	IHL	36	14	12	26	....	....	....	46	....	....	....	....	....	....	....	....	....	....	15	8	9	17	15	....	....	....
1992-93	**San Jose Sharks**	**NHL**	**39**	**7**	**13**	**20**	**6**	**9**	**15**	**10**	**2**	**0**	**1**	**56**	**12.5**	**26**	**16**	**25**	**0**	**–15**	....	....	....	....	....	....	....	....
	Kansas City Blades	IHL	32	15	12	27	....	....	....	25	....	....	....	....	....	....	....	....	....	....	....	....	....	....	....	....	....	....
1993-94	Kansas City Blades	IHL	62	27	21	48	....	....	....	60	....	....	....	....	....	....	....	....	....	....	....	....	....	....	....	....	....	....
1994-95	Chicago Wolves	IHL	47	14	16	30	....	....	....	20	....	....	....	....	....	....	....	....	....	....	....	....	....	....	....	....	....	....
	Peoria Rivermen	IHL	9	5	0	5	....	....	....	4	....	....	....	....	....	....	....	....	....	....	9	5	3	8	2	....	....	....
1995-96	San Francisco Spiders	IHL	20	6	3	9	....	....	....	8	....	....	....	....	....	....	....	....	....	....	....	....	....	....	....	....	....	....
	Jacksonville Lizard Kings	ECHL	3	0	2	2	....	....	....	4	....	....	....	....	....	....	....	....	....	....	18	5	12	17	23	....	....	....
1996-97	South Carolina Stingrays	ECHL	68	54	56	*110	....	....	....	70	....	....	....	....	....	....	....	....	....	....	....	....	....	....	....	....	....	....
	NHL Totals		**44**	**7**	**13**	**20**	**6**	**9**	**15**	**10**	**2**	**0**	**1**	**63**	**11.1**	**27**	**16**	**32**	**0**		....	....	....	....	....	....	....	....

QMJHL Second All-Star Team (1989) • ECHL First All-Star Team (1997)
Signed as a free agent by **Minnesota**, October 1, 1989. Claimed by **San Jose** from **Minnesota** in Dispersal Draft, May 30, 1991.

• COURTNALL, GEOFF

Geoff Courtnall LW – L. 6'1", 195 lbs. b: Duncan, B.C., 8/18/1962.

			REGULAR SEASON																			PLAYOFFS							
Season	Club	League	GP	G	A	Pts	AG	AA	APts	PIM	PP	SH	GW	S	%	TGF	PGF	TGA	PGA	+/–	GP	G	A	Pts	PIM	PP	SH	GW
1980-81	Victoria Cougars	WHL	11	3	4	7	....	....	....	6	....	....	....	....	....	....	....	....	....	....	15	2	1	3	7	....	....	....
1981-82	Victoria Cougars	WHL	72	35	57	90	....	....	....	100	....	....	....	....	....	....	....	....	....	....	4	1	0	1	2	....	....	....
1982-83	Victoria Cougars	WHL	71	41	73	114	....	....	....	186	....	....	....	....	....	....	....	....	....	....	12	6	7	13	42	....	....	....
1983-84	**Boston Bruins**	**NHL**	**4**	**0**	**0**	**0**	**0**	**0**	**0**	**0**	**0**	**0**	**0**	**1**	**0.0**	**1**	**0**	**2**	**0**	**–1**	....	....	....	....	....	....	....	....
	Hershey Bears	AHL	74	14	12	26	....	....	....	51	....	....	....	....	....	....	....	....	....	....	....	....	....	....	....	....	....	....
1984-85	**Boston Bruins**	**NHL**	**64**	**12**	**16**	**28**	**10**	**11**	**21**	**82**	**0**	**0**	**1**	**91**	**13.2**	**35**	**0**	**38**	**0**	**–3**	**5**	**0**	**2**	**2**	**7**	**0**	**0**	**0**
	Hershey Bears	AHL	9	8	4	12	....	....	....	4	....	....	....	....	....	....	....	....	....	....	....	....	....	....	....	....	....	....
1985-86	**Boston Bruins**	**NHL**	**64**	**21**	**16**	**37**	**17**	**11**	**28**	**61**	**2**	**0**	**4**	**161**	**13.0**	**53**	**9**	**43**	**0**	**+1**	**3**	**0**	**0**	**0**	**2**	**0**	**0**	**0**
	Moncton Golden Flames	AHL	12	8	8	16	....	....	....	6	....	....	....	....	....	....	....	....	....	....	....	....	....	....	....	....	....	....
1986-87	**Boston Bruins**	**NHL**	**65**	**13**	**23**	**36**	**11**	**17**	**28**	**117**	**2**	**0**	**1**	**178**	**7.3**	**48**	**11**	**41**	**0**	**–4**	**1**	**0**	**0**	**0**	**0**	**0**	**0**	**0**
1987-88	**Boston Bruins**	**NHL**	**62**	**32**	**26**	**58**	**27**	**18**	**45**	**108**	**8**	**0**	**4**	**220**	**14.5**	**86**	**25**	**37**	**0**	**+24**	....	....	....	....	....	....	....	....
	Edmonton Oilers	**NHL**	**12**	**4**	**4**	**8**	**3**	**3**	**6**	**15**	**0**	**0**	**1**	**32**	**12.5**	**10**	**0**	**9**	**0**	**+1**	**19**	**0**	**3**	**3**	**23**	**0**	**0**	**0**
1988-89	**Washington Capitals**	**NHL**	**79**	**42**	**38**	**80**	**36**	**27**	**63**	**112**	**16**	**0**	**6**	**239**	**17.6**	**114**	**52**	**52**	**1**	**+11**	**6**	**2**	**5**	**7**	**12**	**1**	**0**	**0**
1989-90	Washington Capitals	FrTour	4	4	1	5	....	....	....	4	....	....	....	....	....	....	....	....	....	....	....	....	....	....	....	....	....	....
	Washington Capitals	**NHL**	**80**	**35**	**39**	**74**	**30**	**28**	**58**	**104**	**9**	**0**	**2**	**307**	**11.4**	**114**	**35**	**52**	**0**	**+27**	**15**	**4**	**9**	**13**	**32**	**1**	**0**	**2**
1990-91	**St. Louis Blues**	**NHL**	**66**	**27**	**30**	**57**	**25**	**23**	**48**	**56**	**9**	**0**	**6**	**216**	**12.5**	**85**	**23**	**43**	**0**	**+19**	....	....	....	....	....	....	....	....
	Vancouver Canucks	**NHL**	**11**	**6**	**2**	**8**	**5**	**2**	**7**	**8**	**3**	**0**	**2**	**47**	**12.8**	**20**	**9**	**21**	**7**	**–3**	**6**	**3**	**5**	**8**	**4**	**0**	**0**	**0**
	Canada	WEC-A	10	5	1	6	....	....	....	16	....	....	....	....	....	....	....	....	....	....	....	....	....	....	....	....	....	....

			REGULAR SEASON																		PLAYOFFS							
Season	Club	League	GP	G	A	Pts	AG	AA	APts	PIM	PP	SH	GW	S	%	TGF	PGF	TGA	PGA	+/-	GP	G	A	Pts	PIM	PP	SH	GW
1991-92	**Vancouver Canucks**	**NHL**	**70**	**23**	**34**	**57**	**21**	**26**	**47**	**116**	**12**	**0**	**3**	**281**	**8.2**	**81**	**38**	**50**	**1**	**-6**	**12**	**6**	**8**	**14**	**20**	**2**	**0**	**1**
1992-93	**Vancouver Canucks**	**NHL**	**84**	**31**	**46**	**77**	**26**	**32**	**58**	**167**	**9**	**0**	**11**	**214**	**14.5**	**109**	**27**	**56**	**1**	**+27**	**12**	**4**	**10**	**14**	**12**	**1**	**0**	**1**
1993-94	**Vancouver Canucks**	**NHL**	**82**	**26**	**44**	**70**	**24**	**34**	**58**	**123**	**12**	**1**	**2**	**264**	**9.8**	**114**	**47**	**68**	**16**	**+15**	**24**	**9**	**10**	**19**	**51**	**0**	**1**	**3**
1994-95	**Vancouver Canucks**	**NHL**	**45**	**16**	**18**	**34**	**28**	**26**	**54**	**81**	**7**	**0**	**1**	**144**	**11.1**	**51**	**24**	**30**	**5**	**+2**	**11**	**4**	**2**	**6**	**34**	**3**	**1**	**1**
1995-96	**St. Louis Blues**	**NHL**	**69**	**24**	**16**	**40**	**24**	**13**	**37**	**101**	**7**	**1**	**1**	**228**	**10.5**	**60**	**26**	**57**	**14**	**-9**	**13**	**0**	**3**	**3**	**14**	**0**	**0**	**0**
1996-97	**St. Louis Blues**	**NHL**	**82**	**17**	**40**	**57**	**18**	**35**	**53**	**86**	**4**	**0**	**2**	**203**	**8.4**	**86**	**21**	**64**	**2**	**+3**	**6**	**3**	**1**	**4**	**23**	**1**	**0**	**2**
1997-98	**St. Louis Blues**	**NHL**	**79**	**31**	**31**	**62**	**36**	**30**	**66**	**94**	**6**	**0**	**5**	**189**	**16.4**	**86**	**24**	**51**	**1**	**+12**	**10**	**2**	**8**	**10**	**18**	**1**	**0**	**0**
	NHL Totals		**1018**	**360**	**423**	**783**	**341**	**336**	**677**	**1431**	**106**	**2**	**52**	**3015**	**11.9**	**1153**	**371**	**714**	**48**		**143**	**37**	**66**	**103**	**252**	**10**	**2**	**10**

Signed as a free agent by **Boston**, July 6, 1983. Traded to **Edmonton** by **Boston** with Bill Ranford and future considerations for Andy Moog, March 8, 1988. Rights traded to **Washington** by **Edmonton** for Greg C. Adams, July 22, 1988. Traded to **St. Louis** by **Washington** for Peter Zezel and Mike Lalor, July 13, 1990. Traded to **Vancouver** by **St. Louis** with Robert Dirk, Sergio Momesso, Cliff Ronning and St. Louis' 5th round choice (Brian Loney) in 1992 Entry Draft for Dan Quinn and Garth Butcher, March 5, 1991. Signed as a free agent by **St. Louis**, July 14, 1995.

• COURTNALL, RUSS

Russ Courtnall RW – R. 5'11", 185 lbs. b: Duncan, B.C., 6/2/1965. Toronto's 1st choice, 7th overall, in 1983 Entry Draft.

Season	Club	League	GP	G	A	Pts	AG	AA	APts	PIM	PP	SH	GW	S	%	TGF	PGF	TGA	PGA	+/-	GP	G	A	Pts	PIM	PP	SH	GW
1982-83	Victoria Cougars	WHL	60	36	61	97	....	....	....	33	....	....	....	....	....	....	....	....	....	....	12	11	7	18	6	....	....	....
1983-84	Victoria Cougars	WHL	32	29	37	66	....	....	....	63	....	....	....	....	....	....	....	....	....	....	....	....	....	....	....	....	....	....
	Canada	WJC-A	7	7	6	13	....	....	....	0	....	....	....	....	....	....	....	....	....	....	....	....	....	....	....	....	....	....
	Canada	Nat-Team	16	4	7	11	....	....	....	10	....	....	....	....	....	....	....	....	....	....	....	....	....	....	....	....	....	....
	Canada	Olympics	7	1	3	4	....	....	....	2	....	....	....	....	....	....	....	....	....	....	....	....	....	....	....	....	....	....
	Toronto Maple Leafs	**NHL**	**14**	**3**	**9**	**12**	**2**	**6**	**8**	**6**	**1**	**0**	**0**	**29**	**10.3**	**17**	**3**	**15**	**1**	**0**	....	....	....	....	....	....	....	....
1984-85	**Toronto Maple Leafs**	**NHL**	**69**	**12**	**10**	**22**	**10**	**7**	**17**	**44**	**0**	**2**	**1**	**130**	**9.2**	**34**	**4**	**56**	**3**	**-23**	....	....	....	....	....	....	....	....
1985-86	**Toronto Maple Leafs**	**NHL**	**73**	**22**	**38**	**60**	**18**	**25**	**43**	**52**	**3**	**1**	**4**	**203**	**10.8**	**85**	**10**	**86**	**11**	**0**	**10**	**3**	**6**	**9**	**8**	**1**	**0**	**0**
1986-87	**Toronto Maple Leafs**	**NHL**	**79**	**29**	**44**	**73**	**25**	**32**	**57**	**90**	**3**	**6**	**3**	**282**	**10.3**	**104**	**30**	**110**	**16**	**-20**	**13**	**3**	**4**	**7**	**11**	**1**	**0**	**0**
1987-88	**Toronto Maple Leafs**	**NHL**	**65**	**23**	**26**	**49**	**20**	**18**	**38**	**47**	**6**	**3**	**1**	**212**	**10.8**	**80**	**28**	**78**	**10**	**-16**	**6**	**2**	**1**	**3**	**0**	**0**	**0**	**0**
1988-89	**Toronto Maple Leafs**	**NHL**	**9**	**1**	**1**	**2**	**1**	**1**	**2**	**4**	**0**	**1**	**0**	**11**	**9.1**	**4**	**0**	**7**	**1**	**-2**	....	....	....	....	....	....	....	....
	Montreal Canadiens	**NHL**	**64**	**22**	**17**	**39**	**19**	**12**	**31**	**15**	**7**	**0**	**3**	**136**	**16.2**	**57**	**12**	**35**	**1**	**+11**	**21**	**8**	**5**	**13**	**18**	**1**	**0**	**2**
1989-90	**Montreal Canadiens**	**NHL**	**80**	**27**	**32**	**59**	**23**	**23**	**46**	**27**	**3**	**0**	**2**	**294**	**9.2**	**79**	**12**	**62**	**9**	**+14**	**11**	**5**	**1**	**6**	**10**	**0**	**0**	**0**
1990-91	Montreal Canadiens	FrTour	3	1	0	1	....	....	....	4	....	....	....	....	....	....	....	....	....	....	....	....	....	....	....	....	....	....
	Montreal Canadiens	**NHL**	**79**	**26**	**50**	**76**	**24**	**38**	**62**	**29**	**5**	**1**	**5**	**279**	**9.3**	**100**	**29**	**93**	**27**	**+5**	**13**	**8**	**3**	**11**	**7**	**2**	**2**	**1**
	Canada	WEC-A	2	1	3	4	....	....	....	0	....	....	....	....	....	....	....	....	....	....	....	....	....	....	....	....	....	....
1991-92	Canada	C Cup	8	0	2	2	....	....	....	0	....	....	....	....	....	....	....	....	....	....	....	....	....	....	....	....	....	....
	Montreal Canadiens	**NHL**	**27**	**7**	**14**	**21**	**6**	**11**	**17**	**6**	**0**	**1**	**1**	**63**	**11.1**	**21**	**2**	**19**	**6**	**+6**	**10**	**1**	**1**	**2**	**4**	**0**	**0**	**1**
1992-93	**Minnesota North Stars**	**NHL**	**84**	**36**	**43**	**79**	**30**	**29**	**59**	**49**	**14**	**2**	**3**	**294**	**12.2**	**102**	**41**	**71**	**11**	**+1**	....	....	....	....	....	....	....	....
1993-94	**Dallas Stars**	**NHL**	**84**	**23**	**57**	**80**	**21**	**44**	**65**	**59**	**5**	**0**	**4**	**231**	**10.0**	**108**	**35**	**70**	**3**	**+6**	**9**	**1**	**8**	**9**	**0**	**0**	**0**	**0**
1994-95	**Dallas Stars**	**NHL**	**32**	**7**	**10**	**17**	**12**	**15**	**27**	**13**	**2**	**0**	**1**	**90**	**7.8**	**27**	**10**	**25**	**0**	**-8**	....	....	....	....	....	....	....	....
	Vancouver Canucks	**NHL**	**13**	**4**	**14**	**18**	**7**	**21**	**28**	**4**	**0**	**2**	**1**	**42**	**9.5**	**22**	**6**	**8**	**2**	**+10**	**11**	**4**	**8**	**12**	**21**	**0**	**2**	**1**
1995-96	**Vancouver Canucks**	**NHL**	**81**	**26**	**39**	**65**	**26**	**32**	**58**	**40**	**6**	**4**	**4**	**205**	**12.7**	**101**	**25**	**71**	**20**	**+25**	**6**	**1**	**3**	**4**	**2**	**0**	**0**	**0**
1996-97	**Vancouver Canucks**	**NHL**	**47**	**9**	**19**	**28**	**10**	**17**	**27**	**24**	**1**	**0**	**1**	**101**	**8.9**	**37**	**9**	**39**	**15**	**+4**	....	....	....	....	....	....	....	....
	New York Rangers	**NHL**	**14**	**2**	**5**	**7**	**2**	**4**	**6**	**2**	**1**	**1**	**1**	**24**	**8.3**	**12**	**3**	**13**	**1**	**-3**	**15**	**3**	**4**	**7**	**0**	**1**	**0**	**0**
1997-98	**Los Angeles Kings**	**NHL**	**58**	**12**	**6**	**18**	**14**	**6**	**20**	**27**	**1**	**4**	**4**	**97**	**12.4**	**28**	**4**	**41**	**15**	**-2**	**4**	**0**	**0**	**0**	**2**	**0**	**0**	**0**
	NHL Totals		**972**	**291**	**434**	**725**	**270**	**341**	**611**	**538**	**58**	**28**	**39**	**2723**	**10.7**	**1018**	**263**	**899**	**152**		**129**	**39**	**44**	**83**	**83**	**6**	**4**	**5**

Played in NHL All-Star Game (1994)

Traded to **Montreal** by **Toronto** for John Kordic and Montreal's 6th round choice (Michael Doers) in 1989 Entry Draft, November 7, 1988. Traded to **Minnesota** by **Montreal** for Brian Bellows, August 31, 1992. Transferred to **Dallas** after **Minnesota** franchise relocated, June 9, 1993. Traded to **Vancouver** by **Dallas** for Greg Adams, Dan Kesa and Vancouver's 5th round choice (later traded to LA Kings — LA Kings selected Jason Morgan) in 1995 Entry Draft, April 7, 1995. Traded to **NY Rangers** by **Vancouver** with Esa Tikkanen for Sergei Nemchinov and Brian Noonan, March 8, 1997. Signed as a free agent by **Los Angeles**, November 7, 1997.

• COURVILLE, LARRY

Larry Courville LW – L. 6'1", 180 lbs. b: Timmins, Ont., 4/2/1975. Vancouver's 2nd choice, 61st overall, in 1995 Entry Draft.

Season	Club	League	GP	G	A	Pts	AG	AA	APts	PIM	PP	SH	GW	S	%	TGF	PGF	TGA	PGA	+/-	GP	G	A	Pts	PIM	PP	SH	GW
1991-92	Cornwall Royals	OHL	60	8	12	20	....	....	....	80	....	....	....	....	....	....	....	....	....	....	6	0	0	0	0	....	....	....
1992-93	Newmarket Royals	OHL	64	21	18	39	....	....	....	181	....	....	....	....	....	....	....	....	....	....	7	0	6	6	14	....	....	....
1993-94	Newmarket Royals	OHL	39	20	19	39	....	....	....	134	....	....	....	....	....	....	....	....	....	....	....	....	....	....	....	....	....	....
	Moncton Hawks	AHL	8	2	0	2	....	....	....	37	....	....	....	....	....	....	....	....	....	....	10	2	2	4	27	....	....	....
1994-95	Sarnia Sting	OHL	16	9	9	18	....	....	....	58	....	....	....	....	....	....	....	....	....	....	....	....	....	....	....	....	....	....
	Canada	WJC-A	7	2	3	5	....	....	....	6	....	....	....	....	....	....	....	....	....	....	....	....	....	....	....	....	....	....
	Oshawa Generals	OHL	28	25	30	55	....	....	....	72	....	....	....	....	....	....	....	....	....	....	7	4	10	14	10	....	....	....
1995-96	**Vancouver Canucks**	**NHL**	**3**	**1**	**0**	**1**	**1**	**0**	**1**	**0**	**0**	**0**	**1**	**2**	**50.0**	**1**	**0**	**0**	**0**	**+1**	....	....	....	....	....	....	....	....
	Syracuse Crunch	AHL	71	17	32	49	....	....	....	127	....	....	....	....	....	....	....	....	....	....	14	5	3	8	10	....	....	....
1996-97	**Vancouver Canucks**	**NHL**	**19**	**0**	**2**	**2**	**0**	**2**	**2**	**11**	**0**	**0**	**0**	**11**	**0.0**	**3**	**0**	**7**	**0**	**-4**	....	....	....	....	....	....	....	....
	Syracuse Crunch	AHL	54	20	24	44	....	....	....	103	....	....	....	....	....	....	....	....	....	....	3	0	1	1	20	....	....	....
1997-98	**Vancouver Canucks**	**NHL**	**11**	**0**	**0**	**0**	**0**	**0**	**0**	**5**	**0**	**0**	**0**	**3**	**0.0**	**0**	**0**	**7**	**0**	**-7**	....	....	....	....	....	....	....	....
	Syracuse Crunch	AHL	29	6	12	18	....	....	....	84	....	....	....	....	....	....	....	....	....	....	....	....	....	....	....	....	....	....
	NHL Totals		**33**	**1**	**2**	**3**	**1**	**2**	**3**	**16**	**0**	**0**	**1**	**16**	**6.3**	**4**	**0**	**14**	**0**		....	....	....	....	....	....	....	....

OHL Second All-Star Team (1995)

Re-entered NHL Entry Draft. Originally Winnipeg's 6th choice, 119th overall in 1993 Entry Draft.

• COUTURIER, SYLVAIN

Sylvain Couturier C – L. 6'2", 205 lbs. b: Greenfield Park, Que., 4/23/1968. Los Angeles' 3rd choice, 65th overall, in 1986 Entry Draft.

Season	Club	League	GP	G	A	Pts	AG	AA	APts	PIM	PP	SH	GW	S	%	TGF	PGF	TGA	PGA	+/-	GP	G	A	Pts	PIM	PP	SH	GW
1985-86	Laval Titan	QMJHL	68	21	37	58	....	....	....	64	....	....	....	....	....	....	....	....	....	....	14	1	7	8	28	....	....	....
1986-87	Laval Titan	QMJHL	67	39	51	90	....	....	....	77	....	....	....	....	....	....	....	....	....	....	13	12	14	26	19	....	....	....
1987-88	Laval Titan	QMJHL	67	70	67	137	....	....	....	115	....	....	....	....	....	....	....	....	....	....	....	....	....	....	....	....	....	....
1988-89	**Los Angeles Kings**	**NHL**	**16**	**1**	**3**	**4**	**1**	**2**	**3**	**2**	**1**	**0**	**0**	**15**	**6.7**	**11**	**3**	**11**	**0**	**-3**	....	....	....	....	....	....	....	....
	New Haven Nighthawks	AHL	44	18	20	38	....	....	....	33	....	....	....	....	....	....	....	....	....	....	10	2	2	4	11	....	....	....
1989-90	New Haven Nighthawks	AHL	50	9	8	17	....	....	....	47	....	....	....	....	....	....	....	....	....	....	....	....	....	....	....	....	....	....
1990-91	**Los Angeles Kings**	**NHL**	**3**	**0**	**1**	**1**	**0**	**1**	**1**	**0**	**0**	**0**	**0**	**2**	**0.0**	**1**	**0**	**1**	**0**	**0**	....	....	....	....	....	....	....	....
	Phoenix Roadrunners	IHL	66	50	37	87	....	....	....	49	....	....	....	....	....	....	....	....	....	....	10	8	2	10	10	....	....	....
1991-92	**Los Angeles Kings**	**NHL**	**14**	**3**	**1**	**4**	**3**	**1**	**4**	**2**	**0**	**0**	**0**	**21**	**14.3**	**5**	**0**	**9**	**1**	**-3**	....	....	....	....	....	....	....	....
	Phoenix Roadrunners	IHL	39	19	20	39	....	....	....	68	....	....	....	....	....	....	....	....	....	....	....	....	....	....	....	....	....	....
1992-93	Phoenix Roadrunners	IHL	38	23	16	39	....	....	....	63	....	....	....	....	....	....	....	....	....	....	....	....	....	....	....	....	....	....
	Adirondack Red Wings	AHL	29	17	17	34	....	....	....	12	....	....	....	....	....	....	....	....	....	....	11	3	5	8	10	....	....	....
	Fort Wayne Komets	IHL	....	....	....	....	....	....	....	....	....	....	....	....	....	....	....	....	....	....	4	2	3	5	2	....	....	....
1993-94	Milwaukee Admirals	IHL	80	41	51	92	....	....	....	123	....	....	....	....	....	....	....	....	....	....	4	1	2	3	2	....	....	....
1994-95	Milwaukee Admirals	IHL	77	31	41	72	....	....	....	77	....	....	....	....	....	....	....	....	....	....	15	1	4	5	10	....	....	....
1995-96	Milwaukee Admirals	IHL	82	33	52	85	....	....	....	60	....	....	....	....	....	....	....	....	....	....	5	1	0	1	2	....	....	....
1996-97	Milwaukee Admirals	IHL	79	26	24	50	....	....	....	42	....	....	....	....	....	....	....	....	....	....	3	0	1	1	2	....	....	....
	NHL Totals		**33**	**4**	**5**	**9**	**4**	**4**	**8**	**4**	**1**	**0**	**0**	**38**	**10.5**	**17**	**3**	**21**	**1**		....	....	....	....	....	....	....	....

Traded to **Detroit** by **LA Kings** with Paul Coffey and Jim Hiller for Jimmy Carson, Marc Potvin and Gary Shuchuk, January 29, 1993.

• COWICK, BRUCE

Bruce Cowick LW – L. 6'1", 200 lbs. b: Victoria, B.C., 8/18/1951.

Season	Club	League	GP	G	A	Pts	AG	AA	APts	PIM	PP	SH	GW	S	%	TGF	PGF	TGA	PGA	+/-	GP	G	A	Pts	PIM	PP	SH	GW
1969-70	Victoria Cougars	BCJHL	47	27	40	67	....	....	....	....	....	....	....	....	....	....	....	....	....	....	....	....	....	....	....	....	....	....
1970-71	Victoria Cougars	BCJHL	47	31	44	75	....	....	....	197	....	....	....	....	....	....	....	....	....	....	....	....	....	....	....	....	....	....
1971-72	San Diego Gulls	WHL	65	6	8	14	....	....	....	97	....	....	....	....	....	....	....	....	....	....	4	0	2	2	2	....	....	....
1972-73	San Diego Gulls	WHL	61	17	13	30	....	....	....	165	....	....	....	....	....	....	....	....	....	....	....	....	....	....	....	....	....	....
1973-74	Richmond Robins	AHL	68	14	7	21	....	....	....	130	....	....	....	....	....	....	....	....	....	....	5	1	1	2	9	....	....	....
	Philadelphia Flyers	**NHL**	....	....	....	....	....	....	....	....	....	....	....	....	....	....	....	....	....	....	**8**	**0**	**0**	**0**	**9**	....	....	....
1974-75	**Washington Capitals**	**NHL**	**65**	**5**	**6**	**11**	**5**	**5**	**10**	**41**	**0**	**0**	**0**	**73**	**6.8**	**20**	**3**	**59**	**0**	**-42**	....	....	....	....	....	....	....	....
1975-76	**St. Louis Blues**	**NHL**	**5**	**0**	**0**	**0**	**0**	**0**	**0**	**2**	**0**	**0**	**0**	**3**	**0.0**	**1**	**0**	**0**	**0**	**+1**	....	....	....	....	....	....	....	....
	Providence Reds	AHL	38	3	6	9	....	....	....	38	....	....	....	....	....	....	....	....	....	....	1	0	0	0	0	....	....	....
	NHL Totals		**70**	**5**	**6**	**11**	**5**	**5**	**10**	**43**	**0**	**0**	**0**	**76**	**6.6**	**21**	**3**	**59**	**0**		**8**	**0**	**0**	**0**	**9**	**0**	**0**	**0**

Signed as a free agent by **San Diego** (WHL), October 2, 1971. Traded to **Philadelphia** by **San Diego** (WHL) for Fred Stanfield, Tom Trevalyn, Bob Currier and Bob Hurlbury, July, 1973. Claimed by **Washington** from **Philadelphia** in Expansion Draft, June 12, 1974. Claimed on waivers by **St. Louis** from **Washington**, May 21, 1975.

• COWIE, ROB

Rob Cowie D – L. 6′, 195 lbs. b: Toronto, Ont., 11/3/1967.

			REGULAR SEASON																		PLAYOFFS							
Season	Club	League	GP	G	A	Pts	AG	AA	APts	PIM	PP	SH	GW	S	%	TGF	PGF	TGA	PGA	+/–	GP	G	A	Pts	PIM	PP	SH	GW
1985-86	St. Michael's Buzzers	Jr. B	31	9	23	32	....	....	....	24	....	....	....	....	....	....	....	....	....	....	....	....	....	....	....	....	....	....
1986-87	St. Michael's Buzzers	Jr. B	36	25	32	57	....	....	....	55	....	....	....	....	....	....	....	....	....	....	....	....	....	....	....	....	....	....
1987-88	Northeastern University	H.E.	36	7	8	15	....	....	....	38	....	....	....	....	....	....	....	....	....	....	....	....	....	....	....	....	....	....
1988-89	Northeastern University	H.E.	36	7	34	41	....	....	....	60	....	....	....	....	....	....	....	....	....	....	....	....	....	....	....	....	....	....
1989-90	Northeastern University	H.E.	34	14	31	45	....	....	....	54	....	....	....	....	....	....	....	....	....	....	....	....	....	....	....	....	....	....
1990-91	Northeastern University	H.E.	33	18	23	41	....	....	....	56	....	....	....	....	....	....	....	....	....	....	....	....	....	....	....	....	....	....
1991-92	Moncton Hawks	AHL	64	11	30	41	....	....	....	89	....	....	....	....	....	....	....	....	....	....	5	1	1	2	0	....	....	....
1992-93	Moncton Hawks	AHL	67	12	20	32	....	....	....	91	....	....	....	....	....	....	....	....	....	....	5	3	5	8	2	....	....	....
1993-94	Springfield Indians	AHL	78	17	57	74	....	....	....	124	....	....	....	....	....	....	....	....	....	....	6	3	6	9	4	....	....	....
1994-95	**Los Angeles Kings**	**NHL**	**32**	**2**	**7**	**9**	**4**	**10**	**14**	**20**	**0**	**0**	**0**	**39**	**5.1**	**16**	**2**	**26**	**6**	**–6**	....	....	....	....	....	....	....	....
	Phoenix Roadrunners	IHL	51	14	33	47	....	....	....	71	....	....	....	....	....	....	....	....	....	....	....	....	....	....	....	....	....	....
1995-96	**Los Angeles Kings**	**NHL**	**46**	**5**	**5**	**10**	**5**	**4**	**9**	**32**	**2**	**0**	**0**	**86**	**5.8**	**30**	**6**	**44**	**4**	**–16**	....	....	....	....	....	....	....	....
	Phoenix Roadrunners	IHL	22	2	17	19	....	....	....	48	....	....	....	....	....	....	....	....	....	....	4	1	3	4	0	....	....	....
1996-97	La Chaux-de-Fonds	Switz.	39	18	18	36	....	....	....	100	....	....	....	....	....	....	....	....	....	....	....	....	....	....	....	....	....	....
1997-98	EHC Eisbaren Berlin	Germany	48	11	30	41	....	....	....	74	....	....	....	....	....	....	....	....	....	....	10	3	5	8	16	....	....	....
	NHL Totals		**78**	**7**	**12**	**19**	**9**	**14**	**23**	**52**	**2**	**0**	**0**	**125**	**5.6**	**46**	**8**	**70**	**10**		....	....	....	....	....	....	....	....

Hockey East Second All-Star Team (1989) • Hockey East First All-Star Team (1990) • Hockey East Second All-Star Team (1991)

Signed as a free agent by **Winnipeg**, July 4, 1991. Signed as a free agent by **Hartford**, August 9, 1993. Signed as a free agent by **LA Kings**, July 8, 1994.

• COXE, CRAIG

Craig Coxe LW – L. 6′4″, 210 lbs. b: Chula Vista, CA, 1/21/1964. Detroit's 4th choice, 66th overall, in 1982 Entry Draft.

Season	Club	League	GP	G	A	Pts	AG	AA	APts	PIM	PP	SH	GW	S	%	TGF	PGF	TGA	PGA	+/–	GP	G	A	Pts	PIM	PP	SH	GW
1981-82	St. Albert Saints	AJHL	51	17	48	65	....	....	....	212	....	....	....	....	....	....	....	....	....	....	....	....	....	....	....	....	....	....
1982-83	Belleville Bulls	OHL	64	14	27	41	....	....	....	102	....	....	....	....	....	....	....	....	....	....	4	1	2	3	2	....	....	....
1983-84	Belleville Bulls	OHL	45	17	28	45	....	....	....	90	....	....	....	....	....	....	....	....	....	....	3	2	0	2	4	....	....	....
1984-85	**Vancouver Canucks**	**NHL**	**9**	**0**	**0**	**0**	**0**	**0**	**0**	**49**	**0**	**0**	**0**	**1**	**0.0**	**0**	**0**	**5**	**0**	**–5**	....	....	....	....	....	....	....	....
	Fredericton Express	AHL	62	8	7	15	....	....	....	242	....	....	....	....	....	....	....	....	....	....	4	2	1	3	16	....	....	....
1985-86	**Vancouver Canucks**	**NHL**	**57**	**3**	**5**	**8**	**2**	**3**	**5**	**176**	**1**	**0**	**0**	**48**	**6.3**	**15**	**2**	**26**	**0**	**–13**	**3**	**0**	**0**	**0**	**2**	**0**	**0**	**0**
1986-87	**Vancouver Canucks**	**NHL**	**15**	**1**	**0**	**1**	**1**	**0**	**1**	**31**	**1**	**0**	**0**	**7**	**14.3**	**1**	**1**	**3**	**0**	**–3**	....	....	....	....	....	....	....	....
	Fredericton Express	AHL	46	1	12	13	....	....	....	168	....	....	....	....	....	....	....	....	....	....	....	....	....	....	....	....	....	....
1987-88	**Vancouver Canucks**	**NHL**	**64**	**5**	**12**	**17**	**4**	**9**	**13**	**186**	**1**	**0**	**1**	**43**	**11.6**	**26**	**3**	**24**	**0**	**–1**	....	....	....	....	....	....	....	....
	Calgary Flames	**NHL**	**7**	**2**	**3**	**5**	**2**	**2**	**4**	**32**	**0**	**0**	**0**	**5**	**40.0**	**9**	**0**	**6**	**0**	**+3**	**2**	**1**	**0**	**1**	**16**	**0**	**0**	**0**
1988-89	**St. Louis Blues**	**NHL**	**41**	**0**	**7**	**7**	**0**	**5**	**5**	**127**	**0**	**0**	**0**	**15**	**0.0**	**12**	**0**	**9**	**0**	**+3**	....	....	....	....	....	....	....	....
	Peoria Rivermen	IHL	8	2	7	9	....	....	....	38	....	....	....	....	....	....	....	....	....	....	....	....	....	....	....	....	....	....
1989-90	**Vancouver Canucks**	**NHL**	**25**	**1**	**4**	**5**	**1**	**3**	**4**	**66**	**0**	**0**	**1**	**11**	**9.1**	**8**	**0**	**12**	**0**	**–4**	....	....	....	....	....	....	....	....
	Milwaukee Admirals	IHL	5	0	5	5	....	....	....	4	....	....	....	....	....	....	....	....	....	....	....	....	....	....	....	....	....	....
1990-91	**Vancouver Canucks**	**NHL**	**7**	**0**	**0**	**0**	**0**	**0**	**0**	**27**	**0**	**0**	**0**	**5**	**0.0**	**2**	**0**	**5**	**0**	**–3**	....	....	....	....	....	....	....	....
	Milwaukee Admirals	IHL	36	9	21	30	....	....	....	116	....	....	....	....	....	....	....	....	....	....	6	3	2	5	22	....	....	....
1991-92	**San Jose Sharks**	**NHL**	**10**	**2**	**0**	**2**	**2**	**0**	**2**	**19**	**0**	**0**	**0**	**11**	**18.2**	**5**	**0**	**9**	**0**	**–4**	....	....	....	....	....	....	....	....
	Kansas City Blades	IHL	51	17	21	38	....	....	....	106	....	....	....	....	....	....	....	....	....	....	....	....	....	....	....	....	....	....
	Kalamazoo Wings	IHL	6	4	5	9	....	....	....	13	....	....	....	....	....	....	....	....	....	....	10	2	4	6	37	....	....	....
1992-93	Cincinnati Cyclones	IHL	20	5	3	8	....	....	....	34	....	....	....	....	....	....	....	....	....	....	....	....	....	....	....	....	....	....
	Kalamazoo Wings	IHL	12	1	1	2	....	....	....	8	....	....	....	....	....	....	....	....	....	....	....	....	....	....	....	....	....	....
1993-94	Tulsa Oilers	CHL	64	26	57	83	....	....	....	236	....	....	....	....	....	....	....	....	....	....	11	4	9	13	38	....	....	....
1994-95	Tulsa Oilers	CHL	12	7	7	14	....	....	....	28	....	....	....	....	....	....	....	....	....	....	7	0	1	1	30	....	....	....
1995-96			DID NOT PLAY – RETIRED																									
1996-97	Tulsa Oilers	CHL	64	29	59	88	....	....	....	95	....	....	....	....	....	....	....	....	....	....	5	2	2	4	8	....	....	....
1997-98	Tulsa Oilers	CHL	25	11	22	33	....	....	....	34	....	....	....	....	....	....	....	....	....	....	....	....	....	....	....	....	....	....
	Wichita Thunder	CHL	31	9	29	38	....	....	....	75	....	....	....	....	....	....	....	....	....	....	15	1	10	11	62	....	....	....
	NHL Totals		**235**	**14**	**31**	**45**	**12**	**22**	**34**	**713**	**3**	**0**	**2**	**146**	**9.6**	**78**	**6**	**99**	**0**		**5**	**1**	**0**	**1**	**18**	**0**	**0**	**0**

Signed as a free agent by **Vancouver**, June 26, 1984. Traded to **Calgary** by **Vancouver** for Brian Bradley and Peter Bakovic, March 6, 1988. Traded to **St. Louis** by **Calgary** with Mike Bullard and Tim Corkey for Mark Hunter, Doug Gilmour, Steve Bozek and Michael Dark, September 6, 1988. Traded to **Chicago** by **St. Louis** for Rik Wilson, September 27, 1989. Claimed by **Vancouver** in Waiver Draft, October 2, 1989. Claimed by **San Jose** from **Vancouver** in Expansion Draft, May 30, 1991.

• CRAIG, MIKE

Mike Craig RW – R. 6′1″, 180 lbs. b: St. Mary's, Ont., 6/6/1971. Minnesota's 2nd choice, 28th overall, in 1989 Entry Draft.

Season	Club	League	GP	G	A	Pts	AG	AA	APts	PIM	PP	SH	GW	S	%	TGF	PGF	TGA	PGA	+/–	GP	G	A	Pts	PIM	PP	SH	GW
1987-88	Oshawa Generals	OHL	61	6	10	16	....	....	....	39	....	....	....	....	....	....	....	....	....	....	7	7	0	1	11	....	....	....
1988-89	Oshawa Generals	OHL	63	36	36	72	....	....	....	34	....	....	....	....	....	....	....	....	....	....	6	3	1	4	6	....	....	....
1989-90	Oshawa Generals	OHL	43	36	40	76	....	....	....	85	....	....	....	....	....	....	....	....	....	....	17	10	16	26	46	....	....	....
	Canada	WJC-A	7	3	0	3	....	....	....	8	....	....	....	....	....	....	....	....	....	....	....	....	....	....	....	....	....	....
1990-91	**Minnesota North Stars**	**NHL**	**39**	**8**	**4**	**12**	**7**	**3**	**10**	**32**	**1**	**0**	**2**	**59**	**13.6**	**26**	**7**	**32**	**2**	**–11**	**10**	**1**	**1**	**2**	**20**	**1**	**0**	**1**
	Canada	WJC-A	7	6	5	11	....	....	....	8	....	....	....	....	....	....	....	....	....	....	....	....	....	....	....	....	....	....
1991-92	**Minnesota North Stars**	**NHL**	**67**	**15**	**16**	**31**	**14**	**12**	**26**	**155**	**4**	**0**	**4**	**136**	**11.0**	**47**	**17**	**44**	**2**	**–12**	**4**	**1**	**0**	**1**	**7**	**0**	**0**	**0**
1992-93	**Minnesota North Stars**	**NHL**	**70**	**15**	**23**	**38**	**12**	**16**	**28**	**106**	**7**	**0**	**0**	**131**	**11.5**	**70**	**31**	**50**	**0**	**–11**	....	....	....	....	....	....	....	....
1993-94	**Dallas Stars**	**NHL**	**72**	**13**	**24**	**37**	**12**	**19**	**31**	**139**	**3**	**0**	**2**	**150**	**8.7**	**57**	**16**	**59**	**4**	**–14**	**4**	**0**	**0**	**0**	**2**	**0**	**0**	**0**
1994-95	**Toronto Maple Leafs**	**NHL**	**37**	**5**	**5**	**10**	**9**	**7**	**16**	**12**	**1**	**0**	**1**	**61**	**8.2**	**14**	**2**	**33**	**0**	**–21**	**2**	**0**	**1**	**1**	**2**	**0**	**0**	**0**
1995-96	**Toronto Maple Leafs**	**NHL**	**70**	**8**	**12**	**20**	**8**	**10**	**18**	**42**	**1**	**0**	**1**	**108**	**7.4**	**32**	**2**	**39**	**1**	**–8**	**6**	**0**	**0**	**0**	**18**	**0**	**0**	**0**
1996-97	**Toronto Maple Leafs**	**NHL**	**65**	**7**	**13**	**20**	**7**	**11**	**18**	**62**	**1**	**0**	**0**	**128**	**5.5**	**30**	**6**	**44**	**0**	**–20**	....	....	....	....	....	....	....	....
1997-98	San Antonio Dragons	IHL	12	4	1	5	....	....	....	18	....	....	....	....	....	....	....	....	....	....	....	....	....	....	....	....	....	....
	Kansas City Blades	IHL	59	14	33	47	....	....	....	68	....	....	....	....	....	....	....	....	....	....	11	5	5	10	28	....	....	....
	NHL Totals		**420**	**71**	**97**	**168**	**69**	**78**	**147**	**548**	**18**	**0**	**10**	**773**	**9.2**	**276**	**81**	**301**	**9**		**26**	**2**	**2**	**4**	**49**	**1**	**0**	**1**

WJC-A All-Star Team (1991)

Transferred to **Dallas** after **Minnesota** franchise relocated, June 9, 1993. Signed as a free agent by **Toronto**, July 29, 1994. Signed as a free agent by **San Jose**, June 13, 1998.

• CRAIGHEAD, JOHN

John Craighead RW – R. 6′, 195 lbs. b: Vancouver, B.C., 11/23/1971.

Season	Club	League	GP	G	A	Pts	AG	AA	APts	PIM	PP	SH	GW	S	%	TGF	PGF	TGA	PGA	+/–	GP	G	A	Pts	PIM	PP	SH	GW
1991-92	West Palm Beach Blaze	SHL	39	12	17	29	....	....	....	160	....	....	....	....	....	....	....	....	....	....	....	....	....	....	....	....	....	....
1992-93			STATISTICS NOT AVAILABLE																									
1993-94	Huntington Blizzard	ECHL	9	4	2	6	....	....	....	44	....	....	....	....	....	....	....	....	....	....	....	....	....	....	....	....	....	....
	Richmond Renegades	ECHL	28	18	12	30	....	....	....	89	....	....	....	....	....	....	....	....	....	....	....	....	....	....	....	....	....	....
1994-95	Detroit Vipers	IHL	44	5	7	12	....	....	....	285	....	....	....	....	....	....	....	....	....	....	3	0	1	1	4	....	....	....
1995-96	Detroit Vipers	IHL	63	7	9	16	....	....	....	368	....	....	....	....	....	....	....	....	....	....	10	2	3	5	28	....	....	....
1996-97	**Toronto Maple Leafs**	**NHL**	**5**	**0**	**0**	**0**	**0**	**0**	**0**	**10**	**0**	**0**	**0**	**0**	**0.0**	**0**	**0**	**0**	**0**	**0**	....	....	....	....	....	....	....	....
	St. John's Maple Leafs	AHL	53	9	10	19	....	....	....	318	....	....	....	....	....	....	....	....	....	....	7	1	1	2	22	....	....	....
1997-98	Cleveland Lumberjacks	IHL	49	9	7	16	....	....	....	233	....	....	....	....	....	....	....	....	....	....	....	....	....	....	....	....	....	....
	Quebec Rafales	IHL	13	2	2	4	....	....	....	73	....	....	....	....	....	....	....	....	....	....	....	....	....	....	....	....	....	....
	NHL Totals		**5**	**0**	**0**	**0**	**0**	**0**	**0**	**10**	**0**	**0**	**0**	**0**	**0.0**	**0**	**0**	**0**	**0**		....	....	....	....	....	....	....	....

Signed as a free agent by **Toronto**, July 22, 1996.

• CRAIGWELL, DALE

Dale Craigwell C – L. 5′11″, 180 lbs. b: Toronto, Ont., 4/24/1971. San Jose's 11th choice, 199th overall, in 1991 Entry Draft.

Season	Club	League	GP	G	A	Pts	AG	AA	APts	PIM	PP	SH	GW	S	%	TGF	PGF	TGA	PGA	+/–	GP	G	A	Pts	PIM	PP	SH	GW
1988-89	Oshawa Generals	OHL	55	9	14	23	....	....	....	15	....	....	....	....	....	....	....	....	....	....	....	....	....	....	....	....	....	....
1989-90	Oshawa Generals	OHL	64	22	41	63	....	....	....	39	....	....	....	....	....	....	....	....	....	....	17	7	7	14	11	....	....	....
1990-91	Oshawa Generals	OHL	56	27	68	95	....	....	....	34	....	....	....	....	....	....	....	....	....	....	16	7	16	23	9	....	....	....
	Canada	WJC-A	7	1	2	3	....	....	....	0	....	....	....	....	....	....	....	....	....	....	....	....	....	....	....	....	....	....
1991-92	**San Jose Sharks**	**NHL**	**32**	**5**	**11**	**16**	**5**	**8**	**13**	**8**	**4**	**0**	**2**	**38**	**13.2**	**29**	**10**	**25**	**3**	**–3**	....	....	....	....	....	....	....	....
	Kansas City Blades	IHL	48	6	19	25	....	....	....	29	....	....	....	....	....	....	....	....	....	....	12	4	7	11	4	....	....	....
1992-93	**San Jose Sharks**	**NHL**	**8**	**3**	**1**	**4**	**2**	**1**	**3**	**4**	**0**	**0**	**0**	**7**	**42.9**	**5**	**0**	**9**	**0**	**–4**	....	....	....	....	....	....	....	....
	Kansas City Blades	IHL	60	15	38	53	....	....	....	24	....	....	....	....	....	....	....	....	....	....	12	*7	5	12	2	....	....	....
1993-94	**San Jose Sharks**	**NHL**	**58**	**3**	**6**	**9**	**3**	**5**	**8**	**16**	**0**	**1**	**0**	**35**	**8.6**	**21**	**2**	**51**	**19**	**–13**	....	....	....	....	....	....	....	....
	Kansas City Blades	IHL	5	3	1	4	....	....	....	0	....	....	....	....	....	....	....	....	....	....	....	....	....	....	....	....	....	....
1994-95			DID NOT PLAY – INJURED																									

			REGULAR SEASON																		PLAYOFFS							
Season	Club	League	GP	G	A	Pts	AG	AA	APts	PIM	PP	SH	GW	S	%	TGF	PGF	TGA	PGA	+/-	GP	G	A	Pts	PIM	PP	SH	GW
1995-96	San Francisco Spiders	IHL	75	11	49	60				38											4	2	0	2	0			
1996-97	Kansas City Blades	IHL	82	17	51	68				34											3	1	0	1	0			
1997-98	Kansas City Blades	IHL	81	13	42	55				12											11	2	9	11	2			
	NHL Totals		**98**	**11**	**18**	**29**	**10**	**14**	**24**	**28**	**4**	**1**	**2**	**80**	**13.8**	**55**	**12**	**85**	**22**									

• CRASHLEY, BART

Bart (William) Crashley D – R. 6', 180 lbs. b: Toronto, Ont., 6/15/1946.

Season	Club	League	GP	G	A	Pts	AG	AA	APts	PIM	PP	SH	GW	S	%	TGF	PGF	TGA	PGA	+/-	GP	G	A	Pts	PIM	PP	SH	GW
1962-63	Hamilton Red Wings	OHA	50	1	16	17				18											5	0	0	0	2			
1963-64	Hamilton Red Wings	OHA	46	5	19	24				31																		
	Pittsburgh Hornets	AHL	1	0	0	0				0																		
1964-65	Hamilton Red Wings	OHA	56	11	35	46				40																		
1965-66	Hamilton Red Wings	OHA	46	8	31	39				55																		
	Detroit Red Wings	**NHL**	**1**	**0**	**0**	**0**	**0**	**0**	**0**	**0**																		
1966-67	**Detroit Red Wings**	**NHL**	**2**	**0**	**0**	**0**	**0**	**0**	**0**	**2**																		
	Pittsburgh Hornets	AHL	16	4	2	6				8																		
	Memphis Wings	CHL	49	6	26	32				40											7	1	5	6	4			
1967-68	**Detroit Red Wings**	**NHL**	**57**	**2**	**14**	**16**	**2**	**15**	**17**	**18**	**0**	**0**	**0**	**86**	**2.3**	**68**	**3**	**66**	**7**	**+6**								
	Fort Worth Wings	CHL	13	0	4	4				16											13	3	9	12	12			
1968-69	**Detroit Red Wings**	**NHL**	**1**	**0**	**0**	**0**	**0**	**0**	**0**	**0**	**0**	**0**	**0**	**0**	**0.0**	**0**	**0**	**0**	**0**	**0**								
	Fort Worth Wings	CHL	37	6	14	20				40																		
1969-70	Montreal Voyageurs	AHL	45	4	9	13				4											7	0	0	0	0			
1970-71	Kansas City Blues	CHL	58	5	19	24				28																		
1971-72	Dallas Black Hawks	CHL	56	20	38	58				24											6	0	7	7	5			
1972-73	Los Angeles Sharks	WHA	70	18	27	45				10											6	0	2	2	2			
1973-74	Los Angeles Sharks	WHA	78	4	26	30				16																		
1974-75	**Kansas City Scouts**	**NHL**	**27**	**3**	**6**	**9**	**3**	**5**	**8**	**10**	**1**	**0**	**1**	**39**	**7.7**	**32**	**12**	**44**	**8**	**–16**								
	Detroit Red Wings	**NHL**	**48**	**2**	**15**	**17**	**2**	**12**	**14**	**14**	**0**	**0**	**0**	**43**	**4.7**	**50**	**6**	**62**	**8**	**–10**								
1975-76	**Los Angeles Kings**	**NHL**	**4**	**0**	**1**	**1**	**0**	**1**	**1**	**6**	**0**	**0**	**0**	**2**	**0.0**	**1**	**1**	**11**	**1**	**–10**								
	Fort Worth Texans	CHL	61	11	32	43				61																		
1976-77	Springfield Indians	AHL	18	2	3	5				10																		
	Fort Worth Texans	CHL	23	4	11	15				10																		
1977-78	Binghamton Whalers	AHL	60	4	17	21				18																		
1978-79			DID NOT PLAY																									
1979-80	EC Heraklith Villacher	Austria	29	10	24	34				26																		
	NHL Totals		**140**	**7**	**36**	**43**	**7**	**33**	**40**	**50**	**1**	**0**	**1**	**170**	**4.1**	**151**	**22**	**183**	**24**									
	Other Major League Totals		148	22	53	75				26											6	0	2	2	2			

CHL First All-Star Team (1972) • Named CHL's Top Defenseman (1972)

Traded to **Montreal** by **Detroit** with Pete Mahovlich for Garry Monahan and Doug Piper, June 6, 1969. Selected by **LA Sharks** (WHA) in 1972 WHA General Player Draft, February 12, 1972. Claimed by **NY Islanders** from **Montreal** in Expansion Draft, June 6, 1972. Traded to **Kansas City** by **NY Islanders** with the rights to Larry Hornung for Bob Bourne, September 16, 1974. Traded to **Detroit** by **Kansas City** with Ted Snell and Larry Giroux for Guy Charron and Claude Houde, December 14, 1974. Traded to **LA Kings** by **Detroit** with the rights to Marcel Dionne for Dan Maloney, Terry Harper and LA Kings' 2nd round choice (later traded to Minnesota — Minnesota selected Jim Roberts) in 1976 Amateur Draft, June 23, 1975.

• CRAVEN, MURRAY

Murray Craven LW – L. 6'2", 185 lbs. b: Medicine Hat, Alta., 7/20/1964. Detroit's 1st choice, 17th overall, in 1982 Entry Draft.

Season	Club	League	GP	G	A	Pts	AG	AA	APts	PIM	PP	SH	GW	S	%	TGF	PGF	TGA	PGA	+/-	GP	G	A	Pts	PIM	PP	SH	GW
1980-81	Medicine Hat Tigers	WHL	69	5	10	15				18											5	0	0	0	2			
1981-82	Medicine Hat Tigers	WHL	72	35	46	81				49																		
1982-83	Medicine Hat Tigers	WHL	28	17	29	46				35																		
	Detroit Red Wings	**NHL**	**31**	**4**	**7**	**11**	**3**	**5**	**8**	**6**	**0**	**0**	**1**	**21**	**19.0**	**16**	**0**	**14**	**2**	**+4**								
1983-84	Medicine Hat Tigers	WHL	48	38	56	94				53											4	5	3	8	4			
	Detroit Red Wings	**NHL**	**15**	**0**	**4**	**4**	**0**	**3**	**3**	**6**	**0**	**0**	**0**	**8**	**0.0**	**8**	**0**	**7**	**1**	**+2**								
1984-85	**Philadelphia Flyers**	**NHL**	**80**	**26**	**35**	**61**	**21**	**24**	**45**	**30**	**2**	**2**	**5**	**142**	**18.3**	**99**	**12**	**57**	**15**	**+45**	**19**	**4**	**6**	**10**	**11**	**1**	**1**	**1**
1985-86	**Philadelphia Flyers**	**NHL**	**78**	**21**	**33**	**54**	**17**	**22**	**39**	**34**	**2**	**0**	**6**	**182**	**11.5**	**82**	**17**	**61**	**20**	**+24**	**5**	**0**	**3**	**3**	**4**	**0**	**0**	**0**
1986-87	**Philadelphia Flyers**	**NHL**	**77**	**19**	**30**	**49**	**16**	**22**	**38**	**38**	**5**	**3**	**2**	**98**	**19.4**	**72**	**23**	**64**	**16**	**+1**	**12**	**3**	**1**	**4**	**9**	**2**	**0**	**0**
1987-88	**Philadelphia Flyers**	**NHL**	**72**	**30**	**46**	**76**	**26**	**33**	**59**	**58**	**6**	**2**	**2**	**184**	**16.3**	**112**	**39**	**60**	**20**	**+25**	**7**	**2**	**5**	**7**	**4**	**0**	**0**	**1**
1988-89	**Philadelphia Flyers**	**NHL**	**51**	**9**	**28**	**37**	**8**	**20**	**28**	**52**	**0**	**0**	**2**	**89**	**10.1**	**49**	**14**	**44**	**13**	**+4**	**1**	**0**	**0**	**0**	**0**	**0**	**0**	**0**
1989-90	**Philadelphia Flyers**	**NHL**	**76**	**25**	**50**	**75**	**22**	**36**	**58**	**42**	**7**	**7**	**3**	**175**	**14.3**	**108**	**36**	**90**	**50**	**+2**								
	Canada	WEC-A	9	1	5	6				6																		
1990-91	**Philadelphia Flyers**	**NHL**	**77**	**19**	**47**	**66**	**17**	**36**	**53**	**53**	**6**	**0**	**0**	**170**	**11.2**	**87**	**30**	**82**	**23**	**–2**								
	Canada	WEC-A	9	1	1	2				10																		
1991-92	**Philadelphia Flyers**	**NHL**	**12**	**3**	**3**	**6**	**3**	**2**	**5**	**8**	**1**	**0**	**0**	**19**	**15.8**	**11**	**2**	**8**	**1**	**+2**								
	Hartford Whalers	**NHL**	**61**	**24**	**30**	**54**	**22**	**23**	**45**	**38**	**8**	**4**	**1**	**133**	**18.0**	**72**	**21**	**84**	**29**	**–4**	**7**	**3**	**3**	**6**	**6**	**0**	**1**	**0**
1992-93	**Hartford Whalers**	**NHL**	**67**	**25**	**42**	**67**	**21**	**29**	**50**	**20**	**6**	**3**	**2**	**139**	**18.0**	**106**	**48**	**111**	**49**	**–4**								
	Vancouver Canucks	**NHL**	**10**	**0**	**10**	**10**	**0**	**7**	**7**	**12**	**0**	**0**	**0**	**12**	**0.0**	**18**	**10**	**12**	**7**	**+3**	**12**	**4**	**6**	**10**	**4**	**1**	**0**	**1**
1993-94	**Vancouver Canucks**	**NHL**	**78**	**15**	**40**	**55**	**14**	**31**	**45**	**30**	**2**	**1**	**3**	**115**	**13.0**	**99**	**36**	**77**	**19**	**+5**	**22**	**4**	**9**	**13**	**18**	**0**	**0**	**1**
1994-95	**Chicago Blackhawks**	**NHL**	**16**	**4**	**3**	**7**	**7**	**4**	**11**	**2**	**1**	**0**	**2**	**29**	**13.8**	**10**	**4**	**7**	**3**	**+2**	**16**	**5**	**5**	**10**	**4**	**0**	**0**	**1**
1995-96	**Chicago Blackhawks**	**NHL**	**66**	**18**	**29**	**47**	**18**	**24**	**42**	**36**	**5**	**1**	**7**	**86**	**20.9**	**71**	**16**	**53**	**18**	**+20**	**9**	**1**	**4**	**5**	**2**	**1**	**0**	**0**
1996-97	**Chicago Blackhawks**	**NHL**	**75**	**8**	**27**	**35**	**8**	**24**	**32**	**12**	**2**	**0**	**1**	**122**	**6.6**	**53**	**13**	**63**	**23**	**0**	**2**	**0**	**0**	**0**	**2**	**0**	**0**	**0**
1997-98	**San Jose Sharks**	**NHL**	**67**	**12**	**17**	**29**	**14**	**17**	**31**	**25**	**2**	**3**	**3**	**107**	**11.2**	**51**	**12**	**51**	**16**	**+4**	**6**	**1**	**1**	**2**	**0**	**0**	**0**	**0**
	NHL Totals		**1009**	**262**	**481**	**743**	**237**	**362**	**599**	**502**	**55**	**21**	**40**	**1831**	**14.3**	**1124**	**333**	**953**	**295**		**118**	**27**	**43**	**70**	**64**	**5**	**2**	**5**

Traded to **Philadelphia** by **Detroit** with Joe Paterson for Darryl Sittler, October 10, 1984. Traded to **Hartford** by **Philadelphia** with Philadelphia's 4th round choice (Kevin Smyth) in 1992 Entry Draft for Kevin Dineen, November 13, 1991. Traded to **Vancouver** by **Hartford** with Vancouver's 5th round choice (previously acquired, Vancouver selected Scott Walker) in 1993 Entry Draft for Robert Kron, Vancouver's 3rd round choice (Marek Malik) in 1993 Entry Draft and future considerations (Jim Sandlak, May 17, 1993), March 22, 1993. Traded to **Chicago** by **Vancouver** for Christian Ruutu, March 10, 1995. Traded to **San Jose** by **Chicago** for the rights to Petr Varis and San Jose's 6th round choice in 1998 Entry Draft, July 25, 1997.

• CRAWFORD, BOB

Bob Crawford RW – R. 5'11", 180 lbs. b: Belleville, Ont., 4/6/1959. St. Louis' 2nd choice, 65th overall, in 1979 Entry Draft.

Season	Club	League	GP	G	A	Pts	AG	AA	APts	PIM	PP	SH	GW	S	%	TGF	PGF	TGA	PGA	+/-	GP	G	A	Pts	PIM	PP	SH	GW
1976-77	Cornwall Royals	QMJHL	71	36	34	70				39																		
	United States	WJC-A																										
1977-78	Cornwall Royals	QMJHL	69	54	67	121				29											9	7	5	12	2			
	United States	WJC-A	6	4	9	13				4																		
1978-79	Cornwall Royals	QMJHL	65	62	70	132				43											7	4	7	11	6			
	United States	WJC-A	5	1	2	3				2																		
1979-80	**St. Louis Blues**	**NHL**	**8**	**1**	**0**	**1**	**1**	**0**	**1**	**2**	**0**	**0**	**0**	**12**	**8.3**	**1**	**0**	**7**	**0**	**–6**								
	Salt Lake Golden Eagles	CHL	67	30	21	51				32											13	3	5	8	9			
1980-81	Salt Lake Golden Eagles	CHL	79	35	26	61				27											17	7	8	15	2			
1981-82	**St. Louis Blues**	**NHL**	**3**	**0**	**1**	**1**	**0**	**1**	**1**	**0**	**0**	**0**	**0**	**9**	**0.0**	**1**	**0**	**5**	**0**	**–4**								
	Salt Lake Golden Eagles	CHL	74	54	45	99				43											10	4	2	6	2			
1982-83	**St. Louis Blues**	**NHL**	**27**	**5**	**9**	**14**	**4**	**6**	**10**	**2**	**1**	**0**	**0**	**63**	**7.9**	**17**	**3**	**19**	**0**	**–5**	**4**	**0**	**0**	**0**	**0**	**0**	**0**	**0**
	Salt Lake Golden Eagles	CHL	25	15	23	38				2																		
1983-84	**Hartford Whalers**	**NHL**	**80**	**36**	**25**	**61**	**29**	**17**	**46**	**32**	**5**	**0**	**3**	**179**	**20.1**	**74**	**19**	**56**	**0**	**–1**								
1984-85	**Hartford Whalers**	**NHL**	**45**	**14**	**14**	**28**	**11**	**9**	**20**	**8**	**2**	**0**	**0**	**90**	**15.6**	**36**	**6**	**33**	**0**	**–3**								
1985-86	**Hartford Whalers**	**NHL**	**57**	**14**	**20**	**34**	**11**	**13**	**24**	**16**	**4**	**0**	**2**	**110**	**12.7**	**46**	**12**	**51**	**1**	**–16**								
	New York Rangers	**NHL**	**11**	**1**	**2**	**3**	**1**	**1**	**2**	**10**	**0**	**0**	**0**	**15**	**6.7**	**7**	**0**	**6**	**1**	**+2**	**7**	**0**	**1**	**1**	**8**	**0**	**0**	**0**
	New Haven Nighthawks	AHL	27	7	8	15				6											5	0	0	0	2			

			REGULAR SEASON																		PLAYOFFS							
Season	Club	League	GP	G	A	Pts	AG	AA	APts	PIM	PP	SH	GW	S	%	TGF	PGF	TGA	PGA	+/-	GP	G	A	Pts	PIM	PP	SH	GW
1986-87	**New York Rangers**	**NHL**	**3**	**0**	**0**	**0**	**0**	**0**	**0**	**2**	**0**	**0**	**0**	**1**	**0.0**	**0**	**0**	**1**	**0**	**–1**	....	....	....	....	....	....	....	....
	New Haven Nighthawks	AHL	4	3	0	3	....	....	....	7	....	....	....	....	....	....	....	....	....	....	....	....	....	....	....	....	....	....
	Washington Capitals	**NHL**	**12**	**0**	**0**	**0**	**0**	**0**	**0**	**0**	**0**	**0**	**0**	**14**	**0.0**	**2**	**0**	**2**	**0**	**0**	....	....	....	....	....	....	....	....
	Binghamton Whalers	AHL	5	0	2	2	....	....	....	0	....	....	....	....	....	....	....	....	....	....	....	....	....	....	....	....	....	....
	Salt Lake Golden Eagles	IHL	2	0	1	1	....	....	....	0	....	....	....	....	....	....	....	....	....	....	....	....	....	....	....	....	....	....
1987-88	SG Rosenheim	Germany	19	6	7	13	....	....	....	16	....	....	....	....	....	....	....	....	....	....	....	....	....	....	....	....	....	....
	HC Merano	Italy	23	15	23	38	....	....	....	11	....	....	....	....	....	....	....	....	....	....	....	....	....	....	....	....	....	....
	NHL Totals		**246**	**71**	**71**	**142**	**57**	**47**	**104**	**72**	**12**	**0**	**5**	**493**	**14.4**	**184**	**40**	**180**	**2**		**11**	**0**	**1**	**1**	**8**	**0**	**0**	**0**

CHL First All-Star Team (1982)

Claimed by **Hartford** from **St. Louis** in Waiver Draft, October 13, 1983. Traded to **NY Rangers** by **Hartford** for Mike McEwen, March 11, 1986. Traded to **Washington** by **NY Islanders** with Kelly Miller and Mike Ridley for Bob Carpenter and Washington's 2nd round choice (Jason Prosofsky), January 1, 1987.

• CRAWFORD, BOBBY

Bobby Crawford RW – L. 5'8", 180 lbs. b: Long Island, NY, 5/27/1960.

Season	Club	League	GP	G	A	Pts	AG	AA	APts	PIM	PP	SH	GW	S	%	TGF	PGF	TGA	PGA	+/-	GP	G	A	Pts	PIM	PP	SH	GW
1977-78	Oshawa Generals	OHA	38	21	16	37	....	....	....	2	....	....	....	....	....	....	....	....	....	....	....	....	....	....	....	....	....	....
1978-79	Oshawa Generals	OHA	68	41	58	99	....	....	....	68	....	....	....	....	....	....	....	....	....	....	5	3	3	6	13	....	....	....
1979-80	Oshawa Generals	OHA	68	61	68	129	....	....	....	48	....	....	....	....	....	....	....	....	....	....	7	4	4	8	8	....	....	....
1980-81	**Colorado Rockies**	**NHL**	**15**	**1**	**3**	**4**	**1**	**2**	**3**	**6**	**0**	**0**	**0**	**25**	**4.0**	**8**	**1**	**3**	**0**	**+4**	....	....	....	....	....	....	....	....
	Fort Worth Texans	CHL	61	19	18	37	....	....	....	32	....	....	....	....	....	....	....	....	....	....	5	2	0	2	4	....	....	....
1981-82	Fort Worth Texans	CHL	80	23	31	54	....	....	....	45	....	....	....	....	....	....	....	....	....	....	....	....	....	....	....	....	....	....
1982-83	**Detroit Red Wings**	**NHL**	**1**	**0**	**0**	**0**	**0**	**0**	**0**	**0**	**0**	**0**	**0**	**1**	**0.0**	**0**	**0**	**0**	**0**	**0**	....	....	....	....	....	....	....	....
	Adirondack Red Wings	AHL	76	28	33	61	....	....	....	32	....	....	....	....	....	....	....	....	....	....	6	2	5	7	4	....	....	....
	NHL Totals		**16**	**1**	**3**	**4**	**1**	**2**	**3**	**6**	**0**	**0**	**0**	**26**	**3.8**	**8**	**1**	**3**	**0**		....	....	....	....	....	....	....	....

OHA Second All-Star Team (1980)

Signed as a free agent by **NY Rangers**, November 16, 1979. Traded to **Colorado** by **NY Rangers** to complete transaction that sent Pat Hickey, Lucien Deblois, Mike McEwen and Dean Turner to Colorado (November 2, 1979), January 15, 1980. Signed as a free agent by **Detroit**, June, 1982.

• CRAWFORD, LOU

Lou Crawford LW – L. 6', 185 lbs. b: Belleville, Ont., 11/5/1962.

Season	Club	League	GP	G	A	Pts	AG	AA	APts	PIM	PP	SH	GW	S	%	TGF	PGF	TGA	PGA	+/-	GP	G	A	Pts	PIM	PP	SH	GW
1978-79	Belleville Bulls	Jr. B	45	25	30	55	....	....	....	107	....	....	....	....	....	....	....	....	....	....	....	....	....	....	....	....	....	....
1979-80	Belleville Bulls	OHA	10	7	11	18	....	....	....	60	....	....	....	....	....	....	....	....	....	....	....	....	....	....	....	....	....	....
	Cornwall Royals	QMJHL	24	0	1	1	....	....	....	46	....	....	....	....	....	....	....	....	....	....	....	....	....	....	....	....	....	....
1980-81	Kitchener Rangers	OHA	53	2	7	9	....	....	....	134	....	....	....	....	....	....	....	....	....	....	....	....	....	....	....	....	....	....
1981-82	Kitchener Rangers	OHL	64	11	17	28	....	....	....	243	....	....	....	....	....	....	....	....	....	....	15	3	4	7	71	....	....	....
1982-83	Rochester Americans	AHL	64	5	11	16	....	....	....	142	....	....	....	....	....	....	....	....	....	....	13	1	1	2	7	....	....	....
1983-84	Rochester Americans	AHL	76	7	6	13	....	....	....	234	....	....	....	....	....	....	....	....	....	....	17	2	4	6	87	....	....	....
1984-85	Rochester Americans	AHL	70	8	7	15	....	....	....	213	....	....	....	....	....	....	....	....	....	....	1	0	0	0	10	....	....	....
1985-86	Nova Scotia Oilers	AHL	78	8	11	19	....	....	....	214	....	....	....	....	....	....	....	....	....	....	....	....	....	....	....	....	....	....
1986-87	Nova Scotia Oilers	AHL	35	3	4	7	....	....	....	48	....	....	....	....	....	....	....	....	....	....	....	....	....	....	....	....	....	....
1987-88	Nova Scotia Oilers	AHL	65	15	15	30	....	....	....	170	....	....	....	....	....	....	....	....	....	....	4	1	2	3	9	....	....	....
1988-89	Adirondack Red Wings	AHL	74	23	23	46	....	....	....	179	....	....	....	....	....	....	....	....	....	....	9	0	6	6	32	....	....	....
1989-90	**Boston Bruins**	**NHL**	**7**	**0**	**0**	**0**	**0**	**0**	**0**	**20**	**0**	**0**	**0**	**6**	**0.0**	**2**	**0**	**1**	**0**	**+1**	....	....	....	....	....	....	....	....
	Maine Mariners	AHL	62	15	13	28	....	....	....	162	....	....	....	....	....	....	....	....	....	....	....	....	....	....	....	....	....	....
1990-91	Maine Mariners	AHL	80	18	17	35	....	....	....	215	....	....	....	....	....	....	....	....	....	....	2	0	0	0	5	....	....	....
1991-92	**Boston Bruins**	**NHL**	**19**	**2**	**1**	**3**	**2**	**1**	**3**	**9**	**0**	**0**	**0**	**14**	**14.3**	**4**	**0**	**10**	**0**	**–6**	....	....	....	....	....	....	....	....
	Maine Mariners	AHL	54	17	15	32	....	....	....	171	....	....	....	....	....	....	....	....	....	....	....	....	....	....	....	....	....	....
1992-93	Milwaukee Admirals	IHL	56	16	14	30	....	....	....	108	....	....	....	....	....	....	....	....	....	....	6	2	2	4	8	....	....	....
1993-94	Brantford Smoke	ColHL	21	12	17	29	....	....	....	39	....	....	....	....	....	....	....	....	....	....	7	4	0	4	17	....	....	....
	St. John's Maple Leafs	AHL	3	0	0	0	....	....	....	0	....	....	....	....	....	....	....	....	....	....	....	....	....	....	....	....	....	....
	NHL Totals		**26**	**2**	**1**	**3**	**2**	**1**	**3**	**29**	**0**	**0**	**0**	**20**	**10.0**	**6**	**0**	**11**	**0**		....	....	....	....	....	....	....	....

Signed as a free agent by **Buffalo**, August 23, 1984. Signed as a free agent by **Detroit**, August 11, 1988. Signed as a free agent by **Boston**, July 6, 1984.

• CRAWFORD, MARC

Marc Crawford LW – L. 5'11", 185 lbs. b: Belleville, Ont., 2/13/1961. Vancouver's 2nd choice, 70th overall, in 1980 Entry Draft.

Season	Club	League	GP	G	A	Pts	AG	AA	APts	PIM	PP	SH	GW	S	%	TGF	PGF	TGA	PGA	+/-	GP	G	A	Pts	PIM	PP	SH	GW
1978-79	Cornwall Royals	QMJHL	70	28	41	69	....	....	....	206	....	....	....	....	....	....	....	....	....	....	....	....	....	....	....	....	....	....
1979-80	Cornwall Royals	QMJHL	54	27	36	63	....	....	....	127	....	....	....	....	....	....	....	....	....	....	18	8	20	28	48	....	....	....
1980-81	Cornwall Royals	QMJHL	63	42	57	99	....	....	....	242	....	....	....	....	....	....	....	....	....	....	19	*20	15	35	27	....	....	....
	Canada	WJC-A	5	1	3	4	....	....	....	4	....	....	....	....	....	....	....	....	....	....	....	....	....	....	....	....	....	....
1981-82	**Vancouver Canucks**	**NHL**	**40**	**4**	**8**	**12**	**3**	**5**	**8**	**29**	**0**	**0**	**0**	**57**	**7.0**	**22**	**0**	**22**	**0**	**0**	**14**	**1**	**0**	**1**	**11**	**0**	**0**	**0**
	Dallas Black Hawks	CHL	34	13	21	34	....	....	....	71	....	....	....	....	....	....	....	....	....	....	....	....	....	....	....	....	....	....
1982-83	**Vancouver Canucks**	**NHL**	**41**	**4**	**5**	**9**	**3**	**3**	**6**	**28**	**0**	**0**	**1**	**34**	**11.8**	**19**	**0**	**22**	**0**	**–3**	**3**	**0**	**1**	**1**	**25**	**0**	**0**	**0**
	Fredericton Express	AHL	30	15	9	24	....	....	....	59	....	....	....	....	....	....	....	....	....	....	9	1	3	4	10	....	....	....
1983-84	**Vancouver Canucks**	**NHL**	**19**	**0**	**1**	**1**	**0**	**1**	**1**	**9**	**0**	**0**	**0**	**13**	**0.0**	**3**	**0**	**3**	**0**	**0**	....	....	....	....	....	....	....	....
	Fredericton Express	AHL	56	9	22	31	....	....	....	96	....	....	....	....	....	....	....	....	....	....	7	4	2	6	23	....	....	....
1984-85	**Vancouver Canucks**	**NHL**	**1**	**0**	**0**	**0**	**0**	**0**	**0**	**4**	**0**	**0**	**0**	**0**	**0.0**	**0**	**0**	**5**	**1**	**–4**	....	....	....	....	....	....	....	....
	Fredericton Express	AHL	65	12	29	41	....	....	....	177	....	....	....	....	....	....	....	....	....	....	5	0	1	1	10	....	....	....
1985-86	**Vancouver Canucks**	**NHL**	**54**	**11**	**14**	**25**	**9**	**9**	**18**	**92**	**0**	**0**	**0**	**80**	**13.8**	**35**	**1**	**41**	**0**	**–7**	**3**	**0**	**1**	**1**	**8**	**0**	**0**	**0**
	Fredericton Express	AHL	26	10	14	24	....	....	....	55	....	....	....	....	....	....	....	....	....	....	....	....	....	....	....	....	....	....
1986-87	**Vancouver Canucks**	**NHL**	**21**	**0**	**3**	**3**	**0**	**2**	**2**	**67**	**0**	**0**	**0**	**19**	**0.0**	**5**	**0**	**14**	**1**	**–8**	....	....	....	....	....	....	....	....
	Fredericton Express	AHL	25	8	11	19	....	....	....	21	....	....	....	....	....	....	....	....	....	....	....	....	....	....	....	....	....	....
1987-88	Fredericton Express	AHL	43	5	13	18	....	....	....	90	....	....	....	....	....	....	....	....	....	....	2	0	0	0	14	....	....	....
1988-89	Milwaukee Admirals	IHL	53	23	30	53	....	....	....	166	....	....	....	....	....	....	....	....	....	....	11	2	5	7	26	....	....	....
	NHL Totals		**176**	**19**	**31**	**50**	**15**	**20**	**35**	**229**	**0**	**0**	**1**	**203**	**9.4**	**84**	**1**	**107**	**2**		**20**	**1**	**2**	**3**	**44**	**0**	**0**	**0**

Memorial Cup All-Star Team (1981) • Won Jack Adams Award (1995)

• CREIGHTON, ADAM

Adam Creighton C – L. 6'5", 220 lbs. b: Burlington, Ont., 6/2/1965. Buffalo's 3rd choice, 11th overall, in 1983 Entry Draft.

Season	Club	League	GP	G	A	Pts	AG	AA	APts	PIM	PP	SH	GW	S	%	TGF	PGF	TGA	PGA	+/-	GP	G	A	Pts	PIM	PP	SH	GW
1981-82	Ottawa 67's	OHL	60	15	27	42	....	....	....	73	....	....	....	....	....	....	....	....	....	....	17	7	1	8	40	....	....	....
1982-83	Ottawa 67's	OHL	68	44	46	90	....	....	....	88	....	....	....	....	....	....	....	....	....	....	9	0	2	2	12	....	....	....
1983-84	Ottawa 67's	OHL	56	42	49	91	....	....	....	79	....	....	....	....	....	....	....	....	....	....	13	16	11	27	28	....	....	....
	Buffalo Sabres	**NHL**	**7**	**2**	**2**	**4**	**2**	**1**	**3**	**4**	**0**	**0**	**1**	**8**	**25.0**	**8**	**1**	**7**	**0**	**0**	....	....	....	....	....	....	....	....
1984-85	Ottawa 67's	OHL	10	4	14	18	....	....	....	23	....	....	....	....	....	....	....	....	....	....	5	6	2	8	11	....	....	....
	Canada	WJC-A	7	8	4	12	....	....	....	4	....	....	....	....	....	....	....	....	....	....	....	....	....	....	....	....	....	....
	Buffalo Sabres	**NHL**	**30**	**2**	**8**	**10**	**2**	**5**	**7**	**33**	**1**	**0**	**0**	**20**	**10.0**	**22**	**17**	**12**	**0**	**–7**	....	....	....	....	....	....	....	....
	Rochester Americans	AHL	6	5	3	8	....	....	....	2	....	....	....	....	....	....	....	....	....	....	5	2	1	3	20	....	....	....
1985-86	**Buffalo Sabres**	**NHL**	**19**	**1**	**1**	**2**	**1**	**1**	**2**	**2**	**0**	**0**	**1**	**9**	**11.1**	**5**	**2**	**5**	**0**	**–2**	....	....	....	....	....	....	....	....
	Rochester Americans	AHL	32	17	21	38	....	....	....	27	....	....	....	....	....	....	....	....	....	....	....	....	....	....	....	....	....	....
1986-87	**Buffalo Sabres**	**NHL**	**56**	**18**	**22**	**40**	**16**	**16**	**32**	**26**	**6**	**0**	**3**	**109**	**16.5**	**56**	**18**	**34**	**0**	**+4**	....	....	....	....	....	....	....	....
1987-88	**Buffalo Sabres**	**NHL**	**36**	**10**	**17**	**27**	**9**	**12**	**21**	**87**	**4**	**0**	**1**	**61**	**16.4**	**40**	**13**	**23**	**3**	**+7**	....	....	....	....	....	....	....	....
1988-89	**Buffalo Sabres**	**NHL**	**24**	**7**	**10**	**17**	**6**	**7**	**13**	**44**	**3**	**0**	**1**	**42**	**16.7**	**21**	**10**	**16**	**0**	**–5**	....	....	....	....	....	....	....	....
	Chicago Blackhawks	**NHL**	**43**	**15**	**14**	**29**	**13**	**10**	**23**	**92**	**8**	**0**	**3**	**113**	**13.3**	**48**	**19**	**34**	**1**	**–4**	**15**	**5**	**6**	**11**	**44**	**3**	**1**	**0**
1989-90	**Chicago Blackhawks**	**NHL**	**80**	**34**	**36**	**70**	**29**	**26**	**55**	**224**	**12**	**0**	**3**	**156**	**21.8**	**96**	**35**	**73**	**16**	**+4**	**20**	**3**	**6**	**9**	**59**	**0**	**1**	**0**
1990-91	**Chicago Blackhawks**	**NHL**	**72**	**22**	**29**	**51**	**20**	**22**	**42**	**135**	**10**	**2**	**6**	**127**	**17.3**	**75**	**29**	**51**	**5**	**0**	**6**	**0**	**1**	**1**	**10**	**0**	**0**	**0**
1991-92	**Chicago Blackhawks**	**NHL**	**11**	**6**	**6**	**12**	**5**	**4**	**9**	**16**	**2**	**0**	**0**	**32**	**18.8**	**12**	**3**	**10**	**0**	**–1**	....	....	....	....	....	....	....	....
	New York Islanders	**NHL**	**66**	**15**	**9**	**24**	**14**	**7**	**21**	**102**	**2**	**0**	**2**	**108**	**13.9**	**44**	**8**	**41**	**1**	**–4**	....	....	....	....	....	....	....	....
1992-93	**Tampa Bay Lightning**	**NHL**	**83**	**19**	**20**	**39**	**16**	**14**	**30**	**110**	**7**	**1**	**0**	**168**	**11.3**	**70**	**26**	**76**	**13**	**–19**	....	....	....	....	....	....	....	....
1993-94	**Tampa Bay Lightning**	**NHL**	**53**	**10**	**10**	**20**	**9**	**8**	**17**	**37**	**2**	**0**	**1**	**77**	**13.0**	**37**	**8**	**36**	**0**	**–7**	....	....	....	....	....	....	....	....
1994-95	**St. Louis Blues**	**NHL**	**48**	**14**	**20**	**34**	**25**	**29**	**54**	**74**	**3**	**0**	**1**	**81**	**17.3**	**59**	**14**	**38**	**10**	**+17**	**7**	**2**	**0**	**2**	**16**	**1**	**0**	**1**
1995-96	**St. Louis Blues**	**NHL**	**61**	**11**	**10**	**21**	**11**	**8**	**19**	**78**	**2**	**0**	**3**	**98**	**11.2**	**31**	**8**	**25**	**2**	**0**	**13**	**1**	**1**	**2**	**8**	**0**	**0**	**0**

			REGULAR SEASON																		PLAYOFFS							
Season	Club	League	GP	G	A	Pts	AG	AA	APts	PIM	PP	SH	GW	S	%	TGF	PGF	TGA	PGA	+/–	GP	G	A	Pts	PIM	PP	SH	GW
1996-97	**Chicago Blackhawks**	**NHL**	**19**	**1**	**2**	**3**	**1**	**2**	**3**	**13**	**0**	**0**	**0**	**20**	**5.0**	**5**	**0**	**7**	**0**	**–2**	....	....	....	....	....	....	....	....
	Indianapolis Ice	IHL	6	1	7	8	....	....	....	11	....	....	....	....	....	....	....	....	....	....	....	....	....	....	....	....	....	....
1997-98	Augsburg Panthers	Germany	22	10	9	19	....	....	....	45	....	....	....	....	....	....	....	....	....	....	....	....	....	....	....	....	....	....
	NHL Totals		**708**	**187**	**216**	**403**	**179**	**172**	**351**	**1077**	**62**	**3**	**26**	**1229**	**15.2**	**629**	**211**	**488**	**51**		**61**	**11**	**14**	**25**	**137**	**4**	**2**	**1**

Won Stafford Smythe Memorial Trophy (Memorial Cup Tournament MVP) (1984)

Traded to **Chicago** by **Buffalo** for Rick Vaive, December 26, 1988. Traded to **NY Islanders** by **Chicago** with Steve Thomas for Brent Sutter and Brad Lauer, October 25, 1991. Claimed by **Tampa Bay** from **NY Islanders** in NHL Waiver Draft, October 4, 1992. Traded to **St. Louis** by **Tampa Bay** for Tom Tilley, October 6, 1994. Signed as a free agent by **Chicago**, October 9, 1996.

• CRESSMAN, DAVE

Dave Cressman LW – L. 6'1", 180 lbs. b: Kitchener, Ont., 1/2/1950. Minnesota's 4th choice, 48th overall, in 1970 Amateur Draft.

Season	Club	League	GP	G	A	Pts	AG	AA	APts	PIM	PP	SH	GW	S	%	TGF	PGF	TGA	PGA	+/–	GP	G	A	Pts	PIM	PP	SH	GW
1967-68	Kitchener Rangers	OHA	1	0	3	3	....	....	....	0	....	....	....	....	....	....	....	....	....	....	19	0	1	1	2	....	....	....
1968-69	Kitchener Rangers	OHA	54	29	26	55	....	....	....	33	....	....	....	....	....	....	....	....	....	....	....	....	....	....	....	....	....	....
1969-70	Kitchener Rangers	OHA	50	18	39	57	....	....	....	69	....	....	....	....	....	....	....	....	....	....	....	....	....	....	....	....	....	....
1970-71			DID NOT PLAY																									
1971-72	Galt Hornets	OHA Sr.	40	19	34	53	....	....	....	24	....	....	....	....	....	....	....	....	....	....	....	....	....	....	....	....	....	....
1972-73	Galt Hornets	OHA Sr.	19	2	6	8	....	....	....	20	....	....	....	....	....	....	....	....	....	....	....	....	....	....	....	....	....	....
1973-74	Saginaw Gears	IHL	75	32	35	67	....	....	....	49	....	....	....	....	....	....	....	....	....	....	9	5	3	8	37	....	....	....
1974-75	**Minnesota North Stars**	**NHL**	**5**	**2**	**0**	**2**	**2**	**0**	**2**	**4**	**0**	**0**	**0**	**13**	**15.4**	**3**	**0**	**1**	**0**	**+2**	....	....	....	....	....	....	....	....
	New Haven Nighthawks	AHL	66	11	15	26	....	....	....	41	....	....	....	....	....	....	....	....	....	....	16	7	*14	21	6	....	....	....
1975-76	**Minnesota North Stars**	**NHL**	**80**	**4**	**8**	**12**	**4**	**6**	**10**	**33**	**0**	**0**	**1**	**72**	**5.6**	**15**	**0**	**73**	**54**	**–4**	....	....	....	....	....	....	....	....
1976-77	New Haven Nighthawks	AHL	80	25	31	56	....	....	....	64	....	....	....	....	....	....	....	....	....	....	6	1	0	1	4	....	....	....
1977-78	Cambridge Hornets	OHA Sr.	25	9	11	20	....	....	....	4	....	....	....	....	....	....	....	....	....	....	....	....	....	....	....	....	....	....
	NHL Totals		**85**	**6**	**8**	**14**	**6**	**6**	**12**	**37**	**0**	**0**	**1**	**85**	**7.1**	**18**	**0**	**74**	**54**		....	....	....	....	....	....	....	....

IHL Second All-Star Team (1974)

• CRISP, TERRY

Terry Crisp C – L. 5'10", 180 lbs. b: Parry Sound, Ont., 5/28/1943.

Season	Club	League	GP	G	A	Pts	AG	AA	APts	PIM	PP	SH	GW	S	%	TGF	PGF	TGA	PGA	+/–	GP	G	A	Pts	PIM	PP	SH	GW
1961-62	Niagara Falls Flyers	OHA	50	16	22	38	....	....	....	57	....	....	....	....	....	....	....	....	....	....	10	1	6	7	6	....	....	....
1962-63	Niagara Falls Flyers	OHA	50	39	35	74	....	....	....	68	....	....	....	....	....	....	....	....	....	....	25	16	*24	*40	32	....	....	....
1963-64	Minneapolis Bruins	CHL	42	15	20	35	....	....	....	22	....	....	....	....	....	....	....	....	....	....	....	....	....	....	....	....	....	....
1964-65	Minneapolis Bruins	CHL	70	28	34	62	....	....	....	22	....	....	....	....	....	....	....	....	....	....	5	0	2	2	0	....	....	....
1965-66	**Boston Bruins**	**NHL**	**3**	**0**	**0**	**0**	**0**	**0**	**0**	**0**	....	....	....	....	....	....	....	....	....	....	....	....	....	....	....	....	....	....
	Oklahoma City Blazers	CHL	61	11	22	33	....	....	....	35	....	....	....	....	....	....	....	....	....	....	9	1	5	6	0	....	....	....
1966-67	Oklahoma City Blazers	CHL	69	31	42	73	....	....	....	37	....	....	....	....	....	....	....	....	....	....	11	3	7	10	0	....	....	....
1967-68	**St. Louis Blues**	**NHL**	**73**	**9**	**20**	**29**	**11**	**21**	**32**	**10**	**0**	**1**	**1**	**135**	**6.7**	**47**	**2**	**46**	**10**	**+9**	**18**	**1**	**5**	**6**	**6**	**0**	**0**	**0**
1968-69	**St. Louis Blues**	**NHL**	**57**	**6**	**9**	**15**	**7**	**8**	**15**	**14**	**1**	**1**	**0**	**40**	**15.0**	**19**	**1**	**18**	**8**	**+8**	**12**	**3**	**4**	**7**	**20**	**0**	**2**	**0**
	Kansas City Blues	CHL	4	1	1	2	....	....	....	4	....	....	....	....	....	....	....	....	....	....	....	....	....	....	....	....	....	....
1969-70	**St. Louis Blues**	**NHL**	**26**	**5**	**6**	**11**	**6**	**6**	**12**	**2**	**0**	**0**	**1**	**44**	**11.4**	**19**	**7**	**19**	**7**	**0**	**16**	**2**	**3**	**5**	**2**	**1**	**0**	**0**
	Buffalo Bisons	AHL	51	15	34	49	....	....	....	14	....	....	....	....	....	....	....	....	....	....	....	....	....	....	....	....	....	....
1970-71	**St. Louis Blues**	**NHL**	**54**	**5**	**11**	**16**	**5**	**10**	**15**	**13**	**0**	**1**	**0**	**47**	**10.6**	**23**	**3**	**27**	**10**	**+3**	**6**	**1**	**0**	**1**	**2**	**0**	**0**	**0**
1971-72	**St. Louis Blues**	**NHL**	**75**	**13**	**18**	**31**	**14**	**16**	**30**	**12**	**1**	**6**	**3**	**94**	**13.8**	**45**	**4**	**75**	**41**	**+7**	**11**	**1**	**3**	**4**	**2**	**0**	**0**	**0**
1972-73	**New York Islanders**	**NHL**	**54**	**4**	**16**	**20**	**4**	**13**	**17**	**6**	**0**	**1**	**0**	**72**	**5.6**	**31**	**2**	**70**	**19**	**–22**	....	....	....	....	....	....	....	....
	Philadelphia Flyers	**NHL**	**12**	**1**	**5**	**6**	**1**	**4**	**5**	**2**	**0**	**0**	**0**	**18**	**5.6**	**9**	**0**	**8**	**3**	**+4**	**11**	**3**	**2**	**5**	**2**	**1**	**0**	**0**
1973-74	**Philadelphia Flyers**	**NHL**	**71**	**10**	**21**	**31**	**10**	**18**	**28**	**20**	**1**	**2**	**3**	**88**	**11.4**	**40**	**4**	**31**	**7**	**+12**	**17**	**2**	**2**	**4**	**4**	**0**	**1**	**1**
1974-75	**Philadelphia Flyers**	**NHL**	**71**	**8**	**19**	**27**	**7**	**15**	**22**	**20**	**0**	**1**	**1**	**70**	**11.4**	**37**	**4**	**36**	**14**	**+11**	**9**	**2**	**4**	**6**	**0**	**0**	**0**	**0**
1975-76	**Philadelphia Flyers**	**NHL**	**38**	**6**	**9**	**15**	**6**	**7**	**13**	**28**	**1**	**0**	**1**	**48**	**12.5**	**22**	**1**	**19**	**4**	**+6**	**10**	**0**	**5**	**5**	**2**	**0**	**0**	**0**
1976-77	**Philadelphia Flyers**	**NHL**	**2**	**0**	**0**	**0**	**0**	**0**	**0**	**0**	**0**	**0**	**0**	**0**	**0.0**	**0**	**0**	**0**	**0**	**0**	....	....	....	....	....	....	....	....
	NHL Totals		**536**	**67**	**134**	**201**	**71**	**118**	**189**	**135**	**4**	**13**	**10**	**656**	**10.2**	**292**	**28**	**349**	**123**		**110**	**15**	**28**	**43**	**40**	**2**	**3**	**1**

Claimed by **St. Louis** from **Boston** in Expansion Draft, June 6, 1967. Claimed by **NY Islanders** from **St. Louis** in Expansion Draft, June 6, 1972. Traded to **Philadelphia** by **NY Islanders** for Jean Potvin and future considerations (Glen Irwin, May 18, 1973), March 5, 1973.

• CRISTOFOLI, ED

Ed Cristofoli RW – L. 6'2", 205 lbs. b: Trail, B.C., 5/14/1967. Montreal's 9th choice, 142nd overall, in 1985 Entry Draft.

Season	Club	League	GP	G	A	Pts	AG	AA	APts	PIM	PP	SH	GW	S	%	TGF	PGF	TGA	PGA	+/–	GP	G	A	Pts	PIM	PP	SH	GW
1984-85	Penticton Knights	BCJHL	48	36	34	70	....	....	....	58	....	....	....	....	....	....	....	....	....	....	....	....	....	....	....	....	....	....
1985-86	University of Denver	WCHA	46	10	9	19	....	....	....	32	....	....	....	....	....	....	....	....	....	....	....	....	....	....	....	....	....	....
1986-87	University of Denver	WCHA	40	14	15	29	....	....	....	52	....	....	....	....	....	....	....	....	....	....	....	....	....	....	....	....	....	....
1987-88	University of Denver	WCHA	38	12	27	39	....	....	....	64	....	....	....	....	....	....	....	....	....	....	....	....	....	....	....	....	....	....
1988-89	University of Denver	WCHA	43	20	19	39	....	....	....	50	....	....	....	....	....	....	....	....	....	....	....	....	....	....	....	....	....	....
1989-90	**Montreal Canadiens**	**NHL**	**9**	**0**	**1**	**1**	**0**	**1**	**1**	**4**	**0**	**0**	**0**	**6**	**0.0**	**2**	**0**	**3**	**0**	**–1**	....	....	....	....	....	....	....	....
	Sherbrooke Canadiens	AHL	57	16	19	35	....	....	....	31	....	....	....	....	....	....	....	....	....	....	12	2	4	6	14	....	....	....
1990-91	Fredericton Canadiens	AHL	34	7	16	23	....	....	....	24	....	....	....	....	....	....	....	....	....	....	....	....	....	....	....	....	....	....
	Kansas City Blades	IHL	22	3	1	4	....	....	....	6	....	....	....	....	....	....	....	....	....	....	....	....	....	....	....	....	....	....
	NHL Totals		**9**	**0**	**1**	**1**	**0**	**1**	**1**	**4**	**0**	**0**	**0**	**6**	**0.0**	**2**	**0**	**3**	**0**		....	....	....	....	....	....	....	....

• CROMBEEN, MIKE

Mike Crombeen RW – R. 5'11", 190 lbs. b: Sarnia, Ont., 4/16/1957. Cleveland's 1st choice, 5th overall, in 1977 Amateur Draft.

Season	Club	League	GP	G	A	Pts	AG	AA	APts	PIM	PP	SH	GW	S	%	TGF	PGF	TGA	PGA	+/–	GP	G	A	Pts	PIM	PP	SH	GW
1973-74	Kingston Canadians	OHA	69	19	29	48	....	....	....	59	....	....	....	....	....	....	....	....	....	....	....	....	....	....	....	....	....	....
1974-75	Kingston Canadians	OHA	69	56	58	114	....	....	....	50	....	....	....	....	....	....	....	....	....	....	....	....	....	....	....	....	....	....
1975-76	Kingston Canadians	OHA	57	43	39	82	....	....	....	65	....	....	....	....	....	....	....	....	....	....	7	3	4	7	8	....	....	....
1976-77	Kingston Canadians	OHA	49	42	36	78	....	....	....	16	....	....	....	....	....	....	....	....	....	....	10	5	9	14	23	....	....	....
1977-78	**Cleveland Barons**	**NHL**	**48**	**3**	**4**	**7**	**3**	**3**	**6**	**13**	**2**	**0**	**0**	**65**	**4.6**	**12**	**3**	**35**	**0**	**–26**	....	....	....	....	....	....	....	....
	Salt Lake Golden Eagles	CHL	12	4	4	8	....	....	....	4	....	....	....	....	....	....	....	....	....	....	....	....	....	....	....	....	....	....
	Binghamton Whalers	AHL	13	1	2	3	....	....	....	4	....	....	....	....	....	....	....	....	....	....	....	....	....	....	....	....	....	....
1978-79	**St. Louis Blues**	**NHL**	**37**	**3**	**8**	**11**	**3**	**6**	**9**	**34**	**0**	**0**	**0**	**51**	**5.9**	**20**	**0**	**38**	**5**	**–13**	....	....	....	....	....	....	....	....
	Salt Lake Golden Eagles	CHL	30	6	9	15	....	....	....	48	....	....	....	....	....	....	....	....	....	....	....	....	....	....	....	....	....	....
1979-80	**St. Louis Blues**	**NHL**	**71**	**10**	**12**	**22**	**9**	**9**	**18**	**20**	**1**	**0**	**2**	**98**	**10.2**	**31**	**2**	**54**	**11**	**–14**	**2**	**0**	**0**	**0**	**0**	**0**	**0**	**0**
1980-81	**St. Louis Blues**	**NHL**	**66**	**9**	**14**	**23**	**7**	**10**	**17**	**58**	**0**	**1**	**1**	**91**	**9.9**	**46**	**0**	**65**	**20**	**+1**	**11**	**3**	**0**	**3**	**8**	**0**	**0**	**2**
1981-82	**St. Louis Blues**	**NHL**	**71**	**19**	**8**	**27**	**15**	**5**	**20**	**32**	**0**	**1**	**1**	**99**	**19.2**	**44**	**2**	**87**	**35**	**–10**	**10**	**3**	**1**	**4**	**20**	**0**	**0**	**1**
1982-83	**St. Louis Blues**	**NHL**	**80**	**6**	**11**	**17**	**5**	**8**	**13**	**20**	**0**	**1**	**1**	**71**	**8.5**	**35**	**0**	**78**	**38**	**–5**	**4**	**0**	**1**	**1**	**4**	**0**	**0**	**0**
1983-84	**Hartford Whalers**	**NHL**	**56**	**1**	**4**	**5**	**1**	**3**	**4**	**25**	**0**	**0**	**0**	**46**	**2.2**	**10**	**0**	**51**	**28**	**–13**	....	....	....	....	....	....	....	....
1984-85	**Hartford Whalers**	**NHL**	**46**	**4**	**7**	**11**	**3**	**5**	**8**	**16**	**0**	**1**	**1**	**31**	**12.9**	**17**	**0**	**26**	**9**	**0**	....	....	....	....	....	....	....	....
	Binghamton Whalers	AHL	6	2	1	3	....	....	....	0	....	....	....	....	....	....	....	....	....	....	....	....	....	....	....	....	....	....
	NHL Totals		**475**	**55**	**68**	**123**	**46**	**49**	**95**	**218**	**3**	**4**	**6**	**552**	**10.0**	**215**	**7**	**434**	**146**		**27**	**6**	**2**	**8**	**32**	**0**	**0**	**3**

OHA Second All-Star Team (1976, 1977)

Claimed by **St. Louis** in **Cleveland-Minnesota** Dispersal Draft, June 13, 1978. Claimed by **Hartford** from **St. Louis** in Waiver Draft, October 3, 1983.

• CRONIN, SHAWN

Shawn Cronin D – L. 6'2", 225 lbs. b: Joliet, IL, 8/20/1963.

Season	Club	League	GP	G	A	Pts	AG	AA	APts	PIM	PP	SH	GW	S	%	TGF	PGF	TGA	PGA	+/–	GP	G	A	Pts	PIM	PP	SH	GW
1982-83	University of Illinois-Chicago	CCHA	36	1	5	6	....	....	....	52	....	....	....	....	....	....	....	....	....	....	....	....	....	....	....	....	....	....
1983-84	University of Illinois-Chicago	CCHA	32	0	4	4	....	....	....	41	....	....	....	....	....	....	....	....	....	....	....	....	....	....	....	....	....	....
1984-85	University of Illinois-Chicago	CCHA	31	2	6	8	....	....	....	52	....	....	....	....	....	....	....	....	....	....	....	....	....	....	....	....	....	....
1985-86	University of Illinois-Chicago	CCHA	35	3	8	11	....	....	....	70	....	....	....	....	....	....	....	....	....	....	....	....	....	....	....	....	....	....
1986-87	Salt Lake Golden Eagles	IHL	53	8	16	24	....	....	....	118	....	....	....	....	....	....	....	....	....	....	....	....	....	....	....	....	....	....
	Binghamton Whalers	AHL	12	0	1	1	....	....	....	60	....	....	....	....	....	....	....	....	....	....	10	0	0	0	41	....	....	....
1987-88	Binghamton Whalers	AHL	65	3	8	11	....	....	....	212	....	....	....	....	....	....	....	....	....	....	4	0	0	0	15	....	....	....
1988-89	**Washington Capitals**	**NHL**	**1**	**0**	**0**	**0**	**0**	**0**	**0**	**0**	**0**	**0**	**0**	**0**	**0.0**	**0**	**0**	**0**	**0**	**0**	....	....	....	....	....	....	....	....
	Baltimore Skipjacks	AHL	75	3	9	12	....	....	....	267	....	....	....	....	....	....	....	....	....	....	....	....	....	....	....	....	....	....
1989-90	**Winnipeg Jets**	**NHL**	**61**	**0**	**4**	**4**	**0**	**3**	**3**	**243**	**0**	**0**	**0**	**30**	**0.0**	**27**	**1**	**52**	**10**	**–16**	**5**	**0**	**0**	**0**	**7**	**0**	**0**	**0**
1990-91	**Winnipeg Jets**	**NHL**	**67**	**1**	**5**	**6**	**1**	**4**	**5**	**189**	**0**	**0**	**0**	**40**	**2.5**	**36**	**1**	**69**	**24**	**–10**	....	....	....	....	....	....	....	....
1991-92	**Winnipeg Jets**	**NHL**	**65**	**0**	**4**	**4**	**0**	**3**	**3**	**271**	**0**	**0**	**0**	**25**	**0.0**	**29**	**0**	**51**	**11**	**–11**	**4**	**0**	**0**	**0**	**6**	**0**	**0**	**0**
1992-93	**Philadelphia Flyers**	**NHL**	**35**	**2**	**1**	**3**	**2**	**1**	**3**	**37**	**0**	**0**	**0**	**12**	**16.7**	**14**	**0**	**22**	**8**	**0**	....	....	....	....	....	....	....	....
	Hershey Bears	AHL	7	0	1	1	....	....	....	12	....	....	....	....	....	....	....	....	....	....	....	....	....	....	....	....	....	....
1993-94	**San Jose Sharks**	**NHL**	**34**	**0**	**2**	**2**	**0**	**2**	**2**	**76**	**0**	**0**	**0**	**14**	**0.0**	**13**	**1**	**18**	**8**	**+2**	**14**	**1**	**0**	**1**	**20**	**0**	**0**	**0**

			REGULAR SEASON																		PLAYOFFS							
Season	Club	League	GP	G	A	Pts	AG	AA	APts	PIM	PP	SH	GW	S	%	TGF	PGF	TGA	PGA	+/–	GP	G	A	Pts	PIM	PP	SH	GW
1994-95	**San Jose Sharks**	**NHL**	**29**	**0**	**2**	**2**	**0**	**3**	**3**	**61**	**0**	**0**	**0**	**12**	**0.0**	**12**	**0**	**17**	**5**	**0**	**9**	**0**	**0**	**0**	**5**	**0**	**0**	**0**
1995-96	Fort Wayne Komets	IHL	48	0	1	1	....	....	....	120	....	....	....	....	....	....	....	....	....	....	5	0	0	0	8	....	....	....
1996-97	Fort Wayne Komets	IHL	13	0	1	1	....	....	....	27	....	....	....	....	....	....	....	....	....	....	....	....	....	....	....	....	....	....
	NHL Totals		**292**	**3**	**18**	**21**	**3**	**16**	**19**	**877**	**0**	**0**	**0**	**133**	**2.3**	**131**	**3**	**229**	**66**		**32**	**1**	**0**	**1**	**38**	**0**	**0**	**0**

Signed as a free agent by **Hartford**, March, 1986. Signed as a free agent by **Washington**, June 6, 1988. Signed as a free agent by **Philadelphia**, June 12, 1989. Traded to **Winnipeg** by **Philadelphia** for future considerations, July 21, 1989. Traded to **Quebec** by **Winnipeg** for Dan Lambert, August 25, 1992. Claimed by **Philadelphia** from **Quebec** in NHL Waiver Draft, October 4, 1992. Traded to **San Jose** by **Philadelphia** for cash, August 5, 1993.

• CROSS, CORY

Cory Cross D – L. 6'5", 219 lbs. b: Lloydminster, Alta., 1/3/1971. Tampa Bay's 1st choice, 1st overall, in 1992 Supplemental Draft.

Season	Club	League	GP	G	A	Pts	AG	AA	APts	PIM	PP	SH	GW	S	%	TGF	PGF	TGA	PGA	+/–	GP	G	A	Pts	PIM	PP	SH	GW
1990-91	University of Alberta	CWUAA	20	2	5	7	....	....	....	16	....	....	....	....	....	....	....	....	....	....	....	....	....	....	....	....	....	....
1991-92	University of Alberta	CWUAA	41	4	11	15	....	....	....	82	....	....	....	....	....	....	....	....	....	....	....	....	....	....	....	....	....	....
1992-93	University of Alberta	CWUAA	43	11	28	39	....	....	....	105	....	....	....	....	....	....	....	....	....	....	....	....	....	....	....	....	....	....
	Atlanta Knights	IHL	7	0	1	1	....	....	....	2	....	....	....	....	....	....	....	....	....	....	4	0	0	0	6	....	....	....
1993-94	**Tampa Bay Lightning**	**NHL**	**5**	**0**	**0**	**0**	**0**	**0**	**0**	**6**	**0**	**0**	**0**	**5**	**0.0**	**0**	**0**	**3**	**0**	**–3**	....	....	....	....	....	....	....	....
	Atlanta Knights	IHL	70	4	14	18	....	....	....	72	....	....	....	....	....	....	....	....	....	....	9	1	2	3	14	....	....	....
1994-95	**Tampa Bay Lightning**	**NHL**	**43**	**1**	**5**	**6**	**2**	**7**	**9**	**41**	**0**	**0**	**1**	**35**	**2.9**	**29**	**4**	**37**	**6**	**–6**	....	....	....	....	....	....	....	....
	Atlanta Knights	IHL	41	5	10	15	....	....	....	67	....	....	....	....	....	....	....	....	....	....	....	....	....	....	....	....	....	....
1995-96	**Tampa Bay Lightning**	**NHL**	**75**	**2**	**14**	**16**	**2**	**11**	**13**	**66**	**0**	**0**	**0**	**57**	**3.5**	**51**	**1**	**61**	**15**	**+4**	**6**	**0**	**0**	**0**	**22**	**0**	**0**	**0**
1996-97	**Tampa Bay Lightning**	**NHL**	**72**	**4**	**5**	**9**	**4**	**4**	**8**	**95**	**0**	**0**	**2**	**75**	**5.3**	**54**	**0**	**71**	**23**	**+6**	....	....	....	....	....	....	....	....
	Canada	WC-A	11	0	2	2	....	....	....	49	....	....	....	....	....	....	....	....	....	....	....	....	....	....	....	....	....	....
1997-98	**Tampa Bay Lightning**	**NHL**	**74**	**3**	**6**	**9**	**4**	**6**	**10**	**77**	**0**	**1**	**0**	**72**	**4.2**	**35**	**3**	**80**	**24**	**–24**	....	....	....	....	....	....	....	....
	Canada	WC-A	6	1	0	1	....	....	....	2	....	....	....	....	....	....	....	....	....	....	....	....	....	....	....	....	....	....
	NHL Totals		**269**	**10**	**30**	**40**	**12**	**28**	**40**	**285**	**0**	**1**	**3**	**244**	**4.1**	**169**	**8**	**252**	**68**		**6**	**0**	**0**	**0**	**22**	**0**	**0**	**0**

• CROSSMAN, DOUG

Doug Crossman D – L. 6'2", 190 lbs. b: Peterborough, Ont., 6/13/1960. Chicago's 6th choice, 112th overall, in 1979 Entry Draft.

Season	Club	League	GP	G	A	Pts	AG	AA	APts	PIM	PP	SH	GW	S	%	TGF	PGF	TGA	PGA	+/–	GP	G	A	Pts	PIM	PP	SH	GW
1977-78	Ottawa 67's	OHA	65	4	17	21	....	....	....	17	....	....	....	....	....	....	....	....	....	....	....	....	....	....	....	....	....	....
1978-79	Ottawa 67's	OHA	67	12	51	63	....	....	....	65	....	....	....	....	....	....	....	....	....	....	4	1	3	4	0	....	....	....
1979-80	Ottawa 67's	OHA	66	20	96	116	....	....	....	48	....	....	....	....	....	....	....	....	....	....	11	7	6	13	19	....	....	....
	Canada	WJC-A	5	0	2	2	....	....	....	2	....	....	....	....	....	....	....	....	....	....	....	....	....	....	....	....	....	....
1980-81	**Chicago Black Hawks**	**NHL**	**9**	**0**	**2**	**2**	**0**	**1**	**1**	**2**	**0**	**0**	**0**	**16**	**0.0**	**8**	**1**	**13**	**1**	**–5**	....	....	....	....	....	....	....	....
	New Brunswick Hawks	AHL	70	13	43	56	....	....	....	90	....	....	....	....	....	....	....	....	....	....	13	5	6	11	36	....	....	....
1981-82	**Chicago Black Hawks**	**NHL**	**70**	**12**	**28**	**40**	**9**	**19**	**28**	**24**	**7**	**0**	**1**	**127**	**9.4**	**100**	**40**	**87**	**8**	**–19**	**11**	**0**	**3**	**3**	**4**	**0**	**0**	**0**
1982-83	**Chicago Black Hawks**	**NHL**	**80**	**13**	**40**	**53**	**11**	**28**	**39**	**46**	**6**	**0**	**1**	**134**	**9.7**	**132**	**40**	**90**	**19**	**+21**	**13**	**3**	**7**	**10**	**6**	**1**	**0**	**0**
1983-84	**Philadelphia Flyers**	**NHL**	**78**	**7**	**28**	**35**	**6**	**19**	**25**	**63**	**2**	**0**	**2**	**160**	**4.4**	**114**	**27**	**87**	**23**	**+23**	**3**	**0**	**0**	**0**	**0**	**0**	**0**	**0**
1984-85	**Philadelphia Flyers**	**NHL**	**80**	**4**	**33**	**37**	**3**	**22**	**25**	**65**	**1**	**1**	**1**	**111**	**3.6**	**118**	**29**	**80**	**22**	**+31**	**19**	**4**	**6**	**10**	**38**	**3**	**0**	**0**
1985-86	**Philadelphia Flyers**	**NHL**	**80**	**6**	**37**	**43**	**5**	**25**	**30**	**55**	**2**	**0**	**1**	**134**	**4.5**	**130**	**52**	**110**	**27**	**–5**	**5**	**0**	**1**	**1**	**4**	**0**	**0**	**0**
1986-87	**Philadelphia Flyers**	**NHL**	**78**	**9**	**31**	**40**	**8**	**22**	**30**	**29**	**7**	**0**	**1**	**122**	**7.4**	**122**	**33**	**115**	**44**	**+18**	**26**	**4**	**14**	**18**	**31**	**2**	**0**	**0**
1987-88	Canada	C Cup	8	0	1	1	....	....	....	4	....	....	....	....	....	....	....	....	....	....	....	....	....	....	....	....	....	....
	Philadelphia Flyers	**NHL**	**76**	**9**	**29**	**38**	**8**	**21**	**29**	**43**	**6**	**0**	**0**	**153**	**5.9**	**113**	**28**	**129**	**43**	**–1**	**7**	**1**	**1**	**2**	**8**	**1**	**0**	**0**
1988-89	**Los Angeles Kings**	**NHL**	**74**	**10**	**15**	**25**	**8**	**11**	**19**	**53**	**2**	**0**	**0**	**137**	**7.3**	**106**	**29**	**102**	**14**	**–11**	**2**	**0**	**1**	**1**	**2**	**0**	**0**	**0**
	New Haven Nighthawks	AHL	3	0	0	0	....	....	....	0	....	....	....	....	....	....	....	....	....	....	....	....	....	....	....	....	....	....
1989-90	**New York Islanders**	**NHL**	**80**	**15**	**44**	**59**	**13**	**31**	**44**	**54**	**8**	**0**	**1**	**159**	**9.4**	**155**	**69**	**141**	**58**	**+3**	**5**	**0**	**1**	**1**	**6**	**0**	**0**	**0**
1990-91	**New York Islanders**	**NHL**	**16**	**1**	**6**	**7**	**1**	**5**	**6**	**12**	**1**	**0**	**0**	**30**	**3.3**	**23**	**13**	**20**	**6**	**–4**	....	....	....	....	....	....	....	....
	Hartford Whalers	**NHL**	**41**	**4**	**19**	**23**	**4**	**14**	**18**	**19**	**2**	**0**	**0**	**62**	**6.5**	**57**	**30**	**44**	**4**	**–13**	....	....	....	....	....	....	....	....
	Detroit Red Wings	**NHL**	**17**	**3**	**4**	**7**	**3**	**3**	**6**	**17**	**1**	**0**	**0**	**16**	**18.8**	**24**	**8**	**23**	**1**	**–6**	**6**	**0**	**5**	**5**	**6**	**0**	**0**	**0**
1991-92	**Detroit Red Wings**	**NHL**	**26**	**0**	**8**	**8**	**0**	**6**	**6**	**14**	**0**	**0**	**0**	**21**	**0.0**	**22**	**6**	**9**	**1**	**+8**	....	....	....	....	....	....	....	....
1992-93	**Tampa Bay Lightning**	**NHL**	**40**	**8**	**21**	**29**	**7**	**14**	**21**	**18**	**2**	**0**	**1**	**54**	**14.8**	**51**	**21**	**41**	**7**	**–4**	....	....	....	....	....	....	....	....
	St. Louis Blues	**NHL**	**19**	**2**	**7**	**9**	**2**	**5**	**7**	**10**	**2**	**0**	**0**	**24**	**8.3**	**21**	**10**	**15**	**1**	**–3**	....	....	....	....	....	....	....	....
1993-94	**St. Louis Blues**	**NHL**	**50**	**2**	**7**	**9**	**2**	**5**	**7**	**10**	**1**	**0**	**0**	**30**	**6.7**	**43**	**12**	**40**	**10**	**+1**	....	....	....	....	....	....	....	....
	Peoria Rivermen	IHL	8	3	5	8	....	....	....	0	....	....	....	....	....	....	....	....	....	....	....	....	....	....	....	....	....	....
1994-95	Denver Grizzlies	IHL	77	6	43	49	....	....	....	31	....	....	....	....	....	....	....	....	....	....	17	3	6	9	7	....	....	....
1995-96	Baltimore Bandits	AHL	23	3	12	15	....	....	....	18	....	....	....	....	....	....	....	....	....	....	....	....	....	....	....	....	....	....
	Chicago Wolves	IHL	8	1	4	5	....	....	....	2	....	....	....	....	....	....	....	....	....	....	6	1	1	2	0	....	....	....
	NHL Totals		**914**	**105**	**359**	**464**	**90**	**251**	**341**	**534**	**50**	**1**	**9**	**1490**	**7.0**	**1339**	**448**	**1146**	**289**		**97**	**12**	**39**	**51**	**105**	**7**	**0**	**0**

OHA First All-Star Team (1980)

Traded to **Philadelphia** by **Chicago** with Chicago's 2nd round choice (Scott Mellanby) in 1984 Entry Draft for Behn Wilson, June 8, 1983. Traded to **LA Kings** by **Philadelphia** for Jay Wells, September 29, 1988. Traded to **NY Islanders** by **LA Kings** to complete transaction that sent Mark Fitzpatrick and Wayne McBean to NY Islanders (February 22, 1989), May 23, 1989. Traded to **Hartford** by **NY Islanders** for Ray Ferraro, November 13, 1990. Traded to **Detroit** by **Hartford** for Doug Houda, February 20, 1991. Traded to **Quebec** by **Detroit** with Dennis Vial for cash, June 15, 1992. Claimed by **Tampa Bay** from **Quebec** in Expansion Draft, June 18, 1992. Traded to **St. Louis** by **Tampa Bay** with Basil McRae and Tampa Bay's 4th round choice (Andrei Petrakov) in 1996 Entry Draft for Jason Ruff and future considerations, January 28, 1993.

• CROTEAU, GARY

Gary "Bull" Croteau LW – L. 6', 205 lbs. b: Sudbury, Ont., 6/20/1946.

Season	Club	League	GP	G	A	Pts	AG	AA	APts	PIM	PP	SH	GW	S	%	TGF	PGF	TGA	PGA	+/–	GP	G	A	Pts	PIM	PP	SH	GW
1964-65	St. Lawrence University	ECAC	14	18	13	31	....	....	....	....	....	....	....	....	....	....	....	....	....	....	....	....	....	....	....	....	....	....
1965-66	St. Lawrence University	ECAC	24	20	11	31	....	....	....	12	....	....	....	....	....	....	....	....	....	....	....	....	....	....	....	....	....	....
1966-67	St. Lawrence University	ECAC	27	21	17	38	....	....	....	....	....	....	....	....	....	....	....	....	....	....	....	....	....	....	....	....	....	....
1967-68	St. Lawrence University	ECAC	19	21	19	40	....	....	....	....	....	....	....	....	....	....	....	....	....	....	....	....	....	....	....	....	....	....
1968-69	**Los Angeles Kings**	**NHL**	**11**	**5**	**1**	**6**	**6**	**1**	**7**	**6**	**3**	**0**	**0**	**19**	**26.3**	**10**	**4**	**7**	**0**	**–1**	**11**	**3**	**2**	**5**	**8**	**1**	**0**	**0**
	Springfield Kings	AHL	53	24	20	44	....	....	....	27	....	....	....	....	....	....	....	....	....	....	....	....	....	....	....	....	....	....
1969-70	**Los Angeles Kings**	**NHL**	**3**	**0**	**0**	**0**	**0**	**0**	**0**	**0**	**0**	**0**	**0**	**1**	**0.0**	**0**	**0**	**0**	**0**	**0**	....	....	....	....	....	....	....	....
	Springfield Kings	AHL	52	23	21	44	....	....	....	22	....	....	....	....	....	....	....	....	....	....	....	....	....	....	....	....	....	....
	Detroit Red Wings	**NHL**	**10**	**0**	**2**	**2**	**0**	**2**	**2**	**2**	**0**	**0**	**0**	**5**	**0.0**	**2**	**0**	**3**	**0**	**–1**	....	....	....	....	....	....	....	....
1970-71	**California Golden Seals**	**NHL**	**74**	**15**	**28**	**43**	**16**	**25**	**41**	**12**	**2**	**0**	**1**	**182**	**8.2**	**67**	**9**	**81**	**1**	**–22**	....	....	....	....	....	....	....	....
1971-72	**California Golden Seals**	**NHL**	**73**	**12**	**12**	**24**	**13**	**11**	**24**	**11**	**1**	**0**	**1**	**107**	**11.2**	**35**	**1**	**52**	**0**	**–18**	....	....	....	....	....	....	....	....
1972-73	**California Golden Seals**	**NHL**	**47**	**6**	**15**	**21**	**6**	**13**	**19**	**8**	**1**	**0**	**0**	**77**	**7.8**	**27**	**2**	**38**	**0**	**–13**	....	....	....	....	....	....	....	....
1973-74	**California Golden Seals**	**NHL**	**76**	**14**	**21**	**35**	**14**	**18**	**32**	**16**	**1**	**0**	**2**	**149**	**9.4**	**58**	**9**	**98**	**2**	**–47**	....	....	....	....	....	....	....	....
1974-75	**Kansas City Scouts**	**NHL**	**77**	**8**	**11**	**19**	**7**	**9**	**16**	**16**	**0**	**1**	**1**	**137**	**5.8**	**31**	**6**	**80**	**19**	**–36**	....	....	....	....	....	....	....	....
1975-76	**Kansas City Scouts**	**NHL**	**79**	**19**	**14**	**33**	**18**	**11**	**29**	**12**	**4**	**0**	**1**	**139**	**13.7**	**44**	**12**	**89**	**33**	**–24**	....	....	....	....	....	....	....	....
1976-77	**Colorado Rockies**	**NHL**	**78**	**24**	**27**	**51**	**23**	**22**	**45**	**14**	**5**	**0**	**2**	**145**	**16.6**	**77**	**12**	**92**	**9**	**–18**	....	....	....	....	....	....	....	....
1977-78	**Colorado Rockies**	**NHL**	**62**	**17**	**22**	**39**	**16**	**18**	**34**	**24**	**8**	**0**	**0**	**104**	**16.3**	**68**	**24**	**64**	**5**	**–15**	....	....	....	....	....	....	....	....
1978-79	**Colorado Rockies**	**NHL**	**79**	**23**	**18**	**41**	**21**	**14**	**35**	**18**	**8**	**0**	**1**	**104**	**22.1**	**69**	**24**	**79**	**6**	**–28**	....	....	....	....	....	....	....	....
1979-80	**Colorado Rockies**	**NHL**	**15**	**1**	**4**	**5**	**1**	**3**	**4**	**4**	**1**	**0**	**0**	**6**	**16.7**	**12**	**1**	**15**	**0**	**–4**	....	....	....	....	....	....	....	....
1980-81	Fort Worth Texans	CHL	4	1	1	2	....	....	....	2	....	....	....	....	....	....	....	....	....	....	....	....	....	....	....	....	....	....
	NHL Totals		**684**	**144**	**175**	**319**	**141**	**147**	**288**	**143**	**34**	**1**	**9**	**1175**	**12.3**	**500**	**104**	**698**	**75**		**11**	**3**	**2**	**5**	**8**	**1**	**0**	**0**

ECAC First All-Star Team (1968)

Rights retained by **Toronto** as a territorial exemption (Sudbury-NOHA), September, 1968. Traded to **LA Kings** by **Toronto** with Brian Murphy and Wayne Thomas for Grant Moore and Lou Deveault, September, 1968. Traded to **Detroit** by **LA Kings** with Dale Rolfe and Larry Johnston for Brian Gibbons and Garry Monahan, February 20, 1970. Claimed by **Oakland** from **Detroit** in Intra-League Draft, June 9, 1970. Claimed by **Kansas City** from **California** in Expansion Draft, June 12, 1974. Transferred to **Colorado** after **Kansas City** franchise relocated, July 15, 1976.

• CROWDER, BRUCE

Bruce Crowder RW – R. 6', 180 lbs. b: Essex, Ont., 3/25/1957. Philadelphia's 14th choice, 153rd overall, in 1977 Amateur Draft.

			REGULAR SEASON																		PLAYOFFS							
Season	Club	League	GP	G	A	Pts	AG	AA	APts	PIM	PP	SH	GW	S	%	TGF	PGF	TGA	PGA	+/–	GP	G	A	Pts	PIM	PP	SH	GW
1976-77	University of New Hampshire	ECAC	STATISTICS NOT AVAILABLE																									
1977-78	University of New Hampshire	ECAC	30	10	35	45	....	....	....	58	....	....	....	....	....	....	....	....	....	....	....	....	....	....	....	....	....	....
1978-79	University of New Hampshire	ECAC	35	22	30	52	....	....	....	34	....	....	....	....	....	....	....	....	....	....	....	....	....	....	....	....	....	....
1979-80	Maine Mariners	AHL	49	16	11	27	....	....	....	23	....	....	....	....	....	....	....	....	....	....	11	3	1	4	13	....	....	....
1980-81	Maine Mariners	AHL	68	25	19	44	....	....	....	94	....	....	....	....	....	....	....	....	....	....	20	*11	6	17	20	....	....	....
1981-82	**Boston Bruins**	**NHL**	**63**	**16**	**11**	**27**	**13**	**7**	**20**	**31**	**1**	**0**	**1**	**83**	**19.3**	**39**	**4**	**43**	**1**	**–7**	**11**	**5**	**3**	**8**	**9**	**1**	**0**	**0**
	Erie Blades	AHL	15	6	6	12	....	....	....	6	....	....	....	....	....	....	....	....	....	....	....	....	....	....	....	....	....	....
1982-83	**Boston Bruins**	**NHL**	**80**	**21**	**19**	**40**	**17**	**13**	**30**	**58**	**1**	**0**	**0**	**148**	**14.2**	**72**	**6**	**36**	**0**	**+30**	**17**	**3**	**1**	**4**	**32**	**0**	**0**	**1**
1983-84	**Boston Bruins**	**NHL**	**74**	**6**	**14**	**20**	**5**	**9**	**14**	**44**	**0**	**0**	**0**	**65**	**9.2**	**37**	**2**	**34**	**0**	**+1**	**3**	**0**	**0**	**0**	**0**	**0**	**0**	**0**
1984-85	**Pittsburgh Penguins**	**NHL**	**26**	**4**	**7**	**11**	**3**	**5**	**8**	**23**	**0**	**0**	**0**	**36**	**11.1**	**14**	**0**	**30**	**7**	**–9**	....	....	....	....	....	....	....	....
	NHL Totals		**243**	**47**	**51**	**98**	**38**	**34**	**72**	**156**	**2**	**0**	**1**	**332**	**14.2**	**162**	**12**	**143**	**8**		**31**	**8**	**4**	**12**	**41**	**1**	**0**	**1**

Signed as a free agent by **Boston**, September 28, 1981. Claimed by **Pittsburgh** from **Boston** in Waiver Draft, October 9, 1984.

• CROWDER, KEITH

Keith Crowder RW – R. 6', 190 lbs. b: Windsor, Ont., 1/6/1959. Boston's 4th choice, 57th overall, in 1979 Entry Draft.

Season	Club	League	GP	G	A	Pts	AG	AA	APts	PIM	PP	SH	GW	S	%	TGF	PGF	TGA	PGA	+/–	GP	G	A	Pts	PIM	PP	SH	GW
1976-77	Peterborough Petes	OHA	58	13	19	32	....	....	....	99	....	....	....	....	....	....	....	....	....	....	....	....	....	....	....	....	....	....
1977-78	Peterborough Petes	OHA	58	30	30	60	....	....	....	135	....	....	....	....	....	....	....	....	....	....	14	3	5	8	21	....	....	....
1978-79	Peterborough Petes	OHA	42	25	41	66	....	....	....	76	....	....	....	....	....	....	....	....	....	....	15	12	6	18	40	....	....	....
	Birmingham Bulls	WHA	5	1	0	1	....	....	....	17	....	....	....	....	....	....	....	....	....	....	....	....	....	....	....	....	....	....
1979-80	Binghamton Whalers	AHL	13	4	0	4	....	....	....	15	....	....	....	....	....	....	....	....	....	....	....	....	....	....	....	....	....	....
	Grand Rapids Owls	IHL	20	10	13	23	....	....	....	22	....	....	....	....	....	....	....	....	....	....	....	....	....	....	....	....	....	....
1980-81	**Boston Bruins**	**NHL**	**47**	**13**	**12**	**25**	**11**	**8**	**19**	**172**	**1**	**0**	**1**	**69**	**18.8**	**41**	**5**	**27**	**0**	**+9**	**3**	**2**	**0**	**2**	**9**	**0**	**0**	**0**
	Springfield Indians	AHL	26	12	18	30	....	....	....	34	....	....	....	....	....	....	....	....	....	....	....	....	....	....	....	....	....	....
1981-82	**Boston Bruins**	**NHL**	**71**	**23**	**21**	**44**	**18**	**14**	**32**	**101**	**0**	**0**	**1**	**130**	**17.7**	**65**	**4**	**61**	**0**	**0**	**11**	**2**	**2**	**4**	**14**	**0**	**0**	**0**
1982-83	**Boston Bruins**	**NHL**	**74**	**35**	**39**	**74**	**29**	**27**	**56**	**105**	**10**	**0**	**5**	**156**	**22.4**	**109**	**40**	**48**	**1**	**+22**	**17**	**1**	**6**	**7**	**54**	**1**	**0**	**0**
1983-84	**Boston Bruins**	**NHL**	**63**	**24**	**28**	**52**	**19**	**19**	**38**	**128**	**4**	**0**	**4**	**110**	**21.8**	**77**	**24**	**41**	**0**	**+12**	**3**	**0**	**0**	**0**	**7**	**0**	**0**	**0**
1984-85	**Boston Bruins**	**NHL**	**79**	**32**	**38**	**70**	**26**	**26**	**52**	**142**	**14**	**0**	**1**	**173**	**18.5**	**107**	**35**	**41**	**0**	**+31**	**4**	**3**	**2**	**5**	**19**	**0**	**0**	**1**
1985-86	**Boston Bruins**	**NHL**	**78**	**38**	**46**	**84**	**30**	**31**	**61**	**177**	**20**	**0**	**4**	**184**	**20.7**	**129**	**58**	**59**	**2**	**+14**	**3**	**2**	**0**	**2**	**21**	**0**	**0**	**0**
1986-87	**Boston Bruins**	**NHL**	**58**	**22**	**30**	**52**	**19**	**22**	**41**	**106**	**4**	**0**	**5**	**114**	**19.3**	**76**	**15**	**41**	**0**	**+20**	**4**	**0**	**1**	**1**	**4**	**0**	**0**	**0**
1987-88	**Boston Bruins**	**NHL**	**68**	**17**	**26**	**43**	**15**	**18**	**33**	**173**	**6**	**0**	**3**	**123**	**13.8**	**79**	**24**	**41**	**0**	**+14**	**23**	**3**	**9**	**12**	**44**	**1**	**0**	**0**
1988-89	**Boston Bruins**	**NHL**	**69**	**15**	**18**	**33**	**13**	**13**	**26**	**147**	**5**	**0**	**2**	**121**	**12.4**	**70**	**27**	**37**	**0**	**+6**	**10**	**0**	**2**	**2**	**37**	**0**	**0**	**0**
1989-90	**Los Angeles Kings**	**NHL**	**55**	**4**	**13**	**17**	**3**	**9**	**12**	**93**	**0**	**0**	**1**	**48**	**8.3**	**31**	**0**	**30**	**1**	**+2**	**7**	**1**	**0**	**1**	**9**	**0**	**0**	**0**
	NHL Totals		**662**	**223**	**271**	**494**	**183**	**187**	**370**	**1344**	**64**	**0**	**27**	**1228**	**18.2**	**784**	**232**	**426**	**4**		**85**	**14**	**22**	**36**	**218**	**2**	**0**	**1**
	Other Major League Totals		5	1	0	1	....	....	....	17	....	....	....	....	....	....	....	....	....	....	....	....	....	....	....	....	....	....

Signed as an underage free agent by **Birmingham** (WHA), July, 1978. Signed as a free agent by **LA Kings**, June 28, 1989.

• CROWDER, TROY

Troy Crowder RW – R. 6'4", 220 lbs. b: Sudbury, Ont., 5/3/1968. New Jersey's 6th choice, 108th overall, in 1986 Entry Draft.

Season	Club	League	GP	G	A	Pts	AG	AA	APts	PIM	PP	SH	GW	S	%	TGF	PGF	TGA	PGA	+/–	GP	G	A	Pts	PIM	PP	SH	GW
1985-86	Hamilton Steelhawks	OHL	56	4	4	8	....	....	....	178	....	....	....	....	....	....	....	....	....	....	....	....	....	....	....	....	....	....
1986-87	Belleville Bulls	OHL	21	5	5	10	....	....	....	52	....	....	....	....	....	....	....	....	....	....	....	....	....	....	....	....	....	....
	North Bay Centennials	OHL	35	6	11	17	....	....	....	90	....	....	....	....	....	....	....	....	....	....	23	3	0	12	99	....	....	....
1987-88	North Bay Centennials	OHL	9	1	2	3	....	....	....	44	....	....	....	....	....	....	....	....	....	....	....	....	....	....	....	....	....	....
	Belleville Bulls	OHL	46	12	27	39	....	....	....	103	....	....	....	....	....	....	....	....	....	....	6	2	3	5	24	....	....	....
	Utica Devils	AHL	3	0	0	0	....	....	....	36	....	....	....	....	....	....	....	....	....	....	....	....	....	....	....	....	....	....
	New Jersey Devils	**NHL**	....	....	....	....	....	....	....	....	....	....	....	....	....	....	....	....	....	....	**1**	**0**	**0**	**0**	**12**	....	....	....
1988-89	Utica Devils	AHL	62	6	4	10	....	....	....	152	....	....	....	....	....	....	....	....	....	....	2	0	0	0	25	....	....	....
1989-90	**New Jersey Devils**	**NHL**	**10**	**0**	**0**	**0**	**0**	**0**	**0**	**23**	**0**	**0**	**0**	**4**	**0.0**	**0**	**0**	**0**	**0**	**0**	**2**	**0**	**0**	**0**	**10**	**0**	**0**	**0**
	Nashville Knights	ECHL	3	0	0	0	....	....	....	15	....	....	....	....	....	....	....	....	....	....	....	....	....	....	....	....	....	....
1990-91	**New Jersey Devils**	**NHL**	**59**	**6**	**3**	**9**	**5**	**2**	**7**	**182**	**0**	**0**	**0**	**46**	**13.0**	**15**	**0**	**25**	**0**	**–10**	....	....	....	....	....	....	....	....
1991-92	**Detroit Red Wings**	**NHL**	**7**	**0**	**0**	**0**	**0**	**0**	**0**	**35**	**0**	**0**	**0**	**2**	**0.0**	**1**	**0**	**2**	**1**	**0**	**1**	**0**	**0**	**0**	**0**	**0**	**0**	**0**
1992-93			DID NOT PLAY – INJURED																									
1993-94			DID NOT PLAY – INJURED																									
1994-95	**Los Angeles Kings**	**NHL**	**29**	**1**	**2**	**3**	**2**	**3**	**5**	**99**	**0**	**0**	**0**	**4**	**25.0**	**6**	**0**	**6**	**0**	**0**	....	....	....	....	....	....	....	....
1995-96	**Los Angeles Kings**	**NHL**	**15**	**1**	**0**	**1**	**1**	**0**	**1**	**42**	**0**	**0**	**0**	**11**	**9.1**	**2**	**0**	**5**	**0**	**–3**	....	....	....	....	....	....	....	....
1996-97	**Vancouver Canucks**	**NHL**	**30**	**1**	**2**	**3**	**1**	**2**	**3**	**52**	**0**	**0**	**0**	**11**	**9.1**	**3**	**0**	**9**	**0**	**–6**	....	....	....	....	....	....	....	....
	Syracuse Crunch	AHL	2	0	0	0	....	....	....	0	....	....	....	....	....	....	....	....	....	....	....	....	....	....	....	....	....	....
1997-98	Hannover Scorpions	Germany	19	1	0	1	....	....	....	34	....	....	....	....	....	....	....	....	....	....	3	0	1	1	00	....	....	....
	NHL Totals		**150**	**9**	**7**	**16**	**9**	**7**	**16**	**433**	**0**	**0**	**0**	**78**	**11.5**	**27**	**0**	**47**	**1**		**4**	**0**	**0**	**0**	**22**	**0**	**0**	**0**

Signed as a free agent by **Detroit**, August 27, 1991. Signed as a free agent by **LA Kings**, August 31, 1994. Signed as a free agent by **Vancouver**, October 4, 1996.

• CROWE, PHILIP

Philip Crowe LW – L. 6'2", 230 lbs. b: Nanton, Alta., 4/14/1970.

Season	Club	League	GP	G	A	Pts	AG	AA	APts	PIM	PP	SH	GW	S	%	TGF	PGF	TGA	PGA	+/–	GP	G	A	Pts	PIM	PP	SH	GW
1991-92	Adirondack Red Wings	AHL	6	1	0	1	....	....	....	29	....	....	....	....	....	....	....	....	....	....	....	....	....	....	....	....	....	....
	Columbus Chill	ECHL	32	4	7	11	....	....	....	145	....	....	....	....	....	....	....	....	....	....	....	....	....	....	....	....	....	....
	Toledo Storm	ECHL	2	0	0	0	....	....	....	0	....	....	....	....	....	....	....	....	....	....	5	0	0	0	58	....	....	....
1992-93	Phoenix Roadrunners	IHL	53	3	3	6	....	....	....	190	....	....	....	....	....	....	....	....	....	....	....	....	....	....	....	....	....	....
1993-94	Fort Wayne Komets	IHL	5	0	1	1	....	....	....	26	....	....	....	....	....	....	....	....	....	....	....	....	....	....	....	....	....	....
	Phoenix Roadrunners	IHL	2	0	0	0	....	....	....	0	....	....	....	....	....	....	....	....	....	....	....	....	....	....	....	....	....	....
	Los Angeles Kings	**NHL**	**31**	**0**	**2**	**2**	**0**	**2**	**2**	**77**	**0**	**0**	**0**	**5**	**0.0**	**7**	**0**	**3**	**0**	**+4**	....	....	....	....	....	....	....	....
1994-95	Hershey Bears	AHL	46	11	6	17	....	....	....	132	....	....	....	....	....	....	....	....	....	....	6	0	1	1	19	....	....	....
1995-96	**Philadelphia Flyers**	**NHL**	**16**	**1**	**1**	**2**	**1**	**1**	**2**	**28**	**0**	**0**	**0**	**6**	**16.7**	**3**	**0**	**3**	**0**	**0**	....	....	....	....	....	....	....	....
	Hershey Bears	AHL	39	6	8	14	....	....	....	105	....	....	....	....	....	....	....	....	....	....	5	1	2	3	19	....	....	....
1996-97	**Ottawa Senators**	**NHL**	**26**	**0**	**1**	**1**	**0**	**1**	**1**	**30**	**0**	**0**	**0**	**8**	**0.0**	**3**	**0**	**3**	**0**	**0**	**3**	**0**	**0**	**0**	**16**	**0**	**0**	**0**
	Detroit Vipers	IHL	41	7	7	14	....	....	....	83	....	....	....	....	....	....	....	....	....	....	....	....	....	....	....	....	....	....
1997-98	**Ottawa Senators**	**NHL**	**9**	**3**	**0**	**3**	**4**	**0**	**4**	**24**	**0**	**0**	**1**	**6**	**50.0**	**4**	**0**	**1**	**0**	**+3**	....	....	....	....	....	....	....	....
	Detroit Vipers	IHL	55	6	13	19	....	....	....	160	....	....	....	....	....	....	....	....	....	....	20	5	2	7	48	....	....	....
	NHL Totals		**82**	**4**	**4**	**8**	**5**	**4**	**9**	**159**	**0**	**0**	**1**	**25**	**16.0**	**17**	**0**	**10**	**0**		**3**	**0**	**0**	**0**	**16**	**0**	**0**	**0**

Signed as a free agent by **LA Kings**, November 8, 1993. Signed as a free agent by **Philadelphia**, July 19, 1994. Signed as a free agent by **Ottawa**, July 29, 1996.

• CROWLEY, MIKE

Mike Crowley D – L. 5'11", 175 lbs. b: Bloomington, MN, 7/4/1975. Philadelphia's 5th choice, 140th overall, in 1993 Entry Draft.

Season	Club	League	GP	G	A	Pts	AG	AA	APts	PIM	PP	SH	GW	S	%	TGF	PGF	TGA	PGA	+/–	GP	G	A	Pts	PIM	PP	SH	GW
1992-93	Bloomington-Jefferson High	H.S.	22	10	32	42	....	....	....	18	....	....	....	....	....	....	....	....	....	....	....	....	....	....	....	....	....	....
1993-94	Bloomington-Jefferson High	H.S.	28	23	54	77	....	....	....	26	....	....	....	....	....	....	....	....	....	....	....	....	....	....	....	....	....	....
1994-95	University of Minnesota	WCHA	41	11	27	38	....	....	....	60	....	....	....	....	....	....	....	....	....	....	....	....	....	....	....	....	....	....
	United States	WJC-A	7	0	3	3	....	....	....	8	....	....	....	....	....	....	....	....	....	....	....	....	....	....	....	....	....	....
1995-96	University of Minnesota	WCHA	42	17	46	63	....	....	....	28	....	....	....	....	....	....	....	....	....	....	....	....	....	....	....	....	....	....
	United States	WC-A	8	0	1	1	....	....	....	6	....	....	....	....	....	....	....	....	....	....	....	....	....	....	....	....	....	....
1996-97	University of Minnesota	WCHA	42	9	*47	*56	....	....	....	24	....	....	....	....	....	....	....	....	....	....	....	....	....	....	....	....	....	....
1997-98	**Anaheim Mighty Ducks**	**NHL**	**8**	**2**	**2**	**4**	**2**	**2**	**4**	**8**	**0**	**0**	**1**	**17**	**11.8**	**9**	**1**	**9**	**1**	**0**	....	....	....	....	....	....	....	....
	Cincinnati Mighty Ducks	AHL	76	12	26	38	....	....	....	91	....	....	....	....	....	....	....	....	....	....	....	....	....	....	....	....	....	....
	United States	WC-A	6	1	0	1	....	....	....	0	....	....	....	....	....	....	....	....	....	....	....	....	....	....	....	....	....	....
	NHL Totals		**8**	**2**	**2**	**4**	**2**	**2**	**4**	**8**	**0**	**0**	**1**	**17**	**11.8**	**9**	**1**	**0**	**1**		....	....	....	....	....	....	....	....

WCHA First All-Star Team (1996, 1997) • NCAA West First All-American Team (1996, 1997)

Traded to **Anaheim** by **Philadelphia** with Anatoli Semenov for Brian Wesenberg, March 19, 1996.

• CROWLEY, TED

Ted Crowley D – R. 6'2", 188 lbs. b: Concord, MA, 5/3/1970. Toronto's 4th choice, 69th overall, in 1988 Entry Draft.

Season	Club	League	GP	G	A	Pts	AG	AA	APts	PIM	PP	SH	GW	S	%	TGF	PGF	TGA	PGA	+/–	GP	G	A	Pts	PIM	PP	SH	GW
1987-88	Lawrence Academy	H.S.	23	11	23	34	....	....	....	....	....	....	....	....	....	....	....	....	....	....	....	....	....	....	....	....	....	....
	United States	WJC-A	7	0	1	1	....	....	....	0	....	....	....	....	....	....	....	....	....	....	....	....	....	....	....	....	....	....
1988-89	Lawrence Academy	H.S.	23	12	24	36	....	....	....	....	....	....	....	....	....	....	....	....	....	....	....	....	....	....	....	....	....	....
	United States	WJC-A	7	1	1	2	....	....	....	0	....	....	....	....	....	....	....	....	....	....	....	....	....	....	....	....	....	....
1989-90	Boston College	H.E.	39	7	24	31	....	....	....	34	....	....	....	....	....	....	....	....	....	....	....	....	....	....	....	....	....	....
	United States	WJC-A	7	1	4	5	....	....	....	6	....	....	....	....	....	....	....	....	....	....	....	....	....	....	....	....	....	....

			REGULAR SEASON																		PLAYOFFS							
Season	Club	League	GP	G	A	Pts	AG	AA	APts	PIM	PP	SH	GW	S	%	TGF	PGF	TGA	PGA	+/–	GP	G	A	Pts	PIM	PP	SH	GW
1990-91	Boston College	H.E.	39	12	24	36	....	....	....	61	....	....	....	....	....	....	....	....	....	....	....	....	....	....	....	....	....	....
1991-92	United States	Nat-Team	42	6	7	13	....	....	....	65	....	....	....	....	....	....	....	....	....	....	....	....	....	....	....	....	....	....
	St. John's Maple Leafs	AHL	29	5	4	9	....	....	....	33	....	....	....	....	....	....	....	....	....	....	10	3	1	4	11	....	....	....
1992-93	St. John's Maple Leafs	AHL	79	19	38	57	....	....	....	41	....	....	....	....	....	....	....	....	....	....	9	2	2	4	4	....	....	....
1993-94	United States	Nat-Team	48	9	13	22	....	....	....	80	....	....	....	....	....	....	....	....	....	....	....	....	....	....	....	....	....	....
	United States	Olympics	8	0	2	2	....	....	....	8	....	....	....	....	....	....	....	....	....	....	....	....	....	....	....	....	....	....
	Hartford Whalers	**NHL**	**21**	**1**	**2**	**3**	**1**	**2**	**3**	**10**	**1**	**0**	**0**	**28**	**3.6**	**15**	**3**	**16**	**3**	**–1**	....	....	....	....	....	....	....	....
1994-95	Chicago Wolves	IHL	53	8	23	31	....	....	....	68	....	....	....	....	....	....	....	....	....	....	....	....	....	....	....	....	....	....
	Houston Aeros	IHL	23	4	9	13	....	....	....	35	....	....	....	....	....	....	....	....	....	....	3	0	1	1	0	....	....	....
1995-96	Providence Bruins	AHL	72	12	30	42	....	....	....	47	....	....	....	....	....	....	....	....	....	....	4	1	2	3	2	....	....	....
1996-97	Cincinnati Cyclones	IHL	39	9	9	18	....	....	....	24	....	....	....	....	....	....	....	....	....	....	....	....	....	....	....	....	....	....
	Phoenix Roadrunners	IHL	30	5	8	13	....	....	....	21	....	....	....	....	....	....	....	....	....	....	....	....	....	....	....	....	....	....
1997-98	Springfield Falcons	AHL	78	14	35	49	....	....	....	55	....	....	....	....	....	....	....	....	....	....	4	1	1	2	2	....	....	....
	NHL Totals		**21**	**1**	**2**	**3**	**1**	**2**	**3**	**10**	**1**	**0**	**0**	**28**	**3.6**	**15**	**3**	**16**	**3**		....	....	....	....	....	....	....	....

Hockey East First All-Star Team (1991) • NCAA East Second All-American Team (1991)

Traded to **Hartford** by **Toronto** for Mark Greig and Hartford's 6th round choice (later traded to NY Rangers — NY Rangers selected Yuri Litvinov) in 1994 Entry Draft, January 25, 1994. Signed as a free agent by **Boston**, August 9, 1995. Signed as a free agent by **Phoenix**, June 27, 1997.

• CULHANE, JIM

Jim Culhane D – L. 6', 190 lbs. b: Halleybury, Ont., 3/13/1965. Hartford's 6th choice, 214th overall, in 1984 Entry Draft.

Season	Club	League	GP	G	A	Pts	AG	AA	APts	PIM	PP	SH	GW	S	%	TGF	PGF	TGA	PGA	+/–	GP	G	A	Pts	PIM	PP	SH	GW
1983-84	Western Michigan University	CCHA	42	1	14	15	....	....	....	88	....	....	....	....	....	....	....	....	....	....	....	....	....	....	....	....	....	....
1984-85	Western Michigan University	CCHA	37	2	8	10	....	....	....	84	....	....	....	....	....	....	....	....	....	....	....	....	....	....	....	....	....	....
1985-86	Western Michigan University	CCHA	40	1	21	22	....	....	....	61	....	....	....	....	....	....	....	....	....	....	....	....	....	....	....	....	....	....
1986-87	Western Michigan University	CCHA	43	9	24	33	....	....	....	163	....	....	....	....	....	....	....	....	....	....	....	....	....	....	....	....	....	....
1987-88	Binghamton Whalers	AHL	75	5	17	22	....	....	....	169	....	....	....	....	....	....	....	....	....	....	4	0	0	0	8	....	....	....
1988-89	Binghamton Whalers	AHL	72	6	11	17	....	....	....	200	....	....	....	....	....	....	....	....	....	....	....	....	....	....	....	....	....	....
1989-90	**Hartford Whalers**	**NHL**	**6**	**0**	**1**	**1**	**0**	**1**	**1**	**4**	**0**	**0**	**0**	**6**	**0.0**	**5**	**0**	**3**	**1**	**+3**	....	....	....	....	....	....	....	....
	Binghamton Whalers	AHL	73	6	11	17	....	....	....	69	....	....	....	....	....	....	....	....	....	....	....	....	....	....	....	....	....	....
1990-91	Capital District Islanders	AHL	15	0	0	0	....	....	....	14	....	....	....	....	....	....	....	....	....	....	....	....	....	....	....	....	....	....
	Kansas City Blades	IHL	59	1	8	9	....	....	....	50	....	....	....	....	....	....	....	....	....	....	....	....	....	....	....	....	....	....
1991-92	Capital District Islanders	AHL	37	1	3	4	....	....	....	58	....	....	....	....	....	....	....	....	....	....	....	....	....	....	....	....	....	....
	NHL Totals		**6**	**0**	**1**	**1**	**0**	**1**	**1**	**4**	**0**	**0**	**0**	**6**	**0.0**	**5**	**0**	**3**	**1**		....	....	....	....	....	....	....	....

Signed as a free agent by **NY Islanders**, October, 1990.

• CULLEN, JOHN

John Cullen C – R. 5'10", 182 lbs. b: Fort Erie, Ont., 8/2/1964. Buffalo's 2nd choice, 10th overall, in 1986 Supplemental Draft.

Season	Club	League	GP	G	A	Pts	AG	AA	APts	PIM	PP	SH	GW	S	%	TGF	PGF	TGA	PGA	+/–	GP	G	A	Pts	PIM	PP	SH	GW
1983-84	Boston University	ECAC	40	23	33	56	....	....	....	28	....	....	....	....	....	....	....	....	....	....	....	....	....	....	....	....	....	....
1984-85	Boston University	H.E.	41	27	32	59	....	....	....	46	....	....	....	....	....	....	....	....	....	....	....	....	....	....	....	....	....	....
1985-86	Boston University	H.E.	43	25	49	74	....	....	....	54	....	....	....	....	....	....	....	....	....	....	....	....	....	....	....	....	....	....
1986-87	Boston University	H.E.	36	23	29	52	....	....	....	35	....	....	....	....	....	....	....	....	....	....	....	....	....	....	....	....	....	....
1987-88	Flint Spirits	IHL	81	48	*109	*157	....	....	....	113	....	....	....	....	....	....	....	....	....	....	16	11	*15	26	16	....	....	....
1988-89	**Pittsburgh Penguins**	**NHL**	**79**	**12**	**37**	**49**	**10**	**26**	**36**	**112**	**8**	**0**	**0**	**121**	**9.9**	**75**	**39**	**65**	**4**	**–25**	**11**	**3**	**6**	**9**	**28**	**0**	**0**	**0**
1989-90	**Pittsburgh Penguins**	**NHL**	**72**	**32**	**60**	**92**	**28**	**43**	**71**	**138**	**9**	**0**	**4**	**197**	**16.2**	**120**	**44**	**101**	**12**	**–13**	....	....	....	....	....	....	....	....
	Canada	WEC-A	10	1	3	4	....	....	....	0	....	....	....	....	....	....	....	....	....	....	....	....	....	....	....	....	....	....
1990-91	**Pittsburgh Penguins**	**NHL**	**65**	**31**	**63**	**94**	**29**	**48**	**77**	**83**	**10**	**0**	**2**	**171**	**18.1**	**123**	**49**	**76**	**2**	**0**	....	....	....	....	....	....	....	....
	Hartford Whalers	**NHL**	**13**	**8**	**8**	**16**	**7**	**6**	**13**	**18**	**4**	**0**	**1**	**34**	**23.5**	**21**	**13**	**15**	**1**	**–6**	**6**	**2**	**7**	**9**	**10**	**0**	**0**	**0**
1991-92	**Hartford Whalers**	**NHL**	**77**	**26**	**51**	**77**	**24**	**38**	**62**	**141**	**10**	**0**	**4**	**173**	**15.0**	**100**	**45**	**83**	**0**	**–28**	**7**	**2**	**1**	**3**	**12**	**1**	**0**	**1**
1992-93	**Hartford Whalers**	**NHL**	**19**	**5**	**4**	**9**	**4**	**3**	**7**	**58**	**3**	**0**	**0**	**38**	**13.2**	**12**	**4**	**23**	**0**	**–15**	....	....	....	....	....	....	....	....
	Toronto Maple Leafs	**NHL**	**47**	**13**	**28**	**41**	**11**	**19**	**30**	**53**	**10**	**0**	**1**	**86**	**15.1**	**58**	**38**	**30**	**2**	**–8**	**12**	**2**	**3**	**5**	**0**	**1**	**0**	**0**
1993-94	**Toronto Maple Leafs**	**NHL**	**53**	**13**	**17**	**30**	**12**	**13**	**25**	**67**	**2**	**0**	**4**	**80**	**16.3**	**40**	**10**	**32**	**0**	**–2**	**3**	**0**	**0**	**0**	**0**	**0**	**0**	**0**
1994-95	**Pittsburgh Penguins**	**NHL**	**46**	**13**	**24**	**37**	**23**	**35**	**58**	**66**	**2**	**0**	**1**	**88**	**14.8**	**52**	**13**	**43**	**0**	**–4**	**9**	**0**	**2**	**2**	**8**	**0**	**0**	**0**
1995-96	**Tampa Bay Lightning**	**NHL**	**76**	**16**	**34**	**50**	**16**	**28**	**44**	**65**	**8**	**0**	**3**	**152**	**10.5**	**75**	**26**	**52**	**4**	**+1**	**5**	**3**	**3**	**6**	**0**	**0**	**1**	**0**
1996-97	**Tampa Bay Lightning**	**NHL**	**70**	**18**	**37**	**55**	**19**	**33**	**52**	**95**	**5**	**0**	**2**	**116**	**15.5**	**64**	**28**	**51**	**1**	**–14**	....	....	....	....	....	....	....	....
1997-98	**Tampa Bay Lightning**	**NHL**	DID NOT PLAY																									
	NHL Totals		**617**	**187**	**363**	**550**	**183**	**292**	**475**	**896**	**71**	**0**	**22**	**1256**	**14.9**	**740**	**309**	**571**	**26**		**53**	**12**	**22**	**34**	**58**	**2**	**1**	**1**

Hockey East First All-Star Team (1985, 1986) • NCAA East Second All-American Team (1986) • Hockey East Second All-Star Team (1987) • IHL First All-Star Team (1988) • Won James Gatschene Memorial Trophy (MVP - IHL) (1988) • Shared Garry F. Longman Memorial Trophy (Top Rookie - IHL) with Ed Belfour (1988) • Won Leo P. Lamoureux Memorial Trophy (Top Scorer - IHL) (1988)

Played in NHL All-Star Game (1991, 1992)

Signed as a free agent by **Pittsburgh**, June 21, 1988. Traded to **Hartford** by **Pittsburgh** with Jeff Parker and Zarley Zalapski for Ron Francis, Grant Jennings and Ulf Samuelsson, March 4, 1991. Traded to **Toronto** by **Hartford** for future considerations, November 24, 1992. Signed as a free agent by **Pittsburgh**, August 3, 1994. Signed as a free agent by **Tampa Bay**, September 11, 1995. • Missed entire 1997-98 season recovering from treatment and surgery for non-Hodgkins Lymphoma.

• CULLEN, MATT

Matt Cullen C – L. 6'1", 195 lbs. b: Virginia, MN, 11/2/1976. Anaheim's 2nd choice, 35th overall, in 1996 Entry Draft.

Season	Club	League	GP	G	A	Pts	AG	AA	APts	PIM	PP	SH	GW	S	%	TGF	PGF	TGA	PGA	+/–	GP	G	A	Pts	PIM	PP	SH	GW
1995-96	St. Cloud State Huskies	WCHA	39	12	29	41	....	....	....	28	....	....	....	....	....	....	....	....	....	....	....	....	....	....	....	....	....	....
	United States	WJC-A	6	3	1	4	....	....	....	0	....	....	....	....	....	....	....	....	....	....	....	....	....	....	....	....	....	....
1996-97	St. Cloud State Huskies	WCHA	36	15	30	45	....	....	....	70	....	....	....	....	....	....	....	....	....	....	....	....	....	....	....	....	....	....
	Baltimore Bandits	AHL	6	3	3	6	....	....	....	7	....	....	....	....	....	....	....	....	....	....	3	0	2	2	0	....	....	....
1997-98	**Anaheim Mighty Ducks**	**NHL**	**61**	**6**	**21**	**27**	**7**	**20**	**27**	**23**	**2**	**0**	**0**	**75**	**8.0**	**42**	**8**	**48**	**10**	**–4**	....	....	....	....	....	....	....	....
	Cincinnati Mighty Ducks	AHL	18	15	12	27	....	....	....	2	....	....	....	....	....	....	....	....	....	....	....	....	....	....	....	....	....	....
	NHL Totals		**61**	**6**	**21**	**27**	**7**	**20**	**27**	**23**	**2**	**0**	**0**	**75**	**8.0**	**42**	**8**	**48**	**10**		....	....	....	....	....	....	....	....

WCHA Second All-Star Team (1997)

• CULLEN, RAY

Ray Cullen C – R. 5'11", 180 lbs. b: Ottawa, Ont., 9/20/1941.

Season	Club	League	GP	G	A	Pts	AG	AA	APts	PIM	PP	SH	GW	S	%	TGF	PGF	TGA	PGA	+/–	GP	G	A	Pts	PIM	PP	SH	GW
1958-59	St. Catharines Teepees	OHA	54	19	14	33	....	....	....	46	....	....	....	....	....	....	....	....	....	....	7	1	1	2	0	....	....	....
1959-60	St. Catharines Teepees	OHA	48	*48	29	77	....	....	....	60	....	....	....	....	....	....	....	....	....	....	17	*15	17	*32	20	....	....	....
1960-61	St. Catharines Teepees	OHA	45	24	50	74	....	....	....	56	....	....	....	....	....	....	....	....	....	....	6	2	2	4	10	....	....	....
1961-62	St. Catharines Teepees	OHA	50	36	42	78	....	....	....	63	....	....	....	....	....	....	....	....	....	....	6	4	2	6	0	....	....	....
1962-63	Knoxville Knights	EHL	67	66	43	109	....	....	....	32	....	....	....	....	....	....	....	....	....	....	5	4	1	5	0	....	....	....
1963-64	St. Louis Braves	CHL	63	46	52	98	....	....	....	24	....	....	....	....	....	....	....	....	....	....	....	....	....	....	....	....	....	....
1964-65	Buffalo Bisons	AHL	70	28	36	64	....	....	....	18	....	....	....	....	....	....	....	....	....	....	9	3	6	9	17	....	....	....
1965-66	**New York Rangers**	**NHL**	**8**	**1**	**3**	**4**	**1**	**3**	**4**	**0**	....	....	....	....	....	....	....	....	....	....	....	....	....	....	....	....	....	....
	Baltimore Clippers	AHL	63	27	46	73	....	....	....	40	....	....	....	....	....	....	....	....	....	....	....	....	....	....	....	....	....	....
1966-67	**Detroit Red Wings**	**NHL**	**27**	**8**	**8**	**16**	**10**	**8**	**18**	**8**	....	....	....	....	....	....	....	....	....	....	....	....	....	....	....	....	....	....
	Pittsburgh Hornets	AHL	28	15	14	29	....	....	....	8	....	....	....	....	....	....	....	....	....	....	....	....	....	....	....	....	....	....
1967-68	**Minnesota North Stars**	**NHL**	**67**	**28**	**25**	**53**	**35**	**26**	**61**	**18**	**11**	**0**	**6**	**203**	**13.8**	**67**	**27**	**64**	**0**	**–24**	**14**	**2**	**6**	**8**	**2**	**1**	**0**	**0**
1968-69	**Minnesota North Stars**	**NHL**	**67**	**26**	**38**	**64**	**29**	**36**	**65**	**44**	**3**	**0**	**2**	**195**	**13.3**	**79**	**22**	**85**	**1**	**–27**	....	....	....	....	....	....	....	....
1969-70	**Minnesota North Stars**	**NHL**	**74**	**17**	**28**	**45**	**20**	**28**	**48**	**8**	**3**	**0**	**3**	**143**	**11.9**	**70**	**1**	**50**	**0**	**+19**	**6**	**1**	**4**	**5**	**0**	**0**	**0**	**0**
1970-71	**Vancouver Canucks**	**NHL**	**70**	**12**	**21**	**33**	**13**	**18**	**31**	**42**	**4**	**0**	**3**	**114**	**10.5**	**49**	**24**	**49**	**0**	**–24**	....	....	....	....	....	....	....	....
	NHL Totals		**313**	**92**	**123**	**215**	**108**	**119**	**227**	**120**	**21**	**0**	**14**	**655**	**14.0**	**265**	**74**	**248**	**1**		**20**	**3**	**10**	**13**	**2**	**1**	**0**	**0**

EHL First All-Star Team (1963) • EHL Rookie of the Year (1963) • CHL First All-Star Team (1964) • Won Dudley "Red" Garrett Memorial Award (Top Rookie - AHL) (1965)

Traded to **NY Rangers** by **Chicago** (Buffalo - AHL) with John McKenzie for Dick Meissner, Dave Richardson, Tracy Pratt and Mel Pearson, June, 1965. Claimed by **Detroit** from **NY Rangers** in Intra-League Draft, June 15, 1966. Claimed by **Minnesota** from **Detroit** in Expansion Draft, June 6, 1967. Claimed by **Vancouver** from **Minnesota** in Expansion Draft, June 10, 1970.

• CULLIMORE, JASSEN

Jassen Cullimore D – L. 6'5", 225 lbs. b: Simcoe, Ont., 12/4/1972. Vancouver's 2nd choice, 29th overall, in 1991 Entry Draft.

Season	Club	League	GP	G	A	Pts	AG	AA	APts	PIM	PP	SH	GW	S	%	TGF	PGF	TGA	PGA	+/–	GP	G	A	Pts	PIM	PP	SH	GW
1989-90	Peterborough Petes	OHL	59	2	6	8	....	....	....	61	....	....	....	....	....	....	....	....	....	....	11	0	2	2	8	....	....	....
1990-91	Peterborough Petes	OHL	62	8	16	24	....	....	....	74	....	....	....	....	....	....	....	....	....	....	4	1	0	1	7	....	....	....
1991-92	Peterborough Petes	OHL	54	9	37	46	....	....	....	65	....	....	....	....	....	....	....	....	....	....	10	3	6	9	8	....	....	....
	Canada	WJC-A	7	1	0	1	....	....	....	2	....	....	....	....	....	....	....	....	....	....	....	....	....	....	....	....	....	....
1992-93	Hamilton Canucks	AHL	56	5	7	12	....	....	....	60	....	....	....	....	....	....	....	....	....	....	....	....	....	....	....	....	....	....
1993-94	Hamilton Canucks	AHL	71	8	20	28	....	....	....	86	....	....	....	....	....	....	....	....	....	....	3	0	1	1	2	....	....	....

			REGULAR SEASON																		PLAYOFFS							
Season	Club	League	GP	G	A	Pts	AG	AA	APts	PIM	PP	SH	GW	S	%	TGF	PGF	TGA	PGA	+/–	GP	G	A	Pts	PIM	PP	SH	GW
1994-95	**Vancouver Canucks**	**NHL**	**34**	**1**	**2**	**3**	**2**	**3**	**5**	**39**	**0**	**0**	**0**	**30**	**3.3**	**18**	**2**	**22**	**4**	**–2**	**11**	**0**	**0**	**0**	**12**	**0**	**0**	**0**
	Syracuse Crunch	AHL	33	2	7	9	....	....	....	66	....	....	....	....	....	....	....	....	....	....	....	....	....	....	....	....	....	....
1995-96	**Vancouver Canucks**	**NHL**	**27**	**1**	**1**	**2**	**1**	**1**	**2**	**21**	**0**	**0**	**1**	**12**	**8.3**	**21**	**0**	**23**	**6**	**+4**	....	....	....	....	....	....	....	....
1996-97	**Vancouver Canucks**	**NHL**	**3**	**0**	**0**	**0**	**0**	**0**	**0**	**2**	**0**	**0**	**0**	**2**	**0.0**	**0**	**0**	**3**	**1**	**–2**	....	....	....	....	....	....	....	....
	Montreal Canadiens	**NHL**	**49**	**2**	**6**	**8**	**2**	**5**	**7**	**42**	**0**	**1**	**1**	**52**	**3.8**	**41**	**5**	**47**	**15**	**+4**	**2**	**0**	**0**	**0**	**2**	**0**	**0**	**0**
1997-98	**Montreal Canadiens**	**NHL**	**3**	**0**	**0**	**0**	**0**	**0**	**0**	**4**	**0**	**0**	**0**	**1**	**0.0**	**0**	**0**	**0**	**0**	**0**	....	....	....	....	....	....	....	....
	Tampa Bay Lightning	**NHL**	**25**	**1**	**2**	**3**	**1**	**2**	**3**	**22**	**1**	**0**	**0**	**17**	**5.9**	**15**	**2**	**26**	**9**	**–4**	....	....	....	....	....	....	....	....
	Fredericton Canadiens	AHL	5	1	0	1	....	....	....	8	....	....	....	....	....	....	....	....	....	....	....	....	....	....	....	....	....	....
	NHL Totals		**141**	**5**	**11**	**16**	**6**	**11**	**17**	**130**	**1**	**1**	**2**	**114**	**4.4**	**95**	**9**	**121**	**35**		**13**	**0**	**0**	**0**	**14**	**0**	**0**	**0**

OHL Second All-Star Team (1992)

Traded to **Montreal** by **Vancouver** for Donald Brashear, November 13, 1996. Claimed on waivers by **Tampa Bay** from **Montreal**, January 22, 1998.

• CUMMINS, BARRY

Barry Cummins D – L. 5'9", 175 lbs. b: Regina, Sask., 1/25/1949.

Season	Club	League	GP	G	A	Pts	AG	AA	APts	PIM	PP	SH	GW	S	%	TGF	PGF	TGA	PGA	+/–	GP	G	A	Pts	PIM	PP	SH	GW
1966-67	Regina Pats	SJHL	17	0	3	3	....	....	....	33	....	....	....	....	....	....	....	....	....	....	14	0	4	4	28	....	....	....
1967-68	Regina Pats	SJHL	50	7	13	20	....	....	....	174	....	....	....	....	....	....	....	....	....	....	....	....	....	....	....	....	....	....
1968-69	Regina Pats	SJHL	DID NOT PLAY – INJURED																									
1969-70	Saskatoon Blades	WCJHL	34	9	25	34	....	....	....	123	....	....	....	....	....	....	....	....	....	....	....	....	....	....	....	....	....	....
	Muskegon Mohawks	IHL	8	0	0	0	....	....	....	8	....	....	....	....	....	....	....	....	....	....	....	....	....	....	....	....	....	....
1970-71	Portland Buckaroos	WHL	58	0	1	1	....	....	....	38	....	....	....	....	....	....	....	....	....	....	10	0	0	0	0	....	....	....
1971-72	Portland Buckaroos	WHL	53	0	8	8	....	....	....	78	....	....	....	....	....	....	....	....	....	....	....	....	....	....	....	....	....	....
	Seattle Totems	WHL	17	1	2	3	....	....	....	23	....	....	....	....	....	....	....	....	....	....	....	....	....	....	....	....	....	....
1972-73	Salt Lake Golden Eagles	WHL	72	4	18	22	....	....	....	190	....	....	....	....	....	....	....	....	....	....	9	0	2	2	17	....	....	....
1973-74	**California Golden Seals**	**NHL**	**36**	**1**	**2**	**3**	**1**	**2**	**3**	**39**	**0**	**0**	**0**	**28**	**3.6**	**28**	**0**	**75**	**12**	**–35**	....	....	....	....	....	....	....	....
	Salt Lake Golden Eagles	WHL	37	2	12	14	....	....	....	100	....	....	....	....	....	....	....	....	....	....	5	0	1	1	8	....	....	....
1974-75	Springfield Indians	AHL	73	9	33	42	....	....	....	151	....	....	....	....	....	....	....	....	....	....	....	....	....	....	....	....	....	....
	NHL Totals		**36**	**1**	**2**	**3**	**1**	**2**	**3**	**39**	**0**	**0**	**0**	**28**	**3.6**	**28**	**0**	**75**	**12**			....	....	....	....	....	....	....

Claimed by **Portland** (WHL) from **Montreal** in Reverse Draft, June, 1970. Traded to **Seattle** (WHL) by **Portland** (WHL) for cash, June, 1971. Traded to **California** (Salt Lake-WHL) by **Seattle** (WHL) for $15,000, June, 1972.

• CUMMINS, JIM

Jim Cummins RW – R. 6'2", 219 lbs. b: Dearborn, MI, 5/17/1970. NY Rangers' 5th choice, 67th overall, in 1989 Entry Draft.

Season	Club	League	GP	G	A	Pts	AG	AA	APts	PIM	PP	SH	GW	S	%	TGF	PGF	TGA	PGA	+/–	GP	G	A	Pts	PIM	PP	SH	GW
1988-89	Michigan State Spartans	CCHA	30	3	8	11	....	....	....	98	....	....	....	....	....	....	....	....	....	....	....	....	....	....	....	....	....	....
1989-90	Michigan State Spartans	CCHA	41	8	7	15	....	....	....	94	....	....	....	....	....	....	....	....	....	....	....	....	....	....	....	....	....	....
1990-91	Michigan State Spartans	CCHA	34	9	6	15	....	....	....	110	....	....	....	....	....	....	....	....	....	....	....	....	....	....	....	....	....	....
1991-92	**Detroit Red Wings**	**NHL**	**1**	**0**	**0**	**0**	**0**	**0**	**0**	**7**	**0**	**0**	**0**	**0**	**0.0**	**0**	**0**	**0**	**0**	**0**	....	....	....	....	....	....	....	....
	Adirondack Red Wings	AHL	65	7	13	20	....	....	....	338	....	....	....	....	....	....	....	....	....	....	5	0	0	0	19	....	....	....
1992-93	**Detroit Red Wings**	**NHL**	**7**	**1**	**1**	**2**	**1**	**1**	**2**	**58**	**0**	**0**	**0**	**5**	**20.0**	**2**	**0**	**2**	**0**	**0**	....	....	....	....	....	....	....	....
	Adirondack Red Wings	AHL	43	16	4	20	....	....	....	179	....	....	....	....	....	....	....	....	....	....	9	3	1	4	4	....	....	....
1993-94	**Philadelphia Flyers**	**NHL**	**22**	**1**	**2**	**3**	**1**	**2**	**3**	**71**	**0**	**0**	**0**	**17**	**5.9**	**3**	**0**	**3**	**0**	**0**	....	....	....	....	....	....	....	....
	Hershey Bears	AHL	17	6	6	12	....	....	....	70	....	....	....	....	....	....	....	....	....	....	....	....	....	....	....	....	....	....
	Tampa Bay Lightning	**NHL**	**4**	**0**	**0**	**0**	**0**	**0**	**0**	**13**	**0**	**0**	**0**	**3**	**0.0**	**1**	**0**	**2**	**0**	**–1**	....	....	....	....	....	....	....	....
	Atlanta Knights	IHL	7	4	5	9	....	....	....	14	....	....	....	....	....	....	....	....	....	....	13	1	2	3	90	....	....	....
1994-95	**Tampa Bay Lightning**	**NHL**	**10**	**1**	**0**	**1**	**2**	**0**	**2**	**41**	**0**	**0**	**1**	**3**	**33.3**	**2**	**0**	**5**	**0**	**–3**	....	....	....	....	....	....	....	....
	Chicago Blackhawks	**NHL**	**27**	**3**	**1**	**4**	**5**	**1**	**6**	**117**	**0**	**0**	**0**	**20**	**15.0**	**7**	**0**	**10**	**0**	**–3**	**14**	**1**	**1**	**2**	**4**	**0**	**0**	**1**
1995-96	**Chicago Blackhawks**	**NHL**	**52**	**2**	**4**	**6**	**2**	**3**	**5**	**180**	**0**	**0**	**2**	**34**	**5.9**	**11**	**0**	**12**	**0**	**–1**	**10**	**0**	**0**	**0**	**2**	**0**	**0**	**0**
1996-97	**Chicago Blackhawks**	**NHL**	**65**	**6**	**6**	**12**	**6**	**5**	**11**	**199**	**0**	**0**	**0**	**61**	**9.8**	**20**	**0**	**16**	**0**	**+4**	**6**	**0**	**0**	**0**	**24**	**0**	**0**	**0**
1997-98	**Chicago Blackhawks**	**NHL**	**55**	**0**	**2**	**2**	**0**	**2**	**2**	**178**	**0**	**0**	**0**	**33**	**0.0**	**5**	**0**	**14**	**0**	**–9**	....	....	....	....	....	....	....	....
	Phoenix Coyotes	**NHL**	**20**	**0**	**0**	**0**	**0**	**0**	**0**	**47**	**0**	**0**	**0**	**10**	**0.0**	**2**	**0**	**9**	**0**	**–7**	**3**	**0**	**0**	**0**	**4**	**0**	**0**	**0**
	NHL Totals		**263**	**14**	**16**	**30**	**17**	**14**	**31**	**911**	**0**	**0**	**3**	**186**	**7.5**	**53**	**0**	**73**	**0**		**33**	**1**	**1**	**2**	**34**	**0**	**0**	**1**

Traded to **Detroit** by **NY Rangers** with Kevin Miller and Dennis Vial for Joey Kocur and Per Djoos, March 5, 1991. Traded to **Philadelphia** by **Detroit** with Philadelphia's 4th round choice (previously acquired by Detroit — later traded to Boston — Boston selected Charles Paquette) in 1993 Entry Draft for Greg Johnson and Philadelphia's 5th round choice (Frederic Deschenes) in 1994 Entry Draft, June 20, 1993. Traded to **Tampa Bay** by **Philadelphia** with Philadelphia's 4th round choice in 1995 Entry Draft for Rob DiMaio, March 18, 1994. Traded to **Chicago** by **Tampa Bay** with Tom Tilley and Jeff Buchanan for Paul Ysebaert and Rich Sutter, February 22, 1995. Traded to **Phoenix** by **Chicago** with Keith Carney for Chad Kilger and Jayson More, March 4, 1998.

• CUNNEYWORTH, RANDY

Randy Cunneyworth LW – L. 6', 198 lbs. b: Etobicoke, Ont., 5/10/1961. Buffalo's 9th choice, 167th overall, in 1980 Entry Draft.

Season	Club	League	GP	G	A	Pts	AG	AA	APts	PIM	PP	SH	GW	S	%	TGF	PGF	TGA	PGA	+/–	GP	G	A	Pts	PIM	PP	SH	GW
1979-80	Ottawa 67's	OHA	63	16	25	41	....	....	....	145	....	....	....	....	....	....	....	....	....	....	11	0	1	1	13	....	....	....
1980-81	Ottawa 67's	OHA	67	54	74	128	....	....	....	240	....	....	....	....	....	....	....	....	....	....	15	5	8	13	35	....	....	....
	Buffalo Sabres	**NHL**	**1**	**0**	**0**	**0**	**0**	**0**	**0**	**2**	**0**	**0**	**0**	**1**	**0.0**	**1**	**0**	**1**	**0**	**0**	....	....	....	....	....	....	....	....
	Rochester Americans	AHL	1	0	1	1	....	....	....	2	....	....	....	....	....	....	....	....	....	....	....	....	....	....	....	....	....	....
1981-82	**Buffalo Sabres**	**NHL**	**20**	**2**	**4**	**6**	**2**	**3**	**5**	**47**	**0**	**0**	**0**	**33**	**6.1**	**10**	**0**	**13**	**0**	**–3**	....	....	....	....	....	....	....	....
	Rochester Americans	AHL	57	12	15	27	....	....	....	86	....	....	....	....	....	....	....	....	....	....	9	4	0	4	30	....	....	....
1982-83	Rochester Americans	AHL	78	23	33	56	....	....	....	111	....	....	....	....	....	....	....	....	....	....	16	4	4	8	35	....	....	....
1983-84	Rochester Americans	AHL	54	18	17	35	....	....	....	85	....	....	....	....	....	....	....	....	....	....	17	5	5	10	55	....	....	....
1984-85	Rochester Americans	AHL	72	30	38	68	....	....	....	148	....	....	....	....	....	....	....	....	....	....	5	2	1	3	16	....	....	....
1985-86	**Pittsburgh Penguins**	**NHL**	**75**	**15**	**30**	**45**	**12**	**20**	**32**	**74**	**2**	**2**	**2**	**134**	**11.2**	**68**	**9**	**68**	**21**	**+12**	....	....	....	....	....	....	....	....
1986-87	**Pittsburgh Penguins**	**NHL**	**79**	**26**	**27**	**53**	**23**	**20**	**43**	**142**	**3**	**2**	**5**	**169**	**15.4**	**79**	**12**	**86**	**33**	**+14**	....	....	....	....	....	....	....	....
1987-88	**Pittsburgh Penguins**	**NHL**	**71**	**35**	**39**	**74**	**30**	**28**	**58**	**141**	**14**	**0**	**6**	**229**	**15.3**	**112**	**45**	**69**	**15**	**+13**	....	....	....	....	....	....	....	....
1988-89	**Pittsburgh Penguins**	**NHL**	**70**	**25**	**19**	**44**	**21**	**13**	**34**	**156**	**10**	**0**	**1**	**163**	**15.3**	**76**	**32**	**69**	**3**	**–22**	**11**	**3**	**5**	**8**	**26**	**1**	**0**	**1**
1989-90	**Winnipeg Jets**	**NHL**	**28**	**5**	**6**	**11**	**4**	**4**	**8**	**34**	**2**	**0**	**1**	**51**	**9.8**	**18**	**6**	**19**	**0**	**–7**	....	....	....	....	....	....	....	....
	Hartford Whalers	**NHL**	**43**	**9**	**9**	**18**	**8**	**6**	**14**	**41**	**2**	**0**	**1**	**70**	**12.9**	**29**	**4**	**31**	**2**	**–4**	**4**	**0**	**0**	**0**	**2**	**0**	**0**	**0**
1990-91	**Hartford Whalers**	**NHL**	**32**	**9**	**5**	**14**	**8**	**4**	**12**	**49**	**0**	**0**	**1**	**56**	**16.1**	**18**	**1**	**26**	**3**	**–6**	**1**	**0**	**0**	**0**	**0**	**0**	**0**	**0**
	Springfield Indians	AHL	2	0	0	0	....	....	....	5	....	....	....	....	....	....	....	....	....	....	....	....	....	....	....	....	....	....
1991-92	**Hartford Whalers**	**NHL**	**39**	**7**	**10**	**17**	**6**	**7**	**13**	**71**	**0**	**0**	**1**	**63**	**11.1**	**27**	**6**	**32**	**6**	**–5**	**7**	**3**	**0**	**3**	**9**	**1**	**1**	**1**
1992-93	**Hartford Whalers**	**NHL**	**39**	**5**	**4**	**9**	**4**	**3**	**7**	**63**	**0**	**0**	**1**	**47**	**10.6**	**18**	**0**	**20**	**3**	**–1**	....	....	....	....	....	....	....	....
1993-94	**Hartford Whalers**	**NHL**	**63**	**9**	**8**	**17**	**8**	**6**	**14**	**87**	**0**	**1**	**1**	**121**	**7.4**	**26**	**0**	**38**	**10**	**–2**	....	....	....	....	....	....	....	....
	Chicago Blackhawks	**NHL**	**16**	**4**	**3**	**7**	**4**	**2**	**6**	**13**	**0**	**0**	**1**	**33**	**12.1**	**8**	**1**	**8**	**2**	**+1**	**6**	**0**	**0**	**0**	**8**	**0**	**0**	**0**
1994-95	**Ottawa Senators**	**NHL**	**48**	**5**	**5**	**10**	**9**	**7**	**16**	**68**	**2**	**0**	**0**	**71**	**7.0**	**21**	**2**	**48**	**10**	**–19**	....	....	....	....	....	....	....	....
1995-96	**Ottawa Senators**	**NHL**	**81**	**17**	**19**	**36**	**17**	**15**	**32**	**130**	**4**	**0**	**2**	**142**	**12.0**	**56**	**12**	**92**	**17**	**–31**	....	....	....	....	....	....	....	....
1996-97	**Ottawa Senators**	**NHL**	**76**	**12**	**24**	**36**	**13**	**21**	**34**	**99**	**6**	**0**	**3**	**115**	**10.4**	**57**	**15**	**57**	**8**	**–7**	**7**	**1**	**1**	**2**	**10**	**0**	**0**	**0**
1997-98	**Ottawa Senators**	**NHL**	**71**	**2**	**11**	**13**	**2**	**11**	**13**	**63**	**1**	**0**	**0**	**81**	**2.5**	**24**	**5**	**48**	**15**	**–14**	**6**	**0**	**1**	**1**	**6**	**0**	**0**	**0**
	NHL Totals		**852**	**187**	**223**	**410**	**171**	**170**	**341**	**1280**	**46**	**5**	**26**	**1579**	**11.8**	**646**	**150**	**725**	**148**		**42**	**7**	**7**	**14**	**61**	**2**	**1**	**2**

Traded to **Pittsburgh** by **Buffalo** with Mike Moller for Pat Hughes, October 4, 1985. Traded to **Winnipeg** by **Pittsburgh** with Rick Tabaracci and Dave McLlwain for Jim Kyte, Andrew McBain and Randy Gilhen, June 17, 1989. Traded to **Hartford** by **Winnipeg** for Paul MacDermid, December 13, 1989. Traded to **Chicago** by **Hartford** with Gary Suter and Hartford's 3rd round choice (later traded to Vancouver — Vancouver selected Larry Courville) in 1995 Entry Draft for Frantisek Kucera and Jocelyn Lemieux, March 11, 1994. Signed as a free agent by **Ottawa**, July 15, 1994.

• CUNNINGHAM, JIM

Jim Cunningham LW – L. 5'11", 185 lbs. b: St. Paul, MN, 8/15/1956.

Season	Club	League	GP	G	A	Pts	AG	AA	APts	PIM	PP	SH	GW	S	%	TGF	PGF	TGA	PGA	+/–	GP	G	A	Pts	PIM	PP	SH	GW
1974-75	St. Paul Vulcans	MWJHL	57	21	31	52	....	....	....	183	....	....	....	....	....	....	....	....	....	....	....	....	....	....	....	....	....	....
1975-76	St. Paul Vulcans	MWJHL	47	16	58	74	....	....	....	148	....	....	....	....	....	....	....	....	....	....	....	....	....	....	....	....	....	....
1976-77	Michigan State Spartans	WCHA	34	11	25	36	....	....	....	59	....	....	....	....	....	....	....	....	....	....	....	....	....	....	....	....	....	....
1977-78	**Philadelphia Flyers**	**NHL**	**1**	**0**	**0**	**0**	**0**	**0**	**0**	**4**	**0**	**0**	**0**	**0**	**0.0**	**1**	**0**	**0**	**0**	**+1**	....	....	....	....	....	....	....	....
	Maine Mariners	AHL	48	1	6	7	....	....	....	106	....	....	....	....	....	....	....	....	....	....	8	0	1	1	20	....	....	....
1978-79	Maine Mariners	AHL	78	8	16	24	....	....	....	223	....	....	....	....	....	....	....	....	....	....	10	2	4	6	10	....	....	....
1979-80	Cincinnati Stingers	CHL	5	0	1	1	....	....	....	5	....	....	....	....	....	....	....	....	....	....	....	....	....	....	....	....	....	....
	Maine Mariners	AHL	51	7	19	26	....	....	....	179	....	....	....	....	....	....	....	....	....	....	....	....	....	....	....	....	....	....
	Adirondack Red Wings	AHL	13	2	3	5	....	....	....	78	....	....	....	....	....	....	....	....	....	....	5	1	0	1	16	....	....	....
1980-81	Maine Mariners	AHL	44	3	5	8	....	....	....	141	....	....	....	....	....	....	....	....	....	....	....	....	....	....	....	....	....	....
	NHL Totals		**1**	**0**	**0**	**0**	**0**	**0**	**0**	**4**	**0**	**0**	**0**	**0**	**0.0**	**1**	**0**	**0**	**0**		....	....	....	....	....	....	....	....

Signed as a free agent by **Philadelphia**, September, 1977. Claimed by **Winnipeg** from **Philadelphia** in Expansion Draft, June 13, 1979.

• CURRAN, BRIAN

Brian "Biff" Curran D – L. 6'5", 220 lbs. b: Toronto, Ont., 11/5/1963. Boston's 2nd choice, 22nd overall, in 1982 Entry Draft.

			REGULAR SEASON																		PLAYOFFS							
Season	Club	League	GP	G	A	Pts	AG	AA	APts	PIM	PP	SH	GW	S	%	TGF	PGF	TGA	PGA	+/–	GP	G	A	Pts	PIM	PP	SH	GW
1980-81	Portland Winter Hawks	WHL	59	2	28	30	....	....	....	275	....	....	....	....	....	....	....	....	....	....	7	0	1	1	13	....	....	....
1981-82	Portland Winter Hawks	WHL	51	2	16	18	....	....	....	132	....	....	....	....	....	....	....	....	....	....	14	1	7	8	63	....	....	....
1982-83	Portland Winter Hawks	WHL	56	1	30	31	....	....	....	187	....	....	....	....	....	....	....	....	....	....	14	1	3	4	57	....	....	....
1983-84	**Boston Bruins**	**NHL**	16	1	1	2	1	1	2	57	0	0	0	6	16.7	9	0	11	2	0	3	0	0	0	7	0	0	0
	Hershey Bears	AHL	23	0	2	2	....	....	....	94	....	....	....	....	....	....	....	....	....	....	....	....	....	....	....	....	....	....
1984-85	**Boston Bruins**	**NHL**	56	0	1	1	0	1	1	158	0	0	0	17	0.0	23	0	34	3	–8	....	....	....	....	....	....	....	....
	Hershey Bears	AHL	4	0	0	0	....	....	....	19	....	....	....	....	....	....	....	....	....	....	....	....	....	....	....	....	....	....
1985-86	**Boston Bruins**	**NHL**	43	2	5	7	2	3	5	192	0	0	0	23	8.7	33	0	38	11	+6	2	0	0	0	4	0	0	0
1986-87	**New York Islanders**	**NHL**	68	0	10	10	0	7	7	356	0	0	0	34	0.0	47	1	64	21	+3	8	0	0	0	51	0	0	0
1987-88	**New York Islanders**	**NHL**	22	0	1	1	0	1	1	68	0	0	0	12	0.0	8	0	21	4	–9	....	....	....	....	....	....	....	....
	Springfield Indians	AHL	8	1	0	1	....	....	....	43	....	....	....	....	....	....	....	....	....	....	....	....	....	....	....	....	....	....
	Toronto Maple Leafs	**NHL**	7	0	1	1	0	1	1	19	0	0	0	1	0.0	6	0	3	0	+3	6	0	0	0	41	0	0	0
1988-89	**Toronto Maple Leafs**	**NHL**	47	1	4	5	1	3	4	185	0	0	0	18	5.6	24	0	30	6	0	....	....	....	....	....	....	....	....
1989-90	**Toronto Maple Leafs**	**NHL**	72	2	9	11	2	6	8	301	0	0	0	21	9.5	49	0	70	19	–2	5	0	1	1	19	0	0	0
1990-91	**Toronto Maple Leafs**	**NHL**	4	0	0	0	0	0	0	7	0	0	0	0	0.0	0	0	2	0	–2	....	....	....	....	....	....	....	....
	Newmarket Saints	AHL	6	0	1	1	....	....	....	32	....	....	....	....	....	....	....	....	....	....	....	....	....	....	....	....	....	....
	Buffalo Sabres	**NHL**	17	0	1	1	0	1	1	43	0	0	0	7	0.0	8	0	11	0	–3	....	....	....	....	....	....	....	....
	Rochester Americans	AHL	10	0	0	0	....	....	....	36	....	....	....	....	....	....	....	....	....	....	....	....	....	....	....	....	....	....
1991-92	**Buffalo Sabres**	**NHL**	3	0	0	0	0	0	0	14	0	0	0	1	0.0	1	0	1	0	0	....	....	....	....	....	....	....	....
	Rochester Americans	AHL	36	0	3	3	....	....	....	122	....	....	....	....	....	....	....	....	....	....	....	....	....	....	....	....	....	....
1992-93	Cape Breton Oilers	AHL	61	2	24	26	....	....	....	223	....	....	....	....	....	....	....	....	....	....	12	0	3	3	12	....	....	....
1993-94	**Washington Capitals**	**NHL**	26	1	0	1	1	0	1	61	0	0	0	11	9.1	11	0	14	1	–2	....	....	....	....	....	....	....	....
	Portland Pirates	AHL	46	1	6	7	....	....	....	247	....	....	....	....	....	....	....	....	....	....	15	0	1	1	59	....	....	....
1994-95	Portland Pirates	AHL	59	2	10	12	....	....	....	328	....	....	....	....	....	....	....	....	....	....	7	0	0	0	24	....	....	....
1995-96	Portland Pirates	AHL	34	1	2	3	....	....	....	122	....	....	....	....	....	....	....	....	....	....	....	....	....	....	....	....	....	....
	Michigan K-Wings	IHL	18	0	5	5	....	....	....	55	....	....	....	....	....	....	....	....	....	....	10	0	4	4	38	....	....	....
1996-97	Philadelphia Phantoms	AHL	3	0	0	0	....	....	....	8	....	....	....	....	....	....	....	....	....	....	....	....	....	....	....	....	....	....
1997-98	Monroe Moccasins	WPHL	68	7	17	24	....	....	....	239	....	....	....	....	....	....	....	....	....	....	....	....	....	....	....	....	....	....
	Utah Grizzlies	IHL	1	0	0	0	....	....	....	2	....	....	....	....	....	....	....	....	....	....	....	....	....	....	....	....	....	....
	Las Vegas Thunder	IHL	9	0	2	2	....	....	....	49	....	....	....	....	....	....	....	....	....	....	2	0	0	0	20	....	....	....
	NHL Totals		381	7	33	40	7	24	31	1461	0	0	0	151	4.6	219	1	299	67		24	0	1	1	122	0	0	0

Signed as a free agent by **NY Islanders**, August 29, 1987. Traded to **Toronto** by **NY Islanders** for Toronto's 6th round choice (Pavel Gross) in 1988 Entry Draft, March 8, 1988. Traded to **Buffalo** by **Toronto** with Lou Franceschetti for Mike Foligno and Buffalo's 8th round choice (Thomas Kurcharcik) in 1991 Entry Draft, December 17, 1990. Signed as a free agent by **Edmonton**, October 27, 1992. Signed as a free agent by **Washington**, October 21, 1993.

• CURRIE, DAN

Dan Currie LW – L. 6'2", 195 lbs. b: Burlington, Ont., 3/15/1968. Edmonton's 4th choice, 84th overall, in 1986 Entry Draft.

Season	Club	League	GP	G	A	Pts	AG	AA	APts	PIM	PP	SH	GW	S	%	TGF	PGF	TGA	PGA	+/–	GP	G	A	Pts	PIM	PP	SH	GW
1985-86	Sault Ste. Marie Greyhounds	OHL	66	21	24	45	....	....	....	37	....	....	....	....	....	....	....	....	....	....	....	....	....	....	....	....	....	....
1986-87	Sault Ste. Marie Greyhounds	OHL	66	31	52	83	....	....	....	53	....	....	....	....	....	....	....	....	....	....	4	2	1	3	2	....	....	....
1987-88	Sault Ste. Marie Greyhounds	OHL	57	50	59	109	....	....	....	53	....	....	....	....	....	....	....	....	....	....	6	3	9	12	4	....	....	....
	Canada	WJC-A	7	4	3	7	....	....	....	2	....	....	....	....	....	....	....	....	....	....	....	....	....	....	....	....	....	....
	Nova Scotia Oilers	AHL	3	4	2	6	....	....	....	0	....	....	....	....	....	....	....	....	....	....	5	4	3	7	0	....	....	....
1988-89	Cape Breton Oilers	AHL	77	29	36	65	....	....	....	29	....	....	....	....	....	....	....	....	....	....	....	....	....	....	....	....	....	....
1989-90	Cape Breton Oilers	AHL	77	36	40	76	....	....	....	28	....	....	....	....	....	....	....	....	....	....	6	4	4	8	0	....	....	....
1990-91	**Edmonton Oilers**	**NHL**	5	0	0	0	0	0	0	0	0	0	0	5	0.0	0	0	0	0	0	....	....	....	....	....	....	....	....
	Cape Breton Oilers	AHL	71	47	45	92	....	....	....	51	....	....	....	....	....	....	....	....	....	....	4	3	1	4	8	....	....	....
1991-92	**Edmonton Oilers**	**NHL**	7	1	0	1	1	0	1	0	0	0	0	3	33.3	2	0	3	0	–1	....	....	....	....	....	....	....	....
	Cape Breton Oilers	AHL	66	*50	42	92	....	....	....	39	....	....	....	....	....	....	....	....	....	....	5	4	5	9	4	....	....	....
1992-93	**Edmonton Oilers**	**NHL**	5	0	0	0	0	0	0	4	0	0	0	11	0.0	0	0	4	0	–4	....	....	....	....	....	....	....	....
	Cape Breton Oilers	AHL	75	57	41	98	....	....	....	73	....	....	....	....	....	....	....	....	....	....	16	7	4	11	29	....	....	....
1993-94	**Los Angeles Kings**	**NHL**	5	1	1	2	1	1	2	0	0	0	0	12	8.3	3	0	4	0	–1	....	....	....	....	....	....	....	....
	Phoenix Roadrunners	IHL	74	37	49	86	....	....	....	96	....	....	....	....	....	....	....	....	....	....	....	....	....	....	....	....	....	....
1994-95	Phoenix Roadrunners	IHL	16	2	6	8	....	....	....	8	....	....	....	....	....	....	....	....	....	....	....	....	....	....	....	....	....	....
	Minnesota Moose	IHL	54	18	35	53	....	....	....	34	....	....	....	....	....	....	....	....	....	....	3	0	0	0	2	....	....	....
1995-96	Chicago Wolves	IHL	79	39	34	73	....	....	....	53	....	....	....	....	....	....	....	....	....	....	9	5	4	9	12	....	....	....
1996-97	Chicago Wolves	IHL	55	18	10	28	....	....	....	18	....	....	....	....	....	....	....	....	....	....	....	....	....	....	....	....	....	....
	Fort Wayne Komets	IHL	24	10	12	22	....	....	....	6	....	....	....	....	....	....	....	....	....	....	....	....	....	....	....	....	....	....
1997-98	Fort Wayne Komets	IHL	77	29	22	51	....	....	....	17	....	....	....	....	....	....	....	....	....	....	4	0	2	2	2	....	....	....
	NHL Totals		22	2	1	3	2	1	3	4	0	0	0	31	6.5	5	0	11	0		....	....	....	....	....	....	....	....

OHL First All-Star Team (1988) • AHL Second All-Star Team (1992) • AHL First All-Star Team (1993)

Signed as a free agent by **LA Kings**, July 16, 1993.

• CURRIE, GLEN

Glen Currie C – L. 6'2", 180 lbs. b: Montreal, Que., 7/18/1958. Washington's 5th choice, 38th overall, in 1978 Amateur Draft.

Season	Club	League	GP	G	A	Pts	AG	AA	APts	PIM	PP	SH	GW	S	%	TGF	PGF	TGA	PGA	+/–	GP	G	A	Pts	PIM	PP	SH	GW
1975-76	Laval National	QMJHL	72	15	54	69	....	....	....	20	....	....	....	....	....	....	....	....	....	....	....	....	....	....	....	....	....	....
1976-77	Laval National	QMJHL	72	28	51	79	....	....	....	42	....	....	....	....	....	....	....	....	....	....	7	1	4	5	15	....	....	....
1977-78	Laval National	QMJHL	72	63	82	145	....	....	....	29	....	....	....	....	....	....	....	....	....	....	5	3	1	4	0	....	....	....
1978-79	Port Huron Flags	IHL	69	27	36	63	....	....	....	43	....	....	....	....	....	....	....	....	....	....	7	5	4	9	2	....	....	....
1979-80	**Washington Capitals**	**NHL**	32	2	0	2	2	0	2	2	0	0	0	25	8.0	5	0	15	8	–2	....	....	....	....	....	....	....	....
	Hershey Bears	AHL	45	17	26	43	....	....	....	16	....	....	....	....	....	....	....	....	....	....	....	....	....	....	....	....	....	....
1980-81	**Washington Capitals**	**NHL**	40	5	13	18	4	9	13	16	2	1	0	52	9.6	26	7	43	19	–5	....	....	....	....	....	....	....	....
	Hershey Bears	AHL	35	18	21	39	....	....	....	10	....	....	....	....	....	....	....	....	....	....	....	....	....	....	....	....	....	....
1981-82	**Washington Capitals**	**NHL**	43	7	7	14	6	5	11	14	0	1	0	45	15.6	24	1	47	22	–2	....	....	....	....	....	....	....	....
	Hershey Bears	AHL	31	12	12	24	....	....	....	6	....	....	....	....	....	....	....	....	....	....	....	....	....	....	....	....	....	....
1982-83	**Washington Capitals**	**NHL**	68	11	28	39	9	19	28	20	0	0	2	54	20.4	50	0	50	18	+18	4	0	3	3	4	0	0	0
	Hershey Bears	AHL	12	5	11	16	....	....	....	6	....	....	....	....	....	....	....	....	....	....	....	....	....	....	....	....	....	....
1983-84	**Washington Capitals**	**NHL**	80	12	24	36	10	16	26	20	0	2	2	71	16.9	53	3	56	15	+9	8	1	0	1	0	0	0	0
1984-85	**Washington Capitals**	**NHL**	44	1	5	6	1	3	4	19	0	0	0	27	3.7	14	0	24	12	+2	....	....	....	....	....	....	....	....
	Binghamton Whalers	AHL	17	1	5	6	....	....	....	6	....	....	....	....	....	....	....	....	....	....	8	2	5	7	2	....	....	....
1985-86	**Los Angeles Kings**	**NHL**	12	1	2	3	1	1	2	9	1	0	0	11	9.1	5	1	9	5	0	....	....	....	....	....	....	....	....
	New Haven Nighthawks	AHL	8	0	4	4	....	....	....	2	....	....	....	....	....	....	....	....	....	....	2	0	0	0	10	....	....	....
1986-87	New Haven Nighthawks	AHL	54	12	16	28	....	....	....	16	....	....	....	....	....	....	....	....	....	....	6	2	1	3	0	....	....	....
1987-88	**Los Angeles Kings**	**NHL**	7	0	0	0	0	0	0	0	0	0	0	3	0.0	1	0	3	0	–2	....	....	....	....	....	....	....	....
	New Haven Nighthawks	AHL	55	15	19	34	....	....	....	14	....	....	....	....	....	....	....	....	....	....	....	....	....	....	....	....	....	....
	NHL Totals		326	39	79	118	33	53	86	100	3	4	4	288	13.5	178	12	247	99		12	1	3	4	4	0	0	0

QMJHL Second All-Star Team (1978)

Traded to **LA Kings** by **Washington** for Daryl Evans, September 9, 1995.

• CURRIE, TONY

Tony Currie RW – R. 5'11", 166 lbs. b: Sydney Mines, N.S., 11/12/1957. St. Louis' 4th choice, 63rd overall, in 1977 Amateur Draft.

Season	Club	League	GP	G	A	Pts	AG	AA	APts	PIM	PP	SH	GW	S	%	TGF	PGF	TGA	PGA	+/–	GP	G	A	Pts	PIM	PP	SH	GW
1973-74	Spruce Grove Mets	AJHL	29	20	16	36	....	....	....	35	....	....	....	....	....	....	....	....	....	....	....	....	....	....	....	....	....	....
	Edmonton Oil Kings	WCJHL	22	0	1	1	....	....	....	2	....	....	....	....	....	....	....	....	....	....	....	....	....	....	....	....	....	....
1974-75	Spruce Grove Mets	AJHL	35	36	44	80	....	....	....	73	....	....	....	....	....	....	....	....	....	....	....	....	....	....	....	....	....	....
1975-76	Edmonton Oil Kings	WHL	71	41	40	81	....	....	....	56	....	....	....	....	....	....	....	....	....	....	5	0	1	1	5	....	....	....
1976-77	Portland Winter Hawks	WCJHL	72	73	52	125	....	....	....	50	....	....	....	....	....	....	....	....	....	....	10	4	7	11	14	....	....	....
1977-78	**St. Louis Blues**	**NHL**	22	4	5	9	4	4	8	4	1	0	0	35	11.4	19	8	21	0	–10	....	....	....	....	....	....	....	....
	Salt Lake Golden Eagles	CHL	53	33	17	50	....	....	....	17	....	....	....	....	....	....	....	....	....	....	....	....	....	....	....	....	....	....
1978-79	**St. Louis Blues**	**NHL**	36	4	15	19	4	11	15	0	1	0	2	57	7.0	30	3	36	0	–9	....	....	....	....	....	....	....	....
	Salt Lake Golden Eagles	CHL	28	22	12	34	....	....	....	6	....	....	....	....	....	....	....	....	....	....	....	....	....	....	....	....	....	....
1979-80	**St. Louis Blues**	**NHL**	40	19	14	33	17	11	28	4	2	0	3	70	27.1	42	9	24	0	+9	2	0	0	0	0	0	0	0
	Salt Lake Golden Eagles	CHL	33	24	23	47	....	....	....	17	....	....	....	....	....	....	....	....	....	....	....	....	....	....	....	....	....	....
1980-81	**St. Louis Blues**	**NHL**	61	23	32	55	19	22	41	38	2	0	4	112	20.5	78	17	30	1	+32	11	4	12	16	4	1	0	0

			REGULAR SEASON																		PLAYOFFS							
Season	**Club**	**League**	**GP**	**G**	**A**	**Pts**	**AG**	**AA**	**APts**	**PIM**	**PP**	**SH**	**GW**	**S**	**%**	**TGF**	**PGF**	**TGA**	**PGA**	**+/–**	**GP**	**G**	**A**	**Pts**	**PIM**	**PP**	**SH**	**GW**
1981-82	**St. Louis Blues**	**NHL**	**48**	**18**	**22**	**40**	**14**	**15**	**29**	**17**	**4**	**0**	**2**	**103**	**17.5**	**57**	**15**	**49**	**0**	**–7**	....	....	....	....	....	....	....	....
	Vancouver Canucks	**NHL**	**12**	**5**	**3**	**8**	**4**	**2**	**6**	**2**	**2**	**0**	**0**	**29**	**17.2**	**12**	**2**	**9**	**0**	**+1**	**3**	**0**	**0**	**0**	**10**	**0**	**0**	**0**
1982-83	**Vancouver Canucks**	**NHL**	**8**	**1**	**1**	**2**	**1**	**1**	**2**	**0**	**0**	**0**	**0**	**6**	**16.7**	**3**	**0**	**6**	**0**	**–3**	....	....	....	....	....	....	....	....
	Fredericton Express	AHL	68	47	48	95	....	....	....	16	....	....	....	....	....	....	....	....	....	....	12	5	12	17	6	....	....	....
1983-84	**Vancouver Canucks**	**NHL**	**18**	**3**	**3**	**6**	**2**	**2**	**4**	**2**	**1**	**0**	**0**	**22**	**13.6**	**13**	**4**	**10**	**0**	**–1**	....	....	....	....	....	....	....	....
	Fredericton Express	AHL	12	6	11	17	....	....	....	16	....	....	....	....	....	....	....	....	....	....	....	....	....	....	....	....	....	....
	Hartford Whalers	**NHL**	**32**	**12**	**16**	**28**	**10**	**11**	**21**	**4**	**6**	**0**	**2**	**54**	**22.2**	**40**	**17**	**26**	**0**	**–3**	....	....	....	....	....	....	....	....
1984-85	**Hartford Whalers**	**NHL**	**13**	**3**	**8**	**11**	**2**	**5**	**7**	**12**	**1**	**0**	**0**	**20**	**15.0**	**16**	**7**	**13**	**0**	**–4**	....	....	....	....	....	....	....	....
	Nova Scotia Voyageurs	AHL	53	16	31	47	....	....	....	8	....	....	....	....	....	....	....	....	....	....	6	1	3	4	0	....	....	....
1985-86	Fredericton Express	AHL	75	35	40	75	....	....	....	23	....	....	....	....	....	....	....	....	....	....	6	5	2	7	4	....	....	....
1986-87	Schwenningen EG	Germany	37	28	32	60	....	....	....	86	....	....	....	....	....	....	....	....	....	....	....	....	....	....	....	....	....	....
	Kloten	Switz.	....	4	3	7	....	....	....	....	....	....	....	....	....	....	....	....	....	....	8	4	5	9	....	....	....	....
1987-88	Schwenningen EG	Germany	40	19	44	63	....	....	....	65	....	....	....	....	....	....	....	....	....	....	....	....	....	....	....	....	....	....
1988-89	Varese HC	Italy	49	39	44	83	....	....	....	36	....	....	....	....	....	....	....	....	....	....	....	....	....	....	....	....	....	....
1989-90	Varese HC	Italy	39	25	37	62	....	....	....	21	....	....	....	....	....	....	....	....	....	....	....	....	....	....	....	....	....	....
	NHL Totals		**290**	**92**	**119**	**211**	**77**	**84**	**161**	**83**	**20**	**0**	**13**	**508**	**18.1**	**310**	**82**	**224**	**1**		**16**	**4**	**12**	**16**	**14**	**1**	**0**	**0**

CHL First All-Star Team (1978) • AHL First All-Star Team (1983) • IHL Second All-Star Team (1986)

Traded to **Vancouver** by **St. Louis** with Jim Nill, Rick Heinz and St. Louis' 4th round choice (Shawn Kilroy) in 1982 Entry Draft for Glen Hanlon, March 9, 1982. Signed as a free agent by **Hartford**, January 21, 1984. Claimed on waivers by **Edmonton** from **Hartford**, December 5, 1984. Signed as a free agent by **Quebec**, August 25, 1985.

• CURTALE, TONY

Tony Curtale D – L. 6′, 185 lbs. b: Detroit, MI, 1/29/1962. Calgary's 2nd choice, 31st overall, in 1980 Entry Draft.

1979-80	Brantford Alexanders	OHA	59	10	35	45	....	....	....	227	....	....	....	....	....	....	....	....	....	....	5	0	4	4	4	....	....	....
1980-81	Brantford Alexanders	OHA	59	14	71	85	....	....	....	141	....	....	....	....	....	....	....	....	....	....	6	1	4	5	26	....	....	....
	Calgary Flames	**NHL**	**2**	**0**	**0**	**0**	**0**	**0**	**0**	**0**	**0**	**0**	**0**	**4**	**0.0**	**0**	**0**	**1**	**0**	**–1**	....	....	....	....	....	....	....	....
1981-82	Brantford Alexanders	OHL	36	17	32	49	....	....	....	118	....	....	....	....	....	....	....	....	....	....	8	1	2	3	35	....	....	....
	Oklahoma City Stars	CHL	....	....	....	....	....	....	....	....	....	....	....	....	....	....	....	....	....	....	4	0	2	2	8	....	....	....
1982-83	Colorado Flames	CHL	74	7	22	29	....	....	....	61	....	....	....	....	....	....	....	....	....	....	5	1	0	1	6	....	....	....
1983-84	Peoria Prancers	IHL	2	0	0	0	....	....	....	2	....	....	....	....	....	....	....	....	....	....	....	....	....	....	....	....	....	....
	Colorado Flames	CHL	54	3	20	23	....	....	....	80	....	....	....	....	....	....	....	....	....	....	6	0	4	4	2	....	....	....
1984-85	Peoria Rivermen	IHL	50	5	31	36	....	....	....	81	....	....	....	....	....	....	....	....	....	....	17	1	7	8	43	....	....	....
1985-86	Peoria Rivermen	IHL	70	7	51	58	....	....	....	116	....	....	....	....	....	....	....	....	....	....	11	1	3	4	57	....	....	....
1986-87	Peoria Rivermen	IHL	72	8	21	29	....	....	....	126	....	....	....	....	....	....	....	....	....	....	....	....	....	....	....	....	....	....
	NHL Totals		**2**	**0**	**0**	**0**	**0**	**0**	**0**	**0**	**0**	**0**	**0**	**4**	**0.0**	**0**	**0**	**1**	**0**		....	....	....	....	....	....	....	....

• CURTIS, PAUL

Paul Curtis D – L. 6′, 185 lbs. b: Peterborough, Ont., 9/29/1947.

1963-64	Peterborough Petes	OHA	2	0	1	1	....	....	....	7	....	....	....	....	....	....	....	....	....	....	1	0	0	0	4	....	....	....
1964-65	Peterborough Petes	OHA	56	0	7	7	....	....	....	90	....	....	....	....	....	....	....	....	....	....	12	0	2	2	19	....	....	....
1965-66	Peterborough Petes	OHA	48	3	17	20	....	....	....	116	....	....	....	....	....	....	....	....	....	....	6	1	1	2	9	....	....	....
1966-67	Peterborough Petes	OHA	44	2	8	10	....	....	....	91	....	....	....	....	....	....	....	....	....	....	0	1	2	3	2	....	....	....
1967-68	Houston Apollos	CHL	62	1	8	9	....	....	....	150	....	....	....	....	....	....	....	....	....	....	....	....	....	....	....	....	....	....
1968-69	Houston Apollos	CHL	70	3	27	30	....	....	....	72	....	....	....	....	....	....	....	....	....	....	3	0	0	0	0	....	....	....
1969-70	**Montreal Canadiens**	**NHL**	**1**	**0**	**0**	**0**	**0**	**0**	**0**	**0**	**0**	**0**	**0**	**1**	**0.0**	**0**	**0**	**1**	**0**	**–1**	....	....	....	....	....	....	....	....
	Montreal Voyageurs	AHL	69	3	27	30	....	....	....	52	....	....	....	....	....	....	....	....	....	....	8	0	5	5	4	....	....	....
1970-71	**Los Angeles Kings**	**NHL**	**64**	**1**	**13**	**14**	**1**	**11**	**12**	**82**	**0**	**0**	**0**	**66**	**1.5**	**46**	**2**	**71**	**9**	**–18**	....	....	....	....	....	....	....	....
1971-72	**Los Angeles Kings**	**NHL**	**64**	**1**	**12**	**13**	**1**	**11**	**12**	**57**	**0**	**0**	**0**	**66**	**1.5**	**65**	**1**	**109**	**13**	**–32**	....	....	....	....	....	....	....	....
1972-73	**Los Angeles Kings**	**NHL**	**27**	**0**	**5**	**5**	**0**	**4**	**4**	**16**	**0**	**0**	**0**	**16**	**0.0**	**17**	**0**	**20**	**1**	**–2**	....	....	....	....	....	....	....	....
	St. Louis Blues	**NHL**	**29**	**1**	**4**	**5**	**1**	**3**	**4**	**6**	**0**	**0**	**0**	**37**	**2.7**	**23**	**1**	**22**	**2**	**+2**	**5**	**0**	**0**	**0**	**2**	**0**	**0**	**0**
1973-74	Cincinnati Swords	AHL	42	1	7	8	....	....	....	33	....	....	....	....	....	....	....	....	....	....	....	....	....	....	....	....	....	....
	Providence Reds	AHL	24	2	14	16	....	....	....	4	....	....	....	....	....	....	....	....	....	....	15	5	8	13	22	....	....	....
1974-75	Michigan-Baltimore	WHA	76	4	15	19	....	....	....	32	....	....	....	....	....	....	....	....	....	....	....	....	....	....	....	....	....	....
1975-76	Baltimore Clippers	AHL	54	2	8	10	....	....	....	33	....	....	....	....	....	....	....	....	....	....	....	....	....	....	....	....	....	....
	NHL Totals		**185**	**3**	**34**	**37**	**3**	**29**	**32**	**161**	**0**	**0**	**0**	**186**	**1.6**	**151**	**4**	**223**	**25**		**5**	**0**	**0**	**0**	**2**	**0**	**0**	**0**
	Other Major League Totals		76	4	15	19	....	....	....	32	....	....	....	....	....	....	....	....	....	....	....	....	....	....	....	....	....	....

AHL Second All-Star Team (1970)

Claimed by **LA Kings** from **Montreal** in Intra-League Draft, June 9, 1970. Traded to **St. Louis** by **LA Kings** for Frank St. Marseille, January 22, 1973. Traded to **Buffalo** by **St. Louis** for Jake Rathwell, June 14, 1973. Traded to **NY Rangers** by **Buffalo** for Real Lemieux, January 21, 1974. Signed as a free agent by **Michigan** (WHA), August, 1974. Signed as a free agent by **Baltimore** (AHL), November, 1975.

• CUSSON, JEAN

Jean Cusson LW – L. 5′10″, 170 lbs. b: Verdun, Que., 10/5/1942.

1964-65	University of Montreal	OQAA	15	19	16	35	....	....	....	....	....	....	....	....	....	....	....	....	....	....	....	....	....	....	....	....	....	....
1965-66	Canada	Nat-Team	STATISTICS NOT AVAILABLE																									
1966-67	Canada	Nat-Team	STATISTICS NOT AVAILABLE																									
	Canada	WEC-A	7	3	0	3	....	....	....	0	....	....	....	....	....	....	....	....	....	....	....	....	....	....	....	....	....	....
1967-68	Canada	Nat-Team	....	15	7	22	....	....	....	6	....	....	....	....	....	....	....	....	....	....	....	....	....	....	....	....	....	....
	Ottawa Nationals	OHA Sr.	8	6	6	12	....	....	....	0	....	....	....	....	....	....	....	....	....	....	....	....	....	....	....	....	....	....
	Oakland Seals	**NHL**	**2**	**0**	**0**	**0**	**0**	**0**	**0**	**0**	**0**	**0**	**0**	**1**	**0.0**	**0**	**0**	**1**	**0**	**–1**	....	....	....	....	....	....	....	....
	NHL Totals		**2**	**0**	**0**	**0**	**0**	**0**	**0**	**0**	**0**	**0**	**0**	**1**	**0.0**	**0**	**0**	**1**	**0**		....	....	....	....	....	....	....	....

Signed as a free agent by **Oakland** to three-game amateur tryout contract, March, 1968.

• CYR, DENIS

Denis Cyr RW – L. 5′10″, 180 lbs. b: Verdun, Que., 2/4/1961. Calgary's 1st choice, 13th overall, in 1980 Entry Draft.

1977-78	Montreal Jr. Canadiens	QMJHL	72	46	55	101	....	....	....	25	....	....	....	....	....	....	....	....	....	....	....	....	....	....	....	....	....	....
1978-79	Montreal Jr. Canadiens	QMJHL	70	70	56	126	....	....	....	88	....	....	....	....	....	....	....	....	....	....	11	7	5	12	26	....	....	....
1979-80	Montreal Jr. Canadiens	QMJHL	70	70	76	146	....	....	....	61	....	....	....	....	....	....	....	....	....	....	10	10	13	23	6	....	....	....
1980-81	Montreal Jr. Canadiens	QMJHL	57	50	40	90	....	....	....	53	....	....	....	....	....	....	....	....	....	....	7	6	6	12	37	....	....	....
	Canada	WJC-A	5	2	1	3	....	....	....	0	....	....	....	....	....	....	....	....	....	....	....	....	....	....	....	....	....	....
	Calgary Flames	**NHL**	**10**	**1**	**4**	**5**	**1**	**3**	**4**	**0**	**0**	**0**	**0**	**10**	**10.0**	**9**	**1**	**6**	**0**	**+2**	....	....	....	....	....	....	....	....
1981-82	**Calgary Flames**	**NHL**	**45**	**12**	**10**	**22**	**9**	**7**	**16**	**13**	**2**	**0**	**2**	**71**	**16.9**	**43**	**9**	**29**	**0**	**+5**	....	....	....	....	....	....	....	....
	Oklahoma City Stars	CHL	14	10	4	14	....	....	....	16	....	....	....	....	....	....	....	....	....	....	....	....	....	....	....	....	....	....
1982-83	**Calgary Flames**	**NHL**	**11**	**1**	**1**	**2**	**1**	**1**	**2**	**0**	**0**	**0**	**0**	**15**	**6.7**	**7**	**0**	**6**	**0**	**+1**	....	....	....	....	....	....	....	....
	Chicago Black Hawks	**NHL**	**41**	**7**	**8**	**15**	**6**	**6**	**12**	**2**	**0**	**0**	**0**	**36**	**19.4**	**19**	**2**	**11**	**0**	**+6**	**1**	**0**	**0**	**0**	**0**	**0**	**0**	**0**
1983-84	**Chicago Black Hawks**	**NHL**	**46**	**12**	**13**	**25**	**10**	**9**	**19**	**19**	**6**	**0**	**1**	**72**	**16.7**	**46**	**14**	**33**	**1**	**0**	....	....	....	....	....	....	....	....
	Springfield Indians	AHL	17	4	13	17	....	....	....	11	....	....	....	....	....	....	....	....	....	....	3	0	0	0	0	....	....	....
1984-85	**St. Louis Blues**	**NHL**	**9**	**5**	**3**	**8**	**4**	**2**	**6**	**0**	**0**	**0**	**1**	**12**	**41.7**	**10**	**1**	**11**	**3**	**+1**	**3**	**0**	**0**	**0**	**0**	**0**	**0**	**0**
	Peoria Rivermen	IHL	62	26	51	77	....	....	....	28	....	....	....	....	....	....	....	....	....	....	20	*18	14	*32	14	....	....	....
1985-86	**St. Louis Blues**	**NHL**	**31**	**3**	**4**	**7**	**2**	**3**	**5**	**2**	**0**	**0**	**0**	**21**	**14.3**	**9**	**0**	**22**	**2**	**–11**	....	....	....	....	....	....	....	....
	Peoria Rivermen	IHL	34	15	26	41	....	....	....	15	....	....	....	....	....	....	....	....	....	....	11	5	4	9	2	....	....	....
1986-87	Peoria Rivermen	IHL	81	29	41	70	....	....	....	10	....	....	....	....	....	....	....	....	....	....	....	....	....	....	....	....	....	....
	NHL Totals		**193**	**41**	**43**	**84**	**33**	**31**	**64**	**36**	**8**	**0**	**4**	**237**	**17.3**	**143**	**27**	**118**	**6**		**4**	**0**	**0**	**0**	**0**	**0**	**0**	**0**

QMJHL Second All-Star Team (1979) • QMJHL First All-Star Team (1980)

Traded to **Chicago** by **Calgary** for the rights to Carey Wilson, November 8, 1982. Signed as a free agent by **St. Louis**, September 14, 1984.

• CYR, PAUL

Paul Cyr LW – L. 5′10″, 180 lbs. b: Port Alberni, B.C., 10/31/1963. Buffalo's 2nd choice, 9th overall, in 1982 Entry Draft.

1979-80	Nanaimo Nuggets	BCJHL	60	28	52	80	....	....	....	202	....	....	....	....	....	....	....	....	....	....	....	....	....	....	....	....	....	....
1980-81	Victoria Cougars	WHL	64	36	22	58	....	....	....	85	....	....	....	....	....	....	....	....	....	....	14	6	5	11	46	....	....	....
1981-82	Victoria Cougars	WHL	58	52	56	108	....	....	....	107	....	....	....	....	....	....	....	....	....	....	4	3	2	5	12	....	....	....
	Canada	WJC-A	7	4	6	10	....	....	....	12	....	....	....	....	....	....	....	....	....	....	....	....	....	....	....	....	....	....
1982-83	Victoria Cougars	WHL	20	21	22	43	....	....	....	61	....	....	....	....	....	....	....	....	....	....	....	....	....	....	....	....	....	....
	Canada	WJC-A	7	1	3	4	....	....	....	19	....	....	....	....	....	....	....	....	....	....	....	....	....	....	....	....	....	....
	Buffalo Sabres	**NHL**	**36**	**15**	**12**	**27**	**12**	**8**	**20**	**59**	**5**	**0**	**2**	**65**	**23.1**	**46**	**16**	**36**	**0**	**–6**	**10**	**1**	**3**	**4**	**6**	**1**	**0**	**0**

			REGULAR SEASON																		PLAYOFFS							
Season	Club	League	GP	G	A	Pts	AG	AA	APts	PIM	PP	SH	GW	S	%	TGF	PGF	TGA	PGA	+/–	GP	G	A	Pts	PIM	PP	SH	GW
1983-84	**Buffalo Sabres**	**NHL**	**71**	**16**	**27**	**43**	**13**	**18**	**31**	**52**	**5**	**0**	**1**	**142**	**11.3**	**73**	**30**	**46**	**0**	**–3**	**3**	**0**	**1**	**1**	**0**	**0**	**0**	**0**
1984-85	**Buffalo Sabres**	**NHL**	**71**	**22**	**24**	**46**	**18**	**16**	**34**	**63**	**5**	**0**	**1**	**169**	**13.0**	**73**	**21**	**60**	**1**	**–7**	**5**	**2**	**2**	**4**	**15**	**0**	**0**	**0**
1985-86	**Buffalo Sabres**	**NHL**	**71**	**20**	**31**	**51**	**16**	**21**	**37**	**120**	**4**	**1**	**2**	**151**	**13.2**	**87**	**31**	**61**	**9**	**+4**	....	....	....	....	....	....	....	....
1986-87	**Buffalo Sabres**	**NHL**	**73**	**11**	**16**	**27**	**10**	**12**	**22**	**122**	**0**	**0**	**1**	**131**	**8.4**	**45**	**0**	**99**	**38**	**–16**	....	....	....	....	....	....	....	....
1987-88	**Buffalo Sabres**	**NHL**	**20**	**1**	**1**	**2**	**1**	**1**	**2**	**38**	**0**	**1**	**1**	**20**	**5.0**	**10**	**2**	**18**	**8**	**–2**	....	....	....	....	....	....	....	....
	New York Rangers	**NHL**	**40**	**4**	**13**	**17**	**3**	**9**	**12**	**41**	**1**	**1**	**0**	**72**	**5.6**	**23**	**3**	**35**	**10**	**–5**	....	....	....	....	....	....	....	....
1988-89	**New York Rangers**	**NHL**	**1**	**0**	**0**	**0**	**0**	**0**	**0**	**2**	**0**	**0**	**0**	**0**	**0.0**	**0**	**0**	**0**	**0**	**0**	....	....	....	....	....	....	....	....
1989-90	**New York Rangers**	**NHL**	DID NOT PLAY – INJURED																									
1990-91	**Hartford Whalers**	**NHL**	**70**	**12**	**13**	**25**	**11**	**10**	**21**	**107**	**0**	**1**	**2**	**128**	**9.4**	**37**	**2**	**65**	**22**	**–8**	**6**	**1**	**0**	**1**	**10**	**0**	**0**	**0**
1991-92	**Hartford Whalers**	**NHL**	**17**	**0**	**3**	**3**	**0**	**2**	**2**	**19**	**0**	**0**	**0**	**20**	**0.0**	**4**	**0**	**15**	**7**	**–4**	....	....	....	....	....	....	....	....
	Springfield Indians	AHL	43	11	18	29	....	....	....	30	....	....	....	....	....	....	....	....	....	....	11	0	3	3	12	....	....	....
1992-93	Springfield Indians	AHL	41	7	14	21	....	....	....	44	....	....	....	....	....	....	....	....	....	....	15	3	2	5	12	....	....	....
	NHL Totals		**470**	**101**	**140**	**241**	**84**	**97**	**181**	**623**	**20**	**4**	**10**	**898**	**11.2**	**398**	**105**	**435**	**95**		**24**	**4**	**6**	**10**	**31**	**1**	**0**	**0**

WHL Second All-Star Team (1982)

Traded to **NY Rangers** by **Buffalo** with Buffalo's 10th round choice (Eric Fenton) in 1988 Entry Draft for Mike Donnelly and NY Rangers' 5th round choice (Alexander Mogilny) in 1988 Entry Draft, December 31, 1987. • Missed entire 1988-89 season recovering from off-season knee surgery. Signed as a free agent by **Hartford**, September 30, 1990.

• CZERKAWSKI, MARIUSZ

Mariusz Czerkawski RW – L. 6', 195 lbs. b: Radomsko, Poland, 4/13/1972. Boston's 5th choice, 106th overall, in 1991 Entry Draft.

Season	Club	League	GP	G	A	Pts	AG	AA	APts	PIM	PP	SH	GW	S	%	TGF	PGF	TGA	PGA	+/–	GP	G	A	Pts	PIM	PP	SH	GW
1989-90	Poland	WJC-A	7	1	0	1	....	....	....	4	....	....	....	....	....	....	....	....	....	....	....	....	....	....	....	....	....	....
1990-91	GKS Tychy	Poland	24	25	15	40	....	....	....	....	....	....	....	....	....	....	....	....	....	....	....	....	....	....	....	....	....	....
	Poland	WJC-B	7	12	3	15	....	....	....	2	....	....	....	....	....	....	....	....	....	....	....	....	....	....	....	....	....	....
	Poland	WEC-B	7	6	2	8	....	....	....	4	....	....	....	....	....	....	....	....	....	....	....	....	....	....	....	....	....	....
1991-92	Djurgarden IF Stockholm	Sweden	39	8	5	13	....	....	....	4	....	....	....	....	....	....	....	....	....	....	3	0	0	0	2	....	....	....
	Poland	Olympics	5	0	1	1	....	....	....	4	....	....	....	....	....	....	....	....	....	....	....	....	....	....	....	....	....	....
	Poland	WC-A	6	0	0	0	....	....	....	4	....	....	....	....	....	....	....	....	....	....	....	....	....	....	....	....	....	....
1992-93	Hammarby	Sweden 2	32	39	30	69	....	....	....	74	....	....	....	....	....	....	....	....	....	....	....	....	....	....	....	....	....	....
1993-94	Djurgarden IF Stockholm	Sweden	39	13	21	34	....	....	....	20	....	....	....	....	....	....	....	....	....	....	6	3	1	4	2	....	....	....
	Boston Bruins	**NHL**	**4**	**2**	**1**	**3**	**2**	**1**	**3**	**0**	**1**	**0**	**0**	**11**	**18.2**	**4**	**1**	**5**	**0**	**–2**	**13**	**3**	**3**	**6**	**4**	**1**	**0**	**0**
1994-95	Kiekko-Espoo	Finland	7	9	3	12	....	....	....	10	....	....	....	....	....	....	....	....	....	....	....	....	....	....	....	....	....	....
	Boston Bruins	**NHL**	**47**	**12**	**14**	**26**	**21**	**21**	**42**	**31**	**1**	**0**	**2**	**126**	**9.5**	**42**	**15**	**23**	**0**	**+4**	**5**	**1**	**0**	**1**	**0**	**0**	**0**	**0**
1995-96	**Boston Bruins**	**NHL**	**33**	**5**	**6**	**11**	**5**	**5**	**10**	**10**	**1**	**0**	**0**	**63**	**7.9**	**16**	**1**	**26**	**0**	**–11**	....	....	....	....	....	....	....	....
	Edmonton Oilers	**NHL**	**37**	**12**	**17**	**29**	**12**	**14**	**26**	**8**	**2**	**0**	**1**	**79**	**15.2**	**41**	**10**	**24**	**0**	**+7**	....	....	....	....	....	....	....	....
1996-97	**Edmonton Oilers**	**NHL**	**76**	**26**	**21**	**47**	**28**	**19**	**47**	**16**	**4**	**0**	**3**	**182**	**14.3**	**61**	**18**	**43**	**0**	**0**	**12**	**2**	**1**	**3**	**10**	**0**	**0**	**0**
1997-98	**New York Islanders**	**NHL**	**68**	**12**	**13**	**25**	**14**	**13**	**27**	**23**	**2**	**0**	**1**	**136**	**8.8**	**37**	**6**	**20**	**0**	**+11**	....	....	....	....	....	....	....	....
	NHL Totals		**265**	**69**	**72**	**141**	**82**	**73**	**155**	**88**	**11**	**0**	**7**	**597**	**11.6**	**201**	**51**	**141**	**0**		**30**	**6**	**4**	**10**	**14**	**1**	**0**	**0**

Named Best Player at WJC-B (1990)

Traded to **Edmonton** by **Boston** with Sean Brown and Boston's 1st round choice (Matthieu Descoteaux) in 1996 Entry Draft for Bill Ranford, January 11, 1996. Traded to **NY Islanders** by **Edmonton** for Dan Lacouture, August 25, 1997.

• DACKELL, ANDREAS

Andreas Dackell RW – R. 5'11", 191 lbs. b: Gavle, Sweden, 12/29/1972. Ottawa's 3rd choice, 136th overall, in 1996 Entry Draft.

Season	Club	League	GP	G	A	Pts	AG	AA	APts	PIM	PP	SH	GW	S	%	TGF	PGF	TGA	PGA	+/–	GP	G	A	Pts	PIM	PP	SH	GW
1990-91	Brynas IF Gavle	Sweden	3	0	1	1	....	....	....	2	....	....	....	....	....	....	....	....	....	....	....	....	....	....	....	....	....	....
1991-92	Brynas IF Gavle	Sweden	4	0	0	0	....	....	....	2	....	....	....	....	....	....	....	....	....	....	2	0	1	1	4	....	....	....
1992-93	Brynas IF Gavle	Sweden	40	12	15	27	....	....	....	12	....	....	....	....	....	....	....	....	....	....	10	4	5	9	2	....	....	....
1993-94	Brynas IF Gavle	Sweden	38	12	17	29	....	....	....	47	....	....	....	....	....	....	....	....	....	....	7	2	2	4	8	....	....	....
	Sweden	Olympics	4	0	0	0	....	....	....	0	....	....	....	....	....	....	....	....	....	....	....	....	....	....	....	....	....	....
	Sweden	WC-A	7	2	2	4	....	....	....	25	....	....	....	....	....	....	....	....	....	....	....	....	....	....	....	....	....	....
1994-95	Brynas IF Gavle	Sweden	39	17	16	33	....	....	....	34	....	....	....	....	....	....	....	....	....	....	14	3	3	6	14	....	....	....
	Sweden	WC-A	8	3	4	7	....	....	....	4	....	....	....	....	....	....	....	....	....	....	....	....	....	....	....	....	....	....
1995-96	Brynas IF Gavle	Sweden	22	6	6	12	....	....	....	8	....	....	....	....	....	....	....	....	....	....	....	....	....	....	....	....	....	....
	Sweden	WC-A	6	0	1	1	....	....	....	0	....	....	....	....	....	....	....	....	....	....	....	....	....	....	....	....	....	....
1996-97	**Ottawa Senators**	**NHL**	**79**	**12**	**19**	**31**	**13**	**17**	**30**	**8**	**2**	**0**	**3**	**79**	**15.2**	**53**	**14**	**47**	**2**	**–6**	**7**	**1**	**0**	**1**	**0**	**0**	**0**	**0**
1997-98	**Ottawa Senators**	**NHL**	**82**	**15**	**18**	**33**	**18**	**18**	**36**	**24**	**3**	**2**	**2**	**130**	**11.5**	**58**	**13**	**70**	**14**	**–11**	**11**	**1**	**1**	**2**	**2**	**1**	**0**	**0**
	NHL Totals		**161**	**27**	**37**	**64**	**31**	**35**	**66**	**32**	**5**	**2**	**5**	**209**	**12.9**	**111**	**27**	**117**	**16**		**18**	**2**	**1**	**3**	**2**	**1**	**0**	**0**

• DAHL, KEVIN

Kevin Dahl D – R. 5'11", 190 lbs. b: Regina, Sask., 12/30/1968. Montreal's 12th choice, 230th overall, in 1988 Entry Draft.

Season	Club	League	GP	G	A	Pts	AG	AA	APts	PIM	PP	SH	GW	S	%	TGF	PGF	TGA	PGA	+/–	GP	G	A	Pts	PIM	PP	SH	GW
1986-87	Bowling Green University	CCHA	32	2	6	8	....	....	....	54	....	....	....	....	....	....	....	....	....	....	....	....	....	....	....	....	....	....
1987-88	Bowling Green University	CCHA	44	2	23	25	....	....	....	78	....	....	....	....	....	....	....	....	....	....	....	....	....	....	....	....	....	....
1988-89	Bowling Green University	CCHA	46	9	26	35	....	....	....	51	....	....	....	....	....	....	....	....	....	....	....	....	....	....	....	....	....	....
1989-90	Bowling Green University	CCHA	43	8	22	30	....	....	....	74	....	....	....	....	....	....	....	....	....	....	....	....	....	....	....	....	....	....
1990-91	Fredericton Canadiens	AHL	32	1	15	16	....	....	....	45	....	....	....	....	....	....	....	....	....	....	9	0	1	1	11	....	....	....
	Winston-Salem Thunderbirds	ECHL	36	7	17	24	....	....	....	58	....	....	....	....	....	....	....	....	....	....	....	....	....	....	....	....	....	....
1991-92	Canada	Nat-Team	45	2	15	17	....	....	....	44	....	....	....	....	....	....	....	....	....	....	....	....	....	....	....	....	....	....
	Canada	Olympics	8	2	0	2	....	....	....	6	....	....	....	....	....	....	....	....	....	....	....	....	....	....	....	....	....	....
	Salt Lake Golden Eagles	IHL	13	0	2	2	....	....	....	12	....	....	....	....	....	....	....	....	....	....	5	0	0	0	13	....	....	....
1992-93	**Calgary Flames**	**NHL**	**61**	**2**	**9**	**11**	**2**	**6**	**8**	**56**	**1**	**0**	**0**	**40**	**5.0**	**57**	**3**	**75**	**30**	**+9**	**6**	**0**	**2**	**2**	**8**	**0**	**0**	**0**
1993-94	**Calgary Flames**	**NHL**	**33**	**0**	**3**	**3**	**0**	**2**	**2**	**23**	**0**	**0**	**0**	**20**	**0.0**	**18**	**1**	**34**	**15**	**–2**	**6**	**0**	**0**	**0**	**4**	**0**	**0**	**0**
	Saint John Flames	AHL	2	0	0	0	....	....	....	0	....	....	....	....	....	....	....	....	....	....	....	....	....	....	....	....	....	....
1994-95	**Calgary Flames**	**NHL**	**34**	**4**	**8**	**12**	**7**	**12**	**19**	**38**	**0**	**0**	**0**	**30**	**13.3**	**24**	**0**	**31**	**15**	**+8**	**3**	**0**	**0**	**0**	**0**	**0**	**0**	**0**
1995-96	**Calgary Flames**	**NHL**	**32**	**1**	**1**	**2**	**1**	**1**	**2**	**26**	**0**	**0**	**1**	**17**	**5.9**	**15**	**1**	**23**	**7**	**–2**	**1**	**0**	**0**	**0**	**0**	**0**	**0**	**0**
	Saint John Flames	AHL	23	4	11	15	....	....	....	37	....	....	....	....	....	....	....	....	....	....	....	....	....	....	....	....	....	....
1996-97	**Phoenix Coyotes**	**NHL**	**2**	**0**	**0**	**0**	**0**	**0**	**0**	**0**	**0**	**0**	**0**	**2**	**0.0**	**0**	**0**	**0**	**0**	**0**	....	....	....	....	....	....	....	....
	Las Vegas Thunder	IHL	73	10	21	31	....	....	....	101	....	....	....	....	....	....	....	....	....	....	3	0	0	0	2	....	....	....
1997-98	**Calgary Flames**	**NHL**	**19**	**0**	**1**	**1**	**0**	**1**	**1**	**6**	**0**	**0**	**0**	**17**	**0.0**	**10**	**1**	**19**	**7**	**–3**	....	....	....	....	....	....	....	....
	Chicago Wolves	IHL	45	8	9	17	....	....	....	61	....	....	....	....	....	....	....	....	....	....	20	1	8	9	32	....	....	....
	NHL Totals		**181**	**7**	**22**	**29**	**10**	**22**	**32**	**149**	**1**	**0**	**1**	**126**	**5.6**	**124**	**6**	**182**	**74**		**16**	**0**	**2**	**2**	**12**	**0**	**0**	**0**

Signed as a free agent by **Calgary**, July 27, 1991. Signed as a free agent by **Phoenix**, September 4, 1996.

• DAHLEN, ULF

Ulf Dahlen RW – L. 6'2", 195 lbs. b: Ostersund, Sweden, 1/12/1967. NY Rangers' 1st choice, 7th overall, in 1985 Entry Draft.

Season	Club	League	GP	G	A	Pts	AG	AA	APts	PIM	PP	SH	GW	S	%	TGF	PGF	TGA	PGA	+/–	GP	G	A	Pts	PIM	PP	SH	GW
1983-84	Ostersund	Sweden 2	36	15	11	26	....	....	....	10	....	....	....	....	....	....	....	....	....	....	....	....	....	....	....	....	....	....
1984-85	Ostersund	Sweden 2	36	33	26	59	....	....	....	20	....	....	....	....	....	....	....	....	....	....	....	....	....	....	....	....	....	....
1985-86	IF Bjorkloven Umea	Sweden	22	4	3	7	....	....	....	8	....	....	....	....	....	....	....	....	....	....	....	....	....	....	....	....	....	....
	Sweden	WJC-A	7	3	4	7	....	....	....	4	....	....	....	....	....	....	....	....	....	....	....	....	....	....	....	....	....	....
1986-87	IF Bjorkloven Umea	Sweden	31	9	12	21	....	....	....	20	....	....	....	....	....	....	....	....	....	....	6	6	2	8	4	....	....	....
	Sweden	WJC-A	7	7	8	15	....	....	....	2	....	....	....	....	....	....	....	....	....	....	....	....	....	....	....	....	....	....
1987-88	**New York Rangers**	**NHL**	**70**	**29**	**23**	**52**	**25**	**16**	**41**	**26**	**11**	**0**	**4**	**159**	**18.2**	**73**	**27**	**41**	**0**	**+5**	....	....	....	....	....	....	....	....
	Colorado Rangers	IHL	2	2	2	4	....	....	....	0	....	....	....	....	....	....	....	....	....	....	....	....	....	....	....	....	....	....
1988-89	**New York Rangers**	**NHL**	**56**	**24**	**19**	**43**	**20**	**13**	**33**	**50**	**8**	**0**	**1**	**147**	**16.3**	**64**	**26**	**44**	**0**	**–6**	**4**	**0**	**0**	**0**	**0**	**0**	**0**	**0**
	Sweden	WEC-A	10	2	2	4	....	....	....	4	....	....	....	....	....	....	....	....	....	....	....	....	....	....	....	....	....	....
1989-90	**New York Rangers**	**NHL**	**63**	**18**	**18**	**36**	**16**	**13**	**29**	**30**	**13**	**0**	**4**	**111**	**16.2**	**66**	**38**	**32**	**0**	**–4**	....	....	....	....	....	....	....	....
	Minnesota North Stars	**NHL**	**13**	**2**	**4**	**6**	**2**	**3**	**5**	**0**	**0**	**0**	**0**	**24**	**8.3**	**14**	**4**	**9**	**0**	**+1**	**7**	**1**	**4**	**5**	**2**	**0**	**0**	**0**
1990-91	Minnesota North Stars	FrTour	4	0	0	0	....	....	....	0	....	....	....	....	....	....	....	....	....	....	....	....	....	....	....	....	....	....
	Minnesota North Stars	**NHL**	**66**	**21**	**18**	**39**	**19**	**14**	**33**	**6**	**4**	**0**	**3**	**133**	**15.8**	**55**	**12**	**36**	**0**	**+7**	**15**	**2**	**6**	**8**	**4**	**0**	**0**	**0**
1991-92	Sweden	C Cup	6	2	1	3	....	....	....	5	....	....	....	....	....	....	....	....	....	....	....	....	....	....	....	....	....	....
	Minnesota North Stars	**NHL**	**79**	**36**	**30**	**66**	**33**	**23**	**56**	**10**	**16**	**1**	**5**	**216**	**16.7**	**90**	**39**	**58**	**2**	**–5**	**7**	**0**	**3**	**3**	**2**	**0**	**0**	**0**
1992-93	**Minnesota North Stars**	**NHL**	**83**	**35**	**39**	**74**	**29**	**27**	**56**	**6**	**13**	**0**	**6**	**223**	**15.7**	**100**	**51**	**69**	**0**	**–20**	....	....	....	....	....	....	....	....
1992-93	Sweden	WC-A	6	5	2	7	....	....	....	0	....	....	....	....	....	....	....	....	....	....	....	....	....	....	....	....	....	....
1993-94	**Dallas Stars**	**NHL**	**65**	**19**	**38**	**57**	**18**	**29**	**47**	**10**	**12**	**0**	**3**	**147**	**12.9**	**82**	**43**	**40**	**0**	**–1**	....	....	....	....	....	....	....	....
	San Jose Sharks	**NHL**	**13**	**6**	**6**	**12**	**6**	**5**	**11**	**0**	**3**	**0**	**2**	**43**	**14.0**	**21**	**9**	**12**	**0**	**0**	**14**	**6**	**2**	**8**	**0**	**3**	**0**	**1**
1994-95	**San Jose Sharks**	**NHL**	**46**	**11**	**23**	**34**	**19**	**34**	**53**	**11**	**4**	**1**	**4**	**85**	**12.9**	**48**	**16**	**34**	**0**	**–2**	**11**	**5**	**4**	**9**	**0**	**3**	**0**	**1**
1995-96	**San Jose Sharks**	**NHL**	**59**	**16**	**12**	**28**	**16**	**10**	**26**	**27**	**5**	**0**	**2**	**103**	**15.5**	**45**	**20**	**46**	**0**	**–21**	....	....	....	....	....	....	....	....

Season	Club	League	REGULAR SEASON																		PLAYOFFS							
			GP	G	A	Pts	AG	AA	APts	PIM	PP	SH	GW	S	%	TGF	PGF	TGA	PGA	+/-	GP	G	A	Pts	PIM	PP	SH	GW
1996-97	Sweden	W Cup	4	1	1	2	....	....	....	0	....	....	....	....	....	....	....	....	....	....	....	....	....	....	....	....	....	....
	San Jose Sharks	**NHL**	**43**	**8**	**11**	**19**	**8**	**10**	**18**	**8**	**3**	**0**	**1**	**78**	**10.3**	**33**	**13**	**31**	**0**	**–11**	....	....	....	....	....	....	....	....
	Chicago Blackhawks	**NHL**	**30**	**6**	**8**	**14**	**6**	**7**	**13**	**10**	**1**	**0**	**3**	**53**	**11.3**	**20**	**3**	**8**	**0**	**+9**	**5**	**0**	**1**	**1**	**0**	**0**	**0**	**0**
1997-98	HV-71 Jonkoping	Sweden	29	9	22	31	....	....	....	16	....	....	....	....	....	....	....	....	....	....	5	1	3	4	12	....	....	....
	Sweden	Olympics	4	1	0	1	....	....	....	2	....	....	....	....	....	....	....	....	....	....	....	....	....	....	....	....	....	....
	Sweden	WC-A	10	3	3	6	....	....	....	0	....	....	....	....	....	....	....	....	....	....	....	....	....	....	....	....	....	....
	NHL Totals		**686**	**231**	**249**	**480**	**217**	**204**	**421**	**194**	**93**	**2**	**38**	**1522**	**15.2**	**711**	**301**	**460**	**2**		**63**	**14**	**20**	**34**	**8**	**6**	**0**	**2**

EJC-A All-Star Team (1985) • Named Best Forward at EJC-A (1985) • WJC-A All-Star Team (1987) • Swedish World All-Star Team (1993) • WC-A All-Star Team (1993)

Traded to **Minnesota** by **NY Rangers** with LA Kings' 4th round choice (previously acquired by NY Rangers — Minnesota selected Cal McGowan) in 1990 Entry Draft and future considerations for Mike Gartner, March 6, 1990. Transferred to **Dallas** after **Minnesota** franchise relocated, June 9, 1993. Traded to **San Jose** by **Dallas** with Dallas' 7th round choice (Brad Mehalko) in 1995 Entry Draft for Doug Zmolek, Mike Lalor and cash, March 19, 1994. Traded to **Chicago** by **San Jose** with Chris Terreri and Michal Sykora for Ed Belfour, January 25, 1997.

• DAHLIN, KJELL

Kjell Dahlin RW – L. 6', 175 lbs. b: Timra, Sweden, 2/2/1963. Montreal's 7th choice, 82nd overall, in 1981 Entry Draft.

Season	Club	League	GP	G	A	Pts	AG	AA	APts	PIM	PP	SH	GW	S	%	TGF	PGF	TGA	PGA	+/-	GP	G	A	Pts	PIM	PP	SH	GW
1981-82	Timra IK	Sweden	36	16	7	23	....	....	....	14	....	....	....	....	....	....	....	....	....	....	....	....	....	....	....	....	....	....
	Sweden	WJC-A	7	5	1	6	....	....	....	4	....	....	....	....	....	....	....	....	....	....	....	....	....	....	....	....	....	....
1982-83	Farjestad BK Karlstad	Sweden	32	10	8	18	....	....	....	2	....	....	....	....	....	....	....	....	....	....	7	0	0	0	2	....	....	....
	Sweden	WJC-A	7	3	4	7	....	....	....	....	....	....	....	....	....	....	....	....	....	....	....	....	....	....	....	....	....	....
1983-84	Farjestad BK Karlstad	Sweden	36	19	9	28	....	....	....	16	....	....	....	....	....	....	....	....	....	....	....	....	....	....	....	....	....	....
1984-85	Farjestad BK Karlstad	Sweden	35	21	25	46	....	....	....	10	....	....	....	....	....	....	....	....	....	....	....	....	....	....	....	....	....	....
1985-86	**Montreal Canadiens**	**NHL**	**77**	**32**	**39**	**71**	**26**	**26**	**52**	**4**	**14**	**0**	**3**	**172**	**18.6**	**116**	**52**	**54**	**0**	**+10**	**16**	**2**	**3**	**5**	**4**	**0**	**0**	**0**
1986-87	**Montreal Canadiens**	**NHL**	**41**	**12**	**8**	**20**	**10**	**6**	**16**	**0**	**3**	**1**	**0**	**53**	**22.6**	**26**	**6**	**23**	**0**	**–3**	**8**	**2**	**4**	**6**	**0**	**0**	**0**	**0**
1987-88	**Montreal Canadiens**	**NHL**	**48**	**13**	**12**	**25**	**11**	**9**	**20**	**6**	**2**	**0**	**2**	**51**	**25.5**	**35**	**8**	**23**	**1**	**+5**	**11**	**2**	**4**	**6**	**2**	**0**	**0**	**0**
1988-89	Farjestad BK Karlstad	Sweden	37	23	20	43	....	....	....	24	....	....	....	....	....	....	....	....	....	....	2	1	0	1	0	....	....	....
1989-90	Farjestad BK Karlstad	Sweden	30	26	12	38	....	....	....	12	....	....	....	....	....	....	....	....	....	....	10	4	5	9	6	....	....	....
1990-91	Farjestad BK Karlstad	Sweden	31	9	8	17	....	....	....	14	....	....	....	....	....	....	....	....	....	....	8	4	3	7	2	....	....	....
1991-92	Farjestad BK Karlstad	Sweden	25	6	10	16	....	....	....	10	....	....	....	....	....	....	....	....	....	....	6	4	1	5	4	....	....	....
1992-93	Farjestad BK Karlstad	Sweden	36	4	8	12	....	....	....	4	....	....	....	....	....	....	....	....	....	....	3	2	0	2	4	....	....	....
	NHL Totals		**166**	**57**	**59**	**116**	**47**	**41**	**88**	**10**	**19**	**1**	**5**	**276**	**20.7**	**177**	**66**	**100**	**1**		**35**	**6**	**11**	**17**	**6**	**0**	**0**	**0**

NHL All-Rookie Team (1986)

• DAHLQUIST, CHRIS

Chris Dahlquist D – L. 6'1", 195 lbs. b: Fridley, MN, 12/14/1962.

Season	Club	League	GP	G	A	Pts	AG	AA	APts	PIM	PP	SH	GW	S	%	TGF	PGF	TGA	PGA	+/-	GP	G	A	Pts	PIM	PP	SH	GW
1981-82	Lake Superior State	CCHA	39	4	10	14	....	....	....	62	....	....	....	....	....	....	....	....	....	....	....	....	....	....	....	....	....	....
1982-83	Lake Superior State	CCHA	35	0	12	12	....	....	....	63	....	....	....	....	....	....	....	....	....	....	....	....	....	....	....	....	....	....
1983-84	Lake Superior State	CCHA	40	4	19	23	....	....	....	76	....	....	....	....	....	....	....	....	....	....	....	....	....	....	....	....	....	....
1984-85	Lake Superior State	CCHA	32	4	10	14	....	....	....	18	....	....	....	....	....	....	....	....	....	....	....	....	....	....	....	....	....	....
1985-86	**Pittsburgh Penguins**	**NHL**	**5**	**1**	**2**	**3**	**1**	**1**	**2**	**2**	**0**	**0**	**0**	**5**	**20.0**	**7**	**1**	**6**	**1**	**+1**	....	....	....	....	....	....	....	....
	Baltimore Skipjacks	AHL	65	4	21	25	....	....	....	64	....	....	....	....	....	....	....	....	....	....	....	....	....	....	....	....	....	....
1986-87	**Pittsburgh Penguins**	**NHL**	**19**	**0**	**1**	**1**	**0**	**1**	**1**	**20**	**0**	**0**	**0**	**15**	**0.0**	**13**	**1**	**15**	**1**	**–2**	....	....	....	....	....	....	....	....
	Baltimore Skipjacks	AHL	51	1	16	17	....	....	....	50	....	....	....	....	....	....	....	....	....	....	....	....	....	....	....	....	....	....
1987-88	**Pittsburgh Penguins**	**NHL**	**44**	**3**	**6**	**9**	**3**	**4**	**7**	**69**	**0**	**0**	**0**	**35**	**8.6**	**28**	**1**	**39**	**15**	**+3**	....	....	....	....	....	....	....	....
1988-89	**Pittsburgh Penguins**	**NHL**	**43**	**1**	**5**	**6**	**1**	**4**	**5**	**42**	**0**	**0**	**0**	**27**	**3.7**	**23**	**2**	**45**	**16**	**–8**	**2**	**0**	**0**	**0**	**0**	**0**	**0**	**0**
	Muskegon Lumberjacks	IHL	10	3	6	9	....	....	....	14	....	....	....	....	....	....	....	....	....	....	....	....	....	....	....	....	....	....
1989-90	**Pittsburgh Penguins**	**NHL**	**62**	**4**	**10**	**14**	**3**	**7**	**10**	**56**	**0**	**0**	**0**	**57**	**7.0**	**43**	**0**	**66**	**21**	**–2**	....	....	....	....	....	....	....	....
	Muskegon Lumberjacks	IHL	6	1	1	2	....	....	....	8	....	....	....	....	....	....	....	....	....	....	....	....	....	....	....	....	....	....
	United States	WEC-A	10	1	0	1	....	....	....	18	....	....	....	....	....	....	....	....	....	....	....	....	....	....	....	....	....	....
1990-91	**Pittsburgh Penguins**	**NHL**	**22**	**1**	**2**	**3**	**1**	**2**	**3**	**30**	**0**	**0**	**0**	**15**	**6.7**	**15**	**0**	**20**	**5**	**0**	....	....	....	....	....	....	....	....
	Minnesota North Stars	**NHL**	**42**	**2**	**6**	**8**	**2**	**5**	**7**	**33**	**0**	**0**	**0**	**37**	**5.4**	**32**	**0**	**48**	**15**	**–1**	**23**	**1**	**6**	**7**	**20**	**0**	**0**	**0**
1991-92	**Minnesota North Stars**	**NHL**	**74**	**1**	**13**	**14**	**1**	**10**	**11**	**68**	**0**	**0**	**0**	**63**	**1.6**	**53**	**2**	**91**	**30**	**–10**	**7**	**0**	**0**	**0**	**6**	**0**	**0**	**0**
1992-93	**Calgary Flames**	**NHL**	**74**	**3**	**7**	**10**	**2**	**5**	**7**	**66**	**0**	**0**	**1**	**64**	**4.7**	**54**	**2**	**76**	**24**	**0**	**6**	**3**	**1**	**4**	**4**	**0**	**0**	**0**
1993-94	**Calgary Flames**	**NHL**	**77**	**1**	**11**	**12**	**1**	**8**	**9**	**52**	**0**	**0**	**0**	**57**	**1.8**	**54**	**0**	**83**	**34**	**+5**	**1**	**0**	**0**	**0**	**0**	**0**	**0**	**0**
1994-95	**Ottawa Senators**	**NHL**	**46**	**1**	**7**	**8**	**2**	**10**	**12**	**36**	**1**	**0**	**0**	**45**	**2.2**	**20**	**1**	**65**	**16**	**–30**	....	....	....	....	....	....	....	....
1995-96	**Ottawa Senators**	**NHL**	**24**	**1**	**1**	**2**	**1**	**1**	**2**	**14**	**0**	**0**	**0**	**13**	**7.7**	**11**	**0**	**23**	**5**	**–7**	....	....	....	....	....	....	....	....
	Cincinnati Cyclones	IHL	38	4	8	12	....	....	....	50	....	....	....	....	....	....	....	....	....	....	2	1	3	4	0	....	....	....
1996-97	Las Vegas Thunder	IHL	18	1	4	5	....	....	....	20	....	....	....	....	....	....	....	....	....	....	....	....	....	....	....	....	....	....
	NHL Totals		**532**	**19**	**71**	**90**	**18**	**58**	**76**	**488**	**1**	**0**	**1**	**433**	**4.4**	**353**	**10**	**577**	**183**		**39**	**4**	**7**	**11**	**30**	**0**	**0**	**0**

Signed as a free agent by **Pittsburgh**, May 7, 1985. Traded to **Minnesota** by **Pittsburgh** with Jim Johnson for Larry Murphy and Peter Taglianetti, December 11, 1990. Claimed by **Calgary** from **Minnesota** in NHL Waiver Draft, October 4, 1992. Signed as a free agent by **Ottawa**, July 4, 1994.

• DAIGLE, ALAIN

Alain Daigle RW – R. 5'10", 180 lbs. b: Trois-Rivieres, Que., 8/24/1954. Chicago's 2nd choice, 34th overall, in 1974 Amateur Draft.

Season	Club	League	GP	G	A	Pts	AG	AA	APts	PIM	PP	SH	GW	S	%	TGF	PGF	TGA	PGA	+/-	GP	G	A	Pts	PIM	PP	SH	GW
1970-71	Trois-Rivieres Draveurs	QJHL	62	28	34	62	....	....	....	66	....	....	....	....	....	....	....	....	....	....	11	2	5	7	10	....	....	....
1971-72	Trois-Rivieres Draveurs	QJMHL	60	30	31	61	....	....	....	161	....	....	....	....	....	....	....	....	....	....	2	1	0	1	20	....	....	....
1972-73	Trois-Rivieres Draveurs	QJMHL	61	42	32	74	....	....	....	97	....	....	....	....	....	....	....	....	....	....	....	....	....	....	....	....	....	....
1973-74	Trois-Rivieres Draveurs	QMJHL	67	80	68	148	....	....	....	72	....	....	....	....	....	....	....	....	....	....	....	....	....	....	....	....	....	....
1974-75	**Chicago Black Hawks**	**NHL**	**52**	**5**	**4**	**9**	**5**	**3**	**8**	**6**	**0**	**0**	**0**	**47**	**10.6**	**13**	**0**	**22**	**3**	**–6**	**2**	**0**	**0**	**0**	**0**	**0**	**0**	**0**
1975-76	**Chicago Black Hawks**	**NHL**	**71**	**15**	**9**	**24**	**14**	**7**	**21**	**15**	**8**	**0**	**2**	**85**	**17.6**	**38**	**15**	**41**	**0**	**–18**	**4**	**0**	**0**	**0**	**0**	**0**	**0**	**0**
1976-77	**Chicago Black Hawks**	**NHL**	**73**	**12**	**8**	**20**	**11**	**6**	**17**	**11**	**2**	**0**	**1**	**89**	**13.5**	**38**	**6**	**33**	**0**	**–1**	**1**	**0**	**0**	**0**	**0**	**0**	**0**	**0**
1977-78	**Chicago Black Hawks**	**NHL**	**53**	**6**	**6**	**12**	**6**	**5**	**11**	**13**	**1**	**0**	**0**	**84**	**7.1**	**17**	**2**	**27**	**0**	**–12**	**4**	**0**	**1**	**1**	**0**	**0**	**0**	**0**
1978-79	**Chicago Black Hawks**	**NHL**	**74**	**11**	**14**	**25**	**10**	**11**	**21**	**55**	**0**	**0**	**0**	**80**	**13.8**	**47**	**1**	**59**	**15**	**+2**	**4**	**0**	**0**	**0**	**0**	**0**	**0**	**0**
	New Brunswick Hawks	AHL	5	2	1	3	....	....	....	4	....	....	....	....	....	....	....	....	....	....	....	....	....	....	....	....	....	....
1979-80	**Chicago Black Hawks**	**NHL**	**66**	**7**	**9**	**16**	**6**	**7**	**13**	**22**	**0**	**1**	**0**	**56**	**12.5**	**30**	**2**	**40**	**6**	**–6**	**2**	**0**	**0**	**0**	**0**	**0**	**0**	**0**
1980-81	HC Gap	France	....	22	13	35	....	....	....	....	....	....	....	....	....	....	....	....	....	....	....	....	....	....	....	....	....	....
	New Brunswick Hawks	AHL	15	5	5	10	....	....	....	14	....	....	....	....	....	....	....	....	....	....	7	1	1	2	7	....	....	....
1981-82	ECS Innsbruck	Austria	....	26	15	41	....	....	....	....	....	....	....	....	....	....	....	....	....	....	....	....	....	....	....	....	....	....
1982-83	Sherbrooke Jets	AHL	43	11	22	33	....	....	....	18	....	....	....	....	....	....	....	....	....	....	....	....	....	....	....	....	....	....
	NHL Totals		**389**	**56**	**50**	**106**	**52**	**39**	**91**	**122**	**11**	**1**	**3**	**441**	**12.7**	**183**	**26**	**222**	**24**		**17**	**0**	**1**	**1**	**0**	**0**	**0**	**0**

• DAIGLE, ALEXANDRE

Alexandre Daigle C – L. 6', 195 lbs. b: Montreal, Que., 2/7/1975. Ottawa's 1st choice, 1st overall, in 1993 Entry Draft.

Season	Club	League	GP	G	A	Pts	AG	AA	APts	PIM	PP	SH	GW	S	%	TGF	PGF	TGA	PGA	+/-	GP	G	A	Pts	PIM	PP	SH	GW
1991-92	Victoriaville Tigres	QMJHL	66	35	75	110	....	....	....	63	....	....	....	....	....	....	....	....	....	....	....	....	....	....	....	....	....	....
1992-93	Victoriaville Tigres	QMJHL	53	45	92	137	....	....	....	85	....	....	....	....	....	....	....	....	....	....	6	5	6	11	4	....	....	....
	Canada	WJC-A	7	0	6	6	....	....	....	27	....	....	....	....	....	....	....	....	....	....	....	....	....	....	....	....	....	....
1993-94	**Ottawa Senators**	**NHL**	**84**	**20**	**31**	**51**	**19**	**24**	**43**	**40**	**4**	**0**	**2**	**168**	**11.9**	**69**	**28**	**98**	**12**	**–45**	....	....	....	....	....	....	....	....
1994-95	Victoriaville Tigres	QMJHL	18	14	20	34	....	....	....	16	....	....	....	....	....	....	....	....	....	....	....	....	....	....	....	....	....	....
	Canada	WJC-A	7	2	8	10	....	....	....	4	....	....	....	....	....	....	....	....	....	....	....	....	....	....	....	....	....	....
	Ottawa Senators	**NHL**	**47**	**16**	**21**	**37**	**28**	**31**	**59**	**14**	**4**	**1**	**2**	**105**	**15.2**	**52**	**18**	**62**	**6**	**–22**	....	....	....	....	....	....	....	....
1995-96	**Ottawa Senators**	**NHL**	**50**	**5**	**12**	**17**	**5**	**10**	**15**	**24**	**1**	**0**	**0**	**77**	**6.5**	**29**	**14**	**50**	**5**	**–30**	....	....	....	....	....	....	....	....
1996-97	**Ottawa Senators**	**NHL**	**82**	**26**	**25**	**51**	**28**	**22**	**50**	**33**	**4**	**0**	**5**	**203**	**12.8**	**71**	**30**	**74**	**0**	**–33**	**7**	**0**	**0**	**0**	**2**	**0**	**0**	**0**
1997-98	**Ottawa Senators**	**NHL**	**38**	**7**	**9**	**16**	**8**	**9**	**17**	**8**	**4**	**0**	**2**	**68**	**10.3**	**24**	**11**	**21**	**1**	**–7**	....	....	....	....	....	....	....	....
	Philadelphia Flyers	**NHL**	**37**	**9**	**17**	**26**	**11**	**17**	**28**	**6**	**4**	**0**	**3**	**78**	**11.5**	**32**	**9**	**24**	**0**	**–1**	**5**	**0**	**2**	**2**	**0**	**0**	**0**	**0**
	NHL Totals		**338**	**83**	**115**	**198**	**99**	**113**	**212**	**125**	**21**	**1**	**14**	**699**	**11.9**	**277**	**110**	**329**	**24**		**12**	**0**	**2**	**2**	**2**	**0**	**0**	**0**

QMJHL Second All-Star Team (1992) • Canadian Major Junior Rookie of the Year (1992) • QMJHL First All-Star Team (1993)

Traded to **Philadelphia** by **Ottawa** for Vaclav Prospal, Pat Falloon and Dallas' 2nd round choice (previously acquired, Ottawa selected Chris Bala) in 1998 Entry Draft, January 17, 1998.

• DAIGNEAULT, J.J.

J.J. (Jean Jacques) Daigneault D – L. 5'10", 186 lbs. b: Montreal, Que., 10/12/1965. Vancouver's 1st choice, 10th overall, in 1984 Entry Draft.

Season	Club	League	GP	G	A	Pts	AG	AA	APts	PIM	PP	SH	GW	S	%	TGF	PGF	TGA	PGA	+/-	GP	G	A	Pts	PIM	PP	SH	GW
1981-82	Laval Voisins	QMJHL	64	4	25	29	....	....	....	41	....	....	....	....	....	....	....	....	....	....	18	1	3	4	2	....	....	....
1982-83	Longueuil Chevaliers	QMJHL	70	26	58	84	....	....	....	58	....	....	....	....	....	....	....	....	....	....	15	4	11	15	35	....	....	....
1983-84	Longueuil Chevaliers	QMJHL	10	2	11	13	....	....	....	6	....	....	....	....	....	....	....	....	....	....	14	3	13	16	30	....	....	....
	Canada	WJC-A	7	0	2	2	....	....	....	2	....	....	....	....	....	....	....	....	....	....	....	....	....	....	....	....	....	....
	Canada	Nat-Team	55	5	14	19	....	....	....	40	....	....	....	....	....	....	....	....	....	....	....	....	....	....	....	....	....	....
	Canada	Olympics	7	1	1	2	....	....	....	0	....	....	....	....	....	....	....	....	....	....	....	....	....	....	....	....	....	....
1984-85	**Vancouver Canucks**	**NHL**	**67**	**4**	**23**	**27**	**3**	**16**	**19**	**69**	**2**	**0**	**0**	**93**	**4.3**	**67**	**17**	**67**	**3**	**–14**	....	....	....	....	....	....	....	....

			REGULAR SEASON																		PLAYOFFS							
Season	Club	League	GP	G	A	Pts	AG	AA	APts	PIM	PP	SH	GW	S	%	TGF	PGF	TGA	PGA	+/–	GP	G	A	Pts	PIM	PP	SH	GW
1985-86	Vancouver Canucks	NHL	64	5	23	28	4	15	19	45	4	0	0	114	4.4	68	36	54	2	–20	3	0	2	2	0	0	0	0
1986-87	Philadelphia Flyers	NHL	77	6	16	22	5	12	17	56	0	0	1	82	7.3	72	13	48	1	+12	9	1	0	1	0	0	0	1
1987-88	Philadelphia Flyers	NHL	28	2	2	4	2	1	3	12	2	0	0	20	10.0	13	6	15	0	–8	....	....	....	....	....	....	....	....
	Hershey Bears	AHL	10	1	5	6	....	....	....	8	....	....	....	....	....	....	....	....	....	....	....	....	....	....	....	....	....	....
1988-89	Hershey Bears	AHL	12	0	10	10	....	....	....	13	....	....	....	....	....	....	....	....	....	....	....	....	....	....	....	....	....	....
	Sherbrooke Canadiens	AHL	63	10	33	43	....	....	....	48	....	....	....	....	....	....	....	....	....	....	6	1	3	4	2	....	....	....
1989-90	Montreal Canadiens	NHL	36	2	10	12	2	7	9	14	0	0	1	40	5.0	40	5	27	3	+11	9	0	0	0	2	0	0	0
	Sherbrooke Canadiens	AHL	28	8	19	27	....	....	....	18	....	....	....	....	....	....	....	....	....	....	....	....	....	....	....	....	....	....
1990-91	Montreal Canadiens	FrTour	1	0	0	0	....	....	....	0	....	....	....	....	....	....	....	....	....	....	....	....	....	....	....	....	....	....
	Montreal Canadiens	NHL	51	3	16	19	3	12	15	31	2	0	0	68	4.4	59	14	58	11	–2	5	0	1	1	0	0	0	0
1991-92	Montreal Canadiens	NHL	79	4	14	18	4	11	15	36	2	0	0	108	3.7	78	16	75	29	+16	11	0	3	3	4	0	0	0
1992-93	Montreal Canadiens	NHL	66	8	10	18	7	7	14	57	0	0	1	68	11.8	76	5	76	30	+25	20	1	3	4	22	0	0	0
1993-94	Montreal Canadiens	NHL	68	2	12	14	2	9	11	73	0	0	1	61	3.3	61	1	61	17	+16	7	0	1	1	12	0	0	0
1994-95	Montreal Canadiens	NHL	45	3	5	8	5	7	12	40	0	0	0	36	8.3	34	0	43	11	+2	....	....	....	....	....	....	....	....
1995-96	Montreal Canadiens	NHL	7	0	1	1	0	1	1	6	0	0	0	3	0.0	6	0	8	2	0	....	....	....	....	....	....	....	....
	St. Louis Blues	NHL	37	1	3	4	1	2	3	24	0	0	0	45	2.2	14	6	18	4	–6	....	....	....	....	....	....	....	....
	Worcester IceCats	AHL	9	1	10	11	....	....	....	10	....	....	....	....	....	....	....	....	....	....	....	....	....	....	....	....	....	....
	Pittsburgh Penguins	NHL	13	3	3	6	3	2	5	23	2	0	0	13	23.1	25	11	16	2	0	17	1	9	10	36	1	0	1
1996-97	Pittsburgh Penguins	NHL	53	3	14	17	3	12	15	36	0	0	1	49	6.1	44	11	44	6	–5	....	....	....	....	....	....	....	....
	Anaheim Mighty Ducks	NHL	13	2	9	11	2	8	10	22	0	0	0	13	15.4	22	11	9	3	+5	11	2	7	9	16	1	0	1
1997-98	Anaheim Mighty Ducks	NHL	53	2	15	17	2	15	17	28	1	0	1	74	2.7	47	14	59	16	–10	....	....	....	....	....	....	....	....
	New York Islanders	NHL	18	0	6	6	0	6	6	21	0	0	0	18	0.0	15	3	17	6	+1	....	....	....	....	....	....	....	....
	NHL Totals		775	50	182	232	48	143	191	593	15	0	6	905	5.5	741	169	695	146		92	5	26	31	92	2	0	3

QMJHL First All-Star Team (1983)

Traded to **Philadelphia** by **Vancouver** with Vancouver's 2nd round choice (Kent Hawley) in 1986 Entry Draft for Dave Richter, Rich Sutter and Vancouver's 3rd round choice (previously acquired, Vancouver selected Don Gibson) in 1986 Entry Draft, June 6, 1986. Traded to **Montreal** by **Philadelphia** for Scott Sandelin, November 7, 1988. Traded to **St. Louis** by **Montreal** for Pat Jablonski, November 7, 1995. Traded to **Pittsburgh** by **St. Louis** for Pittsburgh's 6th round choice (Stephen Wagner) in 1996 Entry Draft, March 20, 1996. Traded to **Anaheim** by **Pittsburgh** for Garry Valk, February 21, 1997. Traded to **NY Islanders** by **Anaheim** with Joe Sacco and Mark Janssens for Travis Green, Doug Houda and Tony Tuzzolino, February 6, 1998. Claimed by **Nashville** from **NY Islanders** in Expansion Draft, June 26, 1998.

• DAILEY, BOB

Bob Dailey D – R. 6'5", 220 lbs. b: Kingston, Ont., 5/3/1953. Vancouver's 2nd choice, 9th overall, in 1973 Amateur Draft.

1970-71	Toronto Marlboros	OHA	36	2	3	5	....	....	....	36	....	....	....	....	....	....	....	....	....	....	....	....	....	....	....	....	....	....
1971-72	Toronto Marlboros	OHA	62	11	39	50	....	....	....	135	....	....	....	....	....	....	....	....	....	....	....	....	....	....	....	....	....	....
1972-73	Toronto Marlboros	OHA	60	9	55	64	....	....	....	200	....	....	....	....	....	....	....	....	....	....	16	9	11	20	22	....	....	....
1973-74	Vancouver Canucks	NHL	76	7	17	24	7	15	22	143	0	0	0	124	5.6	82	8	133	27	–32	....	....	....	....	....	....	....	....
1974-75	Vancouver Canucks	NHL	70	12	36	48	11	28	39	103	7	0	1	170	7.1	113	40	98	16	–9	5	1	3	4	14	0	0	0
1975-76	Vancouver Canucks	NHL	67	15	24	39	14	19	33	119	9	0	3	187	8.0	105	38	94	22	–5	2	1	1	2	0	1	0	0
1976-77	Vancouver Canucks	NHL	44	4	16	20	4	13	17	52	2	0	1	100	4.0	56	14	75	17	–16	....	....	....	....	....	....	....	....
	Philadelphia Flyers	NHL	32	5	14	19	5	11	16	38	2	0	0	77	6.5	55	12	33	6	+16	10	4	9	13	15	2	0	0
1977-78	Philadelphia Flyers	NHL	76	21	36	57	20	29	49	62	5	2	2	211	10.0	136	40	77	26	+45	12	1	5	6	22	0	0	0
1978-79	Philadelphia Flyers	NHL	70	9	30	39	8	23	31	63	1	0	1	164	5.5	109	25	87	24	+21	8	1	2	3	14	0	0	0
1979-80	Philadelphia Flyers	NHL	61	13	26	39	12	20	32	71	2	1	4	185	7.0	100	18	74	22	+30	19	4	13	17	22	1	1	2
1980-81	Philadelphia Flyers	NHL	53	7	27	34	6	19	25	141	1	0	0	141	5.0	66	20	57	19	+8	7	0	1	1	18	0	0	0
1981-82	Philadelphia Flyers	NHL	12	1	5	6	1	3	4	22	0	0	0	22	4.5	16	1	16	5	+4	....	....	....	....	....	....	....	....
	NHL Totals		561	94	231	325	88	180	268	814	29	3	12	1381	6.8	838	216	744	184		63	12	34	46	105	4	1	2

OHA Second All-Star Team (1973)

Played in NHL All-Star Game (1978, 1981)

Traded to **Philadelphia** by **Vancouver** for Larry Goodenough and Jack McIlhargey, January 20, 1977.

• DALEY, PAT

Pat Daley LW – L. 6'1", 176 lbs. b: Maryville, France, 3/27/1959. Winnipeg's 4th choice, 82nd overall, in 1979 Entry Draft.

1975-76	Laval National	QMJHL	70	8	11	19	....	....	....	47	....	....	....	....	....	....	....	....	....	....	....	....	....	....	....	....	....	....
1976-77	Laval National	QMJHL	63	23	36	59	....	....	....	135	....	....	....	....	....	....	....	....	....	....	....	....	....	....	....	....	....	....
1977-78	Laval National	QMJHL	69	44	76	120	....	....	....	174	....	....	....	....	....	....	....	....	....	....	....	....	....	....	....	....	....	....
1978-79	Montreal Juniors	QMJHL	67	25	50	75	....	....	....	139	....	....	....	....	....	....	....	....	....	....	....	....	....	....	....	....	....	....
1979-80	Winnipeg Jets	NHL	5	1	0	1	1	0	1	4	0	0	0	6	16.7	2	0	4	0	–2	....	....	....	....	....	....	....	....
	Tulsa Oilers	CHL	65	9	16	25	....	....	....	141	....	....	....	....	....	....	....	....	....	....	3	1	0	1	13	....	....	....
1980-81	Winnipeg Jets	NHL	7	0	0	0	0	0	0	9	0	0	0	4	0.0	1	0	4	0	–3	....	....	....	....	....	....	....	....
	Tulsa Oilers	CHL	68	18	22	40	....	....	....	189	....	....	....	....	....	....	....	....	....	....	8	3	5	8	24	....	....	....
1981-82	Fredericton Express	AHL	71	14	13	27	....	....	....	120	....	....	....	....	....	....	....	....	....	....	....	....	....	....	....	....	....	....
1982-83	ASG Tours	France	STATISTICS NOT AVAILABLE																									
1983-84	ASG Tours	France	STATISTICS NOT AVAILABLE																									
1984-85	ASG Tours	France	....	27	15	42	....	....	....	....	....	....	....	....	....	....	....	....	....	....	....	....	....	....	....	....	....	....
1985-86	Paris Volant	France	STATISTICS NOT AVAILABLE																									
1986-87	Paris Volant	France	STATISTICS NOT AVAILABLE																									
1987-88	HC Gap	France	30	10	8	18	....	....	....	34	....	....	....	....	....	....	....	....	....	....	....	....	....	....	....	....	....	....
1988-89	HC Rouen	France	40	12	23	35	....	....	....	62	....	....	....	....	....	....	....	....	....	....	....	....	....	....	....	....	....	....
	NHL Totals		12	1	0	1	1	0	1	13	0	0	0	10	10.0	3	0	8	0		....	....	....	....	....	....	....	....

QMJHL First All-Star Team (1978)

Signed as a free agent by **Quebec**, July, 1981.

• DALGARNO, BRAD

Brad Dalgarno RW – R. 6'3", 215 lbs. b: Vancouver, B.C., 8/11/1967. NY Islanders' 1st choice, 6th overall, in 1985 Entry Draft.

1983-84	Orillia Travelways	Jr. B	40	17	11	28	....	....	....	59	....	....	....	....	....	....	....	....	....	....	....	....	....	....	....	....	....	....
1984-85	Hamilton Steelhawks	OHA	66	23	30	53	....	....	....	86	....	....	....	....	....	....	....	....	....	....	....	....	....	....	....	....	....	....
1985-86	Hamilton Steelhawks	OHL	54	22	43	65	....	....	....	79	....	....	....	....	....	....	....	....	....	....	....	....	....	....	....	....	....	....
	New York Islanders	NHL	2	1	0	1	1	0	1	0	0	0	0	3	33.3	2	0	1	0	+1	....	....	....	....	....	....	....	....
1986-87	Hamilton Steelhawks	OHL	60	27	32	59	....	....	....	100	....	....	....	....	....	....	....	....	....	....	....	....	....	....	....	....	....	....
	New York Islanders	NHL	....	....	....	....	....	....	....	....	....	....	....	....	....	....	....	....	....	....	1	0	1	1	0	....	....	....
1987-88	New York Islanders	NHL	38	2	8	10	2	6	8	58	0	0	1	39	5.1	19	5	10	0	+4	4	0	0	0	19	0	0	0
	Springfield Indians	AHL	39	13	11	24	....	....	....	76	....	....	....	....	....	....	....	....	....	....	....	....	....	....	....	....	....	....
1988-89	New York Islanders	NHL	55	11	10	21	9	7	16	86	2	0	1	83	13.3	42	14	36	0	–8	....	....	....	....	....	....	....	....
1989-90			DID NOT PLAY – RETIRED																									
1990-91	New York Islanders	NHL	41	3	12	15	3	9	12	24	0	0	1	34	8.8	19	1	28	0	–10	....	....	....	....	....	....	....	....
	Capital District Islanders	AHL	27	6	14	20	....	....	....	26	....	....	....	....	....	....	....	....	....	....	....	....	....	....	....	....	....	....
1991-92	New York Islanders	NHL	15	2	1	3	2	1	3	12	1	0	0	17	11.8	5	2	11	0	–8	....	....	....	....	....	....	....	....
	Capital District Islanders	AHL	14	7	8	15	....	....	....	34	....	....	....	....	....	....	....	....	....	....	....	....	....	....	....	....	....	....
1992-93	New York Islanders	NHL	57	15	17	32	12	12	24	62	2	0	2	62	24.2	50	3	30	0	+17	18	2	2	4	14	0	0	0
	Capital District Islanders	AHL	19	10	4	14	....	....	....	16	....	....	....	....	....	....	....	....	....	....	....	....	....	....	....	....	....	....
1993-94	New York Islanders	NHL	73	11	19	30	10	15	25	62	3	0	1	97	11.3	49	6	38	9	+14	4	0	1	1	4	0	0	0
1994-95	New York Islanders	NHL	22	3	2	5	5	3	8	14	1	1	0	18	16.7	7	1	17	3	–8	....	....	....	....	....	....	....	....
1995-96	New York Islanders	NHL	18	1	2	3	1	2	3	14	0	0	0	11	9.1	4	1	5	0	–2	....	....	....	....	....	....	....	....
	NHL Totals		321	49	71	120	45	55	100	332	9	1	6	364	13.5	197	33	176	12		27	2	4	6	37	0	0	0

• DALLMAN, MARTY

Marty Dallman C – R. 5'10", 180 lbs. b: Niagara Falls, Ont., 2/15/1963. Los Angeles' 3rd choice, 81st overall, in 1981 Entry Draft.

1980-81	RPI Engineers	ECAC	22	8	10	18	....	....	....	6	....	....	....	....	....	....	....	....	....	....	....	....	....	....	....	....	....	....
1981-82	RPI Engineers	ECAC	28	22	18	40	....	....	....	27	....	....	....	....	....	....	....	....	....	....	....	....	....	....	....	....	....	....
1982-83	RPI Engineers	ECAC	27	21	29	50	....	....	....	28	....	....	....	....	....	....	....	....	....	....	....	....	....	....	....	....	....	....
1983-84	RPI Engineers	ECAC	38	30	24	54	....	....	....	32	....	....	....	....	....	....	....	....	....	....	....	....	....	....	....	....	....	....
1984-85	New Haven Nighthawks	AHL	78	18	39	57	....	....	....	26	....	....	....	....	....	....	....	....	....	....	....	....	....	....	....	....	....	....
1985-86	New Haven Nighthawks	AHL	69	23	33	56	....	....	....	92	....	....	....	....	....	....	....	....	....	....	5	0	4	4	4	....	....	....

			REGULAR SEASON																		PLAYOFFS							
Season	Club	League	GP	G	A	Pts	AG	AA	APts	PIM	PP	SH	GW	S	%	TGF	PGF	TGA	PGA	+/-	GP	G	A	Pts	PIM	PP	SH	GW
1986-87	Baltimore Skipjacks	AHL	6	0	1	1	....	....	....	0	....	....	....	....	....	....	....	....	....	....	....	....	....	....	....	....	....	....
	Newmarket Saints	AHL	42	24	24	48	....	....	....	44	....	....	....	....	....	....	....	....	....	....	....	....	....	....	....	....	....	....
1987-88	**Toronto Maple Leafs**	**NHL**	**2**	**0**	**1**	**1**	**0**	**1**	**1**	**0**	**0**	**0**	**0**	**1**	**0.0**	**1**	**0**	**0**	**0**	**+1**	....	....	....	....	....	....	....	....
	Newmarket Saints	AHL	76	50	39	89	....	....	....	52	....	....	....	....	....	....	....	....	....	....	....	....	....	....	....	....	....	....
1988-89	**Toronto Maple Leafs**	**NHL**	**4**	**0**	**0**	**0**	**0**	**0**	**0**	**0**	**0**	**0**	**0**	**2**	**0.0**	**1**	**1**	**0**	**0**	**0**	....	....	....	....	....	....	....	....
	Newmarket Saints	AHL	37	26	20	46	....	....	....	24	....	....	....	....	....	....	....	....	....	....	....	....	....	....	....	....	....	....
1989-90	WEV Wien	Austria	34	36	33	69	....	....	....	89	....	....	....	....	....	....	....	....	....	....	....	....	....	....	....	....	....	....
1990-91	WEV Wien	Austria	39	39	18	57	....	....	....	....	....	....	....	....	....	....	....	....	....	....	....	....	....	....	....	....	....	....
1991-92	WEV Wien	Austria	39	46	23	69	....	....	....	....	....	....	....	....	....	....	....	....	....	....	....	....	....	....	....	....	....	....
1992-93	Zell-am-Zee	Austria	43	30	17	47	....	....	....	....	....	....	....	....	....	....	....	....	....	....	....	....	....	....	....	....	....	....
	Austria	WC-A	6	0	1	1	....	....	....	10	....	....	....	....	....	....	....	....	....	....	....	....	....	....	....	....	....	....
1993-94	EC Graz	Austria	57	35	43	78	....	....	....	....	....	....	....	....	....	....	....	....	....	....	....	....	....	....	....	....	....	....
	Austria	Olympics	7	4	4	8	....	....	....	8	....	....	....	....	....	....	....	....	....	....	....	....	....	....	....	....	....	....
1994-95	HC Fribourg-Gotteron	Switz.	4	1	1	2	....	....	....	4	....	....	....	....	....	....	....	....	....	....	....	....	....	....	....	....	....	....
	South Carolina Stingrays	ECHL	22	11	16	27	....	....	....	22	....	....	....	....	....	....	....	....	....	....	6	5	9	14	4	....	....	....
1995-96	WEV Wien	Austria	33	22	29	51	....	....	....	67	....	....	....	....	....	....	....	....	....	....	....	....	....	....	....	....	....	....
1996-97	Nottingham Panthers	Britain	40	24	32	56	....	....	....	....	....	....	....	....	....	....	....	....	....	....	8	7	4	11	....	....	....	....
1997-98	Nottingham Panthers	Britain	33	13	20	33	....	....	....	12	....	....	....	....	....	....	....	....	....	....	6	3	2	5	0	....	....	....
	NHL Totals		**6**	**0**	**1**	**1**	**0**	**1**	**1**	**0**	**0**	**0**	**0**	**3**	**0.0**	**2**	**1**	**0**	**0**		....	....	....	....	....	....	....	....

ECAC Second All-Star Team (1984) • AHL Second All-Star Team (1988)

Signed as a free agent by **Toronto**, November, 1986

● DALLMAN, ROD

Rod Dallman LW – L. 5'11", 185 lbs. b: Prince Albert, Sask., 1/26/1967. NY Islanders' 8th choice, 118th overall, in 1985 Entry Draft.

Season	Club	League	GP	G	A	Pts	AG	AA	APts	PIM	PP	SH	GW	S	%	TGF	PGF	TGA	PGA	+/-	GP	G	A	Pts	PIM	PP	SH	GW
1983-84	Prince Albert Midgets	Midget	21	14	6	20	....	....	....	69	....	....	....	....	....	....	....	....	....	....	....	....	....	....	....	....	....	....
1984-85	Prince Albert Raiders	WHL	40	8	11	19	....	....	....	133	....	....	....	....	....	....	....	....	....	....	12	3	4	7	51	....	....	....
1985-86	Prince Albert Raiders	WHL	59	20	21	41	....	....	....	198	....	....	....	....	....	....	....	....	....	....	....	....	....	....	....	....	....	....
1986-87	Prince Albert Raiders	WHL	47	13	21	34	....	....	....	240	....	....	....	....	....	....	....	....	....	....	5	0	1	1	32	....	....	....
1987-88	**New York Islanders**	**NHL**	**3**	**1**	**0**	**1**	**1**	**0**	**1**	**6**	**0**	**0**	**0**	**2**	**50.0**	**1**	**0**	**0**	**0**	**+1**	....	....	....	....	....	....	....	....
	Springfield Indians	AHL	59	9	17	26	....	....	....	355	....	....	....	....	....	....	....	....	....	....	....	....	....	....	....	....	....	....
	Peoria Rivermen	IHL	8	3	4	7	....	....	....	18	....	....	....	....	....	....	....	....	....	....	7	0	2	2	65	....	....	....
1988-89	**New York Islanders**	**NHL**	**1**	**0**	**0**	**0**	**0**	**0**	**0**	**15**	**0**	**0**	**0**	**1**	**0.0**	**0**	**0**	**1**	**0**	**–1**	....	....	....	....	....	....	....	....
	Springfield Indians	AHL	67	12	12	24	....	....	....	360	....	....	....	....	....	....	....	....	....	....	....	....	....	....	....	....	....	....
1989-90	Springfield Indians	AHL	43	10	20	30	....	....	....	129	....	....	....	....	....	....	....	....	....	....	15	5	5	10	59	....	....	....
	New York Islanders	**NHL**	....	....	....	....	....	....	....	....	....	....	....	....	....	....	....	....	....	....	**1**	**0**	**1**	**1**	**0**	....	....	....
1990-91	Hershey Bears	AHL	2	0	0	0	....	....	....	0	....	....	....	....	....	....	....	....	....	....	....	....	....	....	....	....	....	....
	San Diego Gulls	IHL	15	3	5	8	....	....	....	85	....	....	....	....	....	....	....	....	....	....	....	....	....	....	....	....	....	....
1991-92	**Philadelphia Flyers**	**NHL**	**2**	**0**	**0**	**0**	**0**	**0**	**0**	**5**	**0**	**0**	**0**	**2**	**0.0**	**0**	**0**	**0**	**0**	**0**	....	....	....	....	....	....	....	....
	Hershey Bears	AHL	31	4	13	17	....	....	....	114	....	....	....	....	....	....	....	....	....	....	....	....	....	....	....	....	....	....
	NHL Totals		**6**	**1**	**0**	**1**	**1**	**0**	**1**	**26**	**0**	**0**	**0**	**5**	**20.0**	**1**	**0**	**1**	**0**		**1**	**0**	**1**	**1**	**0**	**0**	**0**	**0**

Signed as a free agent by **Philadelphia**, July 31, 1990.

● DAMPHOUSSE, VINCENT

Vincent Damphousse C – L. 6'1", 195 lbs. b: Montreal, Que., 12/17/1967. Toronto's 1st choice, 6th overall, in 1986 Entry Draft.

Season	Club	League	GP	G	A	Pts	AG	AA	APts	PIM	PP	SH	GW	S	%	TGF	PGF	TGA	PGA	+/-	GP	G	A	Pts	PIM	PP	SH	GW
1983-84	Laval Voisins	QMJHL	66	29	36	65	....	....	....	25	....	....	....	....	....	....	....	....	....	....	....	....	....	....	....	....	....	....
1984-85	Laval Voisins	QMJHL	68	35	68	103	....	....	....	62	....	....	....	....	....	....	....	....	....	....	....	....	....	....	....	....	....	....
1985-86	Laval Voisins	QMJHL	69	45	110	155	....	....	....	70	....	....	....	....	....	....	....	....	....	....	14	9	27	36	12	....	....	....
1986-87	**Toronto Maple Leafs**	**NHL**	**80**	**21**	**25**	**46**	**18**	**18**	**36**	**26**	**4**	**0**	**1**	**142**	**14.8**	**73**	**10**	**69**	**0**	**–6**	**12**	**1**	**5**	**6**	**8**	**1**	**0**	**0**
1987-88	**Toronto Maple Leafs**	**NHL**	**75**	**12**	**36**	**48**	**10**	**26**	**36**	**40**	**1**	**0**	**2**	**111**	**10.8**	**88**	**9**	**57**	**2**	**+2**	**6**	**0**	**1**	**1**	**10**	**0**	**0**	**0**
1988-89	**Toronto Maple Leafs**	**NHL**	**80**	**26**	**42**	**68**	**22**	**30**	**52**	**75**	**6**	**0**	**4**	**190**	**13.7**	**84**	**22**	**73**	**3**	**–8**	....	....	....	....	....	....	....	....
1989-90	**Toronto Maple Leafs**	**NHL**	**80**	**33**	**61**	**94**	**28**	**44**	**72**	**56**	**9**	**0**	**5**	**229**	**14.4**	**127**	**40**	**87**	**2**	**+2**	**5**	**0**	**2**	**2**	**2**	**0**	**0**	**0**
1990-91	**Toronto Maple Leafs**	**NHL**	**79**	**26**	**47**	**73**	**24**	**36**	**60**	**65**	**10**	**1**	**4**	**247**	**10.5**	**93**	**35**	**99**	**10**	**–31**	....	....	....	....	....	....	....	....
1991-92	**Edmonton Oilers**	**NHL**	**80**	**38**	**51**	**89**	**35**	**38**	**73**	**53**	**12**	**1**	**8**	**247**	**15.4**	**123**	**47**	**88**	**22**	**+10**	**16**	**6**	**8**	**14**	**8**	**1**	**0**	**0**
1992-93	**Montreal Canadiens**	**NHL**	**84**	**39**	**58**	**97**	**33**	**40**	**73**	**98**	**9**	**3**	**8**	**287**	**13.6**	**134**	**50**	**92**	**13**	**+5**	**20**	**11**	**12**	**23**	**16**	**5**	**0**	**3**
1993-94	**Montreal Canadiens**	**NHL**	**84**	**40**	**51**	**91**	**37**	**39**	**76**	**75**	**13**	**0**	**10**	**274**	**14.6**	**117**	**51**	**70**	**4**	**0**	**7**	**1**	**2**	**3**	**8**	**0**	**0**	**0**
1994-95	Ratingen Lions	Germany	11	5	7	12	....	....	....	24	....	....	....	....	....	....	....	....	....	....	....	....	....	....	....	....	....	....
	Montreal Canadiens	**NHL**	**48**	**10**	**30**	**40**	**18**	**44**	**62**	**42**	**4**	**0**	**4**	**123**	**8.1**	**67**	**23**	**32**	**3**	**+15**	....	....	....	....	....	....	....	....
1995-96	**Montreal Canadiens**	**NHL**	**80**	**38**	**56**	**94**	**38**	**46**	**84**	**158**	**11**	**4**	**3**	**254**	**15.0**	**127**	**51**	**97**	**26**	**+5**	**6**	**4**	**4**	**8**	**0**	**0**	**1**	**2**
1996-97	Canada	W Cup	8	2	0	2	....	....	....	8	....	....	....	....	....	....	....	....	....	....	....	....	....	....	....	....	....	....
	Montreal Canadiens	**NHL**	**82**	**27**	**54**	**81**	**29**	**48**	**77**	**82**	**7**	**2**	**3**	**244**	**11.1**	**101**	**30**	**102**	**25**	**–6**	**5**	**0**	**0**	**0**	**2**	**0**	**0**	**0**
1997-98	**Montreal Canadiens**	**NHL**	**76**	**18**	**41**	**59**	**21**	**40**	**61**	**58**	**2**	**1**	**5**	**164**	**11.0**	**87**	**27**	**59**	**13**	**+14**	**10**	**3**	**6**	**9**	**22**	**1**	**0**	**0**
	NHL Totals		**928**	**328**	**552**	**880**	**313**	**449**	**762**	**828**	**88**	**12**	**57**	**2512**	**13.1**	**1199**	**395**	**925**	**123**		**87**	**26**	**40**	**66**	**76**	**8**	**1**	**5**

QMJHL Second All-Star Team (1986)

Played in NHL All-Star Game (1991, 1992)

Traded to **Edmonton** by **Toronto** with Peter Ing, Scott Thornton, Luke Richardson, future considerations and cash for Grant Fuhr, Glenn Anderson and Craig Berube, September 19, 1991. Traded to **Montreal** by **Edmonton** with Edmonton's 4th round choice (Adam Wiesel) in 1993 Entry Draft for Shayne Corson, Brent Gilchrist and Vladimir Vujtek, August 27, 1992.

● DANDENAULT, MATHIEU

Mathieu Dandenault RW – R. 6', 174 lbs. b: Sherbrooke, Que., 2/3/1976. Detroit's 2nd choice, 49th overall, in 1994 Entry Draft.

Season	Club	League	GP	G	A	Pts	AG	AA	APts	PIM	PP	SH	GW	S	%	TGF	PGF	TGA	PGA	+/-	GP	G	A	Pts	PIM	PP	SH	GW
1993-94	Sherbrooke Faucons	QMJHL	67	17	36	53	....	....	....	67	....	....	....	....	....	....	....	....	....	....	12	4	10	14	12	....	....	....
1994-95	Sherbrooke Faucons	QMJHL	67	37	70	107	....	....	....	76	....	....	....	....	....	....	....	....	....	....	7	1	7	8	10	....	....	....
1995-96	**Detroit Red Wings**	**NHL**	**34**	**5**	**7**	**12**	**5**	**6**	**11**	**6**	**1**	**0**	**0**	**32**	**15.6**	**18**	**1**	**11**	**0**	**+6**	....	....	....	....	....	....	....	....
	Adirondack Red Wings	AHL	4	0	0	0	....	....	....	0	....	....	....	....	....	....	....	....	....	....	....	....	....	....	....	....	....	....
1996-97	**Detroit Red Wings**	**NHL**	**65**	**3**	**9**	**12**	**3**	**8**	**11**	**28**	**0**	**0**	**0**	**81**	**3.7**	**31**	**2**	**41**	**2**	**–10**	....	....	....	....	....	....	....	....
1997-98	**Detroit Red Wings**	**NHL**	**68**	**5**	**12**	**17**	**6**	**12**	**18**	**43**	**0**	**0**	**0**	**75**	**6.7**	**30**	**0**	**27**	**2**	**+5**	**3**	**1**	**0**	**1**	**0**	**1**	**0**	**0**
	NHL Totals		**167**	**13**	**28**	**41**	**14**	**26**	**40**	**77**	**1**	**0**	**0**	**188**	**6.9**	**79**	**3**	**79**	**4**		**3**	**1**	**0**	**1**	**0**	**1**	**0**	**0**

● DANEYKO, KEN

Ken Daneyko D – L. 6'1", 215 lbs. b: Windsor, Ont., 4/17/1964. New Jersey's 2nd choice, 18th overall, in 1982 Entry Draft.

Season	Club	League	GP	G	A	Pts	AG	AA	APts	PIM	PP	SH	GW	S	%	TGF	PGF	TGA	PGA	+/-	GP	G	A	Pts	PIM	PP	SH	GW
1980-81	Spokane Flyers	WHL	62	6	13	19	....	....	....	140	....	....	....	....	....	....	....	....	....	....	4	0	0	0	6	....	....	....
1981-82	Spokane Flyers	WHL	26	1	11	12	....	....	....	147	....	....	....	....	....	....	....	....	....	....	....	....	....	....	....	....	....	....
	Seattle Breakers	WHL	38	1	22	23	....	....	....	151	....	....	....	....	....	....	....	....	....	....	14	1	9	10	49	....	....	....
1982-83	Seattle Breakers	WHL	69	17	43	60	....	....	....	150	....	....	....	....	....	....	....	....	....	....	4	1	3	4	14	....	....	....
1983-84	Kamloops Jr. Oilers	WHL	19	6	28	34	....	....	....	52	....	....	....	....	....	....	....	....	....	....	17	4	9	13	28	....	....	....
	New Jersey Devils	**NHL**	**11**	**1**	**4**	**5**	**1**	**3**	**4**	**17**	**0**	**0**	**0**	**17**	**5.9**	**11**	**0**	**15**	**3**	**–1**	....	....	....	....	....	....	....	....
1984-85	**New Jersey Devils**	**NHL**	**1**	**0**	**0**	**0**	**0**	**0**	**0**	**10**	**0**	**0**	**0**	**1**	**0.0**	**0**	**0**	**1**	**0**	**–1**	....	....	....	....	....	....	....	....
	Maine Mariners	AHL	80	4	9	13	....	....	....	206	....	....	....	....	....	....	....	....	....	....	11	1	3	4	36	....	....	....
1985-86	**New Jersey Devils**	**NHL**	**44**	**0**	**10**	**10**	**0**	**7**	**7**	**100**	**0**	**0**	**0**	**48**	**0.0**	**42**	**1**	**56**	**15**	**0**	....	....	....	....	....	....	....	....
	Maine Mariners	AHL	21	3	2	5	....	....	....	75	....	....	....	....	....	....	....	....	....	....	....	....	....	....	....	....	....	....
	Canada	WEC-A	7	0	0	0	....	....	....	0	....	....	....	....	....	....	....	....	....	....	....	....	....	....	....	....	....	....
1986-87	**New Jersey Devils**	**NHL**	**79**	**2**	**12**	**14**	**2**	**9**	**11**	**183**	**0**	**0**	**0**	**113**	**1.8**	**92**	**21**	**129**	**45**	**–13**	....	....	....	....	....	....	....	....
1987-88	**New Jersey Devils**	**NHL**	**80**	**5**	**7**	**12**	**4**	**5**	**9**	**239**	**1**	**0**	**0**	**82**	**6.1**	**67**	**5**	**94**	**29**	**–3**	**20**	**1**	**6**	**7**	**83**	**0**	**0**	**1**
1988-89	**New Jersey Devils**	**NHL**	**80**	**5**	**5**	**10**	**4**	**4**	**8**	**283**	**1**	**0**	**0**	**108**	**4.6**	**56**	**4**	**106**	**32**	**–22**	....	....	....	....	....	....	....	....
	Canada	WEC-A	8	0	0	0	....	....	....	4	....	....	....	....	....	....	....	....	....	....	....	....	....	....	....	....	....	....
1989-90	**New Jersey Devils**	**NHL**	**74**	**6**	**15**	**21**	**5**	**11**	**16**	**219**	**0**	**1**	**1**	**64**	**9.4**	**68**	**1**	**66**	**14**	**+15**	**6**	**2**	**0**	**2**	**21**	**0**	**0**	**0**
1990-91	**New Jersey Devils**	**NHL**	**80**	**4**	**16**	**20**	**4**	**12**	**16**	**249**	**1**	**2**	**1**	**106**	**3.8**	**71**	**10**	**101**	**30**	**–10**	**7**	**0**	**1**	**1**	**10**	**0**	**0**	**0**
1991-92	**New Jersey Devils**	**NHL**	**80**	**1**	**7**	**8**	**1**	**5**	**6**	**170**	**0**	**0**	**0**	**57**	**1.8**	**61**	**1**	**87**	**34**	**+7**	**7**	**0**	**3**	**3**	**16**	**0**	**0**	**0**
1992-93	**New Jersey Devils**	**NHL**	**84**	**2**	**11**	**13**	**2**	**8**	**10**	**236**	**0**	**0**	**0**	**71**	**2.8**	**67**	**1**	**104**	**42**	**+4**	**5**	**0**	**0**	**0**	**8**	**0**	**0**	**0**
1993-94	**New Jersey Devils**	**NHL**	**78**	**1**	**9**	**10**	**1**	**7**	**8**	**176**	**0**	**0**	**1**	**60**	**1.7**	**72**	**0**	**74**	**29**	**+27**	**20**	**0**	**1**	**1**	**45**	**0**	**0**	**0**
1994-95	**New Jersey Devils**	**NHL**	**25**	**1**	**2**	**3**	**2**	**3**	**5**	**54**	**0**	**0**	**0**	**27**	**3.7**	**19**	**0**	**19**	**4**	**+4**	**20**	**1**	**0**	**1**	**22**	**0**	**0**	**0**
1995-96	**New Jersey Devils**	**NHL**	**80**	**2**	**4**	**6**	**2**	**3**	**5**	**115**	**0**	**0**	**0**	**67**	**3.0**	**39**	**1**	**62**	**14**	**–10**	....	....	....	....	....	....	....	....
1996-97	**New Jersey Devils**	**NHL**	**77**	**2**	**7**	**9**	**2**	**6**	**8**	**70**	**0**	**0**	**0**	**63**	**3.2**	**62**	**0**	**56**	**18**	**+24**	**10**	**0**	**0**	**0**	**28**	**0**	**0**	**0**
1997-98	**New Jersey Devils**	**NHL**	**37**	**0**	**1**	**1**	**0**	**1**	**1**	**57**	**0**	**0**	**0**	**18**	**0.0**	**22**	**0**	**25**	**6**	**+3**	**6**	**0**	**1**	**1**	**10**	**0**	**0**	**0**
	NHL Totals		**910**	**32**	**110**	**142**	**30**	**84**	**114**	**2178**	**3**	**3**	**3**	**902**	**3.5**	**749**	**45**	**995**	**315**		**101**	**4**	**12**	**16**	**243**	**0**	**0**	**1**

			REGULAR SEASON																		PLAYOFFS							
Season	Club	League	GP	G	A	Pts	AG	AA	APts	PIM	PP	SH	GW	S	%	TGF	PGF	TGA	PGA	+/–	GP	G	A	Pts	PIM	PP	SH	GW

• DANIELS, JEFF

Jeff Daniels LW – L. 6'1", 200 lbs. b: Oshawa, Ont., 6/24/1968. Pittsburgh's 6th choice, 109th overall, in 1986 Entry Draft.

Season	Club	League	GP	G	A	Pts	AG	AA	APts	PIM	PP	SH	GW	S	%	TGF	PGF	TGA	PGA	+/–	GP	G	A	Pts	PIM	PP	SH	GW
1984-85	Oshawa Generals	OHL	59	7	11	18	....	....	....	16	....	....	....	....	....	....	....	....	....	....	....	....	....	....	....	....	....	....
1985-86	Oshawa Generals	OHL	62	13	19	32	....	....	....	23	....	....	....	....	....	....	....	....	....	....	6	0	1	1	0	....	....	....
1986-87	Oshawa Generals	OHL	54	14	9	23	....	....	....	22	....	....	....	....	....	....	....	....	....	....	15	3	2	5	5	....	....	....
1987-88	Oshawa Generals	OHL	64	29	39	68	....	....	....	59	....	....	....	....	....	....	....	....	....	....	4	2	3	5	0	....	....	....
1988-89	Muskegon Lumberjacks	IHL	58	21	21	42	....	....	....	58	....	....	....	....	....	....	....	....	....	....	11	3	5	8	11	....	....	....
1989-90	Muskegon Lumberjacks	IHL	80	30	47	77	....	....	....	39	....	....	....	....	....	....	....	....	....	....	6	1	1	2	7	....	....	....
1990-91	**Pittsburgh Penguins**	**NHL**	**11**	**0**	**2**	**2**	**0**	**2**	**2**	**2**	**0**	**0**	**0**	**6**	**0.0**	**4**	**0**	**5**	**1**	**0**	....	....	....	....	....	....	....	....
	Muskegon Lumberjacks	IHL	62	23	29	52	....	....	....	18	....	....	....	....	....	....	....	....	....	....	5	1	3	4	2	....	....	....
1991-92	**Pittsburgh Penguins**	**NHL**	**2**	**0**	**0**	**0**	**0**	**0**	**0**	**0**	**0**	**0**	**0**	**0**	**0.0**	**0**	**0**	**0**	**0**	**0**	....	....	....	....	....	....	....	....
	Muskegon Lumberjacks	IHL	44	19	16	35	....	....	....	38	....	....	....	....	....	....	....	....	....	....	10	5	4	9	9	....	....	....
1992-93	**Pittsburgh Penguins**	**NHL**	**58**	**5**	**4**	**9**	**4**	**3**	**7**	**14**	**0**	**0**	**1**	**30**	**16.7**	**18**	**1**	**25**	**3**	**–5**	**12**	**3**	**2**	**5**	**0**	**0**	**0**	**1**
	Cleveland Lumberjacks	IHL	3	2	1	3	....	....	....	0	....	....	....	....	....	....	....	....	....	....	....	....	....	....	....	....	....	....
1993-94	**Pittsburgh Penguins**	**NHL**	**63**	**3**	**5**	**8**	**3**	**4**	**7**	**20**	**0**	**0**	**1**	**46**	**6.5**	**13**	**0**	**16**	**2**	**–1**	....	....	....	....	....	....	....	....
	Florida Panthers	**NHL**	**7**	**0**	**0**	**0**	**0**	**0**	**0**	**0**	**0**	**0**	**0**	**6**	**0.0**	**2**	**0**	**2**	**0**	**0**	....	....	....	....	....	....	....	....
1994-95	**Florida Panthers**	**NHL**	**3**	**0**	**0**	**0**	**0**	**0**	**0**	**0**	**0**	**0**	**0**	**0**	**0.0**	**0**	**0**	**0**	**0**	**0**	....	....	....	....	....	....	....	....
	Detroit Vipers	IHL	25	8	12	20	....	....	....	6	....	....	....	....	....	....	....	....	....	....	5	1	0	1	0	....	....	....
1995-96	Springfield Falcons	AHL	72	22	20	42	....	....	....	32	....	....	....	....	....	....	....	....	....	....	10	3	0	3	2	....	....	....
1996-97	**Hartford Whalers**	**NHL**	**10**	**0**	**2**	**2**	**0**	**2**	**2**	**0**	**0**	**0**	**0**	**6**	**0.0**	**3**	**0**	**1**	**0**	**+2**	....	....	....	....	....	....	....	....
	Springfield Falcons	AHL	38	18	14	32	....	....	....	19	....	....	....	....	....	....	....	....	....	....	16	7	3	10	4	....	....	....
1997-98	**Carolina Hurricanes**	**NHL**	**2**	**0**	**0**	**0**	**0**	**0**	**0**	**0**	**0**	**0**	**0**	**1**	**0.0**	**0**	**0**	**0**	**0**	**0**	....	....	....	....	....	....	....	....
	Beast of New Haven	AHL	71	24	27	51	....	....	....	34	....	....	....	....	....	....	....	....	....	....	3	0	1	1	0	....	....	....
	NHL Totals		**156**	**8**	**13**	**21**	**7**	**11**	**18**	**36**	**0**	**0**	**2**	**95**	**8.4**	**40**	**1**	**49**	**6**		**12**	**3**	**2**	**5**	**0**	**0**	**0**	**1**

Traded to **Florida** by **Pittsburgh** for Greg Hawgood, March 19, 1994. Signed as a free agent by **Hartford**, August 18, 1995. Transferred to **Carolina** after **Hartford** franchise relocated, June 25, 1997. Claimed by **Nashville** from **Carolina** in Expansion Draft, June 26, 1998.

• DANIELS, KIMBI

Kimbi Daniels C – R. 5'10", 175 lbs. b: Brandon, Man., 1/19/1972. Philadelphia's 5th choice, 44th overall, in 1990 Entry Draft.

Season	Club	League	GP	G	A	Pts	AG	AA	APts	PIM	PP	SH	GW	S	%	TGF	PGF	TGA	PGA	+/–	GP	G	A	Pts	PIM	PP	SH	GW
1987-88	West Kildonan North Stars	MJHL	18	5	11	16	....	....	....	28	....	....	....	....	....	....	....	....	....	....	....	....	....	....	....	....	....	....
1988-89	Swift Current Broncos	WHL	68	30	31	61	....	....	....	48	....	....	....	....	....	....	....	....	....	....	12	6	6	12	12	....	....	....
1989-90	Swift Current Broncos	WHL	69	43	51	94	....	....	....	84	....	....	....	....	....	....	....	....	....	....	4	1	3	4	10	....	....	....
1990-91	Swift Current Broncos	WHL	69	54	64	118	....	....	....	68	....	....	....	....	....	....	....	....	....	....	3	4	2	6	6	....	....	....
	Philadelphia Flyers	**NHL**	**2**	**0**	**1**	**1**	**0**	**1**	**1**	**0**	**0**	**0**	**0**	**2**	**0.0**	**1**	**0**	**3**	**0**	**–2**	....	....	....	....	....	....	....	....
1991-92	Seattle Thunderbirds	WHL	19	7	14	21	....	....	....	133	....	....	....	....	....	....	....	....	....	....	15	5	10	15	27	....	....	....
	Canada	WJC-A	7	3	4	7	....	....	....	16	....	....	....	....	....	....	....	....	....	....	....	....	....	....	....	....	....	....
	Philadelphia Flyers	**NHL**	**25**	**1**	**1**	**2**	**1**	**1**	**2**	**4**	**0**	**0**	**1**	**16**	**6.3**	**10**	**1**	**13**	**0**	**–4**	....	....	....	....	....	....	....	....
1992-93	Tri-City Americans	WHL	9	9	12	21	....	....	....	12	....	....	....	....	....	....	....	....	....	....	3	0	1	1	8	....	....	....
1993-94	Salt Lake Golden Eagles	IHL	25	6	9	15	....	....	....	8	....	....	....	....	....	....	....	....	....	....	....	....	....	....	....	....	....	....
	Detroit Falcons	ColHL	23	11	28	39	....	....	....	42	....	....	....	....	....	....	....	....	....	....	....	....	....	....	....	....	....	....
1994-95	Minnesota Moose	IHL	10	1	4	5	....	....	....	2	....	....	....	....	....	....	....	....	....	....	....	....	....	....	....	....	....	....
1995-96	Baltimore Bandits	AHL	7	2	1	3	....	....	....	2	....	....	....	....	....	....	....	....	....	....	....	....	....	....	....	....	....	....
	Jacksonville Lizard Kings	ECHL	26	12	22	34	....	....	....	129	....	....	....	....	....	....	....	....	....	....	....	....	....	....	....	....	....	....
	Charlotte Checkers	ECHL	18	16	14	30	....	....	....	6	....	....	....	....	....	....	....	....	....	....	18	8	6	14	24	....	....	....
1996-97	Charlotte Checkers	ECHL	32	12	24	36	....	....	....	116	....	....	....	....	....	....	....	....	....	....	....	....	....	....	....	....	....	....
	Wheeling Thunderbirds	ECHL	17	5	24	29	....	....	....	10	....	....	....	....	....	....	....	....	....	....	3	1	4	5	6	....	....	....
	Rochester Americans	AHL	6	1	3	4	....	....	....	2	....	....	....	....	....	....	....	....	....	....	....	....	....	....	....	....	....	....
	Hamilton Bulldogs	AHL	3	0	0	0	....	....	....	0	....	....	....	....	....	....	....	....	....	....	16	5	8	13	4	....	....	....
1997-98	Providence Bruins	AHL	32	2	5	7	....	....	....	30	....	....	....	....	....	....	....	....	....	....	....	....	....	....	....	....	....	....
	San Antonio Dragons	IHL	13	2	12	14	....	....	....	20	....	....	....	....	....	....	....	....	....	....	....	....	....	....	....	....	....	....
	Quebec Rafales	IHL	28	7	9	16	....	....	....	69	....	....	....	....	....	....	....	....	....	....	....	....	....	....	....	....	....	....
	NHL Totals		**27**	**1**	**2**	**3**	**1**	**2**	**3**	**4**	**0**	**0**	**1**	**18**	**5.6**	**11**	**1**	**16**	**0**		....	....	....	....	....	....	....	....

• DANIELS, SCOTT

Scott Daniels LW – L. 6'3", 214 lbs. b: Prince Albert, Sask., 9/19/1969. Hartford's 6th choice, 136th overall, in 1989 Entry Draft.

Season	Club	League	GP	G	A	Pts	AG	AA	APts	PIM	PP	SH	GW	S	%	TGF	PGF	TGA	PGA	+/–	GP	G	A	Pts	PIM	PP	SH	GW
1986-87	Kamloops Blazers	WHL	43	6	4	10	....	....	....	68	....	....	....	....	....	....	....	....	....	....	....	....	....	....	....	....	....	....
	New Westminster Bruins	WHL	19	4	7	11	....	....	....	30	....	....	....	....	....	....	....	....	....	....	....	....	....	....	....	....	....	....
1987-88	New Westminster Bruins	WHL	37	6	11	17	....	....	....	157	....	....	....	....	....	....	....	....	....	....	....	....	....	....	....	....	....	....
	Regina Pats	WHL	19	2	3	5	....	....	....	83	....	....	....	....	....	....	....	....	....	....	....	....	....	....	....	....	....	....
1988-89	Regina Pats	WHL	64	21	26	47	....	....	....	241	....	....	....	....	....	....	....	....	....	....	....	....	....	....	....	....	....	....
1989-90	Regina Pats	WHL	52	28	31	59	....	....	....	171	....	....	....	....	....	....	....	....	....	....	....	....	....	....	....	....	....	....
1990-91	Springfield Indians	AHL	40	2	6	8	....	....	....	121	....	....	....	....	....	....	....	....	....	....	....	....	....	....	....	....	....	....
	Louisville IceHawks	ECHL	9	5	3	8	....	....	....	34	....	....	....	....	....	....	....	....	....	....	1	0	2	2	0	....	....	....
1991-92	Springfield Indians	AHL	54	7	15	22	....	....	....	213	....	....	....	....	....	....	....	....	....	....	10	0	0	0	32	....	....	....
1992-93	**Hartford Whalers**	**NHL**	**1**	**0**	**0**	**0**	**0**	**0**	**0**	**19**	**0**	**0**	**0**	**0**	**0.0**	**0**	**0**	**0**	**0**	**0**	....	....	....	....	....	....	....	....
	Springfield Indians	AHL	60	11	12	23	....	....	....	181	....	....	....	....	....	....	....	....	....	....	12	2	7	9	12	....	....	....
1993-94	Springfield Indians	AHL	52	9	11	20	....	....	....	185	....	....	....	....	....	....	....	....	....	....	6	0	1	1	53	....	....	....
1994-95	**Hartford Whalers**	**NHL**	**12**	**0**	**2**	**2**	**0**	**3**	**3**	**55**	**0**	**0**	**0**	**7**	**0.0**	**4**	**0**	**3**	**0**	**+1**	....	....	....	....	....	....	....	....
	Springfield Falcons	AHL	48	9	5	14	....	....	....	277	....	....	....	....	....	....	....	....	....	....	....	....	....	....	....	....	....	....
1995-96	**Hartford Whalers**	**NHL**	**53**	**3**	**4**	**7**	**3**	**3**	**6**	**254**	**0**	**0**	**0**	**43**	**7.0**	**11**	**1**	**14**	**0**	**–4**	....	....	....	....	....	....	....	....
	Springfield Falcons	AHL	6	4	1	5	....	....	....	17	....	....	....	....	....	....	....	....	....	....	....	....	....	....	....	....	....	....
1996-97	**Philadelphia Flyers**	**NHL**	**56**	**5**	**3**	**8**	**5**	**3**	**8**	**237**	**0**	**0**	**2**	**48**	**10.4**	**15**	**0**	**14**	**1**	**+2**	....	....	....	....	....	....	....	....
1997-98	**New Jersey Devils**	**NHL**	**26**	**0**	**3**	**3**	**0**	**3**	**3**	**102**	**0**	**0**	**0**	**17**	**0.0**	**4**	**0**	**3**	**0**	**+1**	**1**	**0**	**0**	**0**	**0**	**0**	**0**	**0**
	NHL Totals		**148**	**8**	**12**	**20**	**8**	**12**	**20**	**667**	**0**	**0**	**2**	**115**	**7.0**	**34**	**1**	**34**	**1**		**1**	**0**	**0**	**0**	**0**	**0**	**0**	**0**

Signed as a free agent by **Philadelphia**, June 27, 1996. Claimed by **New Jersey** from **Philadelphia** in NHL Waiver Draft, September 28, 1997.

• DAOUST, DAN

Dan "Dangerous Danny" Daoust C – L. 5'10", 160 lbs. b: Montreal, Que., 2/29/1960.

Season	Club	League	GP	G	A	Pts	AG	AA	APts	PIM	PP	SH	GW	S	%	TGF	PGF	TGA	PGA	+/–	GP	G	A	Pts	PIM	PP	SH	GW
1977-78	Cornwall Royals	QMJHL	68	24	44	68	....	....	....	74	....	....	....	....	....	....	....	....	....	....	....	....	....	....	....	....	....	....
1978-79	Cornwall Royals	QMJHL	72	42	55	97	....	....	....	85	....	....	....	....	....	....	....	....	....	....	....	....	....	....	....	....	....	....
1979-80	Cornwall Royals	QMJHL	70	40	62	102	....	....	....	82	....	....	....	....	....	....	....	....	....	....	....	....	....	....	....	....	....	....
1980-81	Nova Scotia Voyageurs	AHL	80	38	60	98	....	....	....	106	....	....	....	....	....	....	....	....	....	....	6	1	3	4	10	....	....	....
1981-82	Nova Scotia Voyageurs	AHL	61	25	40	65	....	....	....	75	....	....	....	....	....	....	....	....	....	....	9	5	2	7	11	....	....	....
1982-83	**Montreal Canadiens**	**NHL**	**4**	**0**	**1**	**1**	**0**	**1**	**1**	**4**	**0**	**0**	**0**	**6**	**0.0**	**1**	**0**	**3**	**0**	**–2**	....	....	....	....	....	....	....	....
	Toronto Maple Leafs	**NHL**	**48**	**18**	**33**	**51**	**15**	**23**	**38**	**31**	**9**	**0**	**0**	**119**	**15.1**	**81**	**37**	**53**	**8**	**–1**	....	....	....	....	....	....	....	....
1983-84	**Toronto Maple Leafs**	**NHL**	**78**	**18**	**56**	**74**	**14**	**38**	**52**	**88**	**8**	**0**	**1**	**154**	**11.7**	**116**	**54**	**79**	**1**	**–16**	....	....	....	....	....	....	....	....
1984-85	**Toronto Maple Leafs**	**NHL**	**79**	**17**	**37**	**54**	**14**	**25**	**39**	**98**	**1**	**3**	**2**	**141**	**12.1**	**80**	**20**	**120**	**33**	**–27**	....	....	....	....	....	....	....	....
1985-86	**Toronto Maple Leafs**	**NHL**	**80**	**7**	**13**	**20**	**6**	**9**	**15**	**88**	**1**	**0**	**0**	**92**	**7.6**	**35**	**5**	**101**	**50**	**–21**	**10**	**2**	**2**	**4**	**19**	**0**	**0**	**0**
1986-87	**Toronto Maple Leafs**	**NHL**	**33**	**4**	**3**	**7**	**3**	**2**	**5**	**35**	**0**	**0**	**1**	**25**	**16.0**	**11**	**1**	**16**	**6**	**0**	**13**	**5**	**2**	**7**	**42**	**0**	**0**	**2**
	Newmarket Saints	AHL	1	0	0	0	....	....	....	4	....	....	....	....	....	....	....	....	....	....	....	....	....	....	....	....	....	....
1987-88	**Toronto Maple Leafs**	**NHL**	**67**	**9**	**8**	**17**	**8**	**6**	**14**	**57**	**0**	**0**	**1**	**57**	**15.8**	**21**	**0**	**52**	**24**	**–7**	**4**	**0**	**0**	**0**	**2**	**0**	**0**	**0**
1988-89	**Toronto Maple Leafs**	**NHL**	**68**	**7**	**5**	**12**	**6**	**4**	**10**	**54**	**0**	**2**	**1**	**66**	**10.6**	**20**	**2**	**86**	**48**	**–20**	....	....	....	....	....	....	....	....
1989-90	**Toronto Maple Leafs**	**NHL**	**65**	**7**	**11**	**18**	**6**	**8**	**14**	**89**	**0**	**4**	**0**	**53**	**13.2**	**28**	**2**	**59**	**34**	**+1**	**5**	**0**	**1**	**1**	**20**	**0**	**0**	**0**
1991-92	EC Biel	Switz.	5	5	9	14	....	....	....	8	....	....	....	....	....	....	....	....	....	....	....	....	....	....	....	....	....	....
1992-93	Thurgau	Switz. B	36	23	31	54	....	....	....	....	....	....	....	....	....	....	....	....	....	....	....	....	....	....	....	....	....	....
1993-94	Thurgau	Switz. B	36	21	31	52	....	....	....	....	....	....	....	....	....	....	....	....	....	....	....	....	....	....	....	....	....	....
1994-95	Thurgau	Switz. B	36	23	42	65	....	....	....	105	....	....	....	....	....	....	....	....	....	....	6	7	5	12	41	....	....	....
1995-96	Thurgau	Switz. B	36	25	40	65	....	....	....	50	....	....	....	....	....	....	....	....	....	....	5	3	6	9	10	....	....	....
1996-97	Thurgau	Switz. B	19	10	24	34	....	....	....	20	....	....	....	....	....	....	....	....	....	....	3	1	1	2	8	....	....	....
	NHL Totals		**522**	**87**	**167**	**254**	**72**	**116**	**188**	**544**	**19**	**9**	**6**	**713**	**12.2**	**393**	**121**	**569**	**204**		**32**	**7**	**5**	**12**	**83**	**0**	**0**	**2**

AHL First All-Star Team (1981) • NHL All-Rookie Team (1983)

Signed as a free agent by **Montreal**, March 9, 1981. Traded to **Toronto** by **Montreal** for Toronto's 3rd round choice (later traded to Minnesota — Minnesota selected Ken Hodge Jr.) in 1984 Entry Draft, December 17, 1982.

			REGULAR SEASON																		PLAYOFFS							
Season	Club	League	GP	G	A	Pts	AG	AA	APts	PIM	PP	SH	GW	S	%	TGF	PGF	TGA	PGA	+/-	GP	G	A	Pts	PIM	PP	SH	GW

● **DARBY, CRAIG** Craig Darby C – R. 6'3", 200 lbs. b: Oneida, NY, 9/26/1972. Montreal's 3rd choice, 43rd overall, in 1991 Entry Draft.

Season	Club	League	GP	G	A	Pts	AG	AA	APts	PIM	PP	SH	GW	S	%	TGF	PGF	TGA	PGA	+/-	GP	G	A	Pts	PIM	PP	SH	GW
1990-91	Albany Academy	H.S.	29	32	61	94	....	....	....	....	....	....	....	....	....	....	....	....	....	....	....	....	....	....	....	....	....	....
1991-92	Providence College	H.E.	35	17	24	41	....	....	....	47	....	....	....	....	....	....	....	....	....	....	....	....	....	....	....	....	....	....
1992-93	Providence College	H.E.	35	11	21	32	....	....	....	62	....	....	....	....	....	....	....	....	....	....	....	....	....	....	....	....	....	....
1993-94	Fredericton Canadiens	AHL	66	23	33	56	....	....	....	51	....	....	....	....	....	....	....	....	....	....	....	....	....	....	....	....	....	....
1994-95	**Montreal Canadiens**	**NHL**	**10**	**0**	**2**	**2**	**0**	**3**	**3**	**0**	**0**	**0**	**0**	**4**	**0.0**	**3**	**0**	**8**	**0**	**–5**	....	....	....	....	....	....	....	....
	Fredericton Canadiens	AHL	64	21	47	68	....	....	....	82	....	....	....	....	....	....	....	....	....	....	....	....	....	....	....	....	....	....
	New York Islanders	**NHL**	**3**	**0**	**0**	**0**	**0**	**0**	**0**	**0**	**0**	**0**	**0**	**1**	**0.0**	**0**	**0**	**1**	**0**	**–1**	....	....	....	....	....	....	....	....
1995-96	**New York Islanders**	**NHL**	**10**	**0**	**2**	**2**	**0**	**2**	**2**	**0**	**0**	**0**	**0**	**1**	**0.0**	**2**	**0**	**3**	**0**	**–1**	....	....	....	....	....	....	....	....
	Worcester IceCats	AHL	68	22	28	50	....	....	....	47	....	....	....	....	....	....	....	....	....	....	4	1	1	2	2	....	....	....
1996-97	**Philadelphia Flyers**	**NHL**	**9**	**1**	**4**	**5**	**1**	**4**	**5**	**2**	**0**	**1**	**0**	**13**	**7.7**	**5**	**0**	**4**	**1**	**+2**	....	....	....	....	....	....	....	....
	Philadelphia Phantoms	AHL	59	26	33	59	....	....	....	24	....	....	....	....	....	....	....	....	....	....	10	3	6	9	0	....	....	....
1997-98	**Philadelphia Flyers**	**NHL**	**3**	**1**	**0**	**1**	**1**	**0**	**1**	**0**	**0**	**0**	**0**	**3**	**33.3**	**1**	**0**	**1**	**0**	**0**	....	....	....	....	....	....	....	....
	Philadelphia Phantoms	AHL	77	42	45	87	....	....	....	34	....	....	....	....	....	....	....	....	....	....	20	5	9	14	4	....	....	....
	NHL Totals		**35**	**2**	**8**	**10**	**2**	**9**	**11**	**2**	**0**	**1**	**0**	**22**	**9.1**	**11**	**0**	**17**	**1**		....	....	....	....	....	....	....	....

AHL First All-Star Team (1998)

Traded to **NY Islanders** by **Montreal** with Kirk Muller and Mathieu Schneider for Pierre Turgeon and Vladimir Malakhov, April 5, 1995. Claimed on waivers by **Philadelphia** from **NY Islanders**, June 4, 1996. Claimed by **Nashville** from **Philadelphia** in Expansion Draft, June 26, 1998.

● **DARK, MICHAEL** Michael Dark D – R. 6'3", 210 lbs. b: Sarnia, Ont., 9/17/1963. Montreal's 10th choice, 124th overall, in 1982 Entry Draft.

Season	Club	League	GP	G	A	Pts	AG	AA	APts	PIM	PP	SH	GW	S	%	TGF	PGF	TGA	PGA	+/-	GP	G	A	Pts	PIM	PP	SH	GW
1981-82	Sarnia Sailors	OJHL	41	13	30	43	....	....	....	86	....	....	....	....	....	....	....	....	....	....	....	....	....	....	....	....	....	....
1982-83	RPI Engineers	ECAC	29	3	16	19	....	....	....	54	....	....	....	....	....	....	....	....	....	....	....	....	....	....	....	....	....	....
1983-84	RPI Engineers	ECAC	38	2	12	14	....	....	....	60	....	....	....	....	....	....	....	....	....	....	....	....	....	....	....	....	....	....
1984-85	RPI Engineers	ECAC	36	7	26	33	....	....	....	76	....	....	....	....	....	....	....	....	....	....	....	....	....	....	....	....	....	....
1985-86	RPI Engineers	ECAC	32	7	29	36	....	....	....	58	....	....	....	....	....	....	....	....	....	....	....	....	....	....	....	....	....	....
1986-87	**St. Louis Blues**	**NHL**	**13**	**2**	**0**	**2**	**2**	**0**	**2**	**2**	**0**	**0**	**0**	**4**	**50.0**	**7**	**0**	**7**	**0**	**0**	....	....	....	....	....	....	....	....
	Peoria Rivermen	IHL	42	4	11	15	....	....	....	93	....	....	....	....	....	....	....	....	....	....	....	....	....	....	....	....	....	....
1987-88	**St. Louis Blues**	**NHL**	**30**	**3**	**6**	**9**	**3**	**4**	**7**	**12**	**0**	**0**	**1**	**27**	**11.1**	**11**	**0**	**6**	**1**	**+6**	....	....	....	....	....	....	....	....
	Peoria Rivermen	IHL	37	21	12	33	....	....	....	97	....	....	....	....	....	....	....	....	....	....	2	0	0	0	4	....	....	....
1988-89	Salt Lake Golden Eagles	IHL	36	3	12	15	....	....	....	57	....	....	....	....	....	....	....	....	....	....	....	....	....	....	....	....	....	....
	New Haven Nighthawks	AHL	7	0	4	4	....	....	....	4	....	....	....	....	....	....	....	....	....	....	....	....	....	....	....	....	....	....
1989-90	Peterborough Pirates	Britain	38	42	34	76	....	....	....	*152	....	....	....	....	....	....	....	....	....	....	....	....	....	....	....	....	....	....
	NHL Totals		**43**	**5**	**6**	**11**	**5**	**4**	**9**	**14**	**0**	**0**	**1**	**31**	**16.1**	**18**	**0**	**13**	**1**		....	....	....	....	....	....	....	....

ECAC First All-Star Team (1986) • NCAA East All-American Team (1986)

Traded to **St. Louis** by **Montreal** with Mark Hunter and Montreal's 2nd (Herb Raglan), 3rd (Nelson Emerson), 5th (Dan Brooks) and 6th (Rick Burchill) round choices in 1985 Entry Draft for St. Louis' 1st (Jose Charbonneau), 2nd (Todd Richard), 4th (Martin Desjardins), 5th (Tom Sagissor) and 6th (Donald Defresne) round choices in 1985 Entry Draft, June 15, 1985. Traded to **Calgary** by **St. Louis** with Doug Gilmour, Steve Bozek and Mark Hunter for Mike Bullard, Craig Coxe and Tim Corkery, September 6, 1988.

● **DAVID, RICHARD** Richard David LW – L. 6', 195 lbs. b: Notre Dame de la Salette, Que., 4/8/1958. Montreal's 5th choice, 42nd overall, in 1978 Amateur Draft.

Season	Club	League	GP	G	A	Pts	AG	AA	APts	PIM	PP	SH	GW	S	%	TGF	PGF	TGA	PGA	+/-	GP	G	A	Pts	PIM	PP	SH	GW
1973-74	Hull Festivals	QMJHL	65	24	22	46	....	....	....	16	....	....	....	....	....	....	....	....	....	....	....	....	....	....	....	....	....	....
1974-75	Sorel Black Hawks	QMJHL	34	13	15	28	....	....	....	64	....	....	....	....	....	....	....	....	....	....	....	....	....	....	....	....	....	....
1975-76	Trois-Rivieres Draveurs	QMJHL	73	53	68	121	....	....	....	79	....	....	....	....	....	....	....	....	....	....	....	....	....	....	....	....	....	....
1976-77	Trois-Rivieres Draveurs	QMJHL	66	52	58	110	....	....	....	103	....	....	....	....	....	....	....	....	....	....	....	....	....	....	....	....	....	....
1977-78	Trois-Rivieres Draveurs	QMJHL	69	50	61	111	....	....	....	81	....	....	....	....	....	....	....	....	....	....	13	17	16	33	7	....	....	....
1978-79	Quebec Nordiques	WHA	14	0	4	4	....	....	....	4	....	....	....	....	....	....	....	....	....	....	....	....	....	....	....	....	....	....
	Binghamton Whalers	AHL	10	5	2	7	....	....	....	2	....	....	....	....	....	....	....	....	....	....	....	....	....	....	....	....	....	....
1979-80	**Quebec Nordiques**	**NHL**	**10**	**0**	**0**	**0**	**0**	**0**	**0**	**2**	**0**	**0**	**0**	**10**	**0.0**	**1**	**0**	**3**	**0**	**–2**	....	....	....	....	....	....	....	....
	Syracuse Firebirds	AHL	66	29	32	61	....	....	....	36	....	....	....	....	....	....	....	....	....	....	4	0	1	1	0	....	....	....
1980-81	Rochester Americans	AHL	1	0	0	0	....	....	....	0	....	....	....	....	....	....	....	....	....	....	....	....	....	....	....	....	....	....
	Erie Blades	EHL	32	10	32	42	....	....	....	47	....	....	....	....	....	....	....	....	....	....	8	5	5	10	6	....	....	....
1981-82	**Quebec Nordiques**	**NHL**	**5**	**1**	**1**	**2**	**1**	**1**	**2**	**4**	**0**	**0**	**0**	**6**	**16.7**	**3**	**1**	**5**	**0**	**–3**	**1**	**0**	**0**	**0**	**0**	**0**	**0**	**0**
	Fredericton Express	AHL	74	*51	32	83	....	....	....	18	....	....	....	....	....	....	....	....	....	....	....	....	....	....	....	....	....	....
1982-83	**Quebec Nordiques**	**NHL**	**16**	**3**	**3**	**6**	**2**	**2**	**4**	**4**	**2**	**0**	**1**	**13**	**23.1**	**9**	**3**	**8**	**0**	**–2**	....	....	....	....	....	....	....	....
	Fredericton Express	AHL	48	20	36	56	....	....	....	17	....	....	....	....	....	....	....	....	....	....	12	9	3	12	6	....	....	....
	NHL Totals		**31**	**4**	**4**	**8**	**3**	**3**	**6**	**10**	**2**	**0**	**1**	**20**	**13.8**	**10**	**4**	**10**	**0**		**1**	**0**	**0**	**0**	**0**	**0**	**0**	**0**
	Other Major League Totals		14	0	4	4	....	....	....	4	....	....	....	....	....	....	....	....	....		....	....	....	....	....	....	....	....

QMJHL East First All-Star Team (1976) • AHL Second All-Star Team (1982)

Signed as an underage free agent by **Quebec** (WHA), June, 1978. Rights retained by **Quebec** prior to Expansion Draft, June 9, 1979.

● **DAVIS, KIM** Kim Davis C – L. 5'11", 170 lbs. b: Flin Flon, Man., 10/31/1957. Pittsburgh's 2nd choice, 48th overall, in 1977 Amateur Draft.

Season	Club	League	GP	G	A	Pts	AG	AA	APts	PIM	PP	SH	GW	S	%	TGF	PGF	TGA	PGA	+/-	GP	G	A	Pts	PIM	PP	SH	GW
1974-75	Flin Flon Bombers	WCJHL	64	8	7	15	....	....	....	169	....	....	....	....	....	....	....	....	....	....	....	....	....	....	....	....	....	....
1975-76	Flin Flon Bombers	WCJHL	71	32	45	77	....	....	....	163	....	....	....	....	....	....	....	....	....	....	....	....	....	....	....	....	....	....
1976-77	Flin Flon Bombers	WCJHL	69	56	55	111	....	....	....	250	....	....	....	....	....	....	....	....	....	....	....	....	....	....	....	....	....	....
1977-78	**Pittsburgh Penguins**	**NHL**	**1**	**0**	**0**	**0**	**0**	**0**	**0**	**0**	**0**	**0**	**0**	**0**	**0.0**	**0**	**0**	**0**	**0**	**0**	....	....	....	....	....	....	....	....
	Grand Rapids Owls	IHL	63	28	43	71	....	....	....	191	....	....	....	....	....	....	....	....	....	....	....	....	....	....	....	....	....	....
1978-79	**Pittsburgh Penguins**	**NHL**	**1**	**1**	**0**	**1**	**1**	**0**	**1**	**0**	**0**	**0**	**1**	**1**	**100.0**	**1**	**0**	**1**	**0**	**0**	....	....	....	....	....	....	....	....
	Grand Rapids Owls	IHL	80	44	59	103	....	....	....	235	....	....	....	....	....	....	....	....	....	....	22	12	15	*27	77	....	....	....
1979-80	**Pittsburgh Penguins**	**NHL**	**24**	**3**	**7**	**10**	**3**	**5**	**8**	**43**	**0**	**0**	**1**	**25**	**12.0**	**12**	**2**	**17**	**0**	**–7**	**4**	**0**	**0**	**0**	**0**	**0**	**0**	**0**
	Syracuse Firebirds	AHL	44	13	13	26	....	....	....	62	....	....	....	....	....	....	....	....	....	....	....	....	....	....	....	....	....	....
1980-81	**Pittsburgh Penguins**	**NHL**	**8**	**1**	**0**	**1**	**1**	**0**	**1**	**4**	**0**	**0**	**0**	**2**	**50.0**	**2**	**0**	**5**	**0**	**–3**	....	....	....	....	....	....	....	....
	Binghamton Whalers	AHL	8	1	1	2	....	....	....	26	....	....	....	....	....	....	....	....	....	....	....	....	....	....	....	....	....	....
	Toronto Maple Leafs	**NHL**	**2**	**0**	**0**	**0**	**0**	**0**	**0**	**4**	**0**	**0**	**0**	**2**	**0.0**	**1**	**0**	**2**	**1**	**0**	....	....	....	....	....	....	....	....
	Springfield Indians	AHL	26	5	4	9	....	....	....	56	....	....	....	....	....	....	....	....	....	....	....	....	....	....	....	....	....	....
	New Brunswick Hawks	AHL	32	8	13	21	....	....	....	165	....	....	....	....	....	....	....	....	....	....	2	0	0	0	21	....	....	....
1981-82	New Brunswick Hawks	AHL	79	11	24	35	....	....	....	47	....	....	....	....	....	....	....	....	....	....	14	1	2	3	8	....	....	....
	NHL Totals		**36**	**5**	**7**	**12**	**5**	**5**	**10**	**51**	**0**	**0**	**2**	**30**	**16.7**	**16**	**2**	**25**	**1**		**4**	**0**	**0**	**0**	**0**	**0**	**0**	**0**

Traded to **Toronto** by **Pittsburgh** with Paul Marshall for Dave Burrows and Paul Gardner, November 18, 1980.

● **DAVIS, MAL** Mal Davis LW – L. 5'11", 180 lbs. b: Lockport, N.S., 10/10/1956.

Season	Club	League	GP	G	A	Pts	AG	AA	APts	PIM	PP	SH	GW	S	%	TGF	PGF	TGA	PGA	+/-	GP	G	A	Pts	PIM	PP	SH	GW
1975-76	St. Mary's University	AUAA	20	11	7	18	....	....	....	21	....	....	....	....	....	....	....	....	....	....	....	....	....	....	....	....	....	....
1976-77	St. Mary's University	AUAA	20	16	5	21	....	....	....	2	....	....	....	....	....	....	....	....	....	....	....	....	....	....	....	....	....	....
1977-78	St. Mary's University	AUAA	20	*23	13	36	....	....	....	8	....	....	....	....	....	....	....	....	....	....	....	....	....	....	....	....	....	....
1978-79	**Detroit Red Wings**	**NHL**	**6**	**0**	**0**	**0**	**0**	**0**	**0**	**0**	**0**	**0**	**0**	**1**	**0.0**	**1**	**0**	**3**	**0**	**–2**	....	....	....	....	....	....	....	....
	Kansas City Red Wings	CHL	71	42	24	66	....	....	....	29	....	....	....	....	....	....	....	....	....	....	4	2	0	2	4	....	....	....
1979-80	Adirondack Red Wings	AHL	79	34	31	65	....	....	....	45	....	....	....	....	....	....	....	....	....	....	5	2	2	4	19	....	....	....
1980-81	**Detroit Red Wings**	**NHL**	**5**	**2**	**0**	**2**	**2**	**0**	**2**	**0**	**0**	**0**	**0**	**12**	**16.7**	**5**	**0**	**0**	**0**	**+5**	....	....	....	....	....	....	....	....
	Adirondack Red Wings	AHL	58	23	12	35	....	....	....	48	....	....	....	....	....	....	....	....	....	....	17	0	4	10	9	....	....	....
1981-82	Rochester Americans	AHL	75	32	33	65	....	....	....	14	....	....	....	....	....	....	....	....	....	....	9	2	3	5	2	....	....	....
1982-83	**Buffalo Sabres**	**NHL**	**24**	**8**	**12**	**20**	**7**	**8**	**15**	**0**	**3**	**0**	**3**	**32**	**25.0**	**32**	**15**	**23**	**0**	**–8**	**6**	**1**	**0**	**1**	**0**	**0**	**0**	**0**
	Rochester Americans	AHL	57	43	32	75	....	....	....	15	....	....	....	....	....	....	....	....	....	....	....	....	....	....	....	....	....	....
1983-84	**Buffalo Sabres**	**NHL**	**11**	**2**	**1**	**3**	**2**	**1**	**3**	**4**	**1**	**0**	**0**	**12**	**16.7**	**11**	**5**	**7**	**0**	**–1**	**1**	**0**	**0**	**0**	**0**	**0**	**0**	**0**
	Rochester Americans	AHL	71	55	48	103	....	....	....	53	....	....	....	....	....	....	....	....	....	....	15	6	9	15	33	....	....	....
1984-85	**Buffalo Sabres**	**NHL**	**47**	**17**	**9**	**26**	**14**	**6**	**20**	**26**	**5**	**0**	**5**	**62**	**27.4**	**47**	**20**	**26**	**0**	**+1**	....	....	....	....	....	....	....	....
	Rochester Americans	AHL	6	4	4	8	....	....	....	14	....	....	....	....	....	....	....	....	....	....	....	....	....	....	....	....	....	....
1985-86	**Buffalo Sabres**	**NHL**	**7**	**2**	**0**	**2**	**2**	**0**	**2**	**4**	**2**	**0**	**0**	**5**	**40.0**	**5**	**3**	**3**	**0**	**–1**	....	....	....	....	....	....	....	....
	Rochester Americans	AHL	38	21	15	36	....	....	....	23	....	....	....	....	....	....	....	....	....	....	....	....	....	....	....	....	....	....
1986-87	TPS Turku	Finland	39	24	15	39	....	....	....	93	....	....	....	....	....	....	....	....	....	....	5	3	0	3	13	....	....	....
	Canada	Nat-Team	3	1	3	4	....	....	....	2	....	....	....	....	....	....	....	....	....	....	....	....	....	....	....	....	....	....
1987-88	TPS Turku	Finland	44	32	12	44	....	....	....	68	....	....	....	....	....	....	....	....	....	....	....	....	....	....	....	....	....	....

			REGULAR SEASON																		PLAYOFFS							
Season	Club	League	GP	G	A	Pts	AG	AA	APts	PIM	PP	SH	GW	S	%	TGF	PGF	TGA	PGA	+/–	GP	G	A	Pts	PIM	PP	SH	GW
1988-89	TPS Turku	Finland	34	21	15	36	....	....	....	31	....	....	....	....	....	....	....	....	....	....	10	*9	3	12	4	....	....	....
1989-90	TPS Turku	Finland	38	27	11	38	....	....	....	44	....	....	....	....	....	....	....	....	....	....	8	7	0	7	4	....	....	....
1990-91	TPS Turku	Finland	29	11	6	17	....	....	....	32	....	....	....	....	....	....	....	....	....	....	....	....	....	....	....	....	....	....
	NHL Totals		**100**	**31**	**22**	**53**	**27**	**15**	**42**	**34**	**11**	**0**	**8**	**124**	**25.0**	**101**	**43**	**62**	**0**		**7**	**1**	**0**	**1**	**0**	**0**	**0**	**0**

CHL First All-Star Team (1979) • AHL First All-Star Team (1984)

Signed as a free agent by **Detroit**, October 12, 1978. Signed as a free agent by **Buffalo**, September 2, 1981.

• DAVYDOV, EVGENY

Evgeny Davydov LW – R. 6′, 200 lbs. b: Chelyabinsk, USSR, 5/27/1967. Winnipeg's 14th choice, 235th overall, in 1989 Entry Draft.

1984-85	Chelyabinsk	USSR	5	1	0	1	....	....	....	2	....	....	....	....	....	....	....	....	....	....	....	....	....	....	....	....	....	....
1985-86	Chelyabinsk	USSR	39	11	5	16	....	....	....	22	....	....	....	....	....	....	....	....	....	....	....	....	....	....	....	....	....	....
1986-87	CSKA Moscow	USSR	32	11	2	13	....	....	....	8	....	....	....	....	....	....	....	....	....	....	....	....	....	....	....	....	....	....
1987-88	CSKA Moscow	USSR	44	16	7	23	....	....	....	18	....	....	....	....	....	....	....	....	....	....	....	....	....	....	....	....	....	....
1988-89	CSKA Moscow	USSR	35	9	7	16	....	....	....	4	....	....	....	....	....	....	....	....	....	....	....	....	....	....	....	....	....	....
1989-90	CSKA Moscow	USSR	44	17	6	23	....	....	....	16	....	....	....	....	....	....	....	....	....	....	....	....	....	....	....	....	....	....
1990-91	CSKA Moscow	USSR	44	10	10	20	....	....	....	26	....	....	....	....	....	....	....	....	....	....	....	....	....	....	....	....	....	....
1991-92	CSKA Moscow	CIS	27	13	12	25	....	....	....	14	....	....	....	....	....	....	....	....	....	....	....	....	....	....	....	....	....	....
	Winnipeg Jets	**NHL**	**12**	**4**	**3**	**7**	**4**	**2**	**6**	**8**	**2**	**0**	**0**	**32**	**12.5**	**15**	**5**	**3**	**0**	**+7**	**7**	**2**	**2**	**4**	**2**	**1**	**0**	**0**
1992-93	**Winnipeg Jets**	**NHL**	**79**	**28**	**21**	**49**	**23**	**14**	**37**	**66**	**7**	**0**	**2**	**176**	**15.9**	**72**	**23**	**51**	**0**	**–2**	**4**	**0**	**0**	**0**	**0**	**0**	**0**	**0**
1993-94	**Florida Panthers**	**NHL**	**21**	**2**	**6**	**8**	**2**	**5**	**7**	**8**	**0**	**0**	**0**	**22**	**9.1**	**14**	**6**	**11**	**0**	**–3**	....	....	....	....	....	....	....	....
	Ottawa Senators	**NHL**	**40**	**5**	**7**	**12**	**5**	**5**	**10**	**38**	**1**	**0**	**0**	**44**	**11.4**	**19**	**2**	**23**	**0**	**–6**	....	....	....	....	....	....	....	....
1994-95	**Ottawa Senators**	**NHL**	**3**	**1**	**2**	**3**	**2**	**3**	**5**	**0**	**0**	**0**	**0**	**2**	**50.0**	**3**	**0**	**1**	**0**	**+2**	....	....	....	....	....	....	....	....
	San Diego Gulls	IHL	11	2	1	3	....	....	....	14	....	....	....	....	....	....	....	....	....	....	....	....	....	....	....	....	....	....
	Chicago Wolves	IHL	18	10	12	22	....	....	....	26	....	....	....	....	....	....	....	....	....	....	3	1	0	1	0	....	....	....
1995-96	Amiens SC	France	3	3	0	3	....	....	....	4	....	....	....	....	....	....	....	....	....	....	13	15	9	24	54	....	....	....
1996-97	Brynas IF Gavle	Sweden	46	*30	18	48	....	....	....	103	....	....	....	....	....	....	....	....	....	....	....	....	....	....	....	....	....	....
	NHL Totals		**155**	**40**	**39**	**79**	**36**	**29**	**65**	**120**	**10**	**0**	**2**	**276**	**14.5**	**123**	**36**	**89**	**0**		**11**	**2**	**2**	**4**	**2**	**1**	**0**	**0**

Traded to **Florida** by **Winnipeg** for Florida's 4th round draft choice (later traded to Edmonton — Edmonton selected Adam Copeland) in 1984 Entry Draft. September 30, 1993. Traded to **Ottawa** by **Florida** with Scott Levins and future considerations for Bob Kudelski, January 6, 1994.

• DAWE, JASON

Jason Dawe LW – L. 5′10″, 189 lbs. b: North York, Ont., 5/29/1973. Buffalo's 2nd choice, 35th overall, in 1991 Entry Draft.

1989-90	Peterborough Petes	OHL	50	15	18	33	....	....	....	19	....	....	....	....	....	....	....	....	....	....	12	4	7	11	4	....	....	....
1990-91	Peterborough Petes	OHL	66	43	27	70	....	....	....	43	....	....	....	....	....	....	....	....	....	....	4	3	1	4	0	....	....	....
1991-92	Peterborough Petes	OHL	66	53	55	108	....	....	....	55	....	....	....	....	....	....	....	....	....	....	4	5	0	5	0	....	....	....
1992-93	Peterborough Petes	OHL	59	58	68	126	....	....	....	80	....	....	....	....	....	....	....	....	....	....	21	18	33	51	18	....	....	....
	Canada	WJC-A	7	3	3	6	....	....	....	8	....	....	....	....	....	....	....	....	....	....	....	....	....	....	....	....	....	....
	Rochester Americans	AHL	....	....	....	....	....	....	....	....	....	....	....	....	....	....	....	....	....	....	3	1	0	1	0	....	....	....
1993-94	**Buffalo Sabres**	**NHL**	**32**	**6**	**7**	**13**	**6**	**5**	**11**	**12**	**3**	**0**	**1**	**35**	**17.1**	**18**	**5**	**12**	**0**	**+1**	**6**	**0**	**1**	**1**	**6**	**0**	**0**	**0**
	Rochester Americans	AHL	48	22	14	36	....	....	....	44	....	....	....	....	....	....	....	....	....	....	....	....	....	....	....	....	....	....
1994-95	Rochester Americans	AHL	44	27	19	46	....	....	....	24	....	....	....	....	....	....	....	....	....	....	....	....	....	....	....	....	....	....
	Buffalo Sabres	**NHL**	**42**	**7**	**4**	**11**	**12**	**6**	**18**	**19**	**0**	**1**	**2**	**51**	**13.7**	**15**	**4**	**17**	**0**	**–6**	**5**	**2**	**1**	**3**	**6**	**0**	**0**	**0**
1995-96	**Buffalo Sabres**	**NHL**	**67**	**25**	**25**	**50**	**25**	**20**	**45**	**33**	**8**	**1**	**0**	**130**	**19.2**	**61**	**19**	**58**	**8**	**–8**	....	....	....	....	....	....	....	....
	Rochester Americans	AHL	7	5	4	9	....	....	....	2	....	....	....	....	....	....	....	....	....	....	....	....	....	....	....	....	....	....
	Canada	WC-A	8	3	0	3	....	....	....	2	....	....	....	....	....	....	....	....	....	....	....	....	....	....	....	....	....	....
1996-97	**Buffalo Sabres**	**NHL**	**81**	**22**	**26**	**48**	**23**	**23**	**46**	**32**	**4**	**1**	**3**	**136**	**16.2**	**73**	**19**	**52**	**12**	**+14**	**11**	**2**	**1**	**3**	**6**	**0**	**0**	**0**
1997-98	**Buffalo Sabres**	**NHL**	**68**	**19**	**17**	**36**	**22**	**17**	**39**	**36**	**4**	**1**	**3**	**115**	**16.5**	**51**	**16**	**44**	**19**	**+10**	....	....	....	....	....	....	....	....
	New York Islanders	**NHL**	**13**	**1**	**2**	**3**	**1**	**2**	**3**	**6**	**0**	**0**	**0**	**19**	**5.3**	**5**	**0**	**7**	**0**	**–2**	....	....	....	....	....	....	....	....
	NHL Totals		**303**	**80**	**81**	**161**	**89**	**73**	**162**	**138**	**19**	**4**	**9**	**486**	**16.5**	**223**	**63**	**190**	**39**		**22**	**4**	**3**	**7**	**18**	**0**	**0**	**0**

OHL First All-Star Team (1993) • Canadian Major Junior Second All-Star Team (1993) • Won George Parsons Trophy (Memorial Cup Tournament Most Sportsmanlike Player) (1993)

Traded to **NY Islanders** by **Buffalo** for Jason Holland and Paul Kruse, March 24, 1998.

• DAY, JOE

Joe Day C – L. 5′11″, 180 lbs. b: Chicago, IL, 5/11/1968. Hartford's 8th choice, 186th overall, in 1987 Entry Draft.

1985-86	St. Michael's Buzzers	Jr. B	30	23	18	41	....	....	....	69	....	....	....	....	....	....	....	....	....	....	....	....	....	....	....	....	....	....
1986-87	St. Lawrence University	ECAC	33	9	11	20	....	....	....	25	....	....	....	....	....	....	....	....	....	....	....	....	....	....	....	....	....	....
1987-88	St. Lawrence University	ECAC	30	21	16	37	....	....	....	36	....	....	....	....	....	....	....	....	....	....	....	....	....	....	....	....	....	....
	United States	WJC-A	7	2	1	3	....	....	....	14	....	....	....	....	....	....	....	....	....	....	....	....	....	....	....	....	....	....
1988-89	St. Lawrence University	ECAC	36	21	27	48	....	....	....	44	....	....	....	....	....	....	....	....	....	....	....	....	....	....	....	....	....	....
1989-90	St. Lawrence University	ECAC	32	19	26	45	....	....	....	30	....	....	....	....	....	....	....	....	....	....	....	....	....	....	....	....	....	....
1990-91	Springfield Indians	AHL	75	24	29	53	....	....	....	82	....	....	....	....	....	....	....	....	....	....	18	5	5	10	27	....	....	....
1991-92	**Hartford Whalers**	**NHL**	**24**	**0**	**3**	**3**	**0**	**2**	**2**	**10**	**0**	**0**	**0**	**13**	**0.0**	**3**	**0**	**15**	**10**	**–2**	....	....	....	....	....	....	....	....
	Springfield Indians	AHL	50	33	25	58	....	....	....	92	....	....	....	....	....	....	....	....	....	....	....	....	....	....	....	....	....	....
1992-93	**Hartford Whalers**	**NHL**	**24**	**1**	**7**	**8**	**1**	**5**	**6**	**47**	**0**	**0**	**0**	**10**	**10.0**	**13**	**0**	**27**	**6**	**–8**	....	....	....	....	....	....	....	....
	Springfield Indians	AHL	33	15	20	35	....	....	....	118	....	....	....	....	....	....	....	....	....	....	15	0	8	8	40	....	....	....
1993-94	**New York Islanders**	**NHL**	**24**	**0**	**0**	**0**	**0**	**0**	**0**	**30**	**0**	**0**	**0**	**16**	**0.0**	**4**	**0**	**11**	**0**	**–7**	....	....	....	....	....	....	....	....
	Salt Lake Golden Eagles	IHL	33	16	10	26	....	....	....	153	....	....	....	....	....	....	....	....	....	....	....	....	....	....	....	....	....	....
1994-95	Detroit Vipers	IHL	32	16	10	26	....	....	....	126	....	....	....	....	....	....	....	....	....	....	5	0	2	2	21	....	....	....
1995-96	Detroit Vipers	IHL	53	19	19	38	....	....	....	105	....	....	....	....	....	....	....	....	....	....	....	....	....	....	....	....	....	....
	Las Vegas Thunder	IHL	29	11	17	28	....	....	....	70	....	....	....	....	....	....	....	....	....	....	15	7	3	10	46	....	....	....
1996-97	Baltimore Bandits	AHL	11	3	0	3	....	....	....	22	....	....	....	....	....	....	....	....	....	....	....	....	....	....	....	....	....	....
	Las Vegas Thunder	IHL	30	9	14	23	....	....	....	41	....	....	....	....	....	....	....	....	....	....	3	0	0	0	6	....	....	....
1997-98	Las Vegas Thunder	IHL	82	30	25	55	....	....	....	183	....	....	....	....	....	....	....	....	....	....	4	0	3	3	14	....	....	....
	NHL Totals		**72**	**1**	**10**	**11**	**1**	**7**	**8**	**87**	**0**	**0**	**0**	**39**	**2.6**	**20**	**0**	**53**	**16**		....	....	....	....	....	....	....	....

ECAC Second All-Star Team (1990)

Signed as a free agent by **NY Islanders**, August 24, 1993.

• DAZE, ERIC

Eric Daze LW – L. 6′6″, 222 lbs. b: Montreal, Que., 7/2/1975. Chicago's 5th choice, 90th overall, in 1993 Entry Draft.

1992-93	Beauport Harfangs	QMJHL	68	19	36	55	....	....	....	24	....	....	....	....	....	....	....	....	....	....	....	....	....	....	....	....	....	....
1993-94	Beauport Harfangs	QMJHL	66	59	48	107	....	....	....	31	....	....	....	....	....	....	....	....	....	....	15	16	8	24	2	....	....	....
1994-95	Beauport Harfangs	QMJHL	57	54	45	99	....	....	....	20	....	....	....	....	....	....	....	....	....	....	16	9	12	21	23	....	....	....
	Canada	WJC-A	7	8	2	10	....	....	....	0	....	....	....	....	....	....	....	....	....	....	....	....	....	....	....	....	....	....
	Chicago Blackhawks	**NHL**	**4**	**1**	**1**	**2**	**2**	**1**	**3**	**2**	**0**	**0**	**0**	**1**	**100.0**	**2**	**0**	**0**	**0**	**+2**	**16**	**0**	**1**	**1**	**4**	**0**	**0**	**0**
1995-96	**Chicago Blackhawks**	**NHL**	**80**	**30**	**23**	**53**	**30**	**19**	**49**	**18**	**2**	**0**	**2**	**167**	**18.0**	**76**	**12**	**48**	**0**	**+16**	**10**	**3**	**5**	**8**	**0**	**0**	**0**	**1**
1996-97	**Chicago Blackhawks**	**NHL**	**71**	**22**	**19**	**41**	**23**	**17**	**40**	**16**	**11**	**0**	**4**	**176**	**12.5**	**67**	**26**	**46**	**1**	**–4**	**6**	**2**	**1**	**3**	**2**	**0**	**0**	**0**
1997-98	**Chicago Blackhawks**	**NHL**	**80**	**31**	**11**	**42**	**36**	**11**	**47**	**22**	**10**	**0**	**7**	**216**	**14.4**	**64**	**25**	**39**	**4**	**+4**	....	....	....	....	....	....	....	....
	Canada	WC-A	3	1	4	5	....	....	....	0	....	....	....	....	....	....	....	....	....	....	....	....	....	....	....	....	....	....
	NHL Totals		**235**	**84**	**54**	**138**	**91**	**48**	**139**	**58**	**23**	**0**	**13**	**560**	**15.0**	**209**	**63**	**133**	**5**		**32**	**5**	**7**	**12**	**6**	**0**	**0**	**1**

QMJHL First All-Star Team (1994, 1995) • WJC-A All-Star Team (1995) • Canadian Major Junior Most Sportsmanlike Player of the Year (1995) • NHL All-Rookie Team (1996)

• DEA, BILLY

Billy Dea LW – L. 5′8″, 175 lbs. b: Edmonton, Alta., 4/3/1933.

1949-50	Lethbridge Native Sons	WCJHL	29	20	13	33	....	....	....	4	....	....	....	....	....	....	....	....	....	....	10	4	0	4	0	....	....	....
1950-51	Lethbridge Native Sons	WCJHL	38	25	22	47	....	....	....	6	....	....	....	....	....	....	....	....	....	....	7	3	1	4	0	....	....	....
1951-52	Lethbridge Native Sons	WCJHL	41	44	28	72	....	....	....	10	....	....	....	....	....	....	....	....	....	....	4	2	3	5	0	....	....	....
1952-53	Lethbridge Native Sons	WCJHL	34	34	21	55	....	....	....	53	....	....	....	....	....	....	....	....	....	....	14	*12	9	*21	12	....	....	....
	Saskatoon Quakers	WHL	3	2	1	3	....	....	....	0	....	....	....	....	....	....	....	....	....	....	....	....	....	....	....	....	....	....
1953-54	**New York Rangers**	**NHL**	**14**	**1**	**1**	**2**	**2**	**1**	**3**	**2**	....	....	....	....	....	....	....	....	....	....	....	....	....	....	....	....	....	....
	Vancouver Canucks	WHL	53	21	13	34	....	....	....	8	....	....	....	....	....	....	....	....	....	....	12	6	5	11	4	....	....	....
1954-55	Vancouver Canucks	WHL	59	18	13	31	....	....	....	13	....	....	....	....	....	....	....	....	....	....	4	0	1	1	0	....	....	....
1955-56	Edmonton Flyers	WHL	70	29	42	71	....	....	....	14	....	....	....	....	....	....	....	....	....	....	3	2	1	3	4	....	....	....
1956-57	**Detroit Red Wings**	**NHL**	**69**	**15**	**15**	**30**	**20**	**17**	**37**	**14**	....	....	....	....	....	....	....	....	....	....	**5**	**2**	**0**	**2**	**2**	....	....	....

			REGULAR SEASON																		PLAYOFFS							
Season	Club	League	GP	G	A	Pts	AG	AA	APts	PIM	PP	SH	GW	S	%	TGF	PGF	TGA	PGA	+/–	GP	G	A	Pts	PIM	PP	SH	GW
1957-58	**Detroit Red Wings**	**NHL**	**29**	**4**	**4**	**8**	**5**	**4**	**9**	**6**	....	....	....	....	....	....	....	....	....	....	....	....	....	....	....	....	....	....
	Chicago Black Hawks	**NHL**	**34**	**5**	**8**	**13**	**6**	**9**	**15**	**4**	....	....	....	....	....	....	....	....	....	....	....	....	....	....	....	....	....	....
1958-59	Buffalo Bisons	AHL	70	25	45	70	....	....	....	19	....	....	....	....	....	....	....	....	....	....	11	5	4	9	4	....	....	....
1959-60	Buffalo Bisons	AHL	72	28	26	54	....	....	....	20	....	....	....	....	....	....	....	....	....	....	....	....	....	....	....	....	....	....
1960-61	Buffalo Bisons	AHL	72	35	39	74	....	....	....	10	....	....	....	....	....	....	....	....	....	....	4	1	2	3	0	....	....	....
1961-62	Buffalo Bisons	AHL	70	30	22	52	....	....	....	17	....	....	....	....	....	....	....	....	....	....	11	0	2	2	2	....	....	....
1962-63	Buffalo Bisons	AHL	72	20	12	32	....	....	....	25	....	....	....	....	....	....	....	....	....	....	13	2	8	10	0	....	....	....
1963-64	Buffalo Bisons	AHL	72	25	16	41	....	....	....	4	....	....	....	....	....	....	....	....	....	....	....	....	....	....	....	....	....	....
1964-65	Buffalo Bisons	AHL	72	21	19	40	....	....	....	15	....	....	....	....	....	....	....	....	....	....	9	3	0	3	0	....	....	....
1965-66	Buffalo Bisons	AHL	70	32	23	55	....	....	....	17	....	....	....	....	....	....	....	....	....	....	....	....	....	....	....	....	....	....
1966-67	Buffalo Bisons	AHL	71	25	39	64	....	....	....	5	....	....	....	....	....	....	....	....	....	....	....	....	....	....	....	....	....	....
	Chicago Black Hawks	**NHL**	....	....	....	....	....	....	....	....	....	....	....	....	....	....	....	....	....	....	**2**	**0**	**0**	**0**	**2**	....	....	....
1967-68	**Pittsburgh Penguins**	**NHL**	**73**	**16**	**12**	**28**	**20**	**13**	**33**	**6**	**1**	**0**	**3**	**137**	**11.7**	**47**	**7**	**64**	**9**	**–15**	....	....	....	....	....	....	....	....
1968-69	**Pittsburgh Penguins**	**NHL**	**66**	**10**	**8**	**18**	**11**	**7**	**18**	**4**	**2**	**0**	**1**	**111**	**9.0**	**29**	**5**	**61**	**5**	**–32**	....	....	....	....	....	....	....	....
1969-70	Baltimore Clippers	AHL	7	0	1	1	....	....	....	42	....	....	....	....	....	....	....	....	....	....	....	....	....	....	....	....	....	....
	Detroit Red Wings	**NHL**	**70**	**10**	**3**	**13**	**12**	**3**	**15**	**6**	**0**	**0**	**3**	**63**	**15.9**	**25**	**0**	**30**	**8**	**+3**	**4**	**0**	**1**	**1**	**2**	**0**	**0**	**0**
1970-71	**Detroit Red Wings**	**NHL**	**42**	**6**	**3**	**9**	**6**	**3**	**9**	**2**	**1**	**0**	**0**	**30**	**20.0**	**13**	**1**	**26**	**9**	**–5**	....	....	....	....	....	....	....	....
	Fort Worth Wings	CHL	26	8	15	23	....	....	....	10	....	....	....	....	....	....	....	....	....	....	....	....	....	....	....	....	....	....
1971-72	Tidewater Wings	AHL	72	7	7	14	....	....	....	8	....	....	....	....	....	....	....	....	....	....	4	0	4	4	0	....	....	....
	NHL Totals		**397**	**67**	**54**	**121**	**82**	**57**	**139**	**44**	**4**	**0**	**7**	**341**	**19.6**	**114**	**13**	**181**	**31**		**11**	**2**	**1**	**3**	**6**	**0**	**0**	**0**

Traded to **Detroit** by **NY Rangers** with Aggie Kukklowicz and cash for Dave Creighton and Bronco Horvath, August 18, 1955. Traded to **Chicago** by **Detroit** with Bill Dineen, Lorne Ferguson and Earl Reibel for Nick Mickoski, Bob Bailey, Hec Lalande and John McIntyre, December 17, 1957. Claimed by **Pittsburgh** from **Chicago** in Expansion Draft, June 6, 1967. Traded to **Detroit** by **Pittsburgh** for Mike McMahon, October 28, 1969.

• DEADMARSH, ADAM

Adam Deadmarsh C – R. 6′, 195 lbs. b: Trail, B.C., 5/10/1975. Quebec's 2nd choice, 14th overall, in 1993 Entry Draft.

Season	Club	League	GP	G	A	Pts	AG	AA	APts	PIM	PP	SH	GW	S	%	TGF	PGF	TGA	PGA	+/–	GP	G	A	Pts	PIM	PP	SH	GW
1991-92	Portland Winter Hawks	WHL	68	30	30	60	....	....	....	81	....	....	....	....	....	....	....	....	....	....	6	3	3	6	13	....	....	....
1992-93	Portland Winter Hawks	WHL	58	33	36	69	....	....	....	126	....	....	....	....	....	....	....	....	....	....	16	7	8	15	29	....	....	....
	United States	WJC-A	7	0	0	0	....	....	....	10	....	....	....	....	....	....	....	....	....	....	....	....	....	....	....	....	....	....
1993-94	Portland Winter Hawks	WHL	65	43	56	99	....	....	....	212	....	....	....	....	....	....	....	....	....	....	10	9	8	17	33	....	....	....
	United States	WJC-A	7	0	0	0	....	....	....	8	....	....	....	....	....	....	....	....	....	....	....	....	....	....	....	....	....	....
1994-95	Portland Winter Hawks	WHL	29	28	20	48	....	....	....	129	....	....	....	....	....	....	....	....	....	....	....	....	....	....	....	....	....	....
	United States	WJC-A	7	6	4	10	....	....	....	10	....	....	....	....	....	....	....	....	....	....	....	....	....	....	....	....	....	....
	Quebec Nordiques	**NHL**	**48**	**9**	**8**	**17**	**16**	**12**	**28**	**56**	**0**	**0**	**0**	**48**	**18.8**	**27**	**0**	**12**	**1**	**+16**	**6**	**0**	**1**	**1**	**0**	**0**	**0**	**0**
1995-96	**Colorado Avalanche**	**NHL**	**78**	**21**	**27**	**48**	**21**	**22**	**43**	**142**	**3**	**0**	**2**	**151**	**13.9**	**75**	**18**	**42**	**5**	**+20**	**22**	**5**	**12**	**17**	**25**	**1**	**0**	**0**
1996-97	United States	W Cup	7	2	2	4	....	....	....	8	....	....	....	....	....	....	....	....	....	....	....	....	....	....	....	....	....	....
	Colorado Avalanche	**NHL**	**78**	**33**	**27**	**60**	**35**	**24**	**59**	**136**	**10**	**3**	**4**	**198**	**16.7**	**94**	**39**	**52**	**5**	**+8**	**17**	**3**	**6**	**9**	**24**	**1**	**0**	**1**
1997-98	**Colorado Avalanche**	**NHL**	**73**	**22**	**21**	**43**	**26**	**20**	**46**	**125**	**10**	**0**	**6**	**187**	**11.8**	**70**	**28**	**51**	**9**	**0**	**7**	**2**	**0**	**2**	**4**	**1**	**0**	**0**
	United States	Olympics	4	1	0	1	....	....	....	2	....	....	....	....	....	....	....	....	....	....	....	....	....	....	....	....	....	....
	NHL Totals		**277**	**85**	**83**	**168**	**98**	**78**	**176**	**459**	**23**	**3**	**12**	**584**	**14.6**	**266**	**85**	**157**	**20**		**52**	**10**	**19**	**29**	**53**	**3**	**0**	**1**

Transferred to **Colorado** after **Quebec** franchise relocated, June 21, 1995.

• DEADMARSH, BUTCH

Butch (Ernest Charles) Deadmarsh LW – L. 5′11″, 186 lbs. b: Trail, B.C., 4/5/1950. Buffalo's 2nd choice, 15th overall, in 1970 Amateur Draft.

Season	Club	League	GP	G	A	Pts	AG	AA	APts	PIM	PP	SH	GW	S	%	TGF	PGF	TGA	PGA	+/–	GP	G	A	Pts	PIM	PP	SH	GW
1968-69	Brandon Wheat Kings	WCJHL	47	19	23	42	....	....	....	130	....	....	....	....	....	....	....	....	....	....	5	2	2	4	....	....	....	....
1969-70	Brandon Wheat Kings	WCJHL	54	37	33	70	....	....	....	*301	....	....	....	....	....	....	....	....	....	....	4	3	5	8	20	....	....	....
1970-71	**Buffalo Sabres**	**NHL**	**10**	**0**	**0**	**0**	**0**	**0**	**0**	**9**	**0**	**0**	**0**	**7**	**0.0**	**1**	**1**	**3**	**0**	**–3**	....	....	....	....	....	....	....	....
	Salt Lake Golden Eagles	WHL	59	11	9	20	....	....	....	128	....	....	....	....	....	....	....	....	....	....	....	....	....	....	....	....	....	....
1971-72	**Buffalo Sabres**	**NHL**	**12**	**1**	**1**	**2**	**1**	**1**	**2**	**4**	**0**	**0**	**0**	**10**	**10.0**	**3**	**0**	**13**	**0**	**–10**	....	....	....	....	....	....	....	....
	Cincinnati Swords	AHL	64	34	27	61	....	....	....	145	....	....	....	....	....	....	....	....	....	....	10	6	8	14	33	....	....	....
1972-73	**Buffalo Sabres**	**NHL**	**34**	**1**	**1**	**2**	**1**	**1**	**2**	**26**	**1**	**0**	**0**	**15**	**6.7**	**6**	**2**	**7**	**0**	**–3**	....	....	....	....	....	....	....	....
	Cincinnati Swords	AHL	12	7	4	11	....	....	....	20	....	....	....	....	....	....	....	....	....	....	....	....	....	....	....	....	....	....
	Atlanta Flames	**NHL**	**19**	**1**	**0**	**1**	**1**	**0**	**1**	**8**	**0**	**0**	**0**	**19**	**5.3**	**5**	**1**	**8**	**0**	**–4**	....	....	....	....	....	....	....	....
1973-74	**Atlanta Flames**	**NHL**	**42**	**6**	**1**	**7**	**6**	**1**	**7**	**89**	**0**	**0**	**1**	**49**	**12.2**	**15**	**0**	**14**	**0**	**+1**	**4**	**0**	**0**	**0**	**17**	**0**	**0**	**0**
1974-75	**Kansas City Scouts**	**NHL**	**20**	**3**	**2**	**5**	**3**	**2**	**5**	**19**	**1**	**0**	**1**	**32**	**9.4**	**9**	**2**	**20**	**8**	**–5**	....	....	....	....	....	....	....	....
	Vancouver Blazers	WHA	38	7	8	15	....	....	....	128	....	....	....	....	....	....	....	....	....	....	....	....	....	....	....	....	....	....
1975-76	Calgary Cowboys	WHA	79	26	28	54	....	....	....	196	....	....	....	....	....	....	....	....	....	....	8	0	1	1	14	....	....	....
1976-77	Minnesota Fighting Saints	WHA	35	9	4	13	....	....	....	51	....	....	....	....	....	....	....	....	....	....	....	....	....	....	....	....	....	....
	Calgary Cowboys	WHA	38	13	17	30	....	....	....	77	....	....	....	....	....	....	....	....	....	....	....	....	....	....	....	....	....	....
1977-78	Edmonton Oilers	WHA	20	1	3	4	....	....	....	32	....	....	....	....	....	....	....	....	....	....	....	....	....	....	....	....	....	....
	Cincinnati Stingers	WHA	45	7	6	13	....	....	....	86	....	....	....	....	....	....	....	....	....	....	....	....	....	....	....	....	....	....
	NHL Totals		**137**	**12**	**5**	**17**	**12**	**5**	**17**	**155**	**2**	**0**	**2**	**132**	**9.1**	**39**	**6**	**65**	**8**		**4**	**0**	**0**	**0**	**17**	**0**	**0**	**0**

Traded to **Atlanta** by **Buffalo** for Norm Grafton, February 14, 1973. Selected by **Cincinnati** (WHA), in 1973 WHA Professional Player Draft, June, 1973. Claimed by **Kansas City** from **Atlanta** in Expansion Draft, June 12, 1974. Traded to **Vancouver** (WHA) by **Kansas City** for cash, December, 1974. Transferred to **Calgary** (WHA) after **Vancouver** (WHA) franchise relocated, May 7, 1975. Traded to **Minnesota** (WHA) by **Calgary** (WHA) with Jack Carlson and Dave Antonovich for Jim Harrison, September, 1976. Signed as a free agent by **Calgary** (WHA) after **Minnesota** (WHA) franchise folded, January, 1976. Signed as a free agent by **Edmonton** (WHA) after **Calgary** (WHA) franchise folded, May 31, 1977. Traded to **Cincinnati** (WHA) by **Edmonton** (WHA) for Del Hall and Dennis Sobchuk, December, 1977.

• DEAN, BARRY

Barry Dean LW – L. 6′1″, 195 lbs. b: Maple Creek, Sask., 2/26/1955. Kansas City's 1st choice, 2nd overall, in 1975 Amateur Draft.

Season	Club	League	GP	G	A	Pts	AG	AA	APts	PIM	PP	SH	GW	S	%	TGF	PGF	TGA	PGA	+/–	GP	G	A	Pts	PIM	PP	SH	GW
1971-72	Medicine Hat Tigers	WCJHL	26	2	5	7	....	....	....	46	....	....	....	....	....	....	....	....	....	....	....	....	....	....	....	....	....	....
1972-73	Medicine Hat Tigers	WCJHL	58	23	30	53	....	....	....	208	....	....	....	....	....	....	....	....	....	....	....	....	....	....	....	....	....	....
1973-74	Medicine Hat Tigers	WCJHL	66	23	73	96	....	....	....	213	....	....	....	....	....	....	....	....	....	....	....	....	....	....	....	....	....	....
1974-75	Medicine Hat Tigers	WCJHL	64	40	75	115	....	....	....	159	....	....	....	....	....	....	....	....	....	....	....	....	....	....	....	....	....	....
1975-76	Phoenix Roadrunners	WHA	71	9	25	34	....	....	....	110	....	....	....	....	....	....	....	....	....	....	....	....	....	....	....	....	....	....
1976-77	**Colorado Rockies**	**NHL**	**79**	**14**	**25**	**39**	**13**	**20**	**33**	**92**	**2**	**0**	**0**	**130**	**10.8**	**61**	**15**	**77**	**5**	**–26**	....	....	....	....	....	....	....	....
1977-78	**Philadelphia Flyers**	**NHL**	**56**	**7**	**18**	**25**	**7**	**15**	**22**	**34**	**0**	**0**	**2**	**76**	**9.2**	**36**	**3**	**22**	**1**	**+12**	....	....	....	....	....	....	....	....
1978-79	**Philadelphia Flyers**	**NHL**	**30**	**4**	**13**	**17**	**4**	**10**	**14**	**20**	**0**	**0**	**1**	**52**	**7.7**	**22**	**5**	**22**	**4**	**–1**	....	....	....	....	....	....	....	....
	Maine Mariners	AHL	36	18	17	35	....	....	....	94	....	....	....	....	....	....	....	....	....	....	5	2	1	3	0	....	....	....
1979-80	Maine Mariners	AHL	77	23	26	49	....	....	....	106	....	....	....	....	....	....	....	....	....	....	12	8	9	17	21	....	....	....
1980-81	Wichita Wind	CHL	30	14	14	28	....	....	....	54	....	....	....	....	....	....	....	....	....	....	....	....	....	....	....	....	....	....
1981-82	Fredericton Express	AHL	25	3	10	13	....	....	....	6	....	....	....	....	....	....	....	....	....	....	....	....	....	....	....	....	....	....
	NHL Totals		**165**	**25**	**56**	**81**	**24**	**45**	**69**	**146**	**2**	**0**	**3**	**258**	**9.7**	**119**	**23**	**121**	**10**		....	....	....	....	....	....	....	....
	Other Major League Totals		71	9	25	34	....	....	....	110	....	....	....	....	....	....	....	....	....	....	....	....	....	....	....	....	....	....

WCJHL First All-Star Team (1975)

Selected by **Edmonton** (WHA) in 1975 WHA Amateur Draft, May, 1975. Traded to **Phoenix** (WHA) by **Edmonton** (WHA) for Phoenix's 1st round choice (Blair Chapman) and 3rd round choice (Harold Philipott) in 1976 WHA Amateur Draft, June, 1975. Rights transferred to **Colorado** after **Kansas City** franchise relocated, June, 1976. Traded to **Philadelphia** by **Colorado** for Mark Suzor, August 5, 1977. Claimed by **Philadelphia** as a fill-in during Expansion Draft, June 13, 1979. Traded to **Edmonton** by **Philadelphia** for Ron Areshenkoff and Edmonton's 10th round choice (Bob O'Brien) in 1980 Entry Draft, June 11, 1980.

• DEAN, KEVIN

Kevin Dean D – L. 6′3″, 200 lbs. b: Madison, WI, 4/1/1969. New Jersey's 4th choice, 86th overall, in 1987 Entry Draft.

Season	Club	League	GP	G	A	Pts	AG	AA	APts	PIM	PP	SH	GW	S	%	TGF	PGF	TGA	PGA	+/–	GP	G	A	Pts	PIM	PP	SH	GW
1986-87	Culver Academy	H.S.	25	19	25	44	....	....	....	30	....	....	....	....	....	....	....	....	....	....	....	....	....	....	....	....	....	....
1987-88	Univeristy of New Hampshire	H.E.	27	1	6	7	....	....	....	34	....	....	....	....	....	....	....	....	....	....	....	....	....	....	....	....	....	....
	United States	WJC-A	7	0	0	0	....	....	....	0	....	....	....	....	....	....	....	....	....	....	....	....	....	....	....	....	....	....
1988-89	University of New Hampshire	H.E.	34	1	12	13	....	....	....	28	....	....	....	....	....	....	....	....	....	....	....	....	....	....	....	....	....	....
1989-90	University of New Hampshire	H.E.	39	2	6	8	....	....	....	42	....	....	....	....	....	....	....	....	....	....	....	....	....	....	....	....	....	....
1990-91	University of New Hampshire	H.E.	31	10	12	22	....	....	....	22	....	....	....	....	....	....	....	....	....	....	....	....	....	....	....	....	....	....
	Utica Devils	AHL	7	0	1	1	....	....	....	2	....	....	....	....	....	....	....	....	....	....	....	....	....	....	....	....	....	....
1991-92	Utica Devils	AHL	23	0	3	3	....	....	....	6	....	....	....	....	....	....	....	....	....	....	....	....	....	....	....	....	....	....
	Cincinnati Cyclones	ECHL	30	3	22	25	....	....	....	43	....	....	....	....	....	....	....	....	....	....	9	1	6	7	8	....	....	....
1992-93	Cincinnati Cyclones	IHL	13	2	1	3	....	....	....	15	....	....	....	....	....	....	....	....	....	....	....	....	....	....	....	....	....	....
	Utica Devils	AHL	57	2	16	18	....	....	....	76	....	....	....	....	....	....	....	....	....	....	5	1	0	1	8	....	....	....
1993-94	Albany River Rats	AHL	70	9	33	42	....	....	....	92	....	....	....	....	....	....	....	....	....	....	5	0	2	2	7	....	....	....

			REGULAR SEASON																		PLAYOFFS							
Season	Club	League	GP	G	A	Pts	AG	AA	APts	PIM	PP	SH	GW	S	%	TGF	PGF	TGA	PGA	+/–	GP	G	A	Pts	PIM	PP	SH	GW
1994-95	**New Jersey Devils**	**NHL**	**17**	**0**	**1**	**1**	**0**	**1**	**1**	**4**	**0**	**0**	**0**	**11**	**0.0**	**11**	**0**	**5**	**0**	**+6**	**3**	**0**	**2**	**2**	**0**	**0**	**0**	**0**
	Albany River Rats	AHL	68	5	37	42	....	....	....	66	....	....	....	....	....	....	....	....	....	....	8	0	4	4	4	....	....	....
1995-96	**New Jersey Devils**	**NHL**	**41**	**0**	**6**	**6**	**0**	**5**	**5**	**28**	**0**	**0**	**0**	**29**	**0.0**	**27**	**5**	**22**	**4**	**+4**	....	....	....	....	....	....	....	....
	Albany River Rats	AHL	1	1	0	1	....	....	....	2	....	....	....	....	....	....	....	....	....	....	....	....	....	....	....	....	....	....
1996-97	**New Jersey Devils**	**NHL**	**28**	**2**	**4**	**6**	**2**	**4**	**6**	**6**	**0**	**0**	**0**	**21**	**9.5**	**17**	**1**	**14**	**0**	**+2**	**1**	**1**	**0**	**1**	**0**	**0**	**0**	**1**
	Albany River Rats	AHL	2	0	1	1	....	....	....	4	....	....	....	....	....	....	....	....	....	....	....	....	....	....	....	....	....	....
1997-98	**New Jersey Devils**	**NHL**	**50**	**1**	**8**	**9**	**1**	**8**	**9**	**12**	**1**	**0**	**0**	**28**	**3.6**	**32**	**3**	**26**	**9**	**+12**	**5**	**1**	**0**	**1**	**2**	**0**	**0**	**0**
	Albany River Rats	AHL	2	0	1	1	....	....	....	2	....	....	....	....	....	....	....	....	....	....	....	....	....	....	....	....	....	....
	United States	WC-A	3	0	0	0	....	....	....	0	....	....	....	....	....	....	....	....	....	....	....	....	....	....	....	....	....	....
	NHL Totals		**136**	**3**	**19**	**22**	**3**	**18**	**21**	**50**	**1**	**0**	**0**	**89**	**3.4**	**87**	**9**	**67**	**13**		**9**	**2**	**2**	**4**	**2**	**0**	**0**	**1**

AHL First All-Star Team (1995)

• DEBENEDET, NELSON

Nelson Debenedet LW – L. 6'1", 195 lbs. b: Cordenous, Italy, 12/31/1947.

Season	Club	League	GP	G	A	Pts	AG	AA	APts	PIM	PP	SH	GW	S	%	TGF	PGF	TGA	PGA	+/–	GP	G	A	Pts	PIM	PP	SH	GW
1966-67	Michigan State Spartans	CCHA	27	0	7	7	....	....	....	14	....	....	....	....	....	....	....	....	....	....	....	....	....	....	....	....	....	....
1967-68	Michigan State Spartans	CCHA	29	4	3	7	....	....	....	25	....	....	....	....	....	....	....	....	....	....	....	....	....	....	....	....	....	....
1968-69	Michigan State Spartans	CCHA	28	10	7	17	....	....	....	40	....	....	....	....	....	....	....	....	....	....	....	....	....	....	....	....	....	....
1969-70	Fort Wayne Komets	IHL	8	0	3	3	....	....	....	6	....	....	....	....	....	....	....	....	....	....	....	....	....	....	....	....	....	....
1970-71	University of Toronto	OUAA	15	3	9	12	....	....	....	29	....	....	....	....	....	....	....	....	....	....	....	....	....	....	....	....	....	....
1971-72	Fort Worth Wings	CHL	14	2	4	6	....	....	....	15	....	....	....	....	....	....	....	....	....	....	....	....	....	....	....	....	....	....
	Tidewater Wings	AHL	22	4	3	7	....	....	....	12	....	....	....	....	....	....	....	....	....	....	....	....	....	....	....	....	....	....
	Port Huron Wings	IHL	30	7	5	12	....	....	....	19	....	....	....	....	....	....	....	....	....	....	....	....	....	....	....	....	....	....
1972-73	Virginia Wings	AHL	76	29	27	56	....	....	....	64	....	....	....	....	....	....	....	....	....	....	13	2	5	7	6	....	....	....
1973-74	**Detroit Red Wings**	**NHL**	**15**	**4**	**1**	**5**	**4**	**1**	**5**	**2**	**0**	**0**	**0**	**13**	**30.8**	**9**	**1**	**7**	**0**	**+1**	....	....	....	....	....	....	....	....
	Virginia Wings	AHL	39	8	15	23	....	....	....	40	....	....	....	....	....	....	....	....	....	....	....	....	....	....	....	....	....	....
1974-75	**Pittsburgh Penguins**	**NHL**	**31**	**6**	**3**	**9**	**6**	**2**	**8**	**11**	**1**	**0**	**0**	**28**	**21.4**	**12**	**2**	**17**	**4**	**–3**	....	....	....	....	....	....	....	....
	Hershey Bears	AHL	25	6	6	12	....	....	....	13	....	....	....	....	....	....	....	....	....	....	12	2	4	6	2	....	....	....
1975-76	Hershey Bears	AHL	69	14	19	33	....	....	....	12	....	....	....	....	....	....	....	....	....	....	9	4	5	9	6	....	....	....
	NHL Totals		**46**	**10**	**4**	**14**	**10**	**3**	**13**	**13**	**1**	**0**	**0**	**41**	**24.4**	**21**	**3**	**24**	**4**		....	....	....	....	....	....	....	....

Signed as a free agent by **Detroit**, September, 1971. Traded to **Pittsburgh** by **Detroit** for Hank Nowak and Pittsburgh's 3rd round choice (Dan Mandryk) in 1974 Amateur Draft, May 27, 1974.

• DEBLOIS, LUCIEN

Lucien DeBlois C – R. 5'11", 200 lbs. b: Joliette, Que., 6/21/1957. NY Rangers' 1st choice, 8th overall, in 1977 Amateur Draft.

Season	Club	League	GP	G	A	Pts	AG	AA	APts	PIM	PP	SH	GW	S	%	TGF	PGF	TGA	PGA	+/–	GP	G	A	Pts	PIM	PP	SH	GW
1973-74	Sorel Black Hawks	QMJHL	56	30	35	65	....	....	....	53	....	....	....	....	....	....	....	....	....	....	....	....	....	....	....	....	....	....
1974-75	Sorel Black Hawks	QMJHL	72	46	53	99	....	....	....	62	....	....	....	....	....	....	....	....	....	....	....	....	....	....	....	....	....	....
1975-76	Sorel Black Hawks	QMJHL	70	56	55	111	....	....	....	112	....	....	....	....	....	....	....	....	....	....	5	1	1	2	32	....	....	....
1976-77	Sorel Black Hawks	QMJHL	72	56	78	134	....	....	....	131	....	....	....	....	....	....	....	....	....	....	....	....	....	....	....	....	....	....
1977-78	**New York Rangers**	**NHL**	**71**	**22**	**8**	**30**	**21**	**7**	**28**	**27**	**1**	**0**	**3**	**111**	**19.8**	**61**	**7**	**66**	**1**	**–11**	**3**	**0**	**0**	**0**	**2**	**0**	**0**	**0**
1978-79	**New York Rangers**	**NHL**	**62**	**11**	**17**	**28**	**10**	**13**	**23**	**26**	**0**	**0**	**1**	**106**	**10.4**	**53**	**17**	**47**	**1**	**–10**	**9**	**2**	**0**	**2**	**4**	**1**	**0**	**0**
	New Haven Nighthawks	AHL	7	4	6	10	....	....	....	6	....	....	....	....	....	....	....	....	....	....	....	....	....	....	....	....	....	....
1979-80	**New York Rangers**	**NHL**	**6**	**3**	**1**	**4**	**3**	**1**	**4**	**7**	**0**	**0**	**0**	**16**	**18.8**	**5**	**0**	**7**	**1**	**–1**	....	....	....	....	....	....	....	....
	Colorado Rockies	**NHL**	**70**	**24**	**19**	**43**	**22**	**15**	**37**	**36**	**4**	**0**	**1**	**151**	**15.9**	**57**	**10**	**66**	**1**	**–18**	....	....	....	....	....	....	....	....
1980-81	**Colorado Rockies**	**NHL**	**74**	**26**	**16**	**42**	**21**	**11**	**32**	**78**	**9**	**1**	**2**	**183**	**14.2**	**61**	**22**	**81**	**0**	**–42**	....	....	....	....	....	....	....	....
	Canada	WEC-A	8	3	0	3	....	....	....	4	....	....	....	....	....	....	....	....	....	....	....	....	....	....	....	....	....	....
1981-82	**Winnipeg Jets**	**NHL**	**65**	**25**	**27**	**52**	**20**	**18**	**38**	**87**	**1**	**1**	**2**	**149**	**16.8**	**75**	**7**	**92**	**14**	**–10**	**4**	**2**	**1**	**3**	**4**	**0**	**0**	**0**
1982-83	**Winnipeg Jets**	**NHL**	**79**	**27**	**27**	**54**	**22**	**19**	**41**	**69**	**1**	**3**	**7**	**183**	**14.8**	**74**	**7**	**125**	**33**	**–25**	**3**	**0**	**0**	**0**	**5**	**0**	**0**	**0**
1983-84	**Winnipeg Jets**	**NHL**	**80**	**34**	**45**	**79**	**27**	**31**	**58**	**50**	**8**	**1**	**2**	**195**	**17.4**	**129**	**42**	**119**	**17**	**–15**	**3**	**0**	**1**	**1**	**4**	**0**	**0**	**0**
1984-85	**Montreal Canadiens**	**NHL**	**51**	**12**	**11**	**23**	**10**	**7**	**17**	**20**	**4**	**1**	**2**	**85**	**14.1**	**52**	**18**	**27**	**2**	**+9**	**8**	**2**	**4**	**6**	**4**	**1**	**0**	**0**
1985-86	**Montreal Canadiens**	**NHL**	**61**	**14**	**17**	**31**	**11**	**11**	**22**	**48**	**2**	**0**	**1**	**102**	**13.7**	**51**	**7**	**49**	**8**	**+3**	**11**	**0**	**0**	**0**	**7**	**0**	**0**	**0**
1986-87	**New York Rangers**	**NHL**	**40**	**3**	**8**	**11**	**3**	**6**	**9**	**27**	**1**	**0**	**0**	**45**	**6.7**	**20**	**3**	**27**	**3**	**–7**	**2**	**0**	**0**	**0**	**2**	**0**	**0**	**0**
1987-88	**New York Rangers**	**NHL**	**74**	**9**	**21**	**30**	**8**	**15**	**23**	**103**	**2**	**0**	**0**	**99**	**9.1**	**52**	**15**	**66**	**26**	**–3**	....	....	....	....	....	....	....	....
1988-89	**New York Rangers**	**NHL**	**73**	**9**	**24**	**33**	**8**	**17**	**25**	**107**	**0**	**0**	**2**	**117**	**7.7**	**44**	**0**	**87**	**37**	**–6**	**4**	**0**	**0**	**0**	**4**	**0**	**0**	**0**
1989-90	**Quebec Nordiques**	**NHL**	**70**	**9**	**8**	**17**	**8**	**6**	**14**	**45**	**1**	**0**	**1**	**83**	**10.8**	**28**	**2**	**96**	**41**	**–29**	....	....	....	....	....	....	....	....
1990-91	**Quebec Nordiques**	**NHL**	**14**	**2**	**2**	**4**	**2**	**2**	**4**	**13**	**0**	**0**	**1**	**8**	**25.0**	**6**	**0**	**9**	**4**	**+1**	....	....	....	....	....	....	....	....
	Toronto Maple Leafs	**NHL**	**38**	**10**	**12**	**22**	**9**	**9**	**18**	**30**	**0**	**1**	**0**	**57**	**17.5**	**23**	**0**	**46**	**19**	**–4**	....	....	....	....	....	....	....	....
1991-92	**Toronto Maple Leafs**	**NHL**	**54**	**8**	**11**	**19**	**7**	**8**	**15**	**39**	**0**	**1**	**1**	**75**	**10.7**	**25**	**0**	**51**	**23**	**–3**	....	....	....	....	....	....	....	....
	Winnipeg Jets	**NHL**	**11**	**1**	**2**	**3**	**1**	**1**	**2**	**2**	**0**	**0**	**1**	**15**	**6.7**	**5**	**0**	**5**	**1**	**+1**	**5**	**1**	**0**	**1**	**2**	**0**	**0**	**1**
	NHL Totals		**993**	**249**	**276**	**525**	**213**	**197**	**410**	**814**	**34**	**9**	**27**	**1780**	**14.0**	**821**	**157**	**1066**	**232**		**52**	**7**	**6**	**13**	**38**	**2**	**0**	**1**

QMJHL East First All-Star Team (1976) • QMJHL First All-Star Team (1977)

Traded to **Colorado** by **NY Rangers** with Pat Hickey, Mike McEwen, Dean Turner and future considerations (Bobby Crawford, January 15, 1979) for Barry Beck, November 2, 1979. Traded to **Winnipeg** by **Colorado** for Brent Ashton and Winnipeg's 3rd choice (Dave Kasper) in 1982 Entry Draft, July 15, 1981. Traded to **Montreal** by **Winnipeg** for Perry Turnbull, June 13, 1984. Signed as a free agent by **NY Rangers**, September 8, 1986. Signed as a free agent by **Quebec**, August 2, 1989. Traded to **Toronto** by **Quebec** with Aaron Broten and Michel Petit for Scott Pearson and Toronto's 2nd round choice in 1991 (later traded to Washington — Washington selected Eric Lavigne) and 2nd round choice (Toumos Grondman) in 1992 Entry Draft, Novemeber 17, 1990. Traded to **Winnipeg** by **Toronto** for Mark Osborne, March 10, 1992.

• DEBOL, DAVID

David Debol C – R. 5'11", 175 lbs. b: St. Claire Shores, MI, 3/27/1956. Chicago's 4th choice, 63rd overall, in 1976 Amateur Draft.

Season	Club	League	GP	G	A	Pts	AG	AA	APts	PIM	PP	SH	GW	S	%	TGF	PGF	TGA	PGA	+/–	GP	G	A	Pts	PIM	PP	SH	GW
1975-76	University of Michigan	CCHA	42	39	22	61	....	....	....	22	....	....	....	....	....	....	....	....	....	....	....	....	....	....	....	....	....	....
1976-77	University of Michigan	CCHA	45	43	56	99	....	....	....	40	....	....	....	....	....	....	....	....	....	....	....	....	....	....	....	....	....	....
	United States	WEC-A	8	3	3	6	....	....	....	2	....	....	....	....	....	....	....	....	....	....	....	....	....	....	....	....	....	....
1977-78	University of Michigan	CCHA	46	20	38	58	....	....	....	16	....	....	....	....	....	....	....	....	....	....	....	....	....	....	....	....	....	....
	United States	WEC-A	10	4	4	8	....	....	....	0	....	....	....	....	....	....	....	....	....	....	....	....	....	....	....	....	....	....
	Cincinnati Stingers	WHA	9	3	2	5	....	....	....	2	....	....	....	....	....	....	....	....	....	....	....	....	....	....	....	....	....	....
1978-79	Cincinnati Stingers	WHA	59	10	27	37	....	....	....	9	....	....	....	....	....	....	....	....	....	....	....	....	....	....	....	....	....	....
1979-80	**Hartford Whalers**	**NHL**	**48**	**12**	**14**	**26**	**11**	**11**	**22**	**4**	**0**	**0**	**1**	**96**	**12.5**	**35**	**0**	**41**	**1**	**–5**	**3**	**0**	**0**	**0**	**0**	**0**	**0**	**0**
	Springfield Indians	AHL	16	4	12	16	....	....	....	2	....	....	....	....	....	....	....	....	....	....	....	....	....	....	....	....	....	....
	Cincinnati Stingers	CHL	10	8	8	16	....	....	....	2	....	....	....	....	....	....	....	....	....	....	....	....	....	....	....	....	....	....
1980-81	**Hartford Whalers**	**NHL**	**44**	**14**	**12**	**26**	**12**	**8**	**20**	**0**	**2**	**0**	**0**	**70**	**20.0**	**38**	**6**	**44**	**0**	**–12**	....	....	....	....	....	....	....	....
	Binghamton Whalers	AHL	18	4	11	15	....	....	....	0	....	....	....	....	....	....	....	....	....	....	....	....	....	....	....	....	....	....
	United States	WEC-A	8	5	4	9	....	....	....	14	....	....	....	....	....	....	....	....	....	....	....	....	....	....	....	....	....	....
1981-82	Cincinnati Tigers	CHL	50	16	24	40	....	....	....	6	....	....	....	....	....	....	....	....	....	....	....	....	....	....	....	....	....	....
	Oklahoma City Stars	CHL	21	13	15	28	....	....	....	2	....	....	....	....	....	....	....	....	....	....	4	0	3	3	2	....	....	....
1982-83	Birmingham South Stars	CHL	55	25	28	53	....	....	....	8	....	....	....	....	....	....	....	....	....	....	13	5	5	10	2	....	....	....
	NHL Totals		**92**	**26**	**26**	**52**	**23**	**19**	**42**	**4**	**2**	**0**	**1**	**166**	**15.7**	**73**	**6**	**85**	**1**		**3**	**0**	**0**	**0**	**0**	**0**	**0**	**0**
	Other Major League Totals		68	13	29	42	....	....	....	11	....	....	....	....	....	....	....	....	....		....	....	....	....	....	....	....	....

WCHA Second All-Star Team (1976) • WCHA First All-Star Team (1977) • NCAA West First All-American Team (1977) • NCAA Championship All-Tournament Team (1977)

Selected by **New England** (WHA) in 1976 WHA Amateur Draft, June, 1976. WHA rights traded to **Edmonton** (WHA) by **New England** (WHA) to complete transaction that sent Jack Carlson, Steve Carlson, Dave Keon, Dave Dyden and John Mckenzie to New England, June, 1977. WHA rights traded to **Cincinnati** (WHA) by **Edmonton** (WHA) for Dennis Sobchuk and future considerations, December, 1977. Claimed by **Hartford** from **Cincinnati** (WHA) in WHA Dispersal Draft, June, 1979.

• DEBRUSK, LOUIE

Louie DeBrusk LW – L. 6'2", 215 lbs. b: Cambridge, Ont., 3/19/1971. NY Rangers' 4th choice, 49th overall, in 1989 Entry Draft.

Season	Club	League	GP	G	A	Pts	AG	AA	APts	PIM	PP	SH	GW	S	%	TGF	PGF	TGA	PGA	+/–	GP	G	A	Pts	PIM	PP	SH	GW
1988-89	London Knights	OHL	59	11	11	22	....	....	....	149	....	....	....	....	....	....	....	....	....	....	19	1	1	2	43	....	....	....
1989-90	London Knights	OHL	61	21	19	40	....	....	....	198	....	....	....	....	....	....	....	....	....	....	6	2	2	4	24	....	....	....
1990-91	London Knights	OHL	61	31	33	64	....	....	....	*223	....	....	....	....	....	....	....	....	....	....	7	2	2	4	14	....	....	....
	Binghamton Rangers	AHL	2	0	0	0	....	....	....	7	....	....	....	....	....	....	....	....	....	....	2	0	0	0	9	....	....	....
1991-92	**Edmonton Oilers**	**NHL**	**25**	**2**	**1**	**3**	**2**	**1**	**3**	**124**	**0**	**0**	**1**	**7**	**28.6**	**8**	**0**	**4**	**0**	**+4**	....	....	....	....	....	....	....	....
	Cape Breton Oilers	AHL	28	2	2	4	....	....	....	73	....	....	....	....	....	....	....	....	....	....	....	....	....	....	....	....	....	....
1992-93	**Edmonton Oilers**	**NHL**	**51**	**8**	**2**	**10**	**7**	**1**	**8**	**205**	**0**	**0**	**1**	**33**	**24.2**	**17**	**3**	**30**	**0**	**–16**	....	....	....	....	....	....	....	....
1993-94	**Edmonton Oilers**	**NHL**	**48**	**4**	**6**	**10**	**4**	**5**	**9**	**185**	**0**	**0**	**0**	**27**	**14.8**	**14**	**1**	**22**	**0**	**–9**	....	....	....	....	....	....	....	....
	Cape Breton Oilers	AHL	5	3	1	4	....	....	....	58	....	....	....	....	....	....	....	....	....	....	....	....	....	....	....	....	....	....
1994-95	**Edmonton Oilers**	**NHL**	**34**	**2**	**0**	**2**	**4**	**0**	**4**	**93**	**0**	**0**	**0**	**14**	**14.3**	**3**	**0**	**7**	**0**	**–4**	....	....	....	....	....	....	....	....
1995-96	**Edmonton Oilers**	**NHL**	**38**	**1**	**3**	**4**	**1**	**2**	**3**	**96**	**0**	**0**	**0**	**17**	**5.9**	**4**	**0**	**11**	**0**	**–7**	....	....	....	....	....	....	....	....

			REGULAR SEASON																		PLAYOFFS							
Season	Club	League	GP	G	A	Pts	AG	AA	APts	PIM	PP	SH	GW	S	%	TGF	PGF	TGA	PGA	+/-	GP	G	A	Pts	PIM	PP	SH	GW
1996-97	Edmonton Oilers	NHL	32	2	0	2	2	0	2	94	0	0	0	10	20.0	2	0	8	0	-6	6	0	0	0	4	0	0	0
1997-98	Tampa Bay Lightning	NHL	54	1	2	3	1	2	3	166	0	0	0	14	7.1	5	0	7	0	-2								
	San Antonio Dragons	IHL	17	7	4	11				130																		
	NHL Totals		282	20	14	34	21	11	32	963	0	0	2	122	16.4	53	4	89	0		6	0	0	0	4	0	0	0

Traded to **Edmonton** by **NY Rangers** with Bernie Nicholls and Steven Rice for Mark Messier and future considerations, October 4, 1991.

Signed as a free agent by **Tampa Bay**, September 23, 1997. Traded to **Phoenix** by **Tampa Bay** with Tampa Bay's 5th round choice (Jay Leach) in 1998 Entry Draft for Craig Janney, June 11, 1998.

• DEFAZIO, DEAN

Dean Defazio LW – L. 5'11", 185 lbs. b: Ottawa, Ont., 4/16/1963. Pittsburgh's 8th choice, 175th overall, in 1981 Entry Draft.

Season	Club	League	GP	G	A	Pts	AG	AA	APts	PIM	PP	SH	GW	S	%	TGF	PGF	TGA	PGA	+/-	GP	G	A	Pts	PIM	PP	SH	GW
1979-80	Ottawa Jr. Senators	OJHL	47	27	25	52				80																		
1980-81	Brantford Alexanders	OHL	60	6	13	19				104											6	1	0	1	19			
1981-82	Brantford Alexanders	OHL	10	2	6	8				30																		
	Sudbury Wolves	OHL	50	21	32	53				81																		
1982-83	Oshawa Generals	OHL	52	22	23	45				108											17	8	9	17	16			
1983-84	Pittsburgh Penguins	NHL	22	0	2	2	0	1	1	28	0	0	0	12	0.0	4	0	15	0	-11								
	Baltimore Skipjacks	AHL	46	18	13	31				114											10	2	2	4	19			
1984-85	Baltimore Skipjacks	AHL	78	10	17	27				88											10	2	1	3	64			
1985-86	Baltimore Skipjacks	AHL	75	14	24	38				171																		
1986-87	Newmarket Saints	AHL	76	7	13	20				116																		
1987-88	New Haven Nighthawks	AHL	26	5	12	17				21																		
	Baltimore Skipjacks	AHL	2	1	2	3				75																		
	Flint Spirits	IHL	30	8	6	14				39																		
	NHL Totals		22	0	2	2	0	1	1	28	0	0	0	12	0.0	4	0	15	0									

• DEGRAY, DALE

Dale "Digger" DeGray D – R. 6', 200 lbs. b: Oshawa, Ont., 9/1/1963. Calgary's 7th choice, 162nd overall, in 1981 Entry Draft.

Season	Club	League	GP	G	A	Pts	AG	AA	APts	PIM	PP	SH	GW	S	%	TGF	PGF	TGA	PGA	+/-	GP	G	A	Pts	PIM	PP	SH	GW
1979-80	Oshawa Legionaires	OJHL	42	14	14	28				34																		
	Oshawa Generals	OHA	1	0	0	0				2																		
1980-81	Oshawa Generals	OHL	61	11	10	21				93											8	1	1	2	19			
1981-82	Oshawa Generals	OHL	66	11	23	34				162											12	3	4	7	49			
1982-83	Oshawa Generals	OHL	69	20	30	50				149											17	7	7	14	36			
1983-84	Colorado Flames	CHL	67	16	14	30				67											6	1	1	2	2			
1984-85	Moncton Golden Flames	AHL	77	24	37	61				63																		
1985-86	Calgary Flames	NHL	1	0	0	0	0	0	0	0	0	0	0	1	0.0	1	0	2	0	-1								
	Moncton Golden Flames	AHL	76	10	31	41				128											6	0	1	1	0			
1986-87	Calgary Flames	NHL	27	6	7	13	5	5	10	29	0	0	1	57	10.5	20	1	26	4	-3								
	Moncton Golden Flames	AHL	45	10	22	32				57											5	2	1	3	19			
1987-88	Toronto Maple Leafs	NHL	56	6	18	24	5	13	18	63	1	0	1	122	4.9	62	19	50	11	+4	5	0	1	1	16	0	0	0
	Newmarket Saints	AHL	8	2	10	12				8																		
1988-89	Los Angeles Kings	NHL	63	6	22	28	5	15	20	97	0	0	1	87	6.9	77	18	64	8	+3	8	1	2	3	12	1	0	0
1989-90	New Haven Nighthawks	AHL	16	2	10	12				38																		
	Buffalo Sabres	NHL	6	0	0	0	0	0	0	6	0	0	0	5	0.0	2	0	6	0	-4								
	Rochester Americans	AHL	50	6	25	31				118											17	5	6	11	59			
1990-91	Rochester Americans	AHL	64	9	25	34				121											15	3	4	7	*76			
1991-92	HC Allege	Italy	27	6	22	28				46																		
1992-93	San Diego Gulls	IHL	79	18	64	82				181											14	3	11	14	77			
1993-94	San Diego Gulls	IHL	80	20	50	70				163											9	2	1	3	8			
1994-95	Detroit Vipers	IHL	14	1	8	9				10																		
	Cleveland Lumberjacks	IHL	64	19	49	68				134											4	0	4	4	10			
	Canada	WC-A	6	1	1	2				6																		
1995-96	Cincinnati Cyclones	IHL	79	13	46	59				90											16	1	6	7	35			
1996-97	Manitoba Moose	IHL	44	9	15	24				42																		
	Cincinnati Cyclones	IHL	30	5	16	21				55																		
1997-98	Manitoba Moose	IHL	15	0	7	7				16																		
	Quebec Rafales	IHL	31	4	9	13				27																		
	Cleveland Lumberjacks	IHL	11	1	9	10				4											9	3	7	10	8			
	NHL Totals		153	18	47	65	15	33	48	195	1	0	3	272	6.6	162	38	148	23		13	1	3	4	28	1	0	0

AHL Second All-Star Team (1985) • IHL Second All-Star Team (1993, 1995)

Traded to **Toronto** by **Calgary** for Toronto's 5th round choice (Scott Matusovich) in 1988 Entry Draft, September 17, 1987. Claimed by **LA Kings** from **Toronto** in Waiver Draft, October 3, 1988. Traded to **Buffalo** by **LA Kings** with future considerations for Bob Halkidis and future considerations, November 24, 1989.

• DELORME, GILBERT

Gilbert Delorme D – R. 6'1", 199 lbs. b: Boucherville, Que., 11/25/1962. Montreal's 2nd choice, 18th overall, in 1981 Entry Draft.

Season	Club	League	GP	G	A	Pts	AG	AA	APts	PIM	PP	SH	GW	S	%	TGF	PGF	TGA	PGA	+/-	GP	G	A	Pts	PIM	PP	SH	GW
1978-79	Chicoutimi Sagueneens	QMJHL	72	13	47	60				53																		
1979-80	Chicoutimi Sagueneens	QMJHL	71	25	86	111				68											12	2	10	12	26			
1980-81	Chicoutimi Sagueneens	QMJHL	70	27	79	106				77											12	10	12	22	16			
	Canada	WJC-A	5	1	0	1				0																		
1981-82	Montreal Canadiens	NHL	60	3	8	11	2	5	7	55	0	0	0	80	3.8	55	2	43	9	+19								
1982-83	Montreal Canadiens	NHL	78	12	21	33	10	14	24	89	3	0	2	166	7.2	116	16	83	10	+27	3	0	0	0	2	0	0	0
1983-84	Montreal Canadiens	NHL	27	2	7	9	2	5	7	8	0	0	0	37	5.4	24	2	28	2	-4								
	St. Louis Blues	NHL	44	0	5	5	0	3	3	41	0	0	0	68	0.0	30	6	37	6	-7	11	1	3	4	11	0	0	0
1984-85	St. Louis Blues	NHL	74	2	12	14	2	0	10	53	1	0	0	85	2.4	76	4	97	32	+7	3	0	0	0	0	0	0	0
1985-86	Quebec Nordiques	NHL	64	2	18	20	2	12	14	51	1	0	0	102	2.0	86	26	73	12	-1	2	0	0	0	5	0	0	0
1986-87	Quebec Nordiques	NHL	19	2	0	2	2	0	2	14	0	0	0	22	9.1	13	0	17	3	-1								
	Detroit Red Wings	NHL	24	2	3	5	2	2	4	33	0	0	0	24	8.3	17	0	28	10	-1	16	0	2	2	14	0	0	0
1987-88	Detroit Red Wings	NHL	55	2	8	10	2	6	8	81	0	0	0	46	4.3	45	0	52	16	+9	15	0	3	3	22	0	0	0
1988-89	Detroit Red Wings	NHL	42	1	3	4	1	2	3	51	0	0	0	23	4.3	27	1	46	9	-11	6	0	1	1	2	0	0	0
1989-90	Pittsburgh Penguins	NHL	54	3	7	10	3	5	8	44	0	0	0	37	8.1	46	1	57	15	+3								
1990-91			DID NOT PLAY																									
1991-92	Muskegon Lumberjacks	IHL	60	6	6	12				89											7	2	2	4	12			
	NHL Totals		541	31	92	123	28	62	90	520	5	0	2	690	4.5	535	58	561	124		56	1	9	10	56	0	0	0

QMJHL Second All-Star Team (1981)

Traded to **St. Louis** by **Montreal** with Greg Paslawski and Doug Wickenheiser for Perry Turnbull, December 21, 1983. Traded to **Quebec** by **St. Louis** for Bruce Bell, October 2, 1985. Traded to **Detroit** by **Quebec** with Brent Ashton and Mark Kumpel for Basil McRae, John Ogrodnick and Doug Shedden, January 17, 1987. Signed as a free agent by **Pittsburgh**, June 28, 1990.

• DELORME, RON

Ron "Chief" Delorme C – R. 6'2", 185 lbs. b: North Battleford, Sask., 9/3/1955. Kansas City's 4th choice, 56th overall, in 1975 Amateur Draft.

Season	Club	League	GP	G	A	Pts	AG	AA	APts	PIM	PP	SH	GW	S	%	TGF	PGF	TGA	PGA	+/-	GP	G	A	Pts	PIM	PP	SH	GW
1973-74	Swift Current Broncos	WCJHL	59	19	15	34				96											13	1	2	3	17			
1974-75	Lethbridge Broncos	WHL	69	30	57	87				144											6	1	7	8	20			
1975-76	Lethbridge Broncos	WHL	26	8	12	20				87											7	3	6	9	24			
	Denver-Ottawa	WHA	22	1	3	4				28																		
	Tucson Mavericks	CHL	18	2	5	7				18																		
1976-77	Colorado Rockies	NHL	29	6	4	10	6	3	9	23	0	0	2	31	19.4	16	2	27	2	11								
	Baltimore Clippers	SHL	25	4	6	10				4																		
	Tulsa Oilers	CHL	6	1	2	3				0																		
1977-78	Colorado Rockies	NHL	68	10	11	21	10	9	19	47	0	0	0	76	13.2	35	3	53	1	-20	2	0	0	0	10	0	0	0
1978-79	Colorado Rockies	NHL	77	20	8	28	18	6	24	68	2	0	3	85	23.5	40	4	67	1	-30								
1979-80	Colorado Rockies	NHL	75	19	24	43	17	18	35	76	5	0	4	98	19.4	75	26	73	0	-24								
1980-81	Colorado Rockies	NHL	65	11	16	27	9	11	20	70	3	0	0	65	16.9	58	13	56	0	11								
1981-82	Vancouver Canucks	NHL	59	9	8	17	7	5	12	177	0	0	0	47	19.1	29	0	38	1	-8	15	0	2	2	31	0	0	0

			REGULAR SEASON																		PLAYOFFS							
Season	Club	League	GP	G	A	Pts	AG	AA	APts	PIM	PP	SH	GW	S	%	TGF	PGF	TGA	PGA	+/–	GP	G	A	Pts	PIM	PP	SH	GW
1982-83	**Vancouver Canucks**	**NHL**	**56**	**5**	**8**	**13**	**4**	**6**	**10**	**87**	**0**	**0**	**0**	**38**	**13.2**	**21**	**0**	**27**	**0**	**–6**	**4**	**0**	**0**	**0**	**10**	**0**	**0**	**0**
1983-84	**Vancouver Canucks**	**NHL**	**64**	**2**	**2**	**4**	**2**	**1**	**3**	**68**	**0**	**0**	**0**	**18**	**11.1**	**13**	**0**	**15**	**0**	**–2**	**4**	**1**	**0**	**1**	**8**	**0**	**0**	**0**
1984-85	**Vancouver Canucks**	**NHL**	**31**	**1**	**2**	**3**	**1**	**1**	**2**	**51**	**0**	**0**	**0**	**13**	**7.7**	**4**	**0**	**13**	**1**	**–8**	....	....	....	....	....	....	....	....
	NHL Totals		**524**	**83**	**83**	**166**	**74**	**60**	**134**	**667**	**10**	**0**	**9**	**471**	**17.6**	**291**	**48**	**369**	**6**		**25**	**1**	**2**	**3**	**59**	**0**	**0**	**0**
	Other Major League Totals		22	1	3	4	....	....	....	28	....	....	....	....	....	....	....	....	....		....	....	....	....	....	....	....	....

Selected by **Denver** (WHA) in 1975 WHA Amateur Draft, June, 1975. Rights transferred to **Colorado** after **Kansas City** franchise relocated, July 15, 1976. Claimed by **Vancouver** from **Colorado** in Waiver Draft, October 5, 1981.

• DELPARTE, GUY

Guy Delparte LW – L. 5'10", 175 lbs. b: Sault St. Marie, Ont., 8/30/1949. Montreal's 6th choice, 63rd overall, in 1969 Amateur Draft.

1968-69	St. Catharines Black Hawks	OHA	24	4	11	15	....	....	....	34	....	....	....	....	....	....	....	....	....	....	....	....	....	....	....	....	....	....
	London Knights	OHA	32	6	17	23	....	....	....	62	....	....	....	....	....	....	....	....	....	....	6	1	2	3	20	....	....	....
1969-70	Johnstown Jets	EHL	68	31	39	70	....	....	....	28	....	....	....	....	....	....	....	....	....	....	9	1	5	6	0	....	....	....
1970-71	Johnstown Jets	EHL	67	11	27	38	....	....	....	66	....	....	....	....	....	....	....	....	....	....	10	5	3	8	30	....	....	....
1971-72	Johnstown Jets	EHL	75	25	41	66	....	....	....	66	....	....	....	....	....	....	....	....	....	....	11	5	8	13	8	....	....	....
1972-73	Nova Scotia Voyageurs	AHL	64	8	12	20	....	....	....	42	....	....	....	....	....	....	....	....	....	....	8	0	0	0	2	....	....	....
1973-74	Nova Scotia Voyageurs	AHL	69	8	24	32	....	....	....	107	....	....	....	....	....	....	....	....	....	....	6	0	2	2	17	....	....	....
1974-75	Nova Scotia Voyageurs	AHL	53	10	11	21	....	....	....	127	....	....	....	....	....	....	....	....	....	....	6	1	2	3	14	....	....	....
1975-76	Oklahoma City Blazers	CHL	72	10	14	24	....	....	....	74	....	....	....	....	....	....	....	....	....	....	4	0	3	3	0	....	....	....
1976-77	**Colorado Rockies**	**NHL**	**48**	**1**	**8**	**9**	**1**	**6**	**7**	**18**	**0**	**0**	**0**	**37**	**2.7**	**19**	**1**	**35**	**7**	**–10**	....	....	....	....	....	....	....	....
	Rhode Island Reds	AHL	11	0	3	3	....	....	....	8	....	....	....	....	....	....	....	....	....	....	....	....	....	....	....	....	....	....
1977-78	Maine Mariners	AHL	78	16	21	37	....	....	....	82	....	....	....	....	....	....	....	....	....	....	12	3	1	4	11	....	....	....
1978-79	Maine Mariners	AHL	67	10	26	36	....	....	....	63	....	....	....	....	....	....	....	....	....	....	....	....	....	....	....	....	....	....
1979-80	Maine Mariners	AHL	78	10	20	30	....	....	....	111	....	....	....	....	....	....	....	....	....	....	9	0	3	3	0	....	....	....
1980-81	Springfield Indians	AHL	73	3	7	10	....	....	....	81	....	....	....	....	....	....	....	....	....	....	7	1	3	4	24	....	....	....
	NHL Totals		**48**	**1**	**8**	**9**	**1**	**6**	**7**	**18**	**0**	**0**	**0**	**37**	**2.7**	**19**	**1**	**35**	**7**		....	....	....	....	....	....	....	....

Signed as a free agent by **Colorado**, October 4, 1976.

• DELVECCHIO, ALEX

Alex "Fats" Delvecchio C – L. 6', 195 lbs. b: Fort William, Ont., 12/4/1932. **HHOF**

1947-48	Fort William Rangers	TBJHL	1	0	0	0	....	....	....	0	....	....	....	....	....	....	....	....	....	....	....	....	....	....	....	....	....	....
1948-49	Fort William Rangers	TBJHL	12	16	8	24	....	....	....	*53	....	....	....	....	....	....	....	....	....	....	1	2	0	2	0	....	....	....
1949-50	Fort William Rangers	TBJHL	18	16	*20	36	....	....	....	36	....	....	....	....	....	....	....	....	....	....	5	4	4	8	15	....	....	....
1950-51	Oshawa Generals	OHA	54	49	*72	121	....	....	....	36	....	....	....	....	....	....	....	....	....	....	....	....	....	....	....	....	....	....
	Detroit Red Wings	**NHL**	**1**	**0**	**0**	**0**	**0**	**0**	**0**	**0**	....	....	....	....	....	....	....	....	....	....	....	....	....	....	....	....	....	....
1951-52	**Detroit Red Wings**	**NHL**	**65**	**15**	**22**	**37**	**21**	**29**	**50**	**22**	....	....	....	....	....	....	....	....	....	....	**8**	**0**	**3**	**3**	**4**	....	....	....
	Indianapolis Capitals	AHL	6	3	6	9	....	....	....	4	....	....	....	....	....	....	....	....	....	....	....	....	....	....	....	....	....	....
1952-53	**Detroit Red Wings**	**NHL**	**70**	**16**	**43**	**59**	**25**	**61**	**86**	**28**	....	....	....	....	....	....	....	....	....	....	**6**	**2**	**4**	**6**	**2**	....	....	....
1953-54	**Detroit Red Wings**	**NHL**	**69**	**11**	**18**	**29**	**17**	**24**	**41**	**34**	....	....	....	....	....	....	....	....	....	....	**12**	**2**	**7**	**9**	**7**	....	....	....
1954-55	**Detroit Red Wings**	**NHL**	**69**	**17**	**31**	**48**	**25**	**40**	**65**	**37**	....	....	....	....	....	....	....	....	....	....	**11**	**7**	**8**	**15**	**2**	....	....	....
1955-56	**Detroit Red Wings**	**NHL**	**70**	**25**	**26**	**51**	**37**	**33**	**70**	**24**	....	....	....	....	....	....	....	....	....	....	**10**	**7**	**3**	**10**	**2**	....	....	....
1956-57	**Detroit Red Wings**	**NHL**	**48**	**16**	**25**	**41**	**22**	**29**	**51**	**8**	....	....	....	....	....	....	....	....	....	....	**5**	**3**	**2**	**5**	**2**	....	....	....
1957-58	**Detroit Red Wings**	**NHL**	**70**	**21**	**38**	**59**	**28**	**42**	**70**	**22**	....	....	....	....	....	....	....	....	....	....	**4**	**0**	**1**	**1**	**0**	....	....	....
1958-59	**Detroit Red Wings**	**NHL**	**70**	**19**	**35**	**54**	**24**	**37**	**61**	**6**	....	....	....	....	....	....	....	....	....	....	....	....	....	....	....	....	....	....
1959-60	**Detroit Red Wings**	**NHL**	**70**	**19**	**28**	**47**	**24**	**29**	**53**	**8**	....	....	....	....	....	....	....	....	....	....	**6**	**2**	**6**	**8**	**0**	....	....	....
1960-61	**Detroit Red Wings**	**NHL**	**70**	**27**	**35**	**62**	**33**	**36**	**69**	**26**	....	....	....	....	....	....	....	....	....	....	**11**	**4**	**5**	**9**	**0**	....	....	....
1961-62	**Detroit Red Wings**	**NHL**	**70**	**26**	**43**	**69**	**32**	**44**	**76**	**18**	....	....	....	....	....	....	....	....	....	....	....	....	....	....	....	....	....	....
1962-63	**Detroit Red Wings**	**NHL**	**70**	**20**	**44**	**64**	**25**	**46**	**71**	**8**	....	....	....	....	....	....	....	....	....	....	**11**	**3**	**6**	**9**	**2**	....	....	....
1963-64	**Detroit Red Wings**	**NHL**	**70**	**23**	**30**	**53**	**31**	**33**	**64**	**11**	....	....	....	....	....	....	....	....	....	....	**14**	**3**	**8**	**11**	**0**	....	....	....
1964-65	**Detroit Red Wings**	**NHL**	**68**	**25**	**42**	**67**	**32**	**46**	**78**	**16**	....	....	....	....	....	....	....	....	....	....	**7**	**2**	**3**	**5**	**4**	....	....	....
1965-66	**Detroit Red Wings**	**NHL**	**70**	**31**	**38**	**69**	**38**	**38**	**76**	**16**	....	....	....	....	....	....	....	....	....	....	**12**	**0**	***11**	**11**	**4**	....	....	....
1966-67	**Detroit Red Wings**	**NHL**	**70**	**17**	**38**	**55**	**21**	**39**	**60**	**10**	....	....	....	....	....	....	....	....	....	....	....	....	....	....	....	....	....	....
1967-68	**Detroit Red Wings**	**NHL**	**74**	**22**	**48**	**70**	**27**	**51**	**78**	**14**	**3**	**0**	**2**	**212**	**10.4**	**106**	**28**	**90**	**20**	**+8**	....	....	....	....	....	....	....	....
1968-69	**Detroit Red Wings**	**NHL**	**72**	**25**	**58**	**83**	**28**	**55**	**83**	**8**	**7**	**0**	**2**	**221**	**11.3**	**123**	**28**	**63**	**11**	**+43**	....	....	....	....	....	....	....	....
1969-70	**Detroit Red Wings**	**NHL**	**73**	**21**	**47**	**68**	**24**	**47**	**71**	**24**	**4**	**0**	**3**	**218**	**9.6**	**100**	**36**	**57**	**19**	**+26**	**4**	**0**	**2**	**2**	**0**	**0**	**0**	**0**
1970-71	**Detroit Red Wings**	**NHL**	**77**	**21**	**34**	**55**	**22**	**30**	**52**	**6**	**6**	**0**	**2**	**171**	**12.3**	**87**	**36**	**91**	**22**	**–18**	....	....	....	....	....	....	....	....
1971-72	**Detroit Red Wings**	**NHL**	**75**	**20**	**45**	**65**	**21**	**41**	**62**	**22**	**9**	**0**	**5**	**123**	**16.3**	**90**	**29**	**80**	**0**	**–19**	....	....	....	....	....	....	....	....
1972-73	**Detroit Red Wings**	**NHL**	**77**	**18**	**53**	**71**	**18**	**44**	**62**	**13**	**8**	**0**	**3**	**130**	**13.8**	**109**	**39**	**64**	**0**	**+6**	....	....	....	....	....	....	....	....
1973-74	**Detroit Red Wings**	**NHL**	**11**	**1**	**4**	**5**	**1**	**3**	**4**	**2**	**1**	**0**	**0**	**9**	**11.1**	**8**	**7**	**15**	**1**	**–13**	....	....	....	....	....	....	....	....
	NHL Totals		**1549**	**456**	**825**	**1281**	**576**	**877**	**1453**	**383**	**38**	**0**	**17**	**1084**	**42.1**	**623**	**203**	**460**	**73**		**121**	**35**	**69**	**104**	**29**	**0**	**0**	**0**

NHL Second All-Star Team (1953, 1959) • Won Lady Byng Trophy (1959, 1966, 1969) • Won Lester Patrick Trophy (1974)

Played in NHL All-Star Game (1953, 1954, 1955, 1956, 1957, 1958, 1959, 1961, 1962, 1963, 1964, 1965, 1967)

• DEMARCO, AB JR.

Ab Jr. (Albert) DeMarco D – R. 6', 170 lbs. b: Cleveland, OH, 2/27/1949.

1966-67	North Bay Trappers	NOHA	STATISTICS NOT AVAILABLE																									
1967-68	Kitchener Rangers	OHA	49	9	30	39	....	....	....	24	....	....	....	....	....	....	....	....	....	....	19	13	11	24	21	....	....	....
1968-69	Ottawa Nationals	OHA Sr.	8	4	8	12	....	....	....	7	....	....	....	....	....	....	....	....	....	....	....	....	....	....	....	....	....	....
	Canada	WEC-A	9	1	0	1	....	....	....	6	....	....	....	....	....	....	....	....	....	....	....	....	....	....	....	....	....	....
1969-70	**New York Rangers**	**NHL**	**3**	**0**	**0**	**0**	**0**	**0**	**0**	**0**	**0**	**0**	**0**	**6**	**0.0**	**0**	**0**	**1**	**0**	**–1**	**5**	**0**	**0**	**0**	**2**	**0**	**0**	**0**
	Omaha Knights	CHL	60	6	30	36	....	....	....	19	....	....	....	....	....	....	....	....	....	....	....	....	....	....	....	....	....	....
1970-71	**New York Rangers**	**NHL**	**2**	**0**	**1**	**1**	**0**	**1**	**1**	**0**	**0**	**0**	**0**	**2**	**0.0**	**2**	**0**	**1**	**0**	**+1**	....	....	....	....	....	....	....	....
	Omaha Knights	CHL	54	17	25	42	....	....	....	18	....	....	....	....	....	....	....	....	....	....	....	....	....	....	....	....	....	....
1971-72	**New York Rangers**	**NHL**	**48**	**4**	**7**	**11**	**4**	**6**	**10**	**4**	**1**	**0**	**0**	**95**	**4.2**	**37**	**1**	**22**	**4**	**+18**	**4**	**0**	**1**	**1**	**0**	**0**	**0**	**0**
1972-73	**New York Rangers**	**NHL**	**51**	**4**	**13**	**17**	**4**	**11**	**15**	**15**	**1**	**0**	**2**	**104**	**3.8**	**68**	**5**	**51**	**4**	**+16**	....	....	....	....	....	....	....	....
	St. Louis Blues	**NHL**	**14**	**4**	**9**	**13**	**4**	**8**	**12**	**2**	**2**	**1**	**1**	**51**	**7.8**	**25**	**9**	**17**	**5**	**+4**	**4**	**1**	**1**	**2**	**2**	**1**	**0**	**0**
1973-74	**St. Louis Blues**	**NHL**	**23**	**3**	**9**	**12**	**3**	**8**	**11**	**11**	**1**	**0**	**0**	**71**	**4.2**	**29**	**9**	**15**	**1**	**+6**	....	....	....	....	....	....	....	....
	Pittsburgh Penguins	**NHL**	**34**	**7**	**12**	**19**	**7**	**10**	**17**	**4**	**3**	**0**	**1**	**101**	**6.9**	**54**	**18**	**32**	**1**	**+5**	....	....	....	....	....	....	....	....
1974-75	**Pittsburgh Penguins**	**NHL**	**8**	**2**	**1**	**3**	**2**	**1**	**3**	**4**	**1**	**0**	**0**	**25**	**8.0**	**11**	**2**	**16**	**3**	**–4**	....	....	....	....	....	....	....	....
	Vancouver Canucks	**NHL**	**61**	**10**	**14**	**24**	**9**	**11**	**20**	**21**	**8**	**0**	**1**	**117**	**8.5**	**64**	**38**	**31**	**3**	**–2**	**2**	**0**	**0**	**0**	**0**	**0**	**0**	**0**
1975-76	**Vancouver Canucks**	**NHL**	**34**	**3**	**8**	**11**	**3**	**6**	**9**	**2**	**2**	**0**	**0**	**33**	**9.1**	**22**	**12**	**15**	**2**	**–3**	....	....	....	....	....	....	....	....
	Los Angeles Kings	**NHL**	**30**	**4**	**3**	**7**	**4**	**2**	**6**	**6**	**2**	**0**	**1**	**70**	**5.7**	**27**	**6**	**26**	**2**	**–3**	**9**	**0**	**0**	**0**	**11**	**0**	**0**	**0**
1976-77	**Los Angeles Kings**	**NHL**	**33**	**3**	**3**	**6**	**3**	**2**	**5**	**6**	**0**	**0**	**0**	**82**	**3.7**	**23**	**2**	**33**	**4**	**–8**	**1**	**0**	**0**	**0**	**2**	**0**	**0**	**0**
	Fort Worth Texans	CHL	31	4	15	19	....	....	....	20	....	....	....	....	....	....	....	....	....	....	....	....	....	....	....	....	....	....
1977-78	Edmonton Oilers	WHA	47	6	8	14	....	....	....	20	....	....	....	....	....	....	....	....	....	....	1	0	0	0	0	....	....	....
1978-79	**Boston Bruins**	**NHL**	**3**	**0**	**0**	**0**	**0**	**0**	**0**	**0**	**0**	**0**	**0**	**5**	**0.0**	**1**	**0**	**1**	**0**	**0**	....	....	....	....	....	....	....	....
	NHL Totals		**344**	**44**	**80**	**124**	**43**	**66**	**109**	**75**	**21**	**1**	**6**	**762**	**5.8**	**363**	**102**	**261**	**29**		**25**	**1**	**2**	**3**	**17**	**1**	**0**	**0**
	Other Major League Totals		47	6	8	14	....	....	....	20	....	....	....	....	....	....	....	....	....		1	0	0	0	0	....	....	....

Selected by **Chicago** (WHA) in 1972 WHA General Player Draft, February 12, 1972. Traded to **St. Louis** by **NY Rangers** for Mike Murphy, March 2, 1973. Traded to **Vancouver** by **St. Louis** with Steve Durbano and Bob Kelly for Bryan Watson, Greg Polis and Pittsburgh's 2nd choice (Bob Hess) in 1974 Amateur Draft, January 17, 1974. Traded to **Vancouver** by **Pittsburgh** for Barry Wilkins, November 4, 1974. Traded to **LA Kings** by **Vancouver** for LA Kings' 2nd choice (later traded to Atlanta — Atlanta selected Brian Hill) in 1977 Amateur Draft, January 14, 1976. Traded to **Atlanta** by **LA Kings** for Randy Manery, May 23, 1977. WHA rights transferred to **Edmonton** (WHA) after **Chicago** (WHA) franchise folded, May, 1975. Signed as a free agent by **Boston**, October 23, 1978.

• DEMITRA, PAVOL

Pavol Demitra LW – L. 6', 189 lbs. b: Dubnica, Czech., 11/29/1974. Ottawa's 8th choice, 227th overall, in 1993 Entry Draft.

1991-92	Spartak Dubnica	Czech. 2	28	13	10	23	....	....	....	12	....	....	....	....	....	....	....	....	....	....	....	....	....	....	....	....	....	....
1992-93	Dukla Trencin	Czech.	46	10	18	28	....	....	....	....	....	....	....	....	....	....	....	....	....	....	....	....	....	....	....	....	....	....
	Czech Republic	WJC-A	7	4	4	8	....	....	....	8	....	....	....	....	....	....	....	....	....	....	....	....	....	....	....	....	....	....
	Spartak Dubnica	Czech. 2	4	3	0	3	....	....	....	....	....	....	....	....	....	....	....	....	....	....	....	....	....	....	....	....	....	....
1993-94	**Ottawa Senators**	**NHL**	**12**	**1**	**1**	**2**	**1**	**1**	**2**	**4**	**1**	**0**	**0**	**10**	**10.0**	**3**	**2**	**8**	**0**	**–7**	....	....	....	....	....	....	....	....
	P.E.I. Senators	AHL	41	18	23	41	....	....	....	8	....	....	....	....	....	....	....	....	....	....	....	....	....	....	....	....	....	....
1994-95	**Ottawa Senators**	**NHL**	**16**	**4**	**3**	**7**	**7**	**4**	**11**	**0**	**1**	**0**	**0**	**21**	**19.0**	**11**	**5**	**10**	**0**	**–4**	....	....	....	....	....	....	....	....
	P.E.I. Senators	AHL	61	26	48	74	....	....	....	23	....	....	....	....	....	....	....	....	....	....	5	0	7	7	0	....	....	....

			REGULAR SEASON																		PLAYOFFS							
Season	Club	League	GP	G	A	Pts	AG	AA	APts	PIM	PP	SH	GW	S	%	TGF	PGF	TGA	PGA	+/–	GP	G	A	Pts	PIM	PP	SH	GW
1995-96	**Ottawa Senators**	**NHL**	**31**	**7**	**10**	**17**	**7**	**8**	**15**	**6**	**2**	**0**	**1**	**66**	**10.6**	**24**	**9**	**18**	**0**	**–3**	....	....	....	....	....	....	....	....
	P.E.I. Senators	AHL	48	28	53	81	....	....	....	44	....	....	....	....	....	....	....	....	....	....	....	....	....	....	....	....	....	....
	Slovakia	WC-A	5	1	2	3	....	....	....	2	....	....	....	....	....	....	....	....	....	....	....	....	....	....	....	....	....	....
1996-97	Slovakia	W Cup	3	0	0	0	....	....	....	4	....	....	....	....	....	....	....	....	....	....	....	....	....	....	....	....	....	....
	Dukla Trencin	Slovakia	1	1	1	2	....	....	....	....	....	....	....	....	....	....	....	....	....	....	....	....	....	....	....	....	....	....
	St. Louis Blues	**NHL**	**8**	**3**	**0**	**3**	**3**	**0**	**3**	**2**	**2**	**0**	**1**	**15**	**20.0**	**5**	**2**	**3**	**0**	**0**	**6**	**1**	**3**	**4**	**0**	**0**	**0**	**0**
	Las Vegas Thunder	IHL	22	8	13	21	....	....	....	10	....	....	....	....	....	....	....	....	....	....	....	....	....	....	....	....	....	....
	Grand Rapids Griffins	IHL	42	20	30	50	....	....	....	24	....	....	....	....	....	....	....	....	....	....	....	....	....	....	....	....	....	....
1997-98	**St. Louis Blues**	**NHL**	**61**	**22**	**30**	**52**	**26**	**29**	**55**	**22**	**4**	**4**	**6**	**147**	**15.0**	**72**	**22**	**43**	**4**	**+11**	**10**	**3**	**3**	**6**	**2**	**0**	**0**	**0**
	NHL Totals		**128**	**37**	**44**	**81**	**44**	**42**	**86**	**34**	**10**	**4**	**8**	**259**	**14.3**	**115**	**40**	**82**	**4**		**16**	**4**	**6**	**10**	**8**	**0**	**0**	**0**

Traded to **St. Louis** by **Ottawa** for Christer Olsson, November 27, 1996.

• DEMPSEY, NATHAN

Nathan Dempsey LW – L. 6', 170 lbs. b: Spruce Grove, Alta., 7/14/1974. Toronto's 12th choice, 245th overall, in 1992 Entry Draft.

Season	Club	League	GP	G	A	Pts	AG	AA	APts	PIM	PP	SH	GW	S	%	TGF	PGF	TGA	PGA	+/–	GP	G	A	Pts	PIM	PP	SH	GW
1991-92	Regina Pats	WHL	70	4	22	26	....	....	....	72	....	....	....	....	....	....	....	....	....	....	....	....	....	....	....	....	....	....
1992-93	Regina Pats	WHL	72	12	29	41	....	....	....	95	....	....	....	....	....	....	....	....	....	....	13	3	8	11	14	....	....	....
	St. John's Maple Leafs	AHL	....	....	....	....	....	....	....	....	....	....	....	....	....	....	....	....	....	....	2	0	0	0	0	....	....	....
1993-94	Regina Pats	WHL	56	14	36	50	....	....	....	100	....	....	....	....	....	....	....	....	....	....	4	0	0	0	4	....	....	....
1994-95	St. John's Maple Leafs	AHL	74	7	30	37	....	....	....	91	....	....	....	....	....	....	....	....	....	....	5	1	0	1	11	....	....	....
1995-96	St. John's Maple Leafs	AHL	73	5	15	20	....	....	....	103	....	....	....	....	....	....	....	....	....	....	4	1	0	1	9	....	....	....
1996-97	**Toronto Maple Leafs**	**NHL**	**14**	**1**	**1**	**2**	**1**	**1**	**2**	**2**	**0**	**0**	**0**	**11**	**9.1**	**2**	**0**	**5**	**1**	**–2**	....	....	....	....	....	....	....	....
	St. John's Maple Leafs	AHL	52	8	18	26	....	....	....	108	....	....	....	....	....	....	....	....	....	....	6	1	0	1	4	....	....	....
1997-98	St. John's Maple Leafs	AHL	68	12	16	28	....	....	....	85	....	....	....	....	....	....	....	....	....	....	4	0	0	0	0	....	....	....
	NHL Totals		**14**	**1**	**1**	**2**	**1**	**1**	**2**	**2**	**0**	**0**	**0**	**11**	**9.1**	**2**	**0**	**5**	**1**		....	....	....	....	....	....	....	....

WHL East Second All-Star Team (1994)

• DENNIS, NORM

Norm Dennis C – L. 5'10", 175 lbs. b: Aurora, Ont., 12/10/1942.

Season	Club	League	GP	G	A	Pts	AG	AA	APts	PIM	PP	SH	GW	S	%	TGF	PGF	TGA	PGA	+/–	GP	G	A	Pts	PIM	PP	SH	GW
1961-62	Montreal Jr. Canadiens	OHA	50	28	44	72	....	....	....	56	....	....	....	....	....	....	....	....	....	....	6	2	3	5	14	....	....	....
1962-63	Montreal Jr. Canadiens	OHA	37	23	32	55	....	....	....	59	....	....	....	....	....	....	....	....	....	....	8	1	7	8	6	....	....	....
	Hull-Ottawa Canadiens	EPHL	1	0	0	0	....	....	....	0	....	....	....	....	....	....	....	....	....	....	....	....	....	....	....	....	....	....
1963-64	Omaha Knights	CHL	72	30	22	52	....	....	....	43	....	....	....	....	....	....	....	....	....	....	10	3	2	5	6	....	....	....
1964-65	Cleveland–Hershey	AHL	7	1	1	2	....	....	....	4	....	....	....	....	....	....	....	....	....	....	....	....	....	....	....	....	....	....
	Omaha Knights	CHL	66	30	40	70	....	....	....	59	....	....	....	....	....	....	....	....	....	....	6	2	5	7	11	....	....	....
1965-66	Houston Apollos	CHL	70	23	36	59	....	....	....	82	....	....	....	....	....	....	....	....	....	....	....	....	....	....	....	....	....	....
1966-67	Houston Apollos	CHL	54	13	33	46	....	....	....	25	....	....	....	....	....	....	....	....	....	....	4	0	2	2	0	....	....	....
1967-68	Cleveland Barons	AHL	72	11	25	36	....	....	....	42	....	....	....	....	....	....	....	....	....	....	....	....	....	....	....	....	....	....
1968-69	**St. Louis Blues**	**NHL**	**2**	**0**	**0**	**0**	**0**	**0**	**0**	**2**	**0**	**0**	**0**	**4**	**0.0**	**1**	**0**	**0**	**0**	**+1**	....	....	....	....	....	....	....	....
	Kansas City Blues	CHL	70	23	38	61	....	....	....	65	....	....	....	....	....	....	....	....	....	....	4	0	0	0	11	....	....	....
1969-70	**St. Louis Blues**	**NHL**	**5**	**3**	**0**	**3**	**3**	**0**	**3**	**5**	**0**	**0**	**0**	**8**	**37.5**	**3**	**1**	**2**	**0**	**0**	**2**	**0**	**0**	**0**	**2**	**0**	**0**	**0**
	Kansas City Blues	CHL	62	16	47	63	....	....	....	68	....	....	....	....	....	....	....	....	....	....	....	....	....	....	....	....	....	....
1970-71	**St. Louis Blues**	**NHL**	**4**	**0**	**0**	**0**	**0**	**0**	**0**	**0**	**0**	**0**	**0**	**0**	**0.0**	**0**	**0**	**4**	**0**	**–4**	**3**	**0**	**0**	**0**	**0**	**0**	**0**	**0**
	Kansas City Blues	CHL	70	25	43	68	....	....	....	52	....	....	....	....	....	....	....	....	....	....	....	....	....	....	....	....	....	....
1971-72	**St. Louis Blues**	**NHL**	**1**	**0**	**0**	**0**	**0**	**0**	**0**	**4**	**0**	**0**	**0**	**1**	**0.0**	**0**	**0**	**1**	**0**	**–1**	....	....	....	....	....	....	....	....
	Kansas City Blues	CHL	72	31	47	78	....	....	....	67	....	....	....	....	....	....	....	....	....	....	....	....	....	....	....	....	....	....
1972-73	Denver Spurs	WHL	72	27	50	77	....	....	....	35	....	....	....	....	....	....	....	....	....	....	5	4	1	5	0	....	....	....
1973-74	Providence Reds	AHL	75	23	50	73	....	....	....	43	....	....	....	....	....	....	....	....	....	....	15	2	12	14	19	....	....	....
1974-75	Providence Reds	AHL	36	2	11	13	....	....	....	22	....	....	....	....	....	....	....	....	....	....	3	0	0	0	0	....	....	....
1975-76	Trail Smoke Eaters	WIHL	24	3	8	11	....	....	....	24	....	....	....	....	....	....	....	....	....	....	....	....	....	....	....	....	....	....
1976-77	Trail Smoke Eaters	WIHL	....	0	5	5	....	....	....	4	....	....	....	....	....	....	....	....	....	....	....	....	....	....	....	....	....	....
1977-78	Trail Smoke Eaters	WIHL	....	2	6	0	....	....	....	4	....	....	....	....	....	....	....	....	....	....	....	....	....	....	....	....	....	....
	NHL Totals		**12**	**3**	**0**	**3**	**3**	**0**	**3**	**11**	**0**	**0**	**0**	**13**	**23.1**	**4**	**1**	**7**	**0**		**5**	**0**	**0**	**0**	**2**	**0**	**0**	**0**

CHL First All-Star Team (1971)

Traded to **St. Louis** by **Montreal** for cash, October 28, 1968. Traded to **NY Rangers** by **St. Louis** with Don Borgeson for Bob Kelly, September 8, 1973.

• DEPALMA, LARRY

Larry DePalma LW – L. 6', 195 lbs. b: Trenton, MI, 10/27/1965.

Season	Club	League	GP	G	A	Pts	AG	AA	APts	PIM	PP	SH	GW	S	%	TGF	PGF	TGA	PGA	+/–	GP	G	A	Pts	PIM	PP	SH	GW
1984-85	New Westminster Bruins	WHL	65	14	16	30	....	....	....	87	....	....	....	....	....	....	....	....	....	....	10	1	1	2	25	....	....	....
1985-86	Saskatoon Blades	WHL	65	61	51	112	....	....	....	232	....	....	....	....	....	....	....	....	....	....	13	7	9	16	58	....	....	....
	Minnesota North Stars	**NHL**	**1**	**0**	**0**	**0**	**0**	**0**	**0**	**0**	**0**	**0**	**0**	**0**	**0.0**	**0**	**0**	**0**	**0**	**0**	....	....	....	....	....	....	....	....
1986-87	**Minnesota North Stars**	**NHL**	**56**	**9**	**6**	**15**	**8**	**4**	**12**	**219**	**2**	**0**	**0**	**56**	**16.1**	**20**	**2**	**26**	**1**	**–7**	....	....	....	....	....	....	....	....
	Springfield Indians	AHL	9	2	2	4	....	....	....	82	....	....	....	....	....	....	....	....	....	....	....	....	....	....	....	....	....	....
1987-88	**Minnesota North Stars**	**NHL**	**7**	**1**	**1**	**2**	**1**	**1**	**2**	**15**	**0**	**0**	**0**	**8**	**12.5**	**2**	**0**	**4**	**0**	**–2**	....	....	....	....	....	....	....	....
	Baltimore Skipjacks	AHL	16	8	10	18	....	....	....	121	....	....	....	....	....	....	....	....	....	....	....	....	....	....	....	....	....	....
	Kalamazoo Wings	IHL	22	6	11	17	....	....	....	215	....	....	....	....	....	....	....	....	....	....	....	....	....	....	....	....	....	....
1988-89	**Minnesota North Stars**	**NHL**	**43**	**5**	**7**	**12**	**4**	**5**	**9**	**102**	**1**	**0**	**1**	**42**	**11.9**	**16**	**2**	**28**	**0**	**–14**	**2**	**0**	**0**	**0**	**6**	**0**	**0**	**0**
1989-90	Kalamazoo Wings	IHL	36	7	14	21	....	....	....	218	....	....	....	....	....	....	....	....	....	....	4	1	1	2	32	....	....	....
1990-91	**Minnesota North Stars**	**NHL**	**14**	**3**	**0**	**3**	**3**	**0**	**3**	**26**	**1**	**0**	**1**	**18**	**16.7**	**7**	**3**	**9**	**0**	**–5**	....	....	....	....	....	....	....	....
	Kalamazoo Wings	IHL	55	27	32	59	....	....	....	160	....	....	....	....	....	....	....	....	....	....	11	5	4	9	25	....	....	....
1991-92	Kansas City Blades	IHL	62	28	29	57	....	....	....	188	....	....	....	....	....	....	....	....	....	....	15	7	*13	20	34	....	....	....
1992-93	**San Jose Sharks**	**NHL**	**20**	**2**	**6**	**8**	**2**	**4**	**6**	**41**	**1**	**0**	**0**	**29**	**6.9**	**16**	**10**	**20**	**0**	**–14**	....	....	....	....	....	....	....	....
	Kansas City Blades	IHL	30	11	11	22	....	....	....	83	....	....	....	....	....	....	....	....	....	....	10	1	4	5	20	....	....	....
1993-94	Atlanta Knights	IHL	21	10	10	20	....	....	....	109	....	....	....	....	....	....	....	....	....	....	....	....	....	....	....	....	....	....
	Salt Lake Golden Eagles	IHL	34	4	12	16	....	....	....	125	....	....	....	....	....	....	....	....	....	....	....	....	....	....	....	....	....	....
	Las Vegas Thunder	IHL	1	0	0	0	....	....	....	17	....	....	....	....	....	....	....	....	....	....	....	....	....	....	....	....	....	....
	Pittsburgh Penguins	**NHL**	**7**	**1**	**0**	**1**	**1**	**0**	**1**	**5**	**0**	**0**	**0**	**2**	**50.0**	**1**	**0**	**0**	**0**	**+1**	**1**	**0**	**0**	**0**	**0**	**0**	**0**	**0**
	Cleveland Lumberjacks	IHL	9	4	1	5	....	....	....	49	....	....	....	....	....	....	....	....	....	....	....	....	....	....	....	....	....	....
1994-95	Cleveland Lumberjacks	IHL	25	6	6	12	....	....	....	113	....	....	....	....	....	....	....	....	....	....	....	....	....	....	....	....	....	....
	San Diego Gulls	IHL	30	14	8	22	....	....	....	86	....	....	....	....	....	....	....	....	....	....	2	0	0	0	20	....	....	....
1995-96	Minnesota Moose	IHL	55	9	17	26	....	....	....	173	....	....	....	....	....	....	....	....	....	....	....	....	....	....	....	....	....	....
	NHL Totals		**148**	**21**	**20**	**41**	**19**	**14**	**33**	**408**	**5**	**0**	**2**	**155**	**13.5**	**62**	**17**	**87**	**1**		**3**	**0**	**0**	**0**	**6**	**0**	**0**	**0**

Signed to an amateur try out contract by **Minnesota**, February 17, 1986. Signed as a free agent by **Minnesota**, May 12, 1986. Signed as a free agent by **San Jose**, August 30, 1991. Signed as a free agent by **NY Islanders**, November 29, 1993. Claimed on waivers by **Pittsburgh** from **NY Islanders**, March 9, 1994.

• DERLAGO, BILL

Bill "Billy D." Derlago C – L. 5'10", 194 lbs. b: Birtle, Man., 8/25/1958. Vancouver's 1st choice, 4th overall, in 1978 Amateur Draft.

Season	Club	League	GP	G	A	Pts	AG	AA	APts	PIM	PP	SH	GW	S	%	TGF	PGF	TGA	PGA	+/–	GP	G	A	Pts	PIM	PP	SH	GW
1974-75	Brandon Wheat Kings	WCJHL	17	0	4	4	....	....	....	2	....	....	....	....	....	....	....	....	....	....	5	1	1	2	0	....	....	....
1975-76	Brandon Wheat Kings	WCJHL	68	49	54	103	....	....	....	43	....	....	....	....	....	....	....	....	....	....	5	3	3	6	0	....	....	....
1976-77	Brandon Wheat Kings	WCJHL	72	*96	82	*178	....	....	....	63	....	....	....	....	....	....	....	....	....	....	16	*14	*16	*30	31	....	....	....
1977-78	Brandon Wheat Kings	WCJHL	52	*89	63	152	....	....	....	105	....	....	....	....	....	....	....	....	....	....	8	9	13	22	10	....	....	....
1978-79	**Vancouver Canucks**	**NHL**	**9**	**4**	**4**	**8**	**4**	**3**	**7**	**2**	**1**	**0**	**0**	**28**	**14.3**	**11**	**6**	**7**	**0**	**–2**	....	....	....	....	....	....	....	....
	Dallas Black Hawks	CHL	11	5	8	13	....	....	....	9	....	....	....	....	....	....	....	....	....	....	....	....	....	....	....	....	....	....
1979-80	**Vancouver Canucks**	**NHL**	**54**	**11**	**15**	**26**	**10**	**11**	**21**	**27**	**4**	**0**	**1**	**75**	**14.7**	**37**	**10**	**44**	**0**	**–17**	....	....	....	....	....	....	....	....
	Toronto Maple Leafs	**NHL**	**23**	**5**	**12**	**17**	**5**	**9**	**14**	**13**	**1**	**0**	**0**	**45**	**11.1**	**24**	**8**	**22**	**0**	**–6**	**3**	**0**	**0**	**0**	**4**	**0**	**0**	**0**
1980-81	**Toronto Maple Leafs**	**NHL**	**80**	**35**	**39**	**74**	**29**	**27**	**56**	**26**	**6**	**0**	**3**	**208**	**16.8**	**98**	**24**	**94**	**9**	**–11**	**3**	**1**	**0**	**1**	**2**	**1**	**0**	**0**
1981-82	**Toronto Maple Leafs**	**NHL**	**75**	**34**	**50**	**84**	**27**	**33**	**60**	**42**	**6**	**0**	**2**	**198**	**17.2**	**118**	**29**	**109**	**25**	**+5**	....	....	....	....	....	....	....	....
1982-83	**Toronto Maple Leafs**	**NHL**	**58**	**13**	**24**	**37**	**11**	**17**	**28**	**27**	**5**	**0**	**1**	**135**	**9.6**	**53**	**25**	**66**	**19**	**–19**	**4**	**3**	**0**	**3**	**2**	**2**	**0**	**0**
1983-84	**Toronto Maple Leafs**	**NHL**	**79**	**40**	**20**	**60**	**32**	**14**	**46**	**50**	**8**	**2**	**3**	**210**	**19.0**	**93**	**23**	**105**	**27**	**–8**	....	....	....	....	....	....	....	....
1984-85	**Toronto Maple Leafs**	**NHL**	**62**	**31**	**31**	**62**	**25**	**21**	**46**	**21**	**7**	**5**	**4**	**147**	**21.1**	**86**	**29**	**100**	**28**	**–15**	....	....	....	....	....	....	....	....
1985-86	**Toronto Maple Leafs**	**NHL**	**1**	**0**	**0**	**0**	**0**	**0**	**0**	**0**	**0**	**0**	**0**	**2**	**0.0**	**0**	**0**	**2**	**2**	**0**	....	....	....	....	....	....	....	....
	Boston Bruins	**NHL**	**39**	**5**	**16**	**21**	**4**	**11**	**15**	**15**	**1**	**1**	**1**	**40**	**12.5**	**30**	**7**	**30**	**11**	**+4**	....	....	....	....	....	....	....	....
	Winnipeg Jets	**NHL**	**27**	**5**	**5**	**10**	**4**	**3**	**7**	**6**	**1**	**0**	**0**	**35**	**14.3**	**14**	**4**	**31**	**8**	**–13**	**3**	**1**	**0**	**1**	**0**	**0**	**0**	**0**

			REGULAR SEASON																		PLAYOFFS							
Season	Club	League	GP	G	A	Pts	AG	AA	APts	PIM	PP	SH	GW	S	%	TGF	PGF	TGA	PGA	+/–	GP	G	A	Pts	PIM	PP	SH	GW
1986-87	**Winnipeg Jets**	**NHL**	**30**	**3**	**6**	**9**	**3**	**4**	**7**	**12**	**1**	**0**	**1**	**26**	**11.5**	**17**	**4**	**17**	**1**	**–3**	....	....	....	....	....	....	....	....
	Quebec Nordiques	**NHL**	**18**	**3**	**5**	**8**	**3**	**4**	**7**	**6**	**0**	**0**	**0**	**20**	**15.0**	**8**	**1**	**11**	**0**	**–4**	....	....	....	....	....	....	....	....
	Fredericton Express	AHL	16	7	8	15	....	....	....	2	....	....	....	....	....	....	....	....	....	....	....	....	....	....	....	....	....	....
	NHL Totals		**555**	**189**	**227**	**416**	**157**	**157**	**314**	**247**	**41**	**8**	**16**	**1169**	**16.2**	**589**	**170**	**638**	**130**		**13**	**5**	**0**	**5**	**8**	**3**	**0**	**0**

WCJHL All-Star Team (1977)

Traded to **Toronto** by **Vancouver** with Rick Vaive for Tiger Williams and Jerry Butler, February 18, 1980. Traded to **Boston** by **Toronto** for Tom Fergus, October 11, 1985. Traded to **Winnipeg** by **Boston** for Wade Campbell, January 31, 1986. Traded to **Quebec** by **Winnipeg** for Quebec's 4th round choice (Mark Brownschilde) in 1989 Entry Draft, January 5, 1987.

• DESJARDINS, ERIC

Eric Desjardins D – R. 6'1", 200 lbs. b: Rouyn, Que., 6/14/1969. Montreal's 3rd choice, 38th overall, in 1987 Entry Draft.

Season	Club	League	GP	G	A	Pts	AG	AA	APts	PIM	PP	SH	GW	S	%	TGF	PGF	TGA	PGA	+/–	GP	G	A	Pts	PIM	PP	SH	GW
1986-87	Granby Bisons	QMJHL	66	14	24	38	....	....	....	178	....	....	....	....	....	....	....	....	....	....	8	3	2	5	10	....	....	....
1987-88	Granby Bisons	QMJHL	62	18	49	67	....	....	....	138	....	....	....	....	....	....	....	....	....	....	5	0	3	3	10	....	....	....
	Canada	WJC-A	7	0	0	0	....	....	....	6	....	....	....	....	....	....	....	....	....	....	....	....	....	....	....	....	....	....
	Sherbrooke Canadiens	AHL	3	0	0	0	....	....	....	6	....	....	....	....	....	....	....	....	....	....	4	0	2	2	2	....	....	....
1988-89	**Montreal Canadiens**	**NHL**	**36**	**2**	**12**	**14**	**2**	**8**	**10**	**26**	**1**	**0**	**0**	**39**	**5.1**	**44**	**12**	**26**	**3**	**+9**	**14**	**1**	**1**	**2**	**6**	**1**	**0**	**0**
	Canada	WJC-A	7	1	4	5	....	....	....	6	....	....	....	....	....	....	....	....	....	....	....	....	....	....	....	....	....	....
1989-90	**Montreal Canadiens**	**NHL**	**55**	**3**	**13**	**16**	**3**	**9**	**12**	**51**	**1**	**0**	**0**	**48**	**6.3**	**55**	**4**	**60**	**10**	**+1**	**6**	**0**	**0**	**0**	**10**	**0**	**0**	**0**
1990-91	Montreal Canadiens	FrTour	2	0	0	0	....	....	....	0	....	....	....	....	....	....	....	....	....	....	....	....	....	....	....	....	....	....
	Montreal Canadiens	**NHL**	**62**	**7**	**18**	**25**	**6**	**14**	**20**	**27**	**0**	**0**	**1**	**114**	**6.1**	**79**	**24**	**65**	**17**	**+7**	**13**	**1**	**4**	**5**	**8**	**1**	**0**	**0**
1991-92	Canada	C Cup	8	1	2	3	....	....	....	6	....	....	....	....	....	....	....	....	....	....	....	....	....	....	....	....	....	....
	Montreal Canadiens	**NHL**	**77**	**6**	**32**	**38**	**5**	**24**	**29**	**50**	**4**	**0**	**2**	**141**	**4.3**	**108**	**37**	**83**	**29**	**+17**	**11**	**3**	**3**	**6**	**4**	**1**	**0**	**0**
1992-93	**Montreal Canadiens**	**NHL**	**82**	**13**	**32**	**45**	**11**	**22**	**33**	**98**	**7**	**0**	**1**	**163**	**8.0**	**147**	**41**	**131**	**45**	**+20**	**20**	**4**	**10**	**14**	**23**	**1**	**0**	**1**
1993-94	**Montreal Canadiens**	**NHL**	**84**	**12**	**23**	**35**	**11**	**18**	**29**	**97**	**6**	**1**	**3**	**193**	**6.2**	**99**	**28**	**104**	**32**	**–1**	**7**	**0**	**2**	**2**	**4**	**0**	**0**	**0**
1994-95	**Montreal Canadiens**	**NHL**	**9**	**0**	**6**	**6**	**0**	**9**	**9**	**2**	**0**	**0**	**0**	**14**	**0.0**	**11**	**4**	**11**	**6**	**+2**	....	....	....	....	....	....	....	....
	Philadelphia Flyers	**NHL**	**34**	**5**	**18**	**23**	**9**	**26**	**35**	**12**	**1**	**0**	**1**	**79**	**6.3**	**53**	**15**	**42**	**14**	**+10**	**15**	**4**	**4**	**8**	**10**	**1**	**0**	**2**
1995-96	**Philadelphia Flyers**	**NHL**	**80**	**7**	**40**	**47**	**7**	**33**	**40**	**45**	**5**	**0**	**2**	**184**	**3.8**	**130**	**55**	**95**	**39**	**+19**	**12**	**0**	**6**	**6**	**2**	**0**	**0**	**0**
1996-97	Canada	W Cup	8	1	2	3	....	....	....	4	....	....	....	....	....	....	....	....	....	....	....	....	....	....	....	....	....	....
	Philadelphia Flyers	**NHL**	**82**	**12**	**34**	**46**	**13**	**30**	**43**	**50**	**5**	**1**	**1**	**183**	**6.6**	**121**	**31**	**83**	**18**	**+25**	**19**	**2**	**8**	**10**	**12**	**0**	**0**	**0**
1997-98	**Philadelphia Flyers**	**NHL**	**77**	**6**	**27**	**33**	**7**	**26**	**33**	**36**	**2**	**1**	**0**	**150**	**4.0**	**95**	**30**	**74**	**20**	**+11**	**5**	**0**	**1**	**1**	**0**	**0**	**0**	**0**
	Canada	Olympics	6	0	0	0	....	....	....	2	....	....	....	....	....	....	....	....	....	....	....	....	....	....	....	....	....	....
	NHL Totals		**678**	**73**	**255**	**328**	**74**	**219**	**293**	**494**	**32**	**3**	**11**	**1308**	**5.6**	**942**	**281**	**774**	**233**		**122**	**15**	**39**	**54**	**79**	**5**	**0**	**3**

QMJHL Second All-Star Team (1987) • QMJHL First All-Star Team (1988)

Played in NHL All-Star Game (1992, 1996)

Traded to **Philadelphia** by **Montreal** with Gilbert Dionne and John LeClair for Mark Recchi and Philadelphia's 3rd round choice (Martin Hohenberger) in 1995 Entry Draft, February 9, 1995.

• DESJARDINS, MARTIN

Martin Desjardins C – L. 6', 180 lbs. b: Ste-Rose, Que., 1/28/1967. Montreal's 5th choice, 75th overall, in 1985 Entry Draft.

Season	Club	League	GP	G	A	Pts	AG	AA	APts	PIM	PP	SH	GW	S	%	TGF	PGF	TGA	PGA	+/–	GP	G	A	Pts	PIM	PP	SH	GW
1984-85	Trois-Rivières Draveurs	QMJHL	66	29	34	63	....	....	....	76	....	....	....	....	....	....	....	....	....	....	7	4	6	10	6	....	....	....
1985-86	Trois-Rivières Draveurs	QMJHL	71	49	69	118	....	....	....	103	....	....	....	....	....	....	....	....	....	....	4	2	4	6	4	....	....	....
1986-87	Trois-Rivières Draveurs	QMJHL	52	32	52	84	....	....	....	77	....	....	....	....	....	....	....	....	....	....	....	....	....	....	....	....	....	....
	Longueuil Chevaliers	QMJHL	17	7	10	17	....	....	....	12	....	....	....	....	....	....	....	....	....	....	19	8	10	18	18	....	....	....
1987-88	Sherbrooke Canadiens	AHL	75	34	36	70	....	....	....	117	....	....	....	....	....	....	....	....	....	....	5	1	1	2	8	....	....	....
1988-89	Sherbrooke Canadiens	AHL	70	17	27	44	....	....	....	104	....	....	....	....	....	....	....	....	....	....	6	2	7	9	21	....	....	....
1989-90	**Montreal Canadiens**	**NHL**	**8**	**0**	**2**	**2**	**0**	**1**	**1**	**2**	**0**	**0**	**0**	**7**	**0.0**	**3**	**0**	**9**	**2**	**–4**	....	....	....	....	....	....	....	....
	Sherbrooke Canadiens	AHL	65	21	26	47	....	....	....	72	....	....	....	....	....	....	....	....	....	....	12	4	*13	17	28	....	....	....
1990-91	Montreal Canadiens	FrTour	1	0	0	0	....	....	....	2	....	....	....	....	....	....	....	....	....	....	....	....	....	....	....	....	....	....
	Fredericton Canadiens	AHL	2	0	1	1	....	....	....	6	....	....	....	....	....	....	....	....	....	....	....	....	....	....	....	....	....	....
	Indianapolis Ice	IHL	71	15	42	57	....	....	....	110	....	....	....	....	....	....	....	....	....	....	7	2	1	3	8	....	....	....
1991-92	Indianapolis Ice	IHL	36	4	7	11	....	....	....	52	....	....	....	....	....	....	....	....	....	....	....	....	....	....	....	....	....	....
	NHL Totals		**8**	**0**	**2**	**2**	**0**	**1**	**1**	**2**	**0**	**0**	**0**	**7**	**0.0**	**3**	**0**	**9**	**2**		....	....	....	....	....	....	....	....

Traded to **Chicago** by **Montreal** for future considerations, October 10, 1990.

• DEULING, JARRETT

Jarrett Deuling LW – L. 6', 202 lbs. b: Vernon, B.C., 3/4/1974. NY Islanders' 2nd choice, 56th overall, in 1992 Entry Draft.

Season	Club	League	GP	G	A	Pts	AG	AA	APts	PIM	PP	SH	GW	S	%	TGF	PGF	TGA	PGA	+/–	GP	G	A	Pts	PIM	PP	SH	GW
1990-91	Kamloops Blazers	WHL	48	4	12	16	....	....	....	43	....	....	....	....	....	....	....	....	....	....	12	5	2	7	7	....	....	....
1991-92	Kamloops Blazers	WHL	68	28	26	54	....	....	....	79	....	....	....	....	....	....	....	....	....	....	17	10	6	16	18	....	....	....
1992-93	Kamloops Blazers	WHL	68	31	32	63	....	....	....	93	....	....	....	....	....	....	....	....	....	....	13	6	7	13	14	....	....	....
1993-94	Kamloops Blazers	WHL	70	44	59	103	....	....	....	171	....	....	....	....	....	....	....	....	....	....	18	*13	8	21	43	....	....	....
1994-95	Worcester IceCats	AHL	63	11	8	19	....	....	....	37	....	....	....	....	....	....	....	....	....	....	....	....	....	....	....	....	....	....
1995-96	**New York Islanders**	**NHL**	**14**	**0**	**1**	**1**	**0**	**1**	**1**	**11**	**0**	**0**	**0**	**11**	**0.0**	**3**	**1**	**3**	**0**	**–1**	....	....	....	....	....	....	....	....
	Worcester IceCats	AHL	57	16	7	23	....	....	....	57	....	....	....	....	....	....	....	....	....	....	4	1	2	3	2	....	....	....
1996-97	**New York Islanders**	**NHL**	**1**	**0**	**0**	**0**	**0**	**0**	**0**	**0**	**0**	**0**	**0**	**0**	**0.0**	**0**	**0**	**0**	**0**	**0**	....	....	....	....	....	....	....	....
	Kentucky Thoroughblades	AHL	58	15	31	46	....	....	....	57	....	....	....	....	....	....	....	....	....	....	4	3	0	3	8	....	....	....
1997-98	Milwaukee Admirals	IHL	64	18	18	36	....	....	....	84	....	....	....	....	....	....	....	....	....	....	10	4	3	7	36	....	....	....
	NHL Totals		**15**	**0**	**1**	**1**	**0**	**1**	**1**	**11**	**0**	**0**	**0**	**11**	**0.0**	**3**	**1**	**3**	**0**		....	....	....	....	....	....	....	....

• DEVEREAUX, BOYD

Boyd Devereaux C – L. 6'2", 195 lbs. b: Seaforth, Ont., 4/16/1978. Edmonton's 1st choice, 6th overall, in 1996 Entry Draft.

Season	Club	League	GP	G	A	Pts	AG	AA	APts	PIM	PP	SH	GW	S	%	TGF	PGF	TGA	PGA	+/–	GP	G	A	Pts	PIM	PP	SH	GW
1995-96	Kitchener Rangers	OHL	66	20	38	58	....	....	....	35	....	....	....	....	....	....	....	....	....	....	12	3	7	10	4	....	....	....
1996-97	Kitchener Rangers	OHL	54	28	41	69	....	....	....	37	....	....	....	....	....	....	....	....	....	....	13	4	11	15	8	....	....	....
	Canada	WJC-A	7	4	0	4	....	....	....	0	....	....	....	....	....	....	....	....	....	....	....	....	....	....	....	....	....	....
	Hamilton Bulldogs	AHL	....	....	....	....	....	....	....	....	....	....	....	....	....	....	....	....	....	....	1	0	1	1	0	....	....	....
1997-98	**Edmonton Oilers**	**NHL**	**38**	**1**	**4**	**5**	**1**	**4**	**5**	**6**	**0**	**0**	**0**	**27**	**3.7**	**9**	**0**	**20**	**6**	**–5**	....	....	....	....	....	....	....	....
	Hamilton Bulldogs	AHL	14	5	6	11	....	....	....	6	....	....	....	....	....	....	....	....	....	....	9	1	1	2	8	....	....	....
	NHL Totals		**38**	**1**	**4**	**5**	**1**	**4**	**5**	**6**	**0**	**0**	**0**	**27**	**3.7**	**9**	**0**	**20**	**6**		....	....	....	....	....	....	....	....

Canadian Major Junior Scholastic Player of the Year (1996)

• DEVINE, KEVIN

Kevin Devine LW – L. 5'8", 165 lbs. b: Toronto, Ont., 12/9/1954. Toronto's 7th choice, 121st overall, in 1974 Amateur Draft.

Season	Club	League	GP	G	A	Pts	AG	AA	APts	PIM	PP	SH	GW	S	%	TGF	PGF	TGA	PGA	+/–	GP	G	A	Pts	PIM	PP	SH	GW
1971-72	Toronto Marlboros	OHA	55	5	12	17	....	....	....	86	....	....	....	....	....	....	....	....	....	....	....	....	....	....	....	....	....	....
1972-73	Toronto Marlboros	OHA	58	30	40	70	....	....	....	150	....	....	....	....	....	....	....	....	....	....	....	....	....	....	....	....	....	....
1973-74	Toronto Marlboros	OHA	67	40	29	69	....	....	....	218	....	....	....	....	....	....	....	....	....	....	....	....	....	....	....	....	....	....
1974-75	San Diego Mariners	WHA	46	4	10	14	....	....	....	48	....	....	....	....	....	....	....	....	....	....	10	1	0	1	14	....	....	....
1975-76	San Diego Mariners	WHA	80	21	28	49	....	....	....	102	....	....	....	....	....	....	....	....	....	....	11	3	1	4	36	....	....	....
1976-77	San Diego Mariners	WHA	81	30	20	50	....	....	....	114	....	....	....	....	....	....	....	....	....	....	7	1	3	4	14	....	....	....
1977-78	Indianapolis Racers	WHA	76	19	23	42	....	....	....	141	....	....	....	....	....	....	....	....	....	....	....	....	....	....	....	....	....	....
1978-79	Quebec Nordiques	WHA	5	0	0	0	....	....	....	6	....	....	....	....	....	....	....	....	....	....	....	....	....	....	....	....	....	....
	San Diego Hawks	PHL	58	36	36	72	....	....	....	119	....	....	....	....	....	....	....	....	....	....	....	....	....	....	....	....	....	....
1979-80	Indianapolis Checkers	CHL	79	27	26	53	....	....	....	171	....	....	....	....	....	....	....	....	....	....	7	1	1	2	26	....	....	....
1980-81	Indianapolis Checkers	CHL	80	28	26	54	....	....	....	153	....	....	....	....	....	....	....	....	....	....	5	3	0	3	10	....	....	....
1981-82	Indianapolis Checkers	CHL	80	24	27	51	....	....	....	199	....	....	....	....	....	....	....	....	....	....	13	8	1	9	32	....	....	....
1982-83	**New York Islanders**	**NHL**	**2**	**0**	**1**	**1**	**0**	**1**	**1**	**8**	**0**	**0**	**0**	**3**	**0.0**	**1**	**0**	**0**	**0**	**+1**	....	....	....	....	....	....	....	....
	Indianapolis Checkers	CHL	78	21	27	48	....	....	....	245	....	....	....	....	....	....	....	....	....	....	13	4	7	11	14	....	....	....
1983-84	Indianapolis Checkers	CHL	71	23	30	53	....	....	....	201	....	....	....	....	....	....	....	....	....	....	10	4	3	7	8	....	....	....
1984-85	Indianapolis Checkers	IHL	78	16	35	51	....	....	....	139	....	....	....	....	....	....	....	....	....	....	7	0	4	4	38	....	....	....
	NHL Totals		**2**	**0**	**1**	**1**	**0**	**1**	**1**	**8**	**0**	**0**	**0**	**3**	**0.0**	**1**	**0**	**0**	**0**		....	....	....	....	....	....	....	....
	Other Major League Totals		288	74	81	155	....	....	....	411	....	....	....	....	....	....	....	....	....	....	28	5	4	9	64	....	....	....

Selected by **San Diego** (WHA) in 1974 WHA Amateur Draft, June, 1974. Signed as a free agent by **Edmonton** (WHA) after **San Diego** (WHA) franchise folded, August, 1977. Traded to **Indianapolis** (WHA) by **Edmonton** (WHA) with Blair MacDonald, Barry Wilkins, Rusty Patenaude and Claude St. Sauveur for Dave Inkpen and Mike Zuke, September, 1977. Traded to **Quebec** (WHA) by **Indianapolis** (WHA) for cash, September, 1978. Signed as a free agent by **NY Islanders**, October 9, 1979.

● de VRIES, GREG

Greg de Vries D – L. 6'3", 218 lbs. b: Sundridge, Ont., 1/4/1973.

			REGULAR SEASON																		PLAYOFFS							
Season	Club	League	GP	G	A	Pts	AG	AA	APts	PIM	PP	SH	GW	S	%	TGF	PGF	TGA	PGA	+/–	GP	G	A	Pts	PIM	PP	SH	GW
1991-92	Bowling Green University	CCHA	24	0	3	3	....	....	....	20	....	....	....	....	....	....	....	....	....	....	....	....	....	....	....	....	....	....
1992-93	Niagara Falls Thunder	OHL	62	3	23	26	....	....	....	86	....	....	....	....	....	....	....	....	....	....	4	0	1	1	6	....	....	....
1993-94	Niagara Falls Thunder	OHL	64	5	40	45	....	....	....	135	....	....	....	....	....	....	....	....	....	....	....	....	....	....	....	....	....	....
	Cape Breton Oilers	AHL	9	0	0	0	....	....	....	11	....	....	....	....	....	....	....	....	....	....	1	0	0	0	0	....	....	....
1994-95	Cape Breton Oilers	AHL	77	5	19	24	....	....	....	68	....	....	....	....	....	....	....	....	....	....	....	....	....	....	....	....	....	....
1995-96	**Edmonton Oilers**	**NHL**	**13**	**1**	**1**	**2**	**1**	**1**	**2**	**12**	**0**	**0**	**0**	**8**	**12.5**	**12**	**0**	**14**	**0**	**–2**	....	....	....	....	....	....	....	....
	Cape Breton Oilers	AHL	58	9	30	39	....	....	....	174	....	....	....	....	....	....	....	....	....	....	....	....	....	....	....	....	....	....
1996-97	**Edmonton Oilers**	**NHL**	**37**	**0**	**4**	**4**	**0**	**4**	**4**	**52**	**0**	**0**	**0**	**31**	**0.0**	**23**	**1**	**36**	**12**	**–2**	**12**	**0**	**1**	**1**	**8**	**0**	**0**	**0**
	Hamilton Bulldogs	AHL	34	4	14	18	....	....	....	26	....	....	....	....	....	....	....	....	....	....	....	....	....	....	....	....	....	....
1997-98	**Edmonton Oilers**	**NHL**	**65**	**7**	**4**	**11**	**8**	**4**	**12**	**80**	**1**	**0**	**0**	**53**	**13.2**	**30**	**1**	**65**	**19**	**–17**	**7**	**0**	**0**	**0**	**21**	**0**	**0**	**0**
	NHL Totals		**115**	**8**	**9**	**17**	**9**	**9**	**18**	**144**	**1**	**0**	**0**	**92**	**8.7**	**65**	**2**	**115**	**31**		**19**	**0**	**1**	**1**	**29**	**0**	**0**	**0**

Signed as a free agent by **Edmonton**, March 20, 1994.

● DEZIEL, MICHEL

Michel Deziel LW – L. 5'11", 180 lbs. b: Sorel, Que., 1/31/1954. Buffalo's 3rd choice, 47th overall, in 1974 Amateur Draft.

			REGULAR SEASON																		PLAYOFFS							
Season	Club	League	GP	G	A	Pts	AG	AA	APts	PIM	PP	SH	GW	S	%	TGF	PGF	TGA	PGA	+/–	GP	G	A	Pts	PIM	PP	SH	GW
1970-71	Sorel Black Hawks	QJHL	60	25	22	47	....	....	....	44	....	....	....	....	....	....	....	....	....	....	7	2	5	7	0	....	....	....
1971-72	Sorel Black Hawks	QMJHL	48	29	32	61	....	....	....	30	....	....	....	....	....	....	....	....	....	....	4	0	2	2	2	....	....	....
1972-73	Sorel Black Hawks	QMJHL	64	50	72	122	....	....	....	49	....	....	....	....	....	....	....	....	....	....	....	....	....	....	....	....	....	....
1973-74	Sorel Black Hawks	QMJHL	69	92	135	227	....	....	....	69	....	....	....	....	....	....	....	....	....	....	....	....	....	....	....	....	....	....
1974-75	Hershey Bears	AHL	69	27	24	51	....	....	....	10	....	....	....	....	....	....	....	....	....	....	8	0	3	3	16	....	....	....
	Buffalo Sabres	**NHL**	....	....	....	....	....	....	....	....	....	....	....	....	....	....	....	....	....	....	**1**	**0**	**0**	**0**	**0**	....	....	....
1975-76	Hershey Bears	AHL	71	25	30	55	....	....	....	42	....	....	....	....	....	....	....	....	....	....	4	0	0	0	2	....	....	....
1976-77	Rhode Island Reds	AHL	70	15	28	43	....	....	....	10	....	....	....	....	....	....	....	....	....	....	....	....	....	....	....	....	....	....
1977-78	Binghamton Dusters	AHL	8	2	0	2	....	....	....	2	....	....	....	....	....	....	....	....	....	....	....	....	....	....	....	....	....	....
1978-79			DID NOT PLAY																									
1979-80	Milwaukee Admirals	IHL	9	1	0	1	....	....	....	2	....	....	....	....	....	....	....	....	....	....	....	....	....	....	....	....	....	....
	NHL Totals		**0**	**0**	**0**	**0**	**0**	**0**	**0**	**0**	**0**	**0**	**0**	**0**	**0.0**	**0**	**0**	**0**	**0**		**1**	**0**	**0**	**0**	**0**	**0**	**0**	**0**

QMJHL First All-Star Team (1974)

● DIDUCK, GERALD

Gerald Diduck D – R. 6'2", 217 lbs. b: Edmonton, Alta., 4/6/1965. NY Islanders' 2nd choice, 16th overall, in 1983 Entry Draft.

			REGULAR SEASON																		PLAYOFFS							
Season	Club	League	GP	G	A	Pts	AG	AA	APts	PIM	PP	SH	GW	S	%	TGF	PGF	TGA	PGA	+/–	GP	G	A	Pts	PIM	PP	SH	GW
1981-82	Lethbridge Broncos	WHL	71	1	15	16	....	....	....	81	....	....	....	....	....	....	....	....	....	....	12	0	3	3	27	....	....	....
1982-83	Lethbridge Broncos	WHL	67	8	16	24	....	....	....	151	....	....	....	....	....	....	....	....	....	....	20	3	12	15	49	....	....	....
1983-84	Lethbridge Broncos	WHL	65	10	24	34	....	....	....	133	....	....	....	....	....	....	....	....	....	....	5	1	4	5	27	....	....	....
	Canada	WJC-A	7	0	0	0	....	....	....	4	....	....	....	....	....	....	....	....	....	....	....	....	....	....	....	....	....	....
	Indianapolis Checkers	CHL	....	....	....	....	....	....	....	....	....	....	....	....	....	....	....	....	....	....	10	1	6	7	19	....	....	....
1984-85	**New York Islanders**	**NHL**	**65**	**2**	**8**	**10**	**2**	**5**	**7**	**80**	**0**	**0**	**0**	**52**	**3.8**	**58**	**2**	**62**	**8**	**+2**	....	....	....	....	....	....	....	....
1985-86	**New York Islanders**	**NHL**	**10**	**1**	**2**	**3**	**1**	**1**	**2**	**2**	**0**	**0**	**0**	**6**	**16.7**	**11**	**0**	**8**	**2**	**+5**	....	....	....	....	....	....	....	....
	Springfield Indians	AHL	61	6	14	20	....	....	....	173	....	....	....	....	....	....	....	....	....	....	....	....	....	....	....	....	....	....
1986-87	**New York Islanders**	**NHL**	**30**	**2**	**3**	**5**	**2**	**2**	**4**	**67**	**0**	**0**	**0**	**64**	**3.7**	**28**	**8**	**33**	**10**	**–3**	**14**	**0**	**1**	**1**	**35**	**0**	**0**	**0**
	Springfield Indians	AHL	45	6	8	14	....	....	....	120	....	....	....	....	....	....	....	....	....	....	....	....	....	....	....	....	....	....
1987-88	**New York Islanders**	**NHL**	**68**	**7**	**12**	**19**	**6**	**9**	**15**	**113**	**4**	**0**	**1**	**128**	**5.5**	**82**	**21**	**59**	**20**	**+22**	**6**	**1**	**0**	**1**	**42**	**1**	**0**	**0**
1988-89	**New York Islanders**	**NHL**	**65**	**11**	**21**	**32**	**9**	**15**	**24**	**155**	**6**	**0**	**0**	**132**	**8.3**	**98**	**33**	**88**	**32**	**+9**	....	....	....	....	....	....	....	....
1989-90	**New York Islanders**	**NHL**	**76**	**3**	**17**	**20**	**3**	**12**	**15**	**163**	**1**	**0**	**0**	**102**	**2.9**	**82**	**9**	**101**	**30**	**+2**	**5**	**0**	**0**	**0**	**12**	**0**	**0**	**0**
1990-91	Montreal Canadiens	FrTour	4	0	1	1	....	....	....	31	....	....	....	....	....	....	....	....	....	....	....	....	....	....	....	....	....	....
	Montreal Canadiens	**NHL**	**32**	**1**	**2**	**3**	**1**	**2**	**3**	**39**	**0**	**0**	**0**	**34**	**2.9**	**33**	**1**	**35**	**6**	**+3**	....	....	....	....	....	....	....	....
	Vancouver Canucks	**NHL**	**31**	**3**	**7**	**10**	**3**	**5**	**8**	**66**	**0**	**0**	**1**	**66**	**4.5**	**24**	**6**	**35**	**9**	**–8**	**6**	**1**	**0**	**1**	**11**	**1**	**0**	**0**
1991-92	**Vancouver Canucks**	**NHL**	**77**	**6**	**21**	**27**	**5**	**16**	**21**	**229**	**2**	**0**	**1**	**128**	**4.7**	**78**	**26**	**75**	**20**	**–3**	**5**	**0**	**0**	**0**	**10**	**0**	**0**	**0**
1992-93	**Vancouver Canucks**	**NHL**	**80**	**6**	**14**	**20**	**5**	**10**	**15**	**171**	**0**	**1**	**0**	**92**	**6.5**	**100**	**17**	**82**	**31**	**+32**	**12**	**4**	**2**	**6**	**12**	**0**	**0**	**0**
1993-94	**Vancouver Canucks**	**NHL**	**55**	**1**	**10**	**11**	**1**	**8**	**9**	**72**	**0**	**0**	**0**	**50**	**2.0**	**44**	**6**	**58**	**22**	**+2**	**24**	**1**	**7**	**8**	**22**	**0**	**0**	**0**
1994-95	**Vancouver Canucks**	**NHL**	**22**	**1**	**3**	**4**	**2**	**4**	**6**	**15**	**1**	**0**	**0**	**25**	**4.0**	**12**	**3**	**25**	**8**	**–8**	....	....	....	....	....	....	....	....
	Chicago Blackhawks	**NHL**	**13**	**1**	**0**	**1**	**2**	**0**	**2**	**48**	**1**	**0**	**0**	**42**	**2.4**	**8**	**1**	**5**	**1**	**+3**	**16**	**1**	**3**	**4**	**22**	**0**	**0**	**0**
1995-96	**Hartford Whalers**	**NHL**	**79**	**1**	**9**	**10**	**1**	**7**	**8**	**88**	**0**	**0**	**0**	**93**	**1.1**	**62**	**1**	**88**	**34**	**+7**	....	....	....	....	....	....	....	....
1996-97	**Hartford Whalers**	**NHL**	**56**	**1**	**10**	**11**	**1**	**9**	**10**	**40**	**0**	**0**	**1**	**59**	**1.7**	**40**	**4**	**55**	**10**	**–9**	....	....	....	....	....	....	....	....
	Phoenix Coyotes	**NHL**	**11**	**1**	**2**	**3**	**1**	**2**	**3**	**23**	**1**	**0**	**0**	**21**	**4.8**	**12**	**3**	**9**	**2**	**+2**	**7**	**0**	**0**	**0**	**10**	**0**	**0**	**0**
1997-98	**Phoenix Coyotes**	**NHL**	**78**	**8**	**10**	**18**	**9**	**10**	**19**	**118**	**1**	**0**	**4**	**104**	**7.7**	**62**	**2**	**79**	**33**	**+14**	**6**	**0**	**2**	**2**	**20**	**0**	**0**	**0**
	NHL Totals		**848**	**56**	**151**	**207**	**54**	**117**	**171**	**1489**	**17**	**1**	**8**	**1188**	**4.7**	**834**	**143**	**897**	**278**		**101**	**8**	**15**	**23**	**196**	**2**	**0**	**0**

Traded to **Montreal** by **NY Islanders** for Craig Ludwig, September 4, 1990. Traded to **Vancouver** by **Montreal** for Vancouver's 4th round choice (Vladimir Vujtek) in 1991 Entry Draft, January 12, 1991. Traded to **Chicago** by **Vancouver** for Bogdan Savenko and Hartford's 3rd round choice (previously acquired, Vancouver selected Larry Courville) in 1995 Entry Draft, April 7, 1995. Signed as a free agent by **Hartford**, August 24, 1995. Traded to **Phoenix** by **Hartford** for Chris Murray, March 18, 1997.

● DIETRICH, DON

Don Dietrich D – L. 6'1", 195 lbs. b: Deloraine, Man., 4/5/1961. Chicago's 14th choice, 183rd overall, in 1980 Entry Draft.

			REGULAR SEASON																		PLAYOFFS							
Season	Club	League	GP	G	A	Pts	AG	AA	APts	PIM	PP	SH	GW	S	%	TGF	PGF	TGA	PGA	+/–	GP	G	A	Pts	PIM	PP	SH	GW
1978-79	Brandon Wheat Kings	WHL	69	6	37	43	....	....	....	29	....	....	....	....	....	....	....	....	....	....	....	....	....	....	....	....	....	....
1979-80	Brandon Wheat Kings	WHL	63	15	45	60	....	....	....	56	....	....	....	....	....	....	....	....	....	....	....	....	....	....	....	....	....	....
1980-81	Brandon Wheat Kings	WHL	72	16	64	80	....	....	....	84	....	....	....	....	....	....	....	....	....	....	....	....	....	....	....	....	....	....
1981-82	New Brunswick Hawks	AHL	62	1	5	6	....	....	....	14	....	....	....	....	....	....	....	....	....	....	2	0	0	0	0	....	....	....
1982-83	Springfield Indians	AHL	76	6	26	32	....	....	....	26	....	....	....	....	....	....	....	....	....	....	....	....	....	....	....	....	....	....
1983-84	**Chicago Black Hawks**	**NHL**	**17**	**0**	**5**	**5**	**0**	**3**	**3**	**0**	**0**	**0**	**0**	**22**	**0.0**	**11**	**0**	**16**	**4**	**–1**	....	....	....	....	....	....	....	....
	Springfield Indians	AHL	50	14	21	35	....	....	....	14	....	....	....	....	....	....	....	....	....	....	....	....	....	....	....	....	....	....
1984-85	Maine Mariners	AHL	75	6	21	27	....	....	....	36	....	....	....	....	....	....	....	....	....	....	11	3	4	7	4	....	....	....
1985-86	**New Jersey Devils**	**NHL**	**11**	**0**	**2**	**2**	**0**	**1**	**1**	**10**	**0**	**0**	**0**	**14**	**0.0**	**10**	**3**	**15**	**0**	**–8**	....	....	....	....	....	....	....	....
	Maine Mariners	AHL	68	9	11	20	....	....	....	33	....	....	....	....	....	....	....	....	....	....	3	0	0	0	0	....	....	....
1986-87	Schwenningen ERC	Germany	38	15	30	45	....	....	....	34	....	....	....	....	....	....	....	....	....	....	....	....	....	....	....	....	....	....
	EHC Kloten	Switz.	....	0	1	1	....	....	....	....	....	....	....	....	....	....	....	....	....	....	8	0	1	1	....	....	....	....
1987-88	Schwenningen ERC	Germany	27	5	19	24	....	....	....	10	....	....	....	....	....	....	....	....	....	....	....	....	....	....	....	....	....	....
	Hershey Bears	AHL	3	0	0	0	....	....	....	0	....	....	....	....	....	....	....	....	....	....	....	....	....	....	....	....	....	....
1988-89	Schwenningen ERC	Germany	35	12	23	35	....	....	....	24	....	....	....	....	....	....	....	....	....	....	3	1	0	1	2	....	....	....
1989-90	Canada	Nat-Team	3	0	2	2	....	....	....	2	....	....	....	....	....	....	....	....	....	....	....	....	....	....	....	....	....	....
1990-91	Moncton Hawks	AHL	3	0	2	2	....	....	....	0	....	....	....	....	....	....	....	....	....	....	....	....	....	....	....	....	....	....
	New Haven Nighthawks	AHL	13	0	2	2	....	....	....	0	....	....	....	....	....	....	....	....	....	....	....	....	....	....	....	....	....	....
	Roanoke Valley Rebels	ECHL	2	0	1	1	....	....	....	8	....	....	....	....	....	....	....	....	....	....	....	....	....	....	....	....	....	....
	NHL Totals		**28**	**0**	**7**	**7**	**0**	**4**	**4**	**10**	**0**	**0**	**0**	**36**	**0.0**	**21**	**3**	**31**	**4**		....	....	....	....	....	....	....	....

Traded to **New Jersey** by **Chicago** with Rich Preston for Bob MacMillan and New Jersey's 5th round choice (Rick Herbert) in 1985 Entry Draft, June 12, 1984.

● DILLABOUGH, BOB

Bob Dillabough C – L. 5'10", 180 lbs. b: Belleville, Ont., 4/27/1941. Deceased.

			REGULAR SEASON																		PLAYOFFS							
Season	Club	League	GP	G	A	Pts	AG	AA	APts	PIM	PP	SH	GW	S	%	TGF	PGF	TGA	PGA	+/–	GP	G	A	Pts	PIM	PP	SH	GW
1957-58	Hamilton Tiger Cubs	OHA	2	0	2	2	....	....	....	0	....	....	....	....	....	....	....	....	....	....	5	0	0	0	0	....	....	....
1958-59	Hamilton Tiger Cubs	OHA	54	11	20	31	....	....	....	58	....	....	....	....	....	....	....	....	....	....	....	....	....	....	....	....	....	....
1959-60	Hamilton Tiger Cubs	OHA	48	14	20	34	....	....	....	22	....	....	....	....	....	....	....	....	....	....	....	....	....	....	....	....	....	....
1960-61	Hamilton Red Wings	OHA	48	27	20	47	....	....	....	28	....	....	....	....	....	....	....	....	....	....	12	8	8	16	2	....	....	....
1961-62	**Detroit Red Wings**	**NHL**	**5**	**0**	**0**	**0**	**0**	**0**	**0**	**2**	....	....	....	....	....	....	....	....	....	....	....	....	....	....	....	....	....	....
	Hershey Bears	AHL	5	2	1	3	....	....	....	2	....	....	....	....	....	....	....	....	....	....	....	....	....	....	....	....	....	....
	Sudbury Wolves	EPHL	34	17	16	33	....	....	....	12	....	....	....	....	....	....	....	....	....	....	5	0	1	1	14	....	....	....
1962-63	Edmonton Flyers	WHL	10	2	0	2	....	....	....	4	....	....	....	....	....	....	....	....	....	....	....	....	....	....	....	....	....	....
	Pittsburgh Hornets	AHL	52	15	19	34	....	....	....	32	....	....	....	....	....	....	....	....	....	....	....	....	....	....	....	....	....	....
	Detroit Red Wings	**NHL**	....	....	....	....	....	....	....	....	....	....	....	....	....	....	....	....	....	....	**1**	**0**	**0**	**0**	**0**	....	....	....
1963-64	Pittsburgh Hornets	AHL	72	9	19	28	....	....	....	18	....	....	....	....	....	....	....	....	....	....	5	2	2	4	6	....	....	....
	Detroit Red Wings	**NHL**	....	....	....	....	....	....	....	....	....	....	....	....	....	....	....	....	....	....	**1**	**0**	**0**	**0**	**0**	....	....	....
1964-65	**Detroit Red Wings**	**NHL**	**4**	**0**	**0**	**0**	**0**	**0**	**0**	**2**	....	....	....	....	....	....	....	....	....	....	**4**	**0**	**0**	**0**	**0**	....	....	....
	Pittsburgh Hornets	AHL	52	13	25	38	....	....	....	18	....	....	....	....	....	....	....	....	....	....	4	0	3	3	2	....	....	....
1965-66	**Boston Bruins**	**NHL**	**53**	**7**	**13**	**20**	**8**	**13**	**21**	**18**	....	....	....	....	....	....	....	....	....	....	....	....	....	....	....	....	....	....
1966-67	**Boston Bruins**	**NHL**	**60**	**6**	**12**	**18**	**7**	**12**	**19**	**14**	....	....	....	....	....	....	....	....	....	....	....	....	....	....	....	....	....	....

			REGULAR SEASON																		PLAYOFFS							
Season	Club	League	GP	G	A	Pts	AG	AA	APts	PIM	PP	SH	GW	S	%	TGF	PGF	TGA	PGA	+/–	GP	G	A	Pts	PIM	PP	SH	GW
1967-68	**Pittsburgh Penguins**	**NHL**	**47**	**7**	**12**	**19**	**9**	**13**	**22**	**18**	**1**	**0**	**0**	**70**	**10.0**	**26**	**2**	**35**	**4**	**–7**	....	....	....	....	....	....	....	....
	Baltimore Clippers	AHL	6	1	0	1	....	....	....	2	....	....	....	....	....	....	....	....	....	....	....	....	....	....	....	....	....	....
1968-69	**Pittsburgh Penguins**	**NHL**	**14**	**0**	**0**	**0**	**0**	**0**	**0**	**2**	**0**	**0**	**0**	**2**	**0.0**	**0**	**0**	**7**	**1**	**–6**	....	....	....	....	....	....	....	....
	Oakland Seals	**NHL**	**48**	**7**	**12**	**19**	**8**	**11**	**19**	**4**	**0**	**0**	**3**	**51**	**13.7**	**28**	**0**	**40**	**8**	**–4**	**7**	**3**	**0**	**3**	**0**	**0**	**1**	**0**
1969-70	**Oakland Seals**	**NHL**	**52**	**5**	**5**	**10**	**6**	**5**	**11**	**16**	**1**	**1**	**0**	**45**	**11.1**	**18**	**5**	**49**	**18**	**–18**	**4**	**0**	**0**	**0**	**0**	**0**	**0**	**0**
1970-71	Rochester Americans	AHL	1	0	0	0	....	....	....	2	....	....	....	....	....	....	....	....	....	....	....	....	....	....	....	....	....	....
	Phoenix Roadrunners	WHL	45	3	12	15	....	....	....	14	....	....	....	....	....	....	....	....	....	....	7	1	1	2	0	....	....	....
1971-72	Tidewater Wings	AHL	15	0	0	0	....	....	....	4	....	....	....	....	....	....	....	....	....	....	....	....	....	....	....	....	....	....
1972-73	Cleveland Crusaders	WHA	72	8	8	16	....	....	....	8	....	....	....	....	....	....	....	....	....	....	9	1	0	1	0	....	....	....
1973-74	Toledo Hornets	IHL	51	14	23	37	....	....	....	20	....	....	....	....	....	....	....	....	....	....	2	0	0	0	0	....	....	....
	NHL Totals		**283**	**32**	**54**	**86**	**38**	**54**	**92**	**76**	**2**	**1**	**3**	**168**	**19.0**	**72**	**7**	**131**	**31**		**17**	**3**	**0**	**3**	**0**	**0**	**1**	**0**
	Other Major League Totals		72	8	8	16	....	....	....	8	....	....	....	....	....	....	....	....	....		9	1	0	1	0	....	....	....

Traded to **Boston** by **Detroit** with Al Langlois, Ron Harris and Parker MacDonald for Ab McDonald, Bob McCord and Ken Stephenson, May 31, 1965. Claimed by **Pittsburgh** from **Boston** in Expansion Draft, June 6, 1967. Traded to **Oakland** by **Pittsburgh** for Billy Harris, November 29, 1968. Claimed by **Vancouver** from **Oakland** in Expansion Draft, June 10, 1970. Traded to **Detroit** by **Vancouver** with Irv Spencer for John Cunniff and Gary Bredin, June 8, 1971. Signed as a free agent by **Cleveland** (WHA), August, 1972.

• DILLON, GARY

Gary Dillon C – L. 5'10", 173 lbs. b: Toronto, Ont., 2/28/1959. Colorado's 1st choice, 85th overall, in 1979 Entry Draft.

Season	Club	League	GP	G	A	Pts	AG	AA	APts	PIM	PP	SH	GW	S	%	TGF	PGF	TGA	PGA	+/–	GP	G	A	Pts	PIM	PP	SH	GW
1975-76	Toronto Marlboros	OHA	60	23	46	69	....	....	....	68	....	....	....	....	....	....	....	....	....	....	....	....	....	....	....	....	....	....
1976-77	Toronto Marlboros	OHA	64	40	62	102	....	....	....	77	....	....	....	....	....	....	....	....	....	....	....	....	....	....	....	....	....	....
1977-78	Toronto Marlboros	OHA	64	39	45	84	....	....	....	112	....	....	....	....	....	....	....	....	....	....	....	....	....	....	....	....	....	....
1978-79	Toronto Marlboros	OHA	59	57	63	120	....	....	....	40	....	....	....	....	....	....	....	....	....	....	....	....	....	....	....	....	....	....
1979-80	Fort Worth Texans	CHL	77	30	26	56	....	....	....	34	....	....	....	....	....	....	....	....	....	....	15	8	9	17	2	....	....	....
1980-81	**Colorado Rockies**	**NHL**	**13**	**1**	**1**	**2**	**1**	**1**	**2**	**29**	**0**	**0**	**0**	**15**	**6.7**	**4**	**0**	**10**	**0**	**–6**	....	....	....	....	....	....	....	....
	Fort Worth Texans	CHL	54	9	16	25	....	....	....	28	....	....	....	....	....	....	....	....	....	....	5	2	1	3	2	....	....	....
1981-82	Fredericton Express	AHL	54	18	21	39	....	....	....	68	....	....	....	....	....	....	....	....	....	....	....	....	....	....	....	....	....	....
	NHL Totals		**13**	**1**	**1**	**2**	**1**	**1**	**2**	**29**	**0**	**0**	**0**	**15**	**6.7**	**4**	**0**	**10**	**0**		....	....	....	....	....	....	....	....

OHA First All-Star Team (1979)

Signed as a free agent by **Quebec**, October 7, 1981.

• DILLON, WAYNE

Wayne "Tommy" Dillon C – L. 6', 185 lbs. b: Toronto, Ont., 5/25/1955. NY Rangers' 1st choice, 12th overall, in 1975 Amateur Draft.

Season	Club	League	GP	G	A	Pts	AG	AA	APts	PIM	PP	SH	GW	S	%	TGF	PGF	TGA	PGA	+/–	GP	G	A	Pts	PIM	PP	SH	GW
1971-72	Toronto Marlboros	OHA	56	14	14	28	....	....	....	8	....	....	....	....	....	....	....	....	....	....	....	....	....	....	....	....	....	....
1972-73	Toronto Marlboros	OHA	59	47	60	107	....	....	....	25	....	....	....	....	....	....	....	....	....	....	10	2	10	12	10	....	....	....
1973-74	Toronto Toros	WHA	71	30	35	65	....	....	....	13	....	....	....	....	....	....	....	....	....	....	12	5	6	11	9	....	....	....
1974-75	Toronto Toros	WHA	77	29	66	95	....	....	....	22	....	....	....	....	....	....	....	....	....	....	6	4	4	8	4	....	....	....
1975-76	**New York Rangers**	**NHL**	**79**	**21**	**24**	**45**	**20**	**19**	**39**	**10**	**3**	**0**	**1**	**138**	**15.2**	**67**	**8**	**70**	**0**	**–11**	....	....	....	....	....	....	....	....
1976-77	**New York Rangers**	**NHL**	**78**	**17**	**29**	**46**	**16**	**24**	**40**	**33**	**1**	**0**	**1**	**158**	**10.8**	**58**	**7**	**65**	**0**	**–14**	....	....	....	....	....	....	....	....
1977-78	**New York Rangers**	**NHL**	**59**	**5**	**13**	**18**	**5**	**11**	**16**	**15**	**1**	**0**	**1**	**50**	**10.0**	**25**	**5**	**30**	**2**	**–8**	**3**	**0**	**1**	**1**	**0**	**0**	**0**	**0**
	New Haven Nighthawks	AHL	3	2	0	2	....	....	....	0	....	....	....	....	....	....	....	....	....	....	....	....	....	....	....	....	....	....
1978-79	Birmingham Bulls	WHA	64	12	27	39	....	....	....	43	....	....	....	....	....	....	....	....	....	....	....	....	....	....	....	....	....	....
1979-80	**Winnipeg Jets**	**NHL**	**13**	**0**	**0**	**0**	**0**	**0**	**0**	**2**	**0**	**0**	**0**	**5**	**0.0**	**0**	**0**	**6**	**0**	**–6**	....	....	....	....	....	....	....	....
1980-81	Rapperswill	Switz.	STATISTICS NOT AVAILABLE																									
1981-82	Fredericton Express	AHL	37	7	13	20	....	....	....	25	....	....	....	....	....	....	....	....	....	....	....	....	....	....	....	....	....	....
	NHL Totals		**229**	**43**	**66**	**109**	**41**	**54**	**95**	**60**	**5**	**0**	**3**	**351**	**12.3**	**150**	**20**	**171**	**2**		**3**	**0**	**1**	**1**	**0**	**0**	**0**	**0**
	Other Major League Totals		212	71	128	199	....	....	....	78	....	....	....	....	....	....	....	....	....		18	9	10	19	13	....	....	....

Signed as an underage free agent by **Toronto** (WHA), August, 1973. Transferred to **Birmingham** (WHA) after **Toronto** (WHA) franchise relocated, June 30, 1976. Traded to **Winnipeg** by **NY Rangers** for future considerations, July, 25, 1979.

• DiMAIO, ROB

Rob DiMaio C – R. 5'10", 190 lbs. b: Calgary, Alta., 2/19/1968. NY Islanders' 6th choice, 118th overall, in 1987 Entry Draft.

Season	Club	League	GP	G	A	Pts	AG	AA	APts	PIM	PP	SH	GW	S	%	TGF	PGF	TGA	PGA	+/–	GP	G	A	Pts	PIM	PP	SH	GW
1986-87	Medicine Hat Tigers	WHL	70	27	43	70	....	....	....	130	....	....	....	....	....	....	....	....	....	....	20	7	11	18	46	....	....	....
1987-88	Medicine Hat Tigers	WHL	54	47	43	90	....	....	....	120	....	....	....	....	....	....	....	....	....	....	14	12	19	*31	59	....	....	....
	Canada	WJC-A	7	1	0	1	....	....	....	10	....	....	....	....	....	....	....	....	....	....	....	....	....	....	....	....	....	....
1988-89	**New York Islanders**	**NHL**	**16**	**1**	**0**	**1**	**1**	**0**	**1**	**30**	**0**	**0**	**1**	**16**	**6.3**	**3**	**0**	**17**	**8**	**–6**	....	....	....	....	....	....	....	....
	Springfield Indians	AHL	40	13	18	31	....	....	....	67	....	....	....	....	....	....	....	....	....	....	....	....	....	....	....	....	....	....
1989-90	**New York Islanders**	**NHL**	**7**	**0**	**0**	**0**	**0**	**0**	**0**	**2**	**0**	**0**	**0**	**2**	**0.0**	**0**	**0**	**0**	**0**	**0**	**1**	**1**	**0**	**1**	**4**	**0**	**0**	**0**
	Springfield Indians	AHL	54	25	27	52	....	....	....	69	....	....	....	....	....	....	....	....	....	....	16	4	7	11	45	....	....	....
1990-91	**New York Islanders**	**NHL**	**1**	**0**	**0**	**0**	**0**	**0**	**0**	**0**	**0**	**0**	**0**	**0**	**0.0**	**0**	**0**	**0**	**0**	**0**	....	....	....	....	....	....	....	....
	Capital District Islanders	AHL	12	3	4	7	....	....	....	22	....	....	....	....	....	....	....	....	....	....	....	....	....	....	....	....	....	....
1991-92	**New York Islanders**	**NHL**	**50**	**5**	**2**	**7**	**5**	**1**	**6**	**43**	**0**	**2**	**0**	**43**	**11.6**	**10**	**0**	**57**	**24**	**–23**	....	....	....	....	....	....	....	....
1992-93	**Tampa Bay Lightning**	**NHL**	**54**	**9**	**15**	**24**	**7**	**10**	**17**	**62**	**2**	**0**	**0**	**75**	**12.0**	**32**	**3**	**34**	**5**	**0**	....	....	....	....	....	....	....	....
1993-94	**Tampa Bay Lightning**	**NHL**	**39**	**8**	**7**	**15**	**7**	**5**	**12**	**40**	**2**	**0**	**1**	**51**	**15.7**	**18**	**7**	**17**	**1**	**–5**	....	....	....	....	....	....	....	....
	Philadelphia Flyers	**NHL**	**14**	**3**	**5**	**8**	**3**	**4**	**7**	**6**	**0**	**0**	**1**	**30**	**10.0**	**12**	**1**	**10**	**0**	**+1**	....	....	....	....	....	....	....	....
1994-95	**Philadelphia Flyers**	**NHL**	**36**	**3**	**1**	**4**	**5**	**1**	**6**	**53**	**0**	**0**	**0**	**34**	**8.8**	**12**	**0**	**13**	**9**	**+8**	**15**	**2**	**4**	**6**	**4**	**0**	**1**	**1**
1995-96	**Philadelphia Flyers**	**NHL**	**59**	**6**	**15**	**21**	**6**	**12**	**18**	**58**	**1**	**1**	**0**	**49**	**12.2**	**29**	**5**	**38**	**14**	**0**	**3**	**0**	**0**	**0**	**0**	**0**	**0**	**0**
1996-97	**Boston Bruins**	**NHL**	**72**	**13**	**15**	**28**	**14**	**13**	**27**	**82**	**0**	**3**	**2**	**152**	**8.6**	**45**	**4**	**80**	**18**	**–21**	....	....	....	....	....	....	....	....
1997-98	**Boston Bruins**	**NHL**	**79**	**10**	**17**	**27**	**12**	**17**	**29**	**82**	**0**	**0**	**4**	**112**	**8.9**	**42**	**7**	**64**	**16**	**–13**	**6**	**1**	**0**	**1**	**8**	**0**	**0**	**0**
	NHL Totals		**427**	**58**	**77**	**135**	**60**	**63**	**123**	**458**	**5**	**6**	**9**	**564**	**10.3**	**203**	**27**	**330**	**95**		**25**	**4**	**4**	**8**	**16**	**0**	**1**	**1**

Won Stafford Smythe Memorial Trophy (Memorial Cup Tournament MVP) (1988)

Claimed by **Tampa Bay** from **NY Islanders** in Expansion Draft, June 18, 1992. Traded to **Philadelphia** by **Tampa Bay** for Jim Cummins and Philadelphia's 4th round choice in 1995 Entry Draft, March 18, 1994. Claimed by **San Jose** from **Philadelphia** in NHL Waiver Draft, September 30, 1996. Traded to **Boston** by **San Jose** for Boston's 5th round choice (Adam Nittel) in 1997 Entry Draft, September 30, 1996.

• DINEEN, GARY

Gary Dineen C – L. 5'10", 175 lbs. b: Montreal, Que., 12/24/1943.

Season	Club	League	GP	G	A	Pts	AG	AA	APts	PIM	PP	SH	GW	S	%	TGF	PGF	TGA	PGA	+/–	GP	G	A	Pts	PIM	PP	SH	GW
1960-61	St. Michael's Majors	OHA	12	0	0	0	....	....	....	0	....	....	....	....	....	....	....	....	....	....	6	0	0	0	0	....	....	....
1961-62	St. Michael's College	Tor-Jr.	33	26	*35	*61	....	....	....	19	....	....	....	....	....	....	....	....	....	....	11	7	11	18	0	....	....	....
1962-63	Neil McNeil Maroons	Tor-Jr.	38	32	*63	*95	....	....	....	33	....	....	....	....	....	....	....	....	....	....	16	*13	*23	*36	2	....	....	....
1963-64	Toronto Marlboros	OHA	2	1	5	6	....	....	....	4	....	....	....	....	....	....	....	....	....	....	9	5	12	17	8	....	....	....
	Canada	Olympics	7	3	6	9	....	....	....	10	....	....	....	....	....	....	....	....	....	....	....	....	....	....	....	....	....	....
1964-65	University of British Columbia	WCIAA	STATISTICS NOT AVAILABLE																									
	Canada	WEC-A	7	6	5	11	....	....	....	4	....	....	....	....	....	....	....	....	....	....	....	....	....	....	....	....	....	....
1965-66	Canada	Nat-Team	STATISTICS NOT AVAILABLE																									
1966-67	Canada	Nat-Team	STATISTICS NOT AVAILABLE																									
	Canada	WEC-A	7	1	4	5	....	....	....	6	....	....	....	....	....	....	....	....	....	....	....	....	....	....	....	....	....	....
1967-68	Ottawa Nationals	OHA Sr.	20	7	20	27	....	....	....	4	....	....	....	....	....	....	....	....	....	....	....	....	....	....	....	....	....	....
	Canada	Olympics	7	1	2	3	....	....	....	6	....	....	....	....	....	....	....	....	....	....	....	....	....	....	....	....	....	....
1968-69	**Minnesota North Stars**	**NHL**	**4**	**0**	**1**	**1**	**0**	**1**	**1**	**0**	**0**	**0**	**0**	**2**	**0.0**	**2**	**2**	**2**	**0**	**–2**	....	....	....	....	....	....	....	....
	Memphis South Stars	CHL	63	11	38	49	....	....	....	0	....	....	....	....	....	....	....	....	....	....	....	....	....	....	....	....	....	....
1969-70	Iowa Stars	CHL	15	3	2	5	....	....	....	2	....	....	....	....	....	....	....	....	....	....	....	....	....	....	....	....	....	....
	Springfield Kings	AHL	8	1	2	3	....	....	....	0	....	....	....	....	....	....	....	....	....	....	....	....	....	....	....	....	....	....
	Salt Lake Golden Eagles	WHL	10	1	2	3	....	....	....	0	....	....	....	....	....	....	....	....	....	....	....	....	....	....	....	....	....	....
	San Diego Gulls	WHL	10	1	2	3	....	....	....	0	....	....	....	....	....	....	....	....	....	....	....	....	....	....	....	....	....	....
1970-71	Springfield Kings	AHL	56	12	22	34	....	....	....	28	....	....	....	....	....	....	....	....	....	....	12	4	7	11	6	....	....	....
	NHL Totals		**4**	**0**	**1**	**1**	**0**	**1**	**1**	**0**	**0**	**0**	**0**	**2**	**0.0**	**2**	**2**	**2**	**0**		....	....	....	....	....	....	....	....

Rights traded to **Minnesota** by **Toronto** for cash, June, 1967. Traded to **LA Kings** (Springfield - AHL) by **Minnesota** (Salt Lake-WHL) for cash, January, 1970. Claimed by **Iowa** (CHL) from **LA Kings** (Springfield - AHL) in Reverse Draft, June, 1970.

Season	Club	League	GP	G	A	Pts	AG	AA	APts	PIM	PP	SH	GW	S	%	TGF	PGF	TGA	PGA	+/–	GP	G	A	Pts	PIM	PP	SH	GW
			REGULAR SEASON																		PLAYOFFS							

• DINEEN, GORD

Gord Dineen D – R. 6′, 195 lbs. b: Quebec City, Que., 9/21/1962. NY Islanders' 2nd choice, 42nd overall, in 1981 Entry Draft.

Season	Club	League	GP	G	A	Pts	AG	AA	APts	PIM	PP	SH	GW	S	%	TGF	PGF	TGA	PGA	+/–	GP	G	A	Pts	PIM	PP	SH	GW
1980-81	Sault Ste. Marie Greyhounds	OHA	68	4	26	30	....	....	....	158	....	....	....	....	....	....	....	....	....	....	19	1	7	8	58	....	....	....
1981-82	Sault Ste. Marie Greyhounds	OHL	68	9	45	54	....	....	....	185	....	....	....	....	....	....	....	....	....	....	13	1	2	3	52	....	....	....
1982-83	**New York Islanders**	**NHL**	**2**	**0**	**0**	**0**	**0**	**0**	**0**	**4**	**0**	**0**	**0**	**3**	**0.0**	**1**	**1**	**2**	**0**	**–2**	....	....	....	....	....	....	....	....
	Indianapolis Checkers	CHL	73	10	47	57	....	....	....	78	....	....	....	....	....	....	....	....	....	....	13	2	10	12	29	....	....	....
1983-84	**New York Islanders**	**NHL**	**43**	**1**	**11**	**12**	**1**	**7**	**8**	**32**	**0**	**0**	**0**	**37**	**2.7**	**49**	**2**	**39**	**2**	**+10**	**9**	**1**	**1**	**2**	**28**	**0**	**0**	**0**
	Indianapolis Checkers	CHL	26	4	13	17	....	....	....	63	....	....	....	....	....	....	....	....	....	....	....	....	....	....	....	....	....	....
1984-85	**New York Islanders**	**NHL**	**48**	**1**	**12**	**13**	**1**	**8**	**9**	**89**	**0**	**0**	**0**	**45**	**2.2**	**48**	**2**	**45**	**9**	**+10**	**10**	**0**	**0**	**0**	**26**	**0**	**0**	**0**
	Springfield Indians	AHL	25	1	8	9	....	....	....	46	....	....	....	....	....	....	....	....	....	....	....	....	....	....	....	....	....	....
1985-86	**New York Islanders**	**NHL**	**57**	**1**	**8**	**9**	**1**	**5**	**6**	**81**	**0**	**0**	**0**	**52**	**1.9**	**58**	**1**	**59**	**17**	**+15**	**3**	**0**	**0**	**0**	**2**	**0**	**0**	**0**
	Springfield Indians	AHL	11	2	3	5	....	....	....	20	....	....	....	....	....	....	....	....	....	....	....	....	....	....	....	....	....	....
1986-87	**New York Islanders**	**NHL**	**71**	**4**	**10**	**14**	**3**	**7**	**10**	**110**	**0**	**0**	**0**	**59**	**6.8**	**47**	**0**	**76**	**21**	**–8**	**7**	**0**	**4**	**4**	**4**	**0**	**0**	**0**
1987-88	**New York Islanders**	**NHL**	**57**	**4**	**12**	**16**	**3**	**9**	**12**	**62**	**1**	**0**	**0**	**50**	**8.0**	**63**	**7**	**78**	**31**	**+9**	....	....	....	....	....	....	....	....
	Minnesota North Stars	**NHL**	**13**	**1**	**1**	**2**	**1**	**1**	**2**	**21**	**0**	**0**	**0**	**6**	**16.7**	**9**	**0**	**23**	**9**	**–5**	....	....	....	....	....	....	....	....
1988-89	**Minnesota North Stars**	**NHL**	**2**	**0**	**1**	**1**	**0**	**1**	**1**	**2**	**0**	**0**	**0**	**7**	**0.0**	**1**	**1**	**5**	**1**	**–4**	....	....	....	....	....	....	....	....
	Kalamazoo Wings	IHL	25	2	6	8	....	....	....	49	....	....	....	....	....	....	....	....	....	....	....	....	....	....	....	....	....	....
	Pittsburgh Penguins	**NHL**	**38**	**1**	**2**	**3**	**1**	**1**	**2**	**42**	**0**	**0**	**0**	**25**	**4.0**	**29**	**2**	**43**	**11**	**–5**	**11**	**0**	**2**	**2**	**8**	**0**	**0**	**0**
1989-90	**Pittsburgh Penguins**	**NHL**	**69**	**1**	**8**	**9**	**1**	**6**	**7**	**125**	**0**	**0**	**0**	**38**	**2.6**	**58**	**0**	**83**	**31**	**+6**	....	....	....	....	....	....	....	....
1990-91	**Pittsburgh Penguins**	**NHL**	**9**	**0**	**0**	**0**	**0**	**0**	**0**	**4**	**0**	**0**	**0**	**6**	**0.0**	**4**	**0**	**9**	**1**	**–4**	....	....	....	....	....	....	....	....
	Muskegon Lumberjacks	IHL	40	1	14	15	....	....	....	57	....	....	....	....	....	....	....	....	....	....	5	0	2	2	0	....	....	....
1991-92	**Pittsburgh Penguins**	**NHL**	**1**	**0**	**0**	**0**	**0**	**0**	**0**	**0**	**0**	**0**	**0**	**0**	**0.0**	**1**	**0**	**3**	**0**	**–2**	....	....	....	....	....	....	....	....
	Muskegon Lumberjacks	IHL	79	8	37	45	....	....	....	83	....	....	....	....	....	....	....	....	....	....	14	2	4	6	33	....	....	....
1992-93	**Ottawa Senators**	**NHL**	**32**	**2**	**4**	**6**	**2**	**3**	**5**	**30**	**1**	**0**	**0**	**36**	**5.6**	**25**	**5**	**54**	**15**	**–19**	....	....	....	....	....	....	....	....
	San Diego Gulls	IHL	41	6	23	29	....	....	....	36	....	....	....	....	....	....	....	....	....	....	....	....	....	....	....	....	....	....
1993-94	**Ottawa Senators**	**NHL**	**77**	**0**	**21**	**21**	**0**	**16**	**16**	**89**	**0**	**0**	**0**	**62**	**0.0**	**59**	**9**	**160**	**58**	**–52**	....	....	....	....	....	....	....	....
	San Diego Gulls	IHL	3	0	0	0	....	....	....	2	....	....	....	....	....	....	....	....	....	....	....	....	....	....	....	....	....	....
1994-95	**New York Islanders**	**NHL**	**9**	**0**	**0**	**0**	**0**	**0**	**0**	**2**	**0**	**0**	**0**	**4**	**0.0**	**2**	**0**	**8**	**1**	**–5**	....	....	....	....	....	....	....	....
	Denver Grizzlies	IHL	68	5	27	32	....	....	....	75	....	....	....	....	....	....	....	....	....	....	17	1	6	7	8	....	....	....
1995-96	Utah Grizzlies	IHL	82	1	17	18	....	....	....	89	....	....	....	....	....	....	....	....	....	....	22	0	3	3	14	....	....	....
1996-97	Utah Grizzlies	IHL	81	5	29	34	....	....	....	62	....	....	....	....	....	....	....	....	....	....	7	0	3	3	4	....	....	....
1997-98	Utah Grizzlies	IHL	82	3	34	37	....	....	....	63	....	....	....	....	....	....	....	....	....	....	4	0	2	2	2	....	....	....
	NHL Totals		**528**	**16**	**90**	**106**	**14**	**64**	**78**	**693**	**2**	**0**	**0**	**430**	**3.7**	**454**	**30**	**687**	**207**		**40**	**1**	**7**	**8**	**68**	**0**	**0**	**0**

CHL First All-Star Team (1983) • Won Bob Gassoff Trophy (CHL's Most Improved Defenseman) (1983) • Won Bobby Orr Trophy (CHL's Top Defenseman) (1983) • IHL First All-Star Team (1992) • IHL Second All-Star Team (1998)

Traded to **Minnesota** by **NY Islanders** for Chris Pryor and future considerations, March 8, 1988. Traded to **Pittsburgh** by **Minnesota** with Scott Bjugstad for Ville Siren and Steve Gotaas, December 17, 1988. Signed as a free agent by **Ottawa**, August 31, 1992. Signed as a free agent by **NY Islanders**, July 26, 1994.

• DINEEN, KEVIN

Kevin Dineen RW – R. 5′11″, 190 lbs. b: Quebec City, Que., 10/28/1963. Hartford's 3rd choice, 56th overall, in 1982 Entry Draft.

Season	Club	League	GP	G	A	Pts	AG	AA	APts	PIM	PP	SH	GW	S	%	TGF	PGF	TGA	PGA	+/–	GP	G	A	Pts	PIM	PP	SH	GW
1981-82	University of Denver	WCHA	26	10	10	20	....	....	....	70	....	....	....	....	....	....	....	....	....	....	....	....	....	....	....	....	....	....
1982-83	University of Denver	WCHA	36	16	13	29	....	....	....	108	....	....	....	....	....	....	....	....	....	....	....	....	....	....	....	....	....	....
1983-84	Canada	Nat-Team	52	5	11	16	....	....	....	2	....	....	....	....	....	....	....	....	....	....	....	....	....	....	....	....	....	....
	Canada	Olympics	7	0	0	0	....	....	....	0	....	....	....	....	....	....	....	....	....	....	....	....	....	....	....	....	....	....
1984-85	**Hartford Whalers**	**NHL**	**57**	**25**	**16**	**41**	**20**	**11**	**31**	**120**	**8**	**4**	**2**	**141**	**17.7**	**53**	**14**	**54**	**9**	**–6**	....	....	....	....	....	....	....	....
	Binghamton Whalers	AHL	25	15	8	23	....	....	....	41	....	....	....	....	....	....	....	....	....	....	....	....	....	....	....	....	....	....
	Canada	WEC-A	10	3	2	5	....	....	....	10	....	....	....	....	....	....	....	....	....	....	....	....	....	....	....	....	....	....
1985-86	**Hartford Whalers**	**NHL**	**57**	**33**	**35**	**68**	**26**	**23**	**49**	**124**	**6**	**0**	**8**	**167**	**19.8**	**93**	**25**	**57**	**5**	**+16**	**10**	**6**	**7**	**13**	**18**	**1**	**0**	**2**
1986-87	**Hartford Whalers**	**NHL**	**78**	**40**	**39**	**79**	**35**	**28**	**63**	**110**	**11**	**0**	**7**	**234**	**17.1**	**128**	**50**	**71**	**0**	**+7**	**6**	**2**	**1**	**3**	**31**	**1**	**0**	**0**
	NHL All-Stars	RV'87	2	1	0	1	....	....	....	0	....	....	....	....	....	....	....	....	....	....	....	....	....	....	....	....	....	....
	Canada	WEC-A	9	4	2	6	....	....	....	20	....	....	....	....	....	....	....	....	....	....	....	....	....	....	....	....	....	....
1987-88	Canada	C Cup	3	1	2	3	....	....	....	0	....	....	....	....	....	....	....	....	....	....	....	....	....	....	....	....	....	....
	Hartford Whalers	**NHL**	**74**	**25**	**25**	**50**	**21**	**18**	**39**	**217**	**5**	**0**	**4**	**223**	**11.2**	**86**	**40**	**63**	**3**	**–14**	**6**	**4**	**4**	**8**	**8**	**1**	**0**	**1**
1988-89	**Hartford Whalers**	**NHL**	**79**	**45**	**44**	**89**	**38**	**31**	**69**	**167**	**20**	**1**	**4**	**294**	**15.3**	**122**	**53**	**79**	**4**	**–6**	**4**	**1**	**0**	**1**	**10**	**0**	**0**	**0**
	Canada	WEC-A	10	3	7	10	....	....	....	12	....	....	....	....	....	....	....	....	....	....	....	....	....	....	....	....	....	....
1989-90	**Hartford Whalers**	**NHL**	**67**	**25**	**41**	**66**	**22**	**29**	**51**	**164**	**8**	**2**	**2**	**214**	**11.7**	**90**	**40**	**55**	**12**	**+7**	**6**	**3**	**2**	**5**	**18**	**0**	**0**	**1**
1990-91	**Hartford Whalers**	**NHL**	**61**	**17**	**30**	**47**	**16**	**23**	**39**	**104**	**4**	**0**	**2**	**161**	**10.6**	**59**	**23**	**56**	**5**	**–15**	**6**	**1**	**0**	**1**	**16**	**0**	**0**	**0**
1991-92	**Hartford Whalers**	**NHL**	**16**	**4**	**2**	**6**	**4**	**1**	**5**	**23**	**1**	**0**	**1**	**28**	**14.3**	**7**	**2**	**15**	**4**	**–6**	....	....	....	....	....	....	....	....
	Philadelphia Flyers	**NHL**	**64**	**26**	**30**	**56**	**24**	**23**	**47**	**130**	**5**	**3**	**4**	**197**	**13.2**	**82**	**25**	**77**	**21**	**+1**	....	....	....	....	....	....	....	....
1992-93	**Philadelphia Flyers**	**NHL**	**83**	**35**	**28**	**63**	**29**	**19**	**48**	**201**	**6**	**3**	**7**	**241**	**14.5**	**117**	**27**	**97**	**21**	**+14**	....	....	....	....	....	....	....	....
	Canada	WC-A	8	1	2	3	....	....	....	8	....	....	....	....	....	....	....	....	....	....	....	....	....	....	....	....	....	....
1993-94	**Philadelphia Flyers**	**NHL**	**71**	**19**	**23**	**42**	**18**	**18**	**36**	**113**	**5**	**1**	**2**	**156**	**12.2**	**77**	**21**	**83**	**18**	**–9**	....	....	....	....	....	....	....	....
1994-95	**Philadelphia Flyers**	**NHL**	**40**	**8**	**5**	**13**	**14**	**7**	**21**	**39**	**4**	**0**	**2**	**55**	**14.5**	**22**	**4**	**22**	**3**	**–1**	**15**	**6**	**4**	**10**	**18**	**1**	**0**	**1**
	Houston Aeros	IHL	17	6	4	10	....	....	....	42	....	....	....	....	....	....	....	....	....	....	....	....	....	....	....	....	....	....
1995-96	**Philadelphia Flyers**	**NHL**	**26**	**0**	**2**	**2**	**0**	**2**	**2**	**50**	**0**	**0**	**0**	**31**	**0.0**	**4**	**2**	**12**	**2**	**–8**	....	....	....	....	....	....	....	....
	Hartford Whalers	**NHL**	**20**	**2**	**7**	**9**	**2**	**6**	**8**	**67**	**0**	**0**	**0**	**35**	**5.7**	**18**	**2**	**12**	**3**	**+7**	....	....	....	....	....	....	....	....
1996-97	**Hartford Whalers**	**NHL**	**78**	**19**	**29**	**48**	**20**	**26**	**46**	**141**	**8**	**0**	**5**	**185**	**10.3**	**79**	**31**	**65**	**11**	**–6**	....	....	....	....	....	....	....	....
1997-98	**Carolina Hurricanes**	**NHL**	**54**	**7**	**16**	**23**	**8**	**16**	**24**	**105**	**0**	**0**	**1**	**96**	**7.3**	**31**	**6**	**37**	**5**	**–7**	....	....	....	....	....	....	....	....
	NHL Totals		**925**	**330**	**372**	**702**	**297**	**281**	**578**	**1875**	**91**	**14**	**51**	**2458**	**13.4**	**1068**	**365**	**855**	**126**		**53**	**23**	**18**	**41**	**119**	**4**	**0**	**5**

Won Bud Light/NHL Man of the Year Award (1991)

Played in NHL All-Star Game (1988, 1989)

Traded to **Philadelphia** by **Hartford** for Murray Craven and Philadelphia's 4th round choice (Kevin Smyth) in 1992 Entry Draft, November 13, 1991. Traded to **Hartford** by **Philadelphia** for Hartford's 3rd round choice (Kris Mallette) in 1997 Entry Draft, December 28, 1995. Transferred to **Carolina** after **Hartford** franchise relocated, June 25, 1997.

• DINEEN, PETER

Peter Dineen D – R. 5′11″, 181 lbs. b: Kingston, Ont., 11/19/1960. Philadelphia's 9th choice, 189th overall, in 1980 Entry Draft.

Season	Club	League	GP	G	A	Pts	AG	AA	APts	PIM	PP	SH	GW	S	%	TGF	PGF	TGA	PGA	+/–	GP	G	A	Pts	PIM	PP	SH	GW
1977-78	Seattle Breakers	WCJHL	2	0	0	0	....	....	....	0	....	....	....	....	....	....	....	....	....	....	....	....	....	....	....	....	....	....
1978-79	Kingston Canadians	OHA	60	7	14	21	....	....	....	70	....	....	....	....	....	....	....	....	....	....	11	2	6	8	28	....	....	....
1979-80	Kingston Canadians	OHA	32	4	10	14	....	....	....	54	....	....	....	....	....	....	....	....	....	....	3	0	0	0	13	....	....	....
1980-81	Maine Mariners	AHL	41	6	7	13	....	....	....	100	....	....	....	....	....	....	....	....	....	....	16	1	2	3	82	....	....	....
1981-82	Maine Mariners	AHL	71	6	14	20	....	....	....	156	....	....	....	....	....	....	....	....	....	....	3	0	0	0	2	....	....	....
1982-83	Maine Mariners	AHL	2	0	0	0	....	....	....	0	....	....	....	....	....	....	....	....	....	....	....	....	....	....	....	....	....	....
	Moncton Alpines	AHL	57	0	10	10	....	....	....	76	....	....	....	....	....	....	....	....	....	....	....	....	....	....	....	....	....	....
1983-84	Moncton Alpines	AHL	63	0	10	10	....	....	....	120	....	....	....	....	....	....	....	....	....	....	....	....	....	....	....	....	....	....
	Hershey Bears	AHL	12	0	1	1	....	....	....	32	....	....	....	....	....	....	....	....	....	....	....	....	....	....	....	....	....	....
1984-85	Hershey Bears	AHL	79	4	19	23	....	....	....	144	....	....	....	....	....	....	....	....	....	....	....	....	....	....	....	....	....	....
1985-86	Binghamton Whalers	AHL	11	0	1	1	....	....	....	35	....	....	....	....	....	....	....	....	....	....	....	....	....	....	....	....	....	....
	Moncton Golden Flames	AHL	55	5	13	18	....	....	....	136	....	....	....	....	....	....	....	....	....	....	9	1	0	1	9	....	....	....
1986-87	**Los Angeles Kings**	**NHL**	**11**	**0**	**2**	**2**	**0**	**1**	**1**	**8**	**0**	**0**	**0**	**5**	**0.0**	**4**	**0**	**15**	**2**	**–9**	....	....	....	....	....	....	....	....
	New Haven Nighthawks	AHL	59	2	17	19	....	....	....	140	....	....	....	....	....	....	....	....	....	....	7	0	1	1	27	....	....	....
1987-88	Adirondack Red Wings	AHL	76	8	26	34	....	....	....	137	....	....	....	....	....	....	....	....	....	....	11	0	2	2	20	....	....	....
1988-89	Adirondack Red Wings	AHL	32	2	12	14	....	....	....	61	....	....	....	....	....	....	....	....	....	....	17	2	5	7	22	....	....	....
1989-90	**Detroit Red Wings**	**NHL**	**2**	**0**	**0**	**0**	**0**	**0**	**0**	**5**	**0**	**0**	**0**	**0**	**0.0**	**1**	**0**	**1**	**0**	**0**	....	....	....	....	....	....	....	....
	Adirondack Red Wings	AHL	27	3	6	9	....	....	....	28	....	....	....	....	....	....	....	....	....	....	6	0	1	1	10	....	....	....
1990-91	San Diego Gulls	IHL	24	0	1	1	....	....	....	17	....	....	....	....	....	....	....	....	....	....	....	....	....	....	....	....	....	....
	NHL Totals		**13**	**0**	**2**	**2**	**0**	**1**	**1**	**13**	**0**	**0**	**0**	**5**	**0.0**	**5**	**0**	**16**	**2**		....	....	....	....	....	....	....	....

Traded to **Edmonton** by **Philadelphia** for Bob Hoffmeyer, October 22, 1982. Signed as a free agent by **Boston**, July 16, 1984. Signed as a free agent by **LA Kings**, July 30, 1986. Signed as a free agent by **Detroit**, September 16, 1987.

• DINGMAN, CHRIS Chris Dingman LW – L. 6'4", 225 lbs. b: Edmonton, Alta., 7/6/1976. Calgary's 1st choice, 19th overall, in 1994 Entry Draft.

			REGULAR SEASON																		PLAYOFFS							
Season	Club	League	GP	G	A	Pts	AG	AA	APts	PIM	PP	SH	GW	S	%	TGF	PGF	TGA	PGA	+/-	GP	G	A	Pts	PIM	PP	SH	GW
1992-93	Brandon Wheat Kings	WHL	50	10	17	27	....	....	....	64	....	....	....	....	....	....	....	....	....	....	4	0	0	0	0	....	....	....
1993-94	Brandon Wheat Kings	WHL	45	21	20	41	....	....	....	77	....	....	....	....	....	....	....	....	....	....	13	1	7	8	39	....	....	....
1994-95	Brandon Wheat Kings	WHL	66	40	43	83	....	....	....	201	....	....	....	....	....	....	....	....	....	....	3	1	0	1	9	....	....	....
1995-96	Brandon Wheat Kings	WHL	40	16	29	45	....	....	....	109	....	....	....	....	....	....	....	....	....	....	19	12	11	23	60	....	....	....
	Saint John Flames	AHL	....	....	....	....	....	....	....	....	....	....	....	....	....	....	....	....	....	....	1	0	0	0	0	....	....	....
1996-97	Saint John Flames	AHL	71	5	6	11	....	....	....	195	....	....	....	....	....	....	....	....	....	....	....	....	....	....	....	....	....	....
1997-98	**Calgary Flames**	**NHL**	**70**	**3**	**3**	**6**	**4**	**3**	**7**	**149**	**1**	**0**	**0**	**47**	**6.4**	**13**	**1**	**24**	**1**	**–11**	....	....	....	....	....	....	....	....
	NHL Totals		**70**	**3**	**3**	**6**	**4**	**3**	**7**	**149**	**1**	**0**	**0**	**47**	**6.4**	**13**	**1**	**24**	**1**		....	....	....	....	....	....	....	....

• DIONNE, GILBERT Gilbert Dionne LW – L. 6', 194 lbs. b: Drummondville, Que., 9/19/1970. Montreal's 5th choice, 81st overall, in 1990 Entry Draft.

Season	Club	League	GP	G	A	Pts	AG	AA	APts	PIM	PP	SH	GW	S	%	TGF	PGF	TGA	PGA	+/-	GP	G	A	Pts	PIM	PP	SH	GW
1988-89	Kitchener Rangers	OHL	66	11	33	44	....	....	....	13	....	....	....	....	....	....	....	....	....	....	5	1	1	2	4	....	....	....
1989-90	Kitchener Rangers	OHL	64	48	57	105	....	....	....	85	....	....	....	....	....	....	....	....	....	....	17	13	10	23	22	....	....	....
1990-91	**Montreal Canadiens**	**NHL**	**2**	**0**	**0**	**0**	**0**	**0**	**0**	**0**	**0**	**0**	**0**	**0**	**0.0**	**0**	**0**	**2**	**0**	**–2**	....	....	....	....	....	....	....	....
	Fredericton Canadiens	AHL	77	40	47	87	....	....	....	62	....	....	....	....	....	....	....	....	....	....	9	6	5	11	8	....	....	....
1991-92	**Montreal Canadiens**	**NHL**	**39**	**21**	**13**	**34**	**19**	**10**	**29**	**10**	**7**	**0**	**2**	**90**	**23.3**	**48**	**18**	**23**	**0**	**+7**	**11**	**3**	**4**	**7**	**10**	**1**	**0**	**1**
	Fredericton Canadiens	AHL	29	19	27	46	....	....	....	20	....	....	....	....	....	....	....	....	....	....	....	....	....	....	....	....	....	....
1992-93	**Montreal Canadiens**	**NHL**	**75**	**20**	**28**	**48**	**17**	**19**	**36**	**63**	**6**	**1**	**2**	**145**	**13.8**	**67**	**22**	**45**	**5**	**+5**	**20**	**6**	**6**	**12**	**20**	**1**	**0**	**1**
	Fredericton Canadiens	AHL	3	4	3	7	....	....	....	0	....	....	....	....	....	....	....	....	....	....	....	....	....	....	....	....	....	....
1993-94	**Montreal Canadiens**	**NHL**	**74**	**19**	**26**	**45**	**18**	**20**	**38**	**31**	**3**	**0**	**5**	**162**	**11.7**	**71**	**24**	**59**	**3**	**–9**	**5**	**1**	**2**	**3**	**0**	**0**	**0**	**0**
1994-95	**Montreal Canadiens**	**NHL**	**6**	**0**	**3**	**3**	**0**	**4**	**4**	**2**	**0**	**0**	**0**	**4**	**0.0**	**3**	**1**	**5**	**0**	**–3**	....	....	....	....	....	....	....	....
	Philadelphia Flyers	**NHL**	**20**	**0**	**6**	**6**	**0**	**9**	**9**	**2**	**0**	**0**	**0**	**29**	**0.0**	**9**	**3**	**7**	**0**	**–1**	**3**	**0**	**0**	**0**	**4**	**0**	**0**	**0**
1995-96	**Philadelphia Flyers**	**NHL**	**2**	**0**	**1**	**1**	**0**	**1**	**1**	**0**	**0**	**0**	**0**	**0**	**0.0**	**1**	**0**	**1**	**0**	**0**	....	....	....	....	....	....	....	....
	Florida Panthers	**NHL**	**5**	**1**	**2**	**3**	**1**	**2**	**3**	**0**	**0**	**0**	**0**	**12**	**8.3**	**4**	**1**	**3**	**0**	**0**	....	....	....	....	....	....	....	....
	Carolina Monarchs	AHL	55	43	58	101	....	....	....	29	....	....	....	....	....	....	....	....	....	....	....	....	....	....	....	....	....	....
1996-97	Carolina Monarchs	AHL	72	41	47	88	....	....	....	69	....	....	....	....	....	....	....	....	....	....	....	....	....	....	....	....	....	....
1997-98	Cincinnati Cyclones	IHL	76	42	57	99	....	....	....	54	....	....	....	....	....	....	....	....	....	....	9	3	4	7	28	....	....	....
	NHL Totals		**223**	**61**	**79**	**140**	**55**	**65**	**120**	**108**	**16**	**1**	**9**	**442**	**13.8**	**203**	**69**	**145**	**8**		**39**	**10**	**12**	**22**	**34**	**2**	**0**	**2**

NHL/Upper Deck All-Rookie Team (1992) • AHL Second All-Star Team (1996) • IHL First All-Star Team (1998)

Traded to **Philadelphia** by **Montreal** with Eric Desjardins and John LeClair for Mark Recchi and Philadelphia's 3rd round choice (Martin Hohenberger) in 1995 Entry draft, February 9, 1995. Signed as a free agent by **Florida**, January 29, 1996.

• DIONNE, MARCEL Marcel "Little Beaver" Dionne C – R. 5'9", 190 lbs. b: Drummondville, Que., 8/3/1951. Detroit's 1st choice, 2nd overall, in 1971 Amateur Draft. **HHOF**

Season	Club	League	GP	G	A	Pts	AG	AA	APts	PIM	PP	SH	GW	S	%	TGF	PGF	TGA	PGA	+/-	GP	G	A	Pts	PIM	PP	SH	GW
1968-69	St. Catharines Black Hawks	OHA	48	37	63	100	....	....	....	38	....	....	....	....	....	....	....	....	....	....	....	....	....	....	....	....	....	....
1969-70	St. Catharines Black Hawks	OHA	54	*55	*77	*132	....	....	....	46	....	....	....	....	....	....	....	....	....	....	....	....	....	....	....	....	....	....
1970-71	St. Catharines Black Hawks	OHA	46	62	81	*143	....	....	....	20	....	....	....	....	....	....	....	....	....	....	....	....	....	....	....	....	....	....
1971-72	**Detroit Red Wings**	**NHL**	**78**	**28**	**49**	**77**	**30**	**45**	**75**	**14**	**7**	**0**	**2**	**268**	**10.4**	**107**	**44**	**64**	**1**	**0**	....	....	....	....	....	....	....	....
1972-73	Canada	Summit	DID NOT PLAY																									
	Detroit Red Wings	**NHL**	**77**	**40**	**50**	**90**	**40**	**42**	**82**	**21**	**10**	**0**	**6**	**282**	**14.2**	**116**	**46**	**77**	**3**	**–4**	....	....	....	....	....	....	....	....
1973-74	**Detroit Red Wings**	**NHL**	**74**	**24**	**54**	**78**	**25**	**47**	**72**	**10**	**3**	**0**	**1**	**280**	**8.6**	**106**	**42**	**96**	**1**	**–31**	....	....	....	....	....	....	....	....
1974-75	**Detroit Red Wings**	**NHL**	**80**	**47**	**74**	**121**	**44**	**59**	**103**	**14**	**15**	**10**	**2**	**378**	**12.4**	**167**	**72**	**140**	**30**	**–15**	....	....	....	....	....	....	....	....
1975-76	**Los Angeles Kings**	**NHL**	**80**	**40**	**54**	**94**	**37**	**43**	**80**	**38**	**7**	**1**	**6**	**329**	**12.2**	**116**	**35**	**92**	**13**	**+2**	**9**	**6**	**1**	**7**	**0**	**3**	**0**	**0**
1976-77	Canada	C Cup	7	1	5	6	....	....	....	4	....	....	....	....	....	....	....	....	....	....	....	....	....	....	....	....	....	....
	Los Angeles Kings	**NHL**	**80**	**53**	**69**	**122**	**51**	**56**	**107**	**12**	**14**	**1**	**5**	**378**	**14.0**	**151**	**64**	**91**	**14**	**+10**	**9**	**5**	**9**	**14**	**2**	**1**	**0**	**1**
1977-78	**Los Angeles Kings**	**NHL**	**70**	**36**	**43**	**79**	**35**	**35**	**70**	**37**	**9**	**0**	**4**	**294**	**12.2**	**107**	**43**	**75**	**3**	**–8**	**2**	**0**	**0**	**0**	**0**	**0**	**0**	**0**
	Canada	WEC-A	10	9	3	12	....	....	....	2	....	....	....	....	....	....	....	....	....	....	....	....	....	....	....	....	....	....
1978-79	**Los Angeles Kings**	**NHL**	**80**	**59**	**71**	**130**	**54**	**55**	**109**	**30**	**19**	**0**	**7**	**362**	**16.3**	**169**	**67**	**87**	**8**	**+23**	**2**	**0**	**1**	**1**	**0**	**0**	**0**	**0**
	NHL All-Stars	Chal Cup	2	0	1	1	....	....	....	0	....	....	....	....	....	....	....	....	....	....	....	....	....	....	....	....	....	....
	Canada	WEC-A	7	2	1	3	....	....	....	4	....	....	....	....	....	....	....	....	....	....	....	....	....	....	....	....	....	....
1979-80	**Los Angeles Kings**	**NHL**	**80**	**53**	**84**	***137**	**48**	**65**	**113**	**32**	**17**	**0**	**6**	**348**	**15.2**	**184**	**74**	**80**	**5**	**+35**	**4**	**0**	**3**	**3**	**4**	**0**	**0**	**0**
1980-81	**Los Angeles Kings**	**NHL**	**80**	**58**	**77**	**135**	**48**	**54**	**102**	**70**	**23**	**4**	**9**	**342**	**17.0**	**203**	**76**	**79**	**7**	**+55**	**4**	**1**	**3**	**4**	**7**	**1**	**0**	**0**
1981-82	Canada	C Cup	6	4	1	5	....	....	....	4	....	....	....	....	....	....	....	....	....	....	....	....	....	....	....	....	....	....
	Los Angeles Kings	**NHL**	**78**	**50**	**67**	**117**	**40**	**44**	**84**	**50**	**17**	**1**	**5**	**351**	**14.2**	**149**	**58**	**115**	**14**	**–10**	**10**	**7**	**4**	**11**	**0**	**4**	**0**	**0**
1982-83	**Los Angeles Kings**	**NHL**	**80**	**56**	**51**	**107**	**46**	**35**	**81**	**22**	**17**	**1**	**7**	**345**	**16.2**	**145**	**53**	**86**	**4**	**+10**	....	....	....	....	....	....	....	....
	Canada	WEC-A	10	6	3	9	....	....	....	2	....	....	....	....	....	....	....	....	....	....	....	....	....	....	....	....	....	....
1983-84	**Los Angeles Kings**	**NHL**	**66**	**39**	**53**	**92**	**31**	**36**	**67**	**28**	**13**	**0**	**2**	**278**	**14.0**	**125**	**51**	**72**	**6**	**+8**	....	....	....	....	....	....	....	....
1984-85	**Los Angeles Kings**	**NHL**	**80**	**46**	**80**	**126**	**38**	**54**	**92**	**46**	**16**	**1**	**2**	**316**	**14.6**	**151**	**62**	**90**	**12**	**+11**	**3**	**1**	**2**	**3**	**2**	**1**	**0**	**0**
1985-86	**Los Angeles Kings**	**NHL**	**80**	**36**	**58**	**94**	**29**	**39**	**68**	**42**	**11**	**0**	**4**	**284**	**12.7**	**118**	**42**	**128**	**30**	**–22**	....	....	....	....	....	....	....	....
	Canada	WEC-A	10	4	4	8	....	....	....	8	....	....	....	....	....	....	....	....	....	....	....	....	....	....	....	....	....	....
1986-87	**Los Angeles Kings**	**NHL**	**67**	**24**	**50**	**74**	**21**	**36**	**57**	**54**	**9**	**0**	**2**	**224**	**10.7**	**104**	**44**	**72**	**4**	**–8**	....	....	....	....	....	....	....	....
	New York Rangers	**NHL**	**14**	**4**	**6**	**10**	**3**	**4**	**7**	**6**	**1**	**0**	**0**	**49**	**8.2**	**12**	**5**	**15**	**0**	**–8**	**6**	**1**	**1**	**2**	**2**	**1**	**0**	**0**
1987-88	**New York Rangers**	**NHL**	**67**	**31**	**34**	**65**	**27**	**24**	**51**	**54**	**22**	**0**	**4**	**184**	**16.8**	**90**	**63**	**43**	**2**	**–14**	....	....	....	....	....	....	....	....
1988-89	**New York Rangers**	**NHL**	**37**	**7**	**16**	**23**	**6**	**11**	**17**	**20**	**4**	**0**	**0**	**74**	**9.5**	**37**	**20**	**23**	**0**	**–6**	....	....	....	....	....	....	....	....
	Denver Rangers	IHL	9	0	13	13	....	....	....	6	....	....	....	....	....	....	....	....	....	....	....	....	....	....	....	....	....	....
	NHL Totals		**1348**	**731**	**1040**	**1771**	**653**	**784**	**1437**	**600**	**234**	**19**	**74**	**5366**	**13.6**	**2357**	**961**	**1525**	**157**		**49**	**21**	**24**	**45**	**17**	**11**	**0**	**1**

OHA Second All-Star Team (1970) • OHA First All-Star Team (1971) • Won Lady Byng Trophy (1975, 1977) • NHL First All-Star Team (1977, 1980) • Named Best Forward at WEC-A (1978) • NHL Second All-Star Team (1979, 1981) • Won Lester B. Pearson Award (1979, 1980) • Won Art Ross Trophy (1980)

Played in NHL All-Star Game (1975, 1976, 1977, 1978, 1980, 1981, 1983, 1985)

Rights traded to **LA Kings** by **Detroit** with Bart Crashley for Terry Harper, Dan Maloney and LA Kings 2nd round choice (later traded to Minnesota — Minnesota selected Jim Roberts) in 1976 Amateur Draft, June 23, 1975. Traded to **NY Rangers** by **LA Kings** with Jeff Crossman and LA Kings' 3rd round choice in 1989 Entry Draft (later traded to Minnesota — Minnesota selected Murray Garbutt) in 1989 Entry Draft for Bob Carpenter and Tom Laidlaw, March 10, 1987.

• DI PIETRO, PAUL Paul Di Pietro C – R. 5'9", 181 lbs. b: Sault Ste. Marie, Ont., 9/8/1970. Montreal's 6th choice, 102nd overall, in 1990 Entry Draft.

Season	Club	League	GP	G	A	Pts	AG	AA	APts	PIM	PP	SH	GW	S	%	TGF	PGF	TGA	PGA	+/-	GP	G	A	Pts	PIM	PP	SH	GW
1986-87	Sudbury Wolves	OHL	49	5	11	16	....	....	....	13	....	....	....	....	....	....	....	....	....	....	....	....	....	....	....	....	....	....
1987-88	Sudbury Wolves	OHL	63	25	42	67	....	....	....	27	....	....	....	....	....	....	....	....	....	....	....	....	....	....	....	....	....	....
1988-89	Sudbury Wolves	OHL	57	31	48	79	....	....	....	27	....	....	....	....	....	....	....	....	....	....	....	....	....	....	....	....	....	....
1989-90	Sudbury Wolves	OHL	66	56	63	119	....	....	....	57	....	....	....	....	....	....	....	....	....	....	7	3	6	9	7	....	....	....
1990-91	Fredericton Canadiens	AHL	78	39	31	70	....	....	....	38	....	....	....	....	....	....	....	....	....	....	9	5	6	11	2	....	....	....
1991-92	**Montreal Canadiens**	**NHL**	**33**	**4**	**6**	**10**	**4**	**4**	**8**	**25**	**0**	**0**	**0**	**27**	**14.8**	**13**	**0**	**8**	**0**	**+5**	....	....	....	....	....	....	....	....
	Fredericton Canadiens	AHL	43	26	31	57	....	....	....	52	....	....	....	....	....	....	....	....	....	....	7	3	4	7	8	....	....	....
1992-93	**Montreal Canadiens**	**NHL**	**29**	**4**	**13**	**17**	**3**	**9**	**12**	**14**	**0**	**0**	**0**	**43**	**9.3**	**24**	**3**	**11**	**1**	**+11**	**17**	**8**	**5**	**13**	**8**	**0**	**0**	**1**
	Fredericton Canadiens	AHL	26	8	16	24	....	....	....	16	....	....	....	....	....	....	....	....	....	....	....	....	....	....	....	....	....	....
1993-94	**Montreal Canadiens**	**NHL**	**70**	**13**	**20**	**33**	**12**	**15**	**27**	**37**	**2**	**0**	**0**	**115**	**11.3**	**52**	**10**	**44**	**0**	**–2**	**7**	**2**	**4**	**6**	**2**	**2**	**0**	**1**
1994-95	**Montreal Canadiens**	**NHL**	**22**	**4**	**5**	**9**	**7**	**7**	**14**	**4**	**0**	**0**	**1**	**41**	**9.8**	**15**	**3**	**16**	**1**	**–3**	....	....	....	....	....	....	....	....
	Toronto Maple Leafs	**NHL**	**12**	**1**	**1**	**2**	**2**	**1**	**3**	**6**	**0**	**0**	**0**	**19**	**5.3**	**2**	**0**	**9**	**1**	**–6**	**7**	**1**	**1**	**2**	**0**	**0**	**0**	**0**
1995-96	**Toronto Maple Leafs**	**NHL**	**20**	**4**	**4**	**8**	**4**	**3**	**7**	**4**	**1**	**0**	**0**	**23**	**17.4**	**8**	**2**	**11**	**2**	**–3**	....	....	....	....	....	....	....	....
	St. John's Maple Leafs	AHL	2	2	2	4	....	....	....	0	....	....	....	....	....	....	....	....	....	....	....	....	....	....	....	....	....	....
	Houston Aeros	IHL	36	18	23	41	....	....	....	44	....	....	....	....	....	....	....	....	....	....	....	....	....	....	....	....	....	....
	Las Vegas Thunder	IHL	13	5	6	11	....	....	....	10	....	....	....	....	....	....	....	....	....	....	13	4	8	12	16	....	....	....
1996-97	**Los Angeles Kings**	**NHL**	**6**	**1**	**0**	**1**	**1**	**0**	**1**	**6**	**0**	**0**	**0**	**10**	**10.0**	**1**	**0**	**3**	**0**	**–2**	....	....	....	....	....	....	....	....
	Phoenix Roadrunners	IHL	33	9	20	29	....	....	....	32	....	....	....	....	....	....	....	....	....	....	....	....	....	....	....	....	....	....
	Cincinnati Cyclones	IHL	32	15	14	29	....	....	....	28	....	....	....	....	....	....	....	....	....	....	3	1	1	2	2	....	....	....
	NHL Totals		**192**	**31**	**49**	**80**	**33**	**39**	**72**	**96**	**3**	**0**	**1**	**278**	**11.2**	**115**	**18**	**102**	**5**		**31**	**11**	**10**	**21**	**10**	**2**	**0**	**2**

Traded to **Toronto** by **Montreal** for a Phoenix's 4th round choice (previously acquired, Montreal selected Kim Staal) in 1996 Entry Draft, April 6, 1995. Signed as a free agent by **LA Kings**, July 23, 1996.

• DIRK, ROBERT Robert Dirk D – L. 6'4", 210 lbs. b: Regina, Sask., 8/20/1966. St. Louis' 4th choice, 53rd overall, in 1984 Entry Draft.

Season	Club	League	GP	G	A	Pts	AG	AA	APts	PIM	PP	SH	GW	S	%	TGF	PGF	TGA	PGA	+/-	GP	G	A	Pts	PIM	PP	SH	GW
1982-83	Regina Pats	WHL	1	0	0	0	....	....	....	0	....	....	....	....	....	....	....	....	....	....	....	....	....	....	....	....	....	....
1983-84	Regina Pats	WHL	62	2	10	12	....	....	....	64	....	....	....	....	....	....	....	....	....	....	23	1	12	13	24	....	....	....
1984-85	Regina Pats	WHL	69	10	34	44	....	....	....	97	....	....	....	....	....	....	....	....	....	....	8	0	0	0	4	....	....	....

Season	Club	League	REGULAR SEASON																		PLAYOFFS							
			GP	G	A	Pts	AG	AA	APts	PIM	PP	SH	GW	S	%	TGF	PGF	TGA	PGA	+/–	GP	G	A	Pts	PIM	PP	SH	GW
1985-86	Regina Pats	WHL	72	19	60	79	....	....	....	140	....	....	....	....	....	....	....	....	....	....	10	3	5	8	8	....	....	....
1986-87	Peoria Rivermen	IHL	76	5	17	22	....	....	....	155	....	....	....	....	....	....	....	....	....	....	....	....	....	....	....	....	....	....
1987-88	**St. Louis Blues**	**NHL**	**7**	**0**	**1**	**1**	**0**	**1**	**1**	**16**	**0**	**0**	**0**	**2**	**0.0**	**2**	**0**	**4**	**2**	**0**	**6**	**0**	**1**	**1**	**2**	**0**	**0**	**0**
	Peoria Rivermen	IHL	54	4	21	25	....	....	....	126	....	....	....	....	....	....	....	....	....	....	....	....	....	....	....	....	....	....
1988-89	**St. Louis Blues**	**NHL**	**9**	**0**	**1**	**1**	**0**	**1**	**1**	**11**	**0**	**0**	**0**	**7**	**0.0**	**5**	**0**	**12**	**4**	**–3**	....	....	....	....	....	....	....	....
	Peoria Rivermen	IHL	22	0	2	2	....	....	....	54	....	....	....	....	....	....	....	....	....	....	....	....	....	....	....	....	....	....
1989-90	**St. Louis Blues**	**NHL**	**37**	**1**	**1**	**2**	**1**	**1**	**2**	**128**	**0**	**0**	**0**	**14**	**7.1**	**28**	**0**	**22**	**3**	**+9**	**3**	**0**	**0**	**0**	**0**	**0**	**0**	**0**
	Peoria Rivermen	IHL	24	1	2	3	....	....	....	79	....	....	....	....	....	....	....	....	....	....	....	....	....	....	....	....	....	....
1990-91	**St. Louis Blues**	**NHL**	**41**	**1**	**3**	**4**	**1**	**2**	**3**	**100**	**0**	**0**	**0**	**20**	**5.0**	**31**	**0**	**29**	**0**	**+2**	....	....	....	....	....	....	....	....
	Peoria Rivermen	IHL	3	0	0	0	....	....	....	2	....	....	....	....	....	....	....	....	....	....	....	....	....	....	....	....	....	....
	Vancouver Canucks	**NHL**	**11**	**1**	**0**	**1**	**1**	**0**	**1**	**20**	**0**	**0**	**0**	**9**	**11.1**	**7**	**0**	**16**	**2**	**–7**	**6**	**0**	**0**	**0**	**13**	**0**	**0**	**0**
1991-92	**Vancouver Canucks**	**NHL**	**72**	**2**	**7**	**9**	**2**	**5**	**7**	**126**	**0**	**0**	**0**	**44**	**4.5**	**51**	**0**	**67**	**22**	**+6**	**13**	**0**	**0**	**0**	**20**	**0**	**0**	**0**
1992-93	**Vancouver Canucks**	**NHL**	**69**	**4**	**8**	**12**	**3**	**5**	**8**	**150**	**0**	**0**	**2**	**41**	**9.8**	**66**	**0**	**68**	**27**	**+25**	**9**	**0**	**0**	**0**	**6**	**0**	**0**	**0**
1993-94	**Vancouver Canucks**	**NHL**	**65**	**2**	**3**	**5**	**2**	**2**	**4**	**105**	**0**	**0**	**0**	**38**	**5.3**	**51**	**0**	**58**	**25**	**+18**	....	....	....	....	....	....	....	....
	Chicago Blackhawks	**NHL**	**6**	**0**	**0**	**0**	**0**	**0**	**0**	**26**	**0**	**0**	**0**	**4**	**0.0**	**1**	**0**	**2**	**1**	**0**	**2**	**0**	**0**	**0**	**15**	**0**	**0**	**0**
1994-95	**Anaheim Mighty Ducks**	**NHL**	**38**	**1**	**3**	**4**	**2**	**4**	**6**	**56**	**0**	**0**	**0**	**15**	**6.7**	**27**	**0**	**46**	**16**	**–3**	....	....	....	....	....	....	....	....
1995-96	**Anaheim Mighty Ducks**	**NHL**	**44**	**1**	**2**	**3**	**1**	**2**	**3**	**42**	**0**	**0**	**0**	**20**	**5.0**	**34**	**0**	**46**	**20**	**+8**	....	....	....	....	....	....	....	....
	Montreal Canadiens	**NHL**	**3**	**0**	**0**	**0**	**0**	**0**	**0**	**6**	**0**	**0**	**0**	**0**	**0.0**	**1**	**0**	**1**	**0**	**0**	....	....	....	....	....	....	....	....
1996-97	Detroit Vipers	IHL	48	2	8	10	....	....	....	36	....	....	....	....	....	....	....	....	....	....	....	....	....	....	....	....	....	....
	Chicago Wolves	IHL	31	1	5	6	....	....	....	26	....	....	....	....	....	....	....	....	....	....	3	0	0	0	0	....	....	....
	NHL Totals		**402**	**13**	**29**	**42**	**13**	**23**	**36**	**786**	**0**	**0**	**2**	**214**	**6.1**	**304**	**0**	**371**	**122**		**39**	**0**	**1**	**1**	**56**	**0**	**0**	**0**

WHL East Second All-Star Team (1986)

Traded to **Vancouver** by **St. Louis** with Geoff Courtnall, Sergio Momesso, Cliff Ronning and St. Louis' 5th round choice (Brian Loney) in 1992 Entry Draft for Dan Quinn and Garth Butcher, March 5, 1991. Traded to **Chicago** by **Vancouver** for Chicago's 4th round choice (Mike Dubinsky) in 1994 Entry Draft, March 21, 1994. Traded to **Anaheim** by **Chicago** for Tampa Bay's 4th round choice (previously acquired, Chicago selected Chris Van Dyk) in 1995 Entry Draft, July 12, 1994. Traded to **Montreal** by **Anaheim** for Jim Campbell, January 21, 1996.

• DJOOS, PER

Per Djoos D – R. 5'11", 176 lbs. b: Mora, Sweden, 5/11/1968. Detroit's 7th choice, 127th overall, in 1986 Entry Draft.

Season	Club	League	GP	G	A	Pts	AG	AA	APts	PIM	PP	SH	GW	S	%	TGF	PGF	TGA	PGA	+/–	GP	G	A	Pts	PIM	PP	SH	GW
1984-85	Mora	Sweden 2	20	2	3	5	....	....	....	2	....	....	....	....	....	....	....	....	....	....	....	....	....	....	....	....	....	....
1985-86	Mora	Sweden 2	30	9	5	14	....	....	....	14	....	....	....	....	....	....	....	....	....	....	....	....	....	....	....	....	....	....
1986-87	Brynas IF	Sweden	23	1	2	3	....	....	....	16	....	....	....	....	....	....	....	....	....	....	....	....	....	....	....	....	....	....
1987-88	Brynas IF	Sweden	34	4	11	15	....	....	....	18	....	....	....	....	....	....	....	....	....	....	....	....	....	....	....	....	....	....
	Sweden	WJC-A	7	0	2	2	....	....	....	4	....	....	....	....	....	....	....	....	....	....	....	....	....	....	....	....	....	....
1988-89	Brynas IF	Sweden	40	1	17	18	....	....	....	44	....	....	....	....	....	....	....	....	....	....	....	....	....	....	....	....	....	....
1989-90	Brynas IF	Sweden	37	5	13	18	....	....	....	34	....	....	....	....	....	....	....	....	....	....	5	1	3	4	6	....	....	....
	Sweden	WEC-A	7	1	0	1	....	....	....	10	....	....	....	....	....	....	....	....	....	....	....	....	....	....	....	....	....	....
1990-91	**Detroit Red Wings**	**NHL**	**26**	**0**	**12**	**12**	**0**	**9**	**9**	**16**	**0**	**0**	**0**	**23**	**0.0**	**31**	**7**	**26**	**0**	**–2**	....	....	....	....	....	....	....	....
	Adirondack Red Wings	AHL	20	2	9	11	....	....	....	6	....	....	....	....	....	....	....	....	....	....	....	....	....	....	....	....	....	....
	Binghamton Rangers	AHL	14	1	8	9	....	....	....	10	....	....	....	....	....	....	....	....	....	....	9	2	2	4	4	....	....	....
1991-92	**New York Rangers**	**NHL**	**50**	**1**	**18**	**19**	**1**	**14**	**15**	**40**	**1**	**0**	**1**	**39**	**2.6**	**48**	**15**	**27**	**1**	**+7**	....	....	....	....	....	....	....	....
1992-93	**New York Rangers**	**NHL**	**6**	**1**	**1**	**2**	**1**	**1**	**2**	**2**	**0**	**0**	**0**	**4**	**25.0**	**4**	**1**	**3**	**0**	**0**	....	....	....	....	....	....	....	....
	Binghamton Rangers	AHL	70	16	53	69	....	....	....	75	....	....	....	....	....	....	....	....	....	....	14	2	8	10	8	....	....	....
1993-94	HC Lugano	Switz.	36	10	25	35	....	....	....	36	....	....	....	....	....	....	....	....	....	....	9	0	7	7	4	....	....	....
1994-95	Vastra Frolunda	Sweden	22	5	4	9	....	....	....	12	....	....	....	....	....	....	....	....	....	....	....	....	....	....	....	....	....	....
1995-96	Vastra Frolunda	Sweden	9	0	2	2	....	....	....	2	....	....	....	....	....	....	....	....	....	....	....	....	....	....	....	....	....	....
1996-97	Brynas IF Gavle	Sweden	50	3	15	18	....	....	....	76	....	....	....	....	....	....	....	....	....	....	....	....	....	....	....	....	....	....
1997-98	Brynas IF Gavle	Sweden	44	9	23	32	....	....	....	40	....	....	....	....	....	....	....	....	....	....	3	0	1	1	2	....	....	....
	NHL Totals		**82**	**2**	**31**	**33**	**2**	**24**	**26**	**58**	**1**	**0**	**1**	**66**	**3.0**	**83**	**23**	**56**	**1**		....	....	....	....	....	....	....	....

EJC-A All-Star Team (1986) • AHL Second All-Star Team (1993)

Traded to **NY Rangers** by **Detroit** with Joey Kocur for Kevin Miller, Jim Cummins and Dennis Vial, March 5, 1991.

• DOAK, GARY

Gary Doak D – R. 5'11", 175 lbs. b: Goderich, Ont., 2/26/1946.

Season	Club	League	GP	G	A	Pts	AG	AA	APts	PIM	PP	SH	GW	S	%	TGF	PGF	TGA	PGA	+/–	GP	G	A	Pts	PIM	PP	SH	GW
1962-63	Hamilton Red Wings	OHA	50	3	10	13	....	....	....	83	....	....	....	....	....	....	....	....	....	....	6	0	0	0	17	....	....	....
1963-64	Hamilton Red Wings	OHA	55	2	31	33	....	....	....	162	....	....	....	....	....	....	....	....	....	....	....	....	....	....	....	....	....	....
	Pittsburgh Hornets	AHL	1	0	0	0	....	....	....	0	....	....	....	....	....	....	....	....	....	....	....	....	....	....	....	....	....	....
1964-65	Hamilton Red Wings	OHA	56	8	26	34	....	....	....	216	....	....	....	....	....	....	....	....	....	....	....	....	....	....	....	....	....	....
	Pittsburgh Hornets	AHL	2	1	0	1	....	....	....	4	....	....	....	....	....	....	....	....	....	....	3	0	0	0	4	....	....	....
1965-66	**Detroit Red Wings**	**NHL**	**4**	**0**	**0**	**0**	**0**	**0**	**0**	**12**	....	....	....	....	....	....	....	....	....	....	....	....	....	....	....	....	....	....
	Pittsburgh Hornets	AHL	48	0	6	6	....	....	....	88	....	....	....	....	....	....	....	....	....	....	....	....	....	....	....	....	....	....
	Boston Bruins	**NHL**	**20**	**0**	**8**	**8**	**0**	**8**	**8**	**28**	....	....	....	....	....	....	....	....	....	....	....	....	....	....	....	....	....	....
1966-67	**Boston Bruins**	**NHL**	**29**	**0**	**1**	**1**	**0**	**1**	**1**	**50**	....	....	....	....	....	....	....	....	....	....	....	....	....	....	....	....	....	....
	Oklahoma City Blazers	CHL	17	4	3	7	....	....	....	96	....	....	....	....	....	....	....	....	....	....	....	....	....	....	....	....	....	....
1967-68	**Boston Bruins**	**NHL**	**59**	**2**	**10**	**12**	**2**	**10**	**12**	**100**	**0**	**0**	**1**	**53**	**3.8**	**57**	**0**	**51**	**7**	**+13**	**4**	**0**	**0**	**0**	**4**	**0**	**0**	**0**
1968-69	**Boston Bruins**	**NHL**	**22**	**3**	**3**	**6**	**3**	**3**	**6**	**37**	**0**	**0**	**0**	**22**	**13.6**	**22**	**2**	**13**	**4**	**+11**	....	....	....	....	....	....	....	....
1969-70	**Boston Bruins**	**NHL**	**44**	**1**	**7**	**8**	**1**	**7**	**8**	**63**	**0**	**0**	**1**	**36**	**2.8**	**30**	**1**	**31**	**9**	**+7**	**8**	**0**	**0**	**0**	**9**	**0**	**0**	**0**
	Oklahoma City Blazers	CHL	13	1	5	6	....	....	....	53	....	....	....	....	....	....	....	....	....	....	....	....	....	....	....	....	....	....
1970-71	**Vancouver Canucks**	**NHL**	**77**	**2**	**10**	**12**	**2**	**9**	**11**	**112**	**0**	**0**	**0**	**60**	**3.3**	**69**	**2**	**119**	**47**	**–5**	....	....	....	....	....	....	....	....
1971-72	**Vancouver Canucks**	**NHL**	**6**	**0**	**1**	**1**	**0**	**1**	**1**	**23**	**0**	**0**	**0**	**4**	**0.0**	**3**	**0**	**5**	**1**	**–1**	....	....	....	....	....	....	....	....
	New York Rangers	**NHL**	**49**	**1**	**10**	**11**	**1**	**9**	**10**	**54**	**0**	**0**	**0**	**33**	**3.0**	**40**	**0**	**32**	**8**	**+16**	**12**	**0**	**0**	**0**	**46**	**0**	**0**	**0**
1972-73	**Detroit Red Wings**	**NHL**	**44**	**0**	**5**	**5**	**0**	**4**	**4**	**51**	**0**	**0**	**0**	**28**	**0.0**	**31**	**0**	**30**	**4**	**+5**	....	....	....	....	....	....	....	....
	Boston Bruins	**NHL**	**5**	**0**	**0**	**0**	**0**	**0**	**0**	**2**	**0**	**0**	**0**	**1**	**0.0**	**0**	**0**	**1**	**0**	**–1**	**2**	**0**	**0**	**0**	**2**	**0**	**0**	**0**
1973-74	**Boston Bruins**	**NHL**	**69**	**0**	**4**	**4**	**0**	**3**	**3**	**44**	**0**	**0**	**0**	**30**	**0.0**	**20**	**0**	**27**	**5**	**–2**	....	....	....	....	....	....	....	....
1974-75	**Boston Bruins**	**NHL**	**40**	**0**	**0**	**0**	**0**	**0**	**0**	**30**	**0**	**0**	**0**	**27**	**0.0**	**11**	**0**	**15**	**1**	**–3**	**3**	**0**	**0**	**0**	**4**	**0**	**0**	**0**
1975-76	**Boston Bruins**	**NHL**	**58**	**1**	**6**	**7**	**1**	**5**	**6**	**60**	**0**	**0**	**1**	**70**	**1.4**	**71**	**1**	**58**	**13**	**+25**	**12**	**1**	**0**	**1**	**22**	**0**	**0**	**0**
1976-77	**Boston Bruins**	**NHL**	**76**	**3**	**13**	**16**	**3**	**11**	**14**	**107**	**0**	**0**	**0**	**70**	**4.3**	**91**	**1**	**85**	**10**	**+15**	**14**	**0**	**2**	**2**	**26**	**0**	**0**	**0**
1977-78	**Boston Bruins**	**NHL**	**61**	**4**	**13**	**17**	**4**	**11**	**15**	**50**	**1**	**0**	**2**	**66**	**6.1**	**83**	**3**	**53**	**10**	**+37**	**12**	**1**	**0**	**1**	**4**	**0**	**0**	**1**
1978-79	**Boston Bruins**	**NHL**	**63**	**0**	**11**	**17**	**5**	**8**	**13**	**28**	**1**	**0**	**0**	**64**	**9.4**	**76**	**4**	**71**	**11**	**+12**	**7**	**0**	**2**	**2**	**4**	**0**	**0**	**0**
1979-80	**Boston Bruins**	**NHL**	**52**	**0**	**5**	**5**	**0**	**4**	**4**	**45**	**0**	**0**	**0**	**29**	**0.0**	**41**	**0**	**30**	**3**	**+14**	**4**	**0**	**0**	**0**	**0**	**0**	**0**	**0**
1980-81	**Boston Bruins**	**NHL**	**11**	**0**	**0**	**0**	**0**	**0**	**0**	**12**	**0**	**0**	**0**	**4**	**0.0**	**6**	**0**	**9**	**0**	**–3**	....	....	....	....	....	....	....	....
	NHL Totals		**789**	**23**	**107**	**130**	**22**	**94**	**116**	**908**	**2**	**0**	**5**	**597**	**3.9**	**651**	**14**	**630**	**133**		**78**	**2**	**4**	**6**	**121**	**0**	**0**	**1**

Traded to **Boston** by **Detroit** with Bill Lesuk and future considerations (Steve Atkinson, June, 1966) for Leo Boivin, February 18, 1966. Claimed by **Vancouver** from **Boston** in Expansion Draft, June 10, 1970. Traded to **NY Rangers** by **Vancouver** with Jim Wiste for Dave Balon, Wayne Connelly and Ron Stewart, November 16, 1971. Traded to **Detroit** by **NY Rangers** with Rick Newell for Joe Zanussi and Detroit's 1st round choice (Al Blanchford) in 1972 Amateur Draft, May 24, 1972. Traded to **Boston** by **Detroit** for Garnet Bailey and future considerations (Murray Wing, June 4, 1973), March 1, 1973.

• DOAN, SHANE

Shane Doan RW – R. 6'1", 215 lbs. b: Halkirk, Alta., 10/10/1976. Winnipeg's 1st choice, 7th overall, in 1995 Entry Draft.

Season	Club	League	GP	G	A	Pts	AG	AA	APts	PIM	PP	SH	GW	S	%	TGF	PGF	TGA	PGA	+/–	GP	G	A	Pts	PIM	PP	SH	GW
1992-93	Kamloops Blazers	WHL	51	7	12	19	....	....	....	65	....	....	....	....	....	....	....	....	....	....	13	0	1	1	8	....	....	....
1993-94	Kamloops Blazers	WHL	52	24	24	48	....	....	....	88	....	....	....	....	....	....	....	....	....	....	....	....	....	....	....	....	....	....
1994-95	Kamloops Blazers	WHL	71	37	57	94	....	....	....	106	....	....	....	....	....	....	....	....	....	....	21	6	10	16	16	....	....	....
1995-96	**Winnipeg Jets**	**NHL**	**74**	**7**	**10**	**17**	**7**	**8**	**15**	**101**	**1**	**0**	**3**	**106**	**6.6**	**30**	**8**	**32**	**1**	**–9**	**6**	**0**	**0**	**0**	**6**	**0**	**0**	**0**
1996-97	**Phoenix Coyotes**	**NHL**	**63**	**4**	**8**	**12**	**4**	**7**	**11**	**49**	**0**	**0**	**0**	**100**	**4.0**	**29**	**3**	**29**	**0**	**–3**	**4**	**0**	**0**	**0**	**2**	**0**	**0**	**0**
1997-98	**Phoenix Coyotes**	**NHL**	**33**	**5**	**6**	**11**	**6**	**6**	**12**	**35**	**0**	**0**	**3**	**42**	**11.9**	**10**	**1**	**20**	**0**	**–3**	**6**	**1**	**0**	**1**	**6**	**0**	**0**	**0**
	Springfield Falcons	AHL	39	21	21	42	....	....	....	64	....	....	....	....	....	....	....	....	....	....	....	....	....	....	....	....	....	....
	NHL Totals		**170**	**16**	**24**	**40**	**17**	**21**	**38**	**185**	**1**	**0**	**6**	**248**	**6.5**	**77**	**12**	**81**	**1**		**16**	**1**	**0**	**1**	**14**	**0**	**0**	**0**

Memorial Cup All-Star Team (1995) • Won Stafford Smythe Memorial Trophy (Memorial Cup Tournament MVP) (1995)

Transferred to **Phoenix** after **Winnipeg** franchise relocated, July 1, 1996.

• DOBBIN, BRIAN

Brian Dobbin RW – R. 5'11", 205 lbs. b: Petrolia, Ont., 8/18/1966. Philadelphia's 7th choice, 100th overall, in 1984 Entry Draft.

Season	Club	League	GP	G	A	Pts	AG	AA	APts	PIM	PP	SH	GW	S	%	TGF	PGF	TGA	PGA	+/–	GP	G	A	Pts	PIM	PP	SH	GW
1981-82	Mooretown Flags	Jr. C	38	31	24	55	....	....	....	50	....	....	....	....	....	....	....	....	....	....	....	....	....	....	....	....	....	....
1982-83	Kingston Canadians	OHL	69	16	39	55	....	....	....	35	....	....	....	....	....	....	....	....	....	....	....	....	....	....	....	....	....	....
1983-84	London Knights	OHL	70	30	40	70	....	....	....	70	....	....	....	....	....	....	....	....	....	....	....	....	....	....	....	....	....	....

			REGULAR SEASON																		PLAYOFFS							
Season	Club	League	GP	G	A	Pts	AG	AA	APts	PIM	PP	SH	GW	S	%	TGF	PGF	TGA	PGA	+/–	GP	G	A	Pts	PIM	PP	SH	GW
1984-85	London Knights	OHL	53	42	57	99	....	....	....	63	....	....	....	....	....	....	....	....	....	....	8	7	4	11	2	....	....	....
1985-86	London Knights	OHL	59	38	55	93	....	....	....	113	....	....	....	....	....	....	....	....	....	....	5	2	1	3	9	....	....	....
	Hershey Bears	AHL	2	1	0	1	....	....	....	0	....	....	....	....	....	....	....	....	....	....	18	5	5	10	21	....	....	....
1986-87	**Philadelphia Flyers**	**NHL**	**12**	**2**	**1**	**3**	**2**	**1**	**3**	**14**	**0**	**0**	**0**	**13**	**15.4**	**4**	**1**	**1**	**0**	**+2**	....	....	....	....	....	....	....	....
	Hershey Bears	AHL	52	26	35	61	....	....	....	66	....	....	....	....	....	....	....	....	....	....	5	4	2	6	15	....	....	....
1987-88	**Philadelphia Flyers**	**NHL**	**21**	**3**	**5**	**8**	**3**	**4**	**7**	**6**	**0**	**0**	**1**	**15**	**20.0**	**11**	**4**	**8**	**0**	**–1**	....	....	....	....	....	....	....	....
	Hershey Bears	AHL	54	36	47	83	....	....	....	58	....	....	....	....	....	....	....	....	....	....	12	7	8	15	15	....	....	....
1988-89	**Philadelphia Flyers**	**NHL**	**14**	**0**	**1**	**1**	**0**	**1**	**1**	**8**	**0**	**0**	**0**	**13**	**0.0**	**2**	**0**	**8**	**0**	**–6**	**2**	**0**	**0**	**0**	**17**	**0**	**0**	**0**
	Hershey Bears	AHL	59	43	48	91	....	....	....	61	....	....	....	....	....	....	....	....	....	....	11	7	6	13	12	....	....	....
1989-90	**Philadelphia Flyers**	**NHL**	**9**	**1**	**1**	**2**	**1**	**1**	**2**	**11**	**1**	**0**	**0**	**11**	**9.1**	**4**	**2**	**1**	**0**	**+1**	....	....	....	....	....	....	....	....
	Hershey Bears	AHL	68	38	47	85	....	....	....	58	....	....	....	....	....	....	....	....	....	....	....	....	....	....	....	....	....	....
1990-91	Hershey Bears	AHL	80	35	43	78	....	....	....	82	....	....	....	....	....	....	....	....	....	....	7	1	2	3	7	....	....	....
1991-92	New Haven Nighthawks	AHL	33	16	21	37	....	....	....	20	....	....	....	....	....	....	....	....	....	....	....	....	....	....	....	....	....	....
	Boston Bruins	**NHL**	**7**	**1**	**0**	**1**	**1**	**0**	**1**	**22**	**0**	**0**	**0**	**4**	**25.0**	**1**	**0**	**1**	**0**	**0**	....	....	....	....	....	....	....	....
	Maine Mariners	AHL	33	21	15	36	....	....	....	14	....	....	....	....	....	....	....	....	....	....	....	....	....	....	....	....	....	....
1992-93	Milwaukee Admirals	IHL	80	39	45	84	....	....	....	50	....	....	....	....	....	....	....	....	....	....	6	4	3	7	6	....	....	....
1993-94	Milwaukee Admirals	IHL	81	48	53	101	....	....	....	73	....	....	....	....	....	....	....	....	....	....	4	1	0	1	4	....	....	....
1994-95	Milwaukee Admirals	IHL	76	21	40	61	....	....	....	62	....	....	....	....	....	....	....	....	....	....	9	0	4	4	2	....	....	....
1995-96	Cincinnati Cyclones	IHL	82	28	37	65	....	....	....	97	....	....	....	....	....	....	....	....	....	....	17	2	2	4	14	....	....	....
1996-97	Austin Ice-Bats	WPHL	23	14	18	32	....	....	....	25	....	....	....	....	....	....	....	....	....	....	6	2	5	7	11	....	....	....
1996-97	Muskegon Fury	ColHL	2	0	0	0	....	....	....	2	....	....	....	....	....	....	....	....	....	....	....	....	....	....	....	....	....	....
	Grand Rapids Griffins	IHL	29	4	5	9	....	....	....	39	....	....	....	....	....	....	....	....	....	....	....	....	....	....	....	....	....	....
1997-98	Port Huron Border Cats	UHL	71	38	46	84	....	....	....	54	....	....	....	....	....	....	....	....	....	....	4	2	1	3	2	....	....	....
	NHL Totals		**63**	**7**	**8**	**15**	**7**	**7**	**14**	**61**	**1**	**0**	**1**	**56**	**12.5**	**22**	**7**	**19**	**0**		**2**	**0**	**0**	**0**	**17**	**0**	**0**	**0**

AHL First All-Star Team (1989) • AHL Second All-Star Team (1990) • IHL Second All-Star Team (1994)

Traded to **Boston** by **Philadelphia** with Gord Murphy and Philadelphia's 3rd round choice (Sergei Zholtok) in 1992 Entry Draft for Garry Galley, Wes Walz and future considerations, January 2, 1992.

• DOBSON, JIM

Jim Dobson RW – R. 6'1", 195 lbs. b: Winnipeg, Man., 2/29/1960. Minnesota's 5th choice, 90th overall, in 1979 Entry Draft.

Season	Club	League	GP	G	A	Pts	AG	AA	APts	PIM	PP	SH	GW	S	%	TGF	PGF	TGA	PGA	+/–	GP	G	A	Pts	PIM	PP	SH	GW
1977-78	New Westminster Bruins	WCJHL	12	4	2	6	....	....	....	121	....	....	....	....	....	....	....	....	....	....	11	5	3	8	2	....	....	....
1978-79	Portland Winter Hawks	WHL	71	38	39	77	....	....	....	143	....	....	....	....	....	....	....	....	....	....	....	....	....	....	....	....	....	....
1979-80	Portland Winter Hawks	WHL	72	66	68	134	....	....	....	181	....	....	....	....	....	....	....	....	....	....	....	....	....	....	....	....	....	....
	Minnesota North Stars	**NHL**	**1**	**0**	**0**	**0**	**0**	**0**	**0**	**0**	**0**	**0**	**0**	**0**	**0.0**	**0**	**0**	**0**	**0**	**0**	....	....	....	....	....	....	....	....
1980-81	**Minnesota North Stars**	**NHL**	**1**	**0**	**0**	**0**	**0**	**0**	**0**	**0**	**0**	**0**	**0**	**0**	**0.0**	**0**	**0**	**0**	**0**	**0**	....	....	....	....	....	....	....	....
	Oklahoma City Stars	CHL	35	23	16	39	....	....	....	46	....	....	....	....	....	....	....	....	....	....	....	....	....	....	....	....	....	....
1981-82	**Minnesota North Stars**	**NHL**	**6**	**0**	**0**	**0**	**0**	**0**	**0**	**4**	**0**	**0**	**0**	**5**	**0.0**	**1**	**0**	**1**	**0**	**0**	....	....	....	....	....	....	....	....
	Nashville South Stars	CHL	29	19	13	32	....	....	....	29	....	....	....	....	....	....	....	....	....	....	....	....	....	....	....	....	....	....
	Colorado Rockies	**NHL**	**3**	**0**	**0**	**0**	**0**	**0**	**0**	**2**	**0**	**0**	**0**	**5**	**0.0**	**0**	**0**	**1**	**0**	**–1**	....	....	....	....	....	....	....	....
	Fort Worth Texans	CHL	34	15	12	27	....	....	....	65	....	....	....	....	....	....	....	....	....	....	....	....	....	....	....	....	....	....
1982-83	Birmingham South Stars	CHL	80	36	37	73	....	....	....	100	....	....	....	....	....	....	....	....	....	....	13	8	4	12	4	....	....	....
1983-84	**Quebec Nordiques**	**NHL**	**1**	**0**	**0**	**0**	**0**	**0**	**0**	**0**	**0**	**0**	**0**	**1**	**0.0**	**0**	**0**	**1**	**0**	**–1**	....	....	....	....	....	....	....	....
	Fredericton Express	AHL	75	33	44	77	....	....	....	74	....	....	....	....	....	....	....	....	....	....	7	3	2	5	2	....	....	....
1984-85	Fredericton Express	AHL	21	8	10	18	....	....	....	52	....	....	....	....	....	....	....	....	....	....	5	3	0	3	5	....	....	....
1985-86	New Haven Nighthawks	AHL	29	5	6	11	....	....	....	12	....	....	....	....	....	....	....	....	....	....	1	0	0	0	0	....	....	....
	NHL Totals		**12**	**0**	**0**	**0**	**0**	**0**	**0**	**6**	**0**	**0**	**0**	**11**	**0.0**	**1**	**0**	**3**	**0**		....	....	....	....	....	....	....	....

WHL All-Star Team (1980)

Rights traded to **Colorado** by **Minnesota** with Kevin Maxwell for cash, December 31, 1981. Signed as a free agent by **Minnesota**, September 20, 1982. Traded to **Quebec** by **Minnesota** for Jay Miller, June 29, 1983.

• DOIG, JASON

Jason Doig D – R. 6'3", 216 lbs. b: Montreal, Que., 1/29/1977. Winnipeg's 3rd choice, 34th overall, in 1995 Entry Draft.

Season	Club	League	GP	G	A	Pts	AG	AA	APts	PIM	PP	SH	GW	S	%	TGF	PGF	TGA	PGA	+/–	GP	G	A	Pts	PIM	PP	SH	GW
1993-94	St-Jean Lynx	QMJHL	63	8	17	25	....	....	....	65	....	....	....	....	....	....	....	....	....	....	5	0	2	2	2	....	....	....
1994-95	Laval Titan	QMJHL	55	13	42	55	....	....	....	259	....	....	....	....	....	....	....	....	....	....	20	4	13	17	39	....	....	....
1995-96	Laval Titan	QMJHL	5	3	6	9	....	....	....	20	....	....	....	....	....	....	....	....	....	....	....	....	....	....	....	....	....	....
	Granby Predateurs	QMJHL	24	4	30	34	....	....	....	91	....	....	....	....	....	....	....	....	....	....	20	10	22	32	*110	....	....	....
	Winnipeg Jets	**NHL**	**15**	**1**	**1**	**2**	**1**	**1**	**2**	**28**	**0**	**0**	**0**	**7**	**14.3**	**7**	**0**	**9**	**0**	**–2**	....	....	....	....	....	....	....	....
	Springfield Falcons	AHL	5	0	0	0	....	....	....	28	....	....	....	....	....	....	....	....	....	....	....	....	....	....	....	....	....	....
1996-97	Granby Predateurs	QMJHL	39	14	33	47	....	....	....	211	....	....	....	....	....	....	....	....	....	....	5	0	4	4	27	....	....	....
	Canada	WJC-A	7	0	2	2	....	....	....	37	....	....	....	....	....	....	....	....	....	....	....	....	....	....	....	....	....	....
	Las Vegas Thunder	IHL	6	0	1	1	....	....	....	19	....	....	....	....	....	....	....	....	....	....	....	....	....	....	....	....	....	....
	Springfield Falcons	AHL	5	0	3	3	....	....	....	2	....	....	....	....	....	....	....	....	....	....	17	1	4	5	37	....	....	....
1997-98	**Phoenix Coyotes**	**NHL**	**4**	**0**	**1**	**1**	**0**	**1**	**1**	**12**	**0**	**0**	**0**	**1**	**0.0**	**1**	**0**	**5**	**0**	**–4**	....	....	....	....	....	....	....	....
	Springfield Falcons	AHL	46	2	25	27	....	....	....	153	....	....	....	....	....	....	....	....	....	....	3	0	0	0	2	....	....	....
	NHL Totals		**19**	**1**	**2**	**3**	**1**	**2**	**3**	**40**	**0**	**0**	**0**	**8**	**12.5**	**8**	**0**	**14**	**0**		....	....	....	....	....	....	....	....

Memorial Cup All-Star Team (1996)

Transferred to **Phoenix** after **Winnipeg** franchise relocated, July 1, 1996.

• DOLLAS, BOBBY

Bobby Dollas D – L. 6'2", 212 lbs. b: Montreal, Que., 1/31/1965. Winnipeg's 2nd choice, 14th overall, in 1983 Entry Draft.

Season	Club	League	GP	G	A	Pts	AG	AA	APts	PIM	PP	SH	GW	S	%	TGF	PGF	TGA	PGA	+/–	GP	G	A	Pts	PIM	PP	SH	GW
1982-83	Laval Voisins	QMJHL	63	16	45	61	....	....	....	144	....	....	....	....	....	....	....	....	....	....	11	5	5	10	23	....	....	....
1983-84	Laval Voisins	QMJHL	54	12	33	45	....	....	....	80	....	....	....	....	....	....	....	....	....	....	14	1	8	9	23	....	....	....
	Winnipeg Jets	**NHL**	**1**	**0**	**0**	**0**	**0**	**0**	**0**	**0**	**0**	**0**	**0**	**0**	**0.0**	**0**	**0**	**2**	**0**	**–2**	....	....	....	....	....	....	....	....
1984-85	**Winnipeg Jets**	**NHL**	**9**	**0**	**0**	**0**	**0**	**0**	**0**	**0**	**0**	**0**	**0**	**2**	**0.0**	**8**	**0**	**4**	**0**	**+4**	....	....	....	....	....	....	....	....
	Canada	WJC-A	7	0	2	2	....	....	....	12	....	....	....	....	....	....	....	....	....	....	....	....	....	....	....	....	....	....
	Sherbrooke Canadiens	AHL	8	1	3	4	....	....	....	4	....	....	....	....	....	....	....	....	....	....	17	3	6	9	17	....	....	....
1985-86	**Winnipeg Jets**	**NHL**	**46**	**0**	**5**	**5**	**0**	**3**	**3**	**66**	**0**	**0**	**0**	**50**	**0.0**	**39**	**1**	**50**	**9**	**–3**	**3**	**0**	**0**	**0**	**2**	**0**	**0**	**0**
	Sherbrooke Canadiens	AHL	25	4	7	11	....	....	....	29	....	....	....	....	....	....	....	....	....	....	....	....	....	....	....	....	....	....
1986-87	Sherbrooke Canadiens	AHL	75	6	18	24	....	....	....	87	....	....	....	....	....	....	....	....	....	....	16	2	4	6	13	....	....	....
1987-88	**Quebec Nordiques**	**NHL**	**9**	**0**	**0**	**0**	**0**	**0**	**0**	**2**	**0**	**0**	**0**	**5**	**0.0**	**1**	**0**	**6**	**1**	**–4**	....	....	....	....	....	....	....	....
	Moncton Hawks	AHL	26	4	10	14	....	....	....	20	....	....	....	....	....	....	....	....	....	....	....	....	....	....	....	....	....	....
	Fredericton Express	AHL	33	4	8	12	....	....	....	27	....	....	....	....	....	....	....	....	....	....	15	2	2	4	24	....	....	....
1988-89	**Quebec Nordiques**	**NHL**	**16**	**0**	**3**	**3**	**0**	**2**	**2**	**16**	**0**	**0**	**0**	**11**	**0.0**	**12**	**0**	**29**	**6**	**–11**	....	....	....	....	....	....	....	....
	Halifax Citadels	AHL	57	5	19	24	....	....	....	65	....	....	....	....	....	....	....	....	....	....	4	1	0	1	14	....	....	....
1989-90	Canada	Nat-Team	68	8	29	37	....	....	....	60	....	....	....	....	....	....	....	....	....	....	....	....	....	....	....	....	....	....
1990-91	**Detroit Red Wings**	**NHL**	**56**	**3**	**5**	**8**	**3**	**4**	**7**	**20**	**0**	**0**	**1**	**59**	**5.1**	**44**	**3**	**52**	**17**	**+6**	**7**	**1**	**0**	**1**	**13**	**0**	**0**	**0**
1991-92	**Detroit Red Wings**	**NHL**	**27**	**3**	**1**	**4**	**3**	**1**	**4**	**20**	**0**	**1**	**0**	**26**	**11.5**	**20**	**0**	**19**	**3**	**+4**	**2**	**0**	**1**	**1**	**0**	**0**	**0**	**0**
	Adirondack Red Wings	AHL	19	1	6	7	....	....	....	33	....	....	....	....	....	....	....	....	....	....	18	7	4	11	22	....	....	....
1992-93	**Detroit Red Wings**	**NHL**	**6**	**0**	**0**	**0**	**0**	**0**	**0**	**2**	**0**	**0**	**0**	**5**	**0.0**	**3**	**0**	**4**	**0**	**–1**	....	....	....	....	....	....	....	....
	Adirondack Red Wings	AHL	64	7	36	43	....	....	....	54	....	....	....	....	....	....	....	....	....	....	11	3	8	11	8	....	....	....
1993-94	**Anaheim Mighty Ducks**	**NHL**	**77**	**9**	**11**	**20**	**8**	**8**	**16**	**55**	**1**	**0**	**1**	**121**	**7.4**	**74**	**10**	**74**	**30**	**+20**	....	....	....	....	....	....	....	....
	Canada	WC-A	8	0	1	1	....	....	....	4	....	....	....	....	....	....	....	....	....	....	....	....	....	....	....	....	....	....
1994-95	**Anaheim Mighty Ducks**	**NHL**	**45**	**7**	**13**	**20**	**12**	**19**	**31**	**12**	**3**	**1**	**1**	**70**	**10.0**	**53**	**15**	**64**	**23**	**–3**	....	....	....	....	....	....	....	....
1995-96	**Anaheim Mighty Ducks**	**NHL**	**82**	**8**	**22**	**30**	**8**	**18**	**26**	**64**	**0**	**1**	**1**	**117**	**6.8**	**87**	**17**	**102**	**41**	**+9**	....	....	....	....	....	....	....	....
1996-97	**Anaheim Mighty Ducks**	**NHL**	**79**	**4**	**14**	**18**	**4**	**12**	**16**	**55**	**1**	**0**	**1**	**96**	**4.2**	**88**	**8**	**100**	**37**	**+17**	**11**	**0**	**0**	**0**	**4**	**0**	**0**	**0**
1997-98	**Anaheim Mighty Ducks**	**NHL**	**22**	**0**	**1**	**1**	**0**	**1**	**1**	**27**	**0**	**0**	**0**	**11**	**0.0**	**7**	**1**	**25**	**7**	**–12**	....	....	....	....	....	....	....	....
	Edmonton Oilers	**NHL**	**30**	**2**	**5**	**7**	**2**	**5**	**7**	**22**	**0**	**0**	**0**	**27**	**7.4**	**25**	**7**	**16**	**4**	**+6**	**11**	**0**	**0**	**0**	**16**	**0**	**0**	**0**
	NHL Totals		**505**	**36**	**80**	**116**	**40**	**73**	**113**	**361**	**5**	**3**	**5**	**600**	**6.0**	**461**	**62**	**547**	**178**		**34**	**1**	**1**	**2**	**35**	**0**	**0**	**0**

QMJHL Second All-Star Team (1983) • WJC-A All-Star Team (1985) • Won Eddie Shore Plaque (AHL's Outstanding Defenseman) (1993) • AHL First All-Star Team (1993)

Traded to **Quebec** by **Winnipeg** for Stu Kulak, December 17, 1987. Signed as a free agent by **Detroit**, October 18, 1990. Claimed by **Anaheim** from **Detroit** in Expansion Draft, June 24, 1993. Traded to **Edmonton** by **Anaheim** for Drew Bannister, January 9, 1998. Traded to **Pittsburgh** by **Edmonton** with Tony Hrkac for Josef Beranek, June 11, 1998.

● DOME, ROBERT Robert Dome RW – L. 6', 214 lbs. b: Skalica, Czech., 1/29/1979. Pittsburgh's 1st choice, 17th overall, in 1997 Entry Draft.

			REGULAR SEASON																		PLAYOFFS							
Season	Club	League	GP	G	A	Pts	AG	AA	APts	PIM	PP	SH	GW	S	%	TGF	PGF	TGA	PGA	+/–	GP	G	A	Pts	PIM	PP	SH	GW
1995-96	Utah Grizzlies	IHL	56	10	9	19				28																		
1996-97	Long Beach Ice Dogs	IHL	13	4	6	10				14																		
	Las Vegas Thunder	IHL	43	10	7	17				22																		
1997-98	**Pittsburgh Penguins**	**NHL**	**30**	**5**	**2**	**7**	**6**	**2**	**8**	**12**	**1**	**0**	**0**	**29**	**17.2**	**8**	**1**	**8**	**0**	**–1**								
	Syracuse Crunch	AHL	36	21	25	46				77																		
	NHL Totals		**30**	**5**	**2**	**7**	**6**	**2**	**8**	**12**	**1**	**0**	**0**	**29**	**17.2**	**8**	**1**	**8**	**0**									

● DOMENICHELLI, HNAT Hnat Domenichelli C – L. 6', 175 lbs. b: Edmonton, Alta., 2/17/1976. Hartford's 2nd choice, 83rd overall, in 1994 Entry Draft.

			REGULAR SEASON																		PLAYOFFS							
Season	Club	League	GP	G	A	Pts	AG	AA	APts	PIM	PP	SH	GW	S	%	TGF	PGF	TGA	PGA	+/–	GP	G	A	Pts	PIM	PP	SH	GW
1992-93	Kamloops Blazers	WHL	45	12	8	20				15											11	1	1	2	2			
1993-94	Kamloops Blazers	WHL	69	27	40	67				31											19	10	12	22	0			
1994-95	Kamloops Blazers	WHL	72	52	62	114				34											19	9	9	18	9			
1995-96	Kamloops Blazers	WHL	62	59	89	148				37											16	7	9	16	29			
	Canada	WJC-A	6	2	3	5				6																		
1996-97	**Hartford Whalers**	**NHL**	**13**	**2**	**1**	**3**	**2**	**1**	**3**	**7**	**1**	**0**	**0**	**14**	**14.3**	**4**	**1**	**7**	**0**	**–4**								
	Springfield Falcons	AHL	39	24	24	48				12																		
	Calgary Flames	**NHL**	**10**	**1**	**2**	**3**	**1**	**2**	**3**	**2**	**1**	**0**	**0**	**16**	**6.3**	**4**	**1**	**2**	**0**	**+1**								
	Saint John Flames	AHL	1	1	1	2				0											5	5	0	5	2			
1997-98	**Calgary Flames**	**NHL**	**31**	**9**	**7**	**16**	**11**	**7**	**18**	**6**	**1**	**0**	**1**	**70**	**12.9**	**25**	**6**	**15**	**0**	**+4**								
	Saint John Flames	AHL	48	33	13	46				24											19	7	8	15	14			
	NHL Totals		**54**	**12**	**10**	**22**	**14**	**10**	**24**	**15**	**3**	**0**	**1**	**100**	**12.0**	**33**	**8**	**24**	**0**									

WHL West Second All-Star Team (1995) • WHL West First All-Star Team (1996) • Canadian Major Junior First All-Star Team (1996) • Canadian Major Junior Most Sportsmanlike Player of the Year (1996)

Traded to **Calgary** by **Hartford** with Glen Featherstone, New Jersey's 2nd round choice (previously acquired, Calgary selected Dimitri Kokorev) in 1997 Entry Draft and Vancouver's 3rd round choice (previously acquired, Calgary selected Paul Manning) in 1998 Entry Draft for Steve Chiasson and Colorado's 3rd round choice (previously acquired, Carolina selected Francis Lessard) in 1997 Entry Draft, March 5, 1997.

● DOMI, TIE Tie Domi RW – R. 5'10", 200 lbs. b: Windsor, Ont., 11/1/1969. Toronto's 2nd choice, 27th overall, in 1988 Entry Draft.

			REGULAR SEASON																		PLAYOFFS							
Season	Club	League	GP	G	A	Pts	AG	AA	APts	PIM	PP	SH	GW	S	%	TGF	PGF	TGA	PGA	+/–	GP	G	A	Pts	PIM	PP	SH	GW
1986-87	Peterborough Petes	OHL	18	1	1	2				79																		
1987-88	Peterborough Petes	OHL	60	22	21	43				292											12	3	9	12	24			
1988-89	Peterborough Petes	OHL	43	14	16	30				175											17	10	9	19	70			
1989-90	**Toronto Maple Leafs**	**NHL**	**2**	**0**	**0**	**0**	**0**	**0**	**0**	**42**	**0**	**0**	**0**	**0**	**0.0**	**0**	**0**	**0**	**0**	**0**								
	Newmarket Saints	AHL	57	14	11	25				285																		
1990-91	**New York Rangers**	**NHL**	**28**	**1**	**0**	**1**	**1**	**0**	**1**	**185**	**0**	**0**	**0**	**5**	**20.0**	**2**	**0**	**7**	**0**	**–5**								
	Binghamton Rangers	AHL	25	11	6	17				219											7	3	2	5	16			
1991-92	**New York Rangers**	**NHL**	**42**	**2**	**4**	**6**	**2**	**3**	**5**	**246**	**0**	**0**	**1**	**20**	**10.0**	**8**	**1**	**11**	**0**	**–4**	**6**	**1**	**1**	**2**	**32**	**0**	**0**	**0**
1992-93	**New York Rangers**	**NHL**	**12**	**2**		**2**	**2**	**0**	**2**	**95**	**0**	**0**	**0**	**11**	**18.2**	**3**	**0**	**4**	**0**	**–1**								
	Winnipeg Jets	**NHL**	**49**	**3**	**10**	**13**	**2**	**7**	**9**	**249**	**0**	**0**	**0**	**29**	**10.3**	**23**	**0**	**22**	**1**	**+2**	**6**	**1**	**0**	**1**	**23**	**0**	**0**	**0**
1993-94	**Winnipeg Jets**	**NHL**	**81**	**8**	**11**	**19**	**7**	**8**	**15**	***347**	**0**	**0**	**1**	**98**	**8.2**	**30**	**3**	**36**	**1**	**–8**								
1994-95	**Winnipeg Jets**	**NHL**	**31**	**4**	**4**	**8**	**7**	**6**	**13**	**128**	**0**	**0**	**0**	**34**	**11.8**	**11**	**0**	**17**	**0**	**–6**								
	Toronto Maple Leafs	**NHL**	**9**	**0**	**1**	**1**	**0**	**1**	**1**	**31**	**0**	**0**	**0**	**12**	**0.0**	**3**	**0**	**2**	**0**	**+1**	**7**	**1**	**0**	**1**	**0**	**0**	**0**	**0**
1995-96	**Toronto Maple Leafs**	**NHL**	**72**	**7**	**6**	**13**	**7**	**5**	**12**	**297**	**0**	**0**	**1**	**61**	**11.5**	**23**	**1**	**26**	**1**	**–3**	**6**	**0**	**2**	**2**	**4**	**0**	**0**	**0**
1996-97	**Toronto Maple Leafs**	**NHL**	**80**	**11**	**17**	**28**	**12**	**15**	**27**	**275**	**2**	**0**	**1**	**98**	**11.2**	**38**	**4**	**52**	**1**	**–17**								
1997-98	**Toronto Maple Leafs**	**NHL**	**80**	**4**	**10**	**14**	**5**	**10**	**15**	**365**	**0**	**0**	**0**	**72**	**5.6**	**24**	**1**	**28**	**0**	**–5**								
	NHL Totals		**486**	**42**	**63**	**105**	**45**	**55**	**100**	**2260**	**2**	**0**	**4**	**440**	**9.5**	**165**	**10**	**205**	**4**		**25**	**3**	**3**	**6**	**59**	**0**	**0**	**0**

Traded to **NY Rangers** by **Toronto** with Mark LaForest for Greg Johnston, June 28, 1990. Traded to **Winnipeg** by **NY Rangers** with Kris King for Ed Olczyk, December 28, 1992. Traded to **Toronto** by **Winnipeg** for Mike Eastwood and Toronto's 3rd round choice (Brad Isbister) in 1995 Entry Draft, April 7, 1995.

● DONALDSON, GARY Gary Donaldson RW – R. 5'9", 155 lbs. b: Trail, B.C., 7/15/1952. Chicago's 9th choice, 141st overall, in 1972 Amateur Draft.

			REGULAR SEASON																		PLAYOFFS							
Season	Club	League	GP	G	A	Pts	AG	AA	APts	PIM	PP	SH	GW	S	%	TGF	PGF	TGA	PGA	+/–	GP	G	A	Pts	PIM	PP	SH	GW
1970-71	Penticton Panthers	BCJHL	60	37	53	90				61																		
1971-72	Victoria Cougars	WCJHL	62	31	44	75				53																		
1972-73	Dallas Black Hawks	CHL	71	15	24	39				46											7	2	1	3	14			
1973-74	**Chicago Black Hawks**	**NHL**	**1**	**0**	**0**	**0**	**0**	**0**	**0**	**0**	**0**	**0**	**0**	**3**	**0.0**	**1**	**0**	**0**	**0**	**+1**								
	Dallas Black Hawks	CHL	71	21	21	42				66											10	3	3	6	24			
1974-75	Dallas Black Hawks	CHL	77	24	28	52				46											8	3	1	4	7			
1975-76	Dallas Black Hawks	CHL	68	33	39	72				26											6	2	0	2	0			
1976-77	Oklahoma City Blazers	CHL	74	23	34	57				37																		
	Houston Aeros	WHA	5	0	0	0				6																		
	NHL Totals		**1**	**0**	**0**	**0**	**0**	**0**	**0**	**0**	**0**	**0**	**0**	**3**	**0.0**	**1**	**0**	**0**	**0**									
	Other Major League Totals		5	0	0	0				6																		

Signed as a free agent by **Houston** (WHA), August, 1976.

● DONATELLI, CLARK Clark Donatelli LW – L. 5'10", 180 lbs. b: Providence, RI, 11/22/1967. NY Rangers' 4th choice, 98th overall, in 1984 Entry Draft.

			REGULAR SEASON																		PLAYOFFS							
Season	Club	League	GP	G	A	Pts	AG	AA	APts	PIM	PP	SH	GW	S	%	TGF	PGF	TGA	PGA	+/–	GP	G	A	Pts	PIM	PP	SH	GW
1983-84	Stratford Cullitons	OJHL	38	41	49	90				46																		
	United States	WJC-A	7	1	2	3				6																		
1984-85	Boston University	H.E.	40	17	18	35				46																		
	United States	WJC-A	7	2	3	5				12																		
	United States	WEC-A	10	3	1	4				14																		
1985-86	Boston University	H.E.	43	28	34	62				30																		
	United States	WEC-A	10	3	3	6				8																		
1986-87	Boston University	H.E.	37	15	23	38				46																		
	United States	WEC-A	9	1	2	3				6																		
1987-88	United States	Nat-Team	50	11	27	38				26																		
	United States	Olympics	6	2	1	3				6																		
1988-89			DID NOT PLAY																									
1989-90	**Minnesota North Stars**	**NHL**	**25**	**3**	**3**	**6**	**3**	**2**	**5**	**17**	**0**	**0**	**1**	**25**	**12.0**	**13**	**2**	**23**	**1**	**–11**								
	Kalamazoo Wings	IHL	27	8	9	17				47											4	0	2	2	12			
1990-91	San Diego Gulls	IHL	46	17	10	27				45																		
1991-92	United States	Nat-Team	42	13	25	38				50																		
	United States	Olympics	8	2	1	3				6																		
	Boston Bruins	**NHL**	**10**	**0**	**1**	**1**	**0**	**1**	**1**	**22**	**0**	**0**	**0**	**7**	**0.0**	**1**	**0**	**13**	**4**	**–8**	**2**	**0**	**0**	**0**	**0**	**0**	**0**	**0**
1992-93	Providence Bruins	AHL	57	12	14	26				40											4	2	1	3	2			
1993-94	San Diego Gulls	IHL	50	11	32	43				54											9	0	1	1	23			
1994-95	San Diego Gulls	IHL	70	22	25	47				48											5	0	1	1	6			
1995-96	Los Angeles Ice Dogs	IHL	22	1	3	4				12																		
	Detroit Vipers	IHL	36	0	12	12				40											11	0	2	2	2			
	NHL Totals		**35**	**3**	**4**	**7**	**3**	**3**	**6**	**39**	**0**	**0**	**1**	**32**	**9.4**	**14**	**2**	**36**	**5**		**2**	**0**	**0**	**0**	**0**	**0**	**0**	**0**

Hockey East Second All-Star Team (1986)

Traded to **Edmonton** by **NY Rangers** with Ville Kentala, Reijo Ruotsalainen, Jim Wiemer and future considerations (Stu Kulak, March 10, 1987) for Mike Golden, Don Jackson and Miroslav Horava, October 2, 1986. Signed as a free agent by **Minnesota**, June 20, 1989. Signed as a free agent by **Boston**, March 10, 1992.

● DONATO, TED Ted Donato LW – L. 5'10", 183 lbs. b: Boston, MA, 4/28/1969. Boston's 6th choice, 98th overall, in 1987 Entry Draft.

			REGULAR SEASON																		PLAYOFFS							
Season	Club	League	GP	G	A	Pts	AG	AA	APts	PIM	PP	SH	GW	S	%	TGF	PGF	TGA	PGA	+/–	GP	G	A	Pts	PIM	PP	SH	GW
1986-87	Catholic Memorial High School	H.S.	22	29	34	63				30																		
1987-88	Harvard University	ECAC	28	12	14	26				24																		
	United States	WJC-A	7	3	2	5				18																		
1988-89	Harvard University	ECAC	34	14	37	51				30																		
1989-90	Harvard University	ECAC	16	5	6	11				34																		
1990-91	Harvard University	ECAC	27	19	*37	56				26																		

Season	Club	League	GP	G	A	Pts	AG	AA	APts	PIM	PP	SH	GW	S	%	TGF	PGF	TGA	PGA	+/–	GP	G	A	Pts	PIM	PP	SH	GW
			REGULAR SEASON																		PLAYOFFS							
1991-92	United States	Nat-Team	52	11	22	33	....	....	....	24	....	....	....	....	....	....	....	....	....	....	....	....	....	....	....	....	....	....
	United States	Olympics	8	4	3	7	....	....	....	8	....	....	....	....	....	....	....	....	....	....	....	....	....	....	....	....	....	....
	Boston Bruins	**NHL**	**10**	**1**	**2**	**3**	**1**	**1**	**2**	**8**	**0**	**0**	**0**	**13**	**7.7**	**4**	**0**	**5**	**0**	**–1**	**15**	**3**	**4**	**7**	**4**	**0**	**0**	**1**
1992-93	**Boston Bruins**	**NHL**	**82**	**15**	**20**	**35**	**12**	**14**	**26**	**61**	**3**	**2**	**5**	**118**	**12.7**	**65**	**27**	**60**	**24**	**+2**	**4**	**0**	**1**	**1**	....	**0**	**0**	**0**
1993-94	**Boston Bruins**	**NHL**	**84**	**22**	**32**	**54**	**21**	**25**	**46**	**59**	**9**	**2**	**1**	**158**	**13.9**	**76**	**22**	**72**	**18**	**0**	**13**	**4**	**2**	**6**	**10**	**2**	**0**	**1**
1994-95	TuTo	Finland	14	5	5	10	....	....	....	47	....	....	....	....	....	....	....	....	....	....	....	....	....	....	....	....	....	....
	Boston Bruins	**NHL**	**47**	**10**	**10**	**20**	**18**	**15**	**33**	**10**	**1**	**0**	**1**	**71**	**14.1**	**33**	**8**	**30**	**8**	**+3**	**5**	**0**	**0**	**0**	**4**	**0**	**0**	**0**
1995-96	**Boston Bruins**	**NHL**	**82**	**23**	**26**	**49**	**23**	**21**	**44**	**46**	**7**	**0**	**1**	**152**	**15.1**	**75**	**30**	**60**	**21**	**+6**	**5**	**1**	**2**	**3**	**2**	**1**	**0**	**0**
1996-97	**Boston Bruins**	**NHL**	**67**	**25**	**26**	**51**	**27**	**23**	**50**	**37**	**6**	**2**	**2**	**172**	**14.5**	**76**	**22**	**82**	**19**	**–9**	....	....	....	....	....	....	....	....
	United States	WC-A	8	4	2	6	....	....	....	8	....	....	....	....	....	....	....	....	....	....	....	....	....	....	....	....	....	....
1997-98	**Boston Bruins**	**NHL**	**79**	**16**	**23**	**39**	**19**	**22**	**41**	**54**	**3**	**0**	**5**	**129**	**12.4**	**64**	**20**	**41**	**3**	**+6**	**5**	**0**	**0**	**0**	**2**	**0**	**0**	**0**
	NHL Totals		**451**	**112**	**139**	**251**	**121**	**121**	**242**	**275**	**29**	**6**	**15**	**813**	**13.8**	**393**	**129**	**350**	**93**		**47**	**8**	**9**	**17**	**22**	**3**	**0**	**2**

NCAA Championship All-Tournament Team (1989) • NCAA Championship Tournament MVP (1989) • ECAC First All-Star Team (1991)

• DONNELLY, DAVE

Dave Donnelly C – L. 5'11", 185 lbs. b: Edmonton, Alta., 2/2/1962. Minnesota's 2nd choice, 27th overall, in 1981 Entry Draft.

Season	Club	League	GP	G	A	Pts	AG	AA	APts	PIM	PP	SH	GW	S	%	TGF	PGF	TGA	PGA	+/–	GP	G	A	Pts	PIM	PP	SH	GW
1979-80	St. Albert Saints	AJHL	59	27	33	60	....	....	....	146	....	....	....	....	....	....	....	....	....	....	....	....	....	....	....	....	....	....
1980-81	St. Albert Saints	AJHL	53	39	55	94	....	....	....	243	....	....	....	....	....	....	....	....	....	....	....	19	15	34	....	....	....	....
1981-82	University of North Dakota	WCHA	38	10	15	25	....	....	....	38	....	....	....	....	....	....	....	....	....	....	....	....	....	....	....	....	....	....
1982-83	University of North Dakota	WCHA	34	18	16	34	....	....	....	106	....	....	....	....	....	....	....	....	....	....	....	....	....	....	....	....	....	....
1983-84	Canada	Nat-Team	64	17	13	30	....	....	....	52	....	....	....	....	....	....	....	....	....	....	....	....	....	....	....	....	....	....
	Canada	Olympics	7	1	1	2	....	....	....	12	....	....	....	....	....	....	....	....	....	....	....	....	....	....	....	....	....	....
	Boston Bruins	**NHL**	**16**	**3**	**4**	**7**	**2**	**3**	**5**	**2**	**0**	**0**	**0**	**22**	**13.6**	**15**	**0**	**2**	**0**	**+13**	**3**	**0**	**0**	**0**	**0**	**0**	**0**	**0**
1984-85	**Boston Bruins**	**NHL**	**38**	**6**	**8**	**14**	**5**	**5**	**10**	**46**	**0**	**1**	**1**	**33**	**18.2**	**18**	**0**	**27**	**8**	**–1**	**1**	**0**	**0**	**0**	**0**	**0**	**0**	**0**
	Hershey Bears	AHL	26	11	6	17	....	....	....	28	....	....	....	....	....	....	....	....	....	....	....	....	....	....	....	....	....	....
1985-86	**Boston Bruins**	**NHL**	**8**	**0**	**0**	**0**	**0**	**0**	**0**	**17**	**0**	**0**	**0**	**8**	**0.0**	**5**	**0**	**5**	**3**	**+3**	....	....	....	....	....	....	....	....
1986-87	**Chicago Blackhawks**	**NHL**	**71**	**6**	**12**	**18**	**5**	**9**	**14**	**81**	**0**	**0**	**0**	**64**	**9.4**	**30**	**0**	**59**	**22**	**–7**	**1**	**0**	**0**	**0**	**0**	**0**	**0**	**0**
1987-88	**Edmonton Oilers**	**NHL**	**4**	**0**	**0**	**0**	**0**	**0**	**0**	**4**	**0**	**0**	**0**	**3**	**0.0**	**0**	**0**	**0**	**0**	**0**	....	....	....	....	....	....	....	....
1988-89	KalPa Kuopio	Finland	43	20	22	42	....	....	....	*98	....	....	....	....	....	....	....	....	....	....	....	....	....	....	....	....	....	....
1989-90	EV Landshut	Germany	33	12	21	33	....	....	....	87	....	....	....	....	....	....	....	....	....	....	....	....	....	....	....	....	....	....
1990-91	Maine Mariners	AHL	67	21	30	51	....	....	....	135	....	....	....	....	....	....	....	....	....	....	2	1	2	3	10	....	....	....
	NHL Totals		**137**	**15**	**24**	**39**	**12**	**17**	**29**	**150**	**0**	**1**	**1**	**130**	**11.5**	**68**	**0**	**93**	**33**		**5**	**0**	**0**	**0**	**0**	**0**	**0**	**0**

Rights traded to **Boston** by **Minnesota** with Brad Palmer for Boston agreeing not to select Brian Bellows in 1982 Entry Draft, June 9, 1982. Traded to **Detroit** by **Boston** for Dwight Foster, March 11, 1986. Signed as a free agent by **Chicago**, September, 1986. Traded to **Edmonton** by **Chicago** for future considerations, October 19, 1987.

• DONNELLY, GORD

Gord Donnelly D – R. 6'1", 202 lbs. b: Montreal, Que., 4/5/1962. St. Louis' 3rd choice, 62nd overall, in 1981 Entry Draft.

Season	Club	League	GP	G	A	Pts	AG	AA	APts	PIM	PP	SH	GW	S	%	TGF	PGF	TGA	PGA	+/–	GP	G	A	Pts	PIM	PP	SH	GW
1980-81	Sherbrooke Castors	QMJHL	67	15	23	38	....	....	....	252	....	....	....	....	....	....	....	....	....	....	14	1	2	3	35	....	....	....
1981-82	Sherbrooke Castors	QMJHL	60	8	41	49	....	....	....	250	....	....	....	....	....	....	....	....	....	....	22	2	7	9	106	....	....	....
1982-83	Salt Lake Golden Eagles	CHL	67	3	12	15	....	....	....	222	....	....	....	....	....	....	....	....	....	....	6	1	1	2	8	....	....	....
1983-84	**Quebec Nordiques**	**NHL**	**38**	**0**	**5**	**5**	**0**	**3**	**3**	**60**	**0**	**0**	**0**	**14**	**0.0**	**17**	**1**	**19**	**2**	**–1**	....	....	....	....	....	....	....	....
	Fredericton Express	AHL	30	2	3	5	....	....	....	146	....	....	....	....	....	....	....	....	....	....	7	1	1	2	43	....	....	....
1984-85	**Quebec Nordiques**	**NHL**	**22**	**0**	**0**	**0**	**0**	**0**	**0**	**33**	**0**	**0**	**0**	**9**	**0.0**	**4**	**0**	**3**	**0**	**+1**	....	....	....	....	....	....	....	....
	Fredericton Express	AHL	42	1	5	6	....	....	....	134	....	....	....	....	....	....	....	....	....	....	6	0	1	1	25	....	....	....
1985-86	**Quebec Nordiques**	**NHL**	**36**	**2**	**2**	**4**	**2**	**1**	**3**	**85**	**0**	**0**	**0**	**30**	**6.7**	**11**	**0**	**13**	**2**	**0**	**1**	**0**	**0**	**0**	**0**	**0**	**0**	**0**
	Fredericton Express	AHL	38	3	5	8	....	....	....	103	....	....	....	....	....	....	....	....	....	....	5	0	0	0	33	....	....	....
1986-87	**Quebec Nordiques**	**NHL**	**38**	**0**	**2**	**2**	**0**	**1**	**1**	**143**	**0**	**0**	**0**	**14**	**0.0**	**6**	**0**	**9**	**0**	**–3**	**13**	**0**	**0**	**0**	**53**	**0**	**0**	**0**
1987-88	**Quebec Nordiques**	**NHL**	**63**	**4**	**3**	**7**	**3**	**2**	**5**	**301**	**1**	**0**	**0**	**46**	**8.7**	**10**	**2**	**24**	**0**	**–16**	....	....	....	....	....	....	....	....
1988-89	**Quebec Nordiques**	**NHL**	**16**	**4**	**0**	**4**	**3**	**0**	**3**	**46**	**1**	**0**	**0**	**14**	**28.6**	**5**	**1**	**12**	**0**	**–8**	....	....	....	....	....	....	....	....
	Winnipeg Jets	**NHL**	**57**	**6**	**10**	**16**	**5**	**7**	**12**	**228**	**0**	**0**	**0**	**53**	**11.3**	**25**	**1**	**36**	**0**	**–12**	....	....	....	....	....	....	....	....
1989-90	**Winnipeg Jets**	**NHL**	**55**	**3**	**3**	**6**	**3**	**2**	**5**	**222**	**0**	**0**	**0**	**43**	**7.0**	**17**	**0**	**15**	**1**	**+3**	**6**	**0**	**1**	**1**	**8**	**0**	**0**	**0**
1990-91	**Winnipeg Jets**	**NHL**	**57**	**3**	**4**	**7**	**3**	**3**	**6**	**265**	**0**	**0**	**0**	**35**	**8.6**	**25**	**0**	**40**	**2**	**–13**	....	....	....	....	....	....	....	....
1991-92	**Winnipeg Jets**	**NHL**	**4**	**0**	**0**	**0**	**0**	**0**	**0**	**11**	**0**	**0**	**0**	**5**	**0.0**	**1**	**0**	**6**	**0**	**–5**	....	....	....	....	....	....	....	....
	Buffalo Sabres	**NHL**	**67**	**2**	**3**	**5**	**2**	**2**	**4**	**305**	**0**	**0**	**1**	**25**	**8.0**	**10**	**0**	**17**	**0**	**–7**	**6**	**0**	**1**	**1**	**0**	**0**	**0**	**0**
1992-93	**Buffalo Sabres**	**NHL**	**60**	**3**	**8**	**11**	**2**	**5**	**7**	**221**	**0**	**0**	**0**	**38**	**7.9**	**22**	**0**	**17**	**0**	**+5**	....	....	....	....	....	....	....	....
1993-94	**Buffalo Sabres**	**NHL**	**7**	**0**	**0**	**0**	**0**	**0**	**0**	**31**	**0**	**0**	**0**	**2**	**0.0**	**3**	**0**	**3**	**1**	**+1**	....	....	....	....	....	....	....	....
	Dallas Stars	**NHL**	**18**	**0**	**1**	**1**	**0**	**1**	**1**	**66**	**0**	**0**	**0**	**5**	**0.0**	**2**	**0**	**6**	**0**	**–4**	....	....	....	....	....	....	....	....
1994-95	Kalamazoo Wings	IHL	7	2	2	4	....	....	....	18	....	....	....	....	....	....	....	....	....	....	....	....	....	....	....	....	....	....
	Dallas Stars	**NHL**	**16**	**1**	**0**	**1**	**2**	**0**	**2**	**52**	**0**	**0**	**0**	**9**	**11.1**	**4**	**0**	**3**	**0**	**+1**	....	....	....	....	....	....	....	....
1995-96	Houston Aeros	IHL	73	3	4	7	....	....	....	333	....	....	....	....	....	....	....	....	....	....	....	....	....	....	....	....	....	....
1996-97	Houston Aeros	IHL	5	0	0	0	....	....	....	25	....	....	....	....	....	....	....	....	....	....	....	....	....	....	....	....	....	....
	Chicago Wolves	IHL	59	3	5	8	....	....	....	144	....	....	....	....	....	....	....	....	....	....	4	0	2	2	28	....	....	....
	NHL Totals		**554**	**28**	**41**	**69**	**25**	**27**	**52**	**2069**	**2**	**0**	**1**	**342**	**8.2**	**162**	**5**	**223**	**8**		**26**	**0**	**2**	**2**	**61**	**0**	**0**	**0**

Rights transferred to **Quebec** by **St. Louis** with rights to Claude Julien as compensation for St. Louis' signing Jacques Demers as coach, August 19, 1983. Traded to **Winnipeg** by **Quebec** for Mario Marois, December 6, 1988. Traded to **Buffalo** by **Winnipeg** with Dave McLlwain, Winnipeg's 5th round choice (Yuri Khmylev) in 1992 Entry Draft and future considerations for Darrin Shannon, Mike Hartman and Dean Kennedy, October 11, 1991. Traded to **Dallas** by **Buffalo** for James Black and Dallas' 7th round choice (Steve Webb) in 1994 Entry Draft, December 15, 1993.

• DONNELLY, MIKE

Mike Donnelly LW – L. 5'11", 185 lbs. b: Detroit, MI, 10/10/1963.

Season	Club	League	GP	G	A	Pts	AG	AA	APts	PIM	PP	SH	GW	S	%	TGF	PGF	TGA	PGA	+/–	GP	G	A	Pts	PIM	PP	SH	GW
1982-83	Michigan State Spartans	CCHA	24	7	13	20	....	....	....	8	....	....	....	....	....	....	....	....	....	....	....	....	....	....	....	....	....	....
1983-84	Michigan State Spartans	CCHA	44	18	14	32	....	....	....	40	....	....	....	....	....	....	....	....	....	....	....	....	....	....	....	....	....	....
1984-85	Michigan State Spartans	CCHA	44	26	21	47	....	....	....	48	....	....	....	....	....	....	....	....	....	....	....	....	....	....	....	....	....	....
1985-86	Michigan State Spartans	CCHA	44	*59	38	97	....	....	....	65	....	....	....	....	....	....	....	....	....	....	....	....	....	....	....	....	....	....
1986-87	**New York Rangers**	**NHL**	**5**	**1**	**1**	**2**	**1**	**1**	**2**	**0**	**0**	**0**	**0**	**5**	**20.0**	**3**	**1**	**2**	**0**	**0**	....	....	....	....	....	....	....	....
	New Haven Nighthawks	AHL	58	27	34	61	....	....	....	52	....	....	....	....	....	....	....	....	....	....	7	2	0	2	9	....	....	....
1987-88	**New York Rangers**	**NHL**	**17**	**2**	**2**	**4**	**2**	**1**	**3**	**8**	**0**	**0**	**0**	**30**	**6.7**	**5**	**0**	**11**	**1**	**–5**	....	....	....	....	....	....	....	....
	Colorado Rangers	IHL	8	7	11	18	....	....	....	15	....	....	....	....	....	....	....	....	....	....	....	....	....	....	....	....	....	....
	Buffalo Sabres	**NHL**	**40**	**6**	**8**	**14**	**5**	**6**	**11**	**44**	**0**	**0**	**0**	**69**	**8.7**	**24**	**4**	**25**	**4**	**–1**	....	....	....	....	....	....	....	....
1988-89	**Buffalo Sabres**	**NHL**	**22**	**4**	**6**	**10**	**3**	**4**	**7**	**10**	**0**	**0**	**0**	**25**	**16.0**	**14**	**3**	**13**	**1**	**–1**	....	....	....	....	....	....	....	....
	Rochester Americans	AHL	53	32	37	69	....	....	....	53	....	....	....	....	....	....	....	....	....	....	....	....	....	....	....	....	....	....
1989-90	**Buffalo Sabres**	**NHL**	**12**	**1**	**2**	**3**	**1**	**1**	**2**	**8**	**0**	**0**	**0**	**20**	**5.0**	**5**	**0**	**10**	**1**	**–4**	....	....	....	....	....	....	....	....
	Rochester Americans	AHL	68	43	55	98	....	....	....	71	....	....	....	....	....	....	....	....	....	....	16	*12	7	19	9	....	....	....
1990-91	**Los Angeles Kings**	**NHL**	**53**	**7**	**5**	**12**	**6**	**4**	**10**	**41**	**0**	**0**	**2**	**76**	**9.2**	**22**	**0**	**29**	**10**	**+3**	**12**	**5**	**4**	**9**	**6**	**0**	**0**	**0**
	New Haven Nighthawks	AHL	18	10	6	16	....	....	....	2	....	....	....	....	....	....	....	....	....	....	....	....	....	....	....	....	....	....
1991-92	**Los Angeles Kings**	**NHL**	**80**	**29**	**16**	**45**	**26**	**12**	**38**	**20**	**0**	**1**	**4**	**197**	**14.7**	**54**	**1**	**74**	**26**	**+5**	**6**	**1**	**0**	**1**	**4**	**0**	**0**	**0**
1992-93	**Los Angeles Kings**	**NHL**	**84**	**29**	**40**	**69**	**24**	**27**	**51**	**45**	**8**	**1**	**2**	**244**	**11.9**	**102**	**33**	**83**	**31**	**+17**	**24**	**6**	**7**	**13**	**14**	**0**	**0**	**0**
1993-94	**Los Angeles Kings**	**NHL**	**81**	**21**	**21**	**42**	**20**	**16**	**36**	**34**	**4**	**2**	**3**	**177**	**11.9**	**62**	**15**	**59**	**14**	**+2**	....	....	....	....	....	....	....	....
1994-95	**Los Angeles Kings**	**NHL**	**9**	**1**	**1**	**2**	**2**	**1**	**3**	**4**	**0**	**0**	**0**	**22**	**4.5**	**3**	**2**	**9**	**1**	**–7**	....	....	....	....	....	....	....	....
	Dallas Stars	**NHL**	**35**	**11**	**14**	**25**	**19**	**21**	**40**	**29**	**3**	**0**	**3**	**94**	**11.7**	**30**	**8**	**23**	**4**	**+3**	**5**	**0**	**1**	**1**	**6**	**0**	**0**	**0**
1995-96	**Dallas Stars**	**NHL**	**24**	**2**	**5**	**7**	**2**	**4**	**6**	**10**	**0**	**0**	**0**	**21**	**9.5**	**9**	**2**	**9**	**0**	**–2**	....	....	....	....	....	....	....	....
	Michigan K-Wings	IHL	21	8	15	23	....	....	....	20	....	....	....	....	....	....	....	....	....	....	8	3	0	3	10	....	....	....
1996-97	**New York Islanders**	**NHL**	**3**	**0**	**0**	**0**	**0**	**0**	**0**	**2**	**0**	**0**	**0**	**5**	**0.0**	**0**	**0**	**0**	**0**	**0**	....	....	....	....	....	....	....	....
	Utah Grizzlies	IHL	14	7	2	9	....	....	....	33	....	....	....	....	....	....	....	....	....	....	....	....	....	....	....	....	....	....
	Detroit Vipers	IHL	19	4	4	8	....	....	....	12	....	....	....	....	....	....	....	....	....	....	....	....	....	....	....	....	....	....
1997-98	Detroit Vipers	IHL	6	0	2	2	....	....	....	2	....	....	....	....	....	....	....	....	....	....	....	....	....	....	....	....	....	....
	NHL Totals		**465**	**114**	**121**	**235**	**111**	**98**	**209**	**255**	**15**	**4**	**14**	**985**	**11.6**	**333**	**69**	**347**	**93**		**47**	**12**	**12**	**24**	**30**	**0**	**0**	**0**

CCHA First All-Star Team (1986) • NCAA West First All-American Team (1986) • NCAA Championship All-Tournament Team (1986) • NCAA Chamionship Tournament MVP (1986)

Signed as a free agent by **NY Rangers**, August 15, 1986. Traded to **Buffalo** by **NY Rangers** with Rangers' 5th round choice (Alexander Mogilny) in 1988 Entry Draft for Paul Cyr and Buffalo's 10th round choice (Eric Fenton) in 1988 Entry Draft, December 31, 1987. Traded to **LA Kings** by **Buffalo** for Mikko Makela, September 30, 1990. Traded to **Dallas** by **LA Kings** with LA Kings' 7th round choice (Eoin McInerney) in 1996 Entry Draft for Dallas' 4th round choice (later traded to Washington — Washington selected Justin Davis) in 1996 Entry Draft, February 17, 1995. Signed as a free agent by **NY Islanders**, August 19, 1996.

			REGULAR SEASON																		PLAYOFFS							
Season	Club	League	GP	G	A	Pts	AG	AA	APts	PIM	PP	SH	GW	S	%	TGF	PGF	TGA	PGA	+/–	GP	G	A	Pts	PIM	PP	SH	GW

● DONOVAN, SHEAN Shean Donovan RW – R. 6'2", 200 lbs. b: Timmins, Ont., 1/22/1975. San Jose's 2nd choice, 28th overall, in 1993 Entry Draft.

Season	Club	League	GP	G	A	Pts	AG	AA	APts	PIM	PP	SH	GW	S	%	TGF	PGF	TGA	PGA	+/–	GP	G	A	Pts	PIM	PP	SH	GW
1991-92	Ottawa 67's	OHL	58	11	8	19	....	....	....	14	....	....	....	....	....	....	....	....	....	....	11	1	0	1	5	....	....	....
1992-93	Ottawa 67's	OHL	66	29	23	52	....	....	....	33	....	....	....	....	....	....	....	....	....	....	....	....	....	....	....	....	....	....
1993-94	Ottawa 67's	OHL	62	35	49	84	....	....	....	63	....	....	....	....	....	....	....	....	....	....	17	10	11	21	14	....	....	....
1994-95	Ottawa 67's	OHL	29	22	19	41	....	....	....	41	....	....	....	....	....	....	....	....	....	....	....	....	....	....	....	....	....	....
	Canada	WJC-A	7	0	0	0	....	....	....	6	....	....	....	....	....	....	....	....	....	....	....	....	....	....	....	....	....	....
	San Jose Sharks	**NHL**	**14**	**0**	**0**	**0**	**0**	**0**	**0**	**6**	**0**	**0**	**0**	**13**	**0.0**	**2**	**0**	**11**	**3**	**–6**	**7**	**0**	**1**	**1**	**6**	**0**	**0**	**0**
	Kansas City Blades	IHL	5	0	2	2	....	....	....	7	....	....	....	....	....	....	....	....	....	....	14	5	3	8	23	....	....	....
1995-96	**San Jose Sharks**	**NHL**	**74**	**13**	**8**	**21**	**13**	**7**	**20**	**39**	**0**	**1**	**2**	**73**	**17.8**	**31**	**2**	**62**	**16**	**–17**	....	....	....	....	....	....	....	....
	Kansas City Blades	IHL	4	0	0	0	....	....	....	8	....	....	....	....	....	....	....	....	....	....	5	0	0	0	8	....	....	....
1996-97	**San Jose Sharks**	**NHL**	**73**	**9**	**6**	**15**	**10**	**5**	**15**	**42**	**0**	**1**	**0**	**115**	**7.8**	**24**	**0**	**56**	**14**	**–18**	....	....	....	....	....	....	....	....
	Kentucky Thoroughblades	AHL	3	1	3	4	....	....	....	18	....	....	....	....	....	....	....	....	....	....	....	....	....	....	....	....	....	....
	Canada	WC-A	10	0	1	1	....	....	....	31	....	....	....	....	....	....	....	....	....	....	....	....	....	....	....	....	....	....
1997-98	**San Jose Sharks**	**NHL**	**20**	**3**	**3**	**6**	**4**	**3**	**7**	**22**	**0**	**0**	**0**	**24**	**12.5**	**10**	**0**	**8**	**1**	**+3**	....	....	....	....	....	....	....	....
	Colorado Avalanche	**NHL**	**47**	**5**	**7**	**12**	**6**	**7**	**13**	**48**	**0**	**0**	**0**	**57**	**8.8**	**16**	**0**	**13**	**0**	**+3**	....	....	....	....	....	....	....	....
	NHL Totals		**228**	**30**	**24**	**54**	**33**	**22**	**55**	**157**	**0**	**2**	**2**	**282**	**10.6**	**83**	**2**	**150**	**34**		**7**	**0**	**1**	**1**	**6**	**0**	**0**	**0**

Traded to **Colorado** by **San Jose** with San Jose's 1st round choice (Alex Tanguay) in 1998 Entry Draft for Mike Ricci and Colorado's 2nd round choice (later traded to Buffalo — Buffalo selected Jaroslav Kristek), in 1998 Entry Draft, November 21, 1997.

● DORE, ANDRE Andre "Trap" Dore D – R. 6'2", 200 lbs. b: Montreal, Que., 2/11/1958. NY Rangers' 5th choice, 60th overall, in 1978 Amateur Draft.

Season	Club	League	GP	G	A	Pts	AG	AA	APts	PIM	PP	SH	GW	S	%	TGF	PGF	TGA	PGA	+/–	GP	G	A	Pts	PIM	PP	SH	GW
1975-76	Hull Festivals	QMJHL	59	4	11	15	....	....	....	67	....	....	....	....	....	....	....	....	....	....	....	....	....	....	....	....	....	....
1976-77	Hull Olympiques	QMJHL	72	9	42	51	....	....	....	178	....	....	....	....	....	....	....	....	....	....	3	0	3	3	29	....	....	....
1977-78	Hull Olympiques	QMJHL	15	3	9	12	....	....	....	22	....	....	....	....	....	....	....	....	....	....	....	....	....	....	....	....	....	....
	Trois-Rivieres Draveurs	QMJHL	27	2	14	16	....	....	....	61	....	....	....	....	....	....	....	....	....	....	....	....	....	....	....	....	....	....
	Quebec Remparts	QMJHL	32	6	17	23	....	....	....	51	....	....	....	....	....	....	....	....	....	....	4	0	0	0	2	....	....	....
1978-79	**New York Rangers**	**NHL**	**2**	**0**	**0**	**0**	**0**	**0**	**0**	**0**	**0**	**0**	**0**	**0**	**0.0**	**1**	**0**	**1**	**0**	**0**	....	....	....	....	....	....	....	....
	New Haven Nighthawks	AHL	71	6	23	29	....	....	....	134	....	....	....	....	....	....	....	....	....	....	10	0	3	3	12	....	....	....
1979-80	**New York Rangers**	**NHL**	**2**	**0**	**0**	**0**	**0**	**0**	**0**	**0**	**0**	**0**	**0**	**0**	**0.0**	**0**	**0**	**1**	**0**	**–1**	....	....	....	....	....	....	....	....
	New Haven Nighthawks	AHL	63	9	21	30	....	....	....	99	....	....	....	....	....	....	....	....	....	....	9	1	1	2	20	....	....	....
1980-81	**New York Rangers**	**NHL**	**15**	**1**	**3**	**4**	**1**	**2**	**3**	**15**	**0**	**0**	**0**	**15**	**6.7**	**9**	**0**	**12**	**2**	**–1**	....	....	....	....	....	....	....	....
	New Haven Nighthawks	AHL	58	8	41	49	....	....	....	105	....	....	....	....	....	....	....	....	....	....	....	....	....	....	....	....	....	....
1981-82	**New York Rangers**	**NHL**	**56**	**4**	**16**	**20**	**3**	**11**	**14**	**64**	**0**	**0**	**0**	**40**	**10.0**	**56**	**1**	**57**	**12**	**+10**	**10**	**1**	**1**	**2**	**16**	**0**	**0**	**0**
	Springfield Indians	AHL	23	3	8	11	....	....	....	20	....	....	....	....	....	....	....	....	....	....	....	....	....	....	....	....	....	....
1982-83	**New York Rangers**	**NHL**	**39**	**3**	**12**	**15**	**2**	**8**	**10**	**39**	**0**	**0**	**1**	**33**	**9.1**	**49**	**1**	**39**	**8**	**+17**	....	....	....	....	....	....	....	....
	St. Louis Blues	**NHL**	**38**	**2**	**15**	**17**	**2**	**10**	**12**	**25**	**0**	**0**	**0**	**41**	**4.9**	**53**	**2**	**53**	**11**	**+9**	**4**	**0**	**1**	**1**	**8**	**0**	**0**	**0**
1983-84	**St. Louis Blues**	**NHL**	**55**	**3**	**12**	**15**	**2**	**8**	**10**	**58**	**0**	**0**	**1**	**51**	**5.9**	**54**	**4**	**73**	**26**	**+3**	....	....	....	....	....	....	....	....
	Quebec Nordiques	**NHL**	**25**	**1**	**16**	**17**	**1**	**11**	**12**	**25**	**0**	**0**	**0**	**30**	**3.3**	**32**	**3**	**34**	**6**	**+1**	**9**	**0**	**0**	**0**	**8**	**0**	**0**	**0**
1984-85	**New York Rangers**	**NHL**	**25**	**0**	**7**	**7**	**0**	**5**	**5**	**35**	**0**	**0**	**0**	**14**	**0.0**	**24**	**2**	**27**	**3**	**–2**	....	....	....	....	....	....	....	....
	New Haven Nighthawks	AHL	39	3	22	25	....	....	....	48	....	....	....	....	....	....	....	....	....	....	....	....	....	....	....	....	....	....
1985-86	Hershey Bears	AHL	65	10	18	28	....	....	....	128	....	....	....	....	....	....	....	....	....	....	18	0	6	6	36	....	....	....
	NHL Totals		**257**	**14**	**81**	**95**	**11**	**55**	**66**	**261**	**0**	**0**	**2**	**224**	**6.3**	**278**	**13**	**297**	**68**		**23**	**1**	**2**	**3**	**32**	**0**	**0**	**0**

Traded to **St. Louis** by **NY Rangers** for Vaclav Nedomansky and Glen Hanlon, January 4, 1983. Traded to **Quebec** by **St. Louis** for Dave Pichette, February 10, 1984. Claimed by **NY Rangers** from **Quebec** in Waiver Draft, October 9, 1984.

● DORE, DANIEL Daniel Dore RW – R. 6'3", 202 lbs. b: Ferme-Neuve, Que., 4/9/1970. Quebec's 2nd choice, 5th overall, in 1988 Entry Draft.

Season	Club	League	GP	G	A	Pts	AG	AA	APts	PIM	PP	SH	GW	S	%	TGF	PGF	TGA	PGA	+/–	GP	G	A	Pts	PIM	PP	SH	GW
1986-87	Drummondville Voltigeurs	QMJHL	68	23	41	64	....	....	....	229	....	....	....	....	....	....	....	....	....	....	8	0	1	1	18	....	....	....
1987-88	Drummondville Voltigeurs	QMJHL	64	24	39	63	....	....	....	218	....	....	....	....	....	....	....	....	....	....	17	7	11	18	42	....	....	....
1988-89	Drummondville Voltigeurs	QMJHL	62	33	58	91	....	....	....	236	....	....	....	....	....	....	....	....	....	....	4	2	3	5	14	....	....	....
1989-90	Chicoutimi Sagueneens	QMJHL	24	6	23	29	....	....	....	112	....	....	....	....	....	....	....	....	....	....	6	0	3	3	27	....	....	....
	Quebec Nordiques	**NHL**	**16**	**2**	**3**	**5**	**2**	**2**	**4**	**59**	**1**	**0**	**0**	**5**	**40.0**	**7**	**4**	**11**	**0**	**–8**	....	....	....	....	....	....	....	....
1990-91	**Quebec Nordiques**	**NHL**	**1**	**0**	**0**	**0**	**0**	**0**	**0**	**0**	**0**	**0**	**0**	**0**	**0.0**	**1**	**0**	**0**	**0**	**+1**	....	....	....	....	....	....	....	....
	Halifax Citadels	AHL	50	7	10	17	....	....	....	139	....	....	....	....	....	....	....	....	....	....	....	....	....	....	....	....	....	....
1991-92	Halifax Citadels	AHL	29	4	1	5	....	....	....	45	....	....	....	....	....	....	....	....	....	....	....	....	....	....	....	....	....	....
	Greensboro Monarchs	ECHL	6	1	0	1	....	....	....	34	....	....	....	....	....	....	....	....	....	....	....	....	....	....	....	....	....	....
1992-93	Hershey Bears	AHL	65	12	10	22	....	....	....	192	....	....	....	....	....	....	....	....	....	....	....	....	....	....	....	....	....	....
1993-94	Chatham Wheels	ColHL	4	1	2	3	....	....	....	13	....	....	....	....	....	....	....	....	....	....	....	....	....	....	....	....	....	....
	NHL Totals		**17**	**2**	**3**	**5**	**2**	**2**	**4**	**59**	**1**	**0**	**0**	**5**	**40.0**	**8**	**4**	**11**	**0**		....	....	....	....	....	....	....	....

Signed as a free agent by **Philadelphia**, December 14, 1992.

● DOREY, JIM Jim Dorey D – L. 6'1", 190 lbs. b: Kingston, Ont., 8/17/1947. Toronto's 4th choice, 23rd overall, in 1964 Amateur Draft.

Season	Club	League	GP	G	A	Pts	AG	AA	APts	PIM	PP	SH	GW	S	%	TGF	PGF	TGA	PGA	+/–	GP	G	A	Pts	PIM	PP	SH	GW
1963-64	Niagara Falls Flyers	OHA	21	1	0	1	....	....	....	4	....	....	....	....	....	....	....	....	....	....	....	....	....	....	....	....	....	....
1964-65	Niagara Falls Flyers	OHA	DID NOT PLAY – INJURED																									
1965-66	London Nationals	OHA	47	5	20	25	....	....	....	168	....	....	....	....	....	....	....	....	....	....	....	....	....	....	....	....	....	....
1966-67	London Nationals	OHA	48	8	41	49	....	....	....	*196	....	....	....	....	....	....	....	....	....	....	6	2	7	9	24	....	....	....
1967-68	Rochester Americans	AHL	20	0	3	3	....	....	....	16	....	....	....	....	....	....	....	....	....	....	....	....	....	....	....	....	....	....
	Phoenix Roadrunners	WHL	4	0	0	0	....	....	....	2	....	....	....	....	....	....	....	....	....	....	....	....	....	....	....	....	....	....
	Tulsa Oilers	CHL	35	4	24	28	....	....	....	81	....	....	....	....	....	....	....	....	....	....	11	3	5	8	16	....	....	....
1968-69	**Toronto Maple Leafs**	**NHL**	**61**	**8**	**22**	**30**	**9**	**21**	**30**	**200**	**0**	**1**	**0**	**133**	**6.0**	**80**	**9**	**78**	**16**	**+9**	**4**	**0**	**1**	**1**	**21**	**0**	**0**	**0**
1969-70	**Toronto Maple Leafs**	**NHL**	**46**	**6**	**11**	**17**	**7**	**11**	**18**	**99**	**0**	**0**	**0**	**122**	**4.9**	**48**	**4**	**44**	**9**	**+9**	....	....	....	....	....	....	....	....
1970-71	**Toronto Maple Leafs**	**NHL**	**74**	**7**	**22**	**29**	**7**	**19**	**26**	**198**	**0**	**1**	**1**	**171**	**4.1**	**89**	**19**	**78**	**14**	**+6**	**6**	**0**	**1**	**1**	**19**	**0**	**0**	**0**
1971-72	**Toronto Maple Leafs**	**NHL**	**50**	**4**	**19**	**23**	**4**	**17**	**21**	**56**	**1**	**0**	**2**	**104**	**3.8**	**53**	**7**	**47**	**11**	**+10**	....	....	....	....	....	....	....	....
	New York Rangers	**NHL**	**1**	**0**	**0**	**0**	**0**	**0**	**0**	**0**	**0**	**0**	**0**	**0**	**0.0**	**0**	**0**	**0**	**0**	**0**	**1**	**0**	**0**	**0**	**0**	**0**	**0**	**0**
1972-73	New England Whalers	WHA	75	7	56	63	....	....	....	95	....	....	....	....	....	....	....	....	....	....	15	3	*16	19	*41	....	....	....
1973-74	New England Whalers	WHA	77	6	40	46	....	....	....	134	....	....	....	....	....	....	....	....	....	....	6	0	6	6	26	....	....	....
1974-75	New England Whalers	WHA	31	5	17	22	....	....	....	43	....	....	....	....	....	....	....	....	....	....	....	....	....	....	....	....	....	....
	Toronto Toros	WHA	43	11	23	34	....	....	....	69	....	....	....	....	....	....	....	....	....	....	6	2	6	8	2	....	....	....
1975-76	Toronto Toros	WHA	74	9	51	60	....	....	....	134	....	....	....	....	....	....	....	....	....	....	....	....	....	....	....	....	....	....
1976-77	Quebec Nordiques	WHA	73	13	34	47	....	....	....	102	....	....	....	....	....	....	....	....	....	....	10	0	2	2	28	....	....	....
1977-78	Quebec Nordiques	WHA	26	1	9	10	....	....	....	23	....	....	....	....	....	....	....	....	....	....	11	0	3	3	34	....	....	....
1978-79	Quebec Nordiques	WHA	32	0	2	2	....	....	....	17	....	....	....	....	....	....	....	....	....	....	3	0	0	0	0	....	....	....
	Philadelphia Firebirds	AHL	5	0	1	1	....	....	....	6	....	....	....	....	....	....	....	....	....	....	....	....	....	....	....	....	....	....
1979-80			DID NOT PLAY																									
1980-81	New Haven Nighthawks	AHL	21	0	7	7	....	....	....	30	....	....	....	....	....	....	....	....	....	....	....	....	....	....	....	....	....	....
	NHL Totals		**232**	**25**	**74**	**99**	**27**	**68**	**95**	**553**	**1**	**2**	**3**	**530**	**4.7**	**270**	**39**	**247**	**50**		**11**	**0**	**2**	**2**	**40**	**0**	**0**	**0**
	Other Major League Totals		431	52	232	284	....	....	....	617	....	....	....	....	....	....	....	....	....	....	51	5	33	38	131	....	....	....

WHA Second All-Star Team (1973)

Selected by **Ontario-Ottawa** (WHA) in 1972 WHA General Player Draft, February 12, 1972. Traded to **NY Rangers** by **Toronto** for Pierre Jarry, February 20, 1972. WHA rights traded to **New England** (WHA) by **Ottawa** (WHA) for cash, July, 1972. Traded to **Toronto** (WHA) by **New England** (WHA) to complete transaction that sent Wayne Carlton to New England, December, 1974. Transferred to **Birmingham** (WHA) after **Toronto** (WHA) franchise relocated, June 30, 1976. Traded to **Quebec** (WHA) by **Birmingham** (WHA) for Dale Hoganson, September, 1976.

● DORION, DAN Dan Dorion C – R. 5'9", 180 lbs. b: Astoria, NY, 3/2/1963. New Jersey's 12th choice, 232nd overall, in 1982 Entry Draft.

Season	Club	League	GP	G	A	Pts	AG	AA	APts	PIM	PP	SH	GW	S	%	TGF	PGF	TGA	PGA	+/–	GP	G	A	Pts	PIM	PP	SH	GW
1981-82	Austin Mavericks	USHL	50	52	44	96	....	....	....	20	....	....	....	....	....	....	....	....	....	....	....	....	....	....	....	....	....	....
1982-83	University of Western Michigan	CCHA	34	11	20	31	....	....	....	23	....	....	....	....	....	....	....	....	....	....	....	....	....	....	....	....	....	....
1983-84	University of Western Michigan	CCHA	42	41	50	91	....	....	....	42	....	....	....	....	....	....	....	....	....	....	....	....	....	....	....	....	....	....
1984-85	University of Western Michigan	CCHA	39	21	46	67	....	....	....	28	....	....	....	....	....	....	....	....	....	....	....	....	....	....	....	....	....	....
	United States	WEC-A	5	2	3	5	....	....	....	2	....	....	....	....	....	....	....	....	....	....	....	....	....	....	....	....	....	....
1985-86	University of Western Michigan	CCHA	42	42	62	104	....	....	....	48	....	....	....	....	....	....	....	....	....	....	....	....	....	....	....	....	....	....
	New Jersey Devils	**NHL**	**3**	**1**	**1**	**2**	**1**	**1**	**2**	**0**	**0**	**0**	**0**	**6**	**16.7**	**3**	**0**	**4**	**0**	**–1**	....	....	....	....	....	....	....	....
	Maine Mariners	AHL	....	....	....	....	....	....	....	....	....	....	....	....	....	....	....	....	....	....	5	2	2	4	0	....	....	....
1986-87	Maine Mariners	AHL	70	16	22	38	....	....	....	47	....	....	....	....	....	....	....	....	....	....	....	....	....	....	....	....	....	....

			REGULAR SEASON																		PLAYOFFS							
Season	Club	League	GP	G	A	Pts	AG	AA	APts	PIM	PP	SH	GW	S	%	TGF	PGF	TGA	PGA	+/-	GP	G	A	Pts	PIM	PP	SH	GW
1987-88	**New Jersey Devils**	**NHL**	1	0	0	0	0	0	0	2	0	0	0	0	0.0	0	0	0	0	0	....	....	....	....	....	....	....	....
	Utica Devils	AHL	65	30	35	65	....	....	....	98	....	....	....	....	....	....	....	....	....	....	....	....	....	....	....	....	....	....
1988-89	Maine Mariners	AHL	16	2	3	5	....	....	....	13	....	....	....	....	....	....	....	....	....	....	....	....	....	....	....	....	....	....
	Utica Devils	AHL	15	7	4	11	....	....	....	19	....	....	....	....	....	....	....	....	....	....	....	....	....	....	....	....	....	....
1989-90	HC Fiemme	Italy	29	37	32	69	....	....	....	66	....	....	....	....	....	....	....	....	....	....	1	1	0	1	0	....	....	....
1990-91			DID NOT PLAY																									
1991-92	Nottingham Panthers	Britain	31	63	66	129	....	....	....	....	....	....	....	....	....	....	....	....	....	....	....	....	....	....	....	....	....	....
1992-93	Humberside Seahawks	Britain	19	37	28	65	....	....	....	22	....	....	....	....	....	....	....	....	....	....	....	....	....	....	....	....	....	....
	Nottingham Panthers	Britain	13	36	12	38	....	....	....	16	....	....	....	....	....	....	....	....	....	....	....	....	....	....	....	....	....	....
1993-94	Roanoke Valley Rebels	ECHL	8	3	3	6	....	....	....	4	....	....	....	....	....	....	....	....	....	....	....	....	....	....	....	....	....	....
	Humberside Seahawks	Britain	28	46	39	85	....	....	....	46	....	....	....	....	....	....	....	....	....	....	6	8	5	13	6	....	....	....
	NHL Totals		4	1	1	2	1	1	2	2	0	0	0	6	16.7	3	0	4	0		....	....	....	....	....	....	....	....

CCHA First All-Star Team (1984, 1986) • NCAA West Second All-American Team (1984) • NCAA West First All-American Team (1986)

• DORNHOEFER, GARY

Gary (Gerhardt Otto) Dornhoefer RW – R. 6'1", 190 lbs. b: Kitchener, Ont., 2/2/1943.

Season	Club	League	GP	G	A	Pts	AG	AA	APts	PIM	PP	SH	GW	S	%	TGF	PGF	TGA	PGA	+/-	GP	G	A	Pts	PIM	PP	SH	GW
1961-62	Niagara Falls Flyers	OHA	50	8	31	39	....	....	....	121	....	....	....	....	....	....	....	....	....	....	6	2	3	5	15	....	....	....
1962-63	Niagara Falls Flyers	OHA	38	16	34	50	....	....	....	58	....	....	....	....	....	....	....	....	....	....	25	13	16	29	*89	....	....	....
1963-64	**Boston Bruins**	**NHL**	32	12	10	22	16	11	27	20	....	....	....	....	....	....	....	....	....	....	....	....	....	....	....	....	....	....
	Minneapolis Bruins	CHL	39	21	30	51	....	....	....	67	....	....	....	....	....	....	....	....	....	....	....	....	....	....	....	....	....	....
1964-65	**Boston Bruins**	**NHL**	20	0	1	1	0	1	1	13	....	....	....	....	....	....	....	....	....	....	....	....	....	....	....	....	....	....
	San Francisco Seals	WHL	37	10	25	35	....	....	....	59	....	....	....	....	....	....	....	....	....	....	....	....	....	....	....	....	....	....
1965-66	**Boston Bruins**	**NHL**	10	0	1	1	0	1	1	2	....	....	....	....	....	....	....	....	....	....	....	....	....	....	....	....	....	....
	Hershey Bears	AHL	54	16	20	36	....	....	....	56	....	....	....	....	....	....	....	....	....	....	3	1	1	2	14	....	....	....
1966-67	Hershey Bears	AHL	71	19	22	41	....	....	....	110	....	....	....	....	....	....	....	....	....	....	5	0	1	1	7	....	....	....
1967-68	**Philadelphia Flyers**	**NHL**	65	13	30	43	16	31	47	134	2	0	4	96	13.5	59	18	44	9	+6	3	0	0	0	15	0	0	0
1968-69	**Philadelphia Flyers**	**NHL**	60	8	16	24	9	15	24	80	2	0	0	111	7.2	41	10	51	0	−20	4	0	1	1	20	0	0	0
1969-70	**Philadelphia Flyers**	**NHL**	65	26	29	55	30	29	59	96	4	2	1	146	17.8	71	13	59	3	+2	....	....	....	....	....	....	....	....
1970-71	**Philadelphia Flyers**	**NHL**	57	20	20	40	21	18	39	93	5	0	2	96	20.8	51	15	35	2	+3	2	0	0	0	4	0	0	0
1971-72	**Philadelphia Flyers**	**NHL**	75	17	32	49	18	29	47	183	2	3	2	167	10.2	68	20	77	14	−15	....	....	....	....	....	....	....	....
1972-73	**Philadelphia Flyers**	**NHL**	77	30	49	79	30	41	71	168	3	0	4	187	16.0	109	30	78	16	+17	11	3	3	6	16	1	0	1
1973-74	**Philadelphia Flyers**	**NHL**	57	11	39	50	11	34	45	125	3	0	4	109	10.1	63	23	33	6	+13	14	5	6	11	43	2	1	1
1974-75	**Philadelphia Flyers**	**NHL**	69	17	27	44	16	21	37	102	3	2	4	115	14.8	71	20	35	7	+23	17	5	5	10	33	0	0	2
1975-76	**Philadelphia Flyers**	**NHL**	74	28	35	63	26	28	54	128	13	0	3	152	18.4	86	33	49	10	+14	16	3	4	7	43	1	0	0
1976-77	**Philadelphia Flyers**	**NHL**	79	25	34	59	24	28	52	85	5	0	3	115	21.7	110	20	46	3	+47	9	1	0	1	22	0	0	0
1977-78	**Philadelphia Flyers**	**NHL**	47	7	5	12	7	4	11	62	2	0	0	61	11.5	24	6	22	1	−3	4	0	0	0	7	0	0	0
	NHL Totals		787	214	328	542	224	291	515	1291	44	7	27	1355	15.8	753	208	529	71		80	17	19	36	203	4	1	4

Played in NHL All-Star Game (1973, 1977)

Claimed by **Philadelphia** from **Boston** in Expansion Draft, June 6, 1967.

• DOUGLAS, JORDY

Jordy Douglas LW – L. 6', 200 lbs. b: Winnipeg, Man., 1/20/1958. Toronto's 4th choice, 81st overall, in 1978 Amateur Draft.

Season	Club	League	GP	G	A	Pts	AG	AA	APts	PIM	PP	SH	GW	S	%	TGF	PGF	TGA	PGA	+/-	GP	G	A	Pts	PIM	PP	SH	GW
1975-76	Flin Flon Bombers	WCJHL	72	12	22	34	....	....	....	48	....	....	....	....	....	....	....	....	....	....	....	....	....	....	....	....	....	....
1976-77	Flin Flon Bombers	WCJHL	59	40	23	63	....	....	....	71	....	....	....	....	....	....	....	....	....	....	....	....	....	....	....	....	....	....
1977-78	Flin Flon Bombers	WCJHL	71	60	56	116	....	....	....	131	....	....	....	....	....	....	....	....	....	....	17	14	22	36	20	....	....	....
1978-79	Springfield Indians	AHL	26	7	9	16	....	....	....	21	....	....	....	....	....	....	....	....	....	....	....	....	....	....	....	....	....	....
	New England Whalers	WHA	51	6	10	16	....	....	....	15	....	....	....	....	....	....	....	....	....	....	10	4	0	4	23	....	....	....
1979-80	**Hartford Whalers**	**NHL**	77	33	24	57	30	18	48	39	5	0	5	188	17.6	79	11	84	5	−11	....	....	....	....	....	....	....	....
1980-81	**Hartford Whalers**	**NHL**	55	13	9	22	11	6	17	29	3	0	1	98	13.3	40	7	56	0	−23	....	....	....	....	....	....	....	....
1981-82	**Hartford Whalers**	**NHL**	30	10	7	17	8	5	13	44	4	0	2	74	13.5	25	7	30	1	−11	....	....	....	....	....	....	....	....
	Binghamton Whalers	AHL	2	0	0	0	....	....	....	0	....	....	....	....	....	....	....	....	....	....	....	....	....	....	....	....	....	....
1982-83	**Minnesota North Stars**	**NHL**	68	13	14	27	11	10	21	30	1	0	2	89	14.6	39	6	45	5	−7	5	0	0	0	2	0	0	0
1983-84	**Minnesota North Stars**	**NHL**	14	3	4	7	2	3	5	10	0	0	1	21	14.3	10	0	14	2	−2	....	....	....	....	....	....	....	....
	Winnipeg Jets	**NHL**	17	4	2	6	3	1	4	8	1	0	1	14	28.6	10	2	17	0	−9	1	0	0	0	2	0	0	0
1984-85	**Winnipeg Jets**	**NHL**	7	0	2	2	0	1	1	0	0	0	0	6	0.0	5	2	9	0	−6	....	....	....	....	....	....	....	....
	Sherbrooke Canadiens	AHL	53	23	21	44	....	....	....	16	....	....	....	....	....	....	....	....	....	....	....	....	....	....	....	....	....	....
1985-86	Ilves Tampere	Finland	36	39	14	53	....	....	....	53	....	....	....	....	....	....	....	....	....	....	....	....	....	....	....	....	....	....
1986-87	Ilves Tampere	Finland	31	7	5	12	....	....	....	42	....	....	....	....	....	....	....	....	....	....	....	....	....	....	....	....	....	....
	NHL Totals		268	76	62	138	65	44	109	160	14	0	12	490	15.5	208	35	255	13		6	0	0	0	4	0	0	0
	Other Major League Totals		51	6	10	16	....	....	....	15	....	....	....	....	....	....	....	....	....	....	10	4	0	4	23	....	....	....

Signed as an underage free agent by **New England** (WHA), June, 1978. Reclaimed by **Toronto** from **Hartford** prior to Expansion Draft, June 9, 1979. Claimed as a priority selection by **Hartford**, June 9, 1979. Traded to **Minnesota** by **Hartford** with Hartford's 5th round draft choice (Jiri Poner) in 1984 Entry Draft for Mark Johnson and Kent-Erik Andersson, October 1, 1982. Traded to **Winnipeg** by **Minnesota** for Tim Trimper, January 12, 1984.

• DOUGLAS, KENT

Kent Douglas D – L. 5'10", 180 lbs. b: Cobalt, Ont., 2/6/1936.

Season	Club	League	GP	G	A	Pts	AG	AA	APts	PIM	PP	SH	GW	S	%	TGF	PGF	TGA	PGA	+/-	GP	G	A	Pts	PIM	PP	SH	GW
1954-55	Kitchener Canucks	OHA	21	2	5	7	....	....	....	104	....	....	....	....	....	....	....	....	....	....	....	....	....	....	....	....	....	....
1955-56	Kitchener Canucks	OHA	48	16	22	38	....	....	....	193	....	....	....	....	....	....	....	....	....	....	8	3	1	4	40	....	....	....
	Springfield Indians	AHL	3	1	0	1	....	....	....	4	....	....	....	....	....	....	....	....	....	....	....	....	....	....	....	....	....	....
1956-57	Owen Sound Mercurys	OHA Sr.	52	9	4	13	....	....	....	*205	....	....	....	....	....	....	....	....	....	....	....	....	....	....	....	....	....	....
1957-58	Winnipeg Warriors	WHL	68	10	24	34	....	....	....	135	....	....	....	....	....	....	....	....	....	....	7	0	1	1	25	....	....	....
1958-59	Vancouver Canucks	WHL	48	14	12	26	....	....	....	144	....	....	....	....	....	....	....	....	....	....	....	....	....	....	....	....	....	....
	Springfield Indians	AHL	9	2	4	6	....	....	....	28	....	....	....	....	....	....	....	....	....	....	....	....	....	....	....	....	....	....
1959-60	Springfield Indians	AHL	67	12	18	30	....	....	....	157	....	....	....	....	....	....	....	....	....	....	10	1	4	5	*45	....	....	....
1960-61	Springfield Indians	AHL	65	8	28	36	....	....	....	138	....	....	....	....	....	....	....	....	....	....	8	1	1	2	14	....	....	....
1961-62	Springfield Indians	AHL	59	18	41	59	....	....	....	151	....	....	....	....	....	....	....	....	....	....	11	2	*8	*10	10	....	....	....
1962-63	**Toronto Maple Leafs**	**NHL**	70	7	15	22	9	16	25	105	....	....	....	....	....	....	....	....	....	....	10	1	1	2	2	....	....	....
1963-64	**Toronto Maple Leafs**	**NHL**	43	0	1	1	0	1	1	29	....	....	....	....	....	....	....	....	....	....	....	....	....	....	....	....	....	....
	Rochester Americans	AHL	27	6	13	19	....	....	....	38	....	....	....	....	....	....	....	....	....	....	2	0	1	1	2	....	....	....
1964-65	**Toronto Maple Leafs**	**NHL**	67	5	23	28	6	25	31	129	....	....	....	....	....	....	....	....	....	....	5	0	1	1	19	....	....	....
1965-66	**Toronto Maple Leafs**	**NHL**	64	6	14	20	7	14	21	97	....	....	....	....	....	....	....	....	....	....	4	0	1	1	12	....	....	....
1966-67	**Toronto Maple Leafs**	**NHL**	39	2	12	14	2	12	14	48	....	....	....	....	....	....	....	....	....	....	....	....	....	....	....	....	....	....
	Tulsa Oilers	CHL	13	1	2	3	....	....	....	21	....	....	....	....	....	....	....	....	....	....	....	....	....	....	....	....	....	....
	Rochester Americans	AHL	11	7	9	16	....	....	....	6	....	....	....	....	....	....	....	....	....	....	10	3	3	6	6	....	....	....
1967-68	**Oakland Seals**	**NHL**	40	4	11	15	5	11	16	80	1	0	0	103	3.9	48	20	57	11	−18	....	....	....	....	....	....	....	....
	Detroit Red Wings	**NHL**	36	7	10	17	9	10	19	46	0	0	0	62	11.3	53	3	61	17	+6	....	....	....	....	....	....	....	....
1968-69	**Detroit Red Wings**	**NHL**	69	2	29	31	2	27	29	97	1	0	0	114	1.8	92	28	94	34	+4	....	....	....	....	....	....	....	....
1969-70	Rochester Americans	AHL	64	9	31	40	....	....	....	145	....	....	....	....	....	....	....	....	....	....	....	....	....	....	....	....	....	....
1970-71	Baltimore Clippers	AHL	71	9	36	45	....	....	....	72	....	....	....	....	....	....	....	....	....	....	6	1	3	4	16	....	....	....
1971-72	Baltimore Clippers	AHL	75	6	31	37	....	....	....	180	....	....	....	....	....	....	....	....	....	....	18	0	4	4	26	....	....	....
1972-73	New York Raiders	WHA	60	3	15	18	....	....	....	74	....	....	....	....	....	....	....	....	....	....	....	....	....	....	....	....	....	....
	Long Island Ducks	EHL	1	0	0	0	....	....	....	0	....	....	....	....	....	....	....	....	....	....	....	....	....	....	....	....	....	....
1973-74	Baltimore Clippers	AHL	71	7	46	53	....	....	....	176	....	....	....	....	....	....	....	....	....	....	9	2	4	6	34	....	....	....
1974-75	Baltimore Clippers	AHL	37	5	19	24	....	....	....	67	....	....	....	....	....	....	....	....	....	....	....	....	....	....	....	....	....	....
	Toledo Goaldiggers	IHL	22	2	9	11	....	....	....	10	....	....	....	....	....	....	....	....	....	....	19	2	7	9	6	....	....	....
1975-76	Baltimore Clippers	AHL	66	5	33	38	....	....	....	140	....	....	....	....	....	....	....	....	....	....	....	....	....	....	....	....	....	....
	NHL Totals		428	33	115	148	40	116	156	631	2	0	0	279	11.8	193	51	212	62		19	1	3	4	33	0	0	0
	Other Major League Totals		60	3	15	18	....	....	....	74	....	....	....	....	....	....	....	....	....	....	....	....	....	....	....	....	....	....

AHL First All-Star Team (1962) • Won Eddie Shore Award (Outstanding Defenseman - AHL) (1962) • Won Calder Memorial Trophy (1963) • AHL Second All-Star Team (1971)

Played in NHL All-Star Game (1962, 1963, 1964)

Traded to **Toronto** by **Springfield** (AHL) for Jim Wilcox, Roger Cote, Wally Boyer, Bill White and Don Mattussi, June, 1962. Claimed by **Oakland** from **Toronto** in Expansion Draft, June 6, 1967. Traded to **Detroit** by **Oakland** for John Brenneman, Ted Hampson and Bert Marshall, January 9, 1968. Traded to **Vancouver** by **Detroit** for cash, June 20, 1969. Traded to **Baltimore** (AHL) by **Vancouver** for cash, October 25, 1970. Selected by **NY Raiders** (WHA) in 1972 WHA General Player Draft, February 12, 1972.

• DOURIS, PETER

Peter Douris RW – R. 6'1", 195 lbs. b: Toronto, Ont., 2/19/1966. Winnipeg's 1st choice, 30th overall, in 1984 Entry Draft.

			REGULAR SEASON																		PLAYOFFS							
Season	Club	League	GP	G	A	Pts	AG	AA	APts	PIM	PP	SH	GW	S	%	TGF	PGF	TGA	PGA	+/–	GP	G	A	Pts	PIM	PP	SH	GW
1983-84	University of New Hampshire	ECAC	37	19	15	34	....	....	....	14	....	....	....	....	....	....	....	....	....	....	....	....	....	....	....	....	....	....
1984-85	University of New Hampshire	H.E.	42	27	24	51	....	....	....	34	....	....	....	....	....	....	....	....	....	....	....	....	....	....	....	....	....	....
1985-86	**Winnipeg Jets**	**NHL**	**11**	**0**	**0**	**0**	**0**	**0**	**0**	**0**	**0**	**0**	**0**	**0**	**0.0**	**3**	**0**	**5**	**1**	**–1**	....	....	....	....	....	....	....	....
	Canada	WJC-A	7	4	2	6	....	....	....	6	....	....	....	....	....	....	....	....	....	....	....	....	....	....	....	....	....	....
1986-87	**Winnipeg Jets**	**NHL**	**6**	**0**	**0**	**0**	**0**	**0**	**0**	**0**	**0**	**0**	**0**	**3**	**0.0**	**0**	**0**	**1**	**0**	**–1**	....	....	....	....	....	....	....	....
	Sherbrooke Canadiens	AHL	62	14	28	42	....	....	....	24	....	....	....	....	....	....	....	....	....	....	17	7	*15	*22	16	....	....	....
1987-88	**Winnipeg Jets**	**NHL**	**4**	**0**	**2**	**2**	**0**	**1**	**1**	**0**	**0**	**0**	**0**	**2**	**0.0**	**2**	**0**	**3**	**0**	**–1**	**1**	**0**	**0**	**0**	**0**	**0**	**0**	**0**
	Moncton Hawks	AHL	73	42	37	79	....	....	....	53	....	....	....	....	....	....	....	....	....	....	....	....	....	....	....	....	....	....
1988-89	Peoria Rivermen	IHL	81	28	41	69	....	....	....	32	....	....	....	....	....	....	....	....	....	....	4	1	2	3	0	....	....	....
1989-90	**Boston Bruins**	**NHL**	**36**	**5**	**6**	**11**	**4**	**4**	**8**	**15**	**1**	**0**	**0**	**63**	**7.9**	**19**	**1**	**10**	**0**	**+8**	**8**	**0**	**1**	**1**	**8**	**0**	**0**	**0**
	Maine Mariners	AHL	38	17	20	37	....	....	....	14	....	....	....	....	....	....	....	....	....	....	....	....	....	....	....	....	....	....
1990-91	**Boston Bruins**	**NHL**	**39**	**5**	**2**	**7**	**5**	**2**	**7**	**9**	**1**	**0**	**1**	**46**	**10.9**	**12**	**1**	**23**	**0**	**–12**	**7**	**0**	**1**	**1**	**6**	**0**	**0**	**0**
	Maine Mariners	AHL	35	16	15	31	....	....	....	9	....	....	....	....	....	....	....	....	....	....	2	3	0	3	2	....	....	....
1991-92	**Boston Bruins**	**NHL**	**54**	**10**	**13**	**23**	**9**	**10**	**19**	**10**	**0**	**0**	**1**	**107**	**9.3**	**38**	**0**	**36**	**7**	**+9**	**7**	**2**	**3**	**5**	**0**	**0**	**0**	**1**
	Maine Mariners	AHL	12	4	3	7	....	....	....	2	....	....	....	....	....	....	....	....	....	....	....	....	....	....	....	....	....	....
1992-93	**Boston Bruins**	**NHL**	**19**	**4**	**4**	**8**	**3**	**3**	**6**	**4**	**0**	**1**	**0**	**33**	**12.1**	**11**	**0**	**7**	**1**	**+5**	**4**	**1**	**0**	**1**	**0**	**0**	**0**	**0**
	Providence Bruins	AHL	50	29	26	55	....	....	....	12	....	....	....	....	....	....	....	....	....	....	....	....	....	....	....	....	....	....
1993-94	**Anaheim Mighty Ducks**	**NHL**	**74**	**12**	**22**	**34**	**11**	**17**	**28**	**21**	**1**	**0**	**1**	**142**	**8.5**	**59**	**14**	**55**	**5**	**–5**	....	....	....	....	....	....	....	....
1994-95	**Anaheim Mighty Ducks**	**NHL**	**46**	**10**	**11**	**21**	**18**	**16**	**34**	**12**	**0**	**0**	**4**	**69**	**14.5**	**30**	**0**	**35**	**9**	**+4**	....	....	....	....	....	....	....	....
1995-96	**Anaheim Mighty Ducks**	**NHL**	**31**	**8**	**7**	**15**	**8**	**6**	**14**	**9**	**2**	**0**	**3**	**45**	**17.8**	**17**	**4**	**28**	**12**	**–3**	....	....	....	....	....	....	....	....
1996-97	Milwaukee Admirals	IHL	80	36	36	72	....	....	....	14	....	....	....	....	....	....	....	....	....	....	3	2	2	4	2	....	....	....
1997-98	**Dallas Stars**	**NHL**	**1**	**0**	**0**	**0**	**0**	**0**	**0**	**0**	**0**	**0**	**0**	**3**	**0.0**	**1**	**0**	**2**	**0**	**–1**	....	....	....	....	....	....	....	....
	Michigan K-Wings	IHL	78	26	31	57	....	....	....	29	....	....	....	....	....	....	....	....	....	....	4	0	5	5	2	....	....	....
	NHL Totals		**321**	**54**	**67**	**121**	**58**	**59**	**117**	**80**	**5**	**1**	**10**	**513**	**10.5**	**192**	**20**	**205**	**35**		**27**	**3**	**5**	**8**	**14**	**0**	**0**	**1**

Traded to **St. Louis** by **Winnipeg** for Kent Carlson and St. Louis' 12th round choice (Sergei Kharin) in 1989 Entry Draft and St. Louis' 4th round choice (Scott Levins) in 1990 Entry Draft, September 29, 1988. Signed as a free agent by **Boston**, June 27, 1989. Signed as a free agent by **Anaheim**, July 22, 1993. Signed as a free agent by **Dallas**, July 16, 1997.

• DOWD, JIM

Jim Dowd C – R. 6'1", 190 lbs. b: Brick, NJ, 12/25/1968. New Jersey's 7th choice, 149th overall, in 1987 Entry Draft.

Season	Club	League	GP	G	A	Pts	AG	AA	APts	PIM	PP	SH	GW	S	%	TGF	PGF	TGA	PGA	+/–	GP	G	A	Pts	PIM	PP	SH	GW
1986-87	Brick Township High Scool	H.S.	24	22	33	55	....	....	....	....	....	....	....	....	....	....	....	....	....	....	....	....	....	....	....	....	....	....
1987-88	Lake Superior State	CCHA	45	18	27	45	....	....	....	16	....	....	....	....	....	....	....	....	....	....	....	....	....	....	....	....	....	....
1988-89	Lake Superior State	CCHA	46	24	35	59	....	....	....	40	....	....	....	....	....	....	....	....	....	....	....	....	....	....	....	....	....	....
1989-90	Lake Superior State	CCHA	46	25	*67	92	....	....	....	30	....	....	....	....	....	....	....	....	....	....	....	....	....	....	....	....	....	....
1990-91	Lake Superior State	CCHA	44	24	*54	*78	....	....	....	53	....	....	....	....	....	....	....	....	....	....	....	....	....	....	....	....	....	....
1991-92	**New Jersey Devils**	**NHL**	**1**	**0**	**0**	**0**	**0**	**0**	**0**	**0**	**0**	**0**	**0**	**0**	**0.0**	**0**	**0**	**0**	**0**	**0**	....	....	....	....	....	....	....	....
	Utica Devils	AHL	78	17	42	59	....	....	....	47	....	....	....	....	....	....	....	....	....	....	4	2	2	4	4	....	....	....
1992-93	**New Jersey Devils**	**NHL**	**1**	....	....	....	**0**	**0**	**0**	**0**	**0**	**0**	**0**	**1**	**0.0**	**0**	**0**	**1**	**0**	**–1**	....	....	....	....	....	....	....	....
	Utica Devils	AHL	78	27	45	72	....	....	....	62	....	....	....	....	....	....	....	....	....	....	5	1	7	8	10	....	....	....
1993-94	**New Jersey Devils**	**NHL**	**15**	**5**	**10**	**15**	**5**	**8**	**13**	**0**	**2**	**0**	**0**	**26**	**19.2**	**20**	**9**	**3**	**0**	**+8**	**19**	**2**	**6**	**8**	**8**	**0**	**0**	**0**
	Albany River Rats	AHL	58	26	37	63	....	....	....	76	....	....	....	....	....	....	....	....	....	....	....	....	....	....	....	....	....	....
1994-95	**New Jersey Devils**	**NHL**	**10**	**1**	**4**	**5**	**2**	**6**	**8**	**0**	**1**	**0**	**0**	**14**	**7.1**	**7**	**3**	**9**	**0**	**–5**	**11**	**2**	**1**	**3**	**8**	**0**	**0**	**1**
1995-96	**New Jersey Devils**	**NHL**	**28**	**4**	**9**	**13**	**4**	**7**	**11**	**17**	**0**	**0**	**0**	**41**	**9.8**	**16**	**0**	**20**	**3**	**–1**	....	....	....	....	....	....	....	....
	Vancouver Canucks	**NHL**	**38**	**1**	**6**	**7**	**1**	**5**	**6**	**6**	**0**	**0**	**0**	**35**	**2.9**	**11**	**0**	**27**	**8**	**–8**	**1**	**0**	**0**	**0**	**0**	**0**	**0**	**0**
1996-97	**New York Islanders**	**NHL**	**3**	**0**	**0**	**0**	**0**	**0**	**0**	**0**	**0**	**0**	**0**	**0**	**0.0**	**1**	**1**	**1**	**0**	**–1**	....	....	....	....	....	....	....	....
	Utah Grizzlies	IHL	48	10	21	31	....	....	....	27	....	....	....	....	....	....	....	....	....	....	....	....	....	....	....	....	....	....
	Saint John Flames	AHL	24	5	11	16	....	....	....	18	....	....	....	....	....	....	....	....	....	....	5	1	2	3	0	....	....	....
1997-98	**Calgary Flames**	**NHL**	**48**	**6**	**8**	**14**	**7**	**8**	**15**	**12**	**0**	**1**	**0**	**58**	**10.3**	**24**	**2**	**27**	**15**	**+10**	....	....	....	....	....	....	....	....
	Saint John Flames	AHL	35	8	30	38	....	....	....	20	....	....	....	....	....	....	....	....	....	....	19	3	13	16	10	....	....	....
	NHL Totals		**144**	**17**	**37**	**54**	**19**	**34**	**53**	**35**	**3**	**1**	**0**	**175**	**9.7**	**79**	**15**	**88**	**26**		**31**	**4**	**7**	**11**	**16**	**0**	**0**	**1**

CCHA Second All-Star Team (1990) • NCAA West Second All-American Team (1990) • CCHA First All-Star Team (1991) • NCAA West First All-American Team (1991)

Traded to **Hartford** by **New Jersey** with New Jersey's 2nd round choice (later traded to Calgary – Calgary selected Dmitri Kokorev) in 1997 Entry Draft for Jocelyn Lemieux and Hartford's 2nd round choice in 1998 Entry Draft, December 19, 1995. Traded to **Vancouver** by **Hartford** with Frantisek Kucera and Hartford's 2nd round choice (Ryan Bonni) in 1997 Entry Draft for Jeff Brown and Vancouver's 3rd round choice in 1998 Entry Draft, December 19, 1995. Claimed by **NY Islanders** from **Vancouver** in NHL Waiver Draft, September 30, 1996. Signed as a free agent by **Calgary**, August, 1997. Traded to **Nashville** by **Calgary** for future considerations, June 26, 1998.

• DOYON, MARIO

Mario Doyon D – R. 6', 174 lbs. b: Quebec City, Que., 8/27/1968. Chicago's 5th choice, 119th overall, in 1986 Entry Draft.

Season	Club	League	GP	G	A	Pts	AG	AA	APts	PIM	PP	SH	GW	S	%	TGF	PGF	TGA	PGA	+/–	GP	G	A	Pts	PIM	PP	SH	GW
1985-86	Drummondville Voltigeurs	QMJHL	71	5	14	19	....	....	....	129	....	....	....	....	....	....	....	....	....	....	23	5	4	9	32	....	....	....
1986-87	Drummondville Voltigeurs	QMJHL	65	18	47	65	....	....	....	150	....	....	....	....	....	....	....	....	....	....	8	1	3	4	30	....	....	....
1987-88	Drummondville Voltigeurs	QMJHL	68	23	54	77	....	....	....	233	....	....	....	....	....	....	....	....	....	....	17	3	14	17	46	....	....	....
1988-89	**Chicago Blackhawks**	**NHL**	**7**	**1**	**1**	**2**	**1**	**1**	**2**	**6**	**1**	**0**	**0**	**7**	**14.3**	**4**	**2**	**0**	**0**	**+2**	....	....	....	....	....	....	....	....
	Saginaw Hawks	IHL	71	16	32	48	....	....	....	69	....	....	....	....	....	....	....	....	....	....	6	0	0	0	8	....	....	....
1989-90	Indianapolis Ice	IHL	66	9	25	34	....	....	....	50	....	....	....	....	....	....	....	....	....	....	....	....	....	....	....	....	....	....
	Quebec Nordiques	**NHL**	**9**	**2**	**3**	**5**	**2**	**2**	**4**	**6**	**1**	**0**	**0**	**19**	**10.5**	**11**	**3**	**10**	**1**	**–1**	....	....	....	....	....	....	....	....
	Halifax Citadels	AHL	5	1	2	3	....	....	....	0	....	....	....	....	....	....	....	....	....	....	6	1	3	4	2	....	....	....
1990-91	**Quebec Nordiques**	**NHL**	**12**	**0**	**0**	**0**	**0**	**0**	**0**	**4**	**0**	**0**	**0**	**12**	**0.0**	**8**	**2**	**9**	**0**	**–3**	....	....	....	....	....	....	....	....
	Halifax Citadels	AHL	59	14	23	37	....	....	....	58	....	....	....	....	....	....	....	....	....	....	....	....	....	....	....	....	....	....
1991-92	Halifax Citadels	AHL	9	0	0	0	....	....	....	22	....	....	....	....	....	....	....	....	....	....	....	....	....	....	....	....	....	....
	New Haven Nighthawks	AHL	64	11	29	40	....	....	....	44	....	....	....	....	....	....	....	....	....	....	5	1	1	2	2	....	....	....
1992-93	Halifax Citadels	AHL	79	5	31	36	....	....	....	73	....	....	....	....	....	....	....	....	....	....	....	....	....	....	....	....	....	....
1993-94	Fredericton Canadiens	AHL	56	12	21	33	....	....	....	44	....	....	....	....	....	....	....	....	....	....	....	....	....	....	....	....	....	....
	Kansas City Blades	IHL	5	0	3	3	....	....	....	0	....	....	....	....	....	....	....	....	....	....	....	....	....	....	....	....	....	....
1994-95	Bolzano	Italy	45	13	30	43	....	....	....	91	....	....	....	....	....	....	....	....	....	....	....	....	....	....	....	....	....	....
1995-96	San Francisco Spiders	IHL	74	13	23	36	....	....	....	61	....	....	....	....	....	....	....	....	....	....	4	1	3	4	0	....	....	....
	NHL Totals		**28**	**3**	**4**	**7**	**3**	**3**	**6**	**16**	**2**	**0**	**0**	**38**	**7.9**	**23**	**7**	**19**	**1**		....	....	....	....	....	....	....	....

Traded to **Quebec** by **Chicago** with Everett Sanipass and Dan Vincelette for Greg Millen, Michel Goulet and Quebec's 6th round choice (Kevin St. Jacques) in 1991 Entry Draft, March 5, 1990.

• DRAKE, DALLAS

Dallas Drake C – L. 6', 180 lbs. b: Trail, B.C., 2/4/1969. Detroit's 6th choice, 116th overall, in 1989 Entry Draft.

Season	Club	League	GP	G	A	Pts	AG	AA	APts	PIM	PP	SH	GW	S	%	TGF	PGF	TGA	PGA	+/–	GP	G	A	Pts	PIM	PP	SH	GW
1988-89	Northern Michigan University	WCHA	38	17	22	39	....	....	....	22	....	....	....	....	....	....	....	....	....	....	....	....	....	....	....	....	....	....
1989-90	Northern Michigan University	WCHA	46	13	24	37	....	....	....	42	....	....	....	....	....	....	....	....	....	....	....	....	....	....	....	....	....	....
1990-91	Northern Michigan University	WCHA	44	22	36	58	....	....	....	89	....	....	....	....	....	....	....	....	....	....	....	....	....	....	....	....	....	....
1991-92	Northern Michigan University	WCHA	38	*39	41	*80	....	....	....	46	....	....	....	....	....	....	....	....	....	....	....	....	....	....	....	....	....	....
1992-93	**Detroit Red Wings**	**NHL**	**72**	**18**	**26**	**44**	**15**	**18**	**33**	**93**	**3**	**2**	**5**	**89**	**20.2**	**62**	**11**	**54**	**18**	**+15**	**7**	**3**	**3**	**6**	**6**	**1**	**0**	**0**
1993-94	**Detroit Red Wings**	**NHL**	**47**	**10**	**22**	**32**	**9**	**17**	**26**	**37**	**0**	**1**	**2**	**78**	**12.8**	**48**	**10**	**47**	**14**	**+5**	....	....	....	....	....	....	....	....
	Adirondack Red Wings	AHL	1	2	0	2	....	....	....	0	....	....	....	....	....	....	....	....	....	....	....	....	....	....	....	....	....	....
	Winnipeg Jets	**NHL**	**15**	**3**	**5**	**8**	**3**	**4**	**7**	**12**	**1**	**1**	**1**	**34**	**8.8**	**9**	**2**	**17**	**4**	**–6**	....	....	....	....	....	....	....	....
1994-95	**Winnipeg Jets**	**NHL**	**43**	**8**	**18**	**26**	**14**	**26**	**40**	**30**	**0**	**0**	**1**	**66**	**12.1**	**38**	**7**	**48**	**11**	**–6**	....	....	....	....	....	....	....	....
1995-96	**Winnipeg Jets**	**NHL**	**69**	**19**	**20**	**39**	**19**	**16**	**35**	**36**	**4**	**4**	**2**	**121**	**15.7**	**63**	**16**	**79**	**25**	**–7**	**3**	**0**	**0**	**0**	**0**	**0**	**0**	**0**
1996-97	**Phoenix Coyotes**	**NHL**	**63**	**17**	**19**	**36**	**18**	**17**	**35**	**52**	**5**	**1**	**1**	**113**	**15.0**	**50**	**13**	**53**	**5**	**–11**	**7**	**0**	**1**	**1**	**2**	**0**	**0**	**0**
1997-98	**Phoenix Coyotes**	**NHL**	**60**	**11**	**29**	**40**	**13**	**28**	**41**	**71**	**3**	**0**	**2**	**112**	**9.8**	**59**	**13**	**36**	**7**	**+17**	**4**	**0**	**1**	**1**	**2**	**0**	**0**	**0**
	NHL Totals		**369**	**86**	**139**	**225**	**91**	**126**	**217**	**331**	**16**	**9**	**14**	**613**	**14.0**	**329**	**72**	**334**	**84**		**21**	**3**	**5**	**8**	**10**	**1**	**0**	**0**

WCHA First All-Star Team (1992) • NCAA West First All-American Team (1992)

Traded to **Winnipeg** by **Detroit** with Tim Cheveldae for Bob Essensa and Sergei Bautin, March 8, 1994. Transferred to **Phoenix** after **Winnipeg** franchise relocated, July 1, 1996.

• DRAPER, KRIS

Kris Draper C – L. 5'11", 185 lbs. b: Toronto, Ont., 5/24/1971. Winnipeg's 4th choice, 62nd overall, in 1989 Entry Draft.

Season	Club	League	GP	G	A	Pts	AG	AA	APts	PIM	PP	SH	GW	S	%	TGF	PGF	TGA	PGA	+/–	GP	G	A	Pts	PIM	PP	SH	GW
1987-88	Don Mills Flyers	Midget	40	35	32	67	....	....	....	46	....	....	....	....	....	....	....	....	....	....	....	....	....	....	....	....	....	....
1988-89	Canada	Nat-Team	60	11	15	26	....	....	....	16	....	....	....	....	....	....	....	....	....	....	....	....	....	....	....	....	....	....
1989-90	Canada	Nat-Team	61	12	22	34	....	....	....	44	....	....	....	....	....	....	....	....	....	....	....	....	....	....	....	....	....	....
	Canada	WJC-A	7	0	2	2	....	....	....	4	....	....	....	....	....	....	....	....	....	....	....	....	....	....	....	....	....	....

			REGULAR SEASON																		PLAYOFFS							
Season	**Club**	**League**	**GP**	**G**	**A**	**Pts**	**AG**	**AA**	**APts**	**PIM**	**PP**	**SH**	**GW**	**S**	**%**	**TGF**	**PGF**	**TGA**	**PGA**	**+/–**	**GP**	**G**	**A**	**Pts**	**PIM**	**PP**	**SH**	**GW**
1990-91	Ottawa 67's	OHL	39	19	42	61	....	....	....	35	....	....	....	....	....	....	....	....	....	....	17	8	11	19	20	....	....	....
	Canada	WJC-A	7	1	3	4	....	....	....	0	....	....	....	....	....	....	....	....	....	....	....	....	....	....	....	....	....	....
	Winnipeg Jets	**NHL**	**3**	**1**	**0**	**1**	**1**	**0**	**1**	**5**	**0**	**0**	**0**	**1**	**100.0**	**1**	**0**	**1**	**0**	**0**	....	....	....	....	....	....	....	....
	Moncton Hawks	AHL	7	2	1	3	....	....	....	2	....	....	....	....	....	....	....	....	....	....	....	....	....	....	....	....	....	....
1991-92	**Winnipeg Jets**	**NHL**	**10**	**2**	**0**	**2**	**2**	**0**	**2**	**2**	**0**	**0**	**0**	**19**	**10.5**	**4**	**0**	**6**	**2**	**0**	**2**	**0**	**0**	**0**	**0**	**0**	**0**	**0**
	Moncton Hawks	AHL	61	11	18	29	....	....	....	113	....	....	....	....	....	....	....	....	....	....	4	0	1	1	6	....	....	....
1992-93	**Winnipeg Jets**	**NHL**	**7**	**0**	**0**	**0**	**0**	**0**	**0**	**2**	**0**	**0**	**0**	**5**	**0.0**	**0**	**0**	**8**	**2**	**–6**	....	....	....	....	....	....	....	....
	Moncton Hawks	AHL	67	12	23	35	....	....	....	40	....	....	....	....	....	....	....	....	....	....	5	2	2	4	18	....	....	....
1993-94	**Detroit Red Wings**	**NHL**	**39**	**5**	**8**	**13**	**5**	**6**	**11**	**31**	**0**	**1**	**0**	**55**	**9.1**	**21**	**1**	**19**	**10**	**+11**	**7**	**2**	**2**	**4**	**4**	**0**	**1**	**0**
	Adirondack Red Wings	AHL	46	20	23	43	....	....	....	49	....	....	....	....	....	....	....	....	....	....	....	....	....	....	....	....	....	....
1994-95	**Detroit Red Wings**	**NHL**	**36**	**2**	**6**	**8**	**4**	**9**	**13**	**22**	**0**	**0**	**0**	**44**	**4.5**	**13**	**0**	**23**	**11**	**+1**	**18**	**4**	**1**	**5**	**12**	**0**	**1**	**1**
1995-96	**Detroit Red Wings**	**NHL**	**52**	**7**	**9**	**16**	**7**	**7**	**14**	**32**	**0**	**1**	**0**	**51**	**13.7**	**20**	**0**	**23**	**5**	**+2**	**18**	**4**	**2**	**6**	**18**	**0**	**1**	**0**
1996-97	**Detroit Red Wings**	**NHL**	**76**	**8**	**5**	**13**	**8**	**4**	**12**	**73**	**1**	**0**	**1**	**85**	**9.4**	**17**	**1**	**38**	**11**	**–11**	**20**	**2**	**4**	**6**	**12**	**0**	**1**	**0**
1997-98	**Detroit Red Wings**	**NHL**	**64**	**13**	**10**	**23**	**15**	**10**	**25**	**45**	**1**	**0**	**4**	**96**	**13.5**	**35**	**3**	**43**	**16**	**+5**	**19**	**1**	**3**	**4**	**12**	**0**	**0**	**1**
	NHL Totals		**287**	**38**	**38**	**76**	**42**	**36**	**78**	**212**	**2**	**2**	**5**	**356**	**10.7**	**111**	**5**	**161**	**57**		**84**	**13**	**12**	**25**	**58**	**0**	**4**	**2**

Traded to **Detroit** by **Winnipeg** for future considerations, June 30, 1993.

• DRISCOLL, PETE

Pete Driscoll LW – L. 6′, 190 lbs. b: Kingston, Ont., 10/27/1954. Toronto's 4th choice, 67th overall, in 1974 Amateur Draft.

Season	Club	League	GP	G	A	Pts	AG	AA	APts	PIM	PP	SH	GW	S	%	TGF	PGF	TGA	PGA	+/–	GP	G	A	Pts	PIM	PP	SH	GW
1973-74	Kingston Canadians	OHA	54	13	21	34	....	....	....	216	....	....	....	....	....	....	....	....	....	....	....	....	....	....	....	....	....	....
1974-75	Vancouver Blazers	WHA	21	3	2	5	....	....	....	40	....	....	....	....	....	....	....	....	....	....	....	....	....	....	....	....	....	....
	Tulsa Oilers	CHL	56	9	10	19	....	....	....	183	....	....	....	....	....	....	....	....	....	....	....	....	....	....	....	....	....	....
1975-76	Calgary Cowboys	WHA	75	16	18	34	....	....	....	126	....	....	....	....	....	....	....	....	....	....	10	2	5	7	41	....	....	....
1976-77	Calgary Cowboys	WHA	76	23	29	52	....	....	....	120	....	....	....	....	....	....	....	....	....	....	....	....	....	....	....	....	....	....
1977-78	Quebec Nordiques	WHA	21	3	7	10	....	....	....	28	....	....	....	....	....	....	....	....	....	....	....	....	....	....	....	....	....	....
	Indianapolis Racers	WHA	56	25	21	46	....	....	....	130	....	....	....	....	....	....	....	....	....	....	....	....	....	....	....	....	....	....
1978-79	Indianapolis Racers	WHA	8	3	1	4	....	....	....	17	....	....	....	....	....	....	....	....	....	....	....	....	....	....	....	....	....	....
	Edmonton Oilers	WHA	69	17	23	40	....	....	....	115	....	....	....	....	....	....	....	....	....	....	13	1	6	7	8	....	....	....
1979-80	**Edmonton Oilers**	**NHL**	**39**	**1**	**5**	**6**	**1**	**4**	**5**	**54**	**0**	**0**	**0**	**23**	**4.3**	**10**	**3**	**18**	**0**	**–11**	**3**	**0**	**0**	**0**	**0**	**0**	**0**	**0**
	Houston Apollos	CHL	8	7	4	11	....	....	....	16	....	....	....	....	....	....	....	....	....	....	....	....	....	....	....	....	....	....
1980-81	**Edmonton Oilers**	**NHL**	**21**	**2**	**3**	**5**	**2**	**2**	**4**	**43**	**1**	**0**	**0**	**17**	**11.8**	**11**	**1**	**9**	**0**	**+1**	....	....	....	....	....	....	....	....
	Wichita Wind	CHL	34	11	14	25	....	....	....	75	....	....	....	....	....	....	....	....	....	....	....	....	....	....	....	....	....	....
1981-82	Wichita Wind	CHL	75	25	29	54	....	....	....	229	....	....	....	....	....	....	....	....	....	....	....	....	....	....	....	....	....	....
	NHL Totals		**60**	**3**	**8**	**11**	**3**	**6**	**9**	**97**	**1**	**0**	**0**	**40**	**7.5**	**21**	**4**	**27**	**0**		**3**	**0**	**0**	**0**	**0**	**0**	**0**	**0**
	Other Major League Totals		326	90	101	191	....	....	....	576	....	....	....	....	....	....	....	....	....		23	3	11	14	49	....	....	....

Selected by **Vancouver** (WHA) in 1974 WHA Amateur Draft, June, 1974. Transferred to **Calgary** (WHA) after **Vancouver** (WHA) franchise relocated, May 7, 1975. Signed as a free agent by **Quebec** (WHA) after **Calgary** (WHA) franchise folded, May 31, 1977. Traded to **Indianapolis** (WHA) by **Quebec** (WHA) with Dave Inkpen for cash, December, 1977. Traded to **Edmonton** (WHA) by **Indianapolis** (WHA) with Wayne Gretzky and Eddie Mio for cash, November, 1978. Rights retained by **Edmonton** prior to Expansion Draft, June 9, 1979.

• DRIVER, BRUCE

Bruce Driver D – L. 6′, 185 lbs. b: Toronto, Ont., 4/29/1962. Colorado's 6th choice, 108th overall, in 1981 Entry Draft.

Season	Club	League	GP	G	A	Pts	AG	AA	APts	PIM	PP	SH	GW	S	%	TGF	PGF	TGA	PGA	+/–	GP	G	A	Pts	PIM	PP	SH	GW
1980-81	University of Wisconsin	WCHA	42	5	15	20	....	....	....	42	....	....	....	....	....	....	....	....	....	....	....	....	....	....	....	....	....	....
1981-82	University of Wisconsin	WCHA	46	7	37	44	....	....	....	84	....	....	....	....	....	....	....	....	....	....	....	....	....	....	....	....	....	....
1982-83	University of Wisconsin	WCHA	49	19	42	61	....	....	....	100	....	....	....	....	....	....	....	....	....	....	....	....	....	....	....	....	....	....
1983-84	Canada	Nat-Team	61	11	17	28	....	....	....	44	....	....	....	....	....	....	....	....	....	....	....	....	....	....	....	....	....	....
	Canada	Olympics	7	3	1	4	....	....	....	10	....	....	....	....	....	....	....	....	....	....	....	....	....	....	....	....	....	....
	New Jersey Devils	**NHL**	**4**	**0**	**2**	**2**	**0**	**1**	**1**	**0**	**0**	**0**	**0**	**5**	**0.0**	**4**	**2**	**4**	**0**	**–2**	....	....	....	....	....	....	....	....
	Maine Mariners	AHL	12	2	6	8	....	....	....	15	....	....	....	....	....	....	....	....	....	....	16	0	10	10	8	....	....	....
1984-85	**New Jersey Devils**	**NHL**	**67**	**9**	**23**	**32**	**7**	**16**	**23**	**36**	**3**	**1**	**0**	**143**	**6.3**	**87**	**34**	**98**	**23**	**–22**	....	....	....	....	....	....	....	....
1985-86	**New Jersey Devils**	**NHL**	**40**	**3**	**15**	**18**	**2**	**10**	**12**	**32**	**1**	**0**	**1**	**64**	**4.7**	**63**	**14**	**58**	**18**	**+9**	....	....	....	....	....	....	....	....
	Maine Mariners	AHL	15	4	7	11	....	....	....	16	....	....	....	....	....	....	....	....	....	....	....	....	....	....	....	....	....	....
1986-87	**New Jersey Devils**	**NHL**	**74**	**6**	**28**	**34**	**5**	**20**	**25**	**36**	**0**	**0**	**0**	**132**	**4.5**	**94**	**28**	**122**	**30**	**–26**	....	....	....	....	....	....	....	....
	Canada	WEC-A	8	0	0	0	....	....	....	4	....	....	....	....	....	....	....	....	....	....	....	....	....	....	....	....	....	....
1987-88	**New Jersey Devils**	**NHL**	**74**	**15**	**40**	**55**	**13**	**28**	**41**	**68**	**7**	**0**	**0**	**190**	**7.9**	**131**	**57**	**112**	**45**	**+7**	**20**	**3**	**7**	**10**	**14**	**3**	**0**	**0**
1988-89	**New Jersey Devils**	**NHL**	**27**	**1**	**15**	**16**	**1**	**11**	**12**	**24**	**1**	**0**	**0**	**69**	**1.4**	**39**	**18**	**33**	**12**	**0**	....	....	....	....	....	....	....	....
1989-90	**New Jersey Devils**	**NHL**	**75**	**7**	**46**	**53**	**6**	**33**	**39**	**63**	**1**	**0**	**0**	**185**	**3.8**	**131**	**39**	**119**	**33**	**+6**	**6**	**1**	**5**	**6**	**6**	**0**	**0**	**0**
1990-91	**New Jersey Devils**	**NHL**	**73**	**9**	**36**	**45**	**8**	**27**	**35**	**62**	**7**	**0**	**2**	**195**	**4.6**	**113**	**40**	**96**	**34**	**+11**	**7**	**1**	**2**	**3**	**12**	**1**	**0**	**0**
1991-92	**New Jersey Devils**	**NHL**	**78**	**7**	**35**	**42**	**6**	**26**	**32**	**66**	**3**	**1**	**1**	**205**	**3.4**	**106**	**36**	**101**	**36**	**+5**	**7**	**0**	**4**	**4**	**2**	**0**	**0**	**0**
1992-93	**New Jersey Devils**	**NHL**	**83**	**14**	**40**	**54**	**12**	**27**	**39**	**66**	**6**	**0**	**0**	**177**	**7.9**	**115**	**47**	**94**	**16**	**–10**	**5**	**1**	**3**	**4**	**4**	**0**	**1**	**0**
1993-94	**New Jersey Devils**	**NHL**	**66**	**8**	**24**	**32**	**7**	**19**	**26**	**63**	**3**	**1**	**0**	**109**	**7.3**	**86**	**24**	**51**	**18**	**+29**	**20**	**3**	**5**	**8**	**12**	**2**	**0**	**0**
1994-95	**New Jersey Devils**	**NHL**	**41**	**4**	**12**	**16**	**7**	**18**	**25**	**18**	**1**	**0**	**1**	**62**	**6.5**	**35**	**13**	**31**	**8**	**–1**	**17**	**1**	**6**	**7**	**8**	**1**	**0**	**0**
1995-96	**New York Rangers**	**NHL**	**66**	**3**	**34**	**37**	**3**	**28**	**31**	**42**	**3**	**0**	**0**	**140**	**2.1**	**89**	**45**	**53**	**11**	**+2**	**11**	**0**	**7**	**7**	**4**	**0**	**0**	**0**
1996-97	**New York Rangers**	**NHL**	**79**	**5**	**25**	**30**	**5**	**22**	**27**	**48**	**2**	**0**	**2**	**154**	**3.2**	**85**	**31**	**63**	**17**	**+8**	**15**	**0**	**1**	**1**	**2**	**0**	**0**	**0**
1997-98	**New York Rangers**	**NHL**	**75**	**5**	**15**	**20**	**6**	**15**	**21**	**46**	**1**	**0**	**0**	**116**	**4.3**	**66**	**21**	**65**	**17**	**–3**	....	....	....	....	....	....	....	....
	NHL Totals		**922**	**96**	**390**	**486**	**88**	**301**	**389**	**670**	**39**	**3**	**7**	**1946**	**4.9**	**1244**	**449**	**1100**	**318**		**108**	**10**	**40**	**50**	**64**	**7**	**1**	**0**

WCHA First All-Star Team (1982) • NCAA West First All-American Team (1982) • NCAA Championship All-Tournament Team (1982) • WCHA Second All-Star Team (1983)

Signed as a free agent by **NY Rangers**, September 28, 1995.

• DROLET, RENE

Rene Drolet RW – R. 5′8″, 160 lbs. b: Quebec City, Que., 11/13/1944.

Season	Club	League	GP	G	A	Pts	AG	AA	APts	PIM	PP	SH	GW	S	%	TGF	PGF	TGA	PGA	+/–	GP	G	A	Pts	PIM	PP	SH	GW
1962-63	Quebec Citadelle	QJHL	STATISTICS NOT AVAILABLE																									
	Quebec Aces	AHL	1	0	0	0	....	....	....	0	....	....	....	....	....	....	....	....	....	....	....	....	....	....	....	....	....	....
1963-64	Montreal Jr. Canadiens	OHA	34	13	19	32	....	....	....	9	....	....	....	....	....	....	....	....	....	....	5	2	6	8	4	....	....	....
1964-65	Montreal Jr. Canadiens	OHA	56	35	39	74	....	....	....	16	....	....	....	....	....	....	....	....	....	....	7	1	4	5	6	....	....	....
	Quebec Aces	AHL	3	0	1	1	....	....	....	6	....	....	....	....	....	....	....	....	....	....	....	....	....	....	....	....	....	....
1965-66	Muskegon Zephyrs	IHL	68	42	53	95	....	....	....	24	....	....	....	....	....	....	....	....	....	....	4	2	1	3	2	....	....	....
	Quebec Aces	AHL	1	0	0	0	....	....	....	0	....	....	....	....	....	....	....	....	....	....	....	....	....	....	....	....	....	....
1966-67	Quebec Aces	AHL	48	6	7	13	....	....	....	0	....	....	....	....	....	....	....	....	....	....	5	0	0	0	2	....	....	....
1967-68	Quebec Aces	AHL	61	18	22	40	....	....	....	6	....	....	....	....	....	....	....	....	....	....	15	6	8	14	2	....	....	....
1968-69	Quebec Aces	AHL	61	30	42	72	....	....	....	14	....	....	....	....	....	....	....	....	....	....	15	4	*10	14	28	....	....	....
1969-70	Quebec Aces	AHL	71	32	48	80	....	....	....	42	....	....	....	....	....	....	....	....	....	....	6	2	1	3	2	....	....	....
1970-71	Quebec Aces	AHL	72	20	37	57	....	....	....	26	....	....	....	....	....	....	....	....	....	....	1	1	1	2	0	....	....	....
1971-72	**Philadelphia Flyers**	**NHL**	**1**	**0**	**0**	**0**	**0**	**0**	**0**	**0**	**0**	**0**	**0**	**3**	**0.0**	**0**	**0**	**0**	**0**	**0**	....	....	....	....	....	....	....	....
	Richmond Robins	AHL	74	31	30	61	....	....	....	18	....	....	....	....	....	....	....	....	....	....	....	....	....	....	....	....	....	....
1972-73	Richmond Robins	AHL	76	34	53	87	....	....	....	30	....	....	....	....	....	....	....	....	....	....	4	2	1	3	0	....	....	....
1973-74	Richmond Robins	AHL	76	26	47	73	....	....	....	18	....	....	....	....	....	....	....	....	....	....	5	5	2	7	2	....	....	....
1974-75	**Detroit Red Wings**	**NHL**	**1**	**0**	**0**	**0**	**0**	**0**	**0**	**0**	**0**	**0**	**0**	**0**	**0.0**	**0**	**0**	**0**	**0**	**0**	....	....	....	....	....	....	....	....
	Virginia Wings	AHL	72	26	52	78	....	....	....	36	....	....	....	....	....	....	....	....	....	....	5	1	3	4	2	....	....	....
1975-76	Rochester Americans	AHL	74	23	40	63	....	....	....	42	....	....	....	....	....	....	....	....	....	....	7	0	1	1	0	....	....	....
1976-77	Rochester Americans	AHL	80	28	37	65	....	....	....	42	....	....	....	....	....	....	....	....	....	....	12	5	4	9	4	....	....	....
1977-78	Rochester Americans	AHL	70	24	27	51	....	....	....	20	....	....	....	....	....	....	....	....	....	....	6	5	1	6	2	....	....	....
	NHL Totals		**2**	**0**	**0**	**0**	**0**	**0**	**0**	**0**	**0**	**0**	**0**	**3**	**0.0**	**0**	**0**	**0**	**0**		....	....	....	....	....	....	....	....

IHL Second All-Star Team (1966)

NHL rights transferred to **Philadelphia** after NHL club purchased **Quebec** (AHL) franchise, May 8, 1967. Claimed by **Detroit** (Tidewater - AHL) from **Philadelphia** in Reverse Draft, June 13, 1974.

• DROPPA, IVAN

Ivan Droppa D – L. 6′2″, 209 lbs. b: Liptovsky Mikulas, Czech., 2/1/1972. Chicago's 2nd choice, 37th overall, in 1990 Entry Draft.

Season	Club	League	GP	G	A	Pts	AG	AA	APts	PIM	PP	SH	GW	S	%	TGF	PGF	TGA	PGA	+/–	GP	G	A	Pts	PIM	PP	SH	GW
1990-91	VSZ Kosice	Czech.	54	1	7	8	....	....	....	12	....	....	....	....	....	....	....	....	....	....	....	....	....	....	....	....	....	....
	Czechoslovakia	WJC-A	5	0	1	1	....	....	....	4	....	....	....	....	....	....	....	....	....	....	....	....	....	....	....	....	....	....
1991-92	VSZ Kosice	Czech.	43	4	9	13	....	....	....	24	....	....	....	....	....	....	....	....	....	....	....	....	....	....	....	....	....	....
	Czechoslovakia	WJC-A	6	0	3	3	....	....	....	6	....	....	....	....	....	....	....	....	....	....	....	....	....	....	....	....	....	....
1992-93	Indianapolis Ice	IHL	77	14	29	43	....	....	....	92	....	....	....	....	....	....	....	....	....	....	5	0	1	1	2	....	....	....
1993-94	**Chicago Blackhawks**	**NHL**	**12**	**0**	**1**	**1**	**0**	**1**	**1**	**12**	**0**	**0**	**0**	**13**	**0.0**	**8**	**0**	**7**	**1**	**+2**	....	....	....	....	....	....	....	....
	Indianapolis Ice	IHL	55	9	10	19	....	....	....	71	....	....	....	....	....	....	....	....	....	....	....	....	....	....	....	....	....	....

			REGULAR SEASON																		PLAYOFFS							
Season	Club	League	GP	G	A	Pts	AG	AA	APts	PIM	PP	SH	GW	S	%	TGF	PGF	TGA	PGA	+/–	GP	G	A	Pts	PIM	PP	SH	GW
1994-95	Indianapolis Ice	IHL	67	5	28	33	....	....	....	91	....	....	....	....	....	....	....	....	....	....	....	....	....	....	....	....	....	....
1995-96	**Chicago Blackhawks**	**NHL**	**7**	**0**	**0**	**0**	**0**	**0**	**0**	**2**	**0**	**0**	**0**	**1**	**0.0**	**3**	**0**	**1**	**0**	**+2**	....	....	....	....	....	....	....	....
	Indianapolis Ice	IHL	72	6	30	36	....	....	....	71	....	....	....	....	....	....	....	....	....	....	3	0	1	1	2	....	....	....
1996-97	Slovakia	W Cup	3	0	1	1	....	....	....	2	....	....	....	....	....	....	....	....	....	....	....	....	....	....	....	....	....	....
	Indianapolis Ice	IHL	26	1	13	14	....	....	....	44	....	....	....	....	....	....	....	....	....	....	....	....	....	....	....	....	....	....
	Carolina Monarchs	AHL	47	4	22	26	....	....	....	48	....	....	....	....	....	....	....	....	....	....	....	....	....	....	....	....	....	....
	Slovakia	WC-A	8	0	2	2	....	....	....	6	....	....	....	....	....	....	....	....	....	....	....	....	....	....	....	....	....	....
1997-98	HC Kosice	Slovakia	23	4	14	10	....	....	....	14	....	....	....	....	....	....	....	....	....	....	11	2	4	6	29	....	....	....
	Slovakia	Olympics	4	0	0	0	....	....	....	0	....	....	....	....	....	....	....	....	....	....	....	....	....	....	....	....	....	....
	Slovakia	WC-A	6	0	0	0	....	....	....	8	....	....	....	....	....	....	....	....	....	....	....	....	....	....	....	....	....	....
	NHL Totals		**19**	**0**	**1**	**1**	**0**	**1**	**1**	**14**	**0**	**0**	**0**	**14**	**0.0**	**11**	**0**	**8**	**1**		....	....	....	....	....	....	....	....

EJC-A All-Star Team (1990) • Named Best Defenseman at EJC-A (1990)

Traded to **Florida** by **Chicago** for Alain Nasreddine and a conditional choice in 1999 Entry Draft, December 18, 1996.

• DROUIN, JUDE

Jude Drouin C – R. 5'10", 160 lbs. b: Mont Louis, Que., 10/28/1948. Montreal's 3rd choice, 17th overall, in 1966 Amateur Draft.

Season	Club	League	GP	G	A	Pts	AG	AA	APts	PIM	PP	SH	GW	S	%	TGF	PGF	TGA	PGA	+/–	GP	G	A	Pts	PIM	PP	SH	GW
1965-66	Verdun Maple Leafs	QJHL	38	33	32	65	....	....	....	103	....	....	....	....	....	....	....	....	....	....	....	....	....	....	....	....	....	....
1966-67	Montreal Jr. Canadiens	OHA	47	32	36	68	....	....	....	64	....	....	....	....	....	....	....	....	....	....	3	0	3	3	9	....	....	....
1967-68	Houston Apollos	CHL	68	22	38	60	....	....	....	59	....	....	....	....	....	....	....	....	....	....	....	....	....	....	....	....	....	....
1968-69	**Montreal Canadiens**	**NHL**	**9**	**0**	**1**	**1**	**0**	**1**	**1**	**0**	**0**	**0**	**0**	**3**	**0.0**	**2**	**0**	**1**	**0**	**+1**	....	....	....	....	....	....	....	....
	Houston Apollos	CHL	53	23	31	54	....	....	....	117	....	....	....	....	....	....	....	....	....	....	3	1	1	2	23	....	....	....
1969-70	**Montreal Canadiens**	**NHL**	**3**	**0**	**0**	**0**	**0**	**0**	**0**	**2**	**0**	**0**	**0**	**8**	**0.0**	**0**	**0**	**2**	**0**	**–2**	....	....	....	....	....	....	....	....
	Montreal Voyageurs	AHL	65	37	*69	106	....	....	....	88	....	....	....	....	....	....	....	....	....	....	8	0	6	6	2	....	....	....
1970-71	**Minnesota North Stars**	**NHL**	**75**	**16**	**52**	**68**	**17**	**46**	**63**	**49**	**4**	**0**	**2**	**208**	**7.7**	**88**	**31**	**53**	**1**	**+5**	**12**	**5**	**7**	**12**	**10**	**1**	**0**	**0**
1971-72	**Minnesota North Stars**	**NHL**	**63**	**13**	**43**	**56**	**14**	**39**	**53**	**31**	**3**	**0**	**5**	**213**	**6.1**	**78**	**28**	**46**	**0**	**+4**	**7**	**4**	**4**	**8**	**6**	**1**	**0**	**1**
1972-73	**Minnesota North Stars**	**NHL**	**78**	**27**	**46**	**73**	**27**	**39**	**66**	**61**	**3**	**0**	**5**	**279**	**9.7**	**95**	**21**	**63**	**1**	**+12**	**6**	**1**	**3**	**4**	**0**	**0**	**0**	**0**
1973-74	**Minnesota North Stars**	**NHL**	**65**	**19**	**24**	**43**	**19**	**21**	**40**	**30**	**4**	**0**	**2**	**200**	**9.5**	**55**	**14**	**53**	**1**	**–11**	....	....	....	....	....	....	....	....
1974-75	**Minnesota North Stars**	**NHL**	**38**	**4**	**18**	**22**	**4**	**14**	**18**	**16**	**1**	**0**	**1**	**72**	**5.6**	**30**	**5**	**46**	**2**	**–19**	....	....	....	....	....	....	....	....
	New York Islanders	**NHL**	**40**	**14**	**18**	**32**	**13**	**14**	**27**	**6**	**2**	**0**	**2**	**93**	**15.1**	**47**	**11**	**28**	**0**	**+8**	**17**	**6**	***12**	**18**	**6**	**1**	**0**	**1**
1975-76	**New York Islanders**	**NHL**	**76**	**21**	**41**	**62**	**20**	**32**	**52**	**58**	**10**	**0**	**2**	**153**	**13.7**	**87**	**34**	**35**	**0**	**+18**	**13**	**6**	**9**	**15**	**0**	**1**	**0**	**1**
1976-77	**New York Islanders**	**NHL**	**78**	**24**	**29**	**53**	**23**	**24**	**47**	**27**	**4**	**0**	**2**	**135**	**17.8**	**82**	**20**	**44**	**0**	**+18**	**12**	**5**	**6**	**11**	**6**	**1**	**0**	**0**
1977-78	**New York Islanders**	**NHL**	**56**	**5**	**17**	**22**	**5**	**14**	**19**	**12**	**0**	**0**	**0**	**78**	**6.4**	**40**	**4**	**22**	**0**	**+14**	**5**	**0**	**0**	**0**	**5**	**0**	**0**	**0**
1978-79			DID NOT PLAY																									
1979-80	**Winnipeg Jets**	**NHL**	**78**	**8**	**16**	**24**	**7**	**12**	**19**	**50**	**1**	**2**	**1**	**84**	**9.5**	**38**	**6**	**103**	**33**	**–38**	....	....	....	....	....	....	....	....
1980-81	**Winnipeg Jets**	**NHL**	**7**	**0**	**0**	**0**	**0**	**0**	**0**	**4**	**0**	**0**	**0**	**1**	**0.0**	**0**	**0**	**5**	**3**	**–2**	....	....	....	....	....	....	....	....
	NHL Totals		**666**	**151**	**305**	**456**	**149**	**256**	**405**	**346**	**32**	**2**	**22**	**1527**	**9.9**	**642**	**174**	**501**	**41**		**72**	**27**	**41**	**68**	**33**	**5**	**0**	**3**

AHL First All-Star Team (1970) • Won Dudley "Red" Garrett Memorial Award (Top Rookie - AHL) (1970) • Won John B. Sollenberger Trophy (Top Scorer - AHL) (1970)

Traded to **Minnesota** by **Montreal** for Bill Collins, June 10, 1970. Traded to **NY Islanders** by **Minnesota** for Craig Cameron, January 7, 1975. Signed as a free agent by **Winnipeg**, October 5, 1979.

• DROUIN, P.C.

P.C. Drouin LW – L. 6'2", 208 lbs. b: St. Lambert, Que., 4/22/1974.

Season	Club	League	GP	G	A	Pts	AG	AA	APts	PIM	PP	SH	GW	S	%	TGF	PGF	TGA	PGA	+/–	GP	G	A	Pts	PIM	PP	SH	GW
1992-93	Cornell University	ECAC	23	3	6	9	....	....	....	30	....	....	....	....	....	....	....	....	....	....	....	....	....	....	....	....	....	....
1993-94	Cornell University	ECAC	21	0	13	19	....	....	....	32	....	....	....	....	....	....	....	....	....	....	....	....	....	....	....	....	....	....
1994-95	Cornell University	ECAC	26	4	16	20	....	....	....	48	....	....	....	....	....	....	....	....	....	....	....	....	....	....	....	....	....	....
1995-96	Cornell University	ECAC	31	18	14	32	....	....	....	60	....	....	....	....	....	....	....	....	....	....	....	....	....	....	....	....	....	....
1996-97	**Boston Bruins**	**NHL**	**3**	**0**	**0**	**0**	**0**	**0**	**0**	**0**	**0**	**0**	**0**	**1**	**0.0**	**1**	**0**	**0**	**0**	**+1**	....	....	....	....	....	....	....	....
	Providence Bruins	AHL	42	12	11	23	....	....	....	10	....	....	....	....	....	....	....	....	....	....	....	....	....	....	....	....	....	....
1997-98	Providence Bruins	AHL	7	0	2	2	....	....	....	4	....	....	....	....	....	....	....	....	....	....	....	....	....	....	....	....	....	....
	Charlotte Checkers	ECHL	62	21	46	67	....	....	....	57	....	....	....	....	....	....	....	....	....	....	7	2	4	6	4	....	....	....
	NHL Totals		**3**	**0**	**0**	**0**	**0**	**0**	**0**	**0**	**0**	**0**	**0**	**1**	**0.0**	**1**	**0**	**0**	**0**		....	....	....	....	....	....	....	....

Signed as a free agent by **Boston**, October 14, 1990.

• DRUCE, JOHN

John Druce RW – R. 6'2", 195 lbs. b: Peterborough, Ont., 2/23/1966. Washington's 2nd choice, 40th overall, in 1985 Entry Draft.

Season	Club	League	GP	G	A	Pts	AG	AA	APts	PIM	PP	SH	GW	S	%	TGF	PGF	TGA	PGA	+/–	GP	G	A	Pts	PIM	PP	SH	GW
1984-85	Peterborough Petes	OHL	54	12	14	26	....	....	....	90	....	....	....	....	....	....	....	....	....	....	17	6	2	8	21	....	....	....
1985-86	Peterborough Petes	OHL	49	22	24	46	....	....	....	84	....	....	....	....	....	....	....	....	....	....	16	0	5	5	34	....	....	....
1986-87	Binghamton Whalers	AHL	77	13	9	22	....	....	....	131	....	....	....	....	....	....	....	....	....	....	12	0	3	3	28	....	....	....
1987-88	Binghamton Whalers	AHL	68	32	29	61	....	....	....	82	....	....	....	....	....	....	....	....	....	....	1	0	0	0	0	....	....	....
1988-89	**Washington Capitals**	**NHL**	**48**	**8**	**7**	**15**	**7**	**5**	**12**	**62**	**0**	**0**	**1**	**59**	**13.6**	**22**	**0**	**15**	**0**	**+7**	**1**	**0**	**0**	**0**	**0**	**0**	**0**	**0**
	Baltimore Skipjacks	AHL	16	2	11	13	....	....	....	10	....	....	....	....	....	....	....	....	....	....	....	....	....	....	....	....	....	....
1989-90	Washington Capitals	FrTour	2	0	0	0	....	....	....	2	....	....	....	....	....	....	....	....	....	....	....	....	....	....	....	....	....	....
	Washington Capitals	**NHL**	**45**	**8**	**3**	**11**	**7**	**2**	**9**	**52**	**1**	**0**	**1**	**66**	**12.1**	**15**	**1**	**23**	**6**	**–3**	**15**	**14**	**3**	**17**	**23**	**8**	**1**	**4**
	Baltimore Skipjacks	AHL	26	15	16	31	....	....	....	38	....	....	....	....	....	....	....	....	....	....	....	....	....	....	....	....	....	....
1990-91	**Washington Capitals**	**NHL**	**80**	**22**	**36**	**58**	**20**	**27**	**47**	**46**	**7**	**1**	**4**	**209**	**10.5**	**94**	**38**	**64**	**12**	**+4**	**11**	**1**	**1**	**2**	**7**	**1**	**0**	**0**
1991-92	**Washington Capitals**	**NHL**	**67**	**19**	**18**	**37**	**17**	**14**	**31**	**39**	**1**	**0**	**3**	**129**	**14.7**	**50**	**4**	**35**	**3**	**+14**	**7**	**1**	**0**	**1**	**2**	**0**	**0**	**1**
1992-93	**Winnipeg Jets**	**NHL**	**50**	**6**	**14**	**20**	**5**	**10**	**15**	**37**	**0**	**0**	**0**	**60**	**10.0**	**31**	**2**	**41**	**8**	**–4**	**2**	**0**	**0**	**0**	**0**	**0**	**0**	**0**
1993-94	**Los Angeles Kings**	**NHL**	**55**	**14**	**17**	**31**	**13**	**13**	**26**	**50**	**1**	**1**	**0**	**104**	**13.5**	**50**	**5**	**30**	**1**	**+16**	....	....	....	....	....	....	....	....
	Phoenix Roadrunners	IHL	8	5	6	11	....	....	....	9	....	....	....	....	....	....	....	....	....	....	....	....	....	....	....	....	....	....
1994-95	**Los Angeles Kings**	**NHL**	**43**	**15**	**5**	**20**	**27**	**7**	**34**	**20**	**3**	**0**	**1**	**75**	**20.0**	**30**	**6**	**31**	**4**	**–3**	....	....	....	....	....	....	....	....
1995-96	**Los Angeles Kings**	**NHL**	**64**	**9**	**12**	**21**	**9**	**10**	**19**	**14**	**0**	**0**	**0**	**103**	**8.7**	**23**	**3**	**68**	**22**	**–26**	....	....	....	....	....	....	....	....
	Philadelphia Flyers	**NHL**	**13**	**4**	**4**	**8**	**4**	**3**	**7**	**13**	**0**	**0**	**0**	**25**	**16.0**	**10**	**1**	**3**	**0**	**+6**	**2**	**0**	**2**	**2**	**2**	**0**	**0**	**0**
1996-97	**Philadelphia Flyers**	**NHL**	**43**	**7**	**8**	**15**	**7**	**7**	**14**	**12**	**1**	**0**	**0**	**73**	**9.6**	**16**	**1**	**25**	**5**	**–5**	**13**	**1**	**0**	**1**	**2**	**0**	**1**	**0**
1997-98	**Philadelphia Flyers**	**NHL**	**23**	**1**	**2**	**3**	**1**	**2**	**3**	**2**	**0**	**0**	**0**	**18**	**5.6**	**4**	**0**	**5**	**1**	**0**	**2**	**0**	**0**	**0**	**2**	**0**	**0**	**0**
	Philadelphia Phantoms	AHL	39	21	28	49	....	....	....	45	....	....	....	....	....	....	....	....	....	....	....	....	....	....	....	....	....	....
	NHL Totals		**531**	**113**	**126**	**239**	**117**	**100**	**217**	**347**	**14**	**2**	**10**	**921**	**12.3**	**345**	**61**	**340**	**62**		**53**	**17**	**6**	**23**	**38**	**9**	**2**	**5**

Traded to **Winnipeg** by **Washington** with Toronto's 4th round choice (previously acquired by Washington — later traded to Detroit — Detroit selected John Jakopin) in 1993 Entry Draft for Pat Elynuik, October 1, 1992. Signed as a free agent by **LA Kings**, August 2, 1993. Traded to **Philadelphia** by **LA Kings** with LA Kings' 7th round choice (Todd Fedoruk) in 1997 Entry Draft for LA Kings' 4th round choice (previously acquired, LA Kings selected Mikael Simons) in 1996 Entry Draft, March 19, 1996.

• DRULIA, STAN

Stan Drulia RW – R. 5'11", 190 lbs. b: Elmira, NY, 1/5/1968. Pittsburgh's 11th choice, 214th overall, in 1986 Entry Draft.

Season	Club	League	GP	G	A	Pts	AG	AA	APts	PIM	PP	SH	GW	S	%	TGF	PGF	TGA	PGA	+/–	GP	G	A	Pts	PIM	PP	SH	GW
1984-85	Belleville Bulls	OHL	63	24	31	55	....	....	....	33	....	....	....	....	....	....	....	....	....	....	....	....	....	....	....	....	....	....
1985-86	Belleville Bulls	OHL	66	43	36	79	....	....	....	73	....	....	....	....	....	....	....	....	....	....	24	4	11	15	15	....	....	....
1986-87	Hamilton Steelhawks	OHL	55	27	51	78	....	....	....	26	....	....	....	....	....	....	....	....	....	....	9	4	4	8	2	....	....	....
1987-88	Hamilton Steelhawks	OHL	65	52	69	121	....	....	....	44	....	....	....	....	....	....	....	....	....	....	14	8	16	24	12	....	....	....
1988-89	Niagara Falls Thunder	OHL	47	52	93	145	....	....	....	59	....	....	....	....	....	....	....	....	....	....	17	11	*26	37	18	....	....	....
	Maine Mariners	AHL	3	1	1	2	....	....	....	0	....	....	....	....	....	....	....	....	....	....	....	....	....	....	....	....	....	....
1989-90	Phoenix Roadrunners	IHL	16	6	3	9	....	....	....	2	....	....	....	....	....	....	....	....	....	....	....	....	....	....	....	....	....	....
	Cape Breton Oilers	AHL	31	5	7	12	....	....	....	2	....	....	....	....	....	....	....	....	....	....	....	....	....	....	....	....	....	....
1990-91	Knoxville Cherokees	ECHL	64	*63	77	*140	....	....	....	39	....	....	....	....	....	....	....	....	....	....	3	3	2	5	4	....	....	....
1991-92	New Haven Nighthawks	AHL	77	49	53	102	....	....	....	46	....	....	....	....	....	....	....	....	....	....	5	2	4	6	4	....	....	....
1992-93	**Tampa Bay Lightning**	**NHL**	**24**	**2**	**1**	**3**	**2**	**1**	**3**	**10**	**0**	**0**	**1**	**22**	**9.1**	**10**	**1**	**10**	**2**	**+1**	....	....	....	....	....	....	....	....
	Atlanta Knights	IHL	47	28	26	54	....	....	....	38	....	....	....	....	....	....	....	....	....	....	3	2	3	5	4	....	....	....
1993-94	Atlanta Knights	IHL	79	54	60	114	....	....	....	70	....	....	....	....	....	....	....	....	....	....	14	13	12	25	8	....	....	....
1994-95	Atlanta Knights	IHL	66	41	49	90	....	....	....	60	....	....	....	....	....	....	....	....	....	....	5	1	5	6	2	....	....	....
1995-96	Atlanta Knights	IHL	75	38	56	94	....	....	....	80	....	....	....	....	....	....	....	....	....	....	3	0	2	2	18	....	....	....
1996-97	Detroit Vipers	IHL	73	33	38	71	....	....	....	42	....	....	....	....	....	....	....	....	....	....	21	5	21	26	14	....	....	....
1997-98	Detroit Vipers	IHL	58	25	35	60	....	....	....	50	....	....	....	....	....	....	....	....	....	....	15	2	4	6	16	....	....	....
	NHL Totals		**24**	**2**	**1**	**3**	**2**	**1**	**3**	**10**	**0**	**0**	**1**	**22**	**9.1**	**10**	**1**	**10**	**2**		....	....	....	....	....	....	....	....

OHL First All-Star Team (1989) • ECHL First All-Star Team (1991) • MVP - ECHL (1991) • AHL Second All-Star Team (1992) • IHL First All-Star Team (1994, 1995) • Won "Bud" Poile Trophy (Playoff MVP - IHL) (1994)

Signed as a free agent by **Edmonton**, February 24, 1989. Signed as a free agent by **Tampa Bay**, September 1, 1992.

• DRURY, TED
Ted Drury C – L. 6', 185 lbs. b: Boston, MA, 9/13/1971. Calgary's 2nd choice, 42nd overall, in 1989 Entry Draft.

			REGULAR SEASON																		PLAYOFFS							
Season	Club	League	GP	G	A	Pts	AG	AA	APts	PIM	PP	SH	GW	S	%	TGF	PGF	TGA	PGA	+/–	GP	G	A	Pts	PIM	PP	SH	GW
1988-89	Fairfield Prep College	H.S.	25	35	31	66																						
1989-90	Harvard University	ECAC	17	9	13	22				10																		
	United States	WJC-A	7	2	1	3				2																		
1990-91	Harvard University	ECAC	25	18	18	36				22																		
1991-92	United States	Nat-Team	53	11	23	34				30																		
	United States	Olympics	7	1	1	2				0																		
1992-93	Harvard University	ECAC	31	22	*41	*63				28																		
	United States	WC-A	6	0	0	0				0																		
1993-94	**Calgary Flames**	**NHL**	**34**	**5**	**7**	**12**	5	5	10	26	0	1	1	43	11.6	19	2	28	6	–5								
	United States	Nat-Team	11	1	4	5				11																		
	United States	Olympics	7	1	2	3				2																		
	Hartford Whalers	**NHL**	**16**	**1**	**5**	**6**	1	4	5	10	0	0	0	37	2.7	7	0	20	3	–10								
1994-95	**Hartford Whalers**	**NHL**	**34**	**3**	**6**	**9**	5	9	14	21	0	0	0	31	9.7	13	0	18	2	–3								
	Springfield Falcons	AHL	2	0	1	1				0																		
1995-96	**Ottawa Senators**	**NHL**	**42**	**9**	**7**	**16**	9	6	15	54	1	0	1	80	11.3	20	5	54	20	–19								
1996-97	**Anaheim Mighty Ducks**	**NHL**	**73**	**9**	**9**	**18**	10	8	18	54	1	0	2	114	7.9	25	1	39	6	–9	10	1	0	1	4	0	0	0
1997-98	**Anaheim Mighty Ducks**	**NHL**	**73**	**6**	**10**	**16**	7	10	17	82	0	1	0	110	5.5	25	0	56	21	–10								
	United States	WC-A	6	0	1	1				4																		
	NHL Totals		**272**	**33**	**44**	**77**	37	42	79	247	2	2	4	415	8.0	109	8	215	58		10	1	0	1	4	0	0	0

ECAC First All-Star Team (1993) • NCAA East First All-America Team (1993)

Traded to **Hartford** by **Calgary** with Gary Suter and Paul Ranheim for James Patrick, Zarley Zalapski and Michael Nylander, March 10, 1994. Claimed by **Ottawa** from **Hartford** in NHL Waiver Draft, October 2, 1995. Traded to **Anaheim** by **Ottawa** with the rights to Marc Moro for Jason York and Shaun Van Allen, October 1, 1996.

• DUBE, CHRISTIAN
Christian Dube C – R. 5'11", 170 lbs. b: Sherbrooke, Que., 4/25/1977. NY Rangers' 6th choice, 39th overall, in 1995 Entry Draft.

			REGULAR SEASON																		PLAYOFFS							
Season	Club	League	GP	G	A	Pts	AG	AA	APts	PIM	PP	SH	GW	S	%	TGF	PGF	TGA	PGA	+/–	GP	G	A	Pts	PIM	PP	SH	GW
1993-94	Sherbrooke Faucons	QMJHL	72	31	41	72				22											11	3	2	5	8			
1994-95	Sherbrooke Faucons	QMJHL	71	36	65	101				43											7	1	7	8	8			
1995-96	Sherbrooke Faucons	QMJHL	62	52	93	145				105											7	5	5	10	6			
	Canada	WJC-A	6	4	2	6				0																		
1996-97	Hull Olympiques	QMJHL	19	15	22	37				37											14	7	16	23	14			
	Canada	WJC-A	7	4	3	7				0																		
	New York Rangers	**NHL**	**27**	**1**	**1**	**2**	1	1	2	4	1	0	0	14	7.1	5	4	5	0	–4	**3**	**0**	**0**	**0**	**0**	0	0	0
1997-98	Hartford Wolf Pack	AHL	79	11	46	57				46											9	0	4	4	6			
	NHL Totals		**27**	**1**	**1**	**2**	1	1	2	4	1	0	0	14	7.1	5	4	5	0		3	0	0	0	0	0	0	0

QMJHL First All-Star Team (1996) • Canadian Major Junior First All-Star Team (1996) • Canadian Major Junior Player of the Year (1996) • WJC-A All-Star Team (1997) • Won Stafford Smythe Memorial Trophy (Memorial Cup Tournament MVP) (1997)

• DUBE, NORM
Norm Dube LW – L. 5'11", 185 lbs. b: Sherbrooke, Que., 9/12/1951. Los Angeles' 6th choice, 90th overall, in 1971 Amateur Draft.

			REGULAR SEASON																		PLAYOFFS							
Season	Club	League	GP	G	A	Pts	AG	AA	APts	PIM	PP	SH	GW	S	%	TGF	PGF	TGA	PGA	+/–	GP	G	A	Pts	PIM	PP	SH	GW
1969-70	Sherbrooke Castors	QJHL	52	19	34	53				27																		
1970-71	Sherbrooke Castors	QJHL	62	72	66	138				17											8	4	7	11	10			
1971-72	University of Sherbrooke	QUAA	STATISTICS NOT AVAILABLE																									
1972-73	Springfield Kings	AHL	66	30	30	60				21																		
1973-74	Springfield Kings	AHL	48	32	21	53				10																		
1974-75	**Kansas City Scouts**	**NHL**	**56**	**8**	**10**	**18**	7	8	15	54	2	0	1	77	10.4	28	4	36	0	–12								
	Providence Reds	AHL	14	5	0	5				4																		
1975-76	**Kansas City Scouts**	**NHL**	**1**	**0**	**0**	**0**	0	0	0	0	0	0	0	0	0.0	0	0	0	0	0								
	Springfield Indians	AHL	67	31	38	69				28																		
1976-77	Beauce Jaros	NAHL	29	20	32	52				12																		
	Quebec Nordiques	WHA	39	15	18	33				8											14	3	12	15	11			
1977-78	Quebec Nordiques	WHA	73	16	31	47				17											10	2	2	4	6			
1978-79	Quebec Nordiques	WHA	36	2	13	15				4																		
	Binghamton Whalers	AHL	36	9	24	33				18											8	4	5	9	14			
1979-80	Nova Scotia Voyageurs	AHL	79	40	*61	*101				49											6	4	2	6	2			
	NHL Totals		**57**	**8**	**10**	**18**	7	8	15	54	2	0	1	77	10.4	28	4	36	0									
	Other Major League Totals		148	33	62	95				29											24	5	14	19	17			

QJHL Second All-Star Team (1971) • AHL First All-Star Team (1980) • Won John B. Sollenberger Trophy (Top Scorer - AHL) (1980) • Won Les Cunningham Award (MVP - AHL) (1980)

Selected by **Ontario-Ottawa** (WHA) in 1972 WHA General Player Draft, February 12, 1972. Claimed by **Kansas City** from **LA Kings** in Expansion Draft, June 12, 1974. WHA rights traded to **Quebec** (WHA) by **Birmingham** (WHA) for future considerations, June 30, 1976.

• DUBERMAN, JUSTIN
Justin Duberman RW – R. 6'1", 185 lbs. b: New Haven, CT, 3/23/1970. Montreal's 12th choice, 230th overall, in 1989 Entry Draft.

			REGULAR SEASON																		PLAYOFFS							
Season	Club	League	GP	G	A	Pts	AG	AA	APts	PIM	PP	SH	GW	S	%	TGF	PGF	TGA	PGA	+/–	GP	G	A	Pts	PIM	PP	SH	GW
1987-88	Detroit Compuware	Tier II	56	61	43	104																						
1988-89	University of North Dakota	WCHA	33	3	1	4				30																		
1989-90	University of North Dakota	WCHA	42	10	9	19				50																		
1990-91	University of North Dakota	WCHA	42	19	18	37				68																		
1991-92	University of North Dakota	WCHA	39	17	27	44				90																		
1992-93	Cleveland Lumberjacks	IHL	77	29	42	71				69											4	0	0	0	12			
1993-94	**Pittsburgh Penguins**	**NHL**	**4**	**0**	**0**	**0**	0	0	0	0	0	0	0	2	0.0	1	0	1	0	0								
	Cleveland Lumberjacks	IHL	59	9	13	22				63																		
1994-95	JyP HT	Finland	2	0	0	0				4																		
	Johnstown Chiefs	ECHL	24	13	14	27				30											5	0	7	7	20			
	Chicago Wolves	IHL	13	1	3	4				39																		
1995-96			DID NOT PLAY																									
1996-97	Newcastle Cobras	Britain	30	20	18	38				106											6	2	1	3	16			
1997-98	Newcastle Cobras	Britain	37	8	10	18				28											6	0	2	2	6			
	NHL Totals		**4**	**0**	**0**	**0**	0	0	0	0	0	0	0	2	0.0	1	0	1	0									

Signed as a free agent by **Pittsburgh**, November 2, 1992.

• DUBINSKY, STEVE
Steve Dubinsky C – L. 6', 190 lbs. b: Montreal, Que., 7/9/1970. Chicago's 9th choice, 226th overall, in 1990 Entry Draft.

			REGULAR SEASON																		PLAYOFFS							
Season	Club	League	GP	G	A	Pts	AG	AA	APts	PIM	PP	SH	GW	S	%	TGF	PGF	TGA	PGA	+/–	GP	G	A	Pts	PIM	PP	SH	GW
1989-90	Clarkson University	ECAC	35	7	10	17				24																		
1990-91	Clarkson University	ECAC	39	13	23	36				26																		
1991-92	Clarkson University	ECAC	32	20	31	51				40																		
1992-93	Clarkson University	ECAC	35	18	26	44				58																		
1993-94	**Chicago Blackhawks**	**NHL**	**27**	**2**	**6**	**8**	2	5	7	16	0	0	0	20	10.0	8	1	7	1	+1	**6**	**0**	**0**	**0**	**10**	0	0	0
	Indianapolis Ice	IHL	54	15	25	40				63																		
1994-95	**Chicago Blackhawks**	**NHL**	**16**	**0**	**0**	**0**	0	0	0	8	0	0	0	16	0.0	2	1	6	0	–5								
	Indianapolis Ice	IHL	62	16	11	27				29																		
1995-96	**Chicago Blackhawks**	**NHL**	**43**	**2**	**3**	**5**	2	2	4	14	0	0	0	33	6.1	11	0	12	4	+3								
	Indianapolis Ice	IHL	16	8	8	16				10																		
1996-97	**Chicago Blackhawks**	**NHL**	**5**	**0**	**0**	**0**	0	0	0	0	0	0	0	4	0.0	2	0	1	1	+2	**4**	**1**	**0**	**1**	**4**	0	0	0
	Indianapolis Ice	IHL	77	32	40	72				53											1	3	1	4	0			
1997-98	**Chicago Blackhawks**	**NHL**	**82**	**5**	**13**	**18**	6	13	19	57	0	1	0	112	4.5	22	0	42	14	–6								
	NHL Totals		**173**	**9**	**22**	**31**	10	20	30	95	0	1	0	185	4.9	45	2	68	20		10	1	0	1	14	0	0	0

• DUCHESNE, GAETAN
Gaetan Duchesne LW – L. 5'11", 200 lbs. b: Les Saulles, Que., 7/11/1962. Washington's 8th choice, 152nd overall, in 1981 Entry Draft.

			REGULAR SEASON																		PLAYOFFS							
Season	Club	League	GP	G	A	Pts	AG	AA	APts	PIM	PP	SH	GW	S	%	TGF	PGF	TGA	PGA	+/–	GP	G	A	Pts	PIM	PP	SH	GW
1979-80	Quebec Remparts	QMJHL	46	9	28	37				22											5	0	2	2	9			
1980-81	Quebec Remparts	QMJHL	72	27	45	72				63											7	1	4	5	6			
1981-82	**Washington Capitals**	**NHL**	**74**	**9**	**14**	**23**	7	9	16	46	0	0	1	78	11.5	37	0	65	22	–6								
1982-83	**Washington Capitals**	**NHL**	**77**	**18**	**19**	**37**	15	13	28	52	0	1	6	126	14.3	54	0	54	15	+15	**4**	**1**	**1**	**2**	**4**	0	0	0
	Hershey Bears	AHL	1	1	0	1				0																		

			REGULAR SEASON																		PLAYOFFS							
Season	Club	League	GP	G	A	Pts	AG	AA	APts	PIM	PP	SH	GW	S	%	TGF	PGF	TGA	PGA	+/–	GP	G	A	Pts	PIM	PP	SH	GW
1983-84	**Washington Capitals**	**NHL**	**79**	**17**	**19**	**36**	**14**	**13**	**27**	**29**	**3**	**2**	**1**	**116**	**14.7**	**64**	**6**	**61**	**18**	**+15**	**8**	**2**	**1**	**3**	**2**	**0**	**0**	**1**
1984-85	**Washington Capitals**	**NHL**	**67**	**15**	**23**	**38**	**12**	**16**	**28**	**32**	**0**	**1**	**1**	**84**	**17.9**	**53**	**0**	**56**	**19**	**+16**	**5**	**0**	**1**	**1**	**7**	**0**	**0**	**0**
1985-86	**Washington Capitals**	**NHL**	**80**	**11**	**28**	**39**	**9**	**19**	**28**	**39**	**0**	**1**	**3**	**119**	**9.2**	**57**	**1**	**63**	**17**	**+10**	**9**	**4**	**3**	**7**	**12**	**0**	**1**	**0**
1986-87	**Washington Capitals**	**NHL**	**74**	**17**	**35**	**52**	**15**	**25**	**40**	**53**	**0**	**1**	**4**	**108**	**15.7**	**69**	**1**	**73**	**23**	**+18**	**7**	**3**	**0**	**3**	**14**	**0**	**0**	**0**
1987-88	**Quebec Nordiques**	**NHL**	**80**	**24**	**23**	**47**	**21**	**16**	**37**	**83**	**4**	**1**	**2**	**138**	**17.4**	**61**	**12**	**80**	**39**	**+8**	....	....	....	....	....	....	....	....
1988-89	**Quebec Nordiques**	**NHL**	**70**	**8**	**21**	**29**	**7**	**15**	**22**	**56**	**2**	**1**	**1**	**110**	**7.3**	**49**	**7**	**73**	**31**	**0**	....	....	....	....	....	....	....	....
1989-90	**Minnesota North Stars**	**NHL**	**72**	**12**	**8**	**20**	**10**	**6**	**16**	**33**	**0**	**1**	**1**	**93**	**12.9**	**31**	**0**	**46**	**20**	**+5**	**7**	**0**	**0**	**0**	**6**	**0**	**0**	**0**
1990-91	Minnesota North Stars	FrTour	3	1	0	1	....	....	....	2	....	....	....	....	....	....	....	....	....	....	....	....	....	....	....	....	....	....
	Minnesota North Stars	**NHL**	**68**	**9**	**9**	**18**	**8**	**7**	**15**	**18**	**0**	**0**	**1**	**100**	**9.0**	**31**	**1**	**44**	**18**	**+4**	**23**	**2**	**3**	**5**	**34**	**0**	**0**	**0**
1991-92	**Minnesota North Stars**	**NHL**	**73**	**8**	**15**	**23**	**7**	**11**	**18**	**102**	**0**	**2**	**1**	**106**	**7.5**	**37**	**0**	**56**	**25**	**+6**	**7**	**1**	**0**	**1**	**6**	**0**	**0**	**0**
1992-93	**Minnesota North Stars**	**NHL**	**84**	**16**	**13**	**29**	**13**	**9**	**22**	**30**	**0**	**2**	**3**	**134**	**11.9**	**40**	**0**	**71**	**37**	**+6**	....	....	....	....	....	....	....	....
1993-94	**San Jose Sharks**	**NHL**	**84**	**12**	**18**	**30**	**11**	**14**	**25**	**28**	**0**	**1**	**3**	**121**	**9.9**	**54**	**2**	**78**	**34**	**+8**	**14**	**1**	**4**	**5**	**12**	**0**	**0**	**0**
1994-95	**San Jose Sharks**	**NHL**	**33**	**2**	**7**	**9**	**4**	**10**	**14**	**16**	**0**	**0**	**0**	**48**	**4.2**	**11**	**0**	**32**	**15**	**–6**	....	....	....	....	....	....	....	....
	Florida Panthers	**NHL**	**13**	**1**	**2**	**3**	**2**	**3**	**5**	**0**	**0**	**0**	**0**	**14**	**7.1**	**6**	**0**	**3**	**0**	**+3**	....	....	....	....	....	....	....	....
1995-96			DID NOT PLAY – RETIRED																									
1996-97	Quebec Rafales	IHL	66	10	18	28	....	....	....	54	....	....	....	....	....	....	....	....	....	....	9	5	0	5	4	....	....	....
1997-98	Quebec Rafales	IHL	3	0	0	0	....	....	....	2	....	....	....	....	....	....	....	....	....	....	....	....	....	....	....	....	....	....
	NHL Totals		**1028**	**179**	**254**	**433**	**155**	**186**	**341**	**617**	**9**	**14**	**28**	**1495**	**12.0**	**664**	**30**	**855**	**333**		**84**	**14**	**13**	**27**	**97**	**0**	**1**	**1**

Traded to **Quebec** by **Washington** with Alan Haworth and Washington's 1st round choice (Joe Sakic) in 1987 Entry Draft for Clint Malarchuk and Dale Hunter, June 13, 1987. Traded to **Minnesota** by **Quebec** for Kevin Kamenski, June 9, 1989. Traded to **San Jose** by **Dallas** for San Jose's 6th round choice (later traded back to San Jose — San Jose selected Petri Varis) in 1993 Entry Draft, June 20, 1993. Transferred to **Dallas** after **Minnesota** franchise relocated, June 9, 1993. Traded to **Florida** by **San Jose** for Florida's 6th round choice (Timo Hakanen) in 1995 Entry Draft, April 7, 1995.

• DUCHESNE, STEVE

Steve Duchesne D – L. 5'11", 195 lbs. b: Sept-Iles, Que., 6/30/1965.

1983-84	Drummondville Voltigeurs	QMJHL	67	1	34	35	....	....	....	79	....	....	....	....	....	....	....	....	....	....	....	....	....	....	....	....	....	....
1984-85	Drummondville Voltigeurs	QMJHL	65	22	54	76	....	....	....	94	....	....	....	....	....	....	....	....	....	....	5	4	7	11	8	....	....	....
1985-86	New Haven Nighthawks	AHL	75	14	35	49	....	....	....	76	....	....	....	....	....	....	....	....	....	....	5	0	2	2	9	....	....	....
1986-87	**Los Angeles Kings**	**NHL**	**75**	**13**	**25**	**38**	**11**	**18**	**29**	**74**	**5**	**0**	**2**	**113**	**11.5**	**109**	**27**	**100**	**26**	**+8**	**5**	**2**	**2**	**4**	**4**	**1**	**0**	**0**
1987-88	**Los Angeles Kings**	**NHL**	**71**	**16**	**39**	**55**	**14**	**28**	**42**	**109**	**5**	**0**	**4**	**190**	**8.4**	**126**	**40**	**118**	**32**	**0**	**5**	**1**	**3**	**4**	**14**	**1**	**0**	**0**
1988-89	**Los Angeles Kings**	**NHL**	**79**	**25**	**50**	**75**	**21**	**35**	**56**	**92**	**8**	**5**	**2**	**215**	**11.6**	**169**	**50**	**123**	**35**	**+31**	**11**	**4**	**4**	**8**	**12**	**2**	**0**	**0**
1989-90	**Los Angeles Kings**	**NHL**	**79**	**20**	**42**	**62**	**17**	**30**	**47**	**36**	**6**	**0**	**1**	**224**	**8.9**	**141**	**56**	**115**	**27**	**–3**	**10**	**2**	**9**	**11**	**6**	**1**	**0**	**0**
1990-91	**Los Angeles Kings**	**NHL**	**78**	**21**	**41**	**62**	**19**	**31**	**50**	**66**	**8**	**0**	**3**	**171**	**12.3**	**152**	**58**	**88**	**13**	**+19**	**12**	**4**	**8**	**12**	**8**	**1**	**0**	**0**
1991-92	**Philadelphia Flyers**	**NHL**	**78**	**18**	**38**	**56**	**16**	**29**	**45**	**86**	**7**	**2**	**3**	**229**	**7.9**	**119**	**47**	**104**	**25**	**–7**	....	....	....	....	....	....	....	....
1992-93	**Quebec Nordiques**	**NHL**	**82**	**20**	**62**	**82**	**17**	**43**	**60**	**57**	**8**	**0**	**2**	**227**	**8.8**	**173**	**76**	**98**	**16**	**+15**	**6**	**0**	**5**	**5**	**6**	**0**	**0**	**0**
1993-94	**St. Louis Blues**	**NHL**	**36**	**12**	**19**	**31**	**11**	**15**	**26**	**14**	**8**	**0**	**1**	**115**	**10.4**	**60**	**28**	**45**	**14**	**+1**	**4**	**0**	**2**	**2**	**2**	**0**	**0**	**0**
	Canada	WC-A	6	0	1	1	....	....	....	0	....	....	....	....	....	....	....	....	....	....	....	....	....	....	....	....	....	....
1994-95	**St. Louis Blues**	**NHL**	**47**	**12**	**26**	**38**	**21**	**38**	**59**	**36**	**1**	**0**	**1**	**116**	**10.3**	**83**	**29**	**44**	**19**	**+29**	**7**	**0**	**4**	**4**	**2**	**0**	**0**	**0**
1995-96	**Ottawa Senators**	**NHL**	**62**	**12**	**24**	**36**	**12**	**20**	**32**	**42**	**7**	**0**	**2**	**163**	**7.4**	**82**	**40**	**87**	**22**	**–23**	....	....	....	....	....	....	....	....
	Canada	WC-A	8	1	3	4	....	....	....	4	....	....	....	....	....	....	....	....	....	....	....	....	....	....	....	....	....	....
1996-97	**Ottawa Senators**	**NHL**	**78**	**19**	**28**	**47**	**20**	**25**	**45**	**38**	**10**	**2**	**3**	**208**	**9.1**	**101**	**36**	**94**	**20**	**–9**	**7**	**1**	**4**	**5**	**0**	**1**	**0**	**1**
1997-98	**St. Louis Blues**	**NHL**	**80**	**14**	**42**	**56**	**16**	**41**	**57**	**32**	**5**	**1**	**1**	**153**	**9.2**	**119**	**46**	**82**	**18**	**+9**	**10**	**0**	**4**	**4**	**6**	**0**	**0**	**0**
	NHL Totals		**845**	**202**	**436**	**638**	**195**	**353**	**548**	**682**	**78**	**10**	**25**	**2124**	**9.5**	**1434**	**533**	**1098**	**267**		**77**	**14**	**45**	**59**	**60**	**7**	**0**	**1**

QMJHL First All-Star Team (1985) • NHL All-Rookie Team (1987)

Played in NHL All-Star Game (1989, 1990, 1993)

Signed as a free agent by **LA Kings,** October 1, 1984. Traded to **Philadelphia** by **LA Kings** with Steve Kasper and LA Kings' 4th round choice (Aris Brimanis) in 1991 Entry Draft for Jari Kurri and Jeff Chychrun, May 30, 1991. Traded to **Quebec** by **Philadelphia** with Peter Forsberg, Kerry Huffman, Mike Ricci, Ron Hextall, Chris Simon, Philadelphia's 1st round choice in the 1993 (Jocelyn Thibault) and 1994 (later traded to Toronto — later traded to Washington — Washington selected Nolan Baumgartner) Entry Drafts and cash for Eric Lindros, June 30, 1992. Traded to **St. Louis** by **Quebec** with Denis Chasse for Garth Butcher, Ron Sutter and Bob Bassen, January 23, 1994. Traded to **Ottawa** by **St. Louis** for Ottawa's 2nd round choice (later traded to Buffalo — Buffalo selected Cory Sarich) in 1996 Entry Draft, August 4, 1995. Traded to **St. Louis** by **Ottawa** for Igor Kravchuk, August 25, 1997. Signed as a free agent by **Los Angeles**, July 2, 1998.

• DUDLEY, RICK

Rick Dudley LW – L. 6', 190 lbs. b. Toronto, Ont., 1/31/1949.

1968-69	St. Catharines Black Hawks	OHA	26	8	7	15	....	....	....	43	....	....	....	....	....	....	....	....	....	....	16	2	1	3	46	....	....	....
1969-70	Iowa Stars	CHL	26	3	3	6	....	....	....	36	....	....	....	....	....	....	....	....	....	....	11	0	3	3	4	....	....	....
1970-71	Cleveland Barons	AHL	16	1	0	1	....	....	....	2	....	....	....	....	....	....	....	....	....	....	....	....	....	....	....	....	....	....
	Flint Generals	IHL	15	1	5	6	....	....	....	30	....	....	....	....	....	....	....	....	....	....	....	....	....	....	....	....	....	....
1971-72	Cincinnati Swords	AHL	51	6	23	29	....	....	....	272	....	....	....	....	....	....	....	....	....	....	9	0	4	4	58	....	....	....
1972-73	**Buffalo Sabres**	**NHL**	**6**	**0**	**1**	**1**	**0**	**1**	**1**	**7**	**0**	**0**	**0**	**6**	**0.0**	**1**	**0**	**3**	**0**	**–2**	....	....	....	....	....	....	....	....
	Cincinnati Swords	AHL	64	40	44	84	....	....	....	159	....	....	....	....	....	....	....	....	....	....	15	7	15	22	*56	....	....	....
1973-74	**Buffalo Sabres**	**NHL**	**67**	**13**	**13**	**26**	**13**	**11**	**24**	**71**	**0**	**0**	**2**	**100**	**13.0**	**38**	**2**	**37**	**1**	**0**	....	....	....	....	....	....	....	....
1974-75	**Buffalo Sabres**	**NHL**	**78**	**31**	**39**	**70**	**29**	**31**	**60**	**116**	**4**	**0**	**6**	**226**	**13.7**	**93**	**10**	**54**	**0**	**+29**	**10**	**3**	**1**	**4**	**26**	**1**	**0**	**1**
1975-76	Cincinnati Stingers	WHA	74	43	38	81	....	....	....	156	....	....	....	....	....	....	....	....	....	....	....	....	....	....	....	....	....	....
1976-77	Cincinnati Stingers	WHA	77	41	47	88	....	....	....	102	....	....	....	....	....	....	....	....	....	....	4	0	1	1	7	....	....	....
1977-78	Cincinnati Stingers	WHA	72	30	41	71	....	....	....	156	....	....	....	....	....	....	....	....	....	....	....	....	....	....	....	....	....	....
1978-79	Cincinnati Stingers	WHA	47	17	20	37	....	....	....	102	....	....	....	....	....	....	....	....	....	....	....	....	....	....	....	....	....	....
	Buffalo Sabres	**NHL**	**24**	**5**	**6**	**11**	**5**	**5**	**10**	**2**	**0**	**0**	**1**	**36**	**13.9**	**22**	**0**	**11**	**0**	**+11**	**3**	**1**	**1**	**2**	**2**	**0**	**0**	**0**
1979-80	**Buffalo Sabres**	**NHL**	**66**	**11**	**22**	**33**	**10**	**17**	**27**	**58**	**0**	**0**	**2**	**109**	**10.1**	**51**	**15**	**26**	**1**	**+11**	**12**	**3**	**0**	**3**	**41**	**1**	**0**	**1**
1980-81	**Buffalo Sabres**	**NHL**	**38**	**10**	**13**	**23**	**8**	**9**	**17**	**10**	**2**	**0**	**0**	**49**	**20.4**	**30**	**5**	**18**	**0**	**+7**	....	....	....	....	....	....	....	....
	Winnipeg Jets	**NHL**	**30**	**5**	**5**	**10**	**4**	**3**	**7**	**28**	**0**	**0**	**0**	**53**	**9.4**	**14**	**1**	**35**	**10**	**–12**	....	....	....	....	....	....	....	....
1981-82	Fredericton Express	AHL	7	1	3	4	....	....	....	30	....	....	....	....	....	....	....	....	....	....	....	....	....	....	....	....	....	....
	NHL Totals		**309**	**75**	**99**	**174**	**69**	**77**	**146**	**292**	**6**	**0**	**11**	**579**	**13.0**	**249**	**33**	**184**	**12**		**25**	**7**	**2**	**9**	**69**	**2**	**0**	**2**
	Other Major League Totals		270	131	146	277	....	....	....	516	....	....	....	....	....	....	....	....	....	....	4	0	1	1	7	....	....	....

WHA Second All-Star Team (1977)

Signed as a free agent by **Buffalo**, September, 1971. Selected by **Miami-Philadelphia** (WHA) in 1972 WHA General Player Draft, February 12, 1972. Selected by **LA Sharks** in 1973 WHA Professional Player Draft, June,1973. WHA rights transferred to **Michigan** (WHA) after **LA Sharks** (WHA) franchise relocated, April 11, 1974. Signed as a free agent by **Cincinnati** (WHA) after **Michigan-Baltimore** (WHA) franchise folded, May, 1975. Rights transferred to **Buffalo** by **Cincinnati** (WHA) for NHL club agreeing to buy out remainer of contract, February, 1979. Claimed on waivers by **Winnipeg** from **Buffalo**, January 12, 1981.

• DUFF, DICK

Dick Duff LW – L. 5'9", 166 lbs. b: Kirkland Lake, Ont., 2/18/1936.

1952-53	St. Michael's Majors	OHA	16	3	2	5	....	....	....	2	....	....	....	....	....	....	....	....	....	....	16	6	9	15	15	....	....	....
1953-54	St. Michael's Majors	OHA	59	35	40	75	....	....	....	120	....	....	....	....	....	....	....	....	....	....	8	2	3	5	23	....	....	....
1954-55	St. Michael's Majors	OHA	47	33	20	53	....	....	....	113	....	....	....	....	....	....	....	....	....	....	5	5	2	7	22	....	....	....
	Toronto Maple Leafs	**NHL**	**3**	**0**	**0**	**0**	**0**	**0**	**0**	**2**	....	....	....	....	....	....	....	....	....	....	....	....	....	....	....	....	....	....
1955-56	**Toronto Maple Leafs**	**NHL**	**69**	**18**	**19**	**37**	**26**	**24**	**50**	**74**	....	....	....	....	....	....	....	....	....	....	**5**	**1**	**4**	**5**	**2**	....	....	....
1956-57	**Toronto Maple Leafs**	**NHL**	**70**	**26**	**14**	**40**	**36**	**16**	**52**	**50**	....	....	....	....	....	....	....	....	....	....	....	....	....	....	....	....	....	....
1957-58	**Toronto Maple Leafs**	**NHL**	**65**	**26**	**23**	**49**	**34**	**25**	**59**	**79**	....	....	....	....	....	....	....	....	....	....	....	....	....	....	....	....	....	....
1958-59	**Toronto Maple Leafs**	**NHL**	**69**	**29**	**24**	**53**	**37**	**26**	**63**	**73**	....	....	....	....	....	....	....	....	....	....	**12**	**4**	**3**	**7**	**8**	....	....	....
1959-60	**Toronto Maple Leafs**	**NHL**	**67**	**19**	**22**	**41**	**24**	**23**	**47**	**51**	....	....	....	....	....	....	....	....	....	....	**10**	**2**	**4**	**6**	**6**	....	....	....
1960-61	**Toronto Maple Leafs**	**NHL**	**67**	**16**	**17**	**33**	**20**	**17**	**37**	**54**	....	....	....	....	....	....	....	....	....	....	**5**	**0**	**1**	**1**	**2**	....	....	....
1961-62	**Toronto Maple Leafs**	**NHL**	**51**	**17**	**20**	**37**	**21**	**20**	**41**	**37**	....	....	....	....	....	....	....	....	....	....	**12**	**3**	**10**	**13**	**20**	....	....	....
1962-63	**Toronto Maple Leafs**	**NHL**	**69**	**16**	**19**	**35**	**20**	**20**	**40**	**56**	....	....	....	....	....	....	....	....	....	....	**10**	**4**	**1**	**5**	**2**	....	....	....
1963-64	**Toronto Maple Leafs**	**NHL**	**52**	**7**	**10**	**17**	**9**	**11**	**20**	**59**	....	....	....	....	....	....	....	....	....	....	....	....	....	....	....	....	....	....
	New York Rangers	**NHL**	**14**	**4**	**4**	**8**	**5**	**4**	**9**	**2**	....	....	....	....	....	....	....	....	....	....	....	....	....	....	....	....	....	....
1964-65	**New York Rangers**	**NHL**	**29**	**3**	**9**	**12**	**4**	**10**	**14**	**20**	....	....	....	....	....	....	....	....	....	....	....	....	....	....	....	....	....	....
	Montreal Canadiens	**NHL**	**40**	**9**	**7**	**16**	**11**	**8**	**19**	**16**	....	....	....	....	....	....	....	....	....	....	**13**	**3**	**6**	**9**	**17**	....	....	....
1965-66	**Montreal Canadiens**	**NHL**	**63**	**21**	**24**	**45**	**25**	**24**	**49**	**78**	....	....	....	....	....	....	....	....	....	....	**10**	**2**	**5**	**7**	**2**	....	....	....
1966-67	**Montreal Canadiens**	**NHL**	**51**	**12**	**11**	**23**	**15**	**11**	**26**	**23**	....	....	....	....	....	....	....	....	....	....	**10**	**2**	**3**	**5**	**4**	....	....	....
1967-68	**Montreal Canadiens**	**NHL**	**66**	**25**	**21**	**46**	**31**	**22**	**53**	**21**	**6**	**0**	**8**	**111**	**22.5**	**66**	**18**	**42**	**0**	**+6**	**13**	**3**	**4**	**7**	**4**	**0**	**0**	**1**
1968-69	**Montreal Canadiens**	**NHL**	**68**	**19**	**21**	**40**	**21**	**20**	**41**	**24**	**5**	**0**	**2**	**138**	**13.8**	**64**	**17**	**60**	**0**	**+10**	**14**	**6**	**8**	**14**	**11**	**3**	**1**	**0**
1969-70	**Montreal Canadiens**	**NHL**	**17**	**1**	**1**	**2**	**1**	**1**	**2**	**4**	**0**	**0**	**0**	**21**	**4.8**	**7**	**2**	**10**	**0**	**–5**	....	....	....	....	....	....	....	....
	Los Angeles Kings	**NHL**	**32**	**5**	**8**	**13**	**6**	**8**	**14**	**8**	**0**	**0**	**0**	**37**	**13.5**	**22**	**5**	**33**	**1**	**–15**	....	....	....	....	....	....	....	....

			REGULAR SEASON																		PLAYOFFS							
Season	Club	League	GP	G	A	Pts	AG	AA	APts	PIM	PP	SH	GW	S	%	TGF	PGF	TGA	PGA	+/–	GP	G	A	Pts	PIM	PP	SH	GW
1970-71	Los Angeles Kings	NHL	7	1	0	1	1	0	1	0	0	0	0	4	25.0	1	0	3	0	–2								
	Buffalo Sabres	NHL	53	7	13	20	7	11	18	12	0	0	1	67	10.4	36	2	50	0	–16								
1971-72	Buffalo Sabres	NHL	8	2	2	4	2	2	4	0	0	0	0	5	40.0	6	1	7	0	–2								
	NHL Totals		1030	283	289	572	356	303	659	743	11	0	11	383	73.9	202	45	205	1		114	30	49	79	78	3	1	1

Played in NHL All-Star Game (1956, 1957, 1958, 1962, 1963, 1965, 1967)

Traded to **NY Rangers** by **Toronto** with Arnie Brown, Bob Nevin, Bill Collins and Rod Seiling for Andy Bathgate and Don McKenney, February 22, 1964. Traded to **Montreal** by **NY Rangers** for Bill Hicke, December 22, 1964. Traded to **LA Kings** by **Montreal** for cash, January 23, 1970. Traded to **Buffalo** by **LA Kings** with Eddie Shack for Mike McMahon, December 1, 1970.

• DUFOUR, LUC

Luc Dufour LW – L. 5'11", 180 lbs. b: Chicoutimi, Que., 2/13/1963. Boston's 2nd choice, 35th overall, in 1981 Entry Draft.

Season	Club	League	GP	G	A	Pts	AG	AA	APts	PIM	PP	SH	GW	S	%	TGF	PGF	TGA	PGA	+/–	GP	G	A	Pts	PIM	PP	SH	GW
1980-81	Chicoutimi Sagueneens	QMJHL	69	43	53	96				89											4	1	2	3	8			
1981-82	Chicoutimi Sagueneens	QMJHL	62	55	60	115				94											20	12	19	31	26			
1982-83	Boston Bruins	NHL	73	14	11	25	11	8	19	107	0	0	1	121	11.6	47	2	26	0	+19	17	1	0	1	30	0	0	1
1983-84	Boston Bruins	NHL	41	6	4	10	5	3	8	47	0	0	1	39	15.4	19	1	16	0	+2								
	Hershey Bears	AHL	37	9	19	28				51																		
1984-85	Hershey Bears	AHL	6	1	1	2				10																		
	Quebec Nordiques	NHL	30	2	3	5	2	2	4	27	0	0	0	18	11.1	7	0	12	0	–5								
	Fredericton Express	AHL	12	2	0	2				13																		
	St. Louis Blues	NHL	23	1	3	4	1	2	3	18	0	0	0	38	2.6	5	0	13	0	–8	1	0	0	0	2	0	0	0
1985-86	Maine Mariners	AHL	75	15	20	35				57											5	0	0	0	8			
1986-87	HC Auronzo	Italy	34	35	40	75				52																		
	NHL Totals		167	23	21	44	19	15	34	199	0	0	2	216	10.6	78	3	67	0		18	1	0	1	32	0	0	1

QMJHL First All-Star Team (1982)

Traded to **Quebec** by **Boston** with Boston's 4th round choice (Peter Massey) in 1985 Entry Draft for Louis Sleigher, October 25, 1984. Traded to **St. Louis** by **Quebec** for Alain Lemieux, January 29, 1985.

• DUFOUR, MARC

Marc Dufour RW – R. 6', 175 lbs. b: Trois Rivieres, Que., 9/11/1941.

Season	Club	League	GP	G	A	Pts	AG	AA	APts	PIM	PP	SH	GW	S	%	TGF	PGF	TGA	PGA	+/–	GP	G	A	Pts	PIM	PP	SH	GW
1959-60	Guelph Biltmores	OHA	38	7	13	20				12											5	0	1	1	2			
1960-61	Guelph Royals	OHA	4	0	0	0				0																		
1961-62	Brandon Wheat Kings	MJHL	33	*37	20	57				48											20	*19	14	*33	32			
1962-63	Sudbury Wolves	EPHL	71	50	49	99				27											8	2	7	9	4			
1963-64	New York Rangers	NHL	10	1	0	1	1	0	1	2																		
	Baltimore Clippers	AHL	38	7	16	23				28																		
	Los Angeles Blades	WHL	12	2	3	5				0											6	1	0	1	0			
1964-65	New York Rangers	NHL	2	0	0	0	0	0	0	0																		
	St. Paul Rangers	CHL	69	43	50	93				33											11	4	*14	*18	21			
1965-66	Baltimore Clippers	AHL	65	14	23	37				8																		
1966-67	Vancouver Canucks	WHL	70	19	17	36				18											8	1	1	2	2			
1967-68	Springfield Kings	AHL	65	20	25	45				12											4	3	1	4	0			
1968-69	Los Angeles Kings	NHL	2	0	0	0	0	0	0	0	0	0	0	2	0.0	0	0	1	0	–1								
	Springfield Kings	AHL	70	34	36	70				20																		
1969-70	Springfield Kings	AHL	71	32	53	85				22											14	2	6	8	4			
1970-71	Baltimore Clippers	AHL	69	31	51	82				15											6	0	5	5	0			
1971-72	Baltimore Clippers	AHL	59	15	36	51				12											18	7	6	13	8			
1972-73	Baltimore Clippers	AHL	67	30	32	62				16																		
1973-74	Baltimore Clippers	AHL	74	42	62	104				21											9	4	3	7	2			
1974-75	Baltimore Clippers	AHL	29	8	7	15				12																		
	NHL Totals		14	1	0	1	1	0	1	2	0	0	0	2	50.0	0	0	1	0									

CHL First All-Star Team (1965) • AHL First All-Star Team (1971) • AHL Second All-Star Team (1974)

Claimed by **LA Kings** from **NY Rangers** in Expansion Draft, June 6, 1967. Claimed by **Baltimore** from **LA Kings** (Springfield - AHL) in Reverse Draft, June, 1970. Selected by **Winnipeg** (WHA) in 1972 WHA General Player Draft, February 12, 1972. Traded to **NY Raiders** (WHA) by **Winnipeg** (WHA) for the rights to Danny Johnson, June, 1972. Signed as a free agent by **Baltimore** (AHL) after securing release from **NY Raiders** (WHA), October, 1972.

• DUFRESNE, DONALD

Donald Dufresne D – R. 6'1", 206 lbs. b: Quebec City, Que., 4/10/1967. Montreal's 8th choice, 117th overall, in 1985 Entry Draft.

Season	Club	League	GP	G	A	Pts	AG	AA	APts	PIM	PP	SH	GW	S	%	TGF	PGF	TGA	PGA	+/–	GP	G	A	Pts	PIM	PP	SH	GW
1983-84	Trois-Rivières Draveurs	QMJHL	67	7	12	19				97																		
1984-85	Trois-Rivières Draveurs	QMJHL	65	5	30	35				112											7	1	3	4	12			
1985-86	Trois-Rivières Draveurs	QMJHL	63	8	32	40				160											1	0	0	0	0			
1986-87	Trois-Rivières Draveurs	QMJHL	51	5	21	26				79																		
	Longueuil Chevaliers	QMJHL	16	0	8	8				18											20	1	8	9	38			
1987-88	Sherbrooke Canadiens	AHL	47	1	8	9				107											6	1	0	1	34			
1988-89	Montreal Canadiens	NHL	13	0	1	1	0	1	1	43	0	0	0	5	0.0	5	0	4	2	+3	6	1	1	2	4	0	0	0
	Sherbrooke Canadiens	AHL	47	0	12	12				170																		
1989-90	Montreal Canadiens	NHL	18	0	4	4	0	3	3	23	0	0	0	6	0.0	14	0	14	1	+1	10	0	1	1	18	0	0	0
	Sherbrooke Canadiens	AHL	38	2	11	13				104																		
1990-91	Montreal Canadiens	FrTour	3	0	0	0				29																		
	Montreal Canadiens	NHL	53	2	13	15	2	10	12	55	0	0	0	32	6.3	43	1	46	9	+5	10	0	1	1	21	0	0	0
	Fredericton Canadiens	AHL	10	1	4	5				35											1	0	0	0	0			
1991-92	Montreal Canadiens	NHL	3	0	0	0	0	0	0	2	0	0	0	2	0.0	2	0	0	0	+2								
	Fredericton Canadiens	AHL	31	8	12	20				60											7	0	0	0	10			
1992-93	Montreal Canadiens	NHL	32	1	2	3	1	1	2	32	0	0	0	13	7.7	18	0	19	1	0	2	0	0	0	0	0	0	0
1993-94	Tampa Bay Lightning	NHL	51	2	6	8	2	5	7	48	0	0	0	49	4.1	29	1	40	10	–2								
	Los Angeles Kings	NHL	9	0	0	0	0	0	0	10	0	0	0	7	0.0	3	0	10	2	–5								
1994-95	St. Louis Blues	NHL	22	0	3	3	0	4	4	10	0	0	0	11	0.0	15	1	16	4	+2	3	0	0	0	4	0	0	0
1995-96	St. Louis Blues	NHL	3	0	0	0	0	0	0	4	0	0	0	1	0.0	0	0	2	0	–2								
	Worcester IceCats	AHL	13	1	1	2				14																		
	Edmonton Oilers	NHL	42	1	6	7	1	5	6	16	0	0	0	20	5.0	19	1	27	7	–2								
1996-97	Edmonton Oilers	NHL	22	0	1	1	0	1	1	15	0	0	0	10	0.0	12	1	15	3	–1	3	0	0	0	0	0	0	0
1997-98	Quebec Rafales	IHL	15	0	4	4				20																		
	NHL Totals		268	6	36	42	6	30	36	258	0	0	0	156	3.8	160	5	193	39		34	1	3	4	47	0	0	0

QMJHL Second All-Star Team (1986, 1987)

Traded to **Tampa Bay** by **Montreal** to complete transaction that sent Rob Ramage to Montreal (March 20, 1993), June 20, 1993. Traded to **LA Kings** by **Tampa Bay** for LA Kings' 6th round choice (Daniel Juden) in 1994 Entry Draft, March 19, 1994. Claimed by **St. Louis** from **LA Kings** in NHL Waiver Draft, January 18, 1995. Traded to **Edmonton** by **St. Louis** with Jeff Norton for Igor Kravchuk and Ken Sutton, January 4, 1996.

• DUGGAN, KEN

Ken Duggan D – L. 6'3", 210 lbs. b: Toronto, Ont., 2/21/1963.

Season	Club	League	GP	G	A	Pts	AG	AA	APts	PIM	PP	SH	GW	S	%	TGF	PGF	TGA	PGA	+/–	GP	G	A	Pts	PIM	PP	SH	GW
1982-83	University of Toronto	OUAA	35	0	5	5				32																		
1983-84	University of Toronto	OUAA	47	11	17	28				54																		
1984-85	University of Toronto	OUAA	45	6	19	25				105																		
1985-86	University of Toronto	OUAA	44	13	41	54				111																		
1986-87	New Haven Nighthawks	AHL	13	0	1	1				4																		
	Flint Spirits	IHL	66	2	23	25				51											6	0	2	2	2			
1987-88	Minnesota North Stars	NHL	1	0	0	0	0	0	0	0	0	0	0	0	0.0	0	0	0	0	0								
	Flint Spirits	IHL	1	0	0	0				0																		
1988-89	Canada	Nat-Team	3	0	1	1				2																		
	NHL Totals		1	0	0	0	0	0	0	0	0	0	0	0	0.0	0	0	0	0									

Signed as a free agent by **NY Rangers**, May 22, 1986. Signed as a free agent by **Minnesota**, January, 1988.

• DUGUAY, RON
Ron "Doogie" Duguay C/RW – R. 6'2", 200 lbs. b: Sudbury, Ont., 7/6/1957. NY Rangers' 2nd choice, 13th overall, in 1977 Amateur Draft.

			REGULAR SEASON																		PLAYOFFS							
Season	Club	League	GP	G	A	Pts	AG	AA	APts	PIM	PP	SH	GW	S	%	TGF	PGF	TGA	PGA	+/–	GP	G	A	Pts	PIM	PP	SH	GW
1973-74	Sudbury Wolves	OHA	59	20	20	40	....	....	....	73	....	....	....	....	....	....	....	....	....	....	....	....	....	....	....	....	....	....
1974-75	Sudbury Wolves	OHA	64	26	52	78	....	....	....	43	....	....	....	....	....	....	....	....	....	....	....	....	....	....	....	....	....	....
1975-76	Sudbury Wolves	OHA	61	42	92	134	....	....	....	101	....	....	....	....	....	....	....	....	....	....	17	11	9	20	37	....	....	....
1976-77	Sudbury Wolves	OHA	61	43	66	109	....	....	....	109	....	....	....	....	....	....	....	....	....	....	6	4	3	7	5	....	....	....
	Canada	WJC-A	5	1	4	5	....	....	....	11	....	....	....	....	....	....	....	....	....	....	....	....	....	....	....	....	....	....
1977-78	**New York Rangers**	**NHL**	**71**	**20**	**20**	**40**	**19**	**16**	**35**	**43**	**3**	**0**	**1**	**129**	**15.5**	**65**	**12**	**74**	**4**	**–17**	**3**	**1**	**1**	**2**	**2**	**1**	**0**	**0**
1978-79	**New York Rangers**	**NHL**	**79**	**27**	**36**	**63**	**25**	**28**	**53**	**35**	**1**	**2**	**3**	**178**	**15.2**	**85**	**17**	**84**	**26**	**+10**	**18**	**5**	**4**	**9**	**11**	**0**	**1**	**0**
1979-80	**New York Rangers**	**NHL**	**73**	**28**	**22**	**50**	**25**	**17**	**42**	**37**	**3**	**3**	**2**	**154**	**18.2**	**65**	**8**	**81**	**18**	**–6**	**9**	**5**	**2**	**7**	**11**	**2**	**0**	**0**
1980-81	**New York Rangers**	**NHL**	**50**	**17**	**21**	**38**	**14**	**15**	**29**	**83**	**5**	**1**	**0**	**103**	**16.5**	**54**	**10**	**62**	**20**	**+2**	**14**	**8**	**9**	**17**	**16**	**0**	**1**	**1**
1981-82	Canada	C Cup	7	0	2	2	....	....	....	6	....	....	....	....	....	....	....	....	....	....	....	....	....	....	....	....	....	....
	New York Rangers	**NHL**	**72**	**40**	**36**	**76**	**32**	**24**	**56**	**82**	**10**	**1**	**3**	**202**	**19.8**	**114**	**35**	**89**	**28**	**+18**	**10**	**5**	**1**	**6**	**31**	**1**	**0**	**0**
1982-83	**New York Rangers**	**NHL**	**72**	**19**	**25**	**44**	**16**	**17**	**33**	**58**	**5**	**0**	**2**	**160**	**11.9**	**71**	**16**	**89**	**21**	**–13**	**9**	**2**	**2**	**4**	**28**	**0**	**0**	**0**
1983-84	**Detroit Red Wings**	**NHL**	**80**	**33**	**47**	**80**	**27**	**32**	**59**	**34**	**13**	**1**	**1**	**215**	**15.3**	**128**	**61**	**117**	**24**	**–26**	**4**	**2**	**3**	**5**	**2**	**1**	**0**	**0**
1984-85	**Detroit Red Wings**	**NHL**	**80**	**38**	**51**	**89**	**31**	**35**	**66**	**51**	**11**	**3**	**4**	**201**	**18.9**	**141**	**49**	**128**	**20**	**–16**	**3**	**1**	**0**	**1**	**7**	**1**	**0**	**0**
1985-86	**Detroit Red Wings**	**NHL**	**67**	**19**	**29**	**48**	**15**	**19**	**34**	**26**	**8**	**0**	**2**	**153**	**12.4**	**81**	**32**	**107**	**28**	**–30**	....	....	....	....	....	....	....	....
	Pittsburgh Penguins	**NHL**	**13**	**6**	**7**	**13**	**5**	**5**	**10**	**6**	**3**	**0**	**0**	**33**	**18.2**	**15**	**8**	**23**	**2**	**–14**	....	....	....	....	....	....	....	....
1986-87	**Pittsburgh Penguins**	**NHL**	**40**	**5**	**13**	**18**	**4**	**9**	**13**	**30**	**0**	**0**	**0**	**55**	**9.1**	**23**	**7**	**28**	**4**	**–8**	....	....	....	....	....	....	....	....
	New York Rangers	**NHL**	**34**	**9**	**12**	**21**	**8**	**9**	**17**	**9**	**2**	**1**	**0**	**66**	**13.6**	**33**	**15**	**44**	**18**	**–8**	**6**	**2**	**0**	**2**	**4**	**1**	**0**	**0**
1987-88	**New York Rangers**	**NHL**	**48**	**4**	**4**	**8**	**3**	**3**	**6**	**23**	**0**	**2**	**0**	**59**	**6.8**	**21**	**3**	**54**	**27**	**–9**	....	....	....	....	....	....	....	....
	Colorado Rangers	IHL	2	0	0	0	....	....	....	0	....	....	....	....	....	....	....	....	....	....	....	....	....	....	....	....	....	....
	Los Angeles Kings	**NHL**	**15**	**2**	**6**	**8**	**2**	**4**	**6**	**17**	**0**	**0**	**1**	**21**	**9.5**	**13**	**3**	**17**	**2**	**–5**	**2**	**0**	**0**	**0**	**0**	**0**	**0**	**0**
1988-89	**Los Angeles Kings**	**NHL**	**70**	**7**	**17**	**24**	**6**	**12**	**18**	**48**	**0**	**0**	**0**	**80**	**8.8**	**53**	**0**	**49**	**19**	**+23**	**11**	**0**	**0**	**0**	**6**	**0**	**0**	**0**
1989-90	Mannheimer ERC	Germany	22	11	7	18	....	....	....	38	....	....	....	....	....	....	....	....	....	....	3	0	1	1	20	....	....	....
1990-91	San Diego Gulls	IHL	51	15	24	39	....	....	....	87	....	....	....	....	....	....	....	....	....	....	....	....	....	....	....	....	....	....
1991-92	San Diego Gulls	IHL	60	18	18	36	....	....	....	32	....	....	....	....	....	....	....	....	....	....	4	0	1	1	0	....	....	....
1992-1996			DID NOT PLAY – RETIRED																									
1996-97	San Diego Gulls	WCHL	2	1	1	2	....	....	....	0	....	....	....	....	....	....	....	....	....	....	....	....	....	....	....	....	....	....
1997-98	San Diego Gulls	WCHL	3	0	3	3	....	....	....	2	....	....	....	....	....	....	....	....	....	....	....	....	....	....	....	....	....	....
	NHL Totals		**864**	**274**	**346**	**620**	**232**	**245**	**477**	**582**	**64**	**14**	**19**	**1809**	**15.1**	**962**	**276**	**1046**	**261**		**89**	**31**	**22**	**53**	**118**	**7**	**2**	**1**

Played in NHL All-Star Game (1982)

Traded to **Detroit** by **NY Rangers** with Eddie Mio and Eddie Johnstone for Willie Huber, Mark Osborne and Mike Blaisdell, June 13, 1983. Traded to **Pittsburgh** by **Detroit** for Doug Shedden, March 11, 1986. Traded to **NY Rangers** by **Pittsburgh** for Chris Kontos, January 21, 1987. Traded to LA Kings by **NY Rangers**, February 23, 1988.

• DUNBAR, DALE
Dale Dunbar D – L. 6', 200 lbs. b: Winthrop, MA, 10/14/1961.

1981-82	Boston University	ECAC	6	0	0	0	....	....	....	0	....	....	....	....	....	....	....	....	....	....	....	....	....	....	....	....	....	....
1982-83	Boston University	ECAC	23	1	7	8	....	....	....	36	....	....	....	....	....	....	....	....	....	....	....	....	....	....	....	....	....	....
1983-84	Boston University	ECAC	34	0	15	23	....	....	....	49	....	....	....	....	....	....	....	....	....	....	....	....	....	....	....	....	....	....
1984-85	Boston University	H.E.	39	2	19	21	....	....	....	62	....	....	....	....	....	....	....	....	....	....	....	....	....	....	....	....	....	....
1985-86	**Vancouver Canucks**	**NHL**	**1**	**0**	**0**	**0**	**0**	**0**	**0**	**2**	**0**	**0**	**0**	**0**	**0.0**	**0**	**0**	**0**	**0**	**0**	....	....	....	....	....	....	....	....
	Fredericton Express	AHL	32	2	10	12	....	....	....	26	....	....	....	....	....	....	....	....	....	....	....	....	....	....	....	....	....	....
1986-87	Peoria Rivermen	IHL	46	2	8	10	....	....	....	32	....	....	....	....	....	....	....	....	....	....	....	....	....	....	....	....	....	....
1987-88	Maine Mariners	AHL	66	1	7	8	....	....	....	120	....	....	....	....	....	....	....	....	....	....	9	1	1	2	33	....	....	....
1988-89	**Boston Bruins**	**NHL**	**1**	**0**	**0**	**0**	**0**	**0**	**0**	**0**	**0**	**0**	**0**	**2**	**0.0**	**0**	**0**	**0**	**0**	**0**	....	....	....	....	....	....	....	....
	Maine Mariners	AHL	65	1	9	10	....	....	....	49	....	....	....	....	....	....	....	....	....	....	....	....	....	....	....	....	....	....
	NHL Totals		**2**	**0**	**0**	**0**	**0**	**0**	**0**	**2**	**0**	**0**	**0**	**2**	**0.0**	**0**	**0**	**0**	**0**		....	....	....	....	....	....	....	....

Signed as a free agent by **Vancouver**, May 10, 1985. Signed as a free agent by **Boston**, August 25, 1987

• DUNCAN, IAIN
Iain Duncan LW L. 6'1", 200 lbs. b. Weston, Ont., 8/4/1963. Winnipeg's 8th choice, 134th overall, in 1983 Entry Draft.

1982-83	North York Rangers	OJHL	STATISTICS NOT AVAILABLE																									
1983-84	Bowling Green University	CCHA	44	11	20	31	....	....	....	65	....	....	....	....	....	....	....	....	....	....	....	....	....	....	....	....	....	....
1984-85	Bowling Green University	CCHA	37	9	21	30	....	....	....	105	....	....	....	....	....	....	....	....	....	....	....	....	....	....	....	....	....	....
1985-86	Bowling Green University	CCHA	41	26	26	52	....	....	....	124	....	....	....	....	....	....	....	....	....	....	....	....	....	....	....	....	....	....
1986-87	Bowling Green University	CCHA	39	28	40	68	....	....	....	141	....	....	....	....	....	....	....	....	....	....	....	....	....	....	....	....	....	....
	Winnipeg Jets	**NHL**	**6**	**1**	**2**	**3**	**1**	**1**	**2**	**0**	**0**	**0**	**0**	**7**	**14.3**	**3**	**1**	**1**	**0**	**+1**	**7**	**0**	**2**	**2**	**6**	**0**	**0**	**0**
1987-88	**Winnipeg Jets**	**NHL**	**62**	**19**	**23**	**42**	**16**	**16**	**32**	**73**	**4**	**0**	**4**	**104**	**18.3**	**56**	**13**	**46**	**1**	**–2**	**4**	**0**	**1**	**1**	**0**	**0**	**0**	**0**
	Moncton Hawks	AHL	8	1	3	4	....	....	....	26	....	....	....	....	....	....	....	....	....	....	....	....	....	....	....	....	....	....
1988-89	**Winnipeg Jets**	**NHL**	**57**	**14**	**30**	**44**	**12**	**21**	**33**	**74**	**1**	**0**	**0**	**91**	**15.4**	**65**	**25**	**57**	**0**	**–17**	....	....	....	....	....	....	....	....
1989-90	Moncton Hawks	AHL	49	16	25	41	....	....	....	81	....	....	....	....	....	....	....	....	....	....	....	....	....	....	....	....	....	....
1990-91	**Winnipeg Jets**	**NHL**	**2**	**0**	**0**	**0**	**0**	**0**	**0**	**2**	**0**	**0**	**0**	**2**	**0.0**	**0**	**0**	**1**	**0**	**–1**	....	....	....	....	....	....	....	....
	Moncton Hawks	AHL	66	19	45	64	....	....	....	105	....	....	....	....	....	....	....	....	....	....	8	3	4	7	40	....	....	....
1991-92	Phoenix Roadrunners	IHL	46	12	24	36	....	....	....	103	....	....	....	....	....	....	....	....	....	....	....	....	....	....	....	....	....	....
1992-93	Adirondack Red Wings	AHL	1	0	0	0	....	....	....	2	....	....	....	....	....	....	....	....	....	....	....	....	....	....	....	....	....	....
	Toledo Storm	ECHL	50	40	50	90	....	....	....	190	....	....	....	....	....	....	....	....	....	....	16	9	*19	28	55	....	....	....
1993-94	Toledo Storm	ECHL	8	6	8	14	....	....	....	23	....	....	....	....	....	....	....	....	....	....	14	6	11	17	32	....	....	....
1994-95	Toledo Storm	ECHL	37	9	34	43	....	....	....	133	....	....	....	....	....	....	....	....	....	....	4	1	2	3	10	....	....	....
1995-96			DID NOT PLAY																									
1996-97	Nashville Nighthawks	CHL	12	7	11	18	....	....	....	68	....	....	....	....	....	....	....	....	....	....	....	....	....	....	....	....	....	....
1997-98	Nashville Ice Flyers	CHL	35	4	22	26	....	....	....	77	....	....	....	....	....	....	....	....	....	....	....	....	....	....	....	....	....	....
	NHL Totals		**127**	**34**	**55**	**89**	**29**	**38**	**67**	**149**	**5**	**0**	**4**	**204**	**16.7**	**124**	**39**	**105**	**1**		**11**	**0**	**3**	**3**	**6**	**0**	**0**	**0**

CCHA First All-Star Team (1987) • NHL All-Rookie Team (1988) • ECHL Second All-Star Team (1993)

• DUNCANSON, CRAIG
Craig Duncanson LW – L. 6', 190 lbs. b: Sudbury, Ont., 3/17/1967. Los Angeles' 1st choice, 9th overall, in 1985 Entry Draft.

1982-83	St. Michael's Buzzers	Jr. B	32	14	19	33	....	....	....	68	....	....	....	....	....	....	....	....	....	....	....	....	....	....	....	....	....	....
1983-84	Sudbury Wolves	OHL	62	38	38	76	....	....	....	176	....	....	....	....	....	....	....	....	....	....	....	....	....	....	....	....	....	....
1984-85	Sudbury Wolves	OHL	53	35	28	63	....	....	....	129	....	....	....	....	....	....	....	....	....	....	....	....	....	....	....	....	....	....
1985-86	Sudbury Wolves	OHL	21	12	17	29	....	....	....	55	....	....	....	....	....	....	....	....	....	....	....	....	....	....	....	....	....	....
	Cornwall Royals	OHL	40	31	50	81	....	....	....	135	....	....	....	....	....	....	....	....	....	....	6	4	7	11	2	....	....	....
	Los Angeles Kings	**NHL**	**2**	**0**	**1**	**1**	**0**	**1**	**1**	**0**	**0**	**0**	**0**	**0**	**0.0**	**1**	**0**	**2**	**0**	**–1**	....	....	....	....	....	....	....	....
	New Haven Nighthawks	AHL	....	....	....	....	....	....	....	....	....	....	....	....	....	....	....	....	....	....	2	0	0	0	5	....	....	....
1986-87	Cornwall Royals	OHL	52	22	45	67	....	....	....	88	....	....	....	....	....	....	....	....	....	....	5	4	3	7	20	....	....	....
	Los Angeles Kings	**NHL**	**2**	**0**	**0**	**0**	**0**	**0**	**0**	**24**	**0**	**0**	**0**	**1**	**0.0**	**2**	**2**	**0**	**0**	**0**	....	....	....	....	....	....	....	....
1987-88	**Los Angeles Kings**	**NHL**	**9**	**0**	**0**	**0**	**0**	**0**	**0**	**12**	**0**	**0**	**0**	**8**	**0.0**	**2**	**1**	**6**	**0**	**–5**	....	....	....	....	....	....	....	....
	New Haven Nighthawks	AHL	57	15	25	40	....	....	....	170	....	....	....	....	....	....	....	....	....	....	....	....	....	....	....	....	....	....
1988-89	**Los Angeles Kings**	**NHL**	**5**	**0**	**0**	**0**	**0**	**0**	**0**	**0**	**0**	**0**	**0**	**1**	**0.0**	**0**	**0**	**1**	**0**	**–1**	....	....	....	....	....	....	....	....
	New Haven Nighthawks	AHL	69	25	39	64	....	....	....	200	....	....	....	....	....	....	....	....	....	....	17	4	8	12	60	....	....	....
1989-90	**Los Angeles Kings**	**NHL**	**10**	**3**	**2**	**5**	**3**	**1**	**4**	**9**	**0**	**0**	**0**	**12**	**25.0**	**6**	**0**	**5**	**0**	**+1**	....	....	....	....	....	....	....	....
	New Haven Nighthawks	AHL	51	17	30	47	....	....	....	152	....	....	....	....	....	....	....	....	....	....	....	....	....	....	....	....	....	....
1990-91	**Winnipeg Jets**	**NHL**	**7**	**2**	**0**	**2**	**2**	**0**	**2**	**16**	**0**	**0**	**0**	**6**	**33.3**	**2**	**0**	**7**	**0**	**–5**	....	....	....	....	....	....	....	....
	Moncton Hawks	AHL	58	16	34	50	....	....	....	107	....	....	....	....	....	....	....	....	....	....	9	3	11	14	31	....	....	....
1991-92	Baltimore Skipjacks	AHL	46	20	26	46	....	....	....	98	....	....	....	....	....	....	....	....	....	....	....	....	....	....	....	....	....	....
	Moncton Hawks	AHL	19	12	9	21	....	....	....	6	....	....	....	....	....	....	....	....	....	....	11	6	4	10	10	....	....	....
1992-93	**New York Rangers**	**NHL**	**3**	**0**	**1**	**1**	**0**	**1**	**1**	**0**	**0**	**0**	**0**	**1**	**0.0**	**1**	**0**	**1**	**0**	**0**	....	....	....	....	....	....	....	....
	Binghamton Rangers	AHL	69	35	59	94	....	....	....	126	....	....	....	....	....	....	....	....	....	....	14	7	5	12	9	....	....	....
1993-94	Binghamton Rangers	AHL	70	25	44	69	....	....	....	83	....	....	....	....	....	....	....	....	....	....	....	....	....	....	....	....	....	....
1994-95	Binghamton Rangers	AHL	62	21	43	64	....	....	....	105	....	....	....	....	....	....	....	....	....	....	11	4	4	8	16	....	....	....

Season	Club	League	GP	G	A	Pts	AG	AA	APts	PIM	PP	SH	GW	S	%	TGF	PGF	TGA	PGA	+/–	GP	G	A	Pts	PIM	PP	SH	GW
			REGULAR SEASON																		PLAYOFFS							
1995-96	Orlando Solar Bears	IHL	79	19	24	43	....	....	....	123	....	....	....	....	....	....	....	....	....	....	22	3	10	13	16	....	....	....
1996-97	Fort Wayne Komets	IHL	61	14	24	38	....	....	....	64	....	....	....	....	....	....	....	....	....	....	....	....	....	....	....	....	....	....
	Cincinnati Cyclones	IHL	21	3	11	14	....	....	....	19	....	....	....	....	....	....	....	....	....	....	3	1	1	2	0	....	....	....
	NHL Totals		**38**	**5**	**4**	**9**	**5**	**3**	**8**	**61**	**0**	**0**	**0**	**29**	**17.2**	**14**	**3**	**22**	**0**		....	....	....	....	....	....	....	....

Traded to **Minnesota** by **LA Kings** for Daniel Berthiaume, September 6, 1990. Traded to **Winnipeg** by **Minnesota** for Brian Hunt, September 6, 1990. Traded to **Washington** by **Winnipeg** with Brent Hughes and Simon Wheeldon for Bob Joyce, Tyler Larter and Kent Paynter, May 21, 1991. Signed as a free agent by **NY Rangers**, September 4, 1992.

• DUNDAS, ROCKY

Rocky Dundas RW – R. 6′, 195 lbs. b: Regina, Sask., 1/30/1967. Montreal's 4th choice, 47th overall, in 1985 Entry Draft.

Season	Club	League	GP	G	A	Pts	AG	AA	APts	PIM	PP	SH	GW	S	%	TGF	PGF	TGA	PGA	+/–	GP	G	A	Pts	PIM	PP	SH	GW
1983-84	Kelowna Wings	WHL	72	15	24	39	....	....	....	57	....	....	....	....	....	....	....	....	....	....	....	....	....	....	....	....	....	....
1984-85	Kelowna Wings	WHL	71	32	44	76	....	....	....	117	....	....	....	....	....	....	....	....	....	....	6	1	1	2	14	....	....	....
1985-86	Spokane Chiefs	WHL	71	31	70	101	....	....	....	160	....	....	....	....	....	....	....	....	....	....	9	2	5	7	28	....	....	....
1986-87	Spokane Chiefs	WHL	19	13	17	30	....	....	....	69	....	....	....	....	....	....	....	....	....	....	....	....	....	....	....	....	....	....
	Medicine Hat Tigers	WHL	29	22	24	46	....	....	....	63	....	....	....	....	....	....	....	....	....	....	20	4	8	12	44	....	....	....
1987-88	Baltimore Skipjacks	AHL	9	0	1	1	....	....	....	46	....	....	....	....	....	....	....	....	....	....	....	....	....	....	....	....	....	....
	Sherbrooke Canadiens	AHL	38	9	6	15	....	....	....	104	....	....	....	....	....	....	....	....	....	....	3	0	0	0	7	....	....	....
1988-89	Sherbrooke Canadiens	AHL	63	12	29	41	....	....	....	212	....	....	....	....	....	....	....	....	....	....	2	2	0	2	8	....	....	....
1989-90	**Toronto Maple Leafs**	**NHL**	**5**	**0**	**0**	**0**	**0**	**0**	**0**	**14**	**0**	**0**	**0**	**1**	**0.0**	**1**	**0**	**2**	**0**	**–1**	....	....	....	....	....	....	....	....
	Newmarket Saints	AHL	62	18	15	33	....	....	....	158	....	....	....	....	....	....	....	....	....	....	....	....	....	....	....	....	....	....
	NHL Totals		**5**	**0**	**0**	**0**	**0**	**0**	**0**	**14**	**0**	**0**	**0**	**1**	**0.0**	**1**	**0**	**2**	**0**		....	....	....	....	....	....	....	....

Signed as a free agent by **Toronto**, October 4, 1989.

• DUNLOP, BLAKE

Blake Dunlop C – R. 5′10″, 170 lbs. b: Hamilton, Ont., 4/4/1953. Minnesota's 1st choice, 18th overall, in 1973 Amateur Draft.

Season	Club	League	GP	G	A	Pts	AG	AA	APts	PIM	PP	SH	GW	S	%	TGF	PGF	TGA	PGA	+/–	GP	G	A	Pts	PIM	PP	SH	GW
1969-70	Ottawa 67's	OHA	45	17	15	32	....	....	....	10	....	....	....	....	....	....	....	....	....	....	....	....	....	....	....	....	....	....
1970-71	Ottawa 67's	OHA	62	44	46	90	....	....	....	39	....	....	....	....	....	....	....	....	....	....	....	....	....	....	....	....	....	....
1971-72	Ottawa 67's	OHA	62	32	52	84	....	....	....	41	....	....	....	....	....	....	....	....	....	....	....	....	....	....	....	....	....	....
1972-73	Ottawa 67's	OHA	62	60	*99	*159	....	....	....	50	....	....	....	....	....	....	....	....	....	....	....	....	....	....	....	....	....	....
1973-74	**Minnesota North Stars**	**NHL**	**12**	**0**	**0**	**0**	**0**	**0**	**0**	**2**	**0**	**0**	**0**	**11**	**0.0**	**1**	**0**	**4**	**0**	**–3**	....	....	....	....	....	....	....	....
	New Haven Nighthawks	AHL	59	37	41	78	....	....	....	25	....	....	....	....	....	....	....	....	....	....	10	7	7	14	4	....	....	....
1974-75	**Minnesota North Stars**	**NHL**	**52**	**9**	**18**	**27**	**8**	**14**	**22**	**8**	**2**	**0**	**3**	**82**	**11.0**	**42**	**11**	**38**	**0**	**–7**	....	....	....	....	....	....	....	....
1975-76	**Minnesota North Stars**	**NHL**	**33**	**9**	**11**	**20**	**8**	**9**	**17**	**8**	**1**	**0**	**1**	**55**	**16.4**	**25**	**5**	**29**	**0**	**–9**	....	....	....	....	....	....	....	....
	New Haven Nighthawks	AHL	10	2	10	12	....	....	....	8	....	....	....	....	....	....	....	....	....	....	....	....	....	....	....	....	....	....
1976-77	**Minnesota North Stars**	**NHL**	**3**	**0**	**1**	**1**	**0**	**1**	**1**	**0**	**0**	**0**	**0**	**8**	**0.0**	**1**	**0**	**3**	**0**	**–2**	....	....	....	....	....	....	....	....
	New Haven Nighthawks	AHL	76	33	60	93	....	....	....	16	....	....	....	....	....	....	....	....	....	....	6	2	4	6	14	....	....	....
1977-78	Fort Worth Texans	CHL	6	4	2	6	....	....	....	11	....	....	....	....	....	....	....	....	....	....	....	....	....	....	....	....	....	....
	Philadelphia Flyers	**NHL**	**3**	**0**	**1**	**1**	**0**	**1**	**1**	**0**	**0**	**0**	**0**	**1**	**0.0**	**2**	**0**	**1**	**0**	**+1**	....	....	....	....	....	....	....	....
	Maine Mariners	AHL	62	29	53	82	....	....	....	24	....	....	....	....	....	....	....	....	....	....	10	5	4	9	12	....	....	....
1978-79	**Philadelphia Flyers**	**NHL**	**66**	**20**	**28**	**48**	**18**	**21**	**39**	**16**	**5**	**0**	**5**	**122**	**16.4**	**65**	**14**	**36**	**12**	**+27**	**8**	**1**	**1**	**2**	**4**	**0**	**0**	**0**
	Maine Mariners	AHL	12	9	5	14	....	....	....	6	....	....	....	....	....	....	....	....	....	....	....	....	....	....	....	....	....	....
1979-80	**St. Louis Blues**	**NHL**	**72**	**18**	**27**	**45**	**16**	**21**	**37**	**28**	**8**	**0**	**2**	**101**	**17.8**	**62**	**21**	**49**	**2**	**–6**	**3**	**0**	**2**	**2**	**2**	**0**	**0**	**0**
1980-81	**St. Louis Blues**	**NHL**	**80**	**20**	**67**	**87**	**16**	**47**	**63**	**40**	**6**	**0**	**2**	**134**	**14.9**	**123**	**43**	**67**	**3**	**+16**	**11**	**0**	**3**	**3**	**4**	**0**	**0**	**0**
1981-82	**St. Louis Blues**	**NHL**	**77**	**25**	**53**	**78**	**20**	**35**	**55**	**32**	**10**	**1**	**1**	**129**	**19.4**	**105**	**38**	**86**	**10**	**–9**	**10**	**2**	**2**	**4**	**4**	**0**	**0**	**0**
1982-83	**St. Louis Blues**	**NHL**	**78**	**22**	**44**	**66**	**18**	**30**	**48**	**14**	**8**	**0**	**2**	**135**	**16.3**	**90**	**25**	**86**	**15**	**–6**	**4**	**1**	**1**	**2**	**0**	**1**	**0**	**0**
1983-84	**St. Louis Blues**	**NHL**	**17**	**1**	**10**	**11**	**1**	**7**	**8**	**4**	**0**	**0**	**0**	**18**	**5.6**	**17**	**4**	**25**	**11**	**–1**	....	....	....	....	....	....	....	....
	Detroit Red Wings	**NHL**	**57**	**6**	**14**	**20**	**5**	**9**	**14**	**20**	**1**	**1**	**0**	**67**	**9.0**	**32**	**1**	**63**	**19**	**–13**	**4**	**0**	**1**	**1**	**4**	**0**	**0**	**0**
	NHL Totals		**550**	**130**	**274**	**404**	**110**	**195**	**305**	**172**	**41**	**2**	**16**	**863**	**15.1**	**565**	**162**	**487**	**72**		**40**	**4**	**10**	**14**	**18**	**1**	**0**	**0**

OHA Second All-Star Team (1973) • AHL First All-Star Team (1978) • Won Fred T. Hunt Memorial Trophy (Sportsmanship - AHL) (1978) • Won Les Cunningham Award (MVP - AHL) (1978) • Won Bill Masterton Trophy (1981)

Traded to **Philadelphia** by **Minnesota** with Minnesota's 3rd round choice (Gord Salt) in 1978 Amateur Draft, October 28, 1977. Traded to **St. Louis** by **Philadelphia** with Rick LaPointe for Phil Myre, June 7, 1979. Signed as a free agent by **Detroit**, December 2, 1983.

• DUNN, DAVE

Dave Dunn D – L. 6′2″, 200 lbs. b: Moosomin, Sask., 8/19/1948.

Season	Club	League	GP	G	A	Pts	AG	AA	APts	PIM	PP	SH	GW	S	%	TGF	PGF	TGA	PGA	+/–	GP	G	A	Pts	PIM	PP	SH	GW
1966-67	University of Saskatchewan	WCIAA	14	3	7	10	....	....	....	12	....	....	....	....	....	....	....	....	....	....	....	....	....	....	....	....	....	....
1967-68	University of Saskatchewan	WCIAA	16	2	5	7	....	....	....	21	....	....	....	....	....	....	....	....	....	....	....	....	....	....	....	....	....	....
1968-69	University of Saskatchewan	WCIAA	20	4	10	14	....	....	....	50	....	....	....	....	....	....	....	....	....	....	....	....	....	....	....	....	....	....
1969-70	University of Saskatchewan	WCIAA	14	14	8	22	....	....	....	22	....	....	....	....	....	....	....	....	....	....	....	....	....	....	....	....	....	....
1970-71	Rochester Americans	AHL	56	2	13	15	....	....	....	74	....	....	....	....	....	....	....	....	....	....	....	....	....	....	....	....	....	....
1971-72	Rochester Americans	AHL	8	1	0	1	....	....	....	18	....	....	....	....	....	....	....	....	....	....	....	....	....	....	....	....	....	....
	Seattle Totems	WHL	46	10	12	22	....	....	....	104	....	....	....	....	....	....	....	....	....	....	....	....	....	....	....	....	....	....
1972-73	Seattle Totems	WHL	63	19	56	75	....	....	....	147	....	....	....	....	....	....	....	....	....	....	....	....	....	....	....	....	....	....
1973-74	**Vancouver Canucks**	**NHL**	**68**	**11**	**22**	**33**	**11**	**19**	**30**	**76**	**0**	**0**	**1**	**97**	**11.3**	**56**	**10**	**59**	**0**	**–13**	....	....	....	....	....	....	....	....
1974-75	**Vancouver Canucks**	**NHL**	**1**	**0**	**0**	**0**	**0**	**0**	**0**	**11**	**0**	**0**	**0**	**1**	**0.0**	**0**	**0**	**0**	**0**	**0**	....	....	....	....	....	....	....	....
	Toronto Maple Leafs	**NHL**	**72**	**3**	**11**	**14**	**3**	**9**	**12**	**142**	**0**	**0**	**2**	**76**	**3.9**	**58**	**3**	**86**	**21**	**–10**	**7**	**1**	**1**	**2**	**24**	**0**	**0**	**0**
1975-76	**Toronto Maple Leafs**	**NHL**	**43**	**0**	**8**	**8**	**0**	**6**	**6**	**84**	**0**	**0**	**0**	**43**	**0.0**	**36**	**3**	**51**	**13**	**–5**	**3**	**0**	**0**	**0**	**17**	**0**	**0**	**0**
	Oklahoma City Blazers	CHL	9	1	7	8	....	....	....	10	....	....	....	....	....	....	....	....	....	....	....	....	....	....	....	....	....	....
1976-77	Winnipeg Jets	WHA	40	3	11	14	....	....	....	129	....	....	....	....	....	....	....	....	....	....	20	4	4	8	23	....	....	....
1977-78	Winnipeg Jets	WHA	66	6	20	26	....	....	....	79	....	....	....	....	....	....	....	....	....	....	9	1	2	3	0	....	....	....
	NHL Totals		**184**	**14**	**41**	**55**	**14**	**34**	**48**	**313**	**0**	**0**	**3**	**217**	**6.5**	**150**	**16**	**196**	**34**		**10**	**1**	**1**	**2**	**41**	**0**	**0**	**0**
	Other Major League Totals		106	9	31	40	....	....	....	208	....	....	....	....	....	....	....	....	....	....	29	5	6	11	23	....	....	....

WHL First All-Star Team (1973) • Won Hal Laycoe Cup (WHL Top Defenseman) (1973)

Signed as a free agent by **Vancouver**, November, 1971. Traded to **Toronto** by **Vancouver** for Garry Monahan and John Grisdale, October 18, 1974. Signed as a free agent by **Winnipeg** (WHA), September, 1976.

• DUNN, RICHIE

Richie Dunn D – L. 6′, 200 lbs. b: Boston, MA, 5/12/1957.

Season	Club	League	GP	G	A	Pts	AG	AA	APts	PIM	PP	SH	GW	S	%	TGF	PGF	TGA	PGA	+/–	GP	G	A	Pts	PIM	PP	SH	GW
1975-76	Kingston Canadians	OHA	61	7	18	25	....	....	....	62	....	....	....	....	....	....	....	....	....	....	....	....	....	....	....	....	....	....
1976-77	Windsor Spitfires	OHA	66	5	21	26	....	....	....	98	....	....	....	....	....	....	....	....	....	....	9	0	5	5	4	....	....	....
	United States	WJC-A	....	....	....	....	....	....	....	....	....	....	....	....	....	....	....	....	....	....	....	....	....	....	....	....	....	....
1977-78	**Buffalo Sabres**	**NHL**	**25**	**0**	**3**	**3**	**0**	**2**	**2**	**16**	**0**	**0**	**0**	**23**	**0.0**	**10**	**0**	**13**	**0**	**–3**	**1**	**0**	**0**	**0**	**2**	**0**	**0**	**0**
	Hershey Bears	AHL	54	7	22	29	....	....	....	17	....	....	....	....	....	....	....	....	....	....	....	....	....	....	....	....	....	....
1978-79	**Buffalo Sabres**	**NHL**	**24**	**0**	**3**	**3**	**0**	**2**	**2**	**14**	**0**	**0**	**0**	**18**	**0.0**	**11**	**1**	**12**	**0**	**–2**	....	....	....	....	....	....	....	....
	Hershey Bears	AHL	34	5	18	23	....	....	....	10	....	....	....	....	....	....	....	....	....	....	4	0	1	1	4	....	....	....
1979-80	**Buffalo Sabres**	**NHL**	**80**	**7**	**31**	**38**	**6**	**24**	**30**	**61**	**4**	**0**	**2**	**147**	**4.8**	**100**	**26**	**62**	**13**	**+25**	**14**	**2**	**8**	**10**	**8**	**2**	**0**	**0**
1980-81	**Buffalo Sabres**	**NHL**	**79**	**7**	**42**	**49**	**6**	**29**	**35**	**34**	**4**	**0**	**1**	**175**	**4.0**	**137**	**46**	**90**	**20**	**+21**	**8**	**0**	**5**	**5**	**6**	**0**	**0**	**0**
1981-82	United States	C Cup	6	1	3	4	....	....	....	4	....	....	....	....	....	....	....	....	....	....	....	....	....	....	....	....	....	....
	Buffalo Sabres	**NHL**	**72**	**7**	**19**	**26**	**6**	**13**	**19**	**73**	**0**	**0**	**1**	**122**	**5.7**	**96**	**17**	**103**	**30**	**+6**	**4**	**0**	**1**	**1**	**0**	**0**	**0**	**0**
1982-83	**Calgary Flames**	**NHL**	**80**	**3**	**11**	**14**	**2**	**8**	**10**	**47**	**0**	**0**	**1**	**88**	**3.4**	**75**	**5**	**84**	**10**	**–4**	**9**	**1**	**1**	**2**	**8**	**0**	**0**	**0**
1983-84	**Hartford Whalers**	**NHL**	**63**	**5**	**20**	**25**	**4**	**14**	**18**	**30**	**0**	**0**	**0**	**82**	**6.1**	**76**	**18**	**96**	**18**	**–20**	....	....	....	....	....	....	....	....
1984-85	**Hartford Whalers**	**NHL**	**13**	**1**	**4**	**5**	**1**	**3**	**4**	**2**	**0**	**0**	**0**	**17**	**5.9**	**14**	**1**	**21**	**5**	**–3**	....	....	....	....	....	....	....	....
	Binghamton Whalers	AHL	64	9	39	48	....	....	....	43	....	....	....	....	....	....	....	....	....	....	8	2	2	4	8	....	....	....
1985-86	**Buffalo Sabres**	**NHL**	**29**	**4**	**5**	**9**	**3**	**3**	**6**	**25**	**4**	**0**	**0**	**55**	**7.3**	**33**	**14**	**33**	**9**	**–5**	....	....	....	....	....	....	....	....
	Rochester Americans	AHL	34	6	17	23	....	....	....	12	....	....	....	....	....	....	....	....	....	....	....	....	....	....	....	....	....	....
	United States	WEC-A	10	1	1	2	....	....	....	2	....	....	....	....	....	....	....	....	....	....	....	....	....	....	....	....	....	....
1986-87	**Buffalo Sabres**	**NHL**	**2**	**0**	**1**	**1**	**0**	**1**	**1**	**2**	**0**	**0**	**0**	**1**	**0.0**	**5**	**0**	**2**	**0**	**+2**	....	....	....	....	....	....	....	....
	Rochester Americans	AHL	64	6	26	32	....	....	....	47	....	....	....	....	....	....	....	....	....	....	18	1	6	7	6	....	....	....
1987-88	**Buffalo Sabres**	**NHL**	**12**	**2**	**0**	**2**	**2**	**0**	**2**	**8**	**0**	**0**	**0**	**19**	**10.5**	**7**	**2**	**14**	**2**	**–7**	....	....	....	....	....	....	....	....
	Rochester Americans	AHL	68	12	35	47	....	....	....	52	....	....	....	....	....	....	....	....	....	....	7	3	3	6	2	....	....	....

			REGULAR SEASON																		PLAYOFFS							
Season	Club	League	GP	G	A	Pts	AG	AA	APts	PIM	PP	SH	GW	S	%	TGF	PGF	TGA	PGA	+/–	GP	G	A	Pts	PIM	PP	SH	GW
1988-89	Buffalo Sabres	NHL	4	0	1	1	0	1	1	2	0	0	0	2	0.0	2	1	4	2	–1	....	....	....	....	....	....	....	....
	Rochester Americans	AHL	69	9	35	44	....	....	....	81	....	....	....	....	....	....	....	....	....	....	....	....	....	....	....	....	....	....
1989-90	Rochester Americans	AHL	41	7	7	14	....	....	....	34	....	....	....	....	....	....	....	....	....	....	7	0	4	4	4	....	....	....
	NHL Totals		483	36	140	176	30	100	130	314	12	0	5	749	4.8	566	131	534	109		36	3	15	18	24	2	0	0

AHL First All-Star Team (1985, 1987) • Won Eddie Shore Award (Outstanding Defenseman - AHL) (1985) • AHL Second All-Star Team (1988)

Signed as a free agent by **Buffalo**, October 3, 1977. Traded to **Calgary** by **Buffalo** with Don Edwards and Buffalo's 2nd round choice (Rich Kromm) in 1982 Entry Draft for Calgary's 1st (Paul Cyr) and 2nd (Jens Johansson) round choices in the 1982 Entry Draft and 3rd round choice (John Tucker) in 1983 Entry Draft, June 9, 1982. Traded to **Hartford** by **Calgary** with Joel Quenneville for Mickey Volvcan, July 5, 1983. Signed as a free agent by **Buffalo**, July 10, 1986.

• DUPERE, DENIS

Denis Dupere LW – L. 6'1", 200 lbs. b: Jonquiese, Que., 6/21/1948.

Season	Club	League	GP	G	A	Pts	AG	AA	APts	PIM	PP	SH	GW	S	%	TGF	PGF	TGA	PGA	+/–	GP	G	A	Pts	PIM	PP	SH	GW
1966-67	Kitchener Rangers	OHA	4	1	1	2	....	....	....	0	....	....	....	....	....	....	....	....	....	....	....	....	....	....	....	....	....	....
1967-68	Kitchener Rangers	OHA	54	35	24	59	....	....	....	22	....	....	....	....	....	....	....	....	....	....	19	2	7	9	20	....	....	....
1968-69	Ottawa Nationals	OHA Sr.	5	4	4	8	....	....	....	7	....	....	....	....	....	....	....	....	....	....	....	....	....	....	....	....	....	....
1969-70	Omaha Knights	CHL	72	33	19	52	....	....	....	35	....	....	....	....	....	....	....	....	....	....	12	5	7	12	11	....	....	....
1970-71	Toronto Maple Leafs	NHL	20	1	2	3	1	2	3	4	1	0	0	18	5.6	4	1	8	4	–1	6	0	0	0	0	0	0	0
	Tulsa Oilers	CHL	48	20	34	54	....	....	....	40	....	....	....	....	....	....	....	....	....	....	....	....	....	....	....	....	....	....
1971-72	Toronto Maple Leafs	NHL	77	7	10	17	7	9	16	4	1	0	0	55	12.7	23	6	40	28	+5	5	0	0	0	0	0	0	0
1972-73	Toronto Maple Leafs	NHL	61	13	23	36	13	19	32	10	4	0	0	129	10.1	56	12	66	18	–4	....	....	....	....	....	....	....	....
1973-74	Toronto Maple Leafs	NHL	34	8	9	17	8	8	16	8	2	0	0	53	15.1	28	9	18	2	+3	3	0	0	0	0	0	0	0
1974-75	Washington Capitals	NHL	53	20	15	35	19	12	31	8	8	0	0	133	15.0	44	18	70	3	–41	....	....	....	....	....	....	....	....
	St. Louis Blues	NHL	22	3	6	9	3	5	8	8	1	0	0	35	8.6	13	1	8	0	+4	....	....	....	....	....	....	....	....
1975-76	Kansas City Scouts	NHL	43	6	8	14	6	6	12	16	2	0	0	37	16.2	19	2	26	1	–8	....	....	....	....	....	....	....	....
1976-77	Colorado Rockies	NHL	57	7	11	18	7	9	16	4	1	3	2	60	11.7	30	3	41	17	+3	....	....	....	....	....	....	....	....
	Rhode Island Reds	AHL	4	3	3	6	....	....	....	0	....	....	....	....	....	....	....	....	....	....	....	....	....	....	....	....	....	....
1977-78	Colorado Rockies	NHL	54	15	15	30	14	12	26	4	2	2	4	67	22.4	41	7	40	15	+9	2	1	0	1	0	1	0	0
	Hampton Gulls	AHL	1	2	0	2	....	....	....	0	....	....	....	....	....	....	....	....	....	....	....	....	....	....	....	....	....	....
	Philadelphia Firebirds	AHL	12	3	2	5	....	....	....	10	....	....	....	....	....	....	....	....	....	....	....	....	....	....	....	....	....	....
	NHL Totals		421	80	99	179	78	82	160	66	22	5	6	587	13.6	258	59	317	88		16	1	0	1	0	1	0	0

Played in NHL All-Star Game (1975)

Traded to **Toronto** by **NY Rangers** to complete transaction that sent Tim Horton to NY Rangers, (March 3, 1970), May 18, 1970. Claimed by **Washington** from **Toronto** in Expansion Draft, June 12, 1974. Traded to **St. Louis** by **Washington** for Garnet Bailey and Stan Gilbertson, February 10, 1975. Traded to **Kansas City** by **St. Louis** with Craig Patrick and cash for Lynn Powis and Kansas City's 2nd choice (Brian Sutter) in 1976 Amateur Draft, June 18, 1975. Transferred to **Colorado** when **Kansas City** franchise relocated, July 15, 1976.

• DUPONT, ANDRE

Andre Dupont D – L. 6', 200 lbs. b: Trois Rivieres, Que., 7/27/1949. NY Rangers' 1st choice, 8th overall, in 1969 Amateur Draft.

Season	Club	League	GP	G	A	Pts	AG	AA	APts	PIM	PP	SH	GW	S	%	TGF	PGF	TGA	PGA	+/–	GP	G	A	Pts	PIM	PP	SH	GW
1968-69	Montreal Jr. Canadiens	OHA	38	2	14	16	....	....	....	212	....	....	....	....	....	....	....	....	....	....	14	2	8	10	*76	....	....	....
1969-70	Omaha Knights	CHL	64	11	26	37	....	....	....	258	....	....	....	....	....	....	....	....	....	....	12	1	8	9	*75	....	....	....
1970-71	New York Rangers	NHL	7	1	2	3	1	2	3	21	0	0	0	17	5.9	5	1	3	0	+1	....	....	....	....	....	....	....	....
	Omaha Knights	CHL	54	15	31	46	....	....	....	*308	....	....	....	....	....	....	....	....	....	....	11	0	7	7	*45	....	....	....
1971-72	St. Louis Blues	NHL	60	3	10	13	3	9	12	147	0	0	0	133	2.3	63	1	66	15	+11	11	1	0	1	20	0	0	0
	Providence Reds	AHL	18	1	8	9	....	....	....	95	....	....	....	....	....	....	....	....	....	....	....	....	....	....	....	....	....	....
1972-73	St. Louis Blues	NHL	25	1	6	7	1	5	6	51	0	0	0	38	2.6	24	2	30	8	–2	....	....	....	....	....	....	....	....
	Philadelphia Flyers	NHL	46	3	20	23	3	17	20	164	1	0	1	103	2.9	71	16	63	16	+8	11	1	2	3	29	0	0	0
1973-74	Philadelphia Flyers	NHL	75	3	20	23	3	17	20	216	2	0	1	165	1.8	88	20	49	15	+34	16	4	3	7	67	0	0	0
1974-75	Philadelphia Flyers	NHL	80	11	21	32	10	17	27	276	2	0	4	164	6.7	97	13	70	27	+41	17	3	2	5	49	1	0	2
1975-76	Philadelphia Flyers	NHL	75	9	27	36	8	21	29	214	3	0	2	139	6.5	105	23	72	30	+40	15	2	2	4	46	2	0	0
1976-77	Philadelphia Flyers	NHL	59	10	19	29	10	15	25	168	1	0	0	110	9.1	110	8	61	16	+57	10	1	1	2	35	0	0	0
1977-78	Philadelphia Flyers	NHL	69	2	12	14	2	10	12	225	0	0	0	106	1.9	72	1	66	26	+31	12	2	1	3	13	0	0	0
1978-79	Philadelphia Flyers	NHL	77	3	9	12	3	7	10	135	0	0	0	128	2.3	89	2	95	29	+21	8	0	0	0	17	0	0	0
1979-80	Philadelphia Flyers	NHL	58	1	7	8	1	5	6	107	0	0	0	67	1.5	75	0	49	11	+37	19	0	4	4	50	0	0	0
1980-81	Quebec Nordiques	NHL	63	5	8	13	4	6	10	93	1	1	0	72	6.9	80	8	116	41	+0	1	0	0	0	0	0	0	0
1981-82	Quebec Nordiques	NHL	60	4	12	16	3	8	11	100	0	0	2	62	6.5	78	1	103	29	+3	16	0	3	3	18	0	0	0
1982-83	Quebec Nordiques	NHL	46	3	12	15	2	8	10	69	0	0	0	42	7.1	53	0	64	22	+11	4	0	0	0	8	0	0	0
	NHL Totals		800	59	185	244	54	147	201	1986	10	1	10	1348	4.4	1019	96	907	283		140	14	18	32	352	3	0	2

CHL Second All-Star Team (1970) • Won Ken McKenzie Trophy (CHL's Rookie of the Year) (1970) • CHL First All-Star Team (1971) • Named CHL's Top Defenseman (1971) • Shared Tommy Ivan Trophy (CHL's MVP) with Gerry Ouellette, Peter McDuffe & Joe Zanussi (1971)

Played in NHL All-Star Game (1976)

Traded to **St. Louis** by **NY Rangers** with Jack Egars and Mike Murphy for Gene Carr, Jim Lorentz and Wayne Connelly, November 15, 1971. Traded to **Philadelphia** by **St. Louis** with St. Louis' 3rd round choice (Bob Stumpf) in 1973 Amateur Draft for Brent Hughes and Pierre Plante, December 14, 1972. Traded to **Quebec** by **Philadelphia** for cash and Quebec's 7th round choice (Vladmir Svitek) in 1981 Entry Draft, September 15, 1980.

• DUPONT, JEROME

Jerome "Jerry" Dupont D – L. 6'3", 190 lbs. b: Ottawa, Ont., 2/21/1962. Chicago's 2nd choice, 15th overall, in 1980 Entry Draft.

Season	Club	League	GP	G	A	Pts	AG	AA	APts	PIM	PP	SH	GW	S	%	TGF	PGF	TGA	PGA	+/–	GP	G	A	Pts	PIM	PP	SH	GW
1978-79	Toronto Marlboros	OHA	68	5	21	26	....	....	....	49	....	....	....	....	....	....	....	....	....	....	....	....	....	....	....	....	....	....
1979-80	Toronto Marlboros	OHA	67	7	37	44	....	....	....	88	....	....	....	....	....	....	....	....	....	....	....	....	....	....	....	....	....	....
1980-81	Toronto Marlboros	OHA	67	6	38	44	....	....	....	116	....	....	....	....	....	....	....	....	....	....	5	2	2	4	9	....	....	....
1981-82	Toronto Marlboros	OHL	7	0	8	8	....	....	....	18	....	....	....	....	....	....	....	....	....	....	10	3	9	12	24	....	....	....
	Chicago Black Hawks	NHL	34	0	4	4	0	3	3	51	0	0	0	22	0.0	21	1	22	0	–2	....	....	....	....	....	....	....	....
1982-83	Chicago Black Hawks	NHL	1	0	0	0	0	0	0	0	0	0	0	0	0.0	0	0	0	0	0	....	....	....	....	....	....	....	....
	Springfield Indians	AHL	78	12	22	34	....	....	....	114	....	....	....	....	....	....	....	....	....	....	....	....	....	....	....	....	....	....
1983-84	Chicago Black Hawks	NHL	36	2	2	4	2	1	3	116	0	0	0	28	7.1	13	1	25	2	–11	4	0	0	0	15	0	0	0
	Springfield Indians	AHL	12	2	3	5	....	....	....	65	....	....	....	....	....	....	....	....	....	....	....	....	....	....	....	....	....	....
1984-85	Chicago Black Hawks	NHL	55	3	10	13	2	7	9	105	0	0	1	54	5.6	44	1	47	9	+5	15	0	2	2	41	0	0	0
1985-86	Chicago Black Hawks	NHL	75	2	13	15	2	9	11	173	0	0	0	69	2.9	62	1	108	30	–17	1	0	0	0	0	0	0	0
1986-87	Toronto Maple Leafs	NHL	13	0	0	0	0	0	0	23	0	0	0	5	0.0	3	0	8	0	–5	....	....	....	....	....	....	....	....
	Newmarket Saints	AHL	29	1	8	9	....	....	....	47	....	....	....	....	....	....	....	....	....	....	....	....	....	....	....	....	....	....
	NHL Totals		214	7	29	36	6	20	26	468	0	0	1	178	3.9	143	4	210	41		20	0	2	2	56	0	0	0

Transferred to **Toronto** by **Chicago** with Ken Yaremchuk and Chicago's 4th round choice (Joe Sacco) in 1987 Entry Draft as compensation for Chicago's signing of free agent Gary Nylund, September 6, 1986.

• DUPONT, NORM

Norm Dupont LW – L. 5'10", 185 lbs. b: Montreal, Que., 2/5/1957. Montreal's 1st choice, 18th overall, in 1977 Amateur Draft.

Season	Club	League	GP	G	A	Pts	AG	AA	APts	PIM	PP	SH	GW	S	%	TGF	PGF	TGA	PGA	+/–	GP	G	A	Pts	PIM	PP	SH	GW
1973-74	Montreal Jr. Canadiens	QMJHL	70	55	70	125	....	....	....	4	....	....	....	....	....	....	....	....	....	....	....	....	....	....	....	....	....	....
1974-75	Montreal Jr. Canadiens	QMJHL	72	*84	74	*158	....	....	....	13	....	....	....	....	....	....	....	....	....	....	....	....	....	....	....	....	....	....
1975-76	Montreal Jr. Canadiens	QMJHL	70	69	63	132	....	....	....	8	....	....	....	....	....	....	....	....	....	....	6	7	3	10	0	....	....	....
1976-77	Montreal Jr. Canadiens	QMJHL	71	70	83	153	....	....	....	52	....	....	....	....	....	....	....	....	....	....	13	9	10	19	9	....	....	....
1977-78	Nova Scotia Voyageurs	AHL	81	31	29	60	....	....	....	21	....	....	....	....	....	....	....	....	....	....	....	....	....	....	....	....	....	....
1978-79	Nova Scotia Voyageurs	AHL	48	27	31	58	....	....	....	10	....	....	....	....	....	....	....	....	....	....	10	*7	4	11	2	....	....	....
1979-80	Montreal Canadiens	NHL	35	1	3	4	1	2	3	4	0	0	0	18	5.6	9	0	7	0	+2	8	1	1	2	0	0	0	1
1980-81	Winnipeg Jets	NHL	80	27	26	53	22	18	40	8	8	0	1	215	12.6	71	23	106	1	–57	....	....	....	....	....	....	....	....
1981-82	Winnipeg Jets	NHL	62	13	25	38	10	17	27	22	4	0	2	148	8.8	61	28	59	2	–24	4	2	0	2	0	2	0	0
1982-83	Winnipeg Jets	NHL	39	7	16	23	6	11	17	6	6	0	1	71	9.9	37	23	30	0	–16	1	1	1	2	0	1	0	0
	Sherbrooke Jets	AHL	3	2	1	3	....	....	....	2	....	....	....	....	....	....	....	....	....	....	....	....	....	....	....	....	....	....
1983-84	Hartford Whalers	NHL	40	7	15	22	6	10	16	12	2	0	0	85	8.2	38	9	45	0	–16	....	....	....	....	....	....	....	....
	Binghamton Whalers	AHL	27	14	24	38	....	....	....	6	....	....	....	....	....	....	....	....	....	....	....	....	....	....	....	....	....	....
1984-85	EHC Biel	Switz.	38	41	33	74	....	....	....	....	....	....	....	....	....	....	....	....	....	....	....	3	0	3	....	....	....	....
1985-86	EHC Biel	Switz.	38	43	*49	*92	....	....	....	....	....	....	....	....	....	....	....	....	....	....	....	....	....	....	....	....	....	....
1986-87	EHC Biel	Switz.	38	30	39	69	....	....	....	....	....	....	....	....	....	....	....	....	....	....	....	....	....	....	....	....	....	....
1987-88	EHC Biel	Switz.	37	*50	35	85	....	....	....	....	....	....	....	....	....	....	....	....	....	....	....	....	....	....	....	....	....	....

Season	Club	League	GP	G	A	Pts	AG	AA	APts	PIM	PP	SH	GW	S	%	TGF	PGF	TGA	PGA	+/–	GP	G	A	Pts	PIM	PP	SH	GW
									REGULAR SEASON															PLAYOFFS				
1988-89	EHC Biel	Switz.	38	36	34	70	....	....	....	....	....	....	....	....	....	....	....	....	....	....	2	0	0	0	0	....	....	....
1990-91	EHC Biel	Switz.	39	23	28	51	....	....	....	....	....	....	....	....	....	....	....	....	....	....	....	....	....	....	....	....	....	....
1990-91	EHC Biel	Switz.	25	15	17	32	....	....	....	20	....	....	....	....	....	....	....	....	....	....	....	....	....	....	....	....	....	....
	NHL Totals		**256**	**55**	**85**	**140**	**45**	**58**	**103**	**52**	**20**	**0**	**4**	**537**	**10.2**	**216**	**83**	**247**	**3**		**13**	**4**	**2**	**6**	**0**	**3**	**0**	**1**

QMJHL First All-Star Team (1975) • QMJHL West First All-Star Team (1976) • QMJHL Second All-Star Team (1977) • Won Dudley "Red" Garrett Memorial Award (Top Rookie - AHL) (1978)

Traded to **Winnipeg** by **Montreal** for Winnipeg's 2nd round choice (David Maley) in 1982 Entry Draft, September 26, 1980. Traded to **Hartford** by **Winnipeg** for Hartford's 4th round choice (Chris Mills) in 1984 Entry Draft, July 4, 1983.

• DUPRE, YANICK

Yanick Dupre LW – L. 6', 189 lbs. b: Montreal, Que., 11/20/1972. Deceased. Philadelphia's 2nd choice, 50th overall, in 1991 Entry Draft.

Season	Club	League	GP	G	A	Pts	AG	AA	APts	PIM	PP	SH	GW	S	%	TGF	PGF	TGA	PGA	+/–	GP	G	A	Pts	PIM	PP	SH	GW
1989-90	Chicoutimi Sagueneens	QMJHL	24	5	9	14	....	....	....	27	....	....	....	....	....	....	....	....	....	....	....	....	....	....	....	....	....	....
	Drummondville Voltigeurs	QMJHL	29	10	10	20	....	....	....	42	....	....	....	....	....	....	....	....	....	....	....	....	....	....	....	....	....	....
1990-91	Drummondville Voltigeurs	QMJHL	58	29	38	67	....	....	....	87	....	....	....	....	....	....	....	....	....	....	11	8	5	13	33	....	....	....
1991-92	Drummondville Voltigeurs	QMJHL	28	19	17	36	....	....	....	48	....	....	....	....	....	....	....	....	....	....	....	....	....	....	....	....	....	....
	Verdun National	QMJHL	12	7	14	21	....	....	....	21	....	....	....	....	....	....	....	....	....	....	19	9	9	18	20	....	....	....
	Philadelphia Flyers	**NHL**	**1**	**0**	**0**	**0**	**0**	**0**	**0**	**0**	**0**	**0**	**0**	**0**	**0.0**	**0**	**0**	**0**	**0**	**0**	....	....	....	....	....	....	....	....
1992-93	Hershey Bears	AHL	63	13	24	37	....	....	....	22	....	....	....	....	....	....	....	....	....	....	....	....	....	....	....	....	....	....
1993-94	Hershey Bears	AHL	51	22	20	42	....	....	....	42	....	....	....	....	....	....	....	....	....	....	8	1	3	4	2	....	....	....
1994-95	**Philadelphia Flyers**	**NHL**	**22**	**0**	**0**	**0**	**0**	**0**	**0**	**8**	**0**	**0**	**0**	**21**	**0.0**	**4**	**1**	**11**	**1**	**–7**	....	....	....	....	....	....	....	....
	Hershey Bears	AHL	41	15	19	34	....	....	....	35	....	....	....	....	....	....	....	....	....	....	....	....	....	....	....	....	....	....
1995-96	**Philadelphia Flyers**	**NHL**	**12**	**2**	**0**	**2**	**2**	**0**	**2**	**8**	**0**	**0**	**1**	**10**	**20.0**	**2**	**0**	**2**	**0**	**0**	....	....	....	....	....	....	....	....
	Hershey Bears	AHL	52	20	36	56	....	....	....	81	....	....	....	....	....	....	....	....	....	....	....	....	....	....	....	....	....	....
	NHL Totals		**35**	**2**	**0**	**2**	**2**	**0**	**2**	**16**	**0**	**0**	**1**	**31**	**6.5**	**6**	**1**	**13**	**1**		....	....	....	....	....	....	....	....

• DURBANO, STEVE

Steve Durbano D – L. 6'1", 210 lbs. b: Toronto, Ont., 12/12/1951. NY Rangers' 2nd choice, 13th overall, in 1971 Amateur Draft.

Season	Club	League	GP	G	A	Pts	AG	AA	APts	PIM	PP	SH	GW	S	%	TGF	PGF	TGA	PGA	+/–	GP	G	A	Pts	PIM	PP	SH	GW
1967-68	York Steel	Jr. B	21	1	9	10	....	....	....	....	....	....	....	....	....	....	....	....	....	....	....	....	....	....	....	....	....	....
1968-69	Toronto Marlboros	OHA	45	5	6	11	....	....	....	158	....	....	....	....	....	....	....	....	....	....	4	0	1	1	17	....	....	....
1969-70	Toronto Marlboros	OHA	53	7	25	32	....	....	....	*371	....	....	....	....	....	....	....	....	....	....	....	....	....	....	....	....	....	....
1970-71	Toronto Marlboros	OHA	49	7	32	39	....	....	....	*324	....	....	....	....	....	....	....	....	....	....	....	....	....	....	....	....	....	....
1971-72	Omaha Knights	CHL	70	7	34	41	....	....	....	*402	....	....	....	....	....	....	....	....	....	....	....	....	....	....	....	....	....	....
1972-73	**St. Louis Blues**	**NHL**	**49**	**3**	**18**	**21**	**3**	**15**	**18**	**231**	**0**	**0**	**0**	**83**	**3.6**	**63**	**18**	**51**	**3**	**–3**	**5**	**0**	**2**	**2**	**8**	**0**	**0**	**0**
1973-74	**St. Louis Blues**	**NHL**	**36**	**4**	**5**	**9**	**4**	**4**	**8**	**146**	**2**	**0**	**0**	**40**	**10.0**	**33**	**13**	**21**	**0**	**–1**	....	....	....	....	....	....	....	....
	Pittsburgh Penguins	**NHL**	**33**	**4**	**14**	**18**	**4**	**12**	**16**	**138**	**2**	**0**	**0**	**68**	**5.9**	**51**	**8**	**31**	**5**	**+17**	....	....	....	....	....	....	....	....
1974-75	**Pittsburgh Penguins**	**NHL**	**1**	**0**	**1**	**1**	**0**	**1**	**1**	**10**	**0**	**0**	**0**	**1**	**0.0**	**1**	**1**	**0**	**0**	**0**	....	....	....	....	....	....	....	....
1975-76	**Pittsburgh Penguins**	**NHL**	**32**	**0**	**8**	**8**	**0**	**6**	**6**	***161**	**0**	**0**	**0**	**41**	**0.0**	**31**	**2**	**23**	**3**	**+9**	....	....	....	....	....	....	....	....
	Kansas City Scouts	**NHL**	**37**	**1**	**11**	**12**	**1**	**9**	**10**	***209**	**0**	**0**	**0**	**65**	**1.5**	**29**	**7**	**71**	**19**	**–30**	....	....	....	....	....	....	....	....
1976-77	**Colorado Rockies**	**NHL**	**19**	**0**	**2**	**2**	**0**	**2**	**2**	**129**	**0**	**0**	**0**	**17**	**0.0**	**8**	**0**	**18**	**4**	**–6**	....	....	....	....	....	....	....	....
	Rhode Island Reds	AHL	9	1	2	3	....	....	....	55	....	....	....	....	....	....	....	....	....	....	....	....	....	....	....	....	....	....
1977-78	Birmingham Bulls	WHA	45	6	4	10	....	....	....	284	....	....	....	....	....	....	....	....	....	....	4	0	2	2	16	....	....	....
1978-79	**St. Louis Blues**	**NHL**	**13**	**1**	**1**	**2**	**1**	**1**	**2**	**103**	**0**	**0**	**0**	**18**	**5.6**	**5**	**0**	**12**	**0**	**–7**	....	....	....	....	....	....	....	....
	Salt Lake Golden Eagles	CHL	10	1	4	5	....	....	....	41	....	....	....	....	....	....	....	....	....	....	....	....	....	....	....	....	....	....
	NHL Totals		**220**	**13**	**60**	**73**	**13**	**50**	**63**	**1127**	**4**	**0**	**0**	**333**	**3.9**	**221**	**49**	**227**	**34**		**5**	**0**	**2**	**2**	**8**	**0**	**0**	**0**
	Other Major League Totals		45	6	4	10	....	....	....	284	....	....	....	....	....	....	....	....	....		4	0	2	2	16	....	....	....

OHA Second All-Star Team (1971)

Selected by **Quebec** (WHA) in 1972 WHA General Player Draft, February 12, 1972. Traded to **St. Louis** by **NY Rangers** for Peter McDuffe and Curt Bennett, May 24, 1972. Traded to **Pittsburgh** by **St. Louis** with Ab Demarco and Bob Kelly for Bryan Watson, Greg Polis and Pittsburgh's 2nd round choice (Bob Hess) in 1974 Amateur Draft, January 17, 1974. Traded to **Kansas City** by **Pittsburgh** with Chuck Arnason for Pittsburgh's 1st round choice (Paul Gardner) in 1976 Amateur Draft for Simon Nolet, Ed Gilbert and Kansas City's 1st round choice (Blair Chapman) in 1976 Amateur Draft, January 9, 1976. Transferred to **Colorado** after **Kansas City** franchise relocated, July 15, 1976. WHA rights traded to **Birmingham** (WHA) by **Quebec** (WHA) for cash, June, 1977. Signed as a free agent by **Detroit**, July 14, 1977. Signed as a free agent by **St. Louis**, August 11, 1978.

• DURIS, VITEZSLAV

Vitezslav "Slava" Duris D – L. 6'1", 185 lbs. b: Pizen, Czechoslovakia, 1/5/1954.

Season	Club	League	GP	G	A	Pts	AG	AA	APts	PIM	PP	SH	GW	S	%	TGF	PGF	TGA	PGA	+/–	GP	G	A	Pts	PIM	PP	SH	GW
1977-78	Dukla Jihlava	Czech.	44	3	6	9	....	....	....	47	....	....	....	....	....	....	....	....	....	....	....	....	....	....	....	....	....	....
1978-79	Dukla Jihlava	Czech.	38	3	9	12	....	....	....	24	....	....	....	....	....	....	....	....	....	....	....	....	....	....	....	....	....	....
	Czechoslovakia	WEC-A	8	1	1	2	....	....	....	8	....	....	....	....	....	....	....	....	....	....	....	....	....	....	....	....	....	....
1979-80	Czechoslovakia	Nat-Team	8	1	1	2	....	....	....	8	....	....	....	....	....	....	....	....	....	....	....	....	....	....	....	....	....	....
	Czechoslovakia	Olympics	6	0	1	1	....	....	....	2	....	....	....	....	....	....	....	....	....	....	....	....	....	....	....	....	....	....
1980-81	**Toronto Maple Leafs**	**NHL**	**57**	**1**	**12**	**13**	**1**	**8**	**9**	**50**	**0**	**0**	**0**	**70**	**1.4**	**64**	**1**	**79**	**29**	**+13**	**3**	**0**	**1**	**1**	**2**	**0**	**0**	**0**
1981-82	Cincinnati Tigers	CHL	66	14	41	55	....	....	....	57	....	....	....	....	....	....	....	....	....	....	....	....	....	....	....	....	....	....
1982-83	**Toronto Maple Leafs**	**NHL**	**32**	**2**	**8**	**10**	**2**	**6**	**8**	**12**	**0**	**1**	**0**	**48**	**4.2**	**50**	**15**	**54**	**22**	**+3**	....	....	....	....	....	....	....	....
1983-84			DID NOT PLAY																									
1984-85	ECD Iserlohn	Germany	36	12	19	31	....	....	....	52	....	....	....	....	....	....	....	....	....	....	3	1	1	2	2	....	....	....
1985-86	ECD Iserholn	Germany	STATISTICS NOT AVAILABLE																									
1986-87	ECD Iserlohn	Germany	39	15	27	42	....	....	....	37	....	....	....	....	....	....	....	....	....	....	....	....	....	....	....	....	....	....
1987-88	EV Landshut	Germany	37	4	18	22	....	....	....	37	....	....	....	....	....	....	....	....	....	....	....	....	....	....	....	....	....	....
1988-89	EV Landshut	Germany	32	0	2	2	....	....	....	12	....	....	....	....	....	....	....	....	....	....	....	....	....	....	....	....	....	....
	EHC Freiburg	Germany	10	2	4	6	....	....	....	23	....	....	....	....	....	....	....	....	....	....	....	....	....	....	....	....	....	....
1989-90	EHC Freiburg	Germany	28	4	8	12	....	....	....	17	....	....	....	....	....	....	....	....	....	....	....	....	....	....	....	....	....	....
	NHL Totals		**89**	**3**	**20**	**23**	**3**	**14**	**17**	**62**	**0**	**1**	**0**	**118**	**2.5**	**114**	**16**	**133**	**51**		**3**	**0**	**1**	**1**	**2**	**0**	**0**	**0**

Signed as a free agent by **Toronto**, September 25, 1980.

• DVORAK, MIROSLAV

Miroslav Dvorak D – R. 5'10", 195 lbs. b: Htuboka nad Vitavou, Czech., 10/11/1951. Philadelphia's 3rd choice, 46th overall, in 1982 Entry Draft.

Season	Club	League	GP	G	A	Pts	AG	AA	APts	PIM	PP	SH	GW	S	%	TGF	PGF	TGA	PGA	+/–	GP	G	A	Pts	PIM	PP	SH	GW
1973-74	Dukla Jihlava	Czech.	STATISTICS NOT AVAILABLE																									
	Czechoslovakia	WEC-A	4	0	3	3	....	....	....	4	....	....	....	....	....	....	....	....	....	....	....	....	....	....	....	....	....	....
1974-75	Motor Ceske Budejovice	Czech.	STATISTICS NOT AVAILABLE																									
	Czechoslovakia	WEC-A	10	2	4	6	....	....	....	2	....	....	....	....	....	....	....	....	....	....	....	....	....	....	....	....	....	....
1975-76	Motor Ceske Budejovice	Czech.	STATISTICS NOT AVAILABLE																									
	Czechoslovakia	Olympics	5	0	2	2	....	....	....	2	....	....	....	....	....	....	....	....	....	....	....	....	....	....	....	....	....	....
	Czechoslovakia	WEC-A	8	0	0	0	....	....	....	4	....	....	....	....	....	....	....	....	....	....	....	....	....	....	....	....	....	....
1976-77	Czechoslovakia	C Cup	7	0	1	1	....	....	....	4	....	....	....	....	....	....	....	....	....	....	....	....	....	....	....	....	....	....
	Motor Ceske Budejovice	Czech.	STATISTICS NOT AVAILABLE																									
	Czechoslovakia	WEC-A	9	0	1	1	....	....	....	8	....	....	....	....	....	....	....	....	....	....	....	....	....	....	....	....	....	....
1977-78	Motor Ceske Budejovice	Czech.	43	10	16	26	....	....	....	48	....	....	....	....	....	....	....	....	....	....	....	....	....	....	....	....	....	....
	Czechoslovakia	Nat-Team	16	1	3	4	....	....	....	....	....	....	....	....	....	....	....	....	....	....	10	0	3	3	4	....	....	....
	Czechoslovakia	WEC-A	10	0	3	3	....	....	....	4	....	....	....	....	....	....	....	....	....	....	....	....	....	....	....	....	....	....
1978-79	Motor Ceske Budejovice	Czech.	42	3	19	22	....	....	....	14	....	....	....	....	....	....	....	....	....	....	....	....	....	....	....	....	....	....
	Czechoslovakia	Nat-Team	24	0	3	3	....	....	....	....	....	....	....	....	....	....	....	....	....	....	8	0	0	0	0	....	....	....
	Czechoslovakia	WEC-A	8	0	0	0	....	....	....	0	....	....	....	....	....	....	....	....	....	....	....	....	....	....	....	....	....	....
1979-80	Czechoslovakia	Nat-Team	24	4	5	9	....	....	....	4	....	....	....	....	....	....	....	....	....	....	6	1	1	2	0	....	....	....
	Czechoslovakia	Olympics	6	0	1	1	....	....	....	0	....	....	....	....	....	....	....	....	....	....	....	....	....	....	....	....	....	....
1980-81	Motor Ceske Budejovice	Czech.	44	8	27	35	....	....	....	....	....	....	....	....	....	....	....	....	....	....	....	....	....	....	....	....	....	....
	Czechoslovakia	Nat-Team	28	5	3	8	....	....	....	....	....	....	....	....	....	....	....	....	....	....	8	1	2	3	4	....	....	....
	Czechoslovakia	WEC-A	8	1	2	3	....	....	....	4	....	....	....	....	....	....	....	....	....	....	....	....	....	....	....	....	....	....
1981-82	Czechoslovakia	C Cup	6	0	3	3	....	....	....	2	....	....	....	....	....	....	....	....	....	....	....	....	....	....	....	....	....	....
	Motor Ceske Budejovice	Czech.	38	6	20	26	....	....	....	24	....	....	....	....	....	....	....	....	....	....	....	....	....	....	....	....	....	....
	Czechoslovakia	Nat-Team	35	0	15	15	....	....	....	6	....	....	....	....	....	....	....	....	....	....	10	0	5	5	4	....	....	....
	Czechoslovakia	WEC-A	10	0	5	5	....	....	....	4	....	....	....	....	....	....	....	....	....	....	....	....	....	....	....	....	....	....
1982-83	**Philadelphia Flyers**	**NHL**	**80**	**4**	**33**	**37**	**3**	**23**	**26**	**20**	**2**	**1**	**0**	**112**	**3.6**	**113**	**29**	**83**	**26**	**+27**	**3**	**0**	**1**	**1**	**0**	**0**	**0**	**0**
	Czechoslovakia	WEC-A	10	0	3	3	....	....	....	14	....	....	....	....	....	....	....	....	....	....	....	....	....	....	....	....	....	....
1983-84	**Philadelphia Flyers**	**NHL**	**66**	**4**	**27**	**31**	**3**	**18**	**21**	**27**	**0**	**1**	**0**	**85**	**4.7**	**93**	**18**	**86**	**30**	**+19**	**2**	**0**	**0**	**0**	**2**	**0**	**0**	**0**
1984-85	**Philadelphia Flyers**	**NHL**	**47**	**3**	**14**	**17**	**2**	**9**	**11**	**4**	**0**	**1**	**1**	**51**	**5.9**	**47**	**9**	**32**	**6**	**+12**	**13**	**0**	**1**	**1**	**4**	**0**	**0**	**0**

Season	Club	League	GP	G	A	Pts	AG	AA	APts	PIM	PP	SH	GW	S	%	TGF	PGF	TGA	PGA	+/–	GP	G	A	Pts	PIM	PP	SH	GW
			REGULAR SEASON																		PLAYOFFS							
1985-86	Kassel	Germany																			17	8	23	31	30			
1986-87	Kassel	Germany	STATISTICS NOT AVAILABLE																									
1987-88	Motor Ceske Budejovice	Czech.	39	0	10	10				16																		
	Essen	German 2	18	4	5	9				8																		
	NHL Totals		**193**	**11**	**74**	**85**	**8**	**50**	**58**	**51**	**2**	**3**	**1**	**248**	**4.4**	**253**	**56**	**201**	**62**		**18**	**0**	**2**	**2**	**6**	**0**	**0**	**0**

Named Best Defenseman at EJC-A (1970)

● DVORAK, RADEK

Radek Dvorak LW – R. 6'2", 187 lbs. b: Tabor, Czech., 3/9/1977. Florida's 1st choice, 10th overall, in 1995 Entry Draft.

Season	Club	League	GP	G	A	Pts	AG	AA	APts	PIM	PP	SH	GW	S	%	TGF	PGF	TGA	PGA	+/–	GP	G	A	Pts	PIM	PP	SH	GW
1993-94	Motor Ceske Budejovice	Czech.	8	0	0	0				0																		
1994-95	Motor Ceske Budejovice	Czech.	10	3	5	8				2											9	5	1	6				
1995-96	**Florida Panthers**	**NHL**	**77**	**13**	**14**	**27**	**13**	**11**	**24**	**20**	**0**	**0**	**4**	**126**	**10.3**	**44**	**2**	**38**	**1**	**+5**	**16**	**1**	**3**	**4**	**0**	**0**	**0**	**0**
1996-97	**Florida Panthers**	**NHL**	**78**	**18**	**21**	**39**	**19**	**19**	**38**	**30**	**2**	**0**	**1**	**139**	**12.9**	**56**	**12**	**47**	**1**	**–2**	**3**	**0**	**0**	**0**	**0**	**0**	**0**	**0**
1997-98	**Florida Panthers**	**NHL**	**64**	**12**	**24**	**36**	**14**	**23**	**37**	**33**	**2**	**3**	**0**	**112**	**10.7**	**45**	**5**	**55**	**14**	**–1**								
	NHL Totals		**219**	**43**	**59**	**102**	**46**	**53**	**99**	**83**	**4**	**3**	**5**	**377**	**11.4**	**145**	**19**	**140**	**16**		**19**	**1**	**3**	**4**	**0**	**0**	**0**	**0**

● DWYER, MIKE

Mike Dwyer LW – L. 5'11", 172 lbs. b: Brampton, Ont., 9/16/1957. Colorado's 4th choice, 74th overall, in 1977 Amateur Draft.

Season	Club	League	GP	G	A	Pts	AG	AA	APts	PIM	PP	SH	GW	S	%	TGF	PGF	TGA	PGA	+/–	GP	G	A	Pts	PIM	PP	SH	GW
1975-76	Windsor Spitfires	OHA	42	20	28	48				24																		
1976-77	Niagara Falls Flyers	OHA	59	30	38	68				127																		
	Windsor Spitfires	OHA	5	5	1	6				11																		
1977-78	Phoenix Roadrunners	CHL	25	12	8	20				16																		
	Hampton Gulls	AHL	9	2	1	3				4																		
1978-79	**Colorado Rockies**	**NHL**	**12**	**2**	**3**	**5**	**2**	**2**	**4**	**2**	**0**	**0**	**0**	**10**	**20.0**	**9**	**1**	**12**	**0**	**–4**								
	Philadelphia Firebirds	AHL	60	20	27	47				52																		
1979-80	**Colorado Rockies**	**NHL**	**10**	**0**	**0**	**0**	**0**	**0**	**0**	**19**	**0**	**0**	**0**	**12**	**0.0**	**0**	**0**	**6**	**1**	**–5**								
	Fort Worth Texans	CHL	13	3	4	7				22																		
	Birmingham Bulls	CHL	40	16	18	34				90																		
1980-81	**Calgary Flames**	**NHL**	**4**	**0**	**1**	**1**	**0**	**1**	**1**	**4**	**0**	**0**	**0**	**6**	**0.0**	**1**	**0**	**2**	**0**	**–1**	**1**	**1**	**0**	**1**	**0**	**0**	**0**	**0**
	Birmingham Bulls	CHL	49	16	34	50				135																		
	Wichita Wind	CHL	12	8	8	16				28											15	6	11	17	36			
1981-82	**Calgary Flames**	**NHL**	**5**	**0**	**2**	**2**	**0**	**1**	**1**	**0**	**0**	**0**	**0**	**5**	**0.0**	**3**	**0**	**3**	**0**	**0**								
	Oklahoma City Stars	CHL	28	9	21	30				35																		
1982-83	Colorado Flames	CHL	51	15	33	48				61											6	4	4	8	2			
	NHL Totals		**31**	**2**	**6**	**8**	**2**	**4**	**6**	**25**	**0**	**0**	**0**	**33**	**6.1**	**13**	**1**	**23**	**1**		**1**	**1**	**0**	**1**	**0**	**0**	**0**	**0**

Signed as a free agent by **Calgary**, October 17, 1980.

● DYKHUIS, KARL

Karl Dykhuis D – L. 6'3", 214 lbs. b: Sept-Iles, Que., 7/8/1972. Chicago's 1st choice, 16th overall, in 1990 Entry Draft.

Season	Club	League	GP	G	A	Pts	AG	AA	APts	PIM	PP	SH	GW	S	%	TGF	PGF	TGA	PGA	+/–	GP	G	A	Pts	PIM	PP	SH	GW
1988-89	Hull Olympiques	QMJHL	63	2	29	31				59											9	1	9	10	6			
1989-90	Hull Olympiques	QMJHL	69	10	46	56				119											11	2	5	7	2			
1990-91	Longueuil College-Francais	QMJHL	3	1	4	5				6											8	2	5	7	6			
	Canada	Nat-Team	37	2	9	11				16																		
	Canada	WJC-A	7	0	3	3				2																		
1991-92	Verdun College-Francais	QMJHL	29	5	19	24				55											17	0	12	12	14			
	Canada	Nat-Team	19	1	2	3				16																		
	Canada	WJC-A	7	0	0	0				8																		
	Chicago Blackhawks	**NHL**	**6**	**1**	**3**	**4**	**1**	**2**	**3**	**4**	**1**	**0**	**0**	**12**	**8.3**	**6**	**3**	**6**	**2**	**–1**								
1992-93	**Chicago Blackhawks**	**NHL**	**12**	**0**	**5**	**5**	**0**	**3**	**3**	**0**	**0**	**0**	**0**	**10**	**0.0**	**10**	**3**	**9**	**4**	**+2**								
	Indianapolis Ice	IHL	59	5	18	23				76											5	1	1	2	8			
1993-94	Indianapolis Ice	IHL	73	7	25	32				132																		
1994-95	Indianapolis Ice	IHL	52	2	21	23				63																		
	Philadelphia Flyers	**NHL**	**33**	**2**	**6**	**8**	**4**	**9**	**13**	**37**	**1**	**0**	**1**	**46**	**4.3**	**28**	**4**	**19**	**2**	**+7**	**15**	**4**	**4**	**8**	**14**	**2**	**0**	**2**
	Hershey Bears	AHL	1	0	0	0				0																		
1995-96	**Philadelphia Flyers**	**NHL**	**82**	**5**	**15**	**20**	**5**	**12**	**17**	**101**	**1**	**0**	**0**	**104**	**4.8**	**82**	**24**	**54**	**8**	**+12**	**12**	**2**	**2**	**4**	**22**	**1**	**0**	**0**
1996-97	**Philadelphia Flyers**	**NHL**	**62**	**4**	**15**	**19**	**4**	**13**	**17**	**35**	**2**	**0**	**1**	**101**	**4.0**	**59**	**10**	**59**	**16**	**+6**	**18**	**0**	**3**	**3**	**2**	**0**	**0**	**0**
1997-98	**Tampa Bay Lightning**	**NHL**	**78**	**5**	**9**	**14**	**6**	**9**	**15**	**110**	**0**	**1**	**0**	**91**	**5.5**	**51**	**4**	**80**	**25**	**–8**								
	NHL Totals		**273**	**17**	**53**	**70**	**20**	**48**	**68**	**287**	**5**	**1**	**2**	**364**	**4.7**	**236**	**48**	**227**	**57**		**45**	**6**	**9**	**15**	**38**	**3**	**0**	**2**

QMJHL First All-Star Team (1990)

Traded to **Philadelphia** by **Chicago** for Bob Wilkie and future considerations, February 16, 1995. Traded to **Tampa Bay** by **Philadelphia** with Mikael Renberg for Philadelphia's 1st round choices in 1998 (Simon Gagne), 1999, 2000, and 2001 Entry Drafts (previously acquired by Tampa Bay), August 20, 1997.

● DYKSTRA, STEVEN

Steven Dykstra D – L. 6'2", 190 lbs. b: Edmonton, Alta., 12/1/1962.

Season	Club	League	GP	G	A	Pts	AG	AA	APts	PIM	PP	SH	GW	S	%	TGF	PGF	TGA	PGA	+/–	GP	G	A	Pts	PIM	PP	SH	GW
1981-82	Seattle Breakers	WHL	57	8	26	34				139											10	3	1	4	42			
1982-83	Rochester Americans	AHL	70	2	16	18				100											15	0	5	5	27			
1983-84	Rochester Americans	AHL	63	3	19	22				141											6	0	0	0	46			
1984-85	Flint Generals	IHL	15	1	7	8				36																		
	Rochester Americans	AHL	51	9	23	32				113											2	0	1	1	10			
1985-86	**Buffalo Sabres**	**NHL**	**64**	**4**	**21**	**25**	**3**	**14**	**17**	**108**	**1**	**1**	**0**	**70**	**5.7**	**59**	**9**	**56**	**7**	**+1**								
1986-87	**Buffalo Sabres**	**NHL**	**37**	**0**	**1**	**1**	**0**	**1**	**1**	**179**	**0**	**0**	**0**	**21**	**0.0**	**13**	**0**	**25**	**5**	**–7**								
	Rochester Americans	AHL	18	0	0	0				77																		
1987-88	**Buffalo Sabres**	**NHL**	**27**	**1**	**1**	**2**	**1**	**1**	**2**	**91**	**0**	**0**	**0**	**11**	**9.1**	**16**	**0**	**18**	**2**	**0**								
	Rochester Americans	AHL	7	0	1	1				33																		
	Edmonton Oilers	**NHL**	**15**	**2**	**3**	**5**	**2**	**2**	**4**	**39**	**0**	**0**	**0**	**15**	**13.3**	**14**	**0**	**15**	**2**	**+1**								
1988-89	**Pittsburgh Penguins**	**NHL**	**65**	**1**	**6**	**7**	**1**	**4**	**5**	**126**	**0**	**0**	**0**	**38**	**2.6**	**38**	**2**	**83**	**37**	**–12**	**1**	**0**	**0**	**0**	**2**	**0**	**0**	**0**
1989-90	**Hartford Whalers**	**NHL**	**9**	**0**	**0**	**0**	**0**	**0**	**0**	**2**	**0**	**0**	**0**	**10**	**0.0**	**5**	**0**	**3**	**0**	**+2**								
	Binghamton Whalers	AHL	53	5	17	22				55																		
	Maine Mariners	AHL	16	0	4	4				20																		
1990-91	San Diego Gulls	IHL	72	6	18	24				141																		
1991-92			DID NOT PLAY																									
1992-93			DID NOT PLAY																									
1993-94	Toledo Storm	ECHL	11	3	5	8				37											12	0	2	2	23			
1994-95	Toledo Storm	ECHL	10	1	5	6				19																		
	Fort Worth Fire	CHL	10	0	2	2				12																		
1995-96	Fort Worth Fire	CHL	57	4	12	16				84																		
	NHL Totals		**217**	**8**	**32**	**40**	**7**	**22**	**29**	**545**	**1**	**1**	**0**	**165**	**4.8**	**143**	**11**	**200**	**53**		**1**	**0**	**0**	**0**	**2**	**0**	**0**	**0**

Signed as a free agent by **Buffalo**, December 10, 1982. Traded to **Edmonton** by **Buffalo** with Buffalo's 7th round choice (David Payne) in 1989 Entry Draft for Scott Metcalfe and Edmonton's 9th round choice (Donald Audette) in 1989 Entry Draft, February 11, 1988. Claimed by **Pittsburgh** from **Edmonton** in Waiver Draft, October 3, 1988. Signed as a free agent by **Hartford**, October 9, 1989. Traded to **Boston** by **Hartford** for Jeff Sirrka, March 3, 1990.

● DZIEDZIC, JOE

Joe Dziedzic LW – L. 6'3", 227 lbs. b: Minneapolis, MN, 12/18/1971. Pittsburgh's 2nd choice, 61st overall, in 1990 Entry Draft.

Season	Club	League	GP	G	A	Pts	AG	AA	APts	PIM	PP	SH	GW	S	%	TGF	PGF	TGA	PGA	+/–	GP	G	A	Pts	PIM	PP	SH	GW
1989-90	Edison High School	H.S.	17	29	19	48				10																		
1990-91	University of Minnesota	WCHA	20	6	4	10				20																		
1991-92	University of Minnesota	WCHA	34	8	9	17				68																		
1992-93	University of Minnesota	WCHA	41	11	14	25				62																		
1993-94	University of Minnesota	WCHA	18	7	10	17				48																		
1994-95	Cleveland Lumberjacks	IHL	68	15	15	30				74											4	1	0	1	10			
1995-96	**Pittsburgh Penguins**	**NHL**	**69**	**5**	**5**	**10**	**5**	**4**	**9**	**68**	**0**	**0**	**3**	**44**	**11.4**	**15**	**0**	**21**	**1**	**–5**	**16**	**1**	**2**	**3**	**19**	**0**	**0**	**0**
1996-97	**Pittsburgh Penguins**	**NHL**	**59**	**9**	**9**	**18**	**10**	**8**	**18**	**63**	**0**	**0**	**1**	**85**	**10.6**	**23**	**0**	**27**	**0**	**–4**	**5**	**0**	**1**	**1**	**4**	**0**	**0**	**0**
1997-98	Cleveland Lumberjacks	IHL	65	21	20	41				176											10	3	4	7	28			
	NHL Totals		**128**	**14**	**14**	**28**	**15**	**12**	**27**	**131**	**0**	**0**	**4**	**129**	**10.9**	**38**	**0**	**48**	**1**		**21**	**1**	**3**	**4**	**23**	**0**	**0**	**0**

• EAGLES, MIKE
Mike Eagles C/LW – L. 5'10", 190 lbs. b: Sussex, N.B., 3/7/1963. Quebec's 5th choice, 116th overall, in 1981 Entry Draft.

			REGULAR SEASON																		PLAYOFFS							
Season	Club	League	GP	G	A	Pts	AG	AA	APts	PIM	PP	SH	GW	S	%	TGF	PGF	TGA	PGA	+/–	GP	G	A	Pts	PIM	PP	SH	GW
1980-81	Kitchener Rangers	OHA	56	11	27	38	....	....	....	64	....	....	....	....	....	....	....	....	....	....	18	4	2	6	36	....	....	....
1981-82	Kitchener Rangers	OHL	62	26	40	66	....	....	....	148	....	....	....	....	....	....	....	....	....	....	15	3	11	14	27	....	....	....
1982-83	Kitchener Rangers	OHL	58	26	36	62	....	....	....	133	....	....	....	....	....	....	....	....	....	....	12	5	7	12	27	....	....	....
	Canada	WJC-A	7	2	4	6	....	....	....	2	....	....	....	....	....	....	....	....	....	....	....	....	....	....	....	....	....	....
	Quebec Nordiques	**NHL**	**2**	**0**	**0**	**0**	**0**	**0**	**0**	**2**	**0**	**0**	**0**	**1**	**0.0**	**0**	**0**	**1**	**0**	**–1**	....	....	....	....	....	....	....	....
1983-84	Fredericton Express	AHL	68	13	29	42	....	....	....	85	....	....	....	....	....	....	....	....	....	....	4	0	0	0	5	....	....	....
1984-85	Fredericton Express	AHL	36	4	20	24	....	....	....	80	....	....	....	....	....	....	....	....	....	....	3	0	0	0	2	....	....	....
1985-86	**Quebec Nordiques**	**NHL**	**73**	**11**	**12**	**23**	**9**	**8**	**17**	**49**	**1**	**0**	**1**	**68**	**16.2**	**32**	**2**	**50**	**23**	**+3**	**3**	**0**	**0**	**0**	**2**	**0**	**0**	**0**
1986-87	**Quebec Nordiques**	**NHL**	**73**	**13**	**19**	**32**	**11**	**14**	**25**	**55**	**0**	**2**	**2**	**95**	**13.7**	**44**	**0**	**83**	**24**	**–15**	**4**	**1**	**0**	**1**	**10**	**0**	**0**	**0**
1987-88	**Quebec Nordiques**	**NHL**	**76**	**10**	**10**	**20**	**9**	**7**	**16**	**74**	**1**	**2**	**2**	**89**	**11.2**	**30**	**1**	**82**	**35**	**–18**	....	....	....	....	....	....	....	....
1988-89	**Chicago Blackhawks**	**NHL**	**47**	**5**	**11**	**16**	**4**	**8**	**12**	**44**	**0**	**0**	**0**	**39**	**12.8**	**24**	**0**	**46**	**14**	**–8**	....	....	....	....	....	....	....	....
1989-90	**Chicago Blackhawks**	**NHL**	**23**	**1**	**2**	**3**	**1**	**1**	**2**	**34**	**0**	**0**	**0**	**23**	**4.3**	**6**	**0**	**11**	**1**	**–4**	....	....	....	....	....	....	....	....
	Indianapolis Ice	IHL	24	11	13	24	....	....	....	47	....	....	....	....	....	....	....	....	....	....	13	*10	10	20	34	....	....	....
1990-91	**Winnipeg Jets**	**NHL**	**44**	**0**	**9**	**9**	**0**	**7**	**7**	**79**	**0**	**0**	**0**	**51**	**0.0**	**18**	**0**	**33**	**5**	**–10**	....	....	....	....	....	....	....	....
	Indianapolis Ice	IHL	25	15	14	29	....	....	....	47	....	....	....	....	....	....	....	....	....	....	....	....	....	....	....	....	....	....
1991-92	**Winnipeg Jets**	**NHL**	**65**	**7**	**10**	**17**	**6**	**7**	**13**	**118**	**0**	**1**	**0**	**60**	**11.7**	**21**	**0**	**63**	**25**	**–17**	**7**	**0**	**0**	**0**	**8**	**0**	**0**	**0**
1992-93	**Winnipeg Jets**	**NHL**	**84**	**8**	**18**	**26**	**7**	**12**	**19**	**131**	**1**	**0**	**1**	**67**	**11.9**	**43**	**1**	**91**	**48**	**–1**	**5**	**0**	**1**	**1**	**6**	**0**	**0**	**0**
1993-94	**Winnipeg Jets**	**NHL**	**73**	**4**	**8**	**12**	**4**	**6**	**10**	**96**	**0**	**1**	**0**	**53**	**7.5**	**13**	**1**	**67**	**35**	**–20**	....	....	....	....	....	....	....	....
1994-95	**Winnipeg Jets**	**NHL**	**27**	**2**	**1**	**3**	**4**	**1**	**5**	**40**	**0**	**0**	**0**	**13**	**15.4**	**4**	**0**	**26**	**9**	**–13**	....	....	....	....	....	....	....	....
	Washington Capitals	**NHL**	**13**	**1**	**3**	**4**	**2**	**4**	**6**	**8**	**0**	**0**	**0**	**15**	**6.7**	**8**	**2**	**8**	**4**	**+2**	**7**	**0**	**2**	**2**	**4**	**0**	**0**	**0**
1995-96	**Washington Capitals**	**NHL**	**70**	**4**	**7**	**11**	**4**	**6**	**10**	**75**	**0**	**0**	**0**	**70**	**5.7**	**25**	**0**	**44**	**18**	**–1**	**6**	**1**	**1**	**2**	**2**	**0**	**0**	**0**
1996-97	**Washington Capitals**	**NHL**	**70**	**1**	**7**	**8**	**1**	**6**	**7**	**42**	**0**	**0**	**0**	**38**	**2.6**	**15**	**0**	**31**	**12**	**–4**	....	....	....	....	....	....	....	....
1997-98	**Washington Capitals**	**NHL**	**36**	**1**	**3**	**4**	**1**	**3**	**4**	**16**	**0**	**0**	**0**	**25**	**4.0**	**9**	**0**	**13**	**2**	**–2**	**12**	**0**	**2**	**2**	**2**	**0**	**0**	**0**
	NHL Totals		**776**	**68**	**120**	**188**	**63**	**90**	**153**	**863**	**3**	**6**	**6**	**707**	**9.6**	**292**	**7**	**649**	**255**		**44**	**2**	**6**	**8**	**34**	**0**	**0**	**0**

Traded to **Chicago** by **Quebec** for Bob Mason, July 5, 1988. Traded to **Winnipeg** by **Chicago** for Winnipeg's 4th round choice (Igor Kravchuk) in 1991 Entry Draft, December 14, 1990. Traded to **Washington** by **Winnipeg** with Igor Ulanov for Washington's 3rd (later traded to Dallas — Dallas selected Sergei Gusev) and 5th (Brian Elder) round choices in 1995 Entry Draft, April 7, 1995.

• EAKIN, BRUCE
Bruce Eakin C – L. 5'11", 190 lbs. b: Winnipeg, Man., 9/28/1962. Calgary's 9th choice, 204th overall, in 1981 Entry Draft.

Season	Club	League	GP	G	A	Pts	AG	AA	APts	PIM	PP	SH	GW	S	%	TGF	PGF	TGA	PGA	+/–	GP	G	A	Pts	PIM	PP	SH	GW
1979-80	St. James Canadians	MJHL	48	42	62	104	....	....	....	76	....	....	....	....	....	....	....	....	....	....	....	....	....	....	....	....	....	....
1980-81	Saskatoon Blades	WHL	52	18	46	64	....	....	....	54	....	....	....	....	....	....	....	....	....	....	....	....	....	....	....	....	....	....
1981-82	Saskatoon Blades	WHL	66	42	*125	167	....	....	....	120	....	....	....	....	....	....	....	....	....	....	5	4	6	10	0	....	....	....
	Canada	WJC-A	7	4	7	11	....	....	....	4	....	....	....	....	....	....	....	....	....	....	....	....	....	....	....	....	....	....
	Calgary Flames	**NHL**	**1**	**0**	**0**	**0**	**0**	**0**	**0**	**0**	**0**	**0**	**0**	**0**	**0.0**	**0**	**0**	**2**	**0**	**–2**	....	....	....	....	....	....	....	....
	Oklahoma City Stars	CHL	3	0	3	3	....	....	....	0	....	....	....	....	....	....	....	....	....	....	4	2	0	2	2	....	....	....
1982-83	Colorado Flames	CHL	73	24	46	70	....	....	....	45	....	....	....	....	....	....	....	....	....	....	6	1	6	7	2	....	....	....
1983-84	**Calgary Flames**	**NHL**	**7**	**2**	**1**	**3**	**2**	**1**	**3**	**4**	**0**	**0**	**0**	**8**	**25.0**	**4**	**1**	**4**	**0**	**–1**	....	....	....	....	....	....	....	....
	Colorado Flames	CHL	67	33	69	102	....	....	....	18	....	....	....	....	....	....	....	....	....	....	6	4	2	6	0	....	....	....
1984-85	**Calgary Flames**	**NHL**	**1**	**0**	**0**	**0**	**0**	**0**	**0**	**0**	**0**	**0**	**0**	**0**	**0.0**	**0**	**0**	**0**	**0**	**0**	....	....	....	....	....	....	....	....
	Moncton Golden Flames	AHL	78	35	48	83	....	....	....	60	....	....	....	....	....	....	....	....	....	....	....	....	....	....	....	....	....	....
1985-86	**Detroit Red Wings**	**NHL**	**4**	**0**	**1**	**1**	**0**	**1**	**1**	**0**	**0**	**0**	**0**	**1**	**0.0**	**1**	**0**	**8**	**3**	**–4**	....	....	....	....	....	....	....	....
	Adirondack Red Wings	AHL	25	8	10	18	....	....	....	23	....	....	....	....	....	....	....	....	....	....	....	....	....	....	....	....	....	....
	Nova Scotia Oilers	AHL	14	6	12	18	....	....	....	12	....	....	....	....	....	....	....	....	....	....	....	....	....	....	....	....	....	....
1986-87	Springfield Indians	AHL	11	0	5	5	....	....	....	6	....	....	....	....	....	....	....	....	....	....	....	....	....	....	....	....	....	....
	New Haven Nighthawks	AHL	4	1	2	3	....	....	....	4	....	....	....	....	....	....	....	....	....	....	....	....	....	....	....	....	....	....
1987-88	Kalpa	Finland	36	6	17	23	....	....	....	50	....	....	....	....	....	....	....	....	....	....	....	....	....	....	....	....	....	....
1988-89	Neuss	Germany	23	18	23	41	....	....	....	52	....	....	....	....	....	....	....	....	....	....	....	....	....	....	....	....	....	....
1989-90	Essen-West	Germany	52	58	95	153	....	....	....	80	....	....	....	....	....	....	....	....	....	....	....	....	....	....	....	....	....	....
1990-91	Essen-West	Germany	49	42	69	111	....	....	....	72	....	....	....	....	....	....	....	....	....	....	....	....	....	....	....	....	....	....
1991-92	Nurnberg	Germany	34	17	39	56	....	....	....	40	....	....	....	....	....	....	....	....	....	....	....	....	....	....	....	....	....	....
1992-93	Krefelder EV	Germany	42	28	34	62	....	....	....	84	....	....	....	....	....	....	....	....	....	....	....	....	....	....	....	....	....	....
1993-94	Krefelder EV	Germany	44	19	28	47	....	....	....	80	....	....	....	....	....	....	....	....	....	....	....	....	....	....	....	....	....	....
1994-95	Dusseldorfer EG	Germany	19	5	5	10	....	....	....	4	....	....	....	....	....	....	....	....	....	....	10	2	10	12	12	....	....	....
1995-96	Dusseldorfer EG	Germany	10	0	0	0	....	....	....	8	....	....	....	....	....	....	....	....	....	....	....	....	....	....	....	....	....	....
	Kassel Huskies	Germany	38	15	21	36	....	....	....	44	....	....	....	....	....	....	....	....	....	....	8	3	5	8	4	....	....	....
1996-97	Kassel Huskies	Germany	49	13	34	47	....	....	....	38	....	....	....	....	....	....	....	....	....	....	10	2	7	9	24	....	....	....
1997-98	Kassel Huskies	EuroHL	6	3	1	4	....	....	....	24	....	....	....	....	....	....	....	....	....	....	....	....	....	....	....	....	....	....
	Kassel Huskies	Germany	48	11	22	33	....	....	....	71	....	....	....	....	....	....	....	....	....	....	....	....	....	....	....	....	....	....
	NHL Totals		**13**	**2**	**2**	**4**	**2**	**2**	**4**	**4**	**0**	**0**	**0**	**9**	**22.2**	**5**	**1**	**14**	**3**		....	....	....	....	....	....	....	....

WHL First All-Star Team (1982) • CHL Second All-Star Team (1984)

Signed as a free agent by **Detroit**, July 18, 1985 Traded to **Edmonton** by **Detroit** for Billy Carroll, December 28, 1985.

• EAKINS, DALLAS
Dallas Eakins D – L. 6'2", 195 lbs. b: Dade City, FL, 2/27/1967. Washington's 11th choice, 208th overall, in 1985 Entry Draft.

Season	Club	League	GP	G	A	Pts	AG	AA	APts	PIM	PP	SH	GW	S	%	TGF	PGF	TGA	PGA	+/–	GP	G	A	Pts	PIM	PP	SH	GW
1984-85	Peterborough Petes	OHL	48	0	8	8	....	....	....	96	....	....	....	....	....	....	....	....	....	....	7	0	0	0	18	....	....	....
1985-86	Peterborough Petes	OHL	60	6	16	22	....	....	....	134	....	....	....	....	....	....	....	....	....	....	16	0	1	1	30	....	....	....
1986-87	Peterborough Petes	OHL	54	3	11	14	....	....	....	145	....	....	....	....	....	....	....	....	....	....	12	1	4	5	37	....	....	....
1987-88	Peterborough Petes	OHL	64	11	27	38	....	....	....	129	....	....	....	....	....	....	....	....	....	....	12	3	12	15	16	....	....	....
1988-89	Baltimore Skipjacks	AHL	62	0	10	10	....	....	....	139	....	....	....	....	....	....	....	....	....	....	....	....	....	....	....	....	....	....
1989-90	Moncton Hawks	AHL	75	2	11	13	....	....	....	189	....	....	....	....	....	....	....	....	....	....	....	....	....	....	....	....	....	....
1990-91	Moncton Hawks	AHL	75	1	12	13	....	....	....	132	....	....	....	....	....	....	....	....	....	....	9	0	1	1	44	....	....	....
1991-92	Moncton Hawks	AHL	67	3	13	16	....	....	....	136	....	....	....	....	....	....	....	....	....	....	11	2	1	3	16	....	....	....
1992-93	**Winnipeg Jets**	**NHL**	**14**	**0**	**2**	**2**	**0**	**1**	**1**	**38**	**0**	**0**	**0**	**9**	**0.0**	**10**	**0**	**13**	**5**	**+2**	....	....	....	....	....	....	....	....
	Moncton Hawks	AHL	55	4	6	10	....	....	....	132	....	....	....	....	....	....	....	....	....	....	....	....	....	....	....	....	....	....
1993-94	**Florida Panthers**	**NHL**	**1**	**0**	**0**	**0**	**0**	**0**	**0**	**0**	**0**	**0**	**0**	**2**	**0.0**	**0**	**0**	**1**	**1**	**0**	....	....	....	....	....	....	....	....
	Cincinnati Cyclones	IHL	80	1	18	19	....	....	....	143	....	....	....	....	....	....	....	....	....	....	8	0	1	1	41	....	....	....
1994-95	**Florida Panthers**	**NHL**	**17**	**0**	**1**	**1**	**0**	**1**	**1**	**35**	**0**	**0**	**0**	**3**	**0.0**	**12**	**0**	**12**	**2**	**+2**	....	....	....	....	....	....	....	....
	Cincinnati Cyclones	IHL	59	6	12	18	....	....	....	69	....	....	....	....	....	....	....	....	....	....	....	....	....	....	....	....	....	....
1995-96	**St. Louis Blues**	**NHL**	**16**	**0**	**1**	**1**	**0**	**1**	**1**	**34**	**0**	**0**	**0**	**6**	**0.0**	**4**	**0**	**10**	**4**	**–2**	....	....	....	....	....	....	....	....
	Worcester IceCats	AHL	4	0	0	0	....	....	....	12	....	....	....	....	....	....	....	....	....	....	....	....	....	....	....	....	....	....
	Winnipeg Jets	**NHL**	**2**	**0**	**0**	**0**	**0**	**0**	**0**	**0**	**0**	**0**	**0**	**0**	**0.0**	**1**	**0**	**0**	**0**	**+1**	....	....	....	....	....	....	....	....
1996-97	**Phoenix Coyotes**	**NHL**	**4**	**0**	**0**	**0**	**0**	**0**	**0**	**10**	**0**	**0**	**0**	**2**	**0.0**	**1**	**0**	**4**	**0**	**–3**	....	....	....	....	....	....	....	....
	Springfield Falcons	AHL	38	6	7	13	....	....	....	63	....	....	....	....	....	....	....	....	....	....	....	....	....	....	....	....	....	....
	New York Rangers	**NHL**	**3**	**0**	**0**	**0**	**0**	**0**	**0**	**6**	**0**	**0**	**0**	**2**	**0.0**	**1**	**0**	**2**	**0**	**–1**	**4**	**0**	**0**	**0**	**4**	**0**	**0**	**0**
	Binghamton Rangers	AHL	19	1	7	8	....	....	....	15	....	....	....	....	....	....	....	....	....	....	....	....	....	....	....	....	....	....
1997-98	**Florida Panthers**	**NHL**	**23**	**0**	**1**	**1**	**0**	**1**	**1**	**44**	**0**	**0**	**0**	**16**	**0.0**	**10**	**0**	**9**	**0**	**+1**	....	....	....	....	....	....	....	....
	Beast of New Haven	AHL	4	0	1	1	....	....	....	7	....	....	....	....	....	....	....	....	....	....	....	....	....	....	....	....	....	....
	NHL Totals		**80**	**0**	**5**	**5**	**0**	**4**	**4**	**167**	**0**	**0**	**0**	**40**	**0.0**	**39**	**0**	**51**	**12**		**4**	**0**	**0**	**0**	**4**	**0**	**0**	**0**

Signed as a free agent by **Winnipeg**, October 17, 1989. Signed as a free agent by **Florida**, July 8, 1993. Traded to **St. Louis** by **Florida** for St. Louis' 4th round choice (Ivan Novoseltsev) in 1997 Entry Draft, September 28, 1995. Claimed on waivers by **Winnipeg** from **St. Louis**, March 20, 1996. Transferred to **Phoenix** after **Winnipeg** franchise relocated, July 1, 1996. Traded to **NY Rangers** by **Phoenix** with Mike Eastwood for Jayson More, February 6, 1997. Signed as a free agent by **Florida**, July 30, 1997. Signed as a free agent by **Toronto**, July 14, 1998.

• EASTWOOD, MIKE
Mike Eastwood C – R. 6'3", 205 lbs. b: Ottawa, Ont., 7/1/1967. Toronto's 5th choice, 91st overall, in 1987 Entry Draft.

Season	Club	League	GP	G	A	Pts	AG	AA	APts	PIM	PP	SH	GW	S	%	TGF	PGF	TGA	PGA	+/–	GP	G	A	Pts	PIM	PP	SH	GW
1986-87	Pembroke Lumber Kings	OJHL	STATISTICS NOT AVAILABLE																									
1987-88	Western Michigan University	CCHA	42	5	8	13	....	....	....	14	....	....	....	....	....	....	....	....	....	....	....	....	....	....	....	....	....	....
1988-89	Western Michigan University	CCHA	40	10	13	23	....	....	....	87	....	....	....	....	....	....	....	....	....	....	....	....	....	....	....	....	....	....
1989-90	Western Michigan University	CCHA	40	25	27	52	....	....	....	36	....	....	....	....	....	....	....	....	....	....	....	....	....	....	....	....	....	....
1990-91	Western Michigan University	CCHA	42	29	32	61	....	....	....	84	....	....	....	....	....	....	....	....	....	....	....	....	....	....	....	....	....	....
1991-92	**Toronto Maple Leafs**	**NHL**	**9**	**0**	**2**	**2**	**0**	**1**	**1**	**4**	**0**	**0**	**0**	**6**	**0.0**	**3**	**2**	**5**	**0**	**–4**	....	....	....	....	....	....	....	....
	St. John's Maple Leafs	AHL	61	18	25	43	....	....	....	28	....	....	....	....	....	....	....	....	....	....	16	9	10	19	16	....	....	....
1992-93	**Toronto Maple Leafs**	**NHL**	**12**	**1**	**6**	**7**	**1**	**4**	**5**	**21**	**0**	**0**	**0**	**11**	**9.1**	**9**	**1**	**10**	**0**	**–2**	**10**	**1**	**2**	**3**	**8**	**0**	**0**	**0**
	St. John's Maple Leafs	AHL	60	24	35	59	....	....	....	32	....	....	....	....	....	....	....	....	....	....	....	....	....	....	....	....	....	....
1993-94	**Toronto Maple Leafs**	**NHL**	**54**	**8**	**10**	**18**	**7**	**8**	**15**	**28**	**1**	**0**	**2**	**41**	**19.5**	**24**	**6**	**19**	**3**	**+2**	**18**	**3**	**2**	**5**	**12**	**1**	**0**	**1**

Season	Club	League	GP	G	A	Pts	AG	AA	APts	PIM	PP	SH	GW	S	%	TGF	PGF	TGA	PGA	+/–	GP	G	A	Pts	PIM	PP	SH	GW
			REGULAR SEASON																		PLAYOFFS							
1994-95	**Toronto Maple Leafs**	**NHL**	**36**	**5**	**5**	**10**	**9**	**7**	**16**	**32**	**0**	**0**	**0**	**38**	**13.2**	**13**	**2**	**27**	**4**	**–12**	....	....	....	....	....	....	....	....
	Winnipeg Jets	**NHL**	**13**	**3**	**6**	**9**	**5**	**9**	**14**	**4**	**0**	**0**	**0**	**17**	**17.6**	**12**	**1**	**9**	**1**	**+3**	....	....	....	....	....	....	....	....
1995-96	**Winnipeg Jets**	**NHL**	**80**	**14**	**14**	**28**	**14**	**11**	**25**	**20**	**2**	**0**	**3**	**94**	**14.9**	**45**	**3**	**77**	**21**	**–14**	**6**	**0**	**1**	**1**	**2**	**0**	**0**	**0**
1996-97	**Phoenix Coyotes**	**NHL**	**33**	**1**	**3**	**4**	**1**	**3**	**4**	**4**	**0**	**0**	**0**	**22**	**4.5**	**10**	**0**	**20**	**7**	**–3**	....	....	....	....	....	....	....	....
	New York Rangers	**NHL**	**27**	**1**	**7**	**8**	**1**	**6**	**7**	**10**	**0**	**0**	**0**	**22**	**4.5**	**10**	**0**	**10**	**2**	**+2**	**15**	**1**	**2**	**3**	**22**	**0**	**0**	**0**
1997-98	**New York Rangers**	**NHL**	**48**	**5**	**5**	**10**	**6**	**5**	**11**	**16**	**0**	**0**	**0**	**34**	**14.7**	**12**	**0**	**23**	**9**	**–2**	....	....	....	....	....	....	....	....
	St. Louis Blues	**NHL**	**10**	**1**	**0**	**1**	**1**	**0**	**1**	**6**	**0**	**0**	**1**	**4**	**25.0**	**1**	**0**	**1**	**0**	**0**	**3**	**1**	**0**	**1**	**0**	**0**	**0**	**1**
	NHL Totals		**322**	**39**	**58**	**97**	**45**	**54**	**99**	**145**	**3**	**0**	**6**	**289**	**13.5**	**139**	**15**	**201**	**47**		**52**	**6**	**7**	**13**	**44**	**1**	**0**	**2**

CCHA Second All-Star Team (1991)

Traded to **Winnipeg** by **Toronto** with Toronto's 3rd round choice (Brad Isbister) in 1995 Entry Draft for Tie Domi, April 7, 1995. Transferred to **Phoenix** after **Winnipeg** franchise relocated, July 1, 1996. Traded to **NY Rangers** by **Phoenix** with Dallas Eakins for Jayson More, February 6, 1997. Traded to **St. Louis** by **NY Rangers** for Harry York, March 24, 1998.

• EATOUGH, JEFF

Jeff Eatough RW – R. 5'9", 168 lbs. b: Toronto, Ont., 6/2/1963. Buffalo's 5th choice, 80th overall, in 1981 Entry Draft.

Season	Club	League	GP	G	A	Pts	AG	AA	APts	PIM	PP	SH	GW	S	%	TGF	PGF	TGA	PGA	+/–	GP	G	A	Pts	PIM	PP	SH	GW
1979-80	Niagara Falls Flyers	OHA	6	0	1	1	....	....	....	4	....	....	....	....	....	....	....	....	....	....	....	....	....	....	....	....	....	....
1980-81	Cornwall Royals	QMJHL	68	30	42	72	....	....	....	142	....	....	....	....	....	....	....	....	....	....	18	5	7	12	52	....	....	....
	Canada	WJC-A	5	1	2	3	....	....	....	4	....	....	....	....	....	....	....	....	....	....	....	....	....	....	....	....	....	....
1981-82	Cornwall Royals	OHL	66	53	37	90	....	....	....	180	....	....	....	....	....	....	....	....	....	....	5	0	5	5	21	....	....	....
	Buffalo Sabres	**NHL**	**1**	**0**	**0**	**0**	**0**	**0**	**0**	**0**	**0**	**0**	**0**	**0**	**0.0**	**0**	**0**	**1**	**0**	**–1**	....	....	....	....	....	....	....	....
1982-83	Cornwall Royals	OHL	9	5	3	8	....	....	....	18	....	....	....	....	....	....	....	....	....	....	....	....	....	....	....	....	....	....
	North Bay Centennials	OHL	50	25	24	49	....	....	....	73	....	....	....	....	....	....	....	....	....	....	8	2	5	7	12	....	....	....
1983-84	Rochester Americans	AHL	24	1	5	6	....	....	....	5	....	....	....	....	....	....	....	....	....	....	....	....	....	....	....	....	....	....
	Flint Generals	IHL	5	4	1	5	....	....	....	6	....	....	....	....	....	....	....	....	....	....	....	....	....	....	....	....	....	....
1984-85	Flint Generals	IHL	4	0	1	1	....	....	....	0	....	....	....	....	....	....	....	....	....	....	....	....	....	....	....	....	....	....
	Pinebridge Bucks	ACHL	12	4	8	12	....	....	....	31	....	....	....	....	....	....	....	....	....	....	....	....	....	....	....	....	....	....
	Mohawk Valley Stars	ACHL	42	27	33	60	....	....	....	37	....	....	....	....	....	....	....	....	....	....	....	....	....	....	....	....	....	....
1985-86	Mohawk Valley Comets	ACHL	27	18	19	37	....	....	....	43	....	....	....	....	....	....	....	....	....	....	6	5	8	13	4	....	....	....
	Flint Spirits	IHL	4	1	0	1	....	....	....	2	....	....	....	....	....	....	....	....	....	....	....	....	....	....	....	....	....	....
1986-87	Mohawk Valley Comets	ACHL	53	43	42	85	....	....	....	93	....	....	....	....	....	....	....	....	....	....	13	5	7	12	46	....	....	....
1987-88	Carolina Thunderbirds	ACHL	9	3	8	11	....	....	....	16	....	....	....	....	....	....	....	....	....	....	....	....	....	....	....	....	....	....
	NHL Totals		**1**	**0**	**0**	**0**	**0**	**0**	**0**	**0**	**0**	**0**	**0**	**0**	**0.0**	**0**	**0**	**1**	**0**		....	....	....	....	....	....	....	....

• EAVES, MIKE

Mike Eaves C – R. 5'10", 180 lbs. b: Denver, CO, 6/10/1956. St. Louis' 8th choice, 113th overall, in 1976 Amateur Draft.

Season	Club	League	GP	G	A	Pts	AG	AA	APts	PIM	PP	SH	GW	S	%	TGF	PGF	TGA	PGA	+/–	GP	G	A	Pts	PIM	PP	SH	GW
1973-74	Nepean Raiders	OJHL	54	54	48	*102	....	....	....	....	....	....	....	....	....	....	....	....	....	....	....	....	....	....	....	....	....	....
1974-75	University of Wisconsin	WCHA	38	17	37	54	....	....	....	12	....	....	....	....	....	....	....	....	....	....	....	....	....	....	....	....	....	....
1975-76	University of Wisconsin	WCHA	34	18	25	43	....	....	....	22	....	....	....	....	....	....	....	....	....	....	....	....	....	....	....	....	....	....
	United States	WEC-A	10	2	1	3	....	....	....	0	....	....	....	....	....	....	....	....	....	....	....	....	....	....	....	....	....	....
1976-77	University of Wisconsin	WCHA	45	38	53	81	....	....	....	18	....	....	....	....	....	....	....	....	....	....	....	....	....	....	....	....	....	....
1977-78	University of Wisconsin	WCHA	43	31	*58	*89	....	....	....	16	....	....	....	....	....	....	....	....	....	....	....	....	....	....	....	....	....	....
	United States	WEC-A	10	4	3	7	....	....	....	2	....	....	....	....	....	....	....	....	....	....	....	....	....	....	....	....	....	....
1978-79	**Minnesota North Stars**	**NHL**	**3**	**0**	**0**	**0**	**0**	**0**	**0**	**0**	**0**	**0**	**0**	**5**	**0.0**	**0**	**0**	**3**	**2**	**–1**	....	....	....	....	....	....	....	....
	Oklahoma City Stars	CHL	68	26	61	87	....	....	....	21	....	....	....	....	....	....	....	....	....	....	....	....	....	....	....	....	....	....
1979-80	**Minnesota North Stars**	**NHL**	**56**	**18**	**28**	**46**	**16**	**21**	**37**	**11**	**9**	**0**	**3**	**80**	**22.5**	**62**	**26**	**36**	**3**	**+3**	**15**	**2**	**5**	**7**	**4**	**0**	**0**	**0**
	Oklahoma City Stars	CHL	12	9	8	17	....	....	....	2	....	....	....	....	....	....	....	....	....	....	....	....	....	....	....	....	....	....
1980-81	**Minnesota North Stars**	**NHL**	**48**	**10**	**24**	**34**	**8**	**17**	**25**	**18**	**1**	**1**	**1**	**104**	**9.6**	**53**	**13**	**42**	**3**	**+1**	....	....	....	....	....	....	....	....
1981-82	United States	C Cup	6	3	3	6	....	....	....	4	....	....	....	....	....	....	....	....	....	....	....	....	....	....	....	....	....	....
	Minnesota North Stars	**NHL**	**25**	**11**	**10**	**21**	**9**	**7**	**16**	**0**	**2**	**0**	**1**	**62**	**17.7**	**31**	**10**	**21**	**2**	**+2**	....	....	....	....	....	....	....	....
1982-83	**Minnesota North Stars**	**NHL**	**75**	**16**	**16**	**32**	**13**	**11**	**24**	**21**	**1**	**5**	**2**	**143**	**11.2**	**42**	**2**	**68**	**25**	**–3**	**9**	**0**	**0**	**0**	**0**	**0**	**0**	**0**
1983-84	**Calgary Flames**	**NHL**	**61**	**14**	**36**	**50**	**11**	**24**	**35**	**20**	**3**	**0**	**3**	**118**	**11.9**	**81**	**22**	**68**	**18**	**+9**	**11**	**4**	**4**	**8**	**2**	**1**	**1**	**1**
1984-85	**Calgary Flames**	**NHL**	**56**	**14**	**29**	**43**	**11**	**20**	**31**	**10**	**1**	**2**	**1**	**96**	**14.6**	**63**	**10**	**66**	**27**	**+14**	....	....	....	....	....	....	....	....
1985-86	**Calgary Flames**	**NHL**	....	....	....	....	....	....	....	....	....	....	....	....	....	....	....	....	....	....	**8**	**1**	**1**	**2**	**8**	....	....	....
	NHL Totals		**324**	**83**	**143**	**226**	**68**	**100**	**168**	**80**	**17**	**8**	**11**	**608**	**13.7**	**332**	**83**	**304**	**80**		**43**	**7**	**10**	**17**	**14**	**1**	**1**	**1**

WCHA Second All-Star Team (1977) • NCAA West First All-American Team (1977, 1978) • WCHA First All-Star Team (1978) • CHL Second All-Star Team (1979) • Won Ken McKenzie Trophy (CHL's Rookie of the Year) (1979)

Rights traded to **Cleveland** by **St. Louis** for Len Frig, August 17, 1977. Rights transferred to **Minnesota** Reserve List after **Cleveland-Minnesota** Dispersal Draft, June 15, 1978. Traded to **Calgary** by **Minnesota** with Keith Hanson for Steve Christoff and Calgary's 2nd round choice (Frantisek Musil) in 1983 Entry Draft, June 8, 1983. • Calgary assistant coach came out of retirement as an emergency injury replacement for Carey Wilson, May 4, 1986.

• EAVES, MURRAY

Murray Eaves C – R. 5'10", 185 lbs. b: Calgary, Alta., 5/10/1960. Winnipeg's 3rd choice, 44th overall, in 1980 Entry Draft.

Season	Club	League	GP	G	A	Pts	AG	AA	APts	PIM	PP	SH	GW	S	%	TGF	PGF	TGA	PGA	+/–	GP	G	A	Pts	PIM	PP	SH	GW
1977-78	Windsor Spitfires	OHA	3	0	0	0	....	....	....	0	....	....	....	....	....	....	....	....	....	....	....	....	....	....	....	....	....	....
1978-79	University of Michigan	CCHA	23	12	22	34	....	....	....	14	....	....	....	....	....	....	....	....	....	....	....	....	....	....	....	....	....	....
1979-80	University of Michigan	CCHA	33	36	49	85	....	....	....	34	....	....	....	....	....	....	....	....	....	....	....	....	....	....	....	....	....	....
1980-81	**Winnipeg Jets**	**NHL**	**12**	**1**	**2**	**3**	**1**	**1**	**2**	**5**	**1**	**0**	**0**	**12**	**8.3**	**7**	**2**	**14**	**2**	**–7**	....	....	....	....	....	....	....	....
	Tulsa Oilers	CHL	59	24	34	58	....	....	....	59	....	....	....	....	....	....	....	....	....	....	8	5	5	10	13	....	....	....
1981-82	**Winnipeg Jets**	**NHL**	**2**	**0**	**0**	**0**	**0**	**0**	**0**	**0**	**0**	**0**	**0**	**0**	**0.0**	**0**	**0**	**0**	**0**	**0**	....	....	....	....	....	....	....	....
	Tulsa Oilers	CHL	68	30	49	79	....	....	....	33	....	....	....	....	....	....	....	....	....	....	3	0	2	2	0	....	....	....
1982-83	**Winnipeg Jets**	**NHL**	**26**	**2**	**7**	**9**	**2**	**5**	**7**	**2**	**0**	**0**	**0**	**17**	**11.8**	**9**	**0**	**15**	**1**	**–5**	....	....	....	....	....	....	....	....
	Sherbrooke Jets	AHL	40	25	34	59	....	....	....	16	....	....	....	....	....	....	....	....	....	....	....	....	....	....	....	....	....	....
1983-84	**Winnipeg Jets**	**NHL**	**2**	**0**	**0**	**0**	**0**	**0**	**0**	**0**	**0**	**0**	**0**	**1**	**0.0**	**0**	**0**	**1**	**1**	**0**	**2**	**0**	**0**	**0**	**2**	**0**	**0**	**0**
	Sherbrooke Jets	AHL	78	47	68	115	....	....	....	40	....	....	....	....	....	....	....	....	....	....	....	....	....	....	....	....	....	....
1984-85	**Winnipeg Jets**	**NHL**	**3**	**0**	**3**	**3**	**0**	**2**	**2**	**0**	**0**	**0**	**0**	**2**	**0.0**	**3**	**0**	**0**	**0**	**+3**	**2**	**0**	**1**	**1**	**0**	**0**	**0**	**0**
	Sherbrooke Canadiens	AHL	47	26	42	68	....	....	....	28	....	....	....	....	....	....	....	....	....	....	15	5	13	18	35	....	....	....
1985-86	**Winnipeg Jets**	**NHL**	**4**	**1**	**0**	**1**	**1**	**0**	**1**	**0**	**0**	**0**	**0**	**6**	**16.7**	**1**	**0**	**3**	**0**	**–2**	....	....	....	....	....	....	....	....
	Sherbrooke Canadiens	AHL	68	22	51	73	....	....	....	26	....	....	....	....	....	....	....	....	....	....	....	....	....	....	....	....	....	....
1986-87	Nova Scotia Oilers	AHL	76	26	38	64	....	....	....	46	....	....	....	....	....	....	....	....	....	....	4	1	1	2	2	....	....	....
1987-88	**Detroit Red Wings**	**NHL**	**7**	**0**	**1**	**1**	**0**	**1**	**1**	**2**	**0**	**0**	**0**	**4**	**0.0**	**1**	**0**	**2**	**0**	**–1**	....	....	....	....	....	....	....	....
	Adirondack Red Wings	AHL	65	39	54	93	....	....	....	65	....	....	....	....	....	....	....	....	....	....	11	3	*11	14	8	....	....	....
1988-89	Adirondack Red Wings	AHL	80	46	72	118	....	....	....	11	....	....	....	....	....	....	....	....	....	....	16	*13	12	25	10	....	....	....
1989-90	**Detroit Red Wings**	**NHL**	**1**	**0**	**0**	**0**	**0**	**0**	**0**	**0**	**0**	**0**	**0**	**2**	**0.0**	**0**	**0**	**2**	**0**	**–2**	....	....	....	....	....	....	....	....
	Adirondack Red Wings	AHL	78	40	40	80	....	....	....	35	....	....	....	....	....	....	....	....	....	....	6	2	3	5	2	....	....	....
1990-91	Varese HC	Italy	32	22	37	59	....	....	....	23	....	....	....	....	....	....	....	....	....	....	10	9	9	18	4	....	....	....
1991-92	Varese HC	Italy	26	17	43	60	....	....	....	45	....	....	....	....	....	....	....	....	....	....	....	....	....	....	....	....	....	....
1992-93	EHC Kloten	Switz.	4	2	3	5	....	....	....	2	....	....	....	....	....	....	....	....	....	....	....	....	....	....	....	....	....	....
1992-93	Varese HC	Italy	27	27	*39	*56	....	....	....	8	....	....	....	....	....	....	....	....	....	....	....	....	....	....	....	....	....	....
1993-94	HC Milano	Italy	27	17	39	56	....	....	....	8	....	....	....	....	....	....	....	....	....	....	....	....	....	....	....	....	....	....
1994-95	Houston Aeros	IHL	31	3	9	12	....	....	....	18	....	....	....	....	....	....	....	....	....	....	....	....	....	....	....	....	....	....
	NHL Totals		**57**	**4**	**13**	**17**	**4**	**9**	**13**	**9**	**1**	**0**	**0**	**44**	**9.1**	**21**	**2**	**37**	**4**		**4**	**0**	**1**	**1**	**2**	**0**	**0**	**0**

WCHA Second All-Star Team (1980) • NCAA West First All-American Team (1980) • AHL First All-Star Team (1984) • AHL Second All-Star Team (1989) • Won Fred T. Hunt Memorial Trophy (Sportsmanship - AHL) (1989, 1990)

Traded to **Edmonton** by **Winnipeg** for future considerations, July 3, 1986. Signed as a free agent by **Detroit**, July 1, 1987.

• ECCLESTONE, TIM

Tim Ecclestone LW – R. 5'10", 195 lbs. b: Toronto, Ont., 9/24/1947. NY Rangers' 2nd choice, 9th overall, in 1964 Amateur Draft.

Season	Club	League	GP	G	A	Pts	AG	AA	APts	PIM	PP	SH	GW	S	%	TGF	PGF	TGA	PGA	+/–	GP	G	A	Pts	PIM	PP	SH	GW
1965-66	Etobicoke Indians	Jr. B	STATISTICS NOT AVAILABLE																									
1966-67	Kitchener Rangers	OHA	48	27	37	64	....	....	....	35	....	....	....	....	....	....	....	....	....	....	13	3	12	15	14	....	....	....
1967-68	**St. Louis Blues**	**NHL**	**50**	**6**	**8**	**14**	**7**	**8**	**15**	**16**	**3**	**0**	**0**	**97**	**6.2**	**22**	**4**	**18**	**1**	**+1**	**12**	**1**	**2**	**3**	**2**	**0**	**0**	**0**
	Kansas City Blues	CHL	13	4	4	8	....	....	....	9	....	....	....	....	....	....	....	....	....	....	....	....	....	....	....	....	....	....
1968-69	**St. Louis Blues**	**NHL**	**68**	**11**	**23**	**34**	**12**	**22**	**34**	**31**	**1**	**0**	**4**	**151**	**7.3**	**52**	**8**	**25**	**1**	**+20**	**12**	**2**	**2**	**4**	**20**	**0**	**0**	**0**
1969-70	**St. Louis Blues**	**NHL**	**65**	**16**	**21**	**37**	**18**	**21**	**39**	**59**	**5**	**0**	**2**	**166**	**9.6**	**56**	**17**	**36**	**4**	**+7**	**16**	**3**	**4**	**7**	**48**	**1**	**0**	**1**
1970-71	**St. Louis Blues**	**NHL**	**47**	**15**	**24**	**39**	**16**	**21**	**37**	**34**	**6**	**0**	**4**	**143**	**10.5**	**48**	**22**	**41**	**8**	**–7**	....	....	....	....	....	....	....	....
	Detroit Red Wings	**NHL**	**27**	**4**	**10**	**14**	**4**	**9**	**13**	**13**	**1**	**0**	**0**	**62**	**6.5**	**25**	**8**	**34**	**2**	**–15**	....	....	....	....	....	....	....	....
1971-72	**Detroit Red Wings**	**NHL**	**72**	**18**	**35**	**53**	**19**	**32**	**51**	**33**	**10**	**0**	**1**	**189**	**9.5**	**80**	**30**	**73**	**2**	**–21**	....	....	....	....	....	....	....	....
1972-73	**Detroit Red Wings**	**NHL**	**78**	**18**	**30**	**48**	**18**	**25**	**43**	**28**	**3**	**1**	**2**	**175**	**10.3**	**73**	**17**	**57**	**7**	**+6**	....	....	....	....	....	....	....	....

Season	Club	League	GP	G	A	Pts	AG	AA	APts	PIM	PP	SH	GW	S	%	TGF	PGF	TGA	PGA	+/–	GP	G	A	Pts	PIM	PP	SH	GW
			REGULAR SEASON																		PLAYOFFS							
1973-74	**Detroit Red Wings**	**NHL**	**14**	**0**	**5**	**5**	**0**	**4**	**4**	**6**	**0**	**0**	**0**	**22**	**0.0**	**7**	**3**	**12**	**2**	**–6**	....	....	....	....	....	....	....	....
	Toronto Maple Leafs	**NHL**	**46**	**9**	**14**	**23**	**9**	**12**	**21**	**32**	**1**	**2**	**1**	**79**	**11.4**	**33**	**3**	**30**	**8**	**+8**	**4**	**0**	**1**	**1**	**0**	**0**	**0**	**0**
1974-75	**Toronto Maple Leafs**	**NHL**	**5**	**1**	**1**	**2**	**1**	**1**	**2**	**0**	**0**	**0**	**0**	**3**	**33.3**	**3**	**0**	**3**	**1**	**+1**	....	....	....	....	....	....	....	....
	Atlanta Flames	**NHL**	**62**	**13**	**21**	**34**	**12**	**17**	**29**	**34**	**0**	**1**	**4**	**103**	**12.6**	**47**	**5**	**51**	**16**	**+7**	....	....	....	....	....	....	....	....
1975-76	**Atlanta Flames**	**NHL**	**69**	**6**	**21**	**27**	**6**	**16**	**22**	**30**	**1**	**1**	**0**	**117**	**5.1**	**53**	**7**	**57**	**18**	**+7**	....	....	....	....	....	....	....	....
1976-77	**Atlanta Flames**	**NHL**	**78**	**9**	**18**	**27**	**9**	**15**	**24**	**26**	**0**	**1**	**0**	**116**	**7.8**	**44**	**1**	**65**	**32**	**+10**	**3**	**0**	**2**	**2**	**6**	**0**	**0**	**0**
1977-78	**Atlanta Flames**	**NHL**	**11**	**0**	**2**	**2**	**0**	**2**	**2**	**2**	**0**	**0**	**0**	**11**	**0.0**	**4**	**0**	**4**	**1**	**+1**	**1**	**0**	**0**	**0**	**0**	**0**	**0**	**0**
	Tulsa Oilers	CHL	6	1	3	4	....	....	....	0	....	....	....	....	....	....	....	....	....	....	....	....	....	....	....	....	....	....
	NHL Totals		**692**	**126**	**233**	**359**	**131**	**205**	**336**	**344**	**31**	**6**	**18**	**1434**	**8.8**	**547**	**125**	**506**	**103**		**48**	**6**	**11**	**17**	**76**	**1**	**0**	**1**

Played in NHL All-Star Game (1971)

Traded to **St. Louis** by **NY Rangers** with Gary Sabourin, Bob Plager and Gord Kannegiesser for Rod Seiling, June 6, 1967. Traded to **Detroit** by **St. Louis** with Red Berenson for Garry Unger and Wayne Connelly, February 6, 1971. Traded to **Toronto** by **Detroit** for Pierre Jarry, November 29, 1973. Traded to **Washington** by **Toronto** with Willie Brossart for Rod Seiling, November 2, 1974. Traded to **Atlanta** by **Washington** for cash, November 2, 1974.

• EDBERG, ROLF

Rolf Edberg C – L. 5'10", 174 lbs. b: Stockholm, Sweden, 9/29/1950.

Season	Club	League	GP	G	A	Pts	AG	AA	APts	PIM	PP	SH	GW	S	%	TGF	PGF	TGA	PGA	+/–	GP	G	A	Pts	PIM	PP	SH	GW
1970-71	AIK Solna	Sweden	14	9	9	18	....	....	....	10	....	....	....	....	....	....	....	....	....	....	14	8	4	12	14	....	....	....
1971-72	AIK Solna	Sweden	14	6	9	15	....	....	....	8	....	....	....	....	....	....	....	....	....	....	14	3	4	7	14	....	....	....
1972-73	AIK Solna	Sweden	12	5	2	7	....	....	....	8	....	....	....	....	....	....	....	....	....	....	13	5	3	8	10	....	....	....
1973-74	AIK Solna	Sweden	STATISTICS NOT AVAILABLE																									
1974-75	AIK Solna	Sweden	30	17	15	32	....	....	....	18	....	....	....	....	....	....	....	....	....	....	....	....	....	....	....	....	....	....
1975-76	AIK Solna	Sweden	36	14	13	27	....	....	....	31	....	....	....	....	....	....	....	....	....	....	....	....	....	....	....	....	....	....
1976-77	AIK Solna	Sweden	35	11	14	25	....	....	....	30	....	....	....	....	....	....	....	....	....	....	....	....	....	....	....	....	....	....
	Sweden	WEC-A	10	5	1	6	....	....	....	2	....	....	....	....	....	....	....	....	....	....	....	....	....	....	....	....	....	....
1977-78	AIK Solna	Sweden	23	5	9	14	....	....	....	14	....	....	....	....	....	....	....	....	....	....	5	2	3	5	4	....	....	....
	Sweden	WEC-A	10	7	5	12	....	....	....	4	....	....	....	....	....	....	....	....	....	....	....	....	....	....	....	....	....	....
1978-79	**Washington Capitals**	**NHL**	**76**	**14**	**27**	**41**	**13**	**21**	**34**	**6**	**1**	**0**	**2**	**133**	**10.5**	**59**	**4**	**46**	**2**	**+11**	....	....	....	....	....	....	....	....
	Sweden	WEC-A	6	4	3	7	....	....	....	2	....	....	....	....	....	....	....	....	....	....	....	....	....	....	....	....	....	....
1979-80	**Washington Capitals**	**NHL**	**63**	**23**	**23**	**46**	**21**	**18**	**39**	**12**	**4**	**1**	**7**	**136**	**16.9**	**62**	**15**	**60**	**8**	**–5**	....	....	....	....	....	....	....	....
1980-81	**Washington Capitals**	**NHL**	**45**	**8**	**8**	**16**	**7**	**6**	**13**	**6**	**0**	**0**	**0**	**48**	**16.7**	**19**	**1**	**30**	**13**	**+1**	....	....	....	....	....	....	....	....
1981-82	AIK Solna	Sweden	29	16	11	27	....	....	....	34	....	....	....	....	....	....	....	....	....	....	7	2	0	2	2	....	....	....
1982-83	AIK Solna	Sweden	29	9	15	24	....	....	....	6	....	....	....	....	....	....	....	....	....	....	3	1	1	2	2	....	....	....
1983-84	Hammersby	Sweden 2	STATISTICS NOT AVAILABLE																									
1984-85	Hammersby	Sweden	20	8	4	12	....	....	....	14	....	....	....	....	....	....	....	....	....	....	....	....	....	....	....	....	....	....
	NHL Totals		**184**	**45**	**58**	**103**	**41**	**45**	**86**	**24**	**5**	**1**	**9**	**317**	**14.2**	**140**	**20**	**136**	**23**		....	....	....	....	....	....	....	....

Swedish Player of the Year (1978)

Signed as a free agent by **Washington**, June 10, 1978.

• EDESTRAND, DARRYL

Darryl Edestrand D – L. 5'11", 180 lbs. b: Strathroy, Ont., 11/6/1945.

Season	Club	League	GP	G	A	Pts	AG	AA	APts	PIM	PP	SH	GW	S	%	TGF	PGF	TGA	PGA	+/–	GP	G	A	Pts	PIM	PP	SH	GW
1962-63	Toronto Marlboros	City Jr.	2	0	1	1	....	....	....	2	....	....	....	....	....	....	....	....	....	....	1	0	0	0	0	....	....	....
1963-64	London Nationals	Jr. B	STATISTICS NOT AVAILABLE																									
1964-65	Toronto Marlboros	OHA	5	0	0	0	....	....	....	5	....	....	....	....	....	....	....	....	....	....	....	....	....	....	....	....	....	....
1965-66	London Nationals	OHA	45	4	20	24	....	....	....	132	....	....	....	....	....	....	....	....	....	....	....	....	....	....	....	....	....	....
	Rochester Americans	AHL	17	1	2	3	....	....	....	10	....	....	....	....	....	....	....	....	....	....	4	1	0	1	2	....	....	....
1966-67	Rochester Americans	AHL	7	0	1	1	....	....	....	4	....	....	....	....	....	....	....	....	....	....	....	....	....	....	....	....	....	....
1967-68	**St. Louis Blues**	**NHL**	**12**	**0**	**0**	**0**	**0**	**0**	**0**	**2**	**0**	**0**	**0**	**12**	**0.0**	**5**	**1**	**7**	**1**	**–2**	....	....	....	....	....	....	....	....
	Kansas City Blues	CHL	53	2	32	34	....	....	....	84	....	....	....	....	....	....	....	....	....	....	7	0	3	3	4	....	....	....
1968-69	Quebec Aces	AHL	74	7	23	30	....	....	....	108	....	....	....	....	....	....	....	....	....	....	15	1	5	6	23	....	....	....
1969-70	**Philadelphia Flyers**	**NHL**	**2**	**0**	**0**	**0**	**0**	**0**	**0**	**6**	**0**	**0**	**0**	**3**	**0.0**	**1**	**0**	**2**	**0**	**–1**	....	....	....	....	....	....	....	....
	Quebec Aces	AHL	71	10	30	40	....	....	....	106	....	....	....	....	....	....	....	....	....	....	6	0	1	1	8	....	....	....
1970-71	Hershey Bears	AHL	72	6	30	36	....	....	....	109	....	....	....	....	....	....	....	....	....	....	4	0	0	0	2	....	....	....
1971-72	**Pittsburgh Penguins**	**NHL**	**77**	**10**	**23**	**33**	**11**	**21**	**32**	**52**	**2**	**1**	**3**	**156**	**6.4**	**75**	**18**	**84**	**15**	**–12**	**4**	**0**	**2**	**2**	**0**	**0**	**0**	**0**
1972-73	**Pittsburgh Penguins**	**NHL**	**78**	**15**	**24**	**39**	**15**	**20**	**35**	**88**	**4**	**1**	**2**	**155**	**9.7**	**112**	**16**	**110**	**17**	**+3**	....	....	....	....	....	....	....	....
1973-74	**Pittsburgh Penguins**	**NHL**	**3**	**0**	**0**	**0**	**0**	**0**	**0**	**0**	**0**	**0**	**0**	**0**	**0.0**	**3**	**3**	**2**	**0**	**–2**	....	....	....	....	....	....	....	....
	Boston Bruins	**NHL**	**52**	**3**	**8**	**11**	**3**	**7**	**10**	**20**	**1**	**0**	**2**	**66**	**4.5**	**53**	**2**	**37**	**5**	**+19**	**16**	**1**	**2**	**3**	**15**	**0**	**0**	**0**
1974-75	**Boston Bruins**	**NHL**	**68**	**1**	**9**	**10**	**1**	**7**	**8**	**56**	**0**	**0**	**0**	**86**	**1.2**	**41**	**2**	**34**	**3**	**+8**	**3**	**0**	**1**	**1**	**7**	**0**	**0**	**0**
1975-76	**Boston Bruins**	**NHL**	**77**	**4**	**17**	**21**	**4**	**13**	**17**	**103**	**1**	**0**	**1**	**131**	**3.1**	**85**	**9**	**79**	**10**	**+7**	**12**	**1**	**3**	**4**	**23**	**0**	**0**	**0**
1976-77	**Boston Bruins**	**NHL**	**17**	**0**	**3**	**3**	**0**	**2**	**2**	**16**	**0**	**0**	**0**	**28**	**0.0**	**19**	**1**	**16**	**2**	**+4**	**3**	**0**	**0**	**0**	**2**	**0**	**0**	**0**
	Rochester Americans	AHL	42	4	13	17	....	....	....	62	....	....	....	....	....	....	....	....	....	....	12	1	3	4	8	....	....	....
1977-78	**Boston Bruins**	**NHL**	**1**	**0**	**0**	**0**	**0**	**0**	**0**	**0**	**0**	**0**	**0**	**0**	**0.0**	**0**	**0**	**1**	**0**	**–1**	....	....	....	....	....	....	....	....
	Rochester Americans	AHL	64	6	27	33	....	....	....	28	....	....	....	....	....	....	....	....	....	....	....	....	....	....	....	....	....	....
	Los Angeles Kings	**NHL**	**13**	**0**	**2**	**2**	**0**	**2**	**2**	**15**	**0**	**0**	**0**	**29**	**0.0**	**11**	**1**	**21**	**3**	**–8**	**2**	**1**	**1**	**2**	**4**	**0**	**0**	**0**
1978-79	**Los Angeles Kings**	**NHL**	**55**	**1**	**4**	**5**	**1**	**3**	**4**	**46**	**0**	**0**	**0**	**62**	**1.6**	**45**	**0**	**61**	**8**	**–8**	**2**	**0**	**0**	**0**	**6**	**0**	**0**	**0**
1979-80	Binghamton Whalers	AHL	57	3	17	20	....	....	....	34	....	....	....	....	....	....	....	....	....	....	....	....	....	....	....	....	....	....
	NHL Totals		**455**	**34**	**90**	**124**	**35**	**75**	**110**	**404**	**8**	**2**	**8**	**728**	**4.7**	**450**	**53**	**454**	**64**		**42**	**3**	**9**	**12**	**57**	**0**	**0**	**0**

Claimed by **St. Louis** from **Toronto** in Expansion Draft, June 6, 1967. Traded to **Philadelphia** by **St. Louis** with Gerry Melynk for Lou Angotti and Ian Campbell, June 11, 1968. Traded to **Hershey** (AHL) by **Philadelphia** for cash, June 15, 1970. Traded to **Boston** by **Pittsburgh** for Nick Beverly, October 25, 1973. Traded to **LA Kings** by **Boston** for cash, March 13, 1978. Claimed by **LA Kings** as a fill-in during Expansion Draft, June 13, 1979.

• EDUR, TOM

Tom Edur D – R. 6'1", 185 lbs. b: Toronto, Ont., 11/18/1954. Boston's 4th choice, 54th overall, in 1974 Amateur Draft.

Season	Club	League	GP	G	A	Pts	AG	AA	APts	PIM	PP	SH	GW	S	%	TGF	PGF	TGA	PGA	+/–	GP	G	A	Pts	PIM	PP	SH	GW
1971-72	Markham Waxers	Jr. B	STATISTICS NOT AVAILABLE																									
1972-73	Toronto Marlboros	OHA	57	14	48	62	....	....	....	32	....	....	....	....	....	....	....	....	....	....	10	1	14	15	10	....	....	....
1973-74	Cleveland Crusaders	WHA	76	7	31	38	....	....	....	5	....	....	....	....	....	....	....	....	....	....	5	1	2	3	0	....	....	....
1974-75	Cleveland Crusaders	WHA	61	3	20	23	....	....	....	28	....	....	....	....	....	....	....	....	....	....	5	2	0	2	0	....	....	....
1975-76	Cleveland Crusaders	WHA	80	7	28	35	....	....	....	65	....	....	....	....	....	....	....	....	....	....	3	0	3	3	0	....	....	....
1976-77	**Colorado Rockies**	**NHL**	**80**	**7**	**25**	**32**	**7**	**20**	**27**	**39**	**3**	**0**	**1**	**150**	**4.7**	**113**	**18**	**108**	**27**	**+14**	....	....	....	....	....	....	....	....
1977-78	**Colorado Rockies**	**NHL**	**20**	**5**	**7**	**12**	**5**	**6**	**11**	**10**	**1**	**0**	**0**	**38**	**13.2**	**37**	**7**	**27**	**7**	**+10**	....	....	....	....	....	....	....	....
	Pittsburgh Penguins	**NHL**	**58**	**5**	**38**	**43**	**5**	**31**	**36**	**18**	**2**	**0**	**1**	**135**	**3.7**	**104**	**29**	**106**	**22**	**–9**	....	....	....	....	....	....	....	....
	NHL Totals		**158**	**17**	**70**	**87**	**17**	**57**	**74**	**67**	**6**	**0**	**2**	**323**	**5.3**	**254**	**54**	**241**	**56**		....	....	....	....	....	....	....	....
	Other Major League Totals		217	17	79	96	....	....	....	98	....	....	....	....	....	....	....	....	....	....	13	3	5	8	0	....	....	....

Signed as an underage free agent by **Cleveland** (WHA), August, 1973. Rights traded to **Colorado** by **Boston** for cash, September 7, 1977. Traded to **Pittsburgh** by **Colorado** for Dennis Owchar, December 2, 1977.

• EGELAND, ALLAN

Allan Egeland C – L. 6', 175 lbs. b: Lethbridge, Alta., 1/31/1973. Tampa Bay's 3rd choice, 55th overall, in 1993 Entry Draft.

Season	Club	League	GP	G	A	Pts	AG	AA	APts	PIM	PP	SH	GW	S	%	TGF	PGF	TGA	PGA	+/–	GP	G	A	Pts	PIM	PP	SH	GW
1990-91	Lethbridge Hurricanes	WHL	67	2	16	18	....	....	....	57	....	....	....	....	....	....	....	....	....	....	9	0	0	0	0	....	....	....
1991-92	Tacoma Rockets	WHL	72	35	39	74	....	....	....	135	....	....	....	....	....	....	....	....	....	....	4	0	1	1	18	....	....	....
1992-93	Tacoma Rockets	WHL	71	56	57	113	....	....	....	119	....	....	....	....	....	....	....	....	....	....	7	9	7	16	18	....	....	....
1993-94	Tacoma Rockets	WHL	70	47	76	123	....	....	....	204	....	....	....	....	....	....	....	....	....	....	8	5	3	8	26	....	....	....
1994-95	Atlanta Knights	IHL	60	8	16	24	....	....	....	112	....	....	....	....	....	....	....	....	....	....	5	0	1	1	16	....	....	....
1995-96	**Tampa Bay Lightning**	**NHL**	**5**	**0**	**0**	**0**	**0**	**0**	**0**	**2**	**0**	**0**	**0**	**1**	**0.0**	**0**	**0**	**0**	**0**	**0**	....	....	....	....	....	....	....	....
	Atlanta Knights	IHL	68	22	22	44	....	....	....	182	....	....	....	....	....	....	....	....	....	....	3	0	1	1	0	....	....	....
1996-97	**Tampa Bay Lightning**	**NHL**	**4**	**0**	**0**	**0**	**0**	**0**	**0**	**5**	**0**	**0**	**0**	**1**	**0.0**	**0**	**0**	**3**	**0**	**–3**	....	....	....	....	....	....	....	....
	Adirondack Red Wings	AHL	52	18	32	50	....	....	....	184	....	....	....	....	....	....	....	....	....	....	2	0	1	1	4	....	....	....
1997-98	**Tampa Bay Lightning**	**NHL**	**8**	**0**	**0**	**0**	**0**	**0**	**0**	**9**	**0**	**0**	**0**	**4**	**0.0**	**0**	**0**	**1**	**1**	**0**	....	....	....	....	....	....	....	....
	Adirondack Red Wings	AHL	35	11	22	33	....	....	....	78	....	....	....	....	....	....	....	....	....	....	3	0	2	2	10	....	....	....
	NHL Totals		**17**	**0**	**0**	**0**	**0**	**0**	**0**	**16**	**0**	**0**	**0**	**6**	**0.0**	**0**	**0**	**4**	**1**		....	....	....	....	....	....	....	....

WHL West First All-Star Team (1993) • WHL West Second All-Star Team (1994)

• EGERS, JACK

Jack Egers RW – L. 6'1", 175 lbs. b: Sudbury, Ont., 1/28/1949. NY Rangers' 4th choice, 20th overall, in 1966 Amateur Draft.

			REGULAR SEASON																		PLAYOFFS							
Season	Club	League	GP	G	A	Pts	AG	AA	APts	PIM	PP	SH	GW	S	%	TGF	PGF	TGA	PGA	+/–	GP	G	A	Pts	PIM	PP	SH	GW
1965-66	Kitchener Rangers	OHA	5	1	1	2	....	....	....	2	....	....	....	....	....	....	....	....	....	....	....	....	....	....	....	....	....	....
1966-67	Kitchener Rangers	OHA	40	18	9	27	....	....	....	48	....	....	....	....	....	....	....	....	....	....	9	0	0	0	6	....	....	....
1967-68	Kitchener Rangers	OHA	54	*53	37	90	....	....	....	78	....	....	....	....	....	....	....	....	....	....	13	5	6	11	21	....	....	....
1968-69	Omaha Knights	CHL	59	28	30	58	....	....	....	47	....	....	....	....	....	....	....	....	....	....	7	3	4	7	7	....	....	....
1969-70	**New York Rangers**	**NHL**	**6**	**3**	**0**	**3**	**3**	**0**	**3**	**2**	**2**	**0**	**0**	**18**	**16.7**	**8**	**4**	**4**	**0**	**0**	**5**	**3**	**1**	**4**	**10**	**1**	**0**	**0**
	Omaha Knights	CHL	70	42	48	90	....	....	....	83	....	....	....	....	....	....	....	....	....	....	3	3	3	6	2	....	....	....
1970-71	**New York Rangers**	**NHL**	**60**	**7**	**10**	**17**	**7**	**9**	**16**	**50**	**3**	**0**	**3**	**88**	**0.0**	**32**	**9**	**16**	**1**	**+8**	**3**	**0**	**0**	**0**	**2**	**0**	**0**	**0**
1971-72	**New York Rangers**	**NHL**	**17**	**2**	**1**	**3**	**2**	**1**	**3**	**14**	**1**	**0**	**0**	**13**	**15.4**	**5**	**2**	**1**	**0**	**+2**	....	....	....	....	....	....	....	....
	St. Louis Blues	**NHL**	**63**	**21**	**25**	**46**	**22**	**23**	**45**	**34**	**5**	**0**	**2**	**210**	**10.0**	**70**	**21**	**45**	**1**	**+5**	**11**	**1**	**4**	**5**	**14**	**0**	**0**	**0**
1972-73	**St. Louis Blues**	**NHL**	**78**	**24**	**24**	**48**	**24**	**20**	**44**	**26**	**4**	**0**	**4**	**240**	**10.0**	**84**	**22**	**61**	**0**	**+1**	**5**	**0**	**1**	**1**	**2**	**0**	**0**	**0**
1973-74	**St. Louis Blues**	**NHL**	**6**	**0**	**1**	**1**	**0**	**1**	**1**	**6**	**0**	**0**	**0**	**15**	**0.0**	**4**	**1**	**2**	**0**	**+1**	....	....	....	....	....	....	....	....
	New York Rangers	**NHL**	**28**	**1**	**3**	**4**	**1**	**3**	**4**	**6**	**0**	**0**	**0**	**9**	**11.1**	**10**	**1**	**8**	**0**	**+1**	**8**	**1**	**0**	**1**	**4**	**0**	**0**	**0**
1974-75	**Washington Capitals**	**NHL**	**14**	**3**	**2**	**5**	**3**	**2**	**5**	**8**	**1**	**0**	**1**	**21**	**14.3**	**7**	**4**	**17**	**0**	**–14**	....	....	....	....	....	....	....	....
1975-76	**Washington Capitals**	**NHL**	**12**	**3**	**3**	**6**	**3**	**2**	**5**	**8**	**2**	**0**	**0**	**18**	**16.7**	**9**	**7**	**4**	**0**	**–2**	....	....	....	....	....	....	....	....
	Baltimore Clippers	AHL	15	4	4	8	....	....	....	19	....	....	....	....	....	....	....	....	....	....	....	....	....	....	....	....	....	....
1976-77	Brantford Alexanders	OHA Sr.	30	20	19	39	....	....	....	55	....	....	....	....	....	....	....	....	....	....	....	....	....	....	....	....	....	....
	NHL Totals		**284**	**64**	**69**	**133**	**65**	**61**	**126**	**154**	**18**	**0**	**10**	**632**	**10.1**	**229**	**71**	**158**	**2**		**32**	**5**	**6**	**11**	**32**	**1**	**0**	**0**

OHA First All-Star Team (1968) • CHL First All-Star Team (1970)

Traded to **St. Louis** by **NY Rangers** with Andre Dupont and Mike Murphy for Gene Carr, Jim Lorentz and Wayne Connelly, November 15, 1971. Traded to **NY Rangers** by **St. Louis** for Glen Sather and Rene Villemore, October 28, 1972. Claimed by **Washington** from **NY Rangers** in Expansion Draft, June 12, 1974.

• EHMAN, GERRY

Gerry Ehman RW – R. 6', 190 lbs. b: Cudworth, Sask., 11/3/1932.

			REGULAR SEASON																		PLAYOFFS							
Season	Club	League	GP	G	A	Pts	AG	AA	APts	PIM	PP	SH	GW	S	%	TGF	PGF	TGA	PGA	+/–	GP	G	A	Pts	PIM	PP	SH	GW
1951-52	Flin Flon Bombers	SJHL	50	40	*42	82	....	....	....	18	....	....	....	....	....	....	....	....	....	....	10	4	11	15	0	....	....	....
1952-53	Edmonton Flyers	WHL	22	3	3	6	....	....	....	0	....	....	....	....	....	....	....	....	....	....	....	....	....	....	....	....	....	....
	St. Louis Flyers	AHL	39	3	1	4	....	....	....	8	....	....	....	....	....	....	....	....	....	....	....	....	....	....	....	....	....	....
1953-54	Sherbrooke Saints	QHL	65	13	21	34	....	....	....	29	....	....	....	....	....	....	....	....	....	....	5	0	2	2	0	....	....	....
1954-55	Quebec Aces	QHL	59	14	25	39	....	....	....	58	....	....	....	....	....	....	....	....	....	....	8	2	3	5	12	....	....	....
1955-56	Vancouver Canucks	WHL	15	5	7	12	....	....	....	6	....	....	....	....	....	....	....	....	....	....	15	9	2	11	14	....	....	....
1956-57	Springfield Indians	AHL	64	23	35	58	....	....	....	18	....	....	....	....	....	....	....	....	....	....	....	....	....	....	....	....	....	....
1957-58	**Boston Bruins**	**NHL**	**1**	**1**	**0**	**1**	**1**	**0**	**1**	**0**	....	....	....	....	....	....	....	....	....	....	....	....	....	....	....	....	....	....
	Springfield Indians	AHL	68	40	39	79	....	....	....	32	....	....	....	....	....	....	....	....	....	....	13	10	6	16	8	....	....	....
1958-59	**Detroit Red Wings**	**NHL**	**6**	**0**	**1**	**1**	**0**	**1**	**1**	**4**	....	....	....	....	....	....	....	....	....	....	....	....	....	....	....	....	....	....
	Hershey Bears	AHL	23	8	7	15	....	....	....	4	....	....	....	....	....	....	....	....	....	....	....	....	....	....	....	....	....	....
	Toronto Maple Leafs	**NHL**	**38**	**12**	**13**	**25**	**15**	**14**	**29**	**12**	....	....	....	....	....	....	....	....	....	....	**12**	**6**	**7**	**13**	**8**	....	....	....
1959-60	**Toronto Maple Leafs**	**NHL**	**69**	**12**	**16**	**28**	**15**	**16**	**31**	**26**	....	....	....	....	....	....	....	....	....	....	**9**	**0**	**0**	**0**	**0**	....	....	....
1960-61	**Toronto Maple Leafs**	**NHL**	**14**	**1**	**1**	**2**	**1**	**1**	**2**	**2**	....	....	....	....	....	....	....	....	....	....	....	....	....	....	....	....	....	....
	Rochester Americans	AHL	53	32	23	55	....	....	....	14	....	....	....	....	....	....	....	....	....	....	....	....	....	....	....	....	....	....
1961-62	Rochester Americans	AHL	66	29	37	66	....	....	....	26	....	....	....	....	....	....	....	....	....	....	2	1	1	2	0	....	....	....
1962-63	Rochester Americans	AHL	72	30	40	70	....	....	....	32	....	....	....	....	....	....	....	....	....	....	1	0	0	0	0	....	....	....
1963-64	**Toronto Maple Leafs**	**NHL**	**4**	**1**	**1**	**2**	**1**	**1**	**2**	**0**	....	....	....	....	....	....	....	....	....	....	**9**	**1**	**0**	**1**	**4**	....	....	....
	Rochester Americans	AHL	66	36	40	05	....	....	....	26	....	....	....	....	....	....	....	....	....	....	2	0	1	1	0	....	....	....
1964-65	Rochester Americans	AHL	70	38	49	87	....	....	....	20	....	....	....	....	....	....	....	....	....	....	10	2	5	7	10	....	....	....
1965-66	Rochester Americans	AHL	70	39	49	88	....	....	....	28	....	....	....	....	....	....	....	....	....	....	12	5	4	9	8	....	....	....
1966-67	Rochester Americans	AHL	68	33	36	69	....	....	....	27	....	....	....	....	....	....	....	....	....	....	13	2	7	9	6	....	....	....
1967-68	**Oakland Seals**	**NHL**	**73**	**19**	**25**	**44**	**23**	**26**	**49**	**20**	**6**	**0**	**3**	**189**	**10.1**	**64**	**24**	**49**	**4**	**–5**	....	....	....	....	....	....	....	....
1968-69	**Oakland Seals**	**NHL**	**70**	**21**	**24**	**45**	**24**	**23**	**47**	**12**	**4**	**0**	**3**	**160**	**13.1**	**70**	**18**	**68**	**3**	**–13**	**7**	**2**	**2**	**4**	**0**	**0**	**0**	**0**
1969-70	**Oakland Seals**	**NHL**	**76**	**11**	**19**	**30**	**13**	**19**	**32**	**8**	**3**	**0**	**1**	**156**	**7.1**	**62**	**11**	**73**	**7**	**–25**	**4**	**1**	**1**	**2**	**0**	**1**	**0**	**0**
1970-71	**California Golden Seals**	**NHL**	**78**	**18**	**18**	**36**	**19**	**16**	**35**	**10**	**1**	**0**	**3**	**154**	**11.7**	**54**	**10**	**88**	**4**	**–40**	....	....	....	....	....	....	....	....
	NHL Totals		**429**	**96**	**118**	**214**	**112**	**117**	**220**	**100**	**14**	**0**	**10**	**659**	**14.6**	**240**	**63**	**278**	**18**		**41**	**10**	**10**	**20**	**12**	**1**	**0**	**0**

AHL First All-Star Team (1958, 1964, 1966) • AHL Second All-Star Team (1961) • Won John B. Sollenberger Trophy (Top Scorer - AHL) (1964)

Played in NHL All-Star Game (1964)

Traded to **Boston** (Springfield - AHL) by **Detroit** (Edmonton-WHL) for cash, June, 1955. Traded to **Detroit** by **Springfield** (AHL) for Hank Bassen, Dennis Olson and Bill McCreary, April, 1958. Traded to **Toronto** by **Detroit** for Willie Marshall, December, 1958. Traded to **Oakland** by **Toronto** for Bryan Hextall and J.P. Parise, October 3, 1967.

• EISENHUT, NEIL

Neil Eisenhut C – L. 6'1", 190 lbs. b: Osoyoos, B.C., 2/9/1967. Vancouver's 11th choice, 233rd overall, in 1987 Entry Draft.

			REGULAR SEASON																		PLAYOFFS							
Season	Club	League	GP	G	A	Pts	AG	AA	APts	PIM	PP	SH	GW	S	%	TGF	PGF	TGA	PGA	+/–	GP	G	A	Pts	PIM	PP	SH	GW
1986-87	Langley Eagles	BCJHL	43	41	34	75	....	....	....	28	....	....	....	....	....	....	....	....	....	....	....	....	....	....	....	....	....	....
1987-88	University of North Dakota	WCHA	42	12	20	32	....	....	....	14	....	....	....	....	....	....	....	....	....	....	....	....	....	....	....	....	....	....
1988-89	University of North Dakota	WCHA	41	22	16	38	....	....	....	20	....	....	....	....	....	....	....	....	....	....	....	....	....	....	....	....	....	....
1989-90	University of North Dakota	WCHA	45	22	32	54	....	....	....	46	....	....	....	....	....	....	....	....	....	....	....	....	....	....	....	....	....	....
1990-91	University of North Dakota	WCHA	20	9	15	24	....	....	....	10	....	....	....	....	....	....	....	....	....	....	....	....	....	....	....	....	....	....
1991-92	Milwaukee Admirals	IHL	76	13	23	36	....	....	....	26	....	....	....	....	....	....	....	....	....	....	2	1	2	3	0	....	....	....
1992-93	Hamilton Canucks	AHL	72	22	40	62	....	....	....	41	....	....	....	....	....	....	....	....	....	....	....	....	....	....	....	....	....	....
1993-94	**Vancouver Canucks**	**NHL**	**13**	**1**	**3**	**4**	**1**	**2**	**3**	**21**	**0**	**0**	**0**	**13**	**7.7**	**4**	**0**	**7**	**3**	**0**	....	....	....	....	....	....	....	....
	Hamilton Canucks	AHL	60	17	36	53	....	....	....	30	....	....	....	....	....	....	....	....	....	....	4	1	4	5	0	....	....	....
1994-95	**Calgary Flames**	**NHL**	**3**	**0**	**0**	**0**	**0**	**0**	**0**	**0**	**0**	**0**	**0**	**2**	**0.0**	**0**	**0**	**0**	**0**	**0**	....	....	....	....	....	....	....	....
	Saint John Flames	AHL	75	16	39	55	....	....	....	30	....	....	....	....	....	....	....	....	....	....	5	1	1	2	6	....	....	....
1995-96	Orlando Solar Bears	IHL	59	10	18	28	....	....	....	30	....	....	....	....	....	....	....	....	....	....	....	....	....	....	....	....	....	....
	Binghamton Rangers	AHL	10	3	3	6	....	....	....	2	....	....	....	....	....	....	....	....	....	....	4	3	2	5	0	....	....	....
1996-97	Flint Generals	CoHL	21	10	33	43	....	....	....	20	....	....	....	....	....	....	....	....	....	....	5	1	4	5	8	....	....	....
	Binghamton Rangers	AHL	55	25	26	51	....	....	....	16	....	....	....	....	....	....	....	....	....	....	4	1	2	3	0	....	....	....
1997-98	Krefeld Pinguine	Germany	42	9	13	22	....	....	....	16	....	....	....	....	....	....	....	....	....	....	3	1	2	3	2	....	....	....
	NHL Totals		**16**	**1**	**3**	**4**	**1**	**2**	**3**	**21**	**0**	**0**	**0**	**15**	**6.7**	**4**	**0**	**7**	**3**		....	....	....	....	....	....	....	....

Originally Signed as a free agent by **Calgary**, June 16, 1994.

• EKLUND, PELLE

Pelle Eklund C – L. 5'10", 175 lbs. b: Stockholm, Sweden, 3/22/1963. Philadelphia's 7th choice, 107th overall, in 1983 Entry Draft.

			REGULAR SEASON																		PLAYOFFS							
Season	Club	League	GP	G	A	Pts	AG	AA	APts	PIM	PP	SH	GW	S	%	TGF	PGF	TGA	PGA	+/–	GP	G	A	Pts	PIM	PP	SH	GW
1982-83	AIK Stockholm	Sweden	34	13	17	30	....	....	....	14	....	....	....	....	....	....	....	....	....	....	3	1	4	5	2	....	....	....
	Sweden	WJC-A	7	5	1	6	....	....	....	....	....	....	....	....	....	....	....	....	....	....	....	....	....	....	....	....	....	....
1983-84	AIK Stockholm	Sweden	35	9	18	27	....	....	....	24	....	....	....	....	....	....	....	....	....	....	6	6	7	13	2	....	....	....
	Sweden	Olympics	7	2	6	8	....	....	....	0	....	....	....	....	....	....	....	....	....	....	....	....	....	....	....	....	....	....
1984-85	AIK Stockholm	Sweden	35	16	33	49	....	....	....	10	....	....	....	....	....	....	....	....	....	....	....	....	....	....	....	....	....	....
	Sweden	C Cup	8	1	1	2	....	....	....	0	....	....	....	....	....	....	....	....	....	....	....	....	....	....	....	....	....	....
	Sweden	WEC-A	10	2	4	6	....	....	....	2	....	....	....	....	....	....	....	....	....	....	....	....	....	....	....	....	....	....
1985-86	**Philadelphia Flyers**	**NHL**	**70**	**15**	**51**	**66**	**12**	**34**	**46**	**12**	**8**	**0**	**5**	**141**	**10.6**	**88**	**61**	**33**	**2**	**–4**	**5**	**0**	**2**	**2**	**0**	**0**	**0**	**0**
	Sweden	WEC-A	4	2	1	3	....	....	....	4	....	....	....	....	....	....	....	....	....	....	....	....	....	....	....	....	....	....
1986-87	**Philadelphia Flyers**	**NHL**	**72**	**14**	**41**	**55**	**12**	**30**	**42**	**2**	**5**	**0**	**0**	**127**	**11.0**	**79**	**37**	**47**	**3**	**–2**	**26**	**7**	**20**	**27**	**2**	**2**	**0**	**0**
1987-88	**Philadelphia Flyers**	**NHL**	**71**	**10**	**32**	**42**	**9**	**23**	**32**	**12**	**2**	**0**	**2**	**101**	**9.9**	**71**	**31**	**46**	**0**	**–6**	**7**	**0**	**3**	**3**	**0**	**0**	**0**	**0**
1988-89	**Philadelphia Flyers**	**NHL**	**79**	**18**	**51**	**69**	**15**	**36**	**51**	**23**	**8**	**1**	**2**	**121**	**14.9**	**111**	**60**	**60**	**14**	**+5**	**19**	**3**	**8**	**11**	**2**	**3**	**0**	**1**
1989-90	**Philadelphia Flyers**	**NHL**	**70**	**23**	**39**	**62**	**20**	**28**	**48**	**16**	**5**	**3**	**2**	**126**	**18.3**	**87**	**26**	**65**	**11**	**+7**	....	....	....	....	....	....	....	....
	Sweden	WEC-A	10	1	7	8	....	....	....	4	....	....	....	....	....	....	....	....	....	....	....	....	....	....	....	....	....	....
1990-91	**Philadelphia Flyers**	**NHL**	**73**	**19**	**50**	**69**	**17**	**38**	**55**	**14**	**8**	**0**	**4**	**131**	**14.5**	**98**	**43**	**70**	**13**	**–2**	....	....	....	....	....	....	....	....
	Sweden	WEC-A	10	1	3	4	....	....	....	2	....	....	....	....	....	....	....	....	....	....	....	....	....	....	....	....	....	....
1991-92	**Philadelphia Flyers**	**NHL**	**51**	**7**	**16**	**23**	**6**	**12**	**18**	**4**	**1**	**2**	**1**	**74**	**9.5**	**45**	**18**	**34**	**7**	**0**	....	....	....	....	....	....	....	....
1992-93	**Philadelphia Flyers**	**NHL**	**55**	**11**	**38**	**49**	**9**	**26**	**35**	**16**	**4**	**0**	**0**	**82**	**13.4**	**71**	**21**	**52**	**14**	**+12**	....	....	....	....	....	....	....	....
1993-94	**Philadelphia Flyers**	**NHL**	**48**	**1**	**16**	**17**	**1**	**12**	**13**	**8**	**0**	**0**	**0**	**49**	**2.0**	**31**	**7**	**35**	**10**	**–1**	....	....	....	....	....	....	....	....
	Dallas Stars	**NHL**	**5**	**2**	**1**	**3**	**2**	**1**	**3**	**2**	**0**	**0**	**0**	**4**	**50.0**	**4**	**1**	**4**	**0**	**–1**	**9**	**0**	**3**	**3**	**4**	**0**	**0**	**0**
1994-95	Leksands IF	Sweden	32	13	36	49	....	....	....	12	....	....	....	....	....	....	....	....	....	....	2	0	1	1	4	....	....	....
	Sweden	WC-A	8	1	2	3	....	....	....	0	....	....	....	....	....	....	....	....	....	....	....	....	....	....	....	....	....	....

			REGULAR SEASON																		PLAYOFFS							
Season	Club	League	GP	G	A	Pts	AG	AA	APts	PIM	PP	SH	GW	S	%	TGF	PGF	TGA	PGA	+/–	GP	G	A	Pts	PIM	PP	SH	GW
1995-96	Leksands IF	Sweden	29	3	16	19	....	....	....	6	....	....	....	....	....	....	....	....	....	....	4	1	0	1	2	....	....	....
	Sweden	WC-A	6	0	3	3	....	....	....	4	....	....	....	....	....	....	....	....	....	....	....	....	....	....	....	....	....	....
1996-97	Leksands IF	Sweden	36	6	15	21	....	....	....	10	....	....	....	....	....	....	....	....	....	....	9	2	5	7	4	....	....	....
	NHL Totals		**594**	**120**	**335**	**455**	**103**	**240**	**343**	**109**	**41**	**6**	**16**	**956**	**12.6**	**685**	**305**	**446**	**74**		**66**	**10**	**36**	**46**	**8**	**5**	**0**	**1**

Traded to **Dallas** by **Philadelphia** for Dallas' 8th round choice (Raymond Giroux) in 1984 Entry Draft, March 21, 1994.

• ELDEBRINK, ANDERS

Anders Eldebrink D – R. 5'11", 190 lbs. b: Kalix, Sweden, 12/11/1960.

Season	Club	League	GP	G	A	Pts	AG	AA	APts	PIM	PP	SH	GW	S	%	TGF	PGF	TGA	PGA	+/–	GP	G	A	Pts	PIM	PP	SH	GW
1976-77	Sodertalje SK	Sweden	2	0	0	0	....	....	....	2	....	....	....	....	....	....	....	....	....	....	....	....	....	....	....	....	....	....
1977-78	Sodertalje SK	Sweden	27	4	2	6	....	....	....	14	....	....	....	....	....	....	....	....	....	....	....	....	....	....	....	....	....	....
1978-79	Sodertalje SK	Sweden	STATISTICS NOT AVAILABLE																									
1979-80	Sodertalje SK	Sweden	STATISTICS NOT AVAILABLE																									
1980-81	Sodertalje SK	Sweden	36	5	18	23	....	....	....	37	....	....	....	....	....	....	....	....	....	....	....	....	....	....	....	....	....	....
	Sweden	WEC-A	8	0	0	0	....	....	....	2	....	....	....	....	....	....	....	....	....	....	....	....	....	....	....	....	....	....
1981-82	**Vancouver Canucks**	**NHL**	**38**	**1**	**8**	**9**	**1**	**5**	**6**	**21**	**0**	**0**	**0**	**47**	**2.1**	**38**	**8**	**32**	**0**	**–2**	**13**	**0**	**0**	**0**	**10**	**0**	**0**	**0**
1982-83	**Vancouver Canucks**	**NHL**	**5**	**1**	**1**	**2**	**1**	**1**	**2**	**0**	**0**	**0**	**0**	**5**	**20.0**	**5**	**2**	**4**	**0**	**–1**	....	....	....	....	....	....	....	....
	Fredericton Express	AHL	47	7	26	33	....	....	....	14	....	....	....	....	....	....	....	....	....	....	....	....	....	....	....	....	....	....
	Quebec Nordiques	**NHL**	**12**	**1**	**2**	**3**	**1**	**1**	**2**	**8**	**0**	**0**	**0**	**14**	**7.1**	**11**	**2**	**12**	**2**	**–1**	**1**	**0**	**0**	**0**	**0**	**0**	**0**	**0**
1983-84	Sodertalje SK	Sweden	36	10	17	27	....	....	....	40	....	....	....	....	....	....	....	....	....	....	3	3	0	3	2	....	....	....
1984-85	Sweden	C Cup	8	0	4	4	....	....	....	6	....	....	....	....	....	....	....	....	....	....	....	....	....	....	....	....	....	....
	Sodertalje SK	Sweden	34	10	12	22	....	....	....	20	....	....	....	....	....	....	....	....	....	....	8	2	6	8	*14	....	....	....
	Sweden	WEC-A	8	2	1	3	....	....	....	18	....	....	....	....	....	....	....	....	....	....	....	....	....	....	....	....	....	....
1985-86	Sodertalje SK	Sweden	34	13	16	29	....	....	....	30	....	....	....	....	....	....	....	....	....	....	7	4	2	6	8	....	....	....
	Sweden	WEC-A	7	1	0	1	....	....	....	6	....	....	....	....	....	....	....	....	....	....	....	....	....	....	....	....	....	....
1986-87	Sodertalje SK	Sweden	31	11	15	26	....	....	....	40	....	....	....	....	....	....	....	....	....	....	....	....	....	....	....	....	....	....
	Sweden	WEC-A	10	3	2	5	....	....	....	4	....	....	....	....	....	....	....	....	....	....	....	....	....	....	....	....	....	....
1987-88	Sweden	C Cup	6	1	2	3	....	....	....	4	....	....	....	....	....	....	....	....	....	....	....	....	....	....	....	....	....	....
	Sodertalje SK	Sweden	40	12	18	30	....	....	....	54	....	....	....	....	....	....	....	....	....	....	2	0	0	0	0	....	....	....
	Sweden	Olympics	8	4	6	10	....	....	....	4	....	....	....	....	....	....	....	....	....	....	....	....	....	....	....	....	....	....
1988-89	Sodertalje SK	Sweden	38	13	22	35	....	....	....	42	....	....	....	....	....	....	....	....	....	....	5	5	3	8	10	....	....	....
	Sweden	WEC-A	9	5	3	8	....	....	....	2	....	....	....	....	....	....	....	....	....	....	....	....	....	....	....	....	....	....
1989-90	Sodertalje SK	Sweden	39	10	20	30	....	....	....	32	....	....	....	....	....	....	....	....	....	....	2	0	1	1	8	....	....	....
	Sweden	WEC-A	10	2	5	7	....	....	....	10	....	....	....	....	....	....	....	....	....	....	....	....	....	....	....	....	....	....
1990-91	EHC Kloten	Switz.	34	15	23	38	....	....	....	....	....	....	....	....	....	....	....	....	....	....	10	1	6	7	....	....	....	....
1991-92	EHC Kloten	Switz.	38	16	17	33	....	....	....	22	....	....	....	....	....	....	....	....	....	....	....	....	....	....	....	....	....	....
1992-93	EHC Kloten	Switz.	36	14	26	40	....	....	....	65	....	....	....	....	....	....	....	....	....	....	11	3	8	11	2	....	....	....
1993-94	EHC Kloten	Switz.	36	14	29	43	....	....	....	18	....	....	....	....	....	....	....	....	....	....	12	4	8	12	14	....	....	....
1994-95	EHC Kloten	Switz.	25	8	16	24	....	....	....	16	....	....	....	....	....	....	....	....	....	....	12	1	10	11	10	....	....	....
1995-96	Sodertalje SK	Sweden	32	9	11	20	....	....	....	28	....	....	....	....	....	....	....	....	....	....	4	2	3	5	4	....	....	....
1996-97	EHC Kloten	Switz.	39	10	13	23	....	....	....	22	....	....	....	....	....	....	....	....	....	....	....	....	....	....	....	....	....	....
	NHL Totals		**55**	**3**	**11**	**14**	**3**	**7**	**10**	**29**	**0**	**0**	**0**	**66**	**4.5**	**54**	**12**	**48**	**2**		**14**	**0**	**0**	**0**	**10**	**0**	**0**	**0**

Swedish World All-Star Team (1984, 1985, 1987, 1988, 1989) • Swedish Player of the Year (1985) • WEC-A All-Star Team (1989)

Signed as a free agent by **Vancouver**, May 18, 1981. Traded to **Quebec** by **Vancouver** for John Garrett, February 4, 1983.

• ELIAS, PATRIK

Patrik Elias LW – L. 6', 175 lbs. b: Trebic, Czech., 4/13/1976. New Jersey's 2nd choice, 51st overall, in 1994 Entry Draft.

Season	Club	League	GP	G	A	Pts	AG	AA	APts	PIM	PP	SH	GW	S	%	TGF	PGF	TGA	PGA	+/–	GP	G	A	Pts	PIM	PP	SH	GW
1992-93	Poldi Kladno	Czech.	2	0	0	0	....	....	....	....	....	....	....	....	....	....	....	....	....	....	....	....	....	....	....	....	....	....
1993-94	Poldi Kladno	Czech.	15	1	2	3	....	....	....	....	....	....	....	....	....	....	....	....	....	....	11	2	2	4	....	....	....	....
1994-95	Poldi Kladno	Czech.	28	4	3	7	....	....	....	37	....	....	....	....	....	....	....	....	....	....	7	1	2	3	12	....	....	....
1995-96	**New Jersey Devils**	**NHL**	**1**	**0**	**0**	**0**	**0**	**0**	**0**	**0**	**0**	**0**	**0**	**2**	**0.0**	**1**	**0**	**2**	**0**	**–1**	....	....	....	....	....	....	....	....
	Albany River Rats	AHL	74	27	36	63	....	....	....	83	....	....	....	....	....	....	....	....	....	....	4	1	1	2	2	....	....	....
1996-97	**New Jersey Devils**	**NHL**	**17**	**2**	**3**	**5**	**2**	**3**	**5**	**2**	**0**	**0**	**0**	**23**	**8.7**	**11**	**3**	**12**	**0**	**–4**	**8**	**2**	**3**	**5**	**4**	**1**	**0**	**0**
	Albany River Rats	AHL	57	24	43	67	....	....	....	76	....	....	....	....	....	....	....	....	....	....	6	1	2	3	8	....	....	....
1997-98	**New Jersey Devils**	**NHL**	**74**	**18**	**19**	**37**	**21**	**19**	**40**	**28**	**5**	**0**	**6**	**147**	**12.2**	**60**	**21**	**23**	**2**	**+18**	**4**	**0**	**1**	**1**	**0**	**0**	**0**	**0**
	Albany River Rats	AHL	3	3	0	3	....	....	....	2	....	....	....	....	....	....	....	....	....	....	....	....	....	....	....	....	....	....
	Czech Republic	WC-A	3	1	0	1	....	....	....	0	....	....	....	....	....	....	....	....	....	....	....	....	....	....	....	....	....	....
	NHL Totals		**92**	**20**	**22**	**42**	**23**	**22**	**45**	**30**	**5**	**0**	**6**	**172**	**11.6**	**72**	**24**	**37**	**2**		**12**	**2**	**4**	**6**	**4**	**1**	**0**	**0**

EJC-A All-Star Team (1994) • NHL All-Rookie Team (1998)

• ELIK, TODD

Todd Elik C – L. 6'2", 195 lbs. b: Brampton, Ont., 4/15/1966.

Season	Club	League	GP	G	A	Pts	AG	AA	APts	PIM	PP	SH	GW	S	%	TGF	PGF	TGA	PGA	+/–	GP	G	A	Pts	PIM	PP	SH	GW
1984-85	Kingston Canadians	OHL	34	14	11	25	....	....	....	6	....	....	....	....	....	....	....	....	....	....	....	....	....	....	....	....	....	....
	North Bay Centennials	OHL	23	4	6	10	....	....	....	2	....	....	....	....	....	....	....	....	....	....	4	2	0	2	0	....	....	....
1985-86	North Bay Centennials	OHL	40	12	34	46	....	....	....	20	....	....	....	....	....	....	....	....	....	....	10	7	6	13	0	....	....	....
1986-87	University of Regina	CWUAA	27	26	34	60	....	....	....	137	....	....	....	....	....	....	....	....	....	....	....	....	....	....	....	....	....	....
	Canada	Nat-Team	1	0	0	0	....	....	....	0	....	....	....	....	....	....	....	....	....	....	....	....	....	....	....	....	....	....
1987-88	Colorado Rangers	IHL	81	44	56	100	....	....	....	83	....	....	....	....	....	....	....	....	....	....	12	8	12	20	9	....	....	....
1988-89	Denver Rangers	IHL	28	20	15	35	....	....	....	22	....	....	....	....	....	....	....	....	....	....	....	....	....	....	....	....	....	....
	New Haven Nighthawks	AHL	43	11	25	36	....	....	....	31	....	....	....	....	....	....	....	....	....	....	17	10	12	22	44	....	....	....
1989-90	**Los Angeles Kings**	**NHL**	**48**	**10**	**23**	**33**	**9**	**16**	**25**	**41**	**1**	**0**	**0**	**86**	**11.6**	**40**	**3**	**37**	**4**	**+4**	**10**	**3**	**9**	**12**	**10**	**1**	**0**	**0**
	New Haven Nighthawks	AHL	32	20	23	43	....	....	....	42	....	....	....	....	....	....	....	....	....	....	....	....	....	....	....	....	....	....
1990-91	**Los Angeles Kings**	**NHL**	**74**	**21**	**37**	**58**	**19**	**28**	**47**	**58**	**2**	**0**	**4**	**153**	**13.7**	**78**	**14**	**44**	**0**	**+20**	**12**	**2**	**7**	**9**	**6**	**0**	**0**	**0**
1991-92	**Minnesota North Stars**	**NHL**	**62**	**14**	**32**	**46**	**13**	**24**	**37**	**125**	**4**	**3**	**1**	**118**	**11.9**	**59**	**13**	**63**	**17**	**0**	**5**	**1**	**1**	**2**	**2**	**0**	**0**	**1**
1992-93	**Minnesota North Stars**	**NHL**	**46**	**13**	**18**	**31**	**11**	**12**	**23**	**48**	**4**	**0**	**1**	**76**	**17.1**	**46**	**10**	**45**	**4**	**–5**	....	....	....	....	....	....	....	....
	Edmonton Oilers	**NHL**	**14**	**1**	**9**	**10**	**1**	**6**	**7**	**8**	**0**	**0**	**0**	**28**	**3.6**	**12**	**2**	**9**	**0**	**+1**	....	....	....	....	....	....	....	....
1993-94	**Edmonton Oilers**	**NHL**	**4**	**0**	**0**	**0**	**0**	**0**	**0**	**6**	**0**	**0**	**0**	**5**	**0.0**	**1**	**1**	**0**	**0**	**0**	....	....	....	....	....	....	....	....
	San Jose Sharks	**NHL**	**75**	**25**	**41**	**66**	**23**	**32**	**55**	**89**	**9**	**0**	**4**	**180**	**13.9**	**83**	**34**	**52**	**0**	**–3**	**14**	**5**	**5**	**10**	**12**	**1**	**0**	**0**
1994-95	**San Jose Sharks**	**NHL**	**22**	**7**	**10**	**17**	**12**	**15**	**27**	**18**	**4**	**0**	**0**	**50**	**14.0**	**24**	**6**	**19**	**4**	**+3**	....	....	....	....	....	....	....	....
	St. Louis Blues	**NHL**	**13**	**2**	**4**	**6**	**4**	**6**	**10**	**4**	**0**	**0**	**0**	**26**	**7.7**	**8**	**1**	**3**	**1**	**+5**	**7**	**4**	**3**	**7**	**2**	**1**	**1**	**0**
1995-96	**Boston Bruins**	**NHL**	**59**	**13**	**33**	**46**	**13**	**27**	**40**	**40**	**6**	**0**	**2**	**108**	**12.0**	**62**	**24**	**36**	**0**	**+2**	**4**	**0**	**2**	**2**	**16**	**0**	**0**	**0**
	Providence Bruins	AHL	7	2	7	9	....	....	....	10	....	....	....	....	....	....	....	....	....	....	....	....	....	....	....	....	....	....
1996-97	**Boston Bruins**	**NHL**	**31**	**4**	**12**	**16**	**4**	**11**	**15**	**16**	**1**	**0**	**0**	**72**	**5.6**	**20**	**3**	**29**	**0**	**–12**	....	....	....	....	....	....	....	....
	Providence Bruins	AHL	37	16	29	45	....	....	....	63	....	....	....	....	....	....	....	....	....	....	10	1	6	7	33	....	....	....
1997-98	HC Lugano	Switz.	39	30	36	66	....	....	....	22	....	....	....	....	....	....	....	....	....	....	7	6	5	11	12	....	....	....
	NHL Totals		**448**	**110**	**219**	**329**	**109**	**177**	**286**	**453**	**31**	**3**	**12**	**902**	**12.2**	**433**	**111**	**337**	**30**		**52**	**15**	**27**	**42**	**48**	**3**	**1**	**1**

Signed as a free agent by **NY Rangers**, February 26, 1988. Traded to **LA Kings** by **NY Rangers** with Igor Liba, Michael Boyce and future considerations for Dean Kennedy and Denis Larocque, December 12, 1988. Traded to **Minnesota** by **LA Kings** for Randy Gilhen, Charlie Huddy, Jim Thomson and NY Rangers' 4th round choice (previously acquired, LA Kings selected Alexei Zhitnik) in 1991 Entry Draft, June 22, 1991. Traded to **Edmonton** by **Minnesota** for Brent Gilchrist, March 5, 1993. Claimed on waivers by **San Jose** from **Edmonton**, October 26, 1993. Traded to **St. Louis** by **San Jose** for Kevin Miller, March 23, 1995. Signed as a free agent by **Boston**, August 8, 1995.

• ELLETT, DAVE

Dave Ellett D – L. 6'2", 205 lbs. b: Cleveland, OH, 3/30/1964. Winnipeg's 3rd choice, 75th overall, in 1982 Entry Draft.

Season	Club	League	GP	G	A	Pts	AG	AA	APts	PIM	PP	SH	GW	S	%	TGF	PGF	TGA	PGA	+/–	GP	G	A	Pts	PIM	PP	SH	GW
1981-82	Ottawa Jr. Senators	OJHL	50	9	35	44	....	....	....	....	....	....	....	....	....	....	....	....	....	....	....	....	....	....	....	....	....	....
1982-83	Bowling Green University	CCHA	40	4	13	17	....	....	....	34	....	....	....	....	....	....	....	....	....	....	....	....	....	....	....	....	....	....
1983-84	Bowling Green University	CCHA	43	15	39	54	....	....	....	96	....	....	....	....	....	....	....	....	....	....	....	....	....	....	....	....	....	....
1984-85	**Winnipeg Jets**	**NHL**	**80**	**11**	**27**	**38**	**9**	**18**	**27**	**85**	**3**	**0**	**0**	**146**	**7.5**	**120**	**16**	**99**	**15**	**+20**	**8**	**1**	**5**	**6**	**4**	**1**	**0**	**0**
1985-86	**Winnipeg Jets**	**NHL**	**80**	**15**	**31**	**46**	**12**	**21**	**33**	**96**	**2**	**0**	**1**	**168**	**8.9**	**127**	**39**	**171**	**45**	**–38**	**3**	**0**	**1**	**1**	**0**	**0**	**0**	**0**
1986-87	**Winnipeg Jets**	**NHL**	**78**	**13**	**31**	**44**	**11**	**22**	**33**	**53**	**5**	**0**	**2**	**159**	**8.2**	**111**	**23**	**83**	**14**	**+19**	**10**	**0**	**8**	**8**	**2**	**0**	**0**	**0**
1987-88	United States	C Cup	DID NOT PLAY																									
	Winnipeg Jets	**NHL**	**68**	**13**	**45**	**58**	**11**	**32**	**43**	**106**	**5**	**0**	**1**	**198**	**6.6**	**135**	**74**	**93**	**24**	**–8**	**5**	**1**	**2**	**3**	**10**	**1**	**0**	**0**
1988-89	**Winnipeg Jets**	**NHL**	**75**	**22**	**34**	**56**	**19**	**24**	**43**	**62**	**9**	**2**	**5**	**209**	**10.5**	**145**	**58**	**137**	**32**	**–18**	....	....	....	....	....	....	....	....
	Canada	WEC-A	10	4	2	6	....	....	....	14	....	....	....	....	....	....	....	....	....	....	....	....	....	....	....	....	....	....
1989-90	**Winnipeg Jets**	**NHL**	**77**	**17**	**29**	**46**	**15**	**21**	**36**	**96**	**8**	**0**	**1**	**205**	**8.3**	**130**	**43**	**125**	**23**	**–15**	**7**	**2**	**0**	**2**	**6**	**2**	**0**	**1**
1990-91	**Winnipeg Jets**	**NHL**	**17**	**4**	**7**	**11**	**4**	**5**	**9**	**6**	**1**	**1**	**0**	**41**	**9.8**	**28**	**15**	**19**	**2**	**–4**	....	....	....	....	....	....	....	....
	Toronto Maple Leafs	**NHL**	**60**	**8**	**30**	**38**	**7**	**23**	**30**	**69**	**5**	**0**	**1**	**154**	**5.2**	**98**	**38**	**92**	**28**	**–4**	....	....	....	....	....	....	....	....

Season	Club	League	REGULAR SEASON																		PLAYOFFS							
			GP	G	A	Pts	AG	AA	APts	PIM	PP	SH	GW	S	%	TGF	PGF	TGA	PGA	+/–	GP	G	A	Pts	PIM	PP	SH	GW
1991-92	Toronto Maple Leafs	NHL	79	18	33	51	16	25	41	95	9	1	4	225	8.0	115	52	105	29	–13	....	....	....	....	....	....	....	....
1992-93	Toronto Maple Leafs	NHL	70	6	34	40	5	23	28	46	4	0	1	186	3.2	127	59	68	19	+19	21	4	8	12	8	2	0	0
1993-94	Toronto Maple Leafs	NHL	68	7	36	43	7	28	35	42	5	0	1	146	4.8	114	52	74	18	+6	18	3	15	18	31	3	0	0
1994-95	Toronto Maple Leafs	NHL	33	5	10	15	9	15	24	26	3	0	1	84	6.0	39	16	42	13	–6	7	0	2	2	0	0	0	0
1995-96	Toronto Maple Leafs	NHL	80	3	19	22	3	15	18	59	1	1	0	153	2.0	76	18	95	27	–10	6	0	0	0	4	0	0	0
1996-97	Toronto Maple Leafs	NHL	56	4	10	14	4	9	13	34	0	0	1	83	4.8	48	4	67	15	–8	....	....	....	....	....	....	....	....
	New Jersey Devils	NHL	20	2	5	7	2	4	6	6	1	0	1	22	9.1	20	8	10	0	+2	10	0	3	3	10	0	0	0
1997-98	Boston Bruins	NHL	82	3	20	23	4	19	23	67	2	0	1	129	2.3	85	24	75	17	+3	6	0	1	1	6	0	0	0
	NHL Totals		1023	151	401	552	138	304	442	948	63	5	21	2308	6.5	1518	539	1355	321		101	11	45	56	81	9	0	1

CCHA Second All-Star Team (1984) • NCAA Championship All-Tournament Team (1984)

Played in NHL All-Star Game (1989, 1992)

Traded to **Toronto** by **Winnipeg** with Paul Fenton for Ed Olczyk and Mark Osborne, November 10, 1990. Traded to **New Jersey** by **Toronto** with Doug Gilmour and future considerations for Jason Smith, Steve Sullivan and the rights to Alyn McCauley, February 25, 1997. Signed as a free agent by **Boston**, July 29, 1997.

• ELLIS, RON

Ron Ellis RW – R. 5'9", 195 lbs. b: Lindsay, Ont., 1/8/1945.

Season	Club	League	GP	G	A	Pts	AG	AA	APts	PIM	PP	SH	GW	S	%	TGF	PGF	TGA	PGA	+/–	GP	G	A	Pts	PIM	PP	SH	GW
1960-61	Toronto Marlboros	OHA	3	2	1	3	....	....	....	2	....	....	....	....	....	....	....	....	....	....	....	....	....	....	....	....	....	....
1961-62	Toronto Marlboros	OHA	33	17	12	29	....	....	....	16	....	....	....	....	....	....	....	....	....	....	12	6	5	11	4	....	....	....
1962-63	Toronto Marlboros	OHA	36	21	22	43	....	....	....	8	....	....	....	....	....	....	....	....	....	....	10	9	9	18	2	....	....	....
1963-64	Toronto Marlboros	OHA	54	46	38	84	....	....	....	20	....	....	....	....	....	....	....	....	....	....	9	4	10	14	10	....	....	....
	Toronto Maple Leafs	NHL	1	0	0	0	0	0	0	0	....	....	....	....	....	....	....	....	....	....	....	....	....	....	....	....	....	....
1964-65	Toronto Maple Leafs	NHL	62	23	16	39	29	17	46	14	....	....	....	....	....	....	....	....	....	....	6	3	0	3	2	....	....	....
1965-66	Toronto Maple Leafs	NHL	70	19	23	42	23	23	46	24	....	....	....	....	....	....	....	....	....	....	4	0	0	0	2	....	....	....
1966-67	Toronto Maple Leafs	NHL	67	22	23	45	27	24	51	14	....	....	....	....	....	....	....	....	....	....	12	2	1	3	4	....	....	....
1967-68	Toronto Maple Leafs	NHL	74	28	20	48	35	21	56	8	1	1	5	215	13.0	67	9	57	5	+6	....	....	....	....	....	....	....	....
1968-69	Toronto Maple Leafs	NHL	72	25	21	46	28	20	48	12	4	0	5	180	13.9	73	11	59	2	+5	4	2	1	3	2	1	0	0
1969-70	Toronto Maple Leafs	NHL	76	35	19	54	41	19	60	14	6	1	3	227	15.4	86	18	66	8	+11	....	....	....	....	....	....	....	....
1970-71	Toronto Maple Leafs	NHL	78	24	29	53	25	26	51	10	2	0	2	234	10.3	85	17	58	7	+17	6	1	1	2	2	1	0	0
1971-72	Toronto Maple Leafs	NHL	78	23	24	47	25	22	47	17	4	0	7	191	12.0	83	25	54	3	+7	5	1	1	2	4	1	0	0
1972-73	Canada	Summit	8	0	3	3	....	....	....	8	....	....	....	....	....	....	....	....	....	....	....	....	....	....	....	....	....	....
	Toronto Maple Leafs	NHL	78	22	29	51	22	24	46	22	4	1	2	228	9.6	89	24	83	17	–1	....	....	....	....	....	....	....	....
1973-74	Toronto Maple Leafs	NHL	70	23	25	48	23	22	45	12	3	0	3	158	14.6	75	14	57	4	+8	4	2	1	3	0	0	0	0
1974-75	Toronto Maple Leafs	NHL	79	32	29	61	30	23	53	25	11	0	5	177	18.1	101	26	80	14	+9	7	3	0	3	2	1	0	0
1975-76			DID NOT PLAY – RETIRED																									
1976-77	Canada	WEC-A	10	5	4	9	....	....	....	2	....	....	....	....	....	....	....	....	....	....	....	....	....	....	....	....	....	....
1977-78	Toronto Maple Leafs	NHL	80	26	24	50	25	20	45	17	3	0	5	128	20.3	75	10	73	16	+8	13	3	2	5	0	0	0	2
1978-79	Toronto Maple Leafs	NHL	63	16	12	28	15	9	24	10	4	0	1	97	16.5	44	6	34	3	+7	6	1	1	2	2	0	0	0
1979-80	Toronto Maple Leafs	NHL	59	12	11	23	11	8	19	6	0	1	2	55	21.8	34	1	66	24	–9	3	0	0	0	0	0	0	0
1980-81	Toronto Maple Leafs	NHL	27	2	3	5	2	2	4	2	0	0	0	19	10.5	5	0	18	12	–1	....	....	....	....	....	....	....	....
	NHL Totals		1034	332	308	640	361	280	641	207	42	4	40	1909	17.4	817	161	704	115		70	18	8	26	20	4	0	2

Played in NHL All-Star Game (1964, 1965, 1968, 1970)

• Came out of retirement to play for **Team Canada** in the 1977 World Hockey Championships, April 21, 1977.

• ELORANTA, KARI

Kari Eloranta D – L. 6'2", 200 lbs. b: Lahti, Finland, 2/29/1956.

Season	Club	League	GP	G	A	Pts	AG	AA	APts	PIM	PP	SH	GW	S	%	TGF	PGF	TGA	PGA	+/–	GP	G	A	Pts	PIM	PP	SH	GW
1974-75	Finland	WJC-A	5	0	0	0	....	....	....	4	....	....	....	....	....	....	....	....	....	....	....	....	....	....	....	....	....	....
1975-76	Finland	WJC-A	4	0	1	1	....	....	....	2	....	....	....	....	....	....	....	....	....	....	....	....	....	....	....	....	....	....
1976-77	Reipas	Finland	36	4	6	10	....	....	....	34	....	....	....	....	....	....	....	....	....	....	....	....	....	....	....	....	....	....
1977-78	Reipas	Finland	36	6	6	12	....	....	....	14	....	....	....	....	....	....	....	....	....	....	....	....	....	....	....	....	....	....
1978-79	Leksands IF	Sweden	36	7	10	17	....	....	....	47	....	....	....	....	....	....	....	....	....	....	....	....	....	....	....	....	....	....
	Finland	WEC-A	6	0	0	0	....	....	....	4	....	....	....	....	....	....	....	....	....	....	....	....	....	....	....	....	....	....
1979-80	Leksands IF	Sweden	33	4	5	9	....	....	....	26	....	....	....	....	....	....	....	....	....	....	2	0	0	0	4	....	....	....
	Finland	Olympics	7	0	4	4	....	....	....	0	....	....	....	....	....	....	....	....	....	....	....	....	....	....	....	....	....	....
1980-81	Leksands IF	Sweden	36	2	14	16	....	....	....	35	....	....	....	....	....	....	....	....	....	....	....	....	....	....	....	....	....	....
	Finland	WEC-A	8	1	2	3	....	....	....	6	....	....	....	....	....	....	....	....	....	....	....	....	....	....	....	....	....	....
1981-82	Calgary Flames	NHL	19	0	5	5	0	3	3	14	0	0	0	11	0.0	10	3	21	0	–14	....	....	....	....	....	....	....	....
	Oklahoma City Stars	CHL	39	3	27	30	....	....	....	31	....	....	....	....	....	....	....	....	....	....	....	....	....	....	....	....	....	....
	St. Louis Blues	NHL	12	1	7	8	1	5	6	6	1	0	1	22	4.5	27	13	17	8	+5	5	0	0	0	0	0	0	0
1982-83	Calgary Flames	NHL	80	4	40	44	3	28	31	43	0	0	0	68	5.9	122	13	109	13	+13	9	1	3	4	17	0	0	0
1983-84	Calgary Flames	NHL	78	5	34	39	4	23	27	44	2	0	0	59	8.5	117	29	98	22	+12	6	0	2	2	2	0	0	0
1984-85	Calgary Flames	NHL	65	2	11	13	2	7	9	39	0	0	0	43	4.7	61	7	60	7	+1	....	....	....	....	....	....	....	....
1985-86	HV 71 Jonkoping	Sweden	36	4	16	20	....	....	....	46	....	....	....	....	....	....	....	....	....	....	2	0	0	0	0	....	....	....
	Finland	WEC-A	10	3	1	4	....	....	....	2	....	....	....	....	....	....	....	....	....	....	....	....	....	....	....	....	....	....
1986-87	HV 71 Jonkoping	Sweden	35	3	18	21	....	....	....	34	....	....	....	....	....	....	....	....	....	....	....	....	....	....	....	....	....	....
	Calgary Flames	NHL	13	1	6	7	1	4	5	9	0	0	0	11	9.1	21	6	16	4	+3	6	0	2	2	0	0	0	0
1987-88	HC Lugano	Switz.	36	5	26	31	....	....	....	28	....	....	....	....	....	....	....	....	....	....	7	2	4	6	8	....	....	....
	Finland	Olympics	8	0	6	6	....	....	....	2	....	....	....	....	....	....	....	....	....	....	....	....	....	....	....	....	....	....
1988-89	HC Lugano	Switz.	....	11	18	29	....	....	....	....	....	....	....	....	....	....	....	....	....	....	10	1	6	7	8	....	....	....
	Finland	WEC-A	10	1	3	4	....	....	....	12	....	....	....	....	....	....	....	....	....	....	....	....	....	....	....	....	....	....
1990-91	Reipas	Finland	44	7	18	25	....	....	....	18	....	....	....	....	....	....	....	....	....	....	....	....	....	....	....	....	....	....
1991-92	Finland	C Cup	6	0	1	1	....	....	....	4	....	....	....	....	....	....	....	....	....	....	....	....	....	....	....	....	....	....
	Rogle BK	Switz.	35	5	17	22	....	....	....	22	....	....	....	....	....	....	....	....	....	....	5	0	0	0	22	....	....	....
	Finland	Olympics	8	0	2	2	....	....	....	4	....	....	....	....	....	....	....	....	....	....	....	....	....	....	....	....	....	....
1992-93	Rogle BK	Sweden	38	9	8	17	....	....	....	44	....	....	....	....	....	....	....	....	....	....	....	....	....	....	....	....	....	....
1993-94	Rogle BK	Sweden	40	2	13	15	....	....	....	14	....	....	....	....	....	....	....	....	....	....	3	0	0	0	....	....	....	....
1994-95	Rogle BK	Sweden	17	1	3	4	....	....	....	8	....	....	....	....	....	....	....	....	....	....	....	....	....	....	....	....	....	....
	NHL Totals		267	13	103	116	11	70	81	155	3	0	1	214	6.1	358	71	321	54		26	1	7	8	19	0	0	0

Signed as a free agent by **Calgary**, September 15, 1981. Traded to **St. Louis** by **Calgary** for future considerations, March 8, 1982. Traded to **Calgary** by **St. Louis** for future considerations, June 3, 1982.

• ELYNUIK, PAT

Pat Elynuik RW – R. 6', 185 lbs. b: Foam Lake, Sask., 10/30/1967. Winnipeg's 1st choice, 8th overall, in 1986 Entry Draft.

Season	Club	League	GP	G	A	Pts	AG	AA	APts	PIM	PP	SH	GW	S	%	TGF	PGF	TGA	PGA	+/–	GP	G	A	Pts	PIM	PP	SH	GW
1984-85	Prince Albert Raiders	WHL	70	23	20	43	....	....	....	54	....	....	....	....	....	....	....	....	....	....	13	9	3	12	7	....	....	....
1985-86	Prince Albert Raiders	WHL	68	53	53	106	....	....	....	62	....	....	....	....	....	....	....	....	....	....	20	7	9	16	17	....	....	....
1986-87	Prince Albert Raiders	WHL	64	51	62	113	....	....	....	40	....	....	....	....	....	....	....	....	....	....	8	5	5	10	12	....	....	....
	Canada	WJC-A	6	6	5	11	....	....	....	2	....	....	....	....	....	....	....	....	....	....	....	....	....	....	....	....	....	....
1987-88	Winnipeg Jets	NHL	13	1	3	4	1	2	3	12	0	0	0	12	8.3	7	1	7	3	+2	....	....	....	....	....	....	....	....
	Moncton Hawks	AHL	30	11	18	29	....	....	....	35	....	....	....	....	....	....	....	....	....	....	....	....	....	....	....	....	....	....
1988-89	Winnipeg Jets	NHL	56	26	25	51	22	18	40	29	5	0	6	100	26.0	73	17	53	2	+5	....	....	....	....	....	....	....	....
	Moncton Hawks	AHL	7	8	2	10	....	....	....	2	....	....	....	....	....	....	....	....	....	....	....	....	....	....	....	....	....	....
1989-90	Winnipeg Jets	NHL	80	32	42	74	28	30	58	83	14	0	3	132	24.2	111	37	73	1	+2	7	2	4	6	2	0	0	0
1990-91	Winnipeg Jets	NHL	80	31	34	65	29	26	55	73	16	0	4	150	20.7	100	53	68	0	–13	....	....	....	....	....	....	....	....
1991-92	Winnipeg Jets	NHL	60	25	25	50	23	19	42	65	9	0	1	127	19.7	79	35	46	0	–2	7	2	2	4	4	2	0	0
1992-93	Washington Capitals	NHL	80	22	35	57	18	24	42	66	8	0	1	121	18.2	94	42	49	0	+3	6	2	3	5	19	0	0	0
1993-94	Washington Capitals	NHL	4	1	1	2	1	1	2	0	1	0	0	8	12.5	3	1	5	0	–3	....	....	....	....	....	....	....	....
	Tampa Bay Lightning	NHL	63	12	14	26	11	11	22	64	3	1	1	103	11.7	44	11	53	2	–18	....	....	....	....	....	....	....	....
1994-95	Ottawa Senators	NHL	41	3	7	10	5	10	15	51	0	0	0	58	5.2	21	9	25	2	–11	....	....	....	....	....	....	....	....

			REGULAR SEASON																		PLAYOFFS							
Season	Club	League	GP	G	A	Pts	AG	AA	APts	PIM	PP	SH	GW	S	%	TGF	PGF	TGA	PGA	+/–	GP	G	A	Pts	PIM	PP	SH	GW
1995-96	**Ottawa Senators**	**NHL**	**29**	**1**	**2**	**3**	**1**	**2**	**3**	**16**	**0**	**0**	**0**	**27**	**3.7**	**7**	**0**	**5**	**0**	**+2**	....	....	....	....	....	....	....	....
	Fort Wayne Komets	IHL	42	22	28	50	....	....	....	43	....	....	....	....	....	....	....	....	....	....	....	....	....	....	....	....	....	....
1996-97	Michigan K-Wings	IHL	81	24	34	58	....	....	....	62	....	....	....	....	....	....	....	....	....	....	4	1	0	1	0	....	....	....
	NHL Totals		**506**	**154**	**188**	**342**	**139**	**143**	**282**	**459**	**56**	**1**	**16**	**838**	**18.4**	**547**	**206**	**384**	**10**		**20**	**6**	**9**	**15**	**25**	**2**	**0**	**0**

WHL East All-Star Team (1986, 1987)

Traded to **Washington** by **Winnipeg** for John Druce and Toronto's 4th round choice (previously acquired by Washington — later traded to Detroit — Detroit selected John Jakopin) in 1993 Entry Draft, October 1, 1992. Traded to **Tampa Bay** by **Washington** for future considerations, October 22, 1993. Signed as a free agent by **Ottawa**, June 21, 1994. Signed as a free agent by **Dallas**, September 6, 1996.

• EMERSON, NELSON

Nelson Emerson RW – R. 5'11", 175 lbs. b: Hamilton, Ont., 8/17/1967. New Jersey's 4th choice, 45th overall, in 1985 Entry Draft.

Season	Club	League	GP	G	A	Pts	AG	AA	APts	PIM	PP	SH	GW	S	%	TGF	PGF	TGA	PGA	+/–	GP	G	A	Pts	PIM	PP	SH	GW
1985-86	Stratford Collitons	OJHL	39	54	58	112	....	....	....	91	....	....	....	....	....	....	....	....	....	....	....	....	....	....	....	....	....	....
1986-87	Bowling Green University	CCHA	45	26	35	61	....	....	....	28	....	....	....	....	....	....	....	....	....	....	....	....	....	....	....	....	....	....
1987-88	Bowling Green University	CCHA	45	34	49	83	....	....	....	54	....	....	....	....	....	....	....	....	....	....	....	....	....	....	....	....	....	....
1988-89	Bowling Green University	CCHA	44	22	46	68	....	....	....	46	....	....	....	....	....	....	....	....	....	....	....	....	....	....	....	....	....	....
1989-90	Bowling Green University	CCHA	44	30	52	82	....	....	....	42	....	....	....	....	....	....	....	....	....	....	....	....	....	....	....	....	....	....
	Peoria Rivermen	IHL	3	1	1	2	....	....	....	0	....	....	....	....	....	....	....	....	....	....	....	....	....	....	....	....	....	....
1990-91	**St. Louis Blues**	**NHL**	**4**	**0**	**3**	**3**	**0**	**2**	**2**	**2**	**0**	**0**	**0**	**3**	**0.0**	**3**	**0**	**5**	**0**	**–2**	....	....	....	....	....	....	....	....
	Peoria Rivermen	IHL	73	36	79	115	....	....	....	91	....	....	....	....	....	....	....	....	....	....	17	9	12	21	16	....	....	....
1991-92	**St. Louis Blues**	**NHL**	**79**	**23**	**36**	**59**	**21**	**27**	**48**	**66**	**3**	**0**	**2**	**143**	**16.1**	**80**	**31**	**54**	**0**	**–5**	**6**	**3**	**3**	**6**	**21**	**2**	**0**	**0**
	Canada	WC-A	3	0	1	1	....	....	....	2	....	....	....	....	....	....	....	....	....	....	....	....	....	....	....	....	....	....
1992-93	**St. Louis Blues**	**NHL**	**82**	**22**	**51**	**73**	**18**	**35**	**53**	**62**	**5**	**2**	**4**	**196**	**11.2**	**115**	**62**	**66**	**15**	**+2**	**11**	**1**	**6**	**7**	**6**	**0**	**0**	**0**
1993-94	**Winnipeg Jets**	**NHL**	**83**	**33**	**41**	**74**	**31**	**32**	**63**	**80**	**4**	**5**	**6**	**282**	**11.7**	**112**	**60**	**109**	**19**	**–38**	....	....	....	....	....	....	....	....
	Canada	WC-A	8	2	2	4	....	....	....	4	....	....	....	....	....	....	....	....	....	....	....	....	....	....	....	....	....	....
1994-95	**Winnipeg Jets**	**NHL**	**48**	**14**	**23**	**37**	**25**	**34**	**59**	**26**	**4**	**1**	**1**	**122**	**11.5**	**49**	**19**	**54**	**12**	**–12**	....	....	....	....	....	....	....	....
1995-96	**Hartford Whalers**	**NHL**	**81**	**29**	**29**	**58**	**29**	**24**	**53**	**78**	**12**	**2**	**5**	**247**	**11.7**	**98**	**46**	**78**	**19**	**–7**	....	....	....	....	....	....	....	....
1996-97	**Hartford Whalers**	**NHL**	**66**	**9**	**29**	**38**	**10**	**26**	**36**	**34**	**2**	**1**	**2**	**194**	**4.6**	**61**	**27**	**63**	**8**	**–21**	....	....	....	....	....	....	....	....
1997-98	**Carolina Hurricanes**	**NHL**	**81**	**21**	**24**	**45**	**25**	**23**	**48**	**50**	**6**	**0**	**4**	**203**	**10.3**	**67**	**34**	**53**	**3**	**–17**	....	....	....	....	....	....	....	....
	Canada	WC-A	6	2	1	3	....	....	....	2	....	....	....	....	....	....	....	....	....	....	....	....	....	....	....	....	....	....
	NHL Totals		**524**	**151**	**236**	**387**	**159**	**203**	**362**	**398**	**36**	**11**	**24**	**1390**	**10.9**	**585**	**279**	**482**	**76**		**17**	**4**	**9**	**13**	**27**	**2**	**0**	**0**

NCAA West Second All-American Team (1988) • CCHA First All-Star Team (1988, 1990) • CCHA Second All-Star Team (1989) • NCAA West First All-American Team (1990) • IHL First All-Star Team (1991) • Won Garry F. Longman Memorial Trophy (Top Rookie - IHL) (1991)

Traded to **Winnipeg** by **St. Louis** with Stephane Quintal for Phil Housley, September 24, 1993. Traded to **Hartford** by **Winnipeg** for Darren Turcotte, October 6, 1995. Transferred to **Carolina** after **Hartford** franchise relocated, June 25, 1997.

• EMMA, DAVID

David Emma C – L. 5'11", 180 lbs. b: Cranston, RI, 1/14/1969. New Jersey's 6th choice, 110th overall, in 1989 Entry Draft.

Season	Club	League	GP	G	A	Pts	AG	AA	APts	PIM	PP	SH	GW	S	%	TGF	PGF	TGA	PGA	+/–	GP	G	A	Pts	PIM	PP	SH	GW
1987-88	Boston College	H.E.	30	19	16	35	....	....	....	30	....	....	....	....	....	....	....	....	....	....	....	....	....	....	....	....	....	....
	United States	WJC-A	7	0	0	0	....	....	....	2	....	....	....	....	....	....	....	....	....	....	....	....	....	....	....	....	....	....
1988-89	Boston College	H.E.	36	20	31	51	....	....	....	36	....	....	....	....	....	....	....	....	....	....	....	....	....	....	....	....	....	....
	United States	WJC-A	7	6	2	8	....	....	....	6	....	....	....	....	....	....	....	....	....	....	....	....	....	....	....	....	....	....
1989-90	Boston College	H.E.	42	38	34	*72	....	....	....	46	....	....	....	....	....	....	....	....	....	....	....	....	....	....	....	....	....	....
1990-91	Boston College	H.E.	39	*35	46	*81	....	....	....	44	....	....	....	....	....	....	....	....	....	....	....	....	....	....	....	....	....	....
	United States	WEC-A	10	1	0	1	....	....	....	8	....	....	....	....	....	....	....	....	....	....	....	....	....	....	....	....	....	....
1991-92	United States	Nat-Team	55	15	16	31	....	....	....	32	....	....	....	....	....	....	....	....	....	....	....	....	....	....	....	....	....	....
	United States	Olympics	6	0	1	1	....	....	....	6	....	....	....	....	....	....	....	....	....	....	....	....	....	....	....	....	....	....
	Utica Devils	AHL	15	4	7	11	....	....	....	12	....	....	....	....	....	....	....	....	....	....	4	1	1	2	2	....	....	....
1992-93	**New Jersey Devils**	**NHL**	**2**	**0**	**0**	**0**	**0**	**0**	**0**	**0**	**0**	**0**	**0**	**2**	**0.0**	**0**	**0**	**0**	**0**	**0**	....	....	....	....	....	....	....	....
	Utica Devils	AHL	61	21	40	61	....	....	....	47	....	....	....	....	....	....	....	....	....	....	5	2	1	3	6	....	....	....
1993-94	**New Jersey Devils**	**NHL**	**15**	**5**	**5**	**10**	**5**	**4**	**9**	**2**	**1**	**0**	**2**	**24**	**20.8**	**18**	**7**	**12**	**1**	**0**	....	....	....	....	....	....	....	....
	Albany River Rats	AHL	56	26	29	55	....	....	....	53	....	....	....	....	....	....	....	....	....	....	5	1	2	3	8	....	....	....
1994-95	**New Jersey Devils**	**NHL**	**6**	**0**	**1**	**1**	**0**	**1**	**1**	**0**	**0**	**0**	**0**	**4**	**0.0**	**1**	**0**	**4**	**1**	**–2**	....	....	....	....	....	....	....	....
	Albany River Rats	AHL	1	0	0	0	....	....	....	0	....	....	....	....	....	....	....	....	....	....	....	....	....	....	....	....	....	....
1995-96	Detroit Vipers	IHL	79	30	32	62	....	....	....	75	....	....	....	....	....	....	....	....	....	....	11	5	2	7	2	....	....	....
1996-97	**Boston Bruins**	**NHL**	**5**	**0**	**0**	**0**	**0**	**0**	**0**	**0**	**0**	**0**	**0**	**3**	**0.0**	**0**	**0**	**2**	**1**	**–1**	....	....	....	....	....	....	....	....
	Providence Bruins	AHL	53	10	18	28	....	....	....	24	....	....	....	....	....	....	....	....	....	....	....	....	....	....	....	....	....	....
	Phoenix Roadrunners	IHL	8	0	4	4	....	....	....	4	....	....	....	....	....	....	....	....	....	....	....	....	....	....	....	....	....	....
	NHL Totals		**28**	**5**	**6**	**11**	**5**	**5**	**10**	**2**	**1**	**0**	**2**	**33**	**15.2**	**19**	**7**	**18**	**3**		....	....	....	....	....	....	....	....

Hockey East Second All-Star Team (1989) • Hockey East First All-Star Team (1990, 1991) • NCAA East First All-American Team (1990, 1991) • Won Hobey Baker Memorial Award (Top U.S. Collegiate Player) (1991)

Signed as a free agent by **Boston**, August 27, 1996.

• EMMONS, GARY

Gary Emmons C – R. 6', 185 lbs. b: Winnipeg, Man., 12/30/1963. NY Rangers' 1st choice, 14th overall, in 1986 Supplemental Draft.

Season	Club	League	GP	G	A	Pts	AG	AA	APts	PIM	PP	SH	GW	S	%	TGF	PGF	TGA	PGA	+/–	GP	G	A	Pts	PIM	PP	SH	GW
1983-84	Northern Michigan University	CCHA	40	28	21	49	....	....	....	42	....	....	....	....	....	....	....	....	....	....	....	....	....	....	....	....	....	....
1984-85	Northern Michigan University	CCHA	40	25	28	53	....	....	....	22	....	....	....	....	....	....	....	....	....	....	....	....	....	....	....	....	....	....
1985-86	Northern Michigan University	CCHA	36	45	30	75	....	....	....	34	....	....	....	....	....	....	....	....	....	....	....	....	....	....	....	....	....	....
1986-87	Northern Michigan University	CCHA	35	32	34	66	....	....	....	59	....	....	....	....	....	....	....	....	....	....	....	....	....	....	....	....	....	....
1987-88	Milwaukee Admirals	IHL	13	3	4	7	....	....	....	4	....	....	....	....	....	....	....	....	....	....	....	....	....	....	....	....	....	....
	Nova Scotia Oilers	AHL	59	18	27	45	....	....	....	22	....	....	....	....	....	....	....	....	....	....	....	....	....	....	....	....	....	....
1988-89	Canada	Nat-Team	49	16	26	42	....	....	....	42	....	....	....	....	....	....	....	....	....	....	....	....	....	....	....	....	....	....
1989-90	Kalamazoo Wings	IHL	81	41	59	100	....	....	....	38	....	....	....	....	....	....	....	....	....	....	8	2	7	9	2	....	....	....
1990-91	Kalamazoo Wings	IHL	62	25	33	58	....	....	....	26	....	....	....	....	....	....	....	....	....	....	11	5	8	13	6	....	....	....
1991-92	Kansas City Blades	IHL	80	29	54	83	....	....	....	60	....	....	....	....	....	....	....	....	....	....	15	6	13	19	8	....	....	....
1992-93	Kansas City Blades	IHL	80	37	44	81	....	....	....	80	....	....	....	....	....	....	....	....	....	....	12	*7	6	13	8	....	....	....
1993-94	**San Jose Sharks**	**NHL**	**3**	**1**	**0**	**1**	**1**	**0**	**1**	**0**	**1**	**0**	**0**	**6**	**16.7**	**1**	**1**	**4**	**0**	**–4**	....	....	....	....	....	....	....	....
	Kansas City Blades	IHL	63	20	49	69	....	....	....	28	....	....	....	....	....	....	....	....	....	....	....	....	....	....	....	....	....	....
1994-95	Kansas City Blades	IHL	81	22	38	60	....	....	....	42	....	....	....	....	....	....	....	....	....	....	21	9	19	28	24	....	....	....
1995-96	Kansas City Blades	IHL	73	24	39	63	....	....	....	72	....	....	....	....	....	....	....	....	....	....	1	0	0	0	4	....	....	....
1996-97	Kansas City Blades	IHL	67	15	30	45	....	....	....	36	....	....	....	....	....	....	....	....	....	....	3	0	1	1	4	....	....	....
	NHL Totals		**3**	**1**	**0**	**1**	**1**	**0**	**1**	**0**	**1**	**0**	**0**	**6**	**16.7**	**1**	**1**	**4**	**0**		....	....	....	....	....	....	....	....

WCHA First All-Star Team (1986, 1987) • NCAA West Second All-American Team (1987)

Signed as a free agent by **Edmonton**, July 27, 1987. Signed as a free agent by **Minnesota**, July 11, 1989. Signed as a free agent by **San Jose**, October 19, 1993.

• ENDEAN, CRAIG

Craig Endean LW – L. 5'11", 170 lbs. b: Kamloops, B.C., 4/13/1968. Winnipeg's 5th choice, 92nd overall, in 1986 Entry Draft.

Season	Club	League	GP	G	A	Pts	AG	AA	APts	PIM	PP	SH	GW	S	%	TGF	PGF	TGA	PGA	+/–	GP	G	A	Pts	PIM	PP	SH	GW
1983-84	Seattle Breakers	WHL	67	16	6	22	....	....	....	14	....	....	....	....	....	....	....	....	....	....	5	2	2	4	2	....	....	....
1984-85	Seattle Breakers	WHL	69	37	60	97	....	....	....	28	....	....	....	....	....	....	....	....	....	....	....	....	....	....	....	....	....	....
1985-86	Seattle Thunderbirds	WHL	70	58	70	128	....	....	....	34	....	....	....	....	....	....	....	....	....	....	5	5	1	6	0	....	....	....
1986-87	Seattle Thunderbirds	WHL	17	20	20	40	....	....	....	18	....	....	....	....	....	....	....	....	....	....	....	....	....	....	....	....	....	....
	Regina Pats	WHL	59	49	57	106	....	....	....	16	....	....	....	....	....	....	....	....	....	....	3	5	0	5	4	....	....	....
	Winnipeg Jets	**NHL**	**2**	**0**	**1**	**1**	**0**	**1**	**1**	**0**	**0**	**0**	**0**	**0**	**0.0**	**2**	**0**	**1**	**0**	**+1**	....	....	....	....	....	....	....	....
1987-88	Regina Pats	WHL	69	50	86	136	....	....	....	50	....	....	....	....	....	....	....	....	....	....	4	4	9	13	8	....	....	....
1988-89	Moncton Hawks	AHL	18	3	9	12	....	....	....	16	....	....	....	....	....	....	....	....	....	....	....	....	....	....	....	....	....	....
	Fort Wayne Komets	IHL	34	10	18	28	....	....	....	0	....	....	....	....	....	....	....	....	....	....	10	4	7	11	6	....	....	....
1989-90	Fort Wayne Komets	IHL	20	2	11	13	....	....	....	8	....	....	....	....	....	....	....	....	....	....	....	....	....	....	....	....	....	....
	Adirondack Red Wings	AHL	7	3	3	6	....	....	....	4	....	....	....	....	....	....	....	....	....	....	....	....	....	....	....	....	....	....
1990-91			DID NOT PLAY																									
1991-92	Winston-Salem Thunderbirds	ECHL	54	25	46	71	....	....	....	27	....	....	....	....	....	....	....	....	....	....	4	1	6	7	2	....	....	....
1992-93	Roanoke Valley Rampage	ECHL	37	15	36	51	....	....	....	51	....	....	....	....	....	....	....	....	....	....	....	....	....	....	....	....	....	....
	NHL Totals		**2**	**0**	**1**	**1**	**0**	**1**	**1**	**0**	**0**	**0**	**0**	**0**	**0.0**	**2**	**0**	**1**	**0**		....	....	....	....	....	....	....	....

WHL East Second All-Star Team (1987) • WHL East First All-Star Team (1988)

• ENGBLOM, BRIAN Brian Engblom D – L. 6'2", 200 lbs. b: Winnipeg, Man., 1/27/1957. Montreal's 3rd choice, 22nd overall, in 1975 Amateur Draft.

			REGULAR SEASON																		PLAYOFFS							
Season	Club	League	GP	G	A	Pts	AG	AA	APts	PIM	PP	SH	GW	S	%	TGF	PGF	TGA	PGA	+/–	GP	G	A	Pts	PIM	PP	SH	GW
1972-73	Winnipeg Blues	MJHL	48	17	46	83																						
1973-74	University of Wisconsin	WCHA	36	10	21	31				54																		
1974-75	University of Wisconsin	WCHA	38	13	23	36				58																		
1975-76	Nova Scotia Voyageurs	AHL	73	4	34	38				79											9	1	7	8	26			
1976-77	Nova Scotia Voyageurs	AHL	80	8	42	50				89											11	3	10	13	10			
	Montreal Canadiens	**NHL**																			**2**	**0**	**0**	**0**	**2**			
1977-78	**Montreal Canadiens**	**NHL**	**28**	**1**	**2**	**3**	**1**	**2**	**3**	**23**	**0**	**0**	**0**	**28**	**3.6**	**24**	**0**	**16**	**1**	**+9**	**5**	**0**	**0**	**0**	**2**	**0**	**0**	**0**
	Nova Scotia Voyageurs	AHL	7	1	5	6				4																		
1978-79	**Montreal Canadiens**	**NHL**	**62**	**3**	**11**	**14**	**3**	**8**	**11**	**60**	**0**	**0**	**0**	**60**	**5.0**	**58**	**3**	**38**	**4**	**+21**	**16**	**0**	**1**	**1**	**11**	**0**	**0**	**0**
1979-80	**Montreal Canadiens**	**NHL**	**70**	**3**	**20**	**23**	**3**	**15**	**18**	**43**	**0**	**0**	**0**	**86**	**3.5**	**102**	**4**	**92**	**16**	**+22**	**10**	**2**	**4**	**6**	**6**	**1**	**0**	**1**
1980-81	**Montreal Canadiens**	**NHL**	**80**	**3**	**25**	**28**	**2**	**17**	**19**	**96**	**1**	**0**	**0**	**120**	**2.5**	**138**	**11**	**80**	**16**	**+63**	**3**	**1**	**0**	**1**	**4**	**0**	**0**	**0**
1981-82	Canada	C Cup	5	1	0	1				4																		
	Montreal Canadiens	**NHL**	**76**	**4**	**29**	**33**	**3**	**19**	**22**	**76**	**1**	**0**	**0**	**109**	**3.7**	**167**	**23**	**91**	**25**	**+78**	**5**	**0**	**2**	**2**	**14**	**0**	**0**	**0**
1982-83	**Washington Capitals**	**NHL**	**73**	**5**	**22**	**27**	**4**	**15**	**19**	**59**	**4**	**0**	**0**	**103**	**4.9**	**119**	**22**	**133**	**32**	**–4**	**4**	**0**	**2**	**2**	**2**	**0**	**0**	**0**
	Canada	WEC-A	10	1	2	3				0																		
1983-84	**Washington Capitals**	**NHL**	**6**	**0**	**1**	**1**	**0**	**1**	**1**	**8**	**0**	**0**	**0**	**15**	**0.0**	**6**	**0**	**13**	**3**	**–4**								
	Los Angeles Kings	**NHL**	**74**	**2**	**27**	**29**	**2**	**18**	**20**	**59**	**2**	**0**	**0**	**127**	**1.6**	**120**	**22**	**147**	**40**	**–9**								
1984-85	**Los Angeles Kings**	**NHL**	**79**	**4**	**19**	**23**	**3**	**13**	**16**	**70**	**3**	**0**	**0**	**100**	**4.0**	**99**	**12**	**109**	**20**	**–2**	**3**	**0**	**0**	**0**	**2**	**0**	**0**	**0**
1985-86	**Los Angeles Kings**	**NHL**	**49**	**3**	**13**	**16**	**2**	**9**	**11**	**61**	**0**	**0**	**0**	**53**	**5.7**	**56**	**3**	**98**	**32**	**–13**								
	Buffalo Sabres	**NHL**	**30**	**1**	**4**	**5**	**1**	**3**	**4**	**16**	**0**	**0**	**0**	**24**	**4.2**	**37**	**1**	**43**	**10**	**+3**								
1986-87	**Calgary Flames**	**NHL**	**32**	**0**	**4**	**4**	**0**	**3**	**3**	**28**	**0**	**0**	**0**	**31**	**0.0**	**26**	**0**	**36**	**3**	**–7**								
	NHL Totals		**659**	**29**	**177**	**206**	**24**	**123**	**147**	**599**	**11**	**0**	**0**	**856**	**3.4**	**952**	**101**	**896**	**202**		**48**	**3**	**9**	**12**	**43**	**1**	**0**	**1**

WCHA First All-Star Team (1975) • NCAA West First All-American Team (1975) • AHL First All-Star Team (1977) • Won Eddie Shore Award (Outstanding Defenseman - AHL) (1977) • NHL Plus/Minus Leader (1981) • NHL Second All-Star Team (1982)

Traded to **Washington** by **Montreal** with Rod Langway, Doug Jarvis and Craig Laughlin for Ryan Walter and Rick Green, September 9, 1982. Traded to **LA Kings** by **Washington** with Ken Houston for Larry Murphy, October 18, 1983. Traded to **Buffalo** by **LA Kings** with Doug Smith for Larry Playfair, Seam McKenna and Ken Baumgartner, January 30, 1986. Traded to **Calgary** by **Buffalo** for Jim Korn, October 3, 1986.

• ENGELE, JERRY Jerry Engele D – L. 6', 197 lbs. b: Humboldt, Sask., 11/26/1950.

Season	Club	League	GP	G	A	Pts	AG	AA	APts	PIM	PP	SH	GW	S	%	TGF	PGF	TGA	PGA	+/–	GP	G	A	Pts	PIM	PP	SH	GW
1966-67	Saskatoon Blades	WCJHL	52	1	9	10				62											6	0	0	0	0			
1967-68	Saskatoon Blades	WCJHL	58	0	11	11				153																		
1968-69	Saskatoon Blades	WCJHL	52	0	9	9				155																		
1969-70	Saskatoon Blades	WCJHL	36	0	7	7				164																		
1970-71	Saskatoon Blades	WCJHL	63	2	21	23				181																		
1971-72	St. Petersburg Suns	EHL	72	6	16	22				110											6	1	1	2	19			
1972-73	Sun Coast Suns	EHL	72	7	33	40				171											5	1	0	1	8			
1973-74	Saginaw Gears	IHL	71	1	27	28				150											13	2	5	7	10			
1974-75	New Haven Nighthawks	AHL	75	1	21	22				182											9	0	3	3	44			
1975-76	**Minnesota North Stars**	**NHL**	**17**	**0**	**1**	**1**	**0**	**1**	**1**	**16**	**0**	**0**	**0**	**16**	**0.0**	**3**	**1**	**18**	**4**	**–12**								
	New Haven Nighthawks	AHL	58	1	20	21				232											3	1	0	1	0			
1976-77	**Minnesota North Stars**	**NHL**	**31**	**1**	**7**	**8**	**1**	**6**	**7**	**41**	**0**	**0**	**1**	**36**	**2.8**	**29**	**0**	**29**	**3**	**+3**	**2**	**0**	**1**	**1**	**0**	**0**	**0**	**0**
	New Haven Nighthawks	AHL	52	2	10	12				84																		
1977-78	**Minnesota North Stars**	**NHL**	**52**	**1**	**5**	**6**	**1**	**4**	**5**	**105**	**0**	**1**	**0**	**44**	**2.3**	**37**	**1**	**51**	**5**	**–10**								
	Fort Worth Texans	CHL	3	0	0	0				2																		
1978-79	Nova Scotia Voyageurs	AHL	75	4	24	28				186											9	0	2	2	13			
1979-80	Saskatoon Blades	WHL	DID NOT PLAY – COACHING																									
	NHL Totals		**100**	**2**	**13**	**15**	**2**	**11**	**13**	**162**	**0**	**1**	**1**	**96**	**2.1**	**69**	**2**	**98**	**12**		**2**	**0**	**1**	**1**	**0**	**0**	**0**	**0**

Signed as a free agent by **Minnesota**, June, 1975. Transferred to **Montreal** by **Minnesota** as compensation for Minnesota's signing of free agent Mike Polich, September 6, 1978.

• ENGLISH, JOHN John English D – R. 6'2", 190 lbs. b: Toronto, Ont., 5/13/1966. Los Angeles' 3rd choice, 48th overall, in 1984 Entry Draft.

Season	Club	League	GP	G	A	Pts	AG	AA	APts	PIM	PP	SH	GW	S	%	TGF	PGF	TGA	PGA	+/–	GP	G	A	Pts	PIM	PP	SH	GW
1982-83	St. Michael's Buzzers	Jr. B	34	2	10	12				92																		
1983-84	Sault Ste. Marie Greyhounds	OHL	64	6	11	17				144											16	0	6	6	45			
1984-85	Sault Ste. Marie Greyhounds	OHL	15	0	3	3				61																		
	Hamilton Steelhawks	OHL	41	2	22	24				105											17	3	3	6	43			
1985-86	Hamilton Steelhawks	OHL	12	2	10	12				57																		
	Ottawa 67's	OHL	40	0	28	[illegible]				120																		
1986-87	New Haven Nighthawks	AHL	3	0	0	0				6																		
	Flint Spirits	IHL	18	1	2	3				83											6	1	2	3	12			
1987-88	**Los Angeles Kings**	**NHL**	**3**	**1**	**3**	**4**	**1**	**2**	**3**	**4**	**1**	**0**	**0**	**5**	**20.0**	**6**	**2**	**4**	**2**	**+2**	**1**	**0**	**0**	**0**	**0**	**0**	**0**	**0**
	New Haven Nighthawks	AHL	65	4	22	26				236																		
1988-89	Cape Breton Oilers	AHL	13	0	3	3				80																		
	New Haven Nighthawks	AHL	49	5	19	24				197																		
	NHL Totals		**3**	**1**	**3**	**4**	**1**	**2**	**3**	**4**	**1**	**0**	**0**	**5**	**20.0**	**6**	**2**	**4**	**2**		**1**	**0**	**0**	**0**	**0**	**0**	**0**	**0**

Traded to **Edmonton** by **LA Kings** with Brian Wilks for Jim Weimer and Alan May, March 7, 1989.

• ENNIS, JIM Jim Ennis D – L. 6', 200 lbs. b: Edmonton, Alta., 7/10/1967. Edmonton's 6th choice, 126th overall, in 1986 Entry Draft.

Season	Club	League	GP	G	A	Pts	AG	AA	APts	PIM	PP	SH	GW	S	%	TGF	PGF	TGA	PGA	+/–	GP	G	A	Pts	PIM	PP	SH	GW
1984-85	Sherwood Park Crusaders	AJHL	STATISTICS NOT AVAILABLE																									
1985-86	Boston University	H.E.	40	1	4	5				22																		
1986-87	Boston University	H.E.	26	3	4	7				27																		
1987-88	**Edmonton Oilers**	**NHL**	**5**	**1**	**0**	**1**	**1**	**0**	**1**	**10**	**1**	**0**	**0**	**9**	**11.1**	**4**	**2**	**2**	**0**	**0**								
	Nova Scotia Oilers	AHL	59	8	12	20				102											5	0	1	1	16			
1988-89	Cape Breton Oilers	AHL	67	3	15	18				94																		
1989-90	Binghamton Whalers	AHL	69	3	12	15				61																		
	NHL Totals		**5**	**1**	**0**	**1**	**1**	**0**	**1**	**10**	**1**	**0**	**0**	**9**	**11.1**	**4**	**2**	**2**	**0**									

Traded to **Hartford** by **Edmonton** for Norm MacIver, October 10, 1989.

• ERICKSON, AUT Aut Erickson D – L. 6'1", 188 lbs. b: Lethbridge, Alta., 1/25/1938.

Season	Club	League	GP	G	A	Pts	AG	AA	APts	PIM	PP	SH	GW	S	%	TGF	PGF	TGA	PGA	+/–	GP	G	A	Pts	PIM	PP	SH	GW
1954-55	Lethbridge Native Sons	WCJHL	39	3	2	5				54											11	0	2	2	2			
1955-56	Lethbridge Native Sons	WCJHL	47	6	14	20				68											11	6	2	8	14			
	Saskatoon Quakers	WHL	1	0	0	0				0																		
1956-57	Prince Albert Mintos	SJHL	49	12	15	27				*152											13	4	5	9	4			
1957-58	Prince Albert Mintos	SJHL	47	14	32	46				108											6	0	4	4	7			
	Saskatoon-St. Paul Regals	WHL	2	0	0	0				0																		
1958-59	Calgary Stampeders	WHL	62	4	15	19				93											8	0	1	1	4			
1959-60	**Boston Bruins**	**NHL**	**58**	**1**	**6**	**7**	**1**	**6**	**7**	**29**																		
1960-61	**Boston Bruins**	**NHL**	**68**	**2**	**6**	**8**	**2**	**6**	**8**	**65**																		
1961-62	Buffalo Bisons	AHL	64	7	23	30				[illegible]											11	1	1	2	6			
1962-63	**Chicago Black Hawks**	**NHL**	**3**	**0**	**0**	**0**	**0**	**0**	**0**	**8**																		
	Buffalo Bisons	AHL	68	3	19	22				97											12	0	4	4	25			
1963-64	**Chicago Black Hawks**	**NHL**	**31**	**0**	**1**	**1**	**0**	**1**	**1**	**34**											**6**	**0**	**0**	**0**	**0**			
	Buffalo Bisons	AHL	34	3	13	16				36																		
1964-65	Pittsburgh Hornets	AHL	64	3	19	22				94											4	0	0	0	6			
1965-66	Victoria Cougars	WHL	65	7	14	21				109											14	1	5	6	10			
1966-67	Victoria Cougars	WHL	70	8	28	36				76																		
	Toronto Maple Leafs	**NHL**																			**1**	**0**	**0**	**0**	**2**			
1967-68	**Oakland Seals**	**NHL**	**65**	**4**	**11**	**15**	**5**	**11**	**16**	**46**	**0**	**0**	**0**	**66**	**6.1**	**46**	**4**	**74**	**15**	**–17**								

			REGULAR SEASON																		PLAYOFFS							
Season	Club	League	GP	G	A	Pts	AG	AA	APts	PIM	PP	SH	GW	S	%	TGF	PGF	TGA	PGA	+/–	GP	G	A	Pts	PIM	PP	SH	GW
1968-69	Phoenix Roadrunners	WHL	68	8	29	37	....	....	....	83	....	....	....	....	....	....	....	....	....	....	....	....	....	....	....	....	....	....
1969-70	**Oakland Seals**	**NHL**	**1**	**0**	**0**	**0**	**0**	**0**	**0**	**0**	**0**	**0**	**0**	**1**	**0.0**	**0**	**0**	**2**	**1**	**–1**	....	....	....	....	....	....	....	....
	Phoenix Roadrunners	WHL	18	0	4	4	....	....	....	8	....	....	....	....	....	....	....	....	....	....	....	....	....	....	....	....	....	....
	NHL Totals		**226**	**7**	**24**	**31**	**8**	**24**	**32**	**182**	**0**	**0**	**0**	**67**	**10.4**	**46**	**4**	**76**	**16**		**7**	**0**	**0**	**0**	**2**	**0**	**0**	**0**

WHL Second All-Star Team (1967)

Claimed by **Boston** from **Chicago** in Intra-League Draft, June 10, 1959. Claimed by **Chicago** from **Boston** in Intra-League Draft, June, 1961. Traded to **Detroit** by **Chicago** with Ron Murphy for John Miszuk, Art Stratton and Ian Cushenan, June 9, 1964. Traded to **Toronto** by **Detroit** with Marcel Pronovost, Larry Jeffrey, Ed Joyal and Lowell MacDonald for Billy Harris, Gary Jarrett and Andy Bathgate, May 20, 1965. Claimed by **Oakland** from **Toronto** in Expansion Draft, June 6, 1967.

• ERICKSON, BRYAN

Bryan Erickson RW – R. 5'9", 175 lbs. b: Roseau, MN, 3/7/1960.

Season	Club	League	GP	G	A	Pts	AG	AA	APts	PIM	PP	SH	GW	S	%	TGF	PGF	TGA	PGA	+/–	GP	G	A	Pts	PIM	PP	SH	GW
1978-79	United States	WJC-A	5	2	1	3	....	....	....	6	....	....	....	....	....	....	....	....	....	....	....	....	....	....	....	....	....	....
1979-80	University of Minnesota	WCHA	23	10	15	25	....	....	....	14	....	....	....	....	....	....	....	....	....	....	....	....	....	....	....	....	....	....
	United States	WJC-A	4	2	2	4	....	....	....	2	....	....	....	....	....	....	....	....	....	....	....	....	....	....	....	....	....	....
1980-81	University of Minnesota	WCHA	44	39	47	86	....	....	....	30	....	....	....	....	....	....	....	....	....	....	....	....	....	....	....	....	....	....
1981-82	University of Minnesota	WCHA	35	25	20	45	....	....	....	20	....	....	....	....	....	....	....	....	....	....	....	....	....	....	....	....	....	....
	United States	WEC-A	7	1	1	2	....	....	....	6	....	....	....	....	....	....	....	....	....	....	....	....	....	....	....	....	....	....
1982-83	University of Minnesota	WCHA	42	35	47	82	....	....	....	34	....	....	....	....	....	....	....	....	....	....	....	....	....	....	....	....	....	....
	Hershey Bears	AHL	1	0	1	1	....	....	....	0	....	....	....	....	....	....	....	....	....	....	3	3	0	3	0	....	....	....
1983-84	**Washington Capitals**	**NHL**	**45**	**12**	**17**	**29**	**10**	**12**	**22**	**16**	**4**	**0**	**2**	**66**	**18.2**	**37**	**7**	**20**	**0**	**+10**	**8**	**2**	**3**	**5**	**7**	**1**	**0**	**0**
	Hershey Bears	AHL	31	16	12	28	....	....	....	11	....	....	....	....	....	....	....	....	....	....	....	....	....	....	....	....	....	....
1984-85	United States	C Cup	6	2	2	4	....	....	....	4	....	....	....	....	....	....	....	....	....	....	....	....	....	....	....	....	....	....
	Washington Capitals	**NHL**	**57**	**15**	**13**	**28**	**12**	**9**	**21**	**23**	**1**	**0**	**1**	**79**	**19.0**	**41**	**8**	**25**	**3**	**+11**	....	....	....	....	....	....	....	....
	Binghamton Whalers	AHL	13	6	11	17	....	....	....	8	....	....	....	....	....	....	....	....	....	....	....	....	....	....	....	....	....	....
1985-86	Binghamton Whalers	AHL	7	5	3	8	....	....	....	2	....	....	....	....	....	....	....	....	....	....	....	....	....	....	....	....	....	....
	Los Angeles Kings	**NHL**	**55**	**20**	**23**	**43**	**16**	**15**	**31**	**36**	**6**	**0**	**4**	**108**	**18.5**	**63**	**18**	**58**	**14**	**+1**	....	....	....	....	....	....	....	....
	United States	WEC-A	10	8	1	9	....	....	....	10	....	....	....	....	....	....	....	....	....	....	....	....	....	....	....	....	....	....
	New Haven Nighthawks	AHL	14	8	3	11	....	....	....	11	....	....	....	....	....	....	....	....	....	....	....	....	....	....	....	....	....	....
1986-87	**Los Angeles Kings**	**NHL**	**68**	**20**	**30**	**50**	**17**	**22**	**39**	**26**	**6**	**2**	**4**	**142**	**14.1**	**79**	**34**	**73**	**16**	**–12**	**3**	**1**	**1**	**2**	**0**	**0**	**0**	**0**
	United States	WEC-A	10	4	4	8	....	....	....	8	....	....	....	....	....	....	....	....	....	....	....	....	....	....	....	....	....	....
1987-88	**Los Angeles Kings**	**NHL**	**42**	**6**	**15**	**21**	**5**	**11**	**16**	**20**	**2**	**0**	**0**	**68**	**8.8**	**36**	**15**	**35**	**0**	**–14**	....	....	....	....	....	....	....	....
	New Haven Nighthawks	AHL	3	0	0	0	....	....	....	0	....	....	....	....	....	....	....	....	....	....	....	....	....	....	....	....	....	....
	Pittsburgh Penguins	**NHL**	**11**	**1**	**4**	**5**	**1**	**3**	**4**	**0**	**0**	**0**	**0**	**13**	**7.7**	**8**	**0**	**6**	**0**	**+2**	....	....	....	....	....	....	....	....
1988-89	HC Merano	Italy	38	38	56	94	....	....	....	29	....	....	....	....	....	....	....	....	....	....	....	....	....	....	....	....	....	....
1989-90	Moncton Hawks	AHL	13	4	7	11	....	....	....	4	....	....	....	....	....	....	....	....	....	....	....	....	....	....	....	....	....	....
1990-91	**Winnipeg Jets**	**NHL**	**6**	**0**	**7**	**7**	**0**	**5**	**5**	**0**	**0**	**0**	**0**	**16**	**0.0**	**7**	**4**	**3**	**1**	**+1**	....	....	....	....	....	....	....	....
	Moncton Hawks	AHL	36	18	14	32	....	....	....	16	....	....	....	....	....	....	....	....	....	....	9	9	2	11	6	....	....	....
1991-92	**Winnipeg Jets**	**NHL**	**10**	**2**	**4**	**6**	**2**	**3**	**5**	**0**	**0**	**0**	**1**	**16**	**12.5**	**11**	**1**	**2**	**1**	**+9**	....	....	....	....	....	....	....	....
1992-93	**Winnipeg Jets**	**NHL**	**41**	**4**	**12**	**16**	**3**	**8**	**11**	**14**	**2**	**0**	**1**	**45**	**8.9**	**21**	**5**	**21**	**7**	**+2**	**3**	**0**	**0**	**0**	**0**	**0**	**0**	**0**
	Moncton Hawks	AHL	2	1	1	2	....	....	....	4	....	....	....	....	....	....	....	....	....	....	....	....	....	....	....	....	....	....
1993-94	**Winnipeg Jets**	**NHL**	**16**	**0**	**0**	**0**	**0**	**0**	**0**	**6**	**0**	**0**	**0**	**8**	**0.0**	**0**	**0**	**11**	**4**	**–7**	....	....	....	....	....	....	....	....
	Moncton Hawks	AHL	3	0	1	1	....	....	....	2	....	....	....	....	....	....	....	....	....	....	....	....	....	....	....	....	....	....
	NHL Totals		**351**	**80**	**125**	**205**	**66**	**88**	**154**	**141**	**21**	**2**	**13**	**561**	**14.3**	**303**	**92**	**254**	**46**		**14**	**3**	**4**	**7**	**7**	**1**	**0**	**0**

WCHA Second All-Star Team (1982) • WCHA First All-Star Team (1983)

Signed as a free agent by **Washington**, April 5, 1983. Traded to **LA Kings** by **Washington** for Bruce Shoebottom, October 31, 1985. Traded to **Pittsburgh** by **LA Kings** for Chris Kontos and Pittsburgh's 6th round choice (Micah Aivazoff) in 1988 Entry Draft, February 5, 1988. Signed as a free agent by **Winnipeg**, March 2, 1990.

• ERICKSON, GRANT

Grant Erickson LW. 5'9", 165 lbs. b: Pierceland, Sask., 4/28/1947.

Season	Club	League	GP	G	A	Pts	AG	AA	APts	PIM	PP	SH	GW	S	%	TGF	PGF	TGA	PGA	+/–	GP	G	A	Pts	PIM	PP	SH	GW
1965-66	Estevan Bruins	SJHL	57	30	20	50	....	....	....	....	....	....	....	....	....	....	....	....	....	....	....	....	....	....	....	....	....	....
1966-67	Estevan Bruins	WCJHL	55	35	49	84	....	....	....	49	....	....	....	....	....	....	....	....	....	....	13	6	8	14	8	....	....	....
1967-68	Oklahoma City Blazers	CHL	70	27	34	61	....	....	....	65	....	....	....	....	....	....	....	....	....	....	1	0	1	1	0	....	....	....
1968-69	**Boston Bruins**	**NHL**	**2**	**1**	**0**	**1**	**1**	**0**	**1**	**0**	**0**	**0**	**0**	**2**	**50.0**	**2**	**0**	**0**	**0**	**+2**	....	....	....	....	....	....	....	....
	Oklahoma City Blazers	CHL	64	28	37	65	....	....	....	66	....	....	....	....	....	....	....	....	....	....	4	3	2	5	0	....	....	....
1969-70	**Minnesota North Stars**	**NHL**	**4**	**0**	**0**	**0**	**0**	**0**	**0**	**0**	**0**	**0**	**0**	**4**	**0.0**	**1**	**0**	**4**	**0**	**–3**	....	....	....	....	....	....	....	....
	Iowa Stars	CHL	68	31	38	69	....	....	....	67	....	....	....	....	....	....	....	....	....	....	11	6	3	9	16	....	....	....
1970-71	Cleveland Barons	AHL	57	18	25	43	....	....	....	41	....	....	....	....	....	....	....	....	....	....	8	3	0	3	4	....	....	....
1971-72	Cleveland Barons	AHL	76	26	24	50	....	....	....	45	....	....	....	....	....	....	....	....	....	....	5	0	0	0	4	....	....	....
1972-73	Cleveland Crusaders	WHA	77	15	29	44	....	....	....	23	....	....	....	....	....	....	....	....	....	....	9	2	1	3	2	....	....	....
1973-74	Cleveland Crusaders	WHA	78	23	27	50	....	....	....	26	....	....	....	....	....	....	....	....	....	....	....	....	....	....	....	....	....	....
1974-75	Cleveland Crusaders	WHA	78	12	15	27	....	....	....	24	....	....	....	....	....	....	....	....	....	....	5	0	0	0	0	....	....	....
1975-76	Syracuse Blazers	NAHL	9	5	2	7	....	....	....	6	....	....	....	....	....	....	....	....	....	....	....	....	....	....	....	....	....	....
	Phoenix Roadrunners	WHA	33	4	7	11	....	....	....	6	....	....	....	....	....	....	....	....	....	....	5	0	2	2	0	....	....	....
	Tucson Mavericks	CHL	29	12	10	22	....	....	....	16	....	....	....	....	....	....	....	....	....	....	....	....	....	....	....	....	....	....
1976-77	Rhode Island Reds	AHL	27	3	9	12	....	....	....	11	....	....	....	....	....	....	....	....	....	....	....	....	....	....	....	....	....	....
	Oklahoma City Blazers	CHL	22	6	10	16	....	....	....	2	....	....	....	....	....	....	....	....	....	....	....	....	....	....	....	....	....	....
	NHL Totals		**6**	**1**	**0**	**1**	**1**	**0**	**1**	**0**	**0**	**0**	**0**	**6**	**16.7**	**3**	**0**	**4**	**0**		....	....	....	....	....	....	....	....
	Other Major League Totals		266	54	78	132				79											19	2	3	5	2	....	....	....

Claimed by **Minnesota** from **Boston** in Intra-League Draft, June 11, 1969. Selected by **Calgary-Cleveland** (WHA) in 1972 WHA General Player Draft, February 12, 1972. Traded to **Phoenix** (WHA) by **Cleveland** (WHA) for Rick Newell and Rob Watt, November, 1975. Traded to **Birmingham** (WHA) by **Phoenix** (WHA) for future considerations, August, 1976.

• ERIKSSON, ANDERS

Anders Eriksson D – L. 6'3", 218 lbs. b: Bollnas, Sweden, 1/9/1975. Detroit's 3rd choice, 22nd overall, in 1993 Entry Draft.

Season	Club	League	GP	G	A	Pts	AG	AA	APts	PIM	PP	SH	GW	S	%	TGF	PGF	TGA	PGA	+/–	GP	G	A	Pts	PIM	PP	SH	GW
1992-93	MoDo AIK	Sweden	20	0	2	2	....	....	....	2	....	....	....	....	....	....	....	....	....	....	1	0	0	0	0	....	....	....
1993-94	MoDo AIK	Sweden	38	2	8	10	....	....	....	42	....	....	....	....	....	....	....	....	....	....	11	0	0	0	8	....	....	....
	Sweden	WJC-A	7	1	3	4	....	....	....	10	....	....	....	....	....	....	....	....	....	....	....	....	....	....	....	....	....	....
1994-95	MoDo AIK	Sweden	39	3	6	9	....	....	....	54	....	....	....	....	....	....	....	....	....	....	....	....	....	....	....	....	....	....
	Sweden	WJC-A	7	3	7	10	....	....	....	10	....	....	....	....	....	....	....	....	....	....	....	....	....	....	....	....	....	....
1995-96	**Detroit Red Wings**	**NHL**	**1**	**0**	**0**	**0**	**0**	**0**	**0**	**2**	**0**	**0**	**0**	**0**	**0.0**	**1**	**0**	**0**	**0**	**+1**	**3**	**0**	**0**	**0**	**0**	**0**	**0**	**0**
	Adirondack Red Wings	AHL	75	6	36	42	....	....	....	64	....	....	....	....	....	....	....	....	....	....	3	0	0	0	0	....	....	....
1996-97	**Detroit Red Wings**	**NHL**	**23**	**0**	**6**	**6**	**0**	**5**	**5**	**10**	**0**	**0**	**0**	**27**	**0.0**	**17**	**0**	**13**	**1**	**+5**	....	....	....	....	....	....	....	....
	Adirondack Red Wings	AHL	44	3	25	28	....	....	....	36	....	....	....	....	....	....	....	....	....	....	4	0	1	1	4	....	....	....
1997-98	**Detroit Red Wings**	**NHL**	**66**	**7**	**14**	**21**	**8**	**14**	**22**	**32**	**1**	**0**	**2**	**91**	**7.7**	**58**	**6**	**41**	**10**	**+21**	**18**	**0**	**5**	**5**	**16**	**0**	**0**	**0**
	NHL Totals		**90**	**7**	**20**	**27**	**8**	**19**	**27**	**44**	**1**	**0**	**2**	**118**	**5.9**	**76**	**6**	**54**	**11**		**21**	**0**	**5**	**5**	**16**	**0**	**0**	**0**

WJC-A All-Star Team (1995)

• ERIKSSON, PETER

Peter Eriksson LW – R. 6'4", 218 lbs. b: Kramfors, Sweden, 7/12/1965. Edmonton's 3rd choice, 64th overall, in 1987 Entry Draft.

Season	Club	League	GP	G	A	Pts	AG	AA	APts	PIM	PP	SH	GW	S	%	TGF	PGF	TGA	PGA	+/–	GP	G	A	Pts	PIM	PP	SH	GW
1984-85	Brynas IF	Sweden	34	16	10	26	....	....	....	10	....	....	....	....	....	....	....	....	....	....	....	....	....	....	....	....	....	....
1985-86	HV-71 Jonkoping	Sweden	30	7	8	15	....	....	....	18	....	....	....	....	....	....	....	....	....	....	1	0	0	0	0	....	....	....
1986-87	HV-71 Jonkoping	Sweden	36	14	5	19	....	....	....	16	....	....	....	....	....	....	....	....	....	....	....	....	....	....	....	....	....	....
1987-88	Sweden	C Cup	3	0	0	0	....	....	....	0	....	....	....	....	....	....	....	....	....	....	....	....	....	....	....	....	....	....
	HV-71 Jonkoping	Sweden	37	14	9	23	....	....	....	20	....	....	....	....	....	....	....	....	....	....	2	1	0	1	0	....	....	....
	Sweden	Olympics	3	0	1	1	....	....	....	0	....	....	....	....	....	....	....	....	....	....	....	....	....	....	....	....	....	....
1988-89	HV-71 Jonkoping	Sweden	40	10	27	37	....	....	....	48	....	....	....	....	....	....	....	....	....	....	3	1	2	3	0	....	....	....
	Sweden	WEC-A	7	0	1	1	....	....	....	8	....	....	....	....	....	....	....	....	....	....	....	....	....	....	....	....	....	....
1989-90	**Edmonton Oilers**	**NHL**	**20**	**3**	**3**	**6**	**3**	**2**	**5**	**24**	**1**	**0**	**0**	**23**	**13.0**	**15**	**5**	**11**	**0**	**–1**	....	....	....	....	....	....	....	....
	Cape Breton Oilers	AHL	21	5	12	17	....	....	....	36	....	....	....	....	....	....	....	....	....	....	5	2	2	4	2	....	....	....
1990-91	HV-71 Jonkoping	Sweden	35	15	7	22	....	....	....	58	....	....	....	....	....	....	....	....	....	....	2	1	0	1	2	....	....	....
1991-92	HV-71 Jonkoping	Sweden	34	10	12	22	....	....	....	28	....	....	....	....	....	....	....	....	....	....	3	1	0	1	0	....	....	....
1992-93	HV-71 Jonkoping	Sweden	40	13	15	28	....	....	....	40	....	....	....	....	....	....	....	....	....	....	....	....	....	....	....	....	....	....
1993-94	HV-71 Jonkoping	Sweden	38	6	7	13	....	....	....	34	....	....	....	....	....	....	....	....	....	....	....	....	....	....	....	....	....	....
	NHL Totals		**20**	**3**	**3**	**6**	**3**	**2**	**5**	**24**	**1**	**0**	**0**	**23**	**13.0**	**15**	**5**	**11**	**0**		....	....	....	....	....	....	....	....

Season	Club	League	REGULAR SEASON GP	G	A	Pts	AG	AA	APts	PIM	PP	SH	GW	S	%	TGF	PGF	TGA	PGA	+/–	PLAYOFFS GP	G	A	Pts	PIM	PP	SH	GW

• ERIKSSON, ROLAND

Roland Eriksson C – L. 6′3″, 190 lbs. b: Storatuna, Sweden, 3/1/1954. Minnesota's 8th choice, 131st overall, in 1974 Amateur Draft.

Season	Club	League	GP	G	A	Pts	AG	AA	APts	PIM	PP	SH	GW	S	%	TGF	PGF	TGA	PGA	+/–	GP	G	A	Pts	PIM	PP	SH	GW
1971-72	Tunabro	Sweden	14	5	3	8	....	....	....	6	....	....	....	....	....	....	....	....	....	....	....	....	....	....	....	....	....	....
1972-73	Tunabro	Sweden	14	10	2	12	....	....	....	0	....	....	....	....	....	....	....	....	....	....	6	5	5	10	0	....	....	....
1973-74	Tunabro	Sweden	STATISTICS NOT AVAILABLE																									
	Sweden	WJC-A	5	5	4	9	....	....	....	0	....	....	....	....	....	....	....	....	....	....	....	....	....	....	....	....	....	....
1974-75	Leksands IF	Sweden	28	11	16	27	....	....	....	14	....	....	....	....	....	....	....	....	....	....	5	3	1	4	0	....	....	....
1975-76	Leksands IF	Sweden	36	21	14	35	....	....	....	18	....	....	....	....	....	....	....	....	....	....	10	8	7	15	0	....	....	....
1975-76	Sweden	WEC-A	10	8	7	15	....	....	....	0	....	....	....	....	....	....	....	....	....	....	....	....	....	....	....	....	....	....
1976-77	Sweden	C Cup	5	2	2	4	....	....	....	2	....	....	....	....	....	....	....	....	....	....	....	....	....	....	....	....	....	....
	Minnesota North Stars	**NHL**	**80**	**25**	**44**	**69**	**24**	**36**	**60**	**10**	**10**	**0**	**1**	**249**	**10.0**	**101**	**46**	**85**	**1**	**–29**	**2**	**1**	**0**	**1**	**0**	**0**	**0**	**0**
	Sweden	WEC-A	10	7	6	13	....	....	....	0	....	....	....	....	....	....	....	....	....	....	....	....	....	....	....	....	....	....
1977-78	**Minnesota North Stars**	**NHL**	**78**	**21**	**39**	**60**	**20**	**32**	**52**	**12**	**3**	**0**	**1**	**257**	**8.2**	**85**	**30**	**91**	**7**	**–29**	....	....	....	....	....	....	....	....
	Sweden	WEC-A	10	1	2	3	....	....	....	2	....	....	....	....	....	....	....	....	....	....	....	....	....	....	....	....	....	....
1978-79	**Vancouver Canucks**	**NHL**	**35**	**2**	**12**	**14**	**2**	**9**	**11**	**4**	**0**	**0**	**0**	**69**	**2.9**	**28**	**12**	**28**	**0**	**–12**	....	....	....	....	....	....	....	....
	Winnipeg Jets	WHA	33	5	10	15	....	....	....	2	....	....	....	....	....	....	....	....	....	....	10	1	4	5	0	....	....	....
1979-80	Leksands IF	Sweden	35	18	21	39	....	....	....	12	....	....	....	....	....	....	....	....	....	....	2	3	1	4	0	....	....	....
1980-81	Dusseldorfer EG	Germany	40	31	*55	86	....	....	....	24	....	....	....	....	....	....	....	....	....	....	11	6	15	21	0	....	....	....
	Sweden	WEC-A	8	2	1	3	....	....	....	2	....	....	....	....	....	....	....	....	....	....	....	....	....	....	....	....	....	....
1981-82	Dusseldorfer EG	Germany	37	30	38	68	....	....	....	14	....	....	....	....	....	....	....	....	....	....	....	....	....	....	....	....	....	....
1982-83	Leksands IF	Sweden	36	20	27	47	....	....	....	16	....	....	....	....	....	....	....	....	....	....	....	....	....	....	....	....	....	....
	Sweden	WEC-A	10	2	2	4	....	....	....	2	....	....	....	....	....	....	....	....	....	....	....	....	....	....	....	....	....	....
1983-84	Leksands IF	Sweden	36	20	20	40	....	....	....	20	....	....	....	....	....	....	....	....	....	....	....	....	....	....	....	....	....	....
1984-85	HV-71 Jonkoping	Sweden2	STATISTICS NOT AVAILABLE																									
1985-86	HV-71 Jonkoping	Sweden	35	11	15	26	....	....	....	10	....	....	....	....	....	....	....	....	....	....	2	0	0	0	2	....	....	....
	NHL Totals		**193**	**48**	**95**	**143**	**46**	**77**	**123**	**26**	**13**	**0**	**2**	**575**	**8.3**	**214**	**88**	**204**	**8**		**2**	**1**	**0**	**1**	**0**	**0**	**0**	**0**
	Other Major League Totals		33	5	10	15	....	....	....	2	....	....	....	....	....	....	....	....	....		10	1	4	5	0	....	....	....

WJC-A All-Star Team (1974)

Played in NHL All-Star Game (1978)

Signed as a free agent by **Vancouver**, June 7, 1978. Signed as a free agent by **Winnipeg** (WHA) after being released by **Vancouver**, January, 1979.

• ERIKSSON, THOMAS

Thomas Eriksson D – L. 6′2″, 182 lbs. b: Stockholm, Sweden, 10/16/1959. Philadelphia's 6th choice, 98th overall, in 1979 Entry Draft.

Season	Club	League	GP	G	A	Pts	AG	AA	APts	PIM	PP	SH	GW	S	%	TGF	PGF	TGA	PGA	+/–	GP	G	A	Pts	PIM	PP	SH	GW
1974-75	Djurgarden IF Stockholm	Sweden	11	7	4	11	....	....	....	0	....	....	....	....	....	....	....	....	....	....	....	....	....	....	....	....	....	....
1975-76	Djurgarden IF Stockholm	Sweden	16	6	1	7	....	....	....	8	....	....	....	....	....	....	....	....	....	....	....	....	....	....	....	....	....	....
1976-77	Norsborgs	Sweden	STATISTICS NOT AVAILABLE																									
1977-78	Djurgarden IF Stockholm	Sweden	25	6	4	10	....	....	....	30	....	....	....	....	....	....	....	....	....	....	....	....	....	....	....	....	....	....
1978-79	Djurgarden IF Stockholm	Sweden	35	6	11	17	....	....	....	70	....	....	....	....	....	....	....	....	....	....	....	....	....	....	....	....	....	....
	Sweden	WJC-A	6	2	0	2	....	....	....	13	....	....	....	....	....	....	....	....	....	....	....	....	....	....	....	....	....	....
	Sweden	WEC-A	6	1	1	2	....	....	....	6	....	....	....	....	....	....	....	....	....	....	....	....	....	....	....	....	....	....
1979-80	Djurgarden IF Stockholm	Sweden	36	12	10	22	....	....	....	64	....	....	....	....	....	....	....	....	....	....	....	....	....	....	....	....	....	....
	Sweden	Olympics	7	2	0	2	....	....	....	10	....	....	....	....	....	....	....	....	....	....	....	....	....	....	....	....	....	....
1980-81	**Philadelphia Flyers**	**NHL**	**24**	**1**	**10**	**11**	**1**	**7**	**8**	**14**	**1**	**0**	**0**	**49**	**2.0**	**37**	**15**	**23**	**5**	**+4**	**7**	**0**	**2**	**2**	**6**	**0**	**0**	**0**
	Maine Mariners	AHL	54	11	20	31	....	....		75	....	....	....	....	....	....	....	....	....	....	....	....	....	....	....	....	....	....
1981-82	Sweden	C Cup	3	0	0	0	....	....	....	0	....	....	....	....	....	....	....	....	....	....	....	....	....	....	....	....	....	....
	Philadelphia Flyers	**NHL**	**1**	**0**	**0**	**0**	**0**	**0**	**0**	**4**	**0**	**0**	**0**	**0**	**0.0**	**0**	**0**	**1**	**0**	**–1**	....	....	....	....	....	....	....	....
	Djurgarden IF Stockholm	Sweden	27	7	5	12	....	....	....	48	....	....	....	....	....	....	....	....	....	....	....	....	....	....	....	....	....	....
	Sweden	WEC-A	10	0	0	0	....	....	....	14	....	....	....	....	....	....	....	....	....	....	....	....	....	....	....	....	....	....
1982-83	Djurgarden IF Stockholm	Sweden	32	12	9	21	....	....	....	51	....	....	....	....	....	....	....	....	....	....	8	1	0	1	*26	....	....	....
	Sweden	WEC-A	10	0	1	1	....	....	....	12	....	....	....	....	....	....	....	....	....	....	....	....	....	....	....	....	....	....
1983-84	**Philadelphia Flyers**	**NHL**	**68**	**11**	**33**	**44**	**9**	**22**	**31**	**37**	**2**	**0**	**1**	**110**	**10.0**	**111**	**22**	**80**	**19**	**+28**	**3**	**0**	**1**	**1**	**0**	**0**	**0**	**0**
1984-85	Sweden	C Cup	7	0	3	3	....	....	....	2	....	....	....	....	....	....	....	....	....	....	....	....	....	....	....	....	....	....
	Philadelphia Flyers	**NHL**	**72**	**10**	**20**	**30**	**0**	**20**	**28**	**36**	**4**	**1**	**1**	**125**	**8.0**	**107**	**31**	**67**	**15**	**+24**	**9**	**0**	**0**	**0**	**6**	**0**	**0**	**0**
1985-86	**Philadelphia Flyers**	**NHL**	**43**	**0**	**4**	**4**	**0**	**3**	**3**	**16**	**0**	**0**	**0**	**32**	**0.0**	**15**	**9**	**20**	**2**	**–12**	....	....	....	....	....	....	....	....
1986-87	Djurgarden IF Stockholm	Sweden	34	0	11	10	....	....	....	64	....	....	....	....	....	....	....	....	....	....	....	....	....	....	....	....	....	....
1987-88	Djurgarden IF Stockholm	Sweden	39	13	17	30	....	....	....	36	....	....	....	....	....	....	....	....	....	....	3	0	0	0	2	....	....	....
	Sweden	Olympics	7	0	3	3		....	....	0	....	....	....	....	....	....	....	....	....	....	....	....	....	....	....	....	....	....
1988-89	Djurgarden IF Stockholm	Sweden	38	6	13	19	....	....	....	50	....	....	....	....	....	....	....	....	....	....	8	3	3	6	*20	....	....	....
	Sweden	WEC-A	8	1	1	2	....	....	....	8	....	....	....	....	....	....	....	....	....	....	....	....	....	....	....	....	....	....
1989-90	Djurgarden IF Stockholm	Sweden	39	11	12	23	....	....	....	*106	....	....	....	....	....	....	....	....	....	....	8	2	2	4	*22	....	....	....
	Sweden	WEC-A	9	4	1	5	....	....	....	14	....	....	....	....	....	....	....	....	....	....	....	....	....	....	....	....	....	....
1990-91	Djurgarden IF Stockholm	Sweden	39	16	11	27	....	....	....	62	....	....	....	....	....	....	....	....	....	....	7	3	2	5	12	....	....	....
1991-92	Djurgarden IF Stockholm	Sweden	31	7	7	14	....	....	....	46	....	....	....	....	....	....	....	....	....	....	10	1	0	1	2	....	....	....
1992-93	Djurgarden IF Stockholm	Sweden	37	7	10	17	....	....	....	48	....	....	....	....	....	....	....	....	....	....	6	1	2	3	4	....	....	....
1993-94	Djurgarden IF Stockholm	Sweden	38	5	13	18	....	....	....	46	....	....	....	....	....	....	....	....	....	....	6	1	4	5	....	....	....	....
1994-95	Vasteras IK	Sweden	40	8	7	15	....	....	....	46	....	....	....	....	....	....	....	....	....	....	4	0	1	1	0	....	....	....
	NHL Totals		**208**	**22**	**76**	**98**	**18**	**52**	**70**	**107**	**7**	**1**	**2**	**316**	**7.0**	**270**	**77**	**191**	**41**		**19**	**0**	**3**	**3**	**12**	**0**	**0**	**0**

Swedish World All-Star Team (1980, 1983, 1990, 1991) • NHL All-Rookie Team (1984)

• ERIXON, JAN

Jan "Exit" Erixon LW – L. 6′, 196 lbs. b: Skelleftea, Sweden, 7/8/1962. NY Rangers' 2nd choice, 30th overall, in 1981 Entry Draft.

Season	Club	League	GP	G	A	Pts	AG	AA	APts	PIM	PP	SH	GW	S	%	TGF	PGF	TGA	PGA	+/–	GP	G	A	Pts	PIM	PP	SH	GW
1979-80	Skelleftea AIK	Sweden	15	1	0	1	....	....	....	2	....	....	....	....	....	....	....	....	....	....	....	....	....	....	....	....	....	....
1980-81	Skelleftea AIK	Sweden	32	6	6	12	....	....	....	4	....	....	....	....	....	....	....	....	....	....	3	1	0	1	0	....	....	....
	Sweden	WJC-A	5	1	6	7	....	....	....	2	....	....	....	....	....	....	....	....	....	....	....	....	....	....	....	....	....	....
1981-82	Sweden	C Cup	2	0	0	0	....	....	....	0	....	....	....	....	....	....	....	....	....	....	....	....	....	....	....	....	....	....
	Skelleftea AIK	Sweden	30	7	7	14	....	....	....	26	....	....	....	....	....	....	....	....	....	....	....	....	....	....	....	....	....	....
	Sweden	WEC-A	10	1	4	5	....	....	....	4	....	....	....	....	....	....	....	....	....	....	....	....	....	....	....	....	....	....
1982-83	Skelleftea AIK	Sweden	36	10	19	29	....	....		32	....	....	....	....	....	....	....	....	....	....	....	....	....	....	....	....	....	....
	Sweden	WEC-A	7	4	0	4	....	....	....	8	....	....	....	....	....	....	....	....	....	....	....	....	....	....	....	....	....	....
1983-84	**New York Rangers**	**NHL**	**75**	**5**	**25**	**30**	**4**	**17**	**21**	**16**	**1**	**0**	**0**	**94**	**5.3**	**64**	**5**	**56**	**11**	**+14**	**5**	**2**	**0**	**2**	**4**	**0**	**0**	**1**
1984-85	**New York Rangers**	**NHL**	**66**	**7**	**22**	**29**	**6**	**15**	**21**	**33**	**0**	**1**	**0**	**72**	**9.7**	**53**	**0**	**87**	**23**	**–11**	**2**	**0**	**0**	**0**	**2**	**0**	**0**	**0**
1985-86	**New York Rangers**	**NHL**	**31**	**2**	**17**	**19**	**2**	**11**	**13**	**4**	**0**	**0**	**0**	**33**	**6.1**	**27**	**0**	**29**	**14**	**+12**	**12**	**0**	**1**	**1**	**4**	**0**	**0**	**0**
1986-87	**New York Rangers**	**NHL**	**68**	**8**	**18**	**26**	**7**	**13**	**20**	**24**	**0**	**1**	**1**	**73**	**11.0**	**58**	**5**	**72**	**22**	**+3**	**6**	**1**	**0**	**1**	**0**	**0**	**0**	**0**
1987-88	**New York Rangers**	**NHL**	**70**	**7**	**19**	**26**	**6**	**14**	**20**	**33**	**0**	**1**	**0**	**99**	**7.1**	**42**	**0**	**67**	**28**	**+3**	....	....	....	....	....	....	....	....
1988-89	**New York Rangers**	**NHL**	**44**	**4**	**11**	**15**	**3**	**8**	**11**	**27**	**0**	**0**	**2**	**41**	**9.8**	**27**	**0**	**51**	**21**	**–3**	**4**	**0**	**1**	**1**	**2**	**0**	**0**	**0**
1989-90	**New York Rangers**	**NHL**	**58**	**4**	**9**	**13**	**3**	**6**	**9**	**8**	**0**	**0**	**1**	**61**	**6.6**	**24**	**1**	**59**	**19**	**–17**	**10**	**1**	**0**	**1**	**2**	**0**	**1**	**0**
1990-91	**New York Rangers**	**NHL**	**53**	**7**	**18**	**25**	**6**	**14**	**20**	**8**	**0**	**3**	**0**	**40**	**17.5**	**43**	**0**	**59**	**29**	**+13**	**6**	**1**	**2**	**3**	**0**	**0**	**0**	**0**
1991-92	**New York Rangers**	**NHL**	**46**	**8**	**9**	**17**	**7**	**7**	**14**	**4**	**0**	**1**	**0**	**51**	**15.7**	**32**	**0**	**32**	**13**	**+13**	**13**	**2**	**3**	**5**	**2**	**0**	**1**	**1**
1992-93	**New York Rangers**	**NHL**	**45**	**5**	**11**	**16**	**4**	**8**	**12**	**10**	**0**	**1**	**1**	**36**	**13.9**	**26**	**0**	**29**	**14**	**+11**	....	....	....	....	....	....	....	....
	NHL Totals		**556**	**57**	**159**	**216**	**48**	**113**	**161**	**167**	**1**	**8**	**5**	**600**	**9.5**	**396**	**11**	**541**	**194**		**58**	**7**	**7**	**14**	**16**	**0**	**2**	**2**

WJC-A All-Star Team (1981)

• ERREY, BOB

Bob Errey LW – L. 5′10″, 185 lbs. b: Montreal, Que., 9/21/1964. Pittsburgh's 1st choice, 15th overall, in 1983 Entry Draft.

Season	Club	League	GP	G	A	Pts	AG	AA	APts	PIM	PP	SH	GW	S	%	TGF	PGF	TGA	PGA	+/–	GP	G	A	Pts	PIM	PP	SH	GW
1981-82	Peterborough Petes	OHL	68	29	31	60	....	....	....	39	....	....	....	....	....	....	....	....	....	....	9	3	1	4	9	....	....	....
1982-83	Peterborough Petes	OHL	67	53	47	100	....	....	....	74	....	....	....	....	....	....	....	....	....	....	4	1	3	4	7	....	....	....
1983-84	**Pittsburgh Penguins**	**NHL**	**65**	**9**	**13**	**22**	**7**	**9**	**16**	**29**	**1**	**0**	**0**	**84**	**10.7**	**38**	**5**	**53**	**0**	**–20**	....	....	....	....	....	....	....	....
1984-85	**Pittsburgh Penguins**	**NHL**	**16**	**0**	**2**	**2**	**0**	**1**	**1**	**7**	**0**	**0**	**0**	**12**	**0.0**	**6**	**0**	**14**	**0**	**–8**	....	....	....	....	....	....	....	....
	Baltimore Skipjacks	AHL	59	17	24	41	....	....	....	14	....	....	....	....	....	....	....	....	....	....	8	3	4	7	11	....	....	....
1985-86	**Pittsburgh Penguins**	**NHL**	**37**	**11**	**6**	**17**	**9**	**4**	**13**	**8**	**1**	**0**	**2**	**57**	**19.3**	**26**	**4**	**23**	**2**	**+1**	....	....	....	....	....	....	....	....
	Baltimore Skipjacks	AHL	18	8	7	15	....	....	....	28	....	....	....	....	....	....	....	....	....	....	....	....	....	....	....	....	....	....
1986-87	**Pittsburgh Penguins**	**NHL**	**72**	**16**	**18**	**34**	**14**	**13**	**27**	**40**	**2**	**1**	**1**	**138**	**11.6**	**48**	**6**	**73**	**26**	**–5**	....	....	....	....	....	....	....	....
1987-88	**Pittsburgh Penguins**	**NHL**	**17**	**3**	**6**	**9**	**3**	**4**	**7**	**18**	**0**	**0**	**0**	**18**	**16.7**	**16**	**0**	**12**	**2**	**+6**	....	....	....	....	....	....	....	....
1988-89	**Pittsburgh Penguins**	**NHL**	**76**	**26**	**32**	**58**	**22**	**22**	**44**	**124**	**0**	**3**	**5**	**130**	**20.0**	**104**	**3**	**92**	**31**	**+40**	**11**	**1**	**2**	**3**	**12**	**0**	**0**	**0**
1989-90	**Pittsburgh Penguins**	**NHL**	**78**	**20**	**19**	**39**	**17**	**14**	**31**	**109**	**0**	**1**	**1**	**127**	**15.7**	**70**	**3**	**90**	**26**	**+3**	....	....	....	....	....	....	....	....

			REGULAR SEASON																		PLAYOFFS							
Season	**Club**	**League**	**GP**	**G**	**A**	**Pts**	**AG**	**AA**	**APts**	**PIM**	**PP**	**SH**	**GW**	**S**	**%**	**TGF**	**PGF**	**TGA**	**PGA**	**+/–**	**GP**	**G**	**A**	**Pts**	**PIM**	**PP**	**SH**	**GW**
1990-91	**Pittsburgh Penguins**	**NHL**	**79**	**20**	**22**	**42**	**18**	**17**	**35**	**115**	**0**	**1**	**2**	**131**	**15.3**	**63**	**1**	**72**	**21**	**+11**	**24**	**5**	**2**	**7**	**29**	**0**	**1**	**0**
1991-92	**Pittsburgh Penguins**	**NHL**	**78**	**19**	**16**	**35**	**17**	**12**	**29**	**119**	**0**	**3**	**1**	**122**	**15.6**	**56**	**3**	**72**	**20**	**+1**	**14**	**3**	**0**	**3**	**10**	**0**	**1**	**0**
1992-93	**Pittsburgh Penguins**	**NHL**	**54**	**8**	**6**	**14**	**7**	**4**	**11**	**76**	**0**	**0**	**2**	**79**	**10.1**	**20**	**0**	**33**	**11**	**–2**	....	....	....	....	....	....	....	....
	Buffalo Sabres	**NHL**	**8**	**1**	**3**	**4**	**1**	**2**	**3**	**4**	**0**	**0**	**0**	**9**	**11.1**	**6**	**0**	**4**	**0**	**+2**	**4**	**0**	**1**	**1**	**10**	**0**	**0**	**0**
1993-94	**San Jose Sharks**	**NHL**	**64**	**12**	**18**	**30**	**11**	**14**	**25**	**126**	**5**	**0**	**2**	**89**	**13.5**	**41**	**16**	**54**	**18**	**–11**	**14**	**3**	**2**	**5**	**10**	**1**	**0**	**0**
1994-95	**San Jose Sharks**	**NHL**	**13**	**2**	**2**	**4**	**4**	**3**	**7**	**27**	**0**	**0**	**0**	**19**	**10.5**	**9**	**1**	**5**	**1**	**+4**	....	....	....	....	....	....	....	....
	Detroit Red Wings	**NHL**	**30**	**6**	**11**	**17**	**11**	**16**	**27**	**31**	**0**	**0**	**1**	**53**	**11.3**	**27**	**7**	**16**	**5**	**+9**	**18**	**1**	**5**	**6**	**30**	**1**	**0**	**0**
1995-96	**Detroit Red Wings**	**NHL**	**71**	**11**	**21**	**32**	**11**	**17**	**28**	**66**	**2**	**2**	**2**	**85**	**12.9**	**59**	**4**	**41**	**16**	**+30**	**14**	**0**	**4**	**4**	**8**	**0**	**0**	**0**
1996-97	**Detroit Red Wings**	**NHL**	**36**	**1**	**2**	**3**	**1**	**2**	**3**	**27**	**0**	**0**	**0**	**34**	**2.9**	**9**	**0**	**20**	**8**	**–3**	....	....	....	....	....	....	....	....
	San Jose Sharks	**NHL**	**30**	**3**	**6**	**9**	**3**	**5**	**8**	**20**	**0**	**0**	**0**	**38**	**7.9**	**14**	**0**	**24**	**8**	**–2**	....	....	....	....	....	....	....	....
	Canada	WC-A	11	2	1	3	....	....	....	6	....	....	....	....	....	....	....	....	....	....	....	....	....	....	....	....	....	....
1997-98	**Dallas Stars**	**NHL**	**59**	**2**	**9**	**11**	**2**	**9**	**11**	**46**	**0**	**0**	**0**	**34**	**5.9**	**19**	**0**	**20**	**8**	**+7**	....	....	....	....	....	....	....	....
	New York Rangers	**NHL**	**12**	**0**	**0**	**0**	**0**	**0**	**0**	**7**	**0**	**0**	**0**	**11**	**0.0**	**2**	**1**	**8**	**2**	**–5**	....	....	....	....	....	....	....	....
	NHL Totals		**895**	**170**	**212**	**382**	**158**	**168**	**326**	**1005**	**11**	**11**	**19**	**1270**	**13.4**	**633**	**54**	**726**	**205**		**99**	**13**	**16**	**29**	**109**	**2**	**2**	**0**

OHL First All-Star Team (1983)

Traded to **Buffalo** by **Pittsburgh** for Mike Ramsey, March 22, 1993. Signed as a free agent by **San Jose**, August 17, 1993. Traded to **Detroit** by **San Jose** for Detroit's 5th round choice (Michal Bros) in 1995 Entry Draft, February 27, 1995. Claimed on waivers by **San Jose** from **Detroit**, February 8, 1997. Signed as a free agent by **Dallas**, July 28, 1997. Traded to **NY Rangers** by **Dallas** with Todd Harvey and Dallas' 4th round choice (Boyd Kane) in 1998 Entry Draft for Brian Skrudland, Mike Keane and NY Rangers' 6th round choice (Pavel Patera) in 1998 Entry Draft, March 24, 1998.

• ESAU, LEONARD

Leonard Esau D – R. 6'3", 190 lbs. b: Meadow Lake, Sask., 6/3/1968. Toronto's 5th choice, 86th overall, in 1988 Entry Draft.

Season	Club	League	GP	G	A	Pts	AG	AA	APts	PIM	PP	SH	GW	S	%	TGF	PGF	TGA	PGA	+/–	GP	G	A	Pts	PIM	PP	SH	GW
1988-89	St. Cloud State Huskies	NCAA	35	12	27	39	....	....	....	69	....	....	....	....	....	....	....	....	....	....	....	....	....	....	....	....	....	....
1989-90	St. Cloud State Huskies	NCAA	29	8	11	19	....	....	....	83	....	....	....	....	....	....	....	....	....	....	....	....	....	....	....	....	....	....
1990-91	Newmarket Saints	AHL	76	4	14	18	....	....	....	28	....	....	....	....	....	....	....	....	....	....	....	....	....	....	....	....	....	....
1991-92	**Toronto Maple Leafs**	**NHL**	**2**	**0**	**0**	**0**	**0**	**0**	**0**	**0**	**0**	**0**	**0**	**0**	**0.0**	**0**	**0**	**1**	**1**	**0**	....	....	....	....	....	....	....	....
	St. John's Maple Leafs	AHL	78	9	29	38	....	....	....	68	....	....	....	....	....	....	....	....	....	....	13	0	2	2	14	....	....	....
1992-93	**Quebec Nordiques**	**NHL**	**4**	**0**	**1**	**1**	**0**	**1**	**1**	**2**	**0**	**0**	**0**	**1**	**0.0**	**2**	**0**	**1**	**0**	**+1**	....	....	....	....	....	....	....	....
	Halifax Citadels	AHL	75	11	31	42	....	....	....	79	....	....	....	....	....	....	....	....	....	....	....	....	....	....	....	....	....	....
1993-94	**Calgary Flames**	**NHL**	**6**	**0**	**3**	**3**	**0**	**2**	**2**	**7**	**0**	**0**	**0**	**4**	**0.0**	**6**	**0**	**7**	**0**	**–1**	....	....	....	....	....	....	....	....
	Saint John Flames	AHL	75	12	36	48	....	....	....	129	....	....	....	....	....	....	....	....	....	....	7	2	2	4	6	....	....	....
1994-95	Saint John Flames	AHL	54	13	27	40	....	....	....	73	....	....	....	....	....	....	....	....	....	....	5	0	2	2	0	....	....	....
	Edmonton Oilers	**NHL**	**14**	**0**	**6**	**6**	**0**	**9**	**9**	**15**	**0**	**0**	**0**	**17**	**0.0**	**11**	**4**	**15**	**0**	**–8**	....	....	....	....	....	....	....	....
	Calgary Flames	**NHL**	**1**	**0**	**0**	**0**	**0**	**0**	**0**	**0**	**0**	**0**	**0**	**4**	**0.0**	**0**	**0**	**2**	**0**	**–2**	....	....	....	....	....	....	....	....
	Canada	WC-A	7	0	1	1	....	....	....	2	....	....	....	....	....	....	....	....	....	....	....	....	....	....	....	....	....	....
1995-96	Cincinnati Cyclones	IHL	82	15	21	36	....	....	....	150	....	....	....	....	....	....	....	....	....	....	17	5	6	11	26	....	....	....
1996-97	Milwaukee Admirals	IHL	49	6	16	22	....	....	....	70	....	....	....	....	....	....	....	....	....	....	....	....	....	....	....	....	....	....
	Detroit Vipers	IHL	30	6	8	14	....	....	....	36	....	....	....	....	....	....	....	....	....	....	13	1	4	5	38	....	....	....
1997-98	Milwaukee Admirals	IHL	26	3	9	12	....	....	....	32	....	....	....	....	....	....	....	....	....	....	....	....	....	....	....	....	....	....
	Indianapolis Ice	IHL	55	6	33	39	....	....	....	28	....	....	....	....	....	....	....	....	....	....	5	0	0	0	4	....	....	....
	NHL Totals		**27**	**0**	**10**	**10**	**0**	**12**	**12**	**24**	**0**	**0**	**0**	**26**	**0.0**	**19**	**4**	**26**	**1**		....	....	....	....	....	....	....	....

Traded to **Quebec** by **Toronto** for Ken McRae, July 21, 1992. Signed as a free agent by **Calgary**, September 6, 1993. Claimed by **Edmonton** from **Calgary** in NHL Waiver Draft, January 18, 1995. Claimed on waivers by **Calgary** from **Edmonton**, March 7, 1995. Signed as a free agent by **Florida**, August 31, 1995.

• ESPOSITO, PHIL

Phil Esposito C – L. 6'1", 205 lbs. b: Sault Ste. Marie, Ont., 2/20/1942. **HHOF**

Season	Club	League	GP	G	A	Pts	AG	AA	APts	PIM	PP	SH	GW	S	%	TGF	PGF	TGA	PGA	+/–	GP	G	A	Pts	PIM	PP	SH	GW
1961-62	St. Catharines Teepees	OHA	49	32	39	71	....	....	....	54	....	....	....	....	....	....	....	....	....	....	6	1	4	5	9	....	....	....
	Sault Ste. Marie Thunderbirds	EPHL	6	0	3	3	....	....	....	2	....	....	....	....	....	....	....	....	....	....	....	....	....	....	....	....	....	....
1962-63	St. Louis Braves	EPHL	71	36	54	90	....	....	....	51	....	....	....	....	....	....	....	....	....	....	....	....	....	....	....	....	....	....
1963-64	**Chicago Black Hawks**	**NHL**	**27**	**3**	**2**	**5**	**4**	**2**	**6**	**2**	....	....	....	....	....	....	....	....	....	....	**4**	**0**	**0**	**0**	**0**	....	....	....
	St. Louis Braves	CHL	43	26	54	80	....	....	....	65	....	....	....	....	....	....	....	....	....	....	....	....	....	....	....	....	....	....
1964-65	**Chicago Black Hawks**	**NHL**	**70**	**23**	**32**	**55**	**29**	**35**	**64**	**44**	....	....	....	....	....	....	....	....	....	....	**13**	**3**	**3**	**6**	**15**	....	....	....
1965-66	**Chicago Black Hawks**	**NHL**	**69**	**27**	**26**	**53**	**33**	**26**	**59**	**49**	....	....	....	....	....	....	....	....	....	....	**6**	**1**	**1**	**2**	**2**	....	....	....
1966-67	**Chicago Black Hawks**	**NHL**	**69**	**21**	**40**	**61**	**26**	**41**	**67**	**40**	....	....	....	....	....	....	....	....	....	....	**6**	**0**	**0**	**0**	**7**	....	....	....
1967-68	**Boston Bruins**	**NHL**	**74**	**35**	***49**	**84**	**44**	**52**	**96**	**21**	**9**	**1**	**3**	**284**	**12.3**	**113**	**37**	**69**	**12**	**+19**	**4**	**0**	**3**	**3**	**0**	**0**	**0**	**0**
1968-69	**Boston Bruins**	**NHL**	**74**	**49**	***77**	**126**	**56**	**73**	**129**	**79**	**10**	**2**	**9**	**351**	**14.0**	**164**	**50**	**69**	**11**	**+56**	**10**	***8**	***10**	***18**	**8**	**5**	**2**	**0**
1969-70	**Boston Bruins**	**NHL**	**76**	***43**	**56**	**99**	**50**	**56**	**106**	**50**	**18**	**1**	**5**	**405**	**10.6**	**157**	**80**	**69**	**20**	**+28**	**14**	***13**	***14**	***27**	**16**	**4**	**2**	**0**
1970-71	**Boston Bruins**	**NHL**	**78**	***76**	**76**	***152**	**81**	**68**	**149**	**71**	**25**	**1**	**16**	**550**	**13.8**	**214**	**78**	**72**	**7**	**+71**	**7**	**3**	**7**	**10**	**6**	**2**	**0**	**0**
1971-72	**Boston Bruins**	**NHL**	**76**	***66**	**67**	***133**	**71**	**61**	**132**	**76**	**28**	**2**	**16**	**426**	**15.5**	**186**	**71**	**67**	**7**	**+55**	**15**	**9**	**15**	***24**	**24**	**2**	**0**	**3**
1972-73	Canada	Summit	8	7	6	13	....	....	....	15	....	....	....	....	....	....	....	....	....	....	....	....	....	....	....	....	....	....
	Boston Bruins	**NHL**	**78**	***55**	***75**	***130**	**55**	**63**	**118**	**87**	**19**	**5**	**11**	**411**	**13.4**	**174**	**67**	**117**	**26**	**+16**	**2**	**0**	**1**	**1**	**2**	**0**	**0**	**0**
1973-74	**Boston Bruins**	**NHL**	**78**	**68**	**77**	***145**	**70**	**67**	**137**	**58**	**14**	**4**	**9**	**393**	**17.3**	**201**	**65**	**109**	**24**	**+51**	**16**	**9**	**5**	**14**	**25**	**4**	**0**	**2**
1974-75	**Boston Bruins**	**NHL**	**79**	**61**	**66**	**127**	**57**	**52**	**109**	**62**	**27**	**4**	**8**	**347**	**17.6**	**174**	**79**	**110**	**33**	**+18**	**3**	**4**	**1**	**5**	**0**	**1**	**0**	**0**
1975-76	**Boston Bruins**	**NHL**	**12**	**6**	**10**	**16**	**6**	**8**	**14**	**8**	**3**	**0**	**0**	**57**	**10.5**	**20**	**10**	**16**	**5**	**–1**	....	....	....	....	....	....	....	....
	New York Rangers	**NHL**	**62**	**29**	**38**	**67**	**27**	**30**	**57**	**28**	**16**	**1**	**2**	**217**	**13.4**	**96**	**45**	**104**	**14**	**–39**	....	....	....	....	....	....	....	....
1976-77	Canada	C Cup	7	4	3	7	....	....	....	0	....	....	....	....	....	....	....	....	....	....	....	....	....	....	....	....	....	....
	New York Rangers	**NHL**	**80**	**34**	**46**	**80**	**33**	**37**	**70**	**52**	**15**	**0**	**4**	**344**	**9.9**	**119**	**48**	**114**	**15**	**–28**	....	....	....	....	....	....	....	....
	Canada	WEC-A	10	7	3	10	....	....	....	14	....	....	....	....	....	....	....	....	....	....	....	....	....	....	....	....	....	....
1977-78	**New York Rangers**	**NHL**	**79**	**38**	**43**	**81**	**37**	**35**	**72**	**53**	**21**	**0**	**5**	**259**	**14.7**	**117**	**56**	**98**	**15**	**–22**	**3**	**0**	**1**	**1**	**5**	**0**	**0**	**0**
1978-79	**New York Rangers**	**NHL**	**80**	**42**	**36**	**78**	**38**	**28**	**66**	**37**	**14**	**0**	**7**	**215**	**19.5**	**113**	**35**	**82**	**3**	**–1**	**18**	**8**	**12**	**20**	**20**	**2**	**0**	**2**
1979-80	**New York Rangers**	**NHL**	**80**	**34**	**44**	**78**	**31**	**34**	**65**	**73**	**13**	**0**	**5**	**245**	**13.9**	**118**	**42**	**89**	**0**	**–13**	**9**	**3**	**3**	**6**	**8**	**1**	**0**	**1**
1980-81	**New York Rangers**	**NHL**	**41**	**7**	**13**	**20**	**6**	**9**	**15**	**20**	**3**	**0**	**0**	**91**	**7.7**	**47**	**13**	**54**	**7**	**–13**	....	....	....	....	....	....	....	....
	NHL Totals		**1282**	**717**	**873**	**1590**	**754**	**777**	**1531**	**910**	**235**	**21**	**100**	**4595**	**15.6**	**2013**	**776**	**1239**	**199**		**130**	**61**	**76**	**137**	**138**	**21**	**4**	**8**

NHL Second All-Star Team (1968, 1975) • NHL First All-Star Team (1969, 1970, 1971, 1972, 1973, 1974) • Won Art Ross Trophy (1969, 1971, 1972, 1973, 1974) • Won Hart Trophy (1969, 1974) • Won Lester B. Pearson Award (1971, 1974) • Won Lester Patrick Trophy (1978)

Played in NHL All-Star Game (1969, 1970, 1971, 1972, 1973, 1974, 1975, 1977, 1978, 1980)

Traded to **Boston** by **Chicago** with Ken Hodge and Fred Stanfield for Pit Martin, Jack Norris, and Gilles Marotte, May 15, 1967. Traded to **NY Rangers** by **Boston** with Carol Vadnais for Brad Park, Jean Ratelle and Joe Zanussi, November 7, 1975.

• EVANS, CHRIS

Chris Evans D – L. 5'9", 180 lbs. b: Toronto, Ont., 9/14/1946.

Season	Club	League	GP	G	A	Pts	AG	AA	APts	PIM	PP	SH	GW	S	%	TGF	PGF	TGA	PGA	+/–	GP	G	A	Pts	PIM	PP	SH	GW
1965-66	Markham Waxers	Jr. B	....	12	24	36	....	....	....	....	....	....	....	....	....	....	....	....	....	....	....	....	....	....	....	....	....	....
1966-67	Toronto Marlboros	OHA	48	7	21	28	....	....	....	84	....	....	....	....	....	....	....	....	....	....	17	2	3	5	34	....	....	....
1967-68	Toronto Marlboros	OHA Sr.	39	5	14	19	....	....	....	42	....	....	....	....	....	....	....	....	....	....	....	....	....	....	....	....	....	....
	Tulsa Oilers	CHL	2	0	0	0	....	....	....	0	....	....	....	....	....	....	....	....	....	....	....	....	....	....	....	....	....	....
1968-69	Tulsa Oilers	CHL	70	9	35	44	....	....	....	88	....	....	....	....	....	....	....	....	....	....	7	0	3	3	6	....	....	....
1969-70	**Toronto Maple Leafs**	**NHL**	**2**	**0**	**0**	**0**	**0**	**0**	**0**	**0**	**0**	**0**	**0**	**0**	**0.0**	**0**	**0**	**6**	**1**	**–5**	....	....	....	....	....	....	....	....
	Phoenix Roadrunners	WHL	70	7	16	23	....	....	....	60	....	....	....	....	....	....	....	....	....	....	....	....	....	....	....	....	....	....
1970-71	Kansas City Blues	CHL	71	10	32	42	....	....	....	111	....	....	....	....	....	....	....	....	....	....	....	....	....	....	....	....	....	....
1971-72	**Buffalo Sabres**	**NHL**	**61**	**6**	**18**	**24**	**6**	**16**	**22**	**98**	**2**	**0**	**0**	**99**	**6.1**	**82**	**26**	**91**	**15**	**–20**	....	....	....	....	....	....	....	....
	Cincinnati Swords	AHL	5	0	5	5	....	....	....	2	....	....	....	....	....	....	....	....	....	....	....	....	....	....	....	....	....	....
	St. Louis Blues	**NHL**	**2**	**0**	**0**	**0**	**0**	**0**	**0**	**0**	**0**	**0**	**0**	**0**	**0.0**	**1**	**0**	**1**	**0**	**0**	**7**	**1**	**0**	**1**	**4**	**0**	**0**	**0**
1972-73	**St. Louis Blues**	**NHL**	**77**	**9**	**12**	**21**	**9**	**10**	**19**	**31**	**0**	**2**	**3**	**138**	**6.5**	**44**	**4**	**68**	**26**	**–2**	**5**	**0**	**1**	**1**	**4**	**0**	**0**	**0**
1973-74	**St. Louis Blues**	**NHL**	**54**	**4**	**7**	**11**	**4**	**6**	**10**	**8**	**0**	**1**	**0**	**48**	**8.3**	**14**	**1**	**38**	**30**	**+5**	....	....	....	....	....	....	....	....
	Detroit Red Wings	**NHL**	**23**	**0**	**2**	**2**	**0**	**2**	**2**	**2**	**0**	**0**	**0**	**19**	**0.0**	**5**	**0**	**22**	**13**	**–4**	....	....	....	....	....	....	....	....
1974-75	**Kansas City Scouts**	**NHL**	**2**	**0**	**2**	**2**	**0**	**2**	**2**	**2**	**0**	**0**	**0**	**4**	**0.0**	**3**	**2**	**3**	**1**	**–1**	....	....	....	....	....	....	....	....
	St. Louis Blues	**NHL**	**20**	**0**	**1**	**1**	**0**	**1**	**1**	**2**	**0**	**0**	**0**	**7**	**0.0**	**2**	**0**	**16**	**13**	**–1**	....	....	....	....	....	....	....	....
	Denver Spurs	CHL	31	3	13	16	....	....	....	47	....	....	....	....	....	....	....	....	....	....	2	1	1	2	2	....	....	....
1975-76	Calgary Cowboys	WHA	75	3	20	23	....	....	....	50	....	....	....	....	....	....	....	....	....	....	10	5	5	10	4	....	....	....
1976-77	Calgary Cowboys	WHA	81	7	27	34	....	....	....	60	....	....	....	....	....	....	....	....	....	....	....	....	....	....	....	....	....	....
1977-78	Birmingham Bulls	WHA	12	1	2	3	....	....	....	4	....	....	....	....	....	....	....	....	....	....	....	....	....	....	....	....	....	....
	Quebec Nordiques	WHA	36	0	2	2	....	....	....	22	....	....	....	....	....	....	....	....	....	....	....	....	....	....	....	....	....	....

			REGULAR SEASON																		PLAYOFFS							
Season	Club	League	GP	G	A	Pts	AG	AA	APts	PIM	PP	SH	GW	S	%	TGF	PGF	TGA	PGA	+/–	GP	G	A	Pts	PIM	PP	SH	GW
1978-79	Phoenix Roadrunners	PHL	57	9	41	50				46																		
1979-80			DID NOT PLAY – RETIRED																									
1980-81	Wichita Wind	CHL	6	1	2	3				14																		
	NHL Totals		**241**	**19**	**42**	**61**	**19**	**37**	**56**	**143**	**2**	**3**	**3**	**315**	**6.0**	**151**	**33**	**245**	**99**		**12**	**1**	**1**	**2**	**8**	**0**	**0**	**0**
	Other Major League Totals		204	11	51	62				136											10	5	5	10	4			

Traded to **Phoenix** (WHL) by **Toronto** for cash, May 22, 1970. Claimed by **St. Louis** from **Phoenix** (WHL) in Inter-League Draft, June 9, 1970. Claimed by **Buffalo** from **St. Louis** in Expansion Draft, June 10, 1970. Selected by **New England** (WHA) in 1972 WHA General Player Draft, February 12, 1972. Traded to **St. Louis** by **Buffalo** for George Morrison and St. Louis' 2nd round choice (Larry Carriere) in 1972 Amateur Draft, March 5, 1972. Traded to **Detroit** by **St. Louis** with Bryan Watson and Jean Hamel for Ted Harris, Bill Collins and Garnet Bailey, February 14, 1974. Claimed by **Kansas City** from **Detroit** in Expansion Draft, June 12, 1974. Traded to **St. Louis** by **Kansas City** with Kansas City's 4th round choice (Mike Liut) in 1976 Amateur Draft for Larry Giroux, October 29, 1974. WHA rights traded to **Calgary** (WHA) by **New England** (WHA) for cash, August, 1975. Signed as a free agent by **Edmonton** (WHA) after **Calgary** (WHA) franchise folded, May 31, 1977. Traded to **Birmingham** (WHA) by **Edmonton** (WHA) with Pete Laframboise and Dan Arndt for Lou Nistico and Jeff Jacques, September, 1977. Claimed on waivers by **Quebec** (WHA) from **Birmingham** (WHA), November, 1977.

• EVANS, DARYL

Daryl Evans LW – L. 5'9", 185 lbs. b: Toronto, Ont., 1/12/1961. Los Angeles' 11th choice, 178th overall, in 1980 Entry Draft.

Season	Club	League	GP	G	A	Pts	AG	AA	APts	PIM	PP	SH	GW	S	%	TGF	PGF	TGA	PGA	+/–	GP	G	A	Pts	PIM	PP	SH	GW
1977-78	Seneca Nats	Jr. B	40	25	35	60				50																		
1978-79	Niagara Falls Flyers	OHA	65	38	26	64				110																		
1979-80	Niagara Falls Flyers	OHA	63	43	52	95				47											10	5	13	18	6			
1980-81	Niagara Falls Flyers	OHA	5	3	4	7				11																		
	Brantford Alexanders	OHA	58	58	54	112				50											6	4	5	9	6			
	Saginaw Gears	IHL	3	3	2	5				0																		
1981-82	**Los Angeles Kings**	**NHL**	**14**	**2**	**6**	**8**	**2**	**4**	**6**	**2**	**0**	**0**	**0**	**25**	**8.0**	**13**	**3**	**8**	**0**	**+2**	**10**	**5**	**8**	**13**	**12**	**1**	**0**	**1**
	New Haven Nighthawks	AHL	41	14	14	28				10																		
1982-83	**Los Angeles Kings**	**NHL**	**80**	**18**	**22**	**40**	**15**	**15**	**30**	**21**	**1**	**1**	**0**	**242**	**7.4**	**79**	**28**	**96**	**27**	**–18**								
1983-84	**Los Angeles Kings**	**NHL**	**4**	**0**	**1**	**1**	**0**	**1**	**1**	**0**	**0**	**0**	**0**	**6**	**0.0**	**2**	**1**	**0**	**0**	**+1**								
	New Haven Nighthawks	AHL	69	51	34	85				14																		
1984-85	**Los Angeles Kings**	**NHL**	**7**	**1**	**0**	**1**	**1**	**0**	**1**	**2**	**0**	**0**	**0**	**12**	**8.3**	**3**	**0**	**1**	**0**	**+2**								
	New Haven Nighthawks	AHL	59	22	24	46				12																		
1985-86	**Washington Capitals**	**NHL**	**6**	**0**	**1**	**1**	**0**	**1**	**1**	**0**	**0**	**0**	**0**	**14**	**0.0**	**1**	**1**	**1**	**0**	**–1**								
	Binghamton Whalers	AHL	69	40	52	92				50											5	6	2	8	0			
1986-87	**Toronto Maple Leafs**	**NHL**	**2**	**1**	**0**	**1**	**1**	**0**	**1**	**0**	**1**	**0**	**0**	**2**	**50.0**	**1**	**1**	**2**	**0**	**–2**	**1**	**0**	**0**	**0**	**0**	**0**	**0**	**0**
	Newmarket Saints	AHL	74	27	46	73				17																		
1987-88	Newmarket Saints	AHL	57	29	36	65				10																		
1988-89	Newmarket Saints	AHL	64	29	30	59				16											5	1	1	2	0			
1989-90			DID NOT PLAY																									
1990-91	Whitley Warriors	Britain	6	10	9	19				6											8	18	22	40	6			
	NHL Totals		**113**	**22**	**30**	**52**	**19**	**21**	**40**	**25**	**2**	**1**	**0**	**301**	**7.3**	**99**	**34**	**108**	**27**		**11**	**5**	**8**	**13**	**12**	**1**	**0**	**1**

OHA First All-Star Team (1981) • AHL Second All-Star Team (1984)

Traded to **Washington** by **LA Kings** for Glen Currie, September 9, 1985. Signed as a free agent by **Toronto**, August, 1986.

• EVANS, DOUG

Doug Evans LW – L. 5'9", 185 lbs. b. Peterborough, Ont., 6/2/1963. Winnipeg's 9th choice, 131st overall, in 1989 Entry Draft.

Season	Club	League	GP	G	A	Pts	AG	AA	APts	PIM	PP	SH	GW	S	%	TGF	PGF	TGA	PGA	+/–	GP	G	A	Pts	PIM	PP	SH	GW
1980-81	Peterborough Petes	OHA	51	9	24	33				139																		
1981-82	Peterborough Petes	OHL	56	17	49	66				176											9	0	2	2	41			
1982-83	Peterborough Petes	OHL	65	31	55	86				165											4	0	3	3	23			
1983-84	Peterborough Petes	OHL	61	45	79	124				98											8	4	12	16	26			
1984-85	Peoria Rivermen	IHL	81	36	61	97				189											20	8	11	19	*88			
1985-86	**St. Louis Blues**	**NHL**	**13**	**1**	**0**	**1**	**1**	**0**	**1**	**2**	**0**	**0**	**0**	**12**	**8.3**	**1**	**0**	**1**	**0**	**0**								
	Peoria Rivermen	IHL	60	46	51	97				179											10	4	6	10	32			
1986-87	**St. Louis Blues**	**NHL**	**53**	**3**	**13**	**16**	**3**	**9**	**12**	**91**	**0**	**0**	**0**	**51**	**5.9**	**30**	**0**	**30**	**2**	**+2**	**5**	**0**	**0**	**0**	**10**	**0**	**0**	**0**
	Peoria Rivermen	IHL	18	10	15	25				39																		
1987-88	**St. Louis Blues**	**NHL**	**41**	**5**	**7**	**12**	**4**	**5**	**9**	**49**	**0**	**0**	**1**	**32**	**15.6**	**15**	**0**	**26**	**4**	**–7**	**2**	**0**	**0**	**0**	**0**	**0**	**0**	**0**
	Peoria Rivermen	IHL	11	4	16	20				64																		
1988-89	**St. Louis Blues**	**NHL**	**53**	**7**	**12**	**19**	**6**	**8**	**14**	**81**	**0**	**1**	**0**	**48**	**14.6**	**26**	**0**	**38**	**15**	**+3**	**7**	**1**	**2**	**3**	**16**	**0**	**0**	**0**
1989-90	**St. Louis Blues**	**NHL**	**3**	**0**	**0**	**0**	**0**	**0**	**0**	**0**	**0**	**0**	**0**	**1**	**0.0**	**0**	**0**	**0**	**0**	**0**								
	Peoria Rivermen	IHL	42	19	28	47				128																		
	Winnipeg Jets	**NHL**	**27**	**10**	**8**	**18**	**9**	**6**	**15**	**33**	**2**	**1**	**1**	**36**	**27.8**	**25**	**4**	**17**	**3**	**+7**	**7**	**2**	**2**	**4**	**10**	**0**	**0**	**0**
1990-91	**Winnipeg Jets**	**NHL**	**70**	**7**	**27**	**34**	**6**	**20**	**26**	**108**	**1**	**0**	**0**	**70**	**10.0**	**52**	**8**	**52**	**7**	**–1**								
1991-92	**Winnipeg Jets**	**NHL**	**30**	**7**	**7**	**14**	**6**	**5**	**11**	**68**	**1**	**0**	**0**	**39**	**17.9**	**35**	**16**	**18**	**1**	**+2**	**1**	**0**	**0**	**0**	**2**	**0**	**0**	**0**
	Moncton Hawks	AHL	10	7	8	15				10																		
	Peoria Rivermen	IHL	16	5	14	19				38																		
1992-93	**Philadelphia Flyers**	**NHL**	**65**	**8**	**13**	**21**	**7**	**9**	**16**	**70**	**0**	**0**	**1**	**60**	**13.3**	**33**	**1**	**52**	**11**	**–9**								
1993-94	Peoria Rivermen	IHL	76	27	63	90				108											6	2	6	8	10			
1994-95	Peoria Rivermen	IHL	74	13	39	52				103											9	2	9	11	10			
1995-96	Peoria Rivermen	IHL	74	19	48	67				81											1	0	0	0	0			
1996-97	Peoria Rivermen	ECHL	67	23	59	82				128											10	10	12	22	20			
1997-98	Peoria Rivermen	ECHL	52	27	37	64				98											3	0	1	1	4			
	NHL Totals		**355**	**48**	**87**	**135**	**42**	**62**	**104**	**502**	**4**	**2**	**3**	**349**	**13.8**	**217**	**29**	**234**	**43**		**22**	**3**	**4**	**7**	**38**	**0**	**0**	**0**

IHL First All-Star Team (1986)

Signed as a free agent by **St. Louis**, June 10, 1985. Traded to **Winnipeg** by **St. Louis** for Ron Wilson, January 22, 1990. Traded to **Boston** by **Winnipeg** for Daniel Berthiaume, June 10, 1992. Claimed by **Philadelphia** from **Boston** in Waiver Draft, October 4, 1992.

• EVANS, J. PAUL

J. Paul Evans C – L. 5'9", 185 lbs. b: Toronto, Ont., 5/2/1954. Los Angeles' 3rd choice, 84th overall, in 1974 Amateur Draft.

Season	Club	League	GP	G	A	Pts	AG	AA	APts	PIM	PP	SH	GW	S	%	TGF	PGF	TGA	PGA	+/–	GP	G	A	Pts	PIM	PP	SH	GW
1971-72	Kitchener Rangers	OHA	57	30	38	68				10																		
1972-73	Kitchener Rangers	OHA	63	29	47	76				22																		
1973-74	Kitchener Rangers	OHA	69	52	60	112				45																		
1974-75	Saginaw Gears	IHL	60	21	35	56				42																		
1975-76	Saginaw Gears	IHL	78	32	53	85				65											12	3	10	13	6			
1976-77	Saginaw Gears	IHL	78	50	62	112				53											19	10	*15	25	2			
1977-78	Springfield Indians	AHL	8	4	6	10				6																		
	Maine Mariners	AHL	66	26	35	61				28											12	3	6	9	14			
1978-79	**Philadelphia Flyers**	**NHL**	**44**	**6**	**5**	**11**	**5**	**4**	**9**	**12**	**0**	**0**	**1**	**39**	**15.4**	**14**	**0**	**28**	**11**	**–3**								
	Maine Mariners	AHL	32	16	24	40				36											10	4	*13	*17	10			
1979-80	Maine Mariners	AHL	80	21	56	77				66											12	3	7	10	18			
1980-81	**Philadelphia Flyers**	**NHL**	**1**	**0**	**0**	**0**	**0**	**0**	**0**	**2**	**0**	**0**	**0**	**0**	**0.0**	**0**	**0**	**0**	**0**	**0**								
	Maine Mariners	AHL	78	28	52	80				49											20	4	7	11	36			
1981-82	Maine Mariners	AHL	79	33	57	90				42											4	2	3	5	2			
1982-83	**Philadelphia Flyers**	**NHL**	**58**	**8**	**20**	**28**	**7**	**14**	**21**	**20**	**0**	**1**	**1**	**51**	**15.7**	**45**	**2**	**41**	**14**	**+16**	**1**	**0**	**0**	**0**	**0**	**0**	**0**	**0**
1983-84	Maine Mariners	AHL	76	23	36	59				65											17	3	7	10	4			
1984-85	Maine Mariners	AHL	78	17	36	53				26											11	3	2	5	0			
	NHL Totals		**103**	**14**	**25**	**39**	**12**	**18**	**30**	**34**	**0**	**1**	**2**	**90**	**15.6**	**59**	**2**	**69**	**25**		**1**	**0**	**0**	**0**	**0**	**0**	**0**	**0**

Traded to **Philadelphia** by **LA Kings** to complete transaction that sent Steve Short to LA Kings (June 17, 1977), November 3, 1977.

• EVANS, KEVIN

Kevin Evans LW – L. 5'9", 185 lbs. b: Peterborough, Ont., 7/10/1965.

Season	Club	League	GP	G	A	Pts	AG	AA	APts	PIM	PP	SH	GW	S	%	TGF	PGF	TGA	PGA	+/–	GP	G	A	Pts	PIM	PP	SH	GW
1983-84	Peterborough Bees	Jr. B	39	17	34	51				210																		
1984-85	London Knights	OHL	52	3	7	10				148											6	0	0	0	8			
1985-86	Victoria Cougars	WHL	66	16	39	55				*441																		
	Kalamazoo Wings	IHL	11	3	5	8				97											6	0	0	3	56			
1986-87	Kalamazoo Wings	IHL	73	19	31	50				*648											3	1	0	1	24			
1987-88	Kalamazoo Wings	IHL	54	9	28	37				404											5	1	1	2	46			
1988-89	Kalamazoo Wings	IHL	50	22	34	56				326																		
1989-90	Kalamazoo Wings	IHL	76	30	54	84				346											10	8	4	12	86			

			REGULAR SEASON																		PLAYOFFS							
Season	Club	League	GP	G	A	Pts	AG	AA	APts	PIM	PP	SH	GW	S	%	TGF	PGF	TGA	PGA	+/–	GP	G	A	Pts	PIM	PP	SH	GW
1990-91	**Minnesota North Stars**	**NHL**	**4**	**0**	**0**	**0**	**0**	**0**	**0**	**19**	**0**	**0**	**0**	**2**	**0.0**	**0**	**0**	**3**	**0**	**–3**	....	....	....	....	....	....	....	....
	Kalamazoo Wings	IHL	16	10	12	22	....	....	....	70	....	....	....	....	....	....	....	....	....	....	....	....	....	....	....	....	....	....
1991-92	**San Jose Sharks**	**NHL**	**5**	**0**	**1**	**1**	**0**	**1**	**1**	**25**	**0**	**0**	**0**	**4**	**0.0**	**1**	**0**	**1**	**0**	**0**	....	....	....	....	....	....	....	....
	Kansas City Blades	IHL	66	10	39	49	....	....	....	342	....	....	....	....	....	....	....	....	....	....	14	2	*13	15	70	....	....	....
1992-93	Kalamazoo Wings	IHL	49	7	24	31	....	....	....	283	....	....	....	....	....	....	....	....	....	....	....	....	....	....	....	....	....	....
1993-94	Peoria Rivermen	IHL	67	10	29	39	....	....	....	254	....	....	....	....	....	....	....	....	....	....	4	0	0	0	6	....	....	....
1994-95	Peoria Rivermen	IHL	29	5	9	14	....	....	....	121	....	....	....	....	....	....	....	....	....	....	....	....	....	....	....	....	....	....
	Kansas City Blades	IHL	26	3	6	9	....	....	....	192	....	....	....	....	....	....	....	....	....	....	19	2	4	6	*111	....	....	....
1995-96	Memphis RiverKings	CHL	38	11	32	43	....	....	....	356	....	....	....	....	....	....	....	....	....	....	6	2	9	11	48	....	....	....
1996-97	Mississippi Sea Wolves	ECHL	63	19	27	46	....	....	....	505	....	....	....	....	....	....	....	....	....	....	3	1	1	2	21	....	....	....
1997-98	Mississippi Sea Wolves	ECHL	38	8	18	26	....	....	....	234	....	....	....	....	....	....	....	....	....	....	....	....	....	....	....	....	....	....
	NHL Totals		**9**	**0**	**1**	**1**	**0**	**1**	**1**	**44**	**0**	**0**	**0**	**6**	**0.0**	**1**	**0**	**4**	**0**		....	....	....	....	....	....	....	....

Signed as a free agent by **Minnesota**, August 8, 1988. Claimed by **San Jose** from **Minnesota** in Dispersal Draft, May 30, 1991. Signed as a free agent by **Minnesota**, July 20, 1992.

• EVANS, PAUL E.

Paul E. Evans C/LW – L. 5'11", 175 lbs. b: Peterborough, Ont., 2/24/1955. Toronto's 8th choice, 149th overall, in 1975 Amateur Draft.

Season	Club	League	GP	G	A	Pts	AG	AA	APts	PIM	PP	SH	GW	S	%	TGF	PGF	TGA	PGA	+/–	GP	G	A	Pts	PIM	PP	SH	GW
1973-74	Peterborough Petes	OHA	67	15	30	45	....	....	....	181	....	....	....	....	....	....	....	....	....	....	....	....	....	....	....	....	....	....
	Canada	WJC-A	5	1	0	1	....	....	....	8	....	....	....	....	....	....	....	....	....	....	....	....	....	....	....	....	....	....
1974-75	Peterborough Petes	OHA	70	25	70	95	....	....	....	192	....	....	....	....	....	....	....	....	....	....	....	....	....	....	....	....	....	....
1975-76	Oklahoma City Blazers	CHL	67	7	23	30	....	....	....	179	....	....	....	....	....	....	....	....	....	....	4	0	1	1	24	....	....	....
1976-77	**Toronto Maple Leafs**	**NHL**	**7**	**1**	**1**	**2**	**1**	**1**	**2**	**19**	**0**	**0**	**0**	**10**	**10.0**	**5**	**1**	**1**	**0**	**+3**	**2**	**0**	**0**	**0**	**0**	**0**	**0**	**0**
	Dallas Black Hawks	CHL	71	18	46	64	....	....	....	163	....	....	....	....	....	....	....	....	....	....	5	0	2	2	15	....	....	....
1977-78	**Toronto Maple Leafs**	**NHL**	**4**	**0**	**0**	**0**	**0**	**0**	**0**	**2**	**0**	**0**	**0**	**0**	**0.0**	**0**	**0**	**1**	**0**	**–1**	....	....	....	....	....	....	....	....
	Dallas Black Hawks	CHL	74	16	39	55	....	....	....	116	....	....	....	....	....	....	....	....	....	....	13	1	11	12	20	....	....	....
1978-79	Saginaw Gears	IHL	11	0	11	11	....	....	....	24	....	....	....	....	....	....	....	....	....	....	....	....	....	....	....	....	....	....
	Flint Generals	IHL	38	7	27	34	....	....	....	93	....	....	....	....	....	....	....	....	....	....	....	....	....	....	....	....	....	....
	NHL Totals		**11**	**1**	**1**	**2**	**1**	**1**	**2**	**21**	**0**	**0**	**0**	**10**	**10.0**	**5**	**1**	**2**	**0**		**2**	**0**	**0**	**0**	**0**	**0**	**0**	**0**

IHL First All-Star Team (1977) • AHL Second All-Star Team (1981)

• EVANS, SHAWN

Shawn Evans D – L. 6'3", 195 lbs. b: Kingston, Ont., 9/7/1965. New Jersey's 8th choice, 24th overall, in 1983 Entry Draft.

Season	Club	League	GP	G	A	Pts	AG	AA	APts	PIM	PP	SH	GW	S	%	TGF	PGF	TGA	PGA	+/–	GP	G	A	Pts	PIM	PP	SH	GW
1981-82	Kitchener MW Juniors	Jr. B	21	9	13	22	....	....	....	55	....	....	....	....	....	....	....	....	....	....	....	....	....	....	....	....	....	....
1982-83	Peterborough Petes	OHL	58	7	41	48	....	....	....	116	....	....	....	....	....	....	....	....	....	....	4	2	0	2	12	....	....	....
1983-84	Peterborough Petes	OHL	67	21	88	109	....	....	....	116	....	....	....	....	....	....	....	....	....	....	8	1	16	17	8	....	....	....
1984-85	Peterborough Petes	OHL	66	16	83	99	....	....	....	78	....	....	....	....	....	....	....	....	....	....	16	6	18	24	6	....	....	....
1985-86	**St. Louis Blues**	**NHL**	**7**	**0**	**0**	**0**	**0**	**0**	**0**	**2**	**0**	**0**	**0**	**1**	**0.0**	**2**	**0**	**3**	**0**	**–1**	....	....	....	....	....	....	....	....
	Peoria Rivermen	IHL	55	8	26	34	....	....	....	36	....	....	....	....	....	....	....	....	....	....	....	....	....	....	....	....	....	....
1986-87	Nova Scotia Oilers	AHL	55	7	28	35	....	....	....	29	....	....	....	....	....	....	....	....	....	....	5	0	4	4	6	....	....	....
1987-88	Nova Scotia Oilers	AHL	79	8	62	70	....	....	....	109	....	....	....	....	....	....	....	....	....	....	5	1	1	2	40	....	....	....
1988-89	Springfield Indians	AHL	68	9	50	59	....	....	....	125	....	....	....	....	....	....	....	....	....	....	....	....	....	....	....	....	....	....
1989-90	**New York Islanders**	**NHL**	**2**	**1**	**0**	**1**	**1**	**0**	**1**	**0**	**1**	**0**	**0**	**4**	**25.0**	**3**	**2**	**3**	**1**	**–1**	....	....	....	....	....	....	....	....
	Springfield Indians	AHL	63	6	35	41	....	....	....	102	....	....	....	....	....	....	....	....	....	....	18	6	11	17	35	....	....	....
1990-91	Maine Mariners	AHL	51	9	37	46	....	....	....	44	....	....	....	....	....	....	....	....	....	....	2	0	1	1	0	....	....	....
1991-92	Springfield Indians	AHL	80	11	67	78	....	....	....	81	....	....	....	....	....	....	....	....	....	....	11	0	8	8	16	....	....	....
1992-93	Milwaukee Admirals	IHL	79	13	65	78	....	....	....	83	....	....	....	....	....	....	....	....	....	....	6	0	3	3	6	....	....	....
1993-94	Milano HC	Italy	21	2	12	14	....	....	....	26	....	....	....	....	....	....	....	....	....	....	....	....	....	....	....	....	....	....
1994-95	Milwaukee Admirals	IHL	58	6	34	40	....	....	....	20	....	....	....	....	....	....	....	....	....	....	....	....	....	....	....	....	....	....
	Fort Wayne Komets	IHL	11	2	8	10	....	....	....	6	....	....	....	....	....	....	....	....	....	....	4	1	3	4	2	....	....	....
1995-96	Fort Wayne Komets	IHL	81	5	61	66	....	....	....	78	....	....	....	....	....	....	....	....	....	....	5	3	3	6	2	....	....	....
1996-97	Fort Wayne Komets	IHL	41	7	13	20	....	....	....	34	....	....	....	....	....	....	....	....	....	....	....	....	....	....	....	....	....	....
	Manitoba Moose	IHL	17	2	3	5	....	....	....	4	....	....	....	....	....	....	....	....	....	....	....	....	....	....	....	....	....	....
	Cincinnati Cyclones	IHL	21	3	9	12	....	....	....	24	....	....	....	....	....	....	....	....	....	....	3	0	0	0	14	....	....	....
1997-98	Baton Rouge Kingfish	ECHL	49	5	17	22	....	....	....	40	....	....	....	....	....	....	....	....	....	....	....	....	....	....	....	....	....	....
	Cincinnati Cyclones	IHL	3	0	0	0	....	....	....	2	....	....	....	....	....	....	....	....	....	....	....	....	....	....	....	....	....	....
	NHL Totals		**9**	**1**	**0**	**1**	**1**	**0**	**1**	**2**	**1**	**0**	**0**	**5**	**20.0**	**5**	**2**	**6**	**1**		....	....	....	....	....	....	....	....

OHL Second All-Star Team (1984) • AHL First All-Star Team (1992) • IHL First All-Star Team (1993)

Traded to **St. Louis** by **New Jersey** with New Jersey's 5th round choice (Michael Wolak) in 1986 Entry Draft for Mark Johnson, September 19, 1985. Traded to **Edmonton** by **St. Louis** for Todd Ewen, October 15, 1986. Signed as a free agent by **NY Islanders**, June 20, 1988. Signed as a free agent by **Boston**, December 17, 1990. Signed as a free agent by **Hartford**, August 15, 1991.

• EVASON, DEAN

Dean Evason C – R. 5'10", 180 lbs. b: Flin Flon, Man., 8/22/1964. Washington's 3rd choice, 89th overall, in 1982 Entry Draft.

Season	Club	League	GP	G	A	Pts	AG	AA	APts	PIM	PP	SH	GW	S	%	TGF	PGF	TGA	PGA	+/–	GP	G	A	Pts	PIM	PP	SH	GW
1980-81	Spokane Chiefs	WHL	3	1	1	2	....	....	....	0	....	....	....	....	....	....	....	....	....	....	....	....	....	....	....	....	....	....
1981-82	Spokane Chiefs	WHL	26	8	14	22	....	....	....	65	....	....	....	....	....	....	....	....	....	....	....	....	....	....	....	....	....	....
	Kamloops Blazers	WHL	44	21	55	76	....	....	....	47	....	....	....	....	....	....	....	....	....	....	4	2	1	3	0	....	....	....
1982-83	Kamloops Blazers	WHL	70	71	93	164	....	....	....	102	....	....	....	....	....	....	....	....	....	....	7	5	7	12	18	....	....	....
1983-84	Kamloops Blazers	WHL	57	49	88	137	....	....	....	89	....	....	....	....	....	....	....	....	....	....	17	*21	20	41	33	....	....	....
	Canada	WJC-A	7	6	3	9	....	....	....	0	....	....	....	....	....	....	....	....	....	....	....	....	....	....	....	....	....	....
	Washington Capitals	**NHL**	**2**	**0**	**0**	**0**	**0**	**0**	**0**	**2**	**0**	**0**	**0**	**0**	**0.0**	**0**	**0**	**0**	**0**	**0**	....	....	....	....	....	....	....	....
1984-85	**Washington Capitals**	**NHL**	**15**	**3**	**4**	**7**	**2**	**3**	**5**	**2**	**0**	**0**	**1**	**18**	**16.7**	**11**	**0**	**2**	**0**	**+9**	....	....	....	....	....	....	....	....
	Hartford Whalers	**NHL**	**2**	**0**	**0**	**0**	**0**	**0**	**0**	**0**	**0**	**0**	**1**	**13**	**0.0**	**6**	**0**	**0**	**0**	**+6**	....	....	....	....	....	....	....	....
	Binghamton Whalers	AHL	65	27	49	76	....	....	....	38	....	....	....	....	....	....	....	....	....	....	8	3	5	8	9	....	....	....
1985-86	**Hartford Whalers**	**NHL**	**55**	**20**	**28**	**48**	**16**	**19**	**35**	**65**	**5**	**2**	**4**	**101**	**19.8**	**69**	**21**	**51**	**6**	**+3**	**10**	**1**	**4**	**5**	**10**	**0**	**0**	**0**
	Binghamton Whalers	AHL	26	9	17	26	....	....	....	29	....	....	....	....	....	....	....	....	....	....	....	....	....	....	....	....	....	....
1986-87	**Hartford Whalers**	**NHL**	**80**	**22**	**37**	**59**	**19**	**27**	**46**	**67**	**7**	**2**	**2**	**124**	**17.7**	**83**	**19**	**89**	**30**	**+5**	**5**	**3**	**2**	**5**	**35**	**0**	**0**	**0**
1987-88	**Hartford Whalers**	**NHL**	**77**	**10**	**18**	**28**	**9**	**13**	**22**	**115**	**6**	**0**	**0**	**126**	**7.9**	**44**	**15**	**80**	**22**	**–29**	**6**	**1**	**1**	**2**	**2**	**0**	**0**	**0**
1988-89	**Hartford Whalers**	**NHL**	**67**	**11**	**17**	**28**	**9**	**12**	**21**	**60**	**0**	**0**	**0**	**95**	**11.6**	**38**	**1**	**58**	**12**	**–9**	**4**	**1**	**2**	**3**	**10**	**0**	**1**	**0**
1989-90	**Hartford Whalers**	**NHL**	**78**	**18**	**25**	**43**	**16**	**18**	**34**	**138**	**2**	**2**	**2**	**150**	**12.0**	**61**	**4**	**76**	**26**	**+7**	**7**	**2**	**2**	**4**	**22**	**0**	**0**	**0**
1990-91	**Hartford Whalers**	**NHL**	**75**	**6**	**23**	**29**	**5**	**17**	**22**	**170**	**1**	**0**	**0**	**85**	**7.1**	**39**	**3**	**70**	**28**	**–6**	**6**	**0**	**4**	**4**	**29**	**0**	**0**	**0**
1991-92	**San Jose Sharks**	**NHL**	**74**	**11**	**15**	**26**	**10**	**11**	**21**	**99**	**1**	**0**	**1**	**88**	**12.5**	**39**	**9**	**67**	**15**	**–22**	....	....	....	....	....	....	....	....
1992-93	**San Jose Sharks**	**NHL**	**84**	**12**	**19**	**31**	**10**	**13**	**23**	**132**	**3**	**0**	**1**	**107**	**11.2**	**47**	**13**	**111**	**42**	**–35**	....	....	....	....	....	....	....	....
1993-94	**Dallas Stars**	**NHL**	**80**	**11**	**33**	**44**	**10**	**25**	**35**	**66**	**3**	**2**	**2**	**118**	**9.3**	**66**	**22**	**82**	**26**	**–12**	**9**	**0**	**2**	**2**	**12**	**0**	**0**	**0**
1994-95	**Dallas Stars**	**NHL**	**47**	**8**	**7**	**15**	**14**	**10**	**24**	**48**	**1**	**0**	**0**	**53**	**15.1**	**28**	**2**	**40**	**17**	**+3**	**5**	**1**	**2**	**3**	**12**	**0**	**1**	**0**
1995-96	**Calgary Flames**	**NHL**	**67**	**7**	**7**	**14**	**7**	**6**	**13**	**38**	**1**	**0**	**1**	**68**	**10.3**	**21**	**4**	**50**	**27**	**–6**	**3**	**0**	**1**	**1**	**0**	**0**	**0**	**0**
1996-97	Canada	Nat-Team	56	25	46	71	....	....	....	106	....	....	....	....	....	....	....	....	....	....	....	....	....	....	....	....	....	....
	EV Zug	Switz.	3	0	1	1	....	....	....	2	....	....	....	....	....	....	....	....	....	....	4	0	2	2	4	....	....	....
	Canada	WC-A	11	2	3	5	....	....	....	20	....	....	....	....	....	....	....	....	....	....	....	....	....	....	....	....	....	....
1997-98	EV Landshut	Germany	47	7	23	30	....	....	....	52	....	....	....	....	....	....	....	....	....	....	6	0	3	3	18	....	....	....
	NHL Totals		**803**	**139**	**233**	**372**	**127**	**174**	**301**	**1002**	**30**	**8**	**15**	**1146**	**12.1**	**552**	**113**	**776**	**251**		**55**	**9**	**20**	**29**	**132**	**0**	**2**	**0**

WHL West First All-Star Team (1984)

Traded to **Hartford** by **Washington** with Peter Sidorkiewicz for David Jensen, March 12, 1985. Traded to **San Jose** by **Hartford** for Dan Keczmer, October 2, 1991. Traded to **Dallas** by **San Jose** for San Jose's 6th round choice (previously acquired, San Jose selected Petri Varis) in 1993 Entry Draft, June 26, 1993. Signed as a free agent by **Calgary**, August 1, 1995.

• EWEN, TODD

Todd Ewen RW – R. 6'2", 230 lbs. b: Saskatoon, Sask., 3/22/1966. Edmonton's 9th choice, 168th overall, in 1984 Entry Draft. **HHOF**

Season	Club	League	GP	G	A	Pts	AG	AA	APts	PIM	PP	SH	GW	S	%	TGF	PGF	TGA	PGA	+/–	GP	G	A	Pts	PIM	PP	SH	GW
1982-83	Kamloops Blazers	WHL	3	0	0	0	....	....	....	2	....	....	....	....	....	....	....	....	....	....	2	0	0	0	0	....	....	....
1983-84	New Westminster Bruins	WHL	68	11	13	24	....	....	....	176	....	....	....	....	....	....	....	....	....	....	7	2	1	3	15	....	....	....
1984-85	New Westminster Bruins	WHL	56	11	20	31	....	....	....	304	....	....	....	....	....	....	....	....	....	....	10	1	8	9	60	....	....	....
1985-86	New Westminster Bruins	WHL	60	28	24	52	....	....	....	289	....	....	....	....	....	....	....	....	....	....	....	....	....	....	....	....	....	....
	Maine Mariners	AHL	....	....	....	....	....	....	....	....	....	....	....	....	....	....	....	....	....	....	3	0	0	0	7	....	....	....
1986-87	**St. Louis Blues**	**NHL**	**23**	**2**	**0**	**2**	**2**	**0**	**2**	**84**	**0**	**0**	**0**	**11**	**18.2**	**4**	**0**	**5**	**0**	**–1**	**4**	**0**	**0**	**0**	**23**	**0**	**0**	**0**
	Peoria Rivermen	IHL	16	3	3	6	....	....	....	110	....	....	....	....	....	....	....	....	....	....	....	....	....	....	....	....	....	....
1987-88	**St. Louis Blues**	**NHL**	**64**	**4**	**2**	**6**	**3**	**1**	**4**	**227**	**0**	**0**	**0**	**38**	**10.5**	**8**	**0**	**13**	**0**	**–5**	**6**	**0**	**0**	**0**	**21**	**0**	**0**	**0**
1988-89	**St. Louis Blues**	**NHL**	**34**	**4**	**5**	**9**	**3**	**4**	**7**	**171**	**0**	**0**	**0**	**22**	**18.2**	**14**	**0**	**10**	**0**	**+4**	**2**	**0**	**0**	**0**	**21**	**0**	**0**	**0**

			REGULAR SEASON																		PLAYOFFS							
Season	Club	League	GP	G	A	Pts	AG	AA	APts	PIM	PP	SH	GW	S	%	TGF	PGF	TGA	PGA	+/–	GP	G	A	Pts	PIM	PP	SH	GW
1989-90	St. Louis Blues	NHL	3	0	0	0	0	0	0	11	0	0	0	3	0.0	0	0	2	0	–2	....	....	....	....	....	....	....	....
	Peoria Rivermen	IHL	2	0	0	0	....	....	....	12	....	....	....	....	....	....	....	....	....	....	....	....	....	....	....	....	....	....
	Montreal Canadiens	NHL	41	4	6	10	3	4	7	158	0	0	2	26	15.4	14	0	13	0	+1	10	0	0	0	4	0	0	0
1990-91	Montreal Canadiens	FrTour	2	0	0	0	....	....	....	20	....	....	....	....	....	....	....	....	....	....	....	....	....	....	....	....	....	....
	Montreal Canadiens	NHL	28	3	2	5	3	2	5	128	0	0	0	13	23.1	11	1	6	0	+4	....	....	....	....	....	....	....	....
1991-92	Montreal Canadiens	NHL	46	1	2	3	1	1	2	130	0	0	0	19	5.3	6	0	4	1	+3	3	0	0	0	18	0	0	0
1992-93	Montreal Canadiens	NHL	75	5	9	14	4	6	10	193	0	0	1	59	8.5	27	0	22	1	+6	1	0	0	0	0	0	0	0
1993-94	Anaheim Mighty Ducks	NHL	76	9	9	18	8	7	15	272	0	0	2	59	15.3	31	3	35	0	–7	....	....	....	....	....	....	....	....
1994-95	Anaheim Mighty Ducks	NHL	24	0	0	0	0	0	0	90	0	0	0	14	0.0	6	0	8	0	–2	....	....	....	....	....	....	....	....
1995-96	Anaheim Mighty Ducks	NHL	53	4	3	7	4	2	6	285	0	0	1	52	7.7	11	0	16	0	–5	....	....	....	....	....	....	....	....
1996-97	San Jose Sharks	NHL	51	0	2	2	0	2	2	162	0	0	0	22	0.0	4	0	9	0	–5	....	....	....	....	....	....	....	....
	NHL Totals		518	36	40	76	31	29	60	1911	0	0	6	338	10.7	136	4	143	2		26	0	0	0	87	0	0	0

Traded to **St. Louis** by **Edmonton** for Shawn Evans, October 15, 1986. Traded to **Montreal** by **St. Louis** for future considerations, December 12, 1989. Traded to **Anaheim** by **Montreal** with Patrik Carnback for Anaheim's 3rd round choice (Chris Murray) in 1994 Entry Draft, August 10, 1993. Signed as a free agent by **San Jose**, September 4, 1996.

• FAIRBAIRN, BILL

Bill Fairbairn RW – R. 5'10", 170 lbs. b: Brandon, Man., 1/7/1947.

Season	Club	League	GP	G	A	Pts	AG	AA	APts	PIM	PP	SH	GW	S	%	TGF	PGF	TGA	PGA	+/–	GP	G	A	Pts	PIM	PP	SH	GW
1963-64	Brandon Wheat Kings	MJHL	4	1	1	2	....	....	....	2	....	....	....	....	....	....	....	....	....	....	2	1	0	1	0	....	....	....
1964-65	Brandon Wheat Kings	SJHL	55	28	31	59	....	....	....	26	....	....	....	....	....	....	....	....	....	....	9	6	5	11	11	....	....	....
1965-66	Brandon Wheat Kings	SJHL	60	36	76	112	....	....	....	94	....	....	....	....	....	....	....	....	....	....	13	12	17	29	31	....	....	....
1966-67	Brandon Wheat Kings	WCJHL	55	60	82	142	....	....	....	75	....	....	....	....	....	....	....	....	....	....	13	12	17	29	31	....	....	....
	Omaha Knights	CHL	3	0	0	0	....	....	....	2	....	....	....	....	....	....	....	....	....	....	....	....	....	....	....	....	....	....
1967-68	Omaha Knights	CHL	70	23	33	56	....	....	....	46	....	....	....	....	....	....	....	....	....	....	....	....	....	....	....	....	....	....
1968-69	New York Rangers	NHL	1	0	0	0	0	0	0	0	0	0	0	1	0.0	0	0	1	0	–1	....	....	....	....	....	....	....	....
	Omaha Knights	CHL	68	28	47	75	....	....	....	62	....	....	....	....	....	....	....	....	....	....	7	3	6	9	9	....	....	....
1969-70	New York Rangers	NHL	76	23	33	56	27	33	60	23	3	0	5	153	15.0	88	17	47	0	+24	6	0	1	1	10	0	0	0
1970-71	New York Rangers	NHL	56	7	23	30	7	20	27	32	2	0	1	88	8.0	47	13	38	0	–4	4	0	0	0	0	0	0	0
1971-72	New York Rangers	NHL	78	22	37	59	23	34	57	53	2	4	6	139	15.8	87	12	55	16	+36	16	5	7	12	11	2	0	1
1972-73	New York Rangers	NHL	78	30	33	63	30	28	58	23	5	2	5	174	17.2	102	15	73	22	+36	10	1	8	9	2	0	0	0
1973-74	New York Rangers	NHL	78	18	44	62	18	38	56	12	4	3	3	185	9.7	94	21	88	26	+11	13	3	5	8	6	0	0	0
1974-75	New York Rangers	NHL	80	24	37	61	22	29	51	10	7	2	3	191	12.6	96	24	84	25	+13	3	4	0	4	13	2	1	0
1975-76	New York Rangers	NHL	80	13	15	28	12	12	24	8	2	1	2	160	8.1	54	4	94	30	–14	....	....	....	....	....	....	....	....
1976-77	New York Rangers	NHL	9	1	2	3	1	2	3	0	0	0	0	10	10.0	6	0	10	5	+1	....	....	....	....	....	....	....	....
	Minnesota North Stars	NHL	51	9	20	29	9	16	25	2	0	2	2	83	10.8	55	6	66	16	–1	2	0	1	1	0	0	0	0
1977-78	Minnesota North Stars	NHL	6	0	1	1	0	1	1	0	0	0	0	7	0.0	4	0	7	2	–1	....	....	....	....	....	....	....	....
	St. Louis Blues	NHL	60	14	16	30	13	13	26	10	2	1	1	82	17.1	44	4	72	9	–23	....	....	....	....	....	....	....	....
1978-79	St. Louis Blues	NHL	5	1	0	1	1	0	1	0	0	0	0	8	12.5	1	0	7	4	–2	....	....	....	....	....	....	....	....
	NHL Totals		658	162	261	423	163	226	389	173	27	15	28	1281	12.6	678	116	642	155		54	13	22	35	42	4	1	1

CHL Second All-Star Team (1969)

Traded to **Minnesota** by **NY Rangers** with Nick Beverly for Bill Goldsworthy, November 11, 1976. Claimed on waivers by **St. Louis** from **Minnesota**, October 24, 1977.

• FAIRCHILD, KELLY

Kelly Fairchild C – L. 5'11", 180 lbs. b. Hibbing, MN, 4/9/1973. Los Angeles' 6th choice, 152nd overall, in 1991 Entry Draft.

Season	Club	League	GP	G	A	Pts	AG	AA	APts	PIM	PP	SH	GW	S	%	TGF	PGF	TGA	PGA	+/–	GP	G	A	Pts	PIM	PP	SH	GW
1990-91	Grand Rapids High	H.S.	28	12	17	29	....	....	....	25	....	....	....	....	....	....	....	....	....	....	....	....	....	....	....	....	....	....
1991-92	University of Wisconsin	WCHA	37	11	10	21	....	....	....	45	....	....	....	....	....	....	....	....	....	....	....	....	....	....	....	....	....	....
1992-93	University of Wisconsin	WCHA	42	25	29	54	....	....	....	54	....	....	....	....	....	....	....	....	....	....	....	....	....	....	....	....	....	....
1993-94	University of Wisconsin	WCHA	42	20	44	*64	....	....	....	81	....	....	....	....	....	....	....	....	....	....	....	....	....	....	....	....	....	....
1994-95	St. John's Maple Leafs	AHL	53	27	23	50	....	....	....	51	....	....	....	....	....	....	....	....	....	....	4	0	2	2	4	....	....	....
1995-96	Toronto Maple Leafs	NHL	1	0	1	1	0	1	1	2	0	0	0	1	0.0	1	0	0	0	+1	....	....	....	....	....	....	....	....
	St. John's Maple Leafs	AHL	78	29	49	78	....	....	....	85	....	....	....	....	....	....	....	....	....	....	2	0	1	1	4	....	....	....
1996-97	Toronto Maple Leafs	NHL	22	0	2	2	0	2	2	2	0	0	0	14	0.0	6	1	11	1	–5	....	....	....	....	....	....	....	....
	St. John's Maple Leafs	AHL	29	9	22	31	....	....	....	36	....	....	....	....	....	....	....	....	....	....	....	....	....	....	....	....	....	....
	Orlando Solar Bears	IHL	25	9	6	15	....	....	....	20	....	....	....	....	....	....	....	....	....	....	9	6	5	11	16	....	....	....
1997-98	St. John's Maple Leafs	AHL	17	5	2	7	....	....	....	24	....	....	....	....	....	....	....	....	....	....	....	....	....	....	....	....	....	....
	Orlando Solar Bears	IHL	22	2	6	8	....	....	....	20	....	....	....	....	....	....	....	....	....	....	....	....	....	....	....	....	....	....
	Milwaukee Admirals	IHL	40	20	24	44	....	....	....	32	....	....	....	....	....	....	....	....	....	....	10	5	2	7	4	....	....	....
	NHL Totals		23	0	3	3	0	3	3	4	0	0	0	15	0.0	7	1	11	1		....	....	....	....	....	....	....	....

WCHA First All-Star Team (1994)

Traded to **Toronto** by **LA Kings** with Dixon Ward, Guy Leveque and Shayne Toporowski for Eric Lacroix, Chris Snell and Toronto's 4th round choice (Eric Belanger) in 1996 Entry Draft, October 3, 1994. Signed as a free agent by **Dallas**, July 2, 1998.

• FALKENBERG, BOB

Bob "Steady" Falkenberg D – R. 6', 185 lbs. b: Stettler, Alta., 1/1/1946.

Season	Club	League	GP	G	A	Pts	AG	AA	APts	PIM	PP	SH	GW	S	%	TGF	PGF	TGA	PGA	+/–	GP	G	A	Pts	PIM	PP	SH	GW
1963-64	Edmonton Oil Kings	SJHL	14	3	12	15	....	....	....	0	....	....	....	....	....	....	....	....	....	....	....	....	....	....	....	....	....	....
1964-65	Edmonton Oil Kings	CAHL	STATISTICS NOT AVAILABLE																									
1965-66	Edmonton Oil Kings	ASHL	25	5	8	13	....	....	....	57	....	....	....	....	....	....	....	....	....	....	....	....	....	....	....	....	....	....
	Memphis Wings	CHL	3	0	1	1	....	....	....	0	....	....	....	....	....	....	....	....	....	....	....	....	....	....	....	....	....	....
1966-67	Detroit Red Wings	NHL	16	1	1	2	1	1	2	10	....	....	....	....	....	....	....	....	....	....	....	....	....	....	....	....	....	....
	Pittsburgh Hornets	AHL	53	2	15	17	....	....	....	28	....	....	....	....	....	....	....	....	....	....	....	....	....	....	....	....	....	....
1967-68	Detroit Red Wings	NHL	20	0	3	3	0	3	3	10	0	0	0	14	0.0	11	0	13	0	–2	....	....	....	....	....	....	....	....
	Fort Worth Wings	CHL	48	2	13	15	....	....	....	57	....	....	....	....	....	....	....	....	....	....	....	....	....	....	....	....	....	....
1968-69	Detroit Red Wings	NHL	5	0	0	0	0	0	0	0	0	0	0	0	0.0	0	0	3	0	–3	....	....	....	....	....	....	....	....
	Baltimore Clippers	AHL	4	0	1	1	....	....		0	....	....	....	....	....	....	....	....	....	....	....	....	....	....	....	....	....	....
	Fort Worth Wings	CHL	51	2	8	10	....	....	....	26	....	....	....	....	....	....	....	....	....	....	....	....	....	....	....	....	....	....
1969-70	Cleveland Barons	AHL	58	1	17	18	....	....	....	57	....	....	....	....	....	....	....	....	....	....	....	....	....	....	....	....	....	....
1970-71	Detroit Red Wings	NHL	9	0	1	1	0	1	1	6	0	0	0	4	0.0	2	0	6	1	–3	....	....	....	....	....	....	....	....
	Fort Worth Wings	CHL	61	2	31	33	....	....	....	118	....	....	....	....	....	....	....	....	....	....	4	0	2	2	2	....	....	....
1971-72	Detroit Red Wings	NHL	4	0	0	0	0	0	0	0	0	0	0	3	0.0	3	0	1	0	+2	....	....	....	....	....	....	....	....
	Tidewater Wings	AHL	74	4	21	25	....	....	....	57	....	....	....	....	....	....	....	....	....	....	....	....	....	....	....	....	....	....
1972-73	Alberta Oilers	WHA	76	6	23	29	....	....	....	44	....	....	....	....	....	....	....	....	....	....	....	....	....	....	....	....	....	....
1973-74	Edmonton Oilers	WHA	78	3	14	17	....	....	....	32	....	....	....	....	....	....	....	....	....	....	5	0	2	2	14	....	....	....
1974-75	San Diego Mariners	WHA	78	2	18	20	....	....	....	42	....	....	....	....	....	....	....	....	....	....	10	0	1	1	4	....	....	....
1975-76	San Diego Mariners	WHA	79	3	13	16	....	....	....	31	....	....	....	....	....	....	....	....	....	....	11	1	2	3	6	....	....	....
1976-77	San Diego Mariners	WHA	64	0	6	6	....	....	....	34	....	....	....	....	....	....	....	....	....	....	2	0	0	0	0	....	....	....
1977-78	Edmonton Oilers	WHA	2	0	0	0	....	....	....	0	....	....	....	....	....	....	....	....	....	....	....	....	....	....	....	....	....	....
	NHL Totals		54	1	5	6	1	5	6	26	0	0	0	21	4.8	16	0	23	1		....	....	....	....	....	....	....	....
	Other Major League Totals		377	14	74	88	....	....	....	183	....	....	....	....	....	....	....	....	....		28	1	5	6	24	....	....	....

Selected by **Alberta** (WHA) in the 1972 WHA General Player Draft, February 12, 1972. Traded to **San Diego** (WHA) by **Edmonton** (WHA) to complete transaction that sent Bobby Sheehan to Edmonton, May, 1974. Signed as a free agent by **Edmonton** (WHA) after **San Diego** (WHA) franchise folded, October, 1978.

• FALLOON, PAT

Pat Falloon RW – R. 5'11", 190 lbs. b: Foxwarren, Man., 9/22/1972. San Jose's 1st choice, 2nd overall, in 1991 Entry Draft.

Season	Club	League	GP	G	A	Pts	AG	AA	APts	PIM	PP	SH	GW	S	%	TGF	PGF	TGA	PGA	+/–	GP	G	A	Pts	PIM	PP	SH	GW
1988-89	Spokane Chiefs	WHL	72	22	56	78	....	....	....	41	....	....	....	....	....	....	....	....	....	....	....	....	....	....	....	....	....	....
1989-90	Spokane Chiefs	WHL	71	60	64	124	....	....	....	48	....	....	....	....	....	....	....	....	....	....	6	5	8	13	4	....	....	....
1990-91	Spokane Chiefs	WHL	61	64	74	100	....	....	....	33	....	....	....	....	....	....	....	....	....	....	15	10	14	24	10	....	....	....
1991-92	San Jose Sharks	NHL	79	25	34	59	23	26	49	16	5	0	1	181	13.8	85	29	92	4	–32	....	....	....	....	....	....	....	....
	Canada	WC-A	6	2	1	3	....	....	....	2	....	....	....	....	....	....	....	....	....	....	....	....	....	....	....	....	....	....
1992-93	San Jose Sharks	NHL	41	14	14	28	12	10	22	12	5	1	1	131	10.7	38	13	53	3	–25	....	....	....	....	....	....	....	....
1993-94	San Jose Sharks	NHL	83	22	31	53	21	24	45	18	6	0	1	193	11.4	82	26	61	2	–3	14	1	2	3	6	0	0	0
1994-95	San Jose Sharks	NHL	46	12	7	19	21	10	31	25	0	0	3	91	13.2	28	3	29	0	–4	11	3	1	4	0	0	0	0
1995-96	San Jose Sharks	NHL	9	3	0	3	3	0	3	4	0	0	0	18	16.7	7	1	7	0	–1	....	....	....	....	....	....	....	....
	Philadelphia Flyers	NHL	62	22	26	48	22	21	43	6	9	0	2	152	14.5	64	27	22	0	+15	12	3	2	5	2	2	0	0

Season	Club	League	GP	G	A	Pts	AG	AA	APts	PIM	PP	SH	GW	S	%	TGF	PGF	TGA	PGA	+/–	GP	G	A	Pts	PIM	PP	SH	GW
			REGULAR SEASON																		PLAYOFFS							
1996-97	**Philadelphia Flyers**	**NHL**	**52**	**11**	**12**	**23**	**12**	**11**	**23**	**10**	**2**	**0**	**4**	**124**	**8.9**	**32**	**10**	**30**	**0**	**–8**	**14**	**3**	**1**	**4**	**2**	**1**	**0**	**0**
1997-98	**Philadelphia Flyers**	**NHL**	**30**	**5**	**7**	**12**	**6**	**7**	**13**	**8**	**1**	**0**	**0**	**63**	**7.9**	**22**	**8**	**11**	**0**	**+3**	....	....	....	....	....	....	....	....
	Ottawa Senators	**NHL**	**28**	**3**	**3**	**6**	**4**	**3**	**7**	**8**	**2**	**0**	**0**	**73**	**4.1**	**10**	**5**	**16**	**0**	**–11**	**1**	**0**	**0**	**0**	**0**	**0**	**0**	**0**
	NHL Totals		**430**	**117**	**134**	**251**	**124**	**112**	**236**	**107**	**30**	**1**	**12**	**1026**	**11.4**	**368**	**122**	**321**	**9**		**52**	**10**	**6**	**16**	**10**	**3**	**0**	**0**

WHL West Second All-Star Team (1989) • WHL West First All-Star Team (1991) • Canadian Major Junior Most Sportsmanlike Player of the Year (1991) • Memorial Cup All-Star Team (1991) • Won Stafford Smythe Memorial Trophy (Memorial Cup Tournament MVP) (1991)

Traded to **Philadelphia** by **San Jose** for Martin Spanhel, Philadelphia's 1st round choice (later traded to Phoenix — Phoenix selected Daniel Briere) in 1996 Entry Draft and Philadelphia's 4th round choice (later traded to Buffalo — Buffalo selected Mike Martone), in 1996 Entry Draft, November 16, 1995. Traded to **Ottawa** by **Philadelphia** with Vaclav Prospal and Dallas' 2nd round choice (previously acquired, Ottawa selected Chris Bala) in 1998 Entry Draft for Alexandre Daigle, January 17, 1998.

• FARRISH, DAVE

Dave Farrish D – L. 6'1", 195 lbs. b: Wingham, Ont., 8/1/1956. NY Rangers' 2nd choice, 24th overall, in 1976 Amateur Draft.

Season	Club	League	GP	G	A	Pts	AG	AA	APts	PIM	PP	SH	GW	S	%	TGF	PGF	TGA	PGA	+/–	GP	G	A	Pts	PIM	PP	SH	GW
1973-74	Sudbury Wolves	OHA	58	11	20	31	....	....	....	205	....	....	....	....	....	....	....	....	....	....	....	....	....	....	....	....	....	....
1974-75	Sudbury Wolves	OHA	60	20	44	64	....	....	....	258	....	....	....	....	....	....	....	....	....	....	14	3	4	7	32	....	....	....
1975-76	Sudbury Wolves	OHA	66	26	49	75	....	....	....	155	....	....	....	....	....	....	....	....	....	....	17	3	12	15	22	....	....	....
1976-77	**New York Rangers**	**NHL**	**80**	**2**	**17**	**19**	**2**	**14**	**16**	**102**	**0**	**0**	**0**	**116**	**1.7**	**74**	**0**	**99**	**9**	**–16**	....	....	....	....	....	....	....	....
1977-78	**New York Rangers**	**NHL**	**66**	**3**	**5**	**8**	**3**	**4**	**7**	**62**	**0**	**1**	**0**	**100**	**3.0**	**66**	**1**	**89**	**11**	**–13**	**3**	**0**	**0**	**0**	**0**	**0**	**0**	**0**
	New Haven Nighthawks	AHL	10	0	3	3	....	....	....	4	....	....	....	....	....	....	....	....	....	....	....	....	....	....	....	....	....	....
1978-79	**New York Rangers**	**NHL**	**71**	**1**	**19**	**20**	**1**	**14**	**15**	**61**	**0**	**0**	**1**	**96**	**1.0**	**80**	**2**	**105**	**24**	**–3**	**7**	**0**	**2**	**2**	**14**	**0**	**0**	**0**
1979-80	**Quebec Nordiques**	**NHL**	**4**	**0**	**0**	**0**	**0**	**0**	**0**	**0**	**0**	**0**	**0**	**2**	**0.0**	**0**	**0**	**1**	**1**	**0**	....	....	....	....	....	....	....	....
	Syracuse Firebirds	AHL	14	4	10	14	....	....	....	17	....	....	....	....	....	....	....	....	....	....	....	....	....	....	....	....	....	....
	Toronto Maple Leafs	**NHL**	**20**	**1**	**8**	**9**	**1**	**6**	**7**	**30**	**0**	**0**	**0**	**32**	**3.1**	**29**	**2**	**28**	**6**	**+5**	**3**	**0**	**0**	**0**	**10**	**0**	**0**	**0**
	New Brunswick Hawks	AHL	20	3	1	4	....	....	....	22	....	....	....	....	....	....	....	....	....	....	....	....	....	....	....	....	....	....
1980-81	**Toronto Maple Leafs**	**NHL**	**74**	**2**	**18**	**20**	**2**	**13**	**15**	**90**	**1**	**0**	**0**	**110**	**1.8**	**83**	**15**	**85**	**10**	**–7**	**1**	**0**	**0**	**0**	**0**	**0**	**0**	**0**
1981-82	New Brunswick Hawks	AHL	67	13	24	37	....	....	....	80	....	....	....	....	....	....	....	....	....	....	15	4	5	9	20	....	....	....
1982-83	**Toronto Maple Leafs**	**NHL**	**56**	**4**	**24**	**28**	**3**	**17**	**20**	**38**	**3**	**0**	**0**	**91**	**4.4**	**77**	**33**	**59**	**16**	**+1**	....	....	....	....	....	....	....	....
	St. Catharines Saints	AHL	14	2	12	14	....	....	....	18	....	....	....	....	....	....	....	....	....	....	....	....	....	....	....	....	....	....
1983-84	**Toronto Maple Leafs**	**NHL**	**59**	**4**	**19**	**23**	**3**	**13**	**16**	**57**	**1**	**0**	**0**	**77**	**5.2**	**63**	**27**	**59**	**10**	**–13**	....	....	....	....	....	....	....	....
	St. Catharines Saints	AHL	4	0	2	2	....	....	....	6	....	....	....	....	....	....	....	....	....	....	7	0	1	1	4	....	....	....
1984-85	St. Catharines Saints	AHL	68	4	12	16	....	....	....	56	....	....	....	....	....	....	....	....	....	....	....	....	....	....	....	....	....	....
1985-86	Hershey Bears	AHL	74	5	17	22	....	....	....	78	....	....	....	....	....	....	....	....	....	....	18	0	4	4	24	....	....	....
1986-87	HC Riessersee	Germany	26	7	10	17	....	....	....	74	....	....	....	....	....	....	....	....	....	....	....	....	....	....	....	....	....	....
	HC Davos	Switz.	....	8	9	17	....	....	....	....	....	....	....	....	....	....	....	....	....	....	....	2	*8	10	....	....	....	....
1987-88	VSV Villach	Austria	33	8	43	51	....	....	....	33	....	....	....	....	....	....	....	....	....	....	....	....	....	....	....	....	....	....
	New Haven Nighthawks	AHL	30	4	14	18	....	....	....	26	....	....	....	....	....	....	....	....	....	....	....	....	....	....	....	....	....	....
1988-89	Baltimore Skipjacks	AHL	60	2	13	15	....	....	....	62	....	....	....	....	....	....	....	....	....	....	....	....	....	....	....	....	....	....
1989-90	Moncton Hawks	AHL	1	0	0	0	....	....	....	0	....	....	....	....	....	....	....	....	....	....	....	....	....	....	....	....	....	....
	NHL Totals		**430**	**17**	**110**	**127**	**15**	**81**	**96**	**440**	**5**	**1**	**1**	**624**	**2.7**	**472**	**80**	**525**	**87**		**14**	**0**	**2**	**2**	**24**	**0**	**0**	**0**

OHA First All-Star Team (1976) • AHL First All-Star Team (1982) • Won Eddie Shore Award (Outstanding Defenseman - AHL) (1982)

Claimed by **Quebec** from **NY Rangers** in Expansion Draft, June 13, 1979. Traded to **Toronto** by **Quebec** with Terry Martin for Reggie Thomas, December 13, 1979. Signed as a free agent by **Philadelphia**, October 7, 1985.

• FAUBERT, MARIO

Mario Faubert D – R. 6'1", 175 lbs. b: Valleyfield, Que., 12/2/1954. Pittsburgh's 3rd choice, 62nd overall, in 1974 Amateur Draft.

Season	Club	League	GP	G	A	Pts	AG	AA	APts	PIM	PP	SH	GW	S	%	TGF	PGF	TGA	PGA	+/–	GP	G	A	Pts	PIM	PP	SH	GW
1972-73	St. Louis University	CCHA	38	3	36	39	....	....	....	68	....	....	....	....	....	....	....	....	....	....	....	....	....	....	....	....	....	....
1973-74	St. Louis University	CCHA	40	8	35	43	....	....	....	62	....	....	....	....	....	....	....	....	....	....	....	....	....	....	....	....	....	....
1974-75	**Pittsburgh Penguins**	**NHL**	**10**	**1**	**0**	**1**	**1**	**0**	**1**	**6**	**1**	**0**	**0**	**13**	**7.7**	**4**	**1**	**5**	**0**	**–2**	....	....	....	....	....	....	....	....
	Hershey Bears	AHL	54	13	21	34	....	....	....	76	....	....	....	....	....	....	....	....	....	....	11	2	7	9	4	....	....	....
1975-76	**Pittsburgh Penguins**	**NHL**	**21**	**1**	**8**	**9**	**1**	**6**	**7**	**10**	**1**	**0**	**0**	**22**	**4.5**	**26**	**5**	**19**	**4**	**+6**	....	....	....	....	....	....	....	....
	Hershey Bears	AHL	39	7	16	23	....	....	....	37	....	....	....	....	....	....	....	....	....	....	10	4	6	10	14	....	....	....
1976-77	**Pittsburgh Penguins**	**NHL**	**47**	**2**	**11**	**13**	**2**	**9**	**11**	**32**	**0**	**0**	**0**	**67**	**3.0**	**35**	**13**	**29**	**3**	**–4**	**3**	**1**	**0**	**1**	**2**	**1**	**0**	**0**
	Hershey Bears	AHL	32	8	19	27	....	....	....	42	....	....	....	....	....	....	....	....	....	....	....	....	....	....	....	....	....	....
1977-78	**Pittsburgh Penguins**	**NHL**	**18**	**0**	**6**	**6**	**0**	**5**	**5**	**11**	**0**	**0**	**0**	**26**	**0.0**	**24**	**7**	**17**	**2**	**+2**	....	....	....	....	....	....	....	....
	Binghamton Whalers	AHL	7	0	3	3	....	....	....	12	....	....	....	....	....	....	....	....	....	....	....	....	....	....	....	....	....	....
1978-79	Binghamton Whalers	AHL	73	7	33	40	....	....	....	50	....	....	....	....	....	....	....	....	....	....	10	3	7	10	6	....	....	....
1979-80	**Pittsburgh Penguins**	**NHL**	**49**	**5**	**13**	**18**	**5**	**10**	**15**	**31**	**4**	**0**	**0**	**83**	**6.0**	**49**	**17**	**55**	**4**	**–19**	**2**	**0**	**1**	**1**	**0**	**0**	**0**	**0**
1980-81	**Pittsburgh Penguins**	**NHL**	**72**	**8**	**44**	**52**	**7**	**31**	**38**	**188**	**3**	**0**	**1**	**142**	**5.6**	**123**	**50**	**124**	**33**	**–18**	**5**	**1**	**1**	**2**	**4**	**1**	**0**	**0**
1981-82	**Pittsburgh Penguins**	**NHL**	**14**	**4**	**8**	**12**	**3**	**5**	**8**	**14**	**4**	**0**	**2**	**40**	**10.0**	**22**	**15**	**11**	**2**	**–2**	....	....	....	....	....	....	....	....
	NHL Totals		**231**	**21**	**90**	**111**	**19**	**66**	**85**	**292**	**13**	**0**	**3**	**393**	**5.3**	**283**	**108**	**260**	**48**		**10**	**2**	**2**	**4**	**6**	**2**	**0**	**0**

CCHA Second All-Star Team (1974)

• FAUSS, TED

Ted Fauss D – L. 6'2", 205 lbs. b: Clark Mills, NY, 6/30/1961.

Season	Club	League	GP	G	A	Pts	AG	AA	APts	PIM	PP	SH	GW	S	%	TGF	PGF	TGA	PGA	+/–	GP	G	A	Pts	PIM	PP	SH	GW
1979-80	Clarkson University	ECAC	34	2	4	6	....	....	....	36	....	....	....	....	....	....	....	....	....	....	....	....	....	....	....	....	....	....
1980-81	Clarkson University	ECAC	37	0	5	5	....	....	....	56	....	....	....	....	....	....	....	....	....	....	....	....	....	....	....	....	....	....
1981-82	Clarkson University	ECAC	35	3	6	9	....	....	....	79	....	....	....	....	....	....	....	....	....	....	....	....	....	....	....	....	....	....
1982-83	Clarkson University	ECAC	25	4	6	10	....	....	....	60	....	....	....	....	....	....	....	....	....	....	....	....	....	....	....	....	....	....
	Nova Scotia Voyageurs	AHL	5	0	1	1	....	....	....	11	....	....	....	....	....	....	....	....	....	....	7	0	1	1	6	....	....	....
1983-84	Nova Scotia Voyageurs	AHL	71	4	11	15	....	....	....	123	....	....	....	....	....	....	....	....	....	....	7	0	2	2	28	....	....	....
1984-85	Sherbrooke Canadiens	AHL	77	1	9	10	....	....	....	62	....	....	....	....	....	....	....	....	....	....	17	2	2	4	27	....	....	....
1985-86			DID NOT PLAY																									
1986-87	**Toronto Maple Leafs**	**NHL**	**15**	**0**	**1**	**1**	**0**	**1**	**1**	**11**	**0**	**0**	**0**	**4**	**0.0**	**17**	**0**	**13**	**0**	**+4**	....	....	....	....	....	....	....	....
	Newmarket Saints	AHL	59	0	5	5	....	....	....	81	....	....	....	....	....	....	....	....	....	....	....	....	....	....	....	....	....	....
1987-88	**Toronto Maple Leafs**	**NHL**	**13**	**0**	**1**	**1**	**0**	**1**	**1**	**4**	**0**	**0**	**0**	**2**	**0.0**	**10**	**0**	**7**	**3**	**+6**	....	....	....	....	....	....	....	....
	Newmarket Saints	AHL	49	0	11	11	....	....	....	86	....	....	....	....	....	....	....	....	....	....	....	....	....	....	....	....	....	....
1988-89	Binghamton Whalers	AHL	53	4	11	15	....	....	....	66	....	....	....	....	....	....	....	....	....	....	....	....	....	....	....	....	....	....
1989-1993			DID NOT PLAY																									
1993-94	Utica Bulldogs	ColHL	20	3	4	7	....	....	....	48	....	....	....	....	....	....	....	....	....	....	....	....	....	....	....	....	....	....
1994-95	Utica Bulldogs	ColHL	5	1	1	2	....	....	....	8	....	....	....	....	....	....	....	....	....	....	....	....	....	....	....	....	....	....
	NHL Totals		**28**	**0**	**2**	**2**	**0**	**2**	**2**	**15**	**0**	**0**	**0**	**6**	**0.0**	**27**	**0**	**20**	**3**		....	....	....	....	....	....	....	....

Signed as a free agent by **Montreal**, March, 1983. Signed as a free agent by **Toronto**, July 21, 1986.

• FAUST, ANDRE

Andre Faust C – L. 5'11", 191 lbs. b: Joliette, Que., 10/7/1969. New Jersey's 8th choice, 173rd overall, in 1989 Entry Draft.

Season	Club	League	GP	G	A	Pts	AG	AA	APts	PIM	PP	SH	GW	S	%	TGF	PGF	TGA	PGA	+/–	GP	G	A	Pts	PIM	PP	SH	GW
1988-89	Princeton University	ECAC	27	15	24	39	....	....	....	28	....	....	....	....	....	....	....	....	....	....	....	....	....	....	....	....	....	....
1989-90	Princeton University	ECAC	22	9	28	37	....	....	....	20	....	....	....	....	....	....	....	....	....	....	....	....	....	....	....	....	....	....
1990-91	Princeton University	ECAC	26	15	22	37	....	....	....	51	....	....	....	....	....	....	....	....	....	....	....	....	....	....	....	....	....	....
1991-92	Princeton University	ECAC	27	14	21	35	....	....	....	38	....	....	....	....	....	....	....	....	....	....	....	....	....	....	....	....	....	....
1992-93	**Philadelphia Flyers**	**NHL**	**10**	**2**	**2**	**4**	**2**	**1**	**3**	**4**	**0**	**0**	**0**	**11**	**18.2**	**5**	**0**	**0**	**0**	**+5**	....	....	....	....	....	....	....	....
	Hershey Bears	AHL	62	26	25	51	....	....	....	71	....	....	....	....	....	....	....	....	....	....	....	....	....	....	....	....	....	....
1993-94	**Philadelphia Flyers**	**NHL**	**37**	**8**	**5**	**13**	**7**	**4**	**11**	**10**	**0**	**0**	**1**	**33**	**24.2**	**16**	**1**	**16**	**0**	**–1**	....	....	....	....	....	....	....	....
	Hershey Bears	AHL	13	6	7	13	....	....	....	10	....	....	....	....	....	....	....	....	....	....	10	4	3	7	26	....	....	....
1994-95	Hershey Bears	AHL	55	12	28	40	....	....	....	72	....	....	....	....	....	....	....	....	....	....	6	1	5	6	12	....	....	....
1995-96	Springfield Falcons	AHL	50	19	19	38	....	....	....	40	....	....	....	....	....	....	....	....	....	....	10	5	2	7	6	....	....	....
1996-97	Augsburg Panthers	Germany	46	21	19	40	....	....	....	84	....	....	....	....	....	....	....	....	....	....	4	3	1	4	2	....	....	....
1997-98	Augsburg Panthers	Germany	41	13	20	33	....	....	....	87	....	....	....	....	....	....	....	....	....	....	....	....	....	....	....	....	....	....
	NHL Totals		**47**	**10**	**7**	**17**	**9**	**5**	**14**	**14**	**0**	**0**	**1**	**44**	**22.7**	**21**	**1**	**16**	**0**		....	....	....	....	....	....	....	....

ECAC Second All-Star Team (1990, 1992)

Signed as a free agent by **Philadelphia**, October 5, 1992. Traded to **Winnipeg** by **Philadelphia** for Winnipeg's 7th round choice (later traded to Carolina — Carolina selected Andrew Merrick) in 1997 Entry Draft, September 20, 1995.

Season	Club	League	GP	G	A	Pts	AG	AA	APts	PIM	PP	SH	GW	S	%	TGF	PGF	TGA	PGA	+/–	GP	G	A	Pts	PIM	PP	SH	GW
			REGULAR SEASON																		PLAYOFFS							

• FEAMSTER, DAVE

Dave Feamster D – L. 5'11", 180 lbs. b: Detroit, MI, 9/10/1958. Chicago's 6th choice, 96th overall, in 1978 Amateur Draft.

Season	Club	League	GP	G	A	Pts	AG	AA	APts	PIM	PP	SH	GW	S	%	TGF	PGF	TGA	PGA	+/–	GP	G	A	Pts	PIM	PP	SH	GW
1976-77	Colorado College	CCHA	37	9	28	37	....	....	....	96	....	....	....	....	....	....	....	....	....	....	....	....	....	....	....	....	....	....
1977-78	Colorado College	CCHA	39	8	34	42	....	....	....	92	....	....	....	....	....	....	....	....	....	....	....	....	....	....	....	....	....	....
	United States	WJC-A	6	0	5	5	....	....	....	8	....	....	....	....	....	....	....	....	....	....	....	....	....	....	....	....	....	....
1978-79	Colorado College	CCHA	31	10	37	47	....	....	....	78	....	....	....	....	....	....	....	....	....	....	....	....	....	....	....	....	....	....
1979-80	Colorado College	CCHA	37	17	33	50	....	....	....	135	....	....	....	....	....	....	....	....	....	....	....	....	....	....	....	....	....	....
1980-81	Dallas Black Hawks	CHL	77	12	33	45	....	....	....	117	....	....	....	....	....	....	....	....	....	....	6	2	3	5	23	....	....	....
1981-82	**Chicago Black Hawks**	**NHL**	**29**	**0**	**2**	**2**	**0**	**1**	**1**	**29**	**0**	**0**	**0**	**24**	**0.0**	**25**	**0**	**41**	**10**	**–6**	**15**	**2**	**4**	**6**	**53**	**0**	**0**	**1**
	New Brunswick Hawks	AHL	42	6	30	36	....	....	....	69	....	....	....	....	....	....	....	....	....	....	....	....	....	....	....	....	....	....
1982-83	**Chicago Black Hawks**	**NHL**	**78**	**6**	**12**	**18**	**5**	**8**	**13**	**69**	**0**	**0**	**0**	**68**	**8.8**	**66**	**1**	**61**	**11**	**+15**	**13**	**1**	**0**	**1**	**4**	**0**	**0**	**0**
1983-84	**Chicago Black Hawks**	**NHL**	**46**	**6**	**7**	**13**	**5**	**5**	**10**	**42**	**0**	**0**	**0**	**44**	**13.6**	**33**	**0**	**48**	**7**	**–8**	**5**	**0**	**1**	**1**	**4**	**0**	**0**	**0**
1984-85	**Chicago Black Hawks**	**NHL**	**16**	**1**	**3**	**4**	**1**	**2**	**3**	**14**	**0**	**0**	**0**	**10**	**10.0**	**14**	**0**	**10**	**1**	**+5**	....	....	....	....	....	....	....	....
	NHL Totals		**169**	**13**	**24**	**37**	**11**	**16**	**27**	**154**	**0**	**0**	**0**	**146**	**8.9**	**138**	**1**	**160**	**29**		**33**	**3**	**5**	**8**	**61**	**0**	**0**	**1**

WCHA First All-Star Team (1980) • NCAA West First All-American Team (1980)

• FEATHERSTONE, GLEN

Glen Featherstone D – L. 6'4", 209 lbs. b: Toronto, Ont., 7/8/1968. St. Louis' 4th choice, 73rd overall, in 1986 Entry Draft.

Season	Club	League	GP	G	A	Pts	AG	AA	APts	PIM	PP	SH	GW	S	%	TGF	PGF	TGA	PGA	+/–	GP	G	A	Pts	PIM	PP	SH	GW
1985-86	Windsor Spitfires	OHL	49	0	6	6	....	....	....	135	....	....	....	....	....	....	....	....	....	....	14	1	1	2	23	....	....	....
1986-87	Windsor Spitfires	OHL	47	6	11	17	....	....	....	154	....	....	....	....	....	....	....	....	....	....	14	2	6	8	19	....	....	....
1987-88	Windsor Spitfires	OHL	53	7	27	34	....	....	....	201	....	....	....	....	....	....	....	....	....	....	12	6	9	15	47	....	....	....
1988-89	**St. Louis Blues**	**NHL**	**18**	**0**	**2**	**2**	**0**	**1**	**1**	**22**	**0**	**0**	**0**	**9**	**0.0**	**13**	**0**	**21**	**5**	**–3**	**6**	**0**	**0**	**0**	**25**	**0**	**0**	**0**
	Peoria Rivermen	IHL	37	5	19	24	....	....	....	97	....	....	....	....	....	....	....	....	....	....	....	....	....	....	....	....	....	....
1989-90	**St. Louis Blues**	**NHL**	**58**	**0**	**12**	**12**	**0**	**9**	**9**	**145**	**0**	**0**	**0**	**34**	**0.0**	**46**	**4**	**54**	**11**	**–1**	**12**	**0**	**2**	**2**	**47**	**0**	**0**	**0**
	Peoria Rivermen	IHL	15	1	4	5	....	....	....	43	....	....	....	....	....	....	....	....	....	....	....	....	....	....	....	....	....	....
1990-91	**St. Louis Blues**	**NHL**	**68**	**5**	**15**	**20**	**5**	**11**	**16**	**204**	**1**	**0**	**1**	**59**	**8.5**	**61**	**4**	**41**	**3**	**+19**	**9**	**0**	**0**	**0**	**31**	**0**	**0**	**0**
1991-92	**Boston Bruins**	**NHL**	**7**	**1**	**0**	**1**	**1**	**0**	**1**	**20**	**0**	**0**	**0**	**8**	**12.5**	**5**	**1**	**8**	**2**	**–2**	....	....	....	....	....	....	....	....
1992-93	**Boston Bruins**	**NHL**	**34**	**5**	**5**	**10**	**4**	**3**	**7**	**102**	**1**	**0**	**0**	**33**	**15.2**	**32**	**2**	**27**	**3**	**+6**	....	....	....	....	....	....	....	....
	Providence Bruins	AHL	8	3	4	7	....	....	....	60	....	....	....	....	....	....	....	....	....	....	....	....	....	....	....	....	....	....
1993-94	**Boston Bruins**	**NHL**	**58**	**1**	**8**	**9**	**1**	**6**	**7**	**152**	**0**	**0**	**1**	**55**	**1.8**	**31**	**1**	**41**	**6**	**–5**	**1**	**0**	**0**	**0**	**0**	**0**	**0**	**0**
1994-95	**New York Rangers**	**NHL**	**6**	**1**	**0**	**1**	**2**	**0**	**2**	**18**	**0**	**0**	**0**	**6**	**16.7**	**4**	**0**	**4**	**0**	**0**	....	....	....	....	....	....	....	....
	Hartford Whalers	**NHL**	**13**	**1**	**1**	**2**	**2**	**1**	**3**	**32**	**0**	**0**	**0**	**16**	**6.3**	**4**	**0**	**11**	**0**	**–7**	....	....	....	....	....	....	....	....
1995-96	**Hartford Whalers**	**NHL**	**68**	**2**	**10**	**12**	**2**	**8**	**10**	**138**	**0**	**0**	**1**	**62**	**3.2**	**54**	**2**	**63**	**21**	**+10**	....	....	....	....	....	....	....	....
1996-97	**Hartford Whalers**	**NHL**	**41**	**2**	**5**	**7**	**2**	**4**	**6**	**87**	**0**	**0**	**0**	**40**	**5.0**	**38**	**6**	**42**	**10**	**0**	....	....	....	....	....	....	....	....
	Calgary Flames	**NHL**	**13**	**1**	**3**	**4**	**1**	**3**	**4**	**19**	**0**	**0**	**0**	**27**	**3.7**	**14**	**4**	**11**	**0**	**–1**	....	....	....	....	....	....	....	....
1997-98	Indianapolis Ice	IHL	73	10	28	38	....	....	....	187	....	....	....	....	....	....	....	....	....	....	5	0	3	3	16	....	....	....
	NHL Totals		**384**	**19**	**61**	**80**	**20**	**46**	**66**	**939**	**2**	**0**	**3**	**349**	**5.4**	**302**	**24**	**323**	**61**		**28**	**0**	**2**	**2**	**103**	**0**	**0**	**0**

Signed as a free agent by **Boston**, July 25, 1991. Traded to **NY Rangers** by **Boston** for Daniel Lacroix, August 19, 1994. Traded to **Hartford** by **NY Rangers** with Michael Stewart, NY Rangers' 1st round choice (Jean-Sebastien Giguere) in 1995 Entry Draft and 4th round choice (Steve Wasylko) in 1996 Entry Draft for Pat Verbeek, March 23, 1995. Traded to **Calgary** by **Hartford** with Hnat Domenichelli, New Jersey's 2nd round choice (previously acquired, Calgary selected Dimitri Kokorev) in 1997 Entry Draft and Vancouver's 3rd round choice (previously acquired, Calgary selected Paul Manning) in 1998 Entry Draft for Steve Chiasson and Colorado's 3rd round choice (previously acquired, Carolina selected Francis Lessard) in 1997 Entry Draft, March 5, 1997.

• FEATHERSTONE, TONY

Tony Featherstone RW – R. 5'11", 187 lbs. b: Toronto, Ont., 7/31/1949. Oakland's 1st choice, 7th overall, in 1969 Amateur Draft.

Season	Club	League	GP	G	A	Pts	AG	AA	APts	PIM	PP	SH	GW	S	%	TGF	PGF	TGA	PGA	+/–	GP	G	A	Pts	PIM	PP	SH	GW
1967-68	Peterborough Petes	OHA	43	11	11	22	....	....	....	109	....	....	....	....	....	....	....	....	....	....	5	3	0	3	28	....	....	....
1968-69	Peterborough Petes	OHA	54	29	38	67	....	....	....	167	....	....	....	....	....	....	....	....	....	....	10	3	5	8	56	....	....	....
1969-70	**Oakland Seals**	**NHL**	**9**	**0**	**1**	**1**	**0**	**1**	**1**	**17**	**0**	**0**	**0**	**13**	**0.0**	**1**	**0**	**8**	**0**	**–7**	**2**	**0**	**0**	**0**	**0**	**0**	**0**	**0**
	Providence Reds	AHL	55	15	25	40	....	....	....	78	....	....	....	....	....	....	....	....	....	....	....	....	....	....	....	....	....	....
1970-71	**California Golden Seals**	**NHL**	**67**	**8**	**8**	**16**	**8**	**7**	**15**	**44**	**1**	**0**	**1**	**90**	**8.9**	**38**	**4**	**39**	**1**	**–4**	....	....	....	....	....	....	....	....
1971-72	Nova Scotia Voyageurs	AHL	56	5	10	15	....	....	....	50	....	....	....	....	....	....	....	....	....	....	15	5	4	9	36	....	....	....
1972-73	Nova Scotia Voyageurs	AHL	74	49	54	103	....	....	....	78	....	....	....	....	....	....	....	....	....	....	13	*10	13	23	34	....	....	....
1973-74	**Minnesota North Stars**	**NHL**	**54**	**9**	**12**	**21**	**9**	**10**	**19**	**4**	**0**	**2**	**0**	**92**	**9.8**	**30**	**2**	**53**	**16**	**–9**	....	....	....	....	....	....	....	....
1974-75	Toronto Toros	WHA	76	25	38	63	....	....	....	26	....	....	....	....	....	....	....	....	....	....	6	2	1	3	25	....	....	....
1975-76	Toronto Toros	WHA	32	4	7	11	....	....	....	5	....	....	....	....	....	....	....	....	....	....	....	....	....	....	....	....	....	....
	NHL Totals		**130**	**17**	**21**	**38**	**17**	**18**	**35**	**65**	**1**	**2**	**1**	**195**	**8.7**	**69**	**6**	**100**	**17**		**2**	**0**	**0**	**0**	**0**	**0**	**0**	**0**
	Other Major League Totals		108	29	45	74	....	....	....	31	....	....	....	....	....	....	....	....	....	....	6	2	1	3	25	....	....	....

AHL First All-Star Team (1973)

Traded to **Montreal** by **California** for Ray Martyniuk, October 6, 1971. Traded to **Minnesota** by **Montreal** with Murray Anderson for future considerations, May 29, 1973. Selected by **Toronto** (WHA) in 1973 WHA Professional Player Draft, June, 1973.

• FEDERKO, BERNIE

Bernie Federko C – L. 6', 178 lbs. b: Foam Lake, Sask., 5/12/1956. St. Louis' 1st choice, 7th overall, in 1976 Amateur Draft.

Season	Club	League	GP	G	A	Pts	AG	AA	APts	PIM	PP	SH	GW	S	%	TGF	PGF	TGA	PGA	+/–	GP	G	A	Pts	PIM	PP	SH	GW
1973-74	Saskatoon Blades	WHL	68	22	28	50	....	....	....	19	....	....	....	....	....	....	....	....	....	....	6	0	0	0	2	....	....	....
1974-75	Saskatoon Blades	WHL	66	39	68	107	....	....	....	30	....	....	....	....	....	....	....	....	....	....	17	*15	7	22	8	....	....	....
1975-76	Saskatoon Blades	WHL	72	72	*115	*187	....	....	....	108	....	....	....	....	....	....	....	....	....	....	20	18	*27	*45	8	....	....	....
1976-77	**St. Louis Blues**	**NHL**	**31**	**14**	**9**	**23**	**13**	**7**	**20**	**15**	**6**	**0**	**3**	**67**	**20.9**	**30**	**11**	**25**	**0**	**–6**	**4**	**1**	**1**	**2**	**2**	**0**	**0**	**0**
	Kansas City Blues	CHL	42	30	39	69	....	....	....	41	....	....	....	....	....	....	....	....	....	....	....	....	....	....	....	....	....	....
1977-78	**St. Louis Blues**	**NHL**	**72**	**17**	**24**	**41**	**16**	**20**	**36**	**27**	**4**	**0**	**1**	**128**	**13.3**	**56**	**20**	**71**	**0**	**–35**	....	....	....	....	....	....	....	....
1978-79	**St. Louis Blues**	**NHL**	**74**	**31**	**64**	**95**	**28**	**49**	**77**	**14**	**7**	**0**	**1**	**156**	**19.9**	**118**	**40**	**94**	**1**	**–15**	....	....	....	....	....	....	....	....
1979-80	**St. Louis Blues**	**NHL**	**79**	**38**	**56**	**94**	**34**	**43**	**77**	**24**	**7**	**0**	**4**	**184**	**20.7**	**127**	**45**	**79**	**0**	**+3**	**3**	**1**	**0**	**1**	**2**	**0**	**0**	**0**
1980-81	**St. Louis Blues**	**NHL**	**78**	**31**	**73**	**104**	**26**	**51**	**77**	**47**	**9**	**2**	**4**	**170**	**18.2**	**129**	**52**	**69**	**1**	**+9**	**11**	**8**	**10**	**18**	**2**	**4**	**0**	**1**
1981-82	**St. Louis Blues**	**NHL**	**74**	**30**	**62**	**92**	**24**	**41**	**65**	**70**	**11**	**0**	**6**	**177**	**16.9**	**110**	**44**	**87**	**2**	**–10**	**10**	**3**	**15**	**18**	**10**	**1**	**0**	**1**
1982-83	**St. Louis Blues**	**NHL**	**75**	**24**	**60**	**84**	**20**	**42**	**62**	**24**	**9**	**0**	**1**	**184**	**13.0**	**113**	**45**	**78**	**0**	**–10**	**4**	**2**	**3**	**5**	**0**	**1**	**0**	**0**
1983-84	**St. Louis Blues**	**NHL**	**79**	**41**	**66**	**107**	**33**	**45**	**78**	**43**	**14**	**0**	**4**	**197**	**20.8**	**138**	**58**	**83**	**0**	**–3**	**11**	**4**	**4**	**8**	**10**	**1**	**0**	**1**
1984-85	**St. Louis Blues**	**NHL**	**76**	**30**	**73**	**103**	**25**	**50**	**75**	**27**	**6**	**0**	**3**	**174**	**17.2**	**124**	**45**	**90**	**1**	**–10**	**3**	**0**	**2**	**2**	**4**	**0**	**0**	**0**
1985-86	**St. Louis Blues**	**NHL**	**80**	**34**	**68**	**102**	**27**	**46**	**73**	**34**	**16**	**0**	**2**	**167**	**20.4**	**139**	**56**	**74**	**1**	**+10**	**19**	**7**	**14**	**21**	**17**	**1**	**0**	**1**
1986-87	**St. Louis Blues**	**NHL**	**64**	**20**	**52**	**72**	**17**	**38**	**55**	**32**	**9**	**0**	**3**	**130**	**15.4**	**97**	**48**	**74**	**0**	**–25**	**6**	**3**	**3**	**6**	**18**	**1**	**0**	**0**
1987-88	**St. Louis Blues**	**NHL**	**79**	**20**	**69**	**89**	**17**	**49**	**66**	**52**	**9**	**0**	**2**	**119**	**16.8**	**123**	**55**	**82**	**2**	**–12**	**10**	**2**	**6**	**8**	**18**	**2**	**0**	**0**
1988-89	**St. Louis Blues**	**NHL**	**66**	**22**	**45**	**67**	**19**	**32**	**51**	**54**	**9**	**0**	**6**	**115**	**19.1**	**96**	**46**	**70**	**0**	**–20**	**10**	**4**	**8**	**12**	**0**	**2**	**0**	**0**
1989-90	**Detroit Red Wings**	**NHL**	**73**	**17**	**40**	**57**	**15**	**29**	**44**	**24**	**3**	**0**	**0**	**108**	**15.7**	**77**	**34**	**54**	**3**	**–8**	....	....	....	....	....	....	....	....
	NHL Totals		**1000**	**369**	**761**	**1130**	**314**	**542**	**856**	**487**	**119**	**2**	**40**	**2076**	**17.8**	**1486**	**599**	**1030**	**11**		**91**	**35**	**66**	**101**	**83**	**13**	**0**	**4**

WCJHL All-Star Team (1976) • CHL Second All-Star Team (1977) • Won Ken McKenzie Trophy (CHL's Rookie of the Year) (1977)

Played in NHL All-Star Game (1980, 1981)

Traded to **Detroit** by **St. Louis** with Tony McKegney for Adam Oates and Paul MacLean, June 15, 1989.

• FEDOROV, SERGEI

Sergei Fedorov C – L. 6'1", 200 lbs. b: Pskov, USSR, 12/13/1969. Detroit's 4th choice, 74th overall, in 1989 Entry Draft.

Season	Club	League	GP	G	A	Pts	AG	AA	APts	PIM	PP	SH	GW	S	%	TGF	PGF	TGA	PGA	+/–	GP	G	A	Pts	PIM	PP	SH	GW
1986-87	CSKA Moscow	USSR	29	6	6	12	....	....	....	12	....	....	....	....	....	....	....	....	....	....	....	....	....	....	....	....	....	....
1987-88	CSKA Moscow	USSR	48	7	9	16	....	....	....	20	....	....	....	....	....	....	....	....	....	....	....	....	....	....	....	....	....	....
	Soviet Union	WJC-A	7	5	7	12	....	....	....	0	....	....	....	....	....	....	....	....	....	....	....	....	....	....	....	....	....	....
1988-89	CSKA Moscow	USSR	44	9	8	17	....	....	....	35	....	....	....	....	....	....	....	....	....	....	....	....	....	....	....	....	....	....
	Soviet Union	WJC-A	7	4	8	12	....	....	....	4	....	....	....	....	....	....	....	....	....	....	....	....	....	....	....	....	....	....
	Soviet Union	WEC-A	10	6	3	9	....	....	....	10	....	....	....	....	....	....	....	....	....	....	....	....	....	....	....	....	....	....
1989-90	CSKA Moscow	Fr-Tour	1	0	0	0	....	....	....	2	....	....	....	....	....	....	....	....	....	....	....	....	....	....	....	....	....	....
	CSKA Moscow	USSR	48	19	10	29	....	....	....	22	....	....	....	....	....	....	....	....	....	....	....	....	....	....	....	....	....	....
	CSKA Moscow	Super-S	5	2	2	4	....	....	....	11	....	....	....	....	....	....	....	....	....	....	....	....	....	....	....	....	....	....
	Soviet Union	WEC-A	10	4	2	6	....	....	....	10	....	....	....	....	....	....	....	....	....	....	....	....	....	....	....	....	....	....
1990-91	**Detroit Red Wings**	**NHL**	**77**	**31**	**48**	**79**	**29**	**36**	**65**	**66**	**11**	**3**	**5**	**259**	**12.0**	**100**	**35**	**73**	**19**	**+11**	**7**	**1**	**5**	**6**	**4**	**0**	**0**	**1**
1991-92	Soviet Union	C Cup	5	2	2	4	....	....	....	6	....	....	....	....	....	....	....	....	....	....	....	....	....	....	....	....	....	....
	Detroit Red Wings	**NHL**	**80**	**32**	**54**	**86**	**29**	**41**	**70**	**72**	**7**	**2**	**5**	**249**	**12.9**	**123**	**42**	**75**	**20**	**+26**	**11**	**5**	**5**	**10**	**8**	**1**	**2**	**1**
1992-93	**Detroit Red Wings**	**NHL**	**73**	**34**	**53**	**87**	**28**	**36**	**64**	**72**	**13**	**4**	**3**	**217**	**15.7**	**124**	**52**	**62**	**23**	**+33**	**7**	**3**	**6**	**9**	**23**	**1**	**1**	**0**
1993-94	**Detroit Red Wings**	**NHL**	**82**	**56**	**64**	**120**	**52**	**50**	**102**	**34**	**13**	**4**	**10**	**337**	**16.6**	**170**	**51**	**99**	**28**	**+48**	**7**	**1**	**7**	**8**	**6**	**0**	**0**	**0**
1994-95	**Detroit Red Wings**	**NHL**	**42**	**20**	**30**	**50**	**36**	**44**	**80**	**24**	**7**	**3**	**5**	**147**	**13.6**	**60**	**24**	**33**	**3**	**+6**	**17**	**7**	***17**	***24**	**6**	**3**	**0**	**0**
1995-96	**Detroit Red Wings**	**NHL**	**78**	**39**	**68**	**107**	**39**	**56**	**95**	**48**	**11**	**3**	**11**	**306**	**12.7**	**143**	**56**	**56**	**18**	**+49**	**19**	**2**	***18**	**20**	**10**	**0**	**0**	**2**

			REGULAR SEASON																		PLAYOFFS							
Season	Club	League	GP	G	A	Pts	AG	AA	APts	PIM	PP	SH	GW	S	%	TGF	PGF	TGA	PGA	+/–	GP	G	A	Pts	PIM	PP	SH	GW
1996-97	Russia	W Cup	5	3	3	6	....	....	....	2	....	....	....	....	....	....	....	....	....	....	....	....	....	....	....	....	....	....
	Detroit Red Wings	**NHL**	**74**	**30**	**33**	**63**	**32**	**29**	**61**	**30**	**9**	**2**	**4**	**273**	**11.0**	**94**	**26**	**51**	**12**	**+29**	**20**	**8**	**12**	**20**	**12**	**3**	**0**	**4**
1997-98	**Detroit Red Wings**	**NHL**	**21**	**6**	**11**	**17**	**7**	**11**	**18**	**25**	**2**	**0**	**2**	**68**	**8.8**	**30**	**12**	**14**	**6**	**+10**	**22**	**10**	**10**	**20**	**12**	**2**	**1**	**1**
	Russia	Olympics	6	1	5	6	....	....	....	8	....	....	....	....	....	....	....	....	....	....	....	....	....	....	....	....	....	....
	NHL Totals		**527**	**248**	**361**	**609**	**252**	**303**	**555**	**371**	**73**	**21**	**45**	**1856**	**13.4**	**844**	**298**	**463**	**129**		**110**	**37**	**80**	**117**	**81**	**10**	**4**	**9**

NHL/Upper Deck All-Rookie Team (1991) • NHL First All-Star Team (1994) • Won Frank J. Selke Trophy (1994, 1996) • Won Lester B. Pearson Award (1994) • Won Hart Trophy (1994)
Played in NHL All-Star Game (1992, 1994, 1996)

• FEDOTOV, ANATOLI

Anatoli Fedotov D – L. 5'11", 178 lbs. b: Saratov, USSR, 5/11/1966. Anaheim's 10th choice, 238th overall, in 1993 Entry Draft.

Season	Club	League	GP	G	A	Pts	AG	AA	APts	PIM	PP	SH	GW	S	%	TGF	PGF	TGA	PGA	+/–	GP	G	A	Pts	PIM	PP	SH	GW
1984-85	Kristall Saratov	USSR 2	STATISTICS NOT AVAILABLE																									
	Soviet Union	WJC-A	6	0	2	2	....	....	....	2	....	....	....	....	....	....	....	....	....	....	....	....	....	....	....	....	....	....
1985-86	Moscow Dynamo	USSR	35	0	2	2	....	....	....	10	....	....	....	....	....	....	....	....	....	....	....	....	....	....	....	....	....	....
	Soviet Union	WJC-A	7	1	5	6	....	....	....	0	....	....	....	....	....	....	....	....	....	....	....	....	....	....	....	....	....	....
1986-87	Moscow Dynamo	USSR	18	3	2	5	....	....	....	12	....	....	....	....	....	....	....	....	....	....	....	....	....	....	....	....	....	....
1987-88	Soviet Union	C Cup	8	0	1	1	....	....	....	4	....	....	....	....	....	....	....	....	....	....	....	....	....	....	....	....	....	....
	Moscow Dynamo	USSR	48	2	3	5	....	....	....	38	....	....	....	....	....	....	....	....	....	....	....	....	....	....	....	....	....	....
1988-89	Moscow Dynamo	USSR	40	2	1	3	....	....	....	24	....	....	....	....	....	....	....	....	....	....	....	....	....	....	....	....	....	....
1989-90	Moscow Dynamo	FrTour	1	0	0	0	....	....	....	4	....	....	....	....	....	....	....	....	....	....	....	....	....	....	....	....	....	....
	Moscow Dynamo	USSR	41	2	4	6	....	....	....	22	....	....	....	....	....	....	....	....	....	....	....	....	....	....	....	....	....	....
	Moscow Dynamo	SuperS	3	0	1	1	....	....	....	4	....	....	....	....	....	....	....	....	....	....	....	....	....	....	....	....	....	....
1990-91			DID NOT PLAY																									
1991-92	Moscow Dynamo	CIS	5	0	0	0	....	....	....	4	....	....	....	....	....	....	....	....	....	....	6	1	0	1	4	....	....	....
1992-93	**Winnipeg Jets**	**NHL**	**1**	**0**	**2**	**2**	**0**	**1**	**1**	**0**	**0**	**0**	**0**	**1**	**0.0**	**4**	**2**	**1**	**0**	**+1**	....	....	....	....	....	....	....	....
	Moncton Hawks	AHL	76	10	37	47	....	....	....	99	....	....	....	....	....	....	....	....	....	....	2	0	0	0	0	....	....	....
1993-94	**Anaheim Mighty Ducks**	**NHL**	**3**	**0**	**0**	**0**	**0**	**0**	**0**	**0**	**0**	**0**	**0**	**1**	**0.0**	**1**	**1**	**1**	**0**	**–1**	....	....	....	....	....	....	....	....
	San Diego Gulls	IHL	66	14	12	26	....	....	....	42	....	....	....	....	....	....	....	....	....	....	8	0	1	1	6	....	....	....
1994-95	San Diego Gulls	IHL	53	5	12	17	....	....	....	16	....	....	....	....	....	....	....	....	....	....	....	....	....	....	....	....	....	....
1995-96	Kristov Sarotov	CIS	41	4	8	12	....	....	....	30	....	....	....	....	....	....	....	....	....	....	....	....	....	....	....	....	....	....
1996-97	Tappara Tampere	Finland	44	9	9	18	....	....	....	62	....	....	....	....	....	....	....	....	....	....	3	0	0	0	4	....	....	....
	Russia	WC-A	9	2	2	4	....	....	....	10	....	....	....	....	....	....	....	....	....	....	....	....	....	....	....	....	....	....
1997-98	HV-71 Jonkoping	Sweden	24	0	1	1	....	....	....	44	....	....	....	....	....	....	....	....	....	....	4	0	0	0	4	....	....	....
	NHL Totals		**4**	**0**	**2**	**2**	**0**	**1**	**1**	**0**	**0**	**0**	**0**	**2**	**0.0**	**5**	**3**	**2**	**0**		....	....	....	....	....	....	....	....

Signed as a free agent by **Winnipeg** to AHL contract, July 4, 1991. • NHL ruled that **Winnipeg** had promoted Fedotov illegally and had no claim to his NHL rights. Fedotov entered NHL Entry Draft and was selected by Anaheim, June 26, 1993.

• FEDYK, BRENT

Brent Fedyk LW – R. 6', 194 lbs. b: Yorkton, Sask., 3/8/1967. Detroit's 1st choice, 8th overall, in 1985 Entry Draft.

Season	Club	League	GP	G	A	Pts	AG	AA	APts	PIM	PP	SH	GW	S	%	TGF	PGF	TGA	PGA	+/–	GP	G	A	Pts	PIM	PP	SH	GW
1983-84	Regina Pats	WHL	63	15	28	43	....	....	....	30	....	....	....	....	....	....	....	....	....	....	23	8	7	15	6	....	....	....
1984-85	Regina Pats	WHL	66	35	35	70	....	....	....	48	....	....	....	....	....	....	....	....	....	....	8	5	4	9	0	....	....	....
1985-86	Regina Pats	WHL	50	43	34	77	....	....	....	47	....	....	....	....	....	....	....	....	....	....	5	0	1	1	0	....	....	....
1986-87	Regina Pats	WHL	12	9	6	15	....	....	....	9	....	....	....	....	....	....	....	....	....	....	....	....	....	....	....	....	....	....
	Seattle Thunderbirds	WHL	13	5	11	16	....	....	....	9	....	....	....	....	....	....	....	....	....	....	....	....	....	....	....	....	....	....
	Portland Winter Hawks	WHL	11	5	4	9	....	....	....	6	....	....	....	....	....	....	....	....	....	....	14	5	6	11	0	....	....	....
1987-88	**Detroit Red Wings**	**NHL**	**2**	**0**	**1**	**1**	**0**	**1**	**1**	**2**	**0**	**0**	**0**	**2**	**0.0**	**1**	**0**	**2**	**0**	**–1**	....	....	....	....	....	....	....	....
	Adirondack Red Wings	AHL	34	9	11	20	....	....	....	22	....	....	....	....	....	....	....	....	....	....	5	0	2	2	6	....	....	....
1988-89	**Detroit Red Wings**	**NHL**	**5**	**2**	**0**	**2**	**2**	**0**	**2**	**0**	**1**	**0**	**0**	**6**	**33.3**	**3**	**1**	**3**	**0**	**–1**	....	....	....	....	....	....	....	....
	Adirondack Red Wings	AHL	66	40	28	68	....	....	....	33	....	....	....	....	....	....	....	....	....	....	15	7	8	15	23	....	....	....
1989-90	**Detroit Red Wings**	**NHL**	**27**	**1**	**4**	**5**	**1**	**3**	**4**	**6**	**0**	**0**	**0**	**28**	**3.6**	**11**	**1**	**13**	**2**	**–1**	....	....	....	....	....	....	....	....
	Adirondack Red Wings	AHL	33	14	15	29	....	....	....	24	....	....	....	....	....	....	....	....	....	....	6	2	1	3	4	....	....	....
1990-91	**Detroit Red Wings**	**NHL**	**67**	**16**	**19**	**35**	**15**	**14**	**29**	**38**	**0**	**0**	**1**	**74**	**21.6**	**45**	**0**	**40**	**15**	**+20**	**6**	**1**	**0**	**1**	**2**	**0**	**0**	**1**
1991-92	**Detroit Red Wings**	**NHL**	**61**	**5**	**8**	**13**	**5**	**6**	**11**	**42**	**0**	**0**	**1**	**60**	**8.3**	**20**	**0**	**35**	**10**	**–5**	**1**	**0**	**0**	**0**	**2**	**0**	**0**	**0**
	Adirondack Red Wings	AHL	1	0	2	2	....	....	....	0	....	....	....	....	....	....	....	....	....	....	....	....	....	....	....	....	....	....
1992-93	**Philadelphia Flyers**	**NHL**	**74**	**21**	**38**	**59**	**17**	**26**	**43**	**48**	**4**	**1**	**2**	**167**	**12.6**	**95**	**24**	**73**	**16**	**+14**	....	....	....	....	....	....	....	....
1993-94	**Philadelphia Flyers**	**NHL**	**72**	**20**	**18**	**38**	**19**	**14**	**33**	**74**	**5**	**0**	**1**	**104**	**19.2**	**52**	**11**	**65**	**10**	**–14**	....	....	....	....	....	....	....	....
1994-95	**Philadelphia Flyers**	**NHL**	**30**	**8**	**4**	**12**	**14**	**6**	**20**	**14**	**3**	**0**	**2**	**41**	**19.5**	**23**	**12**	**16**	**3**	**–2**	**9**	**2**	**2**	**4**	**8**	**0**	**0**	**0**
1995-96	**Philadelphia Flyers**	**NHL**	**24**	**10**	**5**	**15**	**10**	**4**	**14**	**24**	**4**	**0**	**0**	**42**	**23.8**	**19**	**4**	**15**	**1**	**+1**	....	....	....	....	....	....	....	....
	Dallas Stars	**NHL**	**41**	**10**	**9**	**19**	**10**	**7**	**17**	**30**	**4**	**0**	**0**	**71**	**14.1**	**28**	**12**	**41**	**8**	**–17**	....	....	....	....	....	....	....	....
1996-97	Michigan K-Wings	IHL	9	1	2	3	....	....	....	4	....	....	....	....	....	....	....	....	....	....	....	....	....	....	....	....	....	....
1997-98	Detroit Vipers	IHL	40	18	23	41	....	....	....	24	....	....	....	....	....	....	....	....	....	....	....	....	....	....	....	....	....	....
	Cincinnati Cyclones	IHL	26	21	13	34	....	....	....	14	....	....	....	....	....	....	....	....	....	....	9	5	5	10	2	....	....	....
	NHL Totals		**403**	**93**	**106**	**199**	**93**	**81**	**174**	**278**	**21**	**1**	**7**	**595**	**15.6**	**297**	**65**	**303**	**65**		**16**	**3**	**2**	**5**	**12**	**0**	**0**	**1**

Traded to **Philadelphia** by **Detroit** for Philadelphia's 4th round choice (later traded to Boston — Boston selected Charles Paquette) in 1993 Entry Draft, October 1, 1992. Traded to **Dallas** by **Philadelphia** for Trent Klatt, December 13, 1995.

• FELIX, CHRIS

Chris Felix D – R. 5'11", 190 lbs. b: Bramalea, Ont., 5/27/1964.

Season	Club	League	GP	G	A	Pts	AG	AA	APts	PIM	PP	SH	GW	S	%	TGF	PGF	TGA	PGA	+/–	GP	G	A	Pts	PIM	PP	SH	GW
1982-83	Sault Ste. Marie Greyhounds	OHL	68	16	57	73	....	....	....	39	....	....	....	....	....	....	....	....	....	....	16	2	12	14	10	....	....	....
1983-84	Sault Ste. Marie Greyhounds	OHL	70	32	61	93	....	....	....	77	....	....	....	....	....	....	....	....	....	....	16	3	20	23	16	....	....	....
1984-85	Sault Ste. Marie Greyhounds	OHL	63	29	72	101	....	....	....	85	....	....	....	....	....	....	....	....	....	....	16	7	*21	28	25	....	....	....
1985-86	Canada	Nat-Team	73	7	33	40	....	....	....	33	....	....	....	....	....	....	....	....	....	....	....	....	....	....	....	....	....	....
1986-87	Canada	Nat-Team	78	14	38	52	....	....	....	36	....	....	....	....	....	....	....	....	....	....	....	....	....	....	....	....	....	....
1987-88	Canada	Nat-Team	62	6	25	31	....	....	....	66	....	....	....	....	....	....	....	....	....	....	....	....	....	....	....	....	....	....
	Canada	Olympics	6	1	2	3	....	....	....	2	....	....	....	....	....	....	....	....	....	....	....	....	....	....	....	....	....	....
	Fort Wayne Komets	IHL	19	5	17	22	....	....	....	24	....	....	....	....	....	....	....	....	....	....	6	4	4	8	0	....	....	....
	Washington Capitals	**NHL**	....	....	....	....	....	....	....	....	....	....	....	....	....	....	....	....	....	....	**1**	**0**	**0**	**0**	**0**	....	....	....
1988-89	**Washington Capitals**	**NHL**	**21**	**0**	**8**	**8**	**0**	**6**	**6**	**8**	**0**	**0**	**0**	**18**	**0.0**	**30**	**13**	**10**	**0**	**+7**	**1**	**0**	**1**	**1**	**0**	**0**	**0**	**0**
	Baltimore Skipjacks	AHL	50	8	29	37	....	....	....	44	....	....	....	....	....	....	....	....	....	....	....	....	....	....	....	....	....	....
1989-90	**Washington Capitals**	**NHL**	**6**	**1**	**0**	**1**	**1**	**0**	**1**	**2**	**1**	**0**	**0**	**3**	**33.3**	**5**	**4**	**7**	**0**	**–6**	....	....	....	....	....	....	....	....
1989-90	Washington	FrTour	4	0	1	1	....	....	....	0	....	....	....	....	....	....	....	....	....	....	....	....	....	....	....	....	....	....
	Baltimore Skipjacks	AHL	73	19	42	61	....	....	....	115	....	....	....	....	....	....	....	....	....	....	12	0	11	11	18	....	....	....
1990-91	**Washington Capitals**	**NHL**	**8**	**0**	**4**	**4**	**0**	**3**	**3**	**0**	**0**	**0**	**0**	**7**	**0.0**	**4**	**3**	**1**	**0**	**0**	....	....	....	....	....	....	....	....
	Baltimore Skipjacks	AHL	27	4	24	28	....	....	....	26	....	....	....	....	....	....	....	....	....	....	6	1	4	5	6	....	....	....
1991-92	IEV Innsbruck	Austria	44	13	41	54	....	....	....	....	....	....	....	....	....	....	....	....	....	....	....	....	....	....	....	....	....	....
1992-93	IEV Innsbruck	Austria	30	8	28	36	....	....	....	....	....	....	....	....	....	....	....	....	....	....	....	....	....	....	....	....	....	....
1993-94	IEV Innsbruck	Austria	45	18	28	46	....	....	....	....	....	....	....	....	....	....	....	....	....	....	....	....	....	....	....	....	....	....
1994-95	Klagenfurter	Germany	26	11	21	32	....	....	....	93	....	....	....	....	....	....	....	....	....	....	7	1	4	5	10	....	....	....
1995-96	Servette	Switz.	35	9	16	25	....	....	....	91	....	....	....	....	....	....	....	....	....	....	3	0	1	1	0	....	....	....
1996-97	Ilves Tampere	Finland	49	2	12	14	....	....	....	50	....	....	....	....	....	....	....	....	....	....	8	0	1	1	22	....	....	....
1997-98	ESV Kaufbeuren	Germany	15	0	4	4	....	....	....	20	....	....	....	....	....	....	....	....	....	....	....	....	....	....	....	....	....	....
	Adler Mannheim	EuroHL	1	0	0	0	....	....	....	2	....	....	....	....	....	....	....	....	....	....	....	....	....	....	....	....	....	....
	Adler Mannheim	Germany	25	0	1	1	....	....	....	6	....	....	....	....	....	....	....	....	....	....	3	1	0	1	0	....	....	....
	NHL Totals		**35**	**1**	**12**	**13**	**1**	**9**	**10**	**10**	**1**	**0**	**0**	**28**	**3.6**	**39**	**20**	**18**	**0**		**2**	**0**	**1**	**1**	**0**	**0**	**0**	**0**

Signed as a free agent by **Washington**, March 1, 1988.

• FELSNER, BRIAN

Brian Felsner LW – L. 5'11", 189 lbs. b: Mt. Clemens, MI, 11/11/1972.

			REGULAR SEASON																		PLAYOFFS							
Season	Club	League	GP	G	A	Pts	AG	AA	APts	PIM	PP	SH	GW	S	%	TGF	PGF	TGA	PGA	+/-	GP	G	A	Pts	PIM	PP	SH	GW
1993-94	Lake Superior State	CCHA	6	1	1	2	....	....	....	6	....	....	....	....	....	....	....	....	....	....	....	....	....	....	....	....	....	....
1994-95	Lake Superior State	CCHA	41	24	28	52	....	....	....	51	....	....	....	....	....	....	....	....	....	....	....	....	....	....	....	....	....	....
1995-96	Lake Superior State	CCHA	38	16	36	52	....	....	....	40	....	....	....	....	....	....	....	....	....	....	....	....	....	....	....	....	....	....
1996-97	Orlando Solar Bears	IHL	75	29	41	70	....	....	....	38	....	....	....	....	....	....	....	....	....	....	7	2	3	5	6	....	....	....
1997-98	**Chicago Blackhawks**	**NHL**	**12**	**1**	**3**	**4**	**1**	**3**	**4**	**12**	....	....	....	....	....	....	....	....	....	....	....	....	....	....	....	....	....	....
	Indianapolis Ice	IHL	53	17	36	53	....	....	....	36	....	....	....	....	....	....	....	....	....	....	....	....	....	....	....	....	....	....
	Milwaukee Admirals	IHL	15	7	8	15	....	....	....	20	....	....	....	....	....	....	....	....	....	....	10	3	9	12	12	....	....	....
	NHL Totals		**12**	**1**	**3**	**4**	**1**	**3**	**4**	**12**	**0**	**0**	**0**	**0**	**0.0**	**0**	**0**	**0**	**0**		....	....	....	....	....	....	....	....

Signed as a free agent by **Chicago**, September 5, 1997.

• FELSNER, DENNY

Denny Felsner LW – L. 6', 195 lbs. b: Warren, MI, 4/29/1970. St. Louis' 3rd choice, 55th overall, in 1989 Entry Draft.

Season	Club	League	GP	G	A	Pts	AG	AA	APts	PIM	PP	SH	GW	S	%	TGF	PGF	TGA	PGA	+/-	GP	G	A	Pts	PIM	PP	SH	GW
1988-89	University of Michigan	CCHA	39	30	19	49	....	....	....	22	....	....	....	....	....	....	....	....	....	....	....	....	....	....	....	....	....	....
1989-90	University of Michigan	CCHA	33	27	16	43	....	....	....	24	....	....	....	....	....	....	....	....	....	....	....	....	....	....	....	....	....	....
1990-91	University of Michigan	CCHA	46	*40	35	75	....	....	....	58	....	....	....	....	....	....	....	....	....	....	....	....	....	....	....	....	....	....
1991-92	University of Michigan	CCHA	44	42	52	94	....	....	....	46	....	....	....	....	....	....	....	....	....	....	....	....	....	....	....	....	....	....
	St. Louis Blues	**NHL**	**3**	**0**	**1**	**1**	**0**	**1**	**1**	**0**	**0**	**0**	**0**	**2**	**0.0**	**1**	**0**	**1**	**0**	**0**	**1**	**0**	**0**	**0**	**0**	**0**	**0**	**0**
1992-93	**St. Louis Blues**	**NHL**	**6**	**0**	**3**	**3**	**0**	**2**	**2**	**2**	**0**	**0**	**0**	**4**	**0.0**	**6**	**0**	**2**	**0**	**+4**	**9**	**2**	**3**	**5**	**2**	**1**	**0**	**0**
	Peoria Rivermen	IHL	29	14	21	35	....	....	....	8	....	....	....	....	....	....	....	....	....	....	....	....	....	....	....	....	....	....
1993-94	**St. Louis Blues**	**NHL**	**6**	**1**	**0**	**1**	**1**	**0**	**1**	**2**	**0**	**0**	**0**	**6**	**16.7**	**3**	**1**	**3**	**0**	**–1**	....	....	....	....	....	....	....	....
	Peoria Rivermen	IHL	6	8	3	11	....	....	....	14	....	....	....	....	....	....	....	....	....	....	....	....	....	....	....	....	....	....
1994-95	**St. Louis Blues**	**NHL**	**3**	**0**	**0**	**0**	**0**	**0**	**0**	**2**	**0**	**0**	**0**	**2**	**0.0**	**0**	**0**	**1**	**0**	**–1**	....	....	....	....	....	....	....	....
	Peoria Rivermen	IHL	25	10	12	22	....	....	....	14	....	....	....	....	....	....	....	....	....	....	8	2	3	5	0	....	....	....
1995-96	Syracuse Crunch	AHL	66	23	34	57	....	....	....	22	....	....	....	....	....	....	....	....	....	....	14	5	12	17	0	....	....	....
1996-97	Chicago Wolves	IHL	39	10	12	22	....	....	....	4	....	....	....	....	....	....	....	....	....	....	....	....	....	....	....	....	....	....
	Milwaukee Admirals	IHL	14	1	3	4	....	....	....	2	....	....	....	....	....	....	....	....	....	....	....	....	....	....	....	....	....	....
1997-98	Chesapeake Icebreakers	ECHL	50	30	37	67	....	....	....	6	....	....	....	....	....	....	....	....	....	....	....	....	....	....	....	....	....	....
	Detroit Vipers	IHL	3	0	0	0	....	....	....	0	....	....	....	....	....	....	....	....	....	....	....	....	....	....	....	....	....	....
	NHL Totals		**18**	**1**	**4**	**5**	**1**	**3**	**4**	**6**	**0**	**0**	**0**	**14**	**7.1**	**10**	**1**	**7**	**0**		**10**	**2**	**3**	**5**	**2**	**1**	**0**	**0**

CCHA First All-Star Team (1991, 1992) • NCAA West Second All-American Team (1991) • NCAA West First All-American Team (1992)

Signed as a free agent by **Vancouver**, August 31, 1995.

• FELTRIN, TONY

Tony Feltrin D – L. 6'1", 184 lbs. b: Ladysmith, B.C., 12/6/1961. Pittsburgh's 3rd choice, 72nd overall, in 1980 Entry Draft.

Season	Club	League	GP	G	A	Pts	AG	AA	APts	PIM	PP	SH	GW	S	%	TGF	PGF	TGA	PGA	+/-	GP	G	A	Pts	PIM	PP	SH	GW
1977-78	Nanaimo Clippers	BCJHL	63	2	13	15	....	....	....	65	....	....	....	....	....	....	....	....	....	....	....	....	....	....	....	....	....	....
1978-79	Victoria Cougars	WHL	47	2	11	13	....	....	....	119	....	....	....	....	....	....	....	....	....	....	7	0	1	1	4	....	....	....
1979-80	Victoria Cougars	WHL	71	6	25	31	....	....	....	138	....	....	....	....	....	....	....	....	....	....	17	0	8	8	21	....	....	....
1980-81	Victoria Cougars	WHL	43	4	25	29	....	....	....	81	....	....	....	....	....	....	....	....	....	....	....	....	....	....	....	....	....	....
	Pittsburgh Penguins	**NHL**	**2**	**0**	**0**	**0**	**0**	**0**	**0**	**0**	**0**	**0**	**0**	**0**	**0.0**	**1**	**0**	**4**	**0**	**–3**	....	....	....	....	....	....	....	....
1981-82	**Pittsburgh Penguins**	**NHL**	**4**	**0**	**0**	**0**	**0**	**0**	**0**	**4**	**0**	**0**	**0**	**3**	**0.0**	**1**	**0**	**4**	**0**	**–3**	....	....	....	....	....	....	....	....
	Erie Blades	AHL	72	4	15	19	....	....	....	117	....	....	....	....	....	....	....	....	....	....	....	....	....	....	....	....	....	....
1982-83	**Pittsburgh Penguins**	**NHL**	**32**	**3**	**3**	**6**	**2**	**2**	**4**	**40**	**0**	**0**	**0**	**36**	**8.3**	**14**	**0**	**30**	**5**	**–11**	....	....	....	....	....	....	....	....
	Baltimore Skipjacks	AHL	31	2	3	5	....	....	....	34	....	....	....	....	....	....	....	....	....	....	....	....	....	....	....	....	....	....
	Muskegon Mohawks	IHL	2	0	0	0	....	....	....	0	....	....	....	....	....	....	....	....	....	....	....	....	....	....	....	....	....	....
1983-84	Baltimore Skipjacks	AHL	4	0	0	0	....	....	....	2	....	....	....	....	....	....	....	....	....	....	....	....	....	....	....	....	....	....
	Salt Lake Golden Eagles	CHL	65	8	22	30	....	....	....	94	....	....	....	....	....	....	....	....	....	....	5	2	0	2	5	....	....	....
1984-85	Salt Lake Golden Eagles	IHL	81	8	19	27	....	....	....	125	....	....	....	....	....	....	....	....	....	....	7	2	1	3	14	....	....	....
1985-86	**New York Rangers**	**NHL**	**10**	**0**	**0**	**0**	**0**	**0**	**0**	**21**	**0**	**0**	**0**	**8**	**0.0**	**3**	**0**	**6**	**0**	**–3**	....	....	....	....	....	....	....	....
	New Haven Nighthawks	AHL	22	0	2	2	....	....	....	38	....	....	....	....	....	....	....	....	....	....	....	....	....	....	....	....	....	....
	NHL Totals		**48**	**3**	**3**	**6**	**2**	**2**	**4**	**65**	**0**	**0**	**0**	**47**	**6.4**	**19**	**0**	**44**	**5**		....	....	....	....	....	....	....	....

Signed as a free agent by **NY Rangers**, October 8, 1985.

• FENTON, PAUL

Paul Fenton LW – L. 5'11", 180 lbs. b: Springfield, MA, 12/22/1959.

Season	Club	League	GP	G	A	Pts	AG	AA	APts	PIM	PP	SH	GW	S	%	TGF	PGF	TGA	PGA	+/-	GP	G	A	Pts	PIM	PP	SH	GW
1979-80	Boston University	ECAC	24	8	17	25	....	....	....	14	....	....	....	....	....	....	....	....	....	....	....	....	....	....	....	....	....	....
1980-81	Boston University	ECAC	5	3	2	5	....	....	....	0	....	....	....	....	....	....	....	....	....	....	....	....	....	....	....	....	....	....
1981-82	Boston University	ECAC	28	20	13	33	....	....	....	20	....	....	....	....	....	....	....	....	....	....	....	....	....	....	....	....	....	....
1982-83	Peoria Prancers	IHL	82	60	51	111	....	....	....	53	....	....	....	....	....	....	....	....	....	....	....	....	....	....	....	....	....	....
	Colorado Flames	CHL	1	0	1	1	....	....	....	0	....	....	....	....	....	....	....	....	....	....	3	2	0	2	2	....	....	....
1983-84	Binghamton Whalers	AHL	78	41	24	65	....	....	....	67	....	....	....	....	....	....	....	....	....	....	....	....	....	....	....	....	....	....
1984-85	**Hartford Whalers**	**NHL**	**33**	**7**	**5**	**12**	**6**	**3**	**9**	**10**	**0**	**0**	**2**	**53**	**13.2**	**17**	**1**	**11**	**1**	**+6**	....	....	....	....	....	....	....	....
	Binghamton Whalers	AHL	45	26	21	47	....	....	....	18	....	....	....	....	....	....	....	....	....	....	....	....	....	....	....	....	....	....
	United States	WEC A	9	2	1	3	....	....	....	8	....	....	....	....	....	....	....	....	....	....	....	....	....	....	....	....	....	....
1985-86	**Hartford Whalers**	**NHL**	**1**	**0**	**0**	**0**	**0**	**0**	**0**	**0**	**0**	**0**	**0**	**3**	**0.0**	**1**	**0**	**0**	**0**	**+1**	....	....	....	....	....	....	....	....
	Binghamton Whalers	AHL	75	53	35	88	....	....	....	87	....	....	....	....	....	....	....	....	....	....	6	2	0	2	2	....	....	....
1986-87	**New York Rangers**	**NHL**	**8**	**0**	**0**	**0**	**0**	**0**	**0**	**2**	**0**	**0**	**0**	**11**	**0.0**	**1**	**0**	**6**	**0**	**–5**	....	....	....	....	....	....	....	....
	New Haven Nighthawks	AHL	70	37	38	75	....	....	....	45	....	....	....	....	....	....	....	....	....	....	7	6	4	10	6	....	....	....
1987-88	**Los Angeles Kings**	**NHL**	**71**	**20**	**23**	**43**	**17**	**16**	**33**	**46**	**8**	**1**	**1**	**166**	**12.0**	**70**	**24**	**72**	**12**	**–14**	**5**	**2**	**1**	**3**	**2**	**1**	**0**	**0**
	New Haven Nighthawks	AHL	5	11	5	16	....	....	....	9	....	....	....	....	....	....	....	....	....	....	....	....	....	....	....	....	....	....
1988-89	**Los Angeles Kings**	**NHL**	**21**	**2**	**3**	**5**	**2**	**2**	**4**	**6**	**0**	**0**	**0**	**26**	**7.7**	**6**	**1**	**6**	**0**	**–1**	....	....	....	....	....	....	....	....
	Winnipeg Jets	**NHL**	**59**	**14**	**9**	**23**	**12**	**6**	**18**	**33**	**1**	**0**	**0**	**109**	**12.8**	**31**	**3**	**44**	**1**	**–15**	....	....	....	....	....	....	....	....
	United States	WEC A	10	1	3	4	....	....	....	14	....	....	....	....	....	....	....	....	....	....	....	....	....	....	....	....	....	....
1989-90	**Winnipeg Jets**	**NHL**	**80**	**32**	**18**	**50**	**28**	**13**	**41**	**40**	**4**	**1**	**1**	**152**	**21.1**	**74**	**11**	**74**	**13**	**+2**	**7**	**2**	**0**	**2**	**23**	**2**	**0**	**0**
1990-91	**Winnipeg Jets**	**NHL**	**17**	**4**	**4**	**8**	**4**	**3**	**7**	**18**	**1**	**0**	**1**	**20**	**14.3**	**11**	**5**	**11**	**1**	**–4**	....	....	....	....	....	....	....	....
	Toronto Maple Leafs	**NHL**	**30**	**5**	**10**	**15**	**5**	**8**	**13**	**0**	**1**	**1**	**0**	**46**	**10.9**	**20**	**3**	**25**	**5**	**–3**	....	....	....	....	....	....	....	....
	Calgary Flames	**NHL**	**31**	**5**	**7**	**12**	**5**	**5**	**10**	**10**	**0**	**1**	**1**	**59**	**8.5**	**20**	**0**	**21**	**3**	**+2**	**5**	**0**	**0**	**0**	**2**	**0**	**0**	**0**
1991-92	**San Jose Sharks**	**NHL**	**60**	**11**	**4**	**15**	**10**	**3**	**13**	**33**	**3**	**2**	**1**	**96**	**11.5**	**21**	**4**	**67**	**11**	**–39**	....	....	....	....	....	....	....	....
	NHL Totals		**411**	**100**	**83**	**183**	**89**	**59**	**148**	**198**	**18**	**6**	**7**	**749**	**13.4**	**272**	**52**	**337**	**47**		**17**	**4**	**1**	**5**	**27**	**3**	**0**	**0**

IHL Second All-Star Team (1983) • AHL First All-Star Team (1986) • AHL Second All-Star Team (1987)

Signed as a free agent by **Hartford**, October 6, 1983. Signed as a free agent by **NY Rangers**, September 11, 1986. Claimed by **LA Kings** from **Montreal** in Waiver Draft, October 5, 1987. Traded to **Winnipeg** by **LA Kings** for Gilles Hamel, November 25, 1988. Traded to **Toronto** by **Winnipeg** with Dave Ellett for Ed Olczyk and Mark Osborne, November 10, 1989. Traded to **Washington** by **Toronto** with John Kordic for Washington's 5th round choice (Alexei Kuashov) in 1991 Entry Draft, January 24, 1991. Traded to **Calgary** by **Washington** for Ken Sabourin, January 24, 1991. Traded to **Hartford** by **Calgary** for future considerations, August 26, 1991. Traded to **San Jose** by **Hartford** for Mike McHugh, October 18, 1991.

• FENYVES, DAVID

David Fenyves D – L. 6', 192 lbs. b: Dunnville, Ont., 4/29/1960.

Season	Club	League	GP	G	A	Pts	AG	AA	APts	PIM	PP	SH	GW	S	%	TGF	PGF	TGA	PGA	+/-	GP	G	A	Pts	PIM	PP	SH	GW
1977-78	Peterborough Petes	OHA	59	3	12	15	....	....	....	36	....	....	....	....	....	....	....	....	....	....	....	....	....	....	....	....	....	....
1978-79	Peterborough Petes	OHA	66	2	23	25	....	....	....	122	....	....	....	....	....	....	....	....	....	....	19	0	5	5	18	....	....	....
1979-80	Peterborough Petes	OHA	66	9	36	45	....	....	....	92	....	....	....	....	....	....	....	....	....	....	14	0	3	3	14	....	....	....
1980-81	Rochester Americans	AHL	77	6	16	22	....	....	....	146	....	....	....	....	....	....	....	....	....	....	....	....	....	....	....	....	....	....
1981-82	Rochester Americans	AHL	73	3	14	17	....	....	....	68	....	....	....	....	....	....	....	....	....	....	5	0	1	1	4	....	....	....
1982-83	**Buffalo Sabres**	**NHL**	**24**	**0**	**8**	**8**	**0**	**6**	**6**	**14**	**0**	**0**	**0**	**20**	**0.0**	**23**	**0**	**39**	**6**	**–10**	**4**	**0**	**0**	**0**	**0**	**0**	**0**	**0**
	Rochester Americans	AHL	51	2	10	21	....	....	....	45	....	....	....	....	....	....	....	....	....	....	....	....	....	....	....	....	....	....
1983-84	**Buffalo Sabres**	**NHL**	**10**	**0**	**4**	**4**	**0**	**3**	**3**	**9**	**0**	**0**	**0**	**4**	**0.0**	**9**	**0**	**4**	**2**	**+7**	**2**	**0**	**0**	**0**	**7**	**0**	**0**	**0**
	Rochester Americans	AHL	70	3	16	19	....	....	....	55	....	....	....	....	....	....	....	....	....	....	16	1	4	5	22	....	....	....
1984-85	**Buffalo Sabres**	**NHL**	**60**	**1**	**8**	**9**	**1**	**5**	**6**	**27**	**0**	**0**	**0**	**50**	**2.0**	**35**	**0**	**52**	**17**	**0**	**5**	**0**	**0**	**0**	**2**	**0**	**0**	**0**
	Rochester Americans	AHL	9	0	3	3	....	....	....	8	....	....	....	....	....	....	....	....	....	....	....	....	....	....	....	....	....	....
1985-86	**Buffalo Sabres**	**NHL**	**47**	**0**	**7**	**7**	**0**	**5**	**5**	**37**	**0**	**0**	**0**	**31**	**0.0**	**42**	**2**	**42**	**14**	**+12**	....	....	....	....	....	....	....	....
1986-87	**Buffalo Sabres**	**NHL**	**7**	**1**	**0**	**1**	**1**	**0**	**1**	**0**	**0**	**0**	**0**	**3**	**33.3**	**3**	**0**	**0**	**0**	**–3**	....	....	....	....	....	....	....	....
	Rochester Americans	AHL	71	6	16	22	....	....	....	57	....	....	....	....	....	....	....	....	....	....	18	3	12	15	10	....	....	....
1987-88	**Philadelphia Flyers**	**NHL**	**5**	**0**	**0**	**0**	**0**	**0**	**0**	**0**	**0**	**0**	**0**	**3**	**0.0**	**3**	**1**	**3**	**0**	**–1**	....	....	....	....	....	....	....	....
	Hershey Bears	AHL	75	11	40	51	....	....	....	47	....	....	....	....	....	....	....	....	....	....	12	1	8	9	10	....	....	....

Season	Club	League	GP	G	A	Pts	AG	AA	APts	PIM	PP	SH	GW	S	%	TGF	PGF	TGA	PGA	+/–	GP	G	A	Pts	PIM	PP	SH	GW
			REGULAR SEASON																		PLAYOFFS							
1988-89	**Philadelphia Flyers**	**NHL**	1	0	1	1	0	1	1	0	0	0	0	0	0.0	1	0	2	1	0	....	....	....	....	....	....	....	....
	Hershey Bears	AHL	79	15	51	66	....	....	....	41	....	....	....	....	....	....	....	....	....	....	12	2	6	8	6	....	....	....
1989-90	**Philadelphia Flyers**	**NHL**	12	0	0	0	0	0	0	4	0	0	0	10	0.0	6	0	12	0	–6	....	....	....	....	....	....	....	....
	Hershey Bears	AHL	66	6	37	43	....	....	....	57	....	....	....	....	....	....	....	....	....	....	....	....	....	....	....	....	....	....
1990-91	**Philadelphia Flyers**	**NHL**	40	1	4	5	1	3	4	28	0	0	0	32	3.1	27	0	26	0	+1	....	....	....	....	....	....	....	....
	Hershey Bears	AHL	29	4	11	15	....	....	....	13	....	....	....	....	....	....	....	....	....	....	7	0	3	3	6	....	....	....
1991-92	Hershey Bears	AHL	68	4	24	28	....	....	....	29	....	....	....	....	....	....	....	....	....	....	6	1	1	2	10	....	....	....
1992-93	Hershey Bears	AHL	42	3	11	14	....	....	....	14	....	....	....	....	....	....	....	....	....	....	....	....	....	....	....	....	....	....
	NHL Totals		206	3	32	35	3	23	26	119	0	0	0	153	2.0	149	3	186	40		11	0	0	0	9	0	0	0

OHA Second All-Star Team (1980) • AHL Second All-Star Team (1987) • Won Jack A. Butterfield Trophy (Playoff MVP - AHL) (1987) • AHL First All-Star Team (1988, 1989) • Won Eddie Shore Award (Outstanding Defenseman - AHL) (1988, 1989)

Signed as a free agent by **Buffalo**, October 31, 1979. Claimed by **Philadelphia** from **Buffalo** in Waiver Draft, October 5, 1987.

• FERGUS, TOM

Tom Fergus C – L. 6'3", 210 lbs. b: Chicago, IL, 6/16/1962. Boston's 2nd choice, 60th overall, in 1980 Entry Draft.

Season	Club	League	GP	G	A	Pts	AG	AA	APts	PIM	PP	SH	GW	S	%	TGF	PGF	TGA	PGA	+/–	GP	G	A	Pts	PIM	PP	SH	GW
1979-80	Peterborough Petes	OHA	63	8	6	14	....	....	....	14	....	....	....	....	....	....	....	....	....	....	14	1	5	6	6	....	....	....
1980-81	Peterborough Petes	OHA	63	43	45	88	....	....	....	33	....	....	....	....	....	....	....	....	....	....	5	1	4	5	2	....	....	....
1981-82	**Boston Bruins**	**NHL**	61	15	24	39	12	16	28	12	2	0	2	116	12.9	58	5	38	0	+15	6	3	0	3	0	2	0	0
1982-83	**Boston Bruins**	**NHL**	80	28	35	63	23	24	47	39	4	0	6	169	16.6	89	16	50	3	+26	15	2	2	4	15	0	0	0
1983-84	**Boston Bruins**	**NHL**	69	25	36	61	20	24	44	12	6	0	3	123	20.3	82	15	63	4	+8	3	2	0	2	9	1	0	0
1984-85	**Boston Bruins**	**NHL**	79	30	43	73	25	29	54	75	4	0	2	183	16.4	108	28	69	3	+14	5	0	0	0	4	0	0	0
	United States	WEC-A	8	4	2	6	....	....	....	14	....	....	....	....	....	....	....	....	....	....	....	....	....	....	....	....	....	....
1985-86	**Toronto Maple Leafs**	**NHL**	78	31	42	73	25	28	53	64	3	2	3	168	18.5	113	30	144	37	–24	10	5	7	12	6	3	0	1
1986-87	**Toronto Maple Leafs**	**NHL**	57	21	28	49	18	20	38	57	2	1	2	119	17.6	71	14	73	17	+1	2	0	1	1	2	0	0	0
	Newmarket Saints	AHL	1	0	1	1	....	....	....	0	....	....	....	....	....	....	....	....	....	....	....	....	....	....	....	....	....	....
1987-88	**Toronto Maple Leafs**	**NHL**	63	19	31	50	16	22	38	81	5	0	0	124	15.3	63	7	69	18	+5	6	2	3	5	2	0	1	0
1988-89	**Toronto Maple Leafs**	**NHL**	80	22	45	67	19	32	51	48	10	1	3	151	14.6	92	37	121	28	–38	....	....	....	....	....	....	....	....
1989-90	**Toronto Maple Leafs**	**NHL**	54	19	26	45	16	19	35	62	4	0	2	120	15.8	72	16	77	3	–18	5	2	1	3	4	0	0	0
1990-91	**Toronto Maple Leafs**	**NHL**	14	5	4	9	5	3	8	8	2	0	0	17	29.4	13	7	11	0	–5	....	....	....	....	....	....	....	....
1991-92	**Toronto Maple Leafs**	**NHL**	11	1	3	4	1	2	3	4	0	0	0	24	4.2	5	3	13	0	–11	....	....	....	....	....	....	....	....
	Vancouver Canucks	**NHL**	44	14	20	34	13	15	28	17	6	0	3	79	17.7	48	20	42	15	+1	13	5	3	8	6	0	0	1
1992-93	**Vancouver Canucks**	**NHL**	36	5	9	14	4	6	10	20	1	1	0	29	17.2	18	3	26	12	+1	....	....	....	....	....	....	....	....
1993-94	SC Zug	Switz.	32	21	29	50	....	....	....	104	....	....	....	....	....	....	....	....	....	....	....	....	....	....	....	....	....	....
1994-95	SC Zug	Switz.	22	12	12	24	....	....	....	56	....	....	....	....	....	....	....	....	....	....	12	3	10	13	16	....	....	....
	NHL Totals		726	235	346	581	197	240	437	499	49	5	26	1422	16.5	832	201	796	140		65	21	17	38	48	6	1	2

Traded to **Toronto** by **Boston** for Bill Derlago, October 11, 1985. Claimed on waivers by **Vancouver** from **Toronto**, December 18, 1991.

• FERGUSON, CRAIG

Craig Ferguson RW – L. 5'11", 190 lbs. b: Castro Valley, CA, 4/8/1970. Montreal's 8th choice, 146th overall, in 1989 Entry Draft.

Season	Club	League	GP	G	A	Pts	AG	AA	APts	PIM	PP	SH	GW	S	%	TGF	PGF	TGA	PGA	+/–	GP	G	A	Pts	PIM	PP	SH	GW
1988-89	Yale University	ECAC	24	11	6	17	....	....	....	20	....	....	....	....	....	....	....	....	....	....	....	....	....	....	....	....	....	....
1989-90	Yale University	ECAC	28	6	13	19	....	....	....	36	....	....	....	....	....	....	....	....	....	....	....	....	....	....	....	....	....	....
1990-91	Yale University	ECAC	29	11	10	21	....	....	....	34	....	....	....	....	....	....	....	....	....	....	....	....	....	....	....	....	....	....
1991-92	Yale University	ECAC	27	9	16	25	....	....	....	26	....	....	....	....	....	....	....	....	....	....	....	....	....	....	....	....	....	....
1992-93	Fredericton Canadiens	AHL	55	15	13	28	....	....	....	20	....	....	....	....	....	....	....	....	....	....	5	0	1	1	2	....	....	....
	Wheeling Thunderbirds	ECHL	9	6	5	11	....	....	....	24	....	....	....	....	....	....	....	....	....	....	....	....	....	....	....	....	....	....
1993-94	**Montreal Canadiens**	**NHL**	2	0	1	1	0	1	1	0	0	0	0	0	0.0	1	0	0	0	+1	....	....	....	....	....	....	....	....
	Fredericton Canadiens	AHL	57	29	32	61	....	....	....	60	....	....	....	....	....	....	....	....	....	....	....	....	....	....	....	....	....	....
1994-95	Fredericton Canadiens	AHL	80	27	35	62	....	....	....	62	....	....	....	....	....	....	....	....	....	....	17	6	2	8	6	....	....	....
	Montreal Canadiens	**NHL**	1	0	0	0	0	0	0	0	0	0	0	3	0.0	0	0	1	1	0	....	....	....	....	....	....	....	....
1995-96	**Montreal Canadiens**	**NHL**	10	1	0	1	1	0	1	2	0	0	0	9	11.1	2	1	7	1	–5	....	....	....	....	....	....	....	....
	Calgary Flames	**NHL**	8	0	0	0	0	0	0	4	0	0	0	11	0.0	0	0	4	0	–4	....	....	....	....	....	....	....	....
	Saint John Flames	AHL	18	5	13	18	....	....	....	8	....	....	....	....	....	....	....	....	....	....	....	....	....	....	....	....	....	....
	Phoenix Roadrunners	IHL	31	6	9	15	....	....	....	25	....	....	....	....	....	....	....	....	....	....	4	0	2	2	6	....	....	....
1996-97	**Florida Panthers**	**NHL**	3	0	0	0	0	0	0	0	0	0	0	5	0.0	0	0	1	0	–1	....	....	....	....	....	....	....	....
	Carolina Monarchs	AHL	74	29	41	70	....	....	....	57	....	....	....	....	....	....	....	....	....	....	....	....	....	....	....	....	....	....
1997-98	Beast of New Haven	AHL	64	24	28	52	....	....	....	41	....	....	....	....	....	....	....	....	....	....	3	2	1	3	2	....	....	....
	NHL Totals		24	1	1	2	1	1	2	6	0	0	0	28	3.6	3	1	13	2		....	....	....	....	....	....	....	....

Traded to **Calgary** by **Montreal** with Yves Sarault for Calgary's 8th round choice (Petr Kubos) in 1997 Entry Draft, November 26, 1995. Traded to **LA Kings** by **Calgary** for Pat Conacher, February 10, 1996. Signed as a free agent by **Florida**, July 24, 1996.

• FERGUSON, GEORGE

George Ferguson C – R. 6', 195 lbs. b: Trenton, Ont., 8/22/1952. Toronto's 1st choice, 11th overall, in 1972 Amateur Draft.

Season	Club	League	GP	G	A	Pts	AG	AA	APts	PIM	PP	SH	GW	S	%	TGF	PGF	TGA	PGA	+/–	GP	G	A	Pts	PIM	PP	SH	GW
1969-70	Peterborough Petes	OHA	49	19	21	40	....	....	....	20	....	....	....	....	....	....	....	....	....	....	....	....	....	....	....	....	....	....
1970-71	Peterborough Petes	OHA	8	2	0	2	....	....	....	19	....	....	....	....	....	....	....	....	....	....	....	....	....	....	....	....	....	....
	Toronto Marlboros	OHA	43	12	15	27	....	....	....	83	....	....	....	....	....	....	....	....	....	....	....	....	....	....	....	....	....	....
1971-72	Toronto Marlboros	OHA	62	36	56	92	....	....	....	104	....	....	....	....	....	....	....	....	....	....	....	....	....	....	....	....	....	....
1972-73	**Toronto Maple Leafs**	**NHL**	72	10	13	23	10	11	21	34	3	0	1	92	10.9	39	7	49	0	–17	....	....	....	....	....	....	....	....
1973-74	**Toronto Maple Leafs**	**NHL**	16	0	4	4	0	3	3	4	0	0	0	19	0.0	7	2	5	1	+1	3	0	1	1	2	0	0	0
	Oklahoma City Blazers	CHL	35	16	33	49	....	....	....	21	....	....	....	....	....	....	....	....	....	....	....	....	....	....	....	....	....	....
1974-75	**Toronto Maple Leafs**	**NHL**	69	19	30	49	18	24	42	61	3	1	5	134	14.2	68	11	57	5	+5	7	1	0	1	7	0	0	0
1975-76	**Toronto Maple Leafs**	**NHL**	79	12	32	44	11	25	36	76	3	2	2	140	8.6	57	13	65	32	+11	10	2	4	6	2	0	0	1
1976-77	**Toronto Maple Leafs**	**NHL**	50	9	15	24	9	12	21	24	0	2	0	73	12.3	35	7	48	20	0	9	0	3	3	7	0	0	0
1977-78	**Toronto Maple Leafs**	**NHL**	73	7	16	23	7	13	20	37	0	0	0	119	5.9	35	1	54	11	–9	13	5	1	6	7	0	0	0
1978-79	**Pittsburgh Penguins**	**NHL**	80	21	29	50	19	22	41	37	0	3	2	201	10.4	74	1	94	31	+10	7	2	1	3	0	0	0	1
1979-80	**Pittsburgh Penguins**	**NHL**	73	21	28	49	19	21	40	36	1	3	3	176	11.9	62	6	93	37	0	5	0	3	3	4	0	0	0
1980-81	**Pittsburgh Penguins**	**NHL**	79	25	18	43	21	13	34	42	7	3	1	181	13.8	73	24	120	41	–30	5	2	6	8	9	0	0	0
1981-82	**Pittsburgh Penguins**	**NHL**	71	22	31	53	17	20	37	45	4	3	0	168	13.1	76	16	116	50	–6	5	0	1	1	0	0	0	0
1982-83	**Pittsburgh Penguins**	**NHL**	7	0	0	0	0	0	0	2	0	0	0	10	0.0	0	0	14	7	–7	....	....	....	....	....	....	....	....
	Minnesota North Stars	**NHL**	65	8	12	20	7	8	15	14	0	1	2	82	9.8	33	3	52	21	–1	9	0	3	3	4	0	0	0
1983-84	**Minnesota North Stars**	**NHL**	63	6	10	16	5	7	12	19	0	0	0	57	10.5	28	1	62	29	–6	13	2	0	2	2	0	0	1
	NHL Totals		797	160	238	398	143	179	322	431	21	18	16	1452	11.0	587	92	829	285		86	14	23	37	44	0	0	3

Traded to **Pittsburgh** by **Toronto** with Randy Carlyle for Dave Burrows, June 14, 1978. Traded to **Minnesota** by **Pittsburgh** with Pittsburgh's 1st round choice (Brian Lawton) in 1983 Entry Draft for Ron Meighan and Anders Hakansson, October 28, 1982.

• FERGUSON, JOHN

John Ferguson LW – L. 5'11", 190 lbs. b: Vancouver, B.C., 9/5/1938.

Season	Club	League	GP	G	A	Pts	AG	AA	APts	PIM	PP	SH	GW	S	%	TGF	PGF	TGA	PGA	+/–	GP	G	A	Pts	PIM	PP	SH	GW
		....	....	....	....	....	....	....	....	....	....	....	....	....	....	....	....	....	....	....	....	....	....	....	....	....	....	....
1956-57	Melville Millionaires	SJHL	51	11	17	28	....	....	....	49	....	....	....	....	....	....	....	....	....	....	....	....	....	....	....	....	....	....
1957-58	Melville Millionaires	SJHL	50	14	30	44	....	....	....	100	....	....	....	....	....	....	....	....	....	....	....	....	....	....	....	....	....	....
1958-59	Melville Millionaires	SJHL	44	32	34	66	....	....	....	83	....	....	....	....	....	....	....	....	....	....	....	....	....	....	....	....	....	....
1959-60	Fort Wayne Komets	IHL	68	32	33	65	....	....	....	126	....	....	....	....	....	....	....	....	....	....	13	1	1	2	17	....	....	....
1960-61	Cleveland Barons	AHL	62	13	21	34	....	....	....	126	....	....	....	....	....	....	....	....	....	....	....	....	....	....	....	....	....	....
1961-62	Cleveland Barons	AHL	70	20	21	41	....	....	....	146	....	....	....	....	....	....	....	....	....	....	6	2	2	4	6	....	....	....
1962-63	Cleveland Barons	AHL	72	38	40	78	....	....	....	179	....	....	....	....	....	....	....	....	....	....	7	3	3	6	17	....	....	....
1963-64	**Montreal Canadiens**	**NHL**	59	18	27	45	24	30	54	125	....	....	....	....	....	....	....	....	....	....	7	0	1	1	25	....	....	....
1964-65	**Montreal Canadiens**	**NHL**	69	17	27	44	22	29	51	156	....	....	....	....	....	....	....	....	....	....	13	3	1	4	28	....	....	....
1965-66	**Montreal Canadiens**	**NHL**	65	11	14	25	13	14	27	153	....	....	....	....	....	....	....	....	....	....	10	2	0	2	*44	....	....	....
1966-67	**Montreal Canadiens**	**NHL**	67	20	22	42	25	23	48	*177	....	....	....	....	....	....	....	....	....	....	10	4	2	6	22	....	....	....
1967-68	**Montreal Canadiens**	**NHL**	61	15	18	33	19	19	38	117	0	0	3	153	9.8	61	12	31	0	+18	13	3	5	8	25	0	0	1

Season	Club	League	GP	G	A	Pts	AG	AA	APts	PIM	PP	SH	GW	S	%	TGF	PGF	TGA	PGA	+/–	Playoffs GP	G	A	Pts	PIM	PP	SH	GW
1968-69	**Montreal Canadiens**	**NHL**	**71**	**29**	**23**	**52**	**33**	**22**	**55**	**185**	**2**	**0**	**7**	**185**	**15.7**	**73**	**6**	**37**	**0**	**+30**	**14**	**4**	**3**	**7**	***80**	**2**	**2**	**0**
1969-70	**Montreal Canadiens**	**NHL**	**48**	**19**	**13**	**32**	**22**	**13**	**35**	**139**	**6**	**0**	**7**	**116**	**16.4**	**51**	**14**	**27**	**1**	**+11**	....	....	....	....	....	....	....	....
1970-71	**Montreal Canadiens**	**NHL**	**60**	**16**	**14**	**30**	**17**	**12**	**29**	**162**	**3**	**0**	**4**	**117**	**13.7**	**48**	**9**	**37**	**0**	**+2**	**18**	**4**	**6**	**10**	**36**	**1**	**0**	**1**
	NHL Totals		**500**	**145**	**158**	**303**	**175**	**162**	**337**	**1214**	**11**	**0**	**21**	**571**	**25.4**	**233**	**41**	**132**	**1**		**85**	**20**	**18**	**38**	**260**	**3**	**2**	**2**

AHL First All-Star Team (1963)

Played in NHL All-Star Game (1965, 1967)

Traded to **Montreal** by **Cleveland** (AHL) for cash, June, 1963.

• FERGUSON, NORM

Norm Ferguson RW – R. 5'9", 165 lbs. b: Sydney, N.S., 10/16/1945.

Season	Club	League	GP	G	A	Pts	AG	AA	APts	PIM	PP	SH	GW	S	%	TGF	PGF	TGA	PGA	+/–	Playoffs GP	G	A	Pts	PIM	PP	SH	GW
1963-64	Lachine Maroons	QJHL	42	32	60	92	....	....	....	12	....	....	....	....	....	....	....	....	....	....	....	....	....	....	....	....	....	....
1964-65	Montreal Jr. Canadiens	OHA	51	17	16	33	....	....	....	17	....	....	....	....	....	....	....	....	....	....	6	2	0	2	0	....	....	....
1965-66	Montreal Jr. Canadiens	OHA	43	16	29	45	....	....	....	27	....	....	....	....	....	....	....	....	....	....	10	4	3	7	2	....	....	....
1966-67	Houston Apollos	CHL	55	8	6	14	....	....	....	20	....	....	....	....	....	....	....	....	....	....	1	0	0	0	0	....	....	....
1967-68	Cleveland Barons	AHL	72	42	33	75	....	....	....	24	....	....	....	....	....	....	....	....	....	....	....	....	....	....	....	....	....	....
1968-69	**Oakland Seals**	**NHL**	**76**	**34**	**20**	**54**	**38**	**19**	**57**	**31**	**7**	**0**	**3**	**217**	**15.7**	**73**	**14**	**68**	**0**	**–9**	**7**	**1**	**4**	**5**	**7**	**0**	**0**	**0**
1969-70	**Oakland Seals**	**NHL**	**72**	**11**	**9**	**20**	**13**	**9**	**22**	**19**	**2**	**0**	**2**	**125**	**8.8**	**31**	**6**	**40**	**0**	**–15**	**3**	**0**	**0**	**0**	**0**	**0**	**0**	**0**
1970-71	**California Golden Seals**	**NHL**	**54**	**14**	**17**	**31**	**15**	**15**	**30**	**9**	**2**	**0**	**2**	**90**	**15.6**	**41**	**9**	**53**	**0**	**–21**	....	....	....	....	....	....	....	....
1971-72	**California Golden Seals**	**NHL**	**77**	**14**	**20**	**34**	**15**	**18**	**33**	**13**	**4**	**0**	**3**	**94**	**14.9**	**51**	**8**	**48**	**0**	**–5**	....	....	....	....	....	....	....	....
1972-73	New York Raiders	WHA	56	28	40	68	....	....	....	8	....	....	....	....	....	....	....	....	....	....	....	....	....	....	....	....	....	....
1973-74	New York-New Jersey	WHA	75	15	21	36	....	....	....	12	....	....	....	....	....	....	....	....	....	....	....	....	....	....	....	....	....	....
1974-75	San Diego Mariners	WHA	78	36	33	69	....	....	....	6	....	....	....	....	....	....	....	....	....	....	10	6	5	11	0	....	....	....
1975-76	San Diego Mariners	WHA	79	37	37	74	....	....	....	12	....	....	....	....	....	....	....	....	....	....	4	2	0	2	9	....	....	....
1976-77	San Diego Mariners	WHA	77	39	32	71	....	....	....	5	....	....	....	....	....	....	....	....	....	....	7	2	4	6	0	....	....	....
1977-78	Edmonton Oilers	WHA	71	26	21	47	....	....	....	2	....	....	....	....	....	....	....	....	....	....	5	0	0	0	0	....	....	....
	NHL Totals		**279**	**73**	**66**	**139**	**81**	**61**	**142**	**72**	**15**	**0**	**10**	**526**	**13.9**	**196**	**37**	**209**	**0**		**10**	**1**	**4**	**5**	**7**	**0**	**0**	**0**
	Other Major League Totals		436	181	184	365	....	....	....	45	....	....	....	....	....	....	....	....	....	....	26	10	9	19	9	....	....	....

Traded to **Oakland** by **Montreal** with Stan Fuller and the rights to Lyle Bradley for Alain Caron, Wally Boyer, Francois Lacombe and Michel Jacques, May 21, 1968. Selected by **NY Raiders** (WHA) in 1972 WHA General Player Draft, February 12, 1972. Claimed by **NY Islanders** from **Oakland** in Expansion Draft, June 6, 1972. Transferred to **San Diego** (WHA) after **New York-New Jersey** franchise relocated, April 30, 1974. Signed as a free agent by **Edmonton** (WHA) after **San Diego** franchise folded, May, 1977.

• FERGUSON, SCOTT

Scott Ferguson D – L. 6'1", 195 lbs. b: Camrose, Alta., 1/6/1973.

Season	Club	League	GP	G	A	Pts	AG	AA	APts	PIM	PP	SH	GW	S	%	TGF	PGF	TGA	PGA	+/–	Playoffs GP	G	A	Pts	PIM	PP	SH	GW
1990-91	Kamloops Blazers	WHL	4	0	0	0	....	....	....	0	....	....	....	....	....	....	....	....	....	....	....	....	....	....	....	....	....	....
1991-92	Kamloops Blazers	WHL	62	4	10	14	....	....	....	138	....	....	....	....	....	....	....	....	....	....	12	0	2	2	21	....	....	....
1992-93	Kamloops Blazers	WHL	71	4	19	23	....	....	....	206	....	....	....	....	....	....	....	....	....	....	13	0	2	2	24	....	....	....
1993-94	Kamloops Blazers	WHL	68	5	49	54	....	....	....	180	....	....	....	....	....	....	....	....	....	....	19	5	11	16	48	....	....	....
1994-95	Cape Breton Oilers	AHL	58	4	6	10	....	....	....	103	....	....	....	....	....	....	....	....	....	....	....	....	....	....	....	....	....	....
	Wheeling Thunderbirds	ECHL	5	1	5	6	....	....	....	16	....	....	....	....	....	....	....	....	....	....	....	....	....	....	....	....	....	....
1995-96	Cape Breton Oilers	AHL	80	5	16	21	....	....	....	196	....	....	....	....	....	....	....	....	....	....	....	....	....	....	....	....	....	....
1996-97	Hamilton Bulldogs	AHL	74	6	14	20	....	....	....	115	....	....	....	....	....	....	....	....	....	....	21	5	7	12	59	....	....	....
1997-98	**Edmonton Oilers**	**NHL**	**1**	**0**	**0**	**0**	**0**	**0**	**0**	**0**	**0**	**0**	**0**	**0**	**0.0**	**2**	**1**	**0**	**0**	**+1**	....	....	....	....	....	....	....	....
	Hamilton Bulldogs	AHL	77	7	17	24	....	....	....	160	....	....	....	....	....	....	....	....	....	....	9	0	3	3	16	....	....	....
	NHL Totals		**1**	**0**	**0**	**0**	**0**	**0**	**0**	**0**	**0**	**0**	**0**	**0**	**0.0**	**2**	**1**	**0**	**0**		....	....	....	....	....	....	....	....

WHL West Second All-Star Team (1994)

Signed as a free agent by **Edmonton**, June 2, 1994. Traded to **Ottawa** by **Edmonton** for Frantisek Musil, March 9, 1998.

• FERNER, MARK

Mark Ferner D – L. 6', 193 lbs. b: Regina, Sask., 9/5/1965. Buffalo's 12th choice, 202nd overall, in 1983 Entry Draft.

Season	Club	League	GP	G	A	Pts	AG	AA	APts	PIM	PP	SH	GW	S	%	TGF	PGF	TGA	PGA	+/–	Playoffs GP	G	A	Pts	PIM	PP	SH	GW
1982-83	Kamloops Jr. Oilers	WHL	69	6	15	21	....	....	....	81	....	....	....	....	....	....	....	....	....	....	7	0	0	0	7	....	....	....
1983-84	Kamloops Jr. Oilers	WHL	72	9	30	39	....	....	....	169	....	....	....	....	....	....	....	....	....	....	14	1	8	9	20	....	....	....
1984-85	Kamloops Blazers	WHL	69	15	39	54	....	....	....	91	....	....	....	....	....	....	....	....	....	....	15	4	9	13	21	....	....	....
1985-86	Rochester Americans	AHL	63	3	14	17	....	....	....	87	....	....	....	....	....	....	....	....	....	....	....	....	....	....	....	....	....	....
1986-87	**Buffalo Sabres**	**NHL**	**13**	**0**	**3**	**3**	**0**	**2**	**2**	**9**	**0**	**0**	**0**	**5**	**0.0**	**7**	**0**	**0**	**1**	**+2**								
	Rochester Americans	AHL	54	0	12	12	....	....	....	157	....	....	....	....	....	....	....	....	....	....	....	....	....	....	....	....	....	....
1987-88	Rochester Americans	AHL	69	1	25	26	....	....	....	165	....	....	....	....	....	....	....	....	....	....	7	1	4	5	31	....	....	....
1988-89	**Buffalo Sabres**	**NHL**	**2**	**0**	**0**	**0**	**0**	**0**	**0**	**2**	**0**	**0**	**0**	**0**	**0.0**	**1**	**0**	**3**	**0**	**–2**	....	....	....	....	....	....	....	....
	Rochester Americans	AHL	55	0	18	18	....	....	....	97	....	....	....	....	....	....	....	....	....	....	....	....	....	....	....	....	....	....
1989-90	**Washington Capitals**	**NHL**	**2**	**0**	**0**	**0**	**0**	**0**	**0**	**0**	**0**	**0**	**0**	**2**	**0.0**	**0**	**0**	**1**	**0**	**–1**	....	....	....	....	....	....	....	....
	Baltimore Skipjacks	AHL	74	7	28	35	....	....	....	76	....	....	....	....	....	....	....	....	....	....	11	1	2	3	21	....	....	....
1990-91	**Washington Capitals**	**NHL**	**7**	**0**	**1**	**1**	**0**	**1**	**1**	**4**	**0**	**0**	**0**	**3**	**0.0**	**2**	**0**	**4**	**0**	**–2**	....	....	....	....	....	....	....	....
	Baltimore Skipjacks	AHL	61	14	40	54	....	....	....	38	....	....	....	....	....	....	....	....	....	....	6	1	4	5	24	....	....	....
1991-92	Baltimore Skipjacks	AHL	57	7	38	45	....	....	....	67	....	....	....	....	....	....	....	....	....	....	....	....	....	....	....	....	....	....
	St. John's Maple Leafs	AHL	15	1	8	9	....	....	....	6	....	....	....	....	....	....	....	....	....	....	14	2	14	16	38	....	....	....
1992-93	New Haven Nighthawks	AHL	34	5	7	12	....	....	....	69	....	....	....	....	....	....	....	....	....	....	....	....	....	....	....	....	....	....
	San Diego Gulls	IHL	26	0	15	15	....	....	....	34	....	....	....	....	....	....	....	....	....	....	11	1	2	3	8	....	....	....
1993-94	**Anaheim Mighty Ducks**	**NHL**	**50**	**3**	**5**	**8**	**3**	**4**	**7**	**30**	**0**	**0**	**0**	**44**	**6.8**	**32**	**4**	**57**	**13**	**–16**	....	....	....	....	....	....	....	....
1994-95	**Anaheim Mighty Ducks**	**NHL**	**14**	**0**	**1**	**1**	**0**	**1**	**1**	**6**	**0**	**0**	**0**	**15**	**0.0**	**10**	**2**	**18**	**6**	**–4**	....	....	....	....	....	....	....	....
	San Diego Gulls	IHL	46	3	12	15	....	....	....	51	....	....	....	....	....	....	....	....	....	....	....	....	....	....	....	....	....	....
	Detroit Red Wings	**NHL**	**3**	**0**	**0**	**0**	**0**	**0**	**0**	**0**	**0**	**0**	**0**	**1**	**0.0**	**2**	**0**	**2**	**0**	**0**	....	....	....	....	....	....	....	....
	Adirondack Red Wings	AHL	3	0	0	0	....	....	....	2	....	....	....	....	....	....	....	....	....	....	1	0	0	0	0	....	....	....
1995-96	Orlando Solar Bears	IHL	43	4	18	22	....	....	....	37	....	....	....	....	....	....	....	....	....	....	23	4	10	14	8	....	....	....
1996-97	Orlando Solar Bears	IHL	61	12	18	30	....	....	....	55	....	....	....	....	....	....	....	....	....	....	....	....	....	....	....	....	....	....
	Long Beach Ice Dogs	IHL	17	2	6	8	....	....	....	31	....	....	....	....	....	....	....	....	....	....	18	3	4	7	6	....	....	....
1997-98	Kassel Huskies	EuroHL	3	0	0	0	....	....	....	0	....	....	....	....	....	....	....	....	....	....	....	....	....	....	....	....	....	....
	Kassel Huskies	Germany	9	1	1	2	....	....	....	12	....	....	....	....	....	....	....	....	....	....	....	....	....	....	....	....	....	....
	Long Beach Ice Dogs	IHL	65	1	30	31	....	....	....	66	....	....	....	....	....	....	....	....	....	....	16	2	11	13	10	....	....	....
	NHL Totals		**91**	**3**	**10**	**13**	**3**	**8**	**11**	**51**	**0**	**0**	**0**	**70**	**4.3**	**54**	**6**	**91**	**20**		....	....	....	....	....	....	....	....

WHL West First All-Star Team (1985)

Traded to **Washington** by **Buffalo** for Scott McCrory, June 1, 1989. Traded to **Toronto** by **Washington** for future considerations, February 27, 1992. Signed as a free agent by **Ottawa**, August 6, 1992. Claimed by **Anaheim** from **Ottawa** in Expansion Draft, June, 24, 1993. Traded to **Detroit** by **Anaheim** with Stu Grimson and Anaheim's 6th round choice (Magnus Nilsson) in 1996 Entry Draft for Mike Sillinger and Jason York, April 4, 1994.

• FERRARO, CHRIS

Chris Ferraro RW – R. 5'10", 185 lbs. b: Port Jefferson, NY, 1/24/1973. NY Rangers' 4th choice, 85th overall, in 1992 Entry Draft.

Season	Club	League	GP	G	A	Pts	AG	AA	APts	PIM	PP	SH	GW	S	%	TGF	PGF	TGA	PGA	+/–	Playoffs GP	G	A	Pts	PIM	PP	SH	GW
1990-91	Dubuque Fighting Saints	USHL	45	53	44	97	....	....	....	....	....	....	....	....	....	....	....	....	....	....	....	....	....	....	....	....	....	....
1991-92	Waterloo Black Hawks	USHL	38	49	50	99	....	....	....	106	....	....	....	....	....	....	....	....	....	....	....	....	....	....	....	....	....	....
	United States	WJC-A	7	4	3	7	....	....	....	2	....	....	....	....	....	....	....	....	....	....	....	....	....	....	....	....	....	....
1992-93	University of Maine	H.E.	39	25	26	51	....	....	....	46	....	....	....	....	....	....	....	....	....	....	....	....	....	....	....	....	....	....
	United States	WJC-A	7	4	7	11	....	....	....	8	....	....	....	....	....	....	....	....	....	....	....	....	....	....	....	....	....	....
1993-94	University of Maine	H.E.	4	0	1	1	....	....	....	8	....	....	....	....	....	....	....	....	....	....	....	....	....	....	....	....	....	....
	United States	Nat-Team	48	8	34	42	....	....	....	58	....	....	....	....	....	....	....	....	....	....	....	....	....	....	....	....	....	....
1994-95	Atlanta Knights	IHL	54	13	14	27	....	....	....	72	....	....	....	....	....	....	....	....	....	....	....	....	....	....	....	....	....	....
	Binghamton Rangers	AHL	13	6	4	10	....	....	....	38	....	....	....	....	....	....	....	....	....	....	10	2	3	5	16	....	....	....
1995-96	**New York Rangers**	**NHL**	**2**	**1**	**0**	**1**	**1**	**0**	**1**	**0**	**1**	**0**	**0**	**4**	**25.0**	**1**	**1**	**3**	**0**	**–3**	....	....	....	....	....	....	....	....
	Binghamton Rangers	AHL	77	32	67	99	....	....	....	208	....	....	....	....	....	....	....	....	....	....	4	4	2	6	13	....	....	....
1996-97	**New York Rangers**	**NHL**	**12**	**1**	**1**	**2**	**1**	**1**	**2**	**6**	**0**	**0**	**0**	**23**	**4.3**	**3**	**2**	**0**	**0**	**+1**	....	....	....	....	....	....	....	....
	Binghamton Rangers	AHL	53	29	34	63	....	....	....	94	....	....	....	....	....	....	....	....	....	....	....	....	....	....	....	....	....	....
1997-98	**Pittsburgh Penguins**	**NHL**	**46**	**3**	**4**	**7**	**4**	**4**	**8**	**43**	**0**	**0**	**0**	**42**	**7.1**	**10**	**1**	**11**	**0**	**–2**	....	....	....	....	....	....	....	....
	NHL Totals		**60**	**5**	**5**	**10**	**6**	**5**	**11**	**49**	**1**	**0**	**0**	**69**	**7.2**	**14**	**4**	**14**	**0**		....	....	....	....	....	....	....	....

Claimed on waivers by **Pittsburgh** from **NY Rangers**, October 1, 1997.

• FERRARO, PETER

Peter Ferraro C – R. 5'10", 185 lbs. b: Port Jefferson, NY, 1/24/1973. NY Rangers' 1st choice, 24th overall, in 1992 Entry Draft.

			REGULAR SEASON																		PLAYOFFS							
Season	Club	League	GP	G	A	Pts	AG	AA	APts	PIM	PP	SH	GW	S	%	TGF	PGF	TGA	PGA	+/–	GP	G	A	Pts	PIM	PP	SH	GW
1990-91	Dubuque Fighting Saints	USHL	29	21	31	52	....	....	....	83	....	....	....	....	....	....	....	....	....	....	....	....	....	....	....	....	....	....
1991-92	Waterloo Black Hawks	USHL	42	48	53	101	....	....	....	168	....	....	....	....	....	....	....	....	....	....	....	....	....	....	....	....	....	....
	United States	WJC-A	7	3	5	8	....	....	....	12	....	....	....	....	....	....	....	....	....	....	....	....	....	....	....	....	....	....
1992-93	University of Maine	H.E.	36	18	32	50	....	....	....	106	....	....	....	....	....	....	....	....	....	....	....	....	....	....	....	....	....	....
	United States	WJC-A	7	7	4	11	....	....	....	8	....	....	....	....	....	....	....	....	....	....	....	....	....	....	....	....	....	....
1993-94	University of Maine	H.E.	4	3	6	9	....	....	....	16	....	....	....	....	....	....	....	....	....	....	....	....	....	....	....	....	....	....
	United States	Nat-Team	60	30	34	64	....	....	....	87	....	....	....	....	....	....	....	....	....	....	....	....	....	....	....	....	....	....
	United States	Olympics	8	6	0	6	....	....	....	6	....	....	....	....	....	....	....	....	....	....	....	....	....	....	....	....	....	....
1994-95	Atlanta Knights	IHL	61	15	24	39	....	....	....	118	....	....	....	....	....	....	....	....	....	....	....	....	....	....	....	....	....	....
	Binghamton Rangers	AHL	12	2	6	8	....	....	....	67	....	....	....	....	....	....	....	....	....	....	11	4	3	7	51	....	....	....
1995-96	**New York Rangers**	**NHL**	**5**	**0**	**1**	**1**	**0**	**1**	**1**	**0**	**0**	**0**	**0**	**6**	**0.0**	**1**	**1**	**6**	**1**	**–5**	....	....	....	....	....	....	....	....
	Binghamton Rangers	AHL	68	48	53	101	....	....	....	157	....	....	....	....	....	....	....	....	....	....	4	1	6	7	22	....	....	....
1996-97	**New York Rangers**	**NHL**	**2**	**0**	**0**	**0**	**0**	**0**	**0**	**0**	**0**	**0**	**0**	**3**	**0.0**	**1**	**0**	**1**	**0**	**0**	**2**	**0**	**0**	**0**	**0**	**0**	**0**	**0**
	Binghamton Rangers	AHL	75	38	39	77	....	....	....	171	....	....	....	....	....	....	....	....	....	....	4	3	1	4	18	....	....	....
1997-98	**Pittsburgh Penguins**	**NHL**	**29**	**3**	**4**	**7**	**4**	**4**	**8**	**12**	**0**	**0**	**0**	**34**	**8.8**	**9**	**0**	**11**	**0**	**–2**	....	....	....	....	....	....	....	....
	New York Rangers	**NHL**	**1**	**0**	**0**	**0**	**0**	**0**	**0**	**2**	**0**	**0**	**0**	**3**	**0.0**	**1**	**1**	**2**	**0**	**–2**	....	....	....	....	....	....	....	....
	Hartford Wolf Pack	AHL	36	17	23	40	....	....	....	54	....	....	....	....	....	....	....	....	....	....	15	8	6	14	59	....	....	....
	NHL Totals		**37**	**3**	**5**	**8**	**4**	**5**	**9**	**14**	**0**	**0**	**0**	**46**	**6.5**	**12**	**2**	**20**	**1**		**2**	**0**	**0**	**0**	**0**	**0**	**0**	**0**

WJC-A All-Star Team (1992) • AHL First All-Star Team (1996)

Claimed on waivers by **Pittsburgh** from **NY Rangers**, October 1, 1997. Claimed on waivers by **NY Rangers** from **Pittsburgh**, January 9, 1997. Signed as a free agent by **Boston**, July 21, 1998.

• FERRARO, RAY

Ray Ferraro C – L. 5'10", 185 lbs. b: Trail, B.C., 8/23/1964. Hartford's 5th choice, 88th overall, in 1982 Entry Draft.

			REGULAR SEASON																		PLAYOFFS							
Season	Club	League	GP	G	A	Pts	AG	AA	APts	PIM	PP	SH	GW	S	%	TGF	PGF	TGA	PGA	+/–	GP	G	A	Pts	PIM	PP	SH	GW
1981-82	Penticton Knights	BCJHL	40	65	67	132	....	....	....	90	....	....	....	....	....	....	....	....	....	....	....	....	....	....	....	....	....	....
1982-83	Portland Winter Hawks	WHL	50	41	49	90	....	....	....	39	....	....	....	....	....	....	....	....	....	....	14	14	10	24	13	....	....	....
1983-84	Brandon Wheat Kings	WHL	72	*108	84	*192	....	....	....	84	....	....	....	....	....	....	....	....	....	....	11	13	15	28	20	....	....	....
1984-85	**Hartford Whalers**	**NHL**	**44**	**11**	**17**	**28**	**9**	**11**	**20**	**40**	**6**	**0**	**2**	**59**	**18.6**	**35**	**15**	**21**	**0**	**–1**	....	....	....	....	....	....	....	....
	Binghamton Whalers	AHL	37	20	13	33	....	....	....	29	....	....	....	....	....	....	....	....	....	....	....	....	....	....	....	....	....	....
1985-86	**Hartford Whalers**	**NHL**	**76**	**30**	**47**	**77**	**24**	**31**	**55**	**57**	**14**	**0**	**0**	**132**	**22.7**	**110**	**41**	**59**	**0**	**+10**	**10**	**3**	**6**	**9**	**4**	**3**	**0**	**0**
1986-87	**Hartford Whalers**	**NHL**	**80**	**27**	**32**	**59**	**23**	**23**	**46**	**42**	**14**	**0**	**2**	**96**	**28.1**	**82**	**44**	**48**	**1**	**–9**	**6**	**1**	**1**	**2**	**8**	**0**	**0**	**0**
1987-88	**Hartford Whalers**	**NHL**	**68**	**21**	**29**	**50**	**18**	**21**	**39**	**81**	**6**	**0**	**2**	**105**	**20.0**	**70**	**29**	**40**	**0**	**+1**	**6**	**1**	**1**	**2**	**6**	**1**	**0**	**0**
1988-89	**Hartford Whalers**	**NHL**	**80**	**41**	**35**	**76**	**35**	**25**	**60**	**86**	**11**	**0**	**7**	**169**	**24.3**	**100**	**29**	**70**	**0**	**+1**	**4**	**2**	**0**	**2**	**4**	**0**	**0**	**0**
	Canada	WEC-A	9	1	5	6	....	....	....	8	....	....	....	....	....	....	....	....	....	....	....	....	....	....	....	....	....	....
1989-90	**Hartford Whalers**	**NHL**	**79**	**25**	**29**	**54**	**22**	**21**	**43**	**109**	**7**	**0**	**4**	**138**	**18.1**	**75**	**31**	**59**	**0**	**–15**	**7**	**0**	**3**	**3**	**2**	**0**	**0**	**0**
1990-91	**Hartford Whalers**	**NHL**	**15**	**2**	**5**	**7**	**2**	**4**	**6**	**18**	**1**	**0**	**0**	**18**	**11.1**	**13**	**6**	**8**	**0**	**–1**	....	....	....	....	....	....	....	....
	New York Islanders	**NHL**	**61**	**19**	**16**	**35**	**17**	**12**	**29**	**52**	**5**	**0**	**1**	**91**	**20.9**	**48**	**14**	**45**	**0**	**–11**	....	....	....	....	....	....	....	....
1991-92	**New York Islanders**	**NHL**	**80**	**40**	**40**	**80**	**37**	**30**	**67**	**92**	**7**	**0**	**4**	**154**	**26.0**	**103**	**23**	**55**	**0**	**+25**	....	....	....	....	....	....	....	....
	Canada	WC-A	6	2	1	3	....	....	....	6	....	....	....	....	....	....	....	....	....	....	....	....	....	....	....	....	....	....
1992-93	**New York Islanders**	**NHL**	**46**	**14**	**13**	**27**	**12**	**9**	**21**	**40**	**3**	**0**	**1**	**72**	**19.4**	**43**	**7**	**36**	**0**	**0**	**18**	**13**	**7**	**20**	**18**	**0**	**0**	**0**
	Capital District Islanders	AHL	1	0	2	2	....	....	....	2	....	....	....	....	....	....	....	....	....	....	....	....	....	....	....	....	....	....
1993-94	**New York Islanders**	**NHL**	**82**	**21**	**32**	**53**	**20**	**25**	**45**	**83**	**5**	**0**	**3**	**136**	**15.4**	**75**	**18**	**58**	**2**	**+1**	**4**	**1**	**0**	**1**	**6**	**0**	**0**	**0**
1994-95	**New York Islanders**	**NHL**	**47**	**22**	**21**	**43**	**39**	**31**	**70**	**30**	**2**	**0**	**1**	**94**	**23.4**	**50**	**9**	**41**	**1**	**+1**	....	....	....	....	....	....	....	....
1995-96	**New York Rangers**	**NHL**	**65**	**25**	**29**	**54**	**25**	**24**	**49**	**82**	**8**	**0**	**4**	**160**	**15.6**	**76**	**27**	**36**	**0**	**+13**	....	....	....	....	....	....	....	....
	Los Angeles Kings	**NHL**	**11**	**4**	**2**	**6**	**4**	**2**	**6**	**10**	**1**	**0**	**0**	**18**	**22.2**	**7**	**3**	**18**	**1**	**–13**	....	....	....	....	....	....	....	....
	Canada	WC-A	8	0	4	4	....	....	....	2	....	....	....	....	....	....	....	....	....	....	....	....	....	....	....	....	....	....
1996-97	**Los Angeles Kings**	**NHL**	**81**	**25**	**21**	**46**	**27**	**19**	**46**	**112**	**11**	**0**	**2**	**152**	**16.4**	**77**	**26**	**73**	**0**	**–22**	....	....	....	....	....	....	....	....
1997-98	**Los Angeles Kings**	**NHL**	**40**	**6**	**9**	**15**	**7**	**9**	**16**	**42**	**0**	**0**	**2**	**45**	**13.3**	**20**	**6**	**24**	**0**	**–10**	**3**	**0**	**1**	**1**	**2**	**0**	**0**	**0**
	NHL Totals		**955**	**333**	**377**	**710**	**321**	**297**	**618**	**976**	**101**	**0**	**35**	**1639**	**20.3**	**984**	**328**	**691**	**5**		**58**	**21**	**19**	**40**	**50**	**4**	**0**	**0**

WHL First All-Star Team (1984)

Played in NHL All-Star Game (1992)

Traded to **NY Islanders** by **Hartford** for Doug Crossman, November 13, 1990. Signed as a free agent by **NY Rangers**, August 9, 1995. Traded to **LA Kings** by **NY Rangers** with Ian Laperriere, Mattias Norstrom, Nathan Lafayette and NY Rangers' 4th round choice (Sean Blanchard) in 1997 Entry Draft for Marty McSorley, Jari Kurri and Shane Churla, March 14, 1996.

• FETISOV, VIACHESLAV

Viacheslav Fetisov D – L. 6'1", 220 lbs. b: Moscow, USSR, 4/20/1958. New Jersey's 15th choice, 150th overall, in 1983 Entry Draft.

			REGULAR SEASON																		PLAYOFFS							
Season	Club	League	GP	G	A	Pts	AG	AA	APts	PIM	PP	SH	GW	S	%	TGF	PGF	TGA	PGA	+/–	GP	G	A	Pts	PIM	PP	SH	GW
1975-76	CSKA Moscow	USSR	1	0	0	0	....	....	....	0	....	....	....	....	....	....	....	....	....	....	....	....	....	....	....	....	....	....
	Soviet Union	WJC-A	4	0	0	0	....	....	....	11	....	....	....	....	....	....	....	....	....	....	....	....	....	....	....	....	....	....
1976-77	CSKA Moscow	USSR	28	3	4	7	....	....	....	14	....	....	....	....	....	....	....	....	....	....	....	....	....	....	....	....	....	....
	Soviet Union	WJC-A	7	3	2	5	....	....	....	4	....	....	....	....	....	....	....	....	....	....	....	....	....	....	....	....	....	....
	Soviet Union	WEC-A	5	3	3	6	....	....	....	2	....	....	....	....	....	....	....	....	....	....	....	....	....	....	....	....	....	....
1977-78	CSKA Moscow	USSR	35	9	18	27	....	....	....	46	....	....	....	....	....	....	....	....	....	....	....	....	....	....	....	....	....	....
	Soviet Union	WJC-A	7	3	5	8	....	....	....	6	....	....	....	....	....	....	....	....	....	....	....	....	....	....	....	....	....	....
	Soviet Union	WEC-A	10	4	6	10	....	....	....	11	....	....	....	....	....	....	....	....	....	....	....	....	....	....	....	....	....	....
1978-79	CSKA Moscow	USSR	29	10	19	29	....	....	....	40	....	....	....	....	....	....	....	....	....	....	....	....	....	....	....	....	....	....
1979-80	CSKA Moscow	USSR	37	10	14	24	....	....	....	46	....	....	....	....	....	....	....	....	....	....	....	....	....	....	....	....	....	....
	CSKA Moscow	SuperS	4	0	1	1	....	....	....	0	....	....	....	....	....	....	....	....	....	....	....	....	....	....	....	....	....	....
	Soviet Union	Olympics	7	5	4	9	....	....	....	10	....	....	....	....	....	....	....	....	....	....	....	....	....	....	....	....	....	....
1980-81	CSKA Moscow	USSR	48	13	16	29	....	....	....	44	....	....	....	....	....	....	....	....	....	....	....	....	....	....	....	....	....	....
	Soviet Union	WEC-A	8	1	4	5	....	....	....	6	....	....	....	....	....	....	....	....	....	....	....	....	....	....	....	....	....	....
1981-82	Soviet Union	C Cup	7	1	7	8	....	....	....	10	....	....	....	....	....	....	....	....	....	....	....	....	....	....	....	....	....	....
	CSKA Moscow	USSR	46	15	26	41	....	....	....	20	....	....	....	....	....	....	....	....	....	....	....	....	....	....	....	....	....	....
	Soviet Union	WEC-A	10	4	3	7	....	....	....	6	....	....	....	....	....	....	....	....	....	....	....	....	....	....	....	....	....	....
1982-83	CSKA Moscow	USSR	43	6	17	23	....	....	....	46	....	....	....	....	....	....	....	....	....	....	....	....	....	....	....	....	....	....
	USSR	SuperS	6	1	4	5	....	....	....	10	....	....	....	....	....	....	....	....	....	....	....	....	....	....	....	....	....	....
	Soviet Union	WEC-A	10	3	7	10	....	....	....	8	....	....	....	....	....	....	....	....	....	....	....	....	....	....	....	....	....	....
1983-84	CSKA Moscow	USSR	44	19	30	49	....	....	....	38	....	....	....	....	....	....	....	....	....	....	....	....	....	....	....	....	....	....
	Soviet Union	Olympics	7	3	8	11	....	....	....	8	....	....	....	....	....	....	....	....	....	....	....	....	....	....	....	....	....	....
1984-85	CSKA Moscow	USSR	20	13	12	25	....	....	....	6	....	....	....	....	....	....	....	....	....	....	....	....	....	....	....	....	....	....
	Soviet Union	WEC-A	10	6	7	13	....	....	....	15	....	....	....	....	....	....	....	....	....	....	....	....	....	....	....	....	....	....
1985-86	CSKA Moscow	USSR	40	15	19	34	....	....	....	12	....	....	....	....	....	....	....	....	....	....	....	....	....	....	....	....	....	....
	CSKA Moscow	SuperS	6	3	3	6	....	....	....	6	....	....	....	....	....	....	....	....	....	....	....	....	....	....	....	....	....	....
	Soviet Union	WEC-A	10	6	9	15	....	....	....	10	....	....	....	....	....	....	....	....	....	....	....	....	....	....	....	....	....	....
1986-87	CSKA Moscow	USSR	39	13	20	33	....	....	....	18	....	....	....	....	....	....	....	....	....	....	....	....	....	....	....	....	....	....
	USSR	RV'87	2	0	1	1	....	....	....	2	....	....	....	....	....	....	....	....	....	....	....	....	....	....	....	....	....	....
	Soviet Union	WEC-A	10	2	8	10	....	....	....	2	....	....	....	....	....	....	....	....	....	....	....	....	....	....	....	....	....	....
1987-88	Soviet Union	C Cup	9	2	5	7	....	....	....	9	....	....	....	....	....	....	....	....	....	....	....	....	....	....	....	....	....	....
	CSKA Moscow	USSR	46	18	17	35	....	....	....	26	....	....	....	....	....	....	....	....	....	....	....	....	....	....	....	....	....	....
	Soviet Union	Olympics	8	4	9	13	....	....	....	6	....	....	....	....	....	....	....	....	....	....	....	....	....	....	....	....	....	....
1988-89	CSKA Moscow	USSR	23	9	8	17	....	....	....	18	....	....	....	....	....	....	....	....	....	....	....	....	....	....	....	....	....	....
	CSKA Moscow	SuperS	7	2	3	5	....	....	....	7	....	....	....	....	....	....	....	....	....	....	....	....	....	....	....	....	....	....
	Soviet Union	WEC-A	10	2	4	6	....	....	....	17	....	....	....	....	....	....	....	....	....	....	....	....	....	....	....	....	....	....
1989-90	**New Jersey Devils**	**NHL**	**72**	**8**	**34**	**42**	**7**	**24**	**31**	**52**	**2**	**0**	**0**	**108**	**7.4**	**107**	**24**	**108**	**34**	**+9**	**6**	**0**	**2**	**2**	**10**	**0**	**0**	**0**
	Soviet Union	WEC-A	8	2	8	10	....	....	....	8	....	....	....	....	....	....	....	....	....	....	....	....	....	....	....	....	....	....
1990-91	**New Jersey Devils**	**NHL**	**67**	**3**	**16**	**19**	**3**	**12**	**15**	**62**	**1**	**0**	**0**	**71**	**4.2**	**64**	**12**	**78**	**31**	**+5**	**7**	**0**	**0**	**0**	**17**	**0**	**0**	**0**
	Utica Devils	AHL	1	1	1	2	....	....	....	0	....	....	....	....	....	....	....	....	....	....	....	....	....	....	....	....	....	....
	Soviet Union	WEC-A	10	3	1	4	....	....	....	4	....	....	....	....	....	....	....	....	....	....	....	....	....	....	....	....	....	....
1991-92	**New Jersey Devils**	**NHL**	**70**	**3**	**23**	**26**	**3**	**17**	**20**	**108**	**0**	**0**	**1**	**70**	**4.3**	**80**	**18**	**66**	**15**	**+11**	**6**	**0**	**3**	**3**	**8**	**0**	**0**	**0**
1992-93	**New Jersey Devils**	**NHL**	**76**	**4**	**23**	**27**	**3**	**16**	**19**	**158**	**1**	**1**	**0**	**63**	**6.3**	**81**	**13**	**80**	**19**	**+7**	**5**	**0**	**2**	**2**	**4**	**0**	**0**	**0**
1993-94	**New Jersey Devils**	**NHL**	**52**	**1**	**14**	**15**	**1**	**11**	**12**	**30**	**0**	**0**	**0**	**36**	**2.8**	**45**	**8**	**37**	**14**	**+14**	**14**	**1**	**0**	**1**	**8**	**0**	**0**	**0**
1994-95	Spartak	CIS	1	0	1	1	....	....	....	4	....	....	....	....	....	....	....	....	....	....	....	....	....	....	....	....	....	....
	New Jersey Devils	**NHL**	**4**	**0**	**1**	**1**	**0**	**1**	**1**	**0**	**0**	**0**	**0**	**1**	**0.0**	**2**	**0**	**4**	**0**	**–2**	....	....	....	....	....	....	....	....
	Detroit Red Wings	**NHL**	**14**	**3**	**11**	**14**	**5**	**16**	**21**	**2**	**3**	**0**	**0**	**36**	**8.3**	**23**	**7**	**15**	**2**	**+3**	**18**	**0**	**8**	**8**	**14**	**0**	**0**	**0**
1995-96	**Detroit Red Wings**	**NHL**	**69**	**7**	**35**	**42**	**7**	**29**	**36**	**96**	**1**	**1**	**1**	**127**	**5.5**	**94**	**27**	**33**	**3**	**+37**	**19**	**1**	**4**	**5**	**34**	**0**	**0**	**1**

			REGULAR SEASON																		PLAYOFFS							
Season	Club	League	GP	G	A	Pts	AG	AA	APts	PIM	PP	SH	GW	S	%	TGF	PGF	TGA	PGA	+/-	GP	G	A	Pts	PIM	PP	SH	GW
1996-97	Russia	W Cup	4	0	2	2	....	....	....	12	....	....	....	....	....	....	....	....	....	....	....	....	....	....	....	....	....	....
	Detroit Red Wings	**NHL**	**64**	**5**	**23**	**28**	**5**	**20**	**25**	**76**	**0**	**0**	**1**	**95**	**5.3**	**71**	**11**	**37**	**3**	**+26**	**20**	**0**	**4**	**4**	**42**	**0**	**0**	**0**
1997-98	**Detroit Red Wings**	**NHL**	**58**	**2**	**12**	**14**	**2**	**12**	**14**	**72**	**0**	**0**	**1**	**55**	**3.6**	**41**	**7**	**34**	**4**	**+4**	**21**	**0**	**3**	**3**	**10**	**0**	**0**	**0**
	NHL Totals		**546**	**36**	**192**	**228**	**36**	**158**	**194**	**656**	**8**	**2**	**4**	**662**	**5.4**	**608**	**127**	**492**	**125**		**116**	**2**	**26**	**28**	**147**	**0**	**0**	**1**

Named Best Defenseman at EJC-A (1976) • WJC-A All-Star Team (1978) • Named Best Defenseman at WJC-A (1978) • WEC-A All-Star Team (1978, 1982, 1983, 1985, 1986, 1987, 1989, 1990, 1991) • Named Best Defenseman at WEC-A (1978, 1982, 1985, 1986, 1989) • USSR First All-Star Team (1979, 1980, 1982, 1983, 1984, 1985, 1986, 1987, 1988) • USSR Player of the Year (1982, 1986) • Leningradskaya-Pravda Trophy (Top Scoring Defenseman) (1984, 1986, 1987, 1988) • Canada Cup All-Star Team (1987)

Played in NHL All-Star Game (1997, 1998)

Re-entered NHL draft. Originally Montreal's 14th choice, 201st overall, in 1978 Amateur Draft. Traded to **Detroit** by **New Jersey** for Detroit's 3rd round choice (David Gosselin) in 1995 Entry Draft, April 3, 1995.

• FIDLER, MIKE

Mike Fidler LW – L. 5'11", 195 lbs. b: Everett, MA, 8/19/1956. California's 3rd choice, 41st overall, in 1976 Amateur Draft.

1974-75	Boston University	ECAC	31	24	24	48	....	....	....	12	....	....	....	....	....	....	....	....	....	....	....	....	....	....	....	....	....	....
1975-76	Boston University	ECAC	29	22	24	46	....	....	....	78	....	....	....	....	....	....	....	....	....	....	....	....	....	....	....	....	....	....
1976-77	**Cleveland Barons**	**NHL**	**46**	**17**	**16**	**33**	**16**	**13**	**29**	**17**	**7**	**0**	**3**	**112**	**15.2**	**50**	**18**	**37**	**0**	**–5**	....	....	....	....	....	....	....	....
	Salt Lake Golden Eagles	CHL	10	12	6	18	....	....	....	0	....	....	....	....	....	....	....	....	....	....	....	....	....	....	....	....	....	....
1977-78	**Cleveland Barons**	**NHL**	**78**	**23**	**28**	**51**	**22**	**23**	**45**	**38**	**4**	**0**	**3**	**181**	**12.7**	**79**	**21**	**71**	**0**	**–13**	....	....	....	....	....	....	....	....
	United States	WEC-A	10	8	2	10	....	....	....	18	....	....	....	....	....	....	....	....	....	....	....	....	....	....	....	....	....	....
1978-79	**Minnesota North Stars**	**NHL**	**59**	**23**	**26**	**49**	**21**	**20**	**41**	**42**	**4**	**0**	**3**	**158**	**14.6**	**56**	**15**	**66**	**0**	**–25**	....	....	....	....	....	....	....	....
	Oklahoma City Stars	CHL	8	6	4	10	....	....	....	7	....	....	....	....	....	....	....	....	....	....	....	....	....	....	....	....	....	....
1979-80	**Minnesota North Stars**	**NHL**	**24**	**5**	**4**	**9**	**5**	**3**	**8**	**13**	**1**	**0**	**0**	**38**	**13.2**	**18**	**4**	**12**	**1**	**+3**	....	....	....	....	....	....	....	....
1980-81	**Minnesota North Stars**	**NHL**	**20**	**5**	**12**	**17**	**4**	**8**	**12**	**6**	**0**	**0**	**0**	**42**	**11.9**	**25**	**10**	**11**	**1**	**+5**	....	....	....	....	....	....	....	....
	Hartford Whalers	**NHL**	**38**	**9**	**9**	**18**	**7**	**6**	**13**	**4**	**2**	**0**	**0**	**59**	**15.3**	**29**	**7**	**38**	**1**	**–15**	....	....	....	....	....	....	....	....
1981-82	**Hartford Whalers**	**NHL**	**2**	**0**	**1**	**1**	**0**	**1**	**1**	**0**	**0**	**0**	**0**	**2**	**0.0**	**2**	**1**	**1**	**0**	**0**	....	....	....	....	....	....	....	....
	Oklahoma City Stars	CHL	6	3	5	8	....	....	....	0	....	....	....	....	....	....	....	....	....	....	....	....	....	....	....	....	....	....
	Erie Blades	AHL	5	1	2	3	....	....	....	0	....	....	....	....	....	....	....	....	....	....	....	....	....	....	....	....	....	....
1982-83	**Chicago Black Hawks**	**NHL**	**4**	**2**	**1**	**3**	**2**	**1**	**3**	**4**	**0**	**0**	**0**	**6**	**33.3**	**3**	**0**	**4**	**0**	**–1**	....	....	....	....	....	....	....	....
	Springfield Indians	AHL	30	10	17	27	....	....	....	38	....	....	....	....	....	....	....	....	....	....	....	....	....	....	....	....	....	....
1983-84	New Haven Nighthawks	AHL	16	6	7	13	....	....	....	6	....	....	....	....	....	....	....	....	....	....	....	....	....	....	....	....	....	....
	NHL Totals		**271**	**84**	**97**	**181**	**77**	**75**	**152**	**124**	**18**	**0**	**9**	**598**	**14.0**	**262**	**76**	**240**	**3**		....	....	....	....	....	....	....	....

Transferred to **Cleveland** after **California** franchise relocated, August 26, 1976. Protected by **Minnesota** prior to **Cleveland-Minnesota** Dispersal Draft, June 15, 1978. Traded to **Hartford** by **Minnesota** for Gordie Roberts, December 16, 1980. Signed as a free agent by **Boston**, December 1, 1981. Signed as a free agent by **Chicago**, November 28, 1982.

• FILIMONOV, DMITRI

Dmitri Filimonov D – R. 6'4", 220 lbs. b: Perm, USSR, 10/14/1971. Winnipeg's 2nd choice, 49th overall, in 1991 Entry Draft.

1990-91	Moscow Dynamo	FrTour	1	0	0	0	....	....	....	0	....	....	....	....	....	....	....	....	....	....	....	....	....	....	....	....	....	....
	Moscow Dynamo	USSR	45	4	6	10	....	....	....	12	....	....	....	....	....	....	....	....	....	....	....	....	....	....	....	....	....	....
	Mosocw Dynamo	SuperS	7	2	1	3	....	....	....	2	....	....	....	....	....	....	....	....	....	....	....	....	....	....	....	....	....	....
1991-92	Soviet Union	C Cup	5	0	0	0	....	....	....	0	....	....	....	....	....	....	....	....	....	....	....	....	....	....	....	....	....	....
	Moscow Dynamo	CIS	38	3	2	5	....	....	....	12	....	....	....	....	....	....	....	....	....	....	....	....	....	....	....	....	....	....
1992-93	Moscow Dynamo	CIS	42	2	3	5	....	....	....	30	....	....	....	....	....	....	....	....	....	....	10	1	2	3	2	....	....	....
1993-94	**Ottawa Senators**	**NHL**	**30**	**1**	**4**	**5**	**1**	**3**	**4**	**18**	**0**	**0**	**0**	**15**	**6.7**	**17**	**3**	**26**	**2**	**–10**	....	....	....	....	....	....	....	....
	P.E.I. Senators	AHL	48	10	16	26	....	....	....	14	....	....	....	....	....	....	....	....	....	....	....	....	....	....	....	....	....	....
1994-95	P.E.I. Senators	AHL	32	6	19	25	....	....	....	14	....	....	....	....	....	....	....	....	....	....	9	0	1	1	2	....	....	....
1995-96	Indianapolis Ice	IHL	10	0	1	1	....	....	....	12	....	....	....	....	....	....	....	....	....	....	....	....	....	....	....	....	....	....
1996-97	Kalpa Kuopio	Finland	27	2	1	3	....	....	....	12	....	....	....	....	....	....	....	....	....	....	....	....	....	....	....	....	....	....
1997-98	Molot-Prikamje Perm	CIS	45	9	10	19	....	....	....	30	....	....	....	....	....	....	....	....	....	....	....	....	....	....	....	....	....	....
	NHL Totals		**30**	**1**	**4**	**5**	**1**	**3**	**4**	**18**	**0**	**0**	**0**	**15**	**6.7**	**17**	**3**	**26**	**2**		....	....	....	....	....	....	....	....

EJC-A All-Star Team (1989)

Rights traded to **Ottawa** by **Winnipeg** for Ottawa's 4th round choice (Ruslam Batyrshin) in 1993 Entry Draft, March 4, 1993.

• FINLEY, JEFF

Jeff Finley D – L. 6'2", 205 lbs. b: Edmonton, Alta., 4/14/1967. NY Islanders' 4th choice, 55th overall, in 1985 Entry Draft.

1983-84	Portland Winter Hawks	WHL	5	0	0	0	....	....	....	5	....	....	....	....	....	....	....	....	....	....	5	0	1	1	4	....	....	....
1984-85	Portland Winter Hawks	WHL	69	6	44	50	....	....	....	57	....	....	....	....	....	....	....	....	....	....	6	1	2	3	2	....	....	....
1985-86	Portland Winter Hawks	WHL	70	11	59	70	....	....	....	83	....	....	....	....	....	....	....	....	....	....	15	1	7	8	16	....	....	....
1986-87	Portland Winter Hawks	WHL	72	13	53	66	....	....	....	113	....	....	....	....	....	....	....	....	....	....	20	1	*21	22	27	....	....	....
1987-88	**New York Islanders**	**NHL**	**10**	**0**	**5**	**5**	**0**	**4**	**4**	**15**	**0**	**0**	**0**	**9**	**0.0**	**15**	**2**	**8**	**0**	**+5**	**1**	**0**	**0**	**0**	**2**	**0**	**0**	**0**
	Springfield Indians	AHL	52	5	18	23	....	....	....	50	....	....	....	....	....	....	....	....	....	....	....	....	....	....	....	....	....	....
1988-89	**New York Islanders**	**NHL**	**4**	**0**	**0**	**0**	**0**	**0**	**0**	**6**	**0**	**0**	**0**	**1**	**0.0**	**2**	**0**	**1**	**0**	**+1**	....	....	....	....	....	....	....	....
	Springfield Indians	AHL	65	3	16	19	....	....	....	55	....	....	....	....	....	....	....	....	....	....	....	....	....	....	....	....	....	....
1989-90	**New York Islanders**	**NHL**	**11**	**0**	**1**	**1**	**0**	**1**	**1**	**0**	**0**	**0**	**0**	**7**	**0.0**	**7**	**0**	**11**	**4**	**0**	**5**	**0**	**2**	**2**	**2**	**0**	**0**	**0**
	Springfield Indians	AHL	57	1	15	16	....	....	....	41	....	....	....	....	....	....	....	....	....	....	13	1	4	5	23	....	....	....
1990-91	**New York Islanders**	**NHL**	**11**	**0**	**0**	**0**	**0**	**0**	**0**	**4**	**0**	**0**	**0**	**0**	**0.0**	**5**	**0**	**11**	**5**	**–1**	....	....	....	....	....	....	....	....
	Capital District Islanders	AHL	67	10	34	44	....	....	....	34	....	....	....	....	....	....	....	....	....	....	....	....	....	....	....	....	....	....
1991-92	**New York Islanders**	**NHL**	**51**	**1**	**10**	**11**	**1**	**7**	**8**	**26**	**0**	**0**	**0**	**25**	**4.0**	**49**	**11**	**69**	**25**	**–6**	....	....	....	....	....	....	....	....
	Capital District Islanders	AHL	20	1	9	10	....	....	....	6	....	....	....	....	....	....	....	....	....	....	....	....	....	....	....	....	....	....
1992-93	Capital District Islanders	AHL	61	6	29	35	....	....	....	34	....	....	....	....	....	....	....	....	....	....	4	0	1	1	0	....	....	....
1993-94	**Philadelphia Flyers**	**NHL**	**55**	**1**	**8**	**9**	**1**	**6**	**7**	**24**	**0**	**0**	**0**	**43**	**2.3**	**45**	**3**	**46**	**20**	**+16**	....	....	....	....	....	....	....	....
1994-95	Hershey Bears	AHL	36	2	9	11	....	....	....	33	....	....	....	....	....	....	....	....	....	....	6	0	1	1	8	....	....	....
1995-96	**Winnipeg Jets**	**NHL**	**65**	**1**	**5**	**6**	**1**	**4**	**5**	**81**	**0**	**0**	**0**	**27**	**3.7**	**44**	**3**	**70**	**27**	**–2**	**6**	**0**	**0**	**0**	**4**	**0**	**0**	**0**
	Springfield Falcons	AHL	14	3	12	15	....	....	....	22	....	....	....	....	....	....	....	....	....	....	....	....	....	....	....	....	....	....
1996-97	**Phoenix Coyotes**	**NHL**	**65**	**3**	**7**	**10**	**3**	**6**	**9**	**40**	**1**	**0**	**1**	**38**	**7.9**	**40**	**2**	**59**	**13**	**–8**	**1**	**0**	**0**	**0**	**2**	**0**	**0**	**0**
1997-98	**New York Rangers**	**NHL**	**63**	**1**	**6**	**7**	**1**	**6**	**7**	**55**	**0**	**0**	**0**	**32**	**3.1**	**33**	**2**	**43**	**9**	**–3**	....	....	....	....	....	....	....	....
	NHL Totals		**335**	**7**	**42**	**49**	**7**	**34**	**41**	**251**	**1**	**0**	**1**	**182**	**3.8**	**240**	**23**	**318**	**103**		**13**	**0**	**2**	**2**	**10**	**0**	**0**	**0**

Traded to **Ottawa** by **NY Islanders** for Chris Luongo, June 30, 1993. Signed as a free agent by **Philadelphia**, July 30, 1993. Traded to **Winnipeg** by **Philadelphia** for Russ Romaniuk, June 27, 1995. Transferred to **Phoenix** after **Winnipeg** franchise relocated, July 1, 1996. Signed as a free agent by **NY Rangers**, August 18, 1997.

• FINN, STEVEN

Steven Finn D – L. 6', 191 lbs. b: Laval, Que., 8/20/1966. Quebec's 3rd choice, 57th overall, in 1984 Entry Draft.

1982-83	Laval Voisins	QMJHL	69	7	30	37	....	....	....	108	....	....	....	....	....	....	....	....	....	....	6	0	2	2	6	....	....	....
1983-84	Laval Voisins	QMJHL	68	7	39	46	....	....	....	159	....	....	....	....	....	....	....	....	....	....	14	1	6	7	27	....	....	....
1984-85	Laval Voisins	QMJHL	61	20	33	53	....	....	....	169	....	....	....	....	....	....	....	....	....	....	....	....	....	....	....	....	....	....
	Fredericton Express	AHL	4	0	0	0	....	....	....	14	....	....	....	....	....	....	....	....	....	....	6	1	1	2	4	....	....	....
1985-86	Laval Voisins	QMJHL	29	4	15	19	....	....	....	111	....	....	....	....	....	....	....	....	....	....	14	6	16	22	57	....	....	....
	Quebec Nordiques	**NHL**	**17**	**0**	**1**	**1**	**0**	**1**	**1**	**28**	**0**	**0**	**0**	**8**	**0.0**	**7**	**0**	**8**	**1**	**0**	....	....	....	....	....	....	....	....
1986-87	**Quebec Nordiques**	**NHL**	**36**	**2**	**5**	**7**	**2**	**4**	**6**	**40**	**0**	**0**	**0**	**36**	**5.6**	**27**	**6**	**31**	**2**	**–8**	**13**	**0**	**2**	**2**	**29**	**0**	**0**	**0**
	Fredericton Express	AHL	38	7	19	26	....	....	....	73	....	....	....	....	....	....	....	....	....	....	....	....	....	....	....	....	....	....
1987-88	**Quebec Nordiques**	**NHL**	**75**	**3**	**7**	**10**	**3**	**5**	**8**	**198**	**1**	**0**	**0**	**70**	**4.3**	**57**	**3**	**86**	**28**	**–4**	....	....	....	....	....	....	....	....
1988-89	**Quebec Nordiques**	**NHL**	**77**	**2**	**6**	**8**	**2**	**4**	**6**	**235**	**0**	**1**	**0**	**86**	**2.3**	**50**	**2**	**97**	**28**	**–21**	....	....	....	....	....	....	....	....
1989-90	**Quebec Nordiques**	**NHL**	**64**	**3**	**9**	**12**	**3**	**6**	**9**	**208**	**1**	**0**	**0**	**74**	**4.1**	**40**	**2**	**94**	**23**	**–33**	....	....	....	....	....	....	....	....
1990-91	**Quebec Nordiques**	**NHL**	**71**	**6**	**13**	**19**	**5**	**10**	**15**	**228**	**0**	**0**	**0**	**91**	**6.6**	**66**	**0**	**116**	**24**	**–28**	....	....	....	....	....	....	....	....
1991-92	**Quebec Nordiques**	**NHL**	**65**	**4**	**7**	**11**	**4**	**5**	**9**	**194**	**0**	**0**	**0**	**63**	**6.3**	**56**	**5**	**81**	**21**	**–9**	....	....	....	....	....	....	....	....
1992-93	**Quebec Nordiques**	**NHL**	**80**	**5**	**9**	**14**	**4**	**6**	**10**	**160**	**0**	**0**	**0**	**61**	**8.2**	**54**	**0**	**71**	**14**	**–3**	**6**	**0**	**1**	**1**	**8**	**0**	**0**	**0**
1993-94	**Quebec Nordiques**	**NHL**	**80**	**4**	**13**	**17**	**4**	**10**	**14**	**159**	**0**	**0**	**1**	**74**	**5.4**	**40**	**2**	**58**	**11**	**–9**	....	....	....	....	....	....	....	....
1994-95	**Quebec Nordiques**	**NHL**	**40**	**0**	**3**	**3**	**0**	**4**	**4**	**64**	**0**	**0**	**0**	**28**	**0.0**	**25**	**0**	**28**	**4**	**+1**	**4**	**0**	**1**	**1**	**2**	**0**	**0**	**0**

			REGULAR SEASON																		PLAYOFFS							
Season	Club	League	GP	G	A	Pts	AG	AA	APts	PIM	PP	SH	GW	S	%	TGF	PGF	TGA	PGA	+/–	GP	G	A	Pts	PIM	PP	SH	GW
1995-96	**Tampa Bay Lightning**	**NHL**	**16**	**0**	**0**	**0**	**0**	**0**	**0**	**24**	**0**	**0**	**0**	**12**	**0.0**	**5**	**0**	**13**	**2**	**–6**	....	....	....	....	....	....	....	....
	Los Angeles Kings	**NHL**	**50**	**3**	**2**	**5**	**3**	**2**	**5**	**102**	**0**	**0**	**0**	**42**	**7.1**	**38**	**1**	**60**	**17**	**–6**	....	....	....	....	....	....	....	....
1996-97	**Los Angeles Kings**	**NHL**	**54**	**2**	**3**	**5**	**2**	**3**	**5**	**84**	**0**	**0**	**1**	**35**	**5.7**	**30**	**0**	**50**	**12**	**–8**	....	....	....	....	....	....	....	....
1997-98	Long Beach Ice Dogs	IHL	75	6	14	20	....	....	....	134	....	....	....	....	....	....	....	....	....	....	17	1	4	5	48	....	....	....
	NHL Totals		**725**	**34**	**78**	**112**	**32**	**60**	**92**	**1724**	**2**	**1**	**2**	**680**	**5.0**	**495**	**21**	**793**	**187**		**23**	**0**	**4**	**4**	**39**	**0**	**0**	**0**

QMJHL First All-Star Team (1984) • QMJHL Second All-Star Team (1985)

Transferred to **Colorado** after **Quebec** franchise relocated, June 21, 1995. Traded to **Tampa Bay** by **Colorado** for Tampa Bay's 4th round choice (Brad Larsen) in 1997 Entry Draft, October 5, 1995. Traded to **LA Kings** by **Tampa Bay** for Michel Petit, November 13, 1995.

• FIORENTINO, PETER

Peter Fiorentino D – R. 6'1", 205 lbs. b: Niagara Falls, Ont., 12/22/1968. NY Rangers' 10th choice, 215th overall, in 1988 Entry Draft.

Season	Club	League	GP	G	A	Pts	AG	AA	APts	PIM	PP	SH	GW	S	%	TGF	PGF	TGA	PGA	+/–	GP	G	A	Pts	PIM	PP	SH	GW
1985-86	Sault Ste. Marie Greyhounds	OHL	58	1	6	7	....	....	....	87	....	....	....	....	....	....	....	....	....	....	....	....	....	....	....	....	....	....
1986-87	Sault Ste. Marie Greyhounds	OHL	64	1	12	13	....	....	....	187	....	....	....	....	....	....	....	....	....	....	....	....	....	....	....	....	....	....
1987-88	Sault Ste. Marie Greyhounds	OHL	65	5	27	32	....	....	....	252	....	....	....	....	....	....	....	....	....	....	6	2	2	4	21	....	....	....
1988-89	Sault Ste. Marie Greyhounds	OHL	55	5	24	29	....	....	....	220	....	....	....	....	....	....	....	....	....	....	....	....	....	....	....	....	....	....
	Denver Rangers	IHL	10	0	0	0	....	....	....	39	....	....	....	....	....	....	....	....	....	....	4	0	0	0	24	....	....	....
1989-90	Flint Spirits	IHL	64	2	7	9	....	....	....	302	....	....	....	....	....	....	....	....	....	....	....	....	....	....	....	....	....	....
1990-91	Binghamton Rangers	AHL	55	2	11	13	....	....	....	361	....	....	....	....	....	....	....	....	....	....	1	0	0	0	0	....	....	....
1991-92	**New York Rangers**	**NHL**	**1**	**0**	**0**	**0**	**0**	**0**	**0**	**0**	**0**	**0**	**0**	**2**	**0.0**	**0**	**0**	**0**	**0**	**0**	....	....	....	....	....	....	....	....
	Binghamton Rangers	AHL	70	2	11	13	....	....	....	340	....	....	....	....	....	....	....	....	....	....	5	0	1	1	24	....	....	....
1992-93	Binghamton Rangers	AHL	64	9	5	14	....	....	....	286	....	....	....	....	....	....	....	....	....	....	13	0	3	3	22	....	....	....
1993-94	Binghamton Rangers	AHL	68	7	15	22	....	....	....	220	....	....	....	....	....	....	....	....	....	....	....	....	....	....	....	....	....	....
1994-95	Binghamton Rangers	AHL	66	9	16	25	....	....	....	183	....	....	....	....	....	....	....	....	....	....	2	0	1	1	11	....	....	....
1995-96	Las Vegas Thunder	IHL	54	5	7	12	....	....	....	192	....	....	....	....	....	....	....	....	....	....	....	....	....	....	....	....	....	....
	Indianapolis Ice	IHL	10	0	0	0	....	....	....	27	....	....	....	....	....	....	....	....	....	....	5	0	0	0	2	....	....	....
1996-97	Binghamton Rangers	AHL	63	1	10	11	....	....	....	191	....	....	....	....	....	....	....	....	....	....	4	0	2	2	0	....	....	....
1997-98	Quebec Rafales	IHL	12	0	2	2	....	....	....	46	....	....	....	....	....	....	....	....	....	....	....	....	....	....	....	....	....	....
	Hartford Wolf Pack	AHL	1	0	0	0	....	....	....	0	....	....	....	....	....	....	....	....	....	....	....	....	....	....	....	....	....	....
	Binghamton Icemen	UHL	35	2	9	11	....	....	....	78	....	....	....	....	....	....	....	....	....	....	5	1	1	2	2	....	....	....
	NHL Totals		**1**	**0**	**0**	**0**	**0**	**0**	**0**	**0**	**0**	**0**	**0**	**2**	**0.0**	**0**	**0**	**0**	**0**		....	....	....	....	....	....	....	....

• FISCHER, RON

Ron Fischer D – R. 6'2", 195 lbs. b: Merritt, B.C., 4/12/1959.

Season	Club	League	GP	G	A	Pts	AG	AA	APts	PIM	PP	SH	GW	S	%	TGF	PGF	TGA	PGA	+/–	GP	G	A	Pts	PIM	PP	SH	GW
1979-80	University of Calgary	CWUAA	33	4	12	16	....	....	....	54	....	....	....	....	....	....	....	....	....	....	....	....	....	....	....	....	....	....
1980-81	University of Calgary	CWUAA	29	7	24	31	....	....	....	63	....	....	....	....	....	....	....	....	....	....	....	....	....	....	....	....	....	....
	Rochester Americans	AHL	4	0	0	0	....	....	....	0	....	....	....	....	....	....	....	....	....	....	....	....	....	....	....	....	....	....
1981-82	**Buffalo Sabres**	**NHL**	**15**	**0**	**7**	**7**	**0**	**5**	**5**	**6**	**0**	**0**	**0**	**16**	**0.0**	**18**	**1**	**22**	**2**	**–3**	....	....	....	....	....	....	....	....
	Rochester Americans	AHL	61	6	20	26	....	....	....	122	....	....	....	....	....	....	....	....	....	....	9	1	2	3	22	....	....	....
1982-83	**Buffalo Sabres**	**NHL**	**3**	**0**	**0**	**0**	**0**	**0**	**0**	**0**	**0**	**0**	**0**	**1**	**0.0**	**1**	**0**	**1**	**0**	**0**	....	....	....	....	....	....	....	....
	Rochester Americans	AHL	40	2	19	21	....	....	....	56	....	....	....	....	....	....	....	....	....	....	....	....	....	....	....	....	....	....
1983-84	Rochester Americans	AHL	80	10	32	42	....	....	....	94	....	....	....	....	....	....	....	....	....	....	15	4	3	7	19	....	....	....
1984-85	Riessersee	Germany	34	9	15	24	....	....	....	53	....	....	....	....	....	....	....	....	....	....	18	11	25	36	36	....	....	....
1985-86	Riessersee	Germany	36	15	35	50	....	....	....	74	....	....	....	....	....	....	....	....	....	....	18	10	25	35	16	....	....	....
1986-87	SB Rosenheim	Germany	41	5	45	50	....	....	....	56	....	....	....	....	....	....	....	....	....	....	7	1	7	8	....	....	....	....
1987-88	SB Rosenheim	Germany	47	19	25	44	....	....	....	89	....	....	....	....	....	....	....	....	....	....	....	....	....	....	....	....	....	....
	West Germany	Olympics	8	1	1	2	....	....	....	6	....	....	....	....	....	....	....	....	....	....	....	....	....	....	....	....	....	....
1988-89	SB Rosenheim	Germany	33	11	32	43	....	....	....	28	....	....	....	....	....	....	....	....	....	....	11	5	12	17	13	....	....	....
	West Germany	WEC-A	10	2	1	3	....	....	....	6	....	....	....	....	....	....	....	....	....	....	....	....	....	....	....	....	....	....
1989-90	SB Rosenheim	Germany	47	19	24	43	....	....	....	34	....	....	....	....	....	....	....	....	....	....	....	....	....	....	....	....	....	....
1990-91	SB Rosenheim	Germany	31	5	16	21	....	....	....	31	....	....	....	....	....	....	....	....	....	....	11	1	8	9	8	....	....	....
1991-92	SB Rosenheim	Germany	41	4	30	34	....	....	....	52	....	....	....	....	....	....	....	....	....	....	....	....	....	....	....	....	....	....
	Germany	Olympics	8	1	3	4	....	....	....	4	....	....	....	....	....	....	....	....	....	....	....	....	....	....	....	....	....	....
	Germany	WC-A	6	1	2	3	....	....	....	4	....	....	....	....	....	....	....	....	....	....	....	....	....	....	....	....	....	....
1992-93	SB Rosenheim	Germany	50	9	51	60	....	....	....	53	....	....	....	....	....	....	....	....	....	....	....	....	....	....	....	....	....	....
1993-94	Star Bulls Rosenheim	Germany	42	10	23	33	....	....	....	26	....	....	....	....	....	....	....	....	....	....	....	....	....	....	....	....	....	....
1994-95	Star Bulls Rosenheim	Germany	29	1	13	14	....	....	....	20	....	....	....	....	....	....	....	....	....	....	....	....	....	....	....	....	....	....
1995-96	Star Bulls Rosenheim	Germany	50	4	38	42	....	....	....	46	....	....	....	....	....	....	....	....	....	....	4	0	1	1	7	....	....	....
	NHL Totals		**18**	**0**	**7**	**7**	**0**	**5**	**5**	**6**	**0**	**0**	**0**	**17**	**0.0**	**19**	**1**	**23**	**2**		....	....	....	....	....	....	....	....

Signed as a free agent by **Buffalo**, March 19, 1981.

• FISHER, CRAIG

Craig Fisher C – L. 6'3", 180 lbs. b: Oshawa, Ont., 6/30/1970. Philadelphia's 3rd choice, 56th overall, in 1988 Entry Draft.

Season	Club	League	GP	G	A	Pts	AG	AA	APts	PIM	PP	SH	GW	S	%	TGF	PGF	TGA	PGA	+/–	GP	G	A	Pts	PIM	PP	SH	GW
1987-88	Ottawa Legionaires	OJHL	36	42	34	76	....	....	....	48	....	....	....	....	....	....	....	....	....	....	....	....	....	....	....	....	....	....
1988-89	University of Miami-Ohio	CCHA	37	22	20	42	....	....	....	37	....	....	....	....	....	....	....	....	....	....	....	....	....	....	....	....	....	....
1989-90	University of Miami-Ohio	CCHA	39	37	29	66	....	....	....	38	....	....	....	....	....	....	....	....	....	....	....	....	....	....	....	....	....	....
	Philadelphia Flyers	**NHL**	**2**	**0**	**0**	**0**	**0**	**0**	**0**	**0**	**0**	**0**	**0**	**5**	**0.0**	**1**	**0**	**1**	**0**	**0**	....	....	....	....	....	....	....	....
1990-91	**Philadelphia Flyers**	**NHL**	**2**	**0**	**0**	**0**	**0**	**0**	**0**	**0**	**0**	**0**	**0**	**2**	**0.0**	**0**	**0**	**0**	**0**	**0**	....	....	....	....	....	....	....	....
	Hershey Bears	AHL	77	43	36	79	....	....	....	46	....	....	....	....	....	....	....	....	....	....	7	5	3	8	2	....	....	....
1991-92	Cape Breton Oilers	AHL	60	20	25	45	....	....	....	28	....	....	....	....	....	....	....	....	....	....	1	0	0	0	0	....	....	....
1992-93	Cape Breton Oilers	AHL	75	32	29	61	....	....	....	74	....	....	....	....	....	....	....	....	....	....	1	0	0	0	2	....	....	....
1993-94	Cape Breton Oilers	AHL	16	5	5	10	....	....	....	11	....	....	....	....	....	....	....	....	....	....	....	....	....	....	....	....	....	....
	Winnipeg Jets	**NHL**	**4**	**0**	**0**	**0**	**0**	**0**	**0**	**2**	**0**	**0**	**0**	**5**	**0.0**	**1**	**0**	**2**	**0**	**–1**	....	....	....	....	....	....	....	....
	Moncton Hawks	AHL	46	26	35	61	....	....	....	36	....	....	....	....	....	....	....	....	....	....	21	11	11	22	28	....	....	....
1994-95	Indianapolis Ice	IHL	77	53	40	93	....	....	....	65	....	....	....	....	....	....	....	....	....	....	....	....	....	....	....	....	....	....
1995-96	Orlando Solar Bears	IHL	82	*74	56	130	....	....	....	81	....	....	....	....	....	....	....	....	....	....	14	10	7	17	6	....	....	....
1996-97	Utah Grizzlies	IHL	15	6	7	13	....	....	....	4	....	....	....	....	....	....	....	....	....	....	....	....	....	....	....	....	....	....
	Florida Panthers	**NHL**	**4**	**0**	**0**	**0**	**0**	**0**	**0**	**0**	**0**	**0**	**0**	**2**	**0.0**	**2**	**0**	**4**	**0**	**–2**	....	....	....	....	....	....	....	....
	Carolina Monarchs	AHL	42	33	29	62	....	....	....	16	....	....	....	....	....	....	....	....	....	....	....	....	....	....	....	....	....	....
1997-98	Kolner Haie	EuroHL	4	0	0	0	....	....	....	4	....	....	....	....	....	....	....	....	....	....	....	....	....	....	....	....	....	....
	Kolner Haie	Germany	34	9	8	17	....	....	....	34	....	....	....	....	....	....	....	....	....	....	....	....	....	....	....	....	....	....
	NHL Totals		**12**	**0**	**0**	**0**	**0**	**0**	**0**	**2**	**0**	**0**	**0**	**14**	**0.0**	**4**	**0**	**7**	**0**		....	....	....	....	....	....	....	....

CCHA First All-Star Team (1990) • IHL First All-Star Team (1996)

Traded to **Edmonton** by **Philadelphia** with Scott Mellanby and Craig Berube for Dave Brown, Corey Foster and Jari Kurri, May 30, 1991. Traded to **Winnipeg** by **Edmonton** for cash, December 9, 1993. Signed as a free agent by **Chicago**, June 9, 1994. Signed as a free agent by **NY Islanders**, July 29, 1996. Traded to **Florida** by **NY Islanders** for cash, December 7, 1996.

• FITCHNER, BOB

Bob Fitchner C – L. 6', 190 lbs. b: Sudbury, Ont., 12/22/1950. Pittsburgh's 6th choice, 77th overall, in 1970 Amateur Draft.

Season	Club	League	GP	G	A	Pts	AG	AA	APts	PIM	PP	SH	GW	S	%	TGF	PGF	TGA	PGA	+/–	GP	G	A	Pts	PIM	PP	SH	GW
1968-69	Brandon Wheat Kings	WCJHL	60	21	24	45	....	....	....	83	....	....	....	....	....	....	....	....	....	....	....	....	....	....	....	....	....	....
1969-70	Brandon Wheat Kings	WCJHL	60	20	44	64	....	....	....	119	....	....	....	....	....	....	....	....	....	....	....	....	....	....	....	....	....	....
1970-71	Amarillo Wranglers	CHL	70	9	10	19	....	....	....	49	....	....	....	....	....	....	....	....	....	....	....	....	....	....	....	....	....	....
1971-72	Hershey Bears	AHL	3	0	0	0	....	....	....	0	....	....	....	....	....	....	....	....	....	....	....	....	....	....	....	....	....	....
	Fort Wayne Komets	IHL	52	11	17	28	....	....	....	106	....	....	....	....	....	....	....	....	....	....	8	0	4	4	31	....	....	....
1972-73	Fort Wayne Komets	IHL	73	26	37	63	....	....	....	157	....	....	....	....	....	....	....	....	....	....	9	4	*10	*14	22	....	....	....
1973-74	Edmonton Oilers	WHA	31	1	2	3	....	....	....	21	....	....	....	....	....	....	....	....	....	....	....	....	....	....	....	....	....	....
	Winston-Salem Polar Bears	SHL	31	16	16	32	....	....	....	107	....	....	....	....	....	....	....	....	....	....	7	3	5	8	6	....	....	....
1974-75	Indianapolis Racers	WHA	78	11	19	30	....	....	....	96	....	....	....	....	....	....	....	....	....	....	....	....	....	....	....	....	....	....
1975-76	Indianapolis Racers	WHA	52	15	16	31	....	....	....	112	....	....	....	....	....	....	....	....	....	....	....	....	....	....	....	....	....	....
	Quebec Nordiques	WHA	21	7	9	16	....	....	....	22	....	....	....	....	....	....	....	....	....	....	5	1	0	1	8	....	....	....
1976-77	Quebec Nordiques	WHA	81	9	30	39	....	....	....	105	....	....	....	....	....	....	....	....	....	....	17	3	3	6	16	....	....	....
1977-78	Quebec Nordiques	WHA	72	15	28	43	....	....	....	76	....	....	....	....	....	....	....	....	....	....	11	1	6	7	10	....	....	....
1978-79	Quebec Nordiques	WHA	72	10	35	45	....	....	....	69	....	....	....	....	....	....	....	....	....	....	4	1	3	4	0	....	....	....

Season	Club	League	GP	G	A	Pts	AG	AA	APts	PIM	PP	SH	GW	S	%	TGF	PGF	TGA	PGA	+/–	GP	G	A	Pts	PIM	PP	SH	GW
			REGULAR SEASON																		PLAYOFFS							
1979-80	**Quebec Nordiques**	**NHL**	70	11	20	31	10	15	25	59	5	1	0	88	12.5	42	10	90	34	–24	....	....	....	....	....	....	....	....
1980-81	Rochester Americans	AHL	34	5	10	15	....	....	....	60	....	....	....	....	....	....	....	....	....	....	....	....	....	....	....	....	....	....
	Quebec Nordiques	**NHL**	8	1	0	1	1	0	1	0	0	0	0	1	100.0	1	0	4	2	–1	3	0	0	0	10	0	0	0
	NHL Totals		78	12	20	32	11	15	26	59	5	1	0	89	13.5	43	10	94	36		3	0	0	0	10	0	0	0
	Other Major League Totals		407	68	139	207	....	....	....	501	....	....	....	....	....	....	....	....	....		37	6	12	18	34	....		....

Signed as a free agent by **Edmonton** (WHA), August, 1973. Claimed by **Indianapolis** (WHA) from **Edmonton** (WHA) in WHA Expansion Draft, June, 1974. Traded to **Quebec** (WHA) by **Indianapolis** (WHA) with Bill Prentice and Michel Dubois for Michel Parizeau, February, 1976. Rights retained by **Quebec** prior to Expansion Draft, June 9, 1979.

• FITZGERALD, RUSTY

Rusty Fitzgerald C – L. 6'1", 210 lbs. b: Minneapolis, MN, 10/4/1972. Pittsburgh's 2nd choice, 38th overall, in 1991 Entry Draft.

Season	Club	League	GP	G	A	Pts	AG	AA	APts	PIM	PP	SH	GW	S	%	TGF	PGF	TGA	PGA	+/–	GP	G	A	Pts	PIM	PP	SH	GW
1990-91	Duluth East High School	H.S.	15	14	11	25	....	....	....	24	....	....	....	....	....	....	....	....	....	....	....	....	....	....	....	....	....	....
1991-92	University of Minnesota-Duluth.	WCHA	37	9	11	20	....	....	....	40	....	....	....	....	....	....	....	....	....	....	....	....	....	....	....	....	....	....
1992-93	University of Minnesota-Duluth.	WCHA	39	24	23	47	....	....	....	48	....	....	....	....	....	....	....	....	....	....	....	....	....	....	....	....	....	....
1993-94	University of Minnesota-Duluth.	WCHA	37	11	25	36	....	....	....	59	....	....	....	....	....	....	....	....	....	....	....	....	....	....	....	....	....	....
1994-95	University of Minnesota-Duluth.	WCHA	34	16	22	38	....	....	....	50	....	....	....	....	....	....	....	....	....	....	....	....	....	....	....	....	....	....
	Pittsburgh Penguins	**NHL**	4	1	0	1	2	0	2	0	0	0	0	5	20.0	2	0	0	0	+2	5	0	0	0	4	0	0	0
	Cleveland Lumberjacks	IHL	2	0	1	1	....	....	....	0	....	....	....	....	....	....	....	....	....	....	3	3	0	3	6	....	....	....
1995-96	**Pittsburgh Penguins**	**NHL**	21	1	2	3	1	2	3	12	0	0	0	15	6.7	9	0	3	1	+7	....	....	....	....	....	....	....	....
	Cleveland Lumberjacks	IHL	46	17	19	36	....	....	....	90	....	....	....	....	....	....	....	....	....	....	1	0	0	0	2	....	....	....
1996-97			DID NOT PLAY – INJURED																									
1997-98	Cleveland Lumberjacks	IHL	34	3	5	8	....	....	....	36	....	....	....	....	....	....	....	....	....	....	1	0	0	0	0	....	....	....
	NHL Totals		25	2	2	4	3	2	5	12	0	0	0	20	10.0	11	0	3	1		5	0	0	0	4	0	0	0

• FITZGERALD, TOM

Tom Fitzgerald RW/C – R. 6'1", 191 lbs. b: Melrose, MA, 8/28/1968. NY Islanders' 1st choice, 17th overall, in 1986 Entry Draft.

Season	Club	League	GP	G	A	Pts	AG	AA	APts	PIM	PP	SH	GW	S	%	TGF	PGF	TGA	PGA	+/–	GP	G	A	Pts	PIM	PP	SH	GW
1985-86	Austin Prep School	H.S.	24	35	38	73	....	....	....	....	....	....	....	....	....	....	....	....	....	....	....	....	....	....	....	....	....	....
1986-87	Providence College	H.E.	27	8	14	22	....	....	....	22	....	....	....	....	....	....	....	....	....	....	....	....	....	....	....	....	....	....
	United States	WJC-A	7	3	0	3	....	....	....	2	....	....	....	....	....	....	....	....	....	....	....	....	....	....	....	....	....	....
1987-88	Providence College	H.E.	36	19	15	34	....	....	....	50	....	....	....	....	....	....	....	....	....	....	....	....	....	....	....	....	....	....
1988-89	**New York Islanders**	**NHL**	23	3	5	8	3	4	7	10	0	0	1	24	12.5	11	0	16	6	+1	....	....	....	....	....	....	....	....
	Springfield Indians	AHL	61	24	18	42	....	....	....	43	....	....	....	....	....	....	....	....	....	....	....	....	....	....	....	....	....	....
	United States	WEC-A	10	0	2	2	....	....	....	12	....	....	....	....	....	....	....	....	....	....	....	....	....	....	....	....	....	....
1989-90	**New York Islanders**	**NHL**	19	2	5	7	2	4	6	4	0	0	1	24	8.3	8	0	17	6	–3	4	1	0	1	4	0	0	0
	Springfield Indians	AHL	53	30	23	53	....	....	....	32	....	....	....	....	....	....	....	....	....	....	14	2	9	11	13	....	....	....
1990-91	**New York Islanders**	**NHL**	41	5	5	10	5	4	9	24	0	0	2	60	8.3	15	0	31	7	–9	....	....	....	....	....	....	....	....
	Capital District Islanders	AHL	27	7	7	14	....	....	....	50	....	....	....	....	....	....	....	....	....	....	....	....	....	....	....	....	....	....
	United States	WEC-A	10	1	0	1	....	....	....	6	....	....	....	....	....	....	....	....	....	....	....	....	....	....	....	....	....	....
1991-92	**New York Islanders**	**NHL**	45	6	11	17	5	8	13	28	0	2	2	71	8.5	23	0	37	11	–3	....	....	....	....	....	....	....	....
	Capital District Islanders	AHL	4	1	1	2	....	....	....	4	....	....	....	....	....	....	....	....	....	....	....	....	....	....	....	....	....	....
1992-93	**New York Islanders**	**NHL**	77	9	18	27	7	12	19	34	0	3	1	83	10.8	32	0	62	28	–2	18	2	5	7	18	0	0	0
1993-94	**Florida Panthers**	**NHL**	83	18	14	32	17	11	28	54	0	3	1	144	12.5	38	4	62	25	–3	....	....	....	....	....	....	....	....
1994-95	**Florida Panthers**	**NHL**	48	3	13	16	5	19	24	31	0	0	0	78	3.8	22	2	37	14	–3	....	....	....	....	....	....	....	....
1995-96	**Florida Panthers**	**NHL**	82	13	21	34	13	17	30	75	1	6	2	141	9.2	43	2	69	25	–3	22	4	4	8	34	0	0	2
1996-97	**Florida Panthers**	**NHL**	71	10	14	24	11	12	23	64	0	2	1	135	7.4	34	0	47	20	+7	5	0	1	1	0	0	0	0
1997-98	**Florida Panthers**	**NHL**	69	10	5	15	12	5	17	57	0	1	1	105	9.5	22	0	59	33	–4	....	....	....	....	....	....	....	....
	Colorado Avalanche	**NHL**	11	2	1	3	2	1	3	22	0	1	0	14	14.3	5	0	9	4	0	7	0	1	1	20	0	0	0
	NHL Totals		569	81	112	193	82	97	179	403	1	18	12	879	9.2	253	8	446	179		56	7	11	18	76	0	0	2

Claimed by **Florida** from **NY Islanders** in Expansion Draft, June 24, 1993. Traded to **Colorado** by **Florida** for the rights to Mark Parrish and Anaheim's 3rd round choice (previously acquired, Florida selected Lance Ward) in 1998 Entry Draft, March 24, 1998. Signed as a free agent by **Nashville**, July 6, 1998.

• FITZPATRICK, RORY

Rory Fitzpatrick D – R. 6'1", 205 lbs. b: Rochester, NY, 1/11/1975. Montreal's 2nd choice, 47th overall, in 1993 Entry Draft.

Season	Club	League	GP	G	A	Pts	AG	AA	APts	PIM	PP	SH	GW	S	%	TGF	PGF	TGA	PGA	+/–	GP	G	A	Pts	PIM	PP	SH	GW
1992-93	Sudbury Wolves	OHL	58	4	20	24	....	....	....	68	....	....	....	....	....	....	....	....	....	....	14	0	0	0	17	....	....	....
1993-94	Sudbury Wolves	OHL	65	12	34	46	....	....	....	112	....	....	....	....	....	....	....	....	....	....	10	2	5	7	10	....	....	....
1994-95	Sudbury Wolves	OHL	56	12	36	48	....	....	....	72	....	....	....	....	....	....	....	....	....	....	18	3	15	18	21	....	....	....
	United States	WJC-A	7	0	2	2	....	....	....	8	....	....	....	....	....	....	....	....	....	....	....	....	....	....	....	....	....	....
	Fredericton Canadiens	AHL	....	....	....	....	....	....	....	....	....	....	....	....	....	....	....	....	....	....	10	1	2	3	5	....	....	....
1995-96	**Montreal Canadiens**	**NHL**	42	0	2	2	0	2	2	18	0	0	0	31	0.0	15	1	27	6	–7	6	1	1	2	0	0	0	0
	Fredericton Canadiens	AHL	18	4	6	10	....	....	....	36	....	....	....	....	....	....	....	....	....	....	....	....	....	....	....	....	....	....
1996-97	**Montreal Canadiens**	**NHL**	6	0	1	1	0	1	1	6	0	0	0	5	0.0	4	0	6	0	–2	....	....	....	....	....	....	....	....
	St. Louis Blues	**NHL**	2	0	0	0	0	0	0	2	0	0	0	1	0.0	0	0	2	0	–2	....	....	....	....	....	....	....	....
	Worcester IceCats	AHL	49	4	13	17	....	....	....	78	....	....	....	....	....	....	....	....	....	....	5	1	2	3	0	....	....	....
1997-98	Worcester IceCats	AHL	62	8	22	30	....	....	....	111	....	....	....	....	....	....	....	....	....	....	11	0	3	3	26	....	....	....
	NHL Totals		50	0	3	3	0	3	3	26	0	0	0	37	0.0	19	1	35	6		6	1	1	2	0	0	0	0

Traded to **St. Louis** by **Montreal** with Pierre Turgeon and Craig Conroy for Murray Baron, Shayne Corson and St. Louis' 5th round choice (Gennady Razin) in 1997 Entry Draft, October 29, 1996.

• FITZPATRICK, ROSS

Ross Fitzpatrick C – L. 6', 195 lbs. b: Penticton, B.C., 10/7/1960. Philadelphia's 7th choice, 147th overall, in 1980 Entry Draft.

Season	Club	League	GP	G	A	Pts	AG	AA	APts	PIM	PP	SH	GW	S	%	TGF	PGF	TGA	PGA	+/–	GP	G	A	Pts	PIM	PP	SH	GW
1977-78	Penticton Panthers	BCJHL	....	63	63	126	....	....	....	....	....	....	....	....	....	....	....	....	....	....	....	....	....	....	....	....	....	....
1977-78	Penticton Panthers	BCJHL	....	63	63	126	....	....	....	....	....	....	....	....	....	....	....	....	....	....	....	....	....	....	....	....	....	....
1978-79	University of Michigan	CCHA	35	16	21	37	....	....	....	31	....	....	....	....	....	....	....	....	....	....	....	....	....	....	....	....	....	....
1978-79	University of Western Michigan	CCHA	35	16	21	37	....	....	....	31	....	....	....	....	....	....	....	....	....	....	....	....	....	....	....	....	....	....
1979-80	University of Western Michigan	CCHA	34	26	33	59	....	....	....	22	....	....	....	....	....	....	....	....	....	....	....	....	....	....	....	....	....	....
1980-81	University of Western Michigan	CCHA	36	28	43	71	....	....	....	22	....	....	....	....	....	....	....	....	....	....	....	....	....	....	....	....	....	....
1981-82	University of Western Michigan	CCHA	33	30	28	58	....	....	....	34	....	....	....	....	....	....	....	....	....	....	....	....	....	....	....	....	....	....
1982-83	**Philadelphia Flyers**	**NHL**	1	0	0	0	0	0	0	0	0	0	0	3	0.0	0	0	1	0	–1	....	....	....	....	....	....	....	....
	Maine Mariners	AHL	66	29	28	57	....	....	....	32	....	....	....	....	....	....	....	....	....	....	15	5	1	6	12	....	....	....
1983-84	**Philadelphia Flyers**	**NHL**	12	4	2	6	3	1	4	0	0	0	1	21	19.0	8	0	4	0	+4	....	....	....	....	....	....	....	....
	Springfield Indians	AHL	45	33	30	63	....	....	....	28	....	....	....	....	....	....	....	....	....	....	4	3	2	5	2	....	....	....
1984-85	**Philadelphia Flyers**	**NHL**	5	1	0	1	1	0	1	0	1	0	0	10	10.0	3	2	4	0	–3	....	....	....	....	....	....	....	....
	Hershey Bears	AHL	35	26	15	41	....	....	....	8	....	....	....	....	....	....	....	....	....	....	....	....	....	....	....	....	....	....
1985-86	**Philadelphia Flyers**	**NHL**	2	0	0	0	0	0	0	0	0	0	0	0	0.0	0	0	1	0	–1	....	....	....	....	....	....	....	....
	Hershey Bears	AHL	77	50	47	97	....	....	....	28	....	....	....	....	....	....	....	....	....	....	17	9	7	16	10	....	....	....
1986-87	Hershey Bears	AHL	66	45	40	85	....	....	....	34	....	....	....	....	....	....	....	....	....	....	5	1	4	5	10	....	....	....
1987-88	Hershey Bears	AHL	35	14	17	31	....	....	....	12	....	....	....	....	....	....	....	....	....	....	12	*11	4	15	8	....	....	....
1988-89	WEV Wien	Austria	38	26	23	49	....	....	....	....	....	....	....	....	....	....	....	....	....	....	....	....	....	....	....	....	....	....
	Hershey Bears	AHL	11	6	9	15	....	....	....	4	....	....	....	....	....	....	....	....	....	....	9	2	2	4	4	....	....	....
1989-90	Hershey Bears	AHL	74	45	*58	103	....	....	....	26	....	....	....	....	....	....	....	....	....	....	....	....	....	....	....	....	....	....
1990-91	Binghamton Rangers	AHL	69	26	29	55	....	....	....	26	....	....	....	....	....	....	....	....	....	....	10	3	1	4	4	....	....	....
1991-92	Binghamton Rangers	AHL	76	34	38	72	....	....	....	32	....	....	....	....	....	....	....	....	....	....	10	1	3	4	2	....	....	....
	NHL Totals		20	5	2	7	4	1	5	0	1	0	1	34	14.7	11	2	10	0		....	....	....	....	....	....	....	....

CCHA First All-Star Team (1981) • AHL Second All-Star Team (1986, 1990)

Signed as a free agent by **NY Rangers**, July 24, 1990.

• FITZPATRICK, SANDY

Sandy (Alexander Stewart) Fitzpatrick C – L. 6'1", 195 lbs. b: Paisley, Scotland, 12/22/1944.

Season	Club	League	GP	G	A	Pts	AG	AA	APts	PIM	PP	SH	GW	S	%	TGF	PGF	TGA	PGA	+/–	GP	G	A	Pts	PIM	PP	SH	GW
1961-62	Guelph Royals	OHA	48	5	7	12	....	....	....	21	....	....	....	....	....	....	....	....	....	....	....	....	....	....	....	....	....	....
1962-63	Guelph Royals	OHA	50	9	25	34	....	....	....	52	....	....	....	....	....	....	....	....	....	....	....	....	....	....	....	....	....	....
1963-64	Kitchener Rangers	OHA	56	23	28	51	....	....	....	61	....	....	....	....	....	....	....	....	....	....	....	....	....	....	....	....	....	....
1964-65	Kitchener Rangers	OHA	56	51	55	106	....	....	....	140	....	....	....	....	....	....	....	....	....	....	....	....	....	....	....	....	....	....
	New York Rangers	**NHL**	4	0	0	0	0	0	0	2	....	....	....	....	....	....	....	....	....	....	....	....	....	....	....	....	....	....
	St. Paul Rangers	CHL	....	....	....	....	....	....	....	....	....	....	....	....	....	....	....	....	....	....	3	0	0	0	0	....	....	....
1965-66	Minnesota Rangers	CHL	68	15	30	45	....	....	....	74	....	....	....	....	....	....	....	....	....	....	7	5	3	8	4	....	....	....
1966-67	Omaha Knights	CHL	49	7	19	26	....	....	....	57	....	....	....	....	....	....	....	....	....	....	11	0	0	0	9	....	....	....

Season	Club	League	REGULAR SEASON GP	G	A	Pts	AG	AA	APts	PIM	PP	SH	GW	S	%	TGF	PGF	TGA	PGA	+/-	PLAYOFFS GP	G	A	Pts	PIM	PP	SH	GW
1967-68	**Minnesota North Stars**	**NHL**	**18**	**3**	**6**	**9**	**4**	**6**	**10**	**6**	**0**	**0**	**0**	**26**	**11.5**	**10**	**2**	**8**	**0**	**0**	**12**	**0**	**0**	**0**	**0**	**0**	**0**	**0**
	Memphis South Stars	CHL	56	15	29	44	....	....	....	56	....	....	....	....	....	....	....	....	....	....	....	....	....	....	....	....	....	....
1968-69	Memphis South Stars	CHL	66	14	26	40	....	....	....	32	....	....	....	....	....	....	....	....	....	....	....	....	....	....	....	....	....	....
1969-70	San Diego Gulls	WHL	67	17	29	46	....	....	....	16	....	....	....	....	....	....	....	....	....	....	3	0	0	0	4	....	....	....
1970-71	San Diego Gulls	WHL	70	13	21	34	....	....	....	41	....	....	....	....	....	....	....	....	....	....	6	0	2	2	2	....	....	....
1971-72	San Diego Gulls	WHL	24	2	5	7	....	....	....	19	....	....	....	....	....	....	....	....	....	....	....	....	....	....	....	....	....	....
	NHL Totals		**22**	**3**	**6**	**9**	**4**	**6**	**10**	**8**	**0**	**0**	**0**	**26**	**11.5**	**10**	**2**	**8**	**0**		**12**	**0**	**0**	**0**	**0**	**0**	**0**	**0**

Claimed by **Minnesota** from **NY Rangers** in Expansion Draft, June 6, 1967.

• FLATLEY, PAT

Pat Flatley RW – R. 6′2″, 197 lbs. b: Toronto, Ont., 10/3/1963. NY Islanders' 1st choice, 21st overall, in 1982 Entry Draft.

Season	Club	League	GP	G	A	Pts	AG	AA	APts	PIM	PP	SH	GW	S	%	TGF	PGF	TGA	PGA	+/-	GP	G	A	Pts	PIM	PP	SH	GW
1981-82	University of Wisconsin	WCHA	17	10	9	19	....	....	....	40	....	....	....	....	....	....	....	....	....	....	....	....	....	....	....	....	....	....
1982-83	University of Wisconsin	WCHA	26	17	24	41	....	....	....	48	....	....	....	....	....	....	....	....	....	....	....	....	....	....	....	....	....	....
	Canada	WJC-A	7	4	0	4	....	....	....	6	....	....	....	....	....	....	....	....	....	....	....	....	....	....	....	....	....	....
	Canada	WEC-A	6	0	0	0	....	....	....	2	....	....	....	....	....	....	....	....	....	....	....	....	....	....	....	....	....	....
1983-84	Canada	Nat-Team	57	31	17	48	....	....	....	136	....	....	....	....	....	....	....	....	....	....	....	....	....	....	....	....	....	....
	Canada	Olympics	7	3	3	6	....	....	....	20	....	....	....	....	....	....	....	....	....	....	....	....	....	....	....	....	....	....
	New York Islanders	**NHL**	**16**	**2**	**7**	**9**	**2**	**5**	**7**	**6**	**1**	**0**	**0**	**17**	**11.8**	**12**	**2**	**7**	**0**	**+3**	**21**	**9**	**6**	**15**	**14**	**1**	**0**	**1**
1984-85	**New York Islanders**	**NHL**	**78**	**20**	**31**	**51**	**16**	**21**	**37**	**106**	**2**	**0**	**4**	**135**	**14.8**	**70**	**10**	**72**	**4**	**–8**	**4**	**1**	**0**	**1**	**6**	**0**	**0**	**0**
1985-86	**New York Islanders**	**NHL**	**73**	**18**	**34**	**52**	**14**	**23**	**37**	**66**	**6**	**0**	**2**	**120**	**15.0**	**75**	**12**	**50**	**7**	**+20**	**3**	**0**	**0**	**0**	**21**	**0**	**0**	**0**
1986-87	**New York Islanders**	**NHL**	**63**	**16**	**35**	**51**	**14**	**25**	**39**	**81**	**6**	**0**	**4**	**113**	**14.2**	**69**	**21**	**45**	**14**	**+17**	**11**	**3**	**2**	**5**	**6**	**0**	**0**	**0**
1987-88	**New York Islanders**	**NHL**	**40**	**9**	**15**	**24**	**8**	**11**	**19**	**28**	**5**	**1**	**0**	**83**	**10.8**	**37**	**16**	**19**	**5**	**+7**	....	....	....	....	....	....	....	....
1988-89	**New York Islanders**	**NHL**	**41**	**10**	**15**	**25**	**8**	**11**	**19**	**31**	**2**	**1**	**1**	**72**	**13.9**	**39**	**14**	**38**	**8**	**–5**	....	....	....	....	....	....	....	....
	Springfield Indians	AHL	2	1	1	2	....	....	....	2	....	....	....	....	....	....	....	....	....	....	....	....	....	....	....	....	....	....
1989-90	**New York Islanders**	**NHL**	**62**	**17**	**32**	**49**	**15**	**23**	**38**	**101**	**4**	**0**	**2**	**136**	**12.5**	**74**	**24**	**52**	**12**	**+10**	**5**	**3**	**0**	**3**	**2**	**2**	**0**	**0**
1990-91	**New York Islanders**	**NHL**	**56**	**20**	**25**	**45**	**18**	**19**	**37**	**74**	**8**	**0**	**4**	**137**	**14.6**	**62**	**21**	**56**	**13**	**–2**	....	....	....	....	....	....	....	....
1991-92	**New York Islanders**	**NHL**	**38**	**8**	**28**	**36**	**7**	**21**	**28**	**31**	**4**	**1**	**0**	**76**	**10.5**	**50**	**9**	**41**	**14**	**+14**	....	....	....	....	....	....	....	....
1992-93	**New York Islanders**	**NHL**	**80**	**13**	**47**	**60**	**11**	**32**	**43**	**63**	**1**	**2**	**1**	**139**	**9.4**	**89**	**19**	**94**	**29**	**+5**	**15**	**2**	**7**	**9**	**12**	**0**	**0**	**0**
1993-94	**New York Islanders**	**NHL**	**64**	**12**	**30**	**42**	**11**	**23**	**34**	**40**	**2**	**1**	**2**	**112**	**10.7**	**64**	**9**	**63**	**20**	**+12**	....	....	....	....	....	....	....	....
1994-95	**New York Islanders**	**NHL**	**45**	**7**	**20**	**27**	**12**	**29**	**41**	**12**	**1**	**0**	**1**	**81**	**8.6**	**45**	**7**	**43**	**14**	**+9**	....	....	....	....	....	....	....	....
1995-96	**New York Islanders**	**NHL**	**56**	**8**	**9**	**17**	**8**	**7**	**15**	**21**	**0**	**0**	**0**	**89**	**9.0**	**25**	**4**	**52**	**7**	**–24**	....	....	....	....	....	....	....	....
1996-97	**New York Rangers**	**NHL**	**68**	**10**	**12**	**22**	**11**	**11**	**22**	**26**	**0**	**0**	**2**	**96**	**10.4**	**32**	**2**	**25**	**1**	**+6**	**11**	**0**	**0**	**0**	**14**	**0**	**0**	**0**
	NHL Totals		**780**	**170**	**340**	**510**	**155**	**261**	**416**	**686**	**42**	**6**	**23**	**1406**	**12.1**	**743**	**170**	**657**	**148**		**70**	**18**	**15**	**33**	**75**	**3**	**0**	**1**

WCHA First All-Star Team (1983) • NCAA West First All-American Team (1983) • NCAA Championship All-Tournament Team (1983)

Signed as a free agent by **NY Rangers**, September 26, 1996.

• FLEMING, GERRY

Gerry Fleming LW – L. 6′5″, 253 lbs. b: Montreal, Que., 10/16/1967.

Season	Club	League	GP	G	A	Pts	AG	AA	APts	PIM	PP	SH	GW	S	%	TGF	PGF	TGA	PGA	+/-	GP	G	A	Pts	PIM	PP	SH	GW
1983-84	Verdun Juniors	QMJHL	52	4	11	15	....	....	....	270	....	....	....	....	....	....	....	....	....	....	3	0	4	4	2	....	....	....
1984-85	Verdun Jr. Canadiens	QMJHL	44	15	23	38	....	....	....	160	....	....	....	....	....	....	....	....	....	....	14	5	6	11	*96	....	....	....
1985-86	Verdun Jr. Canadiens	QMJHL	47	15	21	36	....	....	....	339	....	....	....	....	....	....	....	....	....	....	4	0	1	1	18	....	....	....
1986-87	University of P.E.I.	AUAA	20	19	11	30	....	....	....	73	....	....	....	....	....	....	....	....	....	....	....	....	....	....	....	....	....	....
1987-88	University of P.E.I.	AUAA	23	11	15	26	....	....	....	61	....	....	....	....	....	....	....	....	....	....	....	....	....	....	....	....	....	....
1988-89	University of P.E.I.	AUAA	17	11	23	34	....	....	....	61	....	....	....	....	....	....	....	....	....	....	....	....	....	....	....	....	....	....
1989-90	Fredericton Alpines	NBSHL	24	12	18	30	....	....	....	83	....	....	....	....	....	....	....	....	....	....	....	3	6	9	....	....	....	....
1990-91	University of P.E.I.	AUAA	9	2	6	8	....	....	....	41	....	....	....	....	....	....	....	....	....	....	....	....	....	....	....	....	....	....
1991-92	Charlottetown Islanders	PEI Sr.	STATISTICS NOT AVAILABLE																									
	Fredericton Canadiens	AHL	37	4	6	10	....	....	....	133	....	....	....	....	....	....	....	....	....	....	1	0	0	0	7	....	....	....
1992-93	Fredericton Canadiens	AHL	64	9	17	26	....	....	....	262	....	....	....	....	....	....	....	....	....	....	5	1	2	3	14	....	....	....
1993-94	**Montreal Canadiens**	**NHL**	**5**	**0**	**0**	**0**	**0**	**0**	**0**	**25**	**0**	**0**	**0**	**4**	**0.0**	**0**	**0**	**4**	**0**	**–4**	....	....	....	....	....	....	....	....
	Fredericton Canadiens	AHL	46	6	16	22	....	....	....	188	....	....	....	....	....	....	....	....	....	....	....	....	....	....	....	....	....	....
1994-95	**Montreal Canadiens**	**NHL**	**6**	**0**	**0**	**0**	**0**	**0**	**0**	**17**	**0**	**0**	**0**	**1**	**0.0**	**0**	**0**	**1**	**0**	**–1**	....	....	....	....	....	....	....	....
	Fredericton Canadiens	AHL	16	3	3	6	....	....	....	60	....	....	....	....	....	....	....	....	....	....	10	2	0	2	67	....	....	....
1995-96	Fredericton Canadiens	AHL	40	8	9	17	....	....	....	127	....	....	....	....	....	....	....	....	....	....	10	3	1	4	19	....	....	....
1996-97	Fredericton Canadiens	AHL	40	5	11	16	....	....	....	164	....	....	....	....	....	....	....	....	....	....	....	....	....	....	....	....	....	....
1997-98	Fredericton Canadiens	AHL	28	3	3	6	....	....	....	101	....	....	....	....	....	....	....	....	....	....	1	0	0	0	0	....	....	....
	NHL Totals		**11**	**0**	**0**	**0**	**0**	**0**	**0**	**42**	**0**	**0**	**0**	**5**	**0.0**	**0**	**0**	**5**	**0**		....	....	....	....	....	....	....	....

Signed as a free agent by **Montreal**, February 17, 1992.

• FLEMING, REGGIE

Reggie Fleming D/LW – L. 5′8″, 170 lbs. b: Montreal, Que., 4/21/1936.

Season	Club	League	GP	G	A	Pts	AG	AA	APts	PIM	PP	SH	GW	S	%	TGF	PGF	TGA	PGA	+/-	GP	G	A	Pts	PIM	PP	SH	GW
1953-54	Montreal Jr. Canadiens	QJHL	48	7	7	14	....	....	....	47	....	....	....	....	....	....	....	....	....	....	8	0	0	0	14	....	....	....
1954-55	Montreal Jr. Canadiens	QJHL	44	3	11	14	....	....	....	*139	....	....	....	....	....	....	....	....	....	....	5	0	0	0	11	....	....	....
1955-56	St. Michael's Majors	OHA	42	1	8	9	....	....	....	93	....	....	....	....	....	....	....	....	....	....	8	0	2	2	18	....	....	....
1956-57	Shawinigan Cataracts	QHL	61	2	9	11	....	....	....	109	....	....	....	....	....	....	....	....	....	....	....	....	....	....	....	....	....	....
1957-58	Shawinigan Cataracts	QHL	51	6	15	21	....	....	....	*227	....	....	....	....	....	....	....	....	....	....	8	3	2	5	16	....	....	....
1958-59	Rochester Americans	AHL	70	6	16	22	....	....	....	112	....	....	....	....	....	....	....	....	....	....	5	0	1	1	13	....	....	....
1959-60	**Montreal Canadiens**	**NHL**	**3**	**0**	**0**	**0**	**0**	**0**	**0**	**2**	....	....	....	....	....	....	....	....	....	....	....	....	....	....	....	....	....	....
	Kingston Frontenacs	EPHL	52	19	49	68	....	....	....	91	....	....	....	....	....	....	....	....	....	....	....	....	....	....	....	....	....	....
	Rochester Americans	AHL	9	1	5	6	....	....	....	4	....	....	....	....	....	....	....	....	....	....	....	....	....	....	....	....	....	....
1960-61	**Chicago Black Hawks**	**NHL**	**66**	**4**	**4**	**8**	**5**	**4**	**9**	**145**	....	....	....	....	....	....	....	....	....	....	**12**	**1**	**0**	**1**	**12**	....	....	....
1961-62	**Chicago Black Hawks**	**NHL**	**70**	**7**	**9**	**16**	**8**	**9**	**17**	**71**	....	....	....	....	....	....	....	....	....	....	**12**	**2**	**2**	**4**	**27**	....	....	....
1962-63	**Chicago Black Hawks**	**NHL**	**64**	**7**	**7**	**14**	**9**	**7**	**16**	**99**	....	....	....	....	....	....	....	....	....	....	**6**	**0**	**0**	**0**	**27**	....	....	....
1963-64	**Chicago Black Hawks**	**NHL**	**61**	**3**	**6**	**9**	**4**	**7**	**11**	**140**	....	....	....	....	....	....	....	....	....	....	**7**	**0**	**0**	**0**	**18**	....	....	....
1964-65	**Boston Bruins**	**NHL**	**67**	**18**	**23**	**41**	**23**	**25**	**48**	**136**	....	....	....	....	....	....	....	....	....	....	....	....	....	....	....	....	....	....
1965-66	**Boston Bruins**	**NHL**	**34**	**4**	**6**	**10**	**5**	**6**	**11**	***42**	....	....	....	....	....	....	....	....	....	....	....	....	....	....	....	....	....	....
	New York Rangers	**NHL**	**35**	**10**	**14**	**24**	**12**	**14**	**26**	***124**	....	....	....	....	....	....	....	....	....	....	....	....	....	....	....	....	....	....
1966-67	**New York Rangers**	**NHL**	**61**	**15**	**16**	**31**	**18**	**16**	**34**	**146**	....	....	....	....	....	....	....	....	....	....	**4**	**0**	**2**	**2**	**11**	....	....	....
1967-68	**New York Rangers**	**NHL**	**73**	**17**	**7**	**24**	**21**	**7**	**28**	**132**	**0**	**1**	**0**	**143**	**11.9**	**34**	**0**	**38**	**5**	**+1**	**6**	**0**	**2**	**2**	**4**	**0**	**0**	**0**
1968-69	**New York Rangers**	**NHL**	**72**	**8**	**12**	**20**	**9**	**11**	**20**	**138**	**2**	**0**	**1**	**117**	**6.8**	**36**	**5**	**46**	**2**	**–13**	**3**	**0**	**0**	**0**	**7**	**0**	**0**	**0**
1969-70	**Philadelphia Flyers**	**NHL**	**65**	**9**	**18**	**27**	**10**	**18**	**28**	**134**	**2**	**0**	**1**	**129**	**7.0**	**44**	**11**	**42**	**5**	**–4**	....	....	....	....	....	....	....	....
1970-71	**Buffalo Sabres**	**NHL**	**78**	**6**	**10**	**16**	**6**	**9**	**15**	**159**	**0**	**0**	**0**	**54**	**11.1**	**21**	**3**	**50**	**24**	**–8**	....	....	....	....	....	....	....	....
1971-72	Cincinnati Swords	AHL	11	3	5	8	....	....	....	62	....	....	....	....	....	....	....	....	....	....	....	....	....	....	....	....	....	....
	Salt Lake Golden Eagles	WHL	56	20	28	48	....	....	....	134	....	....	....	....	....	....	....	....	....	....	....	....	....	....	....	....	....	....
1972-73	Chicago Cougars	WHA	74	23	45	68	....	....	....	95	....	....	....	....	....	....	....	....	....	....	....	....	....	....	....	....	....	....
1973-74	Chicago Cougars	WHA	45	2	12	14	....	....	....	49	....	....	....	....	....	....	....	....	....	....	12	0	4	4	12	....	....	....
1974-75	Saginaw Gears	IHL	9	1	6	7	....	....	....	14	....	....	....	....	....	....	....	....	....	....	17	8	13	21	....	....	....	....
1975-76	Milwaukee Admirals	USHL	1	0	0	0	....	....	....	0	....	....	....	....	....	....	....	....	....	....	....	....	....	....	....	....	....	....
1976-77	Milwaukee Admirals	USHL	23	5	21	26	....	....	....	81	....	....	....	....	....	....	....	....	....	....	....	....	....	....	....	....	....	....
	NHL Totals		**749**	**108**	**132**	**240**	**130**	**133**	**263**	**1468**	**4**	**1**	**2**	**443**	**24.4**	**135**	**19**	**176**	**36**		**50**	**3**	**6**	**9**	**106**	**0**	**0**	**0**
	Other Major League Totals		119	25	57	82	....	....	....	144	....	....	....	....	....	....	....	....	....		12	0	4	4	12	....	....	....

Played in NHL All-Star Game (1961)

Traded to **Chicago** by **Montreal** with Cec Hoekstra, Ab McDonald and Bob Courcy for Terry Gray, Glen Skov and the rights to Danny Lewicki, Lorne Ferguson and Bob Bailey, June 7, 1960. Traded to **Boston** by **Chicago** with Ab McDonald for Doug Mohns, June 8, 1964. Traded to **NY Rangers** by **Boston** for John McKenzie, January 10, 1966. Traded to **Philadelphia** by **NY Rangers** for Leon Rochefort and Don Blackburn, June 6, 1969. Claimed by **Buffalo** from **Philadelphia** in Expansion Draft, June 10, 1970. Selected by **LA Sharks** (WHA) in 1972 WHA General Player Draft, February 12, 1972. WHA rights traded to **Chicago** (WHA) by **LA Sharks** (WHA) for cash, August, 1972.

• FLESCH, JOHN

John Flesch LW – L. 6′2″, 200 lbs. b: Sudbury, Ont., 7/15/1953. Atlanta's 5th choice, 69th overall, in 1973 Amateur Draft.

Season	Club	League	GP	G	A	Pts	AG	AA	APts	PIM	PP	SH	GW	S	%	TGF	PGF	TGA	PGA	+/-	GP	G	A	Pts	PIM	PP	SH	GW
1971-72	Sudbury Wolves	NOHA	48	17	24	41	....	....	....	182	....	....	....	....	....	....	....	....	....	....	....	....	....	....	....	....	....	....
1972-73	Lake Superior State University	CCHA	29	28	32	60	....	....	....	108	....	....	....	....	....	....	....	....	....	....	....	....	....	....	....	....	....	....
1973-74	Omaha Knights	CHL	69	27	27	54	....	....	....	98	....	....	....	....	....	....	....	....	....	....	5	1	2	3	4	....	....	....
1974-75	**Minnesota North Stars**	**NHL**	**57**	**8**	**15**	**23**	**7**	**12**	**19**	**47**	**2**	**0**	**1**	**77**	**10.4**	**32**	**5**	**47**	**1**	**–19**	....	....	....	....	....	....	....	....
1975-76	**Minnesota North Stars**	**NHL**	**33**	**3**	**2**	**5**	**3**	**2**	**5**	**47**	**1**	**0**	**0**	**26**	**11.5**	**7**	**2**	**13**	**0**	**–8**	....	....	....	....	....	....	....	....
	New Haven Nighthawks	AHL	31	11	10	21	....	....	....	95	....	....	....	....	....	....	....	....	....	....	3	1	0	1	2	....	....	....

Season	Club	League	GP	G	A	Pts	AG	AA	APts	PIM	PP	SH	GW	S	%	TGF	PGF	TGA	PGA	+/–	PLAYOFFS GP	G	A	Pts	PIM	PP	SH	GW
1976-77	Columbus Owls	IHL	74	34	39	73	....	....	....	210	....	....	....	....	....	....	....	....	....	....	7	1	5	6	15	....	....	....
1977-78	**Pittsburgh Penguins**	**NHL**	**29**	**7**	**5**	**12**	**7**	**4**	**11**	**19**	**0**	**0**	**2**	**34**	**20.6**	**18**	**0**	**25**	**0**	**–7**	....	....	....	....	....	....	....	....
1978-79	Grand Rapids Owls	IHL	67	26	56	82	....	....	....	149	....	....	....	....	....	....	....	....	....	....	22	10	15	25	36	....	....	....
1979-80	**Colorado Rockies**	**NHL**	**5**	**0**	**1**	**1**	**0**	**1**	**1**	**4**	**0**	**0**	**0**	**3**	**0.0**	**3**	**1**	**4**	**1**	**–1**	....	....	....	....	....	....	....	....
	Grand Rapids Owls	IHL	76	39	54	93	....	....	....	66	....	....	....	....	....	....	....	....	....	....	....	....	....	....	....	....	....	....
1980-81	Milwaukee Admirals	IHL	70	27	44	71	....	....	....	70	....	....	....	....	....	....	....	....	....	....	7	1	3	4	6	....	....	....
1981-82	Milwaukee Admirals	IHL	82	39	54	93	....	....	....	45	....	....	....	....	....	....	....	....	....	....	5	2	2	4	4	....	....	....
1982-83	Milwaukee Admirals	IHL	51	24	31	55	....	....	....	56	....	....	....	....	....	....	....	....	....	....	11	5	7	12	10	....	....	....
1983-84	Milwaukee Admirals	IHL	81	43	44	87	....	....	....	27	....	....	....	....	....	....	....	....	....	....	4	0	2	2	0	....	....	....
1984-85	Kalamazoo Wings	IHL	82	38	40	78	....	....	....	72	....	....	....	....	....	....	....	....	....	....	11	9	4	13	2	....	....	....
1985-86	Kalamazoo Wings	IHL	48	15	15	30	....	....	....	33	....	....	....	....	....	....	....	....	....	....	6	0	3	3	2	....	....	....
	NHL Totals		**124**	**18**	**23**	**41**	**17**	**19**	**36**	**117**	**3**	**0**	**3**	**140**	**12.9**	**60**	**8**	**89**	**2**		....	....	....	....	....	....	....	....

IHL Second All-Star Team (1979) • IHL First All-Star Team (1982)

Traded to **Minnesota** by **Atlanta** with Don Martineau for Buster Harvey and Jerry Byers, May 27, 1974. Signed as a free agent by **Pittsburgh**, February 4, 1978. Signed as a free agent by **Colorado**, January 13, 1980.

• FLETCHER, STEVEN

Steven Fletcher LW/D – L. 6'2", 180 lbs. b: Montreal, Que., 3/31/1962. Calgary's 11th choice, 202nd overall, in 1980 Entry Draft.

Season	Club	League	GP	G	A	Pts	AG	AA	APts	PIM	PP	SH	GW	S	%	TGF	PGF	TGA	PGA	+/–	PLAYOFFS GP	G	A	Pts	PIM	PP	SH	GW
1979-80	Hull Olympiques	QMJHL	61	2	14	16	....	....	....	183	....	....	....	....	....	....	....	....	....	....	....	....	....	....	....	....	....	....
1980-81	Hull Olympiques	QMJHL	66	4	13	17	....	....	....	231	....	....	....	....	....	....	....	....	....	....	....	....	....	....	....	....	....	....
1981-82	Hull Olympiques	QMJHL	60	4	20	24	....	....	....	230	....	....	....	....	....	....	....	....	....	....	....	....	....	....	....	....	....	....
1982-83	Sherbrooke Jets	AHL	36	0	1	1	....	....	....	119	....	....	....	....	....	....	....	....	....	....	....	....	....	....	....	....	....	....
	Fort Wayne Komets	IHL	34	1	9	10	....	....	....	115	....	....	....	....	....	....	....	....	....	....	10	1	6	7	45	....	....	....
1983-84	Sherbrooke Jets	AHL	77	3	7	10	....	....	....	208	....	....	....	....	....	....	....	....	....	....	....	....	....	....	....	....	....	....
1984-85	Sherbrooke Canadiens	AHL	50	2	4	6	....	....	....	192	....	....	....	....	....	....	....	....	....	....	13	0	0	0	48	....	....	....
1985-86	Sherbrooke Canadiens	AHL	64	2	12	14	....	....	....	293	....	....	....	....	....	....	....	....	....	....	....	....	....	....	....	....	....	....
1986-87	Sherbrooke Canadiens	AHL	70	15	11	26	....	....	....	261	....	....	....	....	....	....	....	....	....	....	17	5	5	10	*82	....	....	....
1987-88	Sherbrooke Canadiens	AHL	76	8	21	29	....	....	....	338	....	....	....	....	....	....	....	....	....	....	6	2	1	3	28	....	....	....
	Montreal Canadiens	**NHL**	....	....	....	....	....	....	....	....	....	....	....	....	....	....	....	....	....	....	**1**	**0**	**0**	**0**	**5**	....	....	....
1988-89	**Winnipeg Jets**	**NHL**	**3**	**0**	**0**	**0**	**0**	**0**	**0**	**5**	**0**	**0**	**0**	**1**	**0.0**	**0**	**0**	**1**	**0**	**–1**	....	....	....	....	....	....	....	....
	Moncton Hawks	AHL	23	1	1	2	....	....	....	89	....	....	....	....	....	....	....	....	....	....	....	....	....	....	....	....	....	....
	Halifax Citadels	AHL	29	5	8	13	....	....	....	91	....	....	....	....	....	....	....	....	....	....	....	....	....	....	....	....	....	....
1989-90	Hershey Bears	AHL	28	1	1	2	....	....	....	132	....	....	....	....	....	....	....	....	....	....	....	....	....	....	....	....	....	....
1990-91	Fort Wayne Komets	IHL	66	7	9	16	....	....	....	289	....	....	....	....	....	....	....	....	....	....	15	2	0	2	70	....	....	....
1991-92	Fort Wayne Komets	IHL	60	8	3	11	....	....	....	320	....	....	....	....	....	....	....	....	....	....	5	0	0	0	14	....	....	....
1992-93	Fort Wayne Komets	IHL	52	5	6	11	....	....	....	337	....	....	....	....	....	....	....	....	....	....	3	0	0	0	2	....	....	....
1993-94	Fort Wayne Komets	IHL	47	4	6	10	....	....	....	277	....	....	....	....	....	....	....	....	....	....	5	0	0	0	33	....	....	....
1994-95	Fort Wayne Komets	IHL	43	0	2	2	....	....	....	204	....	....	....	....	....	....	....	....	....	....	1	0	0	0	0	....	....	....
1995-96	Fort Wayne Komets	IHL	2	2	0	2	....	....	....	39	....	....	....	....	....	....	....	....	....	....	....	....	....	....	....	....	....	....
	Atlanta Knights	IHL	23	0	1	1	....	....	....	110	....	....	....	....	....	....	....	....	....	....	....	....	....	....	....	....	....	....
	NHL Totals		**3**	**0**	**0**	**0**	**0**	**0**	**0**	**5**	**0**	**0**	**0**	**1**	**0.0**	**0**	**0**	**1**	**0**		**1**	**0**	**0**	**0**	**5**	**0**	**0**	**0**

Signed as a free agent by **Montreal**, August 21, 1984. Signed as a free agent by **Winnipeg**, July 15, 1988. Traded to **Philadelphia** by **Winnipeg** for future considerations, December 12, 1988.

• FLETT, BILL

Bill "Cowboy" Flett RW – R. 6'1", 205 lbs. b: Vermillion, Alta., 7/21/1943.

Season	Club	League	GP	G	A	Pts	AG	AA	APts	PIM	PP	SH	GW	S	%	TGF	PGF	TGA	PGA	+/–	PLAYOFFS GP	G	A	Pts	PIM	PP	SH	GW
1960-61	Melville Millionaires	SJHL	27	16	2	18	....	....	....	14	....	....	....	....	....	....	....	....	....	....	7	3	1	4	10	....	....	....
1961-62	Melville Millionaires	SJHL	STATISTICS NOT AVAILABLE																									
1962-63	Melville Millionaires	SJHL	53	31	54	85	....	....	....	80	....	....	....	....	....	....	....	....	....	....	18	7	11	18	40	....	....	....
1963-64	Rochester Americans	AHL	1	0	0	0	....	....	....	0	....	....	....	....	....	....	....	....	....	....	....	....	....	....	....	....	....	....
	Charlotte Checkers	EHL	41	26	21	47	....	....	....	48	....	....	....	....	....	....	....	....	....	....	3	0	1	1	6	....	....	....
	Denver Invaders	WHL	....	....	....	....	....	....	....	....	....	....	....	....	....	....	....	....	....	....	1	0	0	0	0	....	....	....
1964-65	Tulsa Oilers	CHL	39	8	22	30	....	....	....	58	....	....	....	....	....	....	....	....	....	....	12	1	2	3	6	....	....	....
	Victoria Maple Leafs	WHL	23	1	7	8	....	....	....	14	....	....	....	....	....	....	....	....	....	....	....	....	....	....	....	....	....	....
1965-66	Tulsa Oilers	CHL	55	23	23	46	....	....	....	0	....	....	....	....	....	....	....	....	....	....	....	....	....	....	....	....	....	....
1966-67	Tulsa Oilers	CHL	62	16	28	44	....	....	....	108	....	....	....	....	....	....	....	....	....	....	....	....	....	....	....	....	....	....
1967-68	**Los Angeles Kings**	**NHL**	**73**	**26**	**20**	**46**	**32**	**21**	**53**	**97**	**3**	**0**	**6**	**205**	**12.7**	**74**	**19**	**60**	**9**	**+4**	**7**	**1**	**2**	**3**	**8**	**0**	**0**	**0**
1968-69	**Los Angeles Kings**	**NHL**	**72**	**24**	**25**	**49**	**27**	**23**	**50**	**53**	**4**	**0**	**6**	**198**	**12.1**	**65**	**14**	**77**	**2**	**–24**	**10**	**3**	**4**	**7**	**11**	**1**	**1**	**0**
1969-70	**Los Angeles Kings**	**NHL**	**69**	**14**	**18**	**32**	**16**	**18**	**34**	**70**	**2**	**0**	**0**	**198**	**7.1**	**53**	**15**	**75**	**10**	**–27**	....	....	....	....	....	....	....	....
	Springfield Kings	AHL	5	2	6	8	....	....	....	6	....	....	....	....	....	....	....	....	....	....	....	....	....	....	....	....	....	....
1970-71	**Los Angeles Kings**	**NHL**	**64**	**13**	**24**	**37**	**14**	**21**	**35**	**57**	**5**	**0**	**0**	**182**	**7.1**	**56**	**14**	**82**	**10**	**–30**	....	....	....	....	....	....	....	....
1971-72	**Los Angeles Kings**	**NHL**	**45**	**7**	**12**	**19**	**7**	**11**	**18**	**18**	**1**	**0**	**0**	**113**	**6.2**	**30**	**5**	**55**	**0**	**–30**	....	....	....	....	....	....	....	....
	Philadelphia Flyers	**NHL**	**31**	**11**	**10**	**21**	**12**	**9**	**21**	**26**	**3**	**0**	**1**	**116**	**9.5**	**38**	**11**	**24**	**2**	**+5**	....	....	....	....	....	....	....	....
1972-73	**Philadelphia Flyers**	**NHL**	**69**	**43**	**31**	**74**	**43**	**26**	**69**	**53**	**11**	**3**	**6**	**283**	**15.2**	**119**	**41**	**70**	**23**	**+31**	**11**	**3**	**4**	**7**	**0**	**0**	**1**	**1**
1973-74	**Philadelphia Flyers**	**NHL**	**67**	**17**	**27**	**44**	**17**	**23**	**40**	**51**	**1**	**1**	**5**	**222**	**7.7**	**76**	**24**	**35**	**3**	**+20**	**17**	**0**	**6**	**6**	**21**	**0**	**0**	**0**
1974-75	**Toronto Maple Leafs**	**NHL**	**77**	**15**	**25**	**40**	**14**	**20**	**34**	**38**	**4**	**3**	**2**	**186**	**8.1**	**59**	**17**	**74**	**32**	**0**	**5**	**0**	**0**	**0**	**2**	**0**	**0**	**0**
1975-76	**Atlanta Flames**	**NHL**	**78**	**23**	**17**	**40**	**21**	**13**	**34**	**30**	**1**	**2**	**3**	**171**	**13.5**	**63**	**3**	**69**	**18**	**+9**	**2**	**0**	**0**	**0**	**0**	**0**	**0**	**0**
1976-77	**Atlanta Flames**	**NHL**	**24**	**4**	**4**	**8**	**4**	**3**	**7**	**6**	**1**	**0**	**1**	**35**	**11.4**	**13**	**3**	**14**	**5**	**+1**	....	....	....	....	....	....	....	....
	Edmonton Oilers	WHA	48	34	20	54	....	....	....	20	....	....	....	....	....	....	....	....	....	....	5	0	2	2	2	....	....	....
1977-78	Edmonton Oilers	WHA	74	41	28	69	....	....	....	34	....	....	....	....	....	....	....	....	....	....	....	....	....	....	....	....	....	....
1978-79	Edmonton Oilers	WHA	73	28	36	64	....	....	....	14	....	....	....	....	....	....	....	....	....	....	10	5	2	7	2	....	....	....
1979-80	**Edmonton Oilers**	**NHL**	**20**	**5**	**2**	**7**	**5**	**2**	**7**	**2**	**1**	**0**	**0**	**26**	**19.2**	**12**	**3**	**27**	**1**	**–17**	....	....	....	....	....	....	....	....
	NHL Totals		**689**	**202**	**215**	**417**	**212**	**190**	**402**	**501**	**37**	**9**	**30**	**1935**	**10.4**	**658**	**169**	**662**	**116**		**52**	**7**	**16**	**23**	**42**	**1**	**2**	**1**
	Other Major League Totals		195	103	84	187			....	68	....	....	....	....	....	....	....	....	....	....	15	5	4	9	4	....	....	....

Played in NHL All-Star Game (1971)

Claimed by **LA Kings** from **Toronto** in Expansion Draft, June 6, 1967. Traded to **Philadelphia** by **LA Kings** with Ed Joyal, Jean Potvin and Ross Lonsberry for Bill Lesuk, Jim Johnson and Serge Bernier, January 28, 1972. Traded to **Toronto** by **Philadelphia** for Dave Fortier and Randy Osburn, May 27, 1974. Claimed on waivers by **Atlanta** from **Toronto**, May 20, 1975. Traded to **Edmonton** (WHA) by **Atlanta** for cash, December, 1976. Rights retained by **Edmonton** prior to Expansion Draft, June 9, 1979.

• FLEURY, THEOREN

Theoren Fleury RW – R. 5'6", 160 lbs. b: Oxbow, Sask., 6/29/1968. Calgary's 9th choice, 166th overall, in 1987 Entry Draft.

Season	Club	League	GP	G	A	Pts	AG	AA	APts	PIM	PP	SH	GW	S	%	TGF	PGF	TGA	PGA	+/–	PLAYOFFS GP	G	A	Pts	PIM	PP	SH	GW
1983-84	St. James Canadians	Midget	22	33	31	64	....	....	....	88	....	....	....	....	....	....	....	....	....	....	....	....	....	....	....	....	....	....
1984-85	Moose Jaw Warriors	WHL	71	29	46	75	....	....	....	82	....	....	....	....	....	....	....	....	....	....	....	....	....	....	....	....	....	....
1985-86	Moose Jaw Warriors	WHL	72	43	65	108	....	....	....	124	....	....	....	....	....	....	....	....	....	....	....	....	....	....	....	....	....	....
1986-87	Moose Jaw Warriors	WHL	66	61	68	129	....	....	....	110	....	....	....	....	....	....	....	....	....	....	9	7	9	16	34	....	....	....
	Canada	WJC-A	6	2	3	5	....	....	....	2	....	....	....	....	....	....	....	....	....	....	....	....	....	....	....	....	....	....
1987-88	Moose Jaw Warriors	WHL	65	68	92	*160	....	....	....	235	....	....	....	....	....	....	....	....	....	....	....	....	....	....	....	....	....	....
	Canada	WJC-A	7	6	2	8	....	....	....	4	....	....	....	....	....	....	....	....	....	....	....	....	....	....	....	....	....	....
	Salt Lake Golden Eagles	IHL	2	3	4	7	....	....	....	7	....	....	....	....	....	....	....	....	....	....	8	11	5	16	16	....	....	....
1988-89	**Calgary Flames**	**NHL**	**36**	**14**	**20**	**34**	**12**	**14**	**26**	**46**	**5**	**0**	**3**	**89**	**15.7**	**50**	**25**	**21**	**1**	**+5**	**22**	**5**	**6**	**11**	**24**	**3**	**0**	**3**
	Salt Lake Golden Eagles	IHL	40	37	37	74	....	....	....	81	....	....	....	....	....	....	....	....	....	....	....	....	....	....	....	....	....	....
1989-90	Calgary Flames	FrTour	4	1	0	1	....	....	....	6	....	....	....	....	....	....	....	....	....	....	....	....	....	....	....	....	....	....
	Calgary Flames	**NHL**	**80**	**31**	**35**	**66**	**27**	**25**	**52**	**157**	**9**	**3**	**6**	**200**	**15.5**	**95**	**32**	**48**	**7**	**+22**	**6**	**2**	**3**	**5**	**10**	**0**	**0**	**0**
	Canada	WEC-A	9	4	7	11	....	....	....	10	....	....	....	....	....	....	....	....	....	....	....	....	....	....	....	....	....	....
1990-91	**Calgary Flames**	**NHL**	**79**	**51**	**53**	**104**	**47**	**40**	**87**	**136**	**9**	**7**	**9**	**249**	**20.5**	**155**	**57**	**63**	**13**	**+48**	**7**	**2**	**5**	**7**	**14**	**0**	**0**	**1**
	Canada	WEC-A	8	5	5	10	....	....	....	8	....	....	....	....	....	....	....	....	....	....	....	....	....	....	....	....	....	....
1991-92	Canada	C Cup	7	1	4	5	....	....	....	12	....	....	....	....	....	....	....	....	....	....	....	....	....	....	....	....	....	....
	Calgary Flames	**NHL**	**80**	**33**	**40**	**73**	**30**	**30**	**60**	**133**	**11**	**1**	**6**	**225**	**14.7**	**121**	**53**	**82**	**14**	**0**	....	....	....	....	....	....	....	....
1992-93	**Calgary Flames**	**NHL**	**83**	**34**	**66**	**100**	**28**	**45**	**73**	**88**	**12**	**2**	**4**	**250**	**13.6**	**145**	**61**	**83**	**13**	**+14**	**6**	**5**	**7**	**12**	**27**	**3**	**1**	**0**
1993-94	**Calgary Flames**	**NHL**	**83**	**40**	**45**	**85**	**37**	**35**	**72**	**186**	**16**	**1**	**6**	**278**	**14.4**	**134**	**55**	**81**	**32**	**+30**	**7**	**6**	**4**	**10**	**5**	**1**	**0**	**2**
1994-95	Tappara Tampere	Finland	10	8	9	17	....	....	....	22	....	....	....	....	....	....	....	....	....	....	....	....	....	....	....	....	....	....
	Calgary Flames	**NHL**	**47**	**29**	**29**	**58**	**52**	**43**	**95**	**112**	**9**	**2**	**5**	**173**	**16.8**	**81**	**30**	**60**	**15**	**+6**	**7**	**7**	**7**	**14**	**2**	**2**	**1**	**0**
1995-96	**Calgary Flames**	**NHL**	**80**	**46**	**50**	**96**	**45**	**41**	**86**	**112**	**17**	**5**	**4**	**353**	**13.0**	**126**	**45**	**90**	**26**	**+17**	**4**	**2**	**1**	**3**	**14**	**0**	**0**	**0**

Season	Club	League	REGULAR SEASON GP	G	A	Pts	AG	AA	APts	PIM	PP	SH	GW	S	%	TGF	PGF	TGA	PGA	+/–	PLAYOFFS GP	G	A	Pts	PIM	PP	SH	GW
1996-97	Canada	W Cup	8	4	2	6	....	....	....	8	....	....	....	....	....	....	....	....	....	....	....	....	....	....	....	....	....	....
	Calgary Flames	**NHL**	**81**	**29**	**38**	**67**	**31**	**34**	**65**	**104**	**9**	**2**	**3**	**336**	**8.6**	**103**	**40**	**84**	**9**	**–12**	....	....	....	....	....	....	....	....
1997-98	**Calgary Flames**	**NHL**	**82**	**27**	**51**	**78**	**32**	**50**	**82**	**197**	**3**	**2**	**4**	**282**	**9.6**	**113**	**32**	**109**	**28**	**0**	....	....	....	....	....	....	....	....
	Canada	Olympics	6	1	3	4	....	....	....	2	....	....	....	....	....	....	....	....	....	....	....	....	....	....	....	....	....	....
	NHL Totals		**731**	**334**	**427**	**761**	**341**	**357**	**698**	**1271**	**100**	**25**	**50**	**2435**	**13.7**	**1123**	**430**	**721**	**158**		**59**	**29**	**33**	**62**	**96**	**9**	**2**	**6**

WJC-A All-Star Team (1988) • WHL East Second All-Star Team (1988) • Co-winner of Alka-Seltzer Plus Award with Marty McSorley (1991) • NHL Second All-Star Team (1995)

Played in NHL All-Star Game (1991, 1992, 1996, 1997, 1998)

• FLICHEL, TODD

Todd Flichel D – R. 6'3", 195 lbs. b: Osgoode, Ont., 9/14/1964. Winnipeg's 10th choice, 176th overall, in 1983 Entry Draft.

Season	Club	League	GP	G	A	Pts	AG	AA	APts	PIM	PP	SH	GW	S	%	TGF	PGF	TGA	PGA	+/–	GP	G	A	Pts	PIM	PP	SH	GW
1983-84	Bowling Green University	CCHA	44	1	3	4	....	....	....	12	....	....	....	....	....	....	....	....	....	....	....	....	....	....	....	....	....	....
1984-85	Bowling Green University	CCHA	42	5	7	12	....	....	....	62	....	....	....	....	....	....	....	....	....	....	....	....	....	....	....	....	....	....
1985-86	Bowling Green University	CCHA	42	3	10	13	....	....	....	84	....	....	....	....	....	....	....	....	....	....	....	....	....	....	....	....	....	....
1986-87	Bowling Green University	CCHA	42	4	15	19	....	....	....	77	....	....	....	....	....	....	....	....	....	....	....	....	....	....	....	....	....	....
1987-88	**Winnipeg Jets**	**NHL**	**2**	**0**	**0**	**0**	**0**	**0**	**0**	**2**	**0**	**0**	**0**	**1**	**0.0**	**0**	**0**	**4**	**0**	**–4**	....	....	....	....	....	....	....	....
	Moncton Hawks	AHL	65	5	12	17	....	....	....	102	....	....	....	....	....	....	....	....	....	....	....	....	....	....	....	....	....	....
1988-89	**Winnipeg Jets**	**NHL**	**1**	**0**	**0**	**0**	**0**	**0**	**0**	**0**	**0**	**0**	**0**	**1**	**0.0**	**0**	**0**	**1**	**0**	**–1**	....	....	....	....	....	....	....	....
	Moncton Hawks	AHL	74	2	29	31	....	....	....	81	....	....	....	....	....	....	....	....	....	....	10	1	4	5	25	....	....	....
1989-90	**Winnipeg Jets**	**NHL**	**3**	**0**	**1**	**1**	**0**	**1**	**1**	**2**	**0**	**0**	**0**	**1**	**0.0**	**1**	**0**	**2**	**1**	**0**	....	....	....	....	....	....	....	....
	Moncton Hawks	AHL	65	7	14	21	....	....	....	74	....	....	....	....	....	....	....	....	....	....	....	....	....	....	....	....	....	....
1990-91	Moncton Hawks	AHL	75	8	21	29	....	....	....	44	....	....	....	....	....	....	....	....	....	....	9	0	0	0	8	....	....	....
1991-92	Fort Wayne Komets	IHL	64	3	10	13	....	....	....	79	....	....	....	....	....	....	....	....	....	....	7	0	0	0	2	....	....	....
1992-93	Rochester Americans	AHL	15	1	3	4	....	....	....	4	....	....	....	....	....	....	....	....	....	....	....	....	....	....	....	....	....	....
	Cincinnati Cyclones	IHL	52	5	10	15	....	....	....	46	....	....	....	....	....	....	....	....	....	....	....	....	....	....	....	....	....	....
1993-94	Rochester Americans	AHL	2	0	0	0	....	....	....	0	....	....	....	....	....	....	....	....	....	....	....	....	....	....	....	....	....	....
	NHL Totals		**6**	**0**	**1**	**1**	**0**	**1**	**1**	**4**	**0**	**0**	**0**	**3**	**0.0**	**1**	**0**	**7**	**1**		....	....	....	....	....	....	....	....

• FLOCKHART, ROB

Rob Flockhart LW – L. 6', 185 lbs. b: Sicamous, B.C., 2/6/1956. Vancouver's 2nd choice, 44th overall, in 1976 Amateur Draft.

Season	Club	League	GP	G	A	Pts	AG	AA	APts	PIM	PP	SH	GW	S	%	TGF	PGF	TGA	PGA	+/–	GP	G	A	Pts	PIM	PP	SH	GW
1972-73	The Pas Blue Devils	AJHL	....	35	45	80	....	....	....	92	....	....	....	....	....	....	....	....	....	....	....	....	....	....	....	....	....	....
1973-74	Kamloops Chiefs	WHL	67	13	16	29	....	....	....	49	....	....	....	....	....	....	....	....	....	....	....	....	....	....	....	....	....	....
1974-75	Kamloops Chiefs	WHL	36	19	20	39	....	....	....	52	....	....	....	....	....	....	....	....	....	....	....	....	....	....	....	....	....	....
	Canada	WJC-A	4	1	0	1	....	....	....	6	....	....	....	....	....	....	....	....	....	....	....	....	....	....	....	....	....	....
1975-76	Kamloops Chiefs	WHL	72	51	47	98	....	....	....	91	....	....	....	....	....	....	....	....	....	....	11	3	9	12	32	....	....	....
1976-77	**Vancouver Canucks**	**NHL**	**5**	**0**	**0**	**0**	**0**	**0**	**0**	**0**	**0**	**0**	**0**	**1**	**0.0**	**1**	**0**	**0**	**0**	**+1**	....	....	....	....	....	....	....	....
	Tulsa Oilers	CHL	65	22	32	54	....	....	....	70	....	....	....	....	....	....	....	....	....	....	9	2	6	8	12	....	....	....
1977-78	**Vancouver Canucks**	**NHL**	**24**	**0**	**1**	**1**	**0**	**1**	**1**	**12**	**0**	**0**	**0**	**15**	**0.0**	**5**	**0**	**19**	**0**	**–14**	....	....	....	....	....	....	....	....
	Tulsa Oilers	CHL	43	17	11	28	....	....	....	55	....	....	....	....	....	....	....	....	....	....	7	2	3	5	14	....	....	....
1978-79	**Vancouver Canucks**	**NHL**	**14**	**1**	**1**	**2**	**1**	**1**	**2**	**0**	**0**	**0**	**0**	**10**	**10.0**	**2**	**0**	**8**	**3**	**–3**	....	....	....	....	....	....	....	....
	Dallas Black Hawks	CHL	44	18	27	45	....	....	....	46	....	....	....	....	....	....	....	....	....	....	9	3	3	6	*34	....	....	....
1979-80	**Minnesota North Stars**	**NHL**	**10**	**1**	**3**	**4**	**1**	**2**	**3**	**2**	**0**	**0**	**1**	**10**	**10.0**	**7**	**2**	**9**	**0**	**–4**	**1**	**1**	**0**	**1**	**2**	**0**	**0**	**0**
	Oklahoma City Stars	CHL	67	31	40	71	....	....	....	51	....	....	....	....	....	....	....	....	....	....	....	....	....	....	....	....	....	....
1980-81	**Minnesota North Stars**	**NHL**	**2**	**0**	**0**	**0**	**0**	**0**	**0**	**0**	**0**	**0**	**0**	**1**	**0.0**	**0**	**0**	**2**	**0**	**–2**	....	....	....	....	....	....	....	....
	Oklahoma City Stars	CHL	75	33	42	75	....	....	....	89	....	....	....	....	....	....	....	....	....	....	3	0	1	1	6	....	....	....
1981-82	Nashville South Stars	CHL	79	27	30	57	....	....	....	98	....	....	....	....	....	....	....	....	....	....	3	0	0	0	2	....	....	....
1982-83	Springfield Indians	AHL	74	22	34	56	....	....	....	55	....	....	....	....	....	....	....	....	....	....	....	....	....	....	....	....	....	....
1983-84	Toledo Goaldiggers	IHL	54	33	20	53	....	....	....	33	....	....	....	....	....	....	....	....	....	....	....	....	....	....	....	....	....	....
1984-85	New Haven Nighthawks	AHL	2	0	2	2	....	....	....	0	....	....	....	....	....	....	....	....	....	....	....	....	....	....	....	....	....	....
	Springfield Indians	AHL	14	5	8	13	....	....	....	22	....	....	....	....	....	....	....	....	....	....	....	....	....	....	....	....	....	....
	NHL Totals		**55**	**2**	**5**	**7**	**2**	**4**	**6**	**14**	**0**	**0**	**1**	**37**	**5.4**	**15**	**2**	**38**	**3**		**1**	**1**	**0**	**1**	**2**	**0**	**0**	**0**

CHL First All-Star Team (1980)

Signed as a free agent by **Minnesota**, October 12, 1979. Signed as a free agent by **Chicago**, December 1, 1982.

• FLOCKHART, RON

Ron "Flockey Hockey" Flockhart C – L. 5'11", 190 lbs. b: Smithers, B.C., 10/10/1960.

Season	Club	League	GP	G	A	Pts	AG	AA	APts	PIM	PP	SH	GW	S	%	TGF	PGF	TGA	PGA	+/–	GP	G	A	Pts	PIM	PP	SH	GW
1978-79	Revelstone Grizzlies	BCJHL	61	47	41	88	....	....	....	54	....	....	....	....	....	....	....	....	....	....	....	....	....	....	....	....	....	....
1979-80	Regina Pats	WHL	65	54	76	130	....	....	....	63	....	....	....	....	....	....	....	....	....	....	17	11	23	34	18	....	....	....
1980-81	**Philadelphia Flyers**	**NHL**	**14**	**3**	**7**	**10**	**2**	**5**	**7**	**11**	**0**	**0**	**0**	**24**	**12.5**	**15**	**1**	**8**	**0**	**+6**	**3**	**1**	**0**	**1**	**2**	**0**	**0**	**0**
	Maine Mariners	AHL	59	33	33	66	....	....	....	26	....	....	....	....	....	....	....	....	....	....	....	....	....	....	....	....	....	....
1981-82	**Philadelphia Flyers**	**NHL**	**72**	**33**	**39**	**72**	**26**	**26**	**52**	**44**	**10**	**0**	**2**	**240**	**13.8**	**94**	**32**	**45**	**1**	**+18**	**4**	**0**	**1**	**1**	**2**	**0**	**0**	**0**
1982-83	**Philadelphia Flyers**	**NHL**	**73**	**29**	**31**	**60**	**24**	**21**	**45**	**49**	**3**	**2**	**6**	**241**	**12.0**	**84**	**25**	**62**	**6**	**+3**	**2**	**1**	**1**	**2**	**2**	**1**	**0**	**0**
1983-84	**Philadelphia Flyers**	**NHL**	**8**	**0**	**3**	**3**	**0**	**2**	**2**	**4**	**0**	**0**	**0**	**12**	**0.0**	**6**	**0**	**5**	**0**	**+1**	....	....	....	....	....	....	....	....
	Pittsburgh Penguins	**NHL**	**68**	**27**	**18**	**45**	**22**	**12**	**34**	**40**	**5**	**0**	**1**	**202**	**13.4**	**64**	**16**	**67**	**0**	**–19**	....	....	....	....	....	....	....	....
1984-85	**Pittsburgh Penguins**	**NHL**	**12**	**0**	**5**	**5**	**0**	**3**	**3**	**4**	**0**	**0**	**0**	**20**	**0.0**	**7**	**1**	**6**	**4**	**+4**	....	....	....	....	....	....	....	....
	Montreal Canadiens	**NHL**	**42**	**10**	**12**	**22**	**8**	**8**	**16**	**14**	**1**	**0**	**2**	**58**	**17.2**	**32**	**7**	**23**	**1**	**+3**	**2**	**1**	**1**	**2**	**2**	**0**	**0**	**1**
1985-86	**St. Louis Blues**	**NHL**	**79**	**22**	**45**	**67**	**18**	**30**	**48**	**26**	**5**	**2**	**3**	**199**	**11.1**	**89**	**29**	**52**	**0**	**+8**	**8**	**1**	**3**	**4**	**6**	**0**	**0**	**0**
1986-87	**St. Louis Blues**	**NHL**	**60**	**16**	**19**	**35**	**14**	**14**	**28**	**12**	**2**	**0**	**2**	**101**	**15.8**	**48**	**5**	**52**	**0**	**–9**	....	....	....	....	....	....	....	....
1987-88	**St. Louis Blues**	**NHL**	**21**	**5**	**4**	**9**	**4**	**3**	**7**	**4**	**0**	**0**	**1**	**27**	**18.5**	**16**	**0**	**11**	**0**	**+5**	....	....	....	....	....	....	....	....
1988-89	Peoria Rivermen	IHL	2	0	2	2	....	....	....	0	....	....	....	....	....	....	....	....	....	....	....	....	....	....	....	....	....	....
	Boston Bruins	**NHL**	**4**	**0**	**0**	**0**	**0**	**0**	**0**	**0**	**0**	**0**	**0**	**3**	**0.0**	**0**	**0**	**4**	**1**	**–3**	....	....	....	....	....	....	....	....
	Maine Mariners	AHL	9	5	6	11	....	....	....	0	....	....	....	....	....	....	....	....	....	....	....	....	....	....	....	....	....	....
	Cortina	Italy	31	31	34	65	....	....	....	25	....	....	....	....	....	....	....	....	....	....	....	....	....	....	....	....	....	....
1989-90	HC Bolzano	Italy	36	48	85	133	....	....	....	15	....	....	....	....	....	....	....	....	....	....	9	5	9	14	0	....	....	....
1990-91	HC Bolzano	Italy	33	35	44	79	....	....	....	32	....	....	....	....	....	....	....	....	....	....	10	7	12	19	2	....	....	....
	NHL Totals		**453**	**145**	**183**	**328**	**118**	**124**	**242**	**208**	**26**	**4**	**17**	**1127**	**12.9**	**455**	**116**	**335**	**13**		**19**	**4**	**6**	**10**	**14**	**1**	**0**	**1**

Signed as a free agent by **Philadelphia**, July 2, 1980. Traded to **Pittsburgh** by **Philadelphia** with Andy Brickley, Mark Taylor and Philadelphia's 1st (Roger Belanger) and 3rd (later traded to Vancouver — Vancouver selected Mike Stevens) round choices in 1984 Entry Draft for Rich Sutter and Pittsburgh's 2nd (Greg Smyth) and 3rd (David McLay) round choices in 1984 Entry Draft, October 23, 1983. Traded to **Montreal** by **Pittsburgh** for John Chabot, November 9, 1984. Traded to **St. Louis** by **Montreal** for Perry Ganchar, August 26, 1985. Traded to **Boston** by **St. Louis** for future considerations, February 13, 1989.

• FLOYD, LARRY

Larry Floyd C – L. 5'8", 180 lbs. b: Peterborough, Ont., 5/1/1961.

Season	Club	League	GP	G	A	Pts	AG	AA	APts	PIM	PP	SH	GW	S	%	TGF	PGF	TGA	PGA	+/–	GP	G	A	Pts	PIM	PP	SH	GW
1979-80	Peterborough Petes	OHA	66	21	37	58	....	....	....	54	....	....	....	....	....	....	....	....	....	....	14	6	9	15	10	....	....	....
1980-81	Peterborough Petes	OHA	44	26	37	63	....	....	....	43	....	....	....	....	....	....	....	....	....	....	5	2	2	4	0	....	....	....
1981-82	Peterborough Petes	OHL	39	32	37	69	....	....	....	26	....	....	....	....	....	....	....	....	....	....	9	9	6	15	20	....	....	....
	Rochester Americans	AHL	1	0	2	2	....	....	....	0	....	....	....	....	....	....	....	....	....	....	7	1	1	2	0	....	....	....
1982-83	**New Jersey Devils**	**NHL**	**5**	**1**	**0**	**1**	**1**	**0**	**1**	**2**	**0**	**0**	**0**	**9**	**11.1**	**1**	**0**	**5**	**0**	**–4**	....	....	....	....	....	....	....	....
	Wichita Wind	CHL	75	40	43	83	....	....	....	16	....	....	....	....	....	....	....	....	....	....	....	....	....	....	....	....	....	....
1983-84	**New Jersey Devils**	**NHL**	**7**	**1**	**3**	**4**	**1**	**2**	**3**	**7**	**0**	**0**	**0**	**15**	**6.7**	**4**	**0**	**11**	**3**	**–4**	....	....	....	....	....	....	....	....
	Maine Mariners	AHL	74	37	49	86	....	....	....	40	....	....	....	....	....	....	....	....	....	....	16	9	8	17	4	....	....	....
1984-85	Maine Mariners	AHL	72	30	51	81	....	....	....	24	....	....	....	....	....	....	....	....	....	....	3	0	1	1	2	....	....	....
1985-86	Maine Mariners	AHL	80	29	58	87	....	....	....	25	....	....	....	....	....	....	....	....	....	....	5	3	3	6	0	....	....	....
1986-87	Maine Mariners	AHL	77	30	44	74	....	....	....	50	....	....	....	....	....	....	....	....	....	....	....	....	....	....	....	....	....	....
1987-88	Utica Devils	AHL	28	21	21	42	....	....	....	14	....	....	....	....	....	....	....	....	....	....	....	....	....	....	....	....	....	....
1988-89	Cape Breton Oilers	AHL	70	16	33	49	....	....	....	40	....	....	....	....	....	....	....	....	....	....	....	....	....	....	....	....	....	....
1989-90	Phoenix Roadrunners	IHL	76	39	40	79	....	....	....	50	....	....	....	....	....	....	....	....	....	....	....	....	....	....	....	....	....	....
1990-91	San Diego Gulls	IHL	73	24	54	78	....	....	....	34	....	....	....	....	....	....	....	....	....	....	....	....	....	....	....	....	....	....
1991-92	San Diego Gulls	IHL	71	18	45	63	....	....	....	58	....	....	....	....	....	....	....	....	....	....	4	0	2	2	0	....	....	....
1992-93	San Diego Gulls	IHL	80	27	31	58	....	....	....	28	....	....	....	....	....	....	....	....	....	....	14	3	1	4	4	....	....	....
1993-94	San Diego Gulls	IHL	52	10	20	30	....	....	....	45	....	....	....	....	....	....	....	....	....	....	8	1	0	1	5	....	....	....
	NHL Totals		**12**	**2**	**3**	**5**	**2**	**2**	**4**	**9**	**0**	**0**	**0**	**24**	**8.3**	**5**	**0**	**16**	**3**		....	....	....	....	....	....	....	....

Won Ken McKenzie Trophy (CHL's Rookie of the Year) (1983)

Signed as a free agent by **New Jersey**, September 16, 1982.

• FOGARTY, BRYAN

Bryan Fogarty D – L. 6'2", 206 lbs. b: Brantford, Ont., 6/11/1969. Quebec's 1st choice, 9th overall, in 1987 Entry Draft.

Season	Club	League	GP	G	A	Pts	AG	AA	APts	PIM	PP	SH	GW	S	%	TGF	PGF	TGA	PGA	+/–	Playoffs GP	G	A	Pts	PIM	PP	SH	GW
1985-86	Kingston Canadians	OHL	47	2	19	21				14											10	1	3	4	4			
1986-87	Kingston Canadians	OHL	56	20	50	70				46											12	2	3	5	5			
1987-88	Kingston Canadians	OHL	48	11	36	47				50																		
1988-89	Niagara Falls Thunder	OHL	60	47	*108	*155				88											17	10	22	32	36			
1989-90	Quebec Nordiques	NHL	45	4	10	14	3	7	10	31	2	0	0	93	4.3	39	13	74	1	–47								
	Halifax Citadels	AHL	22	5	14	19				6											6	2	4	6	0			
1990-91	Quebec Nordiques	NHL	45	9	22	31	8	17	25	24	3	0	2	107	8.4	59	25	46	1	–11								
	Halifax Citadels	AHL	5	0	2	2				0																		
1991-92	Quebec Nordiques	NHL	20	3	12	15	3	9	12	16	0	0	0	30	10.0	27	10	32	0	–15								
	Halifax Citadels	AHL	2	0	0	0				2																		
	New Haven Nighthawks	AHL	4	0	1	1				6																		
	Muskegon Lumberjacks	IHL	8	2	4	6				30																		
1992-93	Pittsburgh Penguins	NHL	12	0	4	4	0	3	3	4	0	0	0	11	0.0	11	7	7	0	–3								
	Cleveland Lumberjacks	IHL	15	2	5	7				8											3	0	1	1	17			
1993-94	Atlanta Knights	IHL	8	1	5	6				4																		
	Las Vegas Thunder	IHL	33	3	16	19				38																		
	Kansas City Blades	IHL	3	2	1	3				2																		
	Montreal Canadiens	NHL	13	1	2	3	1	2	3	10	0	0	0	22	4.5	11	3	13	1	–4								
1994-95	Montreal Canadiens	NHL	21	5	2	7	9	3	12	34	3	0	0	41	12.2	15	6	13	1	–3								
1995-96	Minnesota Moose	IHL	17	3	12	15				24																		
	Detroit Vipers	IHL	18	1	5	6				14																		
	HC Davos	Switz.																			3	1	1	2	0			
1996-97	Kansas City Blades	IHL	22	3	9	12				10																		
	Milan 24	Italy	16	8	20	28				30																		
	Milan 24	Alpenliga	7	3	7	10				10																		
1997-98	Hannover Scorpions	Germany	39	8	17	25				75											4	1	0	1	2			
	NHL Totals		156	22	52	74	24	41	65	119	8	0	2	304	7.2	162	64	185	4									

OHL First All-Star Team (1987, 1989) • Canadian Major Junior Defenseman of the Year (1989) • Canadian Major Junior Player of the Year (1989)

Traded to **Pittsburgh** by **Quebec** for Scott Young, March 10, 1992. Signed as a free agent by **Tampa Bay**, September 28, 1993. Signed as a free agent by **Montreal**, February 25, 1994. Signed as a free agent by **Buffalo**, September 8, 1995.

• FOGOLIN, LEE

Lee "Foggie" Fogolin D – R. 6', 200 lbs. b: Chicago, IL, 2/7/1955. Buffalo's 1st choice, 11th overall, in 1974 Amateur Draft.

Season	Club	League	GP	G	A	Pts	AG	AA	APts	PIM	PP	SH	GW	S	%	TGF	PGF	TGA	PGA	+/–	Playoffs GP	G	A	Pts	PIM	PP	SH	GW
1972-73	Oshawa Generals	OHA	55	5	21	26				132																		
1973-74	Oshawa Generals	OHA	47	7	19	26				108																		
1974-75	Buffalo Sabres	NHL	50	2	2	4	2	2	4	59	2	0	0	14	14.3	20	4	18	2	0	8	0	0	0	6	0	0	0
1975-76	Buffalo Sabres	NHL	58	0	9	9	0	7	7	64	0	0	0	61	0.0	62	1	52	6	+15	9	0	4	4	23	0	0	0
	Hershey Bears	AHL	20	1	8	9				61																		
1976-77	United States	C Cup	2	0	0	0				6																		
	Buffalo Sabres	NHL	71	3	15	18	3	12	15	100	1	0	2	76	3.9	71	7	58	3	+9	4	0	0	0	2	0	0	0
1977-78	Buffalo Sabres	NHL	76	0	23	23	0	19	19	98	0	0	0	77	0.0	78	2	75	6	+7	6	0	2	2	23	0	0	0
1978-79	Buffalo Sabres	NHL	74	3	19	22	3	14	17	103	0	0	0	70	4.3	80	0	103	19	–4	3	0	0	0	4	0	0	0
1979-80	Edmonton Oilers	NHL	80	5	10	15	5	8	13	104	0	0	0	90	5.6	74	2	115	35	–8	3	0	0	0	4	0	0	0
1980-81	Edmonton Oilers	NHL	80	13	17	30	11	12	23	139	0	4	1	89	14.6	97	2	136	43	+2	9	0	0	0	12	0	0	0
1981-82	Edmonton Oilers	NHL	80	4	25	29	3	17	20	154	0	0	0	98	4.1	111	1	107	37	+40	5	1	1	2	14	0	1	0
1982-83	Edmonton Oilers	NHL	72	0	18	18	0	12	12	92	0	0	0	66	0.0	93	2	99	32	+24	16	0	5	5	36	0	0	0
1983-84	Edmonton Oilers	NHL	80	5	16	21	4	11	15	125	0	0	0	73	6.8	104	2	99	30	+33	19	1	4	5	23	0	0	0
1984-85	Edmonton Oilers	NHL	79	4	14	18	3	9	12	126	0	1	1	63	6.3	82	2	95	31	+16	18	3	1	4	16	0	0	1
1985-86	Edmonton Oilers	NHL	80	4	22	26	3	15	18	129	0	0	0	71	5.6	102	1	78	24	+47	8	0	2	2	10	0	0	0
1986-87	Edmonton Oilers	NHL	35	1	3	4	1	2	3	17	0	0	0	37	2.7	31	2	40	9	–2								
	Buffalo Sabres	NHL	9	0	2	2	0	1	1	8	0	0	0	5	0.0	4	0	14	8	–2								
	NHL Totals		924	44	195	239	38	141	179	1318	3	5	4	890	4.9	1009	20	1089	205		108	5	19	24	173	0	1	1

Played in NHL All-Star Game (1986)

Claimed by **Edmonton** from **Buffalo** in Expansion Draft, June 13, 1979. Traded to **Buffalo** by **Edmonton** with Mark Napier for Normand Lacombe, Wayne Van Dorp and future considerations, March 6, 1987.

• FOLCO, PETER

Peter Folco D – L. 6', 185 lbs. b: Montreal, Que., 8/13/1953. Vancouver's 10th choice, 131st overall, in 1973 Amateur Draft.

Season	Club	League	GP	G	A	Pts	AG	AA	APts	PIM	PP	SH	GW	S	%	TGF	PGF	TGA	PGA	+/–	Playoffs GP	G	A	Pts	PIM	PP	SH	GW
1969-70	Verdun Maple Leafs	QJHL	43	1	7	8				24											11	0	0	0	2			
1970-71	Verdun Maple Leafs	QJHL	54	8	20	28				22											5	0	1	1	0			
1971-72	Verdun Maple Leafs	QMJHL	40	7	16	23				59											4	0	0	0	7			
1972-73	Quebec Remparts	QMJHL	55	8	47	55				26																		
1973-74	Vancouver Canucks	NHL	2	0	0	0	0	0	0	0	0	0	0	0	0.0	0	0	1	0	–1								
	Seattle Totems	WHL	69	3	26	29				57																		
1974-75	Seattle Totems	CHL	59	4	19	23				101																		
1975-76	Toronto Toros	WHA	19	1	8	9				15																		
	Beauce Jaros	NAHL	51	8	51	59				84											6	0	4	4	4			
1976-77	Birmingham Bulls	WHA	2	0	0	0				0																		
	Beauce Jaros	NAHL	19	5	12	17				28																		
	Philadelphia Firebirds	NAHL	41	0	25	25				28											4	1	1	2	2			
	NHL Totals		2	0	0	0	0	0	0	0	0	0	0	0	0.0	0	0	1	0									
	Other Major League Totals		21	1	8	9				15																		

Signed as a free agent by **Toronto** (WHA), September, 1975. Transferred to **Birmingham** (WHA) after **Toronto** (WHA) franchise relocated, June 30, 1976. Traded to **Philadelphia** (NAHL) by **Birmingham** for cash, December, 1976.

• FOLEY, GERRY

Gerry Foley RW – R. 5'11", 165 lbs. b: Ware, MA, 9/22/1932.

Season	Club	League	GP	G	A	Pts	AG	AA	APts	PIM	PP	SH	GW	S	%	TGF	PGF	TGA	PGA	+/–	Playoffs GP	G	A	Pts	PIM	PP	SH	GW
1951-52	St. Catharines TeePees	OHA	53	13	23	36				41											14	5	6	11	20			
1952-53	Seattle Bombers	WHL	70	29	30	59				46											5	1	2	3	0			
1953-54	Ottawa Senators	QHL	43	9	6	15				57											22	7	4	11	14			
	Pittsburgh Hornets	AHL	16	1	3	4				13																		
1954-55	Toronto Maple Leafs	NHL	4	0	0	0	0	0	0	8																		
	Pittsburgh Hornets	AHL	61	16	21	37				61											10	5	3	8	8			
1955-56	Pittsburgh Hornets	AHL	59	29	29	58				109											3	2	0	2	2			
1956-57	New York Rangers	NHL	69	7	9	16	9	10	19	48											3	0	0	0	0			
1957-58	New York Rangers	NHL	68	2	5	7	3	5	8	43											6	0	1	1	2			
1958-59	Buffalo Bisons	AHL	68	9	22	31				36											11	*5	2	7	15			
1959-60	Springfield Indians	AHL	31	5	13	18				7											10	1	6	7	4			
1960-61	Springfield Indians	AHL	53	15	29	44				27											3	1	4	5	0			
1961-62	Sudbury Wolves	EPHL	58	18	34	52				36											5	2	5	7	0			
1962-63	Springfield Indians	AHL	51	11	13	24				18																		
1963-64	Springfield Indians	AHL	62	8	18	26				26																		
1964-65	Springfield Indians	AHL	71	21	34	55				36																		
1965-66	Springfield Indians	AHL	49	12	14	26				26											6	3	1	4	6			
1966-67	Springfield Indians	AHL	66	26	35	61				31																		
1967-68	Springfield Kings	AHL	71	25	33	58				39											4	1	0	1	0			
1968-69	Los Angeles Kings	NHL	1	0	0	0	0	0	0	0	0	0	0	4	0.0	0	0	1	0	–1								
	Denver Spurs	WHL	51	10	24	34				16																		
	NHL Totals		142	9	14	23	12	15	27	99	0	0	0	4	225.0	0	0	1	0		9	0	1	1	2	0	0	0

Won WHL Rookie of the Year Award (1953)

Traded to **Toronto** by **Cleveland** (AHL) with Bob Bailey and $30,000 for Chuck Blair, June, 1953. Claimed by **NY Rangers** from **Toronto** in Intra-League Draft, June 5, 1956. NHL rights transferred to **LA Kings** after NHL club purchased **Springfield** (AHL) franchise, May, 1967.

• FOLEY, RICK

Rick Foley D – L. 6'4", 223 lbs. b: Niagara Falls, Ont., 9/22/1945.

			REGULAR SEASON																		PLAYOFFS							
Season	Club	League	GP	G	A	Pts	AG	AA	APts	PIM	PP	SH	GW	S	%	TGF	PGF	TGA	PGA	+/–	GP	G	A	Pts	PIM	PP	SH	GW
1962-63	Toronto Marlboros	City Jr.	30	6	24	30	....	....	....	64	....	....	....	....	....	....	....	....	....	....	9	3	5	8	23	....	....	....
1963-64	Toronto Marlboros	OHA	8	0	0	0	....	....	....	17	....	....	....	....	....	....	....	....	....	....	....	....	....	....	....	....	....	....
	Oshawa Generals	OHA	8	0	3	3	....	....	....	42	....	....	....	....	....	....	....	....	....	....	....	....	....	....	....	....	....	....
1964-65	St. Thomas Barons	Jr. B	STATISTICS NOT AVAILABLE																									
1965-66	St. Thomas Barons	Jr. B	STATISTICS NOT AVAILABLE																									
1966-67	Charlotte Checkers	EHL	68	5	42	47	....	....	....	222	....	....	....	....	....	....	....	....	....	....	8	1	4	5	29	....	....	....
1967-68	Jersey–Charlotte	EHL	71	17	78	95	....	....	....	192	....	....	....	....	....	....	....	....	....	....	14	5	7	12	*69	....	....	....
1968-69	Dallas Black Hawks	CHL	2	0	0	0	....	....	....	4	....	....	....	....	....	....	....	....	....	....	....	....	....	....	....	....	....	....
	Portland Buckaroos	WHL	5	0	0	0	....	....	....	10	....	....	....	....	....	....	....	....	....	....	....	....	....	....	....	....	....	....
	Charlotte Checkers	EHL	66	22	58	80	....	....	....	216	....	....	....	....	....	....	....	....	....	....	3	2	0	2	6	....	....	....
1969-70	Portland Buckaroos	WHL	71	7	38	45	....	....	....	227	....	....	....	....	....	....	....	....	....	....	8	0	4	4	65	....	....	....
1970-71	**Chicago Black Hawks**	**NHL**	**2**	**0**	**1**	**1**	**0**	**1**	**1**	**8**	**0**	**0**	**0**	**4**	**0.0**	**1**	**0**	**0**	**0**	**+1**	**4**	**0**	**1**	**1**	**4**	**0**	**0**	**0**
	Portland Buckaroos	WHL	66	17	54	71	....	....	....	*306	....	....	....	....	....	....	....	....	....	....	9	2	9	11	*44	....	....	....
1971-72	**Philadelphia Flyers**	**NHL**	**58**	**11**	**25**	**36**	**12**	**23**	**35**	**168**	**5**	**0**	**0**	**124**	**8.9**	**65**	**33**	**51**	**3**	**–16**	....	....	....	....	....	....	....	....
1972-73	Richmond Robins	AHL	26	6	15	21	....	....	....	69	....	....	....	....	....	....	....	....	....	....	....	....	....	....	....	....	....	....
	San Diego Gulls	WHL	31	5	14	19	....	....	....	110	....	....	....	....	....	....	....	....	....	....	6	2	6	8	*32	....	....	....
1973-74	**Detroit Red Wings**	**NHL**	**7**	**0**	**0**	**0**	**0**	**0**	**0**	**4**	**0**	**0**	**0**	**5**	**0.0**	**3**	**1**	**11**	**2**	**–7**	....	....	....	....	....	....	....	....
	Baltimore Clippers	AHL	65	14	56	70	....	....	....	164	....	....	....	....	....	....	....	....	....	....	9	2	6	8	28	....	....	....
1974-75	Syracuse Eagles	AHL	69	13	40	53	....	....	....	306	....	....	....	....	....	....	....	....	....	....	1	0	2	2	0	....	....	....
1975-76	Toronto Toros	WHA	11	1	2	3	....	....	....	6	....	....	....	....	....	....	....	....	....	....	....	....	....	....	....	....	....	....
	Baltimore Clippers	AHL	4	2	2	4	....	....	....	14	....	....	....	....	....	....	....	....	....	....	....	....	....	....	....	....	....	....
1976-77	Brantford Alexanders	OHA Sr.	17	2	14	16	....	....	....	76	....	....	....	....	....	....	....	....	....	....	....	....	....	....	....	....	....	....
1977-78	Brantford Alexanders	OHA Sr.	6	1	3	4	....	....	....	20	....	....	....	....	....	....	....	....	....	....	....	....	....	....	....	....	....	....
	NHL Totals		**67**	**11**	**26**	**37**	**12**	**24**	**36**	**180**	**5**	**0**	**0**	**133**	**8.3**	**69**	**34**	**62**	**5**		**4**	**0**	**1**	**1**	**4**	**0**	**0**	**0**
	Other Major League Totals		11	1	2	3	....	....	....	6	....	....	....	....	....	....	....	....	....		....	....	....	....	....	....	....	....

EHL South First All-Star Team (1968, 1969) • WHL First All-Star Team (1971)

Claimed by **Portland** (WHL) from **Toronto** in Reverse Draft, June, 1968. Traded to **Philadelphia** by **Chicago** for Andre Lacroix, October 15, 1971. Selected by **Miami-Philadelphia** (WHA) in 1972 WHA General Player Draft, February 12, 1972. Traded to **Detroit** by **Philadelphia** for Serge Lajeunesse, May 15, 1973. Signed as a free agent by **Toronto** (WHA), June, 1975.

• FOLIGNO, MIKE

Mike Foligno RW – R. 6'2", 195 lbs. b: Sudbury, Ont., 1/29/1959. Detroit's 1st choice, 3rd overall, in 1979 Entry Draft.

			REGULAR SEASON																		PLAYOFFS							
Season	Club	League	GP	G	A	Pts	AG	AA	APts	PIM	PP	SH	GW	S	%	TGF	PGF	TGA	PGA	+/–	GP	G	A	Pts	PIM	PP	SH	GW
1975-76	Sudbury Wolves	OHA	57	22	14	36	....	....	....	45	....	....	....	....	....	....	....	....	....	....	....	....	....	....	....	....	....	....
1976-77	Sudbury Wolves	OHA	66	31	44	75	....	....	....	62	....	....	....	....	....	....	....	....	....	....	....	....	....	....	....	....	....	....
1977-78	Sudbury Wolves	OHA	67	47	39	86	....	....	....	112	....	....	....	....	....	....	....	....	....	....	....	....	....	....	....	....	....	....
1978-79	Sudbury Wolves	OHA	68	65	85	*150	....	....	....	98	....	....	....	....	....	....	....	....	....	....	10	5	5	10	14	....	....	....
1979-80	**Detroit Red Wings**	**NHL**	**80**	**36**	**35**	**71**	**33**	**27**	**60**	**109**	**9**	**0**	**0**	**196**	**18.4**	**106**	**33**	**76**	**1**	**–2**	....	....	....	....	....	....	....	....
1980-81	**Detroit Red Wings**	**NHL**	**80**	**28**	**35**	**63**	**23**	**24**	**47**	**210**	**3**	**0**	**5**	**181**	**15.5**	**116**	**38**	**91**	**0**	**–13**	....	....	....	....	....	....	....	....
	Canada	WEC-A	7	2	0	2	....	....	....	8	....	....	....	....	....	....	....	....	....	....	....	....	....	....	....	....	....	....
1981-82	**Detroit Red Wings**	**NHL**	**26**	**13**	**13**	**26**	**10**	**9**	**19**	**28**	**3**	**0**	**0**	**70**	**18.6**	**33**	**6**	**30**	**1**	**–2**	....	....	....	....	....	....	....	....
	Buffalo Sabres	**NHL**	**56**	**20**	**31**	**51**	**16**	**20**	**36**	**149**	**4**	**0**	**6**	**124**	**16.1**	**78**	**17**	**40**	**0**	**+21**	**4**	**2**	**0**	**2**	**9**	**2**	**0**	**0**
1982-83	**Buffalo Sabres**	**NHL**	**66**	**22**	**25**	**47**	**18**	**17**	**35**	**135**	**4**	**0**	**4**	**130**	**16.9**	**76**	**14**	**56**	**3**	**+9**	**10**	**2**	**3**	**5**	**39**	**0**	**0**	**0**
1983-84	**Buffalo Sabres**	**NHL**	**70**	**32**	**31**	**63**	**26**	**21**	**47**	**151**	**6**	**0**	**5**	**183**	**17.5**	**105**	**27**	**46**	**0**	**+32**	**3**	**2**	**1**	**3**	**19**	**0**	**0**	**0**
1984-85	**Buffalo Sabres**	**NHL**	**77**	**27**	**29**	**56**	**22**	**20**	**42**	**154**	**6**	**0**	**6**	**167**	**16.2**	**93**	**27**	**50**	**0**	**+16**	**5**	**1**	**3**	**4**	**12**	**0**	**0**	**0**
1985-86	**Buffalo Sabres**	**NHL**	**79**	**41**	**39**	**80**	**33**	**26**	**59**	**168**	**7**	**1**	**4**	**223**	**18.4**	**121**	**36**	**68**	**8**	**+25**	....	....	....	....	....	....	....	....
	Canada	WEC-A	10	0	5	5	....	....	....	16	....	....	....	....	....	....	....	....	....	....	....	....	....	....	....	....	....	....
1986-87	**Buffalo Sabres**	**NHL**	**75**	**30**	**29**	**59**	**26**	**21**	**47**	**176**	**11**	**1**	**5**	**185**	**16.2**	**96**	**34**	**62**	**13**	**+13**	....	....	....	....	....	....	....	....
	Canada	WEC-A	10	0	4	4	....	....	....	34	....	....	....	....	....	....	....	....	....	....	....	....	....	....	....	....	....	....
1987-88	**Buffalo Sabres**	**NHL**	**74**	**29**	**28**	**57**	**25**	**20**	**45**	**220**	**10**	**0**	**7**	**159**	**18.2**	**92**	**41**	**69**	**7**	**–11**	**6**	**3**	**2**	**5**	**31**	**0**	**0**	**0**
1988-89	**Buffalo Sabres**	**NHL**	**75**	**27**	**22**	**49**	**23**	**15**	**38**	**156**	**11**	**0**	**5**	**144**	**18.8**	**82**	**28**	**65**	**4**	**–7**	**5**	**3**	**1**	**4**	**21**	**1**	**1**	**1**
1989-90	**Buffalo Sabres**	**NHL**	**61**	**15**	**25**	**40**	**13**	**18**	**31**	**99**	**3**	**0**	**1**	**107**	**14.0**	**59**	**11**	**35**	**0**	**+13**	**6**	**0**	**1**	**1**	**12**	**0**	**0**	**0**
1990-91	**Buffalo Sabres**	**NHL**	**31**	**4**	**5**	**9**	**4**	**4**	**8**	**42**	**0**	**0**	**0**	**27**	**14.8**	**17**	**2**	**11**	**0**	**+4**	....	....	....	....	....	....	....	....
	Toronto Maple Leafs	**NHL**	**37**	**8**	**7**	**15**	**7**	**5**	**12**	**65**	**1**	**0**	**0**	**56**	**14.3**	**24**	**4**	**23**	**0**	**–3**	....	....	....	....	....	....	....	....
1991-92	**Toronto Maple Leafs**	**NHL**	**33**	**6**	**8**	**14**	**5**	**6**	**11**	**50**	**2**	**0**	**1**	**41**	**14.6**	**20**	**6**	**21**	**4**	**–3**	....	....	....	....	....	....	....	....
1992-93	**Toronto Maple Leafs**	**NHL**	**55**	**13**	**5**	**18**	**11**	**3**	**14**	**84**	**5**	**0**	**2**	**95**	**13.7**	**29**	**11**	**16**	**0**	**+2**	**18**	**2**	**6**	**8**	**42**	**1**	**0**	**2**
1993-94	**Toronto Maple Leafs**	**NHL**	**4**	**0**	**0**	**0**	**0**	**0**	**0**	**4**	**0**	**0**	**0**	**3**	**0.0**	**1**	**0**	**1**	**0**	**0**	....	....	....	....	....	....	....	....
	Florida Panthers	**NHL**	**39**	**4**	**5**	**9**	**4**	**4**	**8**	**49**	**0**	**0**	**0**	**32**	**12.5**	**17**	**1**	**9**	**0**	**+7**	....	....	....	....	....	....	....	....
	NHL Totals		**1018**	**355**	**372**	**727**	**299**	**260**	**559**	**2049**	**85**	**2**	**51**	**2123**	**16.7**	**1165**	**336**	**769**	**41**		**57**	**15**	**17**	**32**	**185**	**4**	**1**	**3**

OHA First All-Star Team (1979)

Traded to **Buffalo** by **Detroit** with Dale McCourt and Brent Peterson for Danny Gare, Jim Schoenfeld and Derek Smith, December 2, 1981. Traded to **Toronto** by **Buffalo** with Buffalo's 8th round choice (Thomas Kucharcik) in 1991 Entry Draft for Brian Curran and Lou Franceschetti, December 17, 1990. Traded to **Florida** by **Toronto** for cash, November 5, 1993.

• FONTAINE, LEN

Len Fontaine RW – R. 5'7", 165 lbs. b: Quebec City, Que., 2/25/1948.

			REGULAR SEASON																		PLAYOFFS							
Season	Club	League	GP	G	A	Pts	AG	AA	APts	PIM	PP	SH	GW	S	%	TGF	PGF	TGA	PGA	+/–	GP	G	A	Pts	PIM	PP	SH	GW
1967-68	Sarnia Sailors	Jr. B	STATISTICS NOT AVAILABLE																									
1968-69	Port Huron Flags	IHL	53	15	22	37	....	....	....	10	....	....	....	....	....	....	....	....	....	....	3	0	1	1	2	....	....	....
1969-70	Port Huron Flags	IHL	69	20	29	49	....	....	....	16	....	....	....	....	....	....	....	....	....	....	15	3	6	9	4	....	....	....
1970-71	Port Huron Flags	IHL	71	29	40	69	....	....	....	37	....	....	....	....	....	....	....	....	....	....	14	6	6	12	2	....	....	....
1971-72	Port Huron Wings	IHL	70	41	45	86	....	....	....	54	....	....	....	....	....	....	....	....	....	....	15	7	5	12	13	....	....	....
1972-73	**Detroit Red Wings**	**NHL**	**39**	**8**	**10**	**18**	**8**	**8**	**16**	**6**	**1**	**0**	**0**	**37**	**21.6**	**22**	**3**	**21**	**0**	**–2**	....	....	....	....	....	....	....	....
	Virginia Wings	AHL	17	7	10	17	....	....	....	2	....	....	....	....	....	....	....	....	....	....	13	3	11	14	16	....	....	....
1973-74	**Detroit Red Wings**	**NHL**	**7**	**0**	**1**	**1**	**0**	**1**	**1**	**4**	**0**	**0**	**0**	**6**	**0.0**	**2**	**0**	**4**	**0**	**–2**	....	....	....	....	....	....	....	....
	Virginia Wings	AHL	59	24	39	63	....	....	....	33	....	....	....	....	....	....	....	....	....	....	....	....	....	....	....	....	....	....
1974-75	Michigan-Baltimore	WHA	21	1	8	9	....	....	....	6	....	....	....	....	....	....	....	....	....	....	....	....	....	....	....	....	....	....
	Port Huron Flags	IHL	20	19	9	28	....	....	....	12	....	....	....	....	....	....	....	....	....	....	5	1	1	2	0	....	....	....
1975-76	Port Huron Flags	IHL	74	*53	59	*112	....	....	....	57	....	....	....	....	....	....	....	....	....	....	15	10	9	19	20	....	....	....
1976-77	Toledo Goaldiggers	IHL	61	42	37	79	....	....	....	51	....	....	....	....	....	....	....	....	....	....	....	....	....	....	....	....	....	....
1977-78	Toledo Goaldiggers	IHL	74	34	54	88	....	....	....	16	....	....	....	....	....	....	....	....	....	....	17	11	13	24	12	....	....	....
1978-79	Toledo Goaldiggers	IHL	78	29	60	89	....	....	....	30	....	....	....	....	....	....	....	....	....	....	6	3	3	6	0	....	....	....
1979-80	Toledo Goaldiggers	IHL	70	35	43	78	....	....	....	10	....	....	....	....	....	....	....	....	....	....	4	2	1	3	0	....	....	....
1980-81	Toledo Goaldiggers	IHL	16	4	6	10	....	....	....	0	....	....	....	....	....	....	....	....	....	....	....	....	....	....	....	....	....	....
1981-82	Flint Generals	IHL	62	34	47	81	....	....	....	12	....	....	....	....	....	....	....	....	....	....	4	0	0	0	11	....	....	....
1982-83	Flint Generals	IHL	71	21	37	58	....	....	....	10	....	....	....	....	....	....	....	....	....	....	5	0	3	3	0	....	....	....
	NHL Totals		**46**	**8**	**11**	**19**	**8**	**9**	**17**	**10**	**1**	**0**	**0**	**43**	**18.6**	**24**	**3**	**25**	**0**		....	....	....	....	....	....	....	....
	Other Major League Totals		21	1	8	9	....	....	....	6	....	....	....	....	....	....	....	....	....		....	....	....	....	....	....	....	....

IHL Second All-Star Team (1971) • IHL First All-Star Team (1972, 1976) • Won James Gatschene Memorial Trophy (MVP - IHL) (1972, 1976) • Won Leo P. Lamoureux Memorial Trophy (Top Scorer - IHL) (1976)

Selected by **LA Sharks** in 1972 WHA General Player Draft, February 12, 1972. Signed as a free agent by **Detroit**, May, 1972. Transferred to **Michigan** (WHA) after **LA Sharks** (WHA) franchise relocated, April 11, 1974.

• FONTAS, JON

Jon Fontas C – R. 5'10", 185 lbs. b: Arlington, MA, 4/16/1958.

			REGULAR SEASON																		PLAYOFFS							
Season	Club	League	GP	G	A	Pts	AG	AA	APts	PIM	PP	SH	GW	S	%	TGF	PGF	TGA	PGA	+/–	GP	G	A	Pts	PIM	PP	SH	GW
1975-76	University of New Hampshire	ECAC	31	10	23	33	....	....	....	41	....	....	....	....	....	....	....	....	....	....	....	....	....	....	....	....	....	....
1976-77	University of New Hampshire	ECAC	36	27	37	64	....	....	....	16	....	....	....	....	....	....	....	....	....	....	....	....	....	....	....	....	....	....
1977-78	University of New Hampshire	ECAC	30	31	33	64	....	....	....	12	....	....	....	....	....	....	....	....	....	....	....	....	....	....	....	....	....	....
1978-79	Saginaw Gears	IHL	79	36	45	81	....	....	....	32	....	....	....	....	....	....	....	....	....	....	4	2	2	4	0	....	....	....
1979-80	**Minnesota North Stars**	**NHL**	**1**	**0**	**0**	**0**	**0**	**0**	**0**	**0**	**0**	**0**	**0**	**0**	**0.0**	**0**	**0**	**1**	**0**	**–1**	....	....	....	....	....	....	....	....
	Oklahoma City Stars	CHL	68	22	26	48	....	....	....	16	....	....	....	....	....	....	....	....	....	....	....	....	....	....	....	....	....	....
1980-81	**Minnesota North Stars**	**NHL**	**1**	**0**	**0**	**0**	**0**	**0**	**0**	**0**	**0**	**0**	**0**	**0**	**0.0**	**0**	**0**	**0**	**0**	**0**	....	....	....	....	....	....	....	....
	Oklahoma City Stars	CHL	5	1	1	2	....	....	....	0	....	....	....	....	....	....	....	....	....	....	....	....	....	....	....	....	....	....
	Baltimore Clippers	EHL	63	25	47	72	....	....	....	44	....	....	....	....	....	....	....	....	....	....	4	0	2	2	0	....	....	....
1981-82	Jokerit Helsinki	Finland	36	20	23	43	....	....	....	51	....	....	....	....	....	....	....	....	....	....	....	....	....	....	....	....	....	....

Season	Club	League	GP	G	A	Pts	AG	AA	APts	PIM	PP	SH	GW	S	%	TGF	PGF	TGA	PGA	+/–	GP	G	A	Pts	PIM	PP	SH	GW
			REGULAR SEASON																		PLAYOFFS							
1982-83	JoKP	Finland 2	36	25	34	59	....	....	....	57	....	....	....	....	....	....	....	....	....	....	....	....	....	....	....	....	....	....
1983-84	JoKP	Finland 2	36	27	36	63	....	....	....	24	....	....	....	....	....	....	....	....	....	....	....	....	....	....	....	....	....	....
1984-85	Saipa Lappeenranta	Finland	36	12	15	27	....	....	....	44	....	....	....	....	....	....	....	....	....	....	....	....	....	....	....	....	....	....
	NHL Totals		**2**	**0**	**0**	**0**	**0**	**0**	**0**	**0**	**0**	**0**	**0**	**0**	**0.0**	**0**	**0**	**1**	**0**		....	....	....	....	....	....	....	....

Signed as a free agent by **Minnesota**, September, 1979.

• FONTEYNE, VAL
Val Fonteyne LW – L. 5'10", 160 lbs. b. Wetaskiwin, Alta., 12/2/1933.

Season	Club	League	GP	G	A	Pts	AG	AA	APts	PIM	PP	SH	GW	S	%	TGF	PGF	TGA	PGA	+/–	GP	G	A	Pts	PIM	PP	SH	GW
1951-52	Medicine Hat Tigers	WCJHL	41	9	9	18	....	....	....	5	....	....	....	....	....	....	....	....	....	....	....	....	....	....	....	....	....	....
1952-53	Medicine Hat Tigers	WCJHL	31	7	14	21	....	....	....	4	....	....	....	....	....	....	....	....	....	....	4	4	2	6	0	....	....	....
1953-54	Medicine Hat Tigers	WCJHL	36	14	14	28	....	....	....	18	....	....	....	....	....	....	....	....	....	....	10	1	5	6	12	....	....	....
1954-55	New Westminster Royals	WHL	7	0	1	1	....	....	....	0	....	....	....	....	....	....	....	....	....	....	....	....	....	....	....	....	....	....
	Kelowna Packers	OSHL	41	9	10	19	....	....	....	2	....	....	....	....	....	....	....	....	....	....	4	0	0	0	0	....	....	....
1955-56	Seattle Americans	WHL	70	18	18	36	....	....	....	0	....	....	....	....	....	....	....	....	....	....	....	....	....	....	....	....	....	....
1956-57	Seattle Americans	WHL	70	24	40	64	....	....	....	6	....	....	....	....	....	....	....	....	....	....	6	5	1	6	2	....	....	....
1957-58	Seattle Totems	WHL	70	34	41	75	....	....	....	11	....	....	....	....	....	....	....	....	....	....	9	4	4	8	0	....	....	....
1958-59	Seattle Totems	WHL	64	32	49	81	....	....	....	2	....	....	....	....	....	....	....	....	....	....	12	6	5	11	0	....	....	....
1959-60	**Detroit Red Wings**	**NHL**	**69**	**4**	**7**	**11**	**5**	**7**	**12**	**2**	....	....	....	....	....	....	....	....	....	....	**6**	**0**	**4**	**4**	**0**	....	....	....
1960-61	**Detroit Red Wings**	**NHL**	**66**	**6**	**11**	**17**	**7**	**11**	**18**	**4**	....	....	....	....	....	....	....	....	....	....	**11**	**2**	**3**	**5**	**0**	....	....	....
1961-62	**Detroit Red Wings**	**NHL**	**70**	**5**	**5**	**10**	**6**	**5**	**11**	**4**	....	....	....	....	....	....	....	....	....	....	....	....	....	....	....	....	....	....
1962-63	**Detroit Red Wings**	**NHL**	**67**	**6**	**14**	**20**	**7**	**15**	**22**	**2**	....	....	....	....	....	....	....	....	....	....	**11**	**0**	**0**	**0**	**2**	....	....	....
1963-64	**New York Rangers**	**NHL**	**69**	**7**	**18**	**25**	**9**	**20**	**29**	**4**	....	....	....	....	....	....	....	....	....	....	....	....	....	....	....	....	....	....
1964-65	**New York Rangers**	**NHL**	**27**	**0**	**1**	**1**	**0**	**1**	**1**	**2**	....	....	....	....	....	....	....	....	....	....	....	....	....	....	....	....	....	....
	Detroit Red Wings	**NHL**	**16**	**2**	**5**	**7**	**3**	**5**	**8**	**4**	....	....	....	....	....	....	....	....	....	....	**5**	**0**	**1**	**1**	**0**	....	....	....
1965-66	**Detroit Red Wings**	**NHL**	**59**	**5**	**10**	**15**	**6**	**10**	**16**	**0**	....	....	....	....	....	....	....	....	....	....	**12**	**1**	**0**	**1**	**4**	....	....	....
	Pittsburgh Hornets	AHL	12	5	7	12	....	....	....	6	....	....	....	....	....	....	....	....	....	....	....	....	....	....	....	....	....	....
1966-67	**Detroit Red Wings**	**NHL**	**28**	**1**	**1**	**2**	**1**	**1**	**2**	**0**	....	....	....	....	....	....	....	....	....	....	....	....	....	....	....	....	....	....
	Pittsburgh Hornets	AHL	17	5	11	16	....	....	....	0	....	....	....	....	....	....	....	....	....	....	9	3	5	8	4	....	....	....
1967-68	**Pittsburgh Penguins**	**NHL**	**69**	**6**	**28**	**34**	**7**	**29**	**36**	**0**	**0**	**0**	**2**	**114**	**5.3**	**45**	**5**	**71**	**8**	**–23**	....	....	....	....	....	....	....	....
1968-69	**Pittsburgh Penguins**	**NHL**	**74**	**12**	**17**	**29**	**13**	**16**	**29**	**2**	**0**	**1**	**2**	**109**	**11.0**	**44**	**7**	**84**	**22**	**–25**	....	....	....	....	....	....	....	....
1969-70	**Pittsburgh Penguins**	**NHL**	**68**	**11**	**15**	**26**	**13**	**15**	**28**	**2**	**3**	**0**	**1**	**73**	**15.1**	**37**	**11**	**47**	**17**	**–4**	**10**	**0**	**2**	**2**	**0**	**0**	**0**	**0**
1970-71	**Pittsburgh Penguins**	**NHL**	**70**	**4**	**9**	**13**	**4**	**8**	**12**	**0**	**1**	**1**	**0**	**59**	**6.8**	**21**	**2**	**48**	**21**	**–8**	....	....	....	....	....	....	....	....
1971-72	**Pittsburgh Penguins**	**NHL**	**68**	**6**	**13**	**19**	**6**	**12**	**18**	**0**	**1**	**0**	**0**	**35**	**17.1**	**35**	**5**	**50**	**19**	**–1**	**4**	**0**	**0**	**0**	**2**	**0**	**0**	**0**
1972-73	Alberta Oilers	WHA	77	7	32	39	....	....	....	2	....	....	....	....	....	....	....	....	....	....	....	....	....	....	....	....	....	....
1973-74	Edmonton Oilers	WHA	72	9	13	22	....	....	....	2	....	....	....	....	....	....	....	....	....	....	5	1	0	1	0	....	....	....
	NHL Totals		**820**	**75**	**154**	**229**	**87**	**155**	**242**	**26**	**5**	**2**	**5**	**390**	**19.2**	**182**	**30**	**300**	**87**		**59**	**3**	**10**	**13**	**8**	**0**	**0**	**0**
	Other Major League Totals		149	16	45	61	....	....	....	4	....	....	....	....	....	....	....	....	....	....	5	1	0	1	0	....	....	....

WHL Coast Division First All-Star Team (1958, 1959)

Claimed by **NY Rangers** from **Detroit** in Intra-League Draft, June 4, 1963. Claimed on waivers by **Detroit** from **NY Rangers**, February 8, 1965. Claimed by **Pittsburgh** from **Detroit** in Expansion Draft, June 6, 1967. Selected by **Alberta** (WHA) in 1972 WHA General Player Draft, February 12, 1972.

• FOOTE, ADAM
Adam Foote D – R. 6'1", 202 lbs. b: Toronto, Ont., 7/10/1971. Quebec's 2nd choice, 22nd overall, in 1989 Entry Draft.

Season	Club	League	GP	G	A	Pts	AG	AA	APts	PIM	PP	SH	GW	S	%	TGF	PGF	TGA	PGA	+/–	GP	G	A	Pts	PIM	PP	SH	GW
1988-89	Sault Ste. Marie Greyhounds	OHL	66	7	32	30	....	....	....	120	....	....	....	....	....	....	....	....	....	....	....	....	....	....	....	....	....	....
1909-90	Sault Ste. Marie Greyhounds	OHL	61	12	43	55	....	....	....	199	....	....	....	....	....	....	....	....	....	....	....	....	....	....	....	....	....	....
1990-91	Sault Ste. Marie Greyhounds	OHL	59	18	51	69	....	....	....	93	....	....	....	....	....	....	....	....	....	....	14	5	12	17	28	....	....	....
1991-92	**Quebec Nordiques**	**NHL**	**46**	**2**	**5**	**7**	**2**	**4**	**6**	**44**	**0**	**0**	**0**	**55**	**3.6**	**42**	**5**	**66**	**25**	**–4**	....	....	....	....	....	....	....	....
	Halifax Citadels	AHL	6	0	1	1	....	....	....	2	....	....	....	....	....	....	....	....	....	....	....	....	....	....	....	....	....	....
1992-93	**Quebec Nordiques**	**NHL**	**81**	**4**	**12**	**16**	**3**	**8**	**11**	**168**	**0**	**1**	**0**	**54**	**7.4**	**74**	**0**	**101**	**33**	**+6**	**6**	**0**	**1**	**1**	**2**	**0**	**0**	**0**
1993-94	**Quebec Nordiques**	**NHL**	**45**	**2**	**6**	**8**	**2**	**5**	**7**	**67**	**0**	**0**	**0**	**42**	**4.8**	**42**	**3**	**64**	**28**	**+3**	....	....	....	....	....	....	....	....
1994-95	**Quebec Nordiques**	**NHL**	**35**	**0**	**7**	**7**	**0**	**10**	**10**	**52**	**0**	**0**	**0**	**24**	**0.0**	**35**	**1**	**25**	**8**	**+17**	**6**	**0**	**1**	**1**	**14**	**0**	**0**	**0**
1995-96	**Colorado Avalanche**	**NHL**	**73**	**5**	**11**	**16**	**5**	**9**	**14**	**88**	**1**	**0**	**1**	**40**	**10.2**	**68**	**5**	**64**	**28**	**+27**	**22**	**1**	**3**	**4**	**36**	**0**	**0**	**0**
1996-97	Canada	W Cup	8	1	0	1	....	....	....	16	....	....	....	....	....	....	....	....	....	....	....	....	....	....	....	....	....	....
	Colorado Avalanche	**NHL**	**78**	**2**	**19**	**21**	**2**	**17**	**19**	**135**	**0**	**0**	**0**	**60**	**3.3**	**72**	**5**	**69**	**18**	**+16**	**17**	**0**	**4**	**4**	**62**	**0**	**0**	**0**
1997-98	**Colorado Avalanche**	**NHL**	**77**	**3**	**14**	**17**	**4**	**14**	**18**	**124**	**0**	**0**	**1**	**64**	**4.7**	**57**	**1**	**84**	**25**	**–3**	**7**	**0**	**0**	**0**	**23**	**0**	**0**	**0**
	Canada	Olympics	6	0	1	1	....	....	....	4	....	....	....	....	....	....	....	....	....	....	....	....	....	....	....	....	....	....
	NHL Totals		**435**	**18**	**74**	**92**	**18**	**67**	**85**	**678**	**1**	**1**	**2**	**348**	**5.2**	**390**	**20**	**473**	**165**		**58**	**1**	**9**	**10**	**137**	**0**	**0**	**0**

OHL First All-Star Team (1991)

Transferred to **Colorado** after **Quebec** franchise relocated, June 21, 1995.

• FORBES, COLIN
Colin Forbes LW – L. 6'3", 205 lbs. b: New Westminster, B.C., 2/16/1976. Philadelphia's 5th choice, 166th overall, in 1994 Entry Draft.

Season	Club	League	GP	G	A	Pts	AG	AA	APts	PIM	PP	SH	GW	S	%	TGF	PGF	TGA	PGA	+/–	GP	G	A	Pts	PIM	PP	SH	GW
1993-94	Sherwood Park Crusaders	AJHL	47	18	22	40	....	....	....	76	....	....	....	....	....	....	....	....	....	....	....	....	....	....	....	....	....	....
1994-95	Portland Winter Hawks	WHL	72	24	31	55	....	....	....	108	....	....	....	....	....	....	....	....	....	....	9	1	3	4	10	....	....	....
1995-96	Portland Winter Hawks	WHL	72	33	44	77	....	....	....	137	....	....	....	....	....	....	....	....	....	....	7	2	5	7	14	....	....	....
	Hershey Bears	AHL	2	1	0	1	....	....	....	2	....	....	....	....	....	....	....	....	....	....	4	0	2	2	2	....	....	....
1996-97	**Philadelphia Flyers**	**NHL**	**3**	**1**	**0**	**1**	**1**	**0**	**1**	**0**	**0**	**0**	**0**	**3**	**33.3**	**1**	**0**	**1**	**0**	**0**	**3**	**0**	**0**	**0**	**0**	**0**	**0**	**0**
	Philadelphia Phantoms	AHL	74	21	28	49	....	....	....	108	....	....	....	....	....	....	....	....	....	....	10	5	5	10	33	....	....	....
1997-98	**Philadelphia Flyers**	**NHL**	**63**	**12**	**7**	**19**	**14**	**7**	**21**	**59**	**2**	**0**	**2**	**93**	**12.9**	**28**	**2**	**31**	**7**	**+2**	**5**	**0**	**0**	**0**	**2**	**0**	**0**	**0**
	Philadelphia Phantoms	AHL	13	7	4	11	....	....	....	22	....	....	....	....	....	....	....	....	....	....	....	....	....	....	....	....	....	....
	NHL Totals		**66**	**13**	**7**	**20**	**15**	**7**	**22**	**59**	**2**	**0**	**2**	**96**	**13.5**	**29**	**2**	**32**	**7**		**8**	**0**	**0**	**0**	**2**	**0**	**0**	**0**

• FORBES, DAVE
Dave Forbes LW L. 5'10", 180 lbs. b: Montreal, Que., 11/16/1948.

Season	Club	League	GP	G	A	Pts	AG	AA	APts	PIM	PP	SH	GW	S	%	TGF	PGF	TGA	PGA	+/–	GP	G	A	Pts	PIM	PP	SH	GW
1967-68	American International U.	NCAA	5	13	10	23	....	....	....	....	....	....	....	....	....	....	....	....	....	....	....	....	....	....	....	....	....	....
1968-69	American International U.	NCAA	21	32	25	57	....	....	....	....	....	....	....	....	....	....	....	....	....	....	....	....	....	....	....	....	....	....
1969-70	American International U.	NCAA	17	27	15	42	....	....	....	....	....	....	....	....	....	....	....	....	....	....	....	....	....	....	....	....	....	....
1970-71	American International U.	NCAA	21	30	22	52	....	....	....	....	....	....	....	....	....	....	....	....	....	....	....	....	....	....	....	....	....	....
1971-72	Oklahoma City Blazers	CHL	42	8	11	19	....	....	....	83	....	....	....	....	....	....	....	....	....	....	....	....	....	....	....	....	....	....
	Boston Braves	AHL	3	0	0	0	....	....	....	2	....	....	....	....	....	....	....	....	....	....	7	1	0	1	0	....	....	....
	Dayton Gems	IHL	10	5	2	7	....	....	....	29	....	....	....	....	....	....	....	....	....	....	....	....	....	....	....	....	....	....
1972-73	Boston Braves	AHL	27	10	11	21	....	....	....	32	....	....	....	....	....	....	....	....	....	....	10	3	5	8	27	....	....	....
	Dayton Gems	IHL	49	20	29	49	....	....	....	194	....	....	....	....	....	....	....	....	....	....	....	....	....	....	....	....	....	....
1973-74	**Boston Bruins**	**NHL**	**63**	**10**	**16**	**26**	**10**	**14**	**24**	**41**	**0**	**0**	**1**	**64**	**15.6**	**34**	**0**	**25**	**0**	**+9**	**16**	**0**	**2**	**2**	**6**	**0**	**0**	**0**
	Boston Braves	AHL	11	2	6	8	....	....	....	35	....	....	....	....	....	....	....	....	....	....	....	....	....	....	....	....	....	....
1974-75	**Boston Bruins**	**NHL**	**69**	**18**	**12**	**30**	**17**	**9**	**26**	**80**	**0**	**0**	**2**	**89**	**20.2**	**51**	**1**	**31**	**3**	**+22**	**3**	**0**	**0**	**0**	**0**	**0**	**0**	**0**
1975-76	**Boston Bruins**	**NHL**	**79**	**16**	**13**	**29**	**15**	**10**	**25**	**52**	**0**	**4**	**1**	**165**	**9.7**	**48**	**1**	**49**	**17**	**+15**	**12**	**1**	**1**	**2**	**5**	**0**	**1**	**0**
1976-77	**Boston Bruins**	**NHL**	**73**	**9**	**11**	**20**	**9**	**9**	**18**	**47**	**0**	**2**	**1**	**56**	**16.1**	**30**	**0**	**48**	**31**	**+13**	**14**	**0**	**1**	**1**	**2**	**0**	**0**	**0**
1977-78	**Washington Capitals**	**NHL**	**77**	**11**	**11**	**22**	**11**	**9**	**20**	**119**	**0**	**0**	**0**	**143**	**7.7**	**40**	**1**	**97**	**24**	**–34**	....	....	....	....	....	....	....	....
1978-79	**Washington Capitals**	**NHL**	**2**	**0**	**1**	**1**	**0**	**1**	**1**	**2**	**0**	**0**	**0**	**2**	**0.0**	**1**	**0**	**1**	**0**	**0**	....	....	....	....	....	....	....	....
	Cincinnati Stingers	WHA	73	6	5	11	....	....	....	83	....	....	....	....	....	....	....	....	....	....	3	0	1	1	7	....	....	....
1979-80	Binghamton Whalers	AHL	38	15	15	30	....	....	....	47	....	....	....	....	....	....	....	....	....	....	....	....	....	....	....	....	....	....
	NHL Totals		**363**	**64**	**64**	**128**	**62**	**52**	**114**	**341**	**0**	**6**	**5**	**519**	**12.3**	**204**	**3**	**251**	**75**		**45**	**1**	**4**	**5**	**13**	**0**	**1**	**0**
	Other Major League Totals		73	6	5	11	....	....	....	83	....	....	....	....	....	....	....	....	....	....	3	0	1	1	7	....	....	....

Signed as a free agent by **Boston**, September, 1973. Claimed by **Washington** from **Boston** in Waiver Draft, October 10, 1977. Signed as a free agent by **Cincinnati** (WHA) after clearing NHL waivers, October 25, 1977.

• FORBES, MIKE
Mike Forbes D – R. 6'2", 200 lbs. b: Brampton, Ont., 9/20/1957. Boston's 3rd choice, 52nd overall, in 1977 Amateur Draft.

Season	Club	League	GP	G	A	Pts	AG	AA	APts	PIM	PP	SH	GW	S	%	TGF	PGF	TGA	PGA	+/–	GP	G	A	Pts	PIM	PP	SH	GW
1974-75	Kingston Canadians	OHA	64	0	10	10	....	....	....	98	....	....	....	....	....	....	....	....	....	....	....	....	....	....	....	....	....	....
1975-76	Kingston Canadians	OHA	48	4	13	17	....	....	....	117	....	....	....	....	....	....	....	....	....	....	5	0	0	0	5	....	....	....
1976-77	St. Catharines Fincups	OHA	61	12	41	53	....	....	....	134	....	....	....	....	....	....	....	....	....	....	14	1	5	6	41	....	....	....
1977-78	**Boston Bruins**	**NHL**	**32**	**0**	**4**	**4**	**0**	**3**	**3**	**15**	**0**	**0**	**0**	**22**	**0.0**	**14**	**3**	**19**	**3**	**–5**	....	....	....	....	....	....	....	....
	Rochester Americans	AHL	32	3	12	15	....	....	....	65	....	....	....	....	....	....	....	....	....	....	6	0	1	1	22	....	....	....
1978-79	Rochester Americans	AHL	75	4	20	24	....	....	....	97	....	....	....	....	....	....	....	....	....	....	....	....	....	....	....	....	....	....

			REGULAR SEASON																		PLAYOFFS							
Season	Club	League	GP	G	A	Pts	AG	AA	APts	PIM	PP	SH	GW	S	%	TGF	PGF	TGA	PGA	+/-	GP	G	A	Pts	PIM	PP	SH	GW
1979-80	**Edmonton Oilers**	**NHL**	**2**	**0**	**0**	**0**	0	0	0	0	0	0	0	3	0.0	1	0	6	1	–4	....	....	....	....	....	....	....	....
	Houston Apollos	CHL	55	5	30	35	....	....	....	63	....	....	....	....	....	....	....	....	....	....	....	....	....	....	....	....	....	....
1980-81	Wichita Wind	CHL	79	4	44	48	....	....	....	129	....	....	....	....	....	....	....	....	....	....	15	1	16	17	46	....	....	....
1981-82	**Edmonton Oilers**	**NHL**	**16**	**1**	**7**	**8**	1	5	6	26	0	0	0	14	7.1	31	2	16	1	+14	....	....	....	....	....	....	....	....
	Wichita Wind	CHL	49	4	28	32	....	....	....	94	....	....	....	....	....	....	....	....	....	....	6	0	2	2	4	....	....	....
1982-83	Wichita Wind	CHL	75	15	46	61	....	....	....	73	....	....	....	....	....	....	....	....	....	....	....	....	....	....	....	....	....	....
1983-84	Montana Magic	CHL	76	13	38	51	....	....	....	83	....	....	....	....	....	....	....	....	....	....	....	....	....	....	....	....	....	....
1984-85			DID NOT PLAY																									
1985-86	Muskegon Lumberjacks	IHL	14	1	7	8	....	....	....	13	....	....	....	....	....	....	....	....	....	....	13	0	2	2	19	....	....	....
1986-87	Muskegon Lumberjacks	IHL	67	3	22	25	....	....	....	113	....	....	....	....	....	....	....	....	....	....	15	1	10	11	4	....	....	....
	NHL Totals		**50**	**1**	**11**	**12**	1	8	9	41	0	0	0	39	2.6	46	5	41	5		....	....	....	....	....	....	....	....

CHL Second All-Star Team (1983)

Claimed by **Edmonton** from **Boston** in Expansion Draft, June 13, 1979.

• FOREY, CONNIE

Connie Forey LW – L. 6'2", 185 lbs. b: Montreal, Que., 10/18/1950. Pittsburgh's 4th choice, 49th overall, in 1970 Amateur Draft.

Season	Club	League	GP	G	A	Pts	AG	AA	APts	PIM	PP	SH	GW	S	%	TGF	PGF	TGA	PGA	+/-	GP	G	A	Pts	PIM	PP	SH	GW
1968-69	Ottawa 67's	OHA	53	9	10	19	....	....	....	22	....	....	....	....	....	....	....	....	....	....	7	2	1	3	6	....	....	....
1969-70	Ottawa 67's	OHA	54	24	28	52	....	....	....	39	....	....	....	....	....	....	....	....	....	....	....	....	....	....	....	....	....	....
1970-71	Amarillo Wranglers	CHL	67	17	22	39	....	....	....	55	....	....	....	....	....	....	....	....	....	....	....	....	....	....	....	....	....	....
1971-72	Hershey Bears	AHL	39	11	5	16	....	....	....	20	....	....	....	....	....	....	....	....	....	....	4	0	0	0	0	....	....	....
	Fort Wayne Komets	IHL	2	0	0	0	....	....	....	0	....	....	....	....	....	....	....	....	....	....	....	....	....	....	....	....	....	....
1972-73	New Haven Nighthawks	AHL	71	21	18	39	....	....	....	40	....	....	....	....	....	....	....	....	....	....	....	....	....	....	....	....	....	....
1973-74	**St. Louis Blues**	**NHL**	**4**	**0**	**0**	**0**	0	0	0	2	0	0	0	2	0.0	0	0	2	1	–1	....	....	....	....	....	....	....	....
	Denver Spurs	WHL	49	14	12	26	....	....	....	57	....	....	....	....	....	....	....	....	....	....	....	....	....	....	....	....	....	....
1974-75	Mohawk Valley Comets	NAHL	6	1	1	2	....	....	....	10	....	....	....	....	....	....	....	....	....	....	....	....	....	....	....	....	....	....
	NHL Totals		**4**	**0**	**0**	**0**	0	0	0	2	0	0	0	2	0.0	0	0	2	1		....	....	....	....	....	....	....	....

Claimed by **NY Islanders** from **Hershey** (AHL) in Inter-League Draft, June 6, 1972. Traded to **St. Louis** by **NY Islanders** for cash, August, 1973. • Suspended by WHL for remainder of 1973-74 season and all of 1974-75 season for assaulting referee Malcolm Ashford, February 21, 1973.

• FORSBERG, PETER

Peter Forsberg C – L. 6', 190 lbs. b: Ornskoldsvik, Sweden, 7/20/1973. Philadelphia's 1st choice, 6th overall, in 1991 Entry Draft.

Season	Club	League	GP	G	A	Pts	AG	AA	APts	PIM	PP	SH	GW	S	%	TGF	PGF	TGA	PGA	+/-	GP	G	A	Pts	PIM	PP	SH	GW
1990-91	MoDo AIK	Sweden	23	7	10	17	....	....	....	22	....	....	....	....	....	....	....	....	....	....	....	....	....	....	....	....	....	....
1991-92	MoDo AIK	Sweden	39	9	18	27	....	....	....	78	....	....	....	....	....	....	....	....	....	....	....	....	....	....	....	....	....	....
	Sweden	WJC-A	7	3	8	11	....	....	....	30	....	....	....	....	....	....	....	....	....	....	....	....	....	....	....	....	....	....
	Sweden	WC-A	8	4	2	6	....	....	....	6	....	....	....	....	....	....	....	....	....	....	....	....	....	....	....	....	....	....
1992-93	MoDo AIK	Sweden	39	23	24	47	....	....	....	92	....	....	....	....	....	....	....	....	....	....	3	4	1	5	0	....	....	....
	Sweden	WJC-A	7	7	24	31	....	....	....	8	....	....	....	....	....	....	....	....	....	....	....	....	....	....	....	....	....	....
	Sweden	WC-A	8	1	1	2	....	....	....	12	....	....	....	....	....	....	....	....	....	....	....	....	....	....	....	....	....	....
1993-94	MoDo AIK	Sweden	39	18	26	44	....	....	....	82	....	....	....	....	....	....	....	....	....	....	11	9	7	16	14	....	....	....
	Sweden	Olympics	8	2	6	8	....	....	....	6	....	....	....	....	....	....	....	....	....	....	....	....	....	....	....	....	....	....
1994-95	MoDo AIK	Sweden	11	5	9	14	....	....	....	20	....	....	....	....	....	....	....	....	....	....	....	....	....	....	....	....	....	....
	Quebec Nordiques	**NHL**	**47**	**15**	**35**	**50**	27	52	79	16	3	0	3	86	17.4	65	22	40	14	+17	6	2	4	6	4	1	0	0
1995-96	**Colorado Avalanche**	**NHL**	**82**	**30**	**86**	**116**	30	71	101	47	7	3	3	217	13.8	147	55	96	30	+26	22	10	11	21	18	3	0	1
1996-97	Sweden	W Cup	4	1	4	5	....	....	....	6	....	....	....	....	....	....	....	....	....	....	....	....	....	....	....	....	....	....
	Colorado Avalanche	**NHL**	**65**	**28**	**58**	**86**	30	51	81	73	5	4	4	188	14.9	118	42	54	9	+31	14	5	12	17	10	3	0	0
1997-98	**Colorado Avalanche**	**NHL**	**72**	**25**	**66**	**91**	29	65	94	94	7	3	7	202	12.4	121	52	74	11	+6	7	6	5	11	12	2	0	0
	Sweden	Olympics	4	1	4	5	....	....	....	6	....	....	....	....	....	....	....	....	....	....	....	....	....	....	....	....	....	....
	Sweden	WC-A	7	6	5	11	....	....	....	0	....	....	....	....	....	....	....	....	....	....	....	....	....	....	....	....	....	....
	NHL Totals		**266**	**98**	**245**	**343**	116	239	355	230	22	10	17	693	14.1	451	171	264	64		49	23	32	55	44	9	0	1

WJC-A All-Star Team (1993) • Named Best Forward at WJC-A (1993) • NHL/Upper Deck All-Rookie Team (1995) • Won Calder Memorial Trophy (1995) • NHL First All-Star Team (1998)

Played in NHL All-Star Game (1996, 1998)

Traded to **Quebec** by **Philadelphia** with Steve Duchesne, Kerry Huffman, Mike Ricci, Ron Hextall, Chris Simon, Philadelphia's 1st round choice in the 1993 (Jocelyn Thibault) and 1994 (later traded to Toronto — later traded to Washington — Washington selected Nolan Baumgartner) Entry Drafts and cash for Eric Lindros, June 30, 1992. Transferred to **Colorado** after **Quebec** franchise relocated, June 21, 1995.

• FORSLUND, TOMAS

Tomas Forslund RW – L. 5'11", 200 lbs. b: Falun, Sweden, 11/24/1968. Calgary's 4th choice, 85th overall, in 1988 Entry Draft.

Season	Club	League	GP	G	A	Pts	AG	AA	APts	PIM	PP	SH	GW	S	%	TGF	PGF	TGA	PGA	+/-	GP	G	A	Pts	PIM	PP	SH	GW
1986-87	Leksands IF	Sweden	23	3	5	8	....	....	....	4	....	....	....	....	....	....	....	....	....	....	....	....	....	....	....	....	....	....
1987-88	Leksands IF	Sweden	36	9	10	19	....	....	....	22	....	....	....	....	....	....	....	....	....	....	3	1	1	2	2	....	....	....
	Sweden	WJC-A	7	0	0	0	....	....	....	10	....	....	....	....	....	....	....	....	....	....	....	....	....	....	....	....	....	....
1988-89	Leksands IF	Sweden	39	14	16	30	....	....	....	58	....	....	....	....	....	....	....	....	....	....	10	2	4	6	6	....	....	....
1989-90	Leksands IF	Sweden	38	14	21	35	....	....	....	48	....	....	....	....	....	....	....	....	....	....	3	0	1	1	2	....	....	....
1990-91	Leksands IF	Sweden	22	5	10	15	....	....	....	10	....	....	....	....	....	....	....	....	....	....	21	6	9	15	26	....	....	....
1991-92	Sweden	C Cup	6	1	0	1	....	....	....	2	....	....	....	....	....	....	....	....	....	....	....	....	....	....	....	....	....	....
	Calgary Flames	**NHL**	**38**	**5**	**9**	**14**	5	7	12	12	0	0	1	48	10.4	16	0	32	10	–6	....	....	....	....	....	....	....	....
	Salt Lake Golden Eagles	IHL	22	10	6	16	....	....	....	25	....	....	....	....	....	....	....	....	....	....	5	2	2	4	2	....	....	....
1992-93	**Calgary Flames**	**NHL**	**6**	**0**	**2**	**2**	0	1	1	0	0	0	0	3	0.0	2	0	2	0	0	....	....	....	....	....	....	....	....
	Salt Lake Golden Eagles	IHL	63	31	23	54	....	....	....	68	....	....	....	....	....	....	....	....	....	....	....	....	....	....	....	....	....	....
1993-94	Leksands IF	Sweden	38	16	17	33	....	....	....	66	....	....	....	....	....	....	....	....	....	....	....	....	....	....	....	....	....	....
	Sweden	WC-A	5	2	2	4	....	....	....	4	....	....	....	....	....	....	....	....	....	....	....	....	....	....	....	....	....	....
1994-95	Leksands IF	Sweden	34	24	10	34	....	....	....	46	....	....	....	....	....	....	....	....	....	....	3	1	0	1	25	....	....	....
	Sweden	WC-A	8	2	0	2	....	....	....	10	....	....	....	....	....	....	....	....	....	....	....	....	....	....	....	....	....	....
1995-96	Leksands IF	Sweden	35	13	13	26	....	....	....	65	....	....	....	....	....	....	....	....	....	....	5	1	2	3	4	....	....	....
	Sweden	WC-A	6	0	1	1	....	....	....	2	....	....	....	....	....	....	....	....	....	....	....	....	....	....	....	....	....	....
1996-97	Kolner Haie	Germany	48	16	22	38	....	....	....	42	....	....	....	....	....	....	....	....	....	....	4	0	1	1	2	....	....	....
1997-98	Kolner Haie	Germany	46	15	29	44	....	....	....	66	....	....	....	....	....	....	....	....	....	....	3	2	1	3	2	....	....	....
	NHL Totals		**44**	**5**	**11**	**16**	5	8	13	12	0	0	1	51	9.8	18	0	34	10		....	....	....	....	....	....	....	....

• FORSYTH, ALEX

Alex Forsyth C – L. 6'2", 195 lbs. b: Galt, Ont., 1/6/1955. Washington's 1st choice, 18th overall, in 1975 Amateur Draft.

Season	Club	League	GP	G	A	Pts	AG	AA	APts	PIM	PP	SH	GW	S	%	TGF	PGF	TGA	PGA	+/-	GP	G	A	Pts	PIM	PP	SH	GW
1973-74	Kingston Canadians	OHA	58	11	11	22	....	....	....	17	....	....	....	....	....	....	....	....	....	....	....	....	....	....	....	....	....	....
1974-75	Kingston Canadians	OHA	64	27	31	58	....	....	....	72	....	....	....	....	....	....	....	....	....	....	....	....	....	....	....	....	....	....
1975-76	Richmond Robins	AHL	71	7	16	23	....	....	....	24	....	....	....	....	....	....	....	....	....	....	8	2	5	7	0	....	....	....
1976-77	**Washington Capitals**	**NHL**	**1**	**0**	**0**	**0**	0	0	0	0	0	0	0	0	0.0	0	0	0	0	0	....	....	....	....	....	....	....	....
	Springfield Indians	AHL	74	14	33	47	....	....	....	47	....	....	....	....	....	....	....	....	....	....	....	....	....	....	....	....	....	....
1977-78	Tulsa Oilers	CHL	69	15	16	31	....	....	....	29	....	....	....	....	....	....	....	....	....	....	7	0	0	0	0	....	....	....
	NHL Totals		**1**	**0**	**0**	**0**	0	0	0	0	0	0	0	0	0.0	0	0	0	0		....	....	....	....	....	....	....	....

• FORTIER, DAVE

Dave Fortier D – L. 5'11", 190 lbs. b: Sudbury, Ont., 6/17/1951. Toronto's 2nd choice, 23rd overall, in 1971 Amateur Draft.

Season	Club	League	GP	G	A	Pts	AG	AA	APts	PIM	PP	SH	GW	S	%	TGF	PGF	TGA	PGA	+/-	GP	G	A	Pts	PIM	PP	SH	GW
1969-70	Chelmsford Chargers	NOHA	STATISTICS NOT AVAILABLE																									
1970-71	St. Catharines Black Hawks	OHA	60	8	16	24	....	....	....	196	....	....	....	....	....	....	....	....	....	....	....	....	....	....	....	....	....	....
1971-72	Tulsa Oilers	CHL	71	7	20	27	....	....	....	217	....	....	....	....	....	....	....	....	....	....	13	0	8	8	39	....	....	....
1972-73	**Toronto Maple Leafs**	**NHL**	**23**	**1**	**4**	**5**	1	3	4	63	0	0	0	29	3.4	32	0	46	4	–10	....	....	....	....	....	....	....	....
	Tulsa Oilers	CHL	50	2	20	22	....	....	....	148	....	....	....	....	....	....	....	....	....	....	....	....	....	....	....	....	....	....
1973-74	Oklahoma City Blazers	CHL	72	10	38	48	....	....	....	200	....	....	....	....	....	....	....	....	....	....	10	0	1	1	35	....	....	....
1974-75	**New York Islanders**	**NHL**	**65**	**6**	**12**	**18**	6	9	15	79	1	0	0	74	8.1	61	5	48	6	+14	14	0	2	2	33	0	0	0
1975-76	**New York Islanders**	**NHL**	**59**	**0**	**2**	**2**	0	2	2	68	0	0	0	58	0.0	28	2	19	2	+9	6	0	0	0	0	0	0	0

Season	Club	League	GP	G	A	Pts	AG	AA	APts	PIM	PP	SH	GW	S	%	TGF	PGF	TGA	PGA	+/–	GP	G	A	Pts	PIM	PP	SH	GW
			REGULAR SEASON																		PLAYOFFS							
1976-77	**Vancouver Canucks**	**NHL**	**58**	**1**	**3**	**4**	**1**	**2**	**3**	**125**	**0**	**0**	**0**	**46**	**2.2**	**28**	**0**	**58**	**15**	**–15**	....	....	....	....	....	....	....	....
1977-78	Indianapolis Racers	WHA	54	1	15	16	....	....	....	86	....	....	....	....	....	....	....	....	....	....	....	....	....	....	....	....	....	....
1978-79	Erie Blades	NEHL	44	1	22	23	....	....	....	145	....	....	....	....	....	....	....	....	....	....	....	....	....	....	....	....	....	....
	NHL Totals		**205**	**8**	**21**	**29**	**8**	**16**	**24**	**335**	**1**	**0**	**0**	**207**	**3.9**	**149**	**7**	**171**	**27**		**20**	**0**	**2**	**2**	**33**	**0**	**0**	**0**
	Other Major League Totals		54	1	15	16	....	....	....	86	....	....	....	....	....	....	....	....	....	....	....	....	....	....	....	....	....	....

Selected by **Quebec** (WHA) in 1972 WHA General Player Draft, February 13, 1972. Traded to **Philadelphia** by **Toronto** with Randy Osburn for Bill Flett, May 27, 1974. Claimed by **NY Islanders** from **Philadelphia** in Intra-League Draft, June 10, 1974. Traded to **Vancouver** by **NY Islanders** with Ralph Stewart for cash, October 6, 1976. Signed as a free agent by **Indianapolis** (WHA), September, 1977.

• FORTIER, MARC

Marc Fortier C – R. 6', 192 lbs. b: Windsor, Que., 2/26/1966.

Season	Club	League	GP	G	A	Pts	AG	AA	APts	PIM	PP	SH	GW	S	%	TGF	PGF	TGA	PGA	+/–	GP	G	A	Pts	PIM	PP	SH	GW
1983-84	Chicoutimi Sagueneens	QMJHL	67	16	30	46	....	....	....	51	....	....	....	....	....	....	....	....	....	....	....	....	....	....	....	....	....	....
1984-85	Chicoutimi Sagueneens	QMJHL	68	35	63	98	....	....	....	114	....	....	....	....	....	....	....	....	....	....	14	8	4	12	16	....	....	....
1985-86	Chicoutimi Sagueneens	QMJHL	71	47	86	133	....	....	....	49	....	....	....	....	....	....	....	....	....	....	9	2	14	16	12	....	....	....
1986-87	Chicoutimi Sagueneens	QMJHL	65	66	*135	*201	....	....	....	39	....	....	....	....	....	....	....	....	....	....	19	11	*40	*51	20	....	....	....
1987-88	**Quebec Nordiques**	**NHL**	**27**	**4**	**10**	**14**	**3**	**7**	**10**	**12**	**3**	**0**	**1**	**40**	**10.0**	**19**	**11**	**26**	**1**	**–17**	....	....	....	....	....	....	....	....
	Fredericton Express	AHL	50	26	36	62	....	....	....	48	....	....	....	....	....	....	....	....	....	....	....	....	....	....	....	....	....	....
1988-89	**Quebec Nordiques**	**NHL**	**57**	**20**	**19**	**39**	**17**	**13**	**30**	**45**	**2**	**2**	**2**	**90**	**22.2**	**51**	**13**	**79**	**23**	**–18**	....	....	....	....	....	....	....	....
	Halifax Citadels	AHL	16	11	11	22	....	....	....	14	....	....	....	....	....	....	....	....	....	....	....	....	....	....	....	....	....	....
1989-90	**Quebec Nordiques**	**NHL**	**59**	**13**	**17**	**30**	**11**	**12**	**23**	**28**	**3**	**1**	**1**	**89**	**14.6**	**48**	**13**	**58**	**7**	**–16**	....	....	....	....	....	....	....	....
	Halifax Citadels	AHL	15	5	6	11	....	....	....	6	....	....	....	....	....	....	....	....	....	....	....	....	....	....	....	....	....	....
1990-91	**Quebec Nordiques**	**NHL**	**14**	**0**	**4**	**4**	**0**	**3**	**3**	**6**	**0**	**0**	**0**	**13**	**0.0**	**8**	**3**	**8**	**0**	**–3**	....	....	....	....	....	....	....	....
	Halifax Citadels	AHL	58	24	32	56	....	....	....	85	....	....	....	....	....	....	....	....	....	....	....	....	....	....	....	....	....	....
1991-92	**Quebec Nordiques**	**NHL**	**39**	**5**	**9**	**14**	**5**	**7**	**12**	**33**	**2**	**0**	**1**	**42**	**11.9**	**27**	**4**	**30**	**0**	**–7**	....	....	....	....	....	....	....	....
	Halifax Citadels	AHL	16	9	16	25	....	....	....	44	....	....	....	....	....	....	....	....	....	....	....	....	....	....	....	....	....	....
1992-93	**Ottawa Senators**	**NHL**	**10**	**0**	**1**	**1**	**0**	**1**	**1**	**6**	**0**	**0**	**0**	**12**	**0.0**	**2**	**0**	**10**	**1**	**–7**	....	....	....	....	....	....	....	....
	New Haven Nighthawks	AHL	16	9	15	24	....	....	....	42	....	....	....	....	....	....	....	....	....	....	....	....	....	....	....	....	....	....
	Los Angeles Kings	**NHL**	**6**	**0**	**0**	**0**	**0**	**0**	**0**	**5**	**0**	**0**	**0**	**2**	**0.0**	**0**	**0**	**3**	**1**	**–2**	....	....	....	....	....	....	....	....
	Phoenix Roadrunners	IHL	17	4	9	13	....	....	....	34	....	....	....	....	....	....	....	....	....	....	....	....	....	....	....	....	....	....
1993-94	Phoenix Roadrunners	IHL	81	39	61	100	....	....	....	96	....	....	....	....	....	....	....	....	....	....	....	....	....	....	....	....	....	....
1994-95	Canada	Nat-Team	4	1	3	4	....	....	....	0	....	....	....	....	....	....	....	....	....	....	....	....	....	....	....	....	....	....
	Zurich Grasshoppers	Switz.	35	11	40	51	....	....	....	*104	....	....	....	....	....	....	....	....	....	....	5	2	6	8	2	....	....	....
1995-96	Zurich Grasshoppers	Switz.	36	17	*38	55	....	....	....	30	....	....	....	....	....	....	....	....	....	....	4	1	2	3	4	....	....	....
1996-97	Zurich Grasshoppers	Switz.	24	8	19	27	....	....	....	39	....	....	....	....	....	....	....	....	....	....	....	....	....	....	....	....	....	....
	Eisbaren Berlin	Germany	18	3	8	11	....	....	....	10	....	....	....	....	....	....	....	....	....	....	8	5	4	9	2	....	....	....
1997-98	Eisbaren Berlin	Germany	43	8	36	44	....	....	....	38	....	....	....	....	....	....	....	....	....	....	10	2	5	7	6	....	....	....
	NHL Totals		**212**	**42**	**60**	**102**	**36**	**43**	**79**	**135**	**10**	**3**	**5**	**288**	**14.6**	**155**	**44**	**214**	**33**		....	....	....	....	....	....	....	....

QMJHL First All-Star Team (1987)

Signed as a free agent by **Quebec**, February 3, 1987. Signed as a free agent by **Ottawa**, October 1, 1992. Traded to **LA Kings** by **Ottawa** with Jim Thomson for Bob Kudelski and Shawn McCosh, December 19, 1992.

• FORTIN, RAY

Ray Fortin D – L. 5'8", 180 lbs. b: Drummondville, Que., 3/11/1941.

Season	Club	League	GP	G	A	Pts	AG	AA	APts	PIM	PP	SH	GW	S	%	TGF	PGF	TGA	PGA	+/–	GP	G	A	Pts	PIM	PP	SH	GW
1964-65	Drummondville Rockets	Inter-Sr.	STATISTICS NOT AVAILABLE																									
1965-66	Drummondville Aigles	QSHL	42	5	12	17	....	....	....	54	....	....	....	....	....	....	....	....	....	....	....	....	....	....	....	....	....	....
1966-67	Drummondville Aigles	QSHL	40	9	18	27	....	....	....	54	....	....	....	....	....	....	....	....	....	....	....	....	....	....	....	....	....	....
1967-68	**St. Louis Blues**	**NHL**	**24**	**0**	**2**	**2**	**0**	**2**	**2**	**8**	**0**	**0**	**0**	**25**	**0.0**	**10**	**0**	**16**	**3**	**–3**	**3**	**0**	**0**	**0**	**2**	**0**	**0**	**0**
	Kansas City Blues	CHL	22	1	2	3	....	....	....	22	....	....	....	....	....	....	....	....	....	....	....	....	....	....	....	....	....	....
1968-69	**St. Louis Blues**	**NHL**	**11**	**1**	**0**	**1**	**1**	**0**	**1**	**6**	**0**	**0**	**0**	**10**	**10.0**	**7**	**0**	**3**	**0**	**+4**	....	....	....	....	....	....	....	....
	Kansas City Blues	CHL	50	6	18	24	....	....	....	59	....	....	....	....	....	....	....	....	....	....	....	....	....	....	....	....	....	....
1969-70	**St. Louis Blues**	**NHL**	**57**	**1**	**4**	**5**	**1**	**4**	**5**	**19**	**0**	**0**	**0**	**66**	**1.5**	**39**	**4**	**33**	**1**	**+3**	**3**	**0**	**0**	**0**	**6**	**0**	**0**	**0**
1970-71	Springfield Kings	AHL	25	2	14	16	....	....	....	18	....	....	....	....	....	....	....	....	....	....	....	....	....	....	....	....	....	....
	Montreal Voyageurs	AHL	29	4	11	15	....	....	....	20	....	....	....	....	....	....	....	....	....	....	3	0	2	2	4	....	....	....
1971-72	Boston Braves	AHL	76	3	24	27	....	....	....	64	....	....	....	....	....	....	....	....	....	....	8	0	0	0	6	....	....	....
1972-73	Boston Braves	AHL	74	1	20	21	....	....	....	28	....	....	....	....	....	....	....	....	....	....	1	0	0	0	0	....	....	....
1973-74	San Diego Gulls	WHL	69	1	15	16	....	....	....	36	....	....	....	....	....	....	....	....	....	....	4	0	1	1	4	....	....	....
	NHL Totals		**92**	**2**	**6**	**8**	**2**	**6**	**8**	**33**	**0**	**0**	**0**	**101**	**2.0**	**56**	**4**	**52**	**4**		**6**	**0**	**0**	**0**	**8**	**0**	**0**	**0**

CHL Second All-Star Team (1969) • AHL Second All-Star Team (1971)

Signed as a free agent by **St. Louis**, June, 1967. Traded to **LA Kings** by **St. Louis** for Bob Wall, May 11, 1970. Traded to **Montreal** by **LA Kings** with Gord Labossiere for Ralph Backstrom, January 26, 1971. Claimed by **Hershey** (AHL) from **Montreal** in Reverse Draft, June, 1971. Traded to **Boston** by **Hershey** (AHL) for cash, August, 1971.

• FOSTER, COREY

Corey Foster D – L. 6'3", 204 lbs. b: Ottawa, Ont., 10/27/1969. New Jersey's 1st choice, 12th overall, in 1988 Entry Draft.

Season	Club	League	GP	G	A	Pts	AG	AA	APts	PIM	PP	SH	GW	S	%	TGF	PGF	TGA	PGA	+/–	GP	G	A	Pts	PIM	PP	SH	GW
1986-87	Peterborough Petes	OHL	30	3	4	7	....	....	....	4	....	....	....	....	....	....	....	....	....	....	1	0	0	0	0	....	....	....
1987-88	Peterborough Petes	OHL	66	13	31	44	....	....	....	58	....	....	....	....	....	....	....	....	....	....	11	5	9	14	13	....	....	....
1988-89	Peterborough Petes	OHL	55	14	42	56	....	....	....	42	....	....	....	....	....	....	....	....	....	....	17	1	17	18	12	....	....	....
	Canada	WJC-A	7	1	3	4	....	....	....	4	....	....	....	....	....	....	....	....	....	....	....	....	....	....	....	....	....	....
	New Jersey Devils	**NHL**	**2**	**0**	**0**	**0**	**0**	**0**	**0**	**0**	**0**	**0**	**0**	**2**	**0.0**	**0**	**0**	**2**	**0**	**–2**	....	....	....	....	....	....	....	....
1989-90	Cape Breton Oilers	AHL	54	7	17	24	....	....	....	32	....	....	....	....	....	....	....	....	....	....	1	0	0	0	0	....	....	....
1990-91	Cape Breton Oilers	AHL	67	14	11	25	....	....	....	51	....	....	....	....	....	....	....	....	....	....	4	2	4	6	4	....	....	....
1991-92	**Philadelphia Flyers**	**NHL**	**25**	**3**	**4**	**7**	**3**	**3**	**6**	**20**	**1**	**0**	**0**	**67**	**4.5**	**17**	**6**	**25**	**0**	**–14**	....	....	....	....	....	....	....	....
	Hershey Bears	AHL	19	5	9	14	....	....	....	26	....	....	....	....	....	....	....	....	....	....	6	1	1	2	5	....	....	....
1992-93	Hershey Bears	AHL	80	9	25	34	....	....	....	102	....	....	....	....	....	....	....	....	....	....	....	....	....	....	....	....	....	....
1993-94	Hershey Bears	AHL	66	21	37	58	....	....	....	96	....	....	....	....	....	....	....	....	....	....	9	2	5	7	10	....	....	....
1994-95	P.E.I. Senators	AHL	78	13	34	47	....	....	....	61	....	....	....	....	....	....	....	....	....	....	11	2	5	7	12	....	....	....
1995-96	**Pittsburgh Penguins**	**NHL**	**11**	**2**	**2**	**4**	**2**	**2**	**4**	**2**	**1**	**0**	**0**	**8**	**25.0**	**7**	**3**	**6**	**0**	**–2**	**3**	**0**	**0**	**0**	**4**	**0**	**0**	**0**
	Cleveland Lumberjacks	IHL	61	10	36	46	....	....	....	93	....	....	....	....	....	....	....	....	....	....	....	....	....	....	....	....	....	....
1996-97	**New York Islanders**	**NHL**	**7**	**0**	**0**	**0**	**0**	**0**	**0**	**2**	**0**	**0**	**0**	**1**	**0.0**	**1**	**0**	**4**	**1**	**–2**	....	....	....	....	....	....	....	....
	Cleveland Lumberjacks	IHL	51	5	29	34	....	....	....	71	....	....	....	....	....	....	....	....	....	....	14	0	9	9	22	....	....	....
1997-98	Kokudo Toyko	Japan	37	18	13	31	....	....	....	101	....	....	....	....	....	....	....	....	....	....	....	....	....	....	....	....	....	....
	NHL Totals		**45**	**5**	**6**	**11**	**5**	**5**	**10**	**24**	**2**	**0**	**0**	**78**	**6.4**	**25**	**9**	**37**	**1**		**3**	**0**	**0**	**0**	**4**	**0**	**0**	**0**

Traded to **Edmonton** by **New Jersey** for Edmonton's 1st round choice (Jason Miller) in 1989 Entry Draft, June 17, 1989. Traded to **Philadelphia** by **Edmonton** with Dave Brown and Jari Kurri for Craig Fisher, Scott Mellanby and Craig Berube, May 30, 1991. Signed as a free agent by **Ottawa**, June 20, 1994. Signed as a free agent by **Pittsburgh**, August 7, 1995. Claimed by **NY Islanders** from **Pittsburgh** in Waiver Draft, September 30, 1996.

• FOSTER, DWIGHT

Dwight "Dewey" Foster RW – R. 5'10", 190 lbs. b: Toronto, Ont., 4/2/1957. Boston's 1st choice, 16th overall, in 1977 Amateur Draft.

Season	Club	League	GP	G	A	Pts	AG	AA	APts	PIM	PP	SH	GW	S	%	TGF	PGF	TGA	PGA	+/–	GP	G	A	Pts	PIM	PP	SH	GW
1973-74	Kitchener Rangers	OHA	67	23	32	55	....	....	....	61	....	....	....	....	....	....	....	....	....	....	....	....	....	....	....	....	....	....
1974-75	Kitchener Rangers	OHA	70	39	51	90	....	....	....	88	....	....	....	....	....	....	....	....	....	....	....	....	....	....	....	....	....	....
1975-76	Kitchener Rangers	OHA	61	36	58	94	....	....	....	110	....	....	....	....	....	....	....	....	....	....	8	4	6	10	28	....	....	....
1976-77	Kitchener Rangers	OHA	64	60	*83	*143	....	....	....	88	....	....	....	....	....	....	....	....	....	....	3	2	4	6	2	....	....	....
	Canada	WJC-A	7	2	5	7	....	....	....	4	....	....	....	....	....	....	....	....	....	....	....	....	....	....	....	....	....	....
1977-78	Kitchener Rangers	OHA	61	36	58	94	....	....	....	110	....	....	....	....	....	....	....	....	....	....	8	4	6	10	28	....	....	....
	Boston Bruins	**NHL**	**14**	**2**	**1**	**3**	**2**	**1**	**3**	**6**	**0**	**0**	**0**	**24**	**8.3**	**3**	**0**	**2**	**0**	**+1**	....	....	....	....	....	....	....	....
	Rochester Americans	AHL	3	0	3	3	....	....	....	2	....	....	....	....	....	....	....	....	....	....	....	....	....	....	....	....	....	....
1978-79	**Boston Bruins**	**NHL**	**44**	**11**	**13**	**24**	**10**	**10**	**20**	**14**	**2**	**0**	**0**	**57**	**19.3**	**33**	**7**	**34**	**7**	**–1**	**11**	**1**	**3**	**4**	**0**	**0**	**0**	**0**
	Rochester Americans	AHL	21	11	18	29	....	....	....	8	....	....	....	....	....	....	....	....	....	....	....	....	....	....	....	....	....	....
1979-80	**Boston Bruins**	**NHL**	**57**	**10**	**28**	**38**	**9**	**21**	**30**	**42**	**1**	**1**	**2**	**68**	**14.7**	**53**	**7**	**30**	**7**	**+23**	**9**	**3**	**5**	**8**	**2**	**0**	**1**	**1**
	Binghamton Whalers	AHL	7	1	3	4	....	....	....	2	....	....	....	....	....	....	....	....	....	....	....	....	....	....	....	....	....	....
1980-81	**Boston Bruins**	**NHL**	**77**	**24**	**28**	**52**	**20**	**20**	**40**	**62**	**3**	**3**	**5**	**107**	**22.4**	**76**	**12**	**91**	**31**	**+4**	**3**	**1**	**1**	**2**	**0**	**0**	**0**	**0**
1981-82	**Colorado Rockies**	**NHL**	**70**	**12**	**19**	**31**	**9**	**13**	**22**	**41**	**1**	**1**	**0**	**97**	**12.4**	**52**	**10**	**109**	**14**	**–53**	....	....	....	....	....	....	....	....
1982-83	**New Jersey Devils**	**NHL**	**4**	**0**	**0**	**0**	**0**	**0**	**0**	**2**	**0**	**0**	**0**	**2**	**0.0**	**0**	**0**	**1**	**0**	**–1**	....	....	....	....	....	....	....	....
	Wichita Wind	CHL	2	0	1	1	....	....	....	2	....	....	....	....	....	....	....	....	....	....	....	....	....	....	....	....	....	....
	Detroit Red Wings	**NHL**	**58**	**17**	**22**	**39**	**14**	**15**	**29**	**58**	**3**	**1**	**1**	**83**	**20.5**	**65**	**16**	**72**	**15**	**–8**	....	....	....	....	....	....	....	....
1983-84	**Detroit Red Wings**	**NHL**	**52**	**9**	**12**	**21**	**7**	**8**	**15**	**50**	**0**	**2**	**1**	**75**	**12.0**	**36**	**1**	**56**	**17**	**–4**	**3**	**0**	**1**	**1**	**0**	**0**	**0**	**0**

			REGULAR SEASON																		PLAYOFFS							
Season	Club	League	GP	G	A	Pts	AG	AA	APts	PIM	PP	SH	GW	S	%	TGF	PGF	TGA	PGA	+/–	GP	G	A	Pts	PIM	PP	SH	GW
1984-85	**Detroit Red Wings**	**NHL**	**50**	**16**	**16**	**32**	**13**	**11**	**24**	**56**	**0**	**3**	**0**	**69**	**23.2**	**44**	**0**	**69**	**37**	**+12**	**3**	**0**	**0**	**0**	**0**	**0**	**0**	**0**
1985-86	**Detroit Red Wings**	**NHL**	**55**	**6**	**12**	**18**	**5**	**8**	**13**	**48**	**1**	**1**	**0**	**41**	**14.6**	**25**	**2**	**70**	**34**	**–13**	....	....	....	....	....	....	....	....
	Boston Bruins	**NHL**	**13**	**0**	**0**	**0**	**0**	**0**	**0**	**4**	**0**	**0**	**0**	**8**	**0.0**	**2**	**1**	**11**	**5**	**–5**	**3**	**0**	**2**	**2**	**2**	**0**	**0**	**0**
1986-87	**Boston Bruins**	**NHL**	**47**	**4**	**12**	**16**	**3**	**9**	**12**	**37**	**0**	**1**	**0**	**23**	**17.4**	**24**	**0**	**39**	**16**	**+1**	**3**	**0**	**0**	**0**	**0**	**0**	**0**	**0**
	NHL Totals		**541**	**111**	**163**	**274**	**92**	**116**	**208**	**420**	**11**	**13**	**9**	**654**	**17.0**	**413**	**56**	**584**	**183**		**35**	**5**	**12**	**17**	**4**	**0**	**1**	**1**

Signed as a free agent by **Colorado**, July 21, 1981. Transferred to **New Jersey** when **Colorado** franchise relocated, June 30, 1982. Rights traded to **Detroit** by **New Jersey** for cash, October 29, 1982. Traded to **Boston** by **Detroit** for Dave Donnelly, March 11, 1986.

• FOTIU, NICK

Nick "Nicky Boy" Fotiu LW – L. 6'2", 210 lbs. b: Staten Island, NY, 5/25/1952.

1971-72	New Hyde Park Arrows	NYJHL	32	6	17	23	....	....	....	135	....	....	....	....	....	....	....	....	....	....	5	4	4	8	14	....	....	....
1972-73			DID NOT PLAY – INJURED																									
1973-74	Cape Cod Cubs	NAHL	72	12	24	36	....	....	....	*371	....	....	....	....	....	....	....	....	....	....	....	....	....	....	....	....	....	....
1974-75	New England Whalers	WHA	61	2	2	4	....	....	....	144	....	....	....	....	....	....	....	....	....	....	4	2	0	2	27	....	....	....
	Cape Cod Codders	NAHL	5	2	1	3	....	....	....	13	....	....	....	....	....	....	....	....	....	....	....	....	....	....	....	....	....	....
1975-76	New England Whalers	WHA	49	3	2	5	....	....	....	94	....	....	....	....	....	....	....	....	....	....	16	3	2	5	57	....	....	....
	Cape Cod Codders	NAHL	6	2	1	3	....	....	....	15	....	....	....	....	....	....	....	....	....	....	....	....	....	....	....	....	....	....
1976-77	**New York Rangers**	**NHL**	**70**	**4**	**8**	**12**	**4**	**6**	**10**	**174**	**0**	**0**	**0**	**48**	**8.3**	**16**	**0**	**39**	**0**	**–23**	....	....	....	....	....	....	....	....
1977-78	**New York Rangers**	**NHL**	**59**	**2**	**7**	**9**	**2**	**6**	**8**	**105**	**0**	**0**	**0**	**32**	**6.3**	**13**	**0**	**27**	**0**	**–14**	**3**	**0**	**0**	**0**	**5**	**0**	**0**	**0**
	New Haven Nighthawks	AHL	5	1	1	2	....	....	....	9	....	....	....	....	....	....	....	....	....	....	....	....	....	....	....	....	....	....
1978-79	**New York Rangers**	**NHL**	**71**	**3**	**5**	**8**	**3**	**4**	**7**	**190**	**0**	**0**	**1**	**51**	**5.9**	**22**	**1**	**18**	**0**	**+3**	**4**	**0**	**0**	**0**	**6**	**0**	**0**	**0**
1979-80	**Hartford Whalers**	**NHL**	**74**	**10**	**8**	**18**	**9**	**6**	**15**	**107**	**0**	**0**	**0**	**54**	**18.5**	**28**	**0**	**26**	**0**	**+2**	**3**	**0**	**0**	**0**	**6**	**0**	**0**	**0**
1980-81	**Hartford Whalers**	**NHL**	**42**	**4**	**3**	**7**	**3**	**2**	**5**	**79**	**0**	**0**	**0**	**36**	**11.1**	**17**	**1**	**23**	**0**	**–7**	....	....	....	....	....	....	....	....
	New York Rangers	**NHL**	**27**	**5**	**6**	**11**	**4**	**4**	**8**	**91**	**1**	**0**	**0**	**28**	**17.9**	**16**	**1**	**21**	**0**	**–6**	**2**	**0**	**0**	**0**	**4**	**0**	**0**	**0**
1981-82	**New York Rangers**	**NHL**	**70**	**8**	**10**	**18**	**6**	**7**	**13**	**151**	**0**	**0**	**1**	**76**	**10.5**	**22**	**0**	**30**	**1**	**–7**	**10**	**0**	**2**	**2**	**6**	**0**	**0**	**0**
1982-83	**New York Rangers**	**NHL**	**72**	**8**	**13**	**21**	**7**	**9**	**16**	**90**	**1**	**0**	**1**	**61**	**13.1**	**35**	**2**	**27**	**0**	**+6**	**5**	**0**	**1**	**1**	**6**	**0**	**0**	**0**
1983-84	**New York Rangers**	**NHL**	**40**	**7**	**6**	**13**	**6**	**4**	**10**	**115**	**0**	**0**	**2**	**40**	**17.5**	**21**	**0**	**13**	**0**	**+8**	....	....	....	....	....	....	....	....
1984-85	**New York Rangers**	**NHL**	**46**	**4**	**7**	**11**	**3**	**5**	**8**	**54**	**0**	**0**	**1**	**44**	**9.1**	**15**	**0**	**22**	**0**	**–7**	....	....	....	....	....	....	....	....
1985-86	New Haven Nighthawks	AHL	9	4	2	6	....	....	....	21	....	....	....	....	....	....	....	....	....	....	....	....	....	....	....	....	....	....
	Calgary Flames	**NHL**	**9**	**0**	**1**	**1**	**0**	**1**	**1**	**21**	**0**	**0**	**0**	**7**	**0.0**	**1**	**0**	**4**	**0**	**–3**	**11**	**0**	**1**	**1**	**34**	**0**	**0**	**0**
1986-87	**Calgary Flames**	**NHL**	**42**	**5**	**3**	**8**	**4**	**2**	**6**	**145**	**0**	**0**	**1**	**31**	**16.1**	**12**	**0**	**15**	**0**	**–3**	....	....	....	....	....	....	....	....
1987-88	**Philadelphia Flyers**	**NHL**	**23**	**0**	**0**	**0**	**0**	**0**	**0**	**40**	**0**	**0**	**0**	**9**	**0.0**	**0**	**0**	**9**	**0**	**–9**	....	....	....	....	....	....	....	....
1988-89	**Edmonton Oilers**	**NHL**	**1**	**0**	**0**	**0**	**0**	**0**	**0**	**0**	**0**	**0**	**0**	**0**	**0.0**	**1**	**0**	**0**	**0**	**+1**	....	....	....	....	....	....	....	....
1989-90	New Haven Nighthawks	AHL	31	0	3	3	....	....	....	40	....	....	....	....	....	....	....	....	....	....	....	....	....	....	....	....	....	....
	NHL Totals		**646**	**60**	**77**	**137**	**51**	**56**	**107**	**1362**	**2**	**0**	**7**	**517**	**11.6**	**219**	**5**	**274**	**1**		**38**	**0**	**4**	**4**	**67**	**0**	**0**	**0**
	Other Major League Totals		110	5	4	9				238											20	5	2	7	84			

Signed as a free agent by **New England** (WHA), June, 1974. Signed as a free agent by **NY Rangers**, July 23, 1976. Claimed by **Hartford** from **NY Rangers** in Expansion Draft, June 13, 1979. Traded to **NY Rangers** by **Hartford** for NY Rangers' 5th round choice (Bill Maguire) in 1981 Entry Draft, January 15, 1981. Traded to **Calgary** by **NY Rangers** for future considerations, March 11, 1986. Signed as a free agent by **Philadelphia**, October 30, 1987. Signed as a free agent by **Edmonton**, March, 1989.

• FOX, GREG

Greg Fox D – L. 6'2", 190 lbs. b: Port McNeil, B.C., 8/12/1953. Atlanta's 12th choice, 162nd overall, in 1973 Amateur Draft.

1971-72	Kelowna Buckaroos	BCJHL	53	9	35	44	....	....	....	161	....	....	....	....	....	....	....	....	....	....	....	....	....	....	....	....	....	....
1972-73	University of Michigan	CCHA	30	2	15	17	....	....	....	68	....	....	....	....	....	....	....	....	....	....	....	....	....	....	....	....	....	....
1973-74	University of Michigan	CCHA	32	0	11	11	....	....	....	64	....	....	....	....	....	....	....	....	....	....	....	....	....	....	....	....	....	....
1974-75	University of Michigan	CCHA	36	0	19	19	....	....	....	80	....	....	....	....	....	....	....	....	....	....	....	....	....	....	....	....	....	....
1975-76	University of Michigan	CCHA	39	1	21	22	....	....	....	99	....	....	....	....	....	....	....	....	....	....	....	....	....	....	....	....	....	....
1976-77	Tulsa Oilers	CHL	10	1	7	8	....	....	....	6	....	....	....	....	....	....	....	....	....	....	....	....	....	....	....	....	....	....
	Nova Scotia Voyageurs	AHL	56	2	14	16	....	....	....	110	....	....	....	....	....	....	....	....	....	....	12	0	4	4	8	....	....	....
1977-78	**Atlanta Flames**	**NHL**	**16**	**1**	**2**	**3**	**1**	**2**	**3**	**25**	**1**	**0**	**0**	**15**	**6.7**	**14**	**1**	**14**	**6**	**+5**	**2**	**0**	**1**	**1**	**8**	**0**	**0**	**0**
	Nova Scotia Voyageurs	AHL	51	2	10	12	....	....	....	124	....	....	....	....	....	....	....	....	....	....	9	2	3	5	38	....	....	....
1978-79	**Atlanta Flames**	**NHL**	**64**	**0**	**12**	**12**	**0**	**9**	**9**	**70**	**0**	**0**	**0**	**39**	**0.0**	**71**	**0**	**58**	**12**	**+25**	....	....	....	....	....	....	....	....
	Chicago Black Hawks	**NHL**	**14**	**0**	**5**	**5**	**0**	**4**	**4**	**16**	**0**	**0**	**0**	**18**	**0.0**	**19**	**0**	**13**	**3**	**+9**	**4**	**0**	**1**	**1**	**0**	**0**	**0**	**0**
1979-80	**Chicago Black Hawks**	**NHL**	**71**	**4**	**11**	**15**	**4**	**8**	**12**	**73**	**0**	**0**	**1**	**58**	**6.9**	**53**	**0**	**88**	**22**	**–13**	**7**	**0**	**0**	**0**	**8**	**0**	**0**	**0**
1980-81	**Chicago Black Hawks**	**NHL**	**75**	**3**	**16**	**19**	**2**	**11**	**13**	**112**	**0**	**0**	**0**	**69**	**4.3**	**68**	**3**	**111**	**36**	**–10**	**3**	**0**	**1**	**1**	**2**	**0**	**0**	**0**
1981-82	**Chicago Black Hawks**	**NHL**	**79**	**2**	**19**	**21**	**2**	**13**	**15**	**137**	**0**	**0**	**0**	**89**	**2.2**	**94**	**2**	**158**	**53**	**–13**	**15**	**1**	**3**	**4**	**27**	**0**	**0**	**1**
1982-83	**Chicago Black Hawks**	**NHL**	**76**	**0**	**12**	**12**	**0**	**8**	**8**	**81**	**0**	**0**	**0**	**55**	**0.0**	**69**	**2**	**79**	**23**	**+11**	**13**	**0**	**3**	**3**	**22**	**0**	**0**	**0**
1983-84	**Chicago Black Hawks**	**NHL**	**24**	**0**	**5**	**5**	**0**	**3**	**3**	**31**	**0**	**0**	**0**	**15**	**0.0**	**18**	**0**	**22**	**4**	**0**	....	....	....	....	....	....	....	....
	Pittsburgh Penguins	**NHL**	**49**	**2**	**5**	**7**	**2**	**3**	**5**	**66**	**0**	**0**	**0**	**27**	**7.4**	**38**	**1**	**101**	**22**	**–42**	....	....	....	....	....	....	....	....
1984-85	**Pittsburgh Penguins**	**NHL**	**26**	**2**	**5**	**7**	**2**	**3**	**5**	**26**	**0**	**0**	**0**	**14**	**14.3**	**28**	**1**	**38**	**5**	**–6**	....	....	....	....	....	....	....	....
	Baltimore Skipjacks	AHL	36	3	14	17	....	....	....	38	....	....	....	....	....	....	....	....	....	....	15	1	4	5	14	....	....	....
	NHL Totals		**494**	**14**	**92**	**106**	**13**	**64**	**77**	**637**	**1**	**0**	**1**	**399**	**3.5**	**472**	**10**	**682**	**186**		**44**	**1**	**9**	**10**	**67**	**0**	**0**	**1**

Traded to **Chicago** by **Atlanta** with Tom Lysiak, Harold Phillipoff, Pat Ribble and Mile Zaharko for Ivan Bolrirev, Darcy Rota and Phil Russell, March 13, 1979. Traded to **Pittsburgh** by **Chicago** for Randy Boyd, December 6, 1983.

• FOX, JIM

Jim Fox RW – R. 5'8", 185 lbs. b: Coniston, Ont., 5/18/1960. Los Angeles' 2nd choice, 10th overall, in 1980 Entry Draft.

1975-76	North Bay Trappers	Jr. B	44	30	45	75	....	....	....	16	....	....	....	....	....	....	....	....	....	....	....	....	....	....	....	....	....	....
1976-77	North Bay Trappers	Jr. B	38	44	64	*108	....	....	....	4	....	....	....	....	....	....	....	....	....	....	19	*13	*25	*38	....	....	....	....
1977-78	Ottawa 67's	OHA	59	44	83	127	....	....	....	12	....	....	....	....	....	....	....	....	....	....	....	....	....	....	....	....	....	....
1978-79	Ottawa 67's	OHA	53	37	66	103	....	....	....	4	....	....	....	....	....	....	....	....	....	....	4	2	1	3	2	....	....	....
1979-80	Ottawa 67's	OHA	52	65	*101	*166	....	....	....	30	....	....	....	....	....	....	....	....	....	....	11	6	14	20	2	....	....	....
	Canada	WJC-A	5	3	2	5	....	....	....	0	....	....	....	....	....	....	....	....	....	....	....	....	....	....	....	....	....	....
1980-81	**Los Angeles Kings**	**NHL**	**71**	**18**	**25**	**43**	**15**	**17**	**32**	**8**	**2**	**0**	**2**	**92**	**19.6**	**59**	**13**	**47**	**1**	**0**	**4**	**0**	**1**	**1**	**0**	**0**	**0**	**0**
1981-82	**Los Angeles Kings**	**NHL**	**77**	**30**	**38**	**68**	**24**	**25**	**49**	**23**	**5**	**1**	**0**	**157**	**19.1**	**91**	**16**	**93**	**3**	**–15**	**9**	**1**	**4**	**5**	**0**	**0**	**0**	**0**
1982-83	**Los Angeles Kings**	**NHL**	**77**	**28**	**40**	**68**	**23**	**28**	**51**	**8**	**7**	**0**	**1**	**137**	**20.4**	**92**	**29**	**74**	**0**	**–11**	....	....	....	....	....	....	....	....
1983-84	**Los Angeles Kings**	**NHL**	**80**	**30**	**42**	**72**	**24**	**28**	**52**	**26**	**10**	**0**	**5**	**153**	**19.6**	**102**	**30**	**85**	**1**	**–12**	....	....	....	....	....	....	....	....
1984-85	**Los Angeles Kings**	**NHL**	**79**	**30**	**53**	**83**	**25**	**36**	**61**	**10**	**6**	**0**	**2**	**174**	**17.2**	**111**	**26**	**82**	**1**	**+4**	**3**	**0**	**1**	**1**	**0**	**0**	**0**	**0**
1985-86	**Los Angeles Kings**	**NHL**	**39**	**14**	**17**	**31**	**11**	**11**	**22**	**2**	**2**	**0**	**0**	**81**	**17.3**	**44**	**12**	**45**	**4**	**–9**	....	....	....	....	....	....	....	....
	Canada	WEC-A	10	3	2	5	....	....	....	4	....	....	....	....	....	....	....	....	....	....	....	....	....	....	....	....	....	....
1986-87	**Los Angeles Kings**	**NHL**	**76**	**19**	**42**	**61**	**16**	**30**	**46**	**48**	**4**	**0**	**2**	**162**	**11.7**	**82**	**23**	**70**	**1**	**–10**	**5**	**3**	**2**	**5**	**0**	**1**	**0**	**0**
1987-88	**Los Angeles Kings**	**NHL**	**68**	**16**	**35**	**51**	**14**	**25**	**39**	**18**	**2**	**0**	**1**	**120**	**13.3**	**78**	**24**	**62**	**1**	**–7**	**1**	**0**	**0**	**0**	**0**	**0**	**0**	**0**
1988-89			DID NOT PLAY – INJURED																									
1989-90	**Los Angeles Kings**	**NHL**	**11**	**1**	**1**	**2**	**1**	**1**	**2**	**0**	**0**	**0**	**1**	**7**	**14.3**	**3**	**0**	**5**	**1**	**–1**	....	....	....	....	....	....	....	....
	NHL Totals		**578**	**186**	**293**	**479**	**153**	**201**	**354**	**143**	**38**	**1**	**14**	**1083**	**17.2**	**662**	**173**	**563**	**13**		**22**	**4**	**8**	**12**	**0**	**1**	**0**	**0**

OHA First All-Star Team (1980)

• Missed entire 1988-89 season after injuring knee in game vs. Boston, March 10, 1988.

• FRANCESCHETTI, LOU

Lou Franceschetti RW – L. 6', 200 lbs. b: Toronto, Ont., 3/28/1958. Washington's 8th choice, 71st overall, in 1978 Amateur Draft.

1976-77	Niagara Falls Flyers	OHA	61	23	30	53	....	....	....	80	....	....	....	....	....	....	....	....	....	....	....	....	....	....	....	....	....	....
1977-78	Niagara Falls Flyers	OHA	62	40	50	90	....	....	....	46	....	....	....	....	....	....	....	....	....	....	....	....	....	....	....	....	....	....
1978-79	Saginaw Gears	IHL	2	1	1	2	....	....	....	0	....	....	....	....	....	....	....	....	....	....	....	....	....	....	....	....	....	....
	Port Huron Flags	IHL	76	45	58	103	....	....	....	131	....	....	....	....	....	....	....	....	....	....	....	....	....	....	....	....	....	....
1979-80	Port Huron Flags	IHL	15	3	8	11	....	....	....	31	....	....	....	....	....	....	....	....	....	....	....	....	....	....	....	....	....	....
	Hershey Bears	AHL	65	27	29	56	....	....	....	58	....	....	....	....	....	....	....	....	....	....	14	6	9	15	32	....	....	....
1980-81	Hershey Bears	AHL	79	32	36	68	....	....	....	173	....	....	....	....	....	....	....	....	....	....	10	3	7	10	30	....	....	....
1981-82	**Washington Capitals**	**NHL**	**30**	**2**	**10**	**12**	**2**	**7**	**9**	**23**	**0**	**0**	**1**	**25**	**8.0**	**24**	**6**	**22**	**0**	**–4**	....	....	....	....	....	....	....	....
	Hershey Bears	AHL	50	22	33	55	....	....	....	89	....	....	....	....	....	....	....	....	....	....	....	....	....	....	....	....	....	....
1982-83	Hershey Bears	AHL	80	31	44	75	....	....	....	176	....	....	....	....	....	....	....	....	....	....	5	1	2	3	16	....	....	....
1983-84	**Washington Capitals**	**NHL**	**2**	**0**	**0**	**0**	**0**	**0**	**0**	**0**	**0**	**0**	**0**	**2**	**0.0**	**0**	**0**	**2**	**0**	**–2**	**3**	**0**	**0**	**0**	**8**	**0**	**0**	**0**
	Hershey Bears	AHL	73	26	34	60	....	....	....	130	....	....	....	....	....	....	....	....	....	....	....	....	....	....	....	....	....	....
1984-85	**Washington Capitals**	**NHL**	**22**	**4**	**7**	**11**	**3**	**5**	**8**	**45**	**0**	**0**	**1**	**19**	**21.1**	**14**	**0**	**13**	**0**	**+1**	**5**	**1**	**1**	**2**	**15**	**0**	**0**	**0**
	Binghamton Whalers	AHL	52	29	43	72	....	....	....	75	....	....	....	....	....	....	....	....	....	....	....	....	....	....	....	....	....	....
1985-86	**Washington Capitals**	**NHL**	**76**	**7**	**14**	**21**	**6**	**9**	**15**	**131**	**0**	**0**	**2**	**57**	**12.3**	**41**	**1**	**44**	**0**	**–4**	**8**	**0**	**0**	**0**	**15**	**0**	**0**	**0**

			REGULAR SEASON																		PLAYOFFS							
Season	Club	League	GP	G	A	Pts	AG	AA	APts	PIM	PP	SH	GW	S	%	TGF	PGF	TGA	PGA	+/–	GP	G	A	Pts	PIM	PP	SH	GW
1986-87	**Washington Capitals**	**NHL**	**75**	**12**	**9**	**21**	**10**	**6**	**16**	**127**	**0**	**0**	**1**	**77**	**15.6**	**47**	**2**	**62**	**8**	**–9**	**7**	**0**	**0**	**0**	**23**	**0**	**0**	**0**
1987-88	**Washington Capitals**	**NHL**	**59**	**4**	**8**	**12**	**3**	**6**	**9**	**113**	**1**	**0**	**1**	**53**	**7.5**	**24**	**1**	**22**	**1**	**+2**	**4**	**0**	**0**	**0**	**14**	**0**	**0**	**0**
	Binghamton Whalers	AHL	6	2	4	6	....	....	....	4	....	....	....	....	....	....	....	....	....	....	....	....	....	....	....	....	....	....
1988-89	**Washington Capitals**	**NHL**	**63**	**7**	**10**	**17**	**6**	**7**	**13**	**123**	**0**	**0**	**0**	**55**	**12.7**	**28**	**1**	**34**	**3**	**–4**	**6**	**1**	**0**	**1**	**8**	**0**	**0**	**1**
	Baltimore Skipjacks	AHL	10	8	7	15	....	....	....	30	....	....	....	....	....	....	....	....	....	....	....	....	....	....	....	....	....	....
1989-90	**Toronto Maple Leafs**	**NHL**	**80**	**21**	**15**	**36**	**18**	**11**	**29**	**127**	**0**	**2**	**4**	**76**	**27.6**	**57**	**4**	**93**	**28**	**–12**	**5**	**0**	**1**	**1**	**26**	**0**	**0**	**0**
1990-91	**Toronto Maple Leafs**	**NHL**	**16**	**1**	**1**	**2**	**1**	**1**	**2**	**30**	**0**	**0**	**0**	**7**	**14.3**	**4**	**0**	**13**	**7**	**–2**	....	....	....	....	....	....	....	....
	Buffalo Sabres	**NHL**	**35**	**1**	**7**	**8**	**1**	**5**	**6**	**28**	**0**	**0**	**1**	**20**	**5.0**	**22**	**1**	**22**	**3**	**+2**	**6**	**1**	**0**	**1**	**2**	**0**	**0**	**0**
1991-92	**Buffalo Sabres**	**NHL**	**1**	**0**	**0**	**0**	**0**	**0**	**0**	**0**	**0**	**0**	**0**	**0**	**0.0**	**0**	**0**	**0**	**0**	**0**	....	....	....	....	....	....	....	....
	New Haven Nighthawks	AHL	25	6	7	13	....	....	....	59	....	....	....	....	....	....	....	....	....	....	....	....	....	....	....	....	....	....
	Rochester Americans	AHL	49	15	25	40	....	....	....	64	....	....	....	....	....	....	....	....	....	....	15	3	5	8	31	....	....	....
1992-93	Jacksonville Bullets	SHL	4	0	0	0	....	....	....	0	....	....	....	....	....	....	....	....	....	....	....	....	....	....	....	....	....	....
1993-94	Detroit Falcons	ColHL	2	1	1	2	....	....	....	6	....	....	....	....	....	....	....	....	....	....	....	....	....	....	....	....	....	....
1994-95	Minnesota Moose	IHL	4	1	0	1	....	....	....	12	....	....	....	....	....	....	....	....	....	....	3	0	0	0	0	....	....	....
	London Blues	ColHL	37	14	41	55	....	....	....	64	....	....	....	....	....	....	....	....	....	....	5	0	5	5	16	....	....	....
1995-96	Nashville Knights	ECHL	18	5	13	18	....	....	....	39	....	....	....	....	....	....	....	....	....	....	3	0	0	0	2	....	....	....
	NHL Totals		**459**	**59**	**81**	**140**	**50**	**57**	**107**	**747**	**1**	**2**	**11**	**391**	**15.1**	**261**	**16**	**327**	**50**		**44**	**3**	**2**	**5**	**111**	**0**	**0**	**1**

Traded to **Toronto** by **Washington** for Toronto's 5th round choice (Mark Ouimet) in 1990 Entry Draft, June 29, 1989. Traded to **Buffalo** by **Toronto** with Brian Curran for Mike Foligno and Buffalo's 8th round choice (Thomas Kucharcik) in 1991 Entry Draft, December 17, 1990.

• FRANCIS, BOBBY

Bobby Francis C – R. 5'9", 175 lbs. b: North Battleford, Sask., 12/5/1958.

1972-73	Brooklyn Stars	NYMHL	38	36	34	70	....	....	....	44	....	....	....	....	....	....	....	....	....	....	....	....	....	....	....	....	....	....
1973-74	Brooklyn Stars	NYMHL	41	41	53	94	....	....	....	63	....	....	....	....	....	....	....	....	....	....	12	*17	11	*28	24	....	....	....
1974-75	Bronx Shamrocks	NYMHL	40	53	59	112	....	....	....	71	....	....	....	....	....	....	....	....	....	....	....	....	....	....	....	....	....	....
1975-76	Beawick Vikings	NEJHL	40	62	*74	136	....	....	....	61	....	....	....	....	....	....	....	....	....	....	....	....	....	....	....	....	....	....
1976-77	University of New Hampshire	ECAC	DID NOT PLAY – FRESHMAN																		....	....	....	....	....	....	....	....
1977-78	University of New Hampshire	ECAC	40	9	44	53	....	....	....	....	....	....	....	....	....	....	....	....	....	....	....	....	....	....	....	....	....	....
1978-79	University of New Hampshire	ECAC	35	20	46	66	....	....	....	44	....	....	....	....	....	....	....	....	....	....	....	....	....	....	....	....	....	....
1979-80	University of New Hampshire	ECAC	28	19	23	42	....	....	....	30	....	....	....	....	....	....	....	....	....	....	....	....	....	....	....	....	....	....
1980-81	Birmingham Bulls	CHL	18	6	21	27	....	....	....	20	....	....	....	....	....	....	....	....	....	....	....	....	....	....	....	....	....	....
	Muskegon Mohawks	IHL	27	16	17	33	....	....	....	33	....	....	....	....	....	....	....	....	....	....	....	....	....	....	....	....	....	....
1981-82	Oklahoma City Stars	CHL	80	48	66	*114	....	....	....	76	....	....	....	....	....	....	....	....	....	....	4	1	2	3	11	....	....	....
1982-83	Colorado Flames	CHL	26	20	16	36	....	....	....	24	....	....	....	....	....	....	....	....	....	....	....	....	....	....	....	....	....	....
	Detroit Red Wings	**NHL**	**14**	**2**	**0**	**2**	**2**	**0**	**2**	**0**	**0**	**0**	**0**	**4**	**50.0**	**2**	**0**	**3**	**0**	**–1**	....	....	....	....	....	....	....	....
	Adirondack Red Wings	AHL	17	3	8	11	....	....	....	0	....	....	....	....	....	....	....	....	....	....	....	....	....	....	....	....	....	....
1983-84	Colorado Flames	CHL	68	32	50	82	....	....	....	53	....	....	....	....	....	....	....	....	....	....	1	0	1	1	0	....	....	....
1984-85	Salt Lake Golden Eagles	IHL	53	24	16	40	....	....	....	36	....	....	....	....	....	....	....	....	....	....	6	1	1	2	0	....	....	....
1985-86	Salt Lake Golden Eagles	IHL	82	32	44	76	....	....	....	163	....	....	....	....	....	....	....	....	....	....	5	0	4	4	10	....	....	....
1986-87	Salt Lake Golden Eagles	IHL	82	29	69	98	....	....	....	86	....	....	....	....	....	....	....	....	....	....	17	9	8	17	13	....	....	....
	NHL Totals		**14**	**2**	**0**	**2**	**2**	**0**	**2**	**0**	**0**	**0**	**0**	**4**	**50.0**	**2**	**0**	**3**	**0**		....	....	....	....	....	....	....	....

CHL First All-Star Team (1982) • Won Ken McKenzie Trophy (CHL's Rookie of the Year) (1982) • Won Tommy Ivan Trophy (CHL's MVP) (1982)

Signed as a free agent by **Calgary**, October 27, 1980. Traded to **Detroit** by **Calgary** for the rights to Yves Courteau, December 2, 1982.

• FRANCIS, RON

Ron Francis C – L. 6'3", 200 lbs. b: Sault Ste. Marie, Ont., 3/1/1963. Hartford's 1st choice, 4th overall, in 1981 Entry Draft.

1980-81	Sault Ste. Marie Greyhounds	OHA	64	26	43	69	....	....	....	33	....	....	....	....	....	....	....	....	....	....	19	7	8	15	34	....	....	....
1981-82	Sault Ste. Marie Greyhounds	OHL	25	18	30	48	....	....	....	46	....	....	....	....	....	....	....	....	....	....	....	....	....	....	....	....	....	....
	Hartford Whalers	**NHL**	**59**	**25**	**43**	**68**	**20**	**28**	**40**	**51**	**12**	**0**	**1**	**163**	**15.3**	**91**	**38**	**93**	**27**	**–13**	....	....	....	....	....	....	....	....
1982-83	**Hartford Whalers**	**NHL**	**79**	**31**	**59**	**90**	**25**	**41**	**66**	**60**	**4**	**2**	**4**	**212**	**14.6**	**114**	**33**	**120**	**23**	**–25**	....	....	....	....	....	....	....	....
1983-84	**Hartford Whalers**	**NHL**	**72**	**23**	**60**	**83**	**19**	**41**	**60**	**45**	**5**	**0**	**5**	**202**	**11.4**	**119**	**59**	**78**	**8**	**–10**	....	....	....	....	....	....	....	....
1984-85	**Hartford Whalers**	**NHL**	**80**	**24**	**57**	**81**	**20**	**30**	**60**	**66**	**4**	**0**	**1**	**195**	**12.3**	**129**	**63**	**95**	**6**	**–23**	....	....	....	....	....	....	....	....
	Canada	WEC-A	10	2	5	7	....	....	....	2	....	....	....	....	....	....	....	....	....	....	....	....	....	....	....	....	....	....
1985-86	**Hartford Whalers**	**NHL**	**53**	**24**	**53**	**77**	**19**	**36**	**55**	**24**	**7**	**1**	**4**	**120**	**20.0**	**113**	**48**	**64**	**7**	**+8**	**10**	**1**	**2**	**3**	**4**	**0**	**0**	**0**
1986-87	**Hartford Whalers**	**NHL**	**75**	**30**	**63**	**93**	**26**	**46**	**72**	**45**	**7**	**0**	**7**	**189**	**15.9**	**140**	**61**	**70**	**1**	**+10**	**6**	**2**	**2**	**4**	**6**	**1**	**0**	**0**
1987-88	**Hartford Whalers**	**NHL**	**80**	**25**	**50**	**75**	**21**	**36**	**57**	**87**	**11**	**1**	**3**	**172**	**14.5**	**104**	**51**	**71**	**10**	**–8**	**6**	**2**	**5**	**7**	**2**	**1**	**0**	**0**
1988-89	**Hartford Whalers**	**NHL**	**69**	**29**	**48**	**77**	**25**	**34**	**59**	**36**	**8**	**0**	**4**	**156**	**18.6**	**116**	**49**	**83**	**20**	**+4**	**4**	**0**	**2**	**2**	**0**	**0**	**0**	**0**
1989-90	**Hartford Whalers**	**NHL**	**80**	**32**	**69**	**101**	**28**	**49**	**77**	**73**	**15**	**1**	**5**	**170**	**18.8**	**137**	**61**	**77**	**14**	**+13**	**7**	**3**	**3**	**6**	**8**	**1**	**0**	**0**
1990-91	**Hartford Whalers**	**NHL**	**67**	**21**	**55**	**76**	**19**	**42**	**61**	**51**	**10**	**1**	**6**	**149**	**14.1**	**97**	**40**	**70**	**11**	**–2**	....	....	....	....	....	....	....	....
	Pittsburgh Penguins	**NHL**	**14**	**2**	**9**	**11**	**2**	**7**	**9**	**21**	**0**	**0**	**1**	**25**	**8.0**	**22**	**6**	**17**	**1**	**0**	**24**	**7**	**10**	**17**	**24**	**0**	**0**	**4**
1991-92	**Pittsburgh Penguins**	**NHL**	**70**	**21**	**33**	**54**	**19**	**25**	**44**	**30**	**5**	**1**	**2**	**121**	**17.4**	**107**	**44**	**89**	**19**	**–7**	**21**	**8**	***19**	**27**	**6**	**2**	**0**	**2**
1992-93	**Pittsburgh Penguins**	**NHL**	**84**	**24**	**76**	**100**	**20**	**52**	**72**	**68**	**9**	**2**	**4**	**215**	**11.2**	**156**	**84**	**96**	**30**	**+6**	**12**	**6**	**11**	**17**	**19**	**1**	**0**	**1**
1993-94	**Pittsburgh Penguins**	**NHL**	**82**	**27**	**66**	**93**	**25**	**51**	**76**	**62**	**8**	**0**	**2**	**216**	**12.5**	**134**	**60**	**111**	**34**	**–3**	**6**	**0**	**2**	**2**	**6**	**0**	**0**	**0**
1994-95	**Pittsburgh Penguins**	**NHL**	**44**	**11**	***48**	**59**	**19**	**71**	**90**	**18**	**3**	**0**	**1**	**94**	**11.7**	**77**	**25**	**43**	**21**	**+30**	**12**	**6**	**13**	**19**	**4**	**2**	**0**	**0**
1995-96	**Pittsburgh Penguins**	**NHL**	**77**	**27**	***92**	**119**	**27**	**75**	**102**	**56**	**12**	**1**	**4**	**158**	**17.1**	**189**	**92**	**101**	**29**	**+25**	**11**	**3**	**6**	**9**	**4**	**2**	**0**	**1**
1996-97	**Pittsburgh Penguins**	**NHL**	**81**	**27**	**63**	**90**	**29**	**56**	**85**	**20**	**10**	**1**	**2**	**183**	**14.8**	**141**	**50**	**110**	**26**	**+7**	**5**	**1**	**2**	**3**	**2**	**1**	**0**	**0**
1997-98	**Pittsburgh Penguins**	**NHL**	**81**	**25**	**62**	**87**	**29**	**61**	**90**	**20**	**7**	**0**	**5**	**189**	**13.2**	**126**	**50**	**73**	**9**	**+12**	**6**	**1**	**5**	**6**	**2**	**0**	**0**	**0**
	NHL Totals		**1247**	**428**	**1006**	**1434**	**392**	**790**	**1182**	**833**	**137**	**11**	**61**	**2929**	**14.6**	**2112**	**914**	**1470**	**296**		**130**	**40**	**82**	**122**	**87**	**11**	**0**	**8**

Won Alka-Seltzer Plus Award (1995) • Won Frank J. Selke Trophy (1995) • Won Lady Byng Trophy (1995, 1998)

Played in NHL All-Star Game (1983, 1985, 1990, 1996)

Traded to **Pittsburgh** by **Hartford** with Grant Jennings and Ulf Samuelsson for John Cullen, Jeff Parker and Zarley Zalapski, March 4, 1991. Signed as a free agent by **Carolina**, July 13, 1998.

• FRASER, CURT

Curt "Frazz" Fraser LW – L. 6'1", 200 lbs. b: Cincinnati, OH, 1/12/1958. Vancouver's 2nd choice, 22nd overall, in 1978 Amateur Draft.

1973-74	Kelowna Buckeroos	BCJHL	52	32	32	64	....	....	....	85	....	....	....	....	....	....	....	....	....	....	....	....	....	....	....	....	....	....
1974-75	Victoria Cougars	WCJHL	68	17	32	49	....	....	....	105	....	....	....	....	....	....	....	....	....	....	....	....	....	....	....	....	....	....
1975-76	Victoria Cougars	WCJHL	71	43	64	107	....	....	....	167	....	....	....	....	....	....	....	....	....	....	....	....	....	....	....	....	....	....
1976-77	Victoria Cougars	WCJHL	60	34	41	75	....	....	....	82	....	....	....	....	....	....	....	....	....	....	4	4	2	6	4	....	....	....
1977-78	Victoria Cougars	WCJHL	66	48	44	92	....	....	....	256	....	....	....	....	....	....	....	....	....	....	13	10	7	17	28	....	....	....
	Canada	WJC-A	5	0	2	2	....	....	....	0	....	....	....	....	....	....	....	....	....	....	....	....	....	....	....	....	....	....
1978-79	**Vancouver Canucks**	**NHL**	**78**	**16**	**19**	**35**	**15**	**14**	**29**	**116**	**2**	**0**	**2**	**184**	**8.7**	**61**	**7**	**52**	**1**	**–7**	**3**	**0**	**2**	**2**	**6**	**0**	**0**	**0**
1979-80	**Vancouver Canucks**	**NHL**	**78**	**17**	**25**	**42**	**15**	**19**	**34**	**143**	**0**	**0**	**3**	**148**	**11.5**	**58**	**0**	**51**	**0**	**+7**	**4**	**0**	**0**	**0**	**2**	**0**	**0**	**0**
1980-81	**Vancouver Canucks**	**NHL**	**77**	**25**	**24**	**49**	**21**	**17**	**38**	**118**	**7**	**0**	**2**	**188**	**13.3**	**68**	**22**	**65**	**0**	**–19**	**3**	**1**	**0**	**1**	**2**	**0**	**0**	**0**
1981-82	**Vancouver Canucks**	**NHL**	**79**	**28**	**39**	**67**	**22**	**26**	**48**	**175**	**11**	**0**	**5**	**233**	**12.0**	**95**	**28**	**65**	**0**	**+2**	**17**	**3**	**7**	**10**	**98**	**0**	**0**	**0**
1982-83	**Vancouver Canucks**	**NHL**	**36**	**6**	**7**	**13**	**5**	**5**	**10**	**99**	**2**	**0**	**0**	**67**	**9.0**	**25**	**7**	**25**	**0**	**–7**	....	....	....	....	....	....	....	....
	Chicago Black Hawks	**NHL**	**38**	**6**	**13**	**19**	**5**	**9**	**14**	**77**	**0**	**0**	**2**	**42**	**14.3**	**29**	**2**	**25**	**0**	**+2**	**13**	**4**	**4**	**8**	**18**	**1**	**0**	**1**
1983-84	**Chicago Black Hawks**	**NHL**	**29**	**5**	**12**	**17**	**4**	**8**	**12**	**28**	**1**	**0**	**0**	**45**	**11.1**	**25**	**3**	**13**	**0**	**+9**	**5**	**0**	**0**	**0**	**14**	**0**	**0**	**0**
1984-85	**Chicago Black Hawks**	**NHL**	**73**	**25**	**25**	**50**	**20**	**17**	**37**	**109**	**4**	**0**	**5**	**136**	**18.4**	**77**	**8**	**66**	**0**	**+3**	**15**	**6**	**3**	**9**	**36**	**0**	**0**	**1**
1985-86	**Chicago Black Hawks**	**NHL**	**61**	**29**	**39**	**68**	**23**	**26**	**49**	**84**	**7**	**0**	**1**	**144**	**20.1**	**90**	**26**	**53**	**0**	**+11**	**3**	**0**	**1**	**1**	**12**	**0**	**0**	**0**
1986-87	**Chicago Blackhawks**	**NHL**	**75**	**25**	**25**	**50**	**22**	**18**	**40**	**182**	**3**	**0**	**2**	**183**	**13.7**	**69**	**10**	**54**	**0**	**+5**	**2**	**1**	**1**	**2**	**10**	**0**	**0**	**0**
1987-88	United States	C Cup	5	0	1	1	....	....	....	4	....	....	....	....	....	....	....	....	....	....	....	....	....	....	....	....	....	....
	Minnesota North Stars	**NHL**	**10**	**1**	**1**	**2**	**1**	**1**	**2**	**20**	**0**	**0**	**0**	**21**	**4.8**	**6**	**2**	**10**	**0**	**–7**	....	....	....	....	....	....	....	....
	Chicago Blackhawks	**NHL**	**27**	**4**	**6**	**10**	**3**	**4**	**7**	**57**	**1**	**0**	**1**	**51**	**7.8**	**16**	**4**	**28**	**1**	**–13**	....	....	....	....	....	....	....	....
1988-89	**Minnesota North Stars**	**NHL**	**35**	**5**	**5**	**10**	**4**	**4**	**8**	**76**	**1**	**0**	**0**	**58**	**8.6**	**16**	**4**	**27**	**0**	**–15**	....	....	....	....	....	....	....	....
1989-90	**Minnesota North Stars**	**NHL**	**8**	**1**	**0**	**1**	**1**	**0**	**1**	**22**	**0**	**0**	**0**	**7**	**14.3**	**1**	**0**	**6**	**0**	**–5**	....	....	....	....	....	....	....	....
	NHL Totals		**704**	**193**	**240**	**433**	**161**	**168**	**329**	**1306**	**39**	**0**	**23**	**1507**	**12.8**	**625**	**123**	**538**	**2**		**65**	**15**	**18**	**33**	**198**	**1**	**0**	**2**

Traded to **Chicago** by **Vancouver** for Tony Tanti, January 3, 1983. Traded to **Minnesota** by **Chicago** for Dirk Graham, January 4, 1988.

• FRASER, IAIN

Iain Fraser C – L. 5'10", 175 lbs. b: Scarborough, Ont., 8/10/1969. NY Islanders' 10th choice, 233rd overall, in 1989 Entry Draft

1986-87	Oshawa Generals	OHL	5	1	2	3	....	....	....	0	....	....	....	....	....	....	....	....	....	....	....	....	....	....	....	....	....	....
1987-88	Oshawa Generals	OHL	16	4	4	8	....	....	....	22	....	....	....	....	....	....	....	....	....	....	6	2	3	5	2	....	....	....
1988-89	Oshawa Generals	OHL	62	33	57	90	....	....	....	87	....	....	....	....	....	....	....	....	....	....	6	2	8	10	12	....	....	....
1989-90	Oshawa Generals	OHL	56	40	65	105	....	....	....	75	....	....	....	....	....	....	....	....	....	....	17	10	*22	32	8	....	....	....

			REGULAR SEASON																		PLAYOFFS							
Season	**Club**	**League**	**GP**	**G**	**A**	**Pts**	**AG**	**AA**	**APts**	**PIM**	**PP**	**SH**	**GW**	**S**	**%**	**TGF**	**PGF**	**TGA**	**PGA**	**+/–**	**GP**	**G**	**A**	**Pts**	**PIM**	**PP**	**SH**	**GW**
1990-91	Capital District Islanders	AHL	32	5	13	18	....	....	....	16	....	....	....	....	....	....	....	....	....	....	....	....	....	....	....	....	....	....
	Richmond Renegades	ECHL	3	1	1	2	....	....	....	0	....	....	....	....	....	....	....	....	....	....	....	....	....	....	....	....	....	....
1991-92	Capital District Islanders	AHL	45	9	11	20	....	....	....	24	....	....	....	....	....	....	....	....	....	....	....	....	....	....	....	....	....	....
1992-93	**New York Islanders**	**NHL**	**7**	**2**	**2**	**4**	**2**	**1**	**3**	**2**	**1**	**0**	**0**	**7**	**28.6**	**5**	**2**	**4**	**0**	**–1**	....	....	....	....	....	....	....	....
	Capital District Islanders	AHL	74	41	69	110	....	....	....	16	....	....	....	....	....	....	....	....	....	....	4	0	1	1	0	....	....	....
1993-94	**Quebec Nordiques**	**NHL**	**60**	**17**	**20**	**37**	**16**	**15**	**31**	**23**	**2**	**0**	**2**	**109**	**15.6**	**47**	**8**	**52**	**8**	**–5**	....	....	....	....	....	....	....	....
1994-95	**Dallas Stars**	**NHL**	**4**	**0**	**0**	**0**	**0**	**0**	**0**	**0**	**0**	**0**	**0**	**2**	**0.0**	**1**	**0**	**4**	**0**	**–3**	....	....	....	....	....	....	....	....
	Edmonton Oilers	**NHL**	**9**	**3**	**0**	**3**	**5**	**0**	**5**	**0**	**0**	**0**	**0**	**5**	**60.0**	**4**	**0**	**1**	**0**	**+3**	....	....	....	....	....	....	....	....
	Denver Grizzlies	IHL	1	0	0	0	....	....	....	0	....	....	....	....	....	....	....	....	....	....	....	....	....	....	....	....	....	....
	Canada	WC-A	8	2	7	9	....	....	....	8	....	....	....	....	....	....	....	....	....	....	....	....	....	....	....	....	....	....
1995-96	**Winnipeg Jets**	**NHL**	**12**	**1**	**1**	**2**	**1**	**1**	**2**	**4**	**0**	**0**	**0**	**12**	**8.3**	**4**	**0**	**3**	**0**	**+1**	**4**	**0**	**0**	**0**	**0**	**0**	**0**	**0**
	Springfield Falcons	AHL	53	24	47	71	....	....	....	27	....	....	....	....	....	....	....	....	....	....	6	0	6	6	2	....	....	....
1996-97	**San Jose Sharks**	**NHL**	**2**	**0**	**0**	**0**	**0**	**0**	**0**	**2**	**0**	**0**	**0**	**0**	**0.0**	**0**	**0**	**1**	**0**	**–1**	....	....	....	....	....	....	....	....
	Kentucky Thoroughblades	AHL	57	27	33	60	....	....	....	24	....	....	....	....	....	....	....	....	....	....	....	....	....	....	....	....	....	....
1997-98	Kansas City Blades	IHL	77	16	44	60	....	....	....	45	....	....	....	....	....	....	....	....	....	....	11	2	6	8	6	....	....	....
	NHL Totals		**94**	**23**	**23**	**46**	**24**	**17**	**41**	**31**	**3**	**0**	**2**	**135**	**17.0**	**61**	**10**	**65**	**8**		**4**	**0**	**0**	**0**	**0**	**0**	**0**	**0**

Memorial Cup All-Star Team (1990) • Won Stafford Smythe Memorial Trophy (Memorial Cup Tournament MVP) (1990) • AHL Second All-Star Team (1993)

Signed as a free agent by **Quebec**, August 3, 1993. Traded to **Dallas** by **Quebec** for Dallas' 7th round choice (Dan Hinote) in 1996 Entry Draft, January 31, 1995. Claimed on waivers by **Edmonton** from **Dallas**, March 3, 1995. Signed as a free agent by **Winnipeg**, October 11, 1995. Signed as a free agent by **San Jose**, September 1, 1996.

● FRASER, SCOTT

Scott Fraser C – R. 6'1", 178 lbs. b: Moncton, N.B., 5/3/1972. Montreal's 12th choice, 193rd overall, in 1991 Entry Draft.

Season	Club	League	GP	G	A	Pts	AG	AA	APts	PIM	PP	SH	GW	S	%	TGF	PGF	TGA	PGA	+/–	GP	G	A	Pts	PIM	PP	SH	GW
1990-91	Dartmouth College	ECAC	24	10	10	20	....	....	....	30	....	....	....	....	....	....	....	....	....	....	....	....	....	....	....	....	....	....
1991-92	Dartmouth College	ECAC	24	11	7	18	....	....	....	60	....	....	....	....	....	....	....	....	....	....	....	....	....	....	....	....	....	....
1992-93	Dartmouth College	ECAC	26	21	23	44	....	....	....	13	....	....	....	....	....	....	....	....	....	....	....	....	....	....	....	....	....	....
	Canada	Nat-Team	5	1	0	1	....	....	....	0	....	....	....	....	....	....	....	....	....	....	....	....	....	....	....	....	....	....
1993-94	Dartmouth College	ECAC	24	17	13	30	....	....	....	34	....	....	....	....	....	....	....	....	....	....	....	....	....	....	....	....	....	....
	Canada	Nat-Team	4	0	1	1	....	....	....	4	....	....	....	....	....	....	....	....	....	....	....	....	....	....	....	....	....	....
1994-95	Fredericton Canadiens	AHL	65	23	25	48	....	....	....	36	....	....	....	....	....	....	....	....	....	....	16	3	5	8	14	....	....	....
	Wheeling Thunderbirds	ECHL	8	4	2	6	....	....	....	8	....	....	....	....	....	....	....	....	....	....	....	....	....	....	....	....	....	....
1995-96	**Montreal Canadiens**	**NHL**	**15**	**2**	**0**	**2**	**2**	**0**	**2**	**4**	**0**	**0**	**0**	**9**	**22.2**	**3**	**0**	**4**	**0**	**–1**	....	....	....	....	....	....	....	....
	Fredericton Canadiens	AHL	58	37	37	74	....	....	....	43	....	....	....	....	....	....	....	....	....	....	10	9	7	16	2	....	....	....
1996-97	Fredericton Canadiens	AHL	7	3	8	11	....	....	....	0	....	....	....	....	....	....	....	....	....	....	....	....	....	....	....	....	....	....
	Saint John Flames	AHL	37	22	10	32	....	....	....	24	....	....	....	....	....	....	....	....	....	....	....	....	....	....	....	....	....	....
	San Antonio Dragons	IHL	8	0	1	1	....	....	....	2	....	....	....	....	....	....	....	....	....	....	....	....	....	....	....	....	....	....
	Carolina Monarchs	AHL	18	9	19	28	....	....	....	12	....	....	....	....	....	....	....	....	....	....	....	....	....	....	....	....	....	....
1997-98	**Edmonton Oilers**	**NHL**	**29**	**12**	**11**	**23**	**14**	**11**	**25**	**6**	**6**	**0**	**2**	**61**	**19.7**	**30**	**16**	**8**	**0**	**+6**	**11**	**1**	**1**	**2**	**0**	**0**	**0**	**0**
	Hamilton Bulldogs	AHL	50	29	32	61	....	....	....	26	....	....	....	....	....	....	....	....	....	....	....	....	....	....	....	....	....	....
	NHL Totals		**44**	**14**	**11**	**25**	**16**	**11**	**27**	**10**	**6**	**0**	**2**	**70**	**20.0**	**33**	**16**	**12**	**0**		**11**	**1**	**1**	**2**	**0**	**0**	**0**	**0**

ECAC Second All-Star Team (1993)

Traded to **Calgary** by **Montreal** for David Ling and Calgary's 6th round choice in 1998 Entry Draft, October 24, 1996. Signed as a free agent by **Edmonton**, July 28, 1997. Signed as a free agent by **NY Rangers**, July 2, 1998.

● FRAWLEY, DAN

Dan Frawley RW – R. 6'1", 195 lbs. b: Sturgeon Falls, Ont., 6/2/1962. Chicago's 15th choice, 204th overall, in 1980 Entry Draft.

Season	Club	League	GP	G	A	Pts	AG	AA	APts	PIM	PP	SH	GW	S	%	TGF	PGF	TGA	PGA	+/–	GP	G	A	Pts	PIM	PP	SH	GW
1979-80	Sudbury Wolves	OHA	63	21	26	47	....	....	....	67	....	....	....	....	....	....	....	....	....	....	8	0	1	1	2	....	....	....
1980-81	Cornwall Royals	OHA	28	10	14	24	....	....	....	76	....	....	....	....	....	....	....	....	....	....	18	5	12	17	37	....	....	....
1981-82	Cornwall Royals	OHL	64	27	50	77	....	....	....	239	....	....	....	....	....	....	....	....	....	....	5	3	8	11	19	....	....	....
1982-83	Springfield Indians	AHL	80	30	27	57	....	....	....	107	....	....	....	....	....	....	....	....	....	....	....	....	....	....	....	....	....	....
1983-84	**Chicago Black Hawks**	**NHL**	**3**	**0**	**0**	**0**	**0**	**0**	**0**	**0**	**0**	**0**	**0**	**2**	**0.0**	**0**	**0**	**1**	**0**	**–1**	....	....	....	....	....	....	....	....
	Springfield Indians	AHL	69	22	34	56	....	....	....	137	....	....	....	....	....	....	....	....	....	....	4	0	1	1	12	....	....	....
1984-85	**Chicago Black Hawks**	**NHL**	**30**	**4**	**3**	**7**	**3**	**2**	**5**	**64**	**0**	**0**	**1**	**24**	**16.7**	**12**	**0**	**15**	**1**	**–2**	**1**	**0**	**0**	**0**	**0**	**0**	**0**	**0**
	Milwaukee Admirals	IHL	26	11	12	23	....	....	....	125	....	....	....	....	....	....	....	....	....	....	....	....	....	....	....	....	....	....
1985-86	**Pittsburgh Penguins**	**NHL**	**69**	**10**	**11**	**21**	**8**	**7**	**15**	**174**	**4**	**0**	**1**	**79**	**12.7**	**33**	**11**	**42**	**1**	**–19**	....	....	....	....	....	....	....	....
1986-87	**Pittsburgh Penguins**	**NHL**	**78**	**14**	**14**	**28**	**12**	**10**	**22**	**218**	**0**	**0**	**1**	**109**	**12.8**	**41**	**2**	**49**	**0**	**–10**	....	....	....	....	....	....	....	....
1987-88	**Pittsburgh Penguins**	**NHL**	**47**	**6**	**8**	**14**	**5**	**6**	**11**	**152**	**1**	**2**	**1**	**66**	**9.1**	**23**	**2**	**34**	**13**	**0**	....	....	....	....	....	....	....	....
1988-89	**Pittsburgh Penguins**	**NHL**	**46**	**3**	**4**	**7**	**3**	**3**	**6**	**66**	**0**	**0**	**1**	**37**	**8.1**	**15**	**1**	**15**	**0**	**–1**	....	....	....	....	....	....	....	....
	Muskegon Lumberjacks	IHL	24	12	16	28	....	....	....	35	....	....	....	....	....	....	....	....	....	....	14	6	4	10	31	....	....	....
1989-90	Muskegon Lumberjacks	IHL	82	31	47	78	....	....	....	165	....	....	....	....	....	....	....	....	....	....	15	9	12	21	51	....	....	....
1990-91	Rochester Americans	AHL	74	15	31	46	....	....	....	152	....	....	....	....	....	....	....	....	....	....	14	4	7	11	34	....	....	....
1991-92	Rochester Americans	AHL	78	28	23	51	....	....	....	208	....	....	....	....	....	....	....	....	....	....	16	7	5	12	35	....	....	....
1992-93	Rochester Americans	AHL	75	17	27	44	....	....	....	216	....	....	....	....	....	....	....	....	....	....	17	1	7	8	70	....	....	....
1993-94			DID NOT PLAY – RETIRED																									
1994-95	Rochester Americans	AHL	77	12	15	27	....	....	....	194	....	....	....	....	....	....	....	....	....	....	19	5	6	11	8	....	....	....
1995-96	Rochester Americans	AHL	77	11	22	33	....	....	....	115	....	....	....	....	....	....	....	....	....	....	10	2	2	4	8	....	....	....
	NHL Totals		**273**	**37**	**40**	**77**	**31**	**28**	**59**	**674**	**5**	**2**	**5**	**317**	**11.7**	**124**	**16**	**156**	**15**		**1**	**0**	**0**	**0**	**0**	**0**	**0**	**0**

Claimed by **Pittsburgh** from **Chicago** in Waiver Draft, October 7, 1985.

● FREER, MARK

Mark Freer C – L. 5'10", 180 lbs. b: Peterborough, Ont., 7/14/1968.

Season	Club	League	GP	G	A	Pts	AG	AA	APts	PIM	PP	SH	GW	S	%	TGF	PGF	TGA	PGA	+/–	GP	G	A	Pts	PIM	PP	SH	GW
1985-86	Peterborough Petes	OHL	65	16	28	44	....	....	....	24	....	....	....	....	....	....	....	....	....	....	14	3	4	7	13	....	....	....
1986-87	Peterborough Petes	OHL	65	39	43	82	....	....	....	44	....	....	....	....	....	....	....	....	....	....	12	2	6	8	5	....	....	....
	Philadelphia Flyers	**NHL**	**1**	**0**	**1**	**1**	**0**	**1**	**1**	**0**	**0**	**0**	**0**	**0**	**0.0**	**1**	**0**	**0**	**0**	**+1**	....	....	....	....	....	....	....	....
1987-88	Peterborough Petes	OHL	63	38	70	108	....	....	....	63	....	....	....	....	....	....	....	....	....	....	12	5	12	17	4	....	....	....
	Philadelphia Flyers	**NHL**	**1**	**0**	**0**	**0**	**0**	**0**	**0**	**0**	**0**	**0**	**0**	**0**	**0.0**	**0**	**0**	**2**	**0**	**–2**	....	....	....	....	....	....	....	....
1988-89	**Philadelphia Flyers**	**NHL**	**5**	**0**	**1**	**1**	**0**	**1**	**1**	**0**	**0**	**0**	**0**	**1**	**0.0**	**1**	**0**	**1**	**0**	**0**	....	....	....	....	....	....	....	....
	Hershey Bears	AHL	75	30	49	79	....	....	....	77	....	....	....	....	....	....	....	....	....	....	12	4	6	10	2	....	....	....
1989-90	**Philadelphia Flyers**	**NHL**	**2**	**0**	**0**	**0**	**0**	**0**	**0**	**0**	**0**	**0**	**0**	**2**	**0.0**	**0**	**0**	**0**	**0**	**0**	....	....	....	....	....	....	....	....
	Hershey Bears	AHL	65	28	36	64	....	....	....	31	....	....	....	....	....	....	....	....	....	....	....	....	....	....	....	....	....	....
1990-91	Hershey Bears	AHL	77	18	44	62	....	....	....	45	....	....	....	....	....	....	....	....	....	....	7	1	3	4	17	....	....	....
1991-92	**Philadelphia Flyers**	**NHL**	**50**	**6**	**7**	**13**	**5**	**5**	**10**	**18**	**0**	**0**	**2**	**41**	**14.6**	**16**	**1**	**17**	**1**	**–1**	....	....	....	....	....	....	....	....
	Hershey Bears	AHL	31	13	11	24	....	....	....	38	....	....	....	....	....	....	....	....	....	....	6	0	3	3	2	....	....	....
1992-93	**Ottawa Senators**	**NHL**	**63**	**10**	**14**	**24**	**8**	**10**	**18**	**39**	**3**	**3**	**0**	**80**	**12.5**	**42**	**15**	**86**	**24**	**–35**	....	....	....	....	....	....	....	....
1993-94	**Calgary Flames**	**NHL**	**2**	**0**	**0**	**0**	**0**	**0**	**0**	**4**	**0**	**0**	**0**	**0**	**0.0**	**0**	**0**	**0**	**0**	**0**	....	....	....	....	....	....	....	....
	Saint John Flames	AHL	77	33	53	86	....	....	....	45	....	....	....	....	....	....	....	....	....	....	7	2	4	6	16	....	....	....
1994-95	Houston Aeros	IHL	80	38	42	80	....	....	....	54	....	....	....	....	....	....	....	....	....	....	4	0	1	1	4	....	....	....
	Canada	WC-A	6	1	0	1	....	....	....	2	....	....	....	....	....	....	....	....	....	....	....	....	....	....	....	....	....	....
1995-96	Houston Aeros	IHL	80	22	31	53	....	....	....	67	....	....	....	....	....	....	....	....	....	....	....	....	....	....	....	....	....	....
1996-97	Houston Aeros	IHL	81	21	36	57	....	....	....	43	....	....	....	....	....	....	....	....	....	....	12	2	3	5	4	....	....	....
1997-98	Houston Aeros	IHL	74	14	38	52	....	....	....	41	....	....	....	....	....	....	....	....	....	....	4	2	2	4	4	....	....	....
	NHL Totals		**124**	**16**	**23**	**39**	**13**	**17**	**30**	**61**	**3**	**3**	**2**	**124**	**12.9**	**60**	**16**	**106**	**25**		....	....	....	....	....	....	....	....

Signed as a free agent by **Philadelphia**, October 7, 1986. Claimed by **Ottawa** from **Philadelphia** in Expansion Draft, June 18, 1992. Signed as a free agent by **Calgary**, August 10, 1993.

● FRIDAY, TIM

Tim Friday D – R. 6', 190 lbs. b: Burbank, CA, 3/5/1961.

Season	Club	League	GP	G	A	Pts	AG	AA	APts	PIM	PP	SH	GW	S	%	TGF	PGF	TGA	PGA	+/–	GP	G	A	Pts	PIM	PP	SH	GW
1981-82	RPI Engineers	ECAC	25	2	12	14	....	....	....	10	....	....	....	....	....	....	....	....	....	....	....	....	....	....	....	....	....	....
1982-83	RPI Engineers	ECAC	28	3	16	19	....	....	....	10	....	....	....	....	....	....	....	....	....	....	....	....	....	....	....	....	....	....
1983-84	RPI Engineers	ECAC	32	4	14	18	....	....	....	22	....	....	....	....	....	....	....	....	....	....	....	....	....	....	....	....	....	....
1984-85	RPI Engineers	ECAC	36	5	29	34	....	....	....	26	....	....	....	....	....	....	....	....	....	....	....	....	....	....	....	....	....	....
1985-86	**Detroit Red Wings**	**NHL**	**23**	**0**	**3**	**3**	**0**	**2**	**2**	**6**	**0**	**0**	**0**	**13**	**0.0**	**16**	**3**	**23**	**1**	**–9**	....	....	....	....	....	....	....	....
	Adirondack Red Wings	AHL	43	2	31	33	....	....	....	23	....	....	....	....	....	....	....	....	....	....	16	0	6	6	6	....	....	....
	NHL Totals		**23**	**0**	**3**	**3**	**0**	**2**	**2**	**6**	**0**	**0**	**0**	**13**	**0.0**	**16**	**3**	**23**	**1**		....	....	....	....	....	....	....	....

Signed as a free agent by **Detroit**, May 27, 1985.

• FRIDGEN, DAN

Dan Fridgen   LW – L. 5'11", 175 lbs.   b: Arnprior, Ont., 5/18/1959.

Season	Club	League	GP	G	A	Pts	AG	AA	APts	PIM	PP	SH	GW	S	%	TGF	PGF	TGA	PGA	+/–	Playoffs GP	G	A	Pts	PIM	PP	SH	GW
1978-79	Colgate University	ECAC	26	20	12	32	....	....	....	54	....	....	....	....	....	....	....	....	....	....	....	....	....	....	....	....	....	....
1979-80	Colgate University	ECAC	25	19	18	37	....	....	....	74	....	....	....	....	....	....	....	....	....	....	....	....	....	....	....	....	....	....
1980-81	Colgate University	ECAC	33	*37	31	68	....	....	....	*164	....	....	....	....	....	....	....	....	....	....	....	....	....	....	....	....	....	....
1981-82	Colgate University	ECAC	29	*38	17	55	....	....	....	95	....	....	....	....	....	....	....	....	....	....	....	....	....	....	....	....	....	....
	Hartford Whalers	**NHL**	**2**	**0**	**1**	**1**	**0**	**1**	**1**	**0**	**0**	**0**	**0**	**5**	**0.0**	**1**	**1**	**2**	**0**	**–2**	....	....	....	....	....	....	....	....
1982-83	**Hartford Whalers**	**NHL**	**11**	**2**	**2**	**4**	**2**	**1**	**3**	**2**	**0**	**0**	**0**	**12**	**16.7**	**8**	**0**	**6**	**0**	**+2**	....	....	....	....	....	....	....	....
	Binghamton Whalers	AHL	48	22	16	38	....	....	....	24	....	....	....	....	....	....	....	....	....	....	4	1	0	1	12	....	....	....
1983-84	Binghamton Whalers	AHL	77	23	27	50	....	....	....	61	....	....	....	....	....	....	....	....	....	....	....	....	....	....	....	....	....	....
	NHL Totals		**13**	**2**	**3**	**5**	**2**	**2**	**4**	**2**	**0**	**0**	**0**	**17**	**11.8**	**9**	**1**	**8**	**0**		....	....	....	....	....	....	....	....

ECAC Second All-Star Team (1981)

Signed as a free agent by **Hartford**, April 5, 1982.

• FRIEDMAN, DOUG

Doug Friedman   LW – L. 6'1", 195 lbs.   b: Cape Elizabeth, ME, 9/1/1971.   Quebec's 13th choice, 222nd overall, in 1991 Entry Draft.

Season	Club	League	GP	G	A	Pts	AG	AA	APts	PIM	PP	SH	GW	S	%	TGF	PGF	TGA	PGA	+/–	Playoffs GP	G	A	Pts	PIM	PP	SH	GW
1990-91	Boston University	H.E.	36	6	6	12	....	....	....	37	....	....	....	....	....	....	....	....	....	....	....	....	....	....	....	....	....	....
1991-92	Boston University	H.E.	34	11	8	19	....	....	....	42	....	....	....	....	....	....	....	....	....	....	....	....	....	....	....	....	....	....
1992-93	Boston University	H.E.	38	17	24	41	....	....	....	62	....	....	....	....	....	....	....	....	....	....	....	....	....	....	....	....	....	....
1993-94	Boston University	H.E.	41	9	23	32	....	....	....	110	....	....	....	....	....	....	....	....	....	....	....	....	....	....	....	....	....	....
1994-95	Cornwall Aces	AHL	55	6	9	15	....	....	....	56	....	....	....	....	....	....	....	....	....	....	3	0	0	0	0	....	....	....
1995-96	Cornwall Aces	AHL	80	12	22	34	....	....	....	178	....	....	....	....	....	....	....	....	....	....	8	1	1	2	17	....	....	....
1996-97	Hershey Bears	AHL	61	12	21	33	....	....	....	245	....	....	....	....	....	....	....	....	....	....	23	6	9	15	49	....	....	....
1997-98	**Edmonton Oilers**	**NHL**	**16**	**0**	**0**	**0**	**0**	**0**	**0**	**20**	**0**	**0**	**0**	**8**	**0.0**	**3**	**0**	**5**	**2**	**0**	....	....	....	....	....	....	....	....
	Hamilton Bulldogs	AHL	55	19	27	46	....	....	....	235	....	....	....	....	....	....	....	....	....	....	9	4	4	8	40	....	....	....
	NHL Totals		**16**	**0**	**0**	**0**	**0**	**0**	**0**	**20**	**0**	**0**	**0**	**8**	**0.0**	**3**	**0**	**5**	**2**		....	....	....	....	....	....	....	....

Signed as a free agent by **Edmonton**, July 14, 1997. Claimed by **Nashville** from **Edmonton** in Expansion Draft, June 26, 1998. Signed as a free agent by **NY Rangers**, July 2, 1998.

• FRIESEN, JEFF

Jeff Friesen   C – L. 6', 190 lbs.   b: Meadow Lake, Sask., 8/5/1976.   San Jose's 1st choice, 11th overall, in 1994 Entry Draft.

Season	Club	League	GP	G	A	Pts	AG	AA	APts	PIM	PP	SH	GW	S	%	TGF	PGF	TGA	PGA	+/–	Playoffs GP	G	A	Pts	PIM	PP	SH	GW
1991-92	Regina Pats	WHL	4	3	1	4	....	....	....	2	....	....	....	....	....	....	....	....	....	....	....	....	....	....	....	....	....	....
1992-93	Regina Pats	WHL	70	45	38	83	....	....	....	23	....	....	....	....	....	....	....	....	....	....	13	7	10	17	8	....	....	....
1993-94	Regina Pats	WHL	66	51	67	118	....	....	....	48	....	....	....	....	....	....	....	....	....	....	4	3	2	5	2	....	....	....
1994-95	Regina Pats	WHL	25	21	23	44	....	....	....	22	....	....	....	....	....	....	....	....	....	....	....	....	....	....	....	....	....	....
	Canada	WJC-A	7	5	2	7	....	....	....	4	....	....	....	....	....	....	....	....	....	....	....	....	....	....	....	....	....	....
	San Jose Sharks	**NHL**	**48**	**15**	**10**	**25**	**27**	**15**	**42**	**14**	**5**	**1**	**2**	**86**	**17.4**	**40**	**11**	**58**	**21**	**–8**	**11**	**1**	**5**	**6**	**4**	**0**	**0**	**0**
1995-96	**San Jose Sharks**	**NHL**	**79**	**15**	**31**	**46**	**15**	**25**	**40**	**42**	**2**	**0**	**0**	**123**	**12.2**	**73**	**19**	**102**	**29**	**–19**	....	....	....	....	....	....	....	....
	Canada	WC-A	8	2	0	2	....	....	....	6	....	....	....	....	....	....	....	....	....	....	....	....	....	....	....	....	....	....
1996-97	**San Jose Sharks**	**NHL**	**82**	**28**	**34**	**62**	**30**	**30**	**60**	**75**	**6**	**2**	**5**	**200**	**14.0**	**86**	**21**	**96**	**23**	**–8**	....	....	....	....	....	....	....	....
	Canada	WC-A	11	3	4	7	....	....	....	16	....	....	....	....	....	....	....	....	....	....	....	....	....	....	....	....	....	....
1997-98	**San Jose Sharks**	**NHL**	**79**	**31**	**32**	**63**	**36**	**31**	**67**	**40**	**7**	**6**	**7**	**186**	**16.7**	**86**	**30**	**64**	**16**	**+8**	**6**	**0**	**1**	**1**	**2**	**0**	**0**	**0**
	NHL Totals		**288**	**89**	**107**	**196**	**108**	**101**	**209**	**171**	**20**	**9**	**14**	**595**	**15.0**	**285**	**81**	**320**	**89**		**17**	**1**	**6**	**7**	**6**	**0**	**0**	**0**

Canadian Major Junior Rookie of the Year (1993) • NHL/Upper Deck All-Rookie Team (1995)

• FRIEST, RON

Ron Friest   LW – L. 5'11", 185 lbs.   b: Windsor, Ont., 11/4/1958.

Season	Club	League	GP	G	A	Pts	AG	AA	APts	PIM	PP	SH	GW	S	%	TGF	PGF	TGA	PGA	+/–	Playoffs GP	G	A	Pts	PIM	PP	SH	GW
1976-77	Niagara Falls Flyers	OHA	5	1	0	1	....	....	....	2	....	....	....	....	....	....	....	....	....	....	....	....	....	....	....	....	....	....
	Windsor Spitfires	OHA	57	19	18	37	....	....	....	52	....	....	....	....	....	....	....	....	....	....	9	4	3	7	11	....	....	....
1977-78	Windsor Spitfires	OHA	67	11	20	31	....	....	....	197	....	....	....	....	....	....	....	....	....	....	6	1	1	2	9	....	....	....
1978-79	Oklahoma City Stars	CHL	2	0	4	4	....	....	....	0	....	....	....	....	....	....	....	....	....	....	....	....	....	....	....	....	....	....
	Flint Generals	IHL	54	21	18	39	....	....	....	141	....	....	....	....	....	....	....	....	....	....	11	4	3	7	19	....	....	....
1979-80	Oklahoma City Stars	CHL	11	3	3	6	....	....	....	39	....	....	....	....	....	....	....	....	....	....	....	....	....	....	....	....	....	....
	Baltimore Clippers	EHL	48	35	40	75	....	....	....	162	....	....	....	....	....	....	....	....	....	....	10	8	1	9	49	....	....	....
1980-81	**Minnesota North Stars**	**NHL**	**4**	**1**	**0**	**1**	**1**	**0**	**1**	**10**	**0**	**0**	**0**	**6**	**16.7**	**1**	**0**	**3**	**0**	**–2**	....	....	....	....	....	....	....	....
	Oklahoma City Stars	CHL	71	25	20	45	....	....	....	170	....	....	....	....	....	....	....	....	....	....	3	2	1	3	7	....	....	....
1981-82	**Minnesota North Stars**	**NHL**	**10**	**0**	**0**	**0**	**0**	**0**	**0**	**31**	**0**	**0**	**0**	**5**	**0.0**	**1**	**0**	**5**	**0**	**–4**	**2**	**0**	**0**	**0**	**5**	**0**	**0**	**0**
	Nashville South Stars	CHL	68	32	31	63	....	....	....	100	....	....	....	....	....	....	....	....	....	....	....	....	....	....	....	....	....	....
1982-83	**Minnesota North Stars**	**NHL**	**50**	**6**	**7**	**13**	**5**	**5**	**10**	**150**	**0**	**0**	**0**	**44**	**13.6**	**18**	**0**	**22**	**0**	**–4**	**4**	**1**	**0**	**1**	**2**	**0**	**0**	**0**
	NHL Totals		**64**	**7**	**7**	**14**	**6**	**5**	**11**	**191**	**0**	**0**	**0**	**55**	**12.7**	**20**	**0**	**30**	**0**		**6**	**1**	**0**	**1**	**7**	**0**	**0**	**0**

Signed as a free agent by **Minnesota**, June 26, 1980.

• FRIG, LEN

Len Frig   D – R. 5'11", 190 lbs.   b: Lethbridge, Alta., 10/30/1950.   Chicago's 3rd choice, 42nd overall, in 1970 Amateur Draft.

Season	Club	League	GP	G	A	Pts	AG	AA	APts	PIM	PP	SH	GW	S	%	TGF	PGF	TGA	PGA	+/–	Playoffs GP	G	A	Pts	PIM	PP	SH	GW
1969-70	Calgary Centennials	WCJHL	59	9	15	24	....	....	....	119	....	....	....	....	....	....	....	....	....	....	....	....	....	....	....	....	....	....
1970-71	Calgary Centennials	WCJHL	51	13	32	45	....	....	....	175	....	....	....	....	....	....	....	....	....	....	....	....	....	....	....	....	....	....
1971-72	Dallas Black Hawks	CHL	66	4	30	34	....	....	....	224	....	....	....	....	....	....	....	....	....	....	12	1	8	9	22	....	....	....
1972-73	Dallas Black Hawks	CHL	72	10	22	32	....	....	....	105	....	....	....	....	....	....	....	....	....	....	7	1	2	3	14	....	....	....
	Chicago Black Hawks	**NHL**	....	....	....	....	....	....	....	....	**0**	**0**	**0**	**0**	**0.0**	**0**	**0**	**0**	**0**	**0**	**4**	**1**	**1**	**2**	**0**	**1**	**0**	**0**
1973-74	**Chicago Black Hawks**	**NHL**	**66**	**4**	**10**	**14**	**4**	**9**	**13**	**35**	**0**	**0**	**0**	**71**	**5.6**	**46**	**7**	**28**	**5**	**+16**	**7**	**1**	**0**	**1**	**0**	**1**	**0**	**0**
1974-75	**California Golden Seals**	**NHL**	**80**	**3**	**17**	**20**	**3**	**13**	**16**	**127**	**3**	**0**	**0**	**149**	**2.0**	**91**	**17**	**137**	**35**	**–28**	....	....	....	....	....	....	....	....
1975-76	**California Golden Seals**	**NHL**	**62**	**3**	**12**	**15**	**3**	**9**	**12**	**55**	**1**	**0**	**0**	**108**	**2.8**	**69**	**15**	**82**	**23**	**–5**	....	....	....	....	....	....	....	....
1976-77	**Cleveland Barons**	**NHL**	**66**	**2**	**7**	**9**	**2**	**6**	**8**	**213**	**0**	**0**	**0**	**81**	**2.5**	**47**	**1**	**97**	**20**	**–31**	....	....	....	....	....	....	....	....
1977-78	**St. Louis Blues**	**NHL**	**30**	**1**	**3**	**4**	**1**	**2**	**3**	**45**	**0**	**0**	**1**	**32**	**3.1**	**14**	**1**	**32**	**6**	**–13**	....	....	....	....	....	....	....	....
	Salt Lake Golden Eagles	CHL	29	3	7	10	....	....	....	104	....	....	....	....	....	....	....	....	....	....	6	1	0	1	33	....	....	....
1978-79	Salt Lake Golden Eagles	CHL	76	12	32	44	....	....	....	137	....	....	....	....	....	....	....	....	....	....	10	2	3	5	15	....	....	....
1979-80	**St. Louis Blues**	**NHL**	**7**	**0**	**2**	**2**	**0**	**2**	**2**	**4**	**0**	**0**	**0**	**12**	**0.0**	**5**	**0**	**12**	**2**	**–5**	**3**	**0**	**0**	**0**	**0**	**0**	**0**	**0**
	Salt Lake Golden Eagles	CHL	71	7	33	40	....	....	....	89	....	....	....	....	....	....	....	....	....	....	11	1	6	7	4	....	....	....
1980-81	Salt Lake Golden Eagles	CHL	74	9	48	57	....	....	....	194	....	....	....	....	....	....	....	....	....	....	13	1	2	3	29	....	....	....
1981-82			DID NOT PLAY																									
1982-83			DID NOT PLAY																									
1983-84			DID NOT PLAY																									
1984-85	Salt Lake Golden Eagles	IHL	78	3	16	19	....	....	....	110	....	....	....	....	....	....	....	....	....	....	5	0	2	2	11	....	....	....
1985-86	Salt Lake Golden Eagles	IHL	18	0	5	5	....	....	....	24	....	....	....	....	....	....	....	....	....	....	....	....	....	....	....	....	....	....
	NHL Totals		**311**	**13**	**51**	**64**	**13**	**41**	**54**	**479**	**4**	**0**	**1**	**453**	**2.9**	**272**	**41**	**388**	**91**		**14**	**2**	**1**	**3**	**0**	**2**	**0**	**0**

WCJHL All-Star Team (1971) • CHL First All-Star Team (1973, 1979, 1980) • Named CHL's Top Defenseman (1973)

Traded to **California** by **Chicago** with Mike Christie for Ivan Boldirev, May 24, 1974. Transferred to **Cleveland** after **California** franchise relocated, August 26, 1976. Traded to **St. Louis** by **Cleveland** for the rights to Mike Eaves, August 17, 1977.

• FRYCER, MIROSLAV

Miroslav "Mirko" Frycer   RW – L. 6', 200 lbs.   b: Ostrava, Czechoslovakia, 9/27/1959.

Season	Club	League	GP	G	A	Pts	AG	AA	APts	PIM	PP	SH	GW	S	%	TGF	PGF	TGA	PGA	+/–	Playoffs GP	G	A	Pts	PIM	PP	SH	GW
1977-78	TJ Vitovice	Czech.	34	12	10	22	....	....	....	24	....	....	....	....	....	....	....	....	....	....	....	....	....	....	....	....	....	....
	Czechoslovakia	WJC-A	6	2	1	3	....	....	....	2	....	....	....	....	....	....	....	....	....	....	....	....	....	....	....	....	....	....
1978-79	TJ Vitkovice	Czech.	44	22	12	34	....	....	....	....	....	....	....	....	....	....	....	....	....	....	....	....	....	....	....	....	....	....
	Czechoslovakia	WJC-A	6	1	0	1	....	....	....	8	....	....	....	....	....	....	....	....	....	....	....	....	....	....	....	....	....	....
	Czechoslovakia	WEC-A	1	0	0	0	....	....	....	2	....	....	....	....	....	....	....	....	....	....	....	....	....	....	....	....	....	....
1979-80	TJ Vitkovice	Czech.	44	31	15	46	....	....	....	....	....	....	....	....	....	....	....	....	....	....	....	....	....	....	....	....	....	....
	Czechoslovakia	Olympics	6	1	2	3	....	....	....	7	....	....	....	....	....	....	....	....	....	....	....	....	....	....	....	....	....	....
1980-81	TJ Vitkovice	Czech.	34	33	24	57	....	....	....	....	....	....	....	....	....	....	....	....	....	....	....	....	....	....	....	....	....	....
	Czechoslovakia	WEC-A	8	1	2	3	....	....	....	0	....	....	....	....	....	....	....	....	....	....	....	....	....	....	....	....	....	....
1981-82	**Quebec Nordiques**	**NHL**	**49**	**20**	**17**	**37**	**16**	**11**	**27**	**47**	**5**	**0**	**2**	**89**	**22.5**	**49**	**10**	**51**	**0**	**–12**	....	....	....	....	....	....	....	....
	Fredericton Express	AHL	11	9	5	14	....	....	....	16	....	....	....	....	....	....	....	....	....	....	....	....	....	....	....	....	....	....
	Toronto Maple Leafs	**NHL**	**10**	**4**	**6**	**10**	**3**	**4**	**7**	**31**	**1**	**0**	**2**	**23**	**17.4**	**11**	**2**	**16**	**0**	**–7**	....	....	....	....	....	....	....	....
1982-83	**Toronto Maple Leafs**	**NHL**	**67**	**25**	**30**	**55**	**21**	**21**	**42**	**90**	**5**	**0**	**4**	**133**	**18.8**	**81**	**23**	**56**	**0**	**+2**	**4**	**2**	**5**	**7**	**0**	**0**	**0**	**0**
1983-84	**Toronto Maple Leafs**	**NHL**	**47**	**10**	**16**	**26**	**8**	**11**	**19**	**55**	**1**	**0**	**2**	**78**	**12.8**	**39**	**14**	**49**	**0**	**–24**	....	....	....	....	....	....	....	....
1984-85	**Toronto Maple Leafs**	**NHL**	**65**	**25**	**30**	**55**	**20**	**20**	**40**	**55**	**5**	**0**	**1**	**182**	**13.7**	**76**	**22**	**64**	**3**	**–7**	....	....	....	....	....	....	....	....

			REGULAR SEASON																		PLAYOFFS							
Season	Club	League	GP	G	A	Pts	AG	AA	APts	PIM	PP	SH	GW	S	%	TGF	PGF	TGA	PGA	+/–	GP	G	A	Pts	PIM	PP	SH	GW
1985-86	**Toronto Maple Leafs**	**NHL**	**73**	**32**	**43**	**75**	**26**	**29**	**55**	**74**	**7**	**0**	**3**	**201**	**15.9**	**96**	**29**	**94**	**3**	**–24**	**10**	**1**	**3**	**4**	**10**	**0**	**0**	**0**
1986-87	**Toronto Maple Leafs**	**NHL**	**29**	**7**	**8**	**15**	**6**	**6**	**12**	**28**	**3**	**0**	**0**	**52**	**13.5**	**21**	**7**	**30**	**1**	**–15**	....	....	....	....	....	....	....	....
1987-88	**Toronto Maple Leafs**	**NHL**	**38**	**12**	**20**	**32**	**10**	**14**	**24**	**41**	**1**	**0**	**2**	**76**	**15.8**	**45**	**3**	**34**	**0**	**+8**	**3**	**0**	**0**	**0**	**6**	**0**	**0**	**0**
1988-89	**Detroit Red Wings**	**NHL**	**23**	**7**	**8**	**15**	**6**	**6**	**12**	**47**	**2**	**0**	**1**	**40**	**17.5**	**23**	**6**	**23**	**2**	**–4**	....	....	....	....	....	....	....	....
	Edmonton Oilers	**NHL**	**14**	**5**	**5**	**10**	**4**	**4**	**8**	**18**	**2**	**0**	**0**	**33**	**15.2**	**15**	**5**	**8**	**0**	**+2**	....	....	....	....	....	....	....	....
1989-90	EHC Freiburg	Germany	11	4	13	17	....	....	....	18	....	....	....	....	....	....	....	....	....	....	....	....	....	....	....	....	....	....
1990-91	EHC Freiburg	Germany	21	11	24	35	....	....	....	28	....	....	....	....	....	....	....	....	....	....	....	....	....	....	....	....	....	....
	NHL Totals		**415**	**147**	**183**	**330**	**120**	**126**	**246**	**486**	**32**	**0**	**17**	**907**	**16.2**	**456**	**121**	**425**	**9**		**17**	**3**	**8**	**11**	**16**	**0**	**0**	**0**

Played in NHL All-Star Game (1985)

Signed as a free agent by **Quebec**, April 2, 1980. Traded to Toronto to Quebec with Quebec's 7th round choice (Jeff Triano) in 1982 Entry Draft for Wilf Paiement, March 9, 1982. Traded to **Detroit** by **Toronto** for Darren Veitch, June 10, 1988. Traded to **Edmonton** by **Detroit** for Edmonton's 10th round choice (Rick Judson) in 1989 Entry Draft, January 3, 1989.

• FTOREK, ROBBIE

Robbie "Britz" Ftorek C/LW – L. 5'10", 155 lbs. b: Needham, MA, 1/2/1952. **USHOF**

Season	Club	League	GP	G	A	Pts	AG	AA	APts	PIM	PP	SH	GW	S	%	TGF	PGF	TGA	PGA	+/–	GP	G	A	Pts	PIM	PP	SH	GW
1970-71	Halifax Jr. Canadians	NSJHL	STATISTICS NOT AVAILABLE																									
1971-72	United States	Nat-Team	STATISTICS NOT AVAILABLE																									
	United States	Olympics	6	0	2	2	....	....	....	0	....	....	....	....	....	....	....	....	....	....	....	....	....	....	....	....	....	....
	United States	WEC-B	6	7	3	10	....	....	....	....	....	....	....	....	....	....	....	....	....	....	....	....	....	....	....	....	....	....
1972-73	**Detroit Red Wings**	**NHL**	**3**	**0**	**0**	**0**	**0**	**0**	**0**	**0**	**0**	**0**	**0**	**0**	**0.0**	**0**	**0**	**0**	**0**	**0**	....	....	....	....	....	....	....	....
	Virginia Wings	AHL	55	17	42	59	....	....	....	36	....	....	....	....	....	....	....	....	....	....	5	2	2	4	4	....	....	....
1973-74	**Detroit Red Wings**	**NHL**	**12**	**2**	**5**	**7**	**2**	**4**	**6**	**4**	**1**	**0**	**0**	**10**	**20.0**	**9**	**3**	**5**	**0**	**+1**	....	....	....	....	....	....	....	....
	Virginia Wings	AHL	65	24	42	66	....	....	....	37	....	....	....	....	....	....	....	....	....	....	....	....	....	....	....	....	....	....
1974-75	Tulsa Oilers	CHL	11	6	10	16	....	....	....	14	....	....	....	....	....	....	....	....	....	....	....	....	....	....	....	....	....	....
	Phoenix Roadrunners	WHA	53	31	37	68	....	....	....	29	....	....	....	....	....	....	....	....	....	....	5	2	5	7	2	....	....	....
1975-76	Phoenix Roadrunners	WHA	80	41	72	113	....	....	....	109	....	....	....	....	....	....	....	....	....	....	5	1	3	4	2	....	....	....
1976-77	United States	C Cup	5	3	2	5	....	....	....	16	....	....	....	....	....	....	....	....	....	....	....	....	....	....	....	....	....	....
	Phoenix Roadrunners	WHA	80	46	71	117	....	....	....	86	....	....	....	....	....	....	....	....	....	....	....	....	....	....	....	....	....	....
1977-78	Cincinnati Stingers	WHA	80	59	50	109	....	....	....	54	....	....	....	....	....	....	....	....	....	....	....	....	....	....	....	....	....	....
1978-79	Cincinnati Stingers	WHA	80	39	*77	116	....	....	....	87	....	....	....	....	....	....	....	....	....	....	3	3	2	5	6	....	....	....
1979-80	**Quebec Nordiques**	**NHL**	**52**	**18**	**33**	**51**	**16**	**25**	**41**	**28**	**7**	**0**	**3**	**112**	**16.1**	**76**	**30**	**47**	**7**	**+6**	....	....	....	....	....	....	....	....
1980-81	**Quebec Nordiques**	**NHL**	**78**	**24**	**49**	**73**	**20**	**34**	**54**	**104**	**8**	**0**	**3**	**148**	**16.2**	**98**	**41**	**108**	**32**	**–19**	**5**	**1**	**2**	**3**	**17**	**1**	**0**	**0**
1981-82	United States	C Cup	4	0	0	0	....	....	....	0	....	....	....	....	....	....	....	....	....	....	....	....	....	....	....	....	....	....
	New York Rangers	**NHL**	**30**	**8**	**24**	**32**	**6**	**16**	**22**	**24**	**2**	**0**	**2**	**49**	**16.3**	**46**	**7**	**37**	**6**	**+8**	**10**	**7**	**4**	**11**	**11**	**4**	**0**	**1**
	Quebec Nordiques	**NHL**	**19**	**1**	**8**	**9**	**1**	**5**	**6**	**4**	**0**	**0**	**0**	**20**	**5.0**	**11**	**3**	**15**	**5**	**–2**	....	....	....	....	....	....	....	....
1982-83	**New York Rangers**	**NHL**	**61**	**12**	**19**	**31**	**10**	**13**	**23**	**41**	**1**	**0**	**0**	**56**	**21.4**	**45**	**2**	**47**	**15**	**+11**	**4**	**1**	**0**	**1**	**0**	**0**	**0**	**0**
1983-84	**New York Rangers**	**NHL**	**31**	**3**	**2**	**5**	**2**	**1**	**3**	**22**	**0**	**0**	**1**	**7**	**42.9**	**9**	**0**	**7**	**0**	**+2**	....	....	....	....	....	....	....	....
	Tulsa Oilers	CHL	25	11	11	22	....	....	....	10	....	....	....	....	....	....	....	....	....	....	9	4	5	9	2	....	....	....
1984-85	**New York Rangers**	**NHL**	**48**	**9**	**10**	**19**	**7**	**7**	**14**	**35**	**0**	**1**	**1**	**61**	**14.8**	**23**	**0**	**43**	**13**	**–7**	....	....	....	....	....	....	....	....
	New Haven Nighthawks	AHL	17	9	7	16	....	....	....	30	....	....	....	....	....	....	....	....	....	....	....	....	....	....	....	....	....	....
1985-86	New Haven Nighthawks	AHL	1	0	0	0	....	....	....	0	....	....	....	....	....	....	....	....	....	....	....	....	....	....	....	....	....	....
	NHL Totals		**334**	**77**	**150**	**227**	**64**	**105**	**169**	**262**	**19**	**1**	**10**	**463**	**16.6**	**317**	**86**	**309**	**78**		**19**	**9**	**6**	**15**	**28**	**5**	**0**	**1**
	Other Major League Totals		373	216	307	523				365											13	6	10	16	10	....	....	

WEC-B All-Star Team (1972) • WHA Second All-Star Team (1976, 1978) • WHA First All-Star Team (1977, 1979) • Won Gary Davidson Trophy (WHA MVP) (1977)

Selected by **New England** (WHA) in 1972 WHA General Player Draft, February 13, 1972. Signed as a free agent by **Detroit**, October 1, 1972. WHA rights traded to **Phoenix** (WHA) by **New England** (WHA) for cash, June, 1974. Signed as a free agent by **Cincinnati** (WHA) after **Phoenix** (WHA) franchise folded, May 30, 1977. Signed as a free agent by **Quebec**, August 13, 1979. Traded to **NY Rangers** by **Quebec** with Quebec's 8th round choice (Brian Glynn) in 1982 Entry Draft for Jere Gillis and Dean Talafous (later changed to Pat Hickey when Talafous decided to retire), December 30, 1981.

• FULLAN, LARRY

Larry Fullan LW – L. 5'11", 185 lbs. b: Toronto, Ont., 8/11/1949.

Season	Club	League	GP	G	A	Pts	AG	AA	APts	PIM	PP	SH	GW	S	%	TGF	PGF	TGA	PGA	+/–	GP	G	A	Pts	PIM	PP	SH	GW
1967-68	St. Michael's Buzzers	Jr. B	STATISTICS NOT AVAILABLE																									
1968-69	Colgate University	ECAC	DID NOT PLAY – FRESHMAN																									
1969-70	Cornell University	ECAC	12	28	19	47	....	....	....	....	....	....	....	....	....	....	....	....	....	....	....	....	....	....	....	....	....	....
1970-71	Cornell University	ECAC	27	20	32	52	....	....	....	12	....	....	....	....	....	....	....	....	....	....	....	....	....	....	....	....	....	....
1971-72	Cornell University	ECAC	29	20	43	63	....	....	....	28	....	....	....	....	....	....	....	....	....	....	....	....	....	....	....	....	....	....
1972-73	Nova Scotia Voyageurs	AHL	50	4	10	14	....	....	....	4	....	....	....	....	....	....	....	....	....	....	13	2	0	2	4	....	....	....
1973-74	Nova Scotia Voyageurs	AHL	76	37	47	84	....	....	....	19	....	....	....	....	....	....	....	....	....	....	6	2	5	7	10	....	....	....
1974-75	**Washington Capitals**	**NHL**	**4**	**1**	**0**	**1**	**1**	**0**	**1**	**0**	**1**	**0**	**0**	**5**	**20.0**	**1**	**1**	**2**	**0**	**–2**	....	....	....	....	....	....	....	....
	Richmond Robins	AHL	71	23	42	65	....	....	....	38	....	....	....	....	....	....	....	....	....	....	7	2	1	3	24	....	....	....
1975-76	Richmond Robins	AHL	76	18	57	75	....	....	....	26	....	....	....	....	....	....	....	....	....	....	8	2	6	8	2	....	....	....
	NHL Totals		**4**	**1**	**0**	**1**	**1**	**0**	**1**	**0**	**1**	**0**	**0**	**5**	**20.0**	**1**	**1**	**2**	**0**		....	....	....	....	....	....	....	....

ECAC First All-Star Team (1972) • NCAA East First All-American Team (1972)

Signed as a free agent by **Montreal**, June, 1972. Claimed by **Washington** from **Montreal** in Expansion Draft, June 12, 1974.

• FUSCO, MARK

Mark Fusco D – R. 5'9", 175 lbs. b: Burlington, MA, 3/12/1961.

Season	Club	League	GP	G	A	Pts	AG	AA	APts	PIM	PP	SH	GW	S	%	TGF	PGF	TGA	PGA	+/–	GP	G	A	Pts	PIM	PP	SH	GW
1979-80	Harvard University	ECAC	26	13	16	29	....	....	....	20	....	....	....	....	....	....	....	....	....	....	....	....	....	....	....	....	....	....
1980-81	Harvard University	ECAC	23	7	13	20	....	....	....	28	....	....	....	....	....	....	....	....	....	....	....	....	....	....	....	....	....	....
	United States	WJC-A	3	0	0	0	....	....	....	2	....	....	....	....	....	....	....	....	....	....	....	....	....	....	....	....	....	....
1981-82	Harvard University	ECAC	30	11	29	40	....	....	....	46	....	....	....	....	....	....	....	....	....	....	....	....	....	....	....	....	....	....
1982-83	Harvard University	ECAC	33	13	33	46	....	....	....	30	....	....	....	....	....	....	....	....	....	....	....	....	....	....	....	....	....	....
1983-84	United States	Nat-Team	50	4	24	28	....	....	....	20	....	....	....	....	....	....	....	....	....	....	....	....	....	....	....	....	....	....
	United States	Olympics	6	0	0	0	....	....	....	6	....	....	....	....	....	....	....	....	....	....	....	....	....	....	....	....	....	....
	Hartford Whalers	**NHL**	**17**	**0**	**4**	**4**	**0**	**3**	**3**	**2**	**0**	**0**	**0**	**17**	**0.0**	**13**	**2**	**20**	**3**	**–6**	....	....	....	....	....	....	....	....
1984-85	United States	C Cup	1	0	0	0	....	....	....	2	....	....	....	....	....	....	....	....	....	....	....	....	....	....	....	....	....	....
	Hartford Whalers	**NHL**	**63**	**3**	**8**	**11**	**2**	**5**	**7**	**40**	**0**	**0**	**0**	**70**	**4.3**	**53**	**2**	**83**	**17**	**–15**	....	....	....	....	....	....	....	....
	United States	WEC-A	10	0	1	1	....	....	....	4	....	....	....	....	....	....	....	....	....	....	....	....	....	....	....	....	....	....
	NHL Totals		**80**	**3**	**12**	**15**	**2**	**8**	**10**	**42**	**0**	**0**	**0**	**87**	**3.4**	**66**	**4**	**103**	**20**		....	....	....	....	....	....	....	....

ECAC First All-Star Team (1981, 1983) • NCAA East First All-American Team (1981, 1982, 1983) • ECAC Second All-Star Team (1982) • NCAA Championship All-Tournament Team (1983) • Won Hobey Baker Memorial Award (Top U.S. Collegiate Player) (1983)

Signed as a free agent by **Hartford**, February 25, 1984.

• GAETZ, LINK

Link "Missing Link" Gaetz D – L. 6'3", 215 lbs. b: Vancouver, B.C., 10/2/1968. Minnesota's 2nd choice, 40th overall, in 1988 Entry Draft.

Season	Club	League	GP	G	A	Pts	AG	AA	APts	PIM	PP	SH	GW	S	%	TGF	PGF	TGA	PGA	+/–	GP	G	A	Pts	PIM	PP	SH	GW
1985-86	Quesnel Millionaires	BCJHL	15	0	7	7	....	....	....	4	....	....	....	....	....	....	....	....	....	....	....	....	....	....	....	....	....	....
	Abbotsford Pilots	BCJHL	2	0	0	0	....	....	....	2	....	....	....	....	....	....	....	....	....	....	....	....	....	....	....	....	....	....
1986-87	New Westminster Bruins	WHL	44	2	7	9	....	....	....	52	....	....	....	....	....	....	....	....	....	....	....	....	....	....	....	....	....	....
	Merritt Centennials	BCJHL	7	4	2	6	....	....	....	27	....	....	....	....	....	....	....	....	....	....	....	....	....	....	....	....	....	....
	Delta Kings	BCJHL	16	5	10	15	....	....	....	26	....	....	....	....	....	....	....	....	....	....	....	....	....	....	....	....	....	....
1987-88	Spokane Chiefs	WHL	59	9	20	29	....	....	....	313	....	....	....	....	....	....	....	....	....	....	10	2	2	4	70	....	....	....
1988-89	**Minnesota North Stars**	**NHL**	**12**	**0**	**2**	**2**	**0**	**1**	**1**	**53**	**0**	**0**	**0**	**8**	**0.0**	**6**	**1**	**13**	**5**	**–3**	....	....	....	....	....	....	....	....
	Kalamazoo Wings	IHL	37	3	4	7	....	....	....	192	....	....	....	....	....	....	....	....	....	....	5	0	0	0	56	....	....	....
1989-90	**Minnesota North Stars**	**NHL**	**5**	**0**	**0**	**0**	**0**	**0**	**0**	**33**	**0**	**0**	**0**	**4**	**0.0**	**1**	**1**	**5**	**0**	**–5**	....	....	....	....	....	....	....	....
	Kalamazoo Wings	IHL	61	5	16	21	....	....	....	318	....	....	....	....	....	....	....	....	....	....	9	2	2	4	59	....	....	....
1990-91	Minnesota North Stars	FrTour	3	0	0	0	....	....	....	32	....	....	....	....	....	....	....	....	....	....	....	....	....	....	....	....	....	....
	Kansas City Blades	IHL	18	1	10	11	....	....	....	178	....	....	....	....	....	....	....	....	....	....	....	....	....	....	....	....	....	....
	Kalamazoo Wings	IHL	9	0	1	1	....	....	....	44	....	....	....	....	....	....	....	....	....	....	....	....	....	....	....	....	....	....
1991-92	**San Jose Sharks**	**NHL**	**48**	**6**	**6**	**12**	**5**	**4**	**9**	**326**	**3**	**0**	**0**	**73**	**8.2**	**34**	**14**	**52**	**5**	**–27**	....	....	....	....	....	....	....	....
1992-93	Nashville Knights	ECHL	3	1	0	1	....	....	....	10	....	....	....	....	....	....	....	....	....	....	....	....	....	....	....	....	....	....
	Kansas City Blades	IHL	2	0	0	0	....	....	....	14	....	....	....	....	....	....	....	....	....	....	....	....	....	....	....	....	....	....
1993-94	Cape Breton Oilers	AHL	21	0	1	1	....	....	....	140	....	....	....	....	....	....	....	....	....	....	....	....	....	....	....	....	....	....
	Nashville Knights	ECHL	24	1	1	2	....	....	....	261	....	....	....	....	....	....	....	....	....	....	....	....	....	....	....	....	....	....
	West Palm Beach Blaze	SunHL	6	0	3	3	....	....	....	15	....	....	....	....	....	....	....	....	....	....	3	0	1	1	8	....	....	....
1994-95	San Antonio Iguanas	CHL	13	0	3	3	....	....	....	156	....	....	....	....	....	....	....	....	....	....	....	....	....	....	....	....	....	....

										REGULAR SEASON											PLAYOFFS							
Season	Club	League	GP	G	A	Pts	AG	AA	APts	PIM	PP	SH	GW	S	%	TGF	PGF	TGA	PGA	+/-	GP	G	A	Pts	PIM	PP	SH	GW
1995-96	San Francisco Spiders	IHL	3	0	0	0	....	....	....	32	....	....	....	....	....	....	....	....	....	....	....	....	....	....	....	....	....	....
1996-97	Madison Monsters	ColHL	26	2	4	6	....	....	....	178	....	....	....	....	....	....	....	....	....	....	....	....	....	....	....	....	....	....
1997-98	Anchorage Aces	WCHL	11	0	1	1	....	....	....	130	....	....	....	....	....	....	....	....	....	....	....	....	....	....	....	....	....	....
	NHL Totals		**65**	**6**	**8**	**14**	**5**	**5**	**10**	**412**	**3**	**0**	**0**	**85**	**7.1**	**41**	**16**	**70**	**10**		....	....	....	....	....	....	....	....

Claimed by **San Jose** from **Minnesota** in Dispersal Draft, May 30, 1991. Traded to **Edmonton** by **San Jose** for Edmonton's 10th round choice (Tomas Pisa) in 1994 Entry Draft, September 10, 1993.

• GAGE, JODY

Jody Gage RW – R. 6', 190 lbs. b: Toronto, Ont., 11/29/1959. Detroit's 2nd choice, 45th overall, in 1979 Entry Draft.

Season	Club	League	GP	G	A	Pts	AG	AA	APts	PIM	PP	SH	GW	S	%	TGF	PGF	TGA	PGA	+/-	GP	G	A	Pts	PIM	PP	SH	GW
1976-77	St. Catharines Fincups	OHA	47	13	20	33	....	....	....	2	....	....	....	....	....	....	....	....	....	....	....	....	....	....	....	....	....	....
1977-78	Hamilton Fincups	OHA	32	15	18	33	....	....	....	19	....	....	....	....	....	....	....	....	....	....	....	....	....	....	....	....	....	....
	Kitchener Rangers	OHA	36	17	27	44	....	....	....	21	....	....	....	....	....	....	....	....	....	....	9	4	3	7	4	....	....	....
1978-79	Kitchener Rangers	OHA	58	46	43	89	....	....	....	40	....	....	....	....	....	....	....	....	....	....	10	1	2	3	6	....	....	....
1979-80	Adirondack Red Wings	AHL	63	25	21	46	....	....	....	15	....	....	....	....	....	....	....	....	....	....	5	2	1	3	0	....	....	....
1980-81	**Detroit Red Wings**	**NHL**	**16**	**2**	**2**	**4**	**2**	**1**	**3**	**22**	**0**	**0**	**0**	**26**	**7.7**	**7**	**1**	**18**	**2**	**–10**	....	....	....	....	....	....	....	....
	Adirondack Red Wings	AHL	59	17	31	48	....	....	....	44	....	....	....	....	....	....	....	....	....	....	17	9	6	15	12	....	....	....
1981-82	**Detroit Red Wings**	**NHL**	**31**	**9**	**10**	**19**	**7**	**7**	**14**	**2**	**0**	**0**	**1**	**47**	**19.1**	**35**	**4**	**32**	**0**	**–1**	....	....	....	....	....	....	....	....
	Adirondack Red Wings	AHL	47	21	20	41	....	....	....	21	....	....	....	....	....	....	....	....	....	....	....	....	....	....	....	....	....	....
1982-83	Adirondack Red Wings	AHL	65	23	30	53	....	....	....	33	....	....	....	....	....	....	....	....	....	....	6	1	5	6	8	....	....	....
1983-84	**Detroit Red Wings**	**NHL**	**3**	**0**	**0**	**0**	**0**	**0**	**0**	**0**	**0**	**0**	**0**	**1**	**0.0**	**0**	**0**	**0**	**0**	**0**	....	....	....	....	....	....	....	....
	Adirondack Red Wings	AHL	73	40	32	72	....	....	....	32	....	....	....	....	....	....	....	....	....	....	6	3	4	7	2	....	....	....
1984-85	Adirondack Red Wings	AHL	78	27	33	60	....	....	....	55	....	....	....	....	....	....	....	....	....	....	....	....	....	....	....	....	....	....
1985-86	**Buffalo Sabres**	**NHL**	**7**	**3**	**2**	**5**	**2**	**1**	**3**	**0**	**3**	**0**	**0**	**18**	**16.7**	**8**	**3**	**8**	**0**	**–3**	....	....	....	....	....	....	....	....
	Rochester Americans	AHL	73	42	57	99	....	....	....	56	....	....	....	....	....	....	....	....	....	....	....	....	....	....	....	....	....	....
1986-87	Rochester Americans	AHL	70	26	39	65	....	....	....	60	....	....	....	....	....	....	....	....	....	....	17	*14	5	19	24	....	....	....
1987-88	**Buffalo Sabres**	**NHL**	**2**	**0**	**0**	**0**	**0**	**0**	**0**	**0**	**0**	**0**	**0**	**1**	**0.0**	**0**	**0**	**2**	**0**	**–2**	....	....	....	....	....	....	....	....
	Rochester Americans	AHL	76	*60	44	104	....	....	....	46	....	....	....	....	....	....	....	....	....	....	5	2	5	7	10	....	....	....
1988-89	Rochester Americans	AHL	65	31	38	69	....	....	....	60	....	....	....	....	....	....	....	....	....	....	....	....	....	....	....	....	....	....
1989-90	Rochester Americans	AHL	75	45	38	83	....	....	....	42	....	....	....	....	....	....	....	....	....	....	17	4	6	10	12	....	....	....
1990-91	Rochester Americans	AHL	73	42	43	85	....	....	....	34	....	....	....	....	....	....	....	....	....	....	15	6	10	16	14	....	....	....
1991-92	**Buffalo Sabres**	**NHL**	**9**	**0**	**1**	**1**	**0**	**1**	**1**	**2**	**0**	**0**	**0**	**9**	**0.0**	**3**	**2**	**2**	**0**	**–1**	....	....	....	....	....	....	....	....
	Rochester Americans	AHL	67	40	40	80	....	....	....	54	....	....	....	....	....	....	....	....	....	....	16	5	9	14	10	....	....	....
1992-93	Rochester Americans	AHL	71	40	40	80	....	....	....	76	....	....	....	....	....	....	....	....	....	....	9	5	8	13	2	....	....	....
1993-94	Rochester Americans	AHL	44	18	21	39	....	....	....	57	....	....	....	....	....	....	....	....	....	....	....	....	....	....	....	....	....	....
1994-95	Rochester Americans	AHL	23	4	5	9	....	....	....	20	....	....	....	....	....	....	....	....	....	....	2	0	0	0	0	....	....	....
1995-96	Rochester Americans	AHL	16	3	12	15	....	....	....	20	....	....	....	....	....	....	....	....	....	....	....	....	....	....	....	....	....	....
	NHL Totals		**68**	**14**	**15**	**29**	**11**	**10**	**21**	**26**	**3**	**0**	**1**	**102**	**13.7**	**53**	**10**	**62**	**2**		....	....	....	....	....	....	....	....

AHL First All-Star Team (1986, 1988, 1991) • Won Les Cunningham Award (MVP - AHL) (1988)

Signed as a free agent by **Buffalo**, July 31, 1985.

• GAGNE, PAUL

Paul Gagne LW – L. 5'10", 180 lbs. b: Iroquois Falls, Ont., 2/6/1962. Colorado's 1st choice, 19th overall, in 1980 Entry Draft.

Season	Club	League	GP	G	A	Pts	AG	AA	APts	PIM	PP	SH	GW	S	%	TGF	PGF	TGA	PGA	+/-	GP	G	A	Pts	PIM	PP	SH	GW
1978-79	Windsor Spitfires	OHA	67	24	18	42	....	....	....	64	....	....	....	....	....	....	....	....	....	....	7	1	1	2	2	....	....	....
1979-80	Windsor Spitfires	OHA	65	48	53	101	....	....	....	87	....	....	....	....	....	....	....	....	....	....	13	7	8	15	19	....	....	....
1980-81	**Colorado Rockies**	**NHL**	**61**	**25**	**16**	**41**	**21**	**11**	**32**	**12**	**9**	**0**	**2**	**99**	**25.3**	**61**	**26**	**59**	**0**	**–24**	....	....	....	....	....	....	....	....
1981-82	**Colorado Rockies**	**NHL**	**59**	**10**	**12**	**22**	**8**	**8**	**16**	**17**	**2**	**0**	**0**	**104**	**9.6**	**39**	**4**	**65**	**3**	**–27**	....	....	....	....	....	....	....	....
1982-83	**New Jersey Devils**	**NHL**	**53**	**14**	**15**	**29**	**11**	**10**	**21**	**13**	**4**	**0**	**3**	**76**	**18.4**	**40**	**10**	**32**	**0**	**–2**	....	....	....	....	....	....	....	....
	Wichita Wind	CHL	16	1	9	10	....	....	....	9	....	....	....	....	....	....	....	....	....	....	....	....	....	....	....	....	....	....
1983-84	**New Jersey Devils**	**NHL**	**66**	**14**	**18**	**32**	**11**	**12**	**23**	**33**	**3**	**0**	**1**	**109**	**12.8**	**49**	**5**	**68**	**2**	**–22**	....	....	....	....	....	....	....	....
1984-85	**New Jersey Devils**	**NHL**	**79**	**24**	**19**	**43**	**20**	**13**	**33**	**28**	**3**	**0**	**1**	**152**	**15.8**	**62**	**12**	**61**	**0**	**–11**	....	....	....	....	....	....	....	....
1985-86	**New Jersey Devils**	**NHL**	**47**	**19**	**19**	**38**	**15**	**13**	**28**	**14**	**4**	**0**	**3**	**91**	**20.9**	**55**	**15**	**57**	**2**	**–15**	....	....	....	....	....	....	....	....
1986-87			DID NOT PLAY – INJURED																									
1987-88			DID NOT PLAY – INJURED																									
1988-89	**Toronto Maple Leafs**	**NHL**	**16**	**3**	**2**	**5**	**3**	**1**	**4**	**6**	**1**	**0**	**1**	**14**	**21.4**	**8**	**1**	**18**	**3**	**–8**	....	....	....	....	....	....	....	....
	Newmarket Saints	AHL	56	33	41	74	....	....	....	29	....	....	....	....	....	....	....	....	....	....	5	4	4	8	5			
1989-90	Newmarket Saints	AHL	28	13	14	27				11	....	....	....	....	....	....	....	....	....	....	....	....	....	....	....	....	....	....
	New York Islanders	**NHL**	**9**	**1**	**0**	**1**	**1**	**0**	**1**	**4**	**0**	**0**	**0**	**10**	**10.0**	**3**	**0**	**4**	**0**	**–1**	....	....	....	....	....	....	....	....
	Springfield Indians	AHL	36	18	29	47	....	....	....	6	....	....	....	....	....	....	....	....	....	....	13	10	6	16	2	....	....	....
1990-91	EV Landshut	Germany	49	44	37	81	....	....	....	41	....	....	....	....	....	....	....	....	....	....	....	....	....	....	....	....	....	....
1991-92	EV Landshut	Germany	44	30	23	53	....	....	....	49	....	....	....	....	....	....	....	....	....	....	....	....	....	....	....	....	....	....
1992-93	EHC Olten	Switz. B	36	40	24	64	....	....	....	....	....	....	....	....	....	....	....	....	....	....	....	....	....	....	....	....	....	....
1993-94	EHC Olten	Switz.	30	16	16	32	....	....	....	52	....	....	....	....	....	....	....	....	....	....	....	....	....	....	....	....	....	....
1994-95	EHC Olten	Switz.	32	37	30	67	....	....	....	98	....	....	....	....	....	....	....	....	....	....	3	1	1	2	35	....	....	....
1995-96	Zurcher SC	Switz.	8	5	2	7	....	....	....	6	....	....	....	....	....	....	....	....	....	....	4	0	1	1	8	....	....	....
	NHL Totals		**390**	**110**	**101**	**211**	**90**	**68**	**158**	**127**	**26**	**0**	**11**	**655**	**16.8**	**317**	**73**	**364**	**10**		....	....	....	....	....	....	....	....

OHA Second All-Star Team (1980)

Transferred to **New Jersey** after **Colorado** franchise relocated, June 30, 1982. • Suffered serious back injury in game vs. Winnipeg and missed the entire 1986-87 and 1987-88 seasons, March 25, 1986. Signed as a free agent by **Toronto**, July 28, 1988. Traded to **NY Islanders** by **Toronto** with Derek Laxdal and Jack Capuano for Gilles Thibaudeau and Mike Stevens, December 20, 1989.

• GAGNER, DAVE

Dave Gagner C – L. 5'10", 180 lbs. b: Chatham, Ont., 12/11/1964. NY Rangers' 1st choice, 12th overall, in 1983 Entry Draft.

Season	Club	League	GP	G	A	Pts	AG	AA	APts	PIM	PP	SH	GW	S	%	TGF	PGF	TGA	PGA	+/-	GP	G	A	Pts	PIM	PP	SH	GW
1981-82	Brantford Alexanders	OHL	68	30	46	76	....	....	....	31	....	....	....	....	....	....	....	....	....	....	11	3	6	9	6	....	....	....
1982-83	Brantford Alexanders	OHL	70	55	66	121	....	....	....	57	....	....	....	....	....	....	....	....	....	....	8	5	5	10	4	....	....	....
1983-84	Brantford Alexanders	OHL	12	7	13	20	....	....	....	4	....	....	....	....	....	....	....	....	....	....	6	0	4	4	6	....	....	....
	Canada	Nat-Team	50	19	18	37	....	....	....	26	....	....	....	....	....	....	....	....	....	....	....	....	....	....	....	....	....	....
	Canada	WJC-A	7	4	2	6	....	....	....	4	....	....	....	....	....	....	....	....	....	....	....	....	....	....	....	....	....	....
	Canada	Olympics	7	5	2	7	....	....	....	6	....	....	....	....	....	....	....	....	....	....	....	....	....	....	....	....	....	....
1984-85	**New York Rangers**	**NHL**	**38**	**6**	**6**	**12**	**5**	**4**	**9**	**16**	**0**	**1**	**0**	**52**	**11.5**	**20**	**0**	**39**	**3**	**–16**	....	....	....	....	....	....	....	....
	New Haven Nighthawks	AHL	38	13	20	33	....	....	....	23	....	....	....	....	....	....	....	....	....	....	....	....	....	....	....	....	....	....
1985-86	**New York Rangers**	**NHL**	**32**	**4**	**6**	**10**	**3**	**4**	**7**	**19**	**0**	**0**	**0**	**41**	**9.8**	**17**	**0**	**17**	**1**	**+1**	....	....	....	....	....	....	....	....
	New Haven Nighthawks	AHL	16	10	11	21	....	....	....	11	....	....	....	....	....	....	....	....	....	....	4	1	2	3	2	....	....	....
1986-87	**New York Rangers**	**NHL**	**10**	**1**	**4**	**5**	**1**	**3**	**4**	**12**	**0**	**0**	**0**	**16**	**6.3**	**5**	**0**	**7**	**1**	**–1**	....	....	....	....	....	....	....	....
	New Haven Nighthawks	AHL	56	22	41	63	....	....	....	50	....	....	....	....	....	....	....	....	....	....	7	1	5	6	18	....	....	....
1987-88	**Minnesota North Stars**	**NHL**	**51**	**8**	**11**	**19**	**7**	**8**	**15**	**55**	**0**	**2**	**0**	**87**	**9.2**	**27**	**3**	**64**	**26**	**–14**	....	....	....	....	....	....	....	....
	Kalamazoo Wings	IHL	14	16	10	26	....	....	....	26	....	....	....	....	....	....	....	....	....	....	....	....	....	....	....	....	....	....
1988-89	**Minnesota North Stars**	**NHL**	**75**	**35**	**43**	**78**	**30**	**30**	**60**	**104**	**11**	**3**	**3**	**183**	**19.1**	**110**	**40**	**85**	**28**	**+13**	....	....	....	....	....	....	....	....
	Kalamazoo Wings	IHL	1	0	1	1	....	....	....	4	....	....	....	....	....	....	....	....	....	....	....	....	....	....	....	....	....	....
1989-90	**Minnesota North Stars**	**NHL**	**79**	**40**	**38**	**78**	**35**	**27**	**62**	**54**	**10**	**0**	**3**	**238**	**16.8**	**94**	**34**	**67**	**6**	**–1**	**7**	**2**	**3**	**5**	**16**	**1**	**0**	**0**
1990-91	Minnesota North Stars	FrTour	2	0	0	0	....	....	....	2	....	....	....	....	....	....	....	....	....	....	....	....	....	....	....	....	....	....
	Minnesota North Stars	**NHL**	**73**	**40**	**42**	**82**	**37**	**32**	**69**	**114**	**20**	**0**	**5**	**223**	**17.9**	**108**	**46**	**62**	**9**	**+9**	**23**	**12**	**15**	**27**	**28**	**6**	**1**	**1**
1991-92	**Minnesota North Stars**	**NHL**	**78**	**31**	**40**	**71**	**28**	**30**	**58**	**107**	**17**	**0**	**3**	**229**	**13.5**	**99**	**45**	**68**	**0**	**–4**	**7**	**2**	**4**	**6**	**8**	**2**	**0**	**0**
1992-93	**Minnesota North Stars**	**NHL**	**84**	**33**	**43**	**76**	**28**	**29**	**57**	**143**	**17**	**0**	**5**	**230**	**14.3**	**103**	**53**	**63**	**0**	**–13**	....	....	....	....	....	....	....	....
	Canada	WC-A	8	3	1	4	....	....	....	6	....	....	....	....	....	....	....	....	....	....	....	....	....	....	....	....	....	....
1993-94	**Dallas Stars**	**NHL**	**76**	**32**	**29**	**61**	**30**	**22**	**52**	**83**	**10**	**0**	**6**	**213**	**15.0**	**90**	**39**	**38**	**0**	**+13**	**9**	**5**	**1**	**6**	**2**	**3**	**0**	**0**
1994-95	Courmaosta	Italy	3	0	0	0	....	....	....	0	....	....	....	....	....	....	....	....	....	....	....	....	....	....	....	....	....	....
	Courmaosta	EuroHL	1	0	4	4	....	....	....	0	....	....	....	....	....	....	....	....	....	....	....	....	....	....	....	....	....	....
	Dallas Stars	**NHL**	**48**	**14**	**28**	**42**	**25**	**41**	**66**	**42**	**7**	**0**	**2**	**138**	**10.1**	**55**	**25**	**30**	**2**	**+2**	**5**	**1**	**1**	**2**	**4**	**1**	**0**	**0**

			REGULAR SEASON																		PLAYOFFS							
Season	Club	League	GP	G	A	Pts	AG	AA	APts	PIM	PP	SH	GW	S	%	TGF	PGF	TGA	PGA	+/–	GP	G	A	Pts	PIM	PP	SH	GW
1995-96	**Dallas Stars**	NHL	45	14	13	27	14	11	25	44	6	0	2	145	9.7	41	23	37	2	–17	....	....	....	....	....	....	....	....
	Toronto Maple Leafs	NHL	28	7	15	22	7	12	19	59	1	0	1	70	10.0	28	6	35	11	–2	6	0	2	2	6	0	0	0
1996-97	**Calgary Flames**	NHL	82	27	33	60	29	29	58	48	9	0	4	228	11.8	87	31	69	15	+2	....	....	....	....	....	....	....	....
1997-98	**Florida Panthers**	NHL	78	20	28	48	23	27	50	55	5	1	1	165	12.1	63	26	63	5	–21	....	....	....	....	....	....	....	....
	NHL Totals		877	312	379	691	302	309	611	955	113	7	35	2258	13.8	947	371	734	109		57	22	26	48	64	13	1	1

OHL Second All-Star Team (1983)

Played in NHL All-Star Game (1991)

Traded to **Minnesota** by **NY Rangers** with Jay Caulfield for Jari Gronstrand and Paul Boutilier, October 8, 1987. Transferred to **Dallas** after **Minnesota** franchise relocated, June 9, 1993. Traded to **Toronto** by **Dallas** with Dallas' 6th round choice (Dmitriy Yakushin) in 1996 Entry Draft for Benoit Hogue and Randy Wood, January 29, 1996. Traded to **Calgary** by **Toronto** for Calgary's 3rd round choice (Mike Lankshear) in 1996 Entry Draft, June 22, 1996. Signed as a free agent by **Florida**, July 12, 1997.

• GAGNON, GERMAINE

Germaine Gagnon LW – L. 6', 175 lbs. b: Chicoutimi, Que., 12/9/1942.

Season	Club	League	GP	G	A	Pts	AG	AA	APts	PIM	PP	SH	GW	S	%	TGF	PGF	TGA	PGA	+/–	GP	G	A	Pts	PIM	PP	SH	GW
1961-62	Montreal Jr. Canadiens	OHA	48	20	37	57	....	....	....	63	....	....	....	....	....	....	....	....	....	....	6	3	4	7	4	....	....	....
1962-63	Montreal Jr. Canadiens	OHA	50	19	38	57	....	....	....	72	....	....	....	....	....	....	....	....	....	....	10	3	4	7	16	....	....	....
	Hull-Ottawa Canadiens	EPHL	1	0	0	0	....	....	....	0	....	....	....	....	....	....	....	....	....	....	....	....	....	....	....	....	....	....
1963-64	Omaha Knights	CHL	59	10	25	35	....	....	....	32	....	....	....	....	....	....	....	....	....	....	10	7	4	11	6	....	....	....
1964-65	Quebec Aces	AHL	14	2	7	9	....	....	....	10	....	....	....	....	....	....	....	....	....	....	....	....	....	....	....	....	....	....
	Omaha Knights	CHL	55	13	25	38	....	....	....	73	....	....	....	....	....	....	....	....	....	....	6	0	1	1	11	....	....	....
1965-66	Houston Apollos	CHL	64	14	30	44	....	....	....	58	....	....	....	....	....	....	....	....	....	....	....	....	....	....	....	....	....	....
1966-67	Quebec Aces	AHL	7	0	1	1	....	....	....	0	....	....	....	....	....	....	....	....	....	....	....	....	....	....	....	....	....	....
	Providence Reds	AHL	5	0	0	0	....	....	....	0	....	....	....	....	....	....	....	....	....	....	....	....	....	....	....	....	....	....
	Houston Apollos	CHL	30	6	10	16	....	....	....	43	....	....	....	....	....	....	....	....	....	....	5	2	2	4	0	....	....	....
1967-68	Memphis South Stars	CHL	65	26	34	60	....	....	....	23	....	....	....	....	....	....	....	....	....	....	3	0	0	0	0	....	....	....
1968-69	Vancouver Canucks	WHL	61	8	21	29	....	....	....	16	....	....	....	....	....	....	....	....	....	....	8	1	2	3	0	....	....	....
1969-70	Vancouver Canucks	WHL	72	16	27	43	....	....	....	23	....	....	....	....	....	....	....	....	....	....	11	2	3	5	4	....	....	....
1970-71	Montreal Voyageurs	AHL	61	20	28	48	....	....	....	36	....	....	....	....	....	....	....	....	....	....	3	3	1	4	0	....	....	....
1971-72	**Montreal Canadiens**	NHL	4	0	0	0	0	0	0	0	0	0	0	3	0.0	1	0	1	0	0	....	....	....	....	....	....	....	....
	Nova Scotia Voyageurs	AHL	70	25	56	81	....	....	....	34	....	....	....	....	....	....	....	....	....	....	15	5	*15	20	8	....	....	....
1972-73	**New York Islanders**	NHL	63	12	29	41	12	24	36	31	3	1	1	126	9.5	62	14	86	14	–24	....	....	....	....	....	....	....	....
1973-74	**New York Islanders**	NHL	62	8	14	22	8	12	20	8	0	0	0	68	11.8	35	7	49	27	+6	....	....	....	....	....	....	....	....
	Chicago Black Hawks	NHL	14	3	14	17	3	12	15	4	0	0	1	19	15.8	23	2	15	0	+6	11	2	2	4	2	1	0	1
1974-75	**Chicago Black Hawks**	NHL	80	16	35	51	15	28	43	21	8	0	2	97	16.5	85	39	53	12	+5	8	0	1	1	0	0	0	0
1975-76	**Chicago Black Hawks**	NHL	5	0	0	0	0	0	0	2	0	0	0	10	0.0	1	1	1	0	–1	....	....	....	....	....	....	....	....
	Springfield Indians	AHL	4	0	1	1	....	....	....	2	....	....	....	....	....	....	....	....	....	....	....	....	....	....	....	....	....	....
	Kansas City Scouts	NHL	31	1	9	10	1	7	8	6	1	0	0	30	3.3	17	5	28	2	–14	....	....	....	....	....	....	....	....
	New Haven Nighthawks	AHL	26	12	16	28	....	....	....	14	....	....	....	....	....	....	....	....	....	....	3	1	0	1	0	....	....	....
	NHL Totals		259	40	101	141	39	83	122	72	12	1	4	353	11.3	224	68	233	55		19	2	3	5	2	1	0	1

Traded to **NY Islanders** by **Montreal** to complete transaction that sent Denis DeJordy, Tony Featherstone, Murray Anderson, Chico Resch and Alec Campbell to NY Islanders (June 6, 1972), June 26, 1972. Traded to **Chicago** by **NY Islanders** for cash and future considerations (Walt Ledingham, May 24, 1974), March 7, 1974. Claimed on waivers by **Kansas City** from **Chicago**, October 28, 1975.

• GAGNON, SEAN

Sean Gagnon D – L. 6'2", 210 lbs. b: Sault Ste. Marie, Ont., 9/11/1973.

Season	Club	League	GP	G	A	Pts	AG	AA	APts	PIM	PP	SH	GW	S	%	TGF	PGF	TGA	PGA	+/–	GP	G	A	Pts	PIM	PP	SH	GW
1991-92	Sudbury Wolves	OHL	44	3	4	7	....	....	....	60	....	....	....	....	....	....	....	....	....	....	5	0	1	1	0	....	....	....
1992-93	Sudbury Wolves	OHL	6	1	1	2	....	....	....	16	....	....	....	....	....	....	....	....	....	....	....	....	....	....	....	....	....	....
	Ottawa 67's	OHL	33	2	10	12	....	....	....	68	....	....	....	....	....	....	....	....	....	....	....	....	....	....	....	....	....	....
	Sault Ste. Marie Greyhounds	OHL	24	1	5	6	....	....	....	65	....	....	....	....	....	....	....	....	....	....	15	2	2	4	25	....	....	....
1993-94	Sault Ste. Marie Greyhounds	OHL	42	4	12	16	....	....	....	147	....	....	....	....	....	....	....	....	....	....	14	1	1	2	52	....	....	....
1994-95	Dayton Bombers	ECHL	68	9	23	32	....	....	....	339	....	....	....	....	....	....	....	....	....	....	8	0	3	3	69	....	....	....
1995-96	Dayton Bombers	ECHL	68	7	22	29	....	....	....	326	....	....	....	....	....	....	....	....	....	....	3	0	1	1	33	....	....	....
1996-97	Fort Wayne Komets	IHL	72	7	7	14	....	....	....	457	....	....	....	....	....	....	....	....	....	....	....	....	....	....	....	....	....	....
1997-98	**Phoenix Coyotes**	NHL	5	0	1	1	0	1	1	14	0	0	0	3	0.0	2	0	1	0	+1	....	....	....	....	....	....	....	....
	Springfield Falcons	AHL	54	4	13	17	....	....	....	330	....	....	....	....	....	....	....	....	....	....	2	0	1	1	17	....	....	....
	NHL Totals		5	0	1	1	0	1	1	14	0	0	0	3	0.0	2	0	1	0		....	....	....	....	....	....	....	....

Signed as a free agent by **Phoenix**, May 14, 1997.

• GAINEY, BOB

Bob Gainey LW – L. 6'2", 200 lbs. b: Peterborough, Ont., 12/13/1953. Montreal's 1st choice, 8th overall, in 1973 Amateur Draft. **HHOF**

Season	Club	League	GP	G	A	Pts	AG	AA	APts	PIM	PP	SH	GW	S	%	TGF	PGF	TGA	PGA	+/–	GP	G	A	Pts	PIM	PP	SH	GW
1971-72	Peterborough Petes	OHA	4	2	1	3	....	....	....	33	....	....	....	....	....	....	....	....	....	....	....	....	....	....	....	....	....	....
1972-73	Peterborough Petes	OHA	52	22	21	43	....	....	....	99	....	....	....	....	....	....	....	....	....	....	....	....	....	....	....	....	....	....
1973-74	**Montreal Canadiens**	NHL	66	3	7	10	3	6	9	34	0	0	0	55	5.5	19	0	28	0	–9	6	0	0	0	6	0	0	0
	Nova Scotia Voyageurs	AHL	6	2	5	7	....	....	....	4	....	....	....	....	....	....	....	....	....	....	....	....	....	....	....	....	....	....
1974-75	**Montreal Canadiens**	NHL	80	17	20	37	16	16	32	49	1	0	2	132	12.9	66	4	42	3	+23	11	2	4	6	4	0	0	1
1975-76	**Montreal Canadiens**	NHL	78	15	13	28	14	10	24	57	1	2	1	155	9.7	49	2	46	19	+20	13	1	3	4	20	0	0	0
1976-77	Canada	C Cup	5	2	0	2	....	....	....	2	....	....	....	....	....	....	....	....	....	....	....	....	....	....	....	....	....	....
	Montreal Canadiens	NHL	80	14	19	33	13	15	28	41	0	1	3	143	9.8	61	0	41	11	+31	14	4	1	5	25	0	1	1
1977-78	**Montreal Canadiens**	NHL	66	15	16	31	14	13	27	57	0	2	1	140	10.7	50	8	49	18	+11	15	2	7	9	14	0	1	0
1978-79	**Montreal Canadiens**	NHL	79	20	18	38	18	14	32	44	1	1	1	153	13.1	68	1	71	15	+11	16	6	10	16	10	0	0	1
1979-80	**Montreal Canadiens**	NHL	64	14	19	33	13	15	28	32	4	1	3	153	9.2	65	16	72	21	–2	10	1	1	2	4	0	0	1
1980-81	**Montreal Canadiens**	NHL	78	23	24	47	19	17	36	36	5	3	3	181	12.7	86	15	87	29	+13	3	0	0	0	2	0	0	0
1981-82	Canada	C Cup	7	1	3	4	....	....	....	2	....	....	....	....	....	....	....	....	....	....	....	....	....	....	....	....	....	....
	Montreal Canadiens	NHL	79	21	24	45	17	16	33	24	1	3	1	172	12.2	76	4	67	32	+37	5	0	1	1	8	0	0	0
	Canada	WEC-A	10	2	1	3	....	....	....	0	....	....	....	....	....	....	....	....	....	....	....	....	....	....	....	....	....	....
1982-83	**Montreal Canadiens**	NHL	80	12	18	30	10	12	22	43	0	1	3	150	8.0	63	0	92	36	+7	3	0	0	0	4	0	0	0
	Canada	WEC-A	10	0	6	6	....	....	....	2	....	....	....	....	....	....	....	....	....	....	....	....	....	....	....	....	....	....
1983-84	**Montreal Canadiens**	NHL	77	17	22	39	14	15	29	41	0	0	3	125	13.6	65	1	76	22	+10	15	1	5	6	9	0	0	0
1984-85	**Montreal Canadiens**	NHL	79	19	13	32	16	9	25	40	0	3	3	166	11.4	67	1	83	30	+13	12	1	3	4	13	0	0	0
1985-86	**Montreal Canadiens**	NHL	80	20	23	43	16	15	31	20	0	2	4	135	14.8	66	0	94	38	+10	20	5	5	10	12	0	1	3
1986-87	**Montreal Canadiens**	NHL	47	8	8	16	7	6	13	19	0	1	3	73	11.0	27	0	45	18	0	17	1	3	4	6	0	0	0
1987-88	**Montreal Canadiens**	NHL	78	11	11	22	9	8	17	14	0	0	1	101	10.9	34	0	60	34	+8	6	0	1	1	6	0	0	0
1988-89	**Montreal Canadiens**	NHL	49	10	7	17	8	5	13	34	1	0	2	65	15.4	35	1	39	18	+13	16	1	4	5	8	0	0	0
	NHL Totals		1160	239	262	501	207	192	399	585	14	20	34	2099	11.4	897	53	992	344		182	25	48	73	151	0	3	7

Won Frank J. Selke Trophy (1978, 1979, 1980, 1981) • Won Conn Smythe Trophy (1979)

Played in NHL All-Star Game (1977, 1978, 1980, 1981)

• GALANOV, MAXIM

Maxim Galanov D – L. 6'1", 195 lbs. b: Krasnoyarsk, USSR, 3/13/1974. NY Rangers' 3rd choice, 61st overall, in 1993 Entry Draft.

Season	Club	League	GP	G	A	Pts	AG	AA	APts	PIM	PP	SH	GW	S	%	TGF	PGF	TGA	PGA	+/–	GP	G	A	Pts	PIM	PP	SH	GW
1992-93	Lada Togliatti	CIS	41	4	2	6	....	....	....	12	....	....	....	....	....	....	....	....	....	....	10	1	1	2	12	....	....	....
	Russia	WJC-A	7	1	0	1	....	....	....	4	....	....	....	....	....	....	....	....	....	....	....	....	....	....	....	....	....	....
1993-94	Lada Togliatti	CIS	7	1	0	1	....	....	....	4	....	....	....	....	....	....	....	....	....	....	12	1	0	1	8	....	....	....
1994-95	Lada Togliatti	CIS	45	5	6	11	....	....	....	54	....	....	....	....	....	....	....	....	....	....	9	0	1	1	12	....	....	....
1995-96	Binghamton Rangers	AHL	72	17	36	53	....	....	....	24	....	....	....	....	....	....	....	....	....	....	4	1	1	2	0	....	....	....
1996-97	Binghamton Rangers	AHL	73	13	30	43	....	....	....	30	....	....	....	....	....	....	....	....	....	....	3	0	0	0	2	....	....	....
1997-98	**New York Rangers**	NHL	6	0	1	1	0	1	1	2	0	0	0	5	0.0	7	2	4	0	+1	....	....	....	....	....	....	....	....
	Hartford Wolf Pack	AHL	61	6	24	30	....	....	....	22	....	....	....	....	....	....	....	....	....	....	13	3	6	9	2	....	....	....
	NHL Totals		6	0	1	1	0	1	1	2	0	0	0	5	0.0	7	2	4	0		....	....	....	....	....	....	....	....

			REGULAR SEASON																		PLAYOFFS							
Season	Club	League	GP	G	A	Pts	AG	AA	APts	PIM	PP	SH	GW	S	%	TGF	PGF	TGA	PGA	+/–	GP	G	A	Pts	PIM	PP	SH	GW

• GALARNEAU, MICHEL

Michel Galarneau C – R. 6'2", 180 lbs. b: Montreal, Que., 3/1/1961. Hartford's 2nd choice, 29th overall, in 1980 Entry Draft.

Season	Club	League	GP	G	A	Pts	AG	AA	APts	PIM	PP	SH	GW	S	%	TGF	PGF	TGA	PGA	+/–	GP	G	A	Pts	PIM	PP	SH	GW
1978-79	Hull Olympiques	QMJHL	67	22	37	59	....	....	....	70	....	....	....	....	....	....	....	....	....	....	....	....	....	....	....	....	....	....
1979-80	Hull Olympiques	QMJHL	72	39	64	103	....	....	....	49	....	....	....	....	....	....	....	....	....	....	4	3	1	4	12	....	....	....
1980-81	Hull Olympiques	QMJHL	30	9	21	30	....	....	....	48	....	....	....	....	....	....	....	....	....	....	....	....	....	....	....	....	....	....
	Hartford Whalers	**NHL**	**30**	**2**	**6**	**8**	**2**	**4**	**6**	**9**	**0**	**0**	**1**	**19**	**10.5**	**12**	**1**	**23**	**0**	**–12**	....	....	....	....	....	....	....	....
	Binghamton Whalers	AHL	9	1	0	1	....	....	....	4	....	....	....	....	....	....	....	....	....	....	5	0	1	1	0	....	....	....
1981-82	**Hartford Whalers**	**NHL**	**10**	**0**	**0**	**0**	**0**	**0**	**0**	**4**	**0**	**0**	**0**	**10**	**0.0**	**1**	**0**	**8**	**0**	**–7**	....	....	....	....	....	....	....	....
	Binghamton Whalers	AHL	64	15	17	32	....	....	....	52	....	....	....	....	....	....	....	....	....	....	14	2	0	2	2	....	....	....
1982-83	**Hartford Whalers**	**NHL**	**38**	**5**	**4**	**9**	**4**	**3**	**7**	**21**	**0**	**0**	**0**	**29**	**17.2**	**14**	**0**	**22**	**0**	**–8**	....	....	....	....	....	....	....	....
	Binghamton Whalers	AHL	25	4	6	10	....	....	....	20	....	....	....	....	....	....	....	....	....	....	....	....	....	....	....	....	....	....
1983-84	Fredericton Express	AHL	2	0	0	0	....	....	....	0	....	....	....	....	....	....	....	....	....	....	....	....	....	....	....	....	....	....
	Binghamton Whalers	AHL	4	1	0	1	....	....	....	0	....	....	....	....	....	....	....	....	....	....	....	....	....	....	....	....	....	....
	Montana Magic	CHL	66	18	22	40	....	....	....	44	....	....	....	....	....	....	....	....	....	....	....	....	....	....	....	....	....	....
1984-85	HC Amiens Somme	France	STATISTICS NOT AVAILABLE																									
1985-86	HC Amiens Somme	France	STATISTICS NOT AVAILABLE																									
1986-87	HC Amiens Somme	France	30	51	33	84	....	....	....	....	....	....	....	....	....	....	....	....	....	....	....	....	....	....	....	....	....	....
1987-88	HC Amiens Somme	France	30	28	22	50	....	....	....	36	....	....	....	....	....	....	....	....	....	....	....	....	....	....	....	....	....	....
1988-89	HC Amiens Somme	France	3	2	1	3	....	....	....	2	....	....	....	....	....	....	....	....	....	....	....	....	....	....	....	....	....	....
	NHL Totals		**78**	**7**	**10**	**17**	**6**	**7**	**13**	**34**	**0**	**0**	**1**	**58**	**12.1**	**27**	**1**	**53**	**0**		....	....	....	....	....	....	....	....

• GALLANT, GERARD

Gerard Gallant LW – L. 5'10", 190 lbs. b: Summerside, P.E.I., 9/2/1963. Detroit's 4th choice, 107th overall, in 1981 Entry Draft.

Season	Club	League	GP	G	A	Pts	AG	AA	APts	PIM	PP	SH	GW	S	%	TGF	PGF	TGA	PGA	+/–	GP	G	A	Pts	PIM	PP	SH	GW
1979-80	Summerside Islanders	PEI Jr.	45	60	55	115	....	....	....	90	....	....	....	....	....	....	....	....	....	....	....	....	....	....	....	....	....	....
1980-81	Sherbrooke Beavers	QMJHL	68	41	59	100	....	....	....	265	....	....	....	....	....	....	....	....	....	....	14	6	13	19	46	....	....	....
1981-82	Sherbrooke Beavers	QMJHL	58	34	58	92	....	....	....	260	....	....	....	....	....	....	....	....	....	....	22	14	24	38	84	....	....	....
1982-83	St-Jean Beavers	QMJHL	33	28	25	53	....	....	....	139	....	....	....	....	....	....	....	....	....	....	....	....	....	....	....	....	....	....
	Verdun Juniors	QMJHL	29	26	49	75	....	....	....	105	....	....	....	....	....	....	....	....	....	....	15	*14	19	*33	84	....	....	....
1983-84	Adirondack Red Wings	AHL	77	31	33	64	....	....	....	195	....	....	....	....	....	....	....	....	....	....	7	1	3	4	34	....	....	....
1984-85	**Detroit Red Wings**	**NHL**	**32**	**6**	**12**	**18**	**5**	**8**	**13**	**66**	**0**	**0**	**2**	**44**	**13.6**	**26**	**0**	**17**	**0**	**+9**	**3**	**0**	**0**	**0**	**11**	**0**	**0**	**0**
	Adirondack Red Wings	AHL	46	18	29	47	....	....	....	131	....	....	....	....	....	....	....	....	....	....	....	....	....	....	....	....	....	....
1985-86	**Detroit Red Wings**	**NHL**	**52**	**20**	**19**	**39**	**16**	**13**	**29**	**106**	**3**	**1**	**2**	**116**	**17.2**	**58**	**10**	**66**	**8**	**–10**	....	....	....	....	....	....	....	....
1986-87	**Detroit Red Wings**	**NHL**	**80**	**38**	**34**	**72**	**33**	**25**	**58**	**216**	**17**	**0**	**4**	**191**	**19.9**	**106**	**43**	**71**	**3**	**–5**	**16**	**8**	**6**	**14**	**43**	**2**	**0**	**0**
1987-88	**Detroit Red Wings**	**NHL**	**73**	**34**	**39**	**73**	**29**	**28**	**57**	**242**	**10**	**0**	**3**	**197**	**17.3**	**118**	**41**	**58**	**5**	**+24**	**16**	**6**	**9**	**15**	**55**	**1**	**0**	**1**
1988-89	**Detroit Red Wings**	**NHL**	**76**	**39**	**54**	**93**	**33**	**38**	**71**	**230**	**13**	**0**	**7**	**221**	**17.6**	**140**	**52**	**84**	**3**	**+7**	**6**	**1**	**2**	**3**	**40**	**0**	**0**	**0**
	Canada	WEC-A	8	2	3	5	....	....	....	10	....	....	....	....	....	....	....	....	....	....	....	....	....	....	....	....	....	....
1989-90	**Detroit Red Wings**	**NHL**	**69**	**36**	**44**	**80**	**31**	**31**	**62**	**254**	**12**	**3**	**5**	**219**	**16.4**	**120**	**41**	**96**	**11**	**–6**	....	....	....	....	....	....	....	....
1990-91	**Detroit Red Wings**	**NHL**	**45**	**10**	**16**	**26**	**9**	**12**	**21**	**111**	**3**	**0**	**1**	**82**	**12.2**	**57**	**15**	**36**	**0**	**+6**	....	....	....	....	....	....	....	....
1991-92	**Detroit Red Wings**	**NHL**	**69**	**14**	**22**	**36**	**13**	**17**	**30**	**187**	**4**	**0**	**1**	**116**	**12.1**	**61**	**11**	**35**	**1**	**+16**	**11**	**2**	**2**	**4**	**25**	**0**	**0**	**1**
1992-93	**Detroit Red Wings**	**NHL**	**67**	**10**	**20**	**30**	**8**	**14**	**22**	**188**	**0**	**0**	**0**	**81**	**12.3**	**53**	**3**	**30**	**0**	**+20**	**6**	**1**	**2**	**3**	**4**	**0**	**0**	**0**
1993-94	**Tampa Bay Lightning**	**NHL**	**51**	**4**	**9**	**13**	**4**	**7**	**11**	**74**	**1**	**0**	**2**	**45**	**8.9**	**17**	**2**	**22**	**1**	**–6**	....	....	....	....	....	....	....	....
1994-95	**Tampa Bay Lightning**	**NHL**	**1**	**0**	**0**	**0**	**0**	**0**	**0**	**0**	**0**	**0**	**0**	**1**	**0.0**	**0**	**0**	**0**	**0**	**0**	....	....	....	....	....	....	....	....
	Atlanta Knights	IHL	16	3	3	6	....	....	....	31	....	....	....	....	....	....	....	....	....	....	....	....	....	....	....	....	....	....
1995-96	Detroit Vipers	IHL	3	2	1	3	....	....	....	6	....	....	....	....	....	....	....	....	....	....	....	....	....	....	....	....	....	....
	NHL Totals		**615**	**211**	**269**	**480**	**181**	**193**	**374**	**1674**	**63**	**4**	**27**	**1313**	**16.1**	**756**	**218**	**515**	**32**		**58**	**18**	**21**	**39**	**178**	**3**	**0**	**2**

NHL Second All-Star Team (1989)

Signed as a free agent by **Tampa Bay**, July 21, 1993.

• GALLEY, GARRY

Garry "Ga-Ga" Galley D – L. 6', 204 lbs. b: Montreal, Que., 4/16/1963. Los Angeles' 4th choice, 100th overall, in 1983 Entry Draft.

Season	Club	League	GP	G	A	Pts	AG	AA	APts	PIM	PP	SH	GW	S	%	TGF	PGF	TGA	PGA	+/–	GP	G	A	Pts	PIM	PP	SH	GW
1981-82	Bowling Green University	CCHA	42	3	36	39	....	....	....	48	....	....	....	....	....	....	....	....	....	....	....	....	....	....	....	....	....	....
1982-83	Bowling Green University	CCHA	40	17	29	46	....	....	....	40	....	....	....	....	....	....	....	....	....	....	....	....	....	....	....	....	....	....
1983-84	Bowling Green University	CCHA	44	15	52	67	....	....	....	61	....	....	....	....	....	....	....	....	....	....	....	....	....	....	....	....	....	....
1984-85	**Los Angeles Kings**	**NHL**	**78**	**8**	**30**	**38**	**7**	**20**	**27**	**82**	**1**	**1**	**2**	**131**	**6.1**	**101**	**15**	**94**	**11**	**+3**	**3**	**1**	**0**	**1**	**2**	**0**	**0**	**0**
1985-86	**Los Angeles Kings**	**NHL**	**49**	**9**	**13**	**22**	**7**	**9**	**16**	**46**	**1**	**0**	**1**	**57**	**15.8**	**58**	**7**	**75**	**15**	**–9**	....	....	....	....	....	....	....	....
	New Haven Nighthawks	AHL	4	2	6	8	....	....	....	6	....	....	....	....	....	....	....	....	....	....	....	....	....	....	....	....	....	....
1986-87	**Los Angeles Kings**	**NHL**	**30**	**5**	**11**	**16**	**4**	**8**	**12**	**57**	**2**	**0**	**1**	**43**	**11.6**	**28**	**6**	**37**	**6**	**–9**	....	....	....	....	....	....	....	....
	Washington Capitals	**NHL**	**18**	**1**	**10**	**11**	**1**	**7**	**8**	**10**	**1**	**0**	**0**	**27**	**3.7**	**20**	**12**	**5**	**0**	**+3**	**2**	**0**	**0**	**0**	**0**	**0**	**0**	**0**
1987-88	**Washington Capitals**	**NHL**	**58**	**7**	**23**	**30**	**6**	**16**	**22**	**44**	**3**	**0**	**0**	**100**	**7.0**	**63**	**31**	**24**	**3**	**+11**	**13**	**2**	**4**	**6**	**13**	**0**	**0**	**0**
1988-89	**Boston Bruins**	**NHL**	**78**	**8**	**22**	**30**	**7**	**15**	**22**	**80**	**2**	**1**	**0**	**145**	**5.5**	**71**	**24**	**65**	**11**	**–7**	**9**	**0**	**1**	**1**	**33**	**0**	**0**	**0**
1989-90	**Boston Bruins**	**NHL**	**71**	**8**	**27**	**35**	**7**	**19**	**26**	**75**	**1**	**0**	**0**	**142**	**5.6**	**79**	**8**	**85**	**16**	**+2**	**21**	**3**	**3**	**6**	**34**	**1**	**0**	**2**
1990-91	**Boston Bruins**	**NHL**	**70**	**6**	**21**	**27**	**5**	**16**	**21**	**84**	**1**	**0**	**0**	**128**	**4.7**	**79**	**17**	**83**	**21**	**0**	**16**	**1**	**5**	**6**	**17**	**0**	**0**	**0**
1991-92	**Boston Bruins**	**NHL**	**38**	**2**	**12**	**14**	**2**	**9**	**11**	**83**	**1**	**0**	**0**	**51**	**3.9**	**42**	**6**	**50**	**11**	**–3**	....	....	....	....	....	....	....	....
	Philadelphia Flyers	**NHL**	**39**	**3**	**15**	**18**	**3**	**11**	**14**	**34**	**2**	**0**	**1**	**74**	**4.1**	**42**	**11**	**43**	**13**	**+1**	....	....	....	....	....	....	....	....
1992-93	**Philadelphia Flyers**	**NHL**	**83**	**13**	**49**	**62**	**11**	**34**	**45**	**115**	**4**	**1**	**3**	**231**	**5.6**	**146**	**42**	**142**	**56**	**+18**	....	....	....	....	....	....	....	....
	Canada	WC-A	8	1	2	3	....	....	....	0	....	....	....	....	....	....	....	....	....	....	....	....	....	....	....	....	....	....
1993-94	**Philadelphia Flyers**	**NHL**	**81**	**10**	**60**	**70**	**9**	**46**	**55**	**91**	**5**	**1**	**0**	**186**	**5.4**	**145**	**63**	**133**	**40**	**–11**	....	....	....	....	....	....	....	....
1994-95	**Philadelphia Flyers**	**NHL**	**33**	**2**	**20**	**22**	**4**	**29**	**33**	**20**	**1**	**0**	**0**	**66**	**3.0**	**49**	**25**	**34**	**10**	**0**	....	....	....	....	....	....	....	....
	Buffalo Sabres	**NHL**	**14**	**1**	**9**	**10**	**2**	**13**	**15**	**10**	**2**	**0**	**0**	**31**	**3.2**	**29**	**13**	**13**	**1**	**+4**	**5**	**0**	**3**	**3**	**4**	**0**	**0**	**0**
1995-96	**Buffalo Sabres**	**NHL**	**78**	**10**	**44**	**54**	**10**	**36**	**46**	**81**	**7**	**1**	**2**	**175**	**5.7**	**116**	**53**	**94**	**29**	**–2**	....	....	....	....	....	....	....	....
	Canada	WC-A	8	0	2	2	....	....	....	6	....	....	....	....	....	....	....	....	....	....	....	....	....	....	....	....	....	....
1996-97	**Buffalo Sabres**	**NHL**	**71**	**4**	**34**	**38**	**4**	**30**	**34**	**102**	**1**	**1**	**1**	**84**	**4.8**	**83**	**26**	**61**	**14**	**+10**	**12**	**0**	**6**	**6**	**14**	**0**	**0**	**0**
1997-98	**Los Angeles Kings**	**NHL**	**74**	**9**	**28**	**37**	**11**	**27**	**38**	**63**	**7**	**0**	**0**	**128**	**7.0**	**81**	**29**	**66**	**9**	**–5**	**4**	**0**	**1**	**1**	**2**	**0**	**0**	**0**
	NHL Totals		**963**	**106**	**428**	**534**	**100**	**345**	**445**	**1077**	**42**	**6**	**11**	**1799**	**5.9**	**1232**	**388**	**1104**	**266**		**85**	**7**	**23**	**30**	**119**	**1**	**0**	**2**

CCHA First All-Star Team (1983, 1984) • NCAA East First All-American Team (1984) • NCAA Championship All-Tournament Team (1984)

Played in NHL All-Star Game (1991, 1994)

Traded to **Washington** by **LA Kings** for Al Jensen, February 14, 1987. Signed as a free agent by **Boston**, July 8, 1900. Traded to **Philadelphia** by **Boston** with Wes Walz and Boston's 3rd round choice (Milos Holan) in 1993 Entry Draft for Gord Murphy, Brian Dobbin, Philadelphia's 3rd round choice (Sergei Zholtok) in 1992 Entry Draft and 4th round choice (Charles Paquette) in 1993 Entry Draft, January 2, 1992. Traded to **Buffalo** by **Philadelphia** for Petr Svoboda, April 7, 1995. Signed as a free agent by **LA Kings**, July 15, 1997.

• GALLIMORE, JAMIE

Jamie Gallimore RW – R. 6', 180 lbs. b: Edmonton, Alta., 11/28/1957. Minnesota's 5th choice, 97th overall, in 1977 Amateur Draft.

Season	Club	League	GP	G	A	Pts	AG	AA	APts	PIM	PP	SH	GW	S	%	TGF	PGF	TGA	PGA	+/–	GP	G	A	Pts	PIM	PP	SH	GW
1974-75	Kamloops Chiefs	WCJHL	56	3	5	8	....	....	....	50	....	....	....	....	....	....	....	....	....	....	3	0	1	1	27	....	....	....
1975-76	Kamloops Chiefs	WCJHL	28	5	7	12	....	....	....	57	....	....	....	....	....	....	....	....	....	....	1	0	0	0	0	....	....	....
1976-77	Kamloops Chiefs	WCJHL	72	24	22	46	....	....	....	121	....	....	....	....	....	....	....	....	....	....	....	....	....	....	....	....	....	....
1977-78	**Minnesota North Stars**	**NHL**	**2**	**0**	**0**	**0**	**0**	**0**	**0**	**0**	**0**	**0**	**0**	**0**	**0.0**	**0**	**0**	**0**	**0**	**0**	....	....	....	....	....	....	....	....
	Fort Wayne Komets	IHL	23	6	6	12	....	....	....	21	....	....	....	....	....	....	....	....	....	....	....	....	....	....	....	....	....	....
	Fort Worth Texans	CHL	47	8	2	10	....	....	....	24	....	....	....	....	....	....	....	....	....	....	9	0	0	0	29	....	....	....
1978-79	Oklahoma City Stars	CHL	38	8	6	14	....	....	....	26	....	....	....	....	....	....	....	....	....	....	....	....	....	....	....	....	....	....
1979-80	Oklahoma City Stars	CHL	67	5	8	13	....	....	....	35	....	....	....	....	....	....	....	....	....	....	....	....	....	....	....	....	....	....
1980-81			DID NOT PLAY																									
1981-82	Wichita Wind	CHL	3	0	1	1	....	....	....	11	....	....	....	....	....	....	....	....	....	....	....	....	....	....	....	....	....	....
	NHL Totals		**2**	**0**	**0**	**0**	**0**	**0**	**0**	**0**	**0**	**0**	**0**	**0**	**0.0**	**0**	**0**	**0**	**0**		....	....	....	....	....	....	....	....

• GAMBUCCI, GARY

Gary Gambucci C – L. 5'9", 175 lbs. b: Hibbing, MN, 9/27/1946.

Season	Club	League	GP	G	A	Pts	AG	AA	APts	PIM	PP	SH	GW	S	%	TGF	PGF	TGA	PGA	+/–	GP	G	A	Pts	PIM	PP	SH	GW
1965-66	University of Minnesota	WCHA	28	23	17	40	....	....	....	18	....	....	....	....	....	....	....	....	....	....	....	....	....	....	....	....	....	....
1966-67	University of Minnesota	WCHA	29	17	10	27	....	....	....	23	....	....	....	....	....	....	....	....	....	....	....	....	....	....	....	....	....	....
1967-68	University of Minnesota	WCHA	31	12	29	41	....	....	....	31	....	....	....	....	....	....	....	....	....	....	....	....	....	....	....	....	....	....
1968-69	United States	Nat-Team	STATISTICS NOT AVAILABLE																									
	United States	WEC-A	10	1	1	2	....	....	....	6	....	....	....	....	....	....	....	....	....	....	....	....	....	....	....	....	....	....
1969-70	United States	Nat-Team	7	*11	7	18	....	....	....	4	....	....	....	....	....	....	....	....	....	....	....	....	....	....	....	....	....	....
	United States	WEC-B	....	10	8	18	....	....	....	....	....	....	....	....	....	....	....	....	....	....	....	....	....	....	....	....	....	....
	Muskegon Mohawks	IHL	4	2	1	3	....	....	....	5	....	....	....	....	....	....	....	....	....	....	....	....	....	....	....	....	....	....

			REGULAR SEASON																		PLAYOFFS							
Season	Club	League	GP	G	A	Pts	AG	AA	APts	PIM	PP	SH	GW	S	%	TGF	PGF	TGA	PGA	+/–	GP	G	A	Pts	PIM	PP	SH	GW
1970-71	United States	Nat-Team	....	51	47	98	....	....	....	....	....	....	....	....	....	....	....	....	....	....	....	....	....	....	....	....	....	....
	United States	WEC-A	10	7	3	10	....	....	....	4	....	....	....	....	....	....	....	....	....	....	....	....	....	....	....	....	....	....
1971-72	**Minnesota North Stars**	**NHL**	**9**	**1**	**0**	**1**	**1**	**0**	**1**	**0**	**0**	**0**	**0**	**3**	**33.3**	**3**	**1**	**0**	**0**	**+2**	....	....	....	....	....	....	....	....
	Cleveland Barons	AHL	56	10	11	21	....	....	....	37	....	....	....	....	....	....	....	....	....	....	6	0	0	0	10	....	....	....
1972-73	Cleveland-Jacksonville Barons	AHL	75	26	50	76	....	....	....	47	....	....	....	....	....	....	....	....	....	....	....	....	....	....	....	....	....	....
1973-74	**Minnesota North Stars**	**NHL**	**42**	**1**	**7**	**8**	**1**	**6**	**7**	**9**	**0**	**0**	**0**	**26**	**3.8**	**15**	**2**	**12**	**4**	**+5**	....	....	....	....	....	....	....	....
	New Haven Nighthawks	AHL	2	1	2	3	....	....	....	2	....	....	....	....	....	....	....	....	....	....	....	....	....	....	....	....	....	....
	Portland Buckaroos	WHL	21	11	15	26	....	....	....	20	....	....	....	....	....	....	....	....	....	....	....	....	....	....	....	....	....	....
1974-75	Minnesota Fighting Saints	WHA	67	19	18	37	....	....	....	19	....	....	....	....	....	....	....	....	....	....	12	4	0	4	6	....	....	....
1975-76	Minnesota Fighting Saints	WHA	45	10	6	16	....	....	....	14	....	....	....	....	....	....	....	....	....	....	....	....	....	....	....	....	....	....
	United States	WEC-A	10	1	4	5	....	....	....	17	....	....	....	....	....	....	....	....	....	....	....	....	....	....	....	....	....	....
	NHL Totals		**51**	**2**	**7**	**9**	**2**	**6**	**8**	**9**	**0**	**0**	**0**	**29**	**6.9**	**18**	**3**	**12**	**4**		....	....	....	....	....	....	....	....
	Other Major League Totals		112	29	24	53	....	....	....	33	....	....	....	....	....	....	....	....	....		12	4	0	4	6	....	....	....

WCHA Second All-Star Team (1966) • WCHA First All-Star Team (1968) • NCAA West First All-American Team (1968) • WEC-B All-Star Team (1970)

Signed as a free agent by **Montreal**, May, 1971. Traded to **Minnesota** by **Montreal** with Bob Paradise for cash, May, 1971. Selected by **Miami-Philadelphia** (WHA) in 1972 WHA General Player Draft, February 12, 1972. WHA rights transferred to **Vancouver** after **Philadelphia** franchise relocated, May, 1973. WHA rights traded to **Minnesota** (WHA) by **Vancouver** (WHA) for cash, June, 1974.

• GANCHAR, PERRY

Perry Ganchar RW – R. 5'9", 180 lbs. b: Saskatoon, Sask., 10/28/1963. St. Louis' 3rd choice, 113th overall, in 1982 Entry Draft.

Season	Club	League	GP	G	A	Pts	AG	AA	APts	PIM	PP	SH	GW	S	%	TGF	PGF	TGA	PGA	+/–	GP	G	A	Pts	PIM	PP	SH	GW
1977-78	Saskatoon Blades	WCJHL	4	2	0	2	....	....	....	2	....	....	....	....	....	....	....	....	....	....	....	....	....	....	....	....	....	....
1978-79	Saskatoon Royals	SJHL	50	21	33	54	....	....	....	72	....	....	....	....	....	....	....	....	....	....	....	....	....	....	....	....	....	....
	Saskatoon Blades	WHL	14	5	3	8	....	....	....	15	....	....	....	....	....	....	....	....	....	....	....	....	....	....	....	....	....	....
1979-80	Saskatoon Blades	WHL	27	9	14	23	....	....	....	60	....	....	....	....	....	....	....	....	....	....	....	....	....	....	....	....	....	....
1980-81	Saskatoon Blades	WHL	72	26	53	79	....	....	....	117	....	....	....	....	....	....	....	....	....	....	....	....	....	....	....	....	....	....
1981-82	Saskatoon Blades	WHL	53	38	52	90	....	....	....	82	....	....	....	....	....	....	....	....	....	....	5	3	3	6	17	....	....	....
1982-83	Saskatoon Blades	WHL	68	68	48	116	....	....	....	105	....	....	....	....	....	....	....	....	....	....	6	1	4	5	24	....	....	....
	Salt Lake Golden Eagles	CHL	....	....	....	....	....	....	....	....	....	....	....	....	....	....	....	....	....	....	1	0	1	1	0	....	....	....
1983-84	**St. Louis Blues**	**NHL**	**1**	**0**	**0**	**0**	**0**	**0**	**0**	**0**	**0**	**0**	**0**	**0**	**0.0**	**1**	**0**	**0**	**0**	**+1**	**7**	**3**	**1**	**4**	**0**	**2**	**0**	**0**
	Montana Magic	CHL	59	23	22	45	....	....	....	77	....	....	....	....	....	....	....	....	....	....	....	....	....	....	....	....	....	....
1984-85	**St. Louis Blues**	**NHL**	**7**	**0**	**2**	**2**	**0**	**1**	**1**	**0**	**0**	**0**	**0**	**4**	**0.0**	**3**	**0**	**3**	**0**	**0**	....	....	....	....	....	....	....	....
	Peoria Rivermen	IHL	63	41	29	70	....	....	....	114	....	....	....	....	....	....	....	....	....	....	20	4	11	15	49	....	....	....
1985-86	Sherbrooke Canadiens	AHL	75	25	29	54	....	....	....	42	....	....	....	....	....	....	....	....	....	....	....	....	....	....	....	....	....	....
1986-87	Sherbrooke Canadiens	AHL	68	22	29	51	....	....	....	64	....	....	....	....	....	....	....	....	....	....	17	9	8	17	37	....	....	....
1987-88	**Montreal Canadiens**	**NHL**	**1**	**1**	**0**	**1**	**1**	**0**	**1**	**0**	**0**	**0**	**0**	**1**	**100.0**	**1**	**0**	**2**	**0**	**–1**	....	....	....	....	....	....	....	....
	Sherbrooke Canadiens	AHL	28	12	18	30	....	....	....	61	....	....	....	....	....	....	....	....	....	....	....	....	....	....	....	....	....	....
	Pittsburgh Penguins	**NHL**	**30**	**2**	**5**	**7**	**2**	**4**	**6**	**36**	**0**	**0**	**0**	**34**	**5.9**	**12**	**2**	**10**	**0**	**0**	....	....	....	....	....	....	....	....
1988-89	**Pittsburgh Penguins**	**NHL**	**3**	**0**	**0**	**0**	**0**	**0**	**0**	**0**	**0**	**0**	**0**	**3**	**0.0**	**0**	**0**	**3**	**0**	**–3**	....	....	....	....	....	....	....	....
	Muskegon Lumberjacks	IHL	70	39	34	73	....	....	....	114	....	....	....	....	....	....	....	....	....	....	14	7	8	15	6	....	....	....
1989-90	Muskegon Lumberjacks	IHL	79	40	45	85	....	....	....	111	....	....	....	....	....	....	....	....	....	....	14	3	5	8	27	....	....	....
1990-91	Muskegon Lumberjacks	IHL	80	37	38	75	....	....	....	87	....	....	....	....	....	....	....	....	....	....	5	2	1	3	0	....	....	....
1991-92	Muskegon Lumberjacks	IHL	65	29	20	49	....	....	....	65	....	....	....	....	....	....	....	....	....	....	14	9	9	18	18	....	....	....
1992-93	Cleveland Lumberjacks	IHL	79	37	37	74	....	....	....	156	....	....	....	....	....	....	....	....	....	....	3	0	0	0	4	....	....	....
1993-94	Cleveland Lumberjacks	IHL	63	14	17	31	....	....	....	48	....	....	....	....	....	....	....	....	....	....	....	....	....	....	....	....	....	....
1994-95	Cleveland Lumberjacks	IHL	60	11	17	28	....	....	....	56	....	....	....	....	....	....	....	....	....	....	....	....	....	....	....	....	....	....
1995-96	Cleveland Lumberjacks	IHL	1	0	0	0	....	....	....	0	....	....	....	....	....	....	....	....	....	....	....	....	....	....	....	....	....	....
	NHL Totals		**42**	**3**	**7**	**10**	**3**	**5**	**8**	**36**	**0**	**0**	**0**	**42**	**7.1**	**17**	**2**	**18**	**0**		**7**	**3**	**1**	**4**	**0**	**2**	**0**	**0**

IHL Second All-Star Team (1985)

Traded to **Montreal** by **St. Louis** for Ron Flockhart, August 26, 1985. Traded to **Pittsburgh** by **Montreal** for future considerations, December 17, 1987.

• GANS, DAVE

Dave Gans C – R. 5'10", 180 lbs. b: Brantford, Ont., 6/6/1964. Los Angeles' 3rd choice, 64th overall, in 1982 Entry Draft.

Season	Club	League	GP	G	A	Pts	AG	AA	APts	PIM	PP	SH	GW	S	%	TGF	PGF	TGA	PGA	+/–	GP	G	A	Pts	PIM	PP	SH	GW
1980-81	Brantford Penguins	Jr. B	36	46	45	91	....	....	....	146	....	....	....	....	....	....	....	....	....	....	....	....	....	....	....	....	....	....
1981-82	Oshawa Generals	OHL	66	23	51	74	....	....	....	112	....	....	....	....	....	....	....	....	....	....	12	3	6	9	45	....	....	....
1982-83	Oshawa Generals	OHL	64	41	64	105	....	....	....	90	....	....	....	....	....	....	....	....	....	....	17	14	*24	*38	27	....	....	....
	Los Angeles Kings	**NHL**	**3**	**0**	**0**	**0**	**0**	**0**	**0**	**0**	**0**	**0**	**0**	**0**	**0.0**	**0**	**0**	**1**	**0**	**–1**	....	....	....	....	....	....	....	....
1983-84	Oshawa Generals	OHL	62	56	76	132	....	....	....	89	....	....	....	....	....	....	....	....	....	....	6	3	4	7	9	....	....	....
1984-85	Toledo Goaldiggers	IHL	81	52	53	105	....	....	....	65	....	....	....	....	....	....	....	....	....	....	6	4	3	7	26	....	....	....
1985-86	**Los Angeles Kings**	**NHL**	**3**	**0**	**0**	**0**	**0**	**0**	**0**	**2**	**0**	**0**	**0**	**3**	**0.0**	**1**	**0**	**1**	**0**	**0**	....	....	....	....	....	....	....	....
	New Haven Nighthawks	AHL	17	11	12	23	....	....	....	14	....	....	....	....	....	....	....	....	....	....	....	....	....	....	....	....	....	....
	Hershey Bears	AHL	56	24	32	56	....	....	....	88	....	....	....	....	....	....	....	....	....	....	18	10	5	15	60	....	....	....
1986-87	New Haven Nighthawks	AHL	29	10	11	21	....	....	....	20	....	....	....	....	....	....	....	....	....	....	....	....	....	....	....	....	....	....
	Hershey Bears	AHL	20	7	8	15	....	....	....	28	....	....	....	....	....	....	....	....	....	....	5	0	0	0	21	....	....	....
1987-88	Newmarket Saints	AHL	16	2	7	9	....	....	....	11	....	....	....	....	....	....	....	....	....	....	....	....	....	....	....	....	....	....
	NHL Totals		**6**	**0**	**0**	**0**	**0**	**0**	**0**	**2**	**0**	**0**	**0**	**3**	**0.0**	**1**	**0**	**2**	**0**		....	....	....	....	....	....	....	....

Won George Parsons Trophy (Memorial Cup Tournament Most Sportsmanlike Player) (1983)

• GARDINER, BRUCE

Bruce Gardiner C – R. 6'1", 193 lbs. b: Barrie, Ont., 2/11/1971. St. Louis' 6th choice, 131st overall, in 1991 Entry Draft.

Season	Club	League	GP	G	A	Pts	AG	AA	APts	PIM	PP	SH	GW	S	%	TGF	PGF	TGA	PGA	+/–	GP	G	A	Pts	PIM	PP	SH	GW
1990-91	Colgate University	ECAC	27	4	9	13	....	....	....	72	....	....	....	....	....	....	....	....	....	....	....	....	....	....	....	....	....	....
1991-92	Colgate University	ECAC	23	7	8	15	....	....	....	77	....	....	....	....	....	....	....	....	....	....	....	....	....	....	....	....	....	....
1992-93	Colgate University	ECAC	33	17	12	29	....	....	....	64	....	....	....	....	....	....	....	....	....	....	....	....	....	....	....	....	....	....
1993-94	Colgate University	ECAC	33	23	23	46	....	....	....	68	....	....	....	....	....	....	....	....	....	....	....	....	....	....	....	....	....	....
	Peoria Rivermen	IHL	3	0	0	0	....	....	....	0	....	....	....	....	....	....	....	....	....	....	....	....	....	....	....	....	....	....
1994-95	P.E.I. Senators	AHL	72	17	20	37	....	....	....	132	....	....	....	....	....	....	....	....	....	....	7	4	1	5	4	....	....	....
1995-96	P.E.I. Senators	AHL	38	11	13	24	....	....	....	87	....	....	....	....	....	....	....	....	....	....	5	2	4	6	4	....	....	....
1996-97	**Ottawa Senators**	**NHL**	**67**	**11**	**10**	**21**	**12**	**9**	**21**	**49**	**0**	**1**	**2**	**94**	**11.7**	**29**	**1**	**35**	**11**	**+4**	**7**	**0**	**1**	**1**	**2**	**0**	**0**	**0**
1997-98	**Ottawa Senators**	**NHL**	**55**	**7**	**11**	**18**	**8**	**11**	**19**	**50**	**0**	**0**	**0**	**64**	**10.9**	**25**	**0**	**29**	**6**	**+2**	**11**	**1**	**3**	**4**	**2**	**0**	**0**	**1**
	NHL Totals		**122**	**18**	**21**	**39**	**20**	**20**	**40**	**99**	**0**	**1**	**2**	**158**	**11.4**	**54**	**1**	**64**	**17**		**18**	**1**	**4**	**5**	**4**	**0**	**0**	**1**

ECAC Second All-Star Team (1994)

Signed as a free agent by **Ottawa**, June 14, 1994.

• GARDNER, BILL

Bill Gardner C – L. 5'10", 180 lbs. b: Toronto, Ont., 3/18/1960. Chicago's 3rd choice, 49th overall, in 1979 Entry Draft.

Season	Club	League	GP	G	A	Pts	AG	AA	APts	PIM	PP	SH	GW	S	%	TGF	PGF	TGA	PGA	+/–	GP	G	A	Pts	PIM	PP	SH	GW
1976-77	Peterborough Petes	OHA	1	0	0	0	....	....	....	0	....	....	....	....	....	....	....	....	....	....	....	....	....	....	....	....	....	....
1977-78	Peterborough Petes	OHA	65	23	32	55	....	....	....	10	....	....	....	....	....	....	....	....	....	....	....	....	....	....	....	....	....	....
1978-79	Peterborough Petes	OHA	68	33	71	104	....	....	....	19	....	....	....	....	....	....	....	....	....	....	18	4	20	24	6	....	....	....
1979-80	Peterborough Petes	OHA	59	43	63	106	....	....	....	17	....	....	....	....	....	....	....	....	....	....	14	13	14	27	8	....	....	....
	Canada	WJC-A	5	0	4	4	....	....	....	14	....	....	....	....	....	....	....	....	....	....	....	....	....	....	....	....	....	....
1980-81	**Chicago Black Hawks**	**NHL**	**1**	**0**	**0**	**0**	**0**	**0**	**0**	**0**	**0**	**0**	**0**	**0**	**0.0**	**0**	**0**	**0**	**0**	**0**	....	....	....	....	....	....	....	....
	New Brunswick Hawks	AHL	48	19	29	48	....	....	....	12	....	....	....	....	....	....	....	....	....	....	13	5	10	15	0	....	....	....
1981-82	**Chicago Black Hawks**	**NHL**	**69**	**8**	**15**	**23**	**6**	**10**	**16**	**20**	**1**	**4**	**0**	**66**	**12.1**	**31**	**6**	**84**	**50**	**–9**	**15**	**1**	**4**	**5**	**6**	**0**	**0**	**0**
1982-83	**Chicago Black Hawks**	**NHL**	**77**	**15**	**25**	**40**	**12**	**17**	**29**	**12**	**2**	**0**	**2**	**105**	**14.3**	**54**	**6**	**74**	**36**	**+10**	**13**	**1**	**0**	**1**	**9**	**1**	**0**	**0**
1983-84	**Chicago Black Hawks**	**NHL**	**79**	**27**	**21**	**48**	**22**	**14**	**36**	**12**	**3**	**3**	**3**	**114**	**23.7**	**76**	**17**	**97**	**39**	**+1**	**5**	**0**	**1**	**1**	**0**	**0**	**0**	**0**
1984-85	**Chicago Black Hawks**	**NHL**	**74**	**17**	**34**	**51**	**14**	**23**	**37**	**12**	**5**	**1**	**1**	**120**	**14.2**	**68**	**11**	**88**	**38**	**+7**	**12**	**1**	**3**	**4**	**2**	**0**	**0**	**0**
1985-86	**Chicago Black Hawks**	**NHL**	**46**	**3**	**10**	**13**	**2**	**7**	**9**	**6**	**0**	**0**	**0**	**29**	**10.3**	**20**	**1**	**48**	**21**	**–8**	....	....	....	....	....	....	....	....
	Hartford Whalers	**NHL**	**18**	**1**	**8**	**9**	**1**	**5**	**6**	**4**	**0**	**0**	**0**	**12**	**8.3**	**10**	**0**	**18**	**2**	**–6**	....	....	....	....	....	....	....	....
1986-87	**Hartford Whalers**	**NHL**	**8**	**0**	**1**	**1**	**0**	**1**	**1**	**0**	**0**	**0**	**0**	**7**	**0.0**	**1**	**0**	**5**	**2**	**–2**	....	....	....	....	....	....	....	....
	Binghamton Whalers	AHL	50	17	44	61	....	....	....	18	....	....	....	....	....	....	....	....	....	....	13	4	8	12	14	....	....	....
1987-88	**Chicago Blackhawks**	**NHL**	**2**	**1**	**0**	**1**	**1**	**0**	**1**	**2**	**1**	**0**	**0**	**1**	**100.0**	**1**	**1**	**1**	**0**	**–1**	....	....	....	....	....	....	....	....
	Saginaw Hawks	IHL	54	18	49	67	....	....	....	46	....	....	....	....	....	....	....	....	....	....	10	4	4	8	14	....	....	....
1988-89	**Chicago Blackhawks**	**NHL**	**6**	**1**	**1**	**2**	**1**	**1**	**2**	**0**	**1**	**0**	**1**	**4**	**25.0**	**3**	**1**	**0**	**0**	**+2**	....	....	....	....	....	....	....	....
	Saginaw Hawks	IHL	74	27	45	72	....	....	....	10	....	....	....	....	....	....	....	....	....	....	6	3	1	4	0	....	....	....
1989-90			DID NOT PLAY																									

			REGULAR SEASON																		PLAYOFFS							
Season	Club	League	GP	G	A	Pts	AG	AA	APts	PIM	PP	SH	GW	S	%	TGF	PGF	TGA	PGA	+/–	GP	G	A	Pts	PIM	PP	SH	GW
1990-91	EC Graz	Austria	38	35	*48	*83	....	....	....	....	....	....	....	....	....	....	....	....	....	....	....	....	....	....	....	....	....	....
1991-92	EC Graz	Austria	44	23	*74	*97	....	....	....	....	....	....	....	....	....	....	....	....	....	....	....	....	....	....	....	....	....	....
1992-93	IEV Innsbruck	Austria	25	17	32	49	....	....	....	....	....	....	....	....	....	....	....	....	....	....	....	....	....	....	....	....	....	....
	NHL Totals		**380**	**73**	**115**	**188**	**59**	**78**	**137**	**68**	**13**	**8**	**7**	**458**	**15.9**	**264**	**43**	**415**	**188**		**45**	**3**	**8**	**11**	**17**	**1**	**0**	**0**

Memorial Cup All Star Team (1980)

Traded to **Hartford** by **Chicago** for Hartford's 3rd round choice (Mike Dagenais) in 1987 Entry Draft, February 3, 1986. Signed as a free agent by **Chicago**, September 25, 1987.

• GARDNER, DAVE
Dave Gardner C – R. 6', 185 lbs. b: Toronto, Ont., 8/23/1952. Montreal's 3rd choice, 8th overall, in 1972 Amateur Draft.

Season	Club	League	GP	G	A	Pts	AG	AA	APts	PIM	PP	SH	GW	S	%	TGF	PGF	TGA	PGA	+/–	GP	G	A	Pts	PIM	PP	SH	GW
1969-70	St. Michael's Buzzers	Jr. B	36	54	42	96	....	....	....	....	....	....	....	....	....	....	....	....	....	....	....	....	....	....	....	....	....	....
1970-71	Toronto Marlboros	OHA	62	56	*81	137	....	....	....	7	....	....	....	....	....	....	....	....	....	....	....	....	....	....	....	....	....	....
1971-72	Toronto Marlboros	OHA	57	53	*76	*129	....	....	....	16	....	....	....	....	....	....	....	....	....	....	....	....	....	....	....	....	....	....
1972-73	**Montreal Canadiens**	**NHL**	**5**	**1**	**1**	**2**	**1**	**1**	**2**	**0**	**1**	**0**	**0**	**6**	**16.7**	**3**	**3**	**0**	**0**	**0**	....	....	....	....	....	....	....	....
	Nova Scotia Voyageurs	AHL	66	28	44	72	....	....	....	15	....	....	....	....	....	....	....	....	....	....	13	5	6	11	4	....	....	....
1973-74	**Montreal Canadiens**	**NHL**	**31**	**1**	**10**	**11**	**1**	**9**	**10**	**2**	**0**	**0**	**0**	**26**	**3.8**	**14**	**4**	**6**	**0**	**+4**	....	....	....	....	....	....	....	....
	St. Louis Blues	**NHL**	**15**	**5**	**2**	**7**	**5**	**2**	**7**	**6**	**1**	**0**	**0**	**29**	**17.2**	**9**	**3**	**12**	**0**	**–6**	....	....	....	....	....	....	....	....
1974-75	**St. Louis Blues**	**NHL**	**8**	**0**	**2**	**2**	**0**	**2**	**2**	**0**	**0**	**0**	**0**	**8**	**0.0**	**2**	**2**	**3**	**0**	**–3**	....	....	....	....	....	....	....	....
	California Golden Seals	**NHL**	**64**	**16**	**20**	**36**	**15**	**16**	**31**	**6**	**6**	**1**	**0**	**133**	**12.0**	**48**	**18**	**50**	**1**	**–19**	....	....	....	....	....	....	....	....
1975-76	**California Golden Seals**	**NHL**	**74**	**16**	**32**	**48**	**15**	**25**	**40**	**8**	**2**	**0**	**1**	**157**	**10.2**	**74**	**33**	**45**	**0**	**–4**	....	....	....	....	....	....	....	....
1976-77	**Cleveland Barons**	**NHL**	**76**	**16**	**22**	**38**	**15**	**18**	**33**	**9**	**5**	**0**	**3**	**141**	**11.3**	**66**	**39**	**47**	**0**	**–20**	....	....	....	....	....	....	....	....
1977-78	**Cleveland Barons**	**NHL**	**75**	**19**	**25**	**44**	**18**	**20**	**38**	**10**	**3**	**0**	**3**	**106**	**17.9**	**69**	**21**	**65**	**1**	**–16**	....	....	....	....	....	....	....	....
1978-79	Springfield Indians	AHL	10	1	3	4	....	....	....	0	....	....	....	....	....	....	....	....	....	....	....	....	....	....	....	....	....	....
	Tulsa Oilers	CHL	20	4	10	14	....	....	....	2	....	....	....	....	....	....	....	....	....	....	....	....	....	....	....	....	....	....
	Dallas Black Hawks	CHL	39	6	27	33	....	....	....	6	....	....	....	....	....	....	....	....	....	....	9	5	7	12	4	....	....	....
1979-80	**Philadelphia Flyers**	**NHL**	**2**	**1**	**1**	**2**	**1**	**1**	**2**	**0**	**0**	**0**	**0**	**1**	**100.0**	**3**	**0**	**2**	**0**	**+1**	....	....	....	....	....	....	....	....
	Binghamton Whalers	AHL	18	3	9	12	....	....	....	2	....	....	....	....	....	....	....	....	....	....	....	....	....	....	....	....	....	....
	Maine Mariners	AHL	37	20	35	55	....	....	....	16	....	....	....	....	....	....	....	....	....	....	12	2	5	7	4	....	....	....
1980-81	Ambri-Piotta	Switz.	STATISTICS NOT AVAILABLE																									
1981-82	Ambri-Piotta	Switz.	STATISTICS NOT AVAILABLE																									
1982-83	Ambri-Piotta	Switz.	....	36	22	58	....	....	....	....	....	....	....	....	....	....	....	....	....	....	....	....	....	....	....	....	....	....
1983-84	Visp	Switz.	....	41	33	74	....	....	....	....	....	....	....	....	....	....	....	....	....	....	....	....	....	....	....	....	....	....
1984-85	Ambri-Piotta	Switz.	....	51	43	94	....	....	....	....	....	....	....	....	....	....	....	....	....	....	....	....	....	....	....	....	....	....
	NHL Totals		**350**	**75**	**115**	**190**	**71**	**94**	**165**	**41**	**18**	**1**	**7**	**607**	**12.4**	**288**	**123**	**230**	**2**		....	....	....	....	....	....	....	....

OHA Second All Star Team (1971, 1972

Traded to **St. Louis** by **Montreal** for St. Louis' 1st round choice (Doug Risebrough) in 1974 Amateur Draft, March 9, 1974. Traded to **California** by **St. Louis** with Butch Williams for Craig Patrick and Stan Gilbertson, November 11, 1974. Transferred to **Cleveland** after **California** franchise relocated, August 26, 1976. Placed on **Minnesota** Reserve List after **Minnesota-Cleveland** Dispersal Draft, June 15, 1978. Transferred to **LA Kings** by **Minnesota** with Rick Hampton and Steve Jensen as compensation for Minnesota's signing of free agent Gary Sargent, July 15, 1978. Signed as a free agent by **Philadelphia**, January 21, 1980.

• GARDNER, PAUL
Paul Gardner C – L. 6', 195 lbs. b: Toronto, Ont., 3/5/1956. Kansas City's 1st choice, 11th overall, in 1976 Amateur Draft.

Season	Club	League	GP	G	A	Pts	AG	AA	APts	PIM	PP	SH	GW	S	%	TGF	PGF	TGA	PGA	+/–	GP	G	A	Pts	PIM	PP	SH	GW
1974-75	Oshawa Generals	OHA	64	27	36	63	....	....	....	54	....	....	....	....	....	....	....	....	....	....	5	0	0	0	9	....	....	....
1975-76	Oshawa Generals	OHA	65	69	75	144	....	....	....	75	....	....	....	....	....	....	....	....	....	....	4	2	3	5	2	....	....	....
1976-77	**Colorado Rockies**	**NHL**	**60**	**30**	**29**	**59**	**29**	**24**	**53**	**25**	**11**	**0**	**0**	**191**	**15.7**	**71**	**25**	**74**	**0**	**–28**	....	....	....	....	....	....	....	....
	Rhode Island Reds	AHL	14	10	4	14	....	....	....	12	....	....	....	....	....	....	....	....	....	....	....	....	....	....	....	....	....	....
1977-78	**Colorado Rockies**	**NHL**	**46**	**30**	**22**	**52**	**29**	**18**	**47**	**29**	**13**	**0**	**3**	**133**	**22.6**	**73**	**34**	**56**	**0**	**–17**	....	....	....	....	....	....	....	....
1978-79	**Colorado Rockies**	**NHL**	**64**	**23**	**26**	**49**	**21**	**20**	**41**	**32**	**14**	**0**	**0**	**170**	**13.5**	**67**	**36**	**56**	**0**	**–25**	....	....	....	....	....	....	....	....
	Toronto Maple Leafs	**NHL**	**11**	**7**	**2**	**9**	**6**	**2**	**8**	**0**	**2**	**0**	**1**	**20**	**35.0**	**11**	**5**	**6**	**0**	**0**	**6**	**0**	**1**	**1**	**4**	**0**	**0**	**0**
1979-80	**Toronto Maple Leafs**	**NHL**	**45**	**11**	**13**	**24**	**10**	**10**	**20**	**10**	**4**	**0**	**1**	**74**	**14.9**	**36**	**15**	**29**	**0**	**–8**	....	....	....	....	....	....	....	....
	New Brunswick Hawks	AHL	20	11	16	27	....	....	....	14	....	....	....	....	....	....	....	....	....	....	15	10	5	15	12	....	....	....
1980-81	Springfield Indians	AHL	14	9	12	21	....	....	....	6	....	....	....	....	....	....	....	....	....	....	....	....	....	....	....	....	....	....
	Pittsburgh Penguins	**NHL**	**62**	**34**	**40**	**74**	**28**	**28**	**56**	**59**	**18**	**0**	**1**	**183**	**18.6**	**92**	**45**	**52**	**0**	**–5**	**5**	**1**	**0**	**1**	**8**	**1**	**0**	**0**
1981-82	**Pittsburgh Penguins**	**NHL**	**59**	**36**	**33**	**69**	**29**	**22**	**51**	**28**	**21**	**0**	**2**	**157**	**22.9**	**90**	**62**	**46**	**1**	**–7**	**5**	**1**	**5**	**6**	**2**	**1**	**0**	**0**
1982-83	**Pittsburgh Penguins**	**NHL**	**70**	**28**	**27**	**55**	**23**	**19**	**42**	**12**	**20**	**0**	**1**	**155**	**18.1**	**82**	**53**	**52**	**0**	**–23**	....	....	....	....	....	....	....	....
1983-84	**Pittsburgh Penguins**	**NHL**	**16**	**0**	**5**	**5**	**0**	**3**	**3**	**6**	**0**	**0**	**0**	**21**	**0.0**	**8**	**6**	**6**	**0**	**–4**	....	....	....	....	....	....	....	....
	Baltimore Skipjacks	AHL	54	32	48	80	....	....	....	14	....	....	....	....	....	....	....	....	....	....	10	12	10	22	0	....	....	....
1984-85	**Washington Capitals**	**NHL**	**12**	**2**	**4**	**6**	**2**	**3**	**5**	**6**	**2**	**0**	**0**	**17**	**11.8**	**11**	**6**	**6**	**0**	**–1**	....	....	....	....	....	....	....	....
	Binghamton Whalers	AHL	64	*51	79	*130	....	....	....	10	....	....	....	....	....	....	....	....	....	....	5	3	9	12	0	....	....	....
1985-86	**Buffalo Sabres**	**NHL**	**2**	**0**	**0**	**0**	**0**	**0**	**0**	**0**	**0**	**0**	**0**	**4**	**0.0**	**1**	**1**	**3**	**0**	**–3**	....	....	....	....	....	....	....	....
	Rochester Americans	AHL	71	*61	51	*112	....	....	....	16	....	....	....	....	....	....	....	....	....	....	....	....	....	....	....	....	....	....
	NHL Totals		**447**	**201**	**201**	**402**	**177**	**149**	**326**	**207**	**105**	**0**	**9**	**1125**	**17.9**	**551**	**288**	**385**	**1**		**16**	**2**	**6**	**8**	**14**	**2**	**0**	**0**

AHL First All-Star Team (1985, 1986) • Won Fred T. Hunt Memorial Trophy (Sportsmanship - AHL) (1985) • Won John B. Sollenberger Trophy (Top Scorer - AHL) (1985, 1986) • Won Les Cunningham Award (MVP - AHL) (1985, 1986)

Rights transferred to **Colorado** after **Kansas City** relocated, July 15, 1976. Traded to **Toronto** by **Colorado** for Don Ashby and Trevor Johansen, March 13, 1979. Traded to **Pittsburgh** by **Toronto** with Dave Burrows for Kim Davis and Paul Marshall, November 8, 1980. Signed as a free agent by **Washington**, July 17, 1984. Signed as a free agent by **Buffalo**, July 31, 1985.

• GARE, DANNY
Danny Gare RW – R. 5'9", 175 lbs. b: Nelson, B.C., 5/14/1954. Buffalo's 2nd choice, 29th overall, in 1974 Amateur Draft.

Season	Club	League	GP	G	A	Pts	AG	AA	APts	PIM	PP	SH	GW	S	%	TGF	PGF	TGA	PGA	+/–	GP	G	A	Pts	PIM	PP	SH	GW
1971-72	Calgary Centennials	WCJHL	56	10	17	27	....	....	....	15	....	....	....	....	....	....	....	....	....	....	13	1	1	2	2	....	....	....
1972-73	Calgary Centennials	WCJHL	65	45	43	88	....	....	....	107	....	....	....	....	....	....	....	....	....	....	6	5	5	10	18	....	....	....
1973-74	Calgary Centennials	WCJHL	65	68	59	127	....	....	....	238	....	....	....	....	....	....	....	....	....	....	14	10	12	22	53	....	....	....
1974-75	**Buffalo Sabres**	**NHL**	**78**	**31**	**31**	**62**	**29**	**24**	**53**	**75**	**5**	**0**	**2**	**274**	**11.3**	**85**	**12**	**33**	**0**	**+40**	**17**	**7**	**6**	**13**	**19**	**0**	**0**	**1**
1975-76	**Buffalo Sabres**	**NHL**	**79**	**50**	**23**	**73**	**47**	**18**	**65**	**129**	**8**	**1**	**9**	**303**	**16.5**	**113**	**29**	**61**	**9**	**+32**	**9**	**5**	**2**	**7**	**21**	**0**	**0**	**2**
1976-77	Canada	C Cup	1	0	0	0	....	....	....	0	....	....	....	....	....	....	....	....	....	....	....	....	....	....	....	....	....	....
	Buffalo Sabres	**NHL**	**35**	**11**	**15**	**26**	**11**	**12**	**23**	**73**	**3**	**0**	**0**	**92**	**12.0**	**40**	**10**	**25**	**2**	**+7**	**4**	**0**	**0**	**0**	**18**	**0**	**0**	**0**
1977-78	**Buffalo Sabres**	**NHL**	**69**	**39**	**38**	**77**	**38**	**31**	**69**	**95**	**9**	**0**	**2**	**265**	**14.7**	**105**	**28**	**46**	**1**	**+32**	**8**	**4**	**6**	**10**	**37**	**2**	**0**	**0**
1978-79	**Buffalo Sabres**	**NHL**	**71**	**27**	**40**	**67**	**25**	**31**	**56**	**90**	**7**	**0**	**3**	**260**	**10.4**	**99**	**31**	**53**	**3**	**+18**	**3**	**0**	**0**	**0**	**9**	**0**	**0**	**0**
1979-80	**Buffalo Sabres**	**NHL**	**76**	***56**	**33**	**89**	**51**	**25**	**76**	**90**	**17**	**0**	**11**	**270**	**20.7**	**144**	**48**	**48**	**1**	**+49**	**14**	**4**	**7**	**11**	**35**	**4**	**0**	**1**
1980-81	**Buffalo Sabres**	**NHL**	**73**	**46**	**39**	**85**	**38**	**27**	**65**	**109**	**15**	**0**	**7**	**248**	**18.5**	**130**	**52**	**67**	**1**	**+12**	**3**	**3**	**0**	**3**	**8**	**2**	**0**	**1**
1981-82	Canada	C Cup	7	1	5	6	....	....	....	2	....	....	....	....	....	....	....	....	....	....	....	....	....	....	....	....	....	....
	Buffalo Sabres	**NHL**	**22**	**7**	**14**	**21**	**6**	**9**	**15**	**25**	**2**	**0**	**1**	**71**	**9.9**	**30**	**10**	**21**	**1**	**0**	....	....	....	....	....	....	....	....
	Detroit Red Wings	**NHL**	**36**	**13**	**9**	**22**	**10**	**6**	**16**	**74**	**2**	**1**	**0**	**100**	**13.0**	**34**	**6**	**35**	**3**	**–4**	....	....	....	....	....	....	....	....
1982-83	**Detroit Red Wings**	**NHL**	**79**	**26**	**35**	**61**	**21**	**24**	**45**	**107**	**6**	**0**	**3**	**224**	**11.6**	**85**	**20**	**93**	**12**	**–16**	....	....	....	....	....	....	....	....
1983-84	**Detroit Red Wings**	**NHL**	**63**	**13**	**13**	**26**	**10**	**9**	**19**	**147**	**1**	**0**	**2**	**148**	**8.8**	**43**	**2**	**45**	**7**	**+3**	**4**	**2**	**0**	**2**	**38**	**0**	**0**	**0**
1984-85	**Detroit Red Wings**	**NHL**	**71**	**27**	**29**	**56**	**22**	**20**	**42**	**163**	**3**	**0**	**3**	**167**	**16.2**	**83**	**19**	**70**	**11**	**+5**	**2**	**0**	**0**	**0**	**10**	**0**	**0**	**0**
1985-86	**Detroit Red Wings**	**NHL**	**57**	**7**	**9**	**16**	**6**	**6**	**12**	**102**	**1**	**0**	**0**	**108**	**6.5**	**29**	**4**	**69**	**25**	**–19**	....	....	....	....	....	....	....	....
1986-87	**Edmonton Oilers**	**NHL**	**18**	**1**	**3**	**4**	**1**	**2**	**3**	**6**	**0**	**0**	**0**	**22**	**4.5**	**8**	**1**	**5**	**0**	**+2**	....	....	....	....	....	....	....	....
	NHL Totals		**827**	**354**	**331**	**685**	**315**	**244**	**559**	**1285**	**79**	**2**	**43**	**2552**	**13.9**	**1028**	**272**	**671**	**76**		**64**	**25**	**21**	**46**	**195**	**8**	**0**	**5**

WCJHL First All-Star Team (1974) • NHL Second All-Star Team (1980)

Played in NHL All-Star Game (1980, 1981)

Traded to **Detroit** by **Buffalo** with Jim Schoenfeld and Derek Smith for Mike Foligno, Dale McCourt and Brent Peterson, December 2, 1981. Signed as a free agent by **Edmonton**, September, 1986.

• GARLAND, SCOTT
Scott Garland C – R. 6'1", 185 lbs. b: Regina, Sask., 5/16/1952. d: 6/9/1979.

Season	Club	League	GP	G	A	Pts	AG	AA	APts	PIM	PP	SH	GW	S	%	TGF	PGF	TGA	PGA	+/–	GP	G	A	Pts	PIM	PP	SH	GW
1970-71	Montreal Jr. Canadiens	OHA	29	4	8	12	....	....	....	94	....	....	....	....	....	....	....	....	....	....	....	....	....	....	....	....	....	....
1971-72	Peterbourgh Petes	OHA	5	1	0	1	....	....	....	7	....	....	....	....	....	....	....	....	....	....	....	....	....	....	....	....	....	....
	Sarnia Bees	Jr. B	34	9	14	23	....	....	....	159	....	....	....	....	....	....	....	....	....	....	....	....	....	....	....	....	....	....
1972-73	Tulsa Oilers	CHL	62	15	20	35	....	....	....	192	....	....	....	....	....	....	....	....	....	....	....	....	....	....	....	....	....	....
1973-74	Oklahoma City Blazers	CHL	51	11	10	21	....	....	....	106	....	....	....	....	....	....	....	....	....	....	9	0	1	1	14	....	....	....
1974-75	Oklahoma City Blazers	CHL	61	18	27	45	....	....	....	132	....	....	....	....	....	....	....	....	....	....	5	0	2	2	42	....	....	....
1975-76	**Toronto Maple Leafs**	**NHL**	**16**	**4**	**3**	**7**	**4**	**2**	**6**	**8**	**1**	**0**	**0**	**17**	**23.5**	**12**	**3**	**9**	**0**	**0**	**7**	**1**	**2**	**3**	**35**	**1**	**0**	**0**
	Oklahoma City Blazers	CHL	58	19	40	59	....	....	....	53	....	....	....	....	....	....	....	....	....	....	....	....	....	....	....	....	....	....
1976-77	**Toronto Maple Leafs**	**NHL**	**69**	**9**	**20**	**29**	**9**	**16**	**25**	**83**	**3**	**0**	**1**	**84**	**10.7**	**53**	**12**	**59**	**0**	**–18**	....	....	....	....	....	....	....	....

			REGULAR SEASON																		PLAYOFFS							
Season	Club	League	GP	G	A	Pts	AG	AA	APts	PIM	PP	SH	GW	S	%	TGF	PGF	TGA	PGA	+/–	GP	G	A	Pts	PIM	PP	SH	GW
1977-78	Tulsa Oilers	CHL	20	6	7	13	....	....	....	19	....	....	....	....	....	....	....	....	....	....	7	2	0	2	31	....	....	....
1978-79	**Los Angeles Kings**	**NHL**	6	0	1	1	0	1	1	24	0	0	0	1	0.0	1	0	5	0	–4	....	....	....	....	....	....	....	....
	Springfield Indians	AHL	45	11	20	31	....	....	....	114	....	....	....	....	....	....	....	....	....	....	....	....	....	....	....	....	....	....
	NHL Totals		91	13	24	37	13	19	32	115	4	0	1	102	12.7	66	15	73	0		7	1	2	3	35	1	0	0

Signed as a free agent by **Toronto**, September 30, 1973. Traded to **LA Kings** by **Toronto** with Brian Glennie, Kurt Walker and Toronto's 2nd round choice (Mark Hardy) in 1979 Amateur Draft for Dave Hutchison and Lorne Stamler, June 14, 1978.

• GARNER, ROB

Rob Garner C – L. 5′11″, 180 lbs. b: Weston, Ont., 8/17/1958. Pittsburgh's 3rd choice, 75th overall, in 1978 Amateur Draft.

Season	Club	League	GP	G	A	Pts	AG	AA	APts	PIM	PP	SH	GW	S	%	TGF	PGF	TGA	PGA	+/–	GP	G	A	Pts	PIM	PP	SH	GW
1975-76	Markham Waxers	Jr. B	26	18	8	26	....	....	....	34	....	....	....	....	....	....	....	....	....	....	....	....	....	....	....	....	....	....
	Toronto Marlboros	OHA	37	6	8	14	....	....	....	28	....	....	....	....	....	....	....	....	....	....	....	....	....	....	....	....	....	....
1976-77	Toronto Marlboros	OHA	62	31	35	66	....	....	....	58	....	....	....	....	....	....	....	....	....	....	6	2	2	4	13	....	....	....
1977-78	Toronto Marlboros	OHA	48	38	35	73	....	....	....	111	....	....	....	....	....	....	....	....	....	....	5	2	1	3	24	....	....	....
1978-79	Binghamton Whalers	AHL	77	15	19	34	....	....	....	97	....	....	....	....	....	....	....	....	....	....	10	5	3	8	19	....	....	....
1979-80	Cincinnati Stingers	CHL	27	5	8	13	....	....	....	36	....	....	....	....	....	....	....	....	....	....	....	....	....	....	....	....	....	....
	Syracuse Firebirds	AHL	46	12	13	25	....	....	....	21	....	....	....	....	....	....	....	....	....	....	4	0	0	0	21	....	....	....
1980-81	Binghamton Whalers	AHL	62	18	20	38	....	....	....	77	....	....	....	....	....	....	....	....	....	....	6	1	6	7	13	....	....	....
1981-82	Erie Blades	AHL	75	25	27	52	....	....	....	60	....	....	....	....	....	....	....	....	....	....	....	....	....	....	....	....	....	....
1982-83	**Pittsburgh Penguins**	**NHL**	1	0	0	0	0	0	0	0	0	0	0	1	0.0	0	0	0	0	0	....	....	....	....	....	....	....	....
	Baltimore Skipjacks	AHL	70	21	32	53	....	....	....	48	....	....	....	....	....	....	....	....	....	....	....	....	....	....	....	....	....	....
	NHL Totals		1	0	0	0	0	0	0	0	0	0	0	1	0.0	0	0	0	0		....	....	....	....	....	....	....	....

• GARPENLOV, JOHAN

Johan Garpenlov LW – L. 5′11″, 184 lbs. b: Stockholm, Sweden, 3/21/1968. Detroit's 5th choice, 85th overall, in 1986 Entry Draft.

Season	Club	League	GP	G	A	Pts	AG	AA	APts	PIM	PP	SH	GW	S	%	TGF	PGF	TGA	PGA	+/–	GP	G	A	Pts	PIM	PP	SH	GW
1986-87	Djurgarden IF Stockholm	Sweden	29	5	8	13	....	....	....	22	....	....	....	....	....	....	....	....	....	....	2	0	0	0	0	....	....	....
	Sweden	WJC-A	7	2	3	5	....	....	....	6	....	....	....	....	....	....	....	....	....	....	....	....	....	....	....	....	....	....
1987-88	Djurgarden IF Stockholm	Sweden	30	7	10	17	....	....	....	12	....	....	....	....	....	....	....	....	....	....	3	1	3	4	4	....	....	....
	Sweden	WJC-A	7	5	1	6	....	....	....	12	....	....	....	....	....	....	....	....	....	....	....	....	....	....	....	....	....	....
1988-89	Djurgarden IF Stockholm	Sweden	36	12	19	31	....	....	....	20	....	....	....	....	....	....	....	....	....	....	8	3	4	7	10	....	....	....
1989-90	Djurgarden IF Stockholm	Sweden	39	20	13	33	....	....	....	35	....	....	....	....	....	....	....	....	....	....	8	2	4	6	4	....	....	....
	Sweden	WEC-A	10	4	4	8	....	....	....	4	....	....	....	....	....	....	....	....	....	....	....	....	....	....	....	....	....	....
1990-91	**Detroit Red Wings**	**NHL**	71	18	22	40	17	17	34	18	2	0	3	91	19.8	62	14	61	9	–4	6	0	1	1	4	0	0	0
	Sweden	WEC-A	10	4	0	4	....	....	....	6	....	....	....	....	....	....	....	....	....	....	....	....	....	....	....	....	....	....
1991-92	Sweden	C Cup	6	0	1	1	....	....	....	10	....	....	....	....	....	....	....	....	....	....	....	....	....	....	....	....	....	....
	Detroit Red Wings	**NHL**	16	1	1	2	1	1	2	4	0	0	0	13	7.7	8	0	8	2	+2	....	....	....	....	....	....	....	....
	Adirondack Red Wings	AHL	9	3	3	6	....	....	....	6	....	....	....	....	....	....	....	....	....	....	....	....	....	....	....	....	....	....
	San Jose Sharks	**NHL**	12	5	6	11	5	4	9	4	1	0	1	21	23.8	21	8	16	1	–2	....	....	....	....	....	....	....	....
	Sweden	WC-A	8	1	1	2	....	....	....	10	....	....	....	....	....	....	....	....	....	....	....	....	....	....	....	....	....	....
1992-93	**San Jose Sharks**	**NHL**	79	22	44	66	18	30	48	56	14	0	1	171	12.9	95	39	84	2	–26	....	....	....	....	....	....	....	....
1993-94	**San Jose Sharks**	**NHL**	80	18	35	53	17	27	44	28	7	0	3	125	14.4	78	20	49	0	+9	14	4	6	10	6	0	0	2
1994-95	**San Jose Sharks**	**NHL**	13	1	1	2	2	1	3	2	0	0	0	16	6.3	9	1	11	0	–3	....	....	....	....	....	....	....	....
	Florida Panthers	**NHL**	27	3	9	12	5	13	18	0	0	0	0	28	10.7	22	8	10	0	+4	....	....	....	....	....	....	....	....
1995-96	**Florida Panthers**	**NHL**	82	23	28	51	23	23	46	36	8	0	7	130	17.7	70	34	47	1	–10	20	4	2	6	8	0	0	0
1996-97	Sweden	W Cup	4	1	1	2	....	....	....	2	....	....	....	....	....	....	....	....	....	....	....	....	....	....	....	....	....	....
	Florida Panthers	**NHL**	53	11	25	36	12	22	34	47	1	0	1	83	13.3	51	13	29	1	+10	4	2	0	2	4	2	0	1
1997-98	**Florida Panthers**	**NHL**	39	2	3	5	2	3	5	8	0	0	0	43	4.7	18	1	27	4	–6	....	....	....	....	....	....	....	....
	NHL Totals		472	104	174	278	102	141	243	203	33	0	16	721	14.4	434	138	342	20		44	10	9	19	22	2	0	3

Traded to **San Jose** by **Detroit** for Bob McGill and Vancouver's 8th round choice (previously acquired, San Jose selected C.J. Denomme) in 1992 Entry Draft, March 9, 1992. Traded to **Florida** by **San Jose** for future considerations, March 3, 1995.

• GARTNER, MIKE

Mike Gartner RW – R. 6′, 187 lbs. b: Ottawa, Ont., 10/29/1959. Washington's 1st choice, 4th overall, in 1979 Entry Draft.

Season	Club	League	GP	G	A	Pts	AG	AA	APts	PIM	PP	SH	GW	S	%	TGF	PGF	TGA	PGA	+/–	GP	G	A	Pts	PIM	PP	SH	GW
1976-77	Niagara Falls Flyers	OHA	62	33	42	75	....	....	....	125	....	....	....	....	....	....	....	....	....	....	....	....	....	....	....	....	....	....
1977-78	Niagara Falls Flyers	OHA	64	41	49	90	....	....	....	56	....	....	....	....	....	....	....	....	....	....	....	....	....	....	....	....	....	....
	Canada	WJC-A	6	3	3	6	....	....	....	4	....	....	....	....	....	....	....	....	....	....	....	....	....	....	....	....	....	....
1978-79	Cincinnati Stingers	WHA	78	27	25	52	....	....	....	123	....	....	....	....	....	....	....	....	....	....	3	0	2	2	2	....	....	....
1979-80	**Washington Capitals**	**NHL**	77	36	32	68	33	25	58	66	4	0	3	228	15.8	97	23	61	2	+15	....	....	....	....	....	....	....	....
1980-81	**Washington Capitals**	**NHL**	80	48	46	94	40	32	72	100	13	0	3	326	14.7	123	36	97	5	–5	....	....	....	....	....	....	....	....
	Canada	WEC-A	8	4	0	4	....	....	....	8	....	....	....	....	....	....	....	....	....	....	....	....	....	....	....	....	....	....
1981-82	**Washington Capitals**	**NHL**	80	35	45	80	28	30	58	121	5	2	5	300	11.7	122	29	113	9	–11	....	....	....	....	....	....	....	....
	Canada	WEC-A	10	3	2	5	....	....	....	6	....	....	....	....	....	....	....	....	....	....	....	....	....	....	....	....	....	....
1982-83	**Washington Capitals**	**NHL**	73	38	38	76	31	26	57	54	10	1	3	269	14.1	101	33	76	6	–2	4	0	0	0	4	0	0	0
	Canada	WEC-A	10	4	1	5	....	....	....	12	....	....	....	....	....	....	....	....	....	....	....	....	....	....	....	....	....	....
1983-84	**Washington Capitals**	**NHL**	80	40	45	85	32	31	63	90	8	0	7	286	14.0	119	39	60	2	+22	8	3	7	10	16	2	0	0
1984-85	Canada	C Cup	8	3	2	5	....	....	....	10	....	....	....	....	....	....	....	....	....	....	....	....	....	....	....	....	....	....
	Washington Capitals	**NHL**	80	50	52	102	41	35	76	71	17	0	11	330	15.2	143	54	74	2	+17	5	4	3	7	9	1	0	1
1985-86	**Washington Capitals**	**NHL**	74	35	40	75	28	27	55	63	11	2	4	279	12.5	112	48	79	10	–5	9	2	10	12	4	0	0	0
1986-87	**Washington Capitals**	**NHL**	78	41	32	73	36	23	59	61	5	6	10	317	12.9	118	33	98	14	+1	7	4	3	7	14	0	0	0
1987-88	Canada	C Cup	9	2	2	4	....	....	....	6	....	....	....	....	....	....	....	....	....	....	....	....	....	....	....	....	....	....
	Washington Capitals	**NHL**	80	48	33	81	41	23	64	73	19	0	7	316	15.2	135	54	78	17	+20	14	3	4	7	14	1	0	0
1988-89	**Washington Capitals**	**NHL**	56	26	29	55	22	20	42	71	6	0	1	190	13.7	91	30	57	4	+8	....	....	....	....	....	....	....	....
	Minnesota North Stars	**NHL**	13	7	7	14	6	5	11	2	3	0	0	33	21.2	21	9	11	2	+3	5	0	0	0	6	0	0	0
1989-90	**Minnesota North Stars**	**NHL**	67	34	36	70	29	26	55	32	15	4	2	240	14.2	115	47	83	7	–8	....	....	....	....	....	....	....	....
	New York Rangers	**NHL**	12	11	5	16	9	4	13	6	6	0	3	48	22.9	22	10	8	0	+4	10	5	3	8	12	4	0	1
1990-91	**New York Rangers**	**NHL**	79	49	20	69	45	15	60	53	22	1	4	262	18.7	120	57	75	3	–9	6	1	1	2	0	1	0	0
1991-92	**New York Rangers**	**NHL**	76	40	41	81	37	31	68	55	15	0	6	286	14.0	115	46	61	3	+11	13	8	8	16	4	3	0	1
1992-93	**New York Rangers**	**NHL**	84	45	23	68	38	16	54	59	13	0	3	323	13.9	113	44	77	4	–4	....	....	....	....	....	....	....	....
	Canada	WC-A	7	3	4	7	....	....	....	12	....	....	....	....	....	....	....	....	....	....	....	....	....	....	....	....	....	....
1993-94	**New York Rangers**	**NHL**	71	28	24	52	26	19	45	58	10	5	4	245	11.4	82	30	52	11	+11	....	....	....	....	....	....	....	....
	Toronto Maple Leafs	**NHL**	10	6	6	12	6	5	11	4	1	0	0	30	20.0	18	4	6	1	+9	18	5	6	11	14	1	0	3
1994-95	**Toronto Maple Leafs**	**NHL**	38	12	8	20	21	12	33	6	2	1	1	91	13.2	32	9	25	2	0	5	2	2	4	2	0	0	0
1995-96	**Toronto Maple Leafs**	**NHL**	82	35	19	54	35	15	50	52	15	0	4	275	12.7	96	40	51	0	+5	6	4	1	5	4	2	0	1
1996-97	**Phoenix Coyotes**	**NHL**	82	32	31	63	34	27	61	38	13	1	7	271	11.8	93	39	71	6	–11	7	1	2	3	4	0	0	0
1997-98	**Phoenix Coyotes**	**NHL**	60	12	15	27	14	15	29	24	4	0	2	145	8.3	41	12	37	4	–4	5	1	0	1	18	1	0	0
	NHL Totals		1432	708	627	1335	632	462	1094	1159	217	23	90	5090	13.9	2029	726	1350	114		122	43	50	93	125	16	0	7
	Other Major League Totals		78	27	25	52	....	....	....	123	....	....	....	....	....	....	....	....	....	....	3	0	2	2	2	....	....	....

OHA First All-Star Team (1978)

Played in NHL All-Star Game (1981, 1985, 1986, 1988, 1990, 1993, 1996)

Signed as a underage free agent by **Birmingham** (WHA), May, 1978. Traded to **Minnesota** by **Washington** with Larry Murphy for Dino Ciccarelli and Bob Rouse, March 7, 1989. Traded to **NY Rangers** by **Minnesota** for Ulf Dahlen, LA Kings' 4th round choice (previously acquired, Minnesota selected Cal McGowan) in 1990 Entry Draft and future considerations, March 6, 1990. Traded to **Toronto** by **NY Rangers** for Glenn Anderson, the rights to Scott Malone and Toronto's 4th round choice (Alexander Korobolin) in 1994 Entry Draft, March 21, 1994. Traded to **Phoenix** by **Toronto** for Chicago's 4th round choice (previously acquired, Toronto selected Vladimir Antipov) in 1996 Entry Draft, June 22, 1996.

• GASSOFF, BOB

Bob Gassoff D – L. 5′10″, 195 lbs. b: Quesnel, B.C., 4/17/1953. d: 5/27/1977. St. Louis' 3rd choice, 48th overall, in 1973 Amateur Draft.

Season	Club	League	GP	G	A	Pts	AG	AA	APts	PIM	PP	SH	GW	S	%	TGF	PGF	TGA	PGA	+/–	GP	G	A	Pts	PIM	PP	SH	GW
1971-72	Medicine Hat Tigers	WCJHL	64	1	16	17	....	....	....	314	....	....	....	....	....	....	....	....	....	....	7	0	2	2	29	....	....	....
1972-73	Medicine Hat Tigers	WCJHL	68	11	51	62	....	....	....	*388	....	....	....	....	....	....	....	....	....	....	17	2	10	12	*152	....	....	....
1973-74	**St. Louis Blues**	**NHL**	28	0	3	3	0	3	3	84	0	0	0	20	0.0	12	0	31	3	–16	....	....	....	....	....	....	....	....
	Denver Spurs	WHL	45	4	10	14	....	....	....	*301	....	....	....	....	....	....	....	....	....	....	....	....	....	....	....	....	....	....
1974-75	**St. Louis Blues**	**NHL**	60	4	14	18	4	11	15	222	1	0	1	77	5.2	64	4	57	8	+11	2	0	0	0	0	0	0	0
	Denver Spurs	CHL	19	2	11	13	....	....	....	114	....	....	....	....	....	....	....	....	....	....	....	....	....	....	....	....	....	....
1975-76	**St. Louis Blues**	**NHL**	80	1	12	13	1	9	10	306	0	0	0	100	1.0	73	2	106	27	–8	3	0	0	0	6	0	0	0
1976-77	**St. Louis Blues**	**NHL**	77	6	18	24	6	15	21	254	0	0	3	110	5.5	81	0	98	15	–2	4	0	1	1	10	0	0	0
	NHL Totals		245	11	47	58	11	38	49	866	1	0	4	307	3.6	230	6	292	53		9	0	1	1	16	0	0	0

• GASSOFF, BRAD

Brad Gassoff LW – L. 5'11", 195 lbs. b: Quesnel, B.C., 11/13/1955. Vancouver's 2nd choice, 28th overall, in 1975 Amateur Draft.

			REGULAR SEASON																		PLAYOFFS							
Season	Club	League	GP	G	A	Pts	AG	AA	APts	PIM	PP	SH	GW	S	%	TGF	PGF	TGA	PGA	+/-	GP	G	A	Pts	PIM	PP	SH	GW
1972-73	Medicine Hat Tigers	WCJHL	67	13	22	35	....	....	....	122	....	....	....	....	....	....	....	....	....	....	17	3	3	6	67	....	....	....
1973-74	Medicine Hat Tigers	WCJHL	61	16	25	41	....	....	....	245	....	....	....	....	....	....	....	....	....	....	6	1	0	1	22	....	....	....
1974-75	Kamloops Chiefs	WCJHL	69	50	59	109	....	....	....	251	....	....	....	....	....	....	....	....	....	....	6	4	1	5	24	....	....	....
1975-76	**Vancouver Canucks**	**NHL**	**4**	**0**	**0**	**0**	**0**	**0**	**0**	**5**	**0**	**0**	**0**	**3**	**0.0**	**0**	**0**	**2**	**0**	**–2**	....	....	....	....	....	....	....	....
	Tulsa Oilers	CHL	68	36	28	64	....	....	....	295	....	....	....	....	....	....	....	....	....	....	9	*5	6	*11	32	....	....	....
1976-77	**Vancouver Canucks**	**NHL**	**37**	**6**	**4**	**10**	**6**	**3**	**9**	**35**	**1**	**0**	**0**	**53**	**11.3**	**16**	**5**	**35**	**0**	**–24**	....	....	....	....	....	....	....	....
	Tulsa Oilers	CHL	31	12	16	28	....	....	....	58	....	....	....	....	....	....	....	....	....	....	....	....	....	....	....	....	....	....
1977-78	**Vancouver Canucks**	**NHL**	**47**	**9**	**6**	**15**	**9**	**5**	**14**	**70**	**0**	**0**	**1**	**40**	**22.5**	**28**	**3**	**31**	**0**	**–6**	....	....	....	....	....	....	....	....
	Tulsa Oilers	CHL	18	11	9	20	....	....	....	29	....	....	....	....	....	....	....	....	....	....	....	....	....	....	....	....	....	....
1978-79	**Vancouver Canucks**	**NHL**	**34**	**4**	**7**	**11**	**4**	**5**	**9**	**53**	**0**	**0**	**0**	**44**	**9.1**	**13**	**0**	**24**	**0**	**–11**	**3**	**0**	**0**	**0**	**0**	**0**	**0**	**0**
	Dallas Black Hawks	CHL	36	11	20	31	....	....	....	164	....	....	....	....	....	....	....	....	....	....	....	....	....	....	....	....	....	....
1979-80	Dallas Black Hawks	CHL	68	14	48	62	....	....	....	*353	....	....	....	....	....	....	....	....	....	....	....	....	....	....	....	....	....	....
	NHL Totals		**122**	**19**	**17**	**36**	**19**	**13**	**32**	**163**	**1**	**0**	**1**	**140**	**13.6**	**57**	**8**	**92**	**0**		**3**	**0**	**0**	**0**	**0**	**0**	**0**	**0**

CHL Second All-Star Team (1976) • Won Ken McKenzie Trophy (CHL's Rookie of the Year) (1976)

• GATZOS, STEVE

Steve Gatzos RW – R. 5'11", 185 lbs. b: Toronto, Ont., 6/22/1961. Pittsburgh's 1st choice, 28th overall, in 1981 Entry Draft.

Season	Club	League	GP	G	A	Pts	AG	AA	APts	PIM	PP	SH	GW	S	%	TGF	PGF	TGA	PGA	+/-	GP	G	A	Pts	PIM	PP	SH	GW
1978-79	Sault Ste. Marie Greyhounds	OHA	36	3	9	12	....	....	....	26	....	....	....	....	....	....	....	....	....	....	....	....	....	....	....	....	....	....
1979-80	Sault Ste. Marie Greyhounds	OHA	64	36	38	74	....	....	....	64	....	....	....	....	....	....	....	....	....	....	....	....	....	....	....	....	....	....
1980-81	Sault Ste. Marie Greyhounds	OHA	68	78	50	128	....	....	....	114	....	....	....	....	....	....	....	....	....	....	19	16	9	25	23	....	....	....
1981-82	**Pittsburgh Penguins**	**NHL**	**16**	**6**	**8**	**14**	**5**	**5**	**10**	**14**	**1**	**0**	**0**	**36**	**16.7**	**21**	**5**	**16**	**0**	**0**	**1**	**0**	**0**	**0**	**0**	**0**	**0**	**0**
	Erie Blades	AHL	54	18	19	37	....	....	....	67	....	....	....	....	....	....	....	....	....	....	....	....	....	....	....	....	....	....
1982-83	**Pittsburgh Penguins**	**NHL**	**44**	**6**	**7**	**13**	**5**	**5**	**10**	**52**	**2**	**0**	**1**	**70**	**8.6**	**20**	**4**	**33**	**1**	**–16**	....	....	....	....	....	....	....	....
	Baltimore Skipjacks	AHL	12	5	4	9	....	....	....	22	....	....	....	....	....	....	....	....	....	....	....	....	....	....	....	....	....	....
1983-84	**Pittsburgh Penguins**	**NHL**	**23**	**3**	**3**	**6**	**2**	**2**	**4**	**15**	**0**	**0**	**1**	**29**	**10.3**	**10**	**2**	**17**	**0**	**–9**	....	....	....	....	....	....	....	....
	Baltimore Skipjacks	AHL	48	14	19	33	....	....	....	43	....	....	....	....	....	....	....	....	....	....	....	....	....	....	....	....	....	....
1984-85	**Pittsburgh Penguins**	**NHL**	**6**	**0**	**2**	**2**	**0**	**1**	**1**	**2**	**0**	**0**	**0**	**6**	**0.0**	**4**	**1**	**9**	**0**	**–6**	....	....	....	....	....	....	....	....
	Muskegon Mohawks	IHL	24	18	10	28	....	....	....	24	....	....	....	....	....	....	....	....	....	....	....	....	....	....	....	....	....	....
1985-86	Baltimore Skipjacks	AHL	53	25	8	33	....	....	....	34	....	....	....	....	....	....	....	....	....	....	....	....	....	....	....	....	....	....
1986-87			DID NOT PLAY – INJURED																									
1987-88			DID NOT PLAY																									
1988-89	Seipa	Finland	41	27	18	45	....	....	....	62	....	....	....	....	....	....	....	....	....	....	....	....	....	....	....	....	....	....
1989-90	Medvescak	Yugoslav	....	43	16	59	....	....	....	....	....	....	....	....	....	....	....	....	....	....	....	....	....	....	....	....	....	....
1990-91	Fife Flyers	Britain	17	29	24	53	....	....	....	43	....	....	....	....	....	....	....	....	....	....	....	....	....	....	....	....	....	....
	Roanoke Valley Rebels	ECHL	16	14	13	27	....	....	....	2	....	....	....	....	....	....	....	....	....	....	....	....	....	....	....	....	....	....
	NHL Totals		**89**	**15**	**20**	**35**	**12**	**13**	**25**	**83**	**3**	**0**	**2**	**141**	**10.6**	**55**	**12**	**75**	**1**		**1**	**0**	**0**	**0**	**0**	**0**	**0**	**0**

• GAUDREAU, ROB

Rob Gaudreau RW – R. 5'11", 185 lbs. b: Lincoln, RI, 1/20/1970. Pittsburgh's 8th choice, 172nd overall, in 1988 Entry Draft.

Season	Club	League	GP	G	A	Pts	AG	AA	APts	PIM	PP	SH	GW	S	%	TGF	PGF	TGA	PGA	+/-	GP	G	A	Pts	PIM	PP	SH	GW
1988-89	Providence College	H.E.	42	28	29	57			....	32	....	....	....	....	....	....	....	....	....	....	....	....	....	....	....	....	....	....
1989-90	Providence College	H.E.	32	20	18	38	....	....	....	12	....	....	....	....	....	....	....	....	....	....	....	....	....	....	....	....	....	....
	United States	WJC-A	7	3	1	4	....	....	....	6	....	....	....	....	....	....	....	....	....	....	....	....	....	....	....	....	....	....
1990-91	Providence College	H.E.	36	34	27	61	....	....	....	20	....	....	....	....	....	....	....	....	....	....	....	....	....	....	....	....	....	....
1991-92	Providence College	H.E.	36	21	34	55	....	....	....	22	....	....	....	....	....	....	....	....	....	....	....	....	....	....	....	....	....	....
1992-93	**San Jose Sharks**	**NHL**	**59**	**23**	**20**	**43**	**19**	**14**	**33**	**18**	**5**	**2**	**1**	**191**	**12.0**	**76**	**33**	**76**	**15**	**–18**	....	....	....	....	....	....	....	....
	Kansas City Blades	IHL	19	8	6	14	....	....	....	6	....	....	....	....	....	....	....	....	....	....	....	....	....	....	....	....	....	....
	United States	WC-A	5	3	3	6	....	....	....	2	....	....	....	....	....	....	....	....	....	....	....	....	....	....	....	....	....	....
1993-94	**San Jose Sharks**	**NHL**	**84**	**15**	**20**	**35**	**14**	**15**	**29**	**28**	**6**	**0**	**4**	**151**	**9.9**	**61**	**32**	**60**	**21**	**–10**	**14**	**2**	**0**	**2**	**0**	**1**	**1**	**0**
1994-95	**Ottawa Senators**	**NHL**	**36**	**5**	**9**	**14**	**9**	**13**	**22**	**8**	**0**	**0**	**0**	**65**	**7.7**	**26**	**8**	**37**	**3**	**–18**	....	....	....	....	....	....	....	....
1995-96	**Ottawa Senators**	**NHL**	**52**	**8**	**5**	**13**	**8**	**4**	**12**	**15**	**1**	**1**	**0**	**76**	**10.5**	**25**	**9**	**41**	**6**	**–19**	....	....	....	....	....	....	....	....
	P.E.I. Senators	AHL	3	2	0	2	....	....	....	4	....	....	....	....	....	....	....	....	....	....	....	....	....	....	....	....	....	....
1996-97	HC La Chaux-de-Fonds	Switz.	37	19	23	42	....	....	....	62	....	....	....	....	....	....	....	....	....	....	....	....	....	....	....	....	....	....
	NHL Totals		**231**	**51**	**54**	**105**	**50**	**46**	**96**	**69**	**12**	**3**	**5**	**483**	**10.6**	**188**	**82**	**214**	**45**		**14**	**2**	**0**	**2**	**0**	**1**	**1**	**0**

Hockey East Second All-Star Team (1991) • Hockey East First All-Star Team (1992) • NCAA East Second All-American Team (1992)

Rights traded to **Minnesota** by **Pittsburgh** for Richard Zemlak, November 1, 1988. Claimed by **San Jose** from **Minnesota** in Dispersal Draft, May 30, 1991. Claimed by **Ottawa** from **San Jose** in Waiver Draft, January 18, 1995.

• GAULIN, JEAN-MARC

Jean-Marc Gaulin RW – R. 5'10", 180 lbs. b: Balve, Germany, 3/3/1962. Quebec's 2nd choice, 53rd overall, in 1981 Entry Draft.

Season	Club	League	GP	G	A	Pts	AG	AA	APts	PIM	PP	SH	GW	S	%	TGF	PGF	TGA	PGA	+/-	GP	G	A	Pts	PIM	PP	SH	GW
1978-79	Sherbrooke Beavers	QMJHL	71	26	41	67	....	....	....	89	....	....	....	....	....	....	....	....	....	....	....	....	....	....	....	....	....	....
1979-80	Sherbrooke Beavers	QMJHL	16	6	15	21	....	....	....	14	....	....	....	....	....	....	....	....	....	....	....	....	....	....	....	....	....	....
	Sorel Black Hawks	QMJHL	43	15	25	40	....	....	....	105	....	....	....	....	....	....	....	....	....	....	....	....	....	....	....	....	....	....
1980-81	Sorel Black Hawks	QMJHL	70	50	40	90	....	....	....	157	....	....	....	....	....	....	....	....	....	....	7	0	3	3	6	....	....	....
	Canada	WJC-A	5	2	0	2	....	....	....	4	....	....	....	....	....	....	....	....	....	....	....	....	....	....	....	....	....	....
1981-82	Hull Olympiques	QMJHL	56	50	50	100	....	....	....	93	....	....	....	....	....	....	....	....	....	....	11	2	15	17	9	....	....	....
1982-83	**Quebec Nordiques**	**NHL**	**1**	**0**	**0**	**0**	**0**	**0**	**0**	**0**	**0**	**0**	**0**	**0**	**0.0**	**0**	**0**	**0**	**0**	**0**	....	....	....	....	....	....	....	....
	Fredericton Express	AHL	67	11	17	28	....	....	....	58	....	....	....	....	....	....	....	....	....	....	9	0	0	0	21	....	....	....
1983-84	**Quebec Nordiques**	**NHL**	**2**	**0**	**0**	**0**	**0**	**0**	**0**	**0**	**0**	**0**	**0**	**0**	**0.0**	**0**	**0**	**1**	**0**	**–1**	....	....	....	....	....	....	....	....
	Fredericton Express	AHL	62	14	28	42	....	....	....	80	....	....	....	....	....	....	....	....	....	....	7	2	5	7	0	....	....	....
1984-85	**Quebec Nordiques**	**NHL**	**22**	**3**	**3**	**6**	**2**	**2**	**4**	**8**	**0**	**0**	**0**	**24**	**12.5**	**10**	**0**	**8**	**0**	**+2**	**1**	**0**	**0**	**0**	**0**	**0**	**0**	**0**
	Fredericton Express	AHL	27	10	9	19	....	....	....	32	....	....	....	....	....	....	....	....	....	....	5	1	3	4	2	....	....	....
1985-86	**Quebec Nordiques**	**NHL**	**1**	**1**	**0**	**1**	**1**	**0**	**1**	**0**	**0**	**0**	**0**	**2**	**50.0**	**1**	**0**	**1**	**0**	**0**	....	....	....	....	....	....	....	....
	Fredericton Express	AHL	58	16	26	42	....	....	....	66	....	....	....	....	....	....	....	....	....	....	6	2	3	5	31	....	....	....
1986-87	Fredericton Express	AHL	17	1	1	2	....	....	....	15	....	....	....	....	....	....	....	....	....	....	....	....	....	....	....	....	....	....
	Muskegon Lumberjacks	IHL	5	1	3	4	....	....	....	6	....	....	....	....	....	....	....	....	....	....	....	....	....	....	....	....	....	....
1987-88	Mont Blanc	France	23	19	17	36	....	....	....	26	....	....	....	....	....	....	....	....	....	....	....	....	....	....	....	....	....	....
1988-89	Paris Volants	France	43	44	32	76	....	....	....	20	....	....	....	....	....	....	....	....	....	....	....	....	....	....	....	....	....	....
	NHL Totals		**26**	**4**	**3**	**7**	**3**	**2**	**5**	**8**	**0**	**0**	**0**	**26**	**15.4**	**11**	**0**	**10**	**0**		**1**	**0**	**0**	**0**	**0**	**0**	**0**	**0**

QMJHL Second All-Star Team (1981)

• GAUME, DALLAS

Dallas Gaume C – L. 5'10", 185 lbs. b: Innisfal, Alta., 8/27/1963.

Season	Club	League	GP	G	A	Pts	AG	AA	APts	PIM	PP	SH	GW	S	%	TGF	PGF	TGA	PGA	+/-	GP	G	A	Pts	PIM	PP	SH	GW
1982-83	University of Denver	WCHA	37	19	47	66	....	....	....	12	....	....	....	....	....	....	....	....	....	....	....	....	....	....	....	....	....	....
1983-84	University of Denver	WCHA	32	12	25	37	....	....	....	22	....	....	....	....	....	....	....	....	....	....	....	....	....	....	....	....	....	....
1984-85	University of Denver	WCHA	39	15	48	63	....	....	....	28	....	....	....	....	....	....	....	....	....	....	....	....	....	....	....	....	....	....
1985-86	University of Denver	WCHA	47	32	*67	*99	....	....	....	18	....	....	....	....	....	....	....	....	....	....	....	....	....	....	....	....	....	....
1986-87	Binghamton Whalers	AHL	77	18	39	57	....	....	....	31	....	....	....	....	....	....	....	....	....	....	12	1	1	2	7	....	....	....
1987-88	Binghamton Whalers	AHL	63	24	49	73	....	....	....	39	....	....	....	....	....	....	....	....	....	....	4	1	2	3	0	....	....	....
1988-89	**Hartford Whalers**	**NHL**	**4**	**1**	**1**	**2**	**1**	**1**	**2**	**0**	**0**	**0**	**0**	**5**	**20.0**	**2**	**0**	**1**	**0**	**+1**	....	....	....	....	....	....	....	....
	Binghamton Whalers	AHL	57	23	43	66	....	....	....	16	....	....	....	....	....	....	....	....	....	....	....	....	....	....	....	....	....	....
1989-90	Binghamton Whalers	AHL	76	26	39	65	....	....	....	43	....	....	....	....	....	....	....	....	....	....	....	....	....	....	....	....	....	....
1990-91	Trondheim IHK	Norway	8	5	6	11	....	....	....	6	....	....	....	....	....	....	....	....	....	....	....	....	....	....	....	....	....	....
1991-92	Trondheim IHK	Norway	36	34	*43	*77	....	....	....	....	....	....	....	....	....	....	....	....	....	....	....	....	....	....	....	....	....	....
	NHL Totals		**4**	**1**	**1**	**2**	**1**	**1**	**2**	**0**	**0**	**0**	**0**	**5**	**20.0**	**2**	**0**	**1**	**0**		....	....	....	....	....	....	....	....

WCHA First All-Star Team (1986) • NCAA West First All-American Team (1986)

Signed as a free agent by **Hartford**, July 10, 1986.

• GAUTHIER, DANIEL

Daniel Gauthier LW – L. 6'1", 190 lbs. b: Charlemagne, Que., 5/17/1970. Pittsburgh's 3rd choice, 62nd overall, in 1988 Entry Draft.

Season	Club	League	GP	G	A	Pts	AG	AA	APts	PIM	PP	SH	GW	S	%	TGF	PGF	TGA	PGA	+/-	GP	G	A	Pts	PIM	PP	SH	GW
1986-87	Longueuil Chevaliers	QMJHL	64	23	22	45	....	....	....	23	....	....	....	....	....	....	....	....	....	....	18	4	5	9	15	....	....	....
1987-88	Victoriaville Tigers	QMJHL	66	43	47	90	....	....	....	53	....	....	....	....	....	....	....	....	....	....	5	2	1	3	0	....	....	....
1988-89	Victoriaville Tigers	QMJHL	64	41	75	116	....	....	....	84	....	....	....	....	....	....	....	....	....	....	16	12	17	29	30	....	....	....
1989-90	Victoriaville Tigers	QMJHL	62	45	69	114	....	....	....	32	....	....	....	....	....	....	....	....	....	....	16	8	*19	27	16	....	....	....

			REGULAR SEASON																		PLAYOFFS							
Season	**Club**	**League**	**GP**	**G**	**A**	**Pts**	**AG**	**AA**	**APts**	**PIM**	**PP**	**SH**	**GW**	**S**	**%**	**TGF**	**PGF**	**TGA**	**PGA**	**+/–**	**GP**	**G**	**A**	**Pts**	**PIM**	**PP**	**SH**	**GW**
1990-91	Albany Choppers	IHL	1	1	0	1	....	....	....	0	....	....	....	....	....	....	....	....	....	....	....	....	....	....	....	....	....	....
	Knoxville Cherokees	ECHL	61	41	*93	134	....	....	....	40	....	....	....	....	....	....	....	....	....	....	2	0	4	4	4	....	....	....
1991-92	Muskegon Lumberjacks	IHL	68	19	18	37	....	....	....	28	....	....	....	....	....	....	....	....	....	....	9	3	6	9	8	....	....	....
1992-93	Cleveland Lumberjacks	IHL	80	40	66	106	....	....	....	88	....	....	....	....	....	....	....	....	....	....	4	2	2	4	14	....	....	....
1993-94	Cincinnati Cyclones	IHL	74	30	34	64	....	....	....	101	....	....	....	....	....	....	....	....	....	....	10	2	3	5	14	....	....	....
1994-95	**Chicago Blackhawks**	**NHL**	**5**	**0**	**0**	**0**	**0**	**0**	**0**	**0**	**0**	**0**	**0**	**4**	**0.0**	**1**	**0**	**1**	**0**	**0**	....	....	....	....	....	....	....	....
	Indianapolis Ice	IHL	66	22	50	72	....	....	....	53	....	....	....	....	....	....	....	....	....	....	....	....	....	....	....	....	....	....
1995-96	Indianapolis Ice	IHL	70	28	39	67	....	....	....	44	....	....	....	....	....	....	....	....	....	....	....	....	....	....	....	....	....	....
	Peoria Rivermen	IHL	10	3	5	8	....	....	....	10	....	....	....	....	....	....	....	....	....	....	11	4	6	10	6	....	....	....
1996-97	VEU Feldkirch	Austria	40	16	26	42	....	....	....	38	....	....	....	....	....	....	....	....	....	....	....	....	....	....	....	....	....	....
	Frankfurt Lions	Germany	8	1	0	1	....	....	....	6	....	....	....	....	....	....	....	....	....	....	....	....	....	....	....	....	....	....
	Wedemark Scorpions	Germany	2	1	0	1	....	....	....	0	....	....	....	....	....	....	....	....	....	....	....	....	....	....	....	....	....	....
1997-98	VEU Feldkirch	EuroHL	10	4	7	11	....	....	....	6	....	....	....	....	....	....	....	....	....	....	....	....	....	....	....	....	....	....
	NHL Totals		**5**	**0**	**0**	**0**	**0**	**0**	**0**	**0**	**0**	**0**	**0**	**4**	**0.0**	**1**	**0**	**1**	**0**		....	....	....	....	....	....	....	....

ECHL First All-Star Team (1991) • Rookie of the Year - ECHL (1991)

Signed as a free agent by **Florida**, July 14, 1993. Signed as a free agent by **Chicago**, June 14, 1994.

• GAUTHIER, DENIS

Denis Gauthier D – L. 6′2″, 195 lbs. b: Montreal, Que., 10/1/1976. Calgary's 1st choice, 20th overall, in 1995 Entry Draft.

Season	Club	League	GP	G	A	Pts	AG	AA	APts	PIM	PP	SH	GW	S	%	TGF	PGF	TGA	PGA	+/–	GP	G	A	Pts	PIM	PP	SH	GW
1992-93	Drummondville Voltigeurs	QMJHL	60	1	7	8	....	....	....	136	....	....	....	....	....	....	....	....	....	....	10	0	5	5	40	....	....	....
1993-94	Drummondville Voltigeurs	QMJHL	60	0	7	7	....	....	....	176	....	....	....	....	....	....	....	....	....	....	9	2	0	2	41	....	....	....
1994-95	Drummondville Voltigeurs	QMJHL	64	9	31	40	....	....	....	190	....	....	....	....	....	....	....	....	....	....	4	0	5	5	12	....	....	....
1995-96	Drummondville Voltigeurs	QMJHL	53	25	49	74	....	....	....	140	....	....	....	....	....	....	....	....	....	....	6	4	4	8	32	....	....	....
	Canada	WJC-A	6	1	1	2	....	....	....	6	....	....	....	....	....	....	....	....	....	....	....	....	....	....	....	....	....	....
	Saint John Flames	AHL	5	2	0	2	....	....	....	8	....	....	....	....	....	....	....	....	....	....	16	1	6	7	20	....	....	....
1996-97	Saint John Flames	AHL	73	3	28	31	....	....	....	74	....	....	....	....	....	....	....	....	....	....	5	0	0	0	6	....	....	....
1997-98	**Calgary Flames**	**NHL**	**10**	**0**	**0**	**0**	**0**	**0**	**0**	**16**	**0**	**0**	**0**	**3**	**0.0**	**2**	**0**	**7**	**0**	**–5**	....	....	....	....	....	....	....	....
	Saint John Flames	AHL	68	4	20	24	....	....	....	154	....	....	....	....	....	....	....	....	....	....	21	0	4	4	83	....	....	....
	NHL Totals		**10**	**0**	**0**	**0**	**0**	**0**	**0**	**16**	**0**	**0**	**0**	**3**	**0.0**	**2**	**0**	**7**	**0**		....	....	....	....	....	....	....	....

QMJHL First All-Star Team (1996) • Canadian Major Junior First All-Star Team (1996)

• GAUTHIER, JEAN

Jean Gauthier D – R. 6′1″, 190 lbs. b: Montreal, Que., 4/29/1937.

Season	Club	League	GP	G	A	Pts	AG	AA	APts	PIM	PP	SH	GW	S	%	TGF	PGF	TGA	PGA	+/–	GP	G	A	Pts	PIM	PP	SH	GW
1955-56	St. Boniface Canadians	MJHL	23	1	9	10	....	....	....	*99	....	....	....	....	....	....	....	....	....	....	10	2	3	5	*37	....	....	....
1956-57	Fort William Canadians	TBJHL	....	9	16	25	....	....	....	*133	....	....	....	....	....	....	....	....	....	....	....	....	....	....	....	....	....	....
1957-58	Kingston CKLC's	EOHL	46	8	20	28	....	....	....	118	....	....	....	....	....	....	....	....	....	....	7	0	3	3	12	....	....	....
1958-59	Hull-Ottawa Canadiens	EOHL	52	5	5	10	....	....	....	110	....	....	....	....	....	....	....	....	....	....	8	2	3	5	29	....	....	....
1959-60	Hull-Ottawa Canadiens	EPHL	68	2	23	25	....	....	....	152	....	....	....	....	....	....	....	....	....	....	7	0	1	1	8	....	....	....
1960-61	**Montreal Canadiens**	**NHL**	**4**	**0**	**1**	**1**	**0**	**1**	**1**	**8**	....	....	....	....	....	....	....	....	....	....	....	....	....	....	....	....	....	....
	Hull-Ottawa Canadiens	EPHL	64	8	13	21	....	....	....	*138	....	....	....	....	....	....	....	....	....	....	14	0	5	5	*42	....	....	....
1961-62	**Montreal Canadiens**	**NHL**	**12**	**0**	**1**	**1**	**0**	**1**	**1**	**10**	....	....	....	....	....	....	....	....	....	....	....	....	....	....	....	....	....	....
	Hull-Ottawa Canadiens	EPHL	47	11	20	31	....	....	....	85	....	....	....	....	....	....	....	....	....	....	13	5	4	9	*38	....	....	....
1962-63	**Montreal Canadiens**	**NHL**	**65**	**1**	**17**	**18**	**1**	**18**	**19**	**46**	....	....	....	....	....	....	....	....	....	....	**5**	**0**	**0**	**0**	**12**	....	....	....
1963-64	**Montreal Canadiens**	**NHL**	**1**	**0**	**0**	**0**	**0**	**0**	**0**	**2**	....	....	....	....	....	....	....	....	....	....	....	....	....	....	....	....	....	....
	Quebec Aces	AHL	29	3	7	10	....	....	....	58	....	....	....	....	....	....	....	....	....	....	9	1	2	3	4	....	....	....
1964-65	Omaha Knights	CHL	70	14	37	51	....	....	....	182	....	....	....	....	....	....	....	....	....	....	6	4	1	5	10	....	....	....
	Montreal Canadiens	**NHL**	....	....	....	....	....	....	....	....	....	....	....	....	....	....	....	....	....	....	**2**	**0**	**0**	**0**	**4**	....	....	....
1965-66	**Montreal Canadiens**	**NHL**	**2**	**0**	**0**	**0**	**0**	**0**	**0**	**0**	....	....	....	....	....	....	....	....	....	....	....	....	....	....	....	....	....	....
	Quebec Aces	AHL	3	0	0	0	....	....	....	2	....	....	....	....	....	....	....	....	....	....	6	0	3	3	4	....	....	....
	Houston Apollos	CHL	66	13	9	22	....	....	....	4	....	....	....	....	....	....	....	....	....	....	....	....	....	....	....	....	....	....
1966-67	**Montreal Canadiens**	**NHL**	**2**	**0**	**0**	**0**	**0**	**0**	**0**	**2**	....	....	....	....	....	....	....	....	....	....	....	....	....	....	....	....	....	....
	Seattle Totems	WHL	69	9	22	31	....	....	....	68	....	....	....	....	....	....	....	....	....	....	10	1	3	4	12	....	....	....
1967-68	**Philadelphia Flyers**	**NHL**	**65**	**5**	**7**	**12**	**6**	**7**	**13**	**74**	**1**	**1**	**0**	**104**	**4.8**	**54**	**10**	**55**	**11**	**0**	**7**	**1**	**3**	**4**	**6**	**1**	**0**	**0**
1968-69	**Boston Bruins**	**NHL**	**11**	**0**	**2**	**2**	**0**	**2**	**2**	**8**	**0**	**0**	**0**	**10**	**0.0**	**6**	**1**	**9**	**2**	**–2**	....	....	....	....	....	....	....	....
	Providence Reds	AHL	39	5	14	19	....	....	....	58	....	....	....	....	....	....	....	....	....	....	....	....	....	....	....	....	....	....
1969-70	**Montreal Canadiens**	**NHL**	**4**	**0**	**1**	**1**	**0**	**1**	**1**	**0**	**0**	**0**	**0**	**2**	**0.0**	**1**	**0**	**1**	**0**	**0**	....	....	....	....	....	....	....	....
	Montreal Voyageurs	AHL	54	6	22	28	....	....	....	70	....	....	....	....	....	....	....	....	....	....	8	3	2	5	18	....	....	....
1970-71	Montreal Voyageurs	AHL	52	3	19	22	....	....	....	80	....	....	....	....	....	....	....	....	....	....	3	0	1	1	2	....	....	....
1971-72	Baltimore Clippers	AHL	64	3	37	40	....	....	....	104	....	....	....	....	....	....	....	....	....	....	18	5	7	12	38	....	....	....
1972-73	New York Raiders	WHA	31	2	1	3	....	....	....	21	....	....	....	....	....	....	....	....	....	....	....	....	....	....	....	....	....	....
	Long Island Ducks	EHL	4	1	1	2	....	....	....	10	....	....	....	....	....	....	....	....	....	....	....	....	....	....	....	....	....	....
1973-74	Rochester Americans	AHL	41	3	9	12	....	....	....	63	....	....	....	....	....	....	....	....	....	....	5	0	2	2	6	....	....	....
	NHL Totals		**166**	**6**	**29**	**35**	**7**	**30**	**37**	**150**	**1**	**1**	**0**	**116**	**5.2**	**61**	**11**	**65**	**13**		**14**	**1**	**3**	**4**	**22**	**1**	**0**	**0**
	Other Major League Totals		31	2	1	3	....	....	....	21	....	....	....	....	....	....	....	....	....		....	....	....	....	....	....	....	....

CHL First All-Star Team (1965) • CHL Second All-Star Team (1966)

Claimed by **Philadelphia** from **Montreal** in Expansion Draft, June 6, 1967. Claimed by **Boston** from **Philadelphia** in Intra-League Draft, June 12, 1968. Claimed by **Cleveland** (AHL) from **Oklahoma City** (CHL) in Reverse Draft, June 12, 1969. Traded to **Montreal** by **Cleveland** (AHL) for cash, October, 1969. Selected by **Dayton-Houston** (WHA) in 1972 WHA General Player Draft, February 13, 1972. WHA rights traded to **NY Raiders** (WHA) by **Houston** (WHA) for cash and future considerations, August, 1972.

• GAUTHIER, LUC

Luc Gauthier D – R. 5′9″, 195 lbs. b: Longueuil, Que., 4/19/1964.

Season	Club	League	GP	G	A	Pts	AG	AA	APts	PIM	PP	SH	GW	S	%	TGF	PGF	TGA	PGA	+/–	GP	G	A	Pts	PIM	PP	SH	GW
1982-83	Longueuil Chevaliers	QMJHL	67	3	18	21	....	....	....	132	....	....	....	....	....	....	....	....	....	....	15	0	4	4	35	....	....	....
1983-84	Longueuil Chevaliers	QMJHL	70	8	54	62	....	....	....	207	....	....	....	....	....	....	....	....	....	....	17	4	9	13	24	....	....	....
1984-85	Longueuil Chevaliers	QMJHL	60	13	47	60	....	....	....	111	....	....	....	....	....	....	....	....	....	....	....	....	....	....	....	....	....	....
	Flint Generals	IHL	21	1	0	1	....	....	....	20	....	....	....	....	....	....	....	....	....	....	....	....	....	....	....	....	....	....
1985-86	Saginaw Generals	IHL	66	9	29	38	....	....	....	160	....	....	....	....	....	....	....	....	....	....	....	....	....	....	....	....	....	....
1986-87	Sherbrooke Canadiens	AHL	78	5	17	22	....	....	....	8	....	....	....	....	....	....	....	....	....	....	17	2	4	6	31	....	....	....
1987-88	Sherbrooke Canadiens	AHL	61	4	10	14	....	....	....	105	....	....	....	....	....	....	....	....	....	....	6	0	0	0	18	....	....	....
1988-89	Sherbrooke Canadiens	AHL	77	8	20	28	....	....	....	178	....	....	....	....	....	....	....	....	....	....	6	0	0	0	10	....	....	....
1989-90	Sherbrooke Canadiens	AHL	79	3	23	26	....	....	....	139	....	....	....	....	....	....	....	....	....	....	12	0	4	4	35	....	....	....
1990-91	**Montreal Canadiens**	**NHL**	**3**	**0**	**0**	**0**	**0**	**0**	**0**	**2**	**0**	**0**	**0**	**0**	**0.0**	**3**	**0**	**2**	**0**	**+1**	....	....	....	....	....	....	....	....
	Fredericton Canadiens	AHL	69	7	20	27	....	....	....	238	....	....	....	....	....	....	....	....	....	....	9	1	1	2	10	....	....	....
1991-92	Fredericton Canadiens	AHL	80	4	14	18	....	....	....	252	....	....	....	....	....	....	....	....	....	....	7	1	1	2	26	....	....	....
1992-93	Fredericton Canadiens	AHL	78	9	33	42	....	....	....	167	....	....	....	....	....	....	....	....	....	....	5	2	1	3	20	....	....	....
1993-1996	Fredericton Canadiens	AHL	DID NOT PLAY																									
1996-97	Fredericton Canadiens	AHL	2	0	0	0	....	....	....	0	....	....	....	....	....	....	....	....	....	....	....	....	....	....	....	....	....	....
	NHL Totals		**3**	**0**	**0**	**0**	**0**	**0**	**0**	**2**	**0**	**0**	**0**	**0**	**0.0**	**3**	**0**	**2**	**0**		....	....	....	....	....	....	....	....

Signed as a free agent by **Montreal**, October 7, 1986. • Served as assistant coach of the **Fredericton Canadiens** (AHL) from 1993 to 1997.

• GAUVREAU, JOCELYN

Jocelyn Gauvreau D – L. 5′11″, 180 lbs. b: Masham, Que., 3/4/1964. Montreal's 2nd choice, 31st overall, in 1982 Entry Draft.

Season	Club	League	GP	G	A	Pts	AG	AA	APts	PIM	PP	SH	GW	S	%	TGF	PGF	TGA	PGA	+/–	GP	G	A	Pts	PIM	PP	SH	GW
1980-81	Hull Olympiques	QMJHL	54	12	12	24	....	....	....	55	....	....	....	....	....	....	....	....	....	....	....	....	....	....	....	....	....	....
1981-82	Hull Olympiques	QMJHL	19	5	8	13	....	....	....	8	....	....	....	....	....	....	....	....	....	....	....	....	....	....	....	....	....	....
	Granby Bisons	QMJHL	33	12	21	33	....	....	....	66	....	....	....	....	....	....	....	....	....	....	14	3	10	13	16	....	....	....
1982-83	Granby Bisons	QMJHL	68	33	63	96	....	....	....	42	....	....	....	....	....	....	....	....	....	....	....	....	....	....	....	....	....	....
	Nova Scotia Voyageurs	AHL	1	0	0	0	....	....	....	0	....	....	....	....	....	....	....	....	....	....	5	0	1	1	0	....	....	....
1983-84	Granby Bisons	QMJHL	58	19	39	58	....	....	....	55	....	....	....	....	....	....	....	....	....	....	4	2	3	5	0	....	....	....
	Montreal Canadiens	**NHL**	**2**	**0**	**0**	**0**	**0**	**0**	**0**	**0**	**0**	**0**	**0**	**0**	**0.0**	**0**	**0**	**2**	**0**	**–2**	....	....	....	....	....	....	....	....
	Nova Scotia Voyageurs	AHL	1	0	2	2	....	....	....	0	....	....	....	....	....	....	....	....	....	....	3	1	1	2	0	....	....	....
1984-85	Sherbrooke Canadiens	AHL	10	1	2	3	....	....	....	4	....	....	....	....	....	....	....	....	....	....	....	....	....	....	....	....	....	....
	NHL Totals		**2**	**0**	**0**	**0**	**0**	**0**	**0**	**0**	**0**	**0**	**0**	**0**	**0.0**	**0**	**0**	**2**	**0**		....	....	....	....	....	....	....	....

QMJHL Second All-Star Team (1983)

• GAVEY, AARON Aaron Gavey C – L. 6'1", 194 lbs. b: Sudbury, Ont., 2/22/1974. Tampa Bay's 4th choice, 74th overall, in 1992 Entry Draft.

			REGULAR SEASON																		PLAYOFFS							
Season	Club	League	GP	G	A	Pts	AG	AA	APts	PIM	PP	SH	GW	S	%	TGF	PGF	TGA	PGA	+/-	GP	G	A	Pts	PIM	PP	SH	GW
1991-92	Sault Ste. Marie Greyhounds	OHL	48	7	11	18				27											19	5	1	6	10			
1992-93	Sault Ste. Marie Greyhounds	OHL	62	45	39	84				116											18	5	9	14	36			
1993-94	Sault Ste. Marie Greyhounds	OHL	60	42	60	102				116											14	11	10	21	22			
	Canada	WJC-A	7	4	2	6				26																		
1994-95	Atlanta Knights	IHL	66	18	17	35				85											5	0	1	1	9			
1995-96	**Tampa Bay Lightning**	**NHL**	**73**	**8**	**4**	**12**	**8**	**3**	**11**	**56**	**1**	**1**	**2**	**65**	**12.3**	**20**	**6**	**35**	**15**	**–6**	**6**	**0**	**0**	**0**	**4**	**0**	**0**	**0**
1996-97	**Tampa Bay Lightning**	**NHL**	**16**	**1**	**2**	**3**	**1**	**2**	**3**	**12**	**0**	**0**	**0**	**8**	**12.5**	**5**	**0**	**9**	**3**	**–1**								
	Calgary Flames	**NHL**	**41**	**7**	**9**	**16**	**7**	**8**	**15**	**34**	**3**	**0**	**1**	**54**	**13.0**	**27**	**11**	**33**	**6**	**–11**								
1997-98	**Calgary Flames**	**NHL**	**26**	**2**	**3**	**5**	**2**	**3**	**5**	**24**	**0**	**0**	**1**	**27**	**7.4**	**5**	**0**	**15**	**5**	**–5**								
	Saint John Flames	AHL	8	4	3	7				28																		
	NHL Totals		**156**	**18**	**18**	**36**	**18**	**16**	**34**	**126**	**4**	**1**	**4**	**154**	**11.7**	**57**	**17**	**92**	**29**		**6**	**0**	**0**	**0**	**4**	**0**	**0**	**0**

Traded to **Calgary** by **Tampa Bay** for Rick Tabaracci, November 19, 1996. Traded to **Dallas** by **Calgary** for Bob Bassen, July 14, 1998.

• GAVIN, STEWART Stewart Gavin LW – L. 6', 190 lbs. b: Ottawa, Ont., 3/15/1960. Toronto's 4th choice, 74th overall, in 1980 Entry Draft.

Season	Club	League	GP	G	A	Pts	AG	AA	APts	PIM	PP	SH	GW	S	%	TGF	PGF	TGA	PGA	+/-	GP	G	A	Pts	PIM	PP	SH	GW
1976-77	Ottawa 67's	OHA	1	0	0	0				0																		
1977-78	Toronto Marlboros	OHA	67	16	24	40				19																		
1978-79	Toronto Marlboros	OHA	61	24	25	49				83											3	1	0	1	0			
1979-80	Toronto Marlboros	OHA	68	27	30	57				52											4	1	1	2	2			
1980-81	**Toronto Maple Leafs**	**NHL**	**14**	**1**	**2**	**3**	**1**	**1**	**2**	**13**	**0**	**0**	**0**	**13**	**7.7**	**8**	**0**	**10**	**2**	**0**								
	New Brunswick Hawks	AHL	46	7	12	19				42											13	1	0	1	2			
1981-82	**Toronto Maple Leafs**	**NHL**	**38**	**5**	**6**	**11**	**4**	**4**	**8**	**29**	**1**	**0**	**0**	**66**	**7.6**	**32**	**7**	**44**	**13**	**–6**								
1982-83	**Toronto Maple Leafs**	**NHL**	**63**	**6**	**5**	**11**	**5**	**3**	**8**	**44**	**0**	**0**	**0**	**77**	**7.8**	**23**	**1**	**41**	**12**	**–7**	**4**	**0**	**0**	**0**	**0**	**0**	**0**	**0**
	St. Catharines Saints	AHL	6	2	4	6				17																		
1983-84	**Toronto Maple Leafs**	**NHL**	**80**	**10**	**22**	**32**	**8**	**15**	**23**	**90**	**0**	**1**	**3**	**96**	**10.4**	**59**	**2**	**93**	**30**	**–6**								
1984-85	**Toronto Maple Leafs**	**NHL**	**73**	**12**	**13**	**25**	**10**	**9**	**19**	**38**	**0**	**0**	**0**	**148**	**8.1**	**34**	**0**	**76**	**20**	**–22**								
1985-86	**Hartford Whalers**	**NHL**	**76**	**26**	**29**	**55**	**21**	**19**	**40**	**51**	**3**	**3**	**4**	**161**	**16.1**	**86**	**18**	**74**	**18**	**+12**	**10**	**4**	**1**	**5**	**13**	**0**	**0**	**0**
1986-87	**Hartford Whalers**	**NHL**	**79**	**20**	**21**	**41**	**17**	**15**	**32**	**28**	**3**	**2**	**4**	**162**	**12.3**	**83**	**17**	**85**	**29**	**+10**	**6**	**2**	**4**	**6**	**10**	**0**	**0**	**0**
1987-88	**Hartford Whalers**	**NHL**	**56**	**11**	**10**	**21**	**9**	**7**	**16**	**59**	**2**	**3**	**1**	**125**	**8.8**	**38**	**10**	**59**	**14**	**–17**	**6**	**2**	**2**	**4**	**4**	**0**	**0**	**0**
1988-89	**Minnesota North Stars**	**NHL**	**73**	**8**	**18**	**26**	**7**	**13**	**20**	**34**	**0**	**1**	**0**	**129**	**6.2**	**42**	**1**	**69**	**31**	**+3**	**5**	**3**	**1**	**4**	**10**	**0**	**0**	**0**
1989-90	**Minnesota North Stars**	**NHL**	**80**	**12**	**13**	**25**	**10**	**9**	**19**	**76**	**0**	**3**	**1**	**146**	**8.2**	**45**	**0**	**79**	**43**	**+9**	**7**	**0**	**2**	**2**	**12**	**0**	**0**	**0**
1990-91	Minnesota North Stars	FrTour	2	1	0	1				0																		
	Minnesota North Stars	**NHL**	**38**	**4**	**4**	**8**	**4**	**3**	**7**	**36**	**0**	**1**	**0**	**56**	**7.1**	**19**	**0**	**42**	**20**	**–3**	**21**	**3**	**10**	**13**	**20**	**0**	**1**	**1**
1991-92	**Minnesota North Stars**	**NHL**	**35**	**5**	**4**	**9**	**5**	**3**	**8**	**27**	**0**	**1**	**1**	**49**	**10.2**	**13**	**0**	**29**	**16**	**0**	**7**	**0**	**0**	**0**	**6**	**0**	**0**	**0**
1992-93	**Minnesota North Stars**	**NHL**	**63**	**10**	**8**	**18**	**8**	**5**	**13**	**59**	**0**	**0**	**0**	**114**	**8.8**	**30**	**0**	**46**	**12**	**–4**								
1993-94			DID NOT PLAY – RETIRED																									
1994-95	Kansas City Blades	IHL	18	2	2	4				32																		
1995-96	Minnesota Moose	IHL	22	4	7	11				21																		
	NHL Totals		**768**	**130**	**155**	**285**	**109**	**106**	**215**	**584**	**9**	**15**	**14**	**1342**	**9.7**	**512**	**56**	**747**	**260**		**66**	**14**	**20**	**34**	**75**	**0**	**1**	**1**

Traded to **Hartford** by **Toronto** for Chris Kotsopoulos, October 7, 1985. Claimed by **Minnesota** from **Hartford** in Waiver Draft, October 3, 1988.

• GEALE, BOB Bob Geale C – R. 5'11", 175 lbs. b: Edmonton, Alta., 4/17/1962. Pittsburgh's 6th choice, 156th overall, in 1980 Entry Draft.

Season	Club	League	GP	G	A	Pts	AG	AA	APts	PIM	PP	SH	GW	S	%	TGF	PGF	TGA	PGA	+/-	GP	G	A	Pts	PIM	PP	SH	GW
1978-79	Sherwood Park Crusaders	AJHL	60	11	33	44				44																		
1979-80	Portland Winter Hawks	WHL	72	17	29	46				32																		
1980-81	Portland Winter Hawks	WHL	54	30	32	62				54																		
1981-82	Portland Winter Hawks	WHL	72	31	54	85				89											15	8	10	10	20			
1982-83	Baltimore Skipjacks	AHL	50	4	10	14				6																		
1983-84	Baltimore Skipjacks	AHL	74	17	23	40				50											7	1	0	1	2			
1984-85	**Pittsburgh Penguins**	**NHL**	**1**	**0**	**0**	**0**	**0**	**0**	**0**	**2**	**0**	**0**	**0**	**1**	**0.0**	**0**	**0**	**1**	**0**	**–1**								
	Baltimore Skipjacks	AHL	77	20	23	49				42											15	3	8	11	11			
1985-86	Baltimore Skipjacks	AHL	21	5	7	12				9																		
	NHL Totals		**1**	**0**	**0**	**0**	**0**	**0**	**0**	**2**	**0**	**0**	**0**	**1**	**0.0**	**0**	**0**	**1**	**0**									

• GELDART, GARY Gary Geldart D – L. 5'8", 160 lbs. b: Moncton, N.B., 6/14/1950. Minnesota's 7th choice, 89th overall, in 1970 Amateur Draft.

Season	Club	League	GP	G	A	Pts	AG	AA	APts	PIM	PP	SH	GW	S	%	TGF	PGF	TGA	PGA	+/-	GP	G	A	Pts	PIM	PP	SH	GW
1965-66	Moncton Red Wings	Bantam		9	*15	24				*35																		
1966-67	Halifax Canadians	NSJHL	30	4	15	19				58											16	0	4	4	26			
1967-68	Fredericton Jr. Red Wings	NBJHL	4	1	3	4				8											12	1	10	11	25			
	Fredericton Red Wings	NBSHL	29	3	21	24				72											5	2	2	4	7			
1968-69	Hamilton Red Wings	OHA	52	3	30	33				103											5	0	3	3	12			
1969-70	Hamilton Red Wings	OHA	18	1	13	14				29																		
	London Knights	OHA	30	5	28	33				48																		
1970-71	**Minnesota North Stars**	**NHL**	**4**	**0**	**0**	**0**	**0**	**0**	**0**	**5**	**0**	**0**	**0**	**3**	**0.0**	**1**	**0**	**0**	**0**	**+1**								
	Cleveland Barons	AHL	67	5	19	24				84																		
1971-72	Cleveland Barons	AHL	71	3	19	22				44											6	0	3	3	8			
1972-73	Cleveland-Jacksonville Barons	AHL	74	6	32	38				81																		
1973-74	Nova Scotia Voyageurs	AHL	49	1	21	22				59											6	0	2	2	2			
1974-75	Nova Scotia Voyageurs	AHL	65	2	17	19				111											6	0	0	0	9			
1975-76	Nova Scotia Voyageurs	AHL																			9	0	2	2	0			
1976-77	New Haven Nighthawks	AHL	79	6	34	40				110											6	0	0	0	2			
1977-78	New Haven Nighthawks	AHL	9	0	0	0				12											14	0	1	1	32			
	NHL Totals		**4**	**0**	**0**	**0**	**0**	**0**	**0**	**5**	**0**	**0**	**0**	**3**	**0.0**	**1**	**0**	**0**	**0**									

AHL Second All-Star Team (1977)

Traded to **Montreal** by **Minnesota** for cash, September, 1973. • Missed entire 1975-76 regular season after undergoing off-season knee surgery.

• GELINAS, MARTIN Martin Gelinas LW – L. 5'11", 195 lbs. b: Shawinigan, Que., 6/5/1970. Los Angeles' 1st choice, 7th overall, in 1988 Entry Draft.

Season	Club	League	GP	G	A	Pts	AG	AA	APts	PIM	PP	SH	GW	S	%	TGF	PGF	TGA	PGA	+/-	GP	G	A	Pts	PIM	PP	SH	GW
1987-88	Hull Olympiques	QMJHL	65	63	68	131				74											17	15	18	33	32			
1988-89	Hull Olympiques	QMJHL	41	38	39	77				31											9	5	4	9	14			
	Canada	WJC-A	7	0	2	2				8																		
	Edmonton Oilers	**NHL**	**6**	**1**	**2**	**3**	**1**	**1**	**2**	**0**	**0**	**0**	**0**	**14**	**7.1**	**4**	**0**	**5**	**0**	**–1**								
1989-90	**Edmonton Oilers**	**NHL**	**46**	**17**	**8**	**25**	**15**	**6**	**21**	**30**	**5**	**0**	**2**	**71**	**23.9**	**33**	**7**	**26**	**0**	**0**	**20**	**2**	**3**	**5**	**6**	**0**	**0**	**0**
1990-91	**Edmonton Oilers**	**NHL**	**73**	**20**	**20**	**40**	**18**	**15**	**33**	**34**	**4**	**0**	**2**	**124**	**16.1**	**56**	**11**	**52**	**0**	**–7**	**18**	**3**	**6**	**9**	**25**	**0**	**0**	**1**
1991-92	**Edmonton Oilers**	**NHL**	**68**	**11**	**18**	**29**	**10**	**14**	**24**	**62**	**1**	**0**	**0**	**94**	**11.7**	**47**	**6**	**28**	**1**	**+14**	**15**	**1**	**3**	**4**	**10**	**0**	**0**	**0**
1992-93	**Edmonton Oilers**	**NHL**	**65**	**11**	**12**	**23**	**9**	**8**	**17**	**30**	**0**	**0**	**1**	**93**	**11.8**	**39**	**1**	**36**	**1**	**+3**								
1993-94	**Quebec Nordiques**	**NHL**	**31**	**6**	**6**	**12**	**6**	**5**	**11**	**8**	**0**	**0**	**0**	**53**	**11.3**	**17**	**1**	**18**	**0**	**–2**								
	Vancouver Canucks	**NHL**	**33**	**8**	**8**	**16**	**7**	**6**	**13**	**26**	**3**	**0**	**1**	**54**	**14.8**	**26**	**8**	**25**	**1**	**–6**	**24**	**5**	**4**	**9**	**14**	**2**	**0**	**1**
1994-95	**Vancouver Canucks**	**NHL**	**46**	**13**	**10**	**23**	**23**	**15**	**38**	**36**	**1**	**0**	**4**	**75**	**17.3**	**27**	**2**	**30**	**13**	**+8**	**3**	**0**	**1**	**1**	**0**	**0**	**0**	**0**
1995-96	**Vancouver Canucks**	**NHL**	**81**	**30**	**26**	**56**	**30**	**21**	**51**	**59**	**3**	**4**	**5**	**181**	**16.6**	**75**	**9**	**78**	**20**	**+8**	**6**	**1**	**1**	**2**	**12**	**1**	**0**	**0**
1996-97	**Vancouver Canucks**	**NHL**	**74**	**35**	**33**	**68**	**37**	**29**	**66**	**42**	**6**	**1**	**3**	**177**	**19.8**	**89**	**19**	**85**	**21**	**+6**								
1997-98	**Vancouver Canucks**	**NHL**	**24**	**4**	**4**	**8**	**5**	**4**	**9**	**10**	**1**	**1**	**1**	**49**	**8.2**	**16**	**2**	**26**	**6**	**–6**								
	Carolina Hurricanes	**NHL**	**40**	**12**	**14**	**26**	**14**	**14**	**28**	**30**	**2**	**1**	**4**	**98**	**12.2**	**35**	**8**	**29**	**3**	**+1**								
	Canada	WC-A	6	1	0	1				6																		
	NHL Totals		**587**	**168**	**161**	**329**	**175**	**138**	**313**	**367**	**26**	**7**	**23**	**1083**	**15.5**	**464**	**74**	**438**	**66**		**86**	**12**	**18**	**30**	**67**	**3**	**0**	**2**

QMJHL First All-Star Team (1988) • Canadian Major Junior Rookie of the Year (1988) • Won George Parsons Trophy (Memorial Cup Tournament Most Sportsmanlike Player) (1988)

Traded to **Edmonton** by **LA Kings** with Jimmy Carson and LA Kings' 1st round choices in 1989 (previously acquired, New Jersey selected Jason Miller), 1991 (Martin Rucinsky) and 1993 (Nick Stajduhar) Entry Drafts and cash for Wayne Gretzky, Mike Krushelnyski and Marty McSorley, August 9, 1988. Traded to **Quebec** by **Edmonton** with Edmonton's 6th round choice (Nicholas Checco) in 1993 Entry Draft for Scott Pearson, June 20, 1993. Claimed on waivers by **Vancouver** from **Quebec**, January 15, 1994. Traded to **Carolina** by **Vancouver** with Kirk McLean for Sean Burke, Geoff Sanderson and Enrico Ciccone, January 3, 1998.

• GENDRON, JEAN-GUY

Jean-Guy Gendron LW – L. 5'9", 165 lbs. b: Montreal, Que., 8/30/1934.

			REGULAR SEASON																		PLAYOFFS							
Season	Club	League	GP	G	A	Pts	AG	AA	APts	PIM	PP	SH	GW	S	%	TGF	PGF	TGA	PGA	+/–	GP	G	A	Pts	PIM	PP	SH	GW
1951-52	Trois-Rivieres Reds	QJHL	41	9	28	37	....	....	....	77	....	....	....	....	....	....	....	....	....	....	5	0	1	1	16	....	....	....
1952-53	Trois-Rivieres Reds	QJHL	47	19	10	29	....	....	....	98	....	....	....	....	....	....	....	....	....	....	6	2	3	5	12	....	....	....
	Quebec Aces	QSHL	....	....	....	....	....	....	....	....	....	....	....	....	....	....	....	....	....	....	3	0	0	0	0	....	....	....
1953-54	Trois-Rivieres Reds	QJHL	54	42	45	87	....	....	....	*179	....	....	....	....	....	....	....	....	....	....	4	0	1	1	8	....	....	....
1954-55	Providence Reds	AHL	47	24	15	39	....	....	....	38	....	....	....	....	....	....	....	....	....	....	....	....	....	....	....	....	....	....
1955-56	**New York Rangers**	**NHL**	**63**	**5**	**7**	**12**	**7**	**9**	**16**	**38**	....	....	....	....	....	....	....	....	....	....	**5**	**2**	**1**	**3**	**2**	....	....	....
1956-57	**New York Rangers**	**NHL**	**70**	**9**	**6**	**15**	**12**	**7**	**19**	**40**	....	....	....	....	....	....	....	....	....	....	**5**	**0**	**1**	**1**	**6**	....	....	....
1957-58	**New York Rangers**	**NHL**	**70**	**10**	**17**	**27**	**13**	**18**	**31**	**68**	....	....	....	....	....	....	....	....	....	....	**6**	**1**	**0**	**1**	**11**	....	....	....
1958-59	**Boston Bruins**	**NHL**	**60**	**15**	**9**	**24**	**19**	**10**	**29**	**57**	....	....	....	....	....	....	....	....	....	....	**7**	**1**	**0**	**1**	**18**	....	....	....
1959-60	**Boston Bruins**	**NHL**	**67**	**24**	**11**	**35**	**30**	**11**	**41**	**64**	....	....	....	....	....	....	....	....	....	....	....	....	....	....	....	....	....	....
1960-61	**Boston Bruins**	**NHL**	**13**	**1**	**7**	**8**	**1**	**7**	**8**	**24**	....	....	....	....	....	....	....	....	....	....	....	....	....	....	....	....	....	....
	Montreal Canadiens	**NHL**	**53**	**9**	**12**	**21**	**11**	**12**	**23**	**51**	....	....	....	....	....	....	....	....	....	....	**5**	**0**	**0**	**0**	**2**	....	....	....
1961-62	**New York Rangers**	**NHL**	**69**	**14**	**11**	**25**	**17**	**11**	**28**	**71**	....	....	....	....	....	....	....	....	....	....	**6**	**3**	**1**	**4**	**2**	....	....	....
1962-63	**Boston Bruins**	**NHL**	**66**	**21**	**22**	**43**	**26**	**23**	**49**	**42**	....	....	....	....	....	....	....	....	....	....	....	....	....	....	....	....	....	....
1963-64	**Boston Bruins**	**NHL**	**54**	**5**	**13**	**18**	**7**	**14**	**21**	**43**	....	....	....	....	....	....	....	....	....	....	....	....	....	....	....	....	....	....
	Providence Reds	AHL	6	1	1	2	....	....	....	0	....	....	....	....	....	....	....	....	....	....	....	....	....	....	....	....	....	....
1964-65	Quebec Aces	AHL	53	20	14	34	....	....	....	61	....	....	....	....	....	....	....	....	....	....	5	1	1	2	8	....	....	....
1965-66	Quebec Aces	AHL	58	26	35	61	....	....	....	70	....	....	....	....	....	....	....	....	....	....	6	1	0	1	6	....	....	....
1966-67	Quebec Aces	AHL	68	28	45	73	....	....	....	72	....	....	....	....	....	....	....	....	....	....	5	2	1	3	4	....	....	....
1967-68	**Philadelphia Flyers**	**NHL**	**1**	**0**	**1**	**1**	**0**	**1**	**1**	**2**	**0**	**0**	**0**	**2**	**0.0**	**1**	**0**	**0**	**0**	**+1**	....	....	....	....	....	....	....	....
	Quebec Aces	AHL	72	29	58	87	....	....	....	72	....	....	....	....	....	....	....	....	....	....	15	7	*14	*21	24	....	....	....
1968-69	**Philadelphia Flyers**	**NHL**	**74**	**20**	**35**	**55**	**23**	**33**	**56**	**65**	**5**	**1**	**2**	**198**	**10.1**	**80**	**31**	**57**	**0**	**–8**	**4**	**0**	**0**	**0**	**6**	**0**	**0**	**0**
1969-70	**Philadelphia Flyers**	**NHL**	**71**	**23**	**21**	**44**	**27**	**21**	**48**	**54**	**5**	**0**	**1**	**155**	**14.8**	**68**	**20**	**41**	**1**	**+8**	....	....	....	....	....	....	....	....
1970-71	**Philadelphia Flyers**	**NHL**	**76**	**20**	**16**	**36**	**21**	**14**	**35**	**46**	**5**	**0**	**1**	**145**	**13.8**	**53**	**24**	**38**	**0**	**–9**	**4**	**0**	**1**	**1**	**0**	**0**	**0**	**0**
1971-72	**Philadelphia Flyers**	**NHL**	**56**	**6**	**13**	**19**	**6**	**12**	**18**	**36**	**2**	**0**	**0**	**95**	**6.3**	**32**	**9**	**26**	**1**	**–2**	....	....	....	....	....	....	....	....
1972-73	Quebec Nordiques	WHA	63	17	33	50	....	....	....	113	....	....	....	....	....	....	....	....	....	....	....	....	....	....	....	....	....	....
1973-74	Quebec Nordiques	WHA	64	11	8	19	....	....	....	42	....	....	....	....	....	....	....	....	....	....	....	....	....	....	....	....	....	....
	NHL Totals		**863**	**182**	**201**	**383**	**220**	**203**	**423**	**701**	**17**	**1**	**4**	**595**	**30.6**	**234**	**84**	**162**	**2**		**42**	**7**	**4**	**11**	**47**	**0**	**0**	**0**
	Other Major League Totals		127	28	41	69	....	....	....	155	....	....	....	....	....	....	....	....	....	....	....	....	....	....	....	....	....	....

Traded to **NY Rangers** by **Providence** (AHL) for Bill Ezinicki and cash, May 8, 1955. Claimed by **Boston** from **NY Rangers** in Intra-League Draft, June 3, 1958. Traded to **Montreal** by **Boston** for Andre Pronovost, November 27, 1960. Claimed by **NY Rangers** from **Montreal** in Intra-League Draft, June, 1962. NHL rights transferred to **Philadelphia** after NHL club purchased **Quebec** (AHL) franchise, May 8, 1967. Claimed by **Montreal** from **Philadelphia** in Intra-League Draft, June 11, 1969. Traded to **Philadelphia** by **Montreal** for cash, June 12, 1969. Selected by **LA Sharks** (WHA) in 1972 WHA General Player Draft, February 12, 1972. Signed as a free agent by **Quebec** (WHA) after **LA Sharks** (WHA) dropped Gendron from their negotiating list, June, 1972.

• GENDRON, MARTIN

Martin Gendron RW – R. 5'9", 190 lbs. b: Valleyfield, Que., 2/15/1974. Washington's 4th choice, 71st overall, in 1992 Entry Draft.

Season	Club	League	GP	G	A	Pts	AG	AA	APts	PIM	PP	SH	GW	S	%	TGF	PGF	TGA	PGA	+/–	GP	G	A	Pts	PIM	PP	SH	GW
1990-91	St-Hyacinthe Laser	QMJHL	55	34	23	57	....	....	....	33	....	....	....	....	....	....	....	....	....	....	4	1	2	3	0	....	....	....
1991-92	St-Hyacinthe Laser	QMJHL	69	*71	66	137	....	....	....	45	....	....	....	....	....	....	....	....	....	....	6	7	4	11	14	....	....	....
1992-93	St-Hyacinthe Laser	QMJHL	63	73	61	134	....	....	....	44	....	....	....	....	....	....	....	....	....	....	....	....	....	....	....	....	....	....
	Canada	WJC-A	7	5	2	7	....	....	....	2	....	....	....	....	....	....	....	....	....	....	....	....	....	....	....	....	....	....
	Baltimore Skipjacks	AHL	10	1	2	3	....	....	....	2	....	....	....	....	....	....	....	....	....	....	3	0	0	0	0	....	....	....
1993-94	Hull Olympiques	QMJHL	37	39	36	75	....	....	....	18	....	....	....	....	....	....	....	....	....	....	20	*21	17	38	8	....	....	....
	Canada	Nat-Team	19	4	5	9	....	....	....	2	....	....	....	....	....	....	....	....	....	....	....	....	....	....	....	....	....	....
	Canada	WJC-A	7	6	4	10	....	....	....	6	....	....	....	....	....	....	....	....	....	....	....	....	....	....	....	....	....	....
1994-95	**Washington Capitals**	**NHL**	**8**	**2**	**1**	**3**	**4**	**1**	**5**	**2**	**0**	**0**	**0**	**11**	**18.2**	**5**	**0**	**2**	**0**	**+3**	....	....	....	....	....	....	....	....
	Portland Pirates	AHL	72	36	32	68	....	....	....	54	....	....	....	....	....	....	....	....	....	....	4	5	1	6	2	....	....	....
1995-96	**Washington Capitals**	**NHL**	**20**	**2**	**1**	**3**	**2**	**1**	**3**	**8**	**0**	**0**	**0**	**22**	**9.1**	**3**	**1**	**7**	**0**	**–5**	....	....	....	....	....	....	....	....
	Portland Pirates	AHL	48	38	29	67	....	....	....	39	....	....	....	....	....	....	....	....	....	....	22	*15	18	33	8	....	....	....
1996-97	Las Vegas Thunder	IHL	81	51	39	90	....	....	....	20	....	....	....	....	....	....	....	....	....	....	3	2	1	3	0	....	....	....
1997-98	**Chicago Blackhawks**	**NHL**	**2**	**0**	**0**	**0**	**0**	**0**	**0**	**0**	**0**	**0**	**0**	**3**	**0.0**	**0**	**0**	**1**	**0**	**–1**	....	....	....	....	....	....	....	....
	Indianapolis Ice	IHL	17	8	6	14	....	....	....	16	....	....	....	....	....	....	....	....	....	....	....	....	....	....	....	....	....	....
	Milwaukee Admirals	IHL	40	20	19	39	....	....	....	14	....	....	....	....	....	....	....	....	....	....	....	....	....	....	....	....	....	....
	Fredericton Canadiens	AHL	10	5	10	15	....	....	....	4	....	....	....	....	....	....	....	....	....	....	2	0	0	0	4	....	....	....
	NHL Totals		**30**	**4**	**2**	**6**	**6**	**2**	**8**	**10**	**0**	**0**	**0**	**36**	**11.1**	**8**	**1**	**10**	**0**		....	....	....	....	....	....	....	....

QMJHL First All-Star Team (1992) • Canadian Major Junior Most Sportsmanlike Player of the Year (1992) • QMJHL Second All-Star Team (1993) • Canadian Major Junior First All-Star Team (1993)

Traded to **Chicago** by **Washington** with Washington's 6th round choice (Jonathan Pelletier) in 1998 Entry Draft for Chicago's 5th round choice (Erik Wendell) in 1998 Entry Draft, October 10, 1997. Traded to **Montreal** by **Chicago** for David Ling, March 14, 1998.

• GEOFFRION, BERNIE

Bernie "Boom-Boom" Geoffrion RW – R. 5'9", 166 lbs. b: Montreal, Que., 2/14/1931. **HHOF**

Season	Club	League	GP	G	A	Pts	AG	AA	APts	PIM	PP	SH	GW	S	%	TGF	PGF	TGA	PGA	+/–	GP	G	A	Pts	PIM	PP	SH	GW
1946-47	Montreal Concordia Civics	QJHL	26	7	8	15	....	....	....	6	....	....	....	....	....	....	....	....	....	....	....	....	....	....	....	....	....	....
1947-48	Laval Nationale	QJHL	29	20	15	35	....	....	....	49	....	....	....	....	....	....	....	....	....	....	19	10	7	17	22	....	....	....
1948-49	Laval Nationale	QJHL	42	41	35	76	....	....	....	49	....	....	....	....	....	....	....	....	....	....	9	3	6	9	22	....	....	....
1949-50	Laval Nationale	QJHL	34	*52	34	*86	....	....	....	77	....	....	....	....	....	....	....	....	....	....	3	6	0	6	8	....	....	....
	Montreal Royals	QSHL	1	0	0	0	....	....	....	0	....	....	....	....	....	....	....	....	....	....	....	....	....	....	....	....	....	....
1950-51	Montreal Nationale	QJHL	36	54	44	98	....	....	....	80	....	....	....	....	....	....	....	....	....	....	....	....	....	....	....	....	....	....
	Montreal Canadiens	**NHL**	**18**	**8**	**6**	**14**	**11**	**8**	**19**	**9**	....	....	....	....	....	....	....	....	....	....	**11**	**1**	**1**	**2**	**6**	....	....	....
1951-52	**Montreal Canadiens**	**NHL**	**67**	**30**	**24**	**54**	**43**	**31**	**74**	**66**	....	....	....	....	....	....	....	....	....	....	**11**	**3**	**1**	**4**	**6**	....	....	....
1952-53	**Montreal Canadiens**	**NHL**	**65**	**22**	**17**	**39**	**34**	**24**	**58**	**37**	....	....	....	....	....	....	....	....	....	....	**12**	***6**	**4**	**10**	**12**	....	....	....
1953-54	**Montreal Canadiens**	**NHL**	**54**	**29**	**25**	**54**	**45**	**34**	**79**	**87**	....	....	....	....	....	....	....	....	....	....	**11**	**6**	**5**	**11**	**18**	....	....	....
1954-55	**Montreal Canadiens**	**NHL**	**70**	***38**	**37**	***75**	**57**	**48**	**105**	**57**	....	....	....	....	....	....	....	....	....	....	**12**	**8**	**5**	**13**	**8**	....	....	....
1955-56	**Montreal Canadiens**	**NHL**	**59**	**29**	**33**	**62**	**43**	**42**	**85**	**66**	....	....	....	....	....	....	....	....	....	....	**10**	**5**	**9**	**14**	**6**	....	....	....
1956-57	**Montreal Canadiens**	**NHL**	**41**	**19**	**21**	**40**	**26**	**24**	**50**	**18**	....	....	....	....	....	....	....	....	....	....	**10**	***11**	**7**	***18**	**2**	....	....	....
1957-58	**Montreal Canadiens**	**NHL**	**42**	**27**	**23**	**50**	**36**	**25**	**61**	**51**	....	....	....	....	....	....	....	....	....	....	**10**	**6**	**5**	**11**	**2**	....	....	....
1958-59	**Montreal Canadiens**	**NHL**	**59**	**22**	**44**	**66**	**28**	**47**	**75**	**30**	....	....	....	....	....	....	....	....	....	....	**11**	**5**	**8**	**13**	**10**	....	....	....
1959-60	**Montreal Canadiens**	**NHL**	**59**	**30**	**41**	**71**	**38**	**42**	**80**	**36**	....	....	....	....	....	....	....	....	....	....	**8**	**2**	***10**	***12**	**4**	....	....	....
1960-61	**Montreal Canadiens**	**NHL**	**64**	***50**	**45**	***95**	**63**	**46**	**109**	**29**	....	....	....	....	....	....	....	....	....	....	**4**	**2**	**1**	**3**	**0**	....	....	....
1961-62	**Montreal Canadiens**	**NHL**	**62**	**23**	**36**	**59**	**28**	**37**	**65**	**36**	....	....	....	....	....	....	....	....	....	....	**5**	**0**	**1**	**1**	**6**	....	....	....
1962-63	**Montreal Canadiens**	**NHL**	**51**	**23**	**18**	**41**	**28**	**19**	**47**	**73**	....	....	....	....	....	....	....	....	....	....	**5**	**0**	**1**	**1**	**4**	....	....	....
1963-64	**Montreal Canadiens**	**NHL**	**55**	**21**	**18**	**39**	**28**	**20**	**48**	**41**	....	....	....	....	....	....	....	....	....	....	**7**	**1**	**1**	**2**	**4**	....	....	....
1964-65	Quebec Aces	AHL	DID NOT PLAY – COACHING																									
1965-66	Quebec Aces	AHL	DID NOT PLAY – COACHING																									
1966-67	**New York Rangers**	**NHL**	**58**	**17**	**25**	**42**	**21**	**26**	**47**	**42**	....	....	....	....	....	....	....	....	....	....	**4**	**2**	**0**	**2**	**0**	....	....	....
1967-68	**New York Rangers**	**NHL**	**59**	**5**	**16**	**21**	**6**	**17**	**23**	**11**	**4**	**0**	**0**	**84**	**6.0**	**42**	**30**	**11**	**0**	**+1**	**1**	**0**	**1**	**1**	**0**	**0**	**0**	**0**
	NHL Totals		**883**	**393**	**429**	**822**	**535**	**490**	**1025**	**689**	**4**	**0**	**0**	**84**	**467.9**	**42**	**30**	**11**	**0**		**132**	**58**	**60**	**118**	**88**	**0**	**0**	**0**

Won Calder Memorial Trophy (1952) • NHL Second All-Star Team (1955, 1960) • Won Art Ross Trophy (1955, 1961) • NHL First All-Star Team (1961) • Won Hart Trophy (1961)

Played in NHL All-Star Game (1952, 1953, 1954, 1955, 1956, 1958, 1959, 1960, 1961, 1962, 1963)

Claimed on waivers by **NY Rangers** from **Montreal**, June 9, 1966.

• GEOFFRION, DANNY

Danny Geoffrion RW – R. 5'10", 185 lbs. b: Montreal, Que., 1/24/1958. Montreal's 12th choice, 8th overall, in 1978 Amateur Draft.

Season	Club	League	GP	G	A	Pts	AG	AA	APts	PIM	PP	SH	GW	S	%	TGF	PGF	TGA	PGA	+/–	GP	G	A	Pts	PIM	PP	SH	GW
1973-74	Cornwall Royals	QMJHL	28	6	5	11	....	....	....	5	....	....	....	....	....	....	....	....	....	....	....	....	....	....	....	....	....	....
1974-75	Cornwall Royals	QMJHL	71	33	53	86	....	....	....	70	....	....	....	....	....	....	....	....	....	....	....	....	....	....	....	....	....	....
1975-76	Cornwall Royals	QMJHL	53	42	58	100	....	....	....	123	....	....	....	....	....	....	....	....	....	....	....	....	....	....	....	....	....	....
1976-77	Cornwall Royals	QMJHL	65	39	57	96	....	....	....	148	....	....	....	....	....	....	....	....	....	....	....	....	....	....	....	....	....	....
1977-78	Cornwall Royals	QMJHL	71	68	75	143	....	....	....	183	....	....	....	....	....	....	....	....	....	....	9	4	12	16	37	....	....	....
1978-79	Quebec Nordiques	WHA	77	12	14	26	....	....	....	74	....	....	....	....	....	....	....	....	....	....	4	1	2	3	2	....	....	....
1979-80	**Montreal Canadiens**	**NHL**	**32**	**0**	**6**	**6**	**0**	**5**	**5**	**12**	**0**	**0**	**0**	**19**	**0.0**	**9**	**2**	**6**	**0**	**+1**	**2**	**0**	**0**	**0**	**7**	**0**	**0**	**0**
1980-81	**Winnipeg Jets**	**NHL**	**78**	**20**	**26**	**46**	**16**	**18**	**34**	**82**	**3**	**0**	**0**	**142**	**14.1**	**64**	**13**	**84**	**1**	**–32**	....	....	....	....	....	....	....	....

			REGULAR SEASON																		PLAYOFFS							
Season	Club	League	GP	G	A	Pts	AG	AA	APts	PIM	PP	SH	GW	S	%	TGF	PGF	TGA	PGA	+/–	GP	G	A	Pts	PIM	PP	SH	GW
1981-82	**Winnipeg Jets**	**NHL**	**1**	**0**	**0**	**0**	**0**	**0**	**0**	**5**	**0**	**0**	**0**	**2**	**0.0**	**0**	**0**	**0**	**0**	**0**	....	....	....	....	....	....	....	....
	Tulsa Oilers	CHL	63	24	25	49	....	....	....	76	....	....	....	....	....	....	....	....	....	....	3	1	0	1	6	....	....	....
1982-83	Sherbrooke Jets	AHL	80	37	39	76	....	....	....	46	....	....	....	....	....	....	....	....	....	....	....	....	....	....	....	....	....	....
	NHL Totals		**111**	**20**	**32**	**52**	**16**	**23**	**39**	**99**	**3**	**0**	**0**	**163**	**12.3**	**73**	**15**	**90**	**1**		**2**	**0**	**0**	**0**	**7**	**0**	**0**	**0**
	Other Major League Totals		77	12	14	26	....	....	....	74	....	....	....	....	....	....	....	....	....	....	4	1	2	3	2	....	....	....

QMJHL West Division Second All-Star Team (1976)

Signed as an underage free agent by **New England** (WHA), May, 1978. Reclaimed by **Montreal** from **Quebec** prior to Expansion Draft, June 9, 1979. Claimed by **Quebec** from **Montreal** in Waiver Draft, October 8, 1980. Traded to **Winnipeg** by **Quebec** for cash, October 8, 1980.

• GERMAIN, ERIC

Eric Germain D – L. 6'1", 195 lbs. b: Quebec City, Que., 6/26/1966.

Season	Club	League	GP	G	A	Pts	AG	AA	APts	PIM	PP	SH	GW	S	%	TGF	PGF	TGA	PGA	+/–	GP	G	A	Pts	PIM	PP	SH	GW
1983-84	St-Jean Beavers	QMJHL	57	2	15	17	....	....	....	60	....	....	....	....	....	....	....	....	....	....	4	1	0	1	6	....	....	....
1984-85	St-Jean Beavers	QMJHL	66	10	31	41	....	....	....	243	....	....	....	....	....	....	....	....	....	....	5	4	0	4	14	....	....	....
1985-86	St-Jean Castors	QMJHL	66	5	38	43	....	....	....	183	....	....	....	....	....	....	....	....	....	....	10	0	6	6	56	....	....	....
1986-87	Flint Spirits	IHL	21	0	2	2	....	....	....	23	....	....	....	....	....	....	....	....	....	....	....	....	....	....	....	....	....	....
	Fredericton Express	AHL	44	2	8	10	....	....	....	28	....	....	....	....	....	....	....	....	....	....	....	....	....	....	....	....	....	....
1987-88	**Los Angeles Kings**	**NHL**	**4**	**0**	**1**	**1**	**0**	**1**	**1**	**13**	**0**	**0**	**0**	**2**	**0.0**	**6**	**0**	**9**	**1**	**–2**	**1**	**0**	**0**	**0**	**4**	**0**	**0**	**0**
	New Haven Nighthawks	AHL	69	0	10	10	....	....	....	0	....	....	....	....	....	....	....	....	....	....	....	....	....	....	....	....	....	....
1988-89	New Haven Nighthawks	AHL	55	0	9	9	....	....	....	93	....	....	....	....	....	....	....	....	....	....	17	0	3	3	23	....	....	....
1989-90	New Haven Nighthawks	AHL	59	3	12	15	....	....	....	112	....	....	....	....	....	....	....	....	....	....	....	....	....	....	....	....	....	....
1990-91	Binghamton Rangers	AHL	60	4	10	14	....	....	....	144	....	....	....	....	....	....	....	....	....	....	10	0	1	1	14	....	....	....
1991-92	Moncton Hawks	AHL	3	0	2	2	....	....	....	4	....	....	....	....	....	....	....	....	....	....	....	....	....	....	....	....	....	....
	Binghamton Rangers	AHL	47	3	6	9	....	....	....	86	....	....	....	....	....	....	....	....	....	....	3	0	0	0	0	....	....	....
1992-93			DID NOT PLAY																									
1993-94	Binghamton Rangers	AHL	3	0	0	0	....	....	....	6	....	....	....	....	....	....	....	....	....	....	....	....	....	....	....	....	....	....
	Richmond Renegades	ECHL	56	3	16	19	....	....	....	192	....	....	....	....	....	....	....	....	....	....	....	....	....	....	....	....	....	....
1994-95	Richmond Renegades	ECHL	10	0	2	2	....	....	....	55	....	....	....	....	....	....	....	....	....	....	....	....	....	....	....	....	....	....
	Rochester Americans	AHL	18	1	7	8	....	....	....	13	....	....	....	....	....	....	....	....	....	....	5	0	2	2	18	....	....	....
1995-96	Erie Panthers	ECHL	67	4	13	17	....	....	....	245	....	....	....	....	....	....	....	....	....	....	....	....	....	....	....	....	....	....
1996-97	Columbus Cottonmouths	CHL	66	7	15	22	....	....	....	176	....	....	....	....	....	....	....	....	....	....	3	0	0	0	2	....	....	....
1997-98	Columbus Cottonmouths	CHL	57	0	5	5	....	....	....	113	....	....	....	....	....	....	....	....	....	....	13	0	1	1	10	....	....	....
	NHL Totals		**4**	**0**	**1**	**1**	**0**	**1**	**1**	**13**	**0**	**0**	**0**	**2**	**0.0**	**6**	**0**	**9**	**1**		**1**	**0**	**0**	**0**	**4**	**0**	**0**	**0**

Signed as a free agent by **LA Kings**, July 1, 1986. Signed as a free agent by **NY Rangers**, July 11, 1990.

• GERNANDER, KEN

Ken Gernander C – L. 5'10", 180 lbs. b: Coleraine, MN, 6/30/1969. Winnipeg's 4th choice, 96th overall, in 1987 Entry Draft.

Season	Club	League	GP	G	A	Pts	AG	AA	APts	PIM	PP	SH	GW	S	%	TGF	PGF	TGA	PGA	+/–	GP	G	A	Pts	PIM	PP	SH	GW
1986-87	Greenway High School	H.S.	26	35	34	69	....	....	....	....	....	....	....	....	....	....	....	....	....	....	....	....	....	....	....	....	....	....
1987-88	University of Minnesota	WCHA	44	14	14	28	....	....	....	14	....	....	....	....	....	....	....	....	....	....	....	....	....	....	....	....	....	....
1988-89	University of Minnesota	WCHA	44	9	11	20	....	....	....	2	....	....	....	....	....	....	....	....	....	....	....	....	....	....	....	....	....	....
1989-90	University of Minnesota	WCHA	44	32	17	49	....	....	....	24	....	....	....	....	....	....	....	....	....	....	....	....	....	....	....	....	....	....
1990-91	University of Minnesota	WCHA	44	23	20	43	....	....	....	24	....	....	....	....	....	....	....	....	....	....	....	....	....	....	....	....	....	....
1991-92	Fort Wayne Komets	IHL	13	7	6	13	....	....	....	2	....	....	....	....	....	....	....	....	....	....	....	....	....	....	....	....	....	....
	Moncton Hawks	AHL	43	8	18	26	....	....	....	9	....	....	....	....	....	....	....	....	....	....	8	1	1	2	2	....	....	....
1992-93	Moncton Hawks	AHL	71	18	29	47	....	....	....	20	....	....	....	....	....	....	....	....	....	....	5	1	4	5	0	....	....	....
1993-94	Moncton Hawks	AHL	71	22	25	47	....	....	....	12	....	....	....	....	....	....	....	....	....	....	19	6	1	7	0	....	....	....
1994-95	Binghamton Rangers	AHL	80	28	25	53	....	....	....	24	....	....	....	....	....	....	....	....	....	....	11	2	2	4	6	....	....	....
1995-96	**New York Rangers**	**NHL**	**10**	**2**	**3**	**5**	**2**	**2**	**4**	**4**	**2**	**0**	**0**	**10**	**20.0**	**6**	**4**	**5**	**0**	**–3**	**6**	**0**	**0**	**0**	**0**	**0**	**0**	**0**
	Binghamton Rangers	AHL	63	44	29	73	....	....	....	38	....	....	....	....	....	....	....	....	....	....	....	....	....	....	....	....	....	....
1996-97	Binghamton Rangers	AHL	46	13	18	31	....	....	....	30	....	....	....	....	....	....	....	....	....	....	2	0	1	1	0	....	....	....
	New York Rangers	**NHL**	....	....	....	....	....	....	....	....	....	....	....	....	....	....	....	....	....	....	**9**	**0**	**0**	**0**	**0**	....	....	....
1997-98	Hartford Wolf Pack	AHL	80	35	28	63	....	....	....	26	....	....	....	....	....	....	....	....	....	....	12	5	6	11	4	....	....	....
	NHL Totals		**10**	**2**	**3**	**5**	**2**	**2**	**4**	**4**	**2**	**0**	**0**	**10**	**20.0**	**6**	**4**	**5**	**0**		**15**	**0**	**0**	**0**	**0**	**0**	**0**	**0**

Won Fred Hunt Memorial Trophy (Sportsmanship - AHL) (1996)

Signed as a free agent by **NY Rangers**, July 4, 1994.

• GIALLONARDO, MARIO

Mario Giallonardo D – L. 5'11", 201 lbs. b: Toronto, Ont., 9/23/1957.

Season	Club	League	GP	G	A	Pts	AG	AA	APts	PIM	PP	SH	GW	S	%	TGF	PGF	TGA	PGA	+/–	GP	G	A	Pts	PIM	PP	SH	GW
1976-77	Union College	ECAC	....	5	26	31	....	....	....	....	....	....	....	....	....	....	....	....	....	....	....	....	....	....	....	....	....	....
1977-78	Toledo Goaldiggers	IHL	25	1	6	7	....	....	....	34	....	....	....	....	....	....	....	....	....	....	17	0	9	9	28	....	....	....
1978-79	Philadelphia Firebirds	AHL	70	1	18	19	....	....	....	100	....	....	....	....	....	....	....	....	....	....	....	....	....	....	....	....	....	....
1979-80	**Colorado Rockies**	**NHL**	**8**	**0**	**1**	**1**	**0**	**1**	**1**	**2**	**0**	**0**	**0**	**4**	**0.0**	**3**	**0**	**7**	**1**	**–3**	....	....	....	....	....	....	....	....
	Fort Worth Texans	CHL	70	8	25	33	....	....	....	105	....	....	....	....	....	....	....	....	....	....	15	2	4	6	47	....	....	....
1980-81	**Colorado Rockies**	**NHL**	**15**	**0**	**2**	**2**	**0**	**1**	**1**	**4**	**0**	**0**	**0**	**8**	**0.0**	**13**	**0**	**14**	**2**	**+1**	....	....	....	....	....	....	....	....
	Fort Worth Texans	CHL	57	4	18	22	....	....	....	113	....	....	....	....	....	....	....	....	....	....	....	....	....	....	....	....	....	....
1981-82	Fort Worth Texans	CHL	13	0	4	4	....	....	....	20	....	....	....	....	....	....	....	....	....	....	....	....	....	....	....	....	....	....
	NHL Totals		**23**	**0**	**3**	**3**	**0**	**2**	**2**	**6**	**0**	**0**	**0**	**12**	**0.0**	**16**	**0**	**21**	**3**		....	....	....	....	....	....	....	....

Signed as a free agent by **Colorado**, December 21, 1978.

• GIBBS, BARRY

Barry Gibbs D – R. 5'11", 195 lbs. b: Lloydminster, Sask., 9/28/1948. Boston's 1st choice, 1st overall, in 1966 Amateur Draft.

Season	Club	League	GP	G	A	Pts	AG	AA	APts	PIM	PP	SH	GW	S	%	TGF	PGF	TGA	PGA	+/–	GP	G	A	Pts	PIM	PP	SH	GW
1964-65	Estevan Bruins	SJHL	51	3	4	7	....	....	....	56	....	....	....	....	....	....	....	....	....	....	6	0	1	1	6	....	....	....
1965-66	Estevan Bruins	SJHL	59	3	23	26	....	....	....	45	....	....	....	....	....	....	....	....	....	....	12	0	2	2	14	....	....	....
1966-67	Estevan Bruins	WCJHL	56	10	32	42	....	....	....	81	....	....	....	....	....	....	....	....	....	....	13	2	2	4	21	....	....	....
1967-68	**Boston Bruins**	**NHL**	**16**	**0**	**0**	**0**	**0**	**0**	**0**	**2**	**0**	**0**	**0**	**3**	**0.0**	**4**	**0**	**6**	**1**	**–1**	....	....	....	....	....	....	....	....
	Oklahoma City Blazers	CHL	41	7	16	23	....	....	....	154	....	....	....	....	....	....	....	....	....	....	7	1	2	3	24	....	....	....
1968-69	**Boston Bruins**	**NHL**	**8**	**0**	**0**	**0**	**0**	**0**	**0**	**2**	**0**	**0**	**0**	**3**	**0.0**	**2**	**0**	**5**	**0**	**–3**	....	....	....	....	....	....	....	....
	Oklahoma City Blazers	CHL	55	3	25	28	....	....	....	*194	....	....	....	....	....	....	....	....	....	....	12	0	4	4	*53	....	....	....
1969-70	**Minnesota North Stars**	**NHL**	**56**	**3**	**13**	**16**	**3**	**13**	**16**	**182**	**1**	**0**	**1**	**100**	**3.0**	**75**	**7**	**101**	**21**	**–12**	**6**	**1**	**0**	**1**	**7**	**1**	**0**	**0**
1970-71	**Minnesota North Stars**	**NHL**	**68**	**5**	**15**	**20**	**5**	**13**	**18**	**132**	**3**	**0**	**2**	**116**	**4.3**	**62**	**11**	**80**	**19**	**–10**	**12**	**0**	**1**	**1**	**47**	**0**	**0**	**0**
1971-72	**Minnesota North Stars**	**NHL**	**75**	**4**	**20**	**24**	**4**	**18**	**22**	**128**	**1**	**1**	**0**	**160**	**2.5**	**87**	**14**	**94**	**25**	**+4**	**7**	**1**	**1**	**2**	**9**	**0**	**0**	**0**
1972-73	**Minnesota North Stars**	**NHL**	**63**	**10**	**24**	**34**	**10**	**20**	**30**	**54**	**2**	**0**	**0**	**163**	**6.1**	**91**	**15**	**87**	**25**	**+14**	**5**	**1**	**0**	**1**	**0**	**1**	**0**	**0**
1973-74	**Minnesota North Stars**	**NHL**	**76**	**9**	**29**	**38**	**9**	**25**	**34**	**82**	**3**	**0**	**0**	**151**	**6.0**	**109**	**17**	**144**	**35**	**–17**	....	....	....	....	....	....	....	....
1974-75	**Minnesota North Stars**	**NHL**	**37**	**4**	**20**	**24**	**4**	**16**	**20**	**22**	**2**	**0**	**1**	**101**	**4.0**	**64**	**22**	**76**	**21**	**–13**	....	....	....	....	....	....	....	....
	Atlanta Flames	**NHL**	**39**	**3**	**13**	**16**	**3**	**10**	**13**	**39**	**1**	**0**	**2**	**60**	**5.0**	**43**	**11**	**50**	**12**	**–6**	....	....	....	....	....	....	....	....
1975-76	**Atlanta Flames**	**NHL**	**76**	**8**	**21**	**29**	**7**	**16**	**23**	**92**	**1**	**0**	**0**	**125**	**6.4**	**101**	**14**	**110**	**24**	**+1**	**2**	**1**	**0**	**1**	**2**	**0**	**0**	**0**
1976-77	**Atlanta Flames**	**NHL**	**66**	**1**	**16**	**17**	**1**	**13**	**14**	**63**	**0**	**0**	**0**	**81**	**1.2**	**80**	**5**	**103**	**23**	**–5**	**3**	**0**	**0**	**0**	**2**	**0**	**0**	**0**
1977-78	**Atlanta Flames**	**NHL**	**27**	**1**	**5**	**6**	**1**	**4**	**5**	**24**	**0**	**0**	**0**	**42**	**2.4**	**32**	**1**	**40**	**7**	**–2**	....	....	....	....	....	....	....	....
	St. Louis Blues	**NHL**	**51**	**6**	**12**	**18**	**6**	**10**	**16**	**45**	**4**	**0**	**0**	**103**	**5.8**	**82**	**22**	**93**	**22**	**–11**	....	....	....	....	....	....	....	....
1978-79	**St. Louis Blues**	**NHL**	**76**	**2**	**27**	**29**	**2**	**21**	**23**	**46**	**0**	**0**	**0**	**86**	**2.3**	**88**	**5**	**159**	**34**	**–42**	....	....	....	....	....	....	....	....
1979-80	**Los Angeles Kings**	**NHL**	**63**	**2**	**9**	**11**	**2**	**7**	**9**	**32**	**0**	**0**	**0**	**55**	**3.6**	**55**	**2**	**90**	**24**	**–13**	**1**	**0**	**0**	**0**	**0**	**0**	**0**	**0**
1980-81	Houston Apollos	CHL	33	1	6	7	....	....	....	43	....	....	....	....	....	....	....	....	....	....	....	....	....	....	....	....	....	....
	Oklahoma City Stars	CHL	17	0	3	3	....	....	....	16	....	....	....	....	....	....	....	....	....	....	3	0	1	1	9	....	....	....
	NHL Totals		**797**	**58**	**224**	**282**	**57**	**188**	**243**	**945**	**18**	**1**	**6**	**1349**	**4.3**	**975**	**146**	**1238**	**293**		**36**	**4**	**2**	**6**	**67**	**2**	**0**	**0**

CHL First All-Star Team (1969) • Named CHL's Top Defenseman (1969)

Played in NHL All-Star Game (1973)

Traded to **Minnesota** by **Boston** with Tom Williams for Minnesota's 1st round choice (Don Tannahill) and future considerations (Fred O'Donnell), May 7, 1969. Traded to **Atlanta** by **Minnesota** for Dean Talafous and Dwight Bialowas, January 3, 1975. Traded to **St. Louis** by **Atlanta** with Phil Myre and Curt Bennett for Yves Belanger, Dick Redmond, Bob MacMillan and St. Louis' 2nd round choice (Mike Perovich) in 1979 Entry Draft, December 12, 1977. Traded to **NY Islanders** by **St. Louis** with Terry Richardson for future considerations, June 9, 1979. Traded to **LA Kings** by **NY Islanders** for future considerations (Tommy Williams, August 16, 1979), June 9, 1979.

• GIBSON, DON

Don Gibson D – R. 6'1", 210 lbs. b: Deloraine, Man., 12/29/1967. Vancouver's 2nd choice, 49th overall, in 1986 Entry Draft.

Season	Club	League	GP	G	A	Pts	AG	AA	APts	PIM	PP	SH	GW	S	%	TGF	PGF	TGA	PGA	+/–	Playoffs GP	G	A	Pts	PIM	PP	SH	GW
1985-86	Winkler Flyers	MJHL	34	24	29	53	....	....	....	210	....	....	....	....	....	....	....	....	....	....	....	....	....	....	....	....	....	....
1986-87	Michigan State Spartans	CCHA	43	3	3	6	....	....	....	74	....	....	....	....	....	....	....	....	....	....	....	....	....	....	....	....	....	....
1987-88	Michigan State Spartans	CCHA	43	7	12	19	....	....	....	118	....	....	....	....	....	....	....	....	....	....	....	....	....	....	....	....	....	....
1988-89	Michigan State Spartans	CCHA	39	7	10	17	....	....	....	107	....	....	....	....	....	....	....	....	....	....	....	....	....	....	....	....	....	....
1989-90	Michigan State Spartans	CCHA	44	5	22	27	....	....	....	167	....	....	....	....	....	....	....	....	....	....	....	....	....	....	....	....	....	....
	Milwaukee Admirals	IHL	1	0	0	0	....	....	....	4	....	....	....	....	....	....	....	....	....	....	5	0	1	1	41	....	....	....
1990-91	**Vancouver Canucks**	**NHL**	**14**	**0**	**3**	**3**	**0**	**2**	**2**	**20**	**0**	**0**	**0**	**9**	**0.0**	**11**	**1**	**11**	**0**	**–1**	....	....	....	....	....	....	....	....
	Milwaukee Admirals	IHL	21	4	3	7	....	....	....	76	....	....	....	....	....	....	....	....	....	....	....	....	....	....	....	....	....	....
1991-92	Milwaukee Admirals	IHL	35	6	9	15	....	....	....	105	....	....	....	....	....	....	....	....	....	....	4	1	0	1	7	....	....	....
1992-93	Milwaukee Admirals	IHL	68	3	14	17	....	....	....	381	....	....	....	....	....	....	....	....	....	....	6	0	1	1	11	....	....	....
1993-94	Milwaukee Admirals	IHL	43	4	6	10	....	....	....	233	....	....	....	....	....	....	....	....	....	....	3	0	0	0	10	....	....	....
	NHL Totals		**14**	**0**	**3**	**3**	**0**	**2**	**2**	**20**	**0**	**0**	**0**	**9**	**0.0**	**11**	**1**	**11**	**0**		....	....	....	....	....	....	....	....

CCHA Second All-Star Team (1990)

• GIBSON, DOUG

Doug Gibson C – L. 5'10", 175 lbs. b: Peterborough, Ont., 9/28/1953. Boston's 3rd choice, 36th overall, in 1973 Amateur Draft.

Season	Club	League	GP	G	A	Pts	AG	AA	APts	PIM	PP	SH	GW	S	%	TGF	PGF	TGA	PGA	+/–	Playoffs GP	G	A	Pts	PIM	PP	SH	GW
1970-71	Peterborough Petes	OHA	60	27	43	70	....	....	....	13	....	....	....	....	....	....	....	....	....	....	....	....	....	....	....	....	....	....
1971-72	Peterborough Petes	OHA	63	51	48	99	....	....	....	15	....	....	....	....	....	....	....	....	....	....	....	....	....	....	....	....	....	....
1972-73	Peterborough Petes	OHA	63	52	62	114	....	....	....	10	....	....	....	....	....	....	....	....	....	....	14	9	13	22	6	....	....	....
1973-74	**Boston Bruins**	**NHL**	**2**	**0**	**0**	**0**	**0**	**0**	**0**	**0**	**0**	**0**	**0**	**0**	**0.0**	**0**	**0**	**1**	**0**	**–1**	**1**	**0**	**0**	**0**	**0**	**0**	**0**	**0**
	Boston Braves	AHL	76	31	51	82	....	....	....	16	....	....	....	....	....	....	....	....	....	....	....	....	....	....	....	....	....	....
1974-75	Rochester Americans	AHL	75	*44	*72	*116	....	....	....	31	....	....	....	....	....	....	....	....	....	....	12	5	7	12	15	....	....	....
1975-76	**Boston Bruins**	**NHL**	**50**	**7**	**18**	**25**	**7**	**14**	**21**	**0**	**1**	**0**	**1**	**41**	**17.1**	**30**	**5**	**18**	**1**	**+8**	....	....	....	....	....	....	....	....
	Rochester Americans	AHL	17	11	20	31	....	....	....	11	....	....	....	....	....	....	....	....	....	....	....	....	....	....	....	....	....	....
1976-77	Rochester Americans	AHL	78	41	56	97	....	....	....	11	....	....	....	....	....	....	....	....	....	....	12	5	10	15	2	....	....	....
1977-78	**Washington Capitals**	**NHL**	**11**	**2**	**1**	**3**	**2**	**1**	**3**	**0**	**0**	**0**	**0**	**10**	**20.0**	**7**	**1**	**9**	**0**	**–3**	....	....	....	....	....	....	....	....
	Hershey Bears	AHL	71	24	35	59	....	....	....	8	....	....	....	....	....	....	....	....	....	....	....	....	....	....	....	....	....	....
1978-79	Hershey Bears	AHL	22	8	13	21	....	....	....	10	....	....	....	....	....	....	....	....	....	....	....	....	....	....	....	....	....	....
1979-80	Hershey Bears	AHL	72	20	24	44	....	....	....	17	....	....	....	....	....	....	....	....	....	....	16	*12	9	21	0	....	....	....
1980-81	SC Riessersee	Germany	54	31	42	73	....	....	....	8	....	....	....	....	....	....	....	....	....	....	....	....	....	....	....	....	....	....
1981-82	SC Riessersee	Germany	44	20	17	37	....	....	....	12	....	....	....	....	....	....	....	....	....	....	....	....	....	....	....	....	....	....
1982-83	SC Riessersee	Germany	36	14	37	51	....	....	....	7	....	....	....	....	....	....	....	....	....	....	....	....	....	....	....	....	....	....
1983-84	SC Riessersee	Germany	DID NOT PLAY – COACHING																									
	NHL Totals		**63**	**9**	**19**	**28**	**9**	**15**	**24**	**0**	**1**	**0**	**1**	**51**	**17.6**	**37**	**6**	**28**	**1**		**1**	**0**	**0**	**0**	**0**	**0**	**0**	**0**

AHL First All-Star Team (1975, 1977) • Won John B. Sollenberger Trophy (Top Scorer - AHL) (1975) • Won Les Cunningham Award (MVP - AHL) (1975, 1977)

Claimed on waivers by **Washington** from **Boston**, May 29, 1977.

• GIBSON, JOHN

John Gibson D. 6'3", 210 lbs. b: St. Catharines, Ont., 6/2/1959. Los Angeles' 5th choice, 71st overall, in 1979 Entry Draft.

Season	Club	League	GP	G	A	Pts	AG	AA	APts	PIM	PP	SH	GW	S	%	TGF	PGF	TGA	PGA	+/–	Playoffs GP	G	A	Pts	PIM	PP	SH	GW
1976-77	Niagara Falls Flyers	OHA	59	2	13	15	....	....	....	178	....	....	....	....	....	....	....	....	....	....	....	....	....	....	....	....	....	....
1977-78	Niagara Falls Flyers	OHA	60	8	20	28	....	....	....	133	....	....	....	....	....	....	....	....	....	....	....	....	....	....	....	....	....	....
1978-79	Niagara Falls Flyers	OHA	46	15	26	41	....	....	....	218	....	....	....	....	....	....	....	....	....	....	....	....	....	....	....	....	....	....
	Winnipeg Jets	WHA	9	0	1	1	....	....	....	5	....	....	....	....	....	....	....	....	....	....	....	....	....	....	....	....	....	....
1979-80	Niagara Falls Flyers	OHA	6	2	2	4	....	....	....	20	....	....	....	....	....	....	....	....	....	....	....	....	....	....	....	....	....	....
	Binghamton Whalers	AHL	1	0	0	0	....	....	....	0	....	....	....	....	....	....	....	....	....	....	....	....	....	....	....	....	....	....
	Saginaw Gears	IHL	67	13	36	49	....	....	....	293	....	....	....	....	....	....	....	....	....	....	5	1	2	3	38	....	....	....
1980-81	**Los Angeles Kings**	**NHL**	**4**	**0**	**0**	**0**	**0**	**0**	**0**	**21**	**0**	**0**	**0**	**5**	**0.0**	**2**	**1**	**6**	**0**	**–5**	....	....	....	....	....	....	....	....
	Houston Apollos	CHL	33	5	5	10	....	....	....	94	....	....	....	....	....	....	....	....	....	....	....	....	....	....	....	....	....	....
	Birmingham Bulls	CHL	16	6	3	9	....	....	....	42	....	....	....	....	....	....	....	....	....	....	....	....	....	....	....	....	....	....
	Saginaw Gears	IHL	12	0	7	7	....	....	....	82	....	....	....	....	....	....	....	....	....	....	10	0	1	1	55	....	....	....
1981-82	**Los Angeles Kings**	**NHL**	**6**	**0**	**0**	**0**	**0**	**0**	**0**	**18**	**0**	**0**	**0**	**6**	**0.0**	**6**	**0**	**3**	**1**	**+4**	....	....	....	....	....	....	....	....
	New Haven Nighthawks	AHL	7	1	0	1	....	....	....	24	....	....	....	....	....	....	....	....	....	....	....	....	....	....	....	....	....	....
	Toronto Maple Leafs	**NHL**	**27**	**0**	**2**	**2**	**0**	**1**	**1**	**67**	**0**	**0**	**0**	**31**	**0.0**	**18**	**0**	**44**	**13**	**–13**	....	....	....	....	....	....	....	....
	Cincinnati Tigers	CHL	6	1	2	3	....	....	....	30	....	....	....	....	....	....	....	....	....	....	....	....	....	....	....	....	....	....
	New Brunswick Hawks	AHL	12	0	2	2	....	....	....	6	....	....	....	....	....	....	....	....	....	....	15	0	1	1	39	....	....	....
1982-83	St. Catharines Saints	AHL	21	1	4	5	....	....	....	38	....	....	....	....	....	....	....	....	....	....	....	....	....	....	....	....	....	....
1983-84	**Winnipeg Jets**	**NHL**	**11**	**0**	**0**	**0**	**0**	**0**	**0**	**14**	**0**	**0**	**0**	**4**	**0.0**	**11**	**0**	**10**	**1**	**+2**	....	....	....	....	....	....	....	....
	Sherbrooke Jets	AHL	49	4	11	15	....	....	....	174	....	....	....	....	....	....	....	....	....	....	....	....	....	....	....	....	....	....
	NHL Totals		**48**	**0**	**2**	**2**	**0**	**1**	**1**	**120**	**0**	**0**	**0**	**46**	**0.0**	**37**	**1**	**63**	**15**		....	....	....	....	....	....	....	....
	Other Major League Totals		9	0	1	1	....	....	....	5	....	....	....	....	....	....	....	....	....		....	....	....	....	....	....	....	....

IHL First All-Star Team (1980) • Won Governors' Trophy (Top Defenseman - IHL) (1980)

Signed as a free agent by **Winnipeg** (WHA), March, 1979. Traded to **Toronto** by **LA Kings** with Billy Harris for Ian Turnbull, November 11, 1981. Signed as a free agent by **Winnipeg**, September 19, 1983.

• GIFFIN, LEE

Lee Giffin RW – R. 6', 188 lbs. b: Chatham, Ont., 4/1/1967. Pittsburgh's 2nd choice, 23rd overall, in 1985 Entry Draft.

Season	Club	League	GP	G	A	Pts	AG	AA	APts	PIM	PP	SH	GW	S	%	TGF	PGF	TGA	PGA	+/–	Playoffs GP	G	A	Pts	PIM	PP	SH	GW
1982-83	Newmarket Flyers	Jr. B	47	10	21	31	....	....	....	123	....	....	....	....	....	....	....	....	....	....	....	....	....	....	....	....	....	....
1983-84	Oshawa Generals	OHL	70	23	27	50	....	....	....	88	....	....	....	....	....	....	....	....	....	....	7	1	4	5	12	....	....	....
1984-85	Oshawa Generals	OHL	62	36	42	78	....	....	....	78	....	....	....	....	....	....	....	....	....	....	5	1	2	3	2	....	....	....
1985-86	Oshawa Generals	OHL	54	29	37	66	....	....	....	28	....	....	....	....	....	....	....	....	....	....	6	0	5	5	8	....	....	....
1986-87	Oshawa Generals	OHL	48	31	69	100	....	....	....	46	....	....	....	....	....	....	....	....	....	....	23	*17	19	36	14	....	....	....
	Pittsburgh Penguins	**NHL**	**8**	**1**	**1**	**2**	**1**	**1**	**2**	**0**	**0**	**0**	**0**	**8**	**12.5**	**4**	**0**	**2**	**0**	**+2**	....	....	....	....	....	....	....	....
1987-88	**Pittsburgh Penguins**	**NHL**	**19**	**0**	**2**	**2**	**0**	**1**	**1**	**9**	**0**	**0**	**0**	**8**	**0.0**	**5**	**1**	**6**	**0**	**–2**	....	....	....	....	....	....	....	....
	Muskegon Lumberjacks	IHL	48	26	37	63	....	....	....	61	....	....	....	....	....	....	....	....	....	....	6	1	3	4	2	....	....	....
1988-89	Muskegon Lumberjacks	IHL	63	30	44	74	....	....	....	93	....	....	....	....	....	....	....	....	....	....	12	5	7	12	8	....	....	....
1989-90	Flint Spirits	IHL	73	30	44	74	....	....	....	68	....	....	....	....	....	....	....	....	....	....	4	1	2	3	0	....	....	....
1990-91	Kansas City Blades	IHL	60	25	43	68	....	....	....	48	....	....	....	....	....	....	....	....	....	....	....	....	....	....	....	....	....	....
1991-92	Capital District Islanders	AHL	77	19	26	45	....	....	....	58	....	....	....	....	....	....	....	....	....	....	7	3	3	6	18	....	....	....
1992-93	Chatham Wheelers	ColHL	29	14	26	40	....	....	....	65	....	....	....	....	....	....	....	....	....	....	....	....	....	....	....	....	....	....
	Saginaw Wheels	ColHL	....	....	....	....	....	....	....	....	....	....	....	....	....	....	....	....	....	....	5	6	3	9	0	....	....	....
1993-94			DID NOT PLAY																									
1994-95	Saginaw Wheels	ColHL	13	5	7	12	....	....	....	13	....	....	....	....	....	....	....	....	....	....	10	2	13	15	24	....	....	....
1995-96	Saginaw Wheels	ColHL	58	20	47	67	....	....	....	94	....	....	....	....	....	....	....	....	....	....	5	1	2	3	8	....	....	....
1996-97	Mobile Mystics	ECHL	20	7	9	16	....	....	....	4	....	....	....	....	....	....	....	....	....	....	3	1	0	1	0	....	....	....
1997-98	Mobile Mystics	ECHL	45	16	29	45	....	....	....	46	....	....	....	....	....	....	....	....	....	....	3	2	0	2	0	....	....	....
	NHL Totals		**27**	**1**	**3**	**4**	**1**	**2**	**3**	**9**	**0**	**0**	**0**	**16**	**6.3**	**9**	**1**	**8**	**0**		....	....	....	....	....	....	....	....

OHL First All-Star Team (1987)

Traded to **NY Rangers** by **Pittsburgh** for future considerations, September 14, 1989.

• GILBERT, ED

Ed Gilbert C – L. 6', 185 lbs. b: Hamilton, Ont., 3/12/1952. Montreal's 5th choice, 46th overall, in 1972 Amateur Draft.

Season	Club	League	GP	G	A	Pts	AG	AA	APts	PIM	PP	SH	GW	S	%	TGF	PGF	TGA	PGA	+/–	Playoffs GP	G	A	Pts	PIM	PP	SH	GW
1969-70	Hamilton Kilty B's	Jr. B	25	13	9	22	....	....	....	15	....	....	....	....	....	....	....	....	....	....	....	....	....	....	....	....	....	....
	Hamilton Red Wings	OHA	43	8	17	25	....	....	....	10	....	....	....	....	....	....	....	....	....	....	....	....	....	....	....	....	....	....
1970-71	Hamilton Red Wings	OHA	57	20	35	55	....	....	....	28	....	....	....	....	....	....	....	....	....	....	....	....	....	....	....	....	....	....
1971-72	Hamilton Red Wings	OHA	62	33	41	74	....	....	....	40	....	....	....	....	....	....	....	....	....	....	....	....	....	....	....	....	....	....
1972-73	Nova Scotia Voyageurs	AHL	72	21	18	39	....	....	....	20	....	....	....	....	....	....	....	....	....	....	13	4	8	12	2	....	....	....
1973-74	Nova Scotia Voyageurs	AHL	75	30	44	74	....	....	....	40	....	....	....	....	....	....	....	....	....	....	6	0	2	2	0	....	....	....
1974-75	**Kansas City Scouts**	**NHL**	**80**	**16**	**22**	**38**	**15**	**17**	**32**	**14**	**9**	**2**	**0**	**190**	**8.4**	**50**	**19**	**97**	**21**	**–45**	....	....	....	....	....	....	....	....
1975-76	**Kansas City Scouts**	**NHL**	**41**	**4**	**8**	**12**	**4**	**6**	**10**	**8**	**1**	**0**	**0**	**74**	**5.4**	**17**	**5**	**49**	**8**	**–29**	....	....	....	....	....	....	....	....
	Pittsburgh Penguins	**NHL**	**38**	**1**	**1**	**2**	**1**	**1**	**2**	**0**	**0**	**0**	**0**	**18**	**5.6**	**3**	**1**	**20**	**17**	**–1**	....	....	....	....	....	....	....	....

			REGULAR SEASON																		PLAYOFFS							
Season	Club	League	GP	G	A	Pts	AG	AA	APts	PIM	PP	SH	GW	S	%	TGF	PGF	TGA	PGA	+/–	GP	G	A	Pts	PIM	PP	SH	GW
1976-77	**Pittsburgh Penguins**	**NHL**	**7**	**0**	**0**	**0**	**0**	**0**	**0**	**0**	**0**	**0**	**0**	**4**	**0.0**	**0**	**0**	**5**	**2**	**–3**	....	....	....	....	....	....	....	....
	Hershey Bears	AHL	68	20	29	49	....	....	....	12	....	....	....	....	....	....	....	....	....	....	6	1	0	1	0	....	....	....
1977-78			DID NOT PLAY																									
1978-79	Cincinnati Stingers	WHA	29	3	3	6	....	....	....	6	....	....	....	....	....	....	....	....	....	....	....	....	....	....	....	....	....	....
	NHL Totals		**166**	**21**	**31**	**52**	**20**	**24**	**44**	**22**	**10**	**2**	**0**	**286**	**7.3**	**70**	**25**	**171**	**48**		....	....	....	....	....	....	....	....

Selected by **Quebec** (WHA) in 1972 WHA General Player Draft, February 12, 1972. Claimed by **Kansas City** from **Montreal** in Expansion Draft, June 12, 1974. Traded to **Pittsburgh** by **Kansas City** with Simon Nolet and Kansas City's 1st round choice (Blair Chapman) in 1976 Amateur Draft for Steve Durbano, Chuck Arnason and Pittsburgh's 1st round choice (Greg Carroll) in 1976 Amateur Draft, January 9, 1976. Signed as a free agent by **Cincinnati** (WHA), October, 1978.

• GILBERT, GREG

Greg Gilbert LW – L. 6'1", 191 lbs. b: Mississauga, Ont., 1/22/1962. NY Islanders' 5th choice, 80th overall, in 1980 Entry Draft.

Season	Club	League	GP	G	A	Pts	AG	AA	APts	PIM	PP	SH	GW	S	%	TGF	PGF	TGA	PGA	+/–	GP	G	A	Pts	PIM	PP	SH	GW
1979-80	Toronto Marlboros	OHA	68	10	11	21	....	....	....	35	....	....	....	....	....	....	....	....	....	....	....	....	....	....	....	....	....	....
1980-81	Toronto Marlboros	OHA	64	30	37	67	....	....	....	73	....	....	....	....	....	....	....	....	....	....	5	2	6	8	16	....	....	....
1981-82	Toronto Marlboros	OHL	65	41	67	108	....	....	....	119	....	....	....	....	....	....	....	....	....	....	10	4	12	16	23	....	....	....
	New York Islanders	**NHL**	**1**	**1**	**0**	**1**	**1**	**0**	**1**	**0**	**0**	**0**	**0**	**2**	**50.0**	**2**	**0**	**2**	**0**	**0**	**4**	**1**	**1**	**2**	**2**	**0**	**0**	**0**
1982-83	**New York Islanders**	**NHL**	**45**	**8**	**11**	**19**	**7**	**8**	**15**	**30**	**0**	**0**	**0**	**37**	**21.6**	**24**	**1**	**22**	**0**	**+1**	**10**	**1**	**0**	**1**	**14**	**0**	**0**	**0**
	Indianapolis Checkers	CHL	24	11	16	27	....	....	....	23	....	....	....	....	....	....	....	....	....	....	....	....	....	....	....	....	....	....
1983-84	**New York Islanders**	**NHL**	**79**	**31**	**35**	**66**	**25**	**24**	**49**	**59**	**6**	**0**	**2**	**118**	**26.3**	**113**	**23**	**49**	**10**	**+51**	**21**	**5**	**7**	**12**	**39**	**2**	**0**	**1**
1984-85	**New York Islanders**	**NHL**	**58**	**13**	**25**	**38**	**11**	**17**	**28**	**36**	**2**	**0**	**2**	**82**	**15.9**	**54**	**8**	**65**	**15**	**–4**	....	....	....	....	....	....	....	....
1985-86	**New York Islanders**	**NHL**	**60**	**9**	**19**	**28**	**7**	**13**	**20**	**82**	**1**	**0**	**2**	**58**	**15.5**	**50**	**8**	**45**	**8**	**+5**	**2**	**0**	**0**	**0**	**9**	**0**	**0**	**0**
	Springfield Indians	AHL	2	0	0	0	....	....	....	2	....	....	....	....	....	....	....	....	....	....	....	....	....	....	....	....	....	....
1986-87	**New York Islanders**	**NHL**	**51**	**6**	**7**	**13**	**5**	**5**	**10**	**26**	**0**	**0**	**0**	**50**	**12.0**	**24**	**3**	**49**	**16**	**–12**	**10**	**2**	**2**	**4**	**6**	**0**	**0**	**1**
1987-88	**New York Islanders**	**NHL**	**76**	**17**	**28**	**45**	**15**	**20**	**35**	**46**	**1**	**1**	**0**	**77**	**22.1**	**62**	**4**	**71**	**27**	**+14**	**4**	**0**	**0**	**0**	**6**	**0**	**0**	**0**
1988-89	**New York Islanders**	**NHL**	**55**	**8**	**13**	**21**	**7**	**9**	**16**	**45**	**0**	**0**	**1**	**73**	**11.0**	**31**	**0**	**47**	**17**	**+1**	....	....	....	....	....	....	....	....
	Chicago Blackhawks	**NHL**	**4**	**0**	**0**	**0**	**0**	**0**	**0**	**0**	**0**	**0**	**0**	**2**	**0.0**	**2**	**0**	**1**	**0**	**+1**	**15**	**1**	**5**	**6**	**20**	**0**	**0**	**0**
1989-90	**Chicago Blackhawks**	**NHL**	**70**	**12**	**25**	**37**	**10**	**18**	**28**	**54**	**0**	**0**	**3**	**108**	**11.1**	**62**	**2**	**39**	**6**	**+27**	**19**	**5**	**8**	**13**	**34**	**0**	**0**	**0**
1990-91	**Chicago Blackhawks**	**NHL**	**72**	**10**	**15**	**25**	**9**	**11**	**20**	**58**	**1**	**0**	**0**	**98**	**10.2**	**44**	**7**	**42**	**11**	**+6**	**5**	**0**	**1**	**1**	**2**	**0**	**0**	**0**
1991-92	**Chicago Blackhawks**	**NHL**	**50**	**7**	**5**	**12**	**6**	**4**	**10**	**35**	**0**	**0**	**1**	**45**	**15.6**	**24**	**3**	**31**	**6**	**–4**	**10**	**1**	**3**	**4**	**16**	**0**	**0**	**1**
1992-93	**Chicago Blackhawks**	**NHL**	**77**	**13**	**19**	**32**	**11**	**13**	**24**	**57**	**0**	**1**	**2**	**72**	**18.1**	**45**	**2**	**54**	**16**	**+5**	**3**	**0**	**0**	**0**	**0**	**0**	**0**	**0**
1993-94	**New York Rangers**	**NHL**	**76**	**4**	**11**	**15**	**4**	**8**	**12**	**29**	**1**	**0**	**0**	**64**	**6.3**	**27**	**2**	**30**	**2**	**–3**	**23**	**1**	**3**	**4**	**8**	**0**	**0**	**0**
1994-95	**St. Louis Blues**	**NHL**	**46**	**11**	**14**	**25**	**19**	**21**	**40**	**11**	**0**	**0**	**3**	**57**	**19.3**	**38**	**0**	**21**	**5**	**+22**	**7**	**0**	**3**	**3**	**6**	**0**	**0**	**0**
1995-96	**St. Louis Blues**	**NHL**	**17**	**0**	**1**	**1**	**0**	**1**	**1**	**8**	**0**	**0**	**0**	**9**	**0.0**	**1**	**0**	**3**	**1**	**–1**	....	....	....	....	....	....	....	....
	NHL Totals		**837**	**150**	**228**	**378**	**137**	**172**	**309**	**576**	**12**	**2**	**16**	**952**	**15.8**	**603**	**63**	**571**	**140**		**133**	**17**	**33**	**50**	**162**	**2**	**0**	**3**

Traded to **Chicago** by **NY Islanders** for Chicago's 5th round choice (Steve Young) in 1989 Entry Draft, March 7, 1989. Signed as a free agent by **NY Rangers**, July 29, 1993. Claimed by **St. Louis** from **NY Rangers** in Waiver Draft, January 19, 1995.

• GILBERT, ROD

Rod Gilbert RW – R. 5'9", 180 lbs. b: Montreal, Que., 7/1/1941. **HHOF**

Season	Club	League	GP	G	A	Pts	AG	AA	APts	PIM	PP	SH	GW	S	%	TGF	PGF	TGA	PGA	+/–	GP	G	A	Pts	PIM	PP	SH	GW
1957-58	Guelph Biltmores	OHA	32	14	16	30	....	....	....	14	....	....	....	....	....	....	....	....	....	....	....	....	....	....	....	....	....	....
1958-59	Guelph Biltmores	OHA	54	27	34	61	....	....	....	40	....	....	....	....	....	....	....	....	....	....	10	5	4	9	14	....	....	....
1959-60	Guelph Biltmores	OHA	47	39	52	91	....	....	....	40	....	....	....	....	....	....	....	....	....	....	5	3	3	6	4	....	....	....
	Trois-Rivieres Lions	EPHL	3	4	6	10	....	....	....	0	....	....	....	....	....	....	....	....	....	....	5	2	2	4	2	....	....	....
1960-61	Guelph Royals	OHA	47	*54	49	*103	....	....	....	47	....	....	....	....	....	....	....	....	....	....	6	4	4	8	6	....	....	....
	New York Rangers	**NHL**	**1**	**0**	**1**	**1**	**0**	**1**	**1**	**2**	....	....	....	....	....	....	....	....	....	....	....	....	....	....	....	....	....	....
1961-62	**New York Rangers**	**NHL**	**1**	**0**	**0**	**0**	**0**	**0**	**0**	**0**	....	....	....	....	....	....	....	....	....	....	**4**	**2**	**3**	**5**	**4**	....	....	....
	Kitchener-Waterloo Beavers	EPHL	21	12	11	23	....	....	....	22	....	....	....	....	....	....	....	....	....	....	4	0	0	0	4	....	....	....
1962-63	**New York Rangers**	**NHL**	**70**	**11**	**20**	**31**	**13**	**21**	**34**	**20**	....	....	....	....	....	....	....	....	....	....	....	....	....	....	....	....	....	....
1963-64	**New York Rangers**	**NHL**	**70**	**24**	**40**	**64**	**32**	**45**	**77**	**62**	....	....	....	....	....	....	....	....	....	....	....	....	....	....	....	....	....	....
1964-65	**New York Rangers**	**NHL**	**70**	**25**	**36**	**61**	**32**	**39**	**71**	**52**	....	....	....	....	....	....	....	....	....	....	....	....	....	....	....	....	....	....
1965-66	**New York Rangers**	**NHL**	**34**	**10**	**15**	**25**	**12**	**15**	**27**	**20**	....	....	....	....	....	....	....	....	....	....	....	....	....	....	....	....	....	....
1966-67	**New York Rangers**	**NHL**	**64**	**28**	**18**	**46**	**35**	**18**	**53**	**12**	....	....	....	....	....	....	....	....	....	....	**4**	**2**	**2**	**4**	**6**	....	....	....
1967-68	**New York Rangers**	**NHL**	**73**	**29**	**48**	**77**	**36**	**51**	**87**	**12**	**8**	**0**	**6**	**281**	**10.3**	**102**	**32**	**57**	**0**	**+13**	**6**	**5**	**0**	**5**	**4**	**0**	**0**	**0**
1968-69	**New York Rangers**	**NHL**	**66**	**28**	**49**	**77**	**32**	**46**	**78**	**22**	**8**	**0**	**5**	**301**	**9.3**	**103**	**39**	**52**	**0**	**+12**	**4**	**1**	**0**	**1**	**2**	**0**	**0**	**0**
1969-70	**New York Rangers**	**NHL**	**72**	**16**	**37**	**53**	**18**	**37**	**55**	**22**	**3**	**0**	**1**	**230**	**7.0**	**78**	**30**	**47**	**1**	**+2**	**6**	**4**	**5**	**9**	**0**	**3**	**0**	**0**
1970-71	**New York Rangers**	**NHL**	**78**	**30**	**31**	**61**	**31**	**27**	**58**	**65**	**8**	**0**	**5**	**226**	**13.3**	**86**	**25**	**39**	**0**	**+22**	**13**	**4**	**6**	**10**	**8**	**1**	**0**	**1**
1971-72	**New York Rangers**	**NHL**	**73**	**43**	**54**	**97**	**46**	**49**	**95**	**64**	**6**	**0**	**4**	**238**	**18.1**	**147**	**42**	**54**	**0**	**+51**	**16**	**7**	**8**	**15**	**11**	**4**	**0**	**2**
1972-73	Canada	Summit	6	1	3	4	....	....	....	9	....	....	....	....	....	....	....	....	....	....	....	....	....	....	....	....	....	....
	New York Rangers	**NHL**	**76**	**25**	**59**	**84**	**25**	**50**	**75**	**25**	**6**	**0**	**4**	**183**	**13.7**	**106**	**32**	**62**	**0**	**+12**	**10**	**5**	**1**	**6**	**2**	**0**	**0**	**1**
1973-74	**New York Rangers**	**NHL**	**75**	**36**	**41**	**77**	**37**	**36**	**73**	**20**	**16**	**0**	**8**	**168**	**21.4**	**104**	**39**	**54**	**0**	**+11**	**13**	**3**	**5**	**8**	**4**	**1**	**0**	**1**
1974-75	**New York Rangers**	**NHL**	**76**	**36**	**61**	**97**	**33**	**48**	**81**	**22**	**11**	**0**	**1**	**239**	**15.1**	**100**	**34**	**69**	**1**	**+1**	**3**	**1**	**3**	**4**	**2**	**0**	**0**	**0**
1975-76	**New York Rangers**	**NHL**	**70**	**36**	**50**	**86**	**34**	**39**	**73**	**32**	**9**	**0**	**4**	**211**	**17.1**	**112**	**39**	**81**	**0**	**–8**	....	....	....	....	....	....	....	....
1976-77	**New York Rangers**	**NHL**	**77**	**27**	**48**	**75**	**26**	**39**	**65**	**50**	**7**	**0**	**2**	**187**	**14.4**	**95**	**38**	**74**	**0**	**–17**	....	....	....	....	....	....	....	....
	Canada	WEC-A	9	2	2	4	....	....	....	12	....	....	....	....	....	....	....	....	....	....	....	....	....	....	....	....	....	....
1977-78	**New York Rangers**	**NHL**	**19**	**2**	**7**	**9**	**2**	**6**	**8**	**6**	**1**	**0**	**0**	**27**	**7.4**	**17**	**8**	**19**	**0**	**–10**	....	....	....	....	....	....	....	....
	NHL Totals		**1065**	**406**	**615**	**1021**	**444**	**567**	**1011**	**508**	**83**	**0**	**40**	**2291**	**17.7**	**1083**	**388**	**608**	**2**		**79**	**34**	**33**	**67**	**43**	**9**	**0**	**5**

NHL Second All-Star Team (1968) • NHL First All-Star Team (1972) • Won Bill Masterton Trophy (1976) • Won Lester Patrick Trophy (1991)
Played in NHL All-Star Game (1964, 1965, 1966, 1967, 1969, 1970, 1972, 1975, 1977)

• GILBERTSON, STAN

Stan Gilbertson LW – L. 6', 175 lbs. b: Duluth, MN, 10/29/1944.

Season	Club	League	GP	G	A	Pts	AG	AA	APts	PIM	PP	SH	GW	S	%	TGF	PGF	TGA	PGA	+/–	GP	G	A	Pts	PIM	PP	SH	GW
1962-63	Estevan Bruins	SJHL	53	15	9	24	....	....	....	41	....	....	....	....	....	....	....	....	....	....	11	3	2	5	4	....	....	....
1963-64	Estevan Bruins	SJHL	10	4	1	5	....	....	....	6	....	....	....	....	....	....	....	....	....	....	....	....	....	....	....	....	....	....
	Regina Pats	SJHL	58	40	36	76	....	....	....	122	....	....	....	....	....	....	....	....	....	....	19	15	17	32	58	....	....	....
1964-65	Regina Pats	SJHL	53	41	42	83	....	....	....	148	....	....	....	....	....	....	....	....	....	....	12	9	9	18	46	....	....	....
	Minneapolis Bruins	CHL	4	0	1	1	....	....	....	0	....	....	....	....	....	....	....	....	....	....	....	....	....	....	....	....	....	....
1965-66	Clinton Comets	EHL	34	7	12	19	....	....	....	64	....	....	....	....	....	....	....	....	....	....	....	....	....	....	....	....	....	....
	San Francisco Seals	WHL	43	1	8	9	....	....	....	32	....	....	....	....	....	....	....	....	....	....	7	1	1	2	6	....	....	....
1966-67	California Seals	WHL	59	6	11	17	....	....	....	25	....	....	....	....	....	....	....	....	....	....	6	1	3	4	0	....	....	....
1967-68	Vancouver Canucks	WHL	69	18	24	42	....	....	....	35	....	....	....	....	....	....	....	....	....	....	....	....	....	....	....	....	....	....
1968-69	Hershey Bears	AHL	72	27	19	46	....	....	....	28	....	....	....	....	....	....	....	....	....	....	11	7	6	13	6	....	....	....
1969-70	Hershey Bears	AHL	64	24	20	44	....	....	....	18	....	....	....	....	....	....	....	....	....	....	7	3	1	4	6	....	....	....
1970-71	Hershey Bears	AHL	68	31	18	49	....	....	....	50	....	....	....	....	....	....	....	....	....	....	4	2	0	2	0	....	....	....
1971-72	**California Golden Seals**	**NHL**	**78**	**16**	**16**	**32**	**17**	**15**	**32**	**47**	**3**	**0**	**2**	**141**	**11.3**	**61**	**11**	**62**	**6**	**–6**	....	....	....	....	....	....	....	....
1972-73	**California Golden Seals**	**NHL**	**66**	**6**	**15**	**21**	**6**	**13**	**19**	**19**	**3**	**0**	**0**	**110**	**5.5**	**39**	**9**	**64**	**0**	**–34**	....	....	....	....	....	....	....	....
1973-74	**California Golden Seals**	**NHL**	**76**	**18**	**12**	**30**	**18**	**10**	**28**	**39**	**4**	**0**	**2**	**136**	**13.2**	**40**	**7**	**76**	**2**	**–41**	....	....	....	....	....	....	....	....
1974-75	**California Golden Seals**	**NHL**	**15**	**1**	**4**	**5**	**1**	**3**	**4**	**2**	**1**	**0**	**0**	**26**	**3.8**	**11**	**3**	**22**	**6**	**–8**	....	....	....	....	....	....	....	....
	St. Louis Blues	**NHL**	**22**	**1**	**4**	**5**	**1**	**3**	**4**	**4**	**0**	**0**	**0**	**32**	**3.1**	**10**	**2**	**16**	**3**	**–5**	....	....	....	....	....	....	....	....
	Denver Spurs	CHL	10	11	4	15	....	....	....	7	....	....	....	....	....	....	....	....	....	....	....	....	....	....	....	....	....	....
	Washington Capitals	**NHL**	**25**	**11**	**7**	**18**	**10**	**5**	**15**	**12**	**2**	**0**	**1**	**67**	**16.4**	**26**	**8**	**61**	**6**	**–37**	....	....	....	....	....	....	....	....
1975-76	**Washington Capitals**	**NHL**	**31**	**13**	**14**	**27**	**12**	**11**	**23**	**6**	**5**	**0**	**0**	**62**	**21.0**	**39**	**16**	**50**	**2**	**–25**	....	....	....	....	....	....	....	....
	Pittsburgh Penguins	**NHL**	**48**	**13**	**8**	**21**	**12**	**6**	**18**	**6**	**3**	**0**	**1**	**86**	**15.1**	**38**	**9**	**32**	**0**	**–3**	**3**	**1**	**1**	**2**	**2**	**0**	**0**	**0**
1976-77	**Pittsburgh Penguins**	**NHL**	**67**	**6**	**9**	**15**	**6**	**7**	**13**	**13**	**0**	**0**	**0**	**62**	**9.7**	**26**	**0**	**36**	**1**	**–9**	....	....	....	....	....	....	....	....
	NHL Totals		**428**	**85**	**89**	**174**	**83**	**73**	**156**	**148**	**21**	**0**	**6**	**722**	**11.8**	**290**	**65**	**419**	**28**		**3**	**1**	**1**	**2**	**2**	**0**	**0**	**0**

AHL Second All-Star Team (1971)

Traded to **Vancouver** (WHL) by **Boston** for cash, October, 1967. Traded to **Boston** by **Vancouver** (WHL) for cash, June, 1968. Loaned to Hershey (AHL) by **Boston**, October, 1968. Claimed by **California** from **Boston** in Intra-League Draft, June 8, 1971. Traded to **St. Louis** by **California** with Craig Patrick for Dave Gardner and Butch Williams, November 11, 1974. Traded to **Washington** by **St. Louis** with Garnet Bailey for Denis Dupere, February 10, 1975. Traded to **Pittsburgh** by **Washington** for Harvey Bennett, December 16, 1975.

• GILCHRIST, BRENT

Brent Gilchrist LW – L. 5'11", 180 lbs. b: Moose Jaw, Sask., 4/3/1967. Montreal's 6th choice, 79th overall, in 1985 Entry Draft.

Season	Club	League	GP	G	A	Pts	AG	AA	APts	PIM	PP	SH	GW	S	%	TGF	PGF	TGA	PGA	+/–	GP	G	A	Pts	PIM	PP	SH	GW
1983-84	Kelowna Wings	WHL	69	16	11	27	....	....	....	16	....	....	....	....	....	....	....	....	....	....	....	....	....	....	....	....	....	....
1984-85	Kelowna Wings	WHL	51	35	38	73	....	....	....	58	....	....	....	....	....	....	....	....	....	....	6	5	2	7	8	....	....	....
1985-86	Spokane Chiefs	WHL	52	45	45	90	....	....	....	57	....	....	....	....	....	....	....	....	....	....	9	6	7	13	19	....	....	....
1986-87	Spokane Chiefs	WHL	46	45	55	100	....	....	....	71	....	....	....	....	....	....	....	....	....	....	5	2	7	9	6	....	....	....
	Sherbrooke Canadiens	AHL	....	....	....	....	....	....	....	....	....	....	....	....	....	....	....	....	....	....	10	2	7	9	2	....	....	....

			REGULAR SEASON																		PLAYOFFS							
Season	Club	League	GP	G	A	Pts	AG	AA	APts	PIM	PP	SH	GW	S	%	TGF	PGF	TGA	PGA	+/–	GP	G	A	Pts	PIM	PP	SH	GW
1987-88	Sherbrooke Canadiens	AHL	77	26	48	74	....	....	....	83	....	....	....	....	....	....	....	....	....	....	6	1	3	4	6	....	....	....
1988-89	**Montreal Canadiens**	**NHL**	**49**	**8**	**16**	**24**	**7**	**11**	**18**	**16**	**0**	**0**	**2**	**68**	**11.8**	**37**	**7**	**23**	**2**	**+9**	**9**	**1**	**1**	**2**	**10**	**0**	**0**	**0**
	Sherbrooke Canadiens	AHL	7	6	5	11	....	....	....	7	....	....	....	....	....	....	....	....	....	....	....	....	....	....	....	....	....	....
1989-90	**Montreal Canadiens**	**NHL**	**57**	**9**	**15**	**24**	**8**	**11**	**19**	**28**	**1**	**0**	**0**	**80**	**11.3**	**36**	**3**	**38**	**8**	**+3**	**8**	**2**	**0**	**2**	**2**	**0**	**0**	**0**
1990-91	Montreal Canadiens	FrTour	2	0	0	0	....	....	....	12	....	....	....	....	....	....	....	....	....	....	....	....	....	....	....	....	....	....
	Montreal Canadiens	**NHL**	**51**	**6**	**9**	**15**	**5**	**7**	**12**	**10**	**1**	**0**	**1**	**81**	**7.4**	**25**	**1**	**31**	**4**	**–3**	**13**	**5**	**3**	**8**	**6**	**0**	**0**	**1**
1991-92	**Montreal Canadiens**	**NHL**	**79**	**23**	**27**	**50**	**21**	**20**	**41**	**57**	**2**	**0**	**3**	**146**	**15.8**	**75**	**11**	**55**	**20**	**+29**	**11**	**2**	**4**	**6**	**6**	**1**	**0**	**0**
1992-93	**Edmonton Oilers**	**NHL**	**60**	**10**	**10**	**20**	**8**	**7**	**15**	**47**	**2**	**0**	**0**	**94**	**10.6**	**25**	**5**	**45**	**15**	**–10**	....	....	....	....	....	....	....	....
	Minnesota North Stars	**NHL**	**8**	**0**	**1**	**1**	**0**	**1**	**1**	**2**	**0**	**0**	**0**	**12**	**0.0**	**2**	**1**	**5**	**2**	**–2**	....	....	....	....	....	....	....	....
1993-94	**Dallas Stars**	**NHL**	**76**	**17**	**14**	**31**	**16**	**11**	**27**	**31**	**3**	**1**	**5**	**103**	**16.5**	**50**	**8**	**66**	**24**	**0**	**9**	**3**	**1**	**4**	**2**	**1**	**0**	**0**
1994-95	**Dallas Stars**	**NHL**	**32**	**9**	**4**	**13**	**16**	**6**	**22**	**16**	**1**	**3**	**1**	**70**	**12.9**	**18**	**1**	**28**	**8**	**–3**	**5**	**0**	**1**	**1**	**2**	**0**	**0**	**0**
1995-96	**Dallas Stars**	**NHL**	**77**	**20**	**22**	**42**	**20**	**18**	**38**	**36**	**6**	**1**	**2**	**164**	**12.2**	**56**	**13**	**93**	**39**	**–11**	....	....	....	....	....	....	....	....
1996-97	**Dallas Stars**	**NHL**	**67**	**10**	**20**	**30**	**11**	**18**	**29**	**24**	**2**	**0**	**2**	**116**	**8.6**	**47**	**9**	**41**	**9**	**+6**	**6**	**2**	**2**	**4**	**2**	**0**	**0**	**0**
1997-98	**Detroit Red Wings**	**NHL**	**61**	**13**	**14**	**27**	**15**	**14**	**29**	**40**	**5**	**0**	**3**	**124**	**10.5**	**45**	**11**	**43**	**13**	**+4**	**15**	**2**	**1**	**3**	**12**	**0**	**0**	**0**
	NHL Totals		**617**	**125**	**152**	**277**	**127**	**124**	**251**	**307**	**23**	**5**	**19**	**1058**	**11.8**	**416**	**70**	**468**	**144**		**76**	**17**	**13**	**30**	**42**	**2**	**0**	**1**

Traded to **Edmonton** by **Montreal** with Shayne Corson and Vladimir Vujtek for Vincent Damphousse and Edmonton's 4th round choice (Adam Wiesel) in 1993 Entry Draft, August 27, 1992. Traded to **Minnesota** by **Edmonton** for Todd Elik, March 5, 1993. Transferred to **Dallas** after **Minnesota** franchise relocated, June 9, 1993. Signed as a free agent by **Detroit**, August 1, 1997.

• GILES, CURT

Curt "Pengy" Giles D – L. 5'8", 175 lbs. b: The Pas, Man., 11/30/1958. Minnesota's 4th choice, 54th overall, in 1978 Amateur Draft.

Season	Club	League	GP	G	A	Pts	AG	AA	APts	PIM	PP	SH	GW	S	%	TGF	PGF	TGA	PGA	+/–	GP	G	A	Pts	PIM	PP	SH	GW
1975-76	University of Minnesota-Duluth	WCHA	34	5	17	22	....	....	....	76	....	....	....	....	....	....	....	....	....	....	....	....	....	....	....	....	....	....
1976-77	University of Minnesota-Duluth	WCHA	37	12	37	49	....	....	....	64	....	....	....	....	....	....	....	....	....	....	....	....	....	....	....	....	....	....
1977-78	University of Minnesota-Duluth	WCHA	34	11	36	47	....	....	....	62	....	....	....	....	....	....	....	....	....	....	....	....	....	....	....	....	....	....
1978-79	University of Minnesota-Duluth	WCHA	30	3	38	41	....	....	....	38	....	....	....	....	....	....	....	....	....	....	....	....	....	....	....	....	....	....
1979-80	**Minnesota North Stars**	**NHL**	**37**	**2**	**7**	**9**	**2**	**5**	**7**	**31**	**1**	**0**	**1**	**48**	**4.2**	**35**	**11**	**37**	**4**	**–9**	**12**	**2**	**4**	**6**	**10**	**2**	**0**	**0**
	Oklahoma City Stars	CHL	42	4	24	28	....	....	....	35	....	....	....	....	....	....	....	....	....	....	....	....	....	....	....	....	....	....
1980-81	**Minnesota North Stars**	**NHL**	**67**	**5**	**22**	**27**	**4**	**15**	**19**	**56**	**1**	**0**	**1**	**82**	**6.1**	**79**	**20**	**67**	**17**	**+9**	**19**	**1**	**4**	**5**	**14**	**0**	**0**	**0**
1981-82	**Minnesota North Stars**	**NHL**	**74**	**3**	**12**	**15**	**2**	**8**	**10**	**87**	**0**	**0**	**1**	**65**	**4.6**	**92**	**11**	**79**	**13**	**+15**	**4**	**0**	**0**	**0**	**2**	**0**	**0**	**0**
	Canada	WEC-A	10	0	1	1	....	....	....	12	....	....	....	....	....	....	....	....	....	....	....	....	....	....	....	....	....	....
1982-83	**Minnesota North Stars**	**NHL**	**76**	**2**	**21**	**23**	**2**	**14**	**16**	**70**	**0**	**0**	**0**	**78**	**2.6**	**87**	**6**	**94**	**24**	**+11**	**5**	**0**	**2**	**2**	**6**	**0**	**0**	**0**
1983-84	**Minnesota North Stars**	**NHL**	**70**	**6**	**22**	**28**	**5**	**15**	**20**	**59**	**2**	**0**	**0**	**78**	**7.7**	**90**	**24**	**102**	**38**	**+2**	**16**	**1**	**3**	**4**	**25**	**1**	**0**	**0**
1984-85	**Minnesota North Stars**	**NHL**	**77**	**5**	**25**	**30**	**4**	**17**	**21**	**49**	**3**	**0**	**0**	**98**	**5.1**	**99**	**20**	**96**	**20**	**+3**	**9**	**0**	**0**	**0**	**17**	**0**	**0**	**0**
1985-86	**Minnesota North Stars**	**NHL**	**69**	**6**	**21**	**27**	**5**	**14**	**19**	**30**	**0**	**0**	**1**	**59**	**10.2**	**92**	**11**	**101**	**39**	**+19**	**5**	**0**	**1**	**1**	**10**	**0**	**0**	**0**
1986-87	**Minnesota North Stars**	**NHL**	**11**	**0**	**3**	**3**	**0**	**2**	**2**	**4**	**0**	**0**	**0**	**5**	**0.0**	**9**	**0**	**13**	**6**	**+2**	....	....	....	....	....	....	....	....
	New York Rangers	**NHL**	**61**	**2**	**17**	**19**	**2**	**12**	**14**	**50**	**0**	**0**	**0**	**52**	**3.8**	**70**	**5**	**65**	**3**	**+3**	**5**	**0**	**0**	**0**	**6**	**0**	**0**	**0**
1987-88	**New York Rangers**	**NHL**	**13**	**0**	**0**	**0**	**0**	**0**	**0**	**10**	**0**	**0**	**0**	**12**	**0.0**	**7**	**0**	**16**	**4**	**–5**	....	....	....	....	....	....	....	....
	Minnesota North Stars	**NHL**	**59**	**1**	**12**	**13**	**1**	**9**	**10**	**66**	**0**	**0**	**0**	**60**	**1.7**	**44**	**10**	**84**	**22**	**–28**	....	....	....	....	....	....	....	....
1988-89	**Minnesota North Stars**	**NHL**	**76**	**5**	**10**	**15**	**4**	**7**	**11**	**77**	**0**	**1**	**0**	**64**	**7.8**	**61**	**2**	**94**	**37**	**+2**	**5**	**0**	**0**	**0**	**4**	**0**	**0**	**0**
1989-90	**Minnesota North Stars**	**NHL**	**74**	**1**	**12**	**13**	**1**	**9**	**10**	**48**	**0**	**0**	**0**	**55**	**1.8**	**61**	**0**	**88**	**30**	**+3**	**7**	**0**	**1**	**1**	**6**	**0**	**0**	**0**
1990-91	Minnesota North Stars	FrTour	3	0	0	0	....	....	....	4	....	....	....	....	....	....	....	....	....	....	....	....	....	....	....	....	....	....
	Minnesota North Stars	**NHL**	**70**	**4**	**10**	**14**	**4**	**8**	**12**	**48**	**0**	**0**	**0**	**53**	**7.5**	**55**	**2**	**81**	**31**	**+3**	**10**	**1**	**0**	**1**	**16**	**0**	**0**	**0**
1991-92	Canada	Nat-Team	31	3	6	9	....	....	....	37	....	....	....	....	....	....	....	....	....	....	....	....	....	....	....	....	....	....
	Canada	Olympics	8	1	0	1	....	....	....	6	....	....	....	....	....	....	....	....	....	....	....	....	....	....	....	....	....	....
	St. Louis Blues	**NHL**	**13**	**1**	**1**	**2**	**1**	**1**	**2**	**8**	**0**	**0**	**0**	**4**	**25.0**	**7**	**1**	**11**	**2**	**–3**	**3**	**1**	**1**	**2**	**0**	**1**	**0**	**0**
1992-93	**St. Louis Blues**	**NHL**	**48**	**0**	**4**	**4**	**0**	**3**	**3**	**40**	**0**	**0**	**0**	**23**	**0.0**	**26**	**2**	**43**	**17**	**–2**	**3**	**0**	**0**	**0**	**2**	**0**	**0**	**0**
	NHL Totals		**895**	**43**	**199**	**242**	**37**	**139**	**176**	**733**	**7**	**1**	**4**	**836**	**5.1**	**914**	**125**	**1071**	**307**		**103**	**6**	**16**	**22**	**118**	**4**	**0**	**0**

WCHA First All-Star Team (1978, 1979) • NCAA West First All-American Team (1978, 1979)

Traded to **NY Rangers** by **Minnesota** with Tony McKegney and Minnesota's 2nd round choice (Troy Mallette) in 1988 Entry Draft for Bob Brooke, Minnesota's 4th round choice (previously acquired, Minnesota selected Jeffrey Stolp) in 1988 Entry Draft, November 13, 1986. Traded to **Minnesota** by **NY Rangers** for Byron Lomow and future considerations, November 20, 1987. Signed as a free agent by **St. Louis**, February 29, 1992.

• GILHEN, RANDY

Randy Gilhen C – L. 6', 190 lbs. b: Zweibrucken, W. Germany, 6/13/1963. Hartford's 6th choice, 109th overall, in 1982 Entry Draft.

Season	Club	League	GP	G	A	Pts	AG	AA	APts	PIM	PP	SH	GW	S	%	TGF	PGF	TGA	PGA	+/–	GP	G	A	Pts	PIM	PP	SH	GW
1980-81	Saskatoon Blades	WHL	68	10	5	15	....	....	....	154	....	....	....	....	....	....	....	....	....	....	....	....	....	....	....	....	....	....
1981-82	Saskatoon Blades	WHL	25	15	9	24	....	....	....	45	....	....	....	....	....	....	....	....	....	....	....	....	....	....	....	....	....	....
	Winnipeg Warriors	WHL	36	26	28	54	....	....	....	42	....	....	....	....	....	....	....	....	....	....	....	....	....	....	....	....	....	....
1982-83	Winnipeg Warriors	WHL	71	57	44	101	....	....	....	84	....	....	....	....	....	....	....	....	....	....	3	2	2	4	0	....	....	....
	Hartford Whalers	**NHL**	**2**	**0**	**1**	**1**	**0**	**1**	**1**	**0**	**0**	**0**	**0**	**4**	**0.0**	**2**	**1**	**1**	**0**	**0**	....	....	....	....	....	....	....	....
1983-84	Binghamton Whalers	AHL	73	8	12	20	....	....	....	72	....	....	....	....	....	....	....	....	....	....	....	....	....	....	....	....	....	....
1984-85	Salt Lake Golden Eagles	IHL	57	20	20	40	....	....	....	28	....	....	....	....	....	....	....	....	....	....	....	....	....	....	....	....	....	....
	Binghamton Whalers	AHL	18	3	3	6	....	....	....	9	....	....	....	....	....	....	....	....	....	....	8	4	1	5	16	....	....	....
1985-86	Fort Wayne Komets	IHL	82	44	40	84	....	....	....	48	....	....	....	....	....	....	....	....	....	....	15	10	8	18	6	....	....	....
1986-87	**Winnipeg Jets**	**NHL**	**2**	**0**	**0**	**0**	**0**	**0**	**0**	**0**	**0**	**0**	**0**	**3**	**0.0**	**0**	**0**	**2**	**0**	**–2**	....	....	....	....	....	....	....	....
	Sherbrooke Canadiens	AHL	75	36	29	65	....	....	....	44	....	....	....	....	....	....	....	....	....	....	17	7	13	20	10	....	....	....
1987-88	**Winnipeg Jets**	**NHL**	**13**	**3**	**2**	**5**	**3**	**1**	**4**	**15**	**0**	**0**	**0**	**21**	**14.3**	**10**	**0**	**6**	**1**	**+5**	**4**	**1**	**0**	**1**	**10**	**0**	**1**	**1**
	Moncton Hawks	AHL	68	40	47	87	....	....	....	51	....	....	....	....	....	....	....	....	....	....	....	....	....	....	....	....	....	....
1988-89	**Winnipeg Jets**	**NHL**	**64**	**5**	**3**	**8**	**4**	**2**	**6**	**38**	**0**	**1**	**1**	**76**	**6.6**	**19**	**1**	**67**	**25**	**–24**	....	....	....	....	....	....	....	....
1989-90	**Pittsburgh Penguins**	**NHL**	**61**	**5**	**11**	**16**	**4**	**8**	**12**	**54**	**0**	**0**	**1**	**67**	**7.5**	**23**	**1**	**52**	**22**	**–8**	....	....	....	....	....	....	....	....
1990-91	**Pittsburgh Penguins**	**NHL**	**72**	**15**	**10**	**25**	**14**	**8**	**22**	**51**	**1**	**2**	**1**	**112**	**13.4**	**37**	**1**	**60**	**27**	**+3**	**16**	**1**	**0**	**1**	**14**	**0**	**0**	**0**
1991-92	**Los Angeles Kings**	**NHL**	**33**	**3**	**6**	**9**	**3**	**4**	**7**	**14**	**0**	**1**	**0**	**32**	**9.4**	**12**	**0**	**29**	**14**	**–3**	....	....	....	....	....	....	....	....
	New York Rangers	**NHL**	**40**	**7**	**7**	**14**	**6**	**5**	**11**	**14**	**0**	**0**	**0**	**67**	**10.4**	**25**	**0**	**25**	**5**	**+5**	**13**	**1**	**2**	**3**	**2**	**0**	**0**	**0**
1992-93	**New York Rangers**	**NHL**	**33**	**3**	**2**	**5**	**2**	**1**	**3**	**8**	**0**	**1**	**1**	**34**	**8.8**	**10**	**0**	**35**	**17**	**–8**	....	....	....	....	....	....	....	....
	Tampa Bay Lightning	**NHL**	**11**	**0**	**2**	**2**	**0**	**1**	**1**	**6**	**0**	**0**	**0**	**11**	**0.0**	**5**	**0**	**13**	**2**	**–6**	....	....	....	....	....	....	....	....
1993-94	**Florida Panthers**	**NHL**	**20**	**4**	**4**	**8**	**4**	**3**	**7**	**16**	**0**	**0**	**0**	**52**	**7.7**	**14**	**3**	**22**	**12**	**+1**	....	....	....	....	....	....	....	....
	Winnipeg Jets	**NHL**	**40**	**3**	**3**	**6**	**3**	**2**	**5**	**34**	**0**	**0**	**0**	**43**	**7.0**	**9**	**1**	**45**	**24**	**–13**	....	....	....	....	....	....	....	....
1994-95	**Winnipeg Jets**	**NHL**	**44**	**5**	**6**	**11**	**9**	**9**	**18**	**52**	**0**	**1**	**1**	**47**	**10.6**	**15**	**0**	**48**	**16**	**–17**	....	....	....	....	....	....	....	....
1995-96	**Winnipeg Jets**	**NHL**	**22**	**2**	**3**	**5**	**2**	**2**	**4**	**12**	**0**	**0**	**0**	**26**	**7.7**	**9**	**1**	**14**	**7**	**+1**	....	....	....	....	....	....	....	....
1996-97	Manitoba Moose	IHL	79	21	24	45	....	....	....	101	....	....	....	....	....	....	....	....	....	....	....	....	....	....	....	....	....	....
1997-98	Manitoba Moose	IHL	22	4	2	6	....	....	....	14	....	....	....	....	....	....	....	....	....	....	....	....	....	....	....	....	....	....
	NHL Totals		**457**	**55**	**60**	**115**	**54**	**47**	**101**	**314**	**1**	**6**	**5**	**595**	**9.2**	**190**	**9**	**419**	**172**		**33**	**3**	**2**	**5**	**26**	**0**	**1**	**1**

Signed as a free agent by **Winnipeg**, November 8, 1985. Traded to **Pittsburgh** by **Winnipeg** with Jim Kyte and Andrew McBain for Randy Cunneyworth, Rick Tabaracci and Dave McLlwain, June 17, 1989. Claimed by **Minnesota** from **Pittsburgh** in Expansion Draft, May 30, 1991. Traded to **LA Kings** by **Minnesota** with Charlie Huddy, Jim Thomson and NY Rangers' 4th round choice (previously acquired, LA Kings selected Alexei Zhitnik) in 1991 Entry Draft for Todd Elik, June 22, 1991. Traded to **NY Rangers** by **LA Kings** for Corey Millen, December 23, 1991. Traded to **Tampa Bay** by **NY Rangers** for Mike Hartman, March 22, 1993. Claimed by **Florida** from **Tampa Bay** in Expansion Draft, June 24, 1993. Traded to **Winnipeg** by **Florida** for Stu Barnes and St. Louis' 6th round choice (previously acquired, later traded to Edmonton — later returned to Winnipeg — Winnipeg selected Chris Kibermanis) in 1994 Entry Draft, November 25, 1993.

• GILL, HAL

Hal Gill D – L. 6'6", 200 lbs. b: Concord, MA, 4/6/1975. Boston's 8th choice, 207th overall, in 1993 Entry Draft.

Season	Club	League	GP	G	A	Pts	AG	AA	APts	PIM	PP	SH	GW	S	%	TGF	PGF	TGA	PGA	+/–	GP	G	A	Pts	PIM	PP	SH	GW
1992-93	Nashoba-Mass High School	H.S.	20	25	25	50	....	....	....	....	....	....	....	....	....	....	....	....	....	....	....	....	....	....	....	....	....	....
1993-94	Providence College	H.E.	31	1	2	3	....	....	....	26	....	....	....	....	....	....	....	....	....	....	....	....	....	....	....	....	....	....
1994-95	Providence College	H.E.	26	1	3	4	....	....	....	22	....	....	....	....	....	....	....	....	....	....	....	....	....	....	....	....	....	....
1995-96	Providence College	H.E.	39	5	12	17	....	....	....	54	....	....	....	....	....	....	....	....	....	....	....	....	....	....	....	....	....	....
1996-97	Providence College	H.E.	35	5	16	21	....	....	....	52	....	....	....	....	....	....	....	....	....	....	....	....	....	....	....	....	....	....
1997-98	**Boston Bruins**	**NHL**	**68**	**2**	**4**	**6**	**2**	**4**	**6**	**47**	**0**	**0**	**0**	**56**	**3.6**	**35**	**0**	**48**	**17**	**+4**	**6**	**0**	**0**	**0**	**4**	**0**	**0**	**0**
	Providence Bruins	AHL	4	1	0	1	....	....	....	23	....	....	....	....	....	....	....	....	....	....	....	....	....	....	....	....	....	....
	NHL Totals		**68**	**2**	**4**	**6**	**2**	**4**	**6**	**47**	**0**	**0**	**0**	**56**	**3.6**	**35**	**0**	**48**	**17**		**6**	**0**	**0**	**0**	**4**	**0**	**0**	**0**

• GILL, TODD

Todd Gill D – L. 6', 180 lbs. b: Cardinal, Ont., 11/9/1965. Toronto's 2nd choice, 25th overall, in 1984 Entry Draft.

Season	Club	League	GP	G	A	Pts	AG	AA	APts	PIM	PP	SH	GW	S	%	TGF	PGF	TGA	PGA	+/–	GP	G	A	Pts	PIM	PP	SH	GW
1982-83	Windsor Spitfires	OHL	70	12	24	36	....	....	....	108	....	....	....	....	....	....	....	....	....	....	3	0	0	0	11	....	....	....
1983-84	Windsor Spitfires	OHL	68	9	48	57	....	....	....	184	....	....	....	....	....	....	....	....	....	....	3	1	1	2	10	....	....	....
1984-85	Windsor Spitfires	OHL	53	17	40	57	....	....	....	148	....	....	....	....	....	....	....	....	....	....	4	0	1	1	14	....	....	....
	Toronto Maple Leafs	**NHL**	**10**	**1**	**0**	**1**	**1**	**0**	**1**	**13**	**0**	**0**	**0**	**9**	**11.1**	**4**	**0**	**5**	**0**	**–1**	....	....	....	....	....	....	....	....
1985-86	**Toronto Maple Leafs**	**NHL**	**15**	**1**	**2**	**3**	**1**	**1**	**2**	**28**	**0**	**0**	**0**	**9**	**11.1**	**13**	**2**	**12**	**1**	**0**	**1**	**0**	**0**	**0**	**0**	**0**	**0**	**0**
	St. Catharines Saints	AHL	58	8	25	33	....	....	....	90	....	....	....	....	....	....	....	....	....	....	10	1	6	7	17	....	....	....

			REGULAR SEASON																		PLAYOFFS							
Season	Club	League	GP	G	A	Pts	AG	AA	APts	PIM	PP	SH	GW	S	%	TGF	PGF	TGA	PGA	+/–	GP	G	A	Pts	PIM	PP	SH	GW
1986-87	**Toronto Maple Leafs**	**NHL**	**61**	**4**	**27**	**31**	**3**	**20**	**23**	**92**	**1**	**0**	**0**	**51**	**7.8**	**76**	**11**	**82**	**14**	**–3**	**13**	**2**	**2**	**4**	**42**	**0**	**0**	**0**
	Newmarket Saints	AHL	11	1	8	9	....	....	....	33	....	....	....	....	....	....	....	....	....	....	....	....	....	....	....	....	....	....
1987-88	**Toronto Maple Leafs**	**NHL**	**65**	**8**	**17**	**25**	**7**	**12**	**19**	**131**	**1**	**0**	**3**	**109**	**7.3**	**74**	**11**	**108**	**25**	**–20**	**6**	**1**	**3**	**4**	**20**	**1**	**0**	**0**
	Newmarket Saints	AHL	2	0	1	1	....	....	....	2	....	....	....	....	....	....	....	....	....	....	....	....	....	....	....	....	....	....
1988-89	**Toronto Maple Leafs**	**NHL**	**59**	**11**	**14**	**25**	**9**	**10**	**19**	**72**	**0**	**0**	**1**	**92**	**12.0**	**55**	**7**	**57**	**6**	**–3**	....	....	....	....	....	....	....	....
1989-90	**Toronto Maple Leafs**	**NHL**	**48**	**1**	**14**	**15**	**1**	**10**	**11**	**92**	**0**	**0**	**0**	**44**	**2.3**	**43**	**6**	**49**	**4**	**–8**	**5**	**0**	**3**	**3**	**16**	**0**	**0**	**0**
1990-91	**Toronto Maple Leafs**	**NHL**	**72**	**2**	**22**	**24**	**2**	**17**	**19**	**113**	**0**	**0**	**0**	**90**	**2.2**	**66**	**7**	**70**	**16**	**–4**	....	....	....	....	....	....	....	....
1991-92	**Toronto Maple Leafs**	**NHL**	**74**	**2**	**15**	**17**	**2**	**11**	**13**	**91**	**1**	**0**	**0**	**82**	**2.4**	**49**	**6**	**85**	**20**	**–22**	....	....	....	....	....	....	....	....
	Canada	WC-A	6	0	3	3	....	....	....	6	....	....	....	....	....	....	....	....	....	....	....	....	....	....	....	....	....	....
1992-93	**Toronto Maple Leafs**	**NHL**	**69**	**11**	**32**	**43**	**9**	**22**	**31**	**66**	**5**	**0**	**2**	**113**	**9.7**	**94**	**40**	**61**	**11**	**+4**	**21**	**1**	**10**	**11**	**26**	**0**	**0**	**0**
1993-94	**Toronto Maple Leafs**	**NHL**	**45**	**4**	**24**	**28**	**4**	**19**	**23**	**44**	**2**	**0**	**1**	**74**	**5.4**	**80**	**34**	**45**	**7**	**+8**	**18**	**1**	**5**	**6**	**37**	**0**	**0**	**1**
1994-95	**Toronto Maple Leafs**	**NHL**	**47**	**7**	**25**	**32**	**12**	**37**	**49**	**64**	**3**	**1**	**2**	**82**	**8.5**	**58**	**22**	**57**	**13**	**–8**	**7**	**0**	**3**	**3**	**6**	**0**	**0**	**0**
1995-96	**Toronto Maple Leafs**	**NHL**	**74**	**7**	**18**	**25**	**7**	**15**	**22**	**116**	**1**	**0**	**2**	**109**	**6.4**	**71**	**15**	**89**	**18**	**–15**	**6**	**0**	**0**	**0**	**24**	**0**	**0**	**0**
1996-97	**San Jose Sharks**	**NHL**	**79**	**0**	**21**	**21**	**0**	**19**	**19**	**101**	**0**	**0**	**0**	**101**	**0.0**	**75**	**9**	**123**	**37**	**–20**	....	....	....	....	....	....	....	....
1997-98	**San Jose Sharks**	**NHL**	**64**	**8**	**13**	**21**	**9**	**13**	**22**	**31**	**4**	**0**	**1**	**100**	**8.0**	**57**	**18**	**71**	**19**	**–13**	....	....	....	....	....	....	....	....
	St. Louis Blues	**NHL**	**11**	**5**	**4**	**9**	**6**	**4**	**10**	**10**	**3**	**0**	**1**	**22**	**22.7**	**17**	**7**	**9**	**1**	**+2**	**10**	**2**	**2**	**4**	**10**	**1**	**1**	**0**
	NHL Totals		**793**	**72**	**248**	**320**	**73**	**210**	**283**	**1064**	**21**	**1**	**13**	**1087**	**6.6**	**832**	**195**	**932**	**192**		**87**	**7**	**28**	**35**	**181**	**2**	**1**	**1**

Traded to **San Jose** by **Toronto** for Jamie Baker and San Jose's 5th round choice (Peter Cava) in 1996 Entry Draft, June 14, 1996. Traded to **St. Louis** by **San Jose** for Joe Murphy, March 24, 1998.

• GILLEN, DON

Don Gillen RW – R. 6'3", 210 lbs. b: Dodsland, Sask., 12/24/1960. Philadelphia's 5th choice, 77th overall, in 1979 Entry Draft.

Season	Club	League	GP	G	A	Pts	AG	AA	APts	PIM	PP	SH	GW	S	%	TGF	PGF	TGA	PGA	+/–	GP	G	A	Pts	PIM	PP	SH	GW
1977-78	Weyburn Red Wings	SJHL	58	13	24	37	....	....	....	170	....	....	....	....	....	....	....	....	....	....	....	....	....	....	....	....	....	....
1978-79	Brandon Wheat Kings	WHL	64	21	30	51	....	....	....	212	....	....	....	....	....	....	....	....	....	....	22	10	10	20	34	....	....	....
1979-80	Brandon Wheat Kings	WHL	69	31	56	87	....	....	....	372	....	....	....	....	....	....	....	....	....	....	10	5	3	8	43	....	....	....
	Philadelphia Flyers	**NHL**	**1**	**1**	**0**	**1**	**1**	**0**	**1**	**0**	**0**	**0**	**0**	**2**	**50.0**	**1**	**0**	**0**	**0**	**+1**	....	....	....	....	....	....	....	....
	Maine Mariners	AHL	....	....	....	....	....	....	....	....	....	....	....	....	....	....	....	....	....	....	7	1	2	3	19	....	....	....
1980-81	Maine Mariners	AHL	79	30	29	59	....	....	....	255	....	....	....	....	....	....	....	....	....	....	20	4	4	8	49	....	....	....
1981-82	**Hartford Whalers**	**NHL**	**34**	**1**	**4**	**5**	**1**	**3**	**4**	**22**	**0**	**0**	**0**	**25**	**4.0**	**7**	**0**	**18**	**0**	**–11**	....	....	....	....	....	....	....	....
	Binghamton Whalers	AHL	42	20	10	30	....	....	....	100	....	....	....	....	....	....	....	....	....	....	15	6	5	11	23	....	....	....
1982-83	Binghamton Whalers	AHL	80	38	39	77	....	....	....	245	....	....	....	....	....	....	....	....	....	....	1	0	1	1	0	....	....	....
1983-84	Binghamton Whalers	AHL	73	27	37	64	....	....	....	140	....	....	....	....	....	....	....	....	....	....	....	....	....	....	....	....	....	....
	NHL Totals		**35**	**2**	**4**	**6**	**2**	**3**	**5**	**22**	**0**	**0**	**0**	**27**	**7.4**	**8**	**0**	**18**	**0**		....	....	....	....	....	....	....	....

Traded to **Hartford** by **Philadelphia** with Rick MacLeish, Blake Wesley and Philadelphia's 1st (Paul Lawless), 2nd (Mark Paterson) and 3rd (Kevin Dineen) round choices in 1982 Entry Draft for Ray Allison, Fred Arthur and Hartford's 1st (Ron Sutter) and 3rd (Miroslav Dvorak) round choices in 1982 Entry Draft, July 3, 1981.

• GILLIES, CLARK

Clark "Jethro" Gillies LW – L. 6'3", 215 lbs. b: Moose Jaw, Sask., 4/7/1954. NY Islanders' 1st choice, 4th overall, in 1974 Amateur Draft.

Season	Club	League	GP	G	A	Pts	AG	AA	APts	PIM	PP	SH	GW	S	%	TGF	PGF	TGA	PGA	+/–	GP	G	A	Pts	PIM	PP	SH	GW
1971-72	Regina Pats	WCJHL	68	31	48	79	....	....	....	199	....	....	....	....	....	....	....	....	....	....	15	5	10	15	49	....	....	....
1972-73	Regina Pats	WCJHL	68	40	52	92	....	....	....	192	....	....	....	....	....	....	....	....	....	....	4	0	3	3	34	....	....	....
1973-74	Regina Pats	WCJHL	65	46	66	112	....	....	....	179	....	....	....	....	....	....	....	....	....	....	16	9	8	17	32	....	....	....
1974-75	**New York Islanders**	**NHL**	**80**	**25**	**22**	**47**	**23**	**17**	**40**	**66**	**8**	**0**	**4**	**165**	**15.2**	**71**	**21**	**55**	**1**	**–4**	**17**	**4**	**2**	**6**	**36**	**0**	**0**	**2**
1975-76	**New York Islanders**	**NHL**	**80**	**34**	**27**	**61**	**32**	**21**	**53**	**96**	**15**	**0**	**6**	**210**	**16.2**	**113**	**57**	**36**	**0**	**+20**	**13**	**2**	**4**	**6**	**16**	**0**	**0**	**1**
1976-77	**New York Islanders**	**NHL**	**70**	**33**	**22**	**55**	**32**	**18**	**50**	**93**	**12**	**0**	**5**	**215**	**15.3**	**81**	**25**	**39**	**1**	**+18**	**12**	**4**	**4**	**8**	**15**	**0**	**0**	**4**
1977-78	**New York Islanders**	**NHL**	**80**	**35**	**50**	**85**	**34**	**41**	**75**	**76**	**9**	**0**	**2**	**277**	**12.6**	**146**	**54**	**43**	**0**	**+49**	**7**	**2**	**0**	**2**	**15**	**1**	**0**	**0**
1978-79	**New York Islanders**	**NHL**	**75**	**35**	**56**	**91**	**32**	**43**	**75**	**68**	**11**	**0**	**5**	**210**	**16.7**	**148**	**57**	**34**	**0**	**+57**	**10**	**1**	**2**	**3**	**11**	**0**	**0**	**0**
	NHL All-Stars	Chal Cup	3	1	2	3	....	....	....	2	....	....	....	....	....	....	....	....	....	....	....	....	....	....	....	....	....	....
1979-80	**New York Islanders**	**NHL**	**73**	**19**	**35**	**54**	**17**	**27**	**44**	**49**	**7**	**0**	**5**	**175**	**10.9**	**101**	**33**	**39**	**0**	**+29**	**21**	**6**	**10**	**16**	**63**	**1**	**0**	**2**
1980-81	**New York Islanders**	**NHL**	**80**	**33**	**45**	**78**	**27**	**31**	**58**	**99**	**9**	**0**	**3**	**188**	**17.6**	**129**	**47**	**56**	**0**	**+26**	**18**	**6**	**9**	**15**	**28**	**3**	**0**	**0**
1981-82	Canada	C Cup	7	2	5	7	....	....	....	8	....	....	....	....	....	....	....	....	....	....	....	....	....	....	....	....	....	....
	New York Islanders	**NHL**	**79**	**38**	**39**	**77**	**30**	**26**	**50**	**75**	**8**	**0**	**5**	**200**	**19.0**	**123**	**33**	**51**	**0**	**+39**	**19**	**8**	**6**	**14**	**34**	**4**	**0**	**3**
1982-83	**New York Islanders**	**NHL**	**70**	**21**	**20**	**41**	**17**	**14**	**31**	**76**	**4**	**0**	**2**	**145**	**14.5**	**70**	**22**	**39**	**0**	**+9**	**8**	**0**	**2**	**2**	**10**	**0**	**0**	**0**
1983-84	**New York Islanders**	**NHL**	**76**	**12**	**16**	**28**	**10**	**11**	**21**	**65**	**3**	**0**	**2**	**138**	**8.7**	**71**	**14**	**52**	**0**	**+5**	**21**	**12**	**7**	**19**	**19**	**3**	**0**	**0**
1984-85	**New York Islanders**	**NHL**	**54**	**15**	**17**	**32**	**12**	**11**	**23**	**73**	**5**	**0**	**2**	**125**	**12.0**	**54**	**14**	**40**	**0**	**0**	**10**	**1**	**0**	**1**	**9**	**0**	**0**	**0**
1985-86	**New York Islanders**	**NHL**	**55**	**4**	**10**	**14**	**3**	**7**	**10**	**55**	**1**	**0**	**0**	**74**	**5.4**	**26**	**3**	**31**	**0**	**–8**	**3**	**1**	**0**	**1**	**6**	**0**	**0**	**0**
1986-87	**Buffalo Sabres**	**NHL**	**61**	**10**	**17**	**27**	**9**	**12**	**21**	**81**	**1**	**0**	**2**	**106**	**9.4**	**42**	**5**	**37**	**0**	**0**	....	....	....	....	....	....	....	....
1987-88	**Buffalo Sabres**	**NHL**	**25**	**5**	**2**	**7**	**4**	**1**	**5**	**51**	**0**	**0**	**1**	**23**	**21.7**	**12**	**0**	**11**	**0**	**+1**	**5**	**0**	**1**	**1**	**25**	**0**	**0**	**0**
	NHL Totals		**958**	**319**	**378**	**697**	**282**	**280**	**562**	**1023**	**93**	**0**	**44**	**2251**	**14.2**	**1187**	**385**	**563**	**2**		**164**	**47**	**47**	**94**	**287**	**12**	**0**	**12**

WCJHL First All-Star Team (1974) • NHL First All-Star Team (1978, 1979)

Played in NHL All-Star Game (1978)

Claimed by **Buffalo** from **NY Islanders** in Waiver Draft, October 6, 1986.

• GILLIS, JERE

Jere Gillis LW – L. 6', 194 lbs. b: Bend, OR, 1/18/1957. Vancouver's 1st choice, 4th overall, in 1977 Amateur Draft.

Season	Club	League	GP	G	A	Pts	AG	AA	APts	PIM	PP	SH	GW	S	%	TGF	PGF	TGA	PGA	+/–	GP	G	A	Pts	PIM	PP	SH	GW
1973-74	Sherbrooke Beavers	QMJHL	69	21	19	40	....	....	....	96	....	....	....	....	....	....	....	....	....	....	....	....	....	....	....	....	....	....
1974-75	Sherbrooke Beavers	QMJHL	54	38	57	95	....	....	....	89	....	....	....	....	....	....	....	....	....	....	....	....	....	....	....	....	....	....
1975-76	Sherbrooke Beavers	QMJHL	60	47	55	102	....	....	....	38	....	....	....	....	....	....	....	....	....	....	17	8	14	22	27	....	....	....
1976-77	Sherbrooke Beavers	QMJHL	72	55	85	140	....	....	....	80	....	....	....	....	....	....	....	....	....	....	18	11	12	23	40	....	....	....
1977-78	**Vancouver Canucks**	**NHL**	**79**	**23**	**18**	**41**	**22**	**15**	**37**	**35**	**2**	**0**	**2**	**154**	**14.9**	**59**	**15**	**68**	**0**	**–24**	....	....	....	....	....	....	....	....
1978-79	**Vancouver Canucks**	**NHL**	**78**	**13**	**12**	**25**	**12**	**9**	**21**	**33**	**4**	**0**	**3**	**143**	**9.1**	**51**	**12**	**76**	**6**	**–31**	**1**	**0**	**1**	**1**	**0**	**0**	**0**	**0**
1979-80	**Vancouver Canucks**	**NHL**	**67**	**13**	**17**	**30**	**12**	**13**	**25**	**108**	**5**	**1**	**5**	**130**	**10.0**	**57**	**19**	**69**	**31**	**0**	....	....	....	....	....	....	....	....
1980-81	**Vancouver Canucks**	**NHL**	**11**	**0**	**4**	**4**	**0**	**3**	**3**	**4**	**0**	**0**	**0**	**11**	**0.0**	**6**	**0**	**10**	**4**	**0**	....	....	....	....	....	....	....	....
	New York Rangers	**NHL**	**35**	**10**	**10**	**20**	**8**	**7**	**15**	**4**	**1**	**0**	**1**	**63**	**15.9**	**33**	**4**	**24**	**1**	**+6**	**14**	**2**	**5**	**7**	**9**	**0**	**0**	**0**
1981-82	**New York Rangers**	**NHL**	**26**	**3**	**9**	**12**	**2**	**6**	**8**	**16**	**0**	**0**	**1**	**41**	**7.3**	**18**	**0**	**20**	**0**	**–2**	....	....	....	....	....	....	....	....
	Quebec Nordiques	**NHL**	**12**	**2**	**1**	**3**	**2**	**1**	**3**	**0**	**0**	**0**	**1**	**16**	**12.5**	**7**	**0**	**5**	**0**	**+2**	....	....	....	....	....	....	....	....
	Fredericton Express	AHL	28	2	17	19	....	....	....	10	....	....	....	....	....	....	....	....	....	....	....	....	....	....	....	....	....	....
1982-83	**Buffalo Sabres**	**NHL**	**3**	**0**	**0**	**0**	**0**	**0**	**0**	**0**	**0**	**0**	**0**	**3**	**0.0**	**0**	**0**	**6**	**0**	**–6**	....	....	....	....	....	....	....	....
	Rochester Americans	AHL	53	18	24	42	....	....	....	69	....	....	....	....	....	....	....	....	....	....	16	1	7	8	11	....	....	....
1983-84	**Vancouver Canucks**	**NHL**	**37**	**9**	**13**	**22**	**7**	**9**	**16**	**7**	**0**	**1**	**0**	**55**	**16.4**	**29**	**3**	**27**	**3**	**+2**	**4**	**2**	**1**	**3**	**0**	**0**	**0**	**0**
	Fredericton Express	AHL	36	22	28	50	....	....	....	35	....	....	....	....	....	....	....	....	....	....	....	....	....	....	....	....	....	....
1984-85	**Vancouver Canucks**	**NHL**	**37**	**5**	**11**	**16**	**4**	**7**	**11**	**23**	**0**	**0**	**1**	**56**	**8.9**	**25**	**1**	**34**	**3**	**–7**	....	....	....	....	....	....	....	....
	Fredericton Express	AHL	7	2	1	3	....	....	....	2	....	....	....	....	....	....	....	....	....	....	....	....	....	....	....	....	....	....
1985-86	Fredericton Express	AHL	29	4	14	18	....	....	....	21	....	....	....	....	....	....	....	....	....	....	....	....	....	....	....	....	....	....
1986-87	**Philadelphia Flyers**	**NHL**	**1**	**0**	**0**	**0**	**0**	**0**	**0**	**0**	**0**	**0**	**0**	**0**	**0.0**	**0**	**0**	**0**	**0**	**0**	....	....	....	....	....	....	....	....
	Hershey Bears	AHL	47	13	22	35	....	....	....	32	....	....	....	....	....	....	....	....	....	....	5	0	0	0	9	....	....	....
1987-88			DID NOT PLAY																									
1988-89	Solihull Bulls	Britain	18	46	47	93	....	....	....	12	....	....	....	....	....	....	....	....	....	....	....	....	....	....	....	....	....	....
1989-90	Solihull Bulls	Britain	30	50	35	85	....	....	....	16	....	....	....	....	....	....	....	....	....	....	4	2	4	6	6	....	....	....
1990-91	Peterborough Pirates	Britain	6	13	4	17	....	....	....	22	....	....	....	....	....	....	....	....	....	....	....	....	....	....	....	....	....	....
1991-92	Tellford Tigers	Britain	DID NOT PLAY – COACHING																									
	NHL Totals		**386**	**78**	**95**	**173**	**69**	**70**	**139**	**230**	**12**	**2**	**14**	**672**	**11.6**	**285**	**54**	**339**	**48**		**19**	**4**	**7**	**11**	**9**	**0**	**0**	**0**

QMJHL First All-Star Team (1977) • Memorial Cup All-Star Team (1977)

Traded to **NY Rangers** by **Vancouver** with Jeff Bandura for Mario Marois and Jim Mayer, November 11, 1980. Traded to **Quebec** by **NY Rangers** with Dean Talafous (later changed to Pat Hickey when Talafous decided to retire) for Robbie Ftorek and Quebec's 8th round choice (Brian Glynn) in 1982 Entry Draft, December 30, 1981. Signed as a free agent by **Buffalo**, September 11, 1982. Signed as a free agent by **Vancouver**, September 26, 1983. Signed as a free agent by **Philadelphia**, October, 1986.

• GILLIS, MIKE

Mike Gillis LW – L. 6'1", 195 lbs. b: Sudbury, Ont., 12/1/1958. Colorado's 1st choice, 5th overall, in 1978 Amateur Draft.

Season	Club	League	GP	G	A	Pts	AG	AA	APts	PIM	PP	SH	GW	S	%	TGF	PGF	TGA	PGA	+/–	GP	G	A	Pts	PIM	PP	SH	GW
1975-76	Kingston Canadians	OHA	64	16	45	61	....	....	....	34	....	....	....	....	....	....	....	....	....	....	....	....	....	....	....	....	....	....
1976-77	Kingston Canadians	OHA	4	2	2	4	....	....	....	4	....	....	....	....	....	....	....	....	....	....	....	....	....	....	....	....	....	....
1977-78	Kingston Canadians	OHA	43	21	46	67	....	....	....	86	....	....	....	....	....	....	....	....	....	....	5	3	12	15	0	....	....	....
1978-79	**Colorado Rockies**	**NHL**	**30**	**1**	**7**	**8**	**1**	**5**	**6**	**6**	**0**	**0**	**0**	**54**	**1.9**	**14**	**5**	**27**	**0**	**–18**	....	....	....	....	....	....	....	....
	Philadelphia Firebirds	AHL	2	0	0	0	....	....	....	0	....	....	....	....	....	....	....	....	....	....	....	....	....	....	....	....	....	....

Season	Club	League	GP	G	A	Pts	AG	AA	APts	PIM	PP	SH	GW	S	%	TGF	PGF	TGA	PGA	+/–	GP	G	A	Pts	PIM	PP	SH	GW
			REGULAR SEASON																		PLAYOFFS							
1979-80	**Colorado Rockies**	**NHL**	**40**	**4**	**5**	**9**	**4**	**4**	**8**	**22**	**1**	**0**	**0**	**56**	**7.1**	**13**	**1**	**30**	**0**	**–18**	....	....	....	....	....	....	....	....
	Fort Worth Texans	CHL	29	9	13	22	....	....	....	43	....	....	....	....	....	....	....	....	....	....	....	....	....	....	....	....	....	....
1980-81	**Colorado Rockies**	**NHL**	**51**	**11**	**7**	**18**	**9**	**5**	**14**	**54**	**1**	**0**	**2**	**78**	**14.1**	**28**	**3**	**46**	**0**	**–21**	....	....	....	....	....	....	....	....
	Boston Bruins	**NHL**	**17**	**2**	**4**	**6**	**2**	**3**	**5**	**15**	**0**	**0**	**0**	**26**	**7.7**	**12**	**0**	**14**	**0**	**–2**	**1**	**0**	**0**	**0**	**0**	**0**	**0**	**0**
1981-82	**Boston Bruins**	**NHL**	**53**	**9**	**8**	**17**	**7**	**5**	**12**	**54**	**0**	**0**	**0**	**66**	**13.6**	**39**	**1**	**29**	**1**	**+10**	**11**	**1**	**2**	**3**	**6**	**0**	**0**	**0**
1982-83	**Boston Bruins**	**NHL**	**5**	**0**	**1**	**1**	**0**	**1**	**1**	**0**	**0**	**0**	**0**	**2**	**0.0**	**1**	**0**	**0**	**0**	**+1**	**12**	**1**	**3**	**4**	**2**	**0**	**0**	**0**
	Baltimore Skipjacks	AHL	74	32	81	113	....	....	....	33	....	....	....	....	....	....	....	....	....	....	....	....	....	....	....	....	....	....
1983-84	**Boston Bruins**	**NHL**	**50**	**6**	**11**	**17**	**5**	**7**	**12**	**35**	**0**	**0**	**1**	**59**	**10.2**	**25**	**3**	**29**	**0**	**–7**	**3**	**0**	**0**	**0**	**2**	**0**	**0**	**0**
	Hershey Bears	AHL	26	8	21	29	....	....	....	13	....	....	....	....	....	....	....	....	....	....	....	....	....	....	....	....	....	....
	NHL Totals		**246**	**33**	**43**	**76**	**28**	**30**	**58**	**186**	**2**	**0**	**3**	**341**	**9.7**	**132**	**13**	**175**	**1**		**27**	**2**	**5**	**7**	**10**	**0**	**0**	**0**

Claimed by **Colorado** as a fill-in during Expansion Draft, June 13, 1979. Traded to **Boston** by **Colorado** for Bob Miller, February 18, 1981.

• GILLIS, PAUL

Paul Gillis C – L. 5'11", 198 lbs. b: Toronto, Ont., 12/31/1963. Quebec's 2nd choice, 34th overall, in 1982 Entry Draft.

Season	Club	League	GP	G	A	Pts	AG	AA	APts	PIM	PP	SH	GW	S	%	TGF	PGF	TGA	PGA	+/–	GP	G	A	Pts	PIM	PP	SH	GW
1979-80	St. Michael's Buzzers	Jr. B	44	20	36	56	....	....	....	114	....	....	....	....	....	....	....	....	....	....	....	....	....	....	....	....	....	....
1980-81	Niagara Falls Flyers	OHA	59	14	19	33	....	....	....	165	....	....	....	....	....	....	....	....	....	....	....	....	....	....	....	....	....	....
1981-82	Niagara Falls Flyers	OHL	65	27	62	89	....	....	....	247	....	....	....	....	....	....	....	....	....	....	5	1	5	6	26	....	....	....
1982-83	North Bay Centennials	OHL	61	34	52	86	....	....	....	151	....	....	....	....	....	....	....	....	....	....	6	1	3	4	26	....	....	....
	Quebec Nordiques	**NHL**	**7**	**0**	**2**	**2**	**0**	**1**	**1**	**2**	**0**	**0**	**0**	**1**	**0.0**	**2**	**0**	**3**	**0**	**–1**	....	....	....	....	....	....	....	....
1983-84	**Quebec Nordiques**	**NHL**	**57**	**8**	**9**	**17**	**6**	**6**	**12**	**59**	**0**	**0**	**1**	**58**	**13.8**	**32**	**0**	**37**	**15**	**+10**	**1**	**0**	**0**	**0**	**2**	**0**	**0**	**0**
	Fredericton Express	AHL	18	7	8	15	....	....	....	47	....	....	....	....	....	....	....	....	....	....	....	....	....	....	....	....	....	....
1984-85	**Quebec Nordiques**	**NHL**	**77**	**14**	**28**	**42**	**11**	**19**	**30**	**168**	**0**	**0**	**3**	**104**	**13.5**	**59**	**1**	**72**	**26**	**+12**	**18**	**1**	**7**	**8**	**73**	**0**	**0**	**0**
1985-86	**Quebec Nordiques**	**NHL**	**80**	**19**	**24**	**43**	**15**	**16**	**31**	**203**	**0**	**2**	**2**	**136**	**14.0**	**53**	**0**	**95**	**40**	**–2**	**3**	**0**	**2**	**2**	**14**	**0**	**0**	**0**
1986-87	**Quebec Nordiques**	**NHL**	**76**	**13**	**26**	**39**	**11**	**19**	**30**	**267**	**0**	**0**	**3**	**118**	**11.0**	**48**	**0**	**75**	**22**	**–5**	**13**	**2**	**4**	**6**	**65**	**0**	**0**	**0**
1987-88	**Quebec Nordiques**	**NHL**	**80**	**7**	**10**	**17**	**6**	**7**	**13**	**164**	**1**	**0**	**0**	**82**	**8.5**	**30**	**4**	**96**	**41**	**–29**	....	....	....	....	....	....	....	....
1988-89	**Quebec Nordiques**	**NHL**	**79**	**15**	**25**	**40**	**13**	**18**	**31**	**163**	**5**	**0**	**1**	**97**	**15.5**	**63**	**17**	**95**	**35**	**–14**	....	....	....	....	....	....	....	....
1989-90	**Quebec Nordiques**	**NHL**	**71**	**8**	**14**	**22**	**7**	**10**	**17**	**234**	**0**	**1**	**0**	**68**	**11.8**	**28**	**1**	**80**	**29**	**–24**	....	....	....	....	....	....	....	....
1990-91	**Quebec Nordiques**	**NHL**	**49**	**3**	**8**	**11**	**3**	**6**	**9**	**91**	**0**	**1**	**0**	**57**	**5.3**	**20**	**0**	**49**	**10**	**–19**	....	....	....	....	....	....	....	....
	Chicago Blackhawks	**NHL**	**13**	**0**	**5**	**5**	**0**	**4**	**4**	**53**	**0**	**0**	**0**	**9**	**0.0**	**6**	**0**	**5**	**0**	**+1**	**2**	**0**	**0**	**0**	**2**	**0**	**0**	**0**
1991-92	**Chicago Blackhawks**	**NHL**	**2**	**0**	**0**	**0**	**0**	**0**	**0**	**6**	**0**	**0**	**0**	**1**	**0.0**	**0**	**0**	**3**	**0**	**–3**	....	....	....	....	....	....	....	....
	Indianapolis Ice	IHL	42	10	15	25	....	....	....	170	....	....	....	....	....	....	....	....	....	....	....	....	....	....	....	....	....	....
	Hartford Whalers	**NHL**	**12**	**0**	**2**	**2**	**0**	**1**	**1**	**48**	**0**	**0**	**0**	**6**	**0.0**	**2**	**0**	**4**	**2**	**0**	**5**	**0**	**1**	**1**	**0**	**0**	**0**	**0**
1992-93	**Hartford Whalers**	**NHL**	**21**	**1**	**1**	**2**	**1**	**1**	**2**	**40**	**0**	**0**	**0**	**8**	**12.5**	**2**	**0**	**6**	**2**	**–2**	....	....	....	....	....	....	....	....
	NHL Totals		**624**	**88**	**154**	**242**	**73**	**108**	**181**	**1498**	**6**	**4**	**10**	**745**	**11.8**	**345**	**23**	**620**	**222**		**42**	**3**	**14**	**17**	**156**	**0**	**0**	**0**

Traded to **Chicago** by **Quebec** with Dan Vincelette for Ryan McGill and Mike McNeil, March 5, 1991. Traded to **Hartford** by **Chicago** for future considerations, January 27, 1992.

• GILMOUR, DOUG

Doug Gilmour C – L. 5'11", 172 lbs. b: Kingston, Ont., 6/25/1963. St. Louis' 4th choice, 134th overall, in 1982 Entry Draft.

Season	Club	League	GP	G	A	Pts	AG	AA	APts	PIM	PP	SH	GW	S	%	TGF	PGF	TGA	PGA	+/–	GP	G	A	Pts	PIM	PP	SH	GW
1980-81	Cornwall Royals	QMJHL	51	12	23	35	....	....	....	35	....	....	....	....	....	....	....	....	....	....	....	....	....	....	....	....	....	....
	Canada	WJC-A	5	0	0	0	....	....	....	0	....	....	....	....	....	....	....	....	....	....	....	....	....	....	....	....	....	....
1981-82	Cornwall Royals	OHL	67	46	73	119	....	....	....	42	....	....	....	....	....	....	....	....	....	....	5	6	9	15	2	....	....	....
1982-83	Cornwall Royals	OHL	68	70	*107	*177	....	....	....	62	....	....	....	....	....	....	....	....	....	....	8	8	10	18	16	....	....	....
1983-84	**St. Louis Blues**	**NHL**	**80**	**25**	**28**	**53**	**20**	**19**	**39**	**57**	**3**	**1**	**1**	**157**	**15.9**	**74**	**12**	**75**	**19**	**+6**	**11**	**2**	**9**	**11**	**10**	**1**	**0**	**1**
1984-85	**St. Louis Blues**	**NHL**	**78**	**21**	**36**	**57**	**17**	**24**	**41**	**49**	**3**	**1**	**3**	**162**	**13.0**	**75**	**15**	**85**	**28**	**+3**	**3**	**1**	**1**	**2**	**2**	**0**	**0**	**0**
1985-86	**St. Louis Blues**	**NHL**	**74**	**25**	**28**	**53**	**20**	**19**	**39**	**41**	**2**	**1**	**5**	**183**	**13.7**	**80**	**17**	**93**	**27**	**–3**	**19**	**9**	**12**	***21**	**25**	**1**	**2**	**2**
1986-87	**St. Louis Blues**	**NHL**	**80**	**42**	**63**	**105**	**36**	**46**	**82**	**58**	**17**	**1**	**2**	**207**	**20.3**	**134**	**57**	**104**	**25**	**–2**	**6**	**2**	**2**	**4**	**16**	**1**	**0**	**1**
1987-88	Canada	C Cup	8	2	0	2	....	....	....	4	....	....	....	....	....	....	....	....	....	....	....	....	....	....	....	....	....	....
	St. Louis Blues	**NHL**	**72**	**36**	**50**	**86**	**31**	**36**	**67**	**59**	**19**	**2**	**4**	**163**	**22.1**	**110**	**58**	**91**	**26**	**–13**	**10**	**3**	**14**	**17**	**18**	**1**	**0**	**0**
1988-89	**Calgary Flames**	**NHL**	**72**	**26**	**59**	**85**	**22**	**42**	**64**	**44**	**11**	**0**	**5**	**161**	**16.1**	**132**	**50**	**53**	**16**	**+45**	**22**	**11**	**11**	**22**	**20**	**3**	**0**	**3**
1989-90	Calgary Flames	FrTour	4	1	3	4	....	....	....	4	....	....	....	....	....	....	....	....	....	....	....	....	....	....	....	....	....	....
	Calgary Flames	**NHL**	**78**	**24**	**67**	**91**	**21**	**48**	**69**	**54**	**12**	**1**	**3**	**152**	**15.8**	**129**	**48**	**98**	**37**	**+20**	**6**	**3**	**1**	**4**	**8**	**0**	**0**	**1**
	Canada	WEC-A	9	1	4	5	....	....	....	18	....	....	....	....	....	....	....	....	....	....	....	....	....	....	....	....	....	....
1990-91	**Calgary Flames**	**NHL**	**78**	**20**	**61**	**81**	**18**	**46**	**64**	**144**	**2**	**2**	**5**	**135**	**14.8**	**115**	**26**	**98**	**36**	**+27**	**7**	**1**	**1**	**2**	**0**	**0**	**0**	**1**
1991-92	**Calgary Flames**	**NHL**	**38**	**11**	**27**	**38**	**10**	**20**	**30**	**46**	**4**	**1**	**1**	**64**	**17.2**	**54**	**20**	**37**	**15**	**+12**	....	....	....	....	....	....	....	....
	Toronto Maple Leafs	**NHL**	**40**	**15**	**34**	**49**	**14**	**26**	**40**	**32**	**6**	**0**	**3**	**104**	**14.4**	**69**	**21**	**51**	**16**	**+13**	....	....	....	....	....	....	....	....
1992-93	**Toronto Maple Leafs**	**NHL**	**83**	**32**	**95**	**127**	**27**	**65**	**92**	**100**	**15**	**3**	**2**	**211**	**15.2**	**170**	**83**	**85**	**30**	**+32**	**21**	**10**	***25**	**35**	**30**	**4**	**0**	**1**
1993-94	**Toronto Maple Leafs**	**NHL**	**83**	**27**	**84**	**111**	**25**	**65**	**90**	**105**	**10**	**1**	**3**	**167**	**16.2**	**157**	**64**	**100**	**32**	**+25**	**18**	**6**	**22**	**28**	**42**	**5**	**0**	**1**
1994-95	Rapperswil	Switz.	9	2	13	15	....	....	....	16	....	....	....	....	....	....	....	....	....	....	....	....	....	....	....	....	....	....
	Toronto Maple Leafs	**NHL**	**44**	**10**	**23**	**33**	**18**	**34**	**52**	**26**	**3**	**0**	**1**	**73**	**13.7**	**55**	**23**	**49**	**12**	**–5**	**7**	**0**	**6**	**6**	**6**	**0**	**0**	**0**
1995-96	**Toronto Maple Leafs**	**NHL**	**81**	**32**	**40**	**72**	**32**	**33**	**65**	**77**	**10**	**2**	**3**	**180**	**17.8**	**112**	**54**	**91**	**28**	**–5**	**6**	**1**	**7**	**8**	**12**	**1**	**0**	**0**
1996-97	**Toronto Maple Leafs**	**NHL**	**61**	**15**	**45**	**60**	**16**	**40**	**56**	**46**	**2**	**1**	**1**	**103**	**14.6**	**92**	**27**	**88**	**18**	**–5**	....	....	....	....	....	....	....	....
	New Jersey Devils	**NHL**	**20**	**7**	**15**	**22**	**7**	**13**	**20**	**22**	**2**	**0**	**0**	**40**	**17.5**	**29**	**9**	**14**	**1**	**+7**	**10**	**0**	**4**	**4**	**14**	**0**	**0**	**0**
1997-98	**New Jersey Devils**	**NHL**	**63**	**13**	**40**	**53**	**15**	**39**	**54**	**68**	**3**	**0**	**5**	**94**	**13.8**	**81**	**35**	**51**	**15**	**+10**	**6**	**5**	**2**	**7**	**4**	**1**	**0**	**1**
	NHL Totals		**1125**	**381**	**795**	**1176**	**349**	**615**	**964**	**1028**	**124**	**17**	**47**	**2356**	**16.2**	**1668**	**619**	**1263**	**381**		**152**	**54**	**117**	**171**	**207**	**18**	**2**	**12**

OHL First All-Star Team (1983) • Won Frank J. Selke Trophy (1993)

Played in NHL All-Star Game (1993, 1994)

Traded to **Calgary** by **St. Louis** with Mark Hunter, Steve Bozek and Michael Dark for Mike Bullard, Craig Coxe and Tim Corkery, September 6, 1988. Traded to **Toronto** by **Calgary** with Jamie Macoun, Ric Nattress, Kent Manderville and Rick Wamsley for Gary Leeman, Alexander Godynyuk, Jeff Reese, Michel Petit and Craig Berube, January 2, 1992. Traded to **New Jersey** by **Toronto** with Dave Ellett and future considerations for Jason Smith, Steve Sullivan and the rights to Alyn McCauley, February 25, 1997. Signed as a free agent by **Chicago**, July 3, 1998.

• GINGRAS, GASTON

Gaston Gingras D – L. 6'1", 200 lbs. b: Temiscamingue, Que., 2/13/1959. Montreal's 1st choice, 27th overall, in 1979 Entry Draft.

Season	Club	League	GP	G	A	Pts	AG	AA	APts	PIM	PP	SH	GW	S	%	TGF	PGF	TGA	PGA	+/–	GP	G	A	Pts	PIM	PP	SH	GW
1974-75	North Bay Trappers	Jr. B	41	11	27	38	....	....	....	74	....	....	....	....	....	....	....	....	....	....	....	....	....	....	....	....	....	....
1975-76	Kitchener Rangers	OHA	66	13	31	44	....	....	....	94	....	....	....	....	....	....	....	....	....	....	....	....	....	....	....	....	....	....
1976-77	Kitchener Rangers	OHA	59	13	62	75	....	....	....	134	....	....	....	....	....	....	....	....	....	....	3	0	1	1	6	....	....	....
1977-78	Kitchener Rangers	OHA	32	13	24	37	....	....	....	31	....	....	....	....	....	....	....	....	....	....	....	....	....	....	....	....	....	....
	Hamilton Fincups	OHA	29	11	19	30	....	....	....	37	....	....	....	....	....	....	....	....	....	....	15	3	11	14	13	....	....	....
1978-79	Birmingham Bulls	WHA	60	13	21	34	....	....	....	35	....	....	....	....	....	....	....	....	....	....	....	....	....	....	....	....	....	....
1979-80	**Montreal Canadiens**	**NHL**	**34**	**3**	**7**	**10**	**3**	**5**	**8**	**18**	**2**	**0**	**1**	**60**	**5.0**	**45**	**14**	**21**	**1**	**+11**	**10**	**1**	**6**	**7**	**8**	**0**	**0**	**0**
	Nova Scotia Voyageurs	AHL	30	11	27	38	....	....	....	17	....	....	....	....	....	....	....	....	....	....	....	....	....	....	....	....	....	....
1980-81	**Montreal Canadiens**	**NHL**	**55**	**5**	**16**	**21**	**4**	**11**	**15**	**22**	**3**	**0**	**1**	**133**	**3.8**	**65**	**28**	**35**	**3**	**+5**	**1**	**1**	**0**	**1**	**0**	**1**	**0**	**0**
1981-82	**Montreal Canadiens**	**NHL**	**34**	**6**	**18**	**24**	**5**	**12**	**17**	**28**	**3**	**0**	**3**	**89**	**6.7**	**57**	**21**	**30**	**4**	**+10**	**5**	**0**	**1**	**1**	**0**	**0**	**0**	**0**
1982-83	**Montreal Canadiens**	**NHL**	**22**	**1**	**8**	**9**	**1**	**6**	**7**	**8**	**1**	**0**	**1**	**60**	**1.7**	**40**	**11**	**21**	**2**	**+10**	....	....	....	....	....	....	....	....
	Toronto Maple Leafs	**NHL**	**45**	**10**	**18**	**28**	**8**	**12**	**20**	**10**	**4**	**0**	**1**	**95**	**10.5**	**57**	**22**	**39**	**11**	**+7**	**3**	**1**	**2**	**3**	**2**	**0**	**0**	**0**
1983-84	**Toronto Maple Leafs**	**NHL**	**59**	**7**	**20**	**27**	**6**	**14**	**20**	**16**	**4**	**0**	**0**	**125**	**5.6**	**53**	**18**	**77**	**12**	**–30**	....	....	....	....	....	....	....	....
1984-85	**Toronto Maple Leafs**	**NHL**	**5**	**0**	**2**	**2**	**0**	**1**	**1**	**0**	**0**	**0**	**0**	**17**	**0.0**	**4**	**3**	**10**	**2**	**–7**	....	....	....	....	....	....	....	....
	St. Catharines Saints	AHL	36	7	12	19	....	....	....	13	....	....	....	....	....	....	....	....	....	....	....	....	....	....	....	....	....	....
	Sherbrooke Canadiens	AHL	21	3	14	17	....	....	....	6	....	....	....	....	....	....	....	....	....	....	17	5	4	9	4	....	....	....
1985-86	**Montreal Canadiens**	**NHL**	**34**	**8**	**18**	**26**	**6**	**12**	**18**	**12**	**7**	**0**	**0**	**77**	**10.4**	**39**	**16**	**33**	**0**	**–10**	**11**	**2**	**3**	**5**	**4**	**1**	**0**	**0**
	Sherbrooke Canadiens	AHL	42	11	20	31	....	....	....	14	....	....	....	....	....	....	....	....	....	....	....	....	....	....	....	....	....	....
1986-87	**Montreal Canadiens**	**NHL**	**66**	**11**	**34**	**45**	**10**	**25**	**35**	**21**	**7**	**0**	**2**	**173**	**6.4**	**91**	**37**	**56**	**0**	**–2**	**5**	**0**	**2**	**2**	**0**	**0**	**0**	**0**
1987-88	**Montreal Canadiens**	**NHL**	**2**	**0**	**1**	**1**	**0**	**1**	**1**	**2**	**0**	**0**	**0**	**2**	**0.0**	**1**	**0**	**0**	**0**	**+1**	....	....	....	....	....	....	....	....
	St. Louis Blues	**NHL**	**68**	**7**	**22**	**29**	**6**	**16**	**22**	**18**	**3**	**0**	**0**	**131**	**5.3**	**84**	**34**	**52**	**2**	**0**	**10**	**1**	**3**	**4**	**4**	**0**	**0**	**0**
1988-89	**St. Louis Blues**	**NHL**	**52**	**3**	**10**	**13**	**3**	**7**	**10**	**6**	**2**	**0**	**0**	**98**	**3.1**	**58**	**19**	**44**	**6**	**+1**	**7**	**0**	**1**	**1**	**2**	**0**	**0**	**0**
1989-90	EHC Biel	Switz.	36	17	20	37	....	....	....	....	....	....	....	....	....	....	....	....	....	....	6	3	3	6	....	....	....	....
1990-91	EHC Biel	Switz.	13	1	7	8	....	....	....	....	....	....	....	....	....	....	....	....	....	....	....	....	....	....	....	....	....	....
1991-92	HC Lugano	Switz.	38	10	19	29	....	....	....	24	....	....	....	....	....	....	....	....	....	....	....	....	....	....	....	....	....	....
1992-93	Val Gardena	Italy	19	3	24	27	....	....	....	16	....	....	....	....	....	....	....	....	....	....	....	....	....	....	....	....	....	....

Season	Club	League	REGULAR SEASON																		PLAYOFFS							
			GP	G	A	Pts	AG	AA	APts	PIM	PP	SH	GW	S	%	TGF	PGF	TGA	PGA	+/–	GP	G	A	Pts	PIM	PP	SH	GW
1993-94	Val Gardena	Italy	21	3	14	17	....	....	....	14	....	....	....	....	....	....	....	....	....	....	....	....	....	....	....	....	....	....
1994-95	Fredericton Canadiens	AHL	19	3	6	9	....	....	....	4	....	....	....	....	....	....	....	....	....	....	17	2	12	14	8	....	....	....
1995-96	Fredericton Canadiens	AHL	39	2	21	23	....	....	....	18	....	....	....	....	....	....	....	....	....	....	....	....	....	....	....	....	....	....
	NHL Totals		**476**	**61**	**174**	**235**	**52**	**122**	**174**	**161**	**36**	**0**	**9**	**1060**	**5.8**	**594**	**223**	**418**	**43**		**52**	**6**	**18**	**24**	**20**	**2**	**0**	**0**
	Other Major League Totals		60	13	21	34	....	....	....	35	....	....	....	....	....	....	....	....	....	....	....	....	....	....	....	....	....	....

Signed as an underage free agent by **Birmingham** (WHA), June, 1978. Traded to **Toronto** by **Montreal** for Toronto's 2nd round choice (Benoit Brunet) in 1986 Entry Draft, December 17, 1982. Traded to **Montreal** by **Toronto** for Larry Langdon, February 14, 1985. Traded to **St. Louis** by **Montreal** for Larry Trader and future considerations, October 13, 1987.

• GIRARD, BOB

Bob Girard LW – L. 6', 180 lbs. b: Montreal, Que., 4/12/1949.

Season	Club	League	GP	G	A	Pts	AG	AA	APts	PIM	PP	SH	GW	S	%	TGF	PGF	TGA	PGA	+/–	GP	G	A	Pts	PIM	PP	SH	GW
1972-73	Amqui Aces	QSHL	....	18	33	51	....	....	....	....	....	....	....	....	....	....	....	....	....	....	....	....	....	....	....	....	....	....
1973-74	Charlotte Checkers	SHL	23	5	17	22	....	....	....	12	....	....	....	....	....	....	....	....	....	....	....	....	....	....	....	....	....	....
	Salt Lake Golden Eagles	WHL	50	2	19	21	....	....	....	37	....	....	....	....	....	....	....	....	....	....	1	0	0	0	2	....	....	....
1974-75	Salt Lake Golden Eagles	CHL	74	13	32	45	....	....	....	60	....	....	....	....	....	....	....	....	....	....	11	0	2	2	10	....	....	....
1975-76	**California Golden Seals**	**NHL**	**80**	**16**	**26**	**42**	**15**	**20**	**35**	**54**	**3**	**0**	**1**	**137**	**11.7**	**70**	**18**	**74**	**19**	**–3**	....	....	....	....	....	....	....	....
1976-77	**Cleveland Barons**	**NHL**	**68**	**11**	**10**	**21**	**11**	**8**	**19**	**33**	**1**	**1**	**1**	**101**	**10.9**	**37**	**5**	**70**	**14**	**–24**	....	....	....	....	....	....	....	....
	Salt Lake Golden Eagles	CHL	4	2	6	8	....	....	....	0	....	....	....	....	....	....	....	....	....	....	....	....	....	....	....	....	....	....
1977-78	**Cleveland Barons**	**NHL**	**25**	**0**	**4**	**4**	**0**	**3**	**3**	**11**	**0**	**0**	**0**	**24**	**0.0**	**5**	**0**	**22**	**9**	**–8**	....	....	....	....	....	....	....	....
	Washington Capitals	**NHL**	**52**	**9**	**14**	**23**	**9**	**11**	**20**	**6**	**1**	**0**	**2**	**42**	**21.4**	**47**	**4**	**47**	**1**	**–3**	....	....	....	....	....	....	....	....
1978-79	**Washington Capitals**	**NHL**	**79**	**9**	**15**	**24**	**8**	**11**	**19**	**36**	**0**	**0**	**0**	**59**	**15.3**	**42**	**0**	**79**	**22**	**–15**	....	....	....	....	....	....	....	....
1979-80	**Washington Capitals**	**NHL**	**1**	**0**	**0**	**0**	**0**	**0**	**0**	**0**	**0**	**0**	**0**	**0**	**0.0**	**0**	**0**	**1**	**1**	**0**	....	....	....	....	....	....	....	....
	Hershey Bears	AHL	74	15	26	41	....	....	....	63	....	....	....	....	....	....	....	....	....	....	16	5	5	10	6	....	....	....
	NHL Totals		**305**	**45**	**69**	**114**	**43**	**53**	**96**	**140**	**5**	**1**	**4**	**363**	**12.4**	**201**	**27**	**293**	**66**		....	....	....	....	....	....	....	....

Signed as a free agent by **California**, September, 1973. Transferred to **Cleveland** after **California** franchise relocated, August 26, 1976. Traded to **Washington** by **Cleveland** with Cleveland's 2nd round choice (Paul McKinnon) in 1978 Amateur Draft for Walt McKechnie, December 9, 1977. Claimed by **Washington** as a fill-in during Expansion Draft, June 13, 1979.

• GIROUX, LARRY

Larry "Buffalo Head" Giroux D – R. 6', 190 lbs. b: Weyburn, Sask., 8/28/1951.

Season	Club	League	GP	G	A	Pts	AG	AA	APts	PIM	PP	SH	GW	S	%	TGF	PGF	TGA	PGA	+/–	GP	G	A	Pts	PIM	PP	SH	GW
1967-68	Weyburn Red Wings	WCJHL	2	0	0	0	....	....	....	0	....	....	....	....	....	....	....	....	....	....	....	....	....	....	....	....	....	....
1968-69	Weyburn Red Wings	SJHL	STATISTICS NOT AVAILABLE																									
1969-70	Weyburn Red Wings	SJHL	36	14	33	47	....	....	....	96	....	....	....	....	....	....	....	....	....	....	....	....	....	....	....	....	....	....
1970-71	Swift Current Broncos	WCJHL	62	14	28	42	....	....	....	173	....	....	....	....	....	....	....	....	....	....	....	....	....	....	....	....	....	....
1971-72	Kimberley Dynamiters	WIHL	STATISTICS NOT AVAILABLE																									
	Des Moines Oak Leafs	IHL	5	0	1	1	....	....	....	6	....	....	....	....	....	....	....	....	....	....	....	....	....	....	....	....	....	....
1972-73	Denver Spurs	WHL	2	0	1	1	....	....	....	2	....	....	....	....	....	....	....	....	....	....	....	....	....	....	....	....	....	....
	Fort Worth Wings	CHL	72	5	42	47	....	....	....	130	....	....	....	....	....	....	....	....	....	....	4	0	0	0	24	....	....	....
1973-74	**St. Louis Blues**	**NHL**	**74**	**5**	**17**	**22**	**5**	**15**	**20**	**59**	**2**	**0**	**1**	**131**	**3.8**	**63**	**18**	**65**	**6**	**–14**	....	....	....	....	....	....	....	....
1974-75	**Kansas City Scouts**	**NHL**	**21**	**0**	**6**	**6**	**0**	**5**	**5**	**24**	**0**	**0**	**0**	**27**	**0.0**	**21**	**7**	**38**	**4**	**–20**	....	....	....	....	....	....	....	....
	Denver Spurs	CHL	10	1	6	7	....	....	....	37	....	....	....	....	....	....	....	....	....	....	....	....	....	....	....	....	....	....
	Detroit Red Wings	**NHL**	**39**	**2**	**20**	**22**	**2**	**16**	**18**	**60**	**1**	**0**	**1**	**56**	**3.6**	**56**	**24**	**57**	**15**	**–10**	....	....	....	....	....	....	....	....
	Virginia Wings	AHL	14	3	10	13	....	....	....	31	....	....	....	....	....	....	....	....	....	....	....	....	....	....	....	....	....	....
1975-76	**Detroit Red Wings**	**NHL**	**10**	**1**	**1**	**2**	**1**	**1**	**2**	**25**	**0**	**0**	**0**	**9**	**11.1**	**7**	**1**	**21**	**5**	**–10**	....	....	....	....	....	....	....	....
	New Haven Nighthawks	AHL	67	1	24	25	....	....	....	121	....	....	....	....	....	....	....	....	....	....	3	0	0	0	6	....	....	....
1976-77	**Detroit Red Wings**	**NHL**	**2**	**0**	**0**	**0**	**0**	**0**	**0**	**2**	**0**	**0**	**0**	**7**	**0.0**	**1**	**0**	**1**	**0**	**0**	....	....	....	....	....	....	....	....
	Kansas City Blues	CHL	75	11	34	45	....	....	....	194	....	....	....	....	....	....	....	....	....	....	10	0	*8	8	25	....	....	....
1977-78	**Detroit Red Wings**	**NHL**	**5**	**0**	**3**	**3**	**0**	**2**	**2**	**4**	**0**	**0**	**0**	**10**	**0.0**	**5**	**2**	**8**	**0**	**–5**	**2**	**0**	**0**	**0**	**2**	**0**	**0**	**0**
	Kansas City Red Wings	CHL	73	11	49	60	....	....	....	256	....	....	....	....	....	....	....	....	....	....	....	....	....	....	....	....	....	....
1978-79	**St. Louis Blues**	**NHL**	**73**	**5**	**22**	**27**	**5**	**17**	**22**	**111**	**0**	**0**	**1**	**107**	**4.7**	**72**	**5**	**111**	**19**	**–25**	....	....	....	....	....	....	....	....
1979-80	**St. Louis Blues**	**NHL**	**3**	**0**	**0**	**0**	**0**	**0**	**0**	**4**	**0**	**0**	**0**	**6**	**0.0**	**0**	**0**	**4**	**1**	**–3**	....	....	....	....	....	....	....	....
	Salt Lake Golden Eagles	CHL	5	0	1	1	....	....	....	2	....	....	....	....	....	....	....	....	....	....	....	....	....	....	....	....	....	....
	Hartford Whalers	**NHL**	**47**	**2**	**5**	**7**	**2**	**4**	**6**	**44**	**0**	**0**	**0**	**63**	**3.2**	**49**	**1**	**56**	**9**	**+1**	**3**	**0**	**0**	**0**	**2**	**0**	**0**	**0**
	Springfield Indians	AHL	5	0	1	1	....	....	....	14	....	....	....	....	....	....	....	....	....	....	....	....	....	....	....	....	....	....
	NHL Totals		**274**	**15**	**74**	**89**	**15**	**60**	**75**	**333**	**3**	**0**	**3**	**416**	**3.6**	**274**	**58**	**361**	**59**		**5**	**0**	**0**	**0**	**4**	**0**	**0**	**0**

CHL First All-Star Team (1973, 1978) • Named CHL's Top Defenseman (1978)

Signed as a free agent by **St. Louis**, October, 1972. Traded to **Kansas City** by **St. Louis** for Chris Evans and St. Louis' 4th round choice (Mike Liut) in 1976 Amateur Draft, October 29, 1974. Traded to **Detroit** by **Kansas City** with Bart Crashley and Ted Snell for Guy Charron and Claude Houde, December 14, 1974. Claimed by **St. Louis** from **Detroit** in Waiver Draft, October 9, 1978. Signed as a free agent by **Hartford**, December 13, 1979.

• GIROUX, PIERRE

Pierre Giroux C – R. 5'11", 185 lbs. b: Brownsburg, Que., 11/17/1955. Chicago's 4th choice, 61st overall, in 1975 Amateur Draft.

Season	Club	League	GP	G	A	Pts	AG	AA	APts	PIM	PP	SH	GW	S	%	TGF	PGF	TGA	PGA	+/–	GP	G	A	Pts	PIM	PP	SH	GW
1972-73	Sorel Black Hawks	QMJHL	48	4	13	17	....	....	....	25	....	....	....	....	....	....	....	....	....	....	....	....	....	....	....	....	....	....
1973-74	Sorel Black Hawks	QMJHL	41	4	11	15	....	....	....	23	....	....	....	....	....	....	....	....	....	....	....	....	....	....	....	....	....	....
1974-75	Hull Festivals	QMJHL	72	57	61	118	....	....	....	118	....	....	....	....	....	....	....	....	....	....	4	1	3	4	0	....	....	....
1975-76	Dallas Black Hawks	CHL	62	8	14	22	....	....	....	69	....	....	....	....	....	....	....	....	....	....	10	0	1	1	0	....	....	....
1976-77	Flint Generals	IHL	73	21	36	57	....	....	....	87	....	....	....	....	....	....	....	....	....	....	5	2	0	2	0	....	....	....
1977-78	Dallas Black Hawks	CHL	16	2	5	7	....	....	....	2	....	....	....	....	....	....	....	....	....	....	....	....	....	....	....	....	....	....
	Flint Generals	IHL	40	25	23	48	....	....	....	121	....	....	....	....	....	....	....	....	....	....	5	0	0	0	56	....	....	....
1978-79	New Brunswick Hawks	AHL	8	0	2	2	....	....	....	20	....	....	....	....	....	....	....	....	....	....	....	....	....	....	....	....	....	....
	Flint Generals	IHL	70	41	42	83	....	....	....	146	....	....	....	....	....	....	....	....	....	....	11	4	9	13	9	....	....	....
1979-80	Flint Generals	IHL	80	33	38	71	....	....	....	197	....	....	....	....	....	....	....	....	....	....	5	2	1	3	16	....	....	....
1980-81	Flint Generals	IHL	81	55	47	102	....	....	....	303	....	....	....	....	....	....	....	....	....	....	7	5	5	10	0	....	....	....
1981-82	New Haven Nighthawks	AHL	38	6	11	17	....	....	....	114	....	....	....	....	....	....	....	....	....	....	....	....	....	....	....	....	....	....
1982-83	**Los Angeles Kings**	**NHL**	**6**	**1**	**0**	**1**	**1**	**0**	**1**	**17**	**0**	**0**	**0**	**1**	**100.0**	**2**	**1**	**4**	**2**	**–1**	....	....	....	....	....	....	....	....
	New Haven Nighthawks	AHL	62	16	31	47	....	....	....	337	....	....	....	....	....	....	....	....	....	....	9	1	3	4	26	....	....	....
1983-84	Flint Generals	IHL	56	24	37	61	....	....	....	274	....	....	....	....	....	....	....	....	....	....	....	....	....	....	....	....	....	....
	NHL Totals		**6**	**1**	**0**	**1**	**1**	**0**	**1**	**17**	**0**	**0**	**0**	**1**	**100.0**	**2**	**1**	**4**	**2**		....	....	....	....	....	....	....	

IHL First All-Star Team (1981)

Signed as a free agent by **LA Kings**, August 5, 1982.

• GLADNEY, BOB

Bob Gladney D – L. 5'11", 185 lbs. b: Come-by-Chance, Nfld., 8/27/1957. Toronto's 3rd choice, 24th overall, in 1977 Amateur Draft

Season	Club	League	GP	G	A	Pts	AG	AA	APts	PIM	PP	SH	GW	S	%	TGF	PGF	TGA	PGA	+/–	GP	G	A	Pts	PIM	PP	SH	GW
1974-75	Oshawa Generals	OHA	68	12	50	62	....	....	....	04	....	....	....	....	....	....	....	....	....	....	....	....	....	....	....	....	....	....
1975-76	Oshawa Generals	OHA	66	26	52	78	....	....	....	47	....	....	....	....	....	....	....	....	....	....	5	1	4	5	2	....	....	....
1976-77	Oshawa Generals	OHA	54	20	42	62	....	....	....	56	....	....	....	....	....	....	....	....	....	....	....	....	....	....	....	....	....	....
1977-78	Saginaw Gears	IHL	69	15	50	65	....	....	....	35	....	....	....	....	....	....	....	....	....	....	5	1	4	5	2	....	....	....
1978-79	Saginaw Gears	IHL	67	16	42	58	....	....	....	51	....	....	....	....	....	....	....	....	....	....	4	2	3	5	2	....	....	....
1979-80	New Brunswick Hawks	AHL	26	0	6	6	....	....	....	18	....	....	....	....	....	....	....	....	....	....	10	0	2	2	4	....	....	....
1980-81	Saginaw Gears	IHL	78	12	71	83	....	....	....	54	....	....	....	....	....	....	....	....	....	....	13	3	9	12	12	....	....	....
1981-82	Saginaw Gears	IHL	17	4	9	13	....	....	....	10	....	....	....	....	....	....	....	....	....	....	....	....	....	....	....	....	....	....
	New Haven Nighthawks	AHL	63	7	26	33	....	....	....	12	....	....	....	....	....	....	....	....	....	....	4	1	2	3	0	....	....	....
1982-83	**Los Angeles Kings**	**NHL**	**1**	**0**	**0**	**0**	**0**	**0**	**0**	**2**	**0**	**0**	**0**	**2**	**0.0**	**0**	**0**	**2**	**0**	**–2**	....	....	....	....	....	....	....	....
	New Haven Nighthawks	AHL	80	19	47	66	....	....	....	22	....	....	....	....	....	....	....	....			12	0	7	7	8	....	....	....
1983-84	**Pittsburgh Penguins**	**NHL**	**13**	**1**	**5**	**6**	**1**	**3**	**4**	**2**	**0**	**0**	**0**	**15**	**6.7**	**13**	**3**	**12**	**1**	**–1**	....	....	....	....	....	....	....	....
	Baltimore Skipjacks	AHL	9	4	7	11	....	....	....	10	....	....	....	....	....	....	....	....	....	....	....	....	....	....	....	....	....	....
	NHL Totals		**14**	**1**	**5**	**6**	**1**	**3**	**4**	**4**	**0**	**0**	**0**	**17**	**5.9**	**13**	**3**	**14**	**1**		....	....	....	....	....	....	....	....

IHL Second All-Star Team (1981) • AHL First All-Star Team (1983)

Traded to **LA Kings** by **Toronto** with Toronto's 6th round choice (Kevin Stevens) in 1983 Entry Draft for Don Luce, August 10, 1981. Signed as a free agent by **Pittsburgh**, September 12, 1983.

• GLENNIE, BRIAN

Brian "Blunt" Glennie D – L. 6'1", 197 lbs. b: Toronto, Ont., 8/29/1946.

Season	Club	League	GP	G	A	Pts	AG	AA	APts	PIM	PP	SH	GW	S	%	TGF	PGF	TGA	PGA	+/–	GP	G	A	Pts	PIM	PP	SH	GW
1964-65	Toronto Marlboros	OHA	56	2	18	20	....	....	....	84	....	....	....	....	....	....	....	....	....	....	19	0	9	9	22	....	....	....
1965-66	Toronto Marlboros	OHA	48	5	18	23	....	....	....	134	....	....	....	....	....	....	....	....	....	....	14	0	4	4	57	....	....	....
1966-67	Toronto Marlboros	OHA	43	5	39	44	....	....	....	113	....	....	....	....	....	....	....	....	....	....	17	2	12	14	44	....	....	....
1967-68	Ottawa Nationals	OHA Sr.	30	2	10	12	....	....	....	20	....	....	....	....	....	....	....	....	....	....	....	....	....	....	....	....	....	....

Season	Club	League	GP	G	A	Pts	AG	AA	APts	PIM	PP	SH	GW	S	%	TGF	PGF	TGA	PGA	+/–	GP	G	A	Pts	PIM	PP	SH	GW
			REGULAR SEASON																		PLAYOFFS							
1967-68	Canada	Olympics	7	0	1	1	....	....	....	10	....	....	....	....	....	....	....	....	....	....	....	....	....	....	....	....	....	....
1968-69	Rochester Americans	AHL	15	1	1	2	....	....	....	16	....	....	....	....	....	....	....	....	....	....	....	....	....	....	....	....	....	....
	Tulsa Oilers	CHL	25	4	7	11	....	....	....	40	....	....	....	....	....	....	....	....	....	....	7	1	3	4	12	....	....	....
1969-70	**Toronto Maple Leafs**	**NHL**	**52**	**1**	**14**	**15**	**1**	**14**	**15**	**50**	**0**	**0**	**0**	**44**	**2.3**	**44**	**1**	**65**	**18**	**–4**	....	....	....	....	....	....	....	....
1970-71	**Toronto Maple Leafs**	**NHL**	**54**	**0**	**8**	**8**	**0**	**7**	**7**	**31**	**0**	**0**	**0**	**42**	**0.0**	**25**	**1**	**36**	**11**	**–1**	**3**	**0**	**0**	**0**	**0**	**0**	**0**	**0**
1971-72	**Toronto Maple Leafs**	**NHL**	**61**	**2**	**8**	**10**	**2**	**7**	**9**	**44**	**0**	**0**	**1**	**80**	**2.5**	**45**	**0**	**46**	**12**	**+11**	**5**	**0**	**0**	**0**	**25**	**0**	**0**	**0**
1972-73	Canada	Summit	DID NOT PLAY																									
	Toronto Maple Leafs	**NHL**	**44**	**1**	**10**	**11**	**1**	**8**	**9**	**54**	**0**	**0**	**0**	**74**	**1.4**	**50**	**2**	**61**	**15**	**+2**	....	....	....	....	....	....	....	....
1973-74	**Toronto Maple Leafs**	**NHL**	**65**	**4**	**18**	**22**	**4**	**16**	**20**	**100**	**1**	**1**	**0**	**65**	**6.2**	**76**	**2**	**68**	**21**	**+27**	**3**	**0**	**0**	**0**	**10**	**0**	**0**	**0**
1974-75	**Toronto Maple Leafs**	**NHL**	**63**	**1**	**7**	**8**	**1**	**5**	**6**	**110**	**0**	**0**	**0**	**55**	**1.8**	**54**	**2**	**75**	**18**	**–5**	....	....	....	....	....	....	....	....
1975-76	**Toronto Maple Leafs**	**NHL**	**69**	**0**	**8**	**8**	**0**	**6**	**6**	**75**	**0**	**0**	**0**	**65**	**0.0**	**49**	**0**	**51**	**12**	**+10**	**6**	**0**	**1**	**1**	**15**	**0**	**0**	**0**
1976-77	**Toronto Maple Leafs**	**NHL**	**69**	**1**	**10**	**11**	**1**	**8**	**9**	**73**	**0**	**0**	**0**	**63**	**1.6**	**64**	**1**	**87**	**23**	**–1**	**2**	**0**	**0**	**0**	**0**	**0**	**0**	**0**
1977-78	**Toronto Maple Leafs**	**NHL**	**77**	**2**	**15**	**17**	**2**	**12**	**14**	**62**	**0**	**0**	**0**	**64**	**3.1**	**69**	**5**	**63**	**23**	**+24**	**13**	**0**	**0**	**0**	**16**	**0**	**0**	**0**
1978-79	**Los Angeles Kings**	**NHL**	**18**	**2**	**2**	**4**	**2**	**2**	**4**	**22**	**0**	**0**	**1**	**11**	**18.2**	**18**	**0**	**21**	**5**	**+2**	....	....	....	....	....	....	....	....
	NHL Totals		**572**	**14**	**100**	**114**	**14**	**85**	**99**	**621**	**1**	**1**	**2**	**563**	**2.5**	**494**	**14**	**573**	**158**		**32**	**0**	**1**	**1**	**66**	**0**	**0**	**0**

Traded to **LA Kings** by **Toronto** with Scott Walker, Scott Garland, Toronto's 2nd round choice (Mark Hardy) in 1979 Entry Draft and future considerations for Dave Hutchison and Lorne Stamler, June 14, 1978.

• GLENNON, MATT
Matt Glennon LW – L. 6′, 185 lbs. b: Hull, MA, 9/20/1968. Boston's 7th choice, 119th overall, in 1987 Entry Draft.

Season	Club	League	GP	G	A	Pts	AG	AA	APts	PIM	PP	SH	GW	S	%	TGF	PGF	TGA	PGA	+/–	GP	G	A	Pts	PIM	PP	SH	GW
1985-86	Archbishop Williams	H.S.	18	18	22	40	....	....	....	6	....	....	....	....	....	....	....	....	....	....	....	....	....	....	....	....	....	....
1986-87	Archbishop Williams	H.S.	18	22	36	58	....	....	....	20	....	....	....	....	....	....	....	....	....	....	....	....	....	....	....	....	....	....
1987-88	Boston College	H.E.	16	3	3	6	....	....	....	16	....	....	....	....	....	....	....	....	....	....	....	....	....	....	....	....	....	....
1988-89	Boston College	H.E.	16	1	6	7	....	....	....	4	....	....	....	....	....	....	....	....	....	....	....	....	....	....	....	....	....	....
1989-90	Boston College	H.E.	31	7	11	18	....	....	....	16	....	....	....	....	....	....	....	....	....	....	....	....	....	....	....	....	....	....
1990-91	Boston College	H.E.	33	6	9	15	....	....	....	36	....	....	....	....	....	....	....	....	....	....	....	....	....	....	....	....	....	....
1991-92	**Boston Bruins**	**NHL**	**3**	**0**	**0**	**0**	**0**	**0**	**0**	**2**	**0**	**0**	**0**	**2**	**0.0**	**0**	**0**	**0**	**0**	**0**	....	....	....	....	....	....	....	....
	Maine Mariners	AHL	32	6	12	18	....	....	....	13	....	....	....	....	....	....	....	....	....	....	....	....	....	....	....	....	....	....
	Johnstown Chiefs	ECHL	30	9	46	55	....	....	....	77	....	....	....	....	....	....	....	....	....	....	6	2	4	6	25	....	....	....
1992-93	Providence Bruins	AHL	6	1	3	4	....	....	....	4	....	....	....	....	....	....	....	....	....	....	....	....	....	....	....	....	....	....
	NHL Totals		**3**	**0**	**0**	**0**	**0**	**0**	**0**	**2**	**0**	**0**	**0**	**2**	**0.0**	**0**	**0**	**0**	**0**		....	....	....	....	....	....	....	....

• GLOECKNER, LORRY
Lorry Gloeckner D – L. 6′2″, 210 lbs. b: Kindersley, Sask., 1/25/1956. Boston's 8th choice, 34th overall, in 1976 Amateur Draft.

Season	Club	League	GP	G	A	Pts	AG	AA	APts	PIM	PP	SH	GW	S	%	TGF	PGF	TGA	PGA	+/–	GP	G	A	Pts	PIM	PP	SH	GW
1972-73	Nanimo Clippers	BCJHL	35	3	15	18	....	....	....	45	....	....	....	....	....	....	....	....	....	....	....	....	....	....	....	....	....	....
	Victoria Cougars	WCJHL	4	0	0	0	....	....	....	4	....	....	....	....	....	....	....	....	....	....	....	....	....	....	....	....	....	....
1973-74	Victoria Cougars	WCJHL	33	1	7	8	....	....	....	45	....	....	....	....	....	....	....	....	....	....	....	....	....	....	....	....	....	....
1974-75	Victoria Cougars	WCJHL	65	2	12	14	....	....	....	79	....	....	....	....	....	....	....	....	....	....	....	....	....	....	....	....	....	....
1975-76	Victoria Cougars	WCJHL	71	7	48	55	....	....	....	123	....	....	....	....	....	....	....	....	....	....	15	0	8	8	38	....	....	....
1976-77	Victoria Cougars	WCJHL	58	5	22	27	....	....	....	52	....	....	....	....	....	....	....	....	....	....	4	0	2	2	0	....	....	....
1977-78			DID NOT PLAY																									
1978-79	**Detroit Red Wings**	**NHL**	**13**	**0**	**2**	**2**	**0**	**2**	**2**	**6**	**0**	**0**	**0**	**13**	**0.0**	**10**	**0**	**17**	**0**	**–7**	....	....	....	....	....	....	....	....
	Kansas City Red Wings	CHL	51	0	17	17	....	....	....	44	....	....	....	....	....	....	....	....	....	....	4	0	1	1	9	....	....	....
1979-80	Johnstown Red Wings	EHL	63	6	29	35	....	....	....	83	....	....	....	....	....	....	....	....	....	....	....	....	....	....	....	....	....	....
	NHL Totals		**13**	**0**	**2**	**2**	**0**	**2**	**2**	**6**	**0**	**0**	**0**	**13**	**0.0**	**10**	**0**	**17**	**0**		....	....	....	....	....	....	....	....

Signed as a free agent by **Detroit**, October 12, 1978.

• GLOOR, DAN
Dan Gloor C – L. 5′9″, 170 lbs. b: Stratford, Ont., 12/4/1952. Vancouver's 7th choice, 99th overall, in 1972 Amateur Draft.

Season	Club	League	GP	G	A	Pts	AG	AA	APts	PIM	PP	SH	GW	S	%	TGF	PGF	TGA	PGA	+/–	GP	G	A	Pts	PIM	PP	SH	GW
1969-70	Peterborough Petes	OHA	54	38	37	75	....	....	....	17	....	....	....	....	....	....	....	....	....	....	....	....	....	....	....	....	....	....
1970-71	Peterborough Petes	OHA	48	21	48	69	....	....	....	15	....	....	....	....	....	....	....	....	....	....	....	....	....	....	....	....	....	....
1971-72	Peterborough Petes	OHA	63	24	37	61	....	....	....	37	....	....	....	....	....	....	....	....	....	....	....	....	....	....	....	....	....	....
1972-73	Des Moines Capitols	IHL	73	42	51	93	....	....	....	45	....	....	....	....	....	....	....	....	....	....	3	0	1	1	0	....	....	....
1973-74	**Vancouver Canucks**	**NHL**	**2**	**0**	**0**	**0**	**0**	**0**	**0**	**0**	**0**	**0**	**0**	**0**	**0.0**	**0**	**0**	**2**	**0**	**–2**	....	....	....	....	....	....	....	....
	Seattle Totems	WHL	76	36	48	84	....	....	....	26	....	....	....	....	....	....	....	....	....	....	....	....	....	....	....	....	....	....
1974-75	Seattle Totems	CHL	73	21	36	57	....	....	....	28	....	....	....	....	....	....	....	....	....	....	....	....	....	....	....	....	....	....
1975-76	Tulsa Oilers	CHL	65	23	48	71	....	....	....	16	....	....	....	....	....	....	....	....	....	....	9	4	3	7	0	....	....	....
1976-77	Tulsa Oilers	CHL	76	33	43	76	....	....	....	18	....	....	....	....	....	....	....	....	....	....	9	4	5	9	4	....	....	....
1977-78			DID NOT PLAY – RETIRED																									
1978-79	Phoenix Roadrunners	PHL	40	11	21	32	....	....	....	30	....	....	....	....	....	....	....	....	....	....	....	....	....	....	....	....	....	....
	NHL Totals		**2**	**0**	**0**	**0**	**0**	**0**	**0**	**0**	**0**	**0**	**0**	**0**	**0.0**	**0**	**0**	**2**	**0**		....	....	....	....	....	....	....	....

Won Garry F. Longman Memorial Trophy (Top Rookie - IHL) (1973)

• GLOVER, HOWIE
Howie Glover RW – R. 5′11″, 180 lbs. b: Toronto, Ont., 2/14/1935.

Season	Club	League	GP	G	A	Pts	AG	AA	APts	PIM	PP	SH	GW	S	%	TGF	PGF	TGA	PGA	+/–	GP	G	A	Pts	PIM	PP	SH	GW
1952-53	Toronto Marlboros	OHA	19	1	4	5	....	....	....	9	....	....	....	....	....	....	....	....	....	....	6	0	1	1	6	....	....	....
1953-54	Toronto Marlboros	OHA	19	5	3	8	....	....	....	17	....	....	....	....	....	....	....	....	....	....	....	....	....	....	....	....	....	....
	Kitchener Greenshirts	OHA	42	17	9	26	....	....	....	53	....	....	....	....	....	....	....	....	....	....	4	0	0	0	7	....	....	....
1954-55	Kitchener–Barrie	OHA	48	10	9	19	....	....	....	72	....	....	....	....	....	....	....	....	....	....	....	....	....	....	....	....	....	....
1955-56	Toledo-Marion Mercurys	IHL	60	23	23	46	....	....	....	108	....	....	....	....	....	....	....	....	....	....	9	1	3	4	4	....	....	....
	Cleveland Barons	AHL	2	0	1	1	....	....	....	0	....	....	....	....	....	....	....	....	....	....	....	....	....	....	....	....	....	....
1956-57	North Bay Trappers	NOHA	DID NOT PLAY – SUSPENDED																									
1957-58	Winnipeg Warriors	WHL	67	38	34	72	....	....	....	72	....	....	....	....	....	....	....	....	....	....	7	4	1	5	8	....	....	....
1958-59	**Chicago Black Hawks**	**NHL**	**13**	**0**	**1**	**1**	**0**	**1**	**1**	**2**	....	....	....	....	....	....	....	....	....	....	....	....	....	....	....	....	....	....
	Calgary Stampeders	WHL	42	12	22	34	....	....	....	63	....	....	....	....	....	....	....	....	....	....	8	4	3	7	8	....	....	....
1959-60	Buffalo Bisons	AHL	68	31	25	56	....	....	....	95	....	....	....	....	....	....	....	....	....	....	....	....	....	....	....	....	....	....
1960-61	**Detroit Red Wings**	**NHL**	**66**	**21**	**8**	**29**	**26**	**8**	**34**	**46**	....	....	....	....	....	....	....	....	....	....	**11**	**1**	**2**	**3**	**2**	....	....	....
1961-62	**Detroit Red Wings**	**NHL**	**39**	**7**	**8**	**15**	**8**	**8**	**16**	**44**	....	....	....	....	....	....	....	....	....	....	....	....	....	....	....	....	....	....
1962-63	Pittsburgh Hornets	AHL	71	22	30	52	....	....	....	94	....	....	....	....	....	....	....	....	....	....	....	....	....	....	....	....	....	....
1963-64	**New York Rangers**	**NHL**	**25**	**1**	**0**	**1**	**1**	**0**	**1**	**9**	....	....	....	....	....	....	....	....	....	....	....	....	....	....	....	....	....	....
1964-65	Cleveland Barons	AHL	26	21	7	28	....	....	....	49	....	....	....	....	....	....	....	....	....	....	....	....	....	....	....	....	....	....
1965-66	Cleveland Barons	AHL	56	9	14	23	....	....	....	96	....	....	....	....	....	....	....	....	....	....	12	5	0	5	21	....	....	....
1966-67	Cleveland Barons	AHL	48	18	16	34	....	....	....	66	....	....	....	....	....	....	....	....	....	....	5	2	0	2	0	....	....	....
1967-68	Cleveland Barons	AHL	69	41	22	63	....	....	....	121	....	....	....	....	....	....	....	....	....	....	....	....	....	....	....	....	....	....
1968-69	**Montreal Canadiens**	**NHL**	**1**	**0**	**0**	**0**	**0**	**0**	**0**	**0**	**0**	**0**	**0**	**0**	**0.0**	**0**	**0**	**0**	**0**	**0**	....	....	....	....	....	....	....	....
	Cleveland Barons	AHL	73	24	35	59	....	....	....	44	....	....	....	....	....	....	....	....	....	....	5	2	1	3	4	....	....	....
1969-70	Cleveland Barons	AHL	32	12	14	26	....	....	....	49	....	....	....	....	....	....	....	....	....	....	....	....	....	....	....	....	....	....
	NHL Totals		**144**	**29**	**17**	**46**	**35**	**17**	**52**	**101**	**0**	**0**	**0**	**0**	**0.0**	**0**	**0**	**0**	**0**		**11**	**1**	**2**	**3**	**2**	**0**	**0**	**0**

• Suspended for entire 1956-57 season by NOHA for attacking referee Bud McDonald in pre-season game against Sudbury, October, 1956. Claimed by **Chicago** from **Winnipeg** (WHL) in Inter-League Draft, June 3, 1958. Traded to **Detroit** by **Chicago** for Jim Morrison, June 7, 1960. Traded to **NY Rangers** by **Portland** (WHL) for Pat Hannigan, June, 1963. • Suspended by **NY Rangers** for refusing demotion to Baltimore (AHL), January, 1964. Traded to **Montreal** by **NY Rangers** for Ray Brunel and Bev Bell, June, 1964. Traded to **Cleveland** (AHL) by **Montreal** for cash, June, 1964. Traded to **Montreal** by **Cleveland** (AHL) for Jim Mikol and Bill Staub, August, 1968.

• GLYNN, BRIAN
Brian Glynn D – L. 6′4″, 218 lbs. b: Iserlohn, West Germany, 11/23/1967. Calgary's 2nd choice, 37th overall, in 1986 Entry Draft.

Season	Club	League	GP	G	A	Pts	AG	AA	APts	PIM	PP	SH	GW	S	%	TGF	PGF	TGA	PGA	+/–	GP	G	A	Pts	PIM	PP	SH	GW
1984-85	Saskatoon Blades	WHL	12	1	0	1	....	....	....	2	....	....	....	....	....	....	....	....	....	....	3	0	0	0	0	....	....	....
1985-86	Saskatoon Blades	WHL	66	7	25	32	....	....	....	131	....	....	....	....	....	....	....	....	....	....	13	0	3	3	30	....	....	....
1986-87	Saskatoon Blades	WHL	44	2	26	28	....	....	....	163	....	....	....	....	....	....	....	....	....	....	11	1	3	4	19	....	....	....
1987-88	**Calgary Flames**	**NHL**	**67**	**5**	**14**	**19**	**4**	**10**	**14**	**87**	**4**	**0**	**1**	**84**	**6.0**	**71**	**14**	**82**	**23**	**–2**	**1**	**0**	**0**	**0**	**0**	**0**	**0**	**0**
1988-89	**Calgary Flames**	**NHL**	**9**	**0**	**1**	**1**	**0**	**1**	**1**	**19**	**0**	**0**	**0**	**4**	**0.0**	**6**	**1**	**5**	**1**	**+1**	....	....	....	....	....	....	....	....
	Salt Lake Golden Eagles	IHL	31	3	10	13	....	....	....	105	....	....	....	....	....	....	....	....	....	....	14	3	7	10	31	....	....	....
1989-90	**Calgary Flames**	**NHL**	**1**	**0**	**0**	**0**	**0**	**0**	**0**	**0**	**0**	**0**	**0**	**0**	**0.0**	**0**	**0**	**1**	**0**	**–1**	....	....	....	....	....	....	....	....
	Salt Lake Golden Eagles	IHL	80	17	44	61	....	....	....	164	....	....	....	....	....	....	....	....	....	....	....	....	....	....	....	....	....	....
1990-91	Salt Lake Golden Eagles	IHL	8	1	3	4	....	....	....	18	....	....	....	....	....	....	....	....	....	....	....	....	....	....	....	....	....	....
	Minnesota North Stars	**NHL**	**66**	**8**	**11**	**19**	**7**	**8**	**15**	**83**	**3**	**0**	**0**	**111**	**7.2**	**66**	**19**	**52**	**0**	**–5**	**23**	**2**	**6**	**8**	**18**	**2**	**0**	**0**

			REGULAR SEASON																		PLAYOFFS							
Season	Club	League	GP	G	A	Pts	AG	AA	APts	PIM	PP	SH	GW	S	%	TGF	PGF	TGA	PGA	+/–	GP	G	A	Pts	PIM	PP	SH	GW
1991-92	**Minnesota North Stars**	**NHL**	**37**	**2**	**12**	**14**	**2**	**9**	**11**	**24**	**0**	**0**	**0**	**53**	**3.8**	**39**	**13**	**50**	**8**	**–16**	....	....	....	....	....	....	....	....
	Edmonton Oilers	**NHL**	**25**	**2**	**6**	**8**	**2**	**4**	**6**	**6**	**0**	**1**	**0**	**29**	**6.9**	**33**	**7**	**31**	**16**	**+11**	**16**	**4**	**1**	**5**	**12**	**1**	**0**	**1**
1992-93	**Edmonton Oilers**	**NHL**	**64**	**4**	**12**	**16**	**3**	**8**	**11**	**60**	**2**	**0**	**0**	**80**	**5.0**	**49**	**12**	**82**	**32**	**–13**	....	....	....	....	....	....	....	....
1993-94	**Ottawa Senators**	**NHL**	**48**	**2**	**13**	**15**	**2**	**10**	**12**	**41**	**1**	**0**	**0**	**66**	**3.0**	**45**	**17**	**62**	**19**	**–15**	....	....	....	....	....	....	....	....
	Vancouver Canucks	**NHL**	**16**	**0**	**0**	**0**	**0**	**0**	**0**	**12**	**0**	**0**	**0**	**5**	**0.0**	**8**	**2**	**14**	**4**	**–4**	**17**	**0**	**3**	**3**	**10**	**0**	**0**	**0**
1994-95	**Hartford Whalers**	**NHL**	**43**	**1**	**6**	**7**	**2**	**9**	**11**	**32**	**0**	**0**	**0**	**35**	**2.9**	**28**	**2**	**38**	**10**	**–2**	....	....	....	....	....	....	....	....
1995-96	**Hartford Whalers**	**NHL**	**54**	**0**	**4**	**4**	**0**	**3**	**3**	**44**	**0**	**0**	**0**	**46**	**0.0**	**29**	**7**	**44**	**7**	**–15**	....	....	....	....	....	....	....	....
1996-97	**Hartford Whalers**	**NHL**	**1**	**1**	**0**	**1**	**1**	**0**	**1**	**2**	**0**	**0**	**0**	**2**	**50.0**	**3**	**1**	**0**	**0**	**+2**	....	....	....	....	....	....	....	....
	San Antonio Dragons	IHL	62	13	11	24	....	....	....	46	....	....	....	....	....	....	....	....	....	....	9	2	6	8	4	....	....	....
1997-98	Kolner Haie	EuroHL	6	3	2	5	....	....	....	10	....	....	....	....	....	....	....	....	....	....	....	....	....	....	....	....	....	....
	Kolner Haie	Germany	48	10	12	22	....	....	....	59	....	....	....	....	....	....	....	....	....	....	3	0	0	0	16	....	....	....
	NHL Totals		**431**	**25**	**79**	**104**	**23**	**62**	**85**	**410**	**10**	**1**	**1**	**515**	**4.9**	**377**	**95**	**461**	**120**		**57**	**6**	**10**	**16**	**40**	**3**	**0**	**1**

IHL First All-Star Team (1990) • Won Governors' Trophy (Outstanding Defenseman - IHL) (1990)

Traded to **Minnesota** by **Calgary** for Frantisek Musil, October 26, 1990. Traded to **Edmonton** by **Minnesota** for David Shaw, January 21, 1992. Traded to **Ottawa** by **Edmonton** for Ottawa's 8th round choice (Rob Quinn) in 1994 Entry Draft, September 15, 1993. Claimed on waivers by **Vancouver** from **Ottawa**, February 5, 1994. Claimed by **Hartford** from **Vancouver** in Waiver Draft, January 18, 1995. Traded to **Detroit** by **Hartford** with Brendan Shanahan for Paul Coffey, Keith Primeau and Detroit's 1st round choice (Nikos Tselios) in 1997 Entry Draft, October 9, 1996.

• GODDEN, ERNIE

Ernie Godden C – L. 5'8", 160 lbs. b: Keswick, Ont., 3/13/1961. Toronto's 3rd choice, 55th overall, in 1981 Entry Draft.

Season	Club	League	GP	G	A	Pts	AG	AA	APts	PIM	PP	SH	GW	S	%	TGF	PGF	TGA	PGA	+/–	GP	G	A	Pts	PIM	PP	SH	GW
1976-77	Newmarket Saints	OJHL	44	19	24	43	....	....	....	89	....	....	....	....	....	....	....	....	....	....	....	....	....	....	....	....	....	....
1977-78	Newmarket Saints	OJHL	40	20	24	44	....	....	....	67	....	....	....	....	....	....	....	....	....	....	....	....	....	....	....	....	....	....
1978-79	Windsor Spitfires	OHA	64	25	31	56	....	....	....	165	....	....	....	....	....	....	....	....	....	....	....	....	....	....	....	....	....	....
1979-80	Windsor Spitfires	OHA	62	40	41	81	....	....	....	158	....	....	....	....	....	....	....	....	....	....	16	9	7	16	36	....	....	....
1980-81	Windsor Spitfires	OHA	68	87	66	153	....	....	....	185	....	....	....	....	....	....	....	....	....	....	11	13	16	29	44	....	....	....
1981-82	**Toronto Maple Leafs**	**NHL**	**5**	**1**	**1**	**2**	**1**	**1**	**2**	**6**	**0**	**0**	**0**	**5**	**20.0**	**3**	**0**	**2**	**0**	**+1**	....	....	....	....	....	....	....	....
	Cincinnati Tigers	CHL	67	32	37	69	....	....	....	178	....	....	....	....	....	....	....	....	....	....	3	1	0	1	38	....	....	....
1982-83	St. Catharines Saints	AHL	64	27	23	50	....	....	....	106	....	....	....	....	....	....	....	....	....	....	....	....	....	....	....	....	....	....
1983-84	St. Catharines Saints	AHL	78	31	36	67	....	....	....	69	....	....	....	....	....	....	....	....	....	....	7	4	1	5	28	....	....	....
1984-85	Klagenfurter	Germany	39	34	23	57	....	....	....	68	....	....	....	....	....	....	....	....	....	....	....	....	....	....	....	....	....	....
	NHL Totals		**5**	**1**	**1**	**2**	**1**	**1**	**2**	**6**	**0**	**0**	**0**	**5**	**20.0**	**3**	**0**	**2**	**0**		....	....	....	....	....	....	....	....

OHA First All-Star Team (1981)

• GODFREY, WARREN

Warren Godfrey D – L. 6'1", 190 lbs. b: Toronto, Ont., 3/23/1931.

Season	Club	League	GP	G	A	Pts	AG	AA	APts	PIM	PP	SH	GW	S	%	TGF	PGF	TGA	PGA	+/–	GP	G	A	Pts	PIM	PP	SH	GW
1949-50	Galt Black Hawks	OHA	17	4	2	6	....	....	....	8	....	....	....	....	....	....	....	....	....	....	....	....	....	....	....	....	....	....
1950-51	Waterloo Hurricanes	OHA	51	11	14	25	....	....	....	131	....	....	....	....	....	....	....	....	....	....	....	....	....	....	....	....	....	....
1951-52	Tacoma Rockets	PCHL	61	8	17	25	....	....	....	66	....	....	....	....	....	....	....	....	....	....	7	1	0	1	2	....	....	....
1952-53	**Boston Bruins**	**NHL**	**60**	**1**	**13**	**14**	**2**	**18**	**20**	**40**	....	....	....	....	....	....	....	....	....	....	**11**	**0**	**1**	**1**	**2**	....	....	....
1953-54	**Boston Bruins**	**NHL**	**70**	**5**	**9**	**14**	**8**	**12**	**20**	**71**	....	....	....	....	....	....	....	....	....	....	**4**	**0**	**0**	**0**	**4**	....	....	....
1954-55	**Boston Bruins**	**NHL**	**62**	**1**	**17**	**18**	**1**	**22**	**23**	**58**	....	....	....	....	....	....	....	....	....	....	**3**	**0**	**0**	**0**	**0**	....	....	....
1955-56	**Detroit Red Wings**	**NHL**	**67**	**2**	**6**	**8**	**3**	**7**	**10**	**86**	....	....	....	....	....	....	....	....	....	....	....	....	....	....	....	....	....	....
1956-57	**Detroit Red Wings**	**NHL**	**69**	**1**	**8**	**9**	**1**	**9**	**10**	**103**	....	....	....	....	....	....	....	....	....	....	**5**	**0**	**0**	**0**	**6**	....	....	....
1957-58	**Detroit Red Wings**	**NHL**	**67**	**2**	**16**	**18**	**3**	**17**	**20**	**56**	....	....	....	....	....	....	....	....	....	....	**4**	**0**	**0**	**0**	**0**	....	....	....
1958-59	**Detroit Red Wings**	**NHL**	**69**	**6**	**4**	**10**	**8**	**4**	**12**	**44**	....	....	....	....	....	....	....	....	....	....	....	....	....	....	....	....	....	....
1959-60	**Detroit Red Wings**	**NHL**	**69**	**5**	**9**	**14**	**6**	**9**	**15**	**60**	....	....	....	....	....	....	....	....	....	....	**6**	**1**	**0**	**1**	**10**	....	....	....
1960-61	**Detroit Red Wings**	**NHL**	**63**	**3**	**16**	**19**	**4**	**16**	**20**	**62**	....	....	....	....	....	....	....	....	....	....	**11**	**0**	**2**	**2**	**18**	....	....	....
1961-62	**Detroit Red Wings**	**NHL**	**69**	**4**	**13**	**17**	**5**	**13**	**18**	**84**	....	....	....	....	....	....	....	....	....	....	....	....	....	....	....	....	....	....
1962-63	**Boston Bruins**	**NHL**	**66**	**2**	**9**	**11**	**2**	**9**	**11**	**56**	....	....	....	....	....	....	....	....	....	....	....	....	....	....	....	....	....	....
1963-64	**Detroit Red Wings**	**NHL**	**4**	**0**	**0**	**0**	**0**	**0**	**0**	**2**	....	....	....	....	....	....	....	....	....	....	....	....	....	....	....	....	....	....
	Pittsburgh Hornets	AHL	57	6	21	27	....	....	....	53	....	....	....	....	....	....	....	....	....	....	5	1	1	2	0	....	....	....
1964-65	Pittsburgh Hornets	AHL	56	7	25	32	....	....	....	44	....	....	....	....	....	....	....	....	....	....	4	1	2	3	6	....	....	....
	Detroit Red Wings	**NHL**	**11**	**0**	**0**	**0**	**0**	**0**	**0**	**8**	....	....	....	....	....	....	....	....	....	....	**4**	**0**	**1**	**1**	**2**	....	....	....
1965-66	Memphis Wings	CHL	11	0	5	5	....	....	....	10	....	....	....	....	....	....	....	....	....	....	....	....	....	....	....	....	....	....
	Detroit Red Wings	**NHL**	**26**	**0**	**4**	**4**	**0**	**4**	**4**	**22**	....	....	....	....	....	....	....	....	....	....	**4**	**0**	**0**	**0**	**0**	....	....	....
1966-67	Memphis Wings	CHL	2	0	0	0	....	....	....	0	....	....	....	....	....	....	....	....	....	....	....	....	....	....	....	....	....	....
	Detroit Red Wings	**NHL**	**2**	**0**	**0**	**0**	**0**	**0**	**0**	**0**	....	....	....	....	....	....	....	....	....	....	....	....	....	....	....	....	....	....
	Pittsburgh Hornets	AHL	59	2	12	14	....	....	....	54	....	....	....	....	....	....	....	....	....	....	9	2	1	3	14	....	....	....
1967-68	**Detroit Red Wings**	**NHL**	**12**	**0**	**1**	**1**	**0**	**1**	**1**	**0**	**0**	**0**	**0**	**9**	**0.0**	**16**	**0**	**6**	**1**	**+11**	....	....	....	....	....	....	....	....
	Fort Worth Wings	CHL	41	2	13	15	....	....	....	52	....	....	....	....	....	....	....	....	....	....	13	0	3	3	12	....	....	....
1968-69	Rochester Americans	AHL	67	3	17	20	....	....	....	70	....	....	....	....	....	....	....	....	....	....	....	....	....	....	....	....	....	....
	NHL Totals		**786**	**32**	**125**	**157**	**43**	**141**	**184**	**752**	**0**	**0**	**0**	**9**	**355.6**	**16**	**0**	**6**	**1**		**52**	**1**	**4**	**5**	**42**	**0**	**0**	**0**

Played in NHL All-Star Game (1955)

Traded to **Detroit** by **Boston** with Gilles Boisvert, Rene Chevrefils, Norm Corcoran and Ed Sandford for Marcel Bonin, Lorne Davis, Terry Sawchuk and Vic Stasiuk, June 3, 1955. Claimed by **Boston** from **Detroit** in Intra-League Draft, June 4, 1962. Traded to **Detroit** by **Boston** for Gerry Odrowski, October 10, 1963.

• GODIN, EDDY

Eddy Godin RW – L. 5'10", 190 lbs. b: Donnacona, Que., 3/29/1957. Washington's 3rd choice, 39th overall, in 1977 Amateur Draft.

Season	Club	League	GP	G	A	Pts	AG	AA	APts	PIM	PP	SH	GW	S	%	TGF	PGF	TGA	PGA	+/–	GP	G	A	Pts	PIM	PP	SH	GW
1974-75	Quebec Remparts	QMJHL	72	24	33	57	....	....	....	79	....	....	....	....	....	....	....	....	....	....	....	....	....	....	....	....	....	....
1975-76	Quebec Remparts	QMJHL	72	38	62	100	....	....	....	89	....	....	....	....	....	....	....	....	....	....	15	6	14	20	56	....	....	....
1976-77	Quebec Remparts	QMJHL	71	62	83	145	....	....	....	83	....	....	....	....	....	....	....	....	....	....	14	11	11	22	4	....	....	....
1977-78	**Washington Capitals**	**NHL**	**18**	**3**	**3**	**6**	**3**	**2**	**5**	**6**	**0**	**0**	**0**	**23**	**13.0**	**7**	**1**	**20**	**0**	**–14**	....	....	....	....	....	....	....	....
	Hershey Bears	AHL	50	22	20	42	....	....	....	26	....	....	....	....	....	....	....	....	....	....	....	....	....	....	....	....	....	....
1978-79	**Washington Capitals**	**NHL**	**9**	**0**	**3**	**3**	**0**	**2**	**2**	**6**	**0**	**0**	**0**	**10**	**0.0**	**5**	**1**	**0**	**0**	**–2**	....	....	....	....	....	....	....	....
	Hershey Bears	AHL	50	10	15	31	....	....	....	21	....	....	....	....	....	....	....	....	....	....	4	1	1	2	2	....	....	....
1979-80	Hershey Bears	AHL	71	34	27	61	....	....	....	39	....	....	....	....	....	....	....	....	....	....	16	5	9	14	13	....	....	....
1980-81	Hershey Bears	AHL	71	23	24	47	....	....	....	16	....	....	....	....	....	....	....	....	....	....	8	0	3	3	0	....	....	....
1981-82	Hershey Bears	AHL	74	16	23	39	....	....	....	23	....	....	....	....	....	....	....	....	....	....	5	4	1	5	0	....	....	....
1982-83	Hershey Bears	AHL	21	4	2	6	....	....	....	4	....	....	....	....	....	....	....	....	....	....	....	....	....	....	....	....	....	....
	NHL Totals		**27**	**3**	**6**	**9**	**3**	**4**	**7**	**12**	**0**	**0**	**0**	**33**	**9.1**	**12**	**2**	**26**	**0**		....	....	....	....	....	....	....	....

QMJHL East Division Second All-Star Team (1976)

Claimed by **Washington** as a fill-in during Expansion Draft, June 13, 1979.

• GODYNYUK, ALEXANDER

Alexander Godynyuk D – L. 6', 207 lbs. b: Kiev, Ukraine, 1/27/1970. Toronto's 5th choice, 115th overall, in 1990 Entry Draft.

Season	Club	League	GP	G	A	Pts	AG	AA	APts	PIM	PP	SH	GW	S	%	TGF	PGF	TGA	PGA	+/–	GP	G	A	Pts	PIM	PP	SH	GW
1986-87	Sokol Kiev	USSR	9	0	1	1	....	....	....	2	....	....	....	....	....	....	....	....	....	....	....	....	....	....	....	....	....	....
1987-88	Sokol Kiev	USSR	2	0	0	0	....	....	....	2	....	....	....	....	....	....	....	....	....	....	....	....	....	....	....	....	....	....
1988-89	Sokol Kiev	USSR	30	3	3	6	....	....	....	12	....	....	....	....	....	....	....	....	....	....	....	....	....	....	....	....	....	....
	Soviet Union	WJC-A	7	0	1	1	....	....	....	2	....	....	....	....	....	....	....	....	....	....	....	....	....	....	....	....	....	....
1989-90	Sokol Kiev	FrTour	1	0	0	0	....	....	....	2	....	....	....	....	....	....	....	....	....	....	....	....	....	....	....	....	....	....
	Sokol Kiev	USSR	37	3	2	5	....	....	....	31	....	....	....	....	....	....	....	....	....	....	....	....	....	....	....	....	....	....
	Soviet Union	WJC-A	7	3	2	5	....	....	....	4	....	....	....	....	....	....	....	....	....	....	....	....	....	....	....	....	....	....
1990-91	Sokol Kiev	FrTour	1	0	0	0	....	....	....	4	....	....	....	....	....	....	....	....	....	....	....	....	....	....	....	....	....	....
	Sokol Kiev	USSR	19	3	1	4	....	....	....	20	....	....	....	....	....	....	....	....	....	....	....	....	....	....	....	....	....	....
	Toronto Maple Leafs	**NHL**	**18**	**0**	**3**	**3**	**0**	**2**	**2**	**16**	**0**	**0**	**0**	**15**	**0.0**	**7**	**0**	**10**	**0**	**-3**	....	....	....	....	....	....	....	....
	Newmarket Saints	AHL	11	0	1	1	....	....	....	29	....	....	....	....	....	....	....	....	....	....	....	....	....	....	....	....	....	....
1991-92	**Toronto Maple Leafs**	**NHL**	**31**	**3**	**6**	**9**	**3**	**4**	**7**	**59**	**1**	**0**	**1**	**30**	**10.0**	**23**	**3**	**36**	**4**	**–12**	....	....	....	....	....	....	....	....
	Calgary Flames	**NHL**	**6**	**0**	**1**	**1**	**0**	**1**	**1**	**4**	**0**	**0**	**0**	**12**	**0.0**	**3**	**0**	**6**	**1**	**–2**	....	....	....	....	....	....	....	....
	Salt Lake Golden Eagles	IHL	17	2	1	3	....	....	....	24	....	....	....	....	....	....	....	....	....	....	....	....	....	....	....	....	....	....
1992-93	**Calgary Flames**	**NHL**	**27**	**3**	**4**	**7**	**2**	**3**	**5**	**19**	**0**	**0**	**0**	**35**	**8.6**	**31**	**6**	**22**	**3**	**+6**	....	....	....	....	....	....	....	....
1993-94	**Florida Panthers**	**NHL**	**26**	**0**	**10**	**10**	**0**	**8**	**8**	**35**	**0**	**0**	**0**	**43**	**0.0**	**26**	**8**	**18**	**5**	**+5**	....	....	....	....	....	....	....	....
	Hartford Whalers	**NHL**	**43**	**3**	**9**	**12**	**3**	**7**	**10**	**40**	**0**	**0**	**1**	**67**	**4.5**	**42**	**4**	**46**	**16**	**+8**	....	....	....	....	....	....	....	....
1994-95	**Hartford Whalers**	**NHL**	**14**	**0**	**0**	**0**	**0**	**0**	**0**	**8**	**0**	**0**	**0**	**16**	**0.0**	**11**	**0**	**12**	**2**	**+1**	....	....	....	....	....	....	....	....

Season	Club	League	REGULAR SEASON																		PLAYOFFS							
			GP	G	A	Pts	AG	AA	APts	PIM	PP	SH	GW	S	%	TGF	PGF	TGA	PGA	+/–	GP	G	A	Pts	PIM	PP	SH	GW
1995-96	Hartford Whalers	NHL	3	0	0	0	0	0	0	2	0	0	0	1	0.0	1	0	3	1	–1	....	....	....	....	....	....	....	....
	Springfield Falcons	AHL	14	1	3	4	....	....	....	19	....	....	....	....	....	....	....	....	....	....	....	....	....	....	....	....	....	....
	Detroit Vipers	IHL	7	0	3	3	....	....	....	12	....	....	....	....	....	....	....	....	....	....	....	....	....	....	....	....	....	....
	Minnesota Moose	IHL	45	9	17	26	....	....	....	81	....	....	....	....	....	....	....	....	....	....	....	....	....	....	....	....	....	....
1996-97	Hartford Whalers	NHL	55	1	6	7	1	5	6	41	0	0	1	34	2.9	29	1	46	8	–10	....	....	....	....	....	....	....	....
1997-98	Chicago Wolves	IHL	50	5	11	16	....	....	....	85	....	....	....	....	....	....	....	....	....	....	1	0	0	0	0	....	....	....
	NHL Totals		223	10	39	49	9	30	39	224	1	0	3	253	4.0	173	22	199	40		....	....	....	....	....	....	....	....

Named Best Defenseman at EJC-A (1987) • WJC-A All-Star Team (1990) • Named Best Defenseman at WJC-A (1990)

Traded to **Calgary** by **Toronto** with Craig Berube, Gary Leeman, Michel Petit and Jeff Reese for Doug Gilmour, Jamie Macoun, Ric Nattress, Rick Wamsley and Kent Manderville, January 2, 1992. Claimed by **Florida** from **Calgary** in Expansion Draft, June 24, 1993. Traded to **Hartford** by **Florida** for Jim McKenzie, December 16, 1993. Transferred to **Carolina** after **Hartford** franchise relocated, June 25, 1997. Traded to **St. Louis** by **Carolina** with Carolina's 6th round choice in 1998 Entry Draft for Stephen Leach, June 27, 1997.

• GOEGAN, PETE

Pete Goegan D – L. 6'1", 195 lbs. b: Fort William, Ont., 3/6/1934.

Season	Club	League	GP	G	A	Pts	AG	AA	APts	PIM	PP	SH	GW	S	%	TGF	PGF	TGA	PGA	+/–	GP	G	A	Pts	PIM	PP	SH	GW
1951-52	Fort William Canadians	TBJHL	29	2	6	8	....	....	....	84	....	....	....	....	....	....	....	....	....	....	....	....	....	....	....	....	....	....
1952-53	Fort William Canadians	TBJHL	21	12	11	33	....	....	....	108	....	....	....	....	....	....	....	....	....	....	6	2	1	3	14	....	....	....
1953-54	Fort William Canadians	TBJHL	23	4	11	15	....	....	....	147	....	....	....	....	....	....	....	....	....	....	4	1	3	4	8	....	....	....
1954-55	Fort William Beavers	NOHA	STATISTICS NOT AVAILABLE																									
1955-56	Sault Ste. Marie Indians	NOHA	59	6	15	21	....	....	....	104	....	....	....	....	....	....	....	....	....	....	7	2	1	3	6	....	....	....
1956-57	Cleveland Barons	AHL	51	3	17	20	....	....	....	121	....	....	....	....	....	....	....	....	....	....	11	0	0	0	30	....	....	....
1957-58	Cleveland Barons	AHL	55	6	17	23	....	....	....	94	....	....	....	....	....	....	....	....	....	....	....	....	....	....	....	....	....	....
	Detroit Red Wings	NHL	14	0	2	2	0	2	2	28	....	....	....	....	....	....	....	....	....	....	4	0	0	0	18	....	....	....
1958-59	Detroit Red Wings	NHL	67	1	11	12	1	12	13	109	....	....	....	....	....	....	....	....	....	....	....	....	....	....	....	....	....	....
1959-60	Detroit Red Wings	NHL	21	3	0	3	4	0	4	6	....	....	....	....	....	....	....	....	....	....	6	1	0	1	13	....	....	....
	Edmonton Flyers	WHL	40	11	16	27	....	....	....	107	....	....	....	....	....	....	....	....	....	....	....	....	....	....	....	....	....	....
1960-61	Detroit Red Wings	NHL	67	5	29	34	6	30	36	78	....	....	....	....	....	....	....	....	....	....	11	0	1	1	18	....	....	....
1961-62	Detroit Red Wings	NHL	39	5	5	10	6	5	11	24	....	....	....	....	....	....	....	....	....	....	....	....	....	....	....	....	....	....
	New York Rangers	NHL	7	0	2	2	0	2	2	6	....	....	....	....	....	....	....	....	....	....	....	....	....	....	....	....	....	....
	Springfield Indians	AHL	7	0	1	1	....	....	....	12	....	....	....	....	....	....	....	....	....	....	11	3	3	6	20	....	....	....
1962-63	Detroit Red Wings	NHL	62	1	8	9	1	8	9	48	....	....	....	....	....	....	....	....	....	....	11	0	2	2	12	....	....	....
1963-64	Detroit Red Wings	NHL	12	0	0	0	0	0	0	8	....	....	....	....	....	....	....	....	....	....	....	....	....	....	....	....	....	....
	Pittsburgh Hornets	AHL	55	6	17	23	....	....	....	127	....	....	....	....	....	....	....	....	....	....	5	0	0	0	6	....	....	....
1964-65	Detroit Red Wings	NHL	4	1	0	1	1	0	1	2	....	....	....	....	....	....	....	....	....	....	....	....	....	....	....	....	....	....
	Pittsburgh Hornets	AHL	68	9	14	23	....	....	....	163	....	....	....	....	....	....	....	....	....	....	2	0	0	0	2	....	....	....
1965-66	Detroit Red Wings	NHL	13	0	2	2	0	2	2	14	....	....	....	....	....	....	....	....	....	....	1	0	0	0	0	....	....	....
	Pittsburgh Hornets	AHL	52	4	17	21	....	....	....	85	....	....	....	....	....	....	....	....	....	....	....	....	....	....	....	....	....	....
1966-67	Detroit Red Wings	NHL	31	2	6	8	2	6	8	12	....	....	....	....	....	....	....	....	....	....	....	....	....	....	....	....	....	....
	Pittsburgh Hornets	AHL	34	4	16	20	....	....	....	60	....	....	....	....	....	....	....	....	....	....	9	1	5	6	17	....	....	....
1967-68	Minnesota North Stars	NHL	46	1	2	3	1	2	3	30	0	0	0	35	2.9	21	1	45	9	–16	....	....	....	....	....	....	....	....
	Phoenix Roadrunners	WHL	15	2	5	7	....	....	....	18	....	....	....	....	....	....	....	....	....	....	4	0	0	0	0	....	....	....
1968-69	Denver Spurs	WHL	34	1	10	11	....	....	....	40	....	....	....	....	....	....	....	....	....	....	....	....	....	....	....	....	....	....
	Baltimore Clippers	AHL	25	0	4	4	....	....	....	30	....	....	....	....	....	....	....	....	....	....	4	0	1	1	0	....	....	....
	NHL Totals		383	19	67	86	22	69	91	365	0	0	0	35	54.3	21	1	45	9		33	1	3	4	61	0	0	0

Traded to **Detroit** by **Cleveland** (AHL) for Gord Hollingworth, February 20, 1958. Traded to **NY Rangers** by **Detroit** for Noel Price, February 16, 1962. Traded to **Detroit** by **NY Rangers** for Noel Price, October 8, 1962. Claimed by **Minnesota** from **Detroit** in Expansion Draft, June 6, 1967.

• GOERTZ, DAVE

Dave Goertz D – R. 5'11", 210 lbs. b: Edmonton, Alta., 3/28/1965. Pittsburgh's 10th choice, 232nd overall, in 1983 Entry Draft.

Season	Club	League	GP	G	A	Pts	AG	AA	APts	PIM	PP	SH	GW	S	%	TGF	PGF	TGA	PGA	+/–	GP	G	A	Pts	PIM	PP	SH	GW
1981-82	Regina Pats	WHL	67	5	19	24	....	....	....	181	....	....	....	....	....	....	....	....	....	....	....	....	....	....	....	....	....	....
1982-83	Regina Pats	WHL	69	4	22	26	....	....	....	132	....	....	....	....	....	....	....	....	....	....	5	0	2	2	9	....	....	....
1983-84	Prince Albert Raiders	WHL	60	13	47	60	....	....	....	111	....	....	....	....	....	....	....	....	....	....	5	2	3	5	0	....	....	....
	Baltimore Skipjacks	AHL	1	0	0	0	....	....	....	2	....	....	....	....	....	....	....	....	....	....	6	0	0	0	0	....	....	....
1984-85	Prince Albert Raiders	WHL	48	3	48	51	....	....	....	62	....	....	....	....	....	....	....	....	....	....	13	4	14	18	29	....	....	....
	Baltimore Skipjacks	AHL	....	....	....	....	....	....	....	....	....	....	....	....	....	....	....	....	....	....	2	0	2	2	0	....	....	....
1985-86	Baltimore Skipjacks	AHL	74	1	15	16	....	....	....	76	....	....	....	....	....	....	....	....	....	....	....	....	....	....	....	....	....	....
1986-87	Baltimore Skipjacks	AHL	16	0	3	3	....	....	....	8	....	....	....	....	....	....	....	....	....	....	....	....	....	....	....	....	....	....
	Muskegon Lumberjacks	IHL	44	3	17	20	....	....	....	44	....	....	....	....	....	....	....	....	....	....	15	0	4	4	14	....	....	....
1987-88	Pittsburgh Penguins	NHL	2	0	0	0	0	0	0	2	0	0	0	2	0.0	2	0	3	0	–1	....	....	....	....	....	....	....	....
	Muskegon Lumberjacks	IHL	73	8	36	44	....	....	....	87	....	....	....	....	....	....	....	....	....	....	6	0	4	4	14	....	....	....
1988-89	Muskegon Lumberjacks	IHL	74	1	32	33	....	....	....	102	....	....	....	....	....	....	....	....	....	....	14	0	4	4	10	....	....	....
1989-90	Muskegon Lumberjacks	IHL	51	3	18	21	....	....	....	64	....	....	....	....	....	....	....	....	....	....	....	....	....	....	....	....	....	....
1990-91	Muskegon Mohawks	IHL	30	6	10	16	....	....	....	46	....	....	....	....	....	....	....	....	....	....	....	....	....	....	....	....	....	....
	NHL Totals		2	0	0	0	0	0	0	2	0	0	0	2	0.0	2	0	3	0		....	....	....	....	....	....	....	....

Memorial Cup All-Star Team (1985)

• GOLDSWORTHY, BILL

Bill "Goldie" Goldsworthy RW – R. 6', 190 lbs. b: Waterloo, Ont., 8/24/1944. Deceased.

Season	Club	League	GP	G	A	Pts	AG	AA	APts	PIM	PP	SH	GW	S	%	TGF	PGF	TGA	PGA	+/–	GP	G	A	Pts	PIM	PP	SH	GW
1962-63	Niagara Falls Flyers	OHA	50	7	11	18	....	....	....	71	....	....	....	....	....	....	....	....	....	....	25	4	9	13	47	....	....	....
1963-64	Niagara Falls Flyers	OHA	56	21	47	68	....	....	....	91	....	....	....	....	....	....	....	....	....	....	4	0	3	3	4	....	....	....
1964-65	Niagara Falls Flyers	OHA	54	28	27	55	....	....	....	164	....	....	....	....	....	....	....	....	....	....	11	5	11	16	26	....	....	....
	Boston Bruins	NHL	2	0	0	0	0	0	0	0	....	....	....	....	....	....	....	....	....	....	....	....	....	....	....	....	....	....
1965-66	Boston Bruins	NHL	13	3	1	4	4	1	5	6	....	....	....	....	....	....	....	....	....	....	....	....	....	....	....	....	....	....
	Oklahoma City Blazers	CHL	22	2	5	7	....	....	....	65	....	....	....	....	....	....	....	....	....	....	2	1	0	1	4	....	....	....
1966-67	Boston Bruins	NHL	18	3	5	8	4	5	9	21	....	....	....	....	....	....	....	....	....	....	....	....	....	....	....	....	....	....
	Oklahoma City Blazers	CHL	11	4	1	5	....	....	....	14	....	....	....	....	....	....	....	....	....	....	....	....	....	....	....	....	....	....
	Buffalo Bisons	AHL	22	9	11	20	....	....	....	42	....	....	....	....	....	....	....	....	....	....	....	....	....	....	....	....	....	....
1967-68	Minnesota North Stars	NHL	68	14	19	33	17	20	37	68	2	0	0	154	9.1	50	8	50	0	–8	14	*8	7	*15	12	1	0	1
1968-69	Minnesota North Stars	NHL	68	14	10	24	16	9	25	110	4	0	3	196	7.1	37	11	53	0	–27	....	....	....	....	....	....	....	....
	Memphis South Stars	CHL	6	4	0	4	....	....	....	6	....	....	....	....	....	....	....	....	....	....	....	....	....	....	....	....	....	....
1969-70	Minnesota North Stars	NHL	75	36	29	65	42	29	71	89	11	0	4	230	15.7	82	22	69	0	–9	6	4	3	7	6	3	2	0
1970-71	Minnesota North Stars	NHL	77	34	31	65	36	27	63	85	5	1	7	295	11.5	88	31	77	7	–13	7	2	4	6	6	0	0	0
1971-72	Minnesota North Stars	NHL	78	31	31	62	33	28	61	59	6	0	8	295	10.5	91	32	49	1	+11	7	2	3	5	6	0	0	1
1972-73	Canada	Summit	3	1	1	2	....	....	....	4	....	....	....	....	....	....	....	....	....	....	....	....	....	....	....	....	....	....
	Minnesota North Stars	NHL	75	27	33	60	27	28	55	97	8	0	2	260	10.4	96	17	55	0	+24	6	2	2	4	0	1	0	0
1973-74	Minnesota North Stars	NHL	74	48	26	74	49	22	71	73	12	1	4	321	15.0	106	24	93	14	+3	....	....	....	....	....	....	....	....
1974-75	Minnesota North Stars	NHL	71	37	35	72	34	28	62	77	11	1	3	273	13.6	90	28	111	12	–37	....	....	....	....	....	....	....	....
1975-76	Minnesota North Stars	NHL	68	24	22	46	22	17	39	47	6	0	3	174	13.8	60	20	59	0	–19	....	....	....	....	....	....	....	....
1976-77	Minnesota North Stars	NHL	16	2	3	5	2	2	4	6	1	0	0	39	5.1	8	1	25	10	–8	....	....	....	....	....	....	....	....
	New York Rangers	NHL	61	10	12	22	10	10	20	43	0	0	2	96	10.4	34	4	57	10	–17	....	....	....	....	....	....	....	....
1977-78	New York Rangers	NHL	7	0	1	1	0	1	1	12	0	0	0	7	0.0	6	2	3	0	+1	....	....	....	....	....	....	....	....
	New Haven Nighthawks	AHL	4	1	2	3	....	....	....	4	....	....	....	....	....	....	....	....	....	....	....	....	....	....	....	....	....	....
	Indianapolis Racers	WHA	32	8	10	18	....	....	....	10	....	....	....	....	....	....	....	....	....	....	....	....	....	....	....	....	....	....
1978-79	Edmonton Oilers	WHA	17	4	2	6	....	....	....	14	....	....	....	....	....	....	....	....	....	....	4	1	1	2	11	....	....	....
	NHL Totals		771	283	258	541	296	227	523	793	66	3	36	2340	12.1	748	200	701	54		40	18	19	37	30	5	2	2
	Other Major League Totals		49	12	12	24	....	....	....	24	....	....	....	....	....	....	....	....	....	....	4	1	1	2	11	....	....	....

Played in NHL All-Star Game (1970, 1972, 1974, 1976)

Claimed by **Minnesota** from **Boston** in Expansion Draft, June 6, 1967. Selected by **Minnesota** (WHA) in 1972 WHA General Player Draft, February 12, 1972. Traded to **NY Rangers** by **Minnesdota** for Bill Fairbairn and Nick Beverley, November 11, 1976. Traded to **Indianapolis** (WHA) by **NY Rangers** for Frank Spring, December, 1977. Traded to **Edmonton** (WHA) by **Indianapolis** (WHA) for Juha Widing, June, 1978.

• GOLDUP, GLENN

Glenn Goldup RW – L. 6', 190 lbs. b: St. Catharines, Ont., 4/26/1953. Montreal's 2nd choice, 17th overall, in 1973 Amateur Draft.

Season	Club	League	GP	G	A	Pts	AG	AA	APts	PIM	PP	SH	GW	S	%	TGF	PGF	TGA	PGA	+/–	GP	G	A	Pts	PIM	PP	SH	GW
1968-69	Toronto Marlboros	OHA	35	20	20	40	....	....	....	....	....	....	....	....	....	....	....	....	....	....	....	....	....	....	....	....	....	....
1969-70	Markham Waxers	Jr. B	27	22	19	41	....	....	....	....	....	....	....	....	....	....	....	....	....	....	....	....	....	....	....	....	....	....
	Toronto Marlboros	OHA	2	0	1	1	....	....	....	0	....	....	....	....	....	....	....	....	....	....	....	....	....	....	....	....	....	....

Season	Club	League	REGULAR SEASON																		PLAYOFFS							
			GP	G	A	Pts	AG	AA	APts	PIM	PP	SH	GW	S	%	TGF	PGF	TGA	PGA	+/–	GP	G	A	Pts	PIM	PP	SH	GW
1970-71	Toronto Marlboros	OHA	58	12	22	34	....	....	....	82	....	....	....	....	....	....	....	....	....	....	....	....	....	....	....	....	....	....
1971-72	Toronto Marlboros	OHA	63	24	34	58	....	....	....	161	....	....	....	....	....	....	....	....	....	....	....	....	....	....	....	....	....	....
1972-73	Toronto Marlboros	OHA	54	42	53	95	....	....	....	193	....	....	....	....	....	....	....	....	....	....	16	7	11	18	....	....	....	....
1973-74	**Montreal Canadiens**	**NHL**	**6**	**0**	**0**	**0**	**0**	**0**	**0**	**0**	**0**	**0**	**0**	**2**	**0.0**	**0**	**0**	**1**	**0**	**–1**	....	....	....	....	....	....	....	....
	Nova Scotia Voyageurs	AHL	44	18	15	33	....	....	....	64	....	....	....	....	....	....	....	....	....	....	....	....	....	....	....	....	....	....
1974-75	**Montreal Canadiens**	**NHL**	**9**	**0**	**1**	**1**	**0**	**1**	**1**	**2**	**0**	**0**	**0**	**8**	**0.0**	**2**	**0**	**3**	**0**	**–1**	....	....	....	....	....	....	....	....
	Nova Scotia Voyageurs	AHL	49	15	16	31	....	....	....	140	....	....	....	....	....	....	....	....	....	....	5	1	4	5	36	....	....	....
1975-76	**Montreal Canadiens**	**NHL**	**3**	**0**	**0**	**0**	**0**	**0**	**0**	**2**	**0**	**0**	**0**	**1**	**0.0**	**0**	**0**	**1**	**0**	**–1**	....	....	....	....	....	....	....	....
	Nova Scotia Voyageurs	AHL	65	23	22	45	....	....	....	131	....	....	....	....	....	....	....	....	....	....	9	*8	3	11	*33	....	....	....
1976-77	**Los Angeles Kings**	**NHL**	**28**	**7**	**6**	**13**	**7**	**5**	**12**	**29**	**1**	**0**	**2**	**28**	**25.0**	**20**	**2**	**13**	**0**	**+5**	**8**	**2**	**2**	**4**	**2**	**0**	**0**	**0**
	Fort Worth Texans	CHL	7	2	2	4	....	....	....	9	....	....	....	....	....	....	....	....	....	....	....	....	....	....	....	....	....	....
1977-78	**Los Angeles Kings**	**NHL**	**66**	**14**	**18**	**32**	**13**	**15**	**28**	**66**	**0**	**0**	**0**	**108**	**13.0**	**51**	**7**	**52**	**0**	**–8**	**2**	**1**	**0**	**1**	**11**	**0**	**0**	**0**
1978-79	**Los Angeles Kings**	**NHL**	**73**	**15**	**22**	**37**	**14**	**17**	**31**	**89**	**3**	**0**	**1**	**117**	**12.8**	**62**	**11**	**58**	**0**	**–7**	**2**	**0**	**1**	**1**	**9**	**0**	**0**	**0**
1979-80	**Los Angeles Kings**	**NHL**	**55**	**10**	**11**	**21**	**9**	**8**	**17**	**78**	**1**	**0**	**1**	**92**	**10.9**	**40**	**3**	**41**	**0**	**–4**	**4**	**1**	**0**	**1**	**0**	**0**	**0**	**0**
1980-81	**Los Angeles Kings**	**NHL**	**49**	**6**	**9**	**15**	**5**	**6**	**11**	**35**	**0**	**0**	**0**	**64**	**9.4**	**26**	**2**	**26**	**0**	**–2**	....	....	....	....	....	....	....	....
	New Haven Nighthawks	AHL	15	6	2	8	....	....	....	36	....	....	....	....	....	....	....	....	....	....	3	0	0	0	0	....	....	....
1981-82	**Los Angeles Kings**	**NHL**	**2**	**0**	**0**	**0**	**0**	**0**	**0**	**2**	**0**	**0**	**0**	**1**	**0.0**	**0**	**0**	**0**	**0**	**0**	....	....	....	....	....	....	....	....
	New Haven Nighthawks	AHL	51	14	17	31	....	....	....	91	....	....	....	....	....	....	....	....	....	....	4	3	1	4	2	....	....	....
1982-83	New Haven Nighthawks	AHL	28	0	8	8	....	....	....	39	....	....	....	....	....	....	....	....	....	....	....	....	....	....	....	....	....	....
	NHL Totals		**291**	**52**	**67**	**119**	**48**	**52**	**100**	**303**	**5**	**0**	**4**	**421**	**12.4**	**201**	**25**	**195**	**0**		**16**	**4**	**3**	**7**	**22**	**0**	**0**	**0**

AHL Second All-Star Team (1976)

Traded to **LA Kings** by **Montreal** with Montreal's 3rd round choice (later traded to Detroit — Detroit selected Doug Derkson) in 1978 Amateur Draft for LA Kings' 3rd round choice (Moe Robinson) in 1977 Amateur Draft and 1st round choice (Danny Geoffrion) in 1978 Amateur Draft, June 12, 1976.

• GOLUBOVSKY, YAN

Yan Golubovsky D – R. 6'3", 183 lbs. b: Novosibirsk, USSR, 3/9/1976. Detroit's 1st choice, 23rd overall, in 1994 Entry Draft.

Season	Club	League	GP	G	A	Pts	AG	AA	APts	PIM	PP	SH	GW	S	%	TGF	PGF	TGA	PGA	+/–	GP	G	A	Pts	PIM	PP	SH	GW
1993-94	Moscow Dynamo 2	CIS 3	10	0	1	1	....	....	....	....	....	....	....	....	....	....	....	....	....	....	....	....	....	....	....	....	....	....
	Russian Penguins	IHL	8	0	0	0	....	....	....	23	....	....	....	....	....	....	....	....	....	....	....	....	....	....	....	....	....	....
1994-95	Adirondack Red Wings	AHL	57	4	2	6	....	....	....	39	....	....	....	....	....	....	....	....	....	....	....	....	....	....	....	....	....	....
1995-96	Adirondack Red Wings	AHL	71	5	16	21	....	....	....	97	....	....	....	....	....	....	....	....	....	....	3	0	0	0	2	....	....	....
1996-97	Adirondack Red Wings	AHL	62	2	11	13	....	....	....	67	....	....	....	....	....	....	....	....	....	....	4	0	0	0	0	....	....	....
1997-98	**Detroit Red Wings**	**NHL**	**12**	**0**	**2**	**2**	**0**	**2**	**2**	**6**	**0**	**0**	**0**	**9**	**0.0**	**3**	**0**	**2**	**0**	**+1**	....	....	....	....	....	....	....	....
	Adirondack Red Wings	AHL	52	1	15	16	....	....	....	57	....	....	....	....	....	....	....	....	....	....	3	0	0	0	2	....	....	....
	NHL Totals		**12**	**0**	**2**	**2**	**0**	**2**	**2**	**6**	**0**	**0**	**0**	**9**	**0.0**	**3**	**0**	**2**	**0**		....	....	....	....	....	....	....	....

• GONCHAR, SERGEI

Sergei Gonchar D – L. 6'2", 212 lbs. b: Chelyabinsk, USSR, 4/13/1974. Washington's 1st choice, 14th overall, in 1992 Entry Draft.

Season	Club	League	GP	G	A	Pts	AG	AA	APts	PIM	PP	SH	GW	S	%	TGF	PGF	TGA	PGA	+/–	GP	G	A	Pts	PIM	PP	SH	GW
1991-92	Traktor Chelyabinsk	CIS	31	1	0	1	....	....	....	6	....	....	....	....	....	....	....	....	....	....	....	....	....	....	....	....	....	....
1992-93	Moscow Dynamo	CIS	31	1	3	4	....	....	....	70	....	....	....	....	....	....	....	....	....	....	10	0	0	0	12	....	....	....
	Russia	WJC-A	7	0	2	2	....	....	....	10	....	....	....	....	....	....	....	....	....	....	....	....	....	....	....	....	....	....
1993-94	Moscow Dynamo	CIS	44	4	5	9	....	....	....	36	....	....	....	....	....	....	....	....	....	....	10	0	3	3	14	....	....	....
	Portland Pirates	AHL	....	....	....	....	....	....	....	....	....	....	....	....	....	....	....	....	....	....	2	0	0	0	0	....	....	....
1994-95	Portland Pirates	AHL	61	10	32	42	....	....	....	67	....	....	....	....	....	....	....	....	....	....	....	....	....	....	....	....	....	....
	Washington Capitals	**NHL**	**31**	**2**	**5**	**7**	**4**	**7**	**11**	**22**	**0**	**0**	**0**	**38**	**5.3**	**16**	**2**	**11**	**1**	**+4**	**7**	**2**	**2**	**4**	**2**	**0**	**0**	**1**
1995-96	**Washington Capitals**	**NHL**	**78**	**15**	**26**	**41**	**15**	**21**	**36**	**60**	**4**	**0**	**4**	**139**	**10.8**	**95**	**26**	**50**	**6**	**+25**	**6**	**2**	**4**	**6**	**4**	**1**	**0**	**0**
1996-97	Russia	W Cup	4	2	2	4	....	....	....	2	....	....	....	....	....	....	....	....	....	....	....	....	....	....	....	....	....	....
	Washington Capitals	**NHL**	**57**	**13**	**17**	**30**	**14**	**15**	**29**	**36**	**3**	**0**	**3**	**129**	**10.1**	**66**	**20**	**66**	**9**	**–11**	....	....	....	....	....	....	....	....
1997-98	Lada Togliatti	CIS	7	3	2	5	....	....	....	4	....	....	....	....	....	....	....	....	....	....	....	....	....	....	....	....	....	....
	Lada Togliatti	EuroHL	1	1	0	1	....	....	....	2	....	....	....	....	....	....	....	....	....	....	....	....	....	....	....	....	....	....
	Washington Capitals	**NHL**	**72**	**5**	**16**	**21**	**6**	**16**	**22**	**66**	**2**	**0**	**0**	**134**	**3.7**	**65**	**15**	**51**	**3**	**+2**	**21**	**7**	**4**	**11**	**30**	**3**	**1**	**2**
	Russia	Olympics	6	0	2	2	....	....	....	0	....	....	....	....	....	....	....	....	....	....	....	....	....	....	....	....	....	....
	NHL Totals		**238**	**35**	**64**	**99**	**39**	**59**	**98**	**184**	**9**	**0**	**7**	**440**	**8.0**	**242**	**63**	**170**	**19**		**34**	**11**	**10**	**21**	**36**	**4**	**1**	**3**

EJC-A All-Star Team (1992) • Named Best Defenseman at EJC-A (1992)

• GONEAU, DANIEL

Daniel Goneau LW – L. 6', 194 lbs. b: Montreal, Que., 1/16/1976. NY Rangers' 2nd choice, 48th overall, in 1996 Entry Draft.

Season	Club	League	GP	G	A	Pts	AG	AA	APts	PIM	PP	SH	GW	S	%	TGF	PGF	TGA	PGA	+/–	GP	G	A	Pts	PIM	PP	SH	GW
1992-93	Laval Titan	QMJHL	62	16	25	41	....	....	....	44	....	....	....	....	....	....	....	....	....	....	13	0	4	4	4	....	....	....
1993-94	Laval Titan	QMJHL	68	29	57	86	....	....	....	81	....	....	....	....	....	....	....	....	....	....	19	8	21	29	45	....	....	....
1994-95	Laval Titan	QMJHL	56	16	31	47	....	....	....	78	....	....	....	....	....	....	....	....	....	....	20	5	10	15	33	....	....	....
1995-96	Granby Bisons	QMJHL	67	54	51	105	....	....	....	115	....	....	....	....	....	....	....	....	....	....	21	11	22	33	40	....	....	....
1996-97	**New York Rangers**	**NHL**	**41**	**10**	**3**	**13**	**11**	**3**	**14**	**10**	**3**	**0**	**2**	**44**	**22.7**	**19**	**6**	**18**	**0**	**–5**	....	....	....	....	....	....	....	....
	Binghamton Rangers	AHL	39	15	15	30	....	....	....	10	....	....	....	....	....	....	....	....	....	....	....	....	....	....	....	....	....	....
1997-98	**New York Rangers**	**NHL**	**11**	**2**	**0**	**2**	**2**	**0**	**2**	**4**	**0**	**0**	**1**	**13**	**15.4**	**2**	**0**	**6**	**0**	**–4**	....	....	....	....	....	....	....	....
	Hartford Wolf Pack	AHL	66	21	26	47	....	....	....	44	....	....	....	....	....	....	....	....	....	....	13	1	4	5	18	....	....	....
	NHL Totals		**52**	**12**	**3**	**15**	**13**	**3**	**16**	**14**	**3**	**0**	**3**	**57**	**21.1**	**21**	**6**	**24**	**0**		....	....	....	....	....	....	....	....

QMJHL First All-Star Team (1996)

Re-entered NHL Entry Draft. Originally Boston's 2nd choice, 47th overall, in 1994 Entry Draft.

• GOODENOUGH, LARRY

Larry "Izzy" Goodenough D – R. 6', 195 lbs. b: Toronto, Ont., 1/19/1953. Philadelphia's 1st choice, 20th overall, in 1973 Amateur Draft.

Season	Club	League	GP	G	A	Pts	AG	AA	APts	PIM	PP	SH	GW	S	%	TGF	PGF	TGA	PGA	+/–	GP	G	A	Pts	PIM	PP	SH	GW
1971-72	Toronto Marlboros	OHA	62	3	35	38	....	....	....	61	....	....	....	....	....	....	....	....	....	....	....	....	....	....	....	....	....	....
1972-73	London Knights	OHA	59	15	51	66	....	....	....	153	....	....	....	....	....	....	....	....	....	....	10	2	7	9	10	....	....	....
1973-74	Richmond Robins	AHL	75	11	22	33	....	....	....	54	....	....	....	....	....	....	....	....	....	....	5	2	2	4	0	....	....	....
1974-75	Richmond Robins	AHL	57	10	40	50	....	....	....	76	....	....	....	....	....	....	....	....	....	....	....	....	....	....	....	....	....	....
	Philadelphia Flyers	**NHL**	**20**	**3**	**9**	**12**	**3**	**7**	**10**	**0**	**1**	**0**	**0**	**37**	**8.1**	**39**	**17**	**11**	**1**	**+12**	**5**	**0**	**4**	**4**	**2**	**0**	**0**	**0**
1975-76	**Philadelphia Flyers**	**NHL**	**77**	**8**	**34**	**42**	**7**	**27**	**34**	**83**	**5**	**1**	**2**	**149**	**5.4**	**127**	**47**	**52**	**17**	**+45**	**16**	**3**	**11**	**14**	**6**	**1**	**0**	**0**
1976-77	**Philadelphia Flyers**	**NHL**	**32**	**4**	**13**	**17**	**4**	**11**	**15**	**21**	**1**	**0**	**0**	**52**	**7.7**	**46**	**0**	**26**	**5**	**+15**	....	....	....	....	....	....	....	....
	Vancouver Canucks	**NHL**	**30**	**2**	**4**	**6**	**2**	**3**	**5**	**27**	**0**	**0**	**1**	**35**	**5.7**	**27**	**1**	**42**	**11**	**–5**	....	....	....	....	....	....	....	....
1977-78	**Vancouver Canucks**	**NHL**	**42**	**1**	**6**	**7**	**1**	**5**	**6**	**28**	**0**	**0**	**0**	**49**	**2.0**	**26**	**5**	**46**	**9**	**–16**	....	....	....	....	....	....	....	....
	Tulsa Oilers	CHL	32	5	18	23	....	....	....	26	....	....	....	....	....	....	....	....	....	....	5	0	3	3	11	....	....	....
1978-79	**Vancouver Canucks**	**NHL**	**36**	**4**	**9**	**13**	**4**	**7**	**11**	**18**	**2**	**0**	**0**	**75**	**5.3**	**34**	**14**	**37**	**3**	**–14**	**1**	**0**	**0**	**0**	**2**	**0**	**0**	**0**
	Dallas Black Hawks	CHL	31	3	16	19	....	....	....	23	....	....	....	....	....	....	....	....	....	....	....	....	....	....	....	....	....	....
1979-80	**Vancouver Canucks**	**NHL**	**5**	**0**	**2**	**2**	**0**	**2**	**2**	**2**	**0**	**0**	**0**	**9**	**0.0**	**3**	**1**	**3**	**1**	**0**	....	....	....	....	....	....	....	....
	Dallas Black Hawks	CHL	73	4	34	38	....	....	....	55	....	....	....	....	....	....	....	....	....	....	....	....	....	....	....	....	....	....
1980-81	Houston Apollos	CHL	13	2	3	5	....	....	....	2	....	....	....	....	....	....	....	....	....	....	....	....	....	....	....	....	....	....
	Saginaw Gears	IHL	54	10	43	53	....	....	....	32	....	....	....	....	....	....	....	....	....	....	13	1	12	13	20	....	....	....
1981-82	New Haven Nighthawks	AHL	76	3	27	30	....	....	....	60	....	....	....	....	....	....	....	....	....	....	2	0	1	1	9	....	....	....
1982-83	Binghamton Whalers	AHL	58	1	15	16	....	....	....	36	....	....	....	....	....	....	....	....	....	....	3	0	0	0	2	....	....	....
	NHL Totals		**242**	**22**	**77**	**99**	**21**	**62**	**83**	**179**	**9**	**1**	**3**	**406**	**5.4**	**301**	**94**	**217**	**47**		**22**	**3**	**15**	**18**	**10**	**1**	**0**	**0**

IHL First All-Star Team (1981) • Won Governors' Trophy (Top Defenseman - IHL) (1981)

Traded to **Vancouver** by **Philadelphia** with Jack McIlhargey for Bob Dailey, January 20, 1977.

• GORDIOUK, VIKTOR

Viktor Gordiouk LW – R. 5'10", 176 lbs. b: Odintsovo, USSR, 4/11/1970. Buffalo's 6th choice, 142nd overall, in 1990 Entry Draft.

Season	Club	League	GP	G	A	Pts	AG	AA	APts	PIM	PP	SH	GW	S	%	TGF	PGF	TGA	PGA	+/–	GP	G	A	Pts	PIM	PP	SH	GW
1986-87	Soviet Wings	USSR	2	0	0	0	....	....	....	0	....	....	....	....	....	....	....	....	....	....	....	....	....	....	....	....	....	....
1987-88	Soviet Wings	USSR	26	2	2	4	....	....	....	6	....	....	....	....	....	....	....	....	....	....	....	....	....	....	....	....	....	....
1988-89	Soviet Wings	USSR	41	5	1	6	....	....	....	10	....	....	....	....	....	....	....	....	....	....	....	....	....	....	....	....	....	....
1989-90	Soviet Wings	USSR	48	11	4	15	....	....	....	24	....	....	....	....	....	....	....	....	....	....	....	....	....	....	....	....	....	....
1990-91	Soviet Wings	USSR	46	12	10	22	....	....	....	22	....	....	....	....	....	....	....	....	....	....	....	....	....	....	....	....	....	....
1991-92	Soviet Wings	CIS	42	16	7	23	....	....	....	24	....	....	....	....	....	....	....	....	....	....	....	....	....	....	....	....	....	....
1992-93	**Buffalo Sabres**	**NHL**	**16**	**3**	**6**	**9**	**2**	**4**	**6**	**0**	**0**	**0**	**0**	**24**	**12.5**	**14**	**1**	**9**	**0**	**+4**	....	....	....	....	....	....	....	....
	Rochester Americans	AHL	35	11	14	25	....	....	....	8	....	....	....	....	....	....	....	....	....	....	17	9	9	18	4	....	....	....
1993-94	Rochester Americans	AHL	74	28	39	67	....	....	....	26	....	....	....	....	....	....	....	....	....	....	4	3	0	3	2	....	....	....

Season	Club	League	GP	G	A	Pts	AG	AA	APts	PIM	PP	SH	GW	S	%	TGF	PGF	TGA	PGA	+/–	GP	G	A	Pts	PIM	PP	SH	GW
			REGULAR SEASON																		PLAYOFFS							
1994-95	**Buffalo Sabres**	**NHL**	**10**	**0**	**2**	**2**	**0**	**3**	**3**	**0**	**0**	**0**	**0**	**10**	**0.0**	**4**	**3**	**5**	**1**	**–3**	....	....	....	....	....	....	....	....
	Rochester Americans	AHL	63	31	30	61	....	....	....	36	....	....	....	....	....	....	....	....	....	....	3	0	2	2	0	....	....	....
1995-96	Los Angeles Ice Dogs	IHL	68	17	44	61	....	....	....	53	....	....	....	....	....	....	....	....	....	....	....	....	....	....	....	....	....	....
	Utah Grizzlies	IHL	13	4	4	8	....	....	....	6	....	....	....	....	....	....	....	....	....	....	22	4	6	10	14	....	....	....
1996-97	Dusseldorfer EG	Germany	47	20	16	36	....	....	....	26	....	....	....	....	....	....	....	....	....	....	4	0	2	2	2	....	....	....
1997-98	Dusseldorfer EG	Germany	46	14	17	31	....	....	....	20	....	....	....	....	....	....	....	....	....	....	3	0	0	0	2	....	....	....
	NHL Totals		**26**	**3**	**8**	**11**	**2**	**7**	**9**	**0**	**0**	**0**	**0**	**34**	**8.8**	**18**	**4**	**14**	**1**		....	....	....	....	....	....	....	....

• GORENCE, TOM

Tom Gorence RW – R. 6', 190 lbs. b: St. Paul, MN, 3/11/1957. Philadelphia's 2nd choice, 35th overall, in 1977 Amateur Draft.

Season	Club	League	GP	G	A	Pts	AG	AA	APts	PIM	PP	SH	GW	S	%	TGF	PGF	TGA	PGA	+/–	GP	G	A	Pts	PIM	PP	SH	GW
1975-76	University of Minnesota	WCHA	40	16	10	26	....	....	....	24	....	....	....	....	....	....	....	....	....	....	....	....	....	....	....	....	....	....
1976-77	University of Minnesota	WCHA	29	18	19	37	....	....	....	44	....	....	....	....	....	....	....	....	....	....	....	....	....	....	....	....	....	....
1977-78	Maine Mariners	AHL	79	28	25	53	....	....	....	23	....	....	....	....	....	....	....	....	....	....	12	*8	4	12	19	....	....	....
1978-79	Maine Mariners	AHL	31	11	13	24	....	....	....	23	....	....	....	....	....	....	....	....	....	....	....	....	....	....	....	....	....	....
	Philadelphia Flyers	**NHL**	**42**	**13**	**6**	**19**	**12**	**5**	**17**	**10**	**1**	**0**	**3**	**85**	**15.3**	**39**	**4**	**29**	**10**	**+16**	**7**	**3**	**1**	**4**	**0**	**1**	**0**	**0**
1979-80	**Philadelphia Flyers**	**NHL**	**51**	**8**	**13**	**21**	**7**	**10**	**17**	**15**	**0**	**0**	**2**	**89**	**9.0**	**32**	**2**	**24**	**1**	**+7**	**15**	**3**	**3**	**6**	**18**	**1**	**0**	**0**
1980-81	**Philadelphia Flyers**	**NHL**	**79**	**24**	**18**	**42**	**20**	**13**	**33**	**46**	**0**	**3**	**6**	**165**	**14.5**	**56**	**1**	**63**	**25**	**+17**	**12**	**3**	**2**	**5**	**29**	**0**	**0**	**0**
1981-82	United States	C Cup	6	1	1	2	....	....	....	2	....	....	....	....	....	....	....	....	....	....	....	....	....	....	....	....	....	....
	Philadelphia Flyers	**NHL**	**66**	**5**	**8**	**13**	**4**	**5**	**9**	**8**	**0**	**1**	**0**	**88**	**5.7**	**23**	**0**	**67**	**27**	**–17**	**3**	**0**	**0**	**0**	**0**	**0**	**0**	**0**
	United States	WEC-A	7	1	1	2	....	....	....	2	....	....	....	....	....	....	....	....	....	....	....	....	....	....	....	....	....	....
1982-83	**Philadelphia Flyers**	**NHL**	**53**	**7**	**7**	**14**	**6**	**5**	**11**	**10**	**0**	**0**	**0**	**50**	**14.0**	**24**	**0**	**21**	**1**	**+4**	....	....	....	....	....	....	....	....
	Maine Mariners	AHL	10	0	5	5	....	....	....	2	....	....	....	....	....	....	....	....	....	....	17	9	3	12	12	....	....	....
1983-84	**Edmonton Oilers**	**NHL**	**12**	**1**	**1**	**2**	**1**	**1**	**2**	**0**	**0**	**0**	**0**	**7**	**14.3**	**2**	**0**	**2**	**0**	**0**	....	....	....	....	....	....	....	....
	Moncton Alpines	AHL	53	13	14	27	....	....	....	17	....	....	....	....	....	....	....	....	....	....	....	....	....	....	....	....	....	....
1984-85	Maine Mariners	AHL	12	3	1	4	....	....	....	37	....	....	....	....	....	....	....	....	....	....	10	2	3	5	0	....	....	....
1985-86	Hershey Bears	AHL	1	0	0	0	....	....	....	0	....	....	....	....	....	....	....	....	....	....	....	....	....	....	....	....	....	....
	NHL Totals		**303**	**58**	**53**	**111**	**50**	**39**	**89**	**89**	**1**	**4**	**11**	**484**	**12.0**	**176**	**7**	**206**	**64**		**37**	**9**	**6**	**15**	**47**	**2**	**0**	**0**

Signed as a free agent by **Edmonton**, November 1, 1983. Signed as a free agent by **New Jersey**, March 5, 1985.

• GORING, BUTCH

Butch (Robert Thomas) Goring C – L. 5'9", 170 lbs. b: St. Boniface, Man., 10/22/1949. Los Angeles' 4th choice, 51st overall, in 1969 Amateur Draft.

Season	Club	League	GP	G	A	Pts	AG	AA	APts	PIM	PP	SH	GW	S	%	TGF	PGF	TGA	PGA	+/–	GP	G	A	Pts	PIM	PP	SH	GW
1965-66	Winnipeg Rangers	MJHL	3	0	0	0	....	....	....	0	....	....	....	....	....	....	....	....	....	....	3	0	1	1	0	....	....	....
1966-67	Winnipeg Rangers	MJHL	51	35	31	66	....	....	....	2	....	....	....	....	....	....	....	....	....	....	8	2	6	8	0	....	....	....
1967-68	Hull Volants	QSHL	39	16	41	57	....	....	....	4	....	....	....	....	....	....	....	....	....	....	....	....	....	....	....	....	....	....
1968-69	Winnipeg Jets	WCJHL	39	42	33	75	....	....	....	0	....	....	....	....	....	....	....	....	....	....	....	....	....	....	....	....	....	....
	Dauphin Kings	MJHL	....	....	....	....	....	....	....	....	....	....	....	....	....	....	....	....	....	....	12	8	8	16	5	....	....	....
	Regina Pats	SJHL	....	....	....	....	....	....	....	....	....	....	....	....	....	....	....	....	....	....	4	3	1	4	0	....	....	....
1969-70	**Los Angeles Kings**	**NHL**	**59**	**13**	**23**	**36**	**15**	**23**	**38**	**8**	**2**	**0**	**0**	**125**	**10.4**	**48**	**10**	**59**	**6**	**–15**	....	....	....	....	....	....	....	....
	Springfield Kings	AHL	19	13	7	20	....	....	....	0	....	....	....	....	....	....	....	....	....	....	....	....	....	....	....	....	....	....
1970-71	**Los Angeles Kings**	**NHL**	**19**	**2**	**5**	**7**	**2**	**4**	**6**	**2**	**0**	**0**	**0**	**15**	**13.3**	**7**	**1**	**2**	**0**	**+4**	....	....	....	....	....	....	....	....
	Springfield Kings	AHL	40	23	32	55	....	....	....	4	....	....	....	....	....	....	....	....	....	....	12	*11	*14	*25	0	....	....	....
1971-72	**Los Angeles Kings**	**NHL**	**74**	**21**	**29**	**50**	**22**	**26**	**48**	**2**	**3**	**0**	**2**	**137**	**15.3**	**65**	**15**	**64**	**4**	**–10**	....	....	....	....	....	....	....	....
1972-73	**Los Angeles Kings**	**NHL**	**67**	**28**	**31**	**59**	**28**	**26**	**54**	**2**	**4**	**1**	**1**	**148**	**18.9**	**74**	**12**	**63**	**1**	**0**	....	....	....	....	....	....	....	....
1973-74	**Los Angeles Kings**	**NHL**	**70**	**28**	**33**	**61**	**29**	**29**	**58**	**2**	**5**	**3**	**5**	**161**	**17.4**	**76**	**20**	**77**	**23**	**+2**	**5**	**0**	**1**	**1**	**0**	**0**	**0**	**0**
1974-75	**Los Angeles Kings**	**NHL**	**60**	**27**	**33**	**60**	**25**	**26**	**51**	**6**	**6**	**3**	**7**	**134**	**20.1**	**77**	**26**	**51**	**26**	**+26**	**3**	**0**	**0**	**0**	**0**	**0**	**0**	**0**
1975-76	**Los Angeles Kings**	**NHL**	**80**	**33**	**40**	**73**	**31**	**31**	**62**	**8**	**5**	**5**	**2**	**193**	**17.1**	**96**	**37**	**93**	**34**	**0**	**9**	**2**	**3**	**5**	**4**	**1**	**0**	**2**
1976-77	**Los Angeles Kings**	**NHL**	**78**	**30**	**55**	**85**	**29**	**45**	**74**	**6**	**13**	**0**	**3**	**216**	**13.9**	**120**	**56**	**82**	**28**	**+10**	**9**	**7**	**5**	**12**	**0**	**3**	**0**	**2**
1977-78	**Los Angeles Kings**	**NHL**	**80**	**37**	**36**	**73**	**36**	**29**	**65**	**2**	**9**	**3**	**5**	**248**	**14.9**	**101**	**34**	**102**	**31**	**–4**	**2**	**0**	**0**	**0**	**2**	**0**	**0**	**0**
1978-79	**Los Angeles Kings**	**NHL**	**80**	**36**	**51**	**87**	**33**	**39**	**72**	**16**	**13**	**4**	**2**	**217**	**16.6**	**122**	**64**	**119**	**41**	**–20**	**2**	**0**	**0**	**0**	**0**	**0**	**0**	**0**
1979-80	**Los Angeles Kings**	**NHL**	**69**	**20**	**48**	**68**	**18**	**37**	**55**	**12**	**2**	**1**	**1**	**160**	**12.5**	**106**	**59**	**105**	**37**	**–21**	....	....	....	....	....	....	....	....
	New York Islanders	**NHL**	**12**	**6**	**5**	**11**	**5**	**4**	**9**	**2**	**0**	**1**	**0**	**20**	**30.0**	**16**	**3**	**9**	**3**	**+7**	**21**	**7**	**12**	**19**	**2**	**1**	**0**	**0**
1980-81	**New York Islanders**	**NHL**	**78**	**23**	**37**	**60**	**19**	**26**	**45**	**0**	**4**	**1**	**1**	**152**	**15.1**	**82**	**24**	**88**	**34**	**+4**	**18**	**10**	**10**	**20**	**6**	**4**	**2**	**2**
1981-82	Canada	C Cup	7	3	2	5	....	....	....	4	....	....	....	....	....	....	....	....	....	....	....	....	....	....	....	....	....	....
	New York Islanders	**NHL**	**67**	**15**	**17**	**32**	**12**	**11**	**23**	**10**	**1**	**5**	**1**	**63**	**23.8**	**54**	**10**	**76**	**29**	**–3**	**19**	**6**	**5**	**11**	**12**	**1**	**0**	**2**
1982-83	**New York Islanders**	**NHL**	**75**	**19**	**20**	**39**	**16**	**14**	**30**	**8**	**2**	**5**	**4**	**98**	**19.4**	**53**	**5**	**62**	**24**	**+10**	**20**	**4**	**8**	**12**	**4**	**0**	**0**	**1**
1983-84	**New York Islanders**	**NHL**	**71**	**22**	**24**	**46**	**18**	**16**	**34**	**8**	**0**	**5**	**3**	**89**	**24.7**	**61**	**6**	**74**	**28**	**+9**	**21**	**1**	**5**	**6**	**2**	**1**	**0**	**0**
1984-85	**New York Islanders**	**NHL**	**29**	**2**	**5**	**7**	**2**	**3**	**5**	**2**	**0**	**1**	**0**	**19**	**10.5**	**9**	**1**	**33**	**14**	**–11**	....	....	....	....	....	....	....	....
	Boston Bruins	**NHL**	**39**	**13**	**21**	**34**	**11**	**14**	**25**	**6**	**2**	**2**	**2**	**84**	**15.5**	**50**	**19**	**55**	**16**	**–8**	**5**	**1**	**1**	**2**	**0**	**0**	**0**	**0**
1985-86	**Boston Bruins**	**NHL**	DID NOT PLAY – COACHING																									
1986-87	Nova Scotia Oilers	AHL	10	3	5	8	....	....	....	2	....	....	....	....	....	....	....	....	....	....	....	....	....	....	....	....	....	....
	NHL Totals		**1107**	**375**	**513**	**888**	**351**	**403**	**754**	**102**	**71**	**40**	**39**	**2279**	**16.5**	**1217**	**402**	**1214**	**379**		**134**	**38**	**50**	**88**	**32**	**11**	**2**	**9**

Won Bill Masterton Trophy (1978) • Won Lady Byng Trophy (1978) • Won Conn Smythe Trophy (1981)

Played in NHL All-Star Game (1980)

Traded to **NY Islanders** by **LA Kings** for Billy Harris and Dave Lewis, March 10, 1980. Claimed on waivers by **Boston** from **NY Islanders**, January 8, 1985.

• GORMAN, DAVE

Dave Gorman RW – R. 5'11", 185 lbs. b: Oshawa, Ont., 4/8/1955. Montreal's 7th choice, 70th overall, in 1975 Amateur Draft.

Season	Club	League	GP	G	A	Pts	AG	AA	APts	PIM	PP	SH	GW	S	%	TGF	PGF	TGA	PGA	+/–	GP	G	A	Pts	PIM	PP	SH	GW
1971-72	St. Catharines Black Hawks	OHA	58	31	24	55	....	....	....	71	....	....	....	....	....	....	....	....	....	....	....	....	....	....	....	....	....	....
1972-73	St. Catharines Black Hawks	OHA	62	46	57	103	....	....	....	71	....	....	....	....	....	....	....	....	....	....	....	....	....	....	....	....	....	....
1973-74	St. Catharines Black Hawks	OHA	69	53	76	129	....	....	....	78	....	....	....	....	....	....	....	....	....	....	14	6	25	31	....	....	....	....
1974-75	Phoenix Roadrunners	WHA	13	3	5	8	....	....	....	10	....	....	....	....	....	....	....	....	....	....	....	....	....	....	....	....	....	....
	Tulsa Oilers	CHL	58	19	21	40	....	....	....	96	....	....	....	....	....	....	....	....	....	....	1	0	1	1	2	....	....	....
1975-76	Phoenix Roadrunners	WHA	67	11	20	31	....	....	....	28	....	....	....	....	....	....	....	....	....	....	5	0	2	2	24	....	....	....
1976-77	Phoenix Roadrunners	WHA	5	0	0	0	....	....	....	0	....	....	....	....	....	....	....	....	....	....	....	....	....	....	....	....	....	....
	Birmingham Bulls	WHA	52	9	13	22	....	....	....	38	....	....	....	....	....	....	....	....	....	....	....	....	....	....	....	....	....	....
1977-78	Birmingham Bulls	WHA	63	19	21	40	....	....	....	93	....	....	....	....	....	....	....	....	....	....	4	1	1	2	0	....	....	....
	Hampton Gulls	AHL	2	0	0	0	....	....	....	12	....	....	....	....	....	....	....	....	....	....	....	....	....	....	....	....	....	....
1978-79	Birmingham Bulls	WHA	60	14	24	38	....	....	....	18	....	....	....	....	....	....	....	....	....	....	....	....	....	....	....	....	....	....
1979-80	**Atlanta Flames**	**NHL**	**3**	**0**	**0**	**0**	**0**	**0**	**0**	**0**	**0**	**0**	**0**	**1**	**0.0**	**0**	**0**	**1**	**0**	**–1**	....	....	....	....	....	....	....	....
	Birmingham Bulls	CHL	75	22	43	65	....	....	....	75	....	....	....	....	....	....	....	....	....	....	4	1	1	2	2	....	....	....
1980-81	Nova Scotia Voyageurs	AHL	78	43	47	90	....	....	....	82	....	....	....	....	....	....	....	....	....	....	6	1	2	3	8	....	....	....
1981-82	Rochester Americans	AHL	77	26	41	67	....	....	....	131	....	....	....	....	....	....	....	....	....	....	8	3	4	7	11	....	....	....
	NHL Totals		**3**	**0**	**0**	**0**	**0**	**0**	**0**	**0**	**0**	**0**	**0**	**1**	**0.0**	**0**	**0**	**1**	**0**		....	....	....	....	....	....	....	....
	Other Major League Totals		260	56	83	139	....	....	....	187	....	....	....	....	....	....	....	....	....		9	1	3	4	24	....	....	....

OHA Second All-Star Team (1974) • AHL First All-Star Team (1981)

Selected by **Phoenix** (WHA) in1974 WHA Amateur Draft, June, 1974. Traded to **Birmingham** (WHA) by **Phoenix** (WHA) for Jerry Rollins, November, 1976. Signed as a free agent by **Atlanta**, August, 1979. Signed as a free agent by **Buffalo**, June 30, 1981.

• GOSSELIN, BENOIT

Benoit Gosselin LW – L. 5'11", 190 lbs. b: Montreal, Que., 7/19/1957. NY Rangers' 6th choice, 80th overall, in 1977 Amateur Draft.

Season	Club	League	GP	G	A	Pts	AG	AA	APts	PIM	PP	SH	GW	S	%	TGF	PGF	TGA	PGA	+/–	GP	G	A	Pts	PIM	PP	SH	GW
1973-74	Shawinigan Bruins	QMJHL	64	12	17	29	....	....	....	134	....	....	....	....	....	....	....	....	....	....	....	....	....	....	....	....	....	....
1974-75	Shawinigan Bruins	QMJHL	60	48	49	97	....	....	....	153	....	....	....	....	....	....	....	....	....	....	....	....	....	....	....	....	....	....
1975-76	Sorel Black Hawks	QMJHL	63	40	52	92	....	....	....	144	....	....	....	....	....	....	....	....	....	....	3	2	0	2	51	....	....	....
1976-77	Trois-Rivieres Draveurs	QMJHL	74	64	62	126	....	....	....	145	....	....	....	....	....	....	....	....	....	....	6	3	5	8	10	....	....	....
1977-78	**New York Rangers**	**NHL**	**7**	**0**	**0**	**0**	**0**	**0**	**0**	**33**	**0**	**0**	**0**	**4**	**0.0**	**0**	**0**	**3**	**0**	**–3**	....	....	....	....	....	....	....	....
	New Haven Nighthawks	AHL	52	14	12	26	....	....	....	120	....	....	....	....	....	....	....	....	....	....	15	1	6	7	20	....	....	....
1978-79	New Haven Nighthawks	AHL	3	0	0	0	....	....	....	0	....	....	....	....	....	....	....	....	....	....	....	....	....	....	....	....	....	....
	Toledo Goaldiggers	IHL	8	5	3	8	....	....	....	18	....	....	....	....	....	....	....	....	....	....	....	....	....	....	....	....	....	....
	Kalamazoo Wings	IHL	65	35	24	59	....	....	....	81	....	....	....	....	....	....	....	....	....	....	15	8	6	14	60	....	....	....
1979-80	Dayton Gems	IHL	42	37	20	57	....	....	....	72	....	....	....	....	....	....	....	....	....	....	....	....	....	....	....	....	....	....
	Tulsa Oilers	CHL	37	21	15	36	....	....	....	24	....	....	....	....	....	....	....	....	....	....	3	0	0	0	11	....	....	....

Season	Club	League	GP	G	A	Pts	AG	AA	APts	PIM	PP	SH	GW	S	%	TGF	PGF	TGA	PGA	+/-	GP	G	A	Pts	PIM	PP	SH	GW
										REGULAR SEASON											PLAYOFFS							
1980-81	Tulsa Oilers	CHL	66	22	29	51	....	....	....	66	....	....	....	....	....	....	....	....	....	....	2	0	0	0	2	....	....	....
1981-82	Tulsa Oilers	CHL	71	31	23	54	....	....	....	29	....	....	....	....	....	....	....	....	....	....	....	....	....	....	....	....	....	....
1982-83	Sherbrooke Jets	AHL	21	5	2	7	....	....	....	6	....	....	....	....	....	....	....	....	....	....	....	....	....	....	....	....	....	....
	NHL Totals		**7**	**0**	**0**	**0**	**0**	**0**	**0**	**33**	**0**	**0**	**0**	**4**	**0.0**	**0**	**0**	**3**	**0**		....	....	....	....	....	....	....	....

Signed as a free agent by **Winnipeg**, September 25, 1979.

• GOSSELIN, GUY

Guy Gosselin D – R. 5'10", 185 lbs. b: Rochester, MN, 1/6/1964. Winnipeg's 6th choice, 159th overall, in 1982 Entry Draft.

Season	Club	League	GP	G	A	Pts	AG	AA	APts	PIM	PP	SH	GW	S	%	TGF	PGF	TGA	PGA	+/-	GP	G	A	Pts	PIM	PP	SH	GW
1981-82	John Marshall High School	H.S.	22	14	15	29	....	....	....	48	....	....	....	....	....	....	....	....	....	....	....	....	....	....	....	....	....	....
1982-83	University of Minnesota-Duluth	WCHA	4	0	0	0	....	....	....	0	....	....	....	....	....	....	....	....	....	....	....	....	....	....	....	....	....	....
1983-84	University of Minnesota-Duluth	WCHA	37	3	3	6	....	....	....	26	....	....	....	....	....	....	....	....	....	....	....	....	....	....	....	....	....	....
1984-85	University of Minnesota-Duluth	WCHA	47	3	7	10	....	....	....	25	....	....	....	....	....	....	....	....	....	....	....	....	....	....	....	....	....	....
1985-86	University of Minnesota-Duluth	WCHA	39	2	16	18	....	....	....	53	....	....	....	....	....	....	....	....	....	....	....	....	....	....	....	....	....	....
	United States	WEC-A	8	0	0	0	....	....	....	10	....	....	....	....	....	....	....	....	....	....	....	....	....	....	....	....	....	....
1986-87	University of Minnesota-Duluth	WCHA	33	7	8	15	....	....	....	66	....	....	....	....	....	....	....	....	....	....	....	....	....	....	....	....	....	....
1987-88	United States	Nat-Team	50	3	19	22	....	....	....	82	....	....	....	....	....	....	....	....	....	....	....	....	....	....	....	....	....	....
	United States	Olympics	6	0	3	3	....	....	....	2	....	....	....	....	....	....	....	....	....	....	....	....	....	....	....	....	....	....
	Winnipeg Jets	**NHL**	**5**	**0**	**0**	**0**	**0**	**0**	**0**	**6**	**0**	**0**	**0**	**1**	**0.0**	**3**	**0**	**5**	**1**	**–1**	....	....	....	....	....	....	....	....
1988-89	Moncton Hawks	AHL	58	2	8	10	....	....	....	56	....	....	....	....	....	....	....	....	....	....	10	1	1	2	2	....	....	....
1989-90	Moncton Hawks	AHL	70	2	10	12	....	....	....	37	....	....	....	....	....	....	....	....	....	....	....	....	....	....	....	....	....	....
	United States	WEC-A	10	3	0	3	....	....	....	4	....	....	....	....	....	....	....	....	....	....	....	....	....	....	....	....	....	....
1990-91	Skelleftea	Sweden 2	16	0	1	1	....	....	....	8	....	....	....	....	....	....	....	....	....	....	....	....	....	....	....	....	....	....
	United States	WEC-A	10	0	1	1	....	....	....	6	....	....	....	....	....	....	....	....	....	....	....	....	....	....	....	....	....	....
1991-92	United States	Nat-Team	18	1	3	4	....	....	....	20	....	....	....	....	....	....	....	....	....	....	....	....	....	....	....	....	....	....
	United States	Olympics	8	0	0	0	....	....	....	6	....	....	....	....	....	....	....	....	....	....	....	....	....	....	....	....	....	....
1992-93	Skelleftea	Sweden	34	5	10	15	....	....	....	28	....	....	....	....	....	....	....	....	....	....	....	....	....	....	....	....	....	....
1993-94	Kansas City Blades	IHL	19	1	6	7	....	....	....	2	....	....	....	....	....	....	....	....	....	....	....	....	....	....	....	....	....	....
	NHL Totals		**5**	**0**	**0**	**0**	**0**	**0**	**0**	**6**	**0**	**0**	**0**	**1**	**0.0**	**3**	**0**	**5**	**1**		....	....	....	....	....	....	....	....

WCHA Second All-Star Team (1987)

Signed as a free agent by **San Jose**, August 25, 1993.

• GOTAAS, STEVE

Steve Gotaas C – R. 5'10", 180 lbs. b: Camrose, Alta., 5/10/1967. Pittsburgh's 4th choice, 86th overall, in 1985 Entry Draft.

Season	Club	League	GP	G	A	Pts	AG	AA	APts	PIM	PP	SH	GW	S	%	TGF	PGF	TGA	PGA	+/-	GP	G	A	Pts	PIM	PP	SH	GW
1983-84	Prince Albert Raiders	WHL	65	10	22	32	....	....	....	47	....	....	....	....	....	....	....	....	....	....	5	0	1	1	0	....	....	....
1984-85	Prince Albert Raiders	WHL	72	32	41	73	....	....	....	66	....	....	....	....	....	....	....	....	....	....	13	3	6	9	17	....	....	....
1985-86	Prince Albert Raiders	WHL	61	40	61	101	....	....	....	31	....	....	....	....	....	....	....	....	....	....	....	....	....	....	....	....	....	....
1986-87	Prince Albert Raiders	WHL	68	53	55	108	....	....	....	94	....	....	....	....	....	....	....	....	....	....	8	5	6	11	16	....	....	....
1987-88	**Pittsburgh Penguins**	**NHL**	**36**	**5**	**6**	**11**	**4**	**4**	**8**	**45**	**0**	**0**	**1**	**27**	**18.5**	**13**	**0**	**34**	**10**	**–11**	....	....	....	....	....	....	....	....
	Muskegon Lumberjacks	IHL	34	16	22	38	....	....	....	4	....	....	....	....	....	....	....	....	....	....	....	....	....	....	....	....	....	....
1988-89	**Minnesota North Stars**	**NHL**	**12**	**1**	**3**	**4**	**1**	**2**	**3**	**6**	**1**	**0**	**0**	**18**	**5.6**	**5**	**2**	**4**	**0**	**–1**	**3**	**0**	**1**	**1**	**5**	**0**	**0**	**0**
	Muskegon Lumberjacks	IHL	19	9	16	25	....	....	....	34	....	....	....	....	....	....	....	....	....	....	....	....	....	....	....	....	....	....
	Kalamazoo Wings	IHL	30	24	22	46	....	....	....	12	....	....	....	....	....	....	....	....	....	....	5	2	3	5	2	....	....	....
1989-90	Kalamazoo Wings	IHL	1	1	0	1	....	....	....	0	....	....	....	....	....	....	....	....	....	....	2	0	0	0	2	....	....	....
1990-91	**Minnesota North Stars**	**NHL**	**1**	**0**	**0**	**0**	**0**	**0**	**0**	**2**	**0**	**0**	**0**	**2**	**0.0**	**0**	**0**	**1**	**0**	**–1**	....	....	....	....	....	....	....	....
	Kalamazoo Wings	IHL	78	30	49	79	....	....	....	88	....	....	....	....	....	....	....	....	....	....	7	3	5	8	4	....	....	....
1991-92	Kalamazoo Wings	IHL	72	34	29	63	....	....	....	115	....	....	....	....	....	....	....	....	....	....	12	4	10	14	20	....	....	....
1992-93	Dusseldorfer EG	Germany	30	4	16	20	....	....	....	20	....	....	....	....	....	....	....	....	....	....	....	....	....	....	....	....	....	....
	Klagenfurter AC	Austria	11	3	4	7	....	....	....	....	....	....	....	....	....	....	....	....	....	....	....	....	....	....	....	....	....	....
1993-94	Las Vegas Thunder	IHL	39	4	....	17	....	....	....	43	....	....	....	....	....	....	....	....	....	....	4	0	0	0	28	....	....	....
	NHL Totals		**49**	**6**	**9**	**15**	**5**	**6**	**11**	**53**	**1**	**0**	**1**	**47**	**12.8**	**18**	**2**	**39**	**10**		**3**	**0**	**1**	**1**	**5**	**0**	**0**	**0**

Traded to **Minnesota** by **Pittsburgh** with Ville Siren for Gord Dineen and Scott Bjugstad, December 17, 1988.

• GOULD, BOBBY

Bobby Gould RW – R. 6', 195 lbs. b: Petrolia, Ont., 9/2/1957. Atlanta's 1st choice, 118th overall, in 1977 Amateur Draft.

Season	Club	League	GP	G	A	Pts	AG	AA	APts	PIM	PP	SH	GW	S	%	TGF	PGF	TGA	PGA	+/-	GP	G	A	Pts	PIM	PP	SH	GW
1975-76	University of New Hampshire	ECAC	31	13	14	27	....	....	....	16	....	....	....	....	....	....	....	....	....	....	....	....	....	....	....	....	....	....
1976-77	University of New Hampshire	ECAC	[illegible]	24	25	49	....	....	....	36	....	....	....	....	....	....	....	....	....	....	....	....	....	....	....	....	....	....
1977-78	University of New Hampshire	ECAC	30	23	34	57	....	....	....	40	....	....	....	....	....	....	....	....	....	....	....	....	....	....	....	....	....	....
1978-79	University of New Hampshire	ECAC	25	24	17	41	....	....	....	....	....	....	....	....	....	....	....	....	....	....	....	....	....	....	....	....	....	....
	Tulsa Oilers	CHL	5	2	0	2	....	....	....	4	....	....	....	....	....	....	....	....	....	....	....	....	....	....	....	....	....	....
1979-80	**Atlanta Flames**	**NHL**	**1**	**0**	**0**	**0**	**0**	**0**	**0**	**0**	**0**	**0**	**0**	**1**	**0.0**	**0**	**0**	**1**	**0**	**–1**	....	....	....	....	....	....	....	....
	Birmingham Bulls	CHL	79	27	33	60	....	....	....	73	....	....	....	....	....	....	....	....	....	....	4	2	4	6	0	....	....	....
1980-81	**Calgary Flames**	**NHL**	**3**	**0**	**0**	**0**	**0**	**0**	**0**	**0**	**0**	**0**	**0**	**5**	**0.0**	**1**	**0**	**1**	**0**	**0**	**11**	**3**	**1**	**4**	**4**	**0**	**0**	**0**
	Birmingham Bulls	CHL	58	25	25	50	....	....	....	43	....	....	....	....	....	....	....	....	....	....	....	....	....	....	....	....	....	....
	Fort Worth Texans	CHL	18	8	6	14	....	....	....	6	....	....	....	....	....	....	....	....	....	....	5	5	2	7	10	....	....	....
1981-82	**Calgary Flames**	**NHL**	**16**	**3**	**0**	**3**	**2**	**0**	**2**	**4**	**0**	**0**	**1**	**18**	**16.7**	**6**	**0**	**8**	**0**	**–2**	....	....	....	....	....	....	....	....
	Oklahoma City Stars	CHL	1	0	1	1	....	....	....	0	....	....	....	....	....	....	....	....	....	....	....	....	....	....	....	....	....	....
	Washington Capitals	**NHL**	**60**	**18**	**13**	**31**	**14**	**9**	**23**	**69**	**1**	**0**	**1**	**103**	**17.5**	**41**	**4**	**59**	**19**	**–3**	....	....	....	....	....	....	....	....
1982-83	**Washington Capitals**	**NHL**	**80**	**22**	**18**	**40**	**18**	**12**	**30**	**43**	**0**	**0**	**6**	**142**	**15.5**	**55**	**1**	**66**	**20**	**+16**	**4**	**5**	**0**	**5**	**4**	**1**	**0**	**1**
1983-84	**Washington Capitals**	**NHL**	**78**	**21**	**19**	**40**	**17**	**13**	**30**	**74**	**4**	**0**	**4**	**155**	**13.5**	**53**	**7**	**64**	**16**	**–2**	**5**	**0**	**2**	**2**	**4**	**0**	**0**	**0**
1984-85	**Washington Capitals**	**NHL**	**78**	**14**	**19**	**33**	**11**	**13**	**24**	**69**	**0**	**1**	**3**	**114**	**12.3**	**45**	**0**	**56**	**21**	**+10**	**5**	**0**	**1**	**1**	**2**	**0**	**0**	**0**
1985-86	**Washington Capitals**	**NHL**	**79**	**19**	**19**	**38**	**15**	**13**	**28**	**26**	**0**	**3**	**5**	**125**	**15.2**	**49**	**0**	**67**	**25**	**+7**	**9**	**4**	**3**	**7**	**11**	**0**	**0**	**0**
1986-87	**Washington Capitals**	**NHL**	**78**	**23**	**27**	**50**	**20**	**20**	**40**	**74**	**1**	**1**	**2**	**156**	**14.7**	**66**	**1**	**74**	**27**	**+18**	**7**	**0**	**3**	**3**	**8**	**0**	**0**	**0**
1987-88	**Washington Capitals**	**NHL**	**72**	**12**	**14**	**26**	**10**	**10**	**20**	**58**	**0**	**0**	**2**	**119**	**10.1**	**35**	**0**	**64**	**28**	**–1**	**14**	**3**	**1**	**4**	**21**	**0**	**2**	**0**
1988-89	**Washington Capitals**	**NHL**	**75**	**5**	**13**	**18**	**4**	**9**	**13**	**65**	**0**	**1**	**0**	**91**	**5.5**	**29**	**1**	**57**	**27**	**–2**	**6**	**0**	**2**	**2**	**0**	**0**	**0**	**0**
1989-90	**Boston Bruins**	**NHL**	**77**	**8**	**17**	**25**	**7**	**12**	**19**	**92**	**0**	**0**	**2**	**92**	**8.7**	**36**	**2**	**45**	**8**	**–3**	**17**	**0**	**0**	**0**	**4**	**0**	**0**	**0**
1990-91	Maine Mariners	AHL	71	10	15	25	....	....	....	30	....	....	....	....	....	....	....	....	....	....	2	0	0	0	0	....	....	....
	NHL Totals		**697**	**145**	**159**	**304**	**118**	**111**	**229**	**572**	**6**	**6**	**26**	**1121**	**12.9**	**416**	**16**	**562**	**199**		**78**	**15**	**13**	**28**	**58**	**1**	**2**	**1**

ECAC Second All-Star Team (1979)

Transferred to **Calgary** after **Atlanta** franchise relocated, June 24, 1980. Traded to **Washington** by **Calgary** with Randy Holt for Pat Ribble and Washington's 2nd round choice (later traded to Montreal — Montreal selected Todd Francis), November 25, 1981. Traded to **Boston** by **Washington** for Alain Cote, September 29, 1989.

• GOULD, JOHN

John Gould RW – L. 5'11", 197 lbs. b: Beeton, Ont., 4/11/1949.

Season	Club	League	GP	G	A	Pts	AG	AA	APts	PIM	PP	SH	GW	S	%	TGF	PGF	TGA	PGA	+/-	GP	G	A	Pts	PIM	PP	SH	GW
1967-68	London Nationals	OHA	54	19	27	46	....	....	....	14	....	....	....	....	....	....	....	....	....	....	5	1	2	3	13	....	....	....
1968-69	London Knights	OHA	49	30	44	74	....	....	....	20	....	....	....	....	....	....	....	....	....	....	6	1	3	4	0	....	....	....
1969-70	Charlotte Checkers	EHL	69	25	48	73	....	....	....	18	....	....	....	....	....	....	....	....	....	....	11	10	6	16	6	....	....	....
	Tulsa Oilers	CHL	....	....	....	....	....	....	....	....	....	....	....	....	....	....	....	....	....	....	3	1	0	1	0	....	....	....
1970-71	Charlotte Checkers	EHL	72	48	52	100	....	....	....	50	....	....	....	....	....	....	....	....	....	....	13	10	8	18	6	....	....	....
1971-72	**Buffalo Sabres**	**NHL**	**2**	**1**	**0**	**1**	**1**	**0**	**1**	**0**	**0**	**0**	**0**	**3**	**33.3**	**1**	**0**	**2**	**0**	**–1**	....	....	....	....	....	....	....	....
	Cincinnati Swords	AHL	73	26	15	41	....	....	....	34	....	....	....	....	....	....	....	....	....	....	10	4	6	10	6	....	....	....
1972-73	**Buffalo Sabres**	**NHL**	**8**	**0**	**1**	**1**	**0**	**1**	**1**	**0**	**0**	**0**	**0**	**4**	**0.0**	**2**	**0**	**2**	**0**	**0**	....	....	....	....	....	....	....	....
	Cincinnati Swords	AHL	56	30	42	72	....	....	....	71	....	....	....	....	....	....	....	....	....	....	15	*10	6	16	9	....	....	....
1973-74	**Buffalo Sabres**	**NHL**	**30**	**4**	**2**	**6**	**4**	**2**	**6**	**2**	**0**	**0**	**1**	**48**	**8.3**	**12**	**2**	**21**	**4**	**–7**	....	....	....	....	....	....	....	....
	Vancouver Canucks	**NHL**	**45**	**9**	**10**	**19**	**9**	**9**	**18**	**8**	**2**	**0**	**4**	**127**	**7.1**	**38**	**9**	**45**	**12**	**–4**	....	....	....	....	....	....	....	....
1974-75	**Vancouver Canucks**	**NHL**	**78**	**34**	**31**	**65**	**32**	**24**	**56**	**27**	**6**	**0**	**6**	**230**	**14.8**	**101**	**32**	**81**	**19**	**+7**	**5**	**2**	**2**	**4**	**0**	**1**	**0**	**0**
1975-76	**Vancouver Canucks**	**NHL**	**70**	**32**	**27**	**59**	**30**	**21**	**51**	**16**	**6**	**1**	**5**	**225**	**14.2**	**83**	**24**	**69**	**19**	**+9**	**2**	**1**	**0**	**1**	**0**	**0**	**1**	**0**
1976-77	**Vancouver Canucks**	**NHL**	**25**	**7**	**8**	**15**	**7**	**6**	**13**	**2**	**1**	**0**	**2**	**65**	**10.8**	**21**	**3**	**30**	**3**	**–9**	....	....	....	....	....	....	....	....
	Atlanta Flames	**NHL**	**54**	**8**	**15**	**23**	**8**	**12**	**20**	**8**	**1**	**1**	**0**	**113**	**7.1**	**41**	**13**	**37**	**7**	**–2**	**3**	**0**	**0**	**0**	**2**	**0**	**0**	**0**
1977-78	**Atlanta Flames**	**NHL**	**79**	**19**	**28**	**47**	**18**	**23**	**41**	**21**	**2**	**0**	**4**	**133**	**14.3**	**73**	**16**	**88**	**38**	**+7**	**2**	**0**	**0**	**0**	**2**	**0**	**0**	**0**

			REGULAR SEASON																		PLAYOFFS							
Season	Club	League	GP	G	A	Pts	AG	AA	APts	PIM	PP	SH	GW	S	%	TGF	PGF	TGA	PGA	+/–	GP	G	A	Pts	PIM	PP	SH	GW
1978-79	Atlanta Flames	NHL	61	8	7	15	7	5	12	18	0	0	3	67	11.9	30	8	54	28	–4	2	0	0	0	0	0	0	0
1979-80	Buffalo Sabres	NHL	52	9	9	18	8	7	15	11	0	0	2	72	12.5	27	1	17	0	+9	....	....	....	....	....	....	....	....
	Rochester Americans	AHL	13	6	5	11	....	....	....	6	....	....	....	....	....	....	....	....	....	....	4	0	1	1	2	....	....	....
	NHL Totals		504	131	138	269	124	110	234	113	18	2	27	1087	12.1	429	108	446	130		14	3	2	5	4	1	1	0

AHL Second All-Star Team (1973)

Signed as a free agent by **Buffalo**, August, 1971. Traded to **Vancouver** by **Buffalo** with Tracy Pratt for Jerry Korab, December 27, 1973. Traded to **Atlanta** by **Vancouver** with LA Kings' 2nd round choice (previously acquired, Atlanta selected Brian Hill) in 1977 Amateur Draft for Hilliard Graves and Larry Carriere, December 2, 1976. Claimed by **Edmonton** from **Atlanta** in Expansion Draft, June 13, 1979. Traded to **Buffalo** by **Edmonton** for Alex Tidey, November 13, 1979.

• GOULD, LARRY

Larry Gould LW – L. 5'9", 170 lbs. b: Alliston, Ont., 8/16/1952.

Season	Club	League	GP	G	A	Pts	AG	AA	APts	PIM	PP	SH	GW	S	%	TGF	PGF	TGA	PGA	+/–	GP	G	A	Pts	PIM	PP	SH	GW
1969-70	Hamilton Red Wings	OHA	49	21	19	40	....	....	....	81	....	....	....	....	....	....	....	....	....	....	....	....	....	....	....	....	....	....
1970-71	Hamilton Red Wings	OHA	50	21	16	37	....	....	....	73	....	....	....	....	....	....	....	....	....	....	....	....	....	....	....	....	....	....
1971-72	Niagara Falls Flyers	OHA	61	14	20	34	....	....	....	92	....	....	....	....	....	....	....	....	....	....	....	....	....	....	....	....	....	....
1972-73	Des Moines Capitols	IHL	73	30	54	84	....	....	....	89	....	....	....	....	....	....	....	....	....	....	3	2	1	3	0	....	....	....
1973-74	Vancouver Canucks	NHL	2	0	0	0	0	0	0	0	0	0	0	0	0.0	0	0	2	0	–2	....	....	....	....	....	....	....	....
	Seattle Totems	WHL	53	17	32	49	....	....	....	49	....	....	....	....	....	....	....	....	....	....	....	....	....	....	....	....	....	....
1974-75	Seattle Totems	CHL	72	21	41	62	....	....	....	49	....	....	....	....	....	....	....	....	....	....	....	....	....	....	....	....	....	....
1975-76	Buffalo Norsemen	NAHL	71	32	68	100	....	....	....	22	....	....	....	....	....	....	....	....	....	....	....	....	....	....	....	....	....	....
1976-77	Port Huron Flags	IHL	74	35	71	106	....	....	....	37	....	....	....	....	....	....	....	....	....	....	....	....	....	....	....	....	....	....
1977-78	Port Huron Flags	IHL	80	36	69	105	....	....	....	86	....	....	....	....	....	....	....	....	....	....	....	....	....	....	....	....	....	....
1978-79	Port Huron Flags	IHL	59	30	36	66	....	....	....	32	....	....	....	....	....	....	....	....	....	....	....	....	....	....	....	....	....	....
1979-80	Port Huron Flags	IHL	75	25	57	82	....	....	....	35	....	....	....	....	....	....	....	....	....	....	11	3	12	15	4	....	....	....
1980-81	Port Huron Flags	IHL	71	30	63	93	....	....	....	51	....	....	....	....	....	....	....	....	....	....	4	1	1	2	0	....	....	....
1981-82	Muskegon–Flint	IHL	74	33	60	93	....	....	....	24	....	....	....	....	....	....	....	....	....	....	4	2	2	4	2	....	....	....
	NHL Totals		2	0	0	0	0	0	0	0	0	0	0	0	0.0	0	0	2	0		....	....	....	....	....	....	....	....

IHL Second All-Star Team (1977) • IHL First All-Star Team (1978)

Signed as a free agent by **Vancouver**, October, 1973.

• GOULET, MICHEL

Michel Goulet LW – L. 6'1", 195 lbs. b: Peribonka, Que., 4/21/1960. Quebec's 1st choice, 20th overall, in 1979 Entry Draft.

Season	Club	League	GP	G	A	Pts	AG	AA	APts	PIM	PP	SH	GW	S	%	TGF	PGF	TGA	PGA	+/–	GP	G	A	Pts	PIM	PP	SH	GW
1976-77	Quebec Remparts	QMJHL	37	17	18	35	....	....	....	9	....	....	....	....	....	....	....	....	....	....	14	3	8	11	19	....	....	....
1977-78	Quebec Remparts	QMJHL	72	73	62	135	....	....	....	109	....	....	....	....	....	....	....	....	....	....	1	0	1	1	0	....	....	....
1978-79	Birmingham Bulls	WHA	78	28	30	58	....	....	....	65	....	....	....	....	....	....	....	....	....	....	....	....	....	....	....	....	....	....
1979-80	Quebec Nordiques	NHL	77	22	32	54	20	25	45	48	5	0	1	167	13.2	73	24	60	1	–10	....	....	....	....	....	....	....	....
1980-81	Quebec Nordiques	NHL	76	32	39	71	26	27	53	45	3	2	3	265	12.1	101	21	98	18	0	4	3	4	7	7	0	0	1
1981-82	Quebec Nordiques	NHL	80	42	42	84	33	28	61	48	7	6	3	251	16.7	122	21	96	30	+35	16	8	5	13	6	2	2	0
1982-83	Quebec Nordiques	NHL	80	57	48	105	47	33	80	51	10	4	4	256	22.3	138	25	115	33	+31	4	0	0	0	6	0	0	0
	Canada	WEC-A	10	1	8	9	....	....	....	6	....	....	....	....	....	....	....	....	....	....	....	....	....	....	....	....	....	....
1983-84	Quebec Nordiques	NHL	75	56	65	121	45	44	89	76	11	2	16	239	23.4	149	39	58	10	+62	9	2	4	6	17	0	0	0
1984-85	Canada	C Cup	8	5	6	11	....	....	....	0	....	....	....	....	....	....	....	....	....	....	....	....	....	....	....	....	....	....
	Quebec Nordiques	NHL	69	55	40	95	45	27	72	55	17	0	6	257	21.4	120	40	71	1	+10	17	11	10	21	17	7	0	0
1985-86	Quebec Nordiques	NHL	75	53	51	104	43	34	77	64	28	0	3	244	21.7	152	75	71	0	+6	3	1	2	3	10	1	0	0
1986-87	Quebec Nordiques	NHL	75	49	47	96	43	34	77	61	17	0	6	276	17.8	139	63	92	4	–12	13	9	5	14	35	4	0	2
	NHL All-Stars	RV'87	2	0	1	1	....	....	....	0	....	....	....	....	....	....	....	....	....	....	....	....	....	....	....	....	....	....
1987-88	Canada	C Cup	8	2	3	5	....	....	....	0	....	....	....	....	....	....	....	....	....	....	....	....	....	....	....	....	....	....
	Quebec Nordiques	NHL	80	48	58	106	41	41	82	56	29	1	4	284	16.9	150	83	107	9	–31	....	....	....	....	....	....	....	....
1988-89	Quebec Nordiques	NHL	69	26	38	64	22	27	49	67	11	0	2	162	16.0	111	51	84	4	–20	....	....	....	....	....	....	....	....
1989-90	Quebec Nordiques	NHL	57	16	29	45	14	21	35	42	8	0	0	144	11.1	61	31	64	1	–33	....	....	....	....	....	....	....	....
	Chicago Blackhawks	NHL	8	4	1	5	3	1	4	9	1	1	0	10	40.0	6	2	4	1	+1	14	2	4	6	6	0	0	0
1990-91	Chicago Blackhawks	NHL	74	27	38	65	25	29	54	65	9	0	1	167	16.2	93	36	31	1	+27	....	....	....	....	....	....	....	....
1991-92	Chicago Blackhawks	NHL	75	22	41	63	20	31	51	69	9	0	4	176	12.5	89	34	40	5	+20	9	3	4	7	6	0	0	1
1992-93	Chicago Blackhawks	NHL	63	23	21	44	19	14	33	43	10	0	5	125	18.4	62	29	25	2	+10	3	0	1	1	0	0	0	0
1993-94	Chicago Blackhawks	NHL	56	16	14	30	15	11	26	26	3	0	6	120	13.3	49	19	29	0	+1	....	....	....	....	....	....	....	....
	NHL Totals		1089	548	604	1152	461	427	888	825	178	16	64	3143	17.4	1615	593	1045	120		92	39	39	78	110	14	2	4
	Other Major League Totals		78	28	30	58	....	....	....	65	....	....	....	....	....	....	....	....	....		....	....	....	....	....	....	....	....

QMJHL Second All-Star Team (1978) • NHL Second All-Star Team (1983, 1988) • NHL First All-Star Team (1984, 1986, 1987)

Played in NHL All-Star Game (1983, 1984, 1985, 1986, 1988)

Signed as an underage free agent by **Birmingham** (WHA), June, 1978. Traded to **Chicago** by **Quebec** with Greg Millen and Quebec's 6th round choice (Kevin St. Jacques) in 1991 Entry Draft for Mario Doyon, Everett Sanipass and Dan Vincelette, March 5, 1990. • Suffered career-ending head injury in game vs. Montreal, March 16, 1994.

• GOVEDARIS, CHRIS

Chris Govedaris LW – L. 6', 200 lbs. b: Toronto, Ont., 2/2/1970. Hartford's 1st choice, 11th overall, in 1988 Entry Draft.

Season	Club	League	GP	G	A	Pts	AG	AA	APts	PIM	PP	SH	GW	S	%	TGF	PGF	TGA	PGA	+/–	GP	G	A	Pts	PIM	PP	SH	GW
1986-87	Toronto Marlboros	OHL	64	36	28	64	....	....	....	148	....	....	....	....	....	....	....	....	....	....	....	....	....	....	....	....	....	....
1987-88	Toronto Marlboros	OHL	62	42	38	80	....	....	....	118	....	....	....	....	....	....	....	....	....	....	4	2	1	3	10	....	....	....
1988-89	Toronto Marlboros	OHL	49	41	38	79	....	....	....	117	....	....	....	....	....	....	....	....	....	....	6	2	3	5	0	....	....	....
1989-90	Dukes of Hamilton	OHL	23	11	21	32	....	....	....	53	....	....	....	....	....	....	....	....	....	....	....	....	....	....	....	....	....	....
	Hartford Whalers	NHL	12	0	1	1	0	1	1	6	0	0	0	13	0.0	4	2	2	0	0	2	0	0	0	2	0	0	0
	Binghamton Whalers	AHL	14	3	3	6	....	....	....	4	....	....	....	....	....	....	....	....	....	....	....	....	....	....	....	....	....	....
1990-91	Hartford Whalers	NHL	14	1	3	4	1	2	3	4	0	0	1	10	10.0	7	2	10	1	–4	....	....	....	....	....	....	....	....
	Springfield Indians	AHL	56	26	36	62	....	....	....	133	....	....	....	....	....	....	....	....	....	....	9	2	5	7	36	....	....	....
1991-92	Springfield Indians	AHL	43	14	25	39	....	....	....	55	....	....	....	....	....	....	....	....	....	....	11	3	2	5	25	....	....	....
1992-93	Hartford Whalers	NHL	7	1	0	1	1	0	1	0	0	0	0	6	16.7	1	0	3	0	–2	....	....	....	....	....	....	....	....
	Springfield Indians	AHL	65	31	24	55	....	....	....	58	....	....	....	....	....	....	....	....	....	....	15	7	4	11	18	....	....	....
1993-94	Toronto Maple Leafs	NHL	12	2	2	4	2	2	4	14	0	0	0	16	12.5	5	0	1	0	+4	2	0	0	0	0	0	0	0
	St. John's Maple Leafs	AHL	62	35	35	70	....	....	....	76	....	....	....	....	....	....	....	....	....	....	11	6	5	11	22	....	....	....
1994-95	Milwaukee Admirals	IHL	54	34	25	59	....	....	....	71	....	....	....	....	....	....	....	....	....	....	....	....	....	....	....	....	....	....
	Adirondack Red Wings	AHL	24	19	11	30	....	....	....	34	....	....	....	....	....	....	....	....	....	....	4	2	1	3	10	....	....	....
	Canada	WC-A	8	1	0	1	....	....	....	6	....	....	....	....	....	....	....	....	....	....	....	....	....	....	....	....	....	....
1995-96	Minnesota Moose	IHL	81	31	36	67	....	....	....	133	....	....	....	....	....	....	....	....	....	....	....	....	....	....	....	....	....	....
1996-97	Eisbaren Berlin	Germany	48	24	22	46	....	....	....	115	....	....	....	....	....	....	....	....	....	....	8	4	2	6	10	....	....	....
1997-98	Eisbaren Berlin	Germany	45	19	24	43	....	....	....	40	....	....	....	....	....	....	....	....	....	....	10	2	6	8	10	....	....	....
	NHL Totals		45	4	6	10	4	5	9	24	0	0	1	45	8.9	17	4	16	1		4	0	0	0	2	0	0	0

Signed as a free agent by **Toronto**, September 16, 1993. Signed as a free agent by **Winnipeg**, August 14, 1995.

• GOYER, GERRY

Gerry Goyer C – L. 6'2", 196 lbs. b: Belleville, Ont., 10/20/1936.

Season	Club	League	GP	G	A	Pts	AG	AA	APts	PIM	PP	SH	GW	S	%	TGF	PGF	TGA	PGA	+/–	GP	G	A	Pts	PIM	PP	SH	GW
1955-56	Guelph Biltmores	OHA	48	27	36	63	....	....	....	9	....	....	....	....	....	....	....	....	....	....	3	3	0	3	0	....	....	....
1956-57	Guelph Biltmores	OHA	52	17	20	37	....	....	....	12	....	....	....	....	....	....	....	....	....	....	10	4	5	9	8	....	....	....
	Belleville McFarlands	EOHL	1	0	0	0	....	....	....	0	....	....	....	....	....	....	....	....	....	....	....	....	....	....	....	....	....	....
1957-58	Belleville McFarlands	EOHL	45	12	25	37	....	....	....	17	....	....	....	....	....	....	....	....	....	....	....	....	....	....	....	....	....	....
1958-59	Kelowna Packers	OSHL	54	42	50	92	....	....	....	57	....	....	....	....	....	....	....	....	....	....	....	....	....	....	....	....	....	....
	Seattle Totems	WHL	....	....	....	....	....	....	....	....	....	....	....	....	....	....	....	....	....	....	12	4	2	6	2	....	....	....
1959-60	Seattle–Victoria	WHL	71	15	26	41	....	....	....	19	....	....	....	....	....	....	....	....	....	....	11	5	4	9	0	....	....	....
1960-61	Victoria Cougars	WHL	70	31	46	77	....	....	....	28	....	....	....	....	....	....	....	....	....	....	5	0	4	4	0	....	....	....
1961-62	Los Angeles Blades	WHL	53	29	41	70	....	....	....	24	....	....	....	....	....	....	....	....	....	....	....	....	....	....	....	....	....	....
1962-63	Portland Buckaroos	WHL	68	32	56	78	....	....	....	10	....	....	....	....	....	....	....	....	....	....	7	4	5	9	0	....	....	....
1963-64	Portland Buckaroos	WHL	68	26	26	52	....	....	....	25	....	....	....	....	....	....	....	....	....	....	5	1	3	4	0	....	....	....
1964-65	Portland Buckaroos	WHL	70	26	51	77	....	....	....	20	....	....	....	....	....	....	....	....	....	....	10	*7	8	*15	8	....	....	....
1965-66	Portland Buckaroos	WHL	72	31	45	76	....	....	....	16	....	....	....	....	....	....	....	....	....	....	14	8	9	17	4	....	....	....
1966-67	Portland Buckaroos	WHL	71	20	48	68	....	....	....	14	....	....	....	....	....	....	....	....	....	....	4	0	0	0	4	....	....	....
1967-68	Chicago Black Hawks	NHL	40	1	2	3	1	2	3	4	0	0	0	20	5.0	5	1	23	1	–18	3	0	0	0	2	0	0	0
	Dallas Black Hawks	CHL	5	1	5	6	....	....	....	2	....	....	....	....	....	....	....	....	....	....	....	....	....	....	....	....	....	....
1968-69	Portland Buckaroos	WHL	67	12	28	40	....	....	....	28	....	....	....	....	....	....	....	....	....	....	11	1	2	3	0	....	....	....

			REGULAR SEASON																			PLAYOFFS							
Season	Club	League	GP	G	A	Pts	AG	AA	APts	PIM	PP	SH	GW	S	%	TGF	PGF	TGA	PGA	+/–	GP	G	A	Pts	PIM	PP	SH	GW
1969-70	Portland Buckaroos	WHL	2	1	0	1	....	....	....	0	....	....	....	....	....	....	....	....	....	....	....	....	....	....	....	....	....	....
	Rochester Americans	AHL	5	2	5	7	....	....	....	2	....	....	....	....	....	....	....	....	....	....	....	....	....	....	....	....	....	....
	Vancouver Canucks	WHL	58	24	50	74	....	....	....	12	....	....	....	....	....	....	....	....	....	....	11	5	*16	*21	12	....	....	....
1970-71	San Diego Gulls	WHL	72	24	67	91	....	....	....	39	....	....	....	....	....	....	....	....	....	....	6	1	4	5	8	....	....	....
1971-72	San Diego Gulls	WHL	71	22	48	70	....	....	....	27	....	....	....	....	....	....	....	....	....	....	4	0	2	2	0	....	....	....
1972-73	San Diego Gulls	WHL	70	28	41	69	....	....	....	36	....	....	....	....	....	....	....	....	....	....	6	0	1	1	13	....	....	....
1973-74	San Diego Gulls	WHL	68	18	46	64	....	....	....	43	....	....	....	....	....	....	....	....	....	....	4	0	0	0	0	....	....	....
1974-75	Cranbrook Royals	WIHL	45	23	57	80	....	....	....	49	....	....	....	....	....	....	....	....	....	....	....	....	....	....	....	....	....	....
1975-76	Cranbrook Royals	WIHL	25	6	23	29	....	....	....	23	....	....	....	....	....	....	....	....	....	....	....	....	....	....	....	....	....	....
1976-77	Cranbrook Royals	WIHL	....	25	53	65	....	....	....	19	....	....	....	....	....	....	....	....	....	....	....	....	....	....	....	....	....	....
	NHL Totals		**40**	**1**	**2**	**3**	**1**	**2**	**3**	**4**	**0**	**0**	**0**	**20**	**5.0**	**5**	**1**	**23**	**1**		**3**	**0**	**0**	**0**	**2**	**0**	**0**	**0**

WHL Second All-Star Team (1971)

Claimed by **Toronto** from **LA Blades** (WHL) in Intra-League Draft, June 4, 1962. Traded to **Portland** (WHL) by **Toronto** for cash, September, 1962. Traded to **Chicago** by **Portland** (WHL) for cash, October, 1967. Traded to **Portland** (WHL) by **Chicago** for cash, July, 1968. Traded to **Vancouver** (WHL) by **Portland** (WHL) for cash, November, 1969. Traded to **San Diego** (WHL) by **Vancouver** (WHL) for cash, September, 1970.

• GOYETTE, PHIL

Phil Goyette C – L. 5'11", 170 lbs. b: Lachine, Que., 10/31/1933.

Season	Club	League	GP	G	A	Pts	AG	AA	APts	PIM	PP	SH	GW	S	%	TGF	PGF	TGA	PGA	+/–	GP	G	A	Pts	PIM	PP	SH	GW
1950-51	Montreal Nationale	QJHL	44	10	19	29	....	....	....	26	....	....	....	....	....	....	....	....	....	....	3	1	3	4	0	....	....	....
1951-52	Montreal Nationale	QJHL	45	23	28	41	....	....	....	11	....	....	....	....	....	....	....	....	....	....	9	3	5	8	4	....	....	....
1952-53	Montreal Jr. Canadiens	QJHL	44	23	36	59	....	....	....	13	....	....	....	....	....	....	....	....	....	....	7	2	4	6	0	....	....	....
1953-54	Montreal Jr. Canadiens	QJHL	50	43	47	90	....	....	....	19	....	....	....	....	....	....	....	....	....	....	8	4	5	9	0	....	....	....
1954-55	Cincinnati Mohawks	IHL	57	*41	51	*92	....	....	....	17	....	....	....	....	....	....	....	....	....	....	10	6	8	*14	2	....	....	....
	Montreal Royals	QHL	....	....	....	....	....	....	....	....	....	....	....	....	....	....	....	....	....	....	4	0	1	1	0	....	....	....
1955-56	Montreal Royals	QHL	58	19	15	34	....	....	....	4	....	....	....	....	....	....	....	....	....	....	13	*10	7	17	0	....	....	....
1956-57	**Montreal Canadiens**	**NHL**	**14**	**3**	**4**	**7**	**4**	**5**	**9**	**0**	....	....	....	....	....	....	....	....	....	....	**10**	**2**	**1**	**3**	**4**	....	....	....
	Montreal Royals	QHL	47	13	18	31	....	....	....	10	....	....	....	....	....	....	....	....	....	....	....	....	....	....	....	....	....	....
1957-58	**Montreal Canadiens**	**NHL**	**70**	**9**	**37**	**46**	**12**	**41**	**53**	**8**	....	....	....	....	....	....	....	....	....	....	**10**	**4**	**1**	**5**	**4**	....	....	....
1958-59	**Montreal Canadiens**	**NHL**	**63**	**10**	**18**	**28**	**13**	**19**	**32**	**8**	....	....	....	....	....	....	....	....	....	....	**10**	**0**	**4**	**4**	**0**	....	....	....
1959-60	**Montreal Canadiens**	**NHL**	**65**	**21**	**22**	**43**	**26**	**23**	**49**	**4**	....	....	....	....	....	....	....	....	....	....	**8**	**2**	**1**	**3**	**4**	....	....	....
1960-61	**Montreal Canadiens**	**NHL**	**62**	**7**	**4**	**11**	**8**	**4**	**12**	**4**	....	....	....	....	....	....	....	....	....	....	**6**	**3**	**3**	**6**	**0**	....	....	....
1961-62	**Montreal Canadiens**	**NHL**	**69**	**7**	**27**	**34**	**8**	**27**	**35**	**18**	....	....	....	....	....	....	....	....	....	....	**6**	**1**	**4**	**5**	**2**	....	....	....
1962-63	**Montreal Canadiens**	**NHL**	**32**	**5**	**8**	**13**	**6**	**8**	**14**	**2**	....	....	....	....	....	....	....	....	....	....	**2**	**0**	**0**	**0**	**0**	....	....	....
1963-64	**New York Rangers**	**NHL**	**67**	**24**	**41**	**65**	**32**	**46**	**78**	**15**	....	....	....	....	....	....	....	....	....	....	....	....	....	....	....	....	....	....
1964-65	**New York Rangers**	**NHL**	**52**	**12**	**34**	**46**	**15**	**37**	**52**	**6**	....	....	....	....	....	....	....	....	....	....	....	....	....	....	....	....	....	....
1965-66	**New York Rangers**	**NHL**	**60**	**11**	**31**	**42**	**13**	**31**	**44**	**6**	....	....	....	....	....	....	....	....	....	....	....	....	....	....	....	....	....	....
1966-67	**New York Rangers**	**NHL**	**70**	**12**	**49**	**61**	**15**	**51**	**66**	**6**	....	....	....	....	....	....	....	....	....	....	**4**	**1**	**0**	**1**	**0**	....	....	....
1967-68	**New York Rangers**	**NHL**	**73**	**25**	**40**	**65**	**31**	**42**	**73**	**10**	**4**	**0**	**7**	**179**	**14.0**	**78**	**17**	**43**	**0**	**+18**	**6**	**0**	**1**	**1**	**4**	**0**	**0**	**0**
1968-69	**New York Rangers**	**NHL**	**67**	**13**	**32**	**45**	**15**	**30**	**45**	**8**	**2**	**0**	**3**	**135**	**9.6**	**53**	**10**	**34**	**0**	**+9**	**3**	**0**	**0**	**0**	**0**	**0**	**0**	**0**
1969-70	**St. Louis Blues**	**NHL**	**72**	**29**	**49**	**78**	**34**	**49**	**83**	**16**	**13**	**0**	**5**	**152**	**19.1**	**98**	**53**	**42**	**0**	**+3**	**16**	**3**	**11**	**14**	**6**	**1**	**2**	**0**
1970-71	**Buffalo Sabres**	**NHL**	**60**	**15**	**46**	**61**	**16**	**41**	**57**	**6**	**9**	**0**	**1**	**119**	**12.6**	**75**	**39**	**53**	**2**	**–15**	....	....	....	....	....	....	....	....
1971-72	**Buffalo Sabres**	**NHL**	**37**	**3**	**21**	**24**	**3**	**19**	**22**	**14**	**3**	**0**	**0**	**33**	**9.1**	**32**	**19**	**24**	**1**	**–10**	....	....	....	....	....	....	....	....
	New York Rangers	**NHL**	**8**	**1**	**4**	**5**	**1**	**4**	**5**	**0**	**1**	**0**	**0**	**10**	**10.0**	**6**	**3**	**4**	**0**	**–1**	**13**	**1**	**3**	**4**	**2**	**1**	**0**	**0**
	NHL Totals		**941**	**207**	**467**	**674**	**252**	**477**	**729**	**131**	**32**	**0**	**16**	**628**	**33.0**	**342**	**141**	**200**	**3**		**94**	**17**	**29**	**46**	**26**	**2**	**2**	**0**

IHL First All-Star Team (1955) • Won George H. Wilkinson Trophy (Top Scorer - IHL) (1955) • Won James Gatschene Memorial Trophy (MVP - IHL) (1955) • Won Lady Byng Trophy (1970)

Played in NHL All-Star Game (1957, 1958, 1959, 1961)

Claimed by **Montreal** from **Montreal Royals** (QHL) in Intra-League Draft, June 5, 1956. Traded to **NY Rangers** by **Montreal** with Don Marshall and Jacques Plante for Gump Worsley, Dave Balon, Leon Rochefort and Len Ronson, June 4, 1963. Traded to **St. Louis** by **NY Rangers** for Andre Dupont, June 10, 1969. Claimed by **Buffalo** from **St. Louis** in Expansion Draft, June 10, 1970. Traded to **NY Rangers** by **Buffalo** for cash, March, 1972.

• GRADIN, THOMAS

Thomas Gradin C – R. 5'11", 176 lbs. b: Solleftea, Sweden, 2/18/1956. Chicago's 3rd choice, 45th overall, in 1976 Amateur Draft.

Season	Club	League	GP	G	A	Pts	AG	AA	APts	PIM	PP	SH	GW	S	%	TGF	PGF	TGA	PGA	+/–	GP	G	A	Pts	PIM	PP	SH	GW
1972-73	MoDo AIK	Sweden	11	5	1	6	....	....	....	4	....	....	....	....	....	....	....	....	....	....	6	3	1	4	2	....	....	....
1973-74	MoDo AIK	Sweden	STATISTICS NOT AVAILABLE																									
	Sweden	WJC-A	5	3	3	6	....	....	....	2	....	....	....	....	....	....	....	....	....	....	....	....	....	....	....	....	....	....
1974-75	MoDo AIK	Sweden	29	16	15	31	....	....	....	16	....	....	....	....	....	....	....	....	....	....	....	....	....	....	....	....	....	....
	Sweden	WJC-A	....	....	....	....	....	....	....	....	....	....	....	....	....	....	....	....	....	....	....	....	....	....	....	....	....	....
1975-76	MoDo AIK	Sweden	35	16	23	39	....	....	....	23	....	....	....	....	....	....	....	....	....	....	....	....	....	....	....	....	....	....
	Sweden	WJC-A	4	3	1	4	....	....	....	2	....	....	....	....	....	....	....	....	....	....	....	....	....	....	....	....	....	....
1976-77	AIK Solna	Sweden	36	16	12	28	....	....	....	8	....	....	....	....	....	....	....	....	....	....	....	....	....	....	....	....	....	....
1977-78	AIK Solna	Sweden	36	0	15	37	....	....	....	22	....	....	....	....	....	....	....	....	....	....	6	0	*5	5	14	....	....	....
	Sweden	WEC-A	9	2	1	3	....	....	....	0	....	....	....	....	....	....	....	....	....	....	....	....	....	....	....	....	....	....
1978-79	**Vancouver Canucks**	**NHL**	**76**	**20**	**31**	**51**	**18**	**24**	**42**	**22**	**4**	**0**	**4**	**105**	**19.0**	**61**	**16**	**59**	**2**	**–12**	**3**	**4**	**1**	**5**	**4**	**0**	**0**	**0**
1979-80	**Vancouver Canucks**	**NHL**	**80**	**30**	**45**	**75**	**27**	**35**	**62**	**22**	**7**	**0**	**2**	**146**	**20.5**	**106**	**31**	**65**	**4**	**+14**	**4**	**0**	**2**	**2**	**0**	**0**	**0**	**0**
1980-81	**Vancouver Canucks**	**NHL**	**79**	**21**	**48**	**69**	**17**	**34**	**51**	**34**	**4**	**0**	**1**	**158**	**13.3**	**92**	**23**	**67**	**0**	**+2**	**3**	**1**	**3**	**4**	**0**	**0**	**0**	**0**
1981-82	Sweden	C Cup	5	1	2	3	....	....	....	4	....	....	....	....	....	....	....	....	....	....	....	....	....	....	....	....	....	....
	Vancouver Canucks	**NHL**	**76**	**37**	**49**	**86**	**29**	**32**	**61**	**32**	**6**	**3**	**4**	**183**	**20.2**	**116**	**33**	**91**	**23**	**+15**	**17**	**9**	**10**	**19**	**10**	**4**	**0**	**0**
	Sweden	Nat-Team	11	3	4	7	....	....	....	4	....	....	....	....	....	....	....	....	....	....	....	....	....	....	....	....	....	....
1982-83	**Vancouver Canucks**	**NHL**	**80**	**32**	**54**	**86**	**26**	**37**	**63**	**61**	**12**	**2**	**4**	**175**	**18.3**	**120**	**46**	**105**	**14**	**–17**	**4**	**1**	**3**	**4**	**2**	**0**	**0**	**0**
1983-84	**Vancouver Canucks**	**NHL**	**75**	**21**	**57**	**78**	**17**	**39**	**56**	**32**	**11**	**1**	**5**	**170**	**12.4**	**117**	**39**	**97**	**17**	**–2**	**4**	**0**	**1**	**1**	**2**	**0**	**0**	**0**
1984-85	Sweden	C Cup	8	2	2	4	....	....	....	6	....	....	....	....	....	....	....	....	....	....	....	....	....	....	....	....	....	....
	Vancouver Canucks	**NHL**	**76**	**22**	**42**	**64**	**18**	**28**	**46**	**43**	**3**	**0**	**3**	**152**	**14.5**	**97**	**24**	**111**	**16**	**–22**	....	....	....	....	....	....	....	....
1985-86	**Vancouver Canucks**	**NHL**	**71**	**14**	**27**	**41**	**11**	**18**	**29**	**34**	**2**	**1**	**3**	**121**	**11.6**	**77**	**20**	**97**	**24**	**–16**	**3**	**2**	**1**	**3**	**2**	**0**	**0**	**0**
1986-87	**Boston Bruins**	**NHL**	**64**	**12**	**31**	**43**	**10**	**22**	**32**	**18**	**2**	**3**	**3**	**87**	**13.8**	**60**	**12**	**55**	**11**	**+4**	**4**	**0**	**4**	**4**	**0**	**0**	**0**	**0**
1987-88	AIK Solna	Sweden	38	15	18	33	....	....	....	14	....	....	....	....	....	....	....	....	....	....	5	1	1	2	2	....	....	....
1988-89	AIK Solna	Sweden	33	11	21	32	....	....	....	40	....	....	....	....	....	....	....	....	....	....	2	0	1	1	2	....	....	....
1989-90	AIK Solna	Sweden	35	14	15	29	....	....	....	14	....	....	....	....	....	....	....	....	....	....	3	2	0	2	2	....	....	....
	NHL Totals		**677**	**209**	**384**	**593**	**173**	**269**	**442**	**298**	**51**	**10**	**29**	**1297**	**16.1**	**846**	**244**	**747**	**111**		**42**	**17**	**25**	**42**	**20**	**4**	**0**	**0**

Named Best Forward at EJC-A (1974) • WJC-A All-Star Team (1974)

Played in NHL All-Star Game (1985)

Rights traded to **Vancouver** by **Chicago** for Vancouver's 2nd round choice (Steve Ludzik) in 1980 Entry Draft, June 14, 1978. Signed as a free agent by **Boston**, June 24, 1986.

• GRAHAM, DIRK

Dirk Graham LW/RW – R. 5'11", 198 lbs. b: Regina, Sask., 7/29/1959. Vancouver's 5th choice, 89th overall, in 1979 Entry Draft.

Season	Club	League	GP	G	A	Pts	AG	AA	APts	PIM	PP	SH	GW	S	%	TGF	PGF	TGA	PGA	+/–	GP	G	A	Pts	PIM	PP	SH	GW
1975-76	Regina Blues	SJHL	54	36	32	68	....	....	....	82	....	....	....	....	....	....	....	....	....	....	....	....	....	....	....	....	....	....
	Regina Pats	WCJHL	2	0	0	0	....	....	....	0	....	....	....	....	....	....	....	....	....	....	6	1	1	2	5	....	....	....
1976-77	Regina Pats	WCHL	65	37	28	65	....	....	....	66	....	....	....	....	....	....	....	....	....	....	....	....	....	....	....	....	....	....
1977-78	Regina Pats	WCHL	72	49	61	110	....	....	....	87	....	....	....	....	....	....	....	....	....	....	13	15	19	34	37	....	....	....
1978-79	Regina Pats	WHL	71	48	60	108	....	....	....	252	....	....	....	....	....	....	....	....	....	....	....	....	....	....	....	....	....	....
1979-80	Dallas Black Hawks	CHL	62	17	15	32	....	....	....	96	....	....	....	....	....	....	....	....	....	....	....	....	....	....	....	....	....	....
1980-81	Fort Wayne Komets	IHL	6	1	2	3	....	....	....	12	....	....	....	....	....	....	....	....	....	....	....	....	....	....	....	....	....	....
	Toledo Goaldiggers	IHL	61	40	45	85	....	....	....	88	....	....	....	....	....	....	....	....	....	....	....	....	....	....	....	....	....	....
1981-82	Toledo Goaldiggers	IHL	72	49	56	105	....	....	....	68	....	....	....	....	....	....	....	....	....	....	13	10	11	*21	8	....	....	....
1982-83	Toledo Goaldiggers	IHL	78	70	55	125	....	....	....	00	....	....	....	....	....	....	....	....	....	....	11	13	7	*20	30	....	....	....
1983-84	**Minnesota North Stars**	**NHL**	**6**	**1**	**1**	**2**	**1**	**1**	**2**	**0**	**0**	**0**	**0**	**10**	**10.0**	**2**	**0**	**2**	**1**	**+1**	**1**	**0**	**0**	**0**	**2**	**0**	**0**	**0**
	Salt Lake Golden Eagles	CHL	57	37	57	94	....	....	....	72	....	....	....	....	....	....	....	....	....	....	5	3	8	11	2	....	....	....
1984-85	**Minnesota North Stars**	**NHL**	**36**	**12**	**11**	**23**	**10**	**7**	**17**	**23**	**3**	**0**	**1**	**81**	**14.8**	**33**	**7**	**47**	**6**	**–15**	**9**	**0**	**4**	**4**	**7**	**0**	**0**	**0**
	Springfield Indians	AHL	37	20	28	48	....	....	....	41	....	....	....	....	....	....	....	....	....	....	....	....	....	....	....	....	....	....
1985-86	**Minnesota North Stars**	**NHL**	**80**	**22**	**33**	**55**	**18**	**22**	**40**	**87**	**0**	**4**	**3**	**173**	**12.7**	**77**	**13**	**105**	**35**	**–6**	**5**	**3**	**1**	**4**	**2**	**0**	**1**	**2**
1986-87	**Minnesota North Stars**	**NHL**	**76**	**25**	**29**	**54**	**22**	**21**	**43**	**142**	**6**	**5**	**2**	**197**	**12.7**	**73**	**17**	**100**	**42**	**–2**	....	....	....	....	....	....	....	....
	Canada	WEC-A	0	0	0	0	....	....	....	8	....	....	....	....	....	....	....	....	....	....	....	....	....	....	....	....	....	....
1987-88	**Minnesota North Stars**	**NHL**	**28**	**7**	**5**	**12**	**6**	**4**	**10**	**39**	**4**	**0**	**0**	**66**	**10.6**	**20**	**9**	**29**	**7**	**–11**	....	....	....	....	....	....	....	....
	Chicago Blackhawks	**NHL**	**42**	**17**	**19**	**36**	**15**	**14**	**29**	**32**	**6**	**1**	**2**	**107**	**15.9**	**48**	**13**	**47**	**16**	**+4**	**4**	**1**	**2**	**3**	**4**	**0**	**0**	**0**
1988-89	**Chicago Blackhawks**	**NHL**	**80**	**33**	**45**	**78**	**28**	**32**	**60**	**89**	**5**	**10**	**5**	**217**	**15.2**	**106**	**23**	**127**	**52**	**+8**	**16**	**2**	**4**	**6**	**38**	**1**	**0**	**0**

Season	Club	League	REGULAR SEASON GP	G	A	Pts	AG	AA	APts	PIM	PP	SH	GW	S	%	TGF	PGF	TGA	PGA	+/–	PLAYOFFS GP	G	A	Pts	PIM	PP	SH	GW
1989-90	Chicago Blackhawks	NHL	73	22	32	54	19	23	42	102	2	3	1	180	12.2	83	19	95	32	+1	5	1	5	6	2	0	1	0
1990-91	Chicago Blackhawks	NHL	80	24	21	45	22	16	38	88	4	6	7	189	12.7	71	16	74	31	+12	6	1	2	3	17	0	0	0
1991-92	Canada	C Cup	8	3	1	4	....	....	....	0	....	....	....	....	....	....	....	....	....	....	....	....	....	....	....	....	....	....
	Chicago Blackhawks	NHL	80	17	30	47	16	23	39	89	6	1	1	222	7.7	68	20	92	39	–5	18	7	5	12	8	0	0	1
1992-93	Chicago Blackhawks	NHL	84	20	17	37	17	12	29	139	1	2	5	187	10.7	57	5	89	37	0	4	0	0	0	0	0	0	0
1993-94	Chicago Blackhawks	NHL	67	15	18	33	14	14	28	45	0	2	5	122	12.3	50	4	59	26	+13	6	0	1	1	4	0	0	0
1994-95	Chicago Blackhawks	NHL	40	4	9	13	7	13	20	42	1	1	0	68	5.9	22	4	28	12	+2	16	2	3	5	8	0	0	1
	NHL Totals		772	219	270	489	195	202	397	917	38	35	32	1819	12.0	710	150	894	336		90	17	27	44	92	1	2	4

IHL Second All-Star Team (1981) • IHL First All-Star Team (1983) • CHL First All-Star Team (1984) • Won Frank J. Selke Trophy (1991)

Signed as a free agent by **Minnesota**, August 17, 1983. Traded to **Chicago** by **Minnesota** for Curt Fraser, January 4, 1988.

• GRAHAM, PAT

Pat Graham LW – L. 6'1", 190 lbs. b: Toronto, Ont., 5/25/1961. Pittsburgh's 5th choice, 114th overall, in 1980 Entry Draft.

Season	Club	League	GP	G	A	Pts	AG	AA	APts	PIM	PP	SH	GW	S	%	TGF	PGF	TGA	PGA	+/–	GP	G	A	Pts	PIM	PP	SH	GW
1976-77	St. Michael's Buzzers	Jr. B	30	20	20	48	....	....	....	100	....	....	....	....	....	....	....	....	....	....	....	....	....	....	....	....	....	....
1977-78	Toronto Marlboros	OHA	50	5	6	11	....	....	....	41	....	....	....	....	....	....	....	....	....	....	....	....	....	....	....	....	....	....
1978-79	Toronto Marlboros	OHA	49	10	12	22	....	....	....	102	....	....	....	....	....	....	....	....	....	....	....	....	....	....	....	....	....	....
1979-80	Toronto Marlboros	OHA	2	1	0	1	....	....	....	16	....	....	....	....	....	....	....	....	....	....	....	....	....	....	....	....	....	....
1979-80	Niagara Falls Flyers	OHA	59	31	32	63	....	....	....	75	....	....	....	....	....	....	....	....	....	....	....	....	....	....	....	....	....	....
1980-81	Niagara Falls Flyers	OHA	61	40	54	94	....	....	....	118	....	....	....	....	....	....	....	....	....	....	12	4	7	11	40	....	....	....
1981-82	Pittsburgh Penguins	NHL	42	6	8	14	5	5	10	55	0	0	1	51	11.8	27	1	28	1	–1	4	0	0	0	2	0	0	0
	Erie Blades	AHL	9	4	4	8	....	....	....	4	....	....	....	....	....	....	....	....	....	....	....	....	....	....	....	....	....	....
1982-83	Pittsburgh Penguins	NHL	20	1	5	6	1	3	4	16	1	0	0	25	4.0	12	1	17	0	–6	....	....	....	....	....	....	....	....
	Baltimore Skipjacks	AHL	57	16	16	32	....	....	....	32	....	....	....	....	....	....	....	....	....	....	....	....	....	....	....	....	....	....
1983-84	Toronto Maple Leafs	NHL	41	4	4	8	3	3	6	65	0	0	0	46	8.7	12	0	21	0	–9	....	....	....	....	....	....	....	....
	St. Catharines Saints	AHL	25	7	7	14	....	....	....	18	....	....	....	....	....	....	....	....	....	....	7	1	2	3	9	....	....	....
1984-85	Adirondack Red Wings	AHL	27	5	5	10	....	....	....	19	....	....	....	....	....	....	....	....	....	....	....	....	....	....	....	....	....	....
	Braunlage	Germany	24	12	8	20	....	....	....	57	....	....	....	....	....	....	....	....	....	....	....	....	....	....	....	....	....	....
	NHL Totals		103	11	17	28	9	11	20	136	1	0	1	122	9.0	51	2	66	1		4	0	0	0	2	0	0	0

Traded to **Toronto** by **Pittsburgh** with Nick Ricci for Rocky Saganiuk and Vince Tremblay, August 12, 1983.

• GRAHAM, ROD

Rod Graham LW – L. 6', 185 lbs. b: London, Ont., 8/19/1946.

Season	Club	League	GP	G	A	Pts	AG	AA	APts	PIM	PP	SH	GW	S	%	TGF	PGF	TGA	PGA	+/–	GP	G	A	Pts	PIM	PP	SH	GW
1967-68	Kingston Aces	OHA Sr.	37	15	23	38	....	....	....	46	....	....	....	....	....	....	....	....	....	....	....	....	....	....	....	....	....	....
	Oklahoma City Blazers	CHL	....	....	....	....	....	....	....	....	....	....	....	....	....	....	....	....	....	....	4	0	2	2	2	....	....	....
1968-69	Kingston Aces	OHA Sr.	39	26	32	58	....	....	....	94	....	....	....	....	....	....	....	....	....	....	....	....	....	....	....	....	....	....
1969-70	Kingston Aces	OHA Sr.	32	11	14	25	....	....	....	81	....	....	....	....	....	....	....	....	....	....	....	....	....	....	....	....	....	....
1970-71	Kingston Aces	OHA Sr.	32	24	19	43	....	....	....	65	....	....	....	....	....	....	....	....	....	....	....	....	....	....	....	....	....	....
1971-72			DID NOT PLAY																									
1972-73	Rochester Americans	AHL	70	16	22	38	....	....	....	83	....	....	....	....	....	....	....	....	....	....	6	2	1	3	5	....	....	....
1973-74	Rochester Americans	AHL	74	10	41	51	....	....	....	88	....	....	....	....	....	....	....	....	....	....	5	2	1	3	5	....	....	....
1974-75	Boston Bruins	NHL	14	2	1	3	2	1	3	7	1	0	0	7	28.6	6	1	5	0	0	....	....	....	....	....	....	....	....
	Rochester Americans	AHL	57	12	22	34	....	....	....	97	....	....	....	....	....	....	....	....	....	....	11	1	2	3	20	....	....	....
1975-76	Springfield Indians	AHL	70	20	35	55	....	....	....	74	....	....	....	....	....	....	....	....	....	....	....	....	....	....	....	....	....	....
1976-77	Rochester Americans	AHL	70	5	22	27	....	....	....	77	....	....	....	....	....	....	....	....	....	....	12	1	4	5	6	....	....	....
1977-78	Rochester Americans	AHL	73	7	12	19	....	....	....	39	....	....	....	....	....	....	....	....	....	....	6	0	2	2	9	....	....	....
	NHL Totals		14	2	1	3	2	1	3	7	1	0	0	7	28.6	6	1	5	0		....	....	....	....	....	....	....	....

Signed as a free agent by **Rochester** (AHL), September, 1972. Rights transferred to **Boston** after NHL club signed affiliate agreement with **Rochester** (AHL), June 14, 1974.

• GRANATO, TONY

Tony Granato LW – R. 5'10", 185 lbs. b: Downers Grove, IL, 6/25/1964. NY Rangers' 5th choice, 120th overall, in 1982 Entry Draft.

Season	Club	League	GP	G	A	Pts	AG	AA	APts	PIM	PP	SH	GW	S	%	TGF	PGF	TGA	PGA	+/–	GP	G	A	Pts	PIM	PP	SH	GW
1981-82	Northwood Prep School	H.S.	STATISTICS NOT AVAILABLE																									
1982-83	Northwood Prep School	H.S.	STATISTICS NOT AVAILABLE																									
	United States	WJC-A	7	4	0	4	....	....	....	4	....	....	....	....	....	....	....	....	....	....	....	....	....	....	....	....	....	....
1983-84	University of Wisconsin	WCHA	35	14	17	31	....	....	....	48	....	....	....	....	....	....	....	....	....	....	....	....	....	....	....	....	....	....
	United States	WJC-A	7	1	3	4	....	....	....	6	....	....	....	....	....	....	....	....	....	....	....	....	....	....	....	....	....	....
1984-85	University of Wisconsin	WCHA	42	33	34	67	....	....	....	94	....	....	....	....	....	....	....	....	....	....	....	....	....	....	....	....	....	....
	United States	WEC-A	9	4	2	6	....	....	....	10	....	....	....	....	....	....	....	....	....	....	....	....	....	....	....	....	....	....
1985-86	University of Wisconsin	WCHA	33	25	24	49	....	....	....	36	....	....	....	....	....	....	....	....	....	....	....	....	....	....	....	....	....	....
	United States	WEC-A	8	2	7	9	....	....	....	8	....	....	....	....	....	....	....	....	....	....	....	....	....	....	....	....	....	....
1986-87	University of Wisconsin	WCHA	42	28	45	73	....	....	....	64	....	....	....	....	....	....	....	....	....	....	....	....	....	....	....	....	....	....
	United States	WEC-A	9	2	3	5	....	....	....	12	....	....	....	....	....	....	....	....	....	....	....	....	....	....	....	....	....	....
1987-88	United States	Nat-Team	49	40	31	71	....	....	....	55	....	....	....	....	....	....	....	....	....	....	....	....	....	....	....	....	....	....
	United States	Olympics	6	1	7	8	....	....	....	4	....	....	....	....	....	....	....	....	....	....	....	....	....	....	....	....	....	....
	Colorado Rangers	IHL	22	13	14	27	....	....	....	36	....	....	....	....	....	....	....	....	....	....	8	9	4	13	16	....	....	....
1988-89	New York Rangers	NHL	78	36	27	63	31	19	50	140	4	4	3	234	15.4	88	13	92	34	+17	4	1	1	2	21	0	0	0
1989-90	New York Rangers	NHL	37	7	18	25	6	13	19	77	1	0	0	79	8.9	36	11	35	11	+1	....	....	....	....	....	....	....	....
	Los Angeles Kings	NHL	19	5	6	11	4	4	8	45	1	0	0	41	12.2	21	6	23	6	–2	10	5	4	9	12	2	1	2
1990-91	Los Angeles Kings	NHL	68	30	34	64	28	26	54	154	11	1	3	197	15.2	100	26	66	14	+22	12	1	4	5	28	0	0	0
1991-92	United States	C Cup	7	1	2	3	....	....	....	12	....	....	....	....	....	....	....	....	....	....	....	....	....	....	....	....	....	....
	Los Angeles Kings	NHL	80	39	29	68	36	22	58	187	7	2	8	223	17.5	103	30	85	16	+4	6	1	5	6	10	0	0	0
1992-93	Los Angeles Kings	NHL	81	37	45	82	31	31	62	171	14	2	6	247	15.0	121	47	102	27	–1	24	6	11	17	50	1	0	1
1993-94	Los Angeles Kings	NHL	50	7	14	21	7	11	18	150	2	0	0	117	6.0	43	6	45	6	–2	....	....	....	....	....	....	....	....
1994-95	Los Angeles Kings	NHL	33	13	11	24	23	16	39	68	2	0	3	106	12.3	33	6	25	7	+9	....	....	....	....	....	....	....	....
1995-96	Los Angeles Kings	NHL	49	17	18	35	17	15	32	46	5	0	1	156	10.9	45	14	45	9	–5	....	....	....	....	....	....	....	....
1996-97	San Jose Sharks	NHL	76	25	15	40	27	13	40	159	5	1	4	231	10.8	68	18	73	16	–7	....	....	....	....	....	....	....	....
1997-98	San Jose Sharks	NHL	59	16	9	25	19	9	28	70	3	0	2	119	13.4	41	8	36	6	+3	1	0	0	0	0	0	0	0
	NHL Totals		630	232	226	458	229	179	408	1267	55	10	30	1750	13.3	699	185	627	152		57	14	25	39	121	3	1	3

WCHA Second All-Star Team (1985, 1987) • NCAA West Second All-American Team (1985, 1987) • NHL All-Rookie Team (1989) • Won Bill Masterton Memorial Trophy (1997)

Played in NHL All-Star Game (1997)

Traded to **LA Kings** by **NY Rangers** with Tomas Sandstrom for Bernie Nicholls, January 20, 1990. Signed as a free agent by **San Jose**, September 1, 1996.

• GRANT, DANNY

Danny Grant RW – L. 5'10", 188 lbs. b: Fredericton, N.B., 2/21/1946.

Season	Club	League	GP	G	A	Pts	AG	AA	APts	PIM	PP	SH	GW	S	%	TGF	PGF	TGA	PGA	+/–	GP	G	A	Pts	PIM	PP	SH	GW
1959-60	Barkers Point Aces	Bantam	....	....	....	....	....	....	....	....	....	....	....	....	....	....	....	....	....	....	6	*23	3	*26	0	....	....	....
1960-61	Fredericton Bears	Inter-Sr.	....	....	....	....	....	....	....	....	....	....	....	....	....	....	....	....	....	....	10	17	10	27	4	....	....	....
	Fredericton Canadians	Midget	13	*12	2	*14	....	....	....	....	....	....	....	....	....	....	....	....	....	....	2	4	1	5	0	....	....	....
1962-63	Peterborough Petes	OHA	50	12	9	21	....	....	....	8	....	....	....	....	....	....	....	....	....	....	6	0	1	1	0	....	....	....
1963-64	Peterborough Petes	OHA	44	18	21	39	....	....	....	20	....	....	....	....	....	....	....	....	....	....	5	2	2	4	4	....	....	....
1964-65	Peterborough Petes	OHA	56	47	59	106	....	....	....	23	....	....	....	....	....	....	....	....	....	....	12	7	7	14	4	....	....	....
	Quebec Aces	AHL	1	0	1	1	....	....	....	0	....	....	....	....	....	....	....	....	....	....	....	....	....	....	....	....	....	....
1965-66	Montreal Canadiens	NHL	1	0	0	0	0	0	0	0	....	....	....	....	....	....	....	....	....	....	....	....	....	....	....	....	....	....
	Peterborough Petes	OHA	48	*44	52	96	....	....	....	34	....	....	....	....	....	....	....	....	....	....	4	2	5	7	10	....	....	....
1966-67	Houston Apollos	CHL	64	22	28	50	....	....	....	29	....	....	....	....	....	....	....	....	....	....	6	4	4	8	2	....	....	....
1967-68	Montreal Canadiens	NHL	22	3	4	7	4	4	8	10	0	0	0	16	18.8	11	2	6	0	+3	10	0	3	3	5	0	0	0
	Houston Apollos	CHL	19	14	8	22	....	....	....	6	....	....	....	....	....	....	....	....	....	....	....	....	....	....	....	....	....	....
1968-69	Minnesota North Stars	NHL	75	34	31	65	38	29	67	46	11	0	1	189	18.0	77	21	68	0	–12	....	....	....	....	....	....	....	....
1969-70	Minnesota North Stars	NHL	76	29	28	57	34	28	62	23	14	0	2	247	11.7	86	48	51	0	–13	6	0	2	2	4	0	0	0
1970-71	Minnesota North Stars	NHL	78	34	23	57	36	20	56	46	12	0	1	283	12.0	90	34	49	0	+7	12	5	5	10	8	3	0	1
1971-72	Minnesota North Stars	NHL	78	18	25	43	19	23	42	18	6	0	0	212	8.5	73	29	44	0	0	7	2	1	3	0	0	0	0
1972-73	Minnesota North Stars	NHL	78	32	35	67	32	29	61	12	3	0	6	251	12.7	100	23	55	1	+23	6	3	1	4	0	0	0	0
1973-74	Minnesota North Stars	NHL	78	29	35	64	30	30	60	16	3	0	3	185	15.7	92	21	72	0	–1	....	....	....	....	....	....	....	....
1974-75	Detroit Red Wings	NHL	80	50	37	87	47	29	76	28	19	1	5	241	20.7	134	52	119	26	–11	....	....	....	....	....	....	....	....
1975-76	Detroit Red Wings	NHL	39	10	13	23	9	10	19	20	4	1	0	70	14.3	32	13	46	10	–17	....	....	....	....	....	....	....	....
1976-77	Detroit Red Wings	NHL	42	2	10	12	2	8	10	4	0	0	0	62	3.2	14	5	45	2	–34	....	....	....	....	....	....	....	....

			REGULAR SEASON																		PLAYOFFS							
Season	**Club**	**League**	**GP**	**G**	**A**	**Pts**	**AG**	**AA**	**APts**	**PIM**	**PP**	**SH**	**GW**	**S**	**%**	**TGF**	**PGF**	**TGA**	**PGA**	**+/–**	**GP**	**G**	**A**	**Pts**	**PIM**	**PP**	**SH**	**GW**
1977-78	**Detroit Red Wings**	**NHL**	**13**	**2**	**2**	**4**	**2**	**2**	**4**	**6**	**1**	**0**	**0**	**9**	**22.2**	**7**	**4**	**5**	**0**	**–2**	....	....	....	....	....	....	....	....
	Los Angeles Kings	**NHL**	**41**	**10**	**19**	**29**	**10**	**15**	**25**	**2**	**4**	**0**	**0**	**97**	**10.3**	**45**	**13**	**34**	**0**	**–2**								
1978-79	**Los Angeles Kings**	**NHL**	**35**	**10**	**11**	**21**	**9**	**8**	**17**	**8**	**4**	**0**	**1**	**47**	**21.3**	**30**	**13**	**12**	**0**	**+5**	**2**	**0**	**2**	**2**	**2**	**0**	**0**	**0**
1979-80	Fredericton Capitals	NBSHL	DID NOT PLAY – COACHING																		....	....	....	....	....	....	....	....
1980-81	Fredericton Capitals	NBSHL	DID NOT PLAY – COACHING																									
1981-82	Fredericton Express	AHL	18	2	7	9	....	....	....	4	....	....	....	....	....	....	....	....	....	....	....	....	....	....	....	....	....	....
	NHL Totals		**736**	**263**	**273**	**536**	**272**	**235**	**507**	**239**	**81**	**2**	**19**	**1909**	**13.8**	**791**	**278**	**606**	**39**		**43**	**10**	**14**	**24**	**19**	**3**	**0**	**1**

Won Calder Memorial Trophy (1969)

Played in NHL All-Star Game (1969, 1970, 1971)

Traded to **Minnesota** by **Montreal** with Claude Larose for Minnesota's 1st round choice (Dave Gardner) in 1972 Amateur Draft and future considerations (Marshall Johnston, May 25, 1971), June 10, 1968. Traded to **Detroit** by **Minnesota** for Henry Boucha, August 27, 1974. Traded to **LA Kings** by **Detroit** for Montreal's 3rd round choice (acquired earlier, Detroit selected Doug Derkson) and the rights to Barry Long, January 9, 1978.

• GRATTON, BENOIT

Benoit Gratton LW – L. 5'10", 163 lbs. b: Montreal, Que., 12/28/1976. Washington's 6th choice, 105th overall, in 1995 Entry Draft.

Season	Club	League	GP	G	A	Pts	AG	AA	APts	PIM	PP	SH	GW	S	%	TGF	PGF	TGA	PGA	+/–	GP	G	A	Pts	PIM	PP	SH	GW
1993-94	Laval Titan	QMJHL	51	9	14	23	....	....	....	70	....	....	....	....	....	....	....	....	....	....	20	2	1	3	19	....	....	....
1994-95	Laval Titan	QMJHL	71	30	58	88	....	....	....	199	....	....	....	....	....	....	....	....	....	....	20	8	*21	29	42	....	....	....
1995-96	Laval Titan	QMJHL	38	21	39	60	....	....	....	130	....	....	....	....	....	....	....	....	....	....	....	....	....	....	....	....	....	....
	Granby Bisons	QMJHL	27	12	46	58	....	....	....	97	....	....	....	....	....	....	....	....	....	....	21	13	26	39	68	....	....	....
1996-97	Portland Pirates	AHL	76	6	40	46	....	....	....	140	....	....	....	....	....	....	....	....	....	....	5	2	1	3	14	....	....	....
1997-98	**Washington Capitals**	**NHL**	**6**	**0**	**1**	**1**	**0**	**1**	**1**	**6**	**0**	**0**	**0**	**5**	**0.0**	**1**	**0**	**0**	**0**	**+1**	....	....	....	....	....	....	....	....
	Portland Pirates	AHL	58	19	31	50	....	....	....	137	....	....	....	....	....	....	....	....	....	....	8	4	2	6	24	....	....	....
	NHL Totals		**6**	**0**	**1**	**1**	**0**	**1**	**1**	**6**	**0**	**0**	**0**	**5**	**0.0**	**1**	**0**	**0**	**0**		....	....	....	....	....	....	....	....

• GRATTON, CHRIS

Chris Gratton C – L. 6'4", 218 lbs. b: Brantford, Ont., 7/5/1975. Tampa Bay's 1st choice, 3rd overall, in 1993 Entry Draft.

Season	Club	League	GP	G	A	Pts	AG	AA	APts	PIM	PP	SH	GW	S	%	TGF	PGF	TGA	PGA	+/–	GP	G	A	Pts	PIM	PP	SH	GW
1991-92	Kingston Frontenacs	OHL	62	27	29	66	....	....	....	37	....	....	....	....	....	....	....	....	....	....	....	....	....	....	....	....	....	....
1992-93	Kingston Frontenacs	OHL	58	55	54	109	....	....	....	125	....	....	....	....	....	....	....	....	....	....	16	11	18	29	42	....	....	....
	Canada	WJC-A	7	2	2	4	....	....	....	6	....	....	....	....	....	....	....	....	....	....	....	....	....	....	....	....	....	....
1993-94	**Tampa Bay Lightning**	**NHL**	**84**	**13**	**29**	**42**	**12**	**22**	**34**	**123**	**5**	**1**	**2**	**161**	**8.1**	**59**	**27**	**58**	**1**	**–25**	....	....	....	....	....	....	....	....
1994-95	**Tampa Bay Lightning**	**NHL**	**46**	**7**	**20**	**27**	**12**	**29**	**41**	**89**	**2**	**0**	**0**	**91**	**7.7**	**37**	**11**	**28**	**0**	**–2**	....	....	....	....	....	....	....	....
1995-96	**Tampa Bay Lightning**	**NHL**	**82**	**17**	**21**	**38**	**17**	**17**	**34**	**105**	**7**	**0**	**3**	**183**	**9.3**	**64**	**28**	**50**	**1**	**–13**	**6**	**0**	**2**	**2**	**27**	**0**	**0**	**0**
1996-97	**Tampa Bay Lightning**	**NHL**	**82**	**30**	**32**	**62**	**32**	**28**	**60**	**201**	**9**	**0**	**4**	**230**	**13.0**	**81**	**29**	**81**	**1**	**–28**	....	....	....	....	....	....	....	....
	Canada	WC-A	11	0	5	5	....	....	....	14	....	....	....	....	....	....	....	....	....	....	....	....	....	....	....	....	....	....
1997-98	**Philadelphia Flyers**	**NHL**	**82**	**22**	**40**	**62**	**26**	**39**	**65**	**159**	**5**	**0**	**2**	**182**	**12.1**	**82**	**23**	**48**	**0**	**+11**	**5**	**2**	**0**	**2**	**10**	**0**	**0**	**0**
	Canada	WC-A	4	1	0	1	....	....	....	4	....	....	....	....	....	....	....	....	....	....	....	....	....	....	....	....	....	....
	NHL Totals		**376**	**89**	**142**	**231**	**99**	**135**	**234**	**677**	**28**	**1**	**11**	**847**	**10.5**	**323**	**118**	**265**	**3**		**11**	**2**	**2**	**4**	**37**	**0**	**0**	**0**

Signed as a free agent by **Philadelphia**, August 14, 1997.

• GRATTON, DAN

Dan Gratton C – L. 6', 185 lbs. b: Brantford, Ont., 12/7/1966. Los Angeles' 5th choice, 10th overall, in 1985 Entry Draft.

Season	Club	League	GP	G	A	Pts	AG	AA	APts	PIM	PP	SH	GW	S	%	TGF	PGF	TGA	PGA	+/–	GP	G	A	Pts	PIM	PP	SH	GW
1981-82	Guelph Platers	OJHL	40	14	26	40	....	....	....	70	....	....	....	....	....	....	....	....	....	....	....	....	....	....	....	....	....	....
1982-83	Oshawa Generals	OHL	64	15	28	43	....	....	....	55	....	....	....	....	....	....	....	....	....	....	17	6	10	16	11	....	....	....
1983-84	Oshawa Generals	OHL	65	40	34	74	....	....	....	55	....	....	....	....	....	....	....	....	....	....	7	2	5	7	15	....	....	....
1984-85	Oshawa Generals	OHL	56	24	48	72	....	....	....	67	....	....	....	....	....	....	....	....	....	....	5	3	3	6	0	....	....	....
	Canada	WJC-A	7	2	3	5	....	....	....	16	....	....	....	....	....	....	....	....	....	....	....	....	....	....	....	....	....	....
1985-86	Oshawa Generals	OHA	10	3	5	8	....	....	....	15	....	....	....	....	....	....	....	....	....	....	....	....	....	....	....	....	....	....
	Ottawa 67's	OHA	25	18	18	36	....	....	....	19	....	....	....	....	....	....	....	....	....	....	....	....	....	....	....	....	....	....
	Belleville Bulls	OHL	20	12	14	26	....	....	....	11	....	....	....	....	....	....	....	....	....	....	24	*20	9	29	16	....	....	....
1986-87	New Haven Nighthawks	AHL	49	6	10	10	....	....	....	45	....	....	....	....	....	....	....	....	....	....	2	0	0	0	0	....	....	....
1987-88	**Los Angeles Kings**	**NHL**	**7**	**1**	**0**	**1**	**1**	**0**	**1**	**5**	**0**	**0**	**0**	**3**	**33.3**	**1**	**0**	**0**	**0**	**+1**	....	....	....	....	....	....	....	....
	New Haven Nighthawks	AHL	57	18	28	46	....	....	....	77	....	....	....	....	....	....	....	....	....	....	....	....	....	....	....	....	....	....
1988-89	New Haven Nighthawks	AHL	29	5	13	18	....	....	....	41	....	....	....	....	....	....	....	....	....	....	....	....	....	....	....	....	....	....
	Flint Spirits	IHL	20	5	9	14	....	....	....	0	....	....	....	....	....	....	....	....	....	....	....	....	....	....	....	....	....	....
1989-90	Canada	Nat-Team	68	29	37	66	....	....	....	40	....	....	....	....	....	....	....	....	....	....	....	....	....	....	....	....	....	....
1990-91	Minnesota North Stars	FrTour	3	0	1	1	....	....	....	0	....	....	....	....	....	....	....	....	....	....	....	....	....	....	....	....	....	....
	Canada	Nat-Team	8	6	2	8	....	....	....	4	....	....	....	....	....	....	....	....	....	....	....	....	....	....	....	....	....	....
	Kalamazoo Wings	IHL	44	9	11	20	....	....	....	32	....	....	....	....	....	....	....	....	....	....	6	1	0	1	14	....	....	....
1991-92	Innsbruck	Austria	8	6	2	8	....	....	....	....	....	....	....	....	....	....	....	....	....	....	....	....	....	....	....	....	....	....
	Brantford Smoke	ColHL	17	8	12	20	....	....	....	6	....	....	....	....	....	....	....	....	....	....	....	....	....	....	....	....	....	....
1992-93	Brantford Smoke	ColHL	13	9	8	17	....	....	....	0	....	....	....	....	....	....	....	....	....	....	10	2	11	13	4	....	....	....
1993-94	Hamilton Canucks	AHL	2	0	0	0	....	....	....	12	....	....	....	....	....	....	....	....	....	....	....	....	....	....	....	....	....	....
	Brantford Smoke	ColHL	12	9	10	19	....	....	....	16	....	....	....	....	....	....	....	....	....	....	....	....	....	....	....	....	....	....
	HC Fassa	Italy	22	18	14	32	....	....	....	22	....	....	....	....	....	....	....	....	....	....	....	....	....	....	....	....	....	....
1994-95	Slough Jets	Britain	39	84	87	171	....	....	....	142	....	....	....	....	....	....	....	....	....	....	....	....	....	....	....	....	....	....
1995-96	Slough Jets	Britain	34	36	45	81	....	....	....	118	....	....	....	....	....	....	....	....	....	....	....	....	....	....	....	....	....	....
	NHL Totals		**7**	**1**	**0**	**1**	**1**	**0**	**1**	**5**	**0**	**0**	**0**	**3**	**33.3**	**1**	**0**	**0**	**0**		....	....	....	....	....	....	....	....

Signed as a free agent by **Minnesota**, August 22, 1990.

• GRATTON, NORM

Norm Gratton LW – L. 5'11", 165 lbs. b: LaSalle, Que., 12/22/1950. NY Rangers' 1st choice, 11th overall, in 1970 Amateur Draft.

Season	Club	League	GP	G	A	Pts	AG	AA	APts	PIM	PP	SH	GW	S	%	TGF	PGF	TGA	PGA	+/–	GP	G	A	Pts	PIM	PP	SH	GW
1967-68	Thetford Mines	QJHL	50	21	47	68	....	....	....	....	....	....	....	....	....	....	....	....	....	....	....	....	....	....	....	....	....	....
1968-69	Montreal Jr. Canadiens	OHA	53	10	23	33	....	....	....	37	....	....	....	....	....	....	....	....	....	....	14	7	10	17	4	....	....	....
1969-70	Montreal Jr. Canadiens	OHA	54	32	41	73	....	....	....	65	....	....	....	....	....	....	....	....	....	....	....	....	....	....	....	....	....	....
1970-71	Omaha Knights	CHL	70	19	31	50	....	....	....	52	....	....	....	....	....	....	....	....	....	....	11	6	2	8	0	....	....	....
1971-72	**New York Rangers**	**NHL**	**3**	**0**	**1**	**1**	**0**	**1**	**1**	**0**	**0**	**0**	**0**	**2**	**0.0**	**2**	**0**	**1**	**0**	**+1**	....	....	....	....	....	....	....	....
	Omaha Knights	CHL	68	32	42	74	....	....	....	82	....	....	....	....	....	....	....	....	....	....	....	....	....	....	....	....	....	....
1972-73	**Atlanta Flames**	**NHL**	**29**	**3**	**6**	**9**	**3**	**5**	**8**	**12**	**1**	**0**	**0**	**26**	**11.5**	**14**	**6**	**7**	**0**	**+1**	....	....	....	....	....	....	....	....
	Omaha Knights	CHL	11	5	8	13	....	....	....	4	....	....	....	....	....	....	....	....	....	....	....	....	....	....	....	....	....	....
	Buffalo Sabres	**NHL**	**21**	**6**	**5**	**11**	**6**	**4**	**10**	**12**	**2**	**0**	**1**	**26**	**23.1**	**22**	**11**	**11**	**0**	**0**	**6**	**0**	**1**	**1**	**2**	**0**	**0**	**0**
1973-74	**Buffalo Sabres**	**NHL**	**57**	**6**	**11**	**17**	**6**	**9**	**15**	**16**	**2**	**0**	**0**	**53**	**11.3**	**29**	**6**	**33**	**0**	**–10**	....	....	....	....	....	....	....	....
1974-75	**Buffalo Sabres**	**NHL**	**25**	**3**	**6**	**9**	**3**	**5**	**8**	**2**	**1**	**0**	**0**	**16**	**18.8**	**12**	**3**	**7**	**0**	**+2**	....	....	....	....	....	....	....	....
	Minnesota North Stars	**NHL**	**34**	**14**	**12**	**26**	**13**	**9**	**22**	**8**	**4**	**0**	**1**	**88**	**15.9**	**34**	**8**	**37**	**0**	**–11**	....	....	....	....	....	....	....	....
1975-76	**Minnesota North Stars**	**NHL**	**32**	**7**	**3**	**10**	**7**	**2**	**9**	**14**	**3**	**0**	**0**	**51**	**13.7**	**18**	**6**	**24**	**0**	**–12**	....	....	....	....	....	....	....	....
	New Haven Nighthawks	AHL	29	7	7	14	....	....	....	4	....	....	....	....	....	....	....	....	....	....	3	0	0	0	0	....	....	....
1976-77	Maine Nordiques	NAHL	52	15	26	41	....	....	....	16	....	....	....	....	....	....	....	....	....	....	11	1	3	4	0	....	....	....
	NHL Totals		**201**	**39**	**44**	**83**	**38**	**35**	**73**	**64**	**13**	**0**	**2**	**262**	**14.9**	**131**	**40**	**120**	**0**		**6**	**0**	**1**	**1**	**2**	**0**	**0**	**0**

CHL Second All-Star Team (1972)

Claimed by **Atlanta** from **NY Rangers** in Expansion Draft, June 6, 1972. Traded to **Buffalo** by **Atlanta** for Butch Deadmarsh, February 14, 1973. Traded to **Minnesota** by **Buffalo** with Buffalo's 3rd round choice (Ron Zanussi) in 1976 Amateur Draft for Fred Stanfield, January 27, 1975.

• GRAVES, ADAM

Adam Graves C – L. 6', 210 lbs. b: Toronto, Ont., 4/12/1968. Detroit's 2nd choice, 22nd overall, in 1986 Entry Draft.

Season	Club	League	GP	G	A	Pts	AG	AA	APts	PIM	PP	SH	GW	S	%	TGF	PGF	TGA	PGA	+/–	GP	G	A	Pts	PIM	PP	SH	GW
1985-86	Windsor Spitfires	OHL	62	27	37	64	....	....	....	35	....	....	....	....	....	....	....	....	....	....	16	5	11	16	10	....	....	....
1986-87	Windsor Spitfires	OHL	66	45	55	100	....	....	....	70	....	....	....	....	....	....	....	....	....	....	14	9	8	17	32	....	....	....
	Adirondack Red Wings	AHL	....	....	....	....	....	....	....	....	....	....	....	....	....	....	....	....	....	....	5	0	1	1	0	....	....	....
1987-88	Windsor Spitfires	OHL	37	28	32	60	....	....	....	107	....	....	....	....	....	....	....	....	....	....	12	14	18	*32	16	....	....	....
	Canada	WJC-A	7	5	0	5	....	....	....	4	....	....	....	....	....	....	....	....	....	....	....	....	....	....	....	....	....	....
	Detroit Red Wings	**NHL**	**9**	**0**	**1**	**1**	**0**	**1**	**1**	**8**	**0**	**0**	**0**	**9**	**0.0**	**3**	**0**	**6**	**1**	**–2**	....	....	....	....	....	....	....	....
1988-89	**Detroit Red Wings**	**NHL**	**56**	**7**	**5**	**12**	**6**	**4**	**10**	**60**	**0**	**0**	**1**	**60**	**11.7**	**22**	**1**	**26**	**0**	**–5**	**5**	**0**	**0**	**0**	**4**	**0**	**0**	**0**
	Adirondack Red Wings	AHL	14	10	11	21	....	....	....	28	....	....	....	....	....	....	....	....	....	....	14	11	7	18	17	....	....	....
1989-90	**Detroit Red Wings**	**NHL**	**13**	**0**	**1**	**1**	**0**	**1**	**1**	**13**	**0**	**0**	**0**	**10**	**0.0**	**3**	**0**	**10**	**2**	**–5**	....	....	....	....	....	....	....	....
	Edmonton Oilers	**NHL**	**63**	**9**	**12**	**21**	**8**	**9**	**17**	**123**	**1**	**0**	**1**	**84**	**10.7**	**33**	**3**	**25**	**0**	**+5**	**22**	**5**	**6**	**11**	**17**	**0**	**0**	**1**
1990-91	**Edmonton Oilers**	**NHL**	**76**	**7**	**18**	**25**	**6**	**14**	**20**	**127**	**2**	**0**	**1**	**126**	**5.6**	**42**	**10**	**56**	**3**	**–21**	**18**	**2**	**4**	**6**	**22**	**0**	**0**	**0**

			REGULAR SEASON																		PLAYOFFS							
Season	Club	League	GP	G	A	Pts	AG	AA	APts	PIM	PP	SH	GW	S	%	TGF	PGF	TGA	PGA	+/–	GP	G	A	Pts	PIM	PP	SH	GW
1991-92	New York Rangers	NHL	80	26	33	59	24	25	49	139	4	4	4	228	11.4	99	15	81	16	+19	10	5	3	8	22	1	0	1
1992-93	New York Rangers	NHL	84	36	29	65	30	20	50	148	12	1	6	275	13.1	104	29	99	20	–4	....	....	....	....	....	....	....	....
	Canada	WC-A	8	3	3	6	....	....	....	8	....	....	....	....	....	....	....	....	....	....	....	....	....	....	....	....	....	....
1993-94	New York Rangers	NHL	84	52	27	79	49	21	70	127	20	4	4	291	17.9	137	54	85	29	+27	23	10	7	17	24	3	0	0
1994-95	New York Rangers	NHL	47	17	14	31	30	21	51	51	9	0	3	185	9.2	69	30	43	13	+9	10	4	4	8	8	2	0	0
1995-96	New York Rangers	NHL	82	22	36	58	22	29	51	100	9	1	2	266	8.3	121	48	96	41	+18	10	7	1	8	4	6	0	2
1996-97	Canada	W Cup	7	0	1	1	....	....	....	2	....	....	....	....	....	....	....	....	....	....	....	....	....	....	....	....	....	....
	New York Rangers	NHL	82	33	28	61	35	25	60	66	10	4	3	269	12.3	101	26	99	34	+10	15	2	1	3	12	1	0	2
1997-98	New York Rangers	NHL	72	23	12	35	27	12	39	41	10	0	2	226	10.2	60	33	73	16	–30	....	....	....	....	....	....	....	....
	NHL Totals		748	232	216	448	237	182	419	1003	77	14	27	2029	11.4	794	249	699	175		113	35	26	61	113	13	0	6

NHL Second All-Star Team (1994) • Won King Clancy Memorial Trophy (1994)

Played in NHL All-Star Game (1994)

Traded to **Edmonton** by **Detroit** with Petr Klima, Joe Murphy and Jeff Sharples for Jimmy Carson, Kevin McClelland and Edmonton's 5th round choice (later traded to Montreal — Montreal selected Brad Layzell) in 1991 Entry Draft, November 2, 1989. Signed as a free agent by **NY Rangers**, September 3, 1991.

• GRAVES, HILLIARD

Hilliard Graves RW – R. 5'11", 175 lbs. b: Saint John, N.B., 10/18/1950.

1968-69	Charlottetown Islanders	PEI Jr.	38	16	26	42	....	....	....	69	....	....	....	....	....	....	....	....	....	....	14	10	*13	23	26	....	....	....
1969-70	Charlottetown Islanders	PEI Jr.	32	32	*67	*99	....	....	....	55	....	....	....	....	....	....	....	....	....	....	....	....	....	....	....	....	....	....
1970-71	California Golden Seals	NHL	14	0	0	0	0	0	0	0	0	0	0	6	0.0	0	0	2	0	–2	....	....	....	....	....	....	....	....
	Providence Reds	AHL	16	3	1	4	....	....	....	11	....	....	....	....	....	....	....	....	....	....	....	....	....	....	....	....	....	....
1971-72	Baltimore Clippers	AHL	76	14	18	32	....	....	....	67	....	....	....	....	....	....	....	....	....	....	18	5	4	9	33	....	....	....
1972-73	California Golden Seals	NHL	75	27	25	52	27	21	48	34	3	0	3	128	21.1	62	11	66	0	–15	....	....	....	....	....	....	....	....
1973-74	California Golden Seals	NHL	64	11	18	29	11	16	27	48	1	0	1	91	12.1	42	5	70	1	–32	....	....	....	....	....	....	....	....
1974-75	Atlanta Flames	NHL	67	10	19	29	9	15	24	30	3	0	0	79	12.7	47	8	36	0	+3	....	....	....	....	....	....	....	....
1975-76	Atlanta Flames	NHL	80	19	30	49	18	24	42	16	2	0	3	168	11.3	83	25	58	3	+3	2	0	0	0	0	0	0	0
1976-77	Atlanta Flames	NHL	25	8	5	13	8	4	12	17	1	0	2	41	19.5	23	3	21	0	–1	....	....	....	....	....	....	....	....
	Vancouver Canucks	NHL	54	10	20	30	10	16	26	17	2	0	1	91	11.0	49	10	42	5	+2	....	....	....	....	....	....	....	....
1977-78	Vancouver Canucks	NHL	80	21	26	47	20	21	41	18	4	1	2	138	15.2	68	12	96	23	–17	....	....	....	....	....	....	....	....
1978-79	Vancouver Canucks	NHL	62	11	15	26	10	11	21	14	2	0	2	112	9.8	46	10	74	23	–15	....	....	....	....	....	....	....	....
	New Brunswick Hawks	AHL	18	8	15	23	....	....	....	22	....	....	....	....	....	....	....	....	....	....	5	4	5	9	10	....	....	....
1979-80	Winnipeg Jets	NHL	35	1	5	6	1	4	5	15	0	0	0	27	3.7	12	1	30	6	–13	....	....	....	....	....	....	....	....
	Tulsa Oilers	CHL	5	2	3	5	....	....	....	2	....	....	....	....	....	....	....	....	....	....	....	....	....	....	....	....	....	....
	New Brunswick Hawks	AHL	16	3	6	9	....	....	....	5	....	....	....	....	....	....	....	....	....	....	17	8	6	14	4	....	....	....
	NHL Totals		556	118	163	281	114	132	246	209	18	1	14	881	13.4	432	85	495	61		2	0	0	0	0	0	0	0

Signed as a free agent by **California**, October, 1970. Traded to **Atlanta** by **California** for John Stewart, July 18, 1974. Traded to **Vancouver** by **Atlanta** with Larry Carriere for John Gould and LA Kings' 2nd round choice (previously acquired, Atlanta selected Brian Hill) in 1977 Amateur Draft, December 2, 1976. Claimed by **Winnipeg** from **Vancouver** in Expansion Draft, June 13, 1979.

• GRAVES, STEVE

Steve Graves LW – L. 5'10", 175 lbs. b: Trenton, Ont., 4/7/1964. Edmonton's 2nd choice, 41st overall, in 1982 Entry Draft.

1980-81	Ottawa Jr. Senators	OJHL	44	21	17	38	....	....	....	47	....	....	....	....	....	....	....	....	....	....	....	....	....	....	....	....	....	....
1981-82	Sault Ste. Marie Greyhounds	OHL	66	12	15	27	....	....	....	49	....	....	....	....	....	....	....	....	....	....	13	8	5	13	14	....	....	....
1982-83	Sault Ste. Marie Greyhounds	OHL	60	21	20	41	....	....	....	48	....	....	....	....	....	....	....	....	....	....	5	0	0	0	4	....	....	....
1983-84	Sault Ste. Marie Greyhounds	OHL	67	41	48	89	....	....	....	47	....	....	....	....	....	....	....	....	....	....	16	6	8	14	8	....	....	....
	Edmonton Oilers	NHL	2	0	0	0	0	0	0	0	0	0	0	2	0.0	0	0	0	0	0	....	....	....	....	....	....	....	....
1984-85	Nova Scotia Voyageurs	AHL	80	17	15	32	....	....	....	20	....	....	....	....	....	....	....	....	....	....	6	0	1	1	4	....	....	....
1985-86	Nova Scotia Oilers	AHL	78	19	18	37	....	....	....	22	....	....	....	....	....	....	....	....	....	....	....	....	....	....	....	....	....	....
1986-87	Edmonton Oilers	NHL	12	2	0	2	2	0	2	0	0	0	1	12	16.7	2	0	4	0	–2	....	....	....	....	....	....	....	....
	Nova Scotia Oilers	AHL	59	18	10	28	....	....	....	22	....	....	....	....	....	....	....	....	....	....	5	1	1	2	2	....	....	....
1987-88	Edmonton Oilers	NHL	21	3	4	7	3	3	6	10	0	0	0	21	14.3	14	0	1	0	+13	....	....	....	....	....	....	....	....
	Nova Scotia Oilers	AHL	11	6	2	8	....	....	....	4	....	....	....	....	....	....	....	....	....	....	....	....	....	....	....	....	....	....
1988-89	Canada	Nat-Team	3	5	1	6	....	....	....	2	....	....	....	....	....	....	....	....	....	....	....	....	....	....	....	....	....	....
	TPS Turku	Finland	43	16	12	28	....	....	....	48	....	....	....	....	....	....	....	....	....	....	10	2	8	10	12	....	....	....
1989-90	Canada	Nat-Team	53	24	19	43	....	....	....	50	....	....	....	....	....	....	....	....	....	....	....	....	....	....	....	....	....	....
1990-91	New Haven Nighthawks	AHL	3	0	1	1	....	....	....	2	....	....	....	....	....	....	....	....	....	....	....	....	....	....	....	....	....	....
	Phoenix Roadrunners	IHL	56	11	20	31	....	....	....	64	....	....	....	....	....	....	....	....	....	....	5	1	3	4	2	....	....	....
1991-92	HC Asiago	Italy	12	4	6	10	....	....	....	4	....	....	....	....	....	....	....	....	....	....	....	....	....	....	....	....	....	....
	NHL Totals		35	5	4	9	5	3	8	10	0	0	1	35	14.3	16	0	5	0		....	....	....	....	....	....	....	....

OHL Third All-Star Team (1984)

Signed as a free agent by **LA Kings**, July 16, 1990.

• GRAY, TERRY

Terry Gray RW – R. 6', 175 lbs. b: Montreal, Que., 3/21/1938.

1953-54	Montreal Jr. Royals	QJHL	49	3	4	7	....	....	....	63	....	....	....	....	....	....	....	....	....	....	4	0	1	1	12	....	....	....
1954-55	Montreal Jr. Royals	QJHL	DID NOT PLAY – INJURED																									
1955-56	Montreal Nationale	QJHL	46	45	29	74	....	....	....	33	....	....	....	....	....	....	....	....	....	....	....	....	....	....	....	....	....	....
1956-57	Montreal Nationale	QJHL	30	30	24	54	....	....	....	59	....	....	....	....	....	....	....	....	....	....	....	....	....	....	....	....	....	....
	Hull-Ottawa Jr. Canadiens	Ott-Jr.	1	0	0	0	....	....	....	0	....	....	....	....	....	....	....	....	....	....	....	....	....	....	....	....	....	....
	Montreal Royals	QHL	3	1	0	1	....	....	....	0	....	....	....	....	....	....	....	....	....	....	....	....	....	....	....	....	....	....
1957-58	Hull-Ottawa Jr. Canadiens	Ott-Jr.	24	9	11	20	....	....	....	15	....	....	....	....	....	....	....	....	....	....	....	....	....	....	....	....	....	....
	Hull-Ottawa Jr. Canadiens	EOHL	33	13	13	26	....	....	....	15	....	....	....	....	....	....	....	....	....	....	....	....	....	....	....	....	....	....
	Montreal Royals	QHL	1	0	0	0	....	....	....	0	....	....	....	....	....	....	....	....	....	....	....	....	....	....	....	....	....	....
1958-59	Montreal Royals	QHL	19	11	9	20	....	....	....	33	....	....	....	....	....	....	....	....	....	....	....	....	....	....	....	....	....	....
	Rochester Americans	AHL	45	10	14	24	....	....	....	14	....	....	....	....	....	....	....	....	....	....	5	1	2	3	2	....	....	....
1959-60	Sault Ste. Marie Thunderbirds	EPHL	16	4	11	15	....	....	....	19	....	....	....	....	....	....	....	....	....	....	....	....	....	....	....	....	....	....
	Calgary Stampeders	WHL	49	20	14	34	....	....	....	29	....	....	....	....	....	....	....	....	....	....	....	....	....	....	....	....	....	....
	Buffalo Bisons	AHL	3	0	0	0	....	....	....	0	....	....	....	....	....	....	....	....	....	....	....	....	....	....	....	....	....	....
1960-61	Hull-Ottawa Canadiens	EPHL	69	40	37	77	....	....	....	63	....	....	....	....	....	....	....	....	....	....	14	8	*11	*19	13	....	....	....
1961-62	Boston Bruins	NHL	42	8	7	15	10	7	17	15	....	....	....	....	....	....	....	....	....	....	....	....	....	....	....	....	....	....
	Kingston Frontenacs	EPHL	24	9	11	20	....	....	....	24	....	....	....	....	....	....	....	....	....	....	9	*9	6	15	9	....	....	....
1962-63	Cleveland–Quebec	AHL	68	25	25	50	....	....	....	61	....	....	....	....	....	....	....	....	....	....	....	....	....	....	....	....	....	....
1963-64	Montreal Canadiens	NHL	4	0	0	0	0	0	0	6	....	....	....	....	....	....	....	....	....	....	....	....	....	....	....	....	....	....
	Quebec Aces	AHL	55	25	22	47	....	....	....	65	....	....	....	....	....	....	....	....	....	....	4	0	1	1	6	....	....	....
1964-65	Quebec Aces	AHL	72	39	28	67	....	....	....	54	....	....	....	....	....	....	....	....	....	....	5	2	1	3	12	....	....	....
1965-66	Quebec–Pittsburgh	AHL	73	30	33	63	....	....	....	38	....	....	....	....	....	....	....	....	....	....	3	2	0	2	4	....	....	....
1966-67	Pittsburgh Hornets	AHL	63	25	29	54	....	....	....	52	....	....	....	....	....	....	....	....	....	....	9	3	4	7	11	....	....	....
1967-68	Los Angeles Kings	NHL	65	12	16	28	15	17	32	22	3	0	0	113	10.6	40	6	39	2	–3	7	0	2	2	10	0	0	0
1968-69	St. Louis Blues	NHL	8	4	0	4	4	0	4	4	2	0	1	19	21.1	7	3	4	0	0	11	3	2	5	8	1	0	0
	Kansas City Blues	CHL	53	22	28	50	....	....	....	84	....	....	....	....	....	....	....	....	....	....	....	....	....	....	....	....	....	....
1969-70	St. Louis Blues	NHL	28	2	5	7	2	5	7	17	0	0	2	63	3.2	13	1	10	0	+2	16	2	1	3	4	1	1	0
	Kansas City Blues	CHL	22	15	15	30	....	....	....	89	....	....	....	....	....	....	....	....	....	....	....	....	....	....	....	....	....	....
1970-71	Montreal Voyageurs	AHL	63	24	22	46	....	....	....	78	....	....	....	....	....	....	....	....	....	....	3	1	1	2	4	....	....	....
	St. Louis Blues	NHL	....	....	....	....	....	....	....	....	....	....	....	....	....	....	....	....	....	....	1	0	0	0	0	....	....	....
1971-72	Columbus Seals	IHL	DID NOT PLAY – COACHING																									
1972-73	New Haven Nighthawks	AHL	71	25	25	50	....	....	....	40	....	....	....	....	....	....	....	....	....	....	....	....	....	....	....	....	....	....
1973-74	Fort Worth Wings	CHL	60	18	17	35	....	....	....	30	....	....	....	....	....	....	....	....	....	....	....	....	....	....	....	....	....	....
	NHL Totals		147	26	28	54	31	29	60	64	5	0	3	195	13.3	60	10	53	2		35	5	5	10	22	2	1	0

Traded to **Montreal** by **Chicago** with Glen Skov, the rights to Danny Lewicki, Lorne Ferguson and Bob Bailey for Cec Hoekstra, Reggie Fleming, Ab McDonald and Bob Courcy, June 7, 1960. Traded to **Boston** by **Montreal** with Cliff Pennington for Willie O'Ree and Stan Maxwell, June, 1961. Traded to **Quebec** (AHL) by **Boston** for Gary Bergman with Boston holding rights of recall, November, 1962. Traded to **Springfield** (AHL) by **Boston** with Dale Rolfe, Bruce Gamble and Randy Miller for Bob McCord, June, 1963. Traded to **Montreal** by **Springfield** (AHL) with Ted Harris, Bruce Cline, Wayne Larkin and Jeff Chasczewski for the loan of Gary Bergman, Wayne Boddy, Fred Hilts, Brian D. Smith, John Rodger and Lorne O'Donnell, June, 1963. Traded to **Detroit** (Pittsburgh - AHL) by **Quebec** (AHL) for Claude Laforge, March 1, 1966. Claimed by **LA Kings** from **Detroit** in Expansion Draft, June 6, 1967. Traded to **St. Louis** by **LA Kings** for Myron Stankiewicz, June 11, 1968.

			REGULAR SEASON																		PLAYOFFS							
Season	Club	League	GP	G	A	Pts	AG	AA	APts	PIM	PP	SH	GW	S	%	TGF	PGF	TGA	PGA	+/–	GP	G	A	Pts	PIM	PP	SH	GW

• GREEN, RICK Rick Green D – L. 6'3", 220 lbs. b: Belleville, Ont., 2/20/1956. Washington's 1st choice, 1st overall, in 1976 Amateur Draft.

Season	Club	League	GP	G	A	Pts	AG	AA	APts	PIM	PP	SH	GW	S	%	TGF	PGF	TGA	PGA	+/–	GP	G	A	Pts	PIM	PP	SH	GW
1972-73	London Knights	OHA	7	0	1	1	....	....	....	2	....	....	....	....	....	....	....	....	....	....	....	....	....	....	....	....	....	....
1973-74	London Knights	OHA	65	6	30	36	....	....	....	45	....	....	....	....	....	....	....	....	....	....	....	....	....	....	....	....	....	....
1974-75	London Knights	OHA	65	8	45	53	....	....	....	68	....	....	....	....	....	....	....	....	....	....	....	....	....	....	....	....	....	....
1975-76	London Knights	OHA	61	13	47	60	....	....	....	69	....	....	....	....	....	....	....	....	....	....	5	1	0	1	4	....	....	....
1976-77	**Washington Capitals**	**NHL**	**45**	**3**	**12**	**15**	**3**	**10**	**13**	**16**	**1**	**0**	**0**	**89**	**3.4**	**45**	**10**	**58**	**3**	**–20**	....	....	....	....	....	....	....	....
1977-78	**Washington Capitals**	**NHL**	**60**	**5**	**14**	**19**	**5**	**11**	**16**	**67**	**4**	**0**	**1**	**84**	**6.0**	**62**	**20**	**97**	**20**	**–35**	....	....	....	....	....	....	....	....
1978-79	**Washington Capitals**	**NHL**	**71**	**8**	**33**	**41**	**7**	**25**	**32**	**62**	**2**	**1**	**0**	**133**	**6.0**	**103**	**30**	**163**	**45**	**–45**	....	....	....	....	....	....	....	....
	Canada	WEC-A	8	1	1	2	....	....	....	2	....	....	....	....	....	....	....	....	....	....	....	....	....	....	....	....	....	....
1979-80	**Washington Capitals**	**NHL**	**71**	**4**	**20**	**24**	**4**	**15**	**19**	**52**	**0**	**0**	**1**	**105**	**3.8**	**93**	**10**	**126**	**33**	**–10**	....	....	....	....	....	....	....	....
1980-81	**Washington Capitals**	**NHL**	**65**	**8**	**23**	**31**	**7**	**16**	**23**	**91**	**2**	**0**	**1**	**120**	**6.7**	**97**	**29**	**120**	**37**	**–15**	....	....	....	....	....	....	....	....
	Canada	WEC-A	7	1	3	4	....	....	....	2	....	....	....	....	....	....	....	....	....	....	....	....	....	....	....	....	....	....
1981-82	**Washington Capitals**	**NHL**	**65**	**3**	**25**	**28**	**2**	**17**	**19**	**93**	**1**	**0**	**0**	**91**	**3.3**	**108**	**23**	**129**	**32**	**–12**	....	....	....	....	....	....	....	....
	Canada	WEC-A	9	0	3	3	....	....	....	2	....	....	....	....	....	....	....	....	....	....	....	....	....	....	....	....	....	....
1982-83	**Montreal Canadiens**	**NHL**	**66**	**2**	**24**	**26**	**2**	**17**	**19**	**58**	**1**	**0**	**0**	**71**	**2.8**	**103**	**16**	**85**	**21**	**+23**	**3**	**0**	**0**	**0**	**2**	**0**	**0**	**0**
1983-84	**Montreal Canadiens**	**NHL**	**7**	**0**	**1**	**1**	**0**	**1**	**1**	**7**	**0**	**0**	**0**	**10**	**0.0**	**5**	**1**	**10**	**1**	**–5**	**15**	**1**	**2**	**3**	**33**	**0**	**0**	**0**
1984-85	**Montreal Canadiens**	**NHL**	**77**	**1**	**18**	**19**	**1**	**12**	**13**	**30**	**1**	**0**	**0**	**63**	**1.6**	**63**	**9**	**93**	**28**	**–11**	**12**	**0**	**3**	**3**	**14**	**0**	**0**	**0**
1985-86	**Montreal Canadiens**	**NHL**	**46**	**3**	**2**	**5**	**2**	**1**	**3**	**20**	**0**	**0**	**0**	**45**	**6.7**	**45**	**1**	**75**	**22**	**–9**	**18**	**1**	**4**	**5**	**8**	**0**	**0**	**0**
1986-87	**Montreal Canadiens**	**NHL**	**72**	**1**	**9**	**10**	**1**	**6**	**7**	**10**	**0**	**0**	**0**	**38**	**2.6**	**47**	**2**	**83**	**37**	**–1**	**17**	**0**	**4**	**4**	**8**	**0**	**0**	**0**
	NHL All-Stars	RV'87	2	0	0	0	....	....	....	0	....	....	....	....	....	....	....	....	....	....	....	....	....	....	....	....	....	....
1987-88	**Montreal Canadiens**	**NHL**	**59**	**2**	**11**	**13**	**2**	**8**	**10**	**33**	**1**	**0**	**0**	**44**	**4.5**	**64**	**2**	**69**	**28**	**+21**	**11**	**0**	**2**	**2**	**2**	**0**	**0**	**0**
1988-89	**Montreal Canadiens**	**NHL**	**72**	**1**	**14**	**15**	**1**	**10**	**11**	**25**	**0**	**0**	**0**	**42**	**2.4**	**66**	**2**	**57**	**12**	**+19**	**21**	**1**	**1**	**2**	**6**	**0**	**0**	**0**
1989-90	HC Meran	Italy	9	2	6	8	....	....	....	2	....	....	....	....	....	....	....	....	....	....	10	3	6	9	4	....	....	....
	Canada	WEC-A	10	0	0	0	....	....	....	2	....	....	....	....	....	....	....	....	....	....	....	....	....	....	....	....	....	....
1990-91	**Detroit Red Wings**	**NHL**	**65**	**2**	**14**	**16**	**2**	**11**	**13**	**24**	**0**	**0**	**0**	**36**	**5.6**	**66**	**1**	**90**	**35**	**+10**	**3**	**0**	**0**	**0**	**0**	**0**	**0**	**0**
1991-92	**New York Islanders**	**NHL**	**4**	**0**	**0**	**0**	**0**	**0**	**0**	**0**	**0**	**0**	**0**	**2**	**0.0**	**2**	**0**	**6**	**3**	**–1**	....	....	....	....	....	....	....	....
	NHL Totals		**845**	**43**	**220**	**263**	**39**	**160**	**199**	**588**	**13**	**1**	**3**	**973**	**4.4**	**969**	**156**	**1261**	**357**		**100**	**3**	**16**	**19**	**73**	**0**	**0**	**0**

OHA First All-Star Team (1976)

Traded to **Montreal** by **Washington** with Ryan Walter for Brian Engblom, Rod Langway, Doug Jarvis and Craig Laughlin, September 9, 1982. Traded to **Detroit** by **Montreal** for Edmonton's 5th round choice (previously acquired, Montreal selected Brad Layzell) in 1991 Entry Draft, June 15, 1990. Traded to **NY Islanders** by **Detroit** for Alan Kerr and future considerations, May 26, 1991.

• GREEN, TED Ted "Terrible Ted" Green D – R. 5'10", 200 lbs. b: Eriksdale, Man., 3/23/1940.

Season	Club	League	GP	G	A	Pts	AG	AA	APts	PIM	PP	SH	GW	S	%	TGF	PGF	TGA	PGA	+/–	GP	G	A	Pts	PIM	PP	SH	GW
1956-57	St. Boniface Canadians	MJHL	17	1	2	3	....	....	....	76	....	....	....	....	....	....	....	....	....	....	7	0	0	0	10	....	....	....
1957-58	St. Boniface Canadians	MJHL	23	1	4	5	....	....	....	*97	....	....	....	....	....	....	....	....	....	....	23	3	5	8	*70	....	....	....
1958-59	St. Boniface Canadians	MJHL	25	5	11	16	....	....	....	*120	....	....	....	....	....	....	....	....	....	....	9	1	5	6	32	....	....	....
	Winnipeg Braves	MJHL	....	....	....	....	....	....	....	....	....	....	....	....	....	....	....	....	....	....	16	2	6	8	*50	....	....	....
1959-60	Winnipeg Warriors	WHL	70	8	20	28	....	....	....	109	....	....	....	....	....	....	....	....	....	....	....	....	....	....	....	....	....	....
1960-61	**Boston Bruins**	**NHL**	**1**	**0**	**0**	**0**	**0**	**0**	**0**	**2**	....	....	....	....	....	....	....	....	....	....	....	....	....	....	....	....	....	....
	Kingston Frontenacs	EPHL	11	1	5	6	....	....	....	30	....	....	....	....	....	....	....	....	....	....	5	1	0	1	2	....	....	....
	Winnipeg Warriors	WHL	57	1	18	19	....	....	....	127	....	....	....	....	....	....	....	....	....	....	....	....	....	....	....	....	....	....
1961-62	**Boston Bruins**	**NHL**	**66**	**3**	**8**	**11**	**4**	**8**	**12**	**116**	....	....	....	....	....	....	....	....	....	....	....	....	....	....	....	....	....	....
1962-63	**Boston Bruins**	**NHL**	**70**	**1**	**11**	**12**	**1**	**11**	**12**	**117**	....	....	....	....	....	....	....	....	....	....	....	....	....	....	....	....	....	....
1963-64	**Boston Bruins**	**NHL**	**70**	**4**	**10**	**14**	**5**	**11**	**16**	**145**	....	....	....	....	....	....	....	....	....	....	....	....	....	....	....	....	....	....
1964-65	**Boston Bruins**	**NHL**	**70**	**8**	**27**	**35**	**10**	**29**	**39**	**156**	....	....	....	....	....	....	....	....	....	....	....	....	....	....	....	....	....	....
1965-66	**Boston Bruins**	**NHL**	**27**	**5**	**13**	**18**	**6**	**13**	**19**	**113**	....	....	....	....	....	....	....	....	....	....	....	....	....	....	....	....	....	....
1966-67	**Boston Bruins**	**NHL**	**47**	**6**	**10**	**16**	**7**	**10**	**17**	**67**	....	....	....	....	....	....	....	....	....	....	....	....	....	....	....	....	....	....
1967-68	**Boston Bruins**	**NHL**	**72**	**7**	**36**	**43**	**9**	**38**	**47**	**133**	**3**	**0**	**0**	**113**	**6.2**	**113**	**17**	**107**	**25**	**+14**	**4**	**1**	**1**	**2**	**11**	**1**	**0**	**0**
1968-69	**Boston Bruins**	**NHL**	**65**	**8**	**38**	**46**	**9**	**36**	**45**	**99**	**3**	**0**	**0**	**131**	**6.1**	**126**	**41**	**95**	**19**	**+9**	**10**	**2**	**7**	**9**	**18**	**0**	**0**	**0**
1969-70			DID NOT PLAY – INJURED																									
1970-71	**Boston Bruins**	**NHL**	**78**	**5**	**37**	**42**	**5**	**33**	**38**	**60**	**0**	**0**	**0**	**103**	**4.9**	**125**	**1**	**99**	**12**	**+37**	**7**	**1**	**0**	**1**	**25**	**0**	**0**	**0**
1971-72	**Boston Bruins**	**NHL**	**54**	**1**	**16**	**17**	**1**	**15**	**16**	**21**	**0**	**0**	**0**	**41**	**2.4**	**60**	**0**	**58**	**8**	**+10**	**10**	**0**	**0**	**0**	**0**	**0**	**0**	**0**
1972-73	New England Whalers	WHA	78	16	30	46	....	....	....	47	....	....	....	....	....	....	....	....	....	....	12	1	5	6	25	....	....	....
1973-74	New England Whalers	WHA	75	7	26	33	....	....	....	42	....	....	....	....	....	....	....	....	....	....	7	0	4	4	2	....	....	....
1974-75	New England Whalers	WHA	57	6	14	20	....	....	....	29	....	....	....	....	....	....	....	....	....	....	3	0	0	0	2	....	....	....
1975-76	Winnipeg Jets	WHA	79	5	23	28	....	....	....	73	....	....	....	....	....	....	....	....	....	....	11	0	2	2	16	....	....	....
1976-77	Winnipeg Jets	WHA	70	4	21	25	....	....	....	45	....	....	....	....	....	....	....	....	....	....	20	1	3	4	12	....	....	....
1977-78	Winnipeg Jets	WHA	73	4	22	26	....	....	....	52	....	....	....	....	....	....	....	....	....	....	8	0	2	2	2	....	....	....
1978-79	Winnipeg Jets	WHA	20	0	2	2	....	....	....	16	....	....	....	....	....	....	....	....	....	....	....	....	....	....	....	....	....	....
	NHL Totals		**620**	**48**	**206**	**254**	**57**	**204**	**261**	**1029**	**6**	**0**	**0**	**388**	**12.4**	**424**	**59**	**359**	**64**		**31**	**4**	**8**	**12**	**54**	**1**	**0**	**0**
	Other Major League Totals		452	42	138	180	....	....	....	304	....	....	....	....	....	....	....	....	....	....	61	2	16	18	59	....	....	....

NHL Second All-Star Team (1969)

Played in NHL All-Star Game (1965, 1969)

Claimed by **Boston** from **Montreal** (Winnipeg-WHL) in Intra-League Draft, June 7, 1960. • Missed entire 1969-70 season after suffering head injury in exhibition game vs. St. Louis, September 19, 1969. Selected by **Winnipeg** (WHA) in 1972 WHA General Player Draft, February 12, 1972. Rights traded to **New England** (WHA) by **Winnipeg** (WHA) for cash, May, 1972. Traded to **Winnipeg** (WHA) by **New England** (WHA) for future considerations, May, 1975.

• GREEN, TRAVIS Travis Green C – R. 6'1", 193 lbs. b: Castlegar, B.C., 12/20/1970. NY Islanders' 2nd choice, 23rd overall, in 1989 Entry Draft.

Season	Club	League	GP	G	A	Pts	AG	AA	APts	PIM	PP	SH	GW	S	%	TGF	PGF	TGA	PGA	+/–	GP	G	A	Pts	PIM	PP	SH	GW
1986-87	Spokane Chiefs	WHL	64	8	17	25	....	....	....	27	....	....	....	....	....	....	....	....	....	....	3	0	0	0	0	....	....	....
1987-88	Spokane Chiefs	WHL	72	33	54	87	....	....	....	42	....	....	....	....	....	....	....	....	....	....	15	10	10	20	13	....	....	....
1988-89	Spokane Chiefs	WHL	75	51	51	102	....	....	....	79	....	....	....	....	....	....	....	....	....	....	....	....	....	....	....	....	....	....
1989-90	Spokane Chiefs	WHL	50	45	44	89	....	....	....	80	....	....	....	....	....	....	....	....	....	....	....	....	....	....	....	....	....	....
	Medicine Hat Tigers	WHL	25	15	24	39	....	....	....	19	....	....	....	....	....	....	....	....	....	....	3	0	0	0	2	....	....	....
1990-91	Capital District Islanders	AHL	73	21	34	55	....	....	....	26	....	....	....	....	....	....	....	....	....	....	....	....	....	....	....	....	....	....
1991-92	Capital District Islanders	AHL	71	23	27	50	....	....	....	10	....	....	....	....	....	....	....	....	....	....	7	0	4	4	21	....	....	....
1992-93	**New York Islanders**	**NHL**	**61**	**7**	**18**	**25**	**6**	**12**	**18**	**43**	**1**	**0**	**0**	**115**	**6.1**	**42**	**2**	**37**	**1**	**+4**	**12**	**3**	**1**	**4**	**6**	**0**	**0**	**0**
	Capital District Islanders	AHL	20	12	11	23	....	....	....	39	....	....	....	....	....	....	....	....	....	....	....	....	....	....	....	....	....	....
1993-94	**New York Islanders**	**NHL**	**83**	**18**	**22**	**40**	**17**	**17**	**34**	**44**	**1**	**0**	**2**	**164**	**11.0**	**62**	**7**	**48**	**9**	**+16**	**4**	**0**	**0**	**0**	**2**	**0**	**0**	**0**
1994-95	**New York Islanders**	**NHL**	**42**	**5**	**7**	**12**	**9**	**10**	**19**	**25**	**0**	**0**	**0**	**59**	**8.5**	**18**	**2**	**37**	**11**	**–10**	....	....	....	....	....	....	....	....
1995-96	**New York Islanders**	**NHL**	**69**	**25**	**45**	**70**	**25**	**37**	**62**	**42**	**14**	**1**	**2**	**186**	**13.4**	**91**	**43**	**97**	**29**	**–20**	....	....	....	....	....	....	....	....
	Canada	WC-A	8	5	3	8	....	....	....	8	....	....	....	....	....	....	....	....	....	....	....	....	....	....	....	....	....	....
1996-97	**New York Islanders**	**NHL**	**79**	**23**	**41**	**64**	**24**	**36**	**60**	**38**	**10**	**0**	**3**	**177**	**13.0**	**98**	**28**	**82**	**7**	**–5**	....	....	....	....	....	....	....	....
	Canada	WC-A	11	3	6	9	....	....	....	12	....	....	....	....	....	....	....	....	....	....	....	....	....	....	....	....	....	....
1997-98	**New York Islanders**	**NHL**	**54**	**14**	**12**	**26**	**16**	**12**	**28**	**66**	**8**	**0**	**2**	**99**	**14.1**	**40**	**22**	**40**	**3**	**–19**	....	....	....	....	....	....	....	....
	Anaheim Mighty Ducks	**NHL**	**22**	**5**	**11**	**16**	**6**	**11**	**17**	**16**	**1**	**0**	**0**	**42**	**11.9**	**23**	**10**	**26**	**3**	**–10**	....	....	....	....	....	....	....	....
	Canada	WC-A	6	0	3	3	....	....	....	2	....	....	....	....	....	....	....	....	....	....	....	....	....	....	....	....	....	....
	NHL Totals		**410**	**97**	**156**	**253**	**103**	**135**	**238**	**274**	**35**	**1**	**9**	**842**	**11.5**	**374**	**114**	**367**	**63**		**16**	**3**	**1**	**4**	**8**	**0**	**0**	**0**

Traded to **Anaheim** by **NY Islanders** with Doug Houda and Tony Tuzzolino for Joe Sacco, J.J. Daigneault and Mark Janssens, February 6, 1998.

• GREENLAW, JEFF Jeff "Charlie" Greenlaw LW – L. 6'1", 230 lbs. b: Toronto, Ont., 2/28/1968. Washington's 1st choice, 19th overall, in 1986 Entry Draft.

Season	Club	League	GP	G	A	Pts	AG	AA	APts	PIM	PP	SH	GW	S	%	TGF	PGF	TGA	PGA	+/–	GP	G	A	Pts	PIM	PP	SH	GW
1984-85	St. Catharines Falcons	OJHL	33	21	29	50	....	....	....	141	....	....	....	....	....	....	....	....	....	....	....	....	....	....	....	....	....	....
1985-86	Canada	Nat-Team	57	3	16	19	....	....	....	81	....	....	....	....	....	....	....	....	....	....	....	....	....	....	....	....	....	....
	Canada	WJC-A	7	3	1	4	....	....	....	4	....	....	....	....	....	....	....	....	....	....	....	....	....	....	....	....	....	....
1986-87	**Washington Capitals**	**NHL**	**22**	**0**	**3**	**3**	**0**	**2**	**2**	**44**	**0**	**0**	**0**	**9**	**0.0**	**7**	**0**	**6**	**1**	**+2**	....	....	....	....	....	....	....	....
	Binghamton Whalers	AHL	4	0	2	2	....	....	....	0	....	....	....	....	....	....	....	....	....	....	....	....	....	....	....	....	....	....
1987-88	Binghamton Whalers	AHL	56	8	7	15	....	....	....	142	....	....	....	....	....	....	....	....	....	....	1	0	0	0	2	....	....	....
	Washington Capitals	**NHL**	....	....	....	....	....	....	....	....	....	....	....	....	....	....	....	....	....	....	**1**	**0**	**0**	**0**	**19**	....	....	....
1988-89	Baltimore Skipjacks	AHL	55	12	15	27	....	....	....	115	....	....	....	....	....	....	....	....	....	....	....	....	....	....	....	....	....	....
1989-90	Baltimore Skipjacks	AHL	10	3	2	5	....	....	....	26	....	....	....	....	....	....	....	....	....	....	7	1	0	1	13	....	....	....
1990-91	**Washington Capitals**	**NHL**	**10**	**2**	**0**	**2**	**2**	**0**	**2**	**10**	**0**	**0**	**1**	**9**	**22.2**	**4**	**0**	**3**	**0**	**+1**	**1**	**0**	**0**	**0**	**2**	**0**	**0**	**0**
	Baltimore Skipjacks	AHL	50	17	17	34	....	....	....	93	....	....	....	....	....	....	....	....	....	....	3	1	1	2	2	....	....	....

			REGULAR SEASON																		PLAYOFFS							
Season	Club	League	GP	G	A	Pts	AG	AA	APts	PIM	PP	SH	GW	S	%	TGF	PGF	TGA	PGA	+/–	GP	G	A	Pts	PIM	PP	SH	GW
1991-92	**Washington Capitals**	**NHL**	**5**	**0**	**1**	**1**	**0**	**1**	**1**	**34**	**0**	**0**	**0**	**3**	**0.0**	**1**	**0**	**2**	**0**	**–1**	....	....	....	....	....	....	....	....
	Baltimore Skipjacks	AHL	37	6	8	14	....	....	....	57	....	....	....	....	....	....	....	....	....	....	....	....	....	....	....	....	....	....
1992-93	**Washington Capitals**	**NHL**	**16**	**1**	**1**	**2**	**1**	**1**	**2**	**18**	**0**	**0**	**0**	**15**	**6.7**	**2**	**0**	**6**	**1**	**–3**	....	....	....	....	....	....	....	....
	Baltimore Skipjacks	AHL	49	12	14	26	....	....	....	66	....	....	....	....	....	....	....	....	....	....	7	3	1	4	0	....	....	....
1993-94	**Florida Panthers**	**NHL**	**4**	**0**	**1**	**1**	**0**	**1**	**1**	**2**	**0**	**0**	**0**	**6**	**0.0**	**1**	**0**	**2**	**0**	**–1**	....	....	....	....	....	....	....	....
	Cincinnati Cyclones	IHL	55	14	15	29	....	....	....	85	....	....	....	....	....	....	....	....	....	....	11	2	2	4	28	....	....	....
1994-95	Cincinnati Cyclones	IHL	67	10	21	31	....	....	....	117	....	....	....	....	....	....	....	....	....	....	10	2	0	2	22	....	....	....
1995-96	Cincinnati Cyclones	IHL	64	17	15	32	....	....	....	112	....	....	....	....	....	....	....	....	....	....	17	2	4	6	36	....	....	....
1996-97	Cincinnati Cyclones	IHL	27	6	6	12	....	....	....	70	....	....	....	....	....	....	....	....	....	....	1	0	1	1	2	....	....	....
1997-98	Cincinnati Cyclones	IHL	70	6	9	15	....	....	....	130	....	....	....	....	....	....	....	....	....	....	9	0	2	2	36	....	....	....
	NHL Totals		**57**	**3**	**6**	**9**	**3**	**5**	**8**	**108**	**0**	**0**	**1**	**42**	**7.1**	**15**	**0**	**19**	**2**		**2**	**0**	**0**	**0**	**21**	**0**	**0**	**0**

Signed as a free agent by **Florida**, July 14, 1993.

● GREGG, RANDY

Randy Gregg D – L. 6'4", 215 lbs. b: Edmonton, Alta., 2/19/1956.

Season	Club	League	GP	G	A	Pts	AG	AA	APts	PIM	PP	SH	GW	S	%	TGF	PGF	TGA	PGA	+/–	GP	G	A	Pts	PIM	PP	SH	GW
1975-76	University of Alberta	CWUAA	31	3	20	23	....	....	....	49	....	....	....	....	....	....	....	....	....	....	....	....	....	....	....	....	....	....
1976-77	University of Alberta	CWUAA	34	10	23	33	....	....	....	45	....	....	....	....	....	....	....	....	....	....	....	....	....	....	....	....	....	....
1977-78	University of Alberta	CWUAA	30	8	26	34	....	....	....	43	....	....	....	....	....	....	....	....	....	....	....	....	....	....	....	....	....	....
1978-79	University of Alberta	CWUAA	41	11	26	37	....	....	....	67	....	....	....	....	....	....	....	....	....	....	....	....	....	....	....	....	....	....
1979-80	Canada	Nat-Team	56	7	17	24	....	....	....	36	....	....	....	....	....	....	....	....	....	....	....	....	....	....	....	....	....	....
	Canada	Olympics	6	1	1	2	....	....	....	2	....	....	....	....	....	....	....	....	....	....	....	....	....	....	....	....	....	....
1980-81	Kokudo Bunnies	Japan	35	12	18	30	....	....	....	30	....	....	....	....	....	....	....	....	....	....	....	....	....	....	....	....	....	....
1981-82	Kokudo Bunnies	Japan	36	12	20	32	....	....	....	25	....	....	....	....	....	....	....	....	....	....	....	....	....	....	....	....	....	....
	Edmonton Oilers	**NHL**	....	....	....	....	....	....	....	....	....	....	....	....	....	....	....	....	....	....	**4**	**0**	**0**	**0**	**0**	....	....	....
1982-83	**Edmonton Oilers**	**NHL**	**80**	**6**	**22**	**28**	**5**	**15**	**20**	**54**	**0**	**2**	**2**	**94**	**6.4**	**93**	**8**	**106**	**36**	**+15**	**16**	**2**	**4**	**6**	**13**	**0**	**1**	**1**
1983-84	**Edmonton Oilers**	**NHL**	**80**	**13**	**27**	**40**	**10**	**18**	**28**	**56**	**2**	**1**	**2**	**91**	**14.3**	**131**	**15**	**107**	**31**	**+40**	**19**	**3**	**7**	**10**	**21**	**0**	**0**	**1**
1984-85	Canada	C Cup	3	0	1	1	....	....	....	4	....	....	....	....	....	....	....	....	....	....	....	....	....	....	....	....	....	....
	Edmonton Oilers	**NHL**	**57**	**3**	**20**	**23**	**2**	**14**	**16**	**32**	**0**	**0**	**0**	**58**	**5.2**	**78**	**12**	**54**	**15**	**+27**	**17**	**0**	**6**	**6**	**12**	**0**	**0**	**0**
1985-86	**Edmonton Oilers**	**NHL**	**64**	**2**	**26**	**28**	**2**	**17**	**19**	**47**	**0**	**0**	**0**	**55**	**3.6**	**115**	**22**	**85**	**22**	**+30**	**10**	**1**	**0**	**1**	**12**	**0**	**0**	**0**
1986-87	**Edmonton Oilers**	**NHL**	**52**	**8**	**16**	**24**	**7**	**12**	**19**	**42**	**0**	**0**	**2**	**59**	**13.6**	**90**	**12**	**70**	**28**	**+36**	**18**	**3**	**6**	**9**	**17**	**1**	**0**	**1**
1987-88	**Edmonton Oilers**	**NHL**	**15**	**1**	**2**	**3**	**1**	**1**	**2**	**8**	**0**	**0**	**0**	**20**	**5.0**	**18**	**1**	**18**	**5**	**+4**	**19**	**1**	**8**	**9**	**24**	**0**	**0**	**1**
	Canada	Nat-Team	37	2	6	8	....	....	....	37	....	....	....	....	....	....	....	....	....	....	....	....	....	....	....	....	....	....
	Canada	Olympics	8	1	2	3	....	....	....	8	....	....	....	....	....	....	....	....	....	....	....	....	....	....	....	....	....	....
1988-89	**Edmonton Oilers**	**NHL**	**57**	**3**	**15**	**18**	**3**	**11**	**14**	**28**	**1**	**0**	**1**	**42**	**7.1**	**60**	**13**	**74**	**18**	**–9**	**7**	**1**	**0**	**1**	**4**	**0**	**0**	**0**
1989-90	**Edmonton Oilers**	**NHL**	**48**	**4**	**20**	**24**	**3**	**14**	**17**	**42**	**0**	**0**	**0**	**41**	**9.8**	**72**	**14**	**52**	**18**	**+24**	**20**	**2**	**6**	**8**	**16**	**1**	**0**	**0**
1990-91			DID NOT PLAY																									
1991-92	**Vancouver Canucks**	**NHL**	**21**	**1**	**4**	**5**	**1**	**3**	**4**	**24**	**0**	**0**	**0**	**19**	**5.3**	**17**	**2**	**27**	**9**	**–3**	**7**	**0**	**1**	**1**	**8**	**0**	**0**	**0**
	NHL Totals		**474**	**41**	**152**	**193**	**34**	**105**	**139**	**333**	**3**	**3**	**7**	**479**	**8.6**	**674**	**99**	**593**	**182**		**137**	**13**	**38**	**51**	**127**	**2**	**1**	**4**

Signed as a free agent by **Edmonton**, October 18, 1982. Claimed by **Vancouver** from **Edmonton** in Waiver Draft, October 1, 1990.

● GREIG, BRUCE

Bruce Greig LW – L. 6'2", 220 lbs. b: High River, Alta., 5/9/1953. California's 6th choice, 114th overall, in 1973 Amateur Draft.

Season	Club	League	GP	G	A	Pts	AG	AA	APts	PIM	PP	SH	GW	S	%	TGF	PGF	TGA	PGA	+/–	GP	G	A	Pts	PIM	PP	SH	GW
1971-72	Drumheller Miners	AJHL	5	0	1	1	....	....	....	6	....	....	....	....	....	....	....	....	....	....	....	....	....	....	....	....	....	....
	Medicine Hat Tigers	WCJHL	17	3	3	6	....	....	....	11	....	....	....	....	....	....	....	....	....	....	....	....	....	....	....	....	....	....
1972-73	Vancouver Nationals	WCJHL	24	3	3	6	....	....	....	79	....	....	....	....	....	....	....	....	....	....	....	....	....	....	....	....	....	....
1973-74	**California Golden Seals**	**NHL**	**1**	**0**	**0**	**0**	**0**	**0**	**0**	**4**	**0**	**0**	**0**	**0**	**0.0**	**0**	**0**	**0**	**0**	**0**	....	....	....	....	....	....	....	....
	Salt Lake Golden Eagles	WHL	13	1	2	3	....	....	....	36	....	....	....	....	....	....	....	....	....	....	....	....	....	....	....	....	....	....
1974-75	**California Golden Seals**	**NHL**	**8**	**0**	**1**	**1**	**0**	**1**	**1**	**42**	**0**	**0**	**0**	**5**	**0.0**	**1**	**0**	**4**	**0**	**–3**	....	....	....	....	....	....	....	....
1975-76	Salt Lake City Golden Eagles	CHL	1	0	0	0	....	....	....	11	....	....	....	....	....	....	....	....	....	....	....	....	....	....	....	....	....	....
	Flint Generals	IHL	10	0	5	5	....	....	....	77	....	....	....	....	....	....	....	....	....	....	....	....	....	....	....	....	....	....
1976-77	Calgary Cowboys	WHA	7	1	1	2	....	....	....	10	....	....	....	....	....	....	....	....	....	....	....	....	....	....	....	....	....	....
	Greensboro Generals	SHL	33	10	14	24	....	....	....	68	....	....	....	....	....	....	....	....	....	....	....	....	....	....	....	....	....	....
	Tidewater Sharks	SHL	2	0	0	0	....	....	....	2	....	....	....	....	....	....	....	....	....	....	....	....	....	....	....	....	....	....
1977-78	Cincinnati Stingers	WHA	32	3	1	4	....	....	....	57	....	....	....	....	....	....	....	....	....	....	....	....	....	....	....	....	....	....
1978-79	Indianapolis Racers	WHA	21	3	7	10	....	....	....	64	....	....	....	....	....	....	....	....	....	....	....	....	....	....	....	....	....	....
	San Diego Hawks	PHL	40	15	10	25	....	....	....	168	....	....	....	....	....	....	....	....	....	....	....	....	....	....	....	....	....	....
1979-80	Dayton–Toledo	IHL	52	14	23	37	....	....	....	114	....	....	....	....	....	....	....	....	....	....	1	0	0	0	0	....	....	....
1980-81	Salem Raiders	EHL	58	20	32	52	....	....	....	213	....	....	....	....	....	....	....	....	....	....	6	2	2	4	2	....	....	....
1981-82	Dallas Black Hawks	CHL	9	0	3	3	....	....	....	10	....	....	....	....	....	....	....	....	....	....	....	....	....	....	....	....	....	....
	Salem Raiders	ACHL	37	12	20	32	....	....	....	212	....	....	....	....	....	....	....	....	....	....	11	1	6	7	28	....	....	....
1982-83	Virginia Raiders	ACHL	35	8	16	24	....	....	....	133	....	....	....	....	....	....	....	....	....	....	....	....	....	....	....	....	....	....
	Carolina Thunderbirds	ACHL	11	4	5	9	....	....	....	44	....	....	....	....	....	....	....	....	....	....	....	....	....	....	....	....	....	....
1983-84	Pine Bridge–Mohawk Valley	ACHL	37	12	12	24	....	....	....	206	....	....	....	....	....	....	....	....	....	....	5	0	2	2	49	....	....	....
	NHL Totals		**9**	**0**	**1**	**1**	**0**	**1**	**1**	**46**	**0**	**0**	**0**	**5**	**0.0**	**1**	**0**	**4**	**0**		....	....	....	....	....	....	....	....
	Other Major League Totals		60	7	9	16	....	....	....	131	....	....	....	....	....	....	....	....	....		....	....	....	....	....	....	....	....

Selected by **Cleveland** (WHA) in 1973 WHA Amateur Draft, June, 1973. WHA rights traded to **Calgary** (WHA) by **Cleveland** (WHA) for cash, July, 1976. Signed as a free agent by **Cincinnati** (WHA) to 10-game trial contract, January, 1978. Signed as a free agent by **Indianapolis** (WHA), October, 1978.

● GREIG, MARK

Mark Greig RW – R. 5'11", 190 lbs. b: High River, Alta., 1/25/1970. Hartford's 1st choice, 15th overall, in 1990 Entry Draft.

Season	Club	League	GP	G	A	Pts	AG	AA	APts	PIM	PP	SH	GW	S	%	TGF	PGF	TGA	PGA	+/–	GP	G	A	Pts	PIM	PP	SH	GW
1987-88	Lethbridge Hurricanes	WHL	65	9	18	27	....	....	....	38	....	....	....	....	....	....	....	....	....	....	....	....	....	....	....	....	....	....
1988-89	Lethbridge Hurricanes	WHL	71	36	72	108	....	....	....	113	....	....	....	....	....	....	....	....	....	....	8	5	5	10	16	....	....	....
1989-90	Lethbridge Hurricanes	WHL	65	55	80	135	....	....	....	149	....	....	....	....	....	....	....	....	....	....	18	11	21	32	35	....	....	....
1990-91	**Hartford Whalers**	**NHL**	**4**	**0**	**0**	**0**	**0**	**0**	**0**	**0**	**0**	**0**	**0**	**1**	**0.0**	**1**	**0**	**2**	**0**	**–1**	....	....	....	....	....	....	....	....
	Springfield Indians	AHL	73	32	55	87	....	....	....	73	....	....	....	....	....	....	....	....	....	....	17	2	6	8	22	....	....	....
1991-92	**Hartford Whalers**	**NHL**	**17**	**0**	**5**	**5**	**0**	**4**	**4**	**6**	**0**	**0**	**0**	**18**	**0.0**	**12**	**1**	**4**	**0**	**+7**	....	....	....	....	....	....	....	....
	Springfield Indians	AHL	50	20	27	47	....	....	....	38	....	....	....	....	....	....	....	....	....	....	9	1	1	2	20	....	....	....
1992-93	**Hartford Whalers**	**NHL**	**22**	**1**	**7**	**8**	**1**	**5**	**6**	**27**	**0**	**0**	**0**	**16**	**6.3**	**9**	**2**	**18**	**0**	**–11**	....	....	....	....	....	....	....	....
	Springfield Indians	AHL	55	20	38	58	....	....	....	86	....	....	....	....	....	....	....	....	....	....	....	....	....	....	....	....	....	....
1993-94	**Hartford Whalers**	**NHL**	**31**	**4**	**5**	**9**	**4**	**4**	**8**	**31**	**0**	**0**	**0**	**41**	**9.8**	**14**	**3**	**17**	**0**	**–6**	....	....	....	....	....	....	....	....
	Springfield Indians	AHL	4	0	4	4	....	....	....	21	....	....	....	....	....	....	....	....	....	....	....	....	....	....	....	....	....	....
	Toronto Maple Leafs	**NHL**	**13**	**2**	**2**	**4**	**2**	**2**	**4**	**10**	**0**	**0**	**0**	**14**	**14.3**	**5**	**0**	**4**	**0**	**+1**	....	....	....	....	....	....	....	....
	St. John's Maple Leafs	AHL	9	4	6	10	....	....	....	0	....	....	....	....	....	....	....	....	....	....	11	4	2	6	26	....	....	....
1994-95	**Calgary Flames**	**NHL**	**8**	**1**	**1**	**2**	**2**	**1**	**3**	**2**	**0**	**0**	**0**	**5**	**20.0**	**3**	**1**	**1**	**0**	**+1**	....	....	....	....	....	....	....	....
	Saint John Flames	AHL	67	31	50	81	....	....	....	82	....	....	....	....	....	....	....	....	....	....	2	0	1	1	0	....	....	....
1995-96	Atlanta Knights	IHL	71	25	48	73	....	....	....	104	....	....	....	....	....	....	....	....	....	....	3	2	1	3	4	....	....	....
1996-97	Quebec Rafales	IHL	5	1	2	3	....	....	....	0	....	....	....	....	....	....	....	....	....	....	....	....	....	....	....	....	....	....
	Houston Aeros	IHL	59	12	30	42	....	....	....	59	....	....	....	....	....	....	....	....	....	....	13	5	8	13	2	....	....	....
1997-98	Grand Rapids Griffins	IHL	69	26	36	62	....	....	....	103	....	....	....	....	....	....	....	....	....	....	3	0	4	4	4	....	....	....
	NHL Totals		**95**	**8**	**20**	**28**	**9**	**16**	**25**	**76**	**0**	**0**	**0**	**95**	**8.4**	**44**	**7**	**46**	**0**		....	....	....	....	....	....	....	....

WHL East First All-Star Team (1990)

Traded to **Toronto** by **Hartford** with Hartford's 6th round choice (later traded to NY Rangers — NY Rangers selected Yuri Litvinov) in 1994 Entry Draft for Ted Crowley, January 25, 1994. Signed as a free agent by **Calgary**, August 9, 1994.

● GRENIER, LUCIEN

Lucien Grenier RW – L. 5'10", 163 lbs. b: Malartic, Que., 11/3/1946.

Season	Club	League	GP	G	A	Pts	AG	AA	APts	PIM	PP	SH	GW	S	%	TGF	PGF	TGA	PGA	+/–	GP	G	A	Pts	PIM	PP	SH	GW
1963-64	Notre Dame de Grace Monarchs	QJHL	44	19	29	48	....	....	....	19	....	....	....	....	....	....	....	....	....	....	....	....	....	....	....	....	....	....
1964-65	Montreal Jr. Canadiens	OHA	54	17	7	24	....	....	....	23	....	....	....	....	....	....	....	....	....	....	7	1	4	5	4	....	....	....
1965-66	Montreal Jr. Canadiens	OHA	47	32	41	73	....	....	....	42	....	....	....	....	....	....	....	....	....	....	10	4	4	8	0	....	....	....
1966-67	Houston Apollos	CHL	58	16	18	34	....	....	....	20	....	....	....	....	....	....	....	....	....	....	6	1	0	1	2	....	....	....
1967-68	Houston Apollos	CHL	55	10	22	32	....	....	....	22	....	....	....	....	....	....	....	....	....	....	....	....	....	....	....	....	....	....
1968-69	Houston Apollos	CHL	56	17	23	40	....	....	....	22	....	....	....	....	....	....	....	....	....	....	3	1	0	1	0	....	....	....
	Montreal Canadiens	**NHL**	....	....	....	....	....	....	....	....	....	....	....	....	....	....	....	....	....	....	**2**	**0**	**0**	**0**	**0**	....	....	....
1969-70	**Montreal Canadiens**	**NHL**	**23**	**2**	**3**	**5**	**2**	**3**	**5**	**2**	**0**	**0**	**1**	**25**	**8.0**	**12**	**0**	**12**	**1**	**+1**	....	....	....	....	....	....	....	....
	Montreal Voyageurs	AHL	25	12	8	20	....	....	....	4	....	....	....	....	....	....	....	....	....	....	....	....	....	....	....	....	....	....

			REGULAR SEASON																		PLAYOFFS							
Season	Club	League	GP	G	A	Pts	AG	AA	APts	PIM	PP	SH	GW	S	%	TGF	PGF	TGA	PGA	+/–	GP	G	A	Pts	PIM	PP	SH	GW
1970-71	**Los Angeles Kings**	**NHL**	68	9	7	16	9	6	15	12	1	1	1	63	14.3	34	4	48	17	–1	....	....	....	....	....	....	....	....
1971-72	**Los Angeles Kings**	**NHL**	60	3	4	7	3	4	7	4	1	0	0	22	13.6	11	2	20	5	–6	....	....	....	....	....	....	....	....
1972-73			DID NOT PLAY – INJURED																									
1973-74	Omaha Knights	CHL	56	5	5	10	....	....	....	15	....	....	....	....	....	....	....	....	....	....	5	0	1	1	0	....	....	....
1974-75	Omaha Knights	CHL	31	4	3	7	....	....	....	4	....	....	....	....	....	....	....	....	....	....	....	....	....	....	....	....	....	....
	NHL Totals		151	14	14	28	14	13	27	18	2	1	2	110	12.7	57	6	80	23		2	0	0	0	0	0	0	0

Traded to **LA Kings** by **Montreal** with Larry Mickey and Jack Norris for Leon Rochefort, Gregg Boddy and Wayne Thomas, May 22, 1970. Claimed by **Atlanta** from **LA Kings** in Expansion Draft, June 6, 1972.

• GRENIER, RICHARD

Richard Grenier C – L. 5'11", 170 lbs. b: Montreal, Que., 9/18/1952. NY Islanders' 5th choice, 65th overall, in 1972 Amateur Draft.

Season	Club	League	GP	G	A	Pts	AG	AA	APts	PIM	PP	SH	GW	S	%	TGF	PGF	TGA	PGA	+/–	GP	G	A	Pts	PIM	PP	SH	GW
1970-71	Quebec Remparts	QJHL	62	23	76	99	....	....	....	74	....	....	....	....	....	....	....	....	....	....	14	7	7	14	30	....	....	....
1971-72	Verdun Maple Leafs	QMJHL	61	46	56	102	....	....	....	83	....	....	....	....	....	....	....	....	....	....	4	2	1	3	4	....	....	....
1972-73	**New York Islanders**	**NHL**	10	1	1	2	1	1	2	2	0	0	1	18	5.6	2	0	4	0	–2	....	....	....	....	....	....	....	....
	New Haven Nighthawks	AHL	66	19	20	39	....	....	....	50	....	....	....	....	....	....	....	....	....	....	....	....	....	....	....	....	....	....
1973-74	Fort Worth Wings	CHL	70	28	26	54	....	....	....	39	....	....	....	....	....	....	....	....	....	....	5	2	2	7	6	....	....	....
1974-75	Fort Worth Texans	CHL	55	11	14	25	....	....	....	32	....	....	....	....	....	....	....	....	....	....	....	....	....	....	....	....	....	....
	New Haven Nighthawks	AHL	18	3	5	8	....	....	....	5	....	....	....	....	....	....	....	....	....	....	....	....	....	....	....	....	....	....
1975-76	Beauce Jaros	NAHL	73	77	83	160	....	....	....	82	....	....	....	....	....	....	....	....	....	....	12	14	4	18	12	....	....	....
1976-77	Quebec Nordiques	WHA	34	11	9	20	....	....	....	4	....	....	....	....	....	....	....	....	....	....	....	....	....	....	....	....	....	....
	Maine Nordiques	NAHL	41	25	23	48	....	....	....	12	....	....	....	....	....	....	....	....	....	....	12	*12	6	18	2	....	....	....
1977-78	Binghamton Whalers	AHL	75	*46	30	76	....	....	....	37	....	....	....	....	....	....	....	....	....	....	....	....	....	....	....	....	....	....
1978-79	Binghamton Whalers	AHL	68	37	27	64	....	....	....	36	....	....	....	....	....	....	....	....	....	....	10	6	4	10	13	....	....	....
1979-80	Nova Scotia Voyageurs	AHL	11	6	4	10	....	....	....	0	....	....	....	....	....	....	....	....	....	....	6	1	3	4	2	....	....	....
	Vell Feldkirch	Austria	34	60	43	103	....	....	....	68	....	....	....	....	....	....	....	....	....	....	....	....	....	....	....	....	....	....
1980-81	Kiekko Reipas	Finland	36	29	21	50	....	....	....	36	....	....	....	....	....	....	....	....	....	....	....	....	....	....	....	....	....	....
1981-82	EHC Arosa	Switz.	36	*40	13	53	....	....	....	....	....	....	....	....	....	....	....	....	....	....	....	....	....	....	....	....	....	....
1982-83	EHC Arosa	Switz.	....	39	9	48	....	....	....	....	....	....	....	....	....	....	....	....	....	....	....	....	....	....	....	....	....	....
1983-84	VSV Villach	Austria	28	42	47	89	....	....	....	....	....	....	....	....	....	....	....	....	....	....	....	....	....	....	....	....	....	....
1984-85	VSV Villach	Austria	32	29	45	74	....	....	....	38	....	....	....	....	....	....	....	....	....	....	....	....	....	....	....	....	....	....
1985-86	VSV Villach	Austria	41	36	52	88	....	....	....	30	....	....	....	....	....	....	....	....	....	....	....	....	....	....	....	....	....	....
1986-87	VSV Villach	Austria	20	14	21	35	....	....	....	22	....	....	....	....	....	....	....	....	....	....	....	....	....	....	....	....	....	....
1987-88	WEV Wiener	Austria	34	19	26	45	....	....	....	24	....	....	....	....	....	....	....	....	....	....	....	....	....	....	....	....	....	....
1988-89	WEV Wiener	Austria	38	11	25	36	....	....	....	....	....	....	....	....	....	....	....	....	....	....	....	....	....	....	....	....	....	....
	NHL Totals		10	1	1	2	1	1	2	2	0	0	1	18	5.6	2	0	4	0		....	....	....	....	....	....	....	....
	Other Major League Totals		34	11	9	20	....	....	....	4	....	....	....	....	....	....	....	....	....	....	....	....	....	....	....	....	....	....

NAHL First All-Star Team (1976) • NAHL Second All-Star Team (1977)

Selected by **Miami-Philadelphia** (WHA) in 1972 WHA General Player Draft, February 13, 1972. WHA rights traded to **Quebec** (WHA) by **Calgary** (WHA) for future considerations, July, 1976,

• GRESCHNER, RON

Ron Greschner D – L. 6'2", 205 lbs. b: Goodsoil, Sask., 12/22/1954. NY Rangers' 2nd choice, 32nd overall, in 1974 Amateur Draft.

Season	Club	League	GP	G	A	Pts	AG	AA	APts	PIM	PP	SH	GW	S	%	TGF	PGF	TGA	PGA	+/–	GP	G	A	Pts	PIM	PP	SH	GW
1971-72	New Westminster Bruins	WCJHL	44	1	9	10	....	....	....	126	....	....	....	....	....	....	....	....	....	....	....	....	....	....	....	....	....	....
1972-73	New Westminster Bruins	WCJHL	68	22	47	69	....	....	....	169	....	....	....	....	....	....	....	....	....	....	5	2	4	6	19	....	....	....
1973-74	New Westminster Bruins	WCJHL	67	33	70	103	....	....	....	170	....	....	....	....	....	....	....	....	....	....	11	5	6	11	18	....	....	....
1974-75	**New York Rangers**	**NHL**	70	8	37	45	7	29	36	93	0	0	2	122	6.6	128	28	108	16	+8	3	0	1	1	2	0	0	0
	Providence Reds	AHL	7	5	6	11	....	....	....	10	....	....	....	....	....	....	....	....	....	....	....	....	....	....	....	....	....	....
1975-76	**New York Rangers**	**NHL**	77	6	21	27	6	16	22	93	2	0	0	176	3.4	85	21	135	20	–51	....	....	....	....	....	....	....	....
1976-77	**New York Rangers**	**NHL**	80	11	36	47	11	29	40	89	0	2	1	192	5.7	109	8	124	23	0	....	....	....	....	....	....	....	....
1977-78	**New York Rangers**	**NHL**	78	24	48	72	23	39	62	100	8	1	5	180	13.3	145	56	97	11	+3	3	0	0	0	2	0	0	0
1978-79	**New York Rangers**	**NHL**	60	17	36	53	15	28	43	66	8	0	1	153	11.1	102	30	84	12	0	18	7	5	12	16	4	1	3
	NHL All-Stars	Chal Cup	DID NOT PLAY																									
1979-80	**New York Rangers**	**NHL**	76	21	37	58	19	28	47	103	6	1	3	187	11.2	131	62	100	16	–11	9	0	6	6	10	0	0	0
1980-81	**New York Rangers**	**NHL**	74	27	41	68	22	20	51	112	6	0	1	193	14.0	135	42	106	13	0	14	4	8	12	17	1	0	0
1981-82	**New York Rangers**	**NHL**	29	5	11	16	4	7	11	16	0	0	0	49	10.2	42	9	55	11	–11	....	....	....	....	....	....	....	....
1982-83	**New York Rangers**	**NHL**	10	3	5	8	2	3	5	0	1	0	0	12	25.0	9	3	6	0	0	8	2	2	4	12	2	0	0
1983-84	**New York Rangers**	**NHL**	77	12	44	56	10	30	40	117	5	0	0	130	9.2	109	39	67	2	+5	2	1	0	1	2	0	0	0
1984-85	**New York Rangers**	**NHL**	48	16	29	45	13	20	33	42	8	0	2	88	18.2	73	32	62	2	–19	2	0	3	3	12	0	0	0
1985-86	**New York Rangers**	**NHL**	78	20	28	48	16	19	35	104	6	1	2	150	13.3	88	30	56	7	+9	5	3	1	4	11	0	0	0
1986-87	**New York Rangers**	**NHL**	61	6	34	40	5	25	30	62	1	1	1	109	5.5	72	27	62	11	–6	6	0	5	5	0	0	0	0
1987-88	**New York Rangers**	**NHL**	51	1	5	6	1	4	5	82	0	0	0	67	1.5	48	12	64	19	–9	....	....	....	....	....	....	....	....
1988-89	**New York Rangers**	**NHL**	58	1	10	11	1	7	8	94	0	0	0	49	2.0	50	2	68	29	+9	4	0	1	1	6	0	0	0
1989-90	**New York Rangers**	**NHL**	55	1	9	10	1	6	7	53	0	0	0	26	3.8	33	5	51	16	–7	10	0	0	0	16	0	0	0
	NHL Totals		982	179	431	610	156	319	475	1226	51	6	18	1883	9.5	1359	396	1251	208		84	17	32	49	106	7	1	3

WCJHL First All-Star Team (1974)

Played in NHL All-Star Game (1980)

• GRETZKY, BRENT

Brent Gretzky C – L. 5'10", 160 lbs. b: Brantford, Ont., 2/20/1972. Tampa Bay's 3rd choice, 49th overall, in 1992 Entry Draft.

Season	Club	League	GP	G	A	Pts	AG	AA	APts	PIM	PP	SH	GW	S	%	TGF	PGF	TGA	PGA	+/–	GP	G	A	Pts	PIM	PP	SH	GW
1989-90	Belleville Bulls	OHL	66	15	32	47	....	....	....	30	....	....	....	....	....	....	....	....	....	....	11	0	0	0	0	....	....	....
1990-91	Belleville Bulls	OHL	66	26	56	82	....	....	....	25	....	....	....	....	....	....	....	....	....	....	6	3	3	6	2	....	....	....
1991-92	Belleville Bulls	OHL	62	43	78	121	....	....	....	37	....	....	....	....	....	....	....	....	....	....	....	....	....	....	....	....	....	....
1992-93	Atlanta Knights	IHL	77	20	34	54	....	....	....	84	....	....	....	....	....	....	....	....	....	....	9	3	2	5	8	....	....	....
1993-94	**Tampa Bay Lightning**	**NHL**	10	1	2	3	1	2	3	2	0	0	0	14	7.1	3	0	3	0	0	....	....	....	....	....	....	....	....
	Atlanta Knights	IHL	54	17	23	40	....	....	....	30	....	....	....	....	....	....	....	....	....	....	14	1	1	2	2	....	....	....
1994-95	**Tampa Bay Lightning**	**NHL**	3	0	1	1	0	1	1	0	0	0	0	1	0.0	1	1	2	0	–2	....	....	....	....	....	....	....	....
	Atlanta Knights	IHL	67	19	32	51	....	....	....	42	....	....	....	....	....	....	....	....	....	....	5	4	1	5	4	....	....	....
1995-96	St. John's Maple Leafs	AHL	68	13	28	41	....	....	....	40	....	....	....	....	....	....	....	....	....	....	4	0	6	6	0	....	....	....
1996-97	Las Vegas Thunder	IHL	40	5	12	17	....	....	....	8	....	....	....	....	....	....	....	....	....	....	....	....	....	....	....	....	....	....
	Quebec Rafales	IHL	1	0	0	0	....	....	....	0	....	....	....	....	....	....	....	....	....	....	....	....	....	....	....	....	....	....
	Pensacola Ice Pilots	ECHL	22	9	15	24	....	....	....	4	....	....	....	....	....	....	....	....	....	....	12	5	8	13	4	....	....	....
	NHL Totals		13	1	3	4	1	3	4	2	0	0	0	15	6.7	4	1	5	0		....	....	....	....	....	....	....	....

Signed as a free agent by **Toronto**, September 20, 1995.

• GRETZKY, WAYNE

Wayne "The Great One" Gretzky C – L. 6', 185 lbs. b: Brantford, Ont., 1/26/1961.

Season	Club	League	GP	G	A	Pts	AG	AA	APts	PIM	PP	SH	GW	S	%	TGF	PGF	TGA	PGA	+/–	GP	G	A	Pts	PIM	PP	SH	GW
1976-77	Peterborough Petes	OHA	3	0	3	3	....	....	....	0	....	....	....	....	....	....	....	....	....	....	....	....	....	....	....	....	....	....
1977-78	Sault Ste. Marie Greyhounds	OHA	64	70	112	182	....	....	....	14	....	....	....	....	....	....	....	....	....	....	13	6	20	26	0	....	....	....
	Canada	WJC-A	8	8	9	17	....	....	....	2	....	....	....	....	....	....	....	....	....	....	....	....	....	....	....	....	....	....
1978-79	Indianapolis Racers	WHA	8	3	3	6	....	....	....	0	....	....	....	....	....	....	....	....	....	....	....	....	....	....	....	....	....	....
	Edmonton Oilers	WHA	72	43	61	104	....	....	....	19	....	....	....	....	....	....	....	....	....	....	13	*10	10	*20	2	....	....	....
1979-80	**Edmonton Oilers**	**NHL**	79	51	*86	*137	46	66	112	21	13	1	6	284	18.0	155	42	116	18	+15	3	2	1	3	0	0	0	0
1980-81	**Edmonton Oilers**	**NHL**	80	55	*109	*164	46	77	123	28	15	4	3	261	21.1	207	67	118	17	+41	9	7	14	21	4	2	1	1
1981-82	Canada	C Cup	7	5	7	12	....	....	....	2	....	....	....	....	....	....	....	....	....	....	....	....	....	....	....	....	....	....
	Edmonton Oilers	**NHL**	80	*92	*120	*212	74	80	154	26	18	6	12	369	24.9	205	75	123	14	+81	5	5	7	12	8	1	1	1
	Canada	WEC-A	10	6	8	14	....	....	....	0	....	....	....	....	....	....	....	....	....	....	....	....	....	....	....	....	....	....
1982-83	**Edmonton Oilers**	**NHL**	80	*71	*125	*196	59	87	146	59	18	6	9	348	20.4	236	77	134	35	+60	16	12	*26	*38	4	2	3	3
1983-84	**Edmonton Oilers**	**NHL**	74	*87	*118	*205	71	81	152	39	20	12	11	324	26.9	249	70	134	31	+76	19	13	*22	*35	12	2	0	3
1984-85	Canada	C Cup	8	5	7	12	....	....	....	2	....	....	....	....	....	....	....	....	....	....	....	....	....	....	....	....	....	....
	Edmonton Oilers	**NHL**	80	*73	*135	*208	60	92	152	52	8	11	7	358	20.4	249	61	127	37	+98	18	17	*30	*47	4	4	2	3
1985-86	**Edmonton Oilers**	**NHL**	80	52	*163	*215	42	110	152	46	11	3	6	350	14.9	260	69	162	42	+71	10	8	11	19	2	4	1	2
1986-87	**Edmonton Oilers**	**NHL**	79	*62	*121	*183	54	88	142	28	13	7	4	288	21.5	227	64	120	27	+70	21	5	*29	*34	6	2	0	0
	NHL All-Stars	RV'87	2	0	4	4	....	....	....	0	....	....	....	....	....	....	....	....	....	....	....	....	....	....	....	....	....	....
1987-88	**Edmonton Oilers**	**NHL**	64	40	*109	149	34	78	112	24	9	5	3	211	19.0	172	55	99	21	+39	19	12	*31	*43	16	5	1	3
1987-88	Canada	C Cup	9	3	18	21	....	....	....	2	....	....	....	....	....	....	....	....	....	....	....	....	....	....	....	....	....	....
1988-89	**Los Angeles Kings**	**NHL**	78	54	*114	168	46	81	127	26	11	5	5	303	17.8	213	72	169	43	+15	11	5	17	22	0	1	1	0

			REGULAR SEASON																		PLAYOFFS							
Season	Club	League	GP	G	A	Pts	AG	AA	APts	PIM	PP	SH	GW	S	%	TGF	PGF	TGA	PGA	+/–	GP	G	A	Pts	PIM	PP	SH	GW
1989-90	**Los Angeles Kings**	**NHL**	**73**	**40**	***102**	***142**	**35**	**73**	**108**	**42**	**10**	**4**	**4**	**236**	**16.9**	**181**	**59**	**153**	**39**	**+8**	**7**	**3**	**7**	**10**	**0**	**1**	**0**	**0**
1990-91	**Los Angeles Kings**	**NHL**	**78**	**41**	***122**	***163**	**38**	**93**	**131**	**16**	**8**	**0**	**5**	**212**	**19.3**	**200**	**70**	**110**	**10**	**+30**	**12**	**4**	**11**	**15**	**2**	**1**	**0**	**2**
1991-92	Canada	C Cup	7	4	8	12	....	....	....	2	....	....	....	....	....	....	....	....	....	....	....	....	....	....	....	....	....	....
	Los Angeles Kings	**NHL**	**74**	**31**	***90**	**121**	**28**	**68**	**96**	**34**	**12**	**2**	**2**	**215**	**14.4**	**151**	**65**	**114**	**16**	**–12**	**6**	**2**	**5**	**7**	**2**	**1**	**0**	**0**
1992-93	**Los Angeles Kings**	**NHL**	**45**	**16**	**49**	**65**	**13**	**34**	**47**	**6**	**0**	**2**	**1**	**141**	**11.3**	**90**	**36**	**60**	**12**	**+6**	**24**	***15**	***25**	***40**	**4**	**4**	**1**	**3**
1993-94	**Los Angeles Kings**	**NHL**	**81**	**38**	***92**	***130**	**36**	**71**	**107**	**20**	**14**	**4**	**0**	**233**	**16.3**	**162**	**78**	**138**	**29**	**–25**	....	....	....	....	....	....	....	....
1994-95	**Los Angeles Kings**	**NHL**	**48**	**11**	**37**	**48**	**19**	**55**	**74**	**6**	**3**	**0**	**1**	**142**	**7.7**	**63**	**29**	**70**	**16**	**–20**	....	....	....	....	....	....	....	....
1995-96	**Los Angeles Kings**	**NHL**	**62**	**15**	**66**	**81**	**15**	**54**	**69**	**32**	**5**	**0**	**2**	**144**	**10.4**	**97**	**42**	**76**	**14**	**–7**	....	....	....	....	....	....	....	....
	St. Louis Blues	**NHL**	**18**	**8**	**13**	**21**	**8**	**11**	**19**	**2**	**1**	**1**	**1**	**51**	**15.7**	**27**	**13**	**25**	**5**	**–6**	**13**	**2**	**14**	**16**	**0**	**1**	**0**	**1**
1996-97	Canada	W Cup	8	3	4	7	....	....	....	2	....	....	....	....	....	....	....	....	....	....	....	....	....	....	....	....	....	....
	New York Rangers	**NHL**	**82**	**25**	***72**	**97**	**27**	**64**	**91**	**28**	**6**	**0**	**2**	**286**	**8.7**	**125**	**41**	**83**	**11**	**+12**	**15**	**10**	**10**	**20**	**2**	**3**	**0**	**2**
1997-98	**New York Rangers**	**NHL**	**82**	**23**	**67**	**90**	**27**	**66**	**93**	**28**	**6**	**0**	**4**	**201**	**11.4**	**110**	**41**	**85**	**5**	**–11**	....	....	....	....	....	....	....	....
	Canada	Olympics	6	0	4	4	....	....	....	2	....	....	....	....	....	....	....	....	....	....	....	....	....	....	....	....	....	....
	NHL Totals		**1417**	***885**	***1910**	***2795**	**778**	**1429**	**2207**	**563**	**201**	**73**	**88**	**4957**	**17.9**	**3439**	**1126**	**2214**	**442**		**208**	***122**	***260**	***382**	**66**	**34**	**11**	**24**
	Other Major League Totals		80	46	64	110	....	....	....	19	....	....	....	....	....	....	....	....	....	....	13	10	10	20	2	....	....	....

WJC-A All-Star Team (1978) • Named Best Forward at WJC-A (1978 • OHA Second All-Star Team (1978) • WHA Second All-Star Team (1979) • Won Lou Kaplan Trophy (WHA Rookie of the Year) (1979) • Won Hart Trophy (1980, 1981, 1982, 1983, 1984, 1985, 1986, 1987, 1989) • Won Lady Byng Trophy (1980, 1991, 1992, 1994) • NHL Second All-Star Team (1980, 1988, 1989, 1990, 1994, 1997, 1998) • NHL First All-Star Team (1981, 1982, 1983, 1984, 1985, 1986, 1987, 1991) • Won Art Ross Trophy (1981, 1982, 1983, 1984, 1985, 1986, 1987, 1990, 1991, 1994) • NHL record for assists in regular season (1981, 1982, 1983, 1985, 1986) • NHL record for points in regular season (1981, 1982, 1986) • NHL record for goals in regular season (1982) • Won Lester B. Pearson Award (1982, 1983, 1984, 1985, 1987) • WEC-A All-Star Team (1982) • NHL record for assists in one playoff year (1983, 1985, 1988) • NHL record for points in one playoff year (1983, 1985) • Canada Cup All-Star Team (1984, 1987, 1991) • Won Conn Smythe Trophy (1985, 1988) • NHL Plus/Minus Leader (1982, 1984, 1985, 1987) • Selected Chrysler-Dodge/NHL Performer of the Year (1985, 1986, 1987) • Won Dodge Performance of the Year Award (1989) • Won Lester Patrick Trophy (1994)

Played in NHL All-Star Game (1980, 1981, 1982, 1983, 1984, 1985, 1986, 1988, 1989, 1990, 1991, 1992, 1994, 1996, 1997, 1998)

Signed as an underage free agent by **Indianapolis** (WHA), June 12, 1978. Traded to **Edmonton** (WHA) by **Indianapolis** with Eddie Mio and Peter Driscoll for cash, November, 1978. Reclaimed by **Edmonton** as an under-age junior prior to Expansion Draft, June 9, 1979. Claimed as priority selection by **Edmonton**, June 9, 1979. Traded to **LA Kings** by **Edmonton** with Mike Krushelnyski and Marty McSorley for Jimmy Carson, Martin Gelinas, LA Kings' 1st round choices in 1989 (acquired by New Jersey — New Jersey selected Jason Miller), 1991 (Martin Rucinsky) and 1993 (Nick Stajduhar) Entry Drafts and cash, August 9, 1988. Traded to **St. Louis** by **LA Kings** for Craig Johnson, Patrice Tardif, Roman Vopat, St. Louis 5th round choice (Peter Hogan) in 1996 Entry Draft and 1st round choice (Matt Zultek) in 1997 Entry Draft, February 27, 1996. Signed as a free agent by **NY Rangers**, July 21, 1996.

• GRIER, MICHAEL

Michael Grier RW – R. 6'1", 225 lbs. b: Detroit, MI, 1/5/1975. St. Louis' 7th choice, 219th overall, in 1993 Entry Draft.

1992-93	St. Sebastian's High	H.S.	22	16	27	43	....	....	....	32	....	....	....	....	....	....	....	....	....	....	....	....	....	....	....	....	....	....
1993-94	Boston University	H.E.	39	9	9	18	....	....	....	56	....	....	....	....	....	....	....	....	....	....	....	....	....	....	....	....	....	....
1994-95	Boston University	H.E.	37	*29	26	55	....	....	....	85	....	....	....	....	....	....	....	....	....	....	....	....	....	....	....	....	....	....
1995-96	Boston University	H.E.	38	21	25	46	....	....	....	82	....	....	....	....	....	....	....	....	....	....	....	....	....	....	....	....	....	....
1996-97	**Edmonton Oilers**	**NHL**	**79**	**15**	**17**	**32**	**16**	**15**	**31**	**45**	**4**	**0**	**2**	**89**	**16.9**	**52**	**8**	**37**	**0**	**+7**	**12**	**3**	**1**	**4**	**4**	**1**	**0**	**1**
1997-98	**Edmonton Oilers**	**NHL**	**66**	**9**	**6**	**15**	**11**	**6**	**17**	**73**	**1**	**0**	**1**	**90**	**10.0**	**25**	**3**	**28**	**3**	**–3**	**12**	**2**	**2**	**4**	**13**	**0**	**0**	**1**
	NHL Totals		**145**	**24**	**23**	**47**	**27**	**21**	**48**	**118**	**5**	**0**	**3**	**179**	**13.4**	**77**	**11**	**65**	**3**		**24**	**5**	**3**	**8**	**17**	**1**	**0**	**2**

Hockey East First All-Star Team (1995) • NCAA East First All-American Team (1995)

Rights traded to **Edmonton** by **St. Louis** with Curtis Joseph for St. Louis' 1st round choices in 1996 (previously acquired, St. Louis selected Marty Reasoner) and 1997 (later traded to LA Kings — LA Kings selected Matt Zultek) Entry Drafts, August 4, 1995.

• GRIEVE, BRENT

Brent Grieve LW – L. 6'1", 202 lbs. b: Oshawa, Ont., 5/9/1969. NY Islanders' 4th choice, 65th overall, in 1989 Entry Draft.

1986-87	Oshawa Generals	OHL	60	9	19	28	....	....	....	102	....	....	....	....	....	....	....	....	....	....	24	3	8	11	22	....	....	....
1987-88	Oshawa Generals	OHL	55	19	20	39	....	....	....	122	....	....	....	....	....	....	....	....	....	....	7	0	1	1	8	....	....	....
1988-89	Oshawa Generals	OHL	49	34	33	67	....	....	....	105	....	....	....	....	....	....	....	....	....	....	6	4	3	7	4	....	....	....
1989-90	Oshawa Generals	OHL	62	46	47	93	....	....	....	125	....	....	....	....	....	....	....	....	....	....	17	10	10	20	26	....	....	....
1990-91	Capital District Islanders	AHL	61	14	13	27	....	....	....	80	....	....	....	....	....	....	....	....	....	....	....	....	....	....	....	....	....	....
	Kansas City Blades	IHL	5	2	2	4	....	....	....	2	....	....	....	....	....	....	....	....	....	....	....	....	....	....	....	....	....	....
1991-92	Capital District Islanders	AHL	74	34	32	66	....	....	....	84	....	....	....	....	....	....	....	....	....	....	7	3	1	4	16	....	....	....
1992-93	Capital District Islanders	AHL	79	34	28	62	....	....	....	122	....	....	....	....	....	....	....	....	....	....	4	1	1	2	10	....	....	....
1993-94	**New York Islanders**	**NHL**	**3**	**0**	**0**	**0**	**0**	**0**	**0**	**7**	**0**	**0**	**0**	**1**	**0.0**	**0**	**0**	**1**	**1**	**0**	....	....	....	....	....	....	....	....
	Salt Lake Golden Eagles	IHL	22	9	5	14	....	....	....	30	....	....	....	....	....	....	....	....	....	....	....	....	....	....	....	....	....	....
	Edmonton Oilers	**NHL**	**24**	**13**	**5**	**18**	**12**	**4**	**16**	**14**	**4**	**0**	**0**	**53**	**24.5**	**25**	**8**	**13**	**0**	**+4**	....	....	....	....	....	....	....	....
	Cape Breton Oilers	AHL	20	10	11	21	....	....	....	14	....	....	....	....	....	....	....	....	....	....	4	2	4	6	16	....	....	....
1994-95	**Chicago Blackhawks**	**NHL**	**24**	**1**	**5**	**6**	**2**	**7**	**9**	**23**	**0**	**0**	**0**	**30**	**3.3**	**8**	**2**	**4**	**0**	**+2**	....	....	....	....	....	....	....	....
1995-96	**Chicago Blackhawks**	**NHL**	**28**	**2**	**4**	**6**	**2**	**3**	**5**	**28**	**0**	**0**	**0**	**22**	**9.1**	**11**	**0**	**6**	**0**	**+5**	....	....	....	....	....	....	....	....
	Indianapolis Ice	IHL	24	9	10	19	....	....	....	16	....	....	....	....	....	....	....	....	....	....	....	....	....	....	....	....	....	....
	Phoenix Roadrunners	IHL	13	8	11	19	....	....	....	14	....	....	....	....	....	....	....	....	....	....	4	2	1	3	18	....	....	....
1996-97	**Los Angeles Kings**	**NHL**	**18**	**4**	**2**	**6**	**4**	**2**	**6**	**15**	**0**	**0**	**1**	**50**	**8.0**	**7**	**0**	**9**	**0**	**–2**	....	....	....	....	....	....	....	....
	Phoenix Roadrunners	IHL	31	10	14	24	....	....	....	51	....	....	....	....	....	....	....	....	....	....	....	....	....	....	....	....	....	....
	NHL Totals		**97**	**20**	**16**	**36**	**20**	**16**	**36**	**87**	**4**	**0**	**1**	**156**	**12.8**	**51**	**10**	**33**	**1**		....	....	....	....	....	....	....	....

Traded to **Edmonton** by **NY Islanders** for Marc Laforge, December 15, 1993. Signed as a free agent by **Chicago**, July 7, 1994. Signed as a free agent by **LA Kings**, August 2, 1996.

• GRIMSON, STU

Stu "The Grim Reaper" Grimson LW – L. 6'5", 227 lbs. b: Kamloops, B.C., 5/20/1965. Calgary's 11th choice, 143rd overall, in 1985 Entry Draft.

1982-83	Regina Pats	WHL	48	0	1	1	....	....	....	105	....	....	....	....	....	....	....	....	....	....	5	0	0	0	14	....	....	....
1983-84	Regina Pats	WHL	63	8	8	16	....	....	....	131	....	....	....	....	....	....	....	....	....	....	21	0	1	1	29	....	....	....
1984-85	Regina Pats	WHL	71	24	32	56	....	....	....	248	....	....	....	....	....	....	....	....	....	....	8	1	2	3	14	....	....	....
1985-86	University of Manitoba	CWUAA	12	7	4	11	....	....	....	113	....	....	....	....	....	....	....	....	....	....	8	1	1	2	24	....	....	....
1986-87	University of Manitoba	CWUAA	29	8	8	16	....	....	....	67	....	....	....	....	....	....	....	....	....	....	14	4	2	6	28	....	....	....
1987-88	Salt Lake Golden Eagles	IHL	38	9	5	14	....	....	....	268	....	....	....	....	....	....	....	....	....	....	....	....	....	....	....	....	....	....
1988-89	**Calgary Flames**	**NHL**	**1**	**0**	**0**	**0**	**0**	**0**	**0**	**5**	**0**	**0**	**0**	**0**	**0.0**	**0**	**0**	**0**	**0**	**0**	....	....	....	....	....	....	....	....
	Salt Lake Golden Eagles	IHL	72	9	18	27	....	....	....	397	....	....	....	....	....	....	....	....	....	....	14	2	3	5	86	....	....	....
1989-90	**Calgary Flames**	**NHL**	**3**	**0**	**0**	**0**	**0**	**0**	**0**	**17**	**0**	**0**	**0**	**0**	**0.0**	**0**	**0**	**1**	**0**	**–1**	....	....	....	....	....	....	....	....
	Salt Lake Golden Eagles	IHL	62	8	8	16	....	....	....	319	....	....	....	....	....	....	....	....	....	....	4	0	0	0	8	....	....	....
1990-91	**Chicago Blackhawks**	**NHL**	**35**	**0**	**1**	**1**	**0**	**1**	**1**	**183**	**0**	**0**	**0**	**14**	**0.0**	**4**	**0**	**7**	**0**	**–3**	**5**	**0**	**0**	**0**	**46**	**0**	**0**	**0**
1991-92	**Chicago Blackhawks**	**NHL**	**54**	**2**	**2**	**4**	**2**	**1**	**3**	**234**	**0**	**0**	**0**	**23**	**8.7**	**5**	**0**	**8**	**1**	**–2**	**14**	**0**	**1**	**1**	**10**	**0**	**0**	**0**
	Indianapolis Ice	IHL	5	1	1	2	....	....	....	17	....	....	....	....	....	....	....	....	....	....	....	....	....	....	....	....	....	....
1992-93	**Chicago Blackhawks**	**NHL**	**78**	**1**	**1**	**2**	**1**	**1**	**2**	**193**	**1**	**0**	**0**	**14**	**7.1**	**7**	**2**	**3**	**0**	**+2**	**2**	**0**	**0**	**0**	**4**	**0**	**0**	**0**
1993-94	**Anaheim Mighty Ducks**	**NHL**	**77**	**1**	**5**	**6**	**1**	**4**	**5**	**199**	**0**	**0**	**0**	**34**	**2.9**	**17**	**0**	**24**	**1**	**–6**	....	....	....	....	....	....	....	....
1994-95	**Anaheim Mighty Ducks**	**NHL**	**31**	**0**	**1**	**1**	**0**	**1**	**1**	**110**	**0**	**0**	**0**	**14**	**0.0**	**5**	**0**	**12**	**0**	**–7**	....	....	....	....	....	....	....	....
	Detroit Red Wings	**NHL**	**11**	**0**	**0**	**0**	**0**	**0**	**0**	**37**	**0**	**0**	**0**	**4**	**0.0**	**2**	**0**	**6**	**0**	**–4**	**11**	**1**	**0**	**1**	**26**	**0**	**0**	**0**
1995-96	**Detroit Red Wings**	**NHL**	**56**	**0**	**1**	**1**	**0**	**1**	**1**	**128**	**0**	**0**	**0**	**19**	**0.0**	**6**	**0**	**16**	**0**	**–10**	**2**	**0**	**0**	**0**	**0**	**0**	**0**	**0**
1996-97	**Detroit Red Wings**	**NHL**	**1**	**0**	**0**	**0**	**0**	**0**	**0**	**0**	**0**	**0**	**0**	**0**	**0.0**	**0**	**0**	**1**	**0**	**–1**	....	....	....	....	....	....	....	....
	Hartford Whalers	**NHL**	**75**	**2**	**2**	**4**	**2**	**2**	**4**	**218**	**0**	**0**	**0**	**17**	**11.8**	**8**	**0**	**15**	**0**	**–7**	....	....	....	....	....	....	....	....
1997-98	**Carolina Hurricanes**	**NHL**	**82**	**3**	**4**	**7**	**4**	**4**	**8**	**204**	**0**	**0**	**1**	**17**	**17.6**	**10**	**0**	**10**	**0**	**0**	....	....	....	....	....	....	....	....
	NHL Totals		**504**	**9**	**17**	**26**	**10**	**15**	**25**	**1528**	**1**	**0**	**1**	**156**	**5.8**	**64**	**2**	**103**	**2**		**34**	**1**	**1**	**2**	**86**	**0**	**0**	**0**

• Re-entered NHL draft. Originally Detroit's 11th choice, 193rd overall, in 1983 Entry Draft.

Claimed on waivers by **Chicago** from **Calgary**, October 1, 1990. Claimed by **Anaheim** from **Chicago** in Expansion Draft, June 24, 1993. Traded to **Detroit** by **Anaheim** with Mark Ferner and Anaheim's 6th round choice (Magnus Nilsson) in 1996 Entry Draft for Mike Sillinger and Jason York, April 4, 1995. Claimed on waivers by **Hartford** from **Detroit**, October 13, 1996. Transferred to **Carolina** after **Hartford** franchise relocated, June 25, 1997.

• GRISDALE, JOHN

John Grisdale D – R. 6', 195 lbs. b: Geraldton, Ont., 8/23/1948.

1966-67	Dixie Beehives	Jr. B	STATISTICS NOT AVAILABLE																									
1967-68	Michigan Tech Huskies	WCHA	DID NOT PLAY – FRESHMAN																									
1968-69	Michigan Tech Huskies	WCHA	30	7	7	14	....	....	....	45	....	....	....	....	....	....	....	....	....	....	....	....	....	....	....	....	....	....
1969-70	Michigan Tech Huskies	WCHA	33	2	11	13	....	....	....	62	....	....	....	....	....	....	....	....	....	....	....	....	....	....	....	....	....	....
1970-71	Michigan Tech Huskies	WCHA	31	2	23	25	....	....	....	61	....	....	....	....	....	....	....	....	....	....	....	....	....	....	....	....	....	....
	Tulsa Oilers	CHL	4	2	0	2	....	....	....	12	....	....	....	....	....	....	....	....	....	....	....	....	....	....	....	....	....	....
1971-72	Tulsa Oilers	CHL	59	0	15	15	....	....	....	105	....	....	....	....	....	....	....	....	....	....	13	1	3	4	23	....	....	....
1972-73	**Toronto Maple Leafs**	**NHL**	**49**	**1**	**7**	**8**	**1**	**6**	**7**	**76**	**0**	**0**	**0**	**49**	**2.0**	**47**	**2**	**76**	**9**	**–22**	....	....	....	....	....	....	....	....

Season	Club	League	REGULAR SEASON																		PLAYOFFS							
			GP	G	A	Pts	AG	AA	APts	PIM	PP	SH	GW	S	%	TGF	PGF	TGA	PGA	+/–	GP	G	A	Pts	PIM	PP	SH	GW
1973-74	Tulsa Oilers	CHL	71	9	29	38	....	....	....	193	....	....	....	....	....	....	....	....	....	....	....	....	....	....	....	....	....	....
1974-75	**Toronto Maple Leafs**	**NHL**	**2**	**0**	**0**	**0**	**0**	**0**	**0**	**4**	**0**	**0**	**0**	**0**	**0.0**	**0**	**0**	**0**	**0**	**0**	....	....	....	....	....	....	....	....
	Vancouver Canucks	**NHL**	**58**	**1**	**12**	**13**	**1**	**9**	**10**	**91**	**0**	**0**	**0**	**41**	**2.4**	**68**	**6**	**73**	**14**	**+3**	**5**	**0**	**1**	**1**	**13**	**0**	**0**	**0**
1975-76	**Vancouver Canucks**	**NHL**	**38**	**2**	**6**	**8**	**2**	**5**	**7**	**54**	**2**	**0**	**1**	**31**	**6.5**	**37**	**5**	**38**	**10**	**+4**	**2**	**0**	**0**	**0**	**0**	**0**	**0**	**0**
	Tulsa Oilers	CHL	5	1	0	1	....	....	....	13	....	....	....	....	....	....	....	....	....	....	....	....	....	....	....	....	....	....
1976-77	**Vancouver Canucks**	**NHL**	**20**	**0**	**2**	**2**	**0**	**2**	**2**	**20**	**0**	**0**	**0**	**16**	**0.0**	**10**	**0**	**25**	**2**	**–13**	....	....	....	....	....	....	....	....
	Tulsa Oilers	CHL	47	2	23	25	....	....	....	132	....	....	....	....	....	....	....	....	....	....	9	2	4	6	11	....	....	....
1977-78	**Vancouver Canucks**	**NHL**	**42**	**0**	**9**	**9**	**0**	**7**	**7**	**47**	**0**	**0**	**0**	**44**	**0.0**	**45**	**2**	**57**	**16**	**+2**	....	....	....	....	....	....	....	....
1978-79	**Vancouver Canucks**	**NHL**	**41**	**0**	**3**	**3**	**0**	**2**	**2**	**54**	**0**	**0**	**0**	**19**	**0.0**	**20**	**1**	**45**	**3**	**–23**	**3**	**0**	**0**	**0**	**2**	**0**	**0**	**0**
	Dallas Black Hawks	CHL	4	1	0	1	....	....	....	4	....	....	....	....	....	....	....	....	....	....	....	....	....	....	....	....	....	....
	NHL Totals		**250**	**4**	**39**	**43**	**4**	**31**	**35**	**346**	**2**	**0**	**1**	**200**	**2.0**	**227**	**16**	**314**	**54**		**10**	**0**	**1**	**1**	**15**	**0**	**0**	**0**

Signed as a free agent by **Toronto** (Tulsa-CHL) to four-game tryout contract, March, 1971. Traded to **Vancouver** by **Toronto** with Garry Monahan for Dave Dunn, October 16, 1974.

• GROLEAU, FRANCOIS

Francois Groleau D – L. 6′, 197 lbs. b: Longueuil, Que., 1/23/1973. Calgary's 2nd choice, 41st overall, in 1991 Entry Draft.

Season	Club	League	GP	G	A	Pts	AG	AA	APts	PIM	PP	SH	GW	S	%	TGF	PGF	TGA	PGA	+/–	GP	G	A	Pts	PIM	PP	SH	GW
1989-90	Shawinigan Cataractes	QMJHL	65	11	54	65	....	....	....	80	....	....	....	....	....	....	....	....	....	....	6	0	1	1	12	....	....	....
1990-91	Shawinigan Cataractes	QMJHL	70	9	60	69	....	....	....	70	....	....	....	....	....	....	....	....	....	....	6	0	3	3	2	....	....	....
1991-92	Shawinigan Cataractes	QMJHL	65	8	70	78	....	....	....	74	....	....	....	....	....	....	....	....	....	....	10	5	15	20	8	....	....	....
1992-93	St-Jean Lynx	QMJHL	48	7	38	45	....	....	....	66	....	....	....	....	....	....	....	....	....	....	4	0	1	1	14	....	....	....
1993-94	Saint John Flames	AHL	73	8	14	22	....	....	....	49	....	....	....	....	....	....	....	....	....	....	7	0	1	1	2	....	....	....
1994-95	Saint John Flames	AHL	65	6	34	40	....	....	....	28	....	....	....	....	....	....	....	....	....	....	....	....	....	....	....	....	....	....
	Cornwall Aces	AHL	8	1	2	3	....	....	....	7	....	....	....	....	....	....	....	....	....	....	14	2	7	9	16	....	....	....
1995-96	**Montreal Canadiens**	**NHL**	**2**	**0**	**1**	**1**	**0**	**1**	**1**	**2**	**0**	**0**	**0**	**1**	**0.0**	**2**	**0**	**0**	**0**	**+2**	....	....	....	....	....	....	....	....
	San Francisco Spiders	IHL	63	6	26	32	....	....	....	60	....	....	....	....	....	....	....	....	....	....	....	....	....	....	....	....	....	....
	Fredericton Canadiens	AHL	12	3	5	8	....	....	....	10	....	....	....	....	....	....	....	....	....	....	10	1	6	7	14	....	....	....
1996-97	**Montreal Canadiens**	**NHL**	**5**	**0**	**0**	**0**	**0**	**0**	**0**	**4**	**0**	**0**	**0**	**3**	**0.0**	**3**	**0**	**3**	**0**	**0**	....	....	....	....	....	....	....	....
	Fredericton Canadiens	AHL	47	8	24	32	....	....	....	43	....	....	....	....	....	....	....	....	....	....	....	....	....	....	....	....	....	....
1997-98	**Montreal Canadiens**	**NHL**	**1**	**0**	**0**	**0**	**0**	**0**	**0**	**0**	**0**	**0**	**0**	**3**	**0.0**	**1**	**0**	**0**	**0**	**+1**	....	....	....	....	....	....	....	....
	Fredericton Canadiens	AHL	63	14	26	40	....	....	....	70	....	....	....	....	....	....	....	....	....	....	4	0	2	2	4	....	....	....
	NHL Totals		**8**	**0**	**1**	**1**	**0**	**1**	**1**	**6**	**0**	**0**	**0**	**7**	**0.0**	**6**	**0**	**3**	**0**		....	....	....	....	....	....	....	....

QMJHL Second All-Star Team (1990) • QMJHL First All-Star Team (1992)

Traded to **Quebec** by **Calgary** for Ed Ward, March 23, 1995. Signed as a free agent by **Montreal**, June 17, 1995.

• GRONMAN, TUOMAS

Tuomas Gronman D – R. 6′3″, 219 lbs. b: Viitasaari, Finland, 3/22/1974. Quebec's 3rd choice, 29th overall, in 1992 Entry Draft.

Season	Club	League	GP	G	A	Pts	AG	AA	APts	PIM	PP	SH	GW	S	%	TGF	PGF	TGA	PGA	+/–	GP	G	A	Pts	PIM	PP	SH	GW
1991-92	Tacoma Rockets	WHL	61	5	18	23	....	....	....	102	....	....	....	....	....	....	....	....	....	....	4	0	1	1	2	....	....	....
	Finland	WJC-A	7	1	0	1	....	....	....	10	....	....	....	....	....	....	....	....	....	....	....	....	....	....	....	....	....	....
1992-93	Lukko Rauma	Finland	45	2	11	13	....	....	....	46	....	....	....	....	....	....	....	....	....	....	3	1	0	1	2	....	....	....
	Finland	WJC-A	7	1	2	3	....	....	....	14	....	....	....	....	....	....	....	....	....	....	....	....	....	....	....	....	....	....
1993-94	Lukko Rauma	Finland	44	4	12	16	....	....	....	60	....	....	....	....	....	....	....	....	....	....	9	0	1	1	14	....	....	....
	Finland	WJC-A	7	0	4	4	....	....	....	10	....	....	....	....	....	....	....	....	....	....	....	....	....	....	....	....	....	....
1994-95	TPS Turku	Finland	47	4	20	24	....	....	....	66	....	....	....	....	....	....	....	....	....	....	13	2	2	4	43	....	....	....
1995-96	TPS Turku	Finland	32	5	7	12	....	....	....	85	....	....	....	....	....	....	....	....	....	....	11	1	4	5	16	....	....	....
1996-97	**Chicago Blackhawks**	**NHL**	**16**	**0**	**1**	**1**	**0**	**1**	**1**	**13**	**0**	**0**	**0**	**9**	**0.0**	**2**	**0**	**7**	**1**	**–4**	....	....	....	....	....	....	....	....
	Indianapolis Ice	IHL	51	5	16	21	....	....	....	89	....	....	....	....	....	....	....	....	....	....	4	1	1	2	6	....	....	....
1997-98	Indianapolis Ice	IHL	6	0	3	3	....	....	....	6	....	....	....	....	....	....	....	....	....	....	....	....	....	....	....	....	....	....
	Pittsburgh Penguins	**NHL**	**22**	**1**	**2**	**3**	**1**	**2**	**3**	**25**	**1**	**0**	**1**	**33**	**3.0**	**15**	**5**	**7**	**0**	**+3**	**1**	**0**	**0**	**0**	**0**	**0**	**0**	**0**
	Syracuse Crunch	AHL	33	6	14	20	....	....	....	45	....	....	....	....	....	....	....	....	....	....	....	....	....	....	....	....	....	....
	Finland	Olympics	4	0	0	0	....	....	....	2	....	....	....	....	....	....	....	....	....	....	....	....	....	....	....	....	....	....
	NHL Totals		**38**	**1**	**3**	**4**	**1**	**3**	**4**	**38**	**1**	**0**	**1**	**42**	**2.4**	**17**	**5**	**14**	**1**		**1**	**0**	**0**	**0**	**0**	**0**	**0**	**0**

Rights traded to **Chicago** by **Colorado** for Chicago's 2nd round choice (Phillippe Sauve) in 1998 Entry Draft, July 10, 1996. Traded to **Pittsburgh** by **Chicago** for Greg Johnson, October 27, 1997.

• GRONSTRAND, JARI

Jari Gronstrand D – L. 6′3″, 195 lbs. b: Tampere, Finland, 11/14/1962. Minnesota's 8th choice, 96th overall, in 1986 Entry Draft.

Season	Club	League	GP	G	A	Pts	AG	AA	APts	PIM	PP	SH	GW	S	%	TGF	PGF	TGA	PGA	+/–	GP	G	A	Pts	PIM	PP	SH	GW
1982-83	Tappara Tampere	Finland	35	2	2	4	....	....	....	18	....	....	....	....	....	....	....	....	....	....	8	0	0	0	4	....	....	....
1983-84	Tappara Tampere	Finland	32	2	4	6	....	....	....	14	....	....	....	....	....	....	....	....	....	....	9	0	2	2	4	....	....	....
1984-85	Tappara Tampere	Finland	36	1	9	10	....	....	....	27	....	....	....	....	....	....	....	....	....	....	....	....	....	....	....	....	....	....
1985-86	Tappara Tampere	Finland	36	9	5	14	....	....	....	32	....	....	....	....	....	....	....	....	....	....	8	1	2	3	4	....	....	....
	Finland	WEC-A	9	0	2	2	....	....	....	8	....	....	....	....	....	....	....	....	....	....	....	....	....	....	....	....	....	....
1986-87	**Minnesota North Stars**	**NHL**	**47**	**1**	**6**	**7**	**1**	**4**	**5**	**27**	**0**	**0**	**0**	**32**	**3.1**	**42**	**2**	**54**	**18**	**+4**	....	....	....	....	....	....	....	....
1987-88	Finland	C Cup	4	0	0	0	....	....	....	0	....	....	....	....	....	....	....	....	....	....	....	....	....	....	....	....	....	....
	New York Rangers	**NHL**	**62**	**3**	**11**	**14**	**3**	**8**	**11**	**63**	**1**	**0**	**0**	**65**	**4.6**	**62**	**11**	**73**	**30**	**+8**	....	....	....	....	....	....	....	....
	Colorado Rangers	IHL	3	1	3	4	....	....	....	0	....	....	....	....	....	....	....	....	....	....	....	....	....	....	....	....	....	....
1988-89	**Quebec Nordiques**	**NHL**	**25**	**1**	**3**	**4**	**1**	**2**	**3**	**14**	**0**	**0**	**0**	**18**	**5.6**	**20**	**4**	**28**	**3**	**–9**	....	....	....	....	....	....	....	....
	Halifax Citadels	AHL	8	0	1	1	....	....	....	5	....	....	....	....	....	....	....	....	....	....	....	....	....	....	....	....	....	....
1989-90	**Quebec Nordiques**	**NHL**	**7**	**0**	**1**	**1**	**0**	**1**	**1**	**2**	**0**	**0**	**0**	**3**	**0.0**	**3**	**0**	**8**	**4**	**–1**	....	....	....	....	....	....	....	....
	Halifax Citadels	AHL	2	0	0	0	....	....	....	0	....	....	....	....	....	....	....	....	....	....	....	....	....	....	....	....	....	....
	New York Islanders	**NHL**	**41**	**3**	**4**	**7**	**3**	**3**	**6**	**27**	**0**	**0**	**2**	**23**	**13.0**	**21**	**0**	**24**	**3**	**0**	**3**	**0**	**0**	**0**	**4**	**0**	**0**	**0**
	Springfield Indians	AHL	1	0	1	1	....	....	....	0	....	....	....	....	....	....	....	....	....	....	....	....	....	....	....	....	....	....
1990-91	**New York Islanders**	**NHL**	**3**	**0**	**1**	**1**	**0**	**1**	**1**	**2**	**0**	**0**	**0**	**1**	**0.0**	**3**	**1**	**4**	**0**	**–2**	....	....	....	....	....	....	....	....
	Capital District Islanders	AHL	63	13	22	35	....	....	....	40	....	....	....	....	....	....	....	....	....	....	....	....	....	....	....	....	....	....
1991-92	Tappara Tampere	Finland	38	3	7	10	....	....	....	52	....	....	....	....	....	....	....	....	....	....	....	....	....	....	....	....	....	....
1992-93	Tappara Tampere	Finland	46	5	5	10	....	....	....	76	....	....	....	....	....	....	....	....	....	....	....	....	....	....	....	....	....	....
1993-94	Tappara Tampere	Finland	48	5	6	11	....	....	....	34	....	....	....	....	....	....	....	....	....	....	....	....	....	....	....	....	....	....
1994-95	Saxonia	Germany	39	3	7	10	....	....	....	10	....	....	....	....	....	....	....	....	....	....	2	0	1	1	4	....	....	....
	NHL Totals		**185**	**8**	**26**	**34**	**8**	**19**	**27**	**135**	**1**	**0**	**2**	**142**	**5.6**	**151**	**18**	**191**	**58**		**3**	**0**	**0**	**0**	**4**	**0**	**0**	**0**

Finnish First All-Star Team (1986)

Traded to **NY Rangers** by **Minnesota** for Paul Boutilier for Jay Caufield and Dave Gagner, October 8, 1987. Traded to **Quebec** by **NY Rangers** with Bruce Bell, Walt Poddubny and NY Rangers 4th round choice (Eric Dubois) in 1989 Entry Draft for Jason Lafreniere and Normand Rochefort, August 1, 1988. Claimed on waivers by **NY Islanders**, November 21, 1989.

• GROSEK, MICHAL

Michal Grosek LW – R. 6′2″, 207 lbs. b: Vyskov, Czech., 6/1/1975. Winnipeg's 7th choice, 145th overall, in 1993 Entry Draft.

Season	Club	League	GP	G	A	Pts	AG	AA	APts	PIM	PP	SH	GW	S	%	TGF	PGF	TGA	PGA	+/–	GP	G	A	Pts	PIM	PP	SH	GW
1992-93	ZPS Zlin	Czech.	17	1	3	4	....	....	....	....	....	....	....	....	....	....	....	....	....	....	....	....	....	....	....	....	....	....
1993-94	Tacoma Rockets	WHL	30	25	20	45	....	....	....	106	....	....	....	....	....	....	....	....	....	....	7	2	2	4	30	....	....	....
	Winnipeg Jets	**NHL**	**3**	**1**	**0**	**1**	**1**	**0**	**1**	**0**	**0**	**0**	**0**	**4**	**25.0**	**1**	**0**	**2**	**0**	**–1**	....	....	....	....	....	....	....	....
	Moncton Hawks	AHL	20	1	2	3	....	....	....	47	....	....	....	....	....	....	....	....	....	....	2	0	0	0	0	....	....	....
1994-95	**Winnipeg Jets**	**NHL**	**24**	**2**	**2**	**4**	**4**	**3**	**7**	**21**	**0**	**0**	**1**	**27**	**7.4**	**10**	**2**	**11**	**0**	**–3**	....	....	....	....	....	....	....	....
	Springfield Falcons	AHL	45	10	22	32	....	....	....	98	....	....	....	....	....	....	....	....	....	....	....	....	....	....	....	....	....	....
1995-96	**Winnipeg Jets**	**NHL**	**1**	**0**	**0**	**0**	**0**	**0**	**0**	**0**	**0**	**0**	**0**	**1**	**0.0**	**0**	**0**	**1**	**0**	**–1**	....	....	....	....	....	....	....	....
	Springfield Falcons	AHL	39	16	19	35	....	....	....	68	....	....	....	....	....	....	....	....	....	....	....	....	....	....	....	....	....	....
	Buffalo Sabres	**NHL**	**22**	**6**	**4**	**10**	**6**	**3**	**9**	**31**	**2**	**0**	**1**	**33**	**18.2**	**15**	**6**	**11**	**2**	**0**	....	....	....	....	....	....	....	....
1996-97	**Buffalo Sabres**	**NHL**	**82**	**15**	**21**	**36**	**16**	**19**	**35**	**71**	**1**	**0**	**2**	**117**	**12.8**	**65**	**7**	**34**	**1**	**+25**	**12**	**3**	**3**	**6**	**8**	**0**	**0**	**0**
1997-98	**Buffalo Sabres**	**NHL**	**67**	**10**	**20**	**30**	**12**	**19**	**31**	**60**	**2**	**0**	**1**	**114**	**8.8**	**41**	**8**	**24**	**0**	**+9**	**15**	**6**	**4**	**10**	**28**	**2**	**0**	**3**
	NHL Totals		**199**	**34**	**47**	**81**	**39**	**44**	**83**	**183**	**5**	**0**	**5**	**296**	**11.5**	**132**	**23**	**83**	**3**		**27**	**9**	**7**	**16**	**36**	**2**	**0**	**3**

Traded to **Buffalo** by **Winnipeg** with Darryl Shannon for Craig Muni, February 15, 1996.

• GROULX, WAYNE

Wayne Groulx C – R. 6′1″, 185 lbs. b: Welland, Ont., 2/2/1965. Quebec's 7th choice, 179th overall, in 1983 Entry Draft.

Season	Club	League	GP	G	A	Pts	AG	AA	APts	PIM	PP	SH	GW	S	%	TGF	PGF	TGA	PGA	+/–	GP	G	A	Pts	PIM	PP	SH	GW
1981-82	Sault Ste. Marie Greyhounds	OHL	66	25	41	66	....	....	....	66	....	....	....	....	....	....	....	....	....	....	13	6	8	14	8	....	....	....
1982-83	Sault Ste. Marie Greyhounds	OHL	67	44	86	130	....	....	....	54	....	....	....	....	....	....	....	....	....	....	16	7	9	16	13	....	....	....
1983-84	Sault Ste. Marie Greyhounds	OHL	70	59	78	137	....	....	....	48	....	....	....	....	....	....	....	....	....	....	16	14	0	*36	13	....	....	....
1984-85	Sault Ste. Marie Greyhounds	OHL	64	59	85	144	....	....	....	102	....	....	....	....	....	....	....	....	....	....	16	*18	18	*36	24	....	....	....
	Quebec Nordiques	**NHL**	**1**	**0**	**0**	**0**	**0**	**0**	**0**	**0**	**0**	**0**	**0**	**0**	**0.0**	**0**	**0**	**0**	**0**	**0**	....	....	....	....	....	....	....	....

			REGULAR SEASON																		PLAYOFFS							
Season	Club	League	GP	G	A	Pts	AG	AA	APts	PIM	PP	SH	GW	S	%	TGF	PGF	TGA	PGA	+/–	GP	G	A	Pts	PIM	PP	SH	GW
1985-86	Fredericton Express	AHL	15	2	6	8	....	....	....	12	....	....	....	....	....	....	....	....	....	....	....	....	....	....	....	....	....	....
	Muskegon Lumberjacks	IHL	55	22	27	49	....	....	....	56	....	....	....	....	....	....	....	....	....	....	12	4	4	8	26	....	....	....
1986-87	Fredericton Express	AHL	30	11	7	18	....	....	....	8	....	....	....	....	....	....	....	....	....	....	....	....	....	....	....	....	....	....
	Muskegon Lumberjacks	IHL	38	18	22	40	....	....	....	49	....	....	....	....	....	....	....	....	....	....	....	....	....	....	....	....	....	....
1987-88	Kalpa	Finland	27	17	10	27	....	....	....	54	....	....	....	....	....	....	....	....	....	....	....	....	....	....	....	....	....	....
	Baltimore Skipjacks	AHL	5	5	0	5	....	....	....	15	....	....	....	....	....	....	....	....	....	....	....	....	....	....	....	....	....	....
1988-89	Lustenau	Austria	40	40	47	87	....	....	....	....	....	....	....	....	....	....	....	....	....	....	....	....	....	....	....	....	....	....
1989-90	EC Graz	Austria	36	42	41	83	....	....	....	87	....	....	....	....	....	....	....	....	....	....	....	....	....	....	....	....	....	....
1990-91	EC Graz	Austria	32	26	22	48	....	....	....	....	....	....	....	....	....	....	....	....	....	....	....	....	....	....	....	....	....	....
1991-92	EC Graz	Austria	29	14	19	33	....	....	....	....	....	....	....	....	....	....	....	....	....	....	....	....	....	....	....	....	....	....
	Austria	WC-B	7	7	7	14	....	....	....	43	....	....	....	....	....	....	....	....	....	....	....	....	....	....	....	....	....	....
1992-93	EC Graz	Austria	55	*64	38	102	....	....	....	....	....	....	....	....	....	....	....	....	....	....	....	....	....	....	....	....	....	....
	Austria	WC-A	6	0	0	0	....	....	....	10	....	....	....	....	....	....	....	....	....	....	....	....	....	....	....	....	....	....
1993-94	EC Graz	Austria	44	20	17	37	....	....	....	....	....	....	....	....	....	....	....	....	....	....	....	....	....	....	....	....	....	....
	NHL Totals		**1**	**0**	**0**	**0**	**0**	**0**	**0**	**0**	**0**	**0**	**0**	**0**	**0.0**	**0**	**0**	**0**	**0**		....	....	....	....	....	....	....	....

OHL Second All-Star Team (1984) • OHL First All-Star Team (1985)

● GRUDEN, JOHN

John Gruden D – L. 6′, 190 lbs. b: Virginia, MN, 6/4/1970. Boston's 9th choice, 168th overall, in 1990 Entry Draft.

Season	Club	League	GP	G	A	Pts	AG	AA	APts	PIM	PP	SH	GW	S	%	TGF	PGF	TGA	PGA	+/–	GP	G	A	Pts	PIM	PP	SH	GW
1989-90	Waterloo Siskins	OJHL	47	7	39	46	....	....	....	35	....	....	....	....	....	....	....	....	....	....	....	....	....	....	....	....	....	....
1990-91	Ferris State Bulldogs	CCHA	37	4	11	15	....	....	....	27	....	....	....	....	....	....	....	....	....	....	....	....	....	....	....	....	....	....
1991-92	Ferris State Bulldogs	CCHA	37	9	14	23	....	....	....	24	....	....	....	....	....	....	....	....	....	....	....	....	....	....	....	....	....	....
1992-93	Ferris State Bulldogs	CCHA	41	16	14	30	....	....	....	58	....	....	....	....	....	....	....	....	....	....	....	....	....	....	....	....	....	....
1993-94	Ferris State Bulldogs	CCHA	38	11	25	36	....	....	....	52	....	....	....	....	....	....	....	....	....	....	....	....	....	....	....	....	....	....
	Boston Bruins	**NHL**	**7**	**0**	**1**	**1**	**0**	**1**	**1**	**2**	**0**	**0**	**0**	**8**	**0.0**	**2**	**0**	**6**	**1**	**–3**	....	....	....	....	....	....	....	....
1994-95	**Boston Bruins**	**NHL**	**38**	**0**	**6**	**6**	**0**	**9**	**9**	**22**	**0**	**0**	**0**	**30**	**0.0**	**26**	**0**	**23**	**0**	**+3**	....	....	....	....	....	....	....	....
	Providence Bruins	AHL	1	0	1	1	....	....	....	0	....	....	....	....	....	....	....	....	....	....	....	....	....	....	....	....	....	....
1995-96	**Boston Bruins**	**NHL**	**14**	**0**	**0**	**0**	**0**	**0**	**0**	**4**	**0**	**0**	**0**	**12**	**0.0**	**2**	**0**	**5**	**0**	**–3**	**3**	**0**	**1**	**1**	**0**	**0**	**0**	**0**
	Providence Bruins	AHL	39	5	19	24	....	....	....	29	....	....	....	....	....	....	....	....	....	....	....	....	....	....	....	....	....	....
1996-97	Providence Bruins	AHL	78	18	27	45	....	....	....	52	....	....	....	....	....	....	....	....	....	....	10	3	6	9	4	....	....	....
1997-98	Detroit Vipers	IHL	76	13	42	55	....	....	....	74	....	....	....	....	....	....	....	....	....	....	21	1	8	9	14	....	....	....
	NHL Totals		**59**	**0**	**7**	**7**	**0**	**10**	**10**	**28**	**0**	**0**	**0**	**50**	**0.0**	**30**	**0**	**34**	**1**		**3**	**0**	**1**	**1**	**0**	**0**	**0**	**0**

CCHA First All-Star Team (1994) • NCAA West First All-American Team (1994) • IHL Second All-Star Team (1998)

● GRUEN, DANNY

Danny Gruen LW – L. 5′11″, 190 lbs. b: Thunder Bay, Ont., 6/26/1952. Detroit's 3rd choice, 58th overall, in 1972 Amateur Draft.

Season	Club	League	GP	G	A	Pts	AG	AA	APts	PIM	PP	SH	GW	S	%	TGF	PGF	TGA	PGA	+/–	GP	G	A	Pts	PIM	PP	SH	GW
1971-72	Thunder Bay Vulcans	TBJHL	36	30	60	90	....	....	....	....	....	....	....	....	....	....	....	....	....	....	....	....	....	....	....	....	....	....
1972-73	**Detroit Red Wings**	**NHL**	**2**	**0**	**0**	**0**	**0**	**0**	**0**	**0**	**0**	**0**	**0**	**1**	**0.0**	**0**	**0**	**0**	**0**	**0**	....	....	....	....	....	....	....	....
	Fort Worth Wings	CHL	68	35	45	*80	....	....	....	*194	....	....	....	....	....	....	....	....	....	....	4	4	1	5	9	....	....	....
	Virginia Wings	AHL	3	1	1	2	....	....	....	0	....	....	....	....	....	....	....	....	....	....	....	....	....	....	....	....	....	....
1973-74	**Detroit Red Wings**	**NHL**	**18**	**1**	**3**	**4**	**1**	**3**	**4**	**7**	**0**	**0**	**0**	**18**	**5.6**	**9**	**0**	**9**	**0**	**0**	....	....	....	....	....	....	....	....
	Virginia Wings	AHL	57	25	27	52	....	....	....	64	....	....	....	....	....	....	....	....	....	....	....	....	....	....	....	....	....	....
1974-75	Michigan-Baltimore	WHA	34	10	16	26	....	....	....	73	....	....	....	....	....	....	....	....	....	....	....	....	....	....	....	....	....	....
	Winnipeg Jets	WHA	32	9	12	21	....	....	....	21	....	....	....	....	....	....	....	....	....	....	....	....	....	....	....	....	....	....
1975-76	Cleveland Crusaders	WHA	80	26	24	50	....	....	....	72	....	....	....	....	....	....	....	....	....	....	3	0	1	1	0	....	....	....
1976-77	Minnesota Fighting Saints	WHA	34	10	9	19	....	....	....	19	....	....	....	....	....	....	....	....	....	....	....	....	....	....	....	....	....	....
	Calgary Cowboys	WHA	1	1	0	1	....	....	....	0	....	....	....	....	....	....	....	....	....	....	....	....	....	....	....	....	....	....
	Colorado Rockies	**NHL**	**29**	**8**	**10**	**18**	**8**	**8**	**16**	**12**	**2**	**0**	**1**	**60**	**13.3**	**28**	**6**	**31**	**3**	**–6**	....	....	....	....	....	....	....	....
1977-78	Kansas City Red Wings	CHL	30	15	20	35	....	....	....	40	....	....	....	....	....	....	....	....	....	....	....	....	....	....	....	....	....	....
1978-79	Kansas City Red Wings	CHL	65	19	27	46	....	....	....	82	....	....	....	....	....	....	....	....	....	....	4	0	3	3	0	....	....	....
1979-80	Dayton Gems	IHL	7	0	3	3	....	....	....	22	....	....	....	....	....	....	....	....	....	....	....	....	....	....	....	....	....	....
	Muskegon Mohawks	IHL	24	4	22	26	....	....	....	16	....	....	....	....	....	....	....	....	....	....	....	....	....	....	....	....	....	....
	Hampton Aces	EHL	32	12	9	21	....	....	....	20	....	....	....	....	....	....	....	....	....	....	....	....	....	....	....	....	....	....
1980-81			DID NOT PLAY																									
1981-82			DID NOT PLAY																									
1982-83	Thunder Bay Twins	CASH	36	17	48	65	....	....	....	....	....	....	....	....	....	....	....	....	....	....	....	....	....	....	....	....	....	....
	NHL Totals		**49**	**9**	**13**	**22**	**9**	**11**	**20**	**19**	**2**	**0**	**1**	**79**	**11.4**	**37**	**6**	**40**	**3**		....	....	....	....	....	....	....	....
	Other Major League Totals		181	56	61	117	....	....	....	185	....	....	....	....	....	....	....	....	....	....	3	0	1	1	0	....	....	....

Selected by **Edmonton** (WHA) in 1973 WHA Professional Player Draft, June, 1973 Claimed by **Phoenix** (WHA) from **Edmonton** (WHA) in 1974 WHA Expansion Draft, May, 1974. Traded to **Michigan** (WHA) by **Phoenix** (WHA) for Jim Niecamp, May, 1974. Traded to **Winnipeg** (WHA) by **Michigan-Baltimore** (WHA) for future considerations, February, 1975. Selected by **Cleveland** (WHA) from **Michigan-Baltimore** (WHA) in 1975 WHA Dispersal Draft, June, 1975. Transferred to **Minnesota** (WHA) after **Cleveland** (WHA) franchise relocated, July, 1976. Traded to **Calgary** (WHA) by **Minnesota** (WHA) with Butch Deadmarsh and John Arbour for cash, January, 1977. Rights traded to **Colorado** by **Detroit** for cash, February 11, 1977. Signed as a free agent by **Detroit**, August 17, 1977.

● GRUHL, SCOTT

Scott Gruhl LW – L. 5′11″, 185 lbs. b: Port Colborne, Ont., 9/13/1959.

Season	Club	League	GP	G	A	Pts	AG	AA	APts	PIM	PP	SH	GW	S	%	TGF	PGF	TGA	PGA	+/–	GP	G	A	Pts	PIM	PP	SH	GW
1976-77	Northeastern University	H.E.	17	6	4	10	....	....	....	....	....	....	....	....	....	....	....	....	....	....	....	....	....	....	....	....	....	....
1977-78	Northeastern University	H.E.	28	21	38	59	....	....	....	46	....	....	....	....	....	....	....	....	....	....	....	....	....	....	....	....	....	....
1978-79	Sudbury Wolves	OHA	68	35	49	94	....	....	....	78	....	....	....	....	....	....	....	....	....	....	10	5	7	12	15	....	....	....
1979-80	Binghamton Whalers	AHL	4	1	0	1	....	....	....	0	....	....	....	....	....	....	....	....	....	....	....	....	....	....	....	....	....	....
	Saginaw Gears	IHL	75	53	40	93	....	....	....	100	....	....	....	....	....	....	....	....	....	....	7	2	6	8	16	....	....	....
1980-81	Houston Apollos	CHL	4	0	0	0	....	....	....	0	....	....	....	....	....	....	....	....	....	....	....	....	....	....	....	....	....	....
	Saginaw Gears	IHL	77	56	34	90	....	....	....	87	....	....	....	....	....	....	....	....	....	....	13	*11	8	*19	12	....	....	....
1981-82	**Los Angeles Kings**	**NHL**	**7**	**2**	**1**	**3**	**2**	**1**	**3**	**2**	**0**	**0**	**0**	**8**	**25.0**	**5**	**0**	**4**	**0**	**+1**	....	....	....	....	....	....	....	....
	New Haven Nighthawks	AHL	73	28	41	69	....	....	....	107	....	....	....	....	....	....	....	....	....	....	4	0	4	4	2	....	....	....
1982-83	**Los Angeles Kings**	**NHL**	**7**	**0**	**2**	**2**	**0**	**1**	**1**	**4**	**0**	**0**	**0**	**13**	**0.0**	**4**	**0**	**9**	**0**	**–5**	....	....	....	....	....	....	....	....
	New Haven Nighthawks	AHL	68	25	38	63	....	....	....	114	....	....	....	....	....	....	....	....	....	....	12	3	3	6	22	....	....	....
1983-84	Muskegon Mohawks	IHL	56	40	56	96	....	....	....	49	....	....	....	....	....	....	....	....	....	....	....	....	....	....	....	....	....	....
1984-85	Muskegon Mohawks	IHL	82	62	64	126	....	....	....	102	....	....	....	....	....	....	....	....	....	....	17	7	16	23	25	....	....	....
1985-86	Muskegon Lumberjacks	IHL	82	*59	51	110	....	....	....	178	....	....	....	....	....	....	....	....	....	....	14	7	*13	20	22	....	....	....
1986-87	Muskegon Lumberjacks	IHL	67	34	39	73	....	....	....	157	....	....	....	....	....	....	....	....	....	....	15	5	7	12	54	....	....	....
1987-88	**Pittsburgh Penguins**	**NHL**	**6**	**1**	**0**	**1**	**1**	**0**	**1**	**0**	**0**	**0**	**0**	**7**	**14.3**	**1**	**0**	**1**	**0**	**0**	....	....	....	....	....	....	....	....
	Muskegon Lumberjacks	IHL	55	28	47	75	....	....	....	115	....	....	....	....	....	....	....	....	....	....	6	5	1	6	12	....	....	....
1988-89	Muskegon Lumberjacks	IHL	79	37	55	92	....	....	....	163	....	....	....	....	....	....	....	....	....	....	14	8	11	19	37	....	....	....
1989-90	Muskegon Lumberjacks	IHL	80	41	51	92	....	....	....	206	....	....	....	....	....	....	....	....	....	....	15	8	6	14	26	....	....	....
1990-91	Fort Wayne Komets	IHL	59	23	47	70	....	....	....	109	....	....	....	....	....	....	....	....	....	....	19	4	6	10	39	....	....	....
1991-92	Fort Wayne Komets	IHL	78	44	61	105	....	....	....	196	....	....	....	....	....	....	....	....	....	....	6	2	2	4	48	....	....	....
1992-93	Fort Wayne Komets	IHL	73	34	47	81	....	....	....	290	....	....	....	....	....	....	....	....	....	....	12	4	11	15	14	....	....	....
1993-94	Milwaukee Admirals	IHL	28	6	9	15	....	....	....	102	....	....	....	....	....	....	....	....	....	....	....	....	....	....	....	....	....	....
	Kalamazoo Wings	IHL	30	15	12	27	....	....	....	85	....	....	....	....	....	....	....	....	....	....	5	1	4	5	26	....	....	....
1994-95	Richmond Renegades	ECHL	49	31	40	71	....	....	....	288	....	....	....	....	....	....	....	....	....	....	17	9	9	18	68	....	....	....
1995-96	Richmond Renegades	ECHL	60	46	39	85	....	....	....	236	....	....	....	....	....	....	....	....	....	....	7	3	5	8	18	....	....	....
	Fort Wayne Komets	IHL	....	....	....	....	....	....	....	....	....	....	....	....	....	....	....	....	....	....	2	0	1	1	0	....	....	....
	NHL Totals		**20**	**3**	**3**	**6**	**3**	**2**	**5**	**6**	**0**	**0**	**0**	**28**	**10.7**	**10**	**0**	**14**	**0**		....	....	....	....	....	....	....	....

IHL Second All-Star Team (1980, 1986, 1992) • IHL First All-Star Team (1984, 1985) • Won James Gatschene Memorial Trophy (MVP - IHL) (1985)

Signed as a free agent by **LA Kings**, October 11, 1979. Signed as a free agent by **Pittsburgh**, December 14, 1987.

● GRYP, BOB

Bob Gryp LW – L. 6′1″, 190 lbs. b: Chatham, Ont., 5/6/1950. Toronto's 4th choice, 50th overall, in 1970 Amateur Draft.

Season	Club	League	GP	G	A	Pts	AG	AA	APts	PIM	PP	SH	GW	S	%	TGF	PGF	TGA	PGA	+/–	GP	G	A	Pts	PIM	PP	SH	GW
1968-69	Boston University	ECAC	17	9	17	26	....	....	....	18	....	....	....	....	....	....	....	....	....	....	....	....	....	....	....	....	....	....
1969-70	Boston University	ECAC	27	12	17	29	....	....	....	20	....	....	....	....	....	....	....	....	....	....	....	....	....	....	....	....	....	....
1970-71	Boston University	ECAC	30	20	19	39	....	....	....	51	....	....	....	....	....	....	....	....	....	....	....	....	....	....	....	....	....	....
1971-72	Boston University	ECAC	31	9	36	45	....	....	....	14	....	....	....	....	....	....	....	....	....	....	....	....	....	....	....	....	....	....
1972-73	Boston Braves	AHL	76	38	28	66	....	....	....	99	....	....	....	....	....	....	....	....	....	....	7	3	1	4	4	....	....	....

Season	Club	League	GP	G	A	Pts	AG	AA	APts	PIM	PP	SH	GW	S	%	TGF	PGF	TGA	PGA	+/-	GP	G	A	Pts	PIM	PP	SH	GW
			REGULAR SEASON																		PLAYOFFS							
1973-74	**Boston Bruins**	**NHL**	**1**	**0**	**0**	**0**	**0**	**0**	**0**	**0**	**0**	**0**	**0**	**0**	**0.0**	**0**	**0**	**2**	**0**	**–2**	....	....	....	....	....	....	....	....
	Boston Braves	AHL	66	30	18	48	....	....	....	62	....	....	....	....	....	....	....	....	....	....	....	....	....	....	....	....	....	....
1974-75	**Washington Capitals**	**NHL**	**27**	**5**	**8**	**13**	**5**	**6**	**11**	**21**	**0**	**0**	**0**	**43**	**11.6**	**21**	**6**	**44**	**5**	**–24**	....	....	....	....	....	....	....	....
	Richmond Robins	AHL	49	10	11	21	....	....	....	94	....	....	....	....	....	....	....	....	....	....	....	....	....	....	....	....	....	....
1975-76	**Washington Capitals**	**NHL**	**46**	**6**	**5**	**11**	**6**	**4**	**10**	**12**	**0**	**0**	**0**	**52**	**11.5**	**14**	**2**	**45**	**15**	**–18**	....	....	....	....	....	....	....	....
	Richmond Robins	AHL	9	2	2	4	....	....	....	10	....	....	....	....	....	....	....	....	....	....	....	....	....	....	....	....	....	....
	New Haven Nighthawks	AHL	22	10	9	19	....	....	....	28	....	....	....	....	....	....	....	....	....	....	3	0	0	0	14	....	....	....
1976-77	Johnstown Jets	NAHL	2	1	0	1	....	....	....	0	....	....	....	....	....	....	....	....	....	....	....	....	....	....	....	....	....	....
1977-78	Long Beach Sharks-Rockets	PHL	5	1	0	1	....	....	....	14	....	....	....	....	....	....	....	....	....	....	....	....	....	....	....	....	....	....
	NHL Totals		**74**	**11**	**13**	**24**	**11**	**10**	**21**	**33**	**0**	**0**	**0**	**95**	**11.6**	**35**	**8**	**91**	**20**		....	....	....	....	....	....	....	....

Claimed by **Boston** from **Tulsa** (CHL) in Reverse Draft, June, 1972. Claimed by **Washington** from **Boston** in Expansion Draft, June 12, 1974.

● GUAY, FRANCOIS

Francois Guay C – L. 6', 190 lbs. b: Gatineau, Que., 6/8/1968. Buffalo's 9th choice, 152nd overall, in 1986 Entry Draft.

Season	Club	League	GP	G	A	Pts	AG	AA	APts	PIM	PP	SH	GW	S	%	TGF	PGF	TGA	PGA	+/-	GP	G	A	Pts	PIM	PP	SH	GW
1984-85	Laval Voisins	QMJHL	66	13	18	31	....	....	....	21	....	....	....	....	....	....	....	....	....	....	....	....	....	....	....	....	....	....
1985-86	Laval Titan	QMJHL	71	19	55	74	....	....	....	46	....	....	....	....	....	....	....	....	....	....	14	5	6	11	15	....	....	....
1986-87	Laval Titan	QMJHL	63	52	77	129	....	....	....	67	....	....	....	....	....	....	....	....	....	....	14	5	13	18	18	....	....	....
1987-88	Laval Titan	QMJHL	66	60	84	144	....	....	....	142	....	....	....	....	....	....	....	....	....	....	14	10	15	25	10	....	....	....
1988-89	Rochester Americans	AHL	45	6	20	26	....	....	....	34	....	....	....	....	....	....	....	....	....	....	....	....	....	....	....	....	....	....
1989-90	**Buffalo Sabres**	**NHL**	**1**	**0**	**0**	**0**	**0**	**0**	**0**	**0**	**0**	**0**	**0**	**0**	**0.0**	**0**	**0**	**0**	**0**	**0**	....	....	....	....	....	....	....	....
	Rochester Americans	AHL	69	28	35	63	....	....	....	39	....	....	....	....	....	....	....	....	....	....	16	4	8	12	12	....	....	....
1990-91	Rochester Americans	AHL	61	24	39	63	....	....	....	38	....	....	....	....	....	....	....	....	....	....	15	5	5	10	8	....	....	....
1991-92	Innsbruck EV	Austria	40	34	45	79	....	....	....	....	....	....	....	....	....	....	....	....	....	....	....	....	....	....	....	....	....	....
1992-93	Innsbruck EV	Austria	53	43	59	102	....	....	....	....	....	....	....	....	....	....	....	....	....	....	....	....	....	....	....	....	....	....
1993-94	Klagenfurter AC	Austria	46	30	50	80	....	....	....	....	....	....	....	....	....	....	....	....	....	....	....	....	....	....	....	....	....	....
1994-95	Herisau	Switz.	36	23	44	67	....	....	....	83	....	....	....	....	....	....	....	....	....	....	4	1	2	3	14	....	....	....
1995-96	Herisau	Switz. B	36	32	35	67	....	....	....	52	....	....	....	....	....	....	....	....	....	....	....	....	....	....	....	....	....	....
1996-97	Mannheim Eagles	Germany	14	2	8	10	....	....	....	10	....	....	....	....	....	....	....	....	....	....	....	....	....	....	....	....	....	....
1997-98	Mannheim Eagles	EuroHL	4	0	1	1	....	....	....	6	....	....	....	....	....	....	....	....	....	....	....	....	....	....	....	....	....	....
	Mannheim Eagles	Germany	39	8	13	21	....	....	....	41	....	....	....	....	....	....	....	....	....	....	10	0	4	4	6	....	....	....
	NHL Totals		**1**	**0**	**0**	**0**	**0**	**0**	**0**	**0**	**0**	**0**	**0**	**0**	**0.0**	**0**	**0**	**0**	**0**		....	....	....	....	....	....	....	....

● GUAY, PAUL

Paul Guay RW – R. 5'11", 185 lbs. b: Providence, RI, 9/2/1963. Minnesota's 10th choice, 118th overall, in 1981 Entry Draft.

Season	Club	League	GP	G	A	Pts	AG	AA	APts	PIM	PP	SH	GW	S	%	TGF	PGF	TGA	PGA	+/-	GP	G	A	Pts	PIM	PP	SH	GW
1979-80	Mount St. Charles	H.S.	23	18	19	37	....	....	....	....	....	....	....	....	....	....	....	....	....	....	....	....	....	....	....	....	....	....
1980-81	Mount St. Charles	H.S.	23	28	38	66	....	....	....	....	....	....	....	....	....	....	....	....	....	....	....	....	....	....	....	....	....	....
1981-82	Providence College	ECAC	33	23	17	40	....	....	....	38	....	....	....	....	....	....	....	....	....	....	....	....	....	....	....	....	....	....
1982-83	Providence College	ECAC	42	34	31	65	....	....	....	83	....	....	....	....	....	....	....	....	....	....	....	....	....	....	....	....	....	....
1983-84	United States	Nat-Team	62	20	18	38	....	....	....	44	....	....	....	....	....	....	....	....	....	....	....	....	....	....	....	....	....	....
	United States	Olympics	6	1	0	1	....	....	....	8	....	....	....	....	....	....	....	....	....	....	....	....	....	....	....	....	....	....
	Philadelphia Flyers	**NHL**	**14**	**2**	**6**	**8**	**2**	**4**	**6**	**14**	**0**	**0**	**0**	**19**	**10.5**	**11**	**0**	**16**	**6**	**+1**	**3**	**0**	**0**	**0**	**4**	**0**	**0**	**0**
1984-85	**Philadelphia Flyers**	**NHL**	**2**	**0**	**1**	**1**	**0**	**1**	**1**	**0**	**0**	**0**	**0**	**2**	**0.0**	**2**	**0**	**0**	**0**	**+2**	....	....	....	....	....	....	....	....
	Hershey Bears	AHL	74	23	30	53	....	....	....	123	....	....	....	....	....	....	....	....	....	....	....	....	....	....	....	....	....	....
1985-86	**Los Angeles Kings**	**NHL**	**23**	**3**	**3**	**6**	**2**	**2**	**4**	**18**	**0**	**0**	**0**	**18**	**16.7**	**11**	**1**	**20**	**4**	**–6**	....	....	....	....	....	....	....	....
	New Haven Nighthawks	AHL	57	15	36	51	....	....	....	101	....	....	....	....	....	....	....	....	....	....	5	3	0	3	11	....	....	....
1986-87	**Los Angeles Kings**	**NHL**	**35**	**2**	**5**	**7**	**2**	**4**	**6**	**16**	**0**	**0**	**0**	**18**	**11.1**	**9**	**0**	**40**	**17**	**–14**	**2**	**0**	**0**	**0**	**0**	**0**	**0**	**0**
	New Haven Nighthawks	AHL	6	1	3	4	....	....	....	11	....	....	....	....	....	....	....	....	....	....	....	....	....	....	....	....	....	....
1987-88	**Los Angeles Kings**	**NHL**	**33**	**4**	**4**	**8**	**3**	**3**	**6**	**40**	**0**	**0**	**0**	**42**	**9.5**	**11**	**0**	**21**	**3**	**–7**	**4**	**0**	**1**	**1**	**8**	**0**	**0**	**0**
	New Haven Nighthawks	AHL	42	21	26	47	....	....	....	53	....	....	....	....	....	....	....	....	....	....	....	....	....	....	....	....	....	....
1988-89	**Los Angeles Kings**	**NHL**	**2**	**0**	**0**	**0**	**0**	**0**	**0**	**2**	**0**	**0**	**0**	**2**	**0.0**	**0**	**0**	**2**	**0**	**–2**	....	....	....	....	....	....	....	....
	New Haven Nighthawks	AHL	4	4	6	10	....	....	....	20	....	....	....	....	....	....	....	....	....	....	....	....	....	....	....	....	....	....
	Boston Bruins	**NHL**	**5**	**0**	**2**	**2**	**0**	**1**	**1**	**0**	**0**	**0**	**0**	**1**	**0.0**	**2**	**0**	**2**	**0**	**0**	....	....	....	....	....	....	....	....
	Maine Mariners	AHL	61	15	29	44	....	....	....	77	....	....	....	....	....	....	....	....	....	....	....	....	....	....	....	....	....	....
1989-90	Utica Devils	AHL	75	25	30	55	....	....	....	103	....	....	....	....	....	....	....	....	....	....	5	2	2	4	13	....	....	....
1990-91	**New York Islanders**	**NHL**	**3**	**0**	**2**	**2**	**0**	**2**	**2**	**2**	**0**	**0**	**0**	**5**	**0.0**	**3**	**0**	**1**	**0**	**+2**	....	....	....	....	....	....	....	....
	Capital District Islanders	AHL	74	26	35	61	....	....	....	81	....	....	....	....	....	....	....	....	....	....	....	....	....	....	....	....	....	....
1991-92	Milwaukee Admirals	IHL	81	24	33	57	....	....	....	93	....	....	....	....	....	....	....	....	....	....	3	2	1	3	7	....	....	....
1992-93	Springfield Indians	AHL	65	10	32	42	....	....	....	90	....	....	....	....	....	....	....	....	....	....	11	1	2	3	6	....	....	....
	NHL Totals		**117**	**11**	**23**	**34**	**9**	**17**	**26**	**92**	**0**	**0**	**0**	**107**	**10.3**	**49**	**1**	**102**	**30**		**9**	**0**	**1**	**1**	**12**	**0**	**0**	**0**

ECAC Second All-Star Team (1983)

Rights traded to **Philadelphia** by **Minnesota** with Minnesota's 3rd round choice (Darryl Gilmour) in 1985 Entry Draft for Paul Holmgren, February 23, 1984. Traded to **LA Kings** by **Philadelphia** with Philadelphia's 4th round choice (Sylvain Couturier) in 1986 Entry Draft for Steve Soguin and LA Kings' 2nd round choice (Jukka Seppo) in 1986 Entry Draft, October 11, 1985. Traded to **Boston** by **LA Kings** for the rights to Dave Pasin, November 3, 1988. Signed as a free agent by **New Jersey**, August 14, 1989. Signed as a free agent by **NY Islanders**, August 13, 1990.

● GUERARD, DANIEL

Daniel Guerard RW – R. 6'4", 215 lbs. b: LaSalle, Que., 4/9/1974. Ottawa's 5th choice, 98th overall, in 1992 Entry Draft.

Season	Club	League	GP	G	A	Pts	AG	AA	APts	PIM	PP	SH	GW	S	%	TGF	PGF	TGA	PGA	+/-	GP	G	A	Pts	PIM	PP	SH	GW
1991-92	Victoriaville Tigres	QMJHL	31	5	16	21	....	....	....	66	....	....	....	....	....	....	....	....	....	....	....	....	....	....	....	....	....	....
1992-93	Verdun College-Francais	QMJHL	58	31	26	57	....	....	....	131	....	....	....	....	....	....	....	....	....	....	4	1	1	2	17	....	....	....
	New Haven Nighthawks	AHL	2	2	1	3	....	....	....	0	....	....	....	....	....	....	....	....	....	....	....	....	....	....	....	....	....	....
1993-94	Verdun College-Francais	QMJHL	53	31	34	65	....	....	....	169	....	....	....	....	....	....	....	....	....	....	4	3	1	4	4	....	....	....
	P.E.I. Senators	AHL	3	0	0	0	....	....	....	17	....	....	....	....	....	....	....	....	....	....	....	....	....	....	....	....	....	....
1994-95	**Ottawa Senators**	**NHL**	**2**	**0**	**0**	**0**	**0**	**0**	**0**	**0**	**0**	**0**	**0**	**0**	**0.0**	**0**	**0**	**0**	**0**	**0**	....	....	....	....	....	....	....	....
	P.E.I. Senators	AHL	68	20	22	42	....	....	....	95	....	....	....	....	....	....	....	....	....	....	8	0	1	1	16	....	....	....
1995-96	P.E.I. Senators	AHL	42	3	7	10	....	....	....	56	....	....	....	....	....	....	....	....	....	....	....	....	....	....	....	....	....	....
1996-97	Worcester IceCats	AHL	49	8	8	16	....	....	....	50	....	....	....	....	....	....	....	....	....	....	....	....	....	....	....	....	....	....
	NHL Totals		**2**	**0**	**0**	**0**	**0**	**0**	**0**	**0**	**0**	**0**	**0**	**0**	**0.0**	**0**	**0**	**0**	**0**		....	....	....	....	....	....	....	....

● GUERARD, STEPHANE

Stephane Guerard D – L. 6'2", 198 lbs. b: Ste. Elizabeth, Que., 4/12/1968. Quebec's 3rd choice, 41st overall, in 1986 Entry Draft.

Season	Club	League	GP	G	A	Pts	AG	AA	APts	PIM	PP	SH	GW	S	%	TGF	PGF	TGA	PGA	+/-	GP	G	A	Pts	PIM	PP	SH	GW
1984-85	Laurentide Midgets	Midget	36	6	12	18	....	....	....	140	....	....	....	....	....	....	....	....	....	....	....	....	....	....	....	....	....	....
1985-86	Shawinigan Cataracts	QMJHL	59	4	18	22	....	....	....	167	....	....	....	....	....	....	....	....	....	....	3	1	1	2	0	....	....	....
1986-87	Shawinigan Cataracts	QMJHL	31	5	16	21	....	....	....	57	....	....	....	....	....	....	....	....	....	....	12	2	9	11	36	....	....	....
1987-88	**Quebec Nordiques**	**NHL**	**30**	**0**	**0**	**0**	**0**	**0**	**0**	**34**	**0**	**0**	**0**	**12**	**0.0**	**14**	**0**	**24**	**3**	**–7**	....	....	....	....	....	....	....	....
1988-89	Halifax Citadels	AHL	37	1	9	10	....	....	....	140	....	....	....	....	....	....	....	....	....	....	4	0	0	0	8	....	....	....
1989-90	**Quebec Nordiques**	**NHL**	**4**	**0**	**0**	**0**	**0**	**0**	**0**	**6**	**0**	**0**	**0**	**9**	**0.0**	**1**	**0**	**8**	**2**	**–5**	....	....	....	....	....	....	....	....
	Halifax Citadels	AHL	1	0	0	0	....	....	....	5	....	....	....	....	....	....	....	....	....	....	....	....	....	....	....	....	....	....
	NHL Totals		**34**	**0**	**0**	**0**	**0**	**0**	**0**	**40**	**0**	**0**	**0**	**21**	**0.0**	**15**	**0**	**32**	**5**		....	....	....	....	....	....	....	....

Traded to **NY Rangers** by **Quebec** for Miloslav Horava, May 25, 1991. Traded to **Quebec** by **NY Rangers** for cash, September 3, 1991.

● GUERIN, BILL

Bill Guerin RW – R. 6'2", 210 lbs. b: Wilbraham, MA, 11/9/1970. New Jersey's 1st choice, 5th overall, in 1989 Entry Draft.

Season	Club	League	GP	G	A	Pts	AG	AA	APts	PIM	PP	SH	GW	S	%	TGF	PGF	TGA	PGA	+/-	GP	G	A	Pts	PIM	PP	SH	GW
1988-89	Springfield Olympics	NEJHL	31	32	35	67	....	....	....	90	....	....	....	....	....	....	....	....	....	....	....	....	....	....	....	....	....	....
	United States	WJC-A	7	0	3	3	....	....	....	16	....	....	....	....	....	....	....	....	....	....	....	....	....	....	....	....	....	....
1989-90	Boston College	H.E.	39	14	11	25	....	....	....	54	....	....	....	....	....	....	....	....	....	....	....	....	....	....	....	....	....	....
	United States	WJC-A	7	0	0	0	....	....	....	18	....	....	....	....	....	....	....	....	....	....	....	....	....	....	....	....	....	....
1990-91	Boston College	H.E.	38	26	19	45	....	....	....	102	....	....	....	....	....	....	....	....	....	....	....	....	....	....	....	....	....	....
	United States	Nat-Team	46	12	15	27	....	....	....	67	....	....	....	....	....	....	....	....	....	....	....	....	....	....	....	....	....	....
1991-92	**New Jersey Devils**	**NHL**	**5**	**0**	**1**	**1**	**0**	**1**	**1**	**9**	**0**	**0**	**0**	**8**	**0.0**	**1**	**0**	**0**	**0**	**+1**	**6**	**3**	**0**	**3**	**4**	**0**	**0**	**0**
	Utica Devils	AHL	22	13	10	23	....	....	....	6	....	....	....	....	....	....	....	....	....	....	4	1	3	4	14	....	....	....
1992-93	**New Jersey Devils**	**NHL**	**65**	**14**	**20**	**34**	**12**	**14**	**26**	**63**	**0**	**0**	**2**	**123**	**11.4**	**44**	**2**	**30**	**2**	**+14**	**5**	**1**	**1**	**2**	**4**	**0**	**0**	**0**
	Utica Devils	AHL	18	10	7	17	....	....	....	47	....	....	....	....	....	....	....	....	....	....	....	....	....	....	....	....	....	....
1993-94	**New Jersey Devils**	**NHL**	**81**	**25**	**19**	**44**	**23**	**15**	**38**	**101**	**2**	**0**	**3**	**195**	**12.8**	**72**	**16**	**44**	**2**	**+14**	**17**	**2**	**1**	**3**	**35**	**0**	**0**	**1**
1994-95	**New Jersey Devils**	**NHL**	**48**	**12**	**13**	**25**	**21**	**19**	**40**	**72**	**4**	**0**	**3**	**96**	**12.5**	**32**	**6**	**20**	**0**	**+6**	**20**	**3**	**8**	**11**	**30**	**1**	**0**	**0**
1995-96	**New Jersey Devils**	**NHL**	**80**	**23**	**30**	**53**	**23**	**24**	**47**	**116**	**8**	**0**	**6**	**216**	**10.6**	**77**	**26**	**44**	**0**	**+7**	....	....	....	....	....	....	....	....

			REGULAR SEASON																		PLAYOFFS							
Season	Club	League	GP	G	A	Pts	AG	AA	APts	PIM	PP	SH	GW	S	%	TGF	PGF	TGA	PGA	+/-	GP	G	A	Pts	PIM	PP	SH	GW
1996-97	United States	W Cup	7	0	2	2	....	....	....	17	....	....	....	....	....	....	....	....	....	....	....	....	....	....	....	....	....	....
	New Jersey Devils	**NHL**	**82**	**29**	**18**	**47**	**31**	**16**	**47**	**95**	**7**	**0**	**9**	**177**	**16.4**	**59**	**16**	**45**	**0**	**–2**	**8**	**2**	**1**	**3**	**18**	**1**	**0**	**1**
1997-98	**New Jersey Devils**	**NHL**	**19**	**5**	**5**	**10**	**6**	**5**	**11**	**13**	**1**	**0**	**2**	**48**	**10.4**	**14**	**4**	**10**	**0**	**0**	....	....	....	....	....	....	....	....
	Edmonton Oilers	**NHL**	**40**	**13**	**16**	**29**	**15**	**16**	**31**	**80**	**8**	**0**	**2**	**130**	**10.0**	**50**	**25**	**24**	**0**	**+1**	**12**	**7**	**1**	**8**	**17**	**4**	**0**	**0**
	United States	Olympics	4	0	3	3	....	....	....	2	....	....	....	....	....	....	....	....	....	....	....	....	....	....	....	....	....	....
	NHL Totals		**420**	**121**	**122**	**243**	**131**	**110**	**241**	**549**	**30**	**0**	**27**	**993**	**12.2**	**349**	**95**	**217**	**4**		**68**	**18**	**12**	**30**	**108**	**6**	**0**	**2**

Traded to **Edmonton** by **New Jersey** with Valeri Zelepukin for Jason Arnott and Bryan Muir, January 4, 1998.

• GUEVREMONT, JOCELYN

Jocelyn Guevremont D – R. 6'2", 200 lbs. b: Montreal, Que., 3/1/1951. Vancouver's 1st choice, 3rd overall, in 1971 Amateur Draft.

Season	Club	League	GP	G	A	Pts	AG	AA	APts	PIM	PP	SH	GW	S	%	TGF	PGF	TGA	PGA	+/-	GP	G	A	Pts	PIM	PP	SH	GW
1967-68	Laval Saints	QJHL	....	10	20	30	....	....	....	....	....	....	....	....	....	....	....	....	....	....	....	....	....	....	....	....	....	....
1968-69	Montreal Jr. Canadiens	OHA	54	11	40	51	....	....	....	79	....	....	....	....	....	....	....	....	....	....	14	6	*21	27	6	....	....	....
1969-70	Montreal Jr. Canadiens	OHA	54	13	45	58	....	....	....	46	....	....	....	....	....	....	....	....	....	....	....	....	....	....	....	....	....	....
1970-71	Montreal Jr. Canadiens	OHA	60	22	66	88	....	....	....	112	....	....	....	....	....	....	....	....	....	....	....	....	....	....	....	....	....	....
1971-72	**Vancouver Canucks**	**NHL**	**75**	**13**	**38**	**51**	**14**	**35**	**49**	**44**	**3**	**0**	**1**	**210**	**6.2**	**118**	**41**	**137**	**32**	**–28**	....	....	....	....	....	....	....	....
1972-73	Canada	Summit	DID NOT PLAY																									
	Vancouver Canucks	**NHL**	**78**	**16**	**26**	**42**	**16**	**22**	**38**	**46**	**6**	**1**	**0**	**246**	**6.5**	**125**	**37**	**153**	**23**	**–42**	....	....	....	....	....	....	....	....
1973-74	**Vancouver Canucks**	**NHL**	**72**	**15**	**24**	**39**	**15**	**21**	**36**	**34**	**10**	**0**	**1**	**208**	**7.2**	**94**	**35**	**129**	**33**	**–37**	....	....	....	....	....	....	....	....
1974-75	**Vancouver Canucks**	**NHL**	**2**	**0**	**0**	**0**	**0**	**0**	**0**	**0**	**0**	**0**	**0**	**5**	**0.0**	**3**	**3**	**1**	**0**	**–1**	....	....	....	....	....	....	....	....
	Buffalo Sabres	**NHL**	**64**	**7**	**25**	**32**	**6**	**20**	**26**	**32**	**4**	**0**	**0**	**160**	**4.4**	**118**	**29**	**61**	**4**	**+32**	**17**	**0**	**6**	**6**	**14**	**0**	**0**	**0**
1975-76	**Buffalo Sabres**	**NHL**	**80**	**12**	**40**	**52**	**11**	**31**	**42**	**57**	**6**	**0**	**3**	**229**	**5.2**	**173**	**41**	**105**	**20**	**+47**	**9**	**0**	**5**	**5**	**2**	**0**	**0**	**0**
1976-77	**Buffalo Sabres**	**NHL**	**80**	**9**	**29**	**38**	**9**	**24**	**33**	**46**	**2**	**0**	**2**	**210**	**4.3**	**111**	**16**	**86**	**17**	**+26**	**6**	**3**	**4**	**7**	**0**	**1**	**0**	**0**
1977-78	**Buffalo Sabres**	**NHL**	**66**	**7**	**28**	**35**	**7**	**23**	**30**	**46**	**0**	**0**	**1**	**162**	**4.3**	**98**	**22**	**59**	**8**	**+25**	**8**	**1**	**2**	**3**	**2**	**0**	**0**	**0**
1978-79	**Buffalo Sabres**	**NHL**	**34**	**3**	**8**	**11**	**3**	**6**	**9**	**8**	**0**	**0**	**0**	**51**	**5.9**	**25**	**5**	**10**	**2**	**+12**	....	....	....	....	....	....	....	....
1979-80	**New York Rangers**	**NHL**	**20**	**2**	**5**	**7**	**2**	**4**	**6**	**6**	**2**	**0**	**0**	**41**	**4.9**	**17**	**6**	**26**	**3**	**–12**	....	....	....	....	....	....	....	....
	New Haven Nighthawks	AHL	36	7	27	34	....	....	....	18	....	....	....	....	....	....	....	....	....	....	10	0	10	10	10	....	....	....
	NHL Totals		**571**	**84**	**223**	**307**	**83**	**186**	**269**	**319**	**33**	**1**	**8**	**1522**	**5.5**	**882**	**235**	**767**	**142**		**40**	**4**	**17**	**21**	**18**	**1**	**0**	**0**

OHA Second All-Star Team (1970) • OHA First All-Star Team (1971)

Played in NHL All-Star Game (1974)

Traded to **Buffalo** by **Vancouver** with Bryan McSheffrey for Gerry Meehan and Mike Robitaille, October 14, 1974. Traded to **NY Rangers** by **Buffalo** for future considerations, March 12, 1979.

• GUINDON, BOBBY

Bobby Guindon LW – L. 5'9", 175 lbs. b: Labelle, Que., 11/19/1950. Detroit's 2nd choice, 26th overall, in 1970 Amateur Draft.

Season	Club	League	GP	G	A	Pts	AG	AA	APts	PIM	PP	SH	GW	S	%	TGF	PGF	TGA	PGA	+/-	GP	G	A	Pts	PIM	PP	SH	GW
1967-68	St. Jerome Alouettes	QJHL	....	25	35	60	....	....	....	....	....	....	....	....	....	....	....	....	....	....	....	....	....	....	....	....	....	....
1968-69	Montreal Jr. Canadiens	OHA	54	38	40	78	....	....	....	29	....	....	....	....	....	....	....	....	....	....	14	3	6	9	10	....	....	....
1969-70	Montreal Jr. Canadiens	OHA	53	43	51	94	....	....	....	62	....	....	....	....	....	....	....	....	....	....	....	....	....	....	....	....	....	....
1970-71	Fort Worth Wings	CHL	61	12	13	25	....	....	....	15	....	....	....	....	....	....	....	....	....	....	4	0	0	0	7	....	....	....
1971-72	Fort Worth Wings	CHL	72	22	26	48	....	....	....	36	....	....	....	....	....	....	....	....	....	....	7	2	6	8	14	....	....	....
1972-73	Quebec Nordiques	WHA	71	28	28	56	....	....	....	31	....	....	....	....	....	....	....	....	....	....	....	....	....	....	....	....	....	....
1973-74	Quebec Nordiques	WHA	77	31	39	70	....	....	....	30	....	....	....	....	....	....	....	....	....	....	....	....	....	....	....	....	....	....
1974-75	Quebec Nordiques	WHA	69	12	18	30	....	....	....	23	....	....	....	....	....	....	....	....	....	....	15	7	6	13	10	....	....	....
1975-76	Winnipeg Jets	WHA	29	3	3	6	....	....	....	14	....	....	....	....	....	....	....	....	....	....	13	3	3	6	9	....	....	....
1976-77	Winnipeg Jets	WHA	69	10	17	27	....	....	....	19	....	....	....	....	....	....	....	....	....	....	20	4	4	8	9	....	....	....
1977-78	Winnipeg Jets	WHA	77	20	22	42	....	....	....	18	....	....	....	....	....	....	....	....	....	....	9	8	5	13	5	....	....	....
1978-79	Winnipeg Jets	WHA	71	8	18	26	....	....	....	21	....	....	....	....	....	....	....	....	....	....	7	2	1	3	0	....	....	....
1979-80	**Winnipeg Jets**	**NHL**	**6**	**0**	**1**	**1**	**0**	**1**	**1**	**0**	**0**	**0**	**0**	**10**	**0.0**	**4**	**0**	**2**	**0**	**+2**	....	....	....	....	....	....	....	....
	Tulsa Oilers	CHL	36	11	18	29	....	....	....	10	....	....	....	....	....	....	....	....	....	....	....	....	....	....	....	....	....	....
1980-81	Tulsa Oilers	CHL	25	7	2	9	....	....	....	27	....	....	....	....	....	....	....	....	....	....	....	....	....	....	....	....	....	....
	NHL Totals		**6**	**0**	**1**	**1**	**0**	**1**	**1**	**0**	**0**	**0**	**0**	**10**	**0.0**	**4**	**0**	**2**	**0**		....	....	....	....	....	....	....	....
	Other Major League Totals		463	112	145	257	....	....	....	156	....	....	....	....	....	....	....	....	....		64	24	19	43	33	....	....	....

OHA Second All-Star Team (1970) • Won WHA Playoff MVP Trophy (1978)

Selected by **Quebec** (WHA) in 1972 WHA General Player Draft, February 13, 1972. Signed as a free agent by **Winnipeg** (WHA), November, 1975. Rights retained by **Winnipeg** prior to NHL Expansion Draft, June 9, 1979.

• GUOLLA, STEPHEN

Stephen Guolla LW – L. 6', 180 lbs. b: Scarborough, Ont., 3/15/1973. Ottawa's 1st choice, 3rd overall, in 1994 Supplemental Draft.

Season	Club	League	GP	G	A	Pts	AG	AA	APts	PIM	PP	SH	GW	S	%	TGF	PGF	TGA	PGA	+/-	GP	G	A	Pts	PIM	PP	SH	GW
1991-92	Michigan State Spartans	CCHA	33	4	9	13	....	....	....	8	....	....	....	....	....	....	....	....	....	....	....	....	....	....	....	....	....	....
1992-93	Michigan State Spartans	CCHA	39	19	35	54	....	....	....	6	....	....	....	....	....	....	....	....	....	....	....	....	....	....	....	....	....	....
1993-94	Michigan State Spartans	CCHA	41	23	46	69	....	....	....	16	....	....	....	....	....	....	....	....	....	....	....	....	....	....	....	....	....	....
1994-95	Michigan State Spartans	CCHA	40	16	35	51	....	....	....	16	....	....	....	....	....	....	....	....	....	....	....	....	....	....	....	....	....	....
1995-96	P.E.I. Senators	AHL	72	32	48	80	....	....	....	28	....	....	....	....	....	....	....	....	....	....	3	0	0	0	0	....	....	....
1996-97	**San Jose Sharks**	**NHL**	**43**	**13**	**8**	**21**	**14**	**7**	**21**	**14**	**2**	**0**	**1**	**81**	**16.0**	**35**	**7**	**40**	**2**	**–10**	....	....	....	....	....	....	....	....
	Kentucky Thoroughblades	AHL	34	22	22	44	....	....	....	10	....	....	....	....	....	....	....	....	....	....	4	2	1	3	0	....	....	....
1997-98	**San Jose Sharks**	**NHL**	**7**	**1**	**1**	**2**	**1**	**1**	**2**	**0**	**0**	**0**	**0**	**9**	**11.1**	**4**	**3**	**3**	**0**	**–2**	....	....	....	....	....	....	....	....
	Kentucky Thoroughblades	AHL	69	37	63	100	....	....	....	45	....	....	....	....	....	....	....	....	....	....	3	0	0	0	0	....	....	....
	NHL Totals		**50**	**14**	**9**	**23**	**15**	**8**	**23**	**14**	**2**	**0**	**1**	**90**	**15.6**	**39**	**10**	**43**	**2**		....	....	....	....	....	....	....	....

CCHA Second All-Star Team (1994) • NCAA West Second All-American Team (1994) • AHL Second All-Star Team (1998) • Won Les Cunningham Plaque (MVP - AHL) (1998)

Signed as a free agent by **San Jose**, August 22, 1996.

• GUSAROV, ALEXEI

Alexei Gusarov D – L. 6'3", 185 lbs. b: Leningrad, USSR, 7/8/1964. Quebec's 11th choice, 213th overall, in 1988 Entry Draft.

Season	Club	League	GP	G	A	Pts	AG	AA	APts	PIM	PP	SH	GW	S	%	TGF	PGF	TGA	PGA	+/-	GP	G	A	Pts	PIM	PP	SH	GW
1981-82	SKA Leningrad	USSR	20	1	2	3	....	....	....	16	....	....	....	....	....	....	....	....	....	....	....	....	....	....	....	....	....	....
1982-83	SKA Leningrad	USSR	42	2	1	3	....	....	....	32	....	....	....	....	....	....	....	....	....	....	....	....	....	....	....	....	....	....
1983-84	SKA Leningrad	USSR	43	2	3	5	....	....	....	32	....	....	....	....	....	....	....	....	....	....	....	....	....	....	....	....	....	....
	Soviet Union	WJC-A	7	4	5	9	....	....	....	8	....	....	....	....	....	....	....	....	....	....	....	....	....	....	....	....	....	....
1984-85	Soviet Union	C Cup	2	0	0	0	....	....	....	4	....	....	....	....	....	....	....	....	....	....	....	....	....	....	....	....	....	....
	CSKA Moscow	USSR	36	3	2	5	....	....	....	26	....	....	....	....	....	....	....	....	....	....	....	....	....	....	....	....	....	....
	Soviet Union	WEC-A	10	2	1	3	....	....	....	6	....	....	....	....	....	....	....	....	....	....	....	....	....	....	....	....	....	....
1985-86	CSKA Moscow	USSR	40	3	5	8	....	....	....	30	....	....	....	....	....	....	....	....	....	....	....	....	....	....	....	....	....	....
	CSKA Moscow	SuperS	6	1	3	4	....	....	....	4	....	....	....	....	....	....	....	....	....	....	....	....	....	....	....	....	....	....
	Soviet Union	WEC-A	9	1	2	3	....	....	....	8	....	....	....	....	....	....	....	....	....	....	....	....	....	....	....	....	....	....
1986-87	CSKA Moscow	USSR	38	4	7	11	....	....	....	24	....	....	....	....	....	....	....	....	....	....	....	....	....	....	....	....	....	....
	USSR	RV'87	2	0	0	0	....	....	....	0	....	....	....	....	....	....	....	....	....	....	....	....	....	....	....	....	....	....
	Soviet Union	WEC-A	10	1	2	3	....	....	....	8	....	....	....	....	....	....	....	....	....	....	....	....	....	....	....	....	....	....
1987-88	Soviet Union	C Cup	6	1	1	2	....	....	....	6	....	....	....	....	....	....	....	....	....	....	....	....	....	....	....	....	....	....
	CSKA Moscow	USSR	39	3	2	5	....	....	....	28	....	....	....	....	....	....	....	....	....	....	....	....	....	....	....	....	....	....
	Soviet Union	Olympics	8	1	3	4	....	....	....	6	....	....	....	....	....	....	....	....	....	....	....	....	....	....	....	....	....	....
1988-89	CSKA Moscow	USSR	42	5	4	9	....	....	....	37	....	....	....	....	....	....	....	....	....	....	....	....	....	....	....	....	....	....
	CSKA Moscow	SuperS	7	1	3	4	....	....	....	0	....	....	....	....	....	....	....	....	....	....	....	....	....	....	....	....	....	....
	Soviet Union	WEC-A	9	2	1	3	....	....	....	2	....	....	....	....	....	....	....	....	....	....	....	....	....	....	....	....	....	....
1989-90	CSKA Moscow	FrTour	1	0	0	0	....	....	....	2	....	....	....	....	....	....	....	....	....	....	....	....	....	....	....	....	....	....
	CSKA Moscow	USSR	42	4	7	11	....	....	....	42	....	....	....	....	....	....	....	....	....	....	....	....	....	....	....	....	....	....
	CSKA Moscow	SuperS	2	1	1	2	....	....	....	15	....	....	....	....	....	....	....	....	....	....	....	....	....	....	....	....	....	....
	Soviet Union	WEC-A	10	1	3	4	....	....	....	6	....	....	....	....	....	....	....	....	....	....	....	....	....	....	....	....	....	....
1990-91	CSKA Moscow	FrTour	1	0	0	0	....	....	....	0	....	....	....	....	....	....	....	....	....	....	....	....	....	....	....	....	....	....
	CSKA Moscow	USSR	15	0	0	0	....	....	....	12	....	....	....	....	....	....	....	....	....	....	....	....	....	....	....	....	....	....
	Quebec Nordiques	**NHL**	**36**	**3**	**9**	**12**	**3**	**7**	**10**	**12**	**1**	**0**	**0**	**36**	**8.3**	**37**	**6**	**48**	**13**	**–4**	....	....	....	....	....	....	....	....
	Halifax Citadels	AHL	2	0	3	3	....	....	....	2	....	....	....	....	....	....	....	....	....	....	....	....	....	....	....	....	....	....
	Soviet Union	WEC-A	10	1	4	5	....	....	....	2	....	....	....	....	....	....	....	....	....	....	....	....	....	....	....	....	....	....
1991-92	Soviet Union	C Cup	5	0	2	2	....	....	....	0	....	....	....	....	....	....	....	....	....	....	....	....	....	....	....	....	....	....
	Quebec Nordiques	**NHL**	**68**	**5**	**18**	**23**	**5**	**14**	**19**	**22**	**3**	**0**	**1**	**66**	**7.6**	**79**	**16**	**112**	**40**	**–9**	....	....	....	....	....	....	....	....
	Halifax Citadels	AHL	3	0	0	0	....	....	....	0	....	....	....	....	....	....	....	....	....	....	....	....	....	....	....	....	....	....
1992-93	**Quebec Nordiques**	**NHL**	**79**	**8**	**22**	**30**	**7**	**15**	**22**	**57**	**0**	**2**	**1**	**60**	**13.3**	**88**	**2**	**105**	**37**	**+18**	**5**	**0**	**1**	**1**	**0**	**0**	**0**	**0**
1993-94	**Quebec Nordiques**	**NHL**	**76**	**5**	**20**	**25**	**5**	**15**	**20**	**38**	**0**	**1**	**0**	**84**	**6.0**	**87**	**15**	**112**	**43**	**+3**	....	....	....	....	....	....	....	....

Season	Club	League	REGULAR SEASON																		PLAYOFFS							
			GP	G	A	Pts	AG	AA	APts	PIM	PP	SH	GW	S	%	TGF	PGF	TGA	PGA	+/–	GP	G	A	Pts	PIM	PP	SH	GW
1994-95	**Quebec Nordiques**	**NHL**	**14**	**1**	**2**	**3**	**2**	**3**	**5**	**6**	**0**	**0**	**1**	**7**	**14.3**	**11**	**0**	**12**	**0**	**–1**								
1995-96	**Colorado Avalanche**	**NHL**	**65**	**5**	**15**	**20**	**5**	**12**	**17**	**56**	**0**	**0**	**0**	**42**	**11.9**	**72**	**9**	**63**	**29**	**+29**	**21**	**0**	**9**	**9**	**12**	**0**	**0**	**0**
1996-97	**Colorado Avalanche**	**NHL**	**58**	**2**	**12**	**14**	**2**	**11**	**13**	**28**	**0**	**0**	**0**	**33**	**6.1**	**52**	**3**	**63**	**18**	**+4**	**17**	**0**	**3**	**3**	**14**	**0**	**0**	**0**
1997-98	**Colorado Avalanche**	**NHL**	**72**	**4**	**10**	**14**	**5**	**10**	**15**	**42**	**0**	**1**	**1**	**47**	**8.5**	**54**	**2**	**69**	**26**	**+9**	**7**	**0**	**1**	**1**	**6**	**0**	**0**	**0**
	Russia	Olympics	6	0	1	1				8																		
	NHL Totals		**468**	**33**	**108**	**141**	**34**	**87**	**121**	**261**	**4**	**4**	**4**	**375**	**8.8**	**480**	**53**	**581**	**206**		**50**	**0**	**14**	**14**	**32**	**0**	**0**	**0**

EJC-A All-Star Team (1982) • Named Best Defenseman at EJC-A (1982) • WJC-A All-Star Team (1984) • Named Best Defenseman at WJC-A (1984)

Transferred to **Colorado** after **Quebec** franchise relocated, June 21, 1995.

• GUSEV, SERGEI

Sergei Gusev D – L. 6'1", 195 lbs. b: Nizhny Tagil, USSR, 7/31/1975. Dallas' 4th choice, 69th overall, in 1995 Entry Draft.

Season	Club	League	GP	G	A	Pts	AG	AA	APts	PIM	PP	SH	GW	S	%	TGF	PGF	TGA	PGA	+/–	GP	G	A	Pts	PIM	PP	SH	GW
1994-95	CSK Samara	CIS	50	3	5	8				58																		
1995-96	Michigan K-Wings	IHL	73	11	17	28				76																		
1996-97	Michigan K-Wings	IHL	51	7	8	15				44											4	0	4	4	6			
1997-98	**Dallas Stars**	**NHL**	**9**	**0**	**0**	**0**	**0**	**0**	**0**	**2**	**0**	**0**	**0**	**5**	**0.0**	**1**	**1**	**5**	**0**	**–5**								
	Michigan K-Wings	IHL	36	3	6	9				36											4	0	2	2	6			
	NHL Totals		**9**	**0**	**0**	**0**	**0**	**0**	**0**	**2**	**0**	**0**	**0**	**5**	**0.0**	**1**	**1**	**5**	**0**									

• GUSMANOV, RAVIL

Ravil Gusmanov LW – L. 6'3", 185 lbs. b: Naberezhnye Chelny, USSR, 7/25/1972. Winnipeg's 5th choice, 93rd overall, in 1993 Entry Draft.

Season	Club	League	GP	G	A	Pts	AG	AA	APts	PIM	PP	SH	GW	S	%	TGF	PGF	TGA	PGA	+/–	GP	G	A	Pts	PIM	PP	SH	GW
1990-91	Traktor Chelyabinsk	USSR	15	0	0	0				10																		
1991-92	Traktor Chelyabinsk	CIS	38	4	4	8				20																		
	Russia	WJC-A	7	1	1	2				0																		
1992-93	Traktor Chelyabinsk	CIS	39	15	8	23				30											8	4	0	4	2			
1993-94	Traktor Chelyabinsk	CIS	43	18	9	27				51											6	4	3	7	10			
	Russia	Olympics	8	3	1	4				0																		
1994-95	Springfield Falcons	AHL	72	18	15	33				14																		
1995-96	**Winnipeg Jets**	**NHL**	**4**	**0**	**0**	**0**	**0**	**0**	**0**	**0**	**0**	**0**	**0**	**6**	**0.0**	**0**	**0**	**3**	**0**	**–3**								
	Springfield Falcons	AHL	60	36	32	68				20																		
	Indianapolis Ice	IHL	11	6	10	16				4											5	2	3	5	4			
1996-97	Indianapolis Ice	IHL	60	21	27	48				14																		
	Saint John Flames	AHL	12	4	4	8				2											3	0	1	1	2			
1997-98	Chicago Wolves	IHL	56	27	28	55				26											11	1	3	4	19			
	NHL Totals		**4**	**0**	**0**	**0**	**0**	**0**	**0**	**0**	**0**	**0**	**0**	**6**	**0.0**	**0**	**0**	**3**	**0**									

Traded to **Chicago** by **Winnipeg** for Chicago's 4th round choice (later traded to Toronto — Toronto selected Vladimir Antipov) in 1996 Entry Draft, March 20, 1996. Traded to **Calgary** by **Chicago** for Marc Hussey, March 18, 1997.

• GUSTAFSSON, BENGT

Bengt Gustafsson RW – L. 6', 185 lbs. b: Karlskoga, Sweden, 3/23/1958. Washington's 7th choice, 55th overall, in 1978 Amateur Draft.

Season	Club	League	GP	G	A	Pts	AG	AA	APts	PIM	PP	SH	GW	S	%	TGF	PGF	TGA	PGA	+/–	GP	G	A	Pts	PIM	PP	SH	GW
1977-78	Farjestad BK Karlstad	Sweden	32	15	10	25				10											7	2	6	8	10			
	Sweden	WJC-A	7	2	6	8				10																		
1978-79	Farjestad BK Karlstad	Sweden	32	13	11	24				10											3	2	0	2	4			
	Sweden	WEC-A	8	4	2	6				0																		
	Edmonton Oilers	WHA																			2	1	2	3	0			
1979-80	**Washington Capitals**	**NHL**	**80**	**22**	**38**	**60**	**20**	**29**	**49**	**17**	**6**	**1**	**3**	**185**	**11.9**	**91**	**39**	**89**	**20**	**–17**								
1980-81	**Washington Capitals**	**NHL**	**72**	**21**	**34**	**55**	**17**	**24**	**41**	**26**	**4**	**2**	**1**	**170**	**12.4**	**89**	**31**	**61**	**14**	**+11**								
	Sweden	WEC-A	6	3	1	4				8																		
1981-82	**Washington Capitals**	**NHL**	**70**	**26**	**34**	**60**	**21**	**22**	**43**	**40**	**3**	**0**	**2**	**142**	**18.3**	**87**	**29**	**84**	**6**	**–20**								
1982-83	**Washington Capitals**	**NHL**	**67**	**22**	**42**	**64**	**18**	**29**	**47**	**16**	**2**	**0**	**4**	**139**	**15.8**	**90**	**38**	**47**	**4**	**+9**	**4**	**0**	**1**	**1**	**4**	**0**	**0**	**0**
	Sweden	WEC-A	10	2	7	9				6																		
1983-84	**Washington Capitals**	**NHL**	**69**	**32**	**43**	**75**	**26**	**29**	**55**	**16**	**8**	**0**	**5**	**146**	**21.9**	**100**	**33**	**38**	**0**	**+29**	**5**	**2**	**3**	**5**	**0**	**2**	**0**	**0**
1984-85	Sweden	C Cup	5	1	0	4				2																		
	Washington Capitals	**NHL**	**51**	**14**	**29**	**43**	**11**	**20**	**31**	**8**	**6**	**1**	**3**	**98**	**14.3**	**58**	**20**	**32**	**7**	**+13**	**5**	**1**	**3**	**4**	**0**	**1**	**0**	**0**
1985-86	**Washington Capitals**	**NHL**	**70**	**23**	**52**	**75**	**18**	**35**	**53**	**26**	**8**	**4**	**6**	**113**	**20.4**	**111**	**51**	**72**	**21**	**–9**								
1986-87	Bofors IK	Sweden	28	16	26	42				22																		
	Sweden	WEC-A	10	3	8	11				4																		
1987-88	Sweden	C Cup	6	3	0	3				4																		
	Washington Capitals	**NHL**	**78**	**18**	**36**	**54**	**15**	**26**	**41**	**29**	**7**	**5**	**3**	**136**	**13.2**	**99**	**48**	**84**	**35**	**+2**	**14**	**4**	**9**	**13**	**6**	**2**	**0**	**1**
1988-89	**Washington Capitals**	**NHL**	**72**	**18**	**51**	**69**	**15**	**36**	**51**	**18**	**5**	**4**	**6**	**107**	**16.8**	**96**	**36**	**78**	**31**	**+13**	**4**	**2**	**3**	**5**	**6**	**1**	**0**	**0**
1989-90	Farjestad BK Karlstad	Sweden	37	22	24	46				14											10	4	*10	*14	18			
1990-91	Farjestad BK Karlstad	Sweden	37	9	21	30				6											8	3	6	9	2			
	Sweden	WEC-A	10	0	5	5				6																		
1991-92	Farjestad BK Karlstad	Sweden	35	12	20	32				30											6	2	5	7	2			
	Sweden	Olympics	8	0	1	1				0																		
1992-93	Farjestad BK Karlstad	Sweden	40	17	14	31				32											3	0	1	1	2			
1993-94	VEU Feldkirch	Austria	54	20	43	63				24																		
1994-95	VEU Feldkirch	Austria	41	21	42	63				22											13	9	13	22	2			
1995-96	VEU Feldkirch	Austria	36	20	46	66				12											4	1	5	6	2			
1996-97	VEU Feldkirch	Austria	52	24	54	78				10																		
	NHL Totals		**629**	**196**	**359**	**555**	**161**	**250**	**411**	**196**	**49**	**17**	**33**	**1236**	**15.9**	**821**	**325**	**585**	**138**		**32**	**9**	**19**	**28**	**16**	**6**	**0**	**1**
	Other Major League Totals		0	0	0	0				0											2	1	2	3	0			

WJC-A All-Star Team (1977) • Swedish World All-Star Team (1983, 1987)

Signed as a free agent by **Edmonton** (WHA), March, 1979. Claimed by **Washington** from **Edmonton** prior to Expansion Draft, June 9, 1979.

• GUSTAFSSON, PER

Per Gustafsson D – L. 6'2", 190 lbs. b: Osterham, Sweden, 6/6/1970. Florida's 10th choice, 261st overall, in 1994 Entry Draft.

Season	Club	League	GP	G	A	Pts	AG	AA	APts	PIM	PP	SH	GW	S	%	TGF	PGF	TGA	PGA	+/–	GP	G	A	Pts	PIM	PP	SH	GW
1993-94	HV 71 Jonkoping	Sweden	34	9	7	16				10																		
1994-95	HV 71 Jonkoping	Sweden	38	10	6	16				14											13	7	5	12	8			
1995-96	HV 71 Jonkoping	Sweden	34	8	13	21				12											4	3	1	4	2			
	Sweden	WC-A	6	2	2	4				2																		
1996-97	**Florida Panthers**	**NHL**	**58**	**7**	**22**	**29**	**7**	**19**	**26**	**22**	**2**	**0**	**1**	**105**	**6.7**	**66**	**20**	**30**	**5**	**+11**								
	Sweden	WJC-A	0	0	0	0				0																		
1997-98	**Toronto Maple Leafs**	**NHL**	**22**	**1**	**4**	**5**	**1**	**4**	**5**	**10**	**0**	**0**	**0**	**24**	**4.2**	**15**	**5**	**15**	**0**	**–5**								
	St. John's Maple Leafs	AHL	25	7	18	25				10																		
	Ottawa Senators	**NHL**	**9**	**0**	**1**	**1**	**0**	**1**	**1**	**6**	**0**	**0**	**0**	**12**	**0.0**	**7**	**2**	**2**	**0**	**+3**	**1**	**0**	**0**	**0**	**0**	**0**	**0**	**0**
	NHL Totals		**89**	**8**	**27**	**35**	**8**	**24**	**32**	**38**	**2**	**0**	**1**	**141**	**5.7**	**87**	**30**	**53**	**5**		**1**	**0**	**0**	**0**	**0**	**0**	**0**	**0**

Swedish World All-Star Team (1996)

Traded to **Toronto** by **Florida** for Mike Lankshear, June 13, 1997. Traded to **Ottawa** by **Toronto** for Ottawa's 8th round choice (Dwight Wolfe) in 1998 Entry Draft, March 17, 1998.

• GUSTAVSSON, PETER

Peter Gustavsson LW – L. 6'1", 188 lbs. b: Bollebydg, Sweden, 3/30/1958.

Season	Club	League	GP	G	A	Pts	AG	AA	APts	PIM	PP	SH	GW	S	%	TGF	PGF	TGA	PGA	+/–	GP	G	A	Pts	PIM	PP	SH	GW
1977-78	Vastra Frolunda	Sweden	16	1	5	6				0																		
1978-79	Vastra Frolunda	Sweden	35	2	1	3				4																		
1979-80	Vastra Frolunda	Sweden	36	14	8	22				12											8	2	1	3	0			
1980-81	Vastra Frolunda	Sweden	31	13	15	28				19											2	0	1	1	4			
1981-82	**Colorado Rockies**	**NHL**	**2**	**0**	**0**	**0**	**0**	**0**	**0**	**0**	**0**	**0**	**0**	**2**	**0.0**	**0**	**0**	**1**	**0**	**–1**								
	Fort Worth Texans	CHL	59	8	11	19				4																		
1982-83	Vastra Frolunda	Sweden	36	15	13	28				26																		
1983-84	Vastra Frolunda	Sweden	35	13	13	26				8																		
	NHL Totals		**2**	**0**	**0**	**0**	**0**	**0**	**0**	**0**	**0**	**0**	**0**	**2**	**0.0**	**0**	**0**	**1**	**0**									

Signed as a free agent by **Colorado**, May 11, 1981.

● **GUY, KEVAN** Kevan Guy D – R. 6'3", 202 lbs. b: Edmonton, Alta., 7/16/1965. Calgary's 5th choice, 73rd overall, in 1983 Entry Draft.

			REGULAR SEASON																		PLAYOFFS							
Season	Club	League	GP	G	A	Pts	AG	AA	APts	PIM	PP	SH	GW	S	%	TGF	PGF	TGA	PGA	+/–	GP	G	A	Pts	PIM	PP	SH	GW
1982-83	Medicine Hat Tigers	WHL	69	7	20	27	....	....	....	89	....	....	....	....	....	....	....	....	....	....	5	0	3	3	16	....	....	....
1983-84	Medicine Hat Tigers	WHL	72	15	42	57	....	....	....	117	....	....	....	....	....	....	....	....	....	....	14	3	4	7	14	....	....	....
1984-85	Medicine Hat Tigers	WHL	31	7	17	24	....	....	....	46	....	....	....	....	....	....	....	....	....	....	10	1	2	3	2	....	....	....
1985-86	Moncton Golden Flames	AHL	73	4	20	24	....	....	....	56	....	....	....	....	....	....	....	....	....	....	10	0	2	2	6	....	....	....
1986-87	**Calgary Flames**	**NHL**	**24**	**0**	**4**	**4**	**0**	**3**	**3**	**19**	**0**	**0**	**0**	**24**	**0.0**	**19**	**0**	**16**	**5**	**+8**	**4**	**0**	**1**	**1**	**23**	**0**	**0**	**0**
	Moncton Golden Flames	AHL	46	2	10	12	....	....	....	38	....	....	....	....	....	....	....	....	....	....	....	....	....	....	....	....	....	....
1987-88	**Calgary Flames**	**NHL**	**11**	**0**	**3**	**3**	**0**	**2**	**2**	**8**	**0**	**0**	**0**	**4**	**0.0**	**12**	**0**	**14**	**3**	**+1**	....	....	....	....	....	....	....	....
	Salt Lake Golden Eagles	IHL	61	6	30	36	....	....	....	51	....	....	....	....	....	....	....	....	....	....	19	1	6	7	26	....	....	....
1988-89	**Vancouver Canucks**	**NHL**	**45**	**2**	**2**	**4**	**2**	**1**	**3**	**34**	**0**	**0**	**0**	**40**	**5.0**	**19**	**2**	**34**	**3**	**–14**	**1**	**0**	**0**	**0**	**0**	**0**	**0**	**0**
1989-90	**Vancouver Canucks**	**NHL**	**30**	**2**	**5**	**7**	**2**	**4**	**6**	**32**	**0**	**0**	**0**	**44**	**4.5**	**14**	**3**	**27**	**4**	**–12**	....	....	....	....	....	....	....	....
	Milwaukee Admirals	IHL	29	2	11	13	....	....	....	33	....	....	....	....	....	....	....	....	....	....	....	....	....	....	....	....	....	....
1990-91	**Vancouver Canucks**	**NHL**	**39**	**1**	**6**	**7**	**1**	**5**	**6**	**39**	**0**	**0**	**1**	**37**	**2.7**	**30**	**0**	**46**	**10**	**–6**	....	....	....	....	....	....	....	....
	Calgary Flames	**NHL**	**4**	**0**	**0**	**0**	**0**	**0**	**0**	**4**	**0**	**0**	**0**	**6**	**0.0**	**5**	**0**	**6**	**2**	**+1**	....	....	....	....	....	....	....	....
1991-92	**Calgary Flames**	**NHL**	**3**	**0**	**0**	**0**	**0**	**0**	**0**	**2**	**0**	**0**	**0**	**3**	**0.0**	**3**	**0**	**2**	**1**	**+2**	....	....	....	....	....	....	....	....
	Salt Lake Golden Eagles	IHL	60	3	14	17	....	....	....	89	....	....	....	....	....	....	....	....	....	....	5	0	1	1	4	....	....	....
1992-93	HC Graz	Austria	22	1	6	7	....	....	....	....	....	....	....	....	....	....	....	....	....	....	....	....	....	....	....	....	....	....
	Salt Lake Golden Eagles	IHL	33	1	9	10	....	....	....	50	....	....	....	....	....	....	....	....	....	....	....	....	....	....	....	....	....	....
1993-94	Salt Lake Golden Eagles	IHL	62	4	17	21	....	....	....	45	....	....	....	....	....	....	....	....	....	....	....	....	....	....	....	....	....	....
1994-95	Tallahassee Tiger Sharks	ECHL	6	0	5	5	....	....	....	0	....	....	....	....	....	....	....	....	....	....	....	....	....	....	....	....	....	....
	Denver Grizzlies	IHL	3	0	1	1	....	....	....	0	....	....	....	....	....	....	....	....	....	....	....	....	....	....	....	....	....	....
	NHL Totals		**156**	**5**	**20**	**25**	**5**	**15**	**20**	**138**	**0**	**0**	**1**	**158**	**3.2**	**102**	**5**	**145**	**28**		**5**	**0**	**1**	**1**	**23**	**0**	**0**	**0**

Traded to **Vancouver** by **Calgary** with Brian Bradley and Peter Bakovic for Craig Coxe, March 6, 1988. Traded to **Calgary** by **Vancouver** with Ron Stern and future considerations, March 5, 1991. Signed as a free agent by **NY Islanders**, September 18, 1993.

● **HAANPAA, ARI** Ari Haanpaa RW – R. 6'1", 185 lbs. b: Nokla, Finland, 11/28/1965. NY Islanders' 5th choice, 83rd overall, in 1984 Entry Draft.

Season	Club	League	GP	G	A	Pts	AG	AA	APts	PIM	PP	SH	GW	S	%	TGF	PGF	TGA	PGA	+/–	GP	G	A	Pts	PIM	PP	SH	GW
1983-84	Ilves Tampere	Finland	27	0	1	1	....	....	....	8	....	....	....	....	....	....	....	....	....	....	2	0	0	0	2	....	....	....
	Finland	WJC-A	7	5	3	8	....	....	....	8	....	....	....	....	....	....	....	....	....	....	....	....	....	....	....	....	....	....
1984-85	Ilves Tampere	Finland	13	5	0	5	....	....	....	2	....	....	....	....	....	....	....	....	....	....	9	3	1	4	0	....	....	....
	Finland	WJC-A	7	6	1	7	....	....	....	4	....	....	....	....	....	....	....	....	....	....	....	....	....	....	....	....	....	....
1985-86	**New York Islanders**	**NHL**	**18**	**0**	**7**	**7**	**0**	**5**	**5**	**20**	**0**	**0**	**0**	**16**	**0.0**	**8**	**0**	**8**	**0**	**0**	....	....	....	....	....	....	....	....
	Springfield Indians	AHL	20	3	1	4	....	....	....	13	....	....	....	....	....	....	....	....	....	....	....	....	....	....	....	....	....	....
1986-87	**New York Islanders**	**NHL**	**41**	**6**	**4**	**10**	**5**	**3**	**8**	**17**	**0**	**0**	**3**	**45**	**13.3**	**23**	**1**	**14**	**0**	**+8**	**6**	**0**	**0**	**0**	**10**	**0**	**0**	**0**
1987-88	**New York Islanders**	**NHL**	**1**	**0**	**0**	**0**	**0**	**0**	**0**	**0**	**0**	**0**	**0**	**0**	**0.0**	**0**	**0**	**2**	**0**	**–2**	....	....	....	....	....	....	....	....
	Springfield Indians	AHL	61	14	19	33	....	....	....	34	....	....	....	....	....	....	....	....	....	....	....	....	....	....	....	....	....	....
1988-89	Lukko Rauma	Finland	42	28	19	47	....	....	....	36	....	....	....	....	....	....	....	....	....	....	....	....	....	....	....	....	....	....
1989-90	Lukko Rauma	Finland	24	17	9	26	....	....	....	59	....	....	....	....	....	....	....	....	....	....	....	....	....	....	....	....	....	....
1990-91	JYP HT Jyvaskyla	Finland	32	28	17	45	....	....	....	100	....	....	....	....	....	....	....	....	....	....	5	3	1	4	8	....	....	....
1991-92	JYP HT Jyvaskyla	Finland	41	21	20	41	....	....	....	70	....	....	....	....	....	....	....	....	....	....	10	6	2	8	8	....	....	....
1992-93	JYP HT Jyvaskyla	Finland	44	15	11	26	....	....	....	89	....	....	....	....	....	....	....	....	....	....	9	1	2	3	4	....	....	....
1993-94	Tappara Tampere	Finland	42	21	13	34	....	....	....	72	....	....	....	....	....	....	....	....	....	....	10	3	6	9	6	....	....	....
1994-95	Tappara Tampere	Finland	48	12	12	24	....	....	....	67	....	....	....	....	....	....	....	....	....	....	....	....	....	....	....	....	....	....
1995-96	Tappara Tampere	Finland	45	13	16	29	....	....	....	60	....	....	....	....	....	....	....	....	....	....	4	3	0	3	8	....	....	....
1996-97	WEV Wein	Austria	29	15	13	28	....	....	....	39	....	....	....	....	....	....	....	....	....	....	....	....	....	....	....	....	....	....
	NHL Totals		**60**	**6**	**11**	**17**	**5**	**8**	**13**	**37**	**0**	**0**	**3**	**61**	**9.8**	**31**	**1**	**24**	**0**		**6**	**0**	**0**	**0**	**10**	**0**	**0**	**0**

Finnish First All-Star Team (1991)

● **HAAS, DAVID** David Haas LW – L. 6'2", 200 lbs. b: Toronto, Ont., 6/23/1968. Edmonton's 5th choice, 105th overall, in 1986 Entry Draft.

Season	Club	League	GP	G	A	Pts	AG	AA	APts	PIM	PP	SH	GW	S	%	TGF	PGF	TGA	PGA	+/–	GP	G	A	Pts	PIM	PP	SH	GW
1984-85	Don Mills Flyers	Midget	38	38	38	76	....	....	....	80	....	....	....	....	....	....	....	....	....	....	....	....	....	....	....	....	....	....
1985-86	London Knights	OHL	62	4	13	17	....	....	....	91	....	....	....	....	....	....	....	....	....	....	5	0	1	1	0	....	....	....
1986-87	London Knights	OHL	5	1	0	1	....	....	....	5	....	....	....	....	....	....	....	....	....	....	....	....	....	....	....	....	....	....
	Kitchener Rangers	OHL	4	0	1	1	....	....	....	4	....	....	....	....	....	....	....	....	....	....	....	....	....	....	....	....	....	....
	Belleville Bulls	OHL	55	10	13	23	....	....	....	86	....	....	....	....	....	....	....	....	....	....	6	3	0	3	13	....	....	....
1987-88	Belleville Bulls	OHL	5	1	1	2	....	....	....	9	....	....	....	....	....	....	....	....	....	....	....	....	....	....	....	....	....	....
	Windsor Spitfires	OHL	58	59	46	105	....	....	....	237	....	....	....	....	....	....	....	....	....	....	11	9	11	20	50	....	....	....
1988-89	Cape Breton Oilers	AHL	61	9	9	18	....	....	....	325	....	....	....	....	....	....	....	....	....	....	....	....	....	....	....	....	....	....
1989-90	Cape Breton Oilers	AHL	53	6	12	18	....	....	....	230	....	....	....	....	....	....	....	....	....	....	4	2	2	4	15	....	....	....
1990-91	**Edmonton Oilers**	**NHL**	**5**	**1**	**0**	**1**	**1**	**0**	**1**	**0**	**0**	**0**	**0**	**4**	**25.0**	**1**	**0**	**3**	**0**	**–2**	....	....	....	....	....	....	....	....
	Cape Breton Oilers	AHL	60	24	23	47	....	....	....	137	....	....	....	....	....	....	....	....	....	....	3	0	2	2	12	....	....	....
1991-92	Cape Breton Oilers	AHL	16	3	7	10	....	....	....	32	....	....	....	....	....	....	....	....	....	....	....	....	....	....	....	....	....	....
	New Haven Nighthawks	AHL	50	13	23	36	....	....	....	97	....	....	....	....	....	....	....	....	....	....	5	3	0	3	13	....	....	....
1992-93	Cape Breton Oilers	AHL	73	22	56	78	....	....	....	121	....	....	....	....	....	....	....	....	....	....	16	11	13	24	36	....	....	....
1993-94	**Calgary Flames**	**NHL**	**2**	**1**	**1**	**2**	**1**	**1**	**2**	**7**	**0**	**0**	**0**	**3**	**33.3**	**4**	**0**	**2**	**0**	**+2**	....	....	....	....	....	....	....	....
	Saint John Flames	AHL	37	11	17	28	....	....	....	108	....	....	....	....	....	....	....	....	....	....	....	....	....	....	....	....	....	....
	Phoenix Roadrunners	IHL	11	7	4	11	....	....	....	43	....	....	....	....	....	....	....	....	....	....	....	....	....	....	....	....	....	....
1994-95	Courmaosta	Italy	22	14	20	34	....	....	....	64	....	....	....	....	....	....	....	....	....	....	....	....	....	....	....	....	....	....
	Worcester IceCats	AHL	28	11	10	21	....	....	....	88	....	....	....	....	....	....	....	....	....	....	....	....	....	....	....	....	....	....
	Detroit Vipers	IHL	1	0	1	1	....	....	....	0	....	....	....	....	....	....	....	....	....	....	....	....	....	....	....	....	....	....
1995-96	Olimpija Ljubljana	Slovenia	36	49	26	75	....	....	....	84	....	....	....	....	....	....	....	....	....	....	....	....	....	....	....	....	....	....
1996-97	Milan 24	Italy	10	9	8	17	....	....	....	55	....	....	....	....	....	....	....	....	....	....	....	....	....	....	....	....	....	....
	Olimpija Ljubljania	Slovenia	50	*47	48	*95	....	....	....	....	....	....	....	....	....	....	....	....	....	....	....	....	....	....	....	....	....	....
1997-98	Hannover Scorpions	Germany	48	25	28	53	....	....	....	105	....	....	....	....	....	....	....	....	....	....	4	1	1	2	10	....	....	....
	NHL Totals		**7**	**2**	**1**	**3**	**2**	**1**	**3**	**7**	**0**	**0**	**0**	**7**	**28.6**	**5**	**0**	**5**	**0**		....	....	....	....	....	....	....	....

OHL Second All-Star Team (1988)

Signed as a free agent by **Calgary**, August 10, 1993.

● **HABSCHEID, MARC** Marc Habscheid RW/C – R. 6', 185 lbs. b: Swift Current, Sask., 3/1/1963. Edmonton's 6th choice, 113th overall, in 1981 Entry Draft.

Season	Club	League	GP	G	A	Pts	AG	AA	APts	PIM	PP	SH	GW	S	%	TGF	PGF	TGA	PGA	+/–	GP	G	A	Pts	PIM	PP	SH	GW
1980-81	Saskatoon Blades	WHL	72	34	63	97	....	....	....	50	....	....	....	....	....	....	....	....	....	....	....	....	....	....	....	....	....	....
1981-82	Saskatoon Blades	WHL	55	64	87	151	....	....	....	74	....	....	....	....	....	....	....	....	....	....	5	3	4	7	4	....	....	....
	Canada	WJC-A	7	6	6	12	....	....	....	2	....	....	....	....	....	....	....	....	....	....	....	....	....	....	....	....	....	....
	Edmonton Oilers	**NHL**	**7**	**1**	**3**	**4**	**1**	**2**	**3**	**2**	**1**	**0**	**0**	**7**	**14.3**	**6**	**1**	**0**	**0**	**+5**	....	....	....	....	....	....	....	....
	Wichita Wind	CHL	....	....	....	....	....	....	....	....	....	....	....	....	....	....	....	....	....	....	3	0	0	0	0	....	....	....
1982-83	Kamloops Blazers	WHL	6	7	16	23	....	....	....	8	....	....	....	....	....	....	....	....	....	....	....	....	....	....	....	....	....	....
	Edmonton Oilers	**NHL**	**32**	**3**	**10**	**13**	**2**	**7**	**9**	**14**	**0**	**0**	**0**	**19**	**15.8**	**22**	**2**	**7**	**1**	**+14**	....	....	....	....	....	....	....	....
1983-84	**Edmonton Oilers**	**NHL**	**9**	**1**	**0**	**1**	**1**	**0**	**1**	**6**	**0**	**0**	**0**	**6**	**16.7**	**1**	**0**	**5**	**1**	**–3**	....	....	....	....	....	....	....	....
	Moncton Alpines	AHL	71	19	37	56	....	....	....	32	....	....	....	....	....	....	....	....	....	....	....	....	....	....	....	....	....	....
1984-85	**Edmonton Oilers**	**NHL**	**26**	**5**	**3**	**8**	**4**	**2**	**6**	**4**	**2**	**0**	**0**	**30**	**16.7**	**10**	**3**	**9**	**0**	**–2**	....	....	....	....	....	....	....	....
	Nova Scotia Voyageurs	AHL	48	29	29	58	....	....	....	65	....	....	....	....	....	....	....	....	....	....	6	4	3	7	9	....	....	....
1985-86	**Minnesota North Stars**	**NHL**	**6**	**2**	**3**	**5**	**2**	**2**	**4**	**0**	**1**	**0**	**0**	**8**	**25.0**	**7**	**3**	**6**	**0**	**–2**	**2**	**0**	**0**	**0**	**0**	**0**	**0**	**0**
	Springfield Indians	AHL	41	18	32	50	....	....	....	21	....	....	....	....	....	....	....	....	....	....	....	....	....	....	....	....	....	....
1986-87	Canada	Nat-Team	51	29	32	61	....	....	....	70	....	....	....	....	....	....	....	....	....	....	....	....	....	....	....	....	....	....
	Minnesota North Stars	**NHL**	**15**	**2**	**0**	**2**	**2**	**0**	**2**	**2**	**1**	**0**	**0**	**14**	**14.3**	**3**	**2**	**8**	**1**	**–6**	....	....	....	....	....	....	....	....
1987-88	Canada	Nat-Team	61	19	34	53	....	....	....	42	....	....	....	....	....	....	....	....	....	....	....	....	....	....	....	....	....	....
	Canada	Olympics	8	5	3	8	....	....	....	6	....	....	....	....	....	....	....	....	....	....	....	....	....	....	....	....	....	....
	Minnesota North Stars	**NHL**	**16**	**4**	**11**	**15**	**3**	**8**	**11**	**6**	**3**	**0**	**0**	**44**	**9.1**	**20**	**8**	**21**	**5**	**–4**	....	....	....	....	....	....	....	....
1988-89	**Minnesota North Stars**	**NHL**	**76**	**23**	**31**	**54**	**20**	**22**	**42**	**40**	**7**	**3**	**3**	**182**	**12.6**	**83**	**37**	**85**	**41**	**+2**	**5**	**1**	**3**	**4**	**13**	**0**	**0**	**0**
1989-90	**Detroit Red Wings**	**NHL**	**66**	**15**	**11**	**26**	**13**	**8**	**21**	**33**	**0**	**0**	**0**	**114**	**13.2**	**46**	**7**	**48**	**10**	**+1**	....	....	....	....	....	....	....	....
1990-91	**Detroit Red Wings**	**NHL**	**46**	**9**	**8**	**17**	**8**	**6**	**14**	**22**	**0**	**4**	**1**	**54**	**16.7**	**27**	**7**	**49**	**19**	**–10**	**5**	**0**	**0**	**0**	**0**	**0**	**0**	**0**
1991-92	**Calgary Flames**	**NHL**	**46**	**7**	**11**	**18**	**6**	**8**	**14**	**42**	**2**	**0**	**2**	**60**	**11.7**	**25**	**11**	**42**	**17**	**–11**	....	....	....	....	....	....	....	....
	Canada	WC-A	6	1	0	1	....	....	....	4	....	....	....	....	....	....	....	....	....	....	....	....	....	....	....	....	....	....
1992-93	SC Bern	Switz.	36	19	23	42	....	....	....	70	....	....	....	....	....	....	....	....	....	....	5	1	4	5	6	....	....	....
	Canada	Nat-Team	3	0	3	3	....	....	....	11	....	....	....	....	....	....	....	....	....	....	....	....	....	....	....	....	....	....

			REGULAR SEASON																		PLAYOFFS							
Season	Club	League	GP	G	A	Pts	AG	AA	APts	PIM	PP	SH	GW	S	%	TGF	PGF	TGA	PGA	+/–	GP	G	A	Pts	PIM	PP	SH	GW
1993-94	Las Vegas Thunder	IHL	59	14	40	54	....	....	....	49	....	....	....	....	....	....	....	....	....	....	5	1	1	2	15	....	....	....
1994-95	Las Vegas Thunder	IHL	43	11	15	26	....	....	....	38	....	....	....	....	....	....	....	....	....	....	....	....	....	....	....	....	....	....
	EV Zug	Switz.	5	0	1	1	....	....	....	0	....	....	....	....	....	....	....	....	....	....	....	....	....	....	....	....	....	....
1995-96	Augsburg Panthers	Germany	48	14	32	46	....	....	....	73	....	....	....	....	....	....	....	....	....	....	7	4	5	9	4	....	....	....
	NHL Totals		**345**	**72**	**91**	**163**	**62**	**65**	**127**	**171**	**17**	**7**	**6**	**538**	**13.4**	**250**	**81**	**280**	**95**		**12**	**1**	**3**	**4**	**13**	**0**	**0**	**0**

WHL Second All-Star Team (1982)

Traded to **Minnesota** by **Edmonton** with Don Barber and Emanuel Viveiros for Gord Sherven and Don Biggs, December 20, 1985. Signed as a free agent by **Detroit**, June 9, 1989. Traded to **Calgary** by **Detroit** for Brian MacLellan, June 11, 1991.

• HACHBORN, LEN

Len Hachborn C – L. 5′10″, 175 lbs. b: Brantford, Ont., 9/4/1961. Philadelphia's 12th choice, 184th overall, in 1981 Entry Draft.

Season	Club	League	GP	G	A	Pts	AG	AA	APts	PIM	PP	SH	GW	S	%	TGF	PGF	TGA	PGA	+/–	GP	G	A	Pts	PIM	PP	SH	GW
1979-80	Hamilton Kilty B's	Jr. A	43	25	20	45	....	....	....	42	....	....	....	....	....	....	....	....	....	....	....	....	....	....	....	....	....	....
1980-81	Brantford Alexanders	OHA	66	34	52	86	....	....	....	94	....	....	....	....	....	....	....	....	....	....	6	1	5	6	15	....	....	....
1981-82	Brantford Alexanders	OHL	55	43	50	93	....	....	....	141	....	....	....	....	....	....	....	....	....	....	11	15	9	24	13	....	....	....
1982-83	Maine Mariners	AHL	75	28	55	83	....	....	....	32	....	....	....	....	....	....	....	....	....	....	17	2	7	9	2	....	....	....
1983-84	Springfield Indians	AHL	28	18	42	60	....	....	....	15	....	....	....	....	....	....	....	....	....	....	....	....	....	....	....	....	....	....
	Philadelphia Flyers	**NHL**	**38**	**11**	**21**	**32**	**9**	**14**	**23**	**4**	**1**	**0**	**2**	**69**	**15.9**	**41**	**8**	**26**	**1**	**+8**	**3**	**0**	**0**	**0**	**7**	**0**	**0**	**0**
1984-85	**Philadelphia Flyers**	**NHL**	**40**	**5**	**17**	**22**	**4**	**11**	**15**	**23**	**0**	**0**	**0**	**48**	**10.4**	**30**	**2**	**12**	**0**	**+16**	**4**	**0**	**3**	**3**	**0**	**0**	**0**	**0**
	Hershey Bears	AHL	14	6	7	13	....	....	....	14	....	....	....	....	....	....	....	....	....	....	....	....	....	....	....	....	....	....
1985-86	Hershey Bears	AHL	23	12	22	34	....	....	....	34	....	....	....	....	....	....	....	....	....	....	....	....	....	....	....	....	....	....
	Los Angeles Kings	**NHL**	**24**	**4**	**1**	**5**	**3**	**1**	**4**	**2**	**1**	**0**	**0**	**14**	**28.6**	**8**	**3**	**14**	**0**	**–9**	....	....	....	....	....	....	....	....
	New Haven Nighthawks	AHL	12	5	8	13	....	....	....	21	....	....	....	....	....	....	....	....	....	....	3	0	1	1	26	....	....	....
1986-87	Balzano	Italy	35	36	67	103	....	....	....	47	....	....	....	....	....	....	....	....	....	....	....	....	....	....	....	....	....	....
	Hershey Bears	AHL	17	4	10	14	....	....	....	2	....	....	....	....	....	....	....	....	....	....	5	0	2	2	2	....	....	....
1987-88	Maine Mariners	AHL	29	16	17	33	....	....	....	16	....	....	....	....	....	....	....	....	....	....	10	5	7	12	21	....	....	....
1988-89			DID NOT PLAY																									
1989-90	New Haven Nighthawks	AHL	32	13	27	40	....	....	....	15	....	....	....	....	....	....	....	....	....	....	....	....	....	....	....	....	....	....
1990-91	Binghamton Rangers	AHL	50	9	27	36	....	....	....	8	....	....	....	....	....	....	....	....	....	....	4	0	1	1	6	....	....	....
1991-92	San Diego Gulls	IHL	70	34	73	107	....	....	....	124	....	....	....	....	....	....	....	....	....	....	4	0	2	2	17	....	....	....
1992-93	San Diego Gulls	IHL	59	23	36	59	....	....	....	49	....	....	....	....	....	....	....	....	....	....	10	2	2	4	2	....	....	....
1993-94	Krefeld Pinguine	Germany	2	1	1	2	....	....	....	0	....	....	....	....	....	....	....	....	....	....	3	2	0	2	2	....	....	....
1994-95	Houston Aeros	IHL	53	12	30	42	....	....	....	10	....	....	....	....	....	....	....	....	....	....	....	....	....	....	....	....	....	....
	Springfield Indians	AHL	5	2	4	6	....	....	....	2	....	....	....	....	....	....	....	....	....	....	....	....	....	....	....	....	....	....
	Detroit Vipers	IHL	....	....	....	....	....	....	....	....	....	....	....	....	....	....	....	....	....	....	1	0	1	1	0	....	....	....
1995-96			DID NOT PLAY																									
1996-97	Grand Rapids Griffins	IHL	19	2	2	4	....	....	....	6	....	....	....	....	....	....	....	....	....	....	....	....	....	....	....	....	....	....
1997-98	San Diego Gulls	WCHL	45	27	63	90	....	....	....	62	....	....	....	....	....	....	....	....	....	....	12	7	7	14	10	....	....	....
	NHL Totals		**102**	**20**	**39**	**59**	**16**	**26**	**42**	**29**	**2**	**0**	**2**	**131**	**15.3**	**79**	**13**	**52**	**1**		**7**	**0**	**3**	**3**	**7**	**0**	**0**	**0**

IHL Second All-Star Team (1992)

Traded to **LA Kings** by **Philadelphia** for cash, December 6, 1985.

• HADFIELD, VIC

Vic Hadfield LW – L. 6′, 190 lbs. b: Oakville, Ont., 10/4/1940.

Season	Club	League	GP	G	A	Pts	AG	AA	APts	PIM	PP	SH	GW	S	%	TGF	PGF	TGA	PGA	+/–	GP	G	A	Pts	PIM	PP	SH	GW
1958-59	St. Catharines TeePees	OHA	51	6	14	20	....	....	....	72	....	....	....	....	....	....	....	....	....	....	7	1	2	3	12	....	....	....
1959-60	St. Catharines TeePees	OHA	48	19	34	53	....	....	....	130	....	....	....	....	....	....	....	....	....	....	17	11	13	24	*84	....	....	....
	Buffalo Bisons	AHL	1	0	0	0	....	....	....	0	....	....	....	....	....	....	....	....	....	....	....	....	....	....	....	....	....	....
1960-61	Buffalo Bisons	AHL	62	5	16	21	....	....	....	111	....	....	....	....	....	....	....	....	....	....	3	0	0	0	11	....	....	....
1961-62	**New York Rangers**	**NHL**	**44**	**3**	**1**	**4**	**4**	**1**	**5**	**22**	....	....	....	....	....	....	....	....	....	....	**4**	**0**	**0**	**0**	**2**	....	....	....
1962-63	**New York Rangers**	**NHL**	**36**	**5**	**6**	**11**	**6**	**6**	**12**	**32**	....	....	....	....	....	....	....	....	....	....	....	....	....	....	....	....	....	....
	Baltimore Clippers	AHL	29	10	9	19	....	....	....	84	....	....	....	....	....	....	....	....	....	....	....	....	....	....	....	....	....	....
1963-64	**New York Rangers**	**NHL**	**69**	**14**	**11**	**25**	**18**	**12**	**30**	***151**	....	....	....	....	....	....	....	....	....	....	....	....	....	....	....	....	....	....
1964-65	**New York Rangers**	**NHL**	**70**	**18**	**20**	**38**	**23**	**22**	**45**	**102**	....	....	....	....	....	....	....	....	....	....	....	....	....	....	....	....	....	....
1965-66	**New York Rangers**	**NHL**	**67**	**16**	**19**	**35**	**19**	**19**	**38**	**112**	....	....	....	....	....	....	....	....	....	....	....	....	....	....	....	....	....	....
1966-67	**New York Rangers**	**NHL**	**69**	**13**	**20**	**33**	**16**	**21**	**37**	**80**	....	....	....	....	....	....	....	....	....	....	**4**	**1**	**0**	**1**	**17**	....	....	....
1967-68	**New York Rangers**	**NHL**	**59**	**20**	**19**	**39**	**25**	**20**	**45**	**45**	**7**	**0**	**7**	**177**	**11.3**	**60**	**21**	**40**	**0**	**–2**	**6**	**1**	**2**	**3**	**6**	**1**	**0**	**0**
1968-69	**New York Rangers**	**NHL**	**73**	**26**	**40**	**66**	**29**	**38**	**67**	**108**	**10**	**0**	**4**	**321**	**8.1**	**104**	**33**	**59**	**0**	**+12**	**4**	**2**	**1**	**3**	**2**	**0**	**0**	**0**
1969-70	**New York Rangers**	**NHL**	**71**	**20**	**34**	**54**	**23**	**34**	**57**	**69**	**3**	**0**	**5**	**268**	**7.5**	**77**	**26**	**54**	**0**	**–3**	....	....	....	....	....	....	....	....
1970-71	**New York Rangers**	**NHL**	**63**	**22**	**22**	**44**	**23**	**19**	**42**	**38**	**8**	**0**	**1**	**194**	**11.3**	**62**	**20**	**28**	**0**	**+14**	**12**	**8**	**5**	**13**	**46**	**1**	**0**	**1**
1971-72	**New York Rangers**	**NHL**	**78**	**50**	**56**	**106**	**54**	**51**	**105**	**142**	**23**	**0**	**7**	**242**	**20.7**	**156**	**45**	**51**	**0**	**+60**	**16**	**7**	**9**	**16**	**22**	**2**	**0**	**1**
1972-73	Canada	Summit	2	0	0	0	....	....	....	0	....	....	....	....	....	....	....	....	....	....	....	....	....	....	....	....	....	....
	New York Rangers	**NHL**	**63**	**28**	**34**	**62**	**28**	**28**	**56**	**60**	**9**	**0**	**4**	**214**	**13.1**	**93**	**26**	**54**	**0**	**+13**	**9**	**2**	**2**	**4**	**11**	**0**	**0**	**1**
1973-74	**New York Rangers**	**NHL**	**77**	**27**	**28**	**55**	**28**	**24**	**52**	**75**	**12**	**0**	**4**	**201**	**13.4**	**91**	**37**	**54**	**1**	**+1**	**6**	**1**	**0**	**1**	**0**	**0**	**0**	**0**
1974-75	**Pittsburgh Penguins**	**NHL**	**78**	**31**	**42**	**73**	**29**	**33**	**62**	**72**	**7**	**4**	**3**	**253**	**12.3**	**118**	**46**	**80**	**13**	**+5**	**9**	**4**	**2**	**6**	**0**	**0**	**1**	**0**
1975-76	**Pittsburgh Penguins**	**NHL**	**76**	**30**	**35**	**65**	**28**	**28**	**56**	**46**	**3**	**0**	**2**	**203**	**14.8**	**107**	**38**	**77**	**5**	**–3**	**3**	**1**	**0**	**1**	**11**	**0**	**0**	**0**
1976-77	**Pittsburgh Penguins**	**NHL**	**9**	**0**	**2**	**2**	**0**	**2**	**2**	**0**	**0**	**0**	**0**	**9**	**0.0**	**6**	**4**	**1**	**0**	**+1**	....	....	....	....	....	....	....	....
	NHL Totals		**1002**	**323**	**389**	**712**	**353**	**358**	**711**	**1154**	**82**	**4**	**37**	**2082**	**15.5**	**873**	**296**	**498**	**19**		**73**	**27**	**21**	**48**	**117**	**4**	**1**	**3**

NHL Second All-Star Team (1972)

Played in NHL All-Star Game (1965, 1972)

Claimed by **NY Rangers** from **Chicago** in Intra-League Draft, June 14, 1961. Traded to **Pittsburgh** by **NY Rangers** for Nick Beverley, May 27, 1974.

• HAGGERTY, SEAN

Sean Haggerty LW – L. 6′1″, 186 lbs. b: Rye, NY, 2/11/1976. Toronto's 2nd choice, 48th overall, in 1994 Entry Draft.

Season	Club	League	GP	G	A	Pts	AG	AA	APts	PIM	PP	SH	GW	S	%	TGF	PGF	TGA	PGA	+/–	GP	G	A	Pts	PIM	PP	SH	GW
1993-94	Detroit Jr. Red Wings	OHL	60	31	32	63	....	....	....	21	....	....	....	....	....	....	....	....	....	....	17	9	10	19	11	....	....	....
1994-95	Detroit Jr. Red Wings	OHL	61	40	49	89	....	....	....	37	....	....	....	....	....	....	....	....	....	....	21	13	24	37	18	....	....	....
	United States	WJC-A	7	1	6	7	....	....	....	8	....	....	....	....	....	....	....	....	....	....	....	....	....	....	....	....	....	....
1995-96	Detroit Whalers	OHL	66	*60	51	111	....	....	....	78	....	....	....	....	....	....	....	....	....	....	17	15	9	24	30	....	....	....
	Toronto Maple Leafs	**NHL**	**1**	**0**	**0**	**0**	**0**	**0**	**0**	**0**	**0**	**0**	**0**	**0**	**0.0**	**0**	**0**	**0**	**0**	**0**	....	....	....	....	....	....	....	....
	Worcester IceCats	AHL	....	....	....	....	....	....	....	....	....	....	....	....	....	....	....	....	....	....	1	0	0	0	2	....	....	....
1996-97	Kentucky Thoroughblades	AHL	77	13	22	35	....	....	....	60	....	....	....	....	....	....	....	....	....	....	4	1	0	1	4	....	....	....
1997-98	**New York Islanders**	**NHL**	**5**	**0**	**0**	**0**	**0**	**0**	**0**	**0**	**0**	**0**	**0**	**2**	**0.0**	**0**	**0**	**3**	**0**	**–3**	....	....	....	....	....	....	....	....
	Kentucky Thoroughblades	AHL	63	33	20	53	....	....	....	64	....	....	....	....	....	....	....	....	....	....	3	0	2	2	4	....	....	....
	NHL Totals		**6**	**0**	**0**	**0**	**0**	**0**	**0**	**0**	**0**	**0**	**0**	**2**	**0.0**	**0**	**0**	**3**	**0**		....	....	....	....	....	....	....	....

Memorial Cup All-Star Team (1995) • OHL Second All-Star Team (1996) • AHL Second All-Star Team (1998)

Traded to **NY Islanders** by **Toronto** with Darby Hendrickson, Kenny Jonsson and Toronto's 1st round choice (Roberto Luongo) in 1997 Entry Draft for Wendel Clark, Mathieu Schneider and D.J. Smith, March 13, 1996.

• HAGGLUND, ROGER

Roger Hagglund D – L. 6′1″, 175 lbs. b: Bjorklouen, Sweden, 7/2/1961. Deceased. St. Louis' 6th choice, 138th overall, in 1980 Entry Draft.

Season	Club	League	GP	G	A	Pts	AG	AA	APts	PIM	PP	SH	GW	S	%	TGF	PGF	TGA	PGA	+/–	GP	G	A	Pts	PIM	PP	SH	GW
1978-79	IF Bjorkloven	Sweden	24	2	3	5	....	....	....	23	....	....	....	....	....	....	....	....	....	....	....	....	....	....	....	....	....	....
1979-80	IF Bjorkloven	Sweden	21	3	8	11	....	....	....	28	....	....	....	....	....	....	....	....	....	....	....	....	....	....	....	....	....	....
1980-81	IF Bjorkloven	Sweden	27	1	7	8	....	....	....	21	....	....	....	....	....	....	....	....	....	....	....	....	....	....	....	....	....	....
1981-82	IF Bjorkloven	Sweden	35	7	11	18	....	....	....	40	....	....	....	....	....	....	....	....	....	....	6	0	1	1	10	....	....	....
	Sweden	WEC-A	7	0	0	0	....	....	....	0	....	....	....	....	....	....	....	....	....	....	....	....	....	....	....	....	....	....
1982-83	IF Bjorkloven	Sweden	34	6	12	18	....	....	....	64	....	....	....	....	....	....	....	....	....	....	3	0	0	0	0	....	....	....
	Sweden	WEC-A	7	0	3	3	....	....	....	4	....	....	....	....	....	....	....	....	....	....	....	....	....	....	....	....	....	....
1983-84	Vastra Frolunda	Sweden	27	8	7	15	....	....	....	10	....	....	....	....	....	....	....	....	....	....	....	....	....	....	....	....	....	....
1984-85	**Quebec Nordiques**	**NHL**	**3**	**0**	**0**	**0**	**0**	**0**	**0**	**0**	**0**	**0**	**0**	**5**	**0.0**	**2**	**1**	**1**	**0**	**0**	....	....	....	....	....	....	....	....
	Fredericton Express	AHL	34	0	5	5	....	....	....	6	....	....	....	....	....	....	....	....	....	....	....	....	....	....	....	....	....	....
1985-86	IF Bjorkloven	Sweden	31	4	17	21	....	....	....	50	....	....	....	....	....	....	....	....	....	....	....	....	....	....	....	....	....	....

			REGULAR SEASON																		PLAYOFFS							
Season	Club	League	GP	G	A	Pts	AG	AA	APts	PIM	PP	SH	GW	S	%	TGF	PGF	TGA	PGA	+/-	GP	G	A	Pts	PIM	PP	SH	GW
1986-87	IF Bjorkloven	Sweden	28	3	15	18				36											6	1	2	3	8			
1987-88	IF Bjorkloven	Sweden	35	5	14	19				42											7	1	1	2	4			
1988-89	IF Bjorkloven	Sweden	16	1	7	8				40																		
	NHL Totals		3	0	0	0	0	0	0	0	0	0	0	5	0.0	2	1	1	0									

Traded to **Quebec** by **St. Louis** for cash, July, 1984.

• HAGMAN, MATTI

Matti Hagman C – L. 6′1″, 184 lbs. b: Helsinki, Finland, 9/21/1955. Boston's 6th choice, 104th overall, in 1975 Amateur Draft.

Season	Club	League	GP	G	A	Pts	AG	AA	APts	PIM	PP	SH	GW	S	%	TGF	PGF	TGA	PGA	+/-	GP	G	A	Pts	PIM	PP	SH	GW
1972-73	HIFK Helsinki	Finland	13	11	5	16				7																		
1973-74	HIFK Helsinki	Finland	35	30	9	39				20																		
1974-75	HIFK Helsinki	Finland	35	*30	16	46				27																		
	Finland	WJC-A	5	3	2	5				9																		
	Finland	WEC-A	9	2	3	5				4																		
1975-76	HIFK Helsinki	Finland	36	24	34	58				39											4	1	1	2	5			
	Finland	Olympics	6	1	4	5				2																		
	Finland	WEC-A	10	4	7	11				14																		
1976-77	Finland	C Cup	5	2	4	6				6																		
	Boston Bruins	**NHL**	75	11	17	28	11	14	25	0	1	0	0	71	15.5	39	7	26	0	+6	8	0	1	1	0	0	0	0
1977-78	**Boston Bruins**	**NHL**	15	4	1	5	4	1	5	2	3	0	1	13	30.8	9	6	4	0	−1								
	Quebec Nordiques	WHA	53	25	31	56				16																		
	Finland	WEC-A	5	1	2	3				8																		
1978-79	HIFK Helsinki	Finland	36	20	37	57				53											6	1	6	7	4			
1979-80	HIFK Helsinki	Finland	36	*37	*50	*87				26											7	3	10	13	6			
1980-81	**Edmonton Oilers**	**NHL**	75	20	33	53	16	23	39	16	2	0	0	96	20.8	71	19	49	1	+4	9	4	1	5	6	0	0	2
1981-82	Finland	C Cup	5	1	2	3				4																		
	Edmonton Oilers	**NHL**	72	21	38	59	17	25	42	18	5	0	2	94	22.3	92	22	56	1	+15	3	1	0	1	0	0	0	0
1982-83	HIFK Helsinki	Finland	36	23	*41	*64				50											9	*9	*8	*17	11			
	Finland	WEC-A	10	2	5	7				4																		
1983-84	HIFK Helsinki	Finland	37	22	*47	*69				33											2	1	1	2	2			
1984-85	HIFK Helsinki	Finland	34	23	*44	*67				24																		
1985-86	Landshut	Germany	37	26	51	77				26																		
1986-87	HIFK Helsinki	Finland	44	17	51	68				37											3	0	1	1	10			
1987-88	Finland	C Cup	5	1	0	1				0																		
	HIFK Helsinki	Finland	44	17	43	60				37											6	4	5	9	6			
1988-89	HIFK Helsinki	Finland	44	11	30	41				23											2	0	1	1	0			
1989-90	Hockey-Reipas	Finland	44	18	47	65				4											4	2	3	5	0			
1990-91	Hockey-Reipas	Finland	44	15	35	60				24																		
1991-92	HIFK Helsinki	Finland	42	8	20	28				20																		
	NHL Totals		237	56	89	145	48	63	111	36	11	0	3	274	20.4	211	54	135	2		20	5	2	7	6	0	0	2
	Other Major League Totals		53	25	31	56				16																		

Finnish Rookie of the Year (1974) • Finnish First All-Star Team (1980, 1983)

Traded to **Quebec** (WHA) by **Boston** for cash, December, 1977. Signed as a free agent by **Edmonton**, September 11, 1980.

• HAJDU, RICHARD

Richard Hajdu LW – L. 6′1″, 185 lbs. b: Victoria, B.C., 5/10/1965. Buffalo's 5th choice, 34th overall, in 1983 Entry Draft.

Season	Club	League	GP	G	A	Pts	AG	AA	APts	PIM	PP	SH	GW	S	%	TGF	PGF	TGA	PGA	+/-	GP	G	A	Pts	PIM	PP	SH	GW
1981-82	Kamloops Jr. Oilers	WHL	64	19	21	40				50											4	0	0	0	0			
1982-83	Kamloops Jr. Oilers	WHL	70	22	36	58				101											5	0	0	0	4			
1983-84	Victoria Cougars	WHL	42	17	10	27				106																		
1984-85	Victoria Cougars	WHL	24	12	16	28				33																		
	Rochester Americans	AHL	2	0	2	2				0																		
1985-86	**Buffalo Sabres**	**NHL**	3	0	0	0	0	0	0	4	0	0	0	2	0.0	1	0	0	0	+1								
	Rochester Americans	AHL	54	10	27	37				95																		
1986-87	**Buffalo Sabres**	**NHL**	2	0	0	0	0	0	0	0	0	0	0	1	0.0	1	0	0	0	+1								
	Rochester Americans	AHL	58	7	15	22				90											11	1	1	2	9			
1987-88	Rochester Americans	AHL	37	7	11	18				24											1	0	0	0	0			
	Flint Spirits	IHL	17	4	6	10				30																		
1988-89	Canada	Nat-Team	50	14	11	25				22																		
1989-90	Canada	Nat-Team	42	6	10	16				8																		
1990-91	Gosser Ev.	Austria	19	10	7	17																						
	Canada	Nat-Team	27	5	6	11				10																		
1991-92	DID NOT PLAY																											
1992-93	Dallas Freeze	CHL	21	10	14	24				57																		
	NHL Totals		5	0	0	0	0	0	0	4	0	0	0	3	0.0	2	0	0	0									

• HAJT, BILL

Bill Hajt D – L. 6′3″, 215 lbs. b: Borden, Sask., 11/18/1951. Buffalo's 3rd choice, 33rd overall, in 1971 Amateur Draft.

Season	Club	League	GP	G	A	Pts	AG	AA	APts	PIM	PP	SH	GW	S	%	TGF	PGF	TGA	PGA	+/-	GP	G	A	Pts	PIM	PP	SH	GW
1967-68	Saskatoon Blades	WCJHL	60	4	10	14				35																		
1968-69	Saskatoon Blades	WCJHL	60	3	18	21				54																		
1969-70	Saskatoon Blades	WCJHL	60	10	21	31				40											7	2	3	5	8			
1970-71	Saskatoon Blades	WCJHL	66	19	53	72				50											5	1	4	5	2			
1971-72	DID NOT PLAY																											
1972-73	Cincinnati Swords	AHL	69	4	31	35				40											15	2	9	11	14			
1973-74	**Buffalo Sabres**	**NHL**	6	0	2	2	0	2	2	0	0	0	0	4	0.0	6	2	5	0	−1								
	Cincinnati Swords	AHL	66	5	30	35				66											5	0	4	4	4			
1974-75	**Buffalo Sabres**	**NHL**	76	3	26	29	3	20	23	68	1	0	0	107	2.8	132	9	92	16	+47	17	1	4	5	18	0	0	0
1975-76	**Buffalo Sabres**	**NHL**	80	6	21	27	6	16	22	48	0	0	0	117	5.1	132	6	115	28	+39	9	0	1	1	15	0	0	0
1976-77	**Buffalo Sabres**	**NHL**	79	6	20	26	6	16	22	56	0	0	1	106	5.7	123	8	94	18	+39	6	0	1	1	4	0	0	0
1977-78	**Buffalo Sabres**	**NHL**	76	4	18	22	4	15	19	30	0	0	0	78	5.1	98	0	73	11	+36	8	0	0	0	2	0	0	0
1978-79	**Buffalo Sabres**	**NHL**	40	3	8	11	3	6	9	20	0	1	1	53	5.7	39	1	55	13	−4								
1979-80	**Buffalo Sabres**	**NHL**	75	4	12	16	4	9	13	24	0	1	0	63	6.3	76	1	69	30	+36	14	0	5	5	4	0	0	0
1980-81	**Buffalo Sabres**	**NHL**	68	2	19	21	2	13	15	42	0	0	0	58	3.4	94	2	77	23	+38	8	0	2	2	17	0	0	0
1981-82	**Buffalo Sabres**	**NHL**	65	2	9	11	2	6	8	44	0	0	0	58	3.4	61	1	80	31	+11	2	0	0	0	0	0	0	0
1982-83	**Buffalo Sabres**	**NHL**	72	3	12	15	2	8	10	26	0	0	1	52	5.8	69	0	92	29	+6	10	0	0	0	4	0	0	0
1983-84	**Buffalo Sabres**	**NHL**	79	3	24	27	2	16	18	32	0	1	0	53	5.7	92	2	99	34	+25	3	0	0	0	0	0	0	0
1984-85	**Buffalo Sabres**	**NHL**	57	5	13	18	4	9	13	14	1	1	0	53	9.4	69	2	60	25	+32	3	1	3	4	6	0	0	0
1985-86	**Buffalo Sabres**	**NHL**	58	1	16	17	1	11	12	25	0	0	0	42	2.4	67	2	83	35	+17								
1986-87	**Buffalo Sabres**	**NHL**	23	0	2	2	0	1	1	4	0	0	0	11	0.0	16	0	29	13	0								
	NHL Totals		854	42	202	244	39	148	187	433	2	4	3	855	4.9	1074	36	1023	306		80	2	16	18	70	0	0	0

• HAKANSSON, ANDERS

Anders Hakansson LW – L. 6′2″, 190 lbs. b: Munkfors, Sweden, 4/27/1956. St. Louis' 15th choice, 134th overall, in 1976 Amateur Draft.

Season	Club	League	GP	G	A	Pts	AG	AA	APts	PIM	PP	SH	GW	S	%	TGF	PGF	TGA	PGA	+/-	GP	G	A	Pts	PIM	PP	SH	GW
1974-75	AIK Solna	Sweden	2	0	0	0				0																		
1975-76	AIK Solna	Sweden	18	4	4	8				6																		
	Sweden	WJC-A	4	3	1	4				8																		
1976-77	AIK Solna	Sweden	2	0	0	0				0																		
1977-78	AIK Solna	Sweden	27	8	4	12				10																		
1978-79	AIK Solna	Sweden	36	12	8	20				37																		
1979-80	AIK Solna	Sweden	36	14	10	24				32																		
	Sweden	Nat-Team	5	0	2	2				7																		
1980-81	AIK Solna	Sweden	22	5	12	17				18											6	4	1	5	6			
	Sweden	Nat-Team	10	6	1	7				12																		
	Sweden	WEC-A	7	4	0	4				8																		
1981-82	Sweden	C Cup	5	1	1	2				4																		
	Minnesota North Stars	**NHL**	72	12	4	16	9	3	12	29	0	4	1	76	15.8	31	1	55	13	−12	3	0	0	0	2	0	0	0
1982-83	**Minnesota North Stars**	**NHL**	5	0	0	0	0	0	0	9	0	0	0	3	0.0	2	0	5	4	+1								
	Pittsburgh Penguins	**NHL**	62	9	12	21	7	8	15	26	0	0	1	67	13.4	27	0	52	14	−11								

Season	Club	League	GP	G	A	Pts	AG	AA	APts	PIM	PP	SH	GW	S	%	TGF	PGF	TGA	PGA	+/–	GP	G	A	Pts	PIM	PP	SH	GW
			REGULAR SEASON																		PLAYOFFS							
1983-84	Los Angeles Kings	NHL	80	15	17	32	12	12	24	41	0	1	3	117	12.8	43	2	80	32	–7	....	....	....	....	....	....	....	....
1984-85	Sweden	C Cup	8	1	1	2	....	....	....	2	....	....	....	....	....	....	....	....	....	....	....	....	....	....	....	....	....	....
	Los Angeles Kings	NHL	73	12	12	24	10	8	18	28	1	1	1	75	16.0	34	1	52	15	–4	3	0	0	0	0	0	0	0
1985-86	Los Angeles Kings	NHL	38	4	1	5	3	1	4	8	0	0	2	27	14.8	14	0	32	10	–8	....	....	....	....	....	....	....	....
	NHL Totals		330	52	46	98	41	32	73	141	1	6	8	365	14.2	151	4	276	88		6	0	0	0	2	0	0	0

Swedish World All-Star Team (1981)

Signed as a free agent by **Minnesota**, July 22, 1981. Traded to **Pittsburgh** by **Minnesota** with Ron Meighan and Minnesota's 1st round choice (Bob Errey) in 1983 Entry Draft for George Ferguson and Pittsburgh's 1st round choice (Brian Lawton) in 1983 Entry Draft, October 28, 1982. Traded to **LA Kings** by **Pittsburgh** for the rights to Kevin Stevens, September 9, 1983.

• HALE, LARRY

Larry Hale D – L. 6'1", 180 lbs. b: Summerland, B.C., 10/9/1941.

Season	Club	League	GP	G	A	Pts	AG	AA	APts	PIM	PP	SH	GW	S	%	TGF	PGF	TGA	PGA	+/–	GP	G	A	Pts	PIM	PP	SH	GW
1961-62	Edmonton Oil Kings	WCJHL	STATISTICS NOT AVAILABLE																									
1962-63	Minneapolis Millers	IHL	70	5	30	35	....	....	....	49	....	....	....	....	....	....	....	....	....	....	12	1	4	5	14	....	....	....
1963-64	Seattle Totems	WHL	70	5	16	21	....	....	....	46	....	....	....	....	....	....	....	....	....	....	....	....	....	....	....	....	....	....
1964-65	Seattle Totems	WHL	70	3	15	18	....	....	....	66	....	....	....	....	....	....	....	....	....	....	7	0	2	2	6	....	....	....
1965-66	Seattle Totems	WHL	72	3	11	14	....	....	....	36	....	....	....	....	....	....	....	....	....	....	....	....	....	....	....	....	....	....
1966-67	Seattle Totems	WHL	72	3	23	26	....	....	....	50	....	....	....	....	....	....	....	....	....	....	10	2	4	6	13	....	....	....
1967-68	Seattle Totems	WHL	70	9	19	28	....	....	....	41	....	....	....	....	....	....	....	....	....	....	9	1	8	9	10	....	....	....
1968-69	**Philadelphia Flyers**	**NHL**	**67**	**3**	**16**	**19**	**3**	**15**	**18**	**28**	**0**	**0**	**0**	**62**	**4.8**	**55**	**1**	**94**	**16**	**–24**	**4**	**0**	**0**	**0**	**10**	**0**	**0**	**0**
1969-70	**Philadelphia Flyers**	**NHL**	**53**	**1**	**9**	**10**	**1**	**9**	**10**	**28**	**0**	**0**	**0**	**34**	**2.9**	**36**	**0**	**52**	**12**	**–4**	....	....	....	....	....	....	....	....
	Quebec Aces	AHL	20	0	14	14	....	....	....	44	....	....	....	....	....	....	....	....	....	....	....	....	....	....	....	....	....	....
1970-71	**Philadelphia Flyers**	**NHL**	**70**	**1**	**11**	**12**	**1**	**10**	**11**	**34**	**0**	**0**	**1**	**51**	**2.0**	**46**	**1**	**77**	**14**	**–18**	**4**	**0**	**0**	**0**	**2**	**0**	**0**	**0**
1971-72	**Philadelphia Flyers**	**NHL**	**6**	**0**	**1**	**1**	**0**	**1**	**1**	**0**	**0**	**0**	**0**	**2**	**0.0**	**5**	**0**	**11**	**1**	**–5**	....	....	....	....	....	....	....	....
	Richmond Robins	AHL	68	11	33	44	....	....	....	68	....	....	....	....	....	....	....	....	....	....	....	....	....	....	....	....	....	....
1972-73	Houston Aeros	WHA	68	4	26	30	....	....	....	65	....	....	....	....	....	....	....	....	....	....	10	1	2	3	2	....	....	....
1973-74	Houston Aeros	WHA	69	2	14	16	....	....	....	39	....	....	....	....	....	....	....	....	....	....	14	3	2	5	6	....	....	....
1974-75	Houston Aeros	WHA	76	2	18	20	....	....	....	40	....	....	....	....	....	....	....	....	....	....	13	0	4	4	0	....	....	....
1975-76	Houston Aeros	WHA	77	2	12	14	....	....	....	30	....	....	....	....	....	....	....	....	....	....	17	0	5	5	8	....	....	....
1976-77	Houston Aeros	WHA	67	0	14	14	....	....	....	18	....	....	....	....	....	....	....	....	....	....	11	0	2	2	6	....	....	....
1977-78	Houston Aeros	WHA	56	2	11	13	....	....	....	22	....	....	....	....	....	....	....	....	....	....	....	....	....	....	....	....	....	....
1978-79	Spokane Flyers	PHL	54	0	18	18	....	....	....	30	....	....	....	....	....	....	....	....	....	....	....	....	....	....	....	....	....	....
	NHL Totals		**196**	**5**	**37**	**42**	**5**	**35**	**40**	**90**	**0**	**0**	**1**	**149**	**3.4**	**142**	**2**	**234**	**43**		**8**	**0**	**0**	**0**	**12**	**0**	**0**	**0**
	Other Major League Totals		413	12	95	107	....	....	....	214	....	....	....	....	....	....	....	....	....		65	4	15	19	22	....	....	....

WHL Second All-Star Team (1968)

Claimed by **Minnesota** from **Seattle** (WHL) in Inter-Team Draft, June, 1968. Claimed by **Philadelphia** from **Minnesota** in Intra-League Draft, June, 1968. Selected by **Houston** (WHA) in 1972 WHA General Player Draft, February 12, 1972. Claimed by **Atlanta** from **Philadelphia** in Expansion Draft, June 6, 1972.

• HALKIDIS, BOB

Bob Halkidis D – L. 5'11", 205 lbs. b: Toronto, Ont., 3/5/1966. Buffalo's 4th choice, 81st overall, in 1984 Entry Draft.

Season	Club	League	GP	G	A	Pts	AG	AA	APts	PIM	PP	SH	GW	S	%	TGF	PGF	TGA	PGA	+/–	GP	G	A	Pts	PIM	PP	SH	GW
1983-84	London Knights	OHL	51	9	22	31	....	....	....	123	....	....	....	....	....	....	....	....	....	....	8	0	2	2	27	....	....	....
1984-85	London Knights	OHL	62	14	50	64	....	....	....	154	....	....	....	....	....	....	....	....	....	....	8	3	6	9	22	....	....	....
	Buffalo Sabres	**NHL**	....	....	....	....	....	....	....	....	....	....	....	....	....	....	....	....	....	....	**4**	**0**	**0**	**0**	**19**	....	....	....
1985-86	**Buffalo Sabres**	**NHL**	**37**	**1**	**9**	**10**	**1**	**6**	**7**	**115**	**0**	**0**	**0**	**19**	**5.3**	**27**	**2**	**20**	**0**	**–3**	....	....	....	....	....	....	....	....
1986-87	**Buffalo Sabres**	**NHL**	**6**	**1**	**1**	**2**	**1**	**1**	**2**	**19**	**0**	**0**	**0**	**4**	**25.0**	**7**	**0**	**5**	**1**	**+3**	....	....	....	....	....	....	....	....
	Rochester Americans	AHL	59	1	8	9	....	....	....	144	....	....	....	....	....	....	....	....	....	....	8	0	0	0	43	....	....	....
1987-88	**Buffalo Sabres**	**NHL**	**30**	**0**	**3**	**3**	**0**	**2**	**2**	**115**	**0**	**0**	**0**	**26**	**0.0**	**29**	**3**	**26**	**6**	**+6**	**4**	**0**	**0**	**0**	**22**	**0**	**0**	**0**
	Rochester Americans	AHL	15	2	5	7	....	....	....	50	....	....	....	....	....	....	....	....	....	....	....	....	....	....	....	....	....	....
1988-89	**Buffalo Sabres**	**NHL**	**16**	**0**	**1**	**1**	**0**	**1**	**1**	**66**	**0**	**0**	**0**	**9**	**0.0**	**9**	**0**	**17**	**7**	**–1**	....	....	....	....	....	....	....	....
	Rochester Americans	AHL	16	0	6	6	....	....	....	64	....	....	....	....	....	....	....	....	....	....	....	....	....	....	....	....	....	....
1989-90	Rochester Americans	AHL	18	1	13	14	....	....	....	70	....	....	....	....	....	....	....	....	....	....	....	....	....	....	....	....	....	....
	Los Angeles Kings	**NHL**	**20**	**0**	**4**	**4**	**0**	**3**	**3**	**56**	**0**	**0**	**0**	**19**	**0.0**	**23**	**2**	**23**	**6**	**+4**	**8**	**0**	**1**	**1**	**8**	**0**	**0**	**0**
	New Haven Nighthawks	AHL	30	3	17	20	....	....	....	67	....	....	....	....	....	....	....	....	....	....	....	....	....	....	....	....	....	....
1990-91	**Los Angeles Kings**	**NHL**	**34**	**1**	**3**	**4**	**1**	**2**	**3**	**133**	**0**	**0**	**0**	**25**	**4.0**	**35**	**0**	**38**	**11**	**+8**	**3**	**0**	**0**	**0**	**0**	**0**	**0**	**0**
	New Haven Nighthawks	AHL	7	1	3	4	....	....	....	10	....	....	....	....	....	....	....	....	....	....	....	....	....	....	....	....	....	....
	Phoenix Roadrunners	IHL	4	1	5	6	....	....	....	6	....	....	....	....	....	....	....	....	....	....	....	....	....	....	....	....	....	....
1991-92	**Toronto Maple Leafs**	**NHL**	**46**	**3**	**3**	**6**	**3**	**2**	**5**	**145**	**0**	**0**	**0**	**36**	**8.3**	**20**	**1**	**31**	**3**	**–9**	....	....	....	....	....	....	....	....
1992-93	St. John's Maple Leafs	AHL	29	2	13	15	....	....	....	61	....	....	....	....	....	....	....	....	....	....	....	....	....	....	....	....	....	....
	Milwaukee Admirals	IHL	26	0	9	9	....	....	....	79	....	....	....	....	....	....	....	....	....	....	5	0	1	1	27	....	....	....
1993-94	**Detroit Red Wings**	**NHL**	**28**	**1**	**4**	**5**	**1**	**3**	**4**	**93**	**0**	**0**	**0**	**35**	**2.9**	**14**	**0**	**18**	**3**	**–1**	**1**	**0**	**0**	**0**	**2**	**0**	**0**	**0**
	Adirondack Red Wings	AHL	15	0	6	6	....	....	....	46	....	....	....	....	....	....	....	....	....	....	....	....	....	....	....	....	....	....
1994-95	**Detroit Red Wings**	**NHL**	**4**	**0**	**1**	**1**	**0**	**1**	**1**	**6**	**0**	**0**	**0**	**0**	**0.0**	**3**	**0**	**2**	**1**	**+2**	....	....	....	....	....	....	....	....
	Tampa Bay Lightning	**NHL**	**27**	**1**	**3**	**4**	**2**	**4**	**6**	**40**	**0**	**0**	**0**	**25**	**4.0**	**10**	**0**	**23**	**1**	**–12**	....	....	....	....	....	....	....	....
1995-96	**Tampa Bay Lightning**	**NHL**	**3**	**0**	**0**	**0**	**0**	**0**	**0**	**7**	**0**	**0**	**0**	**0**	**0.0**	**0**	**0**	**3**	**2**	**–1**	....	....	....	....	....	....	....	....
	Atlanta Knights	IHL	21	1	7	8	....	....	....	62	....	....	....	....	....	....	....	....	....	....	....	....	....	....	....	....	....	....
	Indianapolis Ice	IHL	3	0	2	2	....	....	....	8	....	....	....	....	....	....	....	....	....	....	....	....	....	....	....	....	....	....
	New York Islanders	**NHL**	**5**	**0**	**0**	**0**	**0**	**0**	**0**	**30**	**0**	**0**	**0**	**2**	**0.0**	**0**	**0**	**3**	**0**	**–3**	....	....	....	....	....	....	....	....
	Utah Grizzlies	IHL	27	0	7	7	....	....	....	72	....	....	....	....	....	....	....	....	....	....	12	1	1	2	36	....	....	....
1996-97	Carolina Monarchs	AHL	41	5	13	18	....	....	....	47	....	....	....	....	....	....	....	....	....	....	....	....	....	....	....	....	....	....
1997-98	Winston-Salem IceHawks	UHL	3	0	1	1	....	....	....	15	....	....	....	....	....	....	....	....	....	....	....	....	....	....	....	....	....	....
	HIFK Helsinki	Finland	29	1	6	7	....	....	....	12	....	....	....	....	....	....	....	....	....	....	9	0	2	2	14	....	....	....
	NHL Totals		**256**	**8**	**32**	**40**	**9**	**25**	**34**	**825**	**0**	**0**	**0**	**200**	**4.0**	**177**	**8**	**217**	**41**		**20**	**0**	**1**	**1**	**51**	**0**	**0**	**0**

OHL First All-Star Team (1985)

Traded to **LA Kings** by **Buffalo** with future considerations for Dale DeGray and future considerations, November 24, 1989. Signed as a free agent by **Toronto**, July 24, 1991. Signed as a free agent by **Detroit**, September 2, 1993. Claimed on waivers by **Tampa Bay** from **Detroit**, February 10, 1995. Claimed on waivers by **Chicago** from **Tampa Bay**, December 6, 1995. Traded to **NY Islanders** by **Chicago** for Danton Cole, February 2, 1996. Signed as a free agent by **Florida**, July 25, 1996.

• HALKO, STEVEN

Steven Halko D – R. 6'1", 195 lbs. b: Etobicoke, Ont., 3/8/1974. Hartford's 10th choice, 225th overall, in 1992 Entry Draft.

Season	Club	League	GP	G	A	Pts	AG	AA	APts	PIM	PP	SH	GW	S	%	TGF	PGF	TGA	PGA	+/–	GP	G	A	Pts	PIM	PP	SH	GW
1991-92	Thornhill Islanders	OJHL	44	15	46	61	....	....	....	43	....	....	....	....	....	....	....	....	....	....	....	....	....	....	....	....	....	....
1992-93	University of Michigan	CCHA	39	1	12	13	....	....	....	12	....	....	....	....	....	....	....	....	....	....	....	....	....	....	....	....	....	....
1993-94	University of Michigan	CCHA	41	2	13	15	....	....	....	32	....	....	....	....	....	....	....	....	....	....	....	....	....	....	....	....	....	....
1994-95	University of Michigan	CCHA	39	2	14	16	....	....	....	20	....	....	....	....	....	....	....	....	....	....	....	....	....	....	....	....	....	....
1995-96	University of Michigan	CCHA	43	4	16	20	....	....	....	32	....	....	....	....	....	....	....	....	....	....	....	....	....	....	....	....	....	....
1996-97	Springfield Falcons	AHL	70	1	5	6	....	....	....	37	....	....	....	....	....	....	....	....	....	....	11	0	2	2	8	....	....	....
1997-98	**Carolina Hurricanes**	**NHL**	**18**	**0**	**2**	**2**	**0**	**2**	**2**	**10**	**0**	**0**	**0**	**7**	**0.0**	**8**	**0**	**12**	**3**	**–1**	....	....	....	....	....	....	....	....
	Beast of New Haven	AHL	65	1	19	20	....	....	....	44	....	....	....	....	....	....	....	....	....	....	1	0	0	0	0	....	....	....
	NHL Totals		**18**	**0**	**2**	**2**	**0**	**2**	**2**	**10**	**0**	**0**	**0**	**7**	**0.0**	**8**	**0**	**12**	**3**		....	....	....	....	....	....	....	....

CCHA Second All-Star Team (1995, 1996) • NCAA Championship All-Tournament Team (1996)

Transferred to **Carolina** after **Hartford** franchise relocated, June 25, 1997.

• HALL, DEL

Del Hall C – L. 5'10", 170 lbs. b: Peterborough, Ont., 5/7/1949.

Season	Club	League	GP	G	A	Pts	AG	AA	APts	PIM	PP	SH	GW	S	%	TGF	PGF	TGA	PGA	+/–	GP	G	A	Pts	PIM	PP	SH	GW
1969-70	Chatham Maroons	OJHL	....	*53	46	99	....	....	....	....	....	....	....	....	....	....	....	....	....	....	....	....	....	....	....	....	....	....
1970-71	St. Clair College	OUAA	22	23	30	53	....	....	....	26	....	....	....	....	....	....	....	....	....	....	....	....	....	....	....	....	....	....
1971-72	**California Golden Seals**	**NHL**	**1**	**0**	**0**	**0**	**0**	**0**	**0**	**0**	**0**	**0**	**0**	**1**	**0.0**	**0**	**0**	**1**	**0**	**–1**	....	....	....	....	....	....	....	....
	Columbus Seals	IHL	64	26	27	53	....	....	....	18	....	....	....	....	....	....	....	....	....	....	....	....	....	....	....	....	....	....
1972-73	**California Golden Seals**	**NHL**	**6**	**0**	**0**	**0**	**0**	**0**	**0**	**0**	**0**	**0**	**0**	**2**	**0.0**	**0**	**0**	**0**	**0**	**0**	....	....	....	....	....	....	....	....
	Salt Lake Golden Eagles	WHL	63	24	18	42	....	....	....	23	....	....	....	....	....	....	....	....	....	....	9	5	4	9	0	....	....	....
1973-74	**California Golden Seals**	**NHL**	**2**	**2**	**0**	**2**	**2**	**0**	**2**	**2**	**0**	**0**	**0**	**4**	**50.0**	**2**	**0**	**2**	**1**	**+1**	....	....	....	....	....	....	....	....
	Salt Lake Golden Eagles	WHL	71	38	41	79	....	....	....	30	....	....	....	....	....	....	....	....	....	....	5	1	0	1	0	....	....	....
1974-75	Salt Lake Golden Eagles	CHL	70	32	32	64	....	....	....	4	....	....	....	....	....	....	....	....	....	....	11	7	8	15	6	....	....	....
1975-76	Phoenix Roadrunners	WHA	80	47	44	91	....	....	....	10	....	....	....	....	....	....	....	....	....	....	5	2	3	5	0	....	....	....

			REGULAR SEASON																		PLAYOFFS							
Season	Club	League	GP	G	A	Pts	AG	AA	APts	PIM	PP	SH	GW	S	%	TGF	PGF	TGA	PGA	+/-	GP	G	A	Pts	PIM	PP	SH	GW
1976-77	Phoenix Roadrunners	WHA	80	38	41	79	....	....	....	30	....	....	....	....	....	....	....	....	....	....	....	....	....	....	....	....	....	....
1977-78	Cincinnati Stingers	WHA	25	4	3	7	....	....	....	4	....	....	....	....	....	....	....	....	....	....	....	....	....	....	....	....	....	....
	Edmonton Oilers	WHA	1	0	0	0	....	....	....	0	....	....	....	....	....	....	....	....	....	....	....	....	....	....	....	....	....	....
	NHL Totals		**9**	**2**	**0**	**2**	**2**	**0**	**2**	**2**	**0**	**0**	**0**	**7**	**28.6**	**2**	**0**	**3**	**1**		....	....	....	....	....	....	....	....
	Other Major League Totals		186	89	88	177	....	....	....	44	....	....	....	....	....	....	....	....	....		5	2	3	5	0	....	....	....

Signed as a free agent by **California**, October, 1971. Selected by **Edmonton** (WHA) in 1972 WHA General Player Draft, February 13, 1972. WHA rights traded to **Phoenix** (WHA) by **Edmonton** (WHA) for cash, June, 1974. Traded to **Cincinnati** (WHA) by **Phoenix** (WHA) for cash, April, 1977. Traded to **Edmonton** (WHA) by **Cincinnati** (WHA) with Dennis Sobchuk for Butch Deadmarsh, December, 1977.

● HALL, MURRAY

Murray Hall RW – R. 6′, 175 lbs. b: Kirkland Lake, Ont., 11/24/1940.

Season	Club	League	GP	G	A	Pts	AG	AA	APts	PIM	PP	SH	GW	S	%	TGF	PGF	TGA	PGA	+/-	GP	G	A	Pts	PIM	PP	SH	GW
1959-60	St. Catharines Black Hawks	OHA	48	17	15	32	....	....	....	22	....	....	....	....	....	....	....	....	....	....	17	2	7	9	6	....	....	....
1960-61	St. Catharines Black Hawks	OHA	48	35	41	76	....	....	....	60	....	....	....	....	....	....	....	....	....	....	6	3	1	4	2	....	....	....
	Sault Ste. Marie Thunderbirds	EPHL	....	....	....	....	....	....	....	....	....	....	....	....	....	....	....	....	....	....	8	0	2	2	2	....	....	....
1961-62	**Chicago Black Hawks**	**NHL**	**2**	**0**	**0**	**0**	**0**	**0**	**0**	**0**	....	....	....	....	....	....	....	....	....	....	....	....	....	....	....	....	....	....
	Buffalo Bisons	AHL	68	20	21	41	....	....	....	41	....	....	....	....	....	....	....	....	....	....	11	3	1	4	4	....	....	....
1962-63	St. Louis Braves	EPHL	71	29	*69	98	....	....	....	41	....	....	....	....	....	....	....	....	....	....	....	....	....	....	....	....	....	....
	Chicago Black Hawks	**NHL**	....	....	....	....	....	....	....	....	....	....	....	....	....	....	....	....	....	....	**4**	**0**	**0**	**0**	**0**	....	....	....
1963-64	**Chicago Black Hawks**	**NHL**	**23**	**2**	**0**	**2**	**3**	**0**	**3**	**4**	....	....	....	....	....	....	....	....	....	....	....	....	....	....	....	....	....	....
	St. Louis Braves	CHL	28	17	40	57	....	....	....	35	....	....	....	....	....	....	....	....	....	....	6	2	4	6	0	....	....	....
1964-65	Pittsburgh Hornets	AHL	72	29	33	62	....	....	....	29	....	....	....	....	....	....	....	....	....	....	4	0	0	0	4	....	....	....
	Detroit Red Wings	**NHL**	....	....	....	....	....	....	....	....	....	....	....	....	....	....	....	....	....	....	**1**	**0**	**0**	**0**	**0**	....	....	....
1965-66	**Detroit Red Wings**	**NHL**	**1**	**0**	**0**	**0**	**0**	**0**	**0**	**0**	....	....	....	....	....	....	....	....	....	....	**1**	**0**	**0**	**0**	**0**	....	....	....
	Pittsburgh Hornets	AHL	70	28	45	73	....	....	....	102	....	....	....	....	....	....	....	....	....	....	3	0	3	3	0	....	....	....
1966-67	Los Angeles Blades	WHL	43	18	28	46	....	....	....	28	....	....	....	....	....	....	....	....	....	....	....	....	....	....	....	....	....	....
	Pittsburgh Hornets	AHL	12	5	11	16	....	....	....	10	....	....	....	....	....	....	....	....	....	....	....	....	....	....	....	....	....	....
	Detroit Red Wings	**NHL**	**12**	**4**	**3**	**7**	**5**	**3**	**8**	**4**	....	....	....	....	....	....	....	....	....	....	....	....	....	....	....	....	....	....
1967-68	**Minnesota North Stars**	**NHL**	**17**	**2**	**1**	**3**	**2**	**1**	**3**	**10**	**0**	**0**	**0**	**18**	**11.1**	**3**	**1**	**9**	**0**	**–7**	....	....	....	....	....	....	....	....
	Memphis South Stars	CHL	12	3	8	11	....	....	....	23	....	....	....	....	....	....	....	....	....	....	....	....	....	....	....	....	....	....
	Rochester Americans	AHL	38	17	14	31	....	....	....	19	....	....	....	....	....	....	....	....	....	....	11	5	9	14	2	....	....	....
1968-69	Vancouver Canucks	WHL	69	28	37	65	....	....	....	34	....	....	....	....	....	....	....	....	....	....	8	2	3	5	0	....	....	....
1969-70	Vancouver Canucks	WHL	72	27	55	82	....	....	....	42	....	....	....	....	....	....	....	....	....	....	11	*10	11	*21	10	....	....	....
1970-71	**Vancouver Canucks**	**NHL**	**77**	**21**	**38**	**59**	**22**	**34**	**56**	**22**	**5**	**0**	**1**	**127**	**16.5**	**84**	**24**	**76**	**0**	**–16**	....	....	....	....	....	....	....	....
1971-72	**Vancouver Canucks**	**NHL**	**32**	**6**	**6**	**12**	**6**	**5**	**11**	**6**	**1**	**0**	**0**	**46**	**13.0**	**20**	**6**	**26**	**0**	**–12**	....	....	....	....	....	....	....	....
	Rochester Americans	AHL	37	10	32	42	....	....	....	70	....	....	....	....	....	....	....	....	....	....	....	....	....	....	....	....	....	....
1972-73	Houston Aeros	WHA	76	28	42	70	....	....	....	84	....	....	....	....	....	....	....	....	....	....	10	4	4	8	18	....	....	....
1973-74	Houston Aeros	WHA	78	30	28	58	....	....	....	25	....	....	....	....	....	....	....	....	....	....	14	9	6	15	6	....	....	....
1974-75	Houston Aeros	WHA	78	18	29	47	....	....	....	28	....	....	....	....	....	....	....	....	....	....	13	7	3	10	8	....	....	....
1975-76	Houston Aeros	WHA	80	20	26	46	....	....	....	18	....	....	....	....	....	....	....	....	....	....	17	1	4	5	0	....	....	....
1976-77	Oklahoma City Blazers	CHL	30	8	13	21	....	....	....	2	....	....	....	....	....	....	....	....	....	....	....	....	....	....	....	....	....	....
1977-78	Brantford Alexanders	OHA Sr.	25	9	20	29	....	....	....	35	....	....	....	....	....	....	....	....	....	....	....	....	....	....	....	....	....	....
	NHL Totals		**164**	**35**	**48**	**83**	**38**	**43**	**81**	**46**	**6**	**0**	**1**	**191**	**18.3**	**107**	**31**	**111**	**0**		**6**	**0**	**0**	**0**	**0**	**0**	**0**	**0**
	Other Major League Totals		312	96	125	221	....	....	....	155	....	....	....	....	....	....	....	....	....		54	21	17	38	32	....	....	....

Played in NHL All-Star Game (1961)

Claimed by **Detroit** from **Chicago** in Intra-Team Draft, June 9, 1964. Traded to **Chicago** by **Detroit** to complete transaction that sent Howie Young to Detroit (December 20, 1966), May 20, 1966. Claimed by **Minnesota** from **Chicago** in Expansion Draft, June 6, 1967. Traded to **Toronto** by **Minnesota** with Ted Taylor, Len Lunde, Don Johns, Duke Harris and the loan of Carl Wetzel for Milan Marcetta and Jean-Paul Parise, December 26, 1967. Traded to **Rochester** (AHL) by **Toronto** for cash, June, 1968. NHL rights transferred to **Vancouver** when owners of **Vancouver** (WHL) club awarded NHL expansion franchise, May 20, 1970. Selected by **Houston** (WHA) in 1972 WHA General Player Draft, February 12, 1972.

● HALL, TAYLOR

Taylor Hall LW – L. 5′11″, 180 lbs. b: Regina, Sask., 2/20/1964. Vancouver's 4th choice, 116th overall, in 1982 Entry Draft.

Season	Club	League	GP	G	A	Pts	AG	AA	APts	PIM	PP	SH	GW	S	%	TGF	PGF	TGA	PGA	+/-	GP	G	A	Pts	PIM	PP	SH	GW
1980-81	Regina Canadians	Midget	26	51	28	79	....	....	....	35	....	....	....	....	....	....	....	....	....	....	....	....	....	....	....	....	....	....
1981-82	Regina Pats	WHL	48	14	15	29	....	....	....	43	....	....	....	....	....	....	....	....	....	....	11	2	3	5	14	....	....	....
1982-83	Regina Pats	WHL	72	37	57	94	....	....	....	78	....	....	....	....	....	....	....	....	....	....	5	0	3	3	12	....	....	....
1983-84	Regina Pats	WHL	69	63	79	142	....	....	....	42	....	....	....	....	....	....	....	....	....	....	23	21	20	41	26	....	....	....
	Vancouver Canucks	**NHL**	**4**	**1**	**0**	**1**	**1**	**0**	**1**	**0**	**0**	**0**	**0**	**3**	**33.3**	**1**	**0**	**3**	**0**	**–2**	....	....	....	....	....	....	....	....
1984-85	**Vancouver Canucks**	**NHL**	**7**	**1**	**4**	**5**	**1**	**3**	**4**	**19**	**0**	**0**	**0**	**14**	**7.1**	**9**	**2**	**10**	**3**	**0**	....	....	....	....	....	....	....	....
1985-86	**Vancouver Canucks**	**NHL**	**19**	**5**	**5**	**10**	**4**	**3**	**7**	**6**	**1**	**0**	**0**	**30**	**16.7**	**12**	**4**	**20**	**1**	**–11**	....	....	....	....	....	....	....	....
	Fredericton Express	AHL	45	21	14	35	....	....	....	28	....	....	....	....	....	....	....	....	....	....	1	0	0	0	0	....	....	....
1986-87	**Vancouver Canucks**	**NHL**	**4**	**0**	**0**	**0**	**0**	**0**	**0**	**0**	**0**	**0**	**0**	**1**	**0.0**	**0**	**0**	**2**	**0**	**–2**	....	....	....	....	....	....	....	....
	Fredericton Express	AHL	36	21	20	41	....	....	....	23	....	....	....	....	....	....	....	....	....	....	....	....	....	....	....	....	....	....
1987-88	**Boston Bruins**	**NHL**	**7**	**0**	**0**	**0**	**0**	**0**	**0**	**4**	**0**	**0**	**0**	**5**	**0.0**	**3**	**1**	**6**	**1**	**–3**	....	....	....	....	....	....	....	....
	Maine Mariners	AHL	71	33	41	74	....	....	....	58	....	....	....	....	....	....	....	....	....	....	10	1	4	5	21	....	....	....
1988-89	Maine Mariners	AHL	8	0	1	1	....	....	....	7	....	....	....	....	....	....	....	....	....	....	....	....	....	....	....	....	....	....
	Newmarket Saints	AHL	9	5	5	10	....	....	....	14	....	....	....	....	....	....	....	....	....	....	....	....	....	....	....	....	....	....
	HC Asiago	Italy	26	25	21	46	....	....	....	60	....	....	....	....	....	....	....	....	....	....	....	....	....	....	....	....	....	....
1989-90	New Haven Nighthawks	AHL	51	14	23	37	....	....	....	10	....	....	....	....	....	....	....	....	....	....	....	....	....	....	....	....	....	....
	Canada	Nat-Team	4	4	2	6	....	....	....	0	....	....	....	....	....	....	....	....	....	....	....	....	....	....	....	....	....	....
1990-91	San Diego Gulls	IHL	44	13	16	29	....	....	....	28	....	....	....	....	....	....	....	....	....	....	....	....	....	....	....	....	....	....
1991-92	Mannheim Eagles	Germany	15	4	6	10	....	....	....	4	....	....	....	....	....	....	....	....	....	....	....	....	....	....	....	....	....	....
1992-93	Tulsa Oilers	CHL	58	35	45	80	....	....	....	64	....	....	....	....	....	....	....	....	....	....	9	3	5	8	16	....	....	....
1993-94	Tulsa Oilers	CHL	64	33	26	59	....	....	....	95	....	....	....	....	....	....	....	....	....	....	11	3	5	8	14	....	....	....
1994-95	Tulsa Oilers	CHL	58	29	39	68	....	....	....	33	....	....	....	....	....	....	....	....	....	....	7	2	3	5	17	....	....	....
1995-96	Tulsa Oilers	CHL	63	27	35	62	....	....	....	52	....	....	....	....	....	....	....	....	....	....	6	1	1	2	14	....	....	....
	NHL Totals		**41**	**7**	**9**	**16**	**6**	**6**	**12**	**29**	**1**	**0**	**0**	**53**	**13.2**	**25**	**7**	**41**	**5**		....	....	....	....	....	....	....	....

WHL East All-Star Team (1984)

Signed as a free agent by **Boston**, July, 1987. Signed as a free agent by **San Diego** (IHL), August, 1990.

● HALLER, KEVIN

Kevin Haller D – L. 6′2″, 195 lbs. b: Trochu, Alta., 12/5/1970. Buffalo's 1st choice, 14th overall, in 1989 Entry Draft.

Season	Club	League	GP	G	A	Pts	AG	AA	APts	PIM	PP	SH	GW	S	%	TGF	PGF	TGA	PGA	+/-	GP	G	A	Pts	PIM	PP	SH	GW
1988-89	Regina Pats	WHL	72	10	31	41	....	....	....	99	....	....	....	....	....	....	....	....	....	....	....	....	....	....	....	....	....	....
1989-90	Regina Pats	WHL	58	16	37	53	....	....	....	93	....	....	....	....	....	....	....	....	....	....	11	2	9	11	16	....	....	....
	Canada	WJC-A	7	2	2	4	....	....	....	8	....	....	....	....	....	....	....	....	....	....	....	....	....	....	....	....	....	....
	Buffalo Sabres	**NHL**	**2**	**0**	**0**	**0**	**0**	**0**	**0**	**0**	**0**	**0**	**0**	**1**	**0.0**	**1**	**0**	**1**	**0**	**0**	....	....	....	....	....	....	....	....
1990-91	**Buffalo Sabres**	**NHL**	**21**	**1**	**8**	**9**	**1**	**6**	**7**	**20**	**1**	**0**	**0**	**42**	**2.4**	**33**	**8**	**20**	**4**	**+9**	**6**	**1**	**4**	**5**	**10**	**0**	**0**	**0**
	Rochester Americans	AHL	52	2	8	10	....	....	....	53	....	....	....	....	....	....	....	....	....	....	10	2	1	3	6	....	....	....
1991-92	**Buffalo Sabres**	**NHL**	**58**	**6**	**15**	**21**	**5**	**11**	**16**	**75**	**2**	**0**	**1**	**76**	**7.9**	**62**	**17**	**66**	**8**	**–13**	....	....	....	....	....	....	....	....
	Rochester Americans	AHL	4	0	0	0	....	....	....	18	....	....	....	....	....	....	....	....	....	....	....	....	....	....	....	....	....	....
	Montreal Canadiens	**NHL**	**8**	**2**	**2**	**4**	**2**	**1**	**3**	**17**	**1**	**0**	**0**	**9**	**22.2**	**11**	**2**	**6**	**1**	**+4**	**9**	**0**	**0**	**0**	**6**	**0**	**0**	**0**
1992-93	**Montreal Canadiens**	**NHL**	**73**	**11**	**14**	**25**	**9**	**10**	**19**	**117**	**6**	**0**	**1**	**126**	**8.7**	**91**	**24**	**72**	**12**	**+7**	**17**	**1**	**6**	**7**	**16**	**1**	**0**	**0**
1993-94	**Montreal Canadiens**	**NHL**	**68**	**4**	**9**	**13**	**4**	**7**	**11**	**118**	**0**	**0**	**1**	**72**	**5.6**	**64**	**11**	**60**	**10**	**+3**	**7**	**1**	**1**	**2**	**19**	**0**	**0**	**0**
1994-95	**Philadelphia Flyers**	**NHL**	**36**	**2**	**8**	**10**	**4**	**12**	**16**	**48**	**0**	**0**	**0**	**26**	**7.7**	**38**	**1**	**36**	**15**	**+16**	**15**	**4**	**4**	**8**	**10**	**0**	**1**	**1**
1995-96	**Philadelphia Flyers**	**NHL**	**69**	**5**	**9**	**14**	**5**	**7**	**12**	**92**	**0**	**2**	**2**	**89**	**5.6**	**65**	**6**	**64**	**23**	**+18**	**6**	**0**	**1**	**1**	**8**	**0**	**0**	**0**
1996-97	**Philadelphia Flyers**	**NHL**	**27**	**0**	**5**	**5**	**0**	**4**	**4**	**37**	**0**	**0**	**0**	**34**	**0.0**	**17**	**0**	**29**	**11**	**–1**	....	....	....	....	....	....	....	....
	Hartford Whalers	**NHL**	**35**	**2**	**6**	**8**	**2**	**5**	**7**	**48**	**0**	**0**	**0**	**43**	**4.7**	**26**	**6**	**43**	**12**	**–11**	....	....	....	....	....	....	....	....
1997-98	**Carolina Hurricanes**	**NHL**	**65**	**3**	**5**	**8**	**4**	**5**	**9**	**94**	**0**	**0**	**0**	**67**	**4.5**	**44**	**3**	**68**	**22**	**–5**	....	....	....	....	....	....	....	....
	NHL Totals		**462**	**36**	**81**	**117**	**36**	**68**	**104**	**666**	**10**	**2**	**5**	**585**	**6.2**	**452**	**78**	**465**	**118**		**60**	**7**	**16**	**23**	**69**	**1**	**1**	**1**

WHL East First All-Star Team (1990)

Traded to **Montreal** by **Buffalo** for Petr Svoboda, March 10, 1992. Traded to **Philadelphia** by **Montreal** for Yves Racine, June 29, 1994. Traded to **Hartford** by **Philadelphia** with Philadelphia's 1st round choice (later traded to San Jose — San Jose selected Scott Hannan) in 1997 Entry Draft and Hartford/Carolina's 7th round choice (previously acquired, Carolina selected Andrew Merrick) in 1997 Entry Draft for Paul Coffey and Hartford's 3rd round choice (Kris Mallette) in 1997 Entry Draft, December 15, 1996. Transferred to **Carolina** after **Hartford** franchise relocated, June 25, 1997.

• HALLIN, MATS

Mats Hallin LW – L. 6'2", 200 lbs. b: Esklistuna, Sweden, 3/9/1958. Washington's 10th choice, 105th overall, in 1978 Amateur Draft.

			REGULAR SEASON																		PLAYOFFS							
Season	Club	League	GP	G	A	Pts	AG	AA	APts	PIM	PP	SH	GW	S	%	TGF	PGF	TGA	PGA	+/-	GP	G	A	Pts	PIM	PP	SH	GW
1976-77	Sodertalje	Sweden	15	2	5	7	....	....	....	23	....	....	....	....	....	....	....	....	....	....	....	....	....	....	....	....	....	....
1977-78	Sodertalje	Sweden	32	6	3	9	....	....	....	58	....	....	....	....	....	....	....	....	....	....	....	....	....	....	....	....	....	....
	Sweden	WJC-A	7	5	3	8	....	....	....	17	....	....	....	....	....	....	....	....	....	....	....	....	....	....	....	....	....	....
1978-79	Sodertalje	Sweden	14	4	7	11	....	....	....	18	....	....	....	....	....	....	....	....	....	....	....	....	....	....	....	....	....	....
1979-80	Sodertalje	Sweden	31	22	19	41	....	....	....	84	....	....	....	....	....	....	....	....	....	....	9	8	5	13	36	....	....	....
1980-81	Sodertalje	Sweden	33	9	11	20	....	....	....	86	....	....	....	....	....	....	....	....	....	....	....	....	....	....	....	....	....	....
1981-82	Indianapolis Checkers	CHL	63	25	32	57	....	....	....	113	....	....	....	....	....	....	....	....	....	....	8	1	5	6	31	....	....	....
1982-83	**New York Islanders**	**NHL**	**30**	**7**	**7**	**14**	**6**	**5**	**11**	**26**	**0**	**0**	**0**	**37**	**18.9**	**25**	**6**	**15**	**0**	**+4**	**7**	**1**	**0**	**1**	**6**	**0**	**0**	**1**
	Indianapolis Checkers	CHL	42	26	27	53	....	....	....	86	....	....	....	....	....	....	....	....	....	....	....	....	....	....	....	....	....	....
1983-84	**New York Islanders**	**NHL**	**40**	**2**	**5**	**7**	**2**	**3**	**5**	**27**	**0**	**0**	**0**	**31**	**6.5**	**12**	**1**	**13**	**0**	**–2**	**6**	**0**	**0**	**0**	**7**	**0**	**0**	**0**
1984-85	**New York Islanders**	**NHL**	**38**	**5**	**0**	**5**	**4**	**0**	**4**	**50**	**0**	**0**	**1**	**22**	**22.7**	**9**	**0**	**16**	**0**	**–7**	**1**	**0**	**0**	**0**	**0**	**0**	**0**	**0**
1985-86	**Minnesota North Stars**	**NHL**	**38**	**3**	**2**	**5**	**2**	**1**	**3**	**86**	**0**	**0**	**1**	**29**	**10.3**	**10**	**1**	**12**	**0**	**–3**	**1**	**0**	**0**	**0**	**0**	**0**	**0**	**0**
	Springfield Indians	AHL	2	1	1	2	....	....	....	0	....	....	....	....	....	....	....	....	....	....	....	....	....	....	....	....	....	....
1986-87	**Minnesota North Stars**	**NHL**	**6**	**0**	**0**	**0**	**0**	**0**	**0**	**4**	**0**	**0**	**0**	**5**	**0.0**	**0**	**0**	**3**	**0**	**–3**	....	....	....	....	....	....	....	....
1987-88	Sodertalje	Sweden	30	10	13	23	....	....	....	50	....	....	....	....	....	....	....	....	....	....	2	0	1	1	6	....	....	....
1988-89	Sodertalje	Sweden	34	10	6	16	....	....	....	68	....	....	....	....	....	....	....	....	....	....	5	1	1	2	8	....	....	....
1990-91	Malmo IF	Sweden	38	13	14	27	....	....	....	48	....	....	....	....	....	....	....	....	....	....	2	0	2	2	2	....	....	....
1991-92	Malmo IF	Sweden	34	4	9	13	....	....	....	68	....	....	....	....	....	....	....	....	....	....	10	1	1	2	10	....	....	....
	NHL Totals		**152**	**17**	**14**	**31**	**14**	**9**	**23**	**193**	**0**	**0**	**2**	**124**	**13.7**	**56**	**8**	**59**	**0**		**15**	**1**	**0**	**1**	**13**	**0**	**0**	**1**

Signed as a free agent by **NY Islanders**, June 12, 1981. Traded to **Minnesota** by **NY Islanders** for Minnesota's 7th round choice (Will Anderson) in 1986 Entry Draft, September 9, 1985.

• HALWARD, DOUG

Doug "Hawk" Halward D – L. 6'1", 200 lbs. b: Toronto, Ont., 11/1/1955. Boston's 1st choice, 14th overall, in 1975 Amateur Draft.

			REGULAR SEASON																		PLAYOFFS							
Season	Club	League	GP	G	A	Pts	AG	AA	APts	PIM	PP	SH	GW	S	%	TGF	PGF	TGA	PGA	+/-	GP	G	A	Pts	PIM	PP	SH	GW
1973-74	Peterborough Petes	OHA	69	1	15	16	....	....	....	103	....	....	....	....	....	....	....	....	....	....	....	....	....	....	....	....	....	....
	Canada	WJC-A	5	0	0	0	....	....	....	2	....	....	....	....	....	....	....	....	....	....	....	....	....	....	....	....	....	....
1974-75	Peterborough Petes	OHA	68	11	52	63	....	....	....	97	....	....	....	....	....	....	....	....	....	....	3	1	2	3	5	....	....	....
1975-76	**Boston Bruins**	**NHL**	**22**	**1**	**5**	**6**	**1**	**4**	**5**	**6**	**1**	**0**	**0**	**30**	**3.3**	**21**	**4**	**25**	**4**	**–4**	**1**	**0**	**0**	**0**	**0**	**0**	**0**	**0**
	Rochester Americans	AHL	54	6	11	17	....	....	....	51	....	....	....	....	....	....	....	....	....	....	4	1	0	1	4	....	....	....
1976-77	**Boston Bruins**	**NHL**	**18**	**2**	**2**	**4**	**2**	**2**	**4**	**6**	**0**	**0**	**0**	**20**	**10.0**	**16**	**0**	**8**	**1**	**+9**	**6**	**0**	**0**	**0**	**4**	**0**	**0**	**0**
	Rochester Americans	AHL	54	4	28	32	....	....	....	26	....	....	....	....	....	....	....	....	....	....	....	....	....	....	....	....	....	....
1977-78	**Boston Bruins**	**NHL**	**25**	**0**	**2**	**2**	**0**	**2**	**2**	**2**	**0**	**0**	**0**	**18**	**0.0**	**9**	**3**	**14**	**9**	**+1**	....	....	....	....	....	....	....	....
	Rochester Americans	AHL	42	8	14	22	....	....	....	17	....	....	....	....	....	....	....	....	....	....	6	0	3	3	2	....	....	....
1978-79	**Los Angeles Kings**	**NHL**	**27**	**1**	**5**	**6**	**1**	**4**	**5**	**13**	**1**	**0**	**0**	**39**	**2.6**	**31**	**11**	**26**	**2**	**–4**	**1**	**0**	**0**	**0**	**12**	**0**	**0**	**0**
	Springfield Indians	AHL	14	5	1	6	....	....	....	10	....	....	....	....	....	....	....	....	....	....	....	....	....	....	....	....	....	....
1979-80	**Los Angeles Kings**	**NHL**	**63**	**11**	**45**	**56**	**10**	**35**	**45**	**52**	**8**	**0**	**0**	**165**	**6.7**	**141**	**49**	**118**	**40**	**+14**	**1**	**0**	**0**	**0**	**2**	**0**	**0**	**0**
1980-81	**Los Angeles Kings**	**NHL**	**51**	**4**	**15**	**19**	**3**	**10**	**13**	**96**	**1**	**0**	**0**	**74**	**5.4**	**69**	**23**	**61**	**13**	**–2**	....	....	....	....	....	....	....	....
	Vancouver Canucks	**NHL**	**7**	**0**	**1**	**1**	**0**	**1**	**1**	**4**	**0**	**0**	**0**	**8**	**0.0**	**7**	**3**	**9**	**0**	**–5**	**2**	**0**	**1**	**1**	**6**	**0**	**0**	**0**
1981-82	**Vancouver Canucks**	**NHL**	**37**	**4**	**13**	**17**	**3**	**9**	**12**	**40**	**1**	**0**	**0**	**75**	**5.3**	**52**	**18**	**46**	**1**	**–11**	**15**	**2**	**4**	**6**	**44**	**0**	**0**	**1**
	Dallas Black Hawks	CHL	22	8	18	26	....	....	....	49	....	....	....	....	....	....	....	....	....	....	....	....	....	....	....	....	....	....
1982-83	**Vancouver Canucks**	**NHL**	**75**	**19**	**33**	**52**	**16**	**23**	**39**	**83**	**11**	**0**	**2**	**199**	**9.5**	**130**	**46**	**124**	**22**	**–18**	**4**	**1**	**0**	**1**	**21**	**0**	**0**	**0**
	Canada	WEC-A	10	1	2	3	....	....	....	6	....	....	....	....	....	....	....	....	....	....	....	....	....	....	....	....	....	....
1983-84	**Vancouver Canucks**	**NHL**	**54**	**7**	**16**	**23**	**6**	**11**	**17**	**35**	**2**	**0**	**1**	**108**	**6.5**	**78**	**27**	**70**	**20**	**+1**	**4**	**3**	**1**	**4**	**2**	**2**	**0**	**0**
1984-85	**Vancouver Canucks**	**NHL**	**71**	**7**	**27**	**34**	**6**	**18**	**24**	**82**	**2**	**1**	**0**	**173**	**4.0**	**110**	**32**	**164**	**44**	**–42**	....	....	....	....	....	....	....	....
	Canada	WEC-A	10	1	2	3	....	....	....	4	....	....	....	....	....	....	....	....	....	....	....	....	....	....	....	....	....	....
1985-86	**Vancouver Canucks**	**NHL**	**70**	**8**	**25**	**33**	**6**	**17**	**23**	**111**	**3**	**0**	**0**	**122**	**6.6**	**98**	**29**	**112**	**24**	**–19**	**3**	**0**	**0**	**0**	**4**	**0**	**0**	**0**
1986-87	**Vancouver Canucks**	**NHL**	**10**	**0**	**3**	**3**	**0**	**2**	**2**	**34**	**0**	**0**	**0**	**21**	**0.0**	**8**	**0**	**22**	**6**	**–8**	....	....	....	....	....	....	....	....
	Detroit Red Wings	**NHL**	**11**	**0**	**3**	**3**	**0**	**2**	**2**	**19**	**0**	**0**	**0**	**8**	**0.0**	**11**	**2**	**5**	**0**	**+4**	....	....	....	....	....	....	....	....
1987-88	**Detroit Red Wings**	**NHL**	**70**	**5**	**21**	**26**	**4**	**15**	**19**	**130**	**3**	**0**	**1**	**88**	**5.7**	**103**	**31**	**96**	**30**	**+6**	**8**	**1**	**4**	**5**	**10**	**0**	**0**	**0**
1988-89	**Detroit Red Wings**	**NHL**	**18**	**0**	**1**	**1**	**0**	**1**	**1**	**36**	**0**	**0**	**0**	**6**	**0.0**	**14**	**1**	**30**	**6**	**–11**	....	....	....	....	....	....	....	....
	Adirondack Red Wings	AHL	4	1	0	1	....	....	....	0	....	....	....	....	....	....	....	....	....	....	....	....	....	....	....	....	....	....
	Edmonton Oilers	**NHL**	**24**	**0**	**7**	**7**	**0**	**5**	**5**	**26**	**0**	**0**	**0**	**8**	**0.0**	**17**	**1**	**23**	**4**	**–3**	**2**	**0**	**0**	**0**	**0**	**0**	**0**	**0**
	NHL Totals		**653**	**69**	**224**	**293**	**58**	**161**	**219**	**774**	**33**	**1**	**4**	**1161**	**5.9**	**916**	**280**	**953**	**226**		**47**	**7**	**10**	**17**	**113**	**2**	**0**	**1**

Traded to **LA Kings** by **Boston** for future considerations, September 18, 1978. Claimed by **LA Kings** as a fill-in during Expansion Draft, June 13, 1979. Traded to **Vancouver** by **LA Kings** for Vancouver's 5th round choice (Ulf Isaksson) in 1982 Entry Draft, March 8, 1981. Traded to **Detroit** by **Vancouver** for Detroit's 6th round choice (Phil Von Steffanelli) in 1988 Entry Draft, November 21, 1986. Traded to **Edmonton** by **Detroit** for Edmonton's 10th round choice (Jason Glickman) in 1989 Entry Draft, January 23, 1989.

• HAMEL, GILLES

Gilles Hamel LW – L. 6'3", 183 lbs. b: Asbestos, Que., 3/18/1960. Buffalo's 5th choice, 74th overall, in 1979 Entry Draft.

			REGULAR SEASON																		PLAYOFFS							
Season	Club	League	GP	G	A	Pts	AG	AA	APts	PIM	PP	SH	GW	S	%	TGF	PGF	TGA	PGA	+/-	GP	G	A	Pts	PIM	PP	SH	GW
1977-78	Laval National	QMJHL	72	44	37	81	....	....	....	68	....	....	....	....	....	....	....	....	....	....	....	....	....	....	....	....	....	....
1978-79	Laval National	QMJHL	72	56	55	111	....	....	....	130	....	....	....	....	....	....	....	....	....	....	....	....	....	....	....	....	....	....
1979-80	Trois-Rivieres Draveurs	QMJHL	12	13	8	21	....	....	....	8	....	....	....	....	....	....	....	....	....	....	....	....	....	....	....	....	....	....
	Chicoutimi Sagueneens	QMJHL	57	73	62	135	....	....	....	87	....	....	....	....	....	....	....	....	....	....	12	10	6	16	20	....	....	....
	Rochester Americans	AHL	....	....	....	....	....	....	....	....	....	....	....	....	....	....	....	....	....	....	1	0	0	0	0	....	....	....
1980-81	**Buffalo Sabres**	**NHL**	**51**	**10**	**9**	**19**	**8**	**6**	**14**	**53**	**2**	**0**	**0**	**56**	**17.9**	**27**	**5**	**30**	**0**	**–8**	**5**	**0**	**1**	**1**	**4**	**0**	**0**	**0**
	Rochester Americans	AHL	14	8	7	15	....	....	....	7	....	....	....	....	....	....	....	....	....	....	....	....	....	....	....	....	....	....
1981-82	**Buffalo Sabres**	**NHL**	**16**	**2**	**7**	**9**	**2**	**5**	**7**	**2**	**0**	**0**	**1**	**17**	**11.8**	**9**	**0**	**10**	**0**	**–1**	....	....	....	....	....	....	....	....
	Rochester Americans	AHL	57	31	44	75	....	....	....	55	....	....	....	....	....	....	....	....	....	....	....	....	....	....	....	....	....	....
1982-83	**Buffalo Sabres**	**NHL**	**66**	**22**	**20**	**42**	**18**	**14**	**32**	**26**	**2**	**0**	**1**	**120**	**18.3**	**53**	**10**	**39**	**0**	**+4**	**9**	**2**	**2**	**4**	**2**	**1**	**0**	**0**
1983-84	**Buffalo Sabres**	**NHL**	**75**	**21**	**23**	**44**	**17**	**16**	**33**	**37**	**4**	**2**	**1**	**135**	**15.6**	**66**	**14**	**53**	**5**	**+4**	**3**	**0**	**2**	**2**	**2**	**0**	**0**	**0**
1984-85	**Buffalo Sabres**	**NHL**	**80**	**18**	**30**	**48**	**15**	**20**	**35**	**36**	**5**	**3**	**4**	**163**	**11.0**	**89**	**31**	**70**	**9**	**–3**	**1**	**0**	**0**	**0**	**0**	**0**	**0**	**0**
1985-86	**Buffalo Sabres**	**NHL**	**77**	**19**	**25**	**44**	**15**	**17**	**32**	**61**	**4**	**3**	**4**	**158**	**12.0**	**58**	**15**	**94**	**24**	**–27**	....	....	....	....	....	....	....	....
1986-87	**Winnipeg Jets**	**NHL**	**79**	**27**	**21**	**48**	**23**	**15**	**38**	**24**	**1**	**1**	**4**	**175**	**15.4**	**65**	**2**	**66**	**6**	**+3**	**8**	**2**	**0**	**2**	**2**	**0**	**0**	**2**
1987-88	**Winnipeg Jets**	**NHL**	**63**	**8**	**11**	**19**	**7**	**8**	**15**	**35**	**1**	**0**	**0**	**106**	**7.5**	**30**	**3**	**44**	**1**	**–16**	**1**	**0**	**0**	**0**	**0**	**0**	**0**	**0**
1988-89	**Winnipeg Jets**	**NHL**	**1**	**0**	**0**	**0**	**0**	**0**	**0**	**0**	**0**	**0**	**0**	**0**	**0.0**	**0**	**0**	**0**	**0**	**0**	....	....	....	....	....	....	....	....
	Moncton Hawks	AHL	14	7	5	12	....	....	....	10	....	....	....	....	....	....	....	....	....	....	....	....	....	....	....	....	....	....
	Los Angeles Kings	**NHL**	**11**	**0**	**1**	**1**	**0**	**1**	**1**	**2**	**0**	**0**	**0**	**11**	**0.0**	**3**	**0**	**6**	**0**	**–3**	....	....	....	....	....	....	....	....
	New Haven Nighthawks	AHL	34	9	9	18	....	....	....	12	....	....	....	....	....	....	....	....	....	....	1	0	0	0	0	....	....	....
	NHL Totals		**519**	**127**	**147**	**274**	**105**	**102**	**207**	**276**	**19**	**9**	**15**	**941**	**13.5**	**400**	**80**	**412**	**45**		**27**	**4**	**5**	**9**	**10**	**1**	**0**	**2**

QMJHL Second All-Star Team (1979) • QMJHL First All-Star Team (1980)

Traded to **Winnipeg** by **Buffalo** for Scott Arniel, June 21, 1988. Traded to **LA Kings** by **Winnipeg** for Paul Fenton, Novemnber 21, 1988.

• HAMEL, JEAN

Jean Hamel D – L. 5'11", 195 lbs. b: Asbestos, Que., 6/6/1952. St. Louis' 2nd choice, 41st overall, in 1972 Amateur Draft.

			REGULAR SEASON																		PLAYOFFS							
Season	Club	League	GP	G	A	Pts	AG	AA	APts	PIM	PP	SH	GW	S	%	TGF	PGF	TGA	PGA	+/-	GP	G	A	Pts	PIM	PP	SH	GW
1969-70	Drummondville Rangers	QJHL	56	4	11	15	....	....	....	75	....	....	....	....	....	....	....	....	....	....	6	1	1	2	20	....	....	....
1970-71	Drummondville Rangers	QJHL	61	7	23	30	....	....	....	109	....	....	....	....	....	....	....	....	....	....	6	1	1	2	8	....	....	....
1971-72	Drummondville Rangers	QMJHL	59	6	29	35	....	....	....	132	....	....	....	....	....	....	....	....	....	....	9	1	0	1	48	....	....	....
1972-73	**St. Louis Blues**	**NHL**	**55**	**2**	**7**	**9**	**2**	**6**	**8**	**24**	**0**	**0**	**0**	**56**	**3.6**	**41**	**1**	**51**	**6**	**–5**	**2**	**0**	**0**	**0**	**0**	**0**	**0**	**0**
	Denver Spurs	WHL	13	0	6	6	....	....	....	22	....	....	....	....	....	....	....	....	....	....	....	....	....	....	....	....	....	....
1973-74	**St. Louis Blues**	**NHL**	**23**	**1**	**1**	**2**	**1**	**1**	**2**	**6**	**0**	**0**	**0**	**21**	**4.8**	**12**	**0**	**17**	**2**	**–3**	....	....	....	....	....	....	....	....
	Denver Spurs	WHL	10	0	2	2	....	....	....	12	....	....	....	....	....	....	....	....	....	....	....	....	....	....	....	....	....	....
	Detroit Red Wings	**NHL**	**22**	**0**	**3**	**3**	**0**	**3**	**3**	**40**	**0**	**0**	**0**	**18**	**0.0**	**23**	**4**	**40**	**9**	**–12**	....	....	....	....	....	....	....	....
1974-75	**Detroit Red Wings**	**NHL**	**80**	**5**	**19**	**24**	**5**	**15**	**20**	**136**	**0**	**0**	**0**	**112**	**4.5**	**95**	**12**	**157**	**34**	**–40**	....	....	....	....	....	....	....	....
1975-76	**Detroit Red Wings**	**NHL**	**77**	**3**	**9**	**12**	**3**	**7**	**10**	**129**	**1**	**0**	**0**	**92**	**3.3**	**64**	**4**	**103**	**30**	**–13**	....	....	....	....	....	....	....	....
1976-77	**Detroit Red Wings**	**NHL**	**71**	**1**	**10**	**11**	**1**	**8**	**9**	**63**	**0**	**0**	**0**	**85**	**1.2**	**44**	**0**	**85**	**23**	**–18**	....	....	....	....	....	....	....	....
1977-78	**Detroit Red Wings**	**NHL**	**32**	**2**	**6**	**8**	**2**	**5**	**7**	**34**	**0**	**0**	**0**	**37**	**5.4**	**23**	**0**	**21**	**1**	**+3**	**7**	**0**	**0**	**0**	**10**	**0**	**0**	**0**
	Kansas City Red Wings	CHL	28	2	10	12	....	....	....	29	....	....	....	....	....	....	....	....	....	....	....	....	....	....	....	....	....	....
1978-79	**Detroit Red Wings**	**NHL**	**52**	**2**	**4**	**6**	**2**	**3**	**5**	**72**	**0**	**0**	**0**	**41**	**4.9**	**28**	**3**	**35**	**1**	**–9**	....	....	....	....	....	....	....	....
1979-80	**Detroit Red Wings**	**NHL**	**49**	**1**	**4**	**5**	**1**	**3**	**4**	**43**	**0**	**0**	**0**	**27**	**3.7**	**19**	**1**	**23**	**3**	**–2**	....	....	....	....	....	....	....	....
1980-81	**Detroit Red Wings**	**NHL**	**68**	**5**	**7**	**12**	**4**	**5**	**9**	**57**	**0**	**0**	**0**	**47**	**10.6**	**32**	**0**	**46**	**13**	**–1**	....	....	....	....	....	....	....	....
	Adirondack Red Wings	AHL	7	1	3	4	....	....	....	36	....	....	....	....	....	....	....	....	....	....	....	....	....	....	....	....	....	....

			REGULAR SEASON																		PLAYOFFS							
Season	Club	League	GP	G	A	Pts	AG	AA	APts	PIM	PP	SH	GW	S	%	TGF	PGF	TGA	PGA	+/–	GP	G	A	Pts	PIM	PP	SH	GW
1981-82	**Quebec Nordiques**	**NHL**	**40**	**1**	**6**	**7**	**1**	**4**	**5**	**32**	**0**	**0**	**1**	**28**	**3.6**	**50**	**1**	**59**	**13**	**+3**	**5**	**0**	**0**	**0**	**16**	**0**	**0**	**0**
	Fredericton Express	AHL	16	2	4	6	....	....	....	19	....	....	....	....	....	....	....	....	....	....	....	....	....	....	....	....	....	....
1982-83	**Quebec Nordiques**	**NHL**	**51**	**2**	**7**	**9**	**2**	**5**	**7**	**38**	**0**	**0**	**0**	**45**	**4.4**	**55**	**0**	**64**	**20**	**+11**	**4**	**0**	**0**	**0**	**2**	**0**	**0**	**0**
1983-84	**Montreal Canadiens**	**NHL**	**79**	**1**	**12**	**13**	**1**	**8**	**9**	**92**	**0**	**0**	**0**	**68**	**1.5**	**84**	**0**	**91**	**14**	**+7**	**15**	**0**	**2**	**2**	**16**	**0**	**0**	**0**
	NHL Totals		**699**	**26**	**95**	**121**	**25**	**73**	**98**	**766**	**1**	**0**	**1**	**677**	**3.8**	**570**	**26**	**792**	**169**		**33**	**0**	**2**	**2**	**44**	**0**	**0**	**0**

QMJHL Second All-Star Team (1972)

Traded to **Detroit** by **St. Louis** with Chris Evans and Bryan Watson for Ted Harris, Bill Collins and Garnet Bailey, February 14, 1974. Claimed as a fill-in by **Detroit** during Expansion Draft, June 13, 1979. Signed as a free agent by **Quebec**, October 6, 1981. Claimed by **Montreal** from **Quebec** in Waiver Draft, October 3, 1983.

• HAMILTON, AL

Al Hamilton D – R. 6'1", 195 lbs. b: Flin Flon, Man., 8/20/1946.

Season	Club	League	GP	G	A	Pts	AG	AA	APts	PIM	PP	SH	GW	S	%	TGF	PGF	TGA	PGA	+/–	GP	G	A	Pts	PIM	PP	SH	GW
1963-64	Edmonton Oil Kings	SJHL	14	4	7	11	....	....	....	26	....	....	....	....	....	....	....	....	....	....	....	....	....	....	....	....	....	....
1964-65	Edmonton Oil Kings	SJHL	STATISTICS NOT AVAILABLE																									
	St. Paul Rangers	CHL	3	0	2	2	....	....	....	0	....	....	....	....	....	....	....	....	....	....	....	....	....	....	....	....	....	....
1965-66	**New York Rangers**	**NHL**	**4**	**0**	**0**	**0**	**0**	**0**	**0**	**0**	....	....	....	....	....	....	....	....	....	....	....	....	....	....	....	....	....	....
	Edmonton Oil Kings	ASHL	....	15	22	37	....	....	....	99	....	....	....	....	....	....	....	....	....	....	....	....	....	....	....	....	....	....
1966-67	Omaha Knights	CHL	68	11	25	36	....	....	....	96	....	....	....	....	....	....	....	....	....	....	12	4	3	7	16	....	....	....
1967-68	**New York Rangers**	**NHL**	**2**	**0**	**0**	**0**	**0**	**0**	**0**	**0**	**0**	**0**	**0**	**0**	**0.0**	**0**	**0**	**0**	**0**	**0**	....	....	....	....	....	....	....	....
	Buffalo Bisons	AHL	72	9	21	30	....	....	....	82	....	....	....	....	....	....	....	....	....	....	5	0	4	4	23	....	....	....
1968-69	**New York Rangers**	**NHL**	**16**	**0**	**0**	**0**	**0**	**0**	**0**	**8**	**0**	**0**	**0**	**9**	**0.0**	**2**	**0**	**3**	**1**	**0**	**1**	**0**	**0**	**0**	**0**	**0**	**0**	**0**
	Buffalo Bisons	AHL	41	4	14	18	....	....	....	61	....	....	....	....	....	....	....	....	....	....	6	0	4	4	12	....	....	....
1969-70	**New York Rangers**	**NHL**	**59**	**0**	**5**	**5**	**0**	**5**	**5**	**54**	**0**	**0**	**0**	**42**	**0.0**	**24**	**3**	**38**	**9**	**–8**	**5**	**0**	**0**	**0**	**2**	**0**	**0**	**0**
1970-71	**Buffalo Sabres**	**NHL**	**69**	**2**	**28**	**30**	**2**	**25**	**27**	**71**	**0**	**0**	**0**	**98**	**2.0**	**81**	**13**	**114**	**23**	**–23**	....	....	....	....	....	....	....	....
1971-72	**Buffalo Sabres**	**NHL**	**76**	**4**	**30**	**34**	**4**	**27**	**31**	**105**	**1**	**0**	**1**	**91**	**4.4**	**93**	**13**	**119**	**27**	**–12**	....	....	....	....	....	....	....	....
1972-73	Alberta Oilers	WHA	78	11	50	61	....	....	....	124	....	....	....	....	....	....	....	....	....	....	....	....	....	....	....	....	....	....
1973-74	Edmonton Oilers	WHA	78	14	45	59	....	....	....	104	....	....	....	....	....	....	....	....	....	....	4	1	1	2	15	....	....	....
1974-75	Edmonton Oilers	WHA	25	1	13	14	....	....	....	42	....	....	....	....	....	....	....	....	....	....	....	....	....	....	....	....	....	....
1975-76	Edmonton Oilers	WHA	54	2	32	34	....	....	....	78	....	....	....	....	....	....	....	....	....	....	4	0	1	1	6	....	....	....
1976-77	Edmonton Oilers	WHA	81	8	37	45	....	....	....	60	....	....	....	....	....	....	....	....	....	....	5	0	4	4	4	....	....	....
1977-78	Edmonton Oilers	WHA	59	11	43	54	....	....	....	46	....	....	....	....	....	....	....	....	....	....	....	....	....	....	....	....	....	....
1978-79	Edmonton Oilers	WHA	80	6	38	44	....	....	....	38	....	....	....	....	....	....	....	....	....	....	13	4	5	9	4	....	....	....
1979-80	**Edmonton Oilers**	**NHL**	**31**	**4**	**15**	**19**	**4**	**11**	**15**	**20**	**1**	**0**	**0**	**34**	**11.8**	**40**	**9**	**40**	**7**	**–2**	**1**	**0**	**0**	**0**	**0**	**0**	**0**	**0**
	Houston Apollos	CHL	4	0	0	0	....	....	....	0	....	....	....	....	....	....	....	....	....	....	....	....	....	....	....	....	....	....
	NHL Totals		**257**	**10**	**78**	**88**	**10**	**68**	**78**	**258**	**2**	**0**	**1**	**274**	**3.6**	**240**	**38**	**314**	**67**		**7**	**0**	**0**	**0**	**2**	**0**	**0**	**0**
	Other Major League Totals		455	53	258	311	....	....	....	492	....	....	....	....	....	....	....	....	....	....	26	5	11	16	29	....	....	....

CHL Second All-Star Team (1967) • WHA Second All-Star Team (1974) • WHA First All-Star Team (1978)

Claimed by **Buffalo** from **NY Rangers** in Expansion Draft, June 10, 1970. Selected by **Alberta** (WHA) in 1972 WHA General Player Draft, February 12, 1972. Rights retained by **Edmonton** prior to Expansion Draft, June 9, 1979.

• HAMILTON, CHUCK

Chuck Hamilton LW – L. 5'11", 175 lbs. b: Kirkland Lake, Ont., 1/18/1939.

Season	Club	League	GP	G	A	Pts	AG	AA	APts	PIM	PP	SH	GW	S	%	TGF	PGF	TGA	PGA	+/–	GP	G	A	Pts	PIM	PP	SH	GW
1956-57	Peterborough Petes	OHA	52	7	11	18	....	....	....	15	....	....	....	....	....	....	....	....	....	....	....	....	....	....	....	....	....	....
1957-58	Peterborough Petes	OHA	52	8	14	22	....	....	....	50	....	....	....	....	....	....	....	....	....	....	5	1	1	2	4	....	....	....
1958-59	Peterborough Petes	OHA	46	18	28	46	....	....	....	47	....	....	....	....	....	....	....	....	....	....	19	7	9	16	16	....	....	....
1959-60	Hull-Ottawa Canadiens	EPHL	66	6	13	19	....	....	....	39	....	....	....	....	....	....	....	....	....	....	7	0	2	2	6	....	....	....
1960-61	Hull-Ottawa Canadiens	EPHL	40	1	7	8	....	....	....	56	....	....	....	....	....	....	....	....	....	....	14	0	2	2	20	....	....	....
1961-62	Hull-Ottawa Canadiens	EPHL	57	5	9	14	....	....	....	50	....	....	....	....	....	....	....	....	....	....	11	1	3	4	4	....	....	....
	Montreal Canadiens	**NHL**	**1**	**0**	**0**	**0**	**0**	**0**	**0**	**0**	....	....	....	....	....	....	....	....	....	....	....	....	....	....	....	....	....	....
1962-63	Hull-Ottawa Canadiens	EPHL	64	17	33	50	....	....	....	51	....	....	....	....	....	....	....	....	....	....	3	0	1	1	6	....	....	....
1963-64	Hershey Bears	AHL	72	8	30	38	....	....	....	31	....	....	....	....	....	....	....	....	....	....	6	0	3	3	2	....	....	....
1964-65	Hershey Bears	AHL	55	7	15	22	....	....	....	47	....	....	....	....	....	....	....	....	....	....	15	2	0	2	4	....	....	....
1965-66	Hershey Bears	AHL	67	7	16	23	....	....	....	24	....	....	....	....	....	....	....	....	....	....	3	0	2	2	0	....	....	....
1966-67	Hershey Bears	AHL	62	9	12	21	....	....	....	20	....	....	....	....	....	....	....	....	....	....	5	0	0	0	0	....	....	....
1967-68	Hershey Bears	AHL	69	8	22	30	....	....	....	65	....	....	....	....	....	....	....	....	....	....	5	0	1	1	18	....	....	....
1968-69	Hershey Bears	AHL	74	28	46	74	....	....	....	46	....	....	....	....	....	....	....	....	....	....	11	2	4	6	16	....	....	....
1969-70	Hershey Bears	AHL	60	10	20	30	....	....	....	8	....	....	....	....	....	....	....	....	....	....	7	1	4	5	0	....	....	....
1970-71			DID NOT PLAY – INJURED																									
1971-72	Denver Spurs	WHL	70	14	18	32	....	....	....	29	....	....	....	....	....	....	....	....	....	....	9	1	3	4	4	....	....	....
1972-73	**St. Louis Blues**	**NHL**	**3**	**0**	**2**	**2**	**0**	**2**	**2**	**2**	**0**	**0**	**0**	**2**	**0.0**	**5**	**0**	**1**	**0**	**+4**	....	....	....	....	....	....	....	....
	Denver Spurs	WHL	47	7	25	32	....	....	....	64	....	....	....	....	....	....	....	....	....	....	5	0	0	0	4	....	....	....
	NHL Totals		**4**	**0**	**2**	**2**	**0**	**2**	**2**	**2**	**0**	**0**	**0**	**2**	**0.0**	**5**	**0**	**1**	**0**		....	....	....	....	....	....	....	....

Rights sold to **Hershey** (AHL) by **Montreal** with Ralph Keller for Mark Reaume, June 4, 1963. Claimed by **Detroit** from **Hershey** (AHL) in Reverse Draft, June 6, 1969. Traded to **Montreal** by **Detroit** for cash, June 11, 1969. Traded to **Hershey** (AHL) by **Montreal** for cash, October, 1969. • Missed entire 1970-71 season after fracturing leg in exhibition game vs. Baltimore (AHL), September 25, 1970. Traded to **St. Louis** (Denver-WHL) by **Hershey** for cash, September, 1971.

• HAMILTON, JIM

Jim Hamilton RW – L. 6', 180 lbs. b: Barrie, Ont., 1/18/1957. Pittsburgh's 1st choice, 30th overall, in 1977 Amateur Draft.

Season	Club	League	GP	G	A	Pts	AG	AA	APts	PIM	PP	SH	GW	S	%	TGF	PGF	TGA	PGA	+/–	GP	G	A	Pts	PIM	PP	SH	GW
1973-74	London Knights	OHA	70	9	14	23	....	....	....	19	....	....	....	....	....	....	....	....	....	....	....	....	....	....	....	....	....	....
1974-75	London Knights	OHA	68	17	24	41	....	....	....	108	....	....	....	....	....	....	....	....	....	....	....	....	....	....	....	....	....	....
1975-76	London Knights	OHA	53	24	23	47	....	....	....	37	....	....	....	....	....	....	....	....	....	....	5	2	2	4	0	....	....	....
1976-77	London Knights	OHA	65	39	53	92	....	....	....	40	....	....	....	....	....	....	....	....	....	....	19	6	5	11	16	....	....	....
1977-78	**Pittsburgh Penguins**	**NHL**	**25**	**2**	**4**	**6**	**2**	**3**	**5**	**2**	**0**	**0**	**0**	**35**	**5.7**	**13**	**3**	**13**	**0**	**–3**	....	....	....	....	....	....	....	....
	Binghamton Whalers	AHL	31	4	4	8	....	....	....	19	....	....	....	....	....	....	....	....	....	....	....	....	....	....	....	....	....	....
	Grand Rapids Owls	IHL	22	7	15	22	....	....	....	12	....	....	....	....	....	....	....	....	....	....	....	....	....	....	....	....	....	....
1978-79	**Pittsburgh Penguins**	**NHL**	**2**	**0**	**0**	**0**	**0**	**0**	**0**	**0**	**0**	**0**	**0**	**3**	**0.0**	**1**	**0**	**1**	**0**	**0**	**5**	**3**	**0**	**3**	**0**	**1**	**0**	**0**
	Binghamton Whalers	AHL	66	25	24	49	....	....	....	34	....	....	....	....	....	....	....	....	....	....	6	2	3	5	2	....	....	....
1979-80	**Pittsburgh Penguins**	**NHL**	**10**	**2**	**0**	**2**	**2**	**0**	**2**	**0**	**0**	**0**	**0**	**12**	**16.7**	**5**	**0**	**11**	**0**	**–6**	....	....	....	....	....	....	....	....
	Syracuse Firebirds	AHL	50	16	19	35	....	....	....	33	....	....	....	....	....	....	....	....	....	....	4	0	1	1	4	....	....	....
1980-81	**Pittsburgh Penguins**	**NHL**	**20**	**1**	**6**	**7**	**1**	**4**	**5**	**18**	**0**	**0**	**0**	**26**	**3.8**	**10**	**1**	**7**	**0**	**+2**	**1**	**0**	**0**	**0**	**0**	**0**	**0**	**0**
	Binghamton Whalers	AHL	28	16	18	34	....	....	....	31	....	....	....	....	....	....	....	....	....	....	....	....	....	....	....	....	....	....
1981-82	**Pittsburgh Penguins**	**NHL**	**11**	**5**	**3**	**8**	**4**	**2**	**6**	**2**	**0**	**0**	**1**	**15**	**33.3**	**9**	**0**	**7**	**0**	**+2**	....	....	....	....	....	....	....	....
	Erie Blades	AHL	57	27	17	44	....	....	....	51	....	....	....	....	....	....	....	....	....	....	....	....	....	....	....	....	....	....
1982-83	**Pittsburgh Penguins**	**NHL**	**5**	**0**	**2**	**2**	**0**	**1**	**1**	**2**	**0**	**0**	**0**	**12**	**0.0**	**2**	**0**	**4**	**0**	**–2**	....	....	....	....	....	....	....	....
	Baltimore Skipjacks	AHL	45	32	10	42	....	....	....	36	....	....	....	....	....	....	....	....	....	....	....	....	....	....	....	....	....	....
1983-84	**Pittsburgh Penguins**	**NHL**	**11**	**2**	**2**	**4**	**2**	**1**	**3**	**4**	**1**	**0**	**0**	**21**	**9.5**	**10**	**2**	**6**	**0**	**+2**	....	....	....	....	....	....	....	....
	Baltimore Skipjacks	AHL	66	34	45	79	....	....	....	54	....	....	....	....	....	....	....	....	....	....	9	6	6	12	0	....	....	....
1984-85	**Pittsburgh Penguins**	**NHL**	**11**	**2**	**1**	**3**	**2**	**1**	**3**	**0**	**0**	**0**	**0**	**19**	**10.5**	**6**	**0**	**15**	**3**	**–6**	....	....	....	....	....	....	....	....
	Baltimore Skipjacks	AHL	16	5	6	11	....	....	....	24	....	....	....	....	....	....	....	....	....	....	....	....	....	....	....	....	....	....
	Muskegon Mohawks	IHL	1	0	0	0	....	....	....	0	....	....	....	....	....	....	....	....	....	....	....	....	....	....	....	....	....	....
	Zurich EC	Switz.	....	17	4	21	....	....	....	....	....	....	....	....	....	....	....	....	....	....	....	0	1	1	....	....	....	....
	NHL Totals		**95**	**14**	**18**	**32**	**13**	**12**	**25**	**28**	**1**	**0**	**1**	**143**	**9.8**	**56**	**6**	**64**	**3**		**6**	**3**	**0**	**3**	**0**	**1**	**0**	**0**

• HAMMARSTROM, INGE

Inge Hammarstrom LW – L. 6', 180 lbs. b: Sundsvall, Sweden, 1/20/1948.

Season	Club	League	GP	G	A	Pts	AG	AA	APts	PIM	PP	SH	GW	S	%	TGF	PGF	TGA	PGA	+/–	GP	G	A	Pts	PIM	PP	SH	GW
1969-70	Brynas IF	Sweden	14	7	4	11	....	....	....	2	....	....	....	....	....	....	....	....	....	....	14	7	1	8	2	....	....	....
1970-71	Brynas IF	Sweden	14	6	11	17	....	....	....	4	....	....	....	....	....	....	....	....	....	....	14	4	2	6	4	....	....	....
	Sweden	WEC-A	7	2	1	3	....	....	....	4	....	....	....	....	....	....	....	....	....	....	....	....	....	....	....	....	....	....
1971-72	Brynas IF	Sweden	28	19	9	28	....	....	....	10	....	....	....	....	....	....	....	....	....	....	10	6	0	6	0	....	....	....
	Sweden	Olympics	6	4	2	6	....	....	....	0	....	....	....	....	....	....	....	....	....	....	....	....	....	....	....	....	....	....
	Sweden	WEC-A	10	6	0	6	....	....	....	0	....	....	....	....	....	....	....	....	....	....	....	....	....	....	....	....	....	....
1972-73	Brynas IF	Sweden	28	18	11	29	....	....	....	14	....	....	....	....	....	....	....	....	....	....	14	10	6	16	8	....	....	....
	Sweden	WEC-A	10	6	3	9	....	....	....	2	....	....	....	....	....	....	....	....	....	....	....	....	....	....	....	....	....	....
1973-74	**Toronto Maple Leafs**	**NHL**	**66**	**20**	**23**	**43**	**20**	**20**	**40**	**14**	**4**	**0**	**4**	**135**	**14.8**	**79**	**21**	**41**	**0**	**+17**	**4**	**1**	**0**	**1**	**0**	**0**	**0**	**0**
1974-75	**Toronto Maple Leafs**	**NHL**	**69**	**21**	**20**	**41**	**19**	**16**	**35**	**23**	**3**	**0**	**2**	**170**	**12.4**	**61**	**15**	**60**	**0**	**–14**	**7**	**1**	**3**	**4**	**4**	**0**	**0**	**1**
1975-76	**Toronto Maple Leafs**	**NHL**	**76**	**19**	**21**	**40**	**18**	**16**	**34**	**21**	**1**	**0**	**5**	**189**	**10.1**	**65**	**15**	**55**	**5**	**0**	....	....	....	....	....	....	....	....

Season	Club	League	GP	G	A	Pts	AG	AA	APts	PIM	PP	SH	GW	S	%	TGF	PGF	TGA	PGA	+/−	GP	G	A	Pts	PIM	PP	SH	GW
1976-77	Sweden	C Cup	5	1	2	3				2																		
	Toronto Maple Leafs	NHL	78	24	17	41	23	14	37	16	5	0	3	154	15.6	80	19	53	0	+8	2	0	0	0	0	0	0	0
1977-78	Toronto Maple Leafs	NHL	3	1	1	2	1	1	2	0	1	0	0	6	16.7	3	2	0	0	+1								
	St. Louis Blues	NHL	70	19	19	38	18	15	33	4	3	0	2	165	11.5	55	16	60	0	−21								
1978-79	St. Louis Blues	NHL	65	12	22	34	11	17	28	8	0	0	1	129	9.3	45	7	51	0	−13								
	Sweden	WEC-A	8	4	1	5				2																		
1979-80	Brynas IF	Sweden	34	16	10	26				30											7	*5	3	*8	6			
1980-81	Brynas IF	Sweden	29	13	8	21				20																		
	Sweden	WEC-A	6	1	1	2				2																		
1981-82	Brynas IF	Sweden	34	10	12	22				20																		
	NHL Totals		427	116	123	239	110	99	209	86	17	0	17	948	12.2	388	95	320	5		13	2	3	5	4	0	0	1

Signed as a free agent by **Toronto**, May 12, 1973. Traded to **St. Louis** by **Toronto** for Jerry Butler, November 1, 1977.

● HAMMOND, KEN
Ken Hammond D – L. 6'1", 190 lbs. b: Port Credit, Ont., 8/22/1963. Los Angeles' 8th choice, 152nd overall, in 1983 Entry Draft.

Season	Club	League	GP	G	A	Pts	AG	AA	APts	PIM	PP	SH	GW	S	%	TGF	PGF	TGA	PGA	+/−	GP	G	A	Pts	PIM	PP	SH	GW
1981-82	RPI Engineers	ECAC	24	2	3	5				54																		
1982-83	RPI Engineers	ECAC	28	17	26	43				8																		
1983-84	RPI Engineers	ECAC	34	5	11	16				72																		
1984-85	RPI Engineers	ECAC	38	11	28	39				90																		
	Los Angeles Kings	NHL	3	1	0	1	1	0	1	0	0	0	1	3	33.3	4	0	5	3	+2	3	0	0	0	4	0	0	0
1985-86	Los Angeles Kings	NHL	3	0	1	1	0	1	1	2	0	0	0	2	0.0	4	1	6	2	−1								
	New Haven Nighthawks	AHL	67	4	12	16				96											4	0	0	0	7			
1986-87	Los Angeles Kings	NHL	10	0	2	2	0	1	1	11																		
	New Haven Nighthawks	AHL	66	1	15	16				76											6	0	1	1	21			
1987-88	Los Angeles Kings	NHL	46	7	9	16	6	6	12	69	1	0	1	52	13.5	47	8	53	13	−1	2	0	0	0	4	0	0	0
	New Haven Nighthawks	AHL	26	3	8	11				27																		
1988-89	Edmonton Oilers	NHL	5	0	1	1	0	1	1	8	0	0	0	1	0.0	2	0	4	0	−2								
	New York Rangers	NHL	3	0	0	0	0	0	0	0	0	0	0	2	0.0	1	0	5	1	−3								
	Denver Rangers	IHL	38	5	18	23				24																		
	Toronto Maple Leafs	NHL	14	0	2	2	0	1	1	12	0	0	0	9	0.0	6	0	23	4	−13								
1989-90	Newmarket Saints	AHL	75	9	45	54				106																		
1990-91	Boston Bruins	NHL	1	1	0	1	1	0	1	2	0	0	0	3	33.3	2	0	0	0	+2	8	0	0	0	10	0	0	0
	Maine Mariners	AHL	80	10	41	51				159											2	0	1	1	16			
1991-92	San Jose Sharks	NHL	46	5	10	15	5	7	12	82	2	0	0	93	5.4	44	12	65	16	−17								
	Vancouver Canucks	NHL																			2	0	0	0	6			
1992-93	Ottawa Senators	NHL	62	4	4	8	3	3	6	104	0	0	0	64	6.3	32	4	101	31	−42								
	New Haven Nighthawks	AHL	4	0	1	1				4																		
1993-94	Providence Bruins	AHL	65	12	45	57				100																		
1994-95	Kansas City Blades	IHL	76	3	24	27				151											21	1	4	5	45			
1995-96	Kansas City Blades	IHL	33	1	7	8				62																		
	NHL Totals		193	18	29	47	16	20	36	290	3	0	2	229	7.9	142	25	262	70		15	0	0	0	24	0	0	0

ECAC First All-Star Team (1985) • NCAA East First All-American Team (1985) • NCAA Championship All-Tournament Team (1985)

Claimed by **Edmonton** from **LA Kings** in Waiver Draft, October 3, 1988. Claimed on waivers by **NY Rangers** from **Edmonton**, November 1, 1988. Traded to **Toronto** by **NY Rangers** for Chris McRae, February 21, 1989. Traded to **Boston** by **Toronto** for cash, August 20, 1990. Signed as a free agent by **San Jose**, August 9, 1991. Traded to **Vancouver** by **San Jose** for Vancouver's 8th round choice (later traded to Detroit — Detroit selected C.J. Denomme) in 1992 Entry Draft, March 9, 1992. Claimed by **Ottawa** from **Vancouver** in Expansion Draft, June 18, 1992.

● HAMPSON, GORD
Gord Hampson LW – L. 6'3", 210 lbs. b: Vancouver, B.C., 2/13/1959.

Season	Club	League	GP	G	A	Pts	AG	AA	APts	PIM	PP	SH	GW	S	%	TGF	PGF	TGA	PGA	+/−	GP	G	A	Pts	PIM	PP	SH	GW
1977-78	University of Michigan	WCHA	36	9	7	16				21																		
1978-79	University of Michigan	WCHA	36	8	6	14				24																		
1979-80	University of Michigan	WCHA	30	7	15	22				22																		
1980-81	University of Michigan	WCHA	40	15	23	38				40																		
1981-82	Oklahoma City Stars	CHL	71	11	23	34				48											1	0	0	0	0			
1982-83	Calgary Flames	NHL	4	0	0	0	0	0	0	6	0	0	0	4	0.0	0	0	2	0	−2								
	Colorado Flames	CHL	51	17	17	34				73											6	2	5	7	4			
1983-84	Colorado Flames	CHL	62	19	25	44				89																		
	NHL Totals		4	0	0	0	0	0	0	6	0	0	0	4	0.0	0	0	2	0									

Signed as a free agent by **Calgary**, June 8, 1981.

● HAMPSON, TED
Ted Hampson C – L. 5'8", 173 lbs. b: Togo, Sask., 12/11/1936.

Season	Club	League	GP	G	A	Pts	AG	AA	APts	PIM	PP	SH	GW	S	%	TGF	PGF	TGA	PGA	+/−	GP	G	A	Pts	PIM	PP	SH	GW
1953-54	Flin Flon Bombers	SJHL																			1	1	0	1	0			
1954-55	Flin Flon Bombers	SJHL	13	6	6	12				4											1	0	0	0	0			
1955-56	Flin Flon Bombers	SJHL	48	51	*62	*113				16											12	*9	*12	*21	4			
1956-57	Flin Flon Bombers	SJHL	55	48	*70	*118				37											10	6	*13	19	4			
	Brandon Regals	WHL	2	1	3	4				0																		
1957-58	Providence Reds	AHL	70	15	25	40				22											5	0	2	2	0			
1958-59	Vancouver Canucks	WHL	66	27	41	68				23											9	1	4	5	0			
1959-60	Toronto Maple Leafs	NHL	41	2	8	10	2	8	10	17																		
	Rochester Americans	AHL	29	6	18	24				9											12	2	4	6	2			
1960-61	New York Rangers	NHL	69	6	14	20	7	14	21	4																		
1961-62	New York Rangers	NHL	68	4	24	28	5	24	29	10																		
1962-63	New York Rangers	NHL	46	4	2	6	5	2	7	2											6	0	1	1	0			
	Baltimore Clippers	AHL	22	12	14	26				4											3	1	2	3	0			
1963-64	Detroit Red Wings	NHL	7	0	1	1	0	1	1	0																		
	Pittsburgh Hornets	AHL	66	15	33	48				6											5	2	2	4	0			
1964-65	Detroit Red Wings	NHL	1	0	0	0	0	0	0	0																		
	Pittsburgh Hornets	AHL	64	15	39	54				39											4	1	2	3	2			
1965-66	Pittsburgh Hornets	AHL	72	20	29	49				6											3	1	0	1	0			
1966-67	Detroit Red Wings	NHL	65	13	35	48	16	36	52	4																		
	Pittsburgh Hornets	AHL	7	1	4	5				2																		
1967-68	Detroit Red Wings	NHL	37	9	18	27	11	19	30	10	0	0	2	75	12.0	38	6	27	3	+8								
	Oakland Seals	NHL	34	8	19	27	10	20	30	4	2	0	1	72	11.1	35	14	39	8	−10								
1968-69	Oakland Seals	NHL	76	26	49	75	29	46	75	6	9	0	3	189	13.8	101	30	89	5	−15	7	3	4	7	2	0	0	0
1969-70	Oakland Seals	NHL	76	17	35	52	20	35	55	13	7	1	0	157	10.8	74	26	87	22	−17	4	1	1	2	0	0	0	0
1970-71	California Golden Seals	NHL	60	10	20	30	10	18	28	14	1	1	0	124	8.1	47	10	89	31	−21								
	Minnesota North Stars	NHL	18	4	6	10	4	5	9	4	1	3	2	34	11.8	11	2	15	0	−1								
1971-72	Minnesota North Stars	NHL	78	5	14	19	5	13	18	6	0	2	0	100	5.0	26	1	61	35	−1	11	3	3	6	0	1	0	0
1972-73	Minnesota Fighting Saints	WHA	76	17	45	62				20											5	0	1	1	0	0	0	0
1973-74	Minnesota Fighting Saints	WHA	77	17	38	55				9											11	4	4	8	4			
1974-75	Minnesota Fighting Saints	WHA	78	17	36	53				14											12	1	7	8	0			
1975-76	Minnesota Fighting Saints	WHA	59	5	15	20				14																		
	Quebec Nordiques	WHA	14	4	10	14				2											5	0	2	2	10			
1976-77			DID NOT PLAY																									
1977-78			DID NOT PLAY																									

			Regular Season																		Playoffs							
Season	Club	League	GP	G	A	Pts	AG	AA	APts	PIM	PP	SH	GW	S	%	TGF	PGF	TGA	PGA	+/-	GP	G	A	Pts	PIM	PP	SH	GW
1978-79	Oklahoma City Stars	CHL	23	2	7	9	....	....	....	4	....	....	....	....	....	....	....	....	....	....	....	....	....	....	....	....	....	....
1979-80	Oklahoma City Stars	CHL	3	0	1	1	....	....	....	0	....	....	....	....	....	....	....	....	....	....	....	....	....	....	....	....	....	....
1980-81	Oklahoma City Stars	CHL	6	0	0	0	....	....	....	12	....	....	....	....	....	....	....	....	....	....	....	....	....	....	....	....	....	....
	NHL Totals		**676**	**108**	**245**	**353**	**124**	**241**	**365**	**94**	**20**	**7**	**8**	**751**	**14.4**	**332**	**89**	**407**	**107**		**35**	**7**	**10**	**17**	**2**	**3**	**0**	**0**
	Other Major League Totals		304	60	144	204	....	....	....	51	....	....	....	....	....	....	....	....	....		33	6	16	22	18	....	....	....

Won Bill Masterton Trophy (1969) • Won Paul Daneau Trophy (WHA Most Gentlemanly Player) (1973)

Played in NHL All-Star Game (1969)

Claimed on waivers by **Toronto** from **NY Rangers**, September 18, 1959. Claimed by **NY Rangers** from **Toronto** in Intra-League Draft, June 8, 1960. Claimed by **Detroit** from **NY Rangers** in Intra-League Draft, June 4, 1963. Traded to **Oakland** by **Detroit** with John Brenneman and Bert Marshall for Kent Douglas, January 9, 1968. Traded to **Minnesota** by **Oakland** with Wayne Muloin for Tom Williams and Dick Redmond, March 7, 1971. Selected by **Winnipeg** (WHA) in 1972 WHA General Player Draft, February 12, 1972. Claimed by **NY Islanders** from **Minnesota** in Expansion Draft, June 6, 1972. WHA rights traded to **Minnesota** (WHA) by **Winnipeg** (WHA) for cash, August, 1972. Signed as a free agent by **Quebec** (WHA) after **Minnesota** (WHA) franchise folded, February 27, 1976. Signed as a free agent by **Minnesota**, January 1, 1979.

• HAMPTON, RICK

Rick Hampton LW/D – L. 6′, 190 lbs. b: King City, Ont., 6/14/1956. California's 1st choice, 3rd overall, in 1974 Amateur Draft.

Season	Club	League	GP	G	A	Pts	AG	AA	APts	PIM	PP	SH	GW	S	%	TGF	PGF	TGA	PGA	+/-	GP	G	A	Pts	PIM	PP	SH	GW
1972-73	St. Catharines Black Hawks	OHA	50	1	20	21	....	....	....	98	....	....	....	....	....	....	....	....	....	....	....	....	....	....	....	....	....	....
1973-74	St. Catharines Black Hawks	OHA	65	25	25	50	....	....	....	110	....	....	....	....	....	....	....	....	....	....	12	3	8	11	....	....	....	....
1974-75	**California Golden Seals**	**NHL**	**78**	**8**	**17**	**25**	**7**	**13**	**20**	**39**	**1**	**1**	**0**	**99**	**8.1**	**64**	**25**	**88**	**9**	**–40**	....	....	....	....	....	....	....	....
1975-76	**California Golden Seals**	**NHL**	**73**	**14**	**37**	**51**	**13**	**29**	**42**	**54**	**8**	**0**	**2**	**106**	**13.2**	**129**	**44**	**107**	**10**	**–12**	....	....	....	....	....	....	....	....
1976-77	**Cleveland Barons**	**NHL**	**57**	**16**	**24**	**40**	**15**	**19**	**34**	**13**	**5**	**0**	**1**	**114**	**14.0**	**72**	**30**	**54**	**1**	**–11**	....	....	....	....	....	....	....	....
	Canada	WEC-A	10	1	2	3	....	....	....	4	....	....	....	....	....	....	....	....	....	....	....	....	....	....	....	....	....	....
1977-78	**Cleveland Barons**	**NHL**	**77**	**18**	**18**	**36**	**17**	**15**	**32**	**19**	**3**	**0**	**0**	**159**	**11.3**	**62**	**23**	**81**	**18**	**–24**	....	....	....	....	....	....	....	....
	Canada	WEC-A	10	0	0	0	....	....	....	9	....	....	....	....	....	....	....	....	....	....	....	....	....	....	....	....	....	....
1978-79	**Los Angeles Kings**	**NHL**	**49**	**3**	**17**	**20**	**3**	**13**	**16**	**22**	**0**	**0**	**0**	**70**	**4.3**	**62**	**8**	**65**	**11**	**0**	**2**	**0**	**0**	**0**	**0**	**0**	**0**	**0**
1979-80	**Los Angeles Kings**	**NHL**	**3**	**0**	**0**	**0**	**0**	**0**	**0**	**0**	**0**	**0**	**0**	**1**	**0.0**	**3**	**0**	**2**	**2**	**+3**	....	....	....	....	....	....	....	....
	Binghamton Whalers	AHL	19	4	5	9	....	....	....	11	....	....	....	....	....	....	....	....	....	....	....	....	....	....	....	....	....	....
1980-81	Houston Apollos	CHL	33	11	13	24	....	....	....	17	....	....	....	....	....	....	....	....	....	....	....	....	....	....	....	....	....	....
	New Brunswick Hawks	AHL	36	4	23	27	....	....	....	37	....	....	....	....	....	....	....	....	....	....	13	0	1	1	30	....	....	....
	NHL Totals		**337**	**59**	**113**	**172**	**55**	**89**	**144**	**147**	**17**	**1**	**3**	**549**	**10.7**	**392**	**130**	**397**	**51**		**2**	**0**	**0**	**0**	**0**	**0**	**0**	**0**

Transferred to **Cleveland** after **California** franchise relocated, August 26, 1976. Placed on **Minnesota** Reserve List prior to Minnesota-Cleveland Dispersal Draft, June 14, 1978. Transferred to **LA Kings** by **Minnesota** with Steve Jensen and Dave Gardner as compensation for Minnesota's signing of free agent Gary Sargent, July, 1978

• HAMR, RADEK

Radek Hamr D – L. 5′11″, 175 lbs. b: Usti-Nad-Labem, Czech., 6/15/1974. Ottawa's 4th choice, 73rd overall, in 1992 Entry Draft.

Season	Club	League	GP	G	A	Pts	AG	AA	APts	PIM	PP	SH	GW	S	%	TGF	PGF	TGA	PGA	+/-	GP	G	A	Pts	PIM	PP	SH	GW
1991-92	Sparta Praha	Czech.	3	0	0	0	....	....	....	....	....	....	....	....	....	....	....	....	....	....	....	....	....	....	....	....	....	....
1992-93	**Ottawa Senators**	**NHL**	**4**	**0**	**0**	**0**	**0**	**0**	**0**	**0**	**0**	**0**	**0**	**2**	**0.0**	**0**	**0**	**5**	**1**	**–4**	....	....	....	....	....	....	....	....
	New Haven Nighthawks	AHL	59	4	21	25	....	....	....	18	....	....	....	....	....	....	....	....	....	....	....	....	....	....	....	....	....	....
1993-94	**Ottawa Senators**	**NHL**	**7**	**0**	**0**	**0**	**0**	**0**	**0**	**0**	**0**	**0**	**0**	**5**	**0.0**	**4**	**4**	**11**	**1**	**–10**	....	....	....	....	....	....	....	....
	P.E.I. Senators	AHL	69	10	26	36	....	....	....	44	....	....	....	....	....	....	....	....	....	....	....	....	....	....	....	....	....	....
1994-95	P.E.I. Senators	AHL	7	0	1	1	....	....	....	2	....	....	....	....	....	....	....	....	....	....	....	....	....	....	....	....	....	....
	Fort Wayne Komets	IHL	58	3	13	16	....	....	....	14	....	....	....	....	....	....	....	....	....	....	1	0	0	0	0	....	....	....
1995-96	Sparta Praha	Czech.	30	2	3	5	....	....	....	....	....	....	....	....	....	....	....	....	....	....	4	0	0	0	....	....	....	....
1996-97	Sparta Praha	Czech.	52	12	23	35	....	....	....	4	....	....	....	....	....	....	....	....	....	....	10	2	5	7	4	....	....	....
1997-98	Vastra Frolunda	Sweden	46	2	12	14	....	....	....	36	....	....	....	....	....	....	....	....	....	....	7	1	2	3	29	....	....	....
	NHL Totals		**11**	**0**	**0**	**0**	**0**	**0**	**0**	**0**	**0**	**0**	**0**	**7**	**0.0**	**4**	**4**	**16**	**2**		....	....	....	....	....	....	....	....

• HAMRLIK, ROMAN

Roman Hamrlik D – L. 6′2″, 200 lbs. b: Gottwaldov, Czech., 4/12/1974. Tampa Bay's 1st choice, 1st overall, in 1992 Entry Draft.

Season	Club	League	GP	G	A	Pts	AG	AA	APts	PIM	PP	SH	GW	S	%	TGF	PGF	TGA	PGA	+/-	GP	G	A	Pts	PIM	PP	SH	GW
1990-91	TJ Zlin	Czech.	14	2	2	4	....	....	....	18	....	....	....	....	....	....	....	....	....	....	....	....	....	....	....	....	....	....
1991-92	ZPS Zlin	Czech.	34	5	5	10	....	....	....	50	....	....	....	....	....	....	....	....	....	....	....	....	....	....	....	....	....	....
	Czechoslovakia	WJC-A	7	3	0	3	....	....	....	8	....	....	....	....	....	....	....	....	....	....	....	....	....	....	....	....	....	....
1992-93	**Tampa Bay Lightning**	**NHL**	**67**	**6**	**15**	**21**	**5**	**10**	**15**	**71**	**1**	**0**	**1**	**113**	**5.3**	**53**	**14**	**66**	**6**	**–21**	....	....	....	....	....	....	....	....
	Atlanta Knights	IHL	2	1	1	2	....	....	....	2	....	....	....	....	....	....	....	....	....	....	....	....	....	....	....	....	....	....
1993-94	**Tampa Bay Lightning**	**NHL**	**64**	**3**	**18**	**21**	**3**	**14**	**17**	**135**	**0**	**0**	**0**	**158**	**1.9**	**58**	**18**	**59**	**5**	**–14**	....	....	....	....	....	....	....	....
	Czech Republic	WC-A	1	0	0	0	....	....	....	0	....	....	....	....	....	....	....	....	....	....	....	....	....	....	....	....	....	....
1994-95	ZPS Zlin	Czech.	2	1	0	1	....	....	....	10	....	....	....	....	....	....	....	....	....	....	....	....	....	....	....	....	....	....
	Tampa Bay Lightning	**NHL**	**48**	**12**	**11**	**23**	**21**	**16**	**37**	**86**	**7**	**1**	**2**	**134**	**9.0**	**55**	**23**	**69**	**19**	**–18**	....	....	....	....	....	....	....	....
1995-96	**Tampa Bay Lightning**	**NHL**	**82**	**16**	**49**	**65**	**16**	**40**	**56**	**103**	**12**	**0**	**2**	**281**	**5.7**	**130**	**66**	**109**	**21**	**–24**	**5**	**0**	**1**	**1**	**4**	**0**	**0**	**0**
1996-97	Czech Republic	W Cup	3	0	0	0	....	....	....	4	....	....	....	....	....	....	....	....	....	....	....	....	....	....	....	....	....	....
	Tampa Bay Lightning	**NHL**	**79**	**12**	**28**	**40**	**13**	**25**	**38**	**57**	**6**	**0**	**0**	**238**	**5.0**	**96**	**37**	**92**	**4**	**–29**	....	....	....	....	....	....	....	....
1997-98	**Tampa Bay Lightning**	**NHL**	**37**	**3**	**12**	**15**	**4**	**12**	**16**	**22**	**1**	**0**	**0**	**86**	**3.5**	**34**	**14**	**45**	**7**	**–18**	....	....	....	....	....	....	....	....
	Edmonton Oilers	**NHL**	**41**	**6**	**20**	**26**	**7**	**19**	**26**	**48**	**4**	**1**	**3**	**112**	**5.4**	**60**	**31**	**40**	**14**	**+3**	**12**	**0**	**6**	**6**	**12**	**0**	**0**	**0**
	Czech Republic	Olympics	6	1	0	1	....	....	....	2	....	....	....	....	....	....	....	....	....	....	....	....	....	....	....	....	....	....
	NHL Totals		**418**	**58**	**153**	**211**	**69**	**136**	**205**	**522**	**31**	**2**	**8**	**1122**	**5.2**	**486**	**203**	**480**	**76**		**17**	**0**	**7**	**7**	**16**	**0**	**0**	**0**

Named Best Defenseman at EJC-A (1991) • EJC-A All-Star Team (1992)

Played in NHL All-Star Game (1996)

Traded to **Edmonton** by **Tampa Bay** with Paul Comrie for Bryan Marchment, Steve Kelly and Jason Bonsignore, December 30, 1997.

• HAMWAY, MARK

Mark Hamway RW – R. 6′, 190 lbs. b: Detroit, MI, 8/9/1961. NY Islanders' 8th choice, 143rd overall, in 1980 Entry Draft.

Season	Club	League	GP	G	A	Pts	AG	AA	APts	PIM	PP	SH	GW	S	%	TGF	PGF	TGA	PGA	+/-	GP	G	A	Pts	PIM	PP	SH	GW
1977-78	Detroit Nats	Midget	75	70	90	160	....	....	....	....	....	....	....	....	....	....	....	....	....	....	....	....	....	....	....	....	....	....
1978-79	Windsor Spitfires	OHA	66	27	42	64	....	....	....	29	....	....	....	....	....	....	....	....	....	....	....	....	....	....	....	....	....	....
1979-80	Michigan State University	WCHA	38	16	28	44	....	....	....	28	....	....	....	....	....	....	....	....	....	....	....	....	....	....	....	....	....	....
1980-81	Michigan State University	WCHA	35	18	15	33	....	....	....	20	....	....	....	....	....	....	....	....	....	....	....	....	....	....	....	....	....	....
1981-82	Michigan State University	CCHA	41	34	31	65	....	....	....	37	....	....	....	....	....	....	....	....	....	....	....	....	....	....	....	....	....	....
1982-83	Michigan State University	CCHA	32	22	21	43	....	....	....	10	....	....	....	....	....	....	....	....	....	....	....	....	....	....	....	....	....	....
1983-84	Indianapolis Checkers	CHL	71	22	32	54	....	....	....	38	....	....	....	....	....	....	....	....	....	....	9	1	1	2	0	....	....	....
1984-85	**New York Islanders**	**NHL**	**2**	**0**	**0**	**0**	**0**	**0**	**0**	**0**	**0**	**0**	**0**	**1**	**0.0**	**0**	**0**	**0**	**0**	**0**	....	....	....	....	....	....	....	....
	Springfield Indians	AHL	75	29	34	63	....	....	....	29	....	....	....	....	....	....	....	....	....	....	4	0	1	1	0	....	....	....
1985-86	**New York Islanders**	**NHL**	**49**	**5**	**12**	**17**	**4**	**8**	**12**	**9**	**1**	**0**	**1**	**50**	**10.0**	**21**	**1**	**26**	**1**	**–5**	**1**	**0**	**0**	**0**	**0**	**0**	**0**	**0**
	Springfield Indians	AHL	14	5	8	13	....	....	....	7	....	....	....	....	....	....	....	....	....	....	....	....	....	....	....	....	....	....
1986-87	**New York Islanders**	**NHL**	**2**	**0**	**1**	**1**	**0**	**1**	**1**	**0**	**0**	**0**	**0**	**1**	**0.0**	**1**	**0**	**2**	**0**	**–1**	....	....	....	....	....	....	....	....
	Springfield Indians	AHL	59	25	31	56	....	....	....	8	....	....	....	....	....	....	....	....	....	....	....	....	....	....	....	....	....	....
	NHL Totals		**53**	**5**	**13**	**18**	**4**	**9**	**13**	**9**	**1**	**0**	**1**	**52**	**9.6**	**22**	**1**	**28**	**1**		**1**	**0**	**0**	**0**	**0**	**0**	**0**	**0**

CCHA Second All-Star Team (1982)

• HANDY, RON

Ron Handy LW – L. 5′11″, 175 lbs. b: Toronto, Ont., 1/15/1963. NY Islanders' 3rd choice, 57th overall, in 1981 Entry Draft.

Season	Club	League	GP	G	A	Pts	AG	AA	APts	PIM	PP	SH	GW	S	%	TGF	PGF	TGA	PGA	+/-	GP	G	A	Pts	PIM	PP	SH	GW
1979-80	Toronto Marlboros	Midget	39	48	60	108	....	....	....	....	....	....	....	....	....	....	....	....	....	....	....	....	....	....	....	....	....	....
1980-81	Sault Ste. Marie Greyhounds	OHA	66	43	43	86	....	....	....	45	....	....	....	....	....	....	....	....	....	....	18	3	5	8	25	....	....	....
1981-82	Sault Ste. Marie Greyhounds	OHL	20	15	10	25	....	....	....	20	....	....	....	....	....	....	....	....	....	....	....	....	....	....	....	....	....	....
	Kingston Canadians	OHL	44	35	38	73	....	....	....	23	....	....	....	....	....	....	....	....	....	....	4	1	1	2	16	....	....	....
1982-83	Kingston Canadians	OHL	67	52	96	148	....	....	....	64	....	....	....	....	....	....	....	....	....	....	....	....	....	....	....	....	....	....
	Indianapolis Checkers	CHL	9	2	7	9	....	....	....	0	....	....	....	....	....	....	....	....	....	....	10	3	8	11	18	....	....	....
1983-84	Indianapolis Checkers	CHL	66	29	46	75	....	....	....	40	....	....	....	....	....	....	....	....	....	....	10	2	5	7	0	....	....	....
1984-85	**New York Islanders**	**NHL**	**10**	**0**	**2**	**2**	**0**	**1**	**1**	**0**	**0**	**0**	**0**	**6**	**0.0**	**4**	**1**	**4**	**0**	**–1**	....	....	....	....	....	....	....	....
	Springfield Indians	AHL	69	29	35	64	....	....	....	38	....	....	....	....	....	....	....	....	....	....	3	2	2	4	0	....	....	....
1985-86	Springfield Indians	AHL	79	31	30	61	....	....	....	66	....	....	....	....	....	....	....	....	....	....	....	....	....	....	....	....	....	....
1986-87	Indianapolis Checkers	IHL	82	*55	80	135	....	....	....	57	....	....	....	....	....	....	....	....	....	....	6	4	3	7	2	....	....	....
1987-88	**St. Louis Blues**	**NHL**	**4**	**0**	**1**	**1**	**0**	**1**	**1**	**0**	**0**	**0**	**0**	**4**	**0.0**	**1**	**0**	**3**	**1**	**–1**	....	....	....	....	....	....	....	....
	Peoria Rivermen	IHL	78	53	63	116	....	....	....	61	....	....	....	....	....	....	....	....	....	....	7	2	3	5	4	....	....	....
1988-89	Peoria Rivermen	IHL	81	43	57	100	....	....	....	24	....	....	....	....	....	....	....	....	....	....	....	....	....	....	....	....	....	....
1989-90	Peoria Rivermen	IHL	82	36	39	75	....	....	....	52	....	....	....	....	....	....	....	....	....	....	5	3	1	4	0	....	....	....
1990-91	Kansas City Blades	IHL	64	42	39	81	....	....	....	41	....	....	....	....	....	....	....	....	....	....	....	....	....	....	....	....	....	....

Season	Club	League	GP	G	A	Pts	AG	AA	APts	PIM	PP	SH	GW	S	%	TGF	PGF	TGA	PGA	+/–	GP	G	A	Pts	PIM	PP	SH	GW
																					colspan playoffs							

REGULAR SEASON / PLAYOFFS

Season	Club	League	GP	G	A	Pts	AG	AA	APts	PIM	PP	SH	GW	S	%	TGF	PGF	TGA	PGA	+/–	P-GP	P-G	P-A	P-Pts	P-PIM	P-PP	P-SH	P-GW
1991-92	Kansas City Blades	IHL	38	16	19	35				30											15	13	8	21	8			
1992-93	Peoria Rivermen	IHL	18	0	7	7				16																		
	Kansas City Blades	IHL	6	1	1	2				2																		
	Wichita Thunder	CHL	11	6	12	18				20																		
1993-94	Wichita Thunder	CHL	57	29	80	109				98											11	12	10	22	12			
1994-95	Sheffield Steelers	Britain	6	8	6	14				2																		
	Denver Grizzlies	IHL	1	0	0	0				0																		
	Wichita Thunder	CHL	46	24	45	69				72											11	15	16	31	4			
1995-96	Huntsville Channel Cats	SHL	3	3	1	4				0																		
	Louisiana IceGators	ECHL	58	20	65	85				34											5	2	4	6	2			
1996-97	Louisiana IceGators	ECHL	66	33	67	100				58											17	5	17	22	0			
1997-98	Huntsville Channel Cats	CHL	46	27	33	60				50											2	0	1	1	0			
NHL Totals			**14**	**0**	**3**	**3**	**0**	**2**	**2**	**0**	**0**	**0**	**0**	**10**	**0.0**	**5**	**1**	**7**	**1**									

CHL Second All-Star Team (1984, 1994) • IHL Second All-Star Team (1987) • IHL First All-Star Team (1988) • Won "Bud" Poile Trophy (Playoff MVP - IHL) (1992) • Won President's Trophy (CHL's Playoff MVP) (1994, 1995)

Signed as a free agent by **St. Louis**, September, 1987.

● **HANGSLEBEN, AL**   Al "Hank" Hangsleben   D – L. 6'1", 195 lbs.   b: Warroad, MN, 2/22/1953.   Montreal's 6th choice, 56th overall, in 1973 Amateur Draft.

Season	Club	League	GP	G	A	Pts	AG	AA	APts	PIM	PP	SH	GW	S	%	TGF	PGF	TGA	PGA	+/–	P-GP	P-G	P-A	P-Pts	P-PIM	P-PP	P-SH	P-GW
1971-72	University of North Dakota	WCHA	36	13	21	34				49																		
1972-73	University of North Dakota	WCHA	36	15	18	33				77																		
1973-74	University of North Dakota	WCHA	34	9	16	25				56																		
	United States	Nat-Team	7	2	3	5				10																		
1974-75	New England Whalers	WHA	26	0	5	5				8											6	0	3	3	19			
	Cape Cod Codders	NAHL	55	4	39	43				130																		
1975-76	New England Whalers	WHA	78	2	23	25				62											13	2	3	5	20			
	Cape Cod Codders	NAHL	1	0	0	0				9																		
1976-77	New England Whalers	WHA	74	13	9	22				79											4	0	0	0	9			
1977-78	New England Whalers	WHA	79	11	18	29				140											14	1	4	5	37			
1978-79	New England Whalers	WHA	77	10	19	29				148											10	1	2	3	12			
1979-80	**Hartford Whalers**	**NHL**	37	3	15	18	3	11	14	69	0	0	1	40	7.5	39	0	44	14	+9								
	Washington Capitals	**NHL**	37	10	7	17	9	5	14	45	2	0	1	67	14.9	43	7	37	2	+1								
1980-81	**Washington Capitals**	**NHL**	76	5	19	24	4	13	17	198	0	0	0	110	4.5	68	10	76	11	–7								
	United States	WEC A	8	1	3	4				22																		
1981-82	**Washington Capitals**	**NHL**	17	1	1	2	1	1	2	19	0	0	0	13	7.7	6	0	14	5	–3								
	Hershey Bears	AHL	6	1	2	3				26																		
	Los Angeles Kings	**NHL**	18	2	6	8	2	4	6	65	0	0	0	18	11.1	10	1	7	1	+3	4	0	0	0	4			
	New Haven Nighthawks	AHL	18	5	4	9				28																		
1982-83	Moncton Alpines	AHL	71	10	16	26				127																		
1983-84	New Haven Nighthawks	AHL	58	1	23	24				88																		
NHL Totals			**185**	**21**	**48**	**69**	**19**	**34**	**53**	**396**	**2**	**0**	**2**	**248**	**8.5**	**166**	**18**	**178**	**33**		**4**	**0**	**0**	**0**	**4**			
Other Major League Totals			334	36	74	110				437											47	4	12	16	97			

WCHA First All-Star Team (1972) • NCAA West First All-American Team (1972)

Selected by **New England** (WHA) in 1973 WHA Amateur Draft, June, 1973. Reclaimed by **Montreal** from **Hartford** prior to Expansion Draft, June 9, 1976. Claimed by **Hartford** from **Montreal** in Expansion Draft, June 13, 1979. Traded to **Washington** by **Hartford** for Tom Rowe, January 17, 1980. Signed as a free agent by **LA Kings**, January 4, 1982. Traded to **Edmonton** by **LA Kings** for Rick Blight, December 7, 1982.

● **HANKINSON, BEN**   Ben Hankinson   RW – R. 6'2", 210 lbs.   b: Edina, MN, 5/1/1969.   New Jersey's 5th choice, 107th overall, in 1987 Entry Draft.

Season	Club	League	GP	G	A	Pts	AG	AA	APts	PIM	PP	SH	GW	S	%	TGF	PGF	TGA	PGA	+/–	P-GP	P-G	P-A	P-Pts	P-PIM	P-PP	P-SH	P-GW
1986-87	Edina High School	H.S.	26	14	20	34																						
1987-88	University of Minnesota	WCHA	24	4	7	11				36																		
1988-89	University of Minnesota	WCHA	43	7	11	18				115																		
1989-90	University of Minnesota	WCHA	46	25	41	66				34																		
1990-91	University of Minnesota	WCHA	40	19	21	40				133																		
1991-92	Utica Devils	AHL	77	17	16	33				188											4	3	1	4	2			
1992-93	**New Jersey Devils**	**NHL**	4	2	1	3	2	1	3	9	0	0	0	3	66.7	4	0	2	0	+2								
	Utica Devils	AHL	75	35	27	62				145											5	2	2	4	6			
1993-94	**New Jersey Devils**	**NHL**	13	1	0	1	1	0	1	23	0	0	1	14	7.1	4	0	4	0	0	2	1	0	1	4	0	0	0
	Albany River Rats	AHL	29	9	14	23				80											5	3	1	4	6			
1994-95	**New Jersey Devils**	**NHL**	8	0	0	0	0	0	0	7	0	0	0	8	0.0	0	0	6	0	–6								
	Albany River Rats	AHL	1	1	0	1				6																		
	Tampa Bay Lightning	**NHL**	18	0	2	2	0	3	3	6	0	0	0	18	0.0	5	0	4	0	+1								
1995-96	Adirondack Red Wings	AHL	75	25	21	46				210											3	0	0	0	8			
1996-97	Grand Rapids Griffins	IHL	68	16	13	29				219											5	2	2	4	4			
1997-98	Orlando Solar Bears	IHL	80	15	15	30				221											14	0	4	4	47			
NHL Totals			**43**	**3**	**3**	**6**	**3**	**4**	**7**	**45**	**0**	**0**	**1**	**43**	**7.0**	**13**	**0**	**16**	**0**		**2**	**1**	**0**	**1**	**4**	**0**	**0**	**0**

WCHA First All-Star Team (1990)

Traded to **Tampa Bay** by **New Jersey** with Alexander Semak for Shawn Chambers and Danton Cole, March 14, 1995. Traded to **Detroit** by **Tampa Bay** with Marc Bergevin for Shawn Burr and Detroit's 3rd round choice (later traded to Boston — Boston selected Jason Doyle) in 1996 Entry Draft, August 17, 1995.

● **HANNA, JOHN**   John Hanna   D – R. 5'11", 175 lbs.   b: Sydney, N.S., 4/5/1935.

Season	Club	League	GP	G	A	Pts	AG	AA	APts	PIM	PP	SH	GW	S	%	TGF	PGF	TGA	PGA	+/–	P-GP	P-G	P-A	P-Pts	P-PIM	P-PP	P-SH	P-GW
1954-55	Trois-Rivieres Flambeaux	QJHL	42	3	6	9				107											9	0	1	1	10			
1955-56	Philadelphia Ramblers	EHL	28	1	4	5				13																		
	Chicoutimi Sagueneens	QJIL	40	3	14	17				101											5	0	0	0	4			
1956-57	Chicoutimi Sagueneens	QHL	43	1	14	15				64											10	1	2	3	10			
1957-58	Trois-Rivieres Lions	QHL	48	3	25	28				66																		
	Providence Reds	AHL	7	0	3	3				24											3	1	1	2	10			
1958-59	**New York Rangers**	**NHL**	70	1	10	11	1	11	12	83																		
1959-60	**New York Rangers**	**NHL**	61	4	8	12	5	8	13	87																		
1960-61	**New York Rangers**	**NHL**	46	1	8	9	1	8	9	34																		
	Springfield Indians	AHL	18	2	2	4				14																		
1961-62	Quebec Aces	AHL	65	0	17	17				85																		
1962-63	Quebec Aces	AHL	70	7	21	28				61																		
1963-64	**Montreal Canadiens**	**NHL**	6	0	0	0	0	0	0	2																		
	Quebec Aces	AHL	58	4	14	18				54											9	0	4	4	10			
	Quebec Aces	AHL	70	9	25	34				83											5	0	0	0	6			
1965-66	Quebec Aces	AHL	69	4	22	26				93											6	0	1	1	20			
1966-67	Quebec Aces	AHL	67	6	20	26				54											4	0	0	0	4			
1967-68	**Philadelphia Flyers**	**NHL**	15	0	0	0	0	0	0	0	0	0	0	4	0.0	2	1	0	0	+1								
	Quebec Aces	AHL	24	1	12	13				27											14	2	6	8	34			
1968-69	Seattle Totems	WHL	71	25	27	52				49											4	0	1	1	2			
1969-70	Seattle Totems	WHL	66	9	33	42				38											6	0	1	1	11			
1970-71	Seattle Totems	WHL	70	20	40	60				68																		

Season	Club	League	REGULAR SEASON																		PLAYOFFS							
			GP	G	A	Pts	AG	AA	APts	PIM	PP	SH	GW	S	%	TGF	PGF	TGA	PGA	+/–	GP	G	A	Pts	PIM	PP	SH	GW
1971-72	Seattle Totems	WHL	36	5	10	15	....	....	....	16	....	....	....	....	....	....	....	....	....	....	....	....	....	....	....	....	....	....
1972-73	Cleveland Crusaders	WHA	66	6	20	26	....	....	....	68	....	....	....	....	....	....	....	....	....	....	....	....	....	....	....	....	....	....
1973-74	Jacksonville Barons	AHL	11	2	4	6	....	....	....	4	....	....	....	....	....	....	....	....	....	....	....	....	....	....	....	....	....	....
	NHL Totals		**198**	**6**	**26**	**32**	**7**	**27**	**34**	**206**	**0**	**0**	**0**	**4**	**150.0**	**2**	**1**	**0**	**0**		....	....	....	....	....	....	....	....
	Other Major League Totals		66	6	20	26	....	....	....	68	....	....	....	....	....	....	....	....	....	....	....	....	....	....	....	....	....	....

QHL Second All-Star Team (1958) • WHL First All-Star Team (1969, 1971) • Won Hal Laycoe Cup (WHL Top Defenseman) (1969, 1971) • Won Leader Cup (WHL - MVP) (1969) • WHL Second All-Star Team (1970)

Traded to **Montreal** by **NY Rangers** for Al Langlois, June 13, 1961. NHL rights transferred to **Philadelphia** after NHL club purchased **Quebec** (AHL) franchise, May 8, 1967. Traded to **Seattle** (WHL) by **Philadelphia** for cash, October, 1968. Selected by **LA Sharks** (WHA) in 1972 WHA General Player Draft, February 12, 1972. WHA rights traded to **Cleveland** (WHA) by **LA Sharks** (WHA) for future considerations, July, 1972.

• HANNAN, DAVE

Dave Hannan C – L. 5′10″, 180 lbs. b: Sudbury, Ont., 11/26/1961. Pittsburgh's 9th choice, 196th overall, in 1981 Entry Draft.

1979-80	Sault Ste. Marie Greyhounds	OHA	28	11	10	21	....	....	....	31	....	....	....	....	....	....	....	....	....	....	....	....	....	....	....	....	....	....
	Brantford Alexanders	OHA	25	5	10	15	....	....	....	26	....	....	....	....	....	....	....	....	....	....	....	....	....	....	....	....	....	....
1980-81	Brantford Alexanders	OHA	56	46	35	81	....	....	....	155	....	....	....	....	....	....	....	....	....	....	6	2	4	6	20	....	....	....
1981-82	**Pittsburgh Penguins**	**NHL**	**1**	**0**	**0**	**0**	**0**	**0**	**0**	**0**	**0**	**0**	**0**	**0**	**0.0**	**0**	**0**	**2**	**0**	**–2**	....	....	....	....	....	....	....	....
	Erie Blades	AHL	76	33	37	70	....	....	....	129	....	....	....	....	....	....	....	....	....	....	....	....	....	....	....	....	....	....
1982-83	**Pittsburgh Penguins**	**NHL**	**74**	**11**	**22**	**33**	**9**	**15**	**24**	**127**	**2**	**0**	**3**	**95**	**11.6**	**44**	**5**	**77**	**10**	**–28**	....	....	....	....	....	....	....	....
	Baltimore Skipjacks	AHL	5	2	2	4	....	....	....	13	....	....	....	....	....	....	....	....	....	....	....	....	....	....	....	....	....	....
1983-84	**Pittsburgh Penguins**	**NHL**	**24**	**2**	**3**	**5**	**2**	**2**	**4**	**33**	**0**	**1**	**1**	**21**	**9.5**	**9**	**0**	**17**	**6**	**–2**	....	....	....	....	....	....	....	....
	Baltimore Skipjacks	AHL	47	18	24	42	....	....	....	98	....	....	....	....	....	....	....	....	....	....	10	2	6	8	27	....	....	....
1984-85	**Pittsburgh Penguins**	**NHL**	**30**	**6**	**7**	**13**	**5**	**5**	**10**	**43**	**0**	**1**	**1**	**38**	**15.8**	**15**	**0**	**30**	**7**	**–8**	....	....	....	....	....	....	....	....
	Baltimore Skipjacks	AHL	49	20	25	45	....	....	....	91	....	....	....	....	....	....	....	....	....	....	....	....	....	....	....	....	....	....
1985-86	**Pittsburgh Penguins**	**NHL**	**75**	**17**	**18**	**35**	**14**	**12**	**26**	**91**	**0**	**3**	**1**	**100**	**17.0**	**47**	**3**	**89**	**41**	**–4**	....	....	....	....	....	....	....	....
1986-87	**Pittsburgh Penguins**	**NHL**	**58**	**10**	**15**	**25**	**9**	**11**	**20**	**56**	**0**	**1**	**2**	**85**	**11.8**	**39**	**2**	**46**	**7**	**–2**	....	....	....	....	....	....	....	....
1987-88	**Pittsburgh Penguins**	**NHL**	**21**	**4**	**3**	**7**	**3**	**2**	**5**	**23**	**0**	**1**	**1**	**34**	**11.8**	**8**	**0**	**27**	**17**	**–2**	....	....	....	....	....	....	....	....
	Edmonton Oilers	**NHL**	**51**	**9**	**11**	**20**	**8**	**8**	**16**	**43**	**0**	**2**	**2**	**62**	**14.5**	**31**	**0**	**28**	**9**	**+12**	**12**	**1**	**1**	**2**	**8**	**0**	**0**	**1**
1988-89	**Pittsburgh Penguins**	**NHL**	**72**	**10**	**20**	**30**	**8**	**14**	**22**	**157**	**2**	**1**	**3**	**72**	**13.9**	**42**	**5**	**97**	**48**	**–12**	**8**	**0**	**1**	**1**	**4**	**0**	**0**	**0**
1989-90	**Toronto Maple Leafs**	**NHL**	**39**	**6**	**9**	**15**	**5**	**6**	**11**	**55**	**0**	**1**	**0**	**39**	**15.4**	**21**	**0**	**44**	**11**	**–12**	**3**	**1**	**0**	**1**	**4**	**0**	**0**	**1**
1990-91	**Toronto Maple Leafs**	**NHL**	**74**	**11**	**23**	**34**	**10**	**17**	**27**	**82**	**0**	**1**	**2**	**72**	**15.3**	**38**	**3**	**80**	**36**	**–9**	....	....	....	....	....	....	....	....
1991-92	**Toronto Maple Leafs**	**NHL**	**35**	**2**	**2**	**4**	**2**	**1**	**3**	**16**	**0**	**1**	**0**	**24**	**8.3**	**9**	**2**	**33**	**16**	**–10**	....	....	....	....	....	....	....	....
	Canada	Nat-Team	3	0	0	0	....	....	....	2	....	....	....	....	....	....	....	....	....	....	....	....	....	....	....	....	....	....
	Canada	Olympics	8	3	5	8	....	....	....	8	....	....	....	....	....	....	....	....	....	....	....	....	....	....	....	....	....	....
	Buffalo Sabres	**NHL**	**12**	**2**	**4**	**6**	**2**	**3**	**5**	**48**	**0**	**2**	**0**	**8**	**25.0**	**9**	**2**	**10**	**4**	**+1**	**7**	**2**	**0**	**2**	**2**	**2**	**0**	**0**
1992-93	**Buffalo Sabres**	**NHL**	**55**	**5**	**15**	**20**	**4**	**10**	**14**	**43**	**0**	**0**	**0**	**43**	**11.6**	**31**	**3**	**44**	**24**	**+8**	**8**	**1**	**1**	**2**	**18**	**0**	**0**	**0**
1993-94	**Buffalo Sabres**	**NHL**	**83**	**6**	**15**	**21**	**6**	**12**	**18**	**53**	**0**	**3**	**1**	**40**	**15.0**	**35**	**0**	**62**	**37**	**+10**	**7**	**1**	**0**	**1**	**6**	**0**	**0**	**1**
1994-95	**Buffalo Sabres**	**NHL**	**42**	**4**	**12**	**16**	**7**	**18**	**25**	**32**	**0**	**2**	**0**	**36**	**11.1**	**23**	**1**	**30**	**11**	**+3**	**5**	**0**	**2**	**2**	**2**	**0**	**0**	**0**
1995-96	**Buffalo Sabres**	**NHL**	**57**	**6**	**10**	**16**	**6**	**8**	**14**	**30**	**1**	**1**	**2**	**40**	**15.0**	**23**	**2**	**53**	**34**	**+2**	....	....	....	....	....	....	....	....
	Colorado Avalanche	**NHL**	**4**	**1**	**0**	**1**	**1**	**0**	**1**	**2**	**0**	**0**	**0**	**41**	**2.4**	**1**	**0**	**2**	**2**	**+1**	**13**	**0**	**2**	**2**	**2**	**0**	**0**	**0**
1996-97	**Ottawa Senators**	**NHL**	**34**	**2**	**2**	**4**	**2**	**2**	**4**	**8**	**0**	**1**	**1**	**16**	**12.5**	**9**	**0**	**22**	**12**	**–1**	....	....	....	....	....	....	....	....
	NHL Totals		**841**	**114**	**191**	**305**	**103**	**146**	**249**	**942**	**5**	**22**	**20**	**866**	**13.2**	**434**	**28**	**793**	**332**		**63**	**6**	**7**	**13**	**46**	**2**	**0**	**3**

Traded to **Edmonton** by **Pittsburgh** with Craig Simpson, Moe Mantha and Chris Joseph for Paul Coffey, Dave Hunter and Wayne Van Dorp, November 24, 1987. Claimed by **Pittsburgh** from **Edmonton** in Waiver Draft, October 3, 1988. Claimed by **Toronto** from **Pittsburgh** in Waiver Draft, October 2, 1989. Traded to **Buffalo** by **Toronto** for Minnesota's 5th round choice (previously acquired, Toronto selected Chris Deruiter) in 1992 Entry Draft, March 10, 1992. Traded to **Colorado** by **Buffalo** for Colorado's 6th round choice (Darren Mortier) in 1996 Entry Draft, March 20, 1996. Signed as a free agent by **Ottawa**, September 13, 1996.

• HANNIGAN, PAT

Pat "Hopalong" Hannigan LW – R. 5′10″, 183 lbs. b: Timmins, Ont., 3/5/1936.

1953-54	Toronto Marlboros	OHA	20	1	2	3	....	....	....	17	....	....	....	....	....	....	....	....	....	....	1	0	0	0	0	....	....	....
1954-55	Toronto Marlboros	OHA	44	13	19	32	....	....	....	40	....	....	....	....	....	....	....	....	....	....	5	2	3	5	2	....	....	....
1955-56	Toronto Marlboros	OHA	46	38	31	69	....	....	....	121	....	....	....	....	....	....	....	....	....	....	8	5	8	13	2	....	....	....
1956-57	Winnipeg Warriors	WHL	67	12	19	31	....	....	....	82	....	....	....	....	....	....	....	....	....	....	....	....	....	....	....	....	....	....
1957-58	New Westminster Royals	WHL	52	26	28	54	....	....	....	67	....	....	....	....	....	....	....	....	....	....	4	1	0	1	2	....	....	....
	Rochester Americans	AHL	8	0	4	4	....	....	....	4	....	....	....	....	....	....	....	....	....	....	....	....	....	....	....	....	....	....
1958-59	New Westminster Royals	WHL	69	37	46	83	....	....	....	73	....	....	....	....	....	....	....	....	....	....	....	....	....	....	....	....	....	....
	Rochester Americans	AHL	....	....	....	....	....	....	....	....	....	....	....	....	....	....	....	....	....	....	4	0	1	1	0	....	....	....
1959-60	**Toronto Maple Leafs**	**NHL**	**1**	**0**	**0**	**0**	**0**	**0**	**0**	**0**	....	....	....	....	....	....	....	....	....	....	....	....	....	....	....	....	....	....
	Rochester Americans	AHL	65	29	33	62	....	....	....	91	....	....	....	....	....	....	....	....	....	....	11	4	6	10	14	....	....	....
1960-61	Rochester Americans	AHL	13	5	6	11	....	....	....	4	....	....	....	....	....	....	....	....	....	....	....	....	....	....	....	....	....	....
	New York Rangers	**NHL**	**53**	**11**	**9**	**20**	**13**	**9**	**22**	**24**	....	....	....	....	....	....	....	....	....	....	....	....	....	....	....	....	....	....
1961-62	**New York Rangers**	**NHL**	**56**	**8**	**14**	**22**	**10**	**14**	**24**	**34**	....	....	....	....	....	....	....	....	....	....	**4**	**0**	**0**	**0**	**2**	....	....	....
1962-63	Baltimore Clippers	AHL	40	16	20	36	....	....	....	35	....	....	....	....	....	....	....	....	....	....	....	....	....	....	....	....	....	....
1963-64	Portland Buckaroos	WHL	34	12	8	20	....	....	....	43	....	....	....	....	....	....	....	....	....	....	....	....	....	....	....	....	....	....
	Buffalo Bisons	AHL	40	9	24	33	....	....	....	20	....	....	....	....	....	....	....	....	....	....	....	....	....	....	....	....	....	....
1964-65	Buffalo Bisons	AHL	72	38	54	92	....	....	....	118	....	....	....	....	....	....	....	....	....	....	9	3	4	7	23	....	....	....
1965-66	Buffalo Bisons	AHL	66	21	43	64	....	....	....	69	....	....	....	....	....	....	....	....	....	....	....	....	....	....	....	....	....	....
1966-67	Buffalo Bisons	AHL	68	18	38	56	....	....	....	37	....	....	....	....	....	....	....	....	....	....	....	....	....	....	....	....	....	....
1967-68	**Philadelphia Flyers**	**NHL**	**65**	**11**	**15**	**26**	**14**	**16**	**30**	**36**	**0**	**0**	**2**	**63**	**17.5**	**35**	**5**	**26**	**2**	**+6**	**7**	**1**	**2**	**3**	**9**	**0**	**0**	**0**
1968-69	**Philadelphia Flyers**	**NHL**	**7**	**0**	**1**	**1**	**0**	**1**	**1**	**22**	**0**	**0**	**0**	**5**	**0.0**	**2**	**0**	**6**	**0**	**–4**	....	....	....	....	....	....	....	....
	Buffalo Bisons	AHL	31	14	25	39	....	....	....	37	....	....	....	....	....	....	....	....	....	....	....	....	....	....	....	....	....	....
	Vancouver Canucks	WHL	12	4	4	8	....	....	....	2	....	....	....	....	....	....	....	....	....	....	6	4	1	5	4	....	....	....
1969-70	Vancouver Canucks	WHL	69	28	42	70	....	....	....	47	....	....	....	....	....	....	....	....	....	....	....	....	....	....	....	....	....	....
1970-71	Phoenix Roadrunners	WHL	10	1	2	3	....	....	....	0	....	....	....	....	....	....	....	....	....	....	....	....	....	....	....	....	....	....
	NHL Totals		**182**	**30**	**39**	**69**	**37**	**40**	**77**	**116**	**0**	**0**	**2**	**68**	**44.1**	**37**	**5**	**32**	**2**		**11**	**1**	**2**	**3**	**11**	**0**	**0**	**0**

WHL Coast Division First All-Star Team (1959) • AHL First All-Star Team (1965)

Traded to **NY Rangers** by **Toronto** with John Wilson for Eddie Shack, November, 1960. Traded to **Portland** (WHL) by **Baltimore** (AHL) for Howie Glover, June, 1963. Traded to **Buffalo** (AHL) by **Portland** (WHL) for Cliff Schmautz, December, 1963. Claimed by **Detroit** from **NY Rangers** (Buffalo - AHL) in Inter-League Draft, June 9, 1964. Claimed on waivers by **Chicago** from **Detroit**, September, 1964. Claimed by **Philadelphia** from **Chicago** in Expansion Draft, June 6, 1967. Traded to **Vancouver** (WHL) by **Philadelphia** for cash, March, 1969. Traded to **Toronto** (Phoenix-WHL) by **Vancouver** (WHL) with Ted McCaskill for Andre Hinse, August, 1970.

• HANSEN, RITCHIE

Ritchie Hansen C – L. 5′10″, 185 lbs. b: Bronx, NY, 10/30/1955. NY Islanders' 12th choice, 119th overall, in 1975 Amateur Draft.

1971-72	Brooklyn Metros	NYMHL	30	19	*52	71	....	....	....	47	....	....	....	....	....	....	....	....	....	....	....	....	....	....	....	....	....	....
1972-73	Sudbury Wolves	OHA	39	13	21	34	....	....	....	26	....	....	....	....	....	....	....	....	....	....	....	....	....	....	....	....	....	....
1973-74	Sudbury Wolves	OHA	62	34	47	81	....	....	....	31	....	....	....	....	....	....	....	....	....	....	....	....	....	....	....	....	....	....
1974-75	Sudbury Wolves	OHA	69	26	46	72	....	....	....	28	....	....	....	....	....	....	....	....	....	....	15	4	13	17	10	....	....	....
1975-76	Erie Blades	NAHL	74	40	41	81	....	....	....	51	....	....	....	....	....	....	....	....	....	....	....	....	....	....	....	....	....	....
	Muskegon Mohawks	IHL	....	....	....	....	....	....	....	....	....	....	....	....	....	....	....	....	....	....	1	1	2	3	2	....	....	....
1976-77	**New York Islanders**	**NHL**	**4**	**1**	**0**	**1**	**1**	**0**	**1**	**0**	**0**	**0**	**0**	**9**	**11.1**	**1**	**0**	**2**	**0**	**–1**	....	....	....	....	....	....	....	....
	Fort Worth Texans	CHL	74	30	47	77	....	....	....	32	....	....	....	....	....	....	....	....	....	....	6	0	3	3	4	....	....	....
1977-78	**New York Islanders**	**NHL**	**2**	**0**	**0**	**0**	**0**	**0**	**0**	**0**	**0**	**0**	**0**	**2**	**0.0**	**1**	**0**	**1**	**0**	**0**	....	....	....	....	....	....	....	....
	Fort Worth Texans	CHL	67	25	53	78	....	....	....	36	....	....	....	....	....	....	....	....	....	....	14	7	*11	18	2	....	....	....
1978-79	**New York Islanders**	**NHL**	**12**	**1**	**6**	**7**	**1**	**5**	**6**	**4**	**0**	**0**	**0**	**10**	**10.0**	**12**	**1**	**2**	**0**	**+9**	....	....	....	....	....	....	....	....
	Fort Worth Texans	CHL	20	4	8	12	....	....	....	4	....	....	....	....	....	....	....	....	....	....	5	1	0	1	0	....	....	....
1979-80	Salt Lake Golden Eagles	CHL	79	27	48	75	....	....	....	31	....	....	....	....	....	....	....	....	....	....	13	6	8	14	4	....	....	....
1980-81	Salt Lake Golden Eagles	CHL	72	27	51	78	....	....	....	43	....	....	....	....	....	....	....	....	....	....	17	5	18	23	19	....	....	....

Season	Club	League	GP	G	A	Pts	AG	AA	APts	PIM	PP	SH	GW	S	%	TGF	PGF	TGA	PGA	+/–	GP	G	A	Pts	PIM	PP	SH	GW
			REGULAR SEASON																		PLAYOFFS							
1981-82	**St. Louis Blues**	**NHL**	**2**	**0**	**2**	**2**	**0**	**1**	**1**	**0**	**0**	**0**	**0**	**4**	**0.0**	**3**	**0**	**1**	**0**	**+2**	....	....	....	....	....	....	....	....
	Salt Lake Golden Eagles	CHL	78	29	*81	110	....	....	....	52	....	....	....	....	....	....	....	....	....	....	10	1	9	10	0	....	....	....
1982-83	Wichita Wind	CHL	70	17	43	60	....	....	....	12	....	....	....	....	....	....	....	....	....	....	....	....	....	....	....	....	....	....
1983-84	Salt Lake Golden Eagles	CHL	63	24	32	56	....	....	....	22	....	....	....	....	....	....	....	....	....	....	5	0	0	0	2	....	....	....
	NHL Totals		**20**	**2**	**8**	**10**	**2**	**6**	**8**	**4**	**0**	**0**	**0**	**25**	**8.0**	**17**	**1**	**6**	**0**		....	....	....	....	....	....	....	....

CHL Second All-Star Team (1978)

Transferred to **Minnesota** by **NY Islanders** as compensation for NY Islander's signing of free agent Jean Potvin, June 10, 1979. Traded to **St. Louis** by **Minnesota** with Bryan Maxwell for St. Louis' 2nd round choice (later traded to Calgary — Calgary selected Dave Reierson) in 1982 Entry Draft, June 10, 1979. Signed as a free agent by **Minnesota**, July 30, 1983.

• HANSEN, TAVIS

Tavis Hansen C – R. 6'1", 180 lbs. b: Prince Albert, Sask., 6/17/1975. Winnipeg's 3rd choice, 58th overall, in 1994 Entry Draft.

Season	Club	League	GP	G	A	Pts	AG	AA	APts	PIM	PP	SH	GW	S	%	TGF	PGF	TGA	PGA	+/–	GP	G	A	Pts	PIM	PP	SH	GW
1993-94	Tacoma Rockets	WHL	71	23	31	54	....	....	....	122	....	....	....	....	....	....	....	....	....	....	8	1	3	4	17	....	....	....
1994-95	Tacoma Rockets	WHL	71	32	41	73	....	....	....	142	....	....	....	....	....	....	....	....	....	....	4	1	1	2	8	....	....	....
	Winnipeg Jets	**NHL**	**1**	**0**	**0**	**0**	**0**	**0**	**0**	**0**	**0**	**0**	**0**	**0**	**0.0**	**0**	**0**	**0**	**0**	**0**	....	....	....	....	....	....	....	....
1995-96	Springfield Falcons	AHL	67	6	16	22	....	....	....	85	....	....	....	....	....	....	....	....	....	....	5	1	2	3	2	....	....	....
1996-97	**Phoenix Coyotes**	**NHL**	**1**	**0**	**0**	**0**	**0**	**0**	**0**	**0**	**0**	**0**	**0**	**0**	**0.0**	**0**	**0**	**0**	**0**	**0**	....	....	....	....	....	....	....	....
	Springfield Falcons	AHL	12	3	1	4	....	....	....	23	....	....	....	....	....	....	....	....	....	....	....	....	....	....	....	....	....	....
1997-98	Springfield Falcons	AHL	73	20	14	34	....	....	....	70	....	....	....	....	....	....	....	....	....	....	4	1	2	3	18	....	....	....
	NHL Totals		**2**	**0**	**0**	**0**	**0**	**0**	**0**	**0**	**0**	**0**	**0**	**0**	**0.0**	**0**	**0**	**0**	**0**		....	....	....	....	....	....	....	....

Transferred to **Phoenix** after **Winnipeg** franchise relocated, July 1, 1996.

• HANSON, DAVE

Dave Hanson D – L. 6', 190 lbs. b: Cumberland, WI, 4/12/1954. Philadelphia's 6th choice, 79th overall, in 1984 Entry Draft.

Season	Club	League	GP	G	A	Pts	AG	AA	APts	PIM	PP	SH	GW	S	%	TGF	PGF	TGA	PGA	+/–	GP	G	A	Pts	PIM	PP	SH	GW
1973-74	St. Paul Vulcans	USHL	56	9	13	22	....	....	....	*220	....	....	....	....	....	....	....	....	....	....	....	....	....	....	....	....	....	....
1974-75	Johnstown Jets	NAHL	72	10	24	34	....	....	....	249	....	....	....	....	....	....	....	....	....	....	....	....	....	....	....	....	....	....
1975-76	Johnstown Jets	NAHL	66	8	21	29	....	....	....	311	....	....	....	....	....	....	....	....	....	....	....	....	....	....	....	....	....	....
1976-77	Minnesota Fighting Saints	WHA	7	0	2	2	....	....	....	35	....	....	....	....	....	....	....	....	....	....	....	....	....	....	....	....	....	....
	Hampton Gulls	SHL	28	5	7	12	....	....	....	188	....	....	....	....	....	....	....	....	....	....	....	....	....	....	....	....	....	....
	Johnstown Jets	NAHL	6	0	3	3	....	....	....	27	....	....	....	....	....	....	....	....	....	....	....	....	....	....	....	....	....	....
	New England Whalers	WHA	1	0	0	0	....	....	....	9	....	....	....	....	....	....	....	....	....	....	1	0	0	0	0	....	....	....
	Rhode Island Reds	AHL	27	2	10	12	....	....	....	98	....	....	....	....	....	....	....	....	....	....	....	....	....	....	....	....	....	....
1977-78	Kansas City Red Wings	CHL	15	0	0	0	....	....	....	41	....	....	....	....	....	....	....	....	....	....	....	....	....	....	....	....	....	....
	Hampton Gulls	AHL	5	0	3	3	....	....	....	8	....	....	....	....	....	....	....	....	....	....	....	....	....	....	....	....	....	....
	Birmingham Bulls	WHA	42	7	16	23	....	....	....	241	....	....	....	....	....	....	....	....	....	....	5	0	1	1	48	....	....	....
1978-79	**Detroit Red Wings**	**NHL**	**11**	**0**	**0**	**0**	**0**	**0**	**0**	**26**	**0**	**0**	**0**	**5**	**0.0**	**2**	**0**	**3**	**0**	**–1**	....	....	....	....	....	....	....	....
	Birmingham Bulls	WHA	53	6	22	28	....	....	....	212	....	....	....	....	....	....	....	....	....	....	....	....	....	....	....	....	....	....
1979-80	Birmingham Bulls	CHL	33	4	6	10	....	....	....	174	....	....	....	....	....	....	....	....	....	....	....	....	....	....	....	....	....	....
	Minnesota North Stars	**NHL**	**22**	**1**	**1**	**2**	**1**	**1**	**2**	**39**	**0**	**0**	**0**	**11**	**9.1**	**2**	**0**	**7**	**0**	**–5**	....	....	....	....	....	....	....	....
	Oklahoma City Stars	CHL	6	0	0	0	....	....	....	12	....	....	....	....	....	....	....	....	....	....	....	....	....	....	....	....	....	....
1980-81	Adirondack Red Wings	AHL	77	11	21	32	....	....	....	267	....	....	....	....	....	....	....	....	....	....	18	1	4	5	30	....	....	....
1981-82	Adirondack Red Wings	AHL	75	11	23	34	....	....	....	206	....	....	....	....	....	....	....	....	....	....	5	1	3	4	23	....	....	....
1982-83	Indianapolis Checkers	CHL	80	18	21	39	....	....	....	285	....	....	....	....	....	....	....	....	....	....	5	1	3	4	2	....	....	....
1983-84	Indianapolis Checkers	CHL	1	0	0	0	....	....	....	0	....	....	....	....	....	....	....	....	....	....	....	....	....	....	....	....	....	....
	Toledo Goaldiggers	IHL	68	11	26	37	....	....	....	120	....	....	....	....	....	....	....	....	....	....	9	1	3	4	33	....	....	....
1984-1987			DID NOT PLAY																									
1987-88	Hershey Bears	AHL	6	0	0	0	....	....	....	0	....	....	....	....	....	....	....	....	....	....	....	....	....	....	....	....	....	....
1988-89	Indianapolis Ice	IHL	3	0	1	1	....	....	....	19	....	....	....	....	....	....	....	....	....	....	....	....	....	....	....	....	....	....
	NHL Totals		**33**	**1**	**1**	**2**	**1**	**1**	**2**	**65**	**0**	**0**	**0**	**16**	**6.3**	**4**	**0**	**10**	**0**		....	....	....	....	....	....	....	....
	Other Major League Totals		103	13	40	53				497											6	0	1	1	48			

Selected by **Minnesota** (WHA) in 1974 WHA Amateur Draft, June, 1974. Signed as a free agent by **New England** (WHA) after **Minnesota** (WHA) franchise folded, March, 1977. Signed as a free agent by **Birmingham** (WHA), September, 1977. Signed as a free agent by **Detroit**, October 4, 1977. Loaned to **Birmingham** (WHA) by **Detroit** with Steve Durbano and future considerations for Vaclav Nedomansky and Tim Sheehy, November 15, 1977. Traded to **Birmingham** (WHA) by **Detroit** for cash, December, 1979. Traded to **Minnesota** by **Detroit** for future considerations, January 3, 1980. Claimed on waivers by **Detroit** from **Minnesota**, June 8, 1980. Signed as a free agent by **NY Islanders**, September 9, 1982.

• HANSON, KEITH

Keith Hanson D – R. 6'5", 215 lbs. b: Ada, MN, 4/26/1957. Minnesota's 8th choice, 145th overall, in 1977 Amateur Draft.

Season	Club	League	GP	G	A	Pts	AG	AA	APts	PIM	PP	SH	GW	S	%	TGF	PGF	TGA	PGA	+/–	GP	G	A	Pts	PIM	PP	SH	GW
1976-77	Austin Prep High School	MJHL	STATISTICS NOT AVAILABLE																									
	United States	WJC-A	DID NOT PLAY																									
1977-78	Northern Michigan University	CCHA	34	16	15	31	....	....	....	77	....	....	....	....	....	....	....	....	....	....	....	....	....	....	....	....	....	....
1978-79			DID NOT PLAY																									
1979-80	Northern Michigan University	CCHA	38	2	13	15	....	....	....	74	....	....	....	....	....	....	....	....	....	....	....	....	....	....	....	....	....	....
1980-81	Northern Michigan University	CCHA	43	8	24	32	....	....	....	95	....	....	....	....	....	....	....	....	....	....	....	....	....	....	....	....	....	....
1981-82	Toledo Goaldiggers	IHL	82	7	37	44	....	....	....	185	....	....	....	....	....	....	....	....	....	....	13	1	3	4	23	....	....	....
1982-83	Birmingham South Stars	CHL	69	4	21	25	....	....	....	187	....	....	....	....	....	....	....	....	....	....	12	0	3	3	29	....	....	....
1983-84	**Calgary Flames**	**NHL**	**25**	**0**	**2**	**2**	**0**	**1**	**1**	**77**	**0**	**0**	**0**	**19**	**0.0**	**15**	**0**	**32**	**4**	**–13**	....	....	....	....	....	....	....	....
	Colorado Flames	CHL	39	5	21	26	....	....	....	64	....	....	....	....	....	....	....	....	....	....	6	2	2	4	16	....	....	....
1984-85	Moncton Golden Flames	AHL	70	5	17	22	....	....	....	145	....	....	....	....	....	....	....	....	....	....	....	....	....	....	....	....	....	....
	NHL Totals		**25**	**0**	**2**	**2**	**0**	**1**	**1**	**77**	**0**	**0**	**0**	**19**	**0.0**	**15**	**0**	**32**	**4**		....	....	....	....	....	....	....	....

Traded to **Calgary** by **Minnesota** with Mike Eaves for Steve Christoff, June 8, 1983.

• HARBARUK, NICK

Nick Harbaruk RW – R. 6', 195 lbs. b: Drohiczyn, Poland, 8/16/1943.

Season	Club	League	GP	G	A	Pts	AG	AA	APts	PIM	PP	SH	GW	S	%	TGF	PGF	TGA	PGA	+/–	GP	G	A	Pts	PIM	PP	SH	GW
1960-61	Toronto Marlboros	OHA	36	4	8	12	....	....	....	58	....	....	....	....	....	....	....	....	....	....	....	....	....	....	....	....	....	....
1961-62	Pittsburgh Hornets	AHL	1	0	0	0	....	....	....	0	....	....	....	....	....	....	....	....	....	....	....	....	....	....	....	....	....	....
	Toronto Marlboros	OHA	31	7	10	17	....	....	....	56	....	....	....	....	....	....	....	....	....	....	12	6	5	11	38	....	....	....
1962-63	Toronto Marlboros	OHA	16	12	8	20	....	....	....	23	....	....	....	....	....	....	....	....	....	....	....	....	....	....	....	....	....	....
1963-64	Toronto Marlboros	OHA	54	15	25	40	....	....	....	71	....	....	....	....	....	....	....	....	....	....	9	2	2	4	9	....	....	....
1964-65	Rochester Americans	AHL	2	0	0	0	....	....	....	0	....	....	....	....	....	....	....	....	....	....	....	....	....	....	....	....	....	....
	Tulsa Oilers	CHL	67	27	43	70	....	....	....	65	....	....	....	....	....	....	....	....	....	....	12	5	8	13	25	....	....	....
1965-66	Tulsa Oilers	CHL	70	20	46	66	....	....	....	97	....	....	....	....	....	....	....	....	....	....	11	1	4	5	10	....	....	....
1966-67	Tulsa Oilers	CHL	70	14	26	40	....	....	....	84	....	....	....	....	....	....	....	....	....	....	....	....	....	....	....	....	....	....
1967-68	Tulsa Oilers	CHL	54	20	30	50	....	....	....	96	....	....	....	....	....	....	....	....	....	....	11	1	6	7	14	....	....	....
1968-69	Vancouver Canucks	WHL	3	1	1	2	....	....	....	2	....	....	....	....	....	....	....	....	....	....	....	....	....	....	....	....	....	....
	Tulsa Oilers	CHL	69	26	19	45	....	....	....	89	....	....	....	....	....	....	....	....	....	....	7	2	5	7	18	....	....	....
1969-70	**Pittsburgh Penguins**	**NHL**	**74**	**5**	**17**	**22**	**6**	**17**	**23**	**56**	**2**	**0**	**1**	**119**	**4.2**	**39**	**11**	**57**	**22**	**–7**	**10**	**3**	**0**	**3**	**20**	**0**	**1**	**0**
1970-71	**Pittsburgh Penguins**	**NHL**	**78**	**13**	**12**	**25**	**14**	**11**	**25**	**108**	**2**	**1**	**1**	**147**	**8.8**	**40**	**4**	**61**	**16**	**–9**	....	....	....	....	....	....	....	....
1971-72	**Pittsburgh Penguins**	**NHL**	**78**	**12**	**17**	**29**	**13**	**15**	**28**	**46**	**3**	**0**	**1**	**140**	**8.6**	**43**	**7**	**72**	**23**	**–13**	**4**	**0**	**1**	**1**	**0**	**0**	**0**	**0**
1972-73	**Pittsburgh Penguins**	**NHL**	**78**	**10**	**15**	**25**	**10**	**13**	**23**	**47**	**0**	**2**	**1**	**96**	**10.4**	**35**	**2**	**63**	**19**	**–11**	....	....	....	....	....	....	....	....
1973-74	**St. Louis Blues**	**NHL**	**56**	**5**	**14**	**19**	**5**	**12**	**17**	**16**	**0**	**1**	**1**	**49**	**10.2**	**25**	**2**	**33**	**14**	**+4**	....	....	....	....	....	....	....	....
1974-75	Indianapolis Racers	WHA	78	20	23	43	....	....	....	52	....	....	....	....	....	....	....	....	....	....	....	....	....	....	....	....	....	....
1975-76	Indianapolis Racers	WHA	76	23	19	42	....	....	....	24	....	....	....	....	....	....	....	....	....	....	7	2	0	2	10	....	....	....
1976-77	Indianapolis Racers	WHA	27	2	2	4	....	....	....	2	....	....	....	....	....	....	....	....	....	....	6	1	1	2	0	....	....	....
	NHL Totals		**364**	**45**	**75**	**120**	**48**	**68**	**116**	**273**	**7**	**4**	**5**	**551**	**8.2**	**182**	**26**	**286**	**94**		**14**	**3**	**1**	**4**	**20**	**0**	**1**	**0**
	Other Major League Totals		181	45	44	89				78											13	3	1	4	10			

Claimed by **Pittsburgh** from **Vancouver** (WHL) in Intra-League Draft, June, 1969. Traded to **St. Louis** by **Pittsburgh** for Bob Johnson, October 4, 1973. Selected by **New England** (WHA) in 1972 WHA General Player Draft, February 12, 1972. WHA rights traded to **Indianapolis** (WHA) by **New England** (WHA), June, 1974.

• HARDING, JEFF

Jeff Harding RW – R. 6'3", 220 lbs. b: Toronto, Ont., 4/6/1969. Philadelphia's 2nd choice, 30th overall, in 1987 Entry Draft.

Season	Club	League	GP	G	A	Pts	AG	AA	APts	PIM	PP	SH	GW	S	%	TGF	PGF	TGA	PGA	+/–	GP	G	A	Pts	PIM	PP	SH	GW
1986-87	St. Michael's Buzzers	Jr. B	22	22	8	30	....	....	....	97	....	....	....	....	....	....	....	....	....	....	....	....	....	....	....	....	....	....
1987-88	Michigan State University	CCHA	43	17	10	27	....	....	....	129	....	....	....	....	....	....	....	....	....	....	....	....	....	....	....	....	....	....
1988-89	**Philadelphia Flyers**	**NHL**	**6**	**0**	**0**	**0**	**0**	**0**	**0**	**29**	**0**	**0**	**0**	**11**	**0.0**	**1**	**0**	**1**	**1**	**+1**	....	....	....	....	....	....	....	....
	Hershey Bears	AHL	34	13	5	18	....	....	....	64	....	....	....	....	....	....	....	....	....	....	8	1	1	2	33	....	....	....

			REGULAR SEASON																		PLAYOFFS							
Season	Club	League	GP	G	A	Pts	AG	AA	APts	PIM	PP	SH	GW	S	%	TGF	PGF	TGA	PGA	+/–	GP	G	A	Pts	PIM	PP	SH	GW
1989-90	**Philadelphia Flyers**	**NHL**	9	0	0	0	0	0	0	18	0	0	0	11	0.0	1	0	2	0	–1	....	....	....	....	....	....	....	....
	Canada	Nat-Team	21	5	6	11	....	....	....	50	....	....	....	....	....	....	....	....	....	....	....	....	....	....	....	....	....	....
	Hershey Bears	AHL	6	0	2	2	....	....	....	2	....	....	....	....	....	....	....	....	....	....	....	....	....	....	....	....	....	....
1990-91	Cape Breton Oilers	AHL	4	1	0	1	....	....	....	2	....	....	....	....	....	....	....	....	....	....	....	....	....	....	....	....	....	....
	Fort Wayne Komets	IHL	11	3	4	7	....	....	....	10	....	....	....	....	....	....	....	....	....	....	....	....	....	....	....	....	....	....
1991-92	Springfield Indians	AHL	17	1	4	5	....	....	....	27	....	....	....	....	....	....	....	....	....	....	....	....	....	....	....	....	....	....
	Kalamazoo K-Wings	IHL	6	1	0	1	....	....	....	63	....	....	....	....	....	....	....	....	....	....	....	....	....	....	....	....	....	....
	NHL Totals		15	0	0	0	0	0	0	47	0	0	0	22	0.0	2	0	3	1		....	....	....	....	....	....	....	....

• HARDY, JOE

Joe "Gypsy Joe" Hardy C – L. 6', 185 lbs. b: Kenogami, Que., 12/5/1945.

Season	Club	League	GP	G	A	Pts	AG	AA	APts	PIM	PP	SH	GW	S	%	TGF	PGF	TGA	PGA	+/–	GP	G	A	Pts	PIM	PP	SH	GW
1966-67	New Haven Blades	EHL	72	28	51	79	....	....	....	77	....	....	....	....	....	....	....	....	....	....	....	....	....	....	....	....	....	....
1967-68	Victoriaville Tigers	QSHL	35	25	35	60	....	....	....	65	....	....	....	....	....	....	....	....	....	....	....	....	....	....	....	....	....	....
1968-69	Victoriaville Tigers	QSHL	45	25	54	79	....	....	....	75	....	....	....	....	....	....	....	....	....	....	....	....	....	....	....	....	....	....
1969-70	**Oakland Seals**	**NHL**	23	5	4	9	6	4	10	20	1	1	1	38	13.2	13	4	20	3	–8	4	0	0	0	0	0	0	0
	Providence Reds	AHL	46	11	27	38	....	....	....	44	....	....	....	....	....	....	....	....	....	....	....	....	....	....	....	....	....	....
	Seattle Totems	WHL	....	....	....	....	....	....	....	....	....	....	....	....	....	....	....	....	....	....	2	1	0	1	4	....	....	....
1970-71	**California Golden Seals**	**NHL**	40	4	10	14	4	9	13	31	1	0	0	43	9.3	18	4	34	6	–14	....	....	....	....	....	....	....	....
1971-72	Nova Scotia Voyageurs	AHL	65	18	42	60	....	....	....	105	....	....	....	....	....	....	....	....	....	....	15	3	7	10	20	....	....	....
1972-73	Cleveland Crusaders	WHA	72	17	33	50	....	....	....	80	....	....	....	....	....	....	....	....	....	....	7	0	2	2	0	....	....	....
1973-74	Chicago Cougars	WHA	77	24	35	59	....	....	....	55	....	....	....	....	....	....	....	....	....	....	17	4	8	12	13	....	....	....
1974-75	Chicago Cougars	WHA	17	1	6	7	....	....	....	8	....	....	....	....	....	....	....	....	....	....	....	....	....	....	....	....	....	....
	Long Island Cougars	NAHL	4	1	2	3	....	....	....	2	....	....	....	....	....	....	....	....	....	....	....	....	....	....	....	....	....	....
	Indianapolis Racers	WHA	32	2	17	19	....	....	....	36	....	....	....	....	....	....	....	....	....	....	....	....	....	....	....	....	....	....
	San Diego Mariners	WHA	12	2	3	5	....	....	....	22	....	....	....	....	....	....	....	....	....	....	3	0	0	0	0	....	....	....
1975-76	Beauce Jaros	NAHL	72	60	*148	*208	....	....	....	98	....	....	....	....	....	....	....	....	....	....	14	4	24	28	44	....	....	....
1976-77	Beauce Jaros	NAHL	22	7	36	43	....	....	....	30	....	....	....	....	....	....	....	....	....	....	....	....	....	....	....	....	....	....
	Binghamton Dusters	NAHL	28	22	28	50	....	....	....	19	....	....	....	....	....	....	....	....	....	....	8	2	8	10	6	....	....	....
1977-78	Binghamton Dusters	AHL	73	24	*63	87	....	....	....	56	....	....	....	....	....	....	....	....	....	....	....	....	....	....	....	....	....	....
	NHL Totals		63	9	14	23	10	13	23	51	2	1	1	81	11.1	31	8	54	9		4	0	0	0	0	0	0	0
	Other Major League Totals		210	46	94	140	....	....	....	201	....	....	....	....	....	....	....	....	....	....	27	4	10	14	13	....	....	....

NAHL First All-Star Team (1976)

Signed as a free agent by **Oakland**, September, 1969. Traded to **Montreal** by **Oakland** for cash, October, 1971. Selected by **Alberta** (WHA) in 1972 WHA General Player Draft, February 12, 1972. WHA rights traded to **Cleveland** (WHA) by **Alberta** (WHA) for future considerations, July, 1972. Traded to **Chicago** (WHA) by **Cleveland** (WHA) for Larry Hillman, August, 1973. Traded to **Indianapolis** (WHA) by **Chicago** (WHA) for future considerations, December, 1974. Traded to **San Diego** (WHA) by **Indianapolis** (WHA) for future considerations, March, 1975.

• HARDY, MARK

Mark Hardy D – L. 5'11", 195 lbs. b: Semaden, Switz., 2/1/1959. Los Angeles' 3rd choice, 30th overall, in 1979 Entry Draft.

Season	Club	League	GP	G	A	Pts	AG	AA	APts	PIM	PP	SH	GW	S	%	TGF	PGF	TGA	PGA	+/–	GP	G	A	Pts	PIM	PP	SH	GW
1975-76	Montreal Jr. Canadiens	QMJHL	64	6	17	23	....	....	....	44	....	....	....	....	....	....	....	....	....	....	....	....	....	....	....	....	....	....
1976-77	Montreal Jr. Canadiens	QMJHL	72	20	40	60	....	....	....	137	....	....	....	....	....	....	....	....	....	....	12	4	8	12	14	....	....	....
1977-78	Montreal Jr. Canadiens	QMJHL	72	25	57	82	....	....	....	150	....	....	....	....	....	....	....	....	....	....	13	3	10	13	22	....	....	....
1978-79	Montreal Jr. Canadiens	QMJHL	67	18	52	70	....	....	....	117	....	....	....	....	....	....	....	....	....	....	11	5	8	13	40	....	....	....
1979-80	**Los Angeles Kings**	**NHL**	15	0	1	1	0	1	1	10	0	0	0	14	0.0	14	1	28	8	–7	4	1	1	2	9	0	0	0
	Binghamton Dusters	AHL	56	3	13	16	....	....	....	32	....	....	....	....	....	....	....	....	....	....	....	....	....	....	....	....	....	....
1980-81	**Los Angeles Kings**	**NHL**	77	5	20	25	4	14	18	77	3	0	1	90	5.6	111	23	108	34	+14	4	1	2	3	4	1	0	0
1981-82	**Los Angeles Kings**	**NHL**	77	6	39	45	5	26	31	130	1	0	0	121	5.0	137	44	137	32	–12	10	1	2	3	9	0	0	0
1982-83	**Los Angeles Kings**	**NHL**	74	5	34	39	4	23	27	101	3	0	1	162	3.1	128	49	143	34	–30	....	....	....	....	....	....	....	....
1983-84	**Los Angeles Kings**	**NHL**	79	8	41	49	6	28	34	122	5	0	1	175	4.6	149	54	165	40	–30	....	....	....	....	....	....	....	....
1984-85	**Los Angeles Kings**	**NHL**	78	14	39	53	11	26	37	97	8	1	2	151	9.3	134	58	120	24	–20	3	0	1	1	2	0	0	0
1985-86	**Los Angeles Kings**	**NHL**	55	6	21	27	5	14	19	71	2	1	1	113	5.3	87	26	112	40	–11	....	....	....	....	....	....	....	....
	Canada	WEC-A	10	3	2	5	....	....	....	12	....	....	....	....	....	....	....	....	....	....	....	....	....	....	....	....	....	....
1986-87	**Los Angeles Kings**	**NHL**	73	3	27	30	3	20	23	120	0	0	0	97	3.1	114	33	98	33	+16	5	1	2	3	10	0	0	0
1987-88	**Los Angeles Kings**	**NHL**	61	6	22	28	5	16	21	99	4	1	1	107	5.6	82	38	106	35	–27	....	....	....	....	....	....	....	....
	New York Rangers	**NHL**	19	2	2	4	2	1	3	31	0	0	0	27	7.4	12	2	26	11	–5	....	....	....	....	....	....	....	....
1988-89	**Minnesota North Stars**	**NHL**	15	2	4	6	2	3	5	26	0	0	1	19	10.5	14	5	20	10	–1	....	....	....	....	....	....	....	....
	New York Rangers	**NHL**	45	2	12	14	2	8	10	45	0	0	0	51	3.9	38	4	64	22	–8	4	0	1	1	31	0	0	0
1989-90	**New York Rangers**	**NHL**	54	0	15	15	0	11	11	94	0	0	0	55	0.0	53	10	64	25	+4	3	0	1	1	2	0	0	0
1990-91	**New York Rangers**	**NHL**	70	1	5	6	1	4	5	89	0	0	0	63	1.6	60	4	85	28	–1	6	0	1	1	30	0	0	0
1991-92	**New York Rangers**	**NHL**	52	1	8	9	1	6	7	65	0	0	1	42	2.4	65	1	43	12	+33	13	0	3	3	31	0	0	0
1992-93	**New York Rangers**	**NHL**	44	1	10	11	1	7	8	85	0	0	0	28	3.6	41	1	56	18	+2	....	....	....	....	....	....	....	....
	Los Angeles Kings	**NHL**	11	0	3	3	0	2	2	4	0	0	0	20	0.0	6	2	14	6	–4	15	1	2	3	30	0	0	0
1993-94	**Los Angeles Kings**	**NHL**	16	0	3	3	0	2	2	27	0	0	0	8	0.0	10	0	17	2	–5	....	....	....	....	....	....	....	....
	Phoenix Roadrunners	IHL	54	5	3	8	....	....	....	48	....	....	....	....	....	....	....	....	....	....	....	....	....	....	....	....	....	....
1994-95	Detroit Vipers	IHL	41	6	21	27	....	....	....	35	....	....	....	....	....	....	....	....	....	....	5	1	1	2	7	....	....	....
	NHL Totals		915	62	306	368	52	212	264	1293	26	3	9	1343	4.6	1255	355	1406	414		67	5	16	21	158	1	0	0

QMJHL First All-Star Team (1978)

Traded to **NY Rangers** by **LA Kings** for Ron Duguay, February 23, 1988. Traded to **Minnesota** by **NY Rangers** for future considerations (Louie Debrusk) June 13, 1988. Traded to **NY Rangers** by **Minnesota** for Larry Bernard and NY Rangers' 5th round choice (Rhys Hollyman) in 1989 Entry Draft, December 9, 1988. Traded to **LA Kings** by **NY Rangers** with Ottawa's 5th round choice (previously acquired, LA Kings selected Frederick Beaubien) in 1993 Entry Draft for John McIntyre, March 22, 1993.

• HARGREAVES, JIM

Jim "Cement Head" Hargreaves D – R. 5'11", 195 lbs. b: Winnipeg, Man., 5/2/1950. Vancouver's 2nd choice, 16th overall, in 1970 Amateur Draft.

Season	Club	League	GP	G	A	Pts	AG	AA	APts	PIM	PP	SH	GW	S	%	TGF	PGF	TGA	PGA	+/–	GP	G	A	Pts	PIM	PP	SH	GW
1968-69	Winnipeg Jets	WCJHL	56	10	19	29	....	....	....	107	....	....	....	....	....	....	....	....	....	....	....	....	....	....	....	....	....	....
1969-70	Winnipeg Jets	WCJHL	55	10	34	44	....	....	....	176	....	....	....	....	....	....	....	....	....	....	....	....	....	....	....	....	....	....
1970-71	**Vancouver Canucks**	**NHL**	7	0	1	1	0	1	1	33	0	0	0	2	0.0	3	1	5	0	–3	....	....	....	....	....	....	....	....
	Rochester Americans	AHL	42	1	10	11	....	....	....	109	....	....	....	....	....	....	....	....	....	....	....	....	....	....	....	....	....	....
1971-72	Rochester Americans	AHL	61	3	10	13	....	....	....	127	....	....	....	....	....	....	....	....	....	....	....	....	....	....	....	....	....	....
1972-73	**Vancouver Canucks**	**NHL**	59	1	6	7	1	5	6	72	0	0	0	40	2.5	29	1	77	18	–31	....	....	....	....	....	....	....	....
	Seattle Totems	WHL	17	1	11	12	....	....	....	43	....	....	....	....	....	....	....	....	....	....	....	....	....	....	....	....	....	....
1973-74	Winnipeg Jets	WHA	53	1	4	5	....	....	....	50	....	....	....	....	....	....	....	....	....	....	....	....	....	....	....	....	....	....
1974-75	Indianapolis Racers	WHA	37	2	5	7	....	....	....	30	....	....	....	....	....	....	....	....	....	....	....	....	....	....	....	....	....	....
	San Diego Mariners	WHA	41	8	10	18	....	....	....	45	....	....	....	....	....	....	....	....	....	....	10	1	0	1	6	....	....	....
1975-76	San Diego Mariners	WHA	43	1	1	2	....	....	....	26	....	....	....	....	....	....	....	....	....	....	5	0	0	0	2	....	....	....
	NHL Totals		66	1	7	8	1	6	7	105	0	0	0	42	2.4	32	2	82	18		....	....	....	....	....	....	....	....
	Other Major League Totals		174	12	20	32	....	....	....	151	....	....	....	....	....	....	....	....	....	....	15	1	0	1	8	....	....	....

WCJHL All-Star Team (1970)

Selected by **Winnipeg** (WHA) in 1972 WHA General Player Draft, February 12, 1972. Selected by **Indianapolis** (WHA) from **Winnipeg** (WHA) in 1974 WHA Expansion Draft, June, 1974. Traded to **San Diego** (WHA) by **Indianapolis** (WHA) for Ken Block, January, 1975.

• HARKINS, BRETT

Brett Harkins LW – L. 6'1", 185 lbs. b: North Ridgeville, OH, 7/2/1970. NY Islanders' 9th choice, 133rd overall, in 1989 Entry Draft.

Season	Club	League	GP	G	A	Pts	AG	AA	APts	PIM	PP	SH	GW	S	%	TGF	PGF	TGA	PGA	+/–	GP	G	A	Pts	PIM	PP	SH	GW
1988-89	Detroit Compuware	NAJHL	38	23	46	69	....	....	....	94	....	....	....	....	....	....	....	....	....	....	....	....	....	....	....	....	....	....
1989-90	Bowling Green University	CCHA	41	11	43	54	....	....	....	45	....	....	....	....	....	....	....	....	....	....	....	....	....	....	....	....	....	....
1990-91	Bowling Green University	CCHA	40	22	38	60	....	....	....	30	....	....	....	....	....	....	....	....	....	....	....	....	....	....	....	....	....	....
1991-92	Bowling Green University	CCHA	34	8	39	47	....	....	....	32	....	....	....	....	....	....	....	....	....	....	....	....	....	....	....	....	....	....
1992-93	Bowling Green University	CCHA	35	19	28	47	....	....	....	28	....	....	....	....	....	....	....	....	....	....	....	....	....	....	....	....	....	....
1993-94	Adirondack Red Wings	AHL	80	22	47	69	....	....	....	23	....	....	....	....	....	....	....	....	....	....	10	1	5	6	4	....	....	....
1994-95	**Boston Bruins**	**NHL**	1	0	1	1	0	1	1	0	0	0	0	1	0.0	2	1	1	0	0	....	....	....	....	....	....	....	....
	Providence Bruins	AHL	80	23	*69	92	....	....	....	32	....	....	....	....	....	....	....	....	....	....	13	8	14	22	4	....	....	....
1995-96	**Florida Panthers**	**NHL**	8	0	3	3	0	2	2	6	0	0	0	4	0.0	6	3	5	0	–2	....	....	....	....	....	....	....	....
	Carolina Monarchs	AHL	55	23	*71	94	....	....	....	44	....	....	....	....	....	....	....	....	....	....	....	....	....	....	....	....	....	....

			REGULAR SEASON																		PLAYOFFS							
Season	Club	League	GP	G	A	Pts	AG	AA	APts	PIM	PP	SH	GW	S	%	TGF	PGF	TGA	PGA	+/-	GP	G	A	Pts	PIM	PP	SH	GW
1996-97	**Boston Bruins**	**NHL**	**44**	**4**	**14**	**18**	**4**	**12**	**16**	**8**	**3**	**0**	**2**	**52**	**7.7**	**28**	**9**	**22**	**0**	**–3**								
	Providence Bruins	AHL	28	9	31	40				32											10	2	10	12	0			
1997-98	Cleveland Lumberjacks	IHL	80	32	62	94				82											10	4	13	17	14			
	NHL Totals		**53**	**4**	**18**	**22**	**4**	**15**	**19**	**14**	**3**	**0**	**2**	**57**	**7.0**	**36**	**13**	**28**	**0**									

Signed as a free agent by **Boston**, July 1, 1994. Signed as a free agent by **Florida**, July 24, 1995. Signed as a free agent by **Boston**, September 4, 1996.

• HARKINS, TODD

Todd Harkins C – R. 6'3", 210 lbs. b: Cleveland, OH, 10/8/1968. Calgary's 2nd choice, 42nd overall, in 1988 Entry Draft.

Season	Club	League	GP	G	A	Pts	AG	AA	APts	PIM	PP	SH	GW	S	%	TGF	PGF	TGA	PGA	+/-	GP	G	A	Pts	PIM	PP	SH	GW
1987-88	University of Miami-Ohio	CCHA	34	9	7	16				133																		
1988-89	University of Miami-Ohio	CCHA	36	8	7	15				77																		
1989-90	University of Miami-Ohio	CCHA	40	27	17	44				78																		
1990-91	Salt Lake Golden Eagles	IHL	79	15	27	42				113											3	0	0	0	0			
1991-92	**Calgary Flames**	**NHL**	**5**	**0**	**0**	**0**	**0**	**0**	**0**	**7**	**0**	**0**	**0**	**4**	**0.0**	**0**	**0**	**2**	**0**	**–2**								
	Salt Lake Golden Eagles	IHL	72	32	30	62				67											5	1	1	2	6			
	United States	WC-A	6	0	4	4				10																		
1992-93	**Calgary Flames**	**NHL**	**15**	**2**	**3**	**5**	**2**	**2**	**4**	**22**	**0**	**0**	**0**	**17**	**11.8**	**7**	**1**	**10**	**0**	**–4**								
	Salt Lake Golden Eagles	IHL	53	13	21	34				90																		
1993-94	Saint John Flames	AHL	38	13	9	22				64																		
	Hartford Whalers	**NHL**	**28**	**1**	**0**	**1**	**1**	**0**	**1**	**49**	**0**	**0**	**0**	**15**	**6.7**	**3**	**0**	**7**	**0**	**–4**								
	Springfield Indians	AHL	1	0	3	3				0																		
1994-95	Chicago Wolves	IHL	52	18	25	43				136																		
	Houston Aeros	IHL	25	9	10	19				77											4	1	1	2	28			
	United States	WC-A	6	1	3	4				28																		
1995-96	Carolina Monarchs	AHL	69	27	28	55				172																		
1996-97	Fort Wayne Komets	IHL	60	12	13	25				131																		
	Phoenix Roadrunners	IHL	16	4	3	7				24																		
1997-98	Dusseldorfer EG	Germany	48	13	22	35				117											3	2	0	2	12			
	NHL Totals		**48**	**3**	**3**	**6**	**3**	**2**	**5**	**78**	**0**	**0**	**0**	**36**	**8.3**	**10**	**1**	**19**	**0**									

Traded to **Hartford** by **Calgary** for Scott Morrow, January 24, 1994. Signed as a free agent by **Florida**, June 6, 1995.

• HARLOCK, DAVID

David Harlock D – L. 6'2", 205 lbs. b: Toronto, Ont., 3/16/1971. New Jersey's 2nd choice, 24th overall, in 1990 Entry Draft.

Season	Club	League	GP	G	A	Pts	AG	AA	APts	PIM	PP	SH	GW	S	%	TGF	PGF	TGA	PGA	+/-	GP	G	A	Pts	PIM	PP	SH	GW
1989-90	University of Michigan	CCHA	42	2	13	15				44																		
1990-91	University of Michigan	CCHA	39	2	8	10				70																		
	Canada	WJC-A	7	0	2	2				2																		
1991-92	University of Michigan	CCHA	44	1	6	7				80																		
1992-93	University of Michigan	CCHA	38	3	9	12				58																		
	Canada	Nat-Team	4	0	0	0				2																		
1993-94	Canada	Nat-Team	41	0	3	3				28																		
	Canada	Olympics	8	0	0	0				8																		
	Toronto Maple Leafs	**NHL**	**6**	**0**	**0**	**0**	**0**	**0**	**0**	**0**	**0**	**0**	**0**	**2**	**0.0**	**3**	**0**	**6**	**1**	**–2**								
	St. John's Maple Leafs	AHL	10	0	3	3				2											9	0	0	0	6			
1994-95	**Toronto Maple Leafs**	**NHL**	**1**	**0**	**0**	**0**	**0**	**0**	**0**	**0**	**0**	**0**	**0**	**0**	**0.0**	**0**	**0**	**1**	**0**	**–1**								
	St. John's Maple Leafs	AHL	58	0	6	6				44											5	0	0	0	0			
1995-96	**Toronto Maple Leafs**	**NHL**	**1**	**0**	**0**	**0**	**0**	**0**	**0**	**0**	**0**	**0**	**0**	**0**	**0.0**	**0**	**0**	**0**	**0**	**0**								
	St. John's Maple Leafs	AHL	77	0	12	12				92											4	0	1	1	2			
1996-97	San Antonio Dragons	IHL	69	3	10	13				82											9	0	0	0	10			
1997-98	**Washington Capitals**	**NHL**	**6**	**0**	**0**	**0**	**0**	**0**	**0**	**4**	**0**	**0**	**0**	**2**	**0.0**	**3**	**0**	**2**	**1**	**+2**								
	Portland Pirates	AHL	71	3	15	18				66											10	2	2	4	6			
	NHL Totals		**14**	**0**	**0**	**0**	**0**	**0**	**0**	**4**	**0**	**0**	**0**	**4**	**0.0**	**6**	**0**	**9**	**2**									

Signed as a free agent by **Toronto**, August 20, 1993. Signed as a free agent by **Washington**, August 20, 1997.

• HARLOW, SCOTT

Scott Harlow LW – L. 6'1", 185 lbs. b: East Bridgewater, MA, 10/11/1963. Montreal's 6th choice, 61st overall, in 1982 Entry Draft.

Season	Club	League	GP	G	A	Pts	AG	AA	APts	PIM	PP	SH	GW	S	%	TGF	PGF	TGA	PGA	+/-	GP	G	A	Pts	PIM	PP	SH	GW
1982-83	Boston College	ECAC	24	6	10	25				19																		
	United States	WJC-A	7	2	2	4				0																		
1983-84	Boston College	ECAC	39	27	20	47				17																		
1984-85	Boston College	H.E.	44	34	38	72				45																		
1985-86	Boston College	H.E.	42	38	41	79				48																		
1986-87	Sherbrooke Canadiens	AHL	66	22	26	48				6											15	5	6	11	6			
1987-88	Sherbrooke Canadiens	AHL	18	6	12	18				8																		
	St. Louis Blues	**NHL**	**1**	**0**	**1**	**1**	**0**	**1**	**1**	**0**	**0**	**0**	**0**	**2**	**0.0**	**2**	**1**	**2**	**0**	**–1**								
	Baltimore Skipjacks	AHL	29	24	27	51				21																		
	Peoria Rivermen	IHL	39	30	25	55				46																		
1988-89	Peoria Rivermen	IHL	45	16	26	42				22																		
	Maine Mariners	AHL	30	16	17	33				8																		
1989-90	Maine Mariners	AHL	80	31	32	63				68																		
1990-91	New Haven Nighthawks	AHL	73	28	28	56				92																		
1991-92	Phoenix Roadrunners	IHL	4	2	0	2				0																		
	Peterborough Pirates	Britain	16	28	23	51				50											7	11	14	25	8			
	NHL Totals		**1**	**0**	**1**	**1**	**0**	**1**	**1**	**0**	**0**	**0**	**0**	**2**	**0.0**	**2**	**1**	**2**	**0**									

Hockey East Second All-Star Team (1985) • Hockey East First All-Star Team (1986) • NCAA East First All-American Team (1986)

Traded to **St. Louis** by **Montreal** for future considerations, January 21, 1988. Traded to **Boston** by **St. Louis** for Phil DeGaetano, February 3, 1989.

• HARPER, TERRY

Terry Harper D – R. 6'1", 200 lbs. b: Regina, Sask., 1/27/1940.

Season	Club	League	GP	G	A	Pts	AG	AA	APts	PIM	PP	SH	GW	S	%	TGF	PGF	TGA	PGA	+/-	GP	G	A	Pts	PIM	PP	SH	GW
1957-58	Regina Pats	SJHL	51	6	10	16				74											12	2	3	5	12			
1958-59	Regina Pats	SJHL	48	1	19	20				79											9	1	2	3	6			
1959-60	Regina Pats	SJHL	59	17	21	38				56											13	3	7	10	6			
1960-61	Montreal Royals	EPHL	69	3	14	17				85																		
1961-62	Hull-Ottawa Canadiens	EPHL	65	2	18	20				101											12	0	1	1	15			
1962-63	**Montreal Canadiens**	**NHL**	**14**	**1**	**1**	**2**	**1**	**1**	**2**	**10**											**5**	**1**	**0**	**1**	**8**			
	Hull-Ottawa Canadiens	EPHL	52	6	31	37				83																		
	Quebec Aces	AHL	3	0	0	0				0																		
1963-64	**Montreal Canadiens**	**NHL**	**70**	**2**	**15**	**17**	**3**	**17**	**20**	**149**											**7**	**0**	**0**	**0**	**6**			
1964-65	**Montreal Canadiens**	**NHL**	**62**	**0**	**7**	**7**	**0**	**8**	**8**	**93**											**13**	**0**	**0**	**0**	**19**			
1965-66	**Montreal Canadiens**	**NHL**	**69**	**1**	**11**	**12**	**1**	**11**	**12**	**91**											**10**	**2**	**3**	**5**	**18**			
1966-67	**Montreal Canadiens**	**NHL**	**56**	**0**	**16**	**16**	**0**	**16**	**10**	**99**											**10**	**0**	**1**	**1**	**15**			
1967-68	**Montreal Canadiens**	**NHL**	**57**	**3**	**8**	**11**	**4**	**8**	**12**	**66**	**0**	**0**	**1**	**47**	**6.4**	**67**	**1**	**48**	**3**	**+21**	**13**	**0**	**1**	**1**	**8**	**0**	**0**	**0**
1968-69	**Montreal Canadiens**	**NHL**	**21**	**0**	**3**	**3**	**0**	**3**	**3**	**37**	**0**	**0**	**0**	**14**	**0.0**	**24**	**1**	**17**	**1**	**+7**	**11**	**0**	**0**	**0**	**8**	**0**	**0**	**0**
	Cleveland Barons	AHL	28	2	4	6				21																		
1969-70	**Montreal Canadiens**	**NHL**	**75**	**4**	**18**	**22**	**5**	**18**	**23**	**109**	**0**	**0**	**0**	**60**	**6.7**	**90**	**1**	**94**	**32**	**+27**								
1970-71	**Montreal Canadiens**	**NHL**	**78**	**1**	**21**	**22**	**1**	**18**	**19**	**116**	**0**	**0**	**0**	**61**	**1.6**	**110**	**0**	**105**	**30**	**+35**	**20**	**0**	**6**	**6**	**28**	**0**	**0**	**0**
1971-72	**Montreal Canadiens**	**NHL**	**52**	**2**	**12**	**14**	**2**	**11**	**13**	**35**	**0**	**0**	**0**	**39**	**5.1**	**53**	**0**	**54**	**10**	**+9**	**5**	**1**	**1**	**2**	**6**	**0**	**0**	**0**
1972-73	**Los Angeles Kings**	**NHL**	**77**	**1**	**8**	**9**	**1**	**7**	**8**	**74**	**0**	**0**	**1**	**64**	**1.6**	**69**	**1**	**83**	**21**	**+6**								
1973-74	**Los Angeles Kings**	**NHL**	**77**	**0**	**17**	**17**	**0**	**15**	**15**	**119**	**0**	**0**	**0**	**114**	**0.0**	**100**	**1**	**102**	**28**	**+25**	**5**	**0**	**0**	**0**	**16**	**0**	**0**	**0**
1974-75	**Los Angeles Kings**	**NHL**	**80**	**5**	**21**	**26**	**5**	**17**	**22**	**120**	**1**	**0**	**0**	**96**	**5.2**	**95**	**1**	**82**	**26**	**+38**	**3**	**0**	**0**	**0**	**2**	**0**	**0**	**0**
1975-76	**Detroit Red Wings**	**NHL**	**69**	**8**	**25**	**33**	**7**	**20**	**27**	**59**	**4**	**0**	**0**	**111**	**7.2**	**102**	**26**	**112**	**42**	**+6**								
1976-77	**Detroit Red Wings**	**NHL**	**52**	**4**	**8**	**12**	**4**	**6**	**10**	**28**	**1**	**0**	**0**	**60**	**6.7**	**40**	**4**	**77**	**18**	**–23**								
1977-78	**Detroit Red Wings**	**NHL**	**80**	**2**	**17**	**19**	**2**	**14**	**16**	**85**	**0**	**0**	**0**	**76**	**2.6**	**88**	**2**	**118**	**51**	**+19**	**7**	**0**	**1**	**1**	**4**	**0**	**0**	**0**

Season	Club	League	REGULAR SEASON																		PLAYOFFS							
			GP	G	A	Pts	AG	AA	APts	PIM	PP	SH	GW	S	%	TGF	PGF	TGA	PGA	+/–	GP	G	A	Pts	PIM	PP	SH	GW
1978-79	**Detroit Red Wings**	**NHL**	51	0	6	6	0	5	5	58	0	0	0	33	0.0	43	2	68	24	–3	....	....	....	....	....	....	....	....
	Kansas City Red Wings	CHL	22	0	13	13	....	....	....	36	....	....	....	....	....	....	....	....	....	....	....	....	....	....	....	....	....	....
1979-80	**St. Louis Blues**	**NHL**	11	1	5	6	1	4	5	6	0	0	0	14	7.1	17	1	12	1	+5	3	0	0	0	2	0	0	0
1980-81	**Colorado Rockies**	**NHL**	15	0	2	2	0	1	1	8	0	0	0	6	0.0	8	1	10	0	–3	....	....	....	....	....	....	....	....
	NHL Totals		1066	35	221	256	37	200	237	1362	6	0	2	795	4.4	906	42	982	287		112	4	13	17	140	0	0	0

Played in NHL All-Star Game (1965, 1967, 1973, 1975)

Traded to **LA Kings** by **Montreal** for LA Kings' 2nd round choice (Gary MacGregor) in 1974 Amateur Draft, 1st (Pierre Mondou) and 3rd (Paul Woods) round choices in 1975 Amateur Draft and 1st round choice (Rod Shutt) in 1976 Amateur Draft, August 22, 1972. Traded to **Detroit** by **LA Kings** with Dan Maloney, Terry Harper and LA Kings' 2nd round choice (later traded to Minnesota — Minnesota selected Jim Roberts) in 1976 Amateur Draft for Bart Crashley and the rights to Marcel Dionne, June 23, 1975. Signed as a free agent by **St. Louis**, March 10, 1980. Signed as a free agent by **Colorado**, February 12, 1981.

• HARRER, TIM

Tim Harrer RW – R. 6′, 185 lbs. b: Bloomington, MN, 5/10/1957. Atlanta's 9th choice, 148th overall, in 1977 Amateur Draft.

1975-76	Bloomington Jr. Stars	MWJHL	11	5	3	8	....	....	....	6	....	....	....	....	....	....	....	....	....	....	....	....	....	....	....	....	....	....
1976-77	University of Minnesota	WCHA	38	14	9	23	....	....	....	37	....	....	....	....	....	....	....	....	....	....	....	....	....	....	....	....	....	....
1977-78	University of Minnesota	WCHA	35	22	21	43	....	....	....	36	....	....	....	....	....	....	....	....	....	....	....	....	....	....	....	....	....	....
1978-79	University of Minnesota	WCHA	43	28	25	53	....	....	....	38	....	....	....	....	....	....	....	....	....	....	....	....	....	....	....	....	....	....
1979-80	University of Minnesota	WCHA	41	53	29	82	....	....	....	50	....	....	....	....	....	....	....	....	....	....	....	....	....	....	....	....	....	....
1980-81	Birmingham Bulls	CHL	28	9	5	14	....	....	....	36	....	....	....	....	....	....	....	....	....	....	....	....	....	....	....	....	....	....
	Hershey Bears	AHL	39	7	6	13	....	....	....	12	....	....	....	....	....	....	....	....	....	....	2	0	0	0	0	....	....	....
1981-82	Oklahoma City Stars	CHL	77	29	27	56	....	....	....	36	....	....	....	....	....	....	....	....	....	....	4	2	2	4	0	....	....	....
1982-83	**Calgary Flames**	**NHL**	3	0	0	0	0	0	0	2	0	0	0	3	0.0	1	0	1	0	0	....	....	....	....	....	....	....	....
	Colorado Flames	CHL	69	33	29	62	....	....	....	28	....	....	....	....	....	....	....	....	....	....	6	3	3	6	4	....	....	....
1983-84	Salt Lake Golden Eagles	CHL	66	42	27	69	....	....	....	46	....	....	....	....	....	....	....	....	....	....	5	1	2	3	5	....	....	....
1984-85	Nova Scotia Voyageurs	AHL	7	0	0	0	....	....	....	0	....	....	....	....	....	....	....	....	....	....	....	....	....	....	....	....	....	....
	Toledo Goaldiggers	IHL	28	6	10	16	....	....	....	28	....	....	....	....	....	....	....	....	....	....	....	....	....	....	....	....	....	....
	EC Graz	Austria	4	3	1	4	....	....	....	2	....	....	....	....	....	....	....	....	....	....	....	....	....	....	....	....	....	....
	NHL Totals		3	0	0	0	0	0	0	2	0	0	0	3	0.0	1	0	1	0		....	....	....	....	....	....	....	....

WCHA First All-Star Team (1980) • NCAA West First All-American Team (1980)

Transferred to **Calgary** after **Atlanta** franchise relocated, June 24, 1980. Signed as a free agent by **Minnesota**, August 1, 1983.

• HARRIS, BILL

Bill Harris RW – L. 6′2″, 195 lbs. b: Toronto, Ont., 1/29/1952. NY Islanders' 1st choice, 1st overall, in 1972 Amateur Draft.

1968-69	Toronto Marlboros	OHA	41	9	18	27	....	....	....	14	....	....	....	....	....	....	....	....	....	....	6	2	2	4	....	....	....	....
1969-70	Toronto Marlboros	OHA	46	13	17	30	....	....	....	75	....	....	....	....	....	....	....	....	....	....	....	....	....	....	....	....	....	....
1970-71	Toronto Marlboros	OHA	48	34	48	82	....	....	....	61	....	....	....	....	....	....	....	....	....	....	....	....	....	....	....	....	....	....
1971-72	Toronto Marlboros	OHA	63	57	72	*129	....	....	....	87	....	....	....	....	....	....	....	....	....	....	....	....	....	....	....	....	....	....
1972-73	**New York Islanders**	**NHL**	78	28	22	50	28	18	46	35	6	0	2	196	14.3	67	19	104	12	–44	....	....	....	....	....	....	....	....
1973-74	**New York Islanders**	**NHL**	78	23	27	50	23	23	46	34	4	0	3	190	12.1	67	21	58	1	–11	....	....	....	....	....	....	....	....
1974-75	**New York Islanders**	**NHL**	80	25	37	62	23	29	52	34	4	0	5	199	12.6	98	31	65	2	+4	17	3	7	10	12	2	0	1
1975-76	**New York Islanders**	**NHL**	80	32	38	70	30	30	60	54	16	0	4	228	14.0	124	63	41	2	+22	13	5	2	7	10	1	0	0
1976-77	**New York Islanders**	**NHL**	80	24	43	67	23	35	58	44	5	1	3	160	15.0	95	28	53	4	+18	12	7	7	14	8	2	0	1
1977-78	**New York Islanders**	**NHL**	80	22	38	60	21	31	52	40	1	1	1	148	14.9	77	7	53	10	+27	7	0	0	0	4	0	0	0
1978-79	**New York Islanders**	**NHL**	80	15	39	54	14	30	44	18	0	0	5	128	11.7	72	5	46	5	+26	10	2	1	3	10	1	0	1
1979-80	**New York Islanders**	**NHL**	67	15	15	30	14	11	25	37	2	1	2	91	16.5	45	6	57	18	0	....	....	....	....	....	....	....	....
	Los Angeles Kings	**NHL**	11	4	3	7	4	2	6	6	1	0	1	22	18.2	12	2	9	3	+4	4	0	0	0	2	0	0	0
1980-81	**Los Angeles Kings**	**NHL**	80	20	29	49	16	20	36	36	1	4	1	150	13.3	82	18	107	42	–1	4	2	1	3	0	0	0	0
1981-82	**Los Angeles Kings**	**NHL**	16	1	3	4	1	2	3	6	0	0	0	11	9.1	10	3	24	8	–9	....	....	....	....	....	....	....	....
	Toronto Maple Leafs	**NHL**	20	2	0	2	2	0	2	4	0	0	0	21	9.5	11	1	29	3	–16	....	....	....	....	....	....	....	....
1982-83	**Toronto Maple Leafs**	**NHL**	76	11	19	30	9	13	22	26	0	1	0	83	13.3	47	1	94	33	–15	4	0	1	1	2	0	0	0
1983-84	**Toronto Maple Leafs**	**NHL**	50	7	10	17	6	7	13	14	0	0	0	68	10.3	25	3	79	37	–20	....	....	....	....	....	....	....	....
	St. Catharines Saints	AHL	2	0	1	1	....	....	....	0	....	....	....	....	....	....	....	....	....	....	....	....	....	....	....	....	....	....
	Los Angeles Kings	**NHL**	21	2	4	6	2	3	5	6	0	0	0	19	10.5	9	0	24	12	–3	....	....	....	....	....	....	....	....
	NHL Totals		897	231	327	558	216	254	470	394	40	8	27	1714	13.5	841	208	843	192		71	19	19	38	48	6	0	3

OHA Second All-Star Team (1971) • OHA First All-Star Team (1972)

Played in NHL All-Star Game (1976)

Traded to **LA Kings** by **NY Islanders** with Dave Lewis for Butch Goring, March 10, 1980. Traded to **Toronto** by **LA Kings** with John Gibson for Ian Turnbull, November 11, 1981. Traded to **LA Kings** by **Toronto** for cash, February 15, 1984.

• HARRIS, BILLY

Billy "Hinky" Harris C – L. 6′, 155 lbs. b: Toronto, Ont., 7/29/1935.

1950-51	Toronto Marlboros	OHA	2	0	1	1	....	....	....	0	....	....	....	....	....	....	....	....	....	....	....	....	....	....	....	....	....	....
1951-52	Toronto Marlboros	OHA	3	0	1	1	....	....	....	0	....	....	....	....	....	....	....	....	....	....	....	....	....	....	....	....	....	....
1952-53	Toronto Marlboros	OHA	56	20	31	51	....	....	....	4	....	....	....	....	....	....	....	....	....	....	7	2	1	3	4	....	....	....
1953-54	Toronto Marlboros	OHA	59	25	39	64	....	....	....	27	....	....	....	....	....	....	....	....	....	....	15	4	6	10	20	....	....	....
1954-55	Toronto Marlboros	OHA	47	37	29	64	....	....	....	26	....	....	....	....	....	....	....	....	....	....	13	*10	*18	*28	11	....	....	....
1955-56	**Toronto Maple Leafs**	**NHL**	70	9	13	22	13	16	29	8	....	....	....	....	....	....	....	....	....	....	5	1	0	1	4	....	....	....
1956-57	**Toronto Maple Leafs**	**NHL**	23	4	6	10	5	7	12	6	....	....	....	....	....	....	....	....	....	....	....	....	....	....	....	....	....	....
	Rochester Americans	AHL	43	5	20	25	....	....	....	15	....	....	....	....	....	....	....	....	....	....	2	0	0	0	4	....	....	....
1957-58	**Toronto Maple Leafs**	**NHL**	68	16	28	44	21	31	52	32	....	....	....	....	....	....	....	....	....	....	....	....	....	....	....	....	....	....
1958-59	**Toronto Maple Leafs**	**NHL**	70	22	30	52	28	32	60	29	....	....	....	....	....	....	....	....	....	....	12	3	4	7	16	....	....	....
1959-60	**Toronto Maple Leafs**	**NHL**	70	13	25	38	16	26	42	29	....	....	....	....	....	....	....	....	....	....	9	0	3	3	4	....	....	....
1960-61	**Toronto Maple Leafs**	**NHL**	66	12	27	39	15	27	42	30	....	....	....	....	....	....	....	....	....	....	5	1	0	1	0	....	....	....
1961-62	**Toronto Maple Leafs**	**NHL**	67	15	10	25	18	10	28	14	....	....	....	....	....	....	....	....	....	....	12	2	1	3	2	....	....	....
1962-63	**Toronto Maple Leafs**	**NHL**	65	8	24	32	10	25	35	22	....	....	....	....	....	....	....	....	....	....	10	0	1	1	0	....	....	....
1963-64	**Toronto Maple Leafs**	**NHL**	63	6	12	18	8	13	21	17	....	....	....	....	....	....	....	....	....	....	9	1	1	2	4	....	....	....
1964-65	**Toronto Maple Leafs**	**NHL**	48	1	6	7	1	6	7	0	....	....	....	....	....	....	....	....	....	....	....	....	....	....	....	....	....	....
	Rochester Americans	AHL	11	4	10	14	....	....	....	6	....	....	....	....	....	....	....	....	....	....	10	5	*12	*17	10	....	....	....
1965-66	**Detroit Red Wings**	**NHL**	24	1	4	5	1	4	5	6	....	....	....	....	....	....	....	....	....	....	....	....	....	....	....	....	....	....
	Pittsburgh Hornets	AHL	42	15	22	37	....	....	....	2	....	....	....	....	....	....	....	....	....	....	3	0	0	0	2	....	....	....
1966-67	Pittsburgh Hornets	AHL	70	34	36	70	....	....	....	29	....	....	....	....	....	....	....	....	....	....	9	2	6	8	6	....	....	....
1967-68	**Oakland Seals**	**NHL**	62	12	17	29	15	18	33	2	1	0	0	106	11.3	42	10	38	0	–6	....	....	....	....	....	....	....	....
1968-69	**Oakland Seals**	**NHL**	19	0	4	4	0	4	4	2	0	0	0	20	0.0	7	1	12	5	–1	....	....	....	....	....	....	....	....
	Pittsburgh Penguins	**NHL**	54	7	13	20	8	12	20	8	2	0	0	61	11.5	30	6	43	1	–18	....	....	....	....	....	....	....	....
1969-70	Canada	Nat-Team	DID NOT PLAY – COACHING																									
	NHL Totals		769	126	219	345	159	231	390	205	3	0	0	187	67.4	79	17	93	6		62	8	10	18	30	0	0	0

Played in NHL All-Star Game (1958, 1962, 1963, 1964)

Traded to **Detroit** by **Toronto** with Andy Bathgate and Gary Jarrett for Marcel Pronovost, Larry Jeffrey, Ed Joyal, Lowell MacDonald and Aut Erickson, May 20, 1965. Claimed by **Oakland** from **Detroit** in Expansion Draft, June 6, 1967. Traded to **Pittsburgh** by **Oakland** for Bob Dillabough, November 29, 1968.

• HARRIS, DUKE

Duke (George Francis) Harris RW – R. 5′10″, 180 lbs. b: Sarnia, Ont., 2/25/1942.

1958-59	St. Catharines Teepees	OHA	51	11	16	27	....	....	....	26	....	....	....	....	....	....	....	....	....	....	7	0	1	1	0	....	....	....
1959-60	St. Catharines Teepees	OHA	48	16	26	42	....	....	....	19	....	....	....	....	....	....	....	....	....	....	16	6	6	12	30	....	....	....
1960-61	St. Catharines Teepees	OHA	48	15	22	37	....	....	....	30	....	....	....	....	....	....	....	....	....	....	6	0	3	3	4	....	....	....
1961-62	St. Catharines Teepees	OHA	9	5	0	5	....	....	....	8	....	....	....	....	....	....	....	....	....	....	....	....	....	....	....	....	....	....
	Guelph Royals	OHA	39	23	37	60	....	....	....	50	....	....	....	....	....	....	....	....	....	....	....	....	....	....	....	....	....	....
	Sault Ste. Marie Thunderbirds	EPHL	7	0	0	0	....	....	....	0	....	....	....	....	....	....	....	....	....	....	....	....	....	....	....	....	....	....
1962-63	St. Louis Braves	EPHL	72	28	31	59	....	....	....	38	....	....	....	....	....	....	....	....	....	....	....	....	....	....	....	....	....	....
1963-64	St. Louis Braves	CHL	72	21	41	62	....	....	....	16	....	....	....	....	....	....	....	....	....	....	6	1	3	4	4	....	....	....
1964-65	Pittsburgh Hornets	AHL	72	19	31	50	....	....	....	16	....	....	....	....	....	....	....	....	....	....	4	0	3	3	6	....	....	....
1965-66	Pittsburgh Hornets	AHL	72	18	23	41	....	....	....	12	....	....	....	....	....	....	....	....	....	....	3	1	1	2	2	....	....	....
1966-67	Pittsburgh Hornets	AHL	70	27	27	54	....	....	....	24	....	....	....	....	....	....	....	....	....	....	9	1	3	4	4	....	....	....

			REGULAR SEASON																		PLAYOFFS							
Season	Club	League	GP	G	A	Pts	AG	AA	APts	PIM	PP	SH	GW	S	%	TGF	PGF	TGA	PGA	+/–	GP	G	A	Pts	PIM	PP	SH	GW
1967-68	**Minnesota North Stars**	**NHL**	**22**	**1**	**4**	**5**	**1**	**4**	**5**	**4**	**0**	**0**	**0**	**43**	**2.3**	**13**	**10**	**13**	**0**	**–10**	....	....	....	....	....	....	....	....
	Fort Worth Wings	CHL	3	1	1	2	....	....	....	0	....	....	....	....	....	....	....	....	....	....	....	....	....	....	....	....	....	....
	Toronto Maple Leafs	**NHL**	**4**	**0**	**0**	**0**	**0**	**0**	**0**	**0**	**0**	**0**	**0**	**7**	**0.0**	**1**	**1**	**4**	**0**	**–4**	....	....	....	....	....	....	....	....
	Rochester Americans	AHL	38	10	27	37	....	....	....	12	....	....	....	....	....	....	....	....	....	....	10	2	3	5	4	....	....	....
1968-69	Vancouver Canucks	WHL	74	23	17	40	....	....	....	18	....	....	....	....	....	....	....	....	....	....	8	3	0	3	2	....	....	....
1969-70	Vancouver Canucks	WHL	71	20	21	41	....	....	....	23	....	....	....	....	....	....	....	....	....	....	11	6	3	9	4	....	....	....
1970-71	Rochester Americans	AHL	70	29	25	54	....	....	....	42	....	....	....	....	....	....	....	....	....	....	....	....	....	....	....	....	....	....
1971-72	Rochester Americans	AHL	74	27	34	61	....	....	....	24	....	....	....	....	....	....	....	....	....	....	....	....	....	....	....	....	....	....
1972-73	Houston Aeros	WHA	75	30	12	42	....	....	....	14	....	....	....	....	....	....	....	....	....	....	10	1	1	2	4	....	....	....
1973-74	Chicago Cougars	WHA	64	14	16	30	....	....	....	20	....	....	....	....	....	....	....	....	....	....	18	6	6	12	2	....	....	....
1974-75	Chicago Cougars	WHA	54	9	19	28	....	....	....	18	....	....	....	....	....	....	....	....	....	....	....	....	....	....	....	....	....	....
	NHL Totals		**26**	**1**	**4**	**5**	**1**	**4**	**5**	**4**	**0**	**0**	**0**	**50**	**2.0**	**14**	**11**	**17**	**0**		....	....	....	....	....	....	....	....
	Other Major League Totals		193	53	47	100	....	....	....	52	....	....	....	....	....	....	....	....	....		28	7	7	14	6	....	....	....

Claimed by **Detroit** from **St. Louis** (CHL) in Intra-League Draft, June 10, 1964. Traded to **Minnesota** by **Detroit** with Bob McCord for Jean-Guy Talbot and Dave Richardson, October 19, 1967. Traded to **Toronto** by **Minnesota** with Don Johns, Murray Hall, Len Lunde, Ted Taylor and the loan of Carl Wetzel for Milan Marcetta and Jean-Paul Parise, December 26, 1967. Traded to **Rochester** (AHL) by **Toronto** for cash, March, 1968. Selected by **Houston** (WHA) in 1972 WHA General Player Draft, February 13, 1972. Traded to **Chicago** (WHA) by **Houston** (WHA) for cash, July, 1973.

• HARRIS, HUGH

Hugh Harris C – L. 6'1", 195 lbs. b: Toronto, Ont., 6/7/1948.

Season	Club	League	GP	G	A	Pts	AG	AA	APts	PIM	PP	SH	GW	S	%	TGF	PGF	TGA	PGA	+/–	GP	G	A	Pts	PIM	PP	SH	GW
1966-67	Weston Dodgers	OJHL	STATISTICS NOT AVAILABLE																									
1967-68	Muskegon Mohawks	IHL	63	16	19	35	....	....	....	72	....	....	....	....	....	....	....	....	....	....	9	2	4	6	4	....	....	....
1968-69	Muskegon Mohawks	IHL	71	33	39	72	....	....	....	83	....	....	....	....	....	....	....	....	....	....	11	3	9	12	6	....	....	....
1969-70	Muskegon Mohawks	IHL	48	31	25	56	....	....	....	35	....	....	....	....	....	....	....	....	....	....	6	2	1	3	6	....	....	....
1970-71	Montreal Voyageurs	AHL	5	3	2	5	....	....	....	4	....	....	....	....	....	....	....	....	....	....	2	0	0	0	14	....	....	....
	Muskegon Mohawks	IHL	63	*39	47	86	....	....	....	86	....	....	....	....	....	....	....	....	....	....	6	3	3	6	0	....	....	....
1971-72	Cincinnati Swords	AHL	71	18	24	42	....	....	....	70	....	....	....	....	....	....	....	....	....	....	9	3	4	7	6	....	....	....
1972-73	**Buffalo Sabres**	**NHL**	**60**	**12**	**26**	**38**	**12**	**22**	**34**	**17**	**0**	**0**	**0**	**121**	**9.9**	**54**	**4**	**41**	**0**	**+9**	**3**	**0**	**0**	**0**	**0**	**0**	**0**	**0**
	Cincinnati Swords	AHL	14	7	7	14	....	....	....	37	....	....	....	....	....	....	....	....	....	....	....	....	....	....	....	....	....	....
1973-74	New England Whalers	WHA	75	24	28	52	....	....	....	78	....	....	....	....	....	....	....	....	....	....	7	0	4	4	11	....	....	....
1974-75	Phoenix Roadrunners	WHA	22	10	10	20	....	....	....	15	....	....	....	....	....	....	....	....	....	....	....	....	....	....	....	....	....	....
	Vancouver Blazers	WHA	58	23	34	57	....	....	....	49	....	....	....	....	....	....	....	....	....	....	....	....	....	....	....	....	....	....
1975-76	Calgary Cowboys	WHA	30	5	9	14	....	....	....	19	....	....	....	....	....	....	....	....	....	....	....	....	....	....	....	....	....	....
	Indianapolis Racers	WHA	41	12	27	39	....	....	....	23	....	....	....	....	....	....	....	....	....	....	7	2	5	7	8	....	....	....
1976-77	Indianapolis Racers	WHA	46	21	35	56	....	....	....	21	....	....	....	....	....	....	....	....	....	....	2	0	0	0	0	....	....	....
1977-78	Indianapolis Racers	WHA	19	1	7	8	....	....	....	6	....	....	....	....	....	....	....	....	....	....	....	....	....	....	....	....	....	....
	Cincinnati Stingers	WHA	45	11	23	34	....	....	....	30	....	....	....	....	....	....	....	....	....	....	....	....	....	....	....	....	....	....
	NHL Totals		**60**	**12**	**26**	**38**	**12**	**22**	**34**	**17**	**0**	**0**	**0**	**121**	**9.9**	**54**	**4**	**41**	**0**		**3**	**0**	**0**	**0**	**0**	**0**	**0**	**0**
	Other Major League Totals		336	107	173	280	....	....	....	241	....	....	....	....	....	....	....	....	....		16	2	9	11	19	....	....	....

IHL First All-Star Team (1971)

Claimed by **Buffalo** from **Montreal** in Intra-League Draft, June 8, 1971. Selected by **Minnesota** (WHA) in 1972 WHA General Player Draft, February 12, 1972. WHA rights traded to **New England** (WHA) by **Minnesota** (WHA) for cash, July, 1973. Traded to **Phoenix** (WHA) by **New England** (WHA) for future considerations, August, 1974. Traded to **Vancouver** (WHA) by **Phoenix** (WHA) for John Migneault, Serge Beaudoin and Pete McNamee, November, 1974. Transferred to **Calgary** (WHA) after **Vancouver** (WHA) franchise relocated, May 7, 1975. Traded to **Indianapolis** (WHA) by **Calgary** (WHA) for future considerations, January, 1976. Traded to **Cincinnati** (WHA) by **Indianapolis** (WHA) with Byron Baltimore for Gilles Marotte and Blaine Stoughton, January, 1978.

• HARRIS, RON

Ron Harris D – R. 5'10", 190 lbs. b: Verdun, Que., 6/30/1942.

Season	Club	League	GP	G	A	Pts	AG	AA	APts	PIM	PP	SH	GW	S	%	TGF	PGF	TGA	PGA	+/–	GP	G	A	Pts	PIM	PP	SH	GW
1960-61	Hamilton Red Wings	OHA	47	1	9	10	....	....	....	63	....	....	....	....	....	....	....	....	....	....	12	0	0	0	45	....	....	....
1961-62	Hamilton Red Wings	OHA	50	7	29	36	....	....	....	65	....	....	....	....	....	....	....	....	....	....	10	3	2	5	25	....	....	....
1962-63	**Detroit Red Wings**	**NHL**	**1**	**0**	**1**	**1**	**0**	**1**	**1**	**0**	....	....	....	....	....	....	....	....	....	....	....	....	....	....	....	....	....	....
	Pittsburgh Hornets	AHL	62	3	18	21	....	....	....	88	....	....	....	....	....	....	....	....	....	....	....	....	....	....	....	....	....	....
1963-64	**Detroit Red Wings**	**NHL**	**3**	**0**	**0**	**0**	**0**	**0**	**0**	**7**	....	....	....	....	....	....	....	....	....	....	....	....	....	....	....	....	....	....
	Cincinnati Wings	CHL	66	4	21	25	....	....	....	129	....	....	....	....	....	....	....	....	....	....	....	....	....	....	....	....	....	....
1964-65	Memphis Wings	CHL	70	18	10	30	....	....	....	75	....	....	....	....	....	....	....	....	....	....	....	....	....	....	....	....	....	....
	Pittsburgh Hornets	AHL	....	....	....	....	....	....	....	....	....	....	....	....	....	....	....	....	....	....	1	0	0	0	0	....	....	....
1965-66	San Francisco Seals	WHL	54	12	16	28	....	....	....	74	....	....	....	....	....	....	....	....	....	....	7	2	1	3	15	....	....	....
1966-67	California Seals	WHL	31	8	9	17	....	....	....	40	....	....	....	....	....	....	....	....	....	....	6	1	0	1	12	....	....	....
1967-68	**Oakland Seals**	**NHL**	**54**	**4**	**6**	**10**	**5**	**6**	**11**	**60**	**1**	**0**	**1**	**87**	**4.6**	**16**	**2**	**42**	**1**	**–27**	....	....	....	....	....	....	....	....
1968-69	**Detroit Red Wings**	**NHL**	**73**	**3**	**13**	**16**	**3**	**12**	**15**	**91**	**0**	**0**	**1**	**74**	**4.1**	**65**	**1**	**59**	**1**	**+6**	....	....	....	....	....	....	....	....
1969-70	**Detroit Red Wings**	**NHL**	**72**	**2**	**19**	**21**	**2**	**19**	**21**	**99**	**0**	**0**	**0**	**126**	**1.6**	**74**	**10**	**59**	**9**	**+14**	**4**	**0**	**0**	**0**	**8**	**0**	**0**	**0**
1970-71	**Detroit Red Wings**	**NHL**	**42**	**2**	**8**	**10**	**2**	**7**	**9**	**65**	**1**	**1**	**0**	**84**	**2.4**	**36**	**8**	**77**	**20**	**–29**	....	....	....	....	....	....	....	....
1971-72	**Detroit Red Wings**	**NHL**	**61**	**1**	**10**	**11**	**1**	**9**	**10**	**80**	**0**	**0**	**0**	**56**	**1.8**	**23**	**2**	**41**	**5**	**–15**	....	....	....	....	....	....	....	....
1972-73	**Atlanta Flames**	**NHL**	**24**	**2**	**4**	**6**	**2**	**3**	**5**	**8**	**1**	**0**	**0**	**36**	**5.6**	**12**	**2**	**16**	**1**	**–5**	....	....	....	....	....	....	....	....
	New York Rangers	**NHL**	**46**	**3**	**10**	**13**	**3**	**8**	**11**	**17**	**1**	**0**	**0**	**73**	**4.1**	**35**	**1**	**41**	**9**	**+2**	**10**	**0**	**3**	**3**	**2**	**0**	**0**	**0**
1973-74	**New York Rangers**	**NHL**	**63**	**2**	**12**	**14**	**2**	**10**	**12**	**25**	**0**	**0**	**0**	**75**	**2.7**	**38**	**1**	**48**	**9**	**–2**	**11**	**3**	**0**	**3**	**14**	**0**	**0**	**2**
1974-75	**New York Rangers**	**NHL**	**34**	**1**	**7**	**8**	**1**	**5**	**6**	**22**	**0**	**0**	**0**	**38**	**2.6**	**25**	**2**	**29**	**6**	**0**	**3**	**1**	**0**	**1**	**9**	**0**	**0**	**1**
1975-76	**New York Rangers**	**NHL**	**3**	**0**	**1**	**1**	**0**	**1**	**1**	**0**	**0**	**0**	**0**	**1**	**0.0**	**1**	**0**	**2**	**0**	**–1**	....	....	....	....	....	....	....	....
	NHL Totals		**476**	**20**	**91**	**111**	**21**	**81**	**102**	**474**	**4**	**1**	**2**	**650**	**3.1**	**325**	**29**	**414**	**61**		**28**	**4**	**3**	**7**	**33**	**0**	**0**	**3**

Traded to **Boston** by **Detroit** with Albert Langlois, Parker McDonald and Bob Dillabough for Ab McDonald, Bob McCord and Ken Stephenson, May 31, 1965. Claimed by **Oakland** from **Boston** in Expansion Draft, June 6, 1967. Traded to **Detroit** by **Oakland** with Bob Baun for Gary Jarrett, Doug Roberts, Howie Young and Chris Worthy, May 27, 1968. Claimed by **Atlanta** from **Detroit** in Expansion Draft, June 6, 1972. Traded to **NY Rangers** by **Atlanta** for Curt Bennett, November 29, 1972.

• HARRIS, TED

Ted Harris D – L. 6'2", 183 lbs. b: Winnipeg, Man., 7/18/1936.

Season	Club	League	GP	G	A	Pts	AG	AA	APts	PIM	PP	SH	GW	S	%	TGF	PGF	TGA	PGA	+/–	GP	G	A	Pts	PIM	PP	SH	GW
1953-54	Winnipeg Monarchs	MJHL	36	4	5	9	....	....	....	94	....	....	....	....	....	....	....	....	....	....	5	1	1	2	10	....	....	....
1954-55	Winnipeg Monarchs	MJHL	32	2	15	17	....	....	....	*137	....	....	....	....	....	....	....	....	....	....	17	1	3	4	57	....	....	....
1955-56	Winnipeg Monarchs	MJHL	20	6	23	29	....	....	....	78	....	....	....	....	....	....	....	....	....	....	4	0	0	0	21	....	....	....
1956-57	Springfield Indians	AHL	2	0	0	0	....	....	....	4	....	....	....	....	....	....	....	....	....	....	....	....	....	....	....	....	....	....
	Philadelphia Ramblers	EHL	61	11	33	44	....	....	....	103	....	....	....	....	....	....	....	....	....	....	13	2	2	4	31	....	....	....
1957-58	Philadelphia Ramblers	EHL	62	10	19	29	....	....	....	82	....	....	....	....	....	....	....	....	....	....	....	....	....	....	....	....	....	....
1958-59	Springfield Indians	AHL	9	0	2	2	....	....	....	11	....	....	....	....	....	....	....	....	....	....	....	....	....	....	....	....	....	....
	Victoria Cougars	WHL	58	4	12	16	....	....	....	82	....	....	....	....	....	....	....	....	....	....	3	0	0	0	4	....	....	....
1959-60	Springfield Indians	AHL	63	4	13	17	....	....	....	100	....	....	....	....	....	....	....	....	....	....	10	0	2	2	16	....	....	....
1960-61	Springfield Indians	AHL	69	4	22	26	....	....	....	76	....	....	....	....	....	....	....	....	....	....	8	0	1	1	18	....	....	....
1961-62	Springfield Indians	AHL	70	2	29	31	....	....	....	142	....	....	....	....	....	....	....	....	....	....	11	3	3	6	14	....	....	....
1962-63	Springfield Indians	AHL	72	8	30	38	....	....	....	172	....	....	....	....	....	....	....	....	....	....	....	....	....	....	....	....	....	....
1963-64	**Montreal Canadiens**	**NHL**	**4**	**0**	**1**	**1**	**0**	**1**	**1**	**0**	....	....	....	....	....	....	....	....	....	....	....	....	....	....	....	....	....	....
	Cleveland Barons	AHL	67	6	23	29	....	....	....	109	....	....	....	....	....	....	....	....	....	....	9	0	5	5	20	....	....	....
1964-65	**Montreal Canadiens**	**NHL**	**68**	**1**	**14**	**15**	**1**	**15**	**16**	**107**	....	....	....	....	....	....	....	....	....	....	**13**	**0**	**5**	**5**	**45**	....	....	....
1965-66	**Montreal Canadiens**	**NHL**	**53**	**0**	**13**	**13**	**0**	**13**	**13**	**87**	....	....	....	....	....	....	....	....	....	....	**10**	**0**	**0**	**0**	**38**	....	....	....
1966-67	**Montreal Canadiens**	**NHL**	**65**	**2**	**16**	**18**	**2**	**16**	**18**	**86**	....	....	....	....	....	....	....	....	....	....	**10**	**0**	**1**	**1**	**19**	....	....	....
1967-68	**Montreal Canadiens**	**NHL**	**67**	**5**	**16**	**21**	**6**	**17**	**23**	**78**	**0**	**0**	**1**	**56**	**8.9**	**74**	**0**	**59**	**8**	**+23**	**13**	**0**	**4**	**4**	**22**	**0**	**0**	**0**
1968-69	**Montreal Canadiens**	**NHL**	**76**	**7**	**18**	**25**	**8**	**17**	**25**	**102**	**0**	**1**	**0**	**82**	**8.5**	**111**	**3**	**108**	**24**	**+24**	**14**	**1**	**2**	**3**	**34**	**0**	**0**	**0**
1969-70	**Montreal Canadiens**	**NHL**	**74**	**3**	**17**	**20**	**3**	**17**	**20**	**116**	**0**	**0**	**0**	**65**	**4.6**	**80**	**1**	**89**	**19**	**+9**	....	....	....	....	....	....	....	....
1970-71	**Minnesota North Stars**	**NHL**	**78**	**2**	**13**	**15**	**2**	**11**	**13**	**130**	**1**	**0**	**0**	**90**	**2.2**	**81**	**3**	**107**	**29**	**0**	**12**	**0**	**4**	**4**	**36**	**0**	**0**	**0**
1971-72	**Minnesota North Stars**	**NHL**	**78**	**2**	**15**	**17**	**2**	**14**	**16**	**77**	**0**	**0**	**0**	**89**	**2.2**	**74**	**3**	**97**	**26**	**0**	**7**	**0**	**1**	**1**	**17**	**0**	**0**	**0**
1972-73	**Minnesota North Stars**	**NHL**	**78**	**7**	**23**	**30**	**7**	**19**	**26**	**83**	**0**	**0**	**1**	**94**	**7.4**	**103**	**2**	**109**	**33**	**+25**	**5**	**0**	**1**	**1**	**15**	**0**	**0**	**0**

			REGULAR SEASON																		PLAYOFFS							
Season	Club	League	GP	G	A	Pts	AG	AA	APts	PIM	PP	SH	GW	S	%	TGF	PGF	TGA	PGA	+/–	GP	G	A	Pts	PIM	PP	SH	GW
1973-74	**Minnesota North Stars**	**NHL**	**12**	**0**	**1**	**1**	**0**	**1**	**1**	**4**	**0**	**0**	**0**	**10**	**0.0**	**6**	**0**	**17**	**3**	**–8**	....	....	....	....	....	....	....	....
	Detroit Red Wings	**NHL**	**41**	**0**	**11**	**11**	**0**	**9**	**9**	**66**	**0**	**0**	**0**	**32**	**0.0**	**62**	**5**	**70**	**9**	**–4**	....	....	....	....	....	....	....	....
	St. Louis Blues	**NHL**	**24**	**0**	**4**	**4**	**0**	**3**	**3**	**16**	**0**	**0**	**0**	**32**	**0.0**	**21**	**0**	**37**	**14**	**–2**	....	....	....	....	....	....	....	....
1974-75	**Philadelphia Flyers**	**NHL**	**70**	**1**	**6**	**7**	**1**	**5**	**6**	**48**	**0**	**0**	**1**	**38**	**2.6**	**52**	**1**	**26**	**2**	**+27**	**16**	**0**	**4**	**4**	**4**	**0**	**0**	**0**
	NHL Totals		**788**	**30**	**168**	**198**	**32**	**158**	**190**	**1000**	**1**	**1**	**3**	**588**	**5.1**	**664**	**18**	**719**	**167**		**100**	**1**	**22**	**23**	**230**	**0**	**0**	**0**

AHL First All-Star Team (1964) • Won Eddie Shore Award (Outstanding Defenseman - AHL) (1964) • NHL Second All-Star Team (1969)

Played in NHL All-Star Game (1965, 1967, 1969, 1971, 1972)

Traded to **Montreal** by **Springfield** (AHL) with Wayne Larkin, Terry Gray, Bruce Cline and John Chasczewski for Wayne Boddy, Fred Hilts, Brian Smith, John Rodger, Lorne O'Donnell and the loan of Gary Bergman, June, 1963. Claimed by **Minnesota** from **Montreal** in Intra-League Draft, June 9, 1970. Traded to **Detroit** by **Minnesota** for Gary Bergman, November 7, 1973. Traded to **St. Louis** by **Detroit** with Bill Collins and Garnett Bailey for Chris Evans, Bryan Watson and Jean Hamel, February 14, 1973. Traded to **Philadelphia** by **St. Louis** for cash, September 16, 1974.

• HARRISON, JIM

Jim "Max" Harrison C – R. 5'11", 185 lbs. b: Bonnyville, Alta., 7/9/1947.

1964-65	Estevan Bruins	SJHL	25	2	5	7	....	....	....	40	....	....	....	....	....	....	....	....	....	....	....	....	....	....	....	....	....	....
1965-66	Estevan Bruins	SJHL	60	39	37	76	....	....	....	119	....	....	....	....	....	....	....	....	....	....	11	8	1	9	21	....	....	....
1966-67	Estevan Bruins	WCJHL	47	34	40	74	....	....	....	179	....	....	....	....	....	....	....	....	....	....	8	2	4	6	38	....	....	....
1967-68	Estevan Bruins	WCJHL	46	32	43	75	....	....	....	222	....	....	....	....	....	....	....	....	....	....	14	*13	*22	*35	....	....	....	....
1968-69	**Boston Bruins**	**NHL**	**16**	**1**	**2**	**3**	**1**	**2**	**3**	**21**	**0**	**0**	**0**	**12**	**8.3**	**4**	**0**	**9**	**0**	**–5**	....	....	....	....	....	....	....	....
	Oklahoma City Blazers	CHL	43	13	13	26	....	....	....	130	....	....	....	....	....	....	....	....	....	....	9	3	2	5	6	....	....	....
1969-70	**Boston Bruins**	**NHL**	**23**	**3**	**1**	**4**	**3**	**1**	**4**	**16**	**0**	**1**	**0**	**19**	**15.8**	**10**	**0**	**9**	**5**	**+6**	....	....	....	....	....	....	....	....
	Toronto Maple Leafs	**NHL**	**31**	**7**	**10**	**17**	**8**	**10**	**18**	**36**	**1**	**0**	**0**	**43**	**16.3**	**21**	**2**	**24**	**7**	**+2**	....	....	....	....	....	....	....	....
1970-71	**Toronto Maple Leafs**	**NHL**	**78**	**13**	**20**	**33**	**14**	**18**	**32**	**108**	**0**	**1**	**1**	**147**	**8.8**	**59**	**11**	**47**	**5**	**+6**	**6**	**0**	**1**	**1**	**33**	**0**	**0**	**0**
1971-72	**Toronto Maple Leafs**	**NHL**	**66**	**19**	**17**	**36**	**20**	**15**	**35**	**104**	**5**	**0**	**0**	**149**	**12.8**	**49**	**10**	**46**	**3**	**–4**	**5**	**1**	**0**	**1**	**10**	**0**	**0**	**1**
1972-73	Alberta Oilers	WHA	66	39	47	86	....	....	....	93	....	....	....	....	....	....	....	....	....	....	....	....	....	....	....	....	....	....
1973-74	Edmonton Oilers	WHA	47	24	25	69	....	....	....	99	....	....	....	....	....	....	....	....	....	....	....	....	....	....	....	....	....	....
1974-75	Canada	Summit	3	0	1	1	....	....	....	9	....	....	....	....	....	....	....	....	....	....	....	....	....	....	....	....	....	....
	Cleveland Crusaders	WHA	60	20	22	42	....	....	....	106	....	....	....	....	....	....	....	....	....	....	5	1	2	3	4	....	....	....
1975-76	Cleveland Crusaders	WHA	59	34	38	72	....	....	....	62	....	....	....	....	....	....	....	....	....	....	3	0	1	1	9	....	....	....
1976-77	**Chicago Black Hawks**	**NHL**	**60**	**18**	**23**	**41**	**17**	**19**	**36**	**97**	**8**	**1**	**3**	**140**	**12.9**	**59**	**20**	**78**	**13**	**–26**	**2**	**0**	**0**	**0**	**0**	**0**	**0**	**0**
1977-78	**Chicago Black Hawks**	**NHL**	**26**	**2**	**8**	**10**	**2**	**7**	**9**	**31**	**1**	**0**	**0**	**43**	**4.7**	**18**	**2**	**21**	**2**	**–3**	....	....	....	....	....	....	....	....
1978-79	**Chicago Black Hawks**	**NHL**	**21**	**4**	**5**	**9**	**4**	**4**	**8**	**22**	**0**	**0**	**0**	**28**	**14.3**	**15**	**1**	**28**	**8**	**–6**	....	....	....	....	....	....	....	....
	New Brunswick Hawks	AHL	2	0	0	0	....	....	....	0	....	....	....	....	....	....	....	....	....	....	....	....	....	....	....	....	....	....
1979-80	**Edmonton Oilers**	**NHL**	**3**	**0**	**0**	**0**	**0**	**0**	**0**	**0**	**0**	**0**	**0**	**3**	**0.0**	**0**	**0**	**2**	**1**	**–1**	....	....	....	....	....	....	....	....
	NHL Totals		**324**	**67**	**86**	**153**	**69**	**76**	**145**	**435**	**15**	**3**	**4**	**584**	**11.5**	**235**	**46**	**264**	**44**		**13**	**1**	**1**	**2**	**43**	**0**	**0**	**1**
	Other Major League Totals		232	117	132	269	....	....	....	360	....	....	....	....	....	....	....	....	....		8	1	3	4	13	....	....	....

Traded to **Toronto** by **Boston** for Wayne Carlton, December 10, 1969. Selected by **Calgary-Cleveland** (WHA) in 1972 WHA General Player Draft, February 12, 1972. WHA rights traded to **Alberta** (WHA) by **Cleveland** (WHA) for cash, May, 1972. Traded to **Cleveland** (WHA) by **Edmonton** (WHA) for Ron Buchanan, October, 1974. Rights traded to **Chicago** by **Toronto** for Chicago's 2nd round choice (Bob Gladney) in 1977 Amateur Draft, September 28, 1976. Traded to **Edmonton** by **Chicago** for future considerations, September 24, 1979.

• HART, GERRY

Gerry Hart D – L. 5'9", 190 lbs. b: Flin Flon, Man., 1/1/1948.

1964-65	Flin Flon Bombers	SJHL	2	0	0	0	....	....	....	0	....	....	....	....	....	....	....	....	....	....	....	....	....	....	....	....	....	....
1965-66	Flin Flon Bombers	SJHL	60	7	10	17	....	....	....	126	....	....	....	....	....	....	....	....	....	....	....	....	....	....	....	....	....	....
1966-67	Flin Flon Bombers	WCJHL	STATISTICS NOT AVAILABLE																									
1967-68	Flin Flon Bombers	WCJHL	58	13	38	51	....	....	....	290	....	....	....	....	....	....	....	....	....	....	15	1	7	8	43	....	....	....
1968-69	**Detroit Red Wings**	**NHL**	**1**	**0**	**0**	**0**	**0**	**0**	**0**	**2**	**0**	**0**	**0**	**0**	**0.0**	**0**	**0**	**0**	**0**	**0**	....	....	....	....	....	....	....	....
	Fort Worth Wings	CHL	26	2	3	5	....	....	....	52	....	....	....	....	....	....	....	....	....	....	....	....	....	....	....	....	....	....
	Baltimore Clippers	AHL	38	2	6	8	....	....	....	88	....	....	....	....	....	....	....	....	....	....	4	0	1	1	23	....	....	....
1969-70	**Detroit Red Wings**	**NHL**	**3**	**0**	**0**	**0**	**0**	**0**	**0**	**2**	**0**	**0**	**0**	**0**	**0.0**	**0**	**0**	**0**	**0**	**0**	....	....	....	....	....	....	....	....
	Fort Worth Wings	CHL	64	2	19	21	....	....	....	226	....	....	....	....	....	....	....	....	....	....	7	0	4	4	26	....	....	....
1970-71	**Detroit Red Wings**	**NHL**	**64**	**2**	**7**	**9**	**2**	**6**	**8**	**148**	**1**	**0**	**1**	**62**	**3.2**	**55**	**2**	**73**	**17**	**–3**	....	....	....	....	....	....	....	....
1971-72	**Detroit Red Wings**	**NHL**	**3**	**0**	**0**	**0**	**0**	**0**	**0**	**0**	**0**	**0**	**0**	**2**	**0.0**	**1**	**0**	**3**	**0**	**–2**	....	....	....	....	....	....	....	....
	Fort Worth Wings	CHL	14	1	4	5	....	....	....	84	....	....	....	....	....	....	....	....	....	....	....	....	....	....	....	....	....	....
	Tidewater Wings	AHL	28	4	9	13	....	....	....	146	....	....	....	....	....	....	....	....	....	....	....	....	....	....	....	....	....	....
1972-73	**New York Islanders**	**NHL**	**47**	**1**	**11**	**12**	**1**	**9**	**10**	**158**	**0**	**0**	**0**	**72**	**1.4**	**50**	**4**	**79**	**15**	**–18**	....	....	....	....	....	....	....	....
1973-74	**New York Islanders**	**NHL**	**70**	**1**	**10**	**11**	**1**	**9**	**10**	**61**	**0**	**0**	**1**	**63**	**1.6**	**40**	**0**	**67**	**10**	**+17**	....	....	....	....	....	....	....	....
1974-75	**New York Islanders**	**NHL**	**71**	**4**	**14**	**18**	**4**	**11**	**15**	**143**	**0**	**1**	**0**	**81**	**4.9**	**81**	**1**	**68**	**16**	**+28**	**17**	**2**	**2**	**4**	**42**	**0**	**0**	**1**
1975-76	**New York Islanders**	**NHL**	**80**	**6**	**18**	**24**	**6**	**14**	**20**	**151**	**0**	**0**	**0**	**110**	**5.5**	**93**	**2**	**82**	**26**	**+35**	**13**	**1**	**3**	**4**	**24**	**0**	**0**	**0**
1976-77	**New York Islanders**	**NHL**	**80**	**4**	**18**	**22**	**4**	**15**	**19**	**98**	**0**	**1**	**0**	**118**	**3.4**	**93**	**1**	**83**	**20**	**+29**	**12**	**0**	**2**	**2**	**23**	**0**	**0**	**0**
1977-78	**New York Islanders**	**NHL**	**78**	**2**	**23**	**25**	**2**	**19**	**21**	**94**	**0**	**0**	**1**	**126**	**1.6**	**101**	**0**	**76**	**19**	**+44**	**7**	**0**	**0**	**0**	**16**	**0**	**0**	**0**
1978-79	**New York Islanders**	**NHL**	**50**	**2**	**14**	**16**	**2**	**11**	**13**	**78**	**0**	**0**	**1**	**56**	**3.6**	**65**	**0**	**45**	**10**	**+30**	**9**	**0**	**2**	**2**	**10**	**0**	**0**	**0**
1979-80	**Quebec Nordiques**	**NHL**	**71**	**3**	**23**	**26**	**3**	**18**	**21**	**59**	**1**	**0**	**0**	**53**	**5.7**	**70**	**9**	**116**	**42**	**–13**	....	....	....	....	....	....	....	....
1980-81	**Quebec Nordiques**	**NHL**	**6**	**0**	**0**	**0**	**0**	**0**	**0**	**10**	**0**	**0**	**0**	**6**	**0.0**	**5**	**0**	**12**	**5**	**–2**	....	....	....	....	....	....	....	....
	Nova Scotia Voyageurs	AHL	2	0	3	3	....	....	....	2	....	....	....	....	....	....	....	....	....	....	....	....	....	....	....	....	....	....
	St. Louis Blues	**NHL**	**63**	**4**	**11**	**15**	**3**	**8**	**11**	**132**	**0**	**0**	**0**	**44**	**9.1**	**67**	**1**	**69**	**12**	**+9**	**10**	**0**	**0**	**0**	**27**	**0**	**0**	**0**
1981-82	**St. Louis Blues**	**NHL**	**35**	**0**	**1**	**1**	**0**	**1**	**1**	**102**	**0**	**0**	**0**	**15**	**0.0**	**32**	**0**	**50**	**13**	**–5**	**10**	**0**	**3**	**3**	**33**	**0**	**0**	**0**
1982-83	**St. Louis Blues**	**NHL**	**8**	**0**	**0**	**0**	**0**	**0**	**0**	**2**	**0**	**0**	**0**	**0**	**0.0**	**0**	**0**	**5**	**2**	**–3**	....	....	....	....	....	....	....	....
	NHL Totals		**730**	**29**	**150**	**179**	**28**	**121**	**149**	**1240**	**2**	**2**	**4**	**808**	**3.6**	**753**	**20**	**828**	**207**		**78**	**3**	**12**	**15**	**175**	**0**	**0**	**1**

WCJHL All-Star Team (1968)

Claimed by **NY Islanders** from **Detroit** in Expansion Draft, June 6, 1972. Claimed by **Quebec** from **NY Islanders** in Expansion Draft, June 13, 1979. Signed as a free agent by **St. Louis**, November 12, 1980.

• HARTMAN, MIKE

Mike Hartman LW – L. 6', 190 lbs. b: Detroit, MI, 2/7/1967. Buffalo's 8th choice, 131st overall, in 1986 Entry Draft.

1984-85	Belleville Bulls	OHL	49	13	12	25	....	....	....	119	....	....	....	....	....	....	....	....	....	....	....	....	....	....	....	....	....	....
1985-86	Belleville Bulls	OHL	4	2	1	3	....	....	....	5	....	....	....	....	....	....	....	....	....	....	....	....	....	....	....	....	....	....
	North Bay Centennials	OHL	53	19	16	35	....	....	....	205	....	....	....	....	....	....	....	....	....	....	10	2	4	6	34	....	....	....
1986-87	North Bay Centennials	OHL	32	15	24	39	....	....	....	144	....	....	....	....	....	....	....	....	....	....	19	7	8	15	88	....	....	....
	United States	WJC-A	6	2	1	3	....	....	....	4	....	....	....	....	....	....	....	....	....	....	....	....	....	....	....	....	....	....
	Buffalo Sabres	**NHL**	**17**	**3**	**3**	**6**	**3**	**2**	**5**	**69**	**0**	**0**	**0**	**19**	**15.8**	**9**	**0**	**7**	**0**	**+2**	....	....	....	....	....	....	....	....
1987-88	**Buffalo Sabres**	**NHL**	**18**	**3**	**1**	**4**	**3**	**1**	**4**	**90**	**0**	**0**	**1**	**24**	**12.5**	**6**	**0**	**10**	**1**	**–3**	**6**	**0**	**0**	**0**	**35**	**0**	**0**	**0**
	Rochester Americans	AHL	57	13	14	27	....	....	....	283	....	....	....	....	....	....	....	....	....	....	4	1	0	1	22	....	....	....
1988-89	**Buffalo Sabres**	**NHL**	**70**	**8**	**9**	**17**	**7**	**6**	**13**	**316**	**1**	**0**	**0**	**91**	**8.8**	**29**	**1**	**20**	**1**	**+9**	**5**	**0**	**0**	**0**	**34**	**0**	**0**	**0**
1989-90	**Buffalo Sabres**	**NHL**	**60**	**11**	**10**	**21**	**9**	**7**	**16**	**211**	**2**	**0**	**3**	**97**	**11.3**	**26**	**2**	**34**	**0**	**–10**	**6**	**0**	**0**	**0**	**18**	**0**	**0**	**0**
1990-91	**Buffalo Sabres**	**NHL**	**60**	**9**	**3**	**12**	**8**	**2**	**10**	**204**	**2**	**0**	**1**	**65**	**13.8**	**21**	**4**	**28**	**1**	**–10**	**2**	**0**	**0**	**0**	**17**	**0**	**0**	**0**
1991-92	**Winnipeg Jets**	**NHL**	**75**	**4**	**4**	**8**	**4**	**3**	**7**	**264**	**0**	**0**	**1**	**89**	**4.5**	**13**	**0**	**23**	**0**	**–10**	**2**	**0**	**0**	**0**	**2**	**0**	**0**	**0**
1992-93	**Tampa Bay Lightning**	**NHL**	**58**	**4**	**4**	**8**	**3**	**3**	**6**	**154**	**0**	**0**	**0**	**74**	**5.4**	**12**	**0**	**19**	**0**	**–7**	....	....	....	....	....	....	....	....
	New York Rangers	**NHL**	**3**	**0**	**0**	**0**	**0**	**0**	**0**	**6**	**0**	**0**	**0**	**3**	**0.0**	**0**	**0**	**0**	**0**	**0**	....	....	....	....	....	....	....	....
1993-94	**New York Rangers**	**NHL**	**35**	**1**	**1**	**2**	**1**	**1**	**2**	**70**	**0**	**0**	**0**	**19**	**5.3**	**3**	**0**	**8**	**0**	**–5**	....	....	....	....	....	....	....	....
1994-95	**New York Rangers**	**NHL**	**1**	**0**	**0**	**0**	**0**	**0**	**0**	**4**	**0**	**0**	**0**	**0**	**0.0**	**0**	**0**	**0**	**0**	**0**	....	....	....	....	....	....	....	....
	Detroit Vipers	IHL	6	1	0	1	....	....	....	52	....	....	....	....	....	....	....	....	....	....	1	0	0	0	0	....	....	....
1995-96	Orlando Solar Bears	IHL	77	14	10	24	....	....	....	243	....	....	....	....	....	....	....	....	....	....	21	2	2	4	31	....	....	....
1996-97	Hershey Bears	AHL	42	5	8	13	....	....	....	116	....	....	....	....	....	....	....	....	....	....	1	0	0	0	0	....	....	....
1997-98	Charlotte Checkers	ECHL	53	30	18	48	....	....	....	79	....	....	....	....	....	....	....	....	....	....	7	4	0	4	11	....	....	....
	NHL Totals		**397**	**43**	**35**	**78**	**38**	**25**	**63**	**1388**	**5**	**0**	**6**	**481**	**8.9**	**119**	**7**	**149**	**3**		**21**	**0**	**0**	**0**	**106**	**0**	**0**	**0**

Traded to **Winnipeg** by **Buffalo** with Darrin Shannon and Dean Kennedy for Dave McLlwain, Gord Donnelly, Winnipeg's 5th round choice (Yuri Khmylev) in 1992 Entry Draft and future considerations, October 11, 1991. Claimed by **Tampa Bay** from **Winnipeg** in Expansion Draft, June 18, 1992. Traded to **NY Rangers** by **Tampa Bay** for Randy Gilhen, March 22, 1993. Signed as a free agent by **Colorado**, September 26, 1996.

			REGULAR SEASON																		PLAYOFFS							
Season	Club	League	GP	G	A	Pts	AG	AA	APts	PIM	PP	SH	GW	S	%	TGF	PGF	TGA	PGA	+/–	GP	G	A	Pts	PIM	PP	SH	GW

• HARTSBURG, CRAIG

Craig Hartsburg D – L. 6'1", 200 lbs. b: Stratford, Ont., 6/29/1959. Minnesota's 1st choice, 6th overall, in 1979 Entry Draft.

Season	Club	League	GP	G	A	Pts	AG	AA	APts	PIM	PP	SH	GW	S	%	TGF	PGF	TGA	PGA	+/–	GP	G	A	Pts	PIM	PP	SH	GW
1975-76	Sault Ste. Marie Greyhounds	OHA	64	9	19	28	....	....	....	65	....	....	....	....	....	....	....	....	....	....	....	....	....	....	....	....	....	....
1976-77	Sault Ste. Marie Greyhounds	OHA	61	29	64	93	....	....	....	142	....	....	....	....	....	....	....	....	....	....	9	0	11	11	27	....	....	....
1977-78	Sault Ste. Marie Greyhounds	OHA	36	15	42	57	....	....	....	101	....	....	....	....	....	....	....	....	....	....	13	4	8	12	24	....	....	....
	Canada	WJC-A	6	1	4	5	....	....	....	8	....	....	....	....	....	....	....	....	....	....	....	....	....	....	....	....	....	....
1978-79	Birmingham Bulls	WHA	77	9	40	49	....	....	....	73	....	....	....	....	....	....	....	....	....	....	....	....	....	....	....	....	....	....
1979-80	**Minnesota North Stars**	**NHL**	**79**	**14**	**30**	**44**	**13**	**23**	**36**	**81**	**7**	**0**	**2**	**202**	**6.9**	**140**	**45**	**118**	**19**	**–2**	**15**	**3**	**1**	**4**	**17**	**2**	**0**	**0**
1980-81	**Minnesota North Stars**	**NHL**	**74**	**13**	**30**	**43**	**11**	**21**	**32**	**124**	**8**	**0**	**2**	**207**	**6.3**	**109**	**48**	**86**	**16**	**–9**	**19**	**3**	**12**	**15**	**16**	**3**	**0**	**0**
1981-82	Canada	C Cup	7	0	1	1	....	....	....	6	....	....	....	....	....	....	....	....	....	....	....	....	....	....	....	....	....	....
	Minnesota North Stars	**NHL**	**76**	**17**	**60**	**77**	**13**	**40**	**53**	**117**	**5**	**0**	**2**	**204**	**8.3**	**159**	**48**	**115**	**15**	**+11**	**4**	**1**	**2**	**3**	**14**	**0**	**0**	**0**
	Canada	WEC-A	10	3	3	6	....	....	....	12	....	....	....	....	....	....	....	....	....	....	....	....	....	....	....	....	....	....
1982-83	**Minnesota North Stars**	**NHL**	**78**	**12**	**50**	**62**	**10**	**35**	**45**	**109**	**3**	**1**	**1**	**200**	**6.0**	**143**	**43**	**121**	**28**	**+7**	**9**	**3**	**8**	**11**	**7**	**2**	**0**	**0**
	Canada	WEC-A	5	1	2	3	....	....	....	2	....	....	....	....	....	....	....	....	....	....	....	....	....	....	....	....	....	....
1983-84	**Minnesota North Stars**	**NHL**	**26**	**7**	**7**	**14**	**6**	**5**	**11**	**37**	**5**	**0**	**0**	**54**	**13.0**	**53**	**22**	**46**	**13**	**–2**	....	....	....	....	....	....	....	....
1984-85	**Minnesota North Stars**	**NHL**	**32**	**7**	**11**	**18**	**6**	**7**	**13**	**54**	**1**	**1**	**1**	**93**	**7.5**	**51**	**18**	**50**	**12**	**–5**	**9**	**5**	**3**	**8**	**14**	**3**	**0**	**0**
1985-86	**Minnesota North Stars**	**NHL**	**75**	**10**	**47**	**57**	**8**	**31**	**39**	**127**	**4**	**0**	**2**	**185**	**5.4**	**161**	**78**	**87**	**11**	**+7**	**5**	**0**	**1**	**1**	**2**	**0**	**0**	**0**
1986-87	**Minnesota North Stars**	**NHL**	**73**	**11**	**50**	**61**	**10**	**36**	**46**	**93**	**4**	**0**	**1**	**189**	**5.8**	**154**	**67**	**101**	**12**	**–2**	....	....	....	....	....	....	....	....
	Canada	WEC-A	10	0	1	1	....	....	....	14	....	....	....	....	....	....	....	....	....	....	....	....	....	....	....	....	....	....
1987-88	Canada	C Cup	9	0	2	2	....	....	....	6	....	....	....	....	....	....	....	....	....	....	....	....	....	....	....	....	....	....
	Minnesota North Stars	**NHL**	**27**	**3**	**16**	**19**	**3**	**11**	**14**	**29**	**2**	**0**	**1**	**83**	**3.6**	**42**	**23**	**30**	**9**	**–2**	....	....	....	....	....	....	....	....
1988-89	**Minnesota North Stars**	**NHL**	**30**	**4**	**14**	**18**	**3**	**10**	**13**	**47**	**1**	**0**	**0**	**75**	**5.3**	**42**	**15**	**37**	**2**	**–8**	....	....	....	....	....	....	....	....
	NHL Totals		**570**	**98**	**315**	**413**	**83**	**219**	**302**	**818**	**40**	**2**	**12**	**1492**	**6.6**	**1054**	**407**	**789**	**137**		**61**	**15**	**27**	**42**	**70**	**10**	**0**	**0**
	Other Major League Totals		77	9	40	49	....	....	....	73	....	....	....	....	....	....	....	....	....	....	....	....	....	....	....	....	....	....

OHA Second All-Star Team (1977) • Named Best Defenseman at WEC-A (1987)

Played in NHL All-Star Game (1980, 1982, 1983)

Signed as an underage free agent by **Birmingham** (WHA), June, 1978.

• HARVEY, DOUG

Doug Harvey D – L. 5'11", 187 lbs. b: Montreal, Que., 12/19/1924. d: 12/26/1989. **HHOF**

Season	Club	League	GP	G	A	Pts	AG	AA	APts	PIM	PP	SH	GW	S	%	TGF	PGF	TGA	PGA	+/–	GP	G	A	Pts	PIM	PP	SH	GW
1942-43	Montreal Navy	City Sr.	4	0	0	0	....	....	....	0	....	....	....	....	....	....	....	....	....	....	....	....	....	....	....	....	....	....
	Montreal Jr. Royals	QJHL	21	4	6	10	....	....	....	17	....	....	....	....	....	....	....	....	....	....	6	3	4	7	10	....	....	....
	Montreal Royals	QSHL	1	0	0	0	....	....	....	0	....	....	....	....	....	....	....	....	....	....	....	....	....	....	....	....	....	....
1943-44	Montreal Royals	QSHL	1	1	1	2	....	....	....	2	....	....	....	....	....	....	....	....	....	....	....	....	....	....	....	....	....	....
	Montreal Jr. Royals	QJHL	13	4	6	10	....	....	....	*34	....	....	....	....	....	....	....	....	....	....	4	2	*6	*8	10	....	....	....
	Montreal Navy	City Sr.	15	4	1	5	....	....	....	24	....	....	....	....	....	....	....	....	....	....	5	3	1	4	15	....	....	....
1944-45	Montreal Navy	City Sr.	3	0	2	2	....	....	....	2	....	....	....	....	....	....	....	....	....	....	6	3	1	4	6	....	....	....
	Montreal Jr. Royals	City Jr.	....	....	....	....	....	....	....	....	....	....	....	....	....	....	....	....	....	....	9	2	2	4	10	....	....	....
1945-46	Montreal Royals	QSHL	34	2	6	8	....	....	....	90	....	....	....	....	....	....	....	....	....	....	11	1	6	7	*37	....	....	....
1946-47	Montreal Royals	QSHL	40	2	26	28	....	....	....	*171	....	....	....	....	....	....	....	....	....	....	11	2	4	6	*62	....	....	....
1947-48	**Montreal Canadiens**	**NHL**	**35**	**4**	**4**	**8**	**6**	**6**	**12**	**32**	....	....	....	....	....	....	....	....	....	....	....	....	....	....	....	....	....	....
	Buffalo Bisons	AHL	24	1	7	8	....	....	....	38	....	....	....	....	....	....	....	....	....	....	....	....	....	....	....	....	....	....
1948-49	**Montreal Canadiens**	**NHL**	**55**	**3**	**13**	**16**	**5**	**21**	**26**	**87**	....	....	....	....	....	....	....	....	....	....	**7**	**0**	**1**	**1**	**10**	....	....	....
1949-50	**Montreal Canadiens**	**NHL**	**70**	**4**	**20**	**24**	**5**	**25**	**30**	**76**	....	....	....	....	....	....	....	....	....	....	**5**	**0**	**2**	**2**	**10**	....	....	....
1950-51	**Montreal Canadiens**	**NHL**	**70**	**5**	**24**	**29**	**7**	**31**	**38**	**93**	....	....	....	....	....	....	....	....	....	....	**11**	**0**	**5**	**5**	**12**	....	....	....
1951-52	**Montreal Canadiens**	**NHL**	**68**	**6**	**23**	**29**	**8**	**30**	**38**	**82**	....	....	....	....	....	....	....	....	....	....	**11**	**0**	**3**	**3**	**8**	....	....	....
1952-53	**Montreal Canadiens**	**NHL**	**69**	**4**	**30**	**34**	**6**	**42**	**48**	**67**	....	....	....	....	....	....	....	....	....	....	**12**	**0**	**5**	**5**	**8**	....	....	....
1953-54	**Montreal Canadiens**	**NHL**	**68**	**8**	**29**	**37**	**12**	**40**	**52**	**110**	....	....	....	....	....	....	....	....	....	....	**10**	**0**	**2**	**2**	**12**	....	....	....
1954-55	**Montreal Canadiens**	**NHL**	**70**	**6**	**43**	**49**	**9**	**56**	**65**	**58**	....	....	....	....	....	....	....	....	....	....	**12**	**0**	**8**	**8**	**6**	....	....	....
1955-56	**Montreal Canadiens**	**NHL**	**62**	**5**	**39**	**44**	**7**	**49**	**56**	**60**	....	....	....	....	....	....	....	....	....	....	**10**	**2**	**5**	**7**	**10**	....	....	....
1956-57	**Montreal Canadiens**	**NHL**	**70**	**6**	**44**	**50**	**8**	**52**	**60**	**92**	....	....	....	....	....	....	....	....	....	....	**10**	**0**	**7**	**7**	**10**	....	....	....
1957-58	**Montreal Canadiens**	**NHL**	**68**	**9**	**32**	**41**	**12**	**35**	**47**	**131**	....	....	....	....	....	....	....	....	....	....	**10**	**2**	**9**	**11**	**16**	....	....	....
1958-59	**Montreal Canadiens**	**NHL**	**61**	**4**	**16**	**20**	**5**	**17**	**22**	**61**	....	....	....	....	....	....	....	....	....	....	**11**	**1**	**11**	**12**	**22**	....	....	....
1959-60	**Montreal Canadiens**	**NHL**	**66**	**6**	**21**	**27**	**7**	**21**	**28**	**45**	....	....	....	....	....	....	....	....	....	....	**8**	**3**	**0**	**3**	**6**	....	....	....
1960-61	**Montreal Canadiens**	**NHL**	**58**	**6**	**33**	**39**	**7**	**34**	**41**	**48**	....	....	....	....	....	....	....	....	....	....	**6**	**0**	**1**	**1**	**8**	....	....	....
1961-62	**New York Rangers**	**NHL**	**69**	**6**	**24**	**30**	**7**	**24**	**31**	**42**	....	....	....	....	....	....	....	....	....	....	**6**	**0**	**1**	**1**	**2**	....	....	....
1962-63	**New York Rangers**	**NHL**	**68**	**4**	**35**	**39**	**5**	**37**	**42**	**92**	....	....	....	....	....	....	....	....	....	....	....	....	....	....	....	....	....	....
1963-64	**New York Rangers**	**NHL**	**14**	**0**	**2**	**2**	**0**	**2**	**2**	**10**	....	....	....	....	....	....	....	....	....	....	....	....	....	....	....	....	....	....
	St. Paul Rangers	CHL	5	2	2	4	....	....	....	6	....	....	....	....	....	....	....	....	....	....	....	....	....	....	....	....	....	....
	Quebec Aces	AHL	52	6	36	42	....	....	....	30	....	....	....	....	....	....	....	....	....	....	9	0	4	4	10	....	....	....
1964-65	Quebec Aces	AHL	64	1	36	37	....	....	....	72	....	....	....	....	....	....	....	....	....	....	4	1	1	2	9	....	....	....
1965-66	Baltimore Clippers	AHL	67	7	32	39	....	....	....	80	....	....	....	....	....	....	....	....	....	....	....	....	....	....	....	....	....	....
1966-67	Baltimore–Pittsburgh	AHL	52	2	18	20	....	....	....	32	....	....	....	....	....	....	....	....	....	....	9	0	0	0	2	....	....	....
	Detroit Red Wings	**NHL**	**2**	**0**	**0**	**0**	**0**	**0**	**0**	**0**	....	....	....	....	....	....	....	....	....	....	....	....	....	....	....	....	....	....
1967-68	Kansas City Blues	CHL	59	4	16	20	....	....	....	12	....	....	....	....	....	....	....	....	....	....	7	0	6	6	6	....	....	....
	St. Louis Blues	**NHL**	....	....	....	....	....	....	....	....	....	....	....	....	....	....	....	....	....	....	**8**	**0**	**4**	**4**	**12**	....	....	....
1968-69	**St. Louis Blues**	**NHL**	**70**	**2**	**20**	**22**	**2**	**19**	**21**	**30**	**1**	**0**	**0**	**46**	**4.3**	**78**	**19**	**76**	**28**	**+11**	....	....	....	....	....	....	....	....
1969-70	Laval Saints	QJHL	DID NOT PLAY – COACHING																									
	NHL Totals		**1113**	**88**	**452**	**540**	**118**	**541**	**659**	**1216**	**1**	**0**	**0**	**46**	**191.3**	**78**	**19**	**76**	**28**		**137**	**8**	**64**	**72**	**152**	**0**	**0**	**0**

NHL First All-Star Team (1952, 1953, 1954, 1955, 1956, 1957, 1958, 1960, 1961, 1962) • Won James Norris Trophy (1955, 1956, 1957, 1958, 1960, 1961, 1962) • NHL Second All-Star Team (1959) • AHL Second All-Star Team (1964)

Played in NHL All-Star Game (1951, 1952, 1953, 1954, 1955, 1956, 1957, 1958, 1959, 1960, 1961, 1962, 1969)

Traded to **NY Rangers** by **Montreal** for Lou Fontinato, June 13, 1961. Signed as a free agent by **Quebec** (AHL), November 26, 1963. Signed as a free agent by **Baltimore** (AHL), June 10, 1965. Traded to **Providence** (AHL) by **Baltimore** (AHL) for cash, December 23, 1966. Signed as a free agent by **Detroit**, January, 1967. Signed as a free agent by **St. Louis**, April, 1968.

• HARVEY, FRED

Fred "Buster" Harvey RW – R. 6', 185 lbs. b: Fredericton, N.B., 4/2/1950. Minnesota's 1st choice, 17th overall, in 1970 Amateur Draft.

Season	Club	League	GP	G	A	Pts	AG	AA	APts	PIM	PP	SH	GW	S	%	TGF	PGF	TGA	PGA	+/–	GP	G	A	Pts	PIM	PP	SH	GW
1964-65	Fredericton Red Wings	Midget	14	17	21	38	....	....	....	....	....	....	....	....	....	....	....	....	....	....	....	....	....	....	....	....	....	....
	Fredericton Lions	Midget	....	....	....	....	....	....	....	....	....	....	....	....	....	....	....	....	....	....	3	1	1	2	8	....	....	....
1965-66	Fredericton Hawks	Midget	25	*33	22	*55	....	....	....	....	....	....	....	....	....	....	....	....	....	....	....	....	....	....	....	....	....	....
1966-67	Halifax Canadians	NSJHL	51	23	51	74	....	....	....	50	....	....	....	....	....	....	....	....	....	....	17	9	18	27	10	....	....	....
1967-68	Fredericton Jr. Red Wings	NBJHL	4	2	4	6	....	....	....	2	....	....	....	....	....	....	....	....	....	....	12	8	8	16	18	....	....	....
	Fredericton Red Wings	NBSHL	6	2	8	10	....	....	....	34	....	....	....	....	....	....	....	....	....	....	5	0	7	7	11	....	....	....
	Halifax Jr. Canadians	NSJHL	....	....	....	....	....	....	....	....	....	....	....	....	....	....	....	....	....	....	3	2	3	5	2	....	....	....
1968-69	Hamilton Red Wings	OHA	49	23	28	51	....	....	....	30	....	....	....	....	....	....	....	....	....	....	5	2	3	5	6	....	....	....
1969-70	Hamilton Red Wings	OHA	54	26	34	60	....	....	....	39	....	....	....	....	....	....	....	....	....	....	....	....	....	....	....	....	....	....
1970-71	**Minnesota North Stars**	**NHL**	**59**	**12**	**8**	**20**	**13**	**7**	**20**	**36**	**4**	**0**	**3**	**154**	**7.8**	**47**	**18**	**42**	**0**	**–13**	**7**	**0**	**0**	**0**	**4**	**0**	**0**	**0**
1971-72	Cleveland Barons	AHL	73	41	54	95	....	....	....	72	....	....	....	....	....	....	....	....	....	....	6	1	2	3	34	....	....	....
	Minnesota North Stars	**NHL**	....	....	....	....	....	....	....	....	....	....	....	....	....	....	....	....	....	....	**1**	**0**	**0**	**0**	**0**	....	....	....
1972-73	**Minnesota North Stars**	**NHL**	**68**	**21**	**34**	**55**	**21**	**28**	**49**	**16**	**3**	**0**	**3**	**184**	**11.4**	**76**	**11**	**44**	**2**	**+23**	**6**	**0**	**2**	**2**	**4**	**0**	**0**	**0**
1973-74	**Minnesota North Stars**	**NHL**	**72**	**16**	**17**	**33**	**16**	**15**	**31**	**14**	**1**	**0**	**3**	**190**	**8.4**	**55**	**2**	**64**	**0**	**–11**	....	....	....	....	....	....	....	....
1974-75	**Atlanta Flames**	**NHL**	**79**	**17**	**27**	**44**	**16**	**21**	**37**	**16**	**4**	**0**	**3**	**156**	**10.9**	**71**	**16**	**52**	**1**	**+4**	....	....	....	....	....	....	....	....
1975-76	**Atlanta Flames**	**NHL**	**1**	**0**	**0**	**0**	**0**	**0**	**0**	**0**	**0**	**0**	**0**	**1**	**0.0**	**0**	**0**	**1**	**1**	**0**	....	....	....	....	....	....	....	....
	Kansas City Scouts	**NHL**	**39**	**5**	**12**	**17**	**5**	**9**	**14**	**6**	**0**	**0**	**0**	**76**	**6.6**	**26**	**4**	**54**	**1**	**–31**	....	....	....	....	....	....	....	....
	Detroit Red Wings	**NHL**	**35**	**8**	**9**	**17**	**7**	**7**	**14**	**25**	**1**	**0**	**0**	**71**	**11.3**	**27**	**4**	**41**	**10**	**–8**	....	....	....	....	....	....	....	....
1976-77	Kansas City Blues	CHL	15	4	12	16	....	....	....	4	....	....	....	....	....	....	....	....	....	....	10	1	3	4	2	....	....	....
	Detroit Red Wings	**NHL**	**54**	**11**	**11**	**22**	**11**	**9**	**20**	**18**	**2**	**3**	**1**	**105**	**10.5**	**31**	**6**	**51**	**13**	**–13**	....	....	....	....	....	....	....	....
1977-78	Philadelphia Firebirds	AHL	71	10	17	27	....	....	....	31	....	....	....	....	....	....	....	....	....	....	4	1	0	1	2	....	....	....
	NHL Totals		**407**	**90**	**118**	**208**	**89**	**96**	**185**	**131**	**15**	**3**	**13**	**937**	**9.6**	**333**	**61**	**349**	**28**		**14**	**0**	**2**	**2**	**8**	**0**	**0**	**0**

OHA Second All-Star Team (1970) • AHL Second All-Star Team (1972)

Traded to **Atlanta** by **Minnesota** with Jerry Byers for John Flesch and Don Martineau, May 27, 1974. Traded to **Kansas City** by **Atlanta** for Richard Lemieux and Kansas City's 2nd round choice (Miles Zaharko) in 1977 Amateur Draft, October 13, 1975. Traded to **Detroit** by **Kansas City** for Phil Roberto, January 14, 1976.

• HARVEY, HUGH

Hugh Harvey C/LW – L. 6', 175 lbs. b: Kingston, Ont., 6/25/1949.

			REGULAR SEASON																		PLAYOFFS							
Season	Club	League	GP	G	A	Pts	AG	AA	APts	PIM	PP	SH	GW	S	%	TGF	PGF	TGA	PGA	+/–	GP	G	A	Pts	PIM	PP	SH	GW
1969-70	Kingston Aces	OHA Sr.	27	17	16	33	....	....	....	51	....	....	....	....	....	....	....	....	....	....	....	....	....	....	....	....	....	....
1970-71	Oklahoma City Blazers	CHL	70	9	18	27	....	....	....	105	....	....	....	....	....	....	....	....	....	....	5	0	1	1	0	....	....	....
1971-72	Oklahoma City Blazers	CHL	10	2	3	5	....	....	....	20	....	....	....	....	....	....	....	....	....	....	....	....	....	....	....	....	....	....
	Dayton Gems	IHL	50	32	25	57	....	....	....	57	....	....	....	....	....	....	....	....	....	....	5	2	0	2	8	....	....	....
1972-73	Hershey Bears	AHL	70	23	27	50	....	....	....	89	....	....	....	....	....	....	....	....	....	....	7	6	2	8	2	....	....	....
1973-74	Hershey Bears	AHL	76	28	38	66	....	....	....	101	....	....	....	....	....	....	....	....	....	....	14	2	3	5	8	....	....	....
1974-75	**Kansas City Scouts**	**NHL**	**8**	**0**	**0**	**0**	**0**	**0**	**0**	**2**	**0**	**0**	**0**	**5**	**0.0**	**0**	**0**	**1**	**0**	**–1**	....	....	....	....	....	....	....	....
	Baltimore Clippers	AHL	36	4	11	15	....	....	....	30	....	....	....	....	....	....	....	....	....	....	....	....	....	....	....	....	....	....
	Fort Worth Texans	CHL	28	9	9	18	....	....	....	20	....	....	....	....	....	....	....	....	....	....	....	....	....	....	....	....	....	....
1975-76	**Kansas City Scouts**	**NHL**	**10**	**1**	**1**	**2**	**1**	**1**	**2**	**2**	**0**	**0**	**0**	**11**	**9.1**	**3**	**1**	**7**	**0**	**–5**	....	....	....	....	....	....	....	....
	Springfield Indians	AHL	44	15	9	24	....	....	....	49	....	....	....	....	....	....	....	....	....	....	....	....	....	....	....	....	....	....
	Baltimore Clippers	AHL	16	7	1	8	....	....	....	10	....	....	....	....	....	....	....	....	....	....	....	....	....	....	....	....	....	....
	NHL Totals		**18**	**1**	**1**	**2**	**1**	**1**	**2**	**4**	**0**	**0**	**0**	**16**	**6.3**	**3**	**1**	**8**	**0**		....	....	....	....	....	....	....	....

Signed as a free agent by **Philadelphia**, June, 1970. Claimed by **Hershey** (AHL) from **Philadelphia** in Reverse Draft, June, 1970. Claimed by **Kansas City** from **Hershey** (AHL) in Inter-League Draft, June 12, 1974.

• HARVEY, TODD

Todd Harvey C – R. 6', 195 lbs. b: Hamilton, Ont., 2/17/1975. Dallas' 1st choice, 9th overall, in 1993 Entry Draft.

Season	Club	League	GP	G	A	Pts	AG	AA	APts	PIM	PP	SH	GW	S	%	TGF	PGF	TGA	PGA	+/–	GP	G	A	Pts	PIM	PP	SH	GW
1991-92	Detroit Ambassadors	OHL	58	21	43	64	....	....	....	141	....	....	....	....	....	....	....	....	....	....	7	3	5	8	30	....	....	....
1992-93	Detroit Jr. Red Wings	OHL	55	50	50	100	....	....	....	83	....	....	....	....	....	....	....	....	....	....	15	9	12	21	39	....	....	....
1993-94	Detroit Jr. Red Wings	OHL	49	34	51	85	....	....	....	75	....	....	....	....	....	....	....	....	....	....	17	10	12	22	26	....	....	....
	Canada	WJC-A	7	4	3	7	....	....	....	6	....	....	....	....	....	....	....	....	....	....	....	....	....	....	....	....	....	....
1994-95	Detroit Jr. Red Wings	OHL	11	8	14	22	....	....	....	12	....	....	....	....	....	....	....	....	....	....	....	....	....	....	....	....	....	....
	Canada	WJC-A	7	6	0	6	....	....	....	4	....	....	....	....	....	....	....	....	....	....	....	....	....	....	....	....	....	....
	Dallas Stars	**NHL**	**40**	**11**	**9**	**20**	**19**	**13**	**32**	**67**	**2**	**0**	**1**	**64**	**17.2**	**26**	**10**	**19**	**0**	**–3**	**5**	**0**	**0**	**0**	**8**	**0**	**0**	**0**
1995-96	**Dallas Stars**	**NHL**	**69**	**9**	**20**	**29**	**9**	**16**	**25**	**136**	**3**	**0**	**1**	**101**	**8.9**	**59**	**21**	**51**	**0**	**–13**	....	....	....	....	....	....	....	....
	Michigan K-Wings	IHL	5	1	3	4	....	....	....	8	....	....	....	....	....	....	....	....	....	....	....	....	....	....	....	....	....	....
1996-97	**Dallas Stars**	**NHL**	**71**	**9**	**22**	**31**	**10**	**19**	**29**	**142**	**1**	**0**	**2**	**99**	**9.1**	**46**	**6**	**21**	**0**	**+19**	**7**	**0**	**1**	**1**	**10**	**0**	**0**	**0**
1997-98	**Dallas Stars**	**NHL**	**59**	**9**	**10**	**19**	**11**	**10**	**21**	**104**	**0**	**0**	**1**	**88**	**10.2**	**25**	**4**	**16**	**0**	**+5**	....	....	....	....	....	....	....	....
	NHL Totals		**239**	**38**	**61**	**99**	**49**	**58**	**107**	**449**	**6**	**0**	**5**	**352**	**10.8**	**156**	**41**	**107**	**0**		**12**	**0**	**1**	**1**	**18**	**0**	**0**	**0**

Traded to **NY Rangers** by **Dallas** with Bob Errey and Dallas' 4th round choice (Boyd Kane) in 1998 Entry Draft for Brian Skrudland, Mike Keane and NY Rangers' 6th round choice (Pavel Patera) in 1998 Entry Draft, March 24, 1998.

• HATCHER, DERIAN

Derian Hatcher D – L. 6'5", 225 lbs. b: Sterling Heights, MI, 6/4/1972. Minnesota's 1st choice, 8th overall, in 1990 Entry Draft.

Season	Club	League	GP	G	A	Pts	AG	AA	APts	PIM	PP	SH	GW	S	%	TGF	PGF	TGA	PGA	+/–	GP	G	A	Pts	PIM	PP	SH	GW
1989-90	North Bay Centennials	OHL	64	14	38	52	....	....	....	81	....	....	....	....	....	....	....	....	....	....	5	2	3	5	8	....	....	....
1990-91	North Bay Centennials	OHL	64	13	49	62	....	....	....	163	....	....	....	....	....	....	....	....	....	....	10	2	10	12	28	....	....	....
1991-92	**Minnesota North Stars**	**NHL**	**43**	**8**	**4**	**12**	**7**	**3**	**10**	**88**	**0**	**0**	**2**	**51**	**15.7**	**35**	**2**	**33**	**7**	**+7**	**5**	**0**	**2**	**2**	**8**	**0**	**0**	**0**
1992-93	**Minnesota North Stars**	**NHL**	**67**	**4**	**15**	**19**	**3**	**10**	**13**	**178**	**0**	**0**	**1**	**73**	**5.5**	**69**	**13**	**109**	**26**	**–27**	....	....	....	....	....	....	....	....
	Kalamazoo Wings	IHL	2	1	2	3	....	....	....	21	....	....	....	....	....	....	....	....	....	....	....	....	....	....	....	....	....	....
	United States	WC-A	6	1	2	3	....	....	....	8	....	....	....	....	....	....	....	....	....	....	....	....	....	....	....	....	....	....
1993-94	**Dallas Stars**	**NHL**	**83**	**12**	**19**	**31**	**11**	**15**	**26**	**211**	**2**	**1**	**2**	**132**	**9.1**	**103**	**16**	**86**	**18**	**+19**	**9**	**0**	**2**	**2**	**14**	**0**	**0**	**0**
1994-95	**Dallas Stars**	**NHL**	**43**	**5**	**11**	**16**	**9**	**16**	**25**	**105**	**2**	**0**	**2**	**74**	**6.8**	**47**	**15**	**43**	**14**	**+3**	....	....	....	....	....	....	....	....
1995-96	**Dallas Stars**	**NHL**	**79**	**8**	**23**	**31**	**8**	**19**	**27**	**129**	**2**	**0**	**1**	**125**	**6.4**	**85**	**12**	**125**	**40**	**–12**	....	....	....	....	....	....	....	....
1996-97	United States	W Cup	6	3	2	5	....	....	....	10	....	....	....	....	....	....	....	....	....	....	....	....	....	....	....	....	....	....
	Dallas Stars	**NHL**	**63**	**3**	**19**	**22**	**3**	**17**	**20**	**97**	**0**	**0**	**0**	**96**	**3.1**	**63**	**4**	**77**	**26**	**+8**	**7**	**0**	**2**	**2**	**20**	**0**	**0**	**0**
1997-98	**Dallas Stars**	**NHL**	**70**	**6**	**25**	**31**	**7**	**24**	**31**	**132**	**3**	**0**	**2**	**74**	**8.1**	**72**	**17**	**62**	**16**	**+9**	**17**	**3**	**3**	**6**	**39**	**2**	**0**	**0**
	United States	Olympics	4	0	0	0	....	....	....	0	....	....	....	....	....	....	....	....	....	....	....	....	....	....	....	....	....	....
	NHL Totals		**448**	**46**	**116**	**162**	**48**	**104**	**152**	**940**	**9**	**1**	**10**	**625**	**7.4**	**474**	**79**	**535**	**147**		**38**	**3**	**9**	**12**	**81**	**2**	**0**	**0**

Played in NHL All-Star Game (1997)

Transferred to **Dallas** after **Minnesota** franchise relocated, June 9, 1993.

• HATCHER, KEVIN

Kevin Hatcher D – R. 6'4", 225 lbs. b: Detroit, MI, 9/9/1966. Washington's 1st choice, 17th overall, in 1984 Entry Draft.

Season	Club	League	GP	G	A	Pts	AG	AA	APts	PIM	PP	SH	GW	S	%	TGF	PGF	TGA	PGA	+/–	GP	G	A	Pts	PIM	PP	SH	GW
1982-83	Detroit Compuware	Midget	75	30	45	75	....	....	....	120	....	....	....	....	....	....	....	....	....	....	....	....	....	....	....	....	....	....
1983-84	North Bay Centennials	OHL	67	10	39	49	....	....	....	61	....	....	....	....	....	....	....	....	....	....	4	2	2	4	11	....	....	....
	United States	WJC-A	7	1	0	1	....	....	....	0	....	....	....	....	....	....	....	....	....	....	....	....	....	....	....	....	....	....
1984-85	North Bay Centennials	OHL	58	26	37	63	....	....	....	75	....	....	....	....	....	....	....	....	....	....	8	3	8	11	9	....	....	....
	Washington Capitals	**NHL**	**2**	**1**	**0**	**1**	**1**	**0**	**1**	**0**	**0**	**1**	**0**	**3**	**33.3**	**3**	**0**	**3**	**1**	**+1**	**1**	**0**	**0**	**0**	**0**	**0**	**0**	**0**
1985-86	**Washington Capitals**	**NHL**	**79**	**9**	**10**	**19**	**7**	**7**	**14**	**119**	**1**	**0**	**1**	**132**	**6.8**	**80**	**6**	**91**	**23**	**+6**	**9**	**1**	**1**	**2**	**19**	**0**	**0**	**0**
1986-87	**Washington Capitals**	**NHL**	**78**	**8**	**16**	**24**	**7**	**12**	**19**	**144**	**1**	**0**	**2**	**100**	**8.0**	**69**	**11**	**113**	**26**	**–29**	**7**	**1**	**0**	**1**	**20**	**0**	**0**	**0**
1987-88	United States	C Cup	5	0	0	0	....	....	....	4	....	....	....	....	....	....	....	....	....	....	....	....	....	....	....	....	....	....
	Washington Capitals	**NHL**	**71**	**14**	**27**	**41**	**12**	**19**	**31**	**137**	**5**	**0**	**3**	**181**	**7.7**	**86**	**28**	**94**	**37**	**+1**	**14**	**5**	**7**	**12**	**55**	**1**	**0**	**1**
1988-89	**Washington Capitals**	**NHL**	**62**	**13**	**27**	**40**	**11**	**19**	**30**	**101**	**3**	**0**	**2**	**148**	**8.8**	**108**	**38**	**83**	**32**	**+19**	**6**	**1**	**4**	**5**	**20**	**1**	**0**	**0**
1989-90	Washington Capitals	FrTour	4	0	1	1	....	....	....	10	....	....	....	....	....	....	....	....	....	....	....	....	....	....	....	....	....	....
	Washington Capitals	**NHL**	**80**	**13**	**41**	**54**	**11**	**29**	**40**	**102**	**4**	**0**	**2**	**240**	**5.4**	**135**	**41**	**129**	**39**	**+4**	**11**	**0**	**8**	**8**	**32**	**0**	**0**	**0**
1990-91	**Washington Capitals**	**NHL**	**79**	**24**	**50**	**74**	**22**	**38**	**60**	**69**	**9**	**2**	**3**	**267**	**9.0**	**138**	**49**	**125**	**26**	**–10**	**11**	**3**	**3**	**6**	**8**	**2**	**0**	**0**
1991-92	United States	C Cup	8	0	4	4	....	....	....	12	....	....	....	....	....	....	....	....	....	....	....	....	....	....	....	....	....	....
	Washington Capitals	**NHL**	**79**	**17**	**37**	**54**	**16**	**28**	**44**	**105**	**8**	**1**	**2**	**246**	**6.9**	**160**	**54**	**118**	**30**	**+18**	**7**	**2**	**4**	**6**	**19**	**0**	**1**	**0**
1992-93	**Washington Capitals**	**NHL**	**83**	**34**	**45**	**79**	**28**	**31**	**59**	**114**	**13**	**1**	**6**	**329**	**10.3**	**162**	**56**	**162**	**49**	**–7**	**6**	**0**	**1**	**1**	**14**	**0**	**0**	**0**
1993-94	**Washington Capitals**	**NHL**	**72**	**16**	**24**	**40**	**15**	**19**	**34**	**108**	**6**	**0**	**3**	**217**	**7.4**	**100**	**33**	**122**	**42**	**–13**	**11**	**3**	**4**	**7**	**37**	**0**	**1**	**0**
1994-95	**Dallas Stars**	**NHL**	**47**	**10**	**19**	**29**	**18**	**28**	**46**	**66**	**3**	**0**	**2**	**138**	**7.2**	**72**	**27**	**64**	**15**	**–4**	**5**	**2**	**1**	**3**	**2**	**1**	**0**	**1**
1995-96	**Dallas Stars**	**NHL**	**74**	**15**	**26**	**41**	**15**	**21**	**36**	**58**	**7**	**0**	**3**	**237**	**6.3**	**105**	**45**	**104**	**20**	**–24**	....	....	....	....	....	....	....	....
1996-97	United States	W Cup	7	0	3	3	....	....	....	4	....	....	....	....	....	....	....	....	....	....	....	....	....	....	....	....	....	....
	Pittsburgh Penguins	**NHL**	**80**	**15**	**39**	**54**	**16**	**35**	**51**	**103**	**9**	**0**	**1**	**199**	**7.5**	**144**	**47**	**117**	**31**	**+11**	**5**	**1**	**1**	**2**	**4**	**1**	**0**	**0**
1997-98	**Pittsburgh Penguins**	**NHL**	**74**	**19**	**29**	**48**	**22**	**28**	**50**	**66**	**13**	**1**	**3**	**169**	**11.2**	**107**	**49**	**78**	**17**	**–3**	**6**	**1**	**0**	**1**	**12**	**1**	**0**	**0**
	United States	Olympics	3	0	2	2	....	....	....	0	....	....	....	....	....	....	....	....	....	....	....	....	....	....	....	....	....	....
	NHL Totals		**960**	**208**	**390**	**598**	**201**	**314**	**515**	**1292**	**82**	**6**	**33**	**2606**	**8.0**	**1469**	**484**	**1403**	**388**		**99**	**20**	**34**	**54**	**242**	**7**	**2**	**2**

OHL Second All-Star Team (1985)

Played in NHL All-Star Game (1990, 1991, 1992, 1996, 1997)

Traded to **Dallas** by **Washington** for Mark Tinordi and Rick Mrozik, January 18, 1995. Traded to **Pittsburgh** by **Dallas** for Sergei Zubov, June 22, 1996.

• HATOUM, ED

Ed Hatoum RW – R. 5'10", 180 lbs. b: Beirut, Lebanon, 12/7/1947.

Season	Club	League	GP	G	A	Pts	AG	AA	APts	PIM	PP	SH	GW	S	%	TGF	PGF	TGA	PGA	+/–	GP	G	A	Pts	PIM	PP	SH	GW
1964-65	Hamilton Red Wings	OHA	17	0	3	3	....	....	....	8	....	....	....	....	....	....	....	....	....	....	....	....	....	....	....	....	....	....
1965-66	Hamilton Red Wings	OHA	48	16	35	51	....	....	....	51	....	....	....	....	....	....	....	....	....	....	5	0	3	3	2	....	....	....
1966-67	Hamilton Red Wings	OHA	45	19	25	44	....	....	....	89	....	....	....	....	....	....	....	....	....	....	17	5	11	16	16	....	....	....
1967-68	Hamilton Red Wings	OHA	50	25	34	59	....	....	....	44	....	....	....	....	....	....	....	....	....	....	11	6	5	11	10	....	....	....
	Fort Worth Wings	CHL	....	....	....	....	....	....	....	....	....	....	....	....	....	....	....	....	....	....	7	0	1	1	0	....	....	....
1968-69	**Detroit Red Wings**	**NHL**	**16**	**2**	**1**	**3**	**2**	**1**	**3**	**2**	**0**	**0**	**1**	**20**	**10.0**	**6**	**1**	**4**	**0**	**+1**	....	....	....	....	....	....	....	....
	Fort Worth Wings	CHL	53	21	28	49	....	....	....	29	....	....	....	....	....	....	....	....	....	....	....	....	....	....	....	....	....	....
	Baltimore Clippers	AHL	3	0	1	1	....	....	....	2	....	....	....	....	....	....	....	....	....	....	4	1	1	2	0	....	....	....
1969-70	**Detroit Red Wings**	**NHL**	**5**	**0**	**2**	**2**	**0**	**2**	**2**	**2**	**0**	**0**	**0**	**1**	**0.0**	**2**	**0**	**1**	**0**	**+1**	....	....	....	....	....	....	....	....
	Fort Worth Wings	CHL	69	15	40	55	....	....	....	32	....	....	....	....	....	....	....	....	....	....	6	2	3	5	0	....	....	....
1970-71	**Vancouver Canucks**	**NHL**	**26**	**1**	**3**	**4**	**1**	**3**	**4**	**21**	**0**	**1**	**0**	**27**	**3.7**	**9**	**4**	**26**	**7**	**–14**	....	....	....	....	....	....	....	....
	Seattle Totems	WHL	29	8	13	21	....	....	....	19	....	....	....	....	....	....	....	....	....	....	....	....	....	....	....	....	....	....
1971-72	Rochester Americans	AHL	67	9	23	32	....	....	....	29	....	....	....	....	....	....	....	....	....	....	....	....	....	....	....	....	....	....
1972-73	Chicago Cougars	WHA	16	1	1	2	....	....	....	2	....	....	....	....	....	....	....	....	....	....	....	....	....	....	....	....	....	....
	Seattle Totems	WHL	45	11	26	37	....	....	....	14	....	....	....	....	....	....	....	....	....	....	....	....	....	....	....	....	....	....

			REGULAR SEASON																		PLAYOFFS							
Season	Club	League	GP	G	A	Pts	AG	AA	APts	PIM	PP	SH	GW	S	%	TGF	PGF	TGA	PGA	+/–	GP	G	A	Pts	PIM	PP	SH	GW
1973-74	Vancouver Blazers	WHA	37	3	12	15	....	....	....	8	....	....	....	....	....	....	....	....	....	....	....	....	....	....	....	....	....	....
	San Diego Gulls	WHL	5	1	0	1	....	....	....	4	....	....	....	....	....	....	....	....	....	....	....	....	....	....	....	....	....	....
1974-75	Nelson Maple Leafs	WIHL	48	25	53	78	....	....	....	18	....	....	....	....	....	....	....	....	....	....	....	....	....	....	....	....	....	....
1975-76	Nelson Maple Leafs	WIHL	4	0	3	3	....	....	....	0	....	....	....	....	....	....	....	....	....	....	....	....	....	....	....	....	....	....
	NHL Totals		**47**	**3**	**6**	**9**	**3**	**6**	**9**	**25**	**0**	**1**	**1**	**48**	**6.3**	**17**	**5**	**31**	**7**		....	....	....	....	....	....	....	....

Claimed by **Vancouver** from **Detroit** in Expansion Draft, June 10, 1970. Loaned to **Seattle** (WHL) by **Vancouver** with Jim Wiste for the remainder of 1971-72 season for Bobby Schmautz, February 9, 1971. Selected by **LA Sharks** (WHA) in 1972 WHA General Player Draft, February 12, 1972. WHA rights traded to **Chicago** (WHA) by **LA Sharks**(WHA) for cash, October, 1972. Traded to **Vancouver** (WHA) by **Chicago** (WHA) for cash, September, 1973.

• HAUER, BRETT

Brett Hauer D – R. 6'2", 200 lbs. b: Richfield, MN, 7/11/1971. Vancouver's 3rd choice, 71st overall, in 1989 Entry Draft.

1988-89	Richfield High School	H.S.	24	8	15	23	....	....	....	70	....	....	....	....	....	....	....	....	....	....	....	....	....	....	....	....	....	....
1989-90	University of Minnesota-Duluth	WCHA	37	2	6	8	....	....	....	44	....	....	....	....	....	....	....	....	....	....	....	....	....	....	....	....	....	....
1990-91	University of Minnesota-Duluth	WCHA	30	1	7	8	....	....	....	54	....	....	....	....	....	....	....	....	....	....	....	....	....	....	....	....	....	....
1991-92	University of Minnesota-Duluth	WCHA	33	8	14	22	....	....	....	40	....	....	....	....	....	....	....	....	....	....	....	....	....	....	....	....	....	....
1992-93	University of Minnesota-Duluth	WCHA	40	10	46	56	....	....	....	52	....	....	....	....	....	....	....	....	....	....	....	....	....	....	....	....	....	....
	United States	WC-A	6	0	0	0	....	....	....	8	....	....	....	....	....	....	....	....	....	....	....	....	....	....	....	....	....	....
1993-94	United States	Nat-Team	57	6	14	20	....	....	....	88	....	....	....	....	....	....	....	....	....	....	....	....	....	....	....	....	....	....
	United States	Olympics	8	0	0	0	....	....	....	10	....	....	....	....	....	....	....	....	....	....	....	....	....	....	....	....	....	....
	Las Vegas Thunder	IHL	21	0	7	7	....	....	....	8	....	....	....	....	....	....	....	....	....	....	1	0	0	0	0	....	....	....
1994-95	AIK Solna	Sweden	37	1	3	4	....	....	....	38	....	....	....	....	....	....	....	....	....	....	....	....	....	....	....	....	....	....
	United States	WC-A	6	2	2	4	....	....	....	4	....	....	....	....	....	....	....	....	....	....	....	....	....	....	....	....	....	....
1995-96	**Edmonton Oilers**	**NHL**	**29**	**4**	**2**	**6**	**4**	**2**	**6**	**30**	**2**	**0**	**1**	**53**	**7.5**	**22**	**7**	**34**	**8**	**–11**	....	....	....	....	....	....	....	....
	Cape Breton Oilers	AHL	17	3	5	8	....	....	....	29	....	....	....	....	....	....	....	....	....	....	....	....	....	....	....	....	....	....
1996-97	Chicago Wolves	IHL	81	10	30	40	....	....	....	50	....	....	....	....	....	....	....	....	....	....	4	2	0	2	4	....	....	....
1997-98	Manitoba Moose	IHL	82	13	48	61	....	....	....	58	....	....	....	....	....	....	....	....	....	....	3	0	0	0	2	....	....	....
	NHL Totals		**29**	**4**	**2**	**6**	**4**	**2**	**6**	**30**	**2**	**0**	**1**	**53**	**7.5**	**22**	**7**	**34**	**8**		....	....	....	....	....	....	....	....

WCHA First All-Star Team (1993) • NCAA West First All-American Team (1993)

Traded to **Edmonton** by **Vancouver** for Edmonton's 7th round choice (Larry Shapley) in 1997 Entry Draft, August 24, 1995.

• HAWERCHUK, DALE

Dale Hawerchuk C – L. 5'11", 190 lbs. b: Toronto, Ont., 4/4/1963. Winnipeg's 1st choice, 1st overall, in 1981 Entry Draft.

1979-80	Cornwall Royals	QMJHL	72	37	66	103	....	....	....	21	....	....	....	....	....	....	....	....	....	....	18	20	25	45	0	....	....	....
1980-81	Cornwall Royals	QMJHL	72	81	102	183	....	....	....	69	....	....	....	....	....	....	....	....	....	....	19	15	20	35	8	....	....	....
	Canada	WJC-A	5	5	4	9	....	....	....	2	....	....	....	....	....	....	....	....	....	....	....	....	....	....	....	....	....	....
1981-82	**Winnipeg Jets**	**NHL**	**80**	**45**	**58**	**103**	**36**	**38**	**74**	**47**	**12**	**0**	**2**	**339**	**13.3**	**144**	**55**	**97**	**4**	**–4**	**4**	**1**	**7**	**8**	**5**	**0**	**0**	**0**
	Canada	WEC-A	10	3	1	4	....	....	....	0	....	....	....	....	....	....	....	....	....	....	....	....	....	....	....	....	....	....
1982-83	**Winnipeg Jets**	**NHL**	**79**	**40**	**51**	**91**	**33**	**35**	**68**	**31**	**13**	**1**	**3**	**297**	**13.5**	**135**	**60**	**107**	**15**	**–17**	**3**	**1**	**4**	**5**	**8**	**1**	**0**	**0**
1983-84	**Winnipeg Jets**	**NHL**	**80**	**37**	**65**	**102**	**30**	**44**	**74**	**73**	**10**	**0**	**4**	**256**	**14.5**	**137**	**46**	**120**	**15**	**–14**	**3**	**1**	**1**	**2**	**0**	**1**	**0**	**0**
1984-85	**Winnipeg Jets**	**NHL**	**80**	**53**	**77**	**130**	**43**	**52**	**95**	**74**	**17**	**3**	**4**	**280**	**18.9**	**172**	**57**	**102**	**9**	**+22**	**3**	**2**	**1**	**3**	**4**	**1**	**0**	**0**
1985-86	**Winnipeg Jets**	**NHL**	**80**	**46**	**59**	**105**	**37**	**40**	**77**	**44**	**18**	**2**	**2**	**313**	**14.7**	**130**	**53**	**128**	**24**	**–27**	**3**	**0**	**3**	**3**	**0**	**0**	**0**	**0**
	Canada	WEC-A	8	2	4	6	....	....	....	4	....	....	....	....	....	....	....	....	....	....	....	....	....	....	....	....	....	....
1986-87	**Winnipeg Jets**	**NHL**	**80**	**47**	**53**	**100**	**41**	**38**	**79**	**52**	**10**	**0**	**4**	**267**	**17.6**	**135**	**41**	**95**	**4**	**+3**	**10**	**5**	**8**	**13**	**4**	**3**	**0**	**0**
	NHL All-Stars	RV'87	2	0	1	1	....	....	....	2	....	....	....	....	....	....	....	....	....	....	....	....	....	....	....	....	....	....
1987-88	Canada	C Cup	9	4	2	6	....	....	....	0	....	....	....	....	....	....	....	....	....	....	....	....	....	....	....	....	....	....
	Winnipeg Jets	**NHL**	**80**	**44**	**77**	**121**	**38**	**55**	**93**	**59**	**20**	**3**	**4**	**292**	**15.1**	**157**	**80**	**104**	**18**	**–9**	**5**	**3**	**4**	**7**	**16**	**2**	**0**	**0**
1988-89	**Winnipeg Jets**	**NHL**	**75**	**41**	**55**	**96**	**35**	**39**	**74**	**28**	**14**	**3**	**4**	**239**	**17.2**	**132**	**53**	**123**	**14**	**–30**	....	....	....	....	....	....	....	....
	Canada	WEC-A	10	4	8	12	....	....	....	6	....	....	....	....	....	....	....	....	....	....	....	....	....	....	....	....	....	....
1989-90	**Winnipeg Jets**	**NHL**	**79**	**26**	**55**	**81**	**22**	**39**	**61**	**60**	**8**	**0**	**2**	**211**	**12.3**	**117**	**44**	**91**	**7**	**–11**	**7**	**3**	**5**	**8**	**2**	**0**	**0**	**1**
1990-91	**Buffalo Sabres**	**NHL**	**80**	**31**	**58**	**89**	**29**	**44**	**73**	**32**	**12**	**0**	**1**	**194**	**16.0**	**116**	**47**	**69**	**2**	**+2**	**6**	**2**	**4**	**6**	**10**	**1**	**0**	**0**
1991-92	Canada	C Cup	8	2	3	5	....	....	....	0	....	....	....	....	....	....	....	....	....	....	....	....	....	....	....	....	....	....
	Buffalo Sabres	**NHL**	**77**	**23**	**75**	**98**	**21**	**57**	**78**	**27**	**13**	**0**	**4**	**242**	**9.5**	**100**	**60**	**91**	**13**	**–22**	**7**	**2**	**5**	**7**	**0**	**0**	**0**	**0**
1992-93	**Buffalo Sabres**	**NHL**	**81**	**16**	**80**	**96**	**13**	**55**	**68**	**52**	**8**	**0**	**2**	**259**	**6.2**	**147**	**87**	**83**	**6**	**–17**	**8**	**5**	**9**	**14**	**2**	**3**	**0**	**0**
1993-94	**Buffalo Sabres**	**NHL**	**81**	**35**	**51**	**86**	**33**	**39**	**72**	**91**	**13**	**1**	**7**	**227**	**15.4**	**130**	**66**	**55**	**1**	**+10**	**7**	**0**	**7**	**7**	**4**	**0**	**0**	**0**
1994-95	**Buffalo Sabres**	**NHL**	**23**	**5**	**11**	**16**	**9**	**16**	**25**	**2**	**2**	**0**	**2**	**56**	**8.9**	**20**	**13**	**9**	**0**	**–2**	**2**	**0**	**0**	**0**	**0**	**0**	**0**	**0**
1995-96	**St. Louis Blues**	**NHL**	**66**	**13**	**28**	**41**	**13**	**23**	**36**	**22**	**5**	**0**	**1**	**136**	**9.6**	**63**	**32**	**32**	**6**	**+5**	....	....	....	....	....	....	....	....
	Philadelphia Flyers	**NHL**	**16**	**4**	**16**	**20**	**4**	**13**	**17**	**4**	**1**	**0**	**1**	**44**	**9.1**	**27**	**9**	**10**	**2**	**+10**	**12**	**3**	**6**	**9**	**12**	**1**	**0**	**0**
1996-97	**Philadelphia Flyers**	**NHL**	**51**	**12**	**22**	**34**	**13**	**19**	**32**	**32**	**6**	**0**	**2**	**102**	**11.8**	**52**	**17**	**26**	**0**	**+9**	**17**	**2**	**5**	**7**	**0**	**1**	**0**	**1**
	NHL Totals		**1188**	**518**	**891**	**1409**	**450**	**646**	**1096**	**730**	**182**	**13**	**49**	**3754**	**13.8**	**1953**	**843**	**1342**	**140**		**97**	**30**	**69**	**99**	**67**	**14**	**0**	**2**

Memorial Cup All-Star Team (1980, 1981) • Won George Parsons Trophy (Memorial Cup Tournament Most Sportsmanlike Player) (1980) • QMJHL First All-Star Team (1981) • Canadian Major Junior Player of the Year (1981) • Won Stafford Smythe Memorial Trophy (Memorial Cup Tournament MVP) (1981) • Won Calder Memorial Trophy (1982) • NHL Second All-Star Team (1985)

Played in NHL All-Star Game (1982, 1985, 1986, 1988, 1997)

Traded to **Buffalo** by **Winnipeg** with Winnipeg's 1st round choice (Brad May) in 1990 Entry Draft and future considerations for Phil Housley, Scott Arniel, Jeff Parker and Buffalo's 1st round choice (Keith Tkachuk) in 1990 Entry Draft, June 16, 1990. Signed as a free agent by **St. Louis**, September 8, 1995. Traded to **Philadelphia** by **St. Louis** for Craig MacTavish, March 15, 1996.

• HAWGOOD, GREG

Greg Hawgood D – L. 5'10", 190 lbs. b: Edmonton, Alta., 8/10/1968. Boston's 9th choice, 202nd overall, in 1986 Entry Draft.

1983-84	Kamloops Blazers	WHL	49	10	23	33	....	....	....	39	....	....	....	....	....	....	....	....	....	....	....	....	....	....	....	....	....	....
1984-85	Kamloops Blazers	WHL	66	25	40	65	....	....	....	72	....	....	....	....	....	....	....	....	....	....	....	....	....	....	....	....	....	....
1985-86	Kamloops Blazers	WHL	71	34	85	119	....	....	....	86	....	....	....	....	....	....	....	....	....	....	16	9	22	31	16	....	....	....
1986-87	Kamloops Blazers	WHL	61	30	93	123	....	....	....	139	....	....	....	....	....	....	....	....	....	....	....	....	....	....	....	....	....	....
	Canada	WJC-A	6	2	2	4	....	....	....	6	....	....	....	....	....	....	....	....	....	....	....	....	....	....	....	....	....	....
1987-88	Kamloops Blazers	WHL	63	48	85	133	....	....	....	142	....	....	....	....	....	....	....	....	....	....	16	10	16	26	33	....	....	....
	Canada	WJC-A	7	1	8	9	....	....	....	6	....	....	....	....	....	....	....	....	....	....	....	....	....	....	....	....	....	....
	Boston Bruins	**NHL**	**1**	**0**	**0**	**0**	**0**	**0**	**0**	**0**	**0**	**0**	**0**	**1**	**0.0**	**0**	**0**	**1**	**0**	**–1**	**3**	**1**	**0**	**1**	**0**	**0**	**0**	**0**
1988-89	**Boston Bruins**	**NHL**	**56**	**16**	**24**	**40**	**14**	**17**	**31**	**84**	**5**	**0**	**0**	**132**	**12.1**	**88**	**31**	**63**	**10**	**+4**	**10**	**0**	**2**	**2**	**2**	**0**	**0**	**0**
	Maine Mariners	AHL	21	2	9	11	....	....	....	41	....	....	....	....	....	....	....	....	....	....	....	....	....	....	....	....	....	....
1989-90	**Boston Bruins**	**NHL**	**77**	**11**	**27**	**38**	**9**	**19**	**28**	**76**	**2**	**0**	**1**	**127**	**8.7**	**67**	**14**	**43**	**2**	**+12**	**15**	**1**	**3**	**4**	**12**	**1**	**0**	**0**
1990-91	Asiago	Italy	2	3	0	3	....	....	....	9	....	....	....	....	....	....	....	....	....	....	....	....	....	....	....	....	....	....
	Maine Mariners	AHL	5	0	1	1	....	....	....	13	....	....	....	....	....	....	....	....	....	....	....	....	....	....	....	....	....	....
	Edmonton Oilers	**NHL**	**6**	**0**	**1**	**1**	**0**	**1**	**1**	**6**	**0**	**0**	**0**	**9**	**0.0**	**3**	**2**	**4**	**1**	**–2**	....	....	....	....	....	....	....	....
	Cape Breton Oilers	AHL	55	10	32	42	....	....	....	73	....	....	....	....	....	....	....	....	....	....	4	0	3	3	23	....	....	....
1991-92	**Edmonton Oilers**	**NHL**	**20**	**2**	**11**	**13**	**2**	**8**	**10**	**22**	**0**	**0**	**0**	**24**	**8.3**	**34**	**4**	**16**	**5**	**+19**	**13**	**0**	**3**	**3**	**23**	**0**	**0**	**0**
	Cape Breton Oilers	AHL	56	20	55	75	....	....	....	26	....	....	....	....	....	....	....	....	....	....	3	2	2	4	0	....	....	....
1992-93	**Edmonton Oilers**	**NHL**	**29**	**5**	**13**	**18**	**4**	**9**	**13**	**35**	**2**	**0**	**0**	**47**	**10.6**	**32**	**9**	**28**	**4**	**–1**	....	....	....	....	....	....	....	....
	Philadelphia Flyers	**NHL**	**40**	**6**	**22**	**28**	**5**	**15**	**20**	**39**	**5**	**0**	**1**	**91**	**6.6**	**57**	**33**	**32**	**1**	**–7**	....	....	....	....	....	....	....	....
1993-94	**Philadelphia Flyers**	**NHL**	**19**	**3**	**12**	**15**	**3**	**9**	**12**	**19**	**3**	**0**	**0**	**37**	**8.1**	**21**	**15**	**4**	**0**	**+2**	....	....	....	....	....	....	....	....
	Florida Panthers	**NHL**	**33**	**2**	**14**	**16**	**2**	**11**	**13**	**9**	**0**	**0**	**1**	**55**	**3.6**	**38**	**20**	**10**	**0**	**+8**	....	....	....	....	....	....	....	....
	Pittsburgh Penguins	**NHL**	**12**	**1**	**2**	**3**	**1**	**2**	**3**	**8**	**1**	**0**	**1**	**20**	**5.0**	**9**	**6**	**4**	**0**	**–1**	**1**	**0**	**0**	**0**	**0**	**0**	**0**	**0**
1994-95	**Pittsburgh Penguins**	**NHL**	**21**	**1**	**4**	**5**	**2**	**6**	**8**	**25**	**1**	**0**	**0**	**17**	**5.9**	**10**	**4**	**4**	**0**	**+2**	....	....	....	....	....	....	....	....
	Cleveland Lumberjacks	IHL	....	....	....	....	....	....	....	....	....	....	....	....	....	....	....	....	....	....	3	1	0	1	4	....	....	....
1995-96	Las Vegas Thunder	IHL	78	20	65	85	....	....	....	101	....	....	....	....	....	....	....	....	....	....	15	5	11	16	24	....	....	....
1996-97	**San Jose Sharks**	**NHL**	**63**	**6**	**12**	**18**	**6**	**11**	**17**	**69**	**3**	**0**	**0**	**83**	**7.2**	**39**	**20**	**44**	**3**	**–22**	....	....	....	....	....	....	....	....
1997-98	Kolner Haie	Germany	4	0	1	1	....	....	....	16	....	....	....	....	....	....	....	....	....	....	....	....	....	....	....	....	....	....
	Kolner Haie	EuroHL	1	0	0	0	....	....	....	2	....	....	....	....	....	....	....	....	....	....	....	....	....	....	....	....	....	....
	Houston Aeros	IHL	81	19	52	71	....	....	....	75	....	....	....	....	....	....	....	....	....	....	4	0	4	4	0	....	....	....
	NHL Totals		**377**	**53**	**142**	**195**	**48**	**108**	**156**	**392**	**22**	**0**	**4**	**643**	**8.2**	**398**	**158**	**253**	**26**		**42**	**2**	**8**	**10**	**37**	**1**	**0**	**0**

WHL West All-Star Team (1986, 1987, 1988) • WJC-A All-Star Team (1988) • Canadian Major Junior Defenseman of the Year (1988) • AHL First All-Star Team (1992) • Won Eddie Shore Plaque (Top Defenseman - AHL) (1992) • IHL First All-Star Team (1996, 1998) • Won Governors' Trophy (Top Defenseman - IHL) (1996)

Traded to **Edmonton** by **Boston** for Vladimir Ruzicka, October 22, 1990. Traded to **Philadelphia** by **Edmonton** with Josef Beranek for Brian Benning, January 16, 1993. Traded to **Florida** by **Philadelphia** for cash, November 30, 1993. Traded to **Pittsburgh** by **Florida** for Jeff Daniels, March 19, 1994. Signed as a free agent by **San Jose**, September 25, 1996.

			REGULAR SEASON																		PLAYOFFS							
Season	Club	League	GP	G	A	Pts	AG	AA	APts	PIM	PP	SH	GW	S	%	TGF	PGF	TGA	PGA	+/–	GP	G	A	Pts	PIM	PP	SH	GW

• HAWKINS, TODD
Todd Hawkins LW/RW – R. 6'1", 195 lbs. b: Kingston, Ont., 8/2/1966. Vancouver's 10th choice, 217th overall, in 1986 Entry Draft.

1984-85	Belleville Bulls	OHL	58	7	16	23	....	....	....	117	....	....	....	....	....	....	....	....	....	....	12	1	0	1	10	....	....	....
1985-86	Belleville Bulls	OHL	60	14	13	27	....	....	....	172	....	....	....	....	....	....	....	....	....	....	24	9	7	16	60	....	....	....
1986-87	Belleville Bulls	OHL	60	47	40	87	....	....	....	187	....	....	....	....	....	....	....	....	....	....	6	3	5	8	16	....	....	....
1987-88	Flint Spirits	IHL	50	13	13	26	....	....	....	337	....	....	....	....	....	....	....	....	....	....	16	3	5	8	*174	....	....	....
	Fredericton Express	AHL	2	0	4	4	....	....	....	11	....	....	....	....	....	....	....	....	....	....	....	....	....	....	....	....	....	....
1988-89	**Vancouver Canucks**	**NHL**	**4**	**0**	**0**	**0**	**0**	**0**	**0**	**9**	**0**	**0**	**0**	**2**	**0.0**	**0**	**0**	**1**	**0**	**–1**	....	....	....	....	....	....	....	....
	Milwaukee Admirals	IHL	63	12	14	26	....	....	....	307	....	....	....	....	....	....	....	....	....	....	9	1	0	1	33	....	....	....
1989-90	**Vancouver Canucks**	**NHL**	**4**	**0**	**0**	**0**	**0**	**0**	**0**	**6**	**0**	**0**	**0**	**3**	**0.0**	**1**	**0**	**2**	**0**	**–1**	....	....	....	....	....	....	....	....
	Milwaukee Admirals	IHL	61	23	17	40	....	....	....	273	....	....	....	....	....	....	....	....	....	....	5	4	1	5	19	....	....	....
1990-91	Newmarket Saints	AHL	22	2	5	7	....	....	....	66	....	....	....	....	....	....	....	....	....	....	....	....	....	....	....	....	....	....
	Milwaukee Admirals	IHL	39	9	11	20	....	....	....	134	....	....	....	....	....	....	....	....	....	....	....	....	....	....	....	....	....	....
1991-92	**Toronto Maple Leafs**	**NHL**	**2**	**0**	**0**	**0**	**0**	**0**	**0**	**0**	**0**	**0**	**0**	**0**	**0.0**	**0**	**0**	**0**	**0**	**0**	....	....	....	....	....	....	....	....
	St. John's Maple Leafs	AHL	66	30	27	57	....	....	....	139	....	....	....	....	....	....	....	....	....	....	7	1	0	1	10	....	....	....
1992-93	St. John's Maple Leafs	AHL	72	21	41	62	....	....	....	103	....	....	....	....	....	....	....	....	....	....	9	1	3	4	10	....	....	....
1993-94	Cleveland Lumberjacks	IHL	76	19	14	33	....	....	....	115	....	....	....	....	....	....	....	....	....	....	....	....	....	....	....	....	....	....
1994-95	Cleveland Lumberjacks	IHL	4	2	0	2	....	....	....	29	....	....	....	....	....	....	....	....	....	....	....	....	....	....	....	....	....	....
	Minnesota Moose	IHL	47	10	8	18	....	....	....	95	....	....	....	....	....	....	....	....	....	....	3	0	1	1	12	....	....	....
1995-96	Cincinnati Cyclones	IHL	73	16	12	28	....	....	....	65	....	....	....	....	....	....	....	....	....	....	17	7	4	11	32	....	....	....
1996-97	Cincinnati Cyclones	IHL	81	13	13	26	....	....	....	162	....	....	....	....	....	....	....	....	....	....	3	0	1	1	2	....	....	....
1997-98	Cincinnati Cyclones	IHL	71	13	23	36	....	....	....	168	....	....	....	....	....	....	....	....	....	....	9	0	3	3	36	....	....	....
	NHL Totals		**10**	**0**	**0**	**0**	**0**	**0**	**0**	**15**	**0**	**0**	**0**	**5**	**0.0**	**1**	**0**	**3**	**0**		....	....	....	....	....	....	....	....

OHL Second All-Star Team (1987)

Traded to **Toronto** by **Vancouver** for Brian Blad, January 22, 1991. Signed as a free agent by **Pittsburgh**, August 20, 1993.

• HAWORTH, ALAN
Alan Haworth C – R. 5'10", 190 lbs. b: Drummondville, Que., 9/1/1960. Buffalo's 6th choice, 95th overall, in 1979 Entry Draft.

1976-77	Chicoutimi Sagueneens	QMJHL	68	11	18	29	....	....	....	15	....	....	....	....	....	....	....	....	....	....	....	....	....	....	....	....	....	....
1977-78	Chicoutimi Sagueneens	QMJHL	59	17	33	50	....	....	....	40	....	....	....	....	....	....	....	....	....	....	....	....	....	....	....	....	....	....
1978-79	Sherbrooke Beavers	QMJHL	70	50	70	120	....	....	....	63	....	....	....	....	....	....	....	....	....	....	12	6	10	16	8	....	....	....
1979-80	Sherbrooke Beavers	QMJHL	45	28	36	64	....	....	....	50	....	....	....	....	....	....	....	....	....	....	15	11	16	27	4	....	....	....
1980-81	**Buffalo Sabres**	**NHL**	**49**	**16**	**20**	**36**	**13**	**14**	**27**	**34**	**4**	**0**	**1**	**72**	**22.2**	**47**	**10**	**43**	**0**	**–6**	**7**	**4**	**4**	**8**	**2**	**3**	**0**	**1**
	Rochester Americans	AHL	21	14	18	32	....	....	....	19	....	....	....	....	....	....	....	....	....	....	....	....	....	....	....	....	....	....
1981-82	**Buffalo Sabres**	**NHL**	**57**	**21**	**18**	**39**	**17**	**12**	**29**	**30**	**3**	**0**	**1**	**114**	**18.4**	**62**	**9**	**47**	**0**	**+6**	**3**	**0**	**1**	**1**	**2**	**0**	**0**	**0**
	Rochester Americans	AHL	14	5	12	17	....	....	....	10	....	....	....	....	....	....	....	....	....	....	....	....	....	....	....	....	....	....
1982-83	**Washington Capitals**	**NHL**	**74**	**23**	**27**	**50**	**19**	**19**	**38**	**34**	**5**	**0**	**2**	**145**	**15.9**	**74**	**21**	**58**	**0**	**–5**	**4**	**0**	**0**	**0**	**2**	**0**	**0**	**0**
1983-84	**Washington Capitals**	**NHL**	**75**	**24**	**31**	**55**	**19**	**21**	**40**	**52**	**7**	**0**	**5**	**164**	**14.6**	**75**	**20**	**41**	**0**	**+14**	**8**	**3**	**2**	**5**	**4**	**1**	**0**	**0**
1984-85	**Washington Capitals**	**NHL**	**76**	**23**	**26**	**49**	**19**	**18**	**37**	**48**	**4**	**0**	**2**	**154**	**14.9**	**65**	**11**	**36**	**1**	**+19**	**5**	**1**	**0**	**1**	**0**	**0**	**0**	**1**
1985-86	**Washington Capitals**	**NHL**	**71**	**34**	**39**	**73**	**27**	**26**	**53**	**72**	**7**	**0**	**5**	**194**	**17.5**	**92**	**17**	**40**	**1**	**+36**	**9**	**4**	**6**	**10**	**11**	**1**	**0**	**0**
1986-87	**Washington Capitals**	**NHL**	**50**	**25**	**16**	**41**	**22**	**12**	**34**	**43**	**9**	**0**	**2**	**143**	**17.5**	**58**	**14**	**44**	**3**	**+3**	**6**	**0**	**3**	**3**	**7**	**0**	**0**	**0**
1987-88	**Quebec Nordiques**	**NHL**	**72**	**23**	**34**	**57**	**20**	**24**	**44**	**112**	**6**	**0**	**2**	**171**	**13.5**	**77**	**26**	**59**	**3**	**–5**	....	....	....	....	....	....	....	....
1988-89	SC Bern	Switz.	36	24	29	53	....	....	....	....	....	....	....	....	....	....	....	....	....	....	11	*8	2	10	....	....	....	....
1989-90	SC Bern	Switz.	36	31	30	61	....	....	....	....	....	....	....	....	....	....	....	....	....	....	....	....	....	....	....	....	....	....
1990-91	SC Bern	Switz.	36	27	16	43	....	....	....	....	....	....	....	....	....	....	....	....	....	....	10	2	5	7	....	....	....	....
1991-92	SC Bern	Switz.	30	16	23	39	....	....	....	100	....	....	....	....	....	....	....	....	....	....	11	7	6	13	15	....	....	....
	NHL Totals		**524**	**189**	**211**	**400**	**156**	**146**	**302**	**425**	**45**	**0**	**20**	**1157**	**16.3**	**550**	**128**	**368**	**8**		**42**	**12**	**16**	**28**	**28**	**5**	**0**	**2**

Traded to **Washington** by **Buffalo** with Buffalo's 3rd round choice (Milan Novy) in 1982 Entry Draft for Washington's 2nd round choice (Mike Anderson) and 4th round choice (Timo Jutila) in 1982 Entry Draft, June 9, 1982. Traded to **Quebec** by **Washington** with Gaetan Duchesne and Washington's 1st round choice (Joe Sakic) in 1987 Entry Draft for Clint Malarchuk and Dale Hunter, June 13, 1987.

• HAWRYLIW, NEIL
Neil Hawryliw RW – L. 5'11", 185 lbs. b: Fielding, Sask., 11/9/1955.

1972-73	Humboldt Broncos	SJHL	STATISTICS NOT AVAILABLE																									
1973-74	Saskatoon Blades	WCJHL	52	23	20	43	....	....	....	28	....	....	....	....	....	....	....	....	....	....	....	....	....	....	....	....	....	....
1974-75	Saskatoon Blades	WCJHL	68	29	38	67	....	....	....	51	....	....	....	....	....	....	....	....	....	....	....	....	....	....	....	....	....	....
1975-76	Saskatoon Blades	WCJHL	72	48	39	87	....	....	....	155	....	....	....	....	....	....	....	....	....	....	20	14	20	34	23	....	....	....
1976-77	Muskegon Mohawks	IHL	38	18	18	36	....	....	....	16	....	....	....	....	....	....	....	....	....	....	7	2	3	5	4	....	....	....
1977-78	Muskegon Mohawks	IHL	75	37	32	69	....	....	....	84	....	....	....	....	....	....	....	....	....	....	5	2	3	5	9	....	....	....
1978-79	Muskegon Mohawks	IHL	13	11	7	18	....	....	....	14	....	....	....	....	....	....	....	....	....	....	....	....	....	....	....	....	....	....
	Fort Worth Texans	CHL	57	9	15	24	....	....	....	87	....	....	....	....	....	....	....	....	....	....	....	....	....	....	....	....	....	....
1979-80	Indianapolis Checkers	CHL	70	26	19	45	....	....	....	56	....	....	....	....	....	....	....	....	....	....	7	4	2	6	6	....	....	....
1980-81	Indianapolis Checkers	CHL	80	37	42	79	....	....	....	61	....	....	....	....	....	....	....	....	....	....	5	0	2	2	7	....	....	....
1981-82	**New York Islanders**	**NHL**	**1**	**0**	**0**	**0**	**0**	**0**	**0**	**0**	**0**	**0**	**0**	**0**	**0.0**	**0**	**0**	**0**	**0**	**0**	....	....	....	....	....	....	....	....
	Indianapolis Checkers	CHL	58	20	14	34	....	....	....	89	....	....	....	....	....	....	....	....	....	....	13	3	11	14	6	....	....	....
1982-83	Muskegon Mohawks	IHL	68	33	24	57	....	....	....	42	....	....	....	....	....	....	....	....	....	....	4	0	1	1	4	....	....	....
	Wichita Wind	CHL	2	2	3	5	....	....	....	0	....	....	....	....	....	....	....	....	....	....	....	....	....	....	....	....	....	....
1983-84	Muskegon Mohawks	IHL	66	25	37	62	....	....	....	36	....	....	....	....	....	....	....	....	....	....	....	....	....	....	....	....	....	....
1984-85	Muskegon Mohawks	IHL	80	17	22	39	....	....	....	93	....	....	....	....	....	....	....	....	....	....	14	2	3	5	29	....	....	....
1985-86	Muskegon Lumberjacks	IHL	14	4	1	5	....	....	....	10	....	....	....	....	....	....	....	....	....	....	....	....	....	....	....	....	....	....
	Kalamazoo Wings	IHL	68	32	23	55	....	....	....	67	....	....	....	....	....	....	....	....	....	....	6	1	3	4	17	....	....	....
1986-87	Kalamazoo Wings	IHL	56	9	23	32	....	....	....	84	....	....	....	....	....	....	....	....	....	....	5	0	1	1	4	....	....	....
	NHL Totals		**1**	**0**	**0**	**0**	**0**	**0**	**0**	**0**	**0**	**0**	**0**	**0**	**0.0**	**0**	**0**	**0**	**0**		....	....	....	....	....	....	....	....

CHL First All-Star Team (1981)

Signed as a free agent by **NY Islanders**, October 10, 1978.

• HAY, DWAYNE
Dwayne Hay LW – L. 6'1", 183 lbs. b: London, Ont., 2/11/1977. Washington's 3rd choice, 43rd overall, in 1995 Entry Draft.

1994-95	Guelph Platers	OHL	65	26	28	54	....	....	....	37	....	....	....	....	....	....	....	....	....	....	14	5	7	12	6	....	....	....
1995-96	Guelph Platers	OHL	60	28	30	58	....	....	....	49	....	....	....	....	....	....	....	....	....	....	16	4	9	13	18	....	....	....
1996-97	Guelph Platers	OHL	32	17	17	34	....	....	....	21	....	....	....	....	....	....	....	....	....	....	11	4	6	10	0	....	....	....
	Canada	WJC-A	7	0	0	0	....	....	....	2	....	....	....	....	....	....	....	....	....	....	....	....	....	....	....	....	....	....
1997-98	**Washington Capitals**	**NHL**	**2**	**0**	**0**	**0**	**0**	**0**	**0**	**2**	**0**	**0**	**0**	**1**	**0.0**	**0**	**0**	**0**	**0**	**0**	....	....	....	....	....	....	....	....
	Portland Pirates	AHL	58	6	7	13	....	....	....	35	....	....	....	....	....	....	....	....	....	....	....	....	....	....	....	....	....	....
	Beast of New Haven	AHL	10	3	2	5	....	....	....	4	....	....	....	....	....	....	....	....	....	....	2	0	0	0	0	....	....	....
	NHL Totals		**2**	**0**	**0**	**0**	**0**	**0**	**0**	**2**	**0**	**0**	**0**	**1**	**0.0**	**0**	**0**	**0**	**0**		....	....	....	....	....	....	....	....

Traded to **Florida** by **Washington** with future considerations for Esa Tikkanen, March 9, 1998.

• HAYEK, PETER
Peter Hayek D – L. 5'10", 200 lbs. b: Minneapolis, MN, 11/16/1957.

1979-80	University of Minnesota	WCHA	41	8	14	22	....	....	....	110	....	....	....	....	....	....	....	....	....	....	....	....	....	....	....	....	....	....
	Baltimore Clippers	EHL	....	....	....	....	....	....	....	....	....	....	....	....	....	....	....	....	....	....	4	0	1	1	6	....	....	....
1980-81	Oklahoma City Stars	CHL	28	5	3	8	....	....	....	16	....	....	....	....	....	....	....	....	....	....	....	....	....	....	....	....	....	....
	Baltimore Clippers	EHL	47	18	22	40	....	....	....	55	....	....	....	....	....	....	....	....	....	....	4	0	1	1	0	....	....	....
1981-82	**Minnesota North Stars**	**NHL**	**1**	**0**	**0**	**0**	**0**	**0**	**0**	**0**	**0**	**0**	**0**	**0**	**0.0**	**0**	**0**	**1**	**0**	**–1**	....	....	....	....	....	....	....	....
	Nashville South Stars	CHL	68	3	12	15	....	....	....	131	....	....	....	....	....	....	....	....	....	....	3	1	0	1	4	....	....	....
1982-83	Birmingham South Stars	CHL	14	0	2	2	....	....	....	15	....	....	....	....	....	....	....	....	....	....	....	....	....	....	....	....	....	....
	NHL Totals		**1**	**0**	**0**	**0**	**0**	**0**	**0**	**0**	**0**	**0**	**0**	**0**	**0.0**	**0**	**0**	**1**	**0**		....	....	....	....	....	....	....	....

Signed as a free agent by **Minnesota**, September, 1981.

• HAYES, CHRIS
Chris Hayes LW – L. 5'10", 180 lbs. b: Rouyn, Que., 8/24/1946.

1964-65	Oshawa Generals	OHA	44	8	7	15	....	....	....	52	....	....	....	....	....	....	....	....	....	....	6	1	2	3	15	....	....	....
1965-66	Oshawa Generals	OHA	44	8	14	22	....	....	....	92	....	....	....	....	....	....	....	....	....	....	17	0	2	2	26	....	....	....
1966-67	Oshawa Generals	OHA	30	3	11	14	....	....	....	57	....	....	....	....	....	....	....	....	....	....	....	....	....	....	....	....	....	....

Season	Club	League	REGULAR SEASON GP	G	A	Pts	AG	AA	APts	PIM	PP	SH	GW	S	%	TGF	PGF	TGA	PGA	+/–	PLAYOFFS GP	G	A	Pts	PIM	PP	SH	GW
1967-68	Loyola College	OQAA	DID NOT PLAY – FRESHMAN																									
1968-69	Loyola College	OQAA	STATISTICS NOT AVAILABLE																									
1969-70	Loyola College	OQAA	35	27	48	75	....	....	....	79	....	....	....	....	....	....	....	....	....	....	....	....	....	....	....	....	....	....
1970-71	Loyola College	OUAA	34	26	54	80	....	....	....	....	....	....	....	....	....	....	....	....	....	....	....	....	....	....	....	....	....	....
1971-72	Oklahoma City Blazers	CHL	72	15	38	53	....	....	....	59	....	....	....	....	....	....	....	....	....	....	6	5	4	9	2	....	....	....
	Boston Bruins	**NHL**	....	....	....	....	....	....	....	....	....	....	....	....	....	....	....	....	....	....	**1**	**0**	**0**	**0**	**0**	....	....	....
1972-73	Boston Braves	AHL	63	9	19	28	....	....	....	31	....	....	....	....	....	....	....	....	....	....	10	2	5	7	4	....	....	....
1973-74	Albuquerque 6-Guns	CHL	71	20	28	40	....	....	....	118	....	....	....	....	....	....	....	....	....	....	....	....	....	....	....	....	....	....
1974-75			DID NOT PLAY																									
1975-76	Mohawk Valley Comets	NAHL	4	1	2	3	....	....	....	2	....	....	....	....	....	....	....	....	....	....	....	....	....	....	....	....	....	....
	NHL Totals		**0**	**0**	**0**	**0**	**0**	**0**	**0**	**0**	**0**	**0**	**0**	**0**	**0.0**	**0**	**0**	**0**	**0**		**1**	**0**	**0**	**0**	**0**	**0**	**0**	**0**

Signed as a free agent by **Boston**, September, 1971.

• HAYWARD, RICK

Rick Hayward D – L. 6', 180 lbs. b: Toledo, OH, 2/25/1966. Montreal's 9th choice, 162nd overall, in 1986 Entry Draft.

Season	Club	League	GP	G	A	Pts	AG	AA	APts	PIM	PP	SH	GW	S	%	TGF	PGF	TGA	PGA	+/–	GP	G	A	Pts	PIM	PP	SH	GW
1983-84	Hull Olympiques	QMJHL	67	6	17	23	....	....	....	220	....	....	....	....	....	....	....	....	....	....	....	....	....	....	....	....	....	....
1984-85	Hull Olympiques	QMJHL	56	7	27	34	....	....	....	367	....	....	....	....	....	....	....	....	....	....	....	....	....	....	....	....	....	....
1985-86	Hull Olympiques	QMJHL	59	3	40	43	....	....	....	354	....	....	....	....	....	....	....	....	....	....	15	2	11	13	*98	....	....	....
1986-87	Sherbrooke Canadiens	AHL	46	2	3	5	....	....	....	153	....	....	....	....	....	....	....	....	....	....	3	0	1	1	15	....	....	....
1987-88	Saginaw Hawks	IHL	24	3	4	7	....	....	....	129	....	....	....	....	....	....	....	....	....	....	....	....	....	....	....	....	....	....
	Salt Lake Golden Eagles	IHL	17	1	3	4	....	....	....	124	....	....	....	....	....	....	....	....	....	....	13	0	1	1	120	....	....	....
1988-89	Salt Lake Golden Eagles	IHL	72	4	20	24	....	....	....	313	....	....	....	....	....	....	....	....	....	....	10	4	3	7	42	....	....	....
1989-90	Salt Lake Golden Eagles	IHL	58	5	13	18	....	....	....	419	....	....	....	....	....	....	....	....	....	....	....	....	....	....	....	....	....	....
1990-91	**Los Angeles Kings**	**NHL**	**4**	**0**	**0**	**0**	**0**	**0**	**0**	**5**	**0**	**0**	**0**	**0**	**0.0**	**1**	**0**	**1**	**0**	**0**	....	....	....	....	....	....	....	....
	Phoenix Roadrunners	IHL	60	9	13	22	....	....	....	369	....	....	....	....	....	....	....	....	....	....	7	1	2	3	44	....	....	....
1991-92	Capital District Islanders	AHL	27	3	8	11	....	....	....	139	....	....	....	....	....	....	....	....	....	....	7	0	0	0	58	....	....	....
1992-93	Moncton Hawks	AHL	47	1	3	4	....	....	....	231	....	....	....	....	....	....	....	....	....	....	....	....	....	....	....	....	....	....
	Capital District Islanders	AHL	19	0	1	1	....	....	....	80	....	....	....	....	....	....	....	....	....	....	4	1	1	2	27	....	....	....
1993-94	Cincinnati Cyclones	IHL	61	2	6	8	....	....	....	302	....	....	....	....	....	....	....	....	....	....	8	0	1	1	*99	....	....	....
1994-95	Cleveland Lumberjacks	IHL	56	1	3	4	....	....	....	269	....	....	....	....	....	....	....	....	....	....	3	0	0	0	13	....	....	....
1995-96	Cleveland Lumberjacks	IHL	53	0	6	6	....	....	....	244	....	....	....	....	....	....	....	....	....	....	3	0	0	0	6	....	....	....
1996-97	Cleveland Lumberjacks	IHL	73	2	10	12	....	....	....	244	....	....	....	....	....	....	....	....	....	....	13	0	0	0	16	....	....	....
1997-98	Cleveland Lumberjacks	IHL	41	1	3	4	....	....	....	191	....	....	....	....	....	....	....	....	....	....	....	....	....	....	....	....	....	....
	Quebec Rafales	IHL	13	0	3	3	....	....	....	108	....	....	....	....	....	....	....	....	....	....	....	....	....	....	....	....	....	....
	NHL Totals		**4**	**0**	**0**	**0**	**0**	**0**	**0**	**5**	**0**	**0**	**0**	**0**	**0.0**	**1**	**0**	**1**	**0**		....	....	....	....	....	....	....	....

Traded to **Calgary** by **Montreal** for Martin Nicoletti, February 20, 1988. Signed as a free agent by **LA Kings**, July 15, 1990. Signed as a free agent by **Winnipeg**, July 30, 1992. Traded to **NY Islanders** by **Winnipeg** for future considerations, February 22, 1993.

• HAZLETT, STEVE

Steve Hazlett LW – L. 5'9", 170 lbs. b: Sarnia, Ont., 12/12/1957. Vancouver's 6th choice, 76th overall, in 1977 Amateur Draft.

Season	Club	League	GP	G	A	Pts	AG	AA	APts	PIM	PP	SH	GW	S	%	TGF	PGF	TGA	PGA	+/–	GP	G	A	Pts	PIM	PP	SH	GW
1975-76	Hamilton Kilty B's	Jr. B	60	50	45	95	....	....	....	30	....	....	....	....	....	....	....	....	....	....	....	....	....	....	....	....	....	....
	Hamilton Fincups	OHA	5	3	4	7	....	....	....	0	....	....	....	....	....	....	....	....	....	....	....	....	....	....	....	....	....	....
1976-77	St. Catharines Black Hawks	OHA	66	42	58	100	....	....	....	56	....	....	....	....	....	....	....	....	....	....	....	....	....	....	....	....	....	....
	Canada	WJC-A	7	6	0	6	....	....	....	6	....	....	....	....	....	....	....	....	....	....	....	....	....	....	....	....	....	....
1977-78	Hamilton Fincups	OHA	27	19	25	44	....	....	....	16	....	....	....	....	....	....	....	....	....	....	....	....	....	....	....	....	....	....
	Tulsa Oilers	CHL	15	1	2	3	....	....	....	10	....	....	....	....	....	....	....	....	....	....	....	....	....	....	....	....	....	....
	Fort Wayne Komets	IHL	4	3	1	4	....	....	....	4	....	....	....	....	....	....	....	....	....	....	....	....	....	....	....	....	....	....
1978-79	Dallas Black Hawks	CHL	76	*44	32	76	....	....	....	36	....	....	....	....	....	....	....	....	....	....	9	7	1	8	2	....	....	....
1979-80	**Vancouver Canucks**	**NHL**	**1**	**0**	**0**	**0**	**0**	**0**	**0**	**0**	**0**	**0**	**0**	**2**	**0.0**	**0**	**0**	**1**	**0**	**–1**	....	....	....	....	....	....	....	....
	Dallas Black Hawks	CHL	61	23	23	46	....	....	....	43	....	....	....	....	....	....	....	....	....	....	....	....	....	....	....	....	....	....
1980-81	Dallas Black Hawks	CHL	60	18	13	31	....	....	....	74	....	....	....	....	....	....	....	....	....	....	5	0	0	0	4	....	....	....
1981-82	Dallas Black Hawks	CHL	71	19	34	53	....	....	....	48	....	....	....	....	....	....	....	....	....	....	16	3	4	7	24	....	....	....
1982-83	Fort Wayne Komets	IHL	18	4	0	13	....	....	....	6	....	....	....	....	....	....	....	....	....	....	....	....	....	....	....	....	....	....
	NHL Totals		**1**	**0**	**0**	**0**	**0**	**0**	**0**	**0**	**0**	**0**	**0**	**2**	**0.0**	**0**	**0**	**1**	**0**		....	....	....	....	....	....	....	....

• HEAD, GALEN

Galen Head RW R. 6'0", 100 lbs. b: Grande Prairie, Alta., 4/16/1947.

Season	Club	League	GP	G	A	Pts	AG	AA	APts	PIM	PP	SH	GW	S	%	TGF	PGF	TGA	PGA	+/–	GP	G	A	Pts	PIM	PP	SH	GW
1965-66	Edmonton Eskimos	ASHL	....	6	5	11	....	....	....	4	....	....	....	....	....	....	....	....	....	....	....	....	....	....	....	....	....	....
1966-67	Edmonton Oil Kings	WCJHL	56	50	42	92	....	....	....	43	....	....	....	....	....	....	....	....	....	....	9	4	8	12	4	....	....	....
1967-68	**Detroit Red Wings**	**NHL**	**1**	**0**	**0**	**0**	**0**	**0**	**0**	**0**	**0**	**0**	**0**	**0**	**0.0**	**0**	**0**	**1**	**0**	**–1**	....	....	....	....	....	....	....	....
	Fort Worth Wings	CHL	4	3	1	4	....	....	....	4	....	....	....	....	....	....	....	....	....	....	2	1	0	1	0	....	....	....
	Johnstown Jets	EHL	70	53	52	105	....	....	....	31	....	....	....	....	....	....	....	....	....	....	3	2	0	2	0	....	....	....
1968-69	Johnstown Jets	EHL	72	*67	54	121	....	....	....	76	....	....	....	....	....	....	....	....	....	....	3	2	0	2	2	....	....	....
1969-70	Salt Lake Golden Eagles	WHL	43	9	12	21	....	....	....	6	....	....	....	....	....	....	....	....	....	....	....	....	....	....	....	....	....	....
1970-71	Johnstown Jets	EHL	67	31	27	58	....	....	....	42	....	....	....	....	....	....	....	....	....	....	10	7	3	10	2	....	....	....
1971-72	Johnstown Jets	EHL	75	37	34	71	....	....	....	43	....	....	....	....	....	....	....	....	....	....	11	2	5	7	2	....	....	....
1972-73	Johnstown Jets	EHL	72	44	33	77	....	....	....	37	....	....	....	....	....	....	....	....	....	....	12	4	6	10	6	....	....	....
1973-74	Johnstown Jets	EHL	74	31	40	71	....	....	....	24	....	....	....	....	....	....	....	....	....	....	12	5	3	8	2	....	....	....
1974-75	Johnstown Jets	NAHL	58	18	23	41	....	....	....	30	....	....	....	....	....	....	....	....	....	....	15	8	10	18	....	....	....	....
1975-76	Johnstown Jets	NAHL	73	27	30	57	....	....	....	44	....	....	....	....	....	....	....	....	....	....	9	3	3	6	8	....	....	....
	NHL Totals		**1**	**0**	**0**	**0**	**0**	**0**	**0**	**0**	**0**	**0**	**0**	**0**	**0.0**	**0**	**0**	**1**	**0**		....	....	....	....	....	....	....	....

EHL North First All-Star Team (1969)

Claimed by **Salt Lake** (WHL) from **Detroit** in Reverse Draft, June 10, 1969.

• HEALEY, PAUL

Paul Healey RW – R. 6'2", 196 lbs. b: Edmonton, Alta., 3/20/1975. Philadelphia's 7th choice, 192nd overall, in 1993 Entry Draft.

Season	Club	League	GP	G	A	Pts	AG	AA	APts	PIM	PP	SH	GW	S	%	TGF	PGF	TGA	PGA	+/–	GP	G	A	Pts	PIM	PP	SH	GW
1992-93	Prince Albert Raiders	WHL	72	12	20	32	....	....	....	66	....	....	....	....	....	....	....	....	....	....	....	....	....	....	....	....	....	....
1993-94	Prince Albert Raiders	WHL	63	23	26	49	....	....	....	70	....	....	....	....	....	....	....	....	....	....	....	....	....	....	....	....	....	....
1994-95	Prince Albert Raiders	WHL	71	43	50	93	....	....	....	67	....	....	....	....	....	....	....	....	....	....	12	3	4	7	2	....	....	....
1995-96	Hershey Bears	AHL	60	7	15	22	....	....	....	35	....	....	....	....	....	....	....	....	....	....	....	....	....	....	....	....	....	....
1996-97	**Philadelphia Flyers**	**NHL**	**2**	**0**	**0**	**0**	**0**	**0**	**0**	**0**	**0**	**0**	**0**	**0**	**0.0**	**0**	**0**	**0**	**0**	**0**	....	....	....	....	....	....	....	....
	Philadelphia Phantoms	AHL	64	21	19	40	....	....	....	56	....	....	....	....	....	....	....	....	....	....	10	4	1	5	10	....	....	....
1997-98	**Philadelphia Flyers**	**NHL**	**4**	**0**	**0**	**0**	**0**	**0**	**0**	**12**	**0**	**0**	**0**	**0**	**0.0**	**0**	**0**	**0**	**0**	**0**	....	....	....	....	....	....	....	....
	Philadelphia Phantoms	AHL	71	34	18	52	....	....	....	48	....	....	....	....	....	....	....	....	....	....	20	6	2	8	4	....	....	....
	NHL Totals		**6**	**0**	**0**	**0**	**0**	**0**	**0**	**12**	**0**	**0**	**0**	**0**	**0.0**	**0**	**0**	**0**	**0**		....	....	....	....	....	....	....	....

WHL East Second All-Star Team (1995)

• HEAPHY, SHAWN

Shawn Heaphy C – L. 5'8", 180 lbs. b: Sudbury, Ont., 11/27/1968. Calgary's 1st choice, 26th overall, in 1989 Supplemental Draft.

Season	Club	League	GP	G	A	Pts	AG	AA	APts	PIM	PP	SH	GW	S	%	TGF	PGF	TGA	PGA	+/–	GP	G	A	Pts	PIM	PP	SH	GW
1984-85	Sudbury AAA	Midget	....	*132	108	*240	....	....	....	....	....	....	....	....	....	....	....	....	....	....	....	....	....	....	....	....	....	....
1985-86	Stratford Cullitons	OJHL	....	50	34	84	....	....	....	....	....	....	....	....	....	....	....	....	....	....	....	....	....	....	....	....	....	....
1986-87	Stratford Cullitons	OJHL	....	*67	63	*130	....	....	....	....	....	....	....	....	....	....	....	....	....	....	....	....	....	....	....	....	....	....
1987-88	Michigan State Spartans	CCHA	44	19	24	43	....	....	....	48	....	....	....	....	....	....	....	....	....	....	....	....	....	....	....	....	....	....
1988-89	Michigan State Spartans	CCHA	47	26	17	43	....	....	....	80	....	....	....	....	....	....	....	....	....	....	....	....	....	....	....	....	....	....
1989-90	Michigan State Spartans	CCHA	45	28	31	59	....	....	....	64	....	....	....	....	....	....	....	....	....	....	....	....	....	....	....	....	....	....
1990-91	Michigan State Spartans	CCHA	39	30	19	49	....	....	....	57	....	....	....	....	....	....	....	....	....	....	....	....	....	....	....	....	....	....
	Salt Lake Golden Eagles	IHL	....	....	....	....	....	....	....	....	....	....	....	....	....	....	....	....	....	....	1	0	0	0	0	....	....	....
1991-92	Salt Lake Golden Eagles	IHL	76	41	36	77	....	....	....	85	....	....	....	....	....	....	....	....	....	....	5	2	2	4	2	....	....	....
1992-93	**Calgary Flames**	**NHL**	**1**	**0**	**0**	**0**	**0**	**0**	**0**	**0**	**0**	**0**	**0**	**2**	**0.0**	**0**	**0**	**0**	**0**	**0**	....	....	....	....	....	....	....	....
	Salt Lake Golden Eagles	IHL	78	29	36	65	....	....	....	63	....	....	....	....	....	....	....	....	....	....	....	....	....	....	....	....	....	....
1993-94	SG Brunico	Alpenliga	28	20	19	39	....	....	....	42	....	....	....	....	....	....	....	....	....	....	....	....	....	....	....	....	....	....
	SG Brunico	Italy	11	10	0	10	....	....	....	15	....	....	....	....	....	....	....	....	....	....	....	....	....	....	....	....	....	....
	Las Vegas Thunder	IHL	37	10	5	15	....	....	....	45	....	....	....	....	....	....	....	....	....	....	5	0	0	0	6	....	....	....
1994-95	Worcester IceCats	AHL	70	23	28	51	....	....	....	50	....	....	....	....	....	....	....	....	....	....	....	....	....	....	....	....	....	....
	NHL Totals		**1**	**0**	**0**	**0**	**0**	**0**	**0**	**0**	**0**	**0**	**0**	**2**	**0.0**	**0**	**0**	**0**	**0**		....	....	....	....	....	....	....	....

			REGULAR SEASON																		PLAYOFFS							
Season	Club	League	GP	G	A	Pts	AG	AA	APts	PIM	PP	SH	GW	S	%	TGF	PGF	TGA	PGA	+/–	GP	G	A	Pts	PIM	PP	SH	GW

• HEASLIP, MARK — Mark Heaslip — RW – R. 5'10", 190 lbs. b: Duluth, MN, 12/26/1951.

1971-72	University of Minnesota-Duluth	WCHA	33	8	18	26	....	....	....	37	....	....	....	....	....	....	....	....	....	....	....	....	....	....	....	....	....	....
1972-73	University of Minnesota-Duluth	WCHA	36	25	20	45	....	....	....	46	....	....	....	....	....	....	....	....	....	....	....	....	....	....	....	....	....	....
1973-74	Springfield Kings	AHL	76	19	31	50	....	....	....	110	....	....	....	....	....	....	....	....	....	....	....	....	....	....	....	....	....	....
1974-75	Springfield Indians	AHL	75	18	39	57	....	....	....	86	....	....	....	....	....	....	....	....	....	....	17	2	11	13	15	....	....	....
1975-76	Fort Worth Texans	CHL	43	7	14	21	....	....	....	32	....	....	....	....	....	....	....	....	....	....	....	....	....	....	....	....	....	....
	Oklahoma City Blazers	CHL	33	3	8	11	....	....	....	16	....	....	....	....	....	....	....	....	....	....	4	0	0	0	12	....	....	....
1976-77	**New York Rangers**	**NHL**	**19**	**1**	**0**	**1**	**1**	**0**	**1**	**31**	**0**	**0**	**0**	**9**	**11.1**	**3**	**0**	**12**	**6**	**–3**	....	....	....	....	....	....	....	....
	New Haven Nighthawks	AHL	24	8	16	24	....	....	....	35	....	....	....	....	....	....	....	....	....	....	6	1	1	2	6	....	....	....
	United States	WEC-A	10	0	1	1	....	....	....	8	....	....	....	....	....	....	....	....	....	....	....	....	....	....	....	....	....	....
1977-78	**New York Rangers**	**NHL**	**29**	**5**	**10**	**15**	**5**	**8**	**13**	**34**	**0**	**0**	**0**	**32**	**15.6**	**23**	**1**	**22**	**3**	**+3**	**3**	**0**	**0**	**0**	**0**	**0**	**0**	**0**
	New Haven Nighthawks	AHL	50	8	23	31	....	....	....	18	....	....	....	....	....	....	....	....	....	....	....	....	....	....	....	....	....	....
1978-79	**Los Angeles Kings**	**NHL**	**69**	**4**	**9**	**13**	**4**	**7**	**11**	**45**	**0**	**0**	**1**	**53**	**7.5**	**29**	**3**	**51**	**15**	**–10**	**2**	**0**	**0**	**0**	**2**	**0**	**0**	**0**
1979-80	Tulsa Oilers	CHL	68	14	18	32	....	....	....	33	....	....	....	....	....	....	....	....	....	....	3	0	0	0	4	....	....	....
	NHL Totals		**117**	**10**	**19**	**29**	**10**	**15**	**25**	**110**	**0**	**0**	**1**	**94**	**10.6**	**55**	**4**	**85**	**24**		**5**	**0**	**0**	**0**	**2**	**0**	**0**	**0**

Signed as a free agent by **LA Kings**, September, 1973. Traded to **NY Rangers** by **LA Kings** for John Campbell, May 28, 1976. Signed as a free agent by **LA Kings**, June 14, 1978. Claimed by **Winnipeg** from **LA Kings** in Expansion Draft, June 13, 1979.

• HEATH, RANDY — Randy Heath — LW – L. 5'8", 160 lbs. b: Vancouver, B.C., 11/11/1964. NY Rangers' 2nd choice, 33rd overall, in 1983 Entry Draft.

1980-81	Vancouver Blue Hawks	BCJHL	50	35	35	70	....	....	....	30	....	....	....	....	....	....	....	....	....	....	....	....	....	....	....	....	....	....
	Portland Winter Hawks	WHL	2	1	0	1	....	....	....	0	....	....	....	....	....	....	....	....	....	....	....	....	....	....	....	....	....	....
1981-82	Portland Winter Hawks	WHL	65	52	47	99	....	....	....	65	....	....	....	....	....	....	....	....	....	....	15	13	19	32	4	....	....	....
1982-83	Portland Winter Hawks	WHL	72	82	69	151	....	....	....	52	....	....	....	....	....	....	....	....	....	....	14	6	12	18	12	....	....	....
1983-84	Portland Winter Hawks	WHL	60	44	46	90	....	....	....	107	....	....	....	....	....	....	....	....	....	....	14	9	12	21	10	....	....	....
	Canada	WJC-A	7	3	6	9	....	....	....	12	....	....	....	....	....	....	....	....	....	....	....	....	....	....	....	....	....	....
1984-85	**New York Rangers**	**NHL**	**12**	**2**	**3**	**5**	**2**	**2**	**4**	**15**	**1**	**0**	**0**	**18**	**11.1**	**8**	**2**	**7**	**0**	**–1**	....	....	....	....	....	....	....	....
	New Haven Nighthawks	AHL	60	23	26	49	....	....	....	29	....	....	....	....	....	....	....	....	....	....	....	....	....	....	....	....	....	....
1985-86	**New York Rangers**	**NHL**	**1**	**0**	**1**	**1**	**0**	**1**	**1**	**0**	**0**	**0**	**0**	**1**	**0.0**	**1**	**0**	**0**	**0**	**+1**	....	....	....	....	....	....	....	....
	New Haven Nighthawks	AHL	77	36	38	74	....	....	....	53	....	....	....	....	....	....	....	....	....	....	5	3	2	5	7	....	....	....
1986-87	Skelleftea	Sweden	36	12	14	26	....	....	....	40	....	....	....	....	....	....	....	....	....	....	....	....	....	....	....	....	....	....
1987-88	Vasteras IK	Sweden	31	26	25	51	....	....	....	50	....	....	....	....	....	....	....	....	....	....	14	11	9	20	12	....	....	....
1988-89	Vasteras IK	Sweden	22	5	10	15	....	....	....	14	....	....	....	....	....	....	....	....	....	....	....	....	....	....	....	....	....	....
	NHL Totals		**13**	**2**	**4**	**6**	**2**	**3**	**5**	**15**	**1**	**0**	**0**	**19**	**10.5**	**9**	**2**	**7**	**0**		....	....	....	....	....	....	....	....

WHL First All-Star Team (1983) • Memorial Cup All-Star Team (1983) • WHL West First All-Star Team (1984)

• HEDBERG, ANDERS — Anders Hedberg — RW – L. 5'11", 175 lbs. b: Ornskoldsvik, Sweden, 2/25/1951.

1969-70	MoDo AIK	Sweden	14	9	*14	23	....	....	....	2	....	....	....	....	....	....	....	....	....	....	....	....	....	....	....	....	....	....
	Sweden	WEC-A	9	2	3	5	....	....	....	0	....	....	....	....	....	....	....	....	....	....	....	....	....	....	....	....	....	....
1970-71	MoDo AIK	Sweden	14	7	6	13	....	....	....	0	....	....	....	....	....	....	....	....	....	....	....	....	....	....	....	....	....	....
1971-72	MoDo AIK	Sweden	2	1	0	1	....	....	....	0	....	....	....	....	....	....	....	....	....	....	....	....	....	....	....	....	....	....
	Sweden	WEC-A	10	6	5	11	....	....	....	4	....	....	....	....	....	....	....	....	....	....	....	....	....	....	....	....	....	....
1972-73	Djurgarden IF Stockholm	Sweden	12	6	3	9	....	....	....	2	....	....	....	....	....	....	....	....	....	....	14	6	7	13	4	....	....	....
	Sweden	WEC-A	10	2	5	7	....	....	....	0	....	....	....	....	....	....	....	....	....	....	....	....	....	....	....	....	....	....
1973-74	Djurgarden IF Stockholm	Sweden	STATISTICS NOT AVAILABLE																									
	Sweden	WEC-A	10	7	3	10	....	....	....	2	....	....	....	....	....	....	....	....	....	....	....	....	....	....	....	....	....	....
1974-75	Winnipeg Jets	WHA	65	53	47	100	....	....	....	45	....	....	....	....	....	....	....	....	....	....	....	....	....	....	....	....	....	....
1975-76	Winnipeg Jets	WHA	76	50	55	105	....	....	....	48	....	....	....	....	....	....	....	....	....	....	13	*13	6	19	15	....	....	....
1976-77	Sweden	C Cup	5	3	2	5	....	....	....	4	....	....	....	....	....	....	....	....	....	....	....	....	....	....	....	....	....	....
	Winnipeg Jets	WHA	68	*70	61	131	....	....	....	48	....	....	....	....	....	....	....	....	....	....	20	13	16	29	13	....	....	....
1977-78	Winnipeg Jets	WHA	77	63	59	122	....	....	....	60	....	....	....	....	....	....	....	....	....	....	9	9	6	15	2	....	....	....
1978-79	**New York Rangers**	**NHL**	**80**	**33**	**45**	**78**	**30**	**34**	**64**	**33**	**6**	**0**	**5**	**214**	**15.4**	**121**	**41**	**72**	**11**	**+19**	**18**	**4**	**5**	**9**	**12**	**0**	**1**	**1**
	NHL All-Stars	Chal Cup	2	0	0	0	....	....	....	0	....	....	....	....	....	....	....	....	....	....	....	....	....	....	....	....	....	....
1979-80	**New York Rangers**	**NHL**	**80**	**32**	**39**	**71**	**29**	**30**	**59**	**21**	**7**	**0**	**4**	**241**	**13.3**	**106**	**35**	**64**	**6**	**+13**	**9**	**3**	**2**	**5**	**7**	**0**	**0**	**1**
1980-81	**New York Rangers**	**NHL**	**80**	**30**	**40**	**70**	**25**	**28**	**53**	**52**	**7**	**1**	**3**	**243**	**12.3**	**110**	**34**	**91**	**15**	**0**	**14**	**8**	**8**	**16**	**6**	**3**	**0**	**0**
1981-82	Sweden	C Cup	5	4	2	6	....	....	....	0	....	....	....	....	....	....	....	....	....	....	....	....	....	....	....	....	....	....
	New York Rangers	**NHL**	**4**	**0**	**1**	**1**	**0**	**1**	**1**	**0**	**0**	**0**	**0**	**8**	**0.0**	**2**	**0**	**6**	**2**	**–2**	....	....	....	....	....	....	....	....
1982-83	**New York Rangers**	**NHL**	**78**	**25**	**34**	**59**	**21**	**23**	**44**	**12**	**4**	**0**	**5**	**163**	**15.3**	**99**	**23**	**63**	**4**	**+17**	**9**	**4**	**8**	**12**	**4**	**1**	**0**	**0**
1983-84	**New York Rangers**	**NHL**	**79**	**32**	**35**	**67**	**26**	**24**	**50**	**16**	**6**	**0**	**2**	**209**	**15.3**	**107**	**32**	**57**	**0**	**+18**	**5**	**1**	**0**	**1**	**0**	**0**	**0**	**0**
1984-85	**New York Rangers**	**NHL**	**64**	**20**	**31**	**51**	**16**	**21**	**37**	**10**	**9**	**0**	**2**	**141**	**14.2**	**86**	**38**	**68**	**5**	**–15**	**3**	**2**	**1**	**3**	**2**	**0**	**0**	**0**
	NHL Totals		**465**	**172**	**225**	**397**	**147**	**161**	**308**	**144**	**39**	**1**	**21**	**1219**	**14.1**	**631**	**203**	**421**	**43**		**58**	**22**	**24**	**46**	**31**	**4**	**1**	**2**
	Other Major League Totals		286	236	222	458	....	....	....	201	....	....	....	....	....	....	....	....	....		42	35	28	63	30	....	....	....

Named Best Forward at EJC-A (1970) • WHA Second All-Star Team (1975) • Won Lou Kaplan Trophy (WHA Rookie of the Year) (1975) • WHA First All-Star Team (1976, 1977, 1978) • Won Bill Masterton Trophy (1985)

Played in NHL All-Star Game (1985)

Signed as a free agent by **Winnipeg** (WHA), May 3, 1974. Signed as a free agent by **NY Rangers**, June 5, 1978.

• HEDICAN, BRET — Bret Hedican — D – L. 6'2", 195 lbs. b: St. Paul, MN, 8/10/1970. St. Louis' 10th choice, 198th overall, in 1988 Entry Draft.

1987-88	North St. Paul High	H.S.	23	15	19	34	....	....	....	16	....	....	....	....	....	....	....	....	....	....	....	....	....	....	....	....	....	....
1988-89	St. Cloud State Huskies	NCAA	28	5	3	8	....	....	....	28	....	....	....	....	....	....	....	....	....	....	....	....	....	....	....	....	....	....
1989-90	St. Cloud State Huskies	NCAA	36	4	17	21	....	....	....	37	....	....	....	....	....	....	....	....	....	....	....	....	....	....	....	....	....	....
1990-91	St. Cloud State Huskies	WCHA	41	21	26	47	....	....	....	26	....	....	....	....	....	....	....	....	....	....	....	....	....	....	....	....	....	....
1991-92	United States	Nat-Team	54	1	8	9	....	....	....	59	....	....	....	....	....	....	....	....	....	....	....	....	....	....	....	....	....	....
	United States	Olympics	8	0	0	0	....	....	....	4	....	....	....	....	....	....	....	....	....	....	....	....	....	....	....	....	....	....
	St. Louis Blues	**NHL**	**4**	**1**	**0**	**1**	**1**	**0**	**1**	**0**	**0**	**0**	**0**	**1**	**100.0**	**6**	**0**	**5**	**0**	**+1**	**5**	**0**	**0**	**0**	**0**	**0**	**0**	**0**
1992-93	**St. Louis Blues**	**NHL**	**42**	**0**	**8**	**8**	**0**	**5**	**5**	**30**	**0**	**0**	**0**	**40**	**0.0**	**30**	**6**	**40**	**14**	**–2**	**10**	**0**	**0**	**0**	**14**	**0**	**0**	**0**
	Peoria Rivermen	IHL	19	0	8	8	....	....	....	10	....	....	....	....	....	....	....	....	....	....	....	....	....	....	....	....	....	....
1993-94	**St. Louis Blues**	**NHL**	**61**	**0**	**11**	**11**	**0**	**8**	**8**	**64**	**0**	**0**	**0**	**78**	**0.0**	**45**	**5**	**59**	**11**	**–8**	....	....	....	....	....	....	....	....
	Vancouver Canucks	**NHL**	**8**	**0**	**1**	**1**	**0**	**1**	**1**	**0**	**0**	**0**	**0**	**10**	**0.0**	**4**	**1**	**3**	**1**	**+1**	**24**	**1**	**6**	**7**	**16**	**0**	**0**	**0**
1994-95	**Vancouver Canucks**	**NHL**	**45**	**2**	**11**	**13**	**4**	**16**	**20**	**34**	**0**	**0**	**0**	**56**	**3.6**	**41**	**6**	**54**	**16**	**–3**	**11**	**0**	**2**	**2**	**6**	**0**	**0**	**0**
1995-96	**Vancouver Canucks**	**NHL**	**77**	**6**	**23**	**29**	**6**	**19**	**25**	**83**	**1**	**0**	**0**	**113**	**5.3**	**84**	**13**	**85**	**22**	**+8**	**6**	**0**	**1**	**1**	**10**	**0**	**0**	**0**
1996-97	**Vancouver Canucks**	**NHL**	**67**	**4**	**15**	**19**	**4**	**13**	**17**	**51**	**2**	**0**	**1**	**93**	**4.3**	**66**	**12**	**78**	**21**	**–3**	....	....	....	....	....	....	....	....
	United States	WC-A	8	0	5	5	....	....	....	10	....	....	....	....	....	....	....	....	....	....	....	....	....	....	....	....	....	....
1997-98	**Vancouver Canucks**	**NHL**	**71**	**3**	**24**	**27**	**4**	**23**	**27**	**79**	**1**	**0**	**0**	**84**	**3.6**	**68**	**10**	**79**	**24**	**+3**	....	....	....	....	....	....	....	....
	NHL Totals		**375**	**16**	**93**	**109**	**19**	**85**	**104**	**341**	**4**	**0**	**1**	**475**	**3.4**	**344**	**53**	**403**	**109**		**56**	**1**	**9**	**10**	**46**	**0**	**0**	**0**

WCHA First All-Star Team (1991)

Traded to **Vancouver** by **St. Louis** with Jeff Brown and Nathan Lafayette for Craig Janney, March 21, 1994.

• HEIDT, MICHAEL — Michael Heidt — D – L. 6'1", 190 lbs. b: Calgary, Alta., 11/4/1963. Los Angeles' 1st choice, 27th overall, in 1982 Entry Draft.

1980-81	Calgary Canucks	AJHL	56	28	63	91	....	....	....	104	....	....	....	....	....	....	....	....	....	....	....	....	....	....	....	....	....	....
	Calgary Wranglers	WHL	12	1	3	4	....	....	....	6	....	....	....	....	....	....	....	....	....	....	22	2	10	12	5	....	....	....
1981-82	Calgary Wranglers	WHL	70	13	44	57	....	....	....	142	....	....	....	....	....	....	....	....	....	....	9	2	3	5	21	....	....	....
1982-83	Calgary Wranglers	WHL	71	30	65	95	....	....	....	101	....	....	....	....	....	....	....	....	....	....	15	0	11	11	44	....	....	....
1983-84	**Los Angeles Kings**	**NHL**	**6**	**0**	**1**	**1**	**0**	**1**	**1**	**7**	**0**	**0**	**0**	**1**	**0.0**	**3**	**0**	**6**	**2**	**–1**	....	....	....	....	....	....	....	....
	New Haven Nighthawks	AHL	54	4	20	24	....	....	....	49	....	....	....	....	....	....	....	....	....	....	....	....	....	....	....	....	....	....
1984-85	New Haven Nighthawks	AHL	4	0	1	1	....	....	....	0	....	....	....	....	....	....	....	....	....	....	....	....	....	....	....	....	....	....
	Toledo Goaldiggers	IHL	4	0	0	0	....	....	....	0	....	....	....	....	....	....	....	....	....	....	....	....	....	....	....	....	....	....
	Nova Scotia Voyageurs	AHL	27	1	7	8	....	....	....	16	....	....	....	....	....	....	....	....	....	....	5	0	2	2	7	....	....	....
1985-86			DID NOT PLAY																									
1986-87	Bayreuth	Germany	52	41	84	125	....	....	....	102	....	....	....	....	....	....	....	....	....	....	....	....	....	....	....	....	....	....

Season	Club	League	REGULAR SEASON																		PLAYOFFS							
			GP	G	A	Pts	AG	AA	APts	PIM	PP	SH	GW	S	%	TGF	PGF	TGA	PGA	+/–	GP	G	A	Pts	PIM	PP	SH	GW
1987-88	Bayreuth	Germany	22	16	29	45	....	....	....	51	....	....	....	....	....	....	....	....	....	....	....	....	....	....	....	....	....	....
	Hedos	Germany	22	9	38	47	....	....	....	20	....	....	....	....	....	....	....	....	....	....	....	....	....	....	....	....	....	....
1988-89	Schwenningen ERC	Germany	36	10	22	32	....	....	....	42	....	....	....	....	....	....	....	....	....	....	2	1	1	2	2	....	....	....
1989-90	Schwenningen ERC	Germany	36	7	37	44	....	....	....	26	....	....	....	....	....	....	....	....	....	....	10	3	8	11	8	....	....	....
1990-91	SB Rosenheim	Germany	34	7	32	39	....	....	....	28	....	....	....	....	....	....	....	....	....	....	11	3	4	7	6	....	....	....
1991-92	SB Rosenheim	Germany	43	18	28	46	....	....	....	18	....	....	....	....	....	....	....	....	....	....	10	2	10	12	2	....	....	....
	Germany	Olympics	8	0	1	1	....	....	....	6	....	....	....	....	....	....	....	....	....	....	....	....	....	....	....	....	....	....
	Germany	WC-A	6	3	0	3	....	....	....	4	....	....	....	....	....	....	....	....	....	....	....	....	....	....	....	....	....	....
1992-93	Mannheim Eagles	Germany	42	10	27	37	....	....	....	20	....	....	....	....	....	....	....	....	....	....	8	4	3	7	6	....	....	....
1993-94	Mannheim Eagles	Germany	44	14	33	47	....	....	....	28	....	....	....	....	....	....	....	....	....	....	4	0	2	2	4	....	....	....
1994-95	Mannheim Eagles	Germany	37	9	25	34	....	....	....	36	....	....	....	....	....	....	....	....	....	....	10	1	9	10	6	....	....	....
1995-96	Mannheim Eagles	Germany	49	5	24	29	....	....	....	26	....	....	....	....	....	....	....	....	....	....	11	3	6	9	6	....	....	....
	Germany	WC-A	6	1	0	1	....	....	....	4	....	....	....	....	....	....	....	....	....	....	....	....	....	....	....	....	....	....
1996-97	Germany	W Cup	4	0	1	1	....	....	....	2	....	....	....	....	....	....	....	....	....	....	....	....	....	....	....	....	....	....
	EV Landshut	Germany	36	4	16	20	....	....	....	18	....	....	....	....	....	....	....	....	....	....	7	1	2	3	8	....	....	....
1997-98	EV Landshut	Germany	14	2	6	8	....	....	....	12	....	....	....	....	....	....	....	....	....	....	....	....	....	....	....	....	....	....
	NHL Totals		**6**	**0**	**1**	**1**	**0**	**1**	**1**	**7**	**0**	**0**	**0**	**1**	**0.0**	**3**	**0**	**6**	**2**		....	....	....	....	....	....	....	....

● HEINDL, BILL

Bill Heindl LW – L. 5′10″, 175 lbs. b: Sherbrooke, Quebec, 5/13/1946. d: 3/1/1992.

Season	Club	League	GP	G	A	Pts	AG	AA	APts	PIM	PP	SH	GW	S	%	TGF	PGF	TGA	PGA	+/–	GP	G	A	Pts	PIM	PP	SH	GW
1963-64	Winnipeg Braves	MJHL	26	7	7	14	....	....	....	18	....	....	....	....	....	....	....	....	....	....	....	....	....	....	....	....	....	....
1964-65	Winnipeg Braves	MJHL	45	27	33	60	....	....	....	22	....	....	....	....	....	....	....	....	....	....	15	5	5	10	10	....	....	....
1965-66	Oshawa Generals	OHA	48	15	26	41	....	....	....	46	....	....	....	....	....	....	....	....	....	....	17	4	5	9	10	....	....	....
1966-67	Clinton Comets	EHL	72	17	20	37	....	....	....	7	....	....	....	....	....	....	....	....	....	....	9	3	2	5	13	....	....	....
1967-68	Clinton Comets	EHL	72	52	53	105	....	....	....	20	....	....	....	....	....	....	....	....	....	....	14	10	5	15	7	....	....	....
1968-69	Canada	Nat-Team	STATISTICS NOT AVAILABLE																									
	Canada	WEC-A	9	4	1	5	....	....	....	2	....	....	....	....	....	....	....	....	....	....	....	....	....	....	....	....	....	....
1969-70	Canada	Nat-Team	STATISTICS NOT AVAILABLE																									
1970-71	**Minnesota North Stars**	**NHL**	**12**	**1**	**1**	**2**	**1**	**1**	**2**	**0**	**0**	**0**	**0**	**18**	**5.6**	**4**	**0**	**5**	**0**	**–1**	....	....	....	....	....	....	....	....
	Cleveland Barons	AHL	60	25	11	36	....	....	....	22	....	....	....	....	....	....	....	....	....	....	8	3	5	8	0	....	....	....
1971-72	**Minnesota North Stars**	**NHL**	**2**	**0**	**0**	**0**	**0**	**0**	**0**	**0**	**0**	**0**	**0**	**1**	**0.0**	**0**	**0**	**0**	**0**	**0**	....	....	....	....	....	....	....	....
	Cleveland Barons	AHL	70	22	25	47	....	....	....	19	....	....	....	....	....	....	....	....	....	....	6	0	3	3	2	....	....	....
1972-73	**New York Rangers**	**NHL**	**4**	**1**	**0**	**1**	**1**	**0**	**1**	**0**	**0**	**0**	**0**	**6**	**16.7**	**1**	**0**	**1**	**1**	**+1**	....	....	....	....	....	....	....	....
	Providence Reds	AHL	66	21	43	64	....	....	....	10	....	....	....	....	....	....	....	....	....	....	4	1	0	1	2	....	....	....
1973-74	Cleveland Crusaders	WHA	67	4	14	18	....	....	....	4	....	....	....	....	....	....	....	....	....	....	5	0	1	1	2	....	....	....
	Jacksonville Barons	AHL	9	3	2	5	....	....	....	0	....	....	....	....	....	....	....	....	....	....	....	....	....	....	....	....	....	....
1974-75	Cape Cod Codders	NAHL	74	23	36	59	....	....	....	8	....	....	....	....	....	....	....	....	....	....	....	....	....	....	....	....	....	....
	NHL Totals		**18**	**2**	**1**	**3**	**2**	**1**	**3**	**0**	**0**	**0**	**0**	**25**	**8.0**	**5**	**0**	**6**	**1**		....	....	....	....	....	....	....	....
	Other Major League Totals		67	4	14	18	....	....	....	4	....	....	....	....	....	....	....	....	....	....	5	0	1	1	2	....	....	....

Claimed by **Minnesota** (Cleveland - AHL) from **Boston** in Reverse Draft, June, 1970. Selected by **Winnipeg** (WHA) in 1972 WHA General Player Draft, February 12, 1972. Claimed by **Atlanta** from **Minnesota** in Expansion Draft, June, 1972. Traded to **NY Rangers** by **Atlanta** for Bill Hogaboom, June, 1972. WHA rights traded to **Cleveland** (WHA) by **Winnipeg** (WHA) for cash, June, 1973.

● HEINZE, STEPHEN

Stephen Heinze RW – R. 5′11″, 202 lbs. b: Lawrence, MA, 1/30/1970. Boston's 2nd choice, 60th overall, in 1988 Entry Draft.

Season	Club	League	GP	G	A	Pts	AG	AA	APts	PIM	PP	SH	GW	S	%	TGF	PGF	TGA	PGA	+/–	GP	G	A	Pts	PIM	PP	SH	GW
1987-88	Lawrence Academy	H.S.	23	30	25	55	....	....	....	....	....	....	....	....	....	....	....	....	....	....	....	....	....	....	....	....	....	....
1988-89	Boston College	H.E.	36	26	23	49	....	....	....	26	....	....	....	....	....	....	....	....	....	....	....	....	....	....	....	....	....	....
1989-90	Boston College	H.E.	40	27	36	63	....	....	....	41	....	....	....	....	....	....	....	....	....	....	....	....	....	....	....	....	....	....
1990-91	Boston College	H.E.	35	21	26	47	....	....	....	35	....	....	....	....	....	....	....	....	....	....	....	....	....	....	....	....	....	....
1991-92	United States	Nat-Team	49	18	15	33	....	....	....	38	....	....	....	....	....	....	....	....	....	....	....	....	....	....	....	....	....	....
	United States	Olympics	8	1	0	1	....	....	....	8	....	....	....	....	....	....	....	....	....	....	....	....	....	....	....	....	....	....
	Boston Bruins	**NHL**	**14**	**3**	**4**	**7**	**3**	**3**	**6**	**6**	**0**	**0**	**2**	**29**	**10.3**	**8**	**0**	**9**	**0**	**–1**	**7**	**0**	**3**	**3**	**17**	**0**	**0**	**0**
1992-93	**Boston Bruins**	**NHL**	**73**	**18**	**13**	**31**	**15**	**9**	**24**	**24**	**0**	**2**	**4**	**146**	**12.3**	**51**	**0**	**51**	**20**	**+20**	**4**	**1**	**1**	**2**	**2**	**0**	**0**	**0**
1993-94	**Boston Bruins**	**NHL**	**77**	**10**	**11**	**21**	**9**	**8**	**17**	**32**	**0**	**2**	**1**	**183**	**5.5**	**37**	**1**	**54**	**10**	**–2**	**13**	**2**	**3**	**5**	**7**	**0**	**0**	**0**
1994-95	**Boston Bruins**	**NHL**	**36**	**7**	**9**	**16**	**12**	**13**	**25**	**23**	**0**	**1**	**0**	**70**	**10.0**	**19**	**0**	**29**	**10**	**0**	**5**	**0**	**0**	**0**	**0**	**0**	**0**	**0**
1995-96	**Boston Bruins**	**NHL**	**76**	**16**	**12**	**28**	**16**	**10**	**26**	**43**	**0**	**1**	**3**	**129**	**12.4**	**34**	**0**	**55**	**18**	**–7**	**5**	**1**	**1**	**2**	**4**	**0**	**1**	**0**
1996-97	**Boston Bruins**	**NHL**	**30**	**17**	**8**	**25**	**18**	**7**	**25**	**27**	**4**	**2**	**2**	**96**	**17.7**	**36**	**8**	**40**	**4**	**–8**	....	....	....	....	....	....	....	....
1997-98	**Boston Bruins**	**NHL**	**61**	**26**	**20**	**46**	**31**	**19**	**50**	**54**	**9**	**0**	**6**	**160**	**16.3**	**58**	**22**	**28**	**0**	**+8**	**6**	**0**	**0**	**0**	**6**	**0**	**0**	**0**
	NHL Totals		**367**	**97**	**77**	**174**	**104**	**69**	**173**	**209**	**13**	**8**	**18**	**813**	**11.9**	**242**	**31**	**266**	**60**		**40**	**4**	**8**	**12**	**36**	**0**	**1**	**0**

Hockey East First All-Star Team (1990) • NCAA East First All-American Team (1990)

● HEISKALA, EARL

Earl Heiskala LW – L. 6′, 185 lbs. b: Kirkland Lake, Ont., 11/30/1942.

Season	Club	League	GP	G	A	Pts	AG	AA	APts	PIM	PP	SH	GW	S	%	TGF	PGF	TGA	PGA	+/–	GP	G	A	Pts	PIM	PP	SH	GW
1960-61	Hamilton Red Wings	OHA	11	1	0	1	....	....	....	6	....	....	....	....	....	....	....	....	....	....	....	....	....	....	....	....	....	....
1961-62	Hamilton Red Wings	OHA	50	10	20	30	....	....	....	71	....	....	....	....	....	....	....	....	....	....	10	1	4	5	10	....	....	....
1962-63	Hamilton Red Wings	OHA	39	12	18	30	....	....	....	81	....	....	....	....	....	....	....	....	....	....	....	....	....	....	....	....	....	....
1963-64	Oakville Oaks	OHA Sr.	1	0	1	1	....	....	....	2	....	....	....	....	....	....	....	....	....	....	....	....	....	....	....	....	....	....
	Cincinnati Wings	CHL	2	0	0	0	....	....	....	6	....	....	....	....	....	....	....	....	....	....	....	....	....	....	....	....	....	....
1964-65	Knoxville Knights	FHL	70	25	39	64	....	....	....	156	....	....	....	....	....	....	....	....	....	....	10	1	4	5	23	....	....	....
1965-66	Seattle Totems	WHL	64	8	10	18	....	....	....	107	....	....	....	....	....	....	....	....	....	....	....	....	....	....	....	....	....	....
1966-67	Seattle Totems	WHL	65	18	22	40	....	....	....	147	....	....	....	....	....	....	....	....	....	....	10	1	2	3	*29	....	....	....
1967-68	Seattle Totems	WHL	71	26	18	44	....	....	....	*157	....	....	....	....	....	....	....	....	....	....	9	2	2	4	8	....	....	....
1968-69	**Philadelphia Flyers**	**NHL**	**21**	**3**	**3**	**6**	**3**	**3**	**6**	**51**	**0**	**0**	**0**	**38**	**7.9**	**9**	**0**	**13**	**0**	**–4**	....	....	....	....	....	....	....	....
	Quebec Aces	AHL	7	1	6	7	....	....	....	8	....	....	....	....	....	....	....	....	....	....	....	....	....	....	....	....	....	....
	Seattle Totems	WHL	34	14	9	23	....	....	....	69	....	....	....	....	....	....	....	....	....	....	4	1	0	1	6	....	....	....
1969-70	**Philadelphia Flyers**	**NHL**	**65**	**8**	**7**	**15**	**9**	**7**	**16**	**171**	**0**	**0**	**0**	**114**	**7.0**	**26**	**1**	**40**	**0**	**–15**	....	....	....	....	....	....	....	....
1970-71	**Philadelphia Flyers**	**NHL**	**41**	**2**	**1**	**3**	**2**	**1**	**3**	**72**	**0**	**0**	**1**	**39**	**5.1**	**6**	**0**	**15**	**0**	**–9**	....	....	....	....	....	....	....	....
	San Diego Gulls	WHL	21	6	5	11	....	....	....	34	....	....	....	....	....	....	....	....	....	....	5	1	0	1	4	....	....	....
1971-72	San Diego Gulls	WHL	72	15	22	37	....	....	....	169	....	....	....	....	....	....	....	....	....	....	4	1	1	2	20	....	....	....
1972-73	Los Angeles Sharks	WHA	70	12	17	29	....	....	....	148	....	....	....	....	....	....	....	....	....	....	5	1	1	2	4	....	....	....
1973-74	Los Angeles Sharks	WHA	24	2	6	8	....	....	....	45	....	....	....	....	....	....	....	....	....	....	....	....	....	....	....	....	....	....
	Greensboro Generals	SHL	4	2	3	5	....	....	....	4	....	....	....	....	....	....	....	....	....	....	....	....	....	....	....	....	....	....
	NHL Totals		**127**	**13**	**11**	**24**	**14**	**11**	**25**	**294**	**0**	**0**	**1**	**191**	**6.8**	**41**	**1**	**68**	**0**		....	....	....	....	....	....	....	....
	Other Major League Totals		94	14	23	37	....	....	....	193	....	....	....	....	....	....	....	....	....	....	5	1	1	2	4	....	....	....

Traded to **Philadelphia** by **Seattle** (WHL) for Art Stratton and loan of Bob Courcy and Ray LaRose, December 23, 1968. Selected by **LA Sharks** (WHA) in 1972 WHA General Player Draft, February 12, 1972.

● HELANDER, PETER

Peter Helander D – L. 6′1″, 185 lbs. b: Stockholm, Sweden, 12/4/1951. Los Angeles' 8th choice, 153rd overall, in 1982 Entry Draft.

Season	Club	League	GP	G	A	Pts	AG	AA	APts	PIM	PP	SH	GW	S	%	TGF	PGF	TGA	PGA	+/–	GP	G	A	Pts	PIM	PP	SH	GW
1974-75	Skelleftea AIK	Sweden	8	0	0	0	....	....	....	8	....	....	....	....	....	....	....	....	....	....	....	....	....	....	....	....	....	....
1975-76	Skelleftea AIK	Sweden	7	1	1	2	....	....	....	6	....	....	....	....	....	....	....	....	....	....	....	....	....	....	....	....	....	....
1976-77	Skelleftea AIK	Sweden	29	5	2	7	....	....	....	26	....	....	....	....	....	....	....	....	....	....	....	....	....	....	....	....	....	....
1977-78	Skelleftea AIK	Sweden	29	0	4	4	....	....	....	40	....	....	....	....	....	....	....	....	....	....	5	0	0	0	8	....	....	....
1978-79	Skelleftea AIK	Sweden	36	7	4	11	....	....	....	40	....	....	....	....	....	....	....	....	....	....	....	....	....	....	....	....	....	....
1979-80	Skelleftea AIK	Sweden	32	6	8	14	....	....	....	01	....	....	....	....	....	....	....	....	....	....	....	....	....	....	....	....	....	....
1980-81	Skelleftea AIK	Sweden	33	6	8	14	....	....	....	59	....	....	....	....	....	....	....	....	....	....	3	1	0	1	11	....	....	....
	Sweden	WEC-A	8	1	2	3	....	....	....	8	....	....	....	....	....	....	....	....	....	....	....	....	....	....	....	....	....	....
1981-82	Sweden	C Cup	5	0	2	2	....	....	....	8	....	....	....	....	....	....	....	....	....	....	....	....	....	....	....	....	....	....
	Skelleftea AIK	Sweden	30	6	2	8	....	....	....	50	....	....	....	....	....	....	....	....	....	....	....	....	....	....	....	....	....	....
	Sweden	WEC-A	10	1	2	3	....	....	....	14	....	....	....	....	....	....	....	....	....	....	....	....	....	....	....	....	....	....
1982-83	**Los Angeles Kings**	**NHL**	**7**	**0**	**1**	**1**	**0**	**1**	**1**	**0**	**0**	**0**	**0**	**2**	**0.0**	**4**	**0**	**10**	**4**	**–2**	....	....	....	....	....	....	....	....
	New Haven Nighthawks	AHL	9	1	3	4	....	....	....	0	....	....	....	....	....	....	....	....	....	....	....	....	....	....	....	....	....	....
	NHL Totals		**7**	**0**	**1**	**1**	**0**	**1**	**1**	**0**	**0**	**0**	**0**	**2**	**0.0**	**4**	**0**	**10**	**4**		....	....	....	....	....	....	....	....

Swedish World All-Star Team (1981, 1982)

● HELENIUS, SAMI

Sami Helenius D – L. 6′5″, 225 lbs. b: Helsinki, Finland, 1/22/1974. Calgary's 5th choice, 102nd overall, in 1992 Entry Draft.

			REGULAR SEASON																		PLAYOFFS							
Season	Club	League	GP	G	A	Pts	AG	AA	APts	PIM	PP	SH	GW	S	%	TGF	PGF	TGA	PGA	+/–	GP	G	A	Pts	PIM	PP	SH	GW
1992-93	Jokerit Helsinki	Finland	1	0	0	0				0																		
	Finland	WJC-A	7	0	1	1				6																		
1993-94	Reipas Laht	Finland	37	2	3	5				46																		
1994-95	Saint John Flames	AHL	69	2	5	7				217																		
1995-96	Saint John Flames	AHL	68	0	3	3				231											10	0	0	0	9			
1996-97	**Calgary Flames**	**NHL**	**3**	**0**	**1**	**1**	**0**	**1**	**1**	**0**	**0**	**0**	**0**	**1**	**0.0**	**2**	**0**	**1**	**0**	**+1**								
	Saint John Flames	AHL	72	5	10	15				218											2	0	0	0	0			
1997-98	Saint John Flames	AHL	63	1	2	3				185																		
	Las Vegas Thunder	IHL	10	0	1	1				19											4	0	0	0	25			
	NHL Totals		**3**	**0**	**1**	**1**	**0**	**1**	**1**	**0**	**0**	**0**	**0**	**1**	**0.0**	**2**	**0**	**1**	**0**									

● HELMINEN, RAIMO

Raimo Helminen C – L. 6′, 185 lbs. b: Tampere, Finland, 3/11/1964. NY Rangers' 2nd choice, 35th overall, in 1984 Entry Draft.

Season	Club	League	GP	G	A	Pts	AG	AA	APts	PIM	PP	SH	GW	S	%	TGF	PGF	TGA	PGA	+/–	GP	G	A	Pts	PIM	PP	SH	GW
1982-83	Ilves-Tampere	Finland	31	2	3	5				0											6	0	0	0	2			
	Finland	WJC-A	7	0	5	5				0																		
1983-84	Ilves-Tampere	Finland	37	17	13	30				14											2	0	0	0	2			
	Finland	WJC-A	7	11	11	22				4																		
	Finland	Olympics	6	0	2	2				2																		
1984-85	Ilves-Tampere	Finland	36	21	36	57				20																		
	Finland	WEC-A	10	4	5	9				2																		
1985-86	**New York Rangers**	**NHL**	**66**	**10**	**30**	**40**	**8**	**20**	**28**	**10**	**4**	**0**	**2**	**125**	**8.0**	**62**	**26**	**37**	**0**	**–1**	**2**	**0**	**0**	**0**	**0**	**0**	**0**	**0**
1986-87	**New York Rangers**	**NHL**	**21**	**2**	**4**	**6**	**2**	**3**	**5**	**2**	**1**	**0**	**0**	**24**	**8.3**	**12**	**7**	**14**	**1**	**–8**								
	New Haven Nighthawks	AHL	6	0	2	2				0																		
	Minnesota North Stars	**NHL**	**6**	**0**	**1**	**1**	**0**	**1**	**1**	**0**	**0**	**0**	**0**	**6**	**0.0**	**3**	**2**	**4**	**0**	**–3**								
1987-88	Finland	C Cup	5	0	3	3				0																		
	Ilves-Tampere	Finland	31	20	23	43				42																		
	Finland	Olympics	7	2	8	10				4																		
1988-89	**New York Islanders**	**NHL**	**24**	**1**	**11**	**12**	**1**	**8**	**9**	**4**	**1**	**0**	**0**	**22**	**4.5**	**18**	**12**	**26**	**5**	**–15**								
	Springfield Indians	AHL	16	6	11	17				0																		
1989-90	Malmo IF	Sweden	29	26	30	56				16																		
	Finland	WEC-A	4	0	0	0				0																		
1990-91	Malmo IF	Sweden	33	12	18	30				14											2	0	1	1	4			
1991-92	Malmo IF	Sweden	40	9	18	27				24											10	1	3	4	4			
	Finland	Olympics	8	1	2	3				0																		
1992-93	Malmo IF	Sweden	40	9	*33	42				59											6	1	0	1	8			
1993-94	Malmo IF	Sweden	38	20	34	*54				26											11	1	7	8	8			
	Finland	Olympics	8	1	5	6				8																		
	Finland	WC-A	8	1	5	6				0																		
1994-95	Malmo IF	Sweden	35	10	19	29				55											7	3	2	5	4			
	Finland	WC-A	8	1	7	8				2																		
1995-96	Malmo IF	Sweden	40	8	19	27				53											5	1	3	4	12			
	Finland	WC-A	6	0	4	4				0																		
1996-97	Finland	W Cup	3	0	2	2				0																		
	Ilves-Tampere	Finland	49	11	*39	50				8											8	1	5	6	2			
	Finland	WC-A	8	0	6	6				0																		
	Finland	WC-A	10	2	9	11				0																		
1997-98	Ilves-Tampere	Finland	46	12	36	48				42											9	3	5	8	10			
	Finland	Olympics	6	2	0	2				2																		
	NHL Totals		**117**	**13**	**46**	**59**	**11**	**32**	**43**	**16**	**6**	**0**	**2**	**177**	**7.3**	**95**	**47**	**81**	**6**		**2**	**0**	**0**	**0**	**0**	**0**	**0**	**0**

WJC-A All-Star Team (1984) • Named Best Forward at WJC-A (1984) • Finnish First All-Star Team (1988, 1997)

Traded to **Minnesota** by **NY Rangers** for future considerations, March 10, 1987. Signed as a free agent by **NY Islanders**, June 1, 1988.

● HENDERSON, ARCHIE

Archie Henderson RW – R. 6′6″, 220 lbs. b: Calgary, Alta., 2/17/1957. Washington's 10th choice, 156th overall, in 1977 Amateur Draft.

Season	Club	League	GP	G	A	Pts	AG	AA	APts	PIM	PP	SH	GW	S	%	TGF	PGF	TGA	PGA	+/–	GP	G	A	Pts	PIM	PP	SH	GW
1974-75	Lethbridge Broncos	WCJHL	65	3	10	13				177																		
1975-76	Lethbridge Broncos	WCJHL	21	1	2	3				110																		
	Victoria Cougars	WHL	31	8	7	15				205																		
1976-77	Victoria Cougars	WCJHL	47	14	10	24				208																		
1977-78	Port Huron Flags	IHL	71	16	16	32				419											15	5	4	9	47			
1978-79	Hershey Bears	AHL	78	17	11	28				337											4	0	1	1	28			
1979-80	Hershey Bears	AHL	8	0	2	2				37																		
	Fort Worth Texans	CHL	49	8	9	17				199											12	2	1	3	*58			
1980-81	**Washington Capitals**	**NHL**	**7**	**1**	**0**	**1**	**1**	**0**	**1**	**28**	**0**	**0**	**0**	**4**	**25.0**	**2**	**0**	**3**	**0**	**–1**								
	Hershey Bears	AHL	60	3	5	8				251											5	0	0	0	6			
1981-82	**Minnesota North Stars**	**NHL**	**1**	**0**	**0**	**0**	**0**	**0**	**0**	**0**	**0**	**0**	**0**	**0**	**0.0**	**0**	**0**	**0**	**0**	**0**								
	Nashville South Stars	CHL	77	12	23	35				*320											3	0	0	0	17			
1982-83	**Hartford Whalers**	**NHL**	**15**	**2**	**1**	**3**	**2**	**1**	**3**	**64**	**0**	**0**	**0**	**7**	**28.6**	**4**	**0**	**6**	**0**	**–2**								
	Binghamton Whalers	AHL	50	8	9	17				172																		
1983-84	New Haven Nighthawks	AHL	48	1	8	9				164																		
1984-85	Nova Scotia Oilers	AHL	71	5	7	12				271											5	0	0	0	30			
1985-86	Maine Mariners	AHL	57	4	6	10				172											5	0	0	0	24			
1986-87	Maine Mariners	AHL	67	4	6	10				246																		
1987-88	Saginaw Hawks	IHL	55	4	9	13				231											10	0	0	0	66			
	NHL Totals		**23**	**3**	**1**	**4**	**3**	**1**	**4**	**92**	**0**	**0**	**0**	**11**	**27.3**	**6**	**0**	**9**	**0**									

Signed as a free agent by **Minnesota**, July 15, 1981. Signed as a free agent by **Hartford**, August 9, 1982. Signed as a free agent by **LA Kings**, August 29, 1983. Signed as a free agent by **New Jersey**, September 11, 1985.

● HENDERSON, PAUL

Paul Henderson RW – R. 5′11″, 180 lbs. b: Kincardine, Ont., 1/28/1943.

Season	Club	League	GP	G	A	Pts	AG	AA	APts	PIM	PP	SH	GW	S	%	TGF	PGF	TGA	PGA	+/–	GP	G	A	Pts	PIM	PP	SH	GW
1960-61	Hamilton Red Wings	OHA	30	1	3	4				9											12	1	1	2	4			
1961-62	Hamilton Red Wings	OHA	50	24	19	43				68											10	4	6	10	13			
1962-63	**Detroit Red Wings**	**NHL**	**2**	**0**	**0**	**0**	**0**	**0**	**0**	**9**																		
	Hamilton Red Wings	OHA	48	*49	27	76				53											3	2	0	2	0			
1963-64	**Detroit Red Wings**	**NHL**	**32**	**3**	**3**	**6**	**4**	**3**	**7**	**14**											**14**	**2**	**3**	**5**	**6**			
	Pittsburgh Hornets	AHL	38	10	14	24				18																		
1964-65	**Detroit Red Wings**	**NHL**	**70**	**8**	**13**	**21**	**10**	**14**	**24**	**30**											**7**	**0**	**2**	**2**	**0**			
1965-66	**Detroit Red Wings**	**NHL**	**69**	**22**	**24**	**46**	**27**	**24**	**51**	**34**											**12**	**3**	**3**	**6**	**10**			
1966-67	**Detroit Red Wings**	**NHL**	**46**	**21**	**19**	**40**	**26**	**20**	**46**	**10**																		
1967-68	**Detroit Red Wings**	**NHL**	**50**	**13**	**20**	**33**	**16**	**21**	**37**	**35**	**4**	**0**	**2**	**134**	**9.7**	**53**	**14**	**42**	**3**	**0**								
	Toronto Maple Leafs	**NHL**	**13**	**5**	**6**	**11**	**6**	**6**	**12**	**8**	**0**	**0**	**1**	**38**	**13.2**	**22**	**3**	**6**	**0**	**+13**								
1968-69	**Toronto Maple Leafs**	**NHL**	**74**	**27**	**32**	**59**	**30**	**30**	**60**	**16**	**4**	**0**	**5**	**223**	**12.1**	**85**	**21**	**53**	**7**	**+18**	**4**	**0**	**1**	**1**	**0**	**0**	**0**	**0**
1969-70	**Toronto Maple Leafs**	**NHL**	**67**	**20**	**22**	**42**	**23**	**22**	**45**	**18**	**5**	**0**	**4**	**213**	**9.4**	**71**	**16**	**41**	**0**	**+14**								
1970-71	**Toronto Maple Leafs**	**NHL**	**72**	**30**	**30**	**60**	**31**	**26**	**57**	**34**	**8**	**0**	**2**	**213**	**14.1**	**86**	**25**	**48**	**1**	**+14**	**6**	**5**	**1**	**6**	**4**	**1**	**0**	**2**
1971-72	**Toronto Maple Leafs**	**NHL**	**73**	**38**	**19**	**57**	**41**	**17**	**58**	**32**	**12**	**1**	**5**	**191**	**19.9**	**92**	**30**	**52**	**4**	**+14**	**5**	**1**	**2**	**3**	**6**	**0**	**0**	**0**
1972-73	Canada	Summit	8	7	3	10				4																		
	Toronto Maple Leafs	**NHL**	**40**	**18**	**16**	**34**	**18**	**13**	**31**	**18**	**2**	**0**	**3**	**105**	**17.1**	**47**	**10**	**36**	**1**	**+2**								
1973-74	**Toronto Maple Leafs**	**NHL**	**69**	**24**	**31**	**55**	**25**	**27**	**52**	**40**	**5**	**0**	**2**	**159**	**15.1**	**85**	**23**	**58**	**5**	**+9**	**4**	**0**	**2**	**2**	**2**	**0**	**0**	**0**
1974-75	Canada	Summit	7	2	1	3				0																		
	Toronto Toros	WHA	58	30	33	63				18																		
1975-76	Toronto Toros	WHA	65	26	29	55				22																		
1976-77	Birmingham Bulls	WHA	81	23	25	48				30																		
1977-78	Birmingham Bulls	WHA	80	37	29	66				22											5	1	1	2	0			
1978-79	Birmingham Bulls	WHA	76	24	27	51				20																		

			REGULAR SEASON																		PLAYOFFS							
Season	Club	League	GP	G	A	Pts	AG	AA	APts	PIM	PP	SH	GW	S	%	TGF	PGF	TGA	PGA	+/–	GP	G	A	Pts	PIM	PP	SH	GW
1979-80	**Atlanta Flames**	**NHL**	30	7	6	13	6	5	11	6	1	0	1	29	24.1	21	7	10	1	+5	4	0	0	0	0	0	0	0
	Birmingham Bulls	CHL	47	17	18	35				10																		
1980-81	Birmingham Bulls	CHL	35	6	11	17				38																		
	NHL Totals		707	236	241	477	263	228	491	304	41	1	25	1305	18.1	562	149	346	22		56	11	14	25	28	1	0	2
	Other Major League Totals		360	140	143	283				112											5	1	1	2	0			

Played in NHL All-Star Game (1972, 1973)

Traded to **Toronto** by **Detroit** with Norm Ullman and Floyd Smith for Frank Mahovlich, Garry Unger, Pete Stemkowski and the rights to Carl Brewer, March 3, 1968. Selected by **Quebec** (WHA) in 1972 WHA General Player Draft, February 12, 1972. WHA rights traded to **Toronto** (WHA) by **Quebec** (WHA) for cash, June, 1974. Transferred to **Birmingham** (WHA) after **Toronto** (WHA) franchise relocated, June 30, 1976. Signed as a free agent by **Atlanta**, September 17, 1979.

• HENDRICKSON, DARBY

Darby Hendrickson C – L. 6', 185 lbs. b: Richfield, MN, 8/28/1972. Toronto's 3rd choice, 73rd overall, in 1990 Entry Draft.

Season	Club	League	GP	G	A	Pts	AG	AA	APts	PIM	PP	SH	GW	S	%	TGF	PGF	TGA	PGA	+/–	GP	G	A	Pts	PIM	PP	SH	GW
1989-90	Richfield High School	H.S.	24	23	27	50				49																		
1990-91	Richfield High School	H.S.	27	32	29	61																						
1991-92	University of Minnesota	WCHA	41	25	28	53				61																		
1992-93	University of Minnesota	WCHA	31	12	15	27				35																		
1993-94	United States	Nat-Team	59	12	16	28				30																		
	United States	Olympics	8	0	0	0				6																		
	Toronto Maple Leafs	**NHL**																			2	0	0	0	0			
	St. John's Maple Leafs	AHL	6	4	1	5				4											3	1	1	2	0			
1994-95	**Toronto Maple Leafs**	**NHL**	8	0	1	1	0	1	1	4	0	0	0	4	0.0	1	0	1	0	0								
	St. John's Maple Leafs	AHL	59	16	20	36				48																		
1995-96	**Toronto Maple Leafs**	**NHL**	46	6	6	12	6	5	11	47	0	0	0	43	14.0	20	1	23	2	–2								
	New York Islanders	**NHL**	16	1	4	5	1	3	4	33	0	0	1	30	3.3	9	2	18	5	–6								
	United States	WC-A	8	1	1	2				4																		
1996-97	**Toronto Maple Leafs**	**NHL**	64	11	6	17	12	5	17	47	0	1	0	105	10.5	24	1	63	20	–20								
	St. John's Maple Leafs	AHL	12	5	4	9				21																		
	United States	WC-A	8	0	1	1				8																		
1997-98	**Toronto Maple Leafs**	**NHL**	80	8	4	12	9	4	13	67	0	0	0	115	7.0	21	0	59	18	–20								
	NHL Totals		214	26	21	47	28	18	46	198	0	1	1	297	8.8	75	4	164	45		2	0	0	0	0	0	0	0

Traded to **NY Islanders** by **Toronto** with Sean Haggerty, Kenny Jonsson and Toronto's 1st round choice (Roberto Luongo) in 1997 Entry Draft for Wendel Clark, Mathieu Schneider and D.J. Smith, March 13, 1996. Traded to **Toronto** by **NY Islanders** for a conditional choice in 1998 Entry Draft, October 10, 1996.

• HENNING, LORNE

Lorne Henning C – L. 5'11", 185 lbs. b: Melfort, Sask., 2/22/1952. NY Islanders' 2nd choice, 17th overall, in 1972 Amateur Draft.

Season	Club	League	GP	G	A	Pts	AG	AA	APts	PIM	PP	SH	GW	S	%	TGF	PGF	TGA	PGA	+/–	GP	G	A	Pts	PIM	PP	SH	GW
1968-69	Estevan Bruins	WCJHL	60	27	27	54				20																		
1969-70	Estevan Bruins	WCJHL	60	40	52	92				33											5	1	1	2	0			
1970-71	Estevan Bruins	WCJHL	66	64	66	130				41											7	5	10	15	7			
1971-72	New Westminster Royals	WCJHL	60	51	63	114				29											5	3	1	4	7			
1972-73	**New York Islanders**	**NHL**	63	7	19	26	7	16	23	14	0	0	0	101	6.9	36	5	60	1	–28								
	New Haven Nighthawks	AHL	4	0	2	2				2																		
1973-74	**New York Islanders**	**NHL**	60	12	15	27	12	13	25	6	2	0	1	96	12.5	38	11	34	0	–7								
	Fort Worth Wings	CHL	8	4	6	10				4																		
1974-75	**New York Islanders**	**NHL**	61	5	6	11	5	5	10	6	0	4	0	45	11.1	18	2	26	17	+7	17	0	2	2	0	0	0	0
1975-76	**New York Islanders**	**NHL**	80	7	10	17	7	8	15	16	0	4	0	84	8.3	25	0	57	38	+6	13	2	0	2	2	1	1	0
1976-77	**New York Islanders**	**NHL**	80	13	18	31	12	15	27	10	0	6	2	103	12.6	48	0	65	38	+21	12	0	1	1	0	0	0	0
1977-78	**New York Islanders**	**NHL**	79	12	15	27	12	12	24	6	0	2	4	79	15.2	34	0	65	41	+10	7	0	0	0	4	0	0	0
1978-79	**New York Islanders**	**NHL**	73	13	20	33	12	15	27	14	0	2	2	70	18.6	41	1	70	47	+17	10	2	0	2	0	0	1	0
1979-80	**New York Islanders**	**NHL**	39	3	6	9	3	5	8	6	0	0	0	45	6.7	11	0	44	23	–10	21	3	4	7	2	0	3	1
1980-81	**New York Islanders**	**NHL**	9	1	2	3	1	1	2	24	0	0	0	15	6.7	5	0	2	1	+4	1	0	0	0	0	0	0	0
	NHL Totals		544	73	111	184	71	90	161	102	2	18	9	638	11.4	256	19	423	206		81	7	7	14	8	1	5	1

• HENRY, CAMILLE

Camille "The Eel" Henry C – L. 5'9", 152 lbs. b: Quebec City, Que., 1/31/1933. d: 9/12/1997.

Season	Club	League	GP	G	A	Pts	AG	AA	APts	PIM	PP	SH	GW	S	%	TGF	PGF	TGA	PGA	+/–	GP	G	A	Pts	PIM	PP	SH	GW
1949-50	Quebec Citadelle	QJHL	1	0	0	0				0																		
1950-51	Quebec Citadelle	QJHL	46	26	23	40				26											22	13	12	25	22			
1951-52	Quebec Citadelle	QJHL	50	*55	59	*114				59											6	*8	4	12	2			
1952-53	Quebec Citadelle	QJHL	46	*46	30	76				43											9	*10	*8	*18	*21			
1953-54	**New York Rangers**	**NHL**	66	24	15	39	37	20	57	10																		
1954-55	**New York Rangers**	**NHL**	21	5	2	7	7	3	10	4																		
	Quebec Aces	QHL	37	20	18	38				2											8	3	1	4	0			
1955-56	Providence Reds	AHL	59	*50	41	91				8											9	*10	6	16	2			
1956-57	**New York Rangers**	**NHL**	36	14	15	29	19	17	36	2											5	2	3	5	0			
	Providence Reds	AHL	29	31	16	47				8																		
1957-58	**New York Rangers**	**NHL**	70	32	24	56	43	26	69	2											6	1	4	5	5			
1958-59	**New York Rangers**	**NHL**	70	23	35	58	29	37	66	2																		
1959-60	**New York Rangers**	**NHL**	49	12	15	27	15	15	30	6																		
1960-61	**New York Rangers**	**NHL**	53	28	25	53	34	25	59	8																		
1961-62	**New York Rangers**	**NHL**	60	23	15	38	28	15	43	8											5	0	0	0	0			
1962-63	**New York Rangers**	**NHL**	60	37	23	60	46	24	70	8																		
1963-64	**New York Rangers**	**NHL**	68	29	26	55	39	29	68	8																		
1964-65	**New York Rangers**	**NHL**	48	21	15	36	27	16	43	20																		
	Chicago Black Hawks	**NHL**	22	5	3	8	6	3	9	2											14	1	0	1	2			
1965-66	St. Louis Braves	CHL	37	14	22	36				4											5	2	1	3	0			
1966-67			DID NOT PLAY																									
1967-68	**New York Rangers**	**NHL**	36	8	12	20	10	13	23	0	1	0	0	39	20.5	36	7	21	0	+8	6	0	0	0	0	0	0	0
	Buffalo Bisons	AHL	22	9	10	19				0																		
1968-69	**St. Louis Blues**	**NHL**	64	17	22	39	19	21	40	8	7	0	1	94	18.1	60	22	24	0	+14	11	2	5	7	0	1	0	0
1969-70	**St. Louis Blues**	**NHL**	4	1	2	3	1	2	3	0	1	0	0	5	20.0	6	2	5	0	–2								
	Kansas City Blues	CHL	15	5	7	12				4																		
	NHL Totals		727	279	249	528	360	266	626	88	9	0	1	138	202.2	101	31	50	0		47	6	12	18	7	1	0	0

Won Calder Memorial Trophy (1954) • AHL First All-Star Team (1956) • NHL Second All-Star Team (1958) • Won Lady Byng Trophy (1958)

Played in NHL All-Star Game (1958, 1963, 1964)

Traded to **Quebec** (QHL) by **NY Rangers** and cash and the loan of Earl Johnson for cash with NY Rangers holding rights of recall, December 5, 1954. Traded to **Chicago** by **NY Rangers** with Don Johns, Wally Chevrier and Billy Taylor for Doug Robinson, Wayne Hillman and John Brenneman, February 4, 1965. Traded to **NY Rangers** by **Chicago** for Paul Shmyr, August 17, 1967. Traded to **St. Louis** by **NY Rangers** with Bill Plager and Robbie Irons for Don Caley and Wayne Rivers, June 13, 1968. Claimed by **Buffalo** (AHL) from **St. Louis** in Reverse Draft, June, 1969. Traded to **St. Louis** by **Buffalo** (AHL) for cash, June, 1969.

• HENRY, DALE

Dale Henry LW – L. 6', 205 lbs. b: Prince Albert, Sask., 9/24/1964. NY Islanders' 10th choice, 163rd overall, in 1983 Entry Draft.

Season	Club	League	GP	G	A	Pts	AG	AA	APts	PIM	PP	SH	GW	S	%	TGF	PGF	TGA	PGA	+/–	GP	G	A	Pts	PIM	PP	SH	GW
1981-82	Saskatoon Blades	WHL	32	5	4	9				50											5	0	0	0	0			
1982-83	Saskatoon Blades	WHL	63	21	19	40				213											3	0	0	0	12			
1983-84	Saskatoon Blades	WHL	71	41	36	77				162																		
1984-85	**New York Islanders**	**NHL**	16	2	1	3	2	1	3	19	0	0	1	9	22.2	9	0	8	0	+1								
	Springfield Indians	AHL	67	11	20	31				133											4	0	0	0	13			
1985-86	**New York Islanders**	**NHL**	7	1	3	4	1	2	3	15	0	0	0	5	20.0	6	0	6	0	0								
	Springfield Indians	AHL	64	14	26	40				162																		
1986-87	**New York Islanders**	**NHL**	19	3	3	6	3	2	5	46	0	0	0	14	21.4	10	0	8	0	+2	8	0	0	0	2	0	0	0
	Springfield Indians	AHL	23	9	14	23				49																		
1987-88	**New York Islanders**	**NHL**	48	5	15	20	4	11	15	115	0	0	0	53	9.4	31	5	18	0	+8	6	1	0	1	17	0	1	0
	Springfield Indians	AHL	24	9	12	21				103																		
1988-89	**New York Islanders**	**NHL**	22	2	2	4	2	1	3	66	0	0	0	20	10.0	9	1	12	0	–4								
	Springfield Indians	AHL	50	13	21	34				83																		
1989-90	**New York Islanders**	**NHL**	20	0	2	2	0	1	1	2	0	0	0	6	0.0	3	0	7	0	–4								
	Springfield Indians	AHL	43	17	14	31				68											18	3	5	8	33			

Season	Club	League	GP	G	A	Pts	AG	AA	APts	PIM	PP	SH	GW	S	%	TGF	PGF	TGA	PGA	+/–	GP	G	A	Pts	PIM	PP	SH	GW
			REGULAR SEASON																		PLAYOFFS							
1990-91	Albany Choppers	IHL	55	16	22	38	....	....	....	87	....	....	....	....	....	....	....	....	....	....	....	....	....	....	....	....	....	....
	Springfield Indians	AHL	20	5	9	14	....	....	....	31	....	....	....	....	....	....	....	....	....	....	18	2	7	9	24	....	....	....
1991-92	Muskegon Lumberjacks	IHL	39	5	17	22	....	....	....	28	....	....	....	....	....	....	....	....	....	....	14	1	4	5	36	....	....	....
1992-93			DID NOT PLAY																									
1993-94	Milwaukee Admirals	IHL	49	5	11	16	....	....	....	104	....	....	....	....	....	....	....	....	....	....	....	....	....	....	....	....	....	....
1994-95	San Antonio Iguanas	CHL	55	28	36	64	....	....	....	120	....	....	....	....	....	....	....	....	....	....	13	6	8	14	25	....	....	....
1995-96	San Antonio Iguanas	CHL	62	27	40	67	....	....	....	177	....	....	....	....	....	....	....	....	....	....	11	3	8	11	14	....	....	....
1996-97	San Antonio Iguanas	CHL	23	12	19	31	....	....	....	48	....	....	....	....	....	....	....	....	....	....	....	....	....	....	....	....	....	....
1997-98	Shreveport Mudbugs	WPHL	66	34	46	80	....	....	....	91	....	....	....	....	....	....	....	....	....	....	8	3	5	8	29	....	....	....
	NHL Totals		**132**	**13**	**26**	**39**	**12**	**18**	**30**	**263**	**0**	**0**	**1**	**107**	**12.1**	**68**	**6**	**59**	**0**		**14**	**1**	**0**	**1**	**19**	**0**	**1**	**0**

• HEPPLE, ALAN

Alan Hepple D – L. 5′9″, 200 lbs. b: Blaydon-on-Tyne, England, 8/16/1963. New Jersey's 9th choice, 169th overall, in 1982 Entry Draft.

Season	Club	League	GP	G	A	Pts	AG	AA	APts	PIM	PP	SH	GW	S	%	TGF	PGF	TGA	PGA	+/–	GP	G	A	Pts	PIM	PP	SH	GW
1980-81	Ottawa 67's	OHL	64	3	13	16	....	....	....	110	....	....	....	....	....	....	....	....	....	....	6	0	1	1	2	....	....	....
1981-82	Ottawa 67's	OHL	66	6	22	28	....	....	....	160	....	....	....	....	....	....	....	....	....	....	17	2	10	12	84	....	....	....
1982-83	Ottawa 67's	OHL	64	10	26	36	....	....	....	168	....	....	....	....	....	....	....	....	....	....	9	2	1	3	24	....	....	....
1983-84	**New Jersey Devils**	**NHL**	**1**	**0**	**0**	**0**	**0**	**0**	**0**	**7**	**0**	**0**	**0**	**0**	**0.0**	**0**	**0**	**1**	**0**	**–1**	....	....	....	....	....	....	....	....
	Maine Mariners	AHL	64	4	23	27	....	....	....	117	....	....	....	....	....	....	....	....	....	....	....	....	....	....	....	....	....	....
1984-85	**New Jersey Devils**	**NHL**	**1**	**0**	**0**	**0**	**0**	**0**	**0**	**0**	**0**	**0**	**0**	**2**	**0.0**	**0**	**0**	**3**	**1**	**–2**	....	....	....	....	....	....	....	....
	Maine Mariners	AHL	80	7	17	24	....	....	....	125	....	....	....	....	....	....	....	....	....	....	11	0	3	3	30	....	....	....
1985-86	**New Jersey Devils**	**NHL**	**1**	**0**	**0**	**0**	**0**	**0**	**0**	**0**	**0**	**0**	**0**	**0**	**0.0**	**2**	**0**	**2**	**0**	**0**	....	....	....	....	....	....	....	....
	Maine Mariners	AHL	69	4	21	25	....	....	....	104	....	....	....	....	....	....	....	....	....	....	5	0	0	0	11	....	....	....
1986-87	Maine Mariners	AHL	74	6	19	25	....	....	....	137	....	....	....	....	....	....	....	....	....	....	....	....	....	....	....	....	....	....
1987-88	Utica Bulldogs	AHL	78	3	16	19	....	....	....	213	....	....	....	....	....	....	....	....	....	....	....	....	....	....	....	....	....	....
1988-89	Newmarket Saints	AHL	72	5	29	34	....	....	....	122	....	....	....	....	....	....	....	....	....	....	5	0	1	1	23	....	....	....
1989-90	Newmarket Saints	AHL	72	6	20	26	....	....	....	90	....	....	....	....	....	....	....	....	....	....	....	....	....	....	....	....	....	....
1990-91	Newmarket Saints	AHL	76	0	18	18	....	....	....	126	....	....	....	....	....	....	....	....	....	....	....	....	....	....	....	....	....	....
1991-92	San Diego Gulls	IHL	82	6	35	41	....	....	....	191	....	....	....	....	....	....	....	....	....	....	4	0	1	1	6	....	....	....
1992-93	San Diego Gulls	IHL	10	0	1	1	....	....	....	27	....	....	....	....	....	....	....	....	....	....	....	....	....	....	....	....	....	....
	Cincinnati Cyclones	IHL	70	7	31	38	....	....	....	201	....	....	....	....	....	....	....	....	....	....	....	....	....	....	....	....	....	....
	NHL Totals		**3**	**0**	**0**	**0**	**0**	**0**	**0**	**7**	**0**	**0**	**0**	**2**	**0.0**	**2**	**0**	**6**	**1**		....	....	....	....	....	....	....	....

Signed as a free agent by **Toronto**, June 24, 1988.

• HERBERS, IAN

Ian Herbers D – L. 6′4″, 225 lbs. b: Jasper, Alta., 7/18/1967. Buffalo's 11th choice, 190th overall, in 1987 Entry Draft.

Season	Club	League	GP	G	A	Pts	AG	AA	APts	PIM	PP	SH	GW	S	%	TGF	PGF	TGA	PGA	+/–	GP	G	A	Pts	PIM	PP	SH	GW
1984-85	Kelowna Rockets	WHL	68	3	14	17	....	....	....	120	....	....	....	....	....	....	....	....	....	....	6	0	1	1	9	....	....	....
1985-86	Spokane Chiefs	WHL	29	1	6	7	....	....	....	85	....	....	....	....	....	....	....	....	....	....	....	....	....	....	....	....	....	....
	Lethbridge Broncos	WHL	32	1	4	5	....	....	....	109	....	....	....	....	....	....	....	....	....	....	10	1	0	1	37	....	....	....
1986-87	Swift Current Broncos	WHL	72	5	8	13	....	....	....	230	....	....	....	....	....	....	....	....	....	....	4	1	1	2	12	....	....	....
1987-88	Swift Current Broncos	WHL	56	5	14	19	....	....	....	238	....	....	....	....	....	....	....	....	....	....	4	0	2	2	4	....	....	....
1988-89	University of Alberta	CWUAA	47	4	22	26	....	....	....	137	....	....	....	....	....	....	....	....	....	....	....	....	....	....	....	....	....	....
1989-90	University of Alberta	CWUAA	45	5	31	36	....	....	....	83	....	....	....	....	....	....	....	....	....	....	....	....	....	....	....	....	....	....
1990-91	University of Alberta	CWUAA	45	6	24	30	....	....	....	87	....	....	....	....	....	....	....	....	....	....	....	....	....	....	....	....	....	....
1991-92	University of Alberta	CWUAA	43	14	34	48	....	....	....	86	....	....	....	....	....	....	....	....	....	....	....	....	....	....	....	....	....	....
1992-93	Cape Breton Oilers	AHL	77	7	15	22	....	....	....	129	....	....	....	....	....	....	....	....	....	....	10	0	1	1	16	....	....	....
1993-94	**Edmonton Oilers**	**NHL**	**22**	**0**	**2**	**2**	**0**	**2**	**2**	**32**	**0**	**0**	**0**	**16**	**0.0**	**9**	**0**	**22**	**7**	**–6**	....	....	....	....	....	....	....	....
	Cape Breton Oilers	AHL	53	7	16	23	....	....	....	122	....	....	....	....	....	....	....	....	....	....	5	0	3	3	12	....	....	....
1994-95	Cape Breton Oilers	AHL	36	1	11	12	....	....	....	104	....	....	....	....	....	....	....	....	....	....	....	....	....	....	....	....	....	....
	Detroit Vipers	IHL	37	1	5	6	....	....	....	46	....	....	....	....	....	....	....	....	....	....	5	1	1	2	6	....	....	....
1995-96	Detroit Vipers	IHL	73	3	11	14	....	....	....	140	....	....	....	....	....	....	....	....	....	....	12	3	5	8	29	....	....	....
1996-97	Detroit Vipers	IHL	67	3	16	19	....	....	....	129	....	....	....	....	....	....	....	....	....	....	21	0	4	4	34	....	....	....
1997-98	Detroit Vipers	IHL	70	6	6	12	....	....	....	100	....	....	....	....	....	....	....	....	....	....	23	0	3	3	54	....	....	....
	NHL Totals		**22**	**0**	**2**	**2**	**0**	**2**	**2**	**32**	**0**	**0**	**0**	**16**	**0.0**	**9**	**0**	**22**	**7**		....	....	....	....	....	....	....	....

Signed as a free agent by **Edmonton**, September 9, 1992.

• HEROUX, YVES

Yves Heroux RW – R. 5′11″, 185 lbs. b: Terrebonne, Que., 4/27/1965. Quebec's 1st choice, 32nd overall, in 1983 Entry Draft.

Season	Club	League	GP	G	A	Pts	AG	AA	APts	PIM	PP	SH	GW	S	%	TGF	PGF	TGA	PGA	+/–	GP	G	A	Pts	PIM	PP	SH	GW
1981-82	Laurentides AAA	Midget	48	53	53	106	....	....	....	84	....	....	....	....	....	....	....	....	....	....	....	....	....	....	....	....	....	....
1982-83	Chicoutimi Sagueneens	QMJHL	70	41	40	81	....	....	....	44	....	....	....	....	....	....	....	....	....	....	5	0	4	4	8	....	....	....
1983-84	Chicoutimi Sagueneens	QMJHL	56	28	25	53	....	....	....	67	....	....	....	....	....	....	....	....	....	....	....	....	....	....	....	....	....	....
	Fredericton Express	AHL	4	0	0	0	....	....	....	0	....	....	....	....	....	....	....	....	....	....	....	....	....	....	....	....	....	....
1984-85	Chicoutimi Sagueneens	QMJHL	66	42	54	96	....	....	....	123	....	....	....	....	....	....	....	....	....	....	14	5	8	13	16	....	....	....
1985-86	Fredericton Express	AHL	31	12	10	22	....	....	....	42	....	....	....	....	....	....	....	....	....	....	2	0	1	1	7	....	....	....
	Muskegon Lumberjacks	IHL	42	14	8	22	....	....	....	41	....	....	....	....	....	....	....	....	....	....	....	....	....	....	....	....	....	....
1986-87	**Quebec Nordiques**	**NHL**	**1**	**0**	**0**	**0**	**0**	**0**	**0**	**0**	**0**	**0**	**0**	**0**	**0.0**	**0**	**0**	**0**	**0**	**0**	....	....	....	....	....	....	....	....
	Fredericton Express	AHL	37	8	6	14	....	....	....	13	....	....	....	....	....	....	....	....	....	....	....	....	....	....	....	....	....	....
	Muskegon Lumberjacks	IHL	25	6	8	14	....	....	....	31	....	....	....	....	....	....	....	....	....	....	2	0	0	0	0	....	....	....
1987-88	Baltimore Skipjacks	AHL	5	0	2	2	....	....	....	2	....	....	....	....	....	....	....	....	....	....	....	....	....	....	....	....	....	....
1988-89	Flint Spirits	IHL	82	43	42	85	....	....	....	98	....	....	....	....	....	....	....	....	....	....	....	....	....	....	....	....	....	....
1989-90	Canada	Nat-Team	65	13	24	37	....	....	....	63	....	....	....	....	....	....	....	....	....	....	....	....	....	....	....	....	....	....
	Peoria Rivermen	IHL	14	3	2	5	....	....	....	42	....	....	....	....	....	....	....	....	....	....	5	2	2	4	0	....	....	....
1990-91	Albany Choppers	IHL	45	22	18	40	....	....	....	46	....	....	....	....	....	....	....	....	....	....	....	....	....	....	....	....	....	....
	Peoria Rivermen	IHL	33	16	8	24	....	....	....	26	....	....	....	....	....	....	....	....	....	....	17	4	4	8	16	....	....	....
1991-92	Peoria Rivermen	IHL	80	41	36	77	....	....	....	72	....	....	....	....	....	....	....	....	....	....	8	5	1	6	6	....	....	....
1992-93	Kalamazoo Wings	IHL	80	38	30	68	....	....	....	86	....	....	....	....	....	....	....	....	....	....	....	....	....	....	....	....	....	....
1993-94	Kalamazoo Wings	IHL	3	0	2	2	....	....	....	4	....	....	....	....	....	....	....	....	....	....	....	....	....	....	....	....	....	....
	Indianapolis Ice	IHL	74	28	30	58	....	....	....	113	....	....	....	....	....	....	....	....	....	....	....	....	....	....	....	....	....	....
1994-95	Worcester IceCats	AHL	7	3	1	4	....	....	....	2	....	....	....	....	....	....	....	....	....	....	....	....	....	....	....	....	....	....
	Atlanta Knights	IHL	66	31	24	55	....	....	....	56	....	....	....	....	....	....	....	....	....	....	5	2	3	5	6	....	....	....
1995-96	Lustenau	Austria	33	23	31	54	....	....	....	62	....	....	....	....	....	....	....	....	....	....	....	....	....	....	....	....	....	....
1996-97	Augsburg Panthers	Germany	20	4	9	13	....	....	....	30	....	....	....	....	....	....	....	....	....	....	....	....	....	....	....	....	....	....
	Schwenningen Wild Wings	Germany	27	11	17	28	....	....	....	34	....	....	....	....	....	....	....	....	....	....	5	0	3	3	12	....	....	....
1997-98	Schwenningen Wild Wings	Germany	50	14	12	26	....	....	....	147	....	....	....	....	....	....	....	....	....	....	....	....	....	....	....	....	....	....
	NHL Totals		**1**	**0**	**0**	**0**	**0**	**0**	**0**	**0**	**0**	**0**	**0**	**0**	**0.0**	**0**	**0**	**0**	**0**		....	....	....	....	....	....	....	....

Signed as a free agent by **St. Louis**, March 13, 1990. Signed as a free agent by **Minnesota**, August 10, 1992.

• HERTER, JASON

Jason Herter D – R. 6′1″, 190 lbs. b: Hafford, Sask., 10/2/1970. Vancouver's 1st choice, 8th overall, in 1989 Entry Draft.

Season	Club	League	GP	G	A	Pts	AG	AA	APts	PIM	PP	SH	GW	S	%	TGF	PGF	TGA	PGA	+/–	GP	G	A	Pts	PIM	PP	SH	GW
1988-89	University of North Dakota	WCHA	41	8	24	32	....	....	....	62	....	....	....	....	....	....	....	....	....	....	....	....	....	....	....	....	....	....
1989-90	University of North Dakota	WCHA	38	11	39	50	....	....	....	40	....	....	....	....	....	....	....	....	....	....	....	....	....	....	....	....	....	....
	Canada	WJC-A	7	0	1	1	....	....	....	2	....	....	....	....	....	....	....	....	....	....	....	....	....	....	....	....	....	....
1990-91	University of North Dakota	WCHA	39	11	26	37	....	....	....	52	....	....	....	....	....	....	....	....	....	....	....	....	....	....	....	....	....	....
1991-92	Milwaukee Admirals	IHL	56	7	18	25	....	....	....	34	....	....	....	....	....	....	....	....	....	....	1	0	0	0	2	....	....	....
1992-93	Hamilton Canucks	AHL	70	7	16	23	....	....	....	68	....	....	....	....	....	....	....	....	....	....	....	....	....	....	....	....	....	....
1993-94	Kalamazoo Wings	IHL	68	14	28	42	....	....	....	92	....	....	....	....	....	....	....	....	....	....	5	3	0	3	14	....	....	....
1994-95	Kalamazoo Wings	IHL	60	12	20	32	....	....	....	70	....	....	....	....	....	....	....	....	....	....	16	2	8	10	10	....	....	....
1995-96	**New York Islanders**	**NHL**	**1**	**0**	**1**	**1**	**0**	**1**	**1**	**0**	**0**	**0**	**0**	**1**	**0.0**	**3**	**2**	**0**	**0**	**+1**	....	....	....	....	....	....	....	....
	Utah Grizzlies	IHL	74	14	31	45	....	....	....	58	....	....	....	....	....	....	....	....	....	....	20	4	10	14	8	....	....	....
1996-97	Kansas City Blades	IHL	71	9	26	35	....	....	....	62	....	....	....	....	....	....	....	....	....	....	3	0	1	1	0	....	....	....
1997-98	Kansas City Blades	IHL	57	6	19	25	....	....	....	55	....	....	....	....	....	....	....	....	....	....	....	....	....	....	....	....	....	....
	Orlando Solar Bears	IHL	8	1	3	4	....	....	....	8	....	....	....	....	....	....	....	....	....	....	17	5	7	12	20	....	....	....
	NHL Totals		**1**	**0**	**1**	**1**	**0**	**1**	**1**	**0**	**0**	**0**	**0**	**1**	**0.0**	**3**	**2**	**0**	**0**		....	....	....	....	....	....	....	....

WCHA Second All-Star Team (1990, 1991)

Signed as a free agent by **Dallas**, August 6, 1993. Traded to **NY Islanders** by **Dallas** for cash, September 21, 1995.

• HERVEY, MATT   Matt Hervey   D – R. 5'11", 205 lbs.   b: Whittier, CA, 5/16/1968.

			REGULAR SEASON																		PLAYOFFS							
Season	Club	League	GP	G	A	Pts	AG	AA	APts	PIM	PP	SH	GW	S	%	TGF	PGF	TGA	PGA	+/–	GP	G	A	Pts	PIM	PP	SH	GW
1983-84	Victoria Cougars	WHL	67	4	19	23	....	....	....	89	....	....	....	....	....	....	....	....	....	....	....	....	....	....	....	....	....	....
1984-85	Victoria Cougars	WHL	14	1	3	4	....	....	....	17	....	....	....	....	....	....	....	....	....	....	....	....	....	....	....	....	....	....
	Lethbridge Broncos	WHL	54	3	9	12	....	....	....	88	....	....	....	....	....	....	....	....	....	....	4	0	1	1	14	....	....	....
1985-86	Lethbridge Broncos	WHL	60	9	17	26	....	....	....	110	....	....	....	....	....	....	....	....	....	....	....	....	....	....	....	....	....	....
1986-87	Seattle Thunderbirds	WHL	66	4	5	9	....	....	....	59	....	....	....	....	....	....	....	....	....	....	....	....	....	....	....	....	....	....
1987-88	Moncton Hawks	AHL	69	9	20	29	....	....	....	265	....	....	....	....	....	....	....	....	....	....	....	....	....	....	....	....	....	....
1988-89	**Winnipeg Jets**	**NHL**	**2**	**0**	**0**	**0**	**0**	**0**	**0**	**4**	**0**	**0**	**0**	**1**	**0.0**	**2**	**0**	**0**	**0**	**+2**	....	....	....	....	....	....	....	....
	Moncton Hawks	AHL	73	8	28	36	....	....	....	295	....	....	....	....	....	....	....	....	....	....	10	1	2	3	42	....	....	....
1989-90	Moncton Hawks	AHL	47	3	13	16	....	....	....	168	....	....	....	....	....	....	....	....	....	....	....	....	....	....	....	....	....	....
1990-91	Moncton Hawks	AHL	71	4	28	32	....	....	....	132	....	....	....	....	....	....	....	....	....	....	7	0	1	1	23	....	....	....
1991-92	**Boston Bruins**	**NHL**	**16**	**0**	**1**	**1**	**0**	**1**	**1**	**55**	**0**	**0**	**0**	**8**	**0.0**	**5**	**0**	**13**	**3**	**–5**	**5**	**0**	**0**	**0**	**6**	....	....	....
	Maine Mariners	AHL	36	1	7	8	....	....	....	47	....	....	....	....	....	....	....	....	....	....	....	....	....	....	....	....	....	....
1992-93	**Tampa Bay Lightning**	**NHL**	**17**	**0**	**4**	**4**	**0**	**3**	**3**	**38**	**0**	**0**	**0**	**18**	**0.0**	**9**	**3**	**14**	**2**	**–6**	....	....	....	....	....	....	....	....
	Atlanta Knights	IHL	49	12	19	31	....	....	....	122	....	....	....	....	....	....	....	....	....	....	9	0	3	3	19	....	....	....
1993-94	Milwaukee Admirals	IHL	27	6	17	23	....	....	....	51	....	....	....	....	....	....	....	....	....	....	....	....	....	....	....	....	....	....
	NHL Totals		**35**	**0**	**5**	**5**	**0**	**4**	**4**	**97**	**0**	**0**	**0**	**27**	**0.0**	**16**	**3**	**27**	**5**		**5**	**0**	**0**	**0**	**6**	**0**	**0**	**0**

Signed as a free agent by **Winnipeg**, September 27, 1988. Signed as a free agent by **Boston**, August 15, 1991. Traded to **Tampa Bay** by **Boston** with Ken Hodge for Darrin Kimble and future considerations, September 4, 1992.

• HESS, BOB   Bob Hess   D – L. 5'11", 180 lbs.   b: Middleton, N.S., 5/19/1955.   St. Louis' 1st choice, 26th overall, in 1974 Amateur Draft.

			REGULAR SEASON																		PLAYOFFS							
Season	Club	League	GP	G	A	Pts	AG	AA	APts	PIM	PP	SH	GW	S	%	TGF	PGF	TGA	PGA	+/–	GP	G	A	Pts	PIM	PP	SH	GW
1971-72	New Westminster Bruins	WCJHL	5	0	0	0	....	....	....	0	....	....	....	....	....	....	....	....	....	....	1	0	0	0	0	....	....	....
1972-73	New Westminster Bruins	WHL	67	6	13	19	....	....	....	29	....	....	....	....	....	....	....	....	....	....	5	0	3	3	4	....	....	....
1973-74	New Westminster Bruins	WHL	68	10	30	40	....	....	....	104	....	....	....	....	....	....	....	....	....	....	11	3	3	6	6	....	....	....
1974-75	**St. Louis Blues**	**NHL**	**76**	**9**	**30**	**39**	**8**	**24**	**32**	**58**	**4**	**0**	**1**	**110**	**8.2**	**98**	**32**	**71**	**12**	**+7**	**1**	**0**	**0**	**0**	**2**	**0**	**0**	**0**
1975-76	**St. Louis Blues**	**NHL**	**78**	**9**	**23**	**32**	**8**	**18**	**26**	**58**	**2**	**2**	**2**	**117**	**7.7**	**106**	**27**	**98**	**22**	**+3**	**1**	**0**	**1**	**1**	**0**	**0**	**0**	**0**
1976-77	Kansas City Blues	CHL	10	1	8	9	....	....	....	16	....	....	....	....	....	....	....	....	....	....	....	....	....	....	....	....	....	....
	St. Louis Blues	**NHL**	**53**	**4**	**18**	**22**	**4**	**15**	**19**	**14**	**1**	**0**	**0**	**88**	**4.5**	**55**	**15**	**44**	**2**	**–2**	**1**	**0**	**0**	**0**	**0**	**0**	**0**	**0**
1977-78	**St. Louis Blues**	**NHL**	**55**	**2**	**12**	**14**	**2**	**10**	**12**	**16**	**0**	**0**	**0**	**101**	**2.0**	**48**	**7**	**45**	**4**	**0**	....	....	....	....	....	....	....	....
	Salt Lake Golden Eagles	CHL	7	1	3	4	....	....	....	4	....	....	....	....	....	....	....	....	....	....	....	....	....	....	....	....	....	....
1978-79	**St. Louis Blues**	**NHL**	**27**	**3**	**4**	**7**	**3**	**3**	**6**	**14**	**0**	**0**	**0**	**42**	**7.1**	**21**	**6**	**38**	**3**	**–20**	....	....	....	....	....	....	....	....
	Salt Lake Golden Eagles	CHL	45	19	29	48	....	....	....	22	....	....	....	....	....	....	....	....	....	....	9	4	6	10	9	....	....	....
1979-80	Salt Lake Golden Eagles	CHL	79	32	42	74	....	....	....	71	....	....	....	....	....	....	....	....	....	....	13	0	8	8	14	....	....	....
1980-81	**St. Louis Blues**	**NHL**	**4**	**0**	**0**	**0**	**0**	**0**	**0**	**4**	**0**	**0**	**0**	**3**	**0.0**	**4**	**0**	**8**	**1**	**–3**	....	....	....	....	....	....	....	....
	Rochester Americans	AHL	70	17	58	75	....	....	....	95	....	....	....	....	....	....	....	....	....	....	....	....	....	....	....	....	....	....
	Buffalo Sabres	**NHL**	....	....	....	....	....	....	....	....	....	....	....	....	....	....	....	....	....	....	**1**	**1**	**0**	**1**	**0**	....	....	....
1981-82	**Buffalo Sabres**	**NHL**	**33**	**0**	**8**	**8**	**0**	**5**	**5**	**14**	**0**	**0**	**0**	**33**	**0.0**	**40**	**10**	**28**	**4**	**+6**	....	....	....	....	....	....	....	....
	Rochester Americans	AHL	22	6	13	19	....	....	....	10	....	....	....	....	....	....	....	....	....	....	9	1	3	4	2	....	....	....
1982-83	Lugano	Switz.	....	14	17	31	....	....	....	....	....	....	....	....	....	....	....	....	....	....	....	....	....	....	....	....	....	....
	Maine Mariners	AHL	13	5	3	8	....	....	....	10	....	....	....	....	....	....	....	....	....	....	17	0	9	9	15	....	....	....
1983-84	EHC Kloten	Switz.	23	6	10	16	....	....	....	....	....	....	....	....	....	....	....	....	....	....	....	....	....	....	....	....	....	....
	Hartford Whalers	**NHL**	**3**	**0**	**0**	**0**	**0**	**0**	**0**	**0**	**0**	**0**	**0**	**3**	**0.0**	**2**	**0**	**1**	**0**	**+1**	....	....	....	....	....	....	....	....
	Indianapolis Checkers	CHL	9	2	6	8	....	....	....	10	....	....	....	....	....	....	....	....	....	....	9	2	4	6	6	....	....	....
1984-85	Salt Lake Golden Eagles	IHL	48	9	21	30	....	....	....	25	....	....	....	....	....	....	....	....	....	....	7	0	7	7	2	....	....	....
	NHL Totals		**329**	**27**	**95**	**122**	**25**	**75**	**100**	**178**	**7**	**2**	**3**	**497**	**5.4**	**374**	**97**	**333**	**48**		**4**	**1**	**1**	**2**	**2**	**0**	**0**	**0**

AHL First All-Star Team (1981)

Traded to **Buffalo** by **St. Louis** with St. Louis' 4th round choice (Anders Wickberg) in 1981 Entry Draft for Bill Stewart, October 30, 1980. Signed as a free agent by **Hartford**, December, 1984.

• HEWARD, JAMIE   Jamie Heward   D – R. 6'2", 207 lbs.   b: Regina, Sask., 3/30/1971.   Pittsburgh's 1st choice, 16th overall, in 1989 Entry Draft.

			REGULAR SEASON																		PLAYOFFS							
Season	Club	League	GP	G	A	Pts	AG	AA	APts	PIM	PP	SH	GW	S	%	TGF	PGF	TGA	PGA	+/–	GP	G	A	Pts	PIM	PP	SH	GW
1987-88	Regina Pats	WHL	68	10	17	27	....	....	....	17	....	....	....	....	....	....	....	....	....	....	4	1	1	2	2	....	....	....
1988-89	Regina Pats	WHL	52	31	28	59	....	....	....	29	....	....	....	....	....	....	....	....	....	....	....	....	....	....	....	....	....	....
1989-90	Regina Pats	WHL	72	14	44	58	....	....	....	42	....	....	....	....	....	....	....	....	....	....	11	2	2	4	10	....	....	....
1990-91	Regina Pats	WHL	71	23	61	84	....	....	....	41	....	....	....	....	....	....	....	....	....	....	8	2	9	11	6	....	....	....
1991-92	Muskegon Lumberjacks	IHL	54	6	21	27	....	....	....	37	....	....	....	....	....	....	....	....	....	....	14	1	4	5	4	....	....	....
1992-93	Cleveland Lumberjacks	IHL	58	9	18	27	....	....	....	64	....	....	....	....	....	....	....	....	....	....	....	....	....	....	....	....	....	....
1993-94	Cleveland Lumberjacks	IHL	73	8	16	24	....	....	....	72	....	....	....	....	....	....	....	....	....	....	....	....	....	....	....	....	....	....
1994-95	Canada	Nat-Team	51	11	35	46	....	....	....	32	....	....	....	....	....	....	....	....	....	....	....	....	....	....	....	....	....	....
	Canada	WC-A	8	0	5	5	....	....	....	6	....	....	....	....	....	....	....	....	....	....	....	....	....	....	....	....	....	....
1995-96	**Toronto Maple Leafs**	**NHL**	**5**	**0**	**0**	**0**	**0**	**0**	**0**	**0**	**0**	**0**	**0**	**8**	**0.0**	**0**	**0**	**1**	**0**	**–1**	....	....	....	....	....	....	....	....
	St. John's Maple Leafs	AHL	73	22	34	56	....	....	....	33	....	....	....	....	....	....	....	....	....	....	3	1	1	2	6	....	....	....
1996-97	**Toronto Maple Leafs**	**NHL**	**20**	**1**	**4**	**5**	**1**	**4**	**5**	**6**	**0**	**0**	**0**	**23**	**4.3**	**12**	**5**	**13**	**0**	**–6**	....	....	....	....	....	....	....	....
	St. John's Maple Leafs	AHL	27	8	19	27	....	....	....	26	....	....	....	....	....	....	....	....	....	....	9	1	3	4	6	....	....	....
1997-98	Philadelphia Phantoms	AHL	72	17	48	65	....	....	....	54	....	....	....	....	....	....	....	....	....	....	20	3	16	19	10	....	....	....
	NHL Totals		**25**	**1**	**4**	**5**	**1**	**4**	**5**	**6**	**0**	**0**	**0**	**31**	**3.2**	**12**	**5**	**14**	**0**		....	....	....	....	....	....	....	....

WHL East First All-Star Team (1991) • AHL First All-Star Team (1996, 1998) • Won Eddie Shore Plaque (Outstanding Defenseman - AHL) (1998)

Signed as a free agent by **Toronto**, May 4, 1995. Signed as a free agent by **Philadelphia**, July 31, 1997.

• HEXTALL, BRYAN JR.   Bryan Jr. Hextall   C – L. 5'11", 185 lbs.   b: Winnipeg, Man., 5/23/1941.   HHOF

			REGULAR SEASON																		PLAYOFFS							
Season	Club	League	GP	G	A	Pts	AG	AA	APts	PIM	PP	SH	GW	S	%	TGF	PGF	TGA	PGA	+/–	GP	G	A	Pts	PIM	PP	SH	GW
1958-59	Brandon Wheat Kings	MJHL	30	19	23	42	....	....	....	15	....	....	....	....	....	....	....	....	....	....	3	1	1	2	0	....	....	....
1959-60	Brandon Wheat Kings	MJHL	29	22	25	47	....	....	....	33	....	....	....	....	....	....	....	....	....	....	22	15	14	29	12	....	....	....
1960-61	Brandon Wheat Kings	MJHL	31	22	35	57	....	....	....	54	....	....	....	....	....	....	....	....	....	....	9	7	7	14	10	....	....	....
	Winnipeg Rangers	MJHL	....	....	....	....	....	....	....	....	....	....	....	....	....	....	....	....	....	....	5	4	1	5	15	....	....	....
1961-62	Kitchener-Waterloo Beavers	EPHL	56	22	23	45	....	....	....	48	....	....	....	....	....	....	....	....	....	....	7	1	0	1	0	....	....	....
1962-63	**New York Rangers**	**NHL**	**21**	**0**	**2**	**2**	**0**	**2**	**2**	**10**	....	....	....	....	....	....	....	....	....	....	....	....	....	....	....	....	....	....
	Baltimore Clippers	AHL	50	8	14	22	....	....	....	26	....	....	....	....	....	....	....	....	....	....	....	....	....	....	....	....	....	....
1963-64	Baltimore Clippers	AHL	54	10	12	22	....	....	....	39	....	....	....	....	....	....	....	....	....	....	....	....	....	....	....	....	....	....
1964-65	Baltimore Clippers	AHL	71	13	30	43	....	....	....	46	....	....	....	....	....	....	....	....	....	....	5	0	2	2	6	....	....	....
1965-66	Vancouver Canucks	WHL	41	8	20	28	....	....	....	37	....	....	....	....	....	....	....	....	....	....	7	3	1	4	23	....	....	....
1966-67	Vancouver Canucks	WHL	61	14	42	56	....	....	....	60	....	....	....	....	....	....	....	....	....	....	8	3	5	8	11	....	....	....
1967-68	Rochester Americans	AHL	72	24	47	71	....	....	....	134	....	....	....	....	....	....	....	....	....	....	11	4	10	14	13	....	....	....
1968-69	Vancouver Canucks	WHL	70	22	56	78	....	....	....	104	....	....	....	....	....	....	....	....	....	....	8	4	7	11	22	....	....	....
1969-70	**Pittsburgh Penguins**	**NHL**	**66**	**12**	**19**	**31**	**14**	**19**	**33**	**87**	**2**	**0**	**2**	**132**	**9.1**	**49**	**12**	**67**	**8**	**–22**	**10**	**0**	**1**	**1**	**34**	**0**	**0**	**0**
1970-71	**Pittsburgh Penguins**	**NHL**	**76**	**16**	**32**	**48**	**17**	**28**	**45**	**133**	**6**	**0**	**2**	**181**	**8.8**	**74**	**32**	**65**	**0**	**–23**	....	....	....	....	....	....	....	....
1971-72	**Pittsburgh Penguins**	**NHL**	**78**	**20**	**24**	**44**	**21**	**22**	**43**	**126**	**5**	**0**	**5**	**145**	**13.8**	**60**	**14**	**72**	**0**	**–26**	**4**	**0**	**2**	**2**	**9**	**0**	**0**	**0**
1972-73	**Pittsburgh Penguins**	**NHL**	**78**	**21**	**33**	**54**	**21**	**28**	**49**	**113**	**6**	**0**	**3**	**169**	**12.4**	**78**	**22**	**79**	**0**	**–23**	....	....	....	....	....	....	....	....
1973-74	**Pittsburgh Penguins**	**NHL**	**37**	**2**	**7**	**9**	**2**	**6**	**8**	**39**	**2**	**0**	**1**	**50**	**4.0**	**11**	**3**	**21**	**0**	**–13**	....	....	....	....	....	....	....	....
	Atlanta Flames	**NHL**	**40**	**2**	**4**	**6**	**2**	**3**	**5**	**55**	**0**	**0**	**0**	**39**	**5.1**	**11**	**1**	**29**	**19**	**0**	**4**	**0**	**1**	**1**	**16**	**0**	**0**	**0**
1974-75	**Atlanta Flames**	**NHL**	**74**	**18**	**16**	**34**	**17**	**13**	**30**	**62**	**3**	**1**	**2**	**120**	**15.0**	**52**	**14**	**78**	**27**	**–13**	....	....	....	....	....	....	....	....
1975-76	**Detroit Red Wings**	**NHL**	**21**	**0**	**4**	**4**	**0**	**3**	**3**	**29**	**0**	**0**	**0**	**17**	**0.0**	**8**	**3**	**22**	**13**	**–4**	....	....	....	....	....	....	....	....
	Minnesota North Stars	**NHL**	**58**	**8**	**20**	**28**	**7**	**16**	**23**	**84**	**3**	**1**	**1**	**89**	**9.0**	**34**	**13**	**47**	**10**	**–16**	....	....	....	....	....	....	....	....
1976-77			DID NOT PLAY																									
1977-78	Brandon Olympics	CSHL	....	7	34	41	....	....	....	45	....	....	....	....	....	....	....	....	....	....	....	....	....	....	....	....	....	....
	NHL Totals		**549**	**99**	**161**	**260**	**101**	**140**	**241**	**738**	**27**	**2**	**16**	**942**	**10.5**	**377**	**114**	**480**	**77**		**18**	**0**	**4**	**4**	**59**	**0**	**0**	**0**

Claimed by **Oakland** from **NY Rangers** in Expansion Draft, June 6, 1967. Traded to **Toronto** by **NY Rangers** with J.P. Parise for Gerry Ehman, October 12, 1967. Traded to **Vancouver** (WHL) by **Toronto** for cash, October, 1968. Traded to **Pittsburgh** by **Vancouver** (WHL) for Paul Andrea, John Arbour and the continued loan of Andy Bathgate for the 1969-70 season, October, 1969. Claimed on waivers by **Atlanta** from **Pittsburgh**, January 6, 1974. Traded to **Detroit** by **Atlanta** for Dave Kryskow, June 5, 1975. Traded to **Minnesota** by **Detroit** for Rick Chinnick, November 21, 1975.

• HEXTALL, DENNIS

Dennis Hextall LW – L. 5'11", 175 lbs. b: Poplar Point, Man., 4/17/1943.

			REGULAR SEASON																		PLAYOFFS							
Season	Club	League	GP	G	A	Pts	AG	AA	APts	PIM	PP	SH	GW	S	%	TGF	PGF	TGA	PGA	+/–	GP	G	A	Pts	PIM	PP	SH	GW
1961-62	Brandon Wheat Kings	MJHL	39	11	18	29	....	....	....	24	....	....	....	....	....	....	....	....	....	....	20	2	6	8	13	....	....	....
1962-63	Brandon Wheat Kings	MJHL	39	21	*46	67	....	....	....	17	....	....	....	....	....	....	....	....	....	....	19	*16	10	26	12	....	....	....
1963-64	University of North Dakota	WCHA	DID NOT PLAY – FRESHMAN																									
1964-65	University of North Dakota	WCHA	33	17	36	53	....	....	....	33	....	....	....	....	....	....	....	....	....	....	....	....	....	....	....	....	....	....
1965-66	University of North Dakota	WCHA	30	19	29	48	....	....	....	30	....	....	....	....	....	....	....	....	....	....	....	....	....	....	....	....	....	....
1966-67	Knoxville Knights	EHL	61	20	56	76	....	....	....	202	....	....	....	....	....	....	....	....	....	....	4	3	2	5	21	....	....	....
1967-68	Omaha Knights	CHL	10	0	2	2	....	....	....	9	....	....	....	....	....	....	....	....	....	....	....	....	....	....	....	....	....	....
	Buffalo Bisons	AHL	51	15	33	48	....	....	....	114	....	....	....	....	....	....	....	....	....	....	5	1	5	6	12	....	....	....
	New York Rangers	**NHL**	....	....	....	....	....	....	....	....	....	....	....	....	....	....	....	....	....	....	**2**	**0**	**0**	**0**	**0**	....	....	....
1968-69	**New York Rangers**	**NHL**	**13**	**1**	**4**	**5**	**1**	**4**	**5**	**25**	**0**	**0**	**0**	**16**	**6.3**	**8**	**1**	**6**	**0**	**+1**	....	....	....	....	....	....	....	....
	Buffalo Bisons	AHL	60	21	44	65	....	....	....	179	....	....	....	....	....	....	....	....	....	....	6	1	3	4	6	....	....	....
1969-70	**Los Angeles Kings**	**NHL**	**28**	**5**	**7**	**12**	**6**	**7**	**13**	**40**	**2**	**0**	**0**	**34**	**14.7**	**18**	**5**	**37**	**1**	**–23**	....	....	....	....	....	....	....	....
	Springfield–Montreal	AHL	39	15	27	42	....	....	....	178	....	....	....	....	....	....	....	....	....	....	8	2	5	7	29	....	....	....
1970-71	**California Golden Seals**	**NHL**	**78**	**21**	**31**	**52**	**22**	**27**	**49**	**217**	**1**	**0**	**3**	**153**	**13.7**	**85**	**12**	**103**	**10**	**–20**	....	....	....	....	....	....	....	....
1971-72	**Minnesota North Stars**	**NHL**	**33**	**6**	**10**	**16**	**6**	**9**	**15**	**49**	**3**	**0**	**1**	**46**	**13.0**	**23**	**7**	**15**	**0**	**+1**	**7**	**0**	**2**	**2**	**19**	**0**	**0**	**0**
	Cleveland Barons	AHL	5	1	1	2	....	....	....	18	....	....	....	....	....	....	....	....	....	....	....	....	....	....	....	....	....	....
1972-73	**Minnesota North Stars**	**NHL**	**78**	**30**	**52**	**82**	**30**	**44**	**74**	**140**	**3**	**0**	**4**	**140**	**21.4**	**109**	**19**	**64**	**3**	**+29**	**6**	**2**	**0**	**2**	**16**	**0**	**0**	**2**
1973-74	**Minnesota North Stars**	**NHL**	**78**	**20**	**62**	**82**	**20**	**54**	**74**	**138**	**2**	**1**	**3**	**152**	**13.2**	**117**	**27**	**98**	**12**	**+4**	....	....	....	....	....	....	....	....
1974-75	**Minnesota North Stars**	**NHL**	**80**	**17**	**57**	**74**	**16**	**45**	**61**	**147**	**4**	**0**	**2**	**161**	**10.6**	**102**	**30**	**138**	**22**	**–44**	....	....	....	....	....	....	....	....
1975-76	**Minnesota North Stars**	**NHL**	**59**	**11**	**35**	**46**	**10**	**28**	**38**	**93**	**2**	**0**	**0**	**93**	**11.8**	**55**	**17**	**72**	**5**	**–29**	....	....	....	....	....	....	....	....
	Detroit Red Wings	**NHL**	**17**	**5**	**9**	**14**	**5**	**7**	**12**	**71**	**0**	**0**	**1**	**32**	**15.6**	**25**	**7**	**24**	**8**	**+2**	....	....	....	....	....	....	....	....
1976-77	**Detroit Red Wings**	**NHL**	**78**	**14**	**32**	**46**	**13**	**26**	**39**	**158**	**5**	**0**	**1**	**129**	**10.9**	**62**	**12**	**109**	**24**	**–35**	....	....	....	....	....	....	....	....
1977-78	**Detroit Red Wings**	**NHL**	**78**	**16**	**33**	**49**	**15**	**27**	**42**	**195**	**2**	**2**	**3**	**89**	**18.0**	**61**	**11**	**89**	**34**	**–5**	**7**	**1**	**1**	**2**	**10**	**0**	**1**	**1**
1978-79	**Detroit Red Wings**	**NHL**	**20**	**4**	**8**	**12**	**4**	**6**	**10**	**33**	**2**	**0**	**0**	**16**	**25.0**	**17**	**4**	**14**	**4**	**+3**	....	....	....	....	....	....	....	....
	Washington Capitals	**NHL**	**26**	**2**	**9**	**11**	**2**	**7**	**9**	**43**	**0**	**0**	**0**	**22**	**9.1**	**17**	**4**	**35**	**9**	**–13**	....	....	....	....	....	....	....	....
1979-80	**Washington Capitals**	**NHL**	**15**	**1**	**1**	**2**	**1**	**1**	**2**	**49**	**0**	**0**	**0**	**17**	**5.9**	**5**	**0**	**15**	**5**	**–5**	....	....	....	....	....	....	....	....
	NHL Totals		**681**	**153**	**350**	**503**	**151**	**292**	**443**	**1398**	**26**	**3**	**18**	**1100**	**13.9**	**704**	**156**	**819**	**137**		**22**	**3**	**3**	**6**	**45**	**0**	**1**	**3**

WCHA Second All-Star Team (1965) • WCHA First All-Star Team (1966) • AHL Second All-Star Team (1969)

Played in NHL All-Star Game (1974, 1975)

Traded to **LA Kings** by **NY Rangers** with Leon Rochefort for Real Lemieux, June 9, 1969. Traded to **Montreal** by **LA Kings** for Dick Duff, January 23, 1970. Traded to **California** by **Montreal** for cash, May 22, 1970. Traded to **Minnesota** by **California** for Joey Johnston and Walt McKechnie, May 20, 1971. Traded to **Detroit** by **Minnesota** for Bill Hogaboam and LA Kings' 2nd round choice (previously acquired, Minnesota selected Jimmy Roberts) in 1976 Amateur Draft, February 23, 1976. Signed as a free agent by **Washington**, February 7, 1979.

• HICKE, BILL

Bill Hicke RW – L. 5'8", 164 lbs. b: Regina, Sask., 3/31/1938.

			REGULAR SEASON																		PLAYOFFS							
Season	Club	League	GP	G	A	Pts	AG	AA	APts	PIM	PP	SH	GW	S	%	TGF	PGF	TGA	PGA	+/–	GP	G	A	Pts	PIM	PP	SH	GW
1954-55	Regina Pats	SJHL	8	3	9	12	....	....	....	7	....	....	....	....	....	....	....	....	....	....	14	6	8	14	4	....	....	....
1955-56	Regina Pats	SJHL	36	33	9	42	....	....	....	51	....	....	....	....	....	....	....	....	....	....	10	6	8	14	10	....	....	....
1956-57	Regina Pats	SJHL	53	52	48	100	....	....	....	94	....	....	....	....	....	....	....	....	....	....	7	5	5	10	14	....	....	....
1957-58	Regina Pats	SJHL	49	*54	43	*97	....	....	....	144	....	....	....	....	....	....	....	....	....	....	12	9	10	19	20	....	....	....
1958-59	Rochester Americans	AHL	69	41	56	*97	....	....	....	41	....	....	....	....	....	....	....	....	....	....	5	1	1	2	12	....	....	....
	Montreal Canadiens	**NHL**	....	....	....	....	....	....	....	....	....	....	....	....	....	....	....	....	....	....	**1**	**0**	**0**	**0**	**0**	....	....	....
1959-60	**Montreal Canadiens**	**NHL**	**43**	**3**	**10**	**13**	**4**	**10**	**14**	**17**	....	....	....	....	....	....	....	....	....	....	**7**	**1**	**2**	**3**	**0**	....	....	....
	Rochester Americans	AHL	14	8	5	13	....	....	....	22	....	....	....	....	....	....	....	....	....	....	....	....	....	....	....	....	....	....
1960-61	**Montreal Canadiens**	**NHL**	**70**	**18**	**27**	**45**	**22**	**27**	**49**	**31**	....	....	....	....	....	....	....	....	....	....	**5**	**2**	**0**	**2**	**19**	....	....	....
1961-62	**Montreal Canadiens**	**NHL**	**70**	**20**	**31**	**51**	**24**	**31**	**55**	**42**	....	....	....	....	....	....	....	....	....	....	**6**	**0**	**2**	**2**	**14**	....	....	....
1962-63	**Montreal Canadiens**	**NHL**	**70**	**17**	**22**	**39**	**21**	**23**	**44**	**39**	....	....	....	....	....	....	....	....	....	....	**5**	**0**	**0**	**0**	**0**	....	....	....
1963-64	**Montreal Canadiens**	**NHL**	**48**	**11**	**9**	**20**	**14**	**10**	**24**	**41**	....	....	....	....	....	....	....	....	....	....	**7**	**0**	**2**	**2**	**2**	....	....	....
1964-65	**Montreal Canadiens**	**NHL**	**17**	**0**	**1**	**1**	**0**	**1**	**1**	**6**	....	....	....	....	....	....	....	....	....	....	....	....	....	....	....	....	....	....
	Cleveland Barons	AHL	6	3	2	5	....	....	....	2	....	....	....	....	....	....	....	....	....	....	....	....	....	....	....	....	....	....
	New York Rangers	**NHL**	**40**	**6**	**11**	**17**	**8**	**12**	**20**	**26**	....	....	....	....	....	....	....	....	....	....	....	....	....	....	....	....	....	....
1965-66	**New York Rangers**	**NHL**	**49**	**9**	**18**	**27**	**11**	**18**	**29**	**21**	....	....	....	....	....	....	....	....	....	....	....	....	....	....	....	....	....	....
	Minnesota Rangers	CHL	3	2	0	2	....	....	....	4	....	....	....	....	....	....	....	....	....	....	....	....	....	....	....	....	....	....
1966-67	**New York Rangers**	**NHL**	**48**	**3**	**4**	**7**	**4**	**4**	**8**	**11**	....	....	....	....	....	....	....	....	....	....	....	....	....	....	....	....	....	....
	Baltimore Clippers	AHL	18	14	14	28	....	....	....	15	....	....	....	....	....	....	....	....	....	....	9	6	*8	*14	23	....	....	....
1967-68	**Oakland Seals**	**NHL**	**52**	**21**	**19**	**40**	**26**	**20**	**46**	**32**	**12**	**0**	**4**	**142**	**14.8**	**50**	**23**	**51**	**2**	**–22**	....	....	....	....	....	....	....	....
1968-69	**Oakland Seals**	**NHL**	**67**	**25**	**36**	**61**	**28**	**34**	**62**	**68**	**4**	**0**	**3**	**171**	**14.6**	**70**	**16**	**67**	**2**	**–11**	**7**	**0**	**3**	**3**	**4**	**0**	**0**	**0**
1969-70	**Oakland Seals**	**NHL**	**69**	**15**	**29**	**44**	**17**	**29**	**46**	**14**	**5**	**0**	**2**	**139**	**10.8**	**67**	**22**	**56**	**1**	**–10**	**4**	**0**	**1**	**1**	**2**	**0**	**0**	**0**
1970-71	**California Golden Seals**	**NHL**	**74**	**18**	**17**	**35**	**19**	**15**	**34**	**41**	**4**	**0**	**1**	**138**	**13.0**	**51**	**11**	**70**	**1**	**–29**	....	....	....	....	....	....	....	....
1971-72	**Pittsburgh Penguins**	**NHL**	**12**	**2**	**0**	**2**	**2**	**0**	**2**	**6**	**1**	**0**	**0**	**19**	**10.5**	**3**	**1**	**8**	**0**	**–6**	....	....	....	....	....	....	....	....
	Tidewater Wings	AHL	16	4	2	6	....	....	....	6	....	....	....	....	....	....	....	....	....	....	....	....	....	....	....	....	....	....
	Fort Worth Wings	CHL	34	9	10	19	....	....	....	51	....	....	....	....	....	....	....	....	....	....	7	0	5	5	12	....	....	....
1972-73	Alberta Oilers	WHA	73	14	24	38	....	....	....	20	....	....	....	....	....	....	....	....	....	....	....	....	....	....	....	....	....	....
	NHL Totals		**729**	**168**	**234**	**402**	**200**	**234**	**434**	**395**	**26**	**0**	**10**	**609**	**27.6**	**241**	**73**	**252**	**6**		**42**	**3**	**10**	**13**	**41**	**0**	**0**	**0**
	Other Major League Totals		73	14	24	38	....	....	....	20	....	....	....	....	....	....	....	....	....	....	....	....	....	....	....	....	....	....

AHL First All-Star Team (1959) • Won Dudley "Red" Garrett Memorial Award (Top Rookie - AHL) (1959) • Won John B. Sollenberger Trophy (Top Scorer - AHL) (1959) • Won Les Cunningham Award (MVP - AHL) (1959)

Played in NHL All-Star Game (1959, 1960, 1969)

Traded to **NY Rangers** by **Montreal** with Jean-Guy Morissette for Dick Duff and Dave McComb, December 21, 1964. Claimed by **Oakland** from **NY Rangers** in Expansion Draft, June 6, 1967. Traded to **Pittsburgh** by **California** for cash, September 7, 1971. Traded to **Detroit** by **Pittsburgh** for cash, November 22, 1971. Signed as a free agent by **Alberta** (WHA), September, 1972.

• HICKE, ERNIE

Ernie Hicke LW – L. 5'11", 185 lbs. b: Regina, Sask., 11/7/1947.

			REGULAR SEASON																		PLAYOFFS							
Season	Club	League	GP	G	A	Pts	AG	AA	APts	PIM	PP	SH	GW	S	%	TGF	PGF	TGA	PGA	+/–	GP	G	A	Pts	PIM	PP	SH	GW
1963-64	Regina Pats	SJHL	41	10	16	26	....	....	....	22	....	....	....	....	....	....	....	....	....	....	19	11	11	22	44	....	....	....
1964-65	Regina Pats	SJHL	48	12	22	34	....	....	....	95	....	....	....	....	....	....	....	....	....	....	12	0	5	5	28	....	....	....
1965-66	Regina Pats	SJHL	51	39	62	101	....	....	....	151	....	....	....	....	....	....	....	....	....	....	5	3	3	6	10	....	....	....
1966-67	Regina Pats	WCJHL	55	37	66	103	....	....	....	184	....	....	....	....	....	....	....	....	....	....	16	7	12	19	60	....	....	....
1967-68	Houston Apollos	CHL	67	16	20	36	....	....	....	142	....	....	....	....	....	....	....	....	....	....	....	....	....	....	....	....	....	....
1968-69	Houston Apollos	CHL	72	29	43	72	....	....	....	146	....	....	....	....	....	....	....	....	....	....	3	0	0	0	7	....	....	....
1969-70	Salt Lake Golden Eagles	WHL	65	29	26	55	....	....	....	83	....	....	....	....	....	....	....	....	....	....	....	....	....	....	....	....	....	....
1970-71	**California Golden Seals**	**NHL**	**78**	**22**	**25**	**47**	**23**	**22**	**45**	**62**	**7**	**0**	**1**	**202**	**10.9**	**68**	**17**	**87**	**0**	**–36**	....	....	....	....	....	....	....	....
1971-72	**California Golden Seals**	**NHL**	**68**	**11**	**12**	**23**	**12**	**11**	**23**	**55**	**3**	**0**	**2**	**111**	**9.9**	**44**	**13**	**46**	**2**	**–13**	....	....	....	....	....	....	....	....
1972-73	**Atlanta Flames**	**NHL**	**58**	**14**	**23**	**37**	**14**	**19**	**33**	**37**	**2**	**0**	**2**	**120**	**11.7**	**51**	**19**	**34**	**0**	**–2**	....	....	....	....	....	....	....	....
	New York Islanders	**NHL**	**1**	**0**	**0**	**0**	**0**	**0**	**0**	**0**	**0**	**0**	**0**	**2**	**0.0**	**1**	**1**	**0**	**0**	**0**	....	....	....	....	....	....	....	....
1973-74	**New York Islanders**	**NHL**	**55**	**6**	**7**	**13**	**6**	**6**	**12**	**26**	**2**	**0**	**1**	**67**	**9.0**	**21**	**5**	**35**	**0**	**–19**	....	....	....	....	....	....	....	....
1974-75	**New York Islanders**	**NHL**	**20**	**2**	**6**	**8**	**2**	**5**	**7**	**40**	**0**	**0**	**0**	**17**	**11.8**	**15**	**1**	**7**	**0**	**+7**	....	....	....	....	....	....	....	....
	Minnesota North Stars	**NHL**	**42**	**15**	**13**	**28**	**14**	**10**	**24**	**51**	**7**	**0**	**1**	**114**	**13.2**	**43**	**11**	**67**	**9**	**–26**	....	....	....	....	....	....	....	....
1975-76	**Minnesota North Stars**	**NHL**	**80**	**23**	**19**	**42**	**21**	**15**	**36**	**77**	**6**	**0**	**4**	**185**	**12.4**	**60**	**16**	**75**	**0**	**–31**	....	....	....	....	....	....	....	....
1976-77	**Minnesota North Stars**	**NHL**	**77**	**30**	**20**	**50**	**29**	**16**	**45**	**41**	**10**	**0**	**5**	**186**	**16.1**	**79**	**31**	**80**	**0**	**–32**	**2**	**1**	**0**	**1**	**0**	**0**	**0**	**0**
1977-78	**Los Angeles Kings**	**NHL**	**41**	**9**	**15**	**24**	**9**	**12**	**21**	**18**	**1**	**0**	**2**	**60**	**15.0**	**37**	**4**	**26**	**0**	**+7**	....	....	....	....	....	....	....	....
	Binghamton Dusters	AHL	21	6	18	24	....	....	....	6	....	....	....	....	....	....	....	....	....	....	....	....	....	....	....	....	....	....
	Springfield Indians	AHL	7	0	1	1	....	....	....	2	....	....	....	....	....	....	....	....	....	....	....	....	....	....	....	....	....	....
1978-79	Dallas Black Hawks	CHL	39	8	24	32	....	....	....	69	....	....	....	....	....	....	....	....	....	....	....	....	....	....	....	....	....	....
1979-80	Dallas Black Hawks	CHL	72	11	26	37	....	....	....	67	....	....	....	....	....	....	....	....	....	....	....	....	....	....	....	....	....	....
	NHL Totals		**520**	**132**	**140**	**272**	**130**	**116**	**246**	**407**	**38**	**0**	**18**	**1064**	**12.4**	**419**	**118**	**457**	**11**		**2**	**1**	**0**	**1**	**0**	**0**	**0**	**0**

Traded to **California** by **Montreal** with Montreal's 1st round choice (Chris Oddleifson) in 1970 Amateur Draft for Francois Lacombe and Oakland's 1st round choice (Guy Lafleur) in 1971 Amateur Draft, May 22, 1970. Claimed by **Atlanta** from **California** in Expansion Draft, June 6, 1972. Traded to **NY Islanders** by **Atlanta** with future considerations (Billy MacMillan, May 29, 1973) for Arnie Brown, February 13, 1973. Traded to **Minnesota** by **NY Islanders** with Doug Rombough for J.P. Parise, January 5, 1975. Signed as a free agent by **LA Kings**, September 16, 1977.

• HICKEY, GREG

Greg Hickey LW – L. 5'10", 160 lbs. b: Toronto, Ont., 3/8/1955. NY Rangers' 2nd choice, 48th overall, in 1975 Amateur Draft.

			REGULAR SEASON																		PLAYOFFS							
Season	Club	League	GP	G	A	Pts	AG	AA	APts	PIM	PP	SH	GW	S	%	TGF	PGF	TGA	PGA	+/–	GP	G	A	Pts	PIM	PP	SH	GW
1972-73	Hamilton Red Wings	OHA	53	13	9	22	....	....	....	65	....	....	....	....	....	....	....	....	....	....	....	....	....	....	....	....	....	....
1973-74	Hamilton Red Wings	OHA	67	30	28	58	....	....	....	63	....	....	....	....	....	....	....	....	....	....	....	....	....	....	....	....	....	....
1974-75	Hamilton Fincups	OHA	66	27	34	61	....	....	....	95	....	....	....	....	....	....	....	....	....	....	....	....	....	....	....	....	....	....

			REGULAR SEASON																		PLAYOFFS							
Season	Club	League	GP	G	A	Pts	AG	AA	APts	PIM	PP	SH	GW	S	%	TGF	PGF	TGA	PGA	+/–	GP	G	A	Pts	PIM	PP	SH	GW
1975-76	Providence Reds	AHL	31	2	6	8				30																		
	Port Huron Flags	IHL	9	2	3	5				2																		
1976-77	New Haven Nighthawks	AHL	4	2	0	2				2																		
	Richmond Wildcats	SHL	28	8	16	24				65																		
	Charlotte Checkers	SHL	11	5	8	13				4																		
1977-78	New York Rangers	NHL	1	0	0	0	0	0	0	0	0	0	0	2	0.0	1	0	2	0	–1								
	New Haven Nighthawks	AHL	68	18	17	35				40											15	3	3	6	14			
1978-79	New Haven Nighthawks	AHL	76	23	40	63				75											10	3	7	10	4			
1979-80	Fort Wayne Komets	IHL	51	21	23	44				34											15	6	6	12	12			
1980-81	Springfield Indians	AHL	74	15	15	30				65											7	2	1	3	21			
1981-82			DID NOT PLAY																									
1982-83	Hampton Roads Gulls	ACHL	19	9	13	22				16																		
	Virginia Raiders	ACHL	17	3	5	8				6											4	0	0	0	0			
	NHL Totals		1	0	0	0	0	0	0	0	0	0	0	2	0.0	1	0	2	0									

• HICKEY, PAT

Pat "Hitch" Hickey LW – L. 6'1", 190 lbs. b: Brantford, Ont., 5/15/1953. NY Rangers' 2nd choice, 30th overall, in 1973 Amateur Draft.

Season	Club	League	GP	G	A	Pts	AG	AA	APts	PIM	PP	SH	GW	S	%	TGF	PGF	TGA	PGA	+/–	GP	G	A	Pts	PIM	PP	SH	GW
1970-71	Hamilton Red Wings	OHA	55	15	17	32				46																		
1971-72	Hamilton Red Wings	OHA	58	21	39	60				78																		
1972-73	Hamilton Red Wings	OHA	61	32	47	79				80																		
1973-74	Toronto Toros	WHA	78	26	29	55				52											12	3	3	6	12			
1974-75	Toronto Toros	WHA	74	34	34	68				50											5	0	1	1	4			
1975-76	New York Rangers	NHL	70	14	22	36	13	17	30	36	0	0	1	157	8.9	50	14	70	5	–29								
1976-77	New York Rangers	NHL	80	23	17	40	22	14	36	35	4	1	1	130	17.7	57	12	62	6	–11								
1977-78	New York Rangers	NHL	80	40	33	73	39	27	66	47	10	1	3	215	18.6	99	39	93	14	–19	3	2	0	2	0	1	0	0
	Canada	WEC-A	10	5	1	6				4																		
1978-79	New York Rangers	NHL	80	34	41	75	31	31	62	56	8	0	1	193	17.6	107	29	78	8	+8	18	1	7	8	6	0	0	0
1979-80	New York Rangers	NHL	7	2	2	4	2	2	4	10	0	0	0	5	40.0	10	3	9	1	–1								
	Colorado Rockies	NHL	24	7	9	16	6	7	13	10	0	0	0	52	13.5	32	5	34	5	–2								
	Toronto Maple Leafs	NHL	45	22	16	38	20	12	32	16	6	0	3	99	22.2	66	20	46	1	+1	3	0	0	0	2	0	0	0
1980-81	Toronto Maple Leafs	NHL	72	16	33	49	13	23	36	49	5	0	1	157	10.2	72	14	87	13	–16	2	0	0	0	0	0	0	0
1981-82	Toronto Maple Leafs	NHL	1	0	0	0	0	0	0	0	0	0	0	0	0.0	0	0	0	0	0								
	New York Rangers	NHL	53	15	14	29	12	9	21	32	3	0	3	77	19.5	47	10	52	0	–15								
	Quebec Nordiques	NHL	7	0	1	1	0	1	1	4	0	0	0	3	0.0	1	0	2	0	–1	15	1	3	4	21	1	0	0
1982-83	St. Louis Blues	NHL	1	0	0	0	0	0	0	0	0	0	0	1	0.0	0	0	0	0	0								
	Salt Lake Golden Eagles	CHL	36	13	12	25				28											6	1	0	1	2			
1983-84	St. Louis Blues	NHL	69	9	11	20	7	7	14	24	0	0	1	78	11.5	31	0	76	42	–3	11	1	1	2	6	0	1	0
1984-85	St. Louis Blues	NHL	57	10	13	23	8	9	17	32	0	3	1	53	18.9	29	0	47	14	–4	3	0	0	0	2	0	0	0
	NHL Totals		646	192	212	404	173	159	332	351	36	5	15	1220	15.7	601	146	656	109		55	5	11	16	37	2	1	0
	Other Major League Totals		152	60	63	123				102											17	3	4	7	16			

Selected by **Toronto** (WHA) in 1973 WHA Amateur Draft, June, 1973. Traded to **Colorado** by **NY Rangers** with Lucien DeBlois, Mike McEwen, Dean Turner and future considerations (Bobby Sheehan) for Barry Beck, November 2, 1979. Traded to **Toronto** by **Colrado** with Wilf Paiement for Lanny McDonald and Joel Quenneville, December 29, 1979. Traded to **NY Rangers** by **Toronto** for NY Rangers' 5th round choice (Sylvain Charland) in 1982 Entry Draft, October 8, 1982. Traded to **Quebec** by **NY Rangers** to complete transaction that sent Robbie Ftorek and draft choice to Quebec, March 8, 1982. Traded to **St. Louis** by **Quebec** for Rick LaPointe, August 4, 1982.

• HICKS, ALEX

Alex Hicks LW – L. 6'1", 195 lbs. b: Calgary, Alta., 9/4/1969.

Season	Club	League	GP	G	A	Pts	AG	AA	APts	PIM	PP	SH	GW	S	%	TGF	PGF	TGA	PGA	+/–	GP	G	A	Pts	PIM	PP	SH	GW
1988-89	U. of Wisconsin-Eau Claire	NCHA	30	21	26	47				42																		
1989-90	U. of Wisconsin-Eau Claire	NCHA	34	31	48	79				30																		
1990-91	U. of Wisconsin-Eau Claire	NCHA	26	22	35	57				43																		
1991-92	U. of Wisconsin-Eau Claire	NCHA	26	24	42	66				63																		
1992-93	Toledo Storm	ECHL	50	26	34	60				100											16	5	10	15	79			
	Adirondack Red Wings	AHL	3	0	0	0				0																		
1993-94	Toledo Storm	ECHL	60	31	49	80				240											14	10	10	20	56			
	Adirondack Red Wings	AHL	8	1	3	4				2											5	0	2	2	2			
1994-95	Las Vegas Thunder	IHL	79	24	42	66				212											9	2	4	6	47			
1995-96	Anaheim Mighty Ducks	NHL	64	10	11	21	10	9	19	37	0	0	2	83	12.0	36	3	29	7	+11								
	Baltimore Bandits	AHL	13	2	10	12				23																		
1996-97	Anaheim Mighty Ducks	NHL	18	2	6	8	2	5	7	14	0	0	0	21	9.5	11	0	14	4	+1								
	Pittsburgh Penguins	NHL	55	5	15	20	5	13	18	76	0	0	3	57	8.8	26	0	42	10	–6	5	0	1	1	2	0	0	0
1997-98	Pittsburgh Penguins	NHL	58	7	13	20	8	13	21	54	0	0	1	78	9.0	28	1	31	8	+4	6	0	0	0	2	0	0	0
	NHL Totals		195	24	45	69	25	40	65	181	0	0	6	239	10.0	101	4	116	29		11	0	1	1	4	0	0	0

NCAA (College Div.) West First All-American Team (1991, 1992)

Signed as a free agent by **Anaheim**, August 17, 1995. Traded to **Pittsburgh** by **Anaheim** with Fredrik Olausson for Shawn Antoski and Dmitri Mironov, November 19, 1996.

• HICKS, DOUG

Doug "Hicksy" Hicks D – L. 6', 185 lbs. b: Cold Lake, Alta., 5/28/1955. Minnesota's 1st choice, 6th overall, in 1974 Amateur Draft.

Season	Club	League	GP	G	A	Pts	AG	AA	APts	PIM	PP	SH	GW	S	%	TGF	PGF	TGA	PGA	+/–	GP	G	A	Pts	PIM	PP	SH	GW
1971-72	Flin Flon Bombers	WCJHL	50	1	4	5				80																		
1972-73	Flin Flon Bombers	WCJHL	65	14	35	49				106																		
1973-74	Flin Flon Bombers	WCJHL	68	13	48	61				102																		
1974-75	Minnesota North Stars	NHL	80	6	12	18	6	9	15	51	1	0	0	76	7.9	59	3	89	8	–25								
1975-76	Minnesota North Stars	NHL	80	5	13	18	5	10	15	54	3	0	1	102	4.9	78	16	81	2	–17								
1976-77	Minnesota North Stars	NHL	79	5	14	19	5	11	16	68	1	1	0	83	6.0	74	14	121	30	–31	2	0	0	0	7	0	0	0
1977-78	Minnesota North Stars	NHL	61	2	9	11	2	7	9	51	0	0	0	81	2.5	48	7	74	5	–28								
	Chicago Black Hawks	NHL	13	1	7	8	1	6	7	2	0	0	0	22	4.5	19	1	16	3	+5	4	1	0	1	2	1	0	0
1978-79	Chicago Black Hawks	NHL	44	1	8	9	1	6	7	15	0	0	0	32	3.1	30	2	43	3	–12								
	New Brunswick Hawks	AHL	6	0	1	1				12																		
	Dallas Black Hawks	CHL	16	1	10	11				60											9	3	6	9	11			
1979-80	Edmonton Oilers	NHL	78	9	31	40	8	24	32	52	5	2	1	122	7.4	137	34	128	43	+18	3	0	0	0	2	0	0	0
1980-81	Edmonton Oilers	NHL	59	5	16	21	4	11	15	76	1	1	0	109	4.6	86	16	76	27	+21	9	1	1	2	4	0	0	0
1981-82	Edmonton Oilers	NHL	49	3	20	23	2	13	15	55	1	0	0	44	6.8	67	11	60	10	+6								
	Washington Capitals	NHL	12	0	1	1	0	1	1	11	0	0	0	6	0.0	3	0	14	4	–7								
1982-83	Washington Capitals	NHL	6	0	0	0	0	0	0	7	0	0	0	6	0.0	0	0	6	3	–3								
	Hershey Bears	AHL	75	2	35	37				44											5	0	2	2	0			
1983-84			STATISTICS NOT AVAILABLE																									
1984-85	Kolner Haie	Germany	38	10	26	36				60											7	0	0	0	9			
1985-86			STATISTICS NOT AVAILABLE																									
1986-87	HC Salzburger	Austria	22	6	17	23				55																		
	NHL Totals		561	37	131	168	34	98	132	442	12	4	2	683	5.4	601	104	708	138		18	2	1	3	15	1	0	0

Traded to **Chicago** by **Minnesota** for future considerations (Pierre Plante, May 4, 1978), March 14, 1978. Claimed by **Edmonton** from **Chicago** in Expansion Draft, June 13, 1979. Traded to **Washington** by **Edmonton** for Todd Bidner, March 9, 1982.

• HICKS, GLENN

Glenn Hicks LW – L. 5'10", 177 lbs. b: Red Deer, Alta., 8/28/1958. Detroit's 1st choice, 28th overall, in 1978 Amateur Draft.

Season	Club	League	GP	G	A	Pts	AG	AA	APts	PIM	PP	SH	GW	S	%	TGF	PGF	TGA	PGA	+/–	GP	G	A	Pts	PIM	PP	SH	GW
1975-76	Flin Flon Bombers	WCJHL	71	16	19	35				103																		
1976-77	Flin Flon Bombers	WCJHL	71	20	31	59				175																		
1977-78	Flin Flon Bombers	WCJHL	72	50	69	119				225																		
1978-79	Winnipeg Jets	WHA	69	6	10	16				48											7	1	1	2	4			
1979-80	Detroit Red Wings	NHL	50	1	2	3	1	2	3	43	0	0	0	52	1.9	13	1	33	0	–21								
1980-81	Detroit Red Wings	NHL	58	5	10	15	4	7	11	84	1	0	0	71	7.0	28	1	31	4	0								
	Adirondack Red Wings	AHL	19	10	6	16				56																		
1981-82	Tulsa Oilers	CHL	78	14	34	48				103											3	0	0	0	7			
1982-83	Birmingham South Stars	CHL	80	13	26	39				40											13	0	7	7	23			
1983-84	Salt Lake Golden Eagles	CHL	62	4	26	30				87											5	0	1	1	16			

			REGULAR SEASON																	PLAYOFFS							
Season	Club	League	GP	G	A	Pts	AG	AA	APts	PIM	PP	SH	GW	S	%	TGF	PGF	TGA	PGA	+/-	GP	G	A	Pts	PIM	PP	SH	GW
1984-85	Springfield Indians	AHL	11	3	4	7	....	....	....	4	....	....	....	....	....	....	....	....	....	....	....	....	....	....	....
	EHC Kloten	Switz.	38	12	17	29	....	....	....	....	....	....	....	....	....	....	....	....	....	....	....	....	....	....	....
1985-86	Salt Lake Golden Eagles	IHL	82	14	40	54	....	....	....	75	....	....	....	....	....	....	....	....	....	....	5	0	4	4	6
	NHL Totals		108	6	12	18	5	9	14	127	1	0	0	123	4.9	41	2	64	4						
	Other Major League Totals		69	6	10	16				48											7	1	1	2	4

Signed as an underage free agent by **Winnipeg** (WHA), June, 1979. Reclaimed by **Detroit** from **Winnipeg** prior to Expansion Draft, June 9, 1979. Signed as a free agent by **Minnesota**, September 2, 1983.

● HICKS, WAYNE   Wayne Hicks   RW – R. 5'11", 185 lbs.   b: Aberdeen, WA, 4/9/1937.

Season	Club	League	GP	G	A	Pts	AG	AA	APts	PIM	PP	SH	GW	S	%	TGF	PGF	TGA	PGA	+/-	GP	G	A	Pts	PIM	PP	SH	GW
1953-54	Calgary Buffalos	WCJHL	6	0	1	1				2											5	0	0	0	0
1954-55	Moose Jaw Canucks	WCJHL	35	4	5	9				12															
1955-56	Yorkton Terriers	SJHL	48	28	25	53				81											5	2	1	3	2
1956-57	Melville Millionaires	SJHL	50	42	38	80				76															
1956-57	Calgary Stampeders	WHL	4	0	0	0				0															
1957-58	Calgary Stampeders	WHL	60	7	14	21				19											14	0	1	1	6
1958-59	Calgary Stampeders	WHL	64	15	20	35				41											8	1	2	3	5
1959-60	Sault Ste. Marie Greyhounds	EPHL	69	30	47	77				64											1	0	1	1	0
	Chicago Black Hawks	**NHL**	....	....	....	....				....											1	0	0	0	2
1960-61	**Chicago Black Hawks**	**NHL**	1	0	0	0	0	0	0	0											1	0	0	0	2
	Buffalo Bisons	AHL	72	20	35	55				57											4	2	2	4	6
1961-62	Buffalo Bisons	AHL	70	22	42	64				74											11	3	3	6	8
	Calgary Stampeders	WHL	4	1	0	1				0															
1962-63	**Boston Bruins**	**NHL**	65	7	9	16	9	9	18	14															
1963-64	**Montreal Canadiens**	**NHL**	2	0	0	0	0	0	0	0															
	Quebec Aces	AHL	70	36	42	78				30											9	4	2	6	12
1964-65	Quebec Aces	AHL	72	38	47	85				52											5	1	0	1	2
1965-66	Quebec Aces	AHL	72	32	49	81				24											6	0	0	0	0
1966-67	Quebec Aces	AHL	72	31	60	91				34											5	1	2	3	2
1967-68	**Philadelphia Flyers**	**NHL**	32	2	7	9	2	7	9	6	1	0	0	41	4.9	15	11	9	0	–5					
	Quebec Aces	AHL	13	4	9	13				13															
	Pittsburgh Penguins	**NHL**	15	4	7	11	5	7	12	2	2	0	1	26	15.4	14	4	8	0	+2					
1968-69	Baltimore Clippers	AHL	65	33	36	69				55											3	0	0	0	0
1969-70	Baltimore Clippers	AHL	64	14	21	35				58											3	0	0	0	0
1970-71	Salt Lake Golden Eagles	WHL	8	1	3	4				5															
	Phoenix Roadrunners	WHL	67	29	32	61				36											10	1	8	9	2
1971-72	Phoenix Roadrunners	WHL	69	17	31	48				59											6	3	3	6	2
1972-73	Phoenix Roadrunners	WHL	67	17	33	50				31											10	4	*12	*16	4
1973-74	Phoenix Roadrunners	WHL	72	27	32	59				23															
	NHL Totals		115	13	23	36	16	23	39	22	3	0	1	67	19.4	29	15	17	0		2	0	1	1	2	0	0	0

AHL Second All-Star Team (1965, 1969) ● AHL First All-Star Team (1967)

Traded to **Montreal** by **Chicago** for Al MacNeil, May, 1962. Claimed by **Boston** from **Montreal** in Intra-League Draft, June, 1962. Traded to **Montreal** by **Boston** for cash, September 28, 1963. NHL rights transferred to **Philadelphia** after NHL club purchased **Quebec** (AHL) franchise, May 8, 1967. Traded to **Pittsburgh** by **Philadelphia** for cash, February 27, 1968. Traded to **Phoenix** (WHL) by **Salt Lake** (WHL) for Rick Charron, November, 1970.

● HIDI, ANDRE   Andre Hidi   LW – L. 6'2", 205 lbs.   b: Toronto, Ont., 6/5/1960.   Colorado's 7th choice, 148th overall, in 1980 Entry Draft.

Season	Club	League	GP	G	A	Pts	AG	AA	APts	PIM	PP	SH	GW	S	%	TGF	PGF	TGA	PGA	+/-	GP	G	A	Pts	PIM	PP	SH	GW
1979-80	Peterborough Petes	OHA	68	30	35	65				49											14	4	8	12	31
	Canada	WJC-A	5	2	0	2				2															
1980-81	Peterborough Petes	OHA	3	1	1	2				2											5	2	3	5	11
	University of Toronto	OUAA	22	12	13	25				32															
1981-82	University of Toronto	OUAA	22	26	26	52				52															
1982-83	University of Toronto	OUAA	24	23	29	52				50															
1983-84	University of Toronto	OUAA	24	30	30	60				66															
	Washington Capitals	**NHL**	1	0	0	0	0	0	0	0	0	0	0	1	0.0	0	0	0	0	0	2	0	0	0	0	0	0	0
1984-85	**Washington Capitals**	**NHL**	6	2	1	3	2	1	3	9	1	0	0	7	28.6	9	5	2	0	+2					
	Binghamton Whalers	AHL	55	12	17	29				57											3	0	1	1	5
1985-86	Binghamton Whalers	AHL	66	19	24	43				104											6	1	4	5	13
	NHL Totals		7	2	1	3	2	1	3	9	1	0	0	8	25.0	9	5	2	0		2	0	0	0	0	0	0	0

Signed as a free agent by **Washington**, March 29, 1984.

● HIEMER, ULI   Uli Hiemer   D – L. 6'1", 190 lbs.   b: Fussen, W. Germany, 9/21/1962.   Colorado's 3rd choice, 48th overall, in 1981 Entry Draft.

Season	Club	League	GP	G	A	Pts	AG	AA	APts	PIM	PP	SH	GW	S	%	TGF	PGF	TGA	PGA	+/-	GP	G	A	Pts	PIM	PP	SH	GW
1979-80	EV Fussen	Germany	44	6	10	16				84															
	West Germany	WJC-A	5	1	4	5				12															
1980-81	EV Fussen	Germany	34	11	11	22				84															
	West Germany	WEC-A	6	0	1	1				14															
1981-82	Kolner Haie	Germany	43	10	23	33				85											9	3	0	3	27
	West Germany	WJC-A	7	1	2	3				21															
	West Germany	WEC-A	2	0	0	0				2															
1982-83	Kolner Haie	Germany	35	8	17	25				69											8	2	6	8	23
	West Germany	WEC-A	9	1	3	4				8															
1983-84	Kolner Haie	Germany	50	23	23	46				93															
	West Germany	Olympics	6	2	0	2				4															
1984-85	West Germany	C Cup	3	0	0	0				0															
	New Jersey Devils	**NHL**	53	5	24	29	4	16	20	70	3	0	0	85	5.9	64	24	56	2	–14					
	West Germany	WEC-A	10	2	1	3				10															
1985-86	**New Jersey Devils**	**NHL**	50	8	16	24	6	11	17	61	6	0	1	100	8.0	70	22	59	10	–1					
	Maine Mariners	AHL	15	5	2	7				19															
1986-87	**New Jersey Devils**	**NHL**	40	6	14	20	5	10	15	45	2	0	1	80	7.5	53	16	46	3	–6					
	Maine Mariners	AHL	26	4	3	7				51															
1987-88	Dusseldorfer EG	Germany	44	12	25	37				102															
1988-89	Dusseldorfer EG	Germany	42	23	28	51				121															
	West Germany	WEC-A	10	2	1	3				8															
1989-90	Dusseldorfer EG	Germany	32	17	25	42				75											10	6	3	9	*46
	West Germany	WEC-A	10	0	1	1				6															
1990-91	Dusseldorfer EG	Germany	44	18	32	50				43											13	3	11	14	22
1991-92	Dusseldorfer EG	Germany	42	8	27	35				67															
	Germany	Olympics	8	0	1	1				12															
	Germany	WC-A	6	3	1	4				26															
1992-93	Dusseldorfer EG	Germany	44	11	28	39				57															
	Germany	WC-A	5	0	1	1				22															
1993-94	Dusseldorfer EG	Germany	44	17	22	39				60															
	Germany	Olympics	6	0	0	0				0															
1994-95	Dusseldorfer EG	Germany	40	9	19	28				54											10	1	9	10	20
	Germany	WC-A	5	0	2	2				2															
1995-96	Dusseldorfer EG	Germany	47	9	22	31				98											13	3	6	9	24
	NHL Totals		143	19	54	73	15	37	52	176	11	0	2	265	7.2	187	62	161	15						

Transferred to **New Jersey** after **Colorado** franchise relocated, June 30, 1982.

• HIGGINS, MATT

Matt Higgins C – L. 6'2", 170 lbs. b: Calgary, Alta., 10/29/1977. Montreal's 1st choice, 18th overall, in 1996 Entry Draft.

			REGULAR SEASON																		PLAYOFFS							
Season	Club	League	GP	G	A	Pts	AG	AA	APts	PIM	PP	SH	GW	S	%	TGF	PGF	TGA	PGA	+/-	GP	G	A	Pts	PIM	PP	SH	GW
1993-94	Moose Jaw Warriors	WHL	64	6	10	16	....	....	....	10	....	....	....	....	....	....	....	....	....	....	....	....	....	....	....	....	....	....
1994-95	Moose Jaw Warriors	WHL	72	36	34	70	....	....	....	26	....	....	....	....	....	....	....	....	....	....	10	1	2	3	2	....	....	....
1995-96	Moose Jaw Warriors	WHL	67	30	33	63	....	....	....	43	....	....	....	....	....	....	....	....	....	....	....	....	....	....	....	....	....	....
1996-97	Moose Jaw Warriors	WHL	71	33	57	90	....	....	....	51	....	....	....	....	....	....	....	....	....	....	12	3	5	8	2	....	....	....
1997-98	**Montreal Canadiens**	**NHL**	**1**	**0**	**0**	**0**	**0**	**0**	**0**	**0**	**0**	**0**	**0**	**1**	**0.0**	**0**	**0**	**1**	**0**	**–1**	....	....	....	....	....	....	....	....
	Fredericton Canadiens	AHL	50	5	22	27	....	....	....	12	....	....	....	....	....	....	....	....	....	....	4	1	2	3	2	....	....	....
	NHL Totals		**1**	**0**	**0**	**0**	**0**	**0**	**0**	**0**	**0**	**0**	**0**	**1**	**0.0**	**0**	**0**	**1**	**0**		....	....	....	....	....	....	....	....

• HIGGINS, PAUL

Paul Higgins RW – R. 6'1", 195 lbs. b: St. John, N.B., 1/13/1962. Toronto's 10th choice, 200th overall, in 1980 Entry Draft.

Season	Club	League	GP	G	A	Pts	AG	AA	APts	PIM	PP	SH	GW	S	%	TGF	PGF	TGA	PGA	+/-	GP	G	A	Pts	PIM	PP	SH	GW
1979-80	Henry Carr Crusaders	H.S.	....	25	38	63	....	....	....	....	....	....	....	....	....	....	....	....	....	....	....	....	....	....	....	....	....	....
1980-81	Toronto Marlboros	OHL	46	4	4	8	....	....	....	178	....	....	....	....	....	....	....	....	....	....	5	0	0	0	52	....	....	....
1981-82	Toronto Marlboros	OHL	6	0	0	0	....	....	....	11	....	....	....	....	....	....	....	....	....	....	....	....	....	....	....	....	....	....
	Kitchener Rangers	OHL	29	3	5	8	....	....	....	119	....	....	....	....	....	....	....	....	....	....	....	....	....	....	....	....	....	....
	Toronto Maple Leafs	**NHL**	**3**	**0**	**0**	**0**	**0**	**0**	**0**	**17**	**0**	**0**	**0**	**0**	**0.0**	**0**	**0**	**1**	**0**	**–1**	....	....	....	....	....	....	....	....
1982-83	**Toronto Maple Leafs**	**NHL**	**22**	**0**	**0**	**0**	**0**	**0**	**0**	**135**	**0**	**0**	**0**	**1**	**0.0**	**1**	**0**	**4**	**0**	**–3**	**1**	**0**	**0**	**0**	**0**	**0**	**0**	**0**
1983-84	Carolina Thunderbirds	ACHL	4	0	1	1	....	....	....	18	....	....	....	....	....	....	....	....	....	....	....	....	....	....	....	....	....	....
	NHL Totals		**25**	**0**	**0**	**0**	**0**	**0**	**0**	**152**	**0**	**0**	**0**	**1**	**0.0**	**1**	**0**	**5**	**0**		**1**	**0**	**0**	**0**	**0**	**0**	**0**	**0**

• HIGGINS, TIM

Tim Higgins RW. 6', 185 lbs. b: Ottawa, Ont., 2/7/1958. Chicago's 1st choice, 10th overall, in 1978 Amateur Draft.

Season	Club	League	GP	G	A	Pts	AG	AA	APts	PIM	PP	SH	GW	S	%	TGF	PGF	TGA	PGA	+/-	GP	G	A	Pts	PIM	PP	SH	GW
1974-75	Ottawa 67's	OHA	22	1	3	4	....	....	....	6	....	....	....	....	....	....	....	....	....	....	....	....	....	....	....	....	....	....
1975-76	Ottawa 67's	OHA	59	15	10	25	....	....	....	59	....	....	....	....	....	....	....	....	....	....	....	....	....	....	....	....	....	....
1976-77	Ottawa 67's	OHA	66	35	52	87	....	....	....	80	....	....	....	....	....	....	....	....	....	....	19	10	14	24	39	....	....	....
1977-78	Ottawa 67's	OHA	50	41	60	101	....	....	....	99	....	....	....	....	....	....	....	....	....	....	16	9	13	22	36	....	....	....
1978-79	**Chicago Black Hawks**	**NHL**	**36**	**7**	**16**	**23**	**6**	**12**	**18**	**30**	**0**	**0**	**1**	**64**	**10.9**	**36**	**7**	**24**	**1**	**+6**	**4**	**0**	**0**	**0**	**0**	**0**	**0**	**0**
	New Brunswick Hawks	AHL	17	3	5	8	....	....	....	14	....	....	....	....	....	....	....	....	....	....	....	....	....	....	....	....	....	....
1979-80	**Chicago Black Hawks**	**NHL**	**74**	**13**	**12**	**25**	**12**	**9**	**21**	**50**	**2**	**0**	**0**	**110**	**11.8**	**37**	**4**	**49**	**1**	**–15**	**7**	**0**	**3**	**3**	**10**	**0**	**0**	**0**
1980-81	**Chicago Black Hawks**	**NHL**	**78**	**24**	**35**	**59**	**20**	**24**	**44**	**86**	**1**	**0**	**1**	**149**	**16.1**	**88**	**13**	**58**	**3**	**+20**	**3**	**0**	**0**	**0**	**0**	**0**	**0**	**0**
1981-82	**Chicago Black Hawks**	**NHL**	**74**	**20**	**30**	**50**	**16**	**20**	**36**	**85**	**6**	**0**	**2**	**114**	**17.5**	**104**	**30**	**80**	**0**	**–6**	**12**	**3**	**1**	**4**	**15**	**0**	**0**	**0**
1982-83	**Chicago Black Hawks**	**NHL**	**64**	**14**	**9**	**23**	**11**	**6**	**17**	**63**	**0**	**0**	**2**	**71**	**19.7**	**33**	**0**	**39**	**2**	**–4**	**13**	**1**	**3**	**4**	**10**	**0**	**0**	**0**
1983-84	**Chicago Black Hawks**	**NHL**	**32**	**1**	**4**	**5**	**1**	**3**	**4**	**21**	**0**	**0**	**1**	**21**	**4.8**	**10**	**0**	**9**	**0**	**+1**	....	....	....	....	....	....	....	....
	New Jersey Devils	**NHL**	**37**	**18**	**10**	**28**	**14**	**7**	**21**	**27**	**3**	**1**	**3**	**72**	**25.0**	**44**	**11**	**41**	**4**	**–4**	....	....	....	....	....	....	....	....
1984-85	**New Jersey Devils**	**NHL**	**71**	**19**	**29**	**48**	**16**	**20**	**36**	**30**	**5**	**0**	**2**	**147**	**12.9**	**73**	**26**	**58**	**1**	**–10**	....	....	....	....	....	....	....	....
1985-86	**New Jersey Devils**	**NHL**	**59**	**9**	**17**	**26**	**7**	**11**	**18**	**47**	**2**	**0**	**1**	**90**	**10.0**	**45**	**5**	**33**	**0**	**+7**	....	....	....	....	....	....	....	....
1986-87	**Detroit Red Wings**	**NHL**	**77**	**12**	**14**	**26**	**10**	**10**	**20**	**124**	**0**	**1**	**1**	**110**	**10.9**	**43**	**1**	**68**	**24**	**–2**	**12**	**0**	**1**	**1**	**16**	**0**	**0**	**0**
1987-88	**Detroit Red Wings**	**NHL**	**62**	**12**	**13**	**25**	**10**	**9**	**19**	**94**	**0**	**1**	**1**	**63**	**19.0**	**35**	**1**	**37**	**8**	**+5**	**13**	**1**	**0**	**1**	**26**	**0**	**0**	**1**
1988-89	**Detroit Red Wings**	**NHL**	**42**	**5**	**9**	**14**	**4**	**6**	**10**	**62**	**0**	**0**	**0**	**45**	**11.1**	**19**	**1**	**27**	**9**	**0**	**1**	**0**	**0**	**0**	**0**	**0**	**0**	**0**
	Adirondack Red Wings	AHL	14	7	4	11	....	....	....	24	....	....	....	....	....	....	....	....	....	....	....	....	....	....	....	....	....	....
	NHL Totals		**706**	**154**	**198**	**352**	**127**	**137**	**264**	**719**	**19**	**3**	**15**	**1056**	**14.6**	**567**	**99**	**523**	**53**		**65**	**5**	**8**	**13**	**77**	**0**	**0**	**1**

Traded to **New Jersey** by **Chicago** for Jeff Larmer, January 11, 1984. Traded to **Detroit** by **New Jersey** for Claude Loiselle, June 25, 1986.

• HILL, AL

Al Hill C – L. 6'1", 175 lbs. b: Nanaimo, B.C., 4/22/1955.

Season	Club	League	GP	G	A	Pts	AG	AA	APts	PIM	PP	SH	GW	S	%	TGF	PGF	TGA	PGA	+/-	GP	G	A	Pts	PIM	PP	SH	GW
1973-74	Nanaimo Nuggets	BCJHL	64	29	41	70	....	....	....	60	....	....	....	....	....	....	....	....	....	....	....	....	....	....	....	....	....	....
1974-75	Victoria Cougars	WHL	70	21	36	57	....	....	....	75	....	....	....	....	....	....	....	....	....	....	12	5	2	7	21	....	....	....
1975-76	Victoria Cougars	WHL	68	26	40	66	....	....	....	172	....	....	....	....	....	....	....	....	....	....	15	5	10	15	94	....	....	....
1976-77	**Philadelphia Flyers**	**NHL**	**9**	**2**	**4**	**6**	**2**	**3**	**5**	**27**	**0**	**0**	**0**	**6**	**33.3**	**8**	**0**	**2**	**0**	**+6**	....	....	....	....	....	....	....	....
	Springfield Indians	AHL	63	13	28	41	....	....	....	125	....	....	....	....	....	....	....	....	....	....	....	....	....	....	....	....	....	....
1977-78	**Philadelphia Flyers**	**NHL**	**3**	**0**	**0**	**0**	**0**	**0**	**0**	**2**	**0**	**0**	**0**	**3**	**0.0**	**0**	**0**	**0**	**0**	**0**	....	....	....	....	....	....	....	....
	Maine Mariners	AHL	80	32	59	91	....	....	....	118	....	....	....	....	....	....	....	....	....	....	12	2	7	9	49	....	....	....
1978-79	**Philadelphia Flyers**	**NHL**	**31**	**5**	**11**	**16**	**5**	**8**	**13**	**28**	**1**	**0**	**1**	**44**	**11.4**	**27**	**3**	**19**	**0**	**+5**	**7**	**1**	**0**	**1**	**2**	**0**	**0**	**0**
	Maine Mariners	AHL	35	11	14	25	....	....	....	59	....	....	....	....	....	....	....	....	....	....	....	....	....	....	....	....	....	....
1979-80	**Philadelphia Flyers**	**NHL**	**61**	**16**	**10**	**26**	**14**	**8**	**22**	**53**	**0**	**0**	**2**	**79**	**20.3**	**50**	**3**	**39**	**6**	**+14**	**19**	**3**	**5**	**8**	**19**	**1**	**0**	**0**
1980-81	**Philadelphia Flyers**	**NHL**	**57**	**10**	**15**	**25**	**8**	**10**	**18**	**45**	**0**	**0**	**2**	**70**	**14.3**	**37**	**4**	**28**	**6**	**+11**	**12**	**2**	**4**	**6**	**18**	**0**	**0**	**1**
1981-82	**Philadelphia Flyers**	**NHL**	**41**	**6**	**13**	**19**	**5**	**9**	**14**	**58**	**0**	**0**	**0**	**50**	**12.0**	**24**	**2**	**42**	**16**	**–4**	**3**	**0**	**0**	**0**	**0**	**0**	**0**	**0**
1982-83	Moncton Alpines	AHL	78	22	22	44	....	....	....	78	....	....	....	....	....	....	....	....	....	....	....	....	....	....	....	....	....	....
1983-84	Maine Mariners	AHL	51	7	17	24	....	....	....	51	....	....	....	....	....	....	....	....	....	....	17	6	12	18	22	....	....	....
1984-85	Hershey Bears	AHL	73	11	30	41	....	....	....	77	....	....	....	....	....	....	....	....	....	....	....	....	....	....	....	....	....	....
1985-86	Hershey Bears	AHL	80	17	40	57	....	....	....	129	....	....	....	....	....	....	....	....	....	....	18	2	6	8	52	....	....	....
1986-87	**Philadelphia Flyers**	**NHL**	**7**	**0**	**2**	**2**	**0**	**1**	**1**	**4**	**0**	**0**	**0**	**2**	**0.0**	**2**	**0**	**1**	**0**	**+1**	**9**	**2**	**1**	**3**	**0**	**0**	**0**	**0**
	Hershey Bears	AHL	76	13	35	48	....	....	....	124	....	....	....	....	....	....	....	....	....	....	5	0	1	1	2	....	....	....
1987-88	**Philadelphia Flyers**	**NHL**	**12**	**1**	**0**	**1**	**1**	**0**	**1**	**10**	**0**	**0**	**0**	**9**	**11.1**	**5**	**0**	**9**	**4**	**0**	**1**	**0**	**1**	**1**	**4**	**0**	**0**	**0**
	Hershey Bears	AHL	57	10	21	31	....	....	....	62	....	....	....	....	....	....	....	....	....	....	10	1	6	7	12	....	....	....
1988-89	Hershey Bears	AHL	62	13	20	33	....	....	....	63	....	....	....	....	....	....	....	....	....	....	8	2	0	2	10	....	....	....
1989-90	Hershey Bears	AHL	DID NOT PLAY – COACHING																									
	NHL Totals		**221**	**40**	**55**	**95**	**35**	**39**	**74**	**227**	**1**	**0**	**5**	**263**	**15.2**	**153**	**12**	**140**	**32**		**51**	**8**	**11**	**19**	**43**	**1**	**0**	**1**

AHL First All-Star Team (1978)

Signed as a free agent by **Philadelphia**, October 22, 1976. Signed as a free agent by **Edmonton**, November 10, 1982. Signed as a free agent by **Philadelphia**, October 8, 1984.

• HILL, BRIAN

Brian Hill RW – R. 6', 175 lbs. b: Regina, Sask., 1/12/1957. Atlanta's 4th choice, 31st overall, in 1977 Amateur Draft.

Season	Club	League	GP	G	A	Pts	AG	AA	APts	PIM	PP	SH	GW	S	%	TGF	PGF	TGA	PGA	+/-	GP	G	A	Pts	PIM	PP	SH	GW
1974-75	Medicine Hat Tigers	WCJHL	39	7	5	12	....	....	....	6	....	....	....	....	....	....	....	....	....	....	....	....	....	....	....	....	....	....
1975-76	Medicine Hat Tigers	WCJHL	70	22	24	46	....	....	....	98	....	....	....	....	....	....	....	....	....	....	9	2	3	5	2	....	....	....
1976-77	Medicine Hat Tigers	WCJHL	72	53	51	104	....	....	....	101	....	....	....	....	....	....	....	....	....	....	....	....	....	....	....	....	....	....
1977-78	Tulsa Oilers	CHL	75	13	26	39	....	....	....	46	....	....	....	....	....	....	....	....	....	....	7	2	2	4	6	....	....	....
1978-79	Tulsa Oilers	CHL	74	26	27	53	....	....	....	58	....	....	....	....	....	....	....	....	....	....	....	....	....	....	....	....	....	....
1979-80	**Hartford Whalers**	**NHL**	**19**	**1**	**1**	**2**	**1**	**1**	**2**	**4**	**0**	**0**	**0**	**17**	**5.9**	**9**	**0**	**10**	**0**	**–1**	....	....	....	....	....	....	....	....
	Springfield Indians	AHL	45	15	19	34	....	....	....	12	....	....	....	....	....	....	....	....	....	....	....	....	....	....	....	....	....	....
1980-81	VEU Fussen	Germany	43	27	24	51	....	....	....	59	....	....	....	....	....	....	....	....	....	....	....	....	....	....	....	....	....	....
1981-82	VEU Feldkirch	Austria	....	20	22	42	....	....	....	....	....	....	....	....	....	....	....	....	....	....	....	6	16	22	....	....	....	....
1982-83	VEU Feldrich	Austria	28	35	37	72	....	....	....	....	....	....	....	....	....	....	....	....	....	....	....	....	....	....	....	....	....	....
1983-84	VEU Feldrich	Austria	STATISTICS NOT AVAILABLE																									
1984-85	VEU Feldkirch	Austria	37	36	31	67	....	....	....	40	....	....	....	....	....	....	....	....	....	....	....	....	....	....	....	....	....	....
1985-86	EHC Feldkirch	Austria	40	35	30	65	....	....	....	35	....	....	....	....	....	....	....	....	....	....	....	....	....	....	....	....	....	....
	Austria	WEC-B	7	3	1	4	....	....	....	2	....	....	....	....	....	....	....	....	....	....	....	....	....	....	....	....	....	....
1986-87	EHC Feldkirch	Austria	38	22	30	52	....	....	....	38	....	....	....	....	....	....	....	....	....	....	....	....	....	....	....	....	....	....
	EHC Chur	Switz.	....	17	17	34	....	....	....	....	....	....	....	....	....	....	....	....	....	....	....	....	....	....	....	....	....	....
	Austria	WEC-B	5	1	0	1	....	....	....	2	....	....	....	....	....	....	....	....	....	....	....	....	....	....	....	....	....	....
1987-88	SC Rapperswill	Switz. B	....	42	42	84	....	....	....	....	....	....	....	....	....	....	....	....	....	....	....	....	....	....	....	....	....	....
	NHL Totals		**19**	**1**	**1**	**2**	**1**	**1**	**2**	**4**	**0**	**0**	**0**	**17**	**5.9**	**9**	**0**	**10**	**0**		....	....	....	....	....	....	....	....

Claimed by **Hartford** from **Atlanta** in Expansion Draft, June 13, 1979.

• HILL, SEAN

Sean Hill D – R. 6', 203 lbs. b: Duluth, MN, 2/14/1970. Montreal's 9th choice, 167th overall, in 1988 Entry Draft.

Season	Club	League	GP	G	A	Pts	AG	AA	APts	PIM	PP	SH	GW	S	%	TGF	PGF	TGA	PGA	+/-	GP	G	A	Pts	PIM	PP	SH	GW
1987-88	East Duluth High School	H.S.	24	10	17	27	....	....	....	....	....	....	....	....	....	....	....	....	....	....	....	....	....	....	....	....	....	....
1988-89	University of Wisconsin	WCHA	45	2	23	25	....	....	....	69	....	....	....	....	....	....	....	....	....	....	....	....	....	....	....	....	....	....
1989-90	University of Wisconsin	WCHA	42	14	39	53	....	....	....	78	....	....	....	....	....	....	....	....	....	....	....	....	....	....	....	....	....	....
	United States	WJC-A	7	0	3	3	....	....	....	10	....	....	....	....	....	....	....	....	....	....	....	....	....	....	....	....	....	....
1990-91	University of Wisconsin	WCHA	37	19	32	51	....	....	....	122	....	....	....	....	....	....	....	....	....	....	....	....	....	....	....	....	....	....
	Montreal Canadiens	**NHL**	....	....	....	....	....	....	....	....	**0**	**0**	**0**	**0**	**0.0**	**0**	**0**	**0**	**0**	**0**	**1**	**0**	**0**	**0**	**0**	**0**	**0**	**0**
	Fredericton Canadiens	AHL	....	....	....	....	....	....	....	....	....	....	....	....	....	....	....	....	....	....	3	0	2	2	2	....	....	....

Season	Club	League	REGULAR SEASON GP	G	A	Pts	AG	AA	APts	PIM	PP	SH	GW	S	%	TGF	PGF	TGA	PGA	+/–	PLAYOFFS GP	G	A	Pts	PIM	PP	SH	GW
1991-92	Fredericton Canadiens	AHL	42	7	20	27	....	....	....	65	....	....	....	....	....	....	....	....	....	....	7	1	3	4	6	....	....	....
	United States	Olympics	8	2	0	2	....	....	....	6	....	....	....	....	....	....	....	....	....	....	....	....	....	....	....	....	....	....
	United States	Nat-Team	12	4	3	7	....	....	....	16	....	....	....	....	....	....	....	....	....	....	....	....	....	....	....	....	....	....
	Montreal Canadiens	**NHL**	....	....	....	....	....	....	....	....	....	....	....	....	....	....	....	....	....	....	**4**	**1**	**0**	**1**	**2**	....	....	....
1992-93	**Montreal Canadiens**	**NHL**	**31**	**2**	**6**	**8**	**2**	**4**	**6**	**54**	**1**	**0**	**1**	**37**	**5.4**	**28**	**8**	**34**	**9**	**–5**	**3**	**0**	**0**	**0**	**4**	**0**	**0**	**0**
	Fredericton Canadiens	AHL	6	1	3	4	....	....	....	10	....	....	....	....	....	....	....	....	....	....	....	....	....	....	....	....	....	....
1993-94	**Anaheim Mighty Ducks**	**NHL**	**68**	**7**	**20**	**27**	**7**	**15**	**22**	**78**	**2**	**1**	**1**	**165**	**4.2**	**72**	**25**	**74**	**15**	**–12**	....	....	....	....	....	....	....	....
	United States	WC-A	8	0	2	2	....	....	....	6	....	....	....	....	....	....	....	....	....	....	....	....	....	....	....	....	....	....
1994-95	**Ottawa Senators**	**NHL**	**45**	**1**	**14**	**15**	**2**	**21**	**23**	**30**	**0**	**0**	**0**	**107**	**0.9**	**50**	**14**	**66**	**19**	**–11**	....	....	....	....	....	....	....	....
1995-96	**Ottawa Senators**	**NHL**	**80**	**7**	**14**	**21**	**7**	**11**	**18**	**94**	**2**	**0**	**2**	**157**	**4.5**	**59**	**13**	**107**	**35**	**–26**	....	....	....	....	....	....	....	....
1996-97	**Ottawa Senators**	**NHL**	**5**	**0**	**0**	**0**	**0**	**0**	**0**	**4**	**0**	**0**	**0**	**9**	**0.0**	**2**	**0**	**3**	**2**	**+1**	....	....	....	....	....	....	....	....
1997-98	**Ottawa Senators**	**NHL**	**13**	**1**	**1**	**2**	**1**	**1**	**2**	**6**	**0**	**0**	**0**	**16**	**6.3**	**5**	**0**	**9**	**1**	**–3**	....	....	....	....	....	....	....	....
	Carolina Hurricanes	**NHL**	**42**	**0**	**5**	**5**	**0**	**5**	**5**	**48**	**0**	**0**	**0**	**37**	**0.0**	**24**	**1**	**31**	**6**	**–2**	....	....	....	....	....	....	....	....
	NHL Totals		**284**	**18**	**60**	**78**	**19**	**57**	**76**	**314**	**5**	**1**	**4**	**528**	**3.4**	**240**	**61**	**324**	**87**		**8**	**1**	**0**	**1**	**6**	**0**	**0**	**0**

WCHA Second All-Star Team (1990, 1991) • NCAA West Second All-American Team (1991)

Claimed by **Anaheim** from **Montreal** in Expansion Draft, June 24, 1993. Traded to **Ottawa** by **Anaheim** with Anaheim's 9th round choice (Frederic Cassivi) in 1994 Entry Draft for Ottawa's 3rd round choice (later traded to Tampa Bay — Tampa Bay selected Vadim Epanchintsev) in 1994 Entry Draft, June 29, 1994. Traded to **Carolina** by **Ottawa** for Chris Murray, November 18, 1997.

• HILLER, JIM

Jim Hiller RW – R. 6', 190 lbs. b: Port Alberni, B.C., 5/15/1969. Los Angeles' 10th choice, 207th overall, in 1989 Entry Draft.

Season	Club	League	GP	G	A	Pts	AG	AA	APts	PIM	PP	SH	GW	S	%	TGF	PGF	TGA	PGA	+/–	GP	G	A	Pts	PIM	PP	SH	GW
1988-89	Melville Millionaires	SJHL	29	24	37	61	....	....	....	49	....	....	....	....	....	....	....	....	....	....	....	....	....	....	....	....	....	....
1989-90	Northern Michigan University	WCHA	39	23	33	56	....	....	....	52	....	....	....	....	....	....	....	....	....	....	....	....	....	....	....	....	....	....
1990-91	Northern Michigan University	WCHA	43	22	41	63	....	....	....	59	....	....	....	....	....	....	....	....	....	....	....	....	....	....	....	....	....	....
1991-92	Northern Michigan University	WCHA	39	28	52	80	....	....	....	115	....	....	....	....	....	....	....	....	....	....	....	....	....	....	....	....	....	....
1992-93	**Los Angeles Kings**	**NHL**	**40**	**6**	**6**	**12**	**5**	**4**	**9**	**90**	**1**	**0**	**2**	**59**	**10.2**	**24**	**4**	**20**	**0**	**0**	....	....	....	....	....	....	....	....
	Phoenix Roadrunners	IHL	3	0	2	2	....	....	....	2	....	....	....	....	....	....	....	....	....	....	....	....	....	....	....	....	....	....
	Detroit Red Wings	**NHL**	**21**	**2**	**6**	**8**	**2**	**4**	**6**	**19**	**0**	**0**	**0**	**24**	**8.3**	**12**	**0**	**5**	**0**	**+7**	**2**	**0**	**0**	**0**	**4**	**0**	**0**	**0**
1993-94	**New York Rangers**	**NHL**	**2**	**0**	**0**	**0**	**0**	**0**	**0**	**7**	**0**	**0**	**0**	**0**	**0.0**	**2**	**1**	**0**	**0**	**+1**	....	....	....	....	....	....	....	....
	Binghamton Rangers	AHL	67	27	34	61	....	....	....	61	....	....	....	....	....	....	....	....	....	....	....	....	....	....	....	....	....	....
1994-95	Binghamton Rangers	AHL	49	15	13	28	....	....	....	44	....	....	....	....	....	....	....	....	....	....	....	....	....	....	....	....	....	....
	Atlanta Knights	IHL	17	5	10	15	....	....	....	28	....	....	....	....	....	....	....	....	....	....	5	0	3	3	8	....	....	....
1995-96	Canada	Nat-Team	53	17	26	43	....	....	....	68	....	....	....	....	....	....	....	....	....	....	....	....	....	....	....	....	....	....
1996-97	Star Bulls Rosenheim	Germany	47	22	27	49	....	....	....	*187	....	....	....	....	....	....	....	....	....	....	3	0	1	1	45	....	....	....
1997-98	Star Bulls Rosenheim	Germany	42	8	19	27	....	....	....	83	....	....	....	....	....	....	....	....	....	....	....	....	....	....	....	....	....	....
	NHL Totals		**63**	**8**	**12**	**20**	**7**	**8**	**15**	**116**	**1**	**0**	**2**	**83**	**9.6**	**38**	**5**	**25**	**0**		**2**	**0**	**0**	**0**	**4**	**0**	**0**	**0**

WCHA Second All-Star Team (1992) • NCAA West Second All-American Team (1992)

Traded to **Detroit** by **LA Kings** with Paul Coffey and Sylvain Courtier for Jimmy Carson, Marc Potvin and Gary Shuchuk, January 29, 1993. Claimed on waivers by **NY Rangers** from **Detroit**, October 12, 1993.

• HILLIER, RANDY

Randy Hillier D – L. 6'1", 192 lbs. b: Toronto, Ont., 3/30/1960. Boston's 4th choice, 102nd overall, in 1980 Entry Draft.

Season	Club	League	GP	G	A	Pts	AG	AA	APts	PIM	PP	SH	GW	S	%	TGF	PGF	TGA	PGA	+/–	GP	G	A	Pts	PIM	PP	SH	GW
1977-78	Sudbury Wolves	OHA	60	1	14	15	....	....	....	67	....	....	....	....	....	....	....	....	....	....	....	....	....	....	....	....	....	....
1978-79	Sudbury Wolves	OHA	61	8	25	33	....	....	....	173	....	....	....	....	....	....	....	....	....	....	10	2	5	7	21	....	....	....
1979-80	Sudbury Wolves	OHA	60	16	49	65	....	....	....	143	....	....	....	....	....	....	....	....	....	....	9	3	6	9	14	....	....	....
1980-81	Springfield Indians	AHL	64	3	17	20	....	....	....	105	....	....	....	....	....	....	....	....	....	....	6	0	2	2	36	....	....	....
1981-82	**Boston Bruins**	**NHL**	**25**	**0**	**8**	**8**	**0**	**5**	**5**	**29**	**0**	**0**	**0**	**17**	**0.0**	**29**	**0**	**25**	**2**	**+6**	**8**	**0**	**1**	**1**	**16**	**0**	**0**	**0**
	Erie Blades	AHL	35	6	13	19	....	....	....	52	....	....	....	....	....	....	....	....	....	....	....	....	....	....	....	....	....	....
1982-83	**Boston Bruins**	**NHL**	**70**	**0**	**10**	**10**	**0**	**7**	**7**	**99**	**0**	**0**	**0**	**45**	**0.0**	**51**	**2**	**42**	**3**	**+10**	**3**	**0**	**0**	**0**	**4**	**0**	**0**	**0**
1983-84	**Boston Bruins**	**NHL**	**69**	**3**	**12**	**15**	**2**	**8**	**10**	**125**	**0**	**0**	**0**	**62**	**4.8**	**46**	**0**	**55**	**4**	**–5**	....	....	....	....	....	....	....	....
1984-85	**Pittsburgh Penguins**	**NHL**	**45**	**2**	**19**	**21**	**2**	**13**	**15**	**56**	**1**	**0**	**1**	**58**	**3.4**	**49**	**4**	**70**	**13**	**–12**	....	....	....	....	....	....	....	....
1985-86	**Pittsburgh Penguins**	**NHL**	**28**	**0**	**3**	**3**	**0**	**2**	**2**	**53**	**0**	**0**	**0**	**22**	**0.0**	**22**	**2**	**27**	**4**	**–3**	....	....	....	....	....	....	....	....
	Baltimore Skipjacks	AHL	8	0	5	5	....	....	....	14	....	....	....	....	....	....	....	....	....	....	....	....	....	....	....	....	....	....
1986-87	**Pittsburgh Penguins**	**NHL**	**55**	**4**	**8**	**12**	**3**	**6**	**9**	**97**	**0**	**0**	**0**	**51**	**7.8**	**46**	**2**	**45**	**13**	**+12**	....	....	....	....	....	....	....	....
1987-88	**Pittsburgh Penguins**	**NHL**	**55**	**1**	**12**	**13**	**1**	**9**	**10**	**144**	**0**	**0**	**0**	**44**	**2.3**	**52**	**10**	**76**	**28**	**–6**	....	....	....	....	....	....	....	....
1988-89	**Pittsburgh Penguins**	**NHL**	**68**	**1**	**23**	**24**	**1**	**16**	**17**	**141**	**0**	**1**	**0**	**37**	**2.7**	**73**	**1**	**107**	**31**	**–4**	**9**	**0**	**1**	**1**	**49**	**0**	**0**	**0**
1989-90	**Pittsburgh Penguins**	**NHL**	**61**	**3**	**12**	**15**	**3**	**9**	**12**	**71**	**0**	**0**	**1**	**45**	**6.7**	**71**	**2**	**82**	**24**	**+11**	....	....	....	....	....	....	....	....
1990-91	**Pittsburgh Penguins**	**NHL**	**31**	**2**	**2**	**4**	**2**	**2**	**4**	**32**	**0**	**0**	**0**	**14**	**14.3**	**31**	**0**	**46**	**12**	**–3**	**8**	**0**	**0**	**0**	**24**	**0**	**0**	**0**
1991-92	**New York Islanders**	**NHL**	**8**	**0**	**0**	**0**	**0**	**0**	**0**	**11**	**0**	**0**	**0**	**5**	**0.0**	**4**	**0**	**10**	**3**	**–3**	....	....	....	....	....	....	....	....
	Buffalo Sabres	**NHL**	**28**	**0**	**1**	**1**	**0**	**1**	**1**	**48**	**0**	**0**	**0**	**18**	**0.0**	**16**	**1**	**37**	**8**	**–14**	....	....	....	....	....	....	....	....
	San Diego Gulls	IHL	6	0	2	2	....	....	....	4	....	....	....	....	....	....	....	....	....	....	....	....	....	....	....	....	....	....
1992-93	Klagenfurter AC	Austria	23	2	9	11	....	....	....	....	....	....	....	....	....	....	....	....	....	....	....	....	....	....	....	....	....	....
	NHL Totals		**543**	**16**	**110**	**126**	**14**	**78**	**92**	**906**	**1**	**1**	**2**	**418**	**3.8**	**490**	**24**	**622**	**145**		**28**	**0**	**2**	**2**	**93**	**0**	**0**	**0**

Traded to **Pittsburgh** by **Boston** for Pittsburgh's 4th round choice (later traded to Quebec — Quebec selected Greg Polak) in 1985 Entry Draft, October 15, 1984. Signed as a free agent by **NY Islanders**, June 30, 1984. Traded to **Buffalo** by **NY Islanders** with Pat LaFontaine, Randy Wood and future considerations for Pierre Turgeon, Uwe Krupp, Benoit Hogue and Dave McLlwain, October 25, 1991.

• HILLMAN, LARRY

Larry Hillman D – L. 6', 185 lbs. b: Kirkland Lake, Ont., 2/5/1937.

Season	Club	League	GP	G	A	Pts	AG	AA	APts	PIM	PP	SH	GW	S	%	TGF	PGF	TGA	PGA	+/–	GP	G	A	Pts	PIM	PP	SH	GW
1952-53	Windsor Spitfires	OHA	56	2	4	6	....	....	....	39	....	....	....	....	....	....	....	....	....	....	....	....	....	....	....	....	....	....
1953-54	Hamilton Tiger Cubs	OHA	58	6	14	20	....	....	....	99	....	....	....	....	....	....	....	....	....	....	7	0	2	2	10	....	....	....
1954-55	Hamilton Tiger Cubs	OHA	49	5	20	25	....	....	....	106	....	....	....	....	....	....	....	....	....	....	3	0	1	1	9	....	....	....
	Detroit Red Wings	**NHL**	**6**	**0**	**0**	**0**	**0**	**0**	**0**	**2**	....	....	....	....	....	....	....	....	....	....	**3**	**0**	**0**	**0**	**0**	....	....	....
1955-56	**Detroit Red Wings**	**NHL**	**47**	**0**	**3**	**3**	**0**	**4**	**4**	**53**	....	....	....	....	....	....	....	....	....	....	**10**	**0**	**1**	**1**	**6**	....	....	....
	Buffalo Bisons	AHL	15	1	3	4	....	....	....	21	....	....	....	....	....	....	....	....	....	....	....	....	....	....	....	....	....	....
1956-57	**Detroit Red Wings**	**NHL**	**16**	**1**	**2**	**3**	**1**	**2**	**3**	**4**	....	....	....	....	....	....	....	....	....	....	....	....	....	....	....	....	....	....
	Edmonton Flyers	WHL	46	4	2	6	....	....	....	87	....	....	....	....	....	....	....	....	....	....	8	0	4	4	2	....	....	....
1957-58	**Boston Bruins**	**NHL**	**70**	**3**	**19**	**22**	**4**	**21**	**25**	**60**	....	....	....	....	....	....	....	....	....	....	**11**	**0**	**2**	**2**	**6**	....	....	....
1958-59	**Boston Bruins**	**NHL**	**55**	**3**	**10**	**13**	**4**	**11**	**15**	**19**	....	....	....	....	....	....	....	....	....	....	**7**	**0**	**1**	**1**	**0**	....	....	....
1959-60	**Boston Bruins**	**NHL**	**2**	**0**	**1**	**1**	**0**	**1**	**1**	**2**	....	....	....	....	....	....	....	....	....	....	....	....	....	....	....	....	....	....
	Providence Reds	AHL	70	12	31	43	....	....	....	159	....	....	....	....	....	....	....	....	....	....	5	0	1	1	4	....	....	....
1960-61	**Toronto Maple Leafs**	**NHL**	**62**	**3**	**10**	**13**	**4**	**10**	**14**	**59**	....	....	....	....	....	....	....	....	....	....	**5**	**0**	**0**	**0**	**0**	....	....	....
1961-62	**Toronto Maple Leafs**	**NHL**	**5**	**0**	**0**	**0**	**0**	**0**	**0**	**4**	....	....	....	....	....	....	....	....	....	....	....	....	....	....	....	....	....	....
	Rochester Americans	AHL	26	1	14	15	....	....	....	16	....	....	....	....	....	....	....	....	....	....	....	....	....	....	....	....	....	....
1962-63	**Toronto Maple Leafs**	**NHL**	**5**	**0**	**0**	**0**	**0**	**0**	**0**	**2**	....	....	....	....	....	....	....	....	....	....	....	....	....	....	....	....	....	....
	Springfield Indians	AHL	65	5	23	28	....	....	....	56	....	....	....	....	....	....	....	....	....	....	....	....	....	....	....	....	....	....
1963-64	**Toronto Maple Leafs**	**NHL**	**33**	**0**	**4**	**4**	**0**	**4**	**4**	**31**	....	....	....	....	....	....	....	....	....	....	**11**	**0**	**0**	**0**	**2**	....	....	....
	Rochester Americans	AHL	32	1	18	19	....	....	....	48	....	....	....	....	....	....	....	....	....	....	....	....	....	....	....	....	....	....
1964-65	**Toronto Maple Leafs**	**NHL**	**2**	**0**	**0**	**0**	**0**	**0**	**0**	**2**	....	....	....	....	....	....	....	....	....	....	....	....	....	....	....	....	....	....
	Rochester Americans	AHL	71	9	43	52	....	....	....	98	....	....	....	....	....	....	....	....	....	....	10	3	5	8	31	....	....	....
1965-66	**Toronto Maple Leafs**	**NHL**	**48**	**3**	**25**	**28**	**4**	**25**	**29**	**34**	....	....	....	....	....	....	....	....	....	....	**4**	**1**	**1**	**2**	**6**	....	....	....
	Rochester Americans	AHL	22	2	20	22	....	....	....	34	....	....	....	....	....	....	....	....	....	....	....	....	....	....	....	....	....	....
1966-67	**Toronto Maple Leafs**	**NHL**	**55**	**4**	**19**	**23**	**5**	**20**	**25**	**40**	....	....	....	....	....	....	....	....	....	....	**12**	**1**	**2**	**3**	**0**	....	....	....
	Rochester Americans	AHL	12	1	12	13	....	....	....	16	....	....	....	....	....	....	....	....	....	....	....	....	....	....	....	....	....	....
1967-68	**Toronto Maple Leafs**	**NHL**	**55**	**3**	**17**	**20**	**4**	**18**	**22**	**13**	**2**	**0**	**1**	**92**	**3.3**	**69**	**19**	**50**	**7**	**+7**	....	....	....	....	....	....	....	....
	Rochester Americans	AHL	6	0	1	1	....	....	....	0	....	....	....	....	....	....	....	....	....	....	....	....	....	....	....	....	....	....
1968-69	**Minnesota North Stars**	**NHL**	**12**	**1**	**5**	**6**	**1**	**5**	**6**	**0**	**1**	**0**	**0**	**20**	**5.0**	**13**	**9**	**12**	**0**	**–8**	....	....	....	....	....	....	....	....
	Montreal Canadiens	**NHL**	**25**	**0**	**5**	**5**	**0**	**5**	**5**	**17**	**0**	**0**	**0**	**14**	**0.0**	**13**	**0**	**15**	**0**	**–2**	**1**	**0**	**0**	**0**	**0**	**0**	**0**	**0**
1969-70	**Philadelphia Flyers**	**NHL**	**76**	**5**	**26**	**31**	**6**	**26**	**32**	**73**	**0**	**0**	**0**	**252**	**2.0**	**62**	**4**	**87**	**31**	**+2**	....	....	....	....	....	....	....	....
1970-71	**Philadelphia Flyers**	**NHL**	**73**	**3**	**13**	**16**	**3**	**11**	**14**	**39**	**0**	**0**	**0**	**177**	**1.7**	**68**	**4**	**79**	**24**	**+9**	**4**	**0**	**2**	**2**	**2**	**0**	**0**	**0**
1971-72	**Los Angeles Kings**	**NHL**	**22**	**1**	**2**	**3**	**1**	**2**	**3**	**11**	**0**	**0**	**0**	**13**	**7.7**	**7**	**0**	**17**	**3**	**–7**	....	....	....	....	....	....	....	....
	Buffalo Sabres	**NHL**	**43**	**1**	**11**	**12**	**1**	**10**	**11**	**58**	**0**	**0**	**0**	**78**	**1.3**	**65**	**19**	**82**	**15**	**–21**	....	....	....	....	....	....	....	....
1972-73	**Buffalo Sabres**	**NHL**	**78**	**5**	**24**	**29**	**5**	**20**	**25**	**56**	**2**	**0**	**0**	**102**	**4.9**	**93**	**36**	**71**	**11**	**–3**	**6**	**0**	**0**	**0**	**8**	**0**	**0**	**0**

Season	Club	League	REGULAR SEASON																		PLAYOFFS							
			GP	G	A	Pts	AG	AA	APts	PIM	PP	SH	GW	S	%	TGF	PGF	TGA	PGA	+/–	GP	G	A	Pts	PIM	PP	SH	GW
1973-74	Cleveland Crusaders	WHA	44	5	21	26				37																		
1974-75	Cleveland Crusaders	WHA	77	0	16	16				83											5	1	3	4	8			
1975-76	Winnipeg Jets	WHA	71	1	12	13				62											12	0	2	2	32			
	NHL Totals		**790**	**36**	**196**	**232**	**43**	**195**	**238**	**579**	**5**	**0**	**1**	**748**	**4.8**	**390**	**91**	**413**	**91**		**74**	**2**	**9**	**11**	**30**	**0**	**0**	**0**
	Other Major League Totals		192	6	49	55				182											17	1	5	6	40			

AHL First All-Star Team (1960, 1965) • Won Eddie Shore Award (Outstanding Defenseman - AHL) (1960)

Played in NHL All-Star Game (1955, 1962, 1963, 1964, 1968)

Claimed by **Chicago** from **Detroit** in Intra-League Draft, June 5, 1957. Claimed on waivers by **Boston** from **Chicago**, October, 1957. Claimed by **Toronto** from **Boston** in Intra-League Draft, June 8, 1960. Claimed by **NY Rangers** from **Toronto** in Intra-League Draft, June, 1968. Claimed by **Minnesota** from **NY Rangers** in Intra-League Draft, June, 1968. Claimed on waivers by **Pittsburgh** from **Minnesota**, November 22, 1968. Traded to **Montreal** by **Pittsburgh** for Jean-Guy Lagace and cash, November 22, 1968. Claimed by **Philadelphia** from **Montreal** in Intra-League Draft, June 11, 1969. Traded to **LA Kings** by **Philadelphia** for Larry Mickey, June 13, 1971. Traded to **Buffalo** by **LA Kings** with Mike Byers for Doug Barrie and Mike Keeler, December 16, 1971. Selected by **Ontario-Ottawa** (WHA) in 1972 WHA General Player Draft, February 12, 1972. WHA rights traded to **Cleveland** (WHA) by **Ottawa** (WHA) for cash, June, 1973. Claimed by **Winnipeg** (WHA) from **Cleveland** (WHA) in WHA Intra-League Draft, June, 1975.

• HILLMAN, WAYNE

Wayne Hillman D – R. 6'1", 205 lbs. b: Kirkland Lake, Ont., 11/13/1938. Deceased.

Season	Club	League	GP	G	A	Pts	AG	AA	APts	PIM	PP	SH	GW	S	%	TGF	PGF	TGA	PGA	+/–	GP	G	A	Pts	PIM	PP	SH	GW
1955-56	St. Catharines Teepees	OHA	43	2	2	4				23											6	1	0	1	4			
1956-57	St. Catharines Teepees	OHA	49	5	9	14				83											14	0	13	13	32			
	Buffalo Bisons	AHL	1	0	0	0				0																		
1957-58	St. Catharines Teepees	OHA	52	13	26	39				160											8	1	5	6	18			
1958-59	St. Catharines Teepees	OHA	49	8	30	38				115											7	0	0	0	21			
	Buffalo Bisons	AHL	1	0	1	1				0																		
1959-60	Buffalo Bisons	AHL	64	1	13	14				48																		
1960-61	Buffalo Bisons	AHL	72	0	18	18				40											4	0	1	1	0			
	Chicago Black Hawks	**NHL**																			**1**	**0**	**0**	**0**	**0**			
1961-62	**Chicago Black Hawks**	**NHL**	**19**	**0**	**2**	**2**	**0**	**2**	**2**	**14**																		
	Buffalo Bisons	AHL	50	2	16	18				43											9	0	1	1	10			
1962-63	**Chicago Black Hawks**	**NHL**	**67**	**3**	**5**	**8**	**4**	**5**	**9**	**74**											**6**	**0**	**2**	**2**	**2**			
1963-64	**Chicago Black Hawks**	**NHL**	**59**	**1**	**4**	**5**	**1**	**4**	**5**	**51**											**7**	**0**	**1**	**1**	**15**			
1964-65	**Chicago Black Hawks**	**NHL**	**19**	**0**	**1**	**1**	**0**	**1**	**1**	**8**																		
	St. Louis Braves	CHL	29	7	12	19				19																		
	New York Rangers	**NHL**	**22**	**1**	**7**	**8**	**1**	**8**	**9**	**26**																		
1965-66	**New York Rangers**	**NHL**	**68**	**3**	**17**	**20**	**4**	**17**	**21**	**70**																		
1966-67	**New York Rangers**	**NHL**	**67**	**2**	**12**	**14**	**2**	**12**	**14**	**43**											**4**	**0**	**0**	**0**	**2**			
1967-68	**New York Rangers**	**NHL**	**62**	**0**	**5**	**5**	**0**	**5**	**5**	**46**	**0**	**0**	**0**	**39**	**0.0**	**49**	**0**	**49**	**9**	**+9**	**2**	**0**	**0**	**0**	**0**	**0**	**0**	**0**
1968-69	**Minnesota North Stars**	**NHL**	**50**	**0**	**8**	**8**	**0**	**7**	**7**	**32**	**0**	**0**	**0**	**44**	**0.0**	**34**	**1**	**73**	**15**	**–25**								
1969-70	**Philadelphia Flyers**	**NHL**	**68**	**3**	**5**	**8**	**3**	**5**	**8**	**69**	**2**	**0**	**0**	**79**	**3.8**	**88**	**17**	**111**	**31**	**–9**								
1970-71	**Philadelphia Flyers**	**NHL**	**69**	**5**	**7**	**12**	**5**	**6**	**11**	**47**	**0**	**0**	**1**	**71**	**7.0**	**57**	**1**	**62**	**18**	**+12**								
1971-72	**Philadelphia Flyers**	**NHL**	**47**	**0**	**3**	**3**	**0**	**3**	**3**	**21**	**0**	**0**	**0**	**18**	**0.0**	**14**	**2**	**38**	**10**	**–16**								
1972-73	**Philadelphia Flyers**	**NHL**	**74**	**0**	**10**	**10**	**0**	**8**	**8**	**33**	**0**	**0**	**0**	**41**	**0.0**	**63**	**1**	**59**	**13**	**+16**	**8**	**0**	**0**	**0**	**0**	**0**	**0**	**0**
1973-74	Cleveland Crusaders	WHA	66	1	7	8				51											5	0	0	0	16			
1974-75	Cleveland Crusaders	WHA	60	2	9	11				37											5	0	2	2	2			
	NHL Totals		**691**	**18**	**86**	**104**	**20**	**83**	**103**	**534**	**2**	**0**	**1**	**292**	**6.2**	**305**	**22**	**302**	**96**		**20**	**0**	**3**	**3**	**19**	**0**	**0**	**0**
	Other Major League Totals		126	3	16	19				88											10	0	2	2	18			

Traded to **NY Rangers** by **Chicago** with Doug Robinson and John Brenneman for Camille Henry, Don Johns, Billy Taylor and Wally Chevrier, February 4, 1965 Traded to **Minnesota** by **NY Rangers** with Don Seguin and Joey Johnston for Dave Balon, June 12, 1968. Traded to **Philadelphia** by **Minnesota** for John Miszuk, May 14, 1969. Signed as a free agent by **Cleveland** (WHA), September, 1973.

• HILWORTH, JOHN

John Hilworth D – R. 6'4", 205 lbs. b: Jasper, Alta., 5/23/1957. Detroit's 3rd choice, 55th overall, in 1977 Amateur Draft.

Season	Club	League	GP	G	A	Pts	AG	AA	APts	PIM	PP	SH	GW	S	%	TGF	PGF	TGA	PGA	+/–	GP	G	A	Pts	PIM	PP	SH	GW
1973-74	Drumheller Miners	AJHL	57	10	28	38				161																		
	Medicine Hat Tigers	WCJHL	13	0	2	2				11																		
1974-75	Medicine Hat Tigers	WCJHL	70	1	12	13				146																		
1975-76	Medicine Hat Tigers	WCJHL	67	3	17	20				257											5	1	1	2	33			
1976-77	Medicine Hat Tigers	WCJHL	70	6	28	34				268																		
1977-78	**Detroit Red Wings**	**NHL**	**5**	**0**	**0**	**0**	**0**	**0**	**0**	**12**	**0**	**0**	**0**	**0**	**0.0**	**3**	**0**	**3**	**0**	**0**								
	Kansas City Red Wings	CHL	63	3	8	11				119																		
1978-79	**Detroit Red Wings**	**NHL**	**37**	**1**	**1**	**2**	**1**	**1**	**2**	**66**	**0**	**0**	**0**	**25**	**4.0**	**5**	**1**	**17**	**0**	**–13**								
	Kansas City Red Wings	CHL	42	2	14	16				107											3	0	0	0	16			
	Kalamazoo Wings	IHL	2	1	2	3				7																		
1979-80	**Detroit Red Wings**	**NHL**	**15**	**0**	**0**	**0**	**0**	**0**	**0**	**11**	**0**	**0**	**0**	**7**	**0.0**	**0**	**0**	**2**	**0**	**–2**								
	Adirondack Red Wings	AHL	29	0	2	2				83																		
	Houston Apollos	CHL	12	2	2	4				36											6	0	3	3	12			
	Johnstown Red Wings	IHL	4	0	4	4				11																		
1980-81	Wichita Wind	CHL	64	3	12	15				144											13	1	3	4	42			
1981-82			DID NOT PLAY																									
1982-83	Fort Wayne Komets	IHL	82	16	46	62				171											10	2	6	8	33			
1983-84	Fort Wayne Komets	IHL	75	10	20	30				124											6	0	0	0	11			
1984-85	Toledo Goaldiggers	IHL	24	2	5	7				48											6	0	0	0	9			
	NHL Totals		**57**	**1**	**1**	**2**	**1**	**1**	**2**	**89**	**0**	**0**	**0**	**32**	**3.1**	**8**	**1**	**22**	**0**									

Claimed on waivers by **Edmonton** from **Detroit**, March, 1980.

• HINDMARCH, DAVE

Dave Hindmarch RW – R. 5'11", 182 lbs. b: Vancouver, B.C., 10/15/1958. Atlanta's 6th choice, 114th overall, in 1978 Amateur Draft.

Season	Club	League	GP	G	A	Pts	AG	AA	APts	PIM	PP	SH	GW	S	%	TGF	PGF	TGA	PGA	+/–	GP	G	A	Pts	PIM	PP	SH	GW
1976-77	University of Alberta	CWUAA	30	16	19	35				8																		
1977-78	University of Alberta	CWUAA	25	11	18	29				13																		
1978-79	University of Alberta	CWUAA	41	33	29	62				40																		
1979-80	Canada	Nat-Team	44	12	11	23				30																		
	Canada	Olympics	6	3	4	7				4																		
1980-81	**Calgary Flames**	**NHL**	**1**	**1**	**0**	**1**	**1**	**0**	**1**	**0**	**0**	**0**	**0**	**1**	**100.0**	**1**	**0**	**1**	**0**	**0**	**6**	**0**	**0**	**0**	**2**	**0**	**0**	**0**
	Birmingham Bulls	CHL	48	15	14	29				18																		
	Rochester Americans	AHL	18	6	2	8				6																		
1981-82	**Calgary Flames**	**NHL**	**9**	**3**	**0**	**3**	**2**	**0**	**2**	**0**	**0**	**0**	**0**	**10**	**30.0**	**4**	**0**	**9**	**1**	**–4**								
	Oklahoma City Stars	CHL	63	27	21	48				21											4	0	1	1	6			
1982-83	**Calgary Flames**	**NHL**	**60**	**11**	**12**	**23**	**9**	**8**	**17**	**23**	**0**	**0**	**1**	**86**	**12.8**	**40**	**0**	**68**	**20**	**–8**	**4**	**0**	**0**	**0**	**4**	**0**	**0**	**0**
1983-84	**Calgary Flames**	**NHL**	**29**	**6**	**5**	**11**	**5**	**3**	**8**	**2**	**0**	**0**	**0**	**49**	**12.2**	**17**	**0**	**27**	**8**	**–2**								
	NHL Totals		**99**	**21**	**17**	**38**	**17**	**11**	**28**	**25**	**0**	**0**	**1**	**146**	**14.4**	**62**	**0**	**105**	**29**		**10**	**0**	**0**	**0**	**6**	**0**	**0**	**0**

Transferred to **Calgary** after **Atlanta** franchise relocated, June 24, 1980.

• HINSE, ANDRE

Andre "Gypsy Joe" Hinse LW – L. 5'9", 175 lbs. b: Trois-Rivieres, Que., 4/19/1945.

Season	Club	League	GP	G	A	Pts	AG	AA	APts	PIM	PP	SH	GW	S	%	TGF	PGF	TGA	PGA	+/–	GP	G	A	Pts	PIM	PP	SH	GW
1964-65	Trois-Rivieres Reds	QJHL	STATISTICS NOT AVAILABLE																									
1965-66	Charlotte Checkers	EHL	69	33	30	63				67											9	3	4	7	23			
1966-67	Charlotte Checkers	EHL	72	41	37	78				33											8	5	8	13	17			
1967-68	**Toronto Maple Leafs**	**NHL**	**4**	**0**	**0**	**0**	**0**	**0**	**0**	**0**	**0**	**0**	**0**	**1**	**0.0**	**1**	**0**	**3**	**0**	**–2**								
	Tulsa Oilers	CHL	61	31	34	65				35											11	*6	6	12	14			
1968-69	Tulsa Oilers	CHL	42	19	23	42				22											7	4	1	5	0			
1969-70	Phoenix Roadrunners	WHL	72	32	36	68				35																		
1970-71	Phoenix Roadrunners	WHL	67	44	49	93				34											5	0	3	3	2			
1971-72	Phoenix Roadrunners	WHL	66	33	43	76				61											6	3	3	6	9			
1972-73	Phoenix Roadrunners	WHL	72	34	42	76				25											10	*8	7	15	7			
1973-74	Houston Aeros	WHA	69	24	56	80				39											14	8	9	17	18			

			REGULAR SEASON																		PLAYOFFS							
Season	**Club**	**League**	**GP**	**G**	**A**	**Pts**	**AG**	**AA**	**APts**	**PIM**	**PP**	**SH**	**GW**	**S**	**%**	**TGF**	**PGF**	**TGA**	**PGA**	**+/–**	**GP**	**G**	**A**	**Pts**	**PIM**	**PP**	**SH**	**GW**
1974-75	Houston Aeros	WHA	75	39	47	86	....	....	....	12	....	....	....	....	....	....	....	....	....	....	11	5	4	9	8	....	....	....
1975-76	Houston Aeros	WHA	70	35	38	73	....	....	....	6	....	....	....	....	....	....	....	....	....	....	17	2	3	5	2	....	....	....
1976-77	Houston Aeros	WHA	26	2	3	5	....	....	....	8	....	....	....	....	....	....	....	....	....	....	....	....	....	....	....	....	....	....
	Phoenix Roadrunners	WHA	16	2	7	9	....	....	....	14	....	....	....	....	....	....	....	....	....	....	....	....	....	....	....	....	....	....
	NHL Totals		**4**	**0**	**0**	**0**	**0**	**0**	**0**	**0**	**0**	**0**	**0**	**1**	**0.0**	**1**	**0**	**3**	**0**		....	....	....	....	....	....	....	....
	Other Major League Totals		256	102	151	253	....	....	....	79	....	....	....	....	....	....	....	....	....		42	15	16	31	28	....	....	....

WHL First All-Star Team (1971, 1972, 1973)

Signed as a free agent by **Toronto**, September, 1966. Traded to **Vancouver** (WHL) by **Toronto** for Ted McCaskill and Pat Hannigan, August, 1970. Traded to **Toronto** by **Vancouver** (WHL) for Doug Brindley, September, 1971. Selected by **Houston** (WHA) in 1972 WHA General Player Draft, February 12, 1972. Traded to **Phoenix** (WHA) by **Houston** (WHA) with Frank Hughes for Al McLeod and John Gray, December, 1971.

• HINTON, DAN

Dan Hinton LW – L. 6'1", 180 lbs. b: Toronto, Ont., 5/24/1953. Chicago's 5th choice, 77th overall, in 1973 Amateur Draft.

Season	Club	League	GP	G	A	Pts	AG	AA	APts	PIM	PP	SH	GW	S	%	TGF	PGF	TGA	PGA	+/–	GP	G	A	Pts	PIM	PP	SH	GW
1971-72	Kitchener Rangers	OHA	56	15	14	29	....	....	....	89	....	....	....	....	....	....	....	....	....	....	....	....	....	....	....	....	....	....
1972-73	Sault Ste. Marie Greyhounds	OHA	47	22	38	60	....	....	....	99	....	....	....	....	....	....	....	....	....	....	....	....	....	....	....	....	....	....
1973-74	Dallas Black Hawks	CHL	65	11	7	18	....	....	....	51	....	....	....	....	....	....	....	....	....	....	10	2	5	7	9	....	....	....
1974-75	Dallas Black Hawks	CHL	74	24	13	37	....	....	....	107	....	....	....	....	....	....	....	....	....	....	10	8	3	11	26	....	....	....
1975-76	Dallas Black Hawks	CHL	75	20	32	52	....	....	....	105	....	....	....	....	....	....	....	....	....	....	10	*5	3	8	23	....	....	....
1976-77	**Chicago Black Hawks**	**NHL**	**14**	**0**	**0**	**0**	**0**	**0**	**0**	**16**	**0**	**0**	**0**	**11**	**0.0**	**4**	**0**	**10**	**1**	**–5**	....	....	....	....	....	....	....	....
	Dallas Black Hawks	CHL	60	13	22	35	....	....	....	77	....	....	....	....	....	....	....	....	....	....	5	1	2	3	6	....	....	....
1977-78	Dallas Black Hawks	CHL	64	20	13	33	....	....	....	57	....	....	....	....	....	....	....	....	....	....	13	2	1	3	12	....	....	....
1978-79	New Brunswick Hawks	AHL	79	21	31	52	....	....	....	56	....	....	....	....	....	....	....	....	....	....	4	2	0	2	7	....	....	....
	NHL Totals		**14**	**0**	**0**	**0**	**0**	**0**	**0**	**16**	**0**	**0**	**0**	**11**	**0.0**	**4**	**0**	**10**	**1**		....	....	....	....	....	....	....	....

• HIRSCH, TOM

Tom Hirsch D – R. 6'4", 210 lbs. b: Minneapolis, MN, 1/27/1963. Minnesota's 4th choice, 33rd overall, in 1981 Entry Draft.

Season	Club	League	GP	G	A	Pts	AG	AA	APts	PIM	PP	SH	GW	S	%	TGF	PGF	TGA	PGA	+/–	GP	G	A	Pts	PIM	PP	SH	GW
1980-81	Patrick Henry High	H.S.	23	42	35	77	....	....	....	....	....	....	....	....	....	....	....	....	....	....	....	....	....	....	....	....	....	....
1981-82	University of Minnesota	WCHA	36	7	16	23	....	....	....	53	....	....	....	....	....	....	....	....	....	....	....	....	....	....	....	....	....	....
	United States	WEC-A	6	1	1	2	....	....	....	0	....	....	....	....	....	....	....	....	....	....	....	....	....	....	....	....	....	....
1982-83	University of Minnesota	WCHA	37	8	23	31	....	....	....	70	....	....	....	....	....	....	....	....	....	....	....	....	....	....	....	....	....	....
1983-84	United States	Nat-Team	56	8	25	33	....	....	....	72	....	....	....	....	....	....	....	....	....	....	....	....	....	....	....	....	....	....
	United States	Olympics	6	1	0	1	....	....	....	10	....	....	....	....	....	....	....	....	....	....	....	....	....	....	....	....	....	....
	Minnesota North Stars	**NHL**	**15**	**1**	**3**	**4**	**1**	**2**	**3**	**20**	**0**	**1**	**0**	**24**	**4.2**	**11**	**4**	**13**	**3**	**–3**	**12**	**0**	**0**	**0**	**6**	**0**	**0**	**0**
1984-85	United States	C Cup	5	0	0	0	....	....	....	0	....	....	....	....	....	....	....	....	....	....	....	....	....	....	....	....	....	....
	Minnesota North Stars	**NHL**	**15**	**0**	**4**	**4**	**0**	**3**	**3**	**10**	**0**	**0**	**0**	**14**	**0.0**	**11**	**2**	**27**	**5**	**–13**	....	....	....	....	....	....	....	....
	Springfield Indians	AHL	19	4	5	9	....	....	....	2	....	....	....	....	....	....	....	....	....	....	....	....	....	....	....	....	....	....
1985-86			DID NOT PLAY – INJURED																									
1986-87			DID NOT PLAY – INJURED																									
1987-88	**Minnesota North Stars**	**NHL**	**1**	**0**	**0**	**0**	**0**	**0**	**0**	**0**	**0**	**0**	**0**	**0**	**0.0**	**1**	**0**	**0**	**0**	**+1**	....	....	....	....	....	....	....	....
	NHL Totals		**31**	**1**	**7**	**8**	**1**	**5**	**6**	**30**	**0**	**1**	**0**	**38**	**2.6**	**23**	**6**	**40**	**8**		**12**	**0**	**0**	**0**	**6**	**0**	**0**	**0**

• Missed entire 1985-86 and 1986-87 seasons after undergoing shoulder surgery, October, 1985.

• HISLOP, JAMIE

Jamie Hislop RW – R. 5'10", 180 lbs. b: Sarnia, Ont., 1/20/1954. Montreal's 13th choice, 140th overall, in 1974 Amateur Draft.

Season	Club	League	GP	G	A	Pts	AG	AA	APts	PIM	PP	SH	GW	S	%	TGF	PGF	TGA	PGA	+/–	GP	G	A	Pts	PIM	PP	SH	GW
1971-72	Stratford Cullitons	OJHL	38	26	30	56	....	....	....	....	....	....	....	....	....	....	....	....	....	....	....	....	....	....	....	....	....	....
1972-73	University of New Hampshire	ECAC	26	5	16	21	....	....	....	....	....	....	....	....	....	....	....	....	....	....	....	....	....	....	....	....	....	....
1973-74	University of New Hampshire	ECAC	31	21	*35	56	....	....	....	30	....	....	....	....	....	....	....	....	....	....	....	....	....	....	....	....	....	....
1974-75	University of New Hampshire	ECAC	31	28	38	66	....	....	....	12	....	....	....	....	....	....	....	....	....	....	....	....	....	....	....	....	....	....
1975-76	University of New Hampshire	ECAC	31	23	43	66	....	....	....	20	....	....	....	....	....	....	....	....	....	....	....	....	....	....	....	....	....	....
1976-77	Cincinnati Stingers	WHA	46	7	19	26	....	....	....	6	....	....	....	....	....	....	....	....	....	....	4	0	1	1	4	....	....	....
	Hampton Gulls	SHL	37	16	17	33	....	....	....	11	....	....	....	....	....	....	....	....	....	....	....	....	....	....	....	....	....	....
1977-78	Cincinnati Stingers	WHA	80	24	43	67	....	....	....	17	....	....	....	....	....	....	....	....	....	....	....	....	....	....	....	....	....	....
1978-79	Cincinnati Stingers	WHA	80	30	40	70	....	....	....	45	....	....	....	....	....	....	....	....	....	....	3	2	4	6	0	....	....	....
1979-80	**Quebec Nordiques**	**NHL**	**80**	**19**	**20**	**39**	**17**	**15**	**32**	**6**	**0**	**1**	**3**	**124**	**15.3**	**64**	**11**	**80**	**14**	**–13**	....	....	....	....	....	....	....	....
1980-81	**Quebec Nordiques**	**NHL**	**50**	**19**	**22**	**41**	**16**	**15**	**31**	**15**	**5**	**0**	**1**	**86**	**22.1**	**66**	**14**	**73**	**17**	**–4**	....	....	....	....	....	....	....	....
	Calgary Flames	**NHL**	**29**	**6**	**9**	**15**	**5**	**6**	**11**	**11**	**0**	**0**	**0**	**31**	**19.4**	**19**	**0**	**36**	**14**	**–3**	**16**	**3**	**0**	**3**	**5**	**1**	**0**	**1**
1981-82	**Calgary Flames**	**NHL**	**80**	**16**	**25**	**41**	**13**	**17**	**30**	**35**	**0**	**2**	**1**	**113**	**14.2**	**60**	**0**	**87**	**28**	**+1**	**3**	**0**	**0**	**0**	**0**	**0**	**0**	**0**
1982-83	**Calgary Flames**	**NHL**	**79**	**14**	**19**	**33**	**11**	**13**	**24**	**17**	**1**	**1**	**0**	**80**	**17.5**	**56**	**1**	**80**	**20**	**–5**	**9**	**0**	**2**	**2**	**6**	**0**	**0**	**0**
1983-84	**Calgary Flames**	**NHL**	**27**	**1**	**8**	**9**	**1**	**5**	**6**	**2**	**0**	**0**	**1**	**18**	**5.6**	**12**	**0**	**15**	**3**	**0**	....	....	....	....	....	....	....	....
	NHL Totals		**345**	**75**	**103**	**178**	**63**	**71**	**134**	**86**	**6**	**4**	**6**	**452**	**16.6**	**277**	**26**	**371**	**96**		**28**	**3**	**2**	**5**	**11**	**1**	**0**	**1**
	Other Major League Totals		206	61	102	163	....	....	....	68	....	....	....	....	....	....	....	....	....		7	2	5	7	4	....	....	....

ECAC First All-Star Team (1975, 1976) • NCAA East First All-American Team (1976)

Signed as a free agent by **Cincinnati** (WHA), July, 1976. Claimed by **Winnipeg** from **Cincinnati** (WHA) in WHA Dispersal Draft, June 22, 1979. Traded to **Quebec** by **Winnipeg** with Barry Legge for Barry Melrose, June 28, 1979. Traded to **Calgary** by **Quebec** for Daniel Bouchard, January 30, 1991.

• HLINKA, IVAN

Ivan Hlinka C – L. 6'2", 220 lbs. b: Most, Czechoslovakia, 1/26/1950.

Season	Club	League	GP	G	A	Pts	AG	AA	APts	PIM	PP	SH	GW	S	%	TGF	PGF	TGA	PGA	+/–	GP	G	A	Pts	PIM	PP	SH	GW
1969-70	Czechoslovakia	WEC-A	4	0	0	0	....	....	....	2	....	....	....	....	....	....	....	....	....	....	....	....	....	....	....	....	....	....
1970-71	Czechoslovakia	WEC-A	10	4	2	6	....	....	....	2	....	....	....	....	....	....	....	....	....	....	....	....	....	....	....	....	....	....
1971-72	Czechoslovakia	Olympics	6	5	3	8	....	....	....	2	....	....	....	....	....	....	....	....	....	....	....	....	....	....	....	....	....	....
	Czechoslovakia	WEC-A	5	2	3	5	....	....	....	0	....	....	....	....	....	....	....	....	....	....	....	....	....	....	....	....	....	....
1972-73	Czechoslovakia	WEC-A	8	2	1	3	....	....	....	0	....	....	....	....	....	....	....	....	....	....	....	....	....	....	....	....	....	....
1973-74	Czechoslovakia	WEC-A	10	9	4	13	....	....	....	2	....	....	....	....	....	....	....	....	....	....	....	....	....	....	....	....	....	....
1974-75	CHZ Litvinov	Czech.	....	36	*42	*78	....	....	....	....	....	....	....	....	....	....	....	....	....	....	....	....	....	....	....	....	....	....
	Czechoslovakia	WEC-A	6	2	4	6	....	....	....	2	....	....	....	....	....	....	....	....	....	....	....	....	....	....	....	....	....	....
1975-76	CHZ Litvinov	Czech.	STATISTICS NOT AVAILABLE																									
	Czechoslovakia	Olympics	5	3	3	6	....	....	....	7	....	....	....	....	....	....	....	....	....	....	....	....	....	....	....	....	....	....
	Czechoslovakia	WEC-A	10	7	8	15	....	....	....	4	....	....	....	....	....	....	....	....	....	....	....	....	....	....	....	....	....	....
1976-77	Czechoslovakia	C Cup	7	2	2	4	....	....	....	12	....	....	....	....	....	....	....	....	....	....	....	....	....	....	....	....	....	....
	CHZ Litvinov	Czech.	STATISTICS NOT AVAILABLE																									
	Czechoslovakia	WEC-A	10	9	3	12	....	....	....	5	....	....	....	....	....	....	....	....	....	....	....	....	....	....	....	....	....	....
1977-78	CHZ Litvinov	Czech.	STATISTICS NOT AVAILABLE																									
	Czechoslovakia	WEC-A	10	4	10	14	....	....	....	4	....	....	....	....	....	....	....	....	....	....	....	....	....	....	....	....	....	....
1978-79	Trecin–Litinov	Czech.	....	17	20	37	....	....	....	....	....	....	....	....	....	....	....	....	....	....	13	4	8	12	....	....	....	....
	Czechoslovakia	WEC-A	8	3	5	8	....	....	....	6	....	....	....	....	....	....	....	....	....	....	....	....	....	....	....	....	....	....
1979-80	CHZ Litvinov	Czech.	STATISTICS NOT AVAILABLE																									
1980-81	CHZ Litvinov	Czech.	41	25	35	60	....	....	....	....	....	....	....	....	....	....	....	....	....	....	28	5	15	20	....	....	....	....
	Czechoslovakia	WEC-A	8	0	3	3	....	....	....	0	....	....	....	....	....	....	....	....	....	....	....	....	....	....	....	....	....	....
1981-82	**Vancouver Canucks**	**NHL**	**72**	**23**	**37**	**60**	**18**	**24**	**42**	**16**	**7**	**0**	**2**	**152**	**15.1**	**81**	**17**	**43**	**0**	**+21**	**12**	**2**	**6**	**8**	**4**	**2**	**0**	**0**
1982-83	**Vancouver Canucks**	**NHL**	**65**	**19**	**44**	**63**	**16**	**30**	**46**	**12**	**8**	**0**	**0**	**147**	**12.9**	**91**	**46**	**48**	**0**	**–3**	**4**	**1**	**4**	**5**	**4**	**0**	**0**	**0**
	NHL Totals		**137**	**42**	**81**	**123**	**34**	**54**	**88**	**28**	**15**	**0**	**2**	**299**	**14.0**	**172**	**63**	**91**	**0**		**16**	**3**	**10**	**13**	**8**	**2**	**0**	**0**

Czechoslovakian Player of the Year (1978) • WEC-A All-Star Team (1978)

Rights traded to **Vancouver** by **Winnipeg** for Brent Ashton and Vancouver's 4th round choice (Tom Martin), July 15, 1981.

Season	Club	League	REGULAR SEASON																		PLAYOFFS							
			GP	G	A	Pts	AG	AA	APts	PIM	PP	SH	GW	S	%	TGF	PGF	TGA	PGA	+/–	GP	G	A	Pts	PIM	PP	SH	GW

● HLUSHKO, TODD

Todd Hlushko C – L. 5′11″, 185 lbs. b: Toronto, Ont., 2/7/1970. Washington's 14th choice, 240th overall, in 1990 Entry Draft.

Season	Club	League	GP	G	A	Pts	AG	AA	APts	PIM	PP	SH	GW	S	%	TGF	PGF	TGA	PGA	+/–	GP	G	A	Pts	PIM	PP	SH	GW
1988-89	Guelph Platers	OHL	66	28	18	46				71											7	5	3	8	18			
1989-90	Owen Sound Platers	OHL	25	9	17	26				31																		
	London Knights	OHL	40	27	17	44				39											6	2	4	6	10			
1990-91	Baltimore Skipjacks	AHL	66	9	14	23				55																		
1991-92	Baltimore Skipjacks	AHL	74	16	35	51				113																		
1992-93	Canada	Nat-Team	58	22	26	48				10																		
1993-94	Canada	Nat-Team	55	22	6	28				61																		
	Canada	Olympics	8	5	0	5				6																		
	Philadelphia Flyers	**NHL**	**2**	**1**	**0**	**1**	**1**	**0**	**1**	**0**	**0**	**0**	**0**	**2**	**50.0**	**1**	**0**	**0**	**0**	**+1**								
	Hershey Bears	AHL	9	6	0	6				4											6	2	1	3	4			
1994-95	**Calgary Flames**	**NHL**	**2**	**0**	**1**	**1**	**0**	**1**	**1**	**2**	**0**	**0**	**0**	**3**	**0.0**	**1**	**0**	**0**	**0**	**+1**	**1**	**0**	**0**	**0**	**2**	**0**	**0**	**0**
	Saint John Flames	AHL	46	22	10	32				36											4	2	2	4	22			
	Canada	WC-A	8	4	0	4				4																		
1995-96	**Calgary Flames**	**NHL**	**4**	**0**	**0**	**0**	**0**	**0**	**0**	**6**	**0**	**0**	**0**	**6**	**0.0**	**1**	**0**	**3**	**2**	**0**								
	Saint John Flames	AHL	35	14	13	27				70											16	8	1	9	26			
1996-97	**Calgary Flames**	**NHL**	**58**	**7**	**11**	**18**	**7**	**10**	**17**	**49**	**0**	**0**	**0**	**76**	**9.2**	**20**	**0**	**36**	**14**	**–2**								
1997-98	**Calgary Flames**	**NHL**	**13**	**0**	**1**	**1**	**0**	**1**	**1**	**27**	**0**	**0**	**0**	**7**	**0.0**	**3**	**0**	**5**	**2**	**0**								
	Saint John Flames	AHL	33	10	14	24				48											21	13	4	17	61			
	NHL Totals		**79**	**8**	**13**	**21**	**8**	**12**	**20**	**84**	**0**	**0**	**0**	**94**	**8.5**	**26**	**0**	**44**	**18**		**1**	**0**	**0**	**0**	**2**	**0**	**0**	**0**

Signed as a free agent by **Philadelphia**, March 7, 1994. Signed as a free agent by **Calgary**, June 17, 1994. Traded to **Pittsburgh** by **Calgary** with German Titov for Ken Wregget and Dave Roche, June 17, 1998.

● HOCKING, JUSTIN

Justin Hocking D – R. 6′4″, 205 lbs. b: Stettler, Alta., 1/9/1974. Los Angeles' 1st choice, 39th overall, in 1992 Entry Draft.

Season	Club	League	GP	G	A	Pts	AG	AA	APts	PIM	PP	SH	GW	S	%	TGF	PGF	TGA	PGA	+/–	GP	G	A	Pts	PIM	PP	SH	GW
1991-92	Spokane Chiefs	WHL	71	4	6	10				309											10	0	3	3	28			
1992-93	Spokane Chiefs	WHL	16	0	1	1				75																		
	Medicine Hat Tigers	WHL	54	1	9	10				119											10	0	1	1	13			
1993-94	Medicine Hat Tigers	WHL	68	7	26	33				236											3	0	0	0	6			
	Los Angeles Kings	**NHL**	**1**	**0**	**0**	**0**	**0**	**0**	**0**	**0**	**0**	**0**	**0**	**0**	**0.0**	**0**	**0**	**0**	**0**	**0**								
	Phoenix Roadrunners	IHL	3	0	0	0				15																		
1994-95	Syracuse Crunch	AHL	7	0	0	0				24																		
	Portland Pirates	AHL	9	0	1	1				34																		
	Knoxville Cherokees	ECHL	20	0	6	6				70											4	0	0	0	26			
	Phoenix Roadrunners	IHL	20	1	1	2				50											1	0	0	0	0			
1995-96	P.E.I. Senators	AHL	74	4	8	12				251											4	0	2	2	5			
1996-97	Worcester IceCats	AHL	68	1	10	11				198											5	0	3	3	2			
1997-98	Worcester IceCats	AHL	79	5	12	17				198											11	1	2	3	19			
	NHL Totals		**1**	**0**	**0**	**0**	**0**	**0**	**0**	**0**	**0**	**0**	**0**	**0**	**0.0**	**0**	**0**	**0**	**0**									

WHL East Second All-Star Team (1994)

Claimed by **Ottawa** from **LA Kings** in Waiver Draft, October 2, 1995.

● HODGE, KEN

Ken Hodge C/RW – L. 6′1″, 200 lbs. b: Windsor, Ont., 4/13/1966. Minnesota's 2nd choice, 46th overall, in 1984 Entry Draft.

Season	Club	League	GP	G	A	Pts	AG	AA	APts	PIM	PP	SH	GW	S	%	TGF	PGF	TGA	PGA	+/–	GP	G	A	Pts	PIM	PP	SH	GW
1983-84	St. John's Prep	H.S.	22	25	38	63																						
1984-85	Boston College	H.E.	41	20	44	64				28																		
1985-86	Boston College	H.E.	21	11	17	28				16																		
1986-87	Boston College	H.E.	37	29	33	62				30																		
1987-88	Kalamazoo Wings	IHL	70	15	35	50				24																		
1988-89	**Minnesota North Stars**	**NHL**	**5**	**1**	**1**	**2**	**1**	**1**	**2**	**0**	**0**	**0**	**0**	**6**	**16.7**	**0**	**0**	**2**	**0**	**+1**								
	Kalamazoo Wings	IHL	72	26	45	71				34											6	1	5	6	16			
1989-90	Kalamazoo Wings	IHL	68	33	53	86				19											10	5	13	18	2			
1990-91	**Boston Bruins**	**NHL**	**70**	**30**	**29**	**59**	**28**	**22**	**50**	**20**	**12**	**2**	**4**	**137**	**21.9**	**80**	**26**	**57**	**14**	**+11**	**15**	**4**	**6**	**10**	**6**	**1**	**0**	**1**
	Maine Mariners	AHL	8	7	10	17				2																		
1991-92	**Boston Bruins**	**NHL**	**42**	**6**	**11**	**17**	**5**	**8**	**13**	**10**	**3**	**1**	**3**	**62**	**9.7**	**29**	**11**	**41**	**15**	**–8**								
	Maine Mariners	AHL	19	6	11	17				4																		
1992-93	**Tampa Bay Lightning**	**NHL**	**25**	**2**	**7**	**9**	**2**	**5**	**7**	**2**	**0**	**0**	**1**	**32**	**6.3**	**14**	**7**	**22**	**9**	**–6**								
	Atlanta Knights	IHL	16	10	17	27				0																		
	San Diego Gulls	IHL	30	11	24	35				16											14	4	6	10	6			
1993-94	Binghamton Rangers	AHL	79	22	56	78				51																		
1994-95	Kansas City Blades	IHL	62	15	25	40				18											17	4	6	10	4			
1995-96	Minnesota Moose	IHL	75	14	40	54				28																		
	Cardiff Lions	Britain	34	16	29	45				6											7	1	4	5	2			
1996-97	Ratingen Lions	Germany	6	1	3	4				0																		
1997-98	Cardiff Devils	Britain	32	10	19	29				18											9	4	10	14	0			
	NHL Totals		**142**	**39**	**48**	**87**	**36**	**36**	**72**	**32**	**15**	**3**	**8**	**237**	**16.5**	**126**	**44**	**122**	**38**		**15**	**4**	**6**	**10**	**6**	**1**	**0**	**1**

NHL All-Rookie Team (1991)

Traded to **Boston** by **Minnesota** for Boston's 4th round choice (Jere Lentinen) in 1992 Entry Draft, August 21, 1990. Traded to **Tampa Bay** by **Boston** with Matt Hervey for Darin Kimble and future considerations, September 4, 1992. Signed as a free agent by **NY Rangers**, September 2, 1993.

● HODGE, KEN

Ken (Kenneth Raymond) Hodge RW – R. 6′2″, 210 lbs. b: Birmingham, England, 6/25/1944.

Season	Club	League	GP	G	A	Pts	AG	AA	APts	PIM	PP	SH	GW	S	%	TGF	PGF	TGA	PGA	+/–	GP	G	A	Pts	PIM	PP	SH	GW
1961-62	St. Catharines Teepees	OHA	31	4	3	7				6											6	1	0	1	6			
1962-63	St. Catharines Black Hawks	OHA	50	23	23	46				97																		
1963-64	St. Catharines Black Hawks	OHA	56	37	51	88				110											13	6	19	25	28			
1964-65	St. Catharines Black Hawks	OHA	55	*63	60	*123				107											5	3	7	10	8			
	Chicago Black Hawks	**NHL**	**1**	**0**	**0**	**0**	**0**	**0**	**0**	**2**																		
	Buffalo Bisons	AHL	2	0	2	2				0											4	0	0	0	4			
1965-66	**Chicago Black Hawks**	**NHL**	**63**	**6**	**17**	**23**	**7**	**17**	**24**	**47**											**5**	**0**	**0**	**0**	**8**			
1966-67	**Chicago Black Hawks**	**NHL**	**69**	**10**	**25**	**35**	**12**	**26**	**38**	**59**											**6**	**0**	**0**	**0**	**4**			
1967-68	**Boston Bruins**	**NHL**	**74**	**25**	**31**	**56**	**31**	**32**	**63**	**31**	**5**	**0**	**3**	**188**	**13.3**	**75**	**12**	**53**	**3**	**+13**	**4**	**3**	**0**	**3**	**2**	**0**	**0**	**0**
1968-69	**Boston Bruins**	**NHL**	**75**	**45**	**45**	**90**	**51**	**42**	**93**	**75**	**9**	**1**	**7**	**236**	**19.1**	**125**	**22**	**60**	**6**	**+49**	**10**	**5**	**7**	**12**	**4**	**2**	**0**	**0**
1969-70	**Boston Bruins**	**NHL**	**72**	**25**	**29**	**54**	**29**	**29**	**58**	**87**	**6**	**0**	**5**	**198**	**12.6**	**82**	**21**	**53**	**7**	**+15**	**14**	**3**	**10**	**13**	**7**	**0**	**1**	**0**
1970-71	**Boston Bruins**	**NHL**	**78**	**43**	**62**	**105**	**45**	**55**	**100**	**113**	**4**	**0**	**7**	**232**	**18.5**	**147**	**20**	**58**	**2**	**+71**	**7**	**2**	**5**	**7**	**6**	**0**	**0**	**0**
1971-72	**Boston Bruins**	**NHL**	**60**	**16**	**40**	**56**	**17**	**37**	**54**	**81**	**0**	**1**	**2**	**140**	**11.4**	**86**	**7**	**40**	**2**	**+41**	**15**	**9**	**8**	**17**	***62**	**2**	**1**	**3**
1972-73	**Boston Bruins**	**NHL**	**73**	**37**	**44**	**81**	**37**	**37**	**74**	**58**	**16**	**0**	**5**	**197**	**18.8**	**136**	**55**	**77**	**6**	**+10**	**5**	**1**	**0**	**1**	**7**	**1**	**0**	**0**
1973-74	**Boston Bruins**	**NHL**	**76**	**50**	**55**	**105**	**51**	**48**	**99**	**43**	**15**	**0**	**11**	**251**	**19.9**	**174**	**60**	**75**	**1**	**+40**	**16**	**6**	**10**	**16**	**16**	**1**	**0**	**1**
1974-75	**Boston Bruins**	**NHL**	**72**	**23**	**43**	**66**	**21**	**34**	**55**	**90**	**16**	**0**	**2**	**175**	**13.1**	**124**	**58**	**59**	**0**	**+7**	**3**	**1**	**1**	**2**	**0**	**1**	**0**	**0**
1975-76	**Boston Bruins**	**NHL**	**72**	**25**	**36**	**61**	**23**	**28**	**51**	**42**	**8**	**0**	**5**	**161**	**15.5**	**100**	**47**	**34**	**0**	**+19**	**12**	**4**	**6**	**10**	**4**	**4**	**0**	**1**
1976-77	**New York Rangers**	**NHL**	**78**	**21**	**41**	**62**	**20**	**33**	**53**	**43**	**6**	**0**	**5**	**141**	**14.9**	**95**	**36**	**78**	**1**	**–18**								
1977-78	**New York Rangers**	**NHL**	**18**	**2**	**4**	**6**	**2**	**3**	**5**	**8**	**1**	**0**	**1**	**13**	**15.4**	**9**	**4**	**11**	**0**	**–6**								
	New Haven Nighthawks	AHL	52	17	29	46				13											15	3	4	7	20			
1978-79			DID NOT PLAY																									
1979-80	Binghamton Dusters	AHL	37	10	20	30				24																		
	NHL Totals		**881**	**328**	**472**	**800**	**346**	**421**	**767**	**779**	**86**	**2**	**53**	**1932**	**17.0**	**1153**	**342**	**598**	**28**		**97**	**34**	**47**	**81**	**120**	**11**	**2**	**5**

NHL First All-Star Team (1971, 1974)

Played in NHL All-Star Game (1971, 1973, 1974)

Traded to **Boston** by **Chicago** with Phil Esposito and Fred Stanfield for Gilles Marotte, Pit Martin and Jack Norris, May 15, 1967. Traded to **NY Rangers** by **Boston** for Rick Middleton, May 26, 1976.

• HODGSON, DAN

Dan Hodgson C – R. 5'10", 175 lbs. b: Fort Vermillon, Alta., 8/29/1965. Toronto's 4th choice, 85th overall, in 1983 Entry Draft.

			REGULAR SEASON																		PLAYOFFS							
Season	Club	League	GP	G	A	Pts	AG	AA	APts	PIM	PP	SH	GW	S	%	TGF	PGF	TGA	PGA	+/–	GP	G	A	Pts	PIM	PP	SH	GW
1980-81	Coquitlam Panthers	BCJHL	39	32	42	74	....	....	....	26	....	....	....	....	....	....	....	....	....	....	....	....	....	....	....	....	....	....
1981-82	Cowichan Valley Capitals	BCJHL	46	45	75	120	....	....	....	30	....	....	....	....	....	....	....	....	....	....	....	....	....	....	....	....	....	....
1982-83	Prince Albert Raiders	WHL	72	56	74	130	....	....	....	66	....	....	....	....	....	....	....	....	....	....	....	....	....	....	....	....	....	....
1983-84	Prince Albert Raiders	WHL	66	62	*119	181	....	....	....	65	....	....	....	....	....	....	....	....	....	....	5	5	3	8	7	....	....	....
	Canada	WJC-A	7	1	4	5	....	....	....	4	....	....	....	....	....	....	....	....	....	....	....	....	....	....	....	....	....	....
1984-85	Prince Albert Raiders	WHL	64	70	*112	182	....	....	....	86	....	....	....	....	....	....	....	....	....	....	13	10	*26	*36	32	....	....	....
	Canada	WJC-A	7	5	2	7	....	....	....	0	....	....	....	....	....	....	....	....	....	....	....	....	....	....	....	....	....	....
1985-86	**Toronto Maple Leafs**	**NHL**	**40**	**13**	**12**	**25**	**10**	**8**	**18**	**12**	**2**	**0**	**0**	**54**	**24.1**	**33**	**9**	**32**	**3**	**–5**	....	....	....	....	....	....	....	....
	St. Catharines Saints	AHL	22	13	16	29	....	....	....	15	....	....	....	....	....	....	....	....	....	....	13	3	9	12	14	....	....	....
1986-87	Newmarket Saints	AHL	20	7	12	19	....	....	....	16	....	....	....	....	....	....	....	....	....	....	....	....	....	....	....	....	....	....
	Vancouver Canucks	**NHL**	**43**	**9**	**13**	**22**	**8**	**9**	**17**	**25**	**4**	**0**	**0**	**42**	**21.4**	**37**	**17**	**29**	**0**	**–9**	....	....	....	....	....	....	....	....
1987-88	**Vancouver Canucks**	**NHL**	**8**	**3**	**7**	**10**	**3**	**5**	**8**	**2**	**1**	**0**	**1**	**7**	**42.9**	**13**	**7**	**5**	**0**	**+1**	....	....	....	....	....	....	....	....
	Fredericton Express	AHL	13	8	18	26	....	....	....	16	....	....	....	....	....	....	....	....	....	....	....	....	....	....	....	....	....	....
1988-89	**Vancouver Canucks**	**NHL**	**23**	**4**	**13**	**17**	**3**	**9**	**12**	**25**	**0**	**0**	**1**	**38**	**10.5**	**29**	**10**	**16**	**0**	**+3**	....	....	....	....	....	....	....	....
	Milwaukee Admirals	IHL	47	27	55	82	....	....	....	47	....	....	....	....	....	....	....	....	....	....	11	6	7	13	10	....	....	....
1989-90	HC Fribourg-Gotteron	Switz.	36	17	22	39	....	....	....	....	....	....	....	....	....	....	....	....	....	....	....	....	....	....	....	....	....	....
1990-91	EC Hedos Munich	Germany	26	11	17	28	....	....	....	23	....	....	....	....	....	....	....	....	....	....	....	....	....	....	....	....	....	....
1991-92	EC Hedos Munich	Germany	44	24	22	46	....	....	....	31	....	....	....	....	....	....	....	....	....	....	....	....	....	....	....	....	....	....
1992-93	SC Langnau	Switz. B	36	31	33	64	....	....	....	....	....	....	....	....	....	....	....	....	....	....	....	....	....	....	....	....	....	....
1993-94	SC Langnau	Switz. B	8	6	7	13	....	....	....	6	....	....	....	....	....	....	....	....	....	....	....	....	....	....	....	....	....	....
1994-95	HC Davos	Switz.	35	23	27	50	....	....	....	32	....	....	....	....	....	....	....	....	....	....	5	1	2	3	4	....	....	....
1995-96	HC Davos	Switz.	33	16	32	48	....	....	....	59	....	....	....	....	....	....	....	....	....	....	5	3	4	7	2	....	....	....
1996-97	HC Davos	Switz.	46	29	32	61	....	....	....	69	....	....	....	....	....	....	....	....	....	....	6	2	3	5	2	....	....	....
1997-98	HC Davos	Switz.	28	11	29	40	....	....	....	18	....	....	....	....	....	....	....	....	....	....	....	....	....	....	....	....	....	....
	NHL Totals		**114**	**29**	**45**	**74**	**24**	**31**	**55**	**64**	**7**	**0**	**2**	**141**	**20.6**	**112**	**43**	**82**	**3**		....	....	....	....	....	....	....	....

WHL East First All-Star Team (1985) • Memorial Cup All-Star Team (1985) • Canadian Major Junior Player of the Year (1985) • Won Stafford Smythe Memorial Trophy (Memorial Cup Tournament MVP) (1985)

Traded to **Vancouver** by **Toronto** with Jim Benning for Rick Lanz, December 2, 1986.

• HODGSON, RICK

Rick Hodgson D – R. 6', 175 lbs. b: Medicine Hat, Alta., 5/23/1956. Atlanta's 4th choice, 46th overall, in 1976 Amateur Draft.

Season	Club	League	GP	G	A	Pts	AG	AA	APts	PIM	PP	SH	GW	S	%	TGF	PGF	TGA	PGA	+/–	GP	G	A	Pts	PIM	PP	SH	GW
1973-74	Calgary Centennials	WCJHL	65	8	44	52	....	....	....	174	....	....	....	....	....	....	....	....	....	....	....	....	....	....	....	....	....	....
1974-75	Calgary Centennials	WCJHL	56	7	36	43	....	....	....	221	....	....	....	....	....	....	....	....	....	....	....	....	....	....	....	....	....	....
	Canada	WJC-A	3	0	1	1	....	....	....	0	....	....	....	....	....	....	....	....	....	....	....	....	....	....	....	....	....	....
1975-76	Calgary Centennials	WCJHL	50	7	48	55	....	....	....	168	....	....	....	....	....	....	....	....	....	....	....	....	....	....	....	....	....	....
1976-77	Tulsa Oilers	CHL	62	3	18	21	....	....	....	101	....	....	....	....	....	....	....	....	....	....	6	0	0	0	6	....	....	....
1977-78	Tulsa Oilers	CHL	76	7	20	27	....	....	....	180	....	....	....	....	....	....	....	....	....	....	7	0	3	3	19	....	....	....
1978-79	Tulsa Oilers	CHL	75	9	17	26	....	....	....	167	....	....	....	....	....	....	....	....	....	....	....	....	....	....	....	....	....	....
1979-80	**Hartford Whalers**	**NHL**	**6**	**0**	**0**	**0**	**0**	**0**	**0**	**6**	**0**	**0**	**0**	**1**	**0.0**	**4**	**0**	**10**	**1**	**–5**	**1**	**0**	**0**	**0**	**0**	**0**	**0**	**0**
	Springfield Indians	AHL	75	7	26	33	....	....	....	186	....	....	....	....	....	....	....	....	....	....	....	....	....	....	....	....	....	....
	NHL Totals		**6**	**0**	**0**	**0**	**0**	**0**	**0**	**6**	**0**	**0**	**0**	**1**	**0.0**	**4**	**0**	**10**	**1**		**1**	**0**	**0**	**0**	**0**	**0**	**0**	**0**

Claimed by **Hartford** from **Atlanta** in Expansion Draft, June 13, 1979. Traded to **Salt Lake** (WHL) by **Boston** for cash, August, 1969.

• HOEKSTRA, ED

Ed Hoekstra C – R. 5'11", 170 lbs. b: Winnipeg, Man., 11/4/1937.

Season	Club	League	GP	G	A	Pts	AG	AA	APts	PIM	PP	SH	GW	S	%	TGF	PGF	TGA	PGA	+/–	GP	G	A	Pts	PIM	PP	SH	GW
1954-55	St. Catharines Teepess	OHA	49	17	21	38	....	....	....	20	....	....	....	....	....	....	....	....	....	....	11	3	2	5	21	....	....	....
1955-56	St. Catharines Teepees	OHA	48	22	31	53	....	....	....	18	....	....	....	....	....	....	....	....	....	....	6	2	0	2	4	....	....	....
1956-57	St. Catharines Teepees	OHA	52	28	42	70	....	....	....	22	....	....	....	....	....	....	....	....	....	....	14	11	*15	26	2	....	....	....
1957-58	St. Catharines Teepees	OHA	49	35	*58	93	....	....	....	28	....	....	....	....	....	....	....	....	....	....	8	2	6	8	4	....	....	....
1958-59	Trois-Rivieres Lions	QHL	58	19	37	56	....	....	....	8	....	....	....	....	....	....	....	....	....	....	8	3	4	7	0	....	....	....
1959-60	Cleveland Barons	AHL	66	20	38	58	....	....	....	4	....	....	....	....	....	....	....	....	....	....	7	4	3	7	0	....	....	....
1960-61	Kitchener-Waterloo Beavers	EPHL	70	32	33	65	....	....	....	18	....	....	....	....	....	....	....	....	....	....	7	2	3	5	0	....	....	....
1961-62	Kitchener-Waterloo Beavers	EPHL	44	23	27	50	....	....	....	16	....	....	....	....	....	....	....	....	....	....	....	....	....	....	....	....	....	....
	Quebec Aces	AHL	22	6	10	16	....	....	....	2	....	....	....	....	....	....	....	....	....	....	....	....	....	....	....	....	....	....
1962-63	Quebec Aces	AHL	30	6	8	14	....	....	....	2	....	....	....	....	....	....	....	....	....	....	....	....	....	....	....	....	....	....
1963-64	Quebec Aces	AHL	71	20	44	64	....	....	....	22	....	....	....	....	....	....	....	....	....	....	6	2	2	4	2	....	....	....
1964-65	Quebec Aces	AHL	71	28	51	79	....	....	....	16	....	....	....	....	....	....	....	....	....	....	5	0	3	3	6	....	....	....
1965-66	Quebec Aces	AHL	61	24	50	74	....	....	....	10	....	....	....	....	....	....	....	....	....	....	6	5	0	5	4	....	....	....
1966-67	Quebec Aces	AHL	7	1	0	1	....	....	....	0	....	....	....	....	....	....	....	....	....	....	....	....	....	....	....	....	....	....
	California Seals	WHL	31	11	7	18	....	....	....	4	....	....	....	....	....	....	....	....	....	....	6	1	3	4	2	....	....	....
1967-68	**Philadelphia Flyers**	**NHL**	**70**	**15**	**21**	**36**	**19**	**22**	**41**	**6**	**5**	**0**	**4**	**126**	**11.9**	**51**	**10**	**51**	**16**	**+6**	**7**	**0**	**1**	**1**	**0**	**0**	**0**	**0**
1968-69	Denver Spurs	WHL	62	20	49	69	....	....	....	4	....	....	....	....	....	....	....	....	....	....	....	....	....	....	....	....	....	....
1969-70	Denver Spurs	WHL	27	9	18	27	....	....	....	2	....	....	....	....	....	....	....	....	....	....	....	....	....	....	....	....	....	....
	Buffalo Bisons	AHL	1	0	0	0	....	....	....	0	....	....	....	....	....	....	....	....	....	....	....	....	....	....	....	....	....	....
1970-71	Denver Spurs	WHL	30	11	11	22	....	....	....	0	....	....	....	....	....	....	....	....	....	....	....	....	....	....	....	....	....	....
	Springfield Kings	AHL	44	13	22	35	....	....	....	4	....	....	....	....	....	....	....	....	....	....	12	4	2	6	4	....	....	....
1971-72	Springfield Kings	AHL	74	16	*69	85	....	....	....	32	....	....	....	....	....	....	....	....	....	....	5	1	1	2	0	....	....	....
1972-73	Houston Aeros	WHA	78	11	28	39	....	....	....	12	....	....	....	....	....	....	....	....	....	....	9	1	2	3	0	....	....	....
1973-74	Houston Aeros	WHA	19	2	0	2	....	....	....	0	....	....	....	....	....	....	....	....	....	....	....	....	....	....	....	....	....	....
	Macon Whoopees	SHL	2	0	5	5	....	....	....	0	....	....	....	....	....	....	....	....	....	....	....	....	....	....	....	....	....	....
	Jacksonville Barons	AHL	29	11	12	23	....	....	....	2	....	....	....	....	....	....	....	....	....	....	....	....	....	....	....	....	....	....
	NHL Totals		**70**	**15**	**21**	**36**	**19**	**22**	**41**	**6**	**5**	**0**	**4**	**126**	**11.9**	**51**	**10**	**51**	**16**		**7**	**0**	**1**	**1**	**0**	**0**	**0**	**0**
	Other Major League Totals		97	13	28	41	....	....	....	12	....	....	....	....	....	....	....	....	....		9	1	2	3	0	....	....	....

Won William Northey Trophy (Top Rookie - QHL) (1959)

Claimed by **NY Rangers** from **Chicago** in Intra-League Draft, June 9, 1959. Traded to **Cleveland** (AHL) by **NY Rangers** with Also Guidolin for Art Stratton, June, 1959. Loaned to **California** (WHL) by **Quebec** (AHL) for Jean-Guy Morissette, January, 1967. NHL rights transferred to **Philadelphia** after NHL club purchased **Quebec** (AHL) franchise, May 8, 1967. Claimed by **Denver** (WHL) from **Philadelphia** in Reverse Draft, June, 1968. Traded to **LA Kings** (Springfield - AHL) by **Denver** (WHL) for Jimmy Peters Jr., December, 1970. Selected by **Houston** (WHA) in 1972 WHA General Player Draft, February 13, 1972.

• HOENE, PHIL

Phil Hoene LW – L. 5'9", 175 lbs. b: Duluth, MN, 3/15/1949.

Season	Club	League	GP	G	A	Pts	AG	AA	APts	PIM	PP	SH	GW	S	%	TGF	PGF	TGA	PGA	+/–	GP	G	A	Pts	PIM	PP	SH	GW
1969-70	University of Minnesota-Duluth	WCHA	18	5	6	11	....	....	....	8	....	....	....	....	....	....	....	....	....	....	....	....	....	....	....	....	....	....
1970-71	University of Minnesota-Duluth	WCHA	34	14	13	27	....	....	....	37	....	....	....	....	....	....	....	....	....	....	....	....	....	....	....	....	....	....
1971-72	Springfield Kings	AHL	65	15	11	26	....	....	....	17	....	....	....	....	....	....	....	....	....	....	2	0	0	0	0	....	....	....
1972-73	**Los Angeles Kings**	**NHL**	**4**	**0**	**1**	**1**	**0**	**1**	**1**	**0**	**0**	**0**	**0**	**3**	**0.0**	**2**	**1**	**0**	**0**	**+1**	....	....	....	....	....	....	....	....
	Springfield Kings	AHL	70	36	44	80	....	....	....	17	....	....	....	....	....	....	....	....	....	....	....	....	....	....	....	....	....	....
1973-74	**Los Angeles Kings**	**NHL**	**31**	**2**	**3**	**5**	**2**	**3**	**5**	**22**	**0**	**0**	**1**	**20**	**10.0**	**6**	**0**	**19**	**8**	**–5**	....	....	....	....	....	....	....	....
	Springfield Kings	AHL	42	19	23	42	....	....	....	20	....	....	....	....	....	....	....	....	....	....	....	....	....	....	....	....	....	....
1974-75	**Los Angeles Kings**	**NHL**	**2**	**0**	**0**	**0**	**0**	**0**	**0**	**0**	**0**	**0**	**0**	**0**	**0.0**	**0**	**0**	**1**	**1**	**0**	....	....	....	....	....	....	....	....
	Springfield Indians	AHL	70	25	30	55	....	....	....	10	....	....	....	....	....	....	....	....	....	....	17	*12	10	*22	8	....	....	....
1975-76	Fort Worth Texans	CHL	76	13	22	35	....	....	....	14	....	....	....	....	....	....	....	....	....	....	....	....	....	....	....	....	....	....
	NHL Totals		**37**	**2**	**4**	**6**	**2**	**4**	**6**	**22**	**0**	**0**	**1**	**23**	**8.7**	**8**	**1**	**20**	**9**		....	....	....	....	....	....	....	....

Signed as a free agent by **LA Kings**, June, 1971.

• HOFFMAN, MIKE

Mike Hoffman LW – L. 5'11", 190 lbs. b: Barrie, Ont., 2/26/1963. Hartford's 3rd choice, 67th overall, in 1981 Entry Draft.

Season	Club	League	GP	G	A	Pts	AG	AA	APts	PIM	PP	SH	GW	S	%	TGF	PGF	TGA	PGA	+/–	GP	G	A	Pts	PIM	PP	SH	GW
1979-80	Barrie Colts	Midget	60	40	35	75	....	....	....	....	....	....	....	....	....	....	....	....	....	....	....	....	....	....	....	....	....	....
1980-81	Brantford Alexanders	OHA	68	15	19	34	....	....	....	71	....	....	....	....	....	....	....	....	....	....	6	1	0	1	5	....	....	....
1981-82	Brantford Alexanders	OHL	66	34	47	81	....	....	....	169	....	....	....	....	....	....	....	....	....	....	11	5	8	13	9	....	....	....
1982-83	Brantford Alexanders	OHL	63	26	49	75	....	....	....	128	....	....	....	....	....	....	....	....	....	....	8	5	4	9	18	....	....	....
	Hartford Whalers	**NHL**	**2**	**0**	**1**	**1**	**0**	**1**	**1**	**0**	**0**	**0**	**0**	**2**	**0.0**	**2**	**0**	**4**	**0**	**–2**	....	....	....	....	....	....	....	....
	Binghamton Whalers	AHL	1	0	0	0	....	....	....	0	....	....	....	....	....	....	....	....	....	....	3	0	1	1	0	....	....	....
1983-84	Binghamton Whalers	AHL	64	11	13	24	....	....	....	92	....	....	....	....	....	....	....	....	....	....	....	....	....	....	....	....	....	....

			REGULAR SEASON																		PLAYOFFS							
Season	Club	League	GP	G	A	Pts	AG	AA	APts	PIM	PP	SH	GW	S	%	TGF	PGF	TGA	PGA	+/–	GP	G	A	Pts	PIM	PP	SH	GW
1984-85	**Hartford Whalers**	**NHL**	**1**	**0**	**0**	**0**	**0**	**0**	**0**	**0**	**0**	**0**	**0**	**0**	**0.0**	**0**	**0**	**0**	**0**	**0**	....	....	....	....	....	....	....	....
	Binghamton Whalers	AHL	76	19	26	45	....	....	....	95	....	....	....	....	....	....	....	....	....	....	8	4	1	5	23	....	....	....
1985-86	**Hartford Whalers**	**NHL**	**6**	**1**	**2**	**3**	**1**	**1**	**2**	**2**	**0**	**0**	**0**	**7**	**14.3**	**3**	**0**	**5**	**0**	**–2**	....	....	....	....	....	....	....	....
	Binghamton Whalers	AHL	40	14	14	28	....	....	....	79	....	....	....	....	....	....	....	....	....	....	2	1	0	1	2	....	....	....
1986-87	Binghamton Whalers	AHL	74	9	32	41	....	....	....	120	....	....	....	....	....	....	....	....	....	....	13	2	2	4	23	....	....	....
1987-88	Flint Spirits	IHL	64	35	28	63	....	....	....	49	....	....	....	....	....	....	....	....	....	....	14	3	7	10	36	....	....	....
1988-89	Flint Spirits	IHL	76	33	39	72	....	....	....	46	....	....	....	....	....	....	....	....	....	....	....	....	....	....	....	....	....	....
	NHL Totals		**9**	**1**	**3**	**4**	**1**	**2**	**3**	**2**	**0**	**0**	**0**	**9**	**11.1**	**5**	**0**	**9**	**0**		....	....	....	....	....	....	....	....

• HOFFMEYER, BOB

Bob Hoffmeyer D – L. 6′, 182 lbs. b: Dodsland, Sask., 7/27/1955. Chicago's 5th choice, 79th overall, in 1975 Amateur Draft.

Season	Club	League	GP	G	A	Pts	AG	AA	APts	PIM	PP	SH	GW	S	%	TGF	PGF	TGA	PGA	+/–	GP	G	A	Pts	PIM	PP	SH	GW
1973-74	Saskatoon Blades	WCJHL	62	2	10	12	....	....	....	198	....	....	....	....	....	....	....	....	....	....	6	0	1	1	20	....	....	....
1974-75	Saskatoon Blades	WCJHL	64	4	38	42	....	....	....	242	....	....	....	....	....	....	....	....	....	....	17	2	10	12	69	....	....	....
1975-76	Dallas Black Hawks	CHL	5	0	0	0	....	....	....	11	....	....	....	....	....	....	....	....	....	....	....	....	....	....	....	....	....	....
	Flint Generals	IHL	67	3	13	16	....	....	....	145	....	....	....	....	....	....	....	....	....	....	4	1	1	2	5	....	....	....
1976-77	Flint Generals	IHL	78	12	51	63	....	....	....	213	....	....	....	....	....	....	....	....	....	....	5	0	7	7	22	....	....	....
1977-78	**Chicago Black Hawks**	**NHL**	**5**	**0**	**1**	**1**	**0**	**1**	**1**	**12**	**0**	**0**	**0**	**3**	**0.0**	**3**	**0**	**5**	**0**	**–2**	....	....	....	....	....	....	....	....
	Dallas Black Hawks	CHL	67	5	11	16	....	....	....	172	....	....	....	....	....	....	....	....	....	....	13	1	3	4	40	....	....	....
1978-79	**Chicago Black Hawks**	**NHL**	**6**	**0**	**2**	**2**	**0**	**2**	**2**	**5**	**0**	**0**	**0**	**3**	**0.0**	**3**	**0**	**8**	**1**	**–4**	....	....	....	....	....	....	....	....
	New Brunswick Hawks	AHL	41	3	6	9	....	....	....	104	....	....	....	....	....	....	....	....	....	....	....	....	....	....	....	....	....	....
1979-80	New Brunswick Hawks	AHL	77	3	20	23	....	....	....	161	....	....	....	....	....	....	....	....	....	....	17	0	3	3	38	....	....	....
1980-81	Schwenningen	Germany	39	22	30	52	....	....	....	122	....	....	....	....	....	....	....	....	....	....	....	....	....	....	....	....	....	....
	Maine Mariners	AHL	2	1	1	2	....	....	....	0	....	....	....	....	....	....	....	....	....	....	20	2	11	13	68	....	....	....
1981-82	**Philadelphia Flyers**	**NHL**	**57**	**7**	**20**	**27**	**6**	**13**	**19**	**142**	**4**	**0**	**0**	**88**	**8.0**	**90**	**28**	**68**	**19**	**+13**	**2**	**0**	**1**	**1**	**25**	**0**	**0**	**0**
	Maine Mariners	AHL	21	6	8	14	....	....	....	57	....	....	....	....	....	....	....	....	....	....	....	....	....	....	....	....	....	....
1982-83	**Philadelphia Flyers**	**NHL**	**35**	**2**	**11**	**13**	**2**	**8**	**10**	**40**	**1**	**0**	**0**	**50**	**4.0**	**38**	**4**	**44**	**17**	**+7**	**1**	**0**	**0**	**0**	**0**	**0**	**0**	**0**
	Maine Mariners	AHL	23	5	10	15	....	....	....	79	....	....	....	....	....	....	....	....	....	....	....	....	....	....	....	....	....	....
1983-84	Maine Mariners	AHL	14	3	1	4	....	....	....	27	....	....	....	....	....	....	....	....	....	....	....	....	....	....	....	....	....	....
	New Jersey Devils	**NHL**	**58**	**4**	**12**	**16**	**3**	**8**	**11**	**61**	**0**	**0**	**0**	**80**	**5.0**	**45**	**2**	**91**	**28**	**–20**	....	....	....	....	....	....	....	....
1984-85	**New Jersey Devils**	**NHL**	**37**	**1**	**6**	**7**	**1**	**4**	**5**	**65**	**0**	**0**	**0**	**37**	**2.7**	**20**	**0**	**50**	**15**	**–15**	....	....	....	....	....	....	....	....
1985-86	Maine Mariners	AHL	8	0	0	0	....	....	....	6	....	....	....	....	....	....	....	....	....	....	5	0	0	0	6	....	....	....
	NHL Totals		**198**	**14**	**52**	**66**	**12**	**36**	**48**	**325**	**5**	**0**	**0**	**261**	**5.4**	**199**	**34**	**266**	**80**		**3**	**0**	**1**	**1**	**25**	**0**	**0**	**0**

Signed as a free agent by **Philadelphia**, November 22, 1981. Claimed by **Edmonton** from **Philadelphia** in Waiver Draft, October 4, 1982. Traded to **Philadelphia** by **Edmonton** for Peter Dineen, October 22, 1982. Signed as a free agent by **New Jersey**, August 15, 1983.

• HOFFORD, JIM

Jim Hofford D – R. 6′, 190 lbs. b: Sudbury, Ont., 10/4/1964. Buffalo's 8th choice, 118th overall, in 1983 Entry Draft.

Season	Club	League	GP	G	A	Pts	AG	AA	APts	PIM	PP	SH	GW	S	%	TGF	PGF	TGA	PGA	+/–	GP	G	A	Pts	PIM	PP	SH	GW
1981-82	Windsor Spitfires	OHA	67	5	9	14	....	....	....	214	....	....	....	....	....	....	....	....	....	....	....	....	....	....	....	....	....	....
1982-83	Windsor Spitfires	OHL	63	8	20	28	....	....	....	173	....	....	....	....	....	....	....	....	....	....	3	0	1	1	15	....	....	....
1983-84	Windsor Spitfires	OHL	1	0	0	0	....	....	....	2	....	....	....	....	....	....	....	....	....	....	....	....	....	....	....	....	....	....
1984-85	Rochester Americans	AHL	71	2	13	15	....	....	....	166	....	....	....	....	....	....	....	....	....	....	5	0	0	0	16	....	....	....
1985-86	**Buffalo Sabres**	**NHL**	**5**	**0**	**0**	**0**	**0**	**0**	**0**	**5**	**0**	**0**	**0**	**3**	**0.0**	**3**	**0**	**5**	**1**	**–1**	....	....	....	....	....	....	....	....
	Rochester Americans	AHL	40	2	7	9	....	....	....	148	....	....	....	....	....	....	....	....	....	....	....	....	....	....	....	....	....	....
1986-87	**Buffalo Sabres**	**NHL**	**12**	**0**	**0**	**0**	**0**	**0**	**0**	**40**	**0**	**0**	**0**	**8**	**0.0**	**8**	**0**	**10**	**1**	**–1**	....	....	....	....	....	....	....	....
	Rochester Americans	AHL	54	1	8	9	....	....	....	204	....	....	....	....	....	....	....	....	....	....	13	1	0	1	57	....	....	....
1987-88	Rochester Americans	AHL	69	3	15	18	....	....	....	322	....	....	....	....	....	....	....	....	....	....	7	0	0	0	28	....	....	....
1988-89	**Los Angeles Kings**	**NHL**	**1**	**0**	**0**	**0**	**0**	**0**	**0**	**2**	**0**	**0**	**0**	**0**	**0.0**	**2**	**0**	**0**	**0**	**+2**	....	....	....	....	....	....	....	....
	Rochester Americans	AHL	34	1	9	10	....	....	....	13	....	....	....	....	....	....	....	....	....	....	....	....	....	....	....	....	....	....
1989-90	Rochester Americans	AHL	52	1	9	10	....	....	....	233	....	....	....	....	....	....	....	....	....	....	17	1	1	2	56	....	....	....
	NHL Totals		**18**	**0**	**0**	**0**	**0**	**0**	**0**	**47**	**0**	**0**	**0**	**11**	**0.0**	**13**	**0**	**15**	**2**		....	....	....	....	....	....	....	....

Claimed by **LA Kings** from **Buffalo** in Waiver Draft, October 3, 1988.

• HOGABOAM, BILL

Bill Hogaboam C – R. 5′11″, 170 lbs. b: Swift Current, Sask., 9/5/1949.

Season	Club	League	GP	G	A	Pts	AG	AA	APts	PIM	PP	SH	GW	S	%	TGF	PGF	TGA	PGA	+/–	GP	G	A	Pts	PIM	PP	SH	GW
1967-68	Swift Current Broncos	WCJHL	40	27	26	53	....	....	....	34	....	....	....	....	....	....	....	....	....	....	....	....	....	....	....	....		
1968-69	Swift Current Broncos	WCJHL	5	5	4	9	....			2	....	....	....	....	....	....	....	....	....	....	....	....	....	....	....	....	....	....
	Oorel Black Hawks	OJHL	STATISTICS NOT AVAILABLE																									
1969-70	Saskatoon Blades	WCJHL	53	27	42	69	....	....	....	8	....	....	....	....	....	....	....	....	....	....	....	....	....	....	....	....	....	....
1970-71	Omaha Knights	CHL	63	12	18	30	....	....	....	12	....	....	....	....	....	....	....	....	....	....	11	2	3	5	8	....	....	....
1971-72	Phoenix Roadrunners	WHL	1	0	1	1	....	....	....	2	....	....	....	....	....	....	....	....	....	....	....	....	....	....	....	....	....	....
	Omaha Knights	CHL	70	30	52	82	....	....	....	36	....	....	....	....	....	....	....	....	....	....	4	1	5	6	0	....	....	....
1972-73	**Atlanta Flames**	**NHL**	**2**	**0**	**0**	**0**	**0**	**0**	**0**	**0**	**0**	**0**	**0**	**0**	**0.0**	**0**	**0**	**0**	**0**	**0**	....	....	....	....	....	....	....	....
	Detroit Red Wings	**NHL**	**4**	**1**	**0**	**1**	**1**	**0**	**1**	**2**	**0**	**0**	**0**	**1**	**100.0**	**1**	**0**	**2**	**0**	**–1**	....	....	....	....	....	....	....	....
	Virginia Wings	AHL	50	16	28	44	....	....	....	14	....	....	....	....	....	....	....	....	....	....	13	6	10	16	10	....	....	....
1973-74	**Detroit Red Wings**	**NHL**	**47**	**18**	**23**	**41**	**18**	**20**	**38**	**12**	**6**	**0**	**0**	**100**	**18.0**	**57**	**20**	**40**	**0**	**–3**	....	....	....	....	....	....	....	....
	Virginia Wings	AHL	23	8	11	19	....	....	....	15	....	....	....	....	....	....	....	....	....	....	....	....	....	....	....	....	....	....
1974-75	**Detroit Red Wings**	**NHL**	**60**	**14**	**27**	**41**	**13**	**21**	**34**	**16**	**6**	**1**	**1**	**129**	**10.9**	**56**	**24**	**79**	**13**	**–34**	....	....	....	....	....	....	....	....
1975-76	**Detroit Red Wings**	**NHL**	**50**	**21**	**16**	**37**	**20**	**13**	**33**	**30**	**6**	**2**	**0**	**116**	**18.1**	**53**	**15**	**54**	**8**	**–8**	....	....	....	....	....	....	....	....
	Minnesota North Stars	**NHL**	**18**	**7**	**7**	**14**	**7**	**5**	**12**	**6**	**1**	**0**	**0**	**44**	**15.9**	**17**	**4**	**17**	**0**	**–4**	....	....	....	....	....	....	....	....
1976-77	**Minnesota North Stars**	**NHL**	**73**	**10**	**15**	**25**	**10**	**12**	**22**	**16**	**0**	**0**	**0**	**120**	**8.3**	**39**	**3**	**53**	**0**	**–17**	**2**	**0**	**0**	**0**	**0**	**0**	**0**	**0**
1977-78	**Minnesota North Stars**	**NHL**	**8**	**1**	**2**	**3**	**1**	**2**	**3**	**4**	**0**	**0**	**0**	**6**	**16.7**	**4**	**0**	**9**	**0**	**–5**	....	....	....	....	....	....	....	....
	Fort Worth Texans	CHL	60	22	44	66	....	....	....	43	....	....	....	....	....	....	....	....	....	....	10	0	7	7	6	....	....	....
1978-79	**Minnesota North Stars**	**NHL**	**10**	**1**	**1**	**2**	**1**	**1**	**2**	**0**	**0**	**0**	**0**	**6**	**16.7**	**4**	**0**	**7**	**2**	**–1**	....	....	....	....	....	....	....	....
	Oklahoma City Stars	CHL	40	21	29	50	....	....	....	18	....	....	....	....	....	....	....	....	....	....	....	....	....	....	....	....	....	....
	Detroit Red Wings	**NHL**	**18**	**4**	**6**	**10**	**4**	**5**	**9**	**4**	**1**	**0**	**1**	**29**	**13.8**	**13**	**3**	**15**	**0**	**–5**	....	....	....	....	....	....	....	....
1979-80	**Detroit Red Wings**	**NHL**	**42**	**3**	**12**	**15**	**3**	**9**	**12**	**10**	**0**	**0**	**1**	**26**	**11.5**	**18**	**0**	**30**	**4**	**–8**	....	....	....	....	....	....	....	....
	Adirondack Red Wings	AHL	25	11	15	26	....	....	....	4	....	....	....	....	....	....	....	....	....	....	....	....	....	....	....	....	....	....
1980-81	Adirondack Red Wings	AHL	73	19	37	56	....	....	....	78	....	....	....	....	....	....	....	....	....	....	18	0	15	15	4	....	....	....
1981-82	Dallas Black Hawks	CHL	67	20	47	67	....	....	....	24	....	....	....	....	....	....	....	....	....	....	16	1	9	10	8	....	....	....
1982-83	Adirondack Red Wings	AHL	77	20	38	58	....	....	....	14	....	....	....	....	....	....	....	....	....	....	6	3	5	8	0	....	....	....
	NHL Totals		**332**	**80**	**109**	**189**	**78**	**88**	**166**	**100**	**20**	**3**	**3**	**577**	**13.9**	**262**	**69**	**306**	**27**		**2**	**0**	**0**	**0**	**0**	**0**	**0**	**0**

Traded to **Atlanta** by **NY Rangers** for Bill Heindl, June, 1972. Traded to **Detroit** by **Atlanta** for Leon Rochefort, November 28, 1972. Traded to **Minnesota** by **Detroit** with LA Kings' 2nd round choice (acquired earlier, Minnesota selected Jimmy Roberts) in 1976 Amateur Draft for Dennis Hextall, February 27, 1976. Signed as a free agent by **Detroit**, February 12, 1979.

• HOGANSON, DALE

Dale Hoganson D – L. 5′10″, 190 lbs. b: North Battleford, Sask., 7/8/1949. Los Angeles' 1st choice, 16th overall, in 1969 Amateur Draft.

Season	Club	League	GP	G	A	Pts	AG	AA	APts	PIM	PP	SH	GW	S	%	TGF	PGF	TGA	PGA	+/–	GP	G	A	Pts	PIM	PP	SH	GW
1964-65	Estevan Bruins	SJHL	3	0	0	0	....	....	....	0	....	....	....	....	....	....	....	....	....	....	2	0	0	0	4	....	....	....
1965-66	Estevan Bruins	SJHL	56	15	18	33	....	....	....	19	....	....	....	....	....	....	....	....	....	....	12	0	0	0	6	....	....	....
1966-67	Estevan Bruins	WCJHL	55	3	17	20	....	....	....	35	....	....	....	....	....	....	....	....	....	....	13	2	3	5	21	....	....	....
1967-68	Estevan Bruins	WCJHL	56	19	40	59	....	....	....	36	....	....	....	....	....	....	....	....	....	....	14	9	13	22	4	....	....	....
1968-69	Estevan Bruins	WCJHL	54	16	44	60	....	....	....	67	....	....	....	....	....	....	....	....	....	....	....	0	3	3	....	....	....	....
1969-70	**Los Angeles Kings**	**NHL**	**49**	**1**	**7**	**8**	**1**	**7**	**8**	**37**	**0**	**0**	**0**	**57**	**1.8**	**37**	**6**	**59**	**7**	**–21**	....	....	....	....	....	....	....	....
	Springfield Kings	AHL	19	2	5	7	....	....	....	43	....	....	....	....	....	....	....	....	....	....	....	....	....	....	....	....	....	....
1970-71	**Los Angeles Kings**	**NHL**	**70**	**4**	**10**	**14**	**4**	**9**	**13**	**52**	**0**	**0**	**0**	**72**	**5.6**	**68**	**5**	**97**	**18**	**–16**	....	....	....	....	....	....	....	....
1971-72	**Los Angeles Kings**	**NHL**	**10**	**1**	**2**	**3**	**1**	**2**	**3**	**14**	**0**	**0**	**0**	**17**	**5.9**	**8**	**1**	**9**	**0**	**–2**	....	....	....	....	....	....	....	....
	Montreal Canadiens	**NHL**	**21**	**0**	**0**	**0**	**0**	**0**	**0**	**2**	**0**	**0**	**0**	**11**	**0.0**	**11**	**0**	**7**	**1**	**+5**	....	....	....	....	....	....	....	....
	Nova Scotia Voyageurs	AHL	13	3	4	7	....	....	....	11	....	....	....	....	....	....	....	....	....	....	....	....	....	....	....	....	....	....
1972-73	**Montreal Canadiens**	**NHL**	**25**	**0**	**2**	**2**	**0**	**2**	**2**	**2**	**0**	**0**	**0**	**17**	**0.0**	**17**	**0**	**13**	**0**	**+4**	....	....	....	....	....	....	....	....
1973-74	Quebec Nordiques	WHA	62	8	33	41	....	....	....	27	....	....	....	....	....	....	....	....	....	....	....	....	....	....	....	....	....	....
1974-75	Quebec Nordiques	WHA	78	9	35	44	....	....	....	47	....	....	....	....	....	....	....	....	....	....	13	1	3	4	4	....	....	....
1975-76	Quebec Nordiques	WHA	45	3	14	17	....	....	....	18	....	....	....	....	....	....	....	....	....	....	5	1	3	4	2	....	....	....
1976-77	Birmingham Bulls	WHA	81	7	48	55	....	....	....	40	....	....	....	....	....	....	....	....	....	....	....	....	....	....	....	....	....	....
1977-78	Birmingham Bulls	WHA	43	1	12	13	....	....	....	29	....	....	....	....	....	....	....	....	....	....	5	0	0	0	7	....	....	....
1978-79	Quebec Nordiques	WHA	69	2	19	21	....	....	....	17	....	....	....	....	....	....	....	....	....	....	4	0	0	0	2	....	....	....
1979-80	**Quebec Nordiques**	**NHL**	**77**	**4**	**36**	**40**	**4**	**28**	**32**	**31**	**0**	**0**	**0**	**99**	**4.0**	**104**	**35**	**140**	**29**	**–42**	....	....	....	....	....	....	....	....

			REGULAR SEASON																		PLAYOFFS							
Season	Club	League	GP	G	A	Pts	AG	AA	APts	PIM	PP	SH	GW	S	%	TGF	PGF	TGA	PGA	+/–	GP	G	A	Pts	PIM	PP	SH	GW
1980-81	**Quebec Nordiques**	**NHL**	**61**	**3**	**14**	**17**	**2**	**10**	**12**	**32**	**1**	**0**	**0**	**56**	**5.4**	**85**	**16**	**114**	**37**	**–8**	**5**	**0**	**3**	**3**	**10**	**0**	**0**	**0**
1981-82	**Quebec Nordiques**	**NHL**	**30**	**0**	**6**	**6**	**0**	**4**	**4**	**16**	**0**	**0**	**0**	**14**	**0.0**	**29**	**1**	**61**	**9**	**–24**	**6**	**0**	**0**	**0**	**2**	**0**	**0**	**0**
	Fredericton Express	AHL	19	2	4	6	....	....	....	18	....	....	....	....	....	....	....	....	....	....	....	....	....	....	....	....	....	....
	NHL Totals		**343**	**13**	**77**	**90**	**12**	**62**	**74**	**186**	**1**	**0**	**0**	**343**	**3.8**	**359**	**64**	**500**	**101**		**11**	**0**	**3**	**3**	**12**	**0**	**0**	**0**
	Other Major League Totals		378	30	161	191	....	....	....	186	....	....	....	....	....	....	....	....	....		27	2	6	8	15	....	....	....

WCJHL All-Star Team (1968, 1969)

Traded to **Montreal** by **LA Kings** with Denis DeJordy, Noel Price and Doug Robinson for Rogie Vachon, November 4, 1971. Selected by **Calgary-Cleveland** (WHA) in 1972 WHA General Player Draft, February 12, 1972. WHA rights traded to **Quebec** (WHA) by **Cleveland** (WHA) for future considerations, June, 1973. Rights traded to **Atlanta** by **Montreal** for cash, May 29, 1973. Traded to **Birmingham** (WHA) by **Quebec** (WHA) for Jim Dorey, June, 1976. Traded to **Quebec** (WHA) by **Birmingham** (WHA) for cash, July 7, 1978. Rights retained by **Quebec** prior to Expansion Draft, June 9, 1979.

• HOGLUND, JONAS

Jonas Hoglund LW – R. 6'3", 200 lbs. b: Hammaro, Swe., 8/29/1972. Calgary's 11th choice, 222nd overall, in 1992 Entry Draft.

Season	Club	League	GP	G	A	Pts	AG	AA	APts	PIM	PP	SH	GW	S	%	TGF	PGF	TGA	PGA	+/–	GP	G	A	Pts	PIM	PP	SH	GW
1988-89	Farjestad BK Karlstad	Sweden	1	0	0	0	....	....	....	0	....	....	....	....	....	....	....	....	....	....	....	....	....	....	....	....	....	....
1989-90	Farjestad BK Karlstad	Sweden	1	0	0	....	....	....	....	0	....	....	....	....	....	....	....	....	....	....	....	....	....	....	....	....	....	....
1990-91	Farjestad BK Karlstad	Sweden	40	5	5	10	....	....	....	4	....	....	....	....	....	....	....	....	....	....	8	1	0	1	0	....	....	....
1991-92	Farjestad BK Karlstad	Sweden	40	14	11	25	....	....	....	6	....	....	....	....	....	....	....	....	....	....	6	2	4	6	2	....	....	....
	Sweden	WJC-A	7	3	2	5	....	....	....	0	....	....	....	....	....	....	....	....	....	....	....	....	....	....	....	....	....	....
1992-93	Farjestad BK Karlstad	Sweden	40	13	13	26	....	....	....	14	....	....	....	....	....	....	....	....	....	....	3	1	0	1	0	....	....	....
1993-94	Farjestad BK Karlstad	Sweden	22	7	2	9	....	....	....	10	....	....	....	....	....	....	....	....	....	....	....	....	....	....	....	....	....	....
1994-95	Farjestad BK Karlstad	Sweden	40	14	12	26	....	....	....	16	....	....	....	....	....	....	....	....	....	....	4	3	2	5	0	....	....	....
1995-96	Farjestad BK Karlstad	Sweden	40	32	11	43	....	....	....	18	....	....	....	....	....	....	....	....	....	....	8	2	1	3	6	....	....	....
1996-97	**Calgary Flames**	**NHL**	**68**	**19**	**16**	**35**	**20**	**14**	**34**	**12**	**3**	**0**	**6**	**189**	**10.1**	**58**	**22**	**41**	**1**	**–4**	....	....	....	....	....	....	....	....
	Sweden	WC-A	11	4	3	7	....	....	....	4	....	....	....	....	....	....	....	....	....	....	....	....	....	....	....	....	....	....
1997-98	**Calgary Flames**	**NHL**	**50**	**6**	**8**	**14**	**7**	**8**	**15**	**16**	**0**	**0**	**0**	**124**	**4.8**	**25**	**4**	**30**	**0**	**–9**	....	....	....	....	....	....	....	....
	Montreal Canadiens	**NHL**	**28**	**6**	**5**	**11**	**7**	**5**	**12**	**6**	**4**	**0**	**0**	**62**	**9.7**	**18**	**9**	**7**	**0**	**+2**	**10**	**2**	**0**	**2**	**0**	**0**	**0**	**0**
	NHL Totals		**146**	**31**	**29**	**60**	**34**	**27**	**61**	**34**	**7**	**0**	**6**	**375**	**8.3**	**101**	**35**	**78**	**1**		**10**	**2**	**0**	**2**	**0**	**0**	**0**	**0**

Traded to **Montreal** by **Calgary** with Zarley Zalapski for Valeri Bure and Montreal's 4th round choice (Shaun Sutter) in 1998 Entry Draft, February 1, 1998

• HOGUE, BENOIT

Benoit Hogue C – L. 5'10", 194 lbs. b: Repentigny, Que., 10/28/1966. Buffalo's 2nd choice, 35th overall, in 1985 Entry Draft.

Season	Club	League	GP	G	A	Pts	AG	AA	APts	PIM	PP	SH	GW	S	%	TGF	PGF	TGA	PGA	+/–	GP	G	A	Pts	PIM	PP	SH	GW
1983-84	St-Jean Castors	QMJHL	59	14	11	25	....	....	....	42	....	....	....	....	....	....	....	....	....	....	....	....	....	....	....	....	....	....
1984-85	St-Jean Castors	QMJHL	63	46	44	90	....	....	....	92	....	....	....	....	....	....	....	....	....	....	....	....	....	....	....	....	....	....
1985-86	St-Jean Castors	QMJHL	65	54	54	108	....	....	....	115	....	....	....	....	....	....	....	....	....	....	9	6	4	10	26	....	....	....
1986-87	Rochester Americans	AHL	52	14	20	34	....	....	....	52	....	....	....	....	....	....	....	....	....	....	12	5	4	9	8	....	....	....
1987-88	**Buffalo Sabres**	**NHL**	**3**	**1**	**1**	**2**	**1**	**1**	**2**	**0**	**0**	**0**	**1**	**3**	**33.3**	**3**	**0**	**0**	**0**	**+3**	....	....	....	....	....	....	....	....
	Rochester Americans	AHL	62	24	31	55	....	....	....	141	....	....	....	....	....	....	....	....	....	....	7	6	1	7	46	....	....	....
1988-89	**Buffalo Sabres**	**NHL**	**69**	**14**	**30**	**44**	**12**	**21**	**33**	**120**	**1**	**2**	**0**	**114**	**12.3**	**65**	**11**	**79**	**20**	**–5**	**5**	**0**	**0**	**0**	**17**	**0**	**0**	**0**
1989-90	**Buffalo Sabres**	**NHL**	**45**	**11**	**7**	**18**	**9**	**5**	**14**	**79**	**1**	**0**	**1**	**73**	**15.1**	**22**	**2**	**24**	**4**	**0**	**3**	**0**	**0**	**0**	**10**	**0**	**0**	**0**
1990-91	**Buffalo Sabres**	**NHL**	**76**	**19**	**28**	**47**	**17**	**21**	**38**	**76**	**1**	**0**	**2**	**134**	**14.2**	**64**	**16**	**61**	**5**	**–8**	**5**	**3**	**1**	**4**	**10**	**0**	**0**	**0**
1991-92	**Buffalo Sabres**	**NHL**	**3**	**0**	**1**	**1**	**0**	**1**	**1**	**0**	**0**	**0**	**0**	**6**	**0.0**	**2**	**0**	**2**	**0**	**0**	....	....	....	....	....	....	....	....
	New York Islanders	**NHL**	**72**	**30**	**45**	**75**	**27**	**34**	**61**	**67**	**8**	**0**	**5**	**143**	**21.0**	**98**	**20**	**65**	**17**	**+30**	....	....	....	....	....	....	....	....
1992-93	**New York Islanders**	**NHL**	**70**	**33**	**42**	**75**	**28**	**29**	**57**	**108**	**5**	**3**	**5**	**147**	**22.4**	**90**	**19**	**88**	**30**	**+13**	**18**	**6**	**6**	**12**	**31**	**0**	**0**	**0**
1993-94	**New York Islanders**	**NHL**	**83**	**36**	**33**	**69**	**34**	**25**	**59**	**73**	**9**	**5**	**3**	**218**	**16.5**	**95**	**30**	**98**	**26**	**–7**	**4**	**0**	**1**	**1**	**4**	**0**	**0**	**0**
1994-95	**New York Islanders**	**NHL**	**33**	**6**	**4**	**10**	**11**	**6**	**17**	**34**	**1**	**0**	**1**	**50**	**12.0**	**25**	**5**	**33**	**13**	**0**	....	....	....	....	....	....	....	....
	Toronto Maple Leafs	**NHL**	**12**	**3**	**3**	**6**	**5**	**4**	**9**	**0**	**1**	**0**	**1**	**16**	**18.8**	**11**	**2**	**9**	**0**	**0**	**7**	**0**	**0**	**0**	**6**	**0**	**0**	**0**
1995-96	**Toronto Maple Leafs**	**NHL**	**44**	**12**	**25**	**37**	**12**	**20**	**32**	**68**	**3**	**0**	**5**	**94**	**12.8**	**49**	**15**	**39**	**11**	**+6**	....	....	....	....	....	....	....	....
	Dallas Stars	**NHL**	**34**	**7**	**20**	**27**	**7**	**16**	**23**	**36**	**2**	**0**	**0**	**61**	**11.5**	**42**	**14**	**29**	**5**	**+4**	....	....	....	....	....	....	....	....
1996-97	**Dallas Stars**	**NHL**	**73**	**19**	**24**	**43**	**20**	**21**	**41**	**54**	**5**	**0**	**5**	**131**	**14.5**	**70**	**15**	**47**	**0**	**+8**	**7**	**2**	**2**	**4**	**6**	**1**	**0**	**0**
1997-98	**Dallas Stars**	**NHL**	**53**	**6**	**16**	**22**	**7**	**16**	**23**	**35**	**3**	**0**	**1**	**55**	**10.9**	**38**	**9**	**22**	**0**	**+7**	**17**	**4**	**2**	**6**	**16**	**1**	**0**	**2**
	NHL Totals		**670**	**197**	**279**	**476**	**190**	**220**	**410**	**750**	**40**	**10**	**30**	**1245**	**15.8**	**674**	**158**	**596**	**131**		**66**	**15**	**12**	**27**	**100**	**2**	**0**	**2**

Traded to **NY Islanders** by **Buffalo** with Pierre Turgeon, Uwe Krupp and Dave McLlwain for Pat Lafontaine, Randy Hillier, Randy Wood and NY Islanders' 4th round choice (Dean Melanson) in 1992 Entry Draft, October 25, 1991. Traded to **Toronto** by **NY Islanders** with NY Islanders' 3rd round choice (Ryan Pepperall) in 1995 Entry Draft and 5th round choice (Brandon Sugden) in 1996 Entry Draft for Eric Fichaud, April 6, 1995. Traded to **Dallas** by **Toronto** with Randy Wood for Dave Gagner and Dallas' 6th round choice (Dmitriy Yakushin) in 1996 Entry Draft, January 29, 1996.

• HOLAN, MILOS

Milos Holan D – L. 5'11", 191 lbs. b: Bilovec, Czech., 4/22/1971. Philadelphia's 3rd choice, 77th overall, in 1993 Entry Draft.

Season	Club	League	GP	G	A	Pts	AG	AA	APts	PIM	PP	SH	GW	S	%	TGF	PGF	TGA	PGA	+/–	GP	G	A	Pts	PIM	PP	SH	GW
1988-89	TJ Vitkovice	Czech.	7	0	0	0	....	....	....	0	....	....	....	....	....	....	....	....	....	....	....	....	....	....	....	....	....	....
1989-90	TJ Vitkovice	Czech.	50	8	8	16	....	....	....	....	....	....	....	....	....	....	....	....	....	....	....	....	....	....	....	....	....	....
	Czechoslovakia	WJC-A	4	2	0	2	....	....	....	2	....	....	....	....	....	....	....	....	....	....	....	....	....	....	....	....	....	....
1990-91	Dukla Trencin	Czech.	53	6	13	19	....	....	....	....	....	....	....	....	....	....	....	....	....	....	....	....	....	....	....	....	....	....
	Czechoslovakia	WJC-A	6	0	2	2	....	....	....	0	....	....	....	....	....	....	....	....	....	....	....	....	....	....	....	....	....	....
1991-92	Dukla Trencin	Czech.	51	13	22	35	....	....	....	32	....	....	....	....	....	....	....	....	....	....	....	....	....	....	....	....	....	....
1992-93	TJ Vitkovice	Czech.	53	35	33	68	....	....	....	....	....	....	....	....	....	....	....	....	....	....	....	....	....	....	....	....	....	....
	Czech Republic	WC-A	8	1	3	4	....	....	....	10	....	....	....	....	....	....	....	....	....	....	....	....	....	....	....	....	....	....
1993-94	**Philadelphia Flyers**	**NHL**	**8**	**1**	**1**	**2**	**1**	**1**	**2**	**4**	**1**	**0**	**0**	**26**	**3.8**	**9**	**6**	**7**	**0**	**–4**	....	....	....	....	....	....	....	....
	Hershey Bears	AHL	27	7	22	29	....	....	....	16	....	....	....	....	....	....	....	....	....	....	....	....	....	....	....	....	....	....
	Czech Republic	WC-A	6	0	3	3	....	....	....	8	....	....	....	....	....	....	....	....	....	....	....	....	....	....	....	....	....	....
1994-95	Hershey Bears	AHL	55	22	27	49	....	....	....	75	....	....	....	....	....	....	....	....	....	....	....	....	....	....	....	....	....	....
	Anaheim Mighty Ducks	**NHL**	**25**	**2**	**8**	**10**	**4**	**12**	**16**	**14**	**1**	**0**	**1**	**93**	**2.2**	**26**	**9**	**17**	**4**	**+4**	....	....	....	....	....	....	....	....
1995-96	**Anaheim Mighty Ducks**	**NHL**	**16**	**2**	**2**	**4**	**2**	**2**	**4**	**24**	**0**	**0**	**0**	**47**	**4.3**	**10**	**3**	**20**	**1**	**–12**	....	....	....	....	....	....	....	....
	NHL Totals		**49**	**5**	**11**	**16**	**7**	**15**	**22**	**42**	**2**	**0**	**1**	**166**	**3.0**	**45**	**18**	**44**	**5**		....	....	....	....	....	....	....	....

Czechoslovakian Player of the Year (1993)

Traded to **Anaheim** by **Philadelphia** for Anatoli Semenov, March 8, 1995.

• HOLBROOK, TERRY

Terry Holbrook RW – R. 6', 185 lbs. b: Petrolia, Ont., 7/11/1950. Los Angeles' 2nd choice, 38th overall, in 1970 Amateur Draft.

Season	Club	League	GP	G	A	Pts	AG	AA	APts	PIM	PP	SH	GW	S	%	TGF	PGF	TGA	PGA	+/–	GP	G	A	Pts	PIM	PP	SH	GW
1969-70	London Knights	OHA	54	13	15	28	....	....	....	13	....	....	....	....	....	....	....	....	....	....	....	....	....	....	....	....	....	....
1970-71	Springfield Kings	AHL	40	2	8	10	....	....	....	8	....	....	....	....	....	....	....	....	....	....	....	....	....	....	....	....	....	....
	Cleveland Barons	AHL	17	1	7	8	....	....	....	0	....	....	....	....	....	....	....	....	....	....	8	0	0	0	0	....	....	....
1971-72	Cleveland Barons	AHL	76	7	22	29	....	....	....	16	....	....	....	....	....	....	....	....	....	....	6	1	0	1	7	....	....	....
1972-73	Cleveland-Jacksonville Barons	AHL	51	22	21	43	....	....	....	12	....	....	....	....	....	....	....	....	....	....	....	....	....	....	....	....	....	....
	Minnesota North Stars	**NHL**	**21**	**2**	**3**	**5**	**2**	**2**	**4**	**0**	**0**	**0**	**1**	**18**	**11.1**	**6**	**0**	**10**	**0**	**–4**	**6**	**0**	**0**	**0**	**0**	**0**	**0**	**0**
1973-74	**Minnesota North Stars**	**NHL**	**22**	**1**	**3**	**4**	**1**	**3**	**4**	**4**	**1**	**0**	**0**	**19**	**5.3**	**8**	**2**	**16**	**7**	**–3**	....	....	....	....	....	....	....	....
	New Haven Nighthawks	AHL	37	15	21	36	....	....	....	18	....	....	....	....	....	....	....	....	....	....	....	....	....	....	....	....	....	....
1974-75	Cleveland Crusaders	WHA	78	10	13	23	....	....	....	7	....	....	....	....	....	....	....	....	....	....	5	0	1	1	0	....	....	....
1975-76	Cleveland Crusaders	WHA	15	1	2	3	....	....	....	6	....	....	....	....	....	....	....	....	....	....	3	0	0	0	0	....	....	....
	NHL Totals		**43**	**3**	**6**	**9**	**3**	**5**	**8**	**4**	**1**	**0**	**1**	**37**	**8.1**	**14**	**2**	**26**	**7**		**6**	**0**	**0**	**0**	**0**	**0**	**0**	**0**
	Other Major League Totals		93	11	15	26	....	....	....	13	....	....	....	....	....	....	....	....	....		8	0	1	1	0	....	....	....

Traded to **Minnesota** by **LA Kings** for Wayne Schultz and rights to Steve Sutherland, March, 1971. Selected by **Calgary-Cleveland** (WHA) in 1972 WHA General Player Draft, February 12, 1972.

• HOLIK, BOBBY

Bobby Holik LW – R. 6'3", 220 lbs. b: Jihlava, Czech., 1/1/1971. Hartford's 1st choice, 10th overall, in 1989 Entry Draft.

Season	Club	League	GP	G	A	Pts	AG	AA	APts	PIM	PP	SH	GW	S	%	TGF	PGF	TGA	PGA	+/–	GP	G	A	Pts	PIM	PP	SH	GW
1987-88	Dukla Jihlava	Czech.	31	5	9	14	....	....	....	16	....	....	....	....	....	....	....	....	....	....	....	....	....	....	....	....	....	....
1988-89	Dukla Jihlava	Czech.	24	7	10	17	....	....	....	32	....	....	....	....	....	....	....	....	....	....	....	....	....	....	....	....	....	....
	Czechoslovakia	WJC-A	7	5	3	8	....	....	....	2	....	....	....	....	....	....	....	....	....	....	....	....	....	....	....	....	....	....
1989-90	Dukla Jihlava	Czech.	42	15	26	41	....	....	....	....	....	....	....	....	....	....	....	....	....	....	....	....	....	....	....	....	....	....
	Czechoslovakia	WJC-A	7	6	5	11	....	....	....	12	....	....	....	....	....	....	....	....	....	....	....	....	....	....	....	....	....	....
1990-91	**Hartford Whalers**	**NHL**	**78**	**21**	**22**	**43**	**19**	**17**	**36**	**113**	**8**	**0**	**3**	**173**	**12.1**	**59**	**14**	**49**	**1**	**–3**	**6**	**0**	**0**	**0**	**7**	**0**	**0**	**0**
1991-92	**Hartford Whalers**	**NHL**	**76**	**21**	**24**	**45**	**19**	**18**	**37**	**44**	**1**	**0**	**2**	**207**	**10.1**	**63**	**6**	**54**	**1**	**+4**	**7**	**0**	**1**	**1**	**6**	**0**	**0**	**0**
1992-93	**New Jersey Devils**	**NHL**	**61**	**20**	**19**	**39**	**17**	**13**	**30**	**76**	**7**	**0**	**4**	**180**	**11.1**	**62**	**24**	**44**	**0**	**–6**	**5**	**1**	**1**	**2**	**6**	**0**	**0**	**0**
	Utica Devils	AHL	1	....	....	....	....	....	....	2	....	....	....	....	....	....	....	....	....	....	....	....	....	....	....	....	....	....

			REGULAR SEASON																		PLAYOFFS							
Season	Club	League	GP	G	A	Pts	AG	AA	APts	PIM	PP	SH	GW	S	%	TGF	PGF	TGA	PGA	+/-	GP	G	A	Pts	PIM	PP	SH	GW
1993-94	New Jersey Devils	NHL	70	13	20	33	12	15	27	72	2	0	3	130	10.0	49	3	18	0	+28	20	0	3	3	6	0	0	0
1994-95	New Jersey Devils	NHL	48	10	10	20	18	15	33	18	0	0	2	84	11.9	26	2	16	1	+9	20	4	4	8	22	2	0	1
1995-96	New Jersey Devils	NHL	63	13	17	30	13	14	27	58	1	0	1	157	8.3	39	8	23	1	+9								
1996-97	Czech Republic	W Cup	3	0	0	0				0																		
	New Jersey Devils	NHL	82	23	39	62	24	35	59	54	5	0	6	192	12.0	80	17	39	0	+24	10	2	3	5	4	1	0	0
1997-98	New Jersey Devils	NHL	82	29	36	65	34	35	69	100	8	0	8	238	12.2	89	37	29	0	+23	5	0	0	0	8	0	0	0
	NHL Totals		560	150	187	337	156	162	318	535	32	0	29	1361	11.0	467	111	272	4		73	7	12	19	59	3	0	1

Played in NHL All Star Game (1998)

Traded to **New Jersey** by **Hartford** with Hartford's 2nd round choice (Jay Pandolfo) in 1993 Entry Draft and future considerations for Sean Burke and Eric Weinrich, August 28, 1992.

• HOLLAND, JASON

Jason Holland D – R. 6'2", 193 lbs. b: Morinville, Alta., 4/30/1976. NY Islanders' 2nd choice, 38th overall, in 1994 Entry Draft.

Season	Club	League	GP	G	A	Pts	AG	AA	APts	PIM	PP	SH	GW	S	%	TGF	PGF	TGA	PGA	+/-	GP	G	A	Pts	PIM	PP	SH	GW
1992-93	Kamloops Blazers	WHL	4	0	0	0				2																		
1993-94	Kamloops Blazers	WHL	59	14	15	29				80											18	2	3	5	4			
1994-95	Kamloops Blazers	WHL	71	9	32	41				65											21	2	7	9	9			
1995-96	Kamloops Blazers	WHL	63	24	33	57				98											16	4	9	13	22			
	Canada	WJC-A	6	2	1	3				4																		
1996-97	New York Islanders	NHL	4	1	0	1	1	0	1	0	0	0	0	3	33.3	3	0	2	0	+1								
	Kentucky Thoroughblades	AHL	72	14	25	39				46											4	0	2	2	0			
1997-98	New York Islanders	NHL	8	0	0	0	0	0	0	4	0	0	0	6	0.0	2	0	7	1	–4								
	Kentucky Thoroughblades	AHL	50	10	16	26				29																		
	Rochester Americans	AHL	9	0	4	4				10											4	0	3	3	4			
	NHL Totals		12	1	0	1	1	0	1	4	0	0	0	9	11.1	5	0	9	1									

WHL West First All-Star Team (1996)

Traded to **Buffalo** by **NY Islanders** with Paul Kruse for Jason Dawe, March 24, 1998.

• HOLLAND, JERRY

Jerry Holland LW – L. 5'10", 180 lbs. b: Beaverlodge, Alta., 8/25/1954. NY Rangers' 3rd choice, 50th overall, in 1974 Amateur Draft.

Season	Club	League	GP	G	A	Pts	AG	AA	APts	PIM	PP	SH	GW	S	%	TGF	PGF	TGA	PGA	+/-	GP	G	A	Pts	PIM	PP	SH	GW
1970-71	Kamloops Blazers	BCJHL	....	33	39	72				50																		
1971-72	Calgary Wranglers	WCJHL	33	17	13	30				23																		
1972-73	Calgary Wranglers	WCJHL	67	51	54	105				66																		
1973-74	Calgary Wranglers	WCJHL	67	55	65	120				54																		
1974-75	New York Rangers	NHL	1	1	0	1	1	0	1	0	0	0	0	1	100.0	1	0	0	0	+1								
	Providence Reds	AHL	67	*44	35	79				44											6	1	2	3	11			
1975-76	New York Rangers	NHL	36	7	4	11	7	3	10	6	2	0	1	50	14.0	18	4	19	0	–5								
	Providence Reds	AHL	28	9	11	20				11											3	0	1	1	0			
1976-77	New Haven Nighthawks	AHL	72	28	34	62				35											6	0	3	3	0			
1977-78	Edmonton Oilers	WHA	22	2	1	3				14																		
	Salt Lake Golden Eagles	CHL	11	5	6	11				11																		
1978-79	Spokane Flyers	WIHL	52	*38	23	61				20																		
	NHL Totals		37	8	4	12	8	3	11	6	2	0	1	51	15.7	19	4	19	0									
	Other Major League Totals		22	2	1	3				14																		

AHL First All-Star Team (1975) • Won Dudley "Red" Garrett Memorial Award (Top Rookie - AHL) (1975)

Selected by **Cincinnati** (WHA) in 1974 WHA Amateur Draft, June, 1974. Signed as a free agent by **Edmonton** (WHA), September, 1977.

• HOLLINGER, TERRY

Terry Hollinger D – L. 6'1", 200 lbs. b: Regina, Sask., 2/24/1971. St. Louis' 7th choice, 153rd overall, in 1991 Entry Draft.

Season	Club	League	GP	G	A	Pts	AG	AA	APts	PIM	PP	SH	GW	S	%	TGF	PGF	TGA	PGA	+/-	GP	G	A	Pts	PIM	PP	SH	GW
1987-88	Regina Pats	WHL	7	1	1	2				4																		
1988-89	Regina Pats	WHL	65	2	27	29				49																		
1989-90	Regina Pats	WHL	70	14	43	57				40											11	1	3	4	10			
1990-91	Regina Pats	WHL	8	1	6	7				6																		
	Lethbridge Hurricanes	WHL	62	9	32	41				113											16	3	14	17	22			
1991-92	Lethbridge Hurricanes	WHL	65	23	62	85				155											5	1	2	3	13			
	Peoria Rivermen	IHL	1	0	2	2				0											5	0	1	1	0			
1992-93	Peoria Rivermen	IHL	72	2	28	30				67											4	1	1	2	0			
1993-94	St. Louis Blues	NHL	2	0	0	0	0	0	0	0	0	0	0	0	0.0	1	0	1	1	+1								
	Peoria Rivermen	IHL	78	12	31	43				96											6	0	3	3	31			
1994-95	St. Louis Blues	NHL	5	0	0	0	0	0	0	2	0	0	0	1	0.0	2	0	4	1	–1								
	Peoria Rivermen	IHL	69	7	25	32				137											4	2	4	6	8			
1995-96	Rochester Americans	AHL	62	5	50	55				71											19	3	11	14	12			
1996-97	Rochester Americans	AHL	73	12	51	63				54											10	2	7	9	27			
1997-98	Worcester IceCats	AHL	55	8	24	32				34																		
	Houston Aeros	IHL	8	1	1	2				6											4	1	2	3	11			
	NHL Totals		7	0	0	0	0	0	0	2	0	0	0	1	0.0	3	0	5	2									

AHL Second All-Star Team (1996) • AHL First All-Star Team (1997)

Signed as a free agent by **Buffalo**, August 23, 1995. Signed as a free agent by **St. Louis**, July 16, 1997.

• HOLLOWAY, BRUCE

Bruce Holloway D – L. 6', 200 lbs. b: Revelstoke, B.C., 6/27/1963. Vancouver's 6th choice, 136th overall, in 1981 Entry Draft.

Season	Club	League	GP	G	A	Pts	AG	AA	APts	PIM	PP	SH	GW	S	%	TGF	PGF	TGA	PGA	+/-	GP	G	A	Pts	PIM	PP	SH	GW
1978-79	Revelstoke Bruins	BCJHL	61	4	14	18				52																		
	Billings Bighorns	WHL	9	0	1	1				0											4	0	0	0	0			
1979-80	Melville Millionaires	SJHL	9	3	2	5				10																		
	Billings Bighorns	WHL	49	1	9	10				6																		
1980-81	Billings Bighorns	WHL	2	0	2	2				0																		
	Regina Pats	WHL	66	6	27	33				61											11	2	5	7	4			
1981-82	Regina Pats	WHL	69	4	28	32				111											2	0	2	2	17			
1982-83	Brandon Wheat Kings	WHL	7	0	5	5				8																		
	Kamloops Junior Oilers	WHL	51	6	53	59				82											7	1	4	5	6			
1983-84	Fredericton Express	AHL	66	3	30	33				29											5	0	0	0	0			
1984-85	Vancouver Canucks	NHL	2	0	0	0	0	0	0	0	0	0	0	0	0.0	0	0	1	0	–1								
	Fredericton Express	AHL	31	2	4	6				16																		
	St. Catharines Saints	AHL	13	1	0	1				0																		
1985-86	Kalamazoo Wings	IHL	38	7	11	18				45																		
	Peoria Rivermen	IHL	29	4	13	17				47											7	2	3	5	2			
	NHL Totals		2	0	0	0	0	0	0	0	0	0	0	0	0.0	0	0	1	0									

• HOLMES, WARREN

Warren Holmes C – L. 6'1", 195 lbs. b: Beeton, Ont., 2/18/1957. Los Angeles' 2nd choice, 85th overall, in 1977 Amateur Draft.

Season	Club	League	GP	G	A	Pts	AG	AA	APts	PIM	PP	SH	GW	S	%	TGF	PGF	TGA	PGA	+/-	GP	G	A	Pts	PIM	PP	SH	GW
1974-75	Ottawa 67's	OHA	54	9	17	26				47																		
1975-76	Ottawa 67's	OHA	28	3	11	14				6																		
1976-77	Ottawa 67's	OHA	36	18	29	47				31											19	11	10	21	23			
1977-78	Saginaw Gears	IHL	78	48	33	81				51											5	3	3	6	14			
1978-79	Springfield Indians	AHL	4	0	0	0				0																		
	Milwaukee Admirals	IHL	31	11	17	20				33																		
	Saginaw Gears	IHL	38	11	18	29				30											4	1	3	4	8			
1979-80	Binghamton Whalers	AHL	2	0	0	0				0																		
	Saginaw Gears	IHL	72	37	55	92				62											7	5	3	8	21			
1980-81	Houston Apollos	CHL	25	7	7	14				18																		
	Saginaw Gears	IHL	40	21	25	46				27											13	8	9	17	19			
1981-82	Los Angeles Kings	NHL	3	0	2	2	0	1	1	0	0	0	0	6	0.0	3	0	3	1	+1								
	New Haven Nighthawks	AHL	73	28	28	56				29											4	1	5	6	0			
1982-83	Los Angeles Kings	NHL	39	8	16	24	7	11	18	7	2	0	0	66	12.1	36	12	56	24	–8								
	New Haven Nighthawks	AHL	35	17	18	35				26																		

Season	Club	League	REGULAR SEASON GP	G	A	Pts	AG	AA	APts	PIM	PP	SH	GW	S	%	TGF	PGF	TGA	PGA	+/–	PLAYOFFS GP	G	A	Pts	PIM	PP	SH	GW
1983-84	**Los Angeles Kings**	**NHL**	**3**	**0**	**0**	**0**	**0**	**0**	**0**	**0**	**0**	**0**	**0**	**3**	**0.0**	**0**	**0**	**4**	**1**	**–3**	....	....	....	....	....	....	....	....
	New Haven Nighthawks	AHL	76	26	35	61	....	....	....	25	....	....	....	....	....	....	....	....	....	....	....	....	....	....	....	....	....	....
1984-85	Flint Generals	IHL	80	23	44	67	....	....	....	70	....	....	....	....	....	....	....	....	....	....	7	3	3	6	11	....	....	....
1985-86	Saginaw Generals	IHL	65	17	20	37	....	....	....	88	....	....	....	....	....	....	....	....	....	....	....	....	....	....	....	....	....	....
	NHL Totals		**45**	**8**	**18**	**26**	**7**	**12**	**19**	**7**	**2**	**0**	**0**	**75**	**10.7**	**39**	**12**	**63**	**26**		....	....	....	....	....	....	....	....

• HOLMGREN, PAUL

Paul Holmgren RW – R. 6'3", 210 lbs. b: St. Paul, MN, 12/2/1955. Philadelphia's 5th choice, 108th overall, in 1975 Amateur Draft.

Season	Club	League	GP	G	A	Pts	AG	AA	APts	PIM	PP	SH	GW	S	%	TGF	PGF	TGA	PGA	+/–	GP	G	A	Pts	PIM	PP	SH	GW
1973-74	St. Paul Saints	MJHL	55	22	59	81	....	....	....	183	....	....	....	....	....	....	....	....	....	....	....	....	....	....	....	....	....	....
	United States	WJC-A	4	0	0	0	....	....	....	8	....	....	....	....	....	....	....	....	....	....	....	....	....	....	....	....	....	....
1974-75	University of Minnesota	WCHA	37	10	21	31	....	....	....	108	....	....	....	....	....	....	....	....	....	....	....	....	....	....	....	....	....	....
1975-76	Minnesota Fighting Saints	WHA	51	14	16	30	....	....	....	121	....	....	....	....	....	....	....	....	....	....	....	....	....	....	....	....	....	....
	Johnstown Jets	NAHL	6	3	12	15	....	....	....	12	....	....	....	....	....	....	....	....	....	....	....	....	....	....	....	....	....	....
	Philadelphia Flyers	**NHL**	**1**	**0**	**0**	**0**	**0**	**0**	**0**	**2**	**0**	**0**	**0**	**1**	**0.0**	**0**	**0**	**0**	**0**	**0**	....	....	....	....	....	....	....	....
	Richmond Robins	AHL	6	4	4	8	....	....	....	23	....	....	....	....	....	....	....	....	....	....	....	....	....	....	....	....	....	....
1976-77	**Philadelphia Flyers**	**NHL**	**59**	**14**	**12**	**26**	**13**	**10**	**23**	**201**	**0**	**0**	**2**	**74**	**18.9**	**43**	**6**	**28**	**1**	**+10**	**10**	**1**	**1**	**2**	**25**	**0**	**0**	**0**
1977-78	**Philadelphia Flyers**	**NHL**	**62**	**16**	**18**	**34**	**15**	**15**	**30**	**190**	**2**	**0**	**1**	**91**	**17.6**	**66**	**11**	**34**	**2**	**+23**	**12**	**1**	**4**	**5**	**26**	**0**	**0**	**0**
1978-79	**Philadelphia Flyers**	**NHL**	**57**	**19**	**10**	**29**	**17**	**8**	**25**	**168**	**4**	**0**	**3**	**122**	**15.6**	**50**	**11**	**37**	**0**	**+2**	**8**	**1**	**5**	**6**	**22**	**0**	**0**	**0**
1979-80	**Philadelphia Flyers**	**NHL**	**74**	**30**	**35**	**65**	**27**	**27**	**54**	**267**	**9**	**0**	**3**	**153**	**19.6**	**99**	**26**	**44**	**6**	**+35**	**18**	**10**	**10**	**20**	**47**	**3**	**0**	**1**
1980-81	**Philadelphia Flyers**	**NHL**	**77**	**22**	**37**	**59**	**18**	**26**	**44**	**306**	**3**	**0**	**2**	**159**	**13.8**	**102**	**30**	**62**	**2**	**+12**	**12**	**5**	**9**	**14**	**49**	**2**	**0**	**1**
1981-82	**Philadelphia Flyers**	**NHL**	**41**	**9**	**22**	**31**	**7**	**15**	**22**	**183**	**4**	**0**	**3**	**71**	**12.7**	**47**	**11**	**27**	**1**	**+10**	**4**	**1**	**2**	**3**	**6**	**0**	**0**	**0**
1982-83	**Philadelphia Flyers**	**NHL**	**77**	**19**	**24**	**43**	**16**	**17**	**33**	**178**	**3**	**0**	**2**	**122**	**15.6**	**77**	**19**	**40**	**0**	**+18**	**3**	**0**	**0**	**0**	**6**	**0**	**0**	**0**
1983-84	**Philadelphia Flyers**	**NHL**	**52**	**9**	**13**	**22**	**7**	**9**	**16**	**105**	**1**	**0**	**1**	**75**	**12.0**	**34**	**1**	**32**	**0**	**+1**	....	....	....	....	....	....	....	....
	Minnesota North Stars	**NHL**	**11**	**2**	**5**	**7**	**2**	**3**	**5**	**46**	**0**	**0**	**0**	**17**	**11.8**	**7**	**0**	**9**	**0**	**–2**	**12**	**0**	**1**	**1**	**6**	**0**	**0**	**0**
1984-85	**Minnesota North Stars**	**NHL**	**16**	**4**	**3**	**7**	**3**	**2**	**5**	**38**	**2**	**0**	**0**	**13**	**30.8**	**10**	**5**	**9**	**0**	**–4**	**3**	**0**	**0**	**0**	**8**	**0**	**0**	**0**
	NHL Totals		**527**	**144**	**179**	**323**	**125**	**132**	**257**	**1684**	**28**	**0**	**17**	**898**	**16.0**	**535**	**120**	**322**	**12**		**82**	**19**	**32**	**51**	**195**	**5**	**0**	**2**
	Other Major League Totals		51	14	16	30	....	....	....	121	....	....	....	....	....	....	....	....	....		....	....	....	....	....	....	....	....

Played in NHL All-Star Game (1981)

Selected by **Edmonton** (WHA) in 1974 WHA Amateur Draft, June, 1974. WHA rights traded to **Minnesota** (WHA) by **Edmonton** (WHA) for cash, July, 1975. Traded to **Minnesota** by **Philadelphia** for the rights to Paul Guay and Minnesota's 3rd round choice (Darryl Gilmour) in 1985 Entry Draft, February 23, 1984.

• HOLMSTROM, TOMAS

Tomas Holmstrom LW – L. 6', 200 lbs. b: Pitea, Sweden, 1/23/1973. Detroit's 9th choice, 257th overall, in 1994 Entry Draft.

Season	Club	League	GP	G	A	Pts	AG	AA	APts	PIM	PP	SH	GW	S	%	TGF	PGF	TGA	PGA	+/–	GP	G	A	Pts	PIM	PP	SH	GW
1994-95	Lulea HF	Sweden	40	14	14	28	....	....	....	56	....	....	....	....	....	....	....	....	....	....	8	1	2	3	20	....	....	....
1995-96	Lulea HF	Sweden	34	12	11	23	....	....	....	78	....	....	....	....	....	....	....	....	....	....	11	6	2	8	22	....	....	....
	Sweden	WC-A	6	1	0	1	....	....	....	12	....	....	....	....	....	....	....	....	....	....	....	....	....	....	....	....	....	....
1996-97	Sweden	W Cup	DID NOT PLAY																									
	Detroit Red Wings	**NHL**	**47**	**6**	**3**	**9**	**6**	**3**	**9**	**33**	**3**	**0**	**0**	**53**	**11.3**	**19**	**10**	**19**	**0**	**–10**	**1**	**0**	**0**	**0**	**0**	**0**	**0**	**0**
	Adirondack Red Wings	AHL	6	3	1	4	....	....	....	7	....	....	....	....	....	....	....	....	....	....	....	....	....	....	....	....	....	....
1997-98	**Detroit Red Wings**	**NHL**	**57**	**5**	**17**	**22**	**6**	**17**	**23**	**44**	**1**	**0**	**1**	**48**	**10.4**	**33**	**10**	**17**	**0**	**+6**	**22**	**7**	**12**	**19**	**16**	**2**	**0**	**0**
	NHL Totals		**104**	**11**	**20**	**31**	**12**	**20**	**32**	**77**	**4**	**0**	**1**	**101**	**10.9**	**52**	**20**	**36**	**0**		**23**	**7**	**12**	**19**	**16**	**2**	**0**	**0**

• HOLST, GREG

Greg Holst C – L. 5'10", 170 lbs. b: Montreal, Que., 2/21/1954. NY Rangers' 8th choice, 139th overall, in 1974 Amateur Draft.

Season	Club	League	GP	G	A	Pts	AG	AA	APts	PIM	PP	SH	GW	S	%	TGF	PGF	TGA	PGA	+/–	GP	G	A	Pts	PIM	PP	SH	GW
1971-72	University of New Brunswick	AUAA	....	7	8	15	....	....	....	26	....	....	....	....	....	....	....	....	....	....	....	....	....	....	....	....	....	....
1972-73	University of New Brunswick	AUAA	....	22	11	33	....	....	....	82	....	....	....	....	....	....	....	....	....	....	....	....	....	....	....	....	....	....
1973-74	Kingston Canadians	OHA	62	33	47	80	....	....	....	121	....	....	....	....	....	....	....	....	....	....	....	....	....	....	....	....	....	....
1974-75	Port Huron Flags	IHL	8	1	0	1	....	....	....	6	....	....	....	....	....	....	....	....	....	....	....	....	....	....	....	....	....	....
	Winston-Salem Polar Bears	SHL	62	33	37	70	....	....	....	112	....	....	....	....	....	....	....	....	....	....	7	5	6	11	42	....	....	....
1975-76	**New York Rangers**	**NHL**	**2**	**0**	**0**	**0**	**0**	**0**	**0**	**0**	**0**	**0**	**0**	**0**	**0.0**	**0**	**0**	**3**	**0**	**–3**	....	....	....	....	....	....	....	....
	Providence Reds	AHL	69	37	44	81	....	....	....	77	....	....	....	....	....	....	....	....	....	....	3	0	0	0	22	....	....	....
1976-77	**New York Rangers**	**NHL**	**5**	**0**	**0**	**0**	**0**	**0**	**0**	**0**	**0**	**0**	**0**	**7**	**0.0**	**0**	**0**	**2**	**0**	**–2**	....	....	....	....	....	....	....	....
	New Haven Nighthawks	AHL	65	21	25	46	....	....	....	90	....	....	....	....	....	....	....	....	....	....	6	2	3	5	2	....	....	....
1977-78	**New York Rangers**	**NHL**	**4**	**0**	**0**	**0**	**0**	**0**	**0**	**0**	**0**	**0**	**0**	**2**	**0.0**	**0**	**0**	**1**	**0**	**–1**	....	....	....	....	....	....	....	....
	New Haven Nighthawks	AHL	65	15	25	40	....	....	....	44	....	....	....	....	....	....	....	....	....	....	15	6	7	13	6	....	....	....
1978-79	IEV Innsbruck	Austria	....	42	26	68	....	....	....	....	....	....	....	....	....	....	....	....	....	....	....	....	....	....	....	....	....	....
1979-80	IEV Innsbruck	Austria	39	37	34	71	....	....	....	63	....	....	....	....	....	....	....	....	....	....	....	....	....	....	....	....	....	....
1980-81	IEV Innsbruck	Austria	33	28	*48	76	....	....	....	70	....	....	....	....	....	....	....	....	....	....	....	....	....	....	....	....	....	....
1981-82	WEV Wien	Austria	....	41	19	60	....	....	....	....	....	....	....	....	....	....	....	....	....	....	....	14	15	*29	....	....	....	....
1982-83	IEV Innsbruck	Austria 2	STATISTICS NOT AVAILABLE																									
1983-84	IEV Innsbruck	Austria	28	36	32	68	....	....	....	....	....	....	....	....	....	....	....	....	....	....	....	....	....	....	....	....	....	....
1984-85	IEV Innsbruck	Austria	39	44	57	101	....	....	....	36	....	....	....	....	....	....	....	....	....	....	....	....	....	....	....	....	....	....
1985-86	IEV Innsbruck	Austria	36	27	24	51	....	....	....	83	....	....	....	....	....	....	....	....	....	....	....	....	....	....	....	....	....	....
1986-87	IEV Innsbruck	Austria	38	39	36	75	....	....	....	50	....	....	....	....	....	....	....	....	....	....	....	....	....	....	....	....	....	....
1987-88	HC Salzburger	Austria	34	31	20	51	....	....	....	24	....	....	....	....	....	....	....	....	....	....	....	....	....	....	....	....	....	....
1988-89	VSV Villach	Austria	46	38	41	79	....	....	....	....	....	....	....	....	....	....	....	....	....	....	....	....	....	....	....	....	....	....
1990-91	VSV Villach	Austria 2	STATISTICS NOT AVAILABLE																									
1990-91	IEV Innsbruck	Austria	34	19	22	41	....	....	....	....	....	....	....	....	....	....	....	....	....	....	....	....	....	....	....	....	....	....
1991-92	IEV Innsbruck	Austria	42	21	30	51	....	....	....	....	....	....	....	....	....	....	....	....	....	....	....	....	....	....	....	....	....	....
1992-93	EC Graz	Austria	25	4	9	13	....	....	....	....	....	....	....	....	....	....	....	....	....	....	....	....	....	....	....	....	....	....
	NHL Totals		**11**	**0**	**0**	**0**	**0**	**0**	**0**	**0**	**0**	**0**	**0**	**9**	**0.0**	**0**	**0**	**6**	**0**		....	....	....	....	....	....	....	....

Won Dudley "Red" Garrett Memorial Award (Top Rookie - AHL) (1976)

• HOLT, GARY

Gary Holt LW – L. 5'9", 175 lbs. b: Sarnia, Ont., 1/1/1952.

Season	Club	League	GP	G	A	Pts	AG	AA	APts	PIM	PP	SH	GW	S	%	TGF	PGF	TGA	PGA	+/–	GP	G	A	Pts	PIM	PP	SH	GW
1969-70	Sudbury Wolves	NOHA	....	37	40	77	....	....	....	106	....	....	....	....	....	....	....	....	....	....	....	....	....	....	....	....	....	....
1970-71	Niagara Falls Flyers	OHA	35	10	14	24	....	....	....	48	....	....	....	....	....	....	....	....	....	....	....	....	....	....	....	....	....	....
1971-72	Niagara Falls Flyers	OHA	64	11	12	23	....	....	....	27	....	....	....	....	....	....	....	....	....	....	....	....	....	....	....	....	....	....
1972-73	Columbus–Port Huron	IHL	75	30	30	60	....	....	....	82	....	....	....	....	....	....	....	....	....	....	11	1	6	7	6	....	....	....
1973-74	**California Golden Seals**	**NHL**	**1**	**0**	**0**	**0**	**0**	**0**	**0**	**0**	**0**	**0**	**0**	**1**	**0.0**	**0**	**0**	**0**	**0**	**0**	....	....	....	....	....	....	....	....
	Salt Lake Golden Eagles	WHL	71	21	26	47	....	....	....	197	....	....	....	....	....	....	....	....	....	....	5	0	0	0	11	....	....	....
1974-75	**California Golden Seals**	**NHL**	**1**	**0**	**1**	**1**	**0**	**1**	**1**	**0**	**0**	**0**	**0**	**2**	**0.0**	**1**	**0**	**0**	**0**	**+1**	....	....	....	....	....	....	....	....
	Salt Lake Golden Eagles	CHL	78	26	39	65	....	....	....	200	....	....	....	....	....	....	....	....	....	....	11	6	4	10	57	....	....	....
1975-76	**California Golden Seals**	**NHL**	**48**	**6**	**5**	**11**	**6**	**4**	**10**	**50**	**1**	**0**	**0**	**59**	**10.2**	**18**	**4**	**24**	**0**	**–10**	....	....	....	....	....	....	....	....
	Salt Lake City Golden Eagles	CHL	21	9	6	15	....	....	....	30	....	....	....	....	....	....	....	....	....	....	4	1	1	2	45	....	....	....
1976-77	**Cleveland Barons**	**NHL**	**2**	**0**	**1**	**1**	**0**	**1**	**1**	**2**	**0**	**0**	**0**	**4**	**0.0**	**1**	**0**	**2**	**0**	**–1**	....	....	....	....	....	....	....	....
	Salt Lake Golden Eagles	CHL	68	17	21	38	....	....	....	*226	....	....	....	....	....	....	....	....	....	....	....	....	....	....	....	....	....	....
1977-78	**St. Louis Blues**	**NHL**	**49**	**7**	**4**	**11**	**7**	**3**	**10**	**81**	**0**	**0**	**1**	**57**	**12.3**	**20**	**1**	**27**	**2**	**–6**	....	....	....	....	....	....	....	....
	Salt Lake Golden Eagles	CHL	24	8	7	15	....	....	....	89	....	....	....	....	....	....	....	....	....	....	....	....	....	....	....	....	....	....
1978-79	Salt Lake Golden Eagles	CHL	72	14	17	31	....	....	....	143	....	....	....	....	....	....	....	....	....	....	8	2	1	3	12	....	....	....
	NHL Totals		**101**	**13**	**11**	**24**	**13**	**9**	**22**	**133**	**1**	**0**	**1**	**123**	**10.6**	**40**	**5**	**53**	**2**		....	....	....	....	....	....	....	....

Traded to **Port Huron** (IHL) by **Columbus** (IHL) with Dave Haley for Marty Reynolds, Randy Prior and loan of Brian Skinner, December, 1972. Signed as a free agent by **California**, September, 1973. Signed as a free agent by **St. Louis**, October 20, 1977.

• HOLT, RANDY

Randy Holt D – R. 5'11", 185 lbs. b: Pembroke, Ont., 1/15/1953. Chicago's 3rd choice, 45th overall, in 1973 Amateur Draft.

Season	Club	League	GP	G	A	Pts	AG	AA	APts	PIM	PP	SH	GW	S	%	TGF	PGF	TGA	PGA	+/–	GP	G	A	Pts	PIM	PP	SH	GW
1970-71	Niagara Falls Flyers	OHA	35	5	7	12	....	....	....	178	....	....	....	....	....	....	....	....	....	....	....	....	....	....	....	....	....	....
1971-72	Niagara Falls Flyers	OHA	27	3	5	8	....	....	....	118	....	....	....	....	....	....	....	....	....	....	....	....	....	....	....	....	....	....
1972-73	Sudbury Wolves	OHA	55	7	42	49	....	....	....	294	....	....	....	....	....	....	....	....	....	....	....	....	....	....	....	....	....	....
1973-74	Dallas Black Hawks	CHL	66	3	15	18	....	....	....	222	....	....	....	....	....	....	....	....	....	....	10	1	2	3	*51	....	....	....
1974-75	**Chicago Black Hawks**	**NHL**	**12**	**0**	**1**	**1**	**0**	**1**	**1**	**13**	**0**	**0**	**0**	**8**	**0.0**	**5**	**1**	**6**	**1**	**–1**	....	....	....	....	....	....	....	....
	Dallas Black Hawks	CHL	65	8	32	40	....	....	....	*411	....	....	....	....	....	....	....	....	....	....	10	0	7	7	*86	....	....	....
1975-76	**Chicago Black Hawks**	**NHL**	**12**	**0**	**0**	**0**	**0**	**0**	**0**	**13**	**0**	**0**	**0**	**5**	**0.0**	**2**	**0**	**15**	**1**	**–12**	....	....	....	....	....	....	....	....
	Dallas Black Hawks	CHL	64	6	46	52	....	....	....	161	....	....	....	....	....	....	....	....	....	....	8	3	2	5	51	....	....	....

Season	Club	League	GP	G	A	Pts	AG	AA	APts	PIM	PP	SH	GW	S	%	TGF	PGF	TGA	PGA	+/–	GP	G	A	Pts	PIM	PP	SH	GW
			REGULAR SEASON																		PLAYOFFS							
1976-77	Chicago Black Hawks	NHL	12	0	3	3	0	2	2	14	0	0	0	7	0.0	8	0	17	5	–4	2	0	0	0	7	0	0	0
	Dallas Black Hawks	CHL	30	0	10	10	....	....	....	90	....	....	....	....	....	....	....	....	....	....	3	0	1	1	25	....	....	....
1977-78	Chicago Black Hawks	NHL	6	0	0	0	0	0	0	20	0	0	0	4	0.0	3	0	10	3	–4	....	....	....	....	....	....	....	....
	Cleveland Barons	NHL	48	1	4	5	1	3	4	229	0	0	0	23	4.3	15	1	40	2	–24	....	....	....	....	....	....	....	....
1978-79	Vancouver Canucks	NHL	22	1	3	4	1	2	3	80	0	0	0	17	5.9	19	0	30	10	–1	....	....	....	....	....	....	....	....
	Los Angeles Kings	NHL	36	0	6	6	0	5	5	202	0	0	0	21	0.0	16	0	21	3	–2	2	0	0	0	4	0	0	0
1979-80	Los Angeles Kings	NHL	42	0	1	1	0	1	1	94	0	0	0	10	0.0	8	0	11	0	–3	....	....	....	....	....	....	....	....
1980-81	Calgary Flames	NHL	48	0	5	5	0	3	3	165	0	0	0	14	0.0	11	0	17	0	–6	13	2	2	4	52	0	0	1
1981-82	Calgary Flames	NHL	8	0	0	0	0	0	0	9	0	0	0	1	0.0	0	0	4	0	–4	....	....	....	....	....	....	....	....
	Washington Capitals	NHL	53	2	6	8	2	4	6	250	0	0	0	32	6.3	37	0	48	4	–7	....	....	....	....	....	....	....	....
1982-83	Washington Capitals	NHL	70	0	8	8	0	6	6	*275	0	0	0	30	0.0	45	0	66	14	–7	4	0	1	1	20	0	0	0
1983-84	Philadelphia Flyers	NHL	26	0	0	0	0	0	0	74	0	0	0	4	0.0	2	0	16	13	–1	....	....	....	....	....	....	....	....
	NHL Totals		395	4	37	41	4	27	31	1438	0	0	0	176	2.3	171	2	301	56		21	2	3	5	83	0	0	1

CHL First All-Star Team (1975)

Traded to **Cleveland** by **Chicago** for Reg Kerr, November 23, 1977. Claimed by **Vancouver** in **Cleveland-Minnesota** Dispersal Draft, June 15, 1978. Traded to **LA Kings** by **Vancouver** for Don Kosak, December 31, 1978. Traded to **Calgary** by **LA Kings** with Bert Wilson for Gary Unger, June 6, 1980. Traded to **Washington** by **Calgary** with Bobby Gould for Washington's 2nd round choice (later traded to Montreal — Montreal selected Todd Francis) in 1983 Entry Draft and Pat Ribble, November 25, 1981. Signed as a free agent by **Philadelphia**, August 30, 1983.

• HOLZINGER, BRIAN

Brian Holzinger C – R. 5'11", 190 lbs. b: Parma, OH, 10/10/1972. Buffalo's 7th choice, 124th overall, in 1991 Entry Draft.

Season	Club	League	GP	G	A	Pts	AG	AA	APts	PIM	PP	SH	GW	S	%	TGF	PGF	TGA	PGA	+/–	GP	G	A	Pts	PIM	PP	SH	GW
1990-91	Detroit Compuware	USJHL	37	45	41	86	....	....	....	16	....	....	....	....	....	....	....	....	....	....	....	....	....	....	....	....	....	....
1991-92	Bowling Green University	CCHA	30	14	8	22	....	....	....	36	....	....	....	....	....	....	....	....	....	....	....	....	....	....	....	....	....	....
	United States	WJC-A	7	1	1	2	....	....	....	2	....	....	....	....	....	....	....	....	....	....	....	....	....	....	....	....	....	....
1992-93	Bowling Green University	CCHA	41	31	26	57	....	....	....	44	....	....	....	....	....	....	....	....	....	....	....	....	....	....	....	....	....	....
1993-94	Bowling Green University	CCHA	38	22	15	37	....	....	....	24	....	....	....	....	....	....	....	....	....	....	....	....	....	....	....	....	....	....
1994-95	Bowling Green University	CCHA	38	35	33	68	....	....	....	42	....	....	....	....	....	....	....	....	....	....	....	....	....	....	....	....	....	....
	Buffalo Sabres	NHL	4	0	3	3	0	4	4	0	0	0	0	3	0.0	4	0	2	0	+2	4	2	1	3	2	1	0	0
1995-96	Buffalo Sabres	NHL	58	10	10	20	10	8	18	37	5	0	1	71	14.1	26	9	47	9	–21	....	....	....	....	....	....	....	....
	Rochester Americans	AHL	17	10	11	21	....	....	....	14	....	....	....	....	....	....	....	....	....	....	19	10	14	24	10	....	....	....
1996-97	Buffalo Sabres	NHL	81	22	29	51	23	26	49	54	2	2	6	142	15.5	75	17	67	18	+9	12	2	5	7	8	0	0	0
1997-98	Bowling Green State	CCHA	37	4	17	21	....	....	....	34	....	....	....	....	....	....	....	....	....	....	....	....	....	....	....	....	....	....
	Buffalo Sabres	NHL	69	14	21	35	16	20	36	36	4	2	1	116	12.1	54	16	58	18	–2	15	4	7	11	18	1	1	0
	NHL Totals		212	46	63	109	49	58	107	127	11	4	8	332	13.9	159	42	174	45		31	8	13	21	28	2	1	0

CCHA Second All-Star Team (1993) • CCHA First All-Star Team (1995) • NCAA West First All-American Team (1995) • Won Hobey Baker Memorial Award (Top U.S. Collegiate Player) (1995)

• HOMENUKE, RON

Ron Homenuke RW – R. 5'10", 180 lbs. b: Hazelton, B.C., 1/5/1952. Vancouver's 4th choice, 51st overall, in 1972 Amateur Draft.

Season	Club	League	GP	G	A	Pts	AG	AA	APts	PIM	PP	SH	GW	S	%	TGF	PGF	TGA	PGA	+/–	GP	G	A	Pts	PIM	PP	SH	GW
1968-69	Calgary Centennials	WCJHL	37	1	6	7	....	....	....	19	....	....	....	....	....	....	....	....	....	....	....	....	....	....	....	....	....	....
1969-70	Calgary Centennials	WCJHL	56	17	14	31	....	....	....	54	....	....	....	....	....	....	....	....	....	....	16	5	2	7	35	....	....	....
1970-71	Calgary Centennials	WCJHL	63	27	33	60	....	....	....	114	....	....	....	....	....	....	....	....	....	....	11	2	3	5	18	....	....	....
1971-72	Calgary Centennials	WCJHL	68	33	62	95	....	....	....	57	....	....	....	....	....	....	....	....	....	....	13	6	5	11	14	....	....	....
1972-73	Vancouver Canucks	NHL	1	0	0	0	0	0	0	0	0	0	0	1	0.0	0	0	3	0	–3	....	....	....	....	....	....	....	....
	Seattle Totems	WHL	67	13	24	37	....	....	....	46	....	....	....	....	....	....	....	....	....	....	....	....	....	....	....	....	....	....
1973-74	Albuquerque 6-Guns	CHL	47	12	15	27	....	....	....	39	....	....	....	....	....	....	....	....	....	....	....	....	....	....	....	....	....	....
1974-75	Seattle Totems	CHL	69	8	27	35	....	....	....	60	....	....	....	....	....	....	....	....	....	....	....	....	....	....	....	....	....	....
1975-76	Nelson Maple Leafs	WIHL	27	8	16	24	....	....	....	30	....	....	....	....	....	....	....	....	....	....	....	....	....	....	....	....	....	....
	NHL Totals		1	0	0	0	0	0	0	0	0	0	0	1	0.0	0	0	3	0		....	....	....	....	....	....	....	....

• HOOVER, RON

Ron Hoover C – L. 6'1", 185 lbs. b: Oakville, Ont., 10/28/1966. Hartford's 7th choice, 158th overall, in 1986 Entry Draft.

Season	Club	League	GP	G	A	Pts	AG	AA	APts	PIM	PP	SH	GW	S	%	TGF	PGF	TGA	PGA	+/–	GP	G	A	Pts	PIM	PP	SH	GW
1985-86	Western Michigan University	CCHA	43	10	23	33	....	....	....	36	....	....	....	....	....	....	....	....	....	....	....	....	....	....	....	....	....	....
1986-87	Western Michigan University	CCHA	34	7	10	17	....	....	....	22	....	....	....	....	....	....	....	....	....	....	....	....	....	....	....	....	....	....
1987-88	Western Michigan University	CCHA	42	39	23	62	....	....	....	40	....	....	....	....	....	....	....	....	....	....	....	....	....	....	....	....	....	....
1988-89	Western Michigan University	CCHA	42	32	27	59	....	....	....	66	....	....	....	....	....	....	....	....	....	....	....	....	....	....	....	....	....	....
1989-90	Boston Bruins	NHL	2	0	0	0	0	0	0	0	0	0	0	2	0.0	0	0	2	0	–2	....	....	....	....	....	....	....	....
	Maine Mariners	AHL	75	28	26	54	....	....	....	57	....	....	....	....	....	....	....	....	....	....	....	....	....	....	....	....	....	....
1990-91	Boston Bruins	NHL	15	4	0	4	4	0	4	31	0	0	1	17	23.5	6	0	6	0	0	8	0	0	0	18	0	0	0
	Maine Mariners	AHL	62	28	16	44	....	....	....	40	....	....	....	....	....	....	....	....	....	....	....	....	....	....	....	....	....	....
1991-92	St. Louis Blues	NHL	1	0	0	0	0	0	0	0	0	0	0	1	0.0	0	0	0	0	0	....	....	....	....	....	....	....	....
	Peoria Rivermen	IHL	71	27	34	61	....	....	....	30	....	....	....	....	....	....	....	....	....	....	10	4	4	8	4	....	....	....
1992-93	Peoria Rivermen	IHL	58	17	13	30	....	....	....	28	....	....	....	....	....	....	....	....	....	....	4	1	1	2	2	....	....	....
1993-94	Peoria Rivermen	IHL	80	26	24	50	....	....	....	89	....	....	....	....	....	....	....	....	....	....	6	0	1	1	10	....	....	....
1994-95	Peoria Rivermen	IHL	76	22	20	42	....	....	....	70	....	....	....	....	....	....	....	....	....	....	9	2	1	3	12	....	....	....
1995-96	Peoria Rivermen	IHL	74	22	15	37	....	....	....	94	....	....	....	....	....	....	....	....	....	....	12	0	3	3	8	....	....	....
	NHL Totals		18	4	0	4	4	0	4	31	0	0	1	20	20.0	6	0	8	0		8	0	0	0	18	0	0	0

CCHA Second All-Star Team (1988)

Signed as a free agent by **Boston**, September 1, 1989. Signed as a free agent by **St. Louis**, July 23, 1991.

• HOPKINS, DEAN

Dean Hopkins RW – R. 6'1", 210 lbs. b: Cobourg, Ont., 6/6/1959. Los Angeles' 2nd choice, 29th overall, in 1979 Entry Draft.

Season	Club	League	GP	G	A	Pts	AG	AA	APts	PIM	PP	SH	GW	S	%	TGF	PGF	TGA	PGA	+/–	GP	G	A	Pts	PIM	PP	SH	GW
1975-76	London Knights	OHA	53	4	14	18	....	....	....	50	....	....	....	....	....	....	....	....	....	....	....	....	....	....	....	....	....	....
1976-77	London Knights	OHA	63	19	26	45	....	....	....	67	....	....	....	....	....	....	....	....	....	....	....	....	....	....	....	....	....	....
1977-78	London Knights	OHA	67	19	34	53	....	....	....	70	....	....	....	....	....	....	....	....	....	....	11	1	5	6	24	....	....	....
1978-79	London Knights	OHA	65	37	55	92	....	....	....	149	....	....	....	....	....	....	....	....	....	....	7	6	0	6	27	....	....	....
1979-80	Los Angeles Kings	NHL	60	8	6	14	7	5	12	39	1	0	2	57	14.0	19	2	33	0	–16	4	0	1	1	5	0	0	0
1980-81	Los Angeles Kings	NHL	67	8	18	26	7	13	20	118	2	0	1	60	13.3	42	2	34	0	+6	4	1	0	1	9	0	0	1
1981-82	Los Angeles Kings	NHL	41	2	13	15	2	9	11	102	0	0	0	55	3.6	21	2	46	7	–20	10	0	4	4	15	0	0	0
1982-83	Los Angeles Kings	NHL	49	5	12	17	4	8	12	43	0	0	0	50	10.0	27	1	32	1	–5	....	....	....	....	....	....	....	....
	New Haven Nighthawks	AHL	20	9	8	17	....	....	....	58	....	....	....	....	....	....	....	....	....	....	....	....	....	....	....	....	....	....
1983-84	New Haven Nighthawks	AHL	79	35	47	82	....	....	....	162	....	....	....	....	....	....	....	....	....	....	....	....	....	....	....	....	....	....
1984-85	New Haven Nighthawks	AHL	20	7	10	17	....	....	....	38	....	....	....	....	....	....	....	....	....	....	....	....	....	....	....	....	....	....
	Nova Scotia Voyageurs	AHL	49	13	17	30	....	....	....	93	....	....	....	....	....	....	....	....	....	....	6	1	2	3	20	....	....	....
1985-86	Edmonton Oilers	NHL	1	0	0	0	0	0	0	0	0	0	0	0	0.0	0	0	0	0	0	....	....	....	....	....	....	....	....
	Nova Scotia Oilers	AHL	60	23	32	55	....	....	....	131	....	....	....	....	....	....	....	....	....	....	....	....	....	....	....	....	....	....
1986-87	Nova Scotia Oilers	AHL	59	20	25	45	....	....	....	84	....	....	....	....	....	....	....	....	....	....	1	0	0	0	5	....	....	....
1987-88	Nova Scotia Oilers	AHL	44	20	22	42	....	....	....	122	....	....	....	....	....	....	....	....	....	....	5	2	5	7	16	....	....	....
1988-89	Quebec Nordiques	NHL	5	0	2	2	0	1	1	4	0	0	0	6	0.0	2	0	1	0	+1	....	....	....	....	....	....	....	....
	Halifax Citadels	AHL	53	18	31	49	....	....	....	116	....	....	....	....	....	....	....	....	....	....	3	0	1	1	6	....	....	....
1989-90	Halifax Citadels	AHL	54	23	32	55	....	....	....	167	....	....	....	....	....	....	....	....	....	....	6	1	4	5	8	....	....	....
1990-91	Halifax Citadels	AHL	3	2	0	2	....	....	....	2	....	....	....	....	....	....	....	....	....	....	....	....	....	....	....	....	....	....
	NHL Totals		223	23	51	74	20	36	56	306	3	0	3	228	10.1	111	7	146	8		18	1	5	6	29	0	0	1

Traded to **Edmonton** by **LA Kings** for cash, November 27, 1984. Traded to **LA Kings** by **Edmonton** for future considerations, May 31, 1985. Signed as a free agent by **Edmonton**, September 27, 1985. Signed as a free agent by **Quebec**, July 30, 1988.

• HOPKINS, LARRY

Larry Hopkins LW – L. 6'1", 215 lbs. b: Oshawa, Ont., 3/17/1954. Atlanta's 9th choice, 152nd overall, in 1974 Amateur Draft.

Season	Club	League	GP	G	A	Pts	AG	AA	APts	PIM	PP	SH	GW	S	%	TGF	PGF	TGA	PGA	+/–	GP	G	A	Pts	PIM	PP	SH	GW
1972-73	Oshawa Generals	OHA	50	5	17	22	....	....	....	9	....	....	....	....	....	....	....	....	....	....	....	....	....	....	....	....	....	....
1973-74	University of Toronto	OUAA	18	3	8	11	....	....	....	10	....	....	....	....	....	....	....	....	....	....	....	....	....	....	....	....	....	....
1974-75	University of Toronto	OUAA	20	1	4	5	....	....	....	2	....	....	....	....	....	....	....	....	....	....	....	....	....	....	....	....	....	....
1975-76	University of Toronto	OUAA	20	7	12	19	....	....	....	6	....	....	....	....	....	....	....	....	....	....	....	....	....	....	....	....	....	....
1976-77	University of Toronto	OUAA	20	12	20	32	....	....	....	10	....	....	....	....	....	....	....	....	....	....	....	....	....	....	....	....	....	....
1977-78	University of Toronto	OUAA	20	14	26	40	....	....	....	12	....	....	....	....	....	....	....	....	....	....	....	....	....	....	....	....	....	....
	Toronto Maple Leafs	NHL	2	0	0	0	0	0	0	0	0	0	0	0	0.0	0	0	0	0	0	....	....	....	....	....	....	....	....
	Dallas Black Hawks	CHL	....	....	....	....	....	....	....	....	....	....	....	....	....	....	....	....	....	....	11	0	1	1	7	....	....	....
1978-79	Saginaw Gears	IHL	80	36	41	77	....	....	....	67	....	....	....	....	....	....	....	....	....	....	....	....	....	....	....	....	....	....

			REGULAR SEASON																		PLAYOFFS							
Season	Club	League	GP	G	A	Pts	AG	AA	APts	PIM	PP	SH	GW	S	%	TGF	PGF	TGA	PGA	+/–	GP	G	A	Pts	PIM	PP	SH	GW
1979-80	**Winnipeg Jets**	**NHL**	**5**	**0**	**0**	**0**	**0**	**0**	**0**	**0**	**0**	**0**	**0**	**3**	**0.0**	**0**	**0**	**3**	**0**	**–3**	....	....	....	....	....	....	....	....
	Tulsa Oilers	CHL	72	29	31	60	....	....	....	33	....	....	....	....	....	....	....	....	....	....	3	0	0	0	0	....	....	....
1980-81	Tulsa Oilers	CHL	79	16	44	60	....	....	....	45	....	....	....	....	....	....	....	....	....	....	8	1	4	5	11	....	....	....
1981-82	**Winnipeg Jets**	**NHL**	**41**	**10**	**15**	**25**	**8**	**10**	**18**	**22**	**0**	**0**	**3**	**52**	**19.2**	**40**	**1**	**46**	**15**	**+8**	**4**	**0**	**0**	**0**	**2**	**0**	**0**	**0**
	Tulsa Oilers	CHL	31	12	18	30	....	....	....	9	....	....	....	....	....	....	....	....	....	....	....	....	....	....	....	....	....	....
1982-83	**Winnipeg Jets**	**NHL**	**12**	**3**	**1**	**4**	**2**	**1**	**3**	**4**	**0**	**0**	**1**	**16**	**18.8**	**10**	**0**	**6**	**1**	**+5**	**2**	**0**	**0**	**0**	**0**	**0**	**0**	**0**
	Sherbrooke Jets	AHL	66	18	30	48	....	....	....	42	....	....	....	....	....	....	....	....	....	....	....	....	....	....	....	....	....	....
	NHL Totals		**60**	**13**	**16**	**29**	**10**	**11**	**21**	**26**	**0**	**0**	**4**	**71**	**18.3**	**50**	**1**	**55**	**16**		**6**	**0**	**0**	**0**	**2**	**0**	**0**	**0**

Signed to an amateur try-out contract by **Toronto**, March 8, 1978. Signed as a free agent by **Winnipeg**, August 15, 1979.

• HORACEK, TONY

Tony Horacek LW – L. 6'4", 210 lbs. b: Vancouver, B.C., 2/3/1967. Philadelphia's 8th choice, 147th overall, in 1985 Entry Draft.

Season	Club	League	GP	G	A	Pts	AG	AA	APts	PIM	PP	SH	GW	S	%	TGF	PGF	TGA	PGA	+/–	GP	G	A	Pts	PIM	PP	SH	GW
1984-85	Kelowna Wings	WHL	67	9	18	27	....	....	....	114	....	....	....	....	....	....	....	....	....	....	6	0	1	1	11	....	....	....
1985-86	Spokane Chiefs	WHL	64	19	28	47	....	....	....	129	....	....	....	....	....	....	....	....	....	....	9	4	5	9	29	....	....	....
1986-87	Spokane Chiefs	WHL	64	23	37	60	....	....	....	177	....	....	....	....	....	....	....	....	....	....	5	1	3	4	18	....	....	....
	Hershey Bears	AHL	....	....	....	....	....	....	....	....	....	....	....	....	....	....	....	....	....	....	1	0	0	0	0	....	....	....
1987-88	Spokane Chiefs	WHL	24	17	23	40	....	....	....	63	....	....	....	....	....	....	....	....	....	....	....	....	....	....	....	....	....	....
	Kamloops Blazers	WHL	26	14	17	31	....	....	....	51	....	....	....	....	....	....	....	....	....	....	18	6	4	10	73	....	....	....
	Hershey Bears	AHL	1	0	0	0	....	....	....	0	....	....	....	....	....	....	....	....	....	....	....	....	....	....	....	....	....	....
1988-89	Hershey Bears	AHL	10	0	0	0	....	....	....	38	....	....	....	....	....	....	....	....	....	....	....	....	....	....	....	....	....	....
	Indianapolis Ice	IHL	43	11	13	24	....	....	....	138	....	....	....	....	....	....	....	....	....	....	....	....	....	....	....	....	....	....
1989-90	**Philadelphia Flyers**	**NHL**	**48**	**5**	**5**	**10**	**4**	**4**	**8**	**117**	**0**	**0**	**1**	**31**	**16.1**	**19**	**0**	**13**	**0**	**+6**	....	....	....	....	....	....	....	....
	Hershey Bears	AHL	12	0	5	5	....	....	....	25	....	....	....	....	....	....	....	....	....	....	....	....	....	....	....	....	....	....
1990-91	**Philadelphia Flyers**	**NHL**	**34**	**3**	**6**	**9**	**3**	**5**	**8**	**49**	**0**	**0**	**1**	**35**	**8.6**	**17**	**0**	**11**	**0**	**+6**	....	....	....	....	....	....	....	....
	Hershey Bears	AHL	19	5	3	8	....	....	....	35	....	....	....	....	....	....	....	....	....	....	4	2	0	2	14	....	....	....
1991-92	**Philadelphia Flyers**	**NHL**	**34**	**1**	**3**	**4**	**1**	**2**	**3**	**51**	**0**	**0**	**0**	**22**	**4.5**	**5**	**0**	**14**	**0**	**–9**	....	....	....	....	....	....	....	....
	Chicago Blackhawks	**NHL**	**12**	**1**	**4**	**5**	**1**	**3**	**4**	**21**	**0**	**0**	**0**	**10**	**10.0**	**5**	**0**	**4**	**1**	**+2**	**2**	**1**	**0**	**1**	**2**	**0**	**0**	**0**
1992-93	Indianapolis Ice	IHL	6	1	1	2	....	....	....	28	....	....	....	....	....	....	....	....	....	....	5	3	2	5	18	....	....	....
1993-94	**Chicago Blackhawks**	**NHL**	**7**	**0**	**0**	**0**	**0**	**0**	**0**	**53**	**0**	**0**	**0**	**2**	**0.0**	**1**	**0**	**0**	**0**	**+1**	....	....	....	....	....	....	....	....
	Indianapolis Ice	IHL	29	6	7	13	....	....	....	63	....	....	....	....	....	....	....	....	....	....	....	....	....	....	....	....	....	....
1994-95	**Chicago Blackhawks**	**NHL**	**19**	**0**	**1**	**1**	**0**	**1**	**1**	**25**	**0**	**0**	**0**	**6**	**0.0**	**1**	**0**	**5**	**0**	**–4**	....	....	....	....	....	....	....	....
	Indianapolis Ice	IHL	51	7	19	26	....	....	....	201	....	....	....	....	....	....	....	....	....	....	....	....	....	....	....	....	....	....
1995-96	Hershey Bears	AHL	34	4	9	13	....	....	....	75	....	....	....	....	....	....	....	....	....	....	5	1	1	2	4	....	....	....
1996-97	Cincinnati Cyclones	IHL	60	4	5	9	....	....	....	158	....	....	....	....	....	....	....	....	....	....	2	0	1	1	2	....	....	....
1997-98	Utah Grizzlies	IHL	5	0	0	0	....	....	....	7	....	....	....	....	....	....	....	....	....	....	....	....	....	....	....	....	....	....
	NHL Totals		**154**	**10**	**19**	**29**	**9**	**15**	**24**	**316**	**0**	**0**	**2**	**106**	**9.4**	**48**	**0**	**47**	**1**		**2**	**1**	**0**	**1**	**2**	**0**	**0**	**0**

Traded to **Chicago** by **Philadelphia** for Ryan McGill, February 7, 1992.

• HORAVA, MILOSLAV

Miloslav Horava D – L. 6', 193 lbs. b: Kladno, Czech., 8/14/1961. Edmonton's 8th choice, 176th overall, in 1981 Entry Draft.

Season	Club	League	GP	G	A	Pts	AG	AA	APts	PIM	PP	SH	GW	S	%	TGF	PGF	TGA	PGA	+/–	GP	G	A	Pts	PIM	PP	SH	GW
1978-79	Poldi Kladno	Czech.	22	1	5	6	....	....	....	2	....	....	....	....	....	....	....	....	....	....	....	....	....	....	....	....	....	....
1979-80	Poldi Kladno	Czech.	44	19	15	34	....	....	....	10	....	....	....	....	....	....	....	....	....	....	....	....	....	....	....	....	....	....
	Czechoslovakia	WJC-A	5	0	1	1	....	....	....	2	....	....	....	....	....	....	....	....	....	....	....	....	....	....	....	....	....	....
1980-81	Poldi Kladno	Czech.	40	13	16	29	....	....	....	22	....	....	....	....	....	....	....	....	....	....	....	....	....	....	....	....	....	....
	Czechoslovakia	WJC-A	5	2	3	5	....	....	....	6	....	....	....	....	....	....	....	....	....	....	....	....	....	....	....	....	....	....
	Czechoslovakia	WEC-A	8	0	6	6	....	....	....	8	....	....	....	....	....	....	....	....	....	....	....	....	....	....	....	....	....	....
1981-82	Czechoslovakia	C Cup	6	2	0	2	....	....	....	2	....	....	....	....	....	....	....	....	....	....	....	....	....	....	....	....	....	....
	Poldi Kladno	Czech.	42	10	12	22	....	....	....	18	....	....	....	....	....	....	....	....	....	....	....	....	....	....	....	....	....	....
	Czechoslovakia	WEC-A	10	0	1	1	....	....	....	2	....	....	....	....	....	....	....	....	....	....	....	....	....	....	....	....	....	....
1982-83	Poldi Kladno	Czech.	40	12	16	28	....	....	....	26	....	....	....	....	....	....	....	....	....	....	....	....	....	....	....	....	....	....
1983-84	Dukla Trencin	Czech.	44	2	15	17	....	....	....	8	....	....	....	....	....	....	....	....	....	....	....	....	....	....	....	....	....	....
	Czechoslovakia	Olympics	7	0	4	4	....	....	....	2	....	....	....	....	....	....	....	....	....	....	....	....	....	....	....	....	....	....
1984-85	Czechoslovakia	C Cup	4	0	1	1	....	....	....	5	....	....	....	....	....	....	....	....	....	....	....	....	....	....	....	....	....	....
	Dukla Trencin	Czech.	42	20	22	42	....	....	....	22	....	....	....	....	....	....	....	....	....	....	....	....	....	....	....	....	....	....
	Czechoslovakia	WEC-A	9	3	2	5	....	....	....	4	....	....	....	....	....	....	....	....	....	....	....	....	....	....	....	....	....	....
1985-86	Poldi Kladno	Czech.	38	17	26	43	....	....	....	14	....	....	....	....	....	....	....	....	....	....	....	....	....	....	....	....	....	....
1986-87	Poldi Kladno	Czech.	29	7	11	18	....	....	....	10	....	....	....	....	....	....	....	....	....	....	....	....	....	....	....	....	....	....
	Czechoslovakia	WEC-A	10	1	4	5	....	....	....	4	....	....	....	....	....	....	....	....	....	....	....	....	....	....	....	....	....	....
1987-88	Czechoslovakia	C Cup	6	1	2	3	....	....	....	4	....	....	....	....	....	....	....	....	....	....	....	....	....	....	....	....	....	....
	Poldi Kladno	Czech.	29	10	18	28	....	....	....	18	....	....	....	....	....	....	....	....	....	....	....	....	....	....	....	....	....	....
	Czechoslovakia	Olympics	8	1	2	3	....	....	....	14	....	....	....	....	....	....	....	....	....	....	....	....	....	....	....	....	....	....
1988-89	Poldi Kladno	Czech.	35	10	16	26	....	....	....	24	....	....	....	....	....	....	....	....	....	....	....	....	....	....	....	....	....	....
	New York Rangers	**NHL**	**6**	**0**	**1**	**1**	**0**	**1**	**1**	**0**	**0**	**0**	**0**	**7**	**0.0**	**2**	**1**	**3**	**0**	**–2**	....	....	....	....	....	....	....	....
1989-90	**New York Rangers**	**NHL**	**45**	**4**	**10**	**14**	**3**	**7**	**10**	**26**	**1**	**0**	**1**	**50**	**8.0**	**44**	**13**	**21**	**0**	**+10**	**2**	**0**	**1**	**1**	**0**	**0**	**0**	**0**
1990-91	**New York Rangers**	**NHL**	**29**	**1**	**6**	**7**	**1**	**5**	**6**	**12**	**0**	**0**	**0**	**27**	**3.7**	**22**	**6**	**15**	**1**	**+2**	....	....	....	....	....	....	....	....
1991-92	MoDo AIK	Sweden	40	3	21	24	....	....	....	60	....	....	....	....	....	....	....	....	....	....	....	....	....	....	....	....	....	....
	Czechoslovakia	Olympics	6	1	0	1	....	....	....	0	....	....	....	....	....	....	....	....	....	....	....	....	....	....	....	....	....	....
1992-93	MoDo AIK	Sweden	38	8	27	35	....	....	....	52	....	....	....	....	....	....	....	....	....	....	....	....	....	....	....	....	....	....
	Czech Republic	WC-A	8	0	3	3	....	....	....	0	....	....	....	....	....	....	....	....	....	....	....	....	....	....	....	....	....	....
1993-94	MoDo AIK	Sweden	29	5	14	19	....	....	....	38	....	....	....	....	....	....	....	....	....	....	....	....	....	....	....	....	....	....
	Czech Republic	Olympics	7	0	0	0	....	....	....	8	....	....	....	....	....	....	....	....	....	....	....	....	....	....	....	....	....	....
1994-95	Slavia Prava	Czech.	38	7	17	24	....	....	....	....	....	....	....	....	....	....	....	....	....	....	....	....	....	....	....	....	....	....
1995-96	Slavia Prava	Czech.	37	7	31	38	....	....	....	....	....	....	....	....	....	....	....	....	....	....	7	0	7	7	....	....	....	....
1996-97	Slavia Praha	Czech.	43	3	23	26	....	....	....	62	....	....	....	....	....	....	....	....	....	....	3	0	1	1	0	....	....	....
1997-98	Karlovy Vary	Czech.	26	4	6	6	....	....	....	8	....	....	....	....	....	....	....	....	....	....	....	....	....	....	....	....	....	....
	NHL Totals		**80**	**5**	**17**	**22**	**4**	**13**	**17**	**38**	**1**	**0**	**1**	**84**	**6.0**	**68**	**20**	**39**	**1**		**2**	**0**	**1**	**1**	**0**	**0**	**0**	**0**

WJC-A All-Star Team (1981) • Named Best Defenseman at WJC-A (1981)

Traded to **NY Rangers** by **Edmonton** with Don Jackson, Mike Golden and future considerations for Reijo Ruotsalainen, Ville Kentala, Clark Donatelli, Jim Wiemer and future considerations (Stu Kulak, October 10, 1987), October 23, 1986. Traded to **Quebec** by **NY Rangers** for Stephane Guerrard, May 25, 1991.

• HORBUL, DOUG

Doug Horbul LW – L. 5'9", 170 lbs. b: Nokomis, Sask., 7/27/1952. NY Rangers' 6th choice, 63rd overall, in 1972 Amateur Draft.

Season	Club	League	GP	G	A	Pts	AG	AA	APts	PIM	PP	SH	GW	S	%	TGF	PGF	TGA	PGA	+/–	GP	G	A	Pts	PIM	PP	SH	GW
1969-70	Saskatoon Blades	WCJHL	60	22	30	52	....	....	....	22	....	....	....	....	....	....	....	....	....	....	....	....	....	....	....	....	....	....
1970-71	Saskatchewan–Calgary	WCJHL	65	32	26	58	....	....	....	36	....	....	....	....	....	....	....	....	....	....	....	....	....	....	....	....	....	....
1971-72	Calgary Centennials	WCJHL	68	39	32	71	....	....	....	38	....	....	....	....	....	....	....	....	....	....	....	....	....	....	....	....	....	....
1972-73	Providence Reds	AHL	10	1	4	5	....	....	....	2	....	....	....	....	....	....	....	....	....	....	....	....	....	....	....	....	....	....
	Omaha Knights	CHL	53	15	11	26	....	....	....	19	....	....	....	....	....	....	....	....	....	....	11	*7	3	*10	2	....	....	....
1973-74	Providence Reds	AHL	75	34	29	63	....	....	....	31	....	....	....	....	....	....	....	....	....	....	15	9	4	13	8	....	....	....
1974-75	**Kansas City Scouts**	**NHL**	**4**	**1**	**0**	**1**	**1**	**0**	**1**	**2**	**0**	**0**	**0**	**5**	**20.0**	**2**	**1**	**4**	**0**	**–3**	....	....	....	....	....	....	....	....
	Baltimore Clippers	AHL	38	16	8	24	....	....	....	11	....	....	....	....	....	....	....	....	....	....	....	....	....	....	....	....	....	....
	Providence Reds	AHL	32	13	12	25	....	....	....	16	....	....	....	....	....	....	....	....	....	....	6	1	2	3	0	....	....	....
1975-76	Springfield Indians	AHL	25	2	1	3	....	....	....	8	....	....	....	....	....	....	....	....	....	....	....	....	....	....	....	....	....	....
	Baltimore Clippers	AHL	43	7	10	17	....	....	....	16	....	....	....	....	....	....	....	....	....	....	....	....	....	....	....	....	....	....
1976-77	Rhode Island Reds	AHL	16	3	4	7	....	....	....	2	....	....	....	....	....	....	....	....	....	....	....	....	....	....	....	....	....	....
	Fort Wayne Komets	IHL	45	14	21	35	....	....	....	14	....	....	....	....	....	....	....	....	....	....	9	4	6	10	0	....	....	....
1977-78	Trail Smoke Eaters	WIHL	....	12	29	41	....	....	....	8	....	....	....	....	....	....	....	....	....	....	....	....	....	....	....	....	....	....
	NHL Totals		**4**	**1**	**0**	**1**	**1**	**0**	**1**	**2**	**0**	**0**	**0**	**5**	**20.0**	**2**	**1**	**4**	**0**		....	....	....	....	....	....	....	....

Claimed by **Kansas City** from **NY Rangers** in Expansion Draft, June 12, 1974.

• HORDY, MIKE

Mike Hordy D – R. 5'10", 180 lbs. b: Thunder Bay, Ont., 10/10/1956. NY Islanders' 5th choice, 86th overall, in 1976 Amateur Draft.

Season	Club	League	GP	G	A	Pts	AG	AA	APts	PIM	PP	SH	GW	S	%	TGF	PGF	TGA	PGA	+/–	GP	G	A	Pts	PIM	PP	SH	GW
1973-74	Thunder Bay Twins	TBJHL	59	11	39	50	....	....	....	34	....	....	....	....	....	....	....	....	....	....	....	....	....	....	....	....	....	....
1974-75	Sault Ste. Marie Greyhounds	OHA	70	18	33	51	....	....	....	59	....	....	....	....	....	....	....	....	....	....	....	....	....	....	....	....	....	....
1975-76	Sault Ste. Marie Greyhounds	OHA	63	17	51	68	....	....	....	84	....	....	....	....	....	....	....	....	....	....	12	2	8	10	8	....	....	....

			REGULAR SEASON																		PLAYOFFS							
Season	**Club**	**League**	**GP**	**G**	**A**	**Pts**	**AG**	**AA**	**APts**	**PIM**	**PP**	**SH**	**GW**	**S**	**%**	**TGF**	**PGF**	**TGA**	**PGA**	**+/–**	**GP**	**G**	**A**	**Pts**	**PIM**	**PP**	**SH**	**GW**
1976-77	Fort Worth Texans	CHL	2	0	0	0	....	....	....	5	....	....	....	....	....	....	....	....	....	....	3	0	0	0	0	....	....	....
	Muskegon Mohawks	IHL	77	16	45	61	....	....	....	38	....	....	....	....	....	....	....	....	....	....	7	2	4	6	2	....	....	....
1977-78	Fort Worth Texans	CHL	76	14	35	49	....	....	....	87	....	....	....	....	....	....	....	....	....	....	14	2	9	11	15	....	....	....
1978-79	**New York Islanders**	**NHL**	**2**	**0**	**0**	**0**	**0**	**0**	**0**	**0**	**0**	**0**	**0**	**2**	**0.0**	**2**	**0**	**2**	**0**	**0**	....	....	....	....	....	....	....	....
	Fort Worth Texans	CHL	74	17	48	65	....	....	....	71	....	....	....	....	....	....	....	....	....	....	5	0	3	3	6	....	....	....
1979-80	**New York Islanders**	**NHL**	**9**	**0**	**0**	**0**	**0**	**0**	**0**	**7**	**0**	**0**	**0**	**8**	**0.0**	**8**	**0**	**9**	**1**	**0**	....	....	....	....	....	....	....	....
	Indianapolis Checkers	CHL	64	4	32	36	....	....	....	43	....	....	....	....	....	....	....	....	....	....	7	0	4	4	2	....	....	....
1980-81	Indianapolis Checkers	CHL	70	10	48	58	....	....	....	103	....	....	....	....	....	....	....	....	....	....	5	1	3	4	6	....	....	....
1981-82	Indianapolis Checkers	CHL	79	17	49	66	....	....	....	86	....	....	....	....	....	....	....	....	....	....	10	4	6	10	15	....	....	....
1982-83	Zurich EC	Switz.	27	16	10	26	....	....	....	40	....	....	....	....	....	....	....	....	....	....	....	....	....	....	....	....	....	....
1983-84	Maine Mariners	AHL	72	11	40	51	....	....	....	31	....	....	....	....	....	....	....	....	....	....	17	2	6	8	4	....	....	....
1984-85	Maine Mariners	AHL	68	1	18	19	....	....	....	46	....	....	....	....	....	....	....	....	....	....	....	....	....	....	....	....	....	....
	NHL Totals		**11**	**0**	**0**	**0**	**0**	**0**	**0**	**7**	**0**	**0**	**0**	**10**	**0.0**	**10**	**0**	**11**	**1**		....	....	....	....	....	....	....	....

CHL Second All-Star Team (1979, 1980, 1981) • CHL First All-Star Team (1982)

Signed as a free agent by **New Jersey**, August 23, 1983.

• HORNUNG, LARRY

Larry Hornung D – L. 6', 190 lbs. b: Weyburn, Sask., 11/10/1945.

1963-64	Flin Flon Bombers	SJHL	57	4	13	17	....	....	....	96	....	....	....	....	....	....	....	....	....	....	7	0	3	3	8	....	....	....
1964-65	Moose Jaw Canucks	SJHL	17	0	7	7	....	....	....	22	....	....	....	....	....	....	....	....	....	....	7	0	0	0	12	....	....	....
1965-66	Weyburn Red Wings	SJHL	58	16	46	62	....	....	....	90	....	....	....	....	....	....	....	....	....	....	18	1	9	10	20	....	....	....
1966-67	Toledo Blades	IHL	72	8	29	37	....	....	....	34	....	....	....	....	....	....	....	....	....	....	10	1	6	7	20	....	....	....
1967-68	Kansas City Blues	CHL	70	7	30	37	....	....	....	74	....	....	....	....	....	....	....	....	....	....	7	0	1	1	0	....	....	....
1968-69	Kansas City Blues	CHL	2	0	1	1	....	....	....	2	....	....	....	....	....	....	....	....	....	....	....	....	....	....	....	....	....	....
	Buffalo Bisons	AHL	60	7	18	25	....	....	....	38	....	....	....	....	....	....	....	....	....	....	6	0	0	0	2	....	....	....
1969-70	Kansas City Blues	CHL	12	2	6	8	....	....	....	10	....	....	....	....	....	....	....	....	....	....	....	....	....	....	....	....	....	....
	Buffalo Bisons	AHL	54	6	26	32	....	....	....	24	....	....	....	....	....	....	....	....	....	....	14	2	4	6	20	....	....	....
1970-71	**St. Louis Blues**	**NHL**	**1**	**0**	**0**	**0**	**0**	**0**	**0**	**0**	**0**	**0**	**0**	**1**	**0.0**	**3**	**0**	**2**	**0**	**+1**	....	....	....	....	....	....	....	....
	Kansas City Blues	CHL	70	3	17	20	....	....	....	49	....	....	....	....	....	....	....	....	....	....	....	....	....	....	....	....	....	....
1971-72	**St. Louis Blues**	**NHL**	**47**	**2**	**9**	**11**	**2**	**8**	**10**	**10**	**0**	**0**	**1**	**60**	**3.3**	**37**	**5**	**50**	**17**	**–1**	**11**	**0**	**2**	**2**	**2**	**0**	**0**	**0**
	Kansas City Blues	CHL	26	2	20	22	....	....	....	23	....	....	....	....	....	....	....	....	....	....	....	....	....	....	....	....	....	....
1972-73	Winnipeg Jets	WHA	77	13	45	58	....	....	....	28	....	....	....	....	....	....	....	....	....	....	14	2	9	11	0	....	....	....
1973-74	Winnipeg Jets	WHA	51	4	19	23	....	....	....	18	....	....	....	....	....	....	....	....	....	....	4	0	0	0	0	....	....	....
1974-75	Winnipeg Jets	WHA	69	7	25	32	....	....	....	21	....	....	....	....	....	....	....	....	....	....	....	....	....	....	....	....	....	....
1975-76	Winnipeg Jets	WHA	76	3	18	21	....	....	....	26	....	....	....	....	....	....	....	....	....	....	13	0	3	3	6	....	....	....
1976-77	Edmonton Oilers	WHA	21	2	1	3	....	....	....	0	....	....	....	....	....	....	....	....	....	....	....	....	....	....	....	....	....	....
	San Diego Mariners	WHA	58	4	9	13	....	....	....	8	....	....	....	....	....	....	....	....	....	....	6	0	0	0	0	....	....	....
1977-78	Winnipeg Jets	WHA	19	1	4	5	....	....	....	2	....	....	....	....	....	....	....	....	....	....	....	....	....	....	....	....	....	....
	NHL Totals		**48**	**2**	**9**	**11**	**2**	**8**	**10**	**10**	**0**	**0**	**1**	**61**	**3.3**	**40**	**5**	**52**	**17**		**11**	**0**	**2**	**2**	**2**	**0**	**0**	**0**
	Other Major League Totals		371	34	121	155	....	....	....	103	....	....	....	....	....	....	....	....	....		37	2	12	14	6	....	....	....

WHA Second All-Star Team (1973)

Traded to **St. Louis** by **Detroit** with Craig Cameron and Dan Giesebrecht for John Brenneman, October 9, 1967. Traded to **NY Rangers** by **St. Louis** for Sheldon Kannegiesser, November, 1969. Traded to **St. Louis** by **NY Rangers** for cash, June, 1969. Selected by **Winnipeg** (WHA) in 1972 WHA General Player Draft, February 12, 1972. Claimed by **NY Islanders** from **St. Louis** in Expansion Draft, June 6, 1972. Claimed by **Edmonton** (WHA) from **Winnipeg** (WHA) in 1976 WHA Intra-League Draft, June, 1976. Traded to **San Diego** (WHA) by **Edmonton** (WHA) for Greg Boddy, November, 1976. Signed as a free agent by **Winnipeg** (WHA) after **San Diego** (WHA) franchise folded, May, 1977.

• HORTON, TIM

Tim (Myles Gilbert) Horton D – R. 5'10", 180 lbs. b: Cochrane, Ont., 1/12/1930. d: 2/14/1974. HHOF

1946-47	Copper Cliff Redmen	NOHA	9	0	0	0	....	....	....	14	....	....	....	....	....	....	....	....	....	....	5	0	1	1	0	....	....	....
1947-48	St. Michael's Majors	OHA	32	6	7	13	....	....	....	*137	....	....	....	....	....	....	....	....	....	....	....	....	....	....	....	....	....	....
1948-49	St. Michael's Majors	OHA	32	9	18	27	....	....	....	95	....	....	....	....	....	....	....	....	....	....	....	....	....	....	....	....	....	....
1949-50	**Toronto Maple Leafs**	**NHL**	**1**	**0**	**0**	**0**	**0**	**0**	**0**	**2**	....	....	....	....	....	....	....	....	....	....	**1**	**0**	**0**	**0**	**2**	....	....	....
	Pittsburgh Hornets	AHL	60	5	18	23	....	....	....	83	....	....	....	....	....	....	....	....	....	....	....	....	....	....	....	....	....	....
1950-51	Pittsburgh Hornets	AHL	68	8	26	34	....	....	....	129	....	....	....	....	....	....	....	....	....	....	13	0	9	9	16	....	....	....
1951-52	**Toronto Maple Leafs**	**NHL**	**4**	**0**	**0**	**0**	**0**	**0**	**0**	**8**	....	....	....	....	....	....	....	....	....	....	....	....	....	....	....	....	....	....
	Pittsburgh Hornets	AHL	64	12	19	31	....	....	....	146	....	....	....	....	....	....	....	....	....	....	11	1	3	4	16	....	....	....
1952-53	**Toronto Maple Leafs**	**NHL**	**70**	**2**	**14**	**16**	**3**	**19**	**22**	**85**	....	....	....	....	....	....	....	....	....	....	....	....	....	....	....	....	....	....
1953-54	**Toronto Maple Leafs**	**NHL**	**70**	**7**	**24**	**31**	**11**	**33**	**44**	**94**	....	....	....	....	....	....	....	....	....	....	**5**	**1**	**1**	**2**	**4**	....	....	....
1954-55	**Toronto Maple Leafs**	**NHL**	**67**	**5**	**9**	**14**	**7**	**11**	**18**	**84**	....	....	....	....	....	....	....	....	....	....	....	....	....	....	....	....	....	....
1955-56	**Toronto Maple Leafs**	**NHL**	**35**	**0**	**5**	**5**	**0**	**6**	**6**	**36**	....	....	....	....	....	....	....	....	....	....	**2**	**0**	**0**	**0**	**4**	....	....	....
1956-57	**Toronto Maple Leafs**	**NHL**	**66**	**6**	**19**	**25**	**8**	**22**	**30**	**72**	....	....	....	....	....	....	....	....	....	....	....	....	....	....	....	....	....	....
1957-58	**Toronto Maple Leafs**	**NHL**	**53**	**6**	**20**	**26**	**8**	**22**	**30**	**39**	....	....	....	....	....	....	....	....	....	....	....	....	....	....	....	....	....	....
1958-59	**Toronto Maple Leafs**	**NHL**	**70**	**5**	**21**	**26**	**6**	**22**	**28**	**76**	....	....	....	....	....	....	....	....	....	....	**12**	**0**	**3**	**3**	**16**	....	....	....
1959-60	**Toronto Maple Leafs**	**NHL**	**70**	**3**	**29**	**32**	**4**	**30**	**34**	**69**	....	....	....	....	....	....	....	....	....	....	**10**	**0**	**1**	**1**	**6**	....	....	....
1960-61	**Toronto Maple Leafs**	**NHL**	**57**	**6**	**15**	**21**	**7**	**15**	**22**	**75**	....	....	....	....	....	....	....	....	....	....	**5**	**0**	**0**	**0**	**0**	....	....	....
1961-62	**Toronto Maple Leafs**	**NHL**	**70**	**10**	**28**	**38**	**12**	**28**	**40**	**88**	....	....	....	....	....	....	....	....	....	....	**12**	**3**	**13**	**16**	**16**	....	....	....
1962-63	**Toronto Maple Leafs**	**NHL**	**70**	**6**	**19**	**25**	**7**	**20**	**27**	**69**	....	....	....	....	....	....	....	....	....	....	**10**	**1**	**3**	**4**	**10**	....	....	....
1963-64	**Toronto Maple Leafs**	**NHL**	**70**	**9**	**20**	**29**	**12**	**22**	**34**	**71**	....	....	....	....	....	....	....	....	....	....	**14**	**0**	**4**	**4**	**20**	....	....	....
1964-65	**Toronto Maple Leafs**	**NHL**	**70**	**12**	**16**	**28**	**15**	**17**	**32**	**95**	....	....	....	....	....	....	....	....	....	....	**6**	**0**	**2**	**2**	**13**	....	....	....
1965-66	**Toronto Maple Leafs**	**NHL**	**70**	**6**	**22**	**28**	**7**	**22**	**29**	**76**	....	....	....	....	....	....	....	....	....	....	**4**	**1**	**0**	**1**	**12**	....	....	....
1966-67	**Toronto Maple Leafs**	**NHL**	**70**	**8**	**17**	**25**	**10**	**17**	**27**	**70**	....	....	....	....	....	....	....	....	....	....	**12**	**3**	**5**	**8**	**25**	....	....	....
1967-68	**Toronto Maple Leafs**	**NHL**	**69**	**4**	**23**	**27**	**5**	**24**	**29**	**82**	**1**	**1**	**0**	**179**	**2.2**	**99**	**15**	**82**	**18**	**+20**	....	....	....	....	....	....	....	....
1968-69	**Toronto Maple Leafs**	**NHL**	**74**	**11**	**29**	**40**	**12**	**27**	**39**	**107**	**3**	**0**	**1**	**169**	**6.5**	**130**	**23**	**119**	**20**	**+14**	**4**	**0**	**0**	**0**	**7**	**0**	**0**	**0**
1969-70	**Toronto Maple Leafs**	**NHL**	**59**	**3**	**19**	**22**	**3**	**19**	**22**	**91**	**1**	**0**	**1**	**116**	**2.6**	**82**	**11**	**90**	**23**	**+4**	....	....	....	....	....	....	....	....
	New York Rangers	**NHL**	**15**	**1**	**5**	**6**	**1**	**5**	**6**	**16**	**1**	**0**	**0**	**41**	**2.4**	**11**	**3**	**21**	**6**	**–7**	**6**	**1**	**1**	**2**	**28**	**0**	**0**	**0**
1970-71	**New York Rangers**	**NHL**	**78**	**2**	**18**	**20**	**2**	**16**	**18**	**57**	**1**	**0**	**1**	**124**	**1.6**	**92**	**17**	**62**	**15**	**+28**	**13**	**1**	**4**	**5**	**14**	**0**	**0**	**0**
1971-72	**Pittsburgh Penguins**	**NHL**	**44**	**2**	**9**	**11**	**2**	**8**	**10**	**40**	**0**	**0**	**1**	**84**	**2.4**	**50**	**7**	**64**	**16**	**+5**	**4**	**0**	**1**	**1**	**2**	**0**	**0**	**0**
1972-73	**Buffalo Sabres**	**NHL**	**69**	**1**	**16**	**17**	**1**	**13**	**14**	**56**	**0**	**0**	**0**	**73**	**1.4**	**81**	**3**	**91**	**25**	**+12**	**6**	**0**	**1**	**1**	**4**	**0**	**0**	**0**
1973-74	**Buffalo Sabres**	**NHL**	**55**	**0**	**6**	**6**	**0**	**5**	**5**	**53**	**0**	**0**	**0**	**59**	**0.0**	**71**	**1**	**86**	**21**	**+5**	....	....	....	....	....	....	....	....
	NHL Totals		**1446**	**115**	**403**	**518**	**143**	**423**	**566**	**1611**	**7**	**1**	**4**	**845**	**13.6**	**616**	**80**	**605**	**150**		**126**	**11**	**39**	**50**	**183**	**0**	**0**	**0**

AHL First All-Star Team (1952) • NHL Second All-Star Team (1954, 1963, 1967) • NHL First All-Star Team (1964, 1968, 1969)

Played in NHL All-Star Game (1954, 1961, 1962, 1963, 1964, 1968, 1969)

Traded to **NY Rangers** by **Toronto** for future considerations (Denis Dupere, May 18, 1970), March 3, 1970. Claimed by **Pittsburgh** from **NY Rangers** in Intra-League Draft, June 8, 1971. Claimed by **Buffalo** from **Pittsburgh** in Intra-League Draft, June 5, 1972.

• HORVATH, BRONCO

Bronco (Joseph) Horvath C – L. 5'11", 185 lbs. b: Port Colborne, Ont., 3/12/1930.

1948-49	Galt Black Hawks	OHA	33	22	18	40	....	....	....	45	....	....	....	....	....	....	....	....	....	....	....	....	....	....	....	....	....	....
1949-50	Galt Black Hawks	OHA	47	20	33	53	....	....	....	91	....	....	....	....	....	....	....	....	....	....	....	....	....	....	....	....	....	....
	Grand Rapids Rockets	EHL	5	6	1	7	....	....	....	12	....	....	....	....	....	....	....	....	....	....	6	2	6	8	8	....	....	....
1950-51	Springfield Indians	AHL	43	12	26	38	....	....	....	37	....	....	....	....	....	....	....	....	....	....	2	0	0	0	0	....	....	....
1951-52	Syracuse Warriors	AHL	50	12	36	48	....	....	....	56	....	....	....	....	....	....	....	....	....	....	....	....	....	....	....	....	....	....
1952-53	Syracuse Warriors	AHL	52	19	40	59	....	....	....	44	....	....	....	....	....	....	....	....	....	....	4	0	0	0	2	....	....	....
1953-54	Springfield Indians	QHL	19	11	14	25	....	....	....	25	....	....	....	....	....	....	....	....	....	....	....	....	....	....	....	....	....	....
	Syracuse Warriors	AHL	40	21	39	60	....	....	....	54	....	....	....	....	....	....	....	....	....	....	....	....	....	....	....	....	....	....
1954-55	Edmonton Flyers	WHL	67	*50	60	*110	....	....	....	71	....	....	....	....	....	....	....	....	....	....	9	*7	4	*11	12	....	....	....
1955-56	**New York Rangers**	**NHL**	**66**	**12**	**17**	**29**	**17**	**21**	**38**	**40**	....	....	....	....	....	....	....	....	....	....	**5**	**1**	**2**	**3**	**4**	....	....	....
1956-57	**New York Rangers**	**NHL**	**7**	**1**	**2**	**3**	**1**	**2**	**3**	**4**	....	....	....	....	....	....	....	....	....	....	....	....	....	....	....	....	....	....
	Montreal Canadiens	**NHL**	**1**	**0**	**0**	**0**	**0**	**0**	**0**	**0**	....	....	....	....	....	....	....	....	....	....	....	....	....	....	....	....	....	....
	Rochester Americans	AHL	56	37	44	81	....	....	....	39	....	....	....	....	....	....	....	....	....	....	10	6	7	13	14	....	....	....
1957-58	**Boston Bruins**	**NHL**	**67**	**30**	**36**	**66**	**40**	**39**	**79**	**71**	....	....	....	....	....	....	....	....	....	....	**12**	**5**	**3**	**8**	**8**	....	....	....
1958-59	**Boston Bruins**	**NHL**	**45**	**19**	**20**	**39**	**24**	**21**	**45**	**58**	....	....	....	....	....	....	....	....	....	....	**7**	**2**	**3**	**5**	**0**	....	....	....
1959-60	**Boston Bruins**	**NHL**	**68**	***39**	**41**	**80**	**49**	**42**	**91**	**60**	....	....	....	....	....	....	....	....	....	....	....	....	....	....	....	....	....	....
1960-61	**Boston Bruins**	**NHL**	**47**	**15**	**15**	**30**	**18**	**15**	**33**	**15**	....	....	....	....	....	....	....	....	....	....	....	....	....	....	....	....	....	....
1961-62	**Chicago Black Hawks**	**NHL**	**68**	**17**	**29**	**46**	**21**	**29**	**50**	**21**	....	....	....	....	....	....	....	....	....	....	**12**	**4**	**1**	**5**	**6**	....	....	....

Season	Club	League	REGULAR SEASON																		PLAYOFFS							
			GP	G	A	Pts	AG	AA	APts	PIM	PP	SH	GW	S	%	TGF	PGF	TGA	PGA	+/–	GP	G	A	Pts	PIM	PP	SH	GW
1962-63	**New York Rangers**	**NHL**	41	7	15	22	9	16	25	34	....	....	....	....	....	....	....	....	....	....	....	....	....	....	....	....	....	....
	Toronto Maple Leafs	**NHL**	10	0	4	4	0	4	4	12	....	....	....	....	....	....	....	....	....	....	....	....	....	....	....	....	....	....
	Rochester Americans	AHL	18	7	15	22	....	....	....	6	....	....	....	....	....	....	....	....	....	....	....	....	....	....	....	....	....	....
1963-64	Rochester Americans	AHL	70	25	59	84	....	....	....	28	....	....	....	....	....	....	....	....	....	....	2	0	0	0	2	....	....	....
1964-65	Rochester Americans	AHL	72	38	68	106	....	....	....	24	....	....	....	....	....	....	....	....	....	....	10	4	5	9	16	....	....	....
1965-66	Rochester Americans	AHL	70	27	48	75	....	....	....	34	....	....	....	....	....	....	....	....	....	....	12	3	7	10	22	....	....	....
1966-67	Rochester Americans	AHL	72	29	49	78	....	....	....	54	....	....	....	....	....	....	....	....	....	....	12	2	7	9	2	....	....	....
1967-68	**Minnesota North Stars**	**NHL**	14	1	6	7	1	6	7	4	0	0	0	12	8.3	14	11	9	0	–6	....	....	....	....	....	....	....	....
	Tulsa Oilers	CHL	4	1	2	3	....	....	....	0	....	....	....	....	....	....	....	....	....	....	....	....	....	....	....	....	....	....
	Rochester Americans	AHL	44	15	29	44	....	....	....	10	....	....	....	....	....	....	....	....	....	....	10	0	7	7	0	....	....	....
1968-69	Rochester Americans	AHL	66	18	30	48	....	....	....	30	....	....	....	....	....	....	....	....	....	....	....	....	....	....	....	....	....	....
1969-70	Rochester Americans	AHL	5	3	1	4	....	....	....	0	....	....	....	....	....	....	....	....	....	....	....	....	....	....	....	....	....	....
	NHL Totals		434	141	185	326	180	195	375	319	0	0	0	12	1175	14	11	9	0		36	12	9	21	18	0	0	0

WHL First All-Star Team (1955) • AHL First All-Star Team (1957) • NHL Second All-Star Team (1960) • AHL Second All-Star Team (1964, 1965)

Played in NHL All-Star Game (1960, 1961)

Traded to **NY Rangers** by **Detroit** with Dave Creighton for Bill Dea and Aggie Kukulwicz, August 18, 1955. Traded to **Montreal** by **NY Rangers** for cash, November 4, 1956. Claimed by **Boston** from **Montreal** in Intra-League Draft, June 5, 1957. Claimed by **Chicago** from **Boston** in Intra-League Draft, June 13, 1961. Claimed by **NY Rangers** from **Chicago** in Intra-League Draft, June 4, 1962. Claimed on waivers by **Toronto** from **NY Rangers**, January, 1963. Traded to **Minnesota** by **Toronto** for cash, January 21, 1968. Traded to **Rochester** (AHL) by **Minnesota** for cash, February 27, 1968.

• HOSPODAR, ED

Ed "Boxcar" Hospodar D – R. 6′2″, 210 lbs. b: Bowling Green, OH, 2/9/1959. NY Rangers' 2nd choice, 34th overall, in 1979 Entry Draft.

1976-77	Ottawa 67's	OHA	51	3	19	22	....	....	....	140	....	....	....	....	....	....	....	....	....	....	....	....	....	....	....	....	....	....
1977-78	Ottawa 67's	OHA	62	7	26	33	....	....	....	172	....	....	....	....	....	....	....	....	....	....	16	3	6	9	78	....	....	....
	United States	WJC-A	6	3	4	7	....	....	....	10	....	....	....	....	....	....	....	....	....	....	....	....	....	....	....	....	....	....
1978-79	Ottawa 67's	OHA	45	7	16	23	....	....	....	131	....	....	....	....	....	....	....	....	....	....	5	0	1	1	39	....	....	....
1979-80	**New York Rangers**	**NHL**	20	0	1	1	0	1	1	76	0	0	0	9	0.0	5	0	7	0	–2	7	1	0	1	42	0	0	1
	New Haven Nighthawks	AHL	25	3	9	12	....	....	....	131	....	....	....	....	....	....	....	....	....	....	5	0	1	1	39	....	....	....
1980-81	**New York Rangers**	**NHL**	61	5	14	19	4	10	14	214	0	0	0	49	10.2	40	4	30	4	+10	12	2	0	2	*93	0	0	0
1981-82	**New York Rangers**	**NHL**	41	3	8	11	2	5	7	152	0	0	0	29	10.3	32	0	44	4	–8	....	....	....	....	....	....	....	....
1982-83	**Hartford Whalers**	**NHL**	72	1	9	10	1	6	7	199	0	0	0	54	1.9	39	0	86	15	–32	....	....	....	....	....	....	....	....
1983-84	**Hartford Whalers**	**NHL**	59	0	9	9	0	6	6	163	0	0	0	55	0.0	44	1	69	9	–17	....	....	....	....	....	....	....	....
1984-85	**Philadelphia Flyers**	**NHL**	50	3	4	7	2	3	5	130	0	0	0	51	5.9	34	1	27	1	+7	18	1	1	2	69	0	0	0
1985-86	**Philadelphia Flyers**	**NHL**	17	3	1	4	2	1	3	55	0	1	0	11	27.3	8	0	9	1	0	....	....	....	....	....	....	....	....
	Minnesota North Stars	**NHL**	43	0	2	2	0	1	1	91	0	0	0	33	0.0	24	0	19	3	+8	2	0	0	0	2	0	0	0
1986-87	**Philadelphia Flyers**	**NHL**	45	2	2	4	2	1	3	136	0	0	1	17	11.8	16	0	26	2	–8	5	0	0	0	2	0	0	0
1987-88	**Buffalo Sabres**	**NHL**	42	0	1	1	0	1	1	98	0	0	0	15	0.0	11	0	14	2	–1	....	....	....	....	....	....	....	....
1988-89	Rochester Americans	AHL	5	0	0	0	....	....	....	10	....	....	....	....	....	....	....	....	....	....	....	....	....	....	....	....	....	....
	NHL Totals		450	17	51	68	13	35	48	1314	0	1	1	323	5.3	253	6	331	41		44	4	1	5	208	0	0	1

OHA Second All-Star Team (1979)

Traded to **Hartford** by **NY Rangers** for Kent-Erik Andersson, October 1, 1982. Signed as a free agent by **Philadelphia**, July 25, 1984. Traded to **Minnesota** by **Philadelphia** with Todd Bergen for Bo Berglumd and Dave Richter, November 29, 1985. Signed as a free agent by **Philadelphia**, June 12, 1986. Claimed by **Buffalo** from **Philadelphia** in Waiver Draft, October 5, 1987.

• HOSSA, MARIAN

Marian Hossa LW – L. 6′1″, 185 lbs. b: Stara Lubovna, Czech., 1/12/1979. Ottawa's 1st choice, 12th overall, in 1997 Entry Draft.

1995-96	Dukla Trencin	Slov-Jr.	53	42	49	91	....	....	....	26	....	....	....	....	....	....	....	....	....	....	....	....	....	....	....	....	....	....
1996-97	Dukla Trencin	Slovakia	46	25	19	44	....	....	....	33	....	....	....	....	....	....	....	....	....	....	7	5	5	10	....	....	....	....
	Slovakia	WJC-A	6	5	2	7	....	....	....	2	....	....	....	....	....	....	....	....	....	....	....	....	....	....	....	....	....	....
	Slovakia	WC-A	8	0	2	2	....	....	....	0	....	....	....	....	....	....	....	....	....	....	....	....	....	....	....	....	....	....
1997-98	Portland Winter Hawks	WHL	53	45	40	85	....	....	....	50	....	....	....	....	....	....	....	....	....	....	16	13	6	19	6	....	....	....
	Slovakia	WJC-A	6	4	4	8	....	....	....	12	....	....	....	....	....	....	....	....	....	....	....	....	....	....	....	....	....	....
	Ottawa Senators	**NHL**	7	0	1	1	0	1	1	0	0	0	0	10	0.0	2	1	2	0	–1	....	....	....	....	....	....	....	....
	NHL Totals		7	0	1	1	0	1	1	0	0	0	0	10	0.0	2	1	2	0		....	....	....	....	....	....	....	....

• HOSTAK, MARTIN

Martin Hostak C – L. 6′3″, 198 lbs. b: Hradec Kralove, Czech., 11/11/1967. Philadelphia's 3rd choice, 62nd overall, in 1987 Entry Draft.

1986-87	Sparta Praha	Czech.	40	7	2	9	....	....	....	2	....	....	....	....	....	....	....	....	....	....	....	....	....	....	....	....	....	....
	Czechoslovakia	WJC-A	7	7	3	10	....	....	....	4	....	....	....	....	....	....	....	....	....	....	....	....	....	....	....	....	....	....
1987-88	Sparta Praha	Czech.	26	8	9	17	....	....	....	4	....	....	....	....	....	....	....	....	....	....	....	....	....	....	....	....	....	....
1988-89	Sparta Praha	Czech.	35	11	15	26	....	....	....	10	....	....	....	....	....	....	....	....	....	....	....	....	....	....	....	....	....	....
1989-90	Sparta Praha	Czech.	55	31	34	65	....	....	....	....	....	....	....	....	....	....	....	....	....	....	....	....	....	....	....	....	....	....
	Czechoslovakia	WEC-A	4	0	0	0	....	....	....	4	....	....	....	....	....	....	....	....	....	....	....	....	....	....	....	....	....	....
1990-91	**Philadelphia Flyers**	**NHL**	50	3	10	13	3	8	11	22	1	0	0	64	4.7	24	7	17	1	+1	....	....	....	....	....	....	....	....
	Hershey Bears	AHL	11	6	2	8	....	....	....	2	....	....	....	....	....	....	....	....	....	....	3	1	0	1	0	....	....	....
1991-92	**Philadelphia Flyers**	**NHL**	5	0	1	1	0	1	1	2	0	0	0	8	0.0	1	0	2	0	–1	....	....	....	....	....	....	....	....
	Hershey Bears	AHL	63	27	36	63	....	....	....	77	....	....	....	....	....	....	....	....	....	....	6	1	2	3	2	....	....	....
1992-93	MoDo AIK	Sweden	40	15	19	34	....	....	....	42	....	....	....	....	....	....	....	....	....	....	3	2	1	3	4	....	....	....
	Czech Republic	WC-A	8	4	4	8	....	....	....	0	....	....	....	....	....	....	....	....	....	....	....	....	....	....	....	....	....	....
1993-94	MoDo AIK	Sweden	34	16	17	33	....	....	....	28	....	....	....	....	....	....	....	....	....	....	....	....	....	....	....	....	....	....
	Czech Republic	Olympics	7	1	0	1	....	....	....	0	....	....	....	....	....	....	....	....	....	....	....	....	....	....	....	....	....	....
1994-95	MoDo AIK	Sweden	40	14	17	31	....	....	....	30	....	....	....	....	....	....	....	....	....	....	....	....	....	....	....	....	....	....
	Czech Republic	WC-A	4	0	0	0	....	....	....	2	....	....	....	....	....	....	....	....	....	....	....	....	....	....	....	....	....	....
1995-96	MoDo AIK	Sweden	36	12	15	27	....	....	....	28	....	....	....	....	....	....	....	....	....	....	8	0	2	2	4	....	....	....
	NHL Totals		55	3	11	14	3	9	12	24	1	0	0	72	4.2	25	7	19	1		....	....	....	....	....	....	....	....

• HOTHAM, GREG

Greg Hotham D – R. 5′11″, 183 lbs. b: London, Ont., 3/7/1956. Toronto's 5th choice, 84th overall, in 1976 Amateur Draft.

1973-74	Aurora Tigers	OJHL	44	10	22	32	....	....	....	120	....	....	....	....	....	....	....	....	....	....	....	....	....	....	....	....	....	....
1974-75	Aurora Tigers	OJHL	27	14	10	24	....	....	....	46	....	....	....	....	....	....	....	....	....	....	....	....	....	....	....	....	....	....
	Kingston Canadians	OHA	31	1	14	15	....	....	....	49	....	....	....	....	....	....	....	....	....	....	8	5	4	9	0	....	....	....
1975-76	Kingston Canadians	OHA	49	10	32	42	....	....	....	72	....	....	....	....	....	....	....	....	....	....	7	1	2	3	10	....	....	....
1976-77	Saginaw Gears	IHL	60	4	33	37	....	....	....	100	....	....	....	....	....	....	....	....	....	....	....	....	....	....	....	....	....	....
1977-78	Saginaw Gears	IHL	80	13	59	72	....	....	....	56	....	....	....	....	....	....	....	....	....	....	....	....	....	....	....	....	....	....
	Dallas Black Hawks	CHL	....	....	....	....	....	....	....	....	....	....	....	....	....	....	....	....	....	....	5	0	2	2	7	....	....	....
1978-79	New Brunswick Hawks	AHL	76	9	27	36	....	....	....	86	....	....	....	....	....	....	....	....	....	....	5	0	2	2	6	....	....	....
1979-80	**Toronto Maple Leafs**	**NHL**	46	3	10	13	3	8	11	10	0	0	0	46	6.5	49	2	56	5	–4	....	....	....	....	....	....	....	....
	New Brunswick Hawks	AHL	21	1	6	7	....	....	....	10	....	....	....	....	....	....	....	....	....	....	17	2	8	10	26	....	....	....
1980-81	**Toronto Maple Leafs**	**NHL**	11	1	1	2	1	1	2	11	0	0	0	8	12.5	14	0	13	3	+4	....	....	....	....	....	....	....	....
	New Brunswick Hawks	AHL	68	8	48	56	....	....	....	80	....	....	....	....	....	....	....	....	....	....	11	1	6	7	16	....	....	....
1981-82	**Toronto Maple Leafs**	**NHL**	3	0	0	0	0	0	0	0	0	0	0	4	0.0	1	0	8	2	–5	....	....	....	....	....	....	....	....
	Cincinnati Tigers	CHL	46	10	33	43	....	....	....	94	....	....	....	....	....	....	....	....	....	....	....	....	....	....	....	....	....	....
	Pittsburgh Penguins	**NHL**	25	4	6	10	3	4	7	16	2	0	0	38	10.5	34	18	28	6	–6	5	0	3	3	6	0	0	0
1982-83	**Pittsburgh Penguins**	**NHL**	58	2	30	32	2	21	23	39	0	0	0	75	2.7	78	26	102	36	–14	....	....	....	....	....	....	....	....
1983-84	**Pittsburgh Penguins**	**NHL**	76	5	25	30	4	17	21	59	3	0	0	120	4.2	101	30	146	50	–25	....	....	....	....	....	....	....	....
1984-85	**Pittsburgh Penguins**	**NHL**	11	0	2	2	0	1	1	4	0	0	0	6	0.0	7	2	9	1	–3	....	....	....	....	....	....	....	....
	Baltimore Skipjacks	AHL	44	4	27	31	....	....	....	43	....	....	....	....	....	....	....	....	....	....	15	4	4	8	34	....	....	....
1985-86	Baltimore Skipjacks	AHL	78	2	26	28	....	....	....	94	....	....	....	....	....	....	....	....	....	....	....	....	....	....	....	....	....	....
1986-87	Newmarket Saints	AHL	51	4	9	13	....	....	....	60	....	....	....	....	....	....	....	....	....	....	....	....	....	....	....	....	....	....

			REGULAR SEASON																		PLAYOFFS							
Season	**Club**	**League**	**GP**	**G**	**A**	**Pts**	**AG**	**AA**	**APts**	**PIM**	**PP**	**SH**	**GW**	**S**	**%**	**TGF**	**PGF**	**TGA**	**PGA**	**+/–**	**GP**	**G**	**A**	**Pts**	**PIM**	**PP**	**SH**	**GW**
1987-88	Newmarket Saints	AHL	78	12	27	39	....	....	....	102	....	....	....	....	....	....	....	....	....	....	....	....	....	....	....	....	....	....
1988-89	Newmarket Saints	AHL	73	9	42	51	....	....	....	62	....	....	....	....	....	....	....	....	....	....	5	1	4	5	0	....	....	....
1989-90	Newmarket Saints	AHL	24	0	8	8	....	....	....	31	....	....	....	....	....	....	....	....	....	....	....	....	....	....	....	....	....	....
	NHL Totals		**230**	**15**	**74**	**89**	**13**	**52**	**65**	**139**	**5**	**0**	**0**	**297**	**5.1**	**284**	**78**	**362**	**103**		**5**	**0**	**3**	**3**	**6**	**0**	**0**	**0**

IHL Second All-Star Team (1978)

Traded to **Pittsburgh** by **Toronto** for Pittsburgh's 6th round choice (Craig Kales) in 1982 Entry Draft, February 3, 1982.

• HOUCK, PAUL

Paul Houck RW – R. 5'11", 185 lbs. b: N. Vancouver, B.C., 8/12/1963. Edmonton's 3rd choice, 71st overall, in 1981 Entry Draft.

1980-81	Kelowna Buckaroos	BCJHL	52	*65	51	*116	....	....	....	39	....	....	....	....	....	....	....	....	....	....	....	....	....	....	....	....	....	....
1981-82	University of Wisconsin	WCHA	43	9	16	25	....	....	....	38	....	....	....	....	....	....	....	....	....	....	....	....	....	....	....	....	....	....
1982-83	University of Wisconsin	WCHA	47	38	33	71	....	....	....	36	....	....	....	....	....	....	....	....	....	....	....	....	....	....	....	....	....	....
1983-84	University of Wisconsin	WCHA	37	20	20	40	....	....	....	29	....	....	....	....	....	....	....	....	....	....	....	....	....	....	....	....	....	....
1984-85	University of Wisconsin	WCHA	39	16	24	40	....	....	....	54	....	....	....	....	....	....	....	....	....	....	....	....	....	....	....	....	....	....
	Nova Scotia Voyageurs	AHL	10	1	0	1	....	....	....	0	....	....	....	....	....	....	....	....	....	....	....	....	....	....	....	....	....	....
1985-86	**Minnesota North Stars**	**NHL**	**3**	**1**	**0**	**1**	**1**	**0**	**1**	**0**	**0**	**0**	**0**	**3**	**33.3**	**1**	**0**	**0**	**0**	**+1**	....	....	....	....	....	....	....	....
	Springfield Indians	AHL	61	15	17	32	....	....	....	27	....	....	....	....	....	....	....	....	....	....	....	....	....	....	....	....	....	....
1986-87	**Minnesota North Stars**	**NHL**	**12**	**0**	**2**	**2**	**0**	**1**	**1**	**2**	**0**	**0**	**0**	**10**	**0.0**	**3**	**0**	**9**	**4**	**–2**	....	....	....	....	....	....	....	....
	Springfield Indians	AHL	64	29	18	47	....	....	....	58	....	....	....	....	....	....	....	....	....	....	....	....	....	....	....	....	....	....
1987-88	**Minnesota North Stars**	**NHL**	**1**	**0**	**0**	**0**	**0**	**0**	**0**	**0**	**0**	**0**	**0**	**1**	**0.0**	**0**	**0**	**0**	**0**	**0**	....	....	....	....	....	....	....	....
	Kalamazoo Wings	IHL	74	27	29	56	....	....	....	73	....	....	....	....	....	....	....	....	....	....	7	3	4	7	8	....	....	....
1988-89	Springfield Indians	AHL	2	1	0	1	....	....	....	0	....	....	....	....	....	....	....	....	....	....	....	....	....	....	....	....	....	....
	Indianapolis Ice	IHL	81	22	37	59	....	....	....	51	....	....	....	....	....	....	....	....	....	....	....	....	....	....	....	....	....	....
	NHL Totals		**16**	**1**	**2**	**3**	**1**	**1**	**2**	**2**	**0**	**0**	**0**	**14**	**7.1**	**4**	**0**	**9**	**4**		....	....	....	....	....	....	....	....

WCHA Second All-Star Team (1983) • NCAA Championship All-Tournament Team (1983)

Signed as a free agent by **NY Rangers**, September, 1971. Traded to **Minnesota** by **Edmonton** for Gilles Meloche, May 31, 1985.

• HOUDA, DOUG

Doug Houda D – R. 6'2", 190 lbs. b: Blairmore, Alta., 6/3/1966. Detroit's 2nd choice, 28th overall, in 1984 Entry Draft.

1982-83	Calgary Wranglers	WHL	71	5	23	28	....	....	....	99	....	....	....	....	....	....	....	....	....	....	16	1	3	4	44	....	....	....
1983-84	Calgary Wranglers	WHL	69	6	30	36	....	....	....	195	....	....	....	....	....	....	....	....	....	....	4	0	0	0	7	....	....	....
1984-85	Calgary Wranglers	WHL	65	20	54	74	....	....	....	182	....	....	....	....	....	....	....	....	....	....	8	3	4	7	29	....	....	....
1985-86	Calgary Wranglers	WHL	16	4	10	14	....	....	....	60	....	....	....	....	....	....	....	....	....	....	....	....	....	....	....	....	....	....
	Medicine Hat Tigers	WHL	35	9	23	32	....	....	....	80	....	....	....	....	....	....	....	....	....	....	25	4	19	23	64	....	....	....
	Detroit Red Wings	**NHL**	**6**	**0**	**0**	**0**	**0**	**0**	**0**	**4**	**0**	**0**	**0**	**5**	**0.0**	**3**	**0**	**11**	**1**	**–7**	....	....	....	....	....	....	....	....
1986-87	Adirondack Red Wings	AHL	77	6	23	29	....	....	....	142	....	....	....	....	....	....	....	....	....	....	11	1	8	9	50	....	....	....
1987-88	**Detroit Red Wings**	**NHL**	**11**	**1**	**1**	**2**	**1**	**1**	**2**	**10**	**0**	**0**	**0**	**10**	**10.0**	**8**	**0**	**9**	**1**	**0**	....	....	....	....	....	....	....	....
	Adirondack Red Wings	AHL	71	10	32	42	....	....	....	169	....	....	....	....	....	....	....	....	....	....	11	0	3	3	44	....	....	....
1988-89	**Detroit Red Wings**	**NHL**	**57**	**2**	**11**	**13**	**2**	**8**	**10**	**67**	**0**	**0**	**0**	**38**	**5.3**	**57**	**0**	**47**	**7**	**+17**	**6**	**0**	**1**	**1**	**0**	**0**	**0**	**0**
	Adirondack Red Wings	AHL	7	0	3	3	....	....	....	8	....	....	....	....	....	....	....	....	....	....	....	....	....	....	....	....	....	....
1989-90	**Detroit Red Wings**	**NHL**	**73**	**2**	**9**	**11**	**2**	**6**	**8**	**127**	**0**	**0**	**0**	**59**	**3.4**	**51**	**0**	**64**	**8**	**–5**	....	....	....	....	....	....	....	....
1990-91	**Detroit Red Wings**	**NHL**	**22**	**0**	**4**	**4**	**0**	**3**	**3**	**43**	**0**	**0**	**0**	**21**	**0.0**	**18**	**2**	**24**	**6**	**–2**	....	....	....	....	....	....	....	....
	Adirondack Red Wings	AHL	38	9	17	26	....	....	....	67	....	....	....	....	....	....	....	....	....	....	....	....	....	....	....	....	....	....
	Hartford Whalers	**NHL**	**19**	**1**	**2**	**3**	**1**	**2**	**3**	**41**	**0**	**0**	**0**	**21**	**4.8**	**14**	**0**	**22**	**5**	**–3**	**6**	**0**	**0**	**0**	**8**	**0**	**0**	**0**
1991-92	**Hartford Whalers**	**NHL**	**56**	**3**	**6**	**9**	**3**	**4**	**7**	**125**	**1**	**0**	**1**	**40**	**7.5**	**38**	**1**	**59**	**20**	**–2**	**6**	**0**	**2**	**2**	**13**	**0**	**0**	**0**
1992-93	**Hartford Whalers**	**NHL**	**60**	**2**	**6**	**8**	**2**	**4**	**6**	**167**	**0**	**0**	**0**	**43**	**4.7**	**42**	**2**	**79**	**20**	**–19**	....	....	....	....	....	....	....	....
1993-94	**Hartford Whalers**	**NHL**	**7**	**0**	**0**	**0**	**0**	**0**	**0**	**23**	**0**	**0**	**0**	**1**	**0.0**	**1**	**0**	**6**	**1**	**–4**	....	....	....	....	....	....	....	....
	Los Angeles Kings	**NHL**	**54**	**2**	**6**	**8**	**2**	**5**	**7**	**165**	**0**	**0**	**0**	**31**	**6.5**	**28**	**0**	**56**	**13**	**–15**	....	....	....	....	....	....	....	....
1994-95	**Buffalo Sabres**	**NHL**	**28**	**1**	**2**	**3**	**2**	**3**	**5**	**68**	**0**	**0**	**0**	**21**	**4.8**	**12**	**1**	**17**	**7**	**+1**	....	....	....	....	....	....	....	....
1995-96	**Buffalo Sabres**	**NHL**	**38**	**1**	**3**	**4**	**1**	**2**	**3**	**52**	**0**	**0**	**0**	**21**	**4.8**	**27**	**0**	**29**	**5**	**+3**	....	....	....	....	....	....	....	....
	Rochester Americans	AHL	21	1	6	7	....	....	....	41	....	....	....	....	....	....	....	....	....	....	19	3	5	8	30	....	....	....
1996-97	**New York Islanders**	**NHL**	**70**	**2**	**8**	**10**	**2**	**7**	**9**	**99**	**0**	**0**	**0**	**29**	**6.9**	**32**	**2**	**42**	**13**	**+1**	....	....	....	....	....	....	....	....
	Utah Grizzlies	IHL	3	0	0	0	....	....	....	7	....	....	....	....	....	....	....	....	....	....	....	....	....	....	....	....	....	....
1997-98	**New York Islanders**	**NHL**	**31**	**1**	**2**	**3**	**1**	**2**	**3**	**47**	**0**	**0**	**0**	**15**	**6.7**	**14**	**2**	**20**	**2**	**–6**	....	....	....	....	....	....	....	....
	Anaheim Mighty Ducks	**NHL**	**24**	**1**	**2**	**3**	**1**	**2**	**3**	**52**	**0**	**1**	**0**	**9**	**11.1**	**13**	**0**	**24**	**6**	**–5**	....	....	....	....	....	....	....	....
	NHL Totals		**556**	**19**	**62**	**81**	**20**	**49**	**69**	**1090**	**1**	**1**	**1**	**364**	**5.2**	**358**	**10**	**509**	**115**		**18**	**0**	**3**	**3**	**21**	**0**	**0**	**0**

WHL East Second All-Star Team (1985) • AHL First All-Star Team (1988)

Traded to **Hartford** by **Detroit** for Doug Crossman, February 20, 1991. Traded to **LA Kings** by **Hartford** for Marc Potvin, November 3, 1993. Traded to **Buffalo** by **LA Kings** for Sean O'Donnell, July 26, 1994. Signed as a free agent by **NY Islanders**, October 26, 1996. Traded to **Anaheim** by **NY Islanders** with Travis Greene and Tony Tuzzolino for Joe Sacco, J.J. Daigneault and Mark Janssens, February 6, 1998.

• HOUDE, CLAUDE

Claude Houde D – L. 6'1", 188 lbs. b: Drummondville, Que., 11/8/1947.

1968-69	Granby Bisons	QSHL	51	15	30	45	....	....	....		....	....	....	....	....	....	....	....	....	....	....	....	....	....	....	....	....	....
1969-70	Granby Bisons	QSHL	STATISTICS NOT AVAILABLE																									
1970-71	Syracuse Blazers	EHL	65	15	19	34	....	....	....	62	....	....	....	....	....	....	....	....	....	....	6	1	0	1	0	....	....	....
1971-72	Providence Reds	AHL	54	3	9	12	....	....	....	26	....	....	....	....	....	....	....	....	....	....	5	0	0	0	5	....	....	....
1972-73	Toledo Hornets	IHL	22	7	4	11	....	....	....	20	....	....	....	....	....	....	....	....	....	....	....	....	....	....	....	....	....	....
	Providence Reds	AHL	55	9	14	23	....	....	....	22	....	....	....	....	....	....	....	....	....	....	3	0	1	1	10	....	....	....
1973-74	Baltimore Clippers	AHL	62	7	17	24	....	....	....	30	....	....	....	....	....	....	....	....	....	....	....	....	....	....	....	....	....	....
	Virginia Wings	AHL	14	2	3	5	....	....	....	6	....	....	....	....	....	....	....	....	....	....	....	....	....	....	....	....	....	....
1974-75	**Kansas City Scouts**	**NHL**	**34**	**3**	**4**	**7**	**3**	**3**	**6**	**20**	**2**	**0**	**1**	**43**	**7.0**	**22**	**7**	**49**	**3**	**–31**	....	....	....	....	....	....	....	....
	Virginia Wings	AHL	25	1	2	3	....	....	....	28	....	....	....	....	....	....	....	....	....	....	....	....	....	....	....	....	....	....
1975-76	**Kansas City Scouts**	**NHL**	**25**	**0**	**2**	**2**	**0**	**2**	**2**	**20**	**0**	**0**	**0**	**16**	**0.0**	**8**	**0**	**28**	**7**	**–13**	....	....	....	....	....	....	....	....
	Springfield Indians	AHL	29	5	9	14	....	....	....	24	....	....	....	....	....	....	....	....	....	....	....	....	....	....	....	....	....	....
1976-77	Beauce Jaros	NAHL	22	6	16	22	....	....	....	10	....	....	....	....	....	....	....	....	....	....	....	....	....	....	....	....	....	....
	NHL Totals		**59**	**3**	**6**	**9**	**3**	**5**	**8**	**40**	**2**	**0**	**1**	**59**	**5.1**	**30**	**7**	**77**	**10**		....	....	....	....	....	....	....	....

Traded to **Detroit** by **NY Rangers** for Brian Lavender, February 28, 1974. Traded to **Kansas City** by **Detroit** with Guy Charron for Bart Crashley, Ted Snell and Larry Giroux, December 14, 1974.

• HOUDE, ERIC

Eric Houde C – L. 5'11", 185 lbs. b: Montreal, Que., 12/19/1976. Montreal's 9th choice, 216th overall, in 1995 Entry Draft.

1993-94	St-Jean Lynx	QMJHL	71	16	16	32	....	....	....	14	....	....	....	....	....	....	....	....	....	....	5	1	1	2	4	....	....	....
1994-95	St-Jean Lynx	QMJHL	40	10	13	23	....	....	....	23	....	....	....	....	....	....	....	....	....	....	....	....	....	....	....	....	....	....
	Halifax Mooseheads	QMJHL	28	13	23	36	....	....	....	8	....	....	....	....	....	....	....	....	....	....	3	2	1	3	4	....	....	....
1995-96	Halifax Mooseheads	QMJHL	69	40	48	88	....	....	....	35	....	....	....	....	....	....	....	....	....	....	6	3	4	7	2	....	....	....
1996-97	**Montreal Canadiens**	**NHL**	**13**	**0**	**2**	**2**	**0**	**2**	**2**	**2**	**0**	**0**	**0**	**1**	**0.0**	**2**	**0**	**1**	**0**	**+1**	....	....	....	....	....	....	....	....
	Fredericton Canadiens	AHL	66	30	36	66	....	....	....	20	....	....	....	....	....	....	....	....	....	....	....	....	....	....	....	....	....	....
1997-98	**Montreal Canadiens**	**NHL**	**9**	**1**	**0**	**1**	**1**	**0**	**1**	**0**	**0**	**0**	**1**	**4**	**25.0**	**1**	**0**	**4**	**0**	**–3**	....	....	....	....	....	....	....	....
	Fredericton Canadiens	AHL	71	28	42	70	....	....	....	24	....	....	....	....	....	....	....	....	....	....	4	5	2	7	4	....	....	....
	NHL Totals		**22**	**1**	**2**	**3**	**1**	**2**	**3**	**2**	**0**	**0**	**1**	**5**	**20.0**	**3**	**0**	**5**	**0**		....	....	....	....	....	....	....	....

• HOUGH, MIKE

Mike Hough LW – L. 6'1", 197 lbs. b: Montreal, Que., 2/6/1963. Quebec's 7th choice, 181st overall, in 1982 Entry Draft.

1981-82	Kitchener Rangers	OHL	58	14	24	38	....	....	....	172	....	....	....	....	....	....	....	....	....	....	14	4	1	5	16	....	....	....
1982-83	Kitchener Rangers	OHL	61	17	27	44	....	....	....	156	....	....	....	....	....	....	....	....	....	....	12	5	4	9	30	....	....	....
1983-84	Fredericton Express	AHL	69	11	16	27	....	....	....	142	....	....	....	....	....	....	....	....	....	....	1	0	0	0	7	....	....	....
1984-85	Fredericton Express	AHL	76	21	27	48	....	....	....	49	....	....	....	....	....	....	....	....	....	....	6	1	1	2	2	....	....	....
1985-86	Fredericton Express	AHL	74	21	33	54	....	....	....	68	....	....	....	....	....	....	....	....	....	....	6	0	3	3	8	....	....	....
1986-87	**Quebec Nordiques**	**NHL**	**56**	**6**	**8**	**14**	**5**	**6**	**11**	**79**	**1**	**1**	**0**	**60**	**10.0**	**25**	**4**	**35**	**6**	**–8**	**9**	**0**	**3**	**3**	**26**	**0**	**0**	**0**
	Fredericton Express	AHL	10	1	3	4	....	....	....	20	....	....	....	....	....	....	....	....	....	....	....	....	....	....	....	....	....	....
1987-88	**Quebec Nordiques**	**NHL**	**17**	**3**	**2**	**5**	**3**	**1**	**4**	**2**	**0**	**0**	**1**	**23**	**13.0**	**7**	**0**	**15**	**0**	**–8**	....	....	....	....	....	....	....	....
	Fredericton Express	AHL	46	16	25	41	....	....	....	133	....	....	....	....	....	....	....	....	....	....	15	4	8	12	55	....	....	....
1988-89	**Quebec Nordiques**	**NHL**	**46**	**9**	**10**	**19**	**8**	**7**	**15**	**39**	**1**	**3**	**3**	**51**	**17.6**	**24**	**2**	**34**	**5**	**–7**	....	....	....	....	....	....	....	....
	Halifax Citadels	AHL	22	11	10	21	....	....	....	87	....	....	....	....	....	....	....	....	....	....	....	....	....	....	....	....	....	....

			REGULAR SEASON																		PLAYOFFS							
Season	Club	League	GP	G	A	Pts	AG	AA	APts	PIM	PP	SH	GW	S	%	TGF	PGF	TGA	PGA	+/–	GP	G	A	Pts	PIM	PP	SH	GW
1989-90	Quebec Nordiques	NHL	43	13	13	26	11	9	20	84	3	1	0	93	14.0	43	16	57	6	–24	....	....	....	....	....	....	....	....
1990-91	Quebec Nordiques	NHL	63	13	20	33	12	15	27	111	1	1	1	106	12.3	57	8	90	34	–7	....	....	....	....	....	....	....	....
1991-92	Quebec Nordiques	NHL	61	16	22	38	15	17	32	77	6	2	1	92	17.4	75	26	69	19	–1	....	....	....	....	....	....	....	....
1992-93	Quebec Nordiques	NHL	77	8	22	30	7	15	22	69	2	1	2	98	8.2	53	9	76	21	–11	6	0	1	1	2	0	0	0
1993-94	Florida Panthers	NHL	78	6	23	29	6	18	24	62	0	1	1	106	5.7	43	0	59	19	+3	....	....	....	....	....	....	....	....
1994-95	Florida Panthers	NHL	48	6	7	13	11	10	21	38	0	0	2	58	10.3	20	1	29	11	+1	....	....	....	....	....	....	....	....
1995-96	Florida Panthers	NHL	64	7	16	23	7	13	20	37	0	1	1	66	10.6	35	0	45	14	+4	22	4	1	5	8	0	0	2
1996-97	Florida Panthers	NHL	69	8	6	14	8	5	13	48	0	0	2	85	9.4	30	0	35	17	+12	5	1	0	1	2	0	0	0
1997-98	New York Islanders	NHL	74	5	7	12	6	7	13	27	0	0	0	44	11.4	21	1	41	17	–4	....	....	....	....	....	....	....	....
	NHL Totals		696	100	156	256	99	123	222	673	14	11	14	882	11.3	433	67	585	169		42	5	5	10	38	0	0	2

Traded to **Washington** by **Quebec** for Reggie Savage and Paul MacDermid, June 20, 1993. Claimed by **Florida** from **Washington** in Expansion Draft, June 24, 1993. Signed as a free agent by **NY Islanders**, July 21, 1997.

• HOULDER, BILL

Bill Houlder D – L. 6'2", 211 lbs. b: Thunder Bay, Ont., 3/11/1967. Washington's 4th choice, 82nd overall, in 1985 Entry Draft.

Season	Club	League	GP	G	A	Pts	AG	AA	APts	PIM	PP	SH	GW	S	%	TGF	PGF	TGA	PGA	+/–	GP	G	A	Pts	PIM	PP	SH	GW
1984-85	North Bay Centennials	OHL	66	4	20	24	....	....	....	37	....	....	....	....	....	....	....	....	....	....	8	0	0	0	2	....	....	....
1985-86	North Bay Centennials	OHL	59	5	30	35	....	....	....	97	....	....	....	....	....	....	....	....	....	....	10	1	6	7	12	....	....	....
1986-87	North Bay Centennials	OHL	62	17	51	68	....	....	....	68	....	....	....	....	....	....	....	....	....	....	22	4	19	23	20	....	....	....
1987-88	Washington Capitals	NHL	30	1	2	3	1	1	2	10	0	0	0	20	5.0	13	0	15	0	–2	....	....	....	....	....	....	....	....
	Fort Wayne Komets	IHL	43	10	14	24	....	....	....	32	....	....	....	....	....	....	....	....	....	....	....	....	....	....	....	....	....	....
1988-89	Washington Capitals	NHL	8	0	3	3	0	2	2	4	0	0	0	5	0.0	11	1	3	0	+7	....	....	....	....	....	....	....	....
	Baltimore Skipjacks	AHL	65	10	36	46	....	....	....	50	....	....	....	....	....	....	....	....	....	....	....	....	....	....	....	....	....	....
1989-90	Washington Capitals	NHL	41	1	11	12	1	8	9	28	0	0	0	49	2.0	56	8	41	1	+8	....	....	....	....	....	....	....	....
1989-90	Washington	FrTour	4	0	0	0	....	....	....	2	....	....	....	....	....	....	....	....	....	....	....	....	....	....	....	....	....	....
	Baltimore Skipjacks	AHL	26	3	7	10	....	....	....	12	....	....	....	....	....	....	....	....	....	....	7	0	2	2	2	....	....	....
1990-91	Buffalo Sabres	NHL	7	0	2	2	0	2	2	4	0	0	0	7	0.0	3	2	3	0	–2	....	....	....	....	....	....	....	....
	Rochester Americans	AHL	69	13	53	66	....	....	....	28	....	....	....	....	....	....	....	....	....	....	15	5	13	18	4	....	....	....
1991-92	Buffalo Sabres	NHL	10	1	0	1	1	0	1	8	0	0	0	18	5.6	6	1	8	1	–2	....	....	....	....	....	....	....	....
	Rochester Americans	AHL	42	8	26	34	....	....	....	16	....	....	....	....	....	....	....	....	....	....	16	5	6	11	4	....	....	....
1992-93	Buffalo Sabres	NHL	15	3	5	8	2	3	5	6	0	0	0	29	10.3	17	2	13	3	+5	8	0	2	2	4	0	0	0
	San Diego Gulls	IHL	64	24	48	72	....	....	....	39	....	....	....	....	....	....	....	....	....	....	....	....	....	....	....	....	....	....
1993-94	Anaheim Mighty Ducks	NHL	80	14	25	39	13	19	32	40	3	0	3	187	7.5	77	31	89	25	–18	....	....	....	....	....	....	....	....
1994-95	St. Louis Blues	NHL	41	5	13	18	9	19	28	20	1	0	0	59	8.5	48	7	28	3	+16	4	1	1	2	0	0	0	0
1995-96	Tampa Bay Lightning	NHL	61	5	23	28	5	19	24	22	3	0	0	90	5.6	60	24	58	23	+1	6	0	1	1	4	0	0	0
1996-97	Tampa Bay Lightning	NHL	79	4	21	25	4	19	23	30	0	0	2	116	3.4	92	14	93	31	+16	....	....	....	....	....	....	....	....
1997-98	San Jose Sharks	NHL	82	7	25	32	8	24	32	48	4	0	2	102	6.9	86	25	80	32	+13	6	1	2	3	2	0	0	0
	NHL Totals		454	41	130	171	44	116	160	220	11	0	7	682	6.0	469	115	431	119		24	2	6	8	10	0	0	0

AHL First All-Star Team (1991) • Won Governor's Trophy (Outstanding Defenseman - IHL) (1993) • IHL First All-Star Team (1993)

Traded to **Buffalo** by **Washington** for Shawn Anderson, September 30, 1990. Claimed by **Anaheim** from **Buffalo** in Expansion Draft, June 24, 1993. Traded to **St. Louis** by **Anaheim** for Jason Marshall, August 29, 1994. Signed as a free agent by **Tampa Bay**, July 26, 1995. Signed as a free agent by **San Jose**, July 16, 1997.

• HOULE, REJEAN

Rejean "Reggie" Houle LW/RW – L. 5'11", 170 lbs. b: Rouyn, Que., 10/25/1949. Montreal's 1st choice, 1st overall, in 1969 Amateur Draft.

Season	Club	League	GP	G	A	Pts	AG	AA	APts	PIM	PP	SH	GW	S	%	TGF	PGF	TGA	PGA	+/–	GP	G	A	Pts	PIM	PP	SH	GW
1966-67	Thetford Mines Canadiens	QJHL	....	30	30	60	....	....	....	....	....	....	....	....	....	....	....	....	....	....	....	....	....	....	....	....	....	....
1967-68	Montreal Jr. Canadiens	OHA	45	27	38	65	....	....	....	102	....	....	....	....	....	....	....	....	....	....	11	12	8	20	10	....	....	....
1968-69	Montreal Jr. Canadiens	OHA	54	53	55	*108	....	....	....	76	....	....	....	....	....	....	....	....	....	....	14	13	10	23	13	....	....	....
1969-70	Montreal Canadiens	NHL	9	0	1	1	0	1	1	0	0	0	0	1	0.0	2	0	1	0	+1	....	....	....	....	....	....	....	....
	Montreal Voyageurs	AHL	27	9	16	25	....	....	....	23	....	....	....	....	....	....	....	....	....	....	8	3	2	5	4	....	....	....
1970-71	Montreal Canadiens	NHL	66	10	9	19	10	8	18	28	1	0	1	87	11.5	37	5	25	0	+7	20	2	5	7	20	0	0	1
1971-72	Montreal Canadiens	NHL	77	11	17	28	12	15	27	21	1	0	1	145	7.6	49	5	38	3	+9	6	0	0	0	2	0	0	0
1972-73	Montreal Canadiens	NHL	72	13	35	48	13	29	42	36	3	0	1	117	11.1	68	11	35	2	+24	17	3	6	9	0	0	0	0
1973-74	Quebec Nordiques	WHA	69	27	35	62	....	....	....	17	....	....	....	....	....	....	....	....	....	....	....	....	....	....	....	....	....	....
1974-75	Canada	Summit	7	1	1	2	....	....	....	2	....	....	....	....	....	....	....	....	....	....	....	....	....	....	....	....	....	....
	Quebec Nordiques	WHA	64	40	52	92	....	....	....	37	....	....	....	....	....	....	....	....	....	....	15	*10	6	16	2	....	....	....
1975-76	Quebec Nordiques	WHA	81	51	52	103	....	....	....	61	....	....	....	....	....	....	....	....	....	....	5	2	0	2	8	....	....	....
1976-77	Montreal Canadiens	NHL	65	22	30	52	21	24	45	24	2	0	3	131	16.8	76	12	30	5	+39	6	0	1	1	4	0	0	0
1977-78	Montreal Canadiens	NHL	76	30	28	58	29	23	52	50	3	0	5	143	21.0	96	23	41	7	+39	15	3	8	11	14	0	0	0
1978-79	Montreal Canadiens	NHL	66	17	34	51	15	26	41	43	6	0	4	105	16.2	78	18	52	8	+16	7	1	5	6	2	0	0	0
1979-80	Montreal Canadiens	NHL	60	18	27	45	16	21	37	68	2	0	3	115	15.7	63	13	55	8	+3	10	4	5	9	12	1	0	0
1980-81	Montreal Canadiens	NHL	77	27	31	58	22	22	44	83	6	1	3	158	17.1	88	18	63	13	+20	3	1	0	1	6	0	0	0
1981-82	Montreal Canadiens	NHL	51	11	32	43	9	21	30	34	2	1	1	81	13.6	59	16	29	4	+18	5	0	4	4	6	0	0	0
1982-83	Montreal Canadiens	NHL	16	2	3	5	2	2	4	8	1	0	0	18	11.1	8	2	3	1	+4	1	0	0	0	0	0	0	0
	NHL Totals		635	161	247	408	149	192	341	395	27	2	22	1101	14.6	624	123	372	51		90	14	34	48	66	1	0	1
	Other Major League Totals		214	118	139	257	....	....	....	115	....	....	....	....	....	....	....	....	....		20	12	6	18	10	....	....	....

OHA First All-Star Team (1969)

Selected by **Quebec** (WHA) in 1972 WHA General Player Draft, February 13, 1972. Signed as a free agent by **Montreal**, June 10, 1976.

• HOUSLEY, PHIL

Phil Housley D – L. 5'10", 185 lbs. b: St. Paul, MN, 3/9/1964. Buffalo's 1st choice, 6th overall, in 1982 Entry Draft.

Season	Club	League	GP	G	A	Pts	AG	AA	APts	PIM	PP	SH	GW	S	%	TGF	PGF	TGA	PGA	+/–	GP	G	A	Pts	PIM	PP	SH	GW
1981-82	South St. Paul High	H.S.	22	31	34	65	....	....	....	18	....	....	....	....	....	....	....	....	....	....	....	....	....	....	....	....	....	....
	United States	WJC-A	7	1	0	1	....	....	....	6	....	....	....	....	....	....	....	....	....	....	....	....	....	....	....	....	....	....
	United States	WEC-A	7	1	0	1	....	....	....	4	....	....	....	....	....	....	....	....	....	....	....	....	....	....	....	....	....	....
1982-83	Buffalo Sabres	NHL	77	19	47	66	16	32	48	39	11	0	2	183	10.4	141	53	98	6	–4	10	3	4	7	2	1	0	0
1983-84	Buffalo Sabres	NHL	75	31	46	77	25	31	56	33	13	2	6	234	13.2	143	57	87	4	+3	3	0	0	0	6	0	0	0
1984-85	United States	C Cup	6	0	2	2	....	....	....	0	....	....	....	....	....	....	....	....	....	....	....	....	....	....	....	....	....	....
	Buffalo Sabres	NHL	73	16	53	69	13	36	49	28	3	0	4	188	8.5	106	45	48	2	+15	5	3	2	5	2	0	0	0
1985-86	Buffalo Sabres	NHL	79	15	47	62	12	31	43	54	7	0	2	180	8.3	111	53	70	3	–9	....	....	....	....	....	....	....	....
	United States	WEC-A	10	2	6	8	....	....	....	4	....	....	....	....	....	....	....	....	....	....	....	....	....	....	....	....	....	....
1986-87	Buffalo Sabres	NHL	78	21	46	67	18	33	51	57	8	1	2	202	10.4	132	48	100	14	–2	....	....	....	....	....	....	....	....
1987-88	United States	C Cup	5	0	2	2	....	....	....	4	....	....	....	....	....	....	....	....	....	....	....	....	....	....	....	....	....	....
	Buffalo Sabres	NHL	74	29	37	66	25	26	51	96	6	0	1	231	12.6	137	61	103	10	–17	6	2	4	6	6	1	0	0
1988-89	Buffalo Sabres	NHL	72	26	44	70	22	31	53	47	5	0	3	178	14.6	148	65	92	15	+6	5	1	3	4	2	0	0	0
	United States	WEC-A	7	3	4	7	....	....	....	2	....	....	....	....	....	....	....	....	....	....	....	....	....	....	....	....	....	....
1989-90	Buffalo Sabres	NHL	80	21	60	81	18	43	61	32	8	1	4	201	10.4	159	68	86	6	+11	6	1	4	5	4	1	0	0
1990-91	Winnipeg Jets	NHL	78	23	53	76	21	40	61	24	12	1	3	206	11.2	134	57	103	13	–13	....	....	....	....	....	....	....	....
1991-92	Winnipeg Jets	NHL	74	23	63	86	21	47	68	92	11	0	4	234	9.8	138	77	81	15	–5	7	1	4	5	0	1	0	1
1992-93	Winnipeg Jets	NHL	80	18	79	97	15	54	69	52	6	0	2	249	7.2	187	91	120	10	–14	6	0	7	7	2	0	0	0
1993-94	St. Louis Blues	NHL	26	7	15	22	7	12	19	12	4	0	1	60	11.7	45	27	30	7	–5	4	2	1	3	4	2	0	0
1994-95	Zurich Grasshoppers	Switz. 2	10	6	8	14	....	....	....	34	....	....	....	....	....	....	....	....	....	....	....	....	....	....	....	....	....	....
	Calgary Flames	NHL	43	8	35	43	14	52	66	18	3	0	0	135	5.9	86	34	36	1	+17	7	0	9	9	0	0	0	0
1995-96	Calgary Flames	NHL	59	16	36	52	16	29	45	22	6	0	1	155	10.3	91	43	59	9	–2	....	....	....	....	....	....	....	....
	New Jersey Devils	NHL	22	1	15	16	1	12	13	8	0	0	0	50	2.0	28	11	22	1	–4	....	....	....	....	....	....	....	....
1996-97	United States	W Cup	1	0	1	1	....	....	....	0	....	....	....	....	....	....	....	....	....	....	....	....	....	....	....	....	....	....
	Washington Capitals	NHL	77	11	29	40	12	26	38	24	3	1	2	167	6.6	97	44	68	5	–10	....	....	....	....	....	....	....	....
1997-98	Washington Capitals	NHL	64	6	25	31	7	24	31	24	4	1	0	116	5.2	75	40	48	3	–10	18	0	4	4	4	0	0	0
	NHL Totals		1131	291	730	1021	263	559	822	662	110	7	37	2969	9.8	1958	874	1251	124		77	13	42	55	32	6	0	1

NHL All-Rookie Team (1983) • NHL Second All-Star Team (1992)

Played in NHL All-Star Game (1984, 1989, 1990, 1991, 1992, 1993)

Traded to **Winnipeg** by **Buffalo** with Scott Arniel, Jeff Parker and Buffalo's 1st round choice (Keith Tkachuk) in 1990 Entry Draft for Dale Hawerchuk, Winnipeg's 1st round choice (Brad May) in 1990 Entry Draft and future considerations, June 16, 1990. Traded to **St. Louis** by **Winnipeg** for Nelson Emerson and Stephane Quintal, September 24, 1993. Traded to **Calgary** by **St. Louis** with St. Louis' 2nd round choice (Steve Begin) in 1996 Entry Draft and 2nd round choice (John Tripp) in 1997 Entry Draft for Al MacInnis and Calgary's 4th round choice (Didier Tremblay) in 1997 Entry Draft, July 4, 1994. Traded to **New Jersey** by **Calgary** with Dan Keczmer for Tommy Albelin, Cale Hulse and Jocelyn Lemieux, February 26, 1996. Signed as a free agent by **Washington**, July 22, 1996. Claimed on waivers by **Calgary** from **Washington**, July 21, 1998.

• HOUSTON, KEN

Ken Houston RW – R. 6'2", 210 lbs. b: Dresden, Ont., 9/15/1953. Atlanta's 6th choice, 85th overall, in 1973 Amateur Draft.

			REGULAR SEASON																		PLAYOFFS							
Season	Club	League	GP	G	A	Pts	AG	AA	APts	PIM	PP	SH	GW	S	%	TGF	PGF	TGA	PGA	+/–	GP	G	A	Pts	PIM	PP	SH	GW
1971-72	Chatham Maroons	Jr. B	48	8	24	32	....	....	....	213	....	....	....	....	....	....	....	....	....	....	....	....	....	....	....	....	....	....
1972-73	Chatham Maroons	Jr. B	52	14	41	55	....	....	....	60	....	....	....	....	....	....	....	....	....	....	....	....	....	....	....	....	....	....
1973-74	Omaha Knights	CHL	71	8	22	30	....	....	....	144	....	....	....	....	....	....	....	....	....	....	5	1	1	2	6	....	....	....
1974-75	Omaha Knights	CHL	78	9	32	41	....	....	....	158	....	....	....	....	....	....	....	....	....	....	6	1	7	8	8	....	....	....
1975-76	**Atlanta Flames**	**NHL**	38	5	6	11	5	5	10	11	1	0	0	49	10.2	18	1	20	0	–3	2	0	0	0	0	0	0	0
	Nova Scotia Voyageurs	AHL	27	14	15	29	....	....	....	56	....	....	....	....	....	....	....	....	....	....	....	....	....	....	....	....	....	....
1976-77	**Atlanta Flames**	**NHL**	78	20	24	44	19	19	38	35	3	0	2	151	13.2	67	8	54	0	+5	3	0	0	0	4	0	0	0
1977-78	**Atlanta Flames**	**NHL**	74	22	16	38	21	13	34	51	2	0	2	147	15.0	54	4	46	0	+4	2	0	0	0	0	0	0	0
1978-79	**Atlanta Flames**	**NHL**	80	21	31	52	19	24	43	135	2	0	2	140	15.0	83	11	68	0	+4	1	0	0	0	16	0	0	0
1979-80	**Atlanta Flames**	**NHL**	80	23	31	54	21	24	45	100	4	0	4	155	14.8	85	15	72	1	–1	4	1	1	2	10	0	0	0
1980-81	**Calgary Flames**	**NHL**	42	15	15	30	12	10	22	93	4	0	4	78	19.2	58	27	32	1	0	16	7	8	15	28	5	0	1
1981-82	**Calgary Flames**	**NHL**	70	22	22	44	17	15	32	91	3	0	0	165	13.3	76	14	64	0	–2	3	1	0	1	4	0	0	0
1982-83	**Washington Capitals**	**NHL**	71	25	14	39	21	10	31	93	9	0	0	139	18.0	70	27	51	0	–8	4	1	0	1	4	0	0	0
1983-84	**Washington Capitals**	**NHL**	4	0	0	0	0	0	0	4	0	0	0	3	0.0	1	0	3	0	–2	....	....	....	....	....	....	....	....
	Los Angeles Kings	**NHL**	33	8	8	16	6	5	11	11	0	0	0	35	22.9	23	3	23	0	–3	....	....	....	....	....	....	....	....
	NHL Totals		**570**	**161**	**167**	**328**	**141**	**125**	**266**	**624**	**28**	**0**	**14**	**1062**	**15.2**	**535**	**110**	**433**	**2**		**35**	**10**	**9**	**19**	**66**	**5**	**0**	**1**

Transferred to **Calgary** after **Atlanta** franchise relocated, June 24, 1980. Traded to **Washington** by **Calgary** with Pat Riggin for Howard Walker, George White, Washington's 6th round choice (Mats Kihlstron) in 1982 Entry Draft, 3rd round choice (Parry Berezan) in 1983 Entry Draft and 2nd round choice (Paul Ranheim) in 1984 Entry Draft, June 9, 1982. Traded to **LA Kings** by **Washington** with Brian Engblom for Larry Murphy, October 19, 1983.

• HOWATT, GARRY

Garry Howatt LW – R. 5'9", 175 lbs. b: Grand Center, Alta., 9/26/1952. NY Islanders' 13th choice, 144th overall, in 1972 Amateur Draft.

			REGULAR SEASON																		PLAYOFFS							
Season	Club	League	GP	G	A	Pts	AG	AA	APts	PIM	PP	SH	GW	S	%	TGF	PGF	TGA	PGA	+/–	GP	G	A	Pts	PIM	PP	SH	GW
1971-72	Victoria Cougars	WCJHL	24	5	15	20	....	....	....	36	....	....	....	....	....	....	....	....	....	....	....	....	....	....	....	....	....	....
	Flin Flon Bombers	WCJHL	36	24	35	59	....	....	....	109	....	....	....	....	....	....	....	....	....	....	7	4	1	5	30	....	....	....
1972-73	**New York Islanders**	**NHL**	8	0	1	1	0	1	1	18	0	0	0	2	0.0	2	0	7	0	–5	....	....	....	....	....	....	....	....
	New Haven Nighthawks	AHL	65	22	27	49	....	....	....	157	....	....	....	....	....	....	....	....	....	....	....	....	....	....	....	....	....	....
1973-74	**New York Islanders**	**NHL**	78	6	11	17	6	9	15	204	0	0	0	84	7.1	43	3	54	1	–13	....	....	....	....	....	....	....	....
1974-75	**New York Islanders**	**NHL**	77	18	30	48	17	24	41	121	1	0	3	126	14.3	75	5	38	0	+32	17	3	3	6	59	0	0	1
1975-76	**New York Islanders**	**NHL**	80	21	13	34	20	10	30	197	0	0	2	115	18.3	60	2	32	0	+26	13	5	5	10	23	0	0	1
1976-77	**New York Islanders**	**NHL**	70	13	15	28	12	12	24	182	1	0	4	91	14.3	48	3	31	0	+14	12	1	1	2	28	0	0	0
1977-78	**New York Islanders**	**NHL**	61	7	12	19	7	10	17	146	0	0	0	60	11.7	38	0	31	0	+7	7	0	1	1	62	0	0	0
1978-79	**New York Islanders**	**NHL**	75	16	12	28	15	9	24	205	0	0	2	81	19.8	49	1	43	1	+6	9	0	1	1	18	0	0	0
1979-80	**New York Islanders**	**NHL**	77	8	11	19	7	8	15	219	0	0	1	62	12.9	32	1	47	13	–3	21	3	1	4	84	0	0	1
1980-81	**New York Islanders**	**NHL**	70	4	15	19	3	10	13	174	0	0	0	48	8.3	33	1	20	0	+12	8	0	2	2	15	0	0	0
1981-82	**Hartford Whalers**	**NHL**	80	18	32	50	14	21	35	242	1	0	2	111	16.2	89	11	84	1	–5	....	....	....	....	....	....	....	....
1982-83	**New Jersey Devils**	**NHL**	38	1	4	5	1	3	4	114	0	0	0	30	3.3	9	1	41	4	–29	....	....	....	....	....	....	....	....
	Wichita Wind	CHL	11	0	5	5	....	....	....	4	....	....	....	....	....	....	....	....	....	....	....	....	....	....	....	....	....	....
1983-84	**New Jersey Devils**	**NHL**	6	0	0	0	0	0	0	14	0	0	0	5	0.0	2	0	4	1	–1	....	....	....	....	....	....	....	....
	Maine Mariners	AHL	63	12	20	32	....	....	....	124	....	....	....	....	....	....	....	....	....	....	17	4	7	11	46	....	....	....
	NHL Totals		**720**	**112**	**156**	**268**	**102**	**117**	**219**	**1836**	**3**	**0**	**14**	**815**	**13.7**	**480**	**28**	**432**	**21**		**87**	**12**	**14**	**26**	**289**	**0**	**0**	**3**

Traded to **Hartford** by **NY Islanders** for Hartford's 5th round choice (Bob Caulfield) in 1983 Entry Draft, October 2, 1981. Traded to **New Jersey** by **Hartford** with Rick Meagher for Morlin Malinowski and the rights to Scott Fusco, October 15, 1982.

• HOWE, GORDIE

Gordie "Mr. Hockey" Howe RW – R. 6', 205 lbs. b: Floral, Sask., 3/31/1928. **HHOF**

			REGULAR SEASON																		PLAYOFFS							
Season	Club	League	GP	G	A	Pts	AG	AA	APts	PIM	PP	SH	GW	S	%	TGF	PGF	TGA	PGA	+/–	GP	G	A	Pts	PIM	PP	SH	GW
1943-44	Saskatoon Lions	SJHL	5	6	*5	11	....	....	....	4	....	....	....	....	....	....	....	....	....	....	2	0	0	0	6	....	....	....
1944-45	Galt Red Wings	OHA	PLAYED EXHIBITION SEASON ONLY																									
1945-46	Omaha Knights	USHL	51	22	26	48	....	....	....	53	....	....	....	....	....	....	....	....	....	....	6	2	1	3	15	....	....	....
1946-47	**Detroit Red Wings**	**NHL**	58	7	15	22	9	21	30	52	....	....	....	....	....	....	....	....	....	....	5	0	0	0	18	....	....	....
1947-48	**Detroit Red Wings**	**NHL**	60	16	28	44	23	41	64	63	....	....	....	....	....	....	....	....	....	....	10	1	1	2	11	....	....	....
1948-49	**Detroit Red Wings**	**NHL**	40	12	25	37	19	40	59	57	....	....	....	....	....	....	....	....	....	....	11	*8	3	*11	19	....	....	....
1949-50	**Detroit Red Wings**	**NHL**	70	35	33	68	48	42	90	69	....	....	....	....	....	....	....	....	....	....	1	0	0	0	7	....	....	....
1950-51	**Detroit Red Wings**	**NHL**	70	*43	*43	*86	60	56	116	74	....	....	....	....	....	....	....	....	....	....	6	4	3	7	4	....	....	....
1951-52	**Detroit Red Wings**	**NHL**	70	*47	39	*86	68	51	119	78	....	....	....	....	....	....	....	....	....	....	8	2	*5	*7	2	....	....	....
1952-53	**Detroit Red Wings**	**NHL**	70	*49	*46	*95	78	65	143	57	....	....	....	....	....	....	....	....	....	....	6	2	5	7	2	....	....	....
1953-54	**Detroit Red Wings**	**NHL**	70	33	*48	*81	51	66	117	109	....	....	....	....	....	....	....	....	....	....	12	4	5	9	*31	....	....	....
1954-55	**Detroit Red Wings**	**NHL**	64	29	33	62	43	43	86	68	....	....	....	....	....	....	....	....	....	....	11	*9	*11	20	24	....	....	....
1955-56	**Detroit Red Wings**	**NHL**	70	38	41	79	56	52	108	100	....	....	....	....	....	....	....	....	....	....	10	3	9	12	8	....	....	....
1956-57	**Detroit Red Wings**	**NHL**	70	*44	45	*89	62	53	115	72	....	....	....	....	....	....	....	....	....	....	5	2	5	7	6	....	....	....
1957-58	**Detroit Red Wings**	**NHL**	64	33	44	77	44	48	92	40	....	....	....	....	....	....	....	....	....	....	4	1	1	2	0	....	....	....
1958-59	**Detroit Red Wings**	**NHL**	70	32	46	78	41	49	90	57	....	....	....	....	....	....	....	....	....	....	....	....	....	....	....	....	....	....
1959-60	**Detroit Red Wings**	**NHL**	70	28	45	73	35	47	82	46	....	....	....	....	....	....	....	....	....	....	6	1	5	6	4	....	....	....
1960-61	**Detroit Red Wings**	**NHL**	64	23	49	72	28	50	78	30	....	....	....	....	....	....	....	....	....	....	11	4	11	*15	10	....	....	....
1961-62	**Detroit Red Wings**	**NHL**	70	33	44	77	41	45	86	54	....	....	....	....	....	....	....	....	....	....	....	....	....	....	....	....	....	....
1962-63	**Detroit Red Wings**	**NHL**	70	*38	48	*86	48	51	99	100	....	....	....	....	....	....	....	....	....	....	11	7	9	*16	22	....	....	....
1963-64	**Detroit Red Wings**	**NHL**	69	26	47	73	35	53	88	70	....	....	....	....	....	....	....	....	....	....	14	*9	10	*19	16	....	....	....
1964-65	**Detroit Red Wings**	**NHL**	70	29	47	76	37	51	88	104	....	....	....	....	....	....	....	....	....	....	7	4	2	6	20	....	....	....
1965-66	**Detroit Red Wings**	**NHL**	70	29	46	75	35	47	82	83	....	....	....	....	....	....	....	....	....	....	12	4	6	10	12	....	....	....
1966-67	**Detroit Red Wings**	**NHL**	69	25	40	65	31	41	72	53	....	....	....	....	....	....	....	....	....	....	....	....	....	....	....	....	....	....
1967-68	**Detroit Red Wings**	**NHL**	74	39	43	82	49	45	94	53	10	0	4	301	13.0	117	34	83	12	+12	....	....	....	....	....	....	....	....
1968-69	**Detroit Red Wings**	**NHL**	76	44	59	103	50	56	106	58	9	0	6	283	15.5	134	35	66	12	+45	....	....	....	....	....	....	....	....
1969-70	**Detroit Red Wings**	**NHL**	76	31	40	71	36	40	76	58	11	4	5	268	11.6	105	38	54	10	+23	4	2	0	2	2	1	0	0
1970-71	**Detroit Red Wings**	**NHL**	63	23	29	52	24	20	50	38	7	1	3	195	11.8	76	24	65	11	–2	....	....	....	....	....	....	....	....
1971-72			DID NOT PLAY – RETIRED																									
1972-73			DID NOT PLAY – RETIRED																									
1973-74	Houston Aeros	WHA	70	31	69	100	....	....	....	46	....	....	....	....	....	....	....	....	....	....	13	3	*14	17	34	....	....	....
1974-75	Canada	Summit	7	3	4	7	....	....	....	2	....	....	....	....	....	....	....	....	....	....	....	....	....	....	....	....	....	....
	Houston Aeros	WHA	75	34	65	99	....	....	....	84	....	....	....	....	....	....	....	....	....	....	13	8	12	20	20	....	....	....
1975-76	Houston Aeros	WHA	78	32	70	102	....	....	....	76	....	....	....	....	....	....	....	....	....	....	17	4	8	12	31	....	....	....
1976-77	Houston Aeros	WHA	62	24	44	68	....	....	....	57	....	....	....	....	....	....	....	....	....	....	11	5	3	8	11	....	....	....
1977-78	New England Whalers	WHA	76	34	62	96	....	....	....	85	....	....	....	....	....	....	....	....	....	....	14	5	5	10	15	....	....	....
1978-79	New England Whalers	WHA	58	19	24	43	....	....	....	51	....	....	....	....	....	....	....	....	....	....	10	3	1	4	4	....	....	....
1979-80	**Hartford Whalers**	**NHL**	80	15	26	41	14	20	34	42	2	0	0	94	16.0	66	11	46	0	+9	3	1	1	2	2	0	0	0
1980-1997			DID NOT PLAY – RETIRED																									
1997-98	Detroit Vipers	IHL	1	0	0	0	....	....	....	0	....	....	....	....	....	....	....	....	....	....	....	....	....	....	....	....	....	....
	NHL Totals		**1767**	**801**	**1049**	**1850**	**1065**	**1199**	**2264**	**1685**	**39**	**5**	**18**	**1141**	**70.2**	**498**	**142**	**314**	**45**		**157**	**68**	**92**	**160**	**220**	**1**	**0**	**0**
	Other Major League Totals		419	174	334	508	....	....	....	399	....	....	....	....	....	....	....	....	....	....	78	28	43	71	115	....	....	....

USHL Second All-Star Team (1946) • NHL Second All-Star Team (1949, 1950, 1956, 1959, 1961, 1962, 1964, 1965, 1967) • NHL First All-Star Team (1951, 1952, 1953, 1954, 1957, 1958, 1960, 1963, 1966, 1968, 1969, 1970) • Won Art Ross Trophy (1951, 1952, 1953, 1954, 1957, 1963) • Won Hart Trophy (1952, 1953, 1957, 1958, 1960, 1963) • Won Lester Patrick Trophy (1967) • WHA First All-Star Team (1974, 1975) • Won Gary Davidson Trophy (WHA MVP) (1974)

Played in NHL All-Star Game (1948, 1949, 1950, 1951, 1952, 1953, 1954, 1955, 1957, 1958, 1959, 1960, 1961, 1962, 1963, 1964, 1965, 1967, 1968, 1969, 1970, 1971, 1980)

• Played exhibition schedule only with **Galt Red Wings** (OHA) in 1944-45 season because of inter-provincial transfer rules. Signed as a free agent by **Houston** (WHA), June, 1973. Signed as a free agent by **New England** (WHA), June, 1977. Rights retained by **Hartford** prior to Expansion Draft, June 9, 1979. Signed to one game contract by **Detroit Vipers** (IHL), September, 1997.

• HOWE, MARK

Mark Howe D – L. 5'11", 185 lbs. b: Detroit, MI, 5/28/1955. Boston's 2nd choice, 25th overall, in 1974 Amateur Draft.

			REGULAR SEASON																		PLAYOFFS							
Season	Club	League	GP	G	A	Pts	AG	AA	APts	PIM	PP	SH	GW	S	%	TGF	PGF	TGA	PGA	+/–	GP	G	A	Pts	PIM	PP	SH	GW
1970-71	Detroit Jr. Red Wings	SOHA	44	37	*70	*107	....	....	....	....	....	....	....	....	....	....	....	....	....	....	....	....	....	....	....	....	....	....
1971-72	Detroit Jr. Red Wings	SOHA	9	5	9	14	....	....	....	....	....	....	....	....	....	....	....	....	....	....	....	....	....	....	....	....	....	....
	United States	Olympics	6	0	0	0	....	....	....	0	....	....	....	....	....	....	....	....	....	....	....	....	....	....	....	....	....	....
1972-73	Toronto Marlboros	OHA	60	38	66	104	....	....	....	27	....	....	....	....	....	....	....	....	....	....	....	....	....	....	....	....	....	....
1973-74	Houston Aeros	WHA	76	38	41	79	....	....	....	20	....	....	....	....	....	....	....	....	....	....	14	9	10	19	4	....	....	....
1974-75	Canada	Summit	7	2	4	6	....	....	....	4	....	....	....	....	....	....	....	....	....	....	....	....	....	....	....	....	....	....
	Houston Aeros	WHA	74	36	40	76	....	....	....	30	....	....	....	....	....	....	....	....	....	....	13	*10	12	*22	0	....	....	....

			REGULAR SEASON																		PLAYOFFS							
Season	Club	League	GP	G	A	Pts	AG	AA	APts	PIM	PP	SH	GW	S	%	TGF	PGF	TGA	PGA	+/–	GP	G	A	Pts	PIM	PP	SH	GW
1975-76	Houston Aeros	WHA	72	39	37	76	....	....	....	38	....	....	....	....	....	....	....	....	....	....	17	6	10	16	18	....	....	....
1976-77	Houston Aeros	WHA	57	23	52	75	....	....	....	46	....	....	....	....	....	....	....	....	....	....	10	4	10	14	2	....	....	....
1977-78	New England Whalers	WHA	70	30	61	91	....	....	....	32	....	....	....	....	....	....	....	....	....	....	14	8	7	15	18	....	....	....
1978-79	New England Whalers	WHA	77	42	65	107	....	....	....	32	....	....	....	....	....	....	....	....	....	....	6	4	2	6	6	....	....	....
1979-80	**Hartford Whalers**	NHL	74	24	56	80	22	43	65	20	5	2	3	178	13.5	137	32	120	29	+14	3	1	2	3	2	0	0	0
1980-81	**Hartford Whalers**	NHL	63	19	46	65	16	32	48	54	7	2	3	172	11.0	137	38	118	29	+10	....	....	....	....	....	....	....	....
1981-82	United States	C Cup	6	0	4	4	....	....	....	2	....	....	....	....	....	....	....	....	....	....	....	....	....	....	....	....	....	....
	Hartford Whalers	NHL	76	8	45	53	6	30	36	18	3	0	1	220	3.6	127	41	119	25	–8	....	....	....	....	....	....	....	....
1982-83	**Philadelphia Flyers**	NHL	76	20	47	67	16	32	48	18	5	5	4	219	9.1	148	40	78	17	+47	3	0	2	2	4	0	0	0
1983-84	**Philadelphia Flyers**	NHL	71	19	34	53	15	23	38	44	3	3	2	184	10.3	114	28	82	26	+30	3	0	0	0	2	0	0	0
1984-85	**Philadelphia Flyers**	NHL	73	18	39	57	15	26	41	31	3	2	1	213	8.5	146	29	98	32	+51	19	3	8	11	6	1	0	1
1985-86	**Philadelphia Flyers**	NHL	77	24	58	82	19	39	58	36	4	7	3	193	12.4	188	46	93	36	+85	5	0	4	4	0	0	0	0
1986-87	**Philadelphia Flyers**	NHL	69	15	43	58	13	31	44	37	2	4	0	148	10.1	152	42	82	29	+57	26	2	10	12	4	0	0	0
1987-88	**Philadelphia Flyers**	NHL	75	19	43	62	16	31	47	62	8	1	4	177	10.7	137	47	108	41	+23	7	3	6	9	4	0	0	0
1988-89	**Philadelphia Flyers**	NHL	52	9	29	38	8	20	28	45	5	1	1	95	9.5	97	44	73	27	+7	19	0	15	15	10	0	0	0
1989-90	**Philadelphia Flyers**	NHL	40	7	21	28	6	15	21	24	3	1	1	63	11.1	65	16	45	18	+22	....	....	....	....	....	....	....	....
1990-91	**Philadelphia Flyers**	NHL	19	0	10	10	0	8	8	8	0	0	0	40	0.0	29	9	23	12	+9	....	....	....	....	....	....	....	....
1991-92	**Philadelphia Flyers**	NHL	42	7	18	25	6	14	20	18	6	0	0	63	11.1	65	20	40	13	+18	....	....	....	....	....	....	....	....
1992-93	**Detroit Red Wings**	NHL	60	3	31	34	2	21	23	22	3	0	0	72	4.2	88	29	52	15	+22	7	1	3	4	2	0	0	0
1993-94	**Detroit Red Wings**	NHL	44	4	20	24	4	15	19	8	1	0	0	72	5.6	54	9	36	7	+16	6	0	1	1	0	0	0	0
1994-95	**Detroit Red Wings**	NHL	18	1	5	6	2	7	9	10	0	0	1	14	7.1	12	6	11	2	–3	3	0	0	0	0	0	0	0
	NHL Totals		929	197	545	742	166	387	553	455	58	28	24	2123	9.3	1696	476	1178	358		101	10	51	61	34	1	0	1
	Other Major League Totals		426	208	296	504	....	....	....	198	....	....	....	....	....	....	....	....	....		74	41	51	92	48	....	....	....

Won Stafford Smythe Memorial Trophy (Memorial Cup Tournament MVP) (1973) • WHA Second All-Star Team (1974) • Won Lou Kaplan Trophy (WHA Rookie of the Year) (1974) • WHA First All-Star Team (1979) • NHL First All-Star Team (1983, 1986, 1987) • NHL Plus/Minus Leader (1986)

Played in NHL All-Star Game (1981, 1983, 1986, 1988)

Selected by **Houston** (WHA) in 1973 WHA Professional Player Draft, June, 1973. Signed as a free agent by **New England** (WHA), June, 1977. Reclaimed by **Boston** from **Hartford** prior to Expansion Draft, June 9, 1979. Claimed as a priority selection by **Hartford**, June 9, 1979. Traded to **Philadelphia** by **Hartford** with Hartford's 3rd round choice (Derrick Smith) for Ken Linseman, Greg Adams and Philadelphia's 1st round choice (David Jensen) and 3rd round choice (Leif Karlsson) in 1982 Entry Draft, August 19, 1982. Signed as a free agent by **Detroit**, July 7, 1992.

• HOWE, MARTY

Marty Howe D – L. 6'1", 195 lbs. b: Detroit, MI, 2/18/1954. Montreal's 2nd choice, 51st overall, in 1974 Amateur Draft.

Season	Club	League	GP	G	A	Pts	AG	AA	APts	PIM	PP	SH	GW	S	%	TGF	PGF	TGA	PGA	+/–	GP	G	A	Pts	PIM	PP	SH	GW
1970-71	Detroit Jr. Red Wings	SOHA	STATISTICS NOT AVAILABLE																									
1971-72	Toronto Marlboros	OHA	56	7	21	28	....	....	....	122	....	....	....	....	....	....	....	....	....	....	....	....	....	....	....	....	....	....
1972-73	Toronto Marlboros	OHA	38	11	17	28	....	....	....	81	....	....	....	....	....	....	....	....	....	....	....	....	....	....	....	....	....	....
1973-74	Houston Aeros	WHA	73	4	20	24	....	....	....	90	....	....	....	....	....	....	....	....	....	....	14	1	5	6	31	....	....	....
1974-75	Canada	Summit	4	0	0	0	....	....	....	12	....	....	....	....	....	....	....	....	....	....	....	....	....	....	....	....	....	....
	Houston Aeros	WHA	75	13	21	34	....	....	....	89	....	....	....	....	....	....	....	....	....	....	11	0	2	2	11	....	....	....
1975-76	Houston Aeros	WHA	80	14	23	37	....	....	....	81	....	....	....	....	....	....	....	....	....	....	16	4	4	8	12	....	....	....
1976-77	Houston Aeros	WHA	80	17	28	45	....	....	....	103	....	....	....	....	....	....	....	....	....	....	11	3	1	4	10	....	....	....
1977-78	New England Whalers	WHA	75	10	10	20	....	....	....	66	....	....	....	....	....	....	....	....	....	....	14	1	1	2	13	....	....	....
1978-79	New England Whalers	WHA	66	9	15	24	....	....	....	31	....	....	....	....	....	....	....	....	....	....	9	0	1	1	8	....	....	....
1979-80	**Hartford Whalers**	NHL	6	0	1	1	0	1	1	4	0	0	0	6	0.0	4	0	6	0	–2	3	1	1	2	0	0	0	0
	Springfield Indians	AHL	31	8	5	13	....	....	....	12	....	....	....	....	....	....	....	....	....	....	....	....	....	....	....	....	....	....
1980-81	**Hartford Whalers**	NHL	12	0	1	1	0	1	1	25	0	0	0	3	0.0	6	1	12	2	–5	....	....	....	....	....	....	....	....
	Binghamton Whalers	AHL	37	4	10	14	....	....	....	34	....	....	....	....	....	....	....	....	....	....	6	0	2	2	6	....	....	....
1981-82	**Hartford Whalers**	NHL	13	0	4	4	0	3	3	2	0	0	0	25	0.0	16	4	21	5	–4	....	....	....	....	....	....	....	....
	Binghamton Whalers	AHL	61	8	38	46	....	....	....	42	....	....	....	....	....	....	....	....	....	....	15	0	8	8	4	....	....	....
1982-83	**Boston Bruins**	NHL	78	1	11	12	1	8	9	24	0	0	0	68	1.5	59	0	38	0	+21	12	0	1	1	9	0	0	0
1983-84	**Hartford Whalers**	NHL	69	0	11	11	0	7	7	34	0	0	0	58	0.0	58	4	60	7	+1	....	....	....	....	....	....	....	....
1984-85	**Hartford Whalers**	NHL	19	1	1	2	1	1	2	10	0	0	0	23	4.3	19	2	25	4	–4	....	....	....	....	....	....	....	....
	Binghamton Whalers	AHL	44	7	12	19	....	....	....	22	....	....	....	....	....	....	....	....	....	....	8	3	2	5	6	....	....	....
1985-1992			DID NOT PLAY – RETIRED																									
1992-93	Flint Bulldogs	ColHL	3	0	1	1	....	....	....	4	....	....	....	....	....	....	....	....	....	....	....	....	....	....	....	....	....	....
	NHL Totals		197	2	29	31	2	21	23	99	0	0	0	183	1.1	162	11	162	18		15	1	2	3	9	0	0	0
	Other Major League Totals		449	67	117	184	....	....	....	460	....	....	....	....	....	....	....	....	....		75	9	14	23	85	....	....	....

WHA Second All-Star Team (1977)

Selected by **Houston** (WHA) in 1973 WHA Professional Player Draft, June, 1973. Rights traded to **Detroit** by **Montreal** for cash and future considerations, February 25, 1977. Signed as a free agent by **New England** (WHA), June, 1977. Rights retained by **Hartford** prior to Expansion Draft, June 9, 1979. Traded to **Boston** by **Hartford** for future considerations, October 1, 1982. Traded to **Hartford** by **Boston** for future considerations, September 29, 1983.

• HOWELL, HARRY

Harry Howell D – L. 6'1", 195 lbs. b: Hamilton, Ont., 12/28/1932. **HHOF**

Season	Club	League	GP	G	A	Pts	AG	AA	APts	PIM	PP	SH	GW	S	%	TGF	PGF	TGA	PGA	+/–	GP	G	A	Pts	PIM	PP	SH	GW
1949-50	Guelph Biltmores	OHA	3	0	1	1	....	....	....	2	....	....	....	....	....	....	....	....	....	....	5	0	1	1	14	....	....	....
1950-51	Guelph Biltmores	OHA	50	6	16	22	....	....	....	77	....	....	....	....	....	....	....	....	....	....	5	1	0	1	6	....	....	....
1951-52	Guelph Biltmores	OHA	51	17	20	37	....	....	....	79	....	....	....	....	....	....	....	....	....	....	23	7	9	16	36	....	....	....
	Cincinnati Mohawks	AHL	1	0	0	0	....	....	....	0	....	....	....	....	....	....	....	....	....	....	....	....	....	....	....	....	....	....
1952-53	**New York Rangers**	NHL	67	3	8	11	5	11	16	46	....	....	....	....	....	....	....	....	....	....	....	....	....	....	....	....	....	....
1953-54	**New York Rangers**	NHL	67	7	9	16	11	12	23	58	....	....	....	....	....	....	....	....	....	....	....	....	....	....	....	....	....	....
1954-55	**New York Rangers**	NHL	70	2	14	16	3	18	21	87	....	....	....	....	....	....	....	....	....	....	....	....	....	....	....	....	....	....
1955-56	**New York Rangers**	NHL	70	3	15	18	4	19	23	77	....	....	....	....	....	....	....	....	....	....	5	0	1	1	4	....	....	....
1956-57	**New York Rangers**	NHL	65	2	10	12	3	12	15	70	....	....	....	....	....	....	....	....	....	....	5	1	0	1	6	....	....	....
1957-58	**New York Rangers**	NHL	70	4	7	11	5	8	13	62	....	....	....	....	....	....	....	....	....	....	6	1	0	1	8	....	....	....
1958-59	**New York Rangers**	NHL	70	4	10	14	5	11	16	101	....	....	....	....	....	....	....	....	....	....	....	....	....	....	....	....	....	....
1959-60	**New York Rangers**	NHL	67	7	6	13	9	6	15	58	....	....	....	....	....	....	....	....	....	....	....	....	....	....	....	....	....	....
1960-61	**New York Rangers**	NHL	70	7	10	17	8	10	18	62	....	....	....	....	....	....	....	....	....	....	....	....	....	....	....	....	....	....
1961-62	**New York Rangers**	NHL	66	6	15	21	7	15	22	89	....	....	....	....	....	....	....	....	....	....	6	0	1	1	8	....	....	....
1962-63	**New York Rangers**	NHL	70	5	20	25	6	21	27	55	....	....	....	....	....	....	....	....	....	....	....	....	....	....	....	....	....	....
1963-64	**New York Rangers**	NHL	70	5	31	36	7	34	41	75	....	....	....	....	....	....	....	....	....	....	....	....	....	....	....	....	....	....
1964-65	**New York Rangers**	NHL	68	2	20	22	3	22	25	63	....	....	....	....	....	....	....	....	....	....	....	....	....	....	....	....	....	....
1965-66	**New York Rangers**	NHL	70	4	29	33	5	29	34	92	....	....	....	....	....	....	....	....	....	....	....	....	....	....	....	....	....	....
1966-67	**New York Rangers**	NHL	70	12	28	40	15	29	44	54	....	....	....	....	....	....	....	....	....	....	4	0	0	0	4	....	....	....
1967-68	**New York Rangers**	NHL	74	5	24	29	6	25	31	62	1	0	2	220	2.3	102	17	99	26	+12	6	1	0	1	0	1	0	1
1968-69	**New York Rangers**	NHL	56	4	7	11	4	7	11	36	1	0	1	140	2.9	63	13	59	11	+2	2	0	0	0	0	0	0	0
1969-70	**Oakland Seals**	NHL	55	4	16	20	5	16	21	52	3	0	3	147	2.7	57	15	75	19	–14	4	0	1	1	2	0	0	0
1970-71	**California Golden Seals**	NHL	28	0	9	9	0	8	8	14	0	0	0	51	0.0	17	4	44	11	–20	....	....	....	....	....	....	....	....
	Los Angeles Kings	NHL	18	3	8	11	3	7	10	4	1	0	0	33	9.1	25	5	23	4	+1	....	....	....	....	....	....	....	....
1971-72	**Los Angeles Kings**	NHL	77	1	17	18	1	15	16	53	0	0	0	138	0.7	83	5	139	27	–34	....	....	....	....	....	....	....	....
1972-73	**Los Angeles Kings**	NHL	73	4	11	15	4	9	13	28	0	0	0	97	4.1	64	4	68	4	–4	....	....	....	....	....	....	....	....
1973-74	New York-New Jersey	WHA	65	3	23	26	....	....	....	24	....	....	....	....	....	....	....	....	....	....	....	....	....	....	....	....	....	....
1974-75	San Diego Mariners	WHA	74	4	10	14	....	....	....	28	....	....	....	....	....	....	....	....	....	....	5	1	0	1	10	....	....	....
1975-76	Calgary Cowboys	WHA	31	0	3	3	....	....	....	6	....	....	....	....	....	....	....	....	....	....	2	0	0	0	2	....	....	....
	NHL Totals		1411	94	324	418	119	344	463	1298	6	0	6	826	11.4	411	63	507	102		38	3	3	6	32	1	0	1
	Other Major League Totals		170	7	36	43	....	....	....	58	....	....	....	....	....	....	....	....	....		7	1	0	1	12	....	....	....

NHL First All-Star Team (1967) • Won James Norris Trophy (1967)

Played in NHL All-Star Game (1954, 1963, 1964, 1965, 1967, 1968, 1970)

Claimed by **Oakland** from **NY Rangers** in Expansion Draft, June 6, 1967. Traded to **LA Kings** by **California** for cash, February 5, 1971. Selected by **NY Raiders** (WHA) in 1972 WHA General Player Draft, February 12, 1972. Transferred to **San Diego** (WHA) after **New York-New Jersey** (WHA) franchise relocated, April 30, 1974. Signed as a free agent by **Calgary** (WHA), January, 1976.

			REGULAR SEASON																		PLAYOFFS							
Season	Club	League	GP	G	A	Pts	AG	AA	APts	PIM	PP	SH	GW	S	%	TGF	PGF	TGA	PGA	+/–	GP	G	A	Pts	PIM	PP	SH	GW

● HOWSE, DON Don Howse LW – L. 6′, 182 lbs. b: Grand Falls, Nfld., 7/28/1952.

1968-69	Grand Falls Cataracts	Nfld.	STATISTICS NOT AVAILABLE																									
1969-70	Ottawa 67's	OHA	50	3	3	6	....	....	....	4	....	....	....	....	....	....	....	....	....	....	....	....	....	....	....	....	....	....
1970-71	Ottawa 67's	OHA	58	5	12	17	....	....	....	4	....	....	....	....	....	....	....	....	....	....	....	....	....	....	....	....	....	....
1971-72	Grand Falls Flyers	Nfld.	STATISTICS NOT AVAILABLE																									
1972-73	Greensboro Generals	EHL	64	35	54	89	....	....	....	39	....	....	....	....	....	....	....	....	....	....	7	0	2	2	0	....	....	....
1973-74	Nova Scotia Voyageurs	AHL	40	6	12	18	....	....	....	2	....	....	....	....	....	....	....	....	....	....	5	0	3	3	9	....	....	....
1974-75	Nova Scotia Voyageurs	AHL	68	30	43	73	....	....	....	50	....	....	....	....	....	....	....	....	....	....	6	1	1	2	2	....	....	....
1975-76	Nova Scotia Voyageurs	AHL	68	24	36	60	....	....	....	34	....	....	....	....	....	....	....	....	....	....	9	2	5	7	9	....	....	....
1976-77	Nova Scotia Voyageurs	AHL	58	13	24	37	....	....	....	39	....	....	....	....	....	....	....	....	....	....	12	2	3	5	8	....	....	....
1977-78	Nova Scotia Voyageurs	AHL	48	7	22	29	....	....	....	12	....	....	....	....	....	....	....	....	....	....	11	1	3	4	18	....	....	....
1978-79	Nova Scotia Voyageurs	AHL	58	19	15	34	....	....	....	65	....	....	....	....	....	....	....	....	....	....	10	4	3	7	6	....	....	....
1979-80	Binghamton Whalers	AHL	38	12	30	42	....	....	....	32	....	....	....	....	....	....	....	....	....	....	....	....	....	....	....	....	....	....
	Los Angeles Kings	**NHL**	**33**	**2**	**5**	**7**	**2**	**4**	**6**	**6**	**0**	**0**	**0**	**46**	**4.3**	**10**	**1**	**36**	**11**	**–16**	**2**	**0**	**0**	**0**	**0**	**0**	**0**	**0**
1980-81	Houston Apollos	CHL	33	5	9	14	....	....	....	27	....	....	....	....	....	....	....	....	....	....	....	....	....	....	....	....	....	....
	Hershey Bears	AHL	37	9	10	19	....	....	....	22	....	....	....	....	....	....	....	....	....	....	10	1	4	5	11	....	....	....
1981-82	Port-aux-Basques Mariners	Nfld.	STATISTICS NOT AVAILABLE																									
	Stephenville Jets	Nfld.	DID NOT PLAY – COACHING																									
	NHL Totals		**33**	**2**	**5**	**7**	**2**	**4**	**6**	**6**	**0**	**0**	**0**	**46**	**4.3**	**10**	**1**	**36**	**11**		**2**	**0**	**0**	**0**	**0**	**0**	**0**	**0**

Signed as a free agent by **Montreal**, June, 1973. Signed as a free agent by **LA Kings**, October, 1979.

● HOWSON, SCOTT Scott (Donald) Howson C – R. 5′11″, 160 lbs. b: Toronto, Ont., 4/9/1960.

1977-78	North York Rangers	OJHL	55	27	31	58	....	....	....	30	....	....	....	....	....	....	....	....	....	....	....	....	....	....	....	....	....	....
1978-79	Kingston Canadians	OHA	58	27	47	74	....	....	....	45	....	....	....	....	....	....	....	....	....	....	11	0	10	10	12	....	....	....
1979-80	Kingston Canadians	OHA	68	38	50	88	....	....	....	52	....	....	....	....	....	....	....	....	....	....	3	0	4	4	0	....	....	....
1980-81	Kingston Canadians	OHA	66	57	83	140	....	....	....	53	....	....	....	....	....	....	....	....	....	....	14	9	10	19	2	....	....	....
1981-82	Indianapolis Checkers	CHL	8	2	1	3	....	....	....	5	....	....	....	....	....	....	....	....	....	....	....	....	....	....	....	....	....	....
	Toledo Goaldiggers	IHL	71	55	65	120	....	....	....	14	....	....	....	....	....	....	....	....	....	....	12	10	9	19	6	....	....	....
1982-83	Indianapolis Checkers	CHL	67	34	40	74	....	....	....	22	....	....	....	....	....	....	....	....	....	....	13	12	9	21	21	....	....	....
1983-84	Indianapolis Checkers	CHL	71	34	34	68	....	....	....	40	....	....	....	....	....	....	....	....	....	....	7	1	3	4	2	....	....	....
1984-85	**New York Islanders**	**NHL**	**8**	**4**	**1**	**5**	**3**	**1**	**4**	**2**	**1**	**0**	**0**	**6**	**66.7**	**6**	**1**	**1**	**0**	**+4**	....	....	....	....	....	....	....	....
	Springfield Indians	AHL	57	20	40	60	....	....	....	31	....	....	....	....	....	....	....	....	....	....	4	1	3	4	2	....	....	....
1985-86	**New York Islanders**	**NHL**	**10**	**1**	**2**	**3**	**1**	**1**	**2**	**2**	**0**	**0**	**0**	**8**	**12.5**	**4**	**0**	**2**	**0**	**+2**	....	....	....	....	....	....	....	....
	Springfield Indians	AHL	53	15	19	34	....	....	....	10	....	....	....	....	....	....	....	....	....	....	....	....	....	....	....	....	....	....
	NHL Totals		**18**	**5**	**3**	**8**	**4**	**2**	**6**	**4**	**1**	**0**	**0**	**14**	**35.7**	**10**	**1**	**3**	**0**		....	....	....	....	....	....	....	....

Won Garry F. Longman Memorial Trophy (Top Rookie - IHL) (1982)
Signed as a free agent by **NY Islanders**, August 25, 1981.

● HOYDA, DAVE Dave Hoyda LW – L. 6′1″, 205 lbs. b: Edmonton, Alta., 5/20/1957. Philadelphia's 3rd choice, 53rd overall, in 1977 Amateur Draft.

1973-74	Edmonton Mets	AJHL	28	0	1	1	....	....	....	56	....	....	....	....	....	....	....	....	....	....	....	....	....	....	....	....	....	....
1974-75	Edmonton Oil Kings	WCJHL	1	0	0	0	....	....	....	2	....	....	....	....	....	....	....	....	....	....	....	....	....	....	....	....	....	....
	Spruce Grove Mets	AJHL	59	25	31	56	....	....	....	141	....	....	....	....	....	....	....	....	....	....	12	7	6	13	42	....	....	....
1975-76	Spruce Grove Mets	AJHL	4	3	3	6	....	....	....	37	....	....	....	....	....	....	....	....	....	....	....	....	....	....	....	....	....	....
	Edmonton Oil Kings	WCJHL	43	5	18	23	....	....	....	170	....	....	....	....	....	....	....	....	....	....	5	0	1	1	23	....	....	....
1976-77	Portland Winterhawks	WCJHL	61	16	26	42	....	....	....	220	....	....	....	....	....	....	....	....	....	....	....	....	....	....	....	....	....	....
1977-78	**Philadelphia Flyers**	**NHL**	**41**	**1**	**3**	**4**	**1**	**2**	**3**	**119**	**0**	**0**	**0**	**8**	**12.5**	**7**	**0**	**12**	**0**	**–5**	**9**	**0**	**0**	**0**	**17**	**0**	**0**	**0**
	Maine Mariners	AHL	31	4	5	9	....	....	....	112	....	....	....	....	....	....	....	....	....	....	....	....	....	....	....	....	....	....
1978-79	**Philadelphia Flyers**	**NHL**	**67**	**3**	**13**	**16**	**3**	**10**	**13**	**130**	**0**	**0**	**0**	**37**	**8.1**	**28**	**0**	**26**	**0**	**+2**	**3**	**0**	**0**	**0**	**0**	**0**	**0**	**0**
1979-80	**Winnipeg Jets**	**NHL**	**15**	**1**	**1**	**2**	**1**	**1**	**2**	**35**	**0**	**0**	**0**	**7**	**14.3**	**2**	**0**	**0**	**0**	**–4**	....	....	....	....	....	....	....	....
	Tulsa Oilers	CHL	32	11	6	17	....	....	....	89	....	....	....	....	....	....	....	....	....	....	....	....	....	....	....	....	....	....
1980-81	**Winnipeg Jets**	**NHL**	**9**	**1**	**0**	**1**	**1**	**0**	**1**	**7**	**0**	**0**	**0**	**2**	**50.0**	**3**	**0**	**3**	**0**	**0**	....	....	....	....	....	....	....	....
	Tulsa Oilers	CHL	42	13	22	35	....	....	....	118	....	....	....	....	....	....	....	....	....	....	....	....	....	....	....	....	....	....
	NHL Totals		**132**	**6**	**17**	**23**	**6**	**13**	**19**	**299**	**0**	**0**	**0**	**54**	**11.1**	**40**	**0**	**47**	**0**		**12**	**0**	**0**	**0**	**17**	**0**	**0**	**0**

Claimed by **Winnipeg** from **Philadelphia** in Expansion Draft, June 13, 1979.

● HRDINA, JIRI Jiri Hrdina C – L. 6′, 195 lbs. b: Prague, Czech., 1/5/1958. Calgary's 8th choice, 159th overall, in 1984 Entry Draft.

1980-81	Sparta Praha	Czech.	42	14	20	34	....	....	....	....	....	....	....	....	....	....	....	....	....	....	....	....	....	....	....	....	....	....
1981-82	Dukla Trencin	Czech.	44	11	27	38	....	....	....	36	....	....	....	....	....	....	....	....	....	....	....	....	....	....	....	....	....	....
	Czechoslovakia	WEC-A	9	1	0	1	....	....	....	4	....	....	....	....	....	....	....	....	....	....	....	....	....	....	....	....	....	....
1982-83	Czechoslovakia	WEC-A	9	1	0	1	....	....	....	4	....	....	....	....	....	....	....	....	....	....	....	....	....	....	....	....	....	....
1983-84	Czechoslovakia	Olympics	7	4	6	10	....	....	....	10	....	....	....	....	....	....	....	....	....	....	....	....	....	....	....	....	....	....
1984-85	Czechoslovakia	C Cup	5	0	1	1	....	....	....	4	....	....	....	....	....	....	....	....	....	....	....	....	....	....	....	....	....	....
	Czechoslovakia	WEC-A	10	2	2	4	....	....	....	4	....	....	....	....	....	....	....	....	....	....	....	....	....	....	....	....	....	....
1985-86	Sparta Praha	Czech.	44	18	19	37	....	....	....	30	....	....	....	....	....	....	....	....	....	....	....	....	....	....	....	....	....	....
	Czechoslovakia	WEC-A	10	7	5	12	....	....	....	14	....	....	....	....	....	....	....	....	....	....	....	....	....	....	....	....	....	....
1986-87	Sparta Praha	Czech.	31	18	18	36	....	....	....	24	....	....	....	....	....	....	....	....	....	....	....	....	....	....	....	....	....	....
	Czechoslovakia	WEC-A	10	3	3	6	....	....	....	6	....	....	....	....	....	....	....	....	....	....	....	....	....	....	....	....	....	....
1987-88	Czechoslovakia	C Cup	6	1	2	3	....	....	....	0	....	....	....	....	....	....	....	....	....	....	....	....	....	....	....	....	....	....
	Sparta Praha	Czech.	22	7	15	22	....	....	....	0	....	....	....	....	....	....	....	....	....	....	....	....	....	....	....	....	....	....
	Czechoslovakia	Olympics	8	2	5	7	....	....	....	4	....	....	....	....	....	....	....	....	....	....	....	....	....	....	....	....	....	....
	Calgary Flames	**NHL**	**9**	**2**	**5**	**7**	**2**	**4**	**6**	**2**	**0**	**0**	**0**	**13**	**15.4**	**11**	**1**	**3**	**0**	**+7**	**1**	**0**	**0**	**0**	**0**	**0**	**0**	**0**
1988-89	**Calgary Flames**	**NHL**	**70**	**22**	**32**	**54**	**19**	**22**	**41**	**26**	**6**	**0**	**2**	**147**	**15.0**	**85**	**37**	**29**	**0**	**+19**	**4**	**0**	**0**	**0**	**0**	**0**	**0**	**0**
1989-90	Calgary Flames	FrTour	3	1	0	1	....	....	....	0	....	....	....	....	....	....	....	....	....	....	....	....	....	....	....	....	....	....
	Calgary Flames	**NHL**	**64**	**12**	**18**	**30**	**10**	**13**	**23**	**31**	**0**	**0**	**3**	**96**	**12.5**	**48**	**7**	**33**	**2**	**+10**	**6**	**0**	**1**	**1**	**2**	**0**	**0**	**0**
	Czechoslovakia	WEC-A	9	1	5	6	....	....	....	8	....	....	....	....	....	....	....	....	....	....	....	....	....	....	....	....	....	....
1990-91	**Calgary Flames**	**NHL**	**14**	**0**	**3**	**3**	**0**	**2**	**2**	**4**	**0**	**0**	**0**	**8**	**0.0**	**5**	**0**	**9**	**0**	**–4**	....	....	....	....	....	....	....	....
	Pittsburgh Penguins	**NHL**	**37**	**6**	**14**	**20**	**5**	**11**	**16**	**13**	**1**	**1**	**0**	**58**	**10.3**	**34**	**7**	**32**	**3**	**–2**	**14**	**2**	**2**	**4**	**6**	**0**	**0**	**1**
1991-92	**Pittsburgh Penguins**	**NHL**	**56**	**3**	**13**	**16**	**3**	**10**	**13**	**16**	**0**	**0**	**1**	**51**	**5.9**	**31**	**0**	**30**	**3**	**+4**	**21**	**0**	**2**	**2**	**16**	**0**	**0**	**0**
	NHL Totals		**250**	**45**	**85**	**130**	**39**	**62**	**101**	**92**	**7**	**1**	**6**	**373**	**12.1**	**214**	**52**	**136**	**8**		**46**	**2**	**5**	**7**	**24**	**0**	**0**	**1**

Traded to **Pittsburgh** by **Calgary** for Jim Kyte, December 13, 1990.

● HRECHKOSY, DAVE Dave Hrechkosy LW – L. 6′2″, 195 lbs. b: Winnipeg, Man., 11/1/1957.

1969-70	West Kildonen North Stars	MJHL	....	28	15	43	....	....	....	36	....	....	....	....	....	....	....	....	....	....	....	....	....	....	....	....	....	....
1970-71	Winnipeg Jets	WCJHL	57	16	21	37	....	....	....	70	....	....	....	....	....	....	....	....	....	....	....	....	....	....	....	....	....	....
1971-72	New Haven Blades	EHL	75	31	34	65	....	....	....	66	....	....	....	....	....	....	....	....	....	....	7	4	5	9	16	....	....	....
	Providence Reds	AHL	7	3	0	3	....	....	....	2	....	....	....	....	....	....	....	....	....	....	....	....	....	....	....	....	....	....
1972-73	Rochester Americans	AHL	70	15	24	39	....	....	....	48	....	....	....	....	....	....	....	....	....	....	4	0	2	2	8	....	....	....
1973-74	**California Golden Seals**	**NHL**	**2**	**0**	**0**	**0**	**0**	**0**	**0**	**0**	**0**	**0**	**0**	**3**	**0.0**	**1**	**0**	**0**	**0**	**+1**	....	....	....	....	....	....	....	....
	Salt Lake Golden Eagles	WHL	78	36	35	71	....	....	....	58	....	....	....	....	....	....	....	....	....	....	5	2	1	3	10	....	....	....
1974-75	**California Golden Seals**	**NHL**	**72**	**29**	**14**	**43**	**27**	**11**	**38**	**25**	**8**	**2**	**6**	**178**	**16.3**	**56**	**12**	**63**	**2**	**–17**	....	....	....	....	....	....	....	....
1975-76	**California Golden Seals**	**NHL**	**38**	**9**	**5**	**14**	**8**	**4**	**12**	**14**	**4**	**0**	**1**	**75**	**12.0**	**26**	**10**	**31**	**0**	**–15**	....	....	....	....	....	....	....	....
	Salt Lake City Golden Eagles	CHL	16	8	3	11	....	....	....	6	....	....	....	....	....	....	....	....	....	....	....	....	....	....	....	....	....	....
	St. Louis Blues	**NHL**	**13**	**3**	**3**	**6**	**3**	**2**	**5**	**0**	**1**	**0**	**0**	**20**	**15.0**	**12**	**4**	**6**	**0**	**+2**	**3**	**1**	**0**	**1**	**2**	**0**	**0**	**0**
1976-77	**St. Louis Blues**	**NHL**	**15**	**1**	**2**	**3**	**1**	**2**	**3**	**2**	**0**	**0**	**0**	**9**	**11.1**	**5**	**1**	**4**	**0**	**0**	....	....	....	....	....	....	....	....
	Kansas City Blues	CHL	45	9	12	21	....	....	....	4	....	....	....	....	....	....	....	....	....	....	10	3	3	6	0	....	....	....
1977-78	Salt Lake Golden Eagles	CHL	55	5	12	17	....	....	....	11	....	....	....	....	....	....	....	....	....	....	....	....	....	....	....	....	....	....

			REGULAR SEASON																		PLAYOFFS							
Season	Club	League	GP	G	A	Pts	AG	AA	APts	PIM	PP	SH	GW	S	%	TGF	PGF	TGA	PGA	+/–	GP	G	A	Pts	PIM	PP	SH	GW
1978-79	Saginaw Gears	IHL	2	0	2	2	....	....	....	0	....	....	....	....	....	....	....	....	....	....	....	....	....	....	....	....	....	....
	New Haven Nighthawks	AHL	61	15	20	35	....	....	....	21	....	....	....	....	....	....	....	....	....	....	10	6	7	13	8	....	....	....
1979-80	New Haven Nighthawks	AHL	1	0	0	0	....	....	....	0	....	....	....	....	....	....	....	....	....	....	....	....	....	....	....	....	....	....
	NHL Totals		**140**	**42**	**24**	**66**	**39**	**19**	**58**	**41**	**13**	**2**	**7**	**285**	**14.7**	**100**	**27**	**104**	**2**		**3**	**1**	**0**	**1**	**2**	**0**	**0**	**0**

Signed as a free agent by **California**, September, 1973. Traded to **St. Louis** by **California** for St. Louis' 5th round choice (Cal Sandbeck) in 1976 Amateur Draft and California's 3rd round choice (previously acquired, California selected Reg Kerr) in 1977 Amateur Draft, March 9, 1976.

• HRKAC, TONY

Tony Hrkac C – L. 5'11", 170 lbs. b: Thunder Bay, Ont., 7/7/1966. St. Louis' 2nd choice, 32nd overall, in 1984 Entry Draft.

Season	Club	League	GP	G	A	Pts	AG	AA	APts	PIM	PP	SH	GW	S	%	TGF	PGF	TGA	PGA	+/–	GP	G	A	Pts	PIM	PP	SH	GW
1983-84	Orillia Travelways	OJHL	42	*52	54	*106	....	....	....	20	....	....	....	....	....	....	....	....	....	....	....	....	....	....	....	....	....	....
1984-85	University of North Dakota	WCHA	36	18	36	54	....	....	....	16	....	....	....	....	....	....	....	....	....	....	....	....	....	....	....	....	....	....
1985-86	Canada	Nat-Team	62	19	30	49	....	....	....	36	....	....	....	....	....	....	....	....	....	....	....	....	....	....	....	....	....	....
1986-87	University of North Dakota	WCHA	48	46	79	125	....	....	....	48	....	....	....	....	....	....	....	....	....	....	....	....	....	....	....	....	....	....
	St. Louis Blues	**NHL**	....	....	....	....	....	....	....	....	....	....	....	....	....	....	....	....	....	....	**3**	**0**	**0**	**0**	**0**	....	....	....
1987-88	**St. Louis Blues**	**NHL**	**67**	**11**	**37**	**48**	**9**	**26**	**35**	**22**	**2**	**1**	**3**	**86**	**12.8**	**60**	**16**	**63**	**24**	**+5**	**10**	**6**	**1**	**7**	**4**	**3**	**1**	**1**
1988-89	**St. Louis Blues**	**NHL**	**70**	**17**	**28**	**45**	**14**	**20**	**34**	**8**	**5**	**0**	**1**	**133**	**12.8**	**66**	**27**	**81**	**32**	**–10**	**4**	**1**	**1**	**2**	**0**	**0**	**0**	**1**
1989-90	**St. Louis Blues**	**NHL**	**28**	**5**	**12**	**17**	**4**	**9**	**13**	**8**	**1**	**0**	**0**	**41**	**12.2**	**28**	**11**	**16**	**0**	**+1**	....	....	....	....	....	....	....	....
	Quebec Nordiques	**NHL**	**22**	**4**	**8**	**12**	**3**	**6**	**9**	**2**	**2**	**0**	**0**	**29**	**13.8**	**17**	**9**	**13**	**0**	**–5**	....	....	....	....	....	....	....	....
	Halifax Citadels	AHL	20	12	21	33	....	....	....	4	....	....	....	....	....	....	....	....	....	....	6	5	9	14	4	....	....	....
1990-91	**Quebec Nordiques**	**NHL**	**70**	**16**	**32**	**48**	**15**	**24**	**39**	**16**	**6**	**0**	**0**	**122**	**13.1**	**69**	**27**	**68**	**4**	**–22**	....	....	....	....	....	....	....	....
	Halifax Citadels	AHL	3	4	1	5	....	....	....	2	....	....	....	....	....	....	....	....	....	....	....	....	....	....	....	....	....	....
1991-92	**San Jose Sharks**	**NHL**	**22**	**2**	**10**	**12**	**2**	**7**	**9**	**4**	**0**	**0**	**0**	**31**	**6.5**	**19**	**8**	**15**	**2**	**–2**	....	....	....	....	....	....	....	....
	Chicago Blackhawks	**NHL**	**18**	**1**	**2**	**3**	**1**	**1**	**2**	**6**	**0**	**0**	**0**	**22**	**4.5**	**11**	**1**	**8**	**2**	**+4**	**3**	**0**	**0**	**0**	**2**	**0**	**0**	**0**
1992-93	Indianapolis Ice	IHL	80	45	*87	*132	....	....	....	70	....	....	....	....	....	....	....	....	....	....	5	0	2	2	2	....	....	....
1993-94	**St. Louis Blues**	**NHL**	**36**	**6**	**5**	**11**	**6**	**4**	**10**	**8**	**1**	**1**	**1**	**43**	**14.0**	**13**	**3**	**25**	**4**	**–11**	**4**	**0**	**0**	**0**	**0**	**0**	**0**	**0**
	Peoria Rivermen	IHL	45	30	51	81	....	....	....	25	....	....	....	....	....	....	....	....	....	....	1	1	2	3	0	....	....	....
1994-95	Milwaukee Admirals	IHL	71	24	67	91	....	....	....	26	....	....	....	....	....	....	....	....	....	....	15	4	9	13	16	....	....	....
1995-96	Milwaukee Admirals	IHL	43	14	28	42	....	....	....	18	....	....	....	....	....	....	....	....	....	....	5	1	3	4	4	....	....	....
1996-97	Milwaukee Admirals	IHL	81	27	61	88	....	....	....	20	....	....	....	....	....	....	....	....	....	....	3	1	1	2	2	....	....	....
1997-98	**Dallas Stars**	**NHL**	**13**	**5**	**3**	**8**	**6**	**3**	**9**	**0**	**3**	**0**	**0**	**14**	**35.7**	**9**	**5**	**4**	**0**	**0**	....	....	....	....	....	....	....	....
	Michigan K-Wings	IHL	20	7	15	22	....	....	....	6	....	....	....	....	....	....	....	....	....	....	....	....	....	....	....	....	....	....
	Edmonton Oilers	**NHL**	**36**	**8**	**11**	**19**	**9**	**11**	**20**	**10**	**4**	**0**	**1**	**43**	**18.6**	**25**	**10**	**12**	**0**	**+3**	**12**	**0**	**3**	**3**	**2**	**0**	**0**	**0**
	NHL Totals		**382**	**75**	**148**	**223**	**69**	**111**	**180**	**84**	**24**	**2**	**6**	**564**	**13.3**	**317**	**117**	**305**	**68**		**36**	**7**	**5**	**12**	**8**	**3**	**1**	**2**

WCHA First All-Star Team (1987) • NCAA West First All-American Team (1987) • NCAA Championship All-Tournament Team (1987) • NCAA Championship Tournament MVP (1987) • Won 1987 Hobey Baker Memorial Award (Top U.S. Collegiate Player) (1987) • Won James Gatschene Memorial Trophy (MVP - IHL) (1993) • Won Leo P. Lamoureux Memorial Trophy (Leading Scorer - IHL) (1993) • IHL First All-Star Team (1993)

Traded to **Quebec** by **St. Louis** with Greg Millen for Jeff Brown, December 13, 1989. Traded to **San Jose** by **Quebec** for Greg Paslawski, May 31, 1991. Traded to **Chicago** by **San Jose** for future considerations, February 7, 1992. Signed as a free agent by **St. Louis**, July 30, 1993. Signed as a free agent by **Dallas**, August 12, 1997. Claimed on waivers by **Edmonton** from **Dallas**, January 6, 1998. Traded to **Pittsburgh** by **Edmonton** with Bobby Dollas for Josef Beranek, June 16, 1998. Claimed by **Nashville** from **Pittsburgh** in Expansion Draft, June 26, 1998.

• HRYCUIK, JIM

Jim Hrycuik C – L. 5'10", 180 lbs. b: Rosthern, Sask., 10/7/1949.

Season	Club	League	GP	G	A	Pts	AG	AA	APts	PIM	PP	SH	GW	S	%	TGF	PGF	TGA	PGA	+/–	GP	G	A	Pts	PIM	PP	SH	GW
1970-71	Moose Jaw Canucks	SSHL	STATISTICS NOT AVAILABLE																									
1971-72	Regina Caps	ASHL	....	21	*39	*60	....	....	....	36	....	....	....	....	....	....	....	....	....	....	....	....	....	....	....	....	....	....
1972-73	Hershey Bears	AHL	36	3	7	10	....	....	....	22	....	....	....	....	....	....	....	....	....	....	....	....	....	....	....	....	....	....
	Fort Wayne Komets	IHL	25	12	11	23	....	....	....	35	....	....	....	....	....	....	....	....	....	....	9	7	5	12	6	....	....	....
1973-74	Hershey Bears	AHL	74	26	49	75	....	....	....	75	....	....	....	....	....	....	....	....	....	....	14	3	11	14	28	....	....	....
1974-75	**Washington Capitals**	**NHL**	**21**	**5**	**5**	**10**	**5**	**4**	**9**	**12**	**1**	**0**	**0**	**29**	**17.2**	**11**	**4**	**19**	**0**	**–12**	....	....	....	....	....	....	....	....
	Richmond Robins	AHL	7	4	3	7	....	....	....	2	....	....	....	....	....	....	....	....	....	....	....	....	....	....	....	....	....	....
1975-76	Richmond Robins	AHL	56	6	13	19	....	....	....	43	....	....	....	....	....	....	....	....	....	....	8	3	1	4	0	....	....	....
	NHL Totals		**21**	**5**	**5**	**10**	**5**	**4**	**9**	**12**	**1**	**0**	**0**	**29**	**17.2**	**11**	**4**	**19**	**0**		....	....	....	....	....	....	....	....

Signed as a free agent by **Hershey** (AHL), September, 1972. Claimed by **Washington** from **Hershey** (AHL) in Intra-League Draft, June 12, 1974.

• HRYNEWICH, TIM

Tim Hrynewich LW – L. 5'11", 190 lbs. b: Leamington, Ont., 10/2/1963. Pittsburgh's 2nd choice, 38th overall, in 1982 Entry Draft.

Season	Club	League	GP	G	A	Pts	AG	AA	APts	PIM	PP	SH	GW	S	%	TGF	PGF	TGA	PGA	+/–	GP	G	A	Pts	PIM	PP	SH	GW
1980-81	Sudbury Wolves	OHA	65	25	17	42	....	....	....	104	....	....	....	....	....	....	....	....	....	....	....	....	....	....	....	....	....	....
1981-82	Sudbury Wolves	OHL	64	29	41	70	....	....	....	144	....	....	....	....	....	....	....	....	....	....	....	....	....	....	....	....	....	....
1982-83	Sudbury Wolves	OHL	23	21	16	37	....	....	....	65	....	....	....	....	....	....	....	....	....	....	....	....	....	....	....	....	....	....
	Pittsburgh Penguins	**NHL**	**30**	**2**	**3**	**5**	**2**	**2**	**4**	**48**	**0**	**0**	**0**	**22**	**9.1**	**9**	**0**	**15**	**0**	**–6**	....	....	....	....	....	....	....	....
	Baltimore Skipjacks	AHL	9	2	1	3	....	....	....	6	....	....	....	....	....	....	....	....	....	....	....	....	....	....	....	....	....	....
1983-84	**Pittsburgh Penguins**	**NHL**	**25**	**4**	**5**	**9**	**3**	**3**	**6**	**34**	**0**	**0**	**2**	**24**	**16.7**	**18**	**1**	**27**	**0**	**–10**	....	....	....	....	....	....	....	....
	Baltimore Skipjacks	AHL	52	13	17	30	....	....	....	65	....	....	....	....	....	....	....	....	....	....	....	....	....	....	....	....	....	....
1984-85	Baltimore Skipjacks	AHL	21	4	3	7	....	....	....	31	....	....	....	....	....	....	....	....	....	....	....	....	....	....	....	....	....	....
	Muskegon Mohawks	IHL	30	10	13	23	....	....	....	42	....	....	....	....	....	....	....	....	....	....	17	8	7	15	39	....	....	....
1985-86	Muskegon Lumberjacks	IHL	67	25	26	51	....	....	....	110	....	....	....	....	....	....	....	....	....	....	....	....	....	....	....	....	....	....
	Toledo Goaldiggers	IHL	13	8	13	21	....	....	....	25	....	....	....	....	....	....	....	....	....	....	....	....	....	....	....	....	....	....
1986-87	Milwaukee Admirals	IHL	82	39	37	76	....	....	....	78	....	....	....	....	....	....	....	....	....	....	6	2	3	5	2	....	....	....
1987-88	Milwaukee Admirals	IHL	28	6	8	14	....	....	....	39	....	....	....	....	....	....	....	....	....	....	....	....	....	....	....	....	....	....
1988-89	Flint Spirits	IHL	5	0	1	1	....	....	....	4	....	....	....	....	....	....	....	....	....	....	....	....	....	....	....	....	....	....
	Fort Wayne Komets	IHL	4	0	1	1	....	....	....	8	....	....	....	....	....	....	....	....	....	....	....	....	....	....	....	....	....	....
	NHL Totals		**55**	**6**	**8**	**14**	**5**	**5**	**10**	**82**	**0**	**0**	**2**	**46**	**13.0**	**27**	**1**	**42**	**0**		....	....	....	....	....	....	....	....

Traded to **Edmonton** by **Pittsburgh** with Marty McSorley for Gilles Meloche, September 12, 1985.

• HUARD, BILL

Bill Huard LW – L. 6'1", 215 lbs. b: Welland, Ont., 6/24/1967.

Season	Club	League	GP	G	A	Pts	AG	AA	APts	PIM	PP	SH	GW	S	%	TGF	PGF	TGA	PGA	+/–	GP	G	A	Pts	PIM	PP	SH	GW
1986-87	Peterborough Petes	OHL	61	14	11	25	....	....	....	61	....	....	....	....	....	....	....	....	....	....	12	5	2	7	19	....	....	....
1987-88	Peterborough Petes	OHL	66	28	33	61	....	....	....	132	....	....	....	....	....	....	....	....	....	....	12	7	8	15	33	....	....	....
1988-89	Carolina Thunderbirds	ECHL	40	27	21	48	....	....	....	177	....	....	....	....	....	....	....	....	....	....	10	7	2	9	70	....	....	....
1989-90	Utica Devils	AHL	27	1	7	8	....	....	....	67	....	....	....	....	....	....	....	....	....	....	5	0	1	1	33	....	....	....
	Nashville Knights	ECHL	34	24	27	51	....	....	....	212	....	....	....	....	....	....	....	....	....	....	....	....	....	....	....	....	....	....
1990-91	Utica Devils	AHL	72	11	16	27	....	....	....	359	....	....	....	....	....	....	....	....	....	....	....	....	....	....	....	....	....	....
1991-92	Utica Devils	AHL	62	9	11	20	....	....	....	233	....	....	....	....	....	....	....	....	....	....	4	1	1	2	4	....	....	....
1992-93	**Boston Bruins**	**NHL**	**2**	**0**	**0**	**0**	**0**	**0**	**0**	**0**	**0**	**0**	**0**	**0**	**0.0**	**0**	**0**	**0**	**0**	**0**	....	....	....	....	....	....	....	....
	Providence Bruins	AHL	72	18	19	37	....	....	....	302	....	....	....	....	....	....	....	....	....	....	6	3	0	3	9	....	....	....
1993-94	**Ottawa Senators**	**NHL**	**63**	**2**	**2**	**4**	**2**	**2**	**4**	**162**	**0**	**0**	**0**	**24**	**8.3**	**7**	**0**	**27**	**1**	**–19**	....	....	....	....	....	....	....	....
1994-95	**Ottawa Senators**	**NHL**	**26**	**1**	**1**	**2**	**2**	**1**	**3**	**64**	**0**	**0**	**0**	**15**	**6.7**	**6**	**0**	**8**	**0**	**–2**	....	....	....	....	....	....	....	....
	Quebec Nordiques	**NHL**	**7**	**2**	**2**	**4**	**4**	**3**	**7**	**13**	**0**	**0**	**0**	**6**	**33.3**	**5**	**0**	**3**	**0**	**+2**	**1**	**0**	**0**	**0**	**0**	**0**	**0**	**0**
1995-96	**Dallas Stars**	**NHL**	**51**	**6**	**6**	**12**	**6**	**5**	**11**	**176**	**0**	**0**	**0**	**34**	**17.6**	**18**	**0**	**15**	**0**	**+3**	....	....	....	....	....	....	....	....
	Michigan K-Wings	IHL	12	1	1	2	....	....	....	74	....	....	....	....	....	....	....	....	....	....	....	....	....	....	....	....	....	....
1996-97	**Dallas Stars**	**NHL**	**40**	**5**	**6**	**11**	**5**	**5**	**10**	**105**	**0**	**0**	**0**	**34**	**14.7**	**11**	**0**	**6**	**0**	**+5**	....	....	....	....	....	....	....	....
1997-98	**Edmonton Oilers**	**NHL**	**30**	**0**	**1**	**1**	**0**	**1**	**1**	**72**	**0**	**0**	**0**	**12**	**0.0**	**5**	**1**	**9**	**0**	**–5**	**4**	**0**	**0**	**0**	**2**	**0**	**0**	**0**
	NHL Totals		**219**	**16**	**18**	**34**	**19**	**17**	**36**	**592**	**0**	**0**	**0**	**125**	**12.8**	**52**	**1**	**68**	**1**		**5**	**0**	**0**	**0**	**2**	**0**	**0**	**0**

Signed as a free agent by **New Jersey**, October 1, 1989. Signed as a free agent by **Boston**, December 4, 1992. Signed as a free agent by **Ottawa**, June 30, 1993. Traded to **Quebec** by **Ottawa** for Mika Stromberg and Quebec's 4th round choice (Kevin Boyd) in 1995 Entry Draft, April 7, 1995. Transferred to **Colorado** after **Quebec** franchise relocated, July 1, 1995. Claimed by **Dallas** from **Colorado** in NHL Waiver Draft, October 2, 1995. Signed as a free agent by **Edmonton**, July 22, 1997.

• HUBER, WILLIE

Willie Huber D – R. 6'5", 228 lbs. b: Strasskirchen, Germany, 1/15/1958. Detroit's 1st choice, 9th overall, in 1978 Amateur Draft.

Season	Club	League	GP	G	A	Pts	AG	AA	APts	PIM	PP	SH	GW	S	%	TGF	PGF	TGA	PGA	+/–	GP	G	A	Pts	PIM	PP	SH	GW
1975-76	Hamilton Fincups	OHA	58	2	8	10	....	....	....	64	....	....	....	....	....	....	....	....	....	....	....	....	....	....	....	....	....	....
1976-77	St. Catharines Fincups	OHA	36	10	24	34	....	....	....	111	....	....	....	....	....	....	....	....	....	....	10	2	4	6	29	....	....	....
	Canada	WJC-A	7	1	2	3	....	....	....	13	....	....	....	....	....	....	....	....	....	....	....	....	....	....	....	....	....	....
1977-78	Hamilton Fincups	OHA	61	12	45	57	....	....	....	168	....	....	....	....	....	....	....	....	....	....	20	6	12	18	45	....	....	....
	Canada	WJC-A	6	0	2	2	....	....	....	2	....	....	....	....	....	....	....	....	....	....	....	....	....	....	....	....	....	....
1978-79	**Detroit Red Wings**	**NHL**	**68**	**7**	**24**	**31**	**6**	**18**	**24**	**114**	**4**	**0**	**2**	**153**	**4.6**	**87**	**38**	**79**	**5**	**–25**	....	....	....	....	....	....	....	....
	Kansas City Red Wings	CHL	10	2	7	9	....	....	....	12	....	....	....	....	....	....	....	....	....	....	....	....	....	....	....	....	....	....

Season	Club	League	REGULAR SEASON GP	G	A	Pts	AG	AA	APts	PIM	PP	SH	GW	S	%	TGF	PGF	TGA	PGA	+/–	PLAYOFFS GP	G	A	Pts	PIM	PP	SH	GW
1979-80	**Detroit Red Wings**	**NHL**	**76**	**17**	**23**	**40**	**15**	**18**	**33**	**164**	**4**	**2**	**2**	**197**	**8.6**	**105**	**26**	**125**	**20**	**–26**	....	....	....	....	....	....	....	....
	Adirondack Red Wings	AHL	4	1	3	4	....	....	....	2	....	....	....	....	....	....	....	....	....	....	....	....	....	....	....	....	....	....
1980-81	**Detroit Red Wings**	**NHL**	**80**	**15**	**34**	**49**	**12**	**24**	**36**	**130**	**3**	**0**	**0**	**207**	**7.2**	**138**	**42**	**158**	**34**	**–28**	....	....	....	....	....	....	....	....
	Canada	WEC-A	7	0	2	2	....	....	....	10	....	....	....	....	....	....	....	....	....	....	....	....	....	....	....	....	....	....
1981-82	**Detroit Red Wings**	**NHL**	**74**	**15**	**30**	**45**	**12**	**20**	**32**	**98**	**5**	**0**	**2**	**270**	**5.6**	**134**	**25**	**163**	**38**	**–16**	....	....	....	....	....	....	....	....
1982-83	**Detroit Red Wings**	**NHL**	**74**	**14**	**29**	**43**	**11**	**20**	**31**	**106**	**3**	**0**	**1**	**241**	**5.8**	**113**	**26**	**154**	**33**	**–34**	....	....	....	....	....	....	....	....
1983-84	**New York Rangers**	**NHL**	**42**	**9**	**14**	**23**	**7**	**9**	**16**	**60**	**4**	**1**	**1**	**92**	**9.8**	**57**	**14**	**72**	**15**	**–14**	**4**	**1**	**1**	**2**	**9**	**0**	**0**	**0**
1984-85	**New York Rangers**	**NHL**	**49**	**3**	**11**	**14**	**2**	**7**	**9**	**55**	**1**	**0**	**0**	**75**	**4.0**	**46**	**10**	**81**	**25**	**–20**	**2**	**1**	**0**	**1**	**2**	**1**	**0**	**0**
1985-86	**New York Rangers**	**NHL**	**70**	**7**	**8**	**15**	**6**	**5**	**11**	**85**	**1**	**0**	**2**	**124**	**5.6**	**62**	**13**	**93**	**33**	**–11**	**16**	**3**	**2**	**5**	**16**	**2**	**0**	**0**
1986-87	**New York Rangers**	**NHL**	**66**	**8**	**22**	**30**	**7**	**16**	**23**	**68**	**3**	**1**	**0**	**117**	**6.8**	**86**	**29**	**88**	**18**	**–13**	**6**	**0**	**2**	**2**	**6**	**0**	**0**	**0**
1987-88	**New York Rangers**	**NHL**	**11**	**1**	**3**	**4**	**1**	**2**	**3**	**14**	**0**	**0**	**0**	**18**	**5.6**	**9**	**2**	**19**	**8**	**–4**	....	....	....	....	....	....	....	....
	Vancouver Canucks	**NHL**	**35**	**4**	**10**	**14**	**3**	**7**	**10**	**40**	**2**	**0**	**0**	**79**	**5.1**	**44**	**17**	**54**	**17**	**–10**	....	....	....	....	....	....	....	....
	Philadelphia Flyers	**NHL**	**10**	**4**	**9**	**13**	**3**	**6**	**9**	**16**	**3**	**0**	**0**	**14**	**28.6**	**19**	**12**	**18**	**9**	**–2**	**5**	**0**	**0**	**0**	**2**	**0**	**0**	**0**
	NHL Totals		**655**	**104**	**217**	**321**	**85**	**152**	**237**	**950**	**33**	**4**	**10**	**1587**	**6.6**	**900**	**254**	**1104**	**255**		**33**	**5**	**5**	**10**	**35**	**3**	**0**	**0**

OHA Second All-Star Team (1978)

Played in NHL All-Star Game (1983)

Traded to **NY Rangers** by **Detroit** with Mike Blaisdell and Mark Osborne for Ron Duguay, Eddie Mio and Eddie Johnstone, June 13, 1983. Traded to **Vancouver** by **NY Rangers** with Larry Melynk for Michel Petit, November 4, 1987. Traded to **Philadelphia** by **Vancouver** for Paul Lawless and future considerations, March 1, 1988.

• HUBICK, GREG

Greg Hubick D – L. 5′11″, 185 lbs. b: Strasbourg, Sask., 11/12/1951. Montreal's 9th choice, 53rd overall, in 1971 Amateur Draft.

Season	Club	League	GP	G	A	Pts	AG	AA	APts	PIM	PP	SH	GW	S	%	TGF	PGF	TGA	PGA	+/–	PO GP	G	A	Pts	PIM	PP	SH	GW
1969-70	Weyburn Red Wings	SJHL	....	9	21	30	....	....	....	61	....	....	....	....	....	....	....	....	....	....	....	....	....	....	....	....	....	....
1970-71	University of Minnesota-Duluth	WCHA	31	7	15	22	....	....	....	69	....	....	....	....	....	....	....	....	....	....	....	....	....	....	....	....	....	....
1971-72	University of Minnesota-Duluth	WCHA	35	7	14	21	....	....	....	36	....	....	....	....	....	....	....	....	....	....	....	....	....	....	....	....	....	....
1972-73	Nova Scotia Voyageurs	AHL	49	6	14	20	....	....	....	17	....	....	....	....	....	....	....	....	....	....	13	2	7	9	13	....	....	....
1973-74	Nova Scotia Voyageurs	AHL	75	11	26	37	....	....	....	44	....	....	....	....	....	....	....	....	....	....	6	0	2	2	0	....	....	....
1974-75	Nova Scotia Voyageurs	AHL	74	9	27	36	....	....	....	93	....	....	....	....	....	....	....	....	....	....	6	4	1	5	0	....	....	....
1975-76	**Toronto Maple Leafs**	**NHL**	**72**	**6**	**8**	**14**	**6**	**6**	**12**	**10**	**0**	**0**	**1**	**54**	**11.1**	**24**	**1**	**31**	**8**	**0**	....	....	....	....	....	....	....	....
1976-77	Dallas Black Hawks	CHL	70	13	22	35	....	....	....	12	....	....	....	....	....	....	....	....	....	....	5	0	1	1	4	....	....	....
1977-78	Dallas Black Hawks	CHL	76	6	15	21	....	....	....	64	....	....	....	....	....	....	....	....	....	....	13	2	2	4	8	....	....	....
1978-79	Dallas Black Hawks	CHL	69	10	16	26	....	....	....	52	....	....	....	....	....	....	....	....	....	....	9	0	5	5	6	....	....	....
1979-80	**Vancouver Canucks**	**NHL**	**5**	**0**	**1**	**1**	**0**	**1**	**1**	**0**	**0**	**0**	**0**	**4**	**0.0**	**1**	**0**	**2**	**0**	**–1**	....	....	....	....	....	....	....	....
	Dallas Black Hawks	CHL	68	3	22	25	....	....	....	59	....	....	....	....	....	....	....	....	....	....	....	....	....	....	....	....	....	....
1980-81	Dallas Black Hawks	CHL	74	8	51	59	....	....	....	46	....	....	....	....	....	....	....	....	....	....	6	0	3	3	8	....	....	....
1981-82	Wichita Wind	CHL	27	0	6	6	....	....	....	26	....	....	....	....	....	....	....	....	....	....	7	1	3	4	12	....	....	....
	NHL Totals		**77**	**6**	**9**	**15**	**6**	**7**	**13**	**10**	**0**	**0**	**1**	**58**	**10.3**	**25**	**1**	**33**	**8**		....	....	....	....	....	....	....	....

CHL First All-Star Team (1979, 1981) • Named CHL's Top Defenseman (1979)

Traded to **Toronto** by **Montreal** for Toronto's 2nd round choice (Doug Jarvis) in 1975 Amateur Draft, June 26, 1975. Signed as a free agent by **Vancouver**, September 7, 1979.

• HUCK, FRAN

Fran Huck C – L. 5′7″, 165 lbs. b: Regina, Sask., 12/4/1945.

Season	Club	League	GP	G	A	Pts	AG	AA	APts	PIM	PP	SH	GW	S	%	TGF	PGF	TGA	PGA	+/–	PO GP	G	A	Pts	PIM	PP	SH	GW
1962-63	Regina Pats	SJHL	20	4	11	15	....	....	....	20	....	....	....	....	....	....	....	....	....	....	6	4	2	6	8	....	....	....
1963-64	Regina Pats	SJHL	62	*86	67	*153	....	....	....	104	....	....	....	....	....	....	....	....	....	....	19	*22	18	*40	60	....	....	....
1964-65	Regina Pats	SJHL	58	*77	59	136	....	....	....	36	....	....	....	....	....	....	....	....	....	....	12	10	13	23	18	....	....	....
1965-66	Canada	Nat-Team	STATISTICS NOT AVAILABLE																									
	Canada	WEC-A	7	4	4	8	....	....	....	8	....	....	....	....	....	....	....	....	....	....	....	....	....	....	....	....	....	....
1966-67	Canada	Nat-Team	STATISTICS NOT AVAILABLE																									
	Canada	WEC-A	7	5	6	11	....	....	....	6	....	....	....	....	....	....	....	....	....	....	....	....	....	....	....	....	....	....
1967-68	Ottawa Nationals	OHA Sr.	....	8	17	25	....	....	....	24	....	....	....	....	....	....	....	....	....	....	....	....	....	....	....	....	....	....
	Canada	Olympics	7	4	5	9	....	....	....	10	....	....	....	....	....	....	....	....	....	....	....	....	....	....	....	....	....	....
1968-69	Canada	Nat-Team	STATISTICS NOT AVAILABLE																									
	Canada	WEC-A	10	3	2	5	....	....	....	12	....	....	....	....	....	....	....	....	....	....	....	....	....	....	....	....	....	....
1969-70	Canada	Nat-Team	STATISTICS NOT AVAILABLE																									
	Montreal Canadiens	**NHL**	**2**	**0**	**0**	**0**	**0**	**0**	**0**	**0**	**0**	**0**	**0**	**2**	**0.0**	**0**	**0**	**0**	**0**	**0**	....	....	....	....	....	....	....	....
	Montreal Voyageurs	AHL	2	1	2	3	....	....	....	0	....	....	....	....	....	....	....	....	....	....	....	....	....	....	....	....	....	....
1970-71	**Montreal Canadiens**	**NHL**	**5**	**1**	**2**	**3**	**1**	**2**	**2**	**0**	**0**	**0**	**0**	**8**	**12.5**	**4**	**0**	**1**	**0**	**+3**	....	....	....	....	....	....	....	....
	Montreal Voyageurs	AHL	31	12	17	29	....	....	....	18	....	....	....	....	....	....	....	....	....	....	....	....	....	....	....	....	....	....
	St. Louis Blues	**NHL**	**29**	**7**	**8**	**15**	**7**	**7**	**14**	**18**	**2**	**0**	**1**	**43**	**16.3**	**21**	**9**	**11**	**0**	**+1**	**6**	**1**	**2**	**3**	**2**	**0**	**0**	**0**
1971-72	Denver Spurs	WHL	72	28	63	91	....	....	....	83	....	....	....	....	....	....	....	....	....	....	9	*9	4	*13	16	....	....	....
1972-73	**St. Louis Blues**	**NHL**	**58**	**16**	**20**	**36**	**16**	**17**	**33**	**20**	**2**	**0**	**2**	**82**	**19.5**	**49**	**10**	**47**	**7**	**–1**	**5**	**2**	**2**	**4**	**0**	**1**	**0**	**0**
1973-74	Winnipeg Jets	WHA	74	26	48	74	....	....	....	68	....	....	....	....	....	....	....	....	....	....	4	0	0	0	2	....	....	....
1974-75	Minnesota Fighting Saints	WHA	78	22	45	67	....	....	....	26	....	....	....	....	....	....	....	....	....	....	12	3	*13	16	6	....	....	....
1975-76	Minnesota Fighting Saints	WHA	59	17	32	49	....	....	....	27	....	....	....	....	....	....	....	....	....	....	....	....	....	....	....	....	....	....
1976-77	Winnipeg Jets	WHA	12	2	2	4	....	....	....	10	....	....	....	....	....	....	....	....	....	....	7	0	2	2	6	....	....	....
1977-78	Winnipeg Jets	WHA	5	0	0	0	....	....	....	2	....	....	....	....	....	....	....	....	....	....	....	....	....	....	....	....	....	....
	NHL Totals		**94**	**24**	**30**	**54**	**24**	**26**	**50**	**38**	**4**	**0**	**3**	**135**	**17.8**	**74**	**19**	**59**	**7**		**11**	**3**	**4**	**7**	**2**	**1**	**0**	**0**
	Other Major League Totals		228	67	127	194	....	....	....	133	....	....	....	....	....	....	....	....	....	....	23	3	15	18	14	....	....	....

WEC-A All-Star Team (1966) • WHL Second All-Star Team (1972) • Won Leader Cup (WHL - MVP) (1972)

Traded to **St. Louis** by **Montreal** for St. Louis' 2nd round choice (Michel Deguise) in 1971 Amateur Draft, January 28, 1971. Selected by **Winnipeg** (WHA) in 1972 WHA General Player Draft, February 12, 1972. Traded to **Minnesota** (WHA) by **Winnipeg** (WHA) for cash, June, 1974. Signed as a free agent by **Winnipeg** (WHA) after **Minnesota** (WHA) franchise folded, June, 1976.

• HUCUL, FRED

Fred Hucul D – L. 5′10″, 170 lbs. b: Tubrose, Sask., 12/4/1931.

Season	Club	League	GP	G	A	Pts	AG	AA	APts	PIM	PP	SH	GW	S	%	TGF	PGF	TGA	PGA	+/–	PO GP	G	A	Pts	PIM	PP	SH	GW
1949-50	Moose Jaw Canucks	WCJHL	27	8	11	19	....	....	....	59	....	....	....	....	....	....	....	....	....	....	4	1	2	3	8	....	....	....
1950-51	Moose Jaw Canucks	WCJHL	37	19	27	46	....	....	....	165	....	....	....	....	....	....	....	....	....	....	....	....	....	....	....	....	....	....
	Chicago Black Hawks	**NHL**	**3**	**1**	**0**	**1**	**1**	**0**	**1**	**2**	....	....	....	....	....	....	....	....	....	....	....	....	....	....	....	....	....	....
	Regina Caps	WCSHL	5	0	2	2	....	....	....	4	....	....	....	....	....	....	....	....	....	....	....	....	....	....	....	....	....	....
1951-52	**Chicago Black Hawks**	**NHL**	**34**	**3**	**7**	**10**	**4**	**9**	**13**	**37**	....	....	....	....	....	....	....	....	....	....	....	....	....	....	....	....	....	....
	St. Louis Flyers	AHL	9	2	3	5	....	....	....	8	....	....	....	....	....	....	....	....	....	....	....	....	....	....	....	....	....	....
1952-53	**Chicago Black Hawks**	**NHL**	**57**	**5**	**7**	**12**	**8**	**10**	**18**	**25**	....	....	....	....	....	....	....	....	....	....	**6**	**1**	**0**	**1**	**10**	....	....	....
1953-54	**Chicago Black Hawks**	**NHL**	**27**	**0**	**3**	**3**	**0**	**4**	**4**	**19**	....	....	....	....	....	....	....	....	....	....	....	....	....	....	....	....	....	....
	Calgary Stampeders	WHL	15	7	4	11	....	....	....	12	....	....	....	....	....	....	....	....	....	....	....	....	....	....	....	....	....	....
	Quebec Aces	QHL	13	4	6	10	....	....	....	26	....	....	....	....	....	....	....	....	....	....	12	1	3	4	10	....	....	....
1954-55	Calgary Stampeders	WHL	51	12	23	35	....	....	....	59	....	....	....	....	....	....	....	....	....	....	....	....	....	....	....	....	....	....
1955-56	Calgary Stampeders	WHL	70	21	38	59	....	....	....	85	....	....	....	....	....	....	....	....	....	....	8	1	4	5	19	....	....	....
1956-57	Buffalo Bisons	AHL	9	0	6	6	....	....	....	11	....	....	....	....	....	....	....	....	....	....	....	....	....	....	....	....	....	....
1957-58	Calgary Stampeders	WHL	61	18	40	58	....	....	....	51	....	....	....	....	....	....	....	....	....	....	14	1	4	5	27	....	....	....
1958-59	Calgary Stampeders	WHL	64	7	36	43	....	....	....	61	....	....	....	....	....	....	....	....	....	....	8	1	0	1	9	....	....	....
1959-60	Calgary Stampeders	WHL	66	7	46	53	....	....	....	32	....	....	....	....	....	....	....	....	....	....	....	....	....	....	....	....	....	....
1960-61	Calgary Stampeders	WHL	67	9	42	51	....	....	....	55	....	....	....	....	....	....	....	....	....	....	5	0	0	0	9	....	....	....
1961-62	Calgary Stampeders	WHL	53	19	37	56	....	....	....	42	....	....	....	....	....	....	....	....	....	....	7	0	4	4	2	....	....	....
1962-63	Calgary Stampeders	WHL	70	16	41	57	....	....	....	56	....	....	....	....	....	....	....	....	....	....	....	....	....	....	....	....	....	....
1963-64	Denver Invaders	WHL	69	8	49	57	....	....	....	58	....	....	....	....	....	....	....	....	....	....	6	3	4	7	6	....	....	....
1964-65	Victoria Cougars	WHL	51	8	20	28	....	....	....	67	....	....	....	....	....	....	....	....	....	....	12	1	4	5	*28	....	....	....
1965-66	Tulsa Oilers	CHL	7	1	0	1	....	....	....	4	....	....	....	....	....	....	....	....	....	....	....	....	....	....	....	....	....	....
	Victoria Cougars	WHL	61	16	43	59	....	....	....	56	....	....	....	....	....	....	....	....	....	....	14	8	7	15	14	....	....	....
1966-67	Victoria Cougars	WHL	13	3	6	9	....	....	....	12	....	....	....	....	....	....	....	....	....	....	....	....	....	....	....	....	....	....
1967-68	**St. Louis Blues**	**NHL**	**43**	**2**	**13**	**15**	**2**	**14**	**16**	**30**	**1**	**0**	**0**	**85**	**2.4**	**46**	**14**	**41**	**6**	**–3**	....	....	....	....	....	....	....	....
1968-69	Kansas City Blues	CHL	2	0	1	1	....	....	....	0	....	....	....	....	....	....	....	....	....	....	....	....	....	....	....	....	....	....
	NHL Totals		**164**	**11**	**30**	**41**	**15**	**37**	**52**	**113**	**1**	**0**	**0**	**85**	**12.9**	**46**	**14**	**41**	**6**		**6**	**1**	**0**	**1**	**10**	**0**	**0**	**0**

WHL First All-Star Team (1956, 1963, 1964, 1966) • WHL Prairie Division First All-Star Team (1958, 1959) • WHL Second All-Star Team (1961, 1962)

Traded to **Calgary** (WHL) by **Chicago** for cash, September, 1954. Traded to **Toronto** by **Calgary** (WHL) for cash, August, 1964. Claimed by **St. Louis** from **Toronto** in Expansion Draft, June 6, 1967.

• HUDDY, CHARLIE

Charlie Huddy D – L. 6', 210 lbs. b: Oshawa, Ont., 6/2/1959.

			REGULAR SEASON																		PLAYOFFS							
Season	Club	League	GP	G	A	Pts	AG	AA	APts	PIM	PP	SH	GW	S	%	TGF	PGF	TGA	PGA	+/-	GP	G	A	Pts	PIM	PP	SH	GW
1977-78	Oshawa Generals	OHA	59	17	18	35	....	....	....	81	....	....	....	....	....	....	....	....	....	....	6	2	1	3	10	....	....	....
1978-79	Oshawa Generals	OHA	64	20	38	58	....	....	....	108	....	....	....	....	....	....	....	....	....	....	5	3	4	7	12	....	....	....
1979-80	Houston Apollos	CHL	79	14	34	48	....	....	....	46	....	....	....	....	....	....	....	....	....	....	6	1	0	1	2	....	....	....
1980-81	**Edmonton Oilers**	**NHL**	12	2	5	7	2	3	5	6	1	0	0	23	8.7	18	4	20	7	+1	....	....	....	....	....	....	....	....
	Wichita Wind	CHL	47	8	36	44	....	....	....	71	....	....	....	....	....	....	....	....	....	....	17	3	11	14	10	....	....	....
1981-82	**Edmonton Oilers**	**NHL**	41	4	11	15	3	7	10	46	0	0	0	84	4.8	51	7	37	10	+17	5	1	2	3	14	0	1	0
	Wichita Wind	CHL	32	7	19	26	....	....	....	51	....	....	....	....	....	....	....	....	....	....	....	....	....	....	....	....	....	....
1982-83	**Edmonton Oilers**	**NHL**	76	20	37	57	16	26	42	58	7	0	2	151	13.2	194	54	98	20	+62	15	1	6	7	10	0	0	0
1983-84	**Edmonton Oilers**	**NHL**	75	8	34	42	6	23	29	43	3	0	0	161	5.0	172	36	103	17	+50	12	1	9	10	8	0	0	0
1984-85	Canada	C Cup	7	0	2	2	....	....	....	2	....	....	....	....	....	....	....	....	....	....	....	....	....	....	....	....	....	....
	Edmonton Oilers	**NHL**	80	7	44	51	6	30	36	46	3	0	1	146	4.8	189	42	123	26	+50	18	3	17	20	17	1	0	0
1985-86	**Edmonton Oilers**	**NHL**	76	6	35	41	5	23	28	55	1	0	0	151	4.0	173	44	128	29	+30	7	0	2	2	0	0	0	0
1986-87	**Edmonton Oilers**	**NHL**	58	4	15	19	3	11	14	35	0	0	0	75	5.3	89	19	61	18	+27	21	1	7	8	21	0	0	0
1987-88	**Edmonton Oilers**	**NHL**	77	13	28	41	11	20	31	71	2	0	2	163	8.0	117	31	94	31	+23	13	4	5	9	10	2	0	0
1988-89	**Edmonton Oilers**	**NHL**	76	11	33	44	9	23	32	52	5	2	0	178	6.2	131	42	115	26	0	7	2	0	2	4	1	0	0
1989-90	**Edmonton Oilers**	**NHL**	70	1	23	24	1	16	17	56	1	0	1	119	0.8	74	19	93	25	–13	22	0	6	6	11	0	0	0
1990-91	**Edmonton Oilers**	**NHL**	53	5	22	27	5	17	22	32	2	0	0	90	5.6	59	9	61	15	+4	18	3	7	10	10	1	0	0
1991-92	**Los Angeles Kings**	**NHL**	56	4	19	23	4	14	18	43	2	1	0	109	3.7	80	24	93	27	–10	6	1	1	2	10	0	0	1
1992-93	**Los Angeles Kings**	**NHL**	82	2	25	27	2	17	19	64	0	0	1	106	1.9	90	5	123	54	+16	23	1	4	5	12	0	0	0
1993-94	**Los Angeles Kings**	**NHL**	79	5	13	18	5	10	15	71	1	0	0	134	3.7	79	7	107	39	+4	....	....	....	....	....	....	....	....
1994-95	**Los Angeles Kings**	**NHL**	9	0	1	1	0	1	1	6	0	0	0	11	0.0	4	0	11	1	–6	....	....	....	....	....	....	....	....
	Buffalo Sabres	**NHL**	32	2	4	6	4	6	10	36	1	0	0	40	5.0	21	2	27	7	–1	3	0	0	0	0	0	0	0
1995-96	**Buffalo Sabres**	**NHL**	52	5	5	10	5	4	9	59	2	0	1	57	8.8	35	5	43	8	–5	....	....	....	....	....	....	....	....
	St. Louis Blues	**NHL**	12	0	0	0	0	0	0	6	0	0	0	13	0.0	6	0	16	3	–7	13	1	0	1	8	0	0	0
1996-97	**Buffalo Sabres**	**NHL**	1	0	0	0	0	0	0	0	0	0	0	0	0.0	0	0	1	0	–1	....	....	....	....	....	....	....	....
	Rochester Americans	AHL	63	6	8	14	....	....	....	36	....	....	....	....	....	....	....	....	....	....	4	0	0	0	0	....	....	....
	NHL Totals		**1017**	**99**	**354**	**453**	**87**	**251**	**338**	**785**	**31**	**3**	**8**	**1811**	**5.5**	**1582**	**350**	**1354**	**363**		**183**	**19**	**66**	**85**	**135**	**5**	**1**	**1**

NHL Plus/Minus Leader (1983)

Signed as a free agent by **Edmonton**, September 14, 1979. Claimed by **Minnesota** from **Edmonton** in Expansion Draft, May 30, 1991. Traded to **LA Kings** by **Minnesota** with Randy Gilhen, Jim Thomson and NY Rangers' 4th round choice (previously acquired, LA Kings selected Alexei Zhitnik) in 1991 Entry Draft for Todd Elik, June 22, 1991. Traded to **Buffalo** by **LA Kings** with Alexei Zhitnik, Robb Stauber and LA Kings' 5th round choice (Marian Menhart) in 1995 Entry Draft for Philippe Boucher, Denis Tsygurov and Grant Fuhr, February 14, 1995. Traded to **St. Louis** by **Buffalo** with Buffalo's 7th round choice (Daniel Corso) in 1996 Entry Draft for Denis Hamel, March 19, 1996. Signed as a free agent by **Buffalo**, September 26, 1996.

• HUDSON, DAVE

Dave Hudson C – L. 6', 185 lbs. b: St. Thomas, Ont., 12/28/1949. Chicago's 6th choice, 71st overall, in 1969 Amateur Draft.

Season	Club	League	GP	G	A	Pts	AG	AA	APts	PIM	PP	SH	GW	S	%	TGF	PGF	TGA	PGA	+/-	GP	G	A	Pts	PIM	PP	SH	GW
1967-68	University of North Dakota	WCHA	33	8	6	14	....	....	....	6	....	....	....	....	....	....	....	....	....	....	....	....	....	....	....	....	....	....
1968-69	University of North Dakota	WCHA	29	16	14	30	....	....	....	16	....	....	....	....	....	....	....	....	....	....	....	....	....	....	....	....	....	....
1969-70	University of North Dakota	WCHA	30	16	13	29	....	....	....	28	....	....	....	....	....	....	....	....	....	....	....	....	....	....	....	....	....	....
1970-71	Dallas Black Hawks	CHL	69	17	37	54	....	....	....	57	....	....	....	....	....	....	....	....	....	....	7	0	1	1	19	....	....	....
1971-72	Dallas Black Hawks	CHL	63	29	34	63	....	....	....	49	....	....	....	....	....	....	....	....	....	....	12	7	7	14	12	....	....	....
1972-73	**New York Islanders**	**NHL**	69	12	19	31	12	16	28	17	4	0	0	111	10.8	40	13	66	0	–39	....	....	....	....	....	....	....	....
1973-74	**New York Islanders**	**NHL**	63	2	10	12	2	9	11	7	0	0	0	43	4.7	19	1	24	0	–6	....	....	....	....	....	....	....	....
	Fort Worth Wings	CHL	10	5	3	8	....	....	....	19	....	....	....	....	....	....	....	....	....	....	....	....	....	....	....	....	....	....
1974-75	**Kansas City Scouts**	**NHL**	70	9	32	41	8	25	33	27	2	0	1	115	7.8	55	17	71	14	–19	....	....	....	....	....	....	....	....
1975-76	**Kansas City Scouts**	**NHL**	74	11	20	31	10	16	26	12	2	0	0	114	9.6	48	9	85	18	–28	....	....	....	....	....	....	....	....
1976-77	**Colorado Rockies**	**NHL**	73	15	21	36	14	17	31	14	1	0	2	89	16.9	51	5	72	23	–3	....	....	....	....	....	....	....	....
	Rhode Island Reds	AHL	5	0	2	2	....	....	....	2	....	....	....	....	....	....	....	....	....	....	....	....	....	....	....	....	....	....
1977-78	**Colorado Rockies**	**NHL**	60	10	22	32	10	18	28	12	1	0	0	89	11.2	44	6	63	20	–5	2	1	1	2	0	0	0	0
	NHL Totals		**409**	**59**	**124**	**183**	**56**	**101**	**157**	**89**	**10**	**0**	**3**	**561**	**10.5**	**257**	**51**	**381**	**75**		**2**	**1**	**1**	**2**	**0**	**0**	**0**	**0**

Claimed by **NY Islanders** from **Chicago** in Expansion Draft, June 6, 1972. Claimed by **Kansas City** from **NY Islanders** in Expansion Draft, June 12, 1974. Transferred to **Colorado** after **Kansas City** franchise relocated, June, 1976.

• HUDSON, LEX

Lex Hudson D – L. 6'3", 184 lbs. b: Winnipeg, Man., 12/31/1955. Pittsburgh's 12th choice, 196th overall, in 1975 Amateur Draft.

Season	Club	League	GP	G	A	Pts	AG	AA	APts	PIM	PP	SH	GW	S	%	TGF	PGF	TGA	PGA	+/-	GP	G	A	Pts	PIM	PP	SH	GW
1974-75	University of Denver	WCHA	35	2	3	5	....	....	....	29	....	....	....	....	....	....	....	....	....	....	....	....	....	....	....	....	....	....
1975-76	University of Denver	WCHA	35	1	13	14	....	....	....	34	....	....	....	....	....	....	....	....	....	....	....	....	....	....	....	....	....	....
1976-77	University of Denver	WCHA	29	0	9	9	....	....	....	32	....	....	....	....	....	....	....	....	....	....	....	....	....	....	....	....	....	....
1977-78	University of Denver	WCHA	40	1	12	13	....	....	....	46	....	....	....	....	....	....	....	....	....	....	....	....	....	....	....	....	....	....
1978-79	**Pittsburgh Penguins**	**NHL**	2	0	0	0	0	0	0	0	0	0	0	1	0.0	2	0	4	2	0	2	0	0	0	0	0	0	0
	Binghamton Whalers	AHL	2	0	0	0	....	....	....	0	....	....	....	....	....	....	....	....	....	....	....	....	....	....	....	....	....	....
	Grand Rapids Owls	IHL	69	6	29	35	....	....	....	63	....	....	....	....	....	....	....	....	....	....	18	2	6	8	18	....	....	....
1979-80	Cincinnati Stingers	CHL	32	1	6	7	....	....	....	21	....	....	....	....	....	....	....	....	....	....	....	....	....	....	....	....	....	....
	Grand Rapids Owls	IHL	8	1	5	6	....	....	....	0	....	....	....	....	....	....	....	....	....	....	....	....	....	....	....	....	....	....
	NHL Totals		**2**	**0**	**0**	**0**	**0**	**0**	**0**	**0**	**0**	**0**	**0**	**1**	**0.0**	**2**	**0**	**4**	**2**		**2**	**0**	**0**	**0**	**0**	**0**	**0**	**0**

WCHA Second All-Star Team (1978)

• HUDSON, MIKE

Mike Hudson C/LW – L. 6'1", 205 lbs. b: Guelph, Ont., 2/6/1967. Chicago's 6th choice, 140th overall, in 1986 Entry Draft.

Season	Club	League	GP	G	A	Pts	AG	AA	APts	PIM	PP	SH	GW	S	%	TGF	PGF	TGA	PGA	+/-	GP	G	A	Pts	PIM	PP	SH	GW
1984-85	Hamilton Steelhawks	OHL	50	10	12	22	....	....	....	13	....	....	....	....	....	....	....	....	....	....	....	....	....	....	....	....	....	....
1985-86	Hamilton Steelhawks	OHL	7	3	2	5	....	....	....	4	....	....	....	....	....	....	....	....	....	....	....	....	....	....	....	....	....	....
	Sudbury Wolves	OHL	59	35	42	77	....	....	....	20	....	....	....	....	....	....	....	....	....	....	4	2	5	7	7	....	....	....
1986-87	Sudbury Wolves	OHL	63	40	57	97	....	....	....	18	....	....	....	....	....	....	....	....	....	....	....	....	....	....	....	....	....	....
1987-88	Saginaw Hawks	IHL	75	18	30	48	....	....	....	44	....	....	....	....	....	....	....	....	....	....	10	2	3	5	20	....	....	....
1988-89	**Chicago Blackhawks**	**NHL**	41	7	16	23	6	11	17	20	0	1	0	45	15.6	28	5	41	6	–12	10	1	2	3	18	1	0	0
	Saginaw Hawks	IHL	30	15	17	32	....	....	....	10	....	....	....	....	....	....	....	....	....	....	....	....	....	....	....	....	....	....
1989-90	**Chicago Blackhawks**	**NHL**	49	9	12	21	8	9	17	56	0	0	3	51	17.6	32	3	38	6	–3	4	0	0	0	2	0	0	0
1990-91	**Chicago Blackhawks**	**NHL**	55	7	9	16	6	7	13	62	0	0	1	53	13.2	24	1	24	6	+5	6	0	2	2	8	0	0	0
	Indianapolis Ice	IHL	3	1	2	3	....	....	....	0	....	....	....	....	....	....	....	....	....	....	....	....	....	....	....	....	....	....
1991-92	**Chicago Blackhawks**	**NHL**	76	14	15	29	13	11	24	92	2	1	2	97	14.4	38	5	59	15	–11	16	3	5	8	26	0	0	0
1992-93	**Chicago Blackhawks**	**NHL**	36	1	6	7	1	4	5	44	0	0	0	33	3.0	13	1	20	2	–6	....	....	....	....	....	....	....	....
	Edmonton Oilers	**NHL**	5	0	1	1	0	1	1	2	0	0	0	2	0.0	2	0	7	4	–1	....	....	....	....	....	....	....	....
1993-94	**New York Rangers**	**NHL**	48	4	7	11	4	5	9	47	0	0	1	48	8.3	18	1	22	0	–5	....	....	....	....	....	....	....	....
1994-95	**Pittsburgh Penguins**	**NHL**	40	2	9	11	4	13	17	34	0	0	1	33	6.1	17	0	27	9	–1	11	0	0	0	6	0	0	0
1995-96	**Toronto Maple Leafs**	**NHL**	27	2	0	2	2	0	2	29	0	0	0	27	7.4	3	0	11	3	–5	....	....	....	....	....	....	....	....
	St. Louis Blues	**NHL**	32	3	12	15	3	10	13	26	0	0	0	32	9.4	18	2	12	3	+7	2	0	1	1	4	0	0	0
1996-97	Phoenix Roadrunners	IHL	33	6	9	15	....	....	....	10	....	....	....	....	....	....	....	....	....	....	....	....	....	....	....	....	....	....
	Phoenix Coyotes	**NHL**	7	0	0	0	0	0	0	2	0	0	0	9	0.0	1	0	5	0	–4	....	....	....	....	....	....	....	....
1997-98	Augsburg Panthers	Germany	15	1	5	6	....	....	....	16	....	....	....	....	....	....	....	....	....	....	....	....	....	....	....	....	....	....
	Adler Mannheim	EuroHL	1	0	0	0	....	....	....	0	....	....	....	....	....	....	....	....	....	....	....	....	....	....	....	....	....	....
	Adler Mannheim	Germany	14	4	3	7	....	....	....	2	....	....	....	....	....	....	....	....	....	....	10	2	5	7	12	....	....	....
	NHL Totals		**416**	**49**	**87**	**136**	**47**	**71**	**118**	**414**	**2**	**2**	**8**	**430**	**11.4**	**194**	**18**	**266**	**54**		**49**	**4**	**10**	**14**	**64**	**1**	**0**	**0**

Traded to **Edmonton** by **Chicago** for Craig Muni, March 22, 1993. Claimed by **NY Rangers** from **Edmonton** in NHL Waiver Draft, October 3, 1993. Claimed by **Pittsburgh** from **NY Rangers** in NHL Waiver Draft, January 18, 1995. Signed as a free agent by **Toronto**, September 22, 1995. Claimed on waivers by **St. Louis** from **Toronto**, January 4, 1996. Signed as a free agent by **Phoenix**, November 12, 1996.

• HUFFMAN, KERRY

Kerry Huffman D – L. 6'2", 200 lbs. b: Peterborough, Ont., 1/3/1968. Philadelphia's 1st choice, 20th overall, in 1986 Entry Draft.

Season	Club	League	GP	G	A	Pts	AG	AA	APts	PIM	PP	SH	GW	S	%	TGF	PGF	TGA	PGA	+/-	GP	G	A	Pts	PIM	PP	SH	GW
1985-86	Guelph Platers	OHL	56	3	24	27	....	....	....	35	....	....	....	....	....	....	....	....	....	....	20	1	10	11	10	....	....	....
1986-87	Guelph Platers	OHL	44	4	31	35	....	....	....	20	....	....	....	....	....	....	....	....	....	....	5	0	2	2	8	....	....	....
	Canada	WJC-A	6	0	1	1	....	....	....	4	....	....	....	....	....	....	....	....	....	....	....	....	....	....	....	....	....	....
	Philadelphia Flyers	**NHL**	9	0	0	0	0	0	0	2	0	0	0	3	0.0	6	1	0	0	+5	....	....	....	....	....	....	....	....
	Hershey Bears	AHL	3	0	1	1	....	....	....	0	....	....	....	....	....	....	....	....	....	....	4	0	0	0	0	....	....	....
1987-88	**Philadelphia Flyers**	**NHL**	52	6	17	23	5	12	17	34	3	0	2	84	7.1	52	19	48	4	–11	2	0	0	0	0	0	0	0

Season	Club	League	GP	G	A	Pts	AG	AA	APts	PIM	PP	SH	GW	S	%	TGF	PGF	TGA	PGA	+/–	GP	G	A	Pts	PIM	PP	SH	GW
			REGULAR SEASON																		PLAYOFFS							
1988-89	**Philadelphia Flyers**	**NHL**	**29**	**0**	**11**	**11**	**0**	**8**	**8**	**31**	**0**	**0**	**0**	**23**	**0.0**	**32**	**14**	**18**	**0**	**0**	....	....	....	....	....	....	....	....
	Hershey Bears	AHL	29	2	13	15	....	....	....	16	....	....	....	....	....	....	....	....	....	....	....	....	....	....	....	....	....	....
1989-90	**Philadelphia Flyers**	**NHL**	**43**	**1**	**12**	**13**	**1**	**9**	**10**	**34**	**0**	**0**	**0**	**70**	**1.4**	**56**	**19**	**41**	**1**	**–3**	....	....	....	....	....	....	....	....
1990-91	**Philadelphia Flyers**	**NHL**	**10**	**1**	**2**	**3**	**1**	**2**	**3**	**10**	**0**	**0**	**1**	**14**	**7.1**	**12**	**1**	**10**	**0**	**+1**	....	....	....	....	....	....	....	....
	Hershey Bears	AHL	45	5	29	34	....	....	....	20	....	....	....	....	....	....	....	....	....	....	7	1	2	3	0	....	....	....
1991-92	**Philadelphia Flyers**	**NHL**	**60**	**14**	**18**	**32**	**13**	**14**	**27**	**41**	**4**	**0**	**2**	**123**	**11.4**	**66**	**20**	**57**	**12**	**+1**	....	....	....	....	....	....	....	....
	Canada	WC-A	6	1	0	1	....	....	....	2	....	....	....	....	....	....	....	....	....	....	....	....	....	....	....	....	....	....
1992-93	**Quebec Nordiques**	**NHL**	**52**	**4**	**18**	**22**	**3**	**12**	**15**	**54**	**3**	**0**	**0**	**86**	**4.7**	**64**	**22**	**56**	**14**	**0**	**3**	**0**	**0**	**0**	**0**	**0**	**0**	**0**
1993-94	**Quebec Nordiques**	**NHL**	**28**	**0**	**6**	**6**	**0**	**5**	**5**	**28**	**0**	**0**	**0**	**44**	**0.0**	**30**	**9**	**20**	**1**	**+2**	....	....	....	....	....	....	....	....
	Ottawa Senators	**NHL**	**34**	**4**	**8**	**12**	**4**	**6**	**10**	**12**	**2**	**1**	**0**	**68**	**5.9**	**25**	**12**	**57**	**14**	**–30**	....	....	....	....	....	....	....	....
1994-95	**Ottawa Senators**	**NHL**	**37**	**2**	**4**	**6**	**4**	**6**	**10**	**46**	**2**	**0**	**0**	**68**	**2.9**	**30**	**9**	**50**	**12**	**–17**	....	....	....	....	....	....	....	....
1995-96	**Ottawa Senators**	**NHL**	**43**	**4**	**11**	**15**	**4**	**9**	**13**	**63**	**3**	**0**	**0**	**88**	**4.5**	**42**	**22**	**44**	**6**	**–18**	....	....	....	....	....	....	....	....
	Philadelphia Flyers	**NHL**	**4**	**1**	**1**	**2**	**1**	**1**	**2**	**6**	**0**	**0**	**1**	**3**	**33.3**	**5**	**3**	**2**	**0**	**0**	**6**	**0**	**0**	**0**	**2**	**0**	**0**	**0**
1996-97	Las Vegas Thunder	IHL	44	5	19	24	....	....	....	38	....	....	....	....	....	....	....	....	....	....	3	0	0	0	2	....	....	....
1997-98	Grand Rapids Griffins	IHL	73	4	23	27	....	....	....	60	....	....	....	....	....	....	....	....	....	....	3	0	0	0	2	....	....	....
	NHL Totals		**401**	**37**	**108**	**145**	**36**	**84**	**120**	**361**	**17**	**1**	**6**	**674**	**5.5**	**420**	**151**	**403**	**64**		**11**	**0**	**0**	**0**	**2**	**0**	**0**	**0**

Won George Parsons Trophy (Memorial Cup Tournament Most Sportsmanlike Player) (1986) • OHL First All-Star Team (1987)

Traded to **Quebec** by **Philadelphia** with Peter Forsberg, Steve Duchesne, Mike Ricci, Ron Hextall, Chris Simon, Philadelphia's 1st round choice in the 1993 (Jocelyn Thibault) and 1994 (later traded to Toronto — later traded to Washington — Washington selected Nolan Baumgartner) — Entry Drafts and cash for Eric Lindros, June 30, 1992. Claimed on waivers by **Ottawa** from **Quebec**, January 15, 1994. Traded to **Philadelphia** by **Ottawa** for future considerations, March 19, 1996.

• HUGHES, BRENT

Brent Hughes LW – L. 5'11", 195 lbs. b: New Westminster, B.C., 4/5/1966.

Season	Club	League	GP	G	A	Pts	AG	AA	APts	PIM	PP	SH	GW	S	%	TGF	PGF	TGA	PGA	+/–	GP	G	A	Pts	PIM	PP	SH	GW
1983-84	New Westminster Bruins	WHL	67	21	18	39	....	....	....	133	....	....	....	....	....	....	....	....	....	....	9	2	2	4	27	....	....	....
1984-85	New Westminster Bruins	WHL	64	25	32	57	....	....	....	135	....	....	....	....	....	....	....	....	....	....	11	2	1	3	37	....	....	....
1985-86	New Westminster Bruins	WHL	71	28	52	80	....	....	....	180	....	....	....	....	....	....	....	....	....	....	....	....	....	....	....	....	....	....
1986-87	New Westminster Bruins	WHL	8	5	4	9	....	....	....	22	....	....	....	....	....	....	....	....	....	....	....	....	....	....	....	....	....	....
	Victoria Cougars	WHL	61	38	61	99	....	....	....	146	....	....	....	....	....	....	....	....	....	....	5	4	1	5	8	....	....	....
1987-88	Moncton Hawks	AHL	73	13	19	32	....	....	....	206	....	....	....	....	....	....	....	....	....	....	....	....	....	....	....	....	....	....
1988-89	**Winnipeg Jets**	**NHL**	**28**	**3**	**2**	**5**	**3**	**1**	**4**	**82**	**0**	**1**	**0**	**37**	**8.1**	**12**	**1**	**18**	**0**	**–7**	....	....	....	....	....	....	....	....
	Moncton Hawks	AHL	54	34	34	68	....	....	....	286	....	....	....	....	....	....	....	....	....	....	10	9	4	13	40	....	....	....
1989-90	**Winnipeg Jets**	**NHL**	**11**	**1**	**2**	**3**	**1**	**1**	**2**	**33**	**0**	**0**	**1**	**7**	**14.3**	**4**	**0**	**8**	**0**	**–4**	....	....	....	....	....	....	....	....
	Moncton Hawks	AHL	65	31	29	60	....	....	....	277	....	....	....	....	....	....	....	....	....	....	....	....	....	....	....	....	....	....
1990-91	Moncton Hawks	AHL	63	21	22	43	....	....	....	144	....	....	....	....	....	....	....	....	....	....	3	0	0	0	7	....	....	....
1991-92	Baltimore Skipjacks	AHL	55	25	29	54	....	....	....	190	....	....	....	....	....	....	....	....	....	....	....	....	....	....	....	....	....	....
	Boston Bruins	**NHL**	**8**	**1**	**1**	**2**	**1**	**1**	**2**	**38**	**0**	**0**	**1**	**10**	**10.0**	**4**	**0**	**4**	**1**	**+1**	**10**	**2**	**0**	**2**	**20**	**0**	**0**	**0**
	Maine Mariners	AHL	12	6	4	10	....	....	....	34	....	....	....	....	....	....	....	....	....	....	....	....	....	....	....	....	....	....
1992-93	**Boston Bruins**	**NHL**	**62**	**5**	**4**	**9**	**4**	**3**	**7**	**191**	**0**	**0**	**0**	**54**	**9.3**	**17**	**0**	**22**	**1**	**–4**	**1**	**0**	**0**	**0**	**2**	**0**	**0**	**0**
1993-94	**Boston Bruins**	**NHL**	**77**	**13**	**11**	**24**	**12**	**8**	**20**	**143**	**1**	**0**	**1**	**100**	**13.0**	**38**	**1**	**27**	**0**	**+10**	**13**	**2**	**1**	**3**	**27**	**0**	**0**	**1**
	Providence Bruins	AHL	6	2	5	7	....	....	....	4	....	....	....	....	....	....	....	....	....	....	....	....	....	....	....	....	....	....
1994-95	**Boston Bruins**	**NHL**	**44**	**6**	**6**	**12**	**11**	**9**	**20**	**139**	**0**	**0**	**0**	**75**	**8.0**	**19**	**0**	**13**	**0**	**+6**	**5**	**0**	**0**	**0**	**4**	**0**	**0**	**0**
1995-96	**Buffalo Sabres**	**NHL**	**76**	**5**	**10**	**15**	**5**	**8**	**13**	**148**	**0**	**0**	**0**	**56**	**8.9**	**21**	**0**	**30**	**0**	**–9**	....	....	....	....	....	....	....	....
1996-97	**New York Islanders**	**NHL**	**51**	**7**	**3**	**10**	**7**	**3**	**10**	**57**	**0**	**0**	**0**	**47**	**14.9**	**12**	**0**	**17**	**1**	**–4**	....	....	....	....	....	....	....	....
	Utah Grizzlies	IHL	5	2	2	4	....	....	....	11	....	....	....	....	....	....	....	....	....	....	....	....	....	....	....	....	....	....
1997-98	Houston Aeros	IHL	79	19	12	31	....	....	....	128	....	....	....	....	....	....	....	....	....	....	4	0	3	3	20	....	....	....
	NHL Totals		**357**	**41**	**39**	**80**	**44**	**34**	**78**	**831**	**1**	**1**	**3**	**386**	**10.6**	**127**	**2**	**139**	**3**		**29**	**4**	**1**	**5**	**53**	**0**	**0**	**1**

Signed as a free agent by **Winnipeg**, June 13, 1988. Traded to **Washington** by **Winnipeg** with Craig Duncanson and Simon Wheeldon for Bob Joyce, Tyler Larter and Kent Paynter, May 21, 1991. Traded to **Boston** by **Washington** with future considerations for John Byce and Dennis Smith, February 24, 1992. Claimed By **Buffalo** from **Boston** in NHL Waiver Draft, October 2, 1995. Signed as a free agent by **NY Islanders**, August 9, 1996.

• HUGHES, BRENT

Brent Hughes D L. 6', 205 lbs. b: Bowmanville, Ont., 6/17/1943.

Season	Club	League	GP	G	A	Pts	AG	AA	APts	PIM	PP	SH	GW	S	%	TGF	PGF	TGA	PGA	+/–	GP	G	A	Pts	PIM	PP	SH	GW
1959-60	Toronto Marlboros	OHA	16	0	1	1	....	....	....	4	....	....	....	....	....	....	....	....	....	....	....	....	....	....	....	....	....	....
1960-61			DID NOT PLAY – INJURED																									
1961-62	St. Catharines Teepees	OHA	41	1	7	8	....	....	....	40	....	....	....	....	....	....	....	....	....	....	6	1	1	2	0	....	....	....
1962-63	St. Catharines Teepees	OHA	50	9	18	27	....	....	....	78	....	....	....	....	....	....	....	....	....	....	....	....	....	....	....	....	....	....
1963-64	New Haven Blades	EHL	53	6	25	31	....	....	....	100	....	....	....	....	....	....	....	....	....	....	5	0	1	1	0	....	....	....
1964-65	Minneapolis Bruins	CHL	68	2	16	18	....	....	....	79	....	....	....	....	....	....	....	....	....	....	5	2	0	2	13	....	....	....
1965-66	Memphis Wings	CHL	70	4	21	25	....	....	....	50	....	....	....	....	....	....	....	....	....	....	....	....	....	....	....	....	....	....
1966-67	Pittsburgh Hornets	AHL	5	2	4	6	....	....	....	4	....	....	....	....	....	....	....	....	....	....	....	....	....	....	....	....	....	....
	Memphis Wings	CHL	62	0	18	18	....	....	....	49	....	....	....	....	....	....	....	....	....	....	7	0	2	2	6	....	....	....
1967-68	**Los Angeles Kings**	**NHL**	**44**	**4**	**10**	**14**	**5**	**10**	**15**	**36**	**2**	**0**	**0**	**72**	**5.6**	**55**	**7**	**44**	**11**	**+15**	**7**	**0**	**0**	**0**	**10**	**0**	**0**	**0**
	Springfield Kings	AHL	25	5	14	19	....	....	....	30	....	....	....	....	....	....	....	....	....	....	....	....	....	....	....	....	....	....
1968-69	**Los Angeles Kings**	**NHL**	**72**	**2**	**19**	**21**	**2**	**18**	**20**	**73**	**0**	**0**	**0**	**116**	**1.7**	**74**	**13**	**101**	**24**	**–16**	**11**	**1**	**3**	**4**	**37**	**0**	**0**	**0**
1969-70	**Los Angeles Kings**	**NHL**	**52**	**1**	**7**	**8**	**1**	**7**	**8**	**108**	**0**	**0**	**0**	**64**	**1.6**	**33**	**3**	**83**	**20**	**–33**	....	....	....	....	....	....	....	....
	Springfield Kings	AHL	3	0	0	0	....	....	....	10	....	....	....	....	....	....	....	....	....	....	12	0	3	3	51	....	....	....
1970-71	**Philadelphia Flyers**	**NHL**	**30**	**1**	**10**	**11**	**1**	**9**	**10**	**21**	**0**	**0**	**0**	**37**	**2.7**	**37**	**14**	**33**	**4**	**–6**	**4**	**0**	**0**	**0**	**6**	**0**	**0**	**0**
	Quebec Aces	AHL	25	4	20	24	....	....	....	34	....	....	....	....	....	....	....	....	....	....	....	....	....	....	....	....	....	....
1971-72	**Philadelphia Flyers**	**NHL**	**63**	**2**	**20**	**22**	**2**	**18**	**20**	**35**	**0**	**0**	**0**	**93**	**2.2**	**77**	**17**	**67**	**13**	**+6**	....	....	....	....	....	....	....	....
	Baltimore Clippers	AHL	10	2	4	6	....	....	....	6	....	....	....	....	....	....	....	....	....	....	....	....	....	....	....	....	....	....
1972-73	**Philadelphia Flyers**	**NHL**	**29**	**2**	**11**	**13**	**2**	**9**	**11**	**32**	**0**	**0**	**0**	**40**	**5.0**	**36**	**11**	**43**	**10**	**–8**	....	....	....	....	....	....	....	....
	St. Louis Blues	**NHL**	**8**	**1**	**1**	**2**	**1**	**1**	**2**	**0**	**0**	**0**	**0**	**16**	**6.3**	**13**	**2**	**12**	**2**	**+1**	....	....	....	....	....	....	....	....
1973-74	**St. Louis Blues**	**NHL**	**2**	**0**	**0**	**0**	**0**	**0**	**0**	**0**	**0**	**0**	**0**	**0**	**0.0**	**0**	**0**	**0**	**0**	**0**	....	....	....	....	....	....	....	....
1973-74	**Detroit Red Wings**	**NHL**	**69**	**1**	**21**	**22**	**1**	**18**	**19**	**92**	**0**	**0**	**0**	**74**	**1.4**	**83**	**20**	**108**	**17**	**–28**	....	....	....	....	....	....	....	....
1974-75	**Kansas City Scouts**	**NHL**	**66**	**1**	**10**	**19**	**1**	**14**	**15**	**43**	**0**	**0**	**0**	**80**	**1.3**	**73**	**11**	**142**	**29**	**–51**	....	....	....	....	....	....	....	....
1975-76	San Diego Mariners	WHA	78	7	28	35	....	....	....	63	....	....	....	....	....	....	....	....	....	....	10	1	5	6	6	....	....	....
1976-77	San Diego Mariners	WHA	62	4	13	17	....	....	....	48	....	....	....	....	....	....	....	....	....	....	7	1	4	5	0	....	....	....
1977-78	Birmingham Bulls	WHA	80	9	35	44	....	....	....	48	....	....	....	....	....	....	....	....	....	....	5	0	0	0	12	....	....	....
1978-79	Birmingham Bulls	WHA	48	3	3	6	....	....	....	21	....	....	....	....	....	....	....	....	....	....	....	....	....	....	....	....	....	....
	Binghamton Whalers	AHL	8	1	2	3	....	....	....	8	....	....	....	....	....	....	....	....	....	....	....	....	....	....	....	....	....	....
1979-80	Cincinnati Stingers	CHL	11	0	1	1	....	....	....	0	....	....	....	....	....	....	....	....	....	....	....	....	....	....	....	....	....	....
	NHL Totals		**435**	**15**	**117**	**132**	**16**	**104**	**120**	**440**	**2**	**0**	**0**	**592**	**2.5**	**481**	**98**	**633**	**130**		**22**	**1**	**3**	**4**	**53**	**0**	**0**	**0**
	Other Major League Totals		268	23	79	102	....	....	....	180	....	....	....	....	....	....	....	....	....	....	22	2	9	11	18	....	....	....

Claimed by **Detroit** (Springfield - AHL) from **Boston** in Reverse Draft, June 9, 1965. Claimed by **LA Kings** from **Detroit** in Expansion Draft, June 6, 1967. Traded to **Philadelphia** by **LA Kings** for Mike Byers, May 20, 1970. Selected by **NY Raiders** (WHA) in 1972 WHA General Player Draft, February 12, 1972. Traded to **St. Louis** by **Philadelphia** with Pierre Plante for Andre Dupont and St. Louis' 3rd round choice (Bob Stumpf) in 1973 Amateur Draft, December 14, 1972. Traded to **Detroit** by **St. Louis** for cash, October 27, 1973. Transferred to **San Diego** (WHA) after **New York-New Jersey** (WHA) franchise relocated, April 30, 1974. Claimed by **Kansas City** from **Detroit** in Expansion Draft, June 12, 1974. Signed as a free agent by **Birmingham** (WHA) after **San Diego** (WHA) franchise folded, June, 1977.

• HUGHES, FRANK

Frank Hughes LW – L. 5'10", 180 lbs. b: Fernie, B.C., 10/1/1949. Toronto's 4th choice, 43rd overall, in 1969 Amateur Draft.

Season	Club	League	GP	G	A	Pts	AG	AA	APts	PIM	PP	SH	GW	S	%	TGF	PGF	TGA	PGA	+/–	GP	G	A	Pts	PIM	PP	SH	GW
1967-68	Edmonton Oil Kings	WCJHL	DID NOT PLAY																									
1968-69	Edmonton Oil Kings	WCJHL	50	18	10	28	....	....	....	10	....	....	....	....	....	....	....	....	....	....	17	10	7	17	....	....	....	....
1969-70	Phoenix Roadrunners	WHL	71	26	42	68	....	....	....	44	....	....	....	....	....	....	....	....	....	....	....	....	....	....	....	....	....	....
1970-71	Phoenix Roadrunners	WHL	68	30	38	68	....	....	....	67	....	....	....	....	....	....	....	....	....	....	10	4	4	8	14	....	....	....
1971-72	**California Golden Seals**	**NHL**	**5**	**0**	**0**	**0**	**0**	**0**	**0**	**0**	**0**	**0**	**0**	**1**	**0.0**	**1**	**1**	**2**	**0**	**–2**	....	....	....	....	....	....	....	....
	Phoenix Roadrunners	WHL	53	34	28	62	....	....	....	41	....	....	....	....	....	....	....	....	....	....	6	2	3	5	13	....	....	....
1972-73	Houston Aeros	WHA	76	22	19	41	....	....	....	41	....	....	....	....	....	....	....	....	....	....	10	4	4	8	2	....	....	....
1973-74	Houston Aeros	WHA	73	42	42	84	....	....	....	47	....	....	....	....	....	....	....	....	....	....	14	9	5	14	9	....	....	....
1974-75	Houston Aeros	WHA	76	48	35	83	....	....	....	35	....	....	....	....	....	....	....	....	....	....	13	6	6	12	2	....	....	....
1975-76	Houston Aeros	WHA	80	31	45	76	....	....	....	26	....	....	....	....	....	....	....	....	....	....	17	5	1	6	20	....	....	....
1976-77	Houston Aeros	WHA	27	3	8	11	....	....	....	2	....	....	....	....	....	....	....	....	....	....	....	....	....	....	....	....	....	....
	Phoenix Roadrunners	WHA	48	24	29	53	....	....	....	20	....	....	....	....	....	....	....	....	....	....	....	....	....	....	....	....	....	....

Season	Club	League	GP	G	A	Pts	AG	AA	APts	PIM	PP	SH	GW	S	%	TGF	PGF	TGA	PGA	+/-	GP	G	A	Pts	PIM	PP	SH	GW
			REGULAR SEASON																		PLAYOFFS							
1977-78	Houston Aeros	WHA	11	3	2	5				2																		
	Phoenix Roadrunners	PHL	40	*33	*41	*74				44																		
1978-79	Tucson Rustlers	PHL	58	35	49	84				32																		
	NHL Totals		5	0	0	0	0	0	0	0	0	0	0	1	0.0	1	1	2	0									
	Other Major League Totals		391	173	180	353				173											54	24	16	40	33			

Claimed by **California** from **Toronto** in Intra-League Draft, June 8, 1971. Selected by **Dayton-Houston** (WHA) in 1972 WHA General Player Draft, February 12, 1972. Claimed by **Atlanta** from **California** in Expansion Draft, June 6, 1972. Traded to **Phoenix** (WHA) by **Houston** (WHA) with Andre Hinse for John Gray and Al McLeod, December, 1976. Signed as a free agent by **Houston** (WHA) after **Phoenix** (WHA) franchise folded, July, 1977.

• HUGHES, HOWIE

Howie Hughes RW – L. 5'9", 180 lbs. b: St. Boniface, Man., 4/4/1939.

Season	Club	League	GP	G	A	Pts	AG	AA	APts	PIM	PP	SH	GW	S	%	TGF	PGF	TGA	PGA	+/-	GP	G	A	Pts	PIM	PP	SH	GW
1955-56	St. Boniface Canadians	MJHL																			1	0	0	0	0			
1956-57	St. Boniface Canadians	MJHL	21	9	13	22				0											3	0	0	0	0			
1957-58	St. Boniface Canadians	MJHL	30	18	15	33				26											21	5	*7	12	6			
1958-59	St. Boniface Canadians	MJHL	27	10	18	28				35											6	1	2	3	14			
	Winnipeg Braves	MJHL																			16	8	5	13	10			
1959-60	St. Paul Saints	IHL	68	35	44	79				33											13	5	8	13	12			
1960-61	Winnipeg Warriors	WHL	68	12	23	35				26																		
1961-62	Seattle Totems	WHL	64	17	22	39				22											2	0	2	2	2			
1962-63	Vancouver Canucks	WHL	40	5	10	15				12											7	0	0	0	2			
1963-64	St. Paul Rangers	CHL	66	30	34	64				37											8	1	3	4	2			
1964-65	Vancouver Canucks	WHL	67	24	26	50				26											5	0	0	0	2			
1965-66	Vancouver Canucks	WHL	65	37	35	72				24											7	3	2	5	0			
1966-67	Seattle Totems	WHL	70	26	45	71				27											10	*6	5	*11	4			
1967-68	**Los Angeles Kings**	**NHL**	**74**	**9**	**14**	**23**	**11**	**15**	**26**	**20**	**1**	**1**	**2**	**119**	**7.6**	**32**	**2**	**58**	**29**	**+1**	**7**	**2**	**0**	**2**	**0**	**1**	**0**	**0**
1968-69	**Los Angeles Kings**	**NHL**	**73**	**16**	**14**	**30**	**18**	**13**	**31**	**10**	**5**	**0**	**3**	**161**	**9.9**	**48**	**8**	**47**	**4**	**−3**	**7**	**0**	**0**	**0**	**2**	**0**	**0**	**0**
1969-70	**Los Angeles Kings**	**NHL**	**21**	**0**	**4**	**4**	**0**	**4**	**4**	**0**	**0**	**0**	**0**	**18**	**0.0**	**9**	**4**	**21**	**10**	**−6**								
1970-71	Springfield Kings	AHL	2	0	1	1				4																		
	Denver Spurs	WHL	62	19	21	40				19											5	2	2	4	8			
1971-72	Seattle Totems	WHL	71	17	29	46				26																		
1972-73	San Diego Gulls	WHL	68	23	25	48				23											6	4	1	5	2			
1973-74	Portland Buckaroos	WHL	75	41	36	77				22											10	3	4	7	2			
1974-75	Seattle Totems	CHL	48	11	15	26				16																		
	NHL Totals		**168**	**25**	**32**	**57**	**29**	**32**	**61**	**30**	**6**	**1**	**5**	**298**	**8.4**	**89**	**14**	**126**	**43**		**14**	**2**	**0**	**2**	**2**	**1**	**0**	**0**

WHL Second All-Star Team (1967) • WHL First All-Star Team (1974)

Claimed by **LA Kings** from **Montreal** in Expansion Draft, June 6, 1967. Claimed by **San Diego** (WHL) from **LA Kings** (Seattle-WHL) in Reverse Draft, June, 1972.

• HUGHES, JACK

Jack Hughes D – R. 6'1", 205 lbs. b: Somerville, MA, 7/20/1957. Colorado's 8th choice, 142nd overall, in 1977 Amateur Draft.

Season	Club	League	GP	G	A	Pts	AG	AA	APts	PIM	PP	SH	GW	S	%	TGF	PGF	TGA	PGA	+/-	GP	G	A	Pts	PIM	PP	SH	GW
1976-77	Harvard University	ECAC	26	5	16	21				16																		
1977-78	Harvard University	ECAC	23	8	19	27				33																		
1978-79	Harvard University	ECAC	25	3	29	32				51																		
1979-80	United States	Nat-Team	49	3	15	18				62																		
	Fort Worth Texans	CHL	29	1	7	8				70											15	1	11	12	40			
1980-81	**Colorado Rockies**	**NHL**	**38**	**2**	**5**	**7**	**2**	**3**	**5**	**91**	**1**	**0**	**0**	**20**	**10.0**	**28**	**2**	**57**	**9**	**−22**								
	Fort Worth Texans	CHL	27	1	7	8				36											5	0	5	5	16			
1981-82	**Colorado Rockies**	**NHL**	**8**	**0**	**0**	**0**	**0**	**0**	**0**	**13**	**0**	**0**	**0**	**1**	**0.0**	**2**	**0**	**9**	**0**	**−7**								
	Fort Worth Texans	CHL	65	7	25	32				158																		
	NHL Totals		**46**	**2**	**5**	**7**	**2**	**3**	**5**	**104**	**1**	**0**	**0**	**21**	**9.5**	**30**	**2**	**66**	**9**									

ECAC First All-Star Team (1977) • ECAC Second All-Star Team (1978)

• HUGHES, JOHN

John Hughes D – L. 5'11", 200 lbs. b: Charlottetown, P.E.I., 3/18/1954. Vancouver's 2nd choice, 41st overall, in 1974 Amateur Draft.

Season	Club	League	GP	G	A	Pts	AG	AA	APts	PIM	PP	SH	GW	S	%	TGF	PGF	TGA	PGA	+/-	GP	G	A	Pts	PIM	PP	SH	GW
1971-72	Toronto Marlboros	OHA	2	0	0	0				0																		
1972-73	Toronto Marlboros	OHA	63	13	42	55				195																		
1973-74	Toronto Marlboros	OHA	67	6	34	40				189																		
1974-75	Phoenix Roadrunners	WHA	72	4	25	29				201																		
1975-76	Cincinnati Stingers	WHA	79	3	34	37				204																		
1976-77	Cincinnati Stingers	WHA	79	3	27	30				113											4	0	0	0	8			
1977-78	Houston Aeros	WHA	79	3	25	28				130											6	1	1	2	6			
1978-79	Indianapolis Racers	WHA	22	3	4	7				48																		
	Edmonton Oilers	WHA	41	2	15	17				81											13	1	0	1	35			
1979-80	**Vancouver Canucks**	**NHL**	**52**	**2**	**11**	**13**	**2**	**8**	**10**	**181**	**0**	**0**	**0**	**49**	**4.1**	**40**	**1**	**49**	**10**	**0**	**4**	**0**	**0**	**0**	**10**	**0**	**0**	**0**
1980-81	**Edmonton Oilers**	**NHL**	**18**	**0**	**3**	**3**	**0**	**2**	**2**	**30**	**0**	**0**	**0**	**9**	**0.0**	**13**	**1**	**26**	**8**	**−6**								
	Wichita Wind	CHL	23	2	4	6				88																		
	New Haven Nighthawks	AHL	14	3	6	9				50											2	0	0	0	8			
	New York Rangers	**NHL**																			**3**	**0**	**1**	**1**	**6**			
1981-82	Springfield Indians	AHL	76	1	33	34				174																		
	NHL Totals		**70**	**2**	**14**	**16**	**2**	**10**	**12**	**211**	**0**	**0**	**0**	**58**	**3.4**	**53**	**2**	**75**	**18**		**7**	**0**	**1**	**1**	**16**	**0**	**0**	**0**
	Other Major League Totals		372	18	130	148				777											23	2	1	3	49			

Selected by **Cincinnati** (WHA) in 1974 WHA Amateur Draft, June, 1974. Loaned to **Phoenix** (WHA) by **Cincinnati** (WHA) for 1974-75 season, July, 1974. Traded to **Houston** (WHA) by **Cincinnati** (WHA) for Craig Norwich and the rights to Dave Taylor, May, 1977. Traded to **Indianapolis** (WHA) by **Houston** (WHA) for cash, July, 1978. Signed as a free agent by **Edmonton** (WHA) after **Indianapolis** (WHA) franchise folded, January, 1979. Reclaimed by **Vancouver** from **Edmonton** prior to Expansion Draft, June 9, 1979. Claimed on waivers by **Edmonton** from **Vancouver**, December 15, 1980. Traded to **NY Rangers** by **Edmonton** for Ray Markham, March 10, 1981.

• HUGHES, PAT

Pat Hughes RW – R. 6'1", 180 lbs. b: Calgary, Alta., 3/25/1955. Montreal's 6th choice, 52nd overall, in 1975 Amateur Draft.

Season	Club	League	GP	G	A	Pts	AG	AA	APts	PIM	PP	SH	GW	S	%	TGF	PGF	TGA	PGA	+/-	GP	G	A	Pts	PIM	PP	SH	GW
1973-74	University of Michigan	WCHA	38	13	7	20				34																		
1974-75	University of Michigan	WCHA	38	24	19	43				64																		
1975-76	University of Michigan	WCHA	35	16	18	34				70																		
1976-77	Nova Scotia Voyageurs	AHL	77	29	39	68				144											12	2	2	4	8			
1977-78	**Montreal Canadiens**	**NHL**	**3**	**0**	**0**	**0**	**0**	**0**	**0**	**2**	**0**	**0**	**0**	**5**	**0.0**	**0**	**0**	**2**	**0**	**−2**								
	Nova Scotia Voyageurs	AHL	74	40	28	68				128											11	5	9	14	24			
1978-79	**Montreal Canadiens**	**NHL**	**41**	**9**	**8**	**17**	**8**	**6**	**14**	**22**	**1**	**0**	**1**	**51**	**17.6**	**19**	**2**	**10**	**0**	**+7**	**8**	**1**	**2**	**3**	**4**	**0**	**0**	**0**
1979-80	**Pittsburgh Penguins**	**NHL**	**76**	**18**	**14**	**32**	**16**	**11**	**27**	**78**	**5**	**0**	**0**	**159**	**11.3**	**45**	**12**	**72**	**1**	**−38**	**5**	**0**	**0**	**0**	**21**	**0**	**0**	**0**
1980-81	**Pittsburgh Penguins**	**NHL**	**58**	**10**	**9**	**19**	**8**	**6**	**14**	**161**	**0**	**0**	**2**	**89**	**11.2**	**32**	**2**	**39**	**0**	**−9**								
	Edmonton Oilers	**NHL**	**2**	**0**	**0**	**0**	**0**	**0**	**0**	**0**	**0**	**0**	**0**	**3**	**0.0**	**0**	**0**	**3**	**0**	**−3**	**5**	**0**	**5**	**5**	**16**	**0**	**0**	**0**
1981-82	**Edmonton Oilers**	**NHL**	**68**	**24**	**22**	**46**	**19**	**15**	**34**	**99**	**4**	**2**	**0**	**167**	**14.4**	**66**	**6**	**63**	**24**	**+21**	**5**	**2**	**1**	**3**	**6**	**0**	**0**	**0**
1982-83	**Edmonton Oilers**	**NHL**	**80**	**25**	**20**	**45**	**21**	**14**	**35**	**85**	**2**	**5**	**7**	**144**	**17.4**	**64**	**6**	**81**	**23**	**0**	**16**	**2**	**5**	**7**	**14**	**0**	**0**	**1**
1983-84	**Edmonton Oilers**	**NHL**	**77**	**27**	**28**	**55**	**22**	**19**	**41**	**61**	**2**	**3**	**3**	**164**	**16.5**	**78**	**7**	**76**	**23**	**+18**	**19**	**2**	**11**	**13**	**12**	**0**	**0**	**0**
1984-85	**Edmonton Oilers**	**NHL**	**73**	**12**	**13**	**25**	**10**	**9**	**19**	**85**	**1**	**1**	**0**	**98**	**12.2**	**43**	**2**	**62**	**14**	**−7**	**10**	**1**	**1**	**2**	**4**	**0**	**0**	**0**
1985-86	**Buffalo Sabres**	**NHL**	**50**	**4**	**9**	**13**	**3**	**6**	**9**	**25**	**0**	**0**	**0**	**51**	**7.8**	**26**	**1**	**42**	**11**	**−6**								
	Rochester Americans	AHL	10	3	3	6				7																		
1986-87	**St. Louis Blues**	**NHL**	**43**	**1**	**5**	**6**	**1**	**4**	**5**	**26**	**0**	**0**	**0**	**30**	**3.3**	**10**	**0**	**27**	**11**	**−6**								
	Hartford Whalers	**NHL**	**2**	**0**	**0**	**0**	**0**	**0**	**0**	**2**	**0**	**0**	**0**	**3**	**0.0**	**0**	**0**	**1**	**0**	**−1**	**3**	**0**	**0**	**0**	**0**	**0**	**0**	**0**
	NHL Totals		**573**	**130**	**128**	**258**	**108**	**90**	**198**	**646**	**15**	**11**	**13**	**964**	**13.5**	**383**	**38**	**478**	**107**		**71**	**8**	**25**	**33**	**77**	**0**	**0**	**1**

AHL Second All-Star Team (1978)

Traded to **Pittsburgh** by **Montreal** with Bob Holland for Denis Herron and Pittsburgh's 2nd round choice (Jocelyn Gauvreau) in 1982 Entry Draft, August 30, 1979. Traded to **Edmonton** by **Pittsburgh** for Pat Price, March 10, 1981. Traded to **Pittsburgh** by **Edmonton** for Mike Moller, October 4, 1985. Traded to **Buffalo** by **Pittsburgh** for Mike Moller and Randy Cunneyworth, October 4, 1985. Claimed by **St. Louis** from **Buffalo** in Waiver Draft, October 6, 1986. Traded to **Hartford** by **St. Louis** for Hartford's 10th round choice (Andy Cesarski) in 1987 Entry Draft, March 10, 1987.

● **HUGHES, RYAN** Ryan Hughes C – L. 6'2", 196 lbs. b: Montreal, Que., 1/17/1972. Quebec's 2nd choice, 22nd overall, in 1990 Entry Draft.

			REGULAR SEASON																		PLAYOFFS							
Season	Club	League	GP	G	A	Pts	AG	AA	APts	PIM	PP	SH	GW	S	%	TGF	PGF	TGA	PGA	+/–	GP	G	A	Pts	PIM	PP	SH	GW
1988-89	Lac St-Louis	Midget	42	25	62	87	....	....	....	48	....	....	....	....	....	....	....	....	....	....	....	....	....	....	....	....	....	....
1989-90	Cornell University	ECAC	27	7	16	23	....	....	....	35	....	....	....	....	....	....	....	....	....	....	....	....	....	....	....	....	....	....
1990-91	Cornell University	ECAC	32	18	34	52	....	....	....	28	....	....	....	....	....	....	....	....	....	....	....	....	....	....	....	....	....	....
1991-92	Cornell University	ECAC	27	8	13	21	....	....	....	36	....	....	....	....	....	....	....	....	....	....	....	....	....	....	....	....	....	....
	Canada	WJC-A	7	0	1	1	....	....	....	0	....	....	....	....	....	....	....	....	....	....	....	....	....	....	....	....	....	....
1992-93	Cornell University	ECAC	26	8	14	22	....	....	....	30	....	....	....	....	....	....	....	....	....	....	....	....	....	....	....	....	....	....
1993-94	Cornwall Aces	AHL	54	17	12	29	....	....	....	24	....	....	....	....	....	....	....	....	....	....	13	2	4	6	6	....	....	....
1994-95	Cornwall Aces	AHL	72	15	24	39	....	....	....	48	....	....	....	....	....	....	....	....	....	....	14	0	7	7	10	....	....	....
1995-96	**Boston Bruins**	**NHL**	**3**	**0**	**0**	**0**	**0**	**0**	**0**	**0**	**0**	**0**	**0**	**2**	**0.0**	**0**	**0**	**0**	**0**	**0**	....	....	....	....	....	....	....	....
	Providence Bruins	AHL	78	22	52	74	....	....	....	89	....	....	....	....	....	....	....	....	....	....	4	1	2	3	20	....	....	....
1996-97	Chicago Wolves	IHL	14	2	6	8	....	....	....	12	....	....	....	....	....	....	....	....	....	....	....	....	....	....	....	....	....	....
	Quebec Rafales	IHL	30	2	3	5	....	....	....	24	....	....	....	....	....	....	....	....	....	....	8	1	1	2	4	....	....	....
	NHL Totals		**3**	**0**	**0**	**0**	**0**	**0**	**0**	**0**	**0**	**0**	**0**	**2**	**0.0**	**0**	**0**	**0**	**0**		....	....	....	....	....	....	....	....

Signed as a free agent by **Boston**, October 6, 1995.

● **HULBIG, JOE** Joe Hulbig LW – L. 6'3", 215 lbs. b: Norwood, MA, 9/29/1973. Edmonton's 1st choice, 13th overall, in 1992 Entry Draft.

			REGULAR SEASON																		PLAYOFFS							
Season	Club	League	GP	G	A	Pts	AG	AA	APts	PIM	PP	SH	GW	S	%	TGF	PGF	TGA	PGA	+/–	GP	G	A	Pts	PIM	PP	SH	GW
1992-93	Providence College	H.E.	26	3	13	16	....	....	....	22	....	....	....	....	....	....	....	....	....	....	....	....	....	....	....	....	....	....
1993-94	Providence College	H.E.	28	6	4	10	....	....	....	36	....	....	....	....	....	....	....	....	....	....	....	....	....	....	....	....	....	....
1994-95	Providence College	H.E.	37	14	21	35	....	....	....	36	....	....	....	....	....	....	....	....	....	....	....	....	....	....	....	....	....	....
1995-96	Providence College	H.E.	31	14	22	36	....	....	....	56	....	....	....	....	....	....	....	....	....	....	....	....	....	....	....	....	....	....
1996-97	**Edmonton Oilers**	**NHL**	**6**	**0**	**0**	**0**	**0**	**0**	**0**	**0**	**0**	**0**	**0**	**4**	**0.0**	**1**	**0**	**2**	**0**	**–1**	**6**	**0**	**1**	**1**	**2**	**0**	**0**	**0**
	Hamilton Bulldogs	AHL	73	18	28	46	....	....	....	59	....	....	....	....	....	....	....	....	....	....	16	6	10	16	6	....	....	....
1997-98	**Edmonton Oilers**	**NHL**	**17**	**2**	**2**	**4**	**2**	**2**	**4**	**2**	**0**	**0**	**1**	**8**	**25.0**	**6**	**2**	**5**	**0**	**–1**	....	....	....	....	....	....	....	....
	Hamilton Bulldogs	AHL	46	15	16	31	....	....	....	52	....	....	....	....	....	....	....	....	....	....	3	0	1	1	2	....	....	....
	NHL Totals		**23**	**2**	**2**	**4**	**2**	**2**	**4**	**2**	**0**	**0**	**1**	**12**	**16.7**	**7**	**2**	**7**	**0**		**6**	**0**	**1**	**1**	**2**	**0**	**0**	**0**

● **HULL, BOBBY** Bobby "The Golden Jet" Hull LW – L. 5'10", 195 lbs. b: Point Anne, Ont., 1/3/1939. **HHOF**

			REGULAR SEASON																		PLAYOFFS							
Season	Club	League	GP	G	A	Pts	AG	AA	APts	PIM	PP	SH	GW	S	%	TGF	PGF	TGA	PGA	+/–	GP	G	A	Pts	PIM	PP	SH	GW
1954-55	Galt Black Hawks	OHA	6	0	0	0	....	....	....	0	....	....	....	....	....	....	....	....	....	....	....	....	....	....	....	....	....	....
1955-56	St. Catharines Teepees	OHA	48	11	7	18	....	....	....	79	....	....	....	....	....	....	....	....	....	....	6	0	2	2	9	....	....	....
1956-57	St. Catharines Teepees	OHA	52	33	28	61	....	....	....	95	....	....	....	....	....	....	....	....	....	....	13	8	8	16	24	....	....	....
1957-58	**Chicago Black Hawks**	**NHL**	**70**	**13**	**34**	**47**	**17**	**37**	**54**	**62**	....	....	....	....	....	....	....	....	....	....	....	....	....	....	....	....	....	....
1958-59	**Chicago Black Hawks**	**NHL**	**70**	**18**	**32**	**50**	**23**	**34**	**57**	**50**	....	....	....	....	....	....	....	....	....	....	**6**	**1**	**1**	**2**	**2**	....	....	....
1959-60	**Chicago Black Hawks**	**NHL**	**70**	***39**	**42**	***81**	**49**	**43**	**92**	**68**	....	....	....	....	....	....	....	....	....	....	**3**	**1**	**0**	**1**	**2**	....	....	....
1960-61	**Chicago Black Hawks**	**NHL**	**67**	**31**	**25**	**56**	**38**	**25**	**63**	**43**	....	....	....	....	....	....	....	....	....	....	**12**	**4**	**10**	**14**	**4**	....	....	....
1961-62	**Chicago Black Hawks**	**NHL**	**70**	***50**	**34**	***84**	**63**	**35**	**98**	**35**	....	....	....	....	....	....	....	....	....	....	**12**	***8**	**6**	**14**	**12**	....	....	....
1962-63	**Chicago Black Hawks**	**NHL**	**65**	**31**	**31**	**62**	**39**	**32**	**71**	**27**	....	....	....	....	....	....	....	....	....	....	**5**	***8**	**2**	**10**	**4**	....	....	....
1963-64	**Chicago Black Hawks**	**NHL**	**70**	***43**	**44**	**87**	**58**	**49**	**107**	**50**	....	....	....	....	....	....	....	....	....	....	**7**	**2**	**5**	**7**	**2**	....	....	....
1964-65	**Chicago Black Hawks**	**NHL**	**61**	**39**	**32**	**71**	**51**	**35**	**86**	**32**	....	....	....	....	....	....	....	....	....	....	**14**	***10**	**7**	***17**	**27**	....	....	....
1965-66	**Chicago Black Hawks**	**NHL**	**65**	***54**	**43**	***97**	**67**	**43**	**110**	**70**	....	....	....	....	....	....	....	....	....	....	**6**	**2**	**2**	**4**	**10**	....	....	....
1966-67	**Chicago Black Hawks**	**NHL**	**66**	***52**	**28**	**80**	**66**	**29**	**95**	**52**	....	....	....	....	....	....	....	....	....	....	**6**	**4**	**2**	**6**	**0**	....	....	....
1967-68	**Chicago Black Hawks**	**NHL**	**71**	***44**	**31**	**75**	**55**	**32**	**87**	**39**	**8**	**2**	**6**	**364**	**12.1**	**105**	**28**	**73**	**10**	**+14**	**11**	**4**	**6**	**10**	**15**	**1**	**1**	**1**
1968-69	**Chicago Black Hawks**	**NHL**	**74**	***58**	**49**	**107**	**66**	**46**	**112**	**48**	**20**	**2**	**11**	**414**	**14.0**	**132**	**49**	**99**	**9**	**–7**	....	....	....	....	....	....	....	....
1969-70	**Chicago Black Hawks**	**NHL**	**61**	**38**	**29**	**67**	**44**	**29**	**73**	**8**	**10**	**2**	**8**	**289**	**13.1**	**90**	**29**	**50**	**9**	**+20**	**8**	**3**	**8**	**11**	**2**	**0**	**0**	**0**
1970-71	**Chicago Black Hawks**	**NHL**	**78**	**44**	**52**	**96**	**46**	**46**	**92**	**32**	**11**	**0**	**11**	**378**	**11.6**	**129**	**49**	**54**	**8**	**+34**	**18**	**11**	**14**	**25**	**16**	**6**	**0**	**4**
1971-72	**Chicago Black Hawks**	**NHL**	**78**	**50**	**43**	**93**	**54**	**39**	**93**	**24**	**8**	**3**	**9**	**336**	**14.9**	**126**	**37**	**47**	**12**	**+54**	**8**	**4**	**4**	**8**	**6**	**0**	**1**	**0**
1972-73	Winnipeg Jets	WHA	63	51	52	103	....	....	....	37	....	....	....	....	....	....	....	....	....	....	14	9	*10	25	16	....	....	....
1973-74	Winnipeg Jets	WHA	75	53	42	95	....	....	....	38	....	....	....	....	....	....	....	....	....	....	4	1	1	2	4	....	....	....
1974-75	Canada	Summit	8	7	2	9	....	....	....	0	....	....	....	....	....	....	....	....	....	....	....	....	....	....	....	....	....	....
	Winnipeg Jets	WHA	78	*77	65	142	....	....	....	41	....	....	....	....	....	....	....	....	....	....	....	....	....	....	....	....	....	....
1975-76	Winnipeg Jets	WHA	80	53	70	123	....	....	....	30	....	....	....	....	....	....	....	....	....	....	13	12	8	20	4	....	....	....
1976-77	Canada	C Cup	7	5	3	8	....	....	....	2	....	....	....	....	....	....	....	....	....	....	....	....	....	....	....	....	....	....
	Winnipeg Jets	WHA	34	21	32	53	....	....	....	14	....	....	....	....	....	....	....	....	....	....	20	13	9	22	2	....	....	....
1977-78	Winnipeg Jets	WHA	77	46	71	117	....	....	....	23	....	....	....	....	....	....	....	....	....	....	9	8	3	11	12	....	....	....
1978-79	Winnipeg Jets	WHA	4	2	3	5	....	....	....	0	....	....	....	....	....	....	....	....	....	....	....	....	....	....	....	....	....	....
1979-80	**Winnipeg Jets**	**NHL**	**18**	**4**	**6**	**10**	**4**	**5**	**9**	**0**	**1**	**0**	**0**	**25**	**16.0**	**18**	**4**	**21**	**0**	**–7**	....	....	....	....	....	....	....	....
	Hartford Whalers	**NHL**	**9**	**2**	**5**	**7**	**2**	**4**	**6**	**0**	**1**	**0**	**0**	**13**	**15.4**	**9**	**2**	**10**	**0**	**–3**	**3**	**0**	**0**	**0**	**0**	**0**	**0**	**0**
	NHL Totals		**1063**	**610**	**560**	**1170**	**742**	**563**	**1305**	**640**	**59**	**9**	**45**	**1819**	**33.5**	**609**	**198**	**354**	**48**		**119**	**62**	**67**	**129**	**102**	**7**	**2**	**5**
	Other Major League Totals		411	303	335	638	....	....	....	183	....	....	....	....	....	....	....	....	....	....	60	43	37	80	38	....	....	....

NHL First All-Star Team (1960, 1962, 1964, 1965, 1966, 1967, 1968, 1969, 1970, 1972) • Won Art Ross Trophy (1960, 1962, 1966) • NHL Second All-Star Team (1963, 1971) • Won Lady Byng Trophy (1965) • Won Hart Trophy (1965, 1966) • Won Lester Patrick Trophy (1969) • WHA First All-Star Team (1973, 1974, 1975) • Won Gary Davidson Trophy (WHA MVP) (1973, 1975) • WHA Second All-Star Team (1976, 1978)

Played in NHL All-Star Game (1960, 1961, 1962, 1963, 1964, 1965, 1967, 1968, 1969, 1970, 1971, 1972)

Selected by **Winnipeg** (WHA) in 1972 WHA General Player Draft, February 12, 1972. Reclaimed by **Chicago** from Winnipeg prior to Expansion Draft, June 9, 1979 Claimed by **Winnipeg** from **Chicago** in Expansion Draft, June 13, 1979. Traded to **Hartford** by **Winnipeg** for future considerations, February 27, 1980.

● **HULL, BRETT** Brett Hull RW – R. 5'10", 201 lbs. b: Belleville, Ont., 8/9/1964. Calgary's 6th choice, 117th overall, in 1984 Entry Draft.

			REGULAR SEASON																		PLAYOFFS							
Season	Club	League	GP	G	A	Pts	AG	AA	APts	PIM	PP	SH	GW	S	%	TGF	PGF	TGA	PGA	+/–	GP	G	A	Pts	PIM	PP	SH	GW
1983-84	Penticton Knights	BCJHL	56	*105	88	*188	....	....	....	20	....	....	....	....	....	....	....	....	....	....	....	....	....	....	....	....	....	....
1984-85	University of Minnesota-Duluth	WCHA	48	32	28	60	....	....	....	24	....	....	....	....	....	....	....	....	....	....	....	....	....	....	....	....	....	....
1985-86	University of Minnesota-Duluth	WCHA	42	52	32	84	....	....	....	46	....	....	....	....	....	....	....	....	....	....	....	....	....	....	....	....	....	....
	United States	WEC-A	10	7	4	11	....	....	....	18	....	....	....	....	....	....	....	....	....	....	....	....	....	....	....	....	....	....
	Calgary Flames	**NHL**	....	....	....	....	....	....	....	....	....	....	....	....	....	....	....	....	....	....	**2**	**0**	**0**	**0**	**0**	....	....	....
1986-87	**Calgary Flames**	**NHL**	**5**	**1**	**0**	**1**	**1**	**0**	**1**	**0**	**0**	**0**	**1**	**5**	**20.0**	**2**	**0**	**3**	**0**	**–1**	**4**	**2**	**1**	**3**	**0**	**0**	**0**	**0**
	Moncton Golden Flames	AHL	67	50	42	92	....	....	....	16	....	....	....	....	....	....	....	....	....	....	3	2	2	4	2	....	....	....
1987-88	**Calgary Flames**	**NHL**	**52**	**26**	**24**	**50**	**22**	**17**	**39**	**12**	**4**	**0**	**3**	**153**	**17.0**	**72**	**27**	**35**	**0**	**+10**	....	....	....	....	....	....	....	....
	St. Louis Blues	**NHL**	**13**	**6**	**8**	**14**	**5**	**6**	**11**	**4**	**2**	**0**	**0**	**58**	**10.3**	**23**	**8**	**11**	**0**	**+4**	**10**	**7**	**2**	**9**	**4**	**4**	**0**	**3**
1988-89	**St. Louis Blues**	**NHL**	**78**	**41**	**43**	**84**	**35**	**30**	**65**	**33**	**16**	**0**	**6**	**305**	**13.4**	**114**	**58**	**73**	**0**	**–17**	**10**	**5**	**5**	**10**	**6**	**1**	**0**	**2**
1989-90	**St. Louis Blues**	**NHL**	**80**	***72**	**41**	**113**	**63**	**29**	**92**	**24**	**27**	**0**	**12**	**385**	**18.7**	**154**	**66**	**90**	**1**	**–1**	**12**	**13**	**8**	**21**	**17**	**7**	**0**	**3**
1990-91	**St. Louis Blues**	**NHL**	**78**	***86**	**45**	**131**	**80**	**34**	**114**	**22**	**29**	**0**	**11**	**389**	**22.1**	**170**	**62**	**86**	**1**	**+23**	**13**	**11**	**8**	**19**	**4**	**3**	**0**	**2**
1991-92	United States	C Cup	8	2	7	9	....	....	....	0	....	....	....	....	....	....	....	....	....	....	....	....	....	....	....	....	....	....
	St. Louis Blues	**NHL**	**73**	***70**	**39**	**109**	**64**	**29**	**93**	**48**	**20**	**5**	**9**	**408**	**17.2**	**146**	**52**	**100**	**4**	**–2**	**6**	**4**	**4**	**8**	**4**	**1**	**1**	**1**
1992-93	**St. Louis Blues**	**NHL**	**80**	**54**	**47**	**101**	**45**	**32**	**77**	**41**	**29**	**0**	**2**	**390**	**13.8**	**140**	**77**	**95**	**5**	**–27**	**11**	**8**	**5**	**13**	**2**	**5**	**0**	**2**
1993-94	**St. Louis Blues**	**NHL**	**81**	**57**	**40**	**97**	**53**	**31**	**84**	**38**	**25**	**3**	**6**	**392**	**14.5**	**136**	**67**	**94**	**22**	**–3**	**4**	**2**	**1**	**3**	**0**	**1**	**0**	**0**
1994-95	**St. Louis Blues**	**NHL**	**48**	**29**	**21**	**50**	**52**	**31**	**83**	**10**	**9**	**3**	**6**	**200**	**14.5**	**77**	**29**	**57**	**22**	**+13**	**7**	**6**	**2**	**8**	**0**	**2**	**0**	**0**
1995-96	**St. Louis Blues**	**NHL**	**70**	**43**	**40**	**83**	**43**	**33**	**76**	**30**	**16**	**5**	**6**	**327**	**13.1**	**110**	**47**	**91**	**32**	**+4**	**13**	**6**	**5**	**11**	**10**	**2**	**1**	**1**
1996-97	United States	W Cup	7	7	4	11	....	....	....	4	....	....	....	....	....	....	....	....	....	....	....	....	....	....	....	....	....	....
	St. Louis Blues	**NHL**	**77**	**42**	**40**	**82**	**45**	**35**	**80**	**10**	**12**	**2**	**6**	**302**	**13.9**	**100**	**34**	**91**	**16**	**–9**	**6**	**2**	**7**	**9**	**2**	**0**	**0**	**0**
1997-98	**St. Louis Blues**	**NHL**	**66**	**27**	**45**	**72**	**32**	**44**	**76**	**26**	**10**	**0**	**6**	**211**	**12.8**	**94**	**37**	**60**	**2**	**–1**	**10**	**3**	**3**	**6**	**2**	**1**	**0**	**1**
	United States	Olympics	4	2	1	3	....	....	....	0	....	....	....	....	....	....	....	....	....	....	....	....	....	....	....	....	....	....
	NHL Totals		**801**	**554**	**433**	**987**	**540**	**351**	**891**	**298**	**199**	**18**	**74**	**3525**	**15.7**	**1338**	**564**	**886**	**105**		**108**	**69**	**51**	**120**	**51**	**27**	**2**	**15**

WCHA First All-Star Team (1986) • AHL First All-Star Team (1987) • Won Dudley "Red" Garrett Memorial Trophy (Top Rookie - AHL) (1987) • NHL First All-Star Team (1990, 1991, 1992) • Won Lady Byng Trophy (1990) • Won Dodge Ram Tough Award (1990, 1991) • Won Hart Memorial Trophy (1991) • Won Lester B. Pearson Award (1991) • Won ProSet/NHL Player of the Year Award (1991) • World Cup All-Star Team (1996)

Played in NHL All-Star Game (1989, 1990, 1992, 1993, 1994, 1996, 1997, 1998)

Traded to **St. Louis** by **Calgary** with Steve Bozek for Rob Ramage and Rick Wamsley, March 7, 1988. Signed as a free agent by **Dallas**, July 3, 1998.

● **HULL, DENNIS** Dennis Hull LW – L. 5'11", 190 lbs. b: Pointe Anne, Ont., 11/19/1944.

			REGULAR SEASON																		PLAYOFFS							
Season	Club	League	GP	G	A	Pts	AG	AA	APts	PIM	PP	SH	GW	S	%	TGF	PGF	TGA	PGA	+/–	GP	G	A	Pts	PIM	PP	SH	GW
1960-61	St. Catharines Teepees	OHA	47	6	4	10	....	....	....	33	....	....	....	....	....	....	....	....	....	....	6	0	1	1	2	....	....	....
1961-62	St. Catharines Teepees	OHA	50	6	12	18	....	....	....	29	....	....	....	....	....	....	....	....	....	....	2	0	0	0	0	....	....	....
1962-63	St. Catharines Black Hawks	OHA	50	19	29	48	....	....	....	73	....	....	....	....	....	....	....	....	....	....	....	....	....	....	....	....	....	....

Season	Club	League	REGULAR SEASON GP	G	A	Pts	AG	AA	APts	PIM	PP	SH	GW	S	%	TGF	PGF	TGA	PGA	+/–	PLAYOFFS GP	G	A	Pts	PIM	PP	SH	GW
1963-64	St. Catharines Black Hawks	OHA	55	48	49	97	....	....	....	123	....	....	....	....	....	....	....	....	....	....	12	4	11	15	50	....	....	....
1964-65	**Chicago Black Hawks**	**NHL**	**55**	**10**	**4**	**14**	**13**	**4**	**17**	**18**	....	....	....	....	....	....	....	....	....	....	**6**	**0**	**0**	**0**	**0**	....	....	....
1965-66	**Chicago Black Hawks**	**NHL**	**25**	**1**	**5**	**6**	**1**	**5**	**6**	**6**	....	....	....	....	....	....	....	....	....	....	**3**	**0**	**0**	**0**	**0**	....	....	....
	St. Louis Braves	CHL	40	11	16	27	....	....	....	14	....	....	....	....	....	....	....	....	....	....	5	2	1	3	0	....	....	....
1966-67	**Chicago Black Hawks**	**NHL**	**70**	**25**	**17**	**42**	**31**	**17**	**48**	**33**	....	....	....	....	....	....	....	....	....	....	**6**	**0**	**1**	**1**	**12**	....	....	....
1967-68	**Chicago Black Hawks**	**NHL**	**74**	**18**	**15**	**33**	**22**	**16**	**38**	**34**	**0**	**0**	**2**	**197**	**9.1**	**40**	**1**	**71**	**12**	**–20**	**11**	**1**	**3**	**4**	**6**	**0**	**0**	**1**
1968-69	**Chicago Black Hawks**	**NHL**	**72**	**30**	**34**	**64**	**34**	**32**	**66**	**25**	**3**	**0**	**3**	**233**	**12.9**	**95**	**21**	**71**	**4**	**+7**	....	....	....	....	....	....	....	....
1969-70	**Chicago Black Hawks**	**NHL**	**76**	**17**	**35**	**52**	**20**	**35**	**55**	**31**	**5**	**0**	**3**	**223**	**7.6**	**74**	**15**	**57**	**2**	**+4**	**8**	**5**	**2**	**7**	**0**	**0**	**1**	**0**
1970-71	**Chicago Black Hawks**	**NHL**	**78**	**40**	**26**	**66**	**42**	**23**	**65**	**16**	**10**	**0**	**7**	**229**	**17.5**	**92**	**27**	**41**	**4**	**+28**	**18**	**7**	**6**	**13**	**2**	**2**	**0**	**1**
1971-72	**Chicago Black Hawks**	**NHL**	**78**	**30**	**39**	**69**	**32**	**36**	**68**	**10**	**8**	**1**	**2**	**270**	**11.1**	**51**	**9**	**30**	**0**	**+12**	**8**	**4**	**2**	**6**	**4**	**1**	**0**	**0**
1972-73	Canada	Summit	4	2	2	4	....	....	....	4	....	....	....	....	....	....	....	....	....	....	....	....	....	....	....	....	....	....
	Chicago Black Hawks	**NHL**	**78**	**39**	**51**	**90**	**39**	**43**	**82**	**27**	**8**	**0**	**7**	**263**	**14.8**	**130**	**30**	**74**	**2**	**+28**	**16**	**9**	***15**	**24**	**4**	**4**	**0**	**1**
1973-74	**Chicago Black Hawks**	**NHL**	**74**	**29**	**39**	**68**	**30**	**34**	**64**	**15**	**5**	**1**	**6**	**220**	**13.2**	**96**	**26**	**46**	**1**	**+25**	**10**	**6**	**3**	**9**	**0**	**1**	**0**	**1**
1974-75	**Chicago Black Hawks**	**NHL**	**69**	**16**	**21**	**37**	**15**	**17**	**32**	**10**	**4**	**0**	**2**	**199**	**8.0**	**56**	**16**	**59**	**5**	**–14**	**5**	**0**	**2**	**2**	**0**	**0**	**0**	**0**
1975-76	**Chicago Black Hawks**	**NHL**	**80**	**27**	**39**	**66**	**25**	**31**	**56**	**28**	**1**	**4**	**4**	**225**	**12.0**	**87**	**21**	**108**	**25**	**–17**	**4**	**0**	**0**	**0**	**0**	**0**	**0**	**0**
1976-77	**Chicago Black Hawks**	**NHL**	**75**	**16**	**17**	**33**	**15**	**14**	**29**	**2**	**3**	**0**	**0**	**207**	**7.7**	**69**	**21**	**82**	**14**	**–20**	**2**	**1**	**0**	**1**	**0**	**1**	**0**	**0**
1977-78	**Detroit Red Wings**	**NHL**	**55**	**5**	**9**	**14**	**5**	**7**	**12**	**6**	**2**	**0**	**1**	**72**	**6.9**	**22**	**8**	**34**	**0**	**–20**	**7**	**0**	**0**	**0**	**2**	**0**	**0**	**0**
	NHL Totals		**959**	**303**	**351**	**654**	**324**	**314**	**638**	**261**	**49**	**6**	**37**	**2338**	**13.0**	**812**	**195**	**673**	**69**		**104**	**33**	**34**	**67**	**30**	**9**	**1**	**4**

NHL Second All-Star Team (1973)

Played in NHL All-Star Game (1969, 1971, 1972, 1973, 1974)

Traded to **Detroit** by **Chicago** for Detroit's 4th round choice (Carey Wilson) in 1980 Amateur (Entry) Draft, December 2, 1977.

• HULL, JODY

Jody Hull RW – R. 6'2", 195 lbs. b: Cambridge, Ont., 2/2/1969. Hartford's 1st choice, 18th overall, in 1987 Entry Draft.

Season	Club	League	GP	G	A	Pts	AG	AA	APts	PIM	PP	SH	GW	S	%	TGF	PGF	TGA	PGA	+/–	GP	G	A	Pts	PIM	PP	SH	GW
1985-86	Peterborough Petes	OHL	61	20	22	42	....	....	....	29	....	....	....	....	....	....	....	....	....	....	16	1	5	6	4	....	....	....
1986-87	Peterborough Petes	OHL	49	18	34	52	....	....	....	22	....	....	....	....	....	....	....	....	....	....	12	4	9	13	14	....	....	....
1987-88	Peterborough Petes	OHL	60	50	44	94	....	....	....	33	....	....	....	....	....	....	....	....	....	....	12	10	8	18	8	....	....	....
	Canada	WJC-A	7	2	1	3	....	....	....	2	....	....	....	....	....	....	....	....	....	....	....	....	....	....	....	....	....	....
1988-89	**Hartford Whalers**	**NHL**	**60**	**16**	**18**	**34**	**14**	**13**	**27**	**10**	**6**	**0**	**2**	**82**	**19.5**	**53**	**12**	**35**	**0**	**+6**	**1**	**0**	**0**	**0**	**2**	**0**	**0**	**0**
1989-90	**Hartford Whalers**	**NHL**	**38**	**7**	**10**	**17**	**6**	**7**	**13**	**21**	**2**	**0**	**0**	**46**	**15.2**	**18**	**3**	**26**	**5**	**–6**	**5**	**0**	**1**	**1**	**2**	**0**	**0**	**0**
	Binghamton Whalers	AHL	21	7	10	17	....	....	....	6	....	....	....	....	....	....	....	....	....	....	....	....	....	....	....	....	....	....
1990-91	**New York Rangers**	**NHL**	**47**	**5**	**8**	**13**	**5**	**6**	**11**	**10**	**0**	**0**	**0**	**57**	**8.8**	**20**	**0**	**27**	**9**	**+2**	....	....	....	....	....	....	....	....
1991-92	**New York Rangers**	**NHL**	**3**	**0**	**0**	**0**	**0**	**0**	**0**	**2**	**0**	**0**	**0**	**4**	**0.0**	**0**	**0**	**5**	**1**	**–4**	....	....	....	....	....	....	....	....
	Binghamton Rangers	AHL	69	34	31	65	....	....	....	28	....	....	....	....	....	....	....	....	....	....	11	5	2	7	4	....	....	....
1992-93	**Ottawa Senators**	**NHL**	**69**	**13**	**21**	**34**	**11**	**14**	**25**	**14**	**5**	**1**	**0**	**134**	**9.7**	**56**	**26**	**72**	**18**	**–24**	....	....	....	....	....	....	....	....
1993-94	**Florida Panthers**	**NHL**	**69**	**13**	**13**	**26**	**12**	**10**	**22**	**8**	**0**	**1**	**5**	**100**	**13.0**	**38**	**1**	**53**	**22**	**+6**	....	....	....	....	....	....	....	....
1994-95	**Florida Panthers**	**NHL**	**46**	**11**	**8**	**19**	**19**	**12**	**31**	**8**	**0**	**0**	**4**	**63**	**17.5**	**23**	**2**	**35**	**13**	**–1**	....	....	....	....	....	....	....	....
1995-96	**Florida Panthers**	**NHL**	**78**	**20**	**17**	**37**	**20**	**14**	**34**	**25**	**2**	**0**	**3**	**120**	**16.7**	**43**	**4**	**60**	**26**	**+5**	**14**	**3**	**2**	**5**	**0**	**0**	**0**	**0**
1996-97	**Florida Panthers**	**NHL**	**67**	**10**	**6**	**16**	**11**	**5**	**16**	**4**	**0**	**1**	**2**	**92**	**10.9**	**20**	**3**	**20**	**4**	**+1**	**5**	**0**	**0**	**0**	**0**	**0**	**0**	**0**
1997-98	**Florida Panthers**	**NHL**	**21**	**2**	**0**	**2**	**2**	**0**	**2**	**4**	**0**	**1**	**0**	**23**	**8.7**	**5**	**0**	**11**	**7**	**+1**	....	....	....	....	....	....	....	....
	Tampa Bay Lightning	**NHL**	**28**	**2**	**4**	**6**	**2**	**4**	**6**	**4**	**0**	**0**	**2**	**28**	**7.1**	**13**	**1**	**22**	**12**	**+2**	....	....	....	....	....	....	....	....
	NHL Totals		**526**	**99**	**105**	**204**	**102**	**85**	**187**	**110**	**15**	**4**	**18**	**749**	**13.2**	**289**	**52**	**366**	**117**		**25**	**3**	**3**	**6**	**4**	**0**	**0**	**0**

OHL Second All-Star Team (1988)

Traded to **NY Rangers** by **Hartford** for Carey Wilson and NY Rangers' 3rd round choice (Mikael Nylander) in the 1991 Entry Draft, July 9, 1990. Traded to **Ottawa** by **NY Rangers** for future considerations, July 28, 1992. Signed as a free agent by **Florida**, August 10, 1993. Traded to **Tampa Bay** by **Florida** with Mark Fitzpatrick for Dino Ciccarelli and Jeff Norton, January 15, 1998.

• HULSE, CALE

Cale Hulse D – R. 6'3", 210 lbs. b: Edmonton, Alta., 11/10/1973. New Jersey's 3rd choice, 66th overall, in 1992 Entry Draft.

Season	Club	League	GP	G	A	Pts	AG	AA	APts	PIM	PP	SH	GW	S	%	TGF	PGF	TGA	PGA	+/–	GP	G	A	Pts	PIM	PP	SH	GW
1991-92	Portland Winter Hawks	WHL	70	4	18	22	....	....	....	250	....	....	....	....	....	....	....	....	....	....	6	0	2	2	27	....	....	....
1992-93	Portland Winter Hawks	WHL	72	10	26	36	....	....	....	284	....	....	....	....	....	....	....	....	....	....	16	4	4	8	65	....	....	....
1993-94	Albany River Rats	AHL	79	7	14	21	....	....	....	186	....	....	....	....	....	....	....	....	....	....	5	0	3	3	11	....	....	....
1994-95	Albany River Rats	AHL	77	5	13	18	....	....	....	215	....	....	....	....	....	....	....	....	....	....	12	1	1	2	17	....	....	....
1995-96	**New Jersey Devils**	**NHL**	**8**	**0**	**0**	**0**	**0**	**0**	**0**	**15**	**0**	**0**	**0**	**5**	**0.0**	**3**	**0**	**5**	**0**	**–2**	....	....	....	....	....	....	....	....
	Albany River Rats	AHL	42	4	23	27	....	....	....	107	....	....	....	....	....	....	....	....	....	....	....	....	....	....	....	....	....	....
	Calgary Flames	**NHL**	**3**	**0**	**0**	**0**	**0**	**0**	**0**	**5**	**0**	**0**	**0**	**4**	**0.0**	**3**	**0**	**0**	**0**	**+3**	**1**	**0**	**0**	**0**	**0**	**0**	**0**	**0**
	Saint John Flames	AHL	13	2	7	9	....	....	....	39	....	....	....	....	....	....	....	....	....	....	....	....	....	....	....	....	....	....
1996-97	**Calgary Flames**	**NHL**	**63**	**1**	**6**	**7**	**1**	**5**	**6**	**91**	**0**	**1**	**0**	**58**	**1.7**	**34**	**2**	**51**	**17**	**–2**	....	....	....	....	....	....	....	....
1997-98	**Calgary Flames**	**NHL**	**79**	**5**	**22**	**27**	**6**	**21**	**27**	**169**	**1**	**1**	**0**	**117**	**4.3**	**66**	**14**	**76**	**25**	**+1**	....	....	....	....	....	....	....	....
	NHL Totals		**153**	**6**	**28**	**34**	**7**	**26**	**33**	**280**	**1**	**2**	**0**	**184**	**3.3**	**106**	**16**	**132**	**42**		**1**	**0**	**0**	**0**	**0**	**0**	**0**	**0**

Traded to **Calgary** by **New Jersey** with Tommy Albelin and Jocelyn Lemieux for Phil Housley and Dan Keczmer, February 26, 1996.

• HUNTER, DALE

Dale Hunter C – L. 5'10", 198 lbs. b: Petrolia, Ont., 7/31/1960. Quebec's 2nd choice, 41st overall, in 1979 Entry Draft.

Season	Club	League	GP	G	A	Pts	AG	AA	APts	PIM	PP	SH	GW	S	%	TGF	PGF	TGA	PGA	+/–	GP	G	A	Pts	PIM	PP	SH	GW
1977-78	Kitchener Rangers	OHA	68	22	42	64	....	....	....	115	....	....	....	....	....	....	....	....	....	....	....	....	....	....	....	....	....	....
1978-79	Sudbury Wolves	OHA	59	42	68	110	....	....	....	188	....	....	....	....	....	....	....	....	....	....	10	4	12	16	47	....	....	....
1979-80	Sudbury Wolves	OHA	61	34	51	85	....	....	....	189	....	....	....	....	....	....	....	....	....	....	9	6	9	15	45	....	....	....
1980-81	**Quebec Nordiques**	**NHL**	**80**	**19**	**44**	**63**	**16**	**31**	**47**	**226**	**2**	**0**	**2**	**152**	**12.5**	**83**	**9**	**107**	**38**	**+5**	**5**	**4**	**2**	**6**	**34**	**0**	**0**	**1**
1981-82	**Quebec Nordiques**	**NHL**	**80**	**22**	**50**	**72**	**17**	**33**	**50**	**272**	**0**	**2**	**1**	**124**	**17.7**	**95**	**9**	**96**	**36**	**+26**	**16**	**3**	**7**	**10**	**52**	**1**	**0**	**2**
1982-83	**Quebec Nordiques**	**NHL**	**80**	**17**	**46**	**63**	**14**	**32**	**46**	**206**	**1**	**2**	**1**	**125**	**13.6**	**92**	**4**	**122**	**44**	**+10**	**4**	**2**	**1**	**3**	**24**	**0**	**1**	**0**
1983-84	**Quebec Nordiques**	**NHL**	**77**	**24**	**55**	**79**	**19**	**37**	**56**	**232**	**7**	**2**	**1**	**123**	**19.5**	**108**	**20**	**76**	**23**	**+35**	**9**	**2**	**3**	**5**	**41**	**0**	**0**	**0**
1984-85	**Quebec Nordiques**	**NHL**	**80**	**20**	**52**	**72**	**16**	**35**	**51**	**209**	**3**	**3**	**3**	**115**	**17.4**	**104**	**21**	**87**	**27**	**+23**	**17**	**4**	**6**	**10**	***97**	**0**	**1**	**2**
1985-86	**Quebec Nordiques**	**NHL**	**80**	**28**	**42**	**70**	**22**	**28**	**50**	**265**	**7**	**0**	**4**	**152**	**18.4**	**98**	**23**	**84**	**15**	**+6**	**3**	**0**	**0**	**0**	**15**	**0**	**0**	**0**
1986-87	**Quebec Nordiques**	**NHL**	**46**	**10**	**29**	**39**	**9**	**21**	**30**	**135**	**0**	**0**	**0**	**53**	**18.9**	**61**	**14**	**52**	**9**	**+4**	**13**	**1**	**7**	**8**	**56**	**1**	**0**	**0**
1987-88	**Washington Capitals**	**NHL**	**79**	**22**	**37**	**59**	**19**	**26**	**45**	**240**	**11**	**0**	**1**	**126**	**17.5**	**109**	**54**	**56**	**8**	**+7**	**14**	**7**	**5**	**12**	**98**	**4**	**0**	**1**
1988-89	**Washington Capitals**	**NHL**	**80**	**20**	**37**	**57**	**17**	**26**	**43**	**219**	**9**	**0**	**3**	**138**	**14.5**	**95**	**46**	**58**	**6**	**–3**	**6**	**0**	**4**	**4**	**29**	**0**	**0**	**0**
1989-90	Washington Capitals	FrTour	4	1	2	3	....	....	....	4	....	....	....	....	....	....	....	....	....	....	....	....	....	....	....	....	....	....
	Washington Capitals	**NHL**	**80**	**23**	**39**	**62**	**20**	**28**	**48**	**233**	**9**	**1**	**6**	**123**	**18.7**	**104**	**37**	**52**	**2**	**+17**	**15**	**4**	**8**	**12**	**61**	**1**	**0**	**0**
1990-91	**Washington Capitals**	**NHL**	**76**	**16**	**30**	**46**	**15**	**23**	**38**	**234**	**9**	**0**	**2**	**106**	**15.1**	**71**	**31**	**63**	**1**	**–22**	**11**	**1**	**9**	**10**	**41**	**0**	**0**	**0**
1991-92	**Washington Capitals**	**NHL**	**80**	**28**	**50**	**78**	**26**	**38**	**64**	**205**	**13**	**0**	**4**	**110**	**25.5**	**124**	**53**	**75**	**2**	**–2**	**7**	**1**	**4**	**5**	**16**	**0**	**0**	**0**
1992-93	**Washington Capitals**	**NHL**	**84**	**20**	**59**	**79**	**17**	**40**	**57**	**198**	**10**	**0**	**2**	**120**	**16.7**	**109**	**50**	**58**	**2**	**+3**	**6**	**7**	**1**	**8**	**35**	**4**	**0**	**1**
1993-94	**Washington Capitals**	**NHL**	**52**	**9**	**29**	**38**	**8**	**22**	**30**	**131**	**1**	**0**	**1**	**61**	**14.8**	**58**	**16**	**51**	**5**	**–4**	**7**	**0**	**3**	**3**	**14**	**0**	**0**	**0**
1994-95	**Washington Capitals**	**NHL**	**45**	**8**	**15**	**23**	**14**	**22**	**36**	**101**	**3**	**0**	**1**	**73**	**11.0**	**36**	**13**	**27**	**0**	**–4**	**7**	**4**	**4**	**8**	**24**	**2**	**0**	**0**
1995-96	**Washington Capitals**	**NHL**	**82**	**13**	**24**	**37**	**13**	**20**	**33**	**112**	**4**	**0**	**3**	**128**	**10.2**	**48**	**15**	**29**	**1**	**+5**	**6**	**1**	**5**	**6**	**24**	**0**	**0**	**0**
1996-97	**Washington Capitals**	**NHL**	**82**	**14**	**32**	**46**	**15**	**28**	**43**	**125**	**3**	**0**	**5**	**110**	**12.7**	**63**	**18**	**47**	**0**	**–2**	....	....	....	....	....	....	....	....
1997-98	**Washington Capitals**	**NHL**	**82**	**8**	**18**	**26**	**9**	**18**	**27**	**103**	**0**	**0**	**1**	**82**	**9.8**	**38**	**2**	**42**	**7**	**+1**	**21**	**0**	**4**	**4**	**30**	**0**	**0**	**0**
	NHL Totals		**1345**	**321**	**688**	**1009**	**286**	**508**	**794**	**3446**	**92**	**10**	**41**	**2021**	**15.9**	**1496**	**435**	**1182**	**226**		**167**	**41**	**73**	**114**	**691**	**13**	**2**	**7**

Played in NHL All-Star Game (1997)

Traded to **Washington** by **Quebec** with Clint Malarchuk for Gaetan Duchesne, Alan Haworth and Washington's 1st round choice (Joe Sakic) in 1987 Entry Draft, June 13, 1987.

• HUNTER, DAVE

Dave Hunter LW – L. 5'11", 195 lbs. b: Petrolia, Ont., 1/1/1958. Montreal's 2nd choice, 17th overall, in 1978 Amateur Draft.

Season	Club	League	GP	G	A	Pts	AG	AA	APts	PIM	PP	SH	GW	S	%	TGF	PGF	TGA	PGA	+/–	GP	G	A	Pts	PIM	PP	SH	GW
1975-76	Sudbury Wolves	OHA	53	7	21	28	....	....	....	117	....	....	....	....	....	....	....	....	....	....	....	....	....	....	....	....	....	....
1976-77	Sudbury Wolves	OHA	62	30	56	86	....	....	....	140	....	....	....	....	....	....	....	....	....	....	6	1	3	4	9	....	....	....
	Canada	WJC-A	7	6	2	8	....	....	....	2	....	....	....	....	....	....	....	....	....	....	....	....	....	....	....	....	....	....
1977-78	Sudbury Wolves	OHA	68	44	44	88	....	....	....	156	....	....	....	....	....	....	....	....	....	....	....	....	....	....	....	....	....	....
1978-79	Edmonton Oilers	WHA	72	7	25	32	....	....	....	134	....	....	....	....	....	....	....	....	....	....	13	2	3	5	42	....	....	....
	Dallas Black Hawks	CHL	6	3	4	7	....	....	....	6	....	....	....	....	....	....	....	....	....	....	....	....	....	....	....	....	....	....
1979-80	**Edmonton Oilers**	**NHL**	**80**	**12**	**31**	**43**	**11**	**24**	**35**	**103**	**1**	**2**	**3**	**109**	**11.0**	**71**	**3**	**78**	**17**	**+7**	**3**	**0**	**0**	**0**	**7**	**0**	**0**	**0**
1980-81	**Edmonton Oilers**	**NHL**	**78**	**12**	**16**	**28**	**10**	**11**	**21**	**98**	**0**	**0**	**3**	**104**	**11.5**	**51**	**1**	**91**	**29**	**–12**	**9**	**0**	**0**	**0**	**28**	**0**	**0**	**0**
1981-82	**Edmonton Oilers**	**NHL**	**63**	**16**	**22**	**38**	**13**	**15**	**28**	**63**	**0**	**0**	**3**	**124**	**12.9**	**72**	**7**	**47**	**15**	**+33**	**5**	**0**	**1**	**1**	**26**	**0**	**0**	**0**
1982-83	**Edmonton Oilers**	**NHL**	**80**	**13**	**18**	**31**	**11**	**12**	**23**	**120**	**0**	**1**	**0**	**113**	**11.5**	**59**	**1**	**67**	**21**	**+12**	**16**	**4**	**7**	**11**	**60**	**0**	**0**	**0**
1983-84	**Edmonton Oilers**	**NHL**	**80**	**22**	**26**	**48**	**18**	**18**	**36**	**90**	**1**	**1**	**3**	**117**	**18.8**	**75**	**3**	**67**	**20**	**+25**	**17**	**5**	**5**	**10**	**14**	**1**	**1**	**0**
1984-85	**Edmonton Oilers**	**NHL**	**80**	**17**	**19**	**36**	**14**	**13**	**27**	**122**	**1**	**1**	**1**	**119**	**14.3**	**51**	**2**	**68**	**18**	**–1**	**18**	**2**	**5**	**7**	**33**	**0**	**0**	**0**
1985-86	**Edmonton Oilers**	**NHL**	**62**	**15**	**22**	**37**	**12**	**15**	**27**	**77**	**0**	**0**	**1**	**110**	**13.6**	**69**	**0**	**45**	**13**	**+37**	**10**	**2**	**3**	**5**	**23**	**0**	**0**	**0**

Season	Club	League	REGULAR SEASON																		PLAYOFFS							
			GP	G	A	Pts	AG	AA	APts	PIM	PP	SH	GW	S	%	TGF	PGF	TGA	PGA	+/–	GP	G	A	Pts	PIM	PP	SH	GW
1986-87	Edmonton Oilers	NHL	77	6	9	15	5	6	11	79	0	1	1	84	7.1	32	0	53	22	+1	21	3	3	6	20	0	0	0
1987-88	Edmonton Oilers	NHL	21	3	3	6	3	2	5	6	0	0	0	18	16.7	8	0	15	8	+1	....	....	....	....	....	....	....	....
	Pittsburgh Penguins	NHL	59	11	18	29	9	13	22	77	0	2	1	115	9.6	50	2	85	45	+8	....	....	....	....	....	....	....	....
1988-89	Winnipeg Jets	NHL	34	3	1	4	3	1	4	61	0	1	0	43	7.0	9	0	18	6	–3	....	....	....	....	....	....	....	....
	Edmonton Oilers	NHL	32	3	5	8	3	4	7	22	0	0	0	44	6.8	12	0	30	13	–5	6	0	0	0	0	0	0	0
	NHL Totals		746	133	190	323	112	134	246	918	3	9	16	1100	12.1	559	19	664	227		105	16	24	40	211	1	1	0
	Other Major League Totals		72	7	25	32	....	....	....	134	....	....	....	....	....	....	....	....	....		13	2	3	5	42	....	....	....

Signed as an underage free agent by **Edmonton** (WHA), June, 1978. Claimed by **Edmonton** from **Montreal** in Expansion Draft, June 13, 1979. Traded to **Pittsburgh** by **Edmonton** with Paul Coffey and Wayne Van Dorp for Craig Simpson, Dave Hanna, Moe Mantha and Chris Joseph, November 24, 1987. Transferred to **Edmonton** by **Pittsburgh** as compensation for Pittsburgh's claiming Dave Hanna in Waiver Draft, October 3, 1988. Claimed by **Winnipeg** from **Edmonton** in Waiver Draft, October 3, 1988. Claimed on waivers by **Edmonton** from **Winnipeg**, January 14, 1989.

• HUNTER, MARK

Mark Hunter RW – R. 6′, 200 lbs. b: Petrolia, Ont., 11/12/1962. Montreal's 1st choice, 7th overall, in 1981 Entry Draft.

Season	Club	League	GP	G	A	Pts	AG	AA	APts	PIM	PP	SH	GW	S	%	TGF	PGF	TGA	PGA	+/–	GP	G	A	Pts	PIM	PP	SH	GW
1979-80	Brantford Alexanders	OHA	66	34	56	90	....	....	....	171	....	....	....	....	....	....	....	....	....	....	11	2	8	10	27	....	....	....
1980-81	Brantford Alexanders	OHA	53	39	40	79	....	....	....	157	....	....	....	....	....	....	....	....	....	....	6	3	3	6	27	....	....	....
1981-82	Montreal Canadiens	NHL	71	18	11	29	14	7	21	143	0	0	5	79	22.8	43	4	29	0	+10	5	0	0	0	20	0	0	0
1982-83	Montreal Canadiens	NHL	31	8	8	16	7	6	13	73	1	0	2	39	20.5	25	2	18	0	+5	....	....	....	....	....	....	....	....
1983-84	Montreal Canadiens	NHL	22	6	4	10	5	3	8	42	1	0	0	24	25.0	14	1	15	0	–2	14	2	1	3	69	0	0	0
1984-85	Montreal Canadiens	NHL	72	21	12	33	17	8	25	123	6	0	3	108	19.4	49	11	51	0	–13	11	0	3	3	13	0	0	0
1985-86	St. Louis Blues	NHL	78	44	30	74	35	20	55	171	11	2	3	204	21.6	108	36	64	7	+15	19	7	7	14	48	2	0	1
1986-87	St. Louis Blues	NHL	74	36	33	69	31	24	55	167	12	0	4	178	20.2	98	44	74	1	–19	5	0	3	3	10	0	0	0
1987-88	St. Louis Blues	NHL	66	32	31	63	27	22	49	136	14	0	0	164	19.5	92	39	60	1	–6	5	2	3	5	24	1	0	0
1988-89	Calgary Flames	NHL	66	22	8	30	19	6	25	194	12	0	2	116	19.0	56	25	27	0	+4	10	2	2	4	23	0	0	0
1989-90	Calgary Flames	FrTour	4	2	0	2	....	....	....	4	....	....	....	....	....	....	....	....	....	....	....	....	....	....	....	....	....	....
	Calgary Flames	NHL	10	2	3	5	2	2	4	39	2	0	0	15	13.3	9	4	5	0	0	....	....	....	....	....	....	....	....
1990-91	Calgary Flames	NHL	57	10	15	25	9	11	20	125	6	0	0	90	11.1	39	16	24	0	–1	....	....	....	....	....	....	....	....
	Hartford Whalers	NHL	11	4	3	7	4	2	6	40	1	0	0	20	20.0	12	3	6	0	+3	6	5	1	6	17	3	0	0
1991-92	Hartford Whalers	NHL	63	10	13	23	9	10	19	159	5	0	0	92	10.9	37	12	39	6	–8	4	0	0	0	6	0	0	0
1992-93	Washington Capitals	NHL	7	0	0	0	0	0	0	14	0	0	0	5	0.0	1	0	0	0	+1	....	....	....	....	....	....	....	....
	Baltimore Skipjacks	AHL	28	13	18	31	....	....	....	66	....	....	....	....	....	....	....	....	....	....	7	3	1	4	12	....	....	....
	NHL Totals		628	213	171	384	179	121	300	1426	71	2	19	1134	18.8	583	197	412	15		79	18	20	38	230	6	0	1

Played in NHL All-Star Game (1986)

Traded to **St. Louis** by **Montreal** with Michael Dark and Montreal's 2nd (Herb Raglan), 3rd (Nelson Emerson), 5th (Dan Brooks) and 6th (Rick Burchill) round choices in 1985 Entry Draft for St. Louis' 1st (Jose Charbonneau), 2nd (Todd Richard), 4th (Martin Desjardins), 5th (Tom Sagissor) and 6th (Donald Dufresne) round choices in 1985 Entry Draft, June 15, 1985. Traded to **Calgary** by **St. Louis** with Doug Gilmour, Steve Bozek and Michael Dark for Mike Bullard, Craig Coxe and Tim Corkery, September 6, 1988. Traded to **Hartford** by **Calgary** for Carey Wilson, March 5, 1991. Traded to **Wasington** by **Hartford** with future considerations (Yvon Corriveau, August 20, 1992) for Nick Kypreos, June 15, 1992.

• HUNTER, TIM

Tim Hunter RW – R. 6′2″, 202 lbs. b: Calgary, Alta., 9/10/1960. Atlanta's 4th choice, 54th overall, in 1979 Entry Draft.

Season	Club	League	GP	G	A	Pts	AG	AA	APts	PIM	PP	SH	GW	S	%	TGF	PGF	TGA	PGA	+/–	GP	G	A	Pts	PIM	PP	SH	GW
1977-78	Kamloops Chiefs	BCJHL	51	9	28	37	....	....	....	266	....	....	....	....	....	....	....	....	....	....	....	....	....	....	....	....	....	....
	Seattle Breakers	WCJHL	3	1	2	3	....	....	....	4	....	....	....	....	....	....	....	....	....	....	....	....	....	....	....	....	....	....
1978-79	Seattle Breakers	WHL	70	8	41	49	....	....	....	300	....	....	....	....	....	....	....	....	....	....	....	....	....	....	....	....	....	....
1979-80	Seattle Breakers	WHL	72	14	53	67	....	....	....	311	....	....	....	....	....	....	....	....	....	....	12	1	2	3	41	....	....	....
1980-81	Birmingham Bulls	CHL	58	3	5	8	....	....	....	*236	....	....	....	....	....	....	....	....	....	....	....	....	....	....	....	....	....	....
	Nova Scotia Voyageurs	AHL	17	0	0	0	....	....	....	62	....	....	....	....	....	....	....	....	....	....	6	0	1	1	45	....	....	....
1981-82	Calgary Flames	NHL	2	0	0	0	0	0	0	9	0	0	0	0	0.0	1	0	1	0	0	....	....	....	....	....	....	....	....
	Oklahoma City Stars	CHL	55	4	12	16	....	....	....	222	....	....	....	....	....	....	....	....	....	....	....	....	....	....	....	....	....	....
1982-83	Calgary Flames	NHL	16	1	0	1	1	0	1	54	0	0	0	7	14.3	3	0	5	0	–2	9	1	0	1	*70	1	0	0
	Colorado Flames	CHL	46	5	12	17	....	....	....	225	....	....	....	....	....	....	....	....	....	....	....	....	....	....	....	....	....	....
1983-84	Calgary Flames	NHL	43	4	4	8	3	3	6	130	0	0	0	22	18.2	20	2	18	0	0	7	0	0	0	21	0	0	0
1984-85	Calgary Flames	NHL	71	11	11	22	9	7	16	259	1	0	1	68	16.2	42	4	24	0	+14	4	0	0	0	24	0	0	0
1985-86	Calgary Flames	NHL	66	8	7	15	6	5	11	291	2	0	2	65	12.3	25	7	27	0	–9	19	0	3	3	108	0	0	0
1986-87	Calgary Flames	NHL	73	6	15	21	5	11	16	*361	0	0	1	66	9.1	52	4	52	3	–1	6	0	0	0	51	0	0	0
1987-88	Calgary Flames	NHL	68	8	5	13	7	4	11	337	0	0	0	60	13.3	22	0	30	0	–8	9	4	0	4	32	0	0	2
1988-89	Calgary Flames	NHL	75	3	9	12	3	6	9	*375	0	0	1	67	4.5	43	0	21	0	+22	19	0	4	4	32	0	0	0
1989-90	Calgary Flames	FrTour	3	2	0	2	....	....	....	0	....	....	....	....	....	....	....	....	....	....	....	....	....	....	....	....	....	....
	Calgary Flames	NHL	67	2	3	5	2	2	4	279	0	0	0	69	2.9	18	0	28	1	–9	6	0	0	0	4	0	0	0
1990-91	Calgary Flames	NHL	34	5	2	7	5	2	7	143	0	0	1	29	17.2	16	0	15	0	+1	7	0	0	0	10	0	0	0
1991-92	Calgary Flames	NHL	30	1	3	4	1	2	3	167	0	0	0	19	5.3	10	0	8	0	+2	....	....	....	....	....	....	....	....
1992-93	Quebec Nordiques	NHL	48	5	3	8	4	2	6	94	0	0	0	28	17.9	13	0	17	0	–4	....	....	....	....	....	....	....	....
	Vancouver Canucks	NHL	26	0	4	4	0	3	3	99	0	0	0	12	0.0	13	0	12	0	+1	11	0	0	0	26	0	0	0
1993-94	Vancouver Canucks	NHL	56	3	4	7	3	3	6	171	0	1	1	41	7.3	11	1	37	20	–7	24	0	0	0	26	0	0	0
1994-95	Vancouver Canucks	NHL	34	3	2	5	5	3	8	120	0	0	0	17	17.6	8	0	10	3	+1	11	0	0	0	22	0	0	0
1995-96	Vancouver Canucks	NHL	60	2	0	2	2	0	2	122	0	0	1	26	7.7	10	2	16	0	–8	....	....	....	....	....	....	....	....
1996-97	San Jose Sharks	NHL	46	0	4	4	0	4	4	135	0	0	0	13	0.0	6	0	7	1	0	....	....	....	....	....	....	....	....
	NHL Totals		815	62	76	138	56	57	113	3146	3	1	8	609	10.2	313	20	328	28		132	5	7	12	426	1	0	2

Claimed by **Tampa Bay** from **Calgary** in Expansion Draft, June 18, 1992. Traded to **Quebec** by **Tampa Bay** for future considerations (Martin Simard, September 14, 1992), June 19, 1992. Claimed on waivers by **Vancouver** from **Quebec**, February 12, 1993. Signed as a free agent by **San Jose**, July 23, 1996.

• HURAS, LARRY

Larry Huras D – L. 6′2″, 200 lbs. b: Listowel, Ont., 7/8/1955. NY Rangers' 5th choice, 84th overall, in 1975 Amateur Draft.

Season	Club	League	GP	G	A	Pts	AG	AA	APts	PIM	PP	SH	GW	S	%	TGF	PGF	TGA	PGA	+/–	GP	G	A	Pts	PIM	PP	SH	GW
1972-73	Kitchener Rangers	OHA	60	0	7	7	....	....	....	55	....	....	....	....	....	....	....	....	....	....	....	....	....	....	....	....	....	....
1973-74	Kitchener Rangers	OHA	67	4	22	26	....	....	....	83	....	....	....	....	....	....	....	....	....	....	....	....	....	....	....	....	....	....
1974-75	Kitchener Rangers	OHA	68	4	28	32	....	....	....	166	....	....	....	....	....	....	....	....	....	....	....	....	....	....	....	....	....	....
1975-76	Providence Reds	AHL	55	0	12	12	....	....	....	102	....	....	....	....	....	....	....	....	....	....	3	0	1	1	9	....	....	....
	Port Huron Flags	IHL	17	3	9	12	....	....	....	49	....	....	....	....	....	....	....	....	....	....	....	....	....	....	....	....	....	....
1976-77	New York Rangers	NHL	2	0	0	0	0	0	0	0	0	0	0	0	0.0	0	0	0	0	0	....	....	....	....	....	....	....	....
	New Haven Nighthawks	AHL	48	0	6	6	....	....	....	82	....	....	....	....	....	....	....	....	....	....	4	0	0	0	0	....	....	....
1977-78	Salt Lake Golden Eagles	CHL	52	5	7	12	....	....	....	55	....	....	....	....	....	....	....	....	....	....	1	0	0	0	0	....	....	....
1978-79	Dallas Black Hawks	CHL	6	0	1	1	....	....	....	21	....	....	....	....	....	....	....	....	....	....	....	....	....	....	....	....	....	....
	Salt Lake Golden Eagles	CHL	32	1	9	10	....	....	....	52	....	....	....	....	....	....	....	....	....	....	7	0	0	0	15	....	....	....
1979-80	Port Huron Flags	IHL	77	3	28	31	....	....	....	106	....	....	....	....	....	....	....	....	....	....	11	1	1	2	27	....	....	....
1980-81	CSG Grenoble	France	STATISTICS NOT AVAILABLE																									
1981-82	CSG Grenoble	France	....	5	10	21	....	....	....	....	....	....	....	....	....	....	....	....	....	....	....	....	....	....	....	....	....	....
	NHL Totals		2	0	0	0	0	0	0	0	0	0	0	0	0.0	0	0	0	0		....	....	....	....	....	....	....	....

Signed as a free agent by **St. Louis**, October 12, 1977.

• HURLBURT, BOB

Bob Hurlburt LW – L. 5′11″, 185 lbs. b: Toronto, Ont., 5/1/1950.

Season	Club	League	GP	G	A	Pts	AG	AA	APts	PIM	PP	SH	GW	S	%	TGF	PGF	TGA	PGA	+/–	GP	G	A	Pts	PIM	PP	SH	GW
1967-68	North York Rangers	OJHL	35	19	11	30	....	....	....	54	....	....	....	....	....	....	....	....	....	....	....	....	....	....	....	....	....	....
1968-69	Kitchener Rangers	OHA	53	9	14	23	....	....	....	76	....	....	....	....	....	....	....	....	....	....	....	....	....	....	....	....	....	....
1969-70	Kitchener Rangers	OHA	54	9	13	22	....	....	....	126	....	....	....	....	....	....	....	....	....	....	....	....	....	....	....	....	....	....
1970-71	Quebec Aces	AHL	72	10	21	31	....	....	....	51	....	....	....	....	....	....	....	....	....	....	1	0	1	1	0	....	....	....
1971-72	Richmond Robins	AHL	69	5	13	18	....	....	....	69	....	....	....	....	....	....	....	....	....	....	....	....	....	....	....	....	....	....
1972-73	Richmond Robins	AHL	71	2	11	13	....	....	....	64	....	....	....	....	....	....	....	....	....	....	2	0	0	0	2	....	....	....
1973-74	San Diego Gulls	WHL	75	20	27	47	....	....	....	51	....	....	....	....	....	....	....	....	....	....	4	0	3	3	2	....	....	....
1974-75	Vancouver Canucks	NHL	1	0	0	0	0	0	0	2	0	0	0	0	0.0	1	0	1	0	0	....	....	....	....	....	....	....	....
	Seattle Totems	CHL	74	16	23	39	....	....	....	68	....	....	....	....	....	....	....	....	....	....	....	....	....	....	....	....	....	....
1975-76			DID NOT PLAY																									
1976-77	Whitby Warriors	OHA Sr.	12	3	4	7	....	....	....	6	....	....	....	....	....	....	....	....	....	....	....	....	....	....	....	....	....	....
	NHL Totals		1	0	0	0	0	0	0	2	0	0	0	0	0.0	1	0	1	0		....	....	....	....	....	....	....	....

Traded to **San Diego** (WHL) by **Richmond** (AHL) with Tom Tremblay and Jim Stanfield for Bruce Cowick, May, 1973. Traded to **Vancouver** by **San Diego** (WHL) for cash, July, 1974.

• HURLBUT, MIKE
Mike Hurlbut D – L. 6'2", 200 lbs. b: Massena, NY, 10/7/1966. NY Rangers' 1st choice, 5th overall, in 1988 Supplemental Draft.

			REGULAR SEASON																		PLAYOFFS							
Season	Club	League	GP	G	A	Pts	AG	AA	APts	PIM	PP	SH	GW	S	%	TGF	PGF	TGA	PGA	+/–	GP	G	A	Pts	PIM	PP	SH	GW
1985-86	St. Lawrence University	ECAC	25	2	10	12	....	....	....	40	....	....	....	....	....	....	....	....	....	....	....	....	....	....	....	....	....	....
1986-87	St. Lawrence University	ECAC	35	8	15	23	....	....	....	44	....	....	....	....	....	....	....	....	....	....	....	....	....	....	....	....	....	....
1987-88	St. Lawrence University	ECAC	38	6	12	18	....	....	....	18	....	....	....	....	....	....	....	....	....	....	....	....	....	....	....	....	....	....
1988-89	St. Lawrence University	ECAC	36	8	25	33	....	....	....	30	....	....	....	....	....	....	....	....	....	....	....	....	....	....	....	....	....	....
	Denver Rangers	IHL	8	0	2	2	....	....	....	13	....	....	....	....	....	....	....	....	....	....	4	1	2	3	2	....	....	....
1989-90	Flint Spirits	IHL	74	3	34	37	....	....	....	38	....	....	....	....	....	....	....	....	....	....	3	0	1	1	2	....	....	....
1990-91	San Diego Gulls	IHL	2	1	0	1	....	....	....	0	....	....	....	....	....	....	....	....	....	....	....	....	....	....	....	....	....	....
	Binghamton Rangers	AHL	33	2	11	13	....	....	....	27	....	....	....	....	....	....	....	....	....	....	3	0	1	1	0	....	....	....
1991-92	Binghamton Rangers	AHL	79	16	39	55	....	....	....	64	....	....	....	....	....	....	....	....	....	....	11	2	7	9	8	....	....	....
1992-93	**New York Rangers**	**NHL**	**23**	**1**	**8**	**9**	**1**	**5**	**6**	**16**	**1**	**0**	**0**	**26**	**3.8**	**27**	**7**	**20**	**4**	**+4**	....	....	....	....	....	....	....	....
	Binghamton Rangers	AHL	45	11	25	36	....	....	....	46	....	....	....	....	....	....	....	....	....	....	14	2	5	7	12	....	....	....
1993-94	**Quebec Nordiques**	**NHL**	**1**	**0**	**0**	**0**	**0**	**0**	**0**	**0**	**0**	**0**	**0**	**1**	**0.0**	**0**	**0**	**1**	**0**	**–1**	....	....	....	....	....	....	....	....
	Cornwall Aces	AHL	77	13	33	46	....	....	....	100	....	....	....	....	....	....	....	....	....	....	13	3	7	10	12	....	....	....
1994-95	Cornwall Aces	AHL	74	11	49	60	....	....	....	69	....	....	....	....	....	....	....	....	....	....	3	1	0	1	15	....	....	....
1995-96	Minnesota Moose	IHL	22	1	4	5	....	....	....	22	....	....	....	....	....	....	....	....	....	....	....	....	....	....	....	....	....	....
	Houston Aeros	IHL	38	3	12	15	....	....	....	33	....	....	....	....	....	....	....	....	....	....	....	....	....	....	....	....	....	....
1996-97	Houston Aeros	IHL	70	11	24	35	....	....	....	62	....	....	....	....	....	....	....	....	....	....	13	5	8	13	12	....	....	....
1997-98	**Buffalo Sabres**	**NHL**	**3**	**0**	**0**	**0**	**0**	**0**	**0**	**2**	**0**	**0**	**0**	**3**	**0.0**	**0**	**0**	**2**	**1**	**–1**	....	....	....	....	....	....	....	....
	Rochester Americans	AHL	45	10	20	30	....	....	....	48	....	....	....	....	....	....	....	....	....	....	4	1	1	2	2	....	....	....
	NHL Totals		**27**	**1**	**8**	**9**	**1**	**5**	**6**	**18**	**1**	**0**	**0**	**30**	**3.3**	**27**	**7**	**23**	**5**		....	....	....	....	....	....	....	....

ECAC First All-Star Team (1989) • NCAA East First All-American Team (1989) • AHL Second All-Star Team (1995)

Traded to **Quebec** by **NY Rangers** for Alexander Karpovtsev, September 7, 1993. Signed as a free agent by **Buffalo**, September 9, 1997.

• HURLEY, PAUL
Paul Hurley D – R. 5'11", 185 lbs. b: Melrose, MA, 7/12/1946.

Season	Club	League	GP	G	A	Pts	AG	AA	APts	PIM	PP	SH	GW	S	%	TGF	PGF	TGA	PGA	+/–	GP	G	A	Pts	PIM	PP	SH	GW
1964-65	Boston College	ECAC	18	22	13	35	....	....	....	....	....	....	....	....	....	....	....	....	....	....	....	....	....	....	....	....	....	....
1965-66	Boston College	ECAC	27	9	26	35	....	....	....	22	....	....	....	....	....	....	....	....	....	....	....	....	....	....	....	....	....	....
1966-67	Boston College	ECAC	28	32	23	55	....	....	....	19	....	....	....	....	....	....	....	....	....	....	....	....	....	....	....	....	....	....
	United States	Nat-Team	21	9	7	16	....	....	....	6	....	....	....	....	....	....	....	....	....	....	....	....	....	....	....	....	....	....
1967-68	Boston College	ECAC	26	14	28	42	....	....	....	22	....	....	....	....	....	....	....	....	....	....	....	....	....	....	....	....	....	....
	United States	Olympics	7	3	3	6	....	....	....	0	....	....	....	....	....	....	....	....	....	....	....	....	....	....	....	....	....	....
1968-69	**Boston Bruins**	**NHL**	**1**	**0**	**1**	**1**	**0**	**1**	**1**	**0**	**0**	**0**	**0**	**5**	**0.0**	**2**	**0**	**2**	**1**	**+1**	....	....	....	....	....	....	....	....
	Oklahoma City Blazers	CHL	6	2	1	3	....	....	....	4	....	....	....	....	....	....	....	....	....	....	....	....	....	....	....	....	....	....
1969-70	Oklahoma City Blazers	CHL	69	6	26	32	....	....	....	109	....	....	....	....	....	....	....	....	....	....	....	....	....	....	....	....	....	....
1970-71	Oklahoma City Blazers	CHL	43	5	12	17	....	....	....	47	....	....	....	....	....	....	....	....	....	....	5	0	1	1	8	....	....	....
1971-72	Boston Braves	AHL	74	7	28	35	....	....	....	65	....	....	....	....	....	....	....	....	....	....	9	0	4	4	8	....	....	....
1972-73	New England Whalers	WHA	78	3	15	18	....	....	....	58	....	....	....	....	....	....	....	....	....	....	15	0	7	7	14	....	....	....
1973-74	New England Whalers	WHA	52	3	11	14	....	....	....	21	....	....	....	....	....	....	....	....	....	....	....	....	....	....	....	....	....	....
1974-75	New England Whalers	WHA	75	3	26	29	....	....	....	36	....	....	....	....	....	....	....	....	....	....	6	0	1	1	4	....	....	....
1975-76	New England Whalers	WHA	10	0	14	14	....	....	....	20	....	....	....	....	....	....	....	....	....	....	4	0	0	0	0	....	....	....
	Edmonton Oilers	WHA	26	1	4	5	....	....	....	14	....	....	....	....	....	....	....	....	....	....	....	....	....	....	....	....	....	....
1976-77	Calgary Cowboys	WHA	34	0	6	6	....	....	....	32	....	....	....	....	....	....	....	....	....	....	....	....	....	....	....	....	....	....
	NHL Totals		**1**	**0**	**1**	**1**	**0**	**1**	**1**	**0**	**0**	**0**	**0**	**5**	**0.0**	**2**	**0**	**2**	**1**		....	....	....	....	....	....	....	....
	Other Major League Totals		275	10	76	86	....	....	....	181	....	....	....	....	....	....	....	....	....	....	25	0	8	8	18	....	....	....

ECAC First All-Star Team (1969) • NCAA East First All-American Team (1969)

Signed as a free agent by **Boston**, March, 1969. Selected by **New England** in 1972 WHA General Player Draft, February 12, 1972. Traded to **Edmonton** by **New England** with future considerations for Kerry Ketter and Steve Carlyle, February 2, 1976. Signed as a free agent by **Calgary**, September, 1976.

• HUSCROFT, JAMIE
Jamie Huscroft D – R. 6'2", 200 lbs. b: Creston, B.C., 1/9/1967. New Jersey's 9th choice, 171st overall, in 1985 Entry Draft.

Season	Club	League	GP	G	A	Pts	AG	AA	APts	PIM	PP	SH	GW	S	%	TGF	PGF	TGA	PGA	+/–	GP	G	A	Pts	PIM	PP	SH	GW
1983-84	Seattle Breakers	WHL	63	0	12	12	....	....	....	77	....	....	....	....	....	....	....	....	....	....	5	0	0	0	15	....	....	....
1984-85	Seattle Breakers	WHL	69	3	13	16	....	....	....	273	....	....	....	....	....	....	....	....	....	....	....	....	....	....	....	....	....	....
1985-86	Seattle Thunderbirds	WHL	66	6	20	26	....	....	....	394	....	....	....	....	....	....	....	....	....	....	5	0	1	1	18	....	....	....
1986-87	Seattle Thunderbirds	WHL	21	1	18	19	....	....	....	99	....	....	....	....	....	....	....	....	....	....	....	....	....	....	....	....	....	....
	Medicine Hat Tigers	WHL	35	4	21	25	....	....	....	170	....	....	....	....	....	....	....	....	....	....	20	0	3	3	*125	....	....	....
1987-88	Utica Devils	AHL	71	5	7	12	....	....	....	316	....	....	....	....	....	....	....	....	....	....	....	....	....	....	....	....	....	....
	Flint Spirits	IHL	3	1	0	1	....	....	....	2	....	....	....	....	....	....	....	....	....	....	16	0	1	1	110	....	....	....
1988-89	**New Jersey Devils**	**NHL**	**15**	**0**	**2**	**2**	**0**	**1**	**1**	**51**	**0**	**0**	**0**	**9**	**0.0**	**6**	**0**	**13**	**4**	**–3**	....	....	....	....	....	....	....	....
	Utica Devils	AHL	41	2	10	12	....	....	....	215	....	....	....	....	....	....	....	....	....	....	5	0	0	0	40	....	....	....
1989-90	**New Jersey Devils**	**NHL**	**42**	**2**	**3**	**5**	**2**	**2**	**4**	**149**	**0**	**0**	**0**	**19**	**10.5**	**7**	**0**	**9**	**0**	**–2**	**5**	**0**	**0**	**0**	**16**	**0**	**0**	**0**
	Utica Devils	AHL	22	3	6	9	....	....	....	122	....	....	....	....	....	....	....	....	....	....	....	....	....	....	....	....	....	....
1990-91	**New Jersey Devils**	**NHL**	**8**	**0**	**1**	**1**	**0**	**1**	**1**	**27**	**0**	**0**	**0**	**3**	**0.0**	**1**	**0**	**0**	**0**	**+1**	**3**	**0**	**0**	**0**	**6**	**0**	**0**	**0**
	Utica Devils	AHL	59	3	15	18	....	....	....	339	....	....	....	....	....	....	....	....	....	....	....	....	....	....	....	....	....	....
1991-92	Utica Devils	AHL	50	4	7	11	....	....	....	224	....	....	....	....	....	....	....	....	....	....	....	....	....	....	....	....	....	....
1992-93	Providence Bruins	AHL	69	2	15	17	....	....	....	257	....	....	....	....	....	....	....	....	....	....	2	0	1	1	6	....	....	....
1993-94	**Boston Bruins**	**NHL**	**36**	**0**	**1**	**1**	**0**	**1**	**1**	**144**	**0**	**0**	**0**	**13**	**0.0**	**8**	**1**	**9**	**0**	**–2**	**4**	**0**	**0**	**0**	**9**	**0**	**0**	**0**
	Providence Bruins	AHL	32	1	10	11	....	....	....	157	....	....	....	....	....	....	....	....	....	....	....	....	....	....	....	....	....	....
1994-95	**Boston Bruins**	**NHL**	**34**	**0**	**6**	**6**	**0**	**9**	**9**	**103**	**0**	**0**	**0**	**30**	**0.0**	**16**	**0**	**21**	**2**	**–3**	**5**	**0**	**0**	**0**	**11**	**0**	**0**	**0**
1995-96	**Calgary Flames**	**NHL**	**70**	**3**	**9**	**12**	**3**	**7**	**10**	**162**	**0**	**0**	**1**	**57**	**5.3**	**37**	**0**	**28**	**5**	**+14**	**4**	**0**	**1**	**1**	**4**	**0**	**0**	**0**
1996-97	**Calgary Flames**	**NHL**	**39**	**0**	**4**	**4**	**0**	**4**	**4**	**117**	**0**	**0**	**0**	**33**	**0.0**	**15**	**0**	**18**	**5**	**+2**	....	....	....	....	....	....	....	....
	Tampa Bay Lightning	**NHL**	**13**	**0**	**1**	**1**	**0**	**1**	**1**	**34**	**0**	**0**	**0**	**7**	**0.0**	**3**	**0**	**8**	**1**	**–4**	....	....	....	....	....	....	....	....
1997-98	**Tampa Bay Lightning**	**NHL**	**44**	**0**	**3**	**3**	**0**	**3**	**3**	**122**	**0**	**0**	**0**	**21**	**0.0**	**11**	**0**	**23**	**8**	**–4**	....	....	....	....	....	....	....	....
	Vancouver Canucks	**NHL**	**7**	**0**	**1**	**1**	**0**	**1**	**1**	**55**	**0**	**0**	**0**	**5**	**0.0**	**3**	**0**	**2**	**1**	**+2**	....	....	....	....	....	....	....	....
	NHL Totals		**308**	**5**	**31**	**36**	**5**	**30**	**35**	**964**	**0**	**0**	**1**	**197**	**2.5**	**107**	**1**	**131**	**26**		**21**	**0**	**1**	**1**	**46**	**0**	**0**	**0**

Signed as a free agent by **Boston**, July 23, 1992. Signed as a free agent by **Calgary**, August 22, 1995. Traded to **Tampa Bay** by **Calgary** for Tyler Moss, March 18, 1997. Traded to **Vancouver** by **Tampa Bay** for Enrico Ciccone, March 14, 1998.

• HUSKA, RYAN
Ryan Huska LW – L. 6'2", 194 lbs. b: Cranbrook, B.C., 7/2/1975. Chicago's 4th choice, 76th overall, in 1993 Entry Draft.

Season	Club	League	GP	G	A	Pts	AG	AA	APts	PIM	PP	SH	GW	S	%	TGF	PGF	TGA	PGA	+/–	GP	G	A	Pts	PIM	PP	SH	GW
1991-92	Kamloops Blazers	WHL	44	4	5	9	....	....	....	23	....	....	....	....	....	....	....	....	....	....	6	0	1	1	0	....	....	....
1992-93	Kamloops Blazers	WHL	68	17	15	32	....	....	....	50	....	....	....	....	....	....	....	....	....	....	13	2	6	8	4	....	....	....
1993-94	Kamloops Blazers	WHL	69	23	31	54	....	....	....	66	....	....	....	....	....	....	....	....	....	....	19	9	5	14	23	....	....	....
1994-95	Kamloops Blazers	WHL	66	27	40	67	....	....	....	78	....	....	....	....	....	....	....	....	....	....	17	7	8	15	12	....	....	....
1995-96	Indianapolis Ice	IHL	28	2	3	5	....	....	....	15	....	....	....	....	....	....	....	....	....	....	5	1	1	2	27	....	....	....
1996-97	Indianapolis Ice	IHL	80	18	12	30	....	....	....	100	....	....	....	....	....	....	....	....	....	....	4	0	0	0	4	....	....	....
1997-98	**Chicago Blackhawks**	**NHL**	**1**	**0**	**0**	**0**	**0**	**0**	**0**	**0**	**0**	**0**	**0**	**0**	**0.0**	**0**	**0**	**0**	**0**	**0**	....	....	....	....	....	....	....	....
	Indianapolis Ice	IHL	80	19	16	35	....	....	....	115	....	....	....	....	....	....	....	....	....	....	5	0	3	3	10	....	....	....
	NHL Totals		**1**	**0**	**0**	**0**	**0**	**0**	**0**	**0**	**0**	**0**	**0**	**0**	**0.0**	**0**	**0**	**0**	**0**		....	....	....	....	....	....	....	....

• HUSTON, RON
Ron "Spike" Huston C – R. 5'9", 170 lbs. b: Manitou, Man., 4/8/1945.

Season	Club	League	GP	G	A	Pts	AG	AA	APts	PIM	PP	SH	GW	S	%	TGF	PGF	TGA	PGA	+/–	GP	G	A	Pts	PIM	PP	SH	GW
1962-63	Brandon Wheat Kings	MJHL	20	5	9	14	....	....	....	4	....	....	....	....	....	....	....	....	....	....	4	0	1	1	0	....	....	....
1963-64	Brandon Wheat Kings	MJHL	30	20	30	50	....	....	....	15	....	....	....	....	....	....	....	....	....	....	20	6	9	15	4	....	....	....
1964-65	Brandon Wheat Kings	MJHL	52	18	21	39	....	....	....	20	....	....	....	....	....	....	....	....	....	....	8	5	1	6	2	....	....	....
1965-66	Cranbrook Royals	WIHL	49	39	42	81	....	....	....	4	....	....	....	....	....	....	....	....	....	....	....	....	....	....	....	....	....	....
1966-67	Cranbrook Royals	WIHL	39	23	36	59	....	....	....	12	....	....	....	....	....	....	....	....	....	....	....	....	....	....	....	....	....	....
1967-68	Cranbrook Royals	WIHL	44	38	43	81	....	....	....	4	....	....	....	....	....	....	....	....	....	....	....	....	....	....	....	....	....	....
1968-69	Portland Buckaroos	WHL	3	0	0	0	....	....	....	0	....	....	....	....	....	....	....	....	....	....	....	....	....	....	....	....	....	....
	Cranbrook Royals	WIHL	47	*45	43	*88	....	....	....	4	....	....	....	....	....	....	....	....	....	....	....	....	....	....	....	....	....	....
1969-70	Seattle Totems	WHL	5	0	2	2	....	....	....	0	....	....	....	....	....	....	....	....	....	....	....	....	....	....	....	....	....	....
	Cranbrook Royals	WIHL	47	*36	*53	*89	....	....	....	10	....	....	....	....	....	....	....	....	....	....	....	....	....	....	....	....	....	....
1970-71	Calgary Stampeders	ASHL	....	23	19	42	....	....	....	2	....	....	....	....	....	....	....	....	....	....	....	....	....	....	....	....	....	....
1971-72	Spokane Jets	WIHL	49	39	47	*86	....	....	....	30	....	....	....	....	....	....	....	....	....	....	....	....	....	....	....	....	....	....

			REGULAR SEASON																		PLAYOFFS							
Season	Club	League	GP	G	A	Pts	AG	AA	APts	PIM	PP	SH	GW	S	%	TGF	PGF	TGA	PGA	+/–	GP	G	A	Pts	PIM	PP	SH	GW
1972-73	Salt Lake Golden Eagles	WHL	72	42	42	84				21											9	6	7	13	2			
1973-74	California Golden Seals	NHL	23	3	10	13	3	9	12	0	0	0	1	29	10.3	22	4	34	4	–12								
	Salt Lake Golden Eagles	WHL	50	20	32	52				4											5	0	2	2	2			
1974-75	California Golden Seals	NHL	56	12	21	33	11	17	28	8	0	0	2	111	10.8	44	7	63	11	–15								
1975-76	Phoenix Roadrunners	WHA	79	22	44	66				4											5	1	1	2	0			
1976-77	Phoenix Roadrunners	WHA	80	20	39	59				10																		
1977-78	Spokane Flyers	WIHL		33	*86	*119																						
1978-79	Spokane Flyers	PHL	49	19	35	54				8																		
	NHL Totals		79	15	31	46	14	26	40	8	0	0	3	140	10.7	66	11	97	15									
	Other Major League Totals		159	42	83	125				14											5	1	1	2	0			

WHL Second All-Star Team (1973) • Won WHL Rookie of the Year Award (1973)

Signed as a free agent by **California**, September, 1972. Rights traded to **Phoenix** (WHA) by **California** with the rights to Del Hall for the rights to Gary Holt, June, 1975.

• HUTCHISON, DAVE

Dave Hutchison D – L. 6'3", 205 lbs. b: London, Ont., 5/2/1952. Los Angeles' 2nd choice, 36th overall, in 1972 Amateur Draft.

Season	Club	League	GP	G	A	Pts	AG	AA	APts	PIM	PP	SH	GW	S	%	TGF	PGF	TGA	PGA	+/–	GP	G	A	Pts	PIM	PP	SH	GW
1969-70	London Knights	OHA	7	1	2	3				30																		
1970-71	London Knights	OHA	54	2	13	15				154																		
1971-72	London Knights	OHA	46	3	11	14				151																		
1972-73	Philadelphia Blazers	WHA	28	0	2	2				34											3	0	0	0	2			
	Rhode Island Reds	EHL	32	7	18	25				158																		
1973-74	Vancouver Blazers	WHA	69	0	13	13				151																		
1974-75	Los Angeles Kings	NHL	68	0	6	6	0	5	5	133	0	0	0	55	0.0	30	0	30	5	+5	2	0	0	0	22	0	0	0
1975-76	Los Angeles Kings	NHL	50	0	10	10	0	8	8	181	0	0	0	61	0.0	37	0	40	7	+4	9	0	3	3	29	0	0	0
1976-77	Los Angeles Kings	NHL	70	6	11	17	6	9	15	220	1	0	3	115	5.2	78	6	80	15	+7	9	1	4	5	17	0	0	0
1977-78	Los Angeles Kings	NHL	44	0	10	10	0	8	8	71	0	0	0	60	0.0	43	0	37	5	+11								
1978-79	Toronto Maple Leafs	NHL	79	4	15	19	4	11	15	235	0	0	0	117	3.4	84	2	65	19	+36	6	0	3	3	23	0	0	0
1979-80	Toronto Maple Leafs	NHL	31	1	6	7	1	5	6	28	0	0	0	21	4.8	18	0	21	4	+1								
	Chicago Black Hawks	NHL	38	0	5	5	0	4	4	73	0	0	0	57	0.0	23	0	29	6	0	6	0	0	0	12	0	0	0
1980-81	Chicago Black Hawks	NHL	59	2	9	11	2	6	8	124	0	0	0	58	3.4	53	1	50	10	+12	2	0	0	0	2	0	0	0
1981-82	Chicago Black Hawks	NHL	66	5	18	23	4	12	16	246	0	1	0	72	6.9	78	0	110	36	+4	14	1	2	3	44	0	0	0
1982-83	New Jersey Devils	NHL	32	1	4	5	1	3	4	102	0	0	0	21	4.8	11	0	38	7	–20								
	Wichita Wind	CHL	2	0	0	0				0																		
1983-84	Toronto Maple Leafs	NHL	47	0	3	3	0	2	2	137	0	0	0	16	0.0	22	0	31	14	+5								
	NHL Totals		584	19	97	116	18	73	91	1550	1	1	3	653	2.9	477	9	531	128		48	2	12	14	149	0	0	0
	Other Major League Totals		97	0	15	15				185											3	0	0	0	2			

Selected by **Miami-Philadelphia** (WHA) in 1972 WHA General Player Draft, February 13, 1972. Transferred to **Vancouver** (WHA) after **Philadelphia** (WHA) franchise relocated, May, 1973. Traded to **Toronto** by **LA Kings** with Lorne Stamler for Brian Glennie, Kurt Walker, Scott Garland and Toronto's 2nd round choice (Mark Hardy) in 1979 Amateur Draft, June 14, 1978. Traded to **Chicago** by **Toronto** for Pat Ribble, January 10, 1980. Traded to **Washington** by **Chicago** with Ted Bulley for Washington's 6th round choice (Jari Torkii) in 1983 Entry Draft and Washington's 5th round choice (Darin Sceviour) in 1984 Entry Draft, August 12, 1982. Claimed by **New Jersey** from **Washington** in Waiver Draft, October 4, 1982. Signed as a free agent by **Toronto**, November 15, 1983.

• HYNES, DAVE

Dave Hynes LW – L. 5'9", 182 lbs. b: Cambridge, MA, 4/17/1951. Boston's 5th choice, 56th overall, in 1971 Amateur Draft.

Season	Club	League	GP	G	A	Pts	AG	AA	APts	PIM	PP	SH	GW	S	%	TGF	PGF	TGA	PGA	+/–	GP	G	A	Pts	PIM	PP	SH	GW
1970-71	Harvard University	ECAC	27	26	26	62				18																		
1971-72	Harvard University	ECAC	25	23	31	54				40																		
1972-73	Harvard University	ECAC	12	15	19	34				12																		
	United States	Nat-Team	7	*9	6	15																						
1973-74	Boston Bruins	NHL	3	0	0	0	0	0	0	0	0	0	0	1	0.0	0	0	0	0	0								
	Boston Braves	AHL	73	35	37	72				22																		
1974-75	Boston Bruins	NHL	19	4	0	4	4	0	4	2	0	0	0	15	26.7	6	0	3	0	+3								
	Rochester Americans	AHL	59	42	35	77				33											12	2	7	9	6			
1975-76	Rochester Americans	AHL	63	37	30	67				20											7	3	2	5	11			
1976-77	New England Whalers	WHA	22	5	4	9				4																		
	Rhode Island Reds	AHL	46	22	15	37				8																		
	United States	WEC-A	10	3	4	7				10																		
1977-78	Springfield Indians	AHL	46	16	30	46				8											4	1	0	1	0			
	NHL Totals		22	4	0	4	4	0	4	2	0	0	0	16	25.0	6	0	3	0									
	Other Major League Totals		22	5	4	9				4																		

ECAC Second All-Star Team (1972) • NCAA East First All-American Team (1972) • AHL First All-Star Team (1976)

Signed as a free agent by **New England** (WHA), August, 1976.

• HYNES, GORD

Gord Hynes D – L. 6'1", 170 lbs. b: Montreal, Que., 7/22/1966. Boston's 5th choice, 115th overall, in 1985 Entry Draft.

Season	Club	League	GP	G	A	Pts	AG	AA	APts	PIM	PP	SH	GW	S	%	TGF	PGF	TGA	PGA	+/–	GP	G	A	Pts	PIM	PP	SH	GW
1983-84	Medicine Hat Tigers	WHL	72	5	14	19				39											14	0	0	0	0			
1984-85	Medicine Hat Tigers	WHL	70	18	45	63				61											10	6	9	15	17			
1985-86	Medicine Hat Tigers	WHL	58	22	39	61				45											25	8	15	23	32			
1986-87	Moncton Golden Flames	AHL	69	2	19	21				21											4	0	0	0	2			
1987-88	Maine Mariners	AHL	69	5	30	35				65											7	1	3	4	4			
1988-89	Canada	Nat-Team	61	8	38	46				44																		
1989-90	Varese	Italy	29	13	36	49				16											3	3	3	6	0			
	Canada	Nat-Team	11	3	1	4				4																		
1990-91	Canada	Nat-Team	57	12	30	42				62																		
1991-92	Canada	Nat-Team	40	12	22	34				50																		
	Canada	Olympics	8	3	3	6				6																		
	Boston Bruins	NHL	15	0	5	5	0	4	4	6	0	0	0	16	0.0	17	0	9	0	+8	12	1	2	3	6	0	0	0
1992-93	Philadelphia Flyers	NHL	37	3	4	7	2	3	5	16	0	0	0	39	7.7	31	5	31	2	–3								
	Hershey Bears	AHL	9	1	3	4				4																		
1993-94	Cincinnati Cyclones	IHL	80	15	43	58				50											11	2	6	8	24			
1994-95	Detroit Vipers	IHL	62	4	35	39				32																		
1995-96	Schwenningen Wild Wings	Germany	49	9	32	41				61											4	0	2	2	10			
1996-97	Schwenningen Wild Wings	Germany	47	15	41	56				82											5	2	5	7	18			
1997-98	Adler Mannheim	Germany	40	5	24	29				95											10	3	4	7	22			
	NHL Totals		52	3	9	12	2	7	9	22	0	0	0	55	5.5	48	5	40	2		12	1	2	3	6	0	0	0

Signed as a free agent by **Philadelphia**, August 25, 1992. Claimed by **Florida** from **Philadelphia** in Expansion Draft, June 24, 1993.

• IAFRATE, AL

Al "Ski's" Iafrate D – L. 6'3", 235 lbs. b: Dearborn, MI, 3/21/1966. Toronto's 1st choice, 4th overall, in 1984 Entry Draft.

Season	Club	League	GP	G	A	Pts	AG	AA	APts	PIM	PP	SH	GW	S	%	TGF	PGF	TGA	PGA	+/–	GP	G	A	Pts	PIM	PP	SH	GW
1983-84	United States	Nat-Team	55	4	17	21				26																		
	United States	Olympics	6	0	0	0				2																		
	Belleville Bulls	OHL	10	2	4	6				2											3	0	1	1	5			
1984-85	Toronto Maple Leafs	NHL	68	5	16	21	4	11	15	51	3	0	0	88	5.7	67	18	83	15	–19								
1985-86	Toronto Maple Leafs	NHL	65	8	25	33	6	17	23	40	2	0	2	94	8.5	92	23	92	13	–10	10	0	3	3	4	0	0	0
1986-87	Toronto Maple Leafs	NHL	80	9	21	30	8	15	23	55	0	0	3	132	6.8	103	12	141	32	–18	13	1	3	4	11	1	0	0
1987-88	Toronto Maple Leafs	NHL	77	22	30	52	19	21	40	80	4	3	4	169	13.0	105	26	141	41	–21	6	3	4	7	6	2	0	0
1988-89	Toronto Maple Leafs	NHL	65	13	20	33	11	14	25	72	1	2	3	105	12.4	89	15	91	20	+3								
1989-90	Toronto Maple Leafs	NHL	75	21	42	63	18	30	48	135	6	1	0	153	13.7	118	33	126	37	–4								
1990-91	Toronto Maple Leafs	NHL	42	3	15	18	3	11	14	113	2	0	0	51	5.9	40	12	57	14	–15								
	Washington Capitals	NHL	30	6	8	14	5	6	11	124	0	1	1	55	10.9	36	4	38	5	–1	10	1	3	4	22	0	0	1
1991-92	Washington Capitals	NHL	78	17	34	51	16	26	42	180	6	0	1	151	11.3	126	36	112	23	+1	7	4	2	6	14	1	0	0
1992-93	Washington Capitals	NHL	81	25	41	66	21	28	49	169	11	1	4	289	8.7	145	48	115	33	+15	6	6	0	6	4	3	0	1
1993-94	Washington Capitals	NHL	67	10	35	45	9	27	36	143	4	0	3	252	4.0	101	02	70	19	+10								
	Boston Bruins	NHL	12	5	8	13	5	6	11	20	2	0	1	47	10.6	26	6	17	3	+6	13	3	1	4	6	1	0	1
1994-95			DID NOT PLAY – INJURED																									
1995-96			DID NOT PLAY – INJURED																									

Season	Club	League	REGULAR SEASON GP	G	A	Pts	AG	AA	APts	PIM	PP	SH	GW	S	%	TGF	PGF	TGA	PGA	+/–	PLAYOFFS GP	G	A	Pts	PIM	PP	SH	GW
1996-97	**San Jose Sharks**	**NHL**	**38**	**6**	**9**	**15**	**6**	**8**	**14**	**91**	**3**	**0**	**0**	**91**	**6.6**	**32**	**9**	**40**	**7**	**–10**	....	....	....	....	....	....	....	....
1997-98	**San Jose Sharks**	**NHL**	**21**	**2**	**7**	**9**	**2**	**7**	**9**	**28**	**2**	**0**	**0**	**37**	**5.4**	**19**	**5**	**15**	**0**	**–1**	**6**	**1**	**0**	**1**	**10**	**1**	**0**	**0**
	United States	WC-A	4	0	2	2	....	....	....	6	....	....	....	....	....	....	....	....	....	....	....	....	....	....	....	....	....	....
	NHL Totals		**799**	**152**	**311**	**463**	**133**	**227**	**360**	**1301**	**46**	**8**	**22**	**1714**	**8.9**	**1099**	**279**	**1146**	**262**		**71**	**19**	**16**	**35**	**77**	**9**	**0**	**3**

NHL Second All-Star Team (1993)

Played in NHL All-Star Game (1988, 1990, 1993, 1994)

Traded to **Washington** by **Toronto** for Peter Zezel and Bob Rouse, January 16, 1991. Traded to **Boston** by **Washington** for Joe Juneau, March 21, 1994. • Missed entire 1994-95 and 1995-96 seasons recovering from knee surgery. Traded to **San Jose** by **Boston** for Jeff Odgers and Pittsburgh's 5th round choice (previously acquired, Boston selected Elias Abrahamsson) in 1996 Entry Draft, June 21, 1996. Claimed by **Nashville** from **San Jose** in Expansion Draft, June 26, 1998. Signed as a free agent by **Carolina**, July 14, 1998.

• IGINLA, JAROME

Jarome Iginla RW – R. 6'1", 193 lbs. b: Edmonton, Alta., 7/1/1977. Dallas' 1st choice, 11th overall, in 1995 Entry Draft.

Season	Club	League	GP	G	A	Pts	AG	AA	APts	PIM	PP	SH	GW	S	%	TGF	PGF	TGA	PGA	+/–	GP	G	A	Pts	PIM	PP	SH	GW
1993-94	Kamloops Blazers	WHL	48	6	23	39	....	....	....	33	....	....	....	....	....	....	....	....	....	....	19	3	6	9	10	....	....	....
1994-95	Kamloops Blazers	WHL	72	33	38	71	....	....	....	111	....	....	....	....	....	....	....	....	....	....	21	7	11	18	34	....	....	....
1995-96	Kamloops Blazers	WHL	63	63	73	136	....	....	....	120	....	....	....	....	....	....	....	....	....	....	16	16	13	29	44	....	....	....
	Canada	WJC-A	6	5	7	12	....	....	....	4	....	....	....	....	....	....	....	....	....	....	....	....	....	....	....	....	....	....
	Calgary Flames	**NHL**	....	....	....	....	....	....	....	....	....	....	....	....	....	....	....	....	....	....	**2**	**1**	**1**	**2**	**0**	....	....	....
1996-97	**Calgary Flames**	**NHL**	**82**	**21**	**29**	**50**	**22**	**26**	**48**	**37**	**8**	**1**	**3**	**169**	**12.4**	**71**	**24**	**70**	**19**	**–4**	....	....	....	....	....	....	....	....
	Canada	WC-A	11	2	3	5	....	....	....	2	....	....	....	....	....	....	....	....	....	....	....	....	....	....	....	....	....	....
1997-98	**Calgary Flames**	**NHL**	**70**	**13**	**19**	**32**	**15**	**19**	**34**	**29**	**0**	**2**	**1**	**154**	**8.4**	**44**	**9**	**53**	**8**	**–10**	....	....	....	....	....	....	....	....
	NHL Totals		**152**	**34**	**48**	**82**	**37**	**45**	**82**	**66**	**8**	**3**	**4**	**323**	**10.5**	**115**	**33**	**123**	**27**		**2**	**1**	**1**	**2**	**0**	**0**	**0**	**0**

Won George Parsons Trophy (Memorial Cup Tournament Most Sportsmanlike Player) (1995) • WJC-A All-Star Team (1996) • Named Best Forward at WJC-A (1996) • WHL West First All-Star Team (1996) • Canadian Major Junior First All-Star Team (1996) • NHL All-Rookie Team (1997)

Traded to **Calgary** by **Dallas** with Corey Millen for Joe Nieuwendyk, December 19, 1995.

• IHNACAK, MIROSLAV

Miroslav Ihnacak LW – L. 5'11", 175 lbs. b: Poprad, CSSR, 11/19/1962. Toronto's 12th choice, 171st overall, in 1982 Entry Draft.

Season	Club	League	GP	G	A	Pts	AG	AA	APts	PIM	PP	SH	GW	S	%	TGF	PGF	TGA	PGA	+/–	GP	G	A	Pts	PIM	PP	SH	GW
1981-82	VSZ Kosice	Czech.	41	22	11	33	....	....	....	28	....	....	....	....	....	....	....	....	....	....	....	....	....	....	....	....	....	....
1982-83	VSZ Kosice	Czech.	42	20	17	37	....	....	....	32	....	....	....	....	....	....	....	....	....	....	....	....	....	....	....	....	....	....
1983-84	VSZ Kosice	Czech.	42	19	25	44	....	....	....	34	....	....	....	....	....	....	....	....	....	....	....	....	....	....	....	....	....	....
1984-85	VSZ Kosice	Czech.	43	35	31	*66	....	....	....	68	....	....	....	....	....	....	....	....	....	....	....	....	....	....	....	....	....	....
1985-86	VSZ Kosice	Czech.	21	16	16	32	....	....	....	....	....	....	....	....	....	....	....	....	....	....	....	....	....	....	....	....	....	....
	Toronto Maple Leafs	**NHL**	**21**	**2**	**4**	**6**	**2**	**3**	**5**	**27**	**1**	**0**	**0**	**25**	**8.0**	**11**	**2**	**16**	**1**	**–6**	....	....	....	....	....	....	....	....
	St. Catharines Saints	AHL	13	4	4	8	....	....	....	2	....	....	....	....	....	....	....	....	....	....	13	8	3	11	10	....	....	....
1986-87	**Toronto Maple Leafs**	**NHL**	**34**	**6**	**5**	**11**	**5**	**4**	**9**	**12**	**0**	**0**	**0**	**65**	**9.2**	**24**	**1**	**20**	**0**	**+3**	**1**	**0**	**0**	**0**	**0**	**0**	**0**	**0**
	Newmarket Saints	AHL	32	11	17	28	....	....	....	6	....	....	....	....	....	....	....	....	....	....	....	....	....	....	....	....	....	....
1987-88	Newmarket Saints	AHL	51	11	17	28	....	....	....	24	....	....	....	....	....	....	....	....	....	....	....	....	....	....	....	....	....	....
1988-89	**Detroit Red Wings**	**NHL**	**1**	**0**	**0**	**0**	**0**	**0**	**0**	**0**	**0**	**0**	**0**	**1**	**0.0**	**1**	**0**	**1**	**0**	**0**	....	....	....	....	....	....	....	....
	Adirondack Red Wings	AHL	62	34	37	71	....	....	....	32	....	....	....	....	....	....	....	....	....	....	13	4	3	7	16	....	....	....
1989-90	Halifax Citadels	AHL	57	33	37	70	....	....	....	43	....	....	....	....	....	....	....	....	....	....	5	1	4	5	6	....	....	....
1990-91	Halifax Citadels	AHL	77	38	57	95	....	....	....	42	....	....	....	....	....	....	....	....	....	....	....	....	....	....	....	....	....	....
1991-92	Preussen Berlin	Germany	26	8	12	20	....	....	....	24	....	....	....	....	....	....	....	....	....	....	....	....	....	....	....	....	....	....
1992-93	Manheimer ERC	Germany	8	2	7	9	....	....	....	2	....	....	....	....	....	....	....	....	....	....	....	....	....	....	....	....	....	....
	Poprod	Czech.	10	7	2	9	....	....	....	2	....	....	....	....	....	....	....	....	....	....	....	....	....	....	....	....	....	....
	EV Zug	Switz.	7	6	3	9	....	....	....	8	....	....	....	....	....	....	....	....	....	....	....	....	....	....	....	....	....	....
1993-94	Milwaukee Admirals	IHL	1	0	0	0	....	....	....	0	....	....	....	....	....	....	....	....	....	....	....	....	....	....	....	....	....	....
1994-95	VSZ Kosice	Czech.	20	13	17	30	....	....	....	16	....	....	....	....	....	....	....	....	....	....	4	6	*14	*20	6	....	....	....
	Slovakia	WC-B	7	7	1	8	....	....	....	2	....	....	....	....	....	....	....	....	....	....	....	....	....	....	....	....	....	....
	NHL Totals		**56**	**8**	**9**	**17**	**7**	**7**	**14**	**39**	**1**	**0**	**0**	**91**	**8.8**	**36**	**3**	**37**	**1**		**1**	**0**	**0**	**0**	**0**	**0**	**0**	**0**

EJC-A All-Star Team (1979)

Signed as a free agent by **Detroit**, November 18, 1988.

• IHNACAK, PETER

Peter Ihnacak C – R. 5'11", 180 lbs. b: Poprad, Czech., 5/3/1957. Toronto's 3rd choice, 25th overall, in 1982 Entry Draft.

Season	Club	League	GP	G	A	Pts	AG	AA	APts	PIM	PP	SH	GW	S	%	TGF	PGF	TGA	PGA	+/–	GP	G	A	Pts	PIM	PP	SH	GW
1976-77	Czechoslovakia	WJC-A	4	2	2	4	....	....	....	0	....	....	....	....	....	....	....	....	....	....	....	....	....	....	....	....	....	....
1977-78	Dukla Jihlava	Czech.	5	0	1	1	....	....	....	4	....	....	....	....	....	....	....	....	....	....	3	0	2	2	2	....	....	....
1978-79	Dukla Jihlava	Czech.	44	22	12	34	....	....	....	....	....	....	....	....	....	....	....	....	....	....	....	....	....	....	....	....	....	....
1979-80	Sparta Praha	Czech.	44	19	28	47	....	....	....	....	....	....	....	....	....	....	....	....	....	....	....	....	....	....	....	....	....	....
1980-81	Sparta Praha	Czech.	44	23	22	45	....	....	....	....	....	....	....	....	....	....	....	....	....	....	....	....	....	....	....	....	....	....
1981-82	Sparta Praha	Czech.	39	16	22	38	....	....	....	50	....	....	....	....	....	....	....	....	....	....	....	....	....	....	....	....	....	....
	Czechoslovakia	WEC-A	5	0	0	0	....	....	....	0	....	....	....	....	....	....	....	....	....	....	....	....	....	....	....	....	....	....
1982-83	**Toronto Maple Leafs**	**NHL**	**80**	**28**	**38**	**66**	**23**	**26**	**49**	**44**	**6**	**0**	**2**	**162**	**17.3**	**95**	**24**	**66**	**1**	**+6**	....	....	....	....	....	....	....	....
1983-84	**Toronto Maple Leafs**	**NHL**	**47**	**10**	**13**	**23**	**8**	**9**	**17**	**24**	**5**	**0**	**0**	**76**	**13.2**	**42**	**13**	**50**	**0**	**–21**	....	....	....	....	....	....	....	....
1984-85	**Toronto Maple Leafs**	**NHL**	**70**	**22**	**22**	**44**	**18**	**15**	**33**	**24**	**8**	**0**	**1**	**115**	**19.1**	**56**	**21**	**61**	**0**	**–26**	....	....	....	....	....	....	....	....
1985-86	**Toronto Maple Leafs**	**NHL**	**63**	**18**	**27**	**45**	**14**	**18**	**32**	**16**	**5**	**0**	**1**	**96**	**18.8**	**65**	**17**	**57**	**0**	**–9**	**10**	**2**	**3**	**5**	**12**	**0**	**0**	**1**
1986-87	**Toronto Maple Leafs**	**NHL**	**58**	**12**	**27**	**39**	**10**	**20**	**30**	**16**	**4**	**0**	**1**	**98**	**12.2**	**61**	**11**	**55**	**10**	**+5**	**13**	**2**	**4**	**6**	**9**	**0**	**0**	**0**
	Newmarket Saints	AHL	8	2	6	8	....	....	....	0	....	....	....	....	....	....	....	....	....	....	....	....	....	....	....	....	....	....
1987-88	**Toronto Maple Leafs**	**NHL**	**68**	**10**	**20**	**30**	**9**	**14**	**23**	**41**	**0**	**0**	**0**	**75**	**13.3**	**48**	**6**	**60**	**12**	**–6**	**5**	**0**	**3**	**3**	**4**	**0**	**0**	**0**
1988-89	**Toronto Maple Leafs**	**NHL**	**26**	**2**	**16**	**18**	**2**	**11**	**13**	**10**	**0**	**0**	**0**	**30**	**6.7**	**26**	**0**	**25**	**2**	**+3**	....	....	....	....	....	....	....	....
	Newmarket Saints	AHL	38	14	16	30	....	....	....	8	....	....	....	....	....	....	....	....	....	....	....	....	....	....	....	....	....	....
1989-90	**Toronto Maple Leafs**	**NHL**	**5**	**0**	**2**	**2**	**0**	**1**	**1**	**0**	**0**	**0**	**0**	**5**	**0.0**	**5**	**1**	**1**	**0**	**+3**	....	....	....	....	....	....	....	....
	Newmarket Saints	AHL	72	26	47	73	....	....	....	40	....	....	....	....	....	....	....	....	....	....	....	....	....	....	....	....	....	....
1990-91	Freiburg	Germany	35	12	37	39	....	....	....	39	....	....	....	....	....	....	....	....	....	....	....	....	....	....	....	....	....	....
1991-92	Freiburg	Germany	41	21	36	57	....	....	....	34	....	....	....	....	....	....	....	....	....	....	....	....	....	....	....	....	....	....
	Kloten	Switz.	1	0	0	0	....	....	....	0	....	....	....	....	....	....	....	....	....	....	....	....	....	....	....	....	....	....
1992-93	Krefelder EV	Germany	15	5	5	10	....	....	....	10	....	....	....	....	....	....	....	....	....	....	....	....	....	....	....	....	....	....
	Ajoie	Switz.	13	3	8	11	....	....	....	10	....	....	....	....	....	....	....	....	....	....	....	....	....	....	....	....	....	....
1993-94	Krefelder EV	Germany	42	10	25	35	....	....	....	25	....	....	....	....	....	....	....	....	....	....	....	....	....	....	....	....	....	....
1994-95	Krefelder EV	Germany	19	7	6	13	....	....	....	8	....	....	....	....	....	....	....	....	....	....	15	2	4	6	6	....	....	....
1995-96	Krefelder EV	Germany	47	9	34	43	....	....	....	22	....	....	....	....	....	....	....	....	....	....	6	0	0	0	2	....	....	....
	NHL Totals		**417**	**102**	**165**	**267**	**84**	**114**	**198**	**175**	**28**	**0**	**5**	**657**	**15.5**	**398**	**93**	**375**	**25**		**28**	**4**	**10**	**14**	**25**	**0**	**0**	**1**

• INGARFIELD, EARL

Earl Ingarfield C – L. 5'11", 185 lbs. b: Lethbridge, Alta., 10/25/1934.

Season	Club	League	GP	G	A	Pts	AG	AA	APts	PIM	PP	SH	GW	S	%	TGF	PGF	TGA	PGA	+/–	GP	G	A	Pts	PIM	PP	SH	GW
1951-52	Lethbridge Native Sons	WCJHL	44	32	15	47	....	....	....	28	....	....	....	....	....	....	....	....	....	....	....	....	....	....	....	....	....	....
1952-53	Lethbridge Native Sons	WCJHL	30	22	25	47	....	....	....	37	....	....	....	....	....	....	....	....	....	....	14	6	3	9	9	....	....	....
1953-54	Lethbridge Native Sons	WCJHL	36	46	42	88	....	....	....	48	....	....	....	....	....	....	....	....	....	....	4	0	2	2	0	....	....	....
1954-55	Lethbridge Native Sons	WCJHL	36	*45	31	*76	....	....	....	45	....	....	....	....	....	....	....	....	....	....	11	5	6	11	7	....	....	....
1954-55	Lethbridge Native Sons	WCJHL	36	*45	31	*76	....	....	....	45	....	....	....	....	....	....	....	....	....	....	11	5	6	11	7	....	....	....
	Vancouver Canucks	WHL	2	0	0	0	....	....	....	0	....	....	....	....	....	....	....	....	....	....	....	....	....	....	....	....	....	....
1955-56	Saskatoon Quakers	WHL	70	15	23	38	....	....	....	46	....	....	....	....	....	....	....	....	....	....	3	0	0	0	0	....	....	....
1956-57	Winnipeg Warriors	WHL	69	21	27	48	....	....	....	41	....	....	....	....	....	....	....	....	....	....	....	....	....	....	....	....	....	....
1957-58	Winnipeg Warriors	WHL	64	39	41	80	....	....	....	25	....	....	....	....	....	....	....	....	....	....	7	2	2	4	2	....	....	....
1958-59	**New York Rangers**	**NHL**	**35**	**1**	**2**	**3**	**1**	**2**	**3**	**10**	....	....	....	....	....	....	....	....	....	....	....	....	....	....	....	....	....	....
1959-60	**New York Rangers**	**NHL**	**20**	**1**	**2**	**3**	**1**	**2**	**3**	**2**	....	....	....	....	....	....	....	....	....	....	....	....	....	....	....	....	....	....
	Cleveland Barons	AHL	40	25	40	65	....	....	....	17	....	....	....	....	....	....	....	....	....	....	7	3	6	9	6	....	....	....
1960-61	**New York Rangers**	**NHL**	**66**	**13**	**21**	**34**	**16**	**21**	**37**	**18**	....	....	....	....	....	....	....	....	....	....	....	....	....	....	....	....	....	....
1961-62	**New York Rangers**	**NHL**	**70**	**26**	**31**	**57**	**32**	**31**	**63**	**18**	....	....	....	....	....	....	....	....	....	....	**6**	**3**	**2**	**5**	**2**	....	....	....
1962-63	**New York Rangers**	**NHL**	**69**	**19**	**24**	**43**	**23**	**25**	**48**	**40**	....	....	....	....	....	....	....	....	....	....	....	....	....	....	....	....	....	....
1963-64	**New York Rangers**	**NHL**	**63**	**15**	**11**	**26**	**20**	**12**	**32**	**26**	....	....	....	....	....	....	....	....	....	....	....	....	....	....	....	....	....	....
1964-65	**New York Rangers**	**NHL**	**69**	**15**	**13**	**28**	**19**	**14**	**33**	**40**	....	....	....	....	....	....	....	....	....	....	....	....	....	....	....	....	....	....
1965-66	**New York Rangers**	**NHL**	**68**	**20**	**16**	**36**	**24**	**16**	**40**	**35**	....	....	....	....	....	....	....	....	....	....	....	....	....	....	....	....	....	....
1966-67	**New York Rangers**	**NHL**	**67**	**12**	**22**	**34**	**15**	**23**	**38**	**12**	....	....	....	....	....	....	....	....	....	....	**4**	**1**	**0**	**1**	**2**	....	....	....
1967-68	**Pittsburgh Penguins**	**NHL**	**50**	**15**	**22**	**37**	**19**	**23**	**42**	**12**	**2**	**1**	**0**	**110**	**13.6**	**51**	**11**	**53**	**6**	**–7**	....	....	....	....	....	....	....	....

			REGULAR SEASON																		PLAYOFFS							
Season	Club	League	GP	G	A	Pts	AG	AA	APts	PIM	PP	SH	GW	S	%	TGF	PGF	TGA	PGA	+/-	GP	G	A	Pts	PIM	PP	SH	GW
1968-69	**Pittsburgh Penguins**	**NHL**	40	8	15	23	9	14	23	4	3	0	0	71	11.3	27	8	36	0	−17	....	....	....	....	....	....	....	....
	Oakland Seals	**NHL**	26	8	15	23	9	14	23	8	3	0	0	60	13.3	32	8	29	4	−1	7	4	6	10	2	0	1	1
1969-70	**Oakland Seals**	**NHL**	54	21	24	45	24	24	48	10	9	0	3	130	16.2	56	22	60	19	−7	4	1	0	1	4	1	0	0
1970-71	**California Golden Seals**	**NHL**	49	5	8	13	5	7	12	4	0	0	0	76	6.6	25	4	59	30	−8	....	....	....	....	....	....	....	....
1971-72	Regina Pats	WCJHL	DID NOT PLAY – COACHING																									
	NHL Totals		**746**	**179**	**226**	**405**	**217**	**228**	**445**	**239**	**17**	**1**	**3**	**447**	**40.0**	**191**	**53**	**237**	**59**		**21**	**9**	**8**	**17**	**10**	**1**	**1**	**1**

Traded to **Montreal** by **NY Rangers** with Noel Price, Gord Labossiere and Dave McComb for Cesare Maniago and Garry Peters, June 8, 1965. Claimed by **NY Rangers** from **Montreal** in Intra-League Draft, June 9, 1965. Claimed by **Pittsburgh** from **NY Rangers** in Expansion Draft, June 6, 1967. Traded to **Oakland** by **Pittsburgh** with Gene Ubriaco and Dick Mattiussi for Bryan Watson, George Swarbrick and Tracy Pratt, January 30, 1969.

• INGARFIELD, EARL JR.

Earl Jr. Ingarfield C – L. 5′11″, 180 lbs. b: New York, NY, 1/30/1959.

1975-76	Swift Current Broncos	SJHL	54	36	30	66	....	....	....	128	....	....	....	....	....	....	....	....	....	....	....	....	....	....	....	....	....	....
1976-77	Regina Pats	WCJHL	25	1	0	1	....	....	....	38	....	....	....	....	....	....	....	....	....	....	....	....	....	....	....	....	....	....
	Lethbridge Broncos	WCJHL	1	0	0	0	....	....	....	0	....	....	....	....	....	....	....	....	....	....	....	....	....	....	....	....	....	....
1977-78	Lethbridge Broncos	WCJHL	65	25	25	50	....	....	....	127	....	....	....	....	....	....	....	....	....	....	....	....	....	....	....	....	....	....
1978-79	Lethbridge Broncos	WHL	70	43	45	88	....	....	....	84	....	....	....	....	....	....	....	....	....	....	....	....	....	....	....	....	....	....
1979-80	**Atlanta Flames**	**NHL**	1	0	0	0	0	0	0	0	0	0	0	7	0.0	0	0	1	0	−1	2	0	1	1	0	0	0	0
	Birmingham Bulls	CHL	75	27	30	57	....	....	....	160	....	....	....	....	....	....	....	....	....	....	2	4	1	5	0	....	....	....
1980-81	**Calgary Flames**	**NHL**	16	2	3	5	2	2	4	6	0	0	0	20	10.0	6	0	8	3	+1	....	....	....	....	....	....	....	....
	Birmingham Bulls	CHL	23	7	9	16	....	....	....	47	....	....	....	....	....	....	....	....	....	....	....	....	....	....	....	....	....	....
	Detroit Red Wings	**NHL**	22	2	1	3	2	1	3	16	0	0	0	18	11.1	5	0	3	0	+2	....	....	....	....	....	....	....	....
1981-82	Adirondack Red Wings	AHL	68	24	19	43	....	....	....	86	....	....	....	....	....	....	....	....	....	....	2	0	1	1	4	....	....	....
1982-83	Adirondack Red Wings	AHL	65	11	26	37	....	....	....	60	....	....	....	....	....	....	....	....	....	....	1	0	1	1	2	....	....	....
1983-84			DID NOT PLAY																									
1984-85			DID NOT PLAY																									
1985-86	Springfield Indians	AHL	18	2	3	5	....	....	....	27	....	....	....	....	....	....	....	....	....	....	....	....	....	....	....	....	....	....
	Indianapolis Checkers	IHL	20	11	6	17	....	....	....	17	....	....	....	....	....	....	....	....	....	....	5	2	3	5	11	....	....	....
1986-87	Peoria Rivermen	IHL	33	8	11	19	....	....	....	18	....	....	....	....	....	....	....	....	....	....	....	....	....	....	....	....	....	....
	NHL Totals		**39**	**4**	**4**	**8**	**4**	**3**	**7**	**22**	**0**	**0**	**0**	**45**	**8.9**	**11**	**0**	**12**	**3**		**2**	**0**	**1**	**1**	**0**	**0**	**0**	**0**

Signed as a free agent by **Atlanta**, October 9, 1979. Transferred to **Calgary** after **Atlanta** franchise relocated, June 30, 1980. Traded to **Detroit** by **Calgary** for Dan Labraaten, February 3, 1981.

• INGLIS, BILL

Bill Inglis C – L. 5′9″, 160 lbs. b: Ottawa, Ont., 5/11/1943.

1961-62	Montreal Jr. Canadiens	OHA	50	22	28	50	....	....	....	27	....	....	....	....	....	....	....	....	....	....	6	3	4	7	2	....	....	....
1962-63	Montreal Jr. Canadiens	OHA	50	30	39	69	....	....	....	64	....	....	....	....	....	....	....	....	....	....	10	5	3	8	2	....	....	....
	Hull-Ottawa Canadiens	EPHL	1	1	0	1	....	....	....	0	....	....	....	....	....	....	....	....	....	....	....	....	....	....	....	....	....	....
1963-64	Omaha Knights	CHL	60	20	16	36	....	....	....	19	....	....	....	....	....	....	....	....	....	....	10	3	3	6	8	....	....	....
1964-65	Omaha Knights	CHL	70	29	34	63	....	....	....	44	....	....	....	....	....	....	....	....	....	....	6	3	0	3	10	....	....	....
1965-66	Houston Apollos	CHL	69	34	36	70	....	....	....	61	....	....	....	....	....	....	....	....	....	....	....	....	....	....	....	....	....	....
1966-67	Houston Apollos	CHL	70	33	34	67	....	....	....	50	....	....	....	....	....	....	....	....	....	....	6	2	4	6	2	....	....	....
1967-68	**Los Angeles Kings**	**NHL**	12	1	1	2	1	1	2	0	0	0	0	17	5.9	5	0	20	9	−6	....	....	....	....	....	....	....	....
	Springfield Kings	AHL	59	22	24	46	....	....	....	44	....	....	....	....	....	....	....	....	....	....	4	0	0	0	7	....	....	....
1968-69	**Los Angeles Kings**	**NHL**	10	0	1	1	0	1	1	0	0	0	0	18	0.0	2	0	6	2	−2	11	1	2	3	4	0	0	0
	Springfield Kings	AHL	57	26	30	56	....	....	....	22	....	....	....	....	....	....	....	....	....	....	....	....	....	....	....	....	....	....
1969-70	Springfield Kings	AHL	72	31	44	75	....	....	....	25	....	....	....	....	....	....	....	....	....	....	14	5	4	9	6	....	....	....
1970-71	**Buffalo Sabres**	**NHL**	14	0	1	1	0	1	1	4	0	0	0	9	0.0	1	1	5	1	−4	....	....	....	....	....	....	....	....
	Salt Lake Golden Eagles	WHL	6	3	0	3	....	....	....	2	....	....	....	....	....	....	....	....	....	....	....	....	....	....	....	....	....	....
1971-72	Salt Lake Golden Eagles	WHL	71	24	36	60	....	....	....	29	....	....	....	....	....	....	....	....	....	....	....	....	....	....	....	....	....	....
1972-73	Cincinnati Swords	AHL	75	40	57	97	....	....	....	29	....	....	....	....	....	....	....	....	....	....	15	8	7	15	12	....	....	....
1973-74	Cincinnati Swords	AHL	76	35	36	71	....	....	....	48	....	....	....	....	....	....	....	....	....	....	5	2	1	3	4	....	....	....
1974-75	Hershey Bears	AHL	72	27	43	70	....	....	....	42	....	....	....	....	....	....	....	....	....	....	12	4	6	10	4	....	....	....
1975-76	Springfield Indians	AHL	70	19	48	67	....	....	....	8	....	....	....	....	....	....	....	....	....	....	....	....	....	....	....	....	....	....
1976-77	Hershey Bears	AHL	75	21	47	68	....	....	....	10	....	....	....	....	....	....	....	....	....	....	6	0	1	1	0	....	....	....
1977-78	Phoenix Roadrunners	CHL	9	3	4	7	....	....	....	0	....	....	....	....	....	....	....	....	....	....	....	....	....	....	....	....	....	....
	Binghamton Dusters	AHL	11	3	3	6	....	....	....	2	....	....	....	....	....	....	....	....	....	....	....	....	....	....	....	....	....	....
	New Haven Nighthawks	AHL	20	1	1	2	....	....	....	0	....	....	....	....	....	....	....	....	....	....	....	....	....	....	....	....	....	....
	NHL Totals		**36**	**1**	**3**	**4**	**1**	**3**	**4**	**4**	**0**	**0**	**0**	**44**	**2.3**	**8**	**1**	**31**	**12**		**11**	**1**	**2**	**3**	**4**	**0**	**0**	**0**

AHL First All-Star Team (1973) • Won Les Cunningham Award (MVP - AHL) (1973)

Claimed by **LA Kings** from **Montreal** in Expansion Draft, June 6, 1967. Claimed by **Montreal** from **LA Kings** in Intra-League Draft, June 9, 1970. Claimed by **Buffalo** from **Montreal** in Intra-League Draft, June 9, 1970.

• INTRANUOVO, RALPH

Ralph Intranuovo C – L. 5′8″, 185 lbs. b: East York, Ont., 12/11/1973. Edmonton's 5th choice, 96th overall, in 1992 Entry Draft.

1990-91	Sault Ste. Marie Greyhounds	OHL	63	25	42	67	....	....	....	22	....	....	....	....	....	....	....	....	....	....	14	7	13	20	17	....	....	....
1991-92	Sault Ste. Marie Greyhounds	OHL	65	50	63	113	....	....	....	44	....	....	....	....	....	....	....	....	....	....	18	10	14	24	12	....	....	....
1992-93	Sault Ste. Marie Greyhounds	OHL	54	31	47	78	....	....	....	61	....	....	....	....	....	....	....	....	....	....	18	10	16	26	30	....	....	....
	Canada	WJC-A	7	3	2	5	....	....	....	4	....	....	....	....	....	....	....	....	....	....	....	....	....	....	....	....	....	....
1993-94	Cape Breton Oilers	AHL	66	21	31	52	....	....	....	39	....	....	....	....	....	....	....	....	....	....	4	1	2	3	2	....	....	....
1994-95	**Edmonton Oilers**	**NHL**	1	0	1	1	0	1	1	0	0	0	0	1	0.0	1	0	0	0	+1	....	....	....	....	....	....	....	....
	Cape Breton Oilers	AHL	70	46	47	93	....	....	....	62	....	....	....	....	....	....	....	....	....	....	....	....	....	....	....	....	....	....
	Canada	WC-A	8	5	1	6	....	....	....	6	....	....	....	....	....	....	....	....	....	....	....	....	....	....	....	....	....	....
1995-96	**Edmonton Oilers**	**NHL**	13	1	2	3	1	2	3	4	0	0	1	19	5.3	6	3	6	0	−3	....	....	....	....	....	....	....	....
	Cape Breton Oilers	AHL	52	34	39	73	....	....	....	84	....	....	....	....	....	....	....	....	....	....	....	....	....	....	....	....	....	....
1996-97	**Toronto Maple Leafs**	**NHL**	3	0	1	1	0	1	1	0	0	0	0	4	0.0	2	0	3	0	−1	....	....	....	....	....	....	....	....
	Edmonton Oilers	**NHL**	5	1	0	1	1	0	1	0	0	0	0	2	50.0	1	0	1	0	0	....	....	....	....	....	....	....	....
	Hamilton Bulldogs	AHL	68	36	40	76	....	....	....	88	....	....	....	....	....	....	....	....	....	....	22	8	4	12	30	....	....	....
1997-98	Manitoba Moose	IHL	81	26	35	61	....	....	....	68	....	....	....	....	....	....	....	....	....	....	3	2	0	2	4	....	....	....
	NHL Totals		**22**	**2**	**4**	**6**	**2**	**4**	**6**	**4**	**0**	**0**	**1**	**26**	**7.7**	**10**	**3**	**10**	**0**		....	....	....	....	....	....	....	....

Memorial Cup All-Star Team (1993) • Won Stafford Smythe Memorial Trophy (Memorial Cup Tournament MVP) (1993) • AHL Second All-Star Team (1995, 1997)

Claimed by **Toronto** from **Edmonton** in Waiver Draft, September 30, 1996. Claimed on waivers by **Edmonton** from **Toronto**, October 25, 1996.

• IRVINE, TED

Ted Irvine LW – L. 6′2″, 195 lbs. b: Winnipeg, Man., 12/8/1944.

1961-62	St. Boniface Canadians	MJHL	36	6	7	13	....	....	....	4	....	....	....	....	....	....	....	....	....	....	4	5	0	5	0	....	....	....
1962-63	St. Boniface Canadians	MJHL	32	*31	23	54	....	....	....	13	....	....	....	....	....	....	....	....	....	....	8	7	5	12	6	....	....	....
	Brandon Wheat Kings	MJHL	....	....	....	....	....	....	....	....	....	....	....	....	....	....	....	....	....	....	4	2	1	3	4	....	....	....
1963-64	St. Boniface Canadians	MJHL	19	17	11	28	....	....	....	19	....	....	....	....	....	....	....	....	....	....	....	....	....	....	....	....	....	....
	Winnipeg Braves	MJHL	10	3	5	8	....	....	....	2	....	....	....	....	....	....	....	....	....	....	....	....	....	....	....	....	....	....
	Boston Bruins	**NHL**	1	0	0	0	0	0	0	0	....	....	....	....	....	....	....	....	....	....	....	....	....	....	....	....	....	....
	Minneapolis Bruins	CHL	3	1	5	6	....	....	....	0	....	....	....	....	....	....	....	....	....	....	4	1	1	2	2	....	....	....
1964-65	Minneapolis Bruins	CHL	68	15	16	31	....	....	....	40	....	....	....	....	....	....	....	....	....	....	5	0	1	1	6	....	....	....
1965-66	Oklahoma City Blazers	CHL	69	26	20	46	....	....	....	27	....	....	....	....	....	....	....	....	....	....	9	*6	3	9	4	....	....	....
1966-67	Oklahoma City Blazers	CHL	63	15	17	32	....	....	....	54	....	....	....	....	....	....	....	....	....	....	11	6	1	7	0	....	....	....
1967-68	**Los Angeles Kings**	**NHL**	73	18	22	40	22	23	45	26	4	1	3	136	13.2	50	9	58	1	−10	6	1	3	4	2	0	0	0
1968-69	**Los Angeles Kings**	**NHL**	76	15	24	39	17	23	40	47	0	0	3	206	7.3	55	8	65	1	−17	11	5	1	6	7	1	1	0
1969-70	**Los Angeles Kings**	**NHL**	58	11	13	24	13	13	26	28	2	0	0	120	9.2	32	4	48	0	−20	....	....	....	....	....	....	....	....
	New York Rangers	**NHL**	17	0	3	3	0	3	3	10	0	0	0	28	0.0	5	1	11	1	−6	6	1	2	3	8	0	1	0
1970-71	**New York Rangers**	**NHL**	76	20	18	38	21	16	37	137	2	0	6	150	13.3	57	8	32	1	+18	12	1	2	3	28	0	0	0
1971-72	**New York Rangers**	**NHL**	78	15	21	36	16	19	35	66	0	0	1	164	9.1	56	3	45	0	+8	16	4	5	9	19	0	0	0
1972-73	**New York Rangers**	**NHL**	53	8	12	20	8	10	18	54	1	0	1	91	8.8	33	5	24	0	+4	10	1	3	4	20	1	0	0
1973-74	**New York Rangers**	**NHL**	75	26	20	46	27	17	44	105	2	0	5	142	18.3	80	4	75	1	+2	13	3	5	8	16	0	0	0
1974-75	**New York Rangers**	**NHL**	79	17	17	34	16	13	29	66	4	0	3	174	9.8	72	11	76	0	−15	3	0	1	1	11	0	0	0

			REGULAR SEASON																		PLAYOFFS							
Season	**Club**	**League**	**GP**	**G**	**A**	**Pts**	**AG**	**AA**	**APts**	**PIM**	**PP**	**SH**	**GW**	**S**	**%**	**TGF**	**PGF**	**TGA**	**PGA**	**+/–**	**GP**	**G**	**A**	**Pts**	**PIM**	**PP**	**SH**	**GW**
1975-76	**St. Louis Blues**	**NHL**	**69**	**10**	**13**	**23**	**9**	**10**	**19**	**80**	**2**	**0**	**2**	**105**	**9.5**	**41**	**5**	**50**	**2**	**–12**	**3**	**0**	**2**	**2**	**2**	**0**	**0**	**0**
1976-77	**St. Louis Blues**	**NHL**	**69**	**14**	**14**	**28**	**13**	**11**	**24**	**38**	**1**	**0**	**2**	**122**	**11.5**	**46**	**3**	**59**	**0**	**–16**	**3**	**0**	**0**	**0**	**2**	**0**	**0**	**0**
1977-78	St. James Braves	CSHL	12	6	6	12	....	....	....	30	....	....	....	....	....	....	....	....	....	....	....	....	....	....	....	....	....	....
	NHL Totals		**724**	**154**	**177**	**331**	**162**	**158**	**320**	**657**	**18**	**1**	**26**	**1438**	**10.7**	**533**	**61**	**543**	**7**		**83**	**16**	**24**	**40**	**115**	**2**	**2**	**0**

Claimed by **LA Kings** from **Boston** in Expansion Draft, June 6, 1967. Traded to **NY Rangers** by **LA Kings** for Real Lemieux and Juha Widing, February 28, 1970. Traded to **St. Louis** by **NY Rangers** with Bert Wilson and Jerry Butler for Bill Collins and John Davidson, June 18, 1975.

• ISAKSSON, ULF

Ulf Isaksson LW – L. 6'1", 185 lbs. b: Norfunda, Sweden, 3/19/1954. Los Angeles' 6th choice, 95th overall, in 1982 Entry Draft.

Season	Club	League	GP	G	A	Pts	AG	AA	APts	PIM	PP	SH	GW	S	%	TGF	PGF	TGA	PGA	+/–	GP	G	A	Pts	PIM	PP	SH	GW
1974-75	AIK Solna	Sweden	30	15	10	25	....	....	....	12	....	....	....	....	....	....	....	....	....	....	....	....	....	....	....	....	....	....
1975-76	AIK Solna	Sweden	36	11	7	18	....	....	....	6	....	....	....	....	....	....	....	....	....	....	....	....	....	....	....	....	....	....
1976-77	AIK Solna	Sweden	36	14	5	19	....	....	....	8	....	....	....	....	....	....	....	....	....	....	....	....	....	....	....	....	....	....
1977-78	AIK Solna	Sweden	34	11	10	21	....	....	....	16	....	....	....	....	....	....	....	....	....	....	6	3	2	5	2	....	....	....
1978-79	AIK Solna	Sweden	34	15	14	29	....	....	....	14	....	....	....	....	....	....	....	....	....	....	....	....	....	....	....	....	....	....
1979-80	AIK Solna	Sweden	36	9	11	20	....	....	....	12	....	....	....	....	....	....	....	....	....	....	....	....	....	....	....	....	....	....
1980-81	AIK Solna	Sweden	35	13	8	21	....	....	....	26	....	....	....	....	....	....	....	....	....	....	6	3	0	3	2	....	....	....
	Sweden	WEC-A	5	0	1	1	....	....	....	4	....	....	....	....	....	....	....	....	....	....	....	....	....	....	....	....	....	....
1981-82	AIK Solna	Sweden	24	9	8	17	....	....	....	16	....	....	....	....	....	....	....	....	....	....	7	*5	2	*7	4	....	....	....
	Sweden	Nat-Team	32	16	14	30	....	....	....	26	....	....	....	....	....	....	....	....	....	....	....	....	....	....	....	....	....	....
	Sweden	WEC-A	10	1	2	3	....	....	....	4	....	....	....	....	....	....	....	....	....	....	....	....	....	....	....	....	....	....
1982-83	**Los Angeles Kings**	**NHL**	**50**	**7**	**15**	**22**	**6**	**10**	**16**	**10**	**0**	**0**	**1**	**71**	**9.9**	**35**	**4**	**32**	**2**	**+1**	....	....	....	....	....	....	....	....
	New Haven Nighthawks	AHL	14	1	3	4	....	....	....	2	....	....	....	....	....	....	....	....	....	....	2	0	0	0	0	....	....	....
1983-84	AIK Solna	Sweden	36	11	11	22	....	....	....	12	....	....	....	....	....	....	....	....	....	....	6	3	2	5	6	....	....	....
1984-85	AIK Solna	Sweden	33	7	8	15	....	....	....	20	....	....	....	....	....	....	....	....	....	....	....	....	....	....	....	....	....	....
	NHL Totals		**50**	**7**	**15**	**22**	**6**	**10**	**16**	**10**	**0**	**0**	**1**	**71**	**9.9**	**35**	**4**	**32**	**2**		....	....	....	....	....	....	....	....

Swedish World All-Star Team (1982)

• ISBISTER, BRAD

Brad Isbister RW – R. 6'2", 198 lbs. b: Edmonton, Alta., 5/7/1977. Winnipeg's 4th choice, 67th overall, in 1995 Entry Draft.

Season	Club	League	GP	G	A	Pts	AG	AA	APts	PIM	PP	SH	GW	S	%	TGF	PGF	TGA	PGA	+/–	GP	G	A	Pts	PIM	PP	SH	GW
1993-94	Portland Winter Hawks	WHL	64	7	10	17	....	....	....	45	....	....	....	....	....	....	....	....	....	....	10	0	2	2	0	....	....	....
1994-95	Portland Winter Hawks	WHL	67	16	20	36	....	....	....	123	....	....	....	....	....	....	....	....	....	....	....	....	....	....	....	....	....	....
1995-96	Portland Winter Hawks	WHL	71	45	44	89	....	....	....	184	....	....	....	....	....	....	....	....	....	....	7	2	4	6	20	....	....	....
1996-97	Portland Winter Hawks	WHL	24	15	18	33	....	....	....	45	....	....	....	....	....	....	....	....	....	....	6	2	1	3	16	....	....	....
	Canada	WJC-A	7	4	3	7	....	....	....	8	....	....	....	....	....	....	....	....	....	....	....	....	....	....	....	....	....	....
	Springfield Falcons	AHL	7	3	1	4	....	....	....	14	....	....	....	....	....	....	....	....	....	....	9	1	2	3	10	....	....	....
1997-98	**Phoenix Coyotes**	**NHL**	**66**	**9**	**8**	**17**	**11**	**8**	**19**	**102**	**1**	**0**	**1**	**115**	**7.8**	**35**	**7**	**27**	**3**	**+4**	**5**	**0**	**0**	**0**	**2**	**0**	**0**	**0**
	Springfield Falcons	AHL	9	8	2	10	....	....	....	36	....	....	....	....	....	....	....	....	....	....	....	....	....	....	....	....	....	....
	NHL Totals		**66**	**9**	**8**	**17**	**11**	**8**	**19**	**102**	**1**	**0**	**1**	**115**	**7.8**	**35**	**7**	**27**	**3**		**5**	**0**	**0**	**0**	**2**	**0**	**0**	**0**

WHL West Second All-Star Team (1997)

Rights transferred to **Phoenix** after **Winnipeg** franchise relocated, July 1, 1996.

• ISSEL, KIM

Kim Issel RW – R. 6'4", 196 lbs. b: Regina, Sask., 9/25/1967. Edmonton's 1st choice, 21st overall, in 1986 Entry Draft.

Season	Club	League	GP	G	A	Pts	AG	AA	APts	PIM	PP	SH	GW	S	%	TGF	PGF	TGA	PGA	+/–	GP	G	A	Pts	PIM	PP	SH	GW
1983-84	Prince Albert Raiders	WHL	31	9	9	18	....	....	....	24	....	....	....	....	....	....	....	....	....	....	5	4	0	4	9	....	....	....
1984-85	Prince Albert Raiders	WHL	44	8	15	23	....	....	....	43	....	....	....	....	....	....	....	....	....	....	....	....	....	....	....	....	....	....
1985-86	Prince Albert Raiders	WHL	68	29	39	68	....	....	....	41	....	....	....	....	....	....	....	....	....	....	19	6	7	13	6	....	....	....
1986-87	Prince Albert Raiders	WHL	70	31	44	75	....	....	....	55	....	....	....	....	....	....	....	....	....	....	6	1	2	3	17	....	....	....
1987-88	Nova Scotia Oilers	AHL	68	2	25	27	....	....	....	31	....	....	....	....	....	....	....	....	....	....	2	1	0	1	10	....	....	....
1988-89	**Edmonton Oilers**	**NHL**	**4**	**0**	**0**	**0**	**0**	**0**	**0**	**0**	**0**	**0**	**0**	**1**	**0.0**	**1**	**0**	**2**	**0**	**–1**	....	....	....	....	....	....	....	....
	Cape Breton Oilers	AHL	65	34	28	62	....	....	....	4	....	....	....	....	....	....	....	....	....	....	....	....	....	....	....	....	....	....
1989-90	Cape Breton Oilers	AHL	62	36	32	68	....	....	....	46	....	....	....	....	....	....	....	....	....	....	6	1	3	4	10	....	....	....
1990-91	Cape Breton Oilers	AHL	24	6	4	10	....	....	....	28	....	....	....	....	....	....	....	....	....	....	....	....	....	....	....	....	....	....
	Kansas City Blades	IHL	13	7	2	9	....	....	....	2	....	....	....	....	....	....	....	....	....	....	....	....	....	....	....	....	....	....
1991-92	VSV Villach	Austria	45	42	49	91	....	....	....	....	....	....	....	....	....	....	....	....	....	....	....	....	....	....	....	....	....	....
1992-93	VSV Villach	Austria	54	39	48	87	....	....	....	....	....	....	....	....	....	....	....	....	....	....	....	....	....	....	....	....	....	....
1993-94	VSV Villach	Austria	33	23	27	50	....	....	....	....	....	....	....	....	....	....	....	....	....	....	....	....	....	....	....	....	....	....
1994-95	Bolzano	Italy	5	0	2	2	....	....	....	2	....	....	....	....	....	....	....	....	....	....	....	....	....	....	....	....	....	....
	Eisbaren Zell a See	Austria	30	31	20	51	....	....	....	80	....	....	....	....	....	....	....	....	....	....	2	3	5	8	6	....	....	....
1995-96	Durham Wasps	Britain	27	31	27	58	....	....	....	63	....	....	....	....	....	....	....	....	....	....	5	4	4	8	8	....	....	....
1996-97	Olimpija Ljubljana	Slovenia	52	25	27	52	....	....	....	....	....	....	....	....	....	....	....	....	....	....	....	....	....	....	....	....	....	....
1997-98	Schwenningen Wild Wings	Germany	6	1	0	1	....	....	....	4	....	....	....	....	....	....	....	....	....	....	....	....	....	....	....	....	....	....
	NHL Totals		**4**	**0**	**0**	**0**	**0**	**0**	**0**	**0**	**0**	**0**	**0**	**1**	**0.0**	**1**	**0**	**2**	**0**		....	....	....	....	....	....	....	....

Traded to **Pittsburgh** by **Edmonton** for Brad Aitken, March 5, 1991. Signed as a free agent by **Vancouver**, August, 1991.

• JACKSON, DANE

Dane Jackson RW – R. 6'1", 200 lbs. b: Castlegar, B.C., 5/17/1970. Vancouver's 3rd choice, 44th overall, in 1988 Entry Draft.

Season	Club	League	GP	G	A	Pts	AG	AA	APts	PIM	PP	SH	GW	S	%	TGF	PGF	TGA	PGA	+/–	GP	G	A	Pts	PIM	PP	SH	GW
1988-89	University of North Dakota	WCHA	30	4	5	9	....	....	....	33	....	....	....	....	....	....	....	....	....	....	....	....	....	....	....	....	....	....
1989-90	University of North Dakota	WCHA	44	15	11	26	....	....	....	56	....	....	....	....	....	....	....	....	....	....	....	....	....	....	....	....	....	....
1990-91	University of North Dakota	WCHA	37	17	9	26	....	....	....	79	....	....	....	....	....	....	....	....	....	....	....	....	....	....	....	....	....	....
1991-92	University of North Dakota	WCHA	39	23	19	42	....	....	....	81	....	....	....	....	....	....	....	....	....	....	....	....	....	....	....	....	....	....
1992-93	Hamilton Canucks	AHL	68	23	20	43	....	....	....	59	....	....	....	....	....	....	....	....	....	....	....	....	....	....	....	....	....	....
1993-94	**Vancouver Canucks**	**NHL**	**12**	**5**	**1**	**6**	**5**	**1**	**6**	**9**	**0**	**0**	**0**	**18**	**27.8**	**10**	**1**	**6**	**0**	**+3**	....	....	....	....	....	....	....	....
	Hamilton Canucks	AHL	60	25	35	60	....	....	....	75	....	....	....	....	....	....	....	....	....	....	4	2	2	4	16	....	....	....
1994-95	**Vancouver Canucks**	**NHL**	**3**	**1**	**0**	**1**	**2**	**0**	**2**	**4**	**0**	**0**	**0**	**6**	**16.7**	**2**	**0**	**3**	**1**	**0**	**6**	**0**	**0**	**0**	**10**	**0**	**0**	**0**
	Syracuse Crunch	AHL	78	30	28	58	....	....	....	162	....	....	....	....	....	....	....	....	....	....	....	....	....	....	....	....	....	....
1995-96	**Buffalo Sabres**	**NHL**	**22**	**5**	**4**	**9**	**5**	**3**	**8**	**41**	**0**	**0**	**1**	**20**	**25.0**	**16**	**2**	**11**	**0**	**+3**	....	....	....	....	....	....	....	....
	Rochester Americans	AHL	50	27	19	46	....	....	....	132	....	....	....	....	....	....	....	....	....	....	19	4	6	10	53	....	....	....
1996-97	Rochester Americans	AHL	78	24	34	58	....	....	....	111	....	....	....	....	....	....	....	....	....	....	10	7	4	11	14	....	....	....
1997-98	**New York Islanders**	**NHL**	**8**	**1**	**1**	**2**	**1**	**1**	**2**	**4**	**0**	**0**	**1**	**5**	**20.0**	**3**	**0**	**2**	**0**	**+1**	....	....	....	....	....	....	....	....
	Rochester Americans	AHL	28	10	13	23	....	....	....	55	....	....	....	....	....	....	....	....	....	....	3	2	2	4	4	....	....	....
	NHL Totals		**45**	**12**	**6**	**18**	**13**	**5**	**18**	**58**	**0**	**0**	**2**	**49**	**24.5**	**31**	**3**	**22**	**1**		**6**	**0**	**0**	**0**	**10**	**0**	**0**	**0**

Signed as a free agent by **Buffalo**, September 20, 1995. Signed as a free agent by **NY Islanders**, July 21, 1997.

• JACKSON, DON

Don Jackson D – L. 6'3", 210 lbs. b: Minneapolis, MN, 9/2/1956. Minnesota's 3rd choice, 39th overall, in 1976 Amateur Draft.

Season	Club	League	GP	G	A	Pts	AG	AA	APts	PIM	PP	SH	GW	S	%	TGF	PGF	TGA	PGA	+/–	GP	G	A	Pts	PIM	PP	SH	GW
1974-75	University of Notre Dame	WCHA	35	2	7	9	....	....	....	29	....	....	....	....	....	....	....	....	....	....	....	....	....	....	....	....	....	....
1975-76	University of Notre Dame	WCHA	30	4	5	9	....	....	....	22	....	....	....	....	....	....	....	....	....	....	....	....	....	....	....	....	....	....
1976-77	University of Notre Dame	WCHA	38	2	9	11	....	....	....	52	....	....	....	....	....	....	....	....	....	....	....	....	....	....	....	....	....	....
1977-78	University of Notre Dame	WCHA	37	10	23	33	....	....	....	69	....	....	....	....	....	....	....	....	....	....	....	....	....	....	....	....	....	....
	Minnesota North Stars	**NHL**	**2**	**0**	**0**	**0**	**0**	**0**	**0**	**2**	**0**	**0**	**0**	**3**	**0.0**	**2**	**0**	**2**	**1**	**+1**	....	....	....	....	....	....	....	....
	United States	WEC-A	10	1	1	2	....	....	....	4	....	....	....	....	....	....	....	....	....	....	....	....	....	....	....	....	....	....
1978-79	**Minnesota North Stars**	**NHL**	**5**	**0**	**0**	**0**	**0**	**0**	**0**	**2**	**0**	**0**	**0**	**6**	**0.0**	**2**	**0**	**4**	**1**	**–1**	....	....	....	....	....	....	....	....
	Oklahoma City Stars	CHL	73	8	23	31	....	....	....	108	....	....	....	....	....	....	....	....	....	....	....	....	....	....	....	....	....	....
	United States	WEC-A	8	0	1	1	....	....	....	16	....	....	....	....	....	....	....	....	....	....	....	....	....	....	....	....	....	....
1979-80	**Minnesota North Stars**	**NHL**	**10**	**0**	**4**	**4**	**0**	**3**	**3**	**18**	**0**	**0**	**0**	**8**	**0.0**	**9**	**0**	**8**	**3**	**+4**	**1**	**0**	**0**	**0**	**0**	**0**	**0**	**0**
	Oklahoma City Stars	CHL	33	5	9	14	....	....	....	54	....	....	....	....	....	....	....	....	....	....	....	....	....	....	....	....	....	....
1980-81	**Minnesota North Stars**	**NHL**	**10**	**0**	**3**	**3**	**0**	**2**	**2**	**19**	**0**	**0**	**0**	**14**	**0.0**	**8**	**0**	**8**	**3**	**+3**	....	....	....	....	....	....	....	....
	Oklahoma City Stars	CHL	59	5	33	38	....	....	....	67	....	....	....	....	....	....	....	....	....	....	3	0	0	0	0	....	....	....
1981-82	**Edmonton Oilers**	**NHL**	**8**	**0**	**0**	**0**	**0**	**0**	**0**	**18**	**0**	**0**	**0**	**4**	**0.0**	**6**	**1**	**6**	**1**	**0**	....	....	....	....	....	....	....	....
	Wichita Wind	CHL	71	7	37	44	....	....	....	116	....	....	....	....	....	....	....	....	....	....	7	0	1	1	21	....	....	....
1982-83	**Edmonton Oilers**	**NHL**	**71**	**2**	**8**	**10**	**2**	**6**	**8**	**136**	**0**	**1**	**1**	**72**	**2.8**	**73**	**2**	**81**	**22**	**+12**	**16**	**3**	**3**	**6**	**30**	**0**	**0**	**0**
	Birmingham South Stars	CHL	4	1	4	5	....	....	....	8	....	....	....	....	....	....	....	....	....	....	....	....	....	....	....	....	....	....
1983-84	**Edmonton Oilers**	**NHL**	**60**	**8**	**12**	**20**	**6**	**8**	**14**	**120**	**0**	**1**	**2**	**57**	**14.0**	**77**	**0**	**66**	**17**	**+28**	**19**	**1**	**2**	**3**	**32**	**0**	**0**	**0**

			REGULAR SEASON																		PLAYOFFS							
Season	Club	League	GP	G	A	Pts	AG	AA	APts	PIM	PP	SH	GW	S	%	TGF	PGF	TGA	PGA	+/–	GP	G	A	Pts	PIM	PP	SH	GW
1984-85	**Edmonton Oilers**	NHL	78	3	17	20	2	11	13	141	0	0	0	47	6.4	81	1	64	11	+27	9	0	0	0	64	0	0	0
1985-86	**Edmonton Oilers**	NHL	45	2	8	10	2	5	7	93	0	0	0	34	5.9	42	3	42	5	+2	8	0	0	0	21	0	0	0
1986-87	**New York Rangers**	NHL	22	1	0	1	1	0	1	91	0	0	0	4	25.0	11	0	14	2	–1	....	....	....	....	....	....	....	....
	NHL Totals		311	16	52	68	13	35	48	640	0	2	3	249	6.4	311	7	295	66		53	4	5	9	147	0	0	0

Traded to **Edmonton** by **Minnesota** with Edmonton's 3rd round choice (previously acquired, Edmonton selected Wally Chapman) in 1982 Entry Draft for the rights to Don Murdoch, August 21, 1981. Traded to **NY Rangers** by **Edmonton** with Mike Golden and Miroslav Horava for Reijo Ruotsalainen, Ville Kentala, Clark Donatelli, Jim Wiemer and future considerations (Stu Kulak, March 10, 1987), October 2, 1986.

• JACKSON, JEFF

Jeff Jackson LW – L. 6'1", 195 lbs. b: Dresden, Ont., 4/24/1965. Toronto's 2nd choice, 28th overall, in 1983 Entry Draft.

Season	Club	League	GP	G	A	Pts	AG	AA	APts	PIM	PP	SH	GW	S	%	TGF	PGF	TGA	PGA	+/–	GP	G	A	Pts	PIM	PP	SH	GW
1981-82	Newmarket Flyers	OHA	45	30	39	69	....	....	....	105	....	....	....	....	....	....	....	....	....	....	....	....	....	....	....	....	....	....
1982-83	Brantford Alexanders	OHL	64	18	25	43	....	....	....	63	....	....	....	....	....	....	....	....	....	....	8	1	1	2	27	....	....	....
1983-84	Brantford Alexanders	OHL	58	27	42	69	....	....	....	78	....	....	....	....	....	....	....	....	....	....	2	0	1	1	0	....	....	....
1984-85	Hamilton Steelhawks	OHL	20	13	14	27	....	....	....	51	....	....	....	....	....	....	....	....	....	....	17	8	12	20	26	....	....	....
	Canada	WJC-A	7	1	7	8	....	....	....	10	....	....	....	....	....	....	....	....	....	....	....	....	....	....	....	....	....	....
	Toronto Maple Leafs	**NHL**	**17**	**0**	**1**	**1**	**0**	**1**	**1**	**24**	**0**	**0**	**0**	**12**	**0.0**	**2**	**0**	**8**	**2**	**–4**	....	....	....	....	....	....	....	....
1985-86	**Toronto Maple Leafs**	**NHL**	**5**	**1**	**2**	**3**	**1**	**1**	**2**	**2**	**0**	**0**	**0**	**2**	**50.0**	**4**	**0**	**1**	**0**	**+3**	....	....	....	....	....	....	....	....
	St. Catharines Saints	AHL	74	17	28	45	....	....	....	122	....	....	....	....	....	....	....	....	....	....	13	5	2	7	30	....	....	....
1986-87	**Toronto Maple Leafs**	**NHL**	**55**	**8**	**7**	**15**	**7**	**5**	**12**	**64**	**0**	**0**	**0**	**42**	**19.0**	**19**	**0**	**36**	**6**	**–11**	....	....	....	....	....	....	....	....
	Newmarket Saints	AHL	7	3	6	9	....	....	....	13	....	....	....	....	....	....	....	....	....	....	....	....	....	....	....	....	....	....
	New York Rangers	**NHL**	**9**	**5**	**1**	**6**	**4**	**1**	**5**	**15**	**2**	**0**	**1**	**16**	**31.3**	**8**	**2**	**10**	**1**	**–3**	**6**	**1**	**1**	**2**	**16**	**0**	**0**	**0**
1987-88	**Quebec Nordiques**	**NHL**	**68**	**9**	**18**	**27**	**8**	**13**	**21**	**103**	**0**	**2**	**3**	**98**	**9.2**	**36**	**1**	**36**	**6**	**+5**	....	....	....	....	....	....	....	....
1988-89	**Quebec Nordiques**	**NHL**	**33**	**4**	**6**	**10**	**3**	**4**	**7**	**28**	**0**	**1**	**2**	**40**	**10.0**	**16**	**2**	**38**	**9**	**–15**	....	....	....	....	....	....	....	....
1989-90	**Quebec Nordiques**	**NHL**	**65**	**8**	**12**	**20**	**7**	**9**	**16**	**71**	**0**	**1**	**0**	**73**	**11.0**	**34**	**3**	**79**	**27**	**–21**	....	....	....	....	....	....	....	....
1990-91	**Quebec Nordiques**	**NHL**	**10**	**3**	**1**	**4**	**3**	**1**	**4**	**4**	**0**	**0**	**0**	**13**	**23.1**	**9**	**0**	**13**	**7**	**+3**	....	....	....	....	....	....	....	....
	Halifax Citadels	AHL	25	8	17	25	....	....	....	45	....	....	....	....	....	....	....	....	....	....	....	....	....	....	....	....	....	....
1991-92	Indianapolis Ice	IHL	18	3	7	10	....	....	....	41	....	....	....	....	....	....	....	....	....	....	....	....	....	....	....	....	....	....
	Chicago Blackhawks	**NHL**	**1**	**0**	**0**	**0**	**0**	**0**	**0**	**2**	**0**	**0**	**0**	**0**	**0.0**	**0**	**0**	**0**	**0**	**0**	....	....	....	....	....	....	....	....
	New Haven Nighthawks	AHL	30	10	14	24	....	....	....	60	....	....	....	....	....	....	....	....	....	....	5	0	5	5	6	....	....	....
	NHL Totals		**263**	**38**	**48**	**86**	**33**	**35**	**68**	**313**	**2**	**4**	**6**	**296**	**12.8**	**128**	**8**	**221**	**58**		**6**	**1**	**1**	**2**	**16**	**0**	**0**	**0**

Traded to **NY Rangers** by **Toronto** with Toronto's 3rd round choice (Rob Zamuner) in 1989 Entry Draft for Mark Osborne, March 5, 1987. Traded to **Quebec** by **NY Rangers** with Terry Carkner for John Ogrodnick and David Shaw, September 30, 1987. Signed as a free agent by **Chicago**, February 19, 1992.

• JACKSON, JIM

Jim Jackson LW – R. 5'9", 190 lbs. b: Oshawa, Ont., 2/1/1960.

Season	Club	League	GP	G	A	Pts	AG	AA	APts	PIM	PP	SH	GW	S	%	TGF	PGF	TGA	PGA	+/–	GP	G	A	Pts	PIM	PP	SH	GW
1976-77	Oshawa Generals	OHA	65	13	40	53	....	....	....	26	....	....	....	....	....	....	....	....	....	....	....	....	....	....	....	....	....	....
1977-78	Oshawa Generals	OHA	68	33	47	80	....	....	....	60	....	....	....	....	....	....	....	....	....	....	6	2	2	4	26	....	....	....
1978-79	Niagara Falls Flyers	OHA	62	26	39	65	....	....	....	73	....	....	....	....	....	....	....	....	....	....	20	6	9	15	16	....	....	....
1979-80	Niagara Falls Flyers	OHA	66	29	57	86	....	....	....	55	....	....	....	....	....	....	....	....	....	....	10	7	8	15	8	....	....	....
1980-81	Richmond Rifles	EHL	58	17	43	60	....	....	....	42	....	....	....	....	....	....	....	....	....	....	10	1	0	1	4	....	....	....
1981-82	Muskegon Mohawks	IHL	82	24	51	75	....	....	....	72	....	....	....	....	....	....	....	....	....	....	....	....	....	....	....	....	....	....
1982-83	**Calgary Flames**	**NHL**	**48**	**8**	**12**	**20**	**7**	**8**	**15**	**7**	**1**	**0**	**1**	**85**	**9.4**	**38**	**4**	**26**	**0**	**+9**	**8**	**2**	**1**	**3**	**2**	**0**	**0**	**0**
	Colorado Flames	CHL	30	10	16	26	....	....	....	4	....	....	....	....	....	....	....	....	....	....	....	....	....	....	....	....	....	....
1983-84	**Calgary Flames**	**NHL**	**49**	**6**	**14**	**20**	**5**	**9**	**14**	**13**	**0**	**1**	**0**	**66**	**9.1**	**33**	**0**	**41**	**9**	**+1**	**6**	**1**	**1**	**2**	**4**	**0**	**1**	**0**
	Colorado Flames	CHL	25	5	27	32	....	....	....	4	....	....	....	....	....	....	....	....	....	....	....	....	....	....	....	....	....	....
1984-85	**Calgary Flames**	**NHL**	**10**	**1**	**4**	**5**	**1**	**3**	**4**	**0**	**0**	**1**	**1**	**10**	**10.0**	**6**	**0**	**8**	**3**	**+1**	....	....	....	....	....	....	....	....
	Moncton Golden Flames	AHL	24	2	5	7	....	....	....	6	....	....	....	....	....	....	....	....	....	....	....	....	....	....	....	....	....	....
1985-86	Rochester Americans	AHL	65	16	32	48	....	....	....	10	....	....	....	....	....	....	....	....	....	....	....	....	....	....	....	....	....	....
1986-87	Rochester Americans	AHL	71	19	38	57	....	....	....	48	....	....	....	....	....	....	....	....	....	....	16	5	4	9	6	....	....	....
1987-88	**Buffalo Sabres**	**NHL**	**5**	**2**	**0**	**2**	**2**	**0**	**2**	**0**	**1**	**0**	**1**	**11**	**18.2**	**3**	**1**	**3**	**1**	**0**	....	....	....	....	....	....	....	....
	Rochester Americans	AHL	74	23	48	71	....	....	....	23	....	....	....	....	....	....	....	....	....	....	7	2	6	8	4	....	....	....
1988-89	Rochester Americans	AHL	73	19	50	69	....	....	....	14	....	....	....	....	....	....	....	....	....	....	....	....	....	....	....	....	....	....
1989-90	Rochester Americans	AHL	77	16	37	53	....	....	....	14	....	....	....	....	....	....	....	....	....	....	9	1	5	6	4	....	....	....
	NHL Totals		**112**	**17**	**30**	**47**	**15**	**20**	**35**	**20**	**2**	**2**	**3**	**172**	**9.9**	**80**	**5**	**77**	**13**		**14**	**3**	**2**	**5**	**6**	**0**	**1**	**0**

IHL Second All-Star Team (1982)

Signed as a free agent by **Calgary**, October 8, 1982. Signed as a free agent by **Buffalo**, September 26, 1985.

• JACOBS, TIM

Tim Jacobs D – L. 5'10", 180 lbs. b: Espanola, Ont., 3/28/1952. California's 5th choice, 70th overall, in 1972 Amateur Draft.

Season	Club	League	GP	G	A	Pts	AG	AA	APts	PIM	PP	SH	GW	S	%	TGF	PGF	TGA	PGA	+/–	GP	G	A	Pts	PIM	PP	SH	GW
1969-70	St. Catharines Black Hawks	OHA	26	0	0	0	....	....	....	6	....	....	....	....	....	....	....	....	....	....	....	....	....	....	....	....	....	....
1970-71	St. Catharines Black Hawks	OHA	60	1	10	11	....	....	....	23	....	....	....	....	....	....	....	....	....	....	....	....	....	....	....	....	....	....
1971-72	St. Catherines Blackhawks	OHA	58	6	19	25	....	....	....	46	....	....	....	....	....	....	....	....	....	....	....	....	....	....	....	....	....	....
1972-73	Salt Lake Golden Eagles	WHL	72	7	14	21	....	....	....	33	....	....	....	....	....	....	....	....	....	....	9	0	1	1	18	....	....	....
1973-74	Salt Lake Golden Eagles	WHL	75	2	26	28	....	....	....	46	....	....	....	....	....	....	....	....	....	....	5	1	2	3	2	....	....	....
1974-75	Springfield Indians	AHL	73	3	31	34	....	....	....	57	....	....	....	....	....	....	....	....	....	....	17	2	13	15	28	....	....	....
1975-76	**California Golden Seals**	**NHL**	**46**	**0**	**10**	**10**	**0**	**8**	**8**	**35**	**0**	**0**	**0**	**46**	**0.0**	**53**	**11**	**61**	**17**	**–2**	....	....	....	....	....	....	....	....
	Salt Lake City Golden Eagles	CHL	30	4	12	16	....	....	....	22	....	....	....	....	....	....	....	....	....	....	....	....	....	....	....	....	....	....
1976-77	Salt Lake Golden Eagles	CHL	71	1	19	20	....	....	....	34	....	....	....	....	....	....	....	....	....	....	....	....	....	....	....	....	....	....
1977-78	Springfield Indians	AHL	78	6	20	26	....	....	....	16	....	....	....	....	....	....	....	....	....	....	4	0	1	1	0	....	....	....
1978-79	Springfield Indians	AHL	80	7	35	42	....	....	....	33	....	....	....	....	....	....	....	....	....	....	....	....	....	....	....	....	....	....
	NHL Totals		**46**	**0**	**10**	**10**	**0**	**8**	**8**	**35**	**0**	**0**	**0**	**46**	**0.0**	**53**	**11**	**61**	**17**		....	....	....	....	....	....	....	....

• JAGR, JAROMIR

Jaromir Jagr RW – L. 6'2", 216 lbs. b: Kladno, Czech., 2/15/1972. Pittsburgh's 1st choice, 5th overall, in 1990 Entry Draft.

Season	Club	League	GP	G	A	Pts	AG	AA	APts	PIM	PP	SH	GW	S	%	TGF	PGF	TGA	PGA	+/–	GP	G	A	Pts	PIM	PP	SH	GW
1988-89	Poldi Kladno	Czech.	39	8	10	18	....	....	....	4	....	....	....	....	....	....	....	....	....	....	....	....	....	....	....	....	....	....
1989-90	Poldi Kladno	Czech.	51	30	29	59	....	....	....	....	....	....	....	....	....	....	....	....	....	....	....	....	....	....	....	....	....	....
	Czechoslovakia	WJC-A	7	5	13	18	....	....	....	6	....	....	....	....	....	....	....	....	....	....	....	....	....	....	....	....	....	....
	Czechoslovakia	WEC-A	10	3	2	5	....	....	....	2	....	....	....	....	....	....	....	....	....	....	....	....	....	....	....	....	....	....
1990-91	**Pittsburgh Penguins**	**NHL**	**80**	**27**	**30**	**57**	**25**	**23**	**48**	**42**	**7**	**0**	**4**	**136**	**19.9**	**68**	**15**	**57**	**0**	**–4**	**24**	**3**	**10**	**13**	**6**	**1**	**0**	**1**
1991-92	Czechoslovakia	C Cup	5	1	0	1	....	....	....	0	....	....	....	....	....	....	....	....	....	....	....	....	....	....	....	....	....	....
	Pittsburgh Penguins	**NHL**	**70**	**32**	**37**	**69**	**29**	**28**	**57**	**34**	**4**	**0**	**4**	**194**	**16.5**	**98**	**18**	**69**	**1**	**+12**	**21**	**11**	**13**	**24**	**6**	**2**	**0**	**4**
1992-93	**Pittsburgh Penguins**	**NHL**	**81**	**34**	**60**	**94**	**28**	**41**	**69**	**61**	**10**	**1**	**9**	**242**	**14.0**	**131**	**43**	**61**	**3**	**+30**	**12**	**5**	**4**	**9**	**23**	**1**	**0**	**1**
1993-94	**Pittsburgh Penguins**	**NHL**	**80**	**32**	**67**	**99**	**30**	**52**	**82**	**61**	**9**	**0**	**6**	**298**	**10.7**	**133**	**41**	**81**	**4**	**+15**	**6**	**2**	**4**	**6**	**16**	**0**	**0**	**1**
	Czech Republic	WC-A	3	0	2	2	....	....	....	2	....	....	....	....	....	....	....	....	....	....	....	....	....	....	....	....	....	....
1994-95	Poldi Kladno	Czech.	11	8	14	22	....	....	....	10	....	....	....	....	....	....	....	....	....	....	....	....	....	....	....	....	....	....
	HC Bolzano	EuroHL	5	8	8	16	....	....	....	4	....	....	....	....	....	....	....	....	....	....	....	....	....	....	....	....	....	....
	HC Bolzano	Italy	1	0	0	0	....	....	....	0	....	....	....	....	....	....	....	....	....	....	....	....	....	....	....	....	....	....
	Schalke	German 2	1	1	10	11	....	....	....	0	....	....	....	....	....	....	....	....	....	....	....	....	....	....	....	....	....	....
	Pittsburgh Penguins	**NHL**	**48**	**32**	**38**	***70**	**57**	**56**	**113**	**37**	**8**	**3**	**7**	**192**	**16.7**	**89**	**29**	**46**	**9**	**+23**	**12**	**10**	**5**	**15**	**6**	**2**	**1**	**1**
1995-96	**Pittsburgh Penguins**	**NHL**	**82**	**62**	**87**	**149**	**61**	**71**	**132**	**96**	**20**	**1**	**12**	**403**	**15.4**	**205**	**90**	**102**	**18**	**+31**	**18**	**11**	**12**	**23**	**18**	**5**	**1**	**1**
1996-97	Czech Republic	W Cup	3	1	0	1	....	....	....	2	....	....	....	....	....	....	....	....	....	....	....	....	....	....	....	....	....	....
	Pittsburgh Penguins	**NHL**	**63**	**47**	**48**	**95**	**50**	**43**	**93**	**40**	**11**	**2**	**6**	**234**	**20.1**	**128**	**41**	**71**	**6**	**+22**	**5**	**4**	**4**	**8**	**4**	**2**	**0**	**0**
1997-98	**Pittsburgh Penguins**	**NHL**	**77**	**35**	**67**	**102**	**41**	**66**	**107**	**64**	**7**	**0**	**8**	**262**	**13.4**	**123**	**46**	**63**	**3**	**+17**	**6**	**4**	**5**	**9**	**2**	**1**	**0**	**0**
	Czech Republic	Olympics	6	1	4	5	....	....	....	2	....	....	....	....	....	....	....	....	....	....	....	....	....	....	....	....	....	....
	NHL Totals		**581**	**301**	**434**	**735**	**321**	**380**	**701**	**435**	**76**	**7**	**56**	**1961**	**15.3**	**975**	**323**	**550**	**44**		**104**	**50**	**57**	**107**	**81**	**14**	**2**	**9**

WJC-A All-Star Team (1990) • NHL/Upper Deck All-Rookie Team (1991) • NHL First All-Star Team (1995, 1996, 1998) • Won Art Ross Trophy (1995, 1998) • NHL Second All-Star Team (1997)
Played in NHL All-Star Game (1992, 1993, 1996, 1998)

• JAKOPIN, JOHN

John Jakopin D – R. 6'5", 220 lbs. b: Toronto, Ont., 5/16/1975. Detroit's 4th choice, 97th overall, in 1993 Entry Draft.

Season	Club	League	GP	G	A	Pts	AG	AA	APts	PIM	PP	SH	GW	S	%	TGF	PGF	TGA	PGA	+/–	GP	G	A	Pts	PIM	PP	SH	GW
			REGULAR SEASON																		PLAYOFFS							
1992-93	St. Michael's Buzzers	Jr. A	45	9	21	30	....	....	....	42	....	....	....	....	....	....	....	....	....	....	....	....	....	....	....	....	....	....
1993-94	Merrimack College	H.E.	36	2	8	10	....	....	....	64	....	....	....	....	....	....	....	....	....	....	....	....	....	....	....	....	....	....
1994-95	Merrimack College	H.E.	37	4	10	14	....	....	....	42	....	....	....	....	....	....	....	....	....	....	....	....	....	....	....	....	....	....
1995-96	Merrimack College	H.E.	32	10	15	25	....	....	....	68	....	....	....	....	....	....	....	....	....	....	....	....	....	....	....	....	....	....
1996-97	Merrimack College	H.E.	31	4	12	16	....	....	....	68	....	....	....	....	....	....	....	....	....	....	....	....	....	....	....	....	....	....
	Adirondack Red Wings	AHL	3	0	0	0	....	....	....	9	....	....	....	....	....	....	....	....	....	....	....	....	....	....	....	....	....	....
1997-98	**Florida Panthers**	**NHL**	**2**	**0**	**0**	**0**	**0**	**0**	**0**	**4**	**0**	**0**	**0**	**1**	**0.0**	**0**	**0**	**4**	**1**	**–3**	....	....	....	....	....	....	....	....
	Beast of New Haven	AHL	60	2	18	20	....	....	....	151	....	....	....	....	....	....	....	....	....	....	3	0	0	0	0	....	....	....
	NHL Totals		**2**	**0**	**0**	**0**	**0**	**0**	**0**	**4**	**0**	**0**	**0**	**1**	**0.0**	**0**	**0**	**4**	**1**		....	....	....	....	....	....	....	....

Signed as a free agent by **Florida**, May 14, 1997.

• JALO, RISTO

Risto Jalo C – L. 5'11", 185 lbs. b: Tampere, Finland, 7/18/1962. Washington's 7th choice, 131st overall, in 1981 Entry Draft.

Season	Club	League	GP	G	A	Pts	AG	AA	APts	PIM	PP	SH	GW	S	%	TGF	PGF	TGA	PGA	+/–	GP	G	A	Pts	PIM	PP	SH	GW
1979-80	Koovee	Finland	32	13	10	23	....	....	....	16	....	....	....	....	....	....	....	....	....	....	....	....	....	....	....	....	....	....
1980-81	Ilves Tampere	Finland	16	3	3	6	....	....	....	2	....	....	....	....	....	....	....	....	....	....	2	0	0	0	0	....	....	....
	Finland	WJC-A	5	1	5	6	....	....	....	6	....	....	....	....	....	....	....	....	....	....	....	....	....	....	....	....	....	....
1981-82	Ilves Tampere	Finland	34	17	20	37	....	....	....	8	....	....	....	....	....	....	....	....	....	....	....	....	....	....	....	....	....	....
	Finland	WJC-A	7	7	8	15	....	....	....	2	....	....	....	....	....	....	....	....	....	....	....	....	....	....	....	....	....	....
1982-83	Ilves Tampere	Finland	33	14	36	50	....	....	....	20	....	....	....	....	....	....	....	....	....	....	2	0	2	2	0	....	....	....
	Finland	WEC-A	10	1	2	3	....	....	....	4	....	....	....	....	....	....	....	....	....	....	....	....	....	....	....	....	....	....
1983-84	Ilves Tampere	Finland	30	13	32	45	....	....	....	30	....	....	....	....	....	....	....	....	....	....	2	2	2	4	0	....	....	....
	Finland	Olympics	6	2	6	8	....	....	....	4	....	....	....	....	....	....	....	....	....	....	....	....	....	....	....	....	....	....
1984-85	Ilves Tampere	Finland	35	17	21	38	....	....	....	18	....	....	....	....	....	....	....	....	....	....	9	3	4	7	5	....	....	....
	Finland	WEC-A	10	2	2	4	....	....	....	2	....	....	....	....	....	....	....	....	....	....	....	....	....	....	....	....	....	....
1985-86	Ilves Tampere	Finland	30	17	31	48	....	....	....	30	....	....	....	....	....	....	....	....	....	....	....	....	....	....	....	....	....	....
	Edmonton Oilers	**NHL**	**3**	**0**	**3**	**3**	**0**	**2**	**2**	**0**	**0**	**0**	**0**	**3**	**0.0**	**5**	**1**	**2**	**0**	**+2**	....	....	....	....	....	....	....	....
1986-87	Ilves Tampere	Finland	44	23	31	54	....	....	....	38	....	....	....	....	....	....	....	....	....	....	....	....	....	....	....	....	....	....
	Finland	WEC-A	9	0	4	4	....	....	....	10	....	....	....	....	....	....	....	....	....	....	....	....	....	....	....	....	....	....
1987-88	Ilves Tampere	Finaland	35	25	35	60	....	....	....	24	....	....	....	....	....	....	....	....	....	....	3	0	2	2	2	....	....	....
1988-89	Ilves Tampere	Finland	22	5	15	20	....	....	....	6	....	....	....	....	....	....	....	....	....	....	5	4	8	12	2	....	....	....
1989-90	Ilves Tampere	Finland	43	18	41	59	....	....	....	36	....	....	....	....	....	....	....	....	....	....	7	1	4	5	4	....	....	....
	Finland	WEC-A	10	1	2	3	....	....	....	0	....	....	....	....	....	....	....	....	....	....	....	....	....	....	....	....	....	....
1990-91	Vita Hasten	Switz. 2	33	15	23	38	....	....	....	34	....	....	....	....	....	....	....	....	....	....	....	....	....	....	....	....	....	....
1991-92	Ilves Tampere	Finland	40	14	18	32	....	....	....	16	....	....	....	....	....	....	....	....	....	....	....	....	....	....	....	....	....	....
1992-93	HC Fassa	Italy	18	14	14	28	....	....	....	4	....	....	....	....	....	....	....	....	....	....	....	....	....	....	....	....	....	....
1993-94	Ilves Tampere	Finland	46	12	23	35	....	....	....	32	....	....	....	....	....	....	....	....	....	....	....	....	....	....	....	....	....	....
1994-95	HPK Hameenlinna	Finland	50	12	33	45	....	....	....	30	....	....	....	....	....	....	....	....	....	....	....	....	....	....	....	....	....	....
1995-96	HPK Hameenlinna	Finland	34	10	21	31	....	....	....	40	....	....	....	....	....	....	....	....	....	....	9	1	3	4	18	....	....	....
1996-97	HPK Hameenlinna	Finland	38	16	26	42	....	....	....	26	....	....	....	....	....	....	....	....	....	....	10	2	4	6	2	....	....	....
1997-98	HPK Hameenlinna	Finland	21	4	10	14	....	....	....	53	....	....	....	....	....	....	....	....	....	....	....	....	....	....	....	....	....	....
	HPK Hameenlinna	EuroHL	3	0	2	2	....	....	....	0	....	....	....	....	....	....	....	....	....	....	....	....	....	....	....	....	....	....
	NHL Totals		**3**	**0**	**3**	**3**	**0**	**2**	**2**	**0**	**0**	**0**	**0**	**3**	**0.0**	**5**	**1**	**2**	**0**		....	....	....	....	....	....	....	....

Finnish First All-Star Team (1984)

Traded to **Edmonton** by **Washington** for Edmonton's 4th round choice (Larry Shaw) in 1985 Entry Draft, March 6, 1984.

• JALONEN, KARI

Kari Jalonen C – R. 6'3", 190 lbs. b: Oulu, Finland, 1/6/1960.

Season	Club	League	GP	G	A	Pts	AG	AA	APts	PIM	PP	SH	GW	S	%	TGF	PGF	TGA	PGA	+/–	GP	G	A	Pts	PIM	PP	SH	GW
1978-79	Karpat Oulu	Finland	36	13	13	26	....	....	....	30	....	....	....	....	....	....	....	....	....	....	....	....	....	....	....	....	....	....
	Finland	WJC-A	6	3	3	6	....	....	....	2	....	....	....	....	....	....	....	....	....	....	....	....	....	....	....	....	....	....
1979-80	Karpat Oulu	Finland	28	23	24	47	....	....	....	16	....	....	....	....	....	....	....	....	....	....	6	3	5	8	2	....	....	....
	Finland	WJC-A	5	3	5	8	....	....	....	0	....	....	....	....	....	....	....	....	....	....	....	....	....	....	....	....	....	....
1980-81	Karpat Oulu	Finland	35	16	34	50	....	....	....	22	....	....	....	....	....	....	....	....	....	....	12	*7	*14	*21	14	....	....	....
	Finland	WEC-A	8	4	3	7	....	....	....	5	....	....	....	....	....	....	....	....	....	....	....	....	....	....	....	....	....	....
1981-82	Finland	C Cup	5	0	1	1	....	....	....	4	....	....	....	....	....	....	....	....	....	....	....	....	....	....	....	....	....	....
	Karpat Oulu	Finland	33	21	26	47	....	....	....	24	....	....	....	....	....	....	....	....	....	....	3	2	5	7	2	....	....	....
	Finland	WEC-A	7	3	4	7	....	....	....	0	....	....	....	....	....	....	....	....	....	....	....	....	....	....	....	....	....	....
1982-83	**Calgary Flames**	**NHL**	**25**	**9**	**3**	**12**	**7**	**2**	**9**	**4**	**0**	**0**	**1**	**32**	**28.1**	**20**	**0**	**12**	**0**	**+8**	**5**	**1**	**0**	**1**	**0**	**0**	**0**	**0**
	Colorado Flames	CHL	33	12	32	44	....	....	....	8	....	....	....	....	....	....	....	....	....	....	....	....	....	....	....	....	....	....
	Finland	WEC-A	6	3	2	5	....	....	....	0	....	....	....	....	....	....	....	....	....	....	....	....	....	....	....	....	....	....
1983-84	**Calgary Flames**	**NHL**	**9**	**0**	**3**	**3**	**0**	**2**	**2**	**0**	**0**	**0**	**0**	**4**	**0.0**	**5**	**0**	**6**	**0**	**–1**	....	....	....	....	....	....	....	....
	Colorado Flames	CHL	1	0	0	0	....	....	....	0	....	....	....	....	....	....	....	....	....	....	....	....	....	....	....	....	....	....
	Edmonton Oilers	**NHL**	**3**	**0**	**0**	**0**	**0**	**0**	**0**	**0**	**0**	**0**	**0**	**0**	**0.0**	**0**	**0**	**2**	**0**	**–2**	....	....	....	....	....	....	....	....
	Karpat Oulu	Finland	14	6	15	21	....	....	....	17	....	....	....	....	....	....	....	....	....	....	10	5	*12	*17	10	....	....	....
1984-85	Karpat Oulu	Finland	21	9	9	18	....	....	....	10	....	....	....	....	....	....	....	....	....	....	....	....	....	....	....	....	....	....
1985-86	Karpat Oulu	Finland	36	19	35	54	....	....	....	46	....	....	....	....	....	....	....	....	....	....	5	2	3	5	14	....	....	....
	Finland	WEC-A	9	4	6	10	....	....	....	6	....	....	....	....	....	....	....	....	....	....	....	....	....	....	....	....	....	....
1986-87	Karpat Oulu	Finland	44	29	*64	*93	....	....	....	30	....	....	....	....	....	....	....	....	....	....	9	3	*7	10	12	....	....	....
	Finland	WEC-A	10	2	3	5	....	....	....	0	....	....	....	....	....	....	....	....	....	....	....	....	....	....	....	....	....	....
1987-88	Skelleftea	Finland	33	18	33	51	....	....	....	33	....	....	....	....	....	....	....	....	....	....	8	5	4	9	6	....	....	....
1988-89	TPS Turku	Finland	44	18	*56	74	....	....	....	40	....	....	....	....	....	....	....	....	....	....	10	4	*14	*18	8	....	....	....
	Finland	WEC-A	10	5	9	14	....	....	....	0	....	....	....	....	....	....	....	....	....	....	....	....	....	....	....	....	....	....
1989-90	TPS Turku	Finland	37	19	31	50	....	....	....	12	....	....	....	....	....	....	....	....	....	....	9	5	8	13	10	....	....	....
1990-91	TPS Turku	Finland	26	4	22	26	....	....	....	18	....	....	....	....	....	....	....	....	....	....	9	3	4	7	2	....	....	....
1991-92	TPS Turku	Finland	44	10	21	31	....	....	....	8	....	....	....	....	....	....	....	....	....	....	3	0	1	1	0	....	....	....
1992-93	Jurkarat	Finland	26	21	45	66	....	....	....	28	....	....	....	....	....	....	....	....	....	....	....	....	....	....	....	....	....	....
	TPS Turku	Finland	6	0	0	0	....	....	....	6	....	....	....	....	....	....	....	....	....	....	9	2	3	5	2	....	....	....
1993-94	Karpat Oulu	Finland	28	21	46	67	....	....	....	22	....	....	....	....	....	....	....	....	....	....	....	....	....	....	....	....	....	....
1994-95	Lukko Rauma	Finland	18	3	10	13	....	....	....	2	....	....	....	....	....	....	....	....	....	....	9	2	1	3	4	....	....	....
	NHL Totals		**37**	**9**	**6**	**15**	**7**	**4**	**11**	**4**	**0**	**0**	**1**	**36**	**25.0**	**25**	**0**	**20**	**0**		**5**	**1**	**0**	**1**	**0**	**0**	**0**	**0**

Finnish Rookie of the Year (1979) • Finnish First All-Star Team (1987, 1989)

Signed as a free agent by **Calgary**, January 21, 1982. Signed as a free agent by **Edmonton**, December, 1984.

• JAMES, VAL

Val (Edwin) James LW – L. 6'2", 205 lbs. b: Ocala, FL, 2/14/1957. Detroit's 15th choice, 184th overall, in 1977 Amateur Draft.

Season	Club	League	GP	G	A	Pts	AG	AA	APts	PIM	PP	SH	GW	S	%	TGF	PGF	TGA	PGA	+/–	GP	G	A	Pts	PIM	PP	SH	GW
1975-76	Quebec Remparts	QMJHL	72	14	19	33	....	....	....	83	....	....	....	....	....	....	....	....	....	....	15	0	6	6	52	....	....	....
1976-77	Quebec Remparts	QMJHL	68	16	16	32	....	....	....	99	....	....	....	....	....	....	....	....	....	....	10	1	1	2	48	....	....	....
1977-78			DID NOT PLAY																									
1978-79	Erie Blades	NEHL	67	14	26	40	....	....	....	112	....	....	....	....	....	....	....	....	....	....	....	....	....	....	....	....	....	....
1979-80	Erie Blades	EHL	69	12	13	25	....	....	....	117	....	....	....	....	....	....	....	....	....	....	9	0	1	1	3	....	....	....
1980-81	Rochester Americans	AHL	3	0	0	0	....	....	....	12	....	....	....	....	....	....	....	....	....	....	....	....	....	....	....	....	....	....
	Erie Blades	EHL	70	3	18	21	....	....	....	179	....	....	....	....	....	....	....	....	....	....	6	1	3	4	30	....	....	....
1981-82	**Buffalo Sabres**	**NHL**	**7**	**0**	**0**	**0**	**0**	**0**	**0**	**16**	**0**	**0**	**0**	**5**	**0.0**	**0**	**0**	**1**	**0**	**–1**	....	....	....	....	....	....	....	....
	Rochester Americans	AHL	65	5	4	9	....	....	....	204	....	....	....	....	....	....	....	....	....	....	6	0	2	2	16	....	....	....
1982-83	Rochester Americans	AHL	68	3	4	7	....	....	....	88	....	....	....	....	....	....	....	....	....	....	16	1	0	1	27	....	....	....
1983-84	Rochester Americans	AHL	62	1	2	3	....	....	....	122	....	....	....	....	....	....	....	....	....	....	....	....	....	....	....	....	....	....
1984-85	Rochester Americans	AHL	55	1	4	5	....	....	....	70	....	....	....	....	....	....	....	....	....	....	3	0	0	0	15	....	....	....
1985-86	St. Catharines Saints	AHL	80	0	3	3	....	....	....	162	....	....	....	....	....	....	....	....	....	....	13	1	1	2	53	....	....	....

							REGULAR SEASON														PLAYOFFS							
Season	Club	League	GP	G	A	Pts	AG	AA	APts	PIM	PP	SH	GW	S	%	TGF	PGF	TGA	PGA	+/-	GP	G	A	Pts	PIM	PP	SH	GW
1986-87	**Toronto Maple Leafs**	**NHL**	**4**	**0**	**0**	**0**	**0**	**0**	**0**	**14**	**0**	**0**	**0**	**0**	**0.0**	**0**	**0**	**0**	**0**	**0**								
	Newmarket Saints	AHL	74	4	3	7				71																		
1987-88	Baltimore Skipjacks	AHL	9	0	0	0				11																		
	Flint Spirits	IHL	8	2	0	2				26																		
	NHL Totals		**11**	**0**	**0**	**0**	**0**	**0**	**0**	**30**	**0**	**0**	**0**	**5**	**0.0**	**0**	**0**	**1**	**0**									

Signed as a free agent by **Buffalo**, July 22, 1981. Signed as a free agent by **Toronto**, October 3, 1985.

• JANNEY, CRAIG

Craig Janney C – L. 6'1", 190 lbs. b: Hartford, CT, 9/26/1967. Boston's 1st choice, 13th overall, in 1986 Entry Draft.

Season	Club	League	GP	G	A	Pts	AG	AA	APts	PIM	PP	SH	GW	S	%	TGF	PGF	TGA	PGA	+/-	GP	G	A	Pts	PIM	PP	SH	GW
1983-84	Deerfield Academy	H.S.	17	33	35	68				6																		
	United States	WJC-A	7	4	2	6				0																		
1985-86	Boston College	H.E.	34	13	14	27				8																		
	United States	WJC-A	3	1	1	2				2																		
1986-87	Boston College	H.E.	37	26	55	81				6																		
	United States	WEC-A	10	1	0	1				0																		
1987-88	United States	Nat-Team	52	26	44	70				6																		
	United States	Olympics	5	3	3	6				2																		
	Boston Bruins	**NHL**	**15**	**7**	**9**	**16**	**6**	**6**	**12**	**0**	**1**	**0**	**1**	**29**	**24.1**	**18**	**7**	**5**	**0**	**+6**	**23**	**6**	**10**	**16**	**11**	**4**	**0**	**1**
1988-89	**Boston Bruins**	**NHL**	**62**	**16**	**46**	**62**	**14**	**32**	**46**	**12**	**2**	**0**	**2**	**95**	**16.8**	**92**	**32**	**41**	**1**	**+20**	**10**	**4**	**9**	**13**	**21**	**0**	**0**	**0**
1989-90	**Boston Bruins**	**NHL**	**55**	**24**	**38**	**62**	**21**	**27**	**48**	**4**	**11**	**0**	**5**	**105**	**22.9**	**88**	**47**	**41**	**3**	**+3**	**18**	**3**	**19**	**22**	**2**	**1**	**0**	**2**
1990-91	**Boston Bruins**	**NHL**	**77**	**26**	**66**	**92**	**24**	**50**	**74**	**8**	**9**	**1**	**5**	**133**	**19.5**	**128**	**54**	**62**	**3**	**+15**	**18**	**4**	**18**	**22**	**11**	**4**	**0**	**0**
1991-92	United States	C Cup	8	4	2	6				0																		
	St. Louis Blues	**NHL**	**25**	**6**	**30**	**36**	**5**	**23**	**28**	**2**	**3**	**0**	**1**	**37**	**16.2**	**44**	**16**	**23**	**0**	**+5**	**6**	**0**	**6**	**6**	**0**	**0**	**0**	**0**
	Boston Bruins	**NHL**	**53**	**12**	**39**	**51**	**11**	**29**	**40**	**20**	**3**	**0**	**1**	**90**	**13.3**	**74**	**30**	**44**	**1**	**+1**								
1992-93	**St. Louis Blues**	**NHL**	**84**	**24**	**82**	**106**	**20**	**56**	**76**	**12**	**8**	**0**	**6**	**137**	**17.5**	**154**	**79**	**80**	**1**	**–4**	**11**	**2**	**9**	**11**	**0**	**1**	**0**	**2**
1993-94	**St. Louis Blues**	**NHL**	**69**	**16**	**68**	**84**	**15**	**53**	**68**	**24**	**8**	**0**	**7**	**95**	**16.8**	**121**	**63**	**72**	**0**	**–14**	**4**	**1**	**3**	**4**	**0**	**0**	**0**	**0**
	United States	WC-A	7	2	5	7				0																		
1994-95	**St. Louis Blues**	**NHL**	**8**	**2**	**5**	**7**	**4**	**7**	**11**	**0**	**1**	**0**	**0**	**9**	**22.2**	**10**	**4**	**4**	**1**	**+3**								
	San Jose Sharks	**NHL**	**27**	**5**	**15**	**20**	**9**	**22**	**31**	**10**	**2**	**0**	**1**	**31**	**16.1**	**30**	**10**	**24**	**0**	**–4**	**11**	**3**	**4**	**7**	**4**	**0**	**0**	**1**
1995-96	**San Jose Sharks**	**NHL**	**71**	**13**	**49**	**62**	**13**	**40**	**53**	**26**	**5**	**0**	**1**	**78**	**16.7**	**87**	**37**	**85**	**0**	**–35**								
	Winnipeg Jets	**NHL**	**13**	**7**	**13**	**20**	**7**	**11**	**18**	**0**	**2**	**0**	**1**	**91**	**7.7**	**24**	**11**	**12**	**1**	**+2**	**6**	**1**	**2**	**3**	**0**	**0**	**0**	**0**
1996-97	**Phoenix Coyotes**	**NHL**	**77**	**15**	**38**	**53**	**16**	**34**	**50**	**26**	**5**	**0**	**1**	**88**	**17.0**	**74**	**21**	**55**	**1**	**–1**	**7**	**0**	**3**	**3**	**4**	**0**	**0**	**0**
1997-98	**Phoenix Coyotes**	**NHL**	**68**	**10**	**43**	**53**	**12**	**42**	**54**	**12**	**4**	**0**	**0**	**72**	**13.9**	**78**	**22**	**52**	**1**	**+5**	**6**	**0**	**3**	**3**	**0**	**0**	**0**	**0**
	NHL Totals		**704**	**183**	**541**	**724**	**177**	**432**	**609**	**156**	**64**	**1**	**32**	**1090**	**16.8**	**1022**	**433**	**600**	**13**		**120**	**24**	**86**	**110**	**53**	**10**	**0**	**6**

Hockey East First All-Star Team (1987) • NCAA East First All-American Team (1987)

Traded to **St. Louis** by **Boston** with Stephane Quintal for Adam Oates, February 7, 1992. Acquired by **Vancouver** from **St. Louis** with St. Louis' 2nd round choice (Dave Scathard) in 1994 Entry Draft as compensation for St. Louis' signing of free agent Petr Nedved, March 14, 1994. Traded to **St. Louis** by **Vancouver** for Jeff Brown, Bret Hedican and Nathan Lafayette, March 21, 1994. Traded to **San Jose** by **St. Louis** with cash for Jeff Norton and future considerations, March 6, 1995. Traded to **Winnipeg** by **San Jose** for Darren Turcotte and Dallas' 2nd round choice (previously acquired, later traded to Chicago — Chicago selected Remi Royer) in 1996 Entry Draft, March 18, 1996. Transferred to **Phoenix** after **Winnipeg** franchise relocated, July 1, 1996. Traded to **Tampa Bay** by **Phoenix** for Louie Debrusk and Tampa Bay's 5th round choice (Jay Leach) in 1998 Entry Draft, June 11, 1998.

• JANSSENS, MARK

Mark Janssens C – L. 6'3", 212 lbs. b: Surrey, B.C., 5/19/1968. NY Rangers' 4th choice, 72nd overall, in 1986 Entry Draft.

Season	Club	League	GP	G	A	Pts	AG	AA	APts	PIM	PP	SH	GW	S	%	TGF	PGF	TGA	PGA	+/-	GP	G	A	Pts	PIM	PP	SH	GW
1984-85	Regina Pats	WHL	70	8	22	30				51																		
1985-86	Regina Pats	WHL	71	25	38	63				146											9	0	2	2	17			
1986-87	Regina Pats	WHL	68	24	38	62				209											3	0	1	1	14			
1987-88	Regina Pats	WHL	71	39	51	90				202											4	3	4	7	6			
	New York Rangers	**NHL**	**1**	**0**	**0**	**0**	**0**	**0**	**0**	**0**	**0**	**0**	**0**	**0**	**0.0**	**0**	**0**	**0**	**0**	**0**								
	Colorado Rangers	IHL	6	2	2	4				24											12	3	2	5	20			
1988-89	**New York Rangers**	**NHL**	**5**	**0**	**0**	**0**	**0**	**0**	**0**	**0**	**0**	**0**	**0**	**4**	**0.0**	**1**	**1**	**5**	**1**	**–4**								
	Denver Rangers	IHL	38	19	19	38				104											4	3	0	3	18			
1989-90	**New York Rangers**	**NHL**	**80**	**5**	**8**	**13**	**4**	**6**	**10**	**161**	**0**	**0**	**0**	**61**	**8.2**	**20**	**1**	**66**	**21**	**–26**	**9**	**2**	**1**	**3**	**10**	**0**	**0**	**1**
1990-91	**New York Rangers**	**NHL**	**67**	**9**	**7**	**16**	**8**	**5**	**13**	**172**	**0**	**0**	**1**	**45**	**20.0**	**23**	**0**	**33**	**9**	**–1**	**6**	**3**	**0**	**3**	**6**	**0**	**0**	**0**
1991-92	**New York Rangers**	**NHL**	**4**	**0**	**0**	**0**	**0**	**0**	**0**	**5**	**0**	**0**	**0**	**0**	**0.0**	**0**	**0**	**1**	**0**	**–1**								
	Binghamton Rangers	AHL	55	10	23	33				109																		
	Minnesota North Stars	**NHL**	**3**	**0**	**0**	**0**	**0**	**0**	**0**	**0**	**0**	**0**	**0**	**1**	**0.0**	**0**	**0**	**1**	**0**	**–1**								
	Kalamazoo Wings	IHL	2	0	0	0				2											11	1	2	3	22			
1992-93	**Hartford Whalers**	**NHL**	**76**	**12**	**17**	**29**	**10**	**12**	**22**	**237**	**0**	**0**	**1**	**63**	**19.0**	**43**	**0**	**83**	**25**	**–15**								
1993-94	**Hartford Whalers**	**NHL**	**84**	**2**	**10**	**12**	**2**	**8**	**10**	**137**	**0**	**0**	**0**	**52**	**3.8**	**20**	**1**	**69**	**29**	**–13**								
1994-95	**Hartford Whalers**	**NHL**	**46**	**2**	**5**	**7**	**4**	**7**	**11**	**93**	**0**	**0**	**0**	**33**	**6.1**	**13**	**0**	**29**	**8**	**8**								
1995-96	**Hartford Whalers**	**NHL**	**81**	**2**	**7**	**9**	**2**	**6**	**8**	**155**	**0**	**0**	**0**	**63**	**3.2**	**14**	**0**	**38**	**11**	**–13**								
1996-97	**Hartford Whalers**	**NHL**	**54**	**2**	**4**	**6**	**2**	**4**	**6**	**90**	**0**	**0**	**0**	**30**	**6.7**	**9**	**1**	**31**	**13**	**–10**								
	Anaheim Mighty Ducks	**NHL**	**12**	**0**	**2**	**2**	**0**	**2**	**2**	**47**	**0**	**0**	**0**	**9**	**0.0**	**4**	**0**	**9**	**2**	**–3**	**11**	**0**	**0**	**0**	**15**	**0**	**0**	**0**
1997-98	**Anaheim Mighty Ducks**	**NHL**	**55**	**4**	**5**	**9**	**5**	**5**	**10**	**116**	**0**	**0**	**1**	**43**	**9.3**	**17**	**1**	**49**	**11**	**–22**								
	New York Islanders	**NHL**	**12**	**0**	**0**	**0**	**0**	**0**	**0**	**34**	**0**	**0**	**0**	**4**	**0.0**	**1**	**0**	**5**	**1**	**–3**								
	Phoenix Coyotes	**NHL**	**7**	**1**	**2**	**3**	**1**	**2**	**3**	**4**	**0**	**0**	**0**	**6**	**16.7**	**6**	**0**	**3**	**1**	**+4**	**1**	**0**	**0**	**0**	**2**	**0**	**0**	**0**
	NHL Totals		**587**	**39**	**67**	**106**	**38**	**57**	**95**	**1251**	**0**	**0**	**3**	**414**	**9.4**	**179**	**5**	**422**	**132**		**27**	**5**	**1**	**6**	**33**	**0**	**0**	**1**

Traded to **Minnesota** by **NY Rangers** for Mario Thyer and Minnesota's 3rd round choice (Maxim Galanov) in 1993 Entry Draft, March 10, 1992. Traded to **Hartford** by **Minnesota** for James Black, September 3, 1992. Traded to **Anaheim** by **Hartford** for Bates Battaglia and Anaheim's 4th round choice (Carolina selected Josef Vasicek) in 1998 Entry Draft, March 18, 1997. Traded to **NY Islanders** by **Anaheim** with Joe Sacco and J.J. Daignealut for Travis Green, Doug Houda and Tony Tuzzolino, February 6, 1998. Traded to **Phoenix** by **NY Islanders** for Phoenix's 9th round choice (Jason Doyle) in 1998 Entry Draft, March 24, 1998. Signed as a free agent by **Chicago**, July 3, 1998.

• JANTUNEN, MARKO

Marko Jantunen C – L. 5'10", 185 lbs. b: Lahti, Finland, 2/14/1971. Calgary's 13th choice, 239th overall, in 1991 Entry Draft.

Season	Club	League	GP	G	A	Pts	AG	AA	APts	PIM	PP	SH	GW	S	%	TGF	PGF	TGA	PGA	+/-	GP	G	A	Pts	PIM	PP	SH	GW
1990-91	Reipas Vipuri	Finland	39	9	20	29				20																		
	Finland	WJC-A	7	3	10	13				12																		
1991-92	Reipas Vipuri	Finland	42	10	14	24				46																		
1992-93	KalPa	Finland	48	21	27	48				63																		
1993-94	TPS Turku	Finland	48	29	29	58				22											11	2	6	8	12			
1994-95	Vastra Frolunda	Sweden	22	15	8	23				22																		
1995-96	Vastra Frolunda	Sweden	40	17	14	31				66											13	8	8	16	10			
1996-97	**Calgary Flames**	**NHL**	**3**	**0**	**0**	**0**	**0**	**0**	**0**	**0**	**0**	**0**	**0**	**7**	**0.0**	**0**	**0**	**1**	**0**	**–1**								
	Saint John Flames	AHL	23	8	16	24				18																		
	Vastra Frolunda	Sweden	13	4	7	11				16											3	2	0	2	16			
	Finland	WC-A	8	1	0	1				6																		
1997-98	Vastra Frolunda	Sweden	43	14	20	34				61											7	1	2	3	2			
	NHL Totals		**3**	**0**	**0**	**0**	**0**	**0**	**0**	**0**	**0**	**0**	**0**	**7**	**0.0**	**0**	**0**	**1**	**0**									

• JARRETT, DOUG

Doug Jarrett D – L. 6'3", 205 lbs. b: London, Ont., 4/22/1944.

Season	Club	League	GP	G	A	Pts	AG	AA	APts	PIM	PP	SH	GW	S	%	TGF	PGF	TGA	PGA	+/-	GP	G	A	Pts	PIM	PP	SH	GW
1960-61	St. Catharines Teepees	OHA	36	2	2	4				78											6	0	0	0	16			
1961-62	St. Catharines Teepees	OHA	49	4	6	10				103											6	0	1	1	10			
1962-63	St. Catharines Teepees	OHA	50	9	18	27				88																		
	Buffalo Bisons	AHL	1	0	0	0				4																		
1963-64	St. Catharines Black Hawks	OHA	54	10	51	61				144											13	5	12	17	22			
	Buffalo Bisons	AHL	1	0	0	0				0																		
1964-65	**Chicago Black Hawks**	**NHL**	**40**	**2**	**15**	**17**	**3**	**16**	**19**	**34**											**11**	**1**	**0**	**1**	**10**			
	St. Louis Braves	CHL	17	3	7	10				23																		
	Buffalo Bisons	AHL	1	0	0	0				0																		
1965-66	**Chicago Black Hawks**	**NHL**	**66**	**4**	**12**	**16**	**5**	**12**	**17**	**71**											**5**	**0**	**1**	**1**	**9**			
1966-67	**Chicago Black Hawks**	**NHL**	**70**	**5**	**21**	**26**	**6**	**22**	**28**	**76**											**6**	**0**	**3**	**3**	**8**			
1967-68	**Chicago Black Hawks**	**NHL**	**74**	**4**	**19**	**23**	**5**	**20**	**25**	**48**	**0**	**1**	**2**	**140**	**2.7**	**71**	**0**	**110**	**24**	**–15**	**11**	**4**	**0**	**4**	**9**	**0**	**0**	**0**
1968-69	**Chicago Black Hawks**	**NHL**	**69**	**0**	**13**	**13**	**0**	**12**	**12**	**58**	**0**	**0**	**0**	**116**	**0.0**	**71**	**0**	**83**	**19**	**+7**								
1969-70	**Chicago Black Hawks**	**NHL**	**72**	**4**	**20**	**24**	**5**	**20**	**25**	**78**	**1**	**0**	**2**	**134**	**3.0**	**81**	**4**	**60**	**16**	**+33**	**8**	**1**	**0**	**1**	**4**	**0**	**0**	**0**
1970-71	**Chicago Black Hawks**	**NHL**	**51**	**1**	**12**	**13**	**1**	**11**	**12**	**46**	**0**	**1**	**0**	**75**	**1.3**	**43**	**4**	**40**	**11**	**+10**	**18**	**1**	**6**	**7**	**14**	**0**	**0**	**0**

			REGULAR SEASON																		PLAYOFFS							
Season	Club	League	GP	G	A	Pts	AG	AA	APts	PIM	PP	SH	GW	S	%	TGF	PGF	TGA	PGA	+/–	GP	G	A	Pts	PIM	PP	SH	GW
1971-72	**Chicago Black Hawks**	**NHL**	**78**	**6**	**23**	**29**	**6**	**21**	**27**	**68**	**2**	**0**	**1**	**123**	**4.9**	**100**	**2**	**71**	**12**	**+39**	**8**	**0**	**2**	**2**	**16**	**0**	**0**	**0**
1972-73	**Chicago Black Hawks**	**NHL**	**49**	**2**	**11**	**13**	**2**	**9**	**11**	**18**	**1**	**0**	**0**	**74**	**2.7**	**53**	**3**	**54**	**13**	**+9**	**15**	**0**	**3**	**3**	**2**	**0**	**0**	**0**
1973-74	**Chicago Black Hawks**	**NHL**	**67**	**5**	**11**	**16**	**5**	**9**	**14**	**45**	**1**	**0**	**1**	**54**	**9.3**	**55**	**5**	**52**	**7**	**+5**	**10**	**0**	**1**	**1**	**6**	**0**	**0**	**0**
1974-75	**Chicago Black Hawks**	**NHL**	**79**	**5**	**21**	**26**	**5**	**17**	**22**	**66**	**0**	**0**	**0**	**124**	**4.0**	**81**	**6**	**90**	**28**	**+13**	**7**	**0**	**0**	**0**	**4**	**0**	**0**	**0**
1975-76	**New York Rangers**	**NHL**	**45**	**0**	**4**	**4**	**0**	**3**	**3**	**19**	**0**	**0**	**0**	**45**	**0.0**	**32**	**0**	**73**	**15**	**–26**	....	....	....	....	....	....	....	....
1976-77	**New York Rangers**	**NHL**	**9**	**0**	**0**	**0**	**0**	**0**	**0**	**4**	**0**	**0**	**0**	**3**	**0.0**	**2**	**0**	**11**	**3**	**–6**	....	....	....	....	....	....	....	....
	New Haven Nighthawks	AHL	40	2	7	9	....	....	....	10	....	....	....	....	....	....	....	....	....	....	....	....	....	....	....	....	....	....
	NHL Totals		**775**	**38**	**182**	**220**	**43**	**172**	**215**	**631**	**5**	**2**	**6**	**896**	**4.2**	**589**	**24**	**644**	**148**		**99**	**7**	**16**	**23**	**82**	**0**	**0**	**0**

Played in NHL All-Star Game (1975)

Traded to **NY Rangers** by **Chicago** for Gilles Villemure, October 28, 1975.

• JARRETT, GARY

Gary Jarrett LW – L. 5'8", 170 lbs. b: Toronto, Ont., 9/3/1942.

Season	Club	League	GP	G	A	Pts	AG	AA	APts	PIM	PP	SH	GW	S	%	TGF	PGF	TGA	PGA	+/–	GP	G	A	Pts	PIM	PP	SH	GW
1959-60	Toronto Marlboros	OHA	48	24	28	52	....	....	....	12	....	....	....	....	....	....	....	....	....	....	4	1	3	4	14	....	....	....
1960-61	Toronto Marlboros	OHA	46	30	20	50	....	....	....	90	....	....	....	....	....	....	....	....	....	....	....	....	....	....	....	....	....	....
	Sudbury Wolves	EPHL	1	0	0	0	....	....	....	0	....	....	....	....	....	....	....	....	....	....	....	....	....	....	....	....	....	....
	Toronto Maple Leafs	**NHL**	**1**	**0**	**0**	**0**	**0**	**0**	**0**	**0**	....	....	....	....	....	....	....	....	....	....	....	....	....	....	....	....	....	....
	Rochester Americans	AHL	6	0	0	0	....	....	....	2	....	....	....	....	....	....	....	....	....	....	....	....	....	....	....	....	....	....
1961-62	Toronto Marlboros	City Jr.	31	*28	27	55	....	....	....	80	....	....	....	....	....	....	....	....	....	....	12	11	*15	26	41	....	....	....
	Rochester Americans	AHL	5	3	1	4	....	....	....	6	....	....	....	....	....	....	....	....	....	....	....	....	....	....	....	....	....	....
1962-63	Sudbury Wolves	EPHL	21	13	14	27	....	....	....	14	....	....	....	....	....	....	....	....	....	....	....	....	....	....	....	....	....	....
	Rochester Americans	AHL	47	6	22	28	....	....	....	19	....	....	....	....	....	....	....	....	....	....	2	1	3	4	0	....	....	....
1963-64	Denver Invaders	WHL	64	22	35	57	....	....	....	37	....	....	....	....	....	....	....	....	....	....	6	2	0	2	6	....	....	....
	Rochester Americans	AHL	5	0	1	1	....	....	....	0	....	....	....	....	....	....	....	....	....	....	....	....	....	....	....	....	....	....
1964-65	Tulsa Oilers	CHL	67	27	29	56	....	....	....	60	....	....	....	....	....	....	....	....	....	....	12	*8	5	13	10	....	....	....
1965-66	Pittsburgh Hornets	AHL	71	24	26	50	....	....	....	30	....	....	....	....	....	....	....	....	....	....	3	1	0	1	4	....	....	....
1966-67	**Detroit Red Wings**	**NHL**	**4**	**0**	**0**	**0**	**0**	**0**	**0**	**0**	....	....	....	....	....	....	....	....	....	....	....	....	....	....	....	....	....	....
	Pittsburgh Hornets	AHL	68	29	42	71	....	....	....	28	....	....	....	....	....	....	....	....	....	....	9	6	3	9	11	....	....	....
1967-68	**Detroit Red Wings**	**NHL**	**68**	**18**	**21**	**39**	**22**	**22**	**44**	**20**	**1**	**0**	**2**	**207**	**8.7**	**52**	**8**	**44**	**4**	**+4**	....	....	....	....	....	....	....	....
1968-69	**Oakland Seals**	**NHL**	**63**	**22**	**23**	**45**	**25**	**22**	**47**	**22**	**3**	**0**	**1**	**201**	**10.9**	**56**	**13**	**52**	**1**	**–8**	**7**	**2**	**1**	**3**	**4**	**0**	**1**	**0**
1969-70	**Oakland Seals**	**NHL**	**75**	**12**	**19**	**31**	**14**	**19**	**33**	**31**	**2**	**0**	**4**	**229**	**5.2**	**45**	**6**	**63**	**0**	**–24**	**4**	**1**	**0**	**1**	**5**	**1**	**0**	**0**
1970-71	**California Golden Seals**	**NHL**	**75**	**15**	**19**	**34**	**16**	**17**	**33**	**40**	**2**	**0**	**2**	**169**	**8.9**	**51**	**9**	**69**	**0**	**–27**	....	....	....	....	....	....	....	....
1971-72	**California Golden Seals**	**NHL**	**55**	**5**	**10**	**15**	**5**	**9**	**14**	**18**	**2**	**0**	**0**	**64**	**7.8**	**21**	**4**	**18**	**1**	**0**	....	....	....	....	....	....	....	....
1972-73	Cleveland Crusaders	WHA	77	40	38	78	....	....	....	79	....	....	....	....	....	....	....	....	....	....	9	8	3	11	19	....	....	....
1973-74	Cleveland Crusaders	WHA	75	31	39	70	....	....	....	68	....	....	....	....	....	....	....	....	....	....	5	1	1	2	13	....	....	....
1974-75	Cleveland Crusaders	WHA	77	17	24	41	....	....	....	70	....	....	....	....	....	....	....	....	....	....	5	0	1	1	0	....	....	....
1975-76	Cleveland Crusaders	WHA	69	16	17	33	....	....	....	22	....	....	....	....	....	....	....	....	....	....	3	0	3	3	2	....	....	....
	NHL Totals		**341**	**72**	**92**	**164**	**82**	**89**	**171**	**131**	**10**	**0**	**9**	**870**	**8.3**	**225**	**40**	**246**	**6**		**11**	**3**	**1**	**4**	**9**	**1**	**1**	**0**
	Other Major League Totals		298	104	118	222	....	....	....	239	....	....	....	....	....	....	....	....	....	....	22	9	8	17	34	....	....	....

WHA Second All-Star Team (1973)

Traded to **Detroit** by **Toronto** with Billy Harris and Andy Bathgate for Lowell MacDonald, Marcel Pronovost, Ed Joyal and Aut Erickson, May 20, 1965. Traded to **Oakland** by **Detroit** with Doug Roberts, Howie Young and Chris Worthy for Bob Baun and Ron Harris, May 27, 1968. Selected by **Alberta** (WHA) in 1972 WHA General Player Draft, February 12, 1972. WHA rights traded to **Cleveland** (WHA) by **Edmonton** (WHA) for cash, August, 1972.

• JARRY, PIERRE

Pierre Jarry LW – L. 5'11", 190 lbs. b: Montreal, Que., 3/30/1949. NY Rangers' 2nd choice, 12th overall, in 1969 Amateur Draft.

Season	Club	League	GP	G	A	Pts	AG	AA	APts	PIM	PP	SH	GW	S	%	TGF	PGF	TGA	PGA	+/–	GP	G	A	Pts	PIM	PP	SH	GW
1966-67	Sherbrooke Castors	QJHL	26	18	15	33	....	....	....	....	....	....	....	....	....	....	....	....	....	....	....	....	....	....	....	....	....	....
1967-68	Ottawa 67's	OHA	50	36	21	57	....	....	....	61	....	....	....	....	....	....	....	....	....	....	....	....	....	....	....	....	....	....
1968-69	Ottawa 67's	OHA	53	41	57	98	....	....	....	74	....	....	....	....	....	....	....	....	....	....	7	5	8	13	11	....	....	....
1969-70	Omaha Knights	CHL	70	26	27	53	....	....	....	62	....	....	....	....	....	....	....	....	....	....	8	1	2	3	22	....	....	....
1970-71	Omaha Knights	CHL	71	*46	46	*92	....	....	....	94	....	....	....	....	....	....	....	....	....	....	11	4	5	9	8	....	....	....
1971-72	**New York Rangers**	**NHL**	**34**	**3**	**3**	**6**	**3**	**3**	**6**	**20**	**0**	**0**	**0**	**32**	**9.4**	**12**	**3**	**7**	**0**	**+2**	....	....	....	....	....	....	....	....
	Toronto Maple Leafs	**NHL**	**18**	**3**	**4**	**7**	**3**	**4**	**7**	**13**	**0**	**0**	**1**	**42**	**7.1**	**8**	**1**	**10**	**0**	**–3**	**5**	**0**	**1**	**1**	**0**	**0**	**0**	**0**
1972-73	**Toronto Maple Leafs**	**NHL**	**74**	**19**	**18**	**37**	**19**	**15**	**34**	**42**	**2**	**0**	**2**	**188**	**10.1**	**47**	**5**	**55**	**0**	**–13**	....	....	....	....	....	....	....	....
1973-74	**Toronto Maple Leafs**	**NHL**	**12**	**2**	**8**	**10**	**2**	**7**	**9**	**10**	**0**	**0**	**0**	**31**	**6.5**	**16**	**1**	**7**	**0**	**+8**	....	....	....	....	....	....	....	....
	Detroit Red Wings	**NHL**	**52**	**15**	**23**	**38**	**15**	**20**	**35**	**17**	**2**	**0**	**0**	**139**	**10.8**	**54**	**16**	**49**	**0**	**–11**	....	....	....	....	....	....	....	....
1974-75	**Detroit Red Wings**	**NHL**	**39**	**8**	**13**	**21**	**7**	**10**	**17**	**4**	**0**	**0**	**1**	**90**	**8.9**	**32**	**15**	**29**	**0**	**–12**	....	....	....	....	....	....	....	....
	Virginia Wings	AHL	20	11	12	23	....	....	....	17	....	....	....	....	....	....	....	....	....	....	....	....	....	....	....	....	....	....
1975-76	**Minnesota North Stars**	**NHL**	**59**	**21**	**18**	**39**	**20**	**14**	**34**	**32**	**3**	**0**	**0**	**143**	**14.7**	**61**	**17**	**53**	**2**	**–7**	....	....	....	....	....	....	....	....
	New Haven Nighthawks	AHL	13	5	7	12	....	....	....	18	....	....	....	....	....	....	....	....	....	....	....	....	....	....	....	....	....	....
1976-77	**Minnesota North Stars**	**NHL**	**21**	**8**	**13**	**21**	**8**	**11**	**19**	**2**	**4**	**0**	**1**	**52**	**15.4**	**26**	**12**	**21**	**1**	**–6**	....	....	....	....	....	....	....	....
1977-78	**Minnesota North Stars**	**NHL**	**35**	**9**	**17**	**26**	**9**	**14**	**23**	**2**	**1**	**0**	**1**	**77**	**11.7**	**32**	**10**	**31**	**0**	**–9**	....	....	....	....	....	....	....	....
	Fort Worth Texans	CHL	15	4	8	12	....	....	....	14	....	....	....	....	....	....	....	....	....	....	....	....	....	....	....	....	....	....
	Edmonton Oilers	WHA	18	4	10	14	....	....	....	4	....	....	....	....	....	....	....	....	....	....	5	1	0	1	4	....	....	....
	NHL Totals		**344**	**88**	**117**	**205**	**86**	**98**	**184**	**142**	**12**	**0**	**6**	**794**	**11.1**	**288**	**80**	**262**	**3**		**5**	**0**	**1**	**1**	**0**	**0**	**0**	**0**
	Other Major League Totals		18	4	10	14	....	....	....	4	....	....	....	....	....	....	....	....	....	....	5	1	0	1	4	....	....	....

CHL First All-Star Team (1971)

Selected by **Chicago** (WHA) in 1972 WHA General Player Draft, February 12, 1972. Traded to **Toronto** by **NY Rangers** for Jim Dorey, February 20, 1972. Traded to **Detroit** by **Toronto** for Tim Ecclestone, November 29, 1973. Traded to **Minnesota** by **Detroit** for Don Martineau, November 25, 1975. Traded to **Edmonton** (WHA) by **Minnesota** with Chris Aherns for future considerations, March, 1978.

• JARVENPAA, HANNU

Hannu Jarvenpaa RW – L. 6', 195 lbs. b: Ilves, Finland, 5/19/1963. Winnipeg's 11th choice, 71st overall, in 1986 Entry Draft.

Season	Club	League	GP	G	A	Pts	AG	AA	APts	PIM	PP	SH	GW	S	%	TGF	PGF	TGA	PGA	+/–	GP	G	A	Pts	PIM	PP	SH	GW
1981-82	Karpat Oulu	Finland	14	11	2	13	....	....	....	18	....	....	....	....	....	....	....	....	....	....	....	....	....	....	....	....	....	....
	Finland	WJC-A	7	4	4	8	....	....	....	6	....	....	....	....	....	....	....	....	....	....	....	....	....	....	....	....	....	....
1982-83	Karpat Oulu	Finland	34	15	8	23	....	....	....	56	....	....	....	....	....	....	....	....	....	....	....	....	....	....	....	....	....	....
	Finland	WJC-A	6	0	1	1	....	....	....	4	....	....	....	....	....	....	....	....	....	....	....	....	....	....	....	....	....	....
1983-84	Karpat Oulu	Finland	37	15	13	28	....	....	....	46	....	....	....	....	....	....	....	....	....	....	....	....	....	....	....	....	....	....
1984-85	Karpat Oulu	Finland	34	12	12	24	....	....	....	45	....	....	....	....	....	....	....	....	....	....	7	2	2	4	2	....	....	....
	Finland	WEC-A	9	1	5	6	....	....	....	6	....	....	....	....	....	....	....	....	....	....	....	....	....	....	....	....	....	....
1985-86	Karpat Oulu	Finland	36	26	9	35	....	....	....	48	....	....	....	....	....	....	....	....	....	....	5	*5	2	7	12	....	....	....
	Finland	WEC-A	9	5	4	9	....	....	....	12	....	....	....	....	....	....	....	....	....	....	....	....	....	....	....	....	....	....
1986-87	**Winnipeg Jets**	**NHL**	**20**	**1**	**8**	**9**	**1**	**6**	**7**	**8**	**0**	**0**	**0**	**36**	**2.8**	**14**	**2**	**16**	**0**	**–4**	....	....	....	....	....	....	....	....
1987-88	**Winnipeg Jets**	**NHL**	**41**	**6**	**11**	**17**	**5**	**8**	**13**	**34**	**1**	**0**	**0**	**52**	**11.5**	**28**	**4**	**25**	**1**	**0**	....	....	....	....	....	....	....	....
	Moncton Hawks	AHL	5	3	1	4	....	....	....	2	....	....	....	....	....	....	....	....	....	....	....	....	....	....	....	....	....	....
1988-89	**Winnipeg Jets**	**NHL**	**53**	**4**	**7**	**11**	**3**	**5**	**8**	**41**	**1**	**0**	**0**	**27**	**14.8**	**15**	**2**	**27**	**0**	**–14**	....	....	....	....	....	....	....	....
	Moncton Hawks	AHL	4	1	0	1	....	....	....	0	....	....	....	....	....	....	....	....	....	....	....	....	....	....	....	....	....	....
	Finland	WEC-A	7	2	1	3	....	....	....	4	....	....	....	....	....	....	....	....	....	....	....	....	....	....	....	....	....	....
1989-90	Lukko Rauma	Finland	38	12	15	27	....	....	....	48	....	....	....	....	....	....	....	....	....	....	....	....	....	....	....	....	....	....
1990-91	Lukko Rauma	Finland	43	27	18	45	....	....	....	54	....	....	....	....	....	....	....	....	....	....	....	....	....	....	....	....	....	....
	Finland	WEC-A	9	2	2	4	....	....	....	22	....	....	....	....	....	....	....	....	....	....	....	....	....	....	....	....	....	....
1991-92	Finland	C Cup	6	0	1	1	....	....	....	4	....	....	....	....	....	....	....	....	....	....	....	....	....	....	....	....	....	....
	Leksands	Sweden	22	4	4	8	....	....	....	28	....	....	....	....	....	....	....	....	....	....	....	....	....	....	....	....	....	....
	Finland	Olympics	8	5	6	11	....	....	....	14	....	....	....	....	....	....	....	....	....	....	....	....	....	....	....	....	....	....
	Finland	WC-A	8	1	3	4	....	....	....	14	....	....	....	....	....	....	....	....	....	....	....	....	....	....	....	....	....	....
1992-93	Jokerit Helsinki	Finland	44	6	8	14	....	....	....	36	....	....	....	....	....	....	....	....	....	....	....	....	....	....	....	....	....	....
1993-94	Keikoo-Espoo Espoo	Finland	44	15	16	31	....	....	....	40	....	....	....	....	....	....	....	....	....	....	....	....	....	....	....	....	....	....
1994-95	Keikoo-Espoo Espoo	Finland	45	9	6	15	....	....	....	20	....	....	....	....	....	....	....	....	....	....	4	0	0	0	2	....	....	....
	NHL Totals		**114**	**11**	**26**	**37**	**9**	**19**	**28**	**83**	**2**	**0**	**0**	**115**	**9.6**	**57**	**8**	**68**	**1**		....	....	....	....	....	....	....	....

• Re-entered NHL draft. Originally Montreal's 11th choice, 145th overall, in 1982 Entry Draft.

• JARVI, IIRO

Iiro Jarvi RW – L. 6'1", 198 lbs. b: Helsinki, Finland, 3/23/1965. Quebec's 3rd choice, 55th overall, in 1983 Entry Draft.

			REGULAR SEASON																		PLAYOFFS							
Season	Club	League	GP	G	A	Pts	AG	AA	APts	PIM	PP	SH	GW	S	%	TGF	PGF	TGA	PGA	+/–	GP	G	A	Pts	PIM	PP	SH	GW
1983-84	HIFK Helsinki	Finland	27	0	6	6	....	....	....	6	....	....	....	....	....	....	....	....	....	....	....	....	....	....	....	....	....	....
	Finland	WJC-A	7	4	3	7	....	....	....	8	....	....	....	....	....	....	....	....	....	....	....	....	....	....	....	....	....	....
1984-85	HIFK Helsinki	Finland	9	0	1	1	....	....	....	2	....	....	....	....	....	....	....	....	....	....	....	....	....	....	....	....	....	....
	Finland	WJC-A	7	1	1	2	....	....	....	2	....	....	....	....	....	....	....	....	....	....	....	....	....	....	....	....	....	....
1985-86	HIFK Helsinki	Finland	29	7	6	13	....	....	....	19	....	....	....	....	....	....	....	....	....	....	10	4	6	10	2	....	....	....
1986-87	HIFK Helsinki	Finland	43	23	30	53	....	....	....	82	....	....	....	....	....	....	....	....	....	....	5	1	5	6	9	....	....	....
	Finland	WEC-A	8	2	0	2	....	....	....	10	....	....	....	....	....	....	....	....	....	....	....	....	....	....	....	....	....	....
1987 88	Finland	C Cup	4	0	0	0	....	....	....	2	....	....	....	....	....	....	....	....	....	....	....	....	....	....	....	....	....	....
	HIFK Helsinki	Finland	44	21	20	41	....	....	....	68	....	....	....	....	....	....	....	....	....	....	5	2	1	3	7	....	....	....
	Finland	Olympics	8	2	5	7	....	....	....	10	....	....	....	....	....	....	....	....	....	....	....	....	....	....	....	....	....	....
1988-89	**Quebec Nordiques**	**NHL**	**75**	**11**	**30**	**41**	**9**	**21**	**30**	**40**	**1**	**0**	**1**	**109**	**10.1**	**61**	**11**	**65**	**2**	**–13**	....	....	....	....	....	....	....	....
	Finland	WEC-A	9	0	2	2	....	....	....	10	....	....	....	....	....	....	....	....	....	....	....	....	....	....	....	....	....	....
1989-90	**Quebec Nordiques**	**NHL**	**41**	**7**	**13**	**20**	**6**	**9**	**15**	**18**	**1**	**0**	**1**	**52**	**13.5**	**29**	**3**	**37**	**0**	**–11**	....	....	....	....	....	....	....	....
	Halifax Citadels	AHL	26	4	13	17	....	....	....	4	....	....	....	....	....	....	....	....	....	....	....	....	....	....	....	....	....	....
1990-91	Klagenfurter	Germany	26	12	21	23	....	....	....	....	....	....	....	....	....	....	....	....	....	....	....	....	....	....	....	....	....	....
	Halifax Citadels	AHL	5	0	2	2	....	....	....	2	....	....	....	....	....	....	....	....	....	....	....	....	....	....	....	....	....	....
1991-92	Finland	C Cup	6	0	0	0	....	....	....	6	....	....	....	....	....	....	....	....	....	....	....	....	....	....	....	....	....	....
	HIFK Helsinki	Finland	43	14	23	37	....	....	....	64	....	....	....	....	....	....	....	....	....	....	....	....	....	....	....	....	....	....
1992-93	HIFK Helsinki	Finland	47	7	23	30	....	....	....	64	....	....	....	....	....	....	....	....	....	....	....	....	....	....	....	....	....	....
1993-94	HIFK Helsinki	Finland	47	13	24	37	....	....	....	113	....	....	....	....	....	....	....	....	....	....	....	....	....	....	....	....	....	....
1994-95	HIFK Helsinki	Finland	50	14	29	43	....	....	....	50	....	....	....	....	....	....	....	....	....	....	3	0	0	0	2	....	....	....
1995-96	HIFK Helsinki	Finland	50	13	30	43	....	....	....	88	....	....	....	....	....	....	....	....	....	....	3	0	2	2	0	....	....	....
	NHL Totals		**116**	**18**	**43**	**61**	**15**	**30**	**45**	**58**	**2**	**0**	**2**	**161**	**11.2**	**90**	**14**	**102**	**2**		....	....	....	....	....	....	....	....

• JARVIS, DOUG

Doug Jarvis C – L. 5'9", 170 lbs. b: Brantford, Ont., 3/24/1955. Toronto's 2nd choice, 24th overall, in 1975 Amateur Draft.

Season	Club	League	GP	G	A	Pts	AG	AA	APts	PIM	PP	SH	GW	S	%	TGF	PGF	TGA	PGA	+/–	GP	G	A	Pts	PIM	PP	SH	GW
1971-72	Brantford Majors	OJHL	11	2	10	12	....	....	....	0	....	....	....	....	....	....	....	....	....	....	....	....	....	....	....	....	....	....
1972-73	Peterborough Petes	OHA	63	20	49	69	....	....	....	14	....	....	....	....	....	....	....	....	....	....	....	....	....	....	....	....	....	....
1973-74	Peterborough Petes	OHA	70	31	53	84	....	....	....	27	....	....	....	....	....	....	....	....	....	....	....	....	....	....	....	....	....	....
	Canada	WJC-A	5	4	1	5	....	....	....	2	....	....	....	....	....	....	....	....	....	....	....	....	....	....	....	....	....	....
1974-75	Peterborough Petes	OHA	64	45	88	133	....	....	....	38	....	....	....	....	....	....	....	....	....	....	11	4	11	15	8	....	....	....
1975-76	**Montreal Canadiens**	**NHL**	**80**	**5**	**30**	**35**	**5**	**24**	**29**	**16**	**0**	**1**	**1**	**92**	**5.4**	**45**	**7**	**45**	**24**	**+17**	**13**	**2**	**1**	**3**	**2**	**0**	**0**	**0**
1976-77	**Montreal Canadiens**	**NHL**	**80**	**16**	**22**	**38**	**15**	**18**	**33**	**14**	**0**	**0**	**2**	**88**	**18.2**	**55**	**0**	**38**	**13**	**+30**	**14**	**0**	**7**	**7**	**2**	**0**	**0**	**0**
1977-78	**Montreal Canadiens**	**NHL**	**80**	**11**	**28**	**39**	**11**	**23**	**34**	**23**	**2**	**2**	**1**	**129**	**8.5**	**52**	**6**	**59**	**25**	**+12**	**15**	**3**	**5**	**8**	**12**	**1**	**0**	**1**
1978-79	**Montreal Canadiens**	**NHL**	**80**	**10**	**13**	**23**	**9**	**10**	**19**	**16**	**0**	**1**	**1**	**117**	**8.5**	**49**	**1**	**60**	**17**	**+5**	**12**	**1**	**3**	**4**	**4**	**0**	**0**	**0**
1979-80	**Montreal Canadiens**	**NHL**	**80**	**13**	**11**	**24**	**12**	**8**	**20**	**28**	**0**	**1**	**3**	**130**	**10.0**	**39**	**1**	**72**	**29**	**–5**	**10**	**4**	**4**	**8**	**2**	**0**	**1**	**0**
1980-81	**Montreal Canadiens**	**NHL**	**80**	**16**	**22**	**38**	**13**	**15**	**28**	**34**	**0**	**2**	**1**	**122**	**13.1**	**52**	**1**	**71**	**32**	**+12**	**3**	**0**	**0**	**0**	**0**	**0**	**0**	**0**
1981-82	**Montreal Canadiens**	**NHL**	**80**	**20**	**28**	**48**	**16**	**19**	**35**	**20**	**1**	**0**	**4**	**127**	**15.7**	**69**	**4**	**67**	**36**	**+34**	**5**	**1**	**0**	**1**	**4**	**0**	**1**	**0**
1982-83	**Washington Capitals**	**NHL**	**80**	**8**	**22**	**30**	**7**	**15**	**22**	**10**	**0**	**1**	**0**	**96**	**8.4**	**42**	**1**	**79**	**26**	**–12**	**4**	**0**	**1**	**1**	**0**	**0**	**0**	**0**
1983-84	**Washington Capitals**	**NHL**	**80**	**13**	**29**	**42**	**10**	**20**	**30**	**12**	**0**	**2**	**0**	**122**	**10.7**	**68**	**14**	**70**	**23**	**+7**	**8**	**2**	**3**	**5**	**6**	**0**	**0**	**0**
1984-85	**Washington Capitals**	**NHL**	**80**	**9**	**28**	**37**	**7**	**19**	**26**	**32**	**1**	**1**	**1**	**103**	**8.7**	**58**	**3**	**73**	**37**	**+19**	**5**	**1**	**0**	**1**	**2**	**0**	**0**	**0**
1985-86	**Washington Capitals**	**NHL**	**25**	**1**	**2**	**3**	**1**	**1**	**2**	**16**	**0**	**0**	**0**	**19**	**5.3**	**7**	**0**	**15**	**3**	**–5**	....	....	....	....	....	....	....	....
	Hartford Whalers	**NHL**	**57**	**8**	**16**	**24**	**6**	**11**	**17**	**20**	**0**	**3**	**0**	**55**	**14.5**	**36**	**0**	**60**	**31**	**+7**	**10**	**0**	**3**	**3**	**4**	**0**	**0**	**0**
1986-87	**Hartford Whalers**	**NHL**	**80**	**9**	**13**	**22**	**8**	**9**	**17**	**20**	**0**	**2**	**2**	**88**	**10.2**	**34**	**1**	**66**	**33**	**0**	**6**	**0**	**0**	**0**	**4**	**0**	**0**	**0**
1987-88	**Hartford Whalers**	**NHL**	**2**	**0**	**0**	**0**	**0**	**0**	**0**	**2**	**0**	**0**	**0**	**2**	**0.0**	**0**	**0**	**2**	**2**	**0**	....	....	....	....	....	....	....	....
	Binghamton Whalers	AHL	24	5	4	9	....	....	....	4	....	....	....	....	....	....	....	....	....	....	....	....	....	....	....	....	....	....
	NHL Totals		**964**	**139**	**264**	**403**	**120**	**192**	**312**	**263**	**4**	**16**	**16**	**1289**	**10.8**	**606**	**39**	**777**	**331**		**105**	**14**	**27**	**41**	**42**	**1**	**2**	**1**

OHA Second All-Star Team (1975) • Won Frank J. Selke Trophy (1984) • Won Bill Masterton Trophy (1987)

Traded to **Montreal** by **Toronto** for Greg Hubick, June 26, 1975. Traded to **Washington** by **Montreal** with Rod Langway, Craig Laughlin and Brian Engblom for Ryan Walter and Rick Green, September 9, 1982. Traded to **Hartford** by **Washington** for Jorgen Petterson, December 6, 1985.

• JARVIS, WES

Wes Jarvis C – L. 5'11", 185 lbs. b: Toronto, Ont., 5/30/1958. Washington's 18th choice, 213th overall, in 1978 Amateur Draft.

Season	Club	League	GP	G	A	Pts	AG	AA	APts	PIM	PP	SH	GW	S	%	TGF	PGF	TGA	PGA	+/–	GP	G	A	Pts	PIM	PP	SH	GW
1974-75	Weston Dodgers	OJHL	38	20	27	47	....	....	....	18	....	....	....	....	....	....	....	....	....	....						....	....	....
1975-76	Sudbury Wolves	OHA	61	[illegible]	40	74	....	....	....	22	....	....	....	....	....	....	....	....	....	....	....	....	....	....	....	....	....	....
1976-77	Sudbury Wolves	OHA	65	36	60	96	....	....	....	24	....	....	....	....	....	....	....	....	....	....	6	3	2	5	7	....	....	....
1977-78	Sudbury Wolves	OHA	21	7	16	23	....	....	....	16	....	....	....	....	....	....	....	....	....	....	....	....	....	....	....	....	....	....
	Windsor Spitfires	OHA	44	27	51	78	....	....	....	37	....	....	....	....	....	....	....	....	....	....	6	0	2	2	0	....	....	....
1978-79	Port Huron Flags	IHL	73	44	65	109	....	....	....	39	....	....	....	....	....	....	....	....	....	....	7	4	4	8	2	....	....	....
1979-80	**Washington Capitals**	**NHL**	**63**	**11**	**15**	**26**	**10**	**11**	**21**	**8**	**0**	**0**	**0**	**43**	**25.6**	**30**	**0**	**48**	**15**	**–3**	....	....	....	....	....	....	....	....
	Hershey Bears	AHL	16	6	14	20	....	....	....	4	....	....	....	....	....	....	....	....	....	....	....	....	....	....	....	....	....	....
1980-81	**Washington Capitals**	**NHL**	**55**	**9**	**14**	**23**	**7**	**10**	**17**	**30**	**0**	**1**	**0**	**61**	**14.8**	**29**	**1**	**58**	**21**	**–9**	....	....	....	....	....	....	....	....
	Hershey Bears	AHL	24	15	25	40	....	....	....	39	....	....	....	....	....	....	....	....	....	....	10	3	13	16	2	....	....	....
1981-82	**Washington Capitals**	**NHL**	**26**	**1**	**12**	**13**	**1**	**8**	**9**	**18**	**0**	**0**	**0**	**22**	**4.5**	**24**	**3**	**25**	**9**	**+5**	....	....	....	....	....	....	....	....
	Hershey Bears	AHL	56	31	61	92	....	....	....	44	....	....	....	....	....	....	....	....	....	....	5	3	4	7	4	....	....	....
1982-83	**Minnesota North Stars**	**NHL**	**3**	**0**	**0**	**0**	**0**	**0**	**0**	**2**	**0**	**0**	**0**	**2**	**0.0**	**0**	**0**	**2**	**0**	**–2**	....	....	....	....	....	....	....	....
	Birmingham South Stars	CHL	75	40	*68	*108	....	....	....	36	....	....	....	....	....	....	....	....	....	....	13	8	8	16	4	....	....	....
1983-84	**Los Angeles Kings**	**NHL**	**61**	**9**	**13**	**22**	**7**	**9**	**16**	**36**	**1**	**1**	**0**	**63**	**14.3**	**24**	**1**	**53**	**23**	**–7**	....	....	....	....	....	....	....	....
1984-85	**Toronto Maple Leafs**	**NHL**	**26**	**0**	**1**	**1**	**0**	**1**	**1**	**2**	**0**	**0**	**0**	**12**	**0.0**	**3**	**0**	**12**	**3**	**–6**	....	....	....	....	....	....	....	....
	St. Catharines Saints	AHL	52	29	44	73	....	....	....	22	....	....	....	....	....	....	....	....	....	....	....	....	....	....	....	....	....	....
1985-86	**Toronto Maple Leafs**	**NHL**	**2**	**1**	**0**	**1**	**1**	**0**	**1**	**2**	**0**	**0**	**0**	**2**	**50.0**	**1**	**0**	**2**	**0**	**–1**	....	....	....	....	....	....	....	....
	St. Catharines Saints	AHL	74	36	60	96	....	....	....	30	....	....	....	....	....	....	....	....	....	....	13	5	8	13	12	....	....	....
1986-87	Newmarket Saints	AHL	70	28	50	78	....	....	....	32	....	....	....	....	....	....	....	....	....	....	....	....	....	....	....	....	....	....
	Toronto Maple Leafs	**NHL**	....	....	....	....	....	....	....	....	....	....	....	....	....	....	....	....	....	....	**2**	**0**	**0**	**0**	**2**	....	....	....
1987-88	**Toronto Maple Leafs**	**NHL**	**1**	**0**	**0**	**0**	**0**	**0**	**0**	**0**	**0**	**0**	**0**	**0**	**0.0**	**0**	**0**	**0**	**0**	**0**	....	....	....	....	....	....	....	....
	Newmarket Saints	AHL	79	25	59	84	....	....	....	48	....	....	....	....	....	....	....	....	....	....	....	....	....	....	....	....	....	....
1988-89	Newmarket Saints	AHL	52	22	31	53	....	....	....	38	....	....	....	....	....	....	....	....	....	....	5	2	4	6	4	....	....	....
1989-90	Newmarket Saints	AHL	36	13	22	35	....	....	....	18	....	....	....	....	....	....	....	....	....	....	....	....	....	....	....	....	....	....
	NHL Totals		**237**	**31**	**55**	**86**	**26**	**39**	**65**	**98**	**1**	**2**	**0**	**205**	**15.1**	**111**	**5**	**200**	**71**		**2**	**0**	**0**	**0**	**2**	**0**	**0**	**0**

IHL Second All-Star Team (1979) • Won Garry F. Longman Memorial Trophy (Top Rookie - IHL) (1979) • CHL First All-Star Team (1983)

Traded to **Minnesota** by **Washington** with Rollie Boutin for Robbie Moore and Minnesota's 11th round choice (Anders Huss) in 1983 Entry Draft, August 4, 1982. Signed as a free agent by **LA Kings**, August 10, 1983. Signed as a free agent by **Toronto**, October 2, 1984.

• JAVANAINEN, ARTO

Arto Javanainen RW – R. 6', 185 lbs. b: Pori, Finland, 4/8/1959. Pittsburgh's 8th choice, 85th overall, in 1984 Entry Draft.

Season	Club	League	GP	G	A	Pts	AG	AA	APts	PIM	PP	SH	GW	S	%	TGF	PGF	TGA	PGA	+/–	GP	G	A	Pts	PIM	PP	SH	GW
1975-76	Assat Pori	Finland	27	0	0	0	....	....	....	0	....	....	....	....	....	....	....	....	....	....	3	0	0	0	0	....	....	....
1976-77	Assat Pori	Finland	34	9	5	14	....	....	....	8	....	....	....	....	....	....	....	....	....	....	....	....	....	....	....	....	....	....
	Finland	WJC-A	7	4	2	6	....	....	....	4	....	....	....	....	....	....	....	....	....	....	....	....	....	....	....	....	....	....
1977-78	Assat Pori	Finland	35	8	8	16	....	....	....	0	....	....	....	....	....	....	....	....	....	....	9	5	4	9	5	....	....	....
	Finland	WJC-A	6	1	7	8	....	....	....	6	....	....	....	....	....	....	....	....	....	....	....	....	....	....	....	....	....	....
1978-79	Assat Pori	Finland	36	31	18	49	....	....	....	36	....	....	....	....	....	....	....	....	....	....	8	7	4	11	7	....	....	....
	Finland	WJC-A	6	2	3	5	....	....	....	0	....	....	....	....	....	....	....	....	....	....	....	....	....	....	....	....	....	....
1979-80	Assat Pori	Finland	36	28	29	57	....	....	....	48	....	....	....	....	....	....	....	....	....	....	7	*7	2	9	10	....	....	....
1980-81	Assat Pori	Finland	36	*37	27	64	....	....	....	40	....	....	....	....	....	....	....	....	....	....	2	1	0	1	2	....	....	....
1981-82	Finland	C Cup	5	1	0	1	....	....	....	2	....	....	....	....	....	....	....	....	....	....	....	....	....	....	....	....	....	....
	Assat Pori	Finland	36	29	27	56	....	....	....	50	....	....	....	....	....	....	....	....	....	....	8	4	4	8	8	....	....	....
	Finland	WEC-A	5	2	1	3	....	....	....	4	....	....	....	....	....	....	....	....	....	....	....	....	....	....	....	....	....	....
1982-83	Assat Pori	Finland	36	28	23	51	....	....	....	56	....	....	....	....	....	....	....	....	....	....	....	....	....	....	....	....	....	....
	Finland	WEC-A	10	1	2	3	....	....	....	8	....	....	....	....	....	....	....	....	....	....	....	....	....	....	....	....	....	....
1983-84	Assat Pori	Finland	37	37	25	62	....	....	....	62	....	....	....	....	....	....	....	....	....	....	....	....	....	....	....	....	....	....
	Finland	Olympics	5	2	3	5	....	....	....	4	....	....	....	....	....	....	....	....	....	....	....	....	....	....	....	....	....	....
1984-85	**Pittsburgh Penguins**	**NHL**	**14**	**4**	**1**	**5**	**3**	**1**	**4**	**2**	**0**	**0**	**0**	**20**	**20.0**	**11**	**0**	**10**	**0**	**+1**	....	....	....	....	....	....	....	....
	Baltimore Skipjacks	AHL	59	26	29	55	....	....	....	15	....	....	....	....	....	....	....	....	....	....	15	5	4	9	2	....	....	....
1985-86	Assat Pori	Finland	36	*44	27	*71	....	....	....	26	....	....	....	....	....	....	....	....	....	....	....	....	....	....	....	....	....	....

Season	Club	League	REGULAR SEASON																		PLAYOFFS							
			GP	G	A	Pts	AG	AA	APts	PIM	PP	SH	GW	S	%	TGF	PGF	TGA	PGA	+/–	GP	G	A	Pts	PIM	PP	SH	GW
1986-87	Assat Pori	Finland	44	37	24	61	....	....	....	80	....	....	....	....	....	....	....	....	....	....	....	....	....	....	....	....	....	....
1988-89	TPS Turku	Finland	44	32	23	55	....	....	....	38	....	....	....	....	....	....	....	....	....	....	6	5	3	8	2	....	....	....
1989-90	Assat Pori	Finland	36	59	39	98	....	....	....	30	....	....	....	....	....	....	....	....	....	....	3	2	1	3	6	....	....	....
1990-91	Assat Pori	Finland	44	*35	18	53	....	....	....	38	....	....	....	....	....	....	....	....	....	....	....	....	....	....	....	....	....	....
1991-92	Assat Pori	Finland	44	20	14	34	....	....	....	22	....	....	....	....	....	....	....	....	....	....	....	....	....	....	....	....	....	....
1992-93	Assat Pori	Finland	45	17	17	34	....	....	....	26	....	....	....	....	....	....	....	....	....	....	....	....	....	....	....	....	....	....
1993-94	Assat Pori	Finland	48	22	19	41	....	....	....	46	....	....	....	....	....	....	....	....	....	....	....	....	....	....	....	....	....	....
	NHL Totals		**14**	**4**	**1**	**5**	**3**	**1**	**4**	**2**	**0**	**0**	**0**	**20**	**20.0**	**11**	**0**	**10**	**0**		....	....	....	....	....	....	....	....

Finnish First All-Star Team (1982, 1986, 1987, 1988)

Re-entered NHL draft. Originally Montreal's 8th choice, 122nd overall, in 1983 Entry Draft.

• JAY, BOB

Bob Jay D – R. 5'11", 190 lbs. b: Burlington, MA, 11/18/1965.

Season	Club	League	GP	G	A	Pts	AG	AA	APts	PIM	PP	SH	GW	S	%	TGF	PGF	TGA	PGA	+/–	GP	G	A	Pts	PIM	PP	SH	GW
1990-91	Fort Wayne Komets	IHL	40	1	8	9	....	....	....	24	....	....	....	....	....	....	....	....	....	....	14	0	3	3	16	....	....	....
1991-92	Fort Wayne Komets	IHL	76	1	19	20	....	....	....	119	....	....	....	....	....	....	....	....	....	....	7	0	2	2	4	....	....	....
1992-93	Fort Wayne Komets	IHL	78	5	21	26	....	....	....	100	....	....	....	....	....	....	....	....	....	....	8	0	2	2	14	....	....	....
1993-94	**Los Angeles Kings**	**NHL**	**3**	**0**	**1**	**1**	**0**	**1**	**1**	**0**	**0**	**0**	**0**	**2**	**0.0**	**1**	**0**	**4**	**1**	**–2**	....	....	....	....	....	....	....	....
	Phoenix Roadrunners	IHL	65	7	15	22	....	....	....	54	....	....	....	....	....	....	....	....	....	....	....	....	....	....	....	....	....	....
1994-95	Detroit Vipers	IHL	57	3	8	11	....	....	....	51	....	....	....	....	....	....	....	....	....	....	5	0	0	0	10	....	....	....
1995-96	Detroit Vipers	IHL	17	2	2	4	....	....	....	22	....	....	....	....	....	....	....	....	....	....	6	0	1	1	16	....	....	....
	NHL Totals		**3**	**0**	**1**	**1**	**0**	**1**	**1**	**0**	**0**	**0**	**0**	**2**	**0.0**	**1**	**0**	**4**	**1**		....	....	....	....	....	....	....	....

Signed as a free agent by **LA Kings**, July 16, 1993. Signed as a free agent by **Detroit Vipers** (IHL), July 20, 1994.

• JEFFREY, LARRY

Larry Jeffrey LW – L. 5'11", 189 lbs. b: Goderich, Ont., 10/12/1940.

Season	Club	League	GP	G	A	Pts	AG	AA	APts	PIM	PP	SH	GW	S	%	TGF	PGF	TGA	PGA	+/–	GP	G	A	Pts	PIM	PP	SH	GW
1957-58	Hamilton Red Wings	OHA	....	....	....	....	....	....	....	....	....	....	....	....	....	....	....	....	....	....	9	0	0	0	0	....	....	....
1958-59	Hamilton Red Wings	OHA	54	21	20	41	....	....	....	149	....	....	....	....	....	....	....	....	....	....	....	....	....	....	....	....	....	....
1959-60	Hamilton Red Wings	OHA	46	14	24	38	....	....	....	84	....	....	....	....	....	....	....	....	....	....	....	....	....	....	....	....	....	....
	Hershey Bears	AHL	5	0	3	3	....	....	....	2	....	....	....	....	....	....	....	....	....	....	....	....	....	....	....	....	....	....
1960-61	Hamilton Red Wings	OHA	48	28	32	60	....	....	....	105	....	....	....	....	....	....	....	....	....	....	12	6	3	9	39	....	....	....
1961-62	**Detroit Red Wings**	**NHL**	**18**	**5**	**3**	**8**	**6**	**3**	**9**	**20**	....	....	....	....	....	....	....	....	....	....	....	....	....	....	....	....	....	....
	Edmonton Flyers	WHL	48	20	22	42	....	....	....	80	....	....	....	....	....	....	....	....	....	....	....	....	....	....	....	....	....	....
1962-63	**Detroit Red Wings**	**NHL**	**53**	**5**	**11**	**16**	**6**	**11**	**17**	**62**	....	....	....	....	....	....	....	....	....	....	**9**	**3**	**3**	**6**	**8**	....	....	....
	Pittsburgh Hornets	AHL	21	14	7	21	....	....	....	12	....	....	....	....	....	....	....	....	....	....	....	....	....	....	....	....	....	....
1963-64	**Detroit Red Wings**	**NHL**	**58**	**10**	**18**	**28**	**13**	**20**	**33**	**87**	....	....	....	....	....	....	....	....	....	....	**14**	**1**	**6**	**7**	**28**	....	....	....
1964-65	**Detroit Red Wings**	**NHL**	**41**	**4**	**2**	**6**	**5**	**2**	**7**	**48**	....	....	....	....	....	....	....	....	....	....	**2**	**0**	**0**	**0**	**0**	....	....	....
1965-66	**Toronto Maple Leafs**	**NHL**	**20**	**1**	**1**	**2**	**1**	**1**	**2**	**22**	....	....	....	....	....	....	....	....	....	....	....	....	....	....	....	....	....	....
	Rochester Americans	AHL	51	10	20	30	....	....	....	36	....	....	....	....	....	....	....	....	....	....	12	6	5	11	4	....	....	....
1966-67	**Toronto Maple Leafs**	**NHL**	**56**	**11**	**17**	**28**	**13**	**17**	**30**	**27**	....	....	....	....	....	....	....	....	....	....	**6**	**0**	**1**	**1**	**4**	....	....	....
1967-68	**New York Rangers**	**NHL**	**47**	**2**	**4**	**6**	**2**	**4**	**6**	**15**	**0**	**0**	**0**	**48**	**4.2**	**10**	**1**	**29**	**7**	**–13**	**3**	**0**	**0**	**0**	**0**	**0**	**0**	**0**
1968-69	**New York Rangers**	**NHL**	**75**	**1**	**6**	**7**	**1**	**6**	**7**	**12**	**0**	**0**	**0**	**31**	**3.2**	**10**	**0**	**33**	**23**	**0**	**4**	**0**	**0**	**0**	**2**	**0**	**0**	**0**
	NHL Totals		**368**	**39**	**62**	**101**	**47**	**64**	**111**	**293**	**0**	**0**	**0**	**79**	**49.4**	**20**	**1**	**62**	**30**		**38**	**4**	**10**	**14**	**42**	**0**	**0**	**0**

Traded to **Toronto** by **Detroit** with Marcel Pronovost, Ed Joyal, Aut Erickson and Lowell MacDonald for Andy Bathgate, Billy Harris and Gary Jarrett, May 20, 1965. Claimed by **Pittsburgh** from **Toronto** in Expansion Draft, June 6, 1967. Traded to **NY Rangers** by **Pittsburgh** for George Konik, Paul Andrea, Dunc McCallum and Frank Francis, June 6, 1967. Traded to **Detroit** by **NY Rangers** for Sandy Snow and Terry Sawchuk, June 17, 1969.

• JELINEK, TOMAS

Tomas Jelinek RW – L. 5'9", 189 lbs. b: Prague, Czech., 4/29/1962. Ottawa's 11th choice, 242nd overall, in 1992 Entry Draft.

Season	Club	League	GP	G	A	Pts	AG	AA	APts	PIM	PP	SH	GW	S	%	TGF	PGF	TGA	PGA	+/–	GP	G	A	Pts	PIM	PP	SH	GW
1979-80	Sparta Praha	Czech.	7	0	1	1	....	....	....	....	....	....	....	....	....	....	....	....	....	....	....	....	....	....	....	....	....	....
1980-81	Dukla Trencin	Czech.	34	5	6	11	....	....	....	....	....	....	....	....	....	....	....	....	....	....	....	....	....	....	....	....	....	....
1981-82	Dukla Trencin	Czech.	36	9	3	12	....	....	....	46	....	....	....	....	....	....	....	....	....	....	....	....	....	....	....	....	....	....
	Czechoslovakia	WJC-A	7	2	2	4	....	....	....	6	....	....	....	....	....	....	....	....	....	....	....	....	....	....	....	....	....	....
1982-83	Sparta Praha	Czech.	40	20	25	45	....	....	....	....	....	....	....	....	....	....	....	....	....	....	....	....	....	....	....	....	....	....
1983-84	Sparta Praha	Czech.	43	13	5	18	....	....	....	48	....	....	....	....	....	....	....	....	....	....	....	....	....	....	....	....	....	....
1984-85	Sparta Praha	Czech.	44	15	4	19	....	....	....	70	....	....	....	....	....	....	....	....	....	....	....	....	....	....	....	....	....	....
1985-86	Sparta Praha	Czech.	40	7	2	9	....	....	....	....	....	....	....	....	....	....	....	....	....	....	....	....	....	....	....	....	....	....
1986-87	Sparta Praha	Czech.	36	7	5	12	....	....	....	58	....	....	....	....	....	....	....	....	....	....	....	....	....	....	....	....	....	....
1987-88	Sparta Praha	Czech.	45	14	11	25	....	....	....	45	....	....	....	....	....	....	....	....	....	....	....	....	....	....	....	....	....	....
1988-89	Sparta Praha	Czech.	45	15	17	32	....	....	....	87	....	....	....	....	....	....	....	....	....	....	....	....	....	....	....	....	....	....
	Czechoslovakia	WEC-A	5	1	1	2	....	....	....	2	....	....	....	....	....	....	....	....	....	....	....	....	....	....	....	....	....	....
1989-90	Motor Ceske Budejovice	Czech.	48	23	20	43	....	....	....	....	....	....	....	....	....	....	....	....	....	....	....	....	....	....	....	....	....	....
	Czechoslovakia	WEC-A	10	1	4	5	....	....	....	14	....	....	....	....	....	....	....	....	....	....	....	....	....	....	....	....	....	....
1990-91	Budejovice	Czech.	51	24	23	47	....	....	....	102	....	....	....	....	....	....	....	....	....	....	....	....	....	....	....	....	....	....
1991-92	Czechoslovakia	C Cup	5	2	3	5	....	....	....	10	....	....	....	....	....	....	....	....	....	....	....	....	....	....	....	....	....	....
	HPK Hameenlinna	Finland	41	24	23	47	....	....	....	*98	....	....	....	....	....	....	....	....	....	....	....	....	....	....	....	....	....	....
	Czechoslovakia	Olympics	8	3	2	5	....	....	....	12	....	....	....	....	....	....	....	....	....	....	....	....	....	....	....	....	....	....
	Czechoslovakia	WC-A	8	4	5	9	....	....	....	10	....	....	....	....	....	....	....	....	....	....	....	....	....	....	....	....	....	....
1992-93	**Ottawa Senators**	**NHL**	**49**	**7**	**6**	**13**	**6**	**4**	**10**	**52**	**0**	**0**	**0**	**60**	**11.7**	**24**	**7**	**38**	**0**	**–21**	....	....	....	....	....	....	....	....
1993-94	P.E.I. Senators	AHL	2	0	0	0	....	....	....	0	....	....	....	....	....	....	....	....	....	....	....	....	....	....	....	....	....	....
	Zuricher	Switz.	8	3	3	6	....	....	....	18	....	....	....	....	....	....	....	....	....	....	....	....	....	....	....	....	....	....
1994-95	Slavia Praha	Czech.	41	11	17	28	....	....	....	....	....	....	....	....	....	....	....	....	....	....	3	0	0	0	0	....	....	....
1995-96	Skoda Plzen	Czech.	37	19	25	44	....	....	....	....	....	....	....	....	....	....	....	....	....	....	3	1	3	4	....	....	....	....
1996-97	ZKZ Plzen	Czech.	51	22	26	48	....	....	....	66	....	....	....	....	....	....	....	....	....	....	....	....	....	....	....	....	....	....
1997-98	Skoda Plzen	Czech.	14	2	5	7	....	....	....	20	....	....	....	....	....	....	....	....	....	....	....	....	....	....	....	....	....	....
	Sparta Praha	Czech.	37	10	13	23	....	....	....	114	....	....	....	....	....	....	....	....	....	....	10	0	5	5	38	....	....	....
	NHL Totals		**49**	**7**	**6**	**13**	**6**	**4**	**10**	**52**	**0**	**0**	**0**	**60**	**11.7**	**24**	**7**	**38**	**0**		....	....	....	....	....	....	....	....

• JENKINS, DEAN

Dean Jenkins RW – R. 6', 190 lbs. b: Billerica, MA, 11/21/1959.

Season	Club	League	GP	G	A	Pts	AG	AA	APts	PIM	PP	SH	GW	S	%	TGF	PGF	TGA	PGA	+/–	GP	G	A	Pts	PIM	PP	SH	GW
1977-78	Lowell University	ECAC	24	11	7	18	....	....	....	28	....	....	....	....	....	....	....	....	....	....	....	....	....	....	....	....	....	....
1978-79	Lowell University	ECAC	33	16	37	53	....	....	....	75	....	....	....	....	....	....	....	....	....	....	....	....	....	....	....	....	....	....
1979-80	Lowell University	ECAC	29	23	42	65	....	....	....	83	....	....	....	....	....	....	....	....	....	....	....	....	....	....	....	....	....	....
1980-81	Lowell University	ECAC	31	23	32	55	....	....	....	83	....	....	....	....	....	....	....	....	....	....	....	....	....	....	....	....	....	....
1981-82	New Haven Nighthawks	AHL	78	13	22	35	....	....	....	147	....	....	....	....	....	....	....	....	....	....	....	....	....	....	....	....	....	....
1982-83	New Haven Nighthawks	AHL	80	29	43	72	....	....	....	50	....	....	....	....	....	....	....	....	....	....	12	6	2	8	40	....	....	....
1983-84	**Los Angeles Kings**	**NHL**	**5**	**0**	**0**	**0**	**0**	**0**	**0**	**2**	**0**	**0**	**0**	**3**	**0.0**	**1**	**1**	**3**	**2**	**–1**	....	....	....	....	....	....	....	....
	New Haven Nighthawks	AHL	64	24	26	50	....	....	....	131	....	....	....	....	....	....	....	....	....	....	....	....	....	....	....	....	....	....
1984-85	Hershey Bears	AHL	64	14	32	46	....	....	....	135	....	....	....	....	....	....	....	....	....	....	....	....	....	....	....	....	....	....
	NHL Totals		**5**	**0**	**0**	**0**	**0**	**0**	**0**	**2**	**0**	**0**	**0**	**3**	**0.0**	**1**	**1**	**3**	**2**		....	....	....	....	....	....	....	....

Signed as a free agent by **LA Kings**, April 30, 1981. Signed as a free agent by **Boston**, October 10, 1984.

• JENNINGS, GRANT

Grant Jennings D – L. 6'3", 210 lbs. b: Hudson Bay, Sask., 5/5/1965.

Season	Club	League	GP	G	A	Pts	AG	AA	APts	PIM	PP	SH	GW	S	%	TGF	PGF	TGA	PGA	+/–	GP	G	A	Pts	PIM	PP	SH	GW
1983-84	Saskatoon Blades	WHL	64	5	13	18	....	....	....	102	....	....	....	....	....	....	....	....	....	....	....	....	....	....	....	....	....	....
1984-85	Saskatoon Blades	WHL	47	10	24	34	....	....	....	134	....	....	....	....	....	....	....	....	....	....	2	1	0	1	2	....	....	....
1985-86	Binghamton Whalers	AHL	51	0	4	4	....	....	....	109	....	....	....	....	....	....	....	....	....	....	....	....	....	....	....	....	....	....
1986-87	Fort Wayne Komets	IHL	3	0	0	0	....	....	....	0	....	....	....	....	....	....	....	....	....	....	....	....	....	....	....	....	....	....
	Binghamton Whalers	AHL	47	1	5	6	....	....	....	125	....	....	....	....	....	....	....	....	....	....	13	0	2	2	17	....	....	....
1987-88	Binghamton Whalers	AHL	56	2	12	14	....	....	....	195	....	....	....	....	....	....	....	....	....	....	3	1	0	1	15	....	....	....
	Washington Capitals	**NHL**	....	....	....	....	....	....	....	....	....	....	....	....	....	....	....	....	....	....	**1**	**0**	**0**	**0**	**0**	....	....	....
1988-89	**Hartford Whalers**	**NHL**	**55**	**3**	**10**	**13**	**3**	**7**	**10**	**159**	**0**	**0**	**0**	**39**	**7.7**	**50**	**1**	**51**	**19**	**+17**	**4**	**1**	**0**	**1**	**17**	**1**	**0**	**0**
	Binghamton Whalers	AHL	2	0	0	0	....	....	....	2	....	....	....	....	....	....	....	....	....	....	....	....	....	....	....	....	....	....
1989-90	**Hartford Whalers**	**NHL**	**64**	**3**	**6**	**9**	**3**	**4**	**7**	**171**	**0**	**0**	**0**	**45**	**6.7**	**39**	**0**	**72**	**29**	**–4**	**7**	**0**	**0**	**0**	**13**	**0**	**0**	**0**
1990-91	**Hartford Whalers**	**NHL**	**44**	**1**	**4**	**5**	**1**	**3**	**4**	**82**	**0**	**0**	**0**	**28**	**3.6**	**17**	**0**	**46**	**16**	**–13**	....	....	....	....	....	....	....	....
	Pittsburgh Penguins	**NHL**	**13**	**1**	**3**	**4**	**1**	**2**	**3**	**26**	**0**	**0**	**0**	**8**	**12.5**	**10**	**0**	**10**	**2**	**+2**	**13**	**1**	**1**	**2**	**16**	**0**	**0**	**0**

										REGULAR SEASON											PLAYOFFS							
Season	Club	League	GP	G	A	Pts	AG	AA	APts	PIM	PP	SH	GW	S	%	TGF	PGF	TGA	PGA	+/–	GP	G	A	Pts	PIM	PP	SH	GW
1991-92	Pittsburgh Penguins	NHL	53	4	5	9	4	4	8	104	0	2	2	35	11.4	28	0	41	12	–1	10	0	0	0	12	0	0	0
1992-93	Pittsburgh Penguins	NHL	58	0	5	5	0	3	3	65	0	0	0	32	0.0	31	0	26	1	+6	12	0	0	0	8	0	0	0
1993-94	Pittsburgh Penguins	NHL	61	2	4	6	2	3	5	126	0	1	1	49	4.1	25	0	44	9	–10	3	0	0	0	2	0	0	0
1994-95	Pittsburgh Penguins	NHL	25	0	4	4	0	6	6	36	0	0	0	16	0.0	20	0	28	10	+2								
	Toronto Maple Leafs	NHL	10	0	2	2	0	3	3	7	0	0	0	9	0.0	2	0	8	0	–6	4	0	0	0	0	0	0	0
1995-96	Buffalo Sabres	NHL	6	0	0	0	0	0	0	28	0	0	0	3	0.0	1	0	1	1	+1								
	Rochester Americans	AHL	9	0	1	1				28																		
	Atlanta Knights	IHL	3	0	0	0				19											3	0	0	0	20			
1996-97	Quebec Rafales	IHL	42	2	10	12				79																		
1997-98	San Antonio Dragons	IHL	44	1	4	5				116																		
	NHL Totals		**389**	**14**	**43**	**57**	**14**	**35**	**49**	**804**	**0**	**3**	**3**	**264**	**5.3**	**223**	**1**	**327**	**99**		**54**	**2**	**1**	**3**	**68**	**1**	**0**	**0**

Signed as a free agent by **Washington**, June 25, 1985. Traded to **Hartford** by **Washington** with Ed Kastelic for Mike Millar and Neil Sheehy, July 6, 1988. Traded to **Pittsburgh** by **Hartford** with Ron Francis and Ulf Samuelsson for John Cullen, Jeff Parker and Zarley Zalapski, March 4, 1991. Traded to **Toronto** by **Pittsburgh** for Drake Berehowsky, April 7, 1995. Signed as a free agent by **Buffalo**, September 20, 1995.

• JENSEN, CHRIS

Chris Jensen RW – R. 5'11", 180 lbs. b: Fort St. John, B.C., 10/28/1963. NY Rangers' 4th choice, 78th overall, in 1982 Entry Draft.

Season	Club	League	GP	G	A	Pts	AG	AA	APts	PIM	PP	SH	GW	S	%	TGF	PGF	TGA	PGA	+/–	GP	G	A	Pts	PIM	PP	SH	GW
1980-81	Kelowna Packers	BCJHL	53	51	45	96				120																		
1981-82	Kelowna Packers	BCJHL	48	46	46	92				212																		
1982-83	University of North Dakota	WCHA	13	3	3	6				28																		
1983-84	University of North Dakota	WCHA	44	24	25	49				100																		
1984-85	University of North Dakota	WCHA	40	25	27	52				80																		
1985-86	University of North Dakota	WCHA	34	25	40	65				53																		
	New York Rangers	NHL	9	1	3	4	1	2	3	0	0	0	1	18	5.6	6	3	2	0	+1								
1986-87	New York Rangers	NHL	37	6	7	13	5	5	10	21	0	1	2	70	8.6	23	2	22	0	–1								
	New Haven Nighthawks	AHL	14	4	9	13				41																		
1987-88	New York Rangers	NHL	7	0	1	1	0	1	1	2	0	0	0	11	0.0	2	0	3	0	–1								
	Colorado Rangers	IHL	43	10	23	33				68											10	3	7	10	8			
1988-89	Hershey Bears	AHL	45	27	31	58				66											10	4	5	9	29			
1989-90	Philadelphia Flyers	NHL	1	0	0	0	0	0	0	2	0	0	0	0	0.0	0	0	1	0	–1								
	Hershey Bears	AHL	43	16	26	42				101																		
1990-91	Philadelphia Flyers	NHL	18	2	1	3	2	1	3	2	0	0	0	22	9.1	7	1	11	0	–5								
	Hershey Bears	AHL	50	26	20	46				83											6	2	2	4	10			
1991-92	Philadelphia Flyers	NHL	2	0	0	0	0	0	0	0	0	0	0	2	0.0	0	0	1	0	–1								
	Hershey Bears	AHL	71	38	33	71				134											6	0	1	1	2			
1992-93	Hershey Bears	AHL	74	33	47	80				95																		
1993-94	Portland Pirates	AHL	56	33	28	61				52											16	6	10	16	22			
1994-95	Portland Pirates	AHL	67	35	42	77				89											7	4	3	7	0			
1995-96	Minnesota Moose	IHL	52	25	19	44				109																		
	Michigan K-Wings	IHL	13	5	5	10				7											6	0	2	2	6			
1996-97	Manitoba Moose	IHL	16	6	4	10				23																		
	Long Beach Ice Dogs	IHL	16	3	5	8				10											15	2	2	4	22			
1997-98	Wheeling Nailers	ECHL	39	14	14	28				120											15	8	4	12	26			
	NHL Totals		**74**	**9**	**12**	**21**	**8**	**9**	**17**	**27**	**0**	**1**	**3**	**123**	**7.3**	**38**	**6**	**40**	**0**									

Traded to **Philadelphia** by **NY Rangers** for Michael Boyce, September 28, 1988.

• JENSEN, DAVID A.

David A. Jensen C – L. 6'1", 195 lbs. b: Newton, MA, 8/19/1965. Hartford's 2nd choice, 20th overall, in 1983 Entry Draft.

Season	Club	League	GP	G	A	Pts	AG	AA	APts	PIM	PP	SH	GW	S	%	TGF	PGF	TGA	PGA	+/–	GP	G	A	Pts	PIM	PP	SH	GW
1982-83	Lawrence Academy	H.S.	25	41	48	89																						
1983-84	United States	Nat-Team	61	22	56	78				6																		
1984-85	Hartford Whalers	NHL	13	0	4	4	0	3	3	6	0	0	0	11	0.0	6	0	7	0	1								
	Binghamton Whalers	AHL	40	8	9	17				2																		
1985-86	Washington Capitals	NHL	5	1	0	1	1	0	1	0	0	0	0	5	20.0	2	0	1	0	+1	4	0	0	0	0	0	0	0
	Binghamton Whalers	AHL	41	17	14	31				4											4	2	4	6	0			
1986-87	Washington Capitals	NHL	46	8	8	16	7	6	13	12	2	0	0	49	16.3	21	5	26	0	–10	7	0	0	0	2	0	0	0
	Binghamton Whalers	AHL	6	2	5	7				0																		
1987-88	Washington Capitals	NHL	5	0	1	1	0	1	1	4	0	0	0	1	0.0	1	0	1	0	0								
	Binghamton Whalers	AHL	9	5	2	7				2																		
	Fort Wayne Komets	IHL	32	10	13	23				8											5	1	1	2	0			
1988-89	Maine Mariners	AHL	18	12	8	20				2																		
1989-90	Maine Mariners	AHL	4	0	2	2				0																		
1990-91	Maine Mariners	AHL	15	2	5	7				0																		
	Cortina d'Ampezzo	Italy	35	27	18	45				8											6	7	7	14	4			
	NHL Totals		**69**	**9**	**13**	**22**	**8**	**10**	**18**	**22**	**2**	**0**	**0**	**66**	**13.6**	**30**	**5**	**35**	**0**		**11**	**0**	**0**	**0**	**2**	**0**	**0**	**0**

Traded to **Washington** by **Hartford** for Dean Evason and Peter Sidorkiewicz, March 12, 1985. Signed as a free agent by **Boston**, August 1, 1988.

• JENSEN, DAVID H.

David H. Jensen D – L. 6'1", 185 lbs. b: Minneapolis, MN, 5/3/1961. Minnesota's 5th choice, 100th overall, in 1980 Entry Draft.

Season	Club	League	GP	G	A	Pts	AG	AA	APts	PIM	PP	SH	GW	S	%	TGF	PGF	TGA	PGA	+/–	GP	G	A	Pts	PIM	PP	SH	GW
1979-80	University of Minnesota	WCHA	33	0	5	5				32																		
	United States	WJC-A	5	0	3	3				4																		
1980-81	University of Minnesota	WCHA	35	0	13	13				64																		
	United States	WJC-A	5	0	0	0				4																		
1981-82	University of Minnesota	WCHA	32	3	13	16				68																		
1982-83	University of Minnesota	WCHA	25	4	14	18				38																		
	Birmingham South Stars	CHL																			2	0	0	0	0			
1983-84	United States	Nat-Team	47	3	15	18				38																		
	Minnesota North Stars	NHL	8	0	1	1	0	1	1	0	0	0	0	5	0.0	6	0	5	1	+2								
	Salt Lake Golden Eagles	CHL	13	0	7	7				6											5	0	1	1	5			
1984-85	Minnesota North Stars	NHL	5	0	1	1	0	1	1	4	0	0	0	3	0.0	2	0	8	1	–5								
	Springfield Indians	AHL	69	13	27	40				63											4	0	1	1	0			
1985-86	Minnesota North Stars	NHL	5	0	0	0	0	0	0	7	0	0	0	1	0.0	1	0	3	0	–2								
	Springfield Indians	AHL	40	4	18	22				31																		
1986-87	Ritten	Italy	40	21	38	59				53																		
1987-88	Tours	France	30	7	19	26				46																		
	NHL Totals		**18**	**0**	**2**	**2**	**0**	**2**	**2**	**11**	**0**	**0**	**0**	**9**	**0.0**	**9**	**0**	**16**	**2**									

• JENSEN, STEVE

Steve Jensen LW – L. 6'2", 190 lbs. b: Minneapolis, MN, 4/14/1955. Minnesota's 4th choice, 58th overall, in 1975 Amateur Draft.

Season	Club	League	GP	G	A	Pts	AG	AA	APts	PIM	PP	SH	GW	S	%	TGF	PGF	TGA	PGA	+/–	GP	G	A	Pts	PIM	PP	SH	GW
1973-74	Michigan Tech Huskies	WCHA	40	17	3	20				32																		
1974-75	Michigan Tech Huskies	WCHA	41	16	32	48				18																		
	United States	Nat-Team	17	4	1	5																						
	United States	WEC-A	9	2	0	2				2																		
1975-76	United States	Nat-Team	64	52	44	96				42																		
	United States	Olympics	6	6	0	6				6																		
	United States	WEC-A	7	4	5	9				8																		
	Minnesota North Stars	NHL	19	7	6	13	7	5	12	6	1	0	1	49	14.3	20	4	23	2	–5								
1976-77	United States	C Cup	5	1	0	1				2																		
	Minnesota North Stars	NHL	78	22	23	45	21	19	40	62	4	2	1	160	13.8	72	11	81	14	–6	2	0	1	1	0	0	0	0
1977-78	Minnesota North Stars	NHL	74	13	17	30	13	14	27	73	2	0	1	132	9.8	47	5	80	8	–30								
	Fort Worth Texans	CHL	3	0	1	1				2																		
	United States	WEC-A	10	3	0	3				2																		
1978-79	Los Angeles Kings	NHL	72	23	8	31	21	6	27	57	2	0	4	114	20.2	40	5	64	1	–28	2	0	0	0	0	0	0	0
	United States	WEC-A	DID NOT PLAY																									
1979-80	Los Angeles Kings	NHL	76	21	15	36	19	11	30	13	4	2	2	149	14.1	58	16	90	9	–39	4	0	0	0	2	0	0	0

			REGULAR SEASON																		PLAYOFFS							
Season	Club	League	GP	G	A	Pts	AG	AA	APts	PIM	PP	SH	GW	S	%	TGF	PGF	TGA	PGA	+/–	GP	G	A	Pts	PIM	PP	SH	GW
1980-81	**Los Angeles Kings**	**NHL**	**74**	**19**	**19**	**38**	**16**	**13**	**29**	**88**	**5**	**1**	**4**	**118**	**16.1**	**57**	**9**	**69**	**15**	**–6**	**4**	**0**	**2**	**2**	**7**	**0**	**0**	**0**
1981-82	**Los Angeles Kings**	**NHL**	**45**	**8**	**19**	**27**	**6**	**13**	**19**	**19**	**1**	**0**	**1**	**78**	**10.3**	**41**	**6**	**69**	**20**	**–14**	....	....	....	....	....	....	....	....
	New Haven Nighthawks	AHL	14	5	8	13	....	....	....	4	....	....	....	....	....	....	....	....	....	....	1	0	0	0	0	....	....	....
	NHL Totals		**438**	**113**	**107**	**220**	**103**	**81**	**184**	**318**	**19**	**5**	**14**	**800**	**14.1**	**335**	**56**	**476**	**69**		**12**	**0**	**3**	**3**	**9**	**0**	**0**	**0**

NCAA Championship All-Tournament Team (1974, 1975)

Transferred to **LA Kings** by **Minnesota** with Dave Gardner and Rick Hampton as compensation for Minnesota's signing of Gary Sargent, July 15, 1978.

• JERRARD, PAUL

Paul Jerrard D – R. 5'10", 185 lbs. b: Winnipeg, Man., 4/20/1965. NY Rangers' 10th choice, 180th overall, in 1983 Entry Draft.

Season	Club	League	GP	G	A	Pts	AG	AA	APts	PIM	PP	SH	GW	S	%	TGF	PGF	TGA	PGA	+/–	GP	G	A	Pts	PIM	PP	SH	GW
1982-83	Notre Dame Hounds	SJHL	60	34	37	71	....	....	....	150	....	....	....	....	....	....	....	....	....	....	....	....	....	....	....	....	....	....
1983-84	Lake Superior State University	CCHA	40	8	18	26	....	....	....	48	....	....	....	....	....	....	....	....	....	....	....	....	....	....	....	....	....	....
1984-85	Lake Superior State University	CCHA	43	9	25	34	....	....	....	61	....	....	....	....	....	....	....	....	....	....	....	....	....	....	....	....	....	....
1985-86	Lake Superior State University	CCHA	40	13	11	24	....	....	....	34	....	....	....	....	....	....	....	....	....	....	....	....	....	....	....	....	....	....
1986-87	Lake Superior State University	CCHA	35	10	19	29	....	....	....	56	....	....	....	....	....	....	....	....	....	....	....	....	....	....	....	....	....	....
1987-88	Colorado Rangers	IHL	77	20	28	48	....	....	....	182	....	....	....	....	....	....	....	....	....	....	11	2	4	6	40	....	....	....
1988-89	**Minnesota North Stars**	**NHL**	**5**	**0**	**0**	**0**	**0**	**0**	**0**	**4**	**0**	**0**	**0**	**8**	**0.0**	**1**	**0**	**0**	**0**	**+1**	....	....	....	....	....	....	....	....
	Kalamazoo Wings	IHL	68	15	25	40	....	....	....	195	....	....	....	....	....	....	....	....	....	....	6	2	1	3	37	....	....	....
	Denver Rangers	IHL	2	1	1	2	....	....	....	21	....	....	....	....	....	....	....	....	....	....	....	....	....	....	....	....	....	....
1989-90	Kalamazoo Wings	IHL	60	9	18	27	....	....	....	134	....	....	....	....	....	....	....	....	....	....	7	1	1	2	11	....	....	....
1990-91	Albany Choppers	IHL	7	0	3	3	....	....	....	30	....	....	....	....	....	....	....	....	....	....	....	....	....	....	....	....	....	....
	Kalamazoo Wings	IHL	62	10	23	33	....	....	....	111	....	....	....	....	....	....	....	....	....	....	7	0	0	0	13	....	....	....
1991-92	Kalamazoo Wings	IHL	76	4	24	28	....	....	....	123	....	....	....	....	....	....	....	....	....	....	12	1	7	8	31	....	....	....
1992-93	Kalamazoo Wings	IHL	80	8	11	19	....	....	....	187	....	....	....	....	....	....	....	....	....	....	....	....	....	....	....	....	....	....
1993-94	Kalamazoo Wings	IHL	24	0	2	2	....	....	....	60	....	....	....	....	....	....	....	....	....	....	....	....	....	....	....	....	....	....
	Milwaukee Admirals	IHL	28	6	3	9	....	....	....	58	....	....	....	....	....	....	....	....	....	....	2	0	0	0	8	....	....	....
1994-95	Hershey Bears	AHL	66	17	11	28	....	....	....	118	....	....	....	....	....	....	....	....	....	....	6	0	1	....	18	....	....	....
	NHL Totals		**5**	**0**	**0**	**0**	**0**	**0**	**0**	**4**	**0**	**0**	**0**	**8**	**0.0**	**1**	**0**	**0**	**0**		....	....	....	....	....	....	....	....

Traded to **Minnesota** by **NY Rangers** with Mark Tinordi, Mike Sullivan and the rights to Bret Barnett for Brian Lawton, Igor Liba and LA Kings' 3rd round choice (previously acquired, Minnesota selected Murray Garbutt) in 1989 Entry Draft, October 11, 1988.

• JIRIK, JAROSLAV

Jaroslav Jirik RW – R. 5'11", 170 lbs. b: Vojnur, Mestac, Czech., 12/10/1939.

Season	Club	League	GP	G	A	Pts	AG	AA	APts	PIM	PP	SH	GW	S	%	TGF	PGF	TGA	PGA	+/–	GP	G	A	Pts	PIM	PP	SH	GW
1962-63	Czechoslovakia	WEC-A	7	4	3	7	....	....	....	9	....	....	....	....	....	....	....	....	....	....	....	....	....	....	....	....	....	....
1963-64	Czechoslovakia	Olympics	7	3	1	4	....	....	....	6	....	....	....	....	....	....	....	....	....	....	....	....	....	....	....	....	....	....
1964-65	Czechoslovakia	WEC-A	7	8	4	12	....	....	....	5	....	....	....	....	....	....	....	....	....	....	....	....	....	....	....	....	....	....
1965-66	Czechoslovakia	WEC-A	7	4	1	5	....	....	....	2	....	....	....	....	....	....	....	....	....	....	....	....	....	....	....	....	....	....
1966-67	Czechoslovakia	WEC-A	6	5	3	8	....	....	....	2	....	....	....	....	....	....	....	....	....	....	....	....	....	....	....	....	....	....
1967-68	Czechoslovakia	Olympics	4	3	3	6	....	....	....	0	....	....	....	....	....	....	....	....	....	....	....	....	....	....	....	....	....	....
1968-69	Czechoslovakia	WEC-A	5	2	3	5	....	....	....	0	....	....	....	....	....	....	....	....	....	....	....	....	....	....	....	....	....	....
1969-70	**St. Louis Blues**	**NHL**	**3**	**0**	**0**	**0**	**0**	**0**	**0**	**0**	**0**	**0**	**0**	**4**	**0.0**	**1**	**0**	**0**	**0**	**+1**	....	....	....	....	....	....	....	....
	Kansas City Blues	CHL	53	19	16	35	....	....	....	11	....	....	....	....	....	....	....	....	....	....	....	....	....	....	....	....	....	....
	NHL Totals		**3**	**0**	**0**	**0**	**0**	**0**	**0**	**0**	**0**	**0**	**0**	**4**	**0.0**	**1**	**0**	**0**	**0**		....	....	....	....	....	....	....	....

WEC-A All-Star Team (1965)

Signed as a free agent by **St. Louis**, June, 1969. • First player from Iron Curtain country to play in NHL.

• JODZIO, RICK

Rick Jodzio LW – L. 6'1", 190 lbs. b: Edmonton, Alta., 6/3/1954. Buffalo's 9th choice, 153rd overall, in 1974 Amateur Draft.

Season	Club	League	GP	G	A	Pts	AG	AA	APts	PIM	PP	SH	GW	S	%	TGF	PGF	TGA	PGA	+/–	GP	G	A	Pts	PIM	PP	SH	GW
1973-74	Downsview Beavers	OJHL	30	7	12	19	....	....	....	166	....	....	....	....	....	....	....	....	....	....	....	....	....	....	....	....	....	....
	Hamilton Red Wings	OHA	30	1	8	9	....	....	....	86	....	....	....	....	....	....	....	....	....	....	....	....	....	....	....	....	....	....
1974-75	Vancouver Blazers	WHA	44	1	3	4	....	....	....	59	....	....	....	....	....	....	....	....	....	....	....	....	....	....	....	....	....	....
	Charlotte Checkers	SHL	37	9	8	17	....	....	....	109	....	....	....	....	....	....	....	....	....	....	1	0	2	2	0	....	....	....
1975-76	Calgary Cowboys	WHA	47	10	7	17	....	....	....	137	....	....	....	....	....	....	....	....	....	....	2	0	0	0	14	....	....	....
	Springfield Indians	AHL	24	2	3	5	....	....	....	37	....	....	....	....	....	....	....	....	....	....	....	....	....	....	....	....	....	....
1976-77	Calgary Cowboys	WHA	46	4	6	10	....	....	....	61	....	....	....	....	....	....	....	....	....	....	....	....	....	....	....	....	....	....
	Tidewater Sharks	SHL	7	3	3	6	....	....	....	4	....	....	....	....	....	....	....	....	....	....	....	....	....	....	....	....	....	....
	Erie Blades	NAHL	15	5	5	10	....	....	....	32	....	....	....	....	....	....	....	....	....	....	9	2	7	9	21	....	....	....
1977-78	**Colorado Rockies**	**NHL**	**32**	**0**	**5**	**5**	**0**	**4**	**4**	**28**	**0**	**0**	**0**	**25**	**0.0**	**14**	**1**	**18**	**0**	**–5**	....	....	....	....	....	....	....	....
	Cleveland Barons	**NHL**	**38**	**2**	**3**	**5**	**2**	**2**	**4**	**43**	**0**	**0**	**1**	**23**	**8.7**	**9**	**0**	**18**	**0**	**–9**	....	....	....	....	....	....	....	....
1978-79	Oklahoma City Stars	CHL	62	4	21	25	....	....	....	117	....	....	....	....	....	....	....	....	....	....	....	....	....	....	....	....	....	....
1979-80	New Brunswick Hawks	AHL	79	13	25	38	....	....	....	113	....	....	....	....	....	....	....	....	....	....	17	2	4	6	43	....	....	....
	NHL Totals		**70**	**2**	**8**	**10**	**2**	**6**	**8**	**71**	**0**	**0**	**1**	**48**	**4.2**	**23**	**1**	**36**	**0**		....	....	....	....	....	....	....	....
	Other Major League Totals		137	15	16	31	....	....	....	257	....	....	....	....	....	....	....	....	....		2	0	0	0	14	....	....	....

Signed as a free agent by **Vancouver** (WHA), January, 1975. • Suspended one year by WHA for intentionally injuring Marc Tardiff in WHA playoff game, April 11, 1976. Traded to **Colorado** by **Buffalo** for cash, September 22, 1977. Traded to **Cleveland** by **Colorado** with Chuck Arnason for Ralph Klassen and Fred Ahern, January 9, 1978. Placed on Reserve List by **Minnesota** after **Cleveland-Minnesota** Dispersal Draft, June 15, 1978.

• JOHANNESEN, GLENN

Glenn Johannesen LW – R. 6'2", 220 lbs. b: Lac La Rouge, Sask., 2/15/1962. NY Islanders' 11th choice, 206th overall, in 1980 Entry Draft.

Season	Club	League	GP	G	A	Pts	AG	AA	APts	PIM	PP	SH	GW	S	%	TGF	PGF	TGA	PGA	+/–	GP	G	A	Pts	PIM	PP	SH	GW
1980-81	Western Michigan University	CCHA	35	2	18	20	....	....	....	65	....	....	....	....	....	....	....	....	....	....	....	....	....	....	....	....	....	....
1981-82	Western Michigan University	CCHA	33	3	10	13	....	....	....	37	....	....	....	....	....	....	....	....	....	....	....	....	....	....	....	....	....	....
1982-83	Western Michigan University	CCHA	32	1	9	10	....	....	....	36	....	....	....	....	....	....	....	....	....	....	....	....	....	....	....	....	....	....
1983-84	Western Michigan University	CCHA	41	4	16	20	....	....	....	80	....	....	....	....	....	....	....	....	....	....	....	....	....	....	....	....	....	....
	Kalamazoo Wings	IHL	3	0	0	0	....	....	....	0	....	....	....	....	....	....	....	....	....	....	....	....	....	....	....	....	....	....
1984-85	Indianapolis Checkers	IHL	51	10	19	29	....	....	....	130	....	....	....	....	....	....	....	....	....	....	....	....	....	....	....	....	....	....
	Springfield Indians	AHL	21	1	3	4	....	....	....	59	....	....	....	....	....	....	....	....	....	....	....	....	....	....	....	....	....	....
1985-86	**New York Islanders**	**NHL**	**2**	**0**	**0**	**0**	**0**	**0**	**0**	**0**	**0**	**0**	**0**	**2**	**0.0**	**0**	**0**	**1**	**0**	**–1**	....	....	....	....	....	....	....	....
	Springfield Indians	AHL	78	8	21	29	....	....	....	187	....	....	....	....	....	....	....	....	....	....	....	....	....	....	....	....	....	....
1986-87	Springfield Indians	AHL	54	10	6	16	....	....	....	156	....	....	....	....	....	....	....	....	....	....	....	....	....	....	....	....	....	....
1987-88	Springfield Indians	AHL	1	0	0	0	....	....	....	0	....	....	....	....	....	....	....	....	....	....	....	....	....	....	....	....	....	....
	Peoria Rivermen	IHL	73	24	29	53	....	....	....	172	....	....	....	....	....	....	....	....	....	....	7	4	3	7	32	....	....	....
1988-89	Springfield Indians	AHL	5	1	1	2	....	....	....	20	....	....	....	....	....	....	....	....	....	....	....	....	....	....	....	....	....	....
	Indianapolis Ice	IHL	76	18	23	41	....	....	....	235	....	....	....	....	....	....	....	....	....	....	....	....	....	....	....	....	....	....
	NHL Totals		**2**	**0**	**0**	**0**	**0**	**0**	**0**	**0**	**0**	**0**	**0**	**2**	**0.0**	**0**	**0**	**1**	**0**		....	....	....	....	....	....	....	....

• JOHANNSON, JOHN

John Johannson C – L. 6'1", 175 lbs. b: Rochester, MN, 10/18/1961. Colorado's 10th choice, 192nd overall, in 1981 Entry Draft.

Season	Club	League	GP	G	A	Pts	AG	AA	APts	PIM	PP	SH	GW	S	%	TGF	PGF	TGA	PGA	+/–	GP	G	A	Pts	PIM	PP	SH	GW
1980-81	University of Wisconsin	WCHA	38	6	12	18	....	....	....	32	....	....	....	....	....	....	....	....	....	....	....	....	....	....	....	....	....	....
	United States	WJC-A	4	3	0	3	....	....	....	0	....	....	....	....	....	....	....	....	....	....	....	....	....	....	....	....	....	....
1981-82	University of Wisconsin	WCHA	47	15	34	49	....	....	....	46	....	....	....	....	....	....	....	....	....	....	....	....	....	....	....	....	....	....
1982-83	University of Wisconsin	WCHA	47	22	41	63	....	....	....	68	....	....	....	....	....	....	....	....	....	....	10	6	11	17	....	....	....	....
1983-84	University of Wisconsin	WCHA	39	21	25	46	....	....	....	32	....	....	....	....	....	....	....	....	....	....	....	....	....	....	....	....	....	....
	New Jersey Devils	**NHL**	**5**	**0**	**0**	**0**	**0**	**0**	**0**	**0**	**0**	**0**	**0**	**4**	**0.0**	**0**	**0**	**2**	**0**	**–2**	....	....	....	....	....	....	....	....
1984-85	WEV Wien	Austria	23	41	43	84	....	....	....	34	....	....	....	....	....	....	....	....	....	....	....	....	....	....	....	....	....	....
	NHL Totals		**5**	**0**	**0**	**0**	**0**	**0**	**0**	**0**	**0**	**0**	**0**	**4**	**0.0**	**0**	**0**	**2**	**0**		....	....	....	....	....	....	....	....

Rights transferred to **New Jersey** after **Colorado** franchise relocated, June 30, 1982.

• JOHANSEN, TREVOR

Trevor Johansen D – R. 5'9", 200 lbs. b: Thunder Bay, Ont., 3/30/1957. Toronto's 2nd choice, 12th overall, in 1977 Amateur Draft.

Season	Club	League	GP	G	A	Pts	AG	AA	APts	PIM	PP	SH	GW	S	%	TGF	PGF	TGA	PGA	+/–	GP	G	A	Pts	PIM	PP	SH	GW
1973-74	Thunder Bay Twins	TBJHL	59	13	31	44	....	....	....	137	....	....	....	....	....	....	....	....	....	....	....	....	....	....	....	....	....	....
1974-75	Toronto Marlboros	OHA	50	9	30	39	....	....	....	175	....	....	....	....	....	....	....	....	....	....	....	....	....	....	....	....	....	....
1975-76	Toronto Marlboros	OHA	61	5	25	30	....	....	....	141	....	....	....	....	....	....	....	....	....	....	....	....	....	....	....	....	....	....
1976-77	Toronto Marlboros	OHA	61	2	34	36	....	....	....	177	....	....	....	....	....	....	....	....	....	....	....	....	....	....	....	....	....	....
	Canada	WJC-A	5	0	0	0	....	....	....	5	....	....	....	....	....	....	....	....	....	....	....	....	....	....	....	....	....	....
1977-78	**Toronto Maple Leafs**	**NHL**	**79**	**2**	**14**	**16**	**2**	**11**	**13**	**82**	**0**	**0**	**0**	**82**	**2.4**	**86**	**0**	**96**	**13**	**+3**	**13**	**0**	**3**	**3**	**21**	**0**	**0**	**0**

			REGULAR SEASON																		PLAYOFFS							
Season	Club	League	GP	G	A	Pts	AG	AA	APts	PIM	PP	SH	GW	S	%	TGF	PGF	TGA	PGA	+/–	GP	G	A	Pts	PIM	PP	SH	GW
1978-79	**Toronto Maple Leafs**	**NHL**	**40**	**1**	**4**	**5**	**1**	**3**	**4**	**48**	**0**	**0**	**0**	**31**	**3.2**	**31**	**2**	**37**	**9**	**+1**								
	New Brunswick Hawks	AHL	24	1	7	8				49																		
	Colorado Rockies	**NHL**	**11**	**1**	**3**	**4**	**1**	**2**	**3**	**16**	**0**	**0**	**0**	**14**	**7.1**	**5**	**0**	**14**	**1**	**–8**								
	Canada	WEC-A	8	2	1	3				4																		
1979-80	**Colorado Rockies**	**NHL**	**62**	**3**	**8**	**11**	**3**	**6**	**9**	**45**	**1**	**0**	**0**	**43**	**7.0**	**47**	**1**	**80**	**17**	**–17**								
1980-81	**Colorado Rockies**	**NHL**	**35**	**0**	**7**	**7**	**0**	**5**	**5**	**18**	**0**	**0**	**0**	**33**	**0.0**	**28**	**1**	**61**	**14**	**–20**								
1981-82	**Los Angeles Kings**	**NHL**	**46**	**3**	**7**	**10**	**2**	**5**	**7**	**69**	**0**	**0**	**0**	**40**	**7.5**	**38**	**1**	**68**	**17**	**–14**								
	Toronto Maple Leafs	**NHL**	**13**	**1**	**3**	**4**	**1**	**2**	**3**	**4**	**0**	**0**	**0**	**14**	**7.1**	**9**	**0**	**34**	**9**	**–16**								
1982-83	Springfield Indians	AHL	6	0	0	0				16																		
	NHL Totals		**286**	**11**	**46**	**57**	**10**	**34**	**44**	**282**	**1**	**0**	**0**	**257**	**4.3**	**244**	**5**	**390**	**80**		**13**	**0**	**3**	**3**	**21**	**0**	**0**	**0**

OHA First All-Star Team (1977)

Traded to **Colorado** by **Toronto** with Don Ashby for Paul Gardner, March 13, 1979. Claimed by **LA Kings** from **Colorado** in Waiver Draft, October 12, 1981. Claimed on waivers by **Toronto** from **LA Kings**, February 19, 1982.

• JOHANSSON, ANDREAS

Andreas Johansson C – L. 6', 205 lbs. b: Hofors, Sweden, 5/19/1973. NY Islanders' 7th choice, 136th overall, in 1991 Entry Draft.

Season	Club	League	GP	G	A	Pts	AG	AA	APts	PIM	PP	SH	GW	S	%	TGF	PGF	TGA	PGA	+/–	GP	G	A	Pts	PIM	PP	SH	GW
1990-91	Falun	Sweden 2	31	12	10	22				38																		
1991-92	Farjestad BK Karlstad	Sweden	30	3	1	4				10											6	0	0	0	4			
	Sweden	WJC-A	7	1	2	3				4																		
1992-93	Farjestad BK Karlstad	Sweden	38	4	7	11				38											2	0	0	0	0			
	Sweden	WJC-A	7	1	5	6				14																		
1993-94	Farjestad BK Karlstad	Sweden	20	3	6	9				6																		
1994-95	Farjestad BK Karlstad	Sweden	36	9	10	19				42											4	0	0	0	10			
	Sweden	WC-A	8	3	6	9				8																		
1995-96	**New York Islanders**	**NHL**	**3**	**0**	**1**	**1**	**0**	**1**	**1**	**0**	**0**	**0**	**0**	**6**	**0.0**	**1**	**0**	**0**	**0**	**+1**								
	Worcester IceCats	AHL	29	5	5	10				32																		
	Utah Grizzlies	IHL	22	4	13	17				28											12	0	5	5	6			
1996-97	Sweden	W Cup	2	0	0	0				2																		
	New York Islanders	**NHL**	**15**	**2**	**2**	**4**	**2**	**2**	**4**	**0**	**1**	**0**	**0**	**21**	**9.5**	**5**	**2**	**9**	**0**	**–6**								
	Pittsburgh Penguins	**NHL**	**27**	**2**	**7**	**9**	**2**	**6**	**8**	**20**	**0**	**0**	**0**	**38**	**5.3**	**11**	**0**	**20**	**3**	**–6**								
	Cleveland Lumberjacks	IHL	10	2	4	6				42											11	1	5	6	8			
1997-98	**Pittsburgh Penguins**	**NHL**	**50**	**5**	**10**	**15**	**6**	**10**	**16**	**20**	**0**	**1**	**0**	**49**	**10.2**	**23**	**2**	**22**	**5**	**+4**	**1**	**0**	**0**	**0**	**0**	**0**	**0**	**0**
	Sweden	Olympics	3	0	0	0				2																		
	NHL Totals		**95**	**9**	**20**	**29**	**10**	**19**	**29**	**40**	**1**	**1**	**0**	**114**	**7.9**	**40**	**4**	**51**	**8**		**1**	**0**	**0**	**0**	**0**	**0**	**0**	**0**

Swedish World All-Star Team (1995)

Traded to **Pittsburgh** by **NY Islanders** with Darius Kasparaitis for Bryan Smolinski, November 17, 1996.

• JOHANSSON, BJORN

Bjorn Johansson D – L. 6', 195 lbs. b: Orebro, Sweden, 1/15/1956. California's 1st choice, 5th overall, in 1976 Amateur Draft.

Season	Club	League	GP	G	A	Pts	AG	AA	APts	PIM	PP	SH	GW	S	%	TGF	PGF	TGA	PGA	+/–	GP	G	A	Pts	PIM	PP	SH	GW
1971-72	Sodertalje	Sweden	27	8	11	19				16																		
1972-73	Sodertalje	Sweden	14	3	4	7				6											13	2	0	2	2			
1973-74	Sodertalje	Sweden	30	15	17	32				10																		
	Sweden	WJC-A	5	0	1	1				2																		
1974-75	Sodertalje	Sweden	28	6	9	15				12																		
	Sweden	WJC-A	....	1	2	3				....																		
1975-76	Orebro	Sweden	36	30	21	51				30																		
	Sweden	WJC-A	4	3	2	5				0																		
1976-77	**Cleveland Barons**	**NHL**	**10**	**1**	**1**	**2**	**1**	**1**	**2**	**4**	**0**	**0**	**0**	**8**	**12.5**	**5**	**0**	**17**	**1**	**–11**								
	Salt Lake Golden Eagles	CHL	56	8	16	24				10																		
1977-78	**Cleveland Barons**	**NHL**	**5**	**0**	**0**	**0**	**0**	**0**	**0**	**6**	**0**	**0**	**0**	**1**	**0.0**	**1**	**0**	**3**	**0**	**–2**								
	Phoenix Roadrunners	CHL	13	0	3	3				15																		
	Binghamton Dusters	AHL	24	0	10	10				6																		
	Rochester Americans	AHL	25	2	10	12				20																		
1978-79	Orebro	Sweden	36	7	15	22				37																		
1979-80	Vastra Frolunda	Sweden	33	8	10	18				46											8	2	1	3	8			
1980-81	Djurgardens Stockholm	Sweden	20	1	3	4				11																		
	NHL Totals		**15**	**1**	**1**	**2**	**1**	**1**	**2**	**10**	**0**	**0**	**0**	**9**	**11.1**	**6**	**0**	**20**	**1**									

Named Best Defenseman at EJC-A (1975) • WJC-A All-Star Team (1976)

Transferred to **Cleveland** after **California** franchise relocated, August 26, 1976.

• JOHANSSON, CALLE

Calle Johansson D – L. 5'11", 200 lbs. b: Goteborg, Sweden, 2/14/1967. Buffalo's 1st choice, 14th overall, in 1985 Entry Draft.

Season	Club	League	GP	G	A	Pts	AG	AA	APts	PIM	PP	SH	GW	S	%	TGF	PGF	TGA	PGA	+/–	GP	G	A	Pts	PIM	PP	SH	GW
1983-84	Vastra Frolunda	Sweden	28	4	4	8				10																		
1984-85	Vastra Frolunda	Sweden	25	8	13	21				16											6	1	2	3	4			
1985-86	Bjorkloven	Sweden	17	1	2	3				4																		
	Sweden	WJC-A	7	1	1	2				6																		
1986-87	Bjorkloven	Sweden	30	2	13	15				20											6	1	3	4	6			
	Sweden	WJC-A	6	0	8	8				6																		
1987-88	**Buffalo Sabres**	**NHL**	**71**	**4**	**38**	**42**	**3**	**27**	**30**	**37**	**2**	**0**	**0**	**93**	**4.3**	**96**	**33**	**90**	**39**	**+12**	**6**	**0**	**1**	**1**	**0**	**0**	**0**	**0**
1988-89	**Buffalo Sabres**	**NHL**	**47**	**2**	**11**	**13**	**2**	**8**	**10**	**33**	**0**	**0**	**1**	**53**	**3.8**	**50**	**12**	**65**	**20**	**–7**								
	Washington Capitals	**NHL**	**12**	**1**	**7**	**8**	**1**	**5**	**6**	**4**	**1**	**0**	**0**	**22**	**4.5**	**13**	**4**	**8**	**0**	**+1**	**6**	**1**	**2**	**3**	**0**	**1**	**0**	**0**
1989-90	Washington Capitals	FrTour	2	0	0	0				0																		
	Washington Capitals	**NHL**	**70**	**8**	**31**	**39**	**7**	**22**	**29**	**25**	**4**	**0**	**2**	**103**	**7.8**	**93**	**36**	**60**	**10**	**+7**	**15**	**1**	**6**	**7**	**4**	**0**	**0**	**0**
1990-91	**Washington Capitals**	**NHL**	**80**	**11**	**41**	**52**	**10**	**31**	**41**	**23**	**2**	**1**	**2**	**128**	**8.6**	**111**	**41**	**82**	**10**	**–2**	**10**	**2**	**7**	**9**	**8**	**1**	**0**	**0**
	Sweden	WEC-A	4	1	1	2				6																		
1991-92	Sweden	C Cup	6	1	2	3				0																		
	Washington Capitals	**NHL**	**80**	**14**	**42**	**56**	**13**	**32**	**45**	**49**	**5**	**2**	**2**	**119**	**11.8**	**140**	**52**	**103**	**17**	**+2**	**7**	**0**	**5**	**5**	**4**	**0**	**0**	**0**
	Sweden	WC-A	5	0	0	0				4																		
1992-93	**Washington Capitals**	**NHL**	**77**	**7**	**38**	**45**	**6**	**26**	**32**	**56**	**6**	**0**	**0**	**133**	**5.3**	**119**	**42**	**107**	**33**	**+3**	**6**	**0**	**5**	**5**	**4**	**0**	**0**	**0**
1993-94	**Washington Capitals**	**NHL**	**84**	**9**	**33**	**42**	**8**	**25**	**33**	**59**	**4**	**0**	**1**	**141**	**6.4**	**100**	**28**	**111**	**42**	**+3**	**6**	**1**	**3**	**4**	**4**	**0**	**0**	**1**
1994-95	EHC Kloten	Switz.	5	1	2	3				8																		
	Washington Capitals	**NHL**	**46**	**5**	**26**	**31**	**9**	**30**	**47**	**35**	**4**	**0**	**2**	**112**	**4.5**	**61**	**33**	**51**	**17**	**–6**	**7**	**3**	**1**	**4**	**0**	**1**	**0**	**0**
1995-96	**Washington Capitals**	**NHL**	**78**	**10**	**25**	**35**	**10**	**20**	**30**	**50**	**4**	**0**	**0**	**182**	**5.5**	**82**	**31**	**75**	**37**	**+13**								
1996-97	Sweden	W Cup	4	1	5	6				8																		
	Washington Capitals	**NHL**	**65**	**6**	**11**	**17**	**6**	**10**	**16**	**16**	**2**	**0**	**0**	**133**	**4.5**	**57**	**15**	**68**	**24**	**–2**								
1997-98	**Washington Capitals**	**NHL**	**73**	**15**	**20**	**35**	**18**	**19**	**37**	**30**	**10**	**1**	**1**	**163**	**9.2**	**80**	**35**	**79**	**23**	**–11**	**21**	**2**	**8**	**10**	**16**	**0**	**0**	**0**
	Sweden	Olympics	4	0	0	0				2																		
	NHL Totals		**783**	**92**	**323**	**415**	**93**	**263**	**356**	**417**	**44**	**4**	**11**	**1382**	**6.7**	**1002**	**362**	**899**	**272**		**84**	**10**	**38**	**48**	**40**	**3**	**0**	**1**

EJC-A All-Star Team (1985) • Named Best Defenseman at WJC-A (1987) • NHL All-Rookie Team (1988) • World Cup All-Star Team (1996)

Traded to **Washington** by **Buffalo** with Buffalo's 2nd round choice (Byron Dafoe) in 1989 Entry Draft for Clint Malarchuk, Grant Ledyard and Washington's 6th round choice (Brian Holzinger) in 1991 Entry Draft, March 7, 1989.

• JOHANSSON, ROGER

Roger Johansson D – L. 6'1", 190 lbs. b: Ljungby, Sweden, 4/17/1967. Calgary's 5th choice, 80th overall, in 1985 Entry Draft.

Season	Club	League	GP	G	A	Pts	AG	AA	APts	PIM	PP	SH	GW	S	%	TGF	PGF	TGA	PGA	+/–	GP	G	A	Pts	PIM	PP	SH	GW
1983-84	Troja	Sweden 2	11	2	2	4				12																		
1984-85	Troja	Sweden 2	30	1	6	7				20											9	0	4	4	8			
1985-86	Troja	Sweden 2	32	5	16	21				42																		
	Sweden	WJC-A	7	1	1	2				8																		
1986-87	Farjestad BK Karlstad	Sweden	31	6	11	17				20											7	1	1	2	8			
	Sweden	WJC-A	7	2	4	6				2																		
1987-88	Farjestad BK Karlstad	Sweden	24	3	11	14				20											9	1	6	7	12			
1988-89	Farjestad BK Karlstad	Sweden	40	5	15	20				38																		
1989-90	Calgary Flames	FrTour	4	0	1	1				6																		
	Calgary Flames	**NHL**	**35**	**0**	**5**	**5**	**0**	**4**	**4**	**48**	**0**	**0**	**0**	**23**	**0.0**	**22**	**0**	**18**	**5**	**+9**								

Season	Club	League	GP	G	A	Pts	AG	AA	APts	PIM	PP	SH	GW	S	%	TGF	PGF	TGA	PGA	+/–	GP	G	A	Pts	PIM	PP	SH	GW
																				REGULAR SEASON				PLAYOFFS				
1990-91	**Calgary Flames**	NHL	38	4	13	17	4	10	14	47	0	0	0	41	9.8	40	4	35	8	+9	....	....	....	....	....	....	....	....
1991-92	Leksands IF	Sweden	22	3	9	12				42																		
1992-93	**Calgary Flames**	NHL	77	4	16	20	3	11	14	62	1	0	0	101	4.0	54	7	47	13	+13	5	0	1	1	2	0	0	0
1993-94	Leksands IF	Sweden	38	6	15	21				56											4	0	1	1	0			
	Sweden	Olympics	8	2	0	2				8																		
	Sweden	WC-A	8	0	3	3				4																		
1994-95	Leksands IF	Sweden	7	0	0	0				14																		
	Chicago Blackhawks	NHL	11	1	0	1	2	0	2	6	0	0	0	10	10.0	4	0	3	0	+1								
1995-96	Farjestad BK Karlstad	Sweden	34	3	4	7				46											8	3	1	4	16			
	Sweden	WC-A	6	1	1	2				6																		
1996-97	Sweden	W Cup	3	0	0	0				0																		
	Farjestad BK Karlstad	Sweden	46	8	15	23				52											14	3	5	8	38			
	Sweden	WC-A	10	0	1	1				16																		
1997-98	Farjestad BK Karlstad	Sweden	46	12	27	39				44											10	2	7	9	38			
	Farjestad BK Karlstad	EuroHL	6	1	1	2				6																		
	NHL Totals		161	9	34	43	9	25	34	163	1	0	0	175	5.1	120	11	103	26		5	0	1	1	2	0	0	0

Claimed by **Chicago** from **Calgary** in Waiver Draft, January 18, 1995.

● JOHNS, DON   Don Johns   D – R. 6', 180 lbs. b: St. George, Ont., 12/13/1937.

Season	Club	League	GP	G	A	Pts	AG	AA	APts	PIM	PP	SH	GW	S	%	TGF	PGF	TGA	PGA	+/–	GP	G	A	Pts	PIM
1956-57	Hull-Ottawa Jr. Canadiens	Ott-Jr.	27	2	3	5				12															
	Hull-Ottawa Jr. Canadiens	QHL	15	0	0	0				0															
	Hull-Ottawa Jr. Canadiens	EOHL	8	0	2	2				2															
1957-58	Fort William Canadians	TBJHL	50	3	14	17				56											4	1	1	2	8
1958-59	Winnipeg Warriors	WHL	60	4	18	22				112											7	1	0	1	18
1959-60	Winnipeg Warriors	WHL	70	3	21	24				72															
1960-61	**New York Rangers**	NHL	63	1	7	8	1	7	8	34															
1961-62	Springfield Indians	AHL	59	3	10	13				14											11	1	4	5	10
1962-63	**New York Rangers**	NHL	6	0	4	4	0	4	4	6															
	Baltimore Clippers	AHL	69	9	17	26				30											3	1	3	4	2
1963-64	**New York Rangers**	NHL	57	1	9	10	1	10	11	26															
	Baltimore Clippers	AHL	12	0	1	1				10															
1964-65	**New York Rangers**	NHL	22	0	1	1	0	1	1	26															
	Baltimore Clippers	AHL	26	2	10	12				28											9	0	2	2	14
	St. Louis Braves	CHL	23	1	5	6				10															
1965-66	**Montreal Canadiens**	NHL	1	0	0	0	0	0	0	0															
	Quebec Aces	AHL	63	2	24	26				78															
1966-67	Quebec Aces	AHL	69	1	15	16				54															
1967-68	**Minnesota North Stars**	NHL	4	0	0	0	0	0	0	6	0	0	0	4	0.0	4	0	6	1	–1					
	Memphis South Stars	CHL	27	0	9	9				22															
	Rochester Americans	AHL	42	1	13	14				32											11	1	1	2	18
1968-69	Vancouver Canucks	WHL	66	1	22	23				102											7	0	3	3	18
	NHL Totals		153	2	21	23	2	22	24	76	0	0	0	4	50.0	4	0	6	1						

Claimed by **NY Rangers** from **Winnipeg** (WHL) in Inter-League Draft, June 7, 1960. Traded to **Chicago** by **NY Rangers** with Camille Henry, Billy Taylor and Wally Chevrier for Doug Robinson, Wayne Hillman and John Brenneman, February 4, 1965. Traded to **Montreal** by **Chicago** for Bryan Watson, June, 1965. Traded to **Minnesota** by **Montreal** for cash, October 5, 1967. Traded to **Toronto** by **Minnesota** with Duke Harris, Murray Hall, Ted Taylor, Len Lunde and the loan of Carl Wetzel for Jean-Paul Parise and Milan Marcetta, December 26, 1967.

● JOHNSON, BRIAN   Brian Johnson   RW – R. 6'1", 185 lbs. b: Montreal, Que., 4/1/1960. Hartford's 7th choice, 107th overall, in 1983 Entry Draft.

Season	Club	League	GP	G	A	Pts	AG	AA	APts	PIM	PP	SH	GW	S	%	TGF	PGF	TGA	PGA	+/–	GP	G	A	Pts	PIM
1977-78	Verdun Eperviers	QJHL	50	11	14	25				145															
1978-79	Verdun Eperviers	QMJHL	71	32	36	68				192											11	1	6	7	61
1979-80	Verdun Eperviers	QMJHL	21	8	27	35				68															
	Sherbrooke Castors	QMJHL	49	32	52	84				144											15	11	15	26	66
1980-81	Adirondack Red Wings	AHL	65	10	21	31				193											8	0	0	0	33
1981-82	Dallas Black Hawks	CHL	79	18	36	54				223											16	4	3	7	*129
1982-83	Adirondack Red Wings	AHL	67	6	16	22				250											6	1	2	3	15
1983-84	**Detroit Red Wings**	NHL	3	0	0	0	0	0	0	5	0	0	0	4	0.0	0	0	3	0	–3					
	Adirondack Red Wings	AHL	58	4	27	31				233											7	0	0	0	40
1984-85			DID NOT PLAY																						
1985-86	Indianapolis Checkers	IHL	13	0	1	1				57															
	Carolina Thunderbirds	ACHL	22	8	11	19				167															
	NHL Totals		3	0	0	0	0	0	0	5	0	0	0	4	0.0	0	0	3	0						

QMJHL Second All-Star Team (1980)
Signed as a free agent by **Detroit**, October 30, 1979.

● JOHNSON, CRAIG   Craig Johnson   LW/C – L. 6'2", 197 lbs. b: St. Paul, MN, 3/8/1972. St. Louis' 2nd choice, 33rd overall, in 1990 Entry Draft.

Season	Club	League	GP	G	A	Pts	AG	AA	APts	PIM	PP	SH	GW	S	%	TGF	PGF	TGA	PGA	+/–	GP	G	A	Pts	PIM	PP	SH	GW
1989-90	Hill-Murray High School	H.S.	23	15	36	51				0																		
1990-91	University of Minnesota	WCHA	33	13	18	31				34																		
1991-92	University of Minnesota	WCHA	41	17	38	55				66																		
1992-93	University of Minnesota	WCHA	42	22	24	46				70																		
	United States	WC-A	6	1	1	2				4																		
1993-94	United States	Nat-Team	54	25	26	51				64																		
	United States	Olympics	8	0	4	4				4																		
1994-95	**St. Louis Blues**	NHL	15	3	3	6	5	4	4	6	0	0	0	19	15.8	11	1	7	1	+4	1	0	0	0	2	0	0	0
	Peoria Rivermen	IHL	16	2	6	8				25											9	0	4	4	10			
1995-96	**St. Louis Blues**	NHL	49	8	7	15	8	6	14	30	1	0	0	69	11.6	22	2	29	5	–4								
	Worcester IceCats	AHL	5	3	0	3				2																		
	Los Angeles Kings	NHL	11	5	4	9	5	3	8	6	3	0	0	28	17.9	10	3	12	1	–4								
	United States	WC-A	6	1	1	2				2																		
1996-97	**Los Angeles Kings**	NHL	31	4	3	7	4	3	7	26	1	0	0	30	13.3	12	2	17	0	–7								
1997-98	**Los Angeles Kings**	NHL	74	17	21	38	20	20	40	42	6	0	2	125	13.6	54	14	43	12	+9	4	1	0	1	4	0	0	0
	NHL Totals		180	37	38	75	42	36	78	110	11	0	2	271	13.7	109	22	108	19		5	1	0	1	6	0	0	0

Traded to **LA Kings** by **St. Louis** with Patrice Tardif, Roman Vopat, St. Louis 5th round choice (Peter Hogan) in 1996 Entry Draft and 1st round choice (Matt Zultek) in 1997 Entry Draft for Wayne Gretzky, February 27, 1996.

● JOHNSON, DANNY   Danny Johnson   C – L. 5'11", 170 lbs. b: Winnipegosis, Man., 10/1/1944. d: 3/6/1993.

Season	Club	League	GP	G	A	Pts	AG	AA	APts	PIM	PP	SH	GW	S	%	TGF	PGF	TGA	PGA	+/–	GP	G	A	Pts	PIM
1962-63	Flin Flon Bombers	SJHL	45	5	14	19				26											6	2	4	6	2
1963-64	Fort Frances Royals	MJHL	26	8	11	19				49											9	6	2	8	24
1964-65	Brandon Wheat Kings	MJHL	56	26	29	55				90															
1965-66	Tulsa Oilers	CHL	67	6	23	29				40											10	2	0	2	4
1966-67	Tulsa–Omaha	CHL	60	11	17	28				30											12	1	4	5	4
1967-68	Tulsa Oilers	CHL	69	19	37	56				42											11	3	2	5	21
1968-69	Tulsa Oilers	CHL	72	34	38	72				63											7	2	6	8	12
1969-70	**Toronto Maple Leafs**	NHL	1	0	0	0	0	0	0	0	0	0	0	0	0.0	0	0	0	0						
	Tulsa Oilers	CHL	72	33	46	79				56											6	3	4	7	4
1970-71	**Vancouver Canucks**	NHL	66	15	11	26	16	10	26	16	0	0	2	76	19.7	34	3	51	5	–15					
	Rochester Americans	AHL	7	2	2	4				4															
1971-72	**Vancouver Canucks**	NHL	11	1	3	4	1	3	4	0	0	0	1	10	10.0	5	0	8	0	–3					
	Detroit Red Wings	NHL	43	2	5	7	2	5	7	8	0	0	0	28	7.1	12	0	14	0	–2					

			REGULAR SEASON																		PLAYOFFS							
Season	Club	League	GP	G	A	Pts	AG	AA	APts	PIM	PP	SH	GW	S	%	TGF	PGF	TGA	PGA	+/–	GP	G	A	Pts	PIM	PP	SH	GW
1972-73	Winnipeg Jets	WHA	76	19	23	42				17											14	4	1	5	0			
1973-74	Winnipeg Jets	WHA	78	16	21	37				20											4	1	0	1	5			
1974-75	Winnipeg Jets	WHA	78	18	14	32				25																		
	NHL Totals		**121**	**18**	**19**	**37**	**19**	**18**	**37**	**24**	**1**	**0**	**3**	**114**	**15.8**	**51**	**3**	**73**	**5**									
	Other Major League Totals		232	53	58	111				62											18	5	1	6	5			

CHL Second All-Star Team (1969, 1970) • Won Tommy Ivan Trophy (CHL's MVP) (1970)

Claimed by **Toronto** from **Tulsa** (CHL) in Inter-League Draft, June, 1966. Claimed by **Vancouver** from **Toronto** in Expansion Draft, June 10, 1970. Claimed on waivers by **Detroit** from **Vancouver**, November 22, 1971. Selected by **NY Raiders** (WHA) in 1972 WHA General Player Draft, February 12, 1972. Rights traded to **Winnipeg** (WHA) by **NY Raiders** (WHA) for rights to Mark Dufour, June, 1972.

• JOHNSON, GREG

Greg Johnson C – L. 5'10", 185 lbs. b: Thunder Bay, Ont., 3/16/1971. Philadelphia's 1st choice, 33rd overall, in 1989 Entry Draft.

Season	Club	League	GP	G	A	Pts	AG	AA	APts	PIM	PP	SH	GW	S	%	TGF	PGF	TGA	PGA	+/–	GP	G	A	Pts	PIM	PP	SH	GW
1988-89	Thunder Bay Flyers	USHL	47	32	64	96				4											12	5	13	18	0			
1989-90	University of North Dakota	WCHA	44	17	38	55				11																		
1990-91	University of North Dakota	WCHA	38	18	*61	79				6																		
	Canada	WJC-A	7	4	2	6				0																		
1991-92	University of North Dakota	WCHA	39	20	*54	74				8																		
1992-93	University of North Dakota	WCHA	34	19	45	64				18																		
	Canada	Nat-Team	23	6	14	20				2																		
	Canada	WC-A	8	1	2	3				2																		
1993-94	**Detroit Red Wings**	**NHL**	**52**	**6**	**11**	**17**	**6**	**8**	**14**	**22**	**1**	**1**	**0**	**48**	**12.5**	**22**	**2**	**37**	**10**	**–7**	**7**	**2**	**2**	**4**	**2**	**1**	**0**	**0**
	Adirondack Red Wings	AHL	3	2	4	6				0											4	0	4	4	2			
	Canada	Nat-Team	6	2	6	8				4																		
	Canada	Olympics	8	0	3	3				0																		
1994-95	**Detroit Red Wings**	**NHL**	**22**	**3**	**5**	**8**	**5**	**7**	**12**	**14**	**2**	**0**	**0**	**32**	**9.4**	**11**	**2**	**9**	**1**	**+1**	**1**	**0**	**0**	**0**	**0**	**0**	**0**	**0**
1995-96	**Detroit Red Wings**	**NHL**	**60**	**18**	**22**	**40**	**18**	**18**	**36**	**30**	**5**	**0**	**2**	**87**	**20.7**	**47**	**16**	**25**	**0**	**+6**	**13**	**3**	**1**	**4**	**8**	**0**	**0**	**0**
1996-97	**Detroit Red Wings**	**NHL**	**43**	**6**	**10**	**16**	**6**	**9**	**15**	**12**	**0**	**0**	**0**	**56**	**10.7**	**19**	**4**	**20**	**0**	**–5**								
	Pittsburgh Penguins	**NHL**	**32**	**7**	**9**	**16**	**7**	**8**	**15**	**14**	**1**	**0**	**0**	**52**	**13.5**	**23**	**5**	**38**	**7**	**–13**	**5**	**1**	**0**	**1**	**2**	**0**	**0**	**0**
1997-98	**Pittsburgh Penguins**	**NHL**	**5**	**1**	**0**	**1**	**1**	**0**	**1**	**2**	**0**	**0**	**0**	**4**	**25.0**	**1**	**0**	**2**	**1**	**0**								
	Chicago Blackhawks	**NHL**	**69**	**11**	**22**	**33**	**13**	**21**	**34**	**38**	**4**	**0**	**3**	**85**	**12.9**	**54**	**13**	**56**	**13**	**–2**								
	NHL Totals		**283**	**52**	**79**	**131**	**56**	**71**	**127**	**132**	**13**	**1**	**5**	**364**	**14.3**	**177**	**42**	**187**	**32**		**26**	**6**	**3**	**9**	**12**	**1**	**0**	**0**

WCHA First All-Star Team (1991, 1992, 1993) • NCAA West First All-American Team (1991, 1993) • NCAA West Second All-American Team (1992)

Traded to **Detroit** by **Philadelphia** with Philadelphia's 5th round choice (Frederic Deschenes) in 1994 Entry Draft for Jim Cummins and Philadelphia's 4th round choice (previously acquired by Detroit — later traded to Boston — Boston selected Charles Paquette) in 1993 Entry Draft, June 20, 1993. Traded to **Pittsburgh** by **Detroit** for Tomas Sandstrom, January 27, 1997. Traded to **Chicago** by **Pittsburgh** for Tuomas Gronman, October 27, 1997. Claimed by **Nashville** from **Chicago** in Expansion Draft, June 26, 1998.

• JOHNSON, JIM

Jim Johnson D – L. 6'1", 190 lbs. b: New Hope, MN, 8/9/1962.

Season	Club	League	GP	G	A	Pts	AG	AA	APts	PIM	PP	SH	GW	S	%	TGF	PGF	TGA	PGA	+/–	GP	G	A	Pts	PIM	PP	SH	GW
1981-82	University of Minnesota-Duluth	WCHA	40	0	10	10				62																		
1982-83	University of Minnesota-Duluth	WCHA	44	3	18	21				118																		
1983-84	University of Minnesota-Duluth	WCHA	43	3	13	16				116																		
1984-85	University of Minnesota-Duluth	WCHA	47	7	29	36				49																		
	United States	WEC-A	9	0	1	1				22																		
1985-86	**Pittsburgh Penguins**	**NHL**	**80**	**3**	**26**	**29**	**2**	**17**	**19**	**115**	**0**	**0**	**0**	**118**	**2.5**	**115**	**22**	**119**	**38**	**+12**								
	United States	WEC-A	9	0	0	0				12																		
1986-87	**Pittsburgh Penguins**	**NHL**	**80**	**5**	**25**	**30**	**4**	**18**	**22**	**116**	**0**	**0**	**1**	**89**	**5.6**	**92**	**18**	**115**	**35**	**–6**								
	United States	WEC-A	10	0	0	0				28																		
1987-88	**Pittsburgh Penguins**	**NHL**	**55**	**1**	**12**	**13**	**1**	**9**	**10**	**87**	**0**	**0**	**0**	**44**	**2.3**	**40**	**4**	**74**	**34**	**–4**								
1988-89	**Pittsburgh Penguins**	**NHL**	**76**	**2**	**14**	**16**	**2**	**10**	**12**	**163**	**1**	**0**	**0**	**70**	**2.9**	**85**	**13**	**114**	**49**	**+7**	**11**	**0**	**5**	**5**	**44**	**0**	**0**	**0**
1989-90	**Pittsburgh Penguins**	**NHL**	**75**	**3**	**13**	**16**	**3**	**9**	**12**	**154**	**1**	**0**	**0**	**72**	**4.2**	**68**	**10**	**111**	**33**	**–20**								
	United States	WEC-A	10	0	5	5				16																		
1990-91	**Pittsburgh Penguins**	**NHL**	**24**	**0**	**5**	**5**	**0**	**4**	**4**	**23**	**0**	**0**	**0**	**22**	**0.0**	**23**	**0**	**35**	**9**	**–3**								
	Minnesota North Stars	**NHL**	**44**	**1**	**9**	**10**	**1**	**7**	**8**	**100**	**0**	**0**	**0**	**61**	**1.6**	**40**	**0**	**42**	**11**	**+9**	**14**	**0**	**1**	**1**	**52**	**0**	**0**	**0**
1991-92	United States	C Cup	8	0	0	0				20																		
	Minnesota North Stars	**NHL**	**71**	**4**	**10**	**14**	**4**	**7**	**11**	**102**	**0**	**0**	**1**	**86**	**4.7**	**72**	**13**	**80**	**32**	**+11**	**7**	**1**	**3**	**4**	**18**	**0**	**0**	**0**
1992-93	**Minnesota North Stars**	**NHL**	**79**	**3**	**20**	**23**	**2**	**14**	**16**	**105**	**1**	**0**	**0**	**67**	**4.5**	**74**	**1**	**100**	**00**	**+9**								
1993-94	**Dallas Stars**	**NHL**	**53**	**0**	**7**	**7**	**0**	**5**	**5**	**51**	**0**	**0**	**0**	**44**	**0.0**	**32**	**0**	**62**	**24**	**–6**								
	Washington Capitals	**NHL**	**8**	**0**	**0**	**0**	**0**	**0**	**0**	**12**	**0**	**0**	**0**	**5**	**0.0**	**6**	**0**	**8**	**1**	**–1**								
1994-95	**Washington Capitals**	**NHL**	**47**	**0**	**13**	**13**	**0**	**19**	**19**	**43**	**0**	**0**	**0**	**46**	**0.0**	**34**	**3**	**34**	**9**	**+6**	**7**	**0**	**2**	**2**	**8**	**0**	**0**	**0**
1995-96	**Washington Capitals**	**NHL**	**66**	**2**	**4**	**6**	**2**	**3**	**5**	**34**	**0**	**0**	**0**	**49**	**4.1**	**25**	**0**	**32**	**4**	**–3**	**6**	**0**	**0**	**0**	**6**	**0**	**0**	**0**
1996-97	**Phoenix Coyotes**	**NHL**	**55**	**3**	**7**	**10**	**3**	**6**	**9**	**74**	**0**	**0**	**0**	**51**	**5.9**	**36**	**0**	**39**	**8**	**+5**	**6**	**0**	**0**	**0**	**4**	**0**	**0**	**0**
1997-98	**Phoenix Coyotes**	**NHL**	**16**	**2**	**1**	**3**	**2**	**1**	**3**	**18**	**0**	**0**	**0**	**17**	**11.8**	**10**	**0**	**11**	**1**	**0**								
	NHL Totals		**829**	**29**	**166**	**195**	**26**	**129**	**155**	**1197**	**3**	**0**	**2**	**841**	**3.4**	**752**	**87**	**976**	**327**		**51**	**1**	**11**	**12**	**132**	**0**	**0**	**0**

Signed as a free agent by **Pittsburgh**, June 9, 1985. Traded to **Minnesota** by **Pittsburgh** with Chris Dahlquist for Larry Murphy and Peter Taglianetti, December 11, 1990. Transferred to **Dallas** after **Minnesota** franchise relocated, June 9, 1993. Traded to **Washington** by **Dallas** for Alan May and Washington's 7th round choice (Jeff Dewar) in 1995 Entry Draft, March 21, 1994. Signed as a free agent by **Phoenix**, July 6, 1996.

• JOHNSON, JIM

Jim Johnson C – L. 5'9", 190 lbs. b: Winnipeg, Man., 11/7/1942.

Season	Club	League	GP	G	A	Pts	AG	AA	APts	PIM	PP	SH	GW	S	%	TGF	PGF	TGA	PGA	+/–	GP	G	A	Pts	PIM	PP	SH	GW
1960-61	Winnipeg Rangers	MJHL	29	15	21	36				12																		
1961-62	Winnipeg Rangers	MJHL	39	22	23	45				48											3	1	1	2	0			
1962-63	Sudbury Wolves	EPHL	70	16	36	52				16											8	1	4	5	2			
1963-64	St. Paul Rangers	CHL	70	21	33	54				14											11	3	5	8	0			
1964-65	**New York Rangers**	**NHL**	**1**	**0**	**0**	**0**	**0**	**0**	**0**	**0**																		
	St. Paul Rangers	CHL	61	19	45	64				14											11	4	6	10	7			
1965-66	**New York Rangers**	**NHL**	**5**	**1**	**0**	**1**	**1**	**0**	**1**	**0**																		
	Minnesota Rangers	CHL	62	24	46	70				12											7	3	2	5	0			
1966-67	**New York Rangers**	**NHL**	**2**	**0**	**0**	**0**	**0**	**0**	**0**	**0**																		
	Omaha Knights	CHL	64	26	46	72				20											12	2	5	7	2			
1967-68	**Philadelphia Flyers**	**NHL**	**13**	**2**	**1**	**3**	**2**	**1**	**3**	**2**	**0**	**0**	**0**	**12**	**16.7**	**3**	**0**	**4**	**0**	**–1**								
	Quebec Aces	AHL	59	27	45	72				14											15	5	8	13	10			
1968-69	**Philadelphia Flyers**	**NHL**	**69**	**17**	**27**	**44**	**19**	**25**	**44**	**20**	**1**	**1**	**5**	**146**	**11.6**	**66**	**7**	**71**	**18**	**–5**	**3**	**0**	**0**	**0**	**2**	**0**	**0**	**0**
1969-70	**Philadelphia Flyers**	**NHL**	**72**	**18**	**30**	**48**	**21**	**30**	**51**	**17**	**2**	**2**	**1**	**168**	**10.7**	**64**	**11**	**65**	**13**	**+1**								
1970-71	**Philadelphia Flyers**	**NHL**	**66**	**16**	**29**	**45**	**17**	**26**	**43**	**16**	**2**	**0**	**2**	**121**	**13.2**	**62**	**11**	**73**	**12**	**–10**	**4**	**0**	**2**	**2**	**0**	**0**	**0**	**0**
	Quebec Aces	AHL	5	0	1	1				0																		
1971-72	**Philadelphia Flyers**	**NHL**	**46**	**13**	**15**	**28**	**14**	**14**	**28**	**12**	**5**	**2**	**1**	**86**	**15.1**	**34**	**12**	**58**	**15**	**–21**								
	Los Angeles Kings	**NHL**	**28**	**8**	**9**	**17**	**8**	**8**	**16**	**6**	**3**	**2**	**0**	**53**	**15.1**	**27**	**5**	**30**	**7**	**–1**								
1972-73	Minnesota Fighting Saints	WHA	33	9	14	23				12											5	2	1	3	2			
1973-74	Minnesota Fighting Saints	WHA	71	15	39	54				30											11	1	4	5	4			
1974-75	Minnesota Fighting Saints	WHA	11	1	3	4				0																		
	Indianapolis Racers	WHA	42	7	15	22				12																		
	NHL Totals		**302**	**75**	**111**	**186**	**82**	**104**	**186**	**73**	**13**	**7**	**9**	**586**	**12.8**	**245**	**46**	**301**	**65**		**7**	**0**	**2**	**2**	**2**	**0**	**0**	**0**
	Other Major League Totals		157	32	71	103				64											16	3	5	8	6			

Claimed by **NY Rangers** from **Baltimore** (AHL) in Inter-League Draft, June 3, 1964. Claimed by **Philadelphia** from **NY Rangers** in Expansion Draft, June 6, 1967. Traded to **LA Kings** by **Philadelphia** with Bill Lesuk and Serge Bernier for Bill Flett, Ed Joyal, Jean Potvin and Ross Lonsberry, January 28, 1972. Selected by **Minnesota** (WHA) in 1972 WHA General Player Draft, February 12, 1972. Traded to **Indianapolis** (WHA) by **Minnesota** (WHA) for Joe Robertson, November, 1974.

• JOHNSON, MARK

Mark Johnson C – L. 5'9", 170 lbs. b: Madison, WI, 9/22/1957. Pittsburgh's 9th choice, 66th overall, in 1977 Amateur Draft.

Season	Club	League	GP	G	A	Pts	AG	AA	APts	PIM	PP	SH	GW	S	%	TGF	PGF	TGA	PGA	+/–	GP	G	A	Pts	PIM	PP	SH	GW
1976-77	University of Wisconsin	WCHA	43	36	44	80				16																		
1977-78	University of Wisconsin	WCHA	42	*48	38	86				24																		
	United States	WEC-A	10	0	2	2				0																		
1978-79	University of Wisconsin	WCHA	40	*41	49	*90				34																		
	United States	WEC-A	2	0	0	0				0																		

			REGULAR SEASON																		PLAYOFFS							
Season	Club	League	GP	G	A	Pts	AG	AA	APts	PIM	PP	SH	GW	S	%	TGF	PGF	TGA	PGA	+/–	GP	G	A	Pts	PIM	PP	SH	GW
1979-80	United States	Nat-Team	53	33	48	81	....	....	....	25	....	....	....	....	....	....	....	....	....	....	....	....	....	....	....	....	....	....
	United States	Olympics	7	5	6	11	....	....	....	6	....	....	....	....	....	....	....	....	....	....	....	....	....	....	....	....	....	....
	Pittsburgh Penguins	**NHL**	**17**	**3**	**5**	**8**	**3**	**4**	**7**	**4**	**1**	**0**	**1**	**32**	**9.4**	**12**	**6**	**10**	**0**	**–4**	**5**	**2**	**2**	**4**	**0**	**1**	**0**	**1**
1980-81	**Pittsburgh Penguins**	**NHL**	**73**	**10**	**23**	**33**	**8**	**16**	**24**	**50**	**0**	**0**	**1**	**109**	**9.2**	**61**	**14**	**71**	**28**	**+4**	**5**	**2**	**1**	**3**	**6**	**1**	**0**	**0**
	United States	WEC-A	5	0	2	2	....	....	....	2	....	....	....	....	....	....	....	....	....	....	....	....	....	....	....	....	....	....
1981-82	United States	C Cup	6	1	3	4	....	....	....	2	....	....	....	....	....	....	....	....	....	....	....	....	....	....	....	....	....	....
	Pittsburgh Penguins	**NHL**	**46**	**10**	**11**	**21**	**8**	**7**	**15**	**30**	**1**	**1**	**0**	**93**	**10.8**	**34**	**7**	**54**	**13**	**–14**	....	....	....	....	....	....	....	....
	Minnesota North Stars	**NHL**	**10**	**2**	**2**	**4**	**2**	**1**	**3**	**10**	**1**	**0**	**0**	**18**	**11.1**	**4**	**3**	**7**	**2**	**–4**	**4**	**2**	**0**	**2**	**0**	**1**	**0**	**0**
	United States	WEC-A	7	1	1	2	....	....	....	6	....	....	....	....	....	....	....	....	....	....	....	....	....	....	....	....	....	....
1982-83	**Hartford Whalers**	**NHL**	**73**	**31**	**38**	**69**	**25**	**26**	**51**	**28**	**5**	**3**	**5**	**167**	**18.6**	**92**	**22**	**116**	**41**	**–5**	....	....	....	....	....	....	....	....
1983-84	**Hartford Whalers**	**NHL**	**79**	**35**	**52**	**87**	**28**	**35**	**63**	**27**	**13**	**1**	**2**	**184**	**19.0**	**117**	**41**	**94**	**4**	**–14**	....	....	....	....	....	....	....	....
1984-85	United States	C Cup	6	2	3	5	....	....	....	0	....	....	....	....	....	....	....	....	....	....	....	....	....	....	....	....	....	....
	Hartford Whalers	**NHL**	**49**	**19**	**28**	**47**	**16**	**19**	**35**	**21**	**10**	**0**	**2**	**107**	**17.8**	**65**	**34**	**58**	**3**	**–24**	....	....	....	....	....	....	....	....
	St. Louis Blues	**NHL**	**17**	**4**	**6**	**10**	**3**	**4**	**7**	**2**	**2**	**0**	**0**	**36**	**11.1**	**16**	**6**	**19**	**7**	**–2**	**3**	**0**	**1**	**1**	**0**	**0**	**0**	**0**
	United States	WEC-A	10	4	1	5	....	....	....	6	....	....	....	....	....	....	....	....	....	....	....	....	....	....	....	....	....	....
1985-86	**New Jersey Devils**	**NHL**	**80**	**21**	**41**	**62**	**17**	**27**	**44**	**16**	**6**	**1**	**3**	**167**	**12.6**	**91**	**45**	**89**	**30**	**–13**	....	....	....	....	....	....	....	....
	United States	WEC-A	10	5	3	8	....	....	....	10	....	....	....	....	....	....	....	....	....	....	....	....	....	....	....	....	....	....
1986-87	**New Jersey Devils**	**NHL**	**68**	**25**	**26**	**51**	**22**	**19**	**41**	**22**	**11**	**2**	**0**	**193**	**13.0**	**86**	**57**	**81**	**31**	**–21**	....	....	....	....	....	....	....	....
	United States	WEC-A	10	3	6	9	....	....	....	8	....	....	....	....	....	....	....	....	....	....	....	....	....	....	....	....	....	....
1987-88	United States	C Cup	5	0	1	1	....	....	....	0	....	....	....	....	....	....	....	....	....	....	....	....	....	....	....	....	....	....
	New Jersey Devils	**NHL**	**54**	**14**	**19**	**33**	**12**	**14**	**26**	**14**	**2**	**3**	**3**	**121**	**11.6**	**60**	**33**	**53**	**16**	**–10**	**18**	**10**	**8**	**18**	**4**	**5**	**0**	**1**
1988-89	**New Jersey Devils**	**NHL**	**40**	**13**	**25**	**38**	**11**	**18**	**29**	**24**	**4**	**0**	**2**	**95**	**13.7**	**56**	**26**	**41**	**10**	**–1**	....	....	....	....	....	....	....	....
1989-90	**New Jersey Devils**	**NHL**	**63**	**16**	**29**	**45**	**14**	**21**	**35**	**12**	**4**	**0**	**1**	**82**	**19.5**	**72**	**16**	**71**	**7**	**–8**	**2**	**0**	**0**	**0**	**0**	**0**	**0**	**0**
	United States	WEC-A	9	2	3	5	....	....	....	2	....	....	....	....	....	....	....	....	....	....	....	....	....	....	....	....	....	....
1990-91	HC Milano	Italy	36	32	45	77	....	....	....	15	....	....	....	....	....	....	....	....	....	....	10	7	16	23	6	....	....	....
1991-92	HC Milano	Italy	2	1	3	4	....	....	....	0	....	....	....	....	....	....	....	....	....	....	....	....	....	....	....	....	....	....
	Zell-am-Zee	Austria	33	23	49	72	....	....	....	....	....	....	....	....	....	....	....	....	....	....	....	....	....	....	....	....	....	....
	NHL Totals		**669**	**203**	**305**	**508**	**169**	**211**	**380**	**260**	**60**	**11**	**20**	**1404**	**14.5**	**766**	**310**	**764**	**192**		**37**	**16**	**12**	**28**	**10**	**8**	**0**	**2**

WCHA First All-Star Team (1978, 1979) • NCAA West First All-American Team (1978, 1979)

Played in NHL All-Star Game (1984)

Traded to **Minnesota** by **Pittsburgh** for Minnesota's 2nd round choice (Tim Hrynewich) in 1982 Entry Draft, March 2, 1982. Traded to **Hartford** by **Minnesota** with Kent-Erik Andersson for Jordy Douglas and Hartford's 5th round choice (Jim Poner) in 1984 Entry Draft, October 1, 1982. Traded to **St. Louis** by **Hartford** with Greg Millen for Mike Luit and Jorgen Petterson, February 21, 1985. Traded to **New Jersey** by **St. Louis** for Shawn Evans and New Jersey's 5th round choice (Michael Wolak) in 1986 Entry Draft, September 19, 1985.

• JOHNSON, MATT

Matt Johnson LW – L. 6'5", 230 lbs. b: Welland, Ont., 11/23/1975. Los Angeles' 2nd choice, 33rd overall, in 1994 Entry Draft.

Season	Club	League	GP	G	A	Pts	AG	AA	APts	PIM	PP	SH	GW	S	%	TGF	PGF	TGA	PGA	+/–	GP	G	A	Pts	PIM	PP	SH	GW
1992-93	Peterborough Petes	OHL	66	8	17	25	....	....	....	211	....	....	....	....	....	....	....	....	....	....	16	1	1	2	56	....	....	....
1993-94	Peterborough Petes	OHL	50	13	24	37	....	....	....	233	....	....	....	....	....	....	....	....	....	....	....	....	....	....	....	....	....	....
1994-95	Peterborough Petes	OHL	14	1	2	3	....	....	....	43	....	....	....	....	....	....	....	....	....	....	....	....	....	....	....	....	....	....
	Los Angeles Kings	**NHL**	**14**	**1**	**0**	**1**	**2**	**0**	**2**	**102**	**0**	**0**	**0**	**4**	**25.0**	**1**	**0**	**1**	**0**	**0**	....	....	....	....	....	....	....	....
1995-96	**Los Angeles Kings**	**NHL**	**1**	**0**	**0**	**0**	**0**	**0**	**0**	**5**	**0**	**0**	**0**	**1**	**0.0**	**0**	**0**	**0**	**0**	**0**	....	....	....	....	....	....	....	....
	Phoenix Roadrunners	IHL	29	4	4	8	....	....	....	87	....	....	....	....	....	....	....	....	....	....	....	....	....	....	....	....	....	....
1996-97	**Los Angeles Kings**	**NHL**	**52**	**1**	**3**	**4**	**1**	**3**	**4**	**194**	**0**	**0**	**0**	**20**	**5.0**	**7**	**0**	**11**	**0**	**–4**	....	....	....	....	....	....	....	....
1997-98	**Los Angeles Kings**	**NHL**	**66**	**2**	**4**	**6**	**2**	**4**	**6**	**249**	**0**	**0**	**0**	**18**	**11.1**	**9**	**0**	**17**	**0**	**–8**	**4**	**0**	**0**	**0**	**6**	**0**	**0**	**0**
	NHL Totals		**133**	**4**	**7**	**11**	**5**	**7**	**12**	**550**	**0**	**0**	**0**	**43**	**9.3**	**17**	**0**	**29**	**0**		**4**	**0**	**0**	**0**	**6**	**0**	**0**	**0**

• JOHNSON, MIKE

Mike Johnson RW – R. 6'2", 190 lbs. b: Scarborough, Ont., 10/3/1974.

Season	Club	League	GP	G	A	Pts	AG	AA	APts	PIM	PP	SH	GW	S	%	TGF	PGF	TGA	PGA	+/–	GP	G	A	Pts	PIM	PP	SH	GW
1993-94	Bowling Green University	CCHA	38	6	14	20	....	....	....	18	....	....	....	....	....	....	....	....	....	....	....	....	....	....	....	....	....	....
1994-95	Bowling Green University	CCHA	37	16	33	49	....	....	....	35	....	....	....	....	....	....	....	....	....	....	....	....	....	....	....	....	....	....
1995-96	Bowling Green University	CCHA	30	12	19	31	....	....	....	22	....	....	....	....	....	....	....	....	....	....	....	....	....	....	....	....	....	....
1996-97	Bowling Green University	CCHA	38	30	32	62	....	....	....	46	....	....	....	....	....	....	....	....	....	....	....	....	....	....	....	....	....	....
	Toronto Maple Leafs	**NHL**	**13**	**2**	**2**	**4**	**2**	**2**	**4**	**4**	**0**	**1**	**1**	**27**	**7.4**	**8**	**1**	**11**	**2**	**–2**	....	....	....	....	....	....	....	....
1997-98	**Toronto Maple Leafs**	**NHL**	**82**	**15**	**32**	**47**	**18**	**31**	**49**	**24**	**5**	**0**	**0**	**143**	**10.5**	**71**	**23**	**65**	**13**	**–4**	....	....	....	....	....	....	....	....
	NHL Totals		**95**	**17**	**34**	**51**	**20**	**33**	**53**	**28**	**5**	**1**	**1**	**170**	**10.0**	**79**	**24**	**76**	**15**		....	....	....	....	....	....	....	....

NHL All-Rookie Team (1998)

Signed as a free agent by **Toronto**, March 16, 1997.

• JOHNSON, RYAN

Ryan Johnson C – L. 6'2", 185 lbs. b: Thunder Bay, Ont., 6/14/1976. Florida's 4th choice, 36th overall, in 1994 Entry Draft.

Season	Club	League	GP	G	A	Pts	AG	AA	APts	PIM	PP	SH	GW	S	%	TGF	PGF	TGA	PGA	+/–	GP	G	A	Pts	PIM	PP	SH	GW
1993-94	Thunder Bay Flyers	USHL	48	14	36	50	....	....	....	28	....	....	....	....	....	....	....	....	....	....	....	....	....	....	....	....	....	....
1994-95	University of North Dakota	WCHA	38	6	22	28	....	....	....	39	....	....	....	....	....	....	....	....	....	....	....	....	....	....	....	....	....	....
1995-96	University of North Dakota	WCHA	21	2	17	19	....	....	....	14	....	....	....	....	....	....	....	....	....	....	....	....	....	....	....	....	....	....
	Canada	Nat-Team	28	5	12	17	....	....	....	14	....	....	....	....	....	....	....	....	....	....	....	....	....	....	....	....	....	....
1996-97	Carolina Monarchs	AHL	79	18	24	42	....	....	....	28	....	....	....	....	....	....	....	....	....	....	....	....	....	....	....	....	....	....
1997-98	**Florida Panthers**	**NHL**	**10**	**0**	**2**	**2**	**0**	**2**	**2**	**0**	**0**	**0**	**0**	**6**	**0.0**	**2**	**0**	**9**	**3**	**–4**	....	....	....	....	....	....	....	....
	Beast of New Haven	AHL	64	19	48	67	....	....	....	12	....	....	....	....	....	....	....	....	....	....	3	0	1	1	0	....	....	....
	NHL Totals		**10**	**0**	**2**	**2**	**0**	**2**	**2**	**0**	**0**	**0**	**0**	**6**	**0.0**	**2**	**0**	**9**	**3**		....	....	....	....	....	....	....	....

• JOHNSON, TERRY

Terry Johnson D – L. 6'3", 210 lbs. b: Calgary, Alta., 11/28/1958.

Season	Club	League	GP	G	A	Pts	AG	AA	APts	PIM	PP	SH	GW	S	%	TGF	PGF	TGA	PGA	+/–	GP	G	A	Pts	PIM	PP	SH	GW
1975-76	Calgary Canucks	AJHL	55	3	13	16	....	....	....	100	....	....	....	....	....	....	....	....	....	....	....	....	....	....	....	....	....	....
1976-77	Calgary Canucks	AJHL	60	5	26	312	....	....	....	31	....	....	....	....	....	....	....	....	....	....	....	....	....	....	....	....	....	....
1977-78	Saskatoon Blades	WCJHL	70	2	20	22	....	....	....	195	....	....	....	....	....	....	....	....	....	....	....	....	....	....	....	....	....	....
1978-79	University of Calgary	CWUAA	24	2	4	6	....	....	....	81	....	....	....	....	....	....	....	....	....	....	3	1	0	1	2	....	....	....
1979-80	**Quebec Nordiques**	**NHL**	**3**	**0**	**0**	**0**	**0**	**0**	**0**	**2**	**0**	**0**	**0**	**0**	**0.0**	**1**	**0**	**1**	**0**	**0**	....	....	....	....	....	....	....	....
	Syracuse Firebirds	AHL	74	0	13	13	....	....	....	163	....	....	....	....	....	....	....	....	....	....	4	0	0	0	7	....	....	....
1980-81	**Quebec Nordiques**	**NHL**	**13**	**0**	**1**	**1**	**0**	**1**	**1**	**46**	**0**	**0**	**0**	**5**	**0.0**	**7**	**0**	**9**	**1**	**–1**	**2**	**0**	**0**	**0**	**0**	**0**	**0**	**0**
	Hershey Bears	AHL	63	1	7	8	....	....	....	207	....	....	....	....	....	....	....	....	....	....	9	0	1	1	14	....	....	....
1981-82	**Quebec Nordiques**	**NHL**	**6**	**0**	**1**	**1**	**0**	**1**	**1**	**5**	**0**	**0**	**0**	**0**	**0.0**	**2**	**0**	**3**	**0**	**–1**	....	....	....	....	....	....	....	....
	Fredericton Express	AHL	43	0	7	7	....	....	....	132	....	....	....	....	....	....	....	....	....	....	....	....	....	....	....	....	....	....
1982-83	**Quebec Nordiques**	**NHL**	**3**	**0**	**0**	**0**	**0**	**0**	**0**	**2**	**0**	**0**	**0**	**0**	**0.0**	**0**	**0**	**0**	**0**	**0**	....	....	....	....	....	....	....	....
	Fredericton Express	AHL	78	2	15	17	....	....	....	181	....	....	....	....	....	....	....	....	....	....	12	1	1	2	12	....	....	....
1983-84	**St. Louis Blues**	**NHL**	**65**	**2**	**6**	**8**	**2**	**4**	**6**	**143**	**0**	**0**	**0**	**38**	**5.3**	**51**	**1**	**78**	**33**	**+5**	**11**	**0**	**1**	**1**	**25**	**0**	**0**	**0**
1984-85	**St. Louis Blues**	**NHL**	**74**	**0**	**7**	**7**	**0**	**5**	**5**	**120**	....	....	....	....	....	....	....	....	....	....	**3**	**0**	**0**	**0**	**19**	....	....	....
1985-86	**St. Louis Blues**	**NHL**	**49**	**0**	**4**	**4**	**0**	**3**	**3**	**87**	**0**	**0**	**0**	**21**	**0.0**	**42**	**1**	**72**	**25**	**–6**	....	....	....	....	....	....	....	....
	Calgary Flames	**NHL**	**24**	**1**	**4**	**5**	**1**	**3**	**4**	**71**	**0**	**0**	**0**	**11**	**9.1**	**19**	**0**	**34**	**12**	**–3**	**17**	**0**	**3**	**3**	**64**	**0**	**0**	**0**
1986-87	**Toronto Maple Leafs**	**NHL**	**48**	**0**	**1**	**1**	**0**	**1**	**1**	**104**	**0**	**0**	**0**	**10**	**0.0**	**27**	**0**	**38**	**6**	**–5**	**2**	**0**	**0**	**0**	**0**	**0**	**0**	**0**
	Newmarket Saints	AHL	24	0	1	1	....	....	....	37	....	....	....	....	....	....	....	....	....	....	....	....	....	....	....	....	....	....
1987-88	Newmarket Saints	AHL	72	3	3	6	....	....	....	174	....	....	....	....	....	....	....	....	....	....	....	....	....	....	....	....	....	....
	Toronto Maple Leafs	**NHL**	....	....	....	....	....	....	....	....	....	....	....	....	....	....	....	....	....	....	**3**	**0**	**0**	**0**	**10**	....	....	....
	NHL Totals		**285**	**3**	**24**	**27**	**3**	**18**	**21**	**580**	**0**	**0**	**0**	**85**	**3.5**	**149**	**2**	**235**	**77**		**38**	**0**	**4**	**4**	**118**	**0**	**0**	**0**

Signed as a free agent by **Quebec**, October 1, 1978. Claimed by **St. Louis** from **Quebec** in Waiver Draft, October 3, 1983. Traded to **Calgary** by **St. Louis** with Joe Mullen and Rik Wilson for Ed Beers, Charlie Bourgeois and Gino Cavallini, February 1, 1986. Traded to **Toronto** by **Calgary** for Jim Korn, October 3, 1986.

• JOHNSTON, BERNIE

Bernie Johnston C – L. 5'11", 185 lbs. b: Toronto, Ont., 9/15/1956.

Season	Club	League	GP	G	A	Pts	AG	AA	APts	PIM	PP	SH	GW	S	%	TGF	PGF	TGA	PGA	+/–	GP	G	A	Pts	PIM	PP	SH	GW
1972-73	Ajax Waxers	OJHL	30	28	42	70	....	....	....	32	....	....	....	....	....	....	....	....	....	....	....	....	....	....	....	....	....	....
1973-74	Toronto Marlboros	OHA	65	10	11	22	....	....	....	21	....	....	....	....	....	....	....	....	....	....	....	....	....	....	....	....	....	....
1974-75	Toronto Marlboros	OHA	47	9	29	38	....	....	....	20	....	....	....	....	....	....	....	....	....	....	3	1	2	3	4	....	....	....
1975-76	Toronto Marlboros	OHA	60	22	39	61	....	....	....	44	....	....	....	....	....	....	....	....	....	....	10	0	4	4	8	....	....	....
1976-77	Syracuse Blazers	NAHL	73	53	71	124	....	....	....	40	....	....	....	....	....	....	....	....	....	....	9	1	9	10	2	....	....	....
1977-78	Maine Mariners	AHL	68	28	29	57	....	....	....	35	....	....	....	....	....	....	....	....	....	....	11	2	7	9	6	....	....	....
1978-79	Maine Mariners	AHL	70	29	*66	*95	....	....	....	40	....	....	....	....	....	....	....	....	....	....	10	2	5	7	8	....	....	....

			REGULAR SEASON																		PLAYOFFS							
Season	Club	League	GP	G	A	Pts	AG	AA	APts	PIM	PP	SH	GW	S	%	TGF	PGF	TGA	PGA	+/–	GP	G	A	Pts	PIM	PP	SH	GW
1979-80	Hartford Whalers	NHL	32	8	13	21	7	10	17	8	0	0	0	54	14.8	33	0	24	0	+9	3	0	1	1	0	0	0	0
	Springfield Indians	AHL	41	18	36	54	....	....	....	25	....	....	....	....	....	....	....	....	....	....	....	....	....	....	....	....	....	....
1980-81	Hartford Whalers	NHL	25	4	11	15	3	8	11	8	0	0	0	34	11.8	18	1	21	0	–4	....	....	....	....	....	....	....	....
	Binghamton Whalers	AHL	38	14	22	36	....	....	....	36	....	....	....	....	....	....	....	....	....	....	3	0	0	0	0	....	....	....
1981-82	Kloten	Switz.	38	24	22	46	....	....	....	....	....	....	....	....	....	....	....	....	....	....	....	....	....	....	....	....	....	....
	Maine Mariners	AHL	....	....	....	....	....	....	....	....	....	....	....	....	....	....	....	....	....	....	4	0	5	5	0	....	....	....
1982-83	Maine Mariners	AHL	11	7	2	9	....	....	....	2	....	....	....	....	....	....	....	....	....	....	8	4	1	5	4	....	....	....
1983-84			STATISTICS NOT AVAILABLE																									
1984-85	Basel	Switz.	32	33	46	79	....	....	....	....	....	....	....	....	....	....	....	....	....	....	....	....	....	....	....	....	....	....
1985-86	Hershey Bears	AHL	15	2	9	11	....	....	....	6	....	....	....	....	....	....	....	....	....	....	18	2	3	5	11	....	....	....
	NHL Totals		57	12	24	36	10	18	28	16	0	0	0	88	13.6	51	1	45	0		3	0	1	1	0	0	0	0

AHL First All-Star Team (1979) • Won John B. Sollenberger Trophy (Top Scorer - AHL) (1979) • Won Fred T. Hunt Memorial Trophy (Sportsmanship - AHL) (1979)

Signed as a free agent by **Philadelphia**, September 28, 1977. Claimed by **Hartford** from **Philadelphia** in Expansion Draft, June 13, 1979.

• JOHNSTON, GREG

Greg Johnston RW – R. 6'1", 205 lbs. b: Barrie, Ont., 1/14/1965. Boston's 4th choice, 42nd overall, in 1983 Entry Draft.

Season	Club	League	GP	G	A	Pts	AG	AA	APts	PIM	PP	SH	GW	S	%	TGF	PGF	TGA	PGA	+/–	GP	G	A	Pts	PIM	PP	SH	GW
1981-82	Barrie Colts	OJHL	42	31	46	77	....	....	....	74	....	....	....	....	....	....	....	....	....	....	....	....	....	....	....	....	....	....
1982-83	Toronto Marlboros	OHL	58	18	19	37	....	....	....	58	....	....	....	....	....	....	....	....	....	....	4	1	0	1	4	....	....	....
1983-84	Toronto Marlboros	OHL	57	38	35	73	....	....	....	67	....	....	....	....	....	....	....	....	....	....	9	4	2	6	13	....	....	....
	Boston Bruins	NHL	15	2	1	3	2	1	3	2	0	0	1	15	13.3	8	1	10	0	–3	....	....	....	....	....	....	....	....
1984-85	Toronto Marlboros	OHL	42	22	28	50	....	....	....	55	....	....	....	....	....	....	....	....	....	....	5	1	3	4	4	....	....	....
	Canada	WJC-A	7	2	0	2	....	....	....	2	....	....	....	....	....	....	....	....	....	....	....	....	....	....	....	....	....	....
	Boston Bruins	NHL	6	0	0	0	0	0	0	0	0	0	0	1	0.0	1	0	2	0	–1	....	....	....	....	....	....	....	....
	Hershey Bears	AHL	3	1	0	1	....	....	....	0	....	....	....	....	....	....	....	....	....	....	....	....	....	....	....	....	....	....
1985-86	Boston Bruins	NHL	20	0	2	2	0	1	1	0	0	0	0	11	0.0	5	0	12	6	–1	....	....	....	....	....	....	....	....
	Moncton Golden Flames	AHL	60	19	26	45	....	....	....	56	....	....	....	....	....	....	....	....	....	....	10	4	6	10	4	....	....	....
1986-87	Boston Bruins	NHL	76	12	15	27	10	11	21	79	0	0	1	131	9.2	45	3	75	26	–7	4	0	0	0	0	0	0	0
1987-88	Maine Mariners	AHL	75	21	32	53	....	....	....	106	....	....	....	....	....	....	....	....	....	....	10	6	4	10	23	....	....	....
	Boston Bruins	NHL	....	....	....	....	....	....	....	....	....	....	....	....	....	....	....	....	....	....	3	0	1	1	2	....	....	....
1988-89	Boston Bruins	NHL	57	11	9	20	9	6	15	32	0	1	5	89	12.4	39	2	48	18	+7	10	1	0	1	6	0	1	0
	Maine Mariners	AHL	15	5	7	12	....	....	....	31	....	....	....	....	....	....	....	....	....	....	....	....	....	....	....	....	....	....
1989-90	Boston Bruins	NHL	9	1	1	2	1	1	2	6	0	0	0	9	11.1	2	0	3	0	–1	5	1	0	1	4	0	0	1
	Maine Mariners	AHL	52	16	26	42	....	....	....	45	....	....	....	....	....	....	....	....	....	....	....	....	....	....	....	....	....	....
1990-91	Toronto Maple Leafs	NHL	1	0	0	0	0	0	0	0	0	0	0	0	0.0	0	0	0	0	0	....	....	....	....	....	....	....	....
	Newmarket Saints	AHL	73	32	50	82	....	....	....	54	....	....	....	....	....	....	....	....	....	....	....	....	....	....	....	....	....	....
1991-92	Toronto Maple Leafs	NHL	3	0	1	1	0	1	1	5	0	0	0	2	0.0	2	0	3	0	–1	....	....	....	....	....	....	....	....
	St. John's Maple Leafs	AHL	63	28	45	73	....	....	....	33	....	....	....	....	....	....	....	....	....	....	16	8	6	14	10	....	....	....
1992-93	Sauerland	Germany	47	49	59	108	....	....	....	70	....	....	....	....	....	....	....	....	....	....	....	....	....	....	....	....	....	....
1993-94	Sauerland	Germany	51	40	60	100	....	....	....	74	....	....	....	....	....	....	....	....	....	....	....	....	....	....	....	....	....	....
1994-95	Kassel Huskies	Germany	42	17	27	44	....	....	....	26	....	....	....	....	....	....	....	....	....	....	9	4	6	10	6	....	....	....
1995-96	Kassel Huskies	Germany	49	16	23	39	....	....	....	75	....	....	....	....	....	....	....	....	....	....	8	0	1	1	12	....	....	....
1996-97	Kassel Huskies	Germany	49	19	22	41	....	....	....	98	....	....	....	....	....	....	....	....	....	....	10	*8	4	12	14	....	....	....
1997-98	Kassel Huskies	EuroHL	6	2	2	4	....	....	....	6	....	....	....	....	....	....	....	....	....	....	....	....	....	....	....	....	....	....
	Kassel Huskies	Germany	43	9	28	37	....	....	....	73	....	....	....	....	....	....	....	....	....	....	....	....	....	....	....	....	....	....
	NHL Totals		187	26	29	55	22	21	43	124	0	1	7	258	10.1	102	6	153	50		22	2	1	3	12	0	1	1

Traded to **NY Rangers** by **Boston** with future considerations for Chris Nilan, June 28, 1990. Traded to **Toronto** by **NY Rangers** for Tie Domi and Mark LaForest, June 28, 1990.

• JOHNSTON, JAY

Jay Johnston D – L. 5'11", 195 lbs. b: Hamilton, Ont., 2/28/1958. Washington's 6th choice, 45th overall, in 1978 Amateur Draft.

Season	Club	League	GP	G	A	Pts	AG	AA	APts	PIM	PP	SH	GW	S	%	TGF	PGF	TGA	PGA	+/–	GP	G	A	Pts	PIM	PP	SH	GW
1975-76	Hamilton Tigers	OJHL	36	1	25	26	....	....	....	70	....	....	....	....	....	....	....	....	....	....	....	....	....	....	....	....	....	....
1976-77	St. Catharines Fincups	OHA	65	8	20	28	....	....	....	146	....	....	....	....	....	....	....	....	....	....	14	0	6	6	49	....	....	....
1977-78	Hamilton Fincups	OHA	48	2	12	14	....	....	....	163	....	....	....	....	....	....	....	....	....	....	18	0	3	3	59	....	....	....
1978-79	Port Huron Flags	IHL	75	5	19	24	....	....	....	409	....	....	....	....	....	....	....	....	....	....	0	0	1	1	21	....	....	....
1979-80	Hershey Bears	AHL	60	3	20	23	....	....	....	220	....	....	....	....	....	....	....	....	....	....	14	0	4	4	42	....	....	....
1980-81	Washington Capitals	NHL	2	0	0	0	0	0	0	9	0	0	0	0	0.0	1	0	1	0	0	....	....	....	....	....	....	....	....
	Hershey Bears	AHL	61	1	11	12	....	....	....	187	....	....	....	....	....	....	....	....	....	....	4	0	0	0	4	....	....	....
1981-82	Washington Capitals	NHL	6	0	0	0	0	0	0	4	0	0	0	3	0.0	1	0	5	2	–2	....	....	....	....	....	....	....	....
	Hershey Bears	AHL	67	4	9	13	....	....	....	228	....	....	....	....	....	....	....	....	....	....	5	0	0	0	22	....	....	....
1982-83	Hershey Bears	AHL	76	3	13	16	....	....	....	148	....	....	....	....	....	....	....	....	....	....	5	0	0	0	14	....	....	....
1983-84	Hershey Bears	AHL	69	1	9	10	....	....	....	231	....	....	....	....	....	....	....	....	....	....	....	....	....	....	....	....	....	....
1984-85	Fort Wayne Komets	IHL	69	1	12	13	....	....	....	211	....	....	....	....	....	....	....	....	....	....	13	1	4	5	36	....	....	....
1985-86	Fort Wayne Komets	IHL	78	1	13	14	....	....	....	176	....	....	....	....	....	....	....	....	....	....	15	0	1	1	47	....	....	....
1986-87	Fort Wayne Komets	IHL	31	0	8	8	....	....	....	92	....	....	....	....	....	....	....	....	....	....	....	....	....	....	....	....	....	....
	NHL Totals		8	0	0	0	0	0	0	13	0	0	0	3	0.0	2	0	6	2		....	....	....	....	....	....	....	....

• JOHNSTON, JOEY

Joey Johnston LW – L. 5'10", 180 lbs. b: Peterborough, Ont., 3/3/1949. NY Rangers' 2nd choice, 8th overall, in 1966 Amateur Draft.

Season	Club	League	GP	G	A	Pts	AG	AA	APts	PIM	PP	SH	GW	S	%	TGF	PGF	TGA	PGA	+/–	GP	G	A	Pts	PIM	PP	SH	GW
1964-65	Peterborough Petes	OHA	3	0	0	0	....	....	....	0	....	....	....	....	....	....	....	....	....	....	....	....	....	....	....	....	....	....
1965-66	Peterborough Petes	OHA	44	8	15	23	....	....	....	91	....	....	....	....	....	....	....	....	....	....	6	0	0	0	10	....	....	....
1966-67	Peterborough Petes	OHA	32	8	19	27	....	....	....	114	....	....	....	....	....	....	....	....	....	....	6	1	3	4	28	....	....	....
1967-68	Buffalo Bisons	AHL	1	0	0	0	....	....	....	0	....	....	....	....	....	....	....	....	....	....	....	....	....	....	....	....	....	....
	Omaha Knights	CHL	70	24	22	46	....	....	....	131	....	....	....	....	....	....	....	....	....	....	....	....	....	....	....	....	....	....
1968-69	Minnesota North Stars	NHL	11	1	0	1	1	0	1	6	0	0	0	17	5.9	2	0	3	0	–1	....	....	....	....	....	....	....	....
	Memphis South Stars	CHL	58	20	37	57	....	....	....	91	....	....	....	....	....	....	....	....	....	....	....	....	....	....	....	....	....	....
1969-70	Iowa Stars	CHL	62	20	37	57	....	....	....	115	....	....	....	....	....	....	....	....	....	....	11	4	6	10	38	....	....	....
1970-71	Cleveland Barons	AHL	72	27	47	74	....	....	....	142	....	....	....	....	....	....	....	....	....	....	8	7	4	11	24	....	....	....
1971-72	California Golden Seals	NHL	77	15	17	32	16	15	31	107	0	0	3	154	9.7	49	3	96	22	–28	....	....	....	....	....	....	....	....
1972-73	California Golden Seals	NHL	71	28	21	49	28	18	46	62	8	1	2	170	16.5	74	20	81	8	–19	....	....	....	....	....	....	....	....
1973-74	California Golden Seals	NHL	78	27	40	67	28	35	63	67	10	2	0	202	13.4	83	21	105	6	–37	....	....	....	....	....	....	....	....
1974-75	California Golden Seals	NHL	62	14	23	37	13	18	31	72	5	0	0	133	10.5	47	19	63	5	–30	....	....	....	....	....	....	....	....
1975-76	Chicago Black Hawks	NHL	32	0	5	5	0	4	4	6	0	0	0	20	0.0	9	4	11	1	–5	....	....	....	....	....	....	....	....
	Dallas Black Hawks	CHL	11	4	2	6	....	....	....	4	....	....	....	....	....	....	....	....	....	....	....	....	....	....	....	....	....	....
	NHL Totals		331	85	106	191	86	90	176	320	23	3	5	696	12.2	264	67	359	42		....	....	....	....	....	....	....	....

AHL First All-Star Team (1971)

Played in NHL All-Star Game (1973, 1974, 1975)

Traded to **Minnesota** by **NY Rangers** with Wayne Hillman and Dan Seguin for Dave Balon, June 12, 1968. Traded to **California** by **Minnesota** with Walt McKechnie for Dennis Hextall, May 20, 1971. Traded to **Chicago** by **California** for Jim Pappin and Chicago's 3rd round choice (Guy Lash) in 1977 Amateur Draft, June 1, 1975.

• JOHNSTON, LARRY

Larry Johnston D – R. 5'11", 195 lbs. b: Kitchener, Ont., 7/20/1943.

Season	Club	League	GP	G	A	Pts	AG	AA	APts	PIM	PP	SH	GW	S	%	TGF	PGF	TGA	PGA	+/–	GP	G	A	Pts	PIM	PP	SH	GW
1962-63	Waterloo Warriors	OJHL	STATISTICS NOT AVAILABLE																									
1963-64	Johnstown Jets	EHL	71	7	39	46	....	....	....	*356	....	....	....	....	....	....	....	....	....	....	10	3	5	8	*50	....	....	....
1964-65	Tulsa Oilers	CHL	57	4	16	20	....	....	....	*262	....	....	....	....	....	....	....	....	....	....	12	0	4	4	41	....	....	....
1965-66	Springfield Indians	AHL	29	2	5	7	....	....	....	58	....	....	....	....	....	....	....	....	....	....	....	....	....	....	....	....	....	....
	Tulsa Oilers	CHL	36	2	6	8	....	....	....	129	....	....	....	....	....	....	....	....	....	....	10	2	2	4	*20	....	....	....
1966-67	Springfield Indians	AHL	59	4	14	18	....	....	....	93	....	....	....	....	....	....	....	....	....	....	....	....	....	....	....	....	....	....
1967-68	Los Angeles Kings	NHL	4	0	0	0	0	0	0	4	0	0	0	2	0.0	0	0	8	1	–7	....	....	....	....	....	....	....	....
	Springfield Kings	AHL	60	2	22	24	....	....	....	*197	....	....	....	....	....	....	....	....	....	....	4	0	2	2	22	....	....	....
1968-69	Springfield Kings	AHL	74	3	21	24	....	....	....	*240	....	....	....	....	....	....	....	....	....	....	....	....	....	....	....	....	....	....
1969-70	Springfield Kings	AHL	52	3	24	27	....	....	....	150	....	....	....	....	....	....	....	....	....	....	....	....	....	....	....	....	....	....
	Fort Worth Wings	CHL	13	1	0	1	....	....	....	60	....	....	....	....	....	....	....	....	....	....	7	0	1	1	7	....	....	....
1970-71	Baltimore Clippers	AHL	58	2	14	16	....	....	....	198	....	....	....	....	....	....	....	....	....	....	6	0	1	1	12	....	....	....
1971-72	Detroit Red Wings	NHL	65	4	20	24	4	18	22	111	0	0	0	59	6.8	87	0	83	16	+20	....	....	....	....	....	....	....	....
	Tidewater Wings	AHL	12	1	1	2	....	....	....	45	....	....	....	....	....	....	....	....	....	....	....	....	....	....	....	....	....	....
1972-73	Detroit Red Wings	NHL	73	1	12	13	1	10	11	169	0	0	1	53	1.9	79	0	87	14	+6	....	....	....	....	....	....	....	....

			REGULAR SEASON																		PLAYOFFS							
Season	Club	League	GP	G	A	Pts	AG	AA	APts	PIM	PP	SH	GW	S	%	TGF	PGF	TGA	PGA	+/-	GP	G	A	Pts	PIM	PP	SH	GW
1973-74	**Detroit Red Wings**	**NHL**	65	2	12	14	2	10	12	139	0	0	1	47	4.3	67	0	116	23	−26	....	....	....	....	....	....	....	....
1974-75	Michigan-Baltimore	WHA	49	0	9	9	....	....	....	93	....	....	....	....	....	....	....	....	....	....	....	....	....	....	....	....	....	....
	Kansas City Scouts	**NHL**	16	0	7	7	0	5	5	10	0	0	0	12	0.0	16	1	36	4	−17	....	....	....	....	....	....	....	....
1975-76	**Kansas City Scouts**	**NHL**	72	2	10	12	2	8	10	112	1	0	0	77	2.6	64	8	150	33	−61	....	....	....	....	....	....	....	....
1976-77	**Colorado Rockies**	**NHL**	25	0	3	3	0	2	2	35	0	0	0	22	0.0	13	0	42	4	−25	....	....	....	....	....	....	....	....
	Maine Nordiques	NAHL	51	4	22	26	....	....	....	62	....	....	....	....	....	....	....	....	....	....	....	....	....	....	....	....	....	....
	NHL Totals		320	9	64	73	9	53	62	580	1	0	2	272	3.3	326	9	522	95		....	....	....	....	....	....	....	....
	Other Major League Totals		49	0	9	9	....	....	....	93	....	....	....	....	....	....	....	....	....		....	....	....	....	....	....	....	....

Traded to **Springfield** (AHL) by **Toronto** with Bill Smith for Bruce Gamble, September, 1965. NHL rights transferred to **LA Kings** after NHL club purchased **Springfield** (AHL) franchise, May, 1967. Traded to **Detroit** by **LA Kings** with Dale Rolfe and Gary Croteau for Garry Monahan and Brian Gibbons, February 20, 1970. Signed as a free agent by **Michigan** (WHA), July, 1974. Signed as a free agent by **Kansas City** after **Michigan-Baltimore** (WHA) franchise folded, March 1, 1975. Transferred to **Colorado** after **Kansas City** franchise relocated, June, 1976.

• JOHNSTON, MARSHALL

Marshall Johnston D – R. 5'11", 175 lbs. b: Birch Hills, Sask., 6/6/1941.

Season	Club	League	GP	G	A	Pts	AG	AA	APts	PIM	PP	SH	GW	S	%	TGF	PGF	TGA	PGA	+/-	GP	G	A	Pts	PIM	PP	SH	GW
1957-58	Prince Albert Mintos	SJHL	49	20	29	49	....	....	....	21	....	....	....	....	....	....	....	....	....	....	5	0	0	0	2	....	....	....
1958-59	Prince Albert Mintos	SJHL	48	31	24	55	....	....	....	17	....	....	....	....	....	....	....	....	....	....	5	1	0	1	4	....	....	....
1959-60	University of Denver	WCHA	DID NOT PLAY – FRESHMAN																									
1960-61	University of Denver	WCHA	....	4	7	11	....	....	....	....	....	....	....	....	....	....	....	....	....	....	....	....	....	....	....	....	....	....
1961-62	University of Denver	WCHA	12	7	1	8	....	....	....	....	....	....	....	....	....	....	....	....	....	....	....	....	....	....	....	....	....	....
1962-63	University of Denver	WCHA	....	6	12	18	....	....	....	....	....	....	....	....	....	....	....	....	....	....	....	....	....	....	....	....	....	....
1963-64	Canada	Nat-Team	STATISTICS NOT AVAILABLE																									
	Canada	Olympics	7	0	3	3				6											....	....	....	....	....	....	....	....
1964-65	Canada	Nat-Team	STATISTICS NOT AVAILABLE																									
	Winnipeg Maroons	SSHL	2	1	2	3	....	....	....	0	....	....	....	....	....	....	....	....	....	....	....	....	....	....	....	....	....	....
1965-66	Canada	Nat-Team	STATISTICS NOT AVAILABLE																									
	Canada	WEC-A	7	3	3	6	....	....	....	4	....	....	....	....	....	....	....	....	....	....	....	....	....	....	....	....	....	....
1966-67	Canada	Nat-Team	STATISTICS NOT AVAILABLE																									
	Canada	WEC-A	7	2	2	4	....	....	....	0	....	....	....	....	....	....	....	....	....	....	....	....	....	....	....	....	....	....
1967-68	Ottawa Nationals	OHA Sr.	....	5	13	18	....	....	....	10	....	....	....	....	....	....	....	....	....	....	....	....	....	....	....	....	....	....
	Canada	Olympics	7	2	5	7	....	....	....	2	....	....	....	....	....	....	....	....	....	....	....	....	....	....	....	....	....	....
	Minnesota North Stars	**NHL**	7	0	0	0	0	0	0	0	0	0	0	5	0.0	4	2	1	0	+1	....	....	....	....	....	....	....	....
1968-69	**Minnesota North Stars**	**NHL**	13	0	0	0	0	0	0	2	0	0	0	12	0.0	1	0	3	0	−2	....	....	....	....	....	....	....	....
	Cleveland Barons	AHL	53	6	20	26	....	....	....	31	....	....	....	....	....	....	....	....	....	....	5	0	4	4	4	....	....	....
1969-70	**Minnesota North Stars**	**NHL**	28	0	5	5	0	5	5	14	0	0	0	48	0.0	31	5	37	12	+1	6	0	0	0	2	0	0	0
	Iowa Stars	CHL	50	1	25	26	....	....	....	42	....	....	....	....	....	....	....	....	....	....	....	....	....	....	....	....	....	....
1970-71	**Minnesota North Stars**	**NHL**	1	0	0	0	0	0	0	0	0	0	0	0	0.0	0	0	0	0	0	....	....	....	....	....	....	....	....
	Cleveland Barons	AHL	69	11	45	56	....	....	....	45	....	....	....	....	....	....	....	....	....	....	8	0	6	6	4	....	....	....
1971-72	**California Golden Seals**	**NHL**	74	2	11	13	2	10	12	4	2	0	0	52	3.8	49	17	78	19	−27	....	....	....	....	....	....	....	....
1972-73	**California Golden Seals**	**NHL**	78	10	20	30	10	17	27	14	0	1	0	93	10.8	69	25	73	28	−1	....	....	....	....	....	....	....	....
1973-74	**California Golden Seals**	**NHL**	50	2	16	18	2	14	16	24	2	0	0	51	3.9	50	12	101	18	−45	....	....	....	....	....	....	....	....
	NHL Totals		251	14	52	66	14	46	60	58	4	1	0	261	5.4	204	61	293	77		6	0	0	0	2	0	0	0

AHL First All-Star Team (1971) • Won Eddie Shore Award (Outstanding Defenseman - AHL) (1971)

Rights traded to **Minnesota** by **NY Rangers** for cash, June, 1967. Traded to **Montreal** by **Minnesota** to complete transaction that sent Danny Grant to Minnesota (June 10, 1968), May 25, 1971. Minnesota received the rights to Bob Murdoch. Traded to **California** by **Montreal** for cash, August 31, 1971.

• JOHNSTON, RANDY

Randy Johnston D – L. 6', 190 lbs. b: Brampton, Ont., 6/2/1958. NY Islanders' 2nd choice, 34th overall, in 1978 Amateur Draft.

Season	Club	League	GP	G	A	Pts	AG	AA	APts	PIM	PP	SH	GW	S	%	TGF	PGF	TGA	PGA	+/-	GP	G	A	Pts	PIM	PP	SH	GW
1975-76	Peterborough Petes	OHA	46	0	5	5	....	....	....	57	....	....	....	....	....	....	....	....	....	....	....	....	....	....	....	....	....	....
1976-77	Peterborough Petes	OHA	66	4	21	25	....	....	....	141	....	....	....	....	....	....	....	....	....	....	4	0	0	0	8	....	....	....
1977-78	Peterborough Petes	OHA	63	4	31	35	....	....	....	79	....	....	....	....	....	....	....	....	....	....	20	1	4	5	34	....	....	....
1978-79	Fort Worth Texans	CHL	76	3	15	18	....	....	....	80	....	....	....	....	....	....	....	....	....	....	5	0	0	0	6	....	....	....
1979-80	**New York Islanders**	**NHL**	4	0	0	0	0	0	0	4	0	0	0	2	0.0	2	0	4	0	−2	....	....	....	....	....	....	....	....
	Indianapolis Checkers	CHL	69	3	27	30	....	....	....	45	....	....	....	....	....	....	....	....	....	....	7	1	0	1	18	....	....	....
1980-81	Indianapolis Checkers	CHL	76	3	20	23	....	....	....	69	....	....	....	....	....	....	....	....	....	....	5	0	0	0	6	....	....	....
1981-82	Indianapolis Checkers	CHL	78	7	34	41	....	....	....	71	....	....	....	....	....	....	....	....	....	....	11	1	5	6	17	....	....	....
1982-83	Indianapolis Checkers	CHL	66	2	15	17	....	....	....	63	....	....	....	....	....	....	....	....	....	....	10	1	2	3	16	....	....	....
	NHL Totals		4	0	0	0	0	0	0	4	0	0	0	2	0.0	2	0	4	0		....	....	....	....	....	....	....	....

• JOHNSTONE, EDDIE

Eddie Johnstone RW – R. 5'9", 175 lbs. b: Brandon, Man., 3/2/1954. NY Rangers' 6th choice, 104th overall, in 1974 Amateur Draft.

Season	Club	League	GP	G	A	Pts	AG	AA	APts	PIM	PP	SH	GW	S	%	TGF	PGF	TGA	PGA	+/-	GP	G	A	Pts	PIM	PP	SH	GW
1970-71	Vernon Essos	BCJHL	50	45	49	94	....	....	....	79	....	....	....	....	....	....	....	....	....	....	....	....	....	....	....	....	....	....
1971-72	Medicine Hat Tigers	WCJHL	27	14	15	29	....	....	....	46	....	....	....	....	....	....	....	....	....	....	....	....	....	....	....	....	....	....
1972-73	Medicine Hat Tigers	WCJHL	68	58	44	102	....	....	....	70	....	....	....	....	....	....	....	....	....	....	17	13	10	23	21	....	....	....
1973-74	Medicine Hat Tigers	WCJHL	68	64	54	118	....	....	....	164	....	....	....	....	....	....	....	....	....	....	5	5	0	5	10	....	....	....
1974-75	Michigan-Baltimore	WHA	23	4	4	8	....	....	....	43	....	....	....	....	....	....	....	....	....	....	....	....	....	....	....	....	....	....
	Greensboro Generals	SHL	25	21	25	46	....	....	....	21	....	....	....	....	....	....	....	....	....	....	....	....	....	....	....	....	....	....
	Providence Reds	AHL	23	7	10	17	....	....	....	35	....	....	....	....	....	....	....	....	....	....	5	0	0	0	0	....	....	....
1975-76	**New York Rangers**	**NHL**	10	2	1	3	2	1	3	4	0	0	0	6	33.3	5	0	1	0	+4	....	....	....	....	....	....	....	....
	Providence Reds	AHL	58	23	33	56	....	....	....	102	....	....	....	....	....	....	....	....	....	....	3	0	0	0	14	....	....	....
1976-77	New Haven Nighthawks	AHL	80	40	58	98	....	....	....	79	....	....	....	....	....	....	....	....	....	....	6	3	6	9	7	....	....	....
1977-78	**New York Rangers**	**NHL**	53	13	13	26	13	11	24	44	2	1	0	93	14.0	38	11	40	10	−3	....	....	....	....	....	....	....	....
	New Haven Nighthawks	AHL	17	10	12	22	....	....	....	20	....	....	....	....	....	....	....	....	....	....	....	....	....	....	....	....	....	....
1978-79	**New York Rangers**	**NHL**	30	5	3	8	5	2	7	27	0	0	0	18	27.8	11	1	19	4	−5	17	5	0	5	10	0	1	1
1979-80	**New York Rangers**	**NHL**	78	14	21	35	13	16	29	60	0	0	3	121	11.6	59	4	69	17	+3	9	0	1	1	25	0	0	0
1980-81	**New York Rangers**	**NHL**	80	30	38	68	25	27	52	100	4	3	5	187	16.0	97	21	85	24	+15	8	2	2	4	4	0	0	1
1981-82	**New York Rangers**	**NHL**	68	30	28	58	24	19	43	57	4	0	3	141	21.3	92	17	89	9	−5	10	2	6	8	25	1	0	0
1982-83	**New York Rangers**	**NHL**	52	15	21	36	12	14	26	27	2	1	1	98	15.3	63	23	50	6	−4	9	4	1	5	19	1	1	0
1983-84	**Detroit Red Wings**	**NHL**	46	12	11	23	10	7	17	54	4	0	0	50	24.0	39	8	34	6	+3	2	0	0	0	0	0	0	0
1984-85	Adirondack Red Wings	AHL	69	27	28	55	....	....	....	70	....	....	....	....	....	....	....	....	....	....	....	....	....	....	....	....	....	....
1985-86	**Detroit Red Wings**	**NHL**	3	1	0	1	1	0	1	2	0	0	0	3	33.3	1	0	2	1	0	....	....	....	....	....	....	....	....
	Adirondack Red Wings	AHL	62	29	31	60	....	....	....	74	....	....	....	....	....	....	....	....	....	....	17	5	7	12	4	....	....	....
1986-87	**Detroit Red Wings**	**NHL**	6	0	0	0	0	0	0	0	0	0	0	0	0.0	2	0	2	1	+1	....	....	....	....	....	....	....	....
	Adirondack Red Wings	AHL	61	30	22	52	....	....	....	83	....	....	....	....	....	....	....	....	....	....	5	1	0	1	2	....	....	....
	NHL Totals		426	122	136	258	105	97	202	375	16	5	12	717	17.0	407	85	391	78		55	13	10	23	83	2	2	2
	Other Major League Totals		23	4	4	8	....	....	....	43	....	....	....	....	....	....	....	....	....		....	....	....	....	....	....	....	....

AHL First All-Star Team (1977)

Played in NHL All-Star Game (1981)

Selected by **Michigan** (WHA) in 1974 WHA Amateur Draft, June, 1974. Claimed by **NY Rangers** as a fill-in during Expansion Draft, June 13, 1979. Traded to **Detroit** by **NY Rangers** with Eddie Mio and Ron Duguay for Mike Blaisdell, Mark Osborne and Willie Huber, June 13, 1983.

• JOKINEN, OLLI

Olli Jokinen C – L. 6'2", 198 lbs. b: Kuopio, Finland, 12/5/1978. Los Angeles' 1st choice, 3rd overall, in 1997 Entry Draft.

Season	Club	League	GP	G	A	Pts	AG	AA	APts	PIM	PP	SH	GW	S	%	TGF	PGF	TGA	PGA	+/-	GP	G	A	Pts	PIM	PP	SH	GW
1995-96	KalPa Kuopio	Finland	25	20	14	34	....	....	....	47	....	....	....	....	....	....	....	....	....	....	7	4	4	8	20	....	....	....
	KalPa Kuopio	Finland	15	1	1	2	....	....	....	2	....	....	....	....	....	....	....	....	....	....	....	....	....	....	....	....	....	....
1996-97	HIFK Helsinki	Finland	50	14	27	41	....	....	....	88	....	....	....	....	....	....	....	....	....	....	....	....	....	....	....	....	....	....
	Finland	WJC-A	6	5	0	5	....	....	....	12	....	....	....	....	....	....	....	....	....	....	....	....	....	....	....	....	....	....
	Finland	WC-A	8	4	2	6	....	....	....	6	....	....	....	....	....	....	....	....	....	....	....	....	....	....	....	....	....	....
1997-98	HIFK Helsinki	Finland	30	11	28	39	....	....	....	8	....	....	....	....	....	....	....	....	....	....	9	7	2	9	2	....	....	....
	Finland	WJC-A	7	4	6	10	....	....	....	6	....	....	....	....	....	....	....	....	....	....	....	....	....	....	....	....	....	....
	Los Angeles Kings	**NHL**	8	0	0	0	0	0	0	6	0	0	0	12	0.0	2	0	7	0	−5	....	....	....	....	....	....	....	....
	Finland	WC-A	10	0	1	1	....	....	....	6	....	....	....	....	....	....	....	....	....	....	....	....	....	....	....	....	....	....
	NHL Totals		8	0	0	0	0	0	0	6	0	0	0	12	0.0	2	0	7	0		....	....	....	....	....	....	....	....

Finnish Rookie of the Year (1997) • WJC-A All-Star Team (1998) • Named Best Forward at WJC-A (1998)

			REGULAR SEASON																		PLAYOFFS							
Season	Club	League	GP	G	A	Pts	AG	AA	APts	PIM	PP	SH	GW	S	%	TGF	PGF	TGA	PGA	+/-	GP	G	A	Pts	PIM	PP	SH	GW

• JOLY, GREG

Greg Joly D – L. 6'1", 190 lbs. b: Calgary, Alta., 5/30/1954. Washington's 1st choice, 1st overall, in 1974 Amateur Draft.

Season	Club	League	GP	G	A	Pts	AG	AA	APts	PIM	PP	SH	GW	S	%	TGF	PGF	TGA	PGA	+/-	GP	G	A	Pts	PIM	PP	SH	GW
1971-72	Regina Pats	WCJHL	67	6	38	44	....	....	....	41	....	....	....	....	....	....	....	....	....	....	....	....	....	....	....	....	....	....
1972-73	Regina Pats	WCJHL	67	14	54	68	....	....	....	94	....	....	....	....	....	....	....	....	....	....	....	....	....	....	....	....	....	....
1973-74	Regina Pats	WCJHL	67	21	71	92	....	....	....	103	....	....	....	....	....	....	....	....	....	....	....	....	....	....	....	....	....	....
1974-75	**Washington Capitals**	**NHL**	44	1	7	8	1	5	6	44	1	0	0	72	1.4	49	19	107	9	-68	....	....	....	....	....	....	....	....
1975-76	**Washington Capitals**	**NHL**	54	8	17	25	7	13	20	28	3	1	1	81	9.9	62	17	105	14	-46	....	....	....	....	....	....	....	....
	Richmond Robins	AHL	3	3	2	5	....	....	....	4	....	....	....	....	....	....	....	....	....	....	....	....	....	....	....	....	....	....
1976-77	**Detroit Red Wings**	**NHL**	53	1	11	12	1	9	10	14	1	0	0	73	1.4	32	16	44	6	-22	....	....	....	....	....	....	....	....
	Springfield Indians	AHL	22	0	8	8	....	....	....	16	....	....	....	....	....	....	....	....	....	....	....	....	....	....	....	....	....	....
1977-78	**Detroit Red Wings**	**NHL**	79	7	20	27	7	16	23	73	2	0	2	134	5.2	82	11	87	12	-4	5	0	0	0	8	0	0	0
1978-79	**Detroit Red Wings**	**NHL**	20	0	4	4	0	3	3	6	0	0	0	13	0.0	13	0	21	0	-8	....	....	....	....	....	....	....	....
1979-80	**Detroit Red Wings**	**NHL**	59	3	10	13	3	8	11	45	0	0	0	50	6.0	45	0	54	7	-2	....	....	....	....	....	....	....	....
	Adirondack Red Wings	AHL	8	3	3	6	....	....	....	10	....	....	....	....	....	....	....	....	....	....	....	....	....	....	....	....	....	....
1980-81	**Detroit Red Wings**	**NHL**	17	0	2	2	0	1	1	10	0	0	0	8	0.0	15	0	25	2	-8	....	....	....	....	....	....	....	....
	Adirondack Red Wings	AHL	62	3	34	37	....	....	....	158	....	....	....	....	....	....	....	....	....	....	17	4	12	16	38	....	....	....
1981-82	**Detroit Red Wings**	**NHL**	37	1	5	6	1	3	4	30	0	1	0	30	3.3	24	1	31	3	-5	....	....	....	....	....	....	....	....
	Adirondack Red Wings	AHL	36	3	22	25	....	....	....	59	....	....	....	....	....	....	....	....	....	....	....	....	....	....	....	....	....	....
1982-83	**Detroit Red Wings**	**NHL**	2	0	0	0	0	0	0	0	0	0	0	3	0.0	1	0	1	0	0	....	....	....	....	....	....	....	....
	Adirondack Red Wings	AHL	71	8	40	48	....	....	....	118	....	....	....	....	....	....	....	....	....	....	6	1	0	1	0	....	....	....
1983-84	Adirondack Red Wings	AHL	78	10	33	43	....	....	....	133	....	....	....	....	....	....	....	....	....	....	7	0	1	1	19	....	....	....
1984-85	Adirondack Red Wings	AHL	76	9	40	49	....	....	....	111	....	....	....	....	....	....	....	....	....	....	....	....	....	....	....	....	....	....
1985-86	Adirondack Red Wings	AHL	65	0	22	22	....	....	....	68	....	....	....	....	....	....	....	....	....	....	16	0	4	4	38	....	....	....
	NHL Totals		365	21	76	97	20	58	78	250	7	2	3	464	4.5	323	64	475	53		5	0	0	0	8	0	0	0

WCJHL First All-Star Team (1973, 1974) • Won Stafford Smythe Memorial Trophy (Memorial Cup Tournament MVP) (1974) • AHL Second All-Star Team (1984) • AHL First All-Star Team (1985)
Traded to **Detroit** by **Washington** for Bryan Watson, November 30, 1976.

• JOLY, YVAN

Yvan Joly RW – R. 5'11", 175 lbs. b: Hawkesbury, Ont., 2/6/1960. Montreal's 7th choice, 100th overall, in 1979 Entry Draft.

Season	Club	League	GP	G	A	Pts	AG	AA	APts	PIM	PP	SH	GW	S	%	TGF	PGF	TGA	PGA	+/-	GP	G	A	Pts	PIM	PP	SH	GW
1976-77	Ottawa 67's	OHA	62	30	26	56	....	....	....	36	....	....	....	....	....	....	....	....	....	....	....	....	....	....	....	....	....	....
1977-78	Ottawa 67's	OHA	64	34	37	71	....	....	....	67	....	....	....	....	....	....	....	....	....	....	....	....	....	....	....	....	....	....
1978-79	Ottawa 67's	OHA	63	53	59	112	....	....	....	45	....	....	....	....	....	....	....	....	....	....	4	0	2	2	6	....	....	....
	Canada	WJC-A	5	2	0	2	....	....	....	2	....	....	....	....	....	....	....	....	....	....	....	....	....	....	....	....	....	....
1979-80	Ottawa 67's	OHA	67	*66	93	159	....	....	....	47	....	....	....	....	....	....	....	....	....	....	11	4	12	16	13	....	....	....
	Canada	WJC-A	5	3	0	3	....	....	....	8	....	....	....	....	....	....	....	....	....	....	....	....	....	....	....	....	....	....
	Montreal Canadiens	**NHL**	....	....	....	....	....	....	....	....	....	....	....	....	....	....	....	....	....	....	1	0	0	0	0	....	....	....
1980-81	**Montreal Canadiens**	**NHL**	1	0	0	0	0	0	0	0	0	0	0	0	0.0	0	0	0	0	0	....	....	....	....	....	....	....	....
	Nova Scotia Voyageurs	AHL	68	14	27	41	....	....	....	74	....	....	....	....	....	....	....	....	....	....	4	1	0	1	0	....	....	....
1981-82	Nova Scotia Voyageurs	AHL	71	20	30	50	....	....	....	75	....	....	....	....	....	....	....	....	....	....	9	2	3	5	8	....	....	....
1982-83	**Montreal Canadiens**	**NHL**	1	0	0	0	0	0	0	0	0	0	0	1	0.0	0	0	1	0	-1	....	....	....	....	....	....	....	....
	Nova Scotia Voyageurs	AHL	76	43	37	80	....	....	....	52	....	....	....	....	....	....	....	....	....	....	7	2	1	3	2	....	....	....
1983-84	Maine Mariners	AHL	39	12	17	29	....	....	....	25	....	....	....	....	....	....	....	....	....	....	14	0	5	5	4	....	....	....
1985-85			DID NOT PLAY																									
1985-86	Indianapolis Checkers	IHL	17	1	6	7	....	....	....	28	....	....	....	....	....	....	....	....	....	....	....	....	....	....	....	....	....	....
	NHL Totals		2	0	0	0	0	0	0	0	0	0	0	1	0.0	0	0	1	0		1	0	0	0	0	0	0	0

OHA Second All-Star Team (1979) • OHA First All-Star Team (1980)

• JOMPHE, JEAN-FRANCOIS

Jean-Francois Jomphe C – L. 6'1", 195 lbs. b: Harve' St. Pierre, Que., 12/28/1972.

Season	Club	League	GP	G	A	Pts	AG	AA	APts	PIM	PP	SH	GW	S	%	TGF	PGF	TGA	PGA	+/-	GP	G	A	Pts	PIM	PP	SH	GW
1990-91	Shawinigan Cataractes	QMJHL	42	17	22	39	....	....	....	14	....	....	....	....	....	....	....	....	....	....	6	2	1	3	2	....	....	....
1991-92	Shawinigan Cataractes	QMJHL	44	28	33	61	....	....	....	69	....	....	....	....	....	....	....	....	....	....	10	6	10	16	10	....	....	....
1992-93	Sherbrooke Faucons	QMJHL	60	43	43	86	....	....	....	86	....	....	....	....	....	....	....	....	....	....	15	10	13	23	18	....	....	....
1993-94	San Diego Gulls	IHL	29	2	3	5	....	....	....	12	....	....	....	....	....	....	....	....	....	....	....	....	....	....	....	....	....	....
	Greensboro Monarchs	ECHL	25	9	9	18	....	....	....	41	....	....	....	....	....	....	....	....	....	....	1	1	0	1	0	....	....	....
1994-95	Canada	Nat-Team	52	33	25	58	....	....	....	85	....	....	....	....	....	....	....	....	....	....	....	....	....	....	....	....	....	....
	Canada	WC-A	8	4	0	4	....	....	....	6	....	....	....	....	....	....	....	....	....	....	....	....	....	....	....	....	....	....
1995-96	**Anaheim Mighty Ducks**	**NHL**	31	2	12	14	2	10	12	39	2	0	0	40	4.3	19	4	14	6	17	....	....	....	....	....	....	....	....
	Baltimore Bandits	AHL	47	21	34	55	....	....	....	70	....	....	....	....	....	....	....	....	....	....	....	....	....	....	....	....	....	....
	Canada	WC-A	8	0	1	1	....	....	....	4	....	....	....	....	....	....	....	....	....	....	....	....	....	....	....	....	....	....
1996-97	**Anaheim Mighty Ducks**	**NHL**	64	7	14	21	7	12	19	53	0	1	0	81	8.6	28	4	49	16	-9	....	....	....	....	....	....	....	....
1997-98	**Anaheim Mighty Ducks**	**NHL**	9	1	3	4	1	3	4	8	0	0	0	8	12.5	4	0	8	5	+1	....	....	....	....	....	....	....	....
	Cincinnati Mighty Ducks	AHL	38	9	19	28	....	....	....	32	....	....	....	....	....	....	....	....	....	....	....	....	....	....	....	....	....	....
	Quebec Rafales	IHL	17	6	4	10	....	....	....	24	....	....	....	....	....	....	....	....	....	....	....	....	....	....	....	....	....	....
	NHL Totals		104	10	29	39	10	25	35	100	2	1	0	135	7.4	51	8	71	27		....	....	....	....	....	....	....	....

Signed as a free agent by **Anaheim**, September 7, 1993. Traded to **Phoenix** by **Anaheim** for Jim McKenzie, June 18, 1998.

• JONATHAN, STAN

Stan Jonathan LW – L. 5'8", 175 lbs. b: Ohsweken, Ont., 9/5/1955. Boston's 5th choice, 86th overall, in 1975 Amateur Draft.

Season	Club	League	GP	G	A	Pts	AG	AA	APts	PIM	PP	SH	GW	S	%	TGF	PGF	TGA	PGA	+/-	GP	G	A	Pts	PIM	PP	SH	GW
1972-73	Peterborough Petes	OHA	64	14	35	49	....	....	....	107	....	....	....	....	....	....	....	....	....	....	....	....	....	....	....	....	....	....
1973-74	Peterborough Petes	OHA	70	19	33	52	....	....	....	127	....	....	....	....	....	....	....	....	....	....	11	4	5	9	14	....	....	....
1974-75	Peterborough Petes	OHA	70	36	39	75	....	....	....	138	....	....	....	....	....	....	....	....	....	....	11	4	5	9	14	....	....	....
1975-76	**Boston Bruins**	**NHL**	1	0	0	0	0	0	0	0	0	0	0	0	0.0	0	0	0	0	0	....	....	....	....	....	....	....	....
	Rochester Americans	AHL	6	1	1	2	....	....	....	0	....	....	....	....	....	....	....	....	....	....	....	....	....	....	....	....	....	....
	Dayton Gems	IHL	69	26	47	73	....	....	....	192	....	....	....	....	....	....	....	....	....	....	15	*13	8	*21	54	....	....	....
1976-77	**Boston Bruins**	**NHL**	69	17	13	30	16	11	27	69	1	0	2	71	23.9	42	2	39	0	+1	14	4	2	6	24	0	0	1
	Rochester Americans	AHL	3	0	0	0	....	....	....	7	....	....	....	....	....	....	....	....	....	....	....	....	....	....	....	....	....	....
1977-78	**Boston Bruins**	**NHL**	68	27	25	52	26	20	46	116	0	0	2	121	22.3	78	11	46	13	+34	15	0	1	1	36	0	0	0
1978-79	**Boston Bruins**	**NHL**	33	6	9	15	5	7	12	96	0	0	1	32	18.8	30	2	22	2	+8	11	4	1	5	12	0	0	0
1979-80	**Boston Bruins**	**NHL**	79	21	19	40	19	15	34	208	0	0	3	108	19.4	80	4	58	2	+20	9	0	0	0	29	0	0	0
1980-81	**Boston Bruins**	**NHL**	74	14	24	38	12	17	29	192	0	0	2	85	16.5	61	4	53	1	+5	3	0	0	0	30	0	0	0
1981-82	**Boston Bruins**	**NHL**	67	6	17	23	5	11	16	57	1	0	0	50	12.0	35	1	30	2	+6	11	0	0	0	6	0	0	0
1982-83	**Boston Bruins**	**NHL**	1	0	0	0	0	0	0	0	0	0	0	1	0.0	0	0	0	0	0	....	....	....	....	....	....	....	....
	Pittsburgh Penguins	**NHL**	19	0	3	3	0	2	2	13	0	0	0	16	0.0	11	0	10	0	-8	....	....	....	....	....	....	....	....
	Baltimore Skipjacks	AHL	48	13	23	36	....	....	....	00	....	....	....	....	....	....	....	....	....	....	....	....	....	....	....	....	....	....
	NHL Totals		411	91	110	201	83	83	166	751	2	0	10	484	18.8	337	24	267	20		63	8	4	12	137	0	0	1

IHL First All-Star Team (1976)
Traded to **Pittsburgh** by **Boston** for future considerations, November 8, 1982.

• JONES, BOB

Bob Jones LW – L. 6'1", 185 lbs. b: Espanola, Ont., 11/27/1945. Detroit's 9th choice, 179th overall, in 1989 Entry Draft.

Season	Club	League	GP	G	A	Pts	AG	AA	APts	PIM	PP	SH	GW	S	%	TGF	PGF	TGA	PGA	+/-	GP	G	A	Pts	PIM	PP	SH	GW
1962-63	Guelph Royals	OHA	49	5	7	12	....	....	....	13	....	....	....	....	....	....	....	....	....	....	....	....	....	....	....	....	....	....
1962-63	Guelph Royals	OHA	49	5	7	12	....	....	....	....	....	....	....	....	....	....	....	....	....	....	....	....	....	....	....	....	....	....
1963-64	Kitchener Rangers	OHA	56	6	12	18	....	....	....	50	....	....	....	....	....	....	....	....	....	....	....	....	....	....	....	....	....	....
1963-64	Kitchener Rangers	OHA	56	6	12	18	....	....	....	....	....	....	....	....	....	....	....	....	....	....	....	....	....	....	....	....	....	....
1964-65	Kitchener Rangers	OHA	56	39	53	92	....	....	....	59	....	....	....	....	....	....	....	....	....	....	....	....	....	....	....	....	....	....
1964-65	Kitchener Rangers	OHA	56	39	53	92	....	....	....	....	....	....	....	....	....	....	....	....	....	....	....	....	....	....	....	....	....	....
1965-66	Kitchener Rangers	OHA	48	24	25	49	....	....	....	57	....	....	....	....	....	....	....	....	....	....	19	11	14	25	10	....	....	....
1966-67	Omaha Knights	CHL	19	0	2	2	....	....	....	10	....	....	....	....	....	....	....	....	....	....	....	....	....	....	....	....	....	....
	Vancouver Canucks	WHL	47	8	9	17	....	....	....	24	....	....	....	....	....	....	....	....	....	....	8	3	2	5	8	....	....	....
1967-68	Buffalo Bisons	AHL	72	21	32	53	....	....	....	38	....	....	....	....	....	....	....	....	....	....	5	2	4	6	4	....	....	....
1968-69	**New York Rangers**	**NHL**	2	0	0	0	0	0	0	0	0	0	0	2	0.0	0	0	0	0	0	....	....	....	....	....	....	....	....
	Buffalo Bisons	AHL	70	19	37	56	....	....	....	92	....	....	....	....	....	....	....	....	....	....	6	2	4	6	4	....	....	....
1969-70	Buffalo Bisons	AHL	71	25	37	62	....	....	....	40	....	....	....	....	....	....	....	....	....	....	14	5	10	15	14	....	....	....
1970-71	Seattle Totems	WHL	72	17	43	60	....	....	....	61	....	....	....	....	....	....	....	....	....	....	....	....	....	....	....	....	....	....

			REGULAR SEASON																		PLAYOFFS							
Season	Club	League	GP	G	A	Pts	AG	AA	APts	PIM	PP	SH	GW	S	%	TGF	PGF	TGA	PGA	+/–	GP	G	A	Pts	PIM	PP	SH	GW
1971-72	Salt Lake Golden Eagles	WHL	27	9	7	16	....	....	....	10	....	....	....	....	....	....	....	....	....	....	....	....	....	....	....	....	....	....
	Portland Buckaroos	WHL	18	4	4	8	....	....	....	9	....	....	....	....	....	....	....	....	....	....	11	2	3	5	16	....	....	....
1972-73	Los Angeles Sharks	WHA	20	2	7	9	....	....	....	8	....	....	....	....	....	....	....	....	....	....	....	....	....	....	....	....	....	....
	New York Raiders	WHA	56	11	12	23	....	....	....	24	....	....	....	....	....	....	....	....	....	....	....	....	....	....	....	....	....	....
1973-74	New York-New Jersey	WHA	78	17	28	45	....	....	....	20	....	....	....	....	....	....	....	....	....	....	....	....	....	....	....	....	....	....
1974-75	Baltimore Stags	WHA	5	0	1	1	....	....	....	8	....	....	....	....	....	....	....	....	....	....	....	....	....	....	....	....	....	....
	Syracuse Blazers	NAHL	67	38	*76	*114	....	....	....	52	....	....	....	....	....	....	....	....	....	....	....	....	....	....	....	....	....	....
1975-76	Indianapolis Racers	WHA	2	0	0	0	....	....	....	0	....	....	....	....	....	....	....	....	....	....	....	....	....	....	....	....	....	....
	Mohawk Valley Comets	NAHL	69	39	70	109	....	....	....	38	....	....	....	....	....	....	....	....	....	....	4	3	1	4	7	....	....	....
	NHL Totals		2	0	0	0	0	0	0	0	0	0	0	2	0.0	0	0	0	0		....	....	....	....	....	....	....	....
	Other Major League Totals		161	30	48	78	....	....	....	60	....	....	....	....	....	....	....	....	....	....	....	....	....	....	....	....	....	....

NAHL First All-Star Team (1975)

Traded to **Salt Lake** (WHL) by **NY Rangers** for Rick Charron, May, 1971. Traded to **Portland** (WHL) by **Salt Lake** (WHL) for cash, February, 1972. Selected by **Dayton-Houston** (WHA) in 1972 WHA General Player Draft, February 12, 1972. WHA rights traded to **LA Sharks** (WHA) by **Houston** (WHA) for future considerations, September, 1972. Traded to **NY Raiders** (WHA) by **LA Sharks** (WHA) with Jarda Krupicka for Alton White, November, 1972. Transferred to **San Diego** (WHA) after **New York-New Jersey** (WHA) franchise relocated, April 30, 1974. Claimed by **Phoenix** (WHA) from **San Diego** in 1974 WHA Expansion Draft, May, 1974. Claimed by **Indianapolis** (WHA) from **Michigan-Baltimore** (WHA) in 1975 WHA Dispersal Draft, June, 1975.

• JONES, BRAD

Brad Jones LW – L. 6', 195 lbs. b: Sterling Heights, MI, 6/26/1965. Winnipeg's 8th choice, 156th overall, in 1984 Entry Draft.

Season	Club	League	GP	G	A	Pts	AG	AA	APts	PIM	PP	SH	GW	S	%	TGF	PGF	TGA	PGA	+/–	GP	G	A	Pts	PIM	PP	SH	GW
1983-84	University of Michigan	CCHA	37	8	26	34	....	....	....	32	....	....	....	....	....	....	....	....	....	....	....	....	....	....	....	....	....	....
1984-85	University of Michigan	CCHA	34	21	27	48	....	....	....	66	....	....	....	....	....	....	....	....	....	....	....	....	....	....	....	....	....	....
1985-86	University of Michigan	CCHA	36	28	39	67	....	....	....	40	....	....	....	....	....	....	....	....	....	....	....	....	....	....	....	....	....	....
1986-87	University of Michigan	CCHA	40	32	46	78	....	....	....	64	....	....	....	....	....	....	....	....	....	....	....	....	....	....	....	....	....	....
	Winnipeg Jets	NHL	4	1	0	1	1	0	1	0	0	0	0	8	12.5	2	0	0	0	+2	....	....	....	....	....	....	....	....
1987-88	United States	Nat-Team	50	27	23	50	....	....	....	59	....	....	....	....	....	....	....	....	....	....	....	....	....	....	....	....	....	....
	Winnipeg Jets	NHL	19	2	5	7	2	4	6	15	0	0	1	33	6.1	9	0	10	3	+2	1	0	0	0	0	0	0	0
1988-89	Winnipeg Jets	NHL	22	6	5	11	5	4	9	6	0	1	0	25	24.0	18	0	20	2	0	....	....	....	....	....	....	....	....
	Moncton Hawks	AHL	44	20	19	39	....	....	....	62	....	....	....	....	....	....	....	....	....	....	7	0	1	1	22	....	....	....
1989-90	Winnipeg Jets	NHL	2	0	0	0	0	0	0	0	0	0	0	0	0.0	0	0	2	0	–2	....	....	....	....	....	....	....	....
	Moncton Hawks	AHL	15	5	6	11	....	....	....	47	....	....	....	....	....	....	....	....	....	....	....	....	....	....	....	....	....	....
	New Haven Nighthawks	AHL	36	8	11	19	....	....	....	71	....	....	....	....	....	....	....	....	....	....	....	....	....	....	....	....	....	....
1990-91	Los Angeles Kings	NHL	53	9	11	20	8	8	16	57	0	1	1	47	19.1	31	1	34	15	+11	8	1	1	2	2	0	0	1
1991-92	Philadelphia Flyers	NHL	48	7	10	17	6	7	13	44	0	0	1	67	10.4	23	0	38	13	–2	....	....	....	....	....	....	....	....
1992-93	Ilves Tampere	Finland	26	10	7	17	....	....	....	62	....	....	....	....	....	....	....	....	....	....	....	....	....	....	....	....	....	....
	New Haven Senators	AHL	4	2	1	3	....	....	....	6	....	....	....	....	....	....	....	....	....	....	....	....	....	....	....	....	....	....
1993-94	Ajoie	Switz.	19	9	12	21	....	....	....	22	....	....	....	....	....	....	....	....	....	....	....	....	....	....	....	....	....	....
1994-95	Springfield Falcons	AHL	61	23	22	45	....	....	....	47	....	....	....	....	....	....	....	....	....	....	....	....	....	....	....	....	....	....
	Fort Wayne Komets	IHL	4	1	1	2	....	....	....	6	....	....	....	....	....	....	....	....	....	....	....	....	....	....	....	....	....	....
	United States	WC-A	5	0	2	2	....	....	....	2	....	....	....	....	....	....	....	....	....	....	....	....	....	....	....	....	....	....
1995-96	Binghamton Rangers	AHL	62	25	27	52	....	....	....	36	....	....	....	....	....	....	....	....	....	....	4	1	1	2	0	....	....	....
1996-97	Frankfurt Lions	Germany	37	14	11	25	....	....	....	89	....	....	....	....	....	....	....	....	....	....	9	5	3	8	8	....	....	....
1997-98	Binghamton Icemen	UHL	55	37	28	65	....	....	....	58	....	....	....	....	....	....	....	....	....	....	5	2	3	5	6	....	....	....
	NHL Totals		148	25	31	56	22	23	45	122	0	2	3	180	13.9	83	1	104	33		9	1	1	2	2	0	0	1

CCHA Second All-Star Team (1986) • CCHA First All-Star Team (1987) • NCAA West Second All-American Team (1987)

Traded to **LA Kings** by **Winnipeg** for Phil Sykes, December 1, 1990. Signed as a free agent by **Philadelphia**, August 6, 1991.

• JONES, JIM

Jim Jones D – L. 5'10", 185 lbs. b: Espanola, Ont., 7/27/1949. Boston's 8th choice, 69th overall, in 1969 Amateur Draft.

Season	Club	League	GP	G	A	Pts	AG	AA	APts	PIM	PP	SH	GW	S	%	TGF	PGF	TGA	PGA	+/–	GP	G	A	Pts	PIM	PP	SH	GW
1966-67	Kitchener Rangers	OHA	44	1	2	3	....	....	....	10	....	....	....	....	....	....	....	....	....	....	13	0	0	0	0	....	....	....
1967-68	Kitchener Rangers	OHA	11	3	1	4	....	....	....	6	....	....	....	....	....	....	....	....	....	....	....	....	....	....	....	....	....	....
	Peterborough Petes	OHA	42	6	19	25	....	....	....	31	....	....	....	....	....	....	....	....	....	....	5	1	3	4	2	....	....	....
1968-69	Peterborough Petes	OHA	54	10	42	52	....	....	....	73	....	....	....	....	....	....	....	....	....	....	10	0	5	5	2	....	....	....
1969-70	Oklahoma City Blazers	CHL	63	4	10	14	....	....	....	54	....	....	....	....	....	....	....	....	....	....	....	....	....	....	....	....	....	....
1970-71	Oklahoma City Blazers	CHL	36	1	2	3	....	....	....	26	....	....	....	....	....	....	....	....	....	....	....	....	....	....	....	....	....	....
1971-72	California Golden Seals	NHL	2	0	0	0	0	0	0	0	0	0	0	0	0.0	1	0	1	0	0	....	....	....	....	....	....	....	....
	Salt Lake Golden Eagles	WHL	28	2	7	9	....	....	....	20	....	....	....	....	....	....	....	....	....	....	....	....	....	....	....	....	....	....
1972-73	Baltimore Clippers	AHL	16	1	2	3	....	....	....	12	....	....	....	....	....	....	....	....	....	....	....	....	....	....	....	....	....	....
	Columbus Seals	IHL	40	3	15	18	....	....	....	52	....	....	....	....	....	....	....	....	....	....	....	....	....	....	....	....	....	....
	Salt Lake Golden Eagles	WHL	17	0	3	3	....	....	....	16	....	....	....	....	....	....	....	....	....	....	9	1	1	2	0	....	....	....
1973-74	Chicago Cougars	WHA	1	0	0	0	....	....	....	0	....	....	....	....	....	....	....	....	....	....	....	....	....	....	....	....	....	....
	Winston-Salem Polar Bears	SHL	49	2	17	19	....	....	....	35	....	....	....	....	....	....	....	....	....	....	7	1	5	6	6	....	....	....
1974-75	Port Huron–Des Moines	IHL	17	1	5	6	....	....	....	14	....	....	....	....	....	....	....	....	....	....	....	....	....	....	....	....	....	....
	Greensboro Generals	SHL	35	7	20	27	....	....	....	18	....	....	....	....	....	....	....	....	....	....	....	....	....	....	....	....	....	....
	Philadelphia Firebirds	NAHL	12	0	1	1	....	....	....	16	....	....	....	....	....	....	....	....	....	....	4	0	1	1	0	....	....	....
1975-76	Roanoke Valley Rebels	SHL	8	0	2	2	....	....	....	4	....	....	....	....	....	....	....	....	....	....	....	....	....	....	....	....	....	....
	NHL Totals		2	0	0	0	0	0	0	0	0	0	0	0	0.0	1	0	1	0		....	....	....	....	....	....	....	....
	Other Major League Totals		1	0	0	0	....	....	....	0	....	....	....	....	....	....	....	....	....	....	....	....	....	....	....	....	....	....

Signed as a free agent by **California**, June, 1971. Signed as a free agent by **Chicago** (WHA), September, 1973.

• JONES, JIMMY

Jimmy Jones RW – R. 5'9", 180 lbs. b: Woodbridge, Ont., 1/2/1953. Boston's 8th choice, 31st overall, in 1973 Amateur Draft.

Season	Club	League	GP	G	A	Pts	AG	AA	APts	PIM	PP	SH	GW	S	%	TGF	PGF	TGA	PGA	+/–	GP	G	A	Pts	PIM	PP	SH	GW
1970-71	Peterborough Petes	OHA	11	0	2	2	....	....	....	2	....	....	....	....	....	....	....	....	....	....	....	....	....	....	....	....	....	....
1971-72	Peterborough Petes	OHA	4	1	2	3	....	....	....	8	....	....	....	....	....	....	....	....	....	....	....	....	....	....	....	....	....	....
1972-73	Peterborough Petes	OHA	63	37	33	70	....	....	....	73	....	....	....	....	....	....	....	....	....	....	13	11	6	17	38	....	....	....
1973-74	Vancouver Blazers	WHA	18	3	2	5	....	....	....	23	....	....	....	....	....	....	....	....	....	....	....	....	....	....	....	....	....	....
	Roanoke Valley Rebels	SHL	60	24	38	62	....	....	....	97	....	....	....	....	....	....	....	....	....	....	....	....	....	....	....	....	....	....
1974-75	Vancouver Blazers	WHA	63	11	7	18	....	....	....	39	....	....	....	....	....	....	....	....	....	....	....	....	....	....	....	....	....	....
	Tulsa Oilers	CHL	9	6	7	13	....	....	....	17	....	....	....	....	....	....	....	....	....	....	....	....	....	....	....	....	....	....
1975-76	Rochester Americans	AHL	66	16	22	38	....	....	....	71	....	....	....	....	....	....	....	....	....	....	7	1	0	1	11	....	....	....
1976-77	Rochester Americans	AHL	74	24	34	58	....	....	....	66	....	....	....	....	....	....	....	....	....	....	....	....	....	....	....	....	....	....
1977-78	Toronto Maple Leafs	NHL	78	4	9	13	4	7	11	23	0	2	1	54	7.4	15	1	53	40	+1	13	1	5	6	7	0	0	0
1978-79	Toronto Maple Leafs	NHL	69	9	9	18	8	7	15	45	0	0	0	63	14.3	26	0	64	40	+2	6	0	0	0	4	0	0	0
1979-80	Toronto Maple Leafs	NHL	1	0	0	0	0	0	0	0	0	0	0	1	0.0	0	0	1	0	–1	....	....	....	....	....	....	....	....
	New Brunswick Hawks	AHL	48	17	17	34	....	....	....	31	....	....	....	....	....	....	....	....	....	....	....	....	....	....	....	....	....	....
1980-81	Rochester Americans	AHL	73	13	15	28	....	....	....	83	....	....	....	....	....	....	....	....	....	....	....	....	....	....	....	....	....	....
	NHL Totals		148	13	18	31	12	14	26	68	0	2	1	118	11.0	41	1	118	80		19	1	5	6	11	0	0	0
	Other Major League Totals		81	14	9	23	....	....	....	62	....	....	....	....	....	....	....	....	....	....	....	....	....	....	....	....	....	....

Selected by **Vancouver** (WHA) in 1973 WHA Amateur Draft, June, 1973. Signed as a free agent by **Toronto**, October 25, 1977. Claimed as a fill-in by **Toronto** during Expansion Draft, June 13, 1979.

• JONES, KEITH

Keith Jones RW – L. 6'2", 200 lbs. b: Brantford, Ont., 11/8/1968. Washington's 7th choice, 141st overall, in 1988 Entry Draft.

Season	Club	League	GP	G	A	Pts	AG	AA	APts	PIM	PP	SH	GW	S	%	TGF	PGF	TGA	PGA	+/–	GP	G	A	Pts	PIM	PP	SH	GW
1987-88	Niagara Falls Canucks	OJHL	40	50	80	130	....	....	....	....	....	....	....	....	....	....	....	....	....	....	....	....	....	....	....	....	....	....
1988-89	Western Michigan University	CCHA	37	9	12	21	....	....	....	51	....	....	....	....	....	....	....	....	....	....	....	....	....	....	....	....	....	....
1989-90	Western Michigan University	CCHA	40	19	18	37	....	....	....	82	....	....	....	....	....	....	....	....	....	....	....	....	....	....	....	....	....	....
1990-91	Western Michigan University	CCHA	41	30	19	49	....	....	....	106	....	....	....	....	....	....	....	....	....	....	....	....	....	....	....	....	....	....
1991-92	Western Michigan University	CCHA	35	25	31	56	....	....	....	77	....	....	....	....	....	....	....	....	....	....	....	....	....	....	....	....	....	....
	Baltimore Skipjacks	AHL	6	2	4	6	....	....	....	0	....	....	....	....	....	....	....	....	....	....	....	....	....	....	....	....	....	....
1992-93	Washington Capitals	NHL	71	12	14	26	10	10	20	124	0	0	3	73	16.4	46	4	24	0	+18	6	0	0	0	10	0	0	0
	Baltimore Skipjacks	AHL	8	7	3	10	....	....	....	4	....	....	....	....	....	....	....	....	....	....	....	....	....	....	....	....	....	....
1993-94	Washington Capitals	NHL	68	16	19	35	15	15	30	149	5	0	1	97	16.5	52	15	33	0	+4	11	0	1	1	36	0	0	0
	Portland Pirates	AHL	6	5	7	12	....	....	....	4	....	....	....	....	....	....	....	....	....	....	....	....	....	....	....	....	....	....
1994-95	Washington Capitals	NHL	40	14	6	20	25	9	34	65	1	0	4	85	16.5	24	6	20	0	–2	7	4	4	8	22	1	0	0
1995-96	Washington Capitals	NHL	68	18	23	41	18	19	37	103	5	0	2	155	11.6	70	26	38	2	+8	2	0	0	0	7	0	0	0

Season	Club	League	GP	G	A	Pts	AG	AA	APts	PIM	PP	SH	GW	S	%	TGF	PGF	TGA	PGA	+/–	GP	G	A	Pts	PIM	PP	SH	GW
			REGULAR SEASON																		PLAYOFFS							
1996-97	**Washington Capitals**	**NHL**	**11**	**2**	**3**	**5**	**2**	**3**	**5**	**13**	**1**	**0**	**0**	**12**	**16.7**	**8**	**2**	**8**	**0**	**–2**	....	....	....	....	....	....	....	....
	Colorado Avalanche	**NHL**	**67**	**23**	**20**	**43**	**24**	**18**	**42**	**105**	**13**	**1**	**7**	**158**	**14.6**	**73**	**35**	**35**	**2**	**+5**	**6**	**3**	**3**	**6**	**4**	**1**	**0**	**0**
1997-98	**Colorado Avalanche**	**NHL**	**23**	**3**	**7**	**10**	**4**	**7**	**11**	**22**	**1**	**0**	**2**	**31**	**9.7**	**18**	**9**	**13**	**0**	**–4**	**7**	**0**	**0**	**0**	**13**	**0**	**0**	**0**
	Hershey Bears	AHL	4	2	1	3	....	....	....	2	....	....	....	....	....	....	....	....	....	....	....	....	....	....	....	....	....	....
	NHL Totals		**348**	**88**	**92**	**180**	**98**	**81**	**179**	**581**	**26**	**1**	**19**	**611**	**14.4**	**291**	**97**	**171**	**4**		**39**	**7**	**8**	**15**	**92**	**2**	**0**	**0**

CCHA First All-Star Team (1992)

Traded to **Colorado** by **Washington** with Washington's 1st round choice (Scott Parker) in 1998 Entry Draft and future considerations for Curtis Leschyshyn and Chris Simon, November 2, 1996.

• JONES, RON

Ron Jones D – L. 6'1", 195 lbs. b: Vermillion, Alta., 4/11/1951. Boston's 1st choice, 6th overall, in 1971 Amateur Draft.

Season	Club	League	GP	G	A	Pts	AG	AA	APts	PIM	PP	SH	GW	S	%	TGF	PGF	TGA	PGA	+/–	GP	G	A	Pts	PIM	PP	SH	GW
1967-68	Edmonton Oil Kings	WCJHL	48	1	5	6	....	....	....	29	....	....	....	....	....	....	....	....	....	....	....	....	....	....	....	....	....	....
1968-69	Edmonton Oil Kings	WCJHL	46	2	11	13	....	....	....	37	....	....	....	....	....	....	....	....	....	....	....	....	....	....	....	....	....	....
1969-70	Edmonton Oil Kings	WCJHL	52	7	33	40	....	....	....	82	....	....	....	....	....	....	....	....	....	....	....	....	....	....	....	....	....	....
1970-71	Edmonton Oil Kings	WCJHL	63	11	40	51	....	....	....	46	....	....	....	....	....	....	....	....	....	....	....	....	....	....	....	....	....	....
1971-72	**Boston Bruins**	**NHL**	**1**	**0**	**0**	**0**	**0**	**0**	**0**	**0**	**0**	**0**	**0**	**3**	**0.0**	**1**	**0**	**0**	**0**	**+1**	....	....	....	....	....	....	....	....
	Boston Braves	AHL	74	6	11	17	....	....	....	36	....	....	....	....	....	....	....	....	....	....	9	0	0	0	7	....	....	....
1972-73	**Boston Bruins**	**NHL**	**7**	**0**	**0**	**0**	**0**	**0**	**0**	**0**	**0**	**0**	**0**	**0**	**0.0**	**3**	**0**	**2**	**0**	**+1**	....	....	....	....	....	....	....	....
	Boston Braves	AHL	55	3	25	28	....	....	....	34	....	....	....	....	....	....	....	....	....	....	5	0	1	1	2	....	....	....
1973-74	**Pittsburgh Penguins**	**NHL**	**25**	**0**	**3**	**3**	**0**	**3**	**3**	**15**	**0**	**0**	**0**	**18**	**0.0**	**21**	**3**	**36**	**4**	**–14**	....	....	....	....	....	....	....	....
	Hershey Bears	AHL	34	0	12	12	....	....	....	23	....	....	....	....	....	....	....	....	....	....	14	0	3	3	6	....	....	....
1974-75	**Washington Capitals**	**NHL**	**19**	**1**	**1**	**2**	**1**	**1**	**2**	**16**	**1**	**0**	**0**	**13**	**7.7**	**21**	**6**	**38**	**9**	**–14**	....	....	....	....	....	....	....	....
	Hershey Bears	AHL	25	0	6	6	....	....	....	37	....	....	....	....	....	....	....	....	....	....	....	....	....	....	....	....	....	....
1975-76	**Washington Capitals**	**NHL**	**2**	**0**	**0**	**0**	**0**	**0**	**0**	**0**	**0**	**0**	**0**	**0**	**0.0**	**0**	**0**	**1**	**0**	**–1**	....	....	....	....	....	....	....	....
	Richmond Robins	AHL	20	0	7	7	....	....	....	8	....	....	....	....	....	....	....	....	....	....	....	....	....	....	....	....	....	....
	Hershey Bears	AHL	53	7	23	30	....	....	....	34	....	....	....	....	....	....	....	....	....	....	10	1	5	6	9	....	....	....
1976-77	Hershey Bears	AHL	36	0	9	9	....	....	....	18	....	....	....	....	....	....	....	....	....	....	6	0	3	3	4	....	....	....
	NHL Totals		**54**	**1**	**4**	**5**	**1**	**4**	**5**	**31**	**1**	**0**	**0**	**34**	**2.9**	**46**	**9**	**77**	**13**		....	....	....	....	....	....	....	....

WCJHL All-Star Team (1971)

Claimed by **Pittsburgh** from **Boston** in Intra-league Draft, June 12, 1973. Traded to **Washington** by **Pittsburgh** for Pete Laframboise, January 21, 1975.

• JONSSON, KENNY

Kenny Jonsson D – L. 6'3", 195 lbs. b: Angelholm, Sweden, 10/6/1974. Toronto's 1st choice, 12th overall, in 1993 Entry Draft.

Season	Club	League	GP	G	A	Pts	AG	AA	APts	PIM	PP	SH	GW	S	%	TGF	PGF	TGA	PGA	+/–	GP	G	A	Pts	PIM	PP	SH	GW
1991-92	Rogle BK	Sweden 2	30	4	11	15	....	....	....	24	....	....	....	....	....	....	....	....	....	....	....	....	....	....	....	....	....	....
1992-93	Rogle BK	Sweden	39	3	10	13	....	....	....	42	....	....	....	....	....	....	....	....	....	....	....	....	....	....	....	....	....	....
	Sweden	WJC-A	7	2	3	5	....	....	....	14	....	....	....	....	....	....	....	....	....	....	....	....	....	....	....	....	....	....
1993-94	Rogle BK	Sweden	36	4	13	17	....	....	....	40	....	....	....	....	....	....	....	....	....	....	3	1	1	2	2	....	....	....
	Sweden	WJC-A	7	3	5	8	....	....	....	8	....	....	....	....	....	....	....	....	....	....	....	....	....	....	....	....	....	....
	Sweden	Olympics	3	1	0	1	....	....	....	0	....	....	....	....	....	....	....	....	....	....	....	....	....	....	....	....	....	....
	Sweden	WC-A	7	0	1	1	....	....	....	6	....	....	....	....	....	....	....	....	....	....	....	....	....	....	....	....	....	....
1994-95	Rogle BK	Sweden	8	3	1	4	....	....	....	20	....	....	....	....	....	....	....	....	....	....	....	....	....	....	....	....	....	....
	Toronto Maple Leafs	**NHL**	**39**	**2**	**7**	**9**	**4**	**10**	**14**	**16**	**0**	**0**	**1**	**50**	**4.0**	**25**	**9**	**26**	**2**	**–8**	**4**	**0**	**0**	**0**	**0**	**0**	**0**	**0**
	St. John's Maple Leafs	AHL	10	2	5	7	....	....	....	2	....	....	....	....	....	....	....	....	....	....	....	....	....	....	....	....	....	....
1995-96	**Toronto Maple Leafs**	**NHL**	**50**	**4**	**22**	**26**	**4**	**18**	**22**	**22**	**3**	**0**	**1**	**90**	**4.4**	**64**	**30**	**26**	**4**	**+12**	....	....	....	....	....	....	....	....
	New York Islanders	**NHL**	**16**	**0**	**4**	**4**	**0**	**3**	**3**	**10**	**0**	**0**	**0**	**40**	**0.0**	**17**	**7**	**20**	**5**	**–5**	....	....	....	....	....	....	....	....
	Sweden	WC-A	6	0	1	1	....	....	....	8	....	....	....	....	....	....	....	....	....	....	....	....	....	....	....	....	....	....
1996-97	Sweden	W Cup	1	0	0	0	....	....	....	4	....	....	....	....	....	....	....	....	....	....	....	....	....	....	....	....	....	....
	New York Islanders	**NHL**	**81**	**3**	**18**	**21**	**3**	**16**	**19**	**24**	**1**	**0**	**0**	**92**	**3.3**	**92**	**16**	**94**	**28**	**+10**	....	....	....	....	....	....	....	....
1997-98	**New York Islanders**	**NHL**	**81**	**14**	**26**	**40**	**16**	**25**	**41**	**58**	**6**	**0**	**2**	**108**	**13.0**	**98**	**40**	**92**	**32**	**–2**	....	....	....	....	....	....	....	....
	NHL Totals		**267**	**23**	**77**	**100**	**27**	**72**	**99**	**130**	**10**	**0**	**4**	**380**	**6.1**	**296**	**102**	**258**	**71**		**4**	**0**	**0**	**0**	**0**	**0**	**0**	**0**

WJC-A All-Star Team (1993, 1994) • Swedish Rookie of the Year (1993)
Named Best Defenseman at WJC-A (1994) • NHL/Upper Deck All-Rookie Team (1995)

Traded to **NY Islanders** by **Toronto** with Sean Haggerty, Darby Hendrickson and Toronto's 1st round choice (Roberto Luongo) in 1997 Entry Draft for Wendel Clark, Mathieu Schneider and D.J. Smith, March 13, 1996.

• JONSSON, TOMAS

Tomas Jonsson D – L. 5'10", 185 lbs. b: Falun, Sweden, 4/12/1960. NY Islanders' 2nd choice, 25th overall, in 1979 Entry Draft.

Season	Club	League	GP	G	A	Pts	AG	AA	APts	PIM	PP	SH	GW	S	%	TGF	PGF	TGA	PGA	+/–	GP	G	A	Pts	PIM	PP	SH	GW
1977-78	MoDo	Sweden	35	8	9	17	....	....	....	45	....	....	....	....	....	....	....	....	....	....	2	0	0	0	4	....	....	....
	Sweden	WJC-A	7	1	2	3	....	....	....	10	....	....	....	....	....	....	....	....	....	....	....	....	....	....	....	....	....	....
1978-79	MoDo	Sweden	34	11	9	20	....	....	....	77	....	....	....	....	....	....	....	....	....	....	5	1	2	3	13	....	....	....
	Sweden	WJC-A	6	1	1	2	....	....	....	4	....	....	....	....	....	....	....	....	....	....	....	....	....	....	....	....	....	....
	Sweden	Nat-Team	15	2	3	5	....	....	....	16	....	....	....	....	....	....	....	....	....	....	....	....	....	....	....	....	....	....
	Sweden	WEC-A	8	1	3	4	....	....	....	8	....	....	....	....	....	....	....	....	....	....	....	....	....	....	....	....	....	....
1979-80	MoDo	Sweden	36	3	13	16	....	....	....	42	....	....	....	....	....	....	....	....	....	....	....	....	....	....	....	....	....	....
	Sweden	WJC-A	5	2	1	3	....	....	....	10	....	....	....	....	....	....	....	....	....	....	....	....	....	....	....	....	....	....
	Sweden	Nat-Team	18	2	4	6	....	....	....	24	....	....	....	....	....	....	....	....	....	....	....	....	....	....	....	....	....	....
	Sweden	Olympics	7	2	2	4	....	....	....	6	....	....	....	....	....	....	....	....	....	....	....	....	....	....	....	....	....	....
1980-81	MoDo	Sweden	35	8	12	20	....	....	....	58	....	....	....	....	....	....	....	....	....	....	....	....	....	....	....	....	....	....
	Sweden	Nat-Team	19	0	2	2	....	....	....	2	....	....	....	....	....	....	....	....	....	....	....	....	....	....	....	....	....	....
	Sweden	WEC-A	1	0	0	0	....	....	....	0	....	....	....	....	....	....	....	....	....	....	....	....	....	....	....	....	....	....
1981-82	Sweden	C Cup	3	0	1	1	....	....	....	4	....	....	....	....	....	....	....	....	....	....	....	....	....	....	....	....	....	....
	New York Islanders	**NHL**	**70**	**9**	**25**	**34**	**7**	**17**	**24**	**51**	**0**	**0**	**1**	**89**	**10.1**	**104**	**20**	**60**	**2**	**+26**	**10**	**0**	**2**	**2**	**21**	**0**	**0**	**0**
1982-83	**New York Islanders**	**NHL**	**72**	**13**	**35**	**48**	**11**	**24**	**35**	**50**	**1**	**0**	**3**	**100**	**13.0**	**118**	**27**	**60**	**9**	**+40**	**20**	**2**	**10**	**12**	**18**	**0**	**0**	**0**
1983-84	**New York Islanders**	**NHL**	**72**	**11**	**36**	**47**	**9**	**24**	**33**	**54**	**2**	**0**	**1**	**122**	**9.0**	**112**	**34**	**82**	**16**	**+12**	**21**	**3**	**5**	**8**	**22**	**2**	**0**	**0**
1984-85	**New York Islanders**	**NHL**	**69**	**16**	**34**	**50**	**13**	**23**	**36**	**58**	**8**	**0**	**4**	**128**	**12.5**	**125**	**47**	**97**	**18**	**–1**	**7**	**1**	**2**	**3**	**10**	**1**	**0**	**0**
1985-86	**New York Islanders**	**NHL**	**77**	**14**	**30**	**44**	**11**	**20**	**31**	**62**	**5**	**1**	**1**	**119**	**11.8**	**132**	**44**	**87**	**15**	**+16**	**3**	**0**	**1**	**1**	**4**	**0**	**0**	**0**
	Sweden	WEC-A	8	0	5	5	....	....	....	10	....	....	....	....	....	....	....	....	....	....	....	....	....	....	....	....	....	....
1986-87	**New York Islanders**	**NHL**	**47**	**6**	**25**	**31**	**5**	**18**	**23**	**36**	**1**	**1**	**0**	**99**	**6.1**	**82**	**42**	**60**	**12**	**–8**	**10**	**1**	**4**	**5**	**6**	**1**	**0**	**0**
1987-88	Sweden	C Cup	6	1	1	2	....	....	....	2	....	....	....	....	....	....	....	....	....	....	....	....	....	....	....	....	....	....
	New York Islanders	**NHL**	**72**	**6**	**41**	**47**	**5**	**29**	**34**	**115**	**1**	**0**	**1**	**121**	**5.0**	**119**	**55**	**72**	**14**	**+6**	**5**	**2**	**2**	**4**	**10**	**1**	**0**	**0**
1988-89	**New York Islanders**	**NHL**	**53**	**9**	**23**	**32**	**8**	**16**	**24**	**34**	**4**	**1**	**1**	**103**	**8.7**	**75**	**42**	**64**	**18**	**–13**	....	....	....	....	....	....	....	....
	Edmonton Oilers	**NHL**	**20**	**1**	**10**	**11**	**1**	**7**	**8**	**22**	**1**	**0**	**0**	**46**	**2.2**	**34**	**20**	**26**	**0**	**–12**	**4**	**2**	**0**	**2**	**6**	**2**	**0**	**0**
1989-90	Leksands IF	Sweden	40	11	15	26	....	....	....	54	....	....	....	....	....	....	....	....	....	....	3	1	1	2	4	....	....	....
	Sweden	WEC-A	8	0	1	1	....	....	....	8	....	....	....	....	....	....	....	....	....	....	....	....	....	....	....	....	....	....
1990-91	Leksands IF	Sweden	22	7	7	14	....	....	....	16	....	....	....	....	....	....	....	....	....	....	....	....	....	....	....	....	....	....
	Sweden	WEC-A	10	0	4	4	....	....	....	8	....	....	....	....	....	....	....	....	....	....	....	....	....	....	....	....	....	....
1991-92	Leksands IF	Sweden	22	6	7	13	....	....	....	26	....	....	....	....	....	....	....	....	....	....	....	....	....	....	....	....	....	....
1992-93	Leksands IF	Sweden	38	8	15	23	....	....	....	90	....	....	....	....	....	....	....	....	....	....	2	1	1	2	4	....	....	....
1993-94	Leksands IF	Sweden	33	4	14	18	....	....	....	38	....	....	....	....	....	....	....	....	....	....	4	0	1	1	6	....	....	....
	Sweden	Olympics	8	1	3	4	....	....	....	10	....	....	....	....	....	....	....	....	....	....	....	....	....	....	....	....	....	....
1994-95	Leksands IF	Sweden	37	8	17	25	....	....	....	38	....	....	....	....	....	....	....	....	....	....	4	1	3	4	27	....	....	....
	Sweden	WC-A	8	0	2	2	....	....	....	12	....	....	....	....	....	....	....	....	....	....	....	....	....	....	....	....	....	....
1995-96	Leksands IF	Sweden	34	5	17	22	....	....	....	24	....	....	....	....	....	....	....	....	....	....	5	0	4	4	2	....	....	....
1996-97	Leksands IF	Sweden	38	8	13	21	....	....	....	42	....	....	....	....	....	....	....	....	....	....	9	2	1	3	4	....	....	....
1997-98	Leksands IF	EuroHL	5	1	3	4	....	....	....	6	....	....	....	....	....	....	....	....	....	....	....	....	....	....	....	....	....	....
	Leksands IF	Sweden	38	7	10	17	....	....	....	34	....	....	....	....	....	....	....	....	....	....	4	0	0	0	12	....	....	....
	NHL Totals		**552**	**85**	**259**	**344**	**70**	**178**	**248**	**482**	**23**	**3**	**12**	**927**	**9.2**	**901**	**331**	**608**	**104**		**80**	**11**	**26**	**37**	**97**	**7**	**0**	**0**

Swedish World All-Star Team (1979, 1980, 1990, 1995) • WJC-A All-Star Team (1980) • Swedish Player of the Year (1995)

Traded to **Edmonton** by **NY Islanders** for future considerations, February 15, 1989.

• JOSEPH, ANTHONY

Anthony Joseph RW – R. 6'4", 203 lbs. b: Cornwall, Ont., 3/1/1969. Winnipeg's 5th choice, 94th overall, in 1988 Entry Draft.

Season	Club	League	GP	G	A	Pts	AG	AA	APts	PIM	PP	SH	GW	S	%	TGF	PGF	TGA	PGA	+/–	GP	G	A	Pts	PIM	PP	SH	GW
1984-85	Cornwall Midgets	Midget	37	33	30	63	....	....	....	48	....	....	....	....	....	....	....	....	....	....	....	....	....	....	....	....	....	....
1985-86	Oshawa Generals	OHL	41	3	1	4	....	....	....	28	....	....	....	....	....	....	....	....	....	....	....	....	....	....	....	....	....	....
1986-87	Oshawa Generals	OHL	44	2	5	7	....	....	....	93	....	....	....	....	....	....	....	....	....	....	19	0	0	0	58	....	....	....

			REGULAR SEASON																		PLAYOFFS							
Season	Club	League	GP	G	A	Pts	AG	AA	APts	PIM	PP	SH	GW	S	%	TGF	PGF	TGA	PGA	+/–	GP	G	A	Pts	PIM	PP	SH	GW
1987-88	Oshawa Generals	OHL	49	9	18	27	....	....	....	126	....	....	....	....	....	....	....	....	....	....	7	0	0	0	9	....	....	....
1988-89	Oshawa Generals	OHL	52	20	16	36	....	....	....	106	....	....	....	....	....	....	....	....	....	....	6	4	2	6	22	....	....	....
	Winnipeg Jets	**NHL**	**2**	**1**	**0**	**1**	**1**	**0**	**1**	**0**	**0**	**0**	**0**	**4**	**25.0**	**1**	**0**	**0**	**0**	**+1**	....	....	....	....	....	....	....	....
1989-90	Tappara Tampere	Finland	5	0	0	0	....	....	....	2	....	....	....	....	....	....	....	....	....	....	....	....	....	....	....	....	....	....
	Moncton Hawks	AHL	61	9	9	18	....	....	....	74	....	....	....	....	....	....	....	....	....	....	....	....	....	....	....	....	....	....
1990-91	Moncton Hawks	AHL	16	4	2	6	....	....	....	79	....	....	....	....	....	....	....	....	....	....	8	0	1	1	31	....	....	....
1991-92	Kalamazoo Wings	IHL	15	2	0	2	....	....	....	51	....	....	....	....	....	....	....	....	....	....	....	....	....	....	....	....	....	....
	Moncton Hawks	AHL	42	6	5	11	....	....	....	118	....	....	....	....	....	....	....	....	....	....	6	0	1	1	25	....	....	....
1992-93			DID NOT PLAY																									
1993-94	Salt Lake Golden Eagles	IHL	43	4	2	6	....	....	....	213	....	....	....	....	....	....	....	....	....	....	....	....	....	....	....	....	....	....
	NHL Totals		**2**	**1**	**0**	**1**	**1**	**0**	**1**	**0**	**0**	**0**	**0**	**4**	**25.0**	**1**	**0**	**0**	**0**		....	....	....	....	....	....	....	....

• JOSEPH, CHRIS

Chris Joseph D – R. 6'2", 202 lbs. b: Burnaby, B.C., 9/10/1969. Pittsburgh's 1st choice, 5th overall, in 1987 Entry Draft.

Season	Club	League	GP	G	A	Pts	AG	AA	APts	PIM	PP	SH	GW	S	%	TGF	PGF	TGA	PGA	+/–	GP	G	A	Pts	PIM	PP	SH	GW
1985-86	Seattle Thunderbirds	WHL	72	4	8	12	....	....	....	50	....	....	....	....	....	....	....	....	....	....	5	0	3	3	12	....	....	....
1986-87	Seattle Thunderbirds	WHL	67	13	45	58	....	....	....	155	....	....	....	....	....	....	....	....	....	....	....	....	....	....	....	....	....	....
	Canada	WJC-A	6	1	1	2	....	....	....	12	....	....	....	....	....	....	....	....	....	....	....	....	....	....	....	....	....	....
1987-88	**Pittsburgh Penguins**	**NHL**	**17**	**0**	**4**	**4**	**0**	**3**	**3**	**12**	**0**	**0**	**0**	**13**	**0.0**	**18**	**6**	**10**	**0**	**+2**	....	....	....	....	....	....	....	....
	Edmonton Oilers	**NHL**	**7**	**0**	**4**	**4**	**0**	**3**	**3**	**6**	**0**	**0**	**0**	**1**	**0.0**	**8**	**5**	**6**	**0**	**–3**	....	....	....	....	....	....	....	....
	Seattle Thunderbirds	WHL	23	5	14	19	....	....	....	49	....	....	....	....	....	....	....	....	....	....	....	....	....	....	....	....	....	....
	Canada	WJC-A	7	1	2	3	....	....	....	6	....	....	....	....	....	....	....	....	....	....	....	....	....	....	....	....	....	....
	Nova Scotia Oilers	AHL	8	0	2	2	....	....	....	8	....	....	....	....	....	....	....	....	....	....	4	0	0	0	9	....	....	....
1988-89	**Edmonton Oilers**	**NHL**	**44**	**4**	**5**	**9**	**3**	**4**	**7**	**54**	**0**	**0**	**0**	**36**	**11.1**	**43**	**6**	**50**	**4**	**–9**	....	....	....	....	....	....	....	....
	Cape Breton Oilers	AHL	5	1	1	2	....	....	....	18	....	....	....	....	....	....	....	....	....	....	....	....	....	....	....	....	....	....
1989-90	**Edmonton Oilers**	**NHL**	**4**	**0**	**2**	**2**	**0**	**1**	**1**	**2**	**0**	**0**	**0**	**5**	**0.0**	**3**	**3**	**2**	**0**	**–2**	....	....	....	....	....	....	....	....
	Cape Breton Oilers	AHL	61	10	20	30	....	....	....	69	....	....	....	....	....	....	....	....	....	....	6	2	1	3	4	....	....	....
1990-91	**Edmonton Oilers**	**NHL**	**49**	**5**	**17**	**22**	**5**	**13**	**18**	**59**	**2**	**0**	**0**	**74**	**6.8**	**59**	**18**	**42**	**4**	**+3**	....	....	....	....	....	....	....	....
1991-92	**Edmonton Oilers**	**NHL**	**7**	**0**	**0**	**0**	**0**	**0**	**0**	**8**	**0**	**0**	**0**	**5**	**0.0**	**5**	**0**	**6**	**0**	**–1**	**5**	**1**	**3**	**4**	**2**	**0**	**0**	**0**
	Cape Breton Oilers	AHL	63	14	29	43	....	....	....	72	....	....	....	....	....	....	....	....	....	....	5	0	2	2	8	....	....	....
1992-93	**Edmonton Oilers**	**NHL**	**33**	**2**	**10**	**12**	**2**	**7**	**9**	**48**	**1**	**0**	**0**	**49**	**4.1**	**31**	**10**	**36**	**6**	**–9**	....	....	....	....	....	....	....	....
1993-94	**Edmonton Oilers**	**NHL**	**10**	**1**	**1**	**2**	**1**	**1**	**2**	**28**	**1**	**0**	**0**	**25**	**4.0**	**11**	**4**	**18**	**3**	**–8**	....	....	....	....	....	....	....	....
	Tampa Bay Lightning	**NHL**	**66**	**10**	**19**	**29**	**9**	**15**	**24**	**108**	**7**	**0**	**0**	**154**	**6.5**	**93**	**38**	**73**	**5**	**–13**	....	....	....	....	....	....	....	....
1994-95	**Pittsburgh Penguins**	**NHL**	**33**	**5**	**10**	**15**	**9**	**15**	**24**	**46**	**3**	**0**	**0**	**73**	**6.8**	**33**	**9**	**24**	**3**	**+3**	**10**	**1**	**1**	**2**	**12**	**0**	**0**	**0**
1995-96	**Pittsburgh Penguins**	**NHL**	**70**	**5**	**14**	**19**	**5**	**11**	**16**	**71**	**0**	**0**	**1**	**94**	**5.3**	**61**	**5**	**62**	**12**	**+6**	**15**	**1**	**0**	**1**	**8**	**0**	**0**	**0**
1996-97	**Vancouver Canucks**	**NHL**	**63**	**3**	**13**	**16**	**3**	**11**	**14**	**62**	**2**	**0**	**1**	**99**	**3.0**	**69**	**24**	**83**	**17**	**–21**	....	....	....	....	....	....	....	....
1997-98	**Philadelphia Flyers**	**NHL**	**15**	**1**	**0**	**1**	**1**	**0**	**1**	**19**	**0**	**0**	**1**	**20**	**5.0**	**10**	**3**	**8**	**2**	**+1**	**1**	**0**	**0**	**0**	**2**	**0**	**0**	**0**
	Philadelphia Phantoms	AHL	6	2	3	5	....	....	....	2	....	....	....	....	....	....	....	....	....	....	....	....	....	....	....	....	....	....
	NHL Totals		**418**	**36**	**99**	**135**	**38**	**84**	**122**	**523**	**16**	**0**	**3**	**648**	**5.6**	**444**	**131**	**420**	**56**		**31**	**3**	**4**	**7**	**24**	**0**	**0**	**0**

WHL West Second All-Star Team (1987)

Traded to **Edmonton** by **Pittsburgh** with Craig Simpson, Dave Hannan and Moe Mantha for Paul Coffey, Dave Hunter and Wayne Van Dorp, November 24, 1987. Traded to **Tampa Bay** by **Edmonton** for Bob Beers, November 11, 1993. Claimed by **Pittsburgh** from **Tampa Bay** in NHL Waiver Draft, January 18, 1995. Claimed by **Vancouver** from **Pittsburgh** in NHL Waiver Draft, September 30, 1996.

• JOVANOVSKI, ED

Ed Jovanovski D – L. 6'2", 205 lbs. b: Windsor, Ont., 6/26/1976. Florida's 1st choice, 1st overall, in 1994 Entry Draft.

Season	Club	League	GP	G	A	Pts	AG	AA	APts	PIM	PP	SH	GW	S	%	TGF	PGF	TGA	PGA	+/–	GP	G	A	Pts	PIM	PP	SH	GW
1993-94	Windsor Spitfires	OHL	62	15	36	51	....	....	....	221	....	....	....	....	....	....	....	....	....	....	4	0	0	0	15	....	....	....
1994-95	Windsor Spitfires	OHL	50	23	42	65	....	....	....	198	....	....	....	....	....	....	....	....	....	....	9	2	7	9	39	....	....	....
	Canada	WJC-A	7	2	0	2	....	....	....	4	....	....	....	....	....	....	....	....	....	....	....	....	....	....	....	....	....	....
1995-96	**Florida Panthers**	**NHL**	**70**	**10**	**11**	**21**	**10**	**9**	**19**	**137**	**2**	**0**	**2**	**116**	**8.6**	**60**	**17**	**50**	**4**	**–3**	**22**	**1**	**8**	**9**	**52**	**0**	**0**	**0**
1996-97	Canada	W Cup	DID NOT PLAY																									
	Florida Panthers	**NHL**	**61**	**7**	**16**	**23**	**7**	**14**	**21**	**172**	**3**	**0**	**1**	**80**	**8.8**	**57**	**16**	**44**	**2**	**–1**	**5**	**0**	**0**	**0**	**4**	**0**	**0**	**0**
1997-98	**Florida Panthers**	**NHL**	**81**	**9**	**14**	**23**	**11**	**14**	**25**	**158**	**2**	**1**	**3**	**142**	**6.3**	**64**	**15**	**69**	**8**	**–12**	....	....	....	....	....	....	....	....
	Canada	WC-A	6	2	1	3	....	....	....	6	....	....	....	....	....	....	....	....	....	....	....	....	....	....	....	....	....	....
	NHL Totals		**212**	**26**	**41**	**67**	**28**	**37**	**65**	**467**	**7**	**1**	**6**	**338**	**7.7**	**181**	**48**	**163**	**14**		**27**	**1**	**8**	**9**	**56**	**0**	**0**	**0**

OHL Second All-Star Team (1994) • OHL First All-Star Team (1995) • NHL All-Rookie Team (1996)

• JOYAL, EDDIE

Eddie Joyal C. 6', 178 lbs. b: Edmonton, Alta., 5/8/1940.

Season	Club	League	GP	G	A	Pts	AG	AA	APts	PIM	PP	SH	GW	S	%	TGF	PGF	TGA	PGA	+/–	GP	G	A	Pts	PIM	PP	SH	GW
1958-59	Edmonton Oil Kings	WCJHL	35	23	23	46	....	....	....	8	....	....	....	....	....	....	....	....	....	....	....	....	....	....	....	....	....	....
1959-60	Edmonton Oil Kings	WCJHL	23	16	22	38	....	....	....	10	....	....	....	....	....	....	....	....	....	....	....	....	....	....	....	....	....	....
	Calgary Stampeders	WHL	1	0	0	0	....	....	....	0	....	....	....	....	....	....	....	....	....	....	....	....	....	....	....	....	....	....
1960-61	Edmonton Flyers	WHL	64	20	27	47	....	....	....	12	....	....	....	....	....	....	....	....	....	....	....	....	....	....	....	....	....	....
1961-62	Edmonton Flyers	WHL	70	37	32	69	....	....	....	14	....	....	....	....	....	....	....	....	....	....	12	*10	8	18	4	....	....	....
1962-63	**Detroit Red Wings**	**NHL**	**14**	**2**	**8**	**10**	**2**	**8**	**10**	**0**	....	....	....	....	....	....	....	....	....	....	**11**	**1**	**0**	**1**	**2**	....	....	....
	Pittsburgh Hornets	AHL	54	29	27	56	....	....	....	6	....	....	....	....	....	....	....	....	....	....	....	....	....	....	....	....	....	....
1963-64	**Detroit Red Wings**	**NHL**	**47**	**10**	**7**	**17**	**13**	**8**	**21**	**6**	....	....	....	....	....	....	....	....	....	....	**14**	**2**	**3**	**5**	**10**	....	....	....
	Pittsburgh Hornets	AHL	5	3	3	6	....	....	....	6	....	....	....	....	....	....	....	....	....	....	....	....	....	....	....	....	....	....
1964-65	**Detroit Red Wings**	**NHL**	**46**	**8**	**14**	**22**	**10**	**15**	**25**	**4**	....	....	....	....	....	....	....	....	....	....	**7**	**1**	**1**	**2**	**4**	....	....	....
	Pittsburgh Hornets	AHL	6	5	3	8	....	....	....	0	....	....	....	....	....	....	....	....	....	....	....	....	....	....	....	....	....	....
1965-66	**Toronto Maple Leafs**	**NHL**	**14**	**0**	**2**	**2**	**0**	**2**	**2**	**2**	....	....	....	....	....	....	....	....	....	....	....	....	....	....	....	....	....	....
	Rochester Americans	AHL	9	9	1	10	....	....	....	6	....	....	....	....	....	....	....	....	....	....	....	....	....	....	....	....	....	....
	Tulsa Oilers	CHL	41	32	25	57	....	....	....	38	....	....	....	....	....	....	....	....	....	....	11	2	5	7	2	....	....	....
1966-67	Rochester Americans	AHL	70	32	51	83	....	....	....	10	....	....	....	....	....	....	....	....	....	....	13	*10	3	13	4	....	....	....
1967-68	**Los Angeles Kings**	**NHL**	**74**	**23**	**34**	**57**	**28**	**36**	**64**	**20**	**5**	**0**	**3**	**226**	**10.2**	**69**	**17**	**55**	**1**	**–2**	**7**	**4**	**1**	**5**	**2**	**3**	**0**	**1**
1968-69	**Los Angeles Kings**	**NHL**	**73**	**33**	**19**	**52**	**37**	**18**	**55**	**24**	**9**	**0**	**5**	**222**	**14.9**	**71**	**20**	**81**	**0**	**–30**	**11**	**3**	**3**	**6**	**0**	**1**	**0**	**0**
1969-70	**Los Angeles Kings**	**NHL**	**59**	**18**	**22**	**40**	**21**	**22**	**43**	**8**	**6**	**1**	**1**	**173**	**10.4**	**47**	**14**	**57**	**7**	**–17**	....	....	....	....	....	....	....	....
1970-71	**Los Angeles Kings**	**NHL**	**69**	**20**	**21**	**41**	**21**	**18**	**39**	**14**	**3**	**0**	**1**	**168**	**11.9**	**57**	**13**	**55**	**1**	**–10**	....	....	....	....	....	....	....	....
1971-72	**Los Angeles Kings**	**NHL**	**44**	**11**	**3**	**14**	**12**	**3**	**15**	**17**	**1**	**0**	**2**	**70**	**15.7**	**22**	**2**	**50**	**0**	**–30**	....	....	....	....	....	....	....	....
	Philadelphia Flyers	**NHL**	**26**	**3**	**4**	**7**	**3**	**4**	**7**	**8**	**2**	**0**	**0**	**41**	**7.3**	**11**	**4**	**20**	**0**	**–13**	....	....	....	....	....	....	....	....
1972-73	Alberta Oilers	WHA	71	22	16	38	....	....	....	16	....	....	....	....	....	....	....	....	....	....	....	....	....	....	....	....	....	....
1973-74	Edmonton Oilers	WHA	45	8	10	18	....	....	....	2	....	....	....	....	....	....	....	....	....	....	5	2	0	2	4	....	....	....
1974-75	Edmonton Oilers	WHA	78	22	25	47	....	....	....	2	....	....	....	....	....	....	....	....	....	....	....	....	....	....	....	....	....	....
1975-76	Edmonton Oilers	WHA	45	5	4	9	....	....	....	6	....	....	....	....	....	....	....	....	....	....	....	....	....	....	....	....	....	....
	NHL Totals		**466**	**128**	**134**	**262**	**147**	**134**	**281**	**103**	**26**	**1**	**12**	**900**	**14.2**	**277**	**70**	**318**	**9**		**50**	**11**	**8**	**19**	**18**	**4**	**0**	**1**
	Other Major League Totals		239	57	55	112	....	....	....	26	....	....	....	....	....	....	....	....	....	....	5	2	0	2	4	....	....	....

CHL Second All-Star Team (1966)

Traded to **Toronto** by **Detroit** with Marcel Pronovost, Larry Jeffrey, Lowell McDonald and Aut Erickson for Andy Bathgate and Gary Jarrett, May 20, 1965. Claimed by **LA Kings** from **Toronto** in Expansion Draft, June 6, 1967. Traded to **Philadelphia** by **LA Kings** with Bill Flett, Jean Potvin and Ross Lonsberry for Bill Lesuk, Jim Johnson and Serge Bernier, January 28, 1972. Selected by **Alberta** (WHA) in 1972 WHA General Player Draft, February 12, 1972.

• JOYCE, BOB

Bob Joyce LW – L. 6', 195 lbs. b: St. John, N.B., 7/11/1966. Boston's 4th choice, 82nd overall, in 1984 Entry Draft.

Season	Club	League	GP	G	A	Pts	AG	AA	APts	PIM	PP	SH	GW	S	%	TGF	PGF	TGA	PGA	+/–	GP	G	A	Pts	PIM	PP	SH	GW
1983-84	Notre Dame Hounds	SJHL	30	33	37	70	....	....	....	....	....	....	....	....	....	....	....	....	....	....	....	....	....	....	....	....	....	....
1984-85	University of North Dakota	WCHA	41	18	16	34	....	....	....	10	....	....	....	....	....	....	....	....	....	....	....	....	....	....	....	....	....	....
1985-86	University of North Dakota	WCHA	38	31	28	59	....	....	....	40	....	....	....	....	....	....	....	....	....	....	....	....	....	....	....	....	....	....
1986-87	University of North Dakota	WCHA	48	*52	37	89	....	....	....	42	....	....	....	....	....	....	....	....	....	....	....	....	....	....	....	....	....	....
1987-88	Canada	Nat-Team	46	12	10	22	....	....	....	28	....	....	....	....	....	....	....	....	....	....	....	....	....	....	....	....	....	....
	Canada	Olympics	4	1	0	1	....	....	....	0	....	....	....	....	....	....	....	....	....	....	....	....	....	....	....	....	....	....
	Boston Bruins	**NHL**	**15**	**7**	**5**	**12**	**6**	**4**	**10**	**10**	**2**	**0**	**0**	**30**	**23.3**	**17**	**5**	**8**	**0**	**+4**	**23**	**8**	**6**	**14**	**18**	**3**	**0**	**1**
1988-89	**Boston Bruins**	**NHL**	**77**	**18**	**31**	**49**	**15**	**22**	**37**	**46**	**7**	**0**	**3**	**142**	**12.7**	**86**	**28**	**51**	**1**	**+8**	**9**	**5**	**2**	**7**	**2**	**0**	**0**	**0**
1989-90	**Boston Bruins**	**NHL**	**23**	**1**	**2**	**3**	**1**	**1**	**2**	**22**	**0**	**0**	**0**	**32**	**3.1**	**7**	**1**	**16**	**2**	**–8**	....	....	....	....	....	....	....	....
	Washington Capitals	**NHL**	**24**	**5**	**8**	**13**	**4**	**6**	**10**	**4**	**1**	**0**	**1**	**30**	**16.7**	**19**	**4**	**13**	**0**	**+2**	**14**	**2**	**1**	**3**	**9**	**0**	**0**	**0**
1990-91	**Washington Capitals**	**NHL**	**17**	**3**	**3**	**6**	**3**	**2**	**5**	**8**	**0**	**0**	**1**	**30**	**10.0**	**11**	**0**	**8**	**0**	**+3**	....	....	....	....	....	....	....	....
	Baltimore Skipjacks	AHL	36	10	8	18	....	....	....	14	....	....	....	....	....	....	....	....	....	....	6	1	0	1	4	....	....	....

Season	Club	League	GP	G	A	Pts	AG	AA	APts	PIM	PP	SH	GW	S	%	TGF	PGF	TGA	PGA	+/-	GP	G	A	Pts	PIM	PP	SH	GW
1991-92	**Winnipeg Jets**	NHL	1	0	0	0	0	0	0	0	0	0	0	0	0.0	0	0	0	0	0								
	Moncton Hawks	AHL	66	19	29	48				51											10	0	5	5	9			
1992-93	**Winnipeg Jets**	NHL	1	0	0	0	0	0	0	0	0	0	0	0	0.0	0	0	0	0	0								
	Moncton Hawks	AHL	75	25	32	57				52											5	0	0	0	2			
1993-94	Las Vegas Thunder	IHL	63	15	18	33				45											5	2	1	3	8			
1994-95	Las Vegas Thunder	IHL	60	15	12	27				52											10	4	3	7	26			
1995-96	Orlando Solar Bears	IHL	55	7	11	18				81											18	2	1	3	12			
1996-97	Orlando Solar Bears	IHL	76	15	33	48				98											5	0	0	0	2			
	NHL Totals		158	34	49	83	29	35	64	90	10	0	5	264	12.9	140	38	96		3	46	15	9	24	29	3	0	1

WCHA First All-Star Team (1987) • NCAA West First All-American Team (1987) • NCAA Championship All-Tournament Team (1987)

Traded to **Washington** by **Boston** for Dave Christian, December 13, 1989. Traded to **Winnipeg** by **Washington** with Tyler Larter and Kent Paynter for Craig Duncanson, Brent Hughes and Simon Wheeldon, May 21, 1991.

● JOYCE, DUANE   Duane Joyce   D – R. 6'2", 203 lbs. b: Pembroke, MA, 5/5/1965.

Season	Club	League	GP	G	A	Pts	AG	AA	APts	PIM	PP	SH	GW	S	%	TGF	PGF	TGA	PGA	+/-	GP	G	A	Pts	PIM	PP	SH	GW
1986-87	Union College	NCAA II							STATISTICS NOT AVAILABLE																				
1987-88	Virginia Lancers	AAHL	42	22	45	67				73											8	3	5	8	6			
	Springfield Indians	AHL	1	1	1	2				0																		
1988-89	Springfield Indians	AHL	3	0	0	0				0																		
1989-90	Kalamazoo Wings	IHL	2	0	0	0				2																		
	Fort Wayne Komets	IHL	66	10	26	36				53																		
	Muskegon Lumberjacks	IHL	13	3	10	13				8											12	3	7	10	13			
1990-91	Kalamazoo Wings	IHL	80	12	32	44				53											11	0	3	3	6			
1991-92	Kansas City Blades	IHL	80	12	32	44				62											15	6	11	17	8			
1992-93	Kansas City Blades	IHL	75	15	25	40				30											12	1	2	3	6			
1993-94	**Dallas Stars**	NHL	3	0	0	0	0	0	0	0	0	0	0	1	0.0	0	0	0	0									
	Kansas City Blades	IHL	43	9	23	32				40																		
1994-95	Kansas City Blades	IHL	71	9	21	30				31											21	2	5	7	4			
1995-96	Cincinnati Cyclones	IHL	49	11	25	36				36																		
	Orlando Solar Bears	IHL	34	3	17	20				18											21	4	6	10	2			
1996-97	Cincinnati Cyclones	IHL	38	3	16	19				12											3	1	2	3	0			
1997-98	Adirondack Red Wings	AHL	66	7	21	28				30																		
	Detroit Vipers	IHL	7	0	2	2				4											15	5	4	9	4			
	NHL Totals		3	0	0	0	0	0	0	0	0	0	0	1	0.0	0	0	0	0									

Signed as a free agent by **San Jose**, August 13, 1991. Signed as a free agent by **Dallas**, December 3, 1993.

● JUHLIN, PATRIK   Patrik Juhlin   LW – L. 6', 194 lbs. b: Huddinge, Sweden, 4/24/1970. Philadelphia's 2nd choice, 34th overall, in 1989 Entry Draft.

Season	Club	League	GP	G	A	Pts	AG	AA	APts	PIM	PP	SH	GW	S	%	TGF	PGF	TGA	PGA	+/-	GP	G	A	Pts	PIM	PP	SH	GW
1988-89	Vasteras IK	Sweden 2	30	29	13	42				18											2	0	0	0	0			
1989-90	Vasteras IK	Sweden	35	10	13	23				18																		
	Sweden	WJC-A	6	1	0	1				0																		
1990-91	Vasteras IK	Sweden	40	13	9	22				24											4	3	1	4	0			
1991-92	Vasteras IK	Sweden	39	15	12	27				40																		
1992-93	Vasteras IK	Sweden	34	14	12	26				22											3	0	1	1	2			
	Sweden	WC-A	8	2	1	3				4																		
1993-94	Vasteras IK	Sweden	40	15	16	31				20											4	1	1	2	2			
	Sweden	Olympics	8	7	1	8				16																		
	Sweden	WC-A	1	0	0	0				0																		
1994-95	Vasteras IK	Sweden	11	5	9	14				8																		
	Philadelphia Flyers	NHL	42	4	3	7	7	4	11	6	0	0	1	44	9.1	10	1	22	0	-13	13	1	0	1	2	0	0	0
1995-96	**Philadelphia Flyers**	NHL	14	3	3	6	3	2	5	17	1	0	0	14	21.4	7	1	2	0	+4	1	0	0	0	0			
	Hershey Bears	AHL	14	5	2	7				8																		
1996-97	Sweden	W Cup	4	0	0	0				2																		
	Philadelphia Phantoms	AHL	70	31	60	91				24											8	7	6	13	4			
1997-98	Jokerit Helsinki	EuroHL	6	2	3	5				2																		
	Jokerit Helsinki	Finland	47	19	9	28				14											7	5	0	5	4			
	NHL Totals		56	7	6	13	10	6	16	23	1	0	1	58	12.1	17	2	24	0		13	1	0	1	2	0	0	0

AHL First All-Star Team (1997)

● JULIEN, CLAUDE   Claude Julien   D – R. 6', 198 lbs. b: Blind River, Ont., 4/23/1960.

Season	Club	League	GP	G	A	Pts	AG	AA	APts	PIM	PP	SH	GW	S	%	TGF	PGF	TGA	PGA	+/-	GP	G	A	Pts	PIM	PP	SH	GW
1977-78	Newmarket Flyers	OJHL	45	18	26	44				137																		
	Oshawa Generals	OHA	11	0	5	5				14																		
1978-79						DID NOT PLAY – INJURED																						
1979-80	Windsor Spitfires	OHA	68	14	37	51				140											16	5	11	16	23			
1980-81	Windsor Spitfires	OHL	3	1	2	3				21																		
	Port Huron Flags	IHL	77	15	40	55				153											4	1	1	2	4			
1981-82	Salt Lake Golden Eagles	CHL	70	4	18	22				134											5	1	4	5	0			
1982-83	Salt Lake Golden Eagles	CHL	76	14	47	61				176											6	3	3	6	16			
1983-84	Milwaukee Admirals	IHL	5	0	3	3				2																		
	Fredericton Express	AHL	57	7	22	29				58											7	0	4	4	6			
1984-85	**Quebec Nordiques**	NHL	1	0	0	0	0	0	0	0	0	0	0	0	0.0	0	0	0	0	0								
	Fredericton Express	AHL	77	6	28	34				97											6	2	4	6	13			
1985-86	**Quebec Nordiques**	NHL	13	0	1	1	0	1	1	25	0	0	0	4	0.0	5	0	4	1	+2								
	Fredericton Express	AHL	49	3	18	21				74											6	1	4	5	19			
1986-87	Fredericton Express	AHL	17	1	6	7				22																		
	Paris Volants	France	36	15	50	65				22																		
1987-88	Baltimore Skipjacks	AHL	30	6	14	20				22																		
	Fredericton Express	AHL	35	1	14	15				52											13	1	3	4	30			
1988-89	Halifax Citadels	AHL	79	8	52	60				72											4	0	2	2	4			
1989-90	Halifax Citadels	AHL	77	6	37	43				65											4	0	1	1	7			
1990-91	Kansas City Blades	IHL	54	7	16	23				43																		
1991-92	Moncton Hawks	AHL	48	2	15	17				10											4	0	1	1	4			
	NHL Totals		14	0	1	1	0	1	1	25	0	0	0	4	0.0	5	0	4	1									

CHL Second All-Star Team (1983) • AHL Second All-Star Team (1989)

Signed as a free agent by **St. Louis**, September 28, 1981. Transferred to **Quebec** by **St. Louis** with the rights to Gord Donnelly as compensation for St. Louis' signing of Jacques Demers as coach, August 19, 1983.

● JUNEAU, JOE   Joe Juneau   C – L. 6', 195 lbs. b: Pont-Rouge, Que., 1/5/1968. Boston's 3rd choice, 81st overall, in 1988 Entry Draft.

Season	Club	League	GP	G	A	Pts	AG	AA	APts	PIM	PP	SH	GW	S	%	TGF	PGF	TGA	PGA	+/-	GP	G	A	Pts	PIM	PP	SH	GW
1987-88	RPI Engineers	ECAC	31	16	29	45				18																		
1988-89	RPI Engineers	ECAC	30	12	23	35				40																		
1989-90	RPI Engineers	ECAC	34	18	*52	*70				31																		
	Canada	Nat-Team	3	0	2	2				4																		
1990-91	RPI Engineers	ECAC	29	23	40	63				68																		
	Canada	Nat-Team	7	2	3	5				0																		
1991-92	Canada	Nat-Team	60	20	49	69				35																		
	Canada	Olympics	8	6	9	15				4																		
	Boston Bruins	NHL	14	5	14	19	5	11	16	4	2	0	0	38	13.2	30	14	11	1	+6	15	4	8	12	21	2	0	0
1992-93	**Boston Bruins**	NHL	84	32	70	102	27	48	75	33	9	0	3	229	14.0	150	64	64	1	+23	4	2	4	6	2	0	0	0
1993-94	**Boston Bruins**	NHL	63	14	58	72	13	45	58	35	4	0	2	142	9.9	115	53	54	3	+11								
	Washington Capitals	NHL	11	5	8	13	6	6	11	8	2	0	0	22	22.7	16	7	9	0	+0	11	4	5	9	6	2	0	1

			REGULAR SEASON																		PLAYOFFS							
Season	**Club**	**League**	**GP**	**G**	**A**	**Pts**	**AG**	**AA**	**APts**	**PIM**	**PP**	**SH**	**GW**	**S**	**%**	**TGF**	**PGF**	**TGA**	**PGA**	**+/–**	**GP**	**G**	**A**	**Pts**	**PIM**	**PP**	**SH**	**GW**
1994-95	**Washington Capitals**	**NHL**	**44**	**5**	**38**	**43**	**9**	**56**	**65**	**8**	**3**	**0**	**0**	**70**	**7.1**	**58**	**33**	**26**	**0**	**–1**	**7**	**2**	**6**	**8**	**2**	**0**	**0**	**0**
1995-96	**Washington Capitals**	**NHL**	**80**	**14**	**50**	**64**	**14**	**41**	**55**	**30**	**7**	**2**	**2**	**176**	**8.0**	**82**	**38**	**69**	**22**	**–3**	**5**	**0**	**7**	**7**	**6**	**0**	**0**	**0**
1996-97	**Washington Capitals**	**NHL**	**58**	**15**	**27**	**42**	**16**	**24**	**40**	**8**	**9**	**1**	**3**	**124**	**12.1**	**60**	**26**	**59**	**14**	**–11**	....	....	....	....	....	....	....	....
1997-98	**Washington Capitals**	**NHL**	**56**	**9**	**22**	**31**	**11**	**21**	**32**	**26**	**4**	**1**	**1**	**87**	**10.3**	**42**	**16**	**43**	**9**	**–8**	**21**	**7**	**10**	**17**	**8**	**1**	**1**	**4**
	NHL Totals		**410**	**99**	**287**	**386**	**100**	**252**	**352**	**150**	**40**	**4**	**11**	**888**	**11.1**	**553**	**251**	**335**	**50**		**63**	**19**	**40**	**59**	**49**	**7**	**1**	**5**

NCAA East First All-American Team (1990) • ECAC Second All-Star Team (1991) • NCAA East Second All-American Team (1991) • NHL/Upper Deck All-Rookie Team (1993)

Traded to **Washington** by **Boston** for Al Iafrate, March 21, 1994.

• JUNKER, STEVE

Steve Junker LW – L. 6', 184 lbs. b: Castlegar, B.C., 6/26/1972. NY Islanders' 5th choice, 92nd overall, in 1991 Entry Draft.

1990-91	Spokane Chiefs	WHL	71	39	38	77	....	....	....	86	....	....	....	....	....	....	....	....	....	....	15	5	13	18	6	....	....	....
1991-92	Spokane Chiefs	WHL	58	28	32	60	....	....	....	110	....	....	....	....	....	....	....	....	....	....	10	6	7	13	18	....	....	....
	Canada	WJC-A	7	2	2	4	....	....	....	4	....	....	....	....	....	....	....	....	....	....	....	....	....	....	....	....	....	....
1992-93	Capital District Islanders	AHL	79	16	31	47	....	....	....	20	....	....	....	....	....	....	....	....	....	....	4	0	0	0	0	....	....	....
	New York Islanders	**NHL**	....	....	....	....	....	....	....	....	....	....	....	....	....	....	....	....	....	....	**3**	**0**	**1**	**1**	**0**	....	....	....
1993-94	**New York Islanders**	**NHL**	**5**	**0**	**0**	**0**	**0**	**0**	**0**	**0**	**0**	**0**	**0**	**2**	**0.0**	**0**	**0**	**2**	**2**	**0**	....	....	....	....	....	....	....	....
	Salt Lake Golden Eagles	IHL	71	9	14	23	....	....	....	36	....	....	....	....	....	....	....	....	....	....	....	....	....	....	....	....	....	....
1994-95	Denver Grizzlies	IHL	72	13	16	29	....	....	....	37	....	....	....	....	....	....	....	....	....	....	11	3	4	7	4	....	....	....
1995-96	Rochester Americans	AHL	29	5	2	7	....	....	....	31	....	....	....	....	....	....	....	....	....	....	....	....	....	....	....	....	....	....
	Detroit Vipers	IHL	22	4	5	9	....	....	....	14	....	....	....	....	....	....	....	....	....	....	....	....	....	....	....	....	....	....
	Los Angeles Ice Dogs	IHL	7	0	3	3	....	....	....	4	....	....	....	....	....	....	....	....	....	....	....	....	....	....	....	....	....	....
1996-97	Canada	Nat-Team	55	15	23	38	....	....	....	24	....	....	....	....	....	....	....	....	....	....	....	....	....	....	....	....	....	....
1997-98	EV Landshut	Germany	39	3	4	7	....	....	....	6	....	....	....	....	....	....	....	....	....	....	6	0	0	0	6	....	....	....
	NHL Totals		**5**	**0**	**0**	**0**	**0**	**0**	**0**	**0**	**0**	**0**	**0**	**2**	**0.0**	**0**	**0**	**2**	**2**		**3**	**0**	**1**	**1**	**0**	**0**	**0**	**0**

• JUTILA, TIMO

Timo Jutila D – L. 5'7", 175 lbs. b: Turku, Finland, 12/24/1963. Buffalo's 6th choice, 68th overall, in 1982 Entry Draft.

1980-81	Tappara Tampere	Finland	36	9	12	21	....	....	....	44	....	....	....	....	....	....	....	....	....	....	8	3	2	5	6	....	....	....
	Finland	WJC-A	5	1	0	1	....	....	....	2	....	....	....	....	....	....	....	....	....	....	....	....	....	....	....	....	....	....
1981-82	Tappara Tampere	Finland	36	8	11	19	....	....	....	41	....	....	....	....	....	....	....	....	....	....	11	0	0	0	16	....	....	....
	Finland	WJC-A	7	1	6	7	....	....	....	14	....	....	....	....	....	....	....	....	....	....	....	....	....	....	....	....	....	....
1982-83	Tappara Tampere	Finland	36	8	14	22	....	....	....	46	....	....	....	....	....	....	....	....	....	....	8	1	3	4	24	....	....	....
	Finland	WJC-A	7	1	1	2	....	....	....	14	....	....	....	....	....	....	....	....	....	....	....	....	....	....	....	....	....	....
1983-84	Tappara Tampere	Finland	37	5	22	27	....	....	....	57	....	....	....	....	....	....	....	....	....	....	9	0	5	5	18	....	....	....
	Finland	Olympics	5	0	0	0	....	....	....	8	....	....	....	....	....	....	....	....	....	....	....	....	....	....	....	....	....	....
1984-85	**Buffalo Sabres**	**NHL**	**10**	**1**	**5**	**6**	**1**	**3**	**4**	**13**	**1**	**0**	**0**	**28**	**3.6**	**15**	**7**	**13**	**0**	**–5**	....	....	....	....	....	....	....	....
	Rochester Americans	AHL	56	13	30	43	....	....	....	26	....	....	....	....	....	....	....	....	....	....	5	2	5	7	2	....	....	....
1985-86	Tappara Tampere	Finland	30	8	11	19	....	....	....	16	....	....	....	....	....	....	....	....	....	....	8	3	6	9	2	....	....	....
1986-87	Tappara Tampere	Finland	44	10	28	38	....	....	....	60	....	....	....	....	....	....	....	....	....	....	9	1	5	6	18	....	....	....
	Finland	WEC-A	9	1	3	4	....	....	....	4	....	....	....	....	....	....	....	....	....	....	....	....	....	....	....	....	....	....
1987-88	Finland	C Cup	5	1	0	1	....	....	....	6	....	....	....	....	....	....	....	....	....	....	....	....	....	....	....	....	....	....
	Tappara Tampere	Finland	44	12	34	46	....	....	....	50	....	....	....	....	....	....	....	....	....	....	10	6	6	12	16	....	....	....
1988-89	Lulea HF	Sweden	35	7	19	26	....	....	....	42	....	....	....	....	....	....	....	....	....	....	3	0	0	0	2	....	....	....
1989-90	Lulea HF	Sweden	36	6	23	29	....	....	....	42	....	....	....	....	....	....	....	....	....	....	5	1	2	3	0	....	....	....
1990-91	Lulea HF	Sweden	40	8	25	33	....	....	....	55	....	....	....	....	....	....	....	....	....	....	5	0	2	2	8	....	....	....
	Finland	WEC-A	10	0	1	1	....	....	....	14	....	....	....	....	....	....	....	....	....	....	....	....	....	....	....	....	....	....
1991-92	Finland	C Cup	6	0	0	0	....	....	....	2	....	....	....	....	....	....	....	....	....	....	....	....	....	....	....	....	....	....
	Lulea HF	Sweden	40	11	26	37	....	....	....	48	....	....	....	....	....	....	....	....	....	....	2	1	0	1	4	....	....	....
	Finland	Olympics	8	2	2	4	....	....	....	2	....	....	....	....	....	....	....	....	....	....	....	....	....	....	....	....	....	....
	Finland	WC-A	8	2	5	7	....	....	....	10	....	....	....	....	....	....	....	....	....	....	....	....	....	....	....	....	....	....
1992-93	Tappara Tampere	Finland	47	10	33	43	....	....	....	54	....	....	....	....	....	....	....	....	....	....	....	....	....	....	....	....	....	....
	Finland	WC-A	6	1	2	3	....	....	....	8	....	....	....	....	....	....	....	....	....	....	....	....	....	....	....	....	....	....
1993-94	Tappara Tampere	Finland	48	13	36	49	....	....	....	30	....	....	....	....	....	....	....	....	....	....	10	2	5	7	12	....	....	....
	Finland	Olympics	8	1	2	3	....	....	....	6	....	....	....	....	....	....	....	....	....	....	....	....	....	....	....	....	....	....
	Finland	WC-A	8	3	4	7	....	....	....	6	....	....	....	....	....	....	....	....	....	....	....	....	....	....	....	....	....	....
1994-95	Tappara Tampere	Finland	50	11	30	41	....	....	....	66	....	....	....	....	....	....	....	....	....	....	....	....	....	....	....	....	....	....
	Finland	WC-A	8	5	2	7	....	....	....	10	....	....	....	....	....	....	....	....	....	....	....	....	....	....	....	....	....	....
1995-96	Tappara Tampere	Finland	49	14	37	51	....	....	....	62	....	....	....	....	....	....	....	....	....	....	4	0	0	0	6	....	....	....
	Finland	WC-A	6	0	1	1	....	....	....	4	....	....	....	....	....	....	....	....	....	....	....	....	....	....	....	....	....	....
1996-97	SC Bern	Switz.	29	8	20	28	....	....	....	26	....	....	....	....	....	....	....	....	....	....	....	....	....	....	....	....	....	....
	Finland	WC-A	8	1	3	4	....	....	....	6	....	....	....	....	....	....	....	....	....	....	....	....	....	....	....	....	....	....
1997-98	Tappara Tampere	Finland	48	7	20	27	....	....	....	77	....	....	....	....	....	....	....	....	....	....	4	1	1	2	2	....	....	....
	NHL Totals		**10**	**1**	**5**	**6**	**1**	**3**	**4**	**13**	**1**	**0**	**0**	**28**	**3.6**	**15**	**7**	**13**	**0**		....	....	....	....	....	....	....	....

Finnish First All-Star Team (1987, 1988, 1993, 1994, 1996) • WC-A All-Star Team (1992, 1994, 1995)

• KACHOWSKI, MARK

Mark Kachowski LW – L. 5'11", 200 lbs. b: Edmonton, Alta., 2/20/1965.

1983-84	Kamloops Blazers	WHL	57	6	9	15	....	....	....	156	....	....	....	....	....	....	....	....	....	....	16	4	2	6	29	....	....	....
1984-85	Kamloops Blazers	WHL	68	22	15	37	....	....	....	185	....	....	....	....	....	....	....	....	....	....	14	6	8	14	38	....	....	....
1985-86	Kamloops Blazers	WHL	61	21	31	52	....	....	....	182	....	....	....	....	....	....	....	....	....	....	16	7	8	15	51	....	....	....
1986-87	Flint Spirits	IHL	75	18	13	31	....	....	....	273	....	....	....	....	....	....	....	....	....	....	6	1	1	2	21	....	....	....
1987-88	**Pittsburgh Penguins**	**NHL**	**38**	**5**	**3**	**8**	**4**	**2**	**6**	**126**	**0**	**0**	**1**	**21**	**23.8**	**9**	**0**	**8**	**0**	**+1**	....	....	....	....	....	....	....	....
	Muskegon Lumberjacks	IHL	25	3	6	9	....	....	....	72	....	....	....	....	....	....	....	....	....	....	5	0	2	2	11	....	....	....
1988-89	**Pittsburgh Penguins**	**NHL**	**12**	**1**	**1**	**2**	**1**	**1**	**2**	**43**	**0**	**0**	**0**	**3**	**33.3**	**3**	**0**	**2**	**0**	**+1**	....	....	....	....	....	....	....	....
	Muskegon Lumberjacks	IHL	57	8	8	16	....	....	....	167	....	....	....	....	....	....	....	....	....	....	8	1	2	3	17	....	....	....
1989-90	**Pittsburgh Penguins**	**NHL**	**14**	**0**	**1**	**1**	**0**	**1**	**1**	**40**	**0**	**0**	**0**	**4**	**0.0**	**4**	**1**	**2**	**0**	**+1**	....	....	....	....	....	....	....	....
	Muskegon Lumberjacks	IHL	61	23	8	31	....	....	....	129	....	....	....	....	....	....	....	....	....	....	12	2	4	6	21	....	....	....
1990-91	Muskegon Lumberjacks	IHL	80	19	21	40	....	....	....	108	....	....	....	....	....	....	....	....	....	....	5	1	1	2	9	....	....	....
1991-92	Muskegon Lumberjacks	IHL	6	0	0	0	....	....	....	9	....	....	....	....	....	....	....	....	....	....	4	2	0	2	16	....	....	....
	NHL Totals		**64**	**6**	**5**	**11**	**5**	**4**	**9**	**209**	**0**	**0**	**1**	**28**	**21.4**	**16**	**1**	**12**	**0**		....	....	....	....	....	....	....	....

Signed as a free agent by **Pittsburgh**, August 31, 1987.

• KAESE, TRENT

Trent Kaese RW – R. 5'11", 225 lbs. b: Nanaimo, B.C., 9/9/1967. Buffalo's 8th choice, 161st overall, in 1985 Entry Draft.

1983-84	Lethbridge Broncos	WHL	64	6	6	12	....	....	....	33	....	....	....	....	....	....	....	....	....	....	1	0	0	0	0	....	....	....
1984-85	Lethbridge Broncos	WHL	67	20	18	38	....	....	....	107	....	....	....	....	....	....	....	....	....	....	4	0	1	1	7	....	....	....
1985-86	Lethbridge Broncos	WHL	67	24	41	65	....	....	....	67	....	....	....	....	....	....	....	....	....	....	10	5	3	8	8	....	....	....
1986-87	Swift Current Broncos	WHL	2	1	0	1	....	....	....	4	....	....	....	....	....	....	....	....	....	....	....	....	....	....	....	....	....	....
	Calgary Wranglers	WHL	68	30	24	54	....	....	....	117	....	....	....	....	....	....	....	....	....	....	....	....	....	....	....	....	....	....
	Flint Spirits	IHL	1	0	0	0	....	....	....	0	....	....	....	....	....	....	....	....	....	....	6	4	1	5	9	....	....	....
1987-88	Rochester Americans	AHL	37	6	11	17	....	....	....	32	....	....	....	....	....	....	....	....	....	....	3	1	2	3	2	....	....	....
	Flint Spirits	IHL	43	11	26	37	....	....	....	58	....	....	....	....	....	....	....	....	....	....	12	6	6	12	21	....	....	....
1988-89	**Buffalo Sabres**	**NHL**	**1**	**0**	**0**	**0**	**0**	**0**	**0**	**0**	**0**	**0**	**0**	**5**	**0.0**	**0**	**0**	**0**	**0**	**0**	....	....	....	....	....	....	....	....
	Rochester Americans	AHL	45	9	11	20	....	....	....	68	....	....	....	....	....	....	....	....	....	....	....	....	....	....	....	....	....	....
	Flint Spirits	IHL	9	2	3	5	....	....	....	61	....	....	....	....	....	....	....	....	....	....	....	....	....	....	....	....	....	....
1989-90	Phoenix Roadrunners	IHL	2	0	1	1	....	....	....	2	....	....	....	....	....	....	....	....	....	....	....	....	....	....	....	....	....	....
	Winston-Salem Thunderbirds	ECHL	57	56	51	107	....	....	....	110	....	....	....	....	....	....	....	....	....	....	8	5	1	6	18	....	....	....
1990-91	Peterborough Pirates	Britain	34	85	44	129	....	....	....	166	....	....	....	....	....	....	....	....	....	....	8	18	7	25	14	....	....	....
1991-92	Columbus Chill	ECHL	28	28	22	50	....	....	....	56	....	....	....	....	....	....	....	....	....	....	....	....	....	....	....	....	....	....
	Peterborough Pirates	Britain	15	18	18	36	....	....	....	36	....	....	....	....	....	....	....	....	....	....	....	....	....	....	....	....	....	....
1992-93	Peterborough Pirates	Britain	36	81	45	126	....	....	....	126	....	....	....	....	....	....	....	....	....	....	6	14	13	27	12	....	....	....

			REGULAR SEASON																		PLAYOFFS							
Season	Club	League	GP	G	A	Pts	AG	AA	APts	PIM	PP	SH	GW	S	%	TGF	PGF	TGA	PGA	+/-	GP	G	A	Pts	PIM	PP	SH	GW
1993-94	Milton Keynes Kings	Britain	43	96	92	188	....	....	....	157	....	....	....	....	....	....	....	....	....	....	6	15	12	27	6	....	....	....
1994-95	Milton Keynes Kings	Britain	11	7	10	17	....	....	....	22	....	....	....	....	....	....	....	....	....	....	....	....	....	....	....	....	....	....
	Blackburn Hawks	Britain	28	50	50	100	....	....	....	80	....	....	....	....	....	....	....	....	....	....	....	....	....	....	....	....	....	....
	NHL Totals		1	0	0	0	0	0	0	0	0	0	0	5	0.0	0	0	0	0		....	....	....	....	....	....	....	....

ECHL First All-Star Team (1990)

• KALLUR, ANDERS

Anders "Andy" Kallur RW – L. 5'11", 185 lbs. b: Ludvika, Sweden, 7/6/1952.

Season	Club	League	GP	G	A	Pts	AG	AA	APts	PIM	PP	SH	GW	S	%	TGF	PGF	TGA	PGA	+/-	GP	G	A	Pts	PIM	PP	SH	GW
1972-73	Tunabro	Sweden	14	3	3	6	....	....	....	4	....	....	....	....	....	....	....	....	....	....	6	3	1	4	0	....	....	....
1973-74			STATISTICS NOT AVAILABLE																									
1974-75	MoDo	Sweden	30	*30	16	46	....	....	....	26	....	....	....	....	....	....	....	....	....	....	....	....	....	....	....	....	....	....
1975-76	MoDo	Sweden	36	11	16	27	....	....	....	33	....	....	....	....	....	....	....	....	....	....	....	....	....	....	....	....	....	....
1976-77	Sodertalje	Sweden	38	14	9	23	....	....	....	26	....	....	....	....	....	....	....	....	....	....	....	....	....	....	....	....	....	....
1977-78	Sodertalje	Sweden	30	5	7	12	....	....	....	10	....	....	....	....	....	....	....	....	....	....	....	....	....	....	....	....	....	....
1978-79	Djurgardens	Sweden	36	25	21	46	....	....	....	32	....	....	....	....	....	....	....	....	....	....	4	3	3	6	2	....	....	....
1979-80	**New York Islanders**	**NHL**	**76**	**22**	**30**	**52**	**20**	**23**	**43**	**16**	**5**	**4**	**2**	**138**	**15.9**	**85**	**31**	**70**	**28**	**+12**	....	....	....	....	....	....	....	....
	Indianapolis Checkers	CHL	2	0	2	2	....	....	....	0	....	....	....	....	....	....	....	....	....	....	....	....	....	....	....	....	....	....
1980-81	**New York Islanders**	**NHL**	**78**	**36**	**28**	**64**	**30**	**20**	**50**	**32**	**7**	**6**	**4**	**163**	**22.1**	**88**	**21**	**79**	**37**	**+25**	**12**	**4**	**3**	**7**	**10**	**0**	**2**	**0**
1981-82	Sweden	C Cup	5	3	1	4	....	....	....	0	....	....	....	....	....	....	....	....	....	....	....	....	....	....	....	....	....	....
	New York Islanders	**NHL**	**58**	**18**	**22**	**40**	**14**	**15**	**29**	**18**	**2**	**3**	**3**	**74**	**24.3**	**49**	**8**	**49**	**13**	**+5**	**19**	**1**	**6**	**7**	**8**	**0**	**1**	**0**
1982-83	**New York Islanders**	**NHL**	**55**	**6**	**8**	**14**	**5**	**6**	**11**	**33**	**1**	**1**	**0**	**77**	**7.8**	**35**	**9**	**32**	**15**	**+9**	**20**	**3**	**12**	**15**	**12**	**1**	**1**	**0**
1983-84	**New York Islanders**	**NHL**	**65**	**9**	**14**	**23**	**7**	**9**	**16**	**24**	**2**	**3**	**1**	**70**	**12.9**	**41**	**8**	**47**	**14**	**0**	**17**	**2**	**2**	**4**	**2**	**0**	**1**	**1**
1984-85	**New York Islanders**	**NHL**	**51**	**10**	**8**	**18**	**8**	**5**	**13**	**26**	**0**	**2**	**2**	**72**	**13.9**	**25**	**2**	**44**	**12**	**–9**	**10**	**2**	**0**	**2**	**0**	**0**	**0**	**0**
	NHL Totals		**383**	**101**	**110**	**211**	**84**	**78**	**162**	**149**	**17**	**19**	**12**	**594**	**17.0**	**323**	**79**	**321**	**119**		**78**	**12**	**23**	**35**	**32**	**1**	**5**	**1**

Swedish World All-Star Team (1979) • Swedish Player of the Year (1979)

Signed as a free agent by **NY Islanders**, August 15, 1979.

• KAMENSKY, VALERI

Valeri Kamensky LW – R. 6'2", 198 lbs. b: Voskresensk, USSR, 4/18/1966. Quebec's 8th choice, 129th overall, in 1988 Entry Draft.

Season	Club	League	GP	G	A	Pts	AG	AA	APts	PIM	PP	SH	GW	S	%	TGF	PGF	TGA	PGA	+/-	GP	G	A	Pts	PIM	PP	SH	GW
1982-83	Khimik	USSR	5	0	0	0	....	....	....	0	....	....	....	....	....	....	....	....	....	....	....	....	....	....	....	....	....	....
1983-84	Khimik	USSR	20	2	2	4	....	....	....	6	....	....	....	....	....	....	....	....	....	....	....	....	....	....	....	....	....	....
1984-85	Khimik	USSR	45	9	3	12	....	....	....	24	....	....	....	....	....	....	....	....	....	....	....	....	....	....	....	....	....	....
	Soviet Union	WJC-A	7	2	2	4	....	....	....	8	....	....	....	....	....	....	....	....	....	....	....	....	....	....	....	....	....	....
1985-86	CSKA Moscow	USSR	40	15	9	24	....	....	....	8	....	....	....	....	....	....	....	....	....	....	....	....	....	....	....	....	....	....
	Soviet Union	WJC-A	7	7	6	13	....	....	....	6	....	....	....	....	....	....	....	....	....	....	....	....	....	....	....	....	....	....
	Soviet Union	WEC-A	9	2	0	2	....	....	....	8	....	....	....	....	....	....	....	....	....	....	....	....	....	....	....	....	....	....
1986-87	CSKA Moscow	USSR	37	13	8	21	....	....	....	16	....	....	....	....	....	....	....	....	....	....	....	....	....	....	....	....	....	....
	USSR	RV'87	2	2	1	3	....	....	....	2	....	....	....	....	....	....	....	....	....	....	....	....	....	....	....	....	....	....
	Soviet Union	WEC-A	10	5	3	8	....	....	....	6	....	....	....	....	....	....	....	....	....	....	....	....	....	....	....	....	....	....
1987-88	Soviet Union	C Cup	9	6	1	7	....	....	....	6	....	....	....	....	....	....	....	....	....	....	....	....	....	....	....	....	....	....
	CSKA Moscow	USSR	51	26	20	46	....	....	....	40	....	....	....	....	....	....	....	....	....	....	....	....	....	....	....	....	....	....
	Soviet Union	Olympics	8	4	2	6	....	....	....	4	....	....	....	....	....	....	....	....	....	....	....	....	....	....	....	....	....	....
1988-89	CSKA Moscow	USSR	40	18	10	28	....	....	....	30	....	....	....	....	....	....	....	....	....	....	....	....	....	....	....	....	....	....
	CSKA Moscow	SuperS	7	2	4	6	....	....	....	4	....	....	....	....	....	....	....	....	....	....	....	....	....	....	....	....	....	....
	Soviet Union	WEC-A	10	4	4	8	....	....	....	8	....	....	....	....	....	....	....	....	....	....	....	....	....	....	....	....	....	....
1989-90	CSKA Moscow	FrTour	1	0	0	0	....	....	....	0	....	....	....	....	....	....	....	....	....	....	....	....	....	....	....	....	....	....
	CSKA Moscow	USSR	45	19	18	37	....	....	....	40	....	....	....	....	....	....	....	....	....	....	....	....	....	....	....	....	....	....
	CSKA Moscow	SuperS	5	1	2	3	....	....	....	6	....	....	....	....	....	....	....	....	....	....	....	....	....	....	....	....	....	....
	Soviet Union	WEC-A	10	7	2	9	....	....	....	20	....	....	....	....	....	....	....	....	....	....	....	....	....	....	....	....	....	....
1990-91	CSKA Moscow	FrTour	1	0	0	0	....	....	....	0	....	....	....	....	....	....	....	....	....	....	....	....	....	....	....	....	....	....
	CSKA Moscow	USSR	46	20	26	46	....	....	....	66	....	....	....	....	....	....	....	....	....	....	....	....	....	....	....	....	....	....
	CSKA Moscow	SuperS	4	2	2	4	....	....	....	0	....	....	....	....	....	....	....	....	....	....	....	....	....	....	....	....	....	....
	Soviet Union	WEC-A	10	6	5	11	....	....	....	10	....	....	....	....	....	....	....	....	....	....	....	....	....	....	....	....	....	....
1991-92	**Quebec Nordiques**	**NHL**	**23**	**7**	**14**	**21**	**6**	**11**	**17**	**14**	**2**	**0**	**1**	**42**	**16.7**	**31**	**13**	**23**	**4**	**–1**	....	....	....	....	....	....	....	....
1992-93	**Quebec Nordiques**	**NHL**	**32**	**15**	**22**	**37**	**12**	**15**	**27**	**14**	**2**	**3**	**0**	**94**	**16.0**	**50**	**13**	**26**	**2**	**+13**	**6**	**0**	**1**	**1**	**6**	**0**	**0**	**0**
1993-94	**Quebec Nordiques**	**NHL**	**76**	**28**	**37**	**65**	**26**	**20**	**55**	**42**	**6**	**0**	**1**	**170**	**16.5**	**90**	**23**	**61**	**6**	**+12**	....	....	....	....	....	....	....	....
	Russia	WC-A	6	5	5	10	....	....	....	12	....	....	....	....	....	....	....	....	....	....	....	....	....	....	....	....	....	....
1994-95	Ambri-Piotta	Switz.	12	13	6	19	....	....	....	2	....	....	....	....	....	....	....	....	....	....	....	....	....	....	....	....	....	....
	Quebec Nordiques	**NHL**	**40**	**10**	**20**	**30**	**18**	**29**	**47**	**22**	**5**	**1**	**5**	**70**	**14.3**	**41**	**16**	**26**	**4**	**+3**	**2**	**1**	**0**	**1**	**0**	**0**	**0**	**0**
1995-96	**Colorado Avalanche**	**NHL**	**81**	**38**	**47**	**85**	**38**	**38**	**76**	**85**	**18**	**1**	**5**	**220**	**17.3**	**125**	**47**	**69**	**5**	**+14**	**22**	**10**	**12**	**22**	**28**	**3**	**0**	**2**
1996-97	**Colorado Avalanche**	**NHL**	**68**	**28**	**38**	**66**	**30**	**34**	**64**	**38**	**8**	**0**	**4**	**165**	**17.0**	**100**	**43**	**52**	**0**	**+5**	**17**	**8**	**14**	**22**	**16**	**5**	**0**	**2**
1997-98	**Colorado Avalanche**	**NHL**	**75**	**26**	**40**	**66**	**31**	**39**	**70**	**60**	**8**	**0**	**4**	**173**	**15.0**	**104**	**48**	**60**	**2**	**–2**	**7**	**2**	**3**	**5**	**18**	**1**	**0**	**0**
	Russia	Olympics	6	1	2	3	....	....	....	0	....	....	....	....	....	....	....	....	....	....	....	....	....	....	....	....	....	....
	NHL Totals		**395**	**152**	**218**	**370**	**161**	**195**	**356**	**275**	**49**	**5**	**20**	**934**	**16.3**	**541**	**203**	**317**	**23**		**54**	**21**	**30**	**51**	**68**	**9**	**0**	**4**

USSR First All-Star Team (1990, 1991) • USSR Player of the Year (1991) • WEC-A All-Star Team (1991) • Named Best Forward at WEC-A (1991)

Played in NHL All-Star Game (1998)

Transferred to **Colorado** after **Quebec** franchise relocated, June 21, 1995.

• KAMINSKI, KEVIN

Kevin Kaminski C – L. 5'10", 190 lbs. b: Churchbridge, Sask., 3/13/1969. Minnesota's 3rd choice, 48th overall, in 1987 Entry Draft.

Season	Club	League	GP	G	A	Pts	AG	AA	APts	PIM	PP	SH	GW	S	%	TGF	PGF	TGA	PGA	+/-	GP	G	A	Pts	PIM	PP	SH	GW
1986-87	Saskatoon Blades	WHL	67	26	44	70	....	....	....	325	....	....	....	....	....	....	....	....	....	....	11	5	6	11	45	....	....	....
1987-88	Saskatoon Blades	WHL	55	38	61	99	....	....	....	247	....	....	....	....	....	....	....	....	....	....	10	5	7	12	37	....	....	....
1988-89	Saskatoon Blades	WHL	52	25	43	68	....	....	....	199	....	....	....	....	....	....	....	....	....	....	8	4	9	13	25	....	....	....
	Minnesota North Stars	**NHL**	**1**	**0**	**0**	**0**	**0**	**0**	**0**	**0**	**0**	**0**	**0**	**0**	**0.0**	**0**	**0**	**0**	**0**	**0**	....	....	....	....	....	....	....	....
1989-90	**Quebec Nordiques**	**NHL**	**1**	**0**	**0**	**0**	**0**	**0**	**0**	**0**	**0**	**0**	**0**	**0**	**0.0**	**0**	**0**	**1**	**0**	**–1**	....	....	....	....	....	....	....	....
	Halifax Citadels	AHL	19	3	4	7	....	....	....	128	....	....	....	....	....	....	....	....	....	....	2	0	0	0	5	....	....	....
1990-91	Halifax Citadels	AHL	7	1	0	1	....	....	....	44	....	....	....	....	....	....	....	....	....	....	....	....	....	....	....	....	....	....
	Fort Wayne Komets	IHL	56	9	15	24	....	....	....	*455	....	....	....	....	....	....	....	....	....	....	19	4	2	6	*169	....	....	....
1991-92	**Quebec Nordiques**	**NHL**	**5**	**0**	**0**	**0**	**0**	**0**	**0**	**45**	**0**	**0**	**0**	**6**	**0.0**	**0**	**0**	**2**	**0**	**–2**	....	....	....	....	....	....	....	....
	Halifax Citadels	AHL	63	18	27	45	....	....	....	329	....	....	....	....	....	....	....	....	....	....	....	....	....	....	....	....	....	....
1992-93	Halifax Citadels	AHL	79	27	37	64	....	....	....	*345	....	....	....	....	....	....	....	....	....	....	....	....	....	....	....	....	....	....
1993-94	**Washington Capitals**	**NHL**	**13**	**0**	**5**	**5**	**0**	**4**	**4**	**87**	**0**	**0**	**0**	**9**	**0.0**	**6**	**0**	**4**	**0**	**+2**	....	....	....	....	....	....	....	....
	Portland Pirates	AHL	39	10	22	32	....	....	....	263	....	....	....	....	....	....	....	....	....	....	16	4	5	9	*91	....	....	....
1994-95	**Washington Capitals**	**NHL**	**27**	**1**	**1**	**2**	**2**	**1**	**3**	**102**	**0**	**0**	**1**	**12**	**8.3**	**6**	**1**	**11**	**0**	**–6**	**5**	**0**	**0**	**0**	**36**	**0**	**0**	**0**
	Portland Pirates	AHL	34	15	20	35	....	....	....	292	....	....	....	....	....	....	....	....	....	....	....	....	....	....	....	....	....	....
1995-96	**Washington Capitals**	**NHL**	**54**	**1**	**2**	**3**	**1**	**2**	**3**	**164**	**0**	**0**	**0**	**17**	**5.9**	**6**	**1**	**6**	**0**	**–1**	**3**	**0**	**0**	**0**	**16**	**0**	**0**	**0**
1996-97	**Washington Capitals**	**NHL**	**38**	**1**	**2**	**3**	**1**	**2**	**3**	**130**	**0**	**0**	**0**	**12**	**8.3**	**7**	**1**	**6**	**0**	**0**	....	....	....	....	....	....	....	....
1997-98	Portland Pirates	AHL	40	8	12	20	....	....	....	242	....	....	....	....	....	....	....	....	....	....	8	2	1	3	69	....	....	....
	NHL Totals		**139**	**3**	**10**	**13**	**4**	**9**	**13**	**528**	**0**	**0**	**1**	**56**	**5.4**	**25**	**3**	**30**	**0**		**8**	**0**	**0**	**0**	**52**	**0**	**0**	**0**

Traded to **Quebec** by **Minnesota** for Gaetan Duchesne, June 19, 1989. Traded to **Washington** by **Quebec** for Mark Matier, June 15, 1993.

• KAMINSKY, YAN

Yan Kaminsky RW – L. 6'1", 176 lbs. b: Penza, USSR, 7/28/1971. Winnipeg's 4th choice, 99th overall, in 1991 Entry Draft.

Season	Club	League	GP	G	A	Pts	AG	AA	APts	PIM	PP	SH	GW	S	%	TGF	PGF	TGA	PGA	+/-	GP	G	A	Pts	PIM	PP	SH	GW
1989-90	Moscow Dynamo	USSR	6	1	0	1	....	....	....	4	....	....	....	....	....	....	....	....	....	....	....	....	....	....	....	....	....	....
	Soviet Union	WJC-A	7	2	0	2	....	....	....	0	....	....	....	....	....	....	....	....	....	....	....	....	....	....	....	....	....	....
1990-91	Moscow Dynamo	USSR	25	10	5	15	....	....	....	2	....	....	....	....	....	....	....	....	....	....	....	....	....	....	....	....	....	....
1991-92	Moscow Dynamo	CIS	42	9	7	16	....	....	....	22	....	....	....	....	....	....	....	....	....	....	....	....	....	....	....	....	....	....
1992-93	Moscow Dynamo	CIS	39	15	14	29	....	....	....	12	....	....	....	....	....	....	....	....	....	....	10	2	5	7	8	....	....	....
	Russia	WC-A	8	2	2	4	....	....	....	4	....	....	....	....	....	....	....	....	....	....	....	....	....	....	....	....	....	....
1993-94	**Winnipeg Jets**	**NHL**	**1**	**0**	**0**	**0**	**0**	**0**	**0**	**0**	**0**	**0**	**0**	**0**	**0.0**	**1**	**0**	**0**	**0**	**+1**	....	....	....	....	....	....	....	....
	Moncton Hawks	AHL	33	9	13	22	....	....	....	6	....	....	....	....	....	....	....	....	....	....	....	....	....	....	....	....	....	....
	New York Islanders	**NHL**	**23**	**2**	**1**	**3**	**2**	**1**	**3**	**4**	**0**	**0**	**0**	**23**	**8.7**	**7**	**0**	**3**	**0**	**+4**	**2**	**0**	**0**	**0**	**4**	**0**	**0**	**0**

			REGULAR SEASON																		PLAYOFFS							
Season	Club	League	GP	G	A	Pts	AG	AA	APts	PIM	PP	SH	GW	S	%	TGF	PGF	TGA	PGA	+/–	GP	G	A	Pts	PIM	PP	SH	GW
1994-95	Denver Grizzlies	IHL	38	17	16	33	....	....	....	14	....	....	....	....	....	....	....	....	....	....	15	6	6	12	0	....	....	....
	New York Islanders	**NHL**	2	1	1	2	2	1	3	0	0	0	0	4	25.0	2	0	0	0	+2	....	....	....	....	....	....	....	....
1995-96	Utah Grizzlies	IHL	16	3	3	6	....	....	....	8	....	....	....	....	....	....	....	....	....	....	21	3	5	8	4	....	....	....
1996-97	Utah Grizzlies	IHL	77	28	27	55	....	....	....	18	....	....	....	....	....	....	....	....	....	....	7	1	4	5	0	....	....	....
	NHL Totals		26	3	2	5	4	2	6	4	0	0	0	27	11.1	10	0	3	0		2	0	0	0	4	0	0	0

Traded to **NY Islanders** by **Winnipeg** for Wayne McBean, February 1, 1994.

• KANNEGIESSER, GORD

Gord Kannegiesser D – L. 6', 190 lbs. b: North Bay, Ont., 12/21/1945.

Season	Club	League	GP	G	A	Pts	AG	AA	APts	PIM	PP	SH	GW	S	%	TGF	PGF	TGA	PGA	+/–	GP	G	A	Pts	PIM	PP	SH	GW
1962-63	Guelph Royals	OHA	45	2	4	6	....	....	....	4	....	....	....	....	....	....	....	....	....	....	....	....	....	....	....	....	....	....
1963-64	Kitchener Rangers	OHA	56	5	7	12	....	....	....	39	....	....	....	....	....	....	....	....	....	....	....	....	....	....	....	....	....	....
1964-65	Kitchener Rangers	OHA	56	1	9	10	....	....	....	49	....	....	....	....	....	....	....	....	....	....	....	....	....	....	....	....	....	....
1965-66	Kitchener Rangers	OHA	46	4	10	14	....	....	....	53	....	....	....	....	....	....	....	....	....	....	19	3	8	11	34	....	....	....
1966-67	Des Moines Oak Leafs	IHL	72	7	30	37	....	....	....	56	....	....	....	....	....	....	....	....	....	....	7	3	2	5	4	....	....	....
1967-68	**St. Louis Blues**	**NHL**	19	0	1	1	0	1	1	13	0	0	0	12	0.0	6	1	11	3	–3	....	....	....	....	....	....	....	....
	Kansas City Blues	CHL	44	5	9	14	....	....	....	29	....	....	....	....	....	....	....	....	....	....	7	0	1	1	8	....	....	....
1968-69	Kansas City Blues	CHL	72	9	18	27	....	....	....	74	....	....	....	....	....	....	....	....	....	....	4	1	0	1	4	....	....	....
1969-70	Kansas City Blues	CHL	68	1	12	13	....	....	....	68	....	....	....	....	....	....	....	....	....	....	....	....	....	....	....	....	....	....
1970-71	Seattle Totems	WHL	39	6	7	13	....	....	....	18	....	....	....	....	....	....	....	....	....	....	....	....	....	....	....	....	....	....
	Omaha Knights	CHL	....	....	....	....	....	....	....	....	....	....	....	....	....	....	....	....	....	....	5	2	1	3	0	....	....	....
1971-72	**St. Louis Blues**	**NHL**	4	0	0	0	0	0	0	2	0	0	0	4	0.0	1	0	2	0	–1	....	....	....	....	....	....	....	....
	Denver Spurs	WHL	70	8	25	33	....	....	....	57	....	....	....	....	....	....	....	....	....	....	9	0	3	3	9	....	....	....
1972-73	Houston Aeros	WHA	45	0	10	10	....	....	....	37	....	....	....	....	....	....	....	....	....	....	9	0	1	1	11	....	....	....
1973-74	Houston Aeros	WHA	78	0	20	20	....	....	....	26	....	....	....	....	....	....	....	....	....	....	3	0	2	2	2	....	....	....
1974-75	Indianapolis Racers	WHA	4	1	4	5	....	....	....	4	....	....	....	....	....	....	....	....	....	....	....	....	....	....	....	....	....	....
	NHL Totals		23	0	1	1	0	1	1	15	0	0	0	16	0.0	7	1	13	3		....	....	....	....	....	....	....	....
	Other Major League Totals		127	1	34	35	....	....	....	67	....	....	....	....	....	....	....	....	....		12	0	3	3	13	....	....	....

Traded to **St. Louis** by **NY Rangers** with Gary Sabourin, Bob Plager and Tim Ecclestone for Rod Seiling, June 6, 1967. Selected by **Dayton-Houston** (WHA) in 1972 WHA General Player Draft, February 12, 1972. Claimed by **Indianapolis** (WHA) from **Houston** (WHA) in WHA Supplemental Draft, June, 1974.

• KANNEGIESSER, SHELDON

Sheldon Kannegiesser D – L. 6', 198 lbs. b: North Bay, Ont., 8/15/1947.

Season	Club	League	GP	G	A	Pts	AG	AA	APts	PIM	PP	SH	GW	S	%	TGF	PGF	TGA	PGA	+/–	GP	G	A	Pts	PIM	PP	SH	GW
1965-66	Kitchener Rangers	OHA	45	1	8	9	....	....	....	19	....	....	....	....	....	....	....	....	....	....	19	1	3	4	29	....	....	....
1966-67	Kitchener Rangers	OHA	48	7	16	23	....	....	....	81	....	....	....	....	....	....	....	....	....	....	13	2	5	7	16	....	....	....
1967-68	Omaha Knights	CHL	20	1	2	3	....	....	....	11	....	....	....	....	....	....	....	....	....	....	....	....	....	....	....	....	....	....
	Buffalo Bisons	AHL	47	4	2	6	....	....	....	20	....	....	....	....	....	....	....	....	....	....	5	0	0	0	0	....	....	....
1968-69	Omaha Knights	CHL	70	8	13	21	....	....	....	104	....	....	....	....	....	....	....	....	....	....	7	1	1	2	6	....	....	....
1969-70	Buffalo Bisons	AHL	17	1	2	3	....	....	....	14	....	....	....	....	....	....	....	....	....	....	....	....	....	....	....	....	....	....
	Kansas City Blues	CHL	36	0	7	7	....	....	....	44	....	....	....	....	....	....	....	....	....	....	....	....	....	....	....	....	....	....
1970-71	Omaha Knights	CHL	46	4	10	14	....	....	....	75	....	....	....	....	....	....	....	....	....	....	....	....	....	....	....	....	....	....
	Pittsburgh Penguins	**NHL**	18	0	2	2	0	2	2	29	0	0	0	14	0.0	10	0	23	4	–9	....	....	....	....	....	....	....	....
	Amarillo Wranglers	CHL	7	2	2	4	....	....	....	4	....	....	....	....	....	....	....	....	....	....	....	....	....	....	....	....	....	....
1971-72	**Pittsburgh Penguins**	**NHL**	54	2	4	6	2	4	6	47	0	0	0	49	4.1	30	0	49	5	–14	....	....	....	....	....	....	....	....
1972-73	**Pittsburgh Penguins**	**NHL**	3	0	0	0	0	0	0	0	0	0	0	4	0.0	0	0	1	0	–1	....	....	....	....	....	....	....	....
	Hershey Bears	AHL	36	3	12	15	....	....	....	31	....	....	....	....	....	....	....	....	....	....	....	....	....	....	....	....	....	....
	New York Rangers	**NHL**	3	0	1	1	0	1	1	4	0	0	0	2	0.0	3	0	0	0	+3	1	0	0	0	2	0	0	0
1973-74	**New York Rangers**	**NHL**	12	1	3	4	1	3	4	6	0	0	0	6	16.7	12	1	8	1	+4	....	....	....	....	....	....	....	....
	Los Angeles Kings	**NHL**	51	3	17	20	3	15	18	49	1	0	0	76	3.9	60	16	50	9	+3	5	0	1	1	0	0	0	0
1974-75	**Los Angeles Kings**	**NHL**	74	2	23	25	2	18	20	57	0	0	0	84	2.4	99	13	60	15	+41	3	0	1	1	4	0	0	0
1975-76	**Los Angeles Kings**	**NHL**	70	4	9	13	4	7	11	36	2	0	0	79	5.1	84	15	78	19	+10	9	0	0	0	4	0	0	0
1976-77	**Los Angeles Kings**	**NHL**	39	1	1	2	1	1	2	28	0	0	1	18	5.6	22	1	37	9	–7	....	....	....	....	....	....	....	....
	Fort Worth Texans	CHL	24	1	7	8	....	....	....	16	....	....	....	....	....	....	....	....	....	....	....	....	....	....	....	....	....	....
1977-78	**Vancouver Canucks**	**NHL**	42	1	7	8	1	6	7	36	0	0	0	21	4.8	41	0	63	15	–7	....	....	....	....	....	....	....	....
	Springfield Indians	AHL	14	2	8	10	....	....	....	19	....	....	....	....	....	....	....	....	....	....	....	....	....	....	....	....	....	....
	NHL Totals		366	14	67	81	14	57	71	292	3	0	1	353	4.0	361	46	369	77		18	0	2	2	10	0	0	0

Traded to **St. Louis** by **NY Rangers** for Larry Hornung, November, 1969. Traded to **Pittsburgh** by **NY Rangers** with Syl Apps Jr. for Glen Sather, January, 1971. Traded to **NY Rangers** by **Pittsburgh** for future considerations (Steve Andrascik, May 16, 1973), March 2, 1973. Traded to **LA Kings** by **NY Rangers** with Mike Murphy and Tom Williams for Gilles Marotte and Real Lemieux, November 30, 1973. Traded to **Vancouver** by **LA Kings** for Larry Carriere, November 21, 1977.

• KAPANEN, SAMI

Sami Kapanen LW – L. 5'10", 170 lbs. b: Vantaa, Finland, 6/14/1973. Hartford's 4th choice, 87th overall, in 1995 Entry Draft.

Season	Club	League	GP	G	A	Pts	AG	AA	APts	PIM	PP	SH	GW	S	%	TGF	PGF	TGA	PGA	+/–	GP	G	A	Pts	PIM	PP	SH	GW
1990-91	KalPa Kuopio	Finland	14	1	2	3	....	....	....	2	....	....	....	....	....	....	....	....	....	....	8	2	1	3	2	....	....	....
1991-92	KalPa Kuopio	Finland	42	15	10	25	....	....	....	8	....	....	....	....	....	....	....	....	....	....	....	....	....	....	....	....	....	....
	Finland	WJC-A	7	1	5	6	....	....	....	8	....	....	....	....	....	....	....	....	....	....	....	....	....	....	....	....	....	....
1992-93	KalPa Kuopio	Finland	37	4	17	21	....	....	....	12	....	....	....	....	....	....	....	....	....	....	....	....	....	....	....	....	....	....
	Finland	WJC-A	7	1	2	3	....	....	....	2	....	....	....	....	....	....	....	....	....	....	....	....	....	....	....	....	....	....
1993-94	KalPa Kuopio	Finland	48	23	32	55	....	....	....	16	....	....	....	....	....	....	....	....	....	....	....	....	....	....	....	....	....	....
	Finland	Olympics	8	1	0	1	....	....	....	2	....	....	....	....	....	....	....	....	....	....	....	....	....	....	....	....	....	....
	Finland	WC-A	8	4	2	6	....	....	....	0	....	....	....	....	....	....	....	....	....	....	....	....	....	....	....	....	....	....
1994-95	HIFK Helsinki	Finland	49	14	28	42	....	....	....	42	....	....	....	....	....	....	....	....	....	....	3	0	0	0	0	....	....	....
	Finland	WC-A	8	2	2	4	....	....	....	6	....	....	....	....	....	....	....	....	....	....	....	....	....	....	....	....	....	....
1995-96	**Hartford Whalers**	**NHL**	35	5	4	9	5	3	8	6	0	0	0	46	10.9	14	1	14	1	0	....	....	....	....	....	....	....	....
	Springfield Falcons	AHL	28	14	17	31	....	....	....	4	....	....	....	....	....	....	....	....	....	....	3	1	2	3	0	....	....	....
	Finland	WC-A	6	2	3	5	....	....	....	2	....	....	....	....	....	....	....	....	....	....	....	....	....	....	....	....	....	....
1996-97	Finland	W Cup	3	0	0	0	....	....	....	4	....	....	....	....	....	....	....	....	....	....	....	....	....	....	....	....	....	....
	Hartford Whalers	**NHL**	45	13	12	25	14	11	25	2	3	0	2	82	15.9	43	7	31	1	+6	....	....	....	....	....	....	....	....
1997-98	**Carolina Hurricanes**	**NHL**	81	26	37	63	31	36	67	16	4	0	5	190	13.7	94	31	59	5	+9	....	....	....	....	....	....	....	....
	Finland	Olympics	6	0	1	1	....	....	....	0	....	....	....	....	....	....	....	....	....	....	....	....	....	....	....	....	....	....
	Finland	WC-A	10	4	3	7	....	....	....	2	....	....	....	....	....	....	....	....	....	....	....	....	....	....	....	....	....	....
	NHL Totals		161	44	53	97	50	50	100	24	7	0	7	318	13.8	151	39	104	7		....	....	....	....	....	....	....	....

Finnish First All-Star Team (1994)

Transferred to **Carolina** after **Hartford** franchise relocated, June 25, 1997.

• KARABIN, LADISLAV

Ladislav Karabin LW – L. 6'1", 189 lbs. b: Spisska Nova Ves, Czech., 2/16/1970. Pittsburgh's 11th choice, 173rd overall, in 1990 Entry Draft.

Season	Club	League	GP	G	A	Pts	AG	AA	APts	PIM	PP	SH	GW	S	%	TGF	PGF	TGA	PGA	+/–	GP	G	A	Pts	PIM	PP	SH	GW
1988-89	Slovan Bratislava	Czech.	31	7	2	9	....	....	....	10	....	....	....	....	....	....	....	....	....	....	....	....	....	....	....	....	....	....
1989-90	Slovan Bratislava	Czech. 2	STATISTICS NOT AVAILABLE																									
	Czechoslovakia	WJC-A	6	2	1	3	....	....	....	6	....	....	....	....	....	....	....	....	....	....	....	....	....	....	....	....	....	....
1990-91	Slovan Bratislava	Czech.	49	21	7	28	....	....	....	57	....	....	....	....	....	....	....	....	....	....	....	....	....	....	....	....	....	....
1991-92	Slovan Bratislava	Czech.	27	4	8	12	....	....	....	10	....	....	....	....	....	....	....	....	....	....	....	....	....	....	....	....	....	....
1992-93	Slovan Bratislava	Czech.	39	21	23	44	....	....	....	....	....	....	....	....	....	....	....	....	....	....	....	....	....	....	....	....	....	....
1993-94	**Pittsburgh Penguins**	**NHL**	9	0	0	0	0	0	0	2	0	0	0	3	0.0	2	0	2	0	0	....	....	....	....	....	....	....	....
	Cleveland Lumberjacks	IHL	58	13	26	39	....	....	....	48	....	....	....	....	....	....	....	....	....	....	....	....	....	....	....	....	....	....
1994-95	Cleveland Lumberjacks	IHL	47	15	25	40	....	....	....	26	....	....	....	....	....	....	....	....	....	....	4	0	0	0	2	....	....	....
1995-96	Rochester Americans	AHL	21	3	5	8	....	....	....	18	....	....	....	....	....	....	....	....	....	....	....	....	....	....	....	....	....	....
	Los Angeles Ice Dogs	IHL	32	6	8	14	....	....	....	58	....	....	....	....	....	....	....	....	....	....	....	....	....	....	....	....	....	....
1996-97	Slovan Bratislava	Slovakia	33	4	10	14	....	....	....	....	....	....	....	....	....	....	....	....	....	....	....	....	....	....	....	....	....	....
1997-98	Slovan Bratislava	Slovakia	6	0	0	0	....	....	....	0	....	....	....	....	....	....	....	....	....	....	5	1	0	1	4	....	....	....
	Slovan Bratislava	EuroHL	2	0	0	0	....	....	....	0	....	....	....	....	....	....	....	....	....	....	....	....	....	....	....	....	....	....
	NHL Totals		9	0	0	0	0	0	0	2	0	0	0	3	0.0	2	0	2	0		....	....	....	....	....	....	....	....

Signed as a free agent by **Buffalo**, September 20, 1995.

Season	Club	League	GP	G	A	Pts	AG	AA	APts	PIM	PP	SH	GW	S	%	TGF	PGF	TGA	PGA	+/–	GP	G	A	Pts	PIM	PP	SH	GW
			REGULAR SEASON																		PLAYOFFS							
● KARAMNOV, VITALI	Vitali Karamnov	LW – L. 6'2", 185 lbs. b: Moscow, USSR, 7/6/1968. St. Louis' 2nd choice, 62nd overall, in 1992 Entry Draft.																										
1986-87	Moscow Dynamo	USSR	4	0	0	0	....	....	....	0	....	....	....	....	....	....	....	....	....	....	....	....	....	....	....	....	....	....
1987-88	Moscow Dynamo	USSR	2	0	1	1	....	....	....	0	....	....	....	....	....	....	....	....	....	....	....	....	....	....	....	....	....	....
1988-89	Dynamo Kharkov	USSR	23	4	1	5	....	....	....	19	....	....	....	....	....	....	....	....	....	....	....	....	....	....	....	....	....	....
1989-90	Torpedo Yaroslavl	USSR	47	6	7	13	....	....	....	32	....	....	....	....	....	....	....	....	....	....	....	....	....	....	....	....	....	....
1990-91	SKA-Torpedo Yaroslavl	FrTour	1	0	1	1	....	....	....	0	....	....	....	....	....	....	....	....	....	....	....	....	....	....	....	....	....	....
	Torpedo Yaroslavl	USSR	45	14	7	21	....	....	....	30	....	....	....	....	....	....	....	....	....	....	....	....	....	....	....	....	....	....
1991-92	Moscow Dynamo	CIS	40	13	19	32	....	....	....	25	....	....	....	....	....	....	....	....	....	....	....	....	....	....	....	....	....	....
1992-93	**St. Louis Blues**	**NHL**	**7**	**0**	**1**	**1**	**0**	**1**	**1**	**0**	**0**	**0**	**0**	**7**	**0.0**	**1**	**0**	**3**	**0**	**–2**	....	....	....	....	....	....	....	....
	Peoria Rivermen	IHL	23	8	12	20	....	....	....	47	....	....	....	....	....	....	....	....	....	....	....	....	....	....	....	....	....	....
1993-94	**St. Louis Blues**	**NHL**	**59**	**9**	**12**	**21**	**8**	**9**	**17**	**51**	**2**	**0**	**1**	**66**	**13.6**	**27**	**3**	**27**	**0**	**–3**	....	....	....	....	....	....	....	....
	Peoria Rivermen	IHL	3	0	1	1	....	....	....	2	....	....	....	....	....	....	....	....	....	....	1	0	1	1	0	....	....	....
1994-95	**St. Louis Blues**	**NHL**	**26**	**3**	**7**	**10**	**5**	**10**	**15**	**14**	**0**	**0**	**0**	**22**	**13.6**	**17**	**1**	**9**	**0**	**+7**	**2**	**0**	**0**	**0**	**2**	**0**	**0**	**0**
	Peoria Rivermen	IHL	15	6	9	15	....	....	....	7	....	....	....	....	....	....	....	....	....	....	....	....	....	....	....	....	....	....
1995-96	JyP HT Jyvaskyla	Finland	24	8	7	15	....	....	....	36	....	....	....	....	....	....	....	....	....	....	....	....	....	....	....	....	....	....
	Russia	WC-A	8	0	2	2	....	....	....	0	....	....	....	....	....	....	....	....	....	....	....	....	....	....	....	....	....	....
1996-97	Berlin Capitals	Germany	4	2	1	3	....	....	....	27	....	....	....	....	....	....	....	....	....	....	....	....	....	....	....	....	....	....
	Krefeld Penguins	Germany	28	7	13	20	....	....	....	80	....	....	....	....	....	....	....	....	....	....	3	1	1	2	25	....	....	....
1997-98	Krefeld Penguins	Germany	31	8	13	21	....	....	....	38	....	....	....	....	....	....	....	....	....	....	3	0	2	2	2	....	....	....
	NHL Totals		**92**	**12**	**20**	**32**	**13**	**20**	**33**	**65**	**2**	**0**	**1**	**95**	**12.6**	**45**	**4**	**39**	**0**		**2**	**0**	**0**	**0**	**2**	**0**	**0**	**0**
● KARIYA, PAUL	Paul Kariya	LW – L. 5'11", 175 lbs. b: Vancouver, B.C., 10/16/1974. Anaheim's 1st choice, 4th overall, in 1993 Entry Draft.																										
1990-91	Penticton Panthers	BCJHL	54	45	67	112	....	....	....	8	....	....	....	....	....	....	....	....	....	....	....	....	....	....	....	....	....	....
1991-92	Penticton Panthers	BCJHL	40	46	86	132	....	....	....	18	....	....	....	....	....	....	....	....	....	....	....	....	....	....	....	....	....	....
	Canada	WJC-A	6	1	1	2	....	....	....	2	....	....	....	....	....	....	....	....	....	....	....	....	....	....	....	....	....	....
1992-93	University of Maine	H.E.	36	24	*69	*93	....	....	....	12	....	....	....	....	....	....	....	....	....	....	....	....	....	....	....	....	....	....
	Canada	WJC-A	7	2	6	8	....	....	....	2	....	....	....	....	....	....	....	....	....	....	....	....	....	....	....	....	....	....
	Canada	WC-A	8	2	7	9	....	....	....	0	....	....	....	....	....	....	....	....	....	....	....	....	....	....	....	....	....	....
1993-94	University of Maine	H.E.	12	8	16	24	....	....	....	4	....	....	....	....	....	....	....	....	....	....	....	....	....	....	....	....	....	....
	Canada	Nat-Team	23	7	34	41	....	....	....	2	....	....	....	....	....	....	....	....	....	....	....	....	....	....	....	....	....	....
	Canada	Olympics	8	3	4	7	....	....	....	2	....	....	....	....	....	....	....	....	....	....	....	....	....	....	....	....	....	....
	Canada	WC-A	8	5	7	12	....	....	....	2	....	....	....	....	....	....	....	....	....	....	....	....	....	....	....	....	....	....
1994-95	**Anaheim Mighty Ducks**	**NHL**	**47**	**18**	**21**	**39**	**32**	**31**	**63**	**4**	**7**	**1**	**3**	**134**	**13.4**	**50**	**22**	**51**	**6**	**–17**	....	....	....	....	....	....	....	....
1995-96	**Anaheim Mighty Ducks**	**NHL**	**82**	**50**	**58**	**108**	**49**	**47**	**96**	**20**	**20**	**3**	**9**	**349**	**14.3**	**132**	**52**	**87**	**16**	**+9**	....	....	....	....	....	....	....	....
	Canada	WC-A	8	4	3	7	....	....	....	2	....	....	....	....	....	....	....	....	....	....	....	....	....	....	....	....	....	....
1996-97	**Anaheim Mighty Ducks**	**NHL**	**69**	**44**	**55**	**99**	**47**	**49**	**96**	**6**	**15**	**3**	**10**	**340**	**12.9**	**133**	**47**	**63**	**13**	**+36**	**11**	**7**	**6**	**13**	**4**	**4**	**0**	**1**
1997-98	**Anaheim Mighty Ducks**	**NHL**	**22**	**17**	**14**	**31**	**20**	**14**	**34**	**23**	**3**	**0**	**2**	**103**	**16.5**	**41**	**8**	**25**	**4**	**+12**	....	....	....	....	....	....	....	....
	NHL Totals		**220**	**129**	**148**	**277**	**148**	**141**	**289**	**53**	**45**	**7**	**24**	**926**	**13.9**	**356**	**129**	**226**	**39**		**11**	**7**	**6**	**13**	**4**	**4**	**0**	**1**

WJC-A All-Star Team (1993) • Hockey East First All-Star Team (1993) • NCAA East First All-American Team (1993) • NCAA Championship All-Tournament Team (1993) • Won Hobey Baker Memorial Award (Top U.S. Collegiate Player) (1993)
WC-A All-Star Team (1994, 1996)
Named Best Forward at WC-A (1994, 1996) • NHL/Upper Deck All-Rookie Team (1995) • NHL First All-Star Team (1996, 1997) • Won Lady Byng Trophy (1996, 1997)
Played in NHL All-Star Game (1996, 1997)

Season	Club	League	GP	G	A	Pts	AG	AA	APts	PIM	PP	SH	GW	S	%	TGF	PGF	TGA	PGA	+/–	GP	G	A	Pts	PIM	PP	SH	GW
● KARJALAINEN, KYOSTI	Kyosti Karjalainen	RW – R. 6'2", 190 lbs. b: Gavle, Sweden, 6/19/1967. Los Angeles' 6th choice, 132nd overall, in 1987 Entry Draft.																										
1986-87	Brynas IF	Sweden	11	3	2	5	....	....	....	0	....	....	....	....	....	....	....	....	....	....	....	....	....	....	....	....	....	....
1987-88	Brynas IF	Sweden	20	2	1	3	....	....	....	10	....	....	....	....	....	....	....	....	....	....	....	....	....	....	....	....	....	....
1988-89	Brynas IF	Sweden	39	20	17	37	....	....	....	16	....	....	....	....	....	....	....	....	....	....	....	....	....	....	....	....	....	....
1989-90	Brynas IF	Sweden	38	17	15	32	....	....	....	16	....	....	....	....	....	....	....	....	....	....	5	0	3	3	0	....	....	....
1990-91	Phoenix Roadrunners	IHL	70	14	35	49	....	....	....	10	....	....	....	....	....	....	....	....	....	....	6	2	3	5	6	....	....	....
1991-92	**Los Angeles Kings**	**NHL**	**28**	**1**	**8**	**9**	**1**	**6**	**7**	**12**	**0**	**0**	**0**	**20**	**5.0**	**15**	**0**	**11**	**0**	**+4**	**3**	**0**	**1**	**1**	**2**	**0**	**0**	**0**
	Phoenix Roadrunners	IHL	43	14	22	36	....	....	....	30	....	....	....	....	....	....	....	....	....	....	....	....	....	....	....	....	....	....
1992-93	Lulea HF	Sweden	39	7	5	12	....	....	....	44	....	....	....	....	....	....	....	....	....	....	11	0	1	1	0	....	....	....
1993-94	Lulea HF	Sweden	36	2	5	7	....	....	....	8	....	....	....	....	....	....	....	....	....	....	....	....	....	....	....	....	....	....
1994-95	MoDo	Sweden	35	7	9	16	....	....	....	20	....	....	....	....	....	....	....	....	....	....	....	....	....	....	....	....	....	....
1995-96	MoDo	Sweden	35	6	7	13	....	....	....	28	....	....	....	....	....	....	....	....	....	....	8	4	3	7	12	....	....	....
	NHL Totals		**28**	**1**	**8**	**9**	**1**	**6**	**7**	**12**	**0**	**0**	**0**	**20**	**5.0**	**15**	**0**	**11**	**0**		**3**	**0**	**1**	**1**	**2**	**0**	**0**	**0**
● KARLANDER, AL	Al Karlander	C – L. 5'8", 170 lbs. b: Lac La H'ache, B.C., 11/5/1946. Detroit's 2nd choice, 17th overall, in 1967 Amateur Draft.																										
1965-66	Michigan Tech Spartans	WCHA	8	9	10	19	....	....	....	6	....	....	....	....	....	....	....	....	....	....	....	....	....	....	....	....	....	....
1966-67	Michigan Tech Spartans	WCHA	29	5	12	17	....	....	....	10	....	....	....	....	....	....	....	....	....	....	....	....	....	....	....	....	....	....
1967-68	Michigan Tech Spartans	WCHA	32	22	13	35	....	....	....	24	....	....	....	....	....	....	....	....	....	....	....	....	....	....	....	....	....	....
1968-69	Michigan Tech Spartans	WCHA	32	31	13	44	....	....	....	24	....	....	....	....	....	....	....	....	....	....	....	....	....	....	....	....	....	....
1969-70	**Detroit Red Wings**	**NHL**	**41**	**5**	**10**	**15**	**6**	**10**	**16**	**6**	**0**	**0**	**0**	**41**	**12.2**	**23**	**2**	**13**	**0**	**+8**	**4**	**0**	**1**	**1**	**0**	**0**	**0**	**0**
	Fort Worth Wings	CHL	24	15	14	29	....	....	....	12	....	....	....	....	....	....	....	....	....	....	....	....	....	....	....	....	....	....
1970-71	**Detroit Red Wings**	**NHL**	**23**	**1**	**4**	**5**	**1**	**4**	**5**	**10**	**1**	**0**	**0**	**9**	**11.1**	**9**	**2**	**3**	**1**	**+5**	....	....	....	....	....	....	....	....
	Fort Worth Wings	CHL	48	30	28	58	....	....	....	40	....	....	....	....	....	....	....	....	....	....	4	2	1	3	2	....	....	....
1971-72	**Detroit Red Wings**	**NHL**	**71**	**15**	**20**	**35**	**16**	**18**	**34**	**29**	**0**	**0**	**5**	**93**	**16.1**	**61**	**9**	**51**	**13**	**+14**	....	....	....	....	....	....	....	....
1972-73	**Detroit Red Wings**	**NHL**	**77**	**15**	**22**	**37**	**15**	**18**	**33**	**25**	**4**	**0**	**4**	**99**	**15.2**	**51**	**5**	**51**	**7**	**+2**	....	....	....	....	....	....	....	....
1973-74	New England Whalers	WHA	77	20	41	61	....	....	....	46	....	....	....	....	....	....	....	....	....	....	7	1	3	4	2	....	....	....
1974-75	New England Whalers	WHA	51	7	14	21	....	....	....	2	....	....	....	....	....	....	....	....	....	....	5	0	3	3	0	....	....	....
	Cape Cod Codders	NAHL	3	1	2	3	....	....	....	0	....	....	....	....	....	....	....	....	....	....	....	....	....	....	....	....	....	....
1975-76	Indianapolis Racers	WHA	79	19	26	45	....	....	....	36	....	....	....	....	....	....	....	....	....	....	3	0	0	0	4	....	....	....
1976-77	Indianapolis Racers	WHA	65	17	28	45	....	....	....	23	....	....	....	....	....	....	....	....	....	....	6	2	1	3	0	....	....	....
	NHL Totals		**212**	**36**	**56**	**92**	**38**	**50**	**88**	**70**	**5**	**0**	**9**	**242**	**14.9**	**144**	**18**	**118**	**21**		**4**	**0**	**1**	**1**	**0**	**0**	**0**	**0**
	Other Major League Totals		272	63	109	172	....	....	....	107	....	....	....	....	....	....	....	....	....		21	3	7	10	6	....	....	....

WCHA Second All-Star Team (1968) • WCHA First All-Star Team (1969) • NCAA West First All-American Team (1969)
Selected by **New England** (WHA) in 1972 WHA General Player Draft, February 12, 1972. Claimed by **Indianapolis** (WHA) from **New England** (WHA) in WHA Intra-League Draft, June, 1975.

Season	Club	League	GP	G	A	Pts	AG	AA	APts	PIM	PP	SH	GW	S	%	TGF	PGF	TGA	PGA	+/–	GP	G	A	Pts	PIM	PP	SH	GW
● KARPA, DAVE	Dave Karpa	D – R. 6'1", 210 lbs. b: Regina, Sask., 5/7/1971. Quebec's 4th choice, 68th overall, in 1991 Entry Draft.																										
1990-91	Ferris State Bulldogs	CCHA	41	6	19	25	....	....	....	109	....	....	....	....	....	....	....	....	....	....	....	....	....	....	....	....	....	....
1991-92	Ferris State Bulldogs	CCHA	34	7	12	19	....	....	....	124	....	....	....	....	....	....	....	....	....	....	....	....	....	....	....	....	....	....
	Quebec Nordiques	**NHL**	**4**	**0**	**0**	**0**	**0**	**0**	**0**	**14**	**0**	**0**	**0**	**2**	**0.0**	**2**	**0**	**0**	**0**	**+2**	....	....	....	....	....	....	....	....
	Halifax Citadels	AHL	2	0	0	0	....	....	....	4	....	....	....	....	....	....	....	....	....	....	....	....	....	....	....	....	....	....
1992-93	**Quebec Nordiques**	**NHL**	**12**	**0**	**1**	**1**	**0**	**1**	**1**	**13**	**0**	**0**	**0**	**2**	**0.0**	**4**	**0**	**10**	**0**	**–6**	**3**	**0**	**0**	**0**	**0**	**0**	**0**	**0**
	Halifax Citadels	AHL	71	4	27	31	....	....	....	167	....	....	....	....	....	....	....	....	....	....	....	....	....	....	....	....	....	....
1993-94	**Quebec Nordiques**	**NHL**	**60**	**5**	**12**	**17**	**5**	**9**	**14**	**148**	**2**	**0**	**0**	**48**	**10.4**	**45**	**8**	**43**	**6**	**0**	....	....	....	....	....	....	....	....
	Cornwall Aces	AHL	1	0	0	0	....	....	....	0	....	....	....	....	....	....	....	....	....	....	12	2	2	4	27	....	....	....
1994-95	**Quebec Nordiques**	**NHL**	**2**	**0**	**0**	**0**	**0**	**0**	**0**	**0**	**0**	**0**	**0**	**1**	**0.0**	**1**	**0**	**2**	**0**	**-1**	....	....	....	....	....	....	....	....
	Cornwall Aces	AHL	6	0	2	2	....	....	....	19	....	....	....	....	....	....	....	....	....	....	....	....	....	....	....	....	....	....
	Anaheim Mighty Ducks	**NHL**	**26**	**1**	**5**	**6**	**2**	**7**	**9**	**91**	**0**	**0**	**0**	**32**	**3.1**	**22**	**0**	**34**	**12**	**0**	....	....	....	....	....	....	....	....
1995-96	**Anaheim Mighty Ducks**	**NHL**	**72**	**3**	**16**	**19**	**3**	**13**	**16**	**270**	**0**	**1**	**1**	**62**	**4.8**	**52**	**4**	**77**	**26**	**–3**	....	....	....	....	....	....	....	....
1996-97	**Anaheim Mighty Ducks**	**NHL**	**69**	**2**	**11**	**13**	**2**	**10**	**12**	**210**	**0**	**0**	**1**	**90**	**2.2**	**54**	**3**	**67**	**27**	**+11**	**8**	**1**	**1**	**2**	**20**	**0**	**0**	**1**
1997-98	**Anaheim Mighty Ducks**	**NHL**	**78**	**1**	**11**	**12**	**1**	**11**	**12**	**217**	**0**	**0**	**0**	**64**	**1.6**	**59**	**2**	**88**	**28**	**–3**	....	....	....	....	....	....	....	....
	NHL Totals		**323**	**12**	**56**	**68**	**13**	**51**	**64**	**963**	**2**	**1**	**2**	**301**	**4.0**	**239**	**17**	**321**	**99**		**11**	**1**	**1**	**2**	**20**	**0**	**0**	**1**

Traded to **Anaheim** by **Quebec** for Anaheim's 4th round choice (later traded to St. Louis — St. Louis selected Jan Horacek) in 1997 Entry Draft, March 9, 1995.

			REGULAR SEASON																		PLAYOFFS							
Season	**Club**	**League**	**GP**	**G**	**A**	**Pts**	**AG**	**AA**	**APts**	**PIM**	**PP**	**SH**	**GW**	**S**	**%**	**TGF**	**PGF**	**TGA**	**PGA**	**+/–**	**GP**	**G**	**A**	**Pts**	**PIM**	**PP**	**SH**	**GW**

• KARPOV, VALERI

Valeri Karpov RW – L. 5'10", 176 lbs. b: Chelyabinsk, USSR, 8/5/1971. Anaheim's 3rd choice, 56th overall, in 1993 Entry Draft.

Season	Club	League	GP	G	A	Pts	AG	AA	APts	PIM	PP	SH	GW	S	%	TGF	PGF	TGA	PGA	+/–	GP	G	A	Pts	PIM	PP	SH	GW
1988-89	Chelyabinsk	USSR	5	0	0	0	....	....	....	0	....	....	....	....	....	....	....	....	....	....	....	....	....	....	....	....	....	....
1989-90	Chelyabinsk	USSR	24	1	2	3	....	....	....	6	....	....	....	....	....	....	....	....	....	....	....	....	....	....	....	....	....	....
1990-91	Chelyabinsk	USSR	25	8	4	12	....	....	....	15	....	....	....	....	....	....	....	....	....	....	....	....	....	....	....	....	....	....
1991-92	Chelyabinsk	CIS	44	16	10	26	....	....	....	34	....	....	....	....	....	....	....	....	....	....	....	....	....	....	....	....	....	....
1992-93	CSKA Moscow	CIS	9	2	6	8	....	....	....	0	....	....	....	....	....	....	....	....	....	....	....	....	....	....	....	....	....	....
	Chelyabinsk	CIS	29	10	15	25	....	....	....	6	....	....	....	....	....	....	....	....	....	....	8	0	1	1	10	....	....	....
	Russia	WC-A	8	4	5	9	....	....	....	0	....	....	....	....	....	....	....	....	....	....	....	....	....	....	....	....	....	....
1993-94	Chelyabinsk	CIS	32	13	16	29	....	....	....	....	....	....	....	....	....	....	....	....	....	....	6	2	5	7	2	....	....	....
	Russia	Olympics	8	3	1	4	....	....	....	2	....	....	....	....	....	....	....	....	....	....	....	....	....	....	....	....	....	....
1994-95	Chelyabinsk	CIS	10	6	8	14	....	....	....	8	....	....	....	....	....	....	....	....	....	....	....	....	....	....	....	....	....	....
	Anaheim Mighty Ducks	**NHL**	**30**	**4**	**7**	**11**	**7**	**10**	**17**	**6**	**0**	**0**	**0**	**48**	**8.3**	**17**	**1**	**20**	**0**	**–4**	....	....	....	....	....	....	....	....
	San Diego Gulls	IHL	5	3	3	6	....	....	....	0	....	....	....	....	....	....	....	....	....	....	....	....	....	....	....	....	....	....
1995-96	**Anaheim Mighty Ducks**	**NHL**	**37**	**9**	**8**	**17**	**9**	**7**	**16**	**10**	**0**	**0**	**1**	**42**	**21.4**	**20**	**4**	**17**	**0**	**–1**	....	....	....	....	....	....	....	....
	Russia	WC-A	8	3	0	3	....	....	....	6	....	....	....	....	....	....	....	....	....	....	....	....	....	....	....	....	....	....
1996-97	**Anaheim Mighty Ducks**	**NHL**	**9**	**1**	**0**	**1**	**1**	**0**	**1**	**16**	**0**	**0**	**0**	**4**	**25.0**	**1**	**0**	**4**	**1**	**–2**	....	....	....	....	....	....	....	....
	Baltimore Bandits	AHL	10	4	8	12	....	....	....	8	....	....	....	....	....	....	....	....	....	....	....	....	....	....	....	....	....	....
	Long Beach Ice Dogs	IHL	30	18	17	35	....	....	....	19	....	....	....	....	....	....	....	....	....	....	18	8	7	15	18	....	....	....
1997-98	Magnitogorsk	CIS	34	11	14	25	....	....	....	20	....	....	....	....	....	....	....	....	....	....	....	....	....	....	....	....	....	....
	NHL Totals		**76**	**14**	**15**	**29**	**17**	**17**	**34**	**32**	**0**	**0**	**1**	**94**	**14.9**	**38**	**5**	**41**	**1**		....	....	....	....	....	....	....	....

CIS First All-Star Team (1993, 1994)

Signed as a free agent by **Calgary**, September 3, 1997.

• KARPOVTSEV, ALEXANDER

Alexander Karpovtsev D – R. 6'1", 205 lbs. b: Moscow, USSR, 4/7/1970. Quebec's 7th choice, 158th overall, in 1990 Entry Draft.

Season	Club	League	GP	G	A	Pts	AG	AA	APts	PIM	PP	SH	GW	S	%	TGF	PGF	TGA	PGA	+/–	GP	G	A	Pts	PIM	PP	SH	GW
1987-88	Moscow Dynamo	USSR	2	0	1	1	....	....	....	10	....	....	....	....	....	....	....	....	....	....	....	....	....	....	....	....	....	....
1989-90	Moscow Dynamo	USSR	35	1	1	2	....	....	....	27	....	....	....	....	....	....	....	....	....	....	....	....	....	....	....	....	....	....
	Soviet Union	WJC-A	7	0	1	1	....	....	....	8	....	....	....	....	....	....	....	....	....	....	....	....	....	....	....	....	....	....
1990-91	Moscow Dynamo	FrTour	1	0	0	0	....	....	....	2	....	....	....	....	....	....	....	....	....	....	....	....	....	....	....	....	....	....
	Moscow Dynamo	USSR	40	0	5	5	....	....	....	15	....	....	....	....	....	....	....	....	....	....	....	....	....	....	....	....	....	....
	Moscow Dynamo	SuperS	7	0	0	0	....	....	....	6	....	....	....	....	....	....	....	....	....	....	....	....	....	....	....	....	....	....
1991-92	Moscow Dynamo	CIS	35	4	2	6	....	....	....	26	....	....	....	....	....	....	....	....	....	....	....	....	....	....	....	....	....	....
1992-93	Moscow Dynamo	CIS	36	3	11	14	....	....	....	100	....	....	....	....	....	....	....	....	....	....	7	2	1	3	0	....	....	....
	Russia	WC-A	8	0	1	1	....	....	....	10	....	....	....	....	....	....	....	....	....	....	....	....	....	....	....	....	....	....
1993-94	**New York Rangers**	**NHL**	**67**	**3**	**15**	**18**	**3**	**12**	**15**	**58**	**1**	**0**	**1**	**78**	**3.8**	**52**	**10**	**41**	**11**	**+12**	**17**	**0**	**4**	**4**	**12**	**0**	**0**	**0**
1994-95	Moscow Dynamo	CIS	13	0	2	2	....	....	....	10	....	....	....	....	....	....	....	....	....	....	....	....	....	....	....	....	....	....
	New York Rangers	**NHL**	**47**	**4**	**8**	**12**	**7**	**12**	**19**	**30**	**1**	**0**	**1**	**82**	**4.9**	**29**	**6**	**34**	**7**	**–4**	**8**	**1**	**0**	**1**	**0**	**0**	**0**	**0**
1995-96	**New York Rangers**	**NHL**	**40**	**2**	**16**	**18**	**2**	**13**	**15**	**26**	**1**	**0**	**1**	**71**	**2.8**	**51**	**18**	**24**	**3**	**+12**	**6**	**0**	**1**	**1**	**4**	**0**	**0**	**0**
1996-97	Russia	W Cup	1	0	0	0	....	....	....	0	....	....	....	....	....	....	....	....	....	....	....	....	....	....	....	....	....	....
	New York Rangers	**NHL**	**77**	**9**	**29**	**38**	**10**	**26**	**36**	**59**	**6**	**1**	**0**	**84**	**10.7**	**88**	**28**	**78**	**19**	**+1**	**13**	**1**	**3**	**4**	**20**	**1**	**0**	**0**
1997-98	**New York Rangers**	**NHL**	**47**	**3**	**7**	**10**	**4**	**7**	**11**	**38**	**1**	**0**	**1**	**46**	**6.5**	**31**	**7**	**35**	**10**	**–1**	....	....	....	....	....	....	....	....
	NHL Totals		**278**	**21**	**75**	**96**	**26**	**70**	**96**	**211**	**10**	**1**	**4**	**361**	**5.8**	**251**	**69**	**212**	**50**		**44**	**2**	**8**	**10**	**36**	**1**	**0**	**0**

Traded to **NY Rangers** by **Quebec** for Mike Hurlbut, September 7, 1993.

• KASATONOV, ALEXEI

Alexei Kasatonov D – L. 6'1", 215 lbs. b: Leningrad, USSR, 10/14/1959. New Jersey's 10th choice, 234th overall, in 1983 Entry Draft.

Season	Club	League	GP	G	A	Pts	AG	AA	APts	PIM	PP	SH	GW	S	%	TGF	PGF	TGA	PGA	+/–	GP	G	A	Pts	PIM	PP	SH	GW
1976-77	SKA Leningrad	USSR	7	0	0	0	....	....	....	0	....	....	....	....	....	....	....	....	....	....	....	....	....	....	....	....	....	....
1977-78	SKA Leningrad	USSR	35	4	7	11	....	....	....	15	....	....	....	....	....	....	....	....	....	....	....	....	....	....	....	....	....	....
	Soviet Union	WJC-A	7	1	2	3	....	....	....	2	....	....	....	....	....	....	....	....	....	....	....	....	....	....	....	....	....	....
1978-79	CSKA Moscow	USSR	40	5	14	19	....	....	....	30	....	....	....	....	....	....	....	....	....	....	....	....	....	....	....	....	....	....
	Soviet Union	WJC-A	6	3	4	7	....	....	....	6	....	....	....	....	....	....	....	....	....	....	....	....	....	....	....	....	....	....
	USSR	Chal Cup	DID NOT PLAY																									
1979-80	CSKA Moscow	USSR	37	5	8	13	....	....	....	26	....	....	....	....	....	....	....	....	....	....	....	....	....	....	....	....	....	....
	CSKA Moscow	SuperS	5	0	4	4	....	....	....	6	....	....	....	....	....	....	....	....	....	....	....	....	....	....	....	....	....	....
	Soviet Union	Olympics	7	2	5	7	....	....	....	8	....	....	....	....	....	....	....	....	....	....	....	....	....	....	....	....	....	....
1980-81	CSKA Moscow	USSR	47	10	12	22	....	....	....	38	....	....	....	....	....	....	....	....	....	....	....	....	....	....	....	....	....	....
	Soviet Union	WEC-A	8	1	3	4	....	....	....	8	....	....	....	....	....	....	....	....	....	....	....	....	....	....	....	....	....	....
1981-82	Soviet Union	C Cup	7	1	10	11	....	....	....	8	....	....	....	....	....	....	....	....	....	....	....	....	....	....	....	....	....	....
	CSKA Moscow	USSR	46	12	27	39	....	....	....	45	....	....	....	....	....	....	....	....	....	....	....	....	....	....	....	....	....	....
	Soviet Union	WEC-A	10	0	3	3	....	....	....	6	....	....	....	....	....	....	....	....	....	....	....	....	....	....	....	....	....	....
1982-83	CSKA Moscow	USSR	44	12	19	31	....	....	....	37	....	....	....	....	....	....	....	....	....	....	....	....	....	....	....	....	....	....
	USSR	SuperS	6	0	3	3	....	....	....	8	....	....	....	....	....	....	....	....	....	....	....	....	....	....	....	....	....	....
	Soviet Union	WEC-A	10	1	10	11	....	....	....	14	....	....	....	....	....	....	....	....	....	....	....	....	....	....	....	....	....	....
1983-84	CSKA Moscow	USSR	39	12	24	36	....	....	....	20	....	....	....	....	....	....	....	....	....	....	....	....	....	....	....	....	....	....
	Soviet Union	Olympics	7	3	3	6	....	....	....	0	....	....	....	....	....	....	....	....	....	....	....	....	....	....	....	....	....	....
1984-85	Soviet Union	C Cup	6	1	4	5	....	....	....	2	....	....	....	....	....	....	....	....	....	....	....	....	....	....	....	....	....	....
	CSKA Moscow	USSR	40	18	18	36	....	....	....	26	....	....	....	....	....	....	....	....	....	....	....	....	....	....	....	....	....	....
	Soviet Union	WEC-A	9	5	6	11	....	....	....	19	....	....	....	....	....	....	....	....	....	....	....	....	....	....	....	....	....	....
1985-86	CSKA Moscow	USSR	40	6	17	23	....	....	....	27	....	....	....	....	....	....	....	....	....	....	....	....	....	....	....	....	....	....
	CSKA Moscow	SuperS	6	1	3	4	....	....	....	4	....	....	....	....	....	....	....	....	....	....	....	....	....	....	....	....	....	....
	Soviet Union	WEC-A	10	3	4	7	....	....	....	4	....	....	....	....	....	....	....	....	....	....	....	....	....	....	....	....	....	....
1986-87	CSKA Moscow	USSR	40	13	17	30	....	....	....	16	....	....	....	....	....	....	....	....	....	....	....	....	....	....	....	....	....	....
	USSR	RV'87	2	1	0	1	....	....	....	2	....	....	....	....	....	....	....	....	....	....	....	....	....	....	....	....	....	....
	Soviet Union	WEC-A	10	3	5	8	....	....	....	8	....	....	....	....	....	....	....	....	....	....	....	....	....	....	....	....	....	....
1987-88	Soviet Union	C Cup	9	1	4	5	....	....	....	4	....	....	....	....	....	....	....	....	....	....	....	....	....	....	....	....	....	....
	CSKA Moscow	USSR	43	8	12	20	....	....	....	8	....	....	....	....	....	....	....	....	....	....	....	....	....	....	....	....	....	....
	Soviet Union	Olympics	7	2	6	8	....	....	....	0	....	....	....	....	....	....	....	....	....	....	....	....	....	....	....	....	....	....
1988-89	CSKA Moscow	USSR	41	8	14	22	....	....	....	8	....	....	....	....	....	....	....	....	....	....	....	....	....	....	....	....	....	....
	CSKA Moscow	SuperS	7	3	2	5	....	....	....	0	....	....	....	....	....	....	....	....	....	....	....	....	....	....	....	....	....	....
	Soviet Union	WEC-A	10	2	0	2	....	....	....	2	....	....	....	....	....	....	....	....	....	....	....	....	....	....	....	....	....	....
1989-90	CSKA Moscow	FrTour	1	1	0	1	....	....	....	0	....	....	....	....	....	....	....	....	....	....	....	....	....	....	....	....	....	....
	CSKA Moscow	USSR	30	6	7	13	....	....	....	16	....	....	....	....	....	....	....	....	....	....	....	....	....	....	....	....	....	....
	New Jersey Devils	**NHL**	**39**	**6**	**15**	**21**	**5**	**11**	**16**	**16**	**1**	**0**	**0**	**60**	**10.0**	**53**	**10**	**46**	**18**	**+15**	**6**	**0**	**3**	**3**	**14**	**0**	**0**	**0**
	Utica Devils	AHL	3	0	2	2	....	....	....	7	....	....	....	....	....	....	....	....	....	....	....	....	....	....	....	....	....	....
1990-91	**New Jersey Devils**	**NHL**	**78**	**10**	**31**	**41**	**9**	**23**	**32**	**76**	**1**	**0**	**3**	**122**	**8.2**	**88**	**15**	**94**	**44**	**+23**	**7**	**1**	**3**	**4**	**10**	**0**	**0**	**0**
	Soviet Union	WEC-A	10	3	3	6	....	....	....	8	....	....	....	....	....	....	....	....	....	....	....	....	....	....	....	....	....	....
1991-92	Soviet Union	C Cup	5	0	1	1	....	....	....	6	....	....	....	....	....	....	....	....	....	....	....	....	....	....	....	....	....	....
	New Jersey Devils	**NHL**	**76**	**12**	**28**	**40**	**11**	**21**	**32**	**70**	**3**	**2**	**1**	**107**	**11.2**	**106**	**28**	**88**	**24**	**+14**	**7**	**1**	**1**	**2**	**12**	**0**	**0**	**0**
1992-93	**New Jersey Devils**	**NHL**	**64**	**3**	**14**	**17**	**2**	**10**	**12**	**57**	**0**	**0**	**0**	**63**	**4.8**	**67**	**3**	**90**	**30**	**+4**	**4**	**0**	**0**	**0**	**0**	**0**	**0**	**0**
1993-94	**Anaheim Mighty Ducks**	**NHL**	**55**	**4**	**18**	**22**	**4**	**14**	**18**	**43**	**1**	**0**	**1**	**81**	**4.9**	**54**	**16**	**60**	**14**	**–8**	....	....	....	....	....	....	....	....
	St. Louis Blues	**NHL**	**8**	**0**	**2**	**2**	**0**	**2**	**2**	**19**	**0**	**0**	**0**	**6**	**0.0**	**13**	**1**	**11**	**4**	**+5**	**4**	**2**	**0**	**2**	**2**	**0**	**0**	**0**
1994-95	CSKA Moscow	CIS	9	2	3	5	....	....	....	6	....	....	....	....	....	....	....	....	....	....	....	....	....	....	....	....	....	....
	Boston Bruins	**NHL**	**44**	**2**	**14**	**16**	**4**	**21**	**25**	**33**	**0**	**1**	**0**	**50**	**4.0**	**52**	**19**	**40**	**5**	**–2**	**5**	**0**	**0**	**0**	**2**	**0**	**0**	**0**
1995-96	**Boston Bruins**	**NHL**	**19**	**1**	**0**	**1**	**1**	**0**	**1**	**12**	**0**	**0**	**0**	**15**	**6.7**	**21**	**0**	**23**	**3**	**+1**	....	....	....	....	....	....	....	....
	Providence Bruins	AHL	16	3	6	9	....	....	....	10	....	....	....	....	....	....	....	....	....	....	....	....	....	....	....	....	....	....
1996-97	CSKA Moscow	Russia	38	3	20	23	....	....	....	68	....	....	....	....	....	....	....	....	....	....	1	0	0	0	0	....	....	....
	NHL Totals		**383**	**38**	**122**	**160**	**36**	**102**	**138**	**326**	**6**	**3**	**5**	**504**	**7.5**	**454**	**92**	**452**	**142**		**33**	**4**	**7**	**11**	**40**	**0**	**0**	**0**

WJC-A All-Star Team (1979) • Named Best Defenseman at WJC-A (1979) • USSR First All-Star Team (1981, 1982, 1983, 1984, 1985, 1986, 1987, 1988) • Canada Cup All-Star Team (1981) • WEC-A All-Star Team (1982, 1983, 1985, 1986, 1991) • Named Best Defenseman at WEC-A (1983)

Played in NHL All-Star Game (1994)

Claimed by **Anaheim** from **New Jersey** in Expansion Draft, June 24, 1993. Traded to **St. Louis** by **Anaheim** for Maxim Bets and St.Louis' 6th round choice (traded back to St. Louis — St. Louis selected Denis Hamel) in 1995 Entry Draft, March 21, 1994. Signed as a free agent by **Boston**, June 22, 1994.

● **KASPARAITIS, DARIUS** Darius Kasparaitis D – L. 5'10", 205 lbs. b: Elektrenai, USSR, 10/16/1972. NY Islanders' 1st choice, 5th overall, in 1992 Entry Draft.

			REGULAR SEASON																		PLAYOFFS							
Season	Club	League	GP	G	A	Pts	AG	AA	APts	PIM	PP	SH	GW	S	%	TGF	PGF	TGA	PGA	+/–	GP	G	A	Pts	PIM	PP	SH	GW
1988-89	Moscow Dynamo	USSR	3	0	0	0	....	....	....	0	....	....	....	....	....	....	....	....	....	....	....	....	....	....	....	....	....	....
1989-90	Moscow Dynamo	USSR	1	0	0	0	....	....	....	0	....	....	....	....	....	....	....	....	....	....	....	....	....	....	....	....	....	....
1990-91	Moscow Dynamo	USSR	17	0	1	1	....	....	....	10	....	....	....	....	....	....	....	....	....	....	....	....	....	....	....	....	....	....
1991-92	Moscow Dynamo	CIS	31	2	10	12	....	....	....	14	....	....	....	....	....	....	....	....	....	....	....	....	....	....	....	....	....	....
	Russia	WJC A	7	1	5	6	....	....	....	8	....	....	....	....	....	....	....	....	....	....	....	....	....	....	....	....	....	....
	Russia	WC-A	6	2	1	3	....	....	....	4	....	....	....	....	....	....	....	....	....	....	....	....	....	....	....	....	....	....
1992-93	Moscow Dynamo	CIS	7	1	3	4	....	....	....	8	....	....	....	....	....	....	....	....	....	....	....	....	....	....	....	....	....	....
	New York Islanders	NHL	79	4	17	21	3	12	15	166	0	0	0	92	4.3	83	0	97	29	+15	18	0	5	5	31	0	0	0
1993-94	New York Islanders	NHL	76	1	10	11	1	8	9	142	0	0	0	81	1.2	57	3	96	36	–6	4	0	0	0	8	0	0	0
1994-95	New York Islanders	NHL	13	0	1	1	0	1	1	22	0	0	0	8	0.0	5	0	17	1	–11	....	....	....	....	....	....	....	....
1995-96	New York Islanders	NHL	46	1	7	8	1	6	7	93	0	0	0	34	2.9	34	2	59	15	–12	....	....	....	....	....	....	....	....
	Russia	WC-A	8	0	2	2	....	....	....	2	....	....	....	....	....	....	....	....	....	....	....	....	....	....	....	....	....	....
1996-97	Russia	W Cup	5	0	2	2	....	....	....	14	....	....	....	....	....	....	....	....	....	....	....	....	....	....	....	....	....	....
	New York Islanders	NHL	18	0	5	5	0	4	4	16	0	0	0	12	0.0	14	0	27	6	–7	....	....	....	....	....	....	....	....
	Pittsburgh Penguins	NHL	57	2	16	18	2	14	16	84	0	0	0	46	4.3	71	4	69	26	+24	5	0	0	0	6	0	0	0
1997-98	Pittsburgh Penguins	NHL	81	4	8	12	5	8	13	127	0	2	0	71	5.6	50	5	58	16	+3	5	0	0	0	8	0	0	0
	Russia	Olympics	6	0	2	2	....	....	....	6	....	....	....	....	....	....	....	....	....	....	....	....	....	....	....	....	....	....
	NHL Totals		370	12	64	76	12	53	65	650	0	2	0	344	3.5	314	14	423	129		32	0	5	5	53	0	0	0

EJC-A All-Star Team (1990) • Named Best Defenseman at WJC-A (1992)

Traded to **Pittsburgh** by **NY Islanders** with Andreas Johansson for Bryan Smolinski, November 17, 1996.

● **KASPER, STEVE** Steve "The Friendly Ghost" Kasper C – L. 5'8", 175 lbs. b: Montreal, Que., 9/28/1961. Boston's 3rd choice, 81st overall, in 1980 Entry Draft.

Season	Club	League	GP	G	A	Pts	AG	AA	APts	PIM	PP	SH	GW	S	%	TGF	PGF	TGA	PGA	+/–	GP	G	A	Pts	PIM	PP	SH	GW
1977-78	Verdun Epeviers	QMJHL	63	26	45	71	....	....	....	16	....	....	....	....	....	....	....	....	....	....	....	....	....	....	....	....	....	....
1978-79	Verdun Epeviers	QMJHL	67	37	67	104	....	....	....	53	....	....	....	....	....	....	....	....	....	....	11	7	6	13	22	....	....	....
1979-80	Sorel Black Hawks	QMJHL	70	57	65	122	....	....	....	117	....	....	....	....	....	....	....	....	....	....	....	....	....	....	....	....	....	....
1980-81	Sorel Black Hawks	QMJHL	2	5	2	7	....	....	....	0	....	....	....	....	....	....	....	....	....	....	....	....	....	....	....	....	....	....
	Boston Bruins	NHL	76	21	35	56	17	24	41	94	5	0	1	165	12.7	82	15	67	9	+9	3	0	1	1	0	0	0	0
1981-82	Boston Bruins	NHL	73	20	31	51	16	20	36	72	1	3	3	151	13.2	68	7	101	22	–18	11	3	6	9	22	1	0	0
1982-83	Boston Bruins	NHL	24	2	6	8	2	4	6	24	0	0	1	26	7.7	11	0	26	7	–8	12	2	1	3	10	0	1	0
1983-84	Boston Bruins	NHL	27	3	11	14	2	7	9	19	0	0	0	39	7.7	18	0	19	4	+3	3	0	0	0	7	0	0	0
1984-85	Boston Bruins	NHL	77	16	24	40	13	16	29	33	0	5	1	144	11.1	52	0	95	31	–12	5	1	0	1	9	0	0	0
1985-86	Boston Bruins	NHL	80	17	23	40	14	15	29	73	1	3	1	149	11.4	57	2	117	52	–10	3	1	0	1	4	0	1	0
1986-87	Boston Bruins	NHL	79	20	30	50	17	22	39	51	4	2	2	110	18.2	67	6	103	38	–4	3	0	2	2	0	0	0	0
1987-88	Boston Bruins	NHL	79	26	44	70	22	31	53	35	9	3	5	166	15.7	100	32	109	40	–1	23	7	6	13	10	0	1	0
1988-89	Boston Bruins	NHL	49	10	16	26	8	11	19	49	2	0	0	82	12.2	38	6	61	27	–2	....	....	....	....	....	....	....	....
	Los Angeles Kings	NHL	29	9	15	24	8	11	19	14	3	2	2	48	18.8	27	8	26	7	0	11	1	5	6	10	0	0	0
1989-90	Los Angeles Kings	NHL	77	17	28	45	15	20	35	27	1	1	4	72	23.6	59	3	102	50	+4	10	1	1	2	2	0	0	0
1990-91	Los Angeles Kings	NHL	67	9	19	28	8	14	22	33	0	1	1	70	12.9	42	1	70	32	+3	10	4	6	10	8	0	1	0
1991-92	Philadelphia Flyers	NHL	16	3	2	5	3	1	4	10	0	1	0	13	23.1	9	0	20	8	–3	....	....	....	....	....	....	....	....
1992-93	Philadelphia Flyers	NHL	21	1	3	4	1	2	3	2	0	1	0	9	11.1	6	0	25	15	–4	....	....	....	....	....	....	....	....
	Tampa Bay Lightning	NHL	47	3	4	7	2	3	5	18	0	0	0	23	13.0	10	0	45	22	–13	....	....	....	....	....	....	....	....
	NHL Totals		821	177	291	468	148	201	349	554	26	22	21	1267	14.0	646	80	986	364		94	20	28	48	82	1	4	0

Won Frank J. Selke Trophy (1982)

Traded to **LA Kings** by **Boston** for Bobby Carpenter, January 23, 1989. Traded to **Philadelphia** by **LA Kings** with Steve Duschesne and LA Kings' 4th round choice (Aris Brimanis) in 1991 Entry Draft for Jari Kurri and Jeff Chychurn, May 30, 1991. Traded to **Tampa Bay** by **Philadelphia** for Dan Vincelette, December 8, 1992.

● **KASTELIC, ED** Ed Kastelic RW/LW – R. 6'4", 215 lbs. b: Toronto, Ont., 1/29/1964. Washington's 4th choice, 110th overall, in 1982 Entry Draft.

Season	Club	League	GP	G	A	Pts	AG	AA	APts	PIM	PP	SH	GW	S	%	TGF	PGF	TGA	PGA	+/–	GP	G	A	Pts	PIM	PP	SH	GW
1980-81	Mississauga Reps	Midget	51	4	10	14	....	....	....	164	....	....	....	....	....	....	....	....	....	....	....	....	....	....	....	....	....	....
1981-82	London Knights	OHL	68	5	18	23	....	....	....	63	....	....	....	....	....	....	....	....	....	....	4	0	1	1	4	....	....	....
1982-83	London Knights	OHL	68	12	11	23	....	....	....	96	....	....	....	....	....	....	....	....	....	....	3	0	0	0	5	....	....	....
1983-84	London Knights	OHL	68	17	16	33	....	....	....	218	....	....	....	....	....	....	....	....	....	....	8	0	2	2	41	....	....	....
1984-85	Moncton Golden Flames	AHL	62	5	11	16	....	....	....	187	....	....	....	....	....	....	....	....	....	....	....	....	....	....	....	....	....	....
	Binghamton Whalers	AHL	4	0	0	0	....	....	....	7	....	....	....	....	....	....	....	....	....	....	....	....	....	....	....	....	....	....
	Fort Wayne Komets	IHL	5	1	0	1	....	....	....	37	....	....	....	....	....	....	....	....	....	....	....	....	....	....	....	....	....	....
1985-86	Washington Capitals	NHL	15	0	0	0	0	0	0	73	0	0	0	2	0.0	3	0	3	0	0	....	....	....	....	....	....	....	....
	Binghamton Whalers	AHL	23	7	9	16	....	....	....	76	....	....	....	....	....	....	....	....	....	....	....	....	....	....	....	....	....	....
1986-87	Washington Capitals	NHL	23	1	1	2	1	1	2	83	1	0	0	15	6.7	9	5	7	0	–3	5	1	0	1	13	1	0	0
	Binghamton Whalers	AHL	48	17	11	28	....	....	....	124	....	....	....	....	....	....	....	....	....	....	....	....	....	....	....	....	....	....
1987-88	Washington Capitals	NHL	35	1	0	1	1	0	1	78	0	0	0	20	5.0	6	0	9	0	–3	1	0	0	0	19	0	0	0
	Binghamton Whalers	AHL	6	4	1	5	....	....	....	6	....	....	....	....	....	....	....	....	....	....	....	....	....	....	....	....	....	....
1988-89	Hartford Whalers	NHL	10	0	2	2	0	1	1	15	0	0	0	6	0.0	2	0	2	0	0	....	....	....	....	....	....	....	....
	Binghamton Whalers	AHL	35	9	6	15	....	....	....	124	....	....	....	....	....	....	....	....	....	....	....	....	....	....	....	....	....	....
1989-90	Hartford Whalers	NHL	67	6	2	8	5	1	6	198	0	0	0	35	17.1	18	1	20	0	–3	2	0	0	0	0	0	0	0
1990-91	Hartford Whalers	NHL	45	2	2	4	2	2	4	211	0	0	0	15	13.3	5	1	11	0	–7	....	....	....	....	....	....	....	....
1991-92	Hartford Whalers	NHL	25	1	3	4	1	2	3	61	0	0	0	4	25.0	7	1	10	0	–4	....	....	....	....	....	....	....	....
1992-93	Phoenix Roadrunners	IHL	57	11	7	18	....	....	....	158	....	....	....	....	....	....	....	....	....	....	....	....	....	....	....	....	....	....
1993-94	Binghamton Rangers	AHL	44	3	6	9	....	....	....	119	....	....	....	....	....	....	....	....	....	....	....	....	....	....	....	....	....	....
1994-95	Olimpija Ljubjana	Slovenia	30	20	15	35	....	....	....	48	....	....	....	....	....	....	....	....	....	....	....	....	....	....	....	....	....	....
1995-96	Olimpija Ljubjana	Slovenia	31	13	17	30	....	....	....	82	....	....	....	....	....	....	....	....	....	....	....	....	....	....	....	....	....	....
1996-97	Olimpija Ljubjana	Slovenia	48	22	26	48	....			....	....	....	....	....	....	....	....	....	....	....			....	....	....	....	....	....
1997-98	Star Bulls Rosenheim	Germany	42	2	4	6	....	....	....	108	....	....	....	....	....	....	....	....	....	....	....	....	....	....	....	....	....	....
	NHL Totals		220	11	10	21	10	7	17	719	1	0	0	97	11.3	50	8	62	0		8	1	0	1	32	1	0	0

Traded to **Hartford** by **Washington** with Grant Jennings for Mike Millar and Neil Sheehy, July 6, 1988.

● **KASZYCKI, MIKE** Mike Kaszycki C – L. 5'9", 190 lbs. b: Milton, Ont., 2/27/1956. NY Islanders' 2nd choice, 32nd overall, in 1976 Amateur Draft.

Season	Club	League	GP	G	A	Pts	AG	AA	APts	PIM	PP	SH	GW	S	%	TGF	PGF	TGA	PGA	+/–	GP	G	A	Pts	PIM	PP	SH	GW
1972-73	Dixie Beehives	OJHL	44	35	54	89	....	....	....	33	....	....	....	....	....	....	....	....	....	....	....	....	....	....	....	....	....	....
1973-74	Dixie Beehives	OJHL	43	44	55	*99	....	....	....	34	....	....	....	....	....	....	....	....	....	....	....	....	....	....	....	....	....	....
1974-75	Toronto Marlboros	OHA	70	41	44	85	....	....	....	48	....	....	....	....	....	....	....	....	....	....	23	11	15	26	21	....	....	....
1975-76	Sault Ste. Marie Greyhounds	OHA	66	51	*119	*170	....	....	....	38	....	....	....	....	....	....	....	....	....	....	12	10	10	20	8	....	....	....
1976-77	Fort Worth Texans	CHL	76	32	55	87	....	....	....	50	....	....	....	....	....	....	....	....	....	....	6	3	3	6	10	....	....	....
1977-78	New York Islanders	NHL	58	13	29	42	13	24	37	24	3	0	2	85	15.3	59	7	37	0	+15	7	1	3	4	4	0	0	0
	Rochester Americans	AHL	6	4	2	6	....	....	....	2	....	....	....	....	....	....	....	....	....	....	....	....	....	....	....	....	....	....
1978-79	New York Islanders	NHL	71	16	18	34	15	14	29	37	2	0	4	89	18.0	46	6	34	1	+7	10	1	3	4	4	0	0	0
1979-80	New York Islanders	NHL	16	1	4	5	1	3	4	15	0	0	0	13	7.7	13	3	7	0	+3	....	....	....	....	....	....	....	....
	Washington Capitals	NHL	28	7	10	17	6	8	14	10	1	0	0	34	20.6	29	10	24	0	–5	....	....	....	....	....	....	....	....
	Toronto Maple Leafs	NHL	25	4	4	8	4	3	7	10	0	0	0	17	23.5	10	1	25	12	–4	2	0	0	0	2	0	0	0
1980-81	Toronto Maple Leafs	NHL	6	0	2	2	0	1	1	2	0	0	0	3	0.0	2	0	1	1	+2	....	....	....	....	....	....	....	....
	Dallas Black Hawks	CHL	42	15	21	36	....	....	....	42	....	....	....	....	....	....	....	....	....	....	6	2	2	4	9	....	....	....
1981-82	New Brunswick Hawks	AHL	80	36	*82	*118	....	....	....	67	....	....	....	....	....	....	....	....	....	....	15	8	*13	*21	17	....	....	....
1982-83	Toronto Maple Leafs	NHL	22	1	13	14	1	9	10	10	0	0	0	19	5.3	20	3	20	3	0	....	....	....	....	....	....	....	....
	St. Catharines Saints	AHL	56	26	42	68	....	....	....	30	....	....	....	....	....	....	....	....	....	....	....	....	....	....	....	....	....	....
1983-84	St. Catharines Saints	AHL	72	39	71	110	....	....	....	51	....	....	....	....	....	....	....	....	....	....	5	1	1	2	7	....	....	....
1984-85	Moncton Golden Flames	AHL	30	9	15	24	....	....	....	8	....	....	....	....	....	....	....	....	....	....	....	....	....	....	....	....	....	....
	HC Langnau	Switz.	22	12	13	25	....	....	....	....	....	....	....	....	....	....	....	....	....	....	....	....	....	....	....	....	....	....

			REGULAR SEASON																		PLAYOFFS							
Season	Club	League	GP	G	A	Pts	AG	AA	APts	PIM	PP	SH	GW	S	%	TGF	PGF	TGA	PGA	+/–	GP	G	A	Pts	PIM	PP	SH	GW
1985-86	Ambri-Piotta	Switz.	36	19	19	38	....	....	....	....	....	....	....	....	....	....	....	....	....	....	....	....	....	....	....	....	....	....
1986-87	Ambri-Piotta	Switz.	36	23	24	47	....	....	....	....	....	....	....	....	....	....	....	....	....	....	4	1	2	3	0	....	....	....
1987-88	Ambri-Piotta	Switz.	30	17	19	36	....	....	....	....	....	....	....	....	....	....	....	....	....	....	....	....	....	....	....	....	....	....
	NHL Totals		226	42	80	122	40	62	102	108	6	0	6	260	16.2	179	30	148	17		19	2	6	8	10	0	0	0

OHA Second All-Star Team (1976) • AHL First All-Star Team (1982) • Won Fred T. Hunt Memorial Trophy (Sportsmanship - AHL) (1982) • Won John B. Sollenberger Trophy (Top Scorer - AHL) (1982) • Won Les Cunningham Award (MVP - AHL) (1982) • AHL Second All-Star Team (1984)

Traded to **Washington** by **NY Islanders** for Gord Lane, December 7, 1979. Traded to **Toronto** by **Washington** for Pat Ribble, February 16, 1980.

• KEA, ED

Ed Kea D – L. 6'3", 200 lbs. b: Collingwood, Ont., 1/19/1948.

Season	Club	League	GP	G	A	Pts	AG	AA	APts	PIM	PP	SH	GW	S	%	TGF	PGF	TGA	PGA	+/–	GP	G	A	Pts	PIM	PP	SH	GW
1967-68	Collingwood Kings	OHA Sr.	2	0	1	1	....	....	....	0	....	....	....	....	....	....	....	....	....	....	....	....	....	....	....	....	....	....
1968-69	Collingwood Kings	OHA Sr.	8	0	1	1	....	....	....	4	....	....	....	....	....	....	....	....	....	....	....	....	....	....	....	....	....	....
1969-70	New Jersey Devils	EHL	52	4	18	22	....	....	....	130	....	....	....	....	....	....	....	....	....	....	....	....	....	....	....	....	....	....
1970-71	Seattle Totems	WHL	5	0	0	0	....	....	....	2	....	....	....	....	....	....	....	....	....	....	....	....	....	....	....	....	....	....
	New Jersey Devils	EHL	74	8	26	34	....	....	....	148	....	....	....	....	....	....	....	....	....	....	....	....	....	....	....	....	....	....
1971-72	St. Petersburg Suns	EHL	63	10	39	49	....	....	....	107	....	....	....	....	....	....	....	....	....	....	6	2	2	4	20	....	....	....
1972-73	Omaha Knights	CHL	68	10	22	32	....	....	....	145	....	....	....	....	....	....	....	....	....	....	11	3	3	6	10	....	....	....
1973-74	**Atlanta Flames**	**NHL**	3	0	2	2	0	2	2	0	0	0	0	3	0.0	3	0	1	0	+2	....	....	....	....	....	....	....	....
	Tulsa Oilers	CHL	51	6	17	23	....	....	....	38	....	....	....	....	....	....	....	....	....	....	....	....	....	....	....	....	....	....
	Omaha Knights	CHL	7	2	1	3	....	....	....	13	....	....	....	....	....	....	....	....	....	....	....	....	....	....	....	....	....	....
1974-75	**Atlanta Flames**	**NHL**	50	1	9	10	1	7	8	39	0	0	0	61	1.6	43	2	40	6	+7	....	....	....	....	....	....	....	....
	Omaha Knights	CHL	21	6	6	12	....	....	....	26	....	....	....	....	....	....	....	....	....	....	....	....	....	....	....	....	....	....
1975-76	**Atlanta Flames**	**NHL**	78	8	19	27	7	15	22	101	1	0	0	125	6.4	93	8	83	19	+21	2	0	0	0	7	0	0	0
1976-77	**Atlanta Flames**	**NHL**	72	4	21	25	4	17	21	63	0	0	0	112	3.6	73	4	90	21	0	3	0	1	1	2	0	0	0
1977-78	**Atlanta Flames**	**NHL**	60	3	23	26	3	19	22	40	0	0	0	78	3.8	79	4	63	13	+25	1	0	0	0	0	0	0	0
1978-79	**Atlanta Flames**	**NHL**	53	6	18	24	5	14	19	40	2	0	1	53	11.3	57	4	64	9	–2	2	0	0	0	0	0	0	0
	Tulsa Oilers	CHL	2	0	3	3	....	....	....	0	....	....	....	....	....	....	....	....	....	....	....	....	....	....	....	....	....	....
1979-80	**St. Louis Blues**	**NHL**	69	3	16	19	3	12	15	79	0	0	1	73	4.1	85	2	90	16	+9	3	0	0	0	2	0	0	0
1980-81	**St. Louis Blues**	**NHL**	74	3	18	21	2	13	15	60	0	0	0	59	5.1	81	2	97	33	+15	11	1	2	3	12	0	0	0
1981-82	**St. Louis Blues**	**NHL**	78	2	14	16	2	9	11	62	0	0	0	89	2.2	87	1	105	38	+19	10	1	1	2	16	0	0	0
1982-83	**St. Louis Blues**	**NHL**	46	0	5	5	0	3	3	24	0	0	0	42	0.0	28	0	47	12	–7	....	....	....	....	....	....	....	....
	Salt Lake Golden Eagles	CHL	9	1	4	5	....	....	....	10	....	....	....	....	....	....	....	....	....	....	....	....	....	....	....	....	....	....
	NHL Totals		583	30	145	175	27	111	138	508	3	0	2	695	4.3	629	27	680	167		32	2	4	6	39	0	0	0

CHL Second All-Star Team (1974)

Signed as a free agent by **Atlanta**, October 6, 1972. Traded to **St. Louis** by **Atlanta** with Don Laurence and Atlanta's 2nd round choice (Hakan Nordin) in 1981 Entry Draft, October 10, 1979.

• KEANE, MIKE

Mike Keane RW – R. 6', 185 lbs. b: Winnipeg, Man., 5/29/1967.

Season	Club	League	GP	G	A	Pts	AG	AA	APts	PIM	PP	SH	GW	S	%	TGF	PGF	TGA	PGA	+/–	GP	G	A	Pts	PIM	PP	SH	GW
1984-85	Moose Jaw Warriors	WHL	65	17	26	43	....	....	....	141	....	....	....	....	....	....	....	....	....	....	....	....	....	....	....	....	....	....
1985-86	Moose Jaw Warriors	WHL	67	34	49	83	....	....	....	162	....	....	....	....	....	....	....	....	....	....	13	6	8	14	9	....	....	....
1986-87	Moose Jaw Warriors	WHL	53	25	45	70	....	....	....	107	....	....	....	....	....	....	....	....	....	....	9	3	9	12	11	....	....	....
	Sherbrooke Canadiens	AHL	....	....	....	....	....	....	....	....	....	....	....	....	....	....	....	....	....	....	9	2	2	4	16	....	....	....
	Canada	WJC-A	6	0	1	1	....	....	....	4	....	....	....	....	....	....	....	....	....	....	....	....	....	....	....	....	....	....
1987-88	Sherbrooke Canadiens	AHL	78	25	43	68	....	....	....	70	....	....	....	....	....	....	....	....	....	....	6	1	1	2	18	....	....	....
1988-89	**Montreal Canadiens**	**NHL**	69	16	19	35	14	13	27	69	5	0	1	90	17.8	62	17	43	7	+9	21	4	3	7	17	2	0	0
1989-90	**Montreal Canadiens**	**NHL**	74	9	15	24	8	11	19	78	1	0	1	92	9.8	41	6	52	17	0	11	0	1	1	8	0	0	0
1990-91	Montreal Canadiens	FrTour	3	0	0	0	....	....	....	6	....	....	....	....	....	....	....	....	....	....	....	....	....	....	....	....	....	....
	Montreal Canadiens	**NHL**	73	13	23	36	12	17	29	50	2	1	2	109	11.9	54	6	54	12	+6	12	3	2	5	6	0	0	0
1991-92	**Montreal Canadiens**	**NHL**	67	11	30	41	10	23	33	64	2	0	2	116	9.5	71	16	51	12	+16	8	1	1	2	16	0	0	0
1992-93	**Montreal Canadiens**	**NHL**	77	15	45	60	12	31	43	95	0	0	1	120	12.5	79	2	74	26	+29	19	2	13	15	6	0	0	0
1993-94	**Montreal Canadiens**	**NHL**	80	16	30	46	15	23	38	119	6	2	2	129	12.4	78	21	77	26	+6	6	3	1	4	4	0	0	0
1994-95	**Montreal Canadiens**	**NHL**	48	10	10	20	18	15	33	15	1	0	0	75	13.3	30	3	37	15	+5	....	....	....	....	....	....	....	....
1995-96	**Montreal Canadiens**	**NHL**	18	0	7	7	0	6	6	6	0	0	0	17	0.0	12	3	21	6	–6	....	....	....	....	....	....	....	....
	Colorado Avalanche	**NHL**	55	10	10	20	10	8	18	40	0	2	2	67	14.9	29	0	40	12	+1	22	3	2	5	16	0	0	1
1996-97	**Colorado Avalanche**	**NHL**	81	10	17	27	11	15	26	63	0	1	1	91	11.0	43	1	55	15	+2	17	3	1	4	24	0	0	1
1997-98	**New York Rangers**	**NHL**	70	8	10	18	9	10	19	47	2	0	0	113	7.1	25	5	56	24	–12	....	....	....	....	....	....	....	....
	Dallas Stars	**NHL**	13	2	3	5	2	3	5	5	0	0	1	15	13.3	6	0	8	2	0	17	4	4	8	0	0	1	1
	NHL Totals		725	120	219	339	121	175	296	651	19	6	13	1034	11.6	530	80	568	174		133	23	28	51	97	2	1	3

Signed as a free agent by **Montreal**, September 25, 1985. Traded to **Colorado** by **Montreal** with Patrick Roy for Andrei Kovalenko, Martin Rucinsky and Jocelyn Thibault, December 6, 1995. Signed as a free agent by **NY Rangers**, July 30, 1997. Traded to **Dallas** by **NY Rangers** with Brian Skrudland and NY Rangers' 6th round choice (Pavel Patera) in 1998 Entry Draft for Todd Harvey, Bob Errey and Dallas' 4th round choice (Boyd Kane) in 1998 Entry Draft, March 24, 1998.

• KEARNS, DENNIS

Dennis Kearns D – L. 5'9", 185 lbs. b: Kingston, Ont., 9/27/1945.

Season	Club	League	GP	G	A	Pts	AG	AA	APts	PIM	PP	SH	GW	S	%	TGF	PGF	TGA	PGA	+/–	GP	G	A	Pts	PIM	PP	SH	GW
1965-66	Kingston Canadians	OJHL	STATISTICS NOT AVAILABLE																									
1966-67	Kingston Aces	OHA Sr.	40	17	14	31	....	....	....	47	....	....	....	....	....	....	....	....	....	....	....	....	....	....	....	....	....	....
1967-68	Portland Buckaroos	WHL	68	5	15	20	....	....	....	62	....	....	....	....	....	....	....	....	....	....	12	2	4	6	2	....	....	....
1968-69	Portland Buckaroos	WHL	74	2	42	44	....	....	....	81	....	....	....	....	....	....	....	....	....	....	11	2	6	8	13	....	....	....
1969-70	Portland Buckaroos	WHL	72	11	42	53	....	....	....	67	....	....	....	....	....	....	....	....	....	....	8	1	6	7	9	....	....	....
1970-71	Dallas Black Hawks	CHL	65	8	44	52	....	....	....	65	....	....	....	....	....	....	....	....	....	....	10	2	5	7	14	....	....	....
1971-72	**Vancouver Canucks**	**NHL**	73	3	26	29	3	24	27	59	2	0	0	103	2.9	79	34	77	5	–27	....	....	....	....	....	....	....	....
1972-73	**Vancouver Canucks**	**NHL**	72	4	33	37	4	28	32	51	2	0	0	113	3.5	98	21	116	13	–26	....	....	....	....	....	....	....	....
1973-74	**Vancouver Canucks**	**NHL**	52	4	13	17	4	11	15	30	2	0	0	61	6.6	52	23	51	11	–11	....	....	....	....	....	....	....	....
1974-75	**Vancouver Canucks**	**NHL**	49	1	11	12	1	9	10	31	1	0	0	71	1.4	73	23	56	11	+5	4	0	0	0	4	0	0	0
1975-76	**Vancouver Canucks**	**NHL**	80	5	46	51	5	36	41	48	1	0	0	118	4.2	126	46	101	15	–6	2	0	1	1	0	0	0	0
1976-77	**Vancouver Canucks**	**NHL**	80	5	55	60	5	45	50	60	2	1	1	121	4.1	116	39	116	14	–25	....	....	....	....	....	....	....	....
	Canada	WEC-A	10	0	1	1	....	....	....	2	....	....	....	....	....	....	....	....	....	....	....	....	....	....	....	....	....	....
1977-78	**Vancouver Canucks**	**NHL**	80	4	43	47	4	35	39	27	1	0	2	101	4.0	115	48	142	35	–40	....	....	....	....	....	....	....	....
	Canada	WEC-A	10	0	1	1	....	....	....	14	....	....	....	....	....	....	....	....	....	....	....	....	....	....	....	....	....	....
1978-79	**Vancouver Canucks**	**NHL**	78	3	31	34	3	24	27	28	0	0	0	102	2.9	95	22	103	7	–23	3	1	1	2	2	1	0	0
1979-80	**Vancouver Canucks**	**NHL**	67	1	18	19	1	14	15	24	0	0	0	66	1.5	70	10	67	9	+2	2	0	0	0	2	0	0	0
1980-81	**Vancouver Canucks**	**NHL**	46	1	14	15	1	10	11	28	0	0	0	43	2.3	43	10	43	3	–7	....	....	....	....	....	....	....	....
	NHL Totals		677	31	290	321	31	236	267	386	11	1	3	899	3.4	867	276	872	123		11	1	2	3	8	1	0	0

WHL Second All-Star Team (1969) • WHL First All-Star Team (1970) • CHL First All-Star Team (1971)

Traded to **Chicago** (Dallas-CHL) by **Portland** (WHL) for cash, August, 1970. Claimed by **Vancouver** from **Chicago** in Intra-League Draft, June 8, 1971.

• KEATING, MIKE

Mike Keating LW – L. 6', 185 lbs. b: Toronto, Ont., 1/21/1957. NY Rangers' 3rd choice, 26th overall, in 1977 Amateur Draft.

Season	Club	League	GP	G	A	Pts	AG	AA	APts	PIM	PP	SH	GW	S	%	TGF	PGF	TGA	PGA	+/–	GP	G	A	Pts	PIM	PP	SH	GW
1973-74	Seneca Flyers	OJHL	44	38	51	89	....	....	....	66	....	....	....	....	....	....	....	....	....	....	....	....	....	....	....	....	....	....
1974-75	Hamilton Fincups	OHA	53	31	24	55	....	....	....	83	....	....	....	....	....	....	....	....	....	....	....	....	....	....	....	....	....	....
1975-76	Hamilton Fincups	OHA	66	42	37	79	....	....	....	82	....	....	....	....	....	....	....	....	....	....	....	....	....	....	....	....	....	....
1976-77	St. Catherines Fincups	OHA	65	52	61	113	....	....	....	96	....	....	....	....	....	....	....	....	....	....	....	....	....	....	....	....	....	....
	Canada	WJC-A	7	0	2	2	....	....	....	4	....	....	....	....	....	....	....	....	....	....	....	....	....	....	....	....	....	....
1977-78	**New York Rangers**	**NHL**	1	0	0	0	0	0	0	0	0	0	0	2	0.0	0	0	1	0	–1	....	....	....	....	....	....	....	....
	New Haven Nighthawks	AHL	62	15	9	24	....	....	....	12	....	....	....	....	....	....	....	....	....	....	2	0	0	0	0	....	....	....
1978-79	New Haven Nighthawks	AHL	1	0	0	0	....	....	....	0	....	....	....	....	....	....	....	....	....	....	....	....	....	....	....	....	....	....
	Toledo Goaldiggers	IHL	66	26	27	53	....	....	....	54	....	....	....	....	....	....	....	....	....	....	6	4	2	6	14	....	....	....
1979-80	Dayton Gems	IHL	3	1	2	3	....	....	....	0	....	....	....	....	....	....	....	....	....	....	....	....	....	....	....	....	....	....
	Toledo Goaldiggers	IHL	63	31	29	60	....	....	....	58	....	....	....	....	....	....	....	....	....	....	4	2	0	2	8	....	....	....
	NHL Totals		1	0	0	0	0	0	0	0	0	0	0	2	0.0	0	0	1	0		....	....	....	....	....	....	....	....

• KECZMER, DAN

Dan Keczmer D – L. 6'1", 190 lbs. b: Mt. Clemens, MI, 5/25/1968. Minnesota's 11th choice, 201st overall, in 1986 Entry Draft.

			REGULAR SEASON																		PLAYOFFS							
Season	Club	League	GP	G	A	Pts	AG	AA	APts	PIM	PP	SH	GW	S	%	TGF	PGF	TGA	PGA	+/-	GP	G	A	Pts	PIM	PP	SH	GW
1985-86	Detroit Little Caesars	Midget	65	6	48	54	....	....	....	116	....	....	....	....	....	....	....	....	....	....	....	....	....	....	....	....	....	....
1986-87	Lake Superior State	CCHA	38	3	5	8	....	....	....	26	....	....	....	....	....	....	....	....	....	....	....	....	....	....	....	....	....	....
1987-88	Lake Superior State	CCHA	41	2	15	17	....	....	....	34	....	....	....	....	....	....	....	....	....	....	....	....	....	....	....	....	....	....
1988-89	Lake Superior State	CCHA	46	3	26	29	....	....	....	68	....	....	....	....	....	....	....	....	....	....	....	....	....	....	....	....	....	....
1989-90	Lake Superior State	CCHA	43	13	23	36	....	....	....	48	....	....	....	....	....	....	....	....	....	....	....	....	....	....	....	....	....	....
	United States	WEC-A	10	0	0	0	....	....	....	2	....	....	....	....	....	....	....	....	....	....	....	....	....	....	....	....	....	....
1990-91	**Minnesota North Stars**	**NHL**	**9**	**0**	**1**	**1**	**0**	**1**	**1**	**6**	**0**	**0**	**0**	**6**	**0.0**	**2**	**0**	**2**	**0**	**0**	....	....	....	....	....	....	....	....
	Kalamazoo Wings	IHL	60	4	20	24	....	....	....	60	....	....	....	....	....	....	....	....	....	....	9	1	2	3	10	....	....	....
1991-92	United States	Nat-Team	51	3	11	14	....	....	....	56	....	....	....	....	....	....	....	....	....	....	....	....	....	....	....	....	....	....
	Hartford Whalers	**NHL**	**1**	**0**	**0**	**0**	**0**	**0**	**0**	**0**	**0**	**0**	**0**	**2**	**0.0**	**1**	**1**	**1**	**0**	**-1**	....	....	....	....	....	....	....	....
	Springfield Indians	AHL	18	3	4	7	....	....	....	10	....	....	....	....	....	....	....	....	....	....	4	0	0	0	6	....	....	....
1992-93	**Hartford Whalers**	**NHL**	**23**	**4**	**4**	**8**	**3**	**3**	**6**	**28**	**2**	**0**	**1**	**38**	**10.5**	**24**	**4**	**23**	**0**	**-3**	....	....	....	....	....	....	....	....
	Springfield Indians	AHL	37	1	13	14	....	....	....	38	....	....	....	....	....	....	....	....	....	....	12	0	4	4	14	....	....	....
1993-94	**Hartford Whalers**	**NHL**	**12**	**0**	**1**	**1**	**0**	**1**	**1**	**12**	**0**	**0**	**0**	**12**	**0.0**	**8**	**4**	**11**	**1**	**-6**	....	....	....	....	....	....	....	....
	Springfield Indians	AHL	7	0	1	1	....	....	....	4	....	....	....	....	....	....	....	....	....	....	....	....	....	....	....	....	....	....
	Calgary Flames	**NHL**	**57**	**1**	**20**	**21**	**1**	**15**	**16**	**48**	**0**	**0**	**0**	**104**	**1.0**	**72**	**37**	**45**	**8**	**-2**	**3**	**0**	**0**	**0**	**4**	**0**	**0**	**0**
1994-95	**Calgary Flames**	**NHL**	**28**	**2**	**3**	**5**	**4**	**4**	**8**	**10**	**0**	**0**	**0**	**33**	**6.1**	**18**	**2**	**13**	**4**	**+7**	**7**	**0**	**1**	**1**	**2**	**0**	**0**	**0**
1995-96	**Calgary Flames**	**NHL**	**13**	**0**	**0**	**0**	**0**	**0**	**0**	**14**	**0**	**0**	**0**	**13**	**0.0**	**3**	**1**	**8**	**0**	**-6**	....	....	....	....	....	....	....	....
	Saint John Flames	AHL	22	3	11	14	....	....	....	14	....	....	....	....	....	....	....	....	....	....	....	....	....	....	....	....	....	....
	Albany River Rats	AHL	17	0	4	4	....	....	....	4	....	....	....	....	....	....	....	....	....	....	1	0	0	0	0	....	....	....
1996-97	**Dallas Stars**	**NHL**	**13**	**0**	**1**	**1**	**0**	**1**	**1**	**6**	**0**	**0**	**0**	**10**	**0.0**	**8**	**0**	**6**	**1**	**+3**	....	....	....	....	....	....	....	....
	Michigan K-Wings	IHL	42	3	17	20	....	....	....	24	....	....	....	....	....	....	....	....	....	....	....	....	....	....	....	....	....	....
1997-98	**Dallas Stars**	**NHL**	**17**	**1**	**2**	**3**	**1**	**2**	**3**	**26**	**0**	**0**	**0**	**9**	**11.1**	**11**	**1**	**5**	**0**	**+5**	**2**	**0**	**0**	**0**	**2**	**0**	**0**	**0**
	Michigan K-Wings	IHL	44	1	11	12	....	....	....	29	....	....	....	....	....	....	....	....	....	....	....	....	....	....	....	....	....	....
	NHL Totals		**173**	**8**	**32**	**40**	**9**	**27**	**36**	**150**	**2**	**0**	**1**	**227**	**3.5**	**147**	**50**	**114**	**14**		**12**	**0**	**1**	**1**	**8**	**0**	**0**	**0**

CCHA Second All-Star Team (1990)

Claimed by **San Jose** from **Minnesota** in Dispersal Draft, May 30, 1991. Traded to **Hartford** by **San Jose** for Dean Evason, October 2, 1991. Traded to **Calgary** by **Hartford** for Jeff Reese, November 19, 1993. Traded to **New Jersey** by **Calgary** with Phil Housley for Tommy Albelin, Cale Hulse and Jocelyn Lemieux, February 26, 1996. Signed as a free agent by **Dallas**, August 19, 1996.

• KEENAN, LARRY

Larry Keenan LW – L. 5'11", 175 lbs. b: North Bay, Ont., 10/1/1940.

Season	Club	League	GP	G	A	Pts	AG	AA	APts	PIM	PP	SH	GW	S	%	TGF	PGF	TGA	PGA	+/-	GP	G	A	Pts	PIM	PP	SH	GW
1957-58	St. Michael's Majors	OHA	3	0	1	1	....	....	....	2	....	....	....	....	....	....	....	....	....	....	....	....	....	....	....	....	....	....
1958-59	St. Michael's Majors	OHA	48	17	12	29	....	....	....	24	....	....	....	....	....	....	....	....	....	....	15	5	4	9	0	....	....	....
1959-60	St. Michael's Majors	OHA	48	21	20	41	....	....	....	34	....	....	....	....	....	....	....	....	....	....	10	8	10	18	0	....	....	....
1960-61	St. Michael's Majors	OHA	48	31	38	69	....	....	....	41	....	....	....	....	....	....	....	....	....	....	20	24	13	37	8	....	....	....
1961-62	**Toronto Maple Leafs**	**NHL**	**2**	**0**	**0**	**0**	**0**	**0**	**0**	**0**	....	....	....	....	....	....	....	....	....	....	....	....	....	....	....	....	....	....
	Rochester Americans	AHL	57	11	19	30	....	....	....	12	....	....	....	....	....	....	....	....	....	....	2	0	0	0	0	....	....	....
1962-63	Rochester Americans	AHL	64	11	28	39	....	....	....	24	....	....	....	....	....	....	....	....	....	....	2	0	1	1	0	....	....	....
1963-64	Denver Invaders	WHL	66	25	30	55	....	....	....	22	....	....	....	....	....	....	....	....	....	....	6	2	2	4	4	....	....	....
1964-65	Victoria Cougars	WHL	67	35	20	55	....	....	....	27	....	....	....	....	....	....	....	....	....	....	12	5	2	7	8	....	....	....
1965-66	Victoria Cougars	WHL	36	8	18	26	....	....	....	6	....	....	....	....	....	....	....	....	....	....	14	2	4	6	2	....	....	....
1966-67	Victoria Cougars	WHL	17	4	10	14	....	....	....	6	....	....	....	....	....	....	....	....	....	....	....	....	....	....	....	....	....	....
1967-68	**St. Louis Blues**	**NHL**	**40**	**12**	**8**	**20**	**15**	**8**	**23**	**4**	**4**	**0**	**2**	**102**	**11.8**	**26**	**9**	**24**	**0**	**-7**	**18**	**4**	**5**	**9**	**4**	**1**	**0**	**2**
1968-69	**St. Louis Blues**	**NHL**	**46**	**5**	**9**	**14**	**6**	**8**	**14**	**6**	**0**	**0**	**2**	**73**	**6.8**	**30**	**3**	**8**	**0**	**+19**	**12**	**4**	**5**	**9**	**8**	**1**	**2**	**0**
	Kansas City Blues	CHL	7	3	1	4	....	....	....	0	....	....	....	....	....	....	....	....	....	....	....	....	....	....	....	....	....	....
1969-70	**St. Louis Blues**	**NHL**	**56**	**10**	**23**	**33**	**12**	**23**	**35**	**8**	**3**	**0**	**0**	**113**	**8.8**	**60**	**26**	**44**	**2**	**-8**	**16**	**7**	**6**	**13**	**0**	**4**	**2**	**0**
	Kansas City Blues	CHL	6	6	2	8	....	....	....	0	....	....	....	....	....	....	....	....	....	....	....	....	....	....	....	....	....	....
1970-71	**St. Louis Blues**	**NHL**	**10**	**1**	**3**	**4**	**1**	**3**	**4**	**0**	**0**	**0**	**0**	**24**	**4.2**	**7**	**3**	**1**	**0**	**+3**	....	....	....	....	....	....	....	....
	Buffalo Sabres	**NHL**	**51**	**7**	**20**	**27**	**7**	**18**	**25**	**6**	**3**	**0**	**2**	**67**	**10.4**	**41**	**9**	**44**	**2**	**-10**	....	....	....	....	....	....	....	....
1971-72	**Buffalo Sabres**	**NHL**	**14**	**2**	**0**	**2**	**2**	**0**	**2**	**2**	**0**	**0**	**0**	**15**	**13.3**	**5**	**1**	**8**	**1**	**-3**	....	....	....	....	....	....	....	....
	Philadelphia Flyers	**NHL**	**14**	**1**	**1**	**2**	**1**	**1**	**2**	**2**	**1**	**0**	**1**	**13**	**7.7**	**4**	**2**	**7**	**1**	**-4**	....	....	....	....	....	....	....	....
	Richmond Robins	AHL	23	3	6	9	....	....	....	0	....	....	....	....	....	....	....	....	....	....	....	....	....	....	....	....	....	....
1972-73	Richmond Robins	AHL	35	15	18	33	....	....	....	8	....	....	....	....	....	....	....	....	....	....	3	1	0	1	0	....	....	....
1973-74	Richmond Robins	AHL	68	22	37	59	....	....	....	20	....	....	....	....	....	....	....	....	....	....	5	1	0	1	0	....	....	....
	NHL Totals		**233**	**38**	**64**	**102**	**44**	**61**	**105**	**28**	**11**	**0**	**7**	**407**	**9.3**	**173**	**53**	**136**	**6**		**46**	**15**	**16**	**31**	**12**	**6**	**4**	**2**

Claimed by **St. Louis** from **Toronto** in Expansion Draft, June 6, 1967. Traded to **Buffalo** by **St. Louis** with Jean-Guy Talbot for Bob Baun, November 4, 1970. Traded to **Philadelphia** by **Buffalo** for Larry Mickey, November 16, 1971.

• KEHOE, RICK

Rick Kehoe RW – R. 5'11", 180 lbs. b: Windsor, Ont., 7/15/1951. Toronto's 1st choice, 22nd overall, in 1971 Amateur Draft.

Season	Club	League	GP	G	A	Pts	AG	AA	APts	PIM	PP	SH	GW	S	%	TGF	PGF	TGA	PGA	+/-	GP	G	A	Pts	PIM	PP	SH	GW
1969-70	London Knights	OHA	23	3	2	5	....	....	....	6	....	....	....	....	....	....	....	....	....	....	....	....	....	....	....	....	....	....
	Hamilton Red Wings	OHA	32	2	4	6	....	....	....	77	....	....	....	....	....	....	....	....	....	....	....	....	....	....	....	....	....	....
1970-71	Hamilton Red Wings	OHA	58	39	41	80	....	....	....	43	....	....	....	....	....	....	....	....	....	....	....	....	....	....	....	....	....	....
1971-72	**Toronto Maple Leafs**	**NHL**	**38**	**8**	**8**	**16**	**8**	**7**	**15**	**4**	**2**	**0**	**0**	**70**	**11.4**	**24**	**5**	**20**	**0**	**-1**	**2**	**0**	**0**	**0**	**2**	**0**	**0**	**0**
	Tulsa Oilers	CHL	32	18	21	39	....	....	....	20	....	....	....	....	....	....	....	....	....	....	....	....	....	....	....	....	....	....
1972-73	**Toronto Maple Leafs**	**NHL**	**77**	**33**	**42**	**75**	**33**	**35**	**68**	**20**	**2**	**0**	**5**	**204**	**16.2**	**98**	**22**	**87**	**0**	**-11**	....	....	....	....	....	....	....	....
1973-74	**Toronto Maple Leafs**	**NHL**	**69**	**18**	**22**	**40**	**18**	**19**	**37**	**8**	**3**	**0**	**3**	**197**	**9.1**	**72**	**12**	**41**	**0**	**+19**	....	....	....	....	....	....	....	....
1974-75	**Pittsburgh Penguins**	**NHL**	**76**	**32**	**31**	**63**	**30**	**24**	**54**	**22**	**3**	**1**	**0**	**240**	**13.3**	**98**	**17**	**64**	**1**	**+18**	**9**	**0**	**2**	**2**	**0**	**0**	**0**	**0**
1975-76	**Pittsburgh Penguins**	**NHL**	**71**	**29**	**47**	**76**	**27**	**37**	**64**	**6**	**5**	**0**	**2**	**180**	**16.1**	**102**	**18**	**75**	**0**	**+9**	**3**	**0**	**0**	**0**	**0**	**0**	**0**	**0**
1976-77	**Pittsburgh Penguins**	**NHL**	**80**	**30**	**27**	**57**	**29**	**22**	**51**	**10**	**7**	**0**	**5**	**250**	**12.0**	**88**	**22**	**71**	**0**	**-5**	**3**	**0**	**2**	**2**	**0**	**0**	**0**	**0**
1977-78	**Pittsburgh Penguins**	**NHL**	**70**	**20**	**21**	**50**	**28**	**17**	**45**	**10**	**7**	**0**	**2**	**177**	**16.4**	**72**	**20**	**75**	**5**	**-18**	....	....	....	....	....	....	....	....
1978-79	**Pittsburgh Penguins**	**NHL**	**57**	**27**	**18**	**45**	**25**	**14**	**39**	**2**	**7**	**0**	**3**	**165**	**16.4**	**73**	**24**	**36**	**1**	**+14**	**7**	**0**	**2**	**2**	**0**	**0**	**0**	**0**
1979-80	**Pittsburgh Penguins**	**NHL**	**79**	**30**	**30**	**60**	**27**	**23**	**50**	**4**	**7**	**0**	**3**	**239**	**12.6**	**86**	**23**	**66**	**0**	**-3**	**5**	**2**	**5**	**7**	**0**	**2**	**0**	**0**
1980-81	**Pittsburgh Penguins**	**NHL**	**80**	**55**	**33**	**88**	**46**	**23**	**69**	**6**	**20**	**0**	**5**	**299**	**18.4**	**135**	**65**	**79**	**0**	**-9**	**5**	**0**	**3**	**3**	**0**	**0**	**0**	**0**
1981-82	**Pittsburgh Penguins**	**NHL**	**71**	**33**	**52**	**85**	**26**	**34**	**60**	**8**	**17**	**0**	**1**	**249**	**13.3**	**119**	**67**	**80**	**1**	**-27**	**5**	**2**	**3**	**5**	**2**	**0**	**0**	**2**
1982-83	**Pittsburgh Penguins**	**NHL**	**75**	**29**	**36**	**65**	**24**	**25**	**49**	**12**	**15**	**0**	**2**	**203**	**14.3**	**99**	**61**	**83**	**0**	**-45**	....	....	....	....	....	....	....	....
1983-84	**Pittsburgh Penguins**	**NHL**	**57**	**18**	**27**	**45**	**14**	**18**	**32**	**8**	**7**	**0**	**3**	**156**	**11.5**	**58**	**25**	**54**	**1**	**-20**	....	....	....	....	....	....	....	....
1984-85	**Pittsburgh Penguins**	**NHL**	**6**	**0**	**2**	**2**	**0**	**1**	**1**	**0**	**0**	**0**	**0**	**7**	**0.0**	**3**	**0**	**3**	**0**	**0**	....	....	....	....	....	....	....	....
	NHL Totals		**906**	**371**	**396**	**767**	**335**	**299**	**634**	**120**	**102**	**1**	**34**	**2636**	**14.1**	**1127**	**381**	**834**	**9**		**30**	**4**	**17**	**21**	**4**	**2**	**0**	**2**

Won Lady Byng Trophy (1981)

Played in NHL All-Star Game (1981, 1983)

Traded to **Pittsburgh** by **Toronto** for Blaine Stoughton and future considerations, September 13, 1974.

• KEKALAINEN, JARMO

Jarmo Kekalainen LW – L. 6', 190 lbs. b: Tampere, Finland, 7/3/1966.

Season	Club	League	GP	G	A	Pts	AG	AA	APts	PIM	PP	SH	GW	S	%	TGF	PGF	TGA	PGA	+/-	GP	G	A	Pts	PIM	PP	SH	GW
1985-86	Ilves Tampere	Finland	29	6	6	12	....	....	....	8	....	....	....	....	....	....	....	....	....	....	....	....	....	....	....	....	....	....
	Finland	WJC-A	7	4	3	7	....	....	....	4	....	....	....	....	....	....	....	....	....	....	....	....	....	....	....	....	....	....
1986-87	Ilves Tampere	Finland	42	3	4	7	....	....	....	4	....	....	....	....	....	....	....	....	....	....	....	....	....	....	....	....	....	....
1987-88	Clarkson University	ECAC	32	7	11	18	....	....	....	38	....	....	....	....	....	....	....	....	....	....	....	....	....	....	....	....	....	....
1988-89	Clarkson University	ECAC	31	19	25	44	....	....	....	47	....	....	....	....	....	....	....	....	....	....	....	....	....	....	....	....	....	....
1989-90	**Boston Bruins**	**NHL**	**11**	**2**	**2**	**4**	**2**	**1**	**3**	**8**	**0**	**0**	**1**	**7**	**28.6**	**4**	**1**	**1**	**0**	**+2**	....	....	....	....	....	....	....	....
	Maine Mariners	AHL	18	5	11	16	....	....	....	6	....	....	....	....	....	....	....	....	....	....	....	....	....	....	....	....	....	....
1990-91	**Boston Bruins**	**NHL**	**16**	**2**	**1**	**3**	**2**	**1**	**3**	**6**	**0**	**0**	**0**	**12**	**16.7**	**7**	**0**	**7**	**0**	**0**	....	....	....	....	....	....	....	....
	Maine Mariners	AHL	11	2	4	6	....	....	....	4	....	....	....	....	....	....	....	....	....	....	1	0	1	1	0	....	....	....
1991-92	Finland	C Cup	5	0	1	1	....	....	....	0	....	....	....	....	....	....	....	....	....	....	....	....	....	....	....	....	....	....
	KalPa Kuopio	Finland	24	2	8	10	....	....	....	24	....	....	....	....	....	....	....	....	....	....	....	....	....	....	....	....	....	....
1992-93	Tappara Tampere	Finland	47	15	12	27	....	....	....	34	....	....	....	....	....	....	....	....	....	....	....	....	....	....	....	....	....	....

			REGULAR SEASON																		PLAYOFFS							
Season	Club	League	GP	G	A	Pts	AG	AA	APts	PIM	PP	SH	GW	S	%	TGF	PGF	TGA	PGA	+/–	GP	G	A	Pts	PIM	PP	SH	GW
1993-94	**Ottawa Senators**	**NHL**	**28**	**1**	**5**	**6**	**1**	**4**	**5**	**14**	**0**	**0**	**0**	**18**	**5.6**	**11**	**1**	**30**	**12**	**–8**	....	....	....	....	....	....	....	....
	P.E.I. Senators	AHL	18	6	6	12	....	....	....	18	....	....	....	....	....	....	....	....	....	....	....	....	....	....	....	....	....	....
1994-95	KalPa Kuopio	Finland	44	8	16	24	....	....	....	12	....	....	....	....	....	....	....	....	....	....	3	0	0	0	0	....	....	....
1995-96	Kalpa Kuopio	Finland	46	11	23	34	....	....	....	16	....	....	....	....	....	....	....	....	....	....	....	....	....	....	....	....	....	....
	NHL Totals		**55**	**5**	**8**	**13**	**5**	**6**	**11**	**28**	**0**	**0**	**1**	**37**	**13.5**	**22**	**2**	**38**	**12**		....	....	....	....	....	....	....	....

ECAC First All-Star Team (1989)

Signed as a free agent by **Boston**, May 3, 1989. Signed as a free agent by **Ottawa**, August 13, 1993.

• KELLGREN, CHRISTER

Christer Kellgren RW – L. 6', 173 lbs. b: Goteborg, Sweden, 8/15/1958.

Season	Club	League	GP	G	A	Pts	AG	AA	APts	PIM	PP	SH	GW	S	%	TGF	PGF	TGA	PGA	+/–	GP	G	A	Pts	PIM	PP	SH	GW
1978-79	Vastra Frolunda	Sweden	14	1	0	1	....	....	....	2	....	....	....	....	....	....	....	....	....	....	....	....	....	....	....	....	....	....
1979-80	Vastra Frolunda	Sweden	27	3	4	7	....	....	....	4	....	....	....	....	....	....	....	....	....	....	8	1	4	5	2	....	....	....
1980-81	Vastra Frolunda	Sweden	36	20	10	30	....	....	....	20	....	....	....	....	....	....	....	....	....	....	2	1	1	2	4	....	....	....
1981-82	**Colorado Rockies**	**NHL**	**5**	**0**	**0**	**0**	**0**	**0**	**0**	**0**	**0**	**0**	**0**	**4**	**0.0**	**1**	**0**	**5**	**0**	**–4**	....	....	....	....	....	....	....	....
	Fort Worth Texans	CHL	60	9	10	19	....	....	....	6	....	....	....	....	....	....	....	....	....	....	....	....	....	....	....	....	....	....
1982-83	Vastra Frolunda	Sweden	36	16	9	25	....	....	....	26	....	....	....	....	....	....	....	....	....	....	....	....	....	....	....	....	....	....
1983-84	Vastra Frolunda	Sweden	36	17	12	29	....	....	....	32	....	....	....	....	....	....	....	....	....	....	....	....	....	....	....	....	....	....
	NHL Totals		**5**	**0**	**0**	**0**	**0**	**0**	**0**	**0**	**0**	**0**	**0**	**4**	**0.0**	**1**	**0**	**5**	**0**		....	....	....	....	....	....	....	....

Signed as a free agent by **Colorado**, May 11, 1981.

• KELLY, BOB

Bob "Battleship" Kelly LW – L. 6'2", 195 lbs. b: Fort William, Ont., 6/6/1946. Toronto's 1st choice, 16th overall, in 1967 Amateur Draft.

Season	Club	League	GP	G	A	Pts	AG	AA	APts	PIM	PP	SH	GW	S	%	TGF	PGF	TGA	PGA	+/–	GP	G	A	Pts	PIM	PP	SH	GW
1966-67	Port Arthur Marrs	TBJHL	STATISTICS NOT AVAILABLE																									
1967-68	Port Huron Flags	IHL	65	11	26	37	....	....	....	216	....	....	....	....	....	....	....	....	....	....	....	....	....	....	....	....	....	....
1968-69	Port Huron–Columbus	IHL	59	9	15	34	....	....	....	55	....	....	....	....	....	....	....	....	....	....	3	1	1	2	2	....	....	....
1969-70	Providence Reds	AHL	65	2	5	7	....	....	....	28	....	....	....	....	....	....	....	....	....	....	....	....	....	....	....	....	....	....
1970-71	Providence Reds	AHL	26	1	0	1	....	....	....	31	....	....	....	....	....	....	....	....	....	....	....	....	....	....	....	....	....	....
	Des Moines Oak Leafs	IHL	24	3	14	17	....	....	....	58	....	....	....	....	....	....	....	....	....	....	....	....	....	....	....	....	....	....
1971-72	Omaha Knights	CHL	3	2	2	4	....	....	....	4	....	....	....	....	....	....	....	....	....	....	....	....	....	....	....	....	....	....
	Oklahoma City Blazers	CHL	6	1	2	3	....	....	....	22	....	....	....	....	....	....	....	....	....	....	....	....	....	....	....	....	....	....
	Des Moines Oak Leafs	IHL	55	26	23	49	....	....	....	123	....	....	....	....	....	....	....	....	....	....	3	0	1	1	0	....	....	....
1972-73	Rochester Americans	AHL	70	27	35	62	....	....	....	206	....	....	....	....	....	....	....	....	....	....	6	4	4	8	18	....	....	....
1973-74	**St. Louis Blues**	**NHL**	**37**	**9**	**8**	**17**	**9**	**7**	**16**	**45**	**2**	**0**	**0**	**70**	**12.9**	**26**	**5**	**20**	**0**	**+1**	....	....	....	....	....	....	....	....
	Pittsburgh Penguins	**NHL**	**30**	**7**	**10**	**17**	**7**	**9**	**16**	**78**	**1**	**0**	**2**	**101**	**6.9**	**29**	**1**	**38**	**5**	**–5**	....	....	....	....	....	....	....	....
1974-75	**Pittsburgh Penguins**	**NHL**	**69**	**27**	**24**	**51**	**25**	**19**	**44**	**120**	**5**	**0**	**1**	**223**	**12.1**	**85**	**18**	**63**	**2**	**+6**	**9**	**5**	**3**	**8**	**17**	**1**	**0**	**0**
1975-76	**Pittsburgh Penguins**	**NHL**	**77**	**25**	**30**	**55**	**23**	**24**	**47**	**149**	**5**	**0**	**4**	**193**	**13.0**	**89**	**11**	**75**	**1**	**+4**	**3**	**0**	**0**	**0**	**2**	**0**	**0**	**0**
1976-77	**Pittsburgh Penguins**	**NHL**	**74**	**10**	**21**	**31**	**10**	**17**	**27**	**115**	**1**	**0**	**1**	**136**	**7.4**	**53**	**4**	**38**	**2**	**+13**	**3**	**1**	**0**	**1**	**4**	**0**	**0**	**0**
1977-78	**Chicago Black Hawks**	**NHL**	**75**	**7**	**11**	**18**	**7**	**9**	**16**	**95**	**0**	**0**	**2**	**155**	**4.5**	**26**	**6**	**47**	**1**	**–26**	**4**	**0**	**0**	**0**	**8**	**0**	**0**	**0**
1978-79	**Chicago Black Hawks**	**NHL**	**63**	**2**	**5**	**7**	**2**	**4**	**6**	**85**	**0**	**0**	**0**	**59**	**3.4**	**11**	**1**	**20**	**0**	**–10**	**4**	**0**	**0**	**0**	**9**	**0**	**0**	**0**
	New Brunswick Hawks	AHL	7	0	0	0	....	....	....	60	....	....	....	....	....	....	....	....	....	....	....	....	....	....	....	....	....	....
1979-80	Cincinnati Stingers	CHL	2	0	0	0	....	....	....	5	....	....	....	....	....	....	....	....	....	....	....	....	....	....	....	....	....	....
	Houston Apollos	CHL	2	0	0	0	....	....	....	10	....	....	....	....	....	....	....	....	....	....	....	....	....	....	....	....	....	....
	NHL Totals		**425**	**87**	**109**	**196**	**83**	**89**	**172**	**687**	**14**	**0**	**10**	**937**	**9.3**	**319**	**46**	**301**	**11**		**23**	**6**	**3**	**9**	**40**	**1**	**0**	**0**

Traded to **NY Rangers** by **Columbus** (IHL) for cash, October, 1970. Traded to **Rochester** (AHL) by **NY Rangers** for $7,500, October, 1972. Traded to **NY Rangers** by **Rochester** (AHL) for Bill Knibbs and $20,000, June, 1973. Traded to **St. Louis** by **NY Rangers** for Norm Dennis and Don Borgson, September 8, 1973. Traded to **Pittsburgh** by **St. Louis** with Steve Durbano and Ab DeMarco for Bryan Watson, Greg Polis and Pittsburgh's 2nd round choice (Bob Hess) in 1974 Amateur Draft, January 17, 1974. Signed as a free agent by **Chicago**, August 17, 1977.

• KELLY, BOB

Bob "Houndog" Kelly LW – L. 5'10", 200 lbs. b: Oakville, Ont., 11/25/1950. Philadelphia's 8th choice, 32nd overall, in 1970 Amateur Draft.

Season	Club	League	GP	G	A	Pts	AG	AA	APts	PIM	PP	SH	GW	S	%	TGF	PGF	TGA	PGA	+/–	GP	G	A	Pts	PIM	PP	SH	GW
1968-69	Oshawa Generals	OHA	54	21	23	44	....	....	....	128	....	....	....	....	....	....	....	....	....	....	....	....	....	....	....	....	....	....
1969-70	Oshawa Generals	OHA	53	21	31	52	....	....	....	117	....	....	....	....	....	....	....	....	....	....	....	....	....	....	....	....	....	....
1970-71	**Philadelphia Flyers**	**NHL**	**76**	**14**	**18**	**32**	**15**	**16**	**31**	**70**	**1**	**0**	**2**	**178**	**7.9**	**52**	**6**	**40**	**1**	**+7**	**4**	**1**	**0**	**1**	**2**	**0**	**0**	**0**
1971-72	**Philadelphia Flyers**	**NHL**	**78**	**14**	**15**	**29**	**15**	**14**	**29**	**157**	**0**	**0**	**3**	**117**	**12.0**	**41**	**1**	**25**	**1**	**+16**	....	....	....	....	....	....	....	....
1972-73	**Philadelphia Flyers**	**NHL**	**77**	**10**	**11**	**21**	**10**	**9**	**19**	**238**	**0**	**0**	**2**	**125**	**8.0**	**35**	**0**	**35**	**1**	**+1**	**11**	**0**	**1**	**1**	**8**	**0**	**0**	**0**
1973-74	**Philadelphia Flyers**	**NHL**	**65**	**4**	**10**	**14**	**4**	**9**	**13**	**130**	**0**	**0**	**1**	**59**	**6.8**	**20**	**0**	**10**	**0**	**+10**	**5**	**0**	**0**	**0**	**11**	**0**	**0**	**0**
1974-75	**Philadelphia Flyers**	**NHL**	**67**	**11**	**18**	**29**	**10**	**14**	**24**	**99**	**0**	**0**	**1**	**106**	**10.4**	**40**	**0**	**19**	**0**	**+21**	**16**	**3**	**3**	**6**	**15**	**0**	**0**	**1**
1975-76	**Philadelphia Flyers**	**NHL**	**79**	**12**	**8**	**20**	**11**	**6**	**17**	**125**	**0**	**0**	**3**	**103**	**11.7**	**36**	**2**	**31**	**0**	**+3**	**16**	**0**	**2**	**2**	**44**	**0**	**0**	**0**
1976-77	**Philadelphia Flyers**	**NHL**	**73**	**22**	**24**	**46**	**21**	**19**	**40**	**117**	**2**	**0**	**5**	**102**	**21.6**	**62**	**3**	**32**	**0**	**+27**	**10**	**0**	**1**	**1**	**18**	**0**	**0**	**0**
1977-78	**Philadelphia Flyers**	**NHL**	**74**	**19**	**13**	**32**	**18**	**11**	**29**	**95**	**0**	**0**	**5**	**96**	**19.8**	**45**	**1**	**29**	**0**	**+15**	**12**	**3**	**5**	**8**	**26**	**0**	**0**	**0**
1978-79	**Philadelphia Flyers**	**NHL**	**77**	**7**	**31**	**38**	**6**	**24**	**30**	**132**	**1**	**0**	**0**	**85**	**8.2**	**53**	**5**	**33**	**0**	**+15**	**8**	**1**	**1**	**2**	**10**	**1**	**0**	**0**
1979-80	**Philadelphia Flyers**	**NHL**	**75**	**15**	**20**	**35**	**14**	**15**	**29**	**122**	**2**	**0**	**2**	**112**	**13.4**	**57**	**5**	**33**	**0**	**+19**	**19**	**1**	**1**	**2**	**38**	**0**	**0**	**0**
1980-81	**Washington Capitals**	**NHL**	**80**	**26**	**36**	**62**	**21**	**25**	**46**	**157**	**8**	**0**	**4**	**125**	**20.8**	**92**	**26**	**79**	**0**	**–13**	....	....	....	....	....	....	....	....
1981-82	**Washington Capitals**	**NHL**	**16**	**0**	**4**	**4**	**0**	**3**	**3**	**12**	**0**	**0**	**0**	**24**	**0.0**	**7**	**3**	**16**	**0**	**–12**	....	....	....	....	....	....	....	....
	NHL Totals		**837**	**154**	**208**	**362**	**145**	**165**	**310**	**1454**	**14**	**0**	**28**	**1232**	**12.5**	**540**	**52**	**382**	**3**		**101**	**9**	**14**	**23**	**172**	**1**	**0**	**1**

Traded to **Washington** by **Philadelphia** for Washington's 3rd round choice (Bill Campbell) in 1982 Entry Draft, August 21, 1980.

• KELLY, DAVE

Dave Kelly RW – R. 6'2", 205 lbs. b: Chatham, Ont., 9/20/1952.

Season	Club	League	GP	G	A	Pts	AG	AA	APts	PIM	PP	SH	GW	S	%	TGF	PGF	TGA	PGA	+/–	GP	G	A	Pts	PIM	PP	SH	GW
1972-73	Providence College	ECAC	22	11	12	23	....	....	....	54	....	....	....	....	....	....	....	....	....	....	....	....	....	....	....	....	....	....
1973-74	Providence College	ECAC	DID NOT PLAY																									
1974-75	Providence College	ECAC	27	21	22	43	....	....	....	66	....	....	....	....	....	....	....	....	....	....	....	....	....	....	....	....	....	....
1975-76	Richmond Robins	AHL	74	21	19	40	....	....	....	149	....	....	....	....	....	....	....	....	....	....	8	3	4	7	19	....	....	....
1976-77	Springfield Indians	AHL	3	0	1	1	....	....	....	0	....	....	....	....	....	....	....	....	....	....	....	....	....	....	....	....	....	....
	Rhode Island Reds	AHL	45	16	19	35	....	....	....	95	....	....	....	....	....	....	....	....	....	....	....	....	....	....	....	....	....	....
	Detroit Red Wings	**NHL**	**16**	**2**	**0**	**2**	**2**	**0**	**2**	**4**	**0**	**0**	**1**	**17**	**11.8**	**3**	**0**	**11**	**0**	**–8**	....	....	....	....	....	....	....	....
	Kansas City Blues	CHL	....	....	....	....	....	....	....	....	....	....	....	....	....	....	....	....	....	....	10	*4	1	5	6	....	....	....
1977-78	Philadelphia Firebirds	AHL	74	15	13	28	....	....	....	89	....	....	....	....	....	....	....	....	....	....	4	3	2	5	2	....	....	....
	NHL Totals		**16**	**2**	**0**	**2**	**2**	**0**	**2**	**4**	**0**	**0**	**1**	**17**	**11.8**	**3**	**0**	**11**	**0**		....	....	....	....	....	....	....	....

Signed as a free agent by **Philadelphia**, August 12, 1975. Traded to **Detroit** by **Philadelphia** with Terry Murray, Bob Ritchie and Steve Coates for Rick Lapointe and Mike Korney, February 17, 1977.

• KELLY, JOHN PAUL

John Paul "Jeep" Kelly LW – L. 6'1", 215 lbs. b: Edmonton, Alta., 11/15/1959. Los Angeles' 4th choice, 50th overall, in 1979 Entry Draft.

Season	Club	League	GP	G	A	Pts	AG	AA	APts	PIM	PP	SH	GW	S	%	TGF	PGF	TGA	PGA	+/–	GP	G	A	Pts	PIM	PP	SH	GW
1975-76	Maple Ridge Raiders	BCJHL	64	34	35	69	....	....	....	68	....	....	....	....	....	....	....	....	....	....	....	....	....	....	....	....	....	....
	New Westminster Bruins	WHL	2	0	0	0	....	....	....	2	....	....	....	....	....	....	....	....	....	....	....	....	....	....	....	....	....	....
1976-77	New Westminster Bruins	WCJHL	68	35	24	59	....	....	....	62	....	....	....	....	....	....	....	....	....	....	5	2	2	4	0	....	....	....
1977-78	New Westminster Bruins	WCJHL	70	26	30	56	....	....	....	124	....	....	....	....	....	....	....	....	....	....	20	10	15	25	51	....	....	....
1978-79	New Westminster Bruins	WHL	70	25	22	47	....	....	....	207	....	....	....	....	....	....	....	....	....	....	5	0	1	1	15	....	....	....
1979-80	**Los Angeles Kings**	**NHL**	**40**	**2**	**5**	**7**	**2**	**4**	**6**	**28**	**0**	**0**	**0**	**31**	**6.5**	**12**	**0**	**18**	**0**	**–6**	**3**	**0**	**0**	**0**	**2**	**0**	**0**	**0**
1980-81	**Los Angeles Kings**	**NHL**	**19**	**3**	**6**	**9**	**2**	**4**	**6**	**8**	**0**	**0**	**0**	**18**	**16.7**	**11**	**0**	**7**	**0**	**+4**	**4**	**0**	**1**	**1**	**25**	**0**	**0**	**0**
	Houston Apollos	CHL	33	11	17	28	....	....	....	31	....	....	....	....	....	....	....	....	....	....	....	....	....	....	....	....	....	....
	Rochester Americans	AHL	16	5	10	15	....	....	....	32	....	....	....	....	....	....	....	....	....	....	....	....	....	....	....	....	....	....
1981-82	**Los Angeles Kings**	**NHL**	**70**	**12**	**11**	**23**	**9**	**7**	**16**	**100**	**0**	**0**	**0**	**92**	**13.0**	**38**	**3**	**61**	**5**	**–21**	**10**	**1**	**0**	**1**	**14**	**1**	**0**	**0**
1982-83	**Los Angeles Kings**	**NHL**	**65**	**16**	**15**	**31**	**13**	**10**	**23**	**52**	**4**	**1**	**2**	**102**	**15.7**	**53**	**9**	**59**	**1**	**–14**	....	....	....	....	....	....	....	....
1983-84	**Los Angeles Kings**	**NHL**	**72**	**7**	**14**	**21**	**6**	**9**	**15**	**73**	**0**	**0**	**0**	**86**	**8.1**	**35**	**1**	**68**	**0**	**–34**	....	....	....	....	....	....	....	....
1984-85	**Los Angeles Kings**	**NHL**	**73**	**8**	**10**	**18**	**7**	**7**	**14**	**55**	**0**	**0**	**2**	**70**	**11.4**	**28**	**2**	**35**	**0**	**–9**	**1**	**0**	**0**	**0**	**0**	**0**	**0**	**0**
1985-86	**Los Angeles Kings**	**NHL**	**61**	**6**	**9**	**15**	**5**	**6**	**11**	**50**	**0**	**0**	**0**	**38**	**15.8**	**27**	**5**	**39**	**0**	**–17**	....	....	....	....	....	....	....	....
	NHL Totals		**400**	**54**	**70**	**124**	**44**	**47**	**91**	**366**	**4**	**1**	**4**	**437**	**12.4**	**204**	**20**	**287**	**6**		**18**	**1**	**1**	**2**	**41**	**1**	**0**	**0**

• KELLY, STEVE

Steve Kelly C – L. 6'1", 190 lbs. b: Vancouver, B.C., 10/26/1976. Edmonton's 1st choice, 6th overall, in 1995 Entry Draft.

Season	Club	League	GP	G	A	Pts	AG	AA	APts	PIM	PP	SH	GW	S	%	TGF	PGF	TGA	PGA	+/–	GP	G	A	Pts	PIM	PP	SH	GW
1992-93	Prince Albert Raiders	WHL	65	11	9	20	....	....	....	75	....	....	....	....	....	....	....	....	....	....	....	....	....	....	....	....	....	....
1993-94	Prince Albert Raiders	WHL	65	19	42	61	....	....	....	106	....	....	....	....	....	....	....	....	....	....	....	....	....	....	....	....	....	....
1994-95	Prince Albert Raiders	WHL	68	31	41	72	....	....	....	153	....	....	....	....	....	....	....	....	....	....	15	7	9	16	35	....	....	....
1995-96	Prince Albert Raiders	WHL	70	27	74	101	....	....	....	203	....	....	....	....	....	....	....	....	....	....	18	13	18	31	47	....	....	....

Season	Club	League	REGULAR SEASON GP	G	A	Pts	AG	AA	APts	PIM	PP	SH	GW	S	%	TGF	PGF	TGA	PGA	+/–	PLAYOFFS GP	G	A	Pts	PIM	PP	SH	GW
1996-97	**Edmonton Oilers**	**NHL**	**8**	**1**	**0**	**1**	**1**	**0**	**1**	**6**	**0**	**0**	**1**	**6**	**16.7**	**2**	**0**	**3**	**0**	**–1**	**6**	**0**	**0**	**0**	**2**	**0**	**0**	**0**
	Hamilton Bulldogs	AHL	48	9	29	38	....	....	....	111	....	....	....	....	....	....	....	....	....	....	11	3	3	6	24	....	....	....
1997-98	**Edmonton Oilers**	**NHL**	**19**	**0**	**2**	**2**	**0**	**2**	**2**	**8**	**0**	**0**	**0**	**5**	**0.0**	**5**	**0**	**9**	**0**	**–4**	....	....	....	....	....	....	....	....
	Hamilton Bulldogs	AHL	11	2	8	10	....	....	....	18	....	....	....	....	....	....	....	....	....	....	....	....	....	....	....	....	....	....
	Tampa Bay Lightning	**NHL**	**24**	**2**	**1**	**3**	**2**	**1**	**3**	**15**	**1**	**0**	**0**	**17**	**11.8**	**6**	**1**	**14**	**0**	**–9**	....	....	....	....	....	....	....	....
	Milwaukee Admirals	IHL	5	0	1	1	....	....	....	19	....	....	....	....	....	....	....	....	....	....	....	....	....	....	....	....	....	....
	Cleveland Lumberjacks	IHL	5	1	1	2	....	....	....	29	....	....	....	....	....	....	....	....	....	....	1	0	1	1	0	....	....	....
	NHL Totals		**51**	**3**	**3**	**6**	**3**	**3**	**6**	**29**	**1**	**0**	**1**	**28**	**10.7**	**13**	**1**	**26**	**0**		**6**	**0**	**0**	**0**	**2**	**0**	**0**	**0**

Traded to **Tampa Bay** by **Edmonton** with Bryan Marchment and Jason Bonsignore for Roman Hamrlik and Paul Comrie, December 30, 1997.

• KEMP, KEVIN

Kevin Kemp D – L. 6', 188 lbs. b: Ottawa, Ont., 5/3/1954. Toronto's 8th choice, 138th overall, in 1974 Amateur Draft.

Season	Club	League	GP	G	A	Pts	AG	AA	APts	PIM	PP	SH	GW	S	%	TGF	PGF	TGA	PGA	+/–	GP	G	A	Pts	PIM	PP	SH	GW
1973-74	Ottawa 67's	OHA	59	4	8	12	....	....	....	205	....	....	....	....	....	....	....	....	....	....	....	....	....	....	....	....	....	....
1974-75	Milwaukee Admirals	USHL	33	4	14	18	....	....	....	59	....	....	....	....	....	....	....	....	....	....	....	....	....	....	....	....	....	....
	Saginaw Gears	IHL	3	0	0	0	....	....	....	0	....	....	....	....	....	....	....	....	....	....	....	....	....	....	....	....	....	....
	Hampton Gulls	SHL	5	0	0	0	....	....	....	17	....	....	....	....	....	....	....	....	....	....	....	....	....	....	....	....	....	....
1975-76	Oklahoma City Blazers	CHL	33	0	1	1	....	....	....	31	....	....	....	....	....	....	....	....	....	....	3	1	0	1	2	....	....	....
1976-77	Saginaw Gears	IHL	50	2	11	13	....	....	....	186	....	....	....	....	....	....	....	....	....	....	19	1	3	4	99	....	....	....
1977-78	Saginaw Gears	IHL	78	10	18	28	....	....	....	267	....	....	....	....	....	....	....	....	....	....	5	0	0	0	28	....	....	....
1978-79	New Brunswick Hawks	AHL	44	1	4	5	....	....	....	113	....	....	....	....	....	....	....	....	....	....	....	....	....	....	....	....	....	....
	Saginaw Gears	IHL	13	0	4	4	....	....	....	28	....	....	....	....	....	....	....	....	....	....	4	1	1	2	6	....	....	....
1979-80	Springfield Indians	AHL	77	0	19	19	....	....	....	180	....	....	....	....	....	....	....	....	....	....	....	....	....	....	....	....	....	....
1980-81	**Hartford Whalers**	**NHL**	**3**	**0**	**0**	**0**	**0**	**0**	**0**	**4**	**0**	**0**	**0**	**5**	**0.0**	**3**	**0**	**4**	**0**	**–1**	....	....	....	....	....	....	....	....
	Binghamton Whalers	AHL	75	0	5	5	....	....	....	204	....	....	....	....	....	....	....	....	....	....	5	0	2	2	4	....	....	....
	NHL Totals		**3**	**0**	**0**	**0**	**0**	**0**	**0**	**4**	**0**	**0**	**0**	**5**	**0.0**	**3**	**0**	**4**	**0**		....	....	....	....	....	....	....	....

Claimed by **Hartford** from **Toronto** in Expansion Draft, June 13, 1979.

• KENADY, CHRIS

Chris Kenady RW – R. 6'2", 195 lbs. b: Mound, MN, 4/10/1973. St. Louis' 8th choice, 175th overall, in 1991 Entry Draft.

Season	Club	League	GP	G	A	Pts	AG	AA	APts	PIM	PP	SH	GW	S	%	TGF	PGF	TGA	PGA	+/–	GP	G	A	Pts	PIM	PP	SH	GW
1990-91	St. Paul Vulcans	USHL	45	16	20	36	....	....	....	57	....	....	....	....	....	....	....	....	....	....	....	....	....	....	....	....	....	....
1991-92	University of Denver	WCHA	36	8	5	13	....	....	....	56	....	....	....	....	....	....	....	....	....	....	....	....	....	....	....	....	....	....
1992-93	University of Denver	WCHA	38	8	16	24	....	....	....	95	....	....	....	....	....	....	....	....	....	....	....	....	....	....	....	....	....	....
1993-94	University of Denver	WCHA	37	14	11	25	....	....	....	125	....	....	....	....	....	....	....	....	....	....	....	....	....	....	....	....	....	....
1994-95	University of Denver	WCHA	39	21	17	38	....	....	....	113	....	....	....	....	....	....	....	....	....	....	....	....	....	....	....	....	....	....
1995-96	Worcester IceCats	AHL	43	9	10	19	....	....	....	58	....	....	....	....	....	....	....	....	....	....	2	0	0	0	0	....	....	....
1996-97	Worcester IceCats	AHL	73	23	26	49	....	....	....	131	....	....	....	....	....	....	....	....	....	....	5	0	1	1	2	....	....	....
1997-98	**St. Louis Blues**	**NHL**	**5**	**0**	**2**	**2**	**0**	**2**	**2**	**0**	**0**	**0**	**0**	**3**	**0.0**	**2**	**0**	**1**	**0**	**+1**	....	....	....	....	....	....	....	....
	Worcester IceCats	AHL	63	23	22	45	....	....	....	84	....	....	....	....	....	....	....	....	....	....	11	1	5	6	26	....	....	....
	NHL Totals		**5**	**0**	**2**	**2**	**0**	**2**	**2**	**0**	**0**	**0**	**0**	**3**	**0.0**	**2**	**0**	**1**	**0**		....	....	....	....	....	....	....	....

• KENNEDY, DEAN

Dean Kennedy D – R. 6'2", 208 lbs. b: Redvers, Sask., 1/18/1963. Los Angeles' 2nd choice, 39th overall, in 1981 Entry Draft.

Season	Club	League	GP	G	A	Pts	AG	AA	APts	PIM	PP	SH	GW	S	%	TGF	PGF	TGA	PGA	+/–	GP	G	A	Pts	PIM	PP	SH	GW
1979-80	Weyburn Red Wings	SJHL	57	12	20	32	....	....	....	64	....	....	....	....	....	....	....	....	....	....	....	....	....	....	....	....	....	....
	Brandon Wheat Kings	WHL	1	0	0	0			....	0	....	....	....	....	....	....	....	....	....	....	....	....	....	....	....	....	....	....
1980-81	Brandon Wheat Kings	WHL	71	3	29	32	....	....	....	157	....	....	....	....	....	....	....	....	....	....	5	0	2	2	7	....	....	....
1981-82	Brandon Wheat Kings	WHL	49	5	38	43	....	....	....	103	....	....	....	....	....	....	....	....	....	....	....	....	....	....	....	....	....	....
1982-83	Brandon Wheat Kings	WHL	14	2	15	17	....	....	....	22	....	....	....	....	....	....	....	....	....	....	....	....	....	....	....	....	....	....
	Los Angeles Kings	**NHL**	**55**	**0**	**12**	**12**	**0**	**8**	**8**	**97**	**0**	**0**	**0**	**53**	**0.0**	**44**	**0**	**72**	**11**	**–17**	....	....	....	....	....	....	....	....
	Saskatoon Blades	WHL	....	....	....	....	....	....	....	....	....	....	....	....	....	....	....	....	....	....	4	0	3	3	0	....	....	....
1983-84	**Los Angeles Kings**	**NHL**	**37**	**1**	**5**	**6**	**1**	**3**	**4**	**50**	**0**	**0**	**0**	**22**	**4.5**	**21**	**0**	**30**	**4**	**–5**	....	....	....	....	....	....	....	....
	New Haven Nighthawks	AHL	26	1	7	8	....	....	....	23	....	....	....	....	....	....	....	....	....	....	....	....	....	....	....	....	....	....
1984-85	New Haven Nighthawks	AHL	76	3	14	17	....	....	....	104	....	....	....	....	....	....	....	....	....	....	....	....	....	....	....	....	....	....
1985-86	**Los Angeles Kings**	**NHL**	**78**	**2**	**10**	**12**	**2**	**7**	**9**	**132**	**0**	**0**	**0**	**59**	**3.4**	**59**	**2**	**90**	**23**	**–10**	....	....	....	....	....	....	....	....
1986-87	**Los Angeles Kings**	**NHL**	**66**	**6**	**14**	**20**	**5**	**10**	**15**	**91**	**0**	**0**	**1**	**59**	**10.2**	**67**	**1**	**85**	**28**	**+9**	**5**	**0**	**2**	**2**	**10**	**0**	**0**	**0**
1987-88	**Los Angeles Kings**	**NHL**	**58**	**1**	**11**	**12**	**1**	**8**	**9**	**158**	**0**	**0**	**0**	**40**	**2.5**	**46**	**0**	**89**	**21**	**–22**	**4**	**0**	**1**	**1**	**10**	**0**	**0**	**0**
1988-89	**Los Angeles Kings**	**NHL**	**25**	**2**	**5**	**7**	**2**	**4**	**6**	**23**	....	....	....	....	....	....	....	....	....	....	....	....	....	....	....	....	....	....
	New York Rangers	**NHL**	**16**	**0**	**1**	**1**	**0**	**1**	**1**	**40**	**0**	**0**	**0**	**7**	**0.0**	**8**	**0**	**9**	**0**	**–1**	....	....	....	....	....	....	....	....
	Los Angeles Kings	**NHL**	**26**	**1**	**3**	**4**	**1**	**2**	**3**	**40**	**0**	**0**	**1**	**38**	**2.6**	**59**	**1**	**61**	**21**	**+18**	**11**	**0**	**2**	**2**	**8**	**0**	**0**	**0**
1989-90	**Buffalo Sabres**	**NHL**	**80**	**2**	**12**	**14**	**2**	**9**	**11**	**53**	**0**	**0**	**0**	**51**	**3.9**	**38**	**1**	**75**	**26**	**–12**	**6**	**1**	**1**	**2**	**12**	**0**	**0**	**0**
1990-91	**Buffalo Sabres**	**NHL**	**64**	**4**	**8**	**12**	**4**	**6**	**10**	**119**	**0**	**0**	**2**	**46**	**8.7**	**57**	**0**	**66**	**14**	**+5**	**2**	**0**	**1**	**1**	**17**	**0**	**0**	**0**
1991-92	**Winnipeg Jets**	**NHL**	**18**	**2**	**4**	**6**	**2**	**3**	**5**	**21**	**0**	**0**	**1**	**20**	**10.0**	**14**	**0**	**21**	**9**	**+2**	**2**	**0**	**0**	**0**	**0**	**0**	**0**	**0**
1992-93	**Winnipeg Jets**	**NHL**	**78**	**1**	**7**	**8**	**1**	**5**	**6**	**105**	**0**	**0**	**1**	**50**	**2.0**	**48**	**0**	**80**	**29**	**–3**	**6**	**0**	**0**	**0**	**2**	**0**	**0**	**0**
1993-94	**Winnipeg Jets**	**NHL**	**76**	**2**	**8**	**10**	**2**	**6**	**8**	**164**	**0**	**0**	**1**	**38**	**5.3**	**30**	**0**	**71**	**19**	**–22**	....	....	....	....	....	....	....	....
1994-95	**Edmonton Oilers**	**NHL**	**40**	**2**	**8**	**10**	**4**	**12**	**16**	**25**	**0**	**0**	**1**	**45**	**4.4**	**29**	**0**	**41**	**14**	**+2**	....	....	....	....	....	....	....	....
	NHL Totals		**717**	**26**	**108**	**134**	**27**	**84**	**111**	**1118**	**0**	**0**	**8**	**528**	**4.9**	**520**	**5**	**790**	**219**		**36**	**1**	**7**	**8**	**59**	**0**	**0**	**0**

Traded to **NY Rangers** by **LA Kings** with Denis Larocque for Igor Liba, Michael Boyce, Todd Elik and future considerations, December 12, 1988. Traded to **LA Kings** by **NY Rangers** for LA Kings' 4th round choice (later traded to Minnesota — Minnesota selected Cal McGowan) in 1990 Entry Draft, February 3, 1989. Traded to **Buffalo** by **LA Kings** for Buffalo's 4th round choice (Keith Redmond) in 1991 Entry Draft, October 4, 1989. Traded to **Winnipeg** by **Buffalo** with Darrin Shannon and Mike Hartman for Dave McLlwain, Gord Donnelly, Winnipeg's 5th round choice (Yuri Khmylev) in 1992 Entry Draft and future considerations, October 11, 1991. Claimed by **Edmonton** from **Winnipeg** in NHL Waiver Draft, January 18, 1995.

• KENNEDY, FORBES

Forbes Kennedy C – L. 5'8", 150 lbs. b: Dorchester, N.B., 8/18/1935.

Season	Club	League	GP	G	A	Pts	AG	AA	APts	PIM	PP	SH	GW	S	%	TGF	PGF	TGA	PGA	+/–	GP	G	A	Pts	PIM	PP	SH	GW
1952-53	Halifax St. Mary's	NSJHL	25	16	11	27	....	....	....	....	....	....	....	....	....	....	....	....	....	....	....	....	....	....	....	....	....	....
1953-54	Montreal Jr. Canadiens	QJHL	54	10	19	30	....	....	....	43	....	....	....	....	....	....	....	....	....	....	8	1	8	9	6	....	....	....
1954-55	Montreal Jr. Canadiens	QJHL	46	7	14	21	....	....	....	118	....	....	....	....	....	....	....	....	....	....	4	0	2	2	4	....	....	....
1955-56	Montreal Jr. Canadiens	QJHL	....	....	....	....	....	....	....	....	....	....	....	....	....	....	....	....	....	....	....	....	....	....	....	....	....	....
	Montreal–Shawinigan	QHL	3	0	3	3	....	....	....	2	....	....	....	....	....	....	....	....	....	....	....	....	....	....	....	....	....	....
1956-57	**Chicago Black Hawks**	**NHL**	**69**	**8**	**13**	**21**	**11**	**15**	**26**	**102**	....	....	....	....	....	....	....	....	....	....	....	....	....	....	....	....	....	....
1957-58	**Detroit Red Wings**	**NHL**	**70**	**11**	**16**	**27**	**14**	**17**	**31**	**135**	....	....	....	....	....	....	....	....	....	....	**4**	**1**	**0**	**1**	**12**	....	....	....
1958-59	**Detroit Red Wings**	**NHL**	**67**	**1**	**4**	**5**	**1**	**4**	**5**	**149**	....	....	....	....	....	....	....	....	....	....	....	....	....	....	....	....	....	....
1959-60	**Detroit Red Wings**	**NHL**	**17**	**1**	**2**	**3**	**1**	**2**	**3**	**8**	....	....	....	....	....	....	....	....	....	....	....	....	....	....	....	....	....	....
	Edmonton Flyers	WHL	30	6	10	16	....	....	....	39	....	....	....	....	....	....	....	....	....	....	....	....	....	....	....	....	....	....
	Hershey Bears	AHL	21	3	11	14	....	....	....	50	....	....	....	....	....	....	....	....	....	....	....	....	....	....	....	....	....	....
1960-61	Spokane Comets	WHL	70	23	38	61	....	....	....	165	....	....	....	....	....	....	....	....	....	....	4	2	1	3	0	....	....	....
1961-62	**Detroit Red Wings**	**NHL**	**14**	**1**	**0**	**1**	**1**	**0**	**1**	**8**	....	....	....	....	....	....	....	....	....	....	....	....	....	....	....	....	....	....
	Edmonton Flyers	WHL	58	23	31	54	....	....	....	124	....	....	....	....	....	....	....	....	....	....	....	....	....	....	....	....	....	....
1962-63	Edmonton Flyers	WHL	23	7	15	22	....	....	....	38	....	....	....	....	....	....	....	....	....	....	....	....	....	....	....	....	....	....
	Boston Bruins	**NHL**	**49**	**12**	**18**	**30**	**15**	**19**	**34**	**46**	....	....	....	....	....	....	....	....	....	....	....	....	....	....	....	....	....	....
1963-64	**Boston Bruins**	**NHL**	**70**	**8**	**17**	**25**	**10**	**19**	**29**	**95**	....	....	....	....	....	....	....	....	....	....	....	....	....	....	....	....	....	....
1964-65	**Boston Bruins**	**NHL**	**52**	**6**	**4**	**10**	**8**	**4**	**12**	**41**	....	....	....	....	....	....	....	....	....	....	....	....	....	....	....	....	....	....
1965-66	**Boston Bruins**	**NHL**	**50**	**4**	**6**	**10**	**5**	**6**	**11**	**55**	....	....	....	....	....	....	....	....	....	....	....	....	....	....	....	....	....	....
	San Francisco Seals	WHL	6	3	3	6	....	....	....	48	....	....	....	....	....	....	....	....	....	....	....	....	....	....	....	....	....	....
1966-67	California Seals	WHL	71	25	41	66	....	....	....	91	....	....	....	....	....	....	....	....	....	....	6	2	0	2	4	....	....	....
1967-68	**Philadelphia Flyers**	**NHL**	**73**	**10**	**18**	**28**	**12**	**19**	**31**	**130**	**1**	**1**	**3**	**100**	**10.0**	**33**	**1**	**50**	**22**	**+4**	**7**	**1**	**4**	**5**	**14**	**0**	**1**	**0**
1968-69	**Philadelphia Flyers**	**NHL**	**59**	**8**	**7**	**15**	**9**	**7**	**16**	***195**	**0**	**0**	**0**	**64**	**12.5**	**21**	**1**	**51**	**6**	**25**	....	....	....	....	....	....	....	....
	Toronto Maple Leafs	**NHL**	**13**	**0**	**3**	**3**	**0**	**3**	**3**	***24**	**0**	**0**	**0**	**7**	**0.0**	**3**	**0**	**4**	**0**	**–1**	**1**	**0**	**0**	**0**	**38**	**0**	**0**	**0**
1969-70	Buffalo Bisons	AHL	19	2	1	3	....	....	....	42	....	....	....	....	....	....	....	....	....	....	4	0	0	0	0	....	....	....
	Omaha Knights	CHL	....	....	....	....	....	....	....	....	....	....	....	....	....	....	....	....	....	....	6	0	1	1	7	....	....	....
1970-71	Halifax Jr. Canadians	NSJHL	DID NOT PLAY – COACHING																									
	NHL Totals		**603**	**70**	**108**	**178**	**87**	**115**	**202**	**988**	**1**	**1**	**3**	**171**	**40.9**	**57**	**2**	**105**	**28**		**12**	**2**	**4**	**6**	**64**	**0**	**1**	**0**

Traded to **Chicago** by **Montreal** for cash, May 24, 1956. Traded to **Detroit** by **Chicago** with Johnny Wilson, Hank Bassen and Bill Preston for Ted Lindsay and Glenn Hall, July, 1957. Traded to **Boston** by **Detroit** for Andre Pronovost, December, 1962. Claimed by **Philadelphia** from **Boston** in Expansion Draft, June 6, 1967. Traded to **Toronto** by **Philadelphia** with Brit Selby for Gerry Meehan, Mike Byers and Bill Sutherland, March 2, 1969. Traded to **Pittsburgh** by **Toronto** for cash, May 30, 1969. Claimed by **NY Rangers** from **Pittsburgh** in Intra-League Draft, June 11, 1969.

• KENNEDY, MIKE

Mike Kennedy C – R. 6'1", 195 lbs. b: Vancouver, B.C., 4/13/1972. Minnesota's 3rd choice, 97th overall, in 1991 Entry Draft.

			REGULAR SEASON																		PLAYOFFS							
Season	Club	League	GP	G	A	Pts	AG	AA	APts	PIM	PP	SH	GW	S	%	TGF	PGF	TGA	PGA	+/–	GP	G	A	Pts	PIM	PP	SH	GW
1989-90	University of British Columbia	CWUAA	9	5	7	12	....	....	....	0	....	....	....	....	....	....	....	....	....	....	....	....	....	....	....	....	....	....
1990-91	University of British Columbia	CWUAA	28	17	17	34	....	....	....	18	....	....	....	....	....	....	....	....	....	....	....	....	....	....	....	....	....	....
1991-92	Seattle Thunderbirds	WHL	71	42	47	89	....	....	....	134	....	....	....	....	....	....	....	....	....	....	15	11	6	17	20	....	....	....
1992-93	Kalamazoo Wings	IHL	77	21	30	51	....	....	....	39	....	....	....	....	....	....	....	....	....	....	....	....	....	....	....	....	....	....
1993-94	Kalamazoo Wings	IHL	63	20	18	38	....	....	....	42	....	....	....	....	....	....	....	....	....	....	3	1	2	3	2	....	....	....
1994-95	**Dallas Stars**	**NHL**	**44**	**6**	**12**	**18**	**11**	**18**	**29**	**33**	**2**	**0**	**0**	**76**	**7.9**	**30**	**5**	**21**	**0**	**+4**	**5**	**0**	**0**	**0**	**9**	**0**	**0**	**0**
	Kalamazoo Wings	IHL	42	20	28	48	....	....	....	29	....	....	....	....	....	....	....	....	....	....	....	....	....	....	....	....	....	....
1995-96	**Dallas Stars**	**NHL**	**61**	**9**	**17**	**26**	**9**	**14**	**23**	**48**	**4**	**0**	**1**	**111**	**8.1**	**38**	**8**	**41**	**4**	**–7**	....	....	....	....	....	....	....	....
1996-97	**Dallas Stars**	**NHL**	**24**	**1**	**6**	**7**	**1**	**5**	**6**	**13**	**0**	**0**	**1**	**26**	**3.8**	**8**	**0**	**5**	**0**	**+3**	....	....	....	....	....	....	....	....
	Michigan K-Wings	IHL	2	0	1	1	....	....	....	2	....	....	....	....	....	....	....	....	....	....	....	....	....	....	....	....	....	....
1997-98	**Toronto Maple Leafs**	**NHL**	**13**	**0**	**1**	**1**	**0**	**1**	**1**	**14**	**0**	**0**	**0**	**12**	**0.0**	**3**	**0**	**5**	**0**	**–2**	....	....	....	....	....	....	....	....
	St. John's Maple Leafs	AHL	49	11	17	28	....	....	....	86	....	....	....	....	....	....	....	....	....	....	....	....	....	....	....	....	....	....
	Dallas Stars	**NHL**	**2**	**0**	**0**	**0**	**0**	**0**	**0**	**2**	**0**	**0**	**0**	**0**	**0.0**	**1**	**0**	**0**	**0**	**+1**	....	....	....	....	....	....	....	....
	NHL Totals		**144**	**16**	**36**	**52**	**21**	**38**	**59**	**110**	**6**	**0**	**2**	**225**	**7.1**	**80**	**13**	**72**	**4**		**5**	**0**	**0**	**0**	**9**	**0**	**0**	**0**

WHL West Second All-Star Team (1992)

Rights transferred to **Dallas** after **Minnesota** franchise relocated, June 9, 1993. Signed as a free agent by **Toronto**, July 2, 1997. Traded to **Dallas** by **Toronto** for Dallas' 8th round choice (Mikhail Travnicek) in 1998 Entry Draft, March 24, 1998.

• KENNEDY, SHELDON

Sheldon Kennedy RW – R. 5'10", 180 lbs. b: Elkhorn, Man., 6/15/1969. Detroit's 5th choice, 80th overall, in 1988 Entry Draft.

Season	Club	League	GP	G	A	Pts	AG	AA	APts	PIM	PP	SH	GW	S	%	TGF	PGF	TGA	PGA	+/–	GP	G	A	Pts	PIM	PP	SH	GW
1986-87	Swift Current Broncos	WHL	49	23	41	64	....	....	....	43	....	....	....	....	....	....	....	....	....	....	4	0	3	3	4	....	....	....
1987-88	Swift Current Broncos	WHL	59	53	64	117	....	....	....	45	....	....	....	....	....	....	....	....	....	....	10	8	9	17	12	....	....	....
	Canada	WJC-A	7	4	2	6	....	....	....	6	....	....	....	....	....	....	....	....	....	....	....	....	....	....	....	....	....	....
1988-89	Swift Current Broncos	WHL	51	58	48	106	....	....	....	92	....	....	....	....	....	....	....	....	....	....	12	9	15	24	22	....	....	....
	Canada	WJC-A	7	3	4	7	....	....	....	14	....	....	....	....	....	....	....	....	....	....	....	....	....	....	....	....	....	....
1989-90	**Detroit Red Wings**	**NHL**	**20**	**2**	**7**	**9**	**2**	**5**	**7**	**10**	**0**	**0**	**1**	**23**	**8.7**	**13**	**3**	**11**	**1**	**0**	....	....	....	....	....	....	....	....
	Adirondack Red Wings	AHL	26	11	15	26	....	....	....	35	....	....	....	....	....	....	....	....	....	....	....	....	....	....	....	....	....	....
1990-91	**Detroit Red Wings**	**NHL**	**7**	**1**	**0**	**1**	**1**	**0**	**1**	**12**	**0**	**0**	**0**	**11**	**9.1**	**4**	**0**	**5**	**0**	**–1**	....	....	....	....	....	....	....	....
	Adirondack Red Wings	AHL	11	1	3	4	....	....	....	8	....	....	....	....	....	....	....	....	....	....	....	....	....	....	....	....	....	....
1991-92	**Detroit Red Wings**	**NHL**	**27**	**3**	**8**	**11**	**3**	**6**	**9**	**24**	**0**	**0**	**1**	**33**	**9.1**	**15**	**1**	**16**	**0**	**–2**	....	....	....	....	....	....	....	....
	Adirondack Red Wings	AHL	46	25	24	49	....	....	....	56	....	....	....	....	....	....	....	....	....	....	16	5	9	14	12	....	....	....
1992-93	**Detroit Red Wings**	**NHL**	**68**	**19**	**11**	**30**	**16**	**8**	**24**	**46**	**1**	**0**	**2**	**110**	**17.3**	**32**	**1**	**37**	**5**	**–1**	**7**	**1**	**1**	**2**	**2**	**0**	**0**	**0**
1993-94	**Detroit Red Wings**	**NHL**	**61**	**6**	**7**	**13**	**6**	**5**	**11**	**30**	**0**	**1**	**0**	**60**	**10.0**	**22**	**0**	**29**	**5**	**–2**	**7**	**1**	**2**	**3**	**0**	**0**	**0**	**0**
1994-95	**Calgary Flames**	**NHL**	**30**	**7**	**8**	**15**	**12**	**12**	**24**	**45**	**1**	**0**	**0**	**44**	**15.9**	**20**	**2**	**18**	**5**	**+5**	**7**	**3**	**1**	**4**	**16**	**0**	**1**	**0**
1995-96	**Calgary Flames**	**NHL**	**41**	**3**	**7**	**10**	**3**	**6**	**9**	**36**	**0**	**0**	**1**	**54**	**5.6**	**20**	**3**	**14**	**0**	**+3**	**3**	**1**	**0**	**1**	**2**	**0**	**0**	**0**
	Saint John Flames	AHL	3	4	0	4	....	....	....	8	....	....	....	....	....	....	....	....	....	....	....	....	....	....	....	....	....	....
1996-97	**Boston Bruins**	**NHL**	**56**	**8**	**10**	**18**	**8**	**9**	**17**	**30**	**0**	**4**	**0**	**65**	**12.3**	**24**	**0**	**54**	**13**	**–17**	....	....	....	....	....	....	....	....
	Providence Bruins	AHL	3	0	1	1	....	....	....	2	....	....	....	....	....	....	....	....	....	....	....	....	....	....	....	....	....	....
	NHL Totals		**310**	**49**	**58**	**107**	**51**	**51**	**102**	**233**	**2**	**5**	**5**	**400**	**12.3**	**150**	**10**	**184**	**29**		**24**	**6**	**4**	**10**	**20**	**0**	**1**	**0**

WHL East Second All-Star Team (1989) • Memorial Cup All-Star Team (1989)

Traded to **Winnipeg** by **Detroit** for Winnipeg's 3rd round choice (Darryl Laplante) in 1995 Entry Draft, May 25, 1994. Claimed by **Calgary** from **Winnipeg** in NHL Waiver Draft, January 18, 1995. Signed as free agent by **Boston**, August 7, 1996.

• KEON, DAVE

Dave Keon C – L. 5'9", 165 lbs. b: Noranda, Que., 3/22/1940. **HHOF**

Season	Club	League	GP	G	A	Pts	AG	AA	APts	PIM	PP	SH	GW	S	%	TGF	PGF	TGA	PGA	+/–	GP	G	A	Pts	PIM	PP	SH	GW
1956-57	St. Michael's Majors	OHA	4	1	3	4	....	....	....	0	....	....	....	....	....	....	....	....	....	....	....	....	....	....	....	....	....	....
1957-58	St. Michael's Majors	OHA	45	23	27	50	....	....	....	29	....	....	....	....	....	....	....	....	....	....	9	8	5	13	10	....	....	....
1958-59	St. Michael's Majors	OHA	47	33	38	71	....	....	....	31	....	....	....	....	....	....	....	....	....	....	15	4	9	13	8	....	....	....
1959-60	St. Michael's Majors	OHA	47	33	38	71	....	....	....	31	....	....	....	....	....	....	....	....	....	....	10	8	10	18	2	....	....	....
	Kitchener-Waterloo Dutchmen	OHA Sr.	1	1	0	1	....	....	....	0	....	....	....	....	....	....	....	....	....	....	....	....	....	....	....	....	....	....
	Sudbury Wolves	EPHL	....	....	....	....	....	....	....	....	....	....	....	....	....	....	....	....	....	....	4	2	2	4	2	....	....	....
1960-61	**Toronto Maple Leafs**	**NHL**	**70**	**20**	**25**	**45**	**24**	**25**	**49**	**6**	....	....	....	....	....	....	....	....	....	....	**5**	**1**	**1**	**2**	**0**	....	....	....
1961-62	**Toronto Maple Leafs**	**NHL**	**64**	**26**	**35**	**61**	**32**	**36**	**68**	**2**	....	....	....	....	....	....	....	....	....	....	**12**	**5**	**3**	**8**	**0**	....	....	....
1962-63	**Toronto Maple Leafs**	**NHL**	**68**	**28**	**28**	**56**	**35**	**29**	**64**	**2**	....	....	....	....	....	....	....	....	....	....	**10**	**7**	**5**	**12**	**0**	....	....	....
1963-64	**Toronto Maple Leafs**	**NHL**	**70**	**23**	**37**	**60**	**31**	**41**	**72**	**6**	....	....	....	....	....	....	....	....	....	....	**14**	**7**	**2**	**9**	**2**	....	....	....
1964-65	**Toronto Maple Leafs**	**NHL**	**65**	**21**	**29**	**50**	**27**	**31**	**58**	**10**	....	....	....	....	....	....	....	....	....	....	**6**	**2**	**2**	**4**	**2**	....	....	....
1965-66	**Toronto Maple Leafs**	**NHL**	**69**	**24**	**30**	**54**	**29**	**30**	**59**	**4**	....	....	....	....	....	....	....	....	....	....	**4**	**0**	**2**	**2**	**0**	....	....	....
1966-67	**Toronto Maple Leafs**	**NHL**	**66**	**19**	**33**	**52**	**23**	**34**	**57**	**2**	....	....	....	....	....	....	....	....	....	....	**12**	**3**	**5**	**8**	**0**	....	....	....
1967-68	**Toronto Maple Leafs**	**NHL**	**67**	**11**	**37**	**48**	**14**	**39**	**53**	**4**	**1**	**0**	**3**	**196**	**5.6**	**72**	**15**	**52**	**11**	**+16**	....	....	....	....	....	....	....	....
1968-69	**Toronto Maple Leafs**	**NHL**	**75**	**27**	**34**	**61**	**30**	**32**	**62**	**12**	**3**	**6**	**6**	**281**	**9.6**	**82**	**12**	**69**	**16**	**+17**	**4**	**1**	**3**	**4**	**2**	**0**	**0**	**1**
1969-70	**Toronto Maple Leafs**	**NHL**	**72**	**32**	**30**	**62**	**37**	**30**	**67**	**6**	**9**	**2**	**4**	**284**	**11.3**	**84**	**34**	**82**	**17**	**–15**	....	....	....	....	....	....	....	....
1970-71	**Toronto Maple Leafs**	**NHL**	**76**	**38**	**38**	**76**	**40**	**34**	**74**	**4**	**5**	**8**	**9**	**277**	**13.7**	**97**	**27**	**63**	**17**	**+24**	**6**	**3**	**2**	**5**	**0**	**0**	**0**	**0**
1971-72	**Toronto Maple Leafs**	**NHL**	**72**	**18**	**30**	**48**	**19**	**27**	**46**	**4**	**2**	**2**	**5**	**265**	**6.8**	**74**	**33**	**60**	**20**	**+1**	**5**	**2**	**3**	**5**	**0**	**0**	**0**	**0**
1972-73	**Toronto Maple Leafs**	**NHL**	**76**	**37**	**36**	**73**	**37**	**30**	**67**	**2**	**8**	**2**	**6**	**277**	**13.4**	**104**	**38**	**81**	**19**	**+4**	....	....	....	....	....	....	....	....
1973-74	**Toronto Maple Leafs**	**NHL**	**74**	**25**	**28**	**53**	**26**	**24**	**50**	**7**	**1**	**2**	**3**	**244**	**10.2**	**68**	**14**	**58**	**17**	**+13**	**4**	**1**	**2**	**3**	**0**	**0**	**0**	**0**
1974-75	**Toronto Maple Leafs**	**NHL**	**78**	**16**	**43**	**59**	**15**	**34**	**49**	**4**	**1**	**1**	**2**	**183**	**8.7**	**84**	**22**	**89**	**30**	**+3**	**7**	**0**	**5**	**5**	**0**	**0**	**0**	**0**
1975-76	Minnesota Fighting Saints	WHA	57	26	38	64	....	....	....	4	....	....	....	....	....	....	....	....	....	....	....	....	....	....	....	....	....	....
	Indianapolis Racers	WHA	12	3	7	10	....	....	....	2	....	....	....	....	....	....	....	....	....	....	7	2	2	4	2	....	....	....
1976-77	Minnesota Fighting Saints	WHA	42	13	38	51	....	....	....	2	....	....	....	....	....	....	....	....	....	....	....	....	....	....	....	....	....	....
	New England Whalers	WHA	34	14	25	39	....	....	....	8	....	....	....	....	....	....	....	....	....	....	5	3	1	4	0	....	....	....
1977-78	New England Whalers	WHA	77	24	38	62	....	....	....	2	....	....	....	....	....	....	....	....	....	....	14	5	11	16	4	....	....	....
1978-79	New England Whalers	WHA	79	22	43	65	....	....	....	2	....	....	....	....	....	....	....	....	....	....	10	3	9	12	2	....	....	....
1979-80	**Hartford Whalers**	**NHL**	**76**	**10**	**52**	**62**	**9**	**40**	**49**	**10**	**0**	**0**	**0**	**146**	**6.8**	**87**	**18**	**107**	**25**	**–13**	**3**	**0**	**1**	**1**	**0**	**0**	**0**	**0**
1980-81	**Hartford Whalers**	**NHL**	**80**	**13**	**34**	**47**	**11**	**24**	**35**	**26**	**2**	**0**	**1**	**131**	**9.9**	**69**	**15**	**116**	**31**	**–31**	....	....	....	....	....	....	....	....
1981-82	**Hartford Whalers**	**NHL**	**78**	**8**	**11**	**19**	**6**	**7**	**13**	**6**	**0**	**1**	**1**	**84**	**9.5**	**26**	**0**	**68**	**11**	**–31**	....	....	....	....	....	....	....	....
	NHL Totals		**1296**	**396**	**590**	**986**	**445**	**547**	**992**	**117**	**32**	**24**	**40**	**2368**	**16.7**	**847**	**228**	**845**	**214**		**92**	**32**	**36**	**68**	**6**	**0**	**0**	**1**
	Other Major League Totals		301	102	189	291	....	....	....	20	....	....	....	....	....	....	....	....	....		36	13	23	36	8	....	....	....

Won Calder Memorial Trophy (1961) • NHL Second All-Star Team (1962, 1971) • Won Lady Byng Trophy (1962, 1963) • Won Conn Smythe Trophy (1967) • Won Paul Daneau Trophy (WHA Most Gentlemanly Player) (1977, 1978)

Played in NHL All-Star Game (1962, 1963, 1964, 1967, 1968, 1970, 1971, 1973)

Selected by **Ontario-Ottawa** (WHA) in 1972 WHA General Player Draft, February 12, 1972. WHA rights transferred to **Toronto** (WHA) after **Ottawa** (WHA) franchise relocated, May, 1973. WHA rights traded to **Minnesota** (WHA) by **Toronto** (WHA) for future considerations, May, 1975. Signed as a free agent by **Indianapolis** (WHA) after **Minnesota** (WHA) franchise folded, February 27, 1976. Traded to **Minnesota** (WHA) by **Indianapolis** (WHA) for Gary MacGregor and future considerations, September, 1976. Traded to **Edmonton** (WHA) by **Minnesota** (WHA) with Mike Antonovich, Bill Butters, Jack Carlson, Steve Carlson, Jean-Louis Levasseur and John McKenzie, January, 1977. Traded to **New England** (WHA) by **Edmonton** (WHA) with Jack Carlson, Steve Carlson, Dave Dryden and John McKenzie for future considerations (Dave Debol, June, 1977), Dan Arndt and cash, January, 1977. Rights retained by **Hartford** prior to Expansion Draft, June 9, 1979.

• KERCH, ALEXANDER

Alexander Kerch LW – R. 5'10", 190 lbs. b: Arkhangelsk, USSR, 3/16/1967. Edmonton's 5th choice, 60th overall, in 1993 Entry Draft.

Season	Club	League	GP	G	A	Pts	AG	AA	APts	PIM	PP	SH	GW	S	%	TGF	PGF	TGA	PGA	+/–	GP	G	A	Pts	PIM	PP	SH	GW
1984-85	Dynamo Riga	USSR	8	0	0	0	....	....	....	6	....	....	....	....	....	....	....	....	....	....	....	....	....	....	....	....	....	....
1985-86	Dynamo Riga	USSR	23	5	2	7	....	....	....	16	....	....	....	....	....	....	....	....	....	....	....	....	....	....	....	....	....	....
1986-87	Dynamo Riga	USSR	26	5	4	9	....	....	....	10	....	....	....	....	....	....	....	....	....	....	....	....	....	....	....	....	....	....
1987-88	Dynamo Riga	USSR	50	14	4	18	....	....	....	28	....	....	....	....	....	....	....	....	....	....	....	....	....	....	....	....	....	....
1988-89	Dynamo Riga	USSR	39	6	7	13	....	....	....	41	....	....	....	....	....	....	....	....	....	....	....	....	....	....	....	....	....	....
	Dynamo Riga	SuperS	7	1	1	2	....	....	....	4	....	....	....	....	....	....	....	....	....	....	....	....	....	....	....	....	....	....
1989-90	Dynamo Riga	FrTour	1	0	0	0	....	....	....	0	....	....	....	....	....	....	....	....	....	....	....	....	....	....	....	....	....	....
	Dynamo Riga	USSR	46	9	11	20	....	....	....	22	....	....	....	....	....	....	....	....	....	....	....	....	....	....	....	....	....	....
1990-91	Dynamo Riga	FrTour	1	0	0	0	....	....	....	0	....	....	....	....	....	....	....	....	....	....	....	....	....	....	....	....	....	....
	HC Riga	USSR	46	16	17	33	....	....	....	46	....	....	....	....	....	....	....	....	....	....	....	....	....	....	....	....	....	....
1991-92	HC Riga	CIS	27	7	9	16	....	....	....	20	....	....	....	....	....	....	....	....	....	....	....	....	....	....	....	....	....	....
1992-93	HC Riga	CIS	42	23	14	37	....	....	....	28	....	....	....	....	....	....	....	....	....	....	2	1	2	3	2	....	....	....
	Latvia	WC-C	7	8	13	21	....	....	....	4	....	....	....	....	....	....	....	....	....	....	....	....	....	....	....	....	....	....

			REGULAR SEASON																		PLAYOFFS							
Season	Club	League	GP	G	A	Pts	AG	AA	APts	PIM	PP	SH	GW	S	%	TGF	PGF	TGA	PGA	+/–	GP	G	A	Pts	PIM	PP	SH	GW
1993-94	**Edmonton Oilers**	**NHL**	**5**	**0**	**0**	**0**	**0**	**0**	**0**	**2**	**0**	**0**	**0**	**4**	**0.0**	**1**	**1**	**8**	**0**	**–8**								
	Cape Breton Oilers	AHL	57	24	38	62				16											4	1	1	2	2			
1994-95	HC Riga	CIS	11	4	0	4				4																		
	Providence Bruins	AHL	1	0	0	0				15											4	0	2	2	0			
1995-96	HK Riga-Alianse	Latvia	29	28	21	49				42																		
	Latvia	WC-B	7	3	6	9				20																		
1996-97	Landsberg	Germany	51	42	54	96				52																		
	Latvia	WC-A	8	4	4	8				6																		
1997-98	Tappara Tampere	Finland	46	14	17	31				57											4	1	0	1	2			
	Latvia	WC-A	6	3	1	4				2																		
	NHL Totals		**5**	**0**	**0**	**0**	**0**	**0**	**0**	**2**	**0**	**0**	**0**	**4**	**0.0**	**1**	**1**	**8**	**0**									

• KERR, ALAN

Alan Kerr RW – R. 5'11", 195 lbs. b: Hazelton, B.C., 3/28/1964. NY Islanders' 4th choice, 84th overall, in 1982 Entry Draft.

Season	Club	League	GP	G	A	Pts	AG	AA	APts	PIM	PP	SH	GW	S	%	TGF	PGF	TGA	PGA	+/–	GP	G	A	Pts	PIM	PP	SH	GW
1981-82	Seattle Breakers	WHL	68	15	18	33				107											10	6	6	12	32			
1982-83	Seattle Breakers	WHL	71	38	53	91				183											4	2	3	5	0			
1983-84	Seattle Breakers	WHL	66	46	66	112				141											5	1	4	5	12			
1984-85	**New York Islanders**	**NHL**	**19**	**3**	**1**	**4**	**2**	**1**	**3**	**24**	**0**	**0**	**0**	**17**	**17.6**	**6**	**0**	**13**	**0**	**–7**	**4**	**1**	**0**	**1**	**4**	**1**	**0**	**0**
	Springfield Indians	AHL	62	32	27	59				140											4	1	2	3	2			
1985-86	**New York Islanders**	**NHL**	**7**	**0**	**1**	**1**	**0**	**1**	**1**	**16**	**0**	**0**	**0**	**9**	**0.0**	**2**	**0**	**1**	**0**	**+1**	**1**	**0**	**0**	**0**	**0**	**0**	**0**	**0**
	Springfield Indians	AHL	71	35	36	71				127																		
1986-87	**New York Islanders**	**NHL**	**72**	**7**	**10**	**17**	**6**	**7**	**13**	**175**	**0**	**1**	**1**	**97**	**7.2**	**28**	**1**	**50**	**13**	**–10**	**14**	**1**	**4**	**5**	**25**	**0**	**0**	**0**
1987-88	**New York Islanders**	**NHL**	**80**	**24**	**34**	**58**	**21**	**24**	**45**	**198**	**4**	**0**	**2**	**196**	**12.2**	**95**	**17**	**74**	**26**	**+30**	**6**	**1**	**0**	**1**	**14**	**0**	**0**	**0**
1988-89	**New York Islanders**	**NHL**	**71**	**20**	**18**	**38**	**17**	**13**	**30**	**144**	**6**	**0**	**4**	**147**	**13.6**	**52**	**8**	**59**	**10**	**–5**								
1989-90	**New York Islanders**	**NHL**	**75**	**15**	**21**	**36**	**13**	**15**	**28**	**129**	**3**	**0**	**1**	**127**	**11.8**	**65**	**15**	**51**	**0**	**–1**	**4**	**0**	**0**	**0**	**10**	**0**	**0**	**0**
1990-91	**New York Islanders**	**NHL**	**2**	**0**	**0**	**0**	**0**	**0**	**0**	**5**	**0**	**0**	**0**	**2**	**0.0**	**0**	**0**	**0**	**0**	**0**								
	Capital District Islanders	AHL	43	11	21	32				131																		
1991-92	**Detroit Red Wings**	**NHL**	**58**	**3**	**8**	**11**	**3**	**6**	**9**	**133**	**0**	**0**	**1**	**41**	**7.3**	**22**	**0**	**23**	**2**	**+1**	**9**	**2**	**0**	**2**	**17**	**0**	**0**	**0**
1992-93	**Winnipeg Jets**	**NHL**	**7**	**0**	**1**	**1**	**0**	**1**	**1**	**2**	**0**	**0**	**0**	**1**	**0.0**	**1**	**0**	**5**	**0**	**–4**								
	Moncton Hawks	AHL	36	6	10	16				85											5	0	2	2	11			
	NHL Totals		**391**	**72**	**94**	**166**	**62**	**68**	**130**	**826**	**13**	**1**	**9**	**637**	**11.3**	**271**	**41**	**276**	**51**		**38**	**5**	**4**	**9**	**70**	**1**	**0**	**0**

WHL West All-Star Team (1984)

Traded to **Detroit** by **NY Islanders** with future considerations for Rick Green, May 26, 1991. Traded to **Winnipeg** by **Detroit** to complete transaction that sent Aaron Ward to Detroit (June 11, 1993), June 19, 1993.

• KERR, REG

Reg Kerr LW – L. 5'10", 180 lbs. b: Oxbow, Sask., 10/16/1957. Cleveland's 3rd choice, 41st overall, in 1977 Amateur Draft.

Season	Club	League	GP	G	A	Pts	AG	AA	APts	PIM	PP	SH	GW	S	%	TGF	PGF	TGA	PGA	+/–	GP	G	A	Pts	PIM	PP	SH	GW
1973-74	Penticton Panthers	BCJHL	60	15	36	51				130																		
1974-75	Kamloops Chiefs	WCJHL	70	28	57	85				87											6	1	7	8	9			
1975-76	Kamloops Chiefs	WCJHL	70	23	58	81				147											12	6	11	17	18			
1976-77	Kamloops Chiefs	WCJHL	72	47	54	101				172											5	2	2	4	16			
1977-78	**Cleveland Barons**	**NHL**	**7**	**0**	**2**	**2**	**0**	**2**	**2**	**7**	**0**	**0**	**0**	**9**	**0.0**	**2**	**0**	**2**	**0**	**0**								
	Phoenix Roadrunners	CHL	11	4	1	5				15																		
	Chicago Black Hawks	**NHL**	**2**	**0**	**2**	**2**	**0**	**2**	**2**	**0**	**0**	**0**	**0**	**2**	**0.0**	**3**	**1**	**0**	**0**	**+2**								
	Dallas Black Hawks	CHL	55	20	21	41				40											13	1	2	3	20			
1978-79	**Chicago Black Hawks**	**NHL**	**73**	**16**	**24**	**40**	**15**	**18**	**33**	**50**	**2**	**2**	**4**	**111**	**14.4**	**54**	**6**	**74**	**19**	**–7**	**4**	**1**	**0**	**1**	**5**	**0**	**0**	**0**
1979-80	**Chicago Black Hawks**	**NHL**	**49**	**9**	**8**	**17**	**8**	**6**	**14**	**17**	**1**	**1**	**0**	**69**	**13.0**	**22**	**3**	**36**	**7**	**–10**								
1980-81	**Chicago Black Hawks**	**NHL**	**70**	**30**	**30**	**60**	**25**	**21**	**46**	**56**	**6**	**0**	**4**	**154**	**19.5**	**85**	**18**	**64**	**7**	**+10**	**3**	**0**	**0**	**0**	**2**	**0**	**0**	**0**
1981-82	**Chicago Black Hawks**	**NHL**	**59**	**11**	**28**	**39**	**9**	**19**	**28**	**39**	**1**	**0**	**1**	**106**	**10.4**	**54**	**3**	**63**	**2**	**–10**								
1982-83	Springfield Indians	AHL	45	7	18	25				13																		
1983-84	**Edmonton Oilers**	**NHL**	**3**	**0**	**0**	**0**	**0**	**0**	**0**	**0**	**0**	**0**	**0**	**3**	**0.0**	**0**	**0**	**4**	**1**	**–3**								
	Moncton Alpines	AHL	63	13	29	42				43																		
	NHL Totals		**263**	**66**	**94**	**160**	**57**	**68**	**125**	**169**	**10**	**3**	**9**	**454**	**14.5**	**220**	**31**	**243**	**36**		**7**	**1**	**0**	**1**	**7**	**0**	**0**	**0**

WCJHL All-Star Team (1977)

Traded to **Chicago** by **Cleveland** for Randy Holt, November 23, 1977. Signed as a free agent by **Edmonton**, November 9, 1983.

• KERR, TIM

Tim Kerr C/RW – R. 6'3", 230 lbs. b: Windsor, Ont., 1/5/1960.

Season	Club	League	GP	G	A	Pts	AG	AA	APts	PIM	PP	SH	GW	S	%	TGF	PGF	TGA	PGA	+/–	GP	G	A	Pts	PIM	PP	SH	GW
1976-77	Windsor Spitfires	OHA	9	2	4	6				7																		
1977-78	Kingston Canadians	OHA	67	14	25	39				33																		
1978-79	Kingston Canadians	OHA	57	17	25	42				27											6	1	1	2	2			
1979-80	Kingston Canadians	OHA	63	40	33	73				39											3	0	1	1	16			
	Maine Mariners	AHL	7	2	4	6				2																		
1980-81	**Philadelphia Flyers**	**NHL**	**68**	**22**	**23**	**45**	**18**	**16**	**34**	**84**	**6**	**0**	**7**	**95**	**23.2**	**55**	**19**	**33**	**0**	**+3**	**10**	**1**	**3**	**4**	**2**	**1**	**0**	**0**
1981-82	**Philadelphia Flyers**	**NHL**	**61**	**21**	**30**	**51**	**17**	**20**	**37**	**138**	**7**	**0**	**2**	**118**	**17.8**	**74**	**15**	**58**	**5**	**+6**	**4**	**0**	**2**	**2**	**2**	**0**	**0**	**0**
1982-83	**Philadelphia Flyers**	**NHL**	**24**	**11**	**8**	**19**	**9**	**6**	**15**	**6**	**0**	**0**	**1**	**49**	**22.4**	**22**	**3**	**15**	**0**	**+4**	**2**	**2**	**0**	**2**	**0**	**0**	**0**	**0**
1983-84	**Philadelphia Flyers**	**NHL**	**79**	**54**	**39**	**93**	**44**	**26**	**70**	**29**	**9**	**0**	**5**	**286**	**18.9**	**138**	**29**	**79**	**0**	**+30**	**3**	**0**	**0**	**0**	**0**	**0**	**0**	**0**
1984-85	**Philadelphia Flyers**	**NHL**	**74**	**54**	**44**	**98**	**44**	**30**	**74**	**57**	**21**	**0**	**9**	**267**	**20.2**	**135**	**52**	**54**	**0**	**+29**	**12**	**10**	**4**	**14**	**13**	**4**	**0**	**1**
1985-86	**Philadelphia Flyers**	**NHL**	**76**	**58**	**26**	**84**	**47**	**17**	**64**	**79**	**34**	**0**	**8**	**285**	**20.4**	**141**	**78**	**68**	**0**	**–5**	**5**	**3**	**3**	**6**	**8**	**1**	**0**	**0**
1986-87	**Philadelphia Flyers**	**NHL**	**75**	**58**	**37**	**95**	**50**	**27**	**77**	**57**	**26**	**0**	**10**	**261**	**22.2**	**139**	**55**	**48**	**2**	**+38**	**12**	**8**	**5**	**13**	**2**	**5**	**0**	**3**
	NHL All-Stars	RV'87	DID NOT PLAY																									
1987-88	**Philadelphia Flyers**	**NHL**	**8**	**3**	**2**	**5**	**3**	**1**	**4**	**12**	**2**	**0**	**0**	**34**	**8.8**	**17**	**11**	**6**	**0**	**0**	**6**	**1**	**3**	**4**	**4**	**1**	**0**	**0**
1988-89	**Philadelphia Flyers**	**NHL**	**69**	**48**	**40**	**88**	**41**	**28**	**69**	**73**	**25**	**0**	**2**	**236**	**20.3**	**121**	**62**	**64**	**1**	**–4**	**19**	**14**	**11**	**25**	**27**	**8**	**0**	**2**
1989-90	**Philadelphia Flyers**	**NHL**	**40**	**24**	**24**	**48**	**21**	**17**	**38**	**34**	**9**	**0**	**2**	**162**	**14.8**	**75**	**34**	**44**	**0**	**–3**								
1990-91	**Philadelphia Flyers**	**NHL**	**27**	**10**	**14**	**24**	**9**	**11**	**20**	**8**	**6**	**0**	**0**	**74**	**13.5**	**33**	**18**	**23**	**0**	**–8**								
1991-92	**New York Rangers**	**NHL**	**32**	**7**	**11**	**18**	**6**	**8**	**14**	**12**	**5**	**0**	**2**	**56**	**12.5**	**27**	**13**	**19**	**0**	**–5**	**8**	**1**	**0**	**1**	**0**	**1**	**0**	**0**
1992-93	**Hartford Whalers**	**NHL**	**22**	**0**	**6**	**6**	**0**	**4**	**4**	**7**	**0**	**0**	**0**	**48**	**0.0**	**17**	**7**	**21**	**0**	**–11**								
	NHL Totals		**655**	**370**	**304**	**674**	**309**	**211**	**520**	**596**	**150**	**0**	**48**	**1971**	**18.8**	**994**	**396**	**532**	**8**		**81**	**40**	**31**	**71**	**58**	**21**	**0**	**6**

NHL Second All-Star Team (1987) • Won Bill Masterton Trophy (1989)

Played in NHL All-Star Game (1984, 1985, 1986)

Signed as a free agent by **Philadelphia**, October 25, 1979. Claimed by **San Jose** from **Philadelphia** in Expansion Draft, May 30, 1991. Traded to **NY Rangers** by **San Jose** for Brian Mullen and future considerations, May 30, 1991. Traded to **Hartford** by **NY Rangers** for future considerations, July 9, 1992.

• KESA, DAN

Dan Kesa RW – R. 6', 198 lbs. b: Vancouver, B.C., 11/23/1971. Vancouver's 4th choice, 95th overall, in 1991 Entry Draft.

Season	Club	League	GP	G	A	Pts	AG	AA	APts	PIM	PP	SH	GW	S	%	TGF	PGF	TGA	PGA	+/–	GP	G	A	Pts	PIM	PP	SH	GW
1990-91	Prince Albert Raiders	WHL	69	30	23	53				116											3	1	1	2	0			
1991-92	Prince Albert Raiders	WHL	62	46	51	97				201											10	9	10	19	27			
1992-93	Hamilton Canucks	AHL	62	16	24	40				76																		
1993-94	**Vancouver Canucks**	**NHL**	**19**	**2**	**4**	**6**	**2**	**3**	**5**	**18**	**1**	**0**	**1**	**18**	**11.1**	**8**	**1**	**15**	**5**	**–3**								
	Hamilton Canucks	AHL	53	37	33	70				33											4	1	4	5	4			
1994-95	Syracuse Crunch	AHL	70	34	44	78				81																		
1995-96	**Dallas Stars**	**NHL**	**3**	**0**	**0**	**0**	**0**	**0**	**0**	**0**	**0**	**0**	**0**	**0**	**0.0**	**0**	**0**	**3**	**2**	**–1**								
	Michigan K-Wings	IHL	15	4	11	15				33																		
	Springfield Falcons	AHL	22	10	5	15				13																		
	Detroit Vipers	IHL	27	9	0	15				22											12	6	4	10	4			
1996-97	Detroit Vipers	IHL	60	22	21	43				19											20	7	5	12	20			
1997-98	Detroit Vipers	IHL	76	40	37	77				40											20	13	5	18	14			
	NHL Totals		**22**	**2**	**4**	**6**	**2**	**3**	**5**	**18**	**1**	**0**	**1**	**18**	**11.1**	**8**	**1**	**18**	**7**									

Traded to **Dallas** by **Vancouver** with Greg Adams and Vancouver's 5th round choice (later traded to LA Kings — LA Kings selected Jason Morgan) in 1995 Entry Draft for Russ Courtnall, April 7, 1995. Traded to **Hartford** by **Dallas** with future considerations for Robert Petrovicky, November 29, 1995.

			REGULAR SEASON																		PLAYOFFS							
Season	Club	League	GP	G	A	Pts	AG	AA	APts	PIM	PP	SH	GW	S	%	TGF	PGF	TGA	PGA	+/–	GP	G	A	Pts	PIM	PP	SH	GW

• KESSELL, RICK

Rick Kessell C – L. 5'10", 175 lbs. b: Toronto, Ont., 7/27/1949. Pittsburgh's 1st choice, 15th overall, in 1969 Amateur Draft.

Season	Club	League	GP	G	A	Pts	AG	AA	APts	PIM	PP	SH	GW	S	%	TGF	PGF	TGA	PGA	+/–	GP	G	A	Pts	PIM	PP	SH	GW
1965-66	Toronto Marlboros	OHA	....	....	....	....	....	....	....	....	....	....	....	....	....	....	....	....	....	....	2	0	0	0	0	....	....	....
1966-67	Markham Marauders	OJHL	35	29	27	56	....	....	....	....	....	....	....	....	....	....	....	....	....	....	....	....	....	....	....	....	....	....
1967-68	Toronto Marlboros	OHA	14	1	3	4	....	....	....	2	....	....	....	....	....	....	....	....	....	....	....	....	....	....	....	....	....	....
	London Knights	OHA	16	2	2	4	....	....	....	0	....	....	....	....	....	....	....	....	....	....	....	....	....	....	....	....	....	....
1968-69	Oshawa Generals	OHA	53	26	*66	92	....	....	....	8	....	....	....	....	....	....	....	....	....	....	....	....	....	....	....	....	....	....
1969-70	**Pittsburgh Penguins**	**NHL**	**8**	**1**	**2**	**3**	**1**	**2**	**3**	**0**	**0**	**0**	**0**	**15**	**6.7**	**5**	**2**	**3**	**0**	**0**	....	....	....	....	....	....	....	....
	Baltimore Clippers	AHL	52	15	21	36	....	....	....	6	....	....	....	....	....	....	....	....	....	....	5	1	1	2	0	....	....	....
1970-71	**Pittsburgh Penguins**	**NHL**	**6**	**0**	**2**	**2**	**0**	**2**	**2**	**2**	**0**	**0**	**0**	**15**	**0.0**	**4**	**0**	**3**	**0**	**+1**	....	....	....	....	....	....	....	....
	Amarillo Wranglers	CHL	62	31	38	69	....	....	....	10	....	....	....	....	....	....	....	....	....	....	....	....	....	....	....	....	....	....
1971-72	**Pittsburgh Penguins**	**NHL**	**3**	**0**	**1**	**1**	**0**	**1**	**1**	**0**	**0**	**0**	**0**	**3**	**0.0**	**1**	**1**	**1**	**0**	**–1**	....	....	....	....	....	....	....	....
	Hershey Bears	AHL	54	24	19	43	....	....	....	12	....	....	....	....	....	....	....	....	....	....	....	....	....	....	....	....	....	....
1972-73	**Pittsburgh Penguins**	**NHL**	**67**	**1**	**13**	**14**	**1**	**11**	**12**	**0**	**0**	**0**	**0**	**35**	**2.9**	**16**	**2**	**26**	**3**	**–9**	....	....	....	....	....	....	....	....
1973-74	**California Golden Seals**	**NHL**	**51**	**2**	**6**	**8**	**2**	**5**	**7**	**4**	**1**	**0**	**0**	**31**	**6.5**	**10**	**1**	**33**	**20**	**–4**	....	....	....	....	....	....	....	....
1974-75	Salt Lake Golden Eagles	CHL	8	1	4	5	....	....	....	2	....	....	....	....	....	....	....	....	....	....	....	....	....	....	....	....	....	....
	New Haven Nighthawks	AHL	60	21	46	67	....	....	....	16	....	....	....	....	....	....	....	....	....	....	16	4	9	13	2	....	....	....
1975-76	Salt Lake City Golden Eagles	CHL	54	16	39	55	....	....	....	19	....	....	....	....	....	....	....	....	....	....	5	2	3	5	2	....	....	....
1976-77	Whitby Warriors	OHA Sr.	34	9	17	26	....	....	....	6	....	....	....	....	....	....	....	....	....	....	....	....	....	....	....	....	....	....
1977-78	Whitby Warriors	OHA Sr.	32	12	17	29	....	....	....	18	....	....	....	....	....	....	....	....	....	....	....	....	....	....	....	....	....	....
	NHL Totals		**135**	**4**	**24**	**28**	**4**	**21**	**25**	**6**	**1**	**0**	**0**	**99**	**4.0**	**36**	**6**	**66**	**23**		....	....	....	....	....	....	....	....

Claimed by **California** (Salt Lake-CHL) from **Pittsburgh** in Reverse Draft, June 13, 1973.

• KETOLA, VELI-PEKKA

Veli-Pekka Ketola C – L. 6'3", 220 lbs. b: Pori, Finland, 3/28/1948.

Season	Club	League	GP	G	A	Pts	AG	AA	APts	PIM	PP	SH	GW	S	%	TGF	PGF	TGA	PGA	+/–	GP	G	A	Pts	PIM	PP	SH	GW
1965-66	Karhut	Finland	19	8	3	11	....	....	....	12	....	....	....	....	....	....	....	....	....	....	....	....	....	....	....	....	....	....
1966-67	Karhut	Finland	22	15	10	25	....	....	....	30	....	....	....	....	....	....	....	....	....	....	....	....	....	....	....	....	....	....
1967-68	Assat Pori	Finland	20	12	13	25	....	....	....	16	....	....	....	....	....	....	....	....	....	....	....	....	....	....	....	....	....	....
	Finland	Olympics	7	2	1	3	....	....	....	10	....	....	....	....	....	....	....	....	....	....	....	....	....	....	....	....	....	....
1968-69	Assat Pori	Finland	20	15	9	24	....	....	....	22	....	....	....	....	....	....	....	....	....	....	....	....	....	....	....	....	....	....
	Finland	WEC-A	8	0	2	2	....	....	....	2	....	....	....	....	....	....	....	....	....	....	....	....	....	....	....	....	....	....
1969-70	Jokerit Helsinki	Finland	22	25	12	37	....	....	....	26	....	....	....	....	....	....	....	....	....	....	....	....	....	....	....	....	....	....
	Assat Pori	Finland	31	25	17	42	....	....	....	31	....	....	....	....	....	....	....	....	....	....	....	....	....	....	....	....	....	....
1970-71	Finland	WEC-A	10	4	3	7	....	....	....	32	....	....	....	....	....	....	....	....	....	....	....	....	....	....	....	....	....	....
	Finland	WEC-A	6	5	1	6	....	....	....	4	....	....	....	....	....	....	....	....	....	....	....	....	....	....	....	....	....	....
1971-72	Assat Pori	Finland	32	16	14	30	....	....	....	25	....	....	....	....	....	....	....	....	....	....	....	....	....	....	....	....	....	....
	Finland	Olympics	6	1	3	4	....	....	....	7	....	....	....	....	....	....	....	....	....	....	....	....	....	....	....	....	....	....
	Finland	WEC-A	9	4	3	7	....	....	....	4	....	....	....	....	....	....	....	....	....	....	....	....	....	....	....	....	....	....
1972-73	Assat Pori	Finland	36	25	16	41	....	....	....	*74	....	....	....	....	....	....	....	....	....	....	10	2	2	4	12	....	....	....
	Finland	WEC-A	10	2	2	4	....	....	....	12	....	....	....	....	....	....	....	....	....	....	....	....	....	....	....	....	....	....
1973-74	Assat Pori	Finland	35	23	21	44	....	....	....	44	....	....	....	....	....	....	....	....	....	....	10	7	3	10	4	....	....	....
	Finland	WEC-A	10	7	3	10	....	....	....	4	....	....	....	....	....	....	....	....	....	....	....	....	....	....	....	....	....	....
1974-75	Winnipeg Jets	WHA	74	23	28	51	....	....	....	25	....	....	....	....	....	....	....	....	....	....	....	....	....	....	....	....	....	....
1975-76	Winnipeg Jets	WHA	80	32	36	68	....	....	....	32	....	....	....	....	....	....	....	....	....	....	13	7	5	12	2	....	....	....
1976-77	Finland	C Cup	5	0	0	0	....	....	....	2	....	....	....	....	....	....	....	....	....	....	....	....	....	....	....	....	....	....
	Calgary Cowboys	WHA	17	4	6	10	....	....	....	2	....	....	....	....	....	....	....	....	....	....	....	....	....	....	....	....	....	....
	Winnipeg Jets	WHA	64	25	29	54	....	....	....	59	....	....	....	....	....	....	....	....	....	....	....	....	....	....	....	....	....	....
1977-78	Assat Pori	Finland	36	27	29	54	....	....	....	59	....	....	....	....	....	....	....	....	....	....	9	*10	*10	*20	22	....	....	....
1978-79	Assat Pori	Finland	36	23	*49	*72	....	....	....	66	....	....	....	....	....	....	....	....	....	....	....	....	....	....	....	....	....	....
1979-80	Assat Pori	Finland	36	22	38	60	....	....	....	61	....	....	....	....	....	....	....	....	....	....	7	3	7	10	*40	....	....	....
1980-81	Assat Pori	Finland	36	23	39	62	....	....	....	61	....	....	....	....	....	....	....	....	....	....	2	0	0	0	2	....	....	....
1981-82	Finland	C Cup	5	0	0	0	....	....	....	6	....	....	....	....	....	....	....	....	....	....	....	....	....	....	....	....	....	....
	Colorado Rockies	**NHL**	**44**	**9**	**5**	**14**	**7**	**3**	**10**	**4**	**4**	**0**	**1**	**42**	**21.4**	**26**	**10**	**33**	**0**	**–17**	....	....	....	....	....	....	....	....
1982-83	KalPa Kuopio	Finland	6	4	8	12	....	....	....	....	....	....	....	....	....	....	....	....	....	....	....	....	....	....	....	....	....	....
	NHL Totals		**44**	**9**	**5**	**14**	**7**	**3**	**10**	**4**	**4**	**0**	**1**	**42**	**21.4**	**26**	**10**	**33**	**0**		....	....	....	....	....	....	....	....
	Other Major League Totals		235	84	99	183	....	....	....	118	....	....	....	....	....	....	....	....	....		13	7	5	12	2	....	....	....

Finnish First All-Star Team (1968, 1970, 1971, 1974, 1978, 1979)

Selected by **Calgary-Cleveland** (WHA) in 1972 WHA General Player Draft, February 12, 1972. WHA rights traded to **Winnipeg** (WHA) by **Cleveland** (WHA) for future considerations, August, 1974. Traded to **Calgary** (WHA) by **Winnipeg** (WHA) with Ron Ward for Mike Ford and Danny Lawson, March, 1977. Signed as a free agent by **Colorado**, July 8, 1981.

• KETTER, KERRY

Kerry Ketter D – L. 6'1", 202 lbs. b: Prince George, B.C., 9/20/1947.

Season	Club	League	GP	G	A	Pts	AG	AA	APts	PIM	PP	SH	GW	S	%	TGF	PGF	TGA	PGA	+/–	GP	G	A	Pts	PIM	PP	SH	GW
1965-66	Edmonton Oil Kings	AJHL	50	3	5	8	....	....	....	14	....	....	....	....	....	....	....	....	....	....	....	....	....	....	....	....	....	....
1966-67	Edmonton Oil Kings	WCJHL	56	4	26	30	....	....	....	99	....	....	....	....	....	....	....	....	....	....	9	1	4	5	22	....	....	....
1967-68	Edmonton Oil Kings	WCJHL	59	11	28	39	....	....	....	169	....	....	....	....	....	....	....	....	....	....	13	1	5	6	26	....	....	....
	Edmonton Nuggets	ASHL	....	1	0	1	....	....	....	0	....	....	....	....	....	....	....	....	....	....	....	0	1	1	12	....	....	....
1968-69	Fort Worth Wings	CHL	62	2	10	12	....	....	....	80	....	....	....	....	....	....	....	....	....	....	....	....	....	....	....	....	....	....
1969-70	Fort Worth Wings	CHL	61	4	8	12	....	....	....	79	....	....	....	....	....	....	....	....	....	....	7	0	0	0	7	....	....	....
1970-71	Baltimore Clippers	AHL	71	2	20	22	....	....	....	102	....	....	....	....	....	....	....	....	....	....	6	2	1	3	10	....	....	....
1971-72	Nova Scotia Voyageurs	AHL	69	2	8	10	....	....	....	108	....	....	....	....	....	....	....	....	....	....	15	2	5	7	50	....	....	....
1972-73	**Atlanta Flames**	**NHL**	**41**	**0**	**2**	**2**	**0**	**2**	**2**	**58**	**0**	**0**	**0**	**31**	**0.0**	**19**	**1**	**26**	**2**	**–6**	....	....	....	....	....	....	....	....
1973-74	Dallas Black Hawks	CHL	65	5	20	25	....	....	....	84	....	....	....	....	....	....	....	....	....	....	5	0	0	0	4	....	....	....
1974-75	Baltimore Clippers	AHL	44	1	7	8	....	....	....	44	....	....	....	....	....	....	....	....	....	....	....	....	....	....	....	....	....	....
	Omaha Knights	CHL	31	2	11	13	....	....	....	36	....	....	....	....	....	....	....	....	....	....	5	0	4	4	2	....	....	....
1975-76	Edmonton Oilers	WHA	48	1	9	10	....	....	....	20	....	....	....	....	....	....	....	....	....	....	....	....	....	....	....	....	....	....
	NHL Totals		**41**	**0**	**2**	**2**	**0**	**2**	**2**	**58**	**0**	**0**	**0**	**31**	**0.0**	**19**	**1**	**26**	**2**		....	....	....	....	....	....	....	....
	Other Major League Totals		48	1	9	10	....	....	....	20	....	....	....	....	....	....	....	....	....		....	....	....	....	....	....	....	....

Traded to **Montreal** by **Detroit** with cash for Leon Rochefort, May 25, 1971. Selected by **Edmonton** (WHA) in 1972 WHA General Player Draft, February 12, 1972. Claimed by **Atlanta** from **Montreal** in Expansion Draft, June 6, 1972. Claimed by **Kansas City** from **Atlanta** in Expansion Draft, June 12, 1974. Traded to **New England** (WHA) by **Edmonton** (WHA) with Steve Carlyle for Paul Hurley and the rights to Clarke Jantze, February, 1976. • Suspended by **New England** (WHA) for refusing to report to team, February, 1976.

• KHARIN, SERGEI

Sergei Kharin RW – L. 5'11", 180 lbs. b: Odintsovo, USSR, 2/20/1963. Winnipeg's 15th choice, 240th overall, in 1989 Entry Draft.

Season	Club	League	GP	G	A	Pts	AG	AA	APts	PIM	PP	SH	GW	S	%	TGF	PGF	TGA	PGA	+/–	GP	G	A	Pts	PIM	PP	SH	GW
1980-81	Soviet Wings	USSR	2	0	0	0	....	....	....	0	....	....	....	....	....	....	....	....	....	....	....	....	....	....	....	....	....	....
1981-82	Soviet Wings	USSR	34	4	3	7	....	....	....	10	....	....	....	....	....	....	....	....	....	....	....	....	....	....	....	....	....	....
1982-83	Soviet Wings	USSR	49	5	5	10	....	....	....	20	....	....	....	....	....	....	....	....	....	....	....	....	....	....	....	....	....	....
	Soviet Union	WJC-A	7	8	2	10	....	....	....	2	....	....	....	....	....	....	....	....	....	....	....	....	....	....	....	....	....	....
1983-84	Soviet Wings	USSR	33	5	3	8	....	....	....	18	....	....	....	....	....	....	....	....	....	....	....	....	....	....	....	....	....	....
1984-85	Soviet Wings	USSR	34	12	8	20	....	....	....	6	....	....	....	....	....	....	....	....	....	....	....	....	....	....	....	....	....	....
1985-86	Soviet Wings	USSR	38	15	14	29	....	....	....	19	....	....	....	....	....	....	....	....	....	....	....	....	....	....	....	....	....	....
1986-87	Soviet Wings	USSR	40	16	11	27	....	....	....	14	....	....	....	....	....	....	....	....	....	....	....	....	....	....	....	....	....	....
1987-88	Soviet Wings	USSR	45	17	13	30	....	....	....	20	....	....	....	....	....	....	....	....	....	....	....	....	....	....	....	....	....	....
1988-89	Soviet Wings	USSR	44	15	9	24	....	....	....	14	....	....	....	....	....	....	....	....	....	....	....	....	....	....	....	....	....	....
1989-90	Soviet Wings	FrTour	1	0	1	1	....	....	....	0	....	....	....	....	....	....	....	....	....	....	....	....	....	....	....	....	....	....
	Soviet Wings	USSR	47	12	5	17	....	....	....	28	....	....	....	....	....	....	....	....	....	....	....	....	....	....	....	....	....	....
	Soviet Wings	SuperS	5	0	2	2	....	....	....	4	....	....	....	....	....	....	....	....	....	....	....	....	....	....	....	....	....	....
1990-91	**Winnipeg Jets**	**NHL**	**7**	**2**	**3**	**5**	**2**	**2**	**4**	**2**	**0**	**0**	**0**	**13**	**15.4**	**8**	**2**	**4**	**0**	**+2**	....	....	....	....	....	....	....	....
	Moncton Hawks	AHL	66	22	18	40	....	....	....	38	....	....	....	....	....	....	....	....	....	....	5	1	0	1	2	....	....	....
1991-92	Halifax Citadels	AHL	40	10	12	22	....	....	....	15	....	....	....	....	....	....	....	....	....	....	....	....	....	....	....	....	....	....
1992-93	Birmingham Bulls	ECHL	2	0	3	3	....	....	....	0	....	....	....	....	....	....	....	....	....	....	....	....	....	....	....	....	....	....
	Cincinnati Cyclones	IHL	60	13	18	31	....	....	....	25	....	....	....	....	....	....	....	....	....	....	....	....	....	....	....	....	....	....
1993-94	Dayton Bombers	ECHL	59	30	59	89	....	....	....	56	....	....	....	....	....	....	....	....	....	....	3	2	0	2	4	....	....	....
1994-95	Cincinnati Cyclones	IHL	56	14	29	43	....	....	....	24	....	....	....	....	....	....	....	....	....	....	1	0	0	0	0	....	....	....
1995-96	Dayton Bombers	ECHL	25	7	9	16	....	....	....	25	....	....	....	....	....	....	....	....	....	....	....	....	....	....	....	....	....	....
	Worcester IceCats	AHL	28	7	12	19	....	....	....	10	....	....	....	....	....	....	....	....	....	....	3	1	1	2	2	....	....	....

			REGULAR SEASON																		PLAYOFFS							
Season	Club	League	GP	G	A	Pts	AG	AA	APts	PIM	PP	SH	GW	S	%	TGF	PGF	TGA	PGA	+/–	GP	G	A	Pts	PIM	PP	SH	GW
1996-97	Port Huron Border Cats	ColHL	49	20	24	44	....	....	....	20	....	....	....	....	....	....	....	....	....	....	....	....	....	....	....	....	....	....
	Muskegon Fury	ColHL	19	12	16	28	....	....	....	12	....	....	....	....	....	....	....	....	....	....	3	2	1	3	6	....	....	....
1997-98	Muskegon Fury	UHL	74	36	86	122	....	....	....	38	....	....	....	....	....	....	....	....	....	....	11	4	15	19	0	....	....	....
	NHL Totals		**7**	**2**	**3**	**5**	**2**	**2**	**4**	**2**	**0**	**0**	**0**	**13**	**15.4**	**8**	**2**	**4**	**0**		....	....	....	....	....	....	....	....

UHL Second All-Star Team (1998)

Traded to **Quebec** by **Winnipeg** for Shawn Anderson, October 22, 1991.

• KHMYLEV, YURI

Yuri Khmylev LW – R. 6'1", 189 lbs. b: Moscow, USSR, 8/9/1964. Buffalo's 7th choice, 108th overall, in 1992 Entry Draft.

Season	Club	League	GP	G	A	Pts	AG	AA	APts	PIM	PP	SH	GW	S	%	TGF	PGF	TGA	PGA	+/–	GP	G	A	Pts	PIM	PP	SH	GW
1981-82	Soviet Wings	USSR	8	2	2	4	....	....	....	2	....	....	....	....	....	....	....	....	....	....	....	....	....	....	....	....	....	....
1982-83	Soviet Wings	USSR	51	9	7	16	....	....	....	14	....	....	....	....	....	....	....	....	....	....	....	....	....	....	....	....	....	....
1983-84	Soviet Wings	USSR	43	7	8	15	....	....	....	10	....	....	....	....	....	....	....	....	....	....	....	....	....	....	....	....	....	....
	Soviet Union	WJC-A	7	2	7	9	....	....	....	0	....	....	....	....	....	....	....	....	....	....	....	....	....	....	....	....	....	....
1984-85	Soviet Wings	USSR	30	11	4	15	....	....	....	24	....	....	....	....	....	....	....	....	....	....	....	....	....	....	....	....	....	....
1985-86	Soviet Wings	USSR	40	24	9	33	....	....	....	22	....	....	....	....	....	....	....	....	....	....	....	....	....	....	....	....	....	....
	Soviet Union	WEC-A	6	2	1	3	....	....	....	4	....	....	....	....	....	....	....	....	....	....	....	....	....	....	....	....	....	....
1986-87	Soviet Wings	USSR	40	15	15	30	....	....	....	48	....	....	....	....	....	....	....	....	....	....	....	....	....	....	....	....	....	....
	USSR	RV'87	2	0	0	0	....	....	....	0	....	....	....	....	....	....	....	....	....	....	....	....	....	....	....	....	....	....
	Soviet Union	WEC-A	10	1	1	2	....	....	....	8	....	....	....	....	....	....	....	....	....	....	....	....	....	....	....	....	....	....
1987-88	Soviet Union	C Cup	9	0	1	1	....	....	....	2	....	....	....	....	....	....	....	....	....	....	....	....	....	....	....	....	....	....
	Soviet Wings	USSR	48	21	8	29	....	....	....	46	....	....	....	....	....	....	....	....	....	....	....	....	....	....	....	....	....	....
1988-89	Soviet Wings	USSR	44	16	18	34	....	....	....	38	....	....	....	....	....	....	....	....	....	....	....	....	....	....	....	....	....	....
	CSKA Moscow	SuperS	2	1	0	1	....	....	....	2	....	....	....	....	....	....	....	....	....	....	....	....	....	....	....	....	....	....
	Soviet Union	WEC-A	8	1	3	4	....	....	....	0	....	....	....	....	....	....	....	....	....	....	....	....	....	....	....	....	....	....
1989-90	Soviet Wings	FrTour	1	1	0	1	....	....	....	0	....	....	....	....	....	....	....	....	....	....	....	....	....	....	....	....	....	....
	Soviet Wings	USSR	44	14	13	27	....	....	....	30	....	....	....	....	....	....	....	....	....	....	....	....	....	....	....	....	....	....
	Soviet Wings	SuperS	5	4	1	5	....	....	....	0	....	....	....	....	....	....	....	....	....	....	....	....	....	....	....	....	....	....
1990-91	Soviet Wings	FrTour	1	0	0	0	....	....	....	0	....	....	....	....	....	....	....	....	....	....	....	....	....	....	....	....	....	....
	Soviet Wings	USSR	45	25	14	39	....	....	....	26	....	....	....	....	....	....	....	....	....	....	....	....	....	....	....	....	....	....
	CSKA Moscow	SuperS	7	3	3	6	....	....	....	0	....	....	....	....	....	....	....	....	....	....	....	....	....	....	....	....	....	....
1991-92	Soviet Wings	CIS	42	19	17	36	....	....	....	20	....	....	....	....	....	....	....	....	....	....	....	....	....	....	....	....	....	....
	Russia	Olympics	8	4	6	10	....	....	....	4	....	....	....	....	....	....	....	....	....	....	....	....	....	....	....	....	....	....
	Russia	WC-A	5	0	1	1	....	....	....	0	....	....	....	....	....	....	....	....	....	....	....	....	....	....	....	....	....	....
1992-93	**Buffalo Sabres**	**NHL**	**68**	**20**	**19**	**39**	**17**	**13**	**30**	**28**	**0**	**3**	**3**	**122**	**16.4**	**75**	**12**	**66**	**9**	**+6**	**8**	**4**	**3**	**7**	**4**	**1**	**0**	**1**
1993-94	**Buffalo Sabres**	**NHL**	**72**	**27**	**31**	**58**	**25**	**24**	**49**	**49**	**11**	**0**	**4**	**171**	**15.8**	**97**	**45**	**54**	**15**	**+13**	**7**	**3**	**1**	**4**	**8**	**0**	**0**	**0**
1994-95	Soviet Wings	IHL	11	2	2	4	....	....	....	4	....	....	....	....	....	....	....	....	....	....	....	....	....	....	....	....	....	....
	Buffalo Sabres	**NHL**	**48**	**8**	**17**	**25**	**14**	**25**	**39**	**14**	**2**	**1**	**1**	**71**	**11.3**	**34**	**5**	**33**	**12**	**+8**	**5**	**0**	**1**	**1**	**8**	**0**	**0**	**0**
1995-96	**Buffalo Sabres**	**NHL**	**66**	**8**	**20**	**28**	**8**	**16**	**24**	**40**	**5**	**1**	**1**	**123**	**6.5**	**48**	**20**	**64**	**24**	**–12**	....	....	....	....	....	....	....	....
	St. Louis Blues	**NHL**	**7**	**0**	**1**	**1**	**0**	**1**	**1**	**0**	**0**	**0**	**0**	**13**	**0.0**	**1**	**0**	**7**	**1**	**–5**	**6**	**1**	**1**	**2**	**4**	**0**	**0**	**1**
1996-97	**St. Louis Blues**	**NHL**	**2**	**1**	**0**	**1**	**1**	**0**	**1**	**2**	**0**	**0**	**0**	**3**	**33.3**	**1**	**0**	**2**	**0**	**–1**	....	....	....	....	....	....	....	....
	Quebec Rafales	IHL	15	1	7	8	....	....	....	4	....	....	....	....	....	....	....	....	....	....	....	....	....	....	....	....	....	....
	Hamilton Bulldogs	AHL	52	5	19	24	....	....	....	43	....	....	....	....	....	....	....	....	....	....	22	6	7	13	12	....	....	....
1997-98	HC Fribourg Gotteron	Switz.	17	5	6	11	....	....	....	2	....	....	....	....	....	....	....	....	....	....	2	1	0	1	0	....	....	....
	NHL Totals		**263**	**64**	**88**	**152**	**65**	**79**	**144**	**133**	**18**	**5**	**9**	**503**	**12.7**	**256**	**82**	**226**	**61**		**26**	**8**	**6**	**14**	**24**	**1**	**0**	**2**

Traded to **St. Louis** by **Buffalo** with Buffalo's 8th round choice (Andrei Podkonicky) in 1996 Entry Draft for Jean-Luc Grand Pierre, Ottawa's 2nd round choice (previously acquired, Buffalo selected Cory Sarich) in 1996 Entry Draft and St. Louis' 3rd round choice (Maxim Afinogenov) in 1997 Entry Draft, March 20, 1996.

• KHRISTICH, DIMITRI

Dimitri Khristich LW/C – R. 6'2", 195 lbs. b: Kiev, USSR, 7/23/1969. Washington's 6th choice, 120th overall, in 1988 Entry Draft.

Season	Club	League	GP	G	A	Pts	AG	AA	APts	PIM	PP	SH	GW	S	%	TGF	PGF	TGA	PGA	+/–	GP	G	A	Pts	PIM	PP	SH	GW
1985-86	Sokol Kiev	USSR	4	0	0	0	....	....	....	0	....	....	....	....	....	....	....	....	....	....	....	....	....	....	....	....	....	....
1986-87	Sokol Kiev	USSR	20	3	0	3	....	....	....	4	....	....	....	....	....	....	....	....	....	....	....	....	....	....	....	....	....	....
1987-88	Sokol Kiev	USSR	37	9	1	10	....	....	....	18	....	....	....	....	....	....	....	....	....	....	....	....	....	....	....	....	....	....
1988-89	Sokol Kiev	USSR	42	17	10	27	....	....	....	15	....	....	....	....	....	....	....	....	....	....	....	....	....	....	....	....	....	....
1989-90	Sokol Kiev	USSR	47	14	22	36	....	....	....	32	....	....	....	....	....	....	....	....	....	....	....	....	....	....	....	....	....	....
	Soviet Union	WEC-A	7	2	3	5	....	....	....	4	....	....	....	....	....	....	....	....	....	....	....	....	....	....	....	....	....	....
1990-91	Sokol Kiev	USSR	28	10	12	22	....	....	....	20	....	....	....	....	....	....	....	....	....	....	....	....	....	....	....	....	....	....
	Washington Capitals	**NHL**	**40**	**13**	**14**	**27**	**12**	**11**	**23**	**21**	**1**	**0**	**0**	**77**	**16.9**	**39**	**5**	**36**	**1**	**–1**	**11**	**1**	**3**	**4**	**6**	**0**	**0**	**0**
	Baltimore Skipjacks	AHL	3	0	0	0	....	....	....	0	....	....	....	....	....	....	....	....	....	....	....	....	....	....	....	....	....	....
1991-92	**Washington Capitals**	**NHL**	**80**	**36**	**37**	**73**	**33**	**28**	**61**	**35**	**14**	**1**	**7**	**188**	**19.1**	**122**	**53**	**61**	**6**	**+24**	**7**	**3**	**2**	**5**	**15**	**3**	**0**	**1**
1992-93	**Washington Capitals**	**NHL**	**64**	**31**	**35**	**66**	**26**	**24**	**50**	**28**	**9**	**1**	**1**	**127**	**24.4**	**116**	**40**	**53**	**6**	**+29**	**6**	**2**	**5**	**7**	**2**	**1**	**0**	**0**
1993-94	**Washington Capitals**	**NHL**	**83**	**29**	**29**	**58**	**27**	**22**	**49**	**73**	**10**	**0**	**4**	**195**	**14.9**	**99**	**36**	**72**	**7**	**–2**	**11**	**2**	**3**	**5**	**10**	**0**	**0**	**0**
1994-95	**Washington Capitals**	**NHL**	**48**	**12**	**14**	**26**	**21**	**21**	**42**	**41**	**8**	**0**	**2**	**92**	**13.0**	**50**	**27**	**27**	**4**	**0**	**7**	**1**	**4**	**5**	**0**	**0**	**0**	**0**
1995-96	**Los Angeles Kings**	**NHL**	**76**	**27**	**37**	**64**	**27**	**30**	**57**	**44**	**12**	**0**	**3**	**204**	**13.2**	**90**	**36**	**57**	**3**	**0**	....	....	....	....	....	....	....	....
1996-97	**Los Angeles Kings**	**NHL**	**75**	**19**	**37**	**56**	**20**	**33**	**53**	**38**	**3**	**0**	**2**	**135**	**14.1**	**84**	**20**	**66**	**10**	**+8**	....	....	....	....	....	....	....	....
1997-98	**Boston Bruins**	**NHL**	**82**	**29**	**37**	**66**	**34**	**36**	**70**	**42**	**13**	**2**	**1**	**144**	**20.1**	**99**	**37**	**42**	**5**	**+25**	**6**	**2**	**2**	**4**	**2**	**2**	**0**	**0**
	NHL Totals		**548**	**196**	**240**	**436**	**200**	**205**	**405**	**322**	**70**	**4**	**20**	**1162**	**16.9**	**699**	**254**	**404**	**42**		**48**	**11**	**19**	**30**	**35**	**6**	**0**	**1**

Played in NHL All-Star Game (1997)

Traded to **LA Kings** by **Washington** with Byron Dafoe for LA Kings' 1st round choice (Alexander Volchkov) and Dallas' 4th round choice (previously acquired, Washington selected Justin Davis) in 1996 Entry Draft, July 8, 1995. Traded to **Boston** by **LA Kings** with Byron Dafoe for Jozef Stumpel, Sandy Moger and Boston's 4th round choice (later traded to New Jersey - New Jersey selected Pierre Dagenais) in 1998 Entry Draft, August 29, 1997.

• KIDD, IAN

Ian Kidd D – R. 5'11", 195 lbs. b: Gresham, OR, 5/11/1964.

Season	Club	League	GP	G	A	Pts	AG	AA	APts	PIM	PP	SH	GW	S	%	TGF	PGF	TGA	PGA	+/–	GP	G	A	Pts	PIM	PP	SH	GW
1985-86	University of North Dakota	WCHA	37	6	16	22	....	....	....	65	....	....	....	....	....	....	....	....	....	....	....	....	....	....	....	....	....	....
1986-87	University of North Dakota	WCHA	47	13	47	60	....	....	....	58	....	....	....	....	....	....	....	....	....	....	....	....	....	....	....	....	....	....
1987-88	**Vancouver Canucks**	**NHL**	**19**	**4**	**7**	**11**	**3**	**5**	**8**	**25**	**3**	**0**	**0**	**22**	**18.2**	**19**	**7**	**15**	**0**	**–3**	....	....	....	....	....	....	....	....
	Fredericton Express	AHL	53	1	21	22	....	....	....	70	....	....	....	....	....	....	....	....	....	....	12	0	4	4	22	....	....	....
1988-89	**Vancouver Canucks**	**NHL**	**1**	**0**	**0**	**0**	**0**	**0**	**0**	**0**	**0**	**0**	**0**	**0**	**0.0**	**0**	**0**	**1**	**0**	**–1**	....	....	....	....	....	....	....	....
	Milwaukee Admirals	IHL	76	13	40	53	....	....	....	124	....	....	....	....	....	....	....	....	....	....	4	0	2	2	7	....	....	....
1989-90	Milwaukee Admirals	IHL	65	11	36	47	....	....	....	86	....	....	....	....	....	....	....	....	....	....	6	2	5	7	0	....	....	....
1990-91	Milwaukee Admirals	IHL	72	5	26	31	....	....	....	41	....	....	....	....	....	....	....	....	....	....	6	0	1	1	2	....	....	....
1991-92	Milwaukee Admirals	IHL	80	9	24	33	....	....	....	75	....	....	....	....	....	....	....	....	....	....	5	0	1	1	11	....	....	....
1992-93	Milwaukee Admirals	IHL	32	3	10	13	....	....	....	36	....	....	....	....	....	....	....	....	....	....	....	....	....	....	....	....	....	....
	Cincinnati Cyclones	IHL	23	6	23	29	....	....	....	10	....	....	....	....	....	....	....	....	....	....	....	....	....	....	....	....	....	....
1993-94	Cincinnati Cyclones	IHL	79	8	30	38	....	....	....	93	....	....	....	....	....	....	....	....	....	....	8	0	3	3	10	....	....	....
1994-95	Chicago Wolves	IHL	22	2	0	2	....	....	....	20	....	....	....	....	....	....	....	....	....	....	....	....	....	....	....	....	....	....
	Cincinnati Cyclones	IHL	13	1	1	2	....	....	....	10	....	....	....	....	....	....	....	....	....	....	8	1	3	4	6	....	....	....
	NHL Totals		**20**	**4**	**7**	**11**	**3**	**5**	**8**	**25**	**3**	**0**	**0**	**22**	**18.2**	**19**	**7**	**16**	**0**		....	....	....	....	....	....	....	....

WCHA First All-Star Team (1987) • NCAA West First All-American Team (1987) • NCAA Championship All-Tournament Team (1987)

Signed as a free agent by **Vancouver**, July 30, 1987.

• KIESSLING, UDO

Udo Kiessling D – L. 5'10", 180 lbs. b: Crimmitschau, Germany, 5/21/1955.

Season	Club	League	GP	G	A	Pts	AG	AA	APts	PIM	PP	SH	GW	S	%	TGF	PGF	TGA	PGA	+/–	GP	G	A	Pts	PIM	PP	SH	GW
1972-73	Rieresee	Germany	40	8	6	14	....	....	....	44	....	....	....	....	....	....	....	....	....	....	....	....	....	....	....	....	....	....
	West Germany	WEC-A	10	0	0	0	....	....	....	6	....	....	....	....	....	....	....	....	....	....	....	....	....	....	....	....	....	....
1973-74	Augsburg	Germany	36	16	6	22	....	....	....	52	....	....	....	....	....	....	....	....	....	....	....	....	....	....	....	....	....	....
1974-75	SB Rosenheim	Germany	34	20	18	38	....	....	....	73	....	....	....	....	....	....	....	....	....	....	....	....	....	....	....	....	....	....
1975-76	SB Rosenheim	Germany	34	30	22	52	....	....	....	72	....	....	....	....	....	....	....	....	....	....	....	....	....	....	....	....	....	....
	West Germany	Olympics	6	0	1	1	....	....	....	8	....	....	....	....	....	....	....	....	....	....	....	....	....	....	....	....	....	....
	West Germany	WEC-A	10	0	1	1	....	....	....	8	....	....	....	....	....	....	....	....	....	....	....	....	....	....	....	....	....	....
1976-77	Kolner	Germany	46	13	21	34	....	....	....	143	....	....	....	....	....	....	....	....	....	....	....	....	....	....	....	....	....	....
	West Germany	WEC-A	10	1	2	3	....	....	....	6	....	....	....	....	....	....	....	....	....	....	....	....	....	....	....	....	....	....
1977-78	Kolner	Germany	39	16	18	34	....	....	....	48	....	....	....	....	....	....	....	....	....	....	....	....	....	....	....	....	....	....
	West Germany	WEC-A	10	0	5	5	....	....	....	10	....	....	....	....	....	....	....	....	....	....	....	....	....	....	....	....	....	....

			REGULAR SEASON																		PLAYOFFS							
Season	Club	League	GP	G	A	Pts	AG	AA	APts	PIM	PP	SH	GW	S	%	TGF	PGF	TGA	PGA	+/–	GP	G	A	Pts	PIM	PP	SH	GW
1978-79	Kolner	Germany	40	28	32	60	....	....	....	78	....	....	....	....	....	....	....	....	....	....	....	....	....	....	....	....	....	....
	West Germany	WEC-A	8	2	4	6	....	....	....	14	....	....	....	....	....	....	....	....	....	....	....	....	....	....	....	....	....	....
1979-80	Dusseldorf	Germany	48	39	44	83	....	....	....	84	....	....	....	....	....	....	....	....	....	....	7	2	2	4	10	....	....	....
	West Germany	Olympics	5	2	2	4	....	....	....	6	....	....	....	....	....	....	....	....	....	....	....	....	....	....	....	....	....	....
1980-81	Dusseldorf	Germany	39	14	29	43	....	....	....	93	....	....	....	....	....	....	....	....	....	....	11	8	4	12	22	....	....	....
1981-82	Dusseldorf	Germany	38	15	22	37	....	....	....	54	....	....	....	....	....	....	....	....	....	....	2	0	0	0	7	....	....	....
	West Germany	WEC-A	7	1	3	4	....	....	....	12	....	....	....	....	....	....	....	....	....	....	....	....	....	....	....	....	....	....
	Minnesota North Stars	**NHL**	**1**	**0**	**0**	**0**	**0**	**0**	**0**	**2**	**0**	**0**	**0**	**1**	**0.0**	**1**	**1**	**0**	**0**	**0**	....	....	....	....	....	....	....	....
1982-83	Fussen	Germany	21	12	13	25	....	....	....	52	....	....	....	....	....	....	....	....	....	....	....	....	....	....	....	....	....	....
	Kolner	Germany	9	4	0	4	....	....	....	2	....	....	....	....	....	....	....	....	....	....	9	3	7	10	18	....	....	....
	West Germany	WEC-A	4	0	1	1	....	....	....	10	....	....	....	....	....	....	....	....	....	....	....	....	....	....	....	....	....	....
1983-84	Kolner	Germany	45	9	19	28	....	....	....	74	....	....	....	....	....	....	....	....	....	....	....	....	....	....	....	....	....	....
	West Germany	Olympics	6	3	1	4	....	....	....	4	....	....	....	....	....	....	....	....	....	....	....	....	....	....	....	....	....	....
1984-85	West Germany	C Cup	4	0	1	1	....	....	....	4	....	....	....	....	....	....	....	....	....	....	....	....	....	....	....	....	....	....
	Kolner	Germany	36	14	26	40	....	....	....	38	....	....	....	....	....	....	....	....	....	....	9	4	*10	14	22	....	....	....
	West Germany	WEC-A	10	0	3	3	....	....	....	16	....	....	....	....	....	....	....	....	....	....	....	....	....	....	....	....	....	....
1985-86	Kolner	Germany	37	18	27	45	....	....	....	41	....	....	....	....	....	....	....	....	....	....	....	....	....	....	....	....	....	....
	West Germany	WEC-A	10	4	2	6	....	....	....	22	....	....	....	....	....	....	....	....	....	....	....	....	....	....	....	....	....	....
1986-87	Kolner	Germany	42	10	34	44	....	....	....	70	....	....	....	....	....	....	....	....	....	....	9	4	11	15	....	....	....	....
	West Germany	WEC-A	10	5	3	8	....	....	....	18	....	....	....	....	....	....	....	....	....	....	....	....	....	....	....	....	....	....
1987-88	Kolner	Germany	46	12	27	39	....	....	....	76	....	....	....	....	....	....	....	....	....	....	....	....	....	....	....	....	....	....
	West Germany	Olympics	8	1	5	6	....	....	....	20	....	....	....	....	....	....	....	....	....	....	....	....	....	....	....	....	....	....
1988-89	Kolner	Germany	31	11	24	35	....	....	....	38	....	....	....	....	....	....	....	....	....	....	9	6	4	10	8	....	....	....
	West Germany	WEC-A	10	2	0	2	....	....	....	12	....	....	....	....	....	....	....	....	....	....	....	....	....	....	....	....	....	....
1989-90	Kolner	Germany	41	8	17	25	....	....	....	55	....	....	....	....	....	....	....	....	....	....	....	....	....	....	....	....	....	....
	West Germany	WEC-A	10	2	1	3	....	....	....	10	....	....	....	....	....	....	....	....	....	....	....	....	....	....	....	....	....	....
1990-91	Kolner	Germany	35	7	13	20	....	....	....	36	....	....	....	....	....	....	....	....	....	....	12	2	4	6	18	....	....	....
	Germany	WEC-A	10	0	1	1	....	....	....	6	....	....	....	....	....	....	....	....	....	....	....	....	....	....	....	....	....	....
1991-92	Kolner Haie	Germany	42	11	23	34	....	....	....	38	....	....	....	....	....	....	....	....	....	....	....	....	....	....	....	....	....	....
	Germany	Olympics	8	0	0	0	....	....	....	6	....	....	....	....	....	....	....	....	....	....	....	....	....	....	....	....	....	....
1992-93	EV Landshut	Germany	44	9	19	28	....	....	....	50	....	....	....	....	....	....	....	....	....	....	....	....	....	....	....	....	....	....
1993-94	EV Landshut	Germany	44	3	16	19	....	....	....	74	....	....	....	....	....	....	....	....	....	....	....	....	....	....	....	....	....	....
1994-95	EV Landshut	Germany	41	7	15	22	....	....	....	40	....	....	....	....	....	....	....	....	....	....	18	3	7	10	22	....	....	....
1995-96	EV Landshut	Germany	50	3	19	22	....	....	....	44	....	....	....	....	....	....	....	....	....	....	7	0	2	2	4	....	....	....
	NHL Totals		**1**	**0**	**0**	**0**	**0**	**0**	**0**	**2**	**0**	**0**	**0**	**1**	**0.0**	**1**	**1**	**0**	**0**		....	....	....	....	....	....	....	....

German Player of the Year (1977, 1984, 1986) • WEC-A All-Star Team (1987)

Signed as a free agent by **Minnesota**, March 5, 1982.

• KILGER, CHAD

Chad Kilger C – L. 6'3", 204 lbs. b: Cornwall, Ont., 11/27/1976. Anaheim's 1st choice, 4th overall, in 1995 Entry Draft.

Season	Club	League	GP	G	A	Pts	AG	AA	APts	PIM	PP	SH	GW	S	%	TGF	PGF	TGA	PGA	+/–	GP	G	A	Pts	PIM	PP	SH	GW
1993-94	Kingston Frontenacs	OHL	66	17	35	52	....	....	....	23	....	....	....	....	....	....	....	....	....	....	6	7	2	9	8	....	....	....
1994-95	Kingston Frontenacs	OHL	65	42	53	95	....	....	....	95	....	....	....	....	....	....	....	....	....	....	6	5	2	7	10	....	....	....
1995-96	**Anaheim Mighty Ducks**	**NHL**	**45**	**5**	**7**	**12**	**5**	**6**	**11**	**22**	**0**	**0**	**1**	**38**	**13.2**	**26**	**4**	**24**	**0**	**–2**	....	....	....	....	....	....	....	....
	Winnipeg Jets	**NHL**	**29**	**2**	**3**	**5**	**2**	**2**	**4**	**12**	**0**	**0**	**0**	**19**	**10.5**	**8**	**0**	**10**	**0**	**–2**	**4**	**1**	**0**	**1**	**0**	**0**	**0**	**1**
1996-97	**Phoenix Coyotes**	**NHL**	**24**	**4**	**3**	**7**	**4**	**3**	**7**	**13**	**1**	**0**	**0**	**30**	**13.3**	**8**	**1**	**12**	**0**	**–5**	....	....	....	....	....	....	....	....
	Springfield Falcons	AHL	52	17	28	45	....	....	....	36	....	....	....	....	....	....	....	....	....	....	16	5	7	12	56	....	....	....
1997-98	**Phoenix Coyotes**	**NHL**	**10**	**0**	**1**	**1**	**0**	**1**	**1**	**4**	**0**	**0**	**0**	**9**	**0.0**	**1**	**0**	**3**	**0**	**–2**	....	....	....	....	....	....	....	....
	Springfield Falcons	AHL	35	14	14	28	....	....	....	33	....	....	....	....	....	....	....	....	....	....	....	....	....	....	....	....	....	....
	Chicago Blackhawks	**NHL**	**22**	**3**	**8**	**11**	**4**	**8**	**12**	**6**	**2**	**0**	**1**	**23**	**13.0**	**17**	**5**	**10**	**0**	**+2**	....	....	....	....	....	....	....	....
	NHL Totals		**130**	**14**	**22**	**36**	**15**	**20**	**35**	**57**	**3**	**0**	**2**	**119**	**11.8**	**60**	**10**	**59**	**0**		**4**	**1**	**0**	**1**	**0**	**0**	**0**	**1**

Traded to **Winnipeg** by **Anaheim** with Oleg Tverdovsky and Anaheim's 3rd round choice (Per-Anton Lundstrom) in 1996 Entry Draft for Teemu Selanne, Marc Chouinard and Winnipeg's 4th round choice (later traded to Toronto — later traded to Montreal — Montreal selected Kim Staal) in 1996 Entry Draft, February 7, 1996. Transferred to **Phoenix** after **Winnipeg** franchise relocated, July 1, 1996. Traded to **Chicago** by **Phoenix** with Jayson More for Keith Carney and Jim Cummins, March 4, 1998.

• KILREA, BRIAN

Brian Kilrea C – R. 5'11", 175 lbs. b: Ottawa, Ont., 10/21/1934.

Season	Club	League	GP	G	A	Pts	AG	AA	APts	PIM	PP	SH	GW	S	%	TGF	PGF	TGA	PGA	+/–	GP	G	A	Pts	PIM	PP	SH	GW
1953-54	Hamilton Tiger Cubs	OHA	58	26	34	60	....	....	....	69	....	....	....	....	....	....	....	....	....	....	6	1	2	3	6	....	....	....
1954-55	Hamilton Tiger Cubs	OHA	49	27	25	52	....	....	....	56	....	....	....	....	....	....	....	....	....	....	3	1	1	2	7	....	....	....
1955-56	Troy Bruins	IHL	60	16	36	52	....	....	....	22	....	....	....	....	....	....	....	....	....	....	5	0	0	0	2	....	....	....
1956-57	Troy Bruins	IHL	60	9	35	44	....	....	....	46	....	....	....	....	....	....	....	....	....	....	....	....	....	....	....	....	....	....
1957-58	**Detroit Red Wings**	**NHL**	**1**	**0**	**0**	**0**	**0**	**0**	**0**	**0**	....	....	....	....	....	....	....	....	....	....	....	....	....	....	....	....	....	....
	Edmonton Flyers	WHL	3	0	0	0	....	....	....	0	....	....	....	....	....	....	....	....	....	....	....	....	....	....	....	....	....	....
	Troy Bruins	IHL	58	30	35	65	....	....	....	25	....	....	....	....	....	....	....	....	....	....	....	....	....	....	....	....	....	....
1958-59	Troy Bruins	IHL	54	33	60	93	....	....	....	44	....	....	....	....	....	....	....	....	....	....	5	2	3	5	17	....	....	....
1959-60	Springfield Indians	AHL	63	14	27	41	....	....	....	26	....	....	....	....	....	....	....	....	....	....	8	0	1	1	4	....	....	....
1960-61	Springfield Indians	AHL	70	20	67	87	....	....	....	47	....	....	....	....	....	....	....	....	....	....	8	1	5	6	2	....	....	....
1961-62	Springfield Indians	AHL	70	20	*73	93	....	....	....	28	....	....	....	....	....	....	....	....	....	....	2	0	1	1	0	....	....	....
1962-63	Springfield Indians	AHL	72	25	50	75	....	....	....	34	....	....	....	....	....	....	....	....	....	....	....	....	....	....	....	....	....	....
1963-64	Springfield Indians	AHL	72	22	61	83	....	....	....	28	....	....	....	....	....	....	....	....	....	....	....	....	....	....	....	....	....	....
1964-65	Springfield Indians	AHL	71	23	54	77	....	....	....	18	....	....	....	....	....	....	....	....	....	....	....	....	....	....	....	....	....	....
1965-66	Springfield Indians	AHL	70	13	47	60	....	....	....	14	....	....	....	....	....	....	....	....	....	....	6	3	1	4	0	....	....	....
1966-67	Springfield Indians	AHL	63	25	38	63	....	....	....	29	....	....	....	....	....	....	....	....	....	....	....	....	....	....	....	....	....	....
1967-68	**Los Angeles Kings**	**NHL**	**25**	**3**	**5**	**8**	**4**	**5**	**9**	**12**	**0**	**0**	**0**	**24**	**12.5**	**11**	**2**	**17**	**4**	**–4**	....	....	....	....	....	....	....	....
	Springfield Kings	AHL	38	7	25	32	....	....	....	14	....	....	....	....	....	....	....	....	....	....	4	0	3	3	0	....	....	....
1968-69	Vancouver Canucks	WHL	1	0	1	1	....	....	....	0	....	....	....	....	....	....	....	....	....	....	....	....	....	....	....	....	....	....
	Rochester Americans	AHL	33	2	11	13	....	....	....	4	....	....	....	....	....	....	....	....	....	....	....	....	....	....	....	....	....	....
	Tulsa Oilers	CHL	24	11	25	36	....	....	....	12	....	....	....	....	....	....	....	....	....	....	4	0	1	1	0	....	....	....
1969-70	Denver Spurs	WHL	32	5	14	19	....	....	....	18	....	....	....	....	....	....	....	....	....	....	....	....	....	....	....	....	....	....
	NHL Totals		**26**	**3**	**5**	**8**	**4**	**5**	**9**	**12**	**0**	**0**	**0**	**24**	**12.5**	**11**	**2**	**17**	**4**		....	....	....	....	....	....	....	....

IHL Second All-Star Team (1959)

NHL rights transferred to **LA Kings** after NHL club purchased **Springfield** (AHL) franchise, May, 1967. Claimed by **Vancouver** (WHL) from **LA Kings** in Reverse Draft, June, 1968. Claimed on waivers by **Denver** (WHL) from **Vancouver** (WHL), January, 1970.

• KIMBLE, DARIN

Darin Kimble RW – R. 6'2", 210 lbs. b: Lucky Lake, Sask., 11/22/1968. Quebec's 5th choice, 66th overall, in 1988 Entry Draft.

Season	Club	League	GP	G	A	Pts	AG	AA	APts	PIM	PP	SH	GW	S	%	TGF	PGF	TGA	PGA	+/–	GP	G	A	Pts	PIM	PP	SH	GW
1985-86	Calgary Wranglers	WHL	37	14	8	22	....	....	....	93	....	....	....	....	....	....	....	....	....	....	....	....	....	....	....	....	....	....
	New Westminster Bruins	WHL	11	1	1	2	....	....	....	22	....	....	....	....	....	....	....	....	....	....	....	....	....	....	....	....	....	....
	Brandon Wheat Kings	WHL	15	1	6	7	....	....	....	39	....	....	....	....	....	....	....	....	....	....	....	....	....	....	....	....	....	....
1986-87	Prince Albert Raiders	WHL	68	17	13	30	....	....	....	190	....	....	....	....	....	....	....	....	....	....	....	....	....	....	....	....	....	....
1987-88	Prince Albert Raiders	WHL	67	35	36	71	....	....	....	307	....	....	....	....	....	....	....	....	....	....	10	3	2	5	4	....	....	....
1988-89	**Quebec Nordiques**	**NHL**	**26**	**3**	**1**	**4**	**3**	**1**	**4**	**149**	**0**	**0**	**0**	**21**	**14.3**	**9**	**1**	**13**	**0**	**–5**	....	....	....	....	....	....	....	....
	Halifax Citadels	AHL	39	8	6	14	....	....	....	188	....	....	....	....	....	....	....	....	....	....	....	....	....	....	....	....	....	....
1989-90	**Quebec Nordiques**	**NHL**	**44**	**5**	**5**	**10**	**4**	**4**	**8**	**185**	**2**	**0**	**1**	**40**	**12.5**	**23**	**8**	**35**	**0**	**–20**	....	....	....	....	....	....	....	....
	Halifax Citadels	AHL	18	6	6	12	....	....	....	37	....	....	....	....	....	....	....	....	....	....	6	1	1	2	61	....	....	....
1990-91	**Quebec Nordiques**	**NHL**	**35**	**2**	**5**	**7**	**2**	**4**	**6**	**114**	**0**	**0**	**0**	**14**	**14.3**	**9**	**0**	**14**	**0**	**–5**	....	....	....	....	....	....	....	....
	Halifax Citadels	AHL	7	1	4	5	....	....	....	20	....	....	....	....	....	....	....	....	....	....	....	....	....	....	....	....	....	....
	St. Louis Blues	**NHL**	**26**	**1**	**1**	**2**	**1**	**1**	**2**	**128**	**0**	**0**	**1**	**14**	**7.1**	**6**	**0**	**4**	**0**	**+2**	**13**	**0**	**0**	**0**	**38**	**0**	**0**	**0**
1991-92	**St. Louis Blues**	**NHL**	**46**	**1**	**3**	**4**	**1**	**2**	**3**	**166**	**0**	**0**	**0**	**12**	**8.3**	**5**	**0**	**9**	**1**	**–3**	**5**	**0**	**0**	**0**	**7**	**0**	**0**	**0**
1992-93	**Boston Bruins**	**NHL**	**55**	**7**	**3**	**10**	**6**	**2**	**8**	**177**	**0**	**0**	**0**	**20**	**35.0**	**16**	**0**	**12**	**0**	**+4**	**4**	**0**	**0**	**0**	**2**	**0**	**0**	**0**
	Providence Bruins	AHL	12	1	4	5	....	....	....	34	....	....	....	....	....	....	....	....	....	....	....	....	....	....	....	....	....	....
1993-94	**Chicago Blackhawks**	**NHL**	**65**	**4**	**2**	**6**	**4**	**2**	**6**	**133**	**0**	**0**	**0**	**17**	**23.5**	**12**	**0**	**10**	**0**	**+2**	**1**	**0**	**0**	**0**	**5**	**0**	**0**	**0**
1994-95	**Chicago Blackhawks**	**NHL**	**14**	**0**	**0**	**0**	**0**	**0**	**0**	**30**	**0**	**0**	**0**	**2**	**0.0**	**1**	**0**	**6**	**0**	**–5**	....	....	....	....	....	....	....	....
1995-96	Indianapolis Ice	IHL	9	1	0	1	....	....	....	15	....	....	....	....	....	....	....	....	....	....	....	....	....	....	....	....	....	....
	Albany River Rats	AHL	60	4	15	19	....	....	....	144	....	....	....	....	....	....	....	....	....	....	3	0	0	0	2	....	....	....

Season	Club	League	REGULAR SEASON GP	G	A	Pts	AG	AA	APts	PIM	PP	SH	GW	S	%	TGF	PGF	TGA	PGA	+/–	PLAYOFFS GP	G	A	Pts	PIM	PP	SH	GW
1996-97	Manitoba Moose	IHL	39	3	4	7	....	....	....	115	....	....	....	....	....	....	....	....	....	....	....	....	....	....	....	....	....	....
	Kansas City Blades	IHL	33	9	9	18	....	....	....	106	....	....	....	....	....	....	....	....	....	....	2	0	0	0	0	....	....	....
1997-98	Kansas City Blades	IHL	16	1	3	4	....	....	....	60	....	....	....	....	....	....	....	....	....	....	....	....	....	....	....	....	....	....
	San Antonio Dragons	IHL	56	6	14	20	....	....	....	143	....	....	....	....	....	....	....	....	....	....	....	....	....	....	....	....	....	....
	NHL Totals		**311**	**23**	**20**	**43**	**21**	**16**	**37**	**1082**	**2**	**0**	**2**	**140**	**16.4**	**81**	**9**	**103**	**1**		**23**	**0**	**0**	**0**	**52**	**0**	**0**	**0**

Traded to **St. Louis** by **Quebec** for Herb Raglan, Tony Twist and Andy Rymsha, February 4, 1991. Traded to **Tampa Bay** by **St. Louis** with Pat Jablonski and Steve Tuttle for future considerations, June 19, 1992. Traded to **Boston** by **Tampa Bay** with future considerations for Ken Hodge and Matt Hervey, September 4, 1992. Signed as a free agent by **Florida**, July 9, 1993. Traded to **Chicago** by **Florida** for Keith Brown, September 30, 1993. Traded to **New Jersey** by **Chicago** for Michael Vukonich and Bill H. Armstrong, November 1, 1995. Signed as a free agent by **Phoenix**, July 28, 1997.

• KINDRACHUK, OREST

Orest Kindrachuk C – L. 5'10", 175 lbs. b: Nanton, Alta., 9/14/1950.

Season	Club	League	GP	G	A	Pts	AG	AA	APts	PIM	PP	SH	GW	S	%	TGF	PGF	TGA	PGA	+/–	GP	G	A	Pts	PIM	PP	SH	GW
1967-68	Saskatoon Blades	WCJHL	58	24	37	61	....	....	....	44	....	....	....	....	....	....	....	....	....	....	....	....	....	....	....	....	....	....
1968-69	Saskatoon Blades	WCJHL	41	21	25	46	....	....	....	33	....	....	....	....	....	....	....	....	....	....	....	....	....	....	....	....	....	....
1969-70	Saskatoon Blades	WCJHL	4	3	4	7	....	....	....	5	....	....	....	....	....	....	....	....	....	....	....	....	....	....	....	....	....	....
1970-71	Saskatoon Blades	WCJHL	61	49	*100	149	....	....	....	103	....	....	....	....	....	....	....	....	....	....	....	....	....	....	....	....	....	....
1971-72	San Diego Gulls	WHL	61	18	36	54	....	....	....	71	....	....	....	....	....	....	....	....	....	....	4	1	1	2	0	....	....	....
1972-73	**Philadelphia Flyers**	**NHL**	**2**	**0**	**0**	**0**	**0**	**0**	**0**	**0**	**0**	**0**	**0**	**0**	**0.0**	**0**	**0**	**0**	**0**	**0**	....	....	....	....	....	....	....	....
	Richmond Robins	AHL	72	35	51	86	....	....	....	133	....	....	....	....	....	....	....	....	....	....	3	0	1	1	10	....	....	....
1973-74	**Philadelphia Flyers**	**NHL**	**71**	**11**	**30**	**41**	**11**	**26**	**37**	**85**	**3**	**1**	**3**	**106**	**10.4**	**49**	**11**	**19**	**0**	**+19**	**17**	**5**	**4**	**9**	**17**	**0**	**0**	**0**
1974-75	**Philadelphia Flyers**	**NHL**	**60**	**10**	**21**	**31**	**9**	**17**	**26**	**72**	**1**	**0**	**2**	**104**	**9.6**	**44**	**8**	**33**	**5**	**+8**	**14**	**0**	**2**	**2**	**12**	**0**	**0**	**0**
1975-76	**Philadelphia Flyers**	**NHL**	**76**	**26**	**49**	**75**	**24**	**39**	**63**	**101**	**5**	**2**	**2**	**181**	**14.4**	**100**	**31**	**61**	**24**	**+32**	**16**	**4**	**7**	**11**	**4**	**1**	**0**	**2**
1976-77	**Philadelphia Flyers**	**NHL**	**78**	**15**	**36**	**51**	**14**	**29**	**43**	**79**	**1**	**1**	**3**	**147**	**10.2**	**75**	**11**	**58**	**16**	**+22**	**10**	**2**	**1**	**3**	**0**	**1**	**0**	**0**
1977-78	**Philadelphia Flyers**	**NHL**	**73**	**17**	**45**	**62**	**16**	**37**	**53**	**128**	**1**	**1**	**4**	**170**	**10.0**	**87**	**14**	**56**	**18**	**+35**	**12**	**5**	**5**	**10**	**13**	**2**	**0**	**1**
1978-79	**Pittsburgh Penguins**	**NHL**	**79**	**18**	**42**	**60**	**16**	**32**	**48**	**84**	**4**	**1**	**0**	**145**	**12.4**	**87**	**26**	**81**	**23**	**+3**	**7**	**4**	**1**	**5**	**7**	**0**	**0**	**1**
1979-80	**Pittsburgh Penguins**	**NHL**	**52**	**17**	**29**	**46**	**15**	**22**	**37**	**63**	**2**	**2**	**1**	**94**	**18.1**	**58**	**14**	**56**	**16**	**+4**	....	....	....	....	....	....	....	....
1980-81	**Pittsburgh Penguins**	**NHL**	**13**	**3**	**9**	**12**	**2**	**6**	**8**	**34**	**1**	**0**	**0**	**35**	**8.6**	**18**	**8**	**17**	**10**	**+3**	....	....	....	....	....	....	....	....
1981-82	**Washington Capitals**	**NHL**	**4**	**1**	**0**	**1**	**1**	**0**	**1**	**2**	**1**	**0**	**0**	**8**	**12.5**	**2**	**1**	**6**	**1**	**–4**	....	....	....	....	....	....	....	....
	NHL Totals		**508**	**118**	**261**	**379**	**108**	**208**	**316**	**648**	**19**	**8**	**15**	**990**	**11.9**	**520**	**124**	**387**	**113**		**76**	**20**	**20**	**40**	**53**	**4**	**0**	**4**

Signed as a free agent by **Philadelphia**, July, 1971. Traded to **Pittsburgh** by **Philadelphia** with Tom Bladon and Ross Lonsberry for Pittsburgh's 1st round choice (Behn Wilson) in 1978 Amateur Draft, June 14, 1978. Signed as a free agent by **Washington**, September 4, 1981.

• KING, DEREK

Derek King LW – L. 6', 212 lbs. b: Hamilton, Ont., 2/11/1967. NY Islanders' 2nd choice, 13th overall, in 1985 Entry Draft.

Season	Club	League	GP	G	A	Pts	AG	AA	APts	PIM	PP	SH	GW	S	%	TGF	PGF	TGA	PGA	+/–	GP	G	A	Pts	PIM	PP	SH	GW
1984-85	Sault Ste. Marie Greyhounds	OHL	63	35	38	73	....	....	....	106	....	....	....	....	....	....	....	....	....	....	16	3	13	16	11	....	....	....
1985-86	Sault Ste. Marie Greyhounds	OHL	25	12	17	29	....	....	....	33	....	....	....	....	....	....	....	....	....	....	....	....	....	....	....	....	....	....
	Oshawa Generals	OHL	19	8	13	21	....	....	....	15	....	....	....	....	....	....	....	....	....	....	6	3	2	5	13	....	....	....
1986-87	Oshawa Generals	OHL	57	53	53	106	....	....	....	74	....	....	....	....	....	....	....	....	....	....	17	14	10	24	40	....	....	....
	New York Islanders	**NHL**	**2**	**0**	**0**	**0**	**0**	**0**	**0**	**0**	**0**	**0**	**0**	**5**	**0.0**	**1**	**0**	**1**	**0**	**0**	....	....	....	....	....	....	....	....
1987-88	**New York Islanders**	**NHL**	**55**	**12**	**24**	**36**	**10**	**17**	**27**	**30**	**1**	**0**	**4**	**94**	**12.8**	**62**	**19**	**36**	**0**	**+7**	**5**	**0**	**2**	**2**	**2**	**0**	**0**	**0**
	Springfield Indians	AHL	10	7	6	13	....	....	....	6	....	....	....	....	....	....	....	....	....	....	....	....	....	....	....	....	....	....
1988-89	**New York Islanders**	**NHL**	**60**	**14**	**29**	**43**	**12**	**20**	**32**	**14**	**4**	**0**	**0**	**103**	**13.6**	**65**	**21**	**34**	**0**	**+10**	....	....	....	....	....	....	....	....
	Springfield Indians	AHL	4	4	0	4	....	....	....	0	....	....	....	....	....	....	....	....	....	....	....	....	....	....	....	....	....	....
1989-90	**New York Islanders**	**NHL**	**46**	**13**	**27**	**40**	**11**	**19**	**30**	**20**	**5**	**0**	**1**	**91**	**14.3**	**55**	**19**	**34**	**0**	**+2**	**4**	**0**	**0**	**0**	**4**	**0**	**0**	**0**
	Springfield Indians	AHL	21	11	12	23	....	....	....	33	....	....	....	....	....	....	....	....	....	....	....	....	....	....	....	....	....	....
1990-91	**New York Islanders**	**NHL**	**66**	**19**	**26**	**45**	**17**	**20**	**37**	**44**	**2**	**0**	**2**	**130**	**14.6**	**63**	**20**	**42**	**0**	**+1**	....	....	....	....	....	....	....	....
1991-92	**New York Islanders**	**NHL**	**80**	**40**	**38**	**78**	**37**	**29**	**66**	**46**	**21**	**0**	**6**	**189**	**21.2**	**107**	**49**	**68**	**0**	**–10**	....	....	....	....	....	....	....	....
	Canada	WC-A	6	1	1	2	....	....	....	6	....	....	....	....	....	....	....	....	....	....	....	....	....	....	....	....	....	....
1992-93	**New York Islanders**	**NHL**	**77**	**38**	**38**	**76**	**32**	**26**	**58**	**47**	**21**	**0**	**7**	**201**	**18.9**	**132**	**66**	**70**	**0**	**–4**	**18**	**3**	**11**	**14**	**14**	**0**	**0**	**0**
1993-94	**New York Islanders**	**NHL**	**78**	**30**	**40**	**70**	**28**	**31**	**59**	**59**	**10**	**0**	**7**	**171**	**17.5**	**112**	**43**	**51**	**0**	**+18**	**4**	**0**	**1**	**1**	**0**	**0**	**0**	**0**
1994-95	**New York Islanders**	**NHL**	**43**	**10**	**16**	**26**	**18**	**24**	**42**	**41**	**7**	**0**	**0**	**118**	**8.5**	**44**	**16**	**34**	**1**	**–5**	....	....	....	....	....	....	....	....
1995-96	**New York Islanders**	**NHL**	**61**	**12**	**20**	**32**	**12**	**16**	**28**	**23**	**5**	**1**	**0**	**154**	**7.8**	**50**	**13**	**52**	**5**	**–10**	....	....	....	....	....	....	....	....
1996-97	**New York Islanders**	**NHL**	**70**	**23**	**30**	**53**	**24**	**27**	**51**	**20**	**5**	**0**	**3**	**153**	**15.0**	**83**	**21**	**68**	**0**	**–6**	....	....	....	....	....	....	....	....
	Hartford Whalers	**NHL**	**12**	**3**	**3**	**6**	**3**	**3**	**6**	**2**	**1**	**0**	**0**	**28**	**10.7**	**13**	**5**	**8**	**0**	**0**	....	....	....	....	....	....	....	....
1997-98	**Toronto Maple Leafs**	**NHL**	**77**	**21**	**25**	**46**	**25**	**24**	**49**	**43**	**4**	**0**	**3**	**166**	**12.7**	**61**	**20**	**48**	**0**	**–7**	....	....	....	....	....	....	....	....
	NHL Totals		**727**	**235**	**316**	**551**	**229**	**256**	**485**	**389**	**86**	**1**	**33**	**1603**	**14.7**	**848**	**312**	**546**	**6**		**31**	**3**	**14**	**17**	**20**	**0**	**0**	**0**

OHL First All-Star Team (1987)

Traded to **Hartford** by **NY Islanders** for Hartford's 5th round choice (Adam Edinger) in 1997 Entry Draft, March 18, 1997. Signed as a free agent by **Toronto**, July 4, 1997.

• KING, KRIS

Kris King LW – L. 5'11", 208 lbs. b: Bracebridge, Ont., 2/18/1966. Washington's 4th choice, 80th overall, in 1984 Entry Draft.

Season	Club	League	GP	G	A	Pts	AG	AA	APts	PIM	PP	SH	GW	S	%	TGF	PGF	TGA	PGA	+/–	GP	G	A	Pts	PIM	PP	SH	GW
1983-84	Peterborough Petes	OHL	62	13	18	31	....	....	....	168	....	....	....	....	....	....	....	....	....	....	8	3	3	6	14	....	....	....
1984-85	Peterborough Petes	OHL	61	18	35	53	....	....	....	222	....	....	....	....	....	....	....	....	....	....	16	2	8	10	28	....	....	....
1985-86	Peterborough Petes	OHL	58	19	40	59	....	....	....	254	....	....	....	....	....	....	....	....	....	....	8	4	0	4	21	....	....	....
1986-87	Peterborough Petes	OHL	46	23	33	56	....	....	....	160	....	....	....	....	....	....	....	....	....	....	12	5	8	13	41	....	....	....
	Binghamton Whalers	AHL	7	0	0	0	....	....	....	18	....	....	....	....	....	....	....	....	....	....	....	....	....	....	....	....	....	....
1987-88	**Detroit Red Wings**	**NHL**	**3**	**1**	**0**	**1**	**1**	**0**	**1**	**2**	**0**	**0**	**0**	**3**	**33.3**	**1**	**0**	**0**	**0**	**+1**	....	....	....	....	....	....	....	....
	Adirondack Red Wings	AHL	76	21	32	53	....	....	....	337	....	....	....	....	....	....	....	....	....	....	10	4	4	8	53	....	....	....
1988-89	**Detroit Red Wings**	**NHL**	**55**	**2**	**3**	**5**	**2**	**2**	**4**	**168**	**0**	**0**	**0**	**34**	**5.9**	**9**	**0**	**16**	**0**	**–7**	**2**	**0**	**0**	**0**	**2**	**0**	**0**	**0**
1989-90	**New York Rangers**	**NHL**	**68**	**6**	**7**	**13**	**5**	**5**	**10**	**286**	**0**	**0**	**0**	**49**	**12.2**	**30**	**0**	**28**	**0**	**+2**	**10**	**0**	**1**	**1**	**38**	**0**	**0**	**0**
1990-91	**New York Rangers**	**NHL**	**72**	**11**	**14**	**25**	**10**	**11**	**21**	**154**	**0**	**0**	**0**	**107**	**10.3**	**35**	**0**	**36**	**0**	**–1**	**6**	**2**	**0**	**2**	**36**	**0**	**0**	**1**
1991-92	**New York Rangers**	**NHL**	**79**	**10**	**9**	**19**	**9**	**7**	**16**	**224**	**0**	**0**	**2**	**97**	**10.3**	**45**	**0**	**32**	**0**	**+13**	**13**	**4**	**1**	**5**	**14**	**0**	**0**	**3**
1992-93	**New York Rangers**	**NHL**	**30**	**0**	**3**	**3**	**0**	**2**	**2**	**67**	**0**	**0**	**0**	**23**	**0.0**	**11**	**0**	**12**	**0**	**–1**	....	....	....	....	....	....	....	....
	Winnipeg Jets	**NHL**	**48**	**8**	**8**	**16**	**7**	**5**	**12**	**136**	**0**	**0**	**1**	**51**	**15.7**	**25**	**0**	**23**	**3**	**+5**	**6**	**1**	**1**	**2**	**4**	**0**	**0**	**0**
1993-94	**Winnipeg Jets**	**NHL**	**83**	**4**	**8**	**12**	**4**	**6**	**10**	**205**	**0**	**0**	**1**	**86**	**4.7**	**20**	**0**	**42**	**0**	**–22**	....	....	....	....	....	....	....	....
1994-95	**Winnipeg Jets**	**NHL**	**48**	**4**	**2**	**6**	**7**	**3**	**10**	**85**	**0**	**0**	**0**	**58**	**6.9**	**22**	**0**	**23**	**1**	**0**	....	....	....	....	....	....	....	....
1995-96	**Winnipeg Jets**	**NHL**	**81**	**9**	**11**	**20**	**9**	**9**	**18**	**151**	**0**	**1**	**2**	**89**	**10.1**	**38**	**0**	**82**	**17**	**–7**	**6**	**0**	**1**	**1**	**4**	**0**	**0**	**0**
1996-97	**Phoenix Coyotes**	**NHL**	**81**	**3**	**11**	**14**	**3**	**10**	**13**	**185**	**0**	**0**	**0**	**57**	**5.3**	**22**	**3**	**31**	**5**	**–7**	**7**	**0**	**0**	**0**	**17**	**0**	**0**	**0**
1997-98	**Toronto Maple Leafs**	**NHL**	**82**	**3**	**3**	**6**	**4**	**3**	**7**	**199**	**0**	**0**	**2**	**53**	**5.7**	**14**	**0**	**40**	**13**	**–13**	....	....	....	....	....	....	....	....
	NHL Totals		**730**	**61**	**79**	**140**	**61**	**63**	**124**	**1862**	**0**	**1**	**8**	**707**	**8.6**	**272**	**3**	**345**	**39**		**49**	**7**	**4**	**11**	**115**	**0**	**0**	**4**

Won King Clancy Memorial Trophy (1996)

Signed as a free agent by **Detroit**, March 23, 1987. Traded to **NY Rangers** by **Detroit** for Chris McRae and Detroit's 5th round choice (previously acquired, Detroit selected Tony Burns) in 1990 Entry Draft, September 7, 1989. Traded to **Winnipeg** by **NY Rangers** with Tie Domi for Ed Olczyk, December 28, 1992. Transferred to **Phoenix** after **Winnipeg** franchise relocated, July 1, 1996. Signed as a free agent by **Toronto**, July 23, 1997.

• KING, STEVEN

Steven King RW – R. 6', 195 lbs. b: Greenwich, RI, 7/22/1969. NY Rangers' 1st choice, 21st overall, in 1991 Supplemental Draft.

Season	Club	League	GP	G	A	Pts	AG	AA	APts	PIM	PP	SH	GW	S	%	TGF	PGF	TGA	PGA	+/–	GP	G	A	Pts	PIM	PP	SH	GW
1989-90	Brown University	ECAC	27	19	8	27	....	....	....	53	....	....	....	....	....	....	....	....	....	....	....	....	....	....	....	....	....	....
1990-91	Brown University	ECAC	27	19	15	34	....	....	....	76	....	....	....	....	....	....	....	....	....	....	....	....	....	....	....	....	....	....
1991-92	Binghamton Rangers	AHL	66	27	15	42	....	....	....	56	....	....	....	....	....	....	....	....	....	....	10	2	0	2	14	....	....	....
1992-93	**New York Rangers**	**NHL**	**24**	**7**	**5**	**12**	**6**	**3**	**9**	**16**	**5**	**0**	**2**	**42**	**16.7**	**25**	**9**	**12**	**0**	**+4**	....	....	....	....	....	....	....	....
	Binghamton Rangers	AHL	53	35	33	68	....	....	....	100	....	....	....	....	....	....	....	....	....	....	14	7	9	16	26	....	....	....
1993-94	**Anaheim Mighty Ducks**	**NHL**	**36**	**8**	**3**	**11**	**7**	**2**	**9**	**44**	**3**	**0**	**1**	**50**	**16.0**	**16**	**5**	**18**	**0**	**–7**	....	....	....	....	....	....	....	....
1994-95			DID NOT PLAY – INJURED																									
1995-96	**Anaheim Mighty Ducks**	**NHL**	**7**	**2**	**0**	**2**	**2**	**0**	**2**	**15**	**1**	**0**	**1**	**5**	**40.0**	**3**	**1**	**3**	**0**	**–1**	....	....	....	....	....	....	....	....
	Baltimore Bandits	AHL	68	40	21	61	....	....	....	95	....	....	....	....	....	....	....	....	....	....	12	7	5	12	20	....	....	....
1996-97	Philadelphia Phantoms	AHL	39	17	10	27	....	....	....	47	....	....	....	....	....	....	....	....	....	....	....	....	....	....	....	....	....	....
	Michigan K-Wings	IHL	39	15	11	26	....	....	....	39	....	....	....	....	....	....	....	....	....	....	4	1	2	3	12	....	....	....
1997-98	Rochester Americans	AHL	28	15	15	30	....	....	....	28	....	....	....	....	....	....	....	....	....	....	4	1	1	2	4	....	....	....
	Cincinnati Cyclones	IHL	41	17	9	26	....	....	....	22	....	....	....	....	....	....	....	....	....	....	....	....	....	....	....	....	....	....
	NHL Totals		**67**	**17**	**8**	**25**	**15**	**5**	**20**	**75**	**9**	**0**	**4**	**97**	**17.5**	**44**	**15**	**33**	**0**		....	....	....	....	....	....	....	....

Claimed by **Anaheim** from **NY Rangers** in Expansion Draft, June 24, 1993. • Missed entire 1994-95 season after having reconstructive surgery on shoulder, January 5, 1994. Signed as a free agent by **Philadelphia**, July 31, 1996.

● KING, WAYNE Wayne King C – R. 5'10", 185 lbs. b: Midland, Ont., 9/4/1951.

			REGULAR SEASON																		PLAYOFFS							
Season	Club	League	GP	G	A	Pts	AG	AA	APts	PIM	PP	SH	GW	S	%	TGF	PGF	TGA	PGA	+/–	GP	G	A	Pts	PIM	PP	SH	GW
1968-69	Niagara Falls Flyers	OHA	4	1	0	1	....	....	....	0	....	....	....	....	....	....	....	....	....	....	....	....	....	....	....	....	....	....
1969-70	Niagara Falls Flyers	OHA	54	8	26	34	....	....	....	61	....	....	....	....	....	....	....	....	....	....	....	....	....	....	....	....	....	....
1970-71	Niagara Falls Flyers	OHA	59	14	18	32	....	....	....	112	....	....	....	....	....	....	....	....	....	....	....	....	....	....	....	....	....	....
1971-72	Columbus Seals	IHL	72	22	29	51	....	....	....	29	....	....	....	....	....	....	....	....	....	....	....	....	....	....	....	....	....	....
1972-73	Salt Lake Golden Eagles	WHL	72	16	27	43	....	....	....	55	....	....	....	....	....	....	....	....	....	....	9	2	5	7	11	....	....	....
1973-74	**California Golden Seals**	**NHL**	**2**	**0**	**0**	**0**	**0**	**0**	**0**	**0**	**0**	**0**	**0**	**2**	**0.0**	**0**	**0**	**2**	**2**	**0**	....	....	....	....	....	....	....	....
	Salt Lake Golden Eagles	WHL	76	34	34	68	....	....	....	72	....	....	....	....	....	....	....	....	....	....	5	1	0	1	9	....	....	....
1974-75	**California Golden Seals**	**NHL**	**25**	**4**	**7**	**11**	**4**	**5**	**9**	**8**	**1**	**0**	**0**	**29**	**13.8**	**20**	**2**	**28**	**0**	**–10**	....	....	....	....	....	....	....	....
1975-76	**California Golden Seals**	**NHL**	**46**	**1**	**11**	**12**	**1**	**9**	**10**	**26**	**1**	**0**	**0**	**46**	**2.2**	**19**	**5**	**17**	**0**	**–3**	....	....	....	....	....	....	....	....
	Salt Lake City Golden Eagles	CHL	20	9	8	17	....	....	....	21	....	....	....	....	....	....	....	....	....	....	5	1	0	1	10	....	....	....
1976-77	Salt Lake Golden Eagles	CHL	51	12	13	25	....	....	....	36	....	....	....	....	....	....	....	....	....	....	....	....	....	....	....	....	....	....
1977-78	Barrie Flyers	OHA Sr.	40	24	16	40	....	....	....	47	....	....	....	....	....	....	....	....	....	....	....	....	....	....	....	....	....	....
	NHL Totals		**73**	**5**	**18**	**23**	**5**	**14**	**19**	**34**	**2**	**0**	**0**	**77**	**6.5**	**39**	**7**	**47**	**2**		....	....	....	....	....	....	....	....

WHL Second All-Star Team (1974)

Signed as a free agent by **California**, October, 1971.

● KINSELLA, BRIAN Brian Kinsella C – R. 5'11", 180 lbs. b: Barrie, Ont., 2/11/1954. Washington's 6th choice, 91st overall, in 1974 Amateur Draft.

Season	Club	League	GP	G	A	Pts	AG	AA	APts	PIM	PP	SH	GW	S	%	TGF	PGF	TGA	PGA	+/–	GP	G	A	Pts	PIM	PP	SH	GW
1971-72	Oshawa Generals	OHA	44	13	19	32	....	....	....	48	....	....	....	....	....	....	....	....	....	....	....	....	....	....	....	....	....	....
1972-73	Oshawa Generals	OHA	48	28	57	85	....	....	....	49	....	....	....	....	....	....	....	....	....	....	....	....	....	....	....	....	....	....
1973-74	Oshawa Generals	OHA	64	36	43	79	....	....	....	95	....	....	....	....	....	....	....	....	....	....	....	....	....	....	....	....	....	....
1974-75	Richmond Robins	AHL	4	0	0	0	....	....	....	6	....	....	....	....	....	....	....	....	....	....	....	....	....	....	....	....	....	....
	Dayton Gems	IHL	40	15	15	30	....	....	....	35	....	....	....	....	....	....	....	....	....	....	....	....	....	....	....	....	....	....
	Kalamazoo Wings	IHL	10	3	7	10	....	....	....	36	....	....	....	....	....	....	....	....	....	....	....	....	....	....	....	....	....	....
1975-76	**Washington Capitals**	**NHL**	**4**	**0**	**1**	**1**	**0**	**1**	**1**	**0**	**0**	**0**	**0**	**11**	**0.0**	**1**	**0**	**3**	**0**	**–2**	....	....	....	....	....	....	....	....
	Springfield Indians	AHL	1	0	0	0	....	....	....	0	....	....	....	....	....	....	....	....	....	....	....	....	....	....	....	....	....	....
	Dayton Gems	IHL	74	43	45	88	....	....	....	43	....	....	....	....	....	....	....	....	....	....	15	10	7	17	12	....	....	....
1976-77	**Washington Capitals**	**NHL**	**6**	**0**	**0**	**0**	**0**	**0**	**0**	**0**	**0**	**0**	**0**	**3**	**0.0**	**0**	**0**	**4**	**2**	**–2**	....	....	....	....	....	....	....	....
	Springfield Indians	AHL	59	26	16	42	....	....	....	36	....	....	....	....	....	....	....	....	....	....	....	....	....	....	....	....	....	....
1977-78	Port Huron Flags	IHL	34	11	19	30	....	....	....	16	....	....	....	....	....	....	....	....	....	....	....	....	....	....	....	....	....	....
1978-79	Port Huron Flags	IHL	72	16	52	68	....	....	....	94	....	....	....	....	....	....	....	....	....	....	7	2	5	7	8	....	....	....
1979-80	Port Huron Flags	IHL	73	43	40	83	....	....	....	61	....	....	....	....	....	....	....	....	....	....	11	7	3	10	16	....	....	....
1980-81	Port Huron Flags	IHL	79	36	40	76	....	....	....	71	....	....	....	....	....	....	....	....	....	....	4	2	0	2	4	....	....	....
1981-82	Toledo Goaldiggers	IHL	80	36	45	81	....	....	....	71	....	....	....	....	....	....	....	....	....	....	12	8	7	15	10	....	....	....
1982-83	Toledo Goaldiggers	IHL	73	31	35	66	....	....	....	37	....	....	....	....	....	....	....	....	....	....	11	6	5	11	2	....	....	....
1983-84	Toledo Goaldiggers	IHL	41	18	19	37	....	....	....	27	....	....	....	....	....	....	....	....	....	....	....	....	....	....	....	....	....	....
	NHL Totals		**10**	**0**	**1**	**1**	**0**	**1**	**1**	**0**	**0**	**0**	**0**	**14**	**0.0**	**1**	**0**	**7**	**2**		....	....	....	....	....	....	....	....

● KIPRUSOFF, MARKO Marko Kiprusoff D – L. 6', 195 lbs. b: Turku, Finland, 6/6/1972. Montreal's 4th choice, 70th overall, in 1994 Entry Draft.

Season	Club	League	GP	G	A	Pts	AG	AA	APts	PIM	PP	SH	GW	S	%	TGF	PGF	TGA	PGA	+/–	GP	G	A	Pts	PIM	PP	SH	GW
1990-91	TPS Turku	Finland	3	0	0	0	....	....	....	0	....	....	....	....	....	....	....	....	....	....	....	....	....	....	....	....	....	....
1991-92	TPS Turku	Finland	23	0	2	2	....	....	....	0	....	....	....	....	....	....	....	....	....	....	....	....	....	....	....	....	....	....
	HPK Hameenlinna	Finland	3	0	0	0	....	....	....	0	....	....	....	....	....	....	....	....	....	....	....	....	....	....	....	....	....	....
	Finland	WJC-A	7	2	2	3	....	....	....	2	....	....	....	....	....	....	....	....	....	....	....	....	....	....	....	....	....	....
1992-93	TPS Turku	Finland	43	3	7	10	....	....	....	14	....	....	....	....	....	....	....	....	....	....	12	2	3	5	6	....	....	....
1993-94	TPS Turku	Finland	48	5	19	24	....	....	....	8	....	....	....	....	....	....	....	....	....	....	11	0	6	6	4	....	....	....
	Finland	Olympics	8	3	3	6	....	....	....	4	....	....	....	....	....	....	....	....	....	....	....	....	....	....	....	....	....	....
	Finland	WC-A	8	2	1	3	....	....	....	2	....	....	....	....	....	....	....	....	....	....	....	....	....	....	....	....	....	....
1994-95	TPS Turku	Finland	50	10	21	31	....	....	....	16	....	....	....	....	....	....	....	....	....	....	13	0	9	9	2	....	....	....
	Finland	WC-A	8	0	3	3	....	....	....	0	....	....	....	....	....	....	....	....	....	....	....	....	....	....	....	....	....	....
1995-96	**Montreal Canadiens**	**NHL**	**24**	**0**	**4**	**4**	**0**	**3**	**3**	**8**	**0**	**0**	**0**	**36**	**0.0**	**15**	**4**	**18**	**4**	**–3**	....	....	....	....	....	....	....	....
	Fredericton Canadiens	AHL	28	4	10	14	....	....	....	2	....	....	....	....	....	....	....	....	....	....	10	2	5	7	2	....	....	....
1996-97	Finland	W Cup	4	0	1	1	....	....	....	0	....	....	....	....	....	....	....	....	....	....	....	....	....	....	....	....	....	....
	Malmo IF	Sweden	50	10	18	28	....	....	....	24	....	....	....	....	....	....	....	....	....	....	4	0	0	0	0	....	....	....
	Finland	WC-A	8	0	2	2	....	....	....	2	....	....	....	....	....	....	....	....	....	....	....	....	....	....	....	....	....	....
1997-98	Malmo IF	Sweden	46	7	16	23	....	....	....	23	....	....	....	....	....	....	....	....	....	....	....	....	....	....	....	....	....	....
	Finland	WC-A	10	2	1	3	....	....	....	4	....	....	....	....	....	....	....	....	....	....	....	....	....	....	....	....	....	....
	NHL Totals		**24**	**0**	**4**	**4**	**0**	**3**	**3**	**8**	**0**	**0**	**0**	**36**	**0.0**	**15**	**4**	**18**	**4**		....	....	....	....	....	....	....	....

● KIRTON, MARK Mark Kirton C – L. 5'10", 170 lbs. b: Regina, Sask., 2/3/1958. Toronto's 2nd choice, 48th overall, in 1978 Amateur Draft.

Season	Club	League	GP	G	A	Pts	AG	AA	APts	PIM	PP	SH	GW	S	%	TGF	PGF	TGA	PGA	+/–	GP	G	A	Pts	PIM	PP	SH	GW
1975-76	Peterborough Petes	OHA	65	22	38	60	....	....	....	10	....	....	....	....	....	....	....	....	....	....	....	....	....	....	....	....	....	....
1976-77	Peterborough Petes	OHA	48	18	24	42	....	....	....	41	....	....	....	....	....	....	....	....	....	....	4	6	1	7	0	....	....	....
1977-78	Peterborough Petes	OHA	68	27	44	71	....	....	....	29	....	....	....	....	....	....	....	....	....	....	21	12	14	26	14	....	....	....
1978-79	New Brunswick Hawks	AHL	80	20	30	50	....	....	....	14	....	....	....	....	....	....	....	....	....	....	5	0	0	0	2	....	....	....
1979-80	**Toronto Maple Leafs**	**NHL**	**2**	**1**	**0**	**1**	**1**	**0**	**1**	**2**	**0**	**0**	**0**	**3**	**33.3**	**1**	**0**	**2**	**1**	**0**	....	....	....	....	....	....	....	....
	New Brunswick Hawks	AHL	61	19	42	61	....	....	....	33	....	....	....	....	....	....	....	....	....	....	17	7	11	18	16	....	....	....
1980-81	**Toronto Maple Leafs**	**NHL**	**11**	**0**	**0**	**0**	**0**	**0**	**0**	**0**	**0**	**0**	**0**	**5**	**0.0**	**1**	**0**	**8**	**6**	**–1**	....	....	....	....	....	....	....	....
	Detroit Red Wings	**NHL**	**50**	**18**	**13**	**31**	**15**	**9**	**24**	**24**	**6**	**1**	**3**	**97**	**18.6**	**41**	**12**	**78**	**19**	**–30**	....	....	....	....	....	....	....	....
1981-82	**Detroit Red Wings**	**NHL**	**74**	**14**	**28**	**42**	**11**	**19**	**30**	**62**	**0**	**1**	**0**	**121**	**11.6**	**65**	**3**	**112**	**32**	**–18**	....	....	....	....	....	....	....	....
1982-83	**Detroit Red Wings**	**NHL**	**10**	**1**	**1**	**2**	**1**	**1**	**2**	**6**	**0**	**0**	**0**	**15**	**6.7**	**4**	**0**	**6**	**1**	**–1**	....	....	....	....	....	....	....	....
	Vancouver Canucks	**NHL**	**31**	**4**	**6**	**10**	**3**	**4**	**7**	**4**	**0**	**0**	**1**	**34**	**11.8**	**17**	**0**	**25**	**13**	**+5**	**4**	**1**	**2**	**3**	**7**	**0**	**0**	**0**
1983-84	**Vancouver Canucks**	**NHL**	**26**	**2**	**3**	**5**	**2**	**2**	**4**	**2**	**0**	**0**	**0**	**26**	**7.7**	**6**	**0**	**33**	**19**	**–8**	....	....	....	....	....	....	....	....
	Fredericton Express	AHL	35	8	10	18	....	....	....	8	....	....	....	....	....	....	....	....	....	....	7	2	3	5	6	....	....	....
1984-85	**Vancouver Canucks**	**NHL**	**62**	**17**	**5**	**22**	**14**	**3**	**17**	**21**	**0**	**1**	**1**	**92**	**18.5**	**28**	**0**	**84**	**34**	**–22**	....	....	....	....	....	....	....	....
	Fredericton Express	AHL	15	5	9	14	....	....	....	18	....	....	....	....	....	....	....	....	....	....	....	....	....	....	....	....	....	....
1985-86	Fredericton Express	AHL	77	23	36	59	....	....	....	33	....	....	....	....	....	....	....	....	....	....	6	2	2	4	4	....	....	....
1986-87	Fredericton Express	AHL	80	27	37	64	....	....	....	20	....	....	....	....	....	....	....	....	....	....	....	....	....	....	....	....	....	....
1987-88	Newmarket Saints	AHL	73	17	30	47	....	....	....	42	....	....	....	....	....	....	....	....	....	....	....	....	....	....	....	....	....	....
1988-89	Newmarket Saints	AHL	37	4	8	12	....	....	....	18	....	....	....	....	....	....	....	....	....	....	....	....	....	....	....	....	....	....
	NHL Totals		**266**	**57**	**56**	**113**	**47**	**38**	**85**	**121**	**6**	**3**	**5**	**393**	**14.5**	**163**	**15**	**348**	**125**		**4**	**1**	**2**	**3**	**7**	**0**	**0**	**0**

Memorial Cup All-Star Team (1978) • Won George Parsons Trophy (Memorial Cup Tournament Most Sportsmanlike Player) (1978)

Traded to **Detroit** by **Toronto** for Jim Rutherford, December 4, 1980. Traded to **Vancouver** by **Detroit** for Ivan Boldirev, January 17, 1983. Signed as a free agent by **Toronto**, August 15, 1987.

● KISIO, KELLY Kelly Kisio C – R. 5'10", 185 lbs. b: Peace River, Alta., 9/18/1959.

Season	Club	League	GP	G	A	Pts	AG	AA	APts	PIM	PP	SH	GW	S	%	TGF	PGF	TGA	PGA	+/–	GP	G	A	Pts	PIM	PP	SH	GW
1976-77	Red Deer Rustlers	AJHL	60	53	48	101	....	....	....	101	....	....	....	....	....	....	....	....	....	....	....	....	....	....	....	....	....	....
1977-78	Red Deer Rustlers	AJHL	58	74	68	142	....	....	....	66	....	....	....	....	....	....	....	....	....	....	....	....	....	....	....	....	....	....
1978-79	Calgary Wranglers	WHL	70	60	61	121	....	....	....	73	....	....	....	....	....	....	....	....	....	....	....	....	....	....	....	....	....	....
1979-80	Calgary Wranglers	WHL	71	65	73	138	....	....	....	64	....	....	....	....	....	....	....	....	....	....	....	....	....	....	....	....	....	....
1980-81	Adirondack Red Wings	AHL	41	10	14	24	....	....	....	43	....	....	....	....	....	....	....	....	....	....	....	....	....	....	....	....	....	....
	Kalamazoo Wings	IHL	31	27	16	43	....	....	....	48	....	....	....	....	....	....	....	....	....	....	8	7	7	14	13	....	....	....
1981-82	Dallas Black Hawks	CHL	78	*62	39	101	....	....	....	59	....	....	....	....	....	....	....	....	....	....	16	*12	*17	*29	38	....	....	....
1982-83	HC Davos	Switz.	40	49	38	87	....	....	....	....	....	....	....	....	....	....	....	....	....	....	....	....	....	....	....	....	....	....
	Detroit Red Wings	**NHL**	**15**	**4**	**3**	**7**	**3**	**2**	**5**	**0**	**0**	**0**	**0**	**16**	**25.0**	**13**	**1**	**14**	**0**	**–2**	....	....	....	....	....	....	....	....
1983-84	**Detroit Red Wings**	**NHL**	**70**	**23**	**37**	**60**	**19**	**25**	**44**	**34**	**1**	**0**	**2**	**146**	**15.8**	**81**	**19**	**47**	**1**	**+16**	**4**	**1**	**0**	**1**	**4**	**0**	**0**	**0**
1984-85	**Detroit Red Wings**	**NHL**	**75**	**20**	**41**	**61**	**16**	**28**	**44**	**56**	**5**	**0**	**0**	**126**	**15.9**	**80**	**19**	**59**	**0**	**+2**	**3**	**0**	**2**	**2**	**2**	**0**	**0**	**0**
1985-86	**Detroit Red Wings**	**NHL**	**76**	**21**	**48**	**69**	**17**	**32**	**49**	**85**	**7**	**3**	**0**	**140**	**15.0**	**94**	**37**	**85**	**7**	**–21**	....	....	....	....	....	....	....	....
1986-87	**New York Rangers**	**NHL**	**70**	**24**	**40**	**64**	**21**	**29**	**50**	**73**	**4**	**2**	**1**	**137**	**17.5**	**87**	**21**	**89**	**18**	**–5**	**4**	**0**	**1**	**1**	**2**	**0**	**0**	**0**
1987-88	**New York Rangers**	**NHL**	**77**	**23**	**55**	**78**	**20**	**39**	**59**	**88**	**9**	**1**	**1**	**145**	**15.9**	**104**	**41**	**80**	**25**	**+8**	....	....	....	....	....	....	....	....
1988-89	**New York Rangers**	**NHL**	**70**	**26**	**36**	**62**	**22**	**25**	**47**	**91**	**2**	**0**	**4**	**128**	**20.3**	**83**	**13**	**70**	**14**	**+14**	**4**	**0**	**0**	**0**	**9**	**0**	**0**	**0**
1989-90	**New York Rangers**	**NHL**	**68**	**22**	**44**	**66**	**19**	**31**	**50**	**105**	**7**	**2**	**1**	**128**	**17.2**	**101**	**43**	**70**	**23**	**+11**	**10**	**2**	**8**	**10**	**8**	**0**	**1**	**0**
1990-91	**New York Rangers**	**NHL**	**51**	**15**	**20**	**35**	**14**	**15**	**29**	**58**	**7**	**1**	**2**	**74**	**20.3**	**46**	**18**	**35**	**10**	**+3**	....	....	....	....	....	....	....	....
1991-92	**San Jose Sharks**	**NHL**	**48**	**11**	**26**	**37**	**10**	**20**	**30**	**54**	**2**	**3**	**2**	**68**	**16.2**	**50**	**18**	**59**	**20**	**–7**	....	....	....	....	....	....	....	....

			REGULAR SEASON																		PLAYOFFS							
Season	Club	League	GP	G	A	Pts	AG	AA	APts	PIM	PP	SH	GW	S	%	TGF	PGF	TGA	PGA	+/–	GP	G	A	Pts	PIM	PP	SH	GW
1992-93	**San Jose Sharks**	**NHL**	78	26	52	78	22	36	58	90	9	2	2	152	17.1	104	46	101	28	–15	....	....	....	....	....	....	....	....
1993-94	**Calgary Flames**	**NHL**	51	7	23	30	7	18	25	28	1	0	1	62	11.3	44	21	35	6	–6	7	0	2	2	8	0	0	0
1994-95	**Calgary Flames**	**NHL**	12	7	4	11	12	6	18	6	5	1	0	26	26.9	13	5	8	2	+2	7	3	2	5	19	1	0	0
	NHL Totals		761	229	429	658	202	306	508	768	59	15	16	1348	17.0	900	302	752	154		39	6	15	21	52	1	1	0

Played in NHL All-Star Game (1993)

Signed as a free agent by **Detroit**, March 2, 1983. Traded to **NY Rangers** by **Detroit** with Lane Lambert and Jim Leavins for Glen Hanlon and NY Rangers' 3rd round choice (Dennis Holland) in 1987 Entry Draft and 3rd round choice (Guy Dupuis) in 1988 Entry Draft, July 26, 1986. Claimed by **Minnesota** from **NY Rangers** in Expansion Draft, May 30, 1991. Traded to **San Jose** by **Minnesota** for Shane Churla, June 3, 1991. Signed as a free agent by **Calgary**, August 18, 1993.

• KITCHEN, BILL

Bill Kitchen D – L. 6'1", 200 lbs. b: Schomberg, Ont., 10/2/1960.

Season	Club	League	GP	G	A	Pts	AG	AA	APts	PIM	PP	SH	GW	S	%	TGF	PGF	TGA	PGA	+/–	GP	G	A	Pts	PIM	PP	SH	GW
1977-78	Ottawa 67's	OHA	67	5	6	11	....	....	....	54	....	....	....	....	....	....	....	....	....	....	....	....	....	....	....	....	....	....
1978-79	Ottawa 67's	OHA	55	3	16	19	....	....	....	188	....	....	....	....	....	....	....	....	....	....	4	0	1	1	14	....	....	....
1979-80	Ottawa 67's	OHA	63	7	19	26	....	....	....	195	....	....	....	....	....	....	....	....	....	....	11	1	8	9	21	....	....	....
	Canada	WJC-A	5	0	1	1	....	....	....	10	....	....	....	....	....	....	....	....	....	....	....	....	....	....	....	....	....	....
	Nova Scotia Voyageurs	AHL	....	....	....	....	....	....	....	....	....	....	....	....	....	....	....	....	....	....	2	0	1	1	0	....	....	....
1980-81	Nova Scotia Voyageurs	AHL	65	2	7	9	....	....	....	135	....	....	....	....	....	....	....	....	....	....	6	0	1	1	5	....	....	....
1981-82	**Montreal Canadiens**	**NHL**	1	0	0	0	0	0	0	7	0	0	0	0	0.0	0	0	2	2	0	3	0	1	1	0	0	0	0
	Nova Scotia Voyageurs	AHL	71	3	17	20	....	....	....	135	....	....	....	....	....	....	....	....	....	....	6	2	0	2	11	....	....	....
1982-83	**Montreal Canadiens**	**NHL**	8	0	0	0	0	0	0	4	0	0	0	2	0.0	2	1	3	0	–2	....	....	....	....	....	....	....	....
	Nova Scotia Voyageurs	AHL	53	3	11	14	....	....	....	71	....	....	....	....	....	....	....	....	....	....	....	....	....	....	....	....	....	....
1983-84	**Montreal Canadiens**	**NHL**	3	0	0	0	0	0	0	2	0	0	0	3	0.0	2	1	4	3	0	....	....	....	....	....	....	....	....
	Nova Scotia Voyageurs	AHL	68	4	20	24	....	....	....	193	....	....	....	....	....	....	....	....	....	....	10	1	1	2	8	....	....	....
1984-85	**Toronto Maple Leafs**	**NHL**	29	1	4	5	1	3	4	27	0	0	0	21	4.8	30	0	48	12	–6	....	....	....	....	....	....	....	....
	St. Catharines Saints	AHL	31	3	7	10	....	....	....	52	....	....	....	....	....	....	....	....	....	....	....	....	....	....	....	....	....	....
1985-86	St. Catharines Saints	AHL	72	7	32	39	....	....	....	109	....	....	....	....	....	....	....	....	....	....	12	0	2	2	19	....	....	....
	NHL Totals		41	1	4	5	1	3	4	40	0	0	0	26	3.8	34	2	57	17		3	0	1	1	0	0	0	0

Signed as a free agent by **Montreal**, October 23, 1979. Signed as a free agent by **Toronto**, August 16, 1984.

• KITCHEN, MIKE

Mike Kitchen D – L. 5'10", 185 lbs. b: Newmarket, Ont., 2/1/1956. Kansas City's 2nd choice, 38th overall, in 1976 Amateur Draft.

Season	Club	League	GP	G	A	Pts	AG	AA	APts	PIM	PP	SH	GW	S	%	TGF	PGF	TGA	PGA	+/–	GP	G	A	Pts	PIM	PP	SH	GW
1973-74	Toronto Marlboros	OHA	69	3	17	20	....	....	....	145	....	....	....	....	....	....	....	....	....	....	....	....	....	....	....	....	....	....
1974-75	Toronto Marlboros	OHA	68	5	30	35	....	....	....	136	....	....	....	....	....	....	....	....	....	....	21	1	9	10	35	....	....	....
1975-76	Toronto Marlboros	OHA	65	6	18	24	....	....	....	148	....	....	....	....	....	....	....	....	....	....	10	0	2	2	26	....	....	....
1976-77	**Colorado Rockies**	**NHL**	60	1	8	9	1	6	7	36	0	0	0	46	2.2	58	6	57	3	–2	....	....	....	....	....	....	....	....
	Rhode Island Reds	AHL	14	0	10	10	....	....	....	14	....	....	....	....	....	....	....	....	....	....	....	....	....	....	....	....	....	....
1977-78	**Colorado Rockies**	**NHL**	61	2	17	19	2	14	16	45	0	0	1	57	3.5	54	3	75	12	–12	2	0	0	0	2	0	0	0
1978-79	**Colorado Rockies**	**NHL**	53	1	4	5	1	3	4	28	0	0	0	22	4.5	25	1	51	8	–19	....	....	....	....	....	....	....	....
1979-80	**Colorado Rockies**	**NHL**	42	1	6	7	1	5	6	25	0	0	0	31	3.2	16	1	29	4	–10	....	....	....	....	....	....	....	....
	Fort Worth Texans	CHL	30	0	9	9	....	....	....	22	....	....	....	....	....	....	....	....	....	....	15	0	1	1	16	....	....	....
1980-81	**Colorado Rockies**	**NHL**	75	1	7	8	1	5	6	100	0	0	0	49	2.0	47	2	104	21	–38	....	....	....	....	....	....	....	....
1981-82	**Colorado Rockies**	**NHL**	63	1	8	9	1	5	6	60	0	0	0	35	2.9	59	0	95	10	–18	....	....	....	....	....	....	....	....
	Fort Worth Texans	CHL	13	1	5	6	....	....	....	16	....	....	....	....	....	....	....	....	....	....	....	....	....	....	....	....	....	....
1982-83	**New Jersey Devils**	**NHL**	77	4	8	12	3	6	9	52	0	1	0	48	8.7	47	0	106	34	–25	....	....	....	....	....	....	....	....
1983-84	**New Jersey Devils**	**NHL**	43	1	4	5	1	3	4	24	0	0	0	37	2.7	21	2	45	11	–15	....	....	....	....	....	....	....	....
1984-85	Maine Mariners	AHL	12	0	1	1	....	....	....	10	....	....	....	....	....	....	....	....	....	....	....	....	....	....	....	....	....	....
	NHL Totals		474	12	62	74	11	47	58	370	0	1	1	323	3.7	327	15	562	111		2	0	0	0	2	0	0	0

OHA First All-Star Team (1975) • Memorial Cup All-Star Team (1985)

Rights transferred to **Colorado** when **Kansas City** franchise relocated, July 15, 1976. Transferred to **New Jersey** after **Colorado** franchise relocated, June 30, 1982.

• KJELLBERG, PATRIK

Patrik Kjellberg LW – L. 6'2", 196 lbs. b: Falun, Sweden 6/17/1969. Montreal's 4th choice, 83rd overall, in 1988 Entry Draft.

Season	Club	League	GP	G	A	Pts	AG	AA	APts	PIM	PP	SH	GW	S	%	TGF	PGF	TGA	PGA	+/–	GP	G	A	Pts	PIM	PP	SH	GW
1986-87	Falun	Sweden 2	27	11	13	24	....	....	....	14	....	....	....	....	....	....	....	....	....	....	....	....	....	....	....	....	....	....
1987-88	Falun	Sweden 2	29	15	10	25	....	....	....	6	....	....	....	....	....	....	....	....	....	....	....	....	....	....	....	....	....	....
1988-89	AIK Solna	Sweden	25	7	9	16	....	....	....	8	....	....	....	....	....	....	....	....	....	....	....	....	....	....	....	....	....	....
1989-90	AIK Solna	Sweden	33	8	16	24	....	....	....	6	....	....	....	....	....	....	....	....	....	....	3	1	0	1	0	....	....	....
1990-91	AIK Solna	Sweden	38	4	11	15	....	....	....	18	....	....	....	....	....	....	....	....	....	....	....	....	....	....	....	....	....	....
1991-92	AIK Solna	Sweden	40	20	13	33	....	....	....	14	....	....	....	....	....	....	....	....	....	....	3	1	0	1	2	....	....	....
	Sweden	Olympics	8	1	3	4	....	....	....	0	....	....	....	....	....	....	....	....	....	....	....	....	....	....	....	....	....	....
	Sweden	WC-A	8	2	2	4	....	....	....	2	....	....	....	....	....	....	....	....	....	....	....	....	....	....	....	....	....	....
1992-93	**Montreal Canadiens**	**NHL**	7	0	0	0	0	0	0	2	0	0	0	7	0.0	0	0	5	2	–3	....	....	....	....	....	....	....	....
	Fredericton Canadiens	AHL	41	10	27	37	....	....	....	14	....	....	....	....	....	....	....	....	....	....	5	2	2	4	0	....	....	....
1993-94	HV-71 Jonkoping	Sweden	40	11	17	28	....	....	....	18	....	....	....	....	....	....	....	....	....	....	....	....	....	....	....	....	....	....
	Sweden	Olympics	8	0	1	1	....	....	....	2	....	....	....	....	....	....	....	....	....	....	....	....	....	....	....	....	....	....
1994-95	HV-71 Jonkoping	Sweden	29	5	15	20	....	....	....	12	....	....	....	....	....	....	....	....	....	....	....	....	....	....	....	....	....	....
1995-96	Djurgarden Stockholm	Sweden	40	9	7	16	....	....	....	10	....	....	....	....	....	....	....	....	....	....	4	0	2	2	2	....	....	....
1996-97	Djurgarden Stockholm	Sweden	49	29	11	40	....	....	....	18	....	....	....	....	....	....	....	....	....	....	4	2	3	5	4	....	....	....
1997-98	Djurgarden Stockholm	Sweden	46	30	18	48	....	....	....	16	....	....	....	....	....	....	....	....	....	....	15	7	3	10	12	....	....	....
	NHL Totals		7	0	0	0	0	0	0	2	0	0	0	7	0.0	0	0	5	2		....	....	....	....	....	....	....	....

EJC-A All-Star Team (1987)

Signed as a free agent by **Nashville**, June 26, 1998.

• KLASSEN, RALPH

Ralph Klassen C – L. 5'11", 175 lbs. b: Humboldt, Sask., 9/15/1955. California's 1st choice, 3rd overall, in 1975 Amateur Draft

Season	Club	League	GP	G	A	Pts	AG	AA	APts	PIM	PP	SH	GW	S	%	TGF	PGF	TGA	PGA	+/–	GP	G	A	Pts	PIM	PP	SH	GW
1970-71	Saskatoon Blades	WCJHL	61	1	8	9	....	....	....	29	....	....	....	....	....	....	....	....	....	....	....	....	....	....	....	....	....	....
1971-72	Saskatoon Blades	WCJHL	62	17	38	55	....	....	....	64	....	....	....	....	....	....	....	....	....	....	....	....	....	....	....	....	....	....
1972-73	Saskatoon Blades	WCJHL	68	19	47	66	....	....	....	80	....	....	....	....	....	....	....	....	....	....	....	....	....	....	....	....	....	....
1973-74	Saskatoon Blades	WCJHL	68	23	54	77	....	....	....	110	....	....	....	....	....	....	....	....	....	....	6	0	3	3	7	....	....	....
1974-75	Saskatoon Blades	WCJHL	41	21	47	68	....	....	....	34	....	....	....	....	....	....	....	....	....	....	17	5	*23	*28	14	....	....	....
	Canada	WJC-A	4	0	3	3	....	....	....	0	....	....	....	....	....	....	....	....	....	....	....	....	....	....	....	....	....	....
1975-76	**California Golden Seals**	**NHL**	71	6	15	21	6	12	18	26	2	0	0	96	6.3	35	11	71	21	–26	....	....	....	....	....	....	....	....
	Salt Lake Golden Eagles	CHL	4	3	3	6	....	....	....	4	....	....	....	....	....	....	....	....	....	....	....	....	....	....	....	....	....	....
1976-77	**Cleveland Barons**	**NHL**	80	14	18	32	13	15	28	23	4	1	1	131	10.7	50	10	100	35	–25	....	....	....	....	....	....	....	....
	Canada	WEC-A	10	1	5	6	....	....	....	0	....	....	....	....	....	....	....	....	....	....	....	....	....	....	....	....	....	....
1977-78	**Cleveland Barons**	**NHL**	13	2	1	3	2	1	3	6	0	1	0	14	14.3	6	0	17	9	–2	....	....	....	....	....	....	....	....
	Colorado Rockies	**NHL**	44	6	9	15	6	7	13	8	3	0	0	47	12.8	37	11	55	10	–19	2	0	0	0	0	0	0	0
1978-79	**Colorado Rockies**	**NHL**	64	6	13	19	5	10	15	12	1	1	2	100	6.0	32	2	87	32	–25	....	....	....	....	....	....	....	....
	Philadelphia Firebirds	AHL	18	3	9	12	....	....	....	2	....	....	....	....	....	....	....	....	....	....	....	....	....	....	....	....	....	....
1979-80	**St. Louis Blues**	**NHL**	80	9	16	25	8	12	20	10	0	0	3	100	9.0	39	0	78	20	–19	3	0	0	0	0	0	0	0
1980-81	**St. Louis Blues**	**NHL**	66	6	12	18	5	8	13	23	0	1	0	65	9.2	29	0	60	26	–5	11	2	0	2	2	0	0	0
1981-82	**St. Louis Blues**	**NHL**	45	3	7	10	2	5	7	6	0	1	1	25	12.0	16	2	40	23	–3	10	2	2	4	10	0	0	0
1982-83	**St. Louis Blues**	**NHL**	29	0	2	2	0	1	1	6	0	0	0	14	0.0	4	0	13	6	–3	....	....	....	....	....	....	....	....
	Salt Lake Golden Eagles	CHL	21	9	10	19	....	....	....	8	....	....	....	....	....	....	....	....	....	....	6	2	6	8	5	....	....	....
1983-84	**St. Louis Blues**	**NHL**	5	0	0	0	0	0	0	0	0	0	0	5	0.0	0	0	6	0	–6	....	....	....	....	....	....	....	....
	NHL Totals		497	52	93	145	47	71	118	120	10	5	7	597	8.7	248	36	526	182		26	4	2	6	12	0	0	0

Transferred to **Cleveland** after **California** franchise relocated, June, 1976. Traded to **Colorado** by **Cleveland** with Fred Ahern for Rick Jodzio and Chuck Arnason, January 9, 1978. Claimed by **Hartford** from **Colorado** in Expansion Draft, June 13, 1979. Traded to **NY Islanders** by **Hartford** for Terry Richardson, June 14, 1979. Traded to **St. Louis** by **NY Islanders** to complete three-team transaction that sent Barry Gibbs to NY Islanders and Tommy Williams to LA Kings (June 9, 1979), June 14, 1979.

• KLATT, TRENT

Trent Klatt RW – R. 6'1", 205 lbs. b: Robbinsdale, MN, 1/30/1971 Washington's 5th choice, 82nd overall, in 1989 Entry Draft.

Season	Club	League	GP	G	A	Pts	AG	AA	APts	PIM	PP	SH	GW	S	%	TGF	PGF	TGA	PGA	+/–	GP	G	A	Pts	PIM	PP	SH	GW
1988-89	Osseo High School	H.S.	22	24	39	63	....	....	....	....	....	....	....	....	....	....	....	....	....	....	....	....	....	....	....	....	....	....
1989-90	University of Minnesota	WCHA	38	22	14	36	....	....	....	16	....	....	....	....	....	....	....	....	....	....	....	....	....	....	....	....	....	....
1990-91	University of Minnesota	WCHA	39	16	28	44	....	....	....	58	....	....	....	....	....	....	....	....	....	....	....	....	....	....	....	....	....	....

			REGULAR SEASON																		PLAYOFFS							
Season	**Club**	**League**	**GP**	**G**	**A**	**Pts**	**AG**	**AA**	**APts**	**PIM**	**PP**	**SH**	**GW**	**S**	**%**	**TGF**	**PGF**	**TGA**	**PGA**	**+/–**	**GP**	**G**	**A**	**Pts**	**PIM**	**PP**	**SH**	**GW**
1991-92	University of Minnesota	WCHA	41	27	36	63	....	....	....	76	....	....	....	....	....	....	....	....	....	....	....	....	....	....	....	....	....	....
	Minnesota North Stars	**NHL**	**1**	**0**	**0**	**0**	**0**	**0**	**0**	**0**	**0**	**0**	**0**	**1**	**0.0**	**1**	**0**	**1**	**0**	**0**	**6**	**0**	**0**	**0**	**2**	**0**	**0**	**0**
1992-93	**Minnesota North Stars**	**NHL**	**47**	**4**	**19**	**23**	**3**	**13**	**16**	**38**	**1**	**0**	**0**	**69**	**5.8**	**31**	**4**	**26**	**1**	**+2**	....	....	....	....	....	....	....	....
	Kalamazoo Wings	IHL	31	8	11	19	....	....	....	18	....	....	....	....	....	....	....	....	....	....	....	....	....	....	....	....	....	....
1993-94	**Dallas Stars**	**NHL**	**61**	**14**	**24**	**38**	**13**	**19**	**32**	**30**	**3**	**0**	**2**	**86**	**16.3**	**55**	**12**	**30**	**0**	**+13**	**9**	**2**	**1**	**3**	**4**	**1**	**0**	**0**
	Kalamazoo Wings	IHL	6	3	2	5	....	....	....	4	....	....	....	....	....	....	....	....	....	....	....	....	....	....	....	....	....	....
1994-95	**Dallas Stars**	**NHL**	**47**	**12**	**10**	**22**	**21**	**15**	**36**	**26**	**5**	**0**	**3**	**91**	**13.2**	**39**	**18**	**23**	**0**	**–2**	**5**	**1**	**0**	**1**	**0**	**1**	**0**	**0**
1995-96	**Dallas Stars**	**NHL**	**22**	**4**	**4**	**8**	**4**	**3**	**7**	**23**	**0**	**0**	**1**	**37**	**10.8**	**14**	**6**	**8**	**0**	**0**	....	....	....	....	....	....	....	....
	Michigan K-Wings	IHL	2	1	2	3	....	....	....	5	....	....	....	....	....	....	....	....	....	....	....	....	....	....	....	....	....	....
	Philadelphia Flyers	**NHL**	**49**	**3**	**8**	**11**	**3**	**7**	**10**	**21**	**0**	**0**	**1**	**64**	**4.7**	**13**	**1**	**15**	**5**	**+2**	**12**	**4**	**1**	**5**	**0**	**0**	**0**	**0**
1996-97	**Philadelphia Flyers**	**NHL**	**76**	**24**	**21**	**45**	**26**	**19**	**45**	**20**	**5**	**5**	**5**	**131**	**18.3**	**63**	**10**	**57**	**13**	**+9**	**19**	**4**	**3**	**7**	**12**	**0**	**0**	**2**
1997-98	**Philadelphia Flyers**	**NHL**	**82**	**14**	**28**	**42**	**16**	**27**	**43**	**16**	**5**	**0**	**3**	**143**	**9.8**	**63**	**18**	**63**	**20**	**+2**	**5**	**0**	**0**	**0**	**0**	**0**	**0**	**0**
	NHL Totals		**385**	**75**	**114**	**189**	**86**	**103**	**189**	**174**	**19**	**5**	**15**	**622**	**12.1**	**279**	**69**	**223**	**39**		**56**	**11**	**5**	**16**	**18**	**2**	**0**	**2**

Traded to **Minnesota** by **Washington** with Steve Maltais for Shawn Chambers, June 21, 1991. Transferred to **Dallas** after **Minnesota** franchise relocated, June 9, 1993. Traded to **Philadelphia** by **Dallas** for Brent Fedyk, December 13, 1995.

• KLEE, KEN

Ken Klee RW – R. 6′1″, 205 lbs. b: Indianapolis, IN, 4/24/1971. Washington's 11th choice, 177th overall, in 1990 Entry Draft.

1989-90	Bowling Green University	CCHA	39	0	5	5	....	....	....	52	....	....	....	....	....	....	....	....	....	....	....	....	....	....	....	....	....	....
1990-91	Bowling Green University	CCHA	37	7	28	35	....	....	....	50	....	....	....	....	....	....	....	....	....	....	....	....	....	....	....	....	....	....
1991-92	Bowling Green University	CCHA	10	0	1	1	....	....	....	14	....	....	....	....	....	....	....	....	....	....	....	....	....	....	....	....	....	....
	United States	WC-A	2	0	0	0	....	....	....	0	....	....	....	....	....	....	....	....	....	....	....	....	....	....	....	....	....	....
1992-93	Baltimore Skipjacks	AHL	77	4	14	18	....	....	....	93	....	....	....	....	....	....	....	....	....	....	7	0	1	1	15	....	....	....
1993-94	Portland Pirates	AHL	65	2	9	11	....	....	....	87	....	....	....	....	....	....	....	....	....	....	17	1	2	3	14	....	....	....
1994-95	**Washington Capitals**	**NHL**	**23**	**3**	**1**	**4**	**5**	**1**	**6**	**41**	**0**	**0**	**0**	**18**	**16.7**	**11**	**0**	**9**	**0**	**+2**	**7**	**0**	**0**	**0**	**4**	**0**	**0**	**0**
	Portland Pirates	AHL	49	5	7	12	....	....	....	89	....	....	....	....	....	....	....	....	....	....	....	....	....	....	....	....	....	....
1995-96	**Washington Capitals**	**NHL**	**66**	**8**	**3**	**11**	**8**	**2**	**10**	**60**	**0**	**1**	**2**	**76**	**10.5**	**28**	**3**	**29**	**3**	**–1**	**1**	**0**	**0**	**0**	**0**	**0**	**0**	**0**
1996-97	**Washington Capitals**	**NHL**	**80**	**3**	**8**	**11**	**3**	**7**	**10**	**115**	**0**	**0**	**2**	**108**	**2.8**	**39**	**0**	**60**	**16**	**–5**	....	....	....	....	....	....	....	....
	United States	WC-A	8	1	0	1	....	....	....	12	....	....	....	....	....	....	....	....	....	....	....	....	....	....	....	....	....	....
1997-98	**Washington Capitals**	**NHL**	**51**	**4**	**2**	**6**	**5**	**2**	**7**	**46**	**0**	**0**	**1**	**44**	**9.1**	**16**	**0**	**22**	**3**	**–3**	**9**	**1**	**0**	**1**	**10**	**0**	**0**	**0**
	NHL Totals		**220**	**18**	**14**	**32**	**21**	**12**	**33**	**262**	**0**	**1**	**5**	**246**	**7.3**	**94**	**3**	**120**	**22**		**17**	**1**	**0**	**1**	**14**	**0**	**0**	**0**

• KLEINENDORST, SCOT

Scot Kleinendorst D – L. 6′3″, 215 lbs. b: Grand Rapids, MN, 1/16/1960. NY Rangers' 3rd choice, 98th overall, in 1980 Entry Draft.

1978-79	Providence College	ECAC	25	4	4	8	....	....	....	27	....	....	....	....	....	....	....	....	....	....	....	....	....	....	....	....	....	....
1979-80	Providence College	ECAC	30	1	12	13	....	....	....	38	....	....	....	....	....	....	....	....	....	....	....	....	....	....	....	....	....	....
1980-81	Providence College	ECAC	32	3	31	34	....	....	....	75	....	....	....	....	....	....	....	....	....	....	....	....	....	....	....	....	....	....
1981-82	Providence College	ECAC	33	11	27	38	....	....	....	85	....	....	....	....	....	....	....	....	....	....	....	....	....	....	....	....	....	....
	United States	WEC-A	4	0	0	0	....	....	....	2	....	....	....	....	....	....	....	....	....	....	....	....	....	....	....	....	....	....
	Springfield Indians	AHL	5	0	4	4	....	....	....	11	....	....	....	....	....	....	....	....	....	....	....	....	....	....	....	....	....	....
1982-83	**New York Rangers**	**NHL**	**30**	**2**	**9**	**11**	**2**	**6**	**8**	**8**	**1**	**0**	**0**	**16**	**12.5**	**31**	**5**	**24**	**5**	**+7**	**6**	**0**	**2**	**2**	**2**	**0**	**0**	**0**
	Tulsa Oilers	CHL	10	0	7	7	....	....	....	2	....	....	....	....	....	....	....	....	....	....	....	....	....	....	....	....	....	....
1983-84	**New York Rangers**	**NHL**	**23**	**0**	**2**	**2**	**0**	**1**	**1**	**35**	**0**	**0**	**0**	**13**	**0.0**	**11**	**1**	**23**	**3**	**–10**	....	....	....	....	....	....	....	....
	Tulsa Oilers	CHL	10	4	5	9	....	....	....	4	....	....	....	....	....	....	....	....	....	....	....	....	....	....	....	....	....	....
1984-85	**Hartford Whalers**	**NHL**	**35**	**1**	**8**	**9**	**1**	**5**	**6**	**69**	**0**	**0**	**0**	**16**	**6.3**	**29**	**1**	**49**	**11**	**–10**	....	....	....	....	....	....	....	....
	Binghamton Whalers	AHL	30	3	7	10	....	....	....	42	....	....	....	....	....	....	....	....	....	....	....	....	....	....	....	....	....	....
1985-86	**Hartford Whalers**	**NHL**	**41**	**2**	**7**	**9**	**2**	**5**	**7**	**62**	**0**	**0**	**0**	**26**	**7.7**	**46**	**0**	**56**	**18**	**+8**	**10**	**0**	**1**	**1**	**18**	**0**	**0**	**0**
1986-87	**Hartford Whalers**	**NHL**	**66**	**3**	**9**	**12**	**3**	**6**	**9**	**130**	**0**	**0**	**0**	**50**	**6.0**	**54**	**0**	**90**	**40**	**+4**	**4**	**1**	**3**	**4**	**20**	**0**	**0**	**0**
1987-88	**Hartford Whalers**	**NHL**	**44**	**3**	**6**	**9**	**3**	**4**	**7**	**86**	**0**	**0**	**0**	**44**	**6.8**	**25**	**0**	**44**	**14**	**–5**	**3**	**1**	**1**	**2**	**0**	**0**	**0**	**0**
1988-89	**Hartford Whalers**	**NHL**	**24**	**0**	**1**	**1**	**0**	**1**	**1**	**36**	**0**	**0**	**0**	**7**	**0.0**	**7**	**0**	**24**	**6**	**–11**	....	....	....	....	....	....	....	....
	Binghamton Whalers	AHL	4	0	1	1	....	....	....	19	....	....	....	....	....	....	....	....	....	....	....	....	....	....	....	....	....	....
	Washington Capitals	**NHL**	**3**	**0**	**1**	**1**	**0**	**1**	**1**	**10**	**0**	**0**	**0**	**0**	**0.0**	**3**	**0**	**4**	**1**	**0**	....	....	....	....	....	....	....	....
1989-90	Washington Capitals	FrTour	3	1	0	1	....	....	....	0	....	....	....	....	....	....	....	....	....	....	....	....	....	....	....	....	....	....
	Washington Capitals	**NHL**	**15**	**1**	**3**	**4**	**1**	**2**	**3**	**16**	**0**	**0**	**0**	**13**	**7.7**	**8**	**0**	**7**	**3**	**+4**	**3**	**0**	**0**	**0**	**0**	**0**	**0**	**0**
	Baltimore Skipjacks	AHL	2	2	0	2	....	....	....	6	....	....	....	....	....	....	....	....	....	....	....	....	....	....	....	....	....	....
	NHL Totals		**281**	**12**	**46**	**58**	**12**	**31**	**43**	**452**	**1**	**0**	**0**	**185**	**6.5**	**214**	**7**	**321**	**101**		**26**	**2**	**7**	**9**	**40**	**0**	**0**	**0**

ECAC Second All-Star Team (1980) • ECAC First All-Star Team (1982)

Traded to **Hartford** by **NY Rangers** for Blaine Stoughton, February 27, 1984. Traded to **Washington** by **Hartford** for Jim Thompson, March 6, 1989.

• KLEMM, JON

Jon Klemm D – R. 6′3″, 200 lbs. b: Cranbrook, B.C., 1/8/1970.

1987-88	Seattle Thunderbirds	WHL	68	6	7	13	....	....	....	24	....	....	....	....	....	....	....	....	....	....	....	....	....	....	....	....	....	....
1988-89	Seattle Thunderbirds	WHL	2	1	1	2	....	....	....	0	....	....	....	....	....	....	....	....	....	....	....	....	....	....	....	....	....	....
	Spokane Chiefs	WHL	66	6	34	40	....	....	....	42	....	....	....	....	....	....	....	....	....	....	....	....	....	....	....	....	....	....
1989-90	Spokane Chiefs	WHL	66	3	28	31	....	....	....	100	....	....	....	....	....	....	....	....	....	....	6	1	1	2	5	....	....	....
1990-91	Spokane Chiefs	WHL	72	7	58	65	....	....	....	65	....	....	....	....	....	....	....	....	....	....	15	3	6	9	8	....	....	....
1991-92	**Quebec Nordiques**	**NHL**	**4**	**0**	**1**	**1**	**0**	**1**	**1**	**0**	**0**	**0**	**0**	**2**	**0.0**	**3**	**0**	**4**	**3**	**+2**	....	....	....	....	....	....	....	....
	Halifax Citadels	AHL	70	6	13	19	....	....	....	40	....	....	....	....	....	....	....	....	....	....	....	....	....	....	....	....	....	....
1992-93	Halifax Citadels	AHL	80	3	20	23	....	....	....	32	....	....	....	....	....	....	....	....	....	....	....	....	....	....	....	....	....	....
1993-94	**Quebec Nordiques**	**NHL**	**7**	**0**	**0**	**0**	**0**	**0**	**0**	**4**	**0**	**0**	**0**	**11**	**0.0**	**1**	**0**	**2**	**0**	**–1**	....	....	....	....	....	....	....	....
	Cornwall Aces	AHL	66	4	26	30	....	....	....	78	....	....	....	....	....	....	....	....	....	....	13	1	2	3	6	....	....	....
1994-95	**Quebec Nordiques**	**NHL**	**4**	**1**	**0**	**1**	**2**	**0**	**2**	**2**	**0**	**0**	**0**	**5**	**20.0**	**3**	**0**	**1**	**1**	**+3**	....	....	....	....	....	....	....	....
	Cornwall Aces	AHL	65	6	13	19	....	....	....	84	....	....	....	....	....	....	....	....	....	....	....	....	....	....	....	....	....	....
1995-96	**Colorado Avalanche**	**NHL**	**56**	**3**	**12**	**15**	**3**	**10**	**13**	**20**	**0**	**1**	**1**	**61**	**4.9**	**43**	**1**	**40**	**10**	**+12**	**15**	**2**	**1**	**3**	**0**	**1**	**0**	**0**
1996-97	**Colorado Avalanche**	**NHL**	**80**	**9**	**15**	**24**	**10**	**13**	**23**	**37**	**1**	**2**	**1**	**103**	**8.7**	**61**	**5**	**61**	**17**	**+12**	**17**	**1**	**1**	**2**	**6**	**0**	**0**	**0**
1997-98	**Colorado Avalanche**	**NHL**	**67**	**6**	**8**	**14**	**7**	**8**	**15**	**30**	**0**	**0**	**0**	**60**	**10.0**	**27**	**0**	**48**	**18**	**–3**	**4**	**0**	**0**	**0**	**0**	**0**	**0**	**0**
	NHL Totals		**218**	**19**	**36**	**55**	**22**	**32**	**54**	**93**	**1**	**3**	**2**	**242**	**7.9**	**138**	**6**	**156**	**49**		**36**	**3**	**2**	**5**	**6**	**1**	**0**	**0**

WHL West Second All-Star Team (1991)

Signed as a free agent by **Quebec**, May 14, 1991. Transferred to **Colorado** after **Quebec** franchise relocated, June 21, 1995.

• KLIMA, PETR

Petr Klima RW/LW – R. 6′, 190 lbs. b: Chomutov, Czech., 12/23/1964. Detroit's 5th choice, 88th overall, in 1983 Entry Draft.

1981-82	CHZ Litvinov	Czech.	18	7	3	10	....	....	....	8	....	....	....	....	....	....	....	....	....	....	....	....	....	....	....	....	....	....
1982-83	CHZ Litvinov	Czech.	44	19	17	36	....	....	....	74	....	....	....	....	....	....	....	....	....	....	....	....	....	....	....	....	....	....
	Czechoslovakia	WJC-A	7	4	4	8	....	....	....	6	....	....	....	....	....	....	....	....	....	....	....	....	....	....	....	....	....	....
1983-84	Dukla Jihlava	Czech.	41	20	16	36	....	....	....	46	....	....	....	....	....	....	....	....	....	....	....	....	....	....	....	....	....	....
	Czechoslovakia	WJC-A	7	6	4	10	....	....	....	22	....	....	....	....	....	....	....	....	....	....	....	....	....	....	....	....	....	....
1984-85	Czechoslovakia	C Cup	5	2	1	3	....	....	....	4	....	....	....	....	....	....	....	....	....	....	....	....	....	....	....	....	....	....
	Dukla Jihlava	Czech.	35	23	22	45	....	....	....	76	....	....	....	....	....	....	....	....	....	....	....	....	....	....	....	....	....	....
1985-86	**Detroit Red Wings**	**NHL**	**74**	**32**	**24**	**56**	**26**	**16**	**42**	**16**	**8**	**0**	**4**	**174**	**18.4**	**82**	**26**	**106**	**11**	**–39**	....	....	....	....	....	....	....	....
1986-87	**Detroit Red Wings**	**NHL**	**77**	**30**	**23**	**53**	**26**	**17**	**43**	**42**	**6**	**0**	**5**	**209**	**14.4**	**78**	**24**	**70**	**7**	**–9**	**13**	**1**	**2**	**3**	**4**	**0**	**0**	**0**
1987-88	**Detroit Red Wings**	**NHL**	**78**	**37**	**25**	**62**	**32**	**18**	**50**	**46**	**6**	**5**	**5**	**174**	**21.3**	**87**	**20**	**76**	**13**	**+4**	**12**	**10**	**8**	**18**	**10**	**2**	**1**	**4**
1988-89	**Detroit Red Wings**	**NHL**	**51**	**25**	**16**	**41**	**21**	**11**	**32**	**44**	**1**	**0**	**3**	**145**	**17.2**	**52**	**5**	**49**	**7**	**+5**	**6**	**2**	**4**	**6**	**19**	**1**	**0**	**0**
	Adirondack Red Wings	AHL	5	5	1	6	....	....	....	4	....	....	....	....	....	....	....	....	....	....	....	....	....	....	....	....	....	....
1989-90	**Detroit Red Wings**	**NHL**	**13**	**5**	**5**	**10**	**4**	**4**	**8**	**6**	**2**	**0**	**0**	**37**	**13.5**	**11**	**5**	**14**	**0**	**–8**	....	....	....	....	....	....	....	....
	Edmonton Oilers	**NHL**	**63**	**25**	**28**	**53**	**22**	**20**	**42**	**66**	**7**	**0**	**3**	**149**	**16.8**	**86**	**35**	**53**	**1**	**–1**	**21**	**5**	**0**	**5**	**8**	**1**	**0**	**1**
1990-91	**Edmonton Oilers**	**NHL**	**70**	**40**	**28**	**68**	**37**	**21**	**58**	**113**	**7**	**1**	**5**	**204**	**19.6**	**97**	**30**	**44**	**1**	**+24**	**18**	**7**	**6**	**13**	**16**	**1**	**0**	**3**
1991-92	**Edmonton Oilers**	**NHL**	**57**	**21**	**13**	**34**	**19**	**10**	**29**	**52**	**5**	**0**	**0**	**107**	**19.6**	**46**	**18**	**48**	**2**	**–18**	**15**	**1**	**4**	**5**	**8**	**0**	**0**	**0**
1992-93	**Edmonton Oilers**	**NHL**	**68**	**32**	**16**	**48**	**27**	**11**	**38**	**100**	**13**	**0**	**2**	**175**	**18.3**	**75**	**33**	**58**	**1**	**–15**	....	....	....	....	....	....	....	....
1993-94	**Tampa Bay Lightning**	**NHL**	**75**	**28**	**27**	**55**	**26**	**21**	**47**	**76**	**10**	**0**	**2**	**167**	**16.8**	**79**	**32**	**62**	**0**	**–15**	....	....	....	....	....	....	....	....
1994-95	Wolfsburg	German 2	12	27	11	38	....	....	....	28	....	....	....	....	....	....	....	....	....	....	....	....	....	....	....	....	....	....
	ZPS Zlin	Czech.	1	1	0	1	....	....	....	0	....	....	....	....	....	....	....	....	....	....	....	....	....	....	....	....	....	....
	Tampa Bay Lightning	**NHL**	**47**	**13**	**13**	**26**	**23**	**19**	**42**	**26**	**4**	**0**	**3**	**75**	**17.3**	**36**	**12**	**37**	**0**	**–13**	....	....	....	....	....	....	....	....
1995-96	**Tampa Bay Lightning**	**NHL**	**67**	**22**	**30**	**52**	**22**	**24**	**46**	**68**	**8**	**0**	**3**	**164**	**13.4**	**85**	**53**	**57**	**0**	**–25**	**4**	**2**	**0**	**2**	**14**	**2**	**0**	**0**

			REGULAR SEASON																		PLAYOFFS							
Season	Club	League	GP	G	A	Pts	AG	AA	APts	PIM	PP	SH	GW	S	%	TGF	PGF	TGA	PGA	+/–	GP	G	A	Pts	PIM	PP	SH	GW
1996-97	**Los Angeles Kings**	**NHL**	**8**	**0**	**4**	**4**	**0**	**4**	**4**	**2**	**0**	**0**	**0**	**12**	**0.0**	**6**	**4**	**9**	**0**	**–7**								
	Pittsburgh Penguins	**NHL**	**9**	**1**	**3**	**4**	**1**	**3**	**4**	**4**	**0**	**0**	**0**	**21**	**4.8**	**7**	**6**	**5**	**0**	**–4**								
	Cleveland Lumberjacks	IHL	19	7	14	21				6																		
	Edmonton Oilers	**NHL**	**16**	**1**	**5**	**6**	**1**	**4**	**5**	**6**	**0**	**0**	**0**	**22**	**4.5**	**11**	**6**	**6**	**0**	**–1**	**6**	**0**	**0**	**0**	**4**	**0**	**0**	**0**
1997-98	Krefeld Pinguine	Germany	38	7	12	19				18																		
	NHL Totals		**773**	**312**	**260**	**572**	**287**	**203**	**490**	**667**	**77**	**6**	**35**	**1835**	**17.0**	**838**	**309**	**694**	**43**		**95**	**28**	**24**	**52**	**83**	**7**	**1**	**8**

EJC-A All-Star Team (1982)

Traded to **Edmonton** by **Detroit** with Joe Murphy, Adam Graves and Jeff Sharples for Jimmy Carson, Kevin McClelland and Edmonton's 5th round choice (later traded to Montreal — Montreal selected Brad Layzell) in 1991 Entry Draft, November 2, 1989. Traded to **Tampa Bay** by **Edmonton** for Tampa Bay's 3rd round choice (Brad Symes) in 1994 Entry Draft, June 16, 1993. Traded to **LA Kings** by **Tampa Bay** for LA Kings' 5th round choice (Jan Sulc) in 1997 Entry Draft, August 22, 1996. Traded to **Pittsburgh** by **LA Kings** for future considerations, October 25, 1996. Signed as a free agent by **Edmonton**, February 26, 1997.

• KLIMOVICH, SERGEI

Sergei Klimovich C – R. 6'3", 189 lbs. b: Novosibirsk, USSR, 3/8/1974. Chicago's 3rd choice, 41st overall, in 1992 Entry Draft.

Season	Club	League	GP	G	A	Pts	AG	AA	APts	PIM	PP	SH	GW	S	%	TGF	PGF	TGA	PGA	+/–	GP	G	A	Pts	PIM	PP	SH	GW
1991-92	Moscow Dynamo	CIS	3	0	0	0				0																		
1992-93	Moscow Dynamo	CIS	30	4	1	5				14											10	1	0	1	2			
	Russia	WJC-A	7	2	2	4				10																		
1993-94	Moscow Dynamo	CIS	39	7	4	11				14											12	2	3	5	6			
1994-95	Moscow Dynamo	CIS	4	1	0	1				2																		
	Indianapolis Ice	IHL	71	14	30	44				20																		
1995-96	Indianapolis Ice	IHL	68	17	21	38				28											5	1	1	2	6			
1996-97	**Chicago Blackhawks**	**NHL**	**1**	**0**	**0**	**0**	**0**	**0**	**0**	**2**	**0**	**0**	**0**	**0**	**0.0**	**0**	**0**	**1**	**1**	**0**								
	Indianapolis Ice	IHL	75	20	37	57				98											3	1	2	3	0			
1997-98	Idaho Steelheads	WCHL	13	5	9	14				18											1	0	0	0	0			
	Las Vegas Thunder	IHL	25	2	8	10				6																		
	Quebec Rafales	IHL	21	1	7	8				8																		
	NHL Totals		**1**	**0**	**0**	**0**	**0**	**0**	**0**	**2**	**0**	**0**	**0**	**0**	**0.0**	**0**	**0**	**1**	**1**									

• KLUZAK, GORD

Gord Kluzak D – L. 6'4", 220 lbs. b: Climax, Sask., 3/4/1964. Boston's 1st choice, 1st overall, in 1982 Entry Draft.

Season	Club	League	GP	G	A	Pts	AG	AA	APts	PIM	PP	SH	GW	S	%	TGF	PGF	TGA	PGA	+/–	GP	G	A	Pts	PIM	PP	SH	GW
1980-81	Billings Bighorns	WHL	68	4	34	38				160											5	0	1	1	4			
1981-82	Billings Bighorns	WHL	38	9	24	33				110																		
	Canada	WJC-A	7	0	1	1				4																		
1982-83	**Boston Bruins**	**NHL**	**70**	**1**	**6**	**7**	**1**	**4**	**5**	**105**	**0**	**0**	**0**	**49**	**2.0**	**37**	**2**	**32**	**3**	**+6**	**17**	**1**	**4**	**5**	**54**	**0**	**0**	**0**
1983-84	**Boston Bruins**	**NHL**	**80**	**10**	**27**	**37**	**8**	**18**	**26**	**135**	**5**	**0**	**3**	**125**	**8.0**	**117**	**40**	**75**	**7**	**+9**	**3**	**0**	**0**	**0**	**0**	**0**	**0**	**0**
1984-85			DID NOT PLAY – INJURED																									
1985-86	**Boston Bruins**	**NHL**	**70**	**8**	**31**	**39**	**6**	**21**	**27**	**155**	**3**	**0**	**0**	**114**	**7.0**	**94**	**30**	**85**	**24**	**+3**	**3**	**1**	**1**	**2**	**16**	**1**	**0**	**0**
1986-87			DID NOT PLAY – INJURED																									
1987-88	**Boston Bruins**	**NHL**	**66**	**6**	**31**	**37**	**5**	**22**	**27**	**135**	**0**	**1**	**0**	**168**	**3.6**	**100**	**29**	**78**	**25**	**+18**	**23**	**4**	**8**	**12**	**59**	**0**	**1**	**1**
1988-89	**Boston Bruins**	**NHL**	**3**	**0**	**1**	**1**	**0**	**1**	**1**	**2**	**0**	**0**	**0**	**4**	**0.0**	**3**	**1**	**5**	**1**	**–2**								
1989-90	**Boston Bruins**	**NHL**	**8**	**0**	**2**	**2**	**0**	**1**	**1**	**11**	**0**	**0**	**0**	**8**	**0.0**	**10**	**2**	**5**	**1**	**+4**								
1990-91	**Boston Bruins**	**NHL**	**2**	**0**	**0**	**0**	**0**	**0**	**0**	**0**	**0**	**0**	**0**	**3**	**0.0**	**3**	**0**	**1**	**0**	**+2**								
	NHL Totals		**299**	**25**	**98**	**123**	**20**	**67**	**87**	**543**	**8**	**1**	**3**	**471**	**5.3**	**364**	**104**	**281**	**61**		**46**	**6**	**10**	**19**	**129**	**1**	**1**	**1**

WHL Second All-Star Team (1982) • WJC-A All-Star Team (1982) • Named Best Defenseman at WJC-A (1982) • Won Bill Masterton Trophy (1990)
• Missed entire 1984-85 and 1986-87 seasons recovering from knee surgery.

• KNIPSCHEER, FRED

Fred Knipscheer C – L. 5'11", 185 lbs. b: Ft. Wayne, IN, 9/3/1969.

Season	Club	League	GP	G	A	Pts	AG	AA	APts	PIM	PP	SH	GW	S	%	TGF	PGF	TGA	PGA	+/–	GP	G	A	Pts	PIM	PP	SH	GW
1990-91	St. Cloud State Huskies	WCHA	40	9	10	19				57																		
1991-92	St. Cloud State Huskies	WCHA	33	15	17	32				48																		
1992-93	St. Cloud State Huskies	WCHA	36	34	26	60				68																		
1993-94	**Boston Bruins**	**NHL**	**11**	**3**	**2**	**5**	**3**	**2**	**5**	**14**	**0**	**0**	**1**	**15**	**20.0**	**7**	**0**	**5**	**1**	**+3**	**12**	**2**	**1**	**3**	**6**	**0**	**0**	**1**
	Providence Bruins	AHL	62	26	13	39				50																		
1994-95	**Boston Bruins**	**NHL**	**16**	**3**	**1**	**4**	**5**	**1**	**6**	**2**	**0**	**0**	**1**	**20**	**15.0**	**9**	**0**	**8**	**0**	**+1**	**4**	**0**	**0**	**0**	**0**	**0**	**0**	**0**
	Providence Bruins	AHL	71	29	34	63				81																		
1995-96	**St. Louis Blues**	**NHL**	**1**	**0**	**0**	**0**	**0**	**0**	**0**	**2**	**0**	**0**	**0**	**2**	**0.0**	**0**	**0**	**0**	**0**	**0**								
	Worcester IceCats	AHL	68	36	37	73				93											3	0	0	0	2			
1996-97	Phoenix Roadrunners	IHL	24	5	11	16				19																		
	Indianapolis Ice	IHL	41	10	9	19				46											4	0	2	2	10			
1997-98	Kentucky Thoroughblades	AHL	17	0	7	7				8											3	0	1	1	7			
	Utah Grizzlies	IHL	58	21	32	53				69											2	0	0	0	4			
	NHL Totals		**28**	**6**	**3**	**9**	**8**	**3**	**11**	**18**	**0**	**0**	**2**	**37**	**16.2**	**16**	**0**	**13**	**1**		**16**	**2**	**1**	**3**	**6**	**0**	**0**	**1**

WCHA First All-Star Team (1993) • NCAA West Second All-American Team (1993)

Signed as a free agent by **Boston**, April 30, 1993. Traded to **St. Louis** by **Boston** for Rick Zombo, October 2, 1995. Signed as a free agent by **Chicago**, August 16, 1996.

• KNUBLE, MICHAEL

Michael Knuble RW – R. 6'3", 208 lbs. b: Toronto, Ont., 7/4/1972. Detroit's 4th choice, 76th overall, in 1991 Entry Draft.

Season	Club	League	GP	G	A	Pts	AG	AA	APts	PIM	PP	SH	GW	S	%	TGF	PGF	TGA	PGA	+/–	GP	G	A	Pts	PIM	PP	SH	GW
1989-90	East Kentwood High	H.S.	29	63	40	103				40																		
1990-91	Kalamazoo Jr. K-Wings	NAJHL	36	18	24	42				30																		
1991-92	University of Michigan	CCHA	43	7	8	15				48																		
1992-93	University of Michigan	CCHA	39	26	16	42				57																		
1993-94	University of Michigan	CCHA	41	32	26	58				71																		
1994-95	University of Michigan	CCHA	34	*38	22	60				62																		
	Adirondack Red Wings	AHL																			3	0	0	0	0			
	United States	WC-A	6	1	2	3				2																		
1995-96	Adirondack Red Wings	AHL	80	22	23	45				59											3	1	0	1	0			
1996-97	**Detroit Red Wings**	**NHL**	**9**	**1**	**0**	**1**	**1**	**0**	**1**	**0**	**0**	**0**	**0**	**10**	**10.0**	**3**	**0**	**4**	**0**	**–1**								
	Adirondack Red Wings	AHL	68	28	35	63				54																		
1997-98	**Detroit Red Wings**	**NHL**	**53**	**7**	**6**	**13**	**8**	**6**	**14**	**16**	**0**	**0**	**0**	**54**	**13.0**	**22**	**0**	**20**	**0**	**+2**	**3**	**0**	**1**	**1**	**0**	**0**	**0**	**0**
	NHL Totals		**62**	**8**	**6**	**14**	**9**	**6**	**15**	**16**	**0**	**0**	**0**	**64**	**12.5**	**25**	**0**	**24**	**0**		**3**	**0**	**1**	**1**	**0**	**0**	**0**	**0**

CCHA Second All-Star Team (1994, 1995) • NCAA West Second All-American Team (1995)

• KNUTSEN, ESPEN

Espen Knutsen C – L. 5'11", 180 lbs. b: Oslo, Norway, 1/12/1972. Hartford's 9th choice, 204th overall, in 1990 Entry Draft.

Season	Club	League	GP	G	A	Pts	AG	AA	APts	PIM	PP	SH	GW	S	%	TGF	PGF	TGA	PGA	+/–	GP	G	A	Pts	PIM	PP	SH	GW
1988-89	Norway	WJC-A	6	0	2	2				6																		
1989-90	Valerengen	Norway	34	22	26	48																						
	Norway	WJC-A	7	2	7	9				6																		
1990-91	Valerengen	Norway	31	30	24	54				42											5	3	4	7				
	Norway	WJC-A	7	1	2	3				4																		
1991-92	Valerengen	Norway	30	28	26	54				37											8	7	8	15				
1992-93	Valerengen	Norway	13	11	13	24				4																		
1993-94	Valerengen	Norway	38	32	26	58				20																		
	Norway	Olympics	7	1	3	4				2																		
	Norway	WC-A	6	3	2	5				0																		
1994-95	Djurgardens IF Stockholm	Sweden	30	6	14	20				18											3	0	1	1	0			
	Norway	WC-A	5	2	1	3				0																		
1995-96	Djurgardens IF Stockholm	Sweden	32	10	23	33				50											4	1	0	1	2			
	Norway	WC-A	5	3	0	3				0																		

			REGULAR SEASON																		PLAYOFFS							
Season	Club	League	GP	G	A	Pts	AG	AA	APts	PIM	PP	SH	GW	S	%	TGF	PGF	TGA	PGA	+/–	GP	G	A	Pts	PIM	PP	SH	GW
1996-97	Djurgardens IF Stockholm	Sweden	39	16	33	49	....	....	....	20	....	....	....	....	....	....	....	....	....	....	4	2	4	6	6	....	....	....
	Norway	WC-A	8	0	5	5	....	....	....	4	....	....	....	....	....	....	....	....	....	....	....	....	....	....	....	....	....	....
1997-98	**Anaheim Mighty Ducks**	**NHL**	**19**	**3**	**0**	**3**	**4**	**0**	**4**	**6**	**1**	**0**	**0**	**21**	**14.3**	**6**	**4**	**12**	**0**	**–10**	....	....	....	....	....	....	....	....
	Cincinnati Mighty Ducks	AHL	41	4	13	17	....	....	....	18	....	....	....	....	....	....	....	....	....	....	....	....	....	....	....	....	....	....
	NHL Totals		**19**	**3**	**0**	**3**	**4**	**0**	**4**	**6**	**1**	**0**	**0**	**21**	**14.3**	**6**	**4**	**12**	**0**		....	....	....	....	....	....	....	....

Norwegian Player of the Year (1994)

Rights traded to **Anaheim** by **Hartford** for Kevin Brown, October 1, 1996.

• KOCUR, JOE

Joe Kocur RW – R. 6′, 205 lbs. b: Calgary, Alta., 12/21/1964. Detroit's 6th choice, 91st overall, in 1983 Entry Draft.

Season	Club	League	GP	G	A	Pts	AG	AA	APts	PIM	PP	SH	GW	S	%	TGF	PGF	TGA	PGA	+/–	GP	G	A	Pts	PIM	PP	SH	GW
1982-83	Saskatoon Blades	WHL	62	23	17	40	....	....	....	289	....	....	....	....	....	....	....	....	....	....	6	2	3	5	25	....	....	....
1983-84	Saskatoon Blades	WHL	69	40	41	81	....	....	....	258	....	....	....	....	....	....	....	....	....	....	....	....	....	....	....	....	....	....
	Adirondack Red Wings	AHL	....	....	....	....	....	....	....	....	....	....	....	....	....	....	....	....	....	....	5	0	0	0	20	....	....	....
1984-85	**Detroit Red Wings**	**NHL**	**17**	**1**	**0**	**1**	**1**	**0**	**1**	**64**	**0**	**0**	**0**	**7**	**14.3**	**3**	**1**	**6**	**0**	**–4**	**3**	**1**	**0**	**1**	**5**	**0**	**0**	**0**
	Adirondack Red Wings	AHL	47	12	7	19	....	....	....	171	....	....	....	....	....	....	....	....	....	....	....	....	....	....	....	....	....	....
1985-86	**Detroit Red Wings**	**NHL**	**59**	**9**	**6**	**15**	**7**	**4**	**11**	***377**	**2**	**0**	**0**	**65**	**13.8**	**25**	**9**	**40**	**0**	**–24**	....	....	....	....	....	....	....	....
	Adirondack Red Wings	AHL	9	6	2	8	....	....	....	34	....	....	....	....	....	....	....	....	....	....	....	....	....	....	....	....	....	....
1986-87	**Detroit Red Wings**	**NHL**	**77**	**9**	**9**	**18**	**8**	**6**	**14**	**276**	**2**	**0**	**2**	**81**	**11.1**	**36**	**8**	**39**	**1**	**–10**	**16**	**2**	**3**	**5**	**71**	**1**	**0**	**2**
1987-88	**Detroit Red Wings**	**NHL**	**63**	**7**	**7**	**14**	**6**	**5**	**11**	**263**	**0**	**0**	**1**	**41**	**17.1**	**21**	**2**	**30**	**0**	**–11**	**10**	**0**	**1**	**1**	**13**	**0**	**0**	**0**
1988-89	**Detroit Red Wings**	**NHL**	**60**	**9**	**9**	**18**	**8**	**6**	**14**	**213**	**1**	**0**	**1**	**76**	**11.8**	**30**	**3**	**31**	**0**	**–4**	**3**	**0**	**1**	**1**	**6**	**0**	**0**	**0**
1989-90	**Detroit Red Wings**	**NHL**	**71**	**16**	**20**	**36**	**14**	**14**	**28**	**268**	**1**	**0**	**5**	**128**	**12.5**	**67**	**4**	**67**	**0**	**–4**	....	....	....	....	....	....	....	....
1990-91	**Detroit Red Wings**	**NHL**	**52**	**5**	**4**	**9**	**5**	**3**	**8**	**253**	**0**	**0**	**0**	**67**	**7.5**	**23**	**3**	**27**	**1**	**–6**	....	....	....	....	....	....	....	....
	New York Rangers	**NHL**	**5**	**0**	**0**	**0**	**0**	**0**	**0**	**36**	**0**	**0**	**0**	**6**	**0.0**	**1**	**0**	**2**	**0**	**–1**	**6**	**0**	**2**	**2**	**21**	**0**	**0**	**0**
1991-92	**New York Rangers**	**NHL**	**51**	**7**	**4**	**11**	**6**	**3**	**9**	**121**	**0**	**0**	**2**	**72**	**9.7**	**21**	**0**	**25**	**0**	**–4**	**12**	**1**	**1**	**2**	**38**	**0**	**0**	**0**
1992-93	**New York Rangers**	**NHL**	**65**	**3**	**6**	**9**	**2**	**4**	**6**	**131**	**2**	**0**	**0**	**43**	**7.0**	**22**	**3**	**28**	**0**	**–9**	....	....	....	....	....	....	....	....
1993-94	**New York Rangers**	**NHL**	**71**	**2**	**1**	**3**	**2**	**1**	**3**	**129**	**0**	**0**	**0**	**43**	**4.7**	**12**	**1**	**20**	**0**	**–9**	**20**	**1**	**1**	**2**	**17**	**0**	**0**	**0**
1994-95	**New York Rangers**	**NHL**	**48**	**1**	**2**	**3**	**2**	**3**	**5**	**71**	**0**	**0**	**0**	**25**	**4.0**	**9**	**0**	**14**	**1**	**–4**	**10**	**0**	**0**	**0**	**8**	**0**	**0**	**0**
1995-96	**New York Rangers**	**NHL**	**38**	**1**	**2**	**3**	**1**	**2**	**3**	**49**	**0**	**0**	**0**	**19**	**5.3**	**4**	**0**	**8**	**0**	**–4**	....	....	....	....	....	....	....	....
	Vancouver Canucks	**NHL**	**7**	**0**	**1**	**1**	**0**	**1**	**1**	**19**	**0**	**0**	**0**	**1**	**0.0**	**1**	**0**	**4**	**0**	**–3**	**1**	**0**	**0**	**0**	**0**	**0**	**0**	**0**
1996-97	San Antonio Dragons	IHL	5	1	1	2	....	....	....	24	....	....	....	....	....	....	....	....	....	....	....	....	....	....	....	....	....	....
	Detroit Red Wings	**NHL**	**34**	**2**	**1**	**3**	**2**	**1**	**3**	**70**	**0**	**0**	**1**	**38**	**5.3**	**5**	**0**	**12**	**0**	**–7**	**19**	**1**	**3**	**4**	**22**	**0**	**0**	**0**
1997-98	**Detroit Red Wings**	**NHL**	**63**	**6**	**5**	**11**	**7**	**5**	**12**	**92**	**0**	**0**	**2**	**53**	**11.3**	**28**	**1**	**20**	**0**	**+7**	**18**	**4**	**0**	**4**	**30**	**0**	**0**	**0**
	NHL Totals		**781**	**78**	**77**	**155**	**71**	**58**	**129**	**2432**	**8**	**0**	**14**	**765**	**10.2**	**308**	**35**	**373**	**3**		**118**	**10**	**12**	**22**	**231**	**1**	**0**	**2**

Traded to **NY Rangers** by **Detroit** with Per Djoos for Kevin Miller, Jim Cummins and Dennis Vial, March 5, 1991. Traded to **Vancouver** by **NY Rangers** for Kay Whitmore, March 20, 1996. Signed as a free agent by **Detroit**, December 27, 1996.

• KOHN, LADISLAV

Ladislav Kohn RW – L. 5′10″, 180 lbs. b: Uherske Hradiste, Czech., 3/4/1975. Calgary's 9th choice, 175th overall, in 1994 Entry Draft.

Season	Club	League	GP	G	A	Pts	AG	AA	APts	PIM	PP	SH	GW	S	%	TGF	PGF	TGA	PGA	+/–	GP	G	A	Pts	PIM	PP	SH	GW
1993-94	Brandon Wheat Kings	WHL	2	0	0	0	....	....	....	0	....	....	....	....	....	....	....	....	....	....	....	....	....	....	....	....	....	....
	Swift Current Broncos	WHL	69	33	35	68	....	....	....	68	....	....	....	....	....	....	....	....	....	....	7	5	4	9	8	....	....	....
1994-95	Swift Current Broncos	WHL	65	32	60	92	....	....	....	122	....	....	....	....	....	....	....	....	....	....	6	2	6	8	14	....	....	....
	Czech Republic	WJC-A	7	0	4	4	....	....	....	8	....	....	....	....	....	....	....	....	....	....	....	....	....	....	....	....	....	....
	Saint John Flames	AHL	1	0	0	0	....	....	....	0	....	....	....	....	....	....	....	....	....	....	....	....	....	....	....	....	....	....
1995-96	**Calgary Flames**	**NHL**	**5**	**1**	**0**	**1**	**1**	**0**	**1**	**2**	**0**	**0**	**0**	**8**	**12.5**	**1**	**0**	**2**	**0**	**–1**	....	....	....	....	....	....	....	....
	Saint John Flames	AHL	73	28	45	73	....	....	....	97	....	....	....	....	....	....	....	....	....	....	16	6	5	11	12	....	....	....
1996-97	Saint John Flames	AHL	76	28	29	57	....	....	....	81	....	....	....	....	....	....	....	....	....	....	5	0	0	0	0	....	....	....
1997-98	**Calgary Flames**	**NHL**	**4**	**0**	**1**	**1**	**0**	**1**	**1**	**0**	**0**	**0**	**0**	**2**	**0.0**	**2**	**0**	**0**	**0**	**+2**	....	....	....	....	....	....	....	....
	Saint John Flames	AHL	65	25	31	56	....	....	....	90	....	....	....	....	....	....	....	....	....	....	21	14	6	20	20	....	....	....
	NHL Totals		**9**	**1**	**1**	**2**	**1**	**1**	**2**	**2**	**0**	**0**	**0**	**10**	**10.0**	**3**	**0**	**2**	**0**		....	....	....	....	....	....	....	....

Traded to **Toronto** by **Calgary** for David Cooper, July 2, 1998.

• KOIVU, SAKU

Saku Koivu C – L. 5′9″, 175 lbs. b: Turku, Finland, 11/23/1974. Montreal's 1st choice, 21st overall, in 1993 Entry Draft.

Season	Club	League	GP	G	A	Pts	AG	AA	APts	PIM	PP	SH	GW	S	%	TGF	PGF	TGA	PGA	+/–	GP	G	A	Pts	PIM	PP	SH	GW
1992-93	TPS Turku	Finland	46	3	7	10	....	....	....	28	....	....	....	....	....	....	....	....	....	....	11	3	2	5	2	....	....	....
	Finland	WJC-A	7	1	8	9	....	....	....	6	....	....	....	....	....	....	....	....	....	....	....	....	....	....	....	....	....	....
	Finland	WC-A	6	0	1	1	....	....	....	2	....	....	....	....	....	....	....	....	....	....	....	....	....	....	....	....	....	....
1993-94	TPS Turku	Finland	47	23	30	53	....	....	....	42	....	....	....	....	....	....	....	....	....	....	11	4	8	12	16	....	....	....
	Finland	WJC-A	7	3	6	9	....	....	....	12	....	....	....	....	....	....	....	....	....	....	....	....	....	....	....	....	....	....
	Finland	Olympics	8	4	3	7	....	....	....	12	....	....	....	....	....	....	....	....	....	....	....	....	....	....	....	....	....	....
	Finland	WC-A	8	5	6	11	....	....	....	4	....	....	....	....	....	....	....	....	....	....	....	....	....	....	....	....	....	....
1994-95	TPS Turku	Finland	45	27	47	74	....	....	....	73	....	....	....	....	....	....	....	....	....	....	13	7	10	17	16	....	....	....
	Finland	WC-A	8	5	5	10	....	....	....	18	....	....	....	....	....	....	....	....	....	....	....	....	....	....	....	....	....	....
1995-96	**Montreal Canadiens**	**NHL**	**82**	**20**	**25**	**45**	**20**	**20**	**40**	**40**	**8**	**3**	**2**	**136**	**14.7**	**63**	**22**	**76**	**28**	**–7**	**6**	**3**	**1**	**4**	**8**	**0**	**0**	**0**
1996-97	Finland	W Cup	4	1	3	4	....	....	....	4	....	....	....	....	....	....	....	....	....	....	....	....	....	....	....	....	....	....
	Montreal Canadiens	**NHL**	**50**	**17**	**39**	**56**	**18**	**35**	**53**	**38**	**5**	**0**	**3**	**135**	**12.6**	**68**	**21**	**51**	**11**	**+7**	**5**	**1**	**3**	**4**	**10**	**0**	**0**	**0**
	Finland	WC-A	6	2	2	4	....	....	....	2	....	....	....	....	....	....	....	....	....	....	....	....	....	....	....	....	....	....
1997-98	**Montreal Canadiens**	**NHL**	**69**	**14**	**43**	**57**	**16**	**42**	**58**	**48**	**2**	**2**	**3**	**145**	**9.7**	**78**	**30**	**51**	**11**	**+8**	**6**	**2**	**3**	**5**	**2**	**1**	**0**	**0**
	Finland	Olympics	6	2	8	10	....	....	....	4	....	....	....	....	....	....	....	....	....	....	....	....	....	....	....	....	....	....
	NHL Totals		**201**	**51**	**107**	**158**	**54**	**97**	**151**	**126**	**15**	**5**	**8**	**416**	**12.3**	**209**	**73**	**178**	**50**		**17**	**6**	**7**	**13**	**20**	**1**	**0**	**0**

WC-A All-Star Team (1994, 1995) • Finnish First All-Star Team (1995) • Finnish Player of the Year (1995) • Named Best Forward at WC-A (1995)

Played in NHL All-Star Game (1998)

• KOLESAR, MARK

Mark Kolesar LW – R. 6′1″, 188 lbs. b: Brampton, Ont., 1/23/1973.

Season	Club	League	GP	G	A	Pts	AG	AA	APts	PIM	PP	SH	GW	S	%	TGF	PGF	TGA	PGA	+/–	GP	G	A	Pts	PIM	PP	SH	GW
1991-92	Brandon Wheat Kings	WHL	56	6	7	13	....	....	....	36	....	....	....	....	....	....	....	....	....	....	....	....	....	....	....	....	....	....
1992-93	Brandon Wheat Kings	WHL	68	27	33	60	....	....	....	110	....	....	....	....	....	....	....	....	....	....	4	0	0	0	4	....	....	....
1993-94	Brandon Wheat Kings	WHL	59	29	37	66	....	....	....	131	....	....	....	....	....	....	....	....	....	....	14	8	3	11	48	....	....	....
1994-95	St. John's Maple Leafs	AHL	65	12	18	30	....	....	....	62	....	....	....	....	....	....	....	....	....	....	5	1	0	1	2	....	....	....
1995-96	**Toronto Maple Leafs**	**NHL**	**21**	**2**	**2**	**4**	**2**	**2**	**4**	**14**	**0**	**0**	**0**	**10**	**20.0**	**4**	**0**	**9**	**5**	**0**	**3**	**1**	**0**	**1**	**2**	**0**	**1**	**0**
	St. John's Maple Leafs	AHL	52	22	13	35	....	....	....	47	....	....	....	....	....	....	....	....	....	....	....	....	....	....	....	....	....	....
1996-97	**Toronto Maple Leafs**	**NHL**	**7**	**0**	**0**	**0**	**0**	**0**	**0**	**0**	**0**	**0**	**0**	**3**	**0.0**	**0**	**0**	**3**	**0**	**–3**	....	....	....	....	....	....	....	....
	St. John's Maple Leafs	AHL	62	22	28	50	....	....	....	64	....	....	....	....	....	....	....	....	....	....	10	1	3	4	6	....	....	....
1997-98	St. John's Maple Leafs	AHL	2	0	0	0	....	....	....	2	....	....	....	....	....	....	....	....	....	....	....	....	....	....	....	....	....	....
	Manitoba Moose	IHL	30	1	9	10	....	....	....	29	....	....	....	....	....	....	....	....	....	....	....	....	....	....	....	....	....	....
	Hamilton Bulldogs	AHL	27	2	12	14	....	....	....	47	....	....	....	....	....	....	....	....	....	....	6	1	1	2	0	....	....	....
	NHL Totals		**28**	**2**	**2**	**4**	**2**	**2**	**4**	**14**	**0**	**0**	**0**	**13**	**15.4**	**4**	**0**	**12**	**5**		**3**	**1**	**0**	**1**	**2**	**0**	**1**	**0**

Signed as a free agent by **Toronto**, May 24, 1994.

• KOLSTAD, DEAN

Dean Kolstad D – L. 6′6″, 220 lbs. b: Edmonton, Alta., 6/16/1968. Minnesota's 3rd choice, 33rd overall, in 1986 Entry Draft.

Season	Club	League	GP	G	A	Pts	AG	AA	APts	PIM	PP	SH	GW	S	%	TGF	PGF	TGA	PGA	+/–	GP	G	A	Pts	PIM	PP	SH	GW
1984-85	New Westminster Bruins	WHL	13	0	0	0	....	....	....	16	....	....	....	....	....	....	....	....	....	....	....	....	....	....	....	....	....	....
	Langley Eagles	BCJHL	25	3	11	14	....	....	....	61	....	....	....	....	....	....	....	....	....	....	....	....	....	....	....	....	....	....
1985-86	New Westminster Bruins	WHL	16	0	5	5	....	....	....	19	....	....	....	....	....	....	....	....	....	....	....	....	....	....	....	....	....	....
	Prince Albert Raiders	WHL	54	2	15	17	....	....	....	80	....	....	....	....	....	....	....	....	....	....	20	5	3	8	26	....	....	....
1986-87	Prince Albert Raiders	WHL	72	17	37	54	....	....	....	112	....	....	....	....	....	....	....	....	....	....	8	1	5	6	8	....	....	....
1987-88	Prince Albert Raiders	WHL	72	14	37	51	....	....	....	121	....	....	....	....	....	....	....	....	....	....	10	0	9	9	20	....	....	....
1988-89	**Minnesota North Stars**	**NHL**	**25**	**1**	**5**	**6**	**1**	**4**	**5**	**42**	**1**	**0**	**0**	**41**	**2.4**	**28**	**12**	**28**	**7**	**–5**	....	....	....	....	....	....	....	....
	Kalamazoo Wings	IHL	51	10	23	33	....	....	....	91	....	....	....	....	....	....	....	....	....	....	6	1	0	1	23	....	....	....
1989-90	Kalamazoo Wings	IHL	77	10	40	50	....	....	....	172	....	....	....	....	....	....	....	....	....	....	10	3	4	7	14	....	....	....
1990-91	Minnesota North Stars	FrTour	3	0	0	0	....	....	....	6	....	....	....	....	....	....	....	....	....	....	....	....	....	....	....	....	....	....
	Minnesota North Stars	**NHL**	**5**	**0**	**0**	**0**	**0**	**0**	**0**	**15**	**0**	**0**	**0**	**9**	**0.0**	**1**	**1**	**2**	**0**	**–2**	....	....	....	....	....	....	....	....
	Kalamazoo Wings	IHL	33	4	8	12	....	....	....	50	....	....	....	....	....	....	....	....	....	....	9	1	6	7	4	....	....	....
1991-92	Kansas City Blades	IHL	74	9	20	29	....	....	....	83	....	....	....	....	....	....	....	....	....	....	15	3	6	9	8	....	....	....

			REGULAR SEASON																		PLAYOFFS							
Season	Club	League	GP	G	A	Pts	AG	AA	APts	PIM	PP	SH	GW	S	%	TGF	PGF	TGA	PGA	+/-	GP	G	A	Pts	PIM	PP	SH	GW
1992-93	San Jose Sharks	NHL	10	0	2	2	0	1	1	12	0	0	0	22	0.0	5	4	11	1	-9	....	....	....	....	....	....	....	....
	Kansas City Blades	IHL	63	9	21	30	....	....	....	79	....	....	....	....	....	....	....	....	....	....	3	0	0	0	2	....	....	....
1993-94	Binghamton Rangers	AHL	68	7	26	33	....	....	....	92	....	....	....	....	....	....	....	....	....	....	....	....	....	....	....	....	....	....
1994-95	Minnesota Moose	IHL	73	6	18	24	....	....	....	71	....	....	....	....	....	....	....	....	....	....	1	0	0	0	2	....	....	....
1995-96	Portland Pirates	AHL	12	1	1	2	....	....	....	14	....	....	....	....	....	....	....	....	....	....	....	....	....	....	....	....	....	....
1996-97	Central Texas Stampede	WPHL	17	2	10	12	....	....	....	44	....	....	....	....	....	....	....	....	....	....	11	4	7	11	12	....	....	....
1997-98	Central Texas Stampede	WPHL	66	14	59	73	....	....	....	92	....	....	....	....	....	....	....	....	....	....	4	2	2	4	10	....	....	....
	NHL Totals		40	1	7	8	1	5	6	69	1	0	0	72	1.4	34	17	41	8		....	....	....	....	....	....	....	....

WHL East Second All-Star Team (1987, 1988) • IHL Second All-Star Team (1990)

Claimed by **San Jose** from **Minnesota** in Dispersal Draft, May 30, 1991.

• KOMADOSKI, NEIL

Neil Komadoski D – L. 6', 200 lbs. b: Winnipeg, Man., 11/5/1951. Los Angeles' 2nd choice, 48th overall, in 1971 Amateur Draft.

Season	Club	League	GP	G	A	Pts	AG	AA	APts	PIM	PP	SH	GW	S	%	TGF	PGF	TGA	PGA	+/-	GP	G	A	Pts	PIM	PP	SH	GW
1968-69	Winnipeg Jets	WCJHL	58	2	8	10	....	....	....	83	....	....	....	....	....	....	....	....	....	....	....	....	....	....	....	....	....	....
1969-70	Winnipeg Jets	WCJHL	53	7	10	17	....	....	....	104	....	....	....	....	....	....	....	....	....	....	....	....	....	....	....	....	....	....
1970-71	Winnipeg Jets	WCJHL	52	15	24	39	....	....	....	116	....	....	....	....	....	....	....	....	....	....	....	....	....	....	....	....	....	....
1971-72	Springfield Kings	AHL	64	7	20	27	....	....	....	87	....	....	....	....	....	....	....	....	....	....	5	0	0	0	8	....	....	....
1972-73	Los Angeles Kings	NHL	62	1	8	9	1	7	8	67	1	0	0	47	2.1	50	3	76	7	-22	....	....	....	....	....	....	....	....
1973-74	Los Angeles Kings	NHL	68	2	4	6	2	3	5	43	0	0	0	53	3.8	32	2	40	6	-4	2	0	0	0	12	0	0	0
1974-75	Los Angeles Kings	NHL	75	4	12	16	4	9	13	69	3	0	0	66	6.1	54	13	38	7	+10	3	0	0	0	2	0	0	0
1975-76	Los Angeles Kings	NHL	80	3	15	18	3	12	15	165	1	0	0	94	3.2	92	5	103	23	+7	9	0	0	0	18	0	0	0
1976-77	Los Angeles Kings	NHL	68	3	9	12	3	7	10	109	0	0	1	76	3.9	57	4	47	11	+17	9	0	2	2	15	0	0	0
1977-78	Los Angeles Kings	NHL	25	0	6	6	0	5	5	24	0	0	0	14	0.0	23	0	19	5	+9	....	....	....	....	....	....	....	....
	Springfield Indians	AHL	5	0	1	1	....	....	....	6	....	....	....	....	....	....	....	....	....	....	....	....	....	....	....	....	....	....
	St. Louis Blues	NHL	33	2	8	10	2	7	9	73	0	0	0	26	7.7	23	4	50	2	-29	....	....	....	....	....	....	....	....
1978-79	St. Louis Blues	NHL	42	1	2	3	1	2	3	30	0	0	0	28	3.6	41	0	46	5	0	....	....	....	....	....	....	....	....
	Salt Lake Golden Eagles	CHL	23	0	2	2	....	....	....	36	....	....	....	....	....	....	....	....	....	....	....	....	....	....	....	....	....	....
1979-80	St. Louis Blues	NHL	49	0	12	12	0	9	9	52	0	0	0	22	0.0	30	0	62	10	-22	....	....	....	....	....	....	....	....
1980-81	Salt Lake Golden Eagles	CHL	12	0	3	3	....	....	....	12	....	....	....	....	....	....	....	....	....	....	....	....	....	....	....	....	....	....
	Oklahoma City Stars	CHL	28	0	10	10	....	....	....	20	....	....	....	....	....	....	....	....	....	....	....	....	....	....	....	....	....	....
	NHL Totals		502	16	76	92	16	61	77	632	5	0	1	426	3.8	402	31	481	76		23	0	2	2	47	0	0	0

Traded to **St. Louis** by **LA Kings** for St. Louis' 2nd round choice (Greg Terrion), January 14, 1978. Claimed by **St. Louis** as a fill-in during Expansion Draft, June 13, 1979.

• KONIK, GEORGE

George Konik D/LW – L. 5'11", 190 lbs. b: Flin Flon, Man., 5/4/1937.

Season	Club	League	GP	G	A	Pts	AG	AA	APts	PIM	PP	SH	GW	S	%	TGF	PGF	TGA	PGA	+/-	GP	G	A	Pts	PIM	PP	SH	GW
1952-53	Flin Flon Bombers	SJHL	5	0	0	0	....	....	....	4	....	....	....	....	....	....	....	....	....	....	....	....	....	....	....	....	....	....
1953-54	Flin Flon Bombers	SJHL	4	0	2	2	....	....	....	4	....	....	....	....	....	....	....	....	....	....	2	0	0	0	0	....	....	....
1954-55	Flin Flon Bombers	SJHL	12	9	5	14	....	....	....	18	....	....	....	....	....	....	....	....	....	....	....	....	....	....	....	....	....	....
1955-56	Flin Flon Bombers	SJHL	37	13	21	34	....	....	....	83	....	....	....	....	....	....	....	....	....	....	12	4	6	10	12	....	....	....
1956-57	Flin Flon Bombers	SJHL	53	35	41	76	....	....	....	73	....	....	....	....	....	....	....	....	....	....	10	5	7	12	7	....	....	....
1957-58	University of Denver	WCHA	DID NOT PLAY – FRESHMAN																									
1958-59	University of Denver	WCHA	28	21	23	44	....	....	....	75	....	....	....	....	....	....	....	....	....	....	....	....	....	....	....	....	....	....
1959-60	University of Denver	WCHA	34	13	28	41	....	....	....	50	....	....	....	....	....	....	....	....	....	....	....	....	....	....	....	....	....	....
1960-61	University of Denver	WCHA	27	12	19	31	....	....	....	40	....	....	....	....	....	....	....	....	....	....	....	....	....	....	....	....	....	....
1961-62	Los Angeles Blades	WHL	43	3	8	11	....	....	....	38	....	....	....	....	....	....	....	....	....	....	....	....	....	....	....	....	....	....
1962-63	Seattle Totems	WHL	42	7	12	19	....	....	....	50	....	....	....	....	....	....	....	....	....	....	17	4	1	5	38	....	....	....
1963-64	Baltimore Clippers	AHL	72	19	22	41	....	....	....	80	....	....	....	....	....	....	....	....	....	....	....	....	....	....	....	....	....	....
1964-65	St. Paul Saints	USHL	STATISTICS NOT AVAILABLE																									
1965-66	Minnesota Rangers	CHL	38	10	20	30	....	....	....	35	....	....	....	....	....	....	....	....	....	....	7	2	5	7	6	....	....	....
1966-67	Omaha Knights	CHL	66	27	47	74	....	....	....	109	....	....	....	....	....	....	....	....	....	....	12	4	8	12	24	....	....	....
1967-68	Pittsburgh Penguins	NHL	52	7	8	15	9	8	17	26	1	0	1	50	14.0	19	4	27	3	-9	....	....	....	....	....	....	....	....
	Baltimore Clippers	AHL	5	0	2	2	....	....	....	7	....	....	....	....	....	....	....	....	....	....	....	....	....	....	....	....	....	....
1968-69	Rochester Mustangs	USHL	STATISTICS NOT AVAILABLE																									
1969-70	United States	Nat-Team	6	3	*5	*8	....	....	....	4	....	....	....	....	....	....	....	....	....	....	....	....	....	....	....	....	....	....
	United States	WEC-B	7	4	7	11	....	....	....	4	....	....	....	....	....	....	....	....	....	....	....	....	....	....	....	....	....	....
1970-71	Rochester Mustangs	USHL	STATISTICS NOT AVAILABLE																									
	United States	WEC-A	9	1	1	2	....	....	....	8	....	....	....	....	....	....	....	....	....	....	....	....	....	....	....	....	....	....
1971-72	Rochester Mustangs	USHL	STATISTICS NOT AVAILABLE																									
1972-73	Minnesota Fighting Saints	WHA	54	4	12	16	....	....	....	34	....	....	....	....	....	....	....	....	....	....	....	....	....	....	....	....	....	....
	NHL Totals		52	7	8	15	9	8	17	26	1	0	1	50	14.0	19	4	27	3		....	....	....	....	....	....	....	....
	Other Major League Totals		54	4	12	16	....	....	....	34	....	....	....	....	....	....	....	....	....	....	....	....	....	....	....	....	....	....

WCHA Second All-Star Team (1960) • NCAA West First All-American Team (1960) • NCAA Championship All-Tournament Team (1960) • WCHA First All-Star Team (1961) • CHL First All-Star Team (1967) • WEC-B All-Star Team (1970) • Named Best Defenseman at WEC-B (1970)

Traded to **Pittsburgh** by **NY Rangers** with Paul Andrea, Dunc McCallum and Frank Francis for Larry Jeffrey, June 6, 1967. Selected by **Minnesota** (WHA) in 1972 WHA General Player Draft, February 12, 1972.

• KONOWALCHUK, STEVE

Steve Konowalchuk C – L. 6'1", 195 lbs. b: Salt Lake City, UT, 11/11/1972. Washington's 5th choice, 58th overall, in 1991 Entry Draft.

Season	Club	League	GP	G	A	Pts	AG	AA	APts	PIM	PP	SH	GW	S	%	TGF	PGF	TGA	PGA	+/-	GP	G	A	Pts	PIM	PP	SH	GW
1990-91	Portland Winter Hawks	WHL	72	43	49	92	....	....	....	78	....	....	....	....	....	....	....	....	....	....	....	....	....	....	....	....	....	....
1991-92	Portland Winter Hawks	WHL	64	51	53	104	....	....	....	95	....	....	....	....	....	....	....	....	....	....	6	3	6	9	12	....	....	....
	United States	WJC-A	7	4	0	4	....	....	....	8	....	....	....	....	....	....	....	....	....	....	....	....	....	....	....	....	....	....
	Washington Capitals	NHL	1	0	0	0	0	0	0	0	0	0	0	1	0.0	0	0	0	0	0	....	....	....	....	....	....	....	....
	Baltimore Skipjacks	AHL	3	1	1	2	....	....	....	0	....	....	....	....	....	....	....	....	....	....	....	....	....	....	....	....	....	....
1992-93	Washington Capitals	NHL	36	4	7	11	3	5	8	16	1	0	1	34	11.8	14	2	8	0	+4	2	0	1	1	0	0	0	0
	Baltimore Skipjacks	AHL	37	18	28	46	....	....	....	74	....	....	....	....	....	....	....	....	....	....	....	....	....	....	....	....	....	....
1993-94	Washington Capitals	NHL	62	12	14	26	11	11	22	33	0	0	0	63	19.0	37	6	29	7	+9	11	0	1	1	10	0	0	0
	Portland Pirates	AHL	8	11	4	15	....	....	....	4	....	....	....	....	....	....	....	....	....	....	....	....	....	....	....	....	....	....
1994-95	Washington Capitals	NHL	46	11	14	25	19	21	40	44	3	3	3	88	12.5	31	3	31	10	+7	7	2	5	7	12	0	1	0
1995-96	Washington Capitals	NHL	70	23	22	45	23	18	41	92	7	1	3	197	11.7	69	25	55	24	+13	2	0	2	2	0	0	0	0
1996-97	United States	W-Cup	1	0	0	0	....	....	....	0	....	....	....	....	....	....	....	....	....	....	....	....	....	....	....	....	....	....
	Washington Capitals	NHL	78	17	25	42	18	22	40	67	2	1	3	155	11.0	52	10	61	16	-3	....	....	....	....	....	....	....	....
1997-98	Washington Capitals	NHL	80	10	24	34	12	23	35	80	2	0	2	131	7.6	57	7	53	12	+9	....	....	....	....	....	....	....	....
	NHL Totals		373	77	106	183	86	100	186	332	15	5	12	669	11.5	260	53	237	69		22	2	9	11	22	0	1	0

WHL First All-Star Team (1992)

• KONROYD, STEVE

Steve Konroyd D – L. 6'1", 195 lbs. b: Scarborough, Ont., 2/10/1961. Calgary's 4th choice, 39th overall, in 1980 Entry Draft.

Season	Club	League	GP	G	A	Pts	AG	AA	APts	PIM	PP	SH	GW	S	%	TGF	PGF	TGA	PGA	+/-	GP	G	A	Pts	PIM	PP	SH	GW
1978-79	Oshawa Generals	OHA	65	4	19	23	....	....	....	63	....	....	....	....	....	....	....	....	....	....	....	....	....	....	....	....	....	....
1979-80	Oshawa Generals	OHA	62	11	23	34	....	....	....	133	....	....	....	....	....	....	....	....	....	....	7	0	2	2	14	....	....	....
1980-81	Calgary Flames	NHL	4	0	0	0	0	0	0	4	0	0	0	0	0.0	1	0	1	0	0	....	....	....	....	....	....	....	....
	Oshawa Generals	OHA	59	19	47	68	....	....	....	232	....	....	....	....	....	....	....	....	....	....	11	3	11	14	35	....	....	....
1981-82	Calgary Flames	NHL	63	3	14	17	2	9	11	78	0	0	1	57	5.3	71	7	73	3	-6	3	0	0	0	12	0	0	0
	Oklahoma City Stars	CHL	14	2	3	5	....	....	....	15	....	....	....	....	....	....	....	....	....	....	....	....	....	....	....	....	....	....
1982-83	Calgary Flames	NHL	79	4	13	17	3	9	12	73	0	0	0	80	5.0	87	1	111	28	+3	9	2	1	3	18	0	0	0
1983-84	Calgary Flames	NHL	80	1	13	14	1	9	10	94	0	1	0	94	1.1	81	0	131	42	-8	8	1	2	3	8	0	0	0
1984-85	Calgary Flames	NHL	64	3	23	26	2	16	18	73	0	0	0	121	2.5	86	15	101	42	+12	4	1	4	5	2	0	1	0
	Canada	WEC-A	10	0	3	3	....	....	....	0	....	....	....	....	....	....	....	....	....	....	....	....	....	....	....	....	....	....
1985-86	Calgary Flames	NHL	59	7	20	27	6	13	19	64	1	0	1	111	6.3	93	17	91	35	+20	....	....	....	....	....	....	....	....
	New York Islanders	NHL	14	0	5	5	0	3	3	16	0	0	0	13	0.0	15	0	13	2	+4	3	0	0	0	6	0	0	0
1986-87	New York Islanders	NHL	72	5	16	21	4	12	16	70	3	0	0	119	4.2	79	13	106	36	-4	14	1	4	5	10	0	0	0
1987-88	New York Islanders	NHL	62	2	15	17	2	11	13	99	1	0	0	105	1.9	81	13	104	42	+10	6	1	0	1	4	0	1	0
1988-89	New York Islanders	NHL	21	1	5	6	1	4	5	2	0	0	0	30	3.3	18	3	42	22	-5	....	....	....	....	....	....	....	....
	Chicago Blackhawks	NHL	57	5	7	12	4	5	9	40	0	0	1	102	4.9	54	1	101	37	-11	16	2	0	2	10	0	1	0
1989-90	Chicago Blackhawks	NHL	75	3	14	17	3	10	13	34	1	0	0	93	3.2	78	1	96	25	+6	20	1	3	4	19	0	0	0

			REGULAR SEASON																		PLAYOFFS							
Season	Club	League	GP	G	A	Pts	AG	AA	APts	PIM	PP	SH	GW	S	%	TGF	PGF	TGA	PGA	+/–	GP	G	A	Pts	PIM	PP	SH	GW
1990-91	**Chicago Blackhawks**	**NHL**	**70**	**0**	**12**	**12**	**0**	**9**	**9**	**40**	**0**	**0**	**0**	**93**	**0.0**	**54**	**3**	**59**	**19**	**+11**	**6**	**1**	**0**	**1**	**8**	**0**	**0**	**0**
	Canada	WEC-A	10	1	3	4	....	....	....	0	....	....	....	....	....	....	....	....	....	....	....	....	....	....	....	....	....	....
1991-92	**Chicago Blackhawks**	**NHL**	**49**	**2**	**14**	**16**	**2**	**11**	**13**	**65**	**0**	**0**	**0**	**70**	**2.9**	**45**	**8**	**52**	**19**	**+4**	....	....	....	....	....	....	....	....
	Hartford Whalers	**NHL**	**33**	**2**	**10**	**12**	**2**	**7**	**9**	**32**	**1**	**0**	**0**	**56**	**3.6**	**32**	**8**	**52**	**23**	**–5**	**7**	**0**	**1**	**1**	**2**	**0**	**0**	**0**
1992-93	**Hartford Whalers**	**NHL**	**59**	**3**	**11**	**14**	**2**	**8**	**10**	**63**	**0**	**0**	**0**	**62**	**4.8**	**49**	**3**	**90**	**28**	**–16**	....	....	....	....	....	....	....	....
	Detroit Red Wings	**NHL**	**6**	**0**	**1**	**1**	**0**	**1**	**1**	**4**	**0**	**0**	**0**	**4**	**0.0**	**3**	**0**	**5**	**3**	**+1**	**1**	**0**	**0**	**0**	**0**	**0**	**0**	**0**
1993-94	**Detroit Red Wings**	**NHL**	**19**	**0**	**0**	**0**	**0**	**0**	**0**	**10**	**0**	**0**	**0**	**12**	**0.0**	**11**	**1**	**10**	**1**	**+1**	....	....	....	....	....	....	....	....
	Ottawa Senators	**NHL**	**8**	**0**	**2**	**2**	**0**	**2**	**2**	**2**	**0**	**0**	**0**	**9**	**0.0**	**7**	**0**	**12**	**1**	**–4**	....	....	....	....	....	....	....	....
1994-95	Chicago Wolves	IHL	16	2	2	4	....	....	....	4	....	....	....	....	....	....	....	....	....	....	3	0	1	1	2	....	....	....
	Calgary Flames	**NHL**	**1**	**0**	**0**	**0**	**0**	**0**	**0**	**0**	**0**	**0**	**0**	**0**	**0.0**	**1**	**0**	**1**	**0**	**0**	....	....	....	....	....	....	....	....
	NHL Totals		**895**	**41**	**195**	**236**	**34**	**139**	**173**	**863**	**7**	**1**	**3**	**1231**	**3.3**	**946**	**94**	**1241**	**408**		**97**	**10**	**15**	**25**	**99**	**0**	**3**	**0**

OHA Second All-Star Team (1981)

Traded to **NY Islanders** by **Calgary** with Richard Kromm for John Tonelli, March 11, 1986. Traded to **Chicago** by **NY Islanders** with Bob Bassen for Marc Bergevin and Gary Nylund, November 25, 1988. Traded to **Hartford** by **Chicago** for Rob Brown, January 24, 1992. Traded to **Detroit** by **Hartford** for Detroit's 6th round choice (traded back to Detroit — Detroit selected Tim Spitzig) in 1993 Entry Draft, March 22, 1993. Traded to **Ottawa** by **Detroit** for Daniel Berthiaume, March 21, 1994. Signed as a free agent by **Calgary**, April 7, 1995.

• KONSTANTINOV, VLADIMIR

Vladimir Konstantinov D – R. 5'11", 190 lbs. b: Murmansk, USSR, 3/19/1967. Detroit's 12th choice, 221st overall, in 1989 Entry Draft.

Season	Club	League	GP	G	A	Pts	AG	AA	APts	PIM	PP	SH	GW	S	%	TGF	PGF	TGA	PGA	+/–	GP	G	A	Pts	PIM	PP	SH	GW
1984-85	CSKA Moscow	USSR	40	1	4	5	....	....	....	10	....	....	....	....	....	....	....	....	....	....	....	....	....	....	....	....	....	....
1985-86	CSKA Moscow	USSR	26	4	3	7	....	....	....	12	....	....	....	....	....	....	....	....	....	....	....	....	....	....	....	....	....	....
	Soviet Union	WJC-A	7	2	4	6	....	....	....	4	....	....	....	....	....	....	....	....	....	....	....	....	....	....	....	....	....	....
	Soviet Union	WEC-A	10	1	1	2	....	....	....	8	....	....	....	....	....	....	....	....	....	....	....	....	....	....	....	....	....	....
1986-87	CSKA Moscow	USSR	35	2	2	4	....	....	....	19	....	....	....	....	....	....	....	....	....	....	....	....	....	....	....	....	....	....
1987-88	CSKA Moscow	USSR	50	3	6	9	....	....	....	32	....	....	....	....	....	....	....	....	....	....	....	....	....	....	....	....	....	....
1988-89	CSKA Moscow	USSR	37	7	8	15	....	....	....	20	....	....	....	....	....	....	....	....	....	....	....	....	....	....	....	....	....	....
	CSKA Moscow	SuperS	7	1	1	2	....	....	....	8	....	....	....	....	....	....	....	....	....	....	....	....	....	....	....	....	....	....
	Soviet Union	WEC-A	8	2	1	3	....	....	....	2	....	....	....	....	....	....	....	....	....	....	....	....	....	....	....	....	....	....
1989-90	CSKA Moscow	FrTour	1	0	0	0	....	....	....	2	....	....	....	....	....	....	....	....	....	....	....	....	....	....	....	....	....	....
	CSKA Moscow	USSR	47	14	14	28	....	....	....	44	....	....	....	....	....	....	....	....	....	....	....	....	....	....	....	....	....	....
	CSKA Moscow	SuperS	5	0	2	2	....	....	....	6	....	....	....	....	....	....	....	....	....	....	....	....	....	....	....	....	....	....
	Soviet Union	WEC-A	10	2	2	4	....	....	....	12	....	....	....	....	....	....	....	....	....	....	....	....	....	....	....	....	....	....
1990-91	CSKA Moscow	FrTour	1	0	0	0	....	....	....	2	....	....	....	....	....	....	....	....	....	....	....	....	....	....	....	....	....	....
	CSKA Moscow	USSR	45	5	12	17	....	....	....	42	....	....	....	....	....	....	....	....	....	....	....	....	....	....	....	....	....	....
	CSKA Moscow	SuperS	7	1	5	6	....	....	....	10	....	....	....	....	....	....	....	....	....	....	....	....	....	....	....	....	....	....
	Soviet Union	WEC-A	10	0	2	2	....	....	....	37	....	....	....	....	....	....	....	....	....	....	....	....	....	....	....	....	....	....
1991-92	**Detroit Red Wings**	**NHL**	**79**	**8**	**26**	**34**	**7**	**20**	**27**	**172**	**1**	**0**	**2**	**108**	**7.4**	**103**	**7**	**103**	**32**	**+25**	**11**	**0**	**1**	**1**	**16**	**0**	**0**	**0**
1992-93	**Detroit Red Wings**	**NHL**	**82**	**5**	**17**	**22**	**4**	**12**	**16**	**137**	**0**	**0**	**0**	**85**	**5.9**	**86**	**1**	**99**	**36**	**+22**	**7**	**0**	**1**	**1**	**8**	**0**	**0**	**0**
1993-94	**Detroit Red Wings**	**NHL**	**80**	**12**	**21**	**33**	**11**	**16**	**27**	**138**	**1**	**3**	**3**	**97**	**12.4**	**93**	**10**	**81**	**28**	**+30**	**7**	**0**	**2**	**2**	**4**	**0**	**0**	**0**
1994-95	Wedemark	German 2	15	13	17	30	....	....	....	51	....	....	....	....	....	....	....	....	....	....	....	....	....	....	....	....	....	....
	Detroit Red Wings	**NHL**	**47**	**3**	**11**	**14**	**5**	**16**	**21**	**101**	**0**	**0**	**0**	**57**	**5.3**	**44**	**6**	**37**	**9**	**+10**	**18**	**1**	**1**	**2**	**22**	**0**	**0**	**1**
1995-96	**Detroit Red Wings**	**NHL**	**81**	**14**	**20**	**34**	**14**	**16**	**30**	**139**	**3**	**1**	**3**	**168**	**8.3**	**113**	**19**	**51**	**17**	**+60**	**19**	**4**	**5**	**9**	**28**	**0**	**1**	**0**
1996-97	**Detroit Red Wings**	**NHL**	**77**	**5**	**33**	**38**	**5**	**29**	**34**	**151**	**0**	**0**	**0**	**141**	**3.5**	**92**	**15**	**59**	**20**	**+38**	**20**	**0**	**4**	**4**	**29**	**0**	**0**	**0**
1997-98	**Detroit Red Wings**	**NHL**	DID NOT PLAY – INJURED																									
	NHL Totals		**446**	**47**	**128**	**175**	**46**	**109**	**155**	**838**	**5**	**4**	**8**	**656**	**7.2**	**531**	**58**	**430**	**142**		**82**	**5**	**14**	**19**	**107**	**0**	**1**	**1**

NHL/Upper Deck All-Rookie Team (1992) • NHL Second All-Star Team (1996) • Won Alka-Seltzer Plus Award (1996)

• KONTOS, CHRIS

Chris Kontos LW/C – L. 6'1", 195 lbs. b: Toronto, Ont., 12/10/1963. NY Rangers' 1st choice, 15th overall, in 1982 Entry Draft.

Season	Club	League	GP	G	A	Pts	AG	AA	APts	PIM	PP	SH	GW	S	%	TGF	PGF	TGA	PGA	+/–	GP	G	A	Pts	PIM	PP	SH	GW
1980-81	Sudbury Wolves	OHA	57	17	27	44	....	....	....	36	....	....	....	....	....	....	....	....	....	....	....	....	....	....	....	....	....	....
1981-82	Sudbury Wolves	OHL	12	6	6	12	....	....	....	18	....	....	....	....	....	....	....	....	....	....	....	....	....	....	....	....	....	....
	Toronto Marlboros	OHL	59	36	56	92	....	....	....	68	....	....	....	....	....	....	....	....	....	....	10	7	9	16	2	....	....	....
1982-83	Toronto Marlboros	OHL	28	21	33	54	....	....	....	23	....	....	....	....	....	....	....	....	....	....	....	....	....	....	....	....	....	....
	New York Rangers	**NHL**	**44**	**8**	**7**	**15**	**7**	**5**	**12**	**33**	**0**	**0**	**0**	**63**	**12.7**	**26**	**1**	**24**	**0**	**+1**	....	....	....	....	....	....	....	....
1983-84	**New York Rangers**	**NHL**	**6**	**0**	**1**	**1**	**0**	**1**	**1**	**8**	**0**	**0**	**0**	**1**	**0.0**	**1**	**0**	**1**	**0**	**0**	....	....	....	....	....	....	....	....
	Tulsa Oilers	CHL	21	5	13	18	....	....	....	8	....	....	....	....	....	....	....	....	....	....	....	....	....	....	....	....	....	....
1984-85	**New York Rangers**	**NHL**	**28**	**4**	**8**	**12**	**3**	**5**	**8**	**24**	**1**	**0**	**0**	**50**	**8.0**	**17**	**4**	**25**	**0**	**–12**	....	....	....	....	....	....	....	....
	New Haven Nighthawks	AHL	48	19	24	43	....	....	....	30	....	....	....	....	....	....	....	....	....	....	....	....	....	....	....	....	....	....
1985-86	Ilves Tampere	Finland	36	16	15	31	....	....	....	30	....	....	....	....	....	....	....	....	....	....	....	....	....	....	....	....	....	....
	New Haven Nighthawks	AHL	21	8	15	23	....	....	....	12	....	....	....	....	....	....	....	....	....	....	5	4	2	6	4	....	....	....
1986-87	**Pittsburgh Penguins**	**NHL**	**31**	**8**	**9**	**17**	**7**	**6**	**13**	**6**	**1**	**0**	**1**	**38**	**21.1**	**24**	**6**	**25**	**1**	**–6**	....	....	....	....	....	....	....	....
	New Haven Nighthawks	AHL	36	14	17	31	....	....	....	29	....	....	....	....	....	....	....	....	....	....	....	....	....	....	....	....	....	....
1987-88	**Pittsburgh Penguins**	**NHL**	**36**	**1**	**7**	**8**	**1**	**5**	**6**	**12**	**0**	**0**	**0**	**17**	**5.9**	**8**	**0**	**23**	**12**	**–3**	....	....	....	....	....	....	....	....
	Muskegon Lumberjacks	IHL	10	3	6	9	....	....	....	8	....	....	....	....	....	....	....	....	....	....	....	....	....	....	....	....	....	....
	Los Angeles Kings	**NHL**	**6**	**2**	**10**	**12**	**2**	**7**	**9**	**2**	**1**	**0**	**0**	**19**	**10.5**	**18**	**10**	**10**	**3**	**+1**	**4**	**1**	**0**	**1**	**4**	**0**	**0**	**0**
	New Haven Nighthawks	AHL	16	8	16	24	....	....	....	4	....	....	....	....	....	....	....	....	....	....	....	....	....	....	....	....	....	....
1988-89	EHC Kloten	Switz.	36	33	22	55	....	....	....	....	....	....	....	....	....	....	....	....	....	....	6	6	2	8	....	....	....	....
	Los Angeles Kings	**NHL**	**7**	**2**	**1**	**3**	**2**	**1**	**3**	**2**	**1**	**0**	**0**	**9**	**22.2**	**7**	**1**	**4**	**0**	**+2**	**11**	**9**	**0**	**9**	**8**	**6**	**0**	**1**
1989-90	**Los Angeles Kings**	**NHL**	**6**	**2**	**2**	**4**	**2**	**1**	**3**	**4**	**0**	**0**	**0**	**9**	**22.2**	**7**	**1**	**3**	**0**	**+3**	**5**	**1**	**0**	**1**	**0**	**0**	**1**	**0**
	New Haven Nighthawks	AHL	42	10	20	30	....	....	....	25	....	....	....	....	....	....	....	....	....	....	....	....	....	....	....	....	....	....
1990-91	Phoenix Roadrunners	IHL	69	26	36	62	....	....	....	19	....	....	....	....	....	....	....	....	....	....	11	9	12	21	0	....	....	....
1991-92	Canada	Nat-Team	26	10	10	20	....	....	....	4	....	....	....	....	....	....	....	....	....	....	....	....	....	....	....	....	....	....
1992-93	**Tampa Bay Lightning**	**NHL**	**66**	**27**	**24**	**51**	**23**	**16**	**39**	**12**	**12**	**1**	**3**	**136**	**19.9**	**74**	**34**	**58**	**11**	**–7**	....	....	....	....	....	....	....	....
1993-94	Canada	Nat-Team	35	16	16	32	....	....	....	12	....	....	....	....	....	....	....	....	....	....	....	....	....	....	....	....	....	....
	Canada	Olympics	8	3	1	4	....	....	....	2	....	....	....	....	....	....	....	....	....	....	....	....	....	....	....	....	....	....
1994-95	Skelleftea	Sweden	36	21	27	48	....	....	....	30	....	....	....	....	....	....	....	....	....	....	5	2	3	5	4	....	....	....
	Canada	Nat-Team	3	0	1	1	....	....	....	4	....	....	....	....	....	....	....	....	....	....	....	....	....	....	....	....	....	....
1995-96	Cincinnati Cyclones	IHL	81	26	44	70	....	....	....	13	....	....	....	....	....	....	....	....	....	....	17	5	8	13	0	....	....	....
1996-97	Cincinnati Cyclones	IHL	11	1	3	4	....	....	....	4	....	....	....	....	....	....	....	....	....	....	....	....	....	....	....	....	....	....
	Quebec Rafales	IHL	19	8	3	11	....	....	....	0	....	....	....	....	....	....	....	....	....	....	....	....	....	....	....	....	....	....
	Manitoba Moose	IHL	40	17	18	35	....	....	....	12	....	....	....	....	....	....	....	....	....	....	....	....	....	....	....	....	....	....
1997-98	ECR Revier Lowen	Germany	26	10	4	14	....	....	....	14	....	....	....	....	....	....	....	....	....	....	....	....	....	....	....	....	....	....
	NHL Totals		**230**	**54**	**69**	**123**	**47**	**47**	**94**	**103**	**16**	**1**	**4**	**342**	**15.8**	**182**	**57**	**173**	**27**		**20**	**11**	**0**	**11**	**12**	**6**	**1**	**1**

Traded to **Pittsburgh** by **NY Rangers** for Ron Duguay, January 21, 1987. Traded to **LA Kings** by **Pittsburgh** with Pittsburgh's 6th round choice (Micah Aivazoff) in 1988 Entry Draft for Bryan Erickson, February 5, 1988. Signed as a free agent by **Tampa Bay**, July 21, 1992. Signed as a free agent by **Florida**, July 7, 1995.

• KORAB, JERRY

Jerry "Kong" Korab D – L. 6'3", 220 lbs. b: Sault Ste. Marie, Ont., 9/15/1948.

Season	Club	League	GP	G	A	Pts	AG	AA	APts	PIM	PP	SH	GW	S	%	TGF	PGF	TGA	PGA	+/–	GP	G	A	Pts	PIM	PP	SH	GW
1966-67	St. Catharines Black Hawks	OHA	43	3	10	13	....	....	....	57	....	....	....	....	....	....	....	....	....	....	4	0	1	1	12	....	....	....
1967-68	St. Catharines Black Hawks	OHA	54	10	34	44	....	....	....	*244	....	....	....	....	....	....	....	....	....	....	5	0	3	3	26	....	....	....
1968-69	Port Huron Flags	IHL	71	18	46	64	....	....	....	284	....	....	....	....	....	....	....	....	....	....	....	....	....	....	....	....	....	....
1969-70	Portland Buckaroos	WHL	65	9	12	21	....	....	....	169	....	....	....	....	....	....	....	....	....	....	....	....	....	....	....	....	....	....
1970-71	**Chicago Black Hawks**	**NHL**	**46**	**4**	**14**	**18**	**4**	**12**	**16**	**152**	**1**	**0**	**1**	**97**	**4.1**	**47**	**1**	**35**	**3**	**+14**	**7**	**1**	**0**	**1**	**20**	**0**	**0**	**0**
	Portland Buckaroos	WHL	20	3	5	8	....	....	....	78	....	....	....	....	....	....	....	....	....	....	....	....	....	....	....	....	....	....
1971-72	**Chicago Black Hawks**	**NHL**	**73**	**9**	**5**	**14**	**10**	**5**	**15**	**95**	**2**	**0**	**1**	**97**	**9.3**	**37**	**12**	**27**	**3**	**+1**	**8**	**0**	**1**	**1**	**20**	**0**	**0**	**0**
1972-73	**Chicago Black Hawks**	**NHL**	**77**	**12**	**15**	**27**	**12**	**13**	**25**	**94**	**0**	**1**	**1**	**127**	**9.4**	**49**	**7**	**53**	**16**	**+5**	**15**	**0**	**0**	**0**	**22**	**0**	**0**	**0**
1973-74	**Vancouver Canucks**	**NHL**	**31**	**4**	**7**	**11**	**4**	**6**	**10**	**64**	**3**	**0**	**0**	**75**	**5.3**	**26**	**13**	**42**	**8**	**–21**	....	....	....	....	....	....	....	....
	Buffalo Sabres	**NHL**	**45**	**6**	**12**	**18**	**6**	**10**	**16**	**73**	**2**	**0**	**0**	**106**	**5.7**	**44**	**6**	**67**	**6**	**–23**	....	....	....	....	....	....	....	....
1974-75	**Buffalo Sabres**	**NHL**	**79**	**12**	**44**	**56**	**11**	**35**	**46**	**184**	**3**	**2**	**1**	**218**	**5.5**	**189**	**61**	**126**	**39**	**+41**	**16**	**3**	**2**	**5**	**32**	**1**	**0**	**0**
1975-76	**Buffalo Sabres**	**NHL**	**65**	**13**	**28**	**41**	**12**	**22**	**34**	**85**	**3**	**0**	**1**	**146**	**8.9**	**122**	**29**	**100**	**25**	**+18**	**9**	**1**	**3**	**4**	**12**	**0**	**0**	**0**
1976-77	**Buffalo Sabres**	**NHL**	**77**	**14**	**33**	**47**	**13**	**27**	**40**	**120**	**4**	**0**	**1**	**185**	**7.6**	**140**	**40**	**96**	**18**	**+22**	**6**	**2**	**4**	**6**	**8**	**1**	**0**	**1**
1977-78	**Buffalo Sabres**	**NHL**	**77**	**7**	**34**	**41**	**7**	**28**	**35**	**119**	**3**	**0**	**2**	**204**	**3.4**	**135**	**26**	**113**	**23**	**+19**	**8**	**0**	**5**	**5**	**6**	**0**	**0**	**0**
1978-79	**Buffalo Sabres**	**NHL**	**78**	**11**	**40**	**51**	**10**	**31**	**41**	**104**	**8**	**1**	**0**	**204**	**5.4**	**131**	**40**	**125**	**39**	**+5**	**3**	**1**	**0**	**1**	**4**	**0**	**0**	**0**
1979-80	**Buffalo Sabres**	**NHL**	**43**	**1**	**10**	**11**	**1**	**8**	**9**	**74**	**0**	**0**	**1**	**55**	**1.8**	**45**	**6**	**46**	**7**	**0**	....	....	....	....	....	....	....	....
	Los Angeles Kings	**NHL**	**11**	**1**	**2**	**3**	**1**	**2**	**3**	**34**	**0**	**0**	**0**	**30**	**3.3**	**10**	**3**	**14**	**4**	**–3**	**3**	**0**	**1**	**1**	**11**	**0**	**0**	**0**
1980-81	**Los Angeles Kings**	**NHL**	**78**	**9**	**43**	**52**	**7**	**30**	**37**	**139**	**3**	**0**	**2**	**120**	**7.5**	**146**	**55**	**118**	**37**	**+10**	**4**	**0**	**0**	**0**	**33**	**0**	**0**	**0**

							REGULAR SEASON															PLAYOFFS							
Season	**Club**	**League**	**GP**	**G**	**A**	**Pts**	**AG**	**AA**	**APts**	**PIM**	**PP**	**SH**	**GW**	**S**	**%**	**TGF**	**PGF**	**TGA**	**PGA**	**+/–**	**GP**	**G**	**A**	**Pts**	**PIM**	**PP**	**SH**	**GW**
1981-82	**Los Angeles Kings**	**NHL**	**50**	**5**	**13**	**18**	**4**	**9**	**13**	**91**	**3**	**0**	**0**	**71**	**7.0**	**70**	**22**	**81**	**14**	**–19**	**10**	**0**	**2**	**2**	**26**	**0**	**0**	**0**
1982-83	**Los Angeles Kings**	**NHL**	**72**	**3**	**26**	**29**	**2**	**18**	**20**	**90**	**1**	**0**	**0**	**132**	**2.3**	**83**	**15**	**109**	**35**	**–6**	....	....	....	....	....	....	....	....
1983-84	**Buffalo Sabres**	**NHL**	**48**	**2**	**9**	**11**	**2**	**6**	**8**	**82**	**1**	**0**	**1**	**41**	**4.9**	**46**	**3**	**45**	**6**	**+4**	**3**	**0**	**0**	**0**	**5**	**0**	**0**	**0**
	Rochester Americans	AHL	4	0	4	4	....	....	....	2	....	....	....	....	....	....	....	....	....	....	....	....	....	....	....	....	....	....
1984-85	**Buffalo Sabres**	**NHL**	**25**	**1**	**6**	**7**	**1**	**4**	**5**	**29**	**0**	**0**	**1**	**30**	**3.3**	**23**	**9**	**27**	**4**	**–9**	**1**	**0**	**0**	**0**	**2**	**0**	**0**	**0**
	Rochester Americans	AHL	3	1	2	3	....	....	....	6	....	....	....	....	....	....	....	....	....	....	....	....	....	....	....	....	....	....
	NHL Totals		**975**	**114**	**341**	**455**	**107**	**266**	**373**	**1629**	**37**	**4**	**13**	**1938**	**5.9**	**1343**	**348**	**1224**	**287**		**93**	**8**	**18**	**26**	**201**	**2**	**0**	**1**

Played in NHL All-Star Game (1975, 1976)

Traded to **Vancouver** by **Chicago** with Gary Smith for Dale Tallon, May 14, 1973. Traded to **Buffalo** by **Vancouver** for John Gould and Tracy Pratt, December 27, 1973. Traded to **LA Kings** by **Buffalo** for LA Kings' 1st round choice (Phil Housley) in 1982 Entry Draft, March 10, 1980. Signed as a free agent by **Minnesota**, October 17, 1983. Claimed on waivers by **Buffalo** from **Minnesota**, October 20, 1983.

• KORDIC, DAN

Dan Kordic LW – L. 6'5", 234 lbs. b: Edmonton, Alta., 4/18/1971. Philadelphia's 9th choice, 88th overall, in 1990 Entry Draft.

Season	Club	League	GP	G	A	Pts	AG	AA	APts	PIM	PP	SH	GW	S	%	TGF	PGF	TGA	PGA	+/–	GP	G	A	Pts	PIM	PP	SH	GW
1987-88	Medicine Hat Tigers	WHL	63	1	5	6	....	....	....	75	....	....	....	....	....	....	....	....	....	....	....	....	....	....	....	....	....	....
1988-89	Medicine Hat Tigers	WHL	70	1	13	14	....	....	....	190	....	....	....	....	....	....	....	....	....	....	....	....	....	....	....	....	....	....
1989-90	Medicine Hat Tigers	WHL	59	4	12	16	....	....	....	182	....	....	....	....	....	....	....	....	....	....	3	0	0	0	9	....	....	....
1990-91	Medicine Hat Tigers	WHL	67	8	15	23	....	....	....	150	....	....	....	....	....	....	....	....	....	....	12	2	6	8	42	....	....	....
1991-92	**Philadelphia Flyers**	**NHL**	**46**	**1**	**3**	**4**	**1**	**2**	**3**	**126**	**0**	**0**	**0**	**27**	**3.7**	**23**	**0**	**32**	**10**	**+1**	....	....	....	....	....	....	....	....
1992-93	Hershey Bears	AHL	14	0	2	2	....	....	....	17	....	....	....	....	....	....	....	....	....	....	....	....	....	....	....	....	....	....
1993-94	**Philadelphia Flyers**	**NHL**	**4**	**0**	**0**	**0**	**0**	**0**	**0**	**5**	**0**	**0**	**0**	**0**	**0.0**	**1**	**0**	**1**	**0**	**0**	....	....	....	....	....	....	....	....
	Hershey Bears	AHL	64	0	4	4	....	....	....	164	....	....	....	....	....	....	....	....	....	....	11	0	3	3	26	....	....	....
1994-95	Hershey Bears	AHL	37	0	2	2	....	....	....	121	....	....	....	....	....	....	....	....	....	....	6	0	1	1	21	....	....	....
1995-96	**Philadelphia Flyers**	**NHL**	**9**	**1**	**0**	**1**	**1**	**0**	**1**	**31**	**0**	**0**	**0**	**2**	**50.0**	**4**	**0**	**3**	**0**	**+1**	....	....	....	....	....	....	....	....
	Hershey Bears	AHL	52	2	6	8	....	....	....	101	....	....	....	....	....	....	....	....	....	....	....	....	....	....	....	....	....	....
1996-97	**Philadelphia Flyers**	**NHL**	**75**	**1**	**4**	**5**	**1**	**4**	**5**	**210**	**0**	**0**	**0**	**21**	**4.8**	**11**	**0**	**12**	**0**	**–1**	**12**	**1**	**0**	**1**	**22**	**0**	**0**	**0**
1997-98	**Philadelphia Flyers**	**NHL**	**61**	**1**	**1**	**2**	**1**	**1**	**2**	**210**	**0**	**0**	**0**	**12**	**8.3**	**4**	**0**	**8**	**0**	**–4**	....	....	....	....	....	....	....	....
	NHL Totals		**195**	**4**	**8**	**12**	**4**	**7**	**11**	**582**	**0**	**0**	**0**	**62**	**6.5**	**43**	**0**	**56**	**10**		**12**	**1**	**0**	**1**	**22**	**0**	**0**	**0**

• KORDIC, JOHN

John Kordic RW – R. 6'2", 210 lbs. b: Edmonton, Alta., 3/22/1965. d: 8/8/1992. Montreal's 6th choice, 80th overall, in 1983 Entry Draft.

Season	Club	League	GP	G	A	Pts	AG	AA	APts	PIM	PP	SH	GW	S	%	TGF	PGF	TGA	PGA	+/–	GP	G	A	Pts	PIM	PP	SH	GW
1981-82	Edmonton K. of C.	Midget	48	23	41	64	....	....	....	178	....	....	....	....	....	....	....	....	....	....	....	....	....	....	....	....	....	....
1982-83	Portland Winter Hawks	WHL	72	3	22	25	....	....	....	235	....	....	....	....	....	....	....	....	....	....	14	1	6	7	30	....	....	....
1983-84	Portland Winter Hawks	WHL	67	9	50	59	....	....	....	232	....	....	....	....	....	....	....	....	....	....	14	0	13	13	56	....	....	....
1984-85	Portland Winter Hawks	WHL	25	6	22	28	....	....	....	73	....	....	....	....	....	....	....	....	....	....	....	....	....	....	....	....	....	....
	Seattle Breakers	WHL	46	17	36	53	....	....	....	154	....	....	....	....	....	....	....	....	....	....	....	....	....	....	....	....	....	....
	Sherbrooke Canadiens	AHL	4	0	0	0	....	....	....	4	....	....	....	....	....	....	....	....	....	....	4	0	0	0	11	....	....	....
1985-86	**Montreal Canadiens**	**NHL**	**5**	**0**	**1**	**1**	**0**	**1**	**1**	**12**	**0**	**0**	**0**	**0**	**0.0**	**1**	**0**	**0**	**0**	**+1**	**18**	**0**	**0**	**0**	**53**	**0**	**0**	**0**
	Sherbrooke Canadiens	AHL	68	3	14	17	....	....	....	238	....	....	....	....	....	....	....	....	....	....	....	....	....	....	....	....	....	....
1986-87	**Montreal Canadiens**	**NHL**	**44**	**5**	**3**	**8**	**4**	**2**	**6**	**151**	**0**	**0**	**0**	**32**	**15.6**	**11**	**0**	**18**	**0**	**–7**	**11**	**2**	**0**	**2**	**19**	**0**	**0**	**1**
	Sherbrooke Canadiens	AHL	10	4	4	8	....	....	....	49	....	....	....	....	....	....	....	....	....	....	....	....	....	....	....	....	....	....
1987-88	**Montreal Canadiens**	**NHL**	**60**	**2**	**6**	**8**	**2**	**4**	**6**	**159**	**0**	**0**	**0**	**17**	**11.8**	**12**	**0**	**12**	**0**	**0**	**7**	**2**	**2**	**4**	**26**	**0**	**0**	**0**
1988-89	**Montreal Canadiens**	**NHL**	**6**	**0**	**0**	**0**	**0**	**0**	**0**	**13**	**0**	**0**	**0**	**2**	**0.0**	**1**	**0**	**2**	**0**	**–1**	....	....	....	....	....	....	....	....
	Toronto Maple Leafs	**NHL**	**46**	**1**	**2**	**3**	**1**	**1**	**2**	**185**	**0**	**0**	**0**	**33**	**3.0**	**7**	**0**	**20**	**0**	**–13**	....	....	....	....	....	....	....	....
1989-90	**Toronto Maple Leafs**	**NHL**	**55**	**9**	**4**	**13**	**0**	**3**	**11**	**252**	**3**	**0**	**0**	**48**	**18.8**	**20**	**4**	**24**	**0**	**–8**	**5**	**0**	**1**	**1**	**33**	**0**	**0**	**0**
1990-91	**Toronto Maple Leafs**	**NHL**	**3**	**0**	**0**	**0**	**0**	**0**	**0**	**9**	**0**	**0**	**0**	**1**	**0.0**	**0**	**0**	**0**	**0**	**0**	....	....	....	....	....	....	....	....
	Newmarket Saints	AHL	8	1	1	2	....	....	....	79	....	....	....	....	....	....	....	....	....	....	....	....	....	....	....	....	....	....
	Washington Capitals	**NHL**	**7**	**0**	**0**	**0**	**0**	**0**	**0**	**101**	**0**	**0**	**0**	**0**	**0.0**	**2**	**0**	**1**	**0**	**+1**	....	....	....	....	....	....	....	....
1991-92	**Quebec Nordiques**	**NHL**	**18**	**0**	**2**	**2**	**0**	**1**	**1**	**115**	**0**	**0**	**0**	**3**	**0.0**	**2**	**0**	**5**	**0**	**–3**	....	....	....	....	....	....	....	....
	Cape Breton Oilers	AHL	12	2	1	3	....	....	....	141	....	....	....	....	....	....	....	....	....	....	5	0	1	1	53	....	....	....
	NHL Totals		**244**	**17**	**18**	**35**	**15**	**12**	**27**	**997**	**3**	**0**	**0**	**136**	**12.5**	**56**	**4**	**82**	**0**		**41**	**4**	**3**	**7**	**131**	**0**	**0**	**1**

WHL West Second All-Star Team (1985)

Traded to **Toronto** by **Montreal** with Montreal's 6th round choice (Michael Doers) in 1989 Entry Draft for Russ Courtnall, November 7, 1988. Traded to **Washington** by **Toronto** with Paul Fenton for Washington's 5th round choice (Alexei Kudashov) in 1991 Entry Draft, January 24, 1991. Signed as a free agent by **Quebec**, October 4, 1991.

• KORN, JIM

Jim Korn D – L. 6'4", 220 lbs. b: Hopkins, MN, 7/28/1957. Detroit's 4th choice, 73rd overall, in 1977 Amateur Draft.

Season	Club	League	GP	G	A	Pts	AG	AA	APts	PIM	PP	SH	GW	S	%	TGF	PGF	TGA	PGA	+/–	GP	G	A	Pts	PIM	PP	SH	GW
1976-77	Providence College	ECAC	29	6	19	15	....	....	....	73	....	....	....	....	....	....	....	....	....	....	....	....	....	....	....	....	....	....
1977-78	Providence College	ECAC	33	7	14	21	....	....	....	47	....	....	....	....	....	....	....	....	....	....	....	....	....	....	....	....	....	....
1978-79	Providence College	ECAC	27	5	19	24	....	....	....	72	....	....	....	....	....	....	....	....	....	....	....	....	....	....	....	....	....	....
	United States	WEC-A	8	0	1	1	....	....	....	8	....	....	....	....	....	....	....	....	....	....	....	....	....	....	....	....	....	....
1979-80	**Detroit Red Wings**	**NHL**	**63**	**5**	**13**	**18**	**5**	**10**	**15**	**108**	**1**	**0**	**1**	**58**	**8.6**	**62**	**5**	**64**	**3**	**–4**	....	....	....	....	....	....	....	....
	Adirondack Red Wings	AHL	14	2	7	9	....	....	....	40	....	....	....	....	....	....	....	....	....	....	....	....	....	....	....	....	....	....
1980-81	**Detroit Red Wings**	**NHL**	**63**	**5**	**15**	**20**	**4**	**10**	**14**	**246**	**1**	**1**	**1**	**82**	**6.1**	**71**	**10**	**82**	**16**	**–5**	....	....	....	....	....	....	....	....
	Adirondack Red Wings	AHL	9	3	7	10	....	....	....	53	....	....	....	....	....	....	....	....	....	....	....	....	....	....	....	....	....	....
	United States	WEC-A	5	0	1	1	....	....	....	6	....	....	....	....	....	....	....	....	....	....	....	....	....	....	....	....	....	....
1981-82	**Detroit Red Wings**	**NHL**	**59**	**1**	**7**	**8**	**1**	**5**	**6**	**104**	**0**	**0**	**0**	**41**	**2.4**	**28**	**2**	**55**	**10**	**–19**	....	....	....	....	....	....	....	....
	Toronto Maple Leafs	**NHL**	**11**	**1**	**3**	**4**	**1**	**2**	**3**	**44**	**0**	**0**	**0**	**10**	**10.0**	**16**	**2**	**23**	**10**	**+1**	....	....	....	....	....	....	....	....
1982-83	**Toronto Maple Leafs**	**NHL**	**80**	**8**	**21**	**29**	**7**	**14**	**21**	**236**	**0**	**3**	**1**	**101**	**7.9**	**93**	**6**	**162**	**48**	**–27**	**3**	**0**	**0**	**0**	**26**	**0**	**0**	**0**
1983-84	**Toronto Maple Leafs**	**NHL**	**65**	**12**	**14**	**26**	**10**	**9**	**19**	**257**	**0**	**0**	**1**	**94**	**12.8**	**61**	**3**	**121**	**30**	**–33**	....	....	....	....	....	....	....	....
1984-85	**Toronto Maple Leafs**	**NHL**	**41**	**5**	**5**	**10**	**4**	**3**	**7**	**171**	**2**	**0**	**1**	**48**	**10.4**	**25**	**7**	**35**	**0**	**–17**	....	....	....	....	....	....	....	....
1985-86			DID NOT PLAY – INJURED																									
1986-87	**Buffalo Sabres**	**NHL**	**52**	**4**	**10**	**14**	**3**	**7**	**10**	**158**	**0**	**0**	**0**	**35**	**11.4**	**24**	**0**	**30**	**3**	**–3**	....	....	....	....	....	....	....	....
1987-88	**New Jersey Devils**	**NHL**	**52**	**8**	**13**	**21**	**7**	**9**	**16**	**140**	**3**	**0**	**0**	**49**	**16.3**	**29**	**13**	**38**	**0**	**–22**	**9**	**0**	**2**	**2**	**71**	**0**	**0**	**0**
1988-89	**New Jersey Devils**	**NHL**	**65**	**15**	**16**	**31**	**13**	**11**	**24**	**212**	**4**	**0**	**3**	**66**	**23.1**	**53**	**11**	**50**	**5**	**–3**	....	....	....	....	....	....	....	....
1989-90	**New Jersey Devils**	**NHL**	**37**	**2**	**3**	**5**	**2**	**2**	**4**	**99**	**0**	**0**	**0**	**18**	**11.1**	**9**	**0**	**14**	**4**	**–1**	....	....	....	....	....	....	....	....
	Calgary Flames	**NHL**	**9**	**0**	**2**	**2**	**0**	**1**	**1**	**26**	**0**	**0**	**0**	**3**	**0.0**	**5**	**0**	**4**	**0**	**+1**	**4**	**1**	**0**	**1**	**12**	**0**	**0**	**0**
	NHL Totals		**597**	**66**	**122**	**188**	**57**	**83**	**140**	**1801**	**11**	**4**	**8**	**604**	**10.9**	**476**	**59**	**678**	**129**		**16**	**1**	**2**	**3**	**109**	**0**	**0**	**0**

ECAC Second All-Star Team (1979)

Traded to **Toronto** by **Detroit** for Toronto's 4th round choice (Craig Coxe) in 1982 Entry Draft and Toronto's 5th round choice (Joey Kocur) in 1983 Entry Draft, March 8, 1982. Traded to **Calgary** by **Toronto** for Terry Johnson, October 3, 1986. Traded to **Buffalo** by **Calgary** for Brian Engblom, October 3, 1986. Traded to **New Jersey** by **Buffalo** for Jan Ludwig, May 22, 1987. Traded to **Calgary** by **New Jersey** for Calgary's 5th round choice (Peter Kuchyna) in 1990 Entry Draft, March 6, 1990.

• KORNEY, MIKE

Mike Korney RW – R. 6'3", 195 lbs. b: Dauphin, Man., 9/15/1953. Detroit's 4th choice, 59th overall, in 1973 Amateur Draft.

Season	Club	League	GP	G	A	Pts	AG	AA	APts	PIM	PP	SH	GW	S	%	TGF	PGF	TGA	PGA	+/–	GP	G	A	Pts	PIM	PP	SH	GW
1970-71	Dauphin Kings	MJHL	45	15	31	46	....	....	....	38	....	....	....	....	....	....	....	....	....	....	....	....	....	....	....	....	....	....
1971-72	Dauphin Kings	MJHL	41	16	33	49	....	....	....	64	....	....	....	....	....	....	....	....	....	....	....	....	....	....	....	....	....	....
1972-73	Winnipeg Jets	WCJHL	68	20	20	40	....	....	....	92	....	....	....	....	....	....	....	....	....	....	....	....	....	....	....	....	....	....
1973-74	**Detroit Red Wings**	**NHL**	**2**	**0**	**0**	**0**	**0**	**0**	**0**	**0**	**0**	**0**	**0**	**1**	**0.0**	**1**	**0**	**4**	**0**	**–3**	....	....	....	....	....	....	....	....
	Virginia Wings	AHL	19	1	1	2	....	....	....	15	....	....	....	....	....	....	....	....	....	....	....	....	....	....	....	....	....	....
	Port Huron Wings	IHL	7	1	0	1	....	....	....	9	....	....	....	....	....	....	....	....	....	....	....	....	....	....	....	....	....	....
	London Lions	Britain	31	15	10	25	....	....	....	33	....	....	....	....	....	....	....	....	....	....	....	....	....	....	....	....	....	....
1974-75	**Detroit Red Wings**	**NHL**	**30**	**8**	**2**	**10**	**7**	**2**	**9**	**18**	**2**	**0**	**1**	**50**	**16.0**	**20**	**3**	**26**	**0**	**–9**	....	....	....	....	....	....	....	....
	Virginia Wings	AHL	2	0	0	0	....	....	....	0	....	....	....	....	....	....	....	....	....	....	....	....	....	....	....	....	....	....
	Providence Reds	AHL	3	1	0	1	....	....	....	0	....	....	....	....	....	....	....	....	....	....	....	....	....	....	....	....	....	....
	Springfield Indians	AHL	1	0	0	0	....	....	....	0	....	....	....	....	....	....	....	....	....	....	....	....	....	....	....	....	....	....
	Hampton Gulls	SHL	13	0	1	1	....	....	....	35	....	....	....	....	....	....	....	....	....	....	....	....	....	....	....	....	....	....
1975-76	**Detroit Red Wings**	**NHL**	**27**	**1**	**7**	**8**	**1**	**5**	**6**	**23**	**0**	**0**	**0**	**21**	**4.8**	**12**	**3**	**17**	**0**	**–8**	....	....	....	....	....	....	....	....
	New Haven Nighthawks	AHL	21	8	9	17	....	....	....	31	....	....	....	....	....	....	....	....	....	....	....	....	....	....	....	....	....	....
	Oklahoma City Blazers	CHL	18	8	6	14	....	....	....	20	....	....	....	....	....	....	....	....	....	....	4	0	0	0	2	....	....	....
1976-77	Kansas City Blues	CHL	74	17	24	41	....	....	....	82	....	....	....	....	....	....	....	....	....	....	10	1	6	7	13	....	....	....
1977-78	Salt Lake Golden Eagles	CHL	54	12	8	20	....	....	....	75	....	....	....	....	....	....	....	....	....	....	6	2	4	6	6	....	....	....
	Maine Mariners	AHL	15	2	4	6	....	....	....	20	....	....	....	....	....	....	....	....	....	....	....	....	....	....	....	....	....	....

			REGULAR SEASON																		PLAYOFFS							
Season	Club	League	GP	G	A	Pts	AG	AA	APts	PIM	PP	SH	GW	S	%	TGF	PGF	TGA	PGA	+/–	GP	G	A	Pts	PIM	PP	SH	GW
1978-79	**New York Rangers**	**NHL**	**18**	**0**	**1**	**1**	**0**	**1**	**1**	**18**	**0**	**0**	**0**	**20**	**0.0**	**14**	**2**	**11**	**3**	**+4**	....	....	....	....	....	....	....	....
	New Haven Nighthawks	AHL	5	1	3	4	....	....	....	0	....	....	....	....	....	....	....	....	....	....	....	....	....	....	....	....	....	....
	Tulsa Oilers	CHL	11	0	9	9	....	....	....	36	....	....	....	....	....	....	....	....	....	....	....	....	....	....	....	....	....	....
1979-80	Syracuse Firebirds	AHL	73	11	16	27	....	....	....	87	....	....	....	....	....	....	....	....	....	....	4	1	2	3	18	....	....	....
1980-81	Cranbrook Royals	WIHL	DID NOT PLAY – COACHING																									
	NHL Totals		**77**	**9**	**10**	**19**	**8**	**8**	**16**	**59**	**2**	**0**	**1**	**92**	**9.8**	**47**	**8**	**58**	**3**		....	....	....	....	....	....	....	....

Traded to **Philadelphia** by **Detroit** with Rick Lapointe for Terry Murray, Bob Ritchie, Steve Coates and Dave Kelly, February 17, 1977. Signed as a free agent by **St. Louis**, July 22, 1978. Traded to **Montreal** by **St. Louis** for the rights to Gord McTavish, October 7, 1978. Claimed by **NY Rangers** from **Montreal** in Waiver Draft, October 9, 1978. Instead of cash, Montreal received the rights to Dan Newman.

• KOROLEV, IGOR

Igor Korolev RW – L. 6'1", 187 lbs. b: Moscow, USSR, 9/6/1970. St. Louis' 1st choice, 38th overall, in 1992 Entry Draft.

Season	Club	League	GP	G	A	Pts	AG	AA	APts	PIM	PP	SH	GW	S	%	TGF	PGF	TGA	PGA	+/–	GP	G	A	Pts	PIM	PP	SH	GW
1988-89	Moscow Dynamo	USSR	1	0	0	0	....	....	....	2	....	....	....	....	....	....	....	....	....	....	....	....	....	....	....	....	....	....
1989-90	Moscow Dynamo	USSR	17	3	2	5	....	....	....	2	....	....	....	....	....	....	....	....	....	....	....	....	....	....	....	....	....	....
1990-91	Moscow Dynamo	FrTour	1	0	2	2	....	....	....	0	....	....	....	....	....	....	....	....	....	....	....	....	....	....	....	....	....	....
	Moscow Dynamo	USSR	38	12	4	16	....	....	....	12	....	....	....	....	....	....	....	....	....	....	....	....	....	....	....	....	....	....
	Moscow Dynamo	SuperS	7	0	1	1	....	....	....	4	....	....	....	....	....	....	....	....	....	....	....	....	....	....	....	....	....	....
1991-92	Soviet Union	C Cup	5	0	0	0	....	....	....	0	....	....	....	....	....	....	....	....	....	....	....	....	....	....	....	....	....	....
	Moscow Dynamo	CIS	39	15	12	27	....	....	....	16	....	....	....	....	....	....	....	....	....	....	....	....	....	....	....	....	....	....
	Russia	WC-A	6	2	1	3	....	....	....	2	....	....	....	....	....	....	....	....	....	....	....	....	....	....	....	....	....	....
1992-93	Moscow Dynamo	CIS	5	1	2	3	....	....	....	4	....	....	....	....	....	....	....	....	....	....	....	....	....	....	....	....	....	....
	St. Louis Blues	**NHL**	**74**	**4**	**23**	**27**	**3**	**16**	**19**	**20**	**2**	**0**	**0**	**76**	**5.3**	**38**	**9**	**31**	**1**	**–1**	**3**	**0**	**0**	**0**	**0**	**0**	**0**	**0**
1993-94	**St. Louis Blues**	**NHL**	**73**	**6**	**10**	**16**	**6**	**8**	**14**	**40**	**0**	**0**	**1**	**93**	**6.5**	**33**	**2**	**45**	**2**	**–12**	**2**	**0**	**0**	**0**	**0**	**0**	**0**	**0**
1994-95	Moscow Dynamo	CIS	13	4	6	10	....	....	....	18	....	....	....	....	....	....	....	....	....	....	....	....	....	....	....	....	....	....
	Winnipeg Jets	**NHL**	**45**	**8**	**22**	**30**	**14**	**32**	**46**	**10**	**1**	**0**	**1**	**85**	**9.4**	**47**	**9**	**37**	**0**	**+1**	....	....	....	....	....	....	....	....
1995-96	**Winnipeg Jets**	**NHL**	**73**	**22**	**29**	**51**	**22**	**24**	**46**	**42**	**8**	**0**	**5**	**165**	**13.3**	**77**	**27**	**51**	**2**	**+1**	**6**	**0**	**3**	**3**	**0**	**0**	**0**	**0**
1996-97	**Phoenix Coyotes**	**NHL**	**41**	**3**	**7**	**10**	**3**	**6**	**9**	**28**	**2**	**0**	**0**	**41**	**7.3**	**22**	**7**	**20**	**0**	**–5**	**1**	**0**	**0**	**0**	**0**	**0**	**0**	**0**
	Michigan K-Wings	IHL	4	2	2	4	....	....	....	0	....	....	....	....	....	....	....	....	....	....	....	....	....	....	....	....	....	....
	Phoenix Roadrunners	IHL	4	2	6	8	....	....	....	4	....	....	....	....	....	....	....	....	....	....	....	....	....	....	....	....	....	....
1997-98	**Toronto Maple Leafs**	**NHL**	**78**	**17**	**22**	**39**	**20**	**21**	**41**	**22**	**6**	**3**	**5**	**97**	**17.5**	**57**	**16**	**69**	**10**	**–18**	....	....	....	....	....	....	....	....
	NHL Totals		**384**	**60**	**113**	**173**	**68**	**107**	**175**	**162**	**19**	**3**	**12**	**557**	**10.8**	**274**	**70**	**253**	**15**		**12**	**0**	**3**	**3**	**0**	**0**	**0**	**0**

Claimed by **Winnipeg** from **St. Louis** in NHL Waiver Draft, January 18, 1995. Transferred to **Phoenix** after **Winnipeg** franchise relocated, July 1, 1996. Signed as a free agent by **Toronto**, September 29, 1997.

• KOROLL, CLIFF

Cliff Koroll RW – R. 6'1", 195 lbs. b: Canora, Sask., 10/1/1946.

Season	Club	League	GP	G	A	Pts	AG	AA	APts	PIM	PP	SH	GW	S	%	TGF	PGF	TGA	PGA	+/–	GP	G	A	Pts	PIM	PP	SH	GW
1965-66	University of Denver	WCHA	32	21	10	31	....	....	....	23	....	....	....	....	....	....	....	....	....	....	....	....	....	....	....	....	....	....
1966-67	University of Denver	WCHA	25	18	19	37	....	....	....	34	....	....	....	....	....	....	....	....	....	....	....	....	....	....	....	....	....	....
1967-68	University of Denver	WCHA	34	18	22	40	....	....	....	55	....	....	....	....	....	....	....	....	....	....	....	....	....	....	....	....	....	....
1968-69	Dallas Black Hawks	CHL	67	28	34	62	....	....	....	50	....	....	....	....	....	....	....	....	....	....	11	2	8	10	15	....	....	....
1969-70	**Chicago Black Hawks**	**NHL**	**73**	**18**	**19**	**37**	**21**	**19**	**40**	**44**	**0**	**0**	**3**	**160**	**11.3**	**58**	**7**	**39**	**3**	**+15**	**8**	**1**	**4**	**5**	**9**	**0**	**0**	**0**
1970-71	**Chicago Black Hawks**	**NHL**	**72**	**16**	**34**	**50**	**17**	**30**	**47**	**85**	**4**	**0**	**3**	**124**	**12.9**	**85**	**23**	**37**	**3**	**+28**	**18**	**7**	**9**	**16**	**18**	**3**	**0**	**1**
1971-72	**Chicago Black Hawks**	**NHL**	**76**	**22**	**23**	**45**	**23**	**21**	**44**	**51**	**4**	**0**	**6**	**136**	**16.2**	**70**	**16**	**34**	**0**	**+20**	**8**	**0**	**0**	**0**	**11**	**0**	**0**	**0**
1972-73	**Chicago Black Hawks**	**NHL**	**77**	**33**	**24**	**57**	**33**	**20**	**53**	**38**	**6**	**1**	**6**	**151**	**21.9**	**87**	**19**	**57**	**6**	**+17**	**16**	**4**	**6**	**10**	**6**	**0**	**0**	**0**
1973-74	**Chicago Black Hawks**	**NHL**	**78**	**21**	**25**	**46**	**21**	**22**	**43**	**32**	**7**	**0**	**3**	**151**	**13.9**	**82**	**18**	**37**	**0**	**+27**	**11**	**2**	**5**	**7**	**13**	**1**	**0**	**0**
1974-75	**Chicago Black Hawks**	**NHL**	**80**	**27**	**32**	**59**	**25**	**25**	**50**	**27**	**11**	**0**	**9**	**164**	**16.5**	**105**	**40**	**61**	**16**	**+20**	**8**	**3**	**5**	**8**	**8**	**2**	**0**	**0**
1975-76	**Chicago Black Hawks**	**NHL**	**80**	**25**	**33**	**58**	**23**	**26**	**49**	**29**	**11**	**1**	**2**	**185**	**13.5**	**94**	**37**	**66**	**15**	**+6**	**4**	**1**	**0**	**1**	**0**	**1**	**0**	**0**
1976-77	**Chicago Black Hawks**	**NHL**	**80**	**15**	**26**	**41**	**14**	**21**	**35**	**25**	**8**	**1**	**1**	**138**	**10.9**	**82**	**28**	**104**	**25**	**–25**	**2**	**0**	**0**	**0**	**0**	**0**	**0**	**0**
1977-78	**Chicago Black Hawks**	**NHL**	**73**	**16**	**15**	**31**	**15**	**12**	**27**	**19**	**1**	**0**	**4**	**100**	**16.0**	**48**	**7**	**45**	**12**	**+8**	**4**	**1**	**0**	**1**	**0**	**0**	**0**	**0**
1978-79	**Chicago Black Hawks**	**NHL**	**78**	**12**	**19**	**31**	**11**	**14**	**25**	**20**	**1**	**2**	**2**	**109**	**11.0**	**62**	**9**	**85**	**35**	**+3**	**4**	**0**	**0**	**0**	**0**	**0**	**0**	**0**
1979-80	**Chicago Black Hawks**	**NHL**	**47**	**3**	**4**	**7**	**3**	**3**	**6**	**6**	**0**	**0**	**0**	**40**	**7.5**	**11**	**0**	**34**	**13**	**–10**	**2**	**0**	**0**	**0**	**2**	**0**	**0**	**0**
	NHL Totals		**814**	**208**	**254**	**462**	**206**	**213**	**419**	**376**	**53**	**5**	**39**	**1458**	**14.3**	**784**	**204**	**599**	**128**		**85**	**19**	**29**	**48**	**67**	**7**	**0**	**1**

WCHA Second All-Star Team (1968)

Rights traded to **Chicago** by **LA Blades** (WHL) for cash, August, 1967.

• KOROLYUK, ALEXANDER

Alexander Korolyuk C – L. 5'9", 170 lbs. b: Moscow, USSR, 1/15/1976. San Jose's 6th choice, 141st overall, in 1994 Entry Draft.

Season	Club	League	GP	G	A	Pts	AG	AA	APts	PIM	PP	SH	GW	S	%	TGF	PGF	TGA	PGA	+/–	GP	G	A	Pts	PIM	PP	SH	GW
1993-94	Soviet Wings	CIS	22	4	4	8	....	....	....	20	....	....	....	....	....	....	....	....	....	....	3	1	0	1	4	....	....	....
1994-95	Soviet Wings	CIS	52	16	13	29	....	....	....	62	....	....	....	....	....	....	....	....	....	....	4	1	2	3	4	....	....	....
	Russia	WJC-A	7	8	2	10	....	....	....	47	....	....	....	....	....	....	....	....	....	....	....	....	....	....	....	....	....	....
1995-96	Soviet Wings	CIS	50	30	19	49	....	....	....	77	....	....	....	....	....	....	....	....	....	....	....	....	....	....	....	....	....	....
	Russia	WJC-A	7	5	2	7	....	....	....	4	....	....	....	....	....	....	....	....	....	....	....	....	....	....	....	....	....	....
1996-97	Soviet Wings	Russia	17	8	5	13	....	....	....	46	....	....	....	....	....	....	....	....	....	....	....	....	....	....	....	....	....	....
	Manitoba Moose	IHL	42	20	16	36	....	....	....	71	....	....	....	....	....	....	....	....	....	....	....	....	....	....	....	....	....	....
	Russia	WC-A	6	2	3	5	....	....	....	6	....	....	....	....	....	....	....	....	....	....	....	....	....	....	....	....	....	....
1997-98	**San Jose Sharks**	**NHL**	**19**	**2**	**3**	**5**	**2**	**3**	**5**	**6**	**1**	**0**	**0**	**23**	**8.7**	**9**	**2**	**12**	**0**	**–5**	....	....	....	....	....	....	....	....
	Kentucky Thoroughblades	AHL	44	16	23	39	....	....	....	96	....	....	....	....	....	....	....	....	....	....	3	0	0	0	0	....	....	....
	NHL Totals		**19**	**2**	**3**	**5**	**2**	**3**	**5**	**6**	**1**	**0**	**0**	**23**	**8.7**	**9**	**2**	**12**	**0**		....	....	....	....	....	....	....	....

• KORTKO, ROGER

Roger Kortko C – L. 5'11", 195 lbs. b: Hafford, Sask., 2/1/1963. NY Islanders' 6th choice, 126th overall, in 1982 Entry Draft.

Season	Club	League	GP	G	A	Pts	AG	AA	APts	PIM	PP	SH	GW	S	%	TGF	PGF	TGA	PGA	+/–	GP	G	A	Pts	PIM	PP	SH	GW
1980-81	Humbolt Broncos	SJHL	60	43	82	125	....	....	....	52	....	....	....	....	....	....	....	....	....	....	....	....	....	....	....	....	....	....
1981-82	Saskatoon Blades	WHL	65	33	51	84	....	....	....	82	....	....	....	....	....	....	....	....	....	....	4	1	4	5	7	....	....	....
1982-83	Saskatoon Blades	WHL	72	62	99	161	....	....	....	79	....	....	....	....	....	....	....	....	....	....	1	1	1	2	5	....	....	....
1983-84	Indianapolis Checkers	CHL	64	16	27	43	....	....	....	48	....	....	....	....	....	....	....	....	....	....	9	1	5	6	9	....	....	....
1984-85	**New York Islanders**	**NHL**	**27**	**2**	**9**	**11**	**2**	**6**	**8**	**9**	**1**	**0**	**0**	**20**	**10.0**	**16**	**2**	**24**	**7**	**–3**	**10**	**0**	**3**	**3**	**17**	**0**	**0**	**0**
	Springfield Indians	AHL	30	8	30	38	....	....	....	6	....	....	....	....	....	....	....	....	....	....	....	....	....	....	....	....	....	....
1985-86	**New York Islanders**	**NHL**	**52**	**5**	**8**	**13**	**4**	**5**	**9**	**19**	**0**	**0**	**1**	**49**	**10.2**	**23**	**0**	**49**	**15**	**–11**	....	....	....	....	....	....	....	....
	Springfield Indians	AHL	12	2	10	12	....	....	....	10	....	....	....	....	....	....	....	....	....	....	....	....	....	....	....	....	....	....
1986-87	Springfield Indians	AHL	75	16	30	46	....	....	....	54	....	....	....	....	....	....	....	....	....	....	....	....	....	....	....	....	....	....
1987-88	Binghamton Whalers	AHL	72	26	45	71	....	....	....	46	....	....	....	....	....	....	....	....	....	....	4	1	1	2	2	....	....	....
1988-89	Binghamton Whalers	AHL	79	22	36	58	....	....	....	28	....	....	....	....	....	....	....	....	....	....	....	....	....	....	....	....	....	....
	NHL Totals		**79**	**7**	**17**	**24**	**6**	**11**	**17**	**28**	**1**	**0**	**1**	**69**	**10.1**	**39**	**2**	**73**	**22**		**10**	**0**	**3**	**3**	**17**	**0**	**0**	**0**

Signed as a free agent by **Hartford**, September 15, 1987.

• KOSTYNSKI, DOUG

Doug Kostynski C – R. 6'1", 170 lbs. b: Castlegar, B.C., 2/23/1963. Boston's 9th choice, 186th overall, in 1982 Entry Draft.

Season	Club	League	GP	G	A	Pts	AG	AA	APts	PIM	PP	SH	GW	S	%	TGF	PGF	TGA	PGA	+/–	GP	G	A	Pts	PIM	PP	SH	GW
1979-80	New Westminster Bruins	WHL	11	1	4	5	....	....	....	12	....	....	....	....	....	....	....	....	....	....	....	....	....	....	....	....	....	....
1980-81	New Westminster Bruins	WHL	64	18	40	58	....	....	....	51	....	....	....	....	....	....	....	....	....	....	....	....	....	....	....	....	....	....
1981-82	Kamloops Jr. Oilers	WHL	53	39	42	81	....	....	....	57	....	....	....	....	....	....	....	....	....	....	3	1	0	1	0	....	....	....
1982-83	Kamloops Jr. Oilers	WHL	75	57	59	116	....	....	....	55	....	....	....	....	....	....	....	....	....	....	7	2	7	9	6	....	....	....
1983-84	**Boston Bruins**	**NHL**	**9**	**3**	**1**	**4**	**2**	**1**	**3**	**2**	**0**	**0**	**0**	**8**	**37.5**	**9**	**0**	**7**	**0**	**+2**	....	....	....	....	....	....	....	....
	Hershey Bears	AHL	67	13	27	40	....	....	....	8	....	....	....	....	....	....	....	....	....	....	....	....	....	....	....	....	....	....
1984-85	**Boston Bruins**	**NHL**	**6**	**0**	**0**	**0**	**0**	**0**	**0**	**2**	**0**	**0**	**0**	**4**	**0.0**	**2**	**0**	**2**	**0**	**0**	....	....	....	....	....	....	....	....
	Hershey Bears	AHL	55	17	27	44	....	....	....	26	....	....	....	....	....	....	....	....	....	....	....	....	....	....	....	....	....	....
1985-86	Moncton Golden Flames	AHL	72	18	36	54	....	....	....	24	....	....	....	....	....	....	....	....	....	....	8	3	1	4	9	....	....	....
1986-87	Moncton Golden Flames	AHL	74	21	45	66	....	....	....	22	....	....	....	....	....	....	....	....	....	....	6	2	1	3	0	....	....	....
1987-88	Adirondack Red Wings	AHL	10	3	3	6	....	....	....	10	....	....	....	....	....	....	....	....	....	....	1	0	0	0	2	....	....	....
1988-89	Saipa	Finland	44	20	32	52	....	....	....	16	....	....	....	....	....	....	....	....	....	....	....	....	....	....	....	....	....	....
1989-90	Saipa	Finland	38	13	18	31	....	....	....	34	....	....	....	....	....	....	....	....	....	....	....	....	....	....	....	....	....	....
	NHL Totals		**15**	**3**	**1**	**4**	**2**	**1**	**3**	**4**	**0**	**0**	**0**	**12**	**25.0**	**11**	**0**	**9**	**0**		....	....	....	....	....	....	....	....

• KOTSOPOULOS, CHRIS

Chris Kotsopoulos D – R. 6'3", 215 lbs. b: Scarborough, Ont., 11/27/1958.

			REGULAR SEASON																		PLAYOFFS							
Season	Club	League	GP	G	A	Pts	AG	AA	APts	PIM	PP	SH	GW	S	%	TGF	PGF	TGA	PGA	+/–	GP	G	A	Pts	PIM	PP	SH	GW
1975-76	Windsor Spitfires	OHA	59	3	13	16	....	....	....	169	....	....	....	....	....	....	....	....	....	....	....	....	....	....	....	....	....	....
1976-77	Acadia University	AUAA	DID NOT PLAY																									
1977-78	Acadia University	AUAA	17	0	7	7	....	....	....	72	....	....	....	....	....	....	....	....	....	....	....	....	....	....	....	....	....	....
1978-79	Toledo Goaldiggers	IHL	62	6	22	28	....	....	....	153	....	....	....	....	....	....	....	....	....	....	6	1	7	8	48	....	....	....
1979-80	New Haven Nighthawks	AHL	75	7	27	34	....	....	....	149	....	....	....	....	....	....	....	....	....	....	10	4	5	9	28	....	....	....
1980-81	**New York Rangers**	**NHL**	**54**	**4**	**12**	**16**	**3**	**8**	**11**	**153**	**0**	**0**	**0**	**104**	**3.8**	**46**	**8**	**62**	**14**	**–10**	**14**	**0**	**3**	**3**	**63**	**0**	**0**	**0**
1981-82	**Hartford Whalers**	**NHL**	**68**	**13**	**20**	**33**	**10**	**13**	**23**	**147**	**5**	**0**	**1**	**153**	**8.5**	**87**	**33**	**108**	**29**	**–25**	....	....	....	....	....	....	....	....
1982-83	**Hartford Whalers**	**NHL**	**68**	**6**	**24**	**30**	**5**	**17**	**22**	**125**	**3**	**0**	**0**	**122**	**4.9**	**89**	**17**	**114**	**21**	**–21**	....	....	....	....	....	....	....	....
1983-84	**Hartford Whalers**	**NHL**	**72**	**5**	**13**	**18**	**4**	**9**	**13**	**118**	**3**	**0**	**0**	**96**	**5.2**	**83**	**11**	**112**	**38**	**–2**	....	....	....	....	....	....	....	....
1984-85	**Hartford Whalers**	**NHL**	**33**	**5**	**3**	**8**	**4**	**2**	**6**	**53**	**1**	**0**	**0**	**39**	**12.8**	**33**	**1**	**55**	**25**	**+2**	....	....	....	....	....	....	....	....
1985-86	**Toronto Maple Leafs**	**NHL**	**61**	**6**	**11**	**17**	**5**	**7**	**12**	**83**	**0**	**0**	**0**	**69**	**8.7**	**76**	**8**	**98**	**25**	**–5**	**10**	**1**	**0**	**1**	**14**	**0**	**0**	**0**
1986-87	**Toronto Maple Leafs**	**NHL**	**43**	**2**	**10**	**12**	**2**	**7**	**9**	**75**	**0**	**0**	**0**	**43**	**4.7**	**49**	**4**	**54**	**17**	**+8**	**7**	**0**	**0**	**0**	**14**	**0**	**0**	**0**
1987-88	**Toronto Maple Leafs**	**NHL**	**21**	**2**	**2**	**4**	**2**	**1**	**3**	**19**	**0**	**0**	**0**	**22**	**9.1**	**16**	**1**	**27**	**9**	**–3**	....	....	....	....	....	....	....	....
1988-89	**Toronto Maple Leafs**	**NHL**	**57**	**1**	**14**	**15**	**1**	**10**	**11**	**44**	**0**	**0**	**0**	**66**	**1.5**	**59**	**17**	**72**	**26**	**–4**	....	....	....	....	....	....	....	....
1989-90	**Detroit Red Wings**	**NHL**	**2**	**0**	**0**	**0**	**0**	**0**	**0**	**10**	**0**	**0**	**0**	**0**	**0.0**	**1**	**0**	**3**	**1**	**–1**	....	....	....	....	....	....	....	....
	Adirondack Red Wings	AHL	24	2	4	6	....	....	....	4	....	....	....	....	....	....	....	....	....	....	4	0	0	0	2	....	....	....
	NHL Totals		**479**	**44**	**109**	**153**	**36**	**74**	**110**	**827**	**12**	**0**	**1**	**714**	**6.2**	**539**	**100**	**705**	**205**		**31**	**1**	**3**	**4**	**91**	**0**	**0**	**0**

Signed as a free agent by **NY Rangers**, July 10, 1980. Traded to **Hartford** by **NY Rangers** with Gerry MacDonald and Doug Sulliman for Mike Rogers and future considerations, October 2, 1981. Traded to **Toronto** by **Hartford** for Stu Gavin, October 7, 1985. Signed as a free agent by **Detroit**, June 23, 1989.

• KOVALENKO, ANDREI

Andrei Kovalenko RW – L. 5'10", 215 lbs. b: Balakovo, USSR, 6/7/1970. Quebec's 6th choice, 148th overall, in 1990 Entry Draft.

Season	Club	League	GP	G	A	Pts	AG	AA	APts	PIM	PP	SH	GW	S	%	TGF	PGF	TGA	PGA	+/–	GP	G	A	Pts	PIM	PP	SH	GW
1988-89	CSKA Moscow	USSR	10	1	0	1	....	....	....	0	....	....	....	....	....	....	....	....	....	....	....	....	....	....	....	....	....	....
1989-90	CSKA Moscow	FrTour	1	0	0	0	....	....	....	4	....	....	....	....	....	....	....	....	....	....	....	....	....	....	....	....	....	....
	CSKA Moscow	USSR	48	8	5	13	....	....	....	20	....	....	....	....	....	....	....	....	....	....	....	....	....	....	....	....	....	....
	Soviet Union	WJC-A	7	5	6	11	....	....	....	8	....	....	....	....	....	....	....	....	....	....	....	....	....	....	....	....	....	....
1990-91	CSKA Moscow	FrTour	1	1	0	1	....	....	....	2	....	....	....	....	....	....	....	....	....	....	....	....	....	....	....	....	....	....
	CSKA Moscow	USSR	45	13	8	21	....	....	....	26	....	....	....	....	....	....	....	....	....	....	....	....	....	....	....	....	....	....
	CSKA Moscow	SuperS	7	6	3	9	....	....	....	2	....	....	....	....	....	....	....	....	....	....	....	....	....	....	....	....	....	....
1991-92	Soviet Union	C Cup	5	1	2	3	....	....	....	10	....	....	....	....	....	....	....	....	....	....	....	....	....	....	....	....	....	....
	CSKA Moscow	CIS	44	19	13	32	....	....	....	32	....	....	....	....	....	....	....	....	....	....	....	....	....	....	....	....	....	....
	Russia	Olympics	8	1	1	2	....	....	....	2	....	....	....	....	....	....	....	....	....	....	....	....	....	....	....	....	....	....
	Russia	WC-A	6	3	1	4	....	....	....	2	....	....	....	....	....	....	....	....	....	....	....	....	....	....	....	....	....	....
1992-93	CSKA Moscow	CIS	3	3	1	4	....	....	....	4	....	....	....	....	....	....	....	....	....	....	....	....	....	....	....	....	....	....
	Quebec Nordiques	**NHL**	**81**	**27**	**41**	**68**	**23**	**28**	**51**	**57**	**8**	**1**	**4**	**153**	**17.6**	**102**	**29**	**62**	**2**	**+13**	**4**	**1**	**0**	**1**	**2**	**0**	**0**	**0**
1993-94	**Quebec Nordiques**	**NHL**	**58**	**16**	**17**	**33**	**15**	**13**	**28**	**46**	**5**	**0**	**4**	**92**	**17.4**	**47**	**17**	**35**	**0**	**–5**	....	....	....	....	....	....	....	....
	Russia	WC-A	6	5	4	9	....	....	....	2	....	....	....	....	....	....	....	....	....	....	....	....	....	....	....	....	....	....
1994-95	Lada Togliatti	CIS	11	9	2	11	....	....	....	14	....	....	....	....	....	....	....	....	....	....	....	....	....	....	....	....	....	....
	Quebec Nordiques	**NHL**	**45**	**14**	**10**	**24**	**25**	**15**	**40**	**31**	**1**	**0**	**3**	**63**	**22.2**	**42**	**10**	**36**	**0**	**–4**	**6**	**0**	**1**	**1**	**2**	**0**	**0**	**0**
1995-96	**Colorado Avalanche**	**NHL**	**26**	**11**	**11**	**22**	**11**	**9**	**20**	**16**	**3**	**0**	**3**	**46**	**23.9**	**31**	**12**	**8**	**0**	**+11**	....	....	....	....	....	....	....	....
	Montreal Canadiens	**NHL**	**51**	**17**	**17**	**34**	**17**	**14**	**31**	**33**	**3**	**0**	**3**	**85**	**20.0**	**56**	**15**	**32**	**0**	**+9**	**6**	**0**	**0**	**0**	**6**	**0**	**0**	**0**
1996-97	Russia	W Cup	5	2	0	2	....	....	....	4	....	....	....	....	....	....	....	....	....	....	....	....	....	....	....	....	....	....
	Edmonton Oilers	**NHL**	**74**	**32**	**27**	**59**	**34**	**24**	**58**	**81**	**14**	**0**	**2**	**103**	**19.8**	**93**	**47**	**51**	**0**	**–5**	**12**	**4**	**3**	**7**	**6**	**3**	**0**	**0**
1997-98	**Edmonton Oilers**	**NHL**	**59**	**6**	**17**	**23**	**7**	**17**	**24**	**28**	**1**	**0**	**2**	**89**	**6.7**	**38**	**19**	**33**	**0**	**–14**	**1**	**0**	**0**	**0**	**2**	**0**	**0**	**0**
	Russia	Olympics	6	4	1	5	....	....	....	14	....	....	....	....	....	....	....	....	....	....	....	....	....	....	....	....	....	....
	NHL Totals		**394**	**123**	**140**	**263**	**132**	**120**	**252**	**292**	**35**	**1**	**21**	**691**	**17.8**	**409**	**149**	**257**	**2**		**29**	**5**	**4**	**9**	**18**	**3**	**0**	**0**

Transferred to **Colorado** after **Quebec** franchise relocated, June 21, 1995. Traded to **Montreal** by **Colorado** with Martin Rucinsky and Jocelyn Thibault for Patrick Roy and Mike Keane, December 6, 1995. Traded to **Edmonton** by **Montreal** for Scott Thornton, September 6, 1996.

• KOVALEV, ALEXEI

Alexei Kovalev RW – L. 6', 210 lbs. b: Togliatti, USSR, 2/24/1973. NY Rangers' 7th choice, 15th overall, in 1991 Entry Draft.

Season	Club	League	GP	G	A	Pts	AG	AA	APts	PIM	PP	SH	GW	S	%	TGF	PGF	TGA	PGA	+/–	GP	G	A	Pts	PIM	PP	SH	GW
1989-90	Moscow Dynamo	USSR	1	0	0	0	....	....	....	0	....	....	....	....	....	....	....	....	....	....	....	....	....	....	....	....	....	....
1990-91	Moscow Dynamo	FrTour	1	0	0	0	....	....	....	0	....	....	....	....	....	....	....	....	....	....	....	....	....	....	....	....	....	....
	Moscow Dynamo	USSR	18	1	2	3	....	....	....	4	....	....	....	....	....	....	....	....	....	....	....	....	....	....	....	....	....	....
	Moscow Dynamo	SuperS	1	0	0	0	....	....	....	0	....	....	....	....	....	....	....	....	....	....	....	....	....	....	....	....	....	....
1991-92	Moscow Dynamo	CIS	33	16	9	25	....	....	....	20	....	....	....	....	....	....	....	....	....	....	....	....	....	....	....	....	....	....
	Russia	WJC-A	7	5	5	10	....	....	....	2	....	....	....	....	....	....	....	....	....	....	....	....	....	....	....	....	....	....
	Russia	Olympics	8	1	2	3	....	....	....	14	....	....	....	....	....	....	....	....	....	....	....	....	....	....	....	....	....	....
	Russia	WC-A	0	0	1	1	....	....	....	0	....	....	....	....	....	....	....	....	....	....	....	....	....	....	....	....	....	....
1992-93	**New York Rangers**	**NHL**	**65**	**20**	**18**	**38**	**17**	**12**	**29**	**79**	**3**	**0**	**3**	**134**	**14.9**	**54**	**15**	**50**	**1**	**–10**	....	....	....	....	....	....	....	....
	Binghamton Rangers	AHL	13	13	11	24	....	....	....	35	....	....	....	....	....	....	....	....	....	....	9	3	5	8	14	....	....	....
1993-94	**New York Rangers**	**NHL**	**76**	**23**	**33**	**56**	**21**	**25**	**46**	**154**	**7**	**0**	**3**	**184**	**12.5**	**80**	**22**	**47**	**7**	**+18**	**23**	**9**	**12**	**21**	**18**	**5**	**0**	**2**
1994-95	Lada Togliatti	CIS	12	8	8	16	....	....	....	49	....	....	....	....	....	....	....	....	....	....	....	....	....	....	....	....	....	....
	New York Rangers	**NHL**	**48**	**13**	**15**	**28**	**23**	**22**	**45**	**30**	**1**	**1**	**1**	**103**	**12.6**	**42**	**11**	**39**	**2**	**–6**	**10**	**4**	**7**	**11**	**10**	**0**	**0**	**0**
1995-96	**New York Rangers**	**NHL**	**81**	**24**	**34**	**58**	**24**	**28**	**52**	**98**	**8**	**1**	**7**	**206**	**11.7**	**85**	**28**	**60**	**8**	**+5**	**11**	**3**	**4**	**7**	**14**	**0**	**0**	**1**
1996-97	Russia	W Cup	5	2	1	3	....	....	....	8	....	....	....	....	....	....	....	....	....	....	....	....	....	....	....	....	....	....
	New York Rangers	**NHL**	**45**	**13**	**22**	**35**	**14**	**19**	**33**	**42**	**1**	**0**	**0**	**110**	**11.8**	**50**	**15**	**33**	**9**	**+11**	....	....	....	....	....	....	....	....
1997-98	**New York Rangers**	**NHL**	**73**	**23**	**30**	**53**	**27**	**29**	**56**	**44**	**8**	**0**	**3**	**173**	**13.3**	**83**	**40**	**65**	**0**	**–22**	....	....	....	....	....	....	....	....
	Russia	WC-A	6	5	2	7	....	....	....	14	....	....	....	....	....	....	....	....	....	....	....	....	....	....	....	....	....	....
	NHL Totals		**388**	**116**	**152**	**268**	**126**	**135**	**261**	**447**	**28**	**2**	**17**	**910**	**12.7**	**394**	**131**	**294**	**27**		**44**	**16**	**23**	**39**	**42**	**5**	**0**	**3**

EJC-A All-Star Team (1991) • Named Best Forward at EJC-A (1991) • WJC-A All-Star Team (1992)

• KOWAL, JOE

Joe Kowal LW – L. 6'5", 212 lbs. b: Toronto, Ont., 2/3/1956. Buffalo's 1st choice, 33rd overall, in 1976 Amateur Draft.

Season	Club	League	GP	G	A	Pts	AG	AA	APts	PIM	PP	SH	GW	S	%	TGF	PGF	TGA	PGA	+/–	GP	G	A	Pts	PIM	PP	SH	GW
1973-74	Whitby Knob Hill Farms	OJHL	38	12	13	25	....	....	....	47	....	....	....	....	....	....	....	....	....	....	....	....	....	....	....	....	....	....
1974-75	Oshawa Generals	OHA	61	18	26	44	....	....	....	93	....	....	....	....	....	....	....	....	....	....	....	....	....	....	....	....	....	....
1975-76	Hamilton Fincups	OHA	52	32	45	77	....	....	....	100	....	....	....	....	....	....	....	....	....	....	....	....	....	....	....	....	....	....
	Oshawa Generals	OHA	4	0	2	2	....	....	....	13	....	....	....	....	....	....	....	....	....	....	....	....	....	....	....	....	....	....
1976-77	**Buffalo Sabres**	**NHL**	**16**	**0**	**5**	**5**	**0**	**4**	**4**	**6**	**0**	**0**	**0**	**6**	**0.0**	**11**	**0**	**8**	**0**	**+3**	....	....	....	....	....	....	....	....
	Hershey Bears	AHL	46	13	17	30	....	....	....	75	....	....	....	....	....	....	....	....	....	....	2	0	0	0	8	....	....	....
1977-78	**Buffalo Sabres**	**NHL**	**6**	**0**	**0**	**0**	**0**	**0**	**0**	**7**	**0**	**0**	**0**	**3**	**0.0**	**1**	**1**	**0**	**0**	**0**	**2**	**0**	**0**	**0**	**0**	**0**	**0**	**0**
	Hershey Bears	AHL	45	14	16	30	....	....	....	48	....	....	....	....	....	....	....	....	....	....	....	....	....	....	....	....	....	....
1978-79	Springfield Indians	AHL	12	3	3	6	....	....	....	10	....	....	....	....	....	....	....	....	....	....	....	....	....	....	....	....	....	....
	Binghamton Whalers	AHL	52	17	31	48	....	....	....	75	....	....	....	....	....	....	....	....	....	....	10	1	1	2	16	....	....	....
1979-80	Rochester Americans	AHL	66	20	27	47	....	....	....	139	....	....	....	....	....	....	....	....	....	....	3	0	0	0	4	....	....	....
1980-81	Nova Scotia Voyageurs	AHL	34	1	10	11	....	....	....	166	....	....	....	....	....	....	....	....	....	....	....	....	....	....	....	....	....	....
	NHL Totals		**22**	**0**	**5**	**5**	**0**	**4**	**4**	**13**	**0**	**0**	**0**	**9**	**0.0**	**12**	**1**	**8**	**0**		**2**	**0**	**0**	**0**	**0**	**0**	**0**	**0**

• KOZAK, DON

Don Kozak RW – R. 5'11", 190 lbs. b: Saskatoon, Sask., 2/2/1952. Los Angeles' 1st choice, 20th overall, in 1972 Amateur Draft.

Season	Club	League	GP	G	A	Pts	AG	AA	APts	PIM	PP	SH	GW	S	%	TGF	PGF	TGA	PGA	+/–	GP	G	A	Pts	PIM	PP	SH	GW
1967-68	Saskatoon Blades	WCJHL	35	9	5	14	....	....	....	10	....	....	....	....	....	....	....	....	....	....	....	....	....	....	....	....	....	....
1968-69	Saskatoon Blades	WCJHL	26	5	6	11	....	....	....	43	....	....	....	....	....	....	....	....	....	....	....	....	....	....	....	....	....	....
1969-70	Swift Current Broncos	WCJHL	56	40	34	74	....	....	....	67	....	....	....	....	....	....	....	....	....	....	....	....	....	....	....	....	....	....
1970-71	Edmonton Oil Kings	WCJHL	66	60	61	121			....	122	....	....	....	....	....	....	....	....	....	....	....	....	....	....	....	....	....	....
1971-72	Edmonton Oil Kings	WCJHL	68	55	50	105	....	....	....	183	....	....	....	....	....	....	....	....	....	....	....	....	....	....	....	....	....	....
1972-73	**Los Angeles Kings**	**NHL**	**72**	**14**	**6**	**20**	**14**	**5**	**19**	**104**	**4**	**0**	**4**	**78**	**17.9**	**27**	**6**	**47**	**1**	**–25**	....	....	....	....	....	....	....	....
1973-74	**Los Angeles Kings**	**NHL**	**76**	**21**	**14**	**35**	**21**	**12**	**33**	**54**	**1**	**0**	**2**	**109**	**19.3**	**55**	**7**	**41**	**0**	**+7**	**5**	**0**	**0**	**0**	**33**	**0**	**0**	**0**
1974-75	**Los Angeles Kings**	**NHL**	**77**	**16**	**15**	**31**	**15**	**12**	**27**	**64**	**2**	**0**	**6**	**109**	**14.7**	**48**	**13**	**30**	**0**	**+5**	**3**	**1**	**1**	**2**	**7**	**0**	**0**	**0**
1975-76	**Los Angeles Kings**	**NHL**	**62**	**20**	**24**	**44**	**19**	**19**	**38**	**94**	**7**	**0**	**4**	**81**	**24.7**	**52**	**11**	**45**	**0**	**–4**	**9**	**1**	**0**	**1**	**12**	**0**	**0**	**1**
1976-77	**Los Angeles Kings**	**NHL**	**79**	**15**	**17**	**32**	**14**	**14**	**28**	**89**	**1**	**0**	**1**	**98**	**15.3**	**46**	**5**	**50**	**0**	**–9**	**9**	**4**	**1**	**5**	**17**	**1**	**0**	**0**
1977-78	**Los Angeles Kings**	**NHL**	**43**	**8**	**5**	**13**	**8**	**4**	**12**	**45**	**0**	**0**	**1**	**54**	**14.8**	**20**	**1**	**15**	**0**	**+4**	....	....	....	....	....	....	....	....
	Springfield Indians	AHL	7	1	4	5	....	....	....	0	....	....	....	....	....	....	....	....	....	....	....	....	....	....	....	....	....	....

Season	Club	League	GP	G	A	Pts	AG	AA	APts	PIM	PP	SH	GW	S	%	TGF	PGF	TGA	PGA	+/–	GP	G	A	Pts	PIM	PP	SH	GW
			REGULAR SEASON																		PLAYOFFS							
1978-79	**Vancouver Canucks**	**NHL**	**28**	**2**	**5**	**7**	**2**	**4**	**6**	**30**	**1**	**0**	**0**	**29**	**6.9**	**13**	**2**	**27**	**1**	**–15**	**3**	**1**	**0**	**1**	**0**	**0**	**0**	**0**
	Tulsa Oilers	CHL	29	15	10	25	....	....	....	44	....	....	....	....	....	....	....	....	....	....	....	....	....	....	....	....	....	....
	Dallas Black Hawks	CHL	7	2	4	6	....	....	....	9	....	....	....	....	....	....	....	....	....	....	....	....	....	....	....	....	....	....
1979-80	Cincinnati Stingers	CHL	33	10	7	17	....	....	....	68	....	....	....	....	....	....	....	....	....	....	....	....	....	....	....	....	....	....
	Springfield Indians	AHL	51	9	17	26	....	....	....	48	....	....	....	....	....	....	....	....	....	....	....	....	....	....	....	....	....	....
1980-81	Binghamton Whalers	AHL	41	5	10	15	....	....	....	37	....	....	....	....	....	....	....	....	....	....	....	....	....	....	....	....	....	....
	NHL Totals		**437**	**96**	**86**	**182**	**93**	**70**	**163**	**480**	**16**	**0**	**18**	**558**	**17.2**	**261**	**45**	**255**	**2**		**29**	**7**	**2**	**9**	**69**	**1**	**0**	**1**

WCJHL Second All-Star Team (1972)

Traded to **Vancouver** by **LA Kings** for Randy Holt, December 31, 1978. Claimed by **Hartford** from **Vancouver** in Expansion Draft, June 13, 1979.

• KOZLOV, VIKTOR

Viktor Kozlov LW – R. 6′5″, 225 lbs. b: Togliatti, USSR, 2/14/1975. San Jose's 1st choice, 6th overall, in 1993 Entry Draft.

Season	Club	League	GP	G	A	Pts	AG	AA	APts	PIM	PP	SH	GW	S	%	TGF	PGF	TGA	PGA	+/–	GP	G	A	Pts	PIM	PP	SH	GW
1990-91	Lada Togliatti	USSR 2	2	2	0	2	....	....	....	0	....	....	....	....	....	....	....	....	....	....	....	....	....	....	....	....	....	....
1991-92	Lada Togliatti	CIS	3	0	0	0	....	....	....	0	....	....	....	....	....	....	....	....	....	....	....	....	....	....	....	....	....	....
1992-93	Moscow Dynamo	CIS	30	6	5	11	....	....	....	4	....	....	....	....	....	....	....	....	....	....	10	3	0	3	0	....	....	....
	Russia	WJC-A	7	2	1	3	....	....	....	2	....	....	....	....	....	....	....	....	....	....	....	....	....	....	....	....	....	....
1993-94	Moscow Dynamo	CIS	42	16	9	25	....	....	....	14	....	....	....	....	....	....	....	....	....	....	7	3	2	5	0	....	....	....
1994-95	Moscow Dynamo	CIS	3	1	1	2	....	....	....	2	....	....	....	....	....	....	....	....	....	....	....	....	....	....	....	....	....	....
	San Jose Sharks	**NHL**	**16**	**2**	**0**	**2**	**4**	**0**	**4**	**2**	**0**	**0**	**0**	**23**	**8.7**	**6**	**3**	**8**	**0**	**–5**	....	....	....	....	....	....	....	....
	Kansas City Blades	IHL	4	1	1	2	....	....	....	0	....	....	....	....	....	....	....	....	....	....	13	4	5	9	12	....	....	....
1995-96	**San Jose Sharks**	**NHL**	**62**	**6**	**13**	**19**	**6**	**11**	**17**	**6**	**1**	**0**	**0**	**107**	**5.6**	**35**	**6**	**45**	**1**	**–15**	....	....	....	....	....	....	....	....
	Kansas City Blades	IHL	15	4	7	11	....	....	....	12	....	....	....	....	....	....	....	....	....	....	....	....	....	....	....	....	....	....
	Russia	WC-A	8	0	3	3	....	....	....	0	....	....	....	....	....	....	....	....	....	....	....	....	....	....	....	....	....	....
1996-97	**San Jose Sharks**	**NHL**	**78**	**16**	**25**	**41**	**17**	**22**	**39**	**40**	**4**	**0**	**4**	**184**	**8.7**	**59**	**18**	**59**	**2**	**–16**	....	....	....	....	....	....	....	....
1997-98	**San Jose Sharks**	**NHL**	**18**	**5**	**2**	**7**	**6**	**2**	**8**	**2**	**2**	**0**	**0**	**51**	**9.8**	**11**	**4**	**9**	**0**	**–2**	....	....	....	....	....	....	....	....
	Florida Panthers	**NHL**	**46**	**12**	**11**	**23**	**14**	**11**	**25**	**14**	**3**	**2**	**0**	**114**	**10.5**	**38**	**11**	**35**	**7**	**–1**	....	....	....	....	....	....	....	....
	Russia	WC-A	6	4	5	9	....	....	....	0	....	....	....	....	....	....	....	....	....	....	....	....	....	....	....	....	....	....
	NHL Totals		**220**	**41**	**51**	**92**	**47**	**46**	**93**	**64**	**10**	**2**	**4**	**479**	**8.6**	**149**	**42**	**156**	**10**		....	....	....	....	....	....	....	....

EJC-A All-Star Team (1993)

Traded to **Florida** by **San Jose** with Florida's 5th round choice (previously acquired, Florida selected Jaroslav Spacek) in 1998 Entry Draft for Dave Lowry and Florida's 1st round choice (later traded to Tampa Bay - Tampa Bay selected Vincent Lecavalier) in 1998 Entry Draft, November 13, 1997.

• KOZLOV, VYACHESLAV

Vyacheslav Kozlov C – L. 5′10″, 180 lbs. b: Voskresensk, USSR, 5/3/1972. Detroit's 2nd choice, 45th overall, in 1990 Entry Draft.

Season	Club	League	GP	G	A	Pts	AG	AA	APts	PIM	PP	SH	GW	S	%	TGF	PGF	TGA	PGA	+/–	GP	G	A	Pts	PIM	PP	SH	GW
1987-88	Khimik	USSR	2	0	0	0	....	....	....	0	....	....	....	....	....	....	....	....	....	....	....	....	....	....	....	....	....	....
1988-89	Khimik	USSR	14	0	1	1	....	....	....	2	....	....	....	....	....	....	....	....	....	....	....	....	....	....	....	....	....	....
1989-90	Khimik	FrTour	DID NOT PLAY																									
	Khimik	USSR	45	14	12	26	....	....	....	38	....	....	....	....	....	....	....	....	....	....	....	....	....	....	....	....	....	....
	Soviet Union	WJC-A	7	4	7	11	....	....	....	0	....	....	....	....	....	....	....	....	....	....	....	....	....	....	....	....	....	....
1990-91	Khimik	FrTour	1	2	0	2	....	....	....	0	....	....	....	....	....	....	....	....	....	....	....	....	....	....	....	....	....	....
	Khimik	USSR	45	11	13	24	....	....	....	46	....	....	....	....	....	....	....	....	....	....	....	....	....	....	....	....	....	....
	Soviet Union	WEC-A	10	3	4	7	....	....	....	10	....	....	....	....	....	....	....	....	....	....	....	....	....	....	....	....	....	....
1991-92	Soviet Union	C Cup	5	1	2	3	....	....	....	6	....	....	....	....	....	....	....	....	....	....	....	....	....	....	....	....	....	....
	CSKA Moscow	CIS	11	6	5	11	....	....	....	12	....	....	....	....	....	....	....	....	....	....	....	....	....	....	....	....	....	....
	Detroit Red Wings	**NHL**	**7**	**0**	**2**	**2**	**0**	**1**	**1**	**2**	**0**	**0**	**0**	**9**	**0.0**	**2**	**0**	**4**	**0**	**–2**	....	....	....	....	....	....	....	....
1992-93	**Detroit Red Wings**	**NHL**	**17**	**4**	**1**	**5**	**3**	**1**	**4**	**14**	**0**	**0**	**0**	**26**	**15.4**	**12**	**2**	**11**	**0**	**–1**	**4**	**0**	**2**	**2**	**2**	**0**	**0**	**0**
	Adirondack Red Wings	AHL	45	23	36	59	....	....	....	54	....	....	....	....	....	....	....	....	....	....	4	1	1	2	4	....	....	....
1993-94	**Detroit Red Wings**	**NHL**	**77**	**34**	**39**	**73**	**32**	**30**	**62**	**50**	**8**	**2**	**6**	**202**	**16.8**	**104**	**28**	**57**	**8**	**+27**	**7**	**2**	**5**	**7**	**12**	**0**	**0**	**0**
	Adirondack Red Wings	AHL	3	0	1	1	....	....	....	15	....	....	....	....	....	....	....	....	....	....	....	....	....	....	....	....	....	....
	Russia	WC-A	1	0	0	0	....	....	....	4	....	....	....	....	....	....	....	....	....	....	....	....	....	....	....	....	....	....
1994-95	CSKA Moscow	CIS	10	3	4	7	....	....	....	14	....	....	....	....	....	....	....	....	....	....	....	....	....	....	....	....	....	....
	Detroit Red Wings	**NHL**	**46**	**13**	**20**	**33**	**23**	**29**	**52**	**45**	**5**	**0**	**3**	**97**	**13.4**	**53**	**18**	**23**	**0**	**+12**	**18**	**9**	**7**	**16**	**10**	**1**	**0**	**4**
1995-96	**Detroit Red Wings**	**NHL**	**82**	**36**	**37**	**73**	**36**	**30**	**66**	**70**	**9**	**0**	**7**	**237**	**15.2**	**101**	**28**	**43**	**3**	**+33**	**19**	**5**	**7**	**12**	**10**	**2**	**0**	**1**
1996-97	Russia	W Cup	5	1	2	3	....	....	....	8	....	....	....	....	....	....	....	....	....	....	....	....	....	....	....	....	....	....
	Detroit Red Wings	**NHL**	**75**	**23**	**22**	**45**	**24**	**19**	**43**	**46**	**3**	**0**	**6**	**211**	**10.9**	**67**	**11**	**35**	**0**	**+21**	**20**	**8**	**5**	**13**	**14**	**4**	**0**	**2**
1997-98	**Detroit Red Wings**	**NHL**	**80**	**25**	**27**	**52**	**29**	**26**	**55**	**46**	**6**	**0**	**1**	**221**	**11.3**	**84**	**27**	**45**	**2**	**+14**	**22**	**6**	**8**	**14**	**10**	**1**	**0**	**4**
	NHL Totals		**384**	**135**	**148**	**283**	**147**	**136**	**283**	**273**	**31**	**2**	**23**	**1003**	**13.5**	**423**	**114**	**218**	**13**		**90**	**30**	**34**	**64**	**58**	**8**	**0**	**11**

EJC-A All-Star Team (1990) • Named Best Forward at EJC-A (1990) • USSR Rookie of the Year (1990)

• KRAKE, SKIP

Skip (Philip Gordon) Krake C – R. 5′11″, 170 lbs. b: North Battleford, Sask., 10/14/1943.

Season	Club	League	GP	G	A	Pts	AG	AA	APts	PIM	PP	SH	GW	S	%	TGF	PGF	TGA	PGA	+/–	GP	G	A	Pts	PIM	PP	SH	GW
1960-61	Estevan Bruins	SJHL	4	3	1	4	....	....	....	4	....	....	....	....	....	....	....	....	....	....	11	0	3	3	0	....	....	....
1961-62	Estevan Bruins	SJHL	STATISTICS NOT AVAILABLE																									
1962-63	Estevan Bruins	SJHL	54	26	37	63	....	....	....	126	....	....	....	....	....	....	....	....	....	....	11	11	10	21	35	....	....	....
1963-64	**Boston Bruins**	**NHL**	**2**	**0**	**0**	**0**	**0**	**0**	**0**	**0**	....	....	....	....	....	....	....	....	....	....	....	....	....	....	....	....	....	....
	Estevan Bruins	SJHL	60	59	56	115	....	....	....	142	....	....	....	....	....	....	....	....	....	....	10	13	9	22	16	....	....	....
1964-65	Minneapolis Bruins	CHL	69	22	24	46	....	....	....	33	....	....	....	....	....	....	....	....	....	....	5	1	2	3	11	....	....	....
1965-66	**Boston Bruins**	**NHL**	**2**	**0**	**0**	**0**	**0**	**0**	**0**	**0**	....	....	....	....	....	....	....	....	....	....	....	....	....	....	....	....	....	....
	Oklahoma City Blazers	CHL	70	24	37	61	....	....	....	97	....	....	....	....	....	....	....	....	....	....	9	4	6	10	11	....	....	....
1966-67	**Boston Bruins**	**NHL**	**15**	**6**	**2**	**8**	**7**	**2**	**9**	**4**	....	....	....	....	....	....	....	....	....	....	....	....	....	....	....	....	....	....
	Oklahoma City Blazers	CHL	49	15	18	33	....	....	....	107	....	....	....	....	....	....	....	....	....	....	....	....	....	....	....	....	....	....
1967-68	**Boston Bruins**	**NHL**	**68**	**5**	**7**	**12**	**6**	**7**	**13**	**13**	**0**	**3**	**0**	**48**	**10.4**	**23**	**2**	**25**	**13**	**+9**	**4**	**0**	**0**	**0**	**2**	**0**	**0**	**0**
1968-69	**Los Angeles Kings**	**NHL**	**30**	**3**	**9**	**12**	**3**	**8**	**11**	**11**	**1**	**0**	**0**	**52**	**5.8**	**15**	**7**	**25**	**7**	**–10**	**6**	**1**	**0**	**1**	**15**	**0**	**0**	**0**
	Springfield Kings	AHL	43	8	23	31	....	....	....	67	....	....	....	....	....	....	....	....	....	....	....	....	....	....	....	....	....	....
1969-70	**Los Angeles Kings**	**NHL**	**58**	**5**	**17**	**22**	**6**	**17**	**23**	**86**	**2**	**1**	**0**	**101**	**5.0**	**30**	**8**	**60**	**13**	**–25**	....	....	....	....	....	....	....	....
1970-71	**Buffalo Sabres**	**NHL**	**74**	**4**	**5**	**9**	**4**	**4**	**8**	**68**	**1**	**0**	**0**	**64**	**6.3**	**15**	**1**	**58**	**23**	**–21**	....	....	....	....	....	....	....	....
1971-72	Salt Lake Golden Eagles	WHL	53	15	36	51	....	....	....	59	....	....	....	....	....	....	....	....	....	....	....	....	....	....	....	....	....	....
1972-73	Cleveland Crusaders	WHA	26	9	10	19	....	....	....	61	....	....	....	....	....	....	....	....	....	....	9	1	2	3	27	....	....	....
1973-74	Cleveland Crusaders	WHA	69	20	36	56	....	....	....	94	....	....	....	....	....	....	....	....	....	....	5	0	1	1	39	....	....	....
1974-75	Cleveland Crusaders	WHA	71	15	23	38	....	....	....	108	....	....	....	....	....	....	....	....	....	....	5	1	1	2	0	....	....	....
1975-76	Edmonton Oilers	WHA	41	8	8	16	....	....	....	55	....	....	....	....	....	....	....	....	....	....	....	....	....	....	....	....	....	....
	NHL Totals		**249**	**23**	**40**	**63**	**26**	**38**	**64**	**182**	**4**	**4**	**0**	**265**	**8.7**	**83**	**18**	**168**	**56**		**10**	**1**	**0**	**1**	**17**	**0**	**0**	**0**
	Other Major League Totals		207	52	77	129	....	....	....	318	....	....	....	....	....	....	....	....	....		19	2	4	6	66	....	....	....

Traded to **LA Kings** by **Boston** for LA Kings' 1st round choice (Reggie Leach) in 1970 Amateur Draft, May 20, 1968. Claimed by **Buffalo** from **LA Kings** in Expansion Draft, June 10, 1970. Selected by **Calgary-Cleveland** (WHA) in 1972 WHA General Player Draft, February 12, 1972. Traded to **Edmonton** (WHA) by **Cleveland** (WHA) for Ray McKay, August, 1975.

• KRAVCHUK, IGOR

Igor Kravchuk D – L. 6′1″, 200 lbs. b: Ufa, USSR, 9/13/1966. Chicago's 5th choice, 71st overall, in 1991 Entry Draft.

Season	Club	League	GP	G	A	Pts	AG	AA	APts	PIM	PP	SH	GW	S	%	TGF	PGF	TGA	PGA	+/–	GP	G	A	Pts	PIM	PP	SH	GW
1982-83	Yulayev	USSR	10	0	0	0	....	....	....	0	....	....	....	....	....	....	....	....	....	....	....	....	....	....	....	....	....	....
1983-84	Yulayev	USSR 2	STATISTICS NOT AVAILABLE																									
1984-85	Yulayev	USSR 2	50	3	2	5	....	....	....	22	....	....	....	....	....	....	....	....	....	....	....	....	....	....	....	....	....	....
	Soviet Union	WJC-A	7	0	3	3	....	....	....	6	....	....	....	....	....	....	....	....	....	....	....	....	....	....	....	....	....	....
1985-86	Yulayev	USSR	21	2	2	4	....	....	....	6	....	....	....	....	....	....	....	....	....	....	....	....	....	....	....	....	....	....
	Soviet Union	WJC-A	7	0	2	2	....	....	....	4	....	....	....	....	....	....	....	....	....	....	....	....	....	....	....	....	....	....
1986-87	Yulayev	USSR	22	0	1	1	....	....	....	8	....	....	....	....	....	....	....	....	....	....	....	....	....	....	....	....	....	....
1987-88	Soviet Union	C Cup	5	0	4	4	....	....	....	2	....	....	....	....	....	....	....	....	....	....	....	....	....	....	....	....	....	....
	CSKA Moscow	USSR	48	1	8	9	....	....	....	12	....	....	....	....	....	....	....	....	....	....	....	....	....	....	....	....	....	....
	Soviet Union	Olympics	6	1	0	1	....	....	....	0	....	....	....	....	....	....	....	....	....	....	....	....	....	....	....	....	....	....
1988-89	CSKA Moscow	USSR	22	3	3	6	....	....	....	2	....	....	....	....	....	....	....	....	....	....	....	....	....	....	....	....	....	....
1989-90	CSKA Moscow	FrTour	1	0	0	0	....	....	....	2	....	....	....	....	....	....	....	....	....	....	....	....	....	....	....	....	....	....
	CSKA Moscow	USSR	48	1	3	4	....	....	....	16	....	....	....	....	....	....	....	....	....	....	....	....	....	....	....	....	....	....
	CSKA Moscow	SuperS	5	0	3	3	....	....	....	0	....	....	....	....	....	....	....	....	....	....	....	....	....	....	....	....	....	....
	Soviet Union	WEC-A	10	1	4	5	....	....	....	8	....	....	....	....	....	....	....	....	....	....	....	....	....	....	....	....	....	....

			REGULAR SEASON																		PLAYOFFS							
Season	Club	League	GP	G	A	Pts	AG	AA	APts	PIM	PP	SH	GW	S	%	TGF	PGF	TGA	PGA	+/–	GP	G	A	Pts	PIM	PP	SH	GW
1990-91	CSKA Moscow	FrTour	1	0	0	0	....	....	....	0	....	....	....	....	....	....	....	....	....	....	....	....	....	....	....	....	....	....
	CSKA Moscow	USSR	41	6	5	11	....	....	....	16	....	....	....	....	....	....	....	....	....	....	....	....	....	....	....	....	....	....
	CSKA Moscow	SuperS	7	0	2	2	....	....	....	0	....	....	....	....	....	....	....	....	....	....	....	....	....	....	....	....	....	....
	Soviet Union	WEC-A	10	1	3	4	....	....	....	8	....	....	....	....	....	....	....	....	....	....	....	....	....	....	....	....	....	....
1991-92	Soviet Union	C Cup	5	0	0	0	....	....	....	2	....	....	....	....	....	....	....	....	....	....	....	....	....	....	....	....	....	....
	CSKA Moscow	CIS	30	3	8	11	....	....	....	6	....	....	....	....	....	....	....	....	....	....	....	....	....	....	....	....	....	....
	Russia	Olympics	8	3	2	5	....	....	....	6	....	....	....	....	....	....	....	....	....	....	....	....	....	....	....	....	....	....
	Chicago Blackhawks	**NHL**	**18**	**1**	**8**	**9**	**1**	**6**	**7**	**4**	**0**	**0**	**1**	**40**	**2.5**	**22**	**9**	**20**	**4**	**–3**	**18**	**2**	**6**	**8**	**8**	**1**	**0**	**0**
1992-93	**Chicago Blackhawks**	**NHL**	**38**	**6**	**9**	**15**	**5**	**6**	**11**	**30**	**3**	**0**	**0**	**101**	**5.9**	**39**	**9**	**29**	**10**	**+11**	....	....	....	....	....	....	....	....
	Edmonton Oilers	**NHL**	**17**	**4**	**8**	**12**	**3**	**5**	**8**	**2**	**1**	**0**	**0**	**42**	**9.5**	**19**	**5**	**28**	**6**	**–8**	....	....	....	....	....	....	....	....
1993-94	**Edmonton Oilers**	**NHL**	**81**	**12**	**38**	**50**	**11**	**29**	**40**	**16**	**5**	**0**	**2**	**197**	**6.1**	**109**	**37**	**113**	**29**	**–12**	....	....	....	....	....	....	....	....
1994-95	**Edmonton Oilers**	**NHL**	**36**	**7**	**11**	**18**	**12**	**16**	**28**	**29**	**3**	**1**	**0**	**93**	**7.5**	**48**	**25**	**52**	**14**	**–15**	....	....	....	....	....	....	....	....
1995-96	**Edmonton Oilers**	**NHL**	**26**	**4**	**4**	**8**	**4**	**3**	**7**	**10**	**3**	**0**	**0**	**59**	**6.8**	**30**	**16**	**35**	**8**	**–13**	....	....	....	....	....	....	....	....
	St. Louis Blues	**NHL**	**40**	**3**	**12**	**15**	**3**	**10**	**13**	**24**	**0**	**0**	**1**	**114**	**2.6**	**47**	**13**	**55**	**15**	**–6**	**10**	**1**	**5**	**6**	**4**	**0**	**0**	**1**
1996-97	**St. Louis Blues**	**NHL**	**82**	**4**	**24**	**28**	**4**	**21**	**25**	**35**	**1**	**0**	**0**	**142**	**2.8**	**95**	**20**	**93**	**25**	**+7**	**2**	**0**	**0**	**0**	**2**	**0**	**0**	**0**
1997-98	**Ottawa Senators**	**NHL**	**81**	**8**	**27**	**35**	**9**	**26**	**35**	**8**	**3**	**1**	**1**	**191**	**4.2**	**85**	**31**	**89**	**16**	**–19**	**11**	**2**	**3**	**5**	**4**	**0**	**0**	**0**
	Russia	Olympics	6	0	2	2	....	....	....	2	....	....	....	....	....	....	....	....	....	....	....	....	....	....	....	....	....	....
	NHL Totals		**419**	**49**	**141**	**190**	**52**	**122**	**174**	**158**	**19**	**2**	**5**	**979**	**5.0**	**494**	**165**	**514**	**127**		**41**	**5**	**14**	**19**	**18**	**1**	**0**	**1**

Played in NHL All-Star Game (1998)

Traded to **Edmonton** by **Chicago** with Dean McAmmond for Joe Murphy, February 24, 1993. Traded to **St. Louis** by **Edmonton** with Ken Sutton for Jeff Norton and Donald Dufresne, January 4, 1996. Traded to **Ottawa** by **St. Louis** for Steve Duchesne, August 25, 1997.

• KRAVETS, MIKHAIL

Mikhail Kravets RW – L. 5'10", 195 lbs. b: Leningrad, USSR, 11/12/1963. San Jose's 13th choice, 243rd overall, in 1991 Entry Draft.

Season	Club	League	GP	G	A	Pts	AG	AA	APts	PIM	PP	SH	GW	S	%	TGF	PGF	TGA	PGA	+/–	GP	G	A	Pts	PIM	PP	SH	GW
1985-86	SKA Leningrad	USSR	38	14	7	21	....	....	....	20	....	....	....	....	....	....	....	....	....	....	....	....	....	....	....	....	....	....
1986-87	SKA Leningrad	USSR	36	16	11	27	....	....	....	37	....	....	....	....	....	....	....	....	....	....	....	....	....	....	....	....	....	....
1987-88	SKA Leningrad	USSR	44	9	5	14	....	....	....	36	....	....	....	....	....	....	....	....	....	....	....	....	....	....	....	....	....	....
1988-89	SKA Leningrad	USSR	43	8	18	26	....	....	....	20	....	....	....	....	....	....	....	....	....	....	....	....	....	....	....	....	....	....
1989-90	SKA Leningrad	FrTour	1	0	0	0	....	....	....	2	....	....	....	....	....	....	....	....	....	....	....	....	....	....	....	....	....	....
	SKA Leningrad	USSR	30	10	14	24	....	....	....	36	....	....	....	....	....	....	....	....	....	....	....	....	....	....	....	....	....	....
1990-91	SKA-Torpedo Yar.	FrTour	1	0	0	0	....	....	....	0	....	....	....	....	....	....	....	....	....	....	....	....	....	....	....	....	....	....
	SKA Leningrad	USSR	25	8	8	16	....	....	....	28	....	....	....	....	....	....	....	....	....	....	....	....	....	....	....	....	....	....
1991-92	**San Jose Sharks**	**NHL**	**1**	**0**	**0**	**0**	**0**	**0**	**0**	**0**	**0**	**0**	**0**	**2**	**0.0**	**0**	**0**	**0**	**0**	**0**	....	....	....	....	....	....	....	....
	Kansas City Blades	IHL	74	10	32	42	....	....	....	172	....	....	....	....	....	....	....	....	....	....	15	6	8	14	12	....	....	....
1992-93	**San Jose Sharks**	**NHL**	**1**	**0**	**0**	**0**	**0**	**0**	**0**	**0**	**0**	**0**	**0**	**0**	**0.0**	**0**	**0**	**1**	**0**	**–1**	....	....	....	....	....	....	....	....
	Kansas City Blades	IHL	71	19	49	68	....	....	....	153	....	....	....	....	....	....	....	....	....	....	10	2	5	7	55	....	....	....
1993-94	Kansas City Blades	IHL	63	14	44	58	....	....	....	171	....	....	....	....	....	....	....	....	....	....	....	....	....	....	....	....	....	....
1994-95	Detroit Vipers	IHL	7	0	0	0	....	....	....	4	....	....	....	....	....	....	....	....	....	....	....	....	....	....	....	....	....	....
	Minnesota Moose	IHL	37	7	15	22	....	....	....	25	....	....	....	....	....	....	....	....	....	....	....	....	....	....	....	....	....	....
	Syracuse Crunch	AHL	7	2	2	4	....	....	....	8	....	....	....	....	....	....	....	....	....	....	....	....	....	....	....	....	....	....
1995-96	Wichita Thunder	CHL	37	14	57	71	....	....	....	89	....	....	....	....	....	....	....	....	....	....	....	....	....	....	....	....	....	....
	Milwaukee Admirals	IHL	7	0	1	1	....	....	....	4	....	....	....	....	....	....	....	....	....	....	....	....	....	....	....	....	....	....
1996-97	Louisiana Ice Gators	ECHL	67	22	45	67	....	....	....	93	....	....	....	....	....	....	....	....	....	....	17	4	9	13	18	....	....	....
1997-98	Baton Rouge Kingfish	ECHL	11	2	9	11	....	....	....	37	....	....	....	....	....	....	....	....	....	....	....	....	....	....	....	....	....	....
	Louisiana IceGators	ECHL	28	8	18	26	....	....	....	41	....	....	....	....	....	....	....	....	....	....	....	....	....	....	....	....	....	....
	New Orleans Brass	ECHL	4	1	0	1	....	....	....	2	....	....	....	....	....	....	....	....	....	....	....	....	....	....	....	....	....	....
	Mississippi Sea Wolves	ECHL	10	4	10	14	....	....	....	25	....	....	....	....	....	....	....	....	....	....	....	....	....	....	....	....	....	....
	NHL Totals		**2**	**0**	**0**	**0**	**0**	**0**	**0**	**0**	**0**	**0**	**0**	**2**	**0.0**	**0**	**0**	**1**	**0**		....	....	....	....	....	....	....	....

• KRENTZ, DALE

Dale Krentz LW – L. 5'11", 190 lbs. b: Steinbach, Man., 12/19/1961.

Season	Club	League	GP	G	A	Pts	AG	AA	APts	PIM	PP	SH	GW	S	%	TGF	PGF	TGA	PGA	+/–	GP	G	A	Pts	PIM	PP	SH	GW
1982-83	Michigan State Spartans	CCHA	42	11	24	35	....	....	....	50	....	....	....	....	....	....	....	....	....	....	....	....	....	....	....	....	....	....
1983-84	Michigan State Spartans	CCHA	44	12	20	32	....	....	....	34	....	....	....	....	....	....	....	....	....	....	....	....	....	....	....	....	....	....
1984-85	Michigan State Spartans	CCHA	44	24	30	54	....	....	....	26	....	....	....	....	....	....	....	....	....	....	....	....	....	....	....	....	....	....
1985-86	Adirondack Red Wings	AHL	79	19	27	46	....	....	....	27	....	....	....	....	....	....	....	....	....	....	13	2	6	8	9	....	....	....
1986-87	**Detroit Red Wings**	**NHL**	**8**	**0**	**0**	**0**	**0**	**0**	**0**	**0**	**0**	**0**	**0**	**5**	**0.0**	**1**	**0**	**3**	**0**	**–2**	....	....	....	....	....	....	....	....
	Adirondack Red Wings	AHL	71	32	39	71	....	....	....	68	....	....	....	....	....	....	....	....	....	....	11	3	4	7	10	....	....	....
1987-88	**Detroit Red Wings**	**NHL**	**6**	**2**	**0**	**2**	**2**	**0**	**2**	**5**	**0**	**0**	**1**	**5**	**40.0**	**5**	**0**	**6**	**3**	**+2**	**2**	**0**	**0**	**0**	**0**	**0**	**0**	**0**
	Adirondack Red Wings	AHL	67	39	43	82	....	....	....	65	....	....	....	....	....	....	....	....	....	....	8	11	4	15	8	....	....	....
1988-89	**Detroit Red Wings**	**NHL**	**16**	**3**	**3**	**6**	**3**	**2**	**5**	**4**	**0**	**0**	**1**	**27**	**11.1**	**9**	**2**	**11**	**1**	**–3**	....	....	....	....	....	....	....	....
	Adirondack Red Wings	AHL	36	21	20	41	....	....	....	30	....	....	....	....	....	....	....	....	....	....	....	....	....	....	....	....	....	....
1989-90	Adirondack Red Wings	AHL	74	38	50	88	....	....	....	36	....	....	....	....	....	....	....	....	....	....	6	2	3	5	11	....	....	....
1990-91	Alder Mannheim	Germany	47	29	29	58	....	....	....	26	....	....	....	....	....	....	....	....	....	....	....	....	....	....	....	....	....	....
1991-92	Alder Mannheim	Germany	44	25	30	55	....	....	....	24	....	....	....	....	....	....	....	....	....	....	....	....	....	....	....	....	....	....
1992-93	Alder Mannheim	Germany	43	20	21	41	....	....	....	48	....	....	....	....	....	....	....	....	....	....	....	....	....	....	....	....	....	....
1993-94	Alder Mannheim	Germany	44	22	22	44	....	....	....	53	....	....	....	....	....	....	....	....	....	....	....	....	....	....	....	....	....	....
1994-95	Alder Mannheim	Germany	42	14	25	39	....	....	....	55	....	....	....	....	....	....	....	....	....	....	10	3	8	11	12	....	....	....
1995-96	Star Bulls Rosenheim	Germany	49	24	29	53	....	....	....	62	....	....	....	....	....	....	....	....	....	....	4	0	1	1	6	....	....	....
	NHL Totals		**30**	**5**	**3**	**8**	**5**	**2**	**7**	**9**	**0**	**0**	**2**	**37**	**13.5**	**15**	**2**	**20**	**4**		**2**	**0**	**0**	**0**	**0**	**0**	**0**	**0**

AHL Second All-Star Team (1988)

Signed as a free agent by **Detroit**, June 5, 1985.

• KRIVOKRASOV, SERGEI

Sergei Krivokrasov RW – L. 5'11", 185 lbs. b: Angarsk, USSR, 4/15/1974. Chicago's 1st choice, 12th overall, in 1992 Entry Draft.

Season	Club	League	GP	G	A	Pts	AG	AA	APts	PIM	PP	SH	GW	S	%	TGF	PGF	TGA	PGA	+/–	GP	G	A	Pts	PIM	PP	SH	GW
1990-91	CSKA Moscow	FrTour	1	0	0	0	....	....	....	0	....	....	....	....	....	....	....	....	....	....	....	....	....	....	....	....	....	....
	CSKA Moscow	USSR	41	4	0	4	....	....	....	8	....	....	....	....	....	....	....	....	....	....	....	....	....	....	....	....	....	....
1991-92	CSKA Moscow	CIS	42	10	8	18	....	....	....	35	....	....	....	....	....	....	....	....	....	....	....	....	....	....	....	....	....	....
	Russia	WJC-A	7	3	3	6	....	....	....	22	....	....	....	....	....	....	....	....	....	....	....	....	....	....	....	....	....	....
1992-93	**Chicago Blackhawks**	**NHL**	**4**	**0**	**0**	**0**	**0**	**0**	**0**	**2**	**0**	**0**	**0**	**0**	**0.0**	**0**	**0**	**2**	**0**	**–2**	....	....	....	....	....	....	....	....
	Indianapolis Ice	IHL	78	36	33	69	....	....	....	157	....	....	....	....	....	....	....	....	....	....	5	3	1	4	2	....	....	....
1993-94	**Chicago Blackhawks**	**NHL**	**9**	**1**	**0**	**1**	**1**	**0**	**1**	**4**	**0**	**0**	**0**	**7**	**14.3**	**1**	**0**	**3**	**0**	**–2**	....	....	....	....	....	....	....	....
	Indianapolis Ice	IHL	53	19	26	45	....	....	....	145	....	....	....	....	....	....	....	....	....	....	....	....	....	....	....	....	....	....
1994-95	Indianapolis Ice	IHL	29	12	15	27	....	....	....	41	....	....	....	....	....	....	....	....	....	....	....	....	....	....	....	....	....	....
	Chicago Blackhawks	**NHL**	**41**	**12**	**7**	**19**	**21**	**10**	**31**	**33**	**6**	**0**	**2**	**72**	**16.7**	**27**	**7**	**12**	**1**	**+9**	**10**	**0**	**0**	**0**	**8**	**0**	**0**	**0**
1995-96	**Chicago Blackhawks**	**NHL**	**46**	**6**	**10**	**16**	**6**	**8**	**14**	**32**	**0**	**0**	**1**	**52**	**11.5**	**26**	**1**	**15**	**0**	**+10**	**5**	**1**	**0**	**1**	**2**	**0**	**0**	**1**
	Indianapolis Ice	IHL	9	4	5	9	....	....	....	28	....	....	....	....	....	....	....	....	....	....	....	....	....	....	....	....	....	....
1996-97	**Chicago Blackhawks**	**NHL**	**67**	**13**	**11**	**24**	**14**	**10**	**24**	**42**	**2**	**0**	**3**	**104**	**12.5**	**31**	**3**	**29**	**0**	**–1**	**6**	**1**	**0**	**1**	**4**	**0**	**0**	**0**
1997-98	**Chicago Blackhawks**	**NHL**	**58**	**10**	**13**	**23**	**12**	**13**	**25**	**33**	**1**	**0**	**2**	**127**	**7.9**	**33**	**7**	**27**	**0**	**–1**	....	....	....	....	....	....	....	....
	Russia	Olympics	6	0	0	0	....	....	....	4	....	....	....	....	....	....	....	....	....	....	....	....	....	....	....	....	....	....
	NHL Totals		**225**	**42**	**41**	**83**	**54**	**41**	**95**	**146**	**9**	**0**	**8**	**362**	**11.6**	**118**	**18**	**88**	**1**		**21**	**2**	**0**	**2**	**14**	**0**	**0**	**1**

Traded to **Nashville** by **Chicago** for future considerations, June 26, 1998.

• KROMM, RICH

Rich Kromm LW – L. 5'11", 180 lbs. b: Trail, B.C., 3/29/1964. Calgary's 2nd choice, 37th overall, in 1982 Entry Draft.

Season	Club	League	GP	G	A	Pts	AG	AA	APts	PIM	PP	SH	GW	S	%	TGF	PGF	TGA	PGA	+/–	GP	G	A	Pts	PIM	PP	SH	GW
1980-81	Windsor Royals	OJHL	39	22	31	53	....	....	....	40	....	....	....	....	....	....	....	....	....	....	....	....	....	....	....	....	....	....
1981-82	Portland Winter Hawks	WHL	60	16	38	54	....	....	....	30	....	....	....	....	....	....	....	....	....	....	14	0	3	3	17	....	....	....
1982-83	Portland Winter Hawks	WHL	72	35	68	103	....	....	....	64	....	....	....	....	....	....	....	....	....	....	14	7	13	20	12	....	....	....
1983-84	Portland Winter Hawks	WHL	10	10	4	14	....	....	....	13	....	....	....	....	....	....	....	....	....	....	....	....	....	....	....	....	....	....
	Calgary Flames	**NHL**	**53**	**11**	**12**	**23**	**9**	**8**	**17**	**27**	**0**	**0**	**3**	**66**	**16.7**	**42**	**0**	**30**	**2**	**+14**	**11**	**1**	**1**	**2**	**9**	**0**	**0**	**0**
1984-85	**Calgary Flames**	**NHL**	**73**	**20**	**32**	**52**	**16**	**22**	**38**	**32**	**1**	**0**	**2**	**140**	**14.3**	**71**	**1**	**58**	**7**	**+19**	**3**	**0**	**1**	**1**	**4**	**0**	**0**	**0**
1985-86	**Calgary Flames**	**NHL**	**63**	**12**	**17**	**29**	**10**	**11**	**21**	**31**	**0**	**0**	**2**	**97**	**12.4**	**51**	**0**	**45**	**3**	**+9**	....	....	....	....	....	....	....	....
	New York Islanders	**NHL**	**14**	**7**	**7**	**14**	**6**	**5**	**11**	**4**	**0**	**0**	**0**	**23**	**30.4**	**22**	**5**	**9**	**0**	**+8**	**3**	**0**	**1**	**1**	**0**	**0**	**0**	**0**
1986-87	**New York Islanders**	**NHL**	**70**	**12**	**17**	**29**	**10**	**12**	**22**	**20**	**0**	**0**	**0**	**110**	**10.9**	**46**	**5**	**68**	**29**	**+2**	**14**	**1**	**3**	**4**	**4**	**0**	**0**	**0**
1987-88	**New York Islanders**	**NHL**	**71**	**5**	**10**	**15**	**4**	**7**	**11**	**20**	**0**	**1**	**1**	**84**	**6.0**	**30**	**1**	**48**	**21**	**+2**	**5**	**0**	**0**	**0**	**5**	**0**	**0**	**0**

			REGULAR SEASON																		PLAYOFFS							
Season	Club	League	GP	G	A	Pts	AG	AA	APts	PIM	PP	SH	GW	S	%	TGF	PGF	TGA	PGA	+/–	GP	G	A	Pts	PIM	PP	SH	GW
1988-89	**New York Islanders**	**NHL**	20	1	6	7	1	4	5	4	0	0	0	12	8.3	7	0	15	5	–3	....	....	....	....	....	....	....	....
	Springfield Indians	AHL	48	21	26	47	....	....	....	15	....	....	....	....	....	....	....	....	....	....	....	....	....	....	....	....	....	....
1989-90	Leksands IF	Sweden	40	8	16	24	....	....	....	28	....	....	....	....	....	....	....	....	....	....	3	3	1	4	0	....	....	....
	Springfield Indians	AHL	9	3	4	7	....	....	....	4	....	....	....	....	....	....	....	....	....	....	16	1	5	6	4	....	....	....
1990-91	**New York Islanders**	**NHL**	6	1	0	1	1	0	1	0	0	1	0	6	16.7	1	0	3	0	–2	....	....	....	....	....	....	....	....
	Capital District Islanders	AHL	76	19	36	55	....	....	....	18	....	....	....	....	....	....	....	....	....	....	....	....	....	....	....	....	....	....
1991-92	**New York Islanders**	**NHL**	1	0	0	0	0	0	0	0	0	0	0	0	0.0	0	0	0	0	0	....	....	....	....	....	....	....	....
	Capital District Islanders	AHL	76	16	39	55	....	....	....	36	....	....	....	....	....	....	....	....	....	....	7	2	3	5	6	....	....	....
1992-93	**New York Islanders**	**NHL**	1	1	2	3	1	1	2	0	0	0	0	2	50.0	3	0	1	1	+3	....	....	....	....	....	....	....	....
	Capital District Islanders	AHL	79	20	34	54	....	....	....	28	....	....	....	....	....	....	....	....	....	....	3	0	0	0	0	....	....	....
	NHL Totals		372	70	103	173	58	70	128	138	1	2	8	540	13.0	273	12	277	68		36	2	6	8	22	0	0	0

Traded to **NY Islanders** by **Calgary** with Steve Konroyd for John Tonelli, March 11, 1986.

• KRON, ROBERT

Robert Kron LW – L. 5'11", 185 lbs. b: Brno, Czech., 2/27/1967. Vancouver's 5th choice, 88th overall, in 1985 Entry Draft.

Season	Club	League	GP	G	A	Pts	AG	AA	APts	PIM	PP	SH	GW	S	%	TGF	PGF	TGA	PGA	+/–	GP	G	A	Pts	PIM	PP	SH	GW
1983-84	Ingstav Brno	Czech. 2	3	0	1	1	....	....	....	0	....	....	....	....	....	....	....	....	....	....	....	....	....	....	....	....	....	....
1984-85	Zetor Brno	Czech.	40	6	8	14	....	....	....	6	....	....	....	....	....	....	....	....	....	....	....	....	....	....	....	....	....	....
	Czechoslovakia	WJC-A	7	3	5	8	....	....	....	4	....	....	....	....	....	....	....	....	....	....	....	....	....	....	....	....	....	....
1985-86	Zetor Brno	Czech.	44	5	6	11	....	....	....	....	....	....	....	....	....	....	....	....	....	....	....	....	....	....	....	....	....	....
	Czechoslovakia	WJC-A	7	3	1	4	....	....	....	6	....	....	....	....	....	....	....	....	....	....	....	....	....	....	....	....	....	....
1986-87	Zetor Brno	Czech.	34	18	11	29	....	....	....	10	....	....	....	....	....	....	....	....	....	....	....	....	....	....	....	....	....	....
	Czechoslovakia	WJC-A	5	1	2	3	....	....	....	4	....	....	....	....	....	....	....	....	....	....	....	....	....	....	....	....	....	....
1987-88	Zetor Brno	Czech.	44	14	7	21	....	....	....	30	....	....	....	....	....	....	....	....	....	....	....	....	....	....	....	....	....	....
1988-89	Dukla Trencin	Czech.	43	28	19	47	....	....	....	26	....	....	....	....	....	....	....	....	....	....	....	....	....	....	....	....	....	....
	Czechoslovakia	WEC-A	10	2	2	4	....	....	....	2	....	....	....	....	....	....	....	....	....	....	....	....	....	....	....	....	....	....
1989-90	Dukla Trencin	Czech.	39	22	22	44	....	....	....	....	....	....	....	....	....	....	....	....	....	....	....	....	....	....	....	....	....	....
	Czechoslovakia	WEC-A	10	0	1	1	....	....	....	0	....	....	....	....	....	....	....	....	....	....	....	....	....	....	....	....	....	....
1990-91	**Vancouver Canucks**	**NHL**	76	12	20	32	11	15	26	21	2	3	0	124	9.7	50	5	77	21	–11	....	....	....	....	....	....	....	....
1991-92	Czechoslovakia	C Cup	5	0	0	0	....	....	....	0	....	....	....	....	....	....	....	....	....	....	....	....	....	....	....	....	....	....
	Vancouver Canucks	**NHL**	36	2	2	4	2	1	3	2	0	0	0	49	4.1	10	1	25	7	–9	11	1	2	3	2	0	1	0
1992-93	**Vancouver Canucks**	**NHL**	32	10	11	21	8	8	16	14	2	2	2	60	16.7	29	3	29	13	+10	....	....	....	....	....	....	....	....
	Hartford Whalers	**NHL**	13	4	2	6	3	1	4	4	2	0	0	37	10.8	8	3	13	3	–5	....	....	....	....	....	....	....	....
1993-94	**Hartford Whalers**	**NHL**	77	24	26	50	22	20	42	8	2	1	3	194	12.4	81	19	90	28	0	....	....	....	....	....	....	....	....
1994-95	**Hartford Whalers**	**NHL**	37	10	8	18	18	12	30	10	3	1	1	88	11.4	29	9	36	13	–3	....	....	....	....	....	....	....	....
1995-96	**Hartford Whalers**	**NHL**	77	22	28	50	22	23	45	6	8	1	3	203	10.8	79	30	70	20	–1	....	....	....	....	....	....	....	....
1996-97	**Hartford Whalers**	**NHL**	68	10	12	22	11	11	22	10	2	0	4	182	5.5	40	9	56	7	–18	....	....	....	....	....	....	....	....
1997-98	**Carolina Hurricanes**	**NHL**	81	16	20	36	19	19	38	12	4	0	2	175	9.1	55	13	67	17	–8	....	....	....	....	....	....	....	....
	NHL Totals		497	110	129	239	116	110	226	87	25	8	15	1112	9.9	381	92	463	129		11	1	2	3	2	0	1	0

Named Best Forward at WJC-A (1987)

Traded to **Hartford** by **Vancouver** with Vancouver's 3rd round choice (Marek Malik) in 1993 Entry Draft and future considerations (Jim Sandlak, May 17, 1993) for Murray Craven and Vancouver's 5th round choice (previously acquired, Vancouver selected Scott Walker) in 1993 Entry Draft, March 22, 1993. Transferred to **Carolina** after **Hartford** franchise relocated, June 25, 1997.

• KROOK, KEVIN

Kevin Krook D – L. 5'11", 187 lbs. b: Cold Lake, Alta., 4/5/1958. Colorado's 10th choice, 142nd overall, in 1978 Amateur Draft.

Season	Club	League	GP	G	A	Pts	AG	AA	APts	PIM	PP	SH	GW	S	%	TGF	PGF	TGA	PGA	+/–	GP	G	A	Pts	PIM	PP	SH	GW
1974-75	Bellingham Bulls	BCJHL	46	18	52	70	....	....	....	250	....	....	....	....	....	....	....	....	....	....	....	....	....	....	....	....	....	....
1975-76	New Westminster Bruins	WCJHL	44	0	9	9	....	....	....	17	....	....	....	....	....	....	....	....	....	....	17	0	1	1	2	....	....	....
1976-77	Calgary Centennials	WCJHL	25	2	8	10	....	....	....	18	....	....	....	....	....	....	....	....	....	....	....	....	....	....	....	....	....	....
	Regina Pats	WCJHL	49	5	26	31	....	....	....	118	....	....	....	....	....	....	....	....	....	....	....	....	....	....	....	....	....	....
1977-78	Regina Pats	WCJHL	57	8	43	51	....	....	....	203	....	....	....	....	....	....	....	....	....	....	13	2	11	13	28	....	....	....
1978-79	**Colorado Rockies**	**NHL**	3	0	0	0	0	0	0	2	0	0	0	0	0.0	0	0	0	0	0	....	....	....	....	....	....	....	....
	Muskegon Mohawks	IHL	39	2	13	15	....	....	....	39	....	....	....	....	....	....	....	....	....	....	....	....	....	....	....	....	....	....
	NHL Totals		3	0	0	0	0	0	0	2	0	0	0	0	0.0	0	0	0	0		....	....	....	....	....	....	....	....

• KROUPA, VLASTIMIL

Vlastimil Kroupa D – L. 6'3", 205 lbs. b: Most, Czech., 4/27/1975. San Jose's 3rd choice, 45th overall, in 1993 Entry Draft.

Season	Club	League	GP	G	A	Pts	AG	AA	APts	PIM	PP	SH	GW	S	%	TGF	PGF	TGA	PGA	+/–	GP	G	A	Pts	PIM	PP	SH	GW
1992-93	Chemopetrol Litvinov	Czech.	9	0	1	1	....	....	....	....	....	....	....	....	....	....	....	....	....	....	....	....	....	....	....	....	....	....
1993-94	**San Jose Sharks**	**NHL**	27	1	3	4	1	2	3	20	0	0	0	16	6.3	19	1	30	6	–6	14	1	2	3	21	0	0	1
	Kansas City Blades	IHL	39	3	12	15	....	....	....	12	....	....	....	....	....	....	....	....	....	....	....	....	....	....	....	....	....	....
1994-95	**San Jose Sharks**	**NHL**	14	0	2	2	0	3	3	16	0	0	0	4	0.0	7	0	20	6	–7	6	0	0	0	4	0	0	0
	Czech Republic	WJC-A	7	4	2	6	....	....	....	10	....	....	....	....	....	....	....	....	....	....	....	....	....	....	....	....	....	....
	Kansas City Blades	IHL	51	4	8	12	....	....	....	49	....	....	....	....	....	....	....	....	....	....	12	2	4	6	22	....	....	....
1995-96	**San Jose Sharks**	**NHL**	27	1	7	8	1	6	7	18	0	0	0	11	9.1	18	2	37	4	–17	....	....	....	....	....	....	....	....
	Kansas City Blades	IHL	39	5	22	27	....	....	....	44	....	....	....	....	....	....	....	....	....	....	5	0	1	1	6	....	....	....
1996-97	**San Jose Sharks**	**NHL**	35	2	6	8	2	5	7	12	2	0	1	24	8.3	22	7	35	3	–17	....	....	....	....	....	....	....	....
	Kentucky Thoroughblades	AHL	5	0	3	3	....	....	....	0	....	....	....	....	....	....	....	....	....	....	....	....	....	....	....	....	....	....
	Czech Republic	WC-A	9	0	4	4	....	....	....	10	....	....	....	....	....	....	....	....	....	....	....	....	....	....	....	....	....	....
1997-98	**New Jersey Devils**	**NHL**	2	0	1	1	0	1	1	0	0	0	0	1	0.0	2	0	1	0	+1	....	....	....	....	....	....	....	....
	Albany River Rats	AHL	71	5	29	34	....	....	....	48	....	....	....	....	....	....	....	....	....	....	12	0	3	3	6	....	....	....
	NHL Totals		105	4	19	23	4	17	21	66	2	0	1	56	7.1	68	10	123	19		20	1	2	3	25	0	0	1

Traded to **New Jersey** by **San Jose** for New Jersey's 3rd round choice in 1998 Entry Draft, August 22, 1997.

• KRULICKI, JIM

Jim Krulicki LW – L. 5'11", 180 lbs. b: Kitchener, Ont., 3/9/1948.

Season	Club	League	GP	G	A	Pts	AG	AA	APts	PIM	PP	SH	GW	S	%	TGF	PGF	TGA	PGA	+/–	GP	G	A	Pts	PIM	PP	SH	GW
1964-65	Kitchener Rangers	OHA	2	0	0	0	....	....	....	0	....	....	....	....	....	....	....	....	....	....	....	....	....	....	....	....	....	....
1965-66	Kitchener Rangers	OHA	48	16	8	24	....	....	....	41	....	....	....	....	....	....	....	....	....	....	19	4	4	8	4	....	....	....
1966-67	Kitchener Rangers	OHA	48	25	24	49	....	....	....	50	....	....	....	....	....	....	....	....	....	....	13	10	3	13	19	....	....	....
	Omaha Knights	CHL	....	....	....	....	....	....	....	....	....	....	....	....	....	....	....	....	....	....	3	0	0	0	0	....	....	....
1967-68	Kitchener Rangers	OHA	51	28	31	59	....	....	....	49	....	....	....	....	....	....	....	....	....	....	19	3	13	16	32	....	....	....
1968-69	Omaha Knights	CHL	32	3	6	9	....	....	....	10	....	....	....	....	....	....	....	....	....	....	....	....	....	....	....	....	....	....
1969-70	Omaha Knights	CHL	72	9	19	28	....	....	....	26	....	....	....	....	....	....	....	....	....	....	12	5	7	12	22	....	....	....
	Buffalo Bisons	AHL	....	....	....	....	....	....	....	....	....	....	....	....	....	....	....	....	....	....	7	3	2	5	5	....	....	....
1970-71	**New York Rangers**	**NHL**	27	0	2	2	0	2	2	6	0	0	0	13	0.0	2	1	9	7	–1	....	....	....	....	....	....	....	....
	Omaha Knights	CHL	9	2	4	6	....	....	....	7	....	....	....	....	....	....	....	....	....	....	....	....	....	....	....	....	....	....
	Detroit Red Wings	**NHL**	14	0	1	1	0	1	1	0	0	0	0	7	0.0	1	1	7	1	–6	....	....	....	....	....	....	....	....
	NHL Totals		41	0	3	3	0	3	3	6	0	0	0	20	0.0	3	2	16	8		....	....	....	....	....	....	....	....

Traded to **Detroit** by **NY Rangers** for Dale Rolfe, March 2, 1971.

• KRUPP, UWE

Uwe Krupp D – R. 6'6", 235 lbs. b: Cologne, West Germany, 6/24/1965. Buffalo's 13th choice, 223rd overall, in 1983 Entry Draft.

Season	Club	League	GP	G	A	Pts	AG	AA	APts	PIM	PP	SH	GW	S	%	TGF	PGF	TGA	PGA	+/–	GP	G	A	Pts	PIM	PP	SH	GW
1982-83	Kolner EC	Germany	11	0	0	0	....	....	....	0	....	....	....	....	....	....	....	....	....	....	....	....	....	....	....	....	....	....
	West Germany	WJC-A	7	0	0	0	....	....	....	0	....	....	....	....	....	....	....	....	....	....	....	....	....	....	....	....	....	....
1983-84	Kolner EC	W. Ger.	26	0	4	4	....	....	....	22	....	....	....	....	....	....	....	....	....	....	....	....	....	....	....	....	....	....
1984-85	Kolner EC	Germany	39	11	8	19	....	....	....	36	....	....	....	....	....	....	....	....	....	....	....	....	....	....	....	....	....	....
	West Germany	WJC-A	7	0	1	1	....	....	....	8	....	....	....	....	....	....	....	....	....	....	....	....	....	....	....	....	....	....
1985-86	Kolner EC	Germany	45	10	21	31	....	....	....	83	....	....	....	....	....	....	....	....	....	....	....	....	....	....	....	....	....	....
	West Germany	WEC-A	3	2	1	3	....	....	....	2	....	....	....	....	....	....	....	....	....	....	....	....	....	....	....	....	....	....
1986-87	**Buffalo Sabres**	**NHL**	26	1	4	5	1	3	4	23	0	0	0	34	2.9	27	5	34	3	–9	....	....	....	....	....	....	....	....
	Rochester Americans	AHL	42	3	19	22	....	....	....	50	....	....	....	....	....	....	....	....	....	....	17	1	11	12	16	....	....	....
1987-88	**Buffalo Sabres**	**NHL**	75	2	9	11	2	6	8	151	0	0	0	84	2.4	83	10	123	49	–1	6	0	0	0	15	0	0	0
1988-89	**Buffalo Sabres**	**NHL**	70	5	13	18	4	9	13	55	0	1	0	51	9.8	66	1	106	41	0	5	0	1	1	4	0	0	0
1989-90	**Buffalo Sabres**	**NHL**	74	3	20	23	3	14	17	85	0	1	1	69	4.3	75	4	86	30	+15	6	0	0	0	4	0	0	0
	West Germany	WEC-A	2	0	0	0	....	....	....	2	....	....	....	....	....	....	....	....	....	....	....	....	....	....	....	....	....	....
1990-91	**Buffalo Sabres**	**NHL**	74	12	32	44	11	24	35	66	6	0	0	138	8.7	126	40	107	35	+14	6	1	1	2	6	1	0	0

			REGULAR SEASON																		PLAYOFFS							
Season	Club	League	GP	G	A	Pts	AG	AA	APts	PIM	PP	SH	GW	S	%	TGF	PGF	TGA	PGA	+/–	GP	G	A	Pts	PIM	PP	SH	GW
1991-92	**Buffalo Sabres**	**NHL**	**8**	**2**	**0**	**2**	**2**	**0**	**2**	**6**	**0**	**0**	**0**	**13**	**15.4**	**9**	**3**	**15**	**9**	**0**	....	....	....	....	....	....	....	....
	New York Islanders	**NHL**	**59**	**6**	**29**	**35**	**5**	**22**	**27**	**43**	**2**	**0**	**0**	**115**	**5.2**	**110**	**29**	**102**	**34**	**+13**	....	....	....	....	....	....	....	....
1992-93	**New York Islanders**	**NHL**	**80**	**9**	**29**	**38**	**7**	**20**	**27**	**67**	**2**	**0**	**2**	**116**	**7.8**	**106**	**35**	**95**	**30**	**+6**	**18**	**1**	**5**	**6**	**12**	**0**	**0**	**0**
1993-94	**New York Islanders**	**NHL**	**41**	**7**	**14**	**21**	**7**	**11**	**18**	**30**	**3**	**0**	**0**	**82**	**8.5**	**59**	**16**	**40**	**8**	**+11**	**4**	**0**	**1**	**1**	**4**	**0**	**0**	**0**
1994-95	Landshut	Germany	5	1	2	3	....	....	....	6	....	....	....	....	....	....	....	....	....	....	....	....	....	....	....	....	....	....
	Quebec Nordiques	**NHL**	**44**	**6**	**17**	**23**	**11**	**25**	**36**	**20**	**3**	**0**	**1**	**102**	**5.9**	**70**	**25**	**45**	**14**	**+14**	**5**	**0**	**2**	**2**	**2**	**0**	**0**	**0**
1995-96	**Colorado Avalanche**	**NHL**	**6**	**0**	**3**	**3**	**0**	**2**	**2**	**4**	**0**	**0**	**0**	**9**	**0.0**	**10**	**3**	**3**	**0**	**+4**	**22**	**4**	**12**	**16**	**33**	**1**	**0**	**2**
1996-97	**Colorado Avalanche**	**NHL**	**60**	**4**	**17**	**21**	**4**	**15**	**19**	**48**	**2**	**0**	**1**	**107**	**3.7**	**70**	**20**	**51**	**13**	**+12**	....	....	....	....	....	....	....	....
1997-98	**Colorado Avalanche**	**NHL**	**78**	**9**	**22**	**31**	**11**	**21**	**32**	**38**	**5**	**0**	**2**	**149**	**6.0**	**82**	**29**	**50**	**18**	**+21**	**7**	**0**	**1**	**1**	**4**	**0**	**0**	**0**
	Germany	Olympics	2	0	2	2	....	....	....	4	....	....	....	....	....	....	....	....	....	....	....	....	....	....	....	....	....	....
	NHL Totals		**695**	**66**	**209**	**275**	**68**	**172**	**240**	**636**	**23**	**2**	**7**	**1069**	**6.2**	**893**	**220**	**857**	**284**		**79**	**6**	**23**	**29**	**84**	**2**	**0**	**2**

Played in NHL All-Star Game (1991)

Traded to **NY Islanders** by **Buffalo** with Pierre Turgeon, Benoit Hogue and Dave McLlwain for Pat Lafontaine, Randy Hillier, Randy Wood and NY Islanders' 4th round choice (Dean Melanson) in 1992 Entry Draft, October 25, 1991. Traded to **Quebec** by **NY Islanders** with NY Islanders' 1st round choice (Wade Belak) in 1994 Entry Draft for Ron Sutter and Quebec's 1st round choice (Brett Lindros) in 1994 Entry Draft, June 28, 1994. Transferred to **Colorado** after **Quebec** franchise relocated, June 21, 1995. Claimed by **Nashville** from **Colorado** in Expansion Draft, June 26, 1998. Signed as a free agent by **Detroit**, July 7, 1998.

• KRUPPKE, GORD

Gord Kruppke D – R. 6'1", 215 lbs. b: Slave Lake, Alta., 4/2/1969. Detroit's 2nd choice, 32nd overall, in 1987 Entry Draft.

Season	Club	League	GP	G	A	Pts	AG	AA	APts	PIM	PP	SH	GW	S	%	TGF	PGF	TGA	PGA	+/–	GP	G	A	Pts	PIM	PP	SH	GW
1985-86	Prince Albert Raiders	WHL	62	1	8	9	....	....	....	81	....	....	....	....	....	....	....	....	....	....	20	4	4	8	22	....	....	....
1986-87	Prince Albert Raiders	WHL	49	2	10	12	....	....	....	129	....	....	....	....	....	....	....	....	....	....	8	0	0	0	9	....	....	....
1987-88	Prince Albert Raiders	WHL	54	8	8	16	....	....	....	113	....	....	....	....	....	....	....	....	....	....	10	0	0	0	46	....	....	....
1988-89	Prince Albert Raiders	WHL	62	6	26	32	....	....	....	254	....	....	....	....	....	....	....	....	....	....	3	0	0	0	11	....	....	....
1989-90	Adirondack Red Wings	AHL	59	2	12	14	....	....	....	103	....	....	....	....	....	....	....	....	....	....	....	....	....	....	....	....	....	....
1990-91	**Detroit Red Wings**	**NHL**	**4**	**0**	**0**	**0**	**0**	**0**	**0**	**0**	**0**	**0**	**0**	**0**	**0.0**	**2**	**0**	**1**	**0**	**+1**	....	....	....	....	....	....	....	....
	Adirondack Red Wings	AHL	45	1	8	9	....	....	....	153	....	....	....	....	....	....	....	....	....	....	....	....	....	....	....	....	....	....
1991-92	Adirondack Red Wings	AHL	65	3	9	12	....	....	....	208	....	....	....	....	....	....	....	....	....	....	16	0	1	1	52	....	....	....
1992-93	**Detroit Red Wings**	**NHL**	**10**	**0**	**0**	**0**	**0**	**0**	**0**	**20**	**0**	**0**	**0**	**7**	**0.0**	**6**	**0**	**6**	**1**	**+1**	....	....	....	....	....	....	....	....
	Adirondack Red Wings	AHL	41	2	12	14	....	....	....	197	....	....	....	....	....	....	....	....	....	....	9	1	2	3	20	....	....	....
1993-94	**Detroit Red Wings**	**NHL**	**9**	**0**	**0**	**0**	**0**	**0**	**0**	**12**	**0**	**0**	**0**	**5**	**0.0**	**4**	**0**	**11**	**3**	**–4**	....	....	....	....	....	....	....	....
	Adirondack Red Wings	AHL	54	2	9	11	....	....	....	210	....	....	....	....	....	....	....	....	....	....	12	1	3	4	32	....	....	....
1994-95	Adirondack Red Wings	AHL	48	2	9	11	....	....	....	157	....	....	....	....	....	....	....	....	....	....	....	....	....	....	....	....	....	....
	St. John's Maple Leafs	AHL	3	0	1	1	....	....	....	6	....	....	....	....	....	....	....	....	....	....	....	....	....	....	....	....	....	....
1995-96	Houston Aeros	IHL	50	0	4	4	....	....	....	119	....	....	....	....	....	....	....	....	....	....	....	....	....	....	....	....	....	....
1996-97	Houston Aeros	IHL	43	0	5	5	....	....	....	91	....	....	....	....	....	....	....	....	....	....	9	0	1	1	14	....	....	....
1997-98	Houston Aeros	IHL	71	2	6	8	....	....	....	171	....	....	....	....	....	....	....	....	....	....	4	0	0	0	27	....	....	....
	NHL Totals		**23**	**0**	**0**	**0**	**0**	**0**	**0**	**32**	**0**	**0**	**0**	**12**	**0.0**	**12**	**0**	**18**	**4**		....	....	....	....	....	....	....	....

WHL East Second All-Star Team (1989)

Traded to **Toronto** by **Detroit** for future considerations, April 7, 1995.

• KRUSE, PAUL

Paul Kruse LW – L. 6', 202 lbs. b: Merritt, B.C., 3/15/1970. Calgary's 6th choice, 83rd overall, in 1990 Entry Draft.

Season	Club	League	GP	G	A	Pts	AG	AA	APts	PIM	PP	SH	GW	S	%	TGF	PGF	TGA	PGA	+/–	GP	G	A	Pts	PIM	PP	SH	GW
1988-89	Kamloops Blazers	WHL	68	8	15	23	....	....	....	209	....	....	....	....	....	....	....	....	....	....	....	....	....	....	....	....	....	....
1989-90	Kamloops Blazers	WHL	67	22	23	45	....	....	....	291	....	....	....	....	....	....	....	....	....	....	17	3	5	8	79	....	....	....
1990-91	**Calgary Flames**	**NHL**	**1**	**0**	**0**	**0**	**0**	**0**	**0**	**7**	**0**	**0**	**0**	**0**	**0.0**	**0**	**0**	**1**	**0**	**–1**	....	....	....	....	....	....	....	....
	Salt Lake Golden Eagles	IHL	83	24	20	44	....	....	....	313	....	....	....	....	....	....	....	....	....	....	4	1	1	2	4	....	....	....
1991-92	**Calgary Flames**	**NHL**	**16**	**3**	**1**	**4**	**3**	**1**	**4**	**65**	**0**	**0**	**0**	**12**	**25.0**	**10**	**1**	**9**	**1**	**+1**	....	....	....	....	....	....	....	....
	Salt Lake Golden Eagles	IHL	57	14	15	29	....	....	....	267	....	....	....	....	....	....	....	....	....	....	5	1	2	3	19	....	....	....
1992-93	**Calgary Flames**	**NHL**	**27**	**2**	**3**	**5**	**2**	**2**	**4**	**41**	**0**	**0**	**0**	**17**	**11.8**	**11**	**0**	**9**	**0**	**+2**	....	....	....	....	....	....	....	....
	Salt Lake Golden Eagles	IHL	35	1	4	5	....	....	....	206	....	....	....	....	....	....	....	....	....	....	....	....	....	....	....	....	....	....
1993-94	**Calgary Flames**	**NHL**	**68**	**3**	**8**	**11**	**3**	**6**	**9**	**185**	**0**	**0**	**0**	**52**	**5.8**	**21**	**0**	**29**	**2**	**–6**	**7**	**0**	**0**	**0**	**14**	**0**	**0**	**0**
1994-95	**Calgary Flames**	**NHL**	**45**	**11**	**5**	**16**	**19**	**7**	**26**	**141**	**0**	**0**	**2**	**52**	**21.2**	**28**	**0**	**16**	**1**	**+13**	**7**	**4**	**2**	**6**	**10**	**0**	**1**	**0**
1995-96	**Calgary Flames**	**NHL**	**75**	**3**	**12**	**15**	**3**	**10**	**13**	**145**	**0**	**0**	**0**	**83**	**3.6**	**26**	**0**	**31**	**0**	**–5**	**3**	**0**	**0**	**0**	**4**	**0**	**0**	**0**
1996-97	**Calgary Flames**	**NHL**	**14**	**2**	**0**	**2**	**2**	**0**	**2**	**30**	**0**	**0**	**1**	**10**	**20.0**	**3**	**0**	**7**	**0**	**–4**	....	....	....	....	....	....	....	....
	New York Islanders	**NHL**	**48**	**4**	**2**	**6**	**4**	**2**	**6**	**111**	**0**	**0**	**0**	**39**	**10.3**	**16**	**1**	**20**	**0**	**–5**	....	....	....	....	....	....	....	....
1997-98	**New York Islanders**	**NHL**	**62**	**6**	**1**	**7**	**7**	**1**	**8**	**138**	**0**	**0**	**2**	**44**	**13.6**	**10**	**0**	**22**	**0**	**–12**	....	....	....	....	....	....	....	....
	Buffalo Sabres	**NHL**	**12**	**1**	**1**	**2**	**1**	**1**	**2**	**49**	**0**	**0**	**0**	**8**	**12.5**	**2**	**0**	**1**	**0**	**+1**	**1**	**1**	**0**	**1**	**4**	**0**	**0**	**0**
	NHL Totals		**368**	**35**	**33**	**68**	**44**	**30**	**74**	**912**	**0**	**0**	**5**	**317**	**11.0**	**127**	**2**	**145**	**4**		**18**	**5**	**2**	**7**	**32**	**0**	**1**	**0**

Traded to **NY Islanders** by **Calgary** for Colorado's 3rd round choice (previously acquired by NY Islanders — later traded to Hartford — Hartford selected Francis Lessard) in 1997 Entry Draft, November 27, 1996. Traded to **Buffalo** by **NY Islanders** with Jason Holland for Jason Dawe, March 24, 1998.

• KRUSHELNYSKI, MIKE

Mike "Krusher" Krushelnyski LW/C – L. 6'2", 200 lbs. b: Montreal, Que., 4/27/1960. Boston's 7th choice, 120th overall, in 1979 Entry Draft.

Season	Club	League	GP	G	A	Pts	AG	AA	APts	PIM	PP	SH	GW	S	%	TGF	PGF	TGA	PGA	+/–	GP	G	A	Pts	PIM	PP	SH	GW
1978-79	Montreal Jr. Canadiens	QMJHL	46	15	29	44	....	....	....	42	....	....	....	....	....	....	....	....	....	....	11	3	4	7	8	....	....	....
1979-80	Montreal Jr. Canadiens	QMJHL	72	39	60	99	....	....	....	78	....	....	....	....	....	....	....	....	....	....	6	2	3	5	2	....	....	....
1980-81	Springfield Indians	AHL	80	25	28	53	....	....	....	47	....	....	....	....	....	....	....	....	....	....	7	1	1	2	29	....	....	....
1981-82	**Boston Bruins**	**NHL**	**17**	**3**	**3**	**6**	**2**	**2**	**4**	**2**	**0**	**1**	**0**	**19**	**15.8**	**8**	**0**	**8**	**0**	**0**	**1**	**0**	**0**	**0**	**2**	**0**	**0**	**0**
	Erie Blades	AHL	62	31	52	83	....	....	....	44	....	....	....	....	....	....	....	....	....	....	....	....	....	....	....	....	....	....
1982-83	**Boston Bruins**	**NHL**	**79**	**23**	**42**	**65**	**19**	**29**	**48**	**43**	**4**	**2**	**1**	**153**	**15.0**	**104**	**10**	**84**	**28**	**+38**	**17**	**8**	**6**	**14**	**12**	**2**	**0**	**0**
1983-84	**Boston Bruins**	**NHL**	**66**	**25**	**20**	**45**	**20**	**14**	**34**	**55**	**3**	**2**	**1**	**152**	**16.4**	**74**	**19**	**72**	**26**	**+9**	**2**	**0**	**0**	**0**	**0**	**0**	**0**	**0**
1984-85	**Edmonton Oilers**	**NHL**	**80**	**43**	**45**	**88**	**35**	**30**	**65**	**60**	**13**	**0**	**4**	**187**	**23.0**	**161**	**38**	**74**	**7**	**+56**	**18**	**5**	**8**	**13**	**22**	**2**	**0**	**2**
1985-86	**Edmonton Oilers**	**NHL**	**54**	**16**	**24**	**40**	**13**	**16**	**29**	**22**	**3**	**0**	**1**	**98**	**16.3**	**74**	**20**	**48**	**5**	**+11**	**10**	**4**	**5**	**9**	**16**	**1**	**0**	**2**
1986-87	**Edmonton Oilers**	**NHL**	**80**	**16**	**35**	**51**	**14**	**25**	**39**	**67**	**4**	**1**	**2**	**89**	**18.0**	**85**	**17**	**46**	**4**	**+26**	**21**	**3**	**4**	**7**	**18**	**0**	**0**	**1**
1987-88	**Edmonton Oilers**	**NHL**	**76**	**20**	**27**	**47**	**17**	**19**	**36**	**64**	**4**	**0**	**0**	**124**	**16.1**	**68**	**11**	**40**	**9**	**+26**	**19**	**4**	**6**	**10**	**12**	**0**	**0**	**0**
1988-89	**Los Angeles Kings**	**NHL**	**78**	**26**	**36**	**62**	**22**	**25**	**47**	**110**	**5**	**0**	**8**	**143**	**18.2**	**109**	**29**	**86**	**15**	**+9**	**11**	**1**	**4**	**5**	**4**	**1**	**0**	**0**
1989-90	**Los Angeles Kings**	**NHL**	**63**	**16**	**25**	**41**	**14**	**18**	**32**	**50**	**2**	**2**	**2**	**101**	**15.8**	**66**	**8**	**67**	**16**	**+7**	**10**	**1**	**3**	**4**	**12**	**0**	**0**	**1**
1990-91	**Los Angeles Kings**	**NHL**	**15**	**1**	**5**	**6**	**1**	**4**	**5**	**10**	**1**	**0**	**0**	**11**	**9.1**	**9**	**1**	**4**	**3**	**+7**	....	....	....	....	....	....	....	....
	Toronto Maple Leafs	**NHL**	**59**	**17**	**22**	**39**	**16**	**17**	**33**	**48**	**2**	**2**	**1**	**98**	**17.3**	**55**	**12**	**55**	**6**	**–6**	....	....	....	....	....	....	....	....
1991-92	**Toronto Maple Leafs**	**NHL**	**72**	**9**	**15**	**24**	**8**	**11**	**19**	**72**	**0**	**2**	**1**	**100**	**9.0**	**50**	**4**	**59**	**8**	**–5**	....	....	....	....	....	....	....	....
1992-93	**Toronto Maple Leafs**	**NHL**	**84**	**19**	**20**	**39**	**16**	**14**	**30**	**62**	**6**	**2**	**3**	**130**	**14.6**	**65**	**25**	**49**	**12**	**+3**	**16**	**3**	**7**	**10**	**8**	**1**	**0**	**0**
1993-94	**Toronto Maple Leafs**	**NHL**	**54**	**5**	**6**	**11**	**5**	**5**	**10**	**28**	**1**	**0**	**1**	**71**	**7.0**	**22**	**1**	**41**	**15**	**–5**	**6**	**0**	**0**	**0**	**0**	**0**	**0**	**0**
1994-95	**Detroit Red Wings**	**NHL**	**20**	**2**	**3**	**5**	**4**	**4**	**8**	**6**	**0**	**0**	**0**	**20**	**10.0**	**8**	**0**	**8**	**3**	**+3**	**8**	**0**	**0**	**0**	**0**	**0**	**0**	**0**
1995-96	Cape Breton Oilers	AHL	50	16	25	41	....	....	....	78	....	....	....	....	....	....	....	....	....	....	....	....	....	....	....	....	....	....
1996-97	Milano 24	Alpenliga	2	0	0	0	....	....	....	0	....	....	....	....	....	....	....	....	....	....	....	....	....	....	....	....	....	....
	NHL Totals		**897**	**241**	**328**	**569**	**206**	**233**	**439**	**699**	**48**	**14**	**25**	**1496**	**16.1**	**958**	**195**	**741**	**157**		**139**	**29**	**43**	**72**	**106**	**7**	**0**	**6**

Played in NHL All-Star Game (1985)

Traded to **Edmonton** by **Boston** for Ken Linseman, June 21, 1984. Traded to **LA Kings** by **Edmonton** with Wayne Gretzky and Marty McSorley for Jimmy Carson, Martin Gelinas, LA Kings' 1st round choices in 1989 (later traded to New Jersey who selected Jason Miller), 1991 (Martin Rucinsky) and 1993 (Nick Stajduhar) Entry Drafts and cash, August 9, 1988. Traded to **Toronto** by **LA Kings** for John McIntyre, November 9, 1990. Signed as a free agent by **Detroit**, August 1, 1994.

• KRUTOV, VLADIMIR

Vladimir Krutov LW – L. 5'9", 195 lbs. b: Moscow, Soviet Union, 6/1/1960. Vancouver's 11th choice, 238th overall, in 1986 Entry Draft.

Season	Club	League	GP	G	A	Pts	AG	AA	APts	PIM	PP	SH	GW	S	%	TGF	PGF	TGA	PGA	+/–	GP	G	A	Pts	PIM	PP	SH	GW
1977-78	CSKA Moscow	USSR	1	0	0	0	....	....	....	0	....	....	....	....	....	....	....	....	....	....	....	....	....	....	....	....	....	....
1978-79	CSKA Moscow	USSR	25	8	3	11	....	....	....	6	....	....	....	....	....	....	....	....	....	....	....	....	....	....	....	....	....	....
	Soviet Union	WJC-A	6	0	0	14	....	....	....	2	....	....	....	....	....	....	....	....	....	....	....	....	....	....	....	....	....	....
1979-80	CSKA Moscow	USSR	40	30	12	42	....	....	....	16	....	....	....	....	....	....	....	....	....	....	....	....	....	....	....	....	....	....
	Soviet Union	WJC-A	5	7	4	11	....	....	....	5	....	....	....	....	....	....	....	....	....	....	....	....	....	....	....	....	....	....
	Soviet Union	Olympics	7	6	5	11	....	....	....	4	....	....	....	....	....	....	....	....	....	....	....	....	....	....	....	....	....	....
1980-81	CSKA Moscow	USSR	47	25	15	40	....	....	....	20	....	....	....	....	....	....	....	....	....	....	....	....	....	....	....	....	....	....
	Soviet Union	WEC-A	8	6	3	9	....	....	....	0	....	....	....	....	....	....	....	....	....	....	....	....	....	....	....	....	....	....
1981-82	Soviet Union	C Cup	7	4	4	8	....	....	....	10	....	....	....	....	....	....	....	....	....	....	....	....	....	....	....	....	....	....
	CSKA Moscow	USSR	46	37	29	66	....	....	....	30	....	....	....	....	....	....	....	....	....	....	....	....	....	....	....	....	....	....
	Soviet Union	WEC-A	10	4	3	7	....	....	....	6	....	....	....	....	....	....	....	....	....	....	....	....	....	....	....	....	....	....

			REGULAR SEASON																		PLAYOFFS							
Season	Club	League	GP	G	A	Pts	AG	AA	APts	PIM	PP	SH	GW	S	%	TGF	PGF	TGA	PGA	+/–	GP	G	A	Pts	PIM	PP	SH	GW
1982-83	CSKA Moscow	USSR	44	32	21	53	....	....	....	34	....	....	....	....	....	....	....	....	....	....	....	....	....	....	....	....	....	....
	USSR	SuperS	6	5	3	8	....	....	....	2	....	....	....	....	....	....	....	....	....	....	....	....	....	....	....	....	....	....
	Soviet Union	WEC-A	10	8	7	15	....	....	....	12	....	....	....	....	....	....	....	....	....	....	....	....	....	....	....	....	....	....
1983-84	CSKA Moscow	USSR	44	37	20	57	....	....	....	20	....	....	....	....	....	....	....	....	....	....	....	....	....	....	....	....	....	....
	Soviet Union	Olympics	7	4	1	5	....	....	....	2	....	....	....	....	....	....	....	....	....	....	....	....	....	....	....	....	....	....
1984-85	Soviet Union	C Cup	6	3	5	8	....	....	....	4	....	....	....	....	....	....	....	....	....	....	....	....	....	....	....	....	....	....
	CSKA Moscow	USSR	40	23	30	53	....	....	....	26	....	....	....	....	....	....	....	....	....	....	....	....	....	....	....	....	....	....
	Soviet Union	WEC-A	10	3	5	8	....	....	....	8	....	....	....	....	....	....	....	....	....	....	....	....	....	....	....	....	....	....
1985-86	CSKA Moscow	USSR	40	31	17	48	....	....	....	10	....	....	....	....	....	....	....	....	....	....	....	....	....	....	....	....	....	....
	CSKA Moscow	SuperS	6	3	6	9	....	....	....	0	....	....	....	....	....	....	....	....	....	....	....	....	....	....	....	....	....	....
	Soviet Union	WEC-A	10	7	10	17	....	....	....	14	....	....	....	....	....	....	....	....	....	....	....	....	....	....	....	....	....	....
1986-87	CSKA Moscow	USSR	39	26	24	50	....	....	....	16	....	....	....	....	....	....	....	....	....	....	....	....	....	....	....	....	....	....
	USSR	RV'87	2	2	0	2	....	....	....	2	....	....	....	....	....	....	....	....	....	....	....	....	....	....	....	....	....	....
	Soviet Union	WEC-A	10	11	3	14	....	....	....	8	....	....	....	....	....	....	....	....	....	....	....	....	....	....	....	....	....	....
1987-88	Soviet Union	C Cup	9	7	7	14	....	....	....	4	....	....	....	....	....	....	....	....	....	....	....	....	....	....	....	....	....	....
	CSKA Moscow	USSR	38	19	23	42	....	....	....	20	....	....	....	....	....	....	....	....	....	....	....	....	....	....	....	....	....	....
	Soviet Union	Olympics	8	6	9	15	....	....	....	0	....	....	....	....	....	....	....	....	....	....	....	....	....	....	....	....	....	....
1988-89	CSKA Moscow	USSR	35	20	21	41	....	....	....	12	....	....	....	....	....	....	....	....	....	....	....	....	....	....	....	....	....	....
	CSKA Moscow	SuperS	5	2	2	4	....	....	....	2	....	....	....	....	....	....	....	....	....	....	....	....	....	....	....	....	....	....
	Soviet Union	WEC-A	10	4	2	6	....	....	....	12	....	....	....	....	....	....	....	....	....	....	....	....	....	....	....	....	....	....
1989-90	**Vancouver Canucks**	**NHL**	**61**	**11**	**23**	**34**	**9**	**16**	**25**	**20**	**2**	**0**	**1**	**81**	**13.6**	**53**	**18**	**45**	**5**	**–5**	....	....	....	....	....	....	....	....
1990-1994			DID NOT PLAY – RETIRED																									
1994-95	Torpedo Nizhny	Russia	51	12	4	16	....	....	....	44	....	....	....	....	....	....	....	....	....	....	....	....	....	....	....	....	....	....
	NHL Totals		**61**	**11**	**23**	**34**	**9**	**16**	**25**	**20**	**2**	**0**	**1**	**81**	**13.6**	**53**	**18**	**45**	**5**		....	....	....	....	....	....	....	....

WJC-A All-Star Team (1979, 1980) • Named Best Forward at WJC-A (1979, 1980) • USSR First All-Star Team (1982, 1983, 1984, 1985, 1986, 1987, 1988) • WEC-A All-Star Team (1983, 1985, 1986, 1987) • Named Best Forward at WEC-A (1986, 1987) • USSR Player of the Year (1987) • Canada Cup All-Star Team (1987)

• KRYGIER, TODD

Todd Krygier LW – L. 6', 185 lbs. b: Chicago Heights, IL, 10/12/1965. Hartford's 1st choice, 16th overall, in 1988 Supplemental Draft.

Season	Club	League	GP	G	A	Pts	AG	AA	APts	PIM	PP	SH	GW	S	%	TGF	PGF	TGA	PGA	+/–	GP	G	A	Pts	PIM	PP	SH	GW
1984-85	University of Connecticut	NCAA	14	14	11	25	....	....	....	12	....	....	....	....	....	....	....	....	....	....	....	....	....	....	....	....	....	....
1985-86	University of Connecticut	NCAA	32	29	27	56	....	....	....	46	....	....	....	....	....	....	....	....	....	....	....	....	....	....	....	....	....	....
1986-87	University of Connecticut	NCAA	28	24	24	48	....	....	....	44	....	....	....	....	....	....	....	....	....	....	....	....	....	....	....	....	....	....
1987-88	University of Connecticut	NCAA	27	32	39	71	....	....	....	28	....	....	....	....	....	....	....	....	....	....	....	....	....	....	....	....	....	....
	New Haven Nighthawks	AHL	13	1	5	6	....	....	....	34	....	....	....	....	....	....	....	....	....	....	....	....	....	....	....	....	....	....
1988-89	Binghamton Whalers	AHL	76	26	42	68	....	....	....	77	....	....	....	....	....	....	....	....	....	....	....	....	....	....	....	....	....	....
1989-90	**Hartford Whalers**	**NHL**	**58**	**18**	**12**	**30**	**16**	**9**	**25**	**52**	**5**	**1**	**3**	**103**	**17.5**	**52**	**9**	**45**	**6**	**+4**	**7**	**2**	**1**	**3**	**4**	**0**	**0**	**0**
	Binghamton Whalers	AHL	12	1	9	10	....	....	....	16	....	....	....	....	....	....	....	....	....	....	....	....	....	....	....	....	....	....
1990-91	**Hartford Whalers**	**NHL**	**72**	**13**	**17**	**30**	**12**	**13**	**25**	**95**	**3**	**0**	**2**	**113**	**11.5**	**42**	**8**	**50**	**17**	**+1**	**6**	**0**	**2**	**2**	**0**	**0**	**0**	**0**
	United States	WEC-A	10	4	4	8	....	....	....	12	....	....	....	....	....	....	....	....	....	....	....	....	....	....	....	....	....	....
1991-92	**Washington Capitals**	**NHL**	**67**	**13**	**17**	**30**	**12**	**13**	**25**	**107**	**1**	**0**	**1**	**127**	**10.2**	**39**	**2**	**39**	**1**	**–1**	**5**	**2**	**1**	**3**	**4**	**0**	**0**	**0**
	United States	WC-A	1	0	0	0	....	....	....	2	....	....	....	....	....	....	....	....	....	....	....	....	....	....	....	....	....	....
1992-93	**Washington Capitals**	**NHL**	**77**	**11**	**12**	**23**	**9**	**8**	**17**	**60**	**0**	**2**	**0**	**133**	**8.3**	**41**	**2**	**64**	**12**	**–13**	**6**	**1**	**1**	**2**	**4**	**0**	**1**	**0**
1993-94	**Washington Capitals**	**NHL**	**66**	**12**	**18**	**30**	**11**	**14**	**25**	**60**	**0**	**1**	**3**	**146**	**8.2**	**41**	**1**	**58**	**14**	**–4**	**5**	**2**	**0**	**2**	**10**	**0**	**0**	**0**
1994-95	**Anaheim Mighty Ducks**	**NHL**	**35**	**11**	**11**	**22**	**19**	**16**	**35**	**10**	**1**	**0**	**1**	**90**	**12.2**	**31**	**6**	**30**	**6**	**+1**	....	....	....	....	....	....	....	....
1995-96	**Anaheim Mighty Ducks**	**NHL**	**60**	**9**	**28**	**37**	**9**	**23**	**32**	**70**	**2**	**1**	**0**	**153**	**5.9**	**46**	**8**	**53**	**6**	**–9**	....	....	....	....	....	....	....	....
	Washington Capitals	**NHL**	**16**	**6**	**5**	**11**	**6**	**4**	**10**	**12**	**1**	**0**	**0**	**28**	**21.4**	**16**	**2**	**6**	**0**	**+8**	**6**	**2**	**0**	**2**	**12**	**0**	**0**	**1**
1996-97	**Washington Capitals**	**NHL**	**47**	**5**	**11**	**16**	**5**	**10**	**15**	**37**	**1**	**0**	**1**	**121**	**4.1**	**24**	**7**	**27**	**0**	**–10**	....	....	....	....	....	....	....	....
	United States	WC-A	8	1	1	2	....	....	....	6	....	....	....	....	....	....	....	....	....	....	....	....	....	....	....	....	....	....
1997-98	**Washington Capitals**	**NHL**	**45**	**2**	**12**	**14**	**2**	**12**	**14**	**30**	**0**	**0**	**1**	**71**	**2.8**	**24**	**6**	**23**	**2**	**–3**	**13**	**1**	**2**	**3**	**6**	**0**	**0**	**1**
	Portland Pirates	AHL	6	3	4	7	....	....	....	6	....	....	....	....	....	....	....	....	....	....	....	....	....	....	....	....	....	....
	NHL Totals		**543**	**100**	**143**	**243**	**101**	**122**	**223**	**533**	**14**	**5**	**12**	**1085**	**9.2**	**356**	**51**	**395**	**64**		**48**	**10**	**7**	**17**	**40**	**0**	**1**	**2**

NCAA (College Div.) East Second All-American Team (1987)

Traded to **Washington** by **Hartford** for future considerations (Washington's 4th round choice — later traded to Calgary — Calgary selected Jason Smith) in 1993 Entry Draft, October 3, 1991. Traded to **Anaheim** by **Washington** for Anaheim's 4th round choice (later traded to Dallas — Dallas selected Mike Hurley) in 1996 Entry Draft, February 2, 1995. Traded to **Washington** by **Anaheim** for Mike Torchia, March 8, 1996.

• KRYSKOW, DAVE

Dave Kryskow LW – L. 5'10", 175 lbs. b: Edmonton, Alta., 12/25/1957. Chicago's 2nd choice, 26th overall, in 1971 Amateur Draft.

Season	Club	League	GP	G	A	Pts	AG	AA	APts	PIM	PP	SH	GW	S	%	TGF	PGF	TGA	PGA	+/–	GP	G	A	Pts	PIM	PP	SH	GW
1969-70	Edmonton Oil Kings	WCJHL	50	12	33	45	....	....	....	81	....	....	....	....	....	....	....	....	....	....	....	....	....	....	....	....	....	....
1970-71	Edmonton Oil Kings	WCJHL	65	42	45	87	....	....	....	149	....	....	....	....	....	....	....	....	....	....	....	....	....	....	....	....	....	....
1971-72	Dallas Black Hawks	CHL	55	9	18	27	....	....	....	85	....	....	....	....	....	....	....	....	....	....	3	0	0	0	0	....	....	....
1972-73	**Chicago Black Hawks**	**NHL**	**11**	**1**	**0**	**1**	**1**	**0**	**1**	**0**	**0**	**0**	**0**	**4**	**25.0**	**3**	**0**	**4**	**0**	**–1**	**3**	**2**	**0**	**2**	**0**	**0**	**0**	**0**
	Dallas Black Hawks	CHL	52	34	28	62	....	....	....	110	....	....	....	....	....	....	....	....	....	....	7	2	3	5	4	....	....	....
1973-74	**Chicago Black Hawks**	**NHL**	**72**	**7**	**12**	**19**	**7**	**10**	**17**	**22**	**0**	**1**	**0**	**60**	**11.7**	**29**	**0**	**28**	**4**	**+5**	**7**	**0**	**0**	**0**	**2**	**0**	**0**	**0**
1974-75	**Washington Capitals**	**NHL**	**51**	**9**	**15**	**24**	**8**	**12**	**20**	**83**	**1**	**1**	**0**	**98**	**9.2**	**40**	**12**	**71**	**15**	**–28**	....	....	....	....	....	....	....	....
	Detroit Red Wings	**NHL**	**18**	**1**	**4**	**5**	**1**	**3**	**4**	**4**	**0**	**0**	**0**	**7**	**14.3**	**4**	**0**	**6**	**0**	**–2**	....	....	....	....	....	....	....	....
1975-76	**Atlanta Flames**	**NHL**	**79**	**15**	**25**	**40**	**14**	**20**	**34**	**65**	**1**	**0**	**2**	**120**	**12.5**	**57**	**6**	**60**	**3**	**–6**	**2**	**0**	**0**	**0**	**2**	**0**	**0**	**0**
1976-77	Calgary Cowboys	WHA	45	16	17	33	....	....	....	47	....	....	....	....	....	....	....	....	....	....	....	....	....	....	....	....	....	....
	Tidewater Sharks	SHL	37	16	23	39	....	....	....	95	....	....	....	....	....	....	....	....	....	....	....	....	....	....	....	....	....	....
1977-78	Winnipeg Jets	WHA	71	20	21	41	....	....	....	16	....	....	....	....	....	....	....	....	....	....	9	4	4	8	2	....	....	....
	NHL Totals		**231**	**33**	**56**	**89**	**31**	**45**	**76**	**174**	**2**	**2**	**2**	**289**	**11.4**	**133**	**18**	**169**	**22**		**12**	**2**	**0**	**2**	**4**	**0**	**0**	**0**
	Other Major League Totals		116	36	38	74	....	....	....	63	....	....	....	....	....	....	....	....	....	....	9	4	4	8	2	....	....	....

CHL First All-Star Team (1973)

Selected by **Edmonton** (WHA) in 1972 WHA General Player Draft, February 12, 1972. Claimed by **Washington** from **Chicago** in Expansion Draft, June 12, 1974. Traded to **Detroit** by **Washington** for Jack Lynch, February 8, 1975. Traded to **Atlanta** by **Detroit** for Bryan Hextall Jr., June 5, 1975. WHA rights traded to **Calgary** (WHA) by **Edmonton** (WHA) for future considerations, September, 1976. Signed as a free agent by **Winnipeg** (WHA) after **Calgary** (WHA) franchise folded, November, 1977.

• KUBINA, PAVEL

Pavel Kubina D – R. 6'3", 213 lbs. b: Celadna, Czech., 4/15/1977. Tampa Bay's 6th choice, 179th overall, in 1996 Entry Draft.

Season	Club	League	GP	G	A	Pts	AG	AA	APts	PIM	PP	SH	GW	S	%	TGF	PGF	TGA	PGA	+/–	GP	G	A	Pts	PIM	PP	SH	GW
1993-94	TJ Vitkovice	Czech. Jr.	35	4	3	7	....	....	....	....	....	....	....	....	....	....	....	....	....	....	....	....	....	....	....	....	....	....
	TJ Vitkovice	Czech.	1	0	0	0	....	....	....	....	....	....	....	....	....	....	....	....	....	....	....	....	....	....	....	....	....	....
1994-95	TJ Vitkovice	Czech. Jr.	20	6	10	16	....	....	....	....	....	....	....	....	....	....	....	....	....	....	....	....	....	....	....	....	....	....
	TJ Vitkovice	Czech.	8	2	0	2	....	....	....	10	....	....	....	....	....	....	....	....	....	....	4	0	0	0	0	....	....	....
1995-96	TJ Vitkovice	Czech.	33	3	4	7	....	....	....	32	....	....	....	....	....	....	....	....	....	....	4	0	0	0	0	....	....	....
	Czech Republic	WJC-A	6	0	2	2	....	....	....	8	....	....	....	....	....	....	....	....	....	....	....	....	....	....	....	....	....	....
	TJ Vitkovice	Czech. Jr.	16	5	10	15	....	....	....	....	....	....	....	....	....	....	....	....	....	....	....	....	....	....	....	....	....	....
1996-97	TJ Vitkovice	Czech.	1	0	0	0	....	....	....	0	....	....	....	....	....	....	....	....	....	....	....	....	....	....	....	....	....	....
	Moose Jaw	WHL	61	12	32	44	....	....	....	116	....	....	....	....	....	....	....	....	....	....	11	2	5	7	27	....	....	....
1997-98	**Tampa Bay Lightning**	**NHL**	**10**	**1**	**2**	**3**	**1**	**2**	**3**	**22**	**0**	**0**	**0**	**8**	**12.5**	**7**	**0**	**12**	**4**	**–1**	....	....	....	....	....	....	....	....
	Adirondack Red Wings	AHL	55	4	8	12	....	....	....	86	....	....	....	....	....	....	....	....	....	....	1	1	0	1	14	....	....	....
	NHL Totals		**10**	**1**	**2**	**3**	**1**	**2**	**3**	**22**	**0**	**0**	**0**	**8**	**12.5**	**7**	**0**	**12**	**4**		....	....	....	....	....	....	....	....

• KUCERA, FRANTISEK

Frantisek Kucera D – R. 6'2", 205 lbs. b: Prague, Czech., 2/3/1968. Chicago's 3rd choice, 77th overall, in 1986 Entry Draft.

Season	Club	League	GP	G	A	Pts	AG	AA	APts	PIM	PP	SH	GW	S	%	TGF	PGF	TGA	PGA	+/–	GP	G	A	Pts	PIM	PP	SH	GW
1985-86	Sparta Praha	Czech.	15	0	0	0	....	....	....	....	....	....	....	....	....	....	....	....	....	....	....	....	....	....	....	....	....	....
1986-87	Sparta Praha	Czech.	40	5	2	7	....	....	....	14	....	....	....	....	....	....	....	....	....	....	....	....	....	....	....	....	....	....
	Czechoslovakia	WJC-A	7	1	2	3	....	....	....	2	....	....	....	....	....	....	....	....	....	....	....	....	....	....	....	....	....	....
1987-88	Sparta Praha	Czech.	46	7	2	9	....	....	....	30	....	....	....	....	....	....	....	....	....	....	....	....	....	....	....	....	....	....
	Czechoslovakia	WJC-A	7	1	2	3	....	....	....	2	....	....	....	....	....	....	....	....	....	....	....	....	....	....	....	....	....	....
1988-89	Dukla Jihlava	Czech.	45	10	9	19	....	....	....	28	....	....	....	....	....	....	....	....	....	....	....	....	....	....	....	....	....	....
	Czechoslovakia	WEC-A	6	0	1	1	....	....	....	6	....	....	....	....	....	....	....	....	....	....	....	....	....	....	....	....	....	....
1989-90	Dukla Jihlava	Czech.	43	9	10	19	....	....	....	....	....	....	....	....	....	....	....	....	....	....	....	....	....	....	....	....	....	....
1990-91	**Chicago Blackhawks**	**NHL**	**40**	**2**	**12**	**14**	**2**	**9**	**11**	**32**	**1**	**0**	**0**	**65**	**3.1**	**38**	**9**	**38**	**12**	**+3**	....	....	....	....	....	....	....	....
	Indianapolis Ice	IHL	35	8	19	27	....	....	....	23	....	....	....	....	....	....	....	....	....	....	7	0	1	1	15	....	....	....

			REGULAR SEASON																		PLAYOFFS							
Season	**Club**	**League**	**GP**	**G**	**A**	**Pts**	**AG**	**AA**	**APts**	**PIM**	**PP**	**SH**	**GW**	**S**	**%**	**TGF**	**PGF**	**TGA**	**PGA**	**+/–**	**GP**	**G**	**A**	**Pts**	**PIM**	**PP**	**SH**	**GW**
1991-92	Czechoslovakia	C Cup	5	0	0	0				4																		
	Chicago Blackhawks	**NHL**	**61**	**3**	**10**	**13**	**3**	**7**	**10**	**36**	**1**	**0**	**1**	**82**	**3.7**	**50**	**12**	**58**	**23**	**+3**	**6**	**0**	**0**	**0**	**0**	**0**	**0**	**0**
	Indianapolis Ice	IHL	7	1	2	3				4																		
1992-93	**Chicago Blackhawks**	**NHL**	**71**	**5**	**14**	**19**	**4**	**10**	**14**	**59**	**1**	**0**	**1**	**117**	**4.3**	**57**	**8**	**54**	**12**	**+7**								
1993-94	**Chicago Blackhawks**	**NHL**	**60**	**4**	**13**	**17**	**4**	**10**	**14**	**34**	**2**	**0**	**0**	**90**	**4.4**	**53**	**6**	**48**	**10**	**+9**								
	Hartford Whalers	**NHL**	**16**	**1**	**3**	**4**	**1**	**2**	**3**	**14**	**1**	**0**	**0**	**32**	**3.1**	**15**	**7**	**27**	**7**	**–12**								
	Czech Republic	WC-A	4	0	0	0				2																		
1994-95	Sparta Praha	Czech.	16	1	2	3				14																		
	Hartford Whalers	**NHL**	**48**	**3**	**17**	**20**	**5**	**25**	**30**	**30**	**0**	**0**	**1**	**73**	**4.1**	**38**	**7**	**38**	**10**	**+3**								
1995-96	**Hartford Whalers**	**NHL**	**30**	**2**	**6**	**8**	**2**	**5**	**7**	**10**	**0**	**0**	**1**	**43**	**4.7**	**22**	**3**	**25**	**3**	**–3**								
	Vancouver Canucks	**NHL**	**24**	**1**	**0**	**1**	**1**	**0**	**1**	**10**	**0**	**0**	**0**	**34**	**2.9**	**20**	**5**	**13**	**3**	**+5**	**6**	**0**	**1**	**1**	**0**	**0**	**0**	**0**
1996-97	**Vancouver Canucks**	**NHL**	**2**	**0**	**0**	**0**	**0**	**0**	**0**	**0**	**0**	**0**	**0**	**3**	**0.0**	**0**	**0**	**1**	**1**	**0**								
	Syracuse Crunch	AHL	42	6	29	35				36																		
	Houston Aeros	IHL	12	0	3	3				20																		
	Philadelphia Flyers	**NHL**	**2**	**0**	**0**	**0**	**0**	**0**	**0**	**2**	**0**	**0**	**0**	**2**	**0.0**	**1**	**1**	**2**	**0**	**–2**								
	Philadelphia Phantoms	AHL	9	1	5	6				2											10	1	6	7	20			
1997-98	Sparta Praha	EuroHL	4	0	1	1				2																		
	Sparta Praha	Czech.	43	8	12	20				49											9	3	1	4	53			
	Czech Republic	Olympics	6	0	0	0				0																		
	NHL Totals		**354**	**21**	**75**	**96**	**22**	**68**	**90**	**227**	**6**	**0**	**4**	**541**	**3.9**	**294**	**58**	**304**	**81**		**12**	**0**	**1**	**1**	**0**	**0**	**0**	**0**

EJC-A All-Star Team (1986)

Traded to **Hartford** by **Chicago** with Jocelyn Lemieux for Gary Suter, Randy Cunneyworth and Hartford's 3rd round choice (later traded to Vancouver — Vancouver selected Larry Courville) in 1995 Entry Draft, March 11, 1994. Traded to **Vancouver** by **Hartford** with Jim Dowd and Hartford's 2nd round choice (Ryan Bonni) in 1997 Entry Draft for Jeff Brown and Vancouver's 3rd round choice (later traded to Calgary — Calgary selected Paul Manning) in 1998 Entry Draft, December 19, 1995. Traded to **Philadelphia** by **Vancouver** for future considerations, March 18, 1997.

• KUDASHOV, ALEXEI

Alexei Kudashov C – R. 6′, 183 lbs. b: Elektrostal, USSR, 7/21/1971. Toronto's 3rd choice, 102nd overall, in 1991 Entry Draft.

Season	Club	League	GP	G	A	Pts	AG	AA	APts	PIM	PP	SH	GW	S	%	TGF	PGF	TGA	PGA	+/–	GP	G	A	Pts	PIM	PP	SH	GW
1989-90	Soviet Wings	FrTour	1	0	0	0				0																		
	Soviet Wings	USSR	45	0	5	5				14																		
	Soviet Union	WJC-A	7	2	1	3				0																		
1990-91	Soviet Wings	FrTour	1	0	0	0				0																		
	Soviet Wings	USSR	45	9	5	14				10																		
1991-92	Soviet Wings	CIS	42	9	16	25				14																		
1992-93	Soviet Wings	CIS	41	8	20	28				24											7	1	3	4	4			
1993-94	Soviet Wings	CIS	1	2	0	2				0																		
	Toronto Maple Leafs	**NHL**	**25**	**1**	**0**	**1**	**1**	**0**	**1**	**4**	**0**	**0**	**0**	**24**	**4.2**	**2**	**0**	**6**	**1**	**–3**								
	St. John's Maple Leafs	AHL	27	7	15	22				21																		
1994-95	St. John's Maple Leafs	AHL	75	25	54	79				17											5	1	4	5	2			
1995-96	Carolina Monarchs	AHL	33	7	22	29				18																		
	Dusseldorfer EG	Germany	9	7	8	15				4											13	5	5	10	14			
1996-97	Dusseldorfer EG	Germany	48	13	16	29				16											4	3	1	4	2			
1997-98	TPS Turku	EuroHL	6	0	2	2				0																		
	TPS Turku	Finland	48	8	31	39				34											4	0	0	0	4			
	Russia	WC-A	3	1	2	3				2																		
	NHL Totals		**25**	**1**	**0**	**1**	**1**	**0**	**1**	**4**	**0**	**0**	**0**	**24**	**4.2**	**2**	**0**	**6**	**1**									

Signed as a free agent by **Florida**, September 10, 1995.

• KUDELSKI, BOB

Bob Kudelski RW – R. 6′1″, 205 lbs. b: Springfield, MA, 3/3/1964. Los Angeles' 1st choice, 2nd overall, in 1986 Supplemental Draft.

Season	Club	League	GP	G	A	Pts	AG	AA	APts	PIM	PP	SH	GW	S	%	TGF	PGF	TGA	PGA	+/–	GP	G	A	Pts	PIM	PP	SH	GW
1983-84	Yale University	ECAC	21	14	12	26				12																		
1984-85	Yale University	ECAC	32	21	23	44				38																		
1985-86	Yale University	ECAC	31	18	23	41				48																		
1986-87	Yale University	ECAC	30	25	22	47				34																		
1987-88	**Los Angeles Kings**	**NHL**	**26**	**0**	**1**	**1**	**0**	**1**	**1**	**8**	**0**	**0**	**0**	**10**	**0.0**	**3**	**1**	**30**	**18**	**–10**								
	New Haven Nighthawks	AHL	50	15	19	34				41																		
1988-89	**Los Angeles Kings**	**NHL**	**14**	**1**	**3**	**4**	**1**	**2**	**3**	**17**	**0**	**0**	**0**	**15**	**6.7**	**6**	**0**	**11**	**0**	**–5**								
	New Haven Nighthawks	AHL	60	32	29	61				43											17	8	5	13	12			
1989-90	**Los Angeles Kings**	**NHL**	**62**	**23**	**13**	**36**	**20**	**9**	**29**	**49**	**2**	**2**	**3**	**135**	**17.0**	**53**	**11**	**60**	**11**	**–7**	**8**	**1**	**2**	**3**	**2**	**0**	**0**	**0**
1990-91	**Los Angeles Kings**	**NHL**	**72**	**23**	**13**	**36**	**21**	**10**	**31**	**46**	**2**	**3**	**3**	**137**	**16.8**	**57**	**7**	**62**	**21**	**+9**	**8**	**3**	**2**	**5**	**2**	**0**	**0**	**0**
1991-92	**Los Angeles Kings**	**NHL**	**80**	**22**	**21**	**43**	**20**	**16**	**36**	**42**	**2**	**1**	**2**	**155**	**14.2**	**58**	**10**	**82**	**19**	**–15**	**6**	**0**	**0**	**0**	**0**	**0**	**0**	**0**
1992-93	**Los Angeles Kings**	**NHL**	**15**	**3**	**3**	**6**	**2**	**2**	**4**	**8**	**0**	**0**	**1**	**12**	**25.0**	**11**	**4**	**12**	**2**	**–3**								
	Ottawa Senators	**NHL**	**48**	**21**	**14**	**35**	**17**	**10**	**27**	**22**	**12**	**0**	**2**	**125**	**16.8**	**54**	**31**	**45**	**0**	**–22**								
1993-94	**Ottawa Senators**	**NHL**	**42**	**26**	**15**	**41**	**24**	**12**	**36**	**14**	**12**	**0**	**1**	**127**	**20.5**	**57**	**25**	**58**	**1**	**–25**								
	Florida Panthers	**NHL**	**44**	**14**	**15**	**29**	**13**	**12**	**25**	**10**	**5**	**0**	**2**	**124**	**11.3**	**41**	**15**	**34**	**0**	**–8**								
1994-95	**Florida Panthers**	**NHL**	**26**	**6**	**3**	**9**	**11**	**4**	**15**	**2**	**3**	**0**	**1**	**29**	**20.7**	**15**	**6**	**7**	**0**	**+2**								
1995-96	**Florida Panthers**	**NHL**	**13**	**0**	**1**	**1**	**0**	**1**	**1**	**0**	**0**	**0**	**0**	**23**	**0.0**	**5**	**1**	**3**	**0**	**+1**								
	Carolina Monarchs	AHL	4	1	0	1				0																		
	NHL Totals		**442**	**139**	**102**	**241**	**129**	**79**	**208**	**218**	**38**	**6**	**15**	**900**	**15.4**	**360**	**111**	**404**	**72**		**22**	**4**	**4**	**8**	**4**	**0**	**0**	**0**

ECAC First All-Star Team (1987)

Played in NHL All-Star Game (1994)

Traded to **Ottawa** by **LA Kings** with Shawn McCosh for Marc Fortier and Jim Thomson, December 19, 1992. Traded to **Florida** by **Ottawa** for Evgeny Davydov, Scott Levins, Florida's 6th round choice (Mike Gaffney) in 1994 Entry Draft and Dallas' 4th round choice (previously acquired, Ottawa selected Kevin Bolibruck) in 1995 Entry Draft, January 6, 1994.

• KULAK, STU

Stu Kulak RW – R. 5′10″, 180 lbs. b: Edmonton, Alta., 3/10/1963. Vancouver's 5th choice, 115th overall, in 1981 Entry Draft.

Season	Club	League	GP	G	A	Pts	AG	AA	APts	PIM	PP	SH	GW	S	%	TGF	PGF	TGA	PGA	+/–	GP	G	A	Pts	PIM	PP	SH	GW
1979-80	Sherwood Park Crusaders	AJHL	53	30	23	53				111																		
	Victoria Cougars	WHL	3	0	0	0				0																		
1980-81	Victoria Cougars	WHL	72	23	24	47				43											15	3	5	8	19			
1981-82	Victoria Cougars	WHL	71	38	50	88				92											4	1	2	3	43			
1982-83	**Vancouver Canucks**	**NHL**	**4**	**1**	**1**	**2**	**1**	**1**	**2**	**0**	**0**	**0**	**0**	**2**	**50.0**	**2**	**0**	**1**	**0**	**+1**								
	Victoria Cougars	WHL	50	29	33	62				130											10	10	9	19	29			
1983-84	Fredericton Express	AHL	52	12	16	28				55											5	0	0	0	59			
1984-85	DID NOT PLAY – INJURED																											
1985-86	Fredericton Express	AHL	3	1	0	1				0											6	2	1	3	0			
	Kalamazoo Wings	IHL	30	14	8	22				38											2	2	0	2	0			
1986-87	**Vancouver Canucks**	**NHL**	**28**	**1**	**1**	**2**	**1**	**1**	**2**	**37**	**1**	**0**	**1**	**24**	**4.2**	**2**	**1**	**13**	**1**	**–11**								
	Edmonton Oilers	**NHL**	**23**	**3**	**1**	**4**	**3**	**1**	**4**	**41**	**0**	**0**	**1**	**30**	**10.0**	**11**	**0**	**8**	**0**	**+3**								
	New York Rangers	**NHL**	**3**	**0**	**0**	**0**	**0**	**0**	**0**	**0**	**0**	**0**	**0**	**2**	**0.0**	**1**	**0**	**2**	**0**	**–1**	**3**	**0**	**0**	**0**	**2**	**0**	**0**	**0**
1987-88	**Quebec Nordiques**	**NHL**	**14**	**1**	**1**	**2**	**1**	**1**	**2**	**28**	**0**	**0**	**0**	**22**	**4.5**	**2**	**0**	**7**	**0**	**–5**								
	Moncton Hawks	AHL	37	9	12	21				58																		
1988-89	**Winnipeg Jets**	**NHL**	**18**	**2**	**0**	**2**	**2**	**0**	**2**	**24**	**1**	**0**	**0**	**18**	**11.1**	**2**	**1**	**7**	**0**	**–6**								
	Moncton Hawks	AHL	51	30	29	59				98											10	5	6	11	16			
1989-90	Moncton Hawks	AHL	36	14	23	37				72																		
1990-91	Kansas City Blades	IHL	47	13	28	41				20																		
1991-92	DID NOT PLAY																											
1992-93	Erie Panthers	ECHL	21	13	8	21				23																		
1993-94	Tulsa Oilers	CHL	59	17	29	46				101											8	0	0	0	28			
1994-95	San Antonio Iguanas	CHL	65	30	38	68				97											13	3	3	6	36			
1995-96	Reno Renegades	WCHL	43	16	25	41				60											3	1	1	2	0			

			REGULAR SEASON																		PLAYOFFS							
Season	Club	League	GP	G	A	Pts	AG	AA	APts	PIM	PP	SH	GW	S	%	TGF	PGF	TGA	PGA	+/–	GP	G	A	Pts	PIM	PP	SH	GW
1996-97	Reno Renegades	WCHL	36	12	18	30	....	....	....	60	....	....	....	....	....	....	....	....	....	....	....	....	....	....	....	....	....	....
	New Mexico Scorpions	WCHL	5	0	0	0	....	....	....	0	....	....	....	....	....	....	....	....	....	....	6	1	1	2	8	....	....	....
1997-98	Reno Renegades	WCHL	63	16	25	41	....	....	....	54	....	....	....	....	....	....	....	....	....	....	3	3	2	5	4	....	....	....
	NHL Totals		**90**	**8**	**4**	**12**	**8**	**4**	**12**	**130**	**2**	**0**	**2**	**98**	**8.2**	**20**	**2**	**38**	**1**		**3**	**0**	**0**	**0**	**2**	**0**	**0**	**0**

• Missed entire 1984-85 season with torn abdominal muscle. Traded to **Edmonton** by **Vancouver** for cash December 11, 1986. Traded to **NY Rangers** by **Edmonton** to complete transaction that sent Reijo Ruotsalanien, Clark Donatelli, Velle Kentala and Jim Wiemer to Edmonton (October 2, 1986), March 10, 1987. Claimed by **Quebec** from **NY Rangers** in Waiver Draft, October 5, 1987. Traded to **Winnipeg** by **Quebec** for Bobby Dollas, December 17,1987.

• KUMPEL, MARK

Mark Kumpel RW – R. 6′, 190 lbs. b: Wakefield, MA, 3/7/1961. Quebec's 4th choice, 108th overall, in 1980 Entry Draft.

Season	Club	League	GP	G	A	Pts	AG	AA	APts	PIM	PP	SH	GW	S	%	TGF	PGF	TGA	PGA	+/–	GP	G	A	Pts	PIM	PP	SH	GW
1979-80	University of Lowell	ECAC	30	18	18	36	....	....	....	12	....	....	....	....	....	....	....	....	....	....	....	....	....	....	....	....	....	....
1980-81	University of Lowell	ECAC	1	2	0	2	....	....	....	0	....	....	....	....	....	....	....	....	....	....	....	....	....	....	....	....	....	....
1981-82	University of Lowell	ECAC	35	17	13	30	....	....	....	23	....	....	....	....	....	....	....	....	....	....	....	....	....	....	....	....	....	....
1982-83	University of Lowell	ECAC	7	8	5	13	....	....	....	0	....	....	....	....	....	....	....	....	....	....	....	....	....	....	....	....	....	....
	United States	Nat-Team	30	14	18	32	....	....	....	6	....	....	....	....	....	....	....	....	....	....	....	....	....	....	....	....	....	....
1983-84	United States	Nat-Team	61	14	19	33	....	....	....	19	....	....	....	....	....	....	....	....	....	....	....	....	....	....	....	....	....	....
	United States	Olympics	6	1	0	1	....	....	....	2	....	....	....	....	....	....	....	....	....	....	....	....	....	....	....	....	....	....
	Fredericton Express	AHL	16	1	1	2	....	....	....	5	....	....	....	....	....	....	....	....	....	....	3	0	0	0	15	....	....	....
1984-85	**Quebec Nordiques**	**NHL**	**42**	**8**	**7**	**15**	**7**	**5**	**12**	**26**	**1**	**0**	**0**	**52**	**15.4**	**23**	**1**	**18**	**0**	**+4**	**18**	**3**	**4**	**7**	**4**	**0**	**0**	**1**
	Fredericton Express	AHL	18	9	6	15	....	....	....	17	....	....	....	....	....	....	....	....	....	....	....	....	....	....	....	....	....	....
1985-86	**Quebec Nordiques**	**NHL**	**47**	**10**	**12**	**22**	**8**	**8**	**16**	**17**	**0**	**0**	**3**	**76**	**13.2**	**37**	**3**	**25**	**1**	**+10**	**2**	**1**	**0**	**1**	**0**	**0**	**0**	**0**
	Fredericton Express	AHL	7	4	2	6	....	....	....	4	....	....	....	....	....	....	....	....	....	....	....	....	....	....	....	....	....	....
1986-87	**Quebec Nordiques**	**NHL**	**40**	**1**	**8**	**9**	**1**	**6**	**7**	**16**	**0**	**0**	**0**	**47**	**2.1**	**15**	**2**	**25**	**0**	**–12**	....	....	....	....	....	....	....	....
	Detroit Red Wings	**NHL**	**5**	**0**	**1**	**1**	**0**	**1**	**1**	**0**	**0**	**0**	**0**	**1**	**0.0**	**2**	**0**	**0**	**0**	**+2**	**8**	**0**	**0**	**0**	**4**	**0**	**0**	**0**
	Adirondack Red Wings	AHL	7	2	3	5	....	....	....	0	....	....	....	....	....	....	....	....	....	....	1	1	0	1	0	....	....	....
1987-88	**Detroit Red Wings**	**NHL**	**13**	**0**	**2**	**2**	**0**	**1**	**1**	**4**	**0**	**0**	**0**	**6**	**0.0**	**2**	**0**	**2**	**0**	**0**	....	....	....	....	....	....	....	....
	Adirondack Red Wings	AHL	4	5	0	5	....	....	....	2	....	....	....	....	....	....	....	....	....	....	....	....	....	....	....	....	....	....
	Winnipeg Jets	**NHL**	**32**	**4**	**4**	**8**	**3**	**3**	**6**	**19**	**0**	**0**	**0**	**36**	**11.1**	**13**	**0**	**11**	**2**	**+4**	**4**	**0**	**0**	**0**	**4**	**0**	**0**	**0**
1988-89	Moncton Hawks	AHL	53	22	23	45	....	....	....	25	....	....	....	....	....	....	....	....	....	....	10	3	4	7	0	....	....	....
1989-90	**Winnipeg Jets**	**NHL**	**56**	**8**	**9**	**17**	**7**	**6**	**13**	**21**	**0**	**1**	**1**	**74**	**10.8**	**29**	**2**	**40**	**8**	**–5**	**7**	**2**	**0**	**2**	**2**	**0**	**0**	**0**
1990-91	**Winnipeg Jets**	**NHL**	**53**	**7**	**3**	**10**	**6**	**2**	**8**	**10**	**0**	**0**	**0**	**65**	**10.8**	**22**	**0**	**39**	**7**	**–10**	....	....	....	....	....	....	....	....
1991-92	Moncton Hawks	AHL	41	11	18	29	....	....	....	12	....	....	....	....	....	....	....	....	....	....	2	0	0	0	0	....	....	....
1992-93	Providence Bruins	AHL	30	5	3	8	....	....	....	14	....	....	....	....	....	....	....	....	....	....	....	....	....	....	....	....	....	....
	NHL Totals		**288**	**38**	**46**	**84**	**32**	**32**	**64**	**113**	**1**	**1**	**4**	**357**	**10.6**	**143**	**8**	**160**	**18**		**39**	**6**	**4**	**10**	**14**	**0**	**0**	**1**

Traded to **Detroit** by **Quebec** with Brent Aston and Gilbert Delorme for Basil McRae, John Ogrondick and Doug Sheddon, January 17, 1987. Traded to **Winnipeg** by **Detroit** for Jim Nill, January 11, 1988.

• KUNTZ, MURRAY

Murray Kuntz LW – L. 5′10″, 180 lbs. b: Ottawa, Ont., 12/19/1945.

Season	Club	League	GP	G	A	Pts	AG	AA	APts	PIM	PP	SH	GW	S	%	TGF	PGF	TGA	PGA	+/–	GP	G	A	Pts	PIM	PP	SH	GW
1965-66	Ottawa Jr. Montagnards	City Jr.	STATISTICS NOT AVAILABLE																									
1966-67	Toledo Blades	IHL	10	5	4	9	....	....	....	4	....	....	....	....	....	....	....	....	....	....	....	....	....	....	....	....	....	....
	New Haven Blades	EHL	36	13	10	23	....	....	....	11	....	....	....	....	....	....	....	....	....	....	....	....	....	....	....	....	....	....
1967-68	New Haven Blades	EHL	72	40	60	100	....	....	....	34	....	....	....	....	....	....	....	....	....	....	10	5	5	10	7	....	....	....
1968-69	New Haven Blades	EHL	25	28	31	59	....	....	....	25	....	....	....	....	....	....	....	....	....	....	10	4	6	10	2	....	....	....
1969-70	New Haven Blades	EHL	74	51	47	98	....	....	....	68	....	....	....	....	....	....	....	....	....	....	11	1	5	6	2	....	....	....
1970-71	Salt Lake Golden Eagles	WHL	68	18	22	40	....	....	....	14	....	....	....	....	....	....	....	....	....	....	....	....	....	....	....	....	....	....
1971-72	Cincinnati Swords	AHL	45	4	9	13	....	....	....	20	....	....	....	....	....	....	....	....	....	....	....	....	....	....	....	....	....	....
1972-73	Cincinnati Swords	AHL	63	35	30	65	....	....	....	10	....	....	....	....	....	....	....	....	....	....	13	4	4	8	6	....	....	....
1973-74	Rochester Americans	AHL	73	*51	31	82	....	....	....	33	....	....	....	....	....	....	....	....	....	....	6	0	3	3	2	....	....	....
1974-75	**St. Louis Blues**	**NHL**	**7**	**1**	**2**	**3**	**1**	**2**	**3**	**0**	**0**	**0**	**0**	**16**	**6.3**	**11**	**2**	**3**	**0**	**+6**	....	....	....	....	....	....	....	....
	Denver Spurs	CHL	26	11	16	27	....	....	....	10	....	....	....	....	....	....	....	....	....	....	....	....	....	....	....	....	....	....
	Syracuse Eagles	AHL	33	14	16	30	....	....	....	38	....	....	....	....	....	....	....	....	....	....	1	1	0	1	0	....	....	....
1975-76	Springfield Indians	AHL	39	17	12	29	....	....	....	10	....	....	....	....	....	....	....	....	....	....	....	....	....	....	....	....	....	....
	Baltimore Clippers	AHL	39	11	6	17	....	....	....	2	....	....	....	....	....	....	....	....	....	....	....	....	....	....	....	....	....	....
1976-77	Maine Nordiques	NAHL	46	19	17	36	....	....	....	8	....	....	....	....	....	....	....	....	....	....	11	2	5	7	2	....	....	....
	Beauce Jaros	NAHL	23	9	17	26	....	....	....	14	....	....	....	....	....	....	....	....	....	....	....	....	....	....	....	....	....	....
	NHL Totals		**7**	**1**	**2**	**3**	**1**	**2**	**3**	**0**	**0**	**0**	**0**	**16**	**6.3**	**11**	**2**	**3**	**0**		....	....	....	....	....	....	....	....

AHL First All-Star Team (1974)

Signed as a free agent by **Buffalo**, September, 1970. Claimed by **Rochester** (AHL) from **Buffalo** in Reverse Draft, June 12, 1973. Traded to **St. Louis** by **Rochester** (AHL) for cash, June, 1974.

• KURRI, JARI

Jari Kurri RW – R. 6′1″, 195 lbs. b: Helsinki, Finland, 5/18/1960. Edmonton's 3rd choice, 69th overall, in 1980 Entry Draft.

Season	Club	League	GP	G	A	Pts	AG	AA	APts	PIM	PP	SH	GW	S	%	TGF	PGF	TGA	PGA	+/–	GP	G	A	Pts	PIM	PP	SH	GW
1977-78	Jokerit Helsinki	Finland	29	2	9	11	....	....	....	12	....	....	....	....	....	....	....	....	....	....	....	....	....	....	....	....	....	....
1978-79	Jokerit Helsinki	Finland	33	16	14	30	....	....	....	12	....	....	....	....	....	....	....	....	....	....	....	....	....	....	....	....	....	....
	Finland	WJC-A	6	2	3	5	....	....	....	2	....	....	....	....	....	....	....	....	....	....	....	....	....	....	....	....	....	....
1979-80	Jokerit Helsinki	Finland	33	23	16	39	....	....	....	22	....	....	....	....	....	....	....	....	....	....	6	7	2	9	13	....	....	....
	Finland	WJC-A	5	4	7	11	....	....	....	0	....	....	....	....	....	....	....	....	....	....	....	....	....	....	....	....	....	....
	Finland	Olympics	7	2	1	3	....	....	....	6	....	....	....	....	....	....	....	....	....	....	....	....	....	....	....	....	....	....
1980-81	**Edmonton Oilers**	**NHL**	**75**	**32**	**43**	**75**	**26**	**30**	**56**	**40**	**9**	**0**	**1**	**202**	**15.8**	**127**	**36**	**66**	**1**	**+26**	**9**	**5**	**7**	**12**	**4**	**0**	**0**	**0**
1981-82	Finland	C Cup	5	0	1	1	....	....	....	0	....	....	....	....	....	....	....	....	....	....	....	....	....	....	....	....	....	....
	Edmonton Oilers	**NHL**	**71**	**32**	**54**	**86**	**25**	**36**	**61**	**32**	**6**	**1**	**5**	**211**	**15.2**	**122**	**26**	**65**	**7**	**+38**	**5**	**2**	**5**	**7**	**10**	**0**	**0**	**0**
	Finland	WEC-A	7	4	3	7	....	....	....	2	....	....	....	....	....	....	....	....	....	....	....	....	....	....	....	....	....	....
1982-83	**Edmonton Oilers**	**NHL**	**80**	**45**	**59**	**104**	**37**	**41**	**78**	**22**	**10**	**1**	**3**	**218**	**20.6**	**148**	**33**	**89**	**21**	**+47**	**16**	**8**	**15**	**23**	**8**	**2**	**2**	**0**
1983-84	**Edmonton Oilers**	**NHL**	**64**	**52**	**61**	**113**	**42**	**41**	**83**	**14**	**10**	**5**	**4**	**194**	**26.8**	**158**	**42**	**95**	**17**	**+38**	**19**	***14**	**14**	**28**	**13**	**4**	**0**	**0**
1984-85	**Edmonton Oilers**	**NHL**	**73**	**71**	**64**	**135**	**58**	**43**	**101**	**30**	**14**	**3**	**13**	**261**	**27.2**	**178**	**38**	**85**	**21**	**+76**	**18**	***19**	**12**	**31**	**6**	**1**	**2**	**2**
1985-86	**Edmonton Oilers**	**NHL**	**78**	***68**	**63**	**131**	**55**	**42**	**97**	**22**	**16**	**6**	**9**	**236**	**28.8**	**187**	**46**	**123**	**27**	**+45**	**10**	**2**	**10**	**12**	**4**	**0**	**1**	**0**
1986-87	**Edmonton Oilers**	**NHL**	**79**	**54**	**54**	**108**	**47**	**39**	**86**	**41**	**7**	**3**	**5**	**88**	**61.4**	**75**	**23**	**38**	**5**	**+19**	**21**	***15**	**10**	**25**	**20**	**4**	**1**	**5**
	NHL All-Stars	RV'87	2	1	1	2	....	....	....	0	....	....	....	....	....	....	....	....	....	....	....	....	....	....	....	....	....	....
1987-88	Finland	C Cup	5	1	1	2	....	....	....	4	....	....	....	....	....	....	....	....	....	....	....	....	....	....	....	....	....	....
	Edmonton Oilers	**NHL**	**80**	**43**	**53**	**96**	**37**	**38**	**75**	**30**	**10**	**3**	**5**	**207**	**20.8**	**137**	**39**	**85**	**12**	**+25**	**19**	***14**	**17**	**31**	**12**	**5**	**0**	**3**
1988-89	**Edmonton Oilers**	**NHL**	**76**	**44**	**58**	**102**	**37**	**41**	**78**	**69**	**10**	**5**	**8**	**214**	**20.6**	**138**	**44**	**102**	**27**	**+19**	**7**	**3**	**5**	**8**	**6**	**0**	**1**	**0**
	Finland	WEC-A	7	5	4	9	....	....	....	4	....	....	....	....	....	....	....	....	....	....	....	....	....	....	....	....	....	....
1989-90	**Edmonton Oilers**	**NHL**	**78**	**33**	**60**	**93**	**28**	**43**	**71**	**48**	**10**	**2**	**2**	**201**	**16.4**	**127**	**44**	**89**	**24**	**+18**	**22**	**10**	**15**	**25**	**18**	**6**	**0**	**3**
1990-91	Milano Devils	Italy	30	27	48	75	....	....	....	6	....	....	....	....	....	....	....	....	....	....	10	10	12	22	2	....	....	....
	Finland	WEC-A	10	6	6	12	....	....	....	2	....	....	....	....	....	....	....	....	....	....	....	....	....	....	....	....	....	....
1991-92	Finland	C Cup	6	2	0	2	....	....	....	7	....	....	....	....	....	....	....	....	....	....	....	....	....	....	....	....	....	....
	Los Angeles Kings	**NHL**	**73**	**23**	**37**	**60**	**21**	**28**	**49**	**24**	**10**	**1**	**3**	**167**	**13.8**	**97**	**41**	**94**	**14**	**–24**	**4**	**1**	**2**	**3**	**4**	**1**	**0**	**0**
1992-93	**Los Angeles Kings**	**NHL**	**82**	**27**	**60**	**87**	**23**	**41**	**64**	**38**	**12**	**2**	**3**	**210**	**12.9**	**138**	**53**	**95**	**29**	**+19**	**24**	**9**	**8**	**17**	**12**	**2**	**2**	**0**
1993-94	**Los Angeles Kings**	**NHL**	**81**	**31**	**46**	**77**	**29**	**36**	**65**	**48**	**14**	**4**	**3**	**198**	**15.7**	**121**	**56**	**124**	**35**	**–24**	....	....	....	....	....	....	....	....
	Finland	WC-A	8	4	6	10	....	....	....	2	....	....	....	....	....	....	....	....	....	....	....	....	....	....	....	....	....	....
1994-95	Jokerit Helsinki	Finland	20	10	9	19	....	....	....	10	....	....	....	....	....	....	....	....	....	....	....	....	....	....	....	....	....	....
	Los Angeles Kings	**NHL**	**38**	**10**	**19**	**29**	**18**	**28**	**46**	**24**	**2**	**0**	**0**	**84**	**11.9**	**37**	**18**	**48**	**12**	**–17**	....	....	....	....	....	....	....	....
1995-96	**Los Angeles Kings**	**NHL**	**57**	**17**	**23**	**40**	**17**	**19**	**36**	**37**	**5**	**1**	**0**	**131**	**13.0**	**66**	**30**	**62**	**14**	**–12**	....	....	....	....	....	....	....	....
	New York Rangers	**NHL**	**14**	**1**	**4**	**5**	**1**	**3**	**4**	**2**	**0**	**0**	**0**	**27**	**3.7**	**8**	**3**	**15**	**6**	**–4**	**11**	**3**	**5**	**8**	**2**	**0**	**1**	**1**

			REGULAR SEASON																		PLAYOFFS							
Season	Club	League	GP	G	A	Pts	AG	AA	APts	PIM	PP	SH	GW	S	%	TGF	PGF	TGA	PGA	+/-	GP	G	A	Pts	PIM	PP	SH	GW
1996-97	Finland	W Cup	4	1	0	1	....	....	....	0	....	....	....	....	....	....	....	....	....	....	....	....	....	....	....	....	....	....
	Anaheim Mighty Ducks	**NHL**	**82**	**13**	**22**	**35**	**14**	**19**	**33**	**12**	**3**	**0**	**3**	**109**	**11.9**	**56**	**13**	**77**	**21**	**–13**	**11**	**1**	**2**	**3**	**4**	**0**	**0**	**0**
1997-98	**Colorado Avalanche**	**NHL**	**70**	**5**	**17**	**22**	**6**	**17**	**23**	**12**	**2**	**0**	**0**	**61**	**8.2**	**38**	**10**	**38**	**16**	**+6**	**4**	**0**	**0**	**0**	**0**	**0**	**0**	**0**
	Finland	Olympics	6	1	4	5	....	....	....	2	....	....	....	....	....	....	....	....	....	....	....	....	....	....	....	....	....	....
	NHL Totals		**1251**	**601**	**797**	**1398**	**521**	**585**	**1106**	**545**	**150**	**37**	**67**	**3019**	**19.9**	**1968**	**595**	**1390**	**309**		**200**	**106**	**127**	**233**	**123**	**25**	**10**	**14**

EJC-A All-Star Team (1978) • Named Best Forward at EJC-A (1978) • NHL Second All-Star Team (1984, 1986, 1989) • Won Lady Byng Memorial Trophy (1985) • NHL First All-Star Team (1985, 1987) • WEC-A All-Star Team (1991) • WC-A All-Star Team (1994)

Played in NHL All-Star Game (1983, 1985, 1986, 1988, 1989, 1990, 1993, 1998)

Traded to **Philadelphia** by **Edmonton** with Dave Brown and Corey Foster for Craig Fisher, Scott Mellanby and Craig Berube, May 30, 1991. Traded to **LA Kings** by **Philadelphia** with Jeff Chychrun for Steve Duchesne, Steve Kasper and LA Kings' 4th round choice (Aris Brimanis) in 1991 Entry Draft, May 30, 1991. Traded to **NY Rangers** by **LA Kings** with Marty McSorley and Shane Churla for Ray Ferraro, Ian Laperriere, Mattias Norstrom, Nathan Lafayette and NY Rangers' 4th round choice (Sean Blanchard) in 1997 Entry Draft, March 14, 1996. Signed as a free agent by **Anaheim**, September 10, 1996. Signed as a free agent by **Colorado**, September 15, 1997.

• KURTENBACH, ORLAND

Orland Kurtenbach C – L. 6'2", 180 lbs. b: Cudworth, Sask., 9/7/1936.

Season	Club	League	GP	G	A	Pts	AG	AA	APts	PIM	PP	SH	GW	S	%	TGF	PGF	TGA	PGA	+/-	GP	G	A	Pts	PIM	PP	SH	GW
1953-54	Prince Albert Mintos	SJHL	47	29	*40	69	....	....	....	48	....	....	....	....	....	....	....	....	....	....	15	11	10	21	14	....	....	....
1954-55	Prince Albert Mintos	SJHL	48	30	41	71	....	....	....	57	....	....	....	....	....	....	....	....	....	....	10	8	7	15	0	....	....	....
	Saskatoon Quakers	WHL	1	0	0	0	....	....	....	0	....	....	....	....	....	....	....	....	....	....	....	....	....	....	....	....	....	....
1955-56	Prince Albert Mintos	SJHL	43	41	38	79	....	....	....	66	....	....	....	....	....	....	....	....	....	....	12	5	10	15	13	....	....	....
	Saskatoon Quakers	WHL	3	0	0	0	....	....	....	4	....	....	....	....	....	....	....	....	....	....	2	0	0	0	0	....	....	....
1956-57	Prince Albert Mintos	SJHL	50	48	54	102	....	....	....	115	....	....	....	....	....	....	....	....	....	....	13	5	11	16	13	....	....	....
1957-58	Vancouver Canucks	WHL	52	15	39	54	....	....	....	58	....	....	....	....	....	....	....	....	....	....	8	3	3	6	8	....	....	....
1958-59	Buffalo Bisons	AHL	70	9	14	23	....	....	....	73	....	....	....	....	....	....	....	....	....	....	7	0	0	0	0	....	....	....
1959-60	Springfield Indians	AHL	14	0	6	6	....	....	....	17	....	....	....	....	....	....	....	....	....	....	....	....	....	....	....	....	....	....
	Vancouver Canucks	WHL	42	11	27	38	....	....	....	51	....	....	....	....	....	....	....	....	....	....	11	1	5	6	11	....	....	....
1960-61	**New York Rangers**	**NHL**	**10**	**0**	**6**	**6**	**0**	**6**	**6**	**2**	....	....	....	....	....	....	....	....	....	....	....	....	....	....	....	....	....	....
	Vancouver Canucks	WHL	55	20	27	47	....	....	....	31	....	....	....	....	....	....	....	....	....	....	....	....	....	....	....	....	....	....
1961-62	**Boston Bruins**	**NHL**	**8**	**0**	**0**	**0**	**0**	**0**	**0**	**6**	....	....	....	....	....	....	....	....	....	....	....	....	....	....	....	....	....	....
	Providence Reds	AHL	64	31	33	64	....	....	....	51	....	....	....	....	....	....	....	....	....	....	3	1	1	2	5	....	....	....
1962-63	San Francisco Seals	WHL	70	30	57	87	....	....	....	94	....	....	....	....	....	....	....	....	....	....	17	4	13	17	*51	....	....	....
1963-64	**Boston Bruins**	**NHL**	**70**	**12**	**25**	**37**	**16**	**28**	**44**	**91**	....	....	....	....	....	....	....	....	....	....	....	....	....	....	....	....	....	....
1964-65	**Boston Bruins**	**NHL**	**64**	**6**	**20**	**26**	**8**	**22**	**30**	**86**	....	....	....	....	....	....	....	....	....	....	....	....	....	....	....	....	....	....
1965-66	**Toronto Maple Leafs**	**NHL**	**70**	**9**	**6**	**15**	**11**	**6**	**17**	**54**	....	....	....	....	....	....	....	....	....	....	**4**	**0**	**0**	**0**	**20**	....	....	....
1966-67	**New York Rangers**	**NHL**	**60**	**11**	**25**	**36**	**13**	**26**	**39**	**58**	....	....	....	....	....	....	....	....	....	....	**3**	**0**	**2**	**2**	**0**	....	....	....
1967-68	**New York Rangers**	**NHL**	**73**	**15**	**20**	**35**	**19**	**21**	**40**	**82**	**2**	**0**	**2**	**175**	**8.6**	**44**	**4**	**52**	**17**	**+5**	**6**	**1**	**0**	**1**	**26**	**0**	**0**	**0**
1968-69	**New York Rangers**	**NHL**	**2**	**0**	**0**	**0**	**0**	**0**	**0**	**2**	**0**	**0**	**0**	**3**	**0.0**	**0**	**0**	**0**	**0**	**0**	....	....	....	....	....	....	....	....
	Omaha Knights	CHL	1	0	0	0	....	....	....	0	....	....	....	....	....	....	....	....	....	....	....	....	....	....	....	....	....	....
1969-70	**New York Rangers**	**NHL**	**53**	**4**	**10**	**14**	**5**	**10**	**15**	**47**	**1**	**0**	**0**	**89**	**4.5**	**26**	**3**	**23**	**4**	**+4**	**6**	**1**	**2**	**3**	**24**	**0**	**0**	**0**
	Buffalo Bisons	AHL	6	1	5	6	....	....	....	2	....	....	....	....	....	....	....	....	....	....	....	....	....	....	....	....	....	....
1970-71	**Vancouver Canucks**	**NHL**	**52**	**21**	**32**	**53**	**22**	**28**	**50**	**84**	**8**	**1**	**4**	**129**	**16.3**	**72**	**21**	**74**	**22**	**–1**	....	....	....	....	....	....	....	....
1971-72	**Vancouver Canucks**	**NHL**	**78**	**24**	**37**	**61**	**26**	**34**	**60**	**48**	**5**	**3**	**1**	**160**	**15.0**	**85**	**25**	**86**	**24**	**–2**	....	....	....	....	....	....	....	....
1972-73	**Vancouver Canucks**	**NHL**	**47**	**9**	**19**	**28**	**9**	**16**	**25**	**38**	**4**	**0**	**1**	**78**	**11.5**	**43**	**9**	**59**	**11**	**–14**	....	....	....	....	....	....	....	....
1973-74	**Vancouver Canucks**	**NHL**	**52**	**8**	**13**	**21**	**8**	**11**	**19**	**30**	**1**	**0**	**2**	**77**	**10.4**	**32**	**11**	**55**	**4**	**–30**	....	....	....	....	....			
1974-75	Seattle Totems	WHL	DID NOT PLAY – COACHING																									
	NHL Totals		**639**	**119**	**213**	**332**	**137**	**208**	**345**	**628**	**21**	**4**	**10**	**711**	**16.7**	**302**	**73**	**349**	**82**		**19**	**2**	**4**	**6**	**70**	**0**	**0**	**0**

Won WHL Coast Division Rookie of the Year Award (1958)

Claimed by **Boston** from **NY Rangers** in Intra-League Draft, June 13, 1961. Traded to **San Francisco** (WHL) by **Boston** for $20,000, July 26, 1962. Traded to **Boston** by **San Francisco** (WHL) for cash, October, 1963. Traded to **Toronto** by **Boston** with Pat Stapleton and Andy Hebenton for Ron Stewart, June 8, 1965. Claimed by **NY Rangers** from **Toronto** in Intra-league Draft, June 15, 1966. Claimed by **Vancouver** from **NY Rangers** in Expansion Draft, June 10, 1970.

• KURVERS, TOM

Tom Kurvers D – L. 6'2", 195 lbs. b: Minneapolis, MN, 9/14/1962. Montreal's 10th choice, 145th overall, in 1981 Entry Draft.

Season	Club	League	GP	G	A	Pts	AG	AA	APts	PIM	PP	SH	GW	S	%	TGF	PGF	TGA	PGA	+/-	GP	G	A	Pts	PIM	PP	SH	GW
1980-81	University of Minnesota-Duluth	WCHA	39	6	24	30	....	....	....	48	....	....	....	....	....	....	....	....	....	....	....	....	....	....	....	....	....	....
1981-82	University of Minnesota-Duluth	WCHA	37	11	31	42	....	....	....	18	....	....	....	....	....	....	....	....	....	....	....	....	....	....	....	....	....	....
	United States	WJC-A	7	3	3	6	....	....	....	16	....	....	....	....	....	....	....	....	....	....	....	....	....	....	....	....	....	....
1982-83	University of Minnesota-Duluth	WCHA	26	4	23	27	....	....	....	24	....	....	....	....	....	....	....	....	....	....	....	....	....	....	....	....	....	....
1983-84	University of Minnesota-Duluth	WCHA	43	18	58	76	....	....	....	46	....	....	....	....	....	....	....	....	....	....	....	....	....	....	....	....	....	....
1984-85	**Montreal Canadiens**	**NHL**	**75**	**10**	**35**	**45**	**8**	**24**	**32**	**30**	**6**	**1**	**3**	**136**	**7.4**	**117**	**45**	**80**	**5**	**–3**	**12**	**0**	**6**	**6**	**6**	**0**	**0**	**0**
1985-86	**Montreal Canadiens**	**NHL**	**62**	**7**	**23**	**30**	**6**	**15**	**21**	**36**	**3**	**0**	**1**	**69**	**10.1**	**76**	**22**	**47**	**2**	**+9**	....	....	....	....	....	....	....	....
1986-87	**Montreal Canadiens**	**NHL**	**1**	**0**	**0**	**0**	**0**	**0**	**0**	**0**	**0**	**0**	**0**	**2**	**0.0**	**1**	**0**	**0**	**0**	**+1**	....	....	....	....	....	....	....	....
	Buffalo Sabres	**NHL**	**55**	**6**	**17**	**23**	**5**	**12**	**17**	**22**	**1**	**0**	**1**	**71**	**8.5**	**70**	**16**	**86**	**22**	**–10**	....	....	....	....	....	....	....	....
	United States	WEC-A	10	3	1	4	....	....	....	11	....	....	....	....	....	....	....	....	....	....	....	....	....	....	....	....	....	....
1987-88	**New Jersey Devils**	**NHL**	**56**	**5**	**29**	**34**	**4**	**21**	**25**	**46**	**2**	**0**	**1**	**88**	**5.7**	**82**	**29**	**61**	**14**	**+6**	**19**	**6**	**9**	**15**	**38**	**3**	**0**	**1**
1988-89	**New Jersey Devils**	**NHL**	**74**	**16**	**50**	**66**	**14**	**36**	**49**	**38**	**5**	**0**	**0**	**190**	**8.4**	**143**	**61**	**81**	**10**	**+11**	....	....	....	....	....	....	....	....
	United States	WEC-A	10	2	2	4	....	....	....	8	....	....	....	....	....	....	....	....	....	....	....	....	....	....	....	....	....	....
1989-90	**New Jersey Devils**	**NHL**	**1**	**0**	**0**	**0**	**0**	**0**	**0**	**0**	**0**	**0**	**0**	**0**	**0.0**	**0**	**0**	**1**	**0**	**–1**	....	....	....	....	....	....	....	....
	Toronto Maple Leafs	**NHL**	**70**	**15**	**37**	**52**	**13**	**26**	**39**	**29**	**9**	**1**	**1**	**156**	**9.6**	**132**	**56**	**117**	**33**	**–8**	**5**	**0**	**3**	**3**	**4**	**0**	**0**	**0**
1990-91	**Toronto Maple Leafs**	**NHL**	**19**	**0**	**3**	**3**	**0**	**2**	**2**	**8**	**0**	**0**	**0**	**23**	**0.0**	**12**	**3**	**22**	**1**	**–12**	....	....	....	....	....	....	....	....
	Vancouver Canucks	**NHL**	**32**	**4**	**23**	**27**	**4**	**17**	**21**	**20**	**3**	**0**	**0**	**76**	**5.3**	**51**	**25**	**49**	**10**	**–13**	**6**	**2**	**2**	**4**	**12**	**1**	**0**	**0**
1991-92	**New York Islanders**	**NHL**	**74**	**9**	**47**	**56**	**8**	**35**	**43**	**30**	**6**	**0**	**1**	**132**	**6.8**	**125**	**71**	**87**	**15**	**–18**	....	....	....	....	....	....	....	....
1992-93	**New York Islanders**	**NHL**	**52**	**8**	**30**	**38**	**7**	**21**	**28**	**38**	**3**	**0**	**0**	**128**	**6.3**	**91**	**44**	**38**	**0**	**+9**	**12**	**0**	**2**	**2**	**6**	**0**	**0**	**0**
	Capital District Islanders	AHL	7	3	4	7	....	....	....	8	....	....	....	....	....	....	....	....	....	....	....	....	....	....	....	....	....	....
1993-94	**New York Islanders**	**NHL**	**66**	**9**	**31**	**40**	**8**	**24**	**32**	**47**	**5**	**0**	**1**	**141**	**6.4**	**94**	**50**	**39**	**2**	**+7**	**3**	**0**	**0**	**0**	**2**	**0**	**0**	**0**
1994-95	**Anaheim Mighty Ducks**	**NHL**	**22**	**4**	**3**	**7**	**7**	**4**	**11**	**6**	**1**	**0**	**1**	**44**	**9.1**	**16**	**4**	**28**	**3**	**–13**	....	....	....	....	....	....	....	....
1995-96	Seibu Tetsudo Tokyo	Japan	20	18	34	52	....	....	....	....	....	....	....	....	....	....	....	....	....	....	....	....	....	....	....	....	....	....
	NHL Totals		**659**	**93**	**328**	**421**	**84**	**236**	**320**	**350**	**44**	**2**	**10**	**1256**	**7.4**	**1010**	**426**	**736**	**117**		**57**	**8**	**22**	**30**	**68**	**4**	**0**	**1**

WCHA First All-Star Team (1984) • NCAA West First All-American Team (1984) • Won Hobey Baker Memorial Award (Top U.S. Collegiate Player) (1984)

Traded to **Buffalo** by **Montreal** for Buffalo's 2nd round choice (Martin St. Amour) in 1988 Entry Draft, November 18, 1986. Traded to **New Jersey** by **Buffalo** for Detroit's 3rd round choice (acquired earlier, Buffalo selected Andrew McVicar) in 1987 Entry Draft, June 13, 1987. Traded to **Toronto** by **New Jersey** for Toronto's 1st round choice (Scott Niedermayer) in 1991 Entry Draft, October 16, 1989. Traded to **Vancouver** by **Toronto** for Brian Bradley, January 12, 1991. Traded to **Minnesota** by **Vancouver** for Dave Babych, June 22, 1991. Traded to **NY Islanders** by **Minnesota** for Craig Ludwig, June 22, 1991. Traded to **Anaheim** by **NY Islanders** for Troy Loney, June 29, 1994.

• KUSHNER, DALE

Dale Kushner RW – L. 6'1", 195 lbs. b: Terrace, B.C., 6/13/1966.

Season	Club	League	GP	G	A	Pts	AG	AA	APts	PIM	PP	SH	GW	S	%	TGF	PGF	TGA	PGA	+/-	GP	G	A	Pts	PIM	PP	SH	GW
1983-84	Fort McMurray Oil Barons	AJHL	44	15	6	21	....	....	....	139	....	....	....	....	....	....	....	....	....	....	....	....	....	....	....	....	....	....
	Prince Albert Raiders	WHL	1	2	0	2	....	....	....	5	....	....	....	....	....	....	....	....	....	....	....	....	....	....	....	....	....	....
1984-85	Prince Albert Raiders	WHL	2	0	0	0	....	....	....	2	....	....	....	....	....	....	....	....	....	....	....	....	....	....	....	....	....	....
	Moose Jaw Warriors	WHL	17	5	2	7	....	....	....	23	....	....	....	....	....	....	....	....	....	....	....	....	....	....	....	....	....	....
	Medicine Hat Tigers	WHL	48	23	17	40	....	....	....	173	....	....	....	....	....	....	....	....	....	....	10	3	3	6	18	....	....	....
1985-86	Medicine Hat Tigers	WHL	66	25	19	44	....	....	....	218	....	....	....	....	....	....	....	....	....	....	25	0	5	5	114	....	....	....
1986-87	Medicine Hat Tigers	WHL	63	34	34	68	....	....	....	250	....	....	....	....	....	....	....	....	....	....	20	8	13	21	57	....	....	....
1987-88	Springfield Indians	AHL	68	13	23	36	....	....	....	201	....	....	....	....	....	....	....	....	....	....	....	....	....	....	....	....	....	....
1988-89	Springfield Indians	AHL	45	5	8	13	....	....	....	132	....	....	....	....	....	....	....	....	....	....	....	....	....	....	....	....	....	....
1989-90	**New York Islanders**	**NHL**	**2**	**0**	**0**	**0**	**0**	**0**	**0**	**2**	**0**	**0**	**0**	**0**	**0.0**	**0**	**0**	**0**	**0**	**0**	....	....	....	....	....	....	....	....
	Springfield Indians	AHL	45	14	11	25	....	....	....	163	....	....	....	....	....	....	....	....	....	....	7	2	3	5	61	....	....	....
1990-91	**Philadelphia Flyers**	**NHL**	**63**	**7**	**11**	**18**	**6**	**8**	**14**	**195**	**1**	**0**	**0**	**59**	**11.9**	**23**	**2**	**25**	**0**	**–4**	....	....	....	....	....	....	....	....
	Hershey Bears	AHL	5	3	4	7	....	....	....	14	....	....	....	....	....	....	....	....	....	....	....	....	....	....	....	....	....	....
1991-92	**Philadelphia Flyers**	**NHL**	**19**	**3**	**2**	**5**	**3**	**1**	**4**	**18**	**0**	**0**	**1**	**19**	**15.8**	**7**	**0**	**12**	**0**	**–5**	....	....	....	....	....	....	....	....
	Hershey Bears	AHL	46	9	7	16	....	....	....	98	....	....	....	....	....	....	....	....	....	....	6	0	2	2	23	....	....	....
1992-93	Hershey Bears	AHL	26	1	7	8	....	....	....	98	....	....	....	....	....	....	....	....	....	....	....	....	....	....	....	....	....	....
	Capital District Islanders	AHL	7	0	1	1	....	....	....	29	....	....	....	....	....	....	....	....	....	....	2	1	0	1	29	....	....	....

							REGULAR SEASON														PLAYOFFS							
Season	Club	League	GP	G	A	Pts	AG	AA	APts	PIM	PP	SH	GW	S	%	TGF	PGF	TGA	PGA	+/–	GP	G	A	Pts	PIM	PP	SH	GW
1993-94	Saint John Flames	AHL	73	20	17	37	....	....	....	199	....	....	....	....	....	....	....	....	....	....	7	2	1	3	28	....	....	....
1994-95	Saint John Flames	AHL	38	13	10	23	....	....	....	97	....	....	....	....	....	....	....	....	....	....	5	0	3	3	14	....	....	....
1995-96	Michigan K-Wings	IHL	49	5	12	17	....	....	....	108	....	....	....	....	....	....	....	....	....	....	6	0	0	0	20	....	....	....
	NHL Totals		**84**	**10**	**13**	**23**	**9**	**9**	**18**	**215**	**1**	**0**	**1**	**78**	**12.8**	**30**	**2**	**37**	**0**		....	....	....	....	....	....	....	....

Memorial Cup All-Star Team (1987)

Signed as a free agent by **NY Islanders**, April 7, 1987. Signed as a free agent by **Philadelphia**, July 31, 1990.

• KUZYK, KEN

Ken Kuzyk RW – R. 6'1", 195 lbs. b: Toronto, Ont., 8/11/1953.

Season	Club	League	GP	G	A	Pts	AG	AA	APts	PIM	PP	SH	GW	S	%	TGF	PGF	TGA	PGA	+/–	GP	G	A	Pts	PIM	PP	SH	GW
1972-73	Boston University	ECAC	28	10	15	25	....	....	....	8	....	....	....	....	....	....	....	....	....	....	....	....	....	....	....	....	....	....
1973-74	Boston University	ECAC	31	8	7	15	....	....	....	26	....	....	....	....	....	....	....	....	....	....	....	....	....	....	....	....	....	....
1974-75	Boston University	ECAC	32	8	16	24	....	....	....	46	....	....	....	....	....	....	....	....	....	....	....	....	....	....	....	....	....	....
1975-76	Boston University	ECAC	30	15	8	23	....	....	....	30	....	....	....	....	....	....	....	....	....	....	....	....	....	....	....	....	....	....
1976-77	**Cleveland Barons**	**NHL**	**13**	**0**	**5**	**5**	**0**	**4**	**4**	**2**	**0**	**0**	**0**	**19**	**0.0**	**9**	**4**	**4**	**0**	**+1**	....	....	....	....	....	....	....	....
	Salt Lake Golden Eagles	CHL	62	33	27	60	....	....	....	10	....	....	....	....	....	....	....	....	....	....	....	....	....	....	....	....	....	....
1977-78	**Cleveland Barons**	**NHL**	**28**	**5**	**4**	**9**	**5**	**3**	**8**	**6**	**0**	**0**	**0**	**49**	**10.2**	**16**	**1**	**16**	**0**	**–1**	....	....	....	....	....	....	....	....
	Binghamton Dusters	AHL	14	1	1	2	....	....	....	2	....	....	....	....	....	....	....	....	....	....	....	....	....	....	....	....	....	....
	Phoenix Roadrunners	CHL	17	10	11	21	....	....	....	2	....	....	....	....	....	....	....	....	....	....	....	....	....	....	....	....	....	....
	Salt Lake Golden Eagles	CHL	14	4	8	12	....	....	....	0	....	....	....	....	....	....	....	....	....	....	6	1	0	1	0	....	....	....
1978-79	Tulsa Oilers	CHL	74	31	32	63	....	....	....	22	....	....	....	....	....	....	....	....	....	....	....	....	....	....	....	....	....	....
1979-80	Cincinnati Stingers	CHL	17	3	7	10	....	....	....	0	....	....	....	....	....	....	....	....	....	....	....	....	....	....	....	....	....	....
	Oklahoma City Stars	CHL	41	10	12	22	....	....	....	11	....	....	....	....	....	....	....	....	....	....	....	....	....	....	....	....	....	....
	Baltimore Clippers	EHL	1	0	0	0	....	....	....	0	....	....	....	....	....	....	....	....	....	....	....	....	....	....	....	....	....	....
	NHL Totals		**41**	**5**	**9**	**14**	**5**	**7**	**12**	**8**	**0**	**0**	**0**	**68**	**7.4**	**25**	**5**	**20**	**0**		....	....	....	....	....	....	....	....

CHL Second All-Star Team (1977)

Signed as a free agent by **Cleveland**, September, 1976. Placed on **Minnesota** Reserve List after **Cleveland-Minnesota** Dispersal Draft, June 15, 1978. Claimed by **Quebec** from **Minnesota** in Expansion Draft, June 13, 1979. Signed as a free agent by **Minnesota**, February 1, 1980.

• KVARTALNOV, DMITRI

Dmitri Kvartalnov LW – L. 5'11", 180 lbs. b: Voskresensk, USSR, 3/25/1966. Boston's 1st choice, 16th overall, in 1992 Entry Draft.

Season	Club	League	GP	G	A	Pts	AG	AA	APts	PIM	PP	SH	GW	S	%	TGF	PGF	TGA	PGA	+/–	GP	G	A	Pts	PIM	PP	SH	GW
1982-83	Khimik	USSR	7	0	0	0	....	....	....	0	....	....	....	....	....	....	....	....	....	....	....	....	....	....	....	....	....	....
1983-84	Khimik	USSR	2	0	0	0	....	....	....	0	....	....	....	....	....	....	....	....	....	....	....	....	....	....	....	....	....	....
1984-85	SKA Kalinen	USSR 2	STATISTICS NOT AVAILABLE																									
1985-86	SKA Kalinen	USSR 2	STATISTICS NOT AVAILABLE																									
1986-87	Khimik	USSR	40	11	6	17	....	....	....	28	....	....	....	....	....	....	....	....	....	....	....	....	....	....	....	....	....	....
1987-88	Khimik	USSR	43	16	11	27	....	....	....	16	....	....	....	....	....	....	....	....	....	....	....	....	....	....	....	....	....	....
1988-89	Khimik	USSR	44	20	12	32	....	....	....	18	....	....	....	....	....	....	....	....	....	....	....	....	....	....	....	....	....	....
	Soviet Union	WEC-A	10	3	3	6	....	....	....	6	....	....	....	....	....	....	....	....	....	....	....	....	....	....	....	....	....	....
1989-90	Khimik	FrTour	1	0	0	0	....	....	....	0	....	....	....	....	....	....	....	....	....	....	....	....	....	....	....	....	....	....
	Khimik	USSR	46	25	29	54	....	....	....	33	....	....	....	....	....	....	....	....	....	....	....	....	....	....	....	....	....	....
	Khimik	SuperS	6	3	4	7	....	....	....	2	....	....	....	....	....	....	....	....	....	....	....	....	....	....	....	....	....	....
1990-91	Khimik	USSR	42	12	10	22	....	....	....	18	....	....	....	....	....	....	....	....	....	....	....	....	....	....	....	....	....	....
	Khimik	SuperS	7	3	5	8	....	....	....	2	....	....	....	....	....	....	....	....	....	....	....	....	....	....	....	....	....	....
	Soviet Union	WEC-A	7	0	1	1	....	....	....	0	....	....	....	....	....	....	....	....	....	....	....	....	....	....	....	....	....	....
1991-92	San Diego Gulls	IHL	77	*60	58	*118	....	....	....	16	....	....	....	....	....	....	....	....	....	....	4	2	0	2	2	....	....	....
1992-93	Khimik	CIS	3	0	0	0	....	....	....	0	....	....	....	....	....	....	....	....	....	....	....	....	....	....	....	....	....	....
	Boston Bruins	**NHL**	**73**	**30**	**42**	**72**	**25**	**29**	**54**	**16**	**11**	**0**	**4**	**226**	**13.3**	**111**	**48**	**54**	**0**	**+9**	**4**	**0**	**0**	**0**	**0**	**0**	**0**	**0**
1993-94	**Boston Bruins**	**NHL**	**39**	**12**	**7**	**19**	**11**	**5**	**16**	**10**	**4**	**0**	**0**	**68**	**17.6**	**24**	**11**	**22**	**0**	**–9**	....	....	....	....	....	....	....	....
	Providence Bruins	AHL	23	13	13	26	....	....	....	8	....	....	....	....	....	....	....	....	....	....	....	....	....	....	....	....	....	....
1994-95	Ambri-Piotta	Switz.	27	24	18	42	....	....	....	30	....	....	....	....	....	....	....	....	....	....	3	2	0	2	2	....	....	....
1995-96	Ambri-Piotta	Switz.	30	21	37	58	....	....	....	36	....	....	....	....	....	....	....	....	....	....	7	6	7	13	10	....	....	....
	Russia	WC-A	8	4	4	8	....	....	....	2	....	....	....	....	....	....	....	....	....	....	....	....	....	....	....	....	....	....
1996-97	Ambri-Piotta	Switz.	44	30	32	62	....	....	....	30	....	....	....	....	....	....	....	....	....	....	....	....	....	....	....	....	....	....
	Klagenfurter AC	Austria	12	10	9	19	....	....	....	6	....	....	....	....	....	....	....	....	....	....	....	....	....	....	....	....	....	....
	NHL Totals		**112**	**42**	**49**	**91**	**36**	**34**	**70**	**26**	**15**	**0**	**4**	**294**	**14.3**	**135**	**59**	**76**	**0**		**4**	**0**	**0**	**0**	**0**	**0**	**0**	**0**

Won Izvestia Trophy (USSR Top Scorer) (1990) • IHL First All-Star Team (1992) • Won Garry F. Longman Memorial Trophy (Top Rookie - IHL) (1992) • Won Leo P. Lamoureux Memorial Trophy (Top Scorer - IHL) (1992) • Won James Gatschene Memorial Trophy (MVP - IHL) (1992)

• KYLLONEN, MARKKU

Markku Kyllonen LW – L. 6'2", 200 lbs. b: Joensuu, Finland, 2/15/1962. Winnipeg's 8th choice, 163rd overall, in 1987 Entry Draft.

Season	Club	League	GP	G	A	Pts	AG	AA	APts	PIM	PP	SH	GW	S	%	TGF	PGF	TGA	PGA	+/–	GP	G	A	Pts	PIM	PP	SH	GW
1980-81	JoKP	Finland 2	33	7	6	13	....	....	....	12	....	....	....	....	....	....	....	....	....	....	....	....	....	....	....	....	....	....
1981-82	JoKP	Finland 2	STATISTICS NOT AVAILABLE																									
1982-83	JoKP	Finland 2	35	16	23	39	....	....	....	8	....	....	....	....	....	....	....	....	....	....	....	....	....	....	....	....	....	....
1983-84	JoKP	Finland 2	33	16	12	28	....	....	....	4	....	....	....	....	....	....	....	....	....	....	....	....	....	....	....	....	....	....
1984-85	JoKP	Finland 2	43	28	27	55	....	....	....	22	....	....	....	....	....	....	....	....	....	....	....	....	....	....	....	....	....	....
1985-86	JoKP	Finland 2	34	15	13	28	....	....	....	14	....	....	....	....	....	....	....	....	....	....	....	....	....	....	....	....	....	....
1986-87	Karpat Oulu	Finland	43	24	16	40	....	....	....	14	....	....	....	....	....	....	....	....	....	....	9	3	2	5	4	....	....	....
1987-88	Karpat Oulu	Finland	43	8	24	32	....	....	....	32	....	....	....	....	....	....	....	....	....	....	....	....	....	....	....	....	....	....
1988-89	**Winnipeg Jets**	**NHL**	**9**	**0**	**2**	**2**	**0**	**1**	**1**	**2**	**0**	**0**	**0**	**7**	**0.0**	**4**	**2**	**5**	**0**	**–3**	....	....	....	....	....	....	....	....
	Moncton Hawks	AHL	60	14	20	34	....	....	....	16	....	....	....	....	....	....	....	....	....	....	5	1	0	1	0	....	....	....
1989-90	JoKP	Finland	42	16	12	28	....	....	....	22	....	....	....	....	....	....	....	....	....	....	....	....	....	....	....	....	....	....
1990-91	JoKP	Finland	44	42	37	79	....	....	....	22	....	....	....	....	....	....	....	....	....	....	....	....	....	....	....	....	....	....
1991-92	JoKP	Finland	37	11	15	26	....	....	....	22	....	....	....	....	....	....	....	....	....	....	....	....	....	....	....	....	....	....
	NHL Totals		**9**	**0**	**2**	**2**	**0**	**1**	**1**	**2**	**0**	**0**	**0**	**7**	**0.0**	**4**	**2**	**5**	**0**		....	....	....	....	....	....	....	....

• KYPREOS, NICK

Nick Kypreos LW – L. 6', 205 lbs. b: Toronto, Ont., 6/4/1966.

Season	Club	League	GP	G	A	Pts	AG	AA	APts	PIM	PP	SH	GW	S	%	TGF	PGF	TGA	PGA	+/–	GP	G	A	Pts	PIM	PP	SH	GW
1983-84	North Bay Centennials	OHL	51	12	11	23	....	....	....	36	....	....	....	....	....	....	....	....	....	....	4	3	2	5	9	....	....	....
1984-85	North Bay Centennials	OHL	64	41	36	77	....	....	....	71	....	....	....	....	....	....	....	....	....	....	8	2	2	4	15	....	....	....
1985-86	North Bay Centennials	OHL	64	62	35	97	....	....	....	112	....	....	....	....	....	....	....	....	....	....	....	....	....	....	....	....	....	....
1986-87	North Bay Centennials	OHL	46	49	41	90	....	....	....	54	....	....	....	....	....	....	....	....	....	....	24	11	5	16	78	....	....	....
	Hershey Bears	AHL	10	0	1	1	....	....	....	4	....	....	....	....	....	....	....	....	....	....	....	....	....	....	....	....	....	....
1987-88	Hershey Bears	AHL	71	24	20	44	....	....	....	101	....	....	....	....	....	....	....	....	....	....	12	0	2	2	17	....	....	....
1988-89	Hershey Bears	AHL	28	12	15	27	....	....	....	19	....	....	....	....	....	....	....	....	....	....	12	4	5	9	11	....	....	....
1989-90	**Washington Capitals**	**NHL**	**31**	**5**	**4**	**9**	**4**	**3**	**7**	**82**	**0**	**0**	**2**	**27**	**18.5**	**13**	**1**	**10**	**0**	**+2**	**7**	**1**	**0**	**1**	**15**	**0**	**0**	**0**
	Baltimore Skipjacks	AHL	14	6	5	11	....	....	....	6	....	....	....	....	....	....	....	....	....	....	7	4	1	5	17	....	....	....
1990-91	**Washington Capitals**	**NHL**	**79**	**9**	**9**	**18**	**8**	**7**	**15**	**196**	**0**	**0**	**3**	**60**	**15.0**	**28**	**0**	**33**	**1**	**–4**	**9**	**0**	**1**	**1**	**38**	**0**	**0**	**0**
1991-92	**Washington Capitals**	**NHL**	**65**	**4**	**6**	**10**	**4**	**4**	**8**	**206**	**0**	**0**	**0**	**28**	**14.3**	**16**	**0**	**19**	**0**	**–3**	....	....	....	....	....	....	....	....
1992-93	**Hartford Whalers**	**NHL**	**75**	**17**	**10**	**27**	**14**	**7**	**21**	**325**	**0**	**0**	**2**	**81**	**21.0**	**44**	**0**	**60**	**11**	**–5**	....	....	....	....	....	....	....	....
1993-94	**Hartford Whalers**	**NHL**	**10**	**0**	**0**	**0**	**0**	**0**	**0**	**37**	**0**	**0**	**0**	**5**	**0.0**	**0**	**0**	**11**	**3**	**–8**	....	....	....	....	....	....	....	....
	New York Rangers	**NHL**	**46**	**3**	**5**	**8**	**3**	**4**	**7**	**102**	**0**	**0**	**1**	**29**	**10.3**	**11**	**0**	**19**	**0**	**–8**	**3**	**0**	**0**	**0**	**2**	**0**	**0**	**0**
1994-95	**New York Rangers**	**NHL**	**40**	**1**	**3**	**4**	**2**	**4**	**6**	**93**	**0**	**0**	**0**	**16**	**6.3**	**6**	**0**	**6**	**0**	**0**	**10**	**0**	**2**	**2**	**6**	**0**	**0**	**0**
1995-96	**New York Rangers**	**NHL**	**42**	**3**	**4**	**7**	**3**	**3**	**6**	**77**	**0**	**0**	**1**	**35**	**8.6**	**9**	**0**	**8**	**0**	**+1**	....	....	....	....	....	....	....	....
	Toronto Maple Leafs	**NHL**	**19**	**1**	**1**	**2**	**1**	**1**	**2**	**30**	**0**	**0**	**0**	**14**	**7.1**	**2**	**0**	**2**	**0**	**0**	**5**	**0**	**0**	**0**	**4**	**0**	**0**	**0**
1996-97	**Toronto Maple Leafs**	**NHL**	**35**	**3**	**2**	**5**	**3**	**2**	**5**	**62**	**0**	**0**	**0**	**18**	**16.7**	**7**	**0**	**6**	**0**	**+1**	....	....	....	....	....	....	....	....
	St. John's Maple Leafs	AHL	4	0	0	0	....	....	....	4	....	....	....	....	....	....	....	....	....	....	....	....	....	....	....	....	....	....
1997-98	**Toronto Maple Leafs**	**NHL**	DID NOT PLAY – INJURED																									
	NHL Totals		**442**	**46**	**44**	**90**	**42**	**35**	**77**	**1210**	**0**	**0**	**9**	**313**	**14.7**	**136**	**1**	**174**	**15**		**34**	**1**	**3**	**4**	**65**	**0**	**0**	**0**

OHL First All-Star Team (1986) • OHL Second All-Star Team (1987)

Signed as a free agent by **Philadelphia,** September 30, 1984. Claimed by **Washington** from **Philadelphia** in NHL Waiver Draft, October 2, 1989. Traded to **Hartford** by **Washington** for Mark Hunter and future considerations (Yvon Corriveau, August 20, 1992), June 15, 1992. Traded to **NY Rangers** by **Hartford** with Steve Larmer, Barry Richter and Hartford's 6th round choice (Yuri Litvinov) in 1994 Entry Draft for Darren Turcotte and James Patrick, November 2, 1993. Traded to **Toronto** by **NY Rangers** for Bill Berg, February 29, 1996. • Suffered season-ending head injury in exhibition game vs. NY Rangers, September 17, 1997.

• KYTE, JIM

Jim Kyte D – L. 6'5", 210 lbs. b: Ottawa, Ont., 3/21/1964. Winnipeg's 1st choice, 12th overall, in 1982 Entry Draft.

			REGULAR SEASON																		PLAYOFFS							
Season	Club	League	GP	G	A	Pts	AG	AA	APts	PIM	PP	SH	GW	S	%	TGF	PGF	TGA	PGA	+/–	GP	G	A	Pts	PIM	PP	SH	GW
1981-82	Cornwall Royals	OHL	52	4	13	17	....	....	....	148	....	....	....	....	....	....	....	....	....	....	5	0	0	0	10	....	....	....
1982-83	Cornwall Royals	OHL	65	6	30	36	....	....	....	195	....	....	....	....	....	....	....	....	....	....	8	0	2	2	24	....	....	....
	Winnipeg Jets	**NHL**	**2**	**0**	**0**	**0**	**0**	**0**	**0**	**0**	**0**	**0**	**0**	**0**	**0.0**	**0**	**0**	**1**	**0**	**–1**	....	....	....	....	....	....	....	....
1983-84	**Winnipeg Jets**	**NHL**	**58**	**1**	**2**	**3**	**1**	**1**	**2**	**55**	**0**	**0**	**0**	**7**	**14.3**	**23**	**0**	**32**	**2**	**–7**	**3**	**0**	**0**	**0**	**11**	**0**	**0**	**0**
1984-85	**Winnipeg Jets**	**NHL**	**71**	**0**	**3**	**3**	**0**	**2**	**2**	**111**	**0**	**0**	**0**	**32**	**0.0**	**27**	**0**	**56**	**3**	**–26**	**8**	**0**	**0**	**0**	**14**	**0**	**0**	**0**
1985-86	**Winnipeg Jets**	**NHL**	**71**	**1**	**3**	**4**	**1**	**2**	**3**	**126**	**0**	**0**	**0**	**28**	**3.6**	**27**	**2**	**52**	**6**	**–21**	**3**	**0**	**0**	**0**	**12**	**0**	**0**	**0**
1986-87	**Winnipeg Jets**	**NHL**	**72**	**5**	**5**	**10**	**4**	**4**	**8**	**162**	**0**	**0**	**1**	**62**	**8.1**	**61**	**1**	**81**	**25**	**+4**	**10**	**0**	**4**	**4**	**36**	**0**	**0**	**0**
1987-88	**Winnipeg Jets**	**NHL**	**51**	**1**	**3**	**4**	**1**	**2**	**3**	**128**	**0**	**0**	**0**	**59**	**1.7**	**38**	**0**	**74**	**37**	**+1**	....	....	....	....	....	....	....	....
1988-89	**Winnipeg Jets**	**NHL**	**74**	**3**	**9**	**12**	**3**	**6**	**9**	**190**	**0**	**0**	**0**	**56**	**5.4**	**38**	**0**	**90**	**27**	**–25**	....	....	....	....	....	....	....	....
1989-90	**Pittsburgh Penguins**	**NHL**	**56**	**3**	**1**	**4**	**3**	**1**	**4**	**125**	**0**	**0**	**0**	**23**	**13.0**	**34**	**1**	**57**	**14**	**–10**	....	....	....	....	....	....	....	....
1990-91	**Pittsburgh Penguins**	**NHL**	**1**	**0**	**0**	**0**	**0**	**0**	**0**	**2**	**0**	**0**	**0**	**0**	**0.0**	**0**	**0**	**0**	**0**	**0**	....	....	....	....	....	....	....	....
	Muskegon Lumberjacks	IHL	25	2	5	7	....	....	....	157	....	....	....	....	....	....	....	....	....	....	....	....	....	....	....	....	....	....
	Calgary Flames	**NHL**	**42**	**0**	**9**	**9**	**0**	**7**	**7**	**153**	**0**	**0**	**0**	**29**	**0.0**	**32**	**0**	**25**	**3**	**+10**	**7**	**0**	**0**	**0**	**7**	**0**	**0**	**0**
1991-92	**Calgary Flames**	**NHL**	**21**	**0**	**1**	**1**	**0**	**1**	**1**	**107**	**0**	**0**	**0**	**13**	**0.0**	**16**	**0**	**18**	**4**	**+2**	....	....	....	....	....	....	....	....
	Salt Lake Golden Eagles	IHL	6	0	1	1	....	....	....	9	....	....	....	....	....	....	....	....	....	....	....	....	....	....	....	....	....	....
1992-93	**Ottawa Senators**	**NHL**	**4**	....	**1**	**1**	**0**	**1**	**1**	**4**	**0**	**0**	**0**	**1**	**0.0**	**1**	**0**	**3**	**2**	**0**	....	....	....	....	....	....	....	....
	New Haven Nighthawks	AHL	63	6	18	24	....	....	....	163	....	....	....	....	....	....	....	....	....	....	....	....	....	....	....	....	....	....
1993-94	Las Vegas Thunder	IHL	75	2	16	18	....	....	....	246	....	....	....	....	....	....	....	....	....	....	4	0	1	1	51	....	....	....
1994-95	Las Vegas Thunder	IHL	76	3	17	20	....	....	....	195	....	....	....	....	....	....	....	....	....	....	....	....	....	....	....	....	....	....
	San Jose Sharks	**NHL**	**18**	**2**	**5**	**7**	**4**	**7**	**11**	**33**	**0**	**0**	**1**	**14**	**14.3**	**12**	**1**	**23**	**5**	**–7**	**11**	**0**	**2**	**2**	**14**	**0**	**0**	**0**
1995-96	**San Jose Sharks**	**NHL**	**57**	**1**	**7**	**8**	**1**	**6**	**7**	**146**	**0**	**0**	**0**	**32**	**3.1**	**33**	**0**	**65**	**20**	**–12**	....	....	....	....	....	....	....	....
1996-97	Kansas City Blades	IHL	76	3	8	11	....	....	....	259	....	....	....	....	....	....	....	....	....	....	3	0	0	0	2	....	....	....
	NHL Totals		**598**	**17**	**49**	**66**	**18**	**40**	**58**	**1342**	**0**	**0**	**2**	**356**	**4.8**	**342**	**5**	**577**	**148**		**42**	**0**	**6**	**6**	**94**	**0**	**0**	**0**

Traded to **Pittsburgh** by **Winnipeg** with Andrew McBain and Randy Gilhen for Randy Cunneyworth, Rick Tabaracci and Dave McLlwain, June 17, 1989. Traded to **Calgary** by **Pittsburgh** for Jiri Hrdina, December 13, 1990. Signed as a free agent by **Ottawa**, September 10, 1992. Signed as a free agent by **San Jose**, March 31, 1995.

• LABATTE, NEIL

Neil Labatte D – L. 6'2", 178 lbs. b: Toronto, Ont., 4/24/1957. St. Louis' 2nd choice, 27th overall, in 1977 Amateur Draft.

Season	Club	League	GP	G	A	Pts	AG	AA	APts	PIM	PP	SH	GW	S	%	TGF	PGF	TGA	PGA	+/–	GP	G	A	Pts	PIM	PP	SH	GW
1974-75	Brown University	ECAC	....	9	6	15	....	....	....	94	....	....	....	....	....	....	....	....	....	....	....	....	....	....	....	....	....	....
1975-76	Brown University	ECAC	13	7	14	21	....	....	....	51	....	....	....	....	....	....	....	....	....	....	....	....	....	....	....	....	....	....
1976-77	Toronto Marlboros	OHA	66	21	32	53	....	....	....	114	....	....	....	....	....	....	....	....	....	....	....	....	....	....	....	....	....	....
1977-78	Salt Lake Golden Eagles	CHL	75	11	25	36	....	....	....	116	....	....	....	....	....	....	....	....	....	....	6	0	2	2	8	....	....	....
1978-79	**St. Louis Blues**	**NHL**	**22**	**0**	**2**	**2**	**0**	**2**	**2**	**13**	**0**	**0**	**0**	**15**	**0.0**	**18**	**0**	**20**	**1**	**–1**	....	....	....	....	....	....	....	....
	Salt Lake Golden Eagles	CHL	37	2	13	15	....	....	....	90	....	....	....	....	....	....	....	....	....	....	....	....	....	....	....	....	....	....
1979-80	Salt Lake Golden Eagles	CHL	70	1	26	27	....	....	....	79	....	....	....	....	....	....	....	....	....	....	10	1	7	8	17	....	....	....
1980-81	Salt Lake Golden Eagles	CHL	55	8	18	26	....	....	....	55	....	....	....	....	....	....	....	....	....	....	....	....	....	....	....	....	....	....
1981-82	**St. Louis Blues**	**NHL**	**4**	**0**	**0**	**0**	**0**	**0**	**0**	**6**	**0**	**0**	**0**	**3**	**0.0**	**0**	**0**	**3**	**0**	**–3**	....	....	....	....	....	....	....	....
	Salt Lake Golden Eagles	CHL	72	7	24	31	....	....	....	86	....	....	....	....	....	....	....	....	....	....	9	2	5	7	21	....	....	....
	NHL Totals		**26**	**0**	**2**	**2**	**0**	**2**	**2**	**19**	**0**	**0**	**0**	**18**	**0.0**	**18**	**0**	**23**	**1**		....	....	....	....	....	....	....	....

• L'ABBE, MOE

Moe L'Abbe RW – L. 5'9", 170 lbs. b: Montreal, Que., 8/12/1947. Chicago's 4th choice, 22nd overall, in 1964 Amateur Draft.

Season	Club	League	GP	G	A	Pts	AG	AA	APts	PIM	PP	SH	GW	S	%	TGF	PGF	TGA	PGA	+/–	GP	G	A	Pts	PIM	PP	SH	GW
1964-65	St. Catharines Black Hawks	OHA	17	3	4	7	....	....	....	7	....	....	....	....	....	....	....	....	....	....	....	....	....	....	....	....	....	....
1965-66	St. Catharines Black Hawks	OHA	11	0	2	2	....	....	....	32	....	....	....	....	....	....	....	....	....	....	6	0	2	2	0	....	....	....
1966-67	St. Catharines Black Hawks	OHA	48	14	17	31	....	....	....	18	....	....	....	....	....	....	....	....	....	....	6	5	4	9	2	....	....	....
1967-68	St. Catharines Black Hawks	OHA	50	27	23	50	....	....	....	28	....	....	....	....	....	....	....	....	....	....	5	3	3	6	0	....	....	....
1968-69	Dallas Black Hawks	CHL	1	0	0	0	....	....	....	0	....	....	....	....	....	....	....	....	....	....	....	....	....	....	....	....	....	....
	Greensboro Generals	EHL	47	20	29	49	....	....	....	22	....	....	....	....	....	....	....	....	....	....	8	5	2	7	2	....	....	....
1969-70	Dallas Black Hawks	CHL	3	1	2	3	....	....	....	2	....	....	....	....	....	....	....	....	....	....	....	....	....	....	....	....	....	....
	Greensboro Generals	EHL	69	52	39	91	....	....	....	28	....	....	....	....	....	....	....	....	....	....	16	7	10	17	2	....	....	....
1970-71	Dallas Black Hawks	CHL	69	17	24	41	....	....	....	8	....	....	....	....	....	....	....	....	....	....	10	1	1	2	4	....	....	....
1971-72	Portland Buckaroos	WHL	5	0	2	2	....	....	....	0	....	....	....	....	....	....	....	....	....	....	....	....	....	....	....	....	....	....
	Flint Generals	IHL	41	17	17	34	....	....	....	10	....	....	....	....	....	....	....	....	....	....	....	....	....	....	....	....	....	....
1972-73	**Chicago Black Hawks**	**NHL**	**5**	**0**	**1**	**1**	**0**	**1**	**1**	**0**	**0**	**0**	**0**	**4**	**0.0**	**2**	**0**	**1**	**0**	**+1**	....	....	....	....	....	....	....	....
	Dallas Black Hawks	CHL	67	28	34	62	....	....	....	18	....	....	....	....	....	....	....	....	....	....	7	4	6	10	0	....	....	....
1973-74	Dallas Black Hawks	CHL	72	24	30	54	....	....	....	8	....	....	....	....	....	....	....	....	....	....	10	4	*7	*11	0	....	....	....
1974-75	Dallas Black Hawks	CHL	28	9	13	22	....	....	....	11	....	....	....	....	....	....	....	....	....	....	....	....	....	....	....	....	....	....
1975-76	Dallas Black Hawks	CHL	76	38	38	76	....	....	....	10	....	....	....	....	....	....	....	....	....	....	10	4	3	7	2	....	....	....
	NHL Totals		**5**	**0**	**1**	**1**	**0**	**1**	**1**	**0**	**0**	**0**	**0**	**4**	**0.0**	**2**	**0**	**1**	**0**		....	....	....	....	....	....	....	....

EHL South First All-Star Team (1970) • CHL First All-Star Team (1973)

• LABELLE, MARC

Marc Labelle LW – L. 6'1", 215 lbs. b: Maniwaki, Que., 12/20/1969.

Season	Club	League	GP	G	A	Pts	AG	AA	APts	PIM	PP	SH	GW	S	%	TGF	PGF	TGA	PGA	+/–	GP	G	A	Pts	PIM	PP	SH	GW
1987-88	Victoriaville Tigres	QMJHL	63	11	14	25	....	....	....	236	....	....	....	....	....	....	....	....	....	....	5	2	4	6	20	....	....	....
1988-89	Victoriaville Tigres	QMJHL	62	9	26	35	....	....	....	202	....	....	....	....	....	....	....	....	....	....	15	6	3	9	30	....	....	....
1989-90	Victoriaville Tigres	QMJHL	56	18	21	39	....	....	....	192	....	....	....	....	....	....	....	....	....	....	16	4	8	12	42	....	....	....
1990-91	Fredericton Canadiens	AHL	25	1	4	5	....	....	....	95	....	....	....	....	....	....	....	....	....	....	4	0	2	2	25	....	....	....
	Richmond Renegades	ECHL	5	1	1	2	....	....	....	37	....	....	....	....	....	....	....	....	....	....	....	....	....	....	....	....	....	....
1991-92	Fredericton Canadiens	AHL	62	7	10	17	....	....	....	238	....	....	....	....	....	....	....	....	....	....	3	0	0	0	6	....	....	....
1992-93	San Diego Gulls	IHL	5	0	2	2	....	....	....	5	....	....	....	....	....	....	....	....	....	....	....	....	....	....	....	....	....	....
	New Haven Nighthawks	AHL	31	5	4	9	....	....	....	124	....	....	....	....	....	....	....	....	....	....	....	....	....	....	....	....	....	....
	Thunder Bay Thunder Hawks	ColHL	9	0	5	5	....	....	....	17	....	....	....	....	....	....	....	....	....	....	7	0	1	1	11	....	....	....
1993-94	Cincinnati Cyclones	IHL	37	2	1	3	....	....	....	133	....	....	....	....	....	....	....	....	....	....	4	0	1	1	6	....	....	....
1994-95	Cincinnati Cyclones	IHL	54	3	4	7	....	....	....	173	....	....	....	....	....	....	....	....	....	....	8	0	0	0	7	....	....	....
1995-96	Cincinnati Cyclones	IHL	57	6	11	17	....	....	....	218	....	....	....	....	....	....	....	....	....	....	....	....	....	....	....	....	....	....
	Milwaukee Admirals	IHL	20	5	3	8	....	....	....	50	....	....	....	....	....	....	....	....	....	....	5	1	1	2	4	....	....	....
1996-97	**Dallas Stars**	**NHL**	**9**	**0**	**0**	**0**	**0**	**0**	**0**	**46**	**0**	**0**	**0**	**2**	**0.0**	**0**	**0**	**4**	**0**	**–4**	....	....	....	....	....	....	....	....
	Milwaukee Admirals	IHL	14	1	1	2	....	....	....	33	....	....	....	....	....	....	....	....	....	....	....	....	....	....	....	....	....	....
	Michigan K-Wings	IHL	46	4	7	11	....	....	....	148	....	....	....	....	....	....	....	....	....	....	3	0	0	0	6	....	....	....
1997-98	Cincinnati Cyclones	IHL	60	2	1	3	....	....	....	160	....	....	....	....	....	....	....	....	....	....	9	0	1	1	38	....	....	....
	NHL Totals		**9**	**0**	**0**	**0**	**0**	**0**	**0**	**46**	**0**	**0**	**0**	**2**	**0.0**	**0**	**0**	**4**	**0**		....	....	....	....	....	....	....	....

Signed as a free agent by **Montreal**, January 21, 1991. Signed as a free agent by **Ottawa**, July 30, 1992. Claimed by **Florida** from **Ottawa** in Expansion Draft, June 24, 1993. Signed as a free agent by **Dallas**, April 15, 1996. Signed as a free agent by **Ottawa**, July 14, 1997.

• LABOSSIERRE, GORD

Gord Labossierre C – R. 6'1", 190 lbs. b: St. Boniface, Man., 1/2/1940.

Season	Club	League	GP	G	A	Pts	AG	AA	APts	PIM	PP	SH	GW	S	%	TGF	PGF	TGA	PGA	+/–	GP	G	A	Pts	PIM	PP	SH	GW
1956-57	Winnipeg Rangers	MJHL	29	20	13	33	....	....	....	57	....	....	....	....	....	....	....	....	....	....	4	1	0	1	6	....	....	....
1957-58	Brandon Rangers	MJHL	30	*44	35	*79	....	....	....	*97	....	....	....	....	....	....	....	....	....	....	....	....	....	....	....	....	....	....
	Saskatoon-St. Paul Regals	WHL	2	0	0	0	....	....	....	2	....	....	....	....	....	....	....	....	....	....	....	....	....	....	....	....	....	....
	St. Boniface Canadians	MJHL	....	....	....	....	....	....	....	....	....	....	....	....	....	....	....	....	....	....	11	10	5	15	*38	....	....	....
1958-59	Saskatoon Quakers	WHL	64	25	19	44	....	....	....	83	....	....	....	....	....	....	....	....	....	....	....	....	....	....	....	....	....	....
1959-60	Edmonton Flyers	WHL	65	20	18	38	....	....	....	72	....	....	....	....	....	....	....	....	....	....	4	0	1	1	4	....	....	....
1960-61	Edmonton Flyers	WHL	20	5	11	16	....	....	....	20	....	....	....	....	....	....	....	....	....	....	....	....	....	....	....	....	....	....
	Winnipeg Warriors	WHL	43	17	17	34	....	....	....	62	....	....	....	....	....	....	....	....	....	....	....	....	....	....	....	....	....	....
1961-62	Sudbury Wolves	EPHL	30	10	11	21	....	....	....	44	....	....	....	....	....	....	....	....	....	....	....	....	....	....	....	....	....	....
	Seattle Totems	WHL	21	4	4	8	....	....	....	12	....	....	....	....	....	....	....	....	....	....	2	0	0	0	0	....	....	....
1962-63	Sudbury Wolves	EPHL	72	34	67	*101	....	....	....	94	....	....	....	....	....	....	....	....	....	....	8	4	5	9	*23	....	....	....
1963-64	**New York Rangers**	**NHL**	**15**	**0**	**0**	**0**	**0**	**0**	**0**	**12**	....	....	....	....	....	....	....	....	....	....	....	....	....	....	....	....	....	....
	Baltimore Clippers	AHL	48	17	17	34	....	....	....	20	....	....	....	....	....	....	....	....	....	....	....	....	....	....	....	....	....	....
1964-65	**New York Rangers**	**NHL**	**1**	**0**	**0**	**0**	**0**	**0**	**0**	**0**	....	....	....	....	....	....	....	....	....	....	....	....	....	....	....	....	....	....
	Baltimore Clippers	AHL	72	38	41	79	....	....	....	72	....	....	....	....	....	....	....	....	....	....	5	1	1	2	6	....	....	....
1965-66	Quebec Aces	AHL	60	31	51	82	....	....	....	137	....	....	....	....	....	....	....	....	....	....	6	0	1	1	14	....	....	....
1966-67	Quebec Aces	AHL	72	40	55	95	....	....	....	71	....	....	....	....	....	....	....	....	....	....	5	2	3	5	18	....	....	....
1967-68	**Los Angeles Kings**	**NHL**	**68**	**13**	**27**	**40**	**16**	**28**	**44**	**31**	**1**	**0**	**3**	**153**	**8.5**	**53**	**6**	**41**	**0**	**+6**	**7**	**2**	**3**	**5**	**24**	**0**	**0**	**0**

			REGULAR SEASON																		PLAYOFFS							
Season	Club	League	GP	G	A	Pts	AG	AA	APts	PIM	PP	SH	GW	S	%	TGF	PGF	TGA	PGA	+/–	GP	G	A	Pts	PIM	PP	SH	GW
1968-69	**Los Angeles Kings**	**NHL**	48	10	18	28	11	17	28	12	2	0	0	97	10.3	29	3	33	0	–7	....	....	....	....	....	....	....	....
	Springfield Kings	AHL	25	13	23	36	....	....	....	40	....	....	....	....	....	....	....	....	....	....	....	....	....	....	....	....	....	....
1969-70	Springfield Kings	AHL	60	30	59	89	....	....	....	94	....	....	....	....	....	....	....	....	....	....	14	2	5	7	21	....	....	....
1970-71	**Los Angeles Kings**	**NHL**	45	11	10	21	11	9	20	16	1	0	0	88	12.5	29	4	48	1	–22	....	....	....	....	....	....	....	....
	Minnesota North Stars	**NHL**	29	8	4	12	8	4	12	4	0	0	1	45	17.8	15	2	16	0	–3	3	0	0	0	4	0	0	0
1971-72	**Minnesota North Stars**	**NHL**	9	2	3	5	2	3	5	0	0	0	0	23	8.7	7	0	5	0	+2	....	....	....	....	....	....	....	....
	Cleveland Barons	AHL	66	40	45	85	....	....	....	71	....	....	....	....	....	....	....	....	....	....	6	4	2	6	4	....	....	....
1972-73	Houston Aeros	WHA	77	36	60	96	....	....	....	56	....	....	....	....	....	....	....	....	....	....	6	1	4	5	8	....	....	....
1973-74	Houston Aeros	WHA	67	19	36	55	....	....	....	30	....	....	....	....	....	....	....	....	....	....	14	7	9	16	20	....	....	....
1974-75	Houston Aeros	WHA	76	23	34	57	....	....	....	40	....	....	....	....	....	....	....	....	....	....	13	6	7	13	4	....	....	....
1975-76	Houston Aeros	WHA	80	24	32	56	....	....	....	18	....	....	....	....	....	....	....	....	....	....	17	2	8	10	14	....	....	....
	NHL Totals		**215**	**44**	**62**	**106**	**48**	**61**	**109**	**75**	**4**	**0**	**4**	**406**	**10.8**	**133**	**15**	**143**	**1**		**10**	**2**	**3**	**5**	**28**	**0**	**0**	**0**
	Other Major League Totals		300	102	162	264	....	....	....	144	....	....	....	....	....	....	....	....	....	....	50	16	28	44	46	....	....	....

AHL First All-Star Team (1967) • Won John B. Sollenberger Trophy (Top Scorer - AHL) (1967) • AHL Second All-Star Team (1970)

Claimed on waivers by **NY Rangers** from **Detroit**, June, 1963. Traded to **Montreal** by **NY Rangers** with Earl Ingerfield, Noel Price and Dave McComb for Garry Peters and Cesare Maniago, June 8, 1965. Claimed by **LA Kings** from **Montreal** in Expansion Draft, June 6, 1967. Traded to **Montreal** by **LA Kings** with Ray Fortin for Ralph Backstrom, January 26, 1971. Traded to **Minnesota** by **Montreal** for Rey Comeau, January 26, 1971. Selected by **Houston** (WHA) in 1972 WHA General Player Draft, February 12, 1972. Traded to **NY Islanders** by **Minnesota** for future considerations for cash, June 6, 1972. Claimed by **Quebec** (WHA) from **Houston** (WHA) in 1976 WHA Intra-League Draft, June, 1976.

• LABRAATEN, DANIEL

Daniel "Rusty" Labraaten LW – R. 6', 190 lbs. b: Leksand, Sweden, 6/9/1951.

Season	Club	League	GP	G	A	Pts	AG	AA	APts	PIM	PP	SH	GW	S	%	TGF	PGF	TGA	PGA	+/–	GP	G	A	Pts	PIM	PP	SH	GW
1969-70	Leksand IF	Sweden	14	8	4	12	....	....	....	0	....	....	....	....	....	....	....	....	....	....	14	6	5	11	4	....	....	....
1970-71	Leksand IF	Sweden	14	7	8	15	....	....	....	2	....	....	....	....	....	....	....	....	....	....	9	6	6	12	9	....	....	....
1971-72	Leksand IF	Sweden	28	12	8	20	....	....	....	12	....	....	....	....	....	....	....	....	....	....	....	....	....	....	....	....	....	....
1972-73	Leksand IF	Sweden	14	8	5	13	....	....	....	20	....	....	....	....	....	....	....	....	....	....	14	9	5	14	5	....	....	....
1973-74	Sweden	Nat-Team	10	3	0	3	....	....	....	8	....	....	....	....	....	....	....	....	....	....	....	....	....	....	....	....	....	....
	Sweden	WEC-A	10	2	0	2	....	....	....	8	....	....	....	....	....	....	....	....	....	....	....	....	....	....	....	....	....	....
1974-75	Leksand IF	Sweden	30	24	14	38	....	....	....	40	....	....	....	....	....	....	....	....	....	....	5	2	0	2	2	....	....	....
	Sweden	WEC-A	10	9	1	10	....	....	....	12	....	....	....	....	....	....	....	....	....	....	....	....	....	....	....	....	....	....
1975-76	Leksand IF	Sweden	16	13	9	22	....	....	....	6	....	....	....	....	....	....	....	....	....	....	4	2	2	4	0	....	....	....
	Sweden	WEC-A	10	5	3	8	....	....	....	6	....	....	....	....	....	....	....	....	....	....	....	....	....	....	....	....	....	....
1976-77	Sweden	C Cup	5	0	1	1	....	....	....	2	....	....	....	....	....	....	....	....	....	....	....	....	....	....	....	....	....	....
	Winnipeg Jets	WHA	64	24	27	51	....	....	....	21	....	....	....	....	....	....	....	....	....	....	20	7	17	24	15	....	....	....
1977-78	Winnipeg Jets	WHA	47	18	16	34	....	....	....	30	....	....	....	....	....	....	....	....	....	....	4	1	1	2	8	....	....	....
1978-79	**Detroit Red Wings**	**NHL**	78	19	19	38	17	14	31	8	7	0	3	112	17.0	58	18	57	0	–17	....	....	....	....	....	....	....	....
	Sweden	WEC-A	8	1	1	2	....	....	....	4	....	....	....	....	....	....	....	....	....	....	....	....	....	....	....	....	....	....
1979-80	**Detroit Red Wings**	**NHL**	76	30	27	57	27	21	48	8	6	0	5	152	19.7	91	26	60	0	+5	....	....	....	....	....	....	....	....
1980-81	**Detroit Red Wings**	**NHL**	44	3	8	11	2	6	8	12	0	0	0	43	7.0	17	3	33	0	–19	....	....	....	....	....	....	....	....
	Calgary Flames	**NHL**	27	9	7	16	7	5	12	13	1	0	0	39	23.1	32	8	23	0	+1	5	1	0	1	4	1	0	1
1981-82	**Calgary Flames**	**NHL**	43	10	12	22	8	8	16	6	1	0	0	60	16.7	32	6	31	1	–4	3	0	0	0	0	0	0	0
1982-83	Leksand IF	Sweden	30	9	10	19	....	....	....	26	....	....	....	....	....	....	....	....	....	....	....	....	....	....	....	....	....	....
1983-84	Leksand IF	Sweden	36	23	21	*44	....	....	....	14	....	....	....	....	....	....	....	....	....	....	....	....	....	....	....	....	....	....
1984-85	Leksand IF	Sweden	27	15	14	29	....	....	....	14	....	....	....	....	....	....	....	....	....	....	....	....	....	....	....	....	....	....
	Sweden	WEC-A	10	2	2	4	....	....	....	6	....	....	....	....	....	....	....	....	....	....	....	....	....	....	....	....	....	....
1985-86	Leksand IF	Sweden	36	20	12	32	....	....	....	18	....	....	....	....	....	....	....	....	....	....	....	....	....	....	....	....	....	....
	Sweden	WEC-A	8	0	3	3	....	....	....	4	....	....	....	....	....	....	....	....	....	....	....	....	....	....	....	....	....	....
1986-87	Leksand IF	Sweden	31	17	14	31	....	....	....	14	....	....	....	....	....	....	....	....	....	....	....	....	....	....	....	....	....	....
1987-88	Leksand IF	Sweden	24	9	7	16	....	....	....	10	....	....	....	....	....	....	....	....	....	....	3	0	0	0	2	....	....	....
	NHL Totals		**268**	**71**	**73**	**144**	**61**	**54**	**115**	**47**	**15**	**0**	**8**	**406**	**17.5**	**230**	**61**	**204**	**1**		**8**	**1**	**0**	**1**	**4**	**1**	**0**	**1**
	Other Major League Totals		111	42	43	85	....	....	....	51	....	....	....	....	....	....	....	....	....	....	24	8	18	26	23	....	....	....

Signed as a free agent by **Winnipeg** (WHA), June, 1976. Signed as a free agent by **Detroit**, October 12, 1978. Traded to **Calgary** by **Detroit** for Earl Ingarfield Jr., February 3, 1981.

• LABRE, YVON

Yvon Labre D – L. 5'11", 190 lbs. b: Sudbury, Ont., 11/29/1949. Pittsburgh's 3rd choice, 38th overall, in 1969 Amateur Draft.

Season	Club	League	GP	G	A	Pts	AG	AA	APts	PIM	PP	SH	GW	S	%	TGF	PGF	TGA	PGA	+/–	GP	G	A	Pts	PIM	PP	SH	GW
1966-67	Markham Waxers	Jr. B	32	0	14	14	....	....	....	....	....	....	....	....	....	....	....	....	....	....	....	....	....	....	....	....	....	....
1967-68	Toronto Marlboros	OHA	43	4	8	12	....	....	....	107	....	....	....	....	....	....	....	....	....	....	5	0	0	0	18	....	....	....
1968-69	Toronto Marlboros	OHA	54	1	16	17	....	....	....	185	....	....	....	....	....	....	....	....	....	....	6	1	1	2	26	....	....	....
1969-70	Baltimore Clippers	AHL	64	1	8	9	....	....	....	111	....	....	....	....	....	....	....	....	....	....	5	0	2	2	38	....	....	....
1970-71	**Pittsburgh Penguins**	**NHL**	21	1	1	2	1	1	2	19	0	0	0	30	3.3	13	2	11	2	+2	....	....	....	....	....	....	....	....
	Amarillo Wranglers	CHL	42	2	9	11	....	....	....	125	....	....	....	....	....	....	....	....	....	....	....	....	....	....	....	....	....	....
1971-72	Hershey Bears	AHL	59	3	9	12	....	....	....	134	....	....	....	....	....	....	....	....	....	....	4	2	1	3	20	....	....	....
1972-73	Hershey Bears	AHL	72	8	29	37	....	....	....	170	....	....	....	....	....	....	....	....	....	....	7	1	3	4	35	....	....	....
1973-74	**Pittsburgh Penguins**	**NHL**	16	1	2	3	1	2	3	13	0	0	0	12	8.3	9	0	17	1	–7	....	....	....	....	....	....	....	....
	Hershey Bears	AHL	56	6	23	29	....	....	....	135	....	....	....	....	....	....	....	....	....	....	14	1	5	6	42	....	....	....
1974-75	**Washington Capitals**	**NHL**	76	4	23	27	4	18	22	182	0	0	0	72	5.6	67	11	136	26	–54	....	....	....	....	....	....	....	....
1975-76	**Washington Capitals**	**NHL**	80	2	20	22	2	16	18	146	0	0	0	110	1.8	83	8	141	28	–38	....	....	....	....	....	....	....	....
1976-77	**Washington Capitals**	**NHL**	62	3	11	14	3	9	12	169	0	2	0	99	3.0	54	4	76	21	–5	....	....	....	....	....	....	....	....
1977-78	**Washington Capitals**	**NHL**	22	0	8	8	0	7	7	41	0	0	0	21	0.0	17	0	22	5	0	....	....	....	....	....	....	....	....
	Hershey Bears	AHL	21	1	6	7	....	....	....	72	....	....	....	....	....	....	....	....	....	....	....	....	....	....	....	....	....	....
1978-79	**Washington Capitals**	**NHL**	51	1	13	14	1	10	11	80	0	0	0	36	2.8	44	2	50	15	+7	....	....	....	....	....	....	....	....
1979-80	**Washington Capitals**	**NHL**	18	0	5	5	0	4	4	38	0	0	0	5	0.0	13	0	16	6	+3	....	....	....	....	....	....	....	....
1980-81	**Washington Capitals**	**NHL**	25	2	4	6	2	3	5	100	0	0	0	13	15.4	20	1	24	3	–2	....	....	....	....	....	....	....	....
	NHL Totals		**371**	**14**	**87**	**101**	**14**	**70**	**84**	**788**	**0**	**2**	**0**	**398**	**3.5**	**320**	**28**	**493**	**107**		....	....	....	....	....	....	....	....

Claimed by **Washington** from **Pittsburgh** in Expansion Draft, June 12, 1974.

• LACHANCE, MICHEL

Michel Lachance D – R. 6', 190 lbs. b: Quebec City, Que., 4/11/1955. Montreal's 9th choice, 106th overall, in 1975 Amateur Draft.

Season	Club	League	GP	G	A	Pts	AG	AA	APts	PIM	PP	SH	GW	S	%	TGF	PGF	TGA	PGA	+/–	GP	G	A	Pts	PIM	PP	SH	GW
1972-73	Quebec Remparts	QMJHL	51	1	8	9	....	....	....	49	....	....	....	....	....	....	....	....	....	....	....	....	....	....	....	....	....	....
1973-74	Quebec Remparts	QMJHL	70	9	63	72	....	....	....	170	....	....	....	....	....	....	....	....	....	....	....	....	....	....	....	....	....	....
1974-75	Quebec–Montreal	QMJHL	65	13	44	57	....	....	....	145	....	....	....	....	....	....	....	....	....	....	....	....	....	....	....	....	....	....
1975-76			DID NOT PLAY																									
1976-77	Greensboro Generals	EHL	40	7	10	17	....	....	....	108	....	....	....	....	....	....	....	....	....	....	....	....	....	....	....	....	....	....
	Baltimore Clippers	AHL	10	0	4	4	....	....	....	16	....	....	....	....	....	....	....	....	....	....	....	....	....	....	....	....	....	....
	Maine Nordiques	NAHL	4	1	0	1	....	....	....	5	....	....	....	....	....	....	....	....	....	....	....	....	....	....	....	....	....	....
1977-78	Milwaukee Admirals	IHL	72	19	23	42	....	....	....	210	....	....	....	....	....	....	....	....	....	....	....	....	....	....	....	....	....	....
1978-79	**Colorado Rockies**	**NHL**	21	0	4	4	0	3	3	22	0	0	0	22	0.0	7	1	18	3	–9	....	....	....	....	....	....	....	....
	Philadelphia Firebirds	AHL	22	1	5	6	....	....	....	42	....	....	....	....	....	....	....	....	....	....	....	....	....	....	....	....	....	....
	Tulsa Oilers	CHL	22	2	5	7	....	....	....	35	....	....	....	....	....	....	....	....	....	....	....	....	....	....	....	....	....	....
	New Brunswick Hawks	AHL	10	4	1	5	....	....	....	0	....	....	....	....	....	....	....	....	....	....	5	0	2	2	4	....	....	....
1979-80	Fort Worth Texans	CHL	76	12	25	37	....	....	....	95	....	....	....	....	....	....	....	....	....	....	....	....	....	....	....	....	....	....
1980-81	Caen	France	....	11	4	15	....	....	....	....	....	....	....	....	....	....	....	....	....	....	....	....	....	....	....	....	....	....
	NHL Totals		**21**	**0**	**4**	**4**	**0**	**3**	**3**	**22**	**0**	**0**	**0**	**22**	**0.0**	**7**	**1**	**18**	**3**		....	....	....	....	....	....	....	....

Won Governors' Trophy (Top Defenseman - IHL) (1978)

Signed as a free agent by **Colorado**, October 13, 1978.

• LACHANCE, SCOTT

Scott Lachance D – L. 6'1", 196 lbs. b: Charlottesville, VA, 10/22/1972. NY Islanders' 1st choice, 4th overall, in 1991 Entry Draft.

Season	Club	League	GP	G	A	Pts	AG	AA	APts	PIM	PP	SH	GW	S	%	TGF	PGF	TGA	PGA	+/–	GP	G	A	Pts	PIM	PP	SH	GW
1990-91	Boston University	H.E.	31	5	19	24	....	....	....	48	....	....	....	....	....	....	....	....	....	....	....	....	....	....	....	....	....	....
1991-92	United States	Nat-Team	36	1	10	11	....	....	....	34	....	....	....	....	....	....	....	....	....	....	....	....	....	....	....	....	....	....
	United States	WJC-A	7	1	4	5	....	....	....	0	....	....	....	....	....	....	....	....	....	....	....	....	....	....	....	....	....	....
	United States	Olympics	8	0	1	1	....	....	....	6	....	....	....	....	....	....	....	....	....	....	....	....	....	....	....	....	....	....
	New York Islanders	**NHL**	17	1	4	5	1	3	4	9	0	0	0	20	5.0	22	3	9	3	+13	....	....	....	....	....	....	....	....
1992-93	**New York Islanders**	**NHL**	75	7	17	24	6	12	18	67	0	1	2	62	11.3	69	2	100	32	–1	....	....	....	....	....	....	....	....
1993-94	**New York Islanders**	**NHL**	74	3	11	14	3	8	11	70	0	0	1	59	5.1	67	10	89	27	–5	3	0	0	0	0	0	0	0
1994-95	**New York Islanders**	**NHL**	26	6	7	13	11	10	21	26	3	0	0	56	10.7	33	14	29	12	+2	....	....	....	....	....	....	....	....

Season	Club	League	REGULAR SEASON GP	G	A	Pts	AG	AA	APts	PIM	PP	SH	GW	S	%	TGF	PGF	TGA	PGA	+/–	PLAYOFFS GP	G	A	Pts	PIM	PP	SH	GW
1995-96	**New York Islanders**	**NHL**	**55**	**3**	**10**	**13**	**3**	**8**	**11**	**54**	**1**	**0**	**0**	**81**	**3.7**	**58**	**17**	**89**	**29**	**–19**	....	....	....	....	....	....	....	....
	United States	WC-A	8	0	0	0	....	....	....	2	....	....	....	....	....	....	....	....	....	....	....	....	....	....	....	....	....	....
1996-97	**New York Islanders**	**NHL**	**81**	**3**	**11**	**14**	**3**	**10**	**13**	**47**	**1**	**0**	**0**	**97**	**3.1**	**72**	**8**	**90**	**19**	**–7**	....	....	....	....	....	....	....	....
	United States	WC-A	8	0	2	2	....	....	....	4	....	....	....	....	....	....	....	....	....	....	....	....	....	....	....	....	....	....
1997-98	**New York Islanders**	**NHL**	**63**	**2**	**11**	**13**	**2**	**11**	**13**	**45**	**1**	**0**	**0**	**62**	**3.2**	**47**	**11**	**64**	**17**	**–11**	....	....	....	....	....	....	....	....
	NHL Totals		**391**	**25**	**71**	**96**	**29**	**62**	**91**	**318**	**6**	**1**	**3**	**437**	**5.7**	**368**	**65**	**470**	**139**		**3**	**0**	**0**	**0**	**0**	**0**	**0**	**0**

WJC-A All-Star Team (1991)

Played in NHL All-Star Game (1997)

• LACOMBE, FRANCOIS

Francois Lacombe D – L. 5'10", 185 lbs. b: Montreal, Que., 2/24/1948.

Season	Club	League	GP	G	A	Pts	AG	AA	APts	PIM	PP	SH	GW	S	%	TGF	PGF	TGA	PGA	+/–	GP	G	A	Pts	PIM	PP	SH	GW
1965-66	Lachine Maroons	QJHL	40	2	14	16	....	....	....	70	....	....	....	....	....	....	....	....	....	....	....	....	....	....	....	....	....	....
1966-67	Lachine Maroons	QJHL	STATISTICS NOT AVAILABLE																									
1967-68	Montreal Jr. Canadiens	OHA	51	1	10	11	....	....	....	59	....	....	....	....	....	....	....	....	....	....	11	0	3	3	4	....	....	....
1968-69	**Oakland Seals**	**NHL**	**72**	**2**	**16**	**18**	**2**	**15**	**17**	**50**	**1**	**0**	**0**	**103**	**1.9**	**80**	**14**	**82**	**6**	**–10**	**3**	**1**	**0**	**1**	**0**	**0**	**0**	**0**
1969-70	**Oakland Seals**	**NHL**	**2**	**0**	**0**	**0**	**0**	**0**	**0**	**0**	**0**	**0**	**0**	**1**	**0.0**	**2**	**0**	**1**	**0**	**+1**	....	....	....	....	....	....	....	....
	Providence Reds	AHL	70	9	16	25	....	....	....	64	....	....	....	....	....	....	....	....	....	....	....	....	....	....	....	....	....	....
1970-71	**Buffalo Sabres**	**NHL**	**1**	**0**	**1**	**1**	**0**	**1**	**1**	**2**	**0**	**0**	**0**	**1**	**0.0**	**1**	**1**	**2**	**0**	**–2**	....	....	....	....	....	....	....	....
	Salt Lake Golden Eagles	WHL	70	11	39	50	....	....	....	89	....	....	....	....	....	....	....	....	....	....	....	....	....	....	....	....	....	....
1971-72	Salt Lake Golden Eagles	WHL	11	2	3	5	....	....	....	22	....	....	....	....	....	....	....	....	....	....	....	....	....	....	....	....	....	....
	Fort Worth Wings	CHL	19	3	5	8	....	....	....	26	....	....	....	....	....	....	....	....	....	....	....	....	....	....	....	....	....	....
	Cincinnati Swords	AHL	35	4	10	14	....	....	....	26	....	....	....	....	....	....	....	....	....	....	10	1	6	7	20	....	....	....
1972-73	Quebec Nordiques	WHA	62	10	18	28	....	....	....	123	....	....	....	....	....	....	....	....	....	....	....	....	....	....	....	....	....	....
1973-74	Quebec Nordiques	WHA	71	9	26	35	....	....	....	41	....	....	....	....	....	....	....	....	....	....	....	....	....	....	....	....	....	....
1974-75	Maine Nordiques	NAHL	4	0	3	3	....	....	....	12	....	....	....	....	....	....	....	....	....	....	....	....	....	....	....	....	....	....
	Quebec Nordiques	WHA	55	7	17	24	....	....	....	54	....	....	....	....	....	....	....	....	....	....	15	0	2	2	14	....	....	....
1975-76	Calgary Cowboys	WHA	71	3	28	31	....	....	....	62	....	....	....	....	....	....	....	....	....	....	8	0	0	0	2	....	....	....
1976-77	Quebec Nordiques	WHA	81	5	22	27	....	....	....	86	....	....	....	....	....	....	....	....	....	....	17	4	3	7	16	....	....	....
1977-78	Quebec Nordiques	WHA	22	1	7	8	....	....	....	12	....	....	....	....	....	....	....	....	....	....	10	1	4	5	2	....	....	....
1978-79	Quebec Nordiques	WHA	78	3	21	24	....	....	....	44	....	....	....	....	....	....	....	....	....	....	4	0	1	1	2	....	....	....
1979-80	**Quebec Nordiques**	**NHL**	**3**	**0**	**0**	**0**	**0**	**0**	**0**	**2**	**0**	**0**	**0**	**2**	**0.0**	**3**	**0**	**5**	**1**	**–1**	....	....	....	....	....	....	....	....
	Syracuse Firebirds	AHL	50	3	26	29	....	....	....	34	....	....	....	....	....	....	....	....	....	....	1	0	0	0	0	....	....	....
	NHL Totals		**78**	**2**	**17**	**19**	**2**	**16**	**18**	**54**	**1**	**0**	**0**	**107**	**1.9**	**86**	**15**	**90**	**7**		**3**	**1**	**0**	**1**	**0**	**0**	**0**	**0**
	Other Major League Totals		440	38	139	177	....	....	....	422	....	....	....	....	....	....	....	....	....	....	54	5	10	15	36	....	....	....

Traded to **Oakland** by **Montreal** with Michel Jacques and cash for Lyle Bradley, May 21, 1968. Traded to **Montreal** by **Oakland** with cash and Oakland's 1st round choice (Guy Lafleur) in 1971 Amateur Draft for Ernie Hickie and Montreal's 1st round choice (Chris Oddleifson) in 1970 Amateur Draft, June 10, 1970. Claimed by **Buffalo** from **Montreal** in Expansion Draft, June 10, 1970. Selected by **Alberta** (WHA) in 1972 WHA General Player Draft, February 12, 1972. WHA rights traded to **Quebec** (WHA) by **Alberta** (WHA) for future considerations, June, 1972. Claimed by **Calgary** (WHA) from **Quebec** (WHA) in WHA Intra-League Draft, June, 1975. Traded to **Quebec** (WHA) by **Calgary** (WHA) for future considerations, August, 1976. Rights retained by **Quebec** prior to Expansion Draft, June 9, 1979.

• LACOMBE, NORMAND

Normand Lacombe RW – R. 6', 205 lbs. b: Pierrefonds, Que., 10/18/1964. Buffalo's 2nd choice, 10th overall, in 1983 Entry Draft.

Season	Club	League	GP	G	A	Pts	AG	AA	APts	PIM	PP	SH	GW	S	%	TGF	PGF	TGA	PGA	+/–	GP	G	A	Pts	PIM	PP	SH	GW
1981-82	University of New Hampshire	ECAC	35	18	16	34	....	....	....	38	....	....	....	....	....	....	....	....	....	....	....	....	....	....	....	....	....	....
1982-83	University of New Hampshire	ECAC	35	18	25	43	....	....	....	48	....	....	....	....	....	....	....	....	....	....	....	....	....	....	....	....	....	....
1983-84	Rochester Americans	AHL	44	10	16	26	....	....	....	45	....	....	....	....	....	....	....	....	....	....	....	....	....	....	....	....	....	....
1984-85	**Buffalo Sabres**	**NHL**	**30**	**2**	**4**	**6**	**2**	**3**	**5**	**25**	**0**	**0**	**0**	**30**	**6.7**	**10**	**1**	**12**	**0**	**–3**	....	....	....	....	....	....	....	....
	Rochester Americans	AHL	33	13	16	29	....	....	....	33	....	....	....	....	....	....	....	....	....	....	5	3	1	4	4	....	....	....
1985-86	**Buffalo Sabres**	**NHL**	**25**	**6**	**7**	**13**	**5**	**5**	**10**	**13**	**3**	**0**	**2**	**38**	**15.8**	**32**	**9**	**16**	**2**	**+9**	....	....	....	....	....	....	....	....
	Rochester Americans	AHL	32	10	13	23	....	....	....	56	....	....	....	....	....	....	....	....	....	....	....	....	....	....	....	....	....	....
1986-87	**Buffalo Sabres**	**NHL**	**39**	**4**	**7**	**11**	**3**	**5**	**8**	**8**	**1**	**0**	**0**	**48**	**8.3**	**18**	**2**	**27**	**2**	**–9**	....	....	....	....	....	....	....	....
	Rochester Americans	AHL	13	6	5	11	....	....	....	4	....	....	....	....	....	....	....	....	....	....	....	....	....	....	....	....	....	....
	Edmonton Oilers	**NHL**	**1**	**0**	**0**	**0**	**0**	**0**	**0**	**2**	**0**	**0**	**0**	**0**	**0.0**	**1**	**0**	**2**	**0**	**–1**	....	....	....	....	....	....	....	....
	Nova Scotia Oilers	AHL	10	3	5	8	....	....	....	4	....	....	....	....	....	....	....	....	....	....	5	1	1	2	6	....	....	....
1987-88	**Edmonton Oilers**	**NHL**	**53**	**8**	**9**	**17**	**7**	**6**	**13**	**36**	**1**	**0**	**2**	**44**	**18.2**	**26**	**2**	**27**	**0**	**–3**	**19**	**3**	**0**	**3**	**28**	**0**	**0**	**1**
1988-89	**Edmonton Oilers**	**NHL**	**64**	**17**	**11**	**28**	**14**	**8**	**22**	**57**	**2**	**0**	**1**	**71**	**23.9**	**45**	**4**	**39**	**0**	**+2**	**7**	**2**	**1**	**3**	**21**	**0**	**0**	**0**
1989-90	**Edmonton Oilers**	**NHL**	**15**	**5**	**2**	**7**	**4**	**1**	**5**	**21**	**0**	**0**	**0**	**15**	**33.3**	**9**	**0**	**5**	**0**	**+4**	....	....	....	....	....	....	....	....
	Philadelphia Flyers	**NHL**	**18**	**0**	**2**	**2**	**0**	**1**	**1**	**7**	**0**	**0**	**0**	**21**	**0.0**	**9**	**0**	**9**	**0**	**0**	....	....	....	....	....	....	....	....
1990-91	**Philadelphia Flyers**	**NHL**	**74**	**11**	**20**	**31**	**10**	**15**	**25**	**27**	**1**	**0**	**1**	**91**	**12.1**	**37**	**1**	**47**	**10**	**–1**	....	....	....	....	....	....	....	....
	NHL Totals		**319**	**53**	**62**	**115**	**45**	**44**	**89**	**196**	**8**	**0**	**6**	**358**	**14.8**	**187**	**19**	**184**	**14**		**26**	**5**	**1**	**6**	**49**	**0**	**0**	**1**

ECAC Second All-Star Team (1983)

Traded to **Edmonton** by **Buffalo** with Wayne Van Dorp and future considerations for Lee Fogolin and Mark Napier, March 6, 1987. Traded to **Philadelphia** by **Edmonton** for future considerations, January 5, 1990.

• LACROIX, ANDRE

Andre Lacroix C – L. 5'8", 175 lbs. b: Lauzon, Que., 6/5/1945.

Season	Club	League	GP	G	A	Pts	AG	AA	APts	PIM	PP	SH	GW	S	%	TGF	PGF	TGA	PGA	+/–	GP	G	A	Pts	PIM	PP	SH	GW
1963-64	Montreal Jr. Canadiens	OHA	34	12	18	30	....	....	....	13	....	....	....	....	....	....	....	....	....	....	17	8	13	21	8	....	....	....
1964-65	Peterborough Petes	OHA	49	45	*74	119	....	....	....	24	....	....	....	....	....	....	....	....	....	....	12	8	12	20	4	....	....	....
	Quebec Aces	AHL	1	0	0	0	....	....	....	0	....	....	....	....	....	....	....	....	....	....	....	....	....	....	....	....	....	....
1965-66	Peterborough Petes	OHA	48	40	*80	*120	....	....	....	20	....	....	....	....	....	....	....	....	....	....	6	4	8	12	6	....	....	....
	Quebec Aces	AHL	2	1	3	4	....	....	....	0	....	....	....	....	....	....	....	....	....	....	....	....	....	....	....	....	....	....
1966-67	Quebec Aces	AHL	67	25	24	49	....	....	....	14	....	....	....	....	....	....	....	....	....	....	5	2	3	5	2	....	....	....
1967-68	**Philadelphia Flyers**	**NHL**	**18**	**6**	**8**	**14**	**7**	**8**	**15**	**6**	**0**	**0**	**1**	**51**	**11.8**	**17**	**4**	**13**	**0**	**0**	**7**	**2**	**3**	**5**	**0**	**1**	**0**	**0**
	Quebec Aces	AHL	54	41	46	87	....	....	....	18	....	....	....	....	....	....	....	....	....	....	....	....	....	....	....	....	....	....
1968-69	**Philadelphia Flyers**	**NHL**	**75**	**24**	**32**	**56**	**27**	**30**	**57**	**4**	**13**	**0**	**1**	**217**	**11.1**	**75**	**32**	**55**	**0**	**–12**	**4**	**0**	**0**	**0**	**0**	**0**	**0**	**0**
1969-70	**Philadelphia Flyers**	**NHL**	**74**	**22**	**36**	**58**	**25**	**36**	**61**	**14**	**6**	**0**	**4**	**175**	**12.6**	**71**	**31**	**46**	**0**	**–6**	....	....	....	....	....	....	....	....
1970-71	**Philadelphia Flyers**	**NHL**	**78**	**20**	**22**	**42**	**21**	**19**	**40**	**12**	**9**	**0**	**4**	**180**	**11.1**	**56**	**30**	**35**	**0**	**–9**	**4**	**0**	**2**	**2**	**0**	**0**	**0**	**0**
1971-72	**Chicago Black Hawks**	**NHL**	**51**	**4**	**7**	**11**	**4**	**6**	**10**	**6**	**1**	**0**	**1**	**34**	**11.8**	**18**	**4**	**10**	**0**	**+4**	**1**	**0**	**0**	**0**	**0**	**0**	**0**	**0**
1972-73	Philadelphia Blazers	WHA	78	50	74	*124	....	....	....	83	....	....	....	....	....	....	....	....	....	....	4	0	2	2	18	....	....	....
1973-74	New York-New Jersey	WHA	78	31	*80	111	....	....	....	54	....	....	....	....	....	....	....	....	....	....	....	....	....	....	....	....	....	....
1974-75	Canada	Summit	8	1	6	7	....	....	....	6	....	....	....	....	....	....	....	....	....	....	....	....	....	....	....	....	....	....
	San Diego Mariners	WHA	78	41	*106	*147	....	....	....	63	....	....	....	....	....	....	....	....	....	....	10	3	9	12	2	....	....	....
1975-76	San Diego Mariners	WHA	80	29	72	101	....	....	....	42	....	....	....	....	....	....	....	....	....	....	11	4	6	10	4	....	....	....
1976-77	San Diego Mariners	WHA	81	32	82	114	....	....	....	79	....	....	....	....	....	....	....	....	....	....	7	1	6	7	6	....	....	....
1977-78	Houston Aeros	WHA	78	36	77	113	....	....	....	57	....	....	....	....	....	....	....	....	....	....	6	2	2	4	0	....	....	....
1978-79	New England Whalers	WHA	78	32	56	88	....	....	....	34	....	....	....	....	....	....	....	....	....	....	10	4	4	8	0	....	....	....
1979-80	**Hartford Whalers**	**NHL**	**29**	**3**	**14**	**17**	**3**	**11**	**14**	**2**	**1**	**0**	**0**	**45**	**6.7**	**22**	**3**	**27**	**2**	**–6**	....	....	....	....	....	....	....	....
	NHL Totals		**325**	**79**	**119**	**198**	**87**	**110**	**197**	**44**	**30**	**0**	**11**	**702**	**11.3**	**259**	**104**	**186**	**2**		**16**	**2**	**5**	**7**	**0**	**1**	**0**	**0**
	Other Major League Totals		551	251	547	798	....	....	....	412	....	....	....	....	....	....	....	....	....	....	48	14	29	43	30	....	....	....

WHA First All-Star Team (1973, 1974, 1975) • Won W. D. (Bill) Hunter Trophy (WHA Scoring Leader) (1973, 1975)

NHL rights transferred to **Philadelphia** after NHL club purchased **Quebec** (AHL) franchise, May 8, 1967. Traded to **Chicago** by **Philadelphia** for Rock Foley, October 15, 1971. Selected by **Quebec** (WHA) in 1972 WHA General Player Draft, February 12, 1972. WHA rights traded to **Miami-Philadelphia** (WHA) by **Quebec** (WHA) for cash, March, 1972. Transferred to **Vancouver** (WHA) after **Philadelphia** franchise relocated, May, 1973. Traded to **NY Raiders** (WHA) by **Vancouver** (WHA) with Dan Herriman and Bernie Parent for Ron Ward and Pete Donnelly, June, 1973. Transferred to **San Diego** (WHA) after **New York-New Jersey** (WHA) franchise relocated, April 30, 1974. Signed as a free agent by **Houston** (WHA) after **San Diego** (WHA) franchise folded, May 30, 1977. Signed as a free agent by **Winnipeg** (WHA) after **Houston** (WHA) franchise folded, July, 1978. Traded to **New England** (WHA) by **Winnipeg** (WHA) for future considerations, August, 1978. Rights retained by **Hartford** prior to Expansion Draft, June 9, 1979.

• LACROIX, DANIEL

Daniel Lacroix LW – L. 6'2", 205 lbs. b: Montreal, Que., 3/11/1969. NY Rangers' 2nd choice, 31st overall, in 1987 Entry Draft.

Season	Club	League	GP	G	A	Pts	AG	AA	APts	PIM	PP	SH	GW	S	%	TGF	PGF	TGA	PGA	+/–	GP	G	A	Pts	PIM	PP	SH	GW
1986-87	Granby Bisons	QMJHL	54	9	16	25	....	....	....	311	....	....	....	....	....	....	....	....	....	....	8	1	2	3	22	....	....	....
1987-88	Granby Bisons	QMJHL	58	24	50	74	....	....	....	468	....	....	....	....	....	....	....	....	....	....	5	0	4	4	12	....	....	....
1988-89	Granby Bisons	QMJHL	70	45	49	94	....	....	....	320	....	....	....	....	....	....	....	....	....	....	4	1	1	2	57	....	....	....
	Denver Rangers	IHL	2	0	1	1	....	....	....	0	....	....	....	....	....	....	....	....	....	....	2	0	1	1	0	....	....	....
1989-90	Flint Spirits	IHL	61	12	16	28	....	....	....	128	....	....	....	....	....	....	....	....	....	....	4	2	0	2	24	....	....	....
1990-91	Binghamton Rangers	AHL	54	7	12	19	....	....	....	237	....	....	....	....	....	....	....	....	....	....	5	1	0	1	24	....	....	....

			REGULAR SEASON																		PLAYOFFS							
Season	Club	League	GP	G	A	Pts	AG	AA	APts	PIM	PP	SH	GW	S	%	TGF	PGF	TGA	PGA	+/–	GP	G	A	Pts	PIM	PP	SH	GW
1991-92	Binghamton Rangers	AHL	52	12	20	32	....	....	....	149	....	....	....	....	....	....	....	....	....	....	11	2	4	6	28	....	....	....
1992-93	Binghamton Rangers	AHL	73	21	22	43	....	....	....	255	....	....	....	....	....	....	....	....	....	....	....	....	....	....	....	....	....	....
1993-94	**New York Rangers**	**NHL**	**4**	**0**	**0**	**0**	**0**	**0**	**0**	**0**	**0**	**0**	**0**	**0**	**0.0**	**0**	**0**	**0**	**0**	**0**	....	....	....	....	....	....	....	....
	Binghamton Rangers	AHL	59	20	23	43	....	....	....	278	....	....	....	....	....	....	....	....	....	....	....	....	....	....	....	....	....	....
1994-95	Providence Bruins	AHL	40	15	11	26	....	....	....	266	....	....	....	....	....	....	....	....	....	....	....	....	....	....	....	....	....	....
	Boston Bruins	**NHL**	**23**	**1**	**0**	**1**	**2**	**0**	**2**	**38**	**0**	**0**	**0**	**14**	**7.1**	**3**	**0**	**7**	**2**	**–2**	....	....	....	....	....	....	....	....
	New York Rangers	**NHL**	**1**	**0**	**0**	**0**	**0**	**0**	**0**	**0**	**0**	**0**	**0**	**0**	**0.0**	**0**	**0**	**0**	**0**	**0**	....	....	....	....	....	....	....	....
1995-96	**New York Rangers**	**NHL**	**25**	**2**	**2**	**4**	**2**	**2**	**4**	**30**	**0**	**0**	**0**	**14**	**14.3**	**6**	**0**	**9**	**2**	**–1**	....	....	....	....	....	....	....	....
	Binghamton Rangers	AHL	26	12	15	27	....	....	....	155	....	....	....	....	....	....	....	....	....	....	....	....	....	....	....	....	....	....
1996-97	**Philadelphia Flyers**	**NHL**	**74**	**7**	**1**	**8**	**7**	**1**	**8**	**163**	**1**	**0**	**0**	**54**	**13.0**	**21**	**1**	**23**	**2**	**–1**	**12**	**0**	**1**	**1**	**22**	**0**	**0**	**0**
1997-98	**Philadelphia Flyers**	**NHL**	**56**	**1**	**4**	**5**	**1**	**4**	**5**	**135**	**0**	**0**	**0**	**28**	**3.6**	**6**	**0**	**6**	**0**	**0**	**4**	**0**	**0**	**0**	**4**	**0**	**0**	**0**
	NHL Totals		**183**	**11**	**7**	**18**	**12**	**7**	**19**	**366**	**1**	**0**	**0**	**110**	**10.0**	**36**	**1**	**45**	**6**		**16**	**0**	**1**	**1**	**26**	**0**	**0**	**0**

Traded to **Boston** by **NY Rangers** for Glen Featherstone, August 19, 1994. Claimed on waivers by **NY Rangers** from **Boston**, March 23, 1995. Signed as a free agent by **Philadelphia**, July 18, 1996.

• LACROIX, ERIC

Eric Lacroix LW – L. 6'1", 205 lbs. b: Montreal, Que., 7/15/1971. Toronto's 6th choice, 136th overall, in 1990 Entry Draft.

Season	Club	League	GP	G	A	Pts	AG	AA	APts	PIM	PP	SH	GW	S	%	TGF	PGF	TGA	PGA	+/–	GP	G	A	Pts	PIM	PP	SH	GW
1989-90	Govenor Dummer High School	H.S.	....	28	13	41	....	....	....	....	....	....	....	....	....	....	....	....	....	....	....	....	....	....	....	....	....	....
1990-91	St. Lawrence University	ECAC	35	13	11	24	....	....	....	35	....	....	....	....	....	....	....	....	....	....	....	....	....	....	....	....	....	....
1991-92	St. Lawrence University	ECAC	34	11	20	31	....	....	....	40	....	....	....	....	....	....	....	....	....	....	....	....	....	....	....	....	....	....
1992-93	St. John's Maple Leafs	AHL	76	15	19	34	....	....	....	59	....	....	....	....	....	....	....	....	....	....	9	5	3	8	4	....	....	....
1993-94	**Toronto Maple Leafs**	**NHL**	**3**	**0**	**0**	**0**	**0**	**0**	**0**	**2**	**0**	**0**	**0**	**3**	**0.0**	**1**	**0**	**1**	**0**	**0**	**2**	**0**	**0**	**0**	**0**	**0**	**0**	**0**
	St. John's Maple Leafs	AHL	59	17	22	39	....	....	....	69	....	....	....	....	....	....	....	....	....	....	11	5	3	8	6	....	....	....
1994-95	St. John's Maple Leafs	AHL	1	0	0	0	....	....	....	2	....	....	....	....	....	....	....	....	....	....	....	....	....	....	....	....	....	....
	Phoenix Roadrunners	IHL	25	7	1	8	....	....	....	31	....	....	....	....	....	....	....	....	....	....	....	....	....	....	....	....	....	....
	Los Angeles Kings	**NHL**	**45**	**9**	**7**	**16**	**16**	**10**	**26**	**54**	**2**	**1**	**1**	**64**	**14.1**	**28**	**3**	**23**	**0**	**+2**	....	....	....	....	....	....	....	....
1995-96	**Los Angeles Kings**	**NHL**	**72**	**16**	**16**	**32**	**16**	**13**	**29**	**110**	**3**	**0**	**1**	**107**	**15.0**	**53**	**12**	**57**	**5**	**–11**	....	....	....	....	....	....	....	....
1996-97	**Colorado Avalanche**	**NHL**	**81**	**18**	**18**	**36**	**19**	**16**	**35**	**26**	**2**	**0**	**4**	**141**	**12.8**	**53**	**9**	**32**	**4**	**+16**	**17**	**1**	**4**	**5**	**19**	**0**	**0**	**0**
1997-98	**Colorado Avalanche**	**NHL**	**82**	**16**	**15**	**31**	**19**	**15**	**34**	**84**	**5**	**0**	**6**	**126**	**12.7**	**41**	**10**	**38**	**7**	**0**	**7**	**0**	**0**	**0**	**6**	**0**	**0**	**0**
	NHL Totals		**283**	**59**	**56**	**115**	**70**	**54**	**124**	**276**	**12**	**1**	**12**	**441**	**13.4**	**176**	**34**	**151**	**16**		**26**	**1**	**4**	**5**	**25**	**0**	**0**	**0**

Traded to **LA Kings** by **Toronto** with Chris Snell and Toronto's 4th round choice (Eric Belanger) in 1996 Entry Draft for Dixon Ward, Guy Leveque, Kelly Fairchild and Shayne Toporowski, October 3, 1994. Traded to **Colorado** by **LA Kings** with LA Kings' 1st round choice (Martin Skoula) in 1998 Entry Draft for Stephane Fiset and Colorado's 1st round choice (Mathieu Biron) in 1998 Entry Draft, June 20, 1996.

• LACROIX, PIERRE

Pierre Lacroix D – L. 5'11", 185 lbs. b: Quebec City, Que., 4/11/1959. Quebec's 5th choice, 104th overall, in 1979 Entry Draft.

Season	Club	League	GP	G	A	Pts	AG	AA	APts	PIM	PP	SH	GW	S	%	TGF	PGF	TGA	PGA	+/–	GP	G	A	Pts	PIM	PP	SH	GW
1975-76	Quebec Remparts	QMJHL	72	7	30	37	....	....	....	90	....	....	....	....	....	....	....	....	....	....	....	....	....	....	....	....	....	....
1976-77	Quebec Remparts	QMJHL	69	10	43	53	....	....	....	61	....	....	....	....	....	....	....	....	....	....	....	....	....	....	....	....	....	....
1977-78	Quebec Remparts	QMJHL	38	11	30	41	....	....	....	35	....	....	....	....	....	....	....	....	....	....	....	....	....	....	....	....	....	....
	Trois Rivieres Draveurs	QMJHL	30	6	24	30	....	....	....	20	....	....	....	....	....	....	....	....	....	....	5	3	5	8	4	....	....	....
1978-79	Trois-Rivieres Draveurs	QMJHL	72	37	100	137	....	....	....	57	....	....	....	....	....	....	....	....	....	....	13	2	10	12	6	....	....	....
1979-80	**Quebec Nordiques**	**NHL**	**76**	**9**	**21**	**30**	**8**	**16**	**24**	**45**	**4**	**0**	**0**	**86**	**10.5**	**78**	**23**	**63**	**2**	**–6**	....	....	....	....	....	....	....	....
1980-81	**Quebec Nordiques**	**NHL**	**61**	**5**	**34**	**39**	**4**	**24**	**28**	**54**	**4**	**0**	**0**	**96**	**5.2**	**110**	**39**	**80**	**18**	**+9**	**5**	**0**	**2**	**2**	**10**	**0**	**0**	**0**
1981-82	**Quebec Nordiques**	**NHL**	**68**	**4**	**23**	**27**	**3**	**15**	**18**	**74**	**1**	**0**	**0**	**73**	**5.5**	**87**	**19**	**73**	**6**	**+1**	**3**	**0**	**0**	**0**	**0**	**0**	**0**	**0**
1982-83	**Quebec Nordiques**	**NHL**	**13**	**0**	**5**	**5**	**0**	**3**	**3**	**6**	**0**	**0**	**0**	**8**	**0.0**	**14**	**3**	**11**	**4**	**+4**	....	....	....	....	....	....	....	....
	Fredericton Express	AHL	6	0	5	5	....	....	....	0	....	....	....	....	....	....	....	....	....	....	....	....	....	....	....	....	....	....
	Hartford Whalers	**NHL**	**56**	**6**	**25**	**31**	**5**	**17**	**22**	**18**	**1**	**0**	**0**	**89**	**6.7**	**81**	**15**	**102**	**17**	**–19**	....	....	....	....	....	....	....	....
	NHL Totals		**274**	**24**	**108**	**132**	**20**	**75**	**95**	**197**	**10**	**0**	**0**	**352**	**6.8**	**370**	**99**	**329**	**47**		**8**	**0**	**2**	**2**	**10**	**0**	**0**	**0**

QMJHL First All-Star Team (1979) • Canadian Major Junior Player of the Year (1979)

Traded to **Hartford** by **Quebec** for Blake Wesley, December 3, 1982.

• LADOUCEUR, RANDY

Randy Ladouceur D – L. 6'2", 220 lbs. b: Brockville, Ont., 6/30/1960.

Season	Club	League	GP	G	A	Pts	AG	AA	APts	PIM	PP	SH	GW	S	%	TGF	PGF	TGA	PGA	+/–	GP	G	A	Pts	PIM	PP	SH	GW
1978-79	Brantford Alexanders	OHA	64	3	17	20	....	....	....	141	....	....	....	....	....	....	....	....	....	....	....	....	....	....	....	....	....	....
1979-80	Brantford Alexanders	OHA	37	6	15	21	....	....	....	125	....	....	....	....	....	....	....	....	....	....	8	0	5	5	18	....	....	....
1980-81	Kalamazoo Wings	IHL	80	7	30	37	....	....	....	52	....	....	....	....	....	....	....	....	....	....	8	1	3	4	10	....	....	....
1981-82	Adirondack Red Wings	AHL	78	4	28	32	....	....	....	78	....	....	....	....	....	....	....	....	....	....	5	1	1	2	6	....	....	....
1982-83	**Detroit Red Wings**	**NHL**	**27**	**0**	**4**	**4**	**0**	**3**	**3**	**16**	**0**	**0**	**0**	**17**	**0.0**	**18**	**2**	**29**	**3**	**–10**	....	....	....	....	....	....	....	....
	Adirondack Red Wings	AHL	48	11	21	32	....	....	....	54	....	....	....	....	....	....	....	....	....	....	....	....	....	....	....	....	....	....
1983-84	**Detroit Red Wings**	**NHL**	**71**	**3**	**17**	**20**	**2**	**12**	**14**	**58**	**0**	**0**	**0**	**89**	**3.4**	**75**	**8**	**107**	**28**	**–12**	**4**	**1**	**0**	**1**	**6**	**0**	**1**	**0**
	Adirondack Red Wings	AHL	11	3	5	8	....	....	....	12	....	....	....	....	....	....	....	....	....	....	....	....	....	....	....	....	....	....
1984-85	**Detroit Red Wings**	**NHL**	**80**	**3**	**27**	**30**	**2**	**18**	**20**	**108**	**1**	**0**	**1**	**83**	**3.6**	**119**	**18**	**147**	**49**	**+3**	**3**	**1**	**0**	**1**	**0**	**0**	**0**	**0**
1985-86	**Detroit Red Wings**	**NHL**	**78**	**5**	**13**	**18**	**4**	**9**	**13**	**196**	**0**	**0**	**1**	**92**	**5.4**	**76**	**12**	**168**	**50**	**–54**	....	....	....	....	....	....	....	....
1986-87	**Detroit Red Wings**	**NHL**	**34**	**3**	**6**	**9**	**3**	**4**	**7**	**70**	**1**	**0**	**1**	**25**	**12.0**	**29**	**3**	**40**	**10**	**–4**	....	....	....	....	....	....	....	....
	Hartford Whalers	**NHL**	**36**	**2**	**3**	**5**	**2**	**2**	**4**	**51**	**0**	**0**	**0**	**29**	**6.9**	**36**	**1**	**38**	**9**	**+6**	**6**	**0**	**2**	**2**	**12**	**0**	**0**	**0**
1987-88	**Hartford Whalers**	**NHL**	**67**	**1**	**7**	**8**	**1**	**5**	**6**	**91**	**0**	**0**	**1**	**37**	**2.7**	**53**	**3**	**64**	**21**	**+7**	**6**	**1**	**1**	**2**	**4**	**0**	**0**	**0**
1988-89	**Hartford Whalers**	**NHL**	**75**	**2**	**5**	**7**	**2**	**4**	**6**	**95**	**0**	**0**	**0**	**56**	**3.6**	**66**	**0**	**115**	**26**	**–23**	**1**	**0**	**0**	**0**	**10**	**0**	**0**	**0**
1989-90	**Hartford Whalers**	**NHL**	**71**	**3**	**12**	**15**	**3**	**9**	**12**	**126**	**0**	**0**	**0**	**45**	**6.7**	**53**	**2**	**87**	**30**	**–6**	**7**	**1**	**0**	**1**	**10**	**0**	**0**	**1**
1990-91	**Hartford Whalers**	**NHL**	**67**	**1**	**3**	**4**	**1**	**2**	**3**	**118**	**0**	**0**	**0**	**44**	**2.3**	**47**	**0**	**85**	**28**	**–10**	**6**	**1**	**4**	**5**	**6**	**0**	**0**	**0**
1991-92	**Hartford Whalers**	**NHL**	**74**	**1**	**9**	**10**	**1**	**7**	**8**	**127**	**0**	**0**	**0**	**59**	**1.7**	**44**	**1**	**77**	**33**	**–1**	**7**	**0**	**1**	**1**	**11**	**0**	**0**	**0**
1992-93	**Hartford Whalers**	**NHL**	**62**	**2**	**4**	**6**	**2**	**3**	**5**	**109**	**0**	**0**	**0**	**37**	**5.4**	**41**	**0**	**85**	**26**	**–18**	....	....	....	....	....	....	....	....
1993-94	**Anaheim Mighty Ducks**	**NHL**	**81**	**1**	**9**	**10**	**1**	**7**	**8**	**74**	**0**	**0**	**0**	**66**	**1.5**	**59**	**0**	**78**	**26**	**+7**	....	....	....	....	....	....	....	....
1994-95	**Anaheim Mighty Ducks**	**NHL**	**44**	**2**	**4**	**6**	**4**	**6**	**10**	**36**	**0**	**0**	**0**	**42**	**4.8**	**29**	**1**	**41**	**15**	**+2**	....	....	....	....	....	....	....	....
1995-96	**Anaheim Mighty Ducks**	**NHL**	**63**	**1**	**3**	**4**	**1**	**2**	**3**	**47**	**0**	**0**	**0**	**48**	**2.1**	**45**	**0**	**66**	**26**	**+5**	....	....	....	....	....	....	....	....
	NHL Totals		**930**	**30**	**126**	**156**	**29**	**93**	**122**	**1322**	**2**	**0**	**4**	**769**	**3.9**	**790**	**51**	**1227**	**380**		**40**	**5**	**8**	**13**	**59**	**0**	**1**	**1**

Signed as a free agent by **Detroit**, November 1, 1979. Traded to **Hartford** by **Detroit** for Dave Barr, January 12, 1987. Claimed by **Anaheim** from **Hartford** in Expansion Draft, June 24, 1993.

• LAFAYETTE, NATHAN

Nathan LaFayette C – R. 6'1", 200 lbs. b: New Westminster, B.C., 2/17/1973. St. Louis' 3rd choice, 65th overall, in 1991 Entry Draft.

Season	Club	League	GP	G	A	Pts	AG	AA	APts	PIM	PP	SH	GW	S	%	TGF	PGF	TGA	PGA	+/–	GP	G	A	Pts	PIM	PP	SH	GW
1989-90	Kingston Frontenacs	OHL	53	6	8	14	....	....	....	14	....	....	....	....	....	....	....	....	....	....	7	0	1	1	0	....	....	....
1990-91	Kingston Frontenacs	OHL	35	13	13	26	....	....	....	10	....	....	....	....	....	....	....	....	....	....	....	....	....	....	....	....	....	....
	Cornwall Royals	OHL	28	16	22	38	....	....	....	25	....	....	....	....	....	....	....	....	....	....	....	....	....	....	....	....	....	....
1991-92	Cornwall Royals	OHL	66	28	45	73	....	....	....	26	....	....	....	....	....	....	....	....	....	....	6	2	5	7	15	....	....	....
1992-93	Newmarket Royals	OHL	58	49	38	87	....	....	....	26	....	....	....	....	....	....	....	....	....	....	7	4	5	9	19	....	....	....
	Canada	WJC-A	7	3	1	4	....	....	....	0	....	....	....	....	....	....	....	....	....	....	....	....	....	....	....	....	....	....
1993-94	**St. Louis Blues**	**NHL**	**38**	**2**	**3**	**5**	**2**	**2**	**4**	**14**	**0**	**0**	**0**	**23**	**8.7**	**10**	**0**	**22**	**3**	**–9**	....	....	....	....	....	....	....	....
	Peoria Rivermen	IHL	27	13	11	24	....	....	....	20	....	....	....	....	....	....	....	....	....	....	....	....	....	....	....	....	....	....
	Vancouver Canucks	**NHL**	**11**	**1**	**1**	**2**	**1**	**1**	**2**	**4**	**0**	**0**	**0**	**11**	**9.1**	**7**	**1**	**10**	**6**	**+2**	**20**	**2**	**7**	**9**	**4**	**0**	**0**	**0**
1994-95	Syracuse Crunch	AHL	27	9	9	18	....	....	....	10	....	....	....	....	....	....	....	....	....	....	....	....	....	....	....	....	....	....
	Vancouver Canucks	**NHL**	**27**	**4**	**4**	**8**	**7**	**6**	**13**	**2**	**0**	**1**	**0**	**30**	**13.3**	**12**	**1**	**19**	**10**	**+2**	....	....	....	....	....	....	....	....
	New York Rangers	**NHL**	**12**	**0**	**0**	**0**	**0**	**0**	**0**	**0**	**0**	**0**	**0**	**5**	**0.0**	**3**	**0**	**2**	**0**	**+1**	**8**	**0**	**0**	**0**	**2**	**0**	**0**	**0**
1995-96	**New York Rangers**	**NHL**	**5**	**0**	**0**	**0**	**0**	**0**	**0**	**2**	**0**	**0**	**0**	**5**	**0.0**	**0**	**0**	**2**	**1**	**–1**	....	....	....	....	....	....	....	....
	Binghamton Rangers	AHL	57	21	27	48	....	....	....	32	....	....	....	....	....	....	....	....	....	....	....	....	....	....	....	....	....	....
	Los Angeles Kings	**NHL**	**12**	**2**	**4**	**6**	**2**	**3**	**5**	**6**	**1**	**0**	**0**	**23**	**8.7**	**7**	**1**	**11**	**2**	**–3**	....	....	....	....	....	....	....	....

Season	Club	League	REGULAR SEASON																		PLAYOFFS							
			GP	G	A	Pts	AG	AA	APts	PIM	PP	SH	GW	S	%	TGF	PGF	TGA	PGA	+/–	GP	G	A	Pts	PIM	PP	SH	GW
1996-97	**Los Angeles Kings**	**NHL**	**15**	**1**	**3**	**4**	**1**	**3**	**4**	**8**	**0**	**1**	**1**	**26**	**3.8**	**5**	**0**	**14**	**1**	**–8**	....	....	....	....	....	....	....	....
	Phoenix Roadrunners	IHL	31	2	5	7	....	....	....	16	....	....	....	....	....	....	....	....	....	....	....	....	....	....	....	....	....	....
	Syracuse Crunch	AHL	26	14	11	25	....	....	....	18	....	....	....	....	....	....	....	....	....	....	3	1	0	1	2	....	....	....
1997-98	**Los Angeles Kings**	**NHL**	**34**	**5**	**3**	**8**	**6**	**3**	**9**	**32**	**1**	**0**	**1**	**60**	**8.3**	**13**	**1**	**12**	**2**	**+2**	**4**	**0**	**0**	**0**	**2**	**0**	**0**	**0**
	Fredericton Canadiens	AHL	28	7	8	15	....	....	....	36	....	....	....	....	....	....	....	....	....	....	....	....	....	....	....	....	....	....
	NHL Totals		**154**	**15**	**18**	**33**	**19**	**18**	**37**	**68**	**2**	**2**	**2**	**183**	**8.2**	**57**	**4**	**92**	**25**		**32**	**2**	**7**	**9**	**8**	**0**	**0**	**0**

Canadian Major Junior Scholastic Player of the Year (1992)

Traded to **Vancouver** by **St. Louis** with Jeff Brown and Bret Hedican for Craig Janney, March 21, 1994. Traded to **NY Rangers** by **Vancouver** for Corey Hirsch, April 7, 1995. Traded to **LA Kings** by **NY Rangers** with Ray Ferraro, Mattias Norstrom, Ian Laperriere and NY Rangers' 4th round choice (Sean Blanchard) in 1997 Entry Draft for Marty McSorley, Jari Kurri and Shane Churla, March 14, 1996.

• LAFLAMME, CHRISTIAN

Christian Laflamme D – R. 6'1", 202 lbs. b: St. Charles, Que., 11/24/1976. Chicago's 2nd choice, 45th overall, in 1995 Entry Draft.

Season	Club	League	GP	G	A	Pts	AG	AA	APts	PIM	PP	SH	GW	S	%	TGF	PGF	TGA	PGA	+/–	GP	G	A	Pts	PIM	PP	SH	GW
1992-93	Verdun College-Francais	QMJHL	69	2	17	19	....	....	....	85	....	....	....	....	....	....	....	....	....	....	3	0	2	2	6	....	....	....
1993-94	Verdun College-Francais	QMJHL	72	4	34	38	....	....	....	85	....	....	....	....	....	....	....	....	....	....	4	0	3	3	4	....	....	....
1994-95	Beauport Harfangs	QMJHL	67	6	41	47	....	....	....	82	....	....	....	....	....	....	....	....	....	....	8	1	4	5	6	....	....	....
1995-96	Beauport Harfangs	QMJHL	41	13	23	36	....	....	....	63	....	....	....	....	....	....	....	....	....	....	20	7	17	24	32	....	....	....
1996-97	**Chicago Blackhawks**	**NHL**	**4**	**0**	**1**	**1**	**0**	**1**	**1**	**2**	**0**	**0**	**0**	**3**	**0.0**	**4**	**0**	**1**	**0**	**+3**	....	....	....	....	....	....	....	....
	Indianapolis Ice	IHL	62	5	15	20	....	....	....	60	....	....	....	....	....	....	....	....	....	....	4	1	1	2	16	....	....	....
1997-98	**Chicago Blackhawks**	**NHL**	**72**	**0**	**11**	**11**	**0**	**11**	**11**	**59**	**0**	**0**	**0**	**75**	**0.0**	**37**	**3**	**25**	**5**	**+14**	....	....	....	....	....	....	....	....
	NHL Totals		**76**	**0**	**12**	**12**	**0**	**12**	**12**	**61**	**0**	**0**	**0**	**78**	**0.0**	**41**	**3**	**26**	**5**		....	....	....	....	....	....	....	....

QMJHL Second All-Star Team (1995)

• LAFLEUR, GUY

Guy "The Flower" Lafleur RW – R. 6', 185 lbs. b: Thurso, Que., 9/20/1951. Montreal's 1st choice, 1st overall, in 1971 Amateur Draft. **HHOF**

Season	Club	League	GP	G	A	Pts	AG	AA	APts	PIM	PP	SH	GW	S	%	TGF	PGF	TGA	PGA	+/–	GP	G	A	Pts	PIM	PP	SH	GW
1966-67	Quebec Aces	QJHL	8	1	1	2	....	....	....	0	....	....	....	....	....	....	....	....	....	....	....	....	....	....	....	....	....	....
1967-68	Quebec Aces	QJHL	43	30	19	49	....	....	....	....	....	....	....	....	....	....	....	....	....	....	....	....	....	....	....	....	....	....
1968-69	Quebec Aces	QJHL	49	50	60	110	....	....	....	83	....	....	....	....	....	....	....	....	....	....	....	....	....	....	....	....	....	....
1969-70	Quebec Remparts	QJHL	56	*103	67	170	....	....	....	105	....	....	....	....	....	....	....	....	....	....	15	*25	18	*43	34	....	....	....
1970-71	Quebec Remparts	QJHL	62	*130	79	*209	....	....	....	135	....	....	....	....	....	....	....	....	....	....	14	*22	*21	*43	24	....	....	....
1971-72	**Montreal Canadiens**	**NHL**	**73**	**29**	**35**	**64**	**31**	**32**	**63**	**48**	**5**	**0**	**5**	**187**	**15.5**	**99**	**27**	**45**	**0**	**+27**	**6**	**1**	**4**	**5**	**2**	**0**	**0**	**0**
1972-73	**Montreal Canadiens**	**NHL**	**69**	**28**	**27**	**55**	**28**	**23**	**51**	**51**	**9**	**0**	**7**	**176**	**15.9**	**80**	**26**	**39**	**1**	**+16**	**17**	**3**	**5**	**8**	**9**	**2**	**0**	**1**
1973-74	**Montreal Canadiens**	**NHL**	**73**	**21**	**35**	**56**	**21**	**30**	**51**	**29**	**3**	**1**	**2**	**167**	**12.6**	**87**	**25**	**54**	**2**	**+10**	**6**	**0**	**1**	**1**	**4**	**0**	**0**	**0**
1974-75	**Montreal Canadiens**	**NHL**	**70**	**53**	**66**	**119**	**49**	**52**	**101**	**37**	**15**	**2**	**11**	**260**	**20.4**	**166**	**59**	**65**	**10**	**+52**	**11**	**12**	**7**	**19**	**15**	**4**	**0**	**4**
1975-76	**Montreal Canadiens**	**NHL**	**80**	**56**	**69**	***125**	**53**	**54**	**107**	**36**	**18**	**0**	**12**	**303**	**18.5**	**179**	**63**	**49**	**1**	**+68**	**13**	**7**	**10**	**17**	**2**	**0**	**0**	**3**
1976-77	Canada	C Cup	7	1	5	6	....	....	....	12	....	....	....	....	....	....	....	....	....	....	....	....	....	....	....	....	....	....
	Montreal Canadiens	**NHL**	**80**	**56**	***80**	***136**	**54**	**65**	**119**	**20**	**14**	**0**	**8**	**291**	**19.2**	**179**	**47**	**43**	**0**	**+89**	**14**	**9**	***17**	***26**	**6**	**1**	**0**	**2**
1977-78	**Montreal Canadiens**	**NHL**	**78**	***60**	**72**	***132**	**58**	**59**	**117**	**26**	**15**	**0**	**12**	**307**	**19.5**	**186**	**57**	**57**	**1**	**+73**	**15**	***10**	**11**	***21**	**16**	**3**	**0**	**2**
1978-79	**Montreal Canadiens**	**NHL**	**80**	**52**	**77**	**129**	**48**	**59**	**107**	**28**	**13**	**0**	**12**	**342**	**15.2**	**178**	**59**	**64**	**1**	**+56**	**16**	**10**	***13**	***23**	**0**	**2**	**0**	**2**
	NHL All-Stars	Chal Cup	3	1	2	3	....	....	....	0	....	....	....	....	....	....	....	....	....	....	....	....	....	....	....	....	....	....
1979-80	**Montreal Canadiens**	**NHL**	**74**	**50**	**75**	**125**	**45**	**58**	**103**	**12**	**15**	**0**	**7**	**323**	**15.5**	**187**	**70**	**81**	**4**	**+40**	**3**	**3**	**1**	**4**	**0**	**0**	**0**	**0**
1980-81	**Montreal Canadiens**	**NHL**	**51**	**27**	**43**	**70**	**22**	**30**	**52**	**29**	**7**	**0**	**7**	**191**	**14.1**	**100**	**44**	**36**	**4**	**+24**	**3**	**0**	**1**	**1**	**2**	**0**	**0**	**0**
	Canada	WEC-A	7	1	0	1	....	....	....	2	....	....	....	....	....	....	....	....	....	....	....	....	....	....	....	....	....	....
1981-82	Canada	C Cup	7	2	9	11	....	....	....	0	....	....	....	....	....	....	....	....	....	....	....	....	....	....	....	....	....	....
	Montreal Canadiens	**NHL**	**66**	**27**	**57**	**84**	**21**	**38**	**59**	**24**	**9**	**0**	**3**	**233**	**11.6**	**111**	**35**	**46**	**3**	**+33**	**5**	**2**	**1**	**3**	**4**	**2**	**0**	**0**
1982-83	**Montreal Canadiens**	**NHL**	**68**	**27**	**49**	**76**	**22**	**34**	**56**	**12**	**9**	**0**	**1**	**177**	**15.3**	**114**	**42**	**66**	**0**	**+6**	**3**	**0**	**2**	**2**	**2**	**0**	**0**	**0**
1983-84	**Montreal Canadiens**	**NHL**	**80**	**30**	**40**	**70**	**24**	**27**	**51**	**19**	**6**	**0**	**6**	**217**	**13.8**	**113**	**46**	**83**	**2**	**–14**	**12**	**0**	**3**	**3**	**5**	**0**	**0**	**0**
1984-85	**Montreal Canadiens**	**NHL**	**19**	**2**	**3**	**5**	**2**	**2**	**4**	**10**	**0**	**0**	**0**	**35**	**5.7**	**13**	**4**	**12**	**0**	**–3**	....	....	....	....	....	....	....	....
1985-1988			DID NOT PLAY – RETIRED																									
1988-89	**New York Rangers**	**NHL**	**67**	**18**	**27**	**45**	**15**	**19**	**34**	**12**	**6**	**0**	**2**	**122**	**14.8**	**73**	**31**	**41**	**0**	**+1**	**4**	**1**	**0**	**1**	**0**	**1**	**0**	**0**
1989-90	**Quebec Nordiques**	**NHL**	**39**	**12**	**22**	**34**	**10**	**16**	**26**	**4**	**6**	**0**	**2**	**100**	**12.0**	**50**	**27**	**38**	**0**	**–15**	....	....	....	....	....	....	....	....
1990-91	**Quebec Nordiques**	**NHL**	**59**	**12**	**16**	**28**	**11**	**12**	**23**	**2**	**3**	**0**	**0**	**90**	**13.3**	**49**	**15**	**44**	**0**	**–10**	....	....	....	....	....	....	....	....
	NHL Totals		**1126**	**560**	**793**	**1353**	**514**	**610**	**1124**	**399**	**153**	**3**	**97**	**3521**	**15.9**	**1964**	**677**	**863**	**29**		**128**	**58**	**76**	**134**	**67**	**15**	**0**	**14**

QJHL First All-Star Team (1970, 1971) • NHL First All-Star Team (1975, 1976, 1977, 1978, 1979, 1980) • Won Art Ross Trophy (1976, 1977, 1978) • Won Lester B. Pearson Award (1976, 1977, 1978) • Won Hart Trophy (1977, 1978) • Won Conn Smythe Trophy (1977) • NHL Plus/Minus Leader (1978)

Played in NHL All-Star Game (1975, 1976, 1977, 1978, 1980, 1991)

Signed as a free agent by **NY Rangers**, September 26, 1988. Signed as a free agent by **Quebec**, July 14, 1989. NY Rangers received Quebec's 5th round choice (Sergei Zubov) as compensation. Claimed by **Minnesota** from **Quebec** in Expansion Draft, May 30, 1991. Traded to **Quebec** by **Minnesota** for Alan Haworth, May 31, 1991.

• LaFONTAINE, PAT

Pat LaFontaine C – R. 5'10", 182 lbs. b: St. Louis, MO, 2/22/1965. NY Islanders' 1st choice, 3rd overall, in 1983 Entry Draft.

Season	Club	League	GP	G	A	Pts	AG	AA	APts	PIM	PP	SH	GW	S	%	TGF	PGF	TGA	PGA	+/–	GP	G	A	Pts	PIM	PP	SH	GW
1981-82	Detroit Compuware	NASHL	79	175	149	324	....	....	....	....	....	....	....	....	....	....	....	....	....	....	....	....	....	....	....	....	....	....
1982-83	Verdun Jr. Canadiens	QMJHL	70	*104	*130	*234	....	....	....	10	....	....	....	....	....	....	....	....	....	....	15	11	*24	*35	4	....	....	....
1983-84	United States	Nat-Team	58	56	55	111	....	....	....	22	....	....	....	....	....	....	....	....	....	....	....	....	....	....	....	....	....	....
	United States	Olympics	6	5	3	8	....	....	....	0	....	....	....	....	....	....	....	....	....	....	....	....	....	....	....	....	....	....
	New York Islanders	**NHL**	**15**	**13**	**6**	**19**	**10**	**4**	**14**	**6**	**1**	**0**	**0**	**35**	**37.1**	**23**	**2**	**12**	**0**	**+9**	**16**	**3**	**6**	**9**	**8**	**0**	**0**	**0**
1984-85	**New York Islanders**	**NHL**	**67**	**19**	**35**	**54**	**16**	**24**	**40**	**32**	**1**	**0**	**1**	**173**	**11.0**	**82**	**14**	**60**	**1**	**+9**	**9**	**1**	**2**	**3**	**4**	**0**	**0**	**0**
1985-86	**New York Islanders**	**NHL**	**65**	**30**	**23**	**53**	**24**	**15**	**39**	**43**	**2**	**0**	**4**	**172**	**17.4**	**74**	**14**	**46**	**2**	**+16**	**3**	**1**	**0**	**1**	**0**	**1**	**0**	**0**
1986-87	**New York Islanders**	**NHL**	**80**	**38**	**32**	**70**	**33**	**23**	**56**	**70**	**19**	**1**	**6**	**219**	**17.4**	**104**	**53**	**71**	**10**	**–10**	**14**	**5**	**7**	**12**	**10**	**1**	**0**	**2**
1987-88	United States	C Cup	5	3	0	3	....	....	....	0	....	....	....	....	....	....	....	....	....	....	....	....	....	....	....	....	....	....
	New York Islanders	**NHL**	**75**	**47**	**45**	**92**	**40**	**32**	**72**	**52**	**15**	**0**	**7**	**242**	**19.4**	**125**	**52**	**67**	**6**	**+12**	**6**	**4**	**5**	**9**	**8**	**1**	**0**	**1**
1988-89	**New York Islanders**	**NHL**	**79**	**45**	**43**	**88**	**38**	**30**	**68**	**26**	**16**	**0**	**4**	**288**	**15.6**	**115**	**52**	**77**	**6**	**–8**	....	....	....	....	....	....	....	....
	United States	WEC-A	10	5	3	8	....	....	....	8	....	....	....	....	....	....	....	....	....	....	....	....	....	....	....	....	....	....
1989-90	**New York Islanders**	**NHL**	**74**	**54**	**51**	**105**	**47**	**36**	**83**	**38**	**13**	**2**	**8**	**286**	**18.9**	**141**	**66**	**98**	**10**	**–13**	**2**	**0**	**1**	**1**	**0**	**0**	**0**	**0**
1990-91	**New York Islanders**	**NHL**	**75**	**41**	**44**	**85**	**38**	**33**	**71**	**42**	**12**	**2**	**5**	**225**	**18.2**	**117**	**45**	**91**	**13**	**–6**	....	....	....	....	....	....	....	....
1991-92	United States	C Cup	6	3	1	4	....	....	....	2	....	....	....	....	....	....	....	....	....	....	....	....	....	....	....	....	....	....
	Buffalo Sabres	**NHL**	**57**	**46**	**47**	**93**	**42**	**35**	**77**	**98**	**23**	**0**	**5**	**203**	**22.7**	**136**	**70**	**67**	**11**	**+10**	**7**	**8**	**3**	**11**	**4**	**5**	**1**	**1**
1992-93	**Buffalo Sabres**	**NHL**	**84**	**53**	**95**	**148**	**44**	**65**	**109**	**63**	**20**	**2**	**7**	**306**	**17.3**	**200**	**88**	**105**	**4**	**+11**	**7**	**2**	**10**	**12**	**0**	**1**	**0**	**0**
1993-94	**Buffalo Sabres**	**NHL**	**16**	**5**	**13**	**18**	**5**	**10**	**15**	**2**	**1**	**0**	**0**	**40**	**12.5**	**30**	**11**	**28**	**5**	**–4**	....	....	....	....	....	....	....	....
1994-95	**Buffalo Sabres**	**NHL**	**22**	**12**	**15**	**27**	**21**	**22**	**43**	**4**	**6**	**1**	**3**	**54**	**22.2**	**41**	**22**	**18**	**1**	**+2**	**5**	**2**	**2**	**4**	**2**	**1**	**0**	**0**
1995-96	**Buffalo Sabres**	**NHL**	**76**	**40**	**51**	**91**	**40**	**42**	**82**	**36**	**15**	**3**	**7**	**224**	**17.9**	**133**	**68**	**90**	**17**	**–8**	....	....	....	....	....	....	....	....
1996-97	United States	W Cup	5	2	2	4	....	....	....	2	....	....	....	....	....	....	....	....	....	....	....	....	....	....	....	....	....	....
	Buffalo Sabres	**NHL**	**13**	**2**	**6**	**8**	**2**	**5**	**7**	**4**	**1**	**0**	**0**	**38**	**5.3**	**11**	**6**	**13**	**0**	**–8**	....	....	....	....	....	....	....	....
1997-98	**New York Rangers**	**NHL**	**67**	**23**	**39**	**62**	**27**	**38**	**65**	**36**	**11**	**0**	**2**	**160**	**14.4**	**75**	**38**	**56**	**3**	**–16**	....	....	....	....	....	....	....	....
	United States	Olympics	4	1	1	2	....	....	....	0	....	....	....	....	....	....	....	....	....	....	....	....	....	....	....	....	....	....
	NHL Totals		**865**	**468**	**545**	**1013**	**427**	**414**	**841**	**552**	**156**	**11**	**59**	**2665**	**17.6**	**1407**	**601**	**899**	**89**		**69**	**26**	**36**	**62**	**36**	**10**	**1**	**4**

QMJHL First All-Star Team (1983) • Canadian Major Junior Player of the Year (1983) • Won Dodge Performer of the Year Award (1990) • NHL Second All-Star Team (1993) • Won Bill Masterton Memorial Trophy (1995)

Played in NHL All-Star Game (1988, 1989, 1990, 1991, 1993)

Traded to **Buffalo** by **NY Islanders** with Randy Hillier, Randy Wood and NY Islanders' 4th round choice (Dean Melanson) in 1992 Entry Draft for Pierre Turgeon, Uwe Krupp, Benoit Hogue and Dave McLlwain, October 25, 1991. Traded to **NY Rangers** by **Buffalo** for NY Rangers' 2nd round choice (Andrew Peters) in 1998 Entry Draft and future considerations, September 29, 1997.

• LaFOREST, BOB

Bob LaForest RW – R. 5'10", 195 lbs. b: Sault Ste. Marie, Ont., 5/19/1963. Los Angeles' 6th choice, 89th overall, in 1983 Entry Draft.

			REGULAR SEASON																		PLAYOFFS							
Season	Club	League	GP	G	A	Pts	AG	AA	APts	PIM	PP	SH	GW	S	%	TGF	PGF	TGA	PGA	+/–	GP	G	A	Pts	PIM	PP	SH	GW
1980-81	Niagara Falls Flyers	OHA	47	10	6	16	....	....	....	21	....	....	....	....	....	....	....	....	....	....	11	1	3	4	18	....	....	....
1981-82	Niagara Falls Flyers	OHL	66	31	40	71	....	....	....	40	....	....	....	....	....	....	....	....	....	....	5	4	5	9	0	....	....	....
1982-83	North Bay Centennials	OHL	65	58	38	96	....	....	....	32	....	....	....	....	....	....	....	....	....	....	8	5	2	7	8	....	....	....
1983-84	**Los Angeles Kings**	**NHL**	**5**	**1**	**0**	**1**	**1**	**0**	**1**	**2**	**1**	**0**	**0**	**15**	**6.7**	**6**	**3**	**6**	**0**	**–3**	....	....	....	....	....	....	....	....
	New Haven Nighthawks	AHL	26	2	7	9	....	....	....	0	....	....	....	....	....	....	....	....	....	....	....	....	....	....	....	....	....	....
	Hershey Bears	AHL	42	11	16	27	....	....	....	10	....	....	....	....	....	....	....	....	....	....	....	....	....	....	....	....	....	....
1984-85	Indianapolis Checkers	IHL	18	3	6	9	....	....	....	0	....	....	....	....	....	....	....	....	....	....	....	....	....	....	....	....	....	....
	Fort Wayne Komets	IHL	3	1	0	1	....	....	....	0	....	....	....	....	....	....	....	....	....	....	....	....	....	....	....	....	....	....
1985-86	Milwaukee Admirals	IHL	3	0	0	0	....	....	....	0	....	....	....	....	....	....	....	....	....	....	....	....	....	....	....	....	....	....
	NHL Totals		**5**	**1**	**0**	**1**	**1**	**0**	**1**	**2**	**1**	**0**	**0**	**15**	**6.7**	**6**	**3**	**6**	**0**		....	....	....	....	....	....	....	....

Traded to **Boston** by **LA Kings** for Marco Baron, January 3, 1984.

• LAFORGE, CLAUDE

Claude Laforge LW – L. 5'9", 172 lbs. b: Sorel, Que., 7/1/1936.

Season	Club	League	GP	G	A	Pts	AG	AA	APts	PIM	PP	SH	GW	S	%	TGF	PGF	TGA	PGA	+/–	GP	G	A	Pts	PIM	PP	SH	GW
1954-55	Montreal Jr. Canadiens	QJHL	45	18	4	22	....	....	....	43	....	....	....	....	....	....	....	....	....	....	5	1	0	1	0	....	....	....
1955-56	Montreal Jr. Canadiens	QJHL	STATISTICS NOT AVAILABLE																									
	Montreal Royals	QHL	2	0	0	0	....	....	....	2	....	....	....	....	....	....	....	....	....	....	....	....	....	....	....	....	....	....
1956-57	Shawinigan Cataracts	QHL	60	12	13	25	....	....	....	10	....	....	....	....	....	....	....	....	....	....	....	....	....	....	....	....	....	....
	Cincinnati Mohawks	IHL	8	5	5	10	....	....	....	2	....	....	....	....	....	....	....	....	....	....	....	....	....	....	....	....	....	....
1957-58	**Montreal Canadiens**	**NHL**	**5**	**0**	**0**	**0**	**0**	**0**	**0**	**0**	....	....	....	....	....	....	....	....	....	....	....	....	....	....	....	....	....	....
	Shawinigan Cataracts	QHL	52	26	27	53	....	....	....	45	....	....	....	....	....	....	....	....	....	....	....	....	....	....	....	....	....	....
	Rochester Americans	AHL	14	7	6	13	....	....	....	10	....	....	....	....	....	....	....	....	....	....	....	....	....	....	....	....	....	....
1958-59	**Detroit Red Wings**	**NHL**	**57**	**2**	**5**	**7**	**3**	**5**	**8**	**18**	....	....	....	....	....	....	....	....	....	....	....	....	....	....	....	....	....	....
	Hershey Bears	AHL	10	4	5	9	....	....	....	16	....	....	....	....	....	....	....	....	....	....	....	....	....	....	....	....	....	....
1959-60	Hershey Bears	AHL	68	27	31	58	....	....	....	38	....	....	....	....	....	....	....	....	....	....	....	....	....	....	....	....	....	....
1960-61	**Detroit Red Wings**	**NHL**	**10**	**1**	**0**	**1**	**1**	**0**	**1**	**2**	....	....	....	....	....	....	....	....	....	....	....	....	....	....	....	....	....	....
	Hershey Bears	AHL	49	20	30	50	....	....	....	55	....	....	....	....	....	....	....	....	....	....	8	2	1	3	*35	....	....	....
1961-62	**Detroit Red Wings**	**NHL**	**38**	**10**	**9**	**19**	**12**	**9**	**21**	**20**	....	....	....	....	....	....	....	....	....	....	....	....	....	....	....	....	....	....
	Hershey Bears	AHL	31	13	13	26	....	....	....	59	....	....	....	....	....	....	....	....	....	....	....	....	....	....	....	....	....	....
1962-63	Pittsburgh Hornets	AHL	50	10	23	33	....	....	....	73	....	....	....	....	....	....	....	....	....	....	....	....	....	....	....	....	....	....
1963-64	**Detroit Red Wings**	**NHL**	**17**	**2**	**3**	**5**	**3**	**3**	**6**	**4**	....	....	....	....	....	....	....	....	....	....	....	....	....	....	....	....	....	....
	Pittsburgh Hornets	AHL	51	19	23	42	....	....	....	59	....	....	....	....	....	....	....	....	....	....	5	1	3	4	4	....	....	....
1964-65	**Detroit Red Wings**	**NHL**	**1**	**0**	**0**	**0**	**0**	**0**	**0**	**2**	....	....	....	....	....	....	....	....	....	....	....	....	....	....	....	....	....	....
	Pittsburgh Hornets	AHL	67	23	32	55	....	....	....	26	....	....	....	....	....	....	....	....	....	....	4	4	2	6	2	....	....	....
1965-66	Pittsburgh–Quebec	AHL	64	13	26	39	....	....	....	38	....	....	....	....	....	....	....	....	....	....	....	....	....	....	....	....	....	....
1966-67	Quebec Aces	AHL	60	16	25	41	....	....	....	46	....	....	....	....	....	....	....	....	....	....	5	4	2	6	0	....	....	....
1967-68	**Philadelphia Flyers**	**NHL**	**63**	**9**	**16**	**25**	**11**	**17**	**28**	**36**	**0**	**0**	**2**	**106**	**8.5**	**39**	**3**	**38**	**10**	**+8**	**5**	**1**	**2**	**3**	**15**	**0**	**0**	**0**
	Quebec Aces	AHL	8	5	4	9	....	....	....	2	....	....	....	....	....	....	....	....	....	....	....	....	....	....	....	....	....	....
1968-69	**Philadelphia Flyers**	**NHL**	**2**	**0**	**0**	**0**	**0**	**0**	**0**	**0**	**0**	**0**	**0**	**1**	**0.0**	**0**	**0**	**3**	**1**	**–2**	....	....	....	....	....	....	....	....
	Quebec Aces	AHL	57	21	31	52	....	....	....	24	....	....	....	....	....	....	....	....	....	....	11	0	7	7	2	....	....	....
1969-70	Quebec Aces	AHL	72	28	39	67	....	....	....	44	....	....	....	....	....	....	....	....	....	....	6	0	2	2	6	....	....	....
1970-71	Denver Spurs	WHL	64	25	28	53	....	....	....	34	....	....	....	....	....	....	....	....	....	....	5	2	3	5	4	....	....	....
1971-72	Denver Spurs	WHL	56	15	31	46	....	....	....	12	....	....	....	....	....	....	....	....	....	....	9	1	5	6	6	....	....	....
1972-73	Denver Spurs	WHL	25	8	11	19	....	....	....	12	....	....	....	....	....	....	....	....	....	....	....	....	....	....	....	....	....	....
	NHL Totals		**193**	**24**	**33**	**57**	**30**	**34**	**64**	**82**	**0**	**0**	**2**	**107**	**22.4**	**39**	**3**	**41**	**11**		**5**	**1**	**2**	**3**	**15**	**0**	**0**	**0**

QHL Second All-Star Team (1958)

Traded to **Detroit** by **Montreal** with Gene Achtymichuk and Bud MacPherson for cash, June 3, 1958. Traded to **Quebec** (AHL) by **Detroit** (Pittsburgh - AHL) for Terry Gray, March 1, 1966. NHL rights transferred to **Philadelphia** after NHL club purchased **Quebec** (AHL) franchise, May 8, 1967. Traded to **Denver** (WHL) by **Philadelphia** for cash, August, 1970.

• LAFORGE, MARC

Marc Laforge LW – L. 6'2", 210 lbs. b: Sudbury, Ont., 1/3/1968. Hartford's 2nd choice, 32nd overall, in 1986 Entry Draft.

Season	Club	League	GP	G	A	Pts	AG	AA	APts	PIM	PP	SH	GW	S	%	TGF	PGF	TGA	PGA	+/–	GP	G	A	Pts	PIM	PP	SH	GW
1984-85	Kingston Canadians	OHL	57	1	5	6	....	....	....	214	....	....	....	....	....	....	....	....	....	....	....	....	....	....	....	....	....	....
1985-86	Kingston Canadians	OHL	60	1	13	14	....	....	....	248	....	....	....	....	....	....	....	....	....	....	10	0	1	1	30	....	....	....
1986-87	Kingston Canadians	OHL	53	2	10	12	....	....	....	224	....	....	....	....	....	....	....	....	....	....	12	1	0	1	79	....	....	....
	Binghamton Whalers	AHL	....	....	....	....	....	....	....	....	....	....	....	....	....	....	....	....	....	....	4	0	0	0	7	....	....	....
1987-88	Sudbury Wolves	OHL	14	0	2	2	....	....	....	68	....	....	....	....	....	....	....	....	....	....	....	....	....	....	....	....	....	....
1988-89	Binghamton Whalers	AHL	38	2	2	4	....	....	....	179	....	....	....	....	....	....	....	....	....	....	....	....	....	....	....	....	....	....
	Indianapolis Ice	IHL	14	0	2	2	....	....	....	138	....	....	....	....	....	....	....	....	....	....	....	....	....	....	....	....	....	....
1989-90	**Hartford Whalers**	**NHL**	**9**	**0**	**0**	**0**	**0**	**0**	**0**	**43**	**0**	**0**	**0**	**0**	**0.0**	**0**	**0**	**1**	**0**	**–1**	....	....	....	....	....	....	....	....
	Binghamton Whalers	AHL	25	2	6	8	....	....	....	111	....	....	....	....	....	....	....	....	....	....	....	....	....	....	....	....	....	....
	Cape Breton Oilers	AHL	3	0	1	1	....	....	....	24	....	....	....	....	....	....	....	....	....	....	3	0	0	0	27	....	....	....
1990-91	Cape Breton Oilers	AHL	49	1	7	8	....	....	....	217	....	....	....	....	....	....	....	....	....	....	....	....	....	....	....	....	....	....
1991-92	Cape Breton Oilers	AHL	59	0	14	14	....	....	....	341	....	....	....	....	....	....	....	....	....	....	4	0	0	0	24	....	....	....
1992-93	Cape Breton Oilers	AHL	77	1	12	13	....	....	....	208	....	....	....	....	....	....	....	....	....	....	15	1	2	3	*78	....	....	....
1993-94	**Edmonton Oilers**	**NHL**	**5**	**0**	**0**	**0**	**0**	**0**	**0**	**21**	**0**	**0**	**0**	**0**	**0.0**	**3**	**0**	**7**	**2**	**–2**	....	....	....	....	....	....	....	....
	Cape Breton Oilers	AHL	14	0	0	0	....	....	....	91	....	....	....	....	....	....	....	....	....	....	....	....	....	....	....	....	....	....
	Salt Lake Golden Eagles	IHL	43	0	2	2	....	....	....	242	....	....	....	....	....	....	....	....	....	....	....	....	....	....	....	....	....	....
1994-95	Cape Breton Oilers	AHL	18	0	1	1	....	....	....	80	....	....	....	....	....	....	....	....	....	....	....	....	....	....	....	....	....	....
	Syracuse Crunch	AHL	39	1	5	6	....	....	....	202	....	....	....	....	....	....	....	....	....	....	....	....	....	....	....	....	....	....
1995-96	Minnesota Moose	IHL	20	0	2	2	....	....	....	102	....	....	....	....	....	....	....	....	....	....	....	....	....	....	....	....	....	....
	NHL Totals		**14**	**0**	**0**	**0**	**0**	**0**	**0**	**64**	**0**	**0**	**0**	**0**	**0.0**	**3**	**0**	**8**	**2**		....	....	....	....	....	....	....	....

Traded to **Edmonton** by **Hartford** for the rights to Cam Brauer, March 6, 1990. Traded to **NY Islanders** by **Edmonton** for Brent Grieve, December 15, 1993.

• LAFRAMBOISE, PETE

Pete Laframboise LW/C – L. 6'2", 185 lbs. b: Ottawa, Ont., 1/18/1950. California's 2nd choice, 19th overall, in 1970 Amateur Draft.

Season	Club	League	GP	G	A	Pts	AG	AA	APts	PIM	PP	SH	GW	S	%	TGF	PGF	TGA	PGA	+/–	GP	G	A	Pts	PIM	PP	SH	GW
1966-67	Oshawa Generals	OHA	1	0	0	0	....	....	....	0	....	....	....	....	....	....	....	....	....	....	....	....	....	....	....	....	....	....
1967-68	Ottawa 67's	OHA	35	6	5	11	....	....	....	36	....	....	....	....	....	....	....	....	....	....	....	....	....	....	....	....	....	....
1968-69	Ottawa 67's	OHA	47	31	39	70	....	....	....	98	....	....	....	....	....	....	....	....	....	....	7	10	4	14	12	....	....	....
1969-70	Ottawa 67's	OHA	54	26	46	72	....	....	....	68	....	....	....	....	....	....	....	....	....	....	....	....	....	....	....	....	....	....
1970-71	Providence Reds	AHL	64	13	19	32	....	....	....	36	....	....	....	....	....	....	....	....	....	....	10	0	2	2	4	....	....	....
1971-72	**California Golden Seals**	**NHL**	**5**	**0**	**0**	**0**	**0**	**0**	**0**	**0**	**0**	**0**	**0**	**3**	**0.0**	**1**	**1**	**6**	**1**	**–5**	....	....	....	....	....	....	....	....
	Baltimore Clippers	AHL	72	37	44	81	....	....	....	95	....	....	....	....	....	....	....	....	....	....	18	5	8	13	24	....	....	....
1972-73	**California Golden Seals**	**NHL**	**77**	**16**	**25**	**41**	**16**	**21**	**37**	**26**	**2**	**0**	**1**	**113**	**14.2**	**56**	**8**	**72**	**0**	**–24**	....	....	....	....	....	....	....	....
1973-74	**California Golden Seals**	**NHL**	**65**	**7**	**7**	**14**	**7**	**6**	**13**	**14**	**0**	**0**	**0**	**67**	**10.4**	**21**	**1**	**52**	**4**	**–28**	....	....	....	....	....	....	....	....
1974-75	**Washington Capitals**	**NHL**	**45**	**5**	**10**	**15**	**5**	**8**	**13**	**22**	**0**	**0**	**0**	**86**	**5.8**	**20**	**3**	**56**	**2**	**–37**	....	....	....	....	....	....	....	....
	Pittsburgh Penguins	**NHL**	**35**	**5**	**13**	**18**	**5**	**10**	**15**	**8**	**3**	**0**	**0**	**33**	**15.2**	**30**	**12**	**18**	**3**	**+3**	**9**	**1**	**0**	**1**	**0**	**0**	**0**	**0**
1975-76	Hershey Bears	AHL	69	18	47	65	....	....	....	79	....	....	....	....	....	....	....	....	....	....	7	2	3	5	6	....	....	....
1976-77	Edmonton Oilers	WHA	17	0	5	5	....	....	....	12	....	....	....	....	....	....	....	....	....	....	....	....	....	....	....	....	....	....
	Springfield Indians	AHL	53	18	50	68	....	....	....	87	....	....	....	....	....	....	....	....	....	....	....	....	....	....	....	....	....	....
1977-78	Springfield Indians	AHL	68	20	50	70	....	....	....	73	....	....	....	....	....	....	....	....	....	....	4	1	1	2	2	....	....	....
1978-79	Binghamton Dusters	AHL	39	8	25	33	....	....	....	18	....	....	....	....	....	....	....	....	....	....	....	....	....	....	....	....	....	....
	NHL Totals		**227**	**33**	**55**	**88**	**33**	**45**	**78**	**70**	**5**	**0**	**1**	**302**	**10.9**	**128**	**25**	**204**	**10**		**9**	**1**	**0**	**1**	**0**	**0**	**0**	**0**
	Other Major League Totals		17	0	5	5	....	....	....	12	....	....	....	....	....	....	....	....	....	....	....	....	....	....	....	....	....	....

AHL First All-Star Team (1972)

Selected by **LA Sharks** in 1972 WHA General Player Draft, February 12, 1972. Claimed by **Washington** from **California** in Expansion Draft, June 12, 1974. Traded to **Pittsburgh** by **Washington** for Ron Jones, January 21, 1975. Signed as a free agent by **Edmonton** (WHA) after **LA Sharks** (WHA) franchise folded, May, 1975. Traded to **Birmingham** (WHA) by **Edmonton** (WHA) with Dan Arndt and Chris Evans for Lou Nistico and Jeff Jacques, September, 1977.

• LAFRENIERE, JASON

Jason Lafreniere C – R. 5'11", 185 lbs. b: St. Catharines, Ont., 12/6/1966. Quebec's 2nd choice, 36th overall, in 1985 Entry Draft.

Season	Club	League	GP	G	A	Pts	AG	AA	APts	PIM	PP	SH	GW	S	%	TGF	PGF	TGA	PGA	+/–	GP	G	A	Pts	PIM	PP	SH	GW
1982-83	Orillia Travelways	Jr. B	48	17	40	57	....	....	....	9	....	....	....	....	....	....	....	....	....	....	....	....	....	....	....	....	....	....
1983-84	Brantford Alexanders	OHL	70	24	57	81	....	....	....	4	....	....	....	....	....	....	....	....	....	....	6	2	4	6	2	....	....	....
1984-85	Hamilton Steelhawks	OHL	59	26	69	95	....	....	....	10	....	....	....	....	....	....	....	....	....	....	17	12	16	28	0	....	....	....

Season	Club	League	GP	G	A	Pts	AG	AA	APts	PIM	PP	SH	GW	S	%	TGF	PGF	TGA	PGA	+/–	GP	G	A	Pts	PIM	PP	SH	GW
			REGULAR SEASON																		PLAYOFFS							
1985-86	Hamilton Steelhawks	OHL	14	12	10	22				2																		
	Belleville Bulls	OHL	48	37	73	110				2											23	10	*22	*32	6			
1986-87	**Quebec Nordiques**	**NHL**	**56**	**13**	**15**	**28**	**11**	**11**	**22**	**8**	**7**	**0**	**1**	**55**	**23.6**	**40**	**23**	**20**	**0**	**–3**	**12**	**1**	**5**	**6**	**2**	**1**	**0**	**0**
	Fredericton Express	AHL	11	3	11	14				0																		
1987-88	**Quebec Nordiques**	**NHL**	**40**	**10**	**19**	**29**	**9**	**14**	**23**	**4**	**5**	**0**	**1**	**54**	**18.5**	**43**	**22**	**22**	**0**	**–1**								
	Fredericton Express	AHL	32	12	19	31				38																		
1988-89	**New York Rangers**	**NHL**	**30**	**8**	**16**	**24**	**7**	**11**	**18**	**6**	**3**	**0**	**0**	**42**	**19.0**	**34**	**15**	**22**	**0**	**–3**	**3**	**0**	**0**	**0**	**17**	**0**	**0**	**0**
	Denver Rangers	IHL	24	10	19	29				17																		
1989-90	Flint Spirits	IHL	41	9	25	34				34																		
	Phoenix Roadrunners	IHL	14	4	9	13				0																		
1990-91	Canada	Nat Team	59	26	33	59				50																		
1991-92	EV Landshut	Germany	23	7	22	29				16																		
	San Diego Gulls	IHL	5	1	2	3				2																		
1992-93	**Tampa Bay Lightning**	**NHL**	**11**	**3**	**3**	**6**	**2**	**2**	**4**	**4**	**1**	**0**	**0**	**17**	**17.6**	**7**	**3**	**10**	**0**	**–6**								
	Atlanta Knights	IHL	63	23	47	70				34											9	3	4	7	22			
1993-94	**Tampa Bay Lightning**	**NHL**	**1**	**0**	**0**	**0**	**0**	**0**	**0**	**0**	**0**	**0**	**0**	**2**	**0.0**	**0**	**0**	**1**	**0**	**–1**								
	Milwaukee Admirals	IHL	52	14	47	61				16																		
1994-95	Courmaosta	Italy	41	25	47	72				24																		
1995-96	Villacher SV	Austria	34	30	26	56				42																		
1996-97	Sheffield Steelers	Britain	22	11	18	29				18											7	4	2	6	4			
	NHL Totals		**146**	**34**	**53**	**87**	**29**	**38**	**67**	**22**	**16**	**0**	**2**	**170**	**20.0**	**124**	**63**	**75**	**0**		**15**	**1**	**5**	**6**	**19**	**1**	**0**	**0**

OHL First All-Star Team (1986)

Traded to **NY Rangers** by **Quebec** with Normand Rochefort for Bruce Bell, Jari Gronstrand, Walt Poddubny and NY Rangers' 4th round choice (Eric Dubois) in 1989 Entry Draft, August 1, 1988. Signed as a free agent by **Tampa Bay**, July 29, 1992.

• LAFRENIERE, ROGER

Roger Lafreniere LW – L. 6', 190 lbs. b: Montreal, Que., 7/24/1942.

Season	Club	League	GP	G	A	Pts	AG	AA	APts	PIM	PP	SH	GW	S	%	TGF	PGF	TGA	PGA	+/–	GP	G	A	Pts	PIM	PP	SH	GW
1961-62	Hamilton Red Wings	OHA	48	4	19	23				76											10	2	4	6	15			
1962-63	**Detroit Red Wings**	**NHL**	**3**	**0**	**0**	**0**	**0**	**0**	**0**	**4**																		
	Pittsburgh Hornets	AHL	65	2	14	16				123																		
1963-64	Cincinnati Wings	CHL	66	3	24	27				112																		
1964-65	Memphis Wings	CHL	2	0	1	1				0																		
	Providence Reds	AHL	57	4	13	17				96																		
1965-66	Buffalo Bisons	AHL	72	1	16	17				76																		
1966-67	Buffalo Bisons	AHL	71	2	16	18				72																		
1967-68	Buffalo Bisons	AHL	5	0	1	1				0																		
	Omaha Knights	CHL	65	10	25	35				129																		
1968-69	Omaha Knights	CHL	70	14	29	43				122											7	1	5	6	16			
1969-70	Denver Spurs	WHL	61	4	19	23				85																		
1970-71	Denver Spurs	WHL	58	5	13	18				47											5	0	1	1	12			
1971-72	Denver Spurs	WHL	71	10	24	34				87											9	0	1	1	8			
1972-73	**St. Louis Blues**	**NHL**	**10**	**0**	**0**	**0**	**0**	**0**	**0**	**0**	**0**	**0**	**0**	**3**	**0.0**	**0**	**0**	**3**	**2**	**–1**								
	Denver Spurs	WHL	53	9	20	29				100											5	0	2	2	8			
1973-74	San Diego Gulls	WHL	70	9	14	23				75											4	1	0	1	0			
1974-75	Roanoke Valley Rebels	SHL	29	2	18	20				24																		
	NHL Totals		**13**	**0**	**0**	**0**	**0**	**0**	**0**	**4**	**0**	**0**	**0**	**3**	**0.0**	**0**	**0**	**3**	**2**									

Claimed by **Buffalo** (AHL) from **Detroit** in Reverse Draft, June 9, 1965. Traded to **St. Louis** (Denver-WHL) by **Buffalo** for cash, October, 1969. Traded to **San Diego** (WHL) by **St. Louis** for cash, September, 1973.

• LAGACE, JEAN-GUY

Jean Guy Lagace D – R. 5'10", 185 lbs. b: L'Abord A Plouffe, Que., 2/5/1945.

Season	Club	League	GP	G	A	Pts	AG	AA	APts	PIM	PP	SH	GW	S	%	TGF	PGF	TGA	PGA	+/–	GP	G	A	Pts	PIM	PP	SH	GW
1963-64	Laval College	QUAA	STATISTICS NOT AVAILABLE																									
1964-65	Montreal Jr. Canadiens	OHA	4	0	0	0				0																		
1965-66	Muskegon Zephyrs	IHL	66	10	33	43				163											4	0	0	0	8			
1966-67	Muskegon Mohawks	IHL	72	14	25	39				162																		
1967-68	Muskegon Mohawks	IHL	65	14	48	62				157											9	2	5	7	42			
1968-69	**Pittsburgh Penguins**	**NHL**	**17**	**0**	**1**	**1**	**0**	**1**	**1**	**14**	**0**	**0**	**0**	**15**	**0.0**	**5**	**0**	**16**	**3**	**–8**								
	Amarillo Wranglers	CHL	49	9	19	28				96																		
1969-70	Baltimore Clippers	AHL	68	7	21	28				138											4	1	2	3	2			
1970-71	**Buffalo Sabres**	**NHL**	**3**	**0**	**0**	**0**	**0**	**0**	**0**	**2**	**0**	**0**	**0**	**3**	**0.0**	**1**	**1**	**1**	**1**	**0**								
	Amarillo Wranglers	CHL	19	1	15	16				61																		
	Salt Lake Golden Eagles	WHL	39	2	13	15				83																		
1971-72	Hershey Bears	AHL	61	11	30	41				117											4	0	0	0	8			
1972-73	**Pittsburgh Penguins**	**NHL**	**31**	**1**	**5**	**6**	**1**	**4**	**5**	**32**	**0**	**0**	**0**	**33**	**3.0**	**23**	**1**	**32**	**2**	**–8**								
	Hershey Bears	AHL	37	7	14	21				54																		
1973-74	**Pittsburgh Penguins**	**NHL**	**31**	**2**	**6**	**8**	**2**	**5**	**7**	**34**	**1**	**1**	**0**	**28**	**7.1**	**15**	**2**	**30**	**5**	**–12**								
1974-75	**Pittsburgh Penguins**	**NHL**	**27**	**1**	**8**	**9**	**1**	**6**	**7**	**39**	**0**	**0**	**1**	**31**	**3.2**	**33**	**4**	**27**	**3**	**+5**								
	Kansas City Scouts	**NHL**	**19**	**2**	**9**	**11**	**2**	**7**	**9**	**22**	**2**	**0**	**0**	**40**	**5.0**	**26**	**13**	**39**	**6**	**–20**								
	Hershey Bears	AHL	6	0	7	7				8																		
1975-76	**Kansas City Scouts**	**NHL**	**69**	**3**	**10**	**13**	**3**	**8**	**11**	**108**	**1**	**1**	**1**	**75**	**4.0**	**65**	**12**	**125**	**34**	**–38**								
1976-77	Birmingham Bulls	WHA	78	2	25	27				110																		
	NHL Totals		**197**	**9**	**39**	**48**	**9**	**31**	**40**	**251**	**4**	**2**	**2**	**225**	**4.0**	**168**	**33**	**270**	**54**									
	Other Major League Totals		78	2	25	27				110																		

Traded to **Pittsburgh** by **Montreal** for Larry Hillman, November 24, 1968. Claimed by **Minnesota** from **Pittsburgh** in Intra-League Draft, June 9, 1970. Claimed by **Buffalo** from **Minnesota** in Expansion Draft, June 10, 1970. Traded to **Pittsburgh** by **Buffalo** for Terry Ball, January 24, 1971. Selected by **LA Sharks** (WHA) in 1972 WHA General Player Draft, February 12, 1972. Traded to **Kansas City** by **Pittsburgh** with Denis Herron for Michel Plasse, Janury 10, 1975. Signed as a free agent by **Birmingham** (WHA) after **LA Sharks** (WHA) franchise folded, September, 1976.

• LAIDLAW, TOM

Tom "Cowboy" Laidlaw D – L. 6'2", 215 lbs. b: Brampton, Ont., 4/15/1958. NY Rangers' 7th choice, 93rd overall, in 1978 Amateur Draft.

Season	Club	League	GP	G	A	Pts	AG	AA	APts	PIM	PP	SH	GW	S	%	TGF	PGF	TGA	PGA	+/–	GP	G	A	Pts	PIM	PP	SH	GW
1977-78	Northern Michigan University	CCHA	STATISTICS NOT AVAILABLE																									
1978-79	Northern Michigan University	CCHA	29	10	20	30				137																		
1979-80	Northern Michigan University	CCHA	39	8	30	38				83																		
	New Haven Nighthawks	AHL	1	0	0	0				0											10	1	6	7	27			
1980-81	**New York Rangers**	**NHL**	**80**	**6**	**23**	**29**	**5**	**16**	**21**	**100**	**1**	**0**	**0**	**101**	**5.9**	**95**	**5**	**113**	**23**	**0**	**14**	**1**	**4**	**5**	**18**	**0**	**0**	**1**
1981-82	**New York Rangers**	**NHL**	**79**	**3**	**18**	**21**	**2**	**12**	**14**	**104**	**1**	**0**	**0**	**62**	**4.8**	**88**	**5**	**113**	**37**	**+7**	**10**	**0**	**3**	**3**	**14**	**0**	**0**	**0**
1982-83	**New York Rangers**	**NHL**	**80**	**0**	**10**	**10**	**0**	**7**	**7**	**75**	**0**	**0**	**0**	**44**	**0.0**	**61**	**1**	**107**	**36**	**–11**	**9**	**1**	**1**	**2**	**10**	**0**	**0**	**0**
1983-84	**New York Rangers**	**NHL**	**79**	**3**	**15**	**18**	**2**	**10**	**12**	**62**	**0**	**0**	**1**	**61**	**4.9**	**72**	**2**	**132**	**52**	**–10**	**5**	**0**	**0**	**0**	**8**	**0**	**0**	**0**
1984-85	**New York Rangers**	**NHL**	**61**	**1**	**11**	**12**	**1**	**7**	**8**	**52**	**0**	**0**	**0**	**37**	**2.7**	**58**	**3**	**96**	**29**	**–12**	**3**	**0**	**2**	**2**	**4**	**0**	**0**	**0**
1985-86	**New York Rangers**	**NHL**	**68**	**6**	**12**	**18**	**5**	**8**	**13**	**103**	**0**	**1**	**0**	**50**	**12.0**	**60**	**0**	**104**	**41**	**–3**	**7**	**0**	**2**	**2**	**12**	**0**	**0**	**0**
1986-87	**New York Rangers**	**NHL**	**63**	**1**	**10**	**11**	**1**	**7**	**8**	**65**	**1**	**0**	**1**	**36**	**2.8**	**58**	**2**	**109**	**35**	**–18**								
	Los Angeles Kings	**NHL**	**11**	**0**	**3**	**3**	**0**	**2**	**2**	**4**	**0**	**0**	**0**	**7**	**0.0**	**10**	**1**	**12**	**4**	**+1**	**5**	**0**	**0**	**0**	**2**	**0**	**0**	**0**
1987-88	**Los Angeles Kings**	**NHL**	**57**	**1**	**12**	**13**	**1**	**9**	**10**	**47**	**0**	**0**	**0**	**30**	**3.3**	**64**	**10**	**85**	**34**	**+3**	**5**	**0**	**2**	**2**	**4**	**0**	**0**	**0**
1988-89	**Los Angeles Kings**	**NHL**	**70**	**3**	**17**	**20**	**3**	**12**	**15**	**63**	**0**	**0**	**1**	**31**	**9.7**	**105**	**4**	**110**	**39**	**+30**	**11**	**2**	**3**	**5**	**6**	**0**	**0**	**0**
1989-90	**Los Angeles Kings**	**NHL**	**57**	**1**	**8**	**9**	**1**	**6**	**7**	**42**	**0**	**0**	**0**	**27**	**3.7**	**61**	**0**	**86**	**29**	**+4**								
1990-91	Phoenix Roadrunners	IHL	4	0	1	1				2																		
	NHL Totals		**705**	**25**	**139**	**164**	**21**	**96**	**117**	**717**	**2**	**1**	**3**	**486**	**5.1**	**732**	**33**	**1067**	**359**		**69**	**4**	**17**	**21**	**78**	**0**	**0**	**1**

CCHA First All-Star Team (1979, 1980) • NCAA Championship All-Tournament Team (1980)

Traded to **LA Kings** by **NY Rangers** with Bob Carpenter for Jeff Crossman, Marcel Dionne and LA Kings' 3rd round choice (later traded to Minnesota — Minnesota selected Murray Garbut) in 1989 Entry Draft, March 10, 1987.

• LAIRD, ROBBIE

Robbie Laird LW – L. 5'9", 165 lbs. b: Regina, Sask., 12/29/1954. Pittsburgh's 6th choice, 116th overall, in 1974 Amateur Draft.

Season	Club	League	GP	G	A	Pts	AG	AA	APts	PIM	PP	SH	GW	S	%	TGF	PGF	TGA	PGA	+/–	GP	G	A	Pts	PIM	PP	SH	GW
1971-72	Regina Pats	WCJHL	1	1	0	1				0																		
1972-73	Regina Pats	WCJHL	68	14	18	32				102																		
1973-74	Regina Pats	WCJHL	68	39	45	84				243																		

			REGULAR SEASON																		PLAYOFFS							
Season	Club	League	GP	G	A	Pts	AG	AA	APts	PIM	PP	SH	GW	S	%	TGF	PGF	TGA	PGA	+/–	GP	G	A	Pts	PIM	PP	SH	GW
1974-75	Fort Wayne Komets	IHL	62	15	28	43	....	....	....	115	....	....	....	....	....	....	....	....	....	....	....	....	....	....	....	....	....	....
1975-76	Fort Wayne Komets	IHL	78	30	38	68	....	....	....	127	....	....	....	....	....	....	....	....	....	....	9	8	4	12	15	....	....	....
1976-77	Fort Wayne Komets	IHL	78	43	46	89	....	....	....	151	....	....	....	....	....	....	....	....	....	....	9	3	3	6	10	....	....	....
1977-78	Fort Wayne Komets	IHL	64	20	22	42	....	....	....	202	....	....	....	....	....	....	....	....	....	....	11	3	6	9	48	....	....	....
1978-79	Fort Wayne Komets	IHL	80	45	62	107	....	....	....	296	....	....	....	....	....	....	....	....	....	....	13	7	10	17	30	....	....	....
1979-80	**Minnesota North Stars**	**NHL**	**1**	**0**	**0**	**0**	**0**	**0**	**0**	**0**	**0**	**0**	**0**	**0**	**0.0**	**0**	**0**	**2**	**0**	**–2**	....	....	....	....	....	....	....	....
	Oklahoma City Stars	CHL	61	26	19	45	....	....	....	160	....	....	....	....	....	....	....	....	....	....	....	....	....	....	....	....	....	....
1980-81	Oklahoma City Stars	CHL	55	24	23	47	....	....	....	137	....	....	....	....	....	....	....	....	....	....	3	1	1	2	8	....	....	....
1981-82	Nashville South Stars	CHL	35	5	13	18	....	....	....	55	....	....	....	....	....	....	....	....	....	....	3	0	1	1	15	....	....	....
1983-84	Fort Wayne Komets	IHL	77	37	46	83	....	....	....	137	....	....	....	....	....	....	....	....	....	....	4	0	1	1	17	....	....	....
1984-85	Fort Wayne Komets	IHL	79	33	34	67	....	....	....	157	....	....	....	....	....	....	....	....	....	....	13	7	5	12	25	....	....	....
1985-86	Fort Wayne Komets	IHL	2	0	0	0	....	....	....	15	....	....	....	....	....	....	....	....	....	....	....	....	....	....	....	....	....	....
1986-87	Fort Wayne Komets	IHL	DID NOT PLAY – COACHING																									
	NHL Totals		**1**	**0**	**0**	**0**	**0**	**0**	**0**	**0**	**0**	**0**	**0**	**0**	**0.0**	**0**	**0**	**2**	**0**		....	....	....	....	....	....	....	....

IHL First All-Star Team (1979)

Signed as a free agent by **Minnesota**, September 15, 1979.

• LAJEUNESSE, SERGE

Serge Lajeunesse D/RW – R. 5′10″, 185 lbs. b: Montreal, Que., 6/11/1950. Detroit's 1st choice, 12th overall, in 1970 Amateur Draft.

Season	Club	League	GP	G	A	Pts	AG	AA	APts	PIM	PP	SH	GW	S	%	TGF	PGF	TGA	PGA	+/–	GP	G	A	Pts	PIM	PP	SH	GW
1967-68	Montreal Beavers	QJHL	....	5	14	19	....	....	....	....	....	....	....	....	....	....	....	....	....	....	....	....	....	....	....	....	....	....
1968-69	Montreal Jr. Canadiens	OHA	54	2	20	22	....	....	....	172	....	....	....	....	....	....	....	....	....	....	14	1	4	5	19	....	....	....
1969-70	Montreal Jr. Canadiens	OHA	54	2	27	29	....	....	....	87	....	....	....	....	....	....	....	....	....	....	....	....	....	....	....	....	....	....
1970-71	**Detroit Red Wings**	**NHL**	**62**	**1**	**3**	**4**	**1**	**3**	**4**	**55**	**0**	**1**	**0**	**76**	**1.3**	**37**	**0**	**70**	**5**	**–28**	....	....	....	....	....	....	....	....
	Fort Worth Wings	CHL	12	1	5	6	....	....	....	21	....	....	....	....	....	....	....	....	....	....	....	....	....	....	....	....	....	....
1971-72	**Detroit Red Wings**	**NHL**	**7**	**0**	**0**	**0**	**0**	**0**	**0**	**20**	**0**	**0**	**0**	**2**	**0.0**	**4**	**0**	**5**	**0**	**–1**	....	....	....	....	....	....	....	....
	Tidewater Wings	AHL	26	4	7	11	....	....	....	26	....	....	....	....	....	....	....	....	....	....	....	....	....	....	....	....	....	....
	Fort Worth Wings	CHL	36	8	11	19	....	....	....	53	....	....	....	....	....	....	....	....	....	....	7	0	2	2	16	....	....	....
1972-73	**Detroit Red Wings**	**NHL**	**28**	**0**	**1**	**1**	**0**	**1**	**1**	**26**	**0**	**0**	**0**	**10**	**0.0**	**7**	**1**	**24**	**3**	**–15**	....	....	....	....	....	....	....	....
	Virginia Wings	AHL	39	7	16	23	....	....	....	69	....	....	....	....	....	....	....	....	....	....	13	2	5	7	23	....	....	....
1973-74	**Philadelphia Flyers**	**NHL**	**1**	**0**	**0**	**0**	**0**	**0**	**0**	**0**	**0**	**0**	**0**	**2**	**0.0**	**0**	**0**	**0**	**0**	**0**	....	....	....	....	....	....	....	....
	Richmond Robins	AHL	75	28	17	45	....	....	....	96	....	....	....	....	....	....	....	....	....	....	5	0	5	5	2	....	....	....
1974-75	**Philadelphia Flyers**	**NHL**	**5**	**0**	**0**	**0**	**0**	**0**	**0**	**2**	**0**	**0**	**0**	**6**	**0.0**	**1**	**0**	**0**	**0**	**+1**	....	....	....	....	....	....	....	....
	Richmond Robins	AHL	66	11	18	29	....	....	....	58	....	....	....	....	....	....	....	....	....	....	7	1	2	3	4	....	....	....
1975-76	Richmond Robins	AHL	57	7	17	24	....	....	....	42	....	....	....	....	....	....	....	....	....	....	3	0	0	0	2	....	....	....
	NHL Totals		**103**	**1**	**4**	**5**	**1**	**4**	**5**	**103**	**0**	**1**	**0**	**96**	**1.0**	**49**	**1**	**99**	**8**		....	....	....	....	....	....	....	....

OHA Second All-Star Team (1969, 1970)

Traded to **Philadelphia** by **Detroit** for Rick Foley, May 15, 1973.

• LAKOVIC, SASHA

Sasha "The Basha" Lakovic LW – L. 6′, 205 lbs. b: Vancouver, B.C., 9/7/1971.

Season	Club	League	GP	G	A	Pts	AG	AA	APts	PIM	PP	SH	GW	S	%	TGF	PGF	TGA	PGA	+/–	GP	G	A	Pts	PIM	PP	SH	GW
1992-93	Brantford–Chatham	ColHL	28	7	5	12	....	....	....	235	....	....	....	....	....	....	....	....	....	....	....	....	....	....	....	....	....	....
	Columbus Chill	ECHL	27	7	9	16	....	....	....	162	....	....	....	....	....	....	....	....	....	....	....	....	....	....	....	....	....	....
	Binghamton Rangers	AHL	3	0	0	0	....	....	....	0	....	....	....	....	....	....	....	....	....	....	....	....	....	....	....	....	....	....
1993-94	Toledo Storm	ECHL	24	5	10	15	....	....	....	198	....	....	....	....	....	....	....	....	....	....	....	....	....	....	....	....	....	....
	Chatham Wheels	ColHL	13	11	7	18	....	....	....	61	....	....	....	....	....	....	....	....	....	....	....	....	....	....	....	....	....	....
1994-95	Tulsa Oilers	CHL	40	20	24	44	....	....	....	214	....	....	....	....	....	....	....	....	....	....	5	1	3	4	88	....	....	....
1995-96	Las Vegas Thunder	IHL	49	1	2	3	....	....	....	416	....	....	....	....	....	....	....	....	....	....	13	1	1	2	*57	....	....	....
1996-97	**Calgary Flames**	**NHL**	**19**	**0**	**1**	**1**	**0**	**1**	**1**	**54**	**0**	**0**	**0**	**10**	**0.0**	**2**	**0**	**3**	**0**	**–1**	....	....	....	....	....	....	....	....
	St. John's Maple Leafs	AHL	18	1	8	9	....	....	....	182	....	....	....	....	....	....	....	....	....	....	....	....	....	....	....	....	....	....
	Las Vegas Thunder	IHL	10	0	0	0	....	....	....	81	....	....	....	....	....	....	....	....	....	....	2	0	0	0	14	....	....	....
1997-98	**New Jersey Devils**	**NHL**	**2**	**0**	**0**	**0**	**0**	**0**	**0**	**5**	**0**	**0**	**0**	**2**	**0.0**	**0**	**0**	**0**	**0**	**0**	....	....	....	....	....	....	....	....
	Albany River Rats	AHL	30	7	6	13	....	....	....	158	....	....	....	....	....	....	....	....	....	....	13	3	4	7	84	....	....	....
	NHL Totals		**21**	**0**	**1**	**1**	**0**	**1**	**1**	**59**	**0**	**0**	**0**	**12**	**0.0**	**2**	**0**	**3**	**0**		....	....	....	....	....	....	....	....

Signed as a free agent by **Calgary**, October 10, 1996. Signed as a free agent by **New Jersey**, September 24, 1997.

• LALONDE, BOBBY

Bobby Lalonde C – L. 5′5″, 155 lbs. b: Montreal, Que., 3/27/1951. Vancouver's 2nd choice, 17th overall, in 1971 Amateur Draft.

Season	Club	League	GP	G	A	Pts	AG	AA	APts	PIM	PP	SH	GW	S	%	TGF	PGF	TGA	PGA	+/–	GP	G	A	Pts	PIM	PP	SH	GW
1967-68	Shawinigan Bruins	QJHL	....	29	29	58	....	....	....	....	....	....	....	....	....	....	....	....	....	....	....	....	....	....	....	....	....	....
1968-69	Montreal Jr. Canadiens	OHA	54	17	27	44	....	....	....	18	....	....	....	....	....	....	....	....	....	....	13	0	5	5	0	....	....	....
1969-70	Montreal Jr. Canadiens	OHA	54	42	42	84	....	....	....	73	....	....	....	....	....	....	....	....	....	....	....	....	....	....	....	....	....	....
1970-71	Montreal Jr. Canadiens	OHA	61	59	68	127	....	....	....	71	....	....	....	....	....	....	....	....	....	....	....	....	....	....	....	....	....	....
1971-72	**Vancouver Canucks**	**NHL**	**27**	**1**	**5**	**6**	**1**	**5**	**6**	**2**	**0**	**0**	**0**	**24**	**4.2**	**9**	**1**	**16**	**0**	**–8**	....	....	....	....	....	....	....	....
	Rochester Americans	AHL	42	14	11	25	....	....	....	19	....	....	....	....	....	....	....	....	....	....	....	....	....	....	....	....	....	....
1972-73	**Vancouver Canucks**	**NHL**	**77**	**20**	**27**	**47**	**20**	**23**	**43**	**32**	**7**	**0**	**6**	**126**	**15.9**	**67**	**21**	**80**	**2**	**–32**	....	....	....	....	....	....	....	....
1973-74	**Vancouver Canucks**	**NHL**	**36**	**3**	**4**	**7**	**3**	**3**	**6**	**18**	**1**	**0**	**1**	**42**	**7.1**	**14**	**3**	**18**	**4**	**–3**	....	....	....	....	....	....	....	....
1974-75	**Vancouver Canucks**	**NHL**	**74**	**17**	**30**	**47**	**16**	**24**	**40**	**48**	**4**	**0**	**1**	**135**	**12.6**	**51**	**10**	**46**	**5**	**0**	**5**	**0**	**0**	**0**	**0**	**0**	**0**	**0**
1975-76	**Vancouver Canucks**	**NHL**	**71**	**14**	**36**	**50**	**13**	**28**	**41**	**46**	**2**	**0**	**2**	**143**	**9.8**	**63**	**8**	**64**	**5**	**–4**	**1**	**0**	**0**	**0**	**2**	**0**	**0**	**0**
	Tulsa Oilers	CHL	4	3	2	5	....	....	....	2	....	....	....	....	....	....	....	....	....	....	....	....	....	....	....	....	....	....
1976-77	**Vancouver Canucks**	**NHL**	**68**	**17**	**15**	**32**	**16**	**12**	**28**	**39**	**3**	**0**	**1**	**115**	**14.8**	**48**	**16**	**44**	**0**	**–12**	....	....	....	....	....	....	....	....
	Tulsa Oilers	CHL	7	2	2	4	....	....	....	0	....	....	....	....	....	....	....	....	....	....	....	....	....	....	....	....	....	....
1977-78	**Atlanta Flames**	**NHL**	**73**	**14**	**23**	**37**	**13**	**19**	**32**	**28**	**0**	**0**	**0**	**94**	**14.9**	**53**	**10**	**38**	**0**	**+5**	**1**	**1**	**0**	**1**	**0**	**0**	**0**	**0**
1978-79	**Atlanta Flames**	**NHL**	**78**	**24**	**32**	**56**	**22**	**24**	**46**	**24**	**6**	**0**	**1**	**135**	**17.8**	**74**	**22**	**68**	**13**	**–3**	**2**	**1**	**0**	**1**	**0**	**1**	**0**	**0**
1979-80	**Atlanta Flames**	**NHL**	**3**	**0**	**1**	**1**	**0**	**1**	**1**	**2**	**0**	**0**	**0**	**2**	**0.0**	**2**	**1**	**2**	**0**	**–1**	....	....	....	....	....	....	....	....
	Boston Bruins	**NHL**	**71**	**10**	**25**	**35**	**9**	**19**	**28**	**28**	**1**	**2**	**0**	**91**	**11.0**	**50**	**4**	**55**	**23**	**+14**	**4**	**0**	**1**	**1**	**2**	**0**	**0**	**0**
1980-81	**Boston Bruins**	**NHL**	**62**	**4**	**12**	**16**	**3**	**8**	**11**	**31**	**0**	**1**	**0**	**42**	**9.5**	**25**	**4**	**49**	**31**	**+3**	**3**	**2**	**1**	**3**	**2**	**0**	**2**	**0**
1981-82	**Calgary Flames**	**NHL**	**1**	**0**	**0**	**0**	**0**	**0**	**0**	**0**	**0**	**0**	**0**	**1**	**0.0**	**2**	**0**	**0**	**0**	**+2**	....	....	....	....	....	....	....	....
	Oklahoma City Stars	CHL	19	6	11	17	....	....	....	36	....	....	....	....	....	....	....	....	....	....	....	....	....	....	....	....	....	....
	NHL Totals		**641**	**124**	**210**	**334**	**116**	**166**	**282**	**298**	**24**	**3**	**12**	**950**	**13.1**	**458**	**100**	**480**	**83**		**16**	**4**	**2**	**6**	**6**	**1**	**2**	**0**

Signed as a free agent by **Atlanta**, September 20, 1977. Claimed by **Atlanta** as a fill-in during Expansion Draft, June 13, 1979. Traded to **Boston** by **Atlanta** for future considerations, October 23, 1979. Signed as a free agent by **Calgary**, October 25, 1981.

• LALONDE, RON

Ron Lalonde C – L. 5′10″, 170 lbs. b: Toronto, Ont., 10/30/1952. Pittsburgh's 4th choice, 56th overall, in 1972 Amateur Draft.

Season	Club	League	GP	G	A	Pts	AG	AA	APts	PIM	PP	SH	GW	S	%	TGF	PGF	TGA	PGA	+/–	GP	G	A	Pts	PIM	PP	SH	GW
1970-71	Peterborough Petes	OHA	44	21	25	46	....	....	....	13	....	....	....	....	....	....	....	....	....	....	....	....	....	....	....	....	....	....
1971-72	Peterborough Petes	OHA	58	26	37	63	....	....	....	36	....	....	....	....	....	....	....	....	....	....	....	....	....	....	....	....	....	....
1972-73	**Pittsburgh Penguins**	**NHL**	**9**	**0**	**0**	**0**	**0**	**0**	**0**	**2**	**0**	**0**	**0**	**2**	**0.0**	**0**	**0**	**1**	**1**	**0**	....	....	....	....	....	....	....	....
	Hershey Bears	AHL	60	16	26	42	....	....	....	34	....	....	....	....	....	....	....	....	....	....	7	1	1	2	0	....	....	....
1973-74	**Pittsburgh Penguins**	**NHL**	**73**	**10**	**17**	**27**	**10**	**15**	**25**	**14**	**0**	**1**	**2**	**70**	**14.3**	**38**	**2**	**41**	**7**	**+2**	....	....	....	....	....	....	....	....
1974-75	**Pittsburgh Penguins**	**NHL**	**24**	**0**	**3**	**3**	**0**	**2**	**2**	**0**	**0**	**0**	**0**	**12**	**0.0**	**7**	**2**	**10**	**6**	**+1**	....	....	....	....	....	....	....	....
	Washington Capitals	**NHL**	**50**	**12**	**14**	**26**	**11**	**11**	**22**	**27**	**4**	**1**	**1**	**67**	**17.9**	**31**	**6**	**89**	**25**	**–39**	....	....	....	....	....	....	....	....
1975-76	**Washington Capitals**	**NHL**	**80**	**9**	**19**	**28**	**8**	**15**	**23**	**19**	**2**	**1**	**0**	**92**	**9.8**	**48**	**6**	**94**	**26**	**–26**	....	....	....	....	....	....	....	....
1976-77	**Washington Capitals**	**NHL**	**76**	**12**	**17**	**29**	**11**	**14**	**25**	**24**	**0**	**0**	**0**	**83**	**14.5**	**44**	**0**	**105**	**41**	**–20**	....	....	....	....	....	....	....	....
1977-78	**Washington Capitals**	**NHL**	**67**	**1**	**5**	**6**	**1**	**4**	**5**	**16**	**0**	**0**	**0**	**48**	**2.1**	**18**	**0**	**71**	**35**	**–18**	....	....	....	....	....	....	....	....
1978-79	**Washington Capitals**	**NHL**	**18**	**1**	**3**	**4**	**1**	**2**	**3**	**4**	**0**	**1**	**0**	**8**	**12.5**	**6**	**0**	**11**	**4**	**–1**	....	....	....	....	....	....	....	....
	Binghamton Dusters	AHL	26	7	7	14	....	....	....	0	....	....	....	....	....	....	....	....	....	....	....	....	....	....	....	....	....	....
	Hershey Bears	AHL	27	6	6	12	....	....	....	0	....	....	....	....	....	....	....	....	....	....	4	1	0	1	2	....	....	....
1979-80	Hershey Bears	AHL	65	13	17	30	....	....	....	22	....	....	....	....	....	....	....	....	....	....	16	2	3	5	6	....	....	....
1980-81	Salzburg	Austria	28	10	9	19	....	....	....	43	....	....	....	....	....	....	....	....	....	....	....	....	....	....	....	....	....	....
	NHL Totals		**397**	**45**	**78**	**123**	**42**	**63**	**105**	**106**	**6**	**4**	**3**	**382**	**11.8**	**192**	**16**	**422**	**145**		....	....	....	....	....	....	....	....

Traded to **Washington** by **Pittsburgh** for Lew Morrison, December 14, 1974.

REGULAR SEASON / PLAYOFFS

• LALOR, MIKE

Mike Lalor D – L. 6', 200 lbs. b: Buffalo, NY, 3/8/1963.

Season	Club	League	GP	G	A	Pts	AG	AA	APts	PIM	PP	SH	GW	S	%	TGF	PGF	TGA	PGA	+/–	GP	G	A	Pts	PIM	PP	SH	GW
1981-82	Brantford Alexanders	OHL	64	3	13	16	....	....	....	114	....	....	....	....	....	....	....	....	....	....	11	0	6	6	11	....	....	....
1982-83	Brantford Alexanders	OHL	65	10	30	40	....	....	....	113	....	....	....	....	....	....	....	....	....	....	8	1	3	4	20	....	....	....
1983-84	Nova Scotia Voyageurs	AHL	67	5	11	16	....	....	....	80	....	....	....	....	....	....	....	....	....	....	12	0	2	2	13	....	....	....
1984-85	Sherbrooke Canadiens	AHL	79	9	23	32	....	....	....	114	....	....	....	....	....	....	....	....	....	....	17	3	5	8	36	....	....	....
1985-86	**Montreal Canadiens**	**NHL**	**62**	**3**	**5**	**8**	**2**	**3**	**5**	**56**	**0**	**0**	**0**	**44**	**6.8**	**41**	**0**	**61**	**16**	**–4**	**17**	**1**	**2**	**3**	**29**	**0**	**0**	**1**
1986-87	**Montreal Canadiens**	**NHL**	**57**	**0**	**10**	**10**	**0**	**7**	**7**	**47**	**0**	**0**	**0**	**58**	**0.0**	**37**	**0**	**48**	**16**	**+5**	**13**	**2**	**1**	**3**	**29**	**0**	**0**	**0**
1987-88	**Montreal Canadiens**	**NHL**	**66**	**1**	**10**	**11**	**1**	**7**	**8**	**113**	**0**	**0**	**0**	**41**	**2.4**	**55**	**1**	**61**	**11**	**+4**	**11**	**0**	**0**	**0**	**11**	**0**	**0**	**0**
1988-89	**Montreal Canadiens**	**NHL**	**12**	**1**	**4**	**5**	**1**	**3**	**4**	**15**	**0**	**0**	**1**	**12**	**8.3**	**8**	**0**	**9**	**0**	**–1**	....	....	....	....	....	....	....	....
	St. Louis Blues	**NHL**	**36**	**1**	**14**	**15**	**1**	**10**	**11**	**54**	**0**	**0**	**1**	**40**	**2.5**	**41**	**1**	**46**	**21**	**+15**	**10**	**1**	**1**	**2**	**14**	**1**	**0**	**0**
1989-90	**St. Louis Blues**	**NHL**	**78**	**0**	**16**	**16**	**0**	**11**	**11**	**81**	**0**	**0**	**0**	**79**	**0.0**	**79**	**2**	**120**	**37**	**–6**	**12**	**0**	**2**	**2**	**31**	**0**	**0**	**0**
1990-91	**Washington Capitals**	**NHL**	**68**	**1**	**5**	**6**	**1**	**4**	**5**	**61**	**0**	**0**	**0**	**49**	**2.0**	**41**	**1**	**74**	**11**	**–23**	**10**	**1**	**2**	**3**	**22**	**0**	**0**	**0**
1991-92	**Washington Capitals**	**NHL**	**64**	**5**	**7**	**12**	**5**	**5**	**10**	**64**	**0**	**0**	**1**	**54**	**9.3**	**54**	**2**	**42**	**4**	**+14**	....	....	....	....	....	....	....	....
	Winnipeg Jets	**NHL**	**15**	**2**	**3**	**5**	**2**	**2**	**4**	**14**	**0**	**0**	**0**	**20**	**10.0**	**16**	**1**	**12**	**8**	**+11**	**7**	**0**	**0**	**0**	**19**	**0**	**0**	**0**
1992-93	**Winnipeg Jets**	**NHL**	**64**	**1**	**8**	**9**	**1**	**5**	**6**	**76**	**0**	**0**	**0**	**75**	**1.3**	**51**	**1**	**87**	**27**	**–10**	**4**	**0**	**2**	**2**	**4**	**0**	**0**	**0**
1993-94	**San Jose Sharks**	**NHL**	**23**	**0**	**2**	**2**	**0**	**2**	**2**	**8**	**0**	**0**	**0**	**19**	**0.0**	**10**	**0**	**20**	**5**	**–5**	....	....	....	....	....	....	....	....
	Dallas Stars	**NHL**	**12**	**0**	**1**	**1**	**0**	**1**	**1**	**6**	**0**	**0**	**0**	**3**	**0.0**	**3**	**0**	**10**	**2**	**–5**	**5**	**0**	**0**	**0**	**6**	**0**	**0**	**0**
1994-95	**Dallas Stars**	**NHL**	**12**	**0**	**0**	**0**	**0**	**0**	**0**	**9**	**0**	**0**	**0**	**6**	**0.0**	**4**	**0**	**4**	**0**	**0**	**3**	**0**	**0**	**0**	**2**	**0**	**0**	**0**
	Kalamazoo Wings	IHL	5	0	1	1	....	....	....	11	....	....	....	....	....	....	....	....	....	....	....	....	....	....	....	....	....	....
1995-96	**Dallas Stars**	**NHL**	**63**	**1**	**2**	**3**	**1**	**2**	**3**	**31**	**0**	**0**	**0**	**46**	**2.2**	**29**	**2**	**49**	**12**	**–10**	....	....	....	....	....	....	....	....
	San Francisco Spiders	IHL	12	2	2	4	....	....	....	6	....	....	....	....	....	....	....	....	....	....	....	....	....	....	....	....	....	....
	United States	WC-A	8	0	0	0	....	....	....	4	....	....	....	....	....	....	....	....	....	....	....	....	....	....	....	....	....	....
1996-97	**Dallas Stars**	**NHL**	**55**	**1**	**1**	**2**	**1**	**1**	**2**	**42**	**0**	**0**	**0**	**32**	**3.1**	**25**	**0**	**35**	**13**	**+3**	....	....	....	....	....	....	....	....
	NHL Totals		**687**	**17**	**88**	**105**	**16**	**63**	**79**	**677**	**0**	**0**	**3**	**578**	**2.9**	**494**	**11**	**678**	**183**		**92**	**5**	**10**	**15**	**167**	**1**	**0**	**1**

Signed as a free agent by **Montreal**, September, 1983. Traded to **St. Louis** by **Montreal** with Montreal's 1st round choice (later traded to Vancouver — Vancouver selected Shawn Antoski) in 1990 Entry Draft for St. Louis' 1st round choice (Turner Stevenson) in 1990 Entry Draft, January 16, 1989. Traded to **Washington** by **St. Louis** with Peter Zezel for Geoff Courtnall, July 13, 1990. Traded to **Winnipeg** by **Washington** for Paul MacDermid, March 2, 1992. Signed as a free agent by **San Jose**, August 13, 1993. Traded to **Dallas** by **San Jose** with Doug Zmolek and cash for Ulf Dahlen and Dallas' 7th round choice (Brad Mehalko) in 1995 Entry Draft, March 19, 1994.

• LAMB, MARK

Mark Lamb C – L. 5'9", 180 lbs. b: Ponteix, Sask., 8/3/1964. Calgary's 5th choice, 72nd overall, in 1982 Entry Draft.

Season	Club	League	GP	G	A	Pts	AG	AA	APts	PIM	PP	SH	GW	S	%	TGF	PGF	TGA	PGA	+/–	GP	G	A	Pts	PIM	PP	SH	GW
1981-82	Billings Bighorns	WHL	72	45	56	101	....	....	....	46	....	....	....	....	....	....	....	....	....	....	5	4	6	10	4	....	....	....
1982-83	Nanaimo Islanders	WHL	30	14	37	51	....	....	....	16	....	....	....	....	....	....	....	....	....	....	....	....	....	....	....	....	....	....
	Medicine Hat Tigers	WHL	46	22	43	65	....	....	....	33	....	....	....	....	....	....	....	....	....	....	5	3	2	5	4	....	....	....
	Colorado Flames	CHL	....	....	....	....	....	....	....	....	....	....	....	....	....	....	....	....	....	....	6	0	2	2	0	....	....	....
1983-84	Medicine Hat Tigers	WHL	72	59	77	136	....	....	....	30	....	....	....	....	....	....	....	....	....	....	14	12	11	23	6	....	....	....
1984-85	Moncton Golden Flames	AHL	80	23	49	72	....	....	....	53	....	....	....	....	....	....	....	....	....	....	....	....	....	....	....	....	....	....
1985-86	**Calgary Flames**	**NHL**	**1**	**0**	**0**	**0**	**0**	**0**	**0**	**0**	**0**	**0**	**0**	**0**	**0.0**	**0**	**0**	**0**	**0**	**0**	....	....	....	....	....	....	....	....
	Moncton Golden Flames	AHL	79	26	50	76	....	....	....	51	....	....	....	....	....	....	....	....	....	....	10	2	6	8	17	....	....	....
1986-87	**Detroit Red Wings**	**NHL**	**22**	**2**	**1**	**3**	**2**	**1**	**3**	**8**	**0**	**0**	**0**	**8**	**25.0**	**5**	**0**	**5**	**0**	**0**	**11**	**0**	**0**	**0**	**11**	**0**	**0**	**0**
	Adirondack Red Wings	AHL	49	14	36	50	....	....	....	45	....	....	....	....	....	....	....	....	....	....	....	....	....	....	....	....	....	....
1987-88	**Edmonton Oilers**	**NHL**	**2**	**0**	**0**	**0**	**0**	**0**	**0**	**0**	**0**	**0**	**0**	**0**	**0.0**	**0**	**0**	**0**	**0**	**0**	....	....	....	....	....	....	....	....
	Nova Scotia Oilers	AHL	69	27	61	88	....	....	....	45	....	....	....	....	....	....	....	....	....	....	5	0	5	5	6	....	....	....
1988-89	**Edmonton Oilers**	**NHL**	**20**	**2**	**8**	**10**	**2**	**6**	**8**	**14**	**1**	**0**	**0**	**20**	**10.0**	**13**	**1**	**9**	**1**	**+4**	**6**	**0**	**2**	**2**	**8**	**0**	**0**	**0**
	Cape Breton Oilers	AHL	54	33	49	82	....	....	....	29	....	....	....	....	....	....	....	....	....	....	....	....	....	....	....	....	....	....
1989-90	**Edmonton Oilers**	**NHL**	**58**	**12**	**16**	**28**	**10**	**11**	**21**	**42**	**2**	**0**	**2**	**81**	**14.8**	**35**	**4**	**31**	**10**	**+10**	**22**	**6**	**11**	**17**	**2**	**1**	**0**	**2**
1990-91	**Edmonton Oilers**	**NHL**	**37**	**4**	**8**	**12**	**4**	**6**	**10**	**25**	**1**	**0**	**1**	**41**	**9.8**	**21**	**3**	**31**	**11**	**–2**	**15**	**0**	**5**	**5**	**20**	**0**	**0**	**0**
1991-92	**Edmonton Oilers**	**NHL**	**59**	**6**	**22**	**28**	**5**	**17**	**22**	**46**	**2**	**0**	**1**	**61**	**9.8**	**41**	**6**	**49**	**18**	**+4**	**16**	**1**	**1**	**2**	**10**	**0**	**0**	**0**
1992-93	**Ottawa Senators**	**NHL**	**71**	**7**	**19**	**26**	**6**	**13**	**19**	**64**	**1**	**0**	**0**	**123**	**5.7**	**50**	**5**	**131**	**46**	**–40**	....	....	....	....	....	....	....	....
1993-94	**Ottawa Senators**	**NHL**	**66**	**11**	**18**	**29**	**10**	**14**	**24**	**56**	**4**	**1**	**1**	**105**	**10.5**	**38**	**11**	**112**	**44**	**–41**	....	....	....	....	....	....	....	....
	Philadelphia Flyers	**NHL**	**19**	**1**	**6**	**7**	**1**	**5**	**6**	**16**	**0**	**0**	**1**	**19**	**5.3**	**9**	**1**	**17**	**8**	**–3**	....	....	....	....	....	....	....	....
1994-95	**Philadelphia Flyers**	**NHL**	**8**	**0**	**2**	**2**	**0**	**3**	**3**	**2**	**0**	**0**	**0**	**7**	**0.0**	**3**	**0**	**4**	**2**	**+1**	....	....	....	....	....	....	....	....
	Montreal Canadiens	**NHL**	**39**	**1**	**0**	**1**	**2**	**0**	**2**	**18**	**0**	**0**	**0**	**23**	**4.3**	**3**	**0**	**29**	**13**	**–13**	....	....	....	....	....	....	....	....
1995-96	**Montreal Canadiens**	**NHL**	**1**	**0**	**0**	**0**	**0**	**0**	**0**	**0**	**0**	**0**	**0**	**0**	**0.0**	**0**	**0**	**0**	**0**	**0**	....	....	....	....	....	....	....	....
	Houston Aeros	IHL	67	17	60	77	....	....	....	65	....	....	....	....	....	....	....	....	....	....	....	....	....	....	....	....	....	....
1996-97	Houston Aeros	IHL	81	25	53	78	....	....	....	83	....	....	....	....	....	....	....	....	....	....	13	3	12	15	10	....	....	....
1997-98	EV Landshut	Germany	46	7	21	28	....	....	....	36	....	....	....	....	....	....	....	....	....	....	6	3	1	4	8	....	....	....
	NHL Totals		**403**	**46**	**100**	**146**	**42**	**76**	**118**	**291**	**11**	**1**	**6**	**488**	**9.4**	**218**	**31**	**418**	**151**		**70**	**7**	**19**	**26**	**51**	**1**	**0**	**2**

WHL East First All-Star Team (1984)

Signed as a free agent by **Detroit**, July 28, 1986. Claimed by **Edmonton** from **Detroit** in Waiver Draft, October 5, 1987. Claimed by **Ottawa** from **Edmonton** in Expansion Draft, June 18, 1992. Traded to **Philadelphia** by **Ottawa** for Claude Boivin and Kirk Daubenspeck, March 5, 1994. Traded to **Montreal** by **Philadelphia** for cash, February 10, 1995.

• LAMBERT, DAN

Dan Lambert D – L. 5'8", 177 lbs. b: St. Boniface, Man., 1/12/1970. Quebec's 7th choice, 106th overall, in 1989 Entry Draft.

Season	Club	League	GP	G	A	Pts	AG	AA	APts	PIM	PP	SH	GW	S	%	TGF	PGF	TGA	PGA	+/–	GP	G	A	Pts	PIM	PP	SH	GW
1986-87	Swift Current Broncos	WHL	68	13	53	66	....	....	....	95	....	....	....	....	....	....	....	....	....	....	4	1	1	2	9	....	....	....
1987-88	Swift Current Broncos	WHL	69	20	63	83	....	....	....	120	....	....	....	....	....	....	....	....	....	....	10	2	10	12	45	....	....	....
1988-89	Swift Current Broncos	WHL	57	25	77	102	....	....	....	158	....	....	....	....	....	....	....	....	....	....	12	9	19	28	12	....	....	....
1989-90	Swift Current Broncos	WHL	50	17	51	68	....	....	....	119	....	....	....	....	....	....	....	....	....	....	4	2	3	5	12	....	....	....
1990-91	**Quebec Nordiques**	**NHL**	**1**	**0**	**0**	**0**	**0**	**0**	**0**	**0**	**0**	**0**	**0**	**0**	**0.0**	**0**	**0**	**0**	**0**	**0**	....	....	....	....	....	....	....	....
	Halifax Citadels	AHL	30	7	13	20	....	....	....	20	....	....	....	....	....	....	....	....	....	....	....	....	....	....	....	....	....	....
	Fort Wayne Komets	IHL	49	10	27	37	....	....	....	65	....	....	....	....	....	....	....	....	....	....	19	4	10	14	20	....	....	....
1991-92	**Quebec Nordiques**	**NHL**	**28**	**6**	**9**	**15**	**5**	**7**	**12**	**22**	**2**	**0**	**0**	**42**	**14.3**	**29**	**13**	**22**	**1**	**–5**	....	....	....	....	....	....	....	....
	Halifax Citadels	AHL	47	3	28	31	....	....	....	33	....	....	....	....	....	....	....	....	....	....	....	....	....	....	....	....	....	....
1992-93	Moncton Hawks	AHL	73	11	30	41	....	....	....	100	....	....	....	....	....	....	....	....	....	....	5	1	2	3	2	....	....	....
1993-94	HIFK Helsinki	Finland	13	1	2	3	....	....	....	8	....	....	....	....	....	....	....	....	....	....	....	....	....	....	....	....	....	....
	Fort Wayne Komets	IHL	62	10	27	37	....	....	....	138	....	....	....	....	....	....	....	....	....	....	18	3	12	15	20	....	....	....
1994-95	San Diego Gulls	IHL	70	6	19	25	....	....	....	95	....	....	....	....	....	....	....	....	....	....	5	0	5	5	10	....	....	....
1995-96	Los Angeles Ice Dogs	IHL	81	22	65	87	....	....	....	121	....	....	....	....	....	....	....	....	....	....	....	....	....	....	....	....	....	....
1996-97	Long Beach Ice Dogs	IHL	71	15	50	65	....	....	....	70	....	....	....	....	....	....	....	....	....	....	18	2	8	10	8	....	....	....
1997-98	Long Beach Ice Dogs	IHL	81	19	59	78	....	....	....	112	....	....	....	....	....	....	....	....	....	....	17	3	14	17	16	....	....	....
	NHL Totals		**29**	**6**	**9**	**15**	**5**	**7**	**12**	**22**	**2**	**0**	**0**	**42**	**14.3**	**29**	**13**	**22**	**1**		....	....	....	....	....	....	....	....

WHL East First All-Star Team (1989, 1990) • Memorial Cup All-Star Team (1989) • Won Stafford Smythe Memorial Trophy (Memorial Cup Tournament MVP) (1989) • IHL Second All-Star Team (1996) • IHL First All-Star Team (1998) • Won Governor's Trophy (Top Defenseman - IHL) (1998)

Traded to **Winnipeg** by **Quebec** for Shawn Cronin, August 25, 1992.

• LAMBERT, DENNY

Denny Lambert LW – L. 5'11", 200 lbs. b: Wawa, Ont., 1/7/1970.

Season	Club	League	GP	G	A	Pts	AG	AA	APts	PIM	PP	SH	GW	S	%	TGF	PGF	TGA	PGA	+/–	GP	G	A	Pts	PIM	PP	SH	GW
1988-89	Sault Ste. Marie Greyhounds	OHL	61	14	15	29	....	....	....	203	....	....	....	....	....	....	....	....	....	....	....	....	....	....	....	....	....	....
1989-90	Sault Ste. Marie Greyhounds	OHL	61	23	29	52	....	....	....	276	....	....	....	....	....	....	....	....	....	....	....	....	....	....	....	....	....	....
1990-91	Sault Ste. Marie Greyhounds	OHL	59	28	39	67	....	....	....	169	....	....	....	....	....	....	....	....	....	....	14	7	9	16	48	....	....	....
1991-92	San Diego Gulls	IHL	71	17	14	31	....	....	....	229	....	....	....	....	....	....	....	....	....	....	3	0	0	0	10	....	....	....
	St. Thomas Wildcats	ColHL	5	2	6	8	....	....	....	9	....	....	....	....	....	....	....	....	....	....	....	....	....	....	....	....	....	....
1992-93	San Diego Gulls	IHL	56	18	12	30	....	....	....	277	....	....	....	....	....	....	....	....	....	....	14	1	1	2	44	....	....	....
1993-94	San Diego Gulls	IHL	79	13	14	27	....	....	....	314	....	....	....	....	....	....	....	....	....	....	6	1	0	1	55	....	....	....
1994-95	San Diego Gulls	IHL	75	25	35	60	....	....	....	222	....	....	....	....	....	....	....	....	....	....	....	....	....	....	....	....	....	....
	Anaheim Mighty Ducks	**NHL**	**13**	**1**	**3**	**4**	**2**	**4**	**6**	**4**	**0**	**0**	**0**	**14**	**7.1**	**7**	**0**	**4**	**0**	**+3**	....	....	....	....	....	....	....	....
1995-96	**Anaheim Mighty Ducks**	**NHL**	**33**	**0**	**8**	**8**	**0**	**7**	**7**	**55**	**0**	**0**	**0**	**28**	**0.0**	**11**	**0**	**13**	**0**	**–2**	....	....	....	....	....	....	....	....
	Baltimore Bandits	AHL	44	14	28	42	....	....	....	126	....	....	....	....	....	....	....	....	....	....	12	3	9	12	39	....	....	....
1996-97	**Ottawa Senators**	**NHL**	**80**	**4**	**16**	**20**	**4**	**14**	**18**	**217**	**0**	**0**	**1**	**58**	**6.9**	**25**	**1**	**28**	**0**	**–4**	**6**	**0**	**1**	**1**	**9**	**0**	**0**	**0**
1997-98	**Ottawa Senators**	**NHL**	**72**	**9**	**10**	**19**	**11**	**10**	**21**	**250**	**0**	**0**	**1**	**76**	**11.8**	**28**	**0**	**24**	**0**	**+4**	**11**	**0**	**0**	**0**	**19**	**0**	**0**	**0**
	NHL Totals		**198**	**14**	**37**	**51**	**17**	**35**	**52**	**526**	**0**	**0**	**2**	**176**	**8.0**	**71**	**1**	**69**	**0**		**17**	**0**	**1**	**1**	**20**	**0**	**0**	**0**

Signed as a free agent by **Anaheim**, August 16, 1993. Signed as a free agent by **Ottawa**, July 29, 1996. Claimed by **Nashville** from **Ottawa** in Expansion Draft, June 26, 1998.

• LAMBERT, LANE

Lane Lambert RW – R. 6', 185 lbs. b: Melfort, Sask., 11/18/1964. Detroit's 2nd choice, 25th overall, in 1983 Entry Draft.

			REGULAR SEASON																		PLAYOFFS							
Season	Club	League	GP	G	A	Pts	AG	AA	APts	PIM	PP	SH	GW	S	%	TGF	PGF	TGA	PGA	+/–	GP	G	A	Pts	PIM	PP	SH	GW
1980-81	Swift Current Broncos	SJHL	55	43	54	97	....	....	....	63	....	....	....	....	....	....	....	....	....	....	....	....	....	....	....	....	....	....
1981-82	Saskatoon Blades	WHL	72	45	69	114	....	....	....	111	....	....	....	....	....	....	....	....	....	....	5	1	1	2	25	....	....	....
1982-83	Saskatoon Blades	WHL	64	59	60	119	....	....	....	126	....	....	....	....	....	....	....	....	....	....	6	4	3	7	7	....	....	....
1983-84	**Detroit Red Wings**	**NHL**	73	20	15	35	16	10	26	115	1	0	2	88	22.7	59	6	58	0	–5	4	0	0	0	10	0	0	0
1984-85	**Detroit Red Wings**	**NHL**	69	14	11	25	11	7	18	104	0	0	1	69	20.3	44	1	46	0	–3	....	....	....	....	....	....	....	....
1985-86	**Detroit Red Wings**	**NHL**	34	2	3	5	2	2	4	130	0	0	0	32	6.3	15	1	42	17	–11	....	....	....	....	....	....	....	....
	Adirondack Red Wings	AHL	45	16	25	41	....	....	....	69	....	....	....	....	....	....	....	....	....	....	16	5	5	10	9	....	....	....
1986-87	**New York Rangers**	**NHL**	18	2	2	4	2	1	3	33	0	0	1	14	14.3	7	0	5	0	+2	....	....	....	....	....	....	....	....
	New Haven Nighthawks	AHL	11	3	3	6	....	....	....	19	....	....	....	....	....	....	....	....	....	....	....	....	....	....	....	....	....	....
	Quebec Nordiques	**NHL**	15	5	5	10	4	4	8	18	0	0	0	29	17.2	17	0	18	0	–1	13	2	4	6	30	0	0	0
1987-88	**Quebec Nordiques**	**NHL**	61	13	28	41	11	20	31	98	0	0	2	98	13.3	53	10	52	9	0	....	....	....	....	....	....	....	....
1988-89	**Quebec Nordiques**	**NHL**	13	2	2	4	2	1	3	23	0	0	0	19	10.5	4	1	9	4	–2	....	....	....	....	....	....	....	....
	Halifax Citadels	AHL	59	25	35	60	....	....	....	162	....	....	....	....	....	....	....	....	....	....	4	0	2	2	2	....	....	....
1989-90	Canada	Nat-Team	54	28	36	64	....	....	....	48	....	....	....	....	....	....	....	....	....	....	....	....	....	....	....	....	....	....
	Dusseldorf	Germany	6	2	6	8	....	....	....	4	....	....	....	....	....	....	....	....	....	....	....	....	....	....	....	....	....	....
1990-91	Canada	Nat-Team	4	0	1	1	....	....	....	0	....	....	....	....	....	....	....	....	....	....	....	....	....	....	....	....	....	....
	Ajoie	Switz. B	36	26	24	50	....	....	....	....	....	....	....	....	....	....	....	....	....	....	10	15	22	37	....	....	....	....
1991-92	Ajoie	Switz.	35	50	38	88	....	....	....	123	....	....	....	....	....	....	....	....	....	....	9	10	5	15	14	....	....	....
1992-93	Ajoie	Switz.	25	22	16	38	....	....	....	28	....	....	....	....	....	....	....	....	....	....	....	....	....	....	....	....	....	....
1993-94	La-Chaux-de-Fonds	Switz. B	36	*40	27	67	....	....	....	....	....	....	....	....	....	....	....	....	....	....	....	....	....	....	....	....	....	....
1994-95	HC Langnau	Switz. B	36	37	44	81	....	....	....	60	....	....	....	....	....	....	....	....	....	....	7	5	4	9	33	....	....	....
1995-96	HC Langnau	Switz. B	33	39	40	*79	....	....	....	....	....	....	....	....	....	....	....	....	....	....	....	....	....	....	....	....	....	....
1996-97	Cleveland Lumberjacks	IHL	75	24	20	44	....	....	....	94	....	....	....	....	....	....	....	....	....	....	13	4	5	9	21	....	....	....
1997-98	Cleveland Lumberjacks	IHL	39	4	10	14	....	....	....	60	....	....	....	....	....	....	....	....	....	....	3	0	0	0	0	....	....	....
	NHL Totals		283	58	66	124	48	45	93	521	1	0	6	349	16.6	199	19	230	30		17	2	4	6	40	0	0	0

WHL Second All-Star Team (1983)

Traded to **NY Rangers** by **Detroit** with Kelly Kisio and Jim Leavins for Glen Hanlon and NY Rangers' 3rd round choice (Dennis Holland) in 1987 Entry Draft and 3rd round choice (Guy Dupuis) in 1988 Entry Draft, July 26, 1986. Traded to **Quebec** by **NY Rangers** for Pat Price, March 5, 1987.

• LAMBERT, YVON

Yvon Lambert LW – L. 6'2", 200 lbs. b: Drummondville, Que., 5/20/1950. Detroit's 3rd choice, 40th overall, in 1970 Amateur Draft.

Season	Club	League	GP	G	A	Pts	AG	AA	APts	PIM	PP	SH	GW	S	%	TGF	PGF	TGA	PGA	+/–	GP	G	A	Pts	PIM	PP	SH	GW
1969-70	Drummondville Rangers	QMJHL	52	50	51	101	....	....	....	89	....	....	....	....	....	....	....	....	....	....	6	7	4	11	6	....	....	....
1970-71	Port Huron Flags	IHL	65	23	18	41	....	....	....	81	....	....	....	....	....	....	....	....	....	....	14	8	1	9	32	....	....	....
1971-72	Nova Scotia Voyageurs	AHL	67	18	21	39	....	....	....	116	....	....	....	....	....	....	....	....	....	....	15	4	4	8	28	....	....	....
1972-73	**Montreal Canadiens**	**NHL**	1	0	0	0	0	0	0	0	0	0	0	1	0.0	0	0	0	0	0	....	....	....	....	....	....	....	....
	Nova Scotia Voyageurs	AHL	76	*52	52	*104	....	....	....	84	....	....	....	....	....	....	....	....	....	....	13	9	9	18	32	....	....	....
1973-74	**Montreal Canadiens**	**NHL**	60	6	10	16	6	9	15	42	0	0	0	34	17.6	24	0	19	0	+5	5	0	0	0	7	0	0	0
1974-75	**Montreal Canadiens**	**NHL**	80	32	35	67	30	28	58	74	10	0	3	150	21.3	122	47	49	0	+26	11	4	2	6	0	2	0	0
1975-76	**Montreal Canadiens**	**NHL**	80	32	35	67	30	28	58	28	12	0	4	156	20.5	99	39	50	0	+10	12	2	3	5	18	0	0	1
1976-77	**Montreal Canadiens**	**NHL**	79	24	28	52	23	23	46	50	2	0	5	128	18.8	91	19	42	0	+30	14	3	3	6	12	1	0	0
1977-78	**Montreal Canadiens**	**NHL**	77	18	22	40	17	18	35	20	7	0	3	107	16.8	64	19	39	4	+10	15	2	4	6	6	1	0	1
1978-79	**Montreal Canadiens**	**NHL**	79	26	40	66	24	31	55	26	5	1	7	133	19.5	111	30	55	4	+30	16	5	6	11	16	2	0	1
1979-80	**Montreal Canadiens**	**NHL**	77	21	32	53	19	25	44	23	7	0	7	104	20.2	80	22	72	17	+3	10	8	4	12	4	1	0	1
1980-81	**Montreal Canadiens**	**NHL**	73	22	32	54	18	22	40	39	4	0	3	117	18.8	85	24	61	7	+7	3	0	0	0	2	0	0	0
1981-82	**Buffalo Sabres**	**NHL**	77	25	39	64	20	26	46	38	14	0	4	108	23.1	102	31	49	0	+22	4	3	0	3	2	1	0	0
1982-83	Rochester Americans	AHL	79	26	22	48	....	....	....	10	....	....	....	....	....	....	....	....	....	....	12	2	4	6	2	....	....	....
1983-84	Rochester Americans	AHL	79	27	43	70	....	....	....	14	....	....	....	....	....	....	....	....	....	....	18	8	11	19	2	....	....	....
1984-85	Verdun Jr. Canadiens	QMJHL	DID NOT PLAY – COACHING																									
	NHL Totals		683	206	273	479	187	210	397	340	61	1	36	1038	19.8	778	231	436	32		90	27	22	49	67	8	0	4

AHL First All-Star Team (1973) • Won John B. Sollenberger Trophy (Top Scorer - AHL) (1973)

Claimed by **Montreal** from **Detroit** (Port Huron - IHL) in Reverse Draft, June 9, 1971. Claimed by **Buffalo** from **Montreal** in Waiver Draft, October 5, 1981.

• LAMBY, DICK

Dick Lamby D – R. 6'1", 200 lbs. b: Auburn, MA, 5/3/1955. St. Louis' 7th choice, 135th overall, in 1975 Amateur Draft.

Season	Club	League	GP	G	A	Pts	AG	AA	APts	PIM	PP	SH	GW	S	%	TGF	PGF	TGA	PGA	+/–	GP	G	A	Pts	PIM	PP	SH	GW
1974-75	Salem State University	NCAA	26	25	32	57	....	....	....	54	....	....	....	....	....	....	....	....	....	....	....	....	....	....	....	....	....	....
1975-76	United States	Nat-Team	63	12	35	47	....	....	....	146	....	....	....	....	....	....	....	....	....	....	....	....	....	....	....	....	....	....
	United States	Olympics	6	0	2	2	....	....	....	12	....	....	....	....	....	....	....	....	....	....	....	....	....	....	....	....	....	....
1976-77	Boston University	ECAC	24	9	36	45	....	....	....	44	....	....	....	....	....	....	....	....	....	....	....	....	....	....	....	....	....	....
1977-78	Boston University	ECAC	30	15	44	59	....	....	....	64	....	....	....	....	....	....	....	....	....	....	....	....	....	....	....	....	....	....
	United States	WEC-A	7	0	2	2	....	....	....	20	....	....	....	....	....	....	....	....	....	....	....	....	....	....	....	....	....	....
1978-79	**St. Louis Blues**	**NHL**	9	0	4	4	0	3	3	12	0	0	0	11	0.0	18	1	14	2	+5	....	....	....	....	....	....	....	....
	Salt Lake Golden Eagles	CHL	60	4	15	19	....	....	....	122	....	....	....	....	....	....	....	....	....	....	10	2	5	7	21	....	....	....
1979-80	**St. Louis Blues**	**NHL**	12	0	1	1	0	1	1	10	0	0	0	12	0.0	9	0	17	1	–7	....	....	....	....	....	....	....	....
	Salt Lake Golden Eagles	CHL	49	3	14	17	....	....	....	93	....	....	....	....	....	....	....	....	....	....	....	....	....	....	....	....	....	....
1980-81	**St. Louis Blues**	**NHL**	1	0	0	0	0	0	0	0	0	0	0	2	0.0	1	0	2	0	–1	....	....	....	....	....	....	....	....
	Salt Lake Golden Eagles	CHL	53	7	30	37	....	....	....	74	....	....	....	....	....	....	....	....	....	....	14	1	5	6	23	....	....	....
1981-82	Fort Worth Texans	CHL	31	4	6	10	....	....	....	41	....	....	....	....	....	....	....	....	....	....	....	....	....	....	....	....	....	....
	Dallas Black Hawks	CHL	22	0	7	7	....	....	....	53	....	....	....	....	....	....	....	....	....	....	....	....	....	....	....	....	....	....
	Muskegon Mohawks	IHL	16	2	5	7	....	....	....	25	....	....	....	....	....	....	....	....	....	....	....	....	....	....	....	....	....	....
	NHL Totals		22	0	5	5	0	4	4	22	0	0	0	25	0.0	28	1	33	3		....	....	....	....	....	....	....	....

NCAA (College Div.) East All-American Team (1974, 1975) • ECAC Second All-Star Team (1978) • NCAA Championship All-Tournament Team (1978)

Traded to **Colorado** by **St. Louis** with Joe Micheletti for Bill Baker, December 4, 1981.

• LAMMENS, HANK

Hank Lammens D – L. 6'2", 210 lbs. b: Brockville, Ont., 2/21/1966. NY Islanders' 10th choice, 160th overall, in 1985 Entry Draft.

Season	Club	League	GP	G	A	Pts	AG	AA	APts	PIM	PP	SH	GW	S	%	TGF	PGF	TGA	PGA	+/–	GP	G	A	Pts	PIM	PP	SH	GW
1983-84	Brockville Braves	OJHL	46	7	11	18	....	....	....	106	....	....	....	....	....	....	....	....	....	....	....	....	....	....	....	....	....	....
1984-85	St. Lawrence University	ECAC	21	17	9	26	....	....	....	16	....	....	....	....	....	....	....	....	....	....	....	....	....	....	....	....	....	....
1985-86	St. Lawrence University	ECAC	30	3	14	17	....	....	....	60	....	....	....	....	....	....	....	....	....	....	....	....	....	....	....	....	....	....
1986-87	St. Lawrence University	ECAC	35	6	13	19	....	....	....	92	....	....	....	....	....	....	....	....	....	....	....	....	....	....	....	....	....	....
1987-88	St. Lawrence University	ECAC	32	3	6	9	....	....	....	64	....	....	....	....	....	....	....	....	....	....	....	....	....	....	....	....	....	....
1988-89	Springfield Indians	AHL	69	1	13	14	....	....	....	55	....	....	....	....	....	....	....	....	....	....	....	....	....	....	....	....	....	....
1989-90	Springfield Indians	AHL	43	0	6	6	....	....	....	27	....	....	....	....	....	....	....	....	....	....	....	....	....	....	....	....	....	....
1990-91	Capital District Islanders	AHL	32	0	5	5	....	....	....	14	....	....	....	....	....	....	....	....	....	....	....	....	....	....	....	....	....	....
	Kansas City Blades	IHL	17	0	1	1	....	....	....	27	....	....	....	....	....	....	....	....	....	....	....	....	....	....	....	....	....	....
1991-92			DID NOT PLAY																									
1992-93	Canada	Nat-Team	64	8	14	22	....	....	....	83	....	....	....	....	....	....	....	....	....	....	....	....	....	....	....	....	....	....
1993-94	**Ottawa Senators**	**NHL**	27	1	2	3	1	2	3	22	0	0	0	6	16.7	10	0	50	20	–20	....	....	....	....	....	....	....	....
	P.E.I. Senators	AHL	50	2	9	11	....	....	....	32	....	....	....	....	....	....	....	....	....	....	....	....	....	....	....	....	....	....
	NHL Totals		27	1	2	3	1	2	3	22	0	0	0	6	16.7	10	0	50	20		....	....	....	....	....	....	....	....

ECAC Second All-Star Team (1987, 1988)

• Missed entire 1991-92 season training for the 1992 Summer Olympic Games. Signed as a free agent by **Ottawa**, June 25, 1993.

• LAMOUREUX, MITCH

Mitch Lamoureux C – L. 5'6", 175 lbs. b: Ottawa, Ont., 8/22/1962. Pittsburgh's 7th choice, 154th overall, in 1981 Entry Draft.

Season	Club	League	GP	G	A	Pts	AG	AA	APts	PIM	PP	SH	GW	S	%	TGF	PGF	TGA	PGA	+/–	GP	G	A	Pts	PIM	PP	SH	GW
1979-80	Oshawa Generals	OHA	67	28	48	76	....	....	....	63	....	....	....	....	....	....	....	....	....	....	7	2	1	3	16	....	....	....
1980-81	Oshawa Generals	OHA	63	50	69	119	....	....	....	256	....	....	....	....	....	....	....	....	....	....	11	11	13	24	57	....	....	....
1981-82	Oshawa Generals	OHL	66	43	78	121	....	....	....	275	....	....	....	....	....	....	....	....	....	....	12	4	17	21	68	....	....	....
1982-83	Baltimore Skipjacks	AHL	80	57	50	107	....	....	....	107	....	....	....	....	....	....	....	....	....	....	....	....	....	....	....	....	....	....
1983-84	**Pittsburgh Penguins**	**NHL**	8	1	1	2	1	1	2	6	0	0	0	13	7.7	4	1	10	1	–6	....	....	....	....	....	....	....	....
	Baltimore Skipjacks	AHL	68	30	38	68	....	....	....	136	....	....	....	....	....	....	....	....	....	....	9	1	3	4	2	....	....	....
1984-85	**Pittsburgh Penguins**	**NHL**	62	10	8	18	8	5	13	53	0	2	0	81	12.3	21	0	50	20	–9	....	....	....	....	....	....	....	....
	Baltimore Skipjacks	AHL	18	10	14	24	....	....	....	34	....	....	....	....	....	....	....	....	....	....	....	....	....	....	....	....	....	....

Season	Club	League	GP	G	A	Pts	AG	AA	APts	PIM	PP	SH	GW	S	%	TGF	PGF	TGA	PGA	+/-	GP	G	A	Pts	PIM	PP	SH	GW
			REGULAR SEASON																		PLAYOFFS							
1985-86	Baltimore Skipjacks	AHL	75	22	31	53				129																		
1986-87	Hershey Bears	AHL	78	43	46	89				122											5	1	2	3	8			
1987-88	**Philadelphia Flyers**	**NHL**	**3**	**0**	**0**	**0**	**0**	**0**	**0**	**0**	**0**	**0**	**0**	**1**	**0.0**	**0**	**0**	**1**	**0**	**–1**								
	Hershey Bears	AHL	78	35	52	87				171											12	9	7	*16	48			
1988-89	Asiago	Italy	8	9	8	17				16																		
	Hershey Bears	AHL	9	9	7	16				14											9	1	4	5	14			
1989-90	Canada	Nat-Team	4	1	2	3				6																		
	Maine Mariners	AHL	10	4	7	11				10																		
1990-91	Zell-am-Zee	Austria	42	36	44	80																						
1991-92	HC Allegne	Italy	11	12	11	23				12																		
1992-93	San Diego Gulls	IHL	71	28	39	67				130											4	0	0	0	11			
1993-94	Hershey Bears	AHL	80	45	60	105				92											11	3	4	7	26			
1994-95	Hershey Bears	AHL	76	39	46	85				112											6	0	2	2	8			
1995-96	Providence Bruins	AHL	63	22	29	51				62											4	2	3	5	2			
1996-97	Providence Bruins	AHL	75	25	29	54				70											3	0	0	0	4			
1997-98	Binghamton Icemen	UHL	16	18	15	33				10																		
	Hershey Bears	AHL	22	4	9	13				22											7	2	4	6	12			
	NHL Totals		**73**	**11**	**9**	**20**	**9**	**6**	**15**	**59**	**0**	**2**	**0**	**95**	**11.6**	**25**	**1**	**61**	**21**									

AHL Second All-Star Team (1983) • Won Dudley "Red" Garrett Memorial Award (Top Rookie - AHL) (1983)

Signed as a free agent by **Philadelphia**, June 30, 1986.

• LAMPMAN, MIKE

Mike Lampman LW – L. 6'2", 195 lbs. b: Lakewood, CA, 4/20/1950. St. Louis' 10th choice, 111th overall, in 1970 Amateur Draft.

Season	Club	League	GP	G	A	Pts	AG	AA	APts	PIM	PP	SH	GW	S	%	TGF	PGF	TGA	PGA	+/-	GP	G	A	Pts	PIM	PP	SH	GW
1967-68	Marquette Iron Rangers	USHL	....	5	5	10				20																		
1968-69	University of Denver	WCHA	DID NOT PLAY – FRESHMAN																									
1969-70	University of Denver	WCHA	28	12	5	17				32																		
1970-71	University of Denver	WCHA	36	24	18	42				77																		
1971-72	University of Denver	WCHA	36	30	13	43				38																		
1972-73	**St. Louis Blues**	**NHL**	**18**	**2**	**3**	**5**	**2**	**2**	**4**	**2**	**0**	**0**	**0**	**18**	**11.1**	**9**	**2**	**3**	**0**	**+4**								
	Denver Spurs	WHL	49	34	19	53				88											5	0	3	3	0			
1973-74	**St. Louis Blues**	**NHL**	**15**	**1**	**0**	**1**	**1**	**0**	**1**	**0**	**1**	**0**	**0**	**19**	**5.3**	**5**	**1**	**3**	**0**	**+1**								
	Denver Spurs	WHL	5	5	6	11				4																		
	Vancouver Canucks	**NHL**	**14**	**1**	**0**	**1**	**1**	**0**	**1**	**0**	**0**	**0**	**0**	**17**	**5.9**	**5**	**0**	**15**	**0**	**–10**								
	Seattle Totems	WHL	30	8	14	22				13																		
1974-75	Richmond Robins	AHL	36	4	5	9				35											6	1	2	3	8			
1975-76	**Washington Capitals**	**NHL**	**27**	**7**	**12**	**19**	**7**	**9**	**16**	**28**	**0**	**0**	**1**	**55**	**12.7**	**23**	**3**	**27**	**1**	**–6**								
	Baltimore Clippers	AHL	35	13	24	37				24																		
1976-77	**Washington Capitals**	**NHL**	**22**	**6**	**5**	**11**	**6**	**4**	**10**	**4**	**1**	**0**	**0**	**47**	**12.8**	**16**	**2**	**18**	**0**	**–4**								
	NHL Totals		**96**	**17**	**20**	**37**	**17**	**15**	**32**	**34**	**2**	**0**	**1**	**156**	**10.9**	**58**	**8**	**66**	**1**									

WHL Second All-Star Team (1973)

Traded to **Vancouver** by **St. Louis** for John Wright, December 10, 1973. Claimed by **Washington** from **Vancouver** in Expansion Draft, June 12, 1974.

• LANDON, LARRY

Larry Landon RW – R. 6', 191 lbs. b: Niagara Falls, Ont., 5/4/1958. Montreal's 11th choice, 137th overall, in 1978 Amateur Draft.

Season	Club	League	GP	G	A	Pts	AG	AA	APts	PIM	PP	SH	GW	S	%	TGF	PGF	TGA	PGA	+/-	GP	G	A	Pts	PIM	PP	SH	GW
1975-76	St. Catharines Fincups	OHA	10	1	1	2				2																		
1976-77	St. Catharines Falcons	OJHL	STATISTICS NOT AVAILABLE																									
1977-78	RPI Engineers	ECAC	29	13	22	35				18																		
1978-79	RPI Engineers	ECAC	28	18	27	45				12																		
1979-80	RPI Engineers	ECAC	28	20	27	47				14																		
1980-81	RPI Engineers	ECAC	28	13	17	30				27																		
	Nova Scotia Voyageurs	AHL	2	0	0	0				0											2	0	0	0	0			
1981-82	Nova Scotia Voyageurs	AHL	69	11	15	26				31											8	1	0	1	0			
1982-83	Nova Scotia Voyageurs	AHL	68	18	25	43				40											7	2	0	2	0			
1983-84	**Montreal Canadiens**	**NHL**	**2**	**0**	**0**	**0**	**0**	**0**	**0**	**0**	**0**	**0**	**0**	**5**	**0.0**	**2**	**0**	**0**	**0**	**+2**								
	Nova Scotia Voyageurs	AHL	79	26	30	56				19											12	7	2	9	2			
1984-85	Sherbrooke Canadiens	AHL	21	7	9	16				2																		
	Toronto Maple Leafs	**NHL**	**7**	**0**	**0**	**0**	**0**	**0**	**0**	**2**	**0**	**0**	**0**	**5**	**0.0**	**2**	**0**	**7**	**1**	**–4**								
	St. Catharines Saints	AHL	44	21	36	57				8																		
	NHL Totals		**9**	**0**	**0**	**0**	**0**	**0**	**0**	**2**	**0**	**0**	**0**	**10**	**0.0**	**4**	**0**	**7**	**1**									

Traded to **Toronto** by **Montreal** for Gaston Gingras, February 14, 1985.

• LANDRY, ERIC

Eric Landry C – L. 5'11", 185 lbs. b: Gatineau, Que., 1/20/1975. San Jose's 8th choice, 193rd overall, in 1994 Entry Draft.

Season	Club	League	GP	G	A	Pts	AG	AA	APts	PIM	PP	SH	GW	S	%	TGF	PGF	TGA	PGA	+/-	GP	G	A	Pts	PIM	PP	SH	GW
1993-94	St-Hyacinthe Laser	QMJHL	69	42	34	76				128											7	4	2	6	13			
1994-95	St-Hyacinthe Laser	QMJHL	68	38	36	74				249											5	2	1	3	10			
1995-96	Cape Breton Oilers	AHL	74	19	33	52				187																		
1996-97	Hamilton Bulldogs	AHL	74	15	17	32				139											22	6	7	13	43			
1997-98	**Calgary Flames**	**NHL**	**12**	**1**	**0**	**1**	**1**	**0**	**1**	**4**	**0**	**0**	**0**	**7**	**14.3**	**3**	**0**	**8**	**3**	**–2**								
	Saint John Flames	AHL	61	17	21	38				194											20	4	6	10	58			
	United States	WC-A	2	0	0	0				0																		
	NHL Totals		**12**	**1**	**0**	**1**	**1**	**0**	**1**	**4**	**0**	**0**	**0**	**7**	**14.3**	**3**	**0**	**8**	**3**									

Signed as a free agent by **Calgary**, August 20, 1997.

• LANE, GORD

Gord Lane D – L. 6'1", 190 lbs. b: Brandon, Man., 3/31/1953. Pittsburgh's 9th choice, 134th overall, in 1973 Amateur Draft.

Season	Club	League	GP	G	A	Pts	AG	AA	APts	PIM	PP	SH	GW	S	%	TGF	PGF	TGA	PGA	+/-	GP	G	A	Pts	PIM	PP	SH	GW
1970-71	Brandon Wheat Kings	WHL	20	0	4	4				53																		
1971-72	Brandon Wheat Kings	WHL	63	7	16	23				106											11	1	2	3	19			
1972-73	New Westminster Bruins	WHL	36	2	13	15				115											5	0	0	0	29			
1973-74	Fort Wayne Komets	IHL	67	1	14	15				214											4	0	1	1	27			
1974-75	Dayton Gems	IHL	50	6	10	16				225											14	1	3	4	31			
1975-76	**Washington Capitals**	**NHL**	**3**	**1**	**0**	**1**	**1**	**0**	**1**	**12**	**1**	**0**	**0**	**2**	**50.0**	**2**	**1**	**6**	**0**	**–5**								
	Hampton Gulls	SHL	12	1	7	8				58																		
	Dayton Gems	IHL	55	12	22	34				227											15	0	11	11	85			
1976-77	**Washington Capitals**	**NHL**	**80**	**2**	**15**	**17**	**2**	**12**	**14**	**207**	**0**	**0**	**0**	**59**	**3.4**	**60**	**1**	**105**	**21**	**–25**								
1977-78	**Washington Capitals**	**NHL**	**69**	**2**	**9**	**11**	**2**	**7**	**9**	**195**	**0**	**0**	**0**	**68**	**2.9**	**40**	**0**	**80**	**21**	**–19**								
	Hershey Bears	AHL	4	0	1	1				8																		
1978-79	**Washington Capitals**	**NHL**	**64**	**3**	**15**	**18**	**3**	**11**	**14**	**147**	**0**	**0**	**0**	**69**	**4.3**	**54**	**1**	**91**	**23**	**–15**								
	Hershey Bears	AHL	5	0	1	1				48																		
1979-80	**Washington Capitals**	**NHL**	**19**	**2**	**4**	**6**	**2**	**3**	**5**	**53**	**0**	**0**	**0**	**16**	**12.5**	**15**	**0**	**21**	**7**	**+1**								
	New York Islanders	**NHL**	**55**	**2**	**14**	**16**	**2**	**11**	**13**	**152**	**0**	**0**	**1**	**60**	**3.3**	**56**	**1**	**57**	**12**	**+10**	**21**	**1**	**3**	**4**	***85**	**0**	**0**	**0**
1980-81	**New York Islanders**	**NHL**	**60**	**3**	**9**	**12**	**2**	**6**	**8**	**124**	**0**	**1**	**1**	**54**	**5.6**	**48**	**1**	**63**	**10**	**–6**	**12**	**1**	**5**	**6**	**32**	**0**	**0**	**0**
1981-82	**New York Islanders**	**NHL**	**51**	**0**	**13**	**13**	**0**	**9**	**9**	**98**	**0**	**0**	**0**	**46**	**0.0**	**55**	**0**	**34**	**5**	**+26**	**19**	**0**	**4**	**4**	**61**	**0**	**0**	**0**
1982-83	**New York Islanders**	**NHL**	**44**	**3**	**4**	**7**	**2**	**3**	**5**	**87**	**0**	**0**	**0**	**44**	**6.8**	**25**	**0**	**31**	**7**	**+1**	**18**	**1**	**2**	**3**	**32**	**0**	**0**	**1**
1983-84	**New York Islanders**	**NHL**	**37**	**0**	**3**	**3**	**0**	**2**	**2**	**70**	**0**	**0**	**0**	**16**	**0.0**	**33**	**0**	**31**	**4**	**+6**	**4**	**0**	**0**	**0**	**2**	**0**	**0**	**0**
1984-85	**New York Islanders**	**NHL**	**57**	**1**	**8**	**9**	**1**	**5**	**6**	**83**	**0**	**0**	**0**	**21**	**4.8**	**45**	**0**	**44**	**9**	**+10**	**1**	**0**	**0**	**0**	**2**	**0**	**0**	**0**
1985-86	Brandon Wheat Kings	WHL	DID NOT PLAY – COACHING																									
1986-87	Springfield Indians	AHL	62	2	6	8				117																		
1987-88	Springfield Indians	AHL	DID NOT PLAY – COACHING																									
	NHL Totals		**539**	**19**	**94**	**113**	**17**	**69**	**86**	**1228**	**1**	**1**	**2**	**455**	**4.2**	**433**	**5**	**563**	**119**		**75**	**3**	**14**	**17**	**214**	**0**	**0**	**1**

Signed as a free agent by **Washington**, October 5, 1976. Traded to **NY Islanders** by **Washington** for Mike Kaszycki, December 7, 1979.

• LANG, ROBERT

Robert Lang C – R. 6'2", 200 lbs. b: Teplice, Czech., 12/19/1970. Los Angeles' 6th choice, 133rd overall, in 1990 Entry Draft.

			REGULAR SEASON																		PLAYOFFS							
Season	Club	League	GP	G	A	Pts	AG	AA	APts	PIM	PP	SH	GW	S	%	TGF	PGF	TGA	PGA	+/–	GP	G	A	Pts	PIM	PP	SH	GW
1988-89	CHZ Litvinov	Czech.	7	3	2	5	....	....	....	0	....	....	....	....	....	....	....	....	....	....	....	....	....	....	....	....	....	....
1989-90	CHZ Litvinov	Czech.	39	11	10	21	....	....	....	....	....	....	....	....	....	....	....	....	....	....	....	....	....	....	....	....	....	....
1990-91	Chemopetrol Litvinov	Czech.	56	26	26	52	....	....	....	38	....	....	....	....	....	....	....	....	....	....	....	....	....	....	....	....	....	....
1991-92	Chemopetrol Litvinov	Czech.	43	12	31	43	....	....	....	34	....	....	....	....	....	....	....	....	....	....	....	....	....	....	....	....	....	....
	Czechoslovakia	Olympics	8	5	8	13	....	....	....	8	....	....	....	....	....	....	....	....	....	....	....	....	....	....	....	....	....	....
	Czechoslovakia	WC-A	8	2	2	4	....	....	....	2	....	....	....	....	....	....	....	....	....	....	....	....	....	....	....	....	....	....
1992-93	**Los Angeles Kings**	**NHL**	**11**	**0**	**5**	**5**	**0**	**3**	**3**	**2**	**0**	**0**	**0**	**3**	**0.0**	**6**	**0**	**9**	**0**	**–3**	....	....	....	....	....	....	....	....
	Phoenix Roadrunners	IHL	38	9	21	30	....	....	....	20	....	....	....	....	....	....	....	....	....	....	....	....	....	....	....	....	....	....
1993-94	**Los Angeles Kings**	**NHL**	**32**	**9**	**10**	**19**	**8**	**8**	**16**	**10**	**0**	**0**	**0**	**41**	**22.0**	**29**	**4**	**20**	**2**	**+7**	....	....	....	....	....	....	....	....
	Phoenix Roadrunners	IHL	44	11	24	35	....	....	....	34	....	....	....	....	....	....	....	....	....	....	....	....	....	....	....	....	....	....
1994-95	CHZ Litvinov	Czech.	16	4	19	23	....	....	....	28	....	....	....	....	....	....	....	....	....	....	....	....	....	....	....	....	....	....
	Los Angeles Kings	**NHL**	**36**	**4**	**8**	**12**	**7**	**12**	**19**	**4**	**0**	**0**	**0**	**38**	**10.5**	**19**	**2**	**27**	**3**	**–7**	....	....	....	....	....	....	....	....
1995-96	**Los Angeles Kings**	**NHL**	**68**	**6**	**16**	**22**	**6**	**13**	**19**	**10**	**0**	**2**	**0**	**71**	**8.5**	**28**	**2**	**54**	**13**	**–15**	....	....	....	....	....	....	....	....
	Czech Republic	WC-A	8	5	4	9	....	....	....	2	....	....	....	....	....	....	....	....	....	....	....	....	....	....	....	....	....	....
1996-97	Czech Republic	W Cup	3	0	0	0	....	....	....	2	....	....	....	....	....	....	....	....	....	....	....	....	....	....	....	....	....	....
	HC Sparta	Czech.	38	14	27	41	....	....	....	30	....	....	....	....	....	....	....	....	....	....	5	1	2	3	4	....	....	....
	Czech Republic	WC-A	8	1	1	2	....	....	....	25	....	....	....	....	....	....	....	....	....	....	....	....	....	....	....	....	....	....
1997-98	**Boston Bruins**	**NHL**	**3**	**0**	**0**	**0**	**0**	**0**	**0**	**2**	**0**	**0**	**0**	**2**	**0.0**	**1**	**0**	**0**	**0**	**+1**	....	....	....	....	....	....	....	....
	Czech Republic	Olympics	6	0	3	3	....	....	....	0	....	....	....	....	....	....	....	....	....	....	....	....	....	....	....	....	....	....
	Pittsburgh Penguins	**NHL**	**51**	**9**	**13**	**22**	**11**	**13**	**24**	**14**	**1**	**1**	**2**	**64**	**14.1**	**32**	**7**	**29**	**10**	**+6**	**6**	**0**	**3**	**3**	**2**	**0**	**0**	**0**
	Houston Aeros	IHL	9	1	7	8	....	....	....	4	....	....	....	....	....	....	....	....	....	....	....	....	....	....	....	....	....	....
	NHL Totals		**201**	**28**	**52**	**80**	**32**	**49**	**81**	**42**	**1**	**3**	**2**	**219**	**12.8**	**115**	**15**	**139**	**28**		**6**	**0**	**3**	**3**	**2**	**0**	**0**	**0**

Signed as a free agent by **Pittsburgh**, September 2, 1997. Claimed by **Boston** from **Pittsburgh** in NHL Waiver Draft, September 28, 1997. Claimed on waivers by **Pittsburgh** from **Boston**, October 25, 1997.

• LANGDON, DARREN

Darren Langdon LW – L. 6'1", 200 lbs. b: Deer Lake, Nfld., 1/8/1971.

Season	Club	League	GP	G	A	Pts	AG	AA	APts	PIM	PP	SH	GW	S	%	TGF	PGF	TGA	PGA	+/–	GP	G	A	Pts	PIM	PP	SH	GW
1991-92	Summerside Lightning	PEI Jr.	44	34	49	83	....	....	....	441	....	....	....	....	....	....	....	....	....	....	....	....	....	....	....	....	....	....
1992-93	Binghamton Rangers	AHL	18	3	4	7	....	....	....	115	....	....	....	....	....	....	....	....	....	....	8	0	1	1	14	....	....	....
	Dayton Bombers	ECHL	54	23	22	45	....	....	....	429	....	....	....	....	....	....	....	....	....	....	3	0	1	1	40	....	....	....
1993-94	Binghamton Rangers	AHL	54	2	7	9	....	....	....	327	....	....	....	....	....	....	....	....	....	....	....	....	....	....	....	....	....	....
1994-95	Binghamton Rangers	AHL	55	6	14	20	....	....	....	296	....	....	....	....	....	....	....	....	....	....	11	1	3	4	*84	....	....	....
	New York Rangers	**NHL**	**18**	**1**	**1**	**2**	**2**	**1**	**3**	**62**	**0**	**0**	**0**	**6**	**16.7**	**5**	**0**	**5**	**0**	**0**	....	....	....	....	....	....	....	....
1995-96	**New York Rangers**	**NHL**	**64**	**7**	**4**	**11**	**7**	**3**	**10**	**175**	**0**	**0**	**1**	**29**	**24.1**	**12**	**0**	**10**	**0**	**+2**	**2**	**0**	**0**	**0**	**0**	**0**	**0**	**0**
	Binghamton Rangers	AHL	1	0	0	0	....	....	....	12	....	....	....	....	....	....	....	....	....	....	....	....	....	....	....	....	....	....
1996-97	**New York Rangers**	**NHL**	**60**	**3**	**6**	**9**	**3**	**5**	**8**	**195**	**0**	**0**	**1**	**24**	**12.5**	**10**	**0**	**11**	**0**	**–1**	**10**	**0**	**0**	**0**	**2**	**0**	**0**	**0**
1997-98	**New York Rangers**	**NHL**	**70**	**3**	**3**	**6**	**4**	**3**	**7**	**197**	**0**	**0**	**0**	**15**	**20.0**	**9**	**0**	**9**	**0**	**0**	....	....	....	....	....	....	....	....
	NHL Totals		**212**	**14**	**14**	**28**	**16**	**12**	**28**	**629**	**0**	**0**	**2**	**74**	**18.9**	**36**	**0**	**35**	**0**		**12**	**0**	**0**	**0**	**2**	**0**	**0**	**0**

Signed as a free agent by **NY Rangers**, August 16, 1993.

• LANGDON, STEVE

Steve Langdon LW – L. 5'11", 175 lbs. b: Toronto, Ont., 12/23/1953. Boston's 5th choice, 63rd overall, in 1973 Amateur Draft.

Season	Club	League	GP	G	A	Pts	AG	AA	APts	PIM	PP	SH	GW	S	%	TGF	PGF	TGA	PGA	+/–	GP	G	A	Pts	PIM	PP	SH	GW
1972-73	London Knights	OHA	72	31	47	78	....	....	....	93	....	....	....	....	....	....	....	....	....	....	....	....	....	....	....	....	....	....
1973-74	Albuquerque 6-Guns	CHL	67	21	13	34	....	....	....	16	....	....	....	....	....	....	....	....	....	....	....	....	....	....	....	....	....	....
1974-75	**Boston Bruins**	**NHL**	**1**	**0**	**1**	**1**	**0**	**1**	**1**	**0**	**0**	**0**	**0**	**0**	**0.0**	**1**	**0**	**0**	**0**	**+1**	....	....	....	....	....	....	....	....
	Rochester Americans	AHL	56	8	11	19	....	....	....	8	....	....	....	....	....	....	....	....	....	....	12	0	2	2	5	....	....	....
	Binghamton Dusters	NAHL	1	3	1	4	....	....	....	0	....	....	....	....	....	....	....	....	....	....	....	....	....	....	....	....	....	....
1975-76	**Boston Bruins**	**NHL**	**4**	**0**	**0**	**0**	**0**	**0**	**0**	**2**	**0**	**0**	**0**	**2**	**0.0**	**0**	**0**	**1**	**0**	**–1**	**4**	**0**	**0**	**0**	**0**	**0**	**0**	**0**
	Rochester Americans	AHL	62	18	11	29	....	....	....	11	....	....	....	....	....	....	....	....	....	....	5	0	1	1	0	....	....	....
1976-77	Rochester Americans	AHL	43	16	15	31	....	....	....	4	....	....	....	....	....	....	....	....	....	....	12	2	5	7	2	....	....	....
1977-78	**Boston Bruins**	**NHL**	**2**	**0**	**0**	**0**	**0**	**0**	**0**	**0**	**0**	**0**	**0**	**1**	**0.0**	**0**	**0**	**1**	**0**	**–1**	....	....	....	....	....	....	....	....
	Rochester Americans	AHL	72	30	27	57	....	....	....	0	....	....	....	....	....	....	....	....	....	....	6	1	3	4	0	....	....	....
1978-79	Rochester Americans	AHL	80	25	23	48	....	....	....	14	....	....	....	....	....	....	....	....	....	....	....	....	....	....	....	....	....	....
	NHL Totals		**7**	**0**	**1**	**1**	**0**	**1**	**1**	**2**	**0**	**0**	**0**	**3**	**0.0**	**1**	**0**	**2**	**0**		**4**	**0**	**0**	**0**	**0**	**0**	**0**	**0**

• LANGENBRUNNER, JAMIE

Jamie Langenbrunner C – R. 5'11", 185 lbs. b: Duluth, MN, 7/24/1975. Dallas' 2nd choice, 35th overall, in 1993 Entry Draft.

Season	Club	League	GP	G	A	Pts	AG	AA	APts	PIM	PP	SH	GW	S	%	TGF	PGF	TGA	PGA	+/–	GP	G	A	Pts	PIM	PP	SH	GW
1992-93	Cloquet High School	H.S.	27	27	62	89	....	....	....	18	....	....	....	....	....	....	....	....	....	....	....	....	....	....	....	....	....	....
1993-94	Peterborough Petes	OHL	62	33	58	91	....	....	....	53	....	....	....	....	....	....	....	....	....	....	7	4	6	10	2	....	....	....
	United States	WJC-A	7	2	0	2	....	....	....	13	....	....	....	....	....	....	....	....	....	....	....	....	....	....	....	....	....	....
1994-95	Peterborough Petes	OHL	62	42	57	99	....	....	....	84	....	....	....	....	....	....	....	....	....	....	11	8	14	22	12	....	....	....
	United States	WJC-A	7	1	1	2	....	....	....	6	....	....	....	....	....	....	....	....	....	....	....	....	....	....	....	....	....	....
	Dallas Stars	**NHL**	**2**	**0**	**0**	**0**	**0**	**0**	**0**	**2**	**0**	**0**	**0**	**1**	**0.0**	**1**	**0**	**1**	**0**	**0**	....	....	....	....	....	....	....	....
	Kalamazoo Wings	IHL	....	....	....	....	....	....	....	....	....	....	....	....	....	....	....	....	....	....	11	1	3	4	2	....	....	....
1995-96	**Dallas Stars**	**NHL**	**12**	**2**	**2**	**4**	**2**	**2**	**4**	**6**	**1**	**0**	**0**	**15**	**13.3**	**7**	**3**	**6**	**0**	**–2**	....	....	....	....	....	....	....	....
	Michigan K-Wings	IHL	59	25	40	65	....	....	....	129	....	....	....	....	....	....	....	....	....	....	10	3	10	13	8	....	....	....
1996-97	**Dallas Stars**	**NHL**	**76**	**13**	**26**	**39**	**14**	**23**	**37**	**51**	**3**	**0**	**3**	**112**	**11.6**	**50**	**15**	**37**	**0**	**–2**	**5**	**1**	**1**	**2**	**14**	**0**	**0**	**1**
1997-98	**Dallas Stars**	**NHL**	**81**	**23**	**29**	**52**	**27**	**28**	**55**	**61**	**8**	**0**	**6**	**159**	**14.5**	**80**	**33**	**42**	**4**	**+9**	**16**	**1**	**4**	**5**	**14**	**0**	**0**	**1**
	United States	Olympics	3	0	0	0	....	....	....	4	....	....	....	....	....	....	....	....	....	....	....	....	....	....	....	....	....	....
	NHL Totals		**171**	**38**	**57**	**95**	**43**	**53**	**96**	**120**	**12**	**0**	**9**	**287**	**13.2**	**138**	**51**	**86**	**4**		**21**	**2**	**5**	**7**	**28**	**0**	**0**	**2**

• LANGEVIN, CHRIS

Chris Langevin LW – L. 6', 190 lbs. b: Montreal, Que., 11/27/1959.

Season	Club	League	GP	G	A	Pts	AG	AA	APts	PIM	PP	SH	GW	S	%	TGF	PGF	TGA	PGA	+/–	GP	G	A	Pts	PIM	PP	SH	GW
1977-78	Chicoutimi Sagueneens	QMJHL	67	8	20	28	....	....	....	183	....	....	....	....	....	....	....	....	....	....	....	....	....	....	....	....	....	....
1978-79	Chicoutimi Sagueneens	QMJHL	65	24	23	47	....	....	....	182	....	....	....	....	....	....	....	....	....	....	4	0	2	2	19	....	....	....
1979-80	Chicoutimi Sagueneens	QMJHL	46	22	30	52	....	....	....	97	....	....	....	....	....	....	....	....	....	....	2	0	3	3	14	....	....	....
1980-81	Saginaw Gears	IHL	75	35	48	83	....	....	....	179	....	....	....	....	....	....	....	....	....	....	13	2	5	7	24	....	....	....
1981-82	Rochester Americans	AHL	33	3	5	8	....	....	....	150	....	....	....	....	....	....	....	....	....	....	9	4	5	9	33	....	....	....
1982-83	Rochester Americans	AHL	71	18	25	43	....	....	....	255	....	....	....	....	....	....	....	....	....	....	11	0	3	3	34	....	....	....
1983-84	**Buffalo Sabres**	**NHL**	**6**	**1**	**0**	**1**	**1**	**0**	**1**	**2**	**0**	**0**	**0**	**4**	**25.0**	**1**	**0**	**3**	**0**	**–2**	....	....	....	....	....	....	....	....
	Rochester Americans	AHL	41	11	14	25	....	....	....	133	....	....	....	....	....	....	....	....	....	....	15	3	2	5	39	....	....	....
1984-85	Rochester Americans	AHL	63	19	21	40	....	....	....	212	....	....	....	....	....	....	....	....	....	....	5	2	1	3	16	....	....	....
1985-86	**Buffalo Sabres**	**NHL**	**16**	**2**	**1**	**3**	**2**	**1**	**3**	**20**	**0**	**0**	**0**	**10**	**20.0**	**7**	**0**	**4**	**0**	**+3**	....	....	....	....	....	....	....	....
	NHL Totals		**22**	**3**	**1**	**4**	**3**	**1**	**4**	**22**	**0**	**0**	**0**	**14**	**21.4**	**8**	**0**	**7**	**0**		....	....	....	....	....	....	....	....

Signed as a free agent by **Buffalo**, October 14, 1983.

• LANGEVIN, DAVE

Dave "The Bammer" Langevin D – L. 6'2", 200 lbs. b: St. Paul, MN, 5/15/1954. NY Islanders' 6th choice, 112th overall, in 1974 Amateur Draft. **USHOF**

Season	Club	League	GP	G	A	Pts	AG	AA	APts	PIM	PP	SH	GW	S	%	TGF	PGF	TGA	PGA	+/–	GP	G	A	Pts	PIM	PP	SH	GW
1972-73	University of Minnesota-Duluth	WCHA	36	6	11	17	....	....	....	74	....	....	....	....	....	....	....	....	....	....	....	....	....	....	....	....	....	....
1973-74	University of Minnesota-Duluth	WCHA	37	2	11	13	....	....	....	56	....	....	....	....	....	....	....	....	....	....	....	....	....	....	....	....	....	....
1974-75	University of Minnesota-Duluth	WCHA	35	8	24	32	....	....	....	91	....	....	....	....	....	....	....	....	....	....	....	....	....	....	....	....	....	....
1975-76	University of Minnesota-Duluth	WCHA	34	19	26	45	....	....	....	82	....	....	....	....	....	....	....	....	....	....	....	....	....	....	....	....	....	....
	United States	WEC-A	10	1	0	1	....	....	....	11	....	....	....	....	....	....	....	....	....	....	....	....	....	....	....	....	....	....
1976-77	Edmonton Oilers	WHA	77	7	16	23	....	....	....	94	....	....	....	....	....	....	....	....	....	....	5	2	1	3	9	....	....	....
1977-78	Edmonton Oilers	WHA	62	6	22	28	....	....	....	90	....	....	....	....	....	....	....	....	....	....	5	0	2	2	10	....	....	....
1978-79	Edmonton Oilers	WHA	77	6	21	27	....	....	....	76	....	....	....	....	....	....	....	....	....	....	13	0	1	1	25	....	....	....
1979-80	**New York Islanders**	**NHL**	**76**	**3**	**13**	**16**	**3**	**10**	**13**	**109**	**0**	**1**	**0**	**82**	**3.7**	**74**	**1**	**77**	**15**	**+11**	**21**	**0**	**3**	**3**	**32**	**0**	**0**	**0**
1980-81	**New York Islanders**	**NHL**	**75**	**1**	**16**	**17**	**1**	**11**	**12**	**122**	**0**	**0**	**0**	**68**	**1.5**	**87**	**3**	**66**	**22**	**+40**	**18**	**0**	**3**	**3**	**25**	**0**	**0**	**0**
1981-82	United States	C Cup	6	0	1	1	....	....	....	8	....	....	....	....	....	....	....	....	....	....	....	....	....	....	....	....	....	....
	New York Islanders	**NHL**	**73**	**1**	**20**	**21**	**1**	**13**	**14**	**82**	**0**	**0**	**0**	**73**	**1.4**	**93**	**2**	**85**	**28**	**+34**	**19**	**2**	**4**	**6**	**16**	**0**	**0**	**1**
1982-83	**New York Islanders**	**NHL**	**73**	**4**	**17**	**21**	**3**	**12**	**15**	**64**	**0**	**0**	**0**	**107**	**3.7**	**74**	**0**	**69**	**17**	**+22**	**8**	**0**	**2**	**2**	**2**	**0**	**0**	**0**
1983-84	**New York Islanders**	**NHL**	**69**	**3**	**16**	**19**	**2**	**11**	**13**	**53**	**0**	**0**	**1**	**89**	**3.4**	**78**	**1**	**72**	**21**	**+26**	**12**	**0**	**4**	**4**	**18**	**0**	**0**	**0**
1984-85	**New York Islanders**	**NHL**	**56**	**0**	**13**	**13**	**0**	**9**	**9**	**35**	**0**	**0**	**0**	**33**	**0.0**	**46**	**1**	**69**	**18**	**–6**	**4**	**0**	**0**	**0**	**4**	**0**	**0**	**0**

			REGULAR SEASON																		PLAYOFFS							
Season	Club	League	GP	G	A	Pts	AG	AA	APts	PIM	PP	SH	GW	S	%	TGF	PGF	TGA	PGA	+/–	GP	G	A	Pts	PIM	PP	SH	GW
1985-86	**Minnesota North Stars**	**NHL**	**80**	**0**	**8**	**8**	**0**	**5**	**5**	**58**	**0**	**0**	**0**	**54**	**0.0**	**55**	**2**	**116**	**46**	**–17**	**5**	**0**	**1**	**1**	**9**	**0**	**0**	**0**
1986-87	**Los Angeles Kings**	**NHL**	**11**	**0**	**4**	**4**	**0**	**3**	**3**	**7**	**0**	**0**	**0**	**5**	**0.0**	**8**	**0**	**17**	**6**	**–3**	....	....	....	....	....	....	....	....
	New Haven Nighthawks	AHL	10	1	1	2	....	....	....	7	....	....	....	....	....	....	....	....	....	....	....	....	....	....	....	....	....	....
	NHL Totals		**513**	**12**	**107**	**119**	**10**	**74**	**84**	**530**	**0**	**1**	**1**	**511**	**2.3**	**515**	**10**	**571**	**173**		**87**	**2**	**17**	**19**	**106**	**0**	**0**	**1**
	Other Major League Totals		216	19	59	78	....	....	....	260	....	....	....	....	....	....	....	....	....		23	2	4	6	44	....	....	....

WCHA Second All-Star Team (1976) • WHA Second All-Star Team (1979)

Played in NHL All-Star Game (1983)

Selected by **Edmonton** (WHA) in 1974 WHA Amateur Draft, June, 1974. Reclaimed by **NY Islanders** from **Edmonton** prior to Expansion Draft, June 9, 1979. Claimed by **Minnesota** from **NY Islanders** in Waiver Draft, October 7, 1985. Signed as a free agent by **LA Kings**, February 4, 1987.

• LANGKOW, DAYMOND

Daymond Langkow C – L. 5'11", 175 lbs. b: Edmonton, Alta, 9/27/1976. Tampa Bay's 1st choice, 5th overall, in 1995 Entry Draft.

Season	Club	League	GP	G	A	Pts	AG	AA	APts	PIM	PP	SH	GW	S	%	TGF	PGF	TGA	PGA	+/–	GP	G	A	Pts	PIM	PP	SH	GW
1992-93	Tri-City Americans	WHL	64	22	42	64	....	....	....	100	....	....	....	....	....	....	....	....	....	....	4	1	0	1	4	....	....	....
1993-94	Tri-City Americans	WHL	61	40	43	83	....	....	....	174	....	....	....	....	....	....	....	....	....	....	4	2	2	4	15	....	....	....
1994-95	Tri-City Americans	WHL	72	*67	73	*140	....	....	....	142	....	....	....	....	....	....	....	....	....	....	17	12	15	27	52	....	....	....
1995-96	Tri-City Americans	WHL	48	30	61	91	....	....	....	103	....	....	....	....	....	....	....	....	....	....	11	14	13	27	20	....	....	....
	Canada	WJC-A	5	3	3	6	....	....	....	2	....	....	....	....	....	....	....	....	....	....	....	....	....	....	....	....	....	....
	Tampa Bay Lightning	**NHL**	**4**	**0**	**1**	**1**	**0**	**1**	**1**	**0**	**0**	**0**	**0**	**4**	**0.0**	**1**	**0**	**2**	**0**	**–1**	....	....	....	....	....	....	....	....
1996-97	**Tampa Bay Lightning**	**NHL**	**79**	**15**	**13**	**28**	**16**	**11**	**27**	**35**	**3**	**1**	**1**	**170**	**8.8**	**48**	**7**	**44**	**4**	**+1**	....	....	....	....	....	....	....	....
	Adirondack Red Wings	AHL	2	1	1	2	....	....	....	0	....	....	....	....	....	....	....	....	....	....	....	....	....	....	....	....	....	....
1997-98	**Tampa Bay Lightning**	**NHL**	**68**	**8**	**14**	**22**	**9**	**14**	**23**	**62**	**2**	**0**	**1**	**156**	**5.1**	**36**	**7**	**63**	**25**	**–9**	....	....	....	....	....	....	....	....
	NHL Totals		**151**	**23**	**28**	**51**	**25**	**26**	**51**	**97**	**5**	**1**	**2**	**330**	**7.0**	**85**	**14**	**109**	**29**		....	....	....	....	....	....	....	....

WHL West First All-Star Team (1995) • Canadian Major Junior First All-Star Team (1995) • WHL West Second All-Star Team (1996)

• LANGLAIS, ALAIN

Alain Langlais LW – L. 5'10", 175 lbs. b: Chicoutimi, Que., 10/9/1950.

Season	Club	League	GP	G	A	Pts	AG	AA	APts	PIM	PP	SH	GW	S	%	TGF	PGF	TGA	PGA	+/–	GP	G	A	Pts	PIM	PP	SH	GW
1969-70	Sorel Epervers	QJHL	49	60	51	111	....	....	....	105	....	....	....	....	....	....	....	....	....	....	10	7	6	13	22	....	....	....
1970-71	Toledo Hornets	IHL	31	8	8	16	....	....	....	50	....	....	....	....	....	....	....	....	....	....	....	....	....	....	....	....	....	....
	Jersey–Long Island	EHL	47	13	20	33	....	....	....	72	....	....	....	....	....	....	....	....	....	....	....	....	....	....	....	....	....	....
1971-72	Long Island Ducks	EHL	75	45	31	76	....	....	....	125	....	....	....	....	....	....	....	....	....	....	....	....	....	....	....	....	....	....
1972-73	Chicoutimi Sagueneens	QSHL	STATISTICS NOT AVAILABLE																									
1973-74	**Minnesota North Stars**	**NHL**	**14**	**3**	**3**	**6**	**3**	**3**	**6**	**8**	**0**	**0**	**0**	**45**	**6.7**	**8**	**0**	**15**	**1**	**–6**	....	....	....	....	....	....	....	....
	Saginaw Gears	IHL	11	3	3	6	....	....	....	14	....	....	....	....	....	....	....	....	....	....	....	....	....	....	....	....	....	....
	New Haven Nighthawks	AHL	45	21	16	37	....	....	....	73	....	....	....	....	....	....	....	....	....	....	10	6	3	9	9	....	....	....
1974-75	**Minnesota North Stars**	**NHL**	**11**	**1**	**1**	**2**	**1**	**1**	**2**	**2**	**0**	**0**	**0**	**15**	**6.7**	**4**	**0**	**7**	**0**	**–3**	....	....	....	....	....	....	....	....
	New Haven Nighthawks	AHL	66	41	29	70	....	....	....	109	....	....	....	....	....	....	....	....	....	....	12	7	6	13	23	....	....	....
1975-76	New Haven Nighthawks	AHL	53	14	17	31	....	....	....	34	....	....	....	....	....	....	....	....	....	....	....	....	....	....	....	....	....	....
	Richmond Robins	AHL	21	7	11	18	....	....	....	27	....	....	....	....	....	....	....	....	....	....	8	1	0	1	10	....	....	....
1976-77	New Haven Nighthawks	AHL	4	0	0	0	....	....	....	4	....	....	....	....	....	....	....	....	....	....	....	....	....	....	....	....	....	....
	Tulsa Oilers	CHL	68	13	22	35	....	....	....	71	....	....	....	....	....	....	....	....	....	....	9	*4	4	8	9	....	....	....
	NHL Totals		**25**	**4**	**4**	**8**	**4**	**4**	**8**	**10**	**0**	**0**	**0**	**60**	**6.7**	**12**	**0**	**22**	**1**		....	....	....	....	....	....	....	....

EHL North First All-Star Team (1972) • AHL Second All-Star Team (1975)

Signed as a free agent by **Minnesota**, September, 1973.

• LANGWAY, ROD

Rod Langway D – L. 6'3", 218 lbs. b: Maag, Formosa, 5/3/1957. Montreal's 3rd choice, 36th overall, in 1977 Amateur Draft.

Season	Club	League	GP	G	A	Pts	AG	AA	APts	PIM	PP	SH	GW	S	%	TGF	PGF	TGA	PGA	+/–	GP	G	A	Pts	PIM	PP	SH	GW
1976-77	University of New Hampshire	ECAC	34	10	43	53	....	....	....	52	....	....	....	....	....	....	....	....	....	....	....	....	....	....	....	....	....	....
1977-78	Birmingham Bulls	WHA	52	3	18	21	....	....	....	52	....	....	....	....	....	....	....	....	....	....	4	0	0	0	9	....	....	....
	Hampton Gulls	AHL	30	6	16	22	....	....	....	50	....	....	....	....	....	....	....	....	....	....	....	....	....	....	....	....	....	....
1978-79	**Montreal Canadiens**	**NHL**	**45**	**3**	**4**	**7**	**3**	**3**	**6**	**30**	**0**	**0**	**0**	**48**	**6.3**	**32**	**1**	**26**	**0**	**+5**	**8**	**0**	**0**	**0**	**16**	**0**	**0**	**0**
	Nova Scotia Voyageurs	AHL	18	6	13	19	....	....	....	29	....	....	....	....	....	....	....	....	....	....	....	....	....	....	....	....	....	....
1979-80	**Montreal Canadiens**	**NHL**	**77**	**7**	**29**	**36**	**6**	**22**	**28**	**81**	**0**	**0**	**1**	**112**	**6.3**	**108**	**7**	**83**	**18**	**+36**	**10**	**3**	**3**	**6**	**2**	**1**	**0**	**0**
1980-81	**Montreal Canadiens**	**NHL**	**80**	**11**	**34**	**45**	**9**	**24**	**33**	**120**	**5**	**1**	**2**	**165**	**6.7**	**136**	**21**	**85**	**23**	**+53**	**3**	**0**	**0**	**0**	**6**	**0**	**0**	**0**
1981-82	United States	C Cup	6	0	1	1	....	....	....	8	....	....	....	....	....	....	....	....	....	....	....	....	....	....	....	....	....	....
	Montreal Canadiens	**NHL**	**66**	**5**	**34**	**39**	**4**	**22**	**26**	**116**	**1**	**0**	**1**	**139**	**3.6**	**133**	**16**	**73**	**22**	**+66**	**5**	**0**	**3**	**3**	**18**	**0**	**0**	**0**
	United States	WEC-A	6	0	2	2	....	....	....	4	....	....	....	....	....	....	....	....	....	....	....	....	....	....	....	....	....	....
1982-83	**Washington Capitals**	**NHL**	**80**	**3**	**29**	**32**	**2**	**20**	**22**	**75**	**1**	**0**	**0**	**126**	**2.4**	**107**	**7**	**135**	**35**	**0**	**4**	**0**	**0**	**0**	**0**	**0**	**0**	**0**
1983-84	**Washington Capitals**	**NHL**	**80**	**9**	**24**	**33**	**7**	**16**	**23**	**61**	**1**	**2**	**2**	**168**	**5.4**	**112**	**18**	**106**	**26**	**+14**	**8**	**0**	**5**	**5**	**7**	**0**	**0**	**0**
1984-85	United States	C Cup	6	1	1	2	....	....	....	8	....	....	....	....	....	....	....	....	....	....	....	....	....	....	....	....	....	....
	Washington Capitals	**NHL**	**79**	**4**	**22**	**26**	**3**	**15**	**18**	**54**	**0**	**0**	**1**	**102**	**3.9**	**99**	**9**	**94**	**39**	**+35**	**5**	**0**	**1**	**1**	**6**	**0**	**0**	**0**
1985-86	**Washington Capitals**	**NHL**	**71**	**1**	**17**	**18**	**1**	**11**	**12**	**61**	**1**	**0**	**0**	**54**	**1.9**	**85**	**3**	**89**	**34**	**+27**	**9**	**1**	**2**	**3**	**6**	**1**	**0**	**0**
1986-87	**Washington Capitals**	**NHL**	**78**	**2**	**25**	**27**	**2**	**18**	**20**	**53**	**0**	**0**	**1**	**76**	**2.6**	**83**	**8**	**95**	**31**	**+11**	**7**	**0**	**1**	**1**	**2**	**0**	**0**	**0**
	NHL All-Stars	RV'87	2	0	0	0	....	....	....	0	....	....	....	....	....	....	....	....	....	....	....	....	....	....	....	....	....	....
1987-88	United States	C Cup	5	0	1	1	....	....	....	6	....	....	....	....	....	....	....	....	....	....	....	....	....	....	....	....	....	....
	Washington Capitals	**NHL**	**63**	**3**	**13**	**16**	**3**	**9**	**12**	**28**	**0**	**0**	**1**	**49**	**6.1**	**47**	**1**	**77**	**32**	**+1**	**6**	**0**	**0**	**0**	**8**	**0**	**0**	**0**
1988-89	**Washington Capitals**	**NHL**	**76**	**2**	**19**	**21**	**2**	**13**	**15**	**65**	**0**	**0**	**0**	**80**	**2.5**	**74**	**4**	**98**	**40**	**+12**	**6**	**0**	**0**	**0**	**6**	**0**	**0**	**0**
1989-90	Washington Capitals	FrTour	4	0	0	0	....	....	....	2	....	....	....	....	....	....	....	....	....	....	....	....	....	....	....	....	....	....
	Washington Capitals	**NHL**	**58**	**0**	**8**	**8**	**0**	**6**	**6**	**39**	**0**	**0**	**0**	**46**	**0.0**	**40**	**1**	**62**	**30**	**+7**	**15**	**1**	**4**	**5**	**12**	**0**	**0**	**1**
1990-91	**Washington Capitals**	**NHL**	**56**	**1**	**7**	**8**	**1**	**5**	**6**	**24**	**0**	**0**	**0**	**32**	**3.1**	**42**	**0**	**52**	**22**	**+12**	**11**	**0**	**2**	**2**	**6**	**0**	**0**	**0**
1991-92	**Washington Capitals**	**NHL**	**64**	**0**	**13**	**13**	**0**	**10**	**10**	**22**	**0**	**0**	**0**	**32**	**0.0**	**55**	**1**	**72**	**29**	**+11**	**7**	**0**	**1**	**1**	**2**	**0**	**0**	**0**
1992-93	**Washington Capitals**	**NHL**	**21**	**0**	**0**	**0**	**0**	**0**	**0**	**20**	**0**	**0**	**0**	**6**	**0.0**	**2**	**0**	**20**	**5**	**–13**	....	....	....	....	....	....	....	....
1993-94			DID NOT PLAY																									
1994-95	Richmond Renegades	ECHL	6	0	0	0	....	....	....	2	....	....	....	....	....	....	....	....	....	....	9	1	1	2	4	....	....	....
1995-96	San Francisco Spiders	IHL	46	1	5	6	....	....	....	38	....	....	....	....	....	....	....	....	....	....	....	....	....	....	....	....	....	....
	NHL Totals		**994**	**51**	**278**	**329**	**43**	**194**	**237**	**849**	**9**	**3**	**9**	**1235**	**4.1**	**1155**	**97**	**1167**	**386**		**104**	**5**	**22**	**27**	**97**	**2**	**0**	**1**
	Other Major League Totals		52	3	18	21	....	....	....	52	....	....	....	....	....	....	....	....	....		4	0	0	0	9	....	....	....

NHL First All-Star Team (1983, 1984) • Won James Norris Trophy (1983, 1984) • Canada Cup All-Star Team (1984) • NHL Second All-Star Team (1985)

Played in NHL All-Star Game (1981, 1982, 1983, 1984, 1985, 1986)

Selected by **Birmingham** (WHA) in 1977 WHA Amateur Draft, May, 1977. Claimed by **Montreal** as a fill-in during Expansion Draft, June 13, 1979. Traded to **Washington** by **Montreal** with Doug Jarvis, Craig Laughlin and Brian Engblom for Ryan Walter and Rick Green, September 9, 1982.

• LANTHIER, JEAN-MARC

Jean-Marc Lanthier RW – R. 6'2", 195 lbs. b: Montreal, Que., 3/27/1963. Vancouver's 2nd choice, 52nd overall, in 1981 Entry Draft.

Season	Club	League	GP	G	A	Pts	AG	AA	APts	PIM	PP	SH	GW	S	%	TGF	PGF	TGA	PGA	+/–	GP	G	A	Pts	PIM	PP	SH	GW
1979-80	Quebec Remparts	QMJHL	63	14	32	46	....	....	....	4	....	....	....	....	....	....	....	....	....	....	5	0	1	1	0	....	....	....
1980-81	Quebec Remparts	QMJHL	37	13	32	45	....	....	....	18	....	....	....	....	....	....	....	....	....	....	....	....	....	....	....	....	....	....
	Sorel Black Hawks	QMJHL	35	6	33	39	....	....	....	29	....	....	....	....	....	....	....	....	....	....	7	1	4	5	4	....	....	....
1981-82	Laval Voisins	QMJHL	60	44	34	78	....	....	....	48	....	....	....	....	....	....	....	....	....	....	18	8	11	19	8	....	....	....
1982-83	Laval Voisins	QMJHL	69	39	71	110	....	....	....	54	....	....	....	....	....	....	....	....	....	....	12	6	17	23	8	....	....	....
1983-84	**Vancouver Canucks**	**NHL**	**11**	**2**	**1**	**3**	**2**	**1**	**3**	**2**	**0**	**0**	**0**	**9**	**22.2**	**6**	**0**	**8**	**0**	**–2**	....	....	....	....	....	....	....	....
	Fredericton Express	AHL	60	25	17	42	....	....	....	29	....	....	....	....	....	....	....	....	....	....	7	4	6	10	0	....	....	....
1984-85	**Vancouver Canucks**	**NHL**	**27**	**6**	**4**	**10**	**5**	**3**	**8**	**13**	**2**	**0**	**1**	**23**	**26.1**	**16**	**3**	**30**	**1**	**–16**	....	....	....	....	....	....	....	....
	Fredericton Express	AHL	50	21	21	42	....	....	....	13	....	....	....	....	....	....	....	....	....	....	4	1	1	2	4	....	....	....
1985-86	**Vancouver Canucks**	**NHL**	**62**	**7**	**10**	**17**	**6**	**7**	**13**	**12**	**3**	**0**	**1**	**50**	**14.0**	**31**	**9**	**39**	**0**	**–17**	....	....	....	....	....	....	....	....
	Fredericton Express	AHL	7	5	5	10	....	....	....	2	....	....	....	....	....	....	....	....	....	....	....	....	....	....	....	....	....	....
1986-87	Fredericton Express	AHL	78	15	38	53	....	....	....	24	....	....	....	....	....	....	....	....	....	....	....	....	....	....	....	....	....	....
1987-88	**Vancouver Canucks**	**NHL**	**5**	**1**	**1**	**2**	**1**	**1**	**2**	**2**	**0**	**0**	**0**	**3**	**33.3**	**2**	**0**	**3**	**0**	**–1**	....	....	....	....	....	....	....	....
	Fredericton Express	AHL	74	35	71	106	....	....	....	37	....	....	....	....	....	....	....	....	....	....	15	3	8	11	14	....	....	....

			REGULAR SEASON																		PLAYOFFS							
Season	Club	League	GP	G	A	Pts	AG	AA	APts	PIM	PP	SH	GW	S	%	TGF	PGF	TGA	PGA	+/-	GP	G	A	Pts	PIM	PP	SH	GW
1988-89	Maine Mariners	AHL	24	7	16	23				16																		
	Utica Devils	AHL	55	23	26	49				22											3	3	0	3	2			
1989-90	Fort Wayne Komets	IHL	7	4	7	11				4																		
	Utica Devils	AHL	50	13	19	32				32											4	1	1	2	2			
	NHL Totals		105	16	16	32	14	12	26	29	5	0	2	85	18.8	55	12	80		1								

Signed as a free agent by **Boston**, July 1, 1988. Traded to **New Jersey** by **Boston** for Dan Dorion, December 9, 1988.

● **LANYON, TED**   Ted Lanyon   D – R. 5'11", 175 lbs.   b: Winnipeg, Man., 6/11/1939.

1957-58	St. Boniface Canadians	MJHL	28	7	14	21				92											23	5	7	12	62			
1958-59	St. Boniface Canadians	MJHL	28	8	12	20				67											9	0	1	1	18			
1959-60	Johnstown Jets	EHL	14	4	3	7				25											13	0	0	0	12			
	St. Paul Saints	IHL	54	4	9	13				50																		
1960-61	Milwaukee Falcons	IHL	15	7	2	9				28																		
1961-62	Minneapolis Millers	IHL	49	6	12	18				88																		
1962-63	Greensboro Generals	EHL	68	15	25	40				104											4	2	1	3	18			
1963-64	Greensboro Generals	EHL	44	8	14	22				96																		
	Cleveland Barons	AHL	1	0	0	0				2																		
1964-65	Omaha Knights	CHL	2	0	0	0				0																		
	Cleveland Barons	AHL	70	9	13	22				37																		
1965-66	Cleveland Barons	AHL	64	5	10	15				55											12	0	5	5	4			
1966-67	Buffalo Bisons	AHL	69	9	13	22				110																		
1967-68	**Pittsburgh Penguins**	**NHL**	5	0	0	0	0	0	0	4	0	0	0	1	0.0	1	0	0	0	+1								
	Baltimore Clippers	AHL	34	1	9	10				22																		
1968-69	Amarillo Wranglers	CHL	58	6	26	32				168																		
1969-70	Baltimore Clippers	AHL	9	1	1	2				13																		
	Greensboro Generals	EHL	47	13	33	46				80											16	5	13	18	18			
1970-71	Greensboro Generals	EHL	70	20	40	60				128											9	0	5	5	2			
	Omaha Knights	CHL																			6	1	0	1	2			
1971-72	Greensboro Generals	EHL	35	8	27	35				39											11	2	2	4	27			
1972-73	Johnstown Jets	EHL	54	7	30	37				69											12	3	6	9	0			
	NHL Totals		5	0	0	0	0	0	0	4	0	0	0	1	0.0	1	0	0	0									

EHL South First All-Star Team (1970, 1971, 1972, 1973)

Traded to **Pittsburgh** by **Cleveland** (AHL) for cash, August, 1966. Loaned to **Buffalo** by **Pittsburgh** for 1966-67 season, October, 1967.

● **LANZ, RICK**   Rick Lanz   D – R. 6'2", 203 lbs.   b: Karlouy Vary, Czech., 9/16/1961.   Vancouver's 1st choice, 7th overall, in 1980 Entry Draft.

1977-78	Oshawa Generals	OHA	65	1	41	42				51																		
1978-79	Oshawa Generals	OHA	65	12	47	59				88											5	1	3	4	14			
1979-80	Oshawa Generals	OHA	52	18	38	56				51											7	2	3	5	6			
	Canada	WJC-A	5	0	1	1				6																		
1980-81	**Vancouver Canucks**	**NHL**	76	7	22	29	6	15	21	40	3	0	1	134	5.2	95	23	86	15	+1	3	0	0	0	4	0	0	0
1981-82	**Vancouver Canucks**	**NHL**	39	3	11	14	2	7	9	48	2	0	0	94	3.2	42	15	50	10	-13								
1982-83	**Vancouver Canucks**	**NHL**	74	10	38	48	8	26	34	46	4	0	2	180	5.6	104	44	69	4	-5	4	2	1	3	0	1	0	0
	Canada	WEC-A	6	0	2	2				2																		
1983-84	**Vancouver Canucks**	**NHL**	79	18	39	57	14	26	40	45	14	0	3	230	7.8	147	60	117	27	-3	4	0	4	4	2	0	0	0
1984-85	**Vancouver Canucks**	**NHL**	57	2	17	19	2	11	13	69	2	0	0	131	1.5	65	21	99	33	-22								
1985-86	**Vancouver Canucks**	**NHL**	75	15	38	53	12	25	37	73	11	0	0	191	7.9	139	60	139	34	-26	3	0	0	0	0	0	0	0
1986-87	**Vancouver Canucks**	**NHL**	17	1	6	7	1	4	5	10	1	0	0	39	2.6	18	10	24	3	-13								
	Toronto Maple Leafs	**NHL**	44	2	19	21	2	14	16	32	1	0	0	91	2.2	76	20	70	18	+4	13	1	3	4	27	0	0	1
1987-88	**Toronto Maple Leafs**	**NHL**	75	6	22	28	5	16	21	65	3	0	0	145	4.1	100	17	137	42	-12	1	0	0	0	2	0	0	0
1988-89	**Toronto Maple Leafs**	**NHL**	32	1	9	10	1	6	7	18	0	0	1	56	1.8	35	13	54	15	-17								
1989-90	Ambri-Piotta	Switz.	36	4	14	18																						
1990-91	Indianapolis Ice	IHL	8	0	5	5				18																		
1991-92	**Chicago Blackhawks**	**NHL**	1	0	0	0	0	0	0	2	0	0	0	0	0.0	1	0	1	0	0								
	Phoenix Roadrunners	IHL	38	7	14	21				21																		
1992-93	Atlanta Knights	IHL	25	6	12	18				30																		
	NHL Totals		569	65	221	286	53	150	203	448	41	0	7	1291	5.0	822	283	846	201		28	3	8	11	35	1	0	1

Traded to **Toronto** by **Vancouver** for Jim Benning and Dan Hodgson, December 2, 1986. Signed as a free agent by **Chicago**, August 13, 1990. Traded to **LA Kings** by **Chicago** for cash, November 29, 1991.

● **LAPERRIERE, DANIEL**   Daniel Laperriere   D – L. 6'1", 195 lbs.   b: Laval, Que., 3/28/1969.   St. Louis' 4th choice, 93rd overall, in 1989 Entry Draft.

1988-89	St. Lawrence University	ECAC	28	0	7	7				10																		
1989-90	St. Lawrence University	ECAC	31	6	19	25				16																		
1990-91	St. Lawrence University	ECAC	34	7	31	38				18																		
1991-92	St. Lawrence University	ECAC	32	8	*45	53				36																		
1992-93	**St. Louis Blues**	**NHL**	5	0	1	1	0	1	1	0	0	0	0	7	0.0	2	1	4	0	-3								
	Peoria Rivermen	IHL	54	4	20	24				28																		
1993-94	**St. Louis Blues**	**NHL**	20	1	3	4	1	2	3	8	1	0	0	20	5.0	14	7	8	0	-1								
	Peoria Rivermen	IHL	56	10	37	47				16											6	0	2	2	4			
1994-95	Peoria Rivermen	IHL	65	19	33	52				42																		
	St. Louis Blues	**NHL**	4	0	0	0	0	0	0	15	0	0	0	0	0.0	2	0	1	0	+1								
	Ottawa Senators	**NHL**	13	1	1	2	2	1	3	0	1	0	0	18	5.6	14	5	15	2	-4								
1995-96	**Ottawa Senators**	**NHL**	6	0	0	0	0	0	0	4	0	0	0	12	0.0	6	2	2	0	+2								
	P.E.I. Senators	AHL	15	2	7	9				4																		
	Atlanta Knights	IHL	15	4	9	13				4																		
	Kansas City Blades	IHL	23	2	6	8				11											5	0	1	1	0			
1996-97	Portland Pirates	AHL	69	14	26	40				33											5	0	2	2	2			
	NHL Totals		48	2	5	7	3	4	7	27	2	0	0	57	3.5	38	15	30	2									

ECAC Second All-Star Team (1991) ● ECAC First All-Star Team (1992) ● NCAA East First All-American Team (1992)

Traded to **Ottawa** by **St. Louis** with St. Louis' 9th round choice (Erik Kaminski) in 1995 Entry Draft for Ottawa's 9th round choice (Libor Zabransky) in 1995 Entry Draft, April 7, 1995. Signed as a free agent by **Washington**, July 12, 1996.

● **LAPERRIERE, IAN**   Ian Laperriere   C – R. 6'1", 195 lbs.   b: Montreal, Que., 1/19/1974.   St. Louis' 6th choice, 158th overall, in 1992 Entry Draft.

1990-91	Drummondville Voltigeurs	QMJHL	65	19	29	48				117											14	2	9	11	48			
1991-92	Drummondville Voltigeurs	QMJHL	70	28	49	77				160											4	2	2	4	9			
1992-93	Drummondville Voltigeurs	QMJHL	60	44	*96	140				188											10	6	13	19	20			
1993-94	**St. Louis Blues**	**NHL**	1	0	0	0	0	0	0	0	0	0	0	0	0	0	0	0	0	0								
	Drummondville	QMJHL	62	41	72	113				150											9	4	6	10	35			
	Peoria Rivermen	IHL																			5	1	3	4	2			
1994-95	Peoria Rivermen	IHL	51	16	32	48				111																		
	St. Louis Blues	**NHL**	37	13	14	27	23	21	44	85	1	0	1	53	24.5	33	3	19	1	+12	7	0	4	4	21	0	0	0

			REGULAR SEASON																		PLAYOFFS							
Season	Club	League	GP	G	A	Pts	AG	AA	APts	PIM	PP	SH	GW	S	%	TGF	PGF	TGA	PGA	+/-	GP	G	A	Pts	PIM	PP	SH	GW
1995-96	**St. Louis Blues**	**NHL**	**33**	**3**	**6**	**9**	**3**	**5**	**8**	**87**	**1**	**0**	**1**	**31**	**9.7**	**11**	**3**	**13**	**1**	**-4**	....	....	....	....	....	....	....	....
	Worcester IceCats	AHL	3	2	1	3	....	....	....	22	....	....	....	....	....	....	....	....	....	....	....	....	....	....	....	....	....	....
	New York Rangers	**NHL**	**28**	**1**	**2**	**3**	**1**	**2**	**3**	**53**	**0**	**0**	**0**	**21**	**4.8**	**3**	**0**	**8**	**0**	**-5**	....	....	....	....	....	....	....	....
	Los Angeles Kings	**NHL**	**10**	**2**	**3**	**5**	**2**	**2**	**4**	**15**	**0**	**0**	**0**	**18**	**11.1**	**7**	**2**	**7**	**0**	**-2**	....	....	....	....	....	....	....	....
1996-97	**Los Angeles Kings**	**NHL**	**62**	**8**	**15**	**23**	**8**	**13**	**21**	**102**	**0**	**1**	**2**	**84**	**9.5**	**25**	**1**	**67**	**18**	**-25**	....	....	....	....	....	....	....	....
1997-98	**Los Angeles Kings**	**NHL**	**77**	**6**	**15**	**21**	**7**	**15**	**22**	**131**	**0**	**1**	**1**	**74**	**8.1**	**32**	**4**	**58**	**30**	**0**	**4**	**1**	**0**	**1**	**6**	**0**	**0**	**0**
	NHL Totals		**248**	**33**	**55**	**88**	**44**	**58**	**102**	**473**	**2**	**2**	**5**	**282**	**11.7**	**111**	**13**	**172**	**50**		**11**	**1**	**4**	**5**	**27**	**0**	**0**	**0**

QMJHL Second All-Star Team (1993)

Traded to **NY Rangers** by **St. Louis** for Stephane Matteau, December 28, 1995. Traded to **LA Kings** by **NY Rangers** with Ray Ferraro, Mattias Norstrom, Nathan Lafayette and NY Rangers' 4th round choice (Sean Blanchard) in 1997 Entry Draft for Marty McSorley, Jari Kurri and Shane Churla, March 14, 1996.

• LAPERRIERE, JACQUES

Jacques Laperriere D – L. 6'2", 180 lbs. b: Rouyn, Que., 11/22/1941. **HHOF**

Season	Club	League	GP	G	A	Pts	AG	AA	APts	PIM	PP	SH	GW	S	%	TGF	PGF	TGA	PGA	+/-	GP	G	A	Pts	PIM	PP	SH	GW
1958-59	Hull-Ottawa Canadiens	EOHL	1	1	1	2	....	....	....	2	....	....	....	....	....	....	....	....	....	....	2	0	0	0	0	....	....	....
1959-60	Brockville Canadiens	Jr. B	STATISTICS NOT AVAILABLE																									
	Hull-Ottawa Canadiens	EPHL	5	0	2	2	....	....	....	0	....	....	....	....	....	....	....	....	....	....	....	....	....	....	....	....	....	....
1960-61	Montreal–Hull-Ottawa	EPHL	5	0	0	0	....	....	....	2	....	....	....	....	....	....	....	....	....	....	3	0	2	2	4	....	....	....
1961-62	Montreal Jr. Canadiens	OHA	48	20	37	57	....	....	....	98	....	....	....	....	....	....	....	....	....	....	6	0	1	1	11	....	....	....
	Hull-Ottawa Canadiens	EPHL	1	0	0	0	....	....	....	4	....	....	....	....	....	....	....	....	....	....	7	1	4	5	6	....	....	....
1962-63	**Montreal Canadiens**	**NHL**	**6**	**0**	**2**	**2**	**0**	**2**	**2**	**2**	....	....	....	....	....	....	....	....	....	....	**5**	**0**	**1**	**1**	**4**	....	....	....
	Hull-Ottawa Canadiens	EPHL	40	8	19	27	....	....	....	51	....	....	....	....	....	....	....	....	....	....	2	0	0	0	0	....	....	....
1963-64	**Montreal Canadiens**	**NHL**	**65**	**2**	**28**	**30**	**3**	**31**	**34**	**102**	....	....	....	....	....	....	....	....	....	....	**7**	**1**	**1**	**2**	**8**	....	....	....
1964-65	**Montreal Canadiens**	**NHL**	**67**	**5**	**22**	**27**	**6**	**24**	**30**	**92**	....	....	....	....	....	....	....	....	....	....	**6**	**1**	**1**	**2**	**16**	....	....	....
1965-66	**Montreal Canadiens**	**NHL**	**57**	**6**	**25**	**31**	**7**	**25**	**32**	**85**	....	....	....	....	....	....	....	....	....	....	....	....	....	....	....	....	....	....
1966-67	**Montreal Canadiens**	**NHL**	**61**	**0**	**20**	**20**	**0**	**21**	**21**	**48**	....	....	....	....	....	....	....	....	....	....	**9**	**0**	**1**	**1**	**9**	....	....	....
1967-68	**Montreal Canadiens**	**NHL**	**72**	**4**	**21**	**25**	**5**	**22**	**27**	**84**	**1**	**0**	**0**	**122**	**3.3**	**110**	**23**	**88**	**24**	**+23**	**13**	**1**	**3**	**4**	**20**	**0**	**0**	**0**
1968-69	**Montreal Canadiens**	**NHL**	**69**	**5**	**26**	**31**	**6**	**24**	**30**	**45**	**0**	**0**	**1**	**166**	**3.0**	**114**	**14**	**85**	**22**	**+37**	**14**	**1**	**3**	**4**	**28**	**1**	**0**	**0**
1969-70	**Montreal Canadiens**	**NHL**	**73**	**6**	**31**	**37**	**7**	**31**	**38**	**98**	**2**	**1**	**1**	**169**	**3.6**	**126**	**34**	**96**	**32**	**+28**	....	....	....	....	....	....	....	....
1970-71	**Montreal Canadiens**	**NHL**	**49**	**0**	**16**	**16**	**0**	**14**	**14**	**20**	**0**	**0**	**0**	**65**	**0.0**	**78**	**9**	**68**	**23**	**+24**	**20**	**4**	**9**	**13**	**12**	**1**	**0**	**1**
1971-72	**Montreal Canadiens**	**NHL**	**73**	**3**	**25**	**28**	**3**	**23**	**26**	**50**	**2**	**0**	**0**	**97**	**3.1**	**116**	**9**	**104**	**33**	**+36**	**4**	**0**	**0**	**0**	**2**	**0**	**0**	**0**
1972-73	**Montreal Canadiens**	**NHL**	**57**	**7**	**16**	**23**	**7**	**13**	**20**	**34**	**2**	**0**	**0**	**88**	**8.0**	**129**	**11**	**64**	**24**	**+78**	**10**	**1**	**3**	**4**	**2**	**0**	**0**	**0**
1973-74	**Montreal Canadiens**	**NHL**	**42**	**2**	**10**	**12**	**2**	**9**	**11**	**14**	**0**	**1**	**0**	**60**	**3.3**	**66**	**7**	**59**	**15**	**+15**	....	....	....	....	....	....	....	....
	NHL Totals		**691**	**40**	**242**	**282**	**46**	**239**	**285**	**674**	**7**	**2**	**2**	**767**	**5.2**	**739**	**107**	**564**	**173**		**88**	**9**	**22**	**31**	**101**	**2**	**0**	**1**

NHL Second All-Star Team (1964, 1970) • Won Calder Memorial Trophy (1964) • NHL First All-Star Team (1965, 1966) • Won James Norris Trophy (1966) • NHL Plus/Minus Leader (1973)

Played in NHL All-Star Game (1964, 1965, 1967, 1968, 1970)

• LAPLANTE, DARRYL

Darryl Laplante C – L. 6'1", 185 lbs. b: Calgary, Alta., 3/28/1977. Detroit's 3rd choice, 58th overall, in 1995 Entry Draft.

Season	Club	League	GP	G	A	Pts	AG	AA	APts	PIM	PP	SH	GW	S	%	TGF	PGF	TGA	PGA	+/-	GP	G	A	Pts	PIM	PP	SH	GW
1994-95	Moose Jaw Warriors	WHL	71	22	24	46	....	....	....	66	....	....	....	....	....	....	....	....	....	....	10	2	2	4	7	....	....	....
1995-96	Moose Jaw Warriors	WHL	72	42	40	82	....	....	....	76	....	....	....	....	....	....	....	....	....	....	....	....	....	....	....	....	....	....
1996-97	Moose Jaw Warriors	WHL	69	38	42	80	....	....	....	79	....	....	....	....	....	....	....	....	....	....	12	2	4	6	15	....	....	....
1997-98	**Detroit Red Wings**	**NHL**	**2**	**0**	**0**	**0**	**0**	**0**	**0**	**0**	**0**	**0**	**0**	**2**	**0.0**	**0**	**0**	**0**	**0**	**0**	....	....	....	....	....	....	....	....
	Adirondack Red Wings	AHL	77	15	10	25	....	....	....	51	....	....	....	....	....	....	....	....	....	....	3	0	1	1	4	....	....	....
	NHL Totals		**2**	**0**	**0**	**0**	**0**	**0**	**0**	**0**	**0**	**0**	**0**	**2**	**0.0**	**0**	**0**	**0**	**0**		....	....	....	....	....	....	....	....

• LAPOINTE, CLAUDE

Claude Lapointe C – L. 5'9", 181 lbs. b: Lachine, Que., 10/11/1968. Quebec's 12th choice, 234th overall, in 1988 Entry Draft.

Season	Club	League	GP	G	A	Pts	AG	AA	APts	PIM	PP	SH	GW	S	%	TGF	PGF	TGA	PGA	+/-	GP	G	A	Pts	PIM	PP	SH	GW
1986-87	Trois-Rivières Draveurs	QMJHL	70	47	57	104	....	....	....	123	....	....	....	....	....	....	....	....	....	....	....	....	....	....	....	....	....	....
1987-88	Laval Titan	QMJHL	69	37	83	120	....	....	....	143	....	....	....	....	....	....	....	....	....	....	13	2	17	19	53	....	....	....
1988-89	Laval Titan	QMJHL	63	32	72	104	....	....	....	158	....	....	....	....	....	....	....	....	....	....	17	5	14	19	66	....	....	....
1989-90	Halifax Citadels	AHL	63	18	19	37	....	....	....	51	....	....	....	....	....	....	....	....	....	....	6	1	1	2	34	....	....	....
1990-91	**Quebec Nordiques**	**NHL**	**13**	**2**	**2**	**4**	**2**	**2**	**4**	**4**	**0**	**0**	**0**	**7**	**28.6**	**6**	**0**	**6**	**3**	**+3**	....	....	....	....	....	....	....	....
	Halifax Citadels	AHL	43	17	17	34	....	....	....	46	....	....	....	....	....	....	....	....	....	....	....	....	....	....	....	....	....	....
1991-92	**Quebec Nordiques**	**NHL**	**78**	**13**	**20**	**33**	**12**	**15**	**27**	**86**	**0**	**2**	**2**	**95**	**13.7**	**42**	**2**	**81**	**33**	**-8**	....	....	....	....	....	....	....	....
1992-93	**Quebec Nordiques**	**NHL**	**74**	**10**	**26**	**36**	**8**	**18**	**26**	**98**	**0**	**0**	**1**	**91**	**11.0**	**52**	**1**	**66**	**20**	**+5**	**6**	**2**	**4**	**6**	**8**	**0**	**0**	**0**
1993-94	**Quebec Nordiques**	**NHL**	**59**	**11**	**17**	**28**	**10**	**13**	**23**	**70**	**1**	**1**	**1**	**73**	**15.1**	**47**	**3**	**59**	**17**	**+2**	....	....	....	....	....	....	....	....
1994-95	**Quebec Nordiques**	**NHL**	**29**	**4**	**8**	**12**	**7**	**12**	**19**	**41**	**0**	**0**	**0**	**40**	**10.0**	**19**	**0**	**19**	**5**	**+5**	**5**	**0**	**0**	**0**	**8**	**0**	**0**	**0**
1995-96	**Colorado Avalanche**	**NHL**	**3**	**0**	**0**	**0**	**0**	**0**	**0**	**0**	**0**	**0**	**0**	**0**	**0.0**	**0**	**0**	**1**	**0**	**-1**	....	....	....	....	....	....	....	....
	Calgary Flames	**NHL**	**32**	**4**	**5**	**9**	**4**	**4**	**8**	**20**	**0**	**2**	**1**	**44**	**9.1**	**15**	**0**	**23**	**10**	**+2**	**2**	**0**	**0**	**0**	**0**	**0**	**0**	**0**
	Saint John Flames	AHL	12	5	3	8	....	....	....	10	....	....	....	....	....	....	....	....	....	....	....	....	....	....	....	....	....	....
1996-97	**New York Islanders**	**NHL**	**73**	**13**	**5**	**18**	**14**	**4**	**18**	**49**	**0**	**3**	**3**	**80**	**16.3**	**33**	**1**	**68**	**24**	**-12**	....	....	....	....	....	....	....	....
	Utah Grizzlies	IHL	9	7	6	13	....	....	....	14	....	....	....	....	....	....	....	....	....	....	....	....	....	....	....	....	....	....
1997-98	**New York Islanders**	**NHL**	**78**	**10**	**10**	**20**	**12**	**10**	**22**	**47**	**0**	**1**	**3**	**82**	**12.2**	**31**	**0**	**57**	**17**	**-9**	....	....	....	....	....	....	....	....
	NHL Totals		**439**	**67**	**93**	**160**	**69**	**78**	**147**	**415**	**1**	**9**	**11**	**512**	**13.1**	**245**	**7**	**380**	**129**		**13**	**2**	**4**	**6**	**16**	**0**	**0**	**0**

Transferred to **Colorado** after **Quebec** franchise relocated, June 21, 1995. Traded to **Calgary** by **Colorado** for Calgary's 7th round choice (Samuel Pahlsson) in 1996 Entry Draft, November 1, 1995. Signed as a free agent by **NY Islanders**, August 14, 1996.

• LAPOINTE, GUY

Guy Lapointe D – L. 6', 205 lbs. b: Montreal, Que., 3/18/1948. **HHOF**

Season	Club	League	GP	G	A	Pts	AG	AA	APts	PIM	PP	SH	GW	S	%	TGF	PGF	TGA	PGA	+/-	GP	G	A	Pts	PIM	PP	SH	GW
1965-66	Verdun Jr. Maple Leafs	QJHL	37	7	13	20	....	....	....	96	....	....	....	....	....	....	....	....	....	....	....	....	....	....	....	....	....	....
1966-67	Verdun Jr. Maple Leafs	QJHL	....	....	....	....	....	....	....	....	....	....	....	....	....	....	....	....	....	....	....	....	....	....	....	....	....	....
1967-68	Montreal Jr. Canadiens	OHA	51	11	27	38	....	....	....	147	....	....	....	....	....	....	....	....	....	....	11	1	6	7	40	....	....	....
1968-69	**Montreal Jr. Canadiens**	**NHL**	**1**	**0**	**0**	**0**	**0**	**0**	**0**	**2**	**0**	**0**	**0**	**0**	**0.0**	**0**	**0**	**0**	**0**	**0**	....	....	....	....	....	....	....	....
	Houston Apollos	CHL	66	3	15	18	....	....	....	120	....	....	....	....	....	....	....	....	....	....	3	1	0	1	6	....	....	....
1969-70	**Montreal Canadiens**	**NHL**	**5**	**0**	**0**	**0**	**0**	**0**	**0**	**4**	**0**	**0**	**0**	**0**	**0.0**	**0**	**0**	**0**	**0**	**0**	....	....	....	....	....	....	....	....
	Montreal Voyageurs	AHL	57	8	30	38	....	....	....	92	....	....	....	....	....	....	....	....	....	....	8	3	5	8	6	....	....	....
1970-71	**Montreal Canadiens**	**NHL**	**78**	**15**	**29**	**44**	**16**	**26**	**42**	**107**	**5**	**0**	**1**	**228**	**6.6**	**131**	**32**	**87**	**16**	**+28**	**20**	**4**	**5**	**9**	**34**	**1**	**0**	**2**
1971-72	**Montreal Canadiens**	**NHL**	**69**	**11**	**38**	**49**	**12**	**35**	**47**	**58**	**4**	**0**	**4**	**227**	**4.8**	**123**	**38**	**78**	**8**	**+15**	**6**	**0**	**1**	**1**	**0**	**0**	**0**	**0**
1972-73	Canada	Summit	7	0	1	1	....	....	....	6	....	....	....	....	....	....	....	....	....	....	....	....	....	....	....	....	....	....
	Montreal Canadiens	**NHL**	**76**	**19**	**35**	**54**	**19**	**29**	**48**	**117**	**3**	**0**	**2**	**196**	**9.7**	**164**	**37**	**92**	**16**	**+51**	**17**	**6**	**7**	**13**	**20**	**2**	**0**	**1**
1973-74	**Montreal Canadiens**	**NHL**	**71**	**13**	**40**	**53**	**13**	**35**	**48**	**63**	**5**	**1**	**2**	**205**	**6.3**	**140**	**40**	**117**	**29**	**+12**	**6**	**0**	**2**	**2**	**4**	**0**	**0**	**0**
1974-75	**Montreal Canadiens**	**NHL**	**80**	**28**	**47**	**75**	**26**	**37**	**63**	**88**	**11**	**1**	**0**	**219**	**12.8**	**186**	**65**	**116**	**41**	**+46**	**11**	**6**	**4**	**10**	**4**	**3**	**1**	**0**
1975-76	**Montreal Canadiens**	**NHL**	**77**	**21**	**47**	**68**	**20**	**37**	**57**	**78**	**8**	**1**	**1**	**317**	**6.6**	**183**	**60**	**88**	**29**	**+64**	**13**	**3**	**3**	**6**	**12**	**1**	**0**	**1**
1976-77	Canada	C Cup	7	0	4	4	....	....	....	2	....	....	....	....	....	....	....	....	....	....	....	....	....	....	....	....	....	....
	Montreal Canadiens	**NHL**	**77**	**25**	**51**	**76**	**24**	**41**	**65**	**53**	**10**	**0**	**6**	**289**	**8.7**	**177**	**41**	**91**	**24**	**+69**	**12**	**3**	**9**	**12**	**4**	**1**	**0**	**0**
1977-78	**Montreal Canadiens**	**NHL**	**49**	**13**	**29**	**42**	**13**	**24**	**37**	**19**	**4**	**0**	**2**	**148**	**8.8**	**115**	**31**	**52**	**14**	**+46**	**14**	**1**	**6**	**7**	**16**	**1**	**0**	**0**
1978-79	**Montreal Canadiens**	**NHL**	**69**	**13**	**42**	**55**	**12**	**32**	**44**	**43**	**6**	**0**	**1**	**209**	**6.2**	**145**	**42**	**98**	**22**	**+27**	**10**	**2**	**6**	**8**	**10**	**1**	**0**	**0**
	NHL All-Stars	Chal Cup	1	0	0	0	....	....	....	0	....	....	....	....	....	....	....	....	....	....	....	....	....	....	....	....	....	....
1979-80	**Montreal Canadiens**	**NHL**	**45**	**6**	**20**	**26**	**5**	**15**	**20**	**29**	**0**	**0**	**0**	**124**	**4.8**	**75**	**23**	**69**	**15**	**-2**	**2**	**0**	**0**	**0**	**0**	**0**	**0**	**0**
1980-81	**Montreal Canadiens**	**NHL**	**33**	**1**	**9**	**10**	**1**	**6**	**7**	**79**	**1**	**0**	**1**	**47**	**2.1**	**39**	**12**	**39**	**6**	**-6**	**1**	**0**	**0**	**0**	**17**	**0**	**0**	**0**
1981-82	**Montreal Canadiens**	**NHL**	**47**	**1**	**19**	**20**	**1**	**13**	**14**	**72**	**0**	**0**	**0**	**97**	**1.0**	**64**	**25**	**59**	**17**	**-3**	....	....	....	....	....	....	....	....
	St. Louis Blues	**NHL**	**8**	**0**	**6**	**6**	**0**	**4**	**4**	**4**	**0**	**0**	**0**	**15**	**0.0**	**15**	**7**	**15**	**4**	**-3**	**7**	**1**	**0**	**1**	**8**	**1**	**0**	**1**
1982-83	**St. Louis Blues**	**NHL**	**54**	**3**	**23**	**26**	**2**	**16**	**18**	**43**	**1**	**1**	**1**	**106**	**2.8**	**69**	**21**	**75**	**15**	**-12**	**4**	**0**	**1**	**1**	**9**	**0**	**0**	**0**
1983-84	**Boston Bruins**	**NHL**	**46**	**2**	**16**	**10**	**2**	**11**	**13**	**34**	**1**	**0**	**1**	**57**	**3.5**	**46**	**17**	**34**	**2**	**-3**	....	....	....	....	....	....	....	....
1984-85			DID NOT PLAY – RETIRED																									
1985-86	Longueuil Chevaliers	QMJHL	DID NOT PLAY – COACHING																									
	NHL Totals		**884**	**171**	**451**	**622**	**166**	**361**	**527**	**893**	**59**	**4**	**22**	**2484**	**6.9**	**1672**	**491**	**1110**	**258**		**123**	**26**	**44**	**70**	**138**	**11**	**1**	**5**

AHL First All-Star Team (1970) • NHL First All-Star Team (1973) • NHL Second All-Star Team (1975, 1976, 1977)

Played in NHL All-Star Game (1973, 1975, 1976, 1977)

Traded to **St. Louis** by **Montreal** for St. Louis' 2nd round choice (Sergio Momesso) in 1983 Entry Draft, March 9, 1982. Signed as a free agent by **Boston**, August 15, 1983

			REGULAR SEASON																		PLAYOFFS							
Season	Club	League	GP	G	A	Pts	AG	AA	APts	PIM	PP	SH	GW	S	%	TGF	PGF	TGA	PGA	+/–	GP	G	A	Pts	PIM	PP	SH	GW

• LAPOINTE, MARTIN

Martin Lapointe RW – R. 5'11", 200 lbs. b: Ville Ste. Pierre, Que., 9/12/1973. Detroit's 12th choice, 10th overall, in 1991 Entry Draft.

Season	Club	League	GP	G	A	Pts	AG	AA	APts	PIM	PP	SH	GW	S	%	TGF	PGF	TGA	PGA	+/–	GP	G	A	Pts	PIM	PP	SH	GW
1989-90	Laval Titan	QMJHL	65	42	54	96	....	....	....	77	....	....	....	....	....	....	....	....	....	....	14	8	17	25	54	....	....	....
1990-91	Laval Titan	QMJHL	64	44	54	98	....	....	....	66	....	....	....	....	....	....	....	....	....	....	13	7	14	21	26	....	....	....
	Canada	WJC-A	7	0	3	3	....	....	....	2	....	....	....	....	....	....	....	....	....	....	....	....	....	....	....	....	....	....
1991-92	Laval Titan	QMJHL	31	25	30	55	....	....	....	84	....	....	....	....	....	....	....	....	....	....	10	4	10	14	32	....	....	....
	Canada	WJC-A	7	4	1	5	....	....	....	10	....	....	....	....	....	....	....	....	....	....	....	....	....	....	....	....	....	....
	Detroit Red Wings	**NHL**	**4**	**0**	**1**	**1**	**0**	**1**	**1**	**5**	**0**	**0**	**0**	**2**	**0.0**	**2**	**0**	**0**	**0**	**+2**	**3**	**0**	**1**	**1**	**4**	**0**	**0**	**0**
	Adirondack Red Wings	AHL	....	....	....	....	....	....	....	....	....	....	....	....	....	....	....	....	....	....	8	2	2	4	4	....	....	....
1992-93	Laval Titan	QMJHL	35	38	51	89	....	....	....	41	....	....	....	....	....	....	....	....	....	....	13	*13	*17	*30	22	....	....	....
	Canada	WJC-A	7	5	4	9	....	....	....	6	....	....	....	....	....	....	....	....	....	....	....	....	....	....	....	....	....	....
	Detroit Red Wings	**NHL**	**3**	**0**	**0**	**0**	**0**	**0**	**0**	**0**	**0**	**0**	**0**	**2**	**0.0**	**0**	**0**	**2**	**0**	**–2**	....	....	....	....	....	....	....	....
	Adirondack Red Wings	AHL	8	1	2	3	....	....	....	9	....	....	....	....	....	....	....	....	....	....	....	....	....	....	....	....	....	....
1993-94	**Detroit Red Wings**	**NHL**	**50**	**8**	**8**	**16**	**7**	**6**	**13**	**55**	**2**	**0**	**0**	**45**	**17.8**	**34**	**4**	**23**	**0**	**+7**	**4**	**0**	**0**	**0**	**6**	**0**	**0**	**0**
	Adirondack Red Wings	AHL	28	25	21	46	....	....	....	47	....	....	....	....	....	....	....	....	....	....	4	1	1	2	8	....	....	....
1994-95	Adirondack Red Wings	AHL	39	29	16	45	....	....	....	80	....	....	....	....	....	....	....	....	....	....	....	....	....	....	....	....	....	....
	Detroit Red Wings	**NHL**	**39**	**4**	**6**	**10**	**7**	**9**	**16**	**73**	**0**	**0**	**1**	**46**	**8.7**	**16**	**2**	**14**	**1**	**+1**	**2**	**0**	**1**	**1**	**8**	**0**	**0**	**0**
1995-96	**Detroit Red Wings**	**NHL**	**58**	**6**	**3**	**9**	**6**	**2**	**8**	**93**	**1**	**0**	**0**	**76**	**7.9**	**22**	**5**	**17**	**0**	**0**	**11**	**1**	**2**	**3**	**12**	**0**	**0**	**0**
1996-97	**Detroit Red Wings**	**NHL**	**78**	**16**	**17**	**33**	**17**	**15**	**32**	**167**	**5**	**1**	**1**	**149**	**10.7**	**52**	**17**	**53**	**4**	**–14**	**20**	**4**	**8**	**12**	**60**	**1**	**0**	**1**
1997-98	**Detroit Red Wings**	**NHL**	**79**	**15**	**19**	**34**	**18**	**19**	**37**	**106**	**4**	**0**	**3**	**154**	**9.7**	**52**	**14**	**42**	**4**	**0**	**21**	**9**	**6**	**15**	**20**	**2**	**1**	**1**
	NHL Totals		**311**	**49**	**54**	**103**	**55**	**52**	**107**	**499**	**12**	**1**	**5**	**474**	**10.3**	**178**	**42**	**151**	**9**		**61**	**14**	**18**	**32**	**110**	**3**	**1**	**2**

QMJHL First All-Star Team (1990, 1993) • QMJHL Second All-Star Team (1991) • Memorial Cup All-Star Team (1993)

• LAPOINTE, RICK

Rick "Jumbo" Lapointe D – L. 6'2", 200 lbs. b: Victoria, B.C., 8/2/1955. Detroit's 1st choice, 5th overall, in 1975 Amateur Draft.

Season	Club	League	GP	G	A	Pts	AG	AA	APts	PIM	PP	SH	GW	S	%	TGF	PGF	TGA	PGA	+/–	GP	G	A	Pts	PIM	PP	SH	GW
1971-72	Nanaimo Clippers	BCJHL	STATISTICS NOT AVAILABLE																									
	Victoria Cougars	WCJHL	4	0	0	0	....	....	....	0	....	....	....	....	....	....	....	....	....	....	....	....	....	....	....	....	....	....
1972-73	Victoria Cougars	WCJHL	39	3	12	15	....	....	....	31	....	....	....	....	....	....	....	....	....	....	....	....	....	....	....	....	....	....
1973-74	Victoria Cougars	WCJHL	66	8	18	26	....	....	....	207	....	....	....	....	....	....	....	....	....	....	....	....	....	....	....	....	....	....
1974-75	Victoria Cougars	WCJHL	67	19	51	70	....	....	....	177	....	....	....	....	....	....	....	....	....	....	12	1	12	13	26	....	....	....
	Canada	WJC-A	5	2	3	5	....	....	....	16	....	....	....	....	....	....	....	....	....	....	....	....	....	....	....	....	....	....
1975-76	**Detroit Red Wings**	**NHL**	**80**	**10**	**23**	**33**	**9**	**18**	**27**	**95**	**2**	**0**	**0**	**106**	**9.4**	**98**	**16**	**121**	**36**	**–3**	....	....	....	....	....	....	....	....
1976-77	**Detroit Red Wings**	**NHL**	**49**	**2**	**11**	**13**	**2**	**9**	**11**	**80**	**1**	**0**	**0**	**59**	**3.4**	**42**	**8**	**59**	**8**	**–17**	....	....	....	....	....	....	....	....
	Kansas City Blues	CHL	6	0	0	0	....	....	....	6	....	....	....	....	....	....	....	....	....	....	....	....	....	....	....	....	....	....
	Philadelphia Flyers	**NHL**	**22**	**1**	**8**	**9**	**1**	**6**	**7**	**39**	**0**	**0**	**1**	**27**	**3.7**	**30**	**2**	**11**	**3**	**+20**	**10**	**0**	**0**	**0**	**7**	**0**	**0**	**0**
1977-78	**Philadelphia Flyers**	**NHL**	**47**	**4**	**16**	**20**	**4**	**13**	**17**	**91**	**1**	**0**	**0**	**56**	**7.1**	**64**	**6**	**32**	**9**	**+35**	**12**	**0**	**3**	**3**	**19**	**0**	**0**	**0**
1978-79	**Philadelphia Flyers**	**NHL**	**77**	**3**	**18**	**21**	**3**	**14**	**17**	**53**	**1**	**1**	**0**	**75**	**4.0**	**81**	**6**	**80**	**20**	**+15**	**7**	**0**	**1**	**1**	**14**	**0**	**0**	**0**
1979-80	**St. Louis Blues**	**NHL**	**80**	**6**	**19**	**25**	**5**	**15**	**20**	**87**	**0**	**0**	**1**	**113**	**5.3**	**108**	**6**	**150**	**24**	**–24**	**3**	**0**	**1**	**1**	**6**	**0**	**0**	**0**
1980-81	**St. Louis Blues**	**NHL**	**80**	**8**	**25**	**33**	**7**	**17**	**24**	**124**	**0**	**0**	**3**	**84**	**9.5**	**129**	**8**	**113**	**28**	**+36**	**8**	**2**	**2**	**4**	**12**	**0**	**0**	**0**
1981-82	**St. Louis Blues**	**NHL**	**71**	**2**	**20**	**22**	**2**	**13**	**15**	**127**	**0**	**0**	**0**	**91**	**2.2**	**84**	**6**	**110**	**26**	**–6**	**3**	**0**	**0**	**0**	**6**	**0**	**0**	**0**
1982-83	**Quebec Nordiques**	**NHL**	**43**	**2**	**9**	**11**	**2**	**6**	**8**	**59**	**0**	**0**	**0**	**48**	**4.2**	**58**	**1**	**68**	**25**	**+14**	....	....	....	....	....	....	....	....
	Fredericton Express	AHL	31	4	14	18	....	....	....	50	....	....	....	....	....	....	....	....	....	....	12	0	6	6	8	....	....	....
1983-84	**Quebec Nordiques**	**NHL**	**22**	**2**	**10**	**12**	**2**	**7**	**9**	**12**	**0**	**0**	**0**	**24**	**8.3**	**30**	**2**	**21**	**2**	**+9**	**3**	**0**	**0**	**0**	**0**	**0**	**0**	**0**
	Fredericton Express	AHL	54	8	22	30	....	....	....	79	....	....	....	....	....	....	....	....	....	....	....	....	....	....	....	....	....	....
1984-85	**Los Angeles Kings**	**NHL**	**73**	**4**	**13**	**17**	**3**	**9**	**12**	**46**	**0**	**0**	**1**	**69**	**5.8**	**74**	**1**	**103**	**20**	**–10**	....	....	....	....	....	....	....	....
1985-86	**Los Angeles Kings**	**NHL**	**20**	**0**	**4**	**4**	**0**	**3**	**3**	**18**	**0**	**0**	**0**	**7**	**0.0**	**10**	**1**	**28**	**6**	**–13**	....	....	....	....	....	....	....	....
	NHL Totals		**664**	**44**	**176**	**220**	**40**	**130**	**170**	**831**	**5**	**1**	**6**	**759**	**5.8**	**808**	**63**	**896**	**207**		**46**	**2**	**7**	**9**	**64**	**0**	**0**	**0**

WJC-A All-Star Team (1975) • WCJHL First All-Star Team (1975) • AHL First All-Star Team (1984)

Traded to **Philadelphia** by **Detroit** with Mike Korney for Terry Murray, Bob Ritchie, Steve Coates and Dave Kelly, February 17, 1977. Traded to **St. Louis** by **Philadelphia** with Blake Dunlop for Phil Myre, June 7, 1979. Traded to **Quebec** by **St. Louis** for Pat Hickey, August 4, 1982. Signed as a free agent by **LA Kings**, October 10, 1984.

• LAPPIN, PETER

Peter Lappin RW – R. 5'11", 180 lbs. b: St. Charles, IL, 12/31/1965. Calgary's 1st choice, 24th overall, in 1987 Supplemental Draft.

Season	Club	League	GP	G	A	Pts	AG	AA	APts	PIM	PP	SH	GW	S	%	TGF	PGF	TGA	PGA	+/–	GP	G	A	Pts	PIM	PP	SH	GW
1984-85	St. Lawrence University	ECAC	32	10	12	22	....	....	....	22	....	....	....	....	....	....	....	....	....	....	....	....	....	....	....	....	....	....
1985-86	St. Lawrence University	ECAC	30	20	26	46	....	....	....	64	....	....	....	....	....	....	....	....	....	....	....	....	....	....	....	....	....	....
1986-87	St. Lawrence University	ECAC	35	34	24	58	....	....	....	32	....	....	....	....	....	....	....	....	....	....	....	....	....	....	....	....	....	....
1987-88	St. Lawrence University	ECAC	30	16	36	52	....	....	....	26	....	....	....	....	....	....	....	....	....	....	....	....	....	....	....	....	....	....
	Salt Lake Golden Eagles	IHL	3	1	1	2	....	....	....	0	....	....	....	....	....	....	....	....	....	....	17	*16	12	*28	11	....	....	....
1988-89	Salt Lake Golden Eagles	IHL	81	48	42	90	....	....	....	50	....	....	....	....	....	....	....	....	....	....	14	*9	9	18	4	....	....	....
1989-90	**Minnesota North Stars**	**NHL**	**6**	**0**	**0**	**0**	**0**	**0**	**0**	**2**	**0**	**0**	**0**	**8**	**0.0**	**1**	**1**	**5**	**0**	**–5**	....	....	....	....	....	....	....	....
	Kalamazoo Wings	IHL	74	45	35	80	....	....	....	42	....	....	....	....	....	....	....	....	....	....	8	5	2	7	4	....	....	....
1990-91	Kalamazoo Wings	IHL	73	20	47	67	....	....	....	74	....	....	....	....	....	....	....	....	....	....	11	5	4	9	8	....	....	....
1991-92	**San Jose Sharks**	**NHL**	**1**	**0**	**0**	**0**	**0**	**0**	**0**	**0**	**0**	**0**	**0**	**2**	**0.0**	**0**	**0**	**0**	**0**	**0**	....	....	....	....	....	....	....	....
	Kansas City Blades	IHL	78	28	30	58	....	....	....	41	....	....	....	....	....	....	....	....	....	....	4	2	1	3	0	....	....	....
	NHL Totals		**7**	**0**	**0**	**0**	**0**	**0**	**0**	**2**	**0**	**0**	**0**	**10**	**0.0**	**1**	**1**	**5**	**0**		....	....	....	....	....	....	....	....

ECAC Second All-Star Team (1987) • ECAC First All-Star Team (1988) • NCAA Championship All-Tournament Team (1988)

Traded to **Minnesota** by **Calgary** for Minnesota's 2nd round choice (later traded to New Jersey — New Jersey selected Chris Gotziaman), September 5, 1989. Claimed by **San Jose** from **Minnesota** in Dispersal Draft, May 30, 1991.

• LARAQUE, GEORGES

Georges Laraque RW – R. 6'3", 235 lbs. b: Montreal, Que., 12/7/1976. Edmonton's 2nd choice, 31st overall, in 1995 Entry Draft.

Season	Club	League	GP	G	A	Pts	AG	AA	APts	PIM	PP	SH	GW	S	%	TGF	PGF	TGA	PGA	+/–	GP	G	A	Pts	PIM	PP	SH	GW
1993-94	St-Jean Lynx	QMJHL	70	11	11	22	....	....	....	142	....	....	....	....	....	....	....	....	....	....	4	0	0	0	7	....	....	....
1994-95	St-Jean Lynx	QMJHL	62	19	22	41	....	....	....	259	....	....	....	....	....	....	....	....	....	....	7	1	1	2	42	....	....	....
1995-96	Laval Titan	QMJHL	11	8	13	21	....	....	....	76	....	....	....	....	....	....	....	....	....	....	....	....	....	....	....	....	....	....
	St-Hyacinthe Laser	QMJHL	8	3	4	7	....	....	....	59	....	....	....	....	....	....	....	....	....	....	....	....	....	....	....	....	....	....
	Granby Bisons	QMJHL	22	9	7	16	....	....	....	125	....	....	....	....	....	....	....	....	....	....	18	7	6	13	104	....	....	....
1996-97	Hamilton Bulldogs	AHL	73	14	20	34	....	....	....	179	....	....	....	....	....	....	....	....	....	....	15	1	3	4	12	....	....	....
1997-98	**Edmonton Oilers**	**NHL**	**11**	**0**	**0**	**0**	**0**	**0**	**0**	**59**	**0**	**0**	**0**	**4**	**0.0**	**2**	**1**	**6**	**1**	**–4**	....	....	....	....	....	....	....	....
	Hamilton Bulldogs	AHL	46	10	20	30	....	....	....	154	....	....	....	....	....	....	....	....	....	....	3	0	0	0	11	....	....	....
	NHL Totals		**11**	**0**	**0**	**0**	**0**	**0**	**0**	**59**	**0**	**0**	**0**	**4**	**0.0**	**2**	**1**	**6**	**1**		....	....	....	....	....	....	....	....

• LARIONOV, IGOR

Igor Larionov C – L. 5'9", 170 lbs. b: Voskresensk, USSR, 12/3/1960. Vancouver's 11th choice, 214th overall, in 1985 Entry Draft.

Season	Club	League	GP	G	A	Pts	AG	AA	APts	PIM	PP	SH	GW	S	%	TGF	PGF	TGA	PGA	+/–	GP	G	A	Pts	PIM	PP	SH	GW
1977-78	Khimik	USSR	6	3	0	3	....	....	....	4	....	....	....	....	....	....	....	....	....	....	....	....	....	....	....	....	....	....
1978-79	Khimik	USSR	32	3	4	7	....	....	....	12	....	....	....	....	....	....	....	....	....	....	....	....	....	....	....	....	....	....
	Soviet Union	WJC-A	5	2	4	6	....	....	....	8	....	....	....	....	....	....	....	....	....	....	....	....	....	....	....	....	....	....
1979-80	Khimik	USSR	42	11	7	18	....	....	....	24	....	....	....	....	....	....	....	....	....	....	....	....	....	....	....	....	....	....
	Soviet Union	WJC-A	5	3	3	6	....	....	....	4	....	....	....	....	....	....	....	....	....	....	....	....	....	....	....	....	....	....
1980-81	Khimik	USSR	43	22	23	45	....	....	....	36	....	....	....	....	....	....	....	....	....	....	....	....	....	....	....	....	....	....
1981-82	Soviet Union	C Cup	7	4	1	5	....	....	....	8	....	....	....	....	....	....	....	....	....	....	....	....	....	....	....	....	....	....
	CSKA Moscow	USSR	46	31	22	53	....	....	....	6	....	....	....	....	....	....	....	....	....	....	....	....	....	....	....	....	....	....
	Soviet Union	WEC-A	10	4	6	10	....	....	....	2	....	....	....	....	....	....	....	....	....	....	....	....	....	....	....	....	....	....
1982-83	CSKA Moscow	USSR	44	20	19	39	....	....	....	20	....	....	....	....	....	....	....	....	....	....	....	....	....	....	....	....	....	....
	USSR	SuperS	6	4	2	6	....	....	....	0	....	....	....	....	....	....	....	....	....	....	....	....	....	....	....	....	....	....
	Soviet Union	WEC-A	9	5	7	12	....	....	....	4	....	....	....	....	....	....	....	....	....	....	....	....	....	....	....	....	....	....
1983-84	CSKA Moscow	USSR	43	15	26	41	....	....	....	30	....	....	....	....	....	....	....	....	....	....	....	....	....	....	....	....	....	....
	Soviet Union	Olympics	6	1	4	5	....	....	....	6	....	....	....	....	....	....	....	....	....	....	....	....	....	....	....	....	....	....
1984-85	Soviet Union	C Cup	5	1	2	3	....	....	....	6	....	....	....	....	....	....	....	....	....	....	....	....	....	....	....	....	....	....
	CSKA Moscow	USSR	40	18	28	46	....	....	....	20	....	....	....	....	....	....	....	....	....	....	....	....	....	....	....	....	....	....
	Soviet Union	WEC-A	10	2	4	6	....	....	....	8	....	....	....	....	....	....	....	....	....	....	....	....	....	....	....	....	....	....
1985-86	CSKA Moscow	USSR	40	21	31	52	....	....	....	33	....	....	....	....	....	....	....	....	....	....	....	....	....	....	....	....	....	....
	Soviet Union	WEC-A	10	7	1	8	....	....	....	4	....	....	....	....	....	....	....	....	....	....	....	....	....	....	....	....	....	....
1986-87	CSKA Moscow	USSR	39	20	26	46	....	....	....	34	....	....	....	....	....	....	....	....	....	....	....	....	....	....	....	....	....	....
	USSR	RV'87	2	0	2	2	....	....	....	0	....	....	....	....	....	....	....	....	....	....	....	....	....	....	....	....	....	....
	Soviet Union	WEC-A	10	4	8	12	....	....	....	2	....	....	....	....	....	....	....	....	....	....	....	....	....	....	....	....	....	....

			REGULAR SEASON																		PLAYOFFS							
Season	**Club**	**League**	**GP**	**G**	**A**	**Pts**	**AG**	**AA**	**APts**	**PIM**	**PP**	**SH**	**GW**	**S**	**%**	**TGF**	**PGF**	**TGA**	**PGA**	**+/–**	**GP**	**G**	**A**	**Pts**	**PIM**	**PP**	**SH**	**GW**
1987-88	Soviet Union	C Cup	9	1	2	3	....	....	....	6	....	....	....	....	....	....	....	....	....	....	....	....	....	....	....	....	....	....
	CSKA Moscow	USSR	51	25	32	57	....	....	....	54	....	....	....	....	....	....	....	....	....	....	....	....	....	....	....	....	....	....
	Soviet Union	Olympics	8	4	9	13	....	....	....	4	....	....	....	....	....	....	....	....	....	....	....	....	....	....	....	....	....	....
1988-89	CSKA Moscow	USSR	31	15	12	27	....	....	....	22	....	....	....	....	....	....	....	....	....	....	....	....	....	....	....	....	....	....
	CSKA Moscow	SuperS	7	0	7	7	....	....	....	6	....	....	....	....	....	....	....	....	....	....	....	....	....	....	....	....	....	....
	Soviet Union	WEC-A	8	3	0	3	....	....	....	11	....	....	....	....	....	....	....	....	....	....	....	....	....	....	....	....	....	....
1989-90	**Vancouver Canucks**	**NHL**	**74**	**17**	**27**	**44**	**15**	**19**	**34**	**20**	**8**	**0**	**2**	**118**	**14.4**	**71**	**26**	**54**	**4**	**–5**	....	....	....	....	....	....	....	....
1990-91	**Vancouver Canucks**	**NHL**	**64**	**13**	**21**	**34**	**12**	**16**	**28**	**14**	**1**	**1**	**0**	**66**	**19.7**	**53**	**7**	**68**	**19**	**–3**	**6**	**1**	**0**	**1**	**6**	**0**	**0**	**0**
1991-92	**Vancouver Canucks**	**NHL**	**72**	**21**	**44**	**65**	**19**	**33**	**52**	**54**	**10**	**3**	**4**	**97**	**21.6**	**88**	**34**	**71**	**24**	**+7**	**13**	**3**	**7**	**10**	**4**	**1**	**0**	**0**
1992-93	Lugano	Switz.	24	10	19	29	....	....	....	44	....	....	....	....	....	....	....	....	....	....	....	....	....	....	....	....	....	....
1993-94	**San Jose Sharks**	**NHL**	**60**	**18**	**38**	**56**	**17**	**29**	**46**	**40**	**3**	**2**	**2**	**72**	**25.0**	**85**	**23**	**51**	**9**	**+20**	**14**	**5**	**13**	**18**	**10**	**0**	**0**	**0**
1994-95	**San Jose Sharks**	**NHL**	**33**	**4**	**20**	**24**	**7**	**29**	**36**	**14**	**0**	**0**	**1**	**69**	**5.8**	**36**	**8**	**37**	**6**	**–3**	**11**	**1**	**8**	**9**	**2**	**0**	**0**	**0**
1995-96	**San Jose Sharks**	**NHL**	**4**	**1**	**1**	**2**	**1**	**1**	**2**	**0**	**1**	**0**	**0**	**5**	**20.0**	**4**	**2**	**11**	**3**	**–6**	....	....	....	....	....	....	....	....
	Detroit Red Wings	**NHL**	**69**	**21**	**50**	**71**	**21**	**41**	**62**	**34**	**9**	**1**	**5**	**108**	**19.4**	**110**	**39**	**37**	**3**	**+37**	**19**	**6**	**7**	**13**	**6**	**3**	**0**	**2**
1996-97	Russia	W Cup	5	0	4	4	....	....	....	2	....	....	....	....	....	....	....	....	....	....	....	....	....	....	....	....	....	....
	Detroit Red Wings	**NHL**	**64**	**12**	**42**	**54**	**13**	**37**	**50**	**26**	**2**	**1**	**4**	**95**	**12.6**	**100**	**37**	**34**	**2**	**+31**	**20**	**4**	**8**	**12**	**8**	**3**	**0**	**1**
1997-98	**Detroit Red Wings**	**NHL**	**69**	**8**	**39**	**47**	**9**	**38**	**47**	**40**	**3**	**0**	**2**	**93**	**8.6**	**68**	**24**	**33**	**3**	**+14**	**22**	**3**	**10**	**13**	**12**	**0**	**0**	**0**
	NHL Totals		**509**	**115**	**282**	**397**	**114**	**243**	**357**	**242**	**37**	**8**	**20**	**723**	**15.9**	**615**	**200**	**396**	**73**		**105**	**23**	**53**	**76**	**48**	**7**	**0**	**3**

WJC-A All-Star Team (1980) • USSR First All-Star (1983, 1986, 1987, 1988)
WEC-A All-Star Team (1983, 1986) • USSR Player of the Year (1988)

Played in NHL All-Star Game (1998)

Claimed by **San Jose** from **Vancouver** in NHL Waiver Draft, October 4, 1992. Traded to **Detroit** by **San Jose** with future considerations for Ray Sheppard, October 24, 1995.

• LARIVIERE, GARRY

Garry Lariviere D – R. 6', 190 lbs. b: St. Catharines, Ont., 12/6/1954. Buffalo's 5th choice, 83rd overall, in 1974 Amateur Draft.

Season	Club	League	GP	G	A	Pts	AG	AA	APts	PIM	PP	SH	GW	S	%	TGF	PGF	TGA	PGA	+/–	GP	G	A	Pts	PIM	PP	SH	GW
1972-73	St. Catharines Black Hawks	OHA	55	5	32	37	....	....	....	140	....	....	....	....	....	....	....	....	....	....	....	....	....	....	....	....	....	....
1973-74	St. Catharines Black Hawks	OHA	60	3	35	38	....	....	....	153	....	....	....	....	....	....	....	....	....	....	....	....	....	....	....	....	....	....
1974-75	Phoenix Roadrunners	WHA	4	0	1	1	....	....	....	28	....	....	....	....	....	....	....	....	....	....	1	0	0	0	0	....	....	....
	Tulsa Oilers	CHL	76	15	38	53	....	....	....	168	....	....	....	....	....	....	....	....	....	....	....	....	....	....	....	....	....	....
1975-76	Phoenix Roadrunners	WHA	79	7	17	24	....	....	....	100	....	....	....	....	....	....	....	....	....	....	5	0	2	2	2	....	....	....
1976-77	Phoenix Roadrunners	WHA	61	7	23	30	....	....	....	48	....	....	....	....	....	....	....	....	....	....	....	....	....	....	....	....	....	....
	Quebec Nordiques	WHA	15	0	3	3	....	....	....	8	....	....	....	....	....	....	....	....	....	....	17	0	10	10	10	....	....	....
1977-78	Quebec Nordiques	WHA	80	7	49	56	....	....	....	78	....	....	....	....	....	....	....	....	....	....	11	3	2	5	4	....	....	....
1978-79	Quebec Nordiques	WHA	50	5	33	38	....	....	....	54	....	....	....	....	....	....	....	....	....	....	4	0	1	1	2	....	....	....
1979-80	**Quebec Nordiques**	**NHL**	**75**	**2**	**19**	**21**	**2**	**15**	**17**	**56**	**1**	**0**	**0**	**73**	**2.7**	**67**	**4**	**117**	**44**	**–10**	....	....	....	....	....	....	....	....
1980-81	**Quebec Nordiques**	**NHL**	**52**	**3**	**13**	**16**	**2**	**9**	**11**	**50**	**1**	**0**	**0**	**58**	**5.2**	**62**	**7**	**81**	**24**	**–2**	....	....	....	....	....	....	....	....
	Edmonton Oilers	**NHL**	**13**	**0**	**2**	**2**	**0**	**1**	**1**	**6**	**0**	**0**	**0**	**8**	**0.0**	**18**	**0**	**12**	**3**	**+9**	**9**	**0**	**3**	**3**	**8**	**0**	**0**	**0**
1981-82	**Edmonton Oilers**	**NHL**	**62**	**1**	**21**	**22**	**1**	**14**	**15**	**41**	**0**	**0**	**0**	**46**	**2.2**	**88**	**2**	**73**	**14**	**+27**	**4**	**0**	**1**	**1**	**0**	**0**	**0**	**0**
1982-83	**Edmonton Oilers**	**NHL**	**17**	**0**	**2**	**2**	**0**	**1**	**1**	**14**	**0**	**0**	**0**	**15**	**0.0**	**22**	**0**	**15**	**6**	**+13**	**1**	**0**	**1**	**1**	**0**	**0**	**0**	**0**
1983-84	St. Catharines Saints	AHL	65	7	35	42	....	....	....	41	....	....	....	....	....	....	....	....	....	....	7	0	3	3	2	....	....	....
1984-85	St. Catharines Saints	AHL	72	4	32	36	....	....	....	47	....	....	....	....	....	....	....	....	....	....	....	....	....	....	....	....	....	....
1985-86	St. Catharines Saints	AHL	52	0	9	9	....	....	....	10	....	....	....	....	....	....	....	....	....	....	6	0	1	1	6	....	....	....
	NHL Totals		**219**	**6**	**57**	**63**	**5**	**40**	**45**	**167**	**2**	**0**	**0**	**200**	**3.0**	**257**	**13**	**298**	**91**		**14**	**0**	**5**	**5**	**8**	**0**	**0**	**0**
	Other Major League Totals		289	26	126	152	....	....	....	316	....	....	....	....	....	....	....	....	....	....	38	3	15	18	18	....	....	....

CHL First All-Star Team (1975) • AHL First All-Star Team (1984) • Won Eddie Shore Award (Outstanding Defenseman - AHL) (1984) • Won Les Cunningham Award (MVP - AHL) (1984)

Selected by **Chicago** (WHA) in 1974 WHA Amateur Draft, May, 1974. Traded to **Phoenix** (WHA) by **Chicago** (WHA) for future considerations, September, 1974. Rights traded to **NY Islanders** by **Buffalo** for cash and future considerations, February 19, 1975. Traded to **Quebec** (WHA) by **Phoenix** (WHA) for cash, March, 1977. Reclaimed by **NY Islanders** from **Quebec** prior to Expansion Draft, June 9, 1979. Claimed as a priority selection by **Quebec**, June 9, 1979. Traded to **Vancouver** by **Quebec** for Mario Marois, March 10, 1981. Traded to **Edmonton** by **Vancouver** with the rights to Lars Gunnar Pettersson for Blair MacDonald and the rights to Ken Berry, March 10, 1981.

• LARMER, JEFF

Jeff Larmer LW – L. 5'10", 175 lbs. b: Peterborough, Ont., 11/10/1962. Colorado's 7th choice, 129th overall, in 1981 Entry Draft.

Season	Club	League	GP	G	A	Pts	AG	AA	APts	PIM	PP	SH	GW	S	%	TGF	PGF	TGA	PGA	+/–	GP	G	A	Pts	PIM	PP	SH	GW
1978-79	Peterborough Bees	OJHL	40	29	23	52	....	....	....	27	....	....	....	....	....	....	....	....	....	....	....	....	....	....	....	....	....	....
1979-80	Kitchener Rangers	OHA	61	19	27	46	....	....	....	80	....	....	....	....	....	....	....	....	....	....	....	....	....	....	....	....	....	....
1980-81	Kitchener Rangers	OHA	68	54	54	108	....	....	....	103	....	....	....	....	....	....	....	....	....	....	16	12	16	28	27	....	....	....
1981-82	Kitchener Rangers	OHL	49	51	44	95	....	....	....	95	....	....	....	....	....	....	....	....	....	....	15	21	14	35	10	....	....	....
	Colorado Rockies	**NHL**	**8**	**1**	**1**	**2**	**1**	**1**	**2**	**8**	**0**	**0**	**0**	**9**	**11.1**	**6**	**0**	**9**	**0**	**–3**	....	....	....	....	....	....	....	....
1982-83	**New Jersey Devils**	**NHL**	**65**	**21**	**24**	**45**	**17**	**17**	**34**	**21**	**5**	**0**	**0**	**123**	**17.1**	**57**	**14**	**49**	**0**	**–6**	....	....	....	....	....	....	....	....
	Wichita Wind	CHL	10	6	5	11	....	....	....	2	....	....	....	....	....	....	....	....	....	....	....	....	....	....	....	....	....	....
1983-84	**New Jersey Devils**	**NHL**	**40**	**6**	**13**	**19**	**5**	**9**	**14**	**8**	**0**	**0**	**0**	**57**	**10.5**	**27**	**6**	**38**	**0**	**–17**	....	....	....	....	....	....	....	....
	Chicago Black Hawks	**NHL**	**36**	**9**	**13**	**22**	**7**	**9**	**16**	**20**	**2**	**0**	**1**	**62**	**14.5**	**34**	**5**	**28**	**2**	**+3**	**5**	**1**	**0**	**1**	**2**	**1**	**0**	**0**
1984-85	**Chicago Black Hawks**	**NHL**	**7**	**0**	**0**	**0**	**0**	**0**	**0**	**0**	**0**	**0**	**0**	**5**	**0.0**	**1**	**0**	**0**	**0**	**+1**	....	....	....	....	....	....	....	....
	Milwaukee Admirals	IHL	61	24	37	61	....	....	....	30	....	....	....	....	....	....	....	....	....	....	....	....	....	....	....	....	....	....
1985-86	**Chicago Black Hawks**	**NHL**	**2**	**0**	**0**	**0**	**0**	**0**	**0**	**0**	**0**	**0**	**0**	**1**	**0.0**	**1**	**0**	**0**	**0**	**+1**	....	....	....	....	....	....	....	....
	Nova Scotia Oilers	AHL	77	20	44	64	....	....	....	46	....	....	....	....	....	....	....	....	....	....	....	....	....	....	....	....	....	....
1986-1989			STATISTICS NOT AVAILABLE																									
1989-90	Solihull Barons	Britain	24	37	36	73	....	....	....	30	....	....	....	....	....	....	....	....	....	....	....	....	....	....	....	....	....	....
	HC Davos	Switz.	....	2	3	5	....	....	....	....	....	....	....	....	....	....	....	....	....	....	....	4	4	8	....	....	....	....
1990-91			DID NOT PLAY																									
1991-92	Milwaukee Admirals	IHL	76	27	35	62	....	....	....	22	....	....	....	....	....	....	....	....	....	....	5	1	4	5	4	....	....	....
1992-93	Milwaukee Admirals	IHL	78	31	34	65	....	....	....	46	....	....	....	....	....	....	....	....	....	....	6	0	2	2	2	....	....	....
1993-94	Milwaukee Admirals	IHL	25	2	9	11	....	....	....	14	....	....	....	....	....	....	....	....	....	....	1	0	0	0	0	....	....	....
	NHL Totals		**158**	**37**	**51**	**88**	**30**	**36**	**66**	**57**	**7**	**0**	**1**	**257**	**14.4**	**128**	**25**	**124**	**2**		**5**	**1**	**0**	**1**	**2**	**1**	**0**	**0**

OHL Second All-Star Team (1982) • Memorial Cup All-Star Team (1982)

Transferred to **New Jersey** after **Colorado** franchise relocated, June 30, 1982. Traded to **Chicago** by **New Jersey** for Tim Higgins, January 11, 1984.

• LARMER, STEVE

Steve Larmer RW – L. 5'11", 195 lbs. b: Peterborough, Ont., 6/16/1961. Chicago's 11th choice, 120th overall, in 1980 Entry Draft.

Season	Club	League	GP	G	A	Pts	AG	AA	APts	PIM	PP	SH	GW	S	%	TGF	PGF	TGA	PGA	+/–	GP	G	A	Pts	PIM	PP	SH	GW
1977-78	Peterborough Petes	OHA	62	24	17	41	....	....	....	51	....	....	....	....	....	....	....	....	....	....	18	5	7	12	27	....	....	....
1978-79	Niagara Falls Flyers	OHA	66	37	47	84	....	....	....	108	....	....	....	....	....	....	....	....	....	....	....	....	....	....	....	....	....	....
1979-80	Niagara Falls Flyers	OHA	67	45	69	114	....	....	....	71	....	....	....	....	....	....	....	....	....	....	10	5	9	14	15	....	....	....
1980-81	Niagara Falls Flyers	OHA	61	55	78	133	....	....	....	73	....	....	....	....	....	....	....	....	....	....	12	13	8	21	24	....	....	....
	Chicago Black Hawks	**NHL**	**4**	**0**	**1**	**1**	**0**	**1**	**1**	**0**	**0**	**0**	**0**	**3**	**0.0**	**3**	**0**	**2**	**0**	**+1**	....	....	....	....	....	....	....	....
1981-82	**Chicago Black Hawks**	**NHL**	**3**	**0**	**0**	**0**	**0**	**0**	**0**	**0**	**0**	**0**	**0**	**1**	**0.0**	**0**	**0**	**0**	**0**	**0**	....	....	....	....	....	....	....	....
	New Brunswick Hawks	AHL	74	38	44	82	....	....	....	46	....	....	....	....	....	....	....	....	....	....	15	6	6	12	0	....	....	....
1982-83	**Chicago Black Hawks**	**NHL**	**80**	**43**	**47**	**90**	**35**	**32**	**67**	**28**	**13**	**0**	**9**	**195**	**22.1**	**154**	**57**	**53**	**0**	**+44**	**11**	**5**	**7**	**12**	**8**	**2**	**0**	**1**
1983-84	**Chicago Black Hawks**	**NHL**	**80**	**35**	**40**	**75**	**28**	**27**	**55**	**34**	**13**	**0**	**3**	**206**	**17.0**	**124**	**47**	**78**	**0**	**–1**	**5**	**2**	**2**	**4**	**7**	**1**	**0**	**0**
1984-85	**Chicago Black Hawks**	**NHL**	**80**	**46**	**40**	**86**	**38**	**27**	**65**	**16**	**14**	**0**	**6**	**206**	**22.3**	**127**	**43**	**68**	**1**	**+17**	**15**	**9**	**13**	**22**	**14**	**5**	**0**	**1**
1985-86	**Chicago Black Hawks**	**NHL**	**80**	**31**	**45**	**76**	**25**	**30**	**55**	**47**	**13**	**1**	**3**	**184**	**16.8**	**132**	**45**	**95**	**17**	**+9**	**3**	**0**	**3**	**3**	**4**	**0**	**0**	**0**
1986-87	**Chicago Blackhawks**	**NHL**	**80**	**28**	**56**	**84**	**24**	**41**	**65**	**22**	**10**	**0**	**4**	**216**	**13.0**	**124**	**38**	**75**	**9**	**+20**	**4**	**0**	**0**	**0**	**2**	**0**	**0**	**0**
1987-88	**Chicago Blackhawks**	**NHL**	**80**	**41**	**48**	**89**	**35**	**34**	**69**	**42**	**21**	**7**	**0**	**245**	**16.7**	**139**	**69**	**111**	**36**	**–5**	**5**	**1**	**6**	**7**	**0**	**1**	**0**	**0**
1988-89	**Chicago Blackhawks**	**NHL**	**80**	**43**	**44**	**87**	**37**	**31**	**68**	**54**	**19**	**1**	**2**	**269**	**16.0**	**136**	**62**	**113**	**41**	**+2**	**16**	**8**	**9**	**17**	**22**	**3**	**0**	**2**
1989-90	**Chicago Blackhawks**	**NHL**	**80**	**31**	**59**	**90**	**27**	**42**	**69**	**40**	**8**	**2**	**4**	**265**	**11.7**	**136**	**40**	**80**	**27**	**+25**	**20**	**7**	**15**	**22**	**2**	**2**	**2**	**2**
1990-91	**Chicago Blackhawks**	**NHL**	**80**	**44**	**57**	**101**	**41**	**43**	**84**	**79**	**17**	**2**	**9**	**231**	**19.0**	**143**	**62**	**72**	**28**	**+37**	**6**	**5**	**1**	**6**	**4**	**1**	**0**	**0**
	Canada	WEC-A	10	5	3	8	....	....	....	4	....	....	....	....	....	....	....	....	....	....	....	....	....	....	....	....	....	....
1991-92	Canada	C Cup	8	6	5	11	....	....	....	4	....	....	....	....	....	....	....	....	....	....	....	....	....	....	....	....	....	....
	Chicago Blackhawks	**NHL**	**80**	**29**	**45**	**74**	**26**	**34**	**60**	**65**	**11**	**2**	**3**	**292**	**9.9**	**113**	**49**	**88**	**34**	**+10**	**18**	**8**	**7**	**15**	**6**	**3**	**0**	**0**

Season	Club	League	GP	G	A	Pts	AG	AA	APts	PIM	PP	SH	GW	S	%	TGF	PGF	TGA	PGA	+/–	GP	G	A	Pts	PIM	PP	SH	GW
			REGULAR SEASON																		PLAYOFFS							
1992-93	**Chicago Blackhawks**	**NHL**	**84**	**35**	**35**	**70**	**29**	**24**	**53**	**48**	**14**	**4**	**6**	**228**	**15.4**	**123**	**56**	**75**	**31**	**+23**	**4**	**0**	**3**	**3**	**0**	**0**	**0**	**0**
1993-94	**New York Rangers**	**NHL**	**68**	**21**	**39**	**60**	**20**	**30**	**50**	**41**	**6**	**4**	**7**	**146**	**14.4**	**87**	**38**	**43**	**8**	**+14**	**23**	**9**	**7**	**16**	**14**	**3**	**0**	**0**
1994-95	**New York Rangers**	**NHL**	**47**	**14**	**15**	**29**	**25**	**22**	**47**	**16**	**3**	**1**	**4**	**116**	**12.1**	**42**	**12**	**37**	**15**	**+8**	**10**	**2**	**2**	**4**	**6**	**0**	**1**	**1**
	NHL Totals		**1006**	**441**	**571**	**1012**	**390**	**418**	**808**	**532**	**162**	**24**	**60**	**2803**	**15.7**	**1583**	**627**	**999**	**247**		**140**	**56**	**75**	**131**	**89**	**21**	**3**	**7**

OHA Second All-Star Team (1981) • AHL Second All-Star Team (1982) • NHL All-Rookie Team (1983) • Won Calder Memorial Trophy (1983)

Played in NHL All-Star Game (1990, 1991)

Traded to **Hartford** by **Chicago** with Bryan Marchment for Eric Weinrich and Patrick Poulin, November 2, 1993. Traded to **NY Rangers** by **Hartford** with Nick Kypreos, Barry Richter and Hartford's 2nd round choice (Yuri Litinov) in 1994 Entry Draft for Darren Turcotte and James Patrick, November 2, 1993.

• LAROCQUE, DENIS

Denis Larocque D – L. 6'1", 195 lbs. b: Hawkesbury, Ont., 10/5/1967. Los Angeles' 2nd choice, 44th overall, in 1986 Entry Draft.

Season	Club	League	GP	G	A	Pts	AG	AA	APts	PIM	PP	SH	GW	S	%	TGF	PGF	TGA	PGA	+/–	GP	G	A	Pts	PIM	PP	SH	GW
1982-83	Hawkesbury Hawks	OJHL	31	0	13	13	....	....	....	83	....	....	....	....	....	....	....	....	....	....	....	....	....	....	....	....	....	....
1983-84	Guelph Platers	OHL	65	1	5	6	....	....	....	74	....	....	....	....	....	....	....	....	....	....	....	....	....	....	....	....	....	....
1984-85	Guelph Platers	OHL	62	1	15	16	....	....	....	67	....	....	....	....	....	....	....	....	....	....	....	....	....	....	....	....	....	....
1985-86	Guelph Platers	OHL	62	2	17	19	....	....	....	144	....	....	....	....	....	....	....	....	....	....	20	1	4	5	44	....	....	....
1986-87	Guelph Platers	OHL	45	4	10	14	....	....	....	82	....	....	....	....	....	....	....	....	....	....	5	0	2	2	9	....	....	....
1987-88	**Los Angeles Kings**	**NHL**	**8**	**0**	**1**	**1**	**0**	**1**	**1**	**18**	**0**	**0**	**0**	**2**	**0.0**	**3**	**0**	**10**	**3**	**–4**	....	....	....	....	....	....	....	....
	New Haven Nighthawks	AHL	58	4	10	14	....	....	....	154	....	....	....	....	....	....	....	....	....	....	....	....	....	....	....	....	....	....
1988-89	New Haven Nighthawks	AHL	15	2	2	4	....	....	....	51	....	....	....	....	....	....	....	....	....	....	....	....	....	....	....	....	....	....
	Denver Rangers	IHL	30	2	8	10	....	....	....	39	....	....	....	....	....	....	....	....	....	....	4	0	2	2	10	....	....	....
1989-90	Flint Spirits	IHL	31	1	2	3	....	....	....	66	....	....	....	....	....	....	....	....	....	....	....	....	....	....	....	....	....	....
	Cape Breton Oilers	AHL	26	2	4	6	....	....	....	39	....	....	....	....	....	....	....	....	....	....	6	0	1	1	2	....	....	....
1990-91	Moncton Hawks	AHL	68	2	9	11	....	....	....	92	....	....	....	....	....	....	....	....	....	....	1	0	0	0	2	....	....	....
1991-92	St. Thomas Wildcats	ColHL	55	9	21	30	....	....	....	133	....	....	....	....	....	....	....	....	....	....	....	....	....	....	....	....	....	....
1992-93	Dayton Bombers	ECHL	5	0	0	0	....	....	....	17	....	....	....	....	....	....	....	....	....	....	....	....	....	....	....	....	....	....
	St. Thomas Wildcats	ColHL	18	1	4	5	....	....	....	17	....	....	....	....	....	....	....	....	....	....	13	1	3	4	24	....	....	....
	NHL Totals		**8**	**0**	**1**	**1**	**0**	**1**	**1**	**18**	**0**	**0**	**0**	**2**	**0.0**	**3**	**0**	**10**	**3**		....	....	....	....	....	....	....	....

Traded to **NY Rangers** by **LA Kings** with Dean Kennedy for Igor Liba, Michael Boyce, Todd Elik and future considerations, December 12, 1988.

• LAROSE, CLAUDE

Claude Larose LW – L. 5'10", 175 lbs. b: St. Jean, Que., 5/17/1955. NY Rangers' 7th choice, 120th overall, in 1975 Amateur Draft.

Season	Club	League	GP	G	A	Pts	AG	AA	APts	PIM	PP	SH	GW	S	%	TGF	PGF	TGA	PGA	+/–	GP	G	A	Pts	PIM	PP	SH	GW
1971-72	Drummondville Rangers	QMJHL	61	9	10	19	....	....	....	2	....	....	....	....	....	....	....	....	....	....	9	0	2	2	0	....	....	....
1972-73	Drummondville Rangers	QMJHL	61	63	50	113	....	....	....	12	....	....	....	....	....	....	....	....	....	....	....	....	....	....	....	....	....	....
1973-74	Drummondville Rangers	QMJHL	68	56	77	133	....	....	....	16	....	....	....	....	....	....	....	....	....	....	....	....	....	....	....	....	....	....
1974-75	Shawinigan Bruins	QMJHL	29	40	45	85	....	....	....	6	....	....	....	....	....	....	....	....	....	....	....	....	....	....	....	....	....	....
	Sherbrooke Beavers	QMJHL	74	69	76	145	....	....	....	12	....	....	....	....	....	....	....	....	....	....	....	....	....	....	....	....	....	....
1975-76	Cincinnati Stingers	WHA	79	28	24	52	....	....	....	19	....	....	....	....	....	....	....	....	....	....	....	....	....	....	....	....	....	....
1976-77	Cincinnati Stingers	WHA	81	30	46	76	....	....	....	8	....	....	....	....	....	....	....	....	....	....	4	2	1	3	0	....	....	....
1977-78	Cincinnati Stingers	WHA	51	11	20	31	....	....	....	6	....	....	....	....	....	....	....	....	....	....	....	....	....	....	....	....	....	....
	Indianapolis Racers	WHA	28	14	16	30	....	....	....	12	....	....	....	....	....	....	....	....	....	....	....	....	....	....	....	....	....	....
1978-79	Indianapolis Racers	WHA	13	5	8	13	....	....	....	0	....	....	....	....	....	....	....	....	....	....	....	....	....	....	....	....	....	....
	New Haven Nighthawks	AHL	42	25	25	50	....	....	....	7	....	....	....	....	....	....	....	....	....	....	10	7	5	12	2	....	....	....
1979-80	**New York Rangers**	**NHL**	**25**	**4**	**7**	**11**	**4**	**5**	**9**	**2**	**0**	**0**	**0**	**50**	**8.0**	**19**	**5**	**19**	**0**	**–5**	....	....	....	....	....	....	....	....
	New Haven Nighthawks	AHL	31	16	27	43	....	....	....	4	....	....	....	....	....	....	....	....	....	....	....	....	....	....	....	....	....	....
1980-81	New Haven Nighthawks	AHL	80	30	27	57	....	....	....	12	....	....	....	....	....	....	....	....	....	....	4	1	2	3	0	....	....	....
1981-82	Springfield Indians	AHL	76	30	36	66	....	....	....	12	....	....	....	....	....	....	....	....	....	....	....	....	....	....	....	....	....	....
	New York Rangers	**NHL**	....	....	....	....	....	....	....	....	....	....	....	....	....	....	....	....	....	....	**2**	**0**	**0**	**0**	**0**	....	....	....
1982-83			DID NOT PLAY																									
1983-84	Sherbrooke Jets	AHL	80	53	67	120	....	....	....	6	....	....	....	....	....	....	....	....	....	....	....	....	....	....	....	....	....	....
1984-85	Sherbrooke Canadiens	AHL	77	36	43	79	....	....	....	4	....	....	....	....	....	....	....	....	....	....	17	*10	6	16	8	....	....	....
1985-86	Sherbrooke Canadiens	AHL	65	38	39	77	....	....	....	2	....	....	....	....	....	....	....	....	....	....	....	....	....	....	....	....	....	....
	NHL Totals		**25**	**4**	**7**	**11**	**4**	**5**	**9**	**2**	**0**	**0**	**0**	**50**	**8.0**	**19**	**5**	**19**	**0**		**2**	**0**	**0**	**0**	**0**	**0**	**0**	**0**
	Other Major League Totals		252	88	114	202	....	....	....	45	....	....	....	....	....	....	....	....	....	....	4	2	1	3	0	....	....	....

QMJHL Second All-Star Team (1973, 1974, 1975) • Memorial Cup All-Star Team (1975) • AHL First All-Star Team (1984) • Won Fred T. Hunt Memorial Trophy (Sportsmanship - AHL) (1984) • Won John B. Sollenberger Trophy (Top Scorer - AHL) (1984)

Played in NHL All-Star Game (1965, 1967, 1969, 1970)

Selected by **Cincinnati** (WHA) in 1975 WHA Amateur Draft, May, 1975. Traded to **Indianapolis** (WHA) by **Cincinnati** (WHA) with Rich Leduc for Darryl Maggs and Reg Thomas, February, 1978. Rights reclaimed by **NY Rangers** after **Indianapolis** (WHA) franchise folded, December 15, 1978.

• LAROSE, CLAUDE

Claude Larose RW – R. 6', 180 lbs. b: Hearst, Ont., 3/2/1942.

Season	Club	League	GP	G	A	Pts	AG	AA	APts	PIM	PP	SH	GW	S	%	TGF	PGF	TGA	PGA	+/–	GP	G	A	Pts	PIM	PP	SH	GW
1959-60	Peterborough Petes	OHA	48	9	10	19	....	....	....	34	....	....	....	....	....	....	....	....	....	....	12	2	7	9	17	....	....	....
1960-61	Peterborough Petes	OHA	46	36	27	63	....	....	....	108	....	....	....	....	....	....	....	....	....	....	5	5	0	5	31	....	....	....
1961-62	Peterborough Petes	OHA	50	18	36	54	....	....	....	150	....	....	....	....	....	....	....	....	....	....	....	....	....	....	....	....	....	....
	Hull-Ottawa Canadiens	EPHL	1	0	1	1	....	....	....	2	....	....	....	....	....	....	....	....	....	....	6	3	1	4	6	....	....	....
1962-63	**Montreal Canadiens**	**NHL**	**4**	**0**	**0**	**0**	**0**	**0**	**0**	**0**	....	....	....	....	....	....	....	....	....	....	....	....	....	....	....	....	....	....
	Hull-Ottawa Canadiens	EPHL	49	19	24	43	....	....	....	42	....	....	....	....	....	....	....	....	....	....	3	1	0	1	2	....	....	....
1963-64	**Montreal Canadiens**	**NHL**	**21**	**1**	**1**	**2**	**1**	**1**	**2**	**43**	....	....	....	....	....	....	....	....	....	....	**2**	**1**	**0**	**1**	**0**	....	....	....
	Omaha Knights	CHL	47	27	22	49	....	....	....	105	....	....	....	....	....	....	....	....	....	....	8	*8	6	14	17	....	....	....
1964-65	**Montreal Canadiens**	**NHL**	**68**	**21**	**16**	**37**	**27**	**17**	**44**	**82**	....	....	....	....	....	....	....	....	....	....	**13**	**0**	**1**	**1**	**14**	....	....	....
1965-66	**Montreal Canadiens**	**NHL**	**64**	**15**	**18**	**33**	**18**	**18**	**36**	**67**	....	....	....	....	....	....	....	....	....	....	**6**	**0**	**1**	**1**	**31**	....	....	....
1966-67	**Montreal Canadiens**	**NHL**	**69**	**19**	**16**	**35**	**23**	**16**	**39**	**82**	....	....	....	....	....	....	....	....	....	....	**10**	**1**	**5**	**6**	**15**	....	....	....
1967-68	**Montreal Canadiens**	**NHL**	**42**	**2**	**9**	**11**	**2**	**9**	**11**	**28**	**0**	**0**	**0**	**70**	**2.9**	**19**	**1**	**18**	**0**	**0**	**12**	**3**	**2**	**5**	**8**	**0**	**0**	**0**
	Houston Apollos	CHL	10	6	7	13	....	....	....	32	....	....	....	....	....	....	....	....	....	....	....	....	....	....	....	....	....	....
1968-69	**Minnesota North Stars**	**NHL**	**67**	**25**	**37**	**62**	**28**	**35**	**63**	**106**	**5**	**0**	**3**	**268**	**9.3**	**82**	**30**	**63**	**1**	**–10**	....	....	....	....	....	....	....	....
1969-70	**Minnesota North Stars**	**NHL**	**75**	**24**	**23**	**47**	**28**	**23**	**51**	**109**	**6**	**1**	**4**	**262**	**9.2**	**77**	**34**	**67**	**7**	**–17**	**6**	**1**	**1**	**2**	**25**	**0**	**0**	**0**
1970-71	**Montreal Canadiens**	**NHL**	**64**	**10**	**13**	**23**	**10**	**11**	**21**	**90**	**0**	**0**	**2**	**120**	**8.3**	**37**	**5**	**40**	**0**	**–8**	**11**	**1**	**0**	**1**	**10**	**0**	**0**	**0**
1971-72	**Montreal Canadiens**	**NHL**	**77**	**20**	**18**	**38**	**21**	**16**	**37**	**64**	**1**	**3**	**4**	**169**	**11.8**	**56**	**4**	**55**	**12**	**+9**	**6**	**2**	**1**	**3**	**23**	**0**	**0**	**0**
1972-73	**Montreal Canadiens**	**NHL**	**73**	**11**	**23**	**34**	**11**	**19**	**30**	**30**	**0**	**0**	**0**	**132**	**8.3**	**62**	**1**	**41**	**9**	**+29**	**17**	**3**	**4**	**7**	**6**	**0**	**0**	**0**
1973-74	**Montreal Canadiens**	**NHL**	**39**	**17**	**7**	**24**	**17**	**6**	**23**	**52**	**1**	**0**	**1**	**71**	**23.9**	**36**	**1**	**27**	**3**	**+11**	**5**	**0**	**2**	**2**	**11**	**0**	**0**	**0**
1974-75	**Montreal Canadiens**	**NHL**	**8**	**1**	**2**	**3**	**1**	**2**	**3**	**6**	**0**	**0**	**0**	**8**	**12.5**	**2**	**0**	**5**	**0**	**–3**	....	....	....	....	....	....	....	....
	St. Louis Blues	**NHL**	**56**	**10**	**17**	**27**	**9**	**13**	**22**	**38**	**0**	**0**	**1**	**146**	**6.8**	**49**	**4**	**39**	**1**	**+7**	**2**	**1**	**1**	**2**	**0**	**0**	**0**	**0**
1975-76	**St. Louis Blues**	**NHL**	**67**	**13**	**25**	**38**	**12**	**20**	**32**	**48**	**3**	**0**	**0**	**169**	**7.7**	**61**	**11**	**44**	**1**	**+7**	**3**	**0**	**0**	**0**	**0**	**0**	**0**	**0**
1976-77	**St. Louis Blues**	**NHL**	**80**	**29**	**19**	**48**	**28**	**15**	**43**	**22**	**1**	**1**	**2**	**212**	**13.7**	**71**	**5**	**67**	**6**	**+5**	**4**	**1**	**0**	**1**	**0**	**0**	**0**	**0**
1977-78	**St. Louis Blues**	**NHL**	**69**	**8**	**13**	**21**	**8**	**11**	**19**	**20**	**2**	**0**	**0**	**116**	**6.9**	**38**	**8**	**57**	**8**	**–19**	....	....	....	....	....	....	....	....
	NHL Totals		**943**	**226**	**257**	**483**	**244**	**232**	**476**	**887**	**19**	**5**	**17**	**1743**	**13.0**	**590**	**104**	**523**	**48**		**97**	**14**	**18**	**32**	**143**	**0**	**0**	**0**

Traded to **Minnesota** by **Montreal** with Danny Grant for Minnesota's 1st round choice (Dave Gardner) in 1972 Amateur Draft, cash, and future considerations (Marshall Johnston, May 25, 1971), June 10, 1968. Traded to **Montreal** by **Minnesota** for Bobby Rousseau, June 10, 1970. Traded to **St. Louis** by **Montreal** for cash, December 5, 1974.

• LAROSE, GUY

Guy Larose C – L. 5'9", 180 lbs. b: Hull, Que., 8/31/1967. Buffalo's 11th choice, 224th overall, in 1985 Entry Draft.

Season	Club	League	GP	G	A	Pts	AG	AA	APts	PIM	PP	SH	GW	S	%	TGF	PGF	TGA	PGA	+/–	GP	G	A	Pts	PIM	PP	SH	GW
1984-85	Guelph Platers	OHL	58	30	30	60	....	....	....	63	....	....	....	....	....	....	....	....	....	....	....	....	....	....	....	....	....	....
1985-86	Guelph Platers	OHL	37	12	36	48	....	....	....	55	....	....	....	....	....	....	....	....	....	....	....	....	....	....	....	....	....	....
	Ottawa 67's	OHL	28	19	25	44	....	....	....	63	....	....	....	....	....	....	....	....	....	....	....	....	....	....	....	....	....	....
1986-87	Ottawa 67's	OHL	66	28	49	77	....	....	....	77	....	....	....	....	....	....	....	....	....	....	11	2	8	10	27	....	....	....
1987-88	Moncton Hawks	AHL	77	22	31	53	....	....	....	127	....	....	....	....	....	....	....	....	....	....	....	....	....	....	....	....	....	....
1988-89	**Winnipeg Jets**	**NHL**	**3**	**0**	**1**	**1**	**0**	**1**	**1**	**6**	**0**	**0**	**0**	**2**	**0.0**	**2**	**0**	**3**	**0**	**–1**	....	....	....	....	....	....	....	....
	Moncton Hawks	AHL	72	32	27	59	....	....	....	176	....	....	....	....	....	....	....	....	....	....	10	4	4	8	37	....	....	....
1989-90	Moncton Hawks	AHL	79	44	26	70	....	....	....	232	....	....	....	....	....	....	....	....	....	....	....	....	....	....	....	....	....	....
1990-91	**Winnipeg Jets**	**NHL**	**7**	**0**	**0**	**0**	**0**	**0**	**0**	**8**	**0**	**0**	**0**	**7**	**0.0**	**1**	**0**	**3**	**1**	**–1**	....	....	....	....	....	....	....	....
	Moncton Hawks	AHL	35	14	10	24	....	....	....	60	....	....	....	....	....	....	....	....	....	....	....	....	....	....	....	....	....	....
	Binghamton Rangers	AHL	34	21	15	36	....	....	....	48	....	....	....	....	....	....	....	....	....	....	10	8	5	13	37	....	....	....

Season	Club	League	REGULAR SEASON GP	G	A	Pts	AG	AA	APts	PIM	PP	SH	GW	S	%	TGF	PGF	TGA	PGA	+/–	PLAYOFFS GP	G	A	Pts	PIM	PP	SH	GW
1991-92	Binghamton Rangers	AHL	30	10	11	21	....	....	....	36	....	....	....	....	....	....	....	....	....	....	....	....	....	....	....	....	....	....
	Toronto Maple Leafs	**NHL**	**34**	**9**	**5**	**14**	**8**	**4**	**12**	**27**	**0**	**0**	**0**	**60**	**15.0**	**21**	**2**	**27**	**0**	**–8**	....	....	....	....	....	....	....	....
	St. John's Maple Leafs	AHL	15	7	7	14	....	....	....	26	....	....	....	....	....	....	....	....	....	....	....	....	....	....	....	....	....	....
1992-93	**Toronto Maple Leafs**	**NHL**	**9**	**0**	**0**	**0**	**0**	**0**	**0**	**8**	**0**	**0**	**0**	**8**	**0.0**	**0**	**0**	**3**	**0**	**–3**	....	....	....	....	....	....	....	....
	St. John's Maple Leafs	AHL	5	0	1	1	....	....	....	8	....	....	....	....	....	....	....	....	....	....	9	5	2	7	6	....	....	....
1993-94	**Toronto Maple Leafs**	**NHL**	**10**	**1**	**2**	**3**	**1**	**2**	**3**	**10**	**0**	**0**	**0**	**9**	**11.1**	**3**	**0**	**5**	**0**	**–2**	....	....	....	....	....	....	....	....
	St. John's Maple Leafs	AHL	23	13	16	29	....	....	....	41	....	....	....	....	....	....	....	....	....	....	....	....	....	....	....	....	....	....
	Calgary Flames	**NHL**	**7**	**0**	**1**	**1**	**0**	**1**	**1**	**4**	**0**	**0**	**0**	**3**	**0.0**	**3**	**0**	**6**	**0**	**3**	....	....	....	....	....	....	....	....
	Saint John Flames	AHL	15	11	11	22	....	....	....	20	....	....	....	....	....	....	....	....	....	....	7	3	2	5	22	....	....	....
1994-95	Providence Bruins	AHL	68	25	33	58	....	....	....	93	....	....	....	....	....	....	....	....	....	....	12	4	6	10	22	....	....	....
	Boston Bruins	**NHL**	....	....	....	....	**-2**	**-1**	**-3**	....	....	....	....	....	....	....	....	....	....	....	**4**	**0**	**0**	**0**	**0**	....	....	....
1995-96	Detroit Vipers	IHL	50	28	15	43	....	....	....	53	....	....	....	....	....	....	....	....	....	....	....	....	....	....	....	....	....	....
	Las Vegas Thunder	IHL	25	10	22	32	....	....	....	54	....	....	....	....	....	....	....	....	....	....	15	3	6	9	14	....	....	....
1996-97	Houston Aeros	IHL	79	29	25	54	....	....	....	108	....	....	....	....	....	....	....	....	....	....	13	6	7	13	12	....	....	....
1997-98	ECR Revier Lowen	Germany	45	11	17	28	....	....	....	73	....	....	....	....	....	....	....	....	....	....	....	....	....	....	....	....	....	....
	NHL Totals		**70**	**10**	**9**	**19**	**7**	**7**	**14**	**63**	**0**	**0**	**0**	**89**	**11.2**	**30**	**2**	**47**	**1**		**4**	**0**	**0**	**0**	**0**	**0**	**0**	**0**

Signed as a free agent by **Winnipeg**, July 16, 1987. Traded to **NY Rangers** by **Winnipeg** for Rudy Poeschek, January 22, 1991. Traded to **Toronto** by **NY Rangers** for Mike Stevens, December 26, 1991. Claimed on waivers by **Calgary** from **Toronto**, January 1, 1994. Signed as a free agent by **Boston**, July 11, 1994.

• LAROUCHE, PIERRE

Pierre "Lucky Pierre" Larouche C – R. 5'11", 175 lbs. b: Taschereau, Que., 11/16/1955. Pittsburgh's 1st choice, 8th overall, in 1974 Amateur Draft.

Season	Club	League	GP	G	A	Pts	AG	AA	APts	PIM	PP	SH	GW	S	%	TGF	PGF	TGA	PGA	+/–	GP	G	A	Pts	PIM	PP	SH	GW
1972-73	Quebec Remparts	QMJHL	20	6	7	13	....	....	....	20	....	....	....	....	....	....	....	....	....	....	....	....	....	....	....	....	....	....
	Sorel Black Hawks	QMJHL	43	47	54	101	....	....	....	24	....	....	....	....	....	....	....	....	....	....	10	7	6	13	2	....	....	....
1973-74	Sorel Black Hawks	QMJHL	67	94	*157	*251	....	....	....	53	....	....	....	....	....	....	....	....	....	....	13	15	18	33	20	....	....	....
1974-75	**Pittsburgh Penguins**	**NHL**	**79**	**31**	**37**	**68**	**29**	**29**	**58**	**52**	**5**	**0**	**4**	**172**	**18.0**	**87**	**17**	**70**	**2**	**+2**	**9**	**2**	**5**	**7**	**2**	**0**	**0**	**1**
1975-76	**Pittsburgh Penguins**	**NHL**	**76**	**53**	**58**	**111**	**50**	**46**	**96**	**33**	**18**	**0**	**3**	**319**	**16.6**	**136**	**43**	**90**	**1**	**+4**	**3**	**0**	**1**	**1**	**0**	**0**	**0**	**0**
1976-77	**Pittsburgh Penguins**	**NHL**	**65**	**29**	**34**	**63**	**28**	**28**	**56**	**14**	**8**	**0**	**6**	**227**	**12.8**	**84**	**27**	**72**	**5**	**–10**	**3**	**0**	**3**	**3**	**0**	**0**	**0**	**0**
	Canada	WEC-A	10	7	8	15	....	....	....	16	....	....	....	....	....	....	....	....	....	....	....	....	....	....	....	....	....	....
1977-78	**Pittsburgh Penguins**	**NHL**	**20**	**6**	**5**	**11**	**6**	**4**	**10**	**0**	**0**	**0**	**0**	**50**	**12.0**	**14**	**2**	**25**	**0**	**–13**	....	....	....	....	....	....	....	....
	Montreal Canadiens	**NHL**	**44**	**17**	**32**	**49**	**16**	**26**	**42**	**11**	**3**	**0**	**1**	**87**	**19.5**	**70**	**17**	**21**	**0**	**+32**	**5**	**2**	**1**	**3**	**4**	**1**	**0**	**1**
1978-79	**Montreal Canadiens**	**NHL**	**36**	**9**	**13**	**22**	**8**	**10**	**18**	**4**	**4**	**0**	**0**	**64**	**14.1**	**33**	**17**	**13**	**0**	**+3**	**6**	**1**	**3**	**4**	**0**	**0**	**0**	**1**
1979-80	**Montreal Canadiens**	**NHL**	**73**	**50**	**41**	**91**	**45**	**32**	**77**	**16**	**12**	**0**	**7**	**220**	**22.7**	**130**	**39**	**55**	**0**	**+36**	**9**	**1**	**7**	**8**	**2**	**0**	**0**	**0**
1980-81	**Montreal Canadiens**	**NHL**	**61**	**25**	**28**	**53**	**21**	**20**	**41**	**28**	**5**	**0**	**2**	**154**	**16.2**	**77**	**25**	**40**	**1**	**+13**	**2**	**0**	**2**	**2**	**0**	**0**	**0**	**0**
1981-82	**Montreal Canadiens**	**NHL**	**22**	**9**	**12**	**21**	**7**	**8**	**15**	**0**	**3**	**0**	**0**	**40**	**22.5**	**24**	**9**	**18**	**0**	**–3**	....	....	....	....	....	....	....	....
	Hartford Whalers	**NHL**	**45**	**25**	**25**	**50**	**20**	**17**	**37**	**12**	**11**	**1**	**1**	**121**	**20.7**	**71**	**30**	**71**	**13**	**–17**	....	....	....	....	....	....	....	....
1982-83	**Hartford Whalers**	**NHL**	**38**	**18**	**22**	**40**	**15**	**15**	**30**	**8**	**4**	**0**	**0**	**114**	**15.8**	**60**	**20**	**67**	**3**	**–24**	....	....	....	....	....	....	....	....
1983-84	**New York Rangers**	**NHL**	**77**	**48**	**33**	**81**	**39**	**22**	**61**	**22**	**19**	**0**	**4**	**241**	**19.9**	**103**	**36**	**98**	**16**	**–15**	**5**	**3**	**1**	**4**	**2**	**2**	**0**	**0**
1984-85	**New York Rangers**	**NHL**	**65**	**24**	**36**	**60**	**20**	**24**	**44**	**8**	**5**	**0**	**3**	**171**	**14.0**	**82**	**26**	**78**	**5**	**–17**	....	....	....	....	....	....	....	....
1985-86	**New York Rangers**	**NHL**	**28**	**20**	**7**	**27**	**16**	**5**	**21**	**4**	**7**	**0**	**2**	**85**	**23.5**	**35**	**10**	**31**	**0**	**–6**	**16**	**8**	**9**	**17**	**2**	**4**	**0**	**1**
	Hershey Bears	AHL	32	22	17	39	....	....	....	16	....	....	....	....	....	....	....	....	....	....	....	....	....	....	....	....	....	....
1986-87	**New York Rangers**	**NHL**	**73**	**28**	**35**	**63**	**24**	**25**	**49**	**12**	**8**	**0**	**3**	**193**	**14.5**	**95**	**35**	**67**	**0**	**–7**	**6**	**3**	**2**	**5**	**4**	**0**	**0**	**1**
1987-88	**New York Rangers**	**NHL**	**10**	**3**	**9**	**12**	**3**	**6**	**9**	**13**	**2**	**0**	**0**	**30**	**10.0**	**14**	**8**	**9**	**0**	**–3**	....	....	....	....	....	....	....	....
	NHL Totals		**812**	**395**	**427**	**822**	**347**	**317**	**664**	**237**	**114**	**1**	**36**	**2288**	**17.3**	**1115**	**301**	**825**	**46**		**64**	**20**	**34**	**54**	**16**	**7**	**0**	**5**

QMJHL Second All-Star Team (1974)

Played in NHL All-Star Game (1976, 1984)

Traded to **Montreal** by **Pittsburgh** with future considerations (Peter Marsh, December 15, 1977) for Pete Mahovlich and Peter Lee, November 29, 1977. Traded to **Hartford** by **Montreal** for a switch of 1st round choices (Montreal selected Petr Svoboda, Hartford selected Sylvain Cote), Hartford's 2nd round choice (later traded to St. Louis — St. Louis selected Brian Benning) in 1984 Entry Draft and a switch of 3rd round choices (Montreal selected Rocky Dundas, Hartford traded choice to Pittsburgh — Pittsburgh selected Bruce Racine) in 1985 Entry Draft, December 21, 1981. Signed as a free agent by **NY Rangers**, September 12, 1983.

• LAROUCHE, STEVE

Steve Larouche C – R. 6', 180 lbs. b: Rouyn, Que., 4/14/1971 Montreal's 3rd choice, 41st overall, in 1989 Entry Draft.

Season	Club	League	GP	G	A	Pts	AG	AA	APts	PIM	PP	SH	GW	S	%	TGF	PGF	TGA	PGA	+/–	GP	G	A	Pts	PIM	PP	SH	GW
1987-88	Trois-Rivières Draveurs	QMJHL	66	11	29	40	....	....	....	25	....	....	....	....	....	....	....	....	....	....	....	....	....	....	....	....	....	....
1988-89	Trois-Rivières Draveurs	QMJHL	70	51	102	153	....	....	....	53	....	....	....	....	....	....	....	....	....	....	4	4	2	6	0	....	....	....
1989-90	Trois-Rivières Draveurs	QMJHL	60	55	90	145	....	....	....	40	....	....	....	....	....	....	....	....	....	....	7	3	5	8	8	....	....	....
	Canada	Nat-Team	1	1	0	1	....	....	....	0	....	....	....	....	....	....	....	....	....	....	....	....	....	....	....	....	....	....
1990-91	Chicoutimi Sagueneens	QMJHL	45	35	41	76	....	....	....	64	....	....	....	....	....	....	....	....	....	....	17	*13	*20	*33	20	....	....	....
1991-92	Fredericton Canadiens	AHL	74	21	35	56	....	....	....	41	....	....	....	....	....	....	....	....	....	....	7	1	0	1	0	....	....	....
1992-93	Fredericton Canadiens	AHL	77	27	65	92	....	....	....	52	....	....	....	....	....	....	....	....	....	....	5	2	5	7	6	....	....	....
1993-94	Atlanta Knights	IHL	80	43	53	96	....	....	....	73	....	....	....	....	....	....	....	....	....	....	14	*16	10	*26	16	....	....	....
1994-95	P.E.I. Senators	AHL	70	*53	48	101	....	....	....	54	....	....	....	....	....	....	....	....	....	....	2	1	0	1	0	....	....	....
	Ottawa Senators	**NHL**	**18**	**8**	**7**	**15**	**14**	**10**	**24**	**6**	**2**	**0**	**2**	**38**	**21.1**	**19**	**9**	**15**	**0**	**–5**	....	....	....	....	....	....	....	....
1995-96	**New York Rangers**	**NHL**	**1**	**0**	**0**	**0**	**0**	**0**	**0**	**0**	**0**	**0**	**0**	**1**	**0.0**	**1**	**1**	**0**	**0**	**0**	....	....	....	....	....	....	....	....
	Binghamton Rangers	AHL	39	20	46	66	....	....	....	47	....	....	....	....	....	....	....	....	....	....	....	....	....	....	....	....	....	....
	Los Angeles Kings	**NHL**	**7**	**1**	**2**	**3**	**1**	**2**	**3**	**4**	**1**	**0**	**0**	**13**	**7.7**	**5**	**2**	**3**	**0**	**0**	....	....	....	....	....	....	....	....
	Phoenix Roadrunners	IHL	33	19	17	36	....	....	....	14	....	....	....	....	....	....	....	....	....	....	4	0	1	1	8	....	....	....
1996-97	Quebec Rafales	IHL	79	49	53	102	....	....	....	78	....	....	....	....	....	....	....	....	....	....	9	3	10	13	18	....	....	....
1997-98	Quebec Rafales	IHL	68	23	44	67	....	....	....	40	....	....	....	....	....	....	....	....	....	....	....	....	....	....	....	....	....	....
	Chicago Wolves	IHL	13	9	10	19	....	....	....	20	....	....	....	....	....	....	....	....	....	....	22	9	11	20	14	....	....	....
	NHL Totals		**26**	**9**	**9**	**18**	**15**	**12**	**27**	**10**	**3**	**0**	**2**	**52**	**17.3**	**25**	**12**	**18**	**0**		....	....	....	....	....	....	....	....

QMJHL Second All-Star Team (1990) • AHL First All-Star Team (1995) • Won Fred Hunt Memorial Trophy (Sportsmanship - AHL) (1995) • Won Les Cunningham Plaque (MVP - AHL) (1995) • IHL First All-Star Team (1997)

Signed as a free agent by **Ottawa**, September 11, 1994. Traded to **NY Rangers** by **Ottawa** for Jean-Yves Roy, October 5, 1995. Traded to **LA Kings** by **NY Rangers** for Chris Snell, January 14, 1996.

• LARSEN, BRAD

Brad Larsen LW – L. 5'11", 212 lbs. b: Nakusp, B.C., 1/28/1977. Colorado's 3rd choice, 87th overall, in 1997 Entry Draft.

Season	Club	League	GP	G	A	Pts	AG	AA	APts	PIM	PP	SH	GW	S	%	TGF	PGF	TGA	PGA	+/–	GP	G	A	Pts	PIM	PP	SH	GW
1993-94	Swift Current Broncos	WHL	64	15	18	33	....	....	....	32	....	....	....	....	....	....	....	....	....	....	7	1	2	3	4	....	....	....
1994-95	Swift Current Broncos	WHL	62	24	33	57	....	....	....	73	....	....	....	....	....	....	....	....	....	....	6	0	1	1	2	....	....	....
1995-96	Swift Current Broncos	WHL	51	30	47	77	....	....	....	67	....	....	....	....	....	....	....	....	....	....	6	3	2	5	13	....	....	....
	Canada	WJC-A	6	1	1	2	....	....	....	4	....	....	....	....	....	....	....	....	....	....	....	....	....	....	....	....	....	....
1996-97	Swift Current Broncos	WHL	61	36	46	82	....	....	....	61	....	....	....	....	....	....	....	....	....	....	....	....	....	....	....	....	....	....
	Canada	WJC-A	7	0	1	1	....	....	....	6	....	....	....	....	....	....	....	....	....	....	....	....	....	....	....	....	....	....
1997-98	**Colorado Avalanche**	**NHL**	**1**	**0**	**0**	**0**	**0**	**0**	**0**	**0**	**0**	**0**	**0**	**0**	**0.0**	**0**	**0**	**0**	**0**	**0**	....	....	....	....	....	....	....	....
	Hershey Bears	AHL	65	12	10	22	....	....	....	80	....	....	....	....	....	....	....	....	....	....	7	3	2	5	2	....	....	....
	NHL Totals		**1**	**0**	**0**	**0**	**0**	**0**	**0**	**0**	**0**	**0**	**0**	**0**	**0.0**	**0**	**0**	**0**	**0**		....	....	....	....	....	....	....	....

WHL East Second All-Star Team (1997)

• Re-entered NHL draft. Originally Ottawa's 3rd choice, 53rd overall, in 1995 Entry Draft.

Rights traded to **Colorado** by **Ottawa** for Janne Laukkanen, January 26, 1996.

• LARSON, REED

Reed Larson D – R. 6', 195 lbs. b: Minneapolis, MN, 7/30/1956. Detroit's 14th choice, 22nd overall, in 1976 Amateur Draft. **USHOF**

Season	Club	League	GP	G	A	Pts	AG	AA	APts	PIM	PP	SH	GW	S	%	TGF	PGF	TGA	PGA	+/–	GP	G	A	Pts	PIM	PP	SH	GW
1974-75	University of Minnesota	WCHA	41	11	17	28	....	....	....	37	....	....	....	....	....	....	....	....	....	....	....	....	....	....	....	....	....	....
1975-76	University of Minnesota	WCHA	42	13	29	42	....	....	....	94	....	....	....	....	....	....	....	....	....	....	....	....	....	....	....	....	....	....
1976-77	University of Minnesota	WCHA	21	10	15	25	....	....	....	30	....	....	....	....	....	....	....	....	....	....	....	....	....	....	....	....	....	....
	Detroit Red Wings	**NHL**	**14**	**0**	**1**	**1**	**0**	**1**	**1**	**23**	**0**	**0**	**0**	**23**	**0.0**	**6**	**0**	**8**	**0**	**–2**	....	....	....	....	....	....	....	....
1977-78	**Detroit Red Wings**	**NHL**	**75**	**19**	**41**	**60**	**18**	**33**	**51**	**95**	**7**	**1**	**4**	**240**	**7.9**	**132**	**45**	**131**	**36**	**–8**	**7**	**0**	**2**	**2**	**4**	**0**	**0**	**0**
1978-79	**Detroit Red Wings**	**NHL**	**79**	**18**	**49**	**67**	**16**	**38**	**54**	**169**	**6**	**2**	**0**	**271**	**6.6**	**124**	**51**	**125**	**32**	**–20**	....	....	....	....	....	....	....	....
1979-80	**Detroit Red Wings**	**NHL**	**80**	**22**	**44**	**66**	**20**	**34**	**54**	**101**	**7**	**0**	**2**	**293**	**7.5**	**149**	**44**	**145**	**33**	**–7**	....	....	....	....	....	....	....	....
1980-81	**Detroit Red Wings**	**NHL**	**78**	**27**	**31**	**58**	**22**	**22**	**44**	**153**	**8**	**0**	**0**	**297**	**9.1**	**122**	**32**	**177**	**52**	**–35**	....	....	....	....	....	....	....	....
	United States	WEC-A	8	5	1	6	....	....	....	6	....	....	....	....	....	....	....	....	....	....	....	....	....	....	....	....	....	....
1981-82	United States	C Cup	5	1	1	2	....	....	....	4	....	....	....	....	....	....	....	....	....	....	....	....	....	....	....	....	....	....
	Detroit Red Wings	**NHL**	**80**	**21**	**39**	**60**	**17**	**26**	**43**	**112**	**4**	**2**	**2**	**311**	**6.8**	**137**	**26**	**161**	**33**	**–17**	....	....	....	....	....	....	....	....
1982-83	**Detroit Red Wings**	**NHL**	**80**	**22**	**52**	**74**	**18**	**36**	**54**	**104**	**7**	**1**	**1**	**271**	**8.1**	**145**	**30**	**159**	**37**	**–7**	....	....	....	....	....	....	....	....

			REGULAR SEASON																		PLAYOFFS							
Season	Club	League	GP	G	A	Pts	AG	AA	APts	PIM	PP	SH	GW	S	%	TGF	PGF	TGA	PGA	+/–	GP	G	A	Pts	PIM	PP	SH	GW
1983-84	**Detroit Red Wings**	**NHL**	**78**	**23**	**39**	**62**	**19**	**26**	**45**	**122**	**10**	**0**	**5**	**262**	**8.8**	**137**	**48**	**136**	**37**	**–10**	**4**	**2**	**0**	**2**	**21**	**2**	**0**	**0**
1984-85	**Detroit Red Wings**	**NHL**	**77**	**17**	**45**	**62**	**14**	**30**	**44**	**139**	**7**	**0**	**0**	**233**	**7.3**	**149**	**47**	**137**	**42**	**+7**	**3**	**1**	**2**	**3**	**20**	**0**	**0**	**0**
1985-86	**Detroit Red Wings**	**NHL**	**67**	**19**	**41**	**60**	**15**	**27**	**42**	**109**	**11**	**0**	**0**	**205**	**9.3**	**131**	**57**	**151**	**41**	**–36**								
	Boston Bruins	**NHL**	**13**	**3**	**4**	**7**	**2**	**3**	**5**	**8**	**1**	**0**	**0**	**41**	**7.3**	**18**	**4**	**12**	**3**	**+5**	**3**	**1**	**0**	**1**	**6**	**1**	**0**	**0**
1986-87	**Boston Bruins**	**NHL**	**66**	**12**	**24**	**36**	**10**	**17**	**27**	**95**	**9**	**0**	**1**	**209**	**5.7**	**117**	**40**	**85**	**17**	**+9**	**4**	**0**	**2**	**2**	**2**	**0**	**0**	**0**
1987-88	**Boston Bruins**	**NHL**	**62**	**10**	**24**	**34**	**9**	**17**	**26**	**93**	**5**	**1**	**1**	**151**	**6.6**	**81**	**23**	**71**	**16**	**+3**	**8**	**0**	**1**	**1**	**6**	**0**	**0**	**0**
	Maine Mariners	AHL	2	2	0	2				4																		
1988-89	**Edmonton Oilers**	**NHL**	**10**	**2**	**7**	**9**	**2**	**5**	**7**	**15**	**0**	**1**	**0**	**19**	**10.5**	**15**	**3**	**13**	**2**	**+1**								
	New York Islanders	**NHL**	**33**	**7**	**13**	**20**	**6**	**9**	**15**	**35**	**6**	**0**	**1**	**77**	**9.1**	**56**	**28**	**47**	**11**	**–8**								
	Minnesota North Stars	**NHL**	**11**	**0**	**9**	**9**	**0**	**6**	**6**	**18**	**0**	**0**	**0**	**19**	**0.0**	**15**	**7**	**12**	**1**	**–3**	**3**	**0**	**0**	**0**	**4**	**0**	**0**	**0**
1989-90	Alleghe-Sile	Italy	34	17	32	49				49											9	7	18	25	2			
	Buffalo Sabres	**NHL**	**1**	**0**	**0**	**0**	**0**	**0**	**0**	**0**	**0**	**0**	**0**	**1**	**0.0**	**4**	**1**	**2**	**0**	**+1**								
1990-91	Alleghe-Sile	Italy	36	13	38	51				24											7	3	7	10	6			
1991-92	Milan	Italy	29	9	21	30				14																		
1992-93			DID NOT PLAY																									
1993-94			DID NOT PLAY																									
1994-95	Minnesota Moose	IHL	9	2	2	4				11																		
	NHL Totals		**904**	**222**	**463**	**685**	**188**	**330**	**518**	**1391**	**88**	**8**	**17**	**2923**	**7.6**	**1538**	**486**	**1572**	**393**		**32**	**4**	**7**	**11**	**63**	**3**	**0**	**0**

NCAA Championship All-Tournament Team (1975) • WCHA First All-Star Team (1976)

Played in NHL All-Star Game (1978, 1980, 1981)

Traded to **Boston** by **Detroit** for Mike O'Connell, March 10, 1986. Signed as a free agent by **Edmonton**, September 30, 1988. Signed as a free agent by **NY Islanders**, December 5, 1988. Traded to **Minnesota** by **NY Islanders** for Minnesota's 7th round choice (Brett Harkins) and future considerations (Mike Keller), March 7, 1989. Signed as a free agent by **Alleghe-Sile** (Italy), August, 1989. Signed as a free agent by **Buffalo**, March 6, 1990.

• LARTER, TYLER

Tyler Larter C – L. 5'10", 185 lbs. b: Charlottetown, P.E.I., 3/12/1968. Washington's 3rd choice, 78th overall, in 1987 Entry Draft.

Season	Club	League	GP	G	A	Pts	AG	AA	APts	PIM	PP	SH	GW	S	%	TGF	PGF	TGA	PGA	+/–	GP	G	A	Pts	PIM	PP	SH	GW
1984-85	Charlottetown Tigers	PEI Jr.	26	24	32	56																						
	Sault Ste. Marie Greyhounds	OHL	64	14	26	40				48											16	3	9	12	12			
1985-86	Sault Ste. Marie Greyhounds	OHL	60	15	40	55				137																		
1986-87	Sault Ste. Marie Greyhounds	OHL	59	34	59	93				122											4	0	2	2	8			
1987-88	Sault Ste. Marie Greyhounds	OHL	65	44	65	109				155											4	3	9	12	8			
1988-89	Baltimore Skipjacks	AHL	71	9	19	28				189																		
1989-90	**Washington Capitals**	**NHL**	**1**	**0**	**0**	**0**	**0**	**0**	**0**	**0**	**0**	**0**	**0**	**2**	**0.0**	**0**	**0**	**1**	**0**	**–1**								
	Baltimore Skipjacks	AHL	79	31	36	67				104											12	5	6	11	57			
1990-91	Baltimore Skipjacks	AHL	62	21	21	42				84											6	1	0	1	13			
1991-92	Moncton Hawks	AHL	68	25	51	76				156											10	5	5	10	33			
	Kalamazoo Wings	IHL	3	0	2	2				4																		
1992-93	VEU Feldkirch	Austria	39	16	25	41																						
	Val Gardenia	Italy	3	2	2	4				2																		
1993-94	Durham Wasps	Britain	2	2	1	3				8																		
	Whitley Warriors	Britain	32	32	30	62				38											5	9	3	12	8			
	NHL Totals		**1**	**0**	**0**	**0**	**0**	**0**	**0**	**0**	**0**	**0**	**0**	**2**	**0.0**	**0**	**0**	**1**	**0**									

Traded to **Winnipeg** by **Washington** with Bob Joyce and Kent Paynter for Craig Duncanson, Brett Hughesw and Simon Wheeldon, May 21, 1991. Claimed by **Minnesota** from **Winnipeg** in Expansion Draft, May 30, 1991. Traded to **Winnipeg** by **Minnesota** for Tony Joseph, October 15, 1991.

• LATAL, JIRI

Jiri Latal D – L. 6', 190 lbs. b: Olomouc, Czech., 2/2/1967. Toronto's 6th choice, 106th overall, in 1985 Entry Draft.

Season	Club	League	GP	G	A	Pts	AG	AA	APts	PIM	PP	SH	GW	S	%	TGF	PGF	TGA	PGA	+/–	GP	G	A	Pts	PIM	PP	SH	GW
1984-85	Sparta Praha	Czech.	28	2	2	4				10																		
	Czechoslovakia	WJC-A	7	0	4	4				2																		
1985-86	Sparta Praha	Czech.	27	3	2	5																						
	Czechoslovakia	WJC-A	7	0	2	2				2																		
1986-87	Sparta Praha	Czech.	12	1	2	3																						
	Czechoslovakia	WJC-A	7	4	2	6				0																		
1987-88	Dukla Trencin	Czech.	46	8	15	23				27																		
1988-89	Dukla Trencin	Czech.	48	6	22	28																						
	Czechoslovakia	WEC-A	1	0	0	0				0																		
1989-90	**Philadelphia Flyers**	**NHL**	**32**	**6**	**13**	**19**	**5**	**9**	**14**	**6**	**3**	**0**	**0**	**59**	**10.2**	**49**	**12**	**33**	**0**	**+4**								
	Hershey Bears	AHL	22	10	18	28				10																		
1990-91	**Philadelphia Flyers**	**NHL**	**50**	**5**	**21**	**26**	**5**	**16**	**21**	**14**	**1**	**0**	**0**	**81**	**6.2**	**46**	**17**	**49**	**1**	**–19**								
1991-92	**Philadelphia Flyers**	**NHL**	**10**	**1**	**2**	**3**	**1**	**1**	**2**	**4**	**0**	**0**	**1**	**22**	**4.5**	**10**	**2**	**7**	**0**	**+1**								
1992-93	VIF Oslo	Norway	STATISTICS NOT AVAILABLE																									
1993-94	VIF Oslo	Norway	STATISTICS NOT AVAILABLE																									
1994-95	HC Olomouc	Czech.	1	0	0	0															1	0	0	0				
	NHL Totals		**92**	**12**	**36**	**48**	**11**	**26**	**37**	**24**	**4**	**0**	**1**	**162**	**7.4**	**105**	**31**	**89**	**1**									

EJC-A All-Star Team (1984) • WJC-A All-Star Team (1987)

Rights traded to **Philadelphia** by **Toronto** for Philadelphia's 3rd round choice (Al Kinsky) in 1990 Entry Draft, August 28, 1989.

• LATOS, JAMES

James Latos RW – R. 6'1", 200 lbs. b: Wakaw, Sask., 1/4/1966.

Season	Club	League	GP	G	A	Pts	AG	AA	APts	PIM	PP	SH	GW	S	%	TGF	PGF	TGA	PGA	+/–	GP	G	A	Pts	PIM	PP	SH	GW
1982-83	Prince Albert Midgets	SJHL	28	11	18	29				20																		
1983-84	Humboldt Broncos	SJHL	53	12	15	27				131																		
1984-85	Saskatoon Blades	WHL	62	9	9	18				120											3	1	1	2	0			
1985-86	Saskatoon Blades	WHL	40	4	7	11				111																		
	Portland Wheat Kings	WHL	21	6	7	13				80											9	1	1	2	32			
1986-87	Portland Wheat Kings	WHL	69	27	18	45				210											20	5	3	8	56			
1987-88	Colorado Rangers	IHL	38	11	12	23				98																		
1988-89	**New York Rangers**	**NHL**	**1**	**0**	**0**	**0**	**0**	**0**	**0**	**0**	**0**	**0**	**0**	**0**	**0.0**	**0**	**0**	**1**	**0**	**–1**								
	Denver Rangers	IHL	37	7	5	12				157											4	0	0	0	17			
1989-90	Flint Spirits	IHL	71	12	15	27				244											4	0	0	0	0			
1990-91	Kansas City Blades	IHL	61	14	14	28				187																		
1991-92	Knoxville Cherokees	ECHL	10	5	2	7				24																		
	Muskegon Lumberjacks	IHL	27	4	4	8				54											6	0	1	1	10			
	St. Thomas Wildcats	ColHL	27	7	13	20				62																		
1992-93	Muskegon Fury	ColHL	59	10	24	34				163											7	2	0	2	4			
	Cleveland Lumberjacks	IHL	1	0	0	0				0																		
1993-94	Wichita Thunder	ColHL	63	19	34	53				227											11	4	5	9	27			
	NHL Totals		**1**	**0**	**0**	**0**	**0**	**0**	**0**	**0**	**0**	**0**	**0**	**0**	**0.0**	**0**	**0**	**1**	**0**									

Signed as a free agent by **NY Rangers**, June 5, 1987.

• LATTA, DAVID

David Latta LW – L. 6'1", 190 lbs. b: Thunder Bay, Ont., 1/3/1967. Quebec's 1st choice, 15th overall, in 1985 Entry Draft.

Season	Club	League	GP	G	A	Pts	AG	AA	APts	PIM	PP	SH	GW	S	%	TGF	PGF	TGA	PGA	+/–	GP	G	A	Pts	PIM	PP	SH	GW
1982-83	Orillia Travelways	OJHL	43	16	25	41				26																		
1983-84	Kitchener Rangers	OHL	66	17	26	43				54											16	3	6	9	9			
1984-85	Kitchener Rangers	OHL	52	38	27	65				26											4	2	4	6	4			
1985-86	Kitchener Rangers	OHL	55	36	34	70				60											5	7	1	8	15			
	Quebec Nordiques	**NHL**	**1**	**0**	**0**	**0**	**0**	**0**	**0**	**0**	**0**	**0**	**0**	**1**	**0.0**	**0**	**0**	**0**	**0**	**0**								
	Fredericton Express	AHL	3	1	0	1				0											5	0	3	3	0			
1986-87	Kitchener Rangers	OHL	50	32	46	78				46											4	0	3	3	2			
	Canada	WJC-A	6	4	6	10				12																		
1987-88	**Quebec Nordiques**	**NHL**	**10**	**0**	**0**	**0**	**0**	**0**	**0**	**0**	**0**	**0**	**0**	**13**	**0.0**	**2**	**1**	**5**	**0**	**–4**								
	Fredericton Express	AHL	34	11	21	32				28											15	9	4	13	24			
1988-89	**Quebec Nordiques**	**NHL**	**24**	**4**	**8**	**12**	**3**	**6**	**9**	**4**	**1**	**0**	**1**	**30**	**13.3**	**16**	**4**	**20**	**0**	**–8**								
	Halifax Citadels	AHL	42	20	26	46				36											4	0	2	2	2			
1989-90	Halifax Citadels	AHL	34	11	5	16				45																		

			REGULAR SEASON																		PLAYOFFS							
Season	Club	League	GP	G	A	Pts	AG	AA	APts	PIM	PP	SH	GW	S	%	TGF	PGF	TGA	PGA	+/–	GP	G	A	Pts	PIM	PP	SH	GW
1990-91	**Quebec Nordiques**	**NHL**	**1**	**0**	**0**	**0**	**0**	**0**	**0**	**0**	**0**	**0**	**0**	**1**	**0.0**	**0**	**0**	**0**	**0**	**0**	....	....	....	....	....	....	....	....
	Halifax Citadels	AHL	22	4	7	11	....	....	....	12	....	....	....	....	....	....	....	....	....	....	....	....	....	....	....	....	....	....
	Canada	Nat-Team	30	5	14	19	....	....	....	24	....	....	....	....	....	....	....	....	....	....	....	....	....	....	....	....	....	....
1991-92	New Haven Nighthawks	AHL	76	18	27	45	....	....	....	100	....	....	....	....	....	....	....	....	....	....	5	1	1	2	4	....	....	....
1992-93	Cincinnati Cyclones	IHL	13	4	7	11	....	....	....	26	....	....	....	....	....	....	....	....	....	....	....	....	....	....	....	....	....	....
1993-94			DID NOT PLAY																									
1994-95			DID NOT PLAY																									
1995-96	Augsburg Panthers	Germany	1	1	0	1	....	....	....	0	....	....	....	....	....	....	....	....	....	....	....	....	....	....	....	....	....	....
	NHL Totals		**36**	**4**	**8**	**12**	**3**	**6**	**9**	**4**	**1**	**0**	**1**	**45**	**8.9**	**18**	**5**	**25**	**0**		....	....	....	....	....	....	....	....
• LAUEN, MIKE	Mike Lauen	RW – R. 6'1", 185 lbs. b: Edina, MN, 2/9/1961. Winnipeg's 8th choice, 135th overall, in 1980 Entry Draft.																										
1979-80	Michigan Tech Huskies	CCHA	35	24	21	45	....	....	....	16	....	....	....	....	....	....	....	....	....	....	....	....	....	....	....	....	....	....
	United States	WJC-A	5	3	2	5	....	....	....	8	....	....	....	....	....	....	....	....	....	....	....	....	....	....	....	....	....	....
1980-81	Michigan Tech Huskies	CCHA	44	24	20	44	....	....	....	14	....	....	....	....	....	....	....	....	....	....	....	....	....	....	....	....	....	....
1981-82	Michigan Tech Huskies	CCHA	30	13	15	28	....	....	....	28	....	....	....	....	....	....	....	....	....	....	....	....	....	....	....	....	....	....
1982-83	Michigan Tech Huskies	CCHA	38	12	17	29	....	....	....	18	....	....	....	....	....	....	....	....	....	....	....	....	....	....	....	....	....	....
	Sherbrooke Jets	AHL	5	0	3	3	....	....	....	0	....	....	....	....	....	....	....	....	....	....	....	....	....	....	....	....	....	....
1983-84	**Winnipeg Jets**	**NHL**	**4**	**0**	**1**	**1**	**0**	**1**	**1**	**0**	**0**	**0**	**0**	**3**	**0.0**	**2**	**0**	**2**	**0**	**0**	....	....	....	....	....	....	....	....
	Sherbrooke Jets	AHL	62	23	29	52	....	....	....	13	....	....	....	....	....	....	....	....	....	....	....	....	....	....	....	....	....	....
1984-85	Sherbrooke Canadiens	AHL	25	6	10	16	....	....	....	2	....	....	....	....	....	....	....	....	....	....	....	....	....	....	....	....	....	....
1985-86	Toledo Goaldiggers	IHL	27	4	10	14	....	....	....	16	....	....	....	....	....	....	....	....	....	....	....	....	....	....	....	....	....	....
	NHL Totals		**4**	**0**	**1**	**1**	**0**	**1**	**1**	**0**	**0**	**0**	**0**	**3**	**0.0**	**2**	**0**	**2**	**0**		....	....	....	....	....	....	....	....
• LAUER, BRAD	Brad Lauer	LW – L. 6', 195 lbs. b: Humboldt, Sask., 10/27/1966. NY Islanders' 3rd choice, 34th overall, in 1985 Entry Draft.																										
1983-84	Regina Pats	WHL	60	5	7	12	....	....	....	51	....	....	....	....	....	....	....	....	....	....	16	0	1	1	24	....	....	....
1984-85	Regina Pats	WHL	72	33	46	79	....	....	....	57	....	....	....	....	....	....	....	....	....	....	8	6	6	12	9	....	....	....
1985-86	Regina Pats	WHL	57	36	38	74	....	....	....	69	....	....	....	....	....	....	....	....	....	....	10	4	5	9	2	....	....	....
1986-87	**New York Islanders**	**NHL**	**61**	**7**	**14**	**21**	**6**	**10**	**16**	**65**	**1**	**0**	**1**	**75**	**9.3**	**31**	**2**	**31**	**2**	**0**	**6**	**2**	**0**	**2**	**4**	**0**	**0**	**0**
1987-88	**New York Islanders**	**NHL**	**69**	**17**	**18**	**35**	**15**	**13**	**28**	**67**	**3**	**0**	**4**	**94**	**18.1**	**44**	**8**	**24**	**1**	**+13**	**5**	**3**	**1**	**4**	**4**	**0**	**0**	**0**
1988-89	**New York Islanders**	**NHL**	**14**	**3**	**2**	**5**	**3**	**1**	**4**	**2**	**0**	**0**	**0**	**21**	**14.3**	**11**	**2**	**11**	**0**	**–2**	....	....	....	....	....	....	....	....
	Springfield Indians	AHL	8	1	5	6	....	....	....	0	....	....	....	....	....	....	....	....	....	....	....	....	....	....	....	....	....	....
1989-90	**New York Islanders**	**NHL**	**63**	**6**	**18**	**24**	**5**	**13**	**18**	**19**	**0**	**0**	**2**	**86**	**7.0**	**41**	**2**	**53**	**19**	**+5**	**4**	**0**	**2**	**2**	**10**	**0**	**0**	**0**
	Springfield Indians	AHL	7	4	2	6	....	....	....	0	....	....	....	....	....	....	....	....	....	....	....	....	....	....	....	....	....	....
1990-91	**New York Islanders**	**NHL**	**44**	**4**	**8**	**12**	**4**	**6**	**10**	**45**	**0**	**1**	**0**	**70**	**5.7**	**22**	**1**	**39**	**12**	**–6**	....	....	....	....	....	....	....	....
	Capital District Islanders	AHL	11	5	11	16	....	....	....	14	....	....	....	....	....	....	....	....	....	....	....	....	....	....	....	....	....	....
1991-92	**New York Islanders**	**NHL**	**8**	**1**	**0**	**1**	**1**	**0**	**1**	**2**	**0**	**1**	**0**	**12**	**8.3**	**2**	**0**	**5**	**1**	**–2**	....	....	....	....	....	....	....	....
	Chicago Blackhawks	**NHL**	**6**	**0**	**0**	**0**	**0**	**0**	**0**	**4**	**0**	**0**	**0**	**6**	**0.0**	**0**	**0**	**3**	**0**	**–3**	**7**	**1**	**1**	**2**	**2**	**0**	**0**	**0**
	Indianapolis Ice	IHL	57	24	30	54	....	....	....	46	....	....	....	....	....	....	....	....	....	....	....	....	....	....	....	....	....	....
1992-93	**Chicago Blackhawks**	**NHL**	**7**	**0**	**1**	**1**	**0**	**1**	**1**	**2**	**0**	**0**	**0**	**8**	**0.0**	**4**	**1**	**4**	**0**	**–1**	....	....	....	....	....	....	....	....
	Indianapolis Ice	IHL	62	*50	41	91	....	....	....	80	....	....	....	....	....	....	....	....	....	....	5	3	1	4	6	....	....	....
1993-94	**Ottawa Senators**	**NHL**	**30**	**2**	**5**	**7**	**2**	**4**	**6**	**6**	**0**	**1**	**0**	**45**	**4.4**	**11**	**2**	**37**	**13**	**–15**	....	....	....	....	....	....	....	....
	Las Vegas Thunder	IHL	32	21	21	42	....	....	....	30	....	....	....	....	....	....	....	....	....	....	4	1	0	1	2	....	....	....
1994-95	Cleveland Lumberjacks	IHL	51	32	27	59	....	....	....	48	....	....	....	....	....	....	....	....	....	....	4	4	2	6	6	....	....	....
1995-96	**Pittsburgh Penguins**	**NHL**	**21**	**4**	**1**	**5**	**4**	**1**	**5**	**6**	**1**	**0**	**1**	**29**	**13.8**	**10**	**1**	**14**	**0**	**–5**	**12**	**1**	**1**	**2**	**4**	**0**	**0**	**0**
	Cleveland Lumberjacks	IHL	53	25	27	52	....	....	....	44	....	....	....	....	....	....	....	....	....	....	....	....	....	....	....	....	....	....
1996-97	Cleveland Lumberjacks	IHL	64	27	21	48	....	....	....	61	....	....	....	....	....	....	....	....	....	....	14	4	6	10	8	....	....	....
1997-98	Cleveland Lumberjacks	IHL	68	22	33	55	....	....	....	74	....	....	....	....	....	....	....	....	....	....	10	0	3	3	12	....	....	....
	NHL Totals		**323**	**44**	**67**	**111**	**40**	**49**	**89**	**218**	**5**	**3**	**8**	**446**	**9.9**	**176**	**19**	**221**	**48**		**34**	**7**	**5**	**12**	**24**	**0**	**0**	**0**

IHL First All-Star Team (1993)

Traded to **Chicago** by **NY Islanders** with Brent Sutter for Adam Creighton and Steve Thomas, October 25, 1991. Signed as a free agent by **Ottawa**, January 3, 1994. Signed as a free agent by **Pittsburgh**, August 10, 1995.

• LAUGHLIN, CRAIG	Craig Laughlin	RW – R. 6', 190 lbs. b: Toronto, Ont., 9/19/1957. Montreal's 17th choice, 162nd overall, in 1977 Amateur Draft.																										
1976-77	Clarkson College	ECAC	33	12	13	25	....	....	....	44	....	....	....	....	....	....	....	....	....	....	....	....	....	....	....	....	....	....
1977-78	Clarkson College	ECAC	30	17	31	48	....	....	....	56	....	....	....	....	....	....	....	....	....	....	....	....	....	....	....	....	....	....
1978-79	Clarkson College	ECAC	30	18	29	47	....	....	....	22	....	....	....	....	....	....	....	....	....	....	....	....	....	....	....	....	....	....
1979-80	Clarkson College	ECAC	34	18	30	48	....	....	....	38	....	....	....	....	....	....	....	....	....	....	....	....	....	....	....	....	....	....
	Nova Scotia Voyageurs	AHL	2	0	0	0	....	....	....	2	....	....	....	....	....	....	....	....	....	....	....	....	....	....	....	....	....	....
1980-81	Nova Scotia Voyageurs	AHL	46	32	29	61	....	....	....	15	....	....	....	....	....	....	....	....	....	....	6	0	1	1	6	....	....	....
1981-82	**Montreal Canadiens**	**NHL**	**36**	**12**	**11**	**23**	**9**	**7**	**16**	**33**	**2**	**0**	**1**	**52**	**23.1**	**36**	**6**	**20**	**0**	**+10**	**3**	**0**	**1**	**1**	**0**	**0**	**0**	**0**
	Nova Scotia Voyageurs	AHL	26	14	15	29	....	....	....	16	....	....	....	....	....	....	....	....	....	....	....	....	....	....	....	....	....	....
1982-83	**Washington Capitals**	**NHL**	**75**	**17**	**27**	**44**	**14**	**19**	**33**	**41**	**5**	**0**	**3**	**128**	**13.3**	**73**	**25**	**57**	**2**	**–7**	**4**	**1**	**0**	**1**	**0**	**0**	**0**	**0**
1983-84	**Washington Capitals**	**NHL**	**80**	**20**	**32**	**52**	**16**	**22**	**38**	**69**	**7**	**0**	**3**	**111**	**18.0**	**77**	**33**	**40**	**0**	**+4**	**8**	**4**	**2**	**6**	**6**	**1**	**0**	**3**
1984-85	**Washington Capitals**	**NHL**	**78**	**16**	**34**	**50**	**13**	**23**	**36**	**38**	**5**	**0**	**3**	**104**	**15.4**	**86**	**29**	**47**	**2**	**+12**	**5**	**0**	**0**	**0**	**2**	**0**	**0**	**0**
1985-86	**Washington Capitals**	**NHL**	**75**	**30**	**45**	**75**	**24**	**30**	**54**	**43**	**10**	**0**	**4**	**114**	**26.3**	**126**	**51**	**53**	**2**	**+24**	**9**	**1**	**2**	**3**	**10**	**0**	**0**	**1**
1986-87	**Washington Capitals**	**NHL**	**80**	**22**	**30**	**52**	**19**	**22**	**41**	**67**	**11**	**0**	**5**	**109**	**20.2**	**89**	**36**	**56**	**0**	**–3**	**1**	**0**	**0**	**0**	**0**	**0**	**0**	**0**
1987-88	**Washington Capitals**	**NHL**	**40**	**5**	**5**	**10**	**4**	**4**	**8**	**26**	**3**	**0**	**1**	**45**	**11.1**	**18**	**8**	**18**	**0**	**–8**	....	....	....	....	....	....	....	....
	Los Angeles Kings	**NHL**	**19**	**4**	**8**	**12**	**3**	**6**	**9**	**6**	**2**	**0**	**0**	**29**	**13.8**	**17**	**7**	**19**	**1**	**–8**	**3**	**0**	**1**	**1**	**2**	**0**	**0**	**0**
1988-89	**Toronto Maple Leafs**	**NHL**	**66**	**10**	**13**	**23**	**8**	**9**	**17**	**41**	**0**	**0**	**0**	**87**	**11.5**	**33**	**4**	**56**	**5**	**–22**	....	....	....	....	....	....	....	....
1989-90	Landshut	Germany	53	32	48	80	....	....	....	90	....	....	....	....	....	....	....	....	....	....	....	....	....	....	....	....	....	....
	NHL Totals		**549**	**136**	**205**	**341**	**110**	**142**	**252**	**384**	**45**	**0**	**20**	**779**	**17.6**	**555**	**199**	**366**	**12**		**33**	**6**	**6**	**12**	**20**	**1**	**0**	**4**

Traded to **Washington** by **Montreal** with Doug Jarvis, Rod Langway and Brian Engblom for Ryan Walter and Rick Green, September 9, 1982. Traded to **LA Kings** by **Washington** for Grant Ledyard, February 9, 1988. Signed as a free agent by **Toronto**, June 10, 1988.

• LAUGHTON, MIKE	Mike Laughton	C – L. 6'2", 185 lbs. b: Nelson, B.C., 2/21/1944.																										
1963-64	Nelson Maple Leafs	WIHL	....	19	27	46	....	....	....	24	....	....	....	....	....	....	....	....	....	....	....	....	....	....	....	....	....	....
1964-65	Nelson Maple Leafs	WIHL	48	35	21	56	....	....	....	44	....	....	....	....	....	....	....	....	....	....	....	....	....	....	....	....	....	....
1965-66	Nelson Maple Leafs	WIHL	45	36	34	70	....	....	....	72	....	....	....	....	....	....	....	....	....	....	....	....	....	....	....	....	....	....
1966-67	Victoria Maple Leafs	WHL	62	16	11	27	....	....	....	37	....	....	....	....	....	....	....	....	....	....	....	....	....	....	....	....	....	....
1967-68	**Oakland Seals**	**NHL**	**35**	**2**	**6**	**8**	**2**	**6**	**8**	**38**	**2**	**0**	**0**	**53**	**3.8**	**13**	**5**	**27**	**2**	**–17**	....	....	....	....	....	....	....	....
	Vancouver Canucks	WHL	23	8	5	13	....	....	....	10	....	....	....	....	....	....	....	....	....	....	....	....	....	....	....	....	....	....
1968-69	**Oakland Seals**	**NHL**	**53**	**20**	**23**	**43**	**23**	**22**	**45**	**22**	**3**	**0**	**5**	**103**	**19.4**	**55**	**8**	**47**	**0**	**0**	**7**	**2**	**3**	**5**	**0**	**0**	**0**	**0**
	Cleveland Barons	AHL	13	2	6	8	....	....	....	6	....	....	....	....	....	....	....	....	....	....	....	....	....	....	....	....	....	....
1969-70	**Oakland Seals**	**NHL**	**76**	**16**	**19**	**35**	**18**	**19**	**37**	**39**	**3**	**0**	**4**	**147**	**10.9**	**50**	**8**	**70**	**0**	**–28**	**4**	**0**	**1**	**1**	**0**	**0**	**0**	**0**
1970-71	**California Golden Seals**	**NHL**	**25**	**1**	**0**	**1**	**1**	**0**	**1**	**2**	**1**	**0**	**0**	**22**	**4.5**	**2**	**1**	**13**	**0**	**–12**	....	....	....	....	....	....	....	....
1971-72	Nova Scotia Voyageurs	AHL	73	23	28	51	....	....	....	6	....	....	....	....	....	....	....	....	....	....	15	3	7	10	12	....	....	....
1972-73	New York Raiders	WHA	67	16	20	36	....	....	....	44	....	....	....	....	....	....	....	....	....	....	....	....	....	....	....	....	....	....
1973-74	New York-New Jersey	WHA	71	20	18	38	....	....	....	34	....	....	....	....	....	....	....	....	....	....	....	....	....	....	....	....	....	....
1974-75	San Diego Mariners	WHA	65	7	9	16	....	....	....	22	....	....	....	....	....	....	....	....	....	....	10	4	1	5	0	....	....	....
	Syracuse Blazers	NAHL	5	0	5	5	....	....	....	2	....	....	....	....	....	....	....	....	....	....	....	....	....	....	....	....	....	....
1975-76			DID NOT PLAY																									
1976-77	Nelson Maple Leafs	WIHL	....	31	47	78	....	....	....	25	....	....	....	....	....	....	....	....	....	....	....	....	....	....	....	....	....	....
1977-78	Nelson Maple Leafs	WIHL	....	4	5	9	....	....	....	2	....	....	....	....	....	....	....	....	....	....	....	....	....	....	....	....	....	....
	NHL Totals		**189**	**39**	**48**	**87**	**44**	**47**	**91**	**101**	**9**	**0**	**9**	**325**	**12.0**	**120**	**22**	**157**	**2**		**11**	**2**	**4**	**6**	**0**	**0**	**0**	**0**
	Other Major League Totals		203	43	47	90	....	....	....	100	....	....	....	....	....	....	....	....	....	....	10	4	1	5	0	....	....	....

Claimed by **Oakland** from **Toronto** in Expansion Draft, June 6, 1967. Traded to **Montreal** by **California** for cash, October, 1971. Selected by **NY Raiders** (WHA) in 1972 WHA General Player Draft, February 12, 1972. Transferred to **San Diego** (WHA) after **New York-New Jersey** (WHA) franchise relocated, April 30, 1974. Claimed by **Calgary** (WHA) from **San Diego** (WHA) in 1975 WHA Intra-League Draft, June, 1975.

• LAUKKANEN, JANNE

Janne Laukkanen D – L. 6', 180 lbs. b: Lahti, Finland, 3/19/1970. Quebec's 8th choice, 156th overall, in 1991 Entry Draft.

			REGULAR SEASON																		PLAYOFFS							
Season	Club	League	GP	G	A	Pts	AG	AA	APts	PIM	PP	SH	GW	S	%	TGF	PGF	TGA	PGA	+/–	GP	G	A	Pts	PIM	PP	SH	GW
1989-90	Ilves Tampere	Finland	39	5	6	11	....	....	....	10	....	....	....	....	....	....	....	....	....	....	....	....	....	....	....	....	....	....
	Finland	WJC-A	7	0	1	1	....	....	....	4	....	....	....	....	....	....	....	....	....	....	....	....	....	....	....	....	....	....
1990-91	Reipas	Finland	44	8	14	22	....	....	....	56	....	....	....	....	....	....	....	....	....	....	....	....	....	....	....	....	....	....
1991-92	Finland	C Cup	6	1	2	3	....	....	....	2	....	....	....	....	....	....	....	....	....	....	....	....	....	....	....	....	....	....
	HPK Hameenlinna	Finland	43	5	14	19	....	....	....	62	....	....	....	....	....	....	....	....	....	....	....	....	....	....	....	....	....	....
	Finland	Olympics	8	0	1	1	....	....	....	6	....	....	....	....	....	....	....	....	....	....	....	....	....	....	....	....	....	....
	Finland	WC-A	8	2	2	4	....	....	....	12	....	....	....	....	....	....	....	....	....	....	....	....	....	....	....	....	....	....
1992-93	HPK Hameenlinna	Finland	47	8	21	29	....	....	....	76	....	....	....	....	....	....	....	....	....	....	12	1	4	5	10	....	....	....
	Finland	WC-A	6	1	0	1	....	....	....	10	....	....	....	....	....	....	....	....	....	....	....	....	....	....	....	....	....	....
1993-94	HPK Hameenlinna	Finland	48	5	24	29	....	....	....	46	....	....	....	....	....	....	....	....	....	....	....	....	....	....	....	....	....	....
	Finland	Olympics	8	0	2	2	....	....	....	12	....	....	....	....	....	....	....	....	....	....	....	....	....	....	....	....	....	....
	Finland	WC-A	8	0	3	3	....	....	....	6	....	....	....	....	....	....	....	....	....	....	....	....	....	....	....	....	....	....
1994-95	Cornwall Aces	AHL	55	8	26	34	....	....	....	41	....	....	....	....	....	....	....	....	....	....	....	....	....	....	....	....	....	....
	Quebec Nordiques	**NHL**	**11**	**0**	**3**	**3**	**0**	**4**	**4**	**4**	**0**	**0**	**0**	**12**	**0.0**	**10**	**4**	**3**	**0**	**+3**	**6**	**1**	**0**	**1**	**2**	**0**	**0**	**0**
1995-96	**Colorado Avalanche**	**NHL**	**3**	**1**	**0**	**1**	**1**	**0**	**1**	**0**	**1**	**0**	**0**	**4**	**25.0**	**3**	**2**	**2**	**0**	**–1**	....	....	....	....	....	....	....	....
	Cornwall Aces	AHL	35	7	20	27	....	....	....	60	....	....	....	....	....	....	....	....	....	....	....	....	....	....	....	....	....	....
	Ottawa Senators	**NHL**	**20**	**0**	**2**	**2**	**0**	**2**	**2**	**14**	**0**	**0**	**0**	**31**	**0.0**	**14**	**8**	**8**	**2**	**0**	....	....	....	....	....	....	....	....
1996-97	Finland	W Cup	4	0	0	0	....	....	....	4	....	....	....	....	....	....	....	....	....	....	....	....	....	....	....	....	....	....
	Ottawa Senators	**NHL**	**76**	**3**	**18**	**21**	**3**	**16**	**19**	**76**	**2**	**0**	**0**	**109**	**2.8**	**83**	**24**	**85**	**12**	**–14**	**7**	**0**	**1**	**1**	**6**	**0**	**0**	**0**
1997-98	**Ottawa Senators**	**NHL**	**60**	**4**	**17**	**21**	**5**	**17**	**22**	**64**	**2**	**0**	**2**	**69**	**5.8**	**45**	**18**	**55**	**13**	**–15**	**11**	**2**	**2**	**4**	**8**	**1**	**0**	**1**
	Finland	Olympics	6	0	0	0	....	....	....	4	....	....	....	....	....	....	....	....	....	....	....	....	....	....	....	....	....	....
	NHL Totals		**170**	**8**	**40**	**48**	**9**	**39**	**48**	**158**	**5**	**0**	**2**	**225**	**3.6**	**155**	**56**	**153**	**27**		**24**	**3**	**3**	**6**	**16**	**1**	**0**	**1**

Finnish First All-Star Team (1993)

Transferred to **Colorado** after **Quebec** franchise relocated, June 21, 1995. Traded to **Ottawa** by **Colorado** for the rights to Brad Larsen, January 26, 1996.

• LAURENCE, DON

Don "Red" Laurence C – R. 5'9", 175 lbs. b: Galt, Ont., 6/27/1957. Atlanta's 3rd choice, 28th overall, in 1977 Amateur Draft.

1973-74	Peterborough Petes	OHA	60	28	15	43	....	....	....	41	....	....	....	....	....	....	....	....	....	....	....	....	....	....	....	....	....	....
1974-75	Peterborough Petes	OHA	69	40	49	89	....	....	....	53	....	....	....	....	....	....	....	....	....	....	....	....	....	....	....	....	....	....
1975-76	Kitchener Rangers	OHA	59	50	36	86	....	....	....	75	....	....	....	....	....	....	....	....	....	....	8	5	3	8	15	....	....	....
1976-77	Kitchener Rangers	OHA	35	43	45	88	....	....	....	14	....	....	....	....	....	....	....	....	....	....	....	....	....	....	....	....	....	....
1977-78	Tulsa Oilers	CHL	39	15	11	26	....	....	....	10	....	....	....	....	....	....	....	....	....	....	7	3	2	5	4	....	....	....
1978-79	**Atlanta Flames**	**NHL**	**59**	**14**	**20**	**34**	**13**	**15**	**28**	**6**	**2**	**0**	**3**	**113**	**12.4**	**47**	**5**	**36**	**2**	**+8**	....	....	....	....	....	....	....	....
	Nova Scotia Voyageurs	AHL	20	7	7	14	....	....	....	9	....	....	....	....	....	....	....	....	....	....	....	....	....	....	....	....	....	....
1979-80	**St. Louis Blues**	**NHL**	**20**	**1**	**2**	**3**	**1**	**2**	**3**	**8**	**0**	**0**	**1**	**35**	**2.9**	**7**	**0**	**14**	**0**	**–7**	....	....	....	....	....	....	....	....
	Salt Lake Golden Eagles	CHL	27	7	15	22	....	....	....	8	....	....	....	....	....	....	....	....	....	....	13	*9	3	12	2	....	....	....
1980-81	Salt Lake Golden Eagles	CHL	71	39	33	72	....	....	....	41	....	....	....	....	....	....	....	....	....	....	17	6	5	11	8	....	....	....
1981-82	Indianapolis Checkers	CHL	77	43	55	98	....	....	....	43	....	....	....	....	....	....	....	....	....	....	13	10	5	15	18	....	....	....
1982-83	Indianapolis Checkers	CHL	80	*43	55	98	....	....	....	33	....	....	....	....	....	....	....	....	....	....	13	11	11	22	2	....	....	....
1983-84	Indianapolis Checkers	CHL	69	41	37	78	....	....	....	42	....	....	....	....	....	....	....	....	....	....	10	*9	4	*13	0	....	....	....
1984-85	Ambri-Piotta	Switz.	....	*25	6	*31	....	....	....	....	....	....	....	....	....	....	....	....	....	....	....	0	1	1	....	....	....	....
1985-86	Ambri-Piotta	Switz.	36	25	13	38	....	....	....	....	....	....	....	....	....	....	....	....	....	....	....	....	....	....	....	....	....	....
1986-87	EV Zug	Switz.	35	*59	20	79	....	....	....	....	....	....	....	....	....	....	....	....	....	....	....	....	....	....	....	....	....	....
1987-88	EV Zug	Switz.	....	28	13	41	....	....	....	....	....	....	....	....	....	....	....	....	....	....	....	....	....	....	....	....	....	....
1988-89	EV Zug	Switz.	35	48	26	*74	....	....	....	....	....	....	....	....	....	....	....	....	....	....	....	....	....	....	....	....	....	....
1989-90	EV Zug	German 2	STATISTICS NOT AVAILABLE																									
1990-91	EV Zug	Germany	28	22	16	38	....	....	....	....	....	....	....	....	....	....	....	....	....	....	....	....	....	....	....	....	....	....
	NHL Totals		**79**	**15**	**22**	**37**	**14**	**17**	**31**	**14**	**2**	**0**	**4**	**148**	**10.1**	**54**	**5**	**50**	**2**		....	....	....	....	....	....	....	....

CHL Second All-Star Team (1983)

Traded to **St. Louis** by **Atlanta** with Ed Kea and Atlanta's 2nd round choice (Hakan Nordin) in 1981 Entry Draft for Garry Unger, October 10, 1979. Signed as a free agent by **NY Islanders**, October 16, 1981.

• LAUS, PAUL

Paul Laus D – R. 6'1", 216 lbs. b: Beamsville, Ont., 9/26/1970. Pittsburgh's 2nd choice, 37th overall, in 1989 Entry Draft.

1987-88	Hamilton Steelhawks	OHL	56	1	9	10	....	....	....	171	....	....	....	....	....	....	....	....	....	....	14	0	0	0	28	....	....	....
1988-89	Niagara Falls Thunder	OHL	49	1	10	11	....	....	....	225	....	....	....	....	....	....	....	....	....	....	15	0	5	5	56	....	....	....
1989-90	Niagara Falls Thunder	OHL	60	13	35	48	....	....	....	231	....	....	....	....	....	....	....	....	....	....	16	6	16	22	71	....	....	....
1990-91	Albany Choppers	IHL	7	0	0	0	....	....	....	7	....	....	....	....	....	....	....	....	....	....	....	....	....	....	....	....	....	....
	Knoxville Cherokees	ECHL	20	6	12	18	....	....	....	83	....	....	....	....	....	....	....	....	....	....	....	....	....	....	....	....	....	....
	Muskegon Lumberjacks	IHL	35	3	4	7	....	....	....	103	....	....	....	....	....	....	....	....	....	....	4	0	0	0	13	....	....	....
1991-92	Muskegon Lumberjacks	IHL	75	0	21	21	....	....	....	248	....	....	....	....	....	....	....	....	....	....	14	2	5	7	70	....	....	....
1992-93	Cleveland Lumberjacks	IHL	76	8	18	26	....	....	....	427	....	....	....	....	....	....	....	....	....	....	4	1	0	1	27	....	....	....
1993-94	**Florida Panthers**	**NHL**	**39**	**2**	**0**	**2**	**2**	**0**	**2**	**109**	**0**	**0**	**1**	**15**	**13.3**	**16**	**1**	**6**	**0**	**+9**	....	....	....	....	....	....	....	....
1994-95	**Florida Panthers**	**NHL**	**37**	**0**	**7**	**7**	**0**	**10**	**10**	**138**	**0**	**0**	**0**	**18**	**0.0**	**29**	**1**	**17**	**1**	**+12**	....	....	....	....	....	....	....	....
1995-96	**Florida Panthers**	**NHL**	**78**	**3**	**6**	**9**	**3**	**5**	**8**	**236**	**0**	**0**	**0**	**45**	**6.7**	**39**	**0**	**57**	**16**	**–2**	**21**	**2**	**6**	**8**	***62**	**0**	**0**	**0**
1996-97	**Florida Panthers**	**NHL**	**77**	**0**	**12**	**12**	**0**	**11**	**11**	**313**	**0**	**0**	**0**	**63**	**0.0**	**44**	**3**	**32**	**4**	**+13**	**5**	**0**	**1**	**1**	**4**	**0**	**0**	**0**
1997-98	**Florida Panthers**	**NHL**	**77**	**0**	**11**	**11**	**0**	**11**	**11**	**293**	**0**	**0**	**0**	**64**	**0.0**	**34**	**4**	**45**	**10**	**–5**	....	....	....	....	....	....	....	....
	NHL Totals		**308**	**5**	**36**	**41**	**5**	**37**	**42**	**1089**	**0**	**0**	**1**	**205**	**2.4**	**162**	**9**	**157**	**31**		**26**	**2**	**7**	**9**	**66**	**0**	**0**	**0**

Claimed by **Florida** from **Pittsburgh** in Expansion Draft, June 24, 1993.

• LAVALLEE, KEVIN

Kevin LaVallee LW – L. 5'8", 180 lbs. b: Sudbury, Ont., 9/16/1961. Calgary's 3rd choice, 32nd overall, in 1980 Entry Draft.

1978-79	Brantford Alexanders	OHA	66	27	23	50	....	....	....	30	....	....	....	....	....	....	....	....	....	....	....	....	....	....	....	....	....	....
1979-80	Brantford Alexanders	OHA	65	65	70	135	....	....	....	50	....	....	....	....	....	....	....	....	....	....	10	10	4	14	7	....	....	....
1980-81	**Calgary Flames**	**NHL**	**77**	**15**	**20**	**35**	**12**	**14**	**26**	**16**	**3**	**0**	**2**	**131**	**11.5**	**69**	**25**	**48**	**0**	**–4**	**8**	**2**	**3**	**5**	**4**	**1**	**0**	**1**
1981-82	**Calgary Flames**	**NHL**	**75**	**32**	**29**	**61**	**25**	**19**	**44**	**30**	**6**	**0**	**3**	**169**	**18.9**	**84**	**15**	**78**	**0**	**–9**	**3**	**0**	**0**	**0**	**7**	**0**	**0**	**0**
1982-83	**Calgary Flames**	**NHL**	**60**	**19**	**16**	**35**	**16**	**11**	**27**	**17**	**1**	**0**	**2**	**139**	**13.7**	**50**	**3**	**53**	**0**	**–6**	**8**	**1**	**3**	**4**	**4**	**0**	**0**	**0**
	Colorado Flames	CHL	5	5	4	9	....	....	....	0	....	....	....	....	....	....	....	....	....	....	....	....	....	....	....	....	....	....
1983-84	**Los Angeles Kings**	**NHL**	**19**	**3**	**3**	**6**	**2**	**2**	**4**	**2**	**0**	**0**	**0**	**41**	**7.3**	**8**	**0**	**15**	**2**	**–5**	....	....	....	....	....	....	....	....
	New Haven Nighthawks	AHL	47	29	23	52	....	....	....	25	....	....	....	....	....	....	....	....	....	....	....	....	....	....	....	....	....	....
1984-85	**St. Louis Blues**	**NHL**	**38**	**15**	**17**	**32**	**12**	**11**	**23**	**8**	**2**	**0**	**1**	**68**	**22.1**	**44**	**9**	**33**	**0**	**+2**	....	....	....	....	....	....	....	....
1985-86	**St. Louis Blues**	**NHL**	**64**	**18**	**20**	**38**	**14**	**13**	**27**	**8**	**7**	**0**	**2**	**129**	**14.0**	**59**	**20**	**31**	**0**	**+8**	**13**	**2**	**2**	**4**	**6**	**0**	**0**	**0**
1986-87	**Pittsburgh Penguins**	**NHL**	**33**	**8**	**20**	**28**	**7**	**14**	**21**	**4**	**5**	**0**	**0**	**80**	**10.0**	**42**	**24**	**20**	**0**	**–2**	....	....	....	....	....	....	....	....
1987-88	ECS Innsbruck	Austria	34	39	33	72	....	....	....	....	....	....	....	....	....	....	....	....	....	....	....	....	....	....	....	....	....	....
	Ambri-Piotta	Switz.	....	4	1	5	....	....	....	....	....	....	....	....	....	....	....	....	....	....	....	....	....	....	....	....	....	....
1988-89	ECS Innsbruck	Austria	40	45	47	92	....	....	....	....	....	....	....	....	....	....	....	....	....	....	....	....	....	....	....	....	....	....
1989-90	ECS Innsbruck	Austria 2	STATISTICS NOT AVAILABLE																									
1990-91	HC Milano	Italy	36	33	50	83	....	....	....	16	....	....	....	....	....	....	....	....	....	....	....	....	....	....	....	....	....	....
1991-92	HC Milano	Austria	28	20	24	44	....	....	....	11	....	....	....	....	....	....	....	....	....	....	....	....	....	....	....	....	....	....
1992-93	Ajoie	Switz.	9	3	7	10	....	....	....	27	....	....	....	....	....	....	....	....	....	....	....	....	....	....	....	....	....	....
	Rattingen Lions	Germany	10	6	12	18	....	....	....	2	....	....	....	....	....	....	....	....	....	....	....	....	....	....	....	....	....	....
1993-94	Dusseldorfer EG	Germany	44	19	19	38	....	....	....	33	....	....	....	....	....	....	....	....	....	....	....	....	....	....	....	....	....	....
1994-95	Dusseldorfer EG	Germany	39	14	14	28	....	....	....	26	....	....	....	....	....	....	....	....	....	....	10	8	4	12	4	....	....	....
1995-96	Hanover Scorpions	Germany	23	16	20	36	....	....	....	22	....	....	....	....	....	....	....	....	....	....	....	....	....	....	....	....	....	....
	HC Davos	Switz.	18	8	10	18	....	....	....	6	....	....	....	....	....	....	....	....	....	....	3	1	1	2	2	....	....	....
	NHL Totals		**366**	**110**	**125**	**235**	**88**	**84**	**172**	**85**	**24**	**0**	**10**	**757**	**14.5**	**356**	**96**	**278**	**2**		**32**	**5**	**8**	**13**	**21**	**1**	**0**	**1**

Traded to **LA Kings** by **Calgary** with Carl Mokosak for Steve Bozek, June 20, 1983. Signed as a free agent by **St. Louis**, September 13, 1984. Signed as a free agent by **Pittsburgh**, September 13, 1986.

			REGULAR SEASON																		PLAYOFFS							
Season	Club	League	GP	G	A	Pts	AG	AA	APts	PIM	PP	SH	GW	S	%	TGF	PGF	TGA	PGA	+/-	GP	G	A	Pts	PIM	PP	SH	GW
● LAVARRE, MARK Mark Lavarre RW – R. 5'11", 170 lbs. b: Evanston, IL, 2/21/1965. Chicago's 7th choice, 123rd overall, in 1983 Entry Draft.																												
1982-83	Stratford Cullitons	OJHL	40	33	62	95				88																		
1983-84	North Bay Centennials	OHL	41	19	22	41				15																		
1984-85	Windsor Spitfires	OHL	46	15	30	45				30											4	0	0	0	0			
1985-86	**Chicago Black Hawks**	**NHL**	2	0	0	0	0	0	0	0	0	0	0	2	0.0	0	0	2	0	-2								
	Nova Scotia Oilers	AHL	62	15	19	34				32																		
1986-87	**Chicago Blackhawks**	**NHL**	58	8	15	23	7	11	18	33	0	0	0	46	17.4	38	1	26	0	+11								
	Nova Scotia Oilers	AHL	17	12	8	20				8																		
1987-88	**Chicago Blackhawks**	**NHL**	18	1	1	2	1	1	2	25	0	0	0	17	5.9	2	0	11	1	-8	1	0	0	0	2	0	0	0
	Saginaw Hawks	IHL	39	27	18	45				121											5	4	3	7	36			
1988-89	Binghamton Whalers	AHL	37	20	21	41				70																		
	NHL Totals		78	9	16	25	8	12	20	58	0	0	0	65	13.8	40	1	39	1		1	0	0	0	2	0	0	0

Traded to **Hartford** by **Chicago** for future considerations, October 6, 1988.

● LAVENDER, BRIAN Brian Lavender LW – L. 6', 174 lbs. b: Edmonton, Alta., 4/20/1947.																												
1965-66	Regina Pats	SJHL	60	32	35	67				90											5	1	2	3	2			
1966-67	Regina Pats	WCJHL	56	39	71	110				100											16	6	14	20	28			
1967-68	Houston Apollos	CHL	49	7	11	18				105																		
1968-69	Houston Apollos	CHL	71	14	29	43				113											3	0	0	0	6			
1969-70	Cleveland Barons	AHL	67	8	13	21				89																		
1970-71	Montreal Voyageurs	AHL	59	7	9	16				38											3	0	0	0	0			
1971-72	**St. Louis Blues**	**NHL**	46	5	11	16	5	10	15	54	0	0	1	68	7.4	24	1	28	3	-2	3	0	0	0	2	0	0	0
	Denver Spurs	WHL	27	14	16	30				73																		
1972-73	**New York Islanders**	**NHL**	43	6	6	12	6	5	11	47	2	0	0	74	8.1	18	4	57	1	-42								
	Detroit Red Wings	**NHL**	26	2	2	4	2	2	4	14	0	0	0	13	15.4	5	0	3	0	+2								
1973-74	**Detroit Red Wings**	**NHL**	4	0	0	0	0	0	0	11	0	0	0	2	0.0	0	0	4	0	-4								
	Virginia Wings	AHL	53	11	19	30				72																		
	Providence Reds	AHL	10	1	6	7				2											14	6	1	7	24			
1974-75	**California Golden Seals**	**NHL**	65	3	7	10	3	5	8	48	0	0	1	30	10.0	19	4	51	26	-10								
1975-76	Denver-Ottawa	WHA	37	2	0	2				7																		
	NHL Totals		184	16	26	42	16	22	38	174	2	0	2	187	8.6	66	9	143	30		3	0	0	0	2	0	0	0
	Other Major League Totals		37	2	0	2				7																		

Claimed by **Minnesota** from **Montreal** in Intra-League Draft, June 8, 1971. Claimed by **St. Louis** (Denver-WHL) from **Minnesota** in Reverse Draft, June 8, 1971. Selected by **Edmonton** (WHA) in 1972 WHA General Player Draft, February 12, 1972. Traded to **NY Islanders** by **St. Louis** for cash, September 1, 1972. Traded to **Detroit** by **NY Islanders** with Ken Murray for Ralph Stewart and Bob Cook, January 17, 1973. Traded to **NY Rangers** by **Detroit** for Claude Houde, February 28, 1974. Traded to **California** by **NY Rangers** for Hartland Monahan, September 23, 1974. WHA rights traded to **Denver** (WHA) by **Edmonton** (WHA) for cash, September, 1975.

● LAVIGNE, ERIC Eric Lavigne D – L. 6'3", 195 lbs. b: Victoriaville, Que., 11/4/1972. Washington's 3rd choice, 25th overall, in 1991 Entry Draft.																												
1989-90	Hull Olympiques	QMJHL	69	7	11	18				203											11	0	0	0	32			
1990-91	Hull Olympiques	QMJHL	66	11	11	22				153											4	0	1	1	16			
1991-92	Hull Olympiques	QMJHL	46	4	17	21				101											6	0	0	0	32			
1992-93	Hull Olympiques	QMJHL	59	7	20	27				221											10	2	4	6	47			
1993-94	Phoenix Roadrunners	IHL	62	3	11	14				168																		
1994-95	Phoenix Roadrunners	IHL	69	4	10	14				233																		
	Los Angeles Kings	**NHL**	1	0	0	0	0	0	0	0	0	0	0	0	0.0	0	0	1	0	-1								
	Detroit Vipers	IHL	1	0	0	0				2											5	0	0	0	26			
1995-96	P.E.I. Senators	AHL	72	5	13	18				154											2	0	0	0	0			
1996-97	Rochester Americans	AHL	46	1	6	7				89											6	0	1	1	21			
1997-98	Rochester Americans	AHL	28	0	1	1				118																		
	Grand Rapids Griffins	IHL	4	0	1	1				13																		
	Cleveland Lumberjacks	IHL	16	0	0	0				34											10	1	1	2	44			
	NHL Totals		1	0	0	0	0	0	0	0	0	0	0	0	0.0	0	0	1	0									

Signed as a free agent by **LA Kings**, October 13, 1993.

● LAVIOLETTE, PETER Peter Laviolette D – L. 6'2", 200 lbs. b: Norwood, MA, 12/7/1964.																												
1985-86	Westfield State	NCAA	19	12	8	20				44																		
1986-87	Indianapolis Checkers	IHL	72	10	20	30				146											5	0	1	1	12			
1987-88	United States	Nat-Team	54	4	20	24				82																		
	United States	Olympics	5	0	2	2				4																		
	Colorado Rangers	IHL	19	2	5	7				27											9	3	5	8	7			
1988-89	**New York Rangers**	**NHL**	12	0	0	0	0	0	0	6	0	0	0	2	0.0	5	0	3	0	+2								
	Denver Rangers	IHL	57	6	19	25				120											3	0	0	0	4			
1989-90	Flint Spirits	IHL	62	6	18	24				82											4	0	0	0	4			
1990-91	Binghamton Rangers	AHL	65	12	24	36				72											10	2	7	9	30			
1991-92	Binghamton Rangers	AHL	50	4	10	14				50											11	2	7	9	9			
1992-93	Providence Bruins	AHL	74	13	42	55				64											6	0	4	4	10			
1993-94	United States	Nat-Team	56	10	25	35				63																		
	United States	Olympics	8	1	0	1				6																		
	San Diego Gulls	IHL	17	3	4	7				20											9	3	0	3	6			
1994-95	Providence Bruins	AHL	65	7	23	30				84											13	2	8	10	17			
1995-96	Providence Bruins	AHL	72	9	17	26				53											4	1	1	2	4			
1996-97	Providence Bruins	AHL	41	6	8	14				40																		
	NHL Totals		12	0	0	0	0	0	0	6	0	0	0	2	0.0	5	0	3	0									

Signed as a free agent by **NY Rangers**, August 12, 1987. Signed as a free agent by **Boston**, September 8, 1992.

● LAVOIE, DOMINIC Dominic Lavoie D – R. 6'2", 205 lbs. b: Montreal, Que., 11/21/1967.																												
1984-85	St-Jean Castors	QMJHL	30	1	1	2				10																		
1985-86	St-Jean Castors	QMJHL	70	12	37	49				99											10	2	3	5	20			
1986-87	St-Jean Castors	QMJHL	64	12	42	54				97											8	2	7	9	2			
1987-88	Peoria Rivermen	IHL	65	7	26	33				54											7	2	2	4	8			
1988-89	**St. Louis Blues**	**NHL**	1	0	0	0	0	0	0	0	0	0	0	1	0.0	2	0	0	0	+2								
	Peoria Rivermen	IHL	69	11	31	42				98											4	0	0	0	4			
1989-90	**St. Louis Blues**	**NHL**	13	1	1	2	1	1	2	16	1	0	0	20	5.0	11	6	10	0	-5								
	Peoria Rivermen	IHL	58	19	23	42				32											5	2	2	4	16			
1990-91	**St. Louis Blues**	**NHL**	6	1	2	3	1	2	3	2	0	0	0	11	9.1	7	0	3	0	+4								
	Peoria Rivermen	IHL	46	15	25	40				72											16	5	7	12	22			
1991-92	**St. Louis Blues**	**NHL**	6	0	1	1				10	0	0	0	11	0.0	4	1	6	0	-3								
	Peoria Rivermen	IHL	58	20	32	52				87											10	3	4	7	12			
1992-93	**Ottawa Senators**	**NHL**	2	0	1	1	0	1	1	0	0	0	0	8	0.0	2	1	1	0	0								
	New Haven Nighthawks	AHL	14	2	7	9				14																		
	Boston Bruins	**NHL**	2	0	0	0	0	0	0	2	0	0	0	7	0.0	2	1	2	0	-1								
	Providence Bruins	AHL	53	16	27	43				62											6	1	2	3	24			
1993-94	**Los Angeles Kings**	**NHL**	8	3	3	6	3	2	5	2	0	0	0	21	14.3	15	12	5	0	-2								
	Phoenix Roadrunners	IHL	58	20	33	53				70																		
	San Diego Gulls	IHL	9	2	2	4				12											8	1	0	1	20			
1994-95	VEU Feldkirch	Austria	28	12	13	25				79											13	4	8	12	22			

			REGULAR SEASON																		PLAYOFFS							
Season	Club	League	GP	G	A	Pts	AG	AA	APts	PIM	PP	SH	GW	S	%	TGF	PGF	TGA	PGA	+/–	GP	G	A	Pts	PIM	PP	SH	GW
1995-96	VEU Feldkirch	Alpenliga	8	5	7	12	....	....	....	14	....	....	....	....	....	....	....	....	....	....	....	....	....	....	....	....	....	....
	VEU Feldkirch	Austria	35	20	33	53	....	....	....	75	....	....	....	....	....	....	....	....	....	....	8	5	7	12	14	....	....	....
1996-97	VEU Feldkirch	Austria	50	20	33	53	....	....	....	75	....	....	....	....	....	....	....	....	....	....	....	....	....	....	....	....	....	....
1997-98	VEU Feldkirch	EuroHL	10	3	7	10	....	....	....	18	....	....	....	....	....	....	....	....	....	....	....	....	....	....	....	....	....	....
	NHL Totals		**38**	**5**	**8**	**13**	**5**	**7**	**12**	**32**	**3**	**0**	**1**	**79**	**6.3**	**43**	**21**	**27**	**0**		....	....	....	....	....	....	....	....

IHL First All-Star Team (1991) • IHL Second All-Star Team (1992)

Signed as a free agent by **St. Louis**, September 22, 1986. Claimed by **Ottawa** from **St. Louis** in Expansion Draft, June 18, 1992. Claimed on waivers by **Boston** from **Ottawa**, November 20, 1992. Signed as a free agent by **LA Kings**, July 16, 1993.

• LAWLESS, PAUL

Paul Lawless LW – L. 5′11″, 185 lbs. b: Scarborough, Ont., 7/2/1964. Hartford's 1st choice, 14th overall, in 1982 Entry Draft.

1980-81	Wexford Raiders	MJHL	40	38	40	78	....	....	....	....	....	....	....	....	....	....	....	....	....	....	....	....	....	....	....	....	....	....
1981-82	Windsor Spitfires	OHL	68	24	25	49	....	....	....	47	....	....	....	....	....	....	....	....	....	....	9	1	1	2	4	....	....	....
1982-83	Windsor Spitfires	OHL	33	15	20	35	....	....	....	25	....	....	....	....	....	....	....	....	....	....	....	....	....	....	....	....	....	....
	Hartford Whalers	**NHL**	**47**	**6**	**9**	**15**	**5**	**6**	**11**	**4**	**1**	**0**	**0**	**84**	**7.1**	**27**	**3**	**55**	**0**	**–31**	....	....	....	....	....	....	....	....
1983-84	Windsor Spitfires	OHL	55	31	49	80	....	....	....	26	....	....	....	....	....	....	....	....	....	....	2	0	1	1	0	....	....	....
	Hartford Whalers	**NHL**	**6**	**0**	**3**	**3**	**0**	**2**	**2**	**0**	**0**	**0**	**0**	**7**	**0.0**	**3**	**1**	**7**	**0**	**–5**	....	....	....	....	....	....	....	....
1984-85	Binghamton Whalers	AHL	8	1	1	2	....	....	....	0	....	....	....	....	....	....	....	....	....	....	....	....	....	....	....	....	....	....
	Salt Lake Golden Eagles	IHL	72	49	48	97	....	....	....	14	....	....	....	....	....	....	....	....	....	....	7	5	3	8	20	....	....	....
1985-86	**Hartford Whalers**	**NHL**	**64**	**17**	**21**	**38**	**14**	**14**	**28**	**20**	**5**	**0**	**1**	**139**	**12.2**	**58**	**16**	**46**	**1**	**–3**	**1**	**0**	**0**	**0**	**0**	**0**	**0**	**0**
1986-87	**Hartford Whalers**	**NHL**	**60**	**22**	**32**	**54**	**19**	**23**	**42**	**14**	**4**	**0**	**2**	**161**	**13.7**	**68**	**11**	**33**	**0**	**+24**	**2**	**0**	**2**	**2**	**2**	**0**	**0**	**0**
1987-88	**Hartford Whalers**	**NHL**	**28**	**4**	**5**	**9**	**3**	**4**	**7**	**16**	**0**	**0**	**1**	**71**	**5.6**	**20**	**6**	**16**	**0**	**–2**	....	....	....	....	....	....	....	....
	Philadelphia Flyers	**NHL**	**8**	**0**	**5**	**5**	**0**	**4**	**4**	**0**	**0**	**0**	**0**	**10**	**0.0**	**7**	**0**	**7**	**0**	**0**	....	....	....	....	....	....	....	....
	Vancouver Canucks	**NHL**	**13**	**0**	**1**	**1**	**0**	**1**	**1**	**0**	**0**	**0**	**0**	**15**	**0.0**	**5**	**2**	**12**	**0**	**–9**	....	....	....	....	....	....	....	....
1988-89	Milwaukee Admirals	IHL	53	30	35	65	....	....	....	58	....	....	....	....	....	....	....	....	....	....	....	....	....	....	....	....	....	....
	Toronto Maple Leafs	**NHL**	**7**	**0**	**0**	**0**	**0**	**0**	**0**	**0**	**0**	**0**	**0**	**11**	**0.0**	**2**	**0**	**4**	**0**	**–2**	....	....	....	....	....	....	....	....
1989-90	**Toronto Maple Leafs**	**NHL**	**6**	**0**	**1**	**1**	**0**	**1**	**1**	**0**	**0**	**0**	**0**	**6**	**0.0**	**3**	**0**	**8**	**1**	**–4**	....	....	....	....	....	....	....	....
	Newmarket Saints	AHL	3	1	0	1	....	....	....	0	....	....	....	....	....	....	....	....	....	....	....	....	....	....	....	....	....	....
1990-91	HC Lausanne	Switz.	36	26	29	55	....	....	....	....	....	....	....	....	....	....	....	....	....	....	10	10	15	25	....	....	....	....
1991-92	Bolzano	Italy	12	7	14	21	....	....	....	4	....	....	....	....	....	....	....	....	....	....	....	....	....	....	....	....	....	....
1992-93	EC Graz	Austria	29	21	27	48	....	....	....	....	....	....	....	....	....	....	....	....	....	....	....	....	....	....	....	....	....	....
	New Haven Nighthawks	AHL	20	10	12	22	....	....	....	63	....	....	....	....	....	....	....	....	....	....	....	....	....	....	....	....	....	....
	Cincinnati Cyclones	IHL	29	29	25	54	....	....	....	64	....	....	....	....	....	....	....	....	....	....	....	....	....	....	....	....	....	....
1993-94	Cincinnati Cyclones	IHL	71	30	27	57	....	....	....	112	....	....	....	....	....	....	....	....	....	....	11	4	4	8	4	....	....	....
1994-95	Cincinnati Cyclones	IHL	64	44	52	96	....	....	....	119	....	....	....	....	....	....	....	....	....	....	10	9	9	18	8	....	....	....
1995-96	Cincinnati Cyclones	IHL	77	27	58	85	....	....	....	99	....	....	....	....	....	....	....	....	....	....	17	4	6	10	16	....	....	....
1996-97	Cincinnati Cyclones	IHL	14	2	10	12	....	....	....	14	....	....	....	....	....	....	....	....	....	....	....	....	....	....	....	....	....	....
1997-98	Austin Ice-Bats	WPHL	1	1	0	1	....	....	....	14	....	....	....	....	....	....	....	....	....	....	....	....	....	....	....	....	....	....
	NHL Totals		**239**	**49**	**77**	**126**	**41**	**55**	**96**	**54**	**10**	**0**	**4**	**504**	**9.7**	**193**	**39**	**188**	**2**		**3**	**0**	**2**	**2**	**2**	**0**	**0**	**0**

OHL Second All-Star Team (1984) • IHL Second All-Star Team (1994)

Traded to **Philadelphia** by **Hartford** for Lindsy Carson, January 22, 1988. Traded to **Vancouver** by **Philadelphia** with Vancouver's 5th round choice (acquired earlier and later traded to Edmonton — Edmonton selected Peter White) in 1989 Entry Draft for Willie Huber, March 1, 1988. Traded to **Toronto** by **Vancouver** for the rights to Peter Deboer, February 27, 1989.

• LAWRENCE, MARK

Mark Lawrence RW – R. 6′4″, 215 lbs. b: Burlington, Ont., 1/27/1972. Minnesota's 4th choice, 118th overall, in 1991 Entry Draft.

1988-89	Niagara Falls Thunder	OHL	63	9	27	36	....	....	....	142	....	....	....	....	....	....	....	....	....	....	....	....	....	....	....	....	....	....
1989-90	Niagara Falls Thunder	OHL	54	15	18	33	....	....	....	123	....	....	....	....	....	....	....	....	....	....	16	2	5	7	42	....	....	....
1990-91	Detroit Ambassadors	OHL	66	27	38	65	....	....	....	53	....	....	....	....	....	....	....	....	....	....	....	....	....	....	....	....	....	....
1991-92	Detroit Ambassadors	OHL	28	19	26	45	....	....	....	54	....	....	....	....	....	....	....	....	....	....	....	....	....	....	....	....	....	....
	North Bay Centennials	OHL	24	13	14	27	....	....	....	21	....	....	....	....	....	....	....	....	....	....	21	*23	12	35	36	....	....	....
1992-93	Dayton Bombers	ECHL	20	8	14	22	....	....	....	46	....	....	....	....	....	....	....	....	....	....	....	....	....	....	....	....	....	....
	Kalamazoo Wings	IHL	57	22	13	35	....	....	....	47	....	....	....	....	....	....	....	....	....	....	....	....	....	....	....	....	....	....
1993-94	Kalamazoo Wings	IHL	64	17	20	37	....	....	....	90	....	....	....	....	....	....	....	....	....	....	....	....	....	....	....	....	....	....
1994-95	Kalamazoo Wings	IHL	77	21	29	50	....	....	....	92	....	....	....	....	....	....	....	....	....	....	16	3	7	10	28	....	....	....
	Dallas Stars	**NHL**	**2**	**0**	**0**	**0**	**0**	**0**	**0**	**0**	**0**	**0**	**0**	**3**	**0.0**	**0**	**0**	**0**	**0**	**0**	....	....	....	....	....	....	....	....
1995-96	**Dallas Stars**	**NHL**	**13**	**0**	**1**	**1**	**0**	**1**	**1**	**17**	**0**	**0**	**0**	**13**	**0.0**	**3**	**0**	**3**	**0**	**0**	....	....	....	....	....	....	....	....
	Michigan K-Wings	IHL	55	15	14	29	....	....	....	92	....	....	....	....	....	....	....	....	....	....	10	3	4	7	30	....	....	....
1996-97	Michigan K-Wings	IHL	68	15	21	36	....	....	....	141	....	....	....	....	....	....	....	....	....	....	4	0	0	0	18	....	....	....
1997-98	**New York Islanders**	**NHL**	**2**	**0**	**0**	**0**	**0**	**0**	**0**	**2**	**0**	**0**	**0**	**4**	**0.0**	**0**	**0**	**0**	**0**	**0**	....	....	....	....	....	....	....	....
	Utah Grizzlies	IHL	80	36	28	64	....	....	....	102	....	....	....	....	....	....	....	....	....	....	4	1	1	2	4	....	....	....
	NHL Totals		**17**	**0**	**1**	**1**	**0**	**1**	**1**	**19**	**0**	**0**	**0**	**20**	**0.0**	**3**	**0**	**3**	**0**		....	....	....	....	....	....	....	....

Rights transferred to **Dallas** after **Minnesota** franchise relocated, June 9, 1993. Signed as a free agent by **NY Islanders**, August 25, 1997.

• LAWSON, DANNY

Danny Lawson RW – R. 5′11″, 180 lbs. b: Toronto, Ont., 10/30/1947.

1964-65	Hamilton Red Wings	OHA	3	0	0	0	....	....	....	2	....	....	....	....	....	....	....	....	....	....	....	....	....	....	....	....	....	....
1965-66	Hamilton Red Wings	OHA	30	7	9	16	....	....	....	4	....	....	....	....	....	....	....	....	....	....	5	1	1	2	2	....	....	....
1966-67	Hamilton Red Wings	OHA	48	25	24	49	....	....	....	27	....	....	....	....	....	....	....	....	....	....	17	15	11	26	11	....	....	....
1967-68	Hamilton Red Wings	OHA	54	52	38	90	....	....	....	26	....	....	....	....	....	....	....	....	....	....	11	8	7	15	11	....	....	....
	Detroit Red Wings	**NHL**	**1**	**0**	**0**	**0**	**0**	**0**	**0**	**0**	**0**	**0**	**0**	**1**	**0.0**	**0**	**0**	**0**	**0**	**0**	....	....	....	....	....	....	....	....
1968-69	**Detroit Red Wings**	**NHL**	**44**	**5**	**7**	**12**	**6**	**7**	**13**	**21**	**0**	**0**	**0**	**58**	**8.6**	**15**	**2**	**15**	**0**	**–2**	....	....	....	....	....	....	....	....
	Fort Worth Wings	CHL	8	4	5	9	....	....	....	0	....	....	....	....	....	....	....	....	....	....	....	....	....	....	....	....	....	....
	Minnesota North Stars	**NHL**	**18**	**3**	**3**	**6**	**3**	**3**	**6**	**4**	**0**	**0**	**0**	**13**	**23.1**	**7**	**1**	**14**	**1**	**–7**	....	....	....	....	....	....	....	....
1969-70	**Minnesota North Stars**	**NHL**	**45**	**9**	**8**	**17**	**10**	**8**	**18**	**19**	**0**	**0**	**0**	**58**	**15.5**	**22**	**1**	**24**	**0**	**–3**	**6**	**0**	**1**	**1**	**2**	**0**	**0**	**0**
	Iowa Stars	CHL	31	12	21	33	....	....	....	8	....	....	....	....	....	....	....	....	....	....	....	....	....	....	....	....	....	....
1970-71	**Minnesota North Stars**	**NHL**	**33**	**1**	**5**	**6**	**1**	**4**	**5**	**2**	**0**	**0**	**0**	**25**	**4.0**	**8**	**0**	**5**	**0**	**+3**	**10**	**0**	**0**	**0**	**0**	**0**	**0**	**0**
	Cleveland Barons	AHL	10	3	4	7	....	....	....	14	....	....	....	....	....	....	....	....	....	....	....	....	....	....	....	....	....	....
1971-72	**Buffalo Sabres**	**NHL**	**78**	**10**	**6**	**16**	**11**	**5**	**16**	**15**	**0**	**1**	**0**	**176**	**5.7**	**29**	**2**	**90**	**40**	**–23**	....	....	....	....	....	....	....	....
1972-73	Philadelphia Blazers	WHA	78	*61	45	106	....	....	....	35	....	....	....	....	....	....	....	....	....	....	4	0	1	1	0	....	....	....
1973-74	Vancouver Blazers	WHA	78	50	38	88	....	....	....	14	....	....	....	....	....	....	....	....	....	....	....	....	....	....	....	....	....	....
1974-75	Vancouver Blazers	WHA	78	33	43	76	....	....	....	19	....	....	....	....	....	....	....	....	....	....	....	....	....	....	....	....	....	....
1975-76	Calgary Cowboys	WHA	80	44	52	96	....	....	....	46	....	....	....	....	....	....	....	....	....	....	9	4	4	8	19	....	....	....
1976-77	Calgary Cowboys	WHA	64	24	19	43	....	....	....	26	....	....	....	....	....	....	....	....	....	....	....	....	....	....	....	....	....	....
	Winnipeg Jets	WHA	14	6	7	13	....	....	....	2	....	....	....	....	....	....	....	....	....	....	13	2	4	6	6	....	....	....
	NHL Totals		**219**	**28**	**29**	**57**	**31**	**27**	**58**	**61**	**0**	**1**	**0**	**331**	**8.5**	**81**	**6**	**148**	**41**		**16**	**0**	**1**	**1**	**2**	**0**	**0**	**0**
	Other Major League Totals		392	218	204	422	....	....	....	142	....	....	....	....	....	....	....	....	....		26	6	9	15	25	....	....	....

OHA First All-Star Team (1968) • WHA First All-Star Team (1973)

Traded to **Minnesota** by **Detroit** for Wayne Connelly, February 15, 1969. Claimed by **Buffalo** from **Minnesota** in Intra-League Draft, June 8, 1971. Selected by **Miami-Philadelphia** (WHA) in 1972 WHA General Player Draft, February 12, 1972. Transferred to **Vancouver** (WHA) after **Philadelphia** (WHA) franchise relocated, May, 1973. Transferred to **Calgary** (WHA) after **Vancouver** (WHA) franchise relocated, May 7, 1975. Traded to **Winnipeg** (WHA) by **Calgary** (WHA) with Mike Ford for Veli Pekka-Ketola and Ron Ward, March, 1977.

• LAWTON, BRIAN

Brian Lawton LW – L. 6′, 180 lbs. b: New Brunswick, NJ, 6/29/1965. Minnesota's 1st choice, 1st overall, in 1983 Entry Draft.

1981-82	Mount St. Charles	H.S.	26	45	43	88	....	....	....	....	....	....	....	....	....	....	....	....	....	....	....	....	....	....	....	....	....	....
1982-83	Mount St. Charles	H.S.	23	40	43	83	....	....	....	....	....	....	....	....	....	....	....	....	....	....	....	....	....	....	....	....	....	....
	United States	Nat-Team	7	3	2	5	....	....	....	6	....	....	....	....	....	....	....	....	....	....	....	....	....	....	....	....	....	....
	United States	WJC-A	7	3	1	4	....	....	....	6	....	....	....	....	....	....	....	....	....	....	....	....	....	....	....	....	....	....
1983-84	**Minnesota North Stars**	**NHL**	**58**	**10**	**21**	**31**	**8**	**14**	**22**	**33**	**0**	**0**	**4**	**74**	**13.5**	**48**	**7**	**42**	**1**	**0**	**5**	**0**	**0**	**0**	**10**	**0**	**0**	**0**
1984-85	United States	C Cup	6	5	0	5	....	....	....	4	....	....	....	....	....	....	....	....	....	....	....	....	....	....	....	....	....	....
	Minnesota North Stars	**NHL**	**40**	**5**	**6**	**11**	**4**	**4**	**8**	**24**	**1**	**0**	**1**	**40**	**12.5**	**21**	**3**	**22**	**2**	**–2**	....	....	....	....	....	....	....	....
	Springfield Indians	AHL	42	14	28	42	....	....	....	37	....	....	....	....	....	....	....	....	....	....	4	1	1	2	2	....	....	....
1985-86	**Minnesota North Stars**	**NHL**	**65**	**18**	**17**	**35**	**14**	**11**	**25**	**36**	**4**	**0**	**7**	**98**	**18.4**	**53**	**10**	**33**	**0**	**+10**	**3**	**0**	**1**	**1**	**2**	**0**	**0**	**0**
1986-87	**Minnesota North Stars**	**NHL**	**66**	**21**	**23**	**44**	**18**	**17**	**35**	**86**	**2**	**0**	**2**	**125**	**16.8**	**66**	**6**	**41**	**1**	**+20**	....	....	....	....	....	....	....	....
	United States	WEC-A	8	3	3	6	....	....	....	14	....	....	....	....	....	....	....	....	....	....	....	....	....	....	....	....	....	....

			REGULAR SEASON																		PLAYOFFS							
Season	Club	League	GP	G	A	Pts	AG	AA	APts	PIM	PP	SH	GW	S	%	TGF	PGF	TGA	PGA	+/–	GP	G	A	Pts	PIM	PP	SH	GW
1987-88	**Minnesota North Stars**	**NHL**	**74**	**17**	**24**	**41**	**15**	**17**	**32**	**71**	**7**	**0**	**1**	**155**	**11.0**	**72**	**35**	**66**	**19**	**–10**	....	....	....	....	....	....	....	....
1988-89	**New York Rangers**	**NHL**	**30**	**7**	**10**	**17**	**6**	**7**	**13**	**39**	**3**	**0**	**0**	**58**	**12.1**	**24**	**6**	**21**	**1**	**–2**	....	....	....	....	....	....	....	....
	Hartford Whalers	**NHL**	**35**	**10**	**16**	**26**	**8**	**11**	**19**	**28**	**7**	**0**	**2**	**70**	**14.3**	**44**	**24**	**29**	**0**	**–9**	**3**	**1**	**0**	**1**	**0**	**0**	**0**	**0**
1989-90	**Hartford Whalers**	**NHL**	**13**	**2**	**1**	**3**	**2**	**1**	**3**	**6**	**1**	**0**	**0**	**17**	**11.8**	**4**	**2**	**4**	**0**	**–2**	....	....	....	....	....	....	....	....
	Quebec Nordiques	**NHL**	**14**	**5**	**6**	**11**	**4**	**4**	**8**	**10**	**3**	**0**	**0**	**25**	**20.0**	**19**	**6**	**22**	**0**	**–9**	....	....	....	....	....	....	....	....
	Boston Bruins	**NHL**	**8**	**0**	**0**	**0**	**0**	**0**	**0**	**14**	**0**	**0**	**0**	**10**	**0.0**	**1**	**1**	**4**	**0**	**–4**	....	....	....	....	....	....	....	....
	Maine Mariners	AHL	5	0	0	0	....	....	....	14	....	....	....	....	....	....	....	....	....	....	....	....	....	....	....	....	....	....
1990-91	Phoenix Roadrunners	IHL	63	26	40	66	....	....	....	108	....	....	....	....	....	....	....	....	....	....	11	4	9	13	40	....	....	....
1991-92	**San Jose Sharks**	**NHL**	**59**	**15**	**22**	**37**	**14**	**17**	**31**	**42**	**7**	**0**	**1**	**131**	**11.5**	**56**	**26**	**68**	**13**	**–25**	....	....	....	....	....	....	....	....
1992-93	**San Jose Sharks**	**NHL**	**21**	**2**	**8**	**10**	**2**	**5**	**7**	**12**	**0**	**0**	**0**	**29**	**6.9**	**19**	**6**	**26**	**4**	**–9**	....	....	....	....	....	....	....	....
	Kansas City Blades	IHL	9	6	4	10	....	....	....	10	....	....	....	....	....	....	....	....	....	....	....	....	....	....	....	....	....	....
	Cincinnati Cyclones	IHL	17	5	11	16	....	....	....	30	....	....	....	....	....	....	....	....	....	....	....	....	....	....	....	....	....	....
	NHL Totals		**483**	**112**	**154**	**266**	**95**	**108**	**203**	**401**	**35**	**0**	**18**	**832**	**13.5**	**427**	**132**	**378**	**41**		**11**	**1**	**1**	**2**	**12**	**0**	**0**	**0**

Traded to **NY Rangers** by **Minnesota** with Igor Liba and the rights to Eric Bennett for Paul Jerrard, Mark Tinordi, the rights to Bret Barnett and Mike Sullivan and LA Kings' 2nd round choice (acquired earlier, Minnesota selected Murray Garbutt) in 1989 Entry Draft, October 11, 1988. Traded to **Hartford** by **NY Rangers** with Norm MacIver and Don Maloney for Carey Wilson and Hartford's 5th round choice (Lubus Rob) in 1990 Entry Draft, December 26, 1988. Claimed on waivers by **Quebec** from **Hartford**, December 1, 1989. Signed as a free agent by **Boston**, February 7, 1990. Signed as a free agent by **LA Kings**, July 27, 1990. Signed as a free agent by **San Jose**, August 9, 1991. Traded to **New Jersey** by **San Jose** for future considerations, January 22, 1993.

• LAXDAL, DEREK

Derek Laxdal RW – R. 6'1", 175 lbs. b: St. Boniface, Man., 2/21/1966. Toronto's 7th choice, 151st overall, in 1984 Entry Draft.

Season	Club	League	GP	G	A	Pts	AG	AA	APts	PIM	PP	SH	GW	S	%	TGF	PGF	TGA	PGA	+/–	GP	G	A	Pts	PIM	PP	SH	GW
1982-83	Portland Winter Hawks	WHL	39	4	9	13	....	....	....	27	....	....	....	....	....	....	....	....	....	....	14	0	2	2	2	....	....	....
1983-84	Brandon Wheat Kings	WHL	70	23	20	43	....	....	....	86	....	....	....	....	....	....	....	....	....	....	12	0	4	4	10	....	....	....
1984-85	Brandon Wheat Kings	WHL	69	61	41	102	....	....	....	74	....	....	....	....	....	....	....	....	....	....	....	....	....	....	....	....	....	....
	Toronto Maple Leafs	**NHL**	**3**	**0**	**0**	**0**	**0**	**0**	**0**	**6**	**0**	**0**	**0**	**3**	**0.0**	**0**	**0**	**1**	**0**	**–1**	....	....	....	....	....	....	....	....
	St. Catharines Saints	AHL	5	3	2	5	....	....	....	2	....	....	....	....	....	....	....	....	....	....	....	....	....	....	....	....	....	....
1985-86	Brandon Wheat Kings	WHL	42	34	35	69	....	....	....	62	....	....	....	....	....	....	....	....	....	....	....	....	....	....	....	....	....	....
	Canada	WJC-A	7	1	4	5	....	....	....	6	....	....	....	....	....	....	....	....	....	....	....	....	....	....	....	....	....	....
	New Westminster Bruins	WHL	18	9	6	15	....	....	....	14	....	....	....	....	....	....	....	....	....	....	....	....	....	....	....	....	....	....
	St. Catharines Saints	AHL	7	0	1	1	....	....	....	15	....	....	....	....	....	....	....	....	....	....	12	1	1	2	24	....	....	....
1986-87	**Toronto Maple Leafs**	**NHL**	**2**	**0**	**0**	**0**	**0**	**0**	**0**	**7**	**0**	**0**	**0**	**0**	**0.0**	**0**	**0**	**1**	**0**	**–1**	....	....	....	....	....	....	....	....
	Newmarket Saints	AHL	78	24	20	44	....	....	....	69	....	....	....	....	....	....	....	....	....	....	....	....	....	....	....	....	....	....
1987-88	**Toronto Maple Leafs**	**NHL**	**5**	**0**	**0**	**0**	**0**	**0**	**0**	**6**	**0**	**0**	**0**	**2**	**0.0**	**1**	**0**	**1**	**0**	**0**	....	....	....	....	....	....	....	....
	Newmarket Saints	AHL	67	18	25	43	....	....	....	81	....	....	....	....	....	....	....	....	....	....	....	....	....	....	....	....	....	....
1988-89	**Toronto Maple Leafs**	**NHL**	**41**	**9**	**6**	**15**	**8**	**4**	**12**	**65**	**1**	**0**	**0**	**41**	**22.0**	**20**	**4**	**28**	**1**	**–11**	....	....	....	....	....	....	....	....
	Newmarket Saints	AHL	34	22	22	44	....	....	....	53	....	....	....	....	....	....	....	....	....	....	2	0	2	2	5	....	....	....
1989-90	Newmarket Saints	AHL	23	7	8	15	....	....	....	52	....	....	....	....	....	....	....	....	....	....	....	....	....	....	....	....	....	....
	New York Islanders	**NHL**	**12**	**3**	**1**	**4**	**3**	**1**	**4**	**6**	**0**	**0**	**0**	**20**	**15.0**	**4**	**0**	**8**	**0**	**–4**	**1**	**0**	**2**	**2**	**2**	**0**	**0**	**0**
	Springfield Indians	AHL	28	13	12	25	....	....	....	42	....	....	....	....	....	....	....	....	....	....	13	8	6	14	47	....	....	....
1990-91	**New York Islanders**	**NHL**	**4**	**0**	**0**	**0**	**0**	**0**	**0**	**0**	**0**	**0**	**0**	**3**	**0.0**	**0**	**0**	**1**	**0**	**–1**	....	....	....	....	....	....	....	....
	Capital District Islanders	AHL	65	14	25	39	....	....	....	75	....	....	....	....	....	....	....	....	....	....	....	....	....	....	....	....	....	....
1991-92	Capital District Islanders	AHL	49	7	7	14	....	....	....	61	....	....	....	....	....	....	....	....	....	....	4	1	1	2	10	....	....	....
1992-93	Canada	Nat-Team	51	13	27	40	....	....	....	71	....	....	....	....	....	....	....	....	....	....	....	....	....	....	....	....	....	....
1993-94				DID NOT PLAY																								
1994-95	Roanoke Express	ECHL	66	32	24	56	....	....	....	144	....	....	....	....	....	....	....	....	....	....	8	2	4	6	25	....	....	....
1995-96	Humberside Hawks	Britain	33	29	29	58	....	....	....	163	....	....	....	....	....	....	....	....	....	....	7	9	4	13	16	....	....	....
1996-97	Nottingham Panthers	Britain	31	14	14	28	....	....	....	54	....	....	....	....	....	....	....	....	....	....	8	1	3	4	27	....	....	....
1997-98	Nottingham Panthers	Britain	44	24	23	47	....	....	....	103	....	....	....	....	....	....	....	....	....	....	6	1	3	4	10	....	....	....
	NHL Totals		**67**	**12**	**7**	**19**	**11**	**5**	**16**	**90**	**1**	**0**	**0**	**69**	**17.4**	**25**	**4**	**40**	**1**		**1**	**0**	**2**	**2**	**2**	**0**	**0**	**0**

Traded to **NY Islanders** by **Toronto** with Jack Capuano and Paul Gagne for Mike Stevens and Gilles Thibaudeau, December 20, 1989.

• LAZARO, JEFF

Jeff Lazaro LW – L. 5'10", 180 lbs. b: Waltham, MA, 3/21/1968.

Season	Club	League	GP	G	A	Pts	AG	AA	APts	PIM	PP	SH	GW	S	%	TGF	PGF	TGA	PGA	+/–	GP	G	A	Pts	PIM	PP	SH	GW
1986-87	University of New Hampshire	H.E.	38	7	14	21	....	....	....	38	....	....	....	....	....	....	....	....	....	....	....	....	....	....	....	....	....	....
1987-88	University of New Hampshire	H.E.	30	4	13	17	....	....	....	48	....	....	....	....	....	....	....	....	....	....	....	....	....	....	....	....	....	....
1988-89	University of New Hampshire	H.E.	31	8	14	22	....	....	....	38	....	....	....	....	....	....	....	....	....	....	....	....	....	....	....	....	....	....
1989-90	University of New Hampshire	H.E.	39	16	19	35	....	....	....	04	....	....	....	....	....	....	....	....	....	....	....	....	....	....	....	....	....	....
1990-91	**Boston Bruins**	**NHL**	**49**	**5**	**13**	**18**	**5**	**10**	**15**	**67**	**1**	**1**	**1**	**73**	**6.8**	**36**	**1**	**37**	**9**	**+7**	**19**	**3**	**2**	**5**	**30**	**0**	**0**	**0**
	Maine Mariners	AHL	26	8	11	19	....	....	....	18	....	....	....	....	....	....	....	....	....	....	....	....	....	....	....	....	....	....
1991-92	**Boston Bruins**	**NHL**	**27**	**3**	**6**	**9**	**3**	**4**	**7**	**31**	**0**	**0**	**0**	**46**	**6.5**	**14**	**0**	**20**	**10**	**+4**	**9**	**0**	**1**	**1**	**2**	**0**	**0**	**0**
	Maine Mariners	AHL	21	8	4	12	....	....	....	32	....	....	....	....	....	....	....	....	....	....	....	....	....	....	....	....	....	....
1992-93	**Ottawa Senators**	**NHL**	**26**	**6**	**4**	**10**	**5**	**3**	**8**	**16**	**0**	**1**	**0**	**38**	**15.8**	**12**	**1**	**30**	**11**	**–8**	....	....	....	....	....	....	....	....
	New Haven Nighthawks	AHL	27	12	13	25	....	....	....	49	....	....	....	....	....	....	....	....	....	....	....	....	....	....	....	....	....	....
	United States	WC-A	4	2	0	2	....	....	....	2	....	....	....	....	....	....	....	....	....	....	....	....	....	....	....	....	....	....
1993-94	Providence Bruins	AHL	16	3	4	7	....	....	....	26	....	....	....	....	....	....	....	....	....	....	....	....	....	....	....	....	....	....
	United States	Nat-Team	43	18	25	43	....	....	....	57	....	....	....	....	....	....	....	....	....	....	....	....	....	....	....	....	....	....
	United States	Olympics	8	2	2	4	....	....	....	4	....	....	....	....	....	....	....	....	....	....	....	....	....	....	....	....	....	....
	United States	WC-A	8	0	0	0	....	....	....	10	....	....	....	....	....	....	....	....	....	....	....	....	....	....	....	....	....	....
1994-95	ATSE Graz	Austria	23	23	23	46	....	....	....	84	....	....	....	....	....	....	....	....	....	....	8	5	6	11	6	....	....	....
1995-96	Ratinger Lowen	Germany	46	25	41	66	....	....	....	54	....	....	....	....	....	....	....	....	....	....	3	0	0	0	8	....	....	....
1996-97	Ratinger Lowen	Germany	44	13	23	36	....	....	....	69	....	....	....	....	....	....	....	....	....	....	7	5	3	8	8	....	....	....
1997-98	New Orleans Brass	ECHL	70	37	64	101	....	....	....	151	....	....	....	....	....	....	....	....	....	....	4	0	4	4	8	....	....	....
	NHL Totals		**102**	**14**	**23**	**37**	**13**	**17**	**30**	**114**	**1**	**2**	**1**	**157**	**8.9**	**62**	**2**	**87**	**30**		**28**	**3**	**3**	**6**	**32**	**0**	**0**	**0**

ECHL First All-Star Team (1998)

Signed as a free agent by **Boston**, September 26, 1990. Claimed by **Ottawa** from **Boston** in Expansion Draft, June 18, 1992.

• LEACH, JAMIE

Jamie Leach RW – R. 6'1", 205 lbs. b: Winnipeg, Man., 8/25/1969. Pittsburgh's 3rd choice, 47th overall, in 1987 Entry Draft.

Season	Club	League	GP	G	A	Pts	AG	AA	APts	PIM	PP	SH	GW	S	%	TGF	PGF	TGA	PGA	+/–	GP	G	A	Pts	PIM	PP	SH	GW
1984-85	Cherry Hill East	H.S.	60	48	51	99	....	....	....	68	....	....	....	....	....	....	....	....	....	....	....	....	....	....	....	....	....	....
1985-86	New Westminster Bruins	WHL	58	8	7	15	....	....	....	20	....	....	....	....	....	....	....	....	....	....	....	....	....	....	....	....	....	....
1986-87	Hamilton Steelhawks	OHL	64	12	19	31	....	....	....	67	....	....	....	....	....	....	....	....	....	....	....	....	....	....	....	....	....	....
1987-88	Hamilton Steelhawks	OHL	64	24	19	43	....	....	....	79	....	....	....	....	....	....	....	....	....	....	14	6	7	13	12	....	....	....
1988-89	Niagara Falls Flyers	OHL	58	45	62	107	....	....	....	47	....	....	....	....	....	....	....	....	....	....	17	9	11	20	25	....	....	....
1989-90	**Pittsburgh Penguins**	**NHL**	**10**	**0**	**3**	**3**	**0**	**2**	**2**	**0**	**0**	**0**	**0**	**10**	**0.0**	**3**	**0**	**0**	**0**	**+3**	....	....	....	....	....	....	....	....
	Muskegon Lumberjacks	IHL	72	22	36	58	....	....	....	39	....	....	....	....	....	....	....	....	....	....	15	9	4	13	14	....	....	....
1990-91	**Pittsburgh Penguins**	**NHL**	**7**	**2**	**0**	**2**	**2**	**0**	**2**	**0**	**0**	**0**	**0**	**8**	**25.0**	**3**	**1**	**3**	**0**	**–1**	....	....	....	....	....	....	....	....
	Muskegon Lumberjacks	IHL	43	33	22	55	....	....	....	26	....	....	....	....	....	....	....	....	....	....	....	....	....	....	....	....	....	....
1991-92	**Pittsburgh Penguins**	**NHL**	**38**	**5**	**4**	**9**	**5**	**3**	**8**	**8**	**1**	**0**	**0**	**32**	**15.6**	**14**	**2**	**14**	**0**	**–2**	....	....	....	....	....	....	....	....
	Muskegon Lumberjacks	IHL	3	1	1	2	....	....	....	2	....	....	....	....	....	....	....	....	....	....	....	....	....	....	....	....	....	....
1992-93	**Pittsburgh Penguins**	**NHL**	**5**	**0**	**0**	**0**	**0**	**0**	**0**	**2**	**0**	**0**	**0**	**2**	**0.0**	**0**	**0**	**2**	**0**	**–2**	....	....	....	....	....	....	....	....
	Cleveland Lumberjacks	IHL	9	5	3	8	....	....	....	2	....	....	....	....	....	....	....	....	....	....	4	1	2	3	0	....	....	....
	Hartford Whalers	**NHL**	**19**	**3**	**2**	**5**	**2**	**1**	**3**	**2**	**0**	**0**	**0**	**17**	**17.6**	**10**	**2**	**13**	**0**	**–5**	....	....	....	....	....	....	....	....
	Springfield Indians	AHL	29	13	15	28	....	....	....	33	....	....	....	....	....	....	....	....	....	....	....	....	....	....	....	....	....	....
1993-94	**Florida Panthers**	**NHL**	**2**	**1**	**0**	**1**	**1**	**0**	**1**	**0**	**0**	**0**	**0**	**2**	**50.0**	**1**	**0**	**3**	**0**	**–2**	....	....	....	....	....	....	....	....
	Cincinnati Cyclones	IHL	74	15	19	34	....	....	....	64	....	....	....	....	....	....	....	....	....	....	11	1	0	1	4	....	....	....
1994-95	Canada	Nat Team	41	12	26	38	....	....	....	26	....	....	....	....	....	....	....	....	....	....	....	....	....	....	....	....	....	....
	Cincinnati Cyclones	IHL	11	0	2	2	....	....	....	9	....	....	....	....	....	....	....	....	....	....	....	....	....	....	....	....	....	....
	San Diego Gulls	IHL	....	....	....	....	....	....	....	....	....	....	....	....	....	....	....	....	....	....	4	0	0	0	0	....	....	....
1995-96	Rochester Americans	AHL	47	12	14	26	....	....	....	52	....	....	....	....	....	....	....	....	....	....	2	0	0	0	0	....	....	....
	South Carolina Stingrays	ECHL	5	6	1	7	....	....	....	4	....	....	....	....	....	....	....	....	....	....	....	....	....	....	....	....	....	....
1996-97	Sheffield Steelers	Britain	36	17	20	37	....	....	....	26	....	....	....	....	....	....	....	....	....	....	8	4	5	9	12	....	....	....
1997-98	Nottingham Panthers	Britain	39	20	24	45	....	....	....	36	....	....	....	....	....	....	....	....	....	....	5	1	1	2	2	....	....	....
	NHL Totals		**81**	**11**	**9**	**20**	**10**	**6**	**16**	**12**	**1**	**0**	**0**	**71**	**15.5**	**31**	**5**	**35**	**0**		....	....	....	....	....	....	....	....

Claimed on waivers by **Hartford** from **Pittsburgh**, November 21, 1992. Signed as a free agent by **Florida**, August 31, 1993.

• LEACH, REGGIE

Reggie "The Riverton Rifle" Leach RW – R. 6', 180 lbs. b: Riverton, Man., 4/23/1950. Boston's 1st choice, 3rd overall, in 1970 Amateur Draft.

			REGULAR SEASON																		PLAYOFFS							
Season	Club	League	GP	G	A	Pts	AG	AA	APts	PIM	PP	SH	GW	S	%	TGF	PGF	TGA	PGA	+/–	GP	G	A	Pts	PIM	PP	SH	GW
1967-68	Flin Flon Bombers	WCJHL	59	*87	44	131	....	....	....	208	....	....	....	....	....	....	....	....	....	....	....	....	....	....	....	....	....	....
1968-69	Flin Flon Bombers	WHL	22	36	10	46	....	....	....	49	....	....	....	....	....	....	....	....	....	....	18	*13	8	21	0	....	....	....
1969-70	Flin Flon Bombers	WHL	57	*65	46	*111	....	....	....	168	....	....	....	....	....	....	....	....	....	....	17	*16	11	27	50	....	....	....
1970-71	**Boston Bruins**	**NHL**	23	2	4	6	2	4	6	0	0	0	0	30	6.7	8	0	1	0	+7	3	0	0	0	0	0	0	0
	Oklahoma City Blazers	CHL	41	24	18	42	....	....	....	32	....	....	....	....	....	....	....	....	....	....	....	....	....	....	....	....	....	....
1971-72	**Boston Bruins**	**NHL**	56	7	13	20	7	12	19	12	0	0	2	66	10.6	25	1	19	0	+5	....	....	....	....	....	....	....	....
	California Golden Seals	**NHL**	17	6	7	13	6	6	12	7	2	0	1	38	15.8	24	4	19	1	+2	....	....	....	....	....	....	....	....
1972-73	**California Golden Seals**	**NHL**	76	23	12	35	23	10	33	45	3	0	4	184	12.5	63	14	92	2	–41	....	....	....	....	....	....	....	....
1973-74	**California Golden Seals**	**NHL**	78	22	24	46	22	21	43	34	2	0	3	214	10.3	67	17	113	2	–61	....	....	....	....	....	....	....	....
1974-75	**Philadelphia Flyers**	**NHL**	80	45	33	78	42	26	68	63	12	0	10	289	15.6	113	38	24	2	+53	17	8	2	10	6	2	0	2
1975-76	**Philadelphia Flyers**	**NHL**	80	*61	30	91	57	24	81	41	10	0	11	335	18.2	152	46	33	0	+73	16	*19	5	*24	8	2	0	2
1976-77	Canada	C Cup	6	1	1	2	....	....	....	4	....	....	....	....	....	....	....	....	....	....	....	....	....	....	....	....	....	....
	Philadelphia Flyers	**NHL**	77	32	14	46	31	11	42	23	10	0	3	237	13.5	77	25	46	0	+6	10	4	5	9	0	0	0	2
1977-78	**Philadelphia Flyers**	**NHL**	72	24	28	52	23	23	46	24	9	0	4	195	12.3	82	25	39	2	+20	12	2	2	4	0	1	0	0
1978-79	**Philadelphia Flyers**	**NHL**	76	34	20	54	31	15	46	20	13	0	6	279	12.2	77	29	52	1	–3	8	5	1	6	0	3	0	2
1979-80	**Philadelphia Flyers**	**NHL**	76	50	26	76	45	20	65	28	5	4	7	328	15.2	99	14	69	24	+40	19	9	7	16	6	2	1	0
1980-81	**Philadelphia Flyers**	**NHL**	79	34	36	70	28	25	53	59	15	1	2	321	10.6	105	39	64	19	+21	9	0	0	0	2	0	0	0
1981-82	**Philadelphia Flyers**	**NHL**	66	26	21	47	21	14	35	18	5	0	5	211	12.3	71	22	51	4	+2	....	....	....	....	....	....	....	....
1982-83	**Detroit Red Wings**	**NHL**	78	15	17	32	12	12	24	13	2	0	0	139	10.8	49	4	64	18	–1	....	....	....	....	....	....	....	....
1983-84	Montana Magic	CHL	76	21	29	50	....	....	....	34	....	....	....	....	....	....	....	....	....	....	....	....	....	....	....	....	....	....
	NHL Totals		934	381	285	666	350	223	573	387	88	5	58	2866	13.3	1012	278	686	75		94	47	22	69	22	10	1	8

WCJHL First All-Star Team (1968, 1969, 1970) • NHL Second All-Star Team (1976) • Won Conn Smythe Trophy (1976)

Played in NHL All-Star Game (1976, 1980)

Traded to **California** by **Boston** with Rick Smith and Bob Stewart for Carol Vadnais and Don O'Donoghe, February 23, 1972. Traded to **Philadelphia** by **California** for Larry Wright, Al MacAdam, Philadelphia's 1st round choice (Ron Chipperfield) and future considerations (George Pesut, December 11, 1974) in 1974 Amateur Draft, May 24, 1974. Signed as a free agent by **Detroit**, August 25, 1982.

• LEACH, STEPHEN

Stephen Leach RW – R. 5'11", 197 lbs. b: Cambridge, MA, 1/16/1966. Washington's 2nd choice, 34th overall, in 1984 Entry Draft.

			REGULAR SEASON																		PLAYOFFS							
Season	Club	League	GP	G	A	Pts	AG	AA	APts	PIM	PP	SH	GW	S	%	TGF	PGF	TGA	PGA	+/–	GP	G	A	Pts	PIM	PP	SH	GW
1983-84	Matignon High School	H.S.	21	27	22	49	....	....	....	49	....	....	....	....	....	....	....	....	....	....	....	....	....	....	....	....	....	....
1984-85	University of New Hampshire	H.E.	41	12	25	37	....	....	....	53	....	....	....	....	....	....	....	....	....	....	....	....	....	....	....	....	....	....
1985-86	University of New Hampshire	H.E.	25	22	6	28	....	....	....	30	....	....	....	....	....	....	....	....	....	....	....	....	....	....	....	....	....	....
	Washington Capitals	**NHL**	11	1	1	2	1	1	2	2	0	0	0	4	25.0	4	0	4	0	0	6	0	1	1	0	0	0	0
1986-87	**Washington Capitals**	**NHL**	15	1	0	1	1	0	1	6	0	0	0	17	5.9	4	0	9	1	–4	....	....	....	....	....	....	....	....
	Binghamton Whalers	AHL	54	18	21	39	....	....	....	39	....	....	....	....	....	....	....	....	....	....	13	3	1	4	6	....	....	....
1987-88	United States	Nat-Team	49	26	20	46	....	....	....	30	....	....	....	....	....	....	....	....	....	....	....	....	....	....	....	....	....	....
	United States	Olympics	6	1	2	3	....	....	....	0	....	....	....	....	....	....	....	....	....	....	....	....	....	....	....	....	....	....
	Washington Capitals	**NHL**	8	1	1	2	1	1	2	17	0	0	1	5	20.0	3	0	1	0	+2	9	2	1	3	0	0	0	1
1988-89	**Washington Capitals**	**NHL**	74	11	19	30	9	13	22	94	4	0	0	145	7.6	45	8	43	2	–4	6	1	0	1	12	1	0	0
1989-90	**Washington Capitals**	**NHL**	70	18	14	32	16	10	26	104	0	0	2	122	14.8	47	1	38	2	+10	14	2	2	4	8	0	0	0
1990-91	**Washington Capitals**	**NHL**	68	11	19	30	10	14	24	99	4	0	1	134	8.2	43	14	38	0	–9	9	1	2	3	8	0	0	0
1991-92	**Boston Bruins**	**NHL**	78	31	29	60	28	22	50	147	12	0	4	243	12.8	100	36	79	7	–8	15	4	0	4	10	0	0	1
1992-93	**Boston Bruins**	**NHL**	79	26	25	51	22	17	39	126	9	0	4	256	10.2	80	28	58	0	–6	4	1	1	2	2	0	0	0
1993-94	**Boston Bruins**	**NHL**	42	5	10	15	5	8	13	74	1	0	1	89	5.6	29	8	31	0	–10	5	0	1	1	2	0	0	0
1994-95	**Boston Bruins**	**NHL**	35	5	6	11	9	9	18	68	1	0	1	82	6.1	18	4	18	1	–3	....	....	....	....	....	....	....	....
1995-96	**Boston Bruins**	**NHL**	59	9	13	22	9	11	20	86	1	0	2	124	7.3	36	2	38	0	–4	....	....	....	....	....	....	....	....
	St. Louis Blues	**NHL**	14	2	4	6	2	3	5	22	0	0	0	33	6.1	10	3	11	1	–3	11	3	2	5	10	1	0	1
1996-97	**St. Louis Blues**	**NHL**	17	2	1	3	2	1	3	24	0	0	0	33	6.1	7	0	9	0	–2	6	0	0	0	33	0	0	0
1997-98	**Carolina Hurricanes**	**NHL**	45	4	5	9	5	5	10	42	1	1	2	60	6.7	11	1	36	7	–19	....	....	....	....	....	....	....	....
	NHL Totals		615	127	147	274	120	115	235	911	33	1	18	1347	9.4	437	105	413	21		85	14	10	24	85	2	0	3

Traded to **Boston** by **Washington** for Randy Burridge, June 21, 1991. Traded to **St. Louis** by **Boston** for Kevin Sawyer and Steve Staios, March 8, 1996. Traded to **Carolina** by **St. Louis** for Alexander Godynyuk and Carolina's 6th round choice in 1998 Entry Draft, June 27, 1997.

• LEAVINS, JIM

Jim Leavins D – L. 5'11", 185 lbs. b: Dinsmore, Sask., 7/28/1960.

			REGULAR SEASON																		PLAYOFFS							
Season	Club	League	GP	G	A	Pts	AG	AA	APts	PIM	PP	SH	GW	S	%	TGF	PGF	TGA	PGA	+/–	GP	G	A	Pts	PIM	PP	SH	GW
1980-81	University of Denver	WCHA	40	8	18	26	....	....	....	18	....	....	....	....	....	....	....	....	....	....	....	....	....	....	....	....	....	....
1981-82	University of Denver	WCHA	41	8	34	42	....	....	....	56	....	....	....	....	....	....	....	....	....	....	....	....	....	....	....	....	....	....
1982-83	University of Denver	WCHA	33	16	24	40	....	....	....	20	....	....	....	....	....	....	....	....	....	....	....	....	....	....	....	....	....	....
1983-84	University of Denver	WCHA	39	13	26	39	....	....	....	38	....	....	....	....	....	....	....	....	....	....	....	....	....	....	....	....	....	....
1984-85	Fort Wayne Komets	IHL	76	5	50	55	....	....	....	57	....	....	....	....	....	....	....	....	....	....	13	3	8	11	10	....	....	....
1985-86	**Detroit Red Wings**	**NHL**	37	2	11	13	2	7	9	26	1	0	0	63	3.2	46	14	69	14	–23	....	....	....	....	....	....	....	....
	Adirondack Red Wings	AHL	36	4	21	25	....	....	....	19	....	....	....	....	....	....	....	....	....	....	....	....	....	....	....	....	....	....
1986-87	**New York Rangers**	**NHL**	4	0	1	1	0	1	1	4	0	0	0	4	0.0	8	4	4	0	0	....	....	....	....	....	....	....	....
	New Haven Nighthawks	AHL	54	7	21	28	....	....	....	16	....	....	....	....	....	....	....	....	....	....	7	0	4	4	2	....	....	....
1987-88	New Haven Nighthawks	AHL	11	2	5	7	....	....	....	8	....	....	....	....	....	....	....	....	....	....	....	....	....	....	....	....	....	....
	Salt Lake Golden Eagles	IHL	68	12	45	57	....	....	....	45	....	....	....	....	....	....	....	....	....	....	16	5	5	10	8	....	....	....
1988-89	Kookoo	Finland	42	12	11	23	....	....	....	39	....	....	....	....	....	....	....	....	....	....	....	....	....	....	....	....	....	....
	Salt Lake Golden Eagles	IHL	25	8	13	21	....	....	....	14	....	....	....	....	....	....	....	....	....	....	14	2	11	13	6	....	....	....
1989-90	Kookoo	Finland	44	7	24	31	....	....	....	36	....	....	....	....	....	....	....	....	....	....	....	....	....	....	....	....	....	....
	Canada	Nat-Team	5	0	2	2	....	....	....	4	....	....	....	....	....	....	....	....	....	....	....	....	....	....	....	....	....	....
	Salt Lake Golden Eagles	IHL	11	0	6	6	....	....	....	2	....	....	....	....	....	....	....	....	....	....	11	0	8	8	2	....	....	....
1990-91	Farjestad BK Karlstad	Sweden	40	9	8	17	....	....	....	24	....	....	....	....	....	....	....	....	....	....	....	....	....	....	....	....	....	....
	Canada	Nat-Team	4	0	1	1	....	....	....	0	....	....	....	....	....	....	....	....	....	....	....	....	....	....	....	....	....	....
1991-92			DID NOT PLAY																									
1992-93	Varese	Italy	17	3	12	15	....	....	....	12	....	....	....	....	....	....	....	....	....	....	....	....	....	....	....	....	....	....
	NHL Totals		41	2	12	14	2	8	10	30	1	0	0	67	3.0	54	18	73	14		....	....	....	....	....	....	....	....

WCHA First All-Star Team (1984) • IHL Second All-Star Team (1988)

Signed as a free agent by **Detroit**, November 9, 1985. Traded to **NY Rangers** by **Detroit** with Kelly Kisio and Lane Lambert for Glen Hanlon and NY Rangers' 3rd round choice in 1987 (Dennis Holland) and 1988 (Guy Dupuis) Entry Drafts, July 29, 1986. Traded to **Calgary** by **NY Rangers** for Don Mercier, November 6, 1987.

• LEBEAU, PATRICK

Patrick Lebeau LW – L. 5'10", 172 lbs. b: St. Jerome, Que., 3/17/1970. Montreal's 9th choice, 167th overall, in 1989 Entry Draft.

			REGULAR SEASON																		PLAYOFFS							
Season	Club	League	GP	G	A	Pts	AG	AA	APts	PIM	PP	SH	GW	S	%	TGF	PGF	TGA	PGA	+/–	GP	G	A	Pts	PIM	PP	SH	GW
1986-87	Shawinigan Cataractes	QMJHL	66	26	52	78	....	....	....	90	....	....	....	....	....	....	....	....	....	....	13	2	6	8	17	....	....	....
1987-88	Shawinigan Cataractes	QMJHL	53	43	56	99	....	....	....	116	....	....	....	....	....	....	....	....	....	....	11	3	9	12	16	....	....	....
1988-89	Shawinigan Cataractes	QMJHL	17	19	17	36	....	....	....	18	....	....	....	....	....	....	....	....	....	....	....	....	....	....	....	....	....	....
	St-Jean Lynx	QMJHL	49	43	70	113	....	....	....	71	....	....	....	....	....	....	....	....	....	....	4	4	3	7	6	....	....	....
1989-90	Victoriaville Tigres	QMJHL	72	68	*106	*174	....	....	....	109	....	....	....	....	....	....	....	....	....	....	16	7	15	22	12	....	....	....
1990-91	**Montreal Canadiens**	**NHL**	2	1	1	2	1	1	2	0	0	0	0	3	33.3	2	1	1	0	0	....	....	....	....	....	....	....	....
	Fredericton Canadiens	AHL	69	50	51	101	....	....	....	32	....	....	....	....	....	....	....	....	....	....	9	4	7	11	8	....	....	....
1991-92	Fredericton Canadiens	AHL	55	33	38	71	....	....	....	48	....	....	....	....	....	....	....	....	....	....	7	4	5	9	10	....	....	....
	Canada	Nat-Team	7	4	2	6	....	....	....	6	....	....	....	....	....	....	....	....	....	....	....	....	....	....	....	....	....	....
	Canada	Olympics	8	1	3	4	....	....	....	4	....	....	....	....	....	....	....	....	....	....	....	....	....	....	....	....	....	....
1992-93	**Calgary Flames**	**NHL**	1	0	0	0	0	0	0	0	0	0	0	0	0.0	0	0	0	0	0	....	....	....	....	....	....	....	....
	Salt Lake Golden Eagles	IHL	75	40	60	100	....	....	....	65	....	....	....	....	....	....	....	....	....	....	....	....	....	....	....	....	....	....
1993-94	**Florida Panthers**	**NHL**	4	1	1	2	1	1	2	4	1	0	0	4	25.0	2	2	0	0	0	....	....	....	....	....	....	....	....
	Cincinnati Cyclones	IHL	74	47	42	89	....	....	....	90	....	....	....	....	....	....	....	....	....	....	11	4	8	12	14	....	....	....
1994-95	Zurich SC	Switz.	36	27	25	52	....	....	....	22	....	....	....	....	....	....	....	....	....	....	5	4	6	10	6	....	....	....

Season	Club	League	REGULAR SEASON GP	G	A	Pts	AG	AA	APts	PIM	PP	SH	GW	S	%	TGF	PGF	TGA	PGA	+/-	PLAYOFFS GP	G	A	Pts	PIM	PP	SH	GW
1995-96	Zurich SC	Switz.	11	6	8	14	....	....	....	0	....	....	....	....	....	....	....	....	....	....	....	....	....	....	....	....	....	....
	Dusseldorfer EG	Germany	17	13	8	21	....	....	....	18	....	....	....	....	....	....	....	....	....	....	13	11	5	16	14	....	....	....
1996-97	Zurich SC	Switz.	38	27	19	46	....	....	....	26	....	....	....	....	....	....	....	....	....	....	4	1	0	1	25	....	....	....
1997-98	HC La Chaux-de-Fonds	Switz.	40	17	45	62	....	....	....	32	....	....	....	....	....	....	....	....	....	....	....	....	....	....	....	....	....	....
	NHL Totals		**7**	**2**	**2**	**4**	**2**	**2**	**4**	**4**	**1**	**0**	**0**	**7**	**28.6**	**4**	**3**	**1**	**0**		....	....	....	....	....	....	....	....

QMJHL First All-Star Team (1990) • AHL Second All-Star Team (1991) • Won Dudley "Red" Garrett Memorial Award (Top Rookie - AHL) (1991)

Traded to **Calgary** by **Montreal** for future considerations, September 27, 1986. Signed as a free agent by **Florida**, July 26, 1993.

• LEBEAU, STEPHAN

Stephan Lebeau C – R. 5'10", 173 lbs. b: St. Jerome, Que., 2/28/1968.

Season	Club	League	GP	G	A	Pts	AG	AA	APts	PIM	PP	SH	GW	S	%	TGF	PGF	TGA	PGA	+/-	GP	G	A	Pts	PIM	PP	SH	GW
1984-85	Shawinigan Cataractes	QMJHL	66	41	38	79	....	....	....	18	....	....	....	....	....	....	....	....	....	....	9	4	5	9	4	....	....	....
1985-86	Shawinigan Cataractes	QMJHL	72	69	77	146	....	....	....	22	....	....	....	....	....	....	....	....	....	....	5	4	2	6	4	....	....	....
1986-87	Shawinigan Cataractes	QMJHL	65	77	90	167	....	....	....	60	....	....	....	....	....	....	....	....	....	....	14	9	20	29	20	....	....	....
1987-88	Shawinigan Cataractes	QMJHL	67	*94	94	188	....	....	....	66	....	....	....	....	....	....	....	....	....	....	11	17	9	26	10	....	....	....
	Sherbrooke Canadiens	AHL	....	....	....	....	....	....	....	....	....	....	....	....	....	....	....	....	....	....	1	0	1	1	0	....	....	....
1988-89	**Montreal Canadiens**	**NHL**	**1**	**0**	**1**	**1**	**0**	**1**	**1**	**2**	**0**	**0**	**0**	**1**	**0.0**	**1**	**0**	**0**	**0**	**+1**	....	....	....	....	....	....	....	....
	Sherbrooke Canadiens	AHL	78	*70	64	*134	....	....	....	47	....	....	....	....	....	....	....	....	....	....	6	1	4	5	8	....	....	....
1989-90	**Montreal Canadiens**	**NHL**	**57**	**15**	**20**	**35**	**13**	**14**	**27**	**11**	**5**	**0**	**3**	**79**	**19.0**	**56**	**18**	**25**	**0**	**+13**	**2**	**3**	**0**	**3**	**0**	**0**	**0**	**1**
1990-91	Montreal Canadiens	FrTour	2	1	0	1	....	....	....	0	....	....	....	....	....	....	....	....	....	....	....	....	....	....	....	....	....	....
	Montreal Canadiens	**NHL**	**73**	**22**	**31**	**53**	**20**	**23**	**43**	**24**	**8**	**0**	**2**	**108**	**20.4**	**70**	**32**	**34**	**0**	**+4**	**7**	**2**	**1**	**3**	**2**	**0**	**0**	**0**
1991-92	**Montreal Canadiens**	**NHL**	**77**	**27**	**31**	**58**	**25**	**23**	**48**	**14**	**13**	**0**	**5**	**178**	**15.2**	**81**	**31**	**34**	**2**	**+18**	**8**	**1**	**3**	**4**	**4**	**1**	**0**	**0**
1992-93	**Montreal Canadiens**	**NHL**	**71**	**31**	**49**	**80**	**26**	**34**	**60**	**20**	**8**	**0**	**7**	**150**	**20.7**	**109**	**29**	**57**	**0**	**+23**	**13**	**3**	**3**	**6**	**6**	**1**	**0**	**1**
1993-94	**Montreal Canadiens**	**NHL**	**34**	**9**	**7**	**16**	**8**	**5**	**13**	**8**	**4**	**0**	**2**	**61**	**14.8**	**26**	**10**	**16**	**1**	**+1**	....	....	....	....	....	....	....	....
	Anaheim Mighty Ducks	**NHL**	**22**	**6**	**4**	**10**	**6**	**3**	**9**	**14**	**2**	**0**	**1**	**37**	**16.2**	**13**	**5**	**13**	**0**	**–5**	....	....	....	....	....	....	....	....
1994-95	**Anaheim Mighty Ducks**	**NHL**	**38**	**8**	**16**	**24**	**14**	**24**	**38**	**12**	**1**	**0**	**2**	**70**	**11.4**	**33**	**8**	**19**	**0**	**+6**	....	....	....	....	....	....	....	....
1995-96	HC Lugano	Switz.	36	25	28	53	....	....	....	10	....	....	....	....	....	....	....	....	....	....	4	2	2	4	0	....	....	....
1996-97	HC Lugano	Switz.	18	14	12	26	....	....	....	12	....	....	....	....	....	....	....	....	....	....	....	....	....	....	....	....	....	....
1997-98	HC La Chaux-de-Fonds	Switz.	40	31	39	70	....	....	....	14	....	....	....	....	....	....	....	....	....	....	....	....	....	....	....	....	....	....
	NHL Totals		**373**	**118**	**159**	**277**	**112**	**127**	**239**	**105**	**41**	**0**	**22**	**684**	**17.3**	**389**	**133**	**198**	**3**		**30**	**9**	**7**	**16**	**12**	**2**	**0**	**2**

QMJHL Second All-Star Team (1987, 1988) • AHL First All-Star Team (1989) • Won Dudley "Red" Garrett Memorial Trophy (Top Rookie - AHL) (1989) • Won John B. Sollenberger Trophy (Top Scorer - AHL) (1989) • Won Les Cunningham Plaque (MVP - AHL) (1989)

Signed as a free agent by **Montreal**, September 27, 1986. Traded to **Anaheim** by **Montreal** for Ron Tugnutt, February 20, 1994.

• LEBLANC, FERN

Fern LeBlanc C – L. 5'9", 170 lbs. b: Gaspesie, Que., 1/12/1956. Detroit's 7th choice, 111th overall, in 1976 Amateur Draft.

Season	Club	League	GP	G	A	Pts	AG	AA	APts	PIM	PP	SH	GW	S	%	TGF	PGF	TGA	PGA	+/-	GP	G	A	Pts	PIM	PP	SH	GW
1974-75	Sherbrooke Castors	QMJHL	22	17	12	29	....	....	....	8	....	....	....	....	....	....	....	....	....	....	....	....	....	....	....	....	....	....
1975-76	Sherbrooke Castors	QMJHL	71	63	71	134	....	....	....	31	....	....	....	....	....	....	....	....	....	....	....	....	....	....	....	....	....	....
1976-77	**Detroit Red Wings**	**NHL**	**3**	**0**	**0**	**0**	**0**	**0**	**0**	**0**	**0**	**0**	**0**	**1**	**0.0**	**0**	**0**	**3**	**0**	**–3**	....	....	....	....	....	....	....	....
	Kalamazoo Wings	IHL	77	39	32	71	....	....	....	57	....	....	....	....	....	....	....	....	....	....	10	9	8	17	4	....	....	....
1977-78	**Detroit Red Wings**	**NHL**	**2**	**0**	**0**	**0**	**0**	**0**	**0**	**0**	**0**	**0**	**0**	**0**	**0.0**	**2**	**0**	**4**	**0**	**–2**	....	....	....	....	....	....	....	....
	Kansas City Red Wings	CHL	69	29	21	50	....	....	....	39	....	....	....	....	....	....	....	....	....	....	....	....	....	....	....	....	....	....
1978-79	**Detroit Red Wings**	**NHL**	**29**	**5**	**6**	**11**	**5**	**5**	**10**	**0**	**1**	**0**	**0**	**27**	**18.5**	**17**	**4**	**12**	**0**	**+1**	....	....	....	....	....	....	....	....
	Kansas City Red Wings	CHL	35	15	26	41	....	....	....	14	....	....	....	....	....	....	....	....	....	....	....	....	....	....	....	....	....	....
1979-1984			STATISTICS NOT AVAILABLE																									
1984-85	EHC Chur	Switz.	36	29	17	46	....	....	....	....	....	....	....	....	....	....	....	....	....	....	....	....	....	....	....	....	....	....
1985-86	EHC Chur	Switz. 2	STATISTICS NOT AVAILABLE																									
1986-87	SC Herisau	Switz. 2	....	*56	41	*97	....	....	....	....	....	....	....	....	....	....	....	....	....	....	....	....	....	....	....	....	....	....
1987-88	HC Ajoie	Switz. 2	....	46	41	*87	....	....	....	....	....	....	....	....	....	....	....	....	....	....	6	3	3	6	....	....	....	....
1988-89	HC Ajoie	Switz.	....	3	3	6	....	....	....	....	....	....	....	....	....	....	....	....	....	....	....	....	....	....	....	....	....	....
	NHL Totals		**34**	**5**	**6**	**11**	**5**	**5**	**10**	**0**	**1**	**0**	**0**	**28**	**17.9**	**19**	**4**	**19**	**0**		....	....	....	....	....	....	....	....

• LEBLANC, J.P.

J.P. (Jean Paul) LeBlanc C – L. 5'10", 170 lbs. b: South Durham, Que., 10/20/1946.

Season	Club	League	GP	G	A	Pts	AG	AA	APts	PIM	PP	SH	GW	S	%	TGF	PGF	TGA	PGA	+/-	GP	G	A	Pts	PIM	PP	SH	GW
1965-66	St. Catharines Black Hawks	OHA	22	9	15	24	....	....	....	6	....	....	....	....	....	....	....	....	....	....	....	....	....	....	....	....	....	....
1966-67	St. Catharines Black Hawks	OHA	48	18	26	44	....	....	....	73	....	....	....	....	....	....	....	....	....	....	6	1	1	2	23	....	....	....
	Columbus Checkers	IHL	2	1	0	1	....	....	....	2	....	....	....	....	....	....	....	....	....	....	....	....	....	....	....	....	....	....
	St. Louis Braves	CHL	1	0	0	0	....	....	....	0	....	....	....	....	....	....	....	....	....	....	....	....	....	....	....	....	....	....
1967-68	Dallas Black Hawks	CHL	66	19	31	50	....	....	....	83	....	....	....	....	....	....	....	....	....	....	5	1	0	1	2	....	....	....
1968-69	**Chicago Black Hawks**	**NHL**	**6**	**1**	**2**	**3**	**1**	**2**	**3**	**0**	**0**	**0**	**0**	**9**	**11.1**	**3**	**0**	**0**	**1**	**+1**	....	....	....	....	....	....	....	....
	Dallas Black Hawks	CHL	67	18	34	52	....	....	....	82	....	....	....	....	....	....	....	....	....	....	11	2	5	7	35	....	....	....
1969-70	Dallas Black Hawks	CHL	68	28	35	63	....	....	....	138	....	....	....	....	....	....	....	....	....	....	....	....	....	....	....	....	....	....
	Portland Buckaroos	WHL	....	....	....	....	....	....	....	....	....	....	....	....	....	....	....	....	....	....	11	0	4	4	22	....	....	....
1970-71	Dallas Black Hawks	CHL	57	13	31	44	....	....	....	61	....	....	....	....	....	....	....	....	....	....	9	3	5	8	7	....	....	....
1971-72	Dallas Black Hawks	CHL	70	22	*68	90	....	....	....	117	....	....	....	....	....	....	....	....	....	....	12	6	7	13	21	....	....	....
1972-73	Los Angeles Sharks	WHA	77	19	50	69	....	....	....	49	....	....	....	....	....	....	....	....	....	....	6	0	5	5	2	....	....	....
1973-74	Los Angeles Sharks	WHA	78	20	46	66	....	....	....	58	....	....	....	....	....	....	....	....	....	....	....	....	....	....	....	....	....	....
1974-75	Baltimore-Michigan	WHA	78	16	33	49	....	....	....	100	....	....	....	....	....	....	....	....	....	....	....	....	....	....	....	....	....	....
1975-76	**Detroit Red Wings**	**NHL**	**46**	**4**	**9**	**13**	**4**	**7**	**11**	**39**	**0**	**0**	**0**	**60**	**6.7**	**23**	**2**	**39**	**13**	**–5**	....	....	....	....	....	....	....	....
1976-77	**Detroit Red Wings**	**NHL**	**74**	**7**	**11**	**18**	**7**	**9**	**16**	**40**	**0**	**0**	**2**	**77**	**9.1**	**27**	**0**	**63**	**20**	**–16**	....	....	....	....	....	....	....	....
1977-78	**Detroit Red Wings**	**NHL**	**3**	**0**	**2**	**2**	**0**	**2**	**2**	**4**	**0**	**0**	**0**	**5**	**0.0**	**3**	**1**	**2**	**1**	**+1**	**2**	**0**	**0**	**0**	**0**	**0**	**0**	**0**
	Kansas City Red Wings	CHL	65	20	35	55	....	....	....	42	....	....	....	....	....	....	....	....	....	....	....	....	....	....	....	....	....	....
1978-79	**Detroit Red Wings**	**NHL**	**24**	**2**	**6**	**8**	**2**	**5**	**7**	**4**	**2**	**0**	**0**	**27**	**7.4**	**10**	**4**	**19**	**6**	**–7**	....	....	....	....	....	....	....	....
	Kansas City Red Wings	CHL	53	20	33	53	....	....	....	72	....	....	....	....	....	....	....	....	....	....	4	0	0	0	0	....	....	....
1979-80	Adirondack Red Wings	AHL	75	18	42	58	....	....	....	69	....	....	....	....	....	....	....	....	....	....	4	1	1	2	2	....	....	....
1980-81	Adirondack Red Wings	AHL	77	12	36	48	....	....	....	106	....	....	....	....	....	....	....	....	....	....	17	5	7	12	27	....	....	....
1981-82	Kalamazoo Wings	IHL	DID NOT PLAY – COACHING																									
	NHL Totals		**153**	**14**	**30**	**44**	**14**	**25**	**39**	**87**	**2**	**0**	**2**	**178**	**7.9**	**66**	**7**	**126**	**41**		**2**	**0**	**0**	**0**	**0**	**0**	**0**	**0**
	Other Major League Totals		233	55	129	184	....	....	....	207	....	....	....	....	....	....	....	....	....	....	6	0	5	5	2	....	....	....

CHL Second All-Star Team (1972, 1979) • CHL First All-Star Team (1978)

Selected by **LA Sharks** in 1972 WHA General Player Draft, February 12, 1972. Signed as a free agent by **Michigan** (WHA) after **LA Sharks** (WHA) franchise folded, April 11, 1974. Traded to **Detroit** by **Chicago** for Detroit's 2nd round choice (Jean Savard) in 1977 Amateur Draft, November 20, 1975.

• LEBLANC, JOHN

John LeBlanc RW – L. 6'1", 190 lbs. b: Campbellton, N.B., 1/21/1964.

Season	Club	League	GP	G	A	Pts	AG	AA	APts	PIM	PP	SH	GW	S	%	TGF	PGF	TGA	PGA	+/-	GP	G	A	Pts	PIM	PP	SH	GW
1981-82	Campbellton Tigers	NBSHL	....	15	29	44	....	....	....	....	....	....	....	....	....	....	....	....	....	....	....	....	....	....	....	....	....	....
1982-83	Mount Allison University	AUAA	20	21	26	47	....	....	....	10	....	....	....	....	....	....	....	....	....	....	....	....	....	....	....	....	....	....
1983-84	Hull Olympiques	QMJHL	69	39	35	74	....	....	....	32	....	....	....	....	....	....	....	....	....	....	....	....	....	....	....	....	....	....
1984-85	University of New Brunswick	AUAA	24	25	34	59	....	....	....	32	....	....	....	....	....	....	....	....	....	....	....	....	....	....	....	....	....	....
1985-86	University of New Brunswick	AUAA	24	38	28	66	....	....	....	35	....	....	....	....	....	....	....	....	....	....	....	....	....	....	....	....	....	....
1986-87	**Vancouver Canucks**	**NHL**	**2**	**1**	**0**	**1**	**1**	**0**	**1**	**0**	**0**	**0**	**0**	**4**	**25.0**	**2**	**0**	**1**	**0**	**+1**	....	....	....	....	....	....	....	....
	Fredericton Express	AHL	75	40	30	70	....	....	....	27	....	....	....	....	....	....	....	....	....	....	....	....	....	....	....	....	....	....
1987-88	**Vancouver Canucks**	**NHL**	**41**	**12**	**10**	**22**	**10**	**7**	**17**	**18**	**3**	**0**	**1**	**86**	**14.0**	**35**	**10**	**38**	**1**	**–12**	....	....	....	....	....	....	....	....
	Fredericton Express	AHL	35	26	25	61	....	....	....	54	....	....	....	....	....	....	....	....	....	....	15	6	7	13	34	....	....	....
1988-89	Milwaukee Admirals	IHL	61	39	31	70	....	....	....	42	....	....	....	....	....	....	....	....	....	....	....	....	....	....	....	....	....	....
	Edmonton Oilers	**NHL**	**2**	**1**	**0**	**1**	**1**	**0**	**1**	**0**	**0**	**0**	**0**	**5**	**20.0**	**1**	**0**	**1**	**0**	**0**	**1**	**0**	**0**	**0**	**0**	**0**	**0**	**0**
	Cape Breton Oilers	AHL	3	4	0	4	....	....	....	0	....	....	....	....	....	....	....	....	....	....	....	....	....	....	....	....	....	....
1989-90	Cape Breton Oilers	AHL	77	*54	34	88	....	....	....	50	....	....	....	....	....	....	....	....	....	....	6	4	0	4	4	....	....	....
1990-91			DID NOT PLAY																									
1991-92	**Winnipeg Jets**	**NHL**	**16**	**6**	**1**	**7**	**5**	**1**	**6**	**6**	**5**	**0**	**1**	**32**	**18.8**	**10**	**9**	**7**	**0**	**–6**	....	....	....	....	....	....	....	....
	Moncton Hawks	AHL	56	31	22	53	....	....	....	24	....	....	....	....	....	....	....	....	....	....	10	3	2	5	8	....	....	....
1992-93	**Winnipeg Jets**	**NHL**	**3**	**0**	**0**	**0**	**0**	**0**	**0**	**2**	**0**	**0**	**0**	**5**	**0.0**	**0**	**0**	**0**	**0**	**0**	....	....	....	....	....	....	....	....
	Moncton Hawks	AHL	77	48	40	88	....	....	....	29	....	....	....	....	....	....	....	....	....	....	5	2	1	3	6	....	....	....
1993-94	**Winnipeg Jets**	**NHL**	**17**	**6**	**2**	**8**	**6**	**2**	**8**	**2**	**1**	**1**	**1**	**29**	**20.7**	**9**	**3**	**8**	**0**	**–2**	....	....	....	....	....	....	....	....
	Moncton Hawks	AHL	41	25	26	51	....	....	....	38	....	....	....	....	....	....	....	....	....	....	20	3	6	9	6	....	....	....

			REGULAR SEASON																		PLAYOFFS							
Season	Club	League	GP	G	A	Pts	AG	AA	APts	PIM	PP	SH	GW	S	%	TGF	PGF	TGA	PGA	+/–	GP	G	A	Pts	PIM	PP	SH	GW
1994-95	**Winnipeg Jets**	**NHL**	**2**	**0**	**0**	**0**	**0**	**0**	**0**	**0**	**0**	**0**	**0**	**0**	**0.0**	**0**	**0**	**0**	**0**	**0**	....	....	....	....	....	....	....	....
	Springfield Falcons	AHL	65	39	34	73	....	....	....	32	....	....	....	....	....	....	....	....	....	....	....	....	....	....	....	....	....	....
1995-96	Orlando Solar Bears	IHL	60	22	24	46	....	....	....	20	....	....	....	....	....	....	....	....	....	....	....	....	....	....	....	....	....	....
	Fort Wayne Komets	IHL	16	12	11	23	....	....	....	4	....	....	....	....	....	....	....	....	....	....	5	0	2	2	14	....	....	....
1996-97	Fort Wayne Komets	IHL	77	30	31	61	....	....	....	22	....	....	....	....	....	....	....	....	....	....	....	....	....	....	....	....	....	....
1997-98	Utah Grizzlies	IHL	69	25	17	42	....	....	....	16	....	....	....	....	....	....	....	....	....	....	2	0	0	0	2	....	....	....
	NHL Totals		**83**	**26**	**13**	**39**	**23**	**10**	**33**	**28**	**9**	**1**	**3**	**161**	**16.1**	**57**	**22**	**55**	**1**		**1**	**0**	**0**	**0**	**0**	**0**	**0**	**0**

Canadian University Player of the Year (1986)

Signed as a free agent by **Vancouver**, April 12, 1986. Traded to **Edmonton** by **Vancouver** with Vancouver's 5th round choice (Peter White) in 1989 Entry Draft for Doug Smith and Gregory C. Adams, March 7, 1989. • Sat out entire 1990-91 season after failing to come to contract terms with Edmonton. Traded to **Winnipeg** by **Edmonton** with Edmonton's 10th round choice (Teemu Numminen) in 1992 Entry Draft for Winnipeg's 5th round choice (Ryan Haggerty) in 1991 Entry Draft, June 12, 1991.

• LeBOUTILLIER, PETER

Peter LeBoutillier RW – R. 6'1", 205 lbs. b: Minnedosa, Man., 1/11/1975. Anaheim's 6th choice, 133rd overall, in 1995 Entry Draft.

Season	Club	League	GP	G	A	Pts	AG	AA	APts	PIM	PP	SH	GW	S	%	TGF	PGF	TGA	PGA	+/–	GP	G	A	Pts	PIM	PP	SH	GW
1992-93	Red Deer Rebels	WHL	67	8	26	34	....	....	....	284	....	....	....	....	....	....	....	....	....	....	2	0	1	1	5	....	....	....
1993-94	Red Deer Rebels	WHL	66	19	20	39	....	....	....	300	....	....	....	....	....	....	....	....	....	....	2	0	1	1	4	....	....	....
1994-95	Red Deer Rebels	WHL	59	27	16	43	....	....	....	159	....	....	....	....	....	....	....	....	....	....	....	....	....	....	....	....	....	....
1995-96	Baltimore Bandits	AHL	68	7	9	16	....	....	....	228	....	....	....	....	....	....	....	....	....	....	11	0	0	0	33	....	....	....
1996-97	**Anaheim Mighty Ducks**	**NHL**	**23**	**1**	**0**	**1**	**1**	**0**	**1**	**121**	**0**	**0**	**0**	**5**	**20.0**	**2**	**0**	**2**	**0**	**0**	....	....	....	....	....	....	....	....
	Baltimore Bandits	AHL	47	6	12	18	....	....	....	175	....	....	....	....	....	....	....	....	....	....	....	....	....	....	....	....	....	....
1997-98	**Anaheim Mighty Ducks**	**NHL**	**12**	**1**	**1**	**2**	**1**	**1**	**2**	**55**	**0**	**0**	**0**	**6**	**16.7**	**2**	**0**	**3**	**0**	**–1**	....	....	....	....	....	....	....	....
	Cincinnati Mighty Ducks	AHL	51	9	11	20	....	....	....	143	....	....	....	....	....	....	....	....	....	....	....	....	....	....	....	....	....	....
	NHL Totals		**35**	**2**	**1**	**3**	**2**	**1**	**3**	**176**	**0**	**0**	**0**	**11**	**18.2**	**4**	**0**	**5**	**0**		....	....	....	....	....	....	....	....

Re-entered NHL draft. Originally NY Islanders' 6th choice, 144th overall, in 1993 Entry Draft.

• LECAINE, BILL

Bill Lecaine LW – R. 6', 172 lbs. b: Moose Jaw, Sask., 3/11/1940.

Season	Club	League	GP	G	A	Pts	AG	AA	APts	PIM	PP	SH	GW	S	%	TGF	PGF	TGA	PGA	+/–	GP	G	A	Pts	PIM	PP	SH	GW
1955-56	Regina Pats	SJHL	1	1	1	2	....	....	....	0	....	....	....	....	....	....	....	....	....	....	....	....	....	....	....	....	....	....
1956-57	Regina Pats	SJHL	48	20	22	42	....	....	....	21	....	....	....	....	....	....	....	....	....	....	7	2	0	2	2	....	....	....
1957-58	Regina Pats	SJHL	39	16	20	36	....	....	....	22	....	....	....	....	....	....	....	....	....	....	12	5	8	13	18	....	....	....
1958-59	University of North Dakota	WCHA	DID NOT PLAY – FRESHMAN																									
1959-60	Minneapolis Millers	IHL	56	25	32	57	....	....	....	62	....	....	....	....	....	....	....	....	....	....	6	1	2	3	0	....	....	....
1960-61	Minneapolis Millers	IHL	68	35	47	82	....	....	....	61	....	....	....	....	....	....	....	....	....	....	8	2	4	6	7	....	....	....
1961-62	Minneapolis–Indianapolis	IHL	54	24	39	63	....	....	....	77	....	....	....	....	....	....	....	....	....	....	....	....	....	....	....	....	....	....
	Portland Buckaroos	WHL	2	0	0	0	....	....	....	0	....	....	....	....	....	....	....	....	....	....	....	....	....	....	....	....	....	....
1962-63	Port Huron Flags	IHL	61	30	43	73	....	....	....	93	....	....	....	....	....	....	....	....	....	....	....	....	....	....	....	....	....	....
1963-64	Port Huron Flags	IHL	70	28	59	87	....	....	....	110	....	....	....	....	....	....	....	....	....	....	7	1	2	3	*42	....	....	....
1964-65	Port Huron Flags	IHL	66	42	59	101	....	....	....	151	....	....	....	....	....	....	....	....	....	....	7	5	4	9	11	....	....	....
1965-66	Port Huron Flags	IHL	65	41	75	116	....	....	....	178	....	....	....	....	....	....	....	....	....	....	7	5	8	13	29	....	....	....
1966-67	Port Huron Flags	IHL	39	26	38	64	....	....	....	160	....	....	....	....	....	....	....	....	....	....	....	....	....	....	....	....	....	....
1967-68	Baltimore Clippers	AHL	69	15	22	37	....	....	....	28	....	....	....	....	....	....	....	....	....	....	....	....	....	....	....	....	....	....
1968-69	**Pittsburgh Penguins**	**NHL**	**4**	**0**	**0**	**0**	**0**	**0**	**0**	**0**	**0**	**0**	**0**	**1**	**0.0**	**0**	**0**	**0**	**0**	**0**	....	....	....	....	....	....	....	....
	Amarillo Wranglers	CHL	51	17	22	39	....	....	....	60	....	....	....	....	....	....	....	....	....	....	....	....	....	....	....	....	....	....
1969-70	Port Huron Flags	IHL	47	25	29	54	....	....	....	100	....	....	....	....	....	....	....	....	....	....	14	5	8	13	8	....	....	....
1970-71	Port Huron Flags	IHL	68	26	30	56	....	....	....	74	....	....	....	....	....	....	....	....	....	....	14	2	13	15	56	....	....	....
1971-72	Port Huron Wings	IHL	39	15	29	44	....	....	....	52	....	....	....	....	....	....	....	....	....	....	14	2	5	7	38	....	....	....
1972-73	Port Huron Wings	IHL	60	28	38	66	....	....	....	63	....	....	....	....	....	....	....	....	....	....	11	3	3	6	18	....	....	....
1974-75	Port Huron Flags	IHL	19	4	5	9	....	....	....	28	....	....	....	....	....	....	....	....	....	....	....	....	....	....	....	....	....	....
	NHL Totals		**4**	**0**	**0**	**0**	**0**	**0**	**0**	**0**	**0**	**0**	**0**	**1**	**0.0**	**0**	**0**	**0**	**0**		....	....	....	....	....	....	....	....

IHL First All-Star Team (1963, 1966) • IHL Second All-Star Team (1965, 1967, 1973)

Traded to **Indianapolis** (IHL) by **Minneapolis** (IHL) for Dan Summers, January, 1962. Signed as a free agent by **Pittsburgh**, August, 1967.

• LeCLAIR, JOHN

John LeClair LW – L. 6'3", 226 lbs. b: St. Albans, VT, 7/5/1969. Montreal's 2nd choice, 33rd overall, in 1987 Entry Draft.

Season	Club	League	GP	G	A	Pts	AG	AA	APts	PIM	PP	SH	GW	S	%	TGF	PGF	TGA	PGA	+/–	GP	G	A	Pts	PIM	PP	SH	GW
1986-87	Bellows Free Academy	H.S.	23	44	40	84	....	....	....	14	....	....	....	....	....	....	....	....	....	....	....	....	....	....	....	....	....	....
1987-88	University of Vermont	ECAC	31	12	22	34	....	....	....	62	....	....	....	....	....	....	....	....	....	....	....	....	....	....	....	....	....	....
	United States	WJC-A	7	4	2	6	....	....	....	12	....	....	....	....	....	....	....	....	....	....	....	....	....	....	....	....	....	....
1988-89	University of Vermont	ECAC	18	9	12	21	....	....	....	40	....	....	....	....	....	....	....	....	....	....	....	....	....	....	....	....	....	....
	United States	WJC-A	7	6	4	10	....	....	....	12	....	....	....	....	....	....	....	....	....	....	....	....	....	....	....	....	....	....
1989-90	University of Vermont	ECAC	10	10	6	16	....	....	....	38	....	....	....	....	....	....	....	....	....	....	....	....	....	....	....	....	....	....
1990-91	University of Vermont	ECAC	33	25	20	45	....	....	....	58	....	....	....	....	....	....	....	....	....	....	....	....	....	....	....	....	....	....
	Montreal Canadiens	**NHL**	**10**	**2**	**5**	**7**	**2**	**4**	**6**	**2**	**0**	**0**	**1**	**12**	**16.7**	**8**	**0**	**7**	**0**	**+1**	**3**	**0**	**0**	**0**	**0**	**0**	**0**	**0**
1991-92	**Montreal Canadiens**	**NHL**	**59**	**8**	**11**	**19**	**7**	**8**	**15**	**14**	**3**	**0**	**0**	**73**	**11.0**	**26**	**4**	**17**	**0**	**+5**	**8**	**1**	**1**	**2**	**4**	**0**	**0**	**0**
	Fredericton Canadiens	AHL	8	7	7	14	....	....	....	10	....	....	....	....	....	....	....	....	....	....	2	0	0	0	4	....	....	....
1992-93	**Montreal Canadiens**	**NHL**	**72**	**19**	**25**	**44**	**16**	**17**	**33**	**33**	**2**	**0**	**2**	**139**	**13.7**	**61**	**6**	**45**	**1**	**+11**	**20**	**4**	**6**	**10**	**14**	**0**	**0**	**3**
1993-94	**Montreal Canadiens**	**NHL**	**74**	**19**	**24**	**43**	**18**	**19**	**37**	**32**	**1**	**0**	**1**	**153**	**12.4**	**63**	**9**	**37**	**0**	**+17**	**7**	**2**	**1**	**3**	**8**	**1**	**0**	**0**
1994-95	**Montreal Canadiens**	**NHL**	**9**	**1**	**4**	**5**	**2**	**6**	**8**	**10**	**1**	**0**	**0**	**18**	**5.6**	**8**	**3**	**8**	**2**	**–1**	....	....	....	....	....	....	....	....
	Philadelphia Flyers	**NHL**	**37**	**25**	**24**	**49**	**44**	**35**	**79**	**20**	**5**	**0**	**7**	**113**	**22.1**	**72**	**22**	**29**	**0**	**+21**	**15**	**5**	**7**	**12**	**4**	**1**	**0**	**1**
1995-96	**Philadelphia Flyers**	**NHL**	**82**	**51**	**46**	**97**	**50**	**38**	**88**	**64**	**19**	**0**	**10**	**270**	**18.9**	**141**	**57**	**63**	**0**	**+21**	**11**	**6**	**5**	**11**	**6**	**4**	**0**	**1**
1996-97	United States	W Cup	7	6	4	10	....	....	....	6	....	....	....	....	....	....	....	....	....	....	....	....	....	....	....	....	....	....
	Philadelphia Flyers	**NHL**	**82**	**50**	**47**	**97**	**53**	**42**	**95**	**58**	**10**	**0**	**5**	**324**	**15.4**	**153**	**43**	**66**	**0**	**+44**	**19**	**9**	**12**	**21**	**10**	**4**	**0**	**3**
1997-98	**Philadelphia Flyers**	**NHL**	**82**	**51**	**36**	**87**	**60**	**35**	**95**	**32**	**16**	**0**	**9**	**303**	**16.8**	**124**	**45**	**49**	**0**	**+30**	**5**	**1**	**1**	**2**	**8**	**1**	**0**	**1**
	United States	Olympics	4	0	1	1	....	....	....	0	....	....	....	....	....	....	....	....	....	....	....	....	....	....	....	....	....	....
	NHL Totals		**507**	**226**	**222**	**448**	**252**	**204**	**456**	**265**	**57**	**0**	**35**	**1405**	**16.1**	**656**	**189**	**321**	**3**		**88**	**28**	**33**	**61**	**54**	**11**	**0**	**9**

ECAC Second All-Star Team (1991) • NHL First All-Star Team (1995, 1998) • NHL Second All-Star Team (1996, 1997) • World Cup All-Star Team (1996) • Won Bud Ice Plus/Minus Award (1997)

Played in NHL All-Star Game (1996, 1997, 1998)

Traded to **Philadelphia** by **Montreal** with Eric Desjardins and Gilbert Dionne for Mark Recchi and Philadelphia's 3rd round choice (Martin Hohenberger) in 1995 Entry Draft, February 9, 1995.

• LECLERC, MIKE

Mike Leclerc LW – L. 6'1", 205 lbs. b: Winnipeg, Man., 11/10/1976. Anaheim's 3rd choice, 55th overall, in 1995 Entry Draft.

Season	Club	League	GP	G	A	Pts	AG	AA	APts	PIM	PP	SH	GW	S	%	TGF	PGF	TGA	PGA	+/–	GP	G	A	Pts	PIM	PP	SH	GW
1992-93	Victoria Cougars	WHL	70	4	11	15	....	....	....	118	....	....	....	....	....	....	....	....	....	....	....	....	....	....	....	....	....	....
1993-94	Victoria Cougars	WHL	68	29	11	40	....	....	....	112	....	....	....	....	....	....	....	....	....	....	....	....	....	....	....	....	....	....
1994-95	Prince George Cougars	WHL	43	20	36	56	....	....	....	78	....	....	....	....	....	....	....	....	....	....	....	....	....	....	....	....	....	....
	Brandon Wheat Kings	WHL	23	5	8	13	....	....	....	50	....	....	....	....	....	....	....	....	....	....	18	10	6	16	33	....	....	....
1995-96	Brandon Wheat Kings	WHL	71	58	53	111	....	....	....	161	....	....	....	....	....	....	....	....	....	....	19	6	19	25	25	....	....	....
1996-97	**Anaheim Mighty Ducks**	**NHL**	**5**	**1**	**1**	**2**	**1**	**1**	**2**	**0**	**0**	**0**	**1**	**3**	**33.3**	**2**	**0**	**0**	**0**	**+2**	**1**	**0**	**0**	**0**	**0**	**0**	**0**	**0**
	Baltimore Bandits	AHL	71	29	27	56	....	....	....	134	....	....	....	....	....	....	....	....	....	....	....	....	....	....	....	....	....	....
1997-98	**Anaheim Mighty Ducks**	**NHL**	**7**	**0**	**0**	**0**	**0**	**0**	**0**	**6**	**0**	**0**	**0**	**11**	**0.0**	**0**	**0**	**6**	**0**	**–6**	....	....	....	....	....	....	....	....
	Cincinnati Mighty Ducks	AHL	48	18	22	40	....	....	....	83	....	....	....	....	....	....	....	....	....	....	....	....	....	....	....	....	....	....
	NHL Totals		**12**	**1**	**1**	**2**	**1**	**1**	**2**	**6**	**0**	**0**	**1**	**14**	**7.1**	**2**	**0**	**6**	**0**		**1**	**0**	**0**	**0**	**0**	**0**	**0**	**0**

WHL East Second All-Star Team (1996)

• LECLERC, RENE

Rene (Renald) Leclerc RW – R. 5'11", 165 lbs. b: Ville de Vanier, Quebec, 11/12/1947. Detroit's 4th choice, 19th overall, in 1964 Amateur Draft.

Season	Club	League	GP	G	A	Pts	AG	AA	APts	PIM	PP	SH	GW	S	%	TGF	PGF	TGA	PGA	+/–	GP	G	A	Pts	PIM	PP	SH	GW
1963-64	Hamilton Red Wings	OHA	3	0	0	0	....	....	....	0	....	....	....	....	....	....	....	....	....	....	....	....	....	....	....	....	....	....
1964-65	Hamilton Red Wings	OHA	5	0	0	0	....	....	....	8	....	....	....	....	....	....	....	....	....	....	....	....	....	....	....	....	....	....
1965-66	Hamilton Red Wings	OHA	21	4	5	9	....	....	....	34	....	....	....	....	....	....	....	....	....	....	....	....	....	....	....	....	....	....
1966-67	Hamilton Red Wings	OHA	48	17	27	44	....	....	....	89	....	....	....	....	....	....	....	....	....	....	17	10	12	22	43	....	....	....
1967-68	Hamilton Red Wings	OHA	54	31	42	73	....	....	....	119	....	....	....	....	....	....	....	....	....	....	11	10	5	15	19	....	....	....
	Fort Worth Wings	CHL	....	....	....	....	....	....	....	....	....	....	....	....	....	....	....	....	....	....	6	1	1	2	2	....	....	....
1968-69	**Detroit Red Wings**	**NHL**	**43**	**2**	**3**	**5**	**2**	**3**	**5**	**62**	**0**	**0**	**0**	**38**	**5.3**	**6**	**0**	**14**	**0**	**–8**	....	....	....	....	....	....	....	....
	Fort Worth Wings	CHL	22	4	5	9	....	....	....	32	....	....	....	....	....	....	....	....	....	....	....	....	....	....	....	....	....	....
1969-70	Fort Worth Wings	CHL	9	1	2	3	....	....	....	27	....	....	....	....	....	....	....	....	....	....	....	....	....	....	....	....	....	....
	Cleveland Barons	AHL	61	16	20	36	....	....	....	108	....	....	....	....	....	....	....	....	....	....	....	....	....	....	....	....	....	....

			REGULAR SEASON																		PLAYOFFS							
Season	Club	League	GP	G	A	Pts	AG	AA	APts	PIM	PP	SH	GW	S	%	TGF	PGF	TGA	PGA	+/-	GP	G	A	Pts	PIM	PP	SH	GW
1970-71	**Detroit Red Wings**	**NHL**	**44**	**8**	**8**	**16**	**8**	**7**	**15**	**43**	**3**	**0**	**1**	**56**	**14.3**	**19**	**4**	**27**	**9**	**–3**								
	Fort Worth Wings	CHL	23	8	14	22				28																		
1971-72	Fort Worth Wings	CHL	2	0	0	0				0																		
	San Diego Gulls	WHL	28	6	7	13				39																		
	Tidewater Wings	AHL	31	6	6	12				57																		
1972-73	Quebec Nordiques	WHA	67	24	28	52				111																		
1973-74	Quebec Nordiques	WHA	53	17	27	44				84																		
1974-75	Quebec Nordiques	WHA	73	18	32	50				85																		
1975-76	Quebec Nordiques	WHA	42	15	17	32				35											14	7	7	14	41			
	Indianapolis Racers	WHA	40	18	21	39				52											7	2	3	5	7			
1976-77	Indianapolis Racers	WHA	68	25	30	55				43											9	1	1	2	4			
1977-78	Indianapolis Racers	WHA	60	12	15	27				31																		
1978-79	Indianapolis Racers	WHA	22	5	7	12				12																		
	Quebec Nordiques	WHA	23	0	0	0				8											4	0	0	0	0			
	NHL Totals		**87**	**10**	**11**	**21**	**10**	**10**	**20**	**105**	**3**	**0**	**1**	**94**	**10.6**	**25**	**4**	**41**	**9**									
	Other Major League Totals		448	134	177	311				461											34	10	11	21	52			

Selected by **Quebec** (WHA) in 1972 WHA General Player Draft, February 12, 1972. Traded to **Indianapolis** (WHA) by **Quebec** (WHA) for Bill Prentice, January, 1976. Signed as a free agent by **Quebec** (WHA) after **Indianapolis** (WHA) franchise folded, December 18, 1978.

• LECUYER, DOUG

Doug Lecuyer LW – L. 5'9", 180 lbs. b: Wainwright, Alta., 3/10/1958. Chicago's 2nd choice, 29th overall, in 1978 Amateur Draft.

1973-74	Edmonton Oil Kings	WCJHL	54	15	22	37				130											5	1	1	2	16			
1974-75	Edmonton Oil Kings	WCJHL	67	33	39	72				284																		
1975-76	Edmonton Oil Kings	WCJHL	61	40	32	72				335											5	2	2	4	52			
1976-77	Portland Wheat Kings	WCJHL	5	6	4	10				10																		
	Calgary Centennials	WCJHL	50	40	42	82				216																		
1977-78	Portland Winter Hawks	WCJHL	65	43	46	89				342																		
1978-79	**Chicago Black Hawks**	**NHL**	**2**	**1**	**0**	**1**	**1**	**0**	**1**	**0**	**0**	**0**	**0**	**9**	**11.1**	**1**	**0**	**2**	**0**	**–1**								
	New Brunswick Hawks	AHL	43	18	29	47				125																		
1979-80	**Chicago Black Hawks**	**NHL**	**53**	**3**	**10**	**13**	**3**	**8**	**11**	**59**	**0**	**0**	**1**	**75**	**4.0**	**25**	**2**	**30**	**0**	**–7**	**7**	**4**	**0**	**4**	**15**	**0**	**0**	**1**
	New Brunswick Hawks	AHL	5	4	3	7				12																		
	Dallas Black Hawks	CHL	5	1	0	1				2																		
1980-81	**Chicago Black Hawks**	**NHL**	**14**	**0**	**0**	**0**	**0**	**0**	**0**	**41**	**0**	**0**	**0**	**10**	**0.0**	**3**	**0**	**7**	**2**	**–2**								
	Winnipeg Jets	**NHL**	**45**	**6**	**17**	**23**	**5**	**12**	**17**	**66**	**0**	**0**	**1**	**61**	**9.8**	**34**	**1**	**74**	**14**	**–27**								
1981-82	Tulsa Oilers	CHL	69	30	38	68				114											3	0	1	1	8			
1982-83	**Pittsburgh Penguins**	**NHL**	**12**	**1**	**4**	**5**	**1**	**3**	**4**	**12**	**0**	**0**	**1**	**8**	**12.5**	**8**	**2**	**8**	**0**	**–2**								
	Baltimore Skipjacks	AHL	63	17	33	50				56																		
	NHL Totals		**126**	**11**	**31**	**42**	**10**	**23**	**33**	**178**	**0**	**0**	**3**	**163**	**6.7**	**71**	**5**	**121**	**16**		**7**	**4**	**0**	**4**	**15**	**0**	**0**	**1**

Traded to **Winnipeg** by **Chicago** with Tim Trimper for Peter Marsh, December 1, 1980. Claimed by **Pittsburgh** from **Winnipeg** in Waiver Draft, October 4, 1982.

• LEDINGHAM, WALT

Walt Ledingham LW – L. 5'11", 180 lbs. b: Weyburn, Sask., 10/26/1950. Chicago's 4th choice, 56th overall, in 1970 Amateur Draft.

1967-68	Weyburn Red Wings	WCJHL	60	22	28	50				30																		
1968-69	University of Minnesota	WCHA	DID NOT PLAY – FRESHMAN																									
1969-70	University of Minnesota	WCHA	27	16	11	27				4																		
1970-71	University of Minnesota	WCHA	33	26	28	54				38																		
1971-72	University of Minnesota	WCHA	35	24	29	53				18																		
1972-73	**Chicago Black Hawks**	**NHL**	**9**	**0**	**1**	**1**	**0**	**1**	**1**	**4**	**0**	**0**	**0**	**7**	**0.0**	**1**	**0**	**1**	**0**	**0**								
	Dallas Black Hawks	CHL	62	22	31	53				55											7	4	3	7	4			
1973-74	Dallas Black Hawks	CHL	59	13	22	35				17											10	5	6	*11	4			
1974-75	**New York Islanders**	**NHL**	**2**	**0**	**1**	**1**	**0**	**1**	**1**	**0**	**0**	**0**	**0**	**2**	**0.0**	**1**	**0**	**4**	**0**	**3**								
	New Haven Nighthawks	AHL	76	30	36	66				44											16	4	10	14	4			
1975-76	Fort Worth Texans	CHL	55	13	19	32				20																		
1976-77	**New York Islanders**	**NHL**	**4**	**0**	**0**	**0**	**0**	**0**	**0**	**0**	**0**	**0**	**0**	**5**	**0.0**	**0**	**0**	**1**	**0**	**–1**								
	Rhode Island Reds	AHL	73	29	57	86				20																		
	NHL Totals		**15**	**0**	**2**	**2**	**0**	**2**	**2**	**4**	**0**	**0**	**0**	**14**	**0.0**	**2**	**0**	**6**	**0**									

WCHA First All-Star Team (1971) • NCAA West First All-American Team (1971, 1972) • WCHA Second All-Star Team (1972) • AHL First All-Star Team (1977)

Traded to **NY Islanders** by **Chicago** to complete transaction that sent Germain Gagnon to Chicago (March 7, 1974), May 24, 1974.

• LEDUC, RICH

Rich LeDuc C – L. 5'11", 170 lbs. b: Ile Perrot, Que., 8/24/1951. California's 2nd choice, 29th overall, in 1971 Amateur Draft.

1969-70	Trois-Rivieres Ducs	QJHL	55	61	90	151				253																		
1970-71	Trois-Rivieres Ducs	QMJHL	59	56	76	132				195											11	9	10	19	59			
1971-72	Cleveland Barons	AHL	14	1	4	5				27																		
	Boston Braves	AHL	61	26	27	53				92											9	3	3	6	34			
1972-73	**Boston Bruins**	**NHL**	**5**	**1**	**1**	**2**	**1**	**1**	**2**	**2**	**0**	**0**	**0**	**12**	**8.3**	**3**	**0**	**4**	**0**	**–1**								
	Boston Braves	AHL	65	31	42	73				75											10	9	5	14	4			
1973-74	**Boston Bruins**	**NHL**	**28**	**3**	**3**	**6**	**3**	**3**	**6**	**12**	**0**	**0**	**0**	**23**	**13.0**	**8**	**0**	**5**	**0**	**+3**	**5**	**0**	**0**	**0**	**9**	**0**	**0**	**0**
	Boston Braves	AHL	29	7	11	18				60																		
1974-75	Cleveland Crusaders	WHA	78	34	31	65				122											5	0	2	2	2			
1975-76	Cleveland Crusaders	WHA	79	36	22	58				76											3	2	1	3	2			
1976-77	Cincinnati Stingers	WHA	81	52	55	107				75											4	1	3	4	16			
1977-78	Cincinnati Stingers	WHA	54	27	31	58				44											4	1	3	4	16			
	Indianapolis Racers	WHA	28	10	15	25				38																		
1978-79	Indianapolis Racers	WHA	13	5	9	14				14																		
	Quebec Nordiques	WHA	61	30	32	62				30											4	0	2	2	0			
1979-80	**Quebec Nordiques**	**NHL**	**75**	**21**	**27**	**48**	**19**	**21**	**40**	**49**	**9**	**1**	**1**	**145**	**14.5**	**68**	**22**	**98**	**17**	**–35**								
1980-81	**Quebec Nordiques**	**NHL**	**22**	**3**	**7**	**10**	**2**	**5**	**7**	**6**	**0**	**0**	**0**	**21**	**14.3**	**13**	**3**	**12**	**4**	**+2**								
	Rochester Americans	AHL	23	5	7	12				35																		
	Oklahoma City Stars	CHL	19	5	8	13				6											3	1	2	3	0			
	NHL Totals		**130**	**28**	**38**	**66**	**25**	**30**	**55**	**69**	**9**	**1**	**1**	**201**	**13.9**	**92**	**25**	**119**	**21**		**5**	**0**	**0**	**0**	**9**	**0**	**0**	**0**
	Other Major League Totals		313	142	140	282				324											16	3	8	11	20			

QJHL Second All-Star Team (1970) • QJHL First All-Star Team (1971)

Traded to **Boston** by **California** with Chris Oddleifson for Ivan Boldirev, November 17, 1971. Selected by **Cleveland** (WHA) in 1973 WHA Professional Player Draft, June, 1973. Traded to **Cincinnati** (WHA) by **Cleveland** (WHA) for cash, June, 1976. Traded to **Indianapolis** (WHA) by **Cincinnati** (WHA) with Claude Andre Larose for Darryl Maggs and Reg Thomas, February, 1978. Traded to **Quebec** (WHA) by **Indianapolis** (WHA) with Kevin Morrison for future considerations, November, 1978. Rights retained by **Quebec** prior to Expansion Draft, June 9, 1979. Signed as a free agent by **Minnesota**, February, 1981.

• LEDYARD, GRANT

Grant "Granville" Ledyard D – L. 6'2", 195 lbs. b: Winnipeg, Man., 11/19/1961.

1980-81	Saskatoon Blades	WHL	71	9	28	37				148																		
1981-82	Fort Garry Blues	MJHL	63	25	45	70				150																		
1982-83	Tulsa Oilers	CHL	80	13	29	42				116																		
1983-84	Tulsa Oilers	CHL	58	9	17	26				71											9	5	4	9	10			
1984-85	**New York Rangers**	**NHL**	**42**	**8**	**12**	**20**	**7**	**0**	**15**	**53**	**1**	**0**	**1**	**91**	**8.8**	**63**	**16**	**50**	**11**	**+8**	**3**	**0**	**2**	**2**	**4**	**0**	**0**	**0**
	New Haven Nighthawks	AHL	36	6	20	26				18																		
	Canada	WEC-A	3	0	1	1				0																		
1985-86	**New York Rangers**	**NHL**	**27**	**2**	**9**	**11**	**2**	**6**	**8**	**20**	**0**	**0**	**0**	**57**	**3.5**	**32**	**13**	**39**	**13**	**–7**								
	Los Angeles Kings	**NHL**	**52**	**7**	**18**	**25**	**6**	**12**	**18**	**78**	**4**	**0**	**2**	**113**	**6.2**	**66**	**21**	**87**	**20**	**–22**								
	Canada	WEC-A	10	0	2	2				10																		
1986-87	**Los Angeles Kings**	**NHL**	**67**	**14**	**23**	**37**	**12**	**17**	**29**	**93**	**5**	**0**	**1**	**144**	**9.7**	**88**	**38**	**120**	**30**	**–40**	**5**	**0**	**0**	**0**	**10**	**0**	**0**	**0**
1987-88	**Los Angeles Kings**	**NHL**	**23**	**1**	**7**	**8**	**1**	**5**	**6**	**52**	**1**	**0**	**0**	**40**	**2.5**	**16**	**7**	**17**	**1**	**–7**								
	New Haven Nighthawks	AHL	3	2	1	3				4																		
	Washington Capitals	**NHL**	**21**	**4**	**3**	**7**	**3**	**2**	**5**	**14**	**1**	**0**	**1**	**41**	**9.8**	**13**	**3**	**17**	**3**	**–4**	**14**	**1**	**0**	**1**	**30**	**0**	**0**	**0**

			REGULAR SEASON																		PLAYOFFS							
Season	Club	League	GP	G	A	Pts	AG	AA	APts	PIM	PP	SH	GW	S	%	TGF	PGF	TGA	PGA	+/–	GP	G	A	Pts	PIM	PP	SH	GW
1988-89	**Washington Capitals**	**NHL**	**61**	**3**	**11**	**14**	**3**	**8**	**11**	**43**	**1**	**0**	**1**	**81**	**3.7**	**49**	**16**	**37**	**5**	**+1**	....	....	....	....	....	....	....	....
	Buffalo Sabres	**NHL**	**13**	**1**	**5**	**6**	**1**	**4**	**5**	**8**	**0**	**0**	**1**	**25**	**4.0**	**13**	**2**	**11**	**1**	**+1**	**5**	**1**	**2**	**3**	**2**	**0**	**0**	**0**
1989-90	**Buffalo Sabres**	**NHL**	**67**	**2**	**13**	**15**	**2**	**9**	**11**	**37**	**0**	**0**	**1**	**91**	**2.2**	**65**	**14**	**53**	**4**	**+2**	....	....	....	....	....	....	....	....
1990-91	**Buffalo Sabres**	**NHL**	**60**	**8**	**23**	**31**	**7**	**17**	**24**	**46**	**2**	**1**	**1**	**118**	**6.8**	**87**	**24**	**65**	**15**	**+13**	**6**	**3**	**3**	**6**	**10**	**0**	**0**	**0**
1991-92	**Buffalo Sabres**	**NHL**	**50**	**5**	**16**	**21**	**5**	**12**	**17**	**45**	**0**	**0**	**0**	**87**	**5.7**	**54**	**10**	**72**	**24**	**–4**	....	....	....	....	....	....	....	....
1992-93	**Buffalo Sabres**	**NHL**	**50**	**2**	**14**	**16**	**2**	**10**	**12**	**45**	**1**	**0**	**0**	**79**	**2.5**	**53**	**4**	**62**	**11**	**–2**	**8**	**0**	**0**	**0**	**8**	**0**	**0**	**0**
	Rochester Americans	AHL	5	0	2	2	....	....	....	8	....	....	....	....	....	....	....	....	....	....	....	....	....	....	....	....	....	....
1993-94	**Dallas Stars**	**NHL**	**84**	**9**	**37**	**46**	**8**	**29**	**37**	**42**	**6**	**0**	**1**	**177**	**5.1**	**137**	**56**	**100**	**26**	**+7**	**9**	**1**	**2**	**3**	**6**	**0**	**0**	**1**
1994-95	**Dallas Stars**	**NHL**	**38**	**5**	**13**	**18**	**9**	**19**	**28**	**20**	**4**	**0**	**0**	**79**	**6.3**	**45**	**22**	**22**	**5**	**+6**	**3**	**0**	**0**	**0**	**2**	**0**	**0**	**0**
1995-96	**Dallas Stars**	**NHL**	**73**	**5**	**19**	**24**	**5**	**15**	**20**	**20**	**2**	**0**	**1**	**123**	**4.1**	**63**	**19**	**97**	**38**	**–15**	....	....	....	....	....	....	....	....
1996-97	**Dallas Stars**	**NHL**	**67**	**1**	**15**	**16**	**1**	**13**	**14**	**61**	**0**	**0**	**0**	**99**	**1.0**	**71**	**11**	**44**	**15**	**+31**	**7**	**0**	**2**	**2**	**0**	**0**	**0**	**0**
1997-98	**Vancouver Canucks**	**NHL**	**49**	**2**	**13**	**15**	**2**	**13**	**15**	**14**	**1**	**0**	**0**	**57**	**3.5**	**35**	**7**	**38**	**8**	**–2**	....	....	....	....	....	....	....	....
	Boston Bruins	**NHL**	**22**	**2**	**7**	**9**	**2**	**7**	**9**	**6**	**1**	**0**	**0**	**33**	**6.1**	**19**	**9**	**17**	**5**	**–2**	**6**	**0**	**0**	**0**	**2**	**0**	**0**	**0**
	NHL Totals		**866**	**81**	**258**	**339**	**78**	**206**	**284**	**697**	**30**	**1**	**11**	**1535**	**5.3**	**969**	**292**	**948**	**235**		**66**	**6**	**11**	**17**	**74**	**0**	**0**	**1**

Won Bob Gassoff Trophy (CHL's Most Improved Defenseman) (1984)

Signed as a free agent by **NY Rangers**, July 7, 1982. Traded to **LA Kings** by **NY Rangers** with Roland Melanson for LA Kings' 4th round choice (Mike Sullivan) in 1987 Entry Draft and Brian MacLellan, December 7, 1985. Traded to **Washington** by **LA Kings** for Craig Laughlin, February 9, 1988. Traded to **Buffalo** by **Washington** with Clint Malarchuk and Washington's 6th round choice (Brian Holzinger) in 1991 Entry Draft for Calle Johansson and Buffalo's 2nd round choice (Byron Dafoe) in 1989 Entry Draft, March 7, 1989. Signed as a free agent by **Dallas**, August 12, 1993. Signed as a free agent by **Vancouver**, July 17, 1997. Traded to **Boston** by **Vancouver** for Boston's 8th round choice (Curtis Valentine) in 1998 Entry Draft, March 3, 1998.

• LEE, EDWARD

Edward (Hubert) Lee RW – R. 6'2", 180 lbs. b: Rochester, NY, 12/17/1961. Quebec's 4th choice, 95th overall, in 1981 Entry Draft.

Season	Club	League	GP	G	A	Pts	AG	AA	APts	PIM	PP	SH	GW	S	%	TGF	PGF	TGA	PGA	+/–	GP	G	A	Pts	PIM	PP	SH	GW
1980-81	Princeton University	ECAC	21	6	8	14	....	....	....	34	....	....	....	....	....	....	....	....	....	....	....	....	....	....	....	....	....	....
1981-82	Princeton University	ECAC	26	12	21	33	....	....	....	46	....	....	....	....	....	....	....	....	....	....	....	....	....	....	....	....	....	....
1982-83	Princeton University	ECAC	25	19	25	44	....	....	....	51	....	....	....	....	....	....	....	....	....	....	....	....	....	....	....	....	....	....
	United States	Nat-Team	5	5	3	8	....	....	....	8	....	....	....	....	....	....	....	....	....	....	....	....	....	....	....	....	....	....
1983-84	Princeton University	ECAC	11	10	18	28	....	....	....	22	....	....	....	....	....	....	....	....	....	....	....	....	....	....	....	....	....	....
	Fredericton Express	AHL	6	0	4	4	....	....	....	4	....	....	....	....	....	....	....	....	....	....	....	....	....	....	....	....	....	....
1984-85	**Quebec Nordiques**	**NHL**	**2**	**0**	**0**	**0**	**0**	**0**	**0**	**5**	**0**	**0**	**0**	**2**	**0.0**	**0**	**0**	**4**	**0**	**–4**	....	....	....	....	....	....	....	....
	Fredericton Express	AHL	21	11	7	18	....	....	....	45	....	....	....	....	....	....	....	....	....	....	....	....	....	....	....	....	....	....
1985-86	Fredericton Express	AHL	6	3	1	4	....	....	....	2	....	....	....	....	....	....	....	....	....	....	....	....	....	....	....	....	....	....
	Springfield Indians	AHL	24	3	4	7	....	....	....	26	....	....	....	....	....	....	....	....	....	....	....	....	....	....	....	....	....	....
	Indianapolis Checkers	IHL	2	0	0	0	....	....	....	0	....	....	....	....	....	....	....	....	....	....	....	....	....	....	....	....	....	....
	NHL Totals		**2**	**0**	**0**	**0**	**0**	**0**	**0**	**5**	**0**	**0**	**0**	**2**	**0.0**	**0**	**0**	**4**	**0**		....	....	....	....	....	....	....	....

Traded to **Minnesota** by **Quebec** for Minnesota's 6th round choice (Scott White) in 1986 Entry Draft, November 15, 1985.

• LEE, PETER

Peter Lee RW – R. 5'9", 180 lbs. b: Ellesmere, England, 1/2/1956. Montreal's 6th choice, 12th overall, in 1976 Amateur Draft.

Season	Club	League	GP	G	A	Pts	AG	AA	APts	PIM	PP	SH	GW	S	%	TGF	PGF	TGA	PGA	+/–	GP	G	A	Pts	PIM	PP	SH	GW
1971-72	Ottawa 67's	OHA	12	1	0	1	....	....	....	0	....	....	....	....	....	....	....	....	....	....	....	....	....	....	....	....	....	....
1972-73	Ottawa 67's	OHA	63	25	51	76	....	....	....	110	....	....	....	....	....	....	....	....	....	....	....	....	....	....	....	....	....	....
1973-74	Ottawa 67's	OHA	69	38	42	80	....	....	....	40	....	....	....	....	....	....	....	....	....	....	....	....	....	....	....	....	....	....
1974-75	Ottawa 67's	OHA	70	*68	58	126	....	....	....	82	....	....	....	....	....	....	....	....	....	....	7	6	5	11	6	....	....	....
1975-76	Ottawa 67's	OHA	66	*81	80	161	....	....	....	59	....	....	....	....	....	....	....	....	....	....	11	7	11	18	15	....	....	....
1976-77	Nova Scotia Voyageurs	AHL	76	33	27	60	....	....	....	88	....	....	....	....	....	....	....	....	....	....	12	5	3	8	6	....	....	....
1977-78	Nova Scotia Voyageurs	AHL	23	8	11	19	....	....	....	25	....	....	....	....	....	....	....	....	....	....	....	....	....	....	....	....	....	....
	Pittsburgh Penguins	**NHL**	**60**	**5**	**13**	**18**	**5**	**11**	**16**	**19**	**1**	**0**	**1**	**89**	**5.6**	**32**	**9**	**34**	**0**	**–11**	....	....	....	....	....	....	....	....
1978-79	**Pittsburgh Penguins**	**NHL**	**80**	**32**	**26**	**58**	**29**	**20**	**49**	**24**	**10**	**0**	**7**	**219**	**14.6**	**85**	**24**	**75**	**1**	**–13**	**7**	**0**	**3**	**3**	**0**	**0**	**0**	**0**
1979-80	**Pittsburgh Penguins**	**NHL**	**74**	**16**	**29**	**45**	**14**	**22**	**36**	**20**	**4**	**0**	**2**	**161**	**9.9**	**64**	**19**	**58**	**0**	**–13**	**4**	**0**	**1**	**1**	**0**	**0**	**0**	**0**
1980-81	**Pittsburgh Penguins**	**NHL**	**80**	**30**	**34**	**64**	**25**	**24**	**49**	**86**	**4**	**1**	**4**	**196**	**15.3**	**86**	**17**	**101**	**32**	**0**	**5**	**0**	**4**	**4**	**4**	**0**	**0**	**0**
1981-82	**Pittsburgh Penguins**	**NHL**	**74**	**18**	**16**	**34**	**14**	**11**	**25**	**98**	**2**	**0**	**3**	**183**	**9.8**	**56**	**8**	**58**	**2**	**–8**	**3**	**0**	**0**	**0**	**0**	**0**	**0**	**0**
1982-83	**Pittsburgh Penguins**	**NHL**	**63**	**13**	**13**	**26**	**11**	**9**	**20**	**10**	**1**	**0**	**1**	**113**	**11.5**	**40**	**5**	**44**	**0**	**–9**	....	....	....	....	....	....	....	....
	Baltimore Skipjacks	AHL	14	11	6	17	....	....	....	12	....	....	....	....	....	....	....	....	....	....	....	....	....	....	....	....	....	....
1983-84	Dusseldorfer EG	Germany	46	25	24	49	....	....	....	56	....	....	....	....	....	....	....	....	....	....	....	....	....	....	....	....	....	....
1984-85	Dusseldorfer EG	Germany	33	29	34	63	....	....	....	55	....	....	....	....	....	....	....	....	....	....	4	3	0	3	24	....	....	....
1985-86	Dusseldorfer EG	Germany	41	47	49	96	....	....	....	58	....	....	....	....	....	....	....	....	....	....	....	....	....	....	....	....	....	....
1986-87	Dusseldorfer EG	Germany	43	40	35	75	....	....	....	77	....	....	....	....	....	....	....	....	....	....	8	7	9	16	....	....	....	....
1987-88	Dusseldorfer EG	Germany	44	35	36	71	....	....	....	42	....	....	....	....	....	....	....	....	....	....	....	....	....	....	....	....	....	....
1988-89	Dusseldorfer EG	Germany	36	31	34	65	....	....	....	46	....	....	....	....	....	....	....	....	....	....	11	*11	7	18	14	....	....	....
1989-90	Dusseldorfer EG	Germany	31	25	26	51	....	....	....	28	....	....	....	....	....	....	....	....	....	....	....	....	....	....	....	....	....	....
1990-91	Dusseldorfer EG	Germany	37	23	26	49	....	....	....	26	....	....	....	....	....	....	....	....	....	....	13	10	5	15	2	....	....	....
	NHL Totals		**431**	**114**	**131**	**245**	**98**	**97**	**195**	**257**	**22**	**1**	**18**	**961**	**11.9**	**363**	**82**	**370**	**35**		**19**	**0**	**8**	**8**	**4**	**0**	**0**	**0**

OHA Second All-Star Team (1975) • OHA First All-Star Team (1976) • Canadian Major Junior Player of the Year (1976)

Traded to **Pittsburgh** by **Montreal** with Pete Mahovlich for Pierre Larouche and future considerations (Peter Marsh, December 15, 1977), November 29, 1977.

• LEEMAN, GARY

Gary Leeman RW – R. 5'11", 175 lbs. b: Toronto, Ont., 2/19/1964. Toronto's 2nd choice, 24th overall, in 1982 Entry Draft.

Season	Club	League	GP	G	A	Pts	AG	AA	APts	PIM	PP	SH	GW	S	%	TGF	PGF	TGA	PGA	+/–	GP	G	A	Pts	PIM	PP	SH	GW
1981-82	Regina Pats	WHL	72	19	41	60	....	....	....	112	....	....	....	....	....	....	....	....	....	....	3	2	2	4	0	....	....	....
1982-83	Regina Pats	WHL	63	24	62	86	....	....	....	88	....	....	....	....	....	....	....	....	....	....	5	1	5	6	4	....	....	....
	Canada	WJC-A	7	1	2	3	....	....	....	2	....	....	....	....	....	....	....	....	....	....	....	....	....	....	....	....	....	....
	Toronto Maple Leafs	**NHL**	....	....	....	....	....	....	....	....	....	....	....	....	....	....	....	....	....	....	**2**	**0**	**0**	**0**	**0**	....	....	....
1983-84	**Toronto Maple Leafs**	**NHL**	**52**	**4**	**8**	**12**	**3**	**5**	**8**	**31**	**1**	**0**	**0**	**41**	**9.8**	**29**	**6**	**38**	**1**	**–14**	....	....	....	....	....	....	....	....
	Canada	WJC-A	7	3	6	9	....	....	....	12	....	....	....	....	....	....	....	....	....	....	....	....	....	....	....	....	....	....
1984-85	**Toronto Maple Leafs**	**NHL**	**53**	**5**	**26**	**31**	**4**	**18**	**22**	**72**	**3**	**0**	**0**	**88**	**5.7**	**50**	**23**	**47**	**8**	**–12**	....	....	....	....	....	....	....	....
	St. Catharines Saints	AHL	7	2	2	4	....	....	....	11	....	....	....	....	....	....	....	....	....	....	....	....	....	....	....	....	....	....
1985-86	**Toronto Maple Leafs**	**NHL**	**53**	**9**	**23**	**32**	**7**	**15**	**22**	**20**	**1**	**1**	**0**	**123**	**7.3**	**47**	**11**	**49**	**12**	**–1**	**10**	**2**	**10**	**12**	**2**	**0**	**0**	**0**
	St. Catharines Saints	AHL	25	15	13	28	....	....	....	6	....	....	....	....	....	....	....	....	....	....	....	....	....	....	....	....	....	....
1986-87	**Toronto Maple Leafs**	**NHL**	**80**	**21**	**31**	**52**	**18**	**22**	**40**	**66**	**4**	**3**	**2**	**196**	**10.7**	**99**	**37**	**107**	**19**	**–26**	**5**	**0**	**1**	**1**	**14**	**0**	**0**	**0**
1987-88	**Toronto Maple Leafs**	**NHL**	**80**	**30**	**31**	**61**	**26**	**22**	**48**	**62**	**6**	**0**	**0**	**234**	**12.8**	**101**	**27**	**103**	**23**	**–6**	**2**	**2**	**0**	**2**	**2**	**2**	**0**	**0**
1988-89	**Toronto Maple Leafs**	**NHL**	**61**	**32**	**43**	**75**	**27**	**30**	**57**	**66**	**7**	**1**	**3**	**195**	**16.4**	**98**	**34**	**74**	**15**	**+5**	....	....	....	....	....	....	....	....
1989-90	**Toronto Maple Leafs**	**NHL**	**80**	**51**	**44**	**95**	**44**	**31**	**75**	**63**	**14**	**1**	**5**	**256**	**19.9**	**144**	**45**	**109**	**14**	**+4**	**5**	**3**	**3**	**6**	**16**	**2**	**0**	**0**
1990-91	**Toronto Maple Leafs**	**NHL**	**52**	**17**	**12**	**29**	**16**	**9**	**25**	**39**	**4**	**0**	**1**	**135**	**12.6**	**48**	**19**	**60**	**6**	**–25**	....	....	....	....	....	....	....	....
1991-92	**Toronto Maple Leafs**	**NHL**	**34**	**7**	**13**	**20**	**6**	**10**	**16**	**44**	**3**	**0**	**0**	**91**	**7.7**	**38**	**17**	**25**	**3**	**–1**	....	....	....	....	....	....	....	....
	Calgary Flames	**NHL**	**29**	**2**	**7**	**9**	**2**	**5**	**7**	**27**	**1**	**0**	**0**	**50**	**4.0**	**19**	**9**	**22**	**1**	**–11**	....	....	....	....	....	....	....	....
1992-93	**Calgary Flames**	**NHL**	**30**	**9**	**5**	**14**	**7**	**3**	**10**	**10**	**0**	**0**	**2**	**49**	**18.4**	**26**	**6**	**15**	**0**	**+5**	....	....	....	....	....	....	....	....
	Montreal Canadiens	**NHL**	**20**	**6**	**12**	**18**	**5**	**8**	**13**	**14**	**1**	**0**	**1**	**36**	**16.7**	**28**	**10**	**10**	**1**	**+9**	**11**	**1**	**2**	**3**	**2**	**0**	**0**	**0**
1993-94	**Montreal Canadiens**	**NHL**	**31**	**4**	**11**	**15**	**4**	**8**	**12**	**17**	**0**	**0**	**0**	**53**	**7.5**	**21**	**8**	**10**	**2**	**+5**	**1**	**0**	**0**	**0**	**0**	**0**	**0**	**0**
	Fredericton Canadiens	AHL	23	18	8	26	....	....	....	16	....	....	....	....	....	....	....	....	....	....	....	....	....	....	....	....	....	....
1994-95	**Vancouver Canucks**	**NHL**	**10**	**2**	**0**	**2**	**4**	**0**	**4**	**0**	**0**	**0**	**1**	**14**	**14.3**	**4**	**0**	**7**	**0**	**–3**	....	....	....	....	....	....	....	....
1995-96	Gardena	Italy	20	7	12	19	....	....	....	59	....	....	....	....	....	....	....	....	....	....	7	2	4	6	12	....	....	....
1996-97	**St. Louis Blues**	**NHL**	**2**	**0**	**1**	**1**	**0**	**1**	**1**	**0**	**0**	**0**	**0**	**3**	**0.0**	**1**	**1**	**0**	**0**	**0**	....	....	....	....	....	....	....	....
	Worcester IceCats	AHL	24	9	7	16	....	....	....	41	....	....	....	....	....	....	....	....	....	....	....	....	....	....	....	....	....	....
	Utah Grizzlies	IHL	15	6	1	7	....	....	....	20	....	....	....	....	....	....	....	....	....	....	4	0	3	3	4	....	....	....
1997-98	Hannover Scorpions	Germany	44	13	38	51	....	....	....	16	....	....	....	....	....	....	....	....	....	....	4	2	0	2	12	....	....	....
	NHL Totals		**667**	**199**	**267**	**466**	**173**	**187**	**360**	**531**	**45**	**6**	**15**	**1564**	**12.7**	**753**	**253**	**676**	**105**		**36**	**8**	**16**	**24**	**36**	**4**	**0**	**0**

WHL First All-Star Team (1983)

Played in NHL All-Star Game (1989)

Traded to **Calgary** by **Toronto** with Craig Berube, Alexander Godynyuk, Michel Petit and Jeff Reese for Doug Gilmour, Jamie Macoun, Ric Nattress, Rick Wamsley and Kent Manderville, January 2, 1992. Traded to **Montreal** by **Calgary** for Brian Skrudland, January 28, 1993. Signed as a free agent by **Vancouver**, January 18, 1995. Signed as a free agent by **St. Louis**, September 26, 1996.

• LEETCH, BRIAN

Brian Leetch D – L. 5'11", 190 lbs. b: Corpus Christi, TX, 3/3/1968. NY Rangers' 1st choice, 9th overall, in 1986 Entry Draft.

			REGULAR SEASON																		PLAYOFFS							
Season	Club	League	GP	G	A	Pts	AG	AA	APts	PIM	PP	SH	GW	S	%	TGF	PGF	TGA	PGA	+/–	GP	G	A	Pts	PIM	PP	SH	GW
1984-85	Avon Old Farms	H.S.	26	30	46	76	....	....	....	15	....	....	....	....	....	....	....	....	....	....	....	....	....	....	....	....	....	....
	United States	WJC-A	7	0	0	0	....	....	....	2	....	....	....	....	....	....	....	....	....	....	....	....	....	....	....	....	....	....
1985-86	Avon Old Farms	H.S.	28	40	44	84	....	....	....	18	....	....	....	....	....	....	....	....	....	....	....	....	....	....	....	....	....	....
	United States	WJC-A	7	1	4	5	....	....	....	2	....	....	....	....	....	....	....	....	....	....	....	....	....	....	....	....	....	....
1986-87	Boston College	H.E.	37	9	38	47	....	....	....	10	....	....	....	....	....	....	....	....	....	....	....	....	....	....	....	....	....	....
	United States	WEC-A	10	4	5	9	....	....	....	4	....	....	....	....	....	....	....	....	....	....	....	....	....	....	....	....	....	....
	United States	WJC-A	7	1	2	3	....	....	....	8	....	....	....	....	....	....	....	....	....	....	....	....	....	....	....	....	....	....
1987-88	United States	Nat-Team	50	13	61	74	....	....	....	38	....	....	....	....	....	....	....	....	....	....	....	....	....	....	....	....	....	....
	United States	Olympics	6	1	5	6	....	....	....	4	....	....	....	....	....	....	....	....	....	....	....	....	....	....	....	....	....	....
	New York Rangers	**NHL**	**17**	**2**	**12**	**14**	**2**	**9**	**11**	**0**	**1**	**0**	**1**	**40**	**5.0**	**35**	**16**	**14**	**0**	**+5**	....	....	....	....	....	....	....	....
1988-89	**New York Rangers**	**NHL**	**68**	**23**	**48**	**71**	**20**	**34**	**54**	**50**	**8**	**3**	**1**	**268**	**8.6**	**155**	**62**	**110**	**25**	**+8**	**4**	**3**	**2**	**5**	**2**	**2**	**0**	**0**
	United States	WEC-A	10	3	4	7	....	....	....	4	....	....	....	....	....	....	....	....	....	....	....	....	....	....	....	....	....	....
1989-90	**New York Rangers**	**NHL**	**72**	**11**	**45**	**56**	**9**	**32**	**41**	**26**	**5**	**0**	**2**	**222**	**5.0**	**128**	**65**	**104**	**23**	**–18**	....	....	....	....	....	....	....	....
1990-91	**New York Rangers**	**NHL**	**80**	**16**	**72**	**88**	**15**	**55**	**70**	**42**	**6**	**0**	**4**	**206**	**7.8**	**178**	**87**	**116**	**27**	**+2**	**6**	**1**	**3**	**4**	**0**	**0**	**0**	**0**
1991-92	United States	C Cup	7	1	3	4	....	....	....	2	....	....	....	....	....	....	....	....	....	....	....	....	....	....	....	....	....	....
	New York Rangers	**NHL**	**80**	**22**	**80**	**102**	**20**	**60**	**80**	**26**	**10**	**1**	**3**	**245**	**9.0**	**193**	**79**	**114**	**25**	**+25**	**13**	**4**	**11**	**15**	**4**	**1**	**1**	**0**
1992-93	**New York Rangers**	**NHL**	**36**	**6**	**30**	**36**	**5**	**21**	**26**	**26**	**2**	**1**	**1**	**150**	**4.0**	**84**	**40**	**58**	**16**	**+2**	....	....	....	....	....	....	....	....
1993-94	**New York Rangers**	**NHL**	**84**	**23**	**56**	**79**	**21**	**43**	**64**	**67**	**17**	**1**	**4**	**328**	**7.0**	**187**	**86**	**118**	**45**	**+28**	**23**	**11**	***23**	***34**	**6**	**4**	**0**	**4**
1994-95	**New York Rangers**	**NHL**	**48**	**9**	**32**	**41**	**16**	**47**	**63**	**18**	**3**	**0**	**2**	**182**	**4.9**	**84**	**38**	**71**	**25**	**0**	**10**	**6**	**8**	**14**	**8**	**3**	**0**	**1**
1995-96	**New York Rangers**	**NHL**	**82**	**15**	**70**	**85**	**15**	**57**	**72**	**30**	**7**	**0**	**3**	**276**	**5.4**	**158**	**78**	**125**	**57**	**+12**	**11**	**1**	**6**	**7**	**4**	**1**	**0**	**0**
1996-97	United States	W Cup	7	0	7	7	....	....	....	4	....	....	....	....	....	....	....	....	....	....	....	....	....	....	....	....	....	....
	New York Rangers	**NHL**	**82**	**20**	**58**	**78**	**21**	**51**	**72**	**40**	**9**	**0**	**2**	**256**	**7.8**	**166**	**59**	**115**	**39**	**+31**	**15**	**2**	**8**	**10**	**6**	**1**	**0**	**1**
1997-98	**New York Rangers**	**NHL**	**76**	**17**	**33**	**50**	**20**	**32**	**52**	**32**	**11**	**0**	**2**	**230**	**7.4**	**117**	**58**	**120**	**25**	**–36**	....	....	....	....	....	....	....	....
	United States	Olympics	4	1	1	2	....	....	....	0	....	....	....	....	....	....	....	....	....	....	....	....	....	....	....	....	....	....
	NHL Totals		**725**	**164**	**536**	**700**	**164**	**441**	**605**	**357**	**79**	**6**	**25**	**2403**	**6.8**	**1485**	**668**	**1065**	**307**		**82**	**28**	**61**	**89**	**30**	**12**	**1**	**6**

WJC-A All-Star Team (1987) • Hockey East First All-Star Team (1987) • NCAA East First All-American Team (1987) • NHL All-Rookie Team (1989) • Won Calder Memorial Trophy (1989) • NHL Second All-Star Team (1991, 1994, 1996) • Won James Norris Memorial Trophy (1992, 1997) • NHL First All-Star Team (1992, 1997) • Won Conn Smythe Trophy (1994)

Played in NHL All-Star Game (1990, 1991, 1992, 1994, 1996, 1997, 1998)

• LEFEBVRE, SYLVAIN

Sylvain Lefebvre D – L. 6'2", 205 lbs. b: Richmond, Que., 10/14/1967.

Season	Club	League	GP	G	A	Pts	AG	AA	APts	PIM	PP	SH	GW	S	%	TGF	PGF	TGA	PGA	+/–	GP	G	A	Pts	PIM	PP	SH	GW
1984-85	Laval Titan	QMJHL	66	7	5	12	....	....	....	31	....	....	....	....	....	....	....	....	....	....	....	....	....	....	....	....	....	....
1985-86	Laval Titan	QMJHL	71	8	17	25	....	....	....	48	....	....	....	....	....	....	....	....	....	....	14	1	0	1	25	....	....	....
1986-87	Laval Titan	QMJHL	70	10	36	46	....	....	....	44	....	....	....	....	....	....	....	....	....	....	15	1	6	7	12	....	....	....
1987-88	Sherbrooke Canadiens	AHL	79	3	24	27	....	....	....	73	....	....	....	....	....	....	....	....	....	....	6	2	3	5	4	....	....	....
1988-89	Sherbrooke Canadiens	AHL	77	15	32	47	....	....	....	119	....	....	....	....	....	....	....	....	....	....	6	1	3	4	4	....	....	....
1989-90	**Montreal Canadiens**	**NHL**	**68**	**3**	**10**	**13**	**3**	**7**	**10**	**61**	**0**	**0**	**0**	**89**	**3.4**	**82**	**10**	**68**	**14**	**+18**	**6**	**0**	**0**	**0**	**2**	**0**	**0**	**0**
1990-91	Montreal Canadiens	FrTour	4	1	0	1	....	....	....	6	....	....	....	....	....	....	....	....	....	....	....	....	....	....	....	....	....	....
	Montreal Canadiens	**NHL**	**63**	**5**	**18**	**23**	**5**	**14**	**19**	**30**	**1**	**0**	**1**	**76**	**6.6**	**62**	**14**	**73**	**14**	**–11**	**11**	**1**	**0**	**1**	**6**	**0**	**0**	**0**
1991-92	**Montreal Canadiens**	**NHL**	**69**	**3**	**14**	**17**	**3**	**11**	**14**	**91**	**0**	**0**	**0**	**85**	**3.5**	**65**	**9**	**64**	**17**	**+9**	**2**	**0**	**0**	**0**	**2**	**0**	**0**	**0**
1992-93	**Toronto Maple Leafs**	**NHL**	**81**	**2**	**12**	**14**	**2**	**8**	**10**	**90**	**0**	**0**	**0**	**81**	**2.5**	**58**	**2**	**85**	**37**	**+8**	**21**	**3**	**3**	**6**	**20**	**0**	**0**	**0**
1993-94	**Toronto Maple Leafs**	**NHL**	**84**	**2**	**9**	**11**	**2**	**7**	**9**	**79**	**0**	**0**	**0**	**96**	**2.1**	**88**	**1**	**100**	**46**	**+33**	**18**	**0**	**3**	**3**	**16**	**0**	**0**	**0**
1994-95	**Quebec Nordiques**	**NHL**	**48**	**2**	**11**	**13**	**4**	**16**	**20**	**17**	**0**	**0**	**0**	**01**	**2.5**	**65**	**13**	**59**	**20**	**+13**	**6**	**0**	**2**	**2**	**2**	**0**	**0**	**0**
1995-96	**Colorado Avalanche**	**NHL**	**75**	**5**	**11**	**16**	**5**	**9**	**14**	**49**	**2**	**0**	**0**	**115**	**4.3**	**81**	**8**	**75**	**28**	**+26**	**22**	**0**	**5**	**5**	**12**	**0**	**0**	**0**
1996-97	**Colorado Avalanche**	**NHL**	**71**	**2**	**11**	**13**	**2**	**10**	**12**	**30**	**1**	**0**	**0**	**77**	**2.6**	**57**	**3**	**60**	**18**	**+12**	**17**	**0**	**0**	**0**	**25**	**0**	**0**	**0**
1997-98	**Colorado Avalanche**	**NHL**	**81**	**0**	**10**	**10**	**0**	**10**	**10**	**48**	**0**	**0**	**0**	**66**	**0.0**	**44**	**2**	**64**	**24**	**+2**	**7**	**0**	**0**	**0**	**4**	**0**	**0**	**0**
	NHL Totals		**640**	**24**	**106**	**130**	**26**	**92**	**118**	**495**	**4**	**0**	**1**	**766**	**3.1**	**602**	**62**	**648**	**218**		**110**	**4**	**13**	**17**	**89**	**0**	**0**	**0**

AHL Second All-Star Team (1989)

Signed as a free agent by **Montreal**, September 24, 1986. Traded to **Toronto** by **Montreal** for Toronto's 3rd round choice (Martin Belanger) in 1994 Entry Draft, August 20, 1992. Traded to **Quebec** by **Toronto** with Wendel Clark, Landon Wilson and Toronto's 1st round choice (Jeffrey Kealty) in 1994 Entry Draft for Mats Sundin, Garth Butcher, Todd Warriner and Philadelphia's 1st round choice (previously acquired by Quebec — later traded to Washington — Washington selected Nolan Baumgartner) in 1994 Entry Draft, June 28, 1994. Transferred to **Colorado** after **Quebec** franchise relocated, June 21, 1995.

• LEFLEY, BRYAN

Bryan Lefley D/LW – L. 6', 195 lbs. b: Grosse Isle, Man., 10/18/1948. d: 10/30/1997.

Season	Club	League	GP	G	A	Pts	AG	AA	APts	PIM	PP	SH	GW	S	%	TGF	PGF	TGA	PGA	+/–	GP	G	A	Pts	PIM	PP	SH	GW
1964-65	Winnipeg Rangers	MJHL	24	3	2	5	....	....	....	8	....	....	....	....	....	....	....	....	....	....	4	0	0	0	0	....	....	....
1965-66	Winnipeg Rangers	MJHL	14	1	1	2	....	....	....	10	....	....	....	....	....	....	....	....	....	....	9	0	2	2	12	....	....	....
1966-67	Warren Intermediates	Inter-Sr.	STATISTICS NOT AVAILABLE																									
1967-68	Winnipeg Rangers	MJHL	STATISTICS NOT AVAILABLE																									
1968-69	Nelson Maple Leafs	WIHL	STATISTICS NOT AVAILABLE																									
1969-70	Omaha Knights	CHL	63	7	9	16	....	....	....	42	....	....	....	....	....	....	....	....	....	....	12	7	3	10	9	....	....	....
1970-71	Omaha Knights	CHL	67	8	25	33	....	....	....	111	....	....	....	....	....	....	....	....	....	....	10	0	3	3	2	....	....	....
1971-72	Omaha Knights	CHL	71	10	20	30	....	....	....	109	....	....	....	....	....	....	....	....	....	....	....	....	....	....	....	....	....	....
1972-73	**New York Islanders**	**NHL**	**63**	**3**	**7**	**10**	**3**	**6**	**9**	**56**	**0**	**0**	**0**	**39**	**7.7**	**31**	**3**	**78**	**11**	**–39**	....	....	....	....	....	....	....	....
1973-74	**New York Islanders**	**NHL**	**7**	**0**	**0**	**0**	**0**	**0**	**0**	**0**	**0**	**0**	**0**	**1**	**0.0**	**1**	**0**	**1**	**0**	**0**	....	....	....	....	....	....	....	....
	Fort Worth Wings	CHL	58	8	36	44	....	....	....	88	....	....	....	....	....	....	....	....	....	....	5	0	1	1	6	....	....	....
1974-75	**Kansas City Scouts**	**NHL**	**29**	**0**	**3**	**3**	**0**	**2**	**2**	**6**	**0**	**0**	**0**	**12**	**0.0**	**13**	**0**	**43**	**7**	**–23**	....	....	....	....	....	....	....	....
	Baltimore Clippers	AHL	9	3	0	3	....	....	....	10	....	....	....	....	....	....	....	....	....	....	....	....	....	....	....	....	....	....
	Providence Reds	AHL	29	3	10	13	....	....	....	32	....	....	....	....	....	....	....	....	....	....	1	0	0	0	2	....	....	....
1975-76	Springfield Indians	AHL	71	4	25	29	....	....	....	48	....	....	....	....	....	....	....	....	....	....	....	....	....	....	....	....	....	....
1976-77	**Colorado Rockies**	**NHL**	**58**	**0**	**6**	**6**	**0**	**5**	**5**	**27**	**0**	**0**	**0**	**40**	**0.0**	**39**	**5**	**68**	**19**	**–15**	....	....	....	....	....	....	....	....
1977-78	**Colorado Rockies**	**NHL**	**71**	**4**	**13**	**17**	**4**	**11**	**15**	**12**	**0**	**1**	**1**	**65**	**6.2**	**34**	**4**	**50**	**18**	**–4**	**2**	**0**	**0**	**0**	**0**	**0**	**0**	**0**
1978-79	Dusseldorfer EG	Germany	51	13	25	30	....	....	....	44	....	....	....	....	....	....	....	....	....	....	....	....	....	....	....	....	....	....
1979-80	Dusseldorfer EG	Germany	45	13	23	36	....	....	....	36	....	....	....	....	....	....	....	....	....	....	....	....	....	....	....	....	....	....
1980-81	Dusseldorfer EG	Germany	2	0	1	1	....	....	....	0	....	....	....	....	....	....	....	....	....	....	....	....	....	....	....	....	....	....
	NHL Totals		**228**	**7**	**29**	**36**	**7**	**24**	**31**	**101**	**0**	**1**	**1**	**157**	**4.5**	**118**	**12**	**240**	**53**		**2**	**0**	**0**	**0**	**0**	**0**	**0**	**0**

CHL First All-Star Team (1974)

Claimed by **NY Islanders** from **NY Rangers** in Expansion Draft, June 6, 1972. Claimed by **Kansas City** from **NY Islanders** in Expansion Draft, June 12, 1974. Transferred to **Colorado** after **Kansas City** franchise relocated, July 15, 1976.

• LEFLEY, CHUCK

Chuck Lefley LW – L. 6'2", 185 lbs. b: Winnipeg, Man., 1/20/1950. Montreal's 2nd choice, 6th overall, in 1970 Amateur Draft.

Season	Club	League	GP	G	A	Pts	AG	AA	APts	PIM	PP	SH	GW	S	%	TGF	PGF	TGA	PGA	+/–	GP	G	A	Pts	PIM	PP	SH	GW
1965-66	Winnipeg Rangers	MJHL	46	19	20	39	....	....	....	10	....	....	....	....	....	....	....	....	....	....	9	4	5	9	2	....	....	....
1966-67	Winnipeg Rangers	MJHL	STATISTICS NOT AVAILABLE																									
1967-68	Canada	Nat-Team	STATISTICS NOT AVAILABLE																									
1968-69	Canada	Nat-Team	STATISTICS NOT AVAILABLE																									
	Canada	WEC-A	7	0	1	1	....	....	....	10	....	....	....	....	....	....	....	....	....	....	....	....	....	....	....	....	....	....
1969-70	Canada	Nat-Team	STATISTICS NOT AVAILABLE																									
	Brandon Wheat Kings	WCJHL	7	6	6	12	....	....	....	0	....	....	....	....	....	....	....	....	....	....	....	....	....	....	....	....	....	....
1970-71	**Montreal Canadiens**	**NHL**	**1**	**0**	**0**	**0**	**0**	**0**	**0**	**0**	**0**	**0**	**0**	**1**	**0.0**	**0**	**0**	**1**	**0**	**–1**	**1**	**0**	**0**	**0**	**0**	**0**	**0**	**0**
	Montreal Voyageurs	AHL	48	16	19	35	....	....	....	53	....	....	....	....	....	....	....	....	....	....	3	1	1	2	2	....	....	....
1971-72	**Montreal Canadiens**	**NHL**	**16**	**0**	**2**	**2**	**0**	**2**	**2**	**0**	**0**	**0**	**0**	**7**	**0.0**	**3**	**0**	**4**	**0**	**–1**	....	....	....	....	....	....	....	....
	Nova Scotia Voyageurs	AHL	45	15	30	45	....	....	....	18	....	....	....	....	....	....	....	....	....	....	15	7	7	14	0	....	....	....
1972-73	**Montreal Canadiens**	**NHL**	**65**	**21**	**25**	**46**	**21**	**21**	**42**	**22**	**1**	**1**	**7**	**99**	**21.2**	**73**	**3**	**35**	**0**	**+35**	**17**	**3**	**5**	**8**	**6**	**0**	**0**	**0**
1973-74	**Montreal Canadiens**	**NHL**	**74**	**23**	**31**	**54**	**23**	**27**	**50**	**34**	**1**	**2**	**2**	**150**	**15.3**	**80**	**11**	**80**	**20**	**+9**	**6**	**0**	**1**	**1**	**0**	**0**	**0**	**0**
1974-75	**Montreal Canadiens**	**NHL**	**18**	**1**	**2**	**3**	**1**	**2**	**3**	**4**	**0**	**0**	**0**	**29**	**3.4**	**10**	**2**	**10**	**2**	**0**	....	....	....	....	....	....	....	....
	St. Louis Blues	**NHL**	**57**	**23**	**26**	**49**	**21**	**20**	**41**	**24**	**5**	**2**	**3**	**151**	**15.2**	**76**	**19**	**65**	**14**	**+6**	**2**	**0**	**0**	**0**	**2**	**0**	**0**	**0**
1975-76	**St. Louis Blues**	**NHL**	**75**	**43**	**42**	**85**	**40**	**33**	**73**	**41**	**4**	**8**	**9**	**207**	**20.8**	**112**	**36**	**99**	**38**	**+15**	**2**	**2**	**1**	**3**	**0**	**0**	**1**	**0**
1976-77	**St. Louis Blues**	**NHL**	**71**	**11**	**30**	**41**	**11**	**24**	**35**	**12**	**3**	**0**	**1**	**156**	**7.1**	**64**	**21**	**60**	**2**	**–15**	**1**	**0**	**1**	**1**	**2**	**0**	**0**	**0**
1977-78	Jokerit Helsinki	Finland	24	11	12	23	....	....	....	12	....	....	....	....	....	....	....	....	....	....	....	....	....	....	....	....	....	....

			REGULAR SEASON																		PLAYOFFS							
Season	**Club**	**League**	**GP**	**G**	**A**	**Pts**	**AG**	**AA**	**APts**	**PIM**	**PP**	**SH**	**GW**	**S**	**%**	**TGF**	**PGF**	**TGA**	**PGA**	**+/–**	**GP**	**G**	**A**	**Pts**	**PIM**	**PP**	**SH**	**GW**
1978-79	Dusseldorfer EG	Germany	26	17	5	22	....	....	....	2	....	....	....	....	....	....	....	....	....	....	....	....	....	....	....	....	....	....
1979-80	**St. Louis Blues**	**NHL**	**28**	**6**	**6**	**12**	**5**	**5**	**10**	**0**	**0**	**0**	**0**	**37**	**16.2**	**21**	**3**	**15**	**2**	**+5**	....	....	....	....	....	....	....	....
1980-81	**St. Louis Blues**	**NHL**	**2**	**0**	**0**	**0**	**0**	**0**	**0**	**0**	**0**	**0**	**0**	**1**	**0.0**	**0**	**0**	**0**	**0**	**0**	....	....	....	....	....	....	....	....
	NHL Totals		**407**	**128**	**164**	**292**	**122**	**134**	**256**	**137**	**14**	**13**	**22**	**838**	**15.3**	**439**	**95**	**369**	**78**		**29**	**5**	**8**	**13**	**10**	**0**	**1**	**0**

Traded to **St. Louis** by **Montreal** for Don Awrey, November 28, 1974.

● LEGGE, BARRY

Barry Legge D – L. 6′, 186 lbs. b: Winnipeg, Man., 10/22/1954. Montreal's 3rd choice, 61st overall, in 1974 Amateur Draft.

			REGULAR SEASON																		PLAYOFFS							
Season	**Club**	**League**	**GP**	**G**	**A**	**Pts**	**AG**	**AA**	**APts**	**PIM**	**PP**	**SH**	**GW**	**S**	**%**	**TGF**	**PGF**	**TGA**	**PGA**	**+/–**	**GP**	**G**	**A**	**Pts**	**PIM**	**PP**	**SH**	**GW**
1970-71	St. James Canadians	MJHL	47	7	22	29	....	....	....	98	....	....	....	....	....	....	....	....	....	....	....	....	....	....	....	....	....	....
1971-72	Winnipeg Jets	WCJHL	61	1	16	17	....	....	....	138	....	....	....	....	....	....	....	....	....	....	....	....	....	....	....	....	....	....
1972-73	Winnipeg Jets	WCJHL	63	10	43	53	....	....	....	161	....	....	....	....	....	....	....	....	....	....	....	....	....	....	....	....	....	....
1973-74	Winnipeg Jets	WCJHL	66	13	34	47	....	....	....	198	....	....	....	....	....	....	....	....	....	....	....	....	....	....	....	....	....	....
1974-75	Michigan-Baltimore	WHA	36	3	18	21	....	....	....	20	....	....	....	....	....	....	....	....	....	....	....	....	....	....	....	....	....	....
	Greensboro Generals	SHL	37	3	16	19	....	....	....	60	....	....	....	....	....	....	....	....	....	....	....	....	....	....	....	....	....	....
1975-76	Denver-Ottawa	WHA	40	6	8	14	....	....	....	15	....	....	....	....	....	....	....	....	....	....	....	....	....	....	....	....	....	....
	Cleveland Crusaders	WHA	35	0	7	7	....	....	....	22	....	....	....	....	....	....	....	....	....	....	3	0	1	1	12	....	....	....
1976-77	Minnesota Fighting Saints	WHA	2	0	0	0	....	....	....	0	....	....	....	....	....	....	....	....	....	....	....	....	....	....	....	....	....	....
	Cincinnati Stingers	WHA	74	7	22	29	....	....	....	39	....	....	....	....	....	....	....	....	....	....	4	0	0	0	0	....	....	....
1977-78	Cincinnati Stingers	WHA	78	7	17	24	....	....	....	114	....	....	....	....	....	....	....	....	....	....	....	....	....	....	....	....	....	....
1978-79	Cincinnati Stingers	WHA	80	3	8	11	....	....	....	131	....	....	....	....	....	....	....	....	....	....	3	0	4	4	0	....	....	....
1979-80	**Quebec Nordiques**	**NHL**	**31**	**0**	**3**	**3**	**0**	**2**	**2**	**18**	**0**	**0**	**0**	**15**	**0.0**	**22**	**0**	**25**	**5**	**+2**	....	....	....	....	....	....	....	....
	Syracuse Firebirds	AHL	5	0	1	1	....	....	....	4	....	....	....	....	....	....	....	....	....	....	....	....	....	....	....	....	....	....
1980-81	**Winnipeg Jets**	**NHL**	**38**	**0**	**6**	**6**	**0**	**4**	**4**	**69**	**0**	**0**	**0**	**14**	**0.0**	**26**	**1**	**68**	**10**	**–33**	....	....	....	....	....	....	....	....
	Tulsa Oilers	CHL	25	2	4	6	....	....	....	88	....	....	....	....	....	....	....	....	....	....	....	....	....	....	....	....	....	....
1981-82	**Winnipeg Jets**	**NHL**	**38**	**1**	**2**	**3**	**1**	**1**	**2**	**57**	**0**	**0**	**0**	**23**	**4.3**	**26**	**0**	**45**	**13**	**–6**	....	....	....	....	....	....	....	....
	Tulsa Oilers	CHL	1	0	1	1	....	....	....	0	....	....	....	....	....	....	....	....	....	....	....	....	....	....	....	....	....	....
	NHL Totals		**107**	**1**	**11**	**12**	**1**	**7**	**8**	**144**	**0**	**0**	**0**	**52**	**1.9**	**74**	**1**	**138**	**28**		....	....	....	....	....	....	....	....
	Other Major League Totals		345	26	80	106	....	....	....	341	....	....	....	....	....	....	....	....	....	....	10	0	5	5	12	....	....	....

Selected by **Michigan** (WHA) in 1974 WHA Amateur Draft, May, 1974. Claimed by **Denver** (WHA) from **Michigan-Baltimore** (WHA) in 1975 WHA Expansion Draft, June, 1975. Traded to **Cleveland** (WHA) by **Denver-Ottawa** (WHA) with Gary McFarlane for cash, January 20, 1976. Signed as a free agent by **Minnesota** (WHA) after **Cleveland** franchise folded, July, 1976. Traded to **Cincinnati** (WHA) by **Minnesota** (WHA) for cash, October, 1976. Claimed by **Winnipeg** from **Cincinnati** (WHA) in 1979 WHA Dispersal Draft, June 8, 1979. Traded to **Quebec** by **Winnipeg** with Jamie Hislop for Barry Melrose, June 28, 1979. Traded to **Winnipeg** by **Quebec** for cash, May 26, 1980.

● LEGGE, RANDY

Randy Legge D – R. 5′11″, 184 lbs. b: Newmarket, Ont., 12/16/1945.

			REGULAR SEASON																		PLAYOFFS							
Season	**Club**	**League**	**GP**	**G**	**A**	**Pts**	**AG**	**AA**	**APts**	**PIM**	**PP**	**SH**	**GW**	**S**	**%**	**TGF**	**PGF**	**TGA**	**PGA**	**+/–**	**GP**	**G**	**A**	**Pts**	**PIM**	**PP**	**SH**	**GW**
1962-63	Guelph Royals	OHA	48	2	4	6	....	....	....	44	....	....	....	....	....	....	....	....	....	....	....	....	....	....	....	....	....	....
1963-64	Kitchener Rangers	OHA	56	6	6	12	....	....	....	150	....	....	....	....	....	....	....	....	....	....	....	....	....	....	....	....	....	....
1964-65	Kitchener Rangers	OHA	42	3	12	15	....	....	....	103	....	....	....	....	....	....	....	....	....	....	....	....	....	....	....	....	....	....
1965-66	Kitchener Rangers	OHA	47	5	24	29	....	....	....	155	....	....	....	....	....	....	....	....	....	....	19	0	3	3	41	....	....	....
1966-67	Fort Wayne Komets	IHL	72	8	40	48	....	....	....	170	....	....	....	....	....	....	....	....	....	....	11	1	6	7	19	....	....	....
1967-68	Omaha Knights	CHL	61	2	17	19	....	....	....	148	....	....	....	....	....	....	....	....	....	....	....	....	....	....	....	....	....	....
1968-69	Omaha Knights	CHL	8	1	3	4	....	....	....	22	....	....	....	....	....	....	....	....	....	....	....	....	....	....	....	....	....	....
	Buffalo Bisons	AHL	57	1	15	16	....	....	....	66	....	....	....	....	....	....	....	....	....	....	6	0	0	0	4	....	....	....
1969-70	Buffalo Bisons	AHL	72	0	18	18	....	....	....	161	....	....	....	....	....	....	....	....	....	....	14	0	3	3	30	....	....	....
1970-71	Seattle Totems	WHL	72	4	17	21	....	....	....	150	....	....	....	....	....	....	....	....	....	....	....	....	....	....	....	....	....	....
1971-72	Providence Reds	AHL	71	2	7	9	....	....	....	73	....	....	....	....	....	....	....	....	....	....	5	1	1	2	6	....	....	....
1972-73	**New York Rangers**	**NHL**	**12**	**0**	**2**	**2**	**0**	**2**	**2**	**2**	**0**	**0**	**0**	**10**	**0.0**	**5**	**0**	**6**	**1**	**0**	....	....	....	....	....	....	....	....
	Providence Reds	AHL	61	3	9	12	....	....	....	126	....	....	....	....	....	....	....	....	....	....	4	1	1	2	2	....	....	....
1973-74	Providence Reds	AHL	75	4	21	25	....	....	....	121	....	....	....	....	....	....	....	....	....	....	15	0	4	4	9	....	....	....
1974-75	Michigan-Baltimore	WHA	78	1	14	15	....	....	....	69	....	....	....	....	....	....	....	....	....	....	....	....	....	....	....	....	....	....
1975-76	Winnipeg Jets	WHA	1	0	0	0	....	....	....	0	....	....	....	....	....	....	....	....	....	....	....	....	....	....	....	....	....	....
	Mohawk Valley Comets	NAHL	24	1	12	13	....	....	....	50	....	....	....	....	....	....	....	....	....	....	....	....	....	....	....	....	....	....
	Cleveland Crusaders	WHA	44	1	8	9	....	....	....	23	....	....	....	....	....	....	....	....	....	....	3	0	0	0	0	....	....	....
1976-77	San Diego Mariners	WHA	69	1	9	10	....	....	....	69	....	....	....	....	....	....	....	....	....	....	7	0	0	0	18	....	....	....
	NHL Totals		**12**	**0**	**2**	**2**	**0**	**2**	**2**	**2**	**0**	**0**	**0**	**10**	**0.0**	**5**	**0**	**6**	**1**		....	....	....	....	....	....	....	....
	Other Major League Totals		192	3	31	34	....	....	....	161	....	....	....	....	....	....	....	....	....	....	10	0	0	0	18	....	....	....

Selected by **Dayton-Houston** (WHA) in 1972 WHA General Player Draft, February 12, 1972. WHA rights traded to **Michigan** (WHA) by **Houston** (WHA) for cash, June, 1974. Selected by **Winnipeg** (WHA) from **Michigan-Baltimore** (WHA) in 1975 WHA Dispersal Draft, June, 1975. Traded to **Cleveland** (WHA) by **Winnipeg** (WHA) for Lyle Moffat, January, 1976. Signed as a free agent by **San Diego** (WHA) after **Cleveland** (WHA) franchise folded, July, 1976.

● LEHMANN, TOMMY

Tommy Lehmann C – L. 6′1″, 185 lbs. b: Stockholm, Sweden, 2/3/1964. Boston's 11th choice, 228th overall, in 1982 Entry Draft.

			REGULAR SEASON																		PLAYOFFS							
Season	**Club**	**League**	**GP**	**G**	**A**	**Pts**	**AG**	**AA**	**APts**	**PIM**	**PP**	**SH**	**GW**	**S**	**%**	**TGF**	**PGF**	**TGA**	**PGA**	**+/–**	**GP**	**G**	**A**	**Pts**	**PIM**	**PP**	**SH**	**GW**
1982-83	AIK-Solna	Sweden	28	1	5	6	....	....	....	2	....	....	....	....	....	....	....	....	....	....	3	0	0	0	0	....	....	....
1983-84	AIK-Solna	Sweden	22	4	5	9	....	....	....	6	....	....	....	....	....	....	....	....	....	....	6	2	2	4	2	....	....	....
1984-85	AIK-Solna	Sweden	34	13	13	26	....	....	....	6	....	....	....	....	....	....	....	....	....	....	....	....	....	....	....	....	....	....
1985-86	AIK-Solna	Sweden	35	11	13	24	....	....	....	12	....	....	....	....	....	....	....	....	....	....	....	....	....	....	....	....	....	....
1986-87	AIK-Solna	Sweden	32	25	15	40	....	....	....	12	....	....	....	....	....	....	....	....	....	....	....	....	....	....	....	....	....	....
1987-88	**Boston Bruins**	**NHL**	**9**	**1**	**3**	**4**	**1**	**2**	**3**	**6**	**0**	**0**	**0**	**5**	**20.0**	**5**	**1**	**4**	**0**	**0**	....	....	....	....	....	....	....	....
	Maine Mariners	AHL	11	3	5	8	....	....	....	2	....	....	....	....	....	....	....	....	....	....	....	....	....	....	....	....	....	....
1988-89	**Boston Bruins**	**NHL**	**26**	**4**	**2**	**6**	**3**	**1**	**4**	**10**	**1**	**1**	**1**	**26**	**15.4**	**13**	**3**	**17**	**0**	**–7**	....	....	....	....	....	....	....	....
	Maine Mariners	AHL	26	1	13	14	....	....	....	12	....	....	....	....	....	....	....	....	....	....	....	....	....	....	....	....	....	....
1989-90	AIK-Solna	Sweden	22	7	9	16	....	....	....	12	....	....	....	....	....	....	....	....	....	....	3	1	1	2	0	....	....	....
	Edmonton Oilers	**NHL**	**1**	**0**	**0**	**0**	**0**	**0**	**0**	**0**	**0**	**0**	**0**	**0**	**0.0**	**1**	**0**	**0**	**0**	**+1**	....	....	....	....	....	....	....	....
	Cape Breton Oilers	AHL	19	6	11	17	....	....	....	7	....	....	....	....	....	....	....	....	....	....	6	2	2	4	2	....	....	....
1990-91	AIK-Solna	Sweden	37	11	14	25	....	....	....	40	....	....	....	....	....	....	....	....	....	....	....	....	....	....	....	....	....	....
1991-92	AIK-Solna	Sweden	38	4	11	15	....	....	....	12	....	....	....	....	....	....	....	....	....	....	3	0	0	0	2	....	....	....
1992-93	MoDo	Sweden	40	7	7	14	....	....	....	22	....	....	....	....	....	....	....	....	....	....	3	1	0	1	2	....	....	....
1993-94			STATISTICS NOT AVAILABLE																									
1994-95	AIK Stockholm	Sweden	35	4	11	15	....	....	....	16	....	....	....	....	....	....	....	....	....	....	....	....	....	....	....	....	....	....
1995-96			STATISTICS NOT AVAILABLE																									
1996-97	Sodertalje SK	Sweden	2	0	0	0	....	....	....	2	....	....	....	....	....	....	....	....	....	....	....	....	....	....	....	....	....	....
	NHL Totals		**36**	**5**	**5**	**10**	**4**	**3**	**7**	**16**	**1**	**1**	**1**	**31**	**16.1**	**19**	**4**	**21**	**0**		....	....	....	....	....	....	....	....

Traded to **Edmonton** by **Boston** for Edmonton's 3rd round choice (Wes Walz) in 1989 Entry Draft, June 17, 1989.

● LEHTINEN, JERE

Jere Lehtinen RW – R. 6′, 192 lbs. b: Espoo, Finland, 6/24/1973. Minnesota's 3rd choice, 88th overall, in 1992 Entry Draft.

			REGULAR SEASON																		PLAYOFFS							
Season	**Club**	**League**	**GP**	**G**	**A**	**Pts**	**AG**	**AA**	**APts**	**PIM**	**PP**	**SH**	**GW**	**S**	**%**	**TGF**	**PGF**	**TGA**	**PGA**	**+/–**	**GP**	**G**	**A**	**Pts**	**PIM**	**PP**	**SH**	**GW**
1990-91	Espoo	Finland 2	32	15	9	24	....	....	....	12	....	....	....	....	....	....	....	....	....	....	....	....	....	....	....	....	....	....
	Finland	WJC-A	4	2	0	2	....	....	....	0	....	....	....	....	....	....	....	....	....	....	....	....	....	....	....	....	....	....
1991-92	Espoo	Finland 2	43	32	17	49	....	....	....	6	....	....	....	....	....	....	....	....	....	....	....	....	....	....	....	....	....	....
	Finland	WJC-A	7	0	2	2	....	....	....	2	....	....	....	....	....	....	....	....	....	....	....	....	....	....	....	....	....	....
	Finland	WC-A	7	1	1	2	....	....	....	0	....	....	....	....	....	....	....	....	....	....	....	....	....	....	....	....	....	....
1992-93	Kiekko-Espoo	Finland	45	13	14	27	....	....	....	6	....	....	....	....	....	....	....	....	....	....	....	....	....	....	....	....	....	....
	Finland	WJC-A	7	6	8	14	....	....	....	10	....	....	....	....	....	....	....	....	....	....	....	....	....	....	....	....	....	....
1993-94	TPS Turku	Finland	42	19	20	39	....	....	....	6	....	....	....	....	....	....	....	....	....	....	11	11	2	13	2	....	....	....
	Finland	Olympics	8	3	0	3	....	....	....	0	....	....	....	....	....	....	....	....	....	....	....	....	....	....	....	....	....	....
	Finland	WC-A	8	3	5	8	....	....	....	4	....	....	....	....	....	....	....	....	....	....	....	....	....	....	....	....	....	....
1994-95	TPS Turku	Finland	39	19	23	42	....	....	....	33	....	....	....	....	....	....	....	....	....	....	13	8	6	14	4	....	....	....
	Finland	WC-A	8	2	5	7	....	....	....	4	....	....	....	....	....	....	....	....	....	....	....	....	....	....	....	....	....	....
1995-96	**Dallas Stars**	**NHL**	**57**	**6**	**22**	**28**	**6**	**18**	**24**	**16**	**0**	**0**	**1**	**109**	**5.5**	**43**	**11**	**37**	**10**	**+5**	....	....	....	....	....	....	....	....
	Michigan K-Wings	IHL	1	1	0	1	....	....	....	0	....	....	....	....	....	....	....	....	....	....	....	....	....	....	....	....	....	....

Season	Club	League	REGULAR SEASON																		PLAYOFFS							
			GP	G	A	Pts	AG	AA	APts	PIM	PP	SH	GW	S	%	TGF	PGF	TGA	PGA	+/-	GP	G	A	Pts	PIM	PP	SH	GW
1996-97	Finland	W Cup	4	2	2	4	....	....	....	0	....	....	....	....	....	....	....	....	....	....	....	....	....	....	....	....	....	....
	Dallas Stars	**NHL**	**63**	**16**	**27**	**43**	**17**	**24**	**41**	**2**	**3**	**1**	**2**	**134**	**11.9**	**57**	**7**	**40**	**16**	**+26**	**7**	**2**	**2**	**4**	**0**	**0**	**0**	**0**
1997-98	**Dallas Stars**	**NHL**	**72**	**23**	**19**	**42**	**27**	**19**	**46**	**20**	**7**	**2**	**6**	**201**	**11.4**	**80**	**30**	**42**	**11**	**+19**	**12**	**3**	**5**	**8**	**2**	**1**	**0**	**0**
	Finland	Olympics	6	4	2	6	....	....	....	2	....	....	....	....	....	....	....	....	....	....	....	....	....	....	....	....	....	....
	NHL Totals		**192**	**45**	**68**	**113**	**50**	**61**	**111**	**38**	**10**	**3**	**9**	**444**	**10.1**	**180**	**48**	**119**	**37**		**19**	**5**	**7**	**12**	**2**	**1**	**0**	**0**

Finnish First All-Star Team (1995) • WC-A All-Star Team (1995) • Won Frank J. Selke Trophy (1998)

Played in NHL All-Star Game (1998)

Rights transferred to **Dallas** after **Minnesota** franchise relocated, June 9, 1993.

• LEHTO, PETTERI

Petteri Lehto D – L. 5'11", 195 lbs. b: Turku, Finland, 3/13/1961.

Season	Club	League	GP	G	A	Pts	AG	AA	APts	PIM	PP	SH	GW	S	%	TGF	PGF	TGA	PGA	+/-	GP	G	A	Pts	PIM	PP	SH	GW
1980-81	TPS Turku	Finland	31	0	2	2	....	....	....	16	....	....	....	....	....	....	....	....	....	....	....	....	....	....	....	....	....	....
1981-82	Lukko Rauma	Finland	34	3	8	11	....	....	....	24	....	....	....	....	....	....	....	....	....	....	....	....	....	....	....	....	....	....
1982-83	TPS Turku	Finland	33	3	6	9	....	....	....	52	....	....	....	....	....	....	....	....	....	....	3	0	0	0	2	....	....	....
1983-84	TPS Turku	Finland	36	8	10	18	....	....	....	32	....	....	....	....	....	....	....	....	....	....	10	2	1	3	8	....	....	....
	Finland	Olympics	6	2	2	4	....	....	....	10	....	....	....	....	....	....	....	....	....	....	....	....	....	....	....	....	....	....
1984-85	**Pittsburgh Penguins**	**NHL**	**6**	**0**	**0**	**0**	**0**	**0**	**0**	**4**	**0**	**0**	**0**	**5**	**0.0**	**2**	**0**	**6**	**0**	**–4**	....	....	....	....	....	....	....	....
	Baltimore Skipjacks	AHL	52	3	18	21	....	....	....	55	....	....	....	....	....	....	....	....	....	....	....	....	....	....	....	....	....	....
1985-86	TPS Turku	Finland	33	3	10	13	....	....	....	62	....	....	....	....	....	....	....	....	....	....	7	0	2	2	10	....	....	....
1986-87	TPS Turku	Finland	22	1	5	6	....	....	....	30	....	....	....	....	....	....	....	....	....	....	....	....	....	....	....	....	....	....
1987-88	KalPa Kuopio	Finland	32	3	11	14	....	....	....	32	....	....	....	....	....	....	....	....	....	....	....	....	....	....	....	....	....	....
1988-89	TPS Turku	Finland	40	2	9	11	....	....	....	20	....	....	....	....	....	....	....	....	....	....	10	0	0	0	4	....	....	....
	NHL Totals		**6**	**0**	**0**	**0**	**0**	**0**	**0**	**4**	**0**	**0**	**0**	**5**	**0.0**	**2**	**0**	**6**	**0**		....	....	....	....	....	....	....	....

Signed as a free agent by **Pittsburgh**, July, 1984.

• LEHTONEN, ANTERO

Antero Lehtonen LW – L. 6', 185 lbs. b: Tampere, Finland, 4/12/1954.

Season	Club	League	GP	G	A	Pts	AG	AA	APts	PIM	PP	SH	GW	S	%	TGF	PGF	TGA	PGA	+/-	GP	G	A	Pts	PIM	PP	SH	GW
1971-72	Tappara-Tampere	Finland	1	0	0	0	....	....	....	2	....	....	....	....	....	....	....	....	....	....	....	....	....	....	....	....	....	....
1972-73	Tappara-Tampere	Finland	36	20	5	25	....	....	....	23	....	....	....	....	....	....	....	....	....	....	....	....	....	....	....	....	....	....
1973-74	Tappara-Tempere	Finland	36	9	7	16	....	....	....	10	....	....	....	....	....	....	....	....	....	....	....	....	....	....	....	....	....	....
	Finland	WJC-A	5	1	2	3	....	....	....	6	....	....	....	....	....	....	....	....	....	....	....	....	....	....	....	....	....	....
1974-75	Tappara-Tempere	Finland	36	26	7	33	....	....	....	26	....	....	....	....	....	....	....	....	....	....	....	....	....	....	....	....	....	....
1975-76	Tappara-Tempere	Finland	36	19	11	30	....	....	....	21	....	....	....	....	....	....	....	....	....	....	4	0	2	2	8	....	....	....
1976-77	TPS Turku	Finland	36	26	12	38	....	....	....	12	....	....	....	....	....	....	....	....	....	....	8	4	1	5	4	....	....	....
	Finland	WEC-A	9	1	1	2	....	....	....	6	....	....	....	....	....	....	....	....	....	....	....	....	....	....	....	....	....	....
1977-78	TPS Turku	Finland	35	23	13	36	....	....	....	38	....	....	....	....	....	....	....	....	....	....	8	3	5	8	4	....	....	....
1978-79	Tappara-Tempere	Finland	36	35	19	54	....	....	....	43	....	....	....	....	....	....	....	....	....	....	10	8	5	13	6	....	....	....
	Finland	WEC-A	8	3	3	6	....	....	....	0	....	....	....	....	....	....	....	....	....	....	....	....	....	....	....	....	....	....
1979-80	**Washington Capitals**	**NHL**	**65**	**9**	**12**	**21**	**8**	**9**	**17**	**14**	**2**	**0**	**1**	**101**	**8.9**	**30**	**3**	**31**	**0**	**–4**	....	....	....	....	....	....	....	....
	Hershey Bears	AHL	4	3	0	3	....	....	....	2	....	....	....	....	....	....	....	....	....	....	....	....	....	....	....	....	....	....
1980-81	Tappara-Tempere	Finland	27	13	7	20	....	....	....	24	....	....	....	....	....	....	....	....	....	....	8	7	3	10	6	....	....	....
	Finland	WEC-A	8	0	4	4	....	....	....	0	....	....	....	....	....	....	....	....	....	....	....	....	....	....	....	....	....	....
1981-82	TPS Turku	Finland	36	14	8	22	....	....	....	35	....	....	....	....	....	....	....	....	....	....	7	2	1	3	6	....	....	....
1982-83	TPS Turku	Finland	36	11	10	21	....	....	....	16	....	....	....	....	....	....	....	....	....	....	3	4	0	4	0	....	....	....
1983-84	TPS Turku	Finland	30	8	13	21	....	....	....	14	....	....	....	....	....	....	....	....	....	....	9	1	1	2	4	....	....	....
1984-85	JyP-Jyvaskyla	Finland 2	35	35	25	60	....	....	....	16	....	....	....	....	....	....	....	....	....	....	....	....	....	....	....	....	....	....
1985-86	JyP-Jyvaskyla	Finland	36	24	12	36	....	....	....	18	....	....	....	....	....	....	....	....	....	....	....	....	....	....	....	....	....	....
1986-87	JyP Jyvaskyla	Finland	39	10	8	18	....	....	....	20	....	....	....	....	....	....	....	....	....	....	....	....	....	....	....	....	....	....
	NHL Totals		**65**	**9**	**12**	**21**	**8**	**9**	**17**	**14**	**2**	**0**	**1**	**101**	**8.9**	**30**	**3**	**31**	**0**		....	....	....	....	....	....	....	....

Finnish First All-Star Team (1979)

Signed as a free agent by **Washington**, September 16, 1979.

• LEHVONEN, HENRI

Henri "Hank" Lehvonen D – L. 5'11", 200 lbs. b: Sarnia, Ont., 8/26/1950. Minnesota"s 5th choice, 62nd overall, in 1970 Amateur Draft.

Season	Club	League	GP	G	A	Pts	AG	AA	APts	PIM	PP	SH	GW	S	%	TGF	PGF	TGA	PGA	+/-	GP	G	A	Pts	PIM	PP	SH	GW
1967-68	Peterborough Petes	OHA	12	0	3	3	....	....	....	6	....	....	....	....	....	....	....	....	....	....	....	....	....	....	....	....	....	....
	Kitchener Rangers	OHA	24	2	11	13	....	....	....	8	....	....	....	....	....	....	....	....	....	....	17	3	12	15	12	....	....	....
1968-69	Kitchener Rangers	OHA	51	12	21	33	....	....	....	20	....	....	....	....	....	....	....	....	....	....	....	....	....	....	....	....	....	....
1969-70	Kitchener Rangers	OHA	29	2	9	11	....	....	....	25	....	....	....	....	....	....	....	....	....	....	....	....	....	....	....	....	....	....
1970-71	Clinton Comets	EHL	3	0	0	0	....	....	....	0	....	....	....	....	....	....	....	....	....	....	....	....	....	....	....	....	....	....
	Port Huron Flags	IHL	51	4	21	25	....	....	....	29	....	....	....	....	....	....	....	....	....	....	14	1	3	4	6	....	....	....
1971-72	Port Huron Wings	IHL	9	0	6	6	....	....	....	6	....	....	....	....	....	....	....	....	....	....	....	....	....	....	....	....	....	....
1972-73	Port Huron Wings	IHL	66	10	38	48	....	....	....	83	....	....	....	....	....	....	....	....	....	....	11	2	2	4	10	....	....	....
1973-74			DID NOT PLAY																									
1974-75	**Kansas City Scouts**	**NHL**	**4**	**0**	**0**	**0**	**0**	**0**	**0**	**0**	**0**	**0**	**0**	**2**	**0.0**	**5**	**0**	**1**	**0**	**+4**	....	....	....	....	....	....	....	....
	Port Huron Flags	IHL	58	6	29	35	....	....	....	94	....	....	....	....	....	....	....	....	....	....	5	3	2	5	2	....	....	....
1975-76	Port Huron Flags	IHL	16	1	6	7	....	....	....	18	....	....	....	....	....	....	....	....	....	....	....	....	....	....	....	....	....	....
	Toledo Goaldiggers	IHL	35	3	10	13	....	....	....	22	....	....	....	....	....	....	....	....	....	....	4	2	3	5	6	....	....	....
1976-77	Port Huron Flags	IHL	41	0	12	12	....	....	....	18	....	....	....	....	....	....	....	....	....	....	....	....	....	....	....	....	....	....
1977-78			DID NOT PLAY																									
1978-79	Jokerit Helsinki	Finland	36	5	5	10	....	....	....	39	....	....	....	....	....	....	....	....	....	....	....	....	....	....	....	....	....	....
1979-80	Jokerit Helsinki	Finland	35	3	10	13	....	....	....	69	....	....	....	....	....	....	....	....	....	....	....	....	....	....	....	....	....	....
1980-81	Ilves Tampere	Finland	35	0	4	4	....	....	....	40	....	....	....	....	....	....	....	....	....	....	2	0	0	0	6	....	....	....
1981-82	Ilves Tampere	Finland	16	1	1	2	....	....	....	20	....	....	....	....	....	....	....	....	....	....	....	....	....	....	....	....	....	....
	NHL Totals		**4**	**0**	**0**	**0**	**0**	**0**	**0**	**0**	**0**	**0**	**0**	**2**	**0.0**	**5**	**0**	**1**	**0**		....	....	....	....	....	....	....	....

Signed as a free agent by **Kansas City** (Port Huron - IHL), November 15, 1974.

• LEINONEN, MIKKO

Mikko "Breeze" Leinonen C – L. 6', 175 lbs. b: Tampere, Finland, 7/15/1955.

Season	Club	League	GP	G	A	Pts	AG	AA	APts	PIM	PP	SH	GW	S	%	TGF	PGF	TGA	PGA	+/-	GP	G	A	Pts	PIM	PP	SH	GW
1973-74	Tappara Tampere	Finland	35	26	13	39	....	....	....	30	....	....	....	....	....	....	....	....	....	....	....	....	....	....	....	....	....	....
	Finland	WJC-A	5	4	1	5	....	....	....	2	....	....	....	....	....	....	....	....	....	....	....	....	....	....	....	....	....	....
1974-75	Tappara Tampere	Finland	34	17	11	28	....	....	....	14	....	....	....	....	....	....	....	....	....	....	....	....	....	....	....	....	....	....
	Finland	WJC-A	5	0	3	3	....	....	....	2	....	....	....	....	....	....	....	....	....	....	....	....	....	....	....	....	....	....
1975-76	Tappara Tampere	Finland	36	23	24	47	....	....	....	42	....	....	....	....	....	....	....	....	....	....	4	1	1	2	8	....	....	....
1976-77	Tappara Tampere	Finland	33	23	24	47	....	....	....	43	....	....	....	....	....	....	....	....	....	....	6	7	4	11	6	....	....	....
1977-78	MoDo	Finland	36	19	26	45	....	....	....	51	....	....	....	....	....	....	....	....	....	....	2	0	0	0	4	....	....	....
	Finland	WEC-A	8	0	1	1	....	....	....	4	....	....	....	....	....	....	....	....	....	....	....	....	....	....	....	....	....	....
1978-79	MoDo	Finland	34	10	19	29	....	....	....	32	....	....	....	....	....	....	....	....	....	....	6	2	*7	9	4	....	....	....
	Finland	WEC-A	8	1	1	2	....	....	....	4	....	....	....	....	....	....	....	....	....	....	....	....	....	....	....	....	....	....
1979-80	Karpat Oulu	Finland	36	32	20	52	....	....	....	40	....	....	....	....	....	....	....	....	....	....	6	2	2	4	4	....	....	....
	Finland	Olympics	7	6	4	10	....	....	....	0	....	....	....	....	....	....	....	....	....	....	....	....	....	....	....	....	....	....
1980-81	Karpat Oulu	Finland	36	16	36	52	....	....	....	43	....	....	....	....	....	....	....	....	....	....	12	3	7	10	14	....	....	....
	Finland	WEC-A	8	5	3	8	....	....	....	2	....	....	....	....	....	....	....	....	....	....	....	....	....	....	....	....	....	....
1981-82	Finland	C Cup	6	0	1	1	....	....	....	0	....	....	....	....	....	....	....	....	....	....	....	....	....	....	....	....	....	....
	New York Rangers	**NHL**	**53**	**11**	**20**	**31**	**9**	**13**	**22**	**18**	**2**	**0**	**3**	**67**	**16.4**	**45**	**10**	**33**	**0**	**+2**	**7**	**1**	**6**	**7**	**20**	**0**	**0**	**0**
	Springfield Indians	AHL	6	4	2	6	....	....	....	2	....	....	....	....	....	....	....	....	....	....	....	....	....	....	....	....	....	....
1982-83	**New York Rangers**	**NHL**	**78**	**17**	**34**	**51**	**14**	**23**	**37**	**23**	**3**	**0**	**0**	**135**	**12.6**	**87**	**34**	**48**	**7**	**+12**	**7**	**1**	**3**	**4**	**4**	**1**	**0**	**0**
1983-84	**New York Rangers**	**NHL**	**28**	**3**	**23**	**26**	**2**	**16**	**18**	**28**	**0**	**0**	**1**	**39**	**7.7**	**35**	**13**	**26**	**8**	**+4**	**5**	**0**	**2**	**2**	**4**	**0**	**0**	**0**
	Tulsa Oilers	CHL	33	15	23	38	....	....	....	38	....	....	....	....	....	....	....	....	....	....	....	....	....	....	....	....	....	....
1984-85	**Washington Capitals**	**NHL**	**3**	**0**	**1**	**1**	**0**	**1**	**1**	**2**	**0**	**0**	**0**	**5**	**0.0**	**2**	**0**	**1**	**0**	**+1**	**1**	**0**	**0**	**0**	**0**	**0**	**0**	**0**
	Karpat Oulu	Finland	35	19	15	34	....	....	....	*70	....	....	....	....	....	....	....	....	....	....	7	2	3	5	6	....	....	....
1985-86	Karpat Oulu	Finland	36	6	17	23	....	....	....	40	....	....	....	....	....	....	....	....	....	....	5	1	1	2	0	....	....	....
	NHL Totals		**162**	**31**	**78**	**109**	**25**	**53**	**78**	**71**	**5**	**0**	**4**	**246**	**12.6**	**169**	**57**	**108**	**15**		**20**	**2**	**11**	**13**	**28**	**1**	**0**	**0**

Finnish First All-Star Team (1981)

• LEITER, BOBBY Bobby Leiter C – L. 5'9", 175 lbs. b: Winnipeg, Man., 3/22/1941.

Season	Club	League	GP	G	A	Pts	AG	AA	APts	PIM	PP	SH	GW	S	%	TGF	PGF	TGA	PGA	+/-	GP	G	A	Pts	PIM	PP	SH	GW
			REGULAR SEASON																		PLAYOFFS							
1958-59	Winnipeg Braves	MJHL	31	14	21	35	....	....	....	8	....	....	....	....	....	....	....	....	....	....	24	6	*18	24	16	....	....	....
1959-60	Winnipeg Braves	MJHL	31	22	31	53	....	....	....	48	....	....	....	....	....	....	....	....	....	....	4	1	2	3	2	....	....	....
	Winnipeg Warriors	WHL	1	0	0	0	....	....	....	0	....	....	....	....	....	....	....	....	....	....	....	....	....	....	....	....	....	....
1960-61	Winnipeg Braves	MJHL	30	20	14	34	....	....	....	31	....	....	....	....	....	....	....	....	....	....	3	0	3	3	0	....	....	....
	Winnipeg Warriors	WHL	5	1	3	4	....	....	....	0	....	....	....	....	....	....	....	....	....	....	....	....	....	....	....	....	....	....
1961-62	Kingston Frontenacs	EPHL	69	24	32	56	....	....	....	61	....	....	....	....	....	....	....	....	....	....	11	8	8	*16	8	....	....	....
1962-63	**Boston Bruins**	**NHL**	**51**	**9**	**13**	**22**	**11**	**14**	**25**	**34**	....	....	....	....	....	....	....	....	....	....	....	....	....	....	....	....	....	....
	Kingston Frontenacs	EPHL	20	15	23	38	....	....	....	17	....	....	....	....	....	....	....	....	....	....	....	....	....	....	....	....	....	....
1963-64	**Boston Bruins**	**NHL**	**56**	**6**	**13**	**19**	**8**	**14**	**22**	**43**	....	....	....	....	....	....	....	....	....	....	....	....	....	....	....	....	....	....
	Hershey Bears	AHL	15	6	6	12	....	....	....	6	....	....	....	....	....	....	....	....	....	....	6	2	4	6	2	....	....	....
1964-65	**Boston Bruins**	**NHL**	**18**	**3**	**1**	**4**	**4**	**1**	**5**	**6**	....	....	....	....	....	....	....	....	....	....	....	....	....	....	....	....	....	....
1965-66	**Boston Bruins**	**NHL**	**9**	**2**	**1**	**3**	**2**	**1**	**3**	**2**	....	....	....	....	....	....	....	....	....	....	....	....	....	....	....	....	....	....
	Hershey Bears	AHL	45	9	23	32	....	....	....	16	....	....	....	....	....	....	....	....	....	....	3	1	2	3	2	....	....	....
1966-67	San Francisco	WHL	20	2	8	10	....	....	....	10	....	....	....	....	....	....	....	....	....	....	1	0	0	0	0	....	....	....
1967-68	Hershey Bears	AHL	72	22	48	70	....	....	....	57	....	....	....	....	....	....	....	....	....	....	5	0	0	0	4	....	....	....
1968-69	**Boston Bruins**	**NHL**	**1**	**0**	**0**	**0**	**0**	**0**	**0**	**0**	**0**	**0**	**0**	**0**	**0.0**	**0**	**0**	**0**	**0**	**0**	....	....	....	....	....	....	....	....
	Hershey Bears	AHL	72	26	33	59	....	....	....	35	....	....	....	....	....	....	....	....	....	....	11	2	8	10	12	....	....	....
1969-70	Hershey Bears	AHL	72	21	41	62	....	....	....	51	....	....	....	....	....	....	....	....	....	....	7	3	2	5	4	....	....	....
1970-71	Hershey Bears	AHL	72	33	36	69	....	....	....	26	....	....	....	....	....	....	....	....	....	....	4	0	2	2	4	....	....	....
1971-72	**Pittsburgh Penguins**	**NHL**	**78**	**14**	**17**	**31**	**15**	**15**	**30**	**18**	**5**	**0**	**3**	**147**	**9.5**	**42**	**15**	**54**	**2**	**–25**	**4**	**3**	**0**	**3**	**0**	**1**	**0**	**0**
1972-73	**Atlanta Flames**	**NHL**	**78**	**26**	**34**	**60**	**26**	**28**	**54**	**19**	**5**	**0**	**3**	**174**	**14.9**	**72**	**14**	**71**	**1**	**–12**	....	....	....	....	....	....	....	....
1973-74	**Atlanta Flames**	**NHL**	**78**	**26**	**26**	**52**	**27**	**22**	**49**	**10**	**10**	**0**	**4**	**178**	**14.6**	**76**	**34**	**46**	**0**	**–4**	**4**	**0**	**0**	**0**	**2**	**0**	**0**	**0**
1974-75	**Atlanta Flames**	**NHL**	**52**	**10**	**18**	**28**	**9**	**14**	**23**	**8**	**6**	**0**	**1**	**96**	**10.4**	**42**	**22**	**35**	**0**	**–15**	....	....	....	....	....	....	....	....
1975-76	**Atlanta Flames**	**NHL**	**26**	**2**	**3**	**5**	**2**	**2**	**4**	**4**	**1**	**0**	**0**	**26**	**7.7**	**12**	**4**	**8**	**0**	**0**	....	....	....	....	....	....	....	....
	Calgary Cowboys	WHA	51	17	17	34	....	....	....	8	....	....	....	....	....	....	....	....	....	....	3	2	0	2	0	....	....	....
	NHL Totals		**447**	**98**	**126**	**224**	**104**	**111**	**215**	**144**	**27**	**0**	**11**	**621**	**15.8**	**244**	**89**	**214**	**3**		**8**	**3**	**0**	**3**	**2**	**1**	**0**	**0**
	Other Major League Totals		51	17	17	34	....	....	....	8	....	....	....	....	....	....	....	....	....		3	2	0	2	0	....	....	....

AHL Second All-Star Team (1971)

Traded to **Pittsburgh** by **Boston** for cash, May, 1971. Selected by **Winnipeg** (WHA) in 1972 WHA General Player Draft, February 12, 1972., 1975. Claimed by **Atlanta** from **Pittsburgh** in Expansion Draft, June 6, 1972. WHA rights traded to **Calgary** (WHA) by **Winnipeg** (WHA) for future considerations, June, 1975.

• LEITER, KEN Ken Leiter D – L. 6'1", 195 lbs. b: Detroit, MI, 4/19/1961. NY Islanders' 6th choice, 101st overall, in 1980 Entry Draft.

Season	Club	League	GP	G	A	Pts	AG	AA	APts	PIM	PP	SH	GW	S	%	TGF	PGF	TGA	PGA	+/-	GP	G	A	Pts	PIM	PP	SH	GW
1979-80	Michigan State Spartans	WCHA	38	0	10	10	....	....	....	96	....	....	....	....	....	....	....	....	....	....	....	....	....	....	....	....	....	....
1980-81	Michigan State Spartans	WCHA	31	2	12	14	....	....	....	48	....	....	....	....	....	....	....	....	....	....	....	....	....	....	....	....	....	....
1981-82	Michigan State Spartans	CCHA	31	7	13	20	....	....	....	50	....	....	....	....	....	....	....	....	....	....	....	....	....	....	....	....	....	....
1982-83	Michigan State Spartans	CCHA	40	3	28	31	....	....	....	47	....	....	....	....	....	....	....	....	....	....	....	....	....	....	....	....	....	....
1983-84	Indianapolis Checkers	CHL	68	10	26	36	....	....	....	46	....	....	....	....	....	....	....	....	....	....	10	3	4	7	0	....	....	....
1984-85	**New York Islanders**	**NHL**	**5**	**0**	**2**	**2**	**0**	**1**	**1**	**2**	**0**	**0**	**0**	**9**	**0.0**	**5**	**0**	**6**	**1**	**0**	....	....	....	....	....	....	....	....
	Springfield Indians	AHL	39	3	12	15	....	....	....	12	....	....	....	....	....	....	....	....	....	....	4	0	3	3	2	....	....	....
1985-86	**New York Islanders**	**NHL**	**9**	**1**	**1**	**2**	**1**	**1**	**2**	**6**	**0**	**0**	**0**	**9**	**11.1**	**10**	**1**	**8**	**0**	**+1**	....	....	....	....	....	....	....	....
	Springfield Indians	AHL	68	7	27	34	....	....	....	51	....	....	....	....	....	....	....	....	....	....	....	....	....	....	....	....	....	....
1986-87	**New York Islanders**	**NHL**	**74**	**9**	**20**	**29**	**8**	**14**	**22**	**30**	**4**	**0**	**0**	**159**	**5.7**	**85**	**30**	**64**	**11**	**+2**	**11**	**0**	**5**	**5**	**6**	**0**	**0**	**0**
1987-88	**New York Islanders**	**NHL**	**51**	**4**	**13**	**17**	**3**	**9**	**12**	**24**	**1**	**0**	**1**	**104**	**3.8**	**62**	**19**	**40**	**15**	**+18**	**4**	**0**	**1**	**1**	**2**	**0**	**0**	**0**
	Springfield Indians	AHL	2	0	4	4	....	....	....	0	....	....	....	....	....	....	....	....	....	....	....	....	....	....	....	....	....	....
1988-89			DID NOT PLAY																									
1989-90	**Minnesota North Stars**	**NHL**	**4**	**0**	**0**	**0**	**0**	**0**	**0**	**0**	**0**	**0**	**0**	**5**	**0.0**	**2**	**1**	**3**	**0**	**–2**	....	....	....	....	....	....	....	....
	Kalamazoo Wings	IHL	4	1	1	2	....	....	....	0	....	....	....	....	....	....	....	....	....	....	....	....	....	....	....	....	....	....
	NHL Totals		**143**	**14**	**36**	**50**	**12**	**25**	**37**	**62**	**5**	**0**	**1**	**286**	**4.9**	**164**	**51**	**121**	**27**		**15**	**0**	**6**	**6**	**8**	**0**	**0**	**0**

CCHA First All-Star Team (1983)

Claimed by **Minnesota** from **NY Islanders** in Waiver Draft, October 2, 1989.

• LEMAIRE, JACQUES Jacques Lemaire C – L. 5'10", 180 lbs. b: LaSalle, Que., 9/7/1945. **HHOF**

Season	Club	League	GP	G	A	Pts	AG	AA	APts	PIM	PP	SH	GW	S	%	TGF	PGF	TGA	PGA	+/-	GP	G	A	Pts	PIM	PP	SH	GW
1962-63	Lachine Maroons	QJHL	42	41	63	*104	....	....	....	....	....	....	....	....	....	....	....	....	....	....	....	....	....	....	....	....	....	....
1963-64	Montreal Jr. Canadiens	OHA	42	25	30	55	....	....	....	17	....	....	....	....	....	....	....	....	....	....	17	10	6	16	4	....	....	....
1964-65	Montreal Jr. Canadiens	OHA	56	25	47	72	....	....	....	52	....	....	....	....	....	....	....	....	....	....	7	1	5	6	0	....	....	....
	Quebec Aces	AHL	1	0	0	0	....	....	....	0	....	....	....	....	....	....	....	....	....	....	....	....	....	....	....	....	....	....
1965-66	Montreal Jr. Canadiens	OHA	48	41	52	93	....	....	....	69	....	....	....	....	....	....	....	....	....	....	10	11	2	13	14	....	....	....
1966-67	Houston Apollos	CHL	69	19	30	49	....	....	....	19	....	....	....	....	....	....	....	....	....	....	6	0	1	1	0	....	....	....
1967-68	**Montreal Canadiens**	**NHL**	**69**	**22**	**20**	**42**	**27**	**21**	**48**	**16**	**3**	**1**	**3**	**182**	**12.1**	**58**	**8**	**37**	**2**	**+15**	**13**	**7**	**6**	**13**	**6**	**2**	**0**	**2**
1968-69	**Montreal Canadiens**	**NHL**	**75**	**29**	**34**	**63**	**33**	**32**	**65**	**29**	**5**	**0**	**4**	**330**	**8.8**	**102**	**27**	**51**	**7**	**+31**	**14**	**4**	**2**	**6**	**6**	**1**	**0**	**0**
1969-70	**Montreal Canadiens**	**NHL**	**69**	**32**	**28**	**60**	**37**	**28**	**65**	**16**	**13**	**0**	**5**	**237**	**13.5**	**92**	**25**	**49**	**1**	**+19**	....	....	....	....	....	....	....	....
1970-71	**Montreal Canadiens**	**NHL**	**78**	**28**	**28**	**56**	**29**	**25**	**54**	**18**	**6**	**0**	**3**	**252**	**11.1**	**85**	**22**	**63**	**0**	**0**	**20**	**9**	**10**	**19**	**17**	**4**	**0**	**1**
1971-72	**Montreal Canadiens**	**NHL**	**77**	**32**	**49**	**81**	**34**	**45**	**79**	**26**	**8**	**0**	**7**	**266**	**12.0**	**129**	**42**	**52**	**2**	**+37**	**6**	**2**	**1**	**3**	**2**	**0**	**0**	**0**
1972-73	**Montreal Canadiens**	**NHL**	**77**	**44**	**51**	**95**	**44**	**43**	**87**	**16**	**9**	**0**	**5**	**294**	**15.0**	**145**	**37**	**50**	**1**	**+59**	**17**	**7**	**13**	**20**	**2**	**3**	**0**	**1**
1973-74	**Montreal Canadiens**	**NHL**	**66**	**29**	**38**	**67**	**30**	**33**	**63**	**10**	**10**	**0**	**7**	**219**	**13.2**	**95**	**34**	**59**	**2**	**+4**	**6**	**0**	**4**	**4**	**2**	**0**	**0**	**0**
1974-75	**Montreal Canadiens**	**NHL**	**80**	**36**	**56**	**92**	**33**	**44**	**77**	**20**	**12**	**0**	**8**	**260**	**13.8**	**138**	**63**	**53**	**3**	**+25**	**11**	**5**	**7**	**12**	**4**	**1**	**0**	**0**
1975-76	**Montreal Canadiens**	**NHL**	**61**	**20**	**32**	**52**	**19**	**25**	**44**	**20**	**6**	**0**	**3**	**226**	**8.8**	**86**	**32**	**32**	**4**	**+26**	**13**	**3**	**3**	**6**	**2**	**1**	**1**	**1**
1976-77	**Montreal Canadiens**	**NHL**	**75**	**34**	**41**	**75**	**33**	**33**	**66**	**22**	**5**	**2**	**4**	**272**	**12.5**	**138**	**31**	**48**	**11**	**+70**	**14**	**7**	**12**	**19**	**6**	**1**	**0**	**3**
1977-78	**Montreal Canadiens**	**NHL**	**76**	**36**	**61**	**97**	**35**	**50**	**85**	**14**	**6**	**0**	**5**	**310**	**11.6**	**143**	**41**	**60**	**12**	**+54**	**15**	**6**	**8**	**14**	**10**	**0**	**0**	**1**
1978-79	**Montreal Canadiens**	**NHL**	**50**	**24**	**31**	**55**	**22**	**24**	**46**	**10**	**6**	**1**	**4**	**203**	**11.8**	**82**	**26**	**53**	**6**	**+9**	**16**	***11**	**12**	***23**	**6**	**6**	**0**	**2**
1979-80	HC Sierre	Switz.	DID NOT PLAY – COACHING																									
	NHL Totals		**853**	**366**	**469**	**835**	**376**	**403**	**779**	**217**	**89**	**4**	**58**	**3051**	**12.0**	**1293**	**388**	**607**	**51**		**145**	**61**	**78**	**139**	**63**	**19**	**1**	**11**

Won Jack Adams Award (1994)

Played in NHL All-Star Game (1970, 1973)

• LEMAY, MOE Moe Lemay LW – L. 5'11", 185 lbs. b: Saskatoon, Sask., 2/18/1962. Vancouver's 4th choice, 105th overall, in 1981 Entry Draft.

Season	Club	League	GP	G	A	Pts	AG	AA	APts	PIM	PP	SH	GW	S	%	TGF	PGF	TGA	PGA	+/-	GP	G	A	Pts	PIM	PP	SH	GW
1979-80	Ottawa 67's	OHA	62	16	23	39	....	....	....	20	....	....	....	....	....	....	....	....	....	....	10	2	3	5	19	....	....	....
1980-81	Ottawa 67's	OHA	63	32	45	77	....	....	....	102	....	....	....	....	....	....	....	....	....	....	7	3	5	8	17	....	....	....
1981-82	Ottawa 67's	OHL	62	*68	70	138	....	....	....	48	....	....	....	....	....	....	....	....	....	....	17	9	*19	28	18	....	....	....
	Canada	WJC-A	7	2	0	2	....	....	....	4	....	....	....	....	....	....	....	....	....	....	....	....	....	....	....	....	....	....
	Vancouver Canucks	**NHL**	**5**	**1**	**2**	**3**	**1**	**1**	**2**	**0**	**1**	**0**	**0**	**14**	**7.1**	**7**	**3**	**3**	**0**	**+1**	....	....	....	....	....	....	....	....
1982-83	**Vancouver Canucks**	**NHL**	**44**	**11**	**9**	**20**	**9**	**6**	**15**	**41**	**3**	**0**	**1**	**72**	**15.3**	**37**	**13**	**30**	**0**	**–6**	....	....	....	....	....	....	....	....
	Fredericton Express	AHL	26	7	8	15	....	....	....	6	....	....	....	....	....	....	....	....	....	....	9	0	2	2	10	....	....	....
1983-84	**Vancouver Canucks**	**NHL**	**56**	**12**	**18**	**30**	**10**	**12**	**22**	**38**	**1**	**0**	**1**	**109**	**11.0**	**48**	**7**	**38**	**1**	**+4**	**4**	**0**	**0**	**0**	**12**	**0**	**0**	**0**
	Fredericton Express	AHL	23	9	7	16	....	....	....	32	....	....	....	....	....	....	....	....	....	....	....	....	....	....	....	....	....	....
1984-85	**Vancouver Canucks**	**NHL**	**74**	**21**	**31**	**52**	**17**	**21**	**38**	**68**	**4**	**1**	**2**	**162**	**13.0**	**72**	**18**	**69**	**4**	**–11**	....	....	....	....	....	....	....	....
1985-86	**Vancouver Canucks**	**NHL**	**48**	**16**	**15**	**31**	**13**	**10**	**23**	**92**	**6**	**0**	**1**	**112**	**14.3**	**42**	**17**	**39**	**0**	**–14**	....	....	....	....	....	....	....	....
1986-87	**Vancouver Canucks**	**NHL**	**52**	**9**	**17**	**26**	**8**	**12**	**20**	**128**	**2**	**0**	**0**	**86**	**10.5**	**38**	**7**	**34**	**1**	**–2**	....	....	....	....	....	....	....	....
	Edmonton Oilers	**NHL**	**10**	**1**	**2**	**3**	**1**	**1**	**2**	**36**	**0**	**0**	**0**	**7**	**14.3**	**6**	**0**	**4**	**0**	**+2**	**9**	**2**	**1**	**3**	**11**	**0**	**0**	**1**
1987-88	**Edmonton Oilers**	**NHL**	**4**	**0**	**0**	**0**	**0**	**0**	**0**	**2**	**0**	**0**	**0**	**5**	**0.0**	**0**	**0**	**1**	**0**	**–1**	....	....	....	....	....	....	....	....
	Nova Scotia Oilers	AHL	39	14	25	39	....	....	....	89	....	....	....	....	....	....	....	....	....	....	....	....	....	....	....	....	....	....
	Boston Bruins	**NHL**	**2**	**0**	**0**	**0**	**0**	**0**	**0**	**0**	**0**	**0**	**0**	**2**	**0.0**	**0**	**0**	**2**	**0**	**–2**	**15**	**4**	**2**	**6**	**32**	**0**	**0**	**0**
	Maine Mariners	AHL	11	5	6	11	....	....	....	14	....	....	....	....	....	....	....	....	....	....	3	2	1	3	22	....	....	....

			REGULAR SEASON																		PLAYOFFS							
Season	Club	League	GP	G	A	Pts	AG	AA	APts	PIM	PP	SH	GW	S	%	TGF	PGF	TGA	PGA	+/–	GP	G	A	Pts	PIM	PP	SH	GW
1988-89	**Boston Bruins**	NHL	12	0	0	0	0	0	0	23	0	0	0	6	0.0	2	0	7	0	–5	....	....	....	....	....	....	....	....
	Maine Mariners	AHL	13	6	2	8	....	....	....	32	....	....	....	....	....	....	....	....	....	....	....	....	....	....	....	....	....	....
	Winnipeg Jets	NHL	10	1	0	1	1	0	1	14	0	0	0	15	6.7	2	0	6	1	–3	....	....	....	....	....	....	....	....
	Moncton Hawks	AHL	16	9	11	20	....	....	....	21	....	....	....	....	....	....	....	....	....	....	10	3	6	9	25	....	....	....
	NHL Totals		317	72	94	166	60	63	123	442	17	1	5	590	12.2	254	65	233	7		28	6	3	9	55	0	0	1

OHL First All-Star Team (1982)

Traded to **Edmonton** by **Vancouver** for Raimo Summanen, March 10, 1987. Traded to **Boston** by **Edmonton** for Alan May, March 8, 1988. Traded to **Winnipeg** by **Boston** for Ray Neufeld, December 30, 1988.

• LEMELIN, ROGER

Roger Lemelin D – R. 6'3", 215 lbs. b: Iroquois Falls, Ont., 2/6/1954. Kansas City's 4th choice, 56th overall, in 1974 Amateur Draft.

Season	Club	League	GP	G	A	Pts	AG	AA	APts	PIM	PP	SH	GW	S	%	TGF	PGF	TGA	PGA	+/–	GP	G	A	Pts	PIM	PP	SH	GW
1972-73	London Knights	OHA	62	6	12	18	....	....	....	92	....	....	....	....	....	....	....	....	....	....	....	....	....	....	....	....	....	....
1973-74	London Knights	OHA	48	10	30	40	....	....	....	100	....	....	....	....	....	....	....	....	....	....	....	....	....	....	....	....	....	....
1974-75	**Kansas City Scouts**	NHL	8	0	1	1	0	1	1	6	0	0	0	4	0.0	3	1	13	2	–9	....	....	....	....	....	....	....	....
	Baltimore Clippers	AHL	36	1	13	14	....	....	....	59	....	....	....	....	....	....	....	....	....	....	....	....	....	....	....	....	....	....
	Springfield Indians	AHL	23	1	3	4	....	....	....	24	....	....	....	....	....	....	....	....	....	....	17	2	2	4	36	....	....	....
1975-76	**Kansas City Scouts**	NHL	11	0	0	0	0	0	0	0	0	0	0	1	0.0	2	0	5	2	–1	....	....	....	....	....	....	....	....
	Springfield Indians	AHL	53	4	14	18	....	....	....	83	....	....	....	....	....	....	....	....	....	....	....	....	....	....	....	....	....	....
1976-77	**Colorado Rockies**	NHL	14	1	1	2	1	1	2	21	0	0	0	25	4.0	10	0	21	5	–6	....	....	....	....	....	....	....	....
	Rhode Island Reds	AHL	47	2	8	10	....	....	....	73	....	....	....	....	....	....	....	....	....	....	....	....	....	....	....	....	....	....
1977-78	**Colorado Rockies**	NHL	3	0	0	0	0	0	0	0	0	0	0	0	0.0	0	0	0	0	0	....	....	....	....	....	....	....	....
	Phoenix Roadrunners	CHL	27	1	5	6	....	....	....	72	....	....	....	....	....	....	....	....	....	....	....	....	....	....	....	....	....	....
	Hampton Gulls	AHL	16	1	4	5	....	....	....	22	....	....	....	....	....	....	....	....	....	....	....	....	....	....	....	....	....	....
	Philadelphia Firebirds	AHL	33	0	5	5	....	....	....	52	....	....	....	....	....	....	....	....	....	....	....	....	....	....	....	....	....	....
1978-79	Hampton Aces	NEHL	38	4	12	16	....	....	....	109	....	....	....	....	....	....	....	....	....	....	....	....	....	....	....	....	....	....
1979-80	Hershey Bears	AHL	3	0	1	1	....	....	....	2	....	....	....	....	....	....	....	....	....	....	15	0	1	1	62	....	....	....
	Hampton Aces	EHL	5	0	1	1	....	....	....	20	....	....	....	....	....	....	....	....	....	....	....	....	....	....	....	....	....	....
1980-81	Hershey Bears	AHL	12	0	2	2	....	....	....	14	....	....	....	....	....	....	....	....	....	....	....	....	....	....	....	....	....	....
	Oklahoma City Stars	CHL	11	0	1	1	....	....	....	6	....	....	....	....	....	....	....	....	....	....	....	....	....	....	....	....	....	....
	Hampton Aces	EHL	21	0	6	6	....	....	....	24	....	....	....	....	....	....	....	....	....	....	....	....	....	....	....	....	....	....
1981-82			DID NOT PLAY																									
1982-83			DID NOT PLAY																									
1983-84	Muskegon Mohawks	IHL	57	3	13	16	....	....	....	65	....	....	....	....	....	....	....	....	....	....	....	....	....	....	....	....	....	....
	NHL Totals		36	1	2	3	1	2	3	27	0	0	0	30	3.3	15	1	39	9		....	....	....	....	....	....	....	....

Transferred to **Colorado** after **Kansas City** franchise relocated, July 15, 1976.

• LEMIEUX, ALAIN

Alain Lemieux C – L. 6', 185 lbs. b: Montreal, Que., 5/24/1961. St. Louis' 4th choice, 96th overall, in 1980 Entry Draft.

Season	Club	League	GP	G	A	Pts	AG	AA	APts	PIM	PP	SH	GW	S	%	TGF	PGF	TGA	PGA	+/–	GP	G	A	Pts	PIM	PP	SH	GW
1978-79	Chicoutimi Sagueneens	QMJHL	31	15	27	42	....	....	....	5	....	....	....	....	....	....	....	....	....	....	....	....	....	....	....	....	....	....
	Montreal Jr. Canadiens	QMJHL	39	7	5	12	....	....	....	2	....	....	....	....	....	....	....	....	....	....	....	....	....	....	....	....	....	....
1979-80	Chicoutimi Sagueneens	QMJHL	72	47	95	142	....	....	....	36	....	....	....	....	....	....	....	....	....	....	12	8	12	20	8	....	....	....
1980-81	Chicoutimi Sagueneens	QMJHL	1	0	0	0	....	....	....	2	....	....	....	....	....	....	....	....	....	....	....	....	....	....	....	....	....	....
	Trois-Rivieres Draveurs	QMJHL	69	68	98	166	....	....	....	62	....	....	....	....	....	....	....	....	....	....	19	18	*31	*49	38	....	....	....
1981-82	**St. Louis Blues**	NHL	3	0	1	1	0	1	1	0	0	0	0	7	0.0	2	0	3	0	–1	....	....	....	....	....	....	....	....
	Salt Lake Golden Eagles	CHL	74	41	42	83	....	....	....	61	....	....	....	....	....	....	....	....	....	....	10	6	4	10	14	....	....	....
1982-83	**St. Louis Blues**	NHL	42	9	25	34	7	17	24	18	1	0	0	71	12.7	42	6	46	0	–10	4	0	1	1	0	0	0	0
	Salt Lake Golden Eagles	CHL	29	20	24	44	....	....	....	35	....	....	....	....	....	....	....	....	....	....	....	....	....	....	....	....	....	....
1983-84	**St. Louis Blues**	NHL	17	4	5	9	3	3	6	6	1	0	0	14	28.6	10	2	8	0	0	....	....	....	....	....	....	....	....
	Montana Magic	CHL	38	28	41	69	....	....	....	36	....	....	....	....	....	....	....	....	....	....	....	....	....	....	....	....	....	....
	Springfield Indians	AHL	14	11	14	25	....	....	....	18	....	....	....	....	....	....	....	....	....	....	4	0	3	3	2	....	....	....
1984-85	**St. Louis Blues**	NHL	19	4	2	6	3	1	4	0	0	0	1	11	36.4	11	2	7	0	+2	....	....	....	....	....	....	....	....
	Peoria Rivermen	IHL	2	1	0	1	....	....	....	0	....	....	....	....	....	....	....	....	....	....	....	....	....	....	....	....	....	....
	Quebec Nordiques	NHL	30	11	11	22	3	7	10	12	2	0	2	48	22.9	35	17	19	0	–1	14	3	3	6	0	2	0	0
1985-86	**Quebec Nordiques**	NHL	7	0	0	0	0	0	0	2	0	0	0	1	0.0	0	0	1	0	–1	1	1	2	3	0	1	0	0
	Fredericton Express	AHL	64	29	45	74	....	....	....	54	....	....	....	....	....	....	....	....	....	....	5	5	2	7	5	....	....	....
1986-87	**Pittsburgh Penguins**	NHL	1	0	0	0	0	0	0	0	0	0	0	0	0.0	0	0	1	0	–1	....	....	....	....	....	....	....	....
	Baltimore Skipjacks	AHL	72	41	56	97	....	....	....	62	....	....	....	....	....	....	....	....	....	....	....	....	....	....	....	....	....	....
	EHC Chur	Switz.	2	0	1	1	....	....	....	....	....	....	....	....	....	....	....	....	....	....	....	....	....	....	....	....	....	....
1987-88	Hershey Bears	AHL	20	8	10	18	....	....	....	10	....	....	....	....	....	....	....	....	....	....	....	....	....	....	....	....	....	....
	Baltimore Skipjacks	AHL	16	2	14	16	....	....	....	4	....	....	....	....	....	....	....	....	....	....	....	....	....	....	....	....	....	....
	Springfield Indians	AHL	15	7	10	17	....	....	....	4	....	....	....	....	....	....	....	....	....	....	....	....	....	....	....	....	....	....
1988-89	Indianapolis Ice	IHL	29	18	26	44	....	....	....	90	....	....	....	....	....	....	....	....	....	....	....	....	....	....	....	....	....	....
	Karpat Oulu	Finland	16	4	9	13	....	....	....	16	....	....	....	....	....	....	....	....	....	....	....	....	....	....	....	....	....	....
	Saipa	Finland	5	1	4	5	....	....	....	4	....	....	....	....	....	....	....	....	....	....	....	....	....	....	....	....	....	....
1989-90			DID NOT PLAY																									
1990-91	Milwaukee Admirals	IHL	30	8	21	29	....	....	....	30	....	....	....	....	....	....	....	....	....	....	6	2	5	7	12	....	....	....
	Albany Choppers	IHL	33	5	36	41	....	....	....	24	....	....	....	....	....	....	....	....	....	....	....	....	....	....	....	....	....	....
	NHL Totals		119	28	44	72	22	29	51	38	4	0	3	152	18.4	100	27	85	0		19	4	6	10	0	3	0	0

QMJHL Second All-Star Team (1981) • AHL Second All-Star Team (1987)

Traded to **Quebec** by **St. Louis** for Luc Dufour, January 29, 1985. Signed as a free agent by **Pittsburgh**, December, 1986.

• LEMIEUX, BOB

Bob Lemieux D – L. 6'1", 195 lbs. b: Montreal, Que., 12/16/1944.

Season	Club	League	GP	G	A	Pts	AG	AA	APts	PIM	PP	SH	GW	S	%	TGF	PGF	TGA	PGA	+/–	GP	G	A	Pts	PIM	PP	SH	GW
1962-63	Montreal Jr. Canadiens	OHA	50	5	12	17	....	....	....	135	....	....	....	....	....	....	....	....	....	....	10	4	1	5	24	....	....	....
	Hull-Ottawa Canadiens	EPHL	1	0	0	0	....	....	....	0	....	....	....	....	....	....	....	....	....	....	....	....	....	....	....	....	....	....
1963-64	Montreal Jr. Canadiens	OHA	56	7	33	40	....	....	....	*219	....	....	....	....	....	....	....	....	....	....	17	2	8	10	58	....	....	....
1964-65	Montreal Jr. Canadiens	OHA	52	3	20	23	....	....	....	132	....	....	....	....	....	....	....	....	....	....	7	0	1	1	12	....	....	....
1965-66	Houston Apollos	CHL	2	0	0	0	....	....	....	2	....	....	....	....	....	....	....	....	....	....	....	....	....	....	....	....	....	....
	Muskegon Zephyrs	IHL	70	14	44	58	....	....	....	199	....	....	....	....	....	....	....	....	....	....	4	0	2	2	24	....	....	....
1966-67	Seattle Totems	WHL	72	10	13	23	....	....	....	117	....	....	....	....	....	....	....	....	....	....	10	2	2	4	14	....	....	....
1967-68	**Oakland Seals**	NHL	19	0	1	1	0	1	1	12	....	....	....	....	....	....	....	....	....	....	....	....	....	....	....	....	....	....
	Vancouver Canucks	WHL	44	10	21	31	....	....	....	70	....	....	....	....	....	....	....	....	....	....	....	....	....	....	....	....	....	....
1968-69	Vancouver Canucks	WHL	65	3	12	15	....	....	....	115	....	....	....	....	....	....	....	....	....	....	7	0	2	2	4	....	....	....
1969-70	Vancouver Canucks	WHL	59	7	10	17	....	....	....	92	....	....	....	....	....	....	....	....	....	....	11	1	0	1	2	....	....	....
	NHL Totals		19	0	1	1	0	1	1	12	0	0	0	0	0.0	0	0	0	0		....	....	....	....	....	....	....	....

IHL First All-Star Team (1966) • Won Governors' Trophy (Top Defenseman - IHL) (1966)

Claimed by **Oakland** from **Montreal** in Expansion Draft, June 6, 1967.

• LEMIEUX, CLAUDE

Claude Lemieux RW – R. 6'1", 215 lbs. b: Buckingham, Que., 7/16/1965. Montreal's 4th choice, 26th overall, in 1983 Entry Draft.

Season	Club	League	GP	G	A	Pts	AG	AA	APts	PIM	PP	SH	GW	S	%	TGF	PGF	TGA	PGA	+/–	GP	G	A	Pts	PIM	PP	SH	GW
1982-83	Trois-Rivières Draveurs	QMJHL	62	28	38	66	....	....	....	187	....	....	....	....	....	....	....	....	....	....	4	1	0	1	30	....	....	....
1983-84	Verdun Jr. Canadiens	QMJHL	51	41	45	86	....	....	....	225	....	....	....	....	....	....	....	....	....	....	9	8	12	20	63	....	....	....
	Montreal Canadiens	NHL	8	1	1	2	1	1	2	12	0	0	0	7	14.3	2	0	4	0	2	....	....	....	....	....	....	....	....
	Nova Scotia Voyageurs	AHL	....	....	....	....	....	....	....	....	....	....	....	....	....	....	....	....	....	....	2	1	0	1	0	....	....	....
1984-85	Verdun Jr. Canadiens	QMJHL	52	58	66	124	....	....	....	152	....	....	....	....	....	....	....	....	....	....	14	23	17	40	38	....	....	....
	Canada	WJC-A	6	3	2	5	....	....	....	6	....	....	....	....	....	....	....	....	....	....	....	....	....	....	....	....	....	....
	Montreal Canadiens	NHL	1	0	1	1	0	1	1	7	0	0	0	0	0.0	1	0	0	0	+1	....	....	....	....	....	....	....	....
1985-86	**Montreal Canadiens**	NHL	10	1	2	3	1	1	2	22	1	0	0	16	6.3	5	1	10	0	–6	20	10	6	16	68	4	0	4
	Sherbrooke Canadiens	AHL	58	21	32	53	....	....	....	145	....	....	....	....	....	....	....	....	....	....	....	....	....	....	....	....	....	....
1986-87	**Montreal Canadiens**	NHL	76	27	26	53	23	19	42	156	5	0	1	184	14.7	91	31	60	0	0	17	4	9	13	41	2	0	0
	NHL All-Stars	RV'87	2	0	0	0	....	....	....	4	....	....	....	....	....	....	....	....	....	....	....	....	....	....	....	....	....	....
1987-88	Canada	C Cup	6	1	1	2	....	....	....	4	....	....	....	....	....	....	....	....	....	....	....	....	....	....	....	....	....	....
	Montreal Canadiens	NHL	78	31	30	61	27	21	48	137	6	0	3	241	12.9	102	32	55	1	+16	11	3	2	5	20	0	0	2
1988-89	**Montreal Canadiens**	NHL	69	29	22	51	25	15	40	136	7	0	3	220	13.2	73	26	33	0	+14	18	4	3	7	58	0	0	0

			REGULAR SEASON																		PLAYOFFS							
Season	Club	League	GP	G	A	Pts	AG	AA	APts	PIM	PP	SH	GW	S	%	TGF	PGF	TGA	PGA	+/–	GP	G	A	Pts	PIM	PP	SH	GW
1989-90	Montreal Canadiens	NHL	39	8	10	18	7	7	14	106	3	0	1	104	7.7	26	11	24	1	–8	11	1	3	4	38	0	0	1
1990-91	New Jersey Devils	NHL	78	30	17	47	28	13	41	105	10	0	2	271	11.1	71	24	57	2	–8	7	4	0	4	34	2	0	1
1991-92	New Jersey Devils	NHL	74	41	27	68	38	20	58	109	13	1	8	296	13.9	110	33	73	5	+9	7	4	3	7	26	1	0	0
1992-93	New Jersey Devils	NHL	77	30	51	81	25	35	60	155	13	0	3	311	9.6	122	46	74	1	+3	5	2	0	2	19	1	0	0
1993-94	New Jersey Devils	NHL	79	18	26	44	17	20	37	86	5	0	5	181	9.9	73	20	63	23	+13	20	7	11	18	44	0	0	2
1994-95	New Jersey Devils	NHL	45	6	13	19	11	19	30	86	1	0	1	117	5.1	36	10	33	9	+2	20	*13	3	16	20	0	0	3
1995-96	Colorado Avalanche	NHL	79	39	32	71	39	26	65	117	9	2	10	315	12.4	117	39	78	14	+14	19	5	7	12	55	3	0	0
1996-97	Canada	W Cup	8	1	1	2	....	....	....	19	....	....	....	....	....	....	....	....	....	....	....	....	....	....	....	....	....	....
	Colorado Avalanche	NHL	45	11	17	28	12	15	27	43	5	0	4	168	6.5	51	20	35	0	–4	17	*13	10	23	32	4	0	4
1997-98	Colorado Avalanche	NHL	78	26	27	53	31	26	57	115	11	1	1	261	10.0	95	45	58	1	–7	7	3	3	6	8	1	0	1
	NHL Totals		836	298	302	600	285	239	524	1392	89	4	42	2692	11.1	975	338	657	57		179	73	60	133	463	18	0	18

QMJHL Second All-Star Team (1984) • QMJHL First All-Star Team (1985) • Won Conn Smythe Trophy (1995)

Traded to **New Jersey** by **Montreal** for Sylvain Turgeon, September 4, 1990. Traded to **NY Islanders** by **New Jersey** for Steve Thomas, October 3, 1995. Traded to **Colorado** by **NY Islanders** for Wendel Clark, October 3, 1995.

• LEMIEUX, JACQUES

Jacques Lemieux D – R. 6′2″, 190 lbs. b: Matane, Que., 4/8/1943.

Season	Club	League	GP	G	A	Pts	AG	AA	APts	PIM	PP	SH	GW	S	%	TGF	PGF	TGA	PGA	+/–	GP	G	A	Pts	PIM	PP	SH	GW
1963-64	Rouyn-Noranda Alouettes	NOHA	STATISTICS NOT AVAILABLE																									
	Omaha Knights	CHL	2	0	0	0	....	....	....	0	....	....	....	....	....	....	....	....	....	....	....	....	....	....	....	....	....	....
1964-65	Rouyn-Noranda Alouettes	NOHA	STATISTICS NOT AVAILABLE																									
	Omaha Knights	CHL	14	0	3	3	....	....	....	13	....	....	....	....	....	....	....	....	....	....	6	0	2	2	14	....	....	....
1965-66	Houston Apollos	CHL	70	7	19	26	....	....	....	59	....	....	....	....	....	....	....	....	....	....	....	....	....	....	....	....	....	....
1966-67	Cleveland Barons	AHL	68	6	30	36	....	....	....	47	....	....	....	....	....	....	....	....	....	....	5	0	2	2	6	....	....	....
1967-68	Los Angeles Kings	NHL	16	0	3	3	0	3	3	8	0	0	0	5	0.0	10	4	9	6	+3	....	....	....	....	....	....	....	....
1968-69	Denver Spurs	WHL	25	5	8	13	....	....	....	16	....	....	....	....	....	....	....	....	....	....	....	....	....	....	....	....	....	....
	Springfield Kings	AHL	51	4	31	35	....	....	....	6	....	....	....	....	....	....	....	....	....	....	....	....	....	....	....	....	....	....
	Los Angeles Kings	NHL	....	....	....	....	....	....	....	....	....	....	....	....	....	....	....	....	....	....	1	0	0	0	0	....	....	....
1969-70	Los Angeles Kings	NHL	3	0	1	1	0	1	1	0	0	0	0	0	0.0	1	0	1	0	0	....	....	....	....	....	....	....	....
	Springfield Kings	AHL	7	0	0	0	....	....	....	2	....	....	....	....	....	....	....	....	....	....	....	....	....	....	....	....	....	....
	Denver Spurs	WHL	7	1	0	1	....	....	....	4	....	....	....	....	....	....	....	....	....	....	....	....	....	....	....	....	....	....
	NHL Totals		19	0	4	4	0	4	4	8	0	0	0	5	0.0	11	4	10	6		1	0	0	0	0	0	0	0

Claimed by **LA Kings** from **Montreal** in Expansion Draft, June 6, 1967.

• LEMIEUX, JEAN

Jean Lemieux D – R. 6′1″, 180 lbs. b: Noranda, Que., 5/31/1952. Atlanta's 3rd choice, 34th overall, in 1972 Amateur Draft.

Season	Club	League	GP	G	A	Pts	AG	AA	APts	PIM	PP	SH	GW	S	%	TGF	PGF	TGA	PGA	+/–	GP	G	A	Pts	PIM	PP	SH	GW
1969-70	Sherbrooke Castors	QJHL	54	7	23	30	....	....	....	32	....	....	....	....	....	....	....	....	....	....	....	....	....	....	....	....	....	....
1970-71	Sherbrooke Castors	QJHL	62	18	37	55	....	....	....	52	....	....	....	....	....	....	....	....	....	....	11	2	5	7	4	....	....	....
1971-72	Sherbrooke Castors	QMJHL	61	20	50	70	....	....	....	32	....	....	....	....	....	....	....	....	....	....	4	1	4	5	15	....	....	....
1972-73	Omaha Knights	CHL	64	10	32	42	....	....	....	35	....	....	....	....	....	....	....	....	....	....	11	4	5	9	0	....	....	....
1973-74	Atlanta Flames	NHL	32	3	5	8	3	4	7	6	2	0	0	58	5.2	29	9	24	0	–4	3	1	1	2	0	1	0	0
	Nova Scotia Voyageurs	AHL	24	3	7	10	....	....	....	6	....	....	....	....	....	....	....	....	....	....	....	....	....	....	....	....	....	....
1974-75	Atlanta Flames	NHL	75	3	24	27	3	19	22	19	1	0	2	140	2.1	78	20	65	4	–3	....	....	....	....	....	....	....	....
1975-76	Atlanta Flames	NHL	33	4	9	13	4	7	11	10	1	0	0	51	7.8	36	15	17	0	+4	....	....	....	....	....	....	....	....
	Washington Capitals	NHL	33	6	14	20	6	11	17	2	5	0	1	65	9.2	37	15	49	6	–21	....	....	....	....	....	....	....	....
	Nova Scotia Voyageurs	AHL	11	1	9	10	....	....	....	2	....	....	....	....	....	....	....	....	....	....	....	....	....	....	....	....	....	....
1976-77	Washington Capitals	NHL	15	4	4	8	4	3	7	2	2	0	0	19	21.1	17	10	17	1	–9	....	....	....	....	....	....	....	....
	Springfield Indians	AHL	65	17	28	45	....	....	....	11	....	....	....	....	....	....	....	....	....	....	....	....	....	....	....	....	....	....
1977-78	Washington Capitals	NHL	16	3	7	10	3	6	9	0	3	0	0	24	12.5	15	11	16	0	–12	....	....	....	....	....	....	....	....
	Hershey Bears	AHL	55	7	25	32	....	....	....	12	....	....	....	....	....	....	....	....	....	....	....	....	....	....	....	....	....	....
1978-79	Nova Scotia Voyageurs	AHL	63	6	37	43	....	....	....	14	....	....	....	....	....	....	....	....	....	....	10	1	8	9	2	....	....	....
	NHL Totals		204	23	63	86	23	50	73	39	14	0	3	357	6.4	212	80	188	11		3	1	1	2	0	1	0	0

Traded to **Washington** by **Atlanta** with Gerry Meehan and Buffalo's 1st round choice (acquired earlier, Washington selected Greg Carroll) in 1976 Amateur Draft for Bill Clement, January 22, 1976.

• LEMIEUX, JOCELYN

Jocelyn Lemieux RW – L. 5′10″, 200 lbs. b: Mont-Laurier, Que., 11/18/1967. St. Louis' 1st choice, 10th overall, in 1986 Entry Draft.

Season	Club	League	GP	G	A	Pts	AG	AA	APts	PIM	PP	SH	GW	S	%	TGF	PGF	TGA	PGA	+/–	GP	G	A	Pts	PIM	PP	SH	GW
1984-85	Laval Titan	QMJHL	68	13	19	32	....	....	....	92	....	....	....	....	....	....	....	....	....	....	....	....	....	....	....	....	....	....
1985-86	Laval Titan	QMJHL	71	57	68	125	....	....	....	131	....	....	....	....	....	....	....	....	....	....	14	9	15	24	37	....	....	....
1986-87	St. Louis Blues	NHL	53	10	8	18	9	6	15	94	1	0	1	48	20.8	32	1	31	1	+1	5	0	1	1	6	0	0	0
1987-88	St. Louis Blues	NHL	23	1	0	1	1	0	1	42	0	0	0	19	5.3	5	0	10	0	–5	5	0	0	0	15	0	0	0
	Peoria Rivermen	IHL	8	0	5	5	....	....	....	35	....	....	....	....	....	....	....	....	....	....	....	....	....	....	....	....	....	....
1988-89	Montreal Canadiens	NHL	1	0	1	1	0	1	1	0	0	0	0	0	0.0	0	0	1	0	–1	....	....	....	....	....	....	....	....
	Sherbrooke Canadiens	AHL	73	25	28	53	....	....	....	134	....	....	....	....	....	....	....	....	....	....	4	3	1	4	6	....	....	....
1989-90	Montreal Canadiens	NHL	34	4	2	6	3	1	4	61	0	0	1	34	11.8	13	0	14	0	–1	....	....	....	....	....	....	....	....
	Chicago Blackhawks	NHL	39	10	11	21	9	8	17	47	1	0	1	78	12.8	28	3	29	4	0	18	1	8	9	28	0	0	0
1990-91	Chicago Blackhawks	NHL	67	6	7	13	5	5	10	119	1	1	2	89	6.7	24	5	34	8	–7	4	0	0	0	0	0	0	0
1991-92	Chicago Blackhawks	NHL	78	6	10	16	5	7	12	80	0	0	1	103	5.8	29	4	31	4	–2	18	3	1	4	33	0	0	2
1992-93	Chicago Blackhawks	NHL	81	10	21	31	8	14	22	111	1	0	2	117	8.5	37	3	29	0	+5	4	1	0	1	2	0	0	0
1993-94	Chicago Blackhawks	NHL	66	12	8	20	11	6	17	63	0	0	0	129	9.3	35	1	29	0	+5	....	....	....	....	....	....	....	....
	Hartford Whalers	NHL	16	6	1	7	6	1	7	19	0	0	2	22	27.3	8	0	20	4	–8	....	....	....	....	....	....	....	....
1994-95	Hartford Whalers	NHL	41	6	5	11	11	7	18	32	0	0	1	78	7.7	16	0	25	2	–7	....	....	....	....	....	....	....	....
1995-96	Hartford Whalers	NHL	29	1	2	3	1	2	3	31	0	0	0	43	2.3	7	0	18	0	–11	....	....	....	....	....	....	....	....
	New Jersey Devils	NHL	18	0	1	1	0	1	1	4	0	0	0	20	0.0	3	0	10	0	–7	....	....	....	....	....	....	....	....
	Calgary Flames	NHL	20	4	4	8	4	3	7	10	0	0	0	27	14.8	10	0	15	4	–1	4	0	0	0	0	0	0	0
1996-97	Long Beach Ice Dogs	IHL	28	4	10	14	....	....	....	54	....	....	....	....	....	....	....	....	....	....	....	....	....	....	....	....	....	....
	Phoenix Coyotes	NHL	2	1	0	1	1	0	1	0	0	0	1	4	25.0	1	0	1	0	0	2	0	0	0	4	0	0	0
1997-98	Phoenix Coyotes	NHL	30	3	3	6	4	3	7	27	1	0	0	32	9.4	9	1	8	0	0	....	....	....	....	....	....	....	....
	Springfield Falcons	AHL	6	3	1	4	....	....	....	0	....	....	....	....	....	....	....	....	....	....	4	2	2	4	2	....	....	....
	Long Beach Ice Dogs	IHL	10	3	5	8	....	....	....	24	....	....	....	....	....	....	....	....	....	....	....	....	....	....	....	....	....	....
	NHL Totals		598	80	84	164	78	65	143	740	5	1	12	843	9.5	257	18	305	27		60	5	10	15	88	0	0	2

QMJHL First All-Star Team (1986)

Traded to **Montreal** by **St. Louis** with Darrell May and St. Louis' 2nd round choice (Patrice Brisebois) in the 1989 Entry Draft for Sergio Momesso and Vincent Riendeau, August 9, 1988. Traded to **Chicago** by **Montreal** for Chicago's 3rd round choice (Charles Poulin) in 1990 Entry Draft, January 5, 1990. Traded to **Hartford** by **Chicago** with Frantisek Kucera for Gary Suter, Randy Cunneyworth and Hartford's 3rd round choice (later traded to Vancouver — Vancouver selected Larry Courville) in 1995 Entry Draft, March 11, 1994. Traded to **New Jersey** by **Hartford** with Hartford's 2nd round choice in 1998 Entry Draft for Jim Dowd and New Jersey's 2nd round choice (later traded to Calgary — Calgary selected Dmitri Kokorev) in 1997 Entry Draft, December 19, 1995. Traded to **Calgary** by **New Jersey** with Tommy Albelin and Cale Hulse for Phil Housley and Dan Keczmer, February 26, 1996. Signed as a free agent by **Phoenix**, March 18, 1997.

• LEMIEUX, MARIO

Mario "The Magnificent" Lemieux C – R. 6′4″, 225 lbs. b: Montreal, Que., 10/5/1965. Pittsburgh's 1st choice, 1st overall, in 1984 Entry Draft.

Season	Club	League	GP	G	A	Pts	AG	AA	APts	PIM	PP	SH	GW	S	%	TGF	PGF	TGA	PGA	+/–	GP	G	A	Pts	PIM	PP	SH	GW
1981-82	Laval Titan	QMJHL	64	30	66	96	....	....	....	22	....	....	....	....	....	....	....	....	....	....	18	5	9	14	31	....	....	....
1982-83	Laval Titan	QMJHL	66	84	100	184	....	....	....	76	....	....	....	....	....	....	....	....	....	....	12	14	18	32	18	....	....	....
	Canada	WJC-A	7	5	5	10	....	....	....	12	....	....	....	....	....	....	....	....	....	....	....	....	....	....	....	....	....	....
1983-84	Laval Titan	QMJHL	70	*133	*149	*282	....	....	....	92	....	....	....	....	....	....	....	....	....	....	14	*29	*23	*52	29	....	....	....
1984-85	Pittsburgh Penguins	NHL	73	43	57	100	35	39	74	54	11	0	2	209	20.6	125	46	114	0	–35	....	....	....	....	....	....	....	....
	Canada	WEC-A	9	4	6	10	....	....	....	2	....	....	....	....	....	....	....	....	....	....	....	....	....	....	....	....	....	....
1985-86	Pittsburgh Penguins	NHL	79	48	93	141	39	63	102	43	17	0	4	276	17.4	173	81	100	2	–6	....	....	....	....	....	....	....	....
1986-87	Pittsburgh Penguins	NHL	63	54	53	107	47	38	85	57	19	0	4	267	20.2	133	51	72	3	+13	....	....	....	....	....	....	....	....
	NHL All-Stars	RV'87	2	0	3	3	....	....	....	0	....	....	....	....	....	....	....	....	....	....	....	....	....	....	....	....	....	....
1987-88	Canada	C Cup	9	11	7	18	....	....	....	8	....	....	....	....	....	....	....	....	....	....	....	....	....	....	....	....	....	....
	Pittsburgh Penguins	NHL	77	*70	98	*168	60	70	130	92	22	10	7	382	18.3	211	106	121	39	+23	....	....	....	....	....	....	....	....
1988-89	Pittsburgh Penguins	NHL	76	*85	*114	*199	73	81	154	100	31	13	8	313	27.2	254	110	163	60	+41	11	12	7	19	16	7	1	0
1989-90	Pittsburgh Penguins	NHL	59	45	78	123	39	56	95	78	14	3	4	226	19.9	151	67	134	32	–18	....	....	....	....	....	....	....	....
1990-91	Pittsburgh Penguins	NHL	26	19	26	45	17	20	37	30	6	1	2	89	21.3	61	25	29	1	+8	23	16	*28	*44	16	6	2	0
1991-92	Pittsburgh Penguins	NHL	64	44	87	*131	40	66	106	94	12	4	5	249	17.7	182	70	99	14	+27	15	*16	18	*34	2	8	2	5
1992-93	Pittsburgh Penguins	NHL	60	69	91	*160	58	63	121	38	16	6	10	286	24.1	203	82	89	23	+55	11	8	10	18	10	3	1	1

			REGULAR SEASON																		PLAYOFFS							
Season	Club	League	GP	G	A	Pts	AG	AA	APts	PIM	PP	SH	GW	S	%	TGF	PGF	TGA	PGA	+/–	GP	G	A	Pts	PIM	PP	SH	GW
1993-94	Pittsburgh Penguins	NHL	22	17	20	37	16	15	31	32	7	0	4	92	18.5	42	19	31	6	–2	6	4	3	7	2	1	0	0
1994-95			DID NOT PLAY																									
1995-96	Pittsburgh Penguins	NHL	70	*69	*92	*161	68	75	143	54	31	8	8	338	20.4	197	102	113	28	+10	18	11	16	27	33	3	1	2
1996-97	Pittsburgh Penguins	NHL	76	50	*72	*122	53	64	117	65	15	3	7	327	15.3	156	54	102	27	+27	5	3	3	6	4	0	0	0
	NHL Totals		745	613	881	1494	545	650	1195	737	201	48	65	3054	20.1	1888	813	1167	235		89	70	85	155	83	28	7	8

QMJHL Second All-Star Team (1983) • QMJHL First All-Star Team (1984) • Canadian Major Junior Player of the Year (1984) • Won Calder Memorial Trophy (1985) • NHL All-Rookie Team (1985) • NHL Second All Star Team (1986, 1987, 1992) • Won Lester B. Pearson Award (1986, 1988, 1993, 1996) • Canada Cup All-Star Team (1987) • Won Hart Trophy (1988, 1993, 1996) • Won Art Ross Trophy (1988, 1989, 1992, 1993, 1996, 1997) • NHL First All-Star Team (1988, 1989, 1993, 1996, 1997) • Won Dodge Performance of the Year Award (1988) • Won Dodge Performer of the Year Award (1988, 1989) • Won Dodge Ram Tough Award (1989) • Won Conn Smythe Trophy (1991, 1992) • Won ProSet/NHL Player of the Year Award (1992) • Won Bill Masterton Memorial Trophy (1993) • Won Alka-Seltzer Plus Award (1993)

Played in NHL All-Star Game (1985, 1986, 1988, 1989, 1990, 1992, 1996, 1997)

• LEMIEUX, REAL

Real Lemieux LW – L. 5'11", 180 lbs. b: Victoriaville, Que., 1/3/1945. Deceased.

Season	Club	League	GP	G	A	Pts	AG	AA	APts	PIM	PP	SH	GW	S	%	TGF	PGF	TGA	PGA	+/–	GP	G	A	Pts	PIM	PP	SH	GW
1963-64	Hamilton Red Wings	OHA	42	20	24	44	....	....	....	58	....	....	....	....	....	....	....	....	....	....	....	....	....	....	....	....	....	....
1964-65	Hamilton Red Wings	OHA	48	48	40	88	....	....	....	64	....	....	....	....	....	....	....	....	....	....	....	....	....	....	....	....	....	....
	Memphis Wings	CHL	8	5	7	12	....	....	....	0	....	....	....	....	....	....	....	....	....	....	....	....	....	....	....	....	....	....
1965-66	Memphis Wings	CHL	53	11	15	26	....	....	....	68	....	....	....	....	....	....	....	....	....	....	....	....	....	....	....	....	....	....
1966-67	Detroit Red Wings	NHL	1	0	0	0	0	0	0	0	....	....	....	....	....	....	....	....	....	....	....	....	....	....	....	....	....	....
	Memphis Wings	CHL	68	28	34	62	....	....	....	*211	....	....	....	....	....	....	....	....	....	....	7	4	0	4	7	....	....	....
1967-68	Los Angeles Kings	NHL	74	12	23	35	15	24	39	60	5	1	0	129	9.3	60	16	77	31	–2	7	1	1	2	0	0	0	0
1968-69	Los Angeles Kings	NHL	75	11	29	40	12	27	39	68	2	0	2	134	8.2	66	14	97	23	–22	11	1	3	4	10	1	0	0
1969-70	New York Rangers	NHL	55	4	6	10	5	6	11	51	0	0	0	49	8.2	19	1	24	7	+1	....	....	....	....	....	....	....	....
	Los Angeles Kings	NHL	18	2	4	6	2	4	6	10	0	0	1	28	7.1	10	2	14	5	–1	....	....	....	....	....	....	....	....
1970-71	Los Angeles Kings	NHL	43	3	6	9	3	5	8	22	0	0	1	36	8.3	22	2	39	12	–7	....	....	....	....	....	....	....	....
	Springfield Kings	AHL	33	14	22	36	....	....	....	25	....	....	....	....	....	....	....	....	....	....	....	....	....	....	....	....	....	....
1971-72	Los Angeles Kings	NHL	78	13	25	38	14	23	37	28	2	0	0	102	12.7	56	12	103	19	–40	....	....	....	....	....	....	....	....
1972-73	Los Angeles Kings	NHL	74	5	10	15	5	8	13	19	1	1	0	43	11.6	29	3	45	18	–1	....	....	....	....	....	....	....	....
1973-74	Los Angeles Kings	NHL	20	0	0	0	0	0	0	0	0	0	0	2	0.0	2	0	13	11	0	....	....	....	....	....	....	....	....
	New York Rangers	NHL	7	0	0	0	0	0	0	0	0	0	0	0	0.0	0	0	1	0	–1	....	....	....	....	....	....	....	....
	Buffalo Sabres	NHL	11	1	1	2	1	1	2	4	0	0	0	4	25.0	3	0	4	1	0	....	....	....	....	....	....	....	....
	NHL Totals		456	51	104	155	57	98	155	262	10	2	4	527	9.7	267	50	417	127		18	2	4	6	10	1	0	0

Claimed by **LA Kings** from **Detroit** in Expansion Draft, June 6, 1967. Traded to **NY Rangers** by **LA Kings** for Leon Rochefort and Dennis Hextall, June 9, 1969. Traded to **LA Kings** by **NY Rangers** with Juha Widing for Ted Irvine, February 28, 1970. Traded to **NY Rangers** by **LA Kings** with Gilles Marotte for Sheldon Kannegiesser, Mike Murphy and Tom Williams, November 30, 1973. Traded to **Buffalo** by **NY Rangers** for Paul Curtis, January 21, 1974.

• LEMIEUX, RICHARD

Richard Lemieux C – L. 5'8", 155 lbs. b: Temiscamingue, Que., 4/19/1951. Vancouver's 3rd choice, 39th overall, in 1971 Amateur Draft.

Season	Club	League	GP	G	A	Pts	AG	AA	APts	PIM	PP	SH	GW	S	%	TGF	PGF	TGA	PGA	+/–	GP	G	A	Pts	PIM	PP	SH	GW
1967-68	Thetford Mines Canadiens	QJHL	....	28	32	60	....	....	....	....	....	....	....	....	....	....	....	....	....	....	....	....	....	....	....	....	....	....
1968-69	Montreal Jr. Canadiens	OHA	51	10	28	38	....	....	....	51	....	....	....	....	....	....	....	....	....	....	14	6	12	18	6	....	....	....
1969-70	Montreal Jr. Canadiens	OHA	50	29	43	72	....	....	....	75	....	....	....	....	....	....	....	....	....	....	....	....	....	....	....	....	....	....
1970-71	Montreal Jr. Canadiens	OHA	15	11	23	34	....	....	....	35	....	....	....	....	....	....	....	....	....	....	....	....	....	....	....	....	....	....
1971-72	Vancouver Canucks	NHL	42	7	9	16	7	8	15	4	0	0	0	82	8.5	23	0	36	0	–13	....	....	....	....	....	....	....	....
	Rochester Americans	AHL	34	12	12	24	....	....	....	30	....	....	....	....	....	....	....	....	....	....	....	....	....	....	....	....	....	....
1972-73	Vancouver Canucks	NHL	78	17	35	52	17	29	46	41	3	0	2	138	12.3	73	23	80	5	–25	....	....	....	....	....	....	....	....
1973-74	Vancouver Canucks	NHL	72	5	17	22	5	15	20	23	1	0	0	73	6.8	28	6	49	3	–24	....	....	....	....	....	....	....	....
1974-75	Kansas City Scouts	NHL	79	10	20	30	9	16	25	64	3	0	1	131	7.6	48	16	68	1	–35	....	....	....	....	....	....	....	....
1975-76	Kansas City Scouts	NHL	2	0	0	0	0	0	0	0	0	0	0	1	0.0	0	0	0	0	0	....	....	....	....	....	....	....	....
	Atlanta Flames	NHL	1	0	1	1	0	1	1	0	0	0	0	1	0.0	2	0	0	0	+2	2	0	0	0	0	0	0	0
	Nova Scotia Voyageurs	AHL	60	25	23	48	....	....	....	37	....	....	....	....	....	....	....	....	....	....	9	*8	6	14	4	....	....	....
1976-77	Calgary Cowboys	WHA	33	6	11	17	....	....	....	9	....	....	....	....	....	....	....	....	....	....	....	....	....	....	....	....	....	....
	NHL Totals		274	39	82	121	38	69	107	132	7	0	3	426	9.2	174	45	233	9		2	0	0	0	0	0	0	0
	Other Major League Totals		33	6	11	17	....	....	....	9	....	....	....	....	....	....	....	....	....	....	....	....	....	....	....	....	....	....

Selected by **LA Sharks** (WHA) in 1972 WHA General Player Draft, February 12, 1972. WHA rights transferred to **Michigan** (WHA) after **LA Sharks** (WHA) franchise relocated, April 11, 1974. Claimed by **Kansas City** from **Vancouver** in Expansion Draft, June 12, 1974. Traded to **Atlanta** by **Kansas City** with future considerations for Buster Harvey, October 13, 1975. Signed as a free agent by **Calgary** (WHA) after **Michigan-Baltimore** (WHA) franchise folded, June, 1976.

• LENARDON, TIM

Tim Lenardon C – L. 6'2", 185 lbs. b: Trail, B.C., 5/11/1962.

Season	Club	League	GP	G	A	Pts	AG	AA	APts	PIM	PP	SH	GW	S	%	TGF	PGF	TGA	PGA	+/–	GP	G	A	Pts	PIM	PP	SH	GW
1981-82	Trail Smoke Eaters	BCJHL	40	48	61	138	....	....	....	....	....	....	....	....	....	....	....	....	....	....	....	....	....	....	....	....	....	....
1982-83	Trail Smoke Eaters	BCJHL	38	86	86	172	....	....	....	....	....	....	....	....	....	....	....	....	....	....	....	....	....	....	....	....	....	....
1983-84	Brandon University	GPAC	24	22	21	43	....	....	....	36	....	....	....	....	....	....	....	....	....	....	....	....	....	....	....	....	....	....
1984-85	Brandon University	GPAC	24	20	39	59	....	....	....	42	....	....	....	....	....	....	....	....	....	....	....	....	....	....	....	....	....	....
1985-86	Brandon University	CWUAA	28	27	40	67	....	....	....	54	....	....	....	....	....	....	....	....	....	....	....	....	....	....	....	....	....	....
1986-87	New Jersey Devils	NHL	7	1	1	2	1	1	2	0	0	0	0	13	7.7	3	0	5	0	–2	....	....	....	....	....	....	....	....
	Maine Mariners	AHL	61	28	35	63	....	....	....	30	....	....	....	....	....	....	....	....	....	....	....	....	....	....	....	....	....	....
1987-88	Utica Devils	AHL	79	38	53	91	....	....	....	72	....	....	....	....	....	....	....	....	....	....	....	....	....	....	....	....	....	....
1988-89	Utica Devils	AHL	63	28	27	55	....	....	....	48	....	....	....	....	....	....	....	....	....	....	....	....	....	....	....	....	....	....
	Milwaukee Admirals	IHL	15	6	5	11	....	....	....	27	....	....	....	....	....	....	....	....	....	....	10	2	3	5	25	....	....	....
1989-90	Vancouver Canucks	NHL	8	1	0	1	1	0	1	4	0	0	0	9	11.1	1	0	4	1	–2	....	....	....	....	....	....	....	....
	Milwaukee Admirals	IHL	66	32	36	68	....	....	....	134	....	....	....	....	....	....	....	....	....	....	6	1	1	2	4	....	....	....
1990-91	HC Flemme	Italy	36	23	28	51	....	....	....	50	....	....	....	....	....	....	....	....	....	....	10	8	18	26	0	....	....	....
1991-92	Kalamazoo Wings	IHL	73	27	24	51	....	....	....	37	....	....	....	....	....	....	....	....	....	....	12	5	5	10	4	....	....	....
1992-93	Kalamazoo Wings	IHL	60	12	18	30	....	....	....	56	....	....	....	....	....	....	....	....	....	....	....	....	....	....	....	....	....	....
	NHL Totals		15	2	1	3	2	1	3	4	0	0	0	22	9.1	4	0	9	1		....	....	....	....	....	....	....	....

Signed as a free agent by **New Jersey**, August 6, 1986. Traded to **Vancouver** by **New Jersey** for Claude Vilgrain, March 7, 1989. Signed as a free agent by **Minnesota**, July 25, 1991.

• LEROUX, FRANCOIS

Francois Leroux D – L. 6'6", 235 lbs. b: Ste.-Adele, Que., 4/18/1970. Edmonton's 1st choice, 19th overall, in 1988 Entry Draft.

Season	Club	League	GP	G	A	Pts	AG	AA	APts	PIM	PP	SH	GW	S	%	TGF	PGF	TGA	PGA	+/–	GP	G	A	Pts	PIM	PP	SH	GW
1987-88	St-Jean Lynx	QMJHL	58	3	8	11	....	....	....	143	....	....	....	....	....	....	....	....	....	....	7	2	0	2	21	....	....	....
1988-89	St-Jean Lynx	QMJHL	57	8	34	42	....	....	....	185	....	....	....	....	....	....	....	....	....	....	....	....	....	....	....	....	....	....
	Edmonton Oilers	NHL	2	0	0	0	0	0	0	0	0	0	0	0	0.0	1	0	0	0	+1	....	....	....	....	....	....	....	....
1989-90	Victoriaville Tigres	QMJHL	54	4	33	37	....	....	....	169	....	....	....	....	....	....	....	....	....	....	....	....	....	....	....	....	....	....
	Edmonton Oilers	NHL	3	0	1	1	0	1	1	0	0	0	0	0	0.0	1	0	3	0	–2	....	....	....	....	....	....	....	....
1990-91	Edmonton Oilers	NHL	1	0	2	2	0	2	2	0	0	0	0	1	0.0	2	0	1	0	+1	....	....	....	....	....	....	....	....
	Cape Breton Oilers	AHL	71	2	7	9	....	....	....	124	....	....	....	....	....	....	....	....	....	....	4	0	1	1	19	....	....	....
1991-92	Edmonton Oilers	NHL	4	0	0	0	0	0	0	7	0	0	0	0	0.0	2	1	2	0	–1	....	....	....	....	....	....	....	....
	Cape Breton Oilers	AHL	61	7	22	29	....	....	....	114	....	....	....	....	....	....	....	....	....	....	5	0	0	0	8	....	....	....
1992-93	Edmonton Oilers	NHL	1	0	0	0	0	0	0	4	0	0	0	0	0.0	0	0	1	1	0	....	....	....	....	....	....	....	....
	Cape Breton Oilers	AHL	55	10	24	34	....	....	....	139	....	....	....	....	....	....	....	....	....	....	16	0	5	5	29	....	....	....
1993-94	Ottawa Senators	NHL	23	0	1	1	0	1	1	70	0	0	0	8	0.0	6	0	13	3	–4	....	....	....	....	....	....	....	....
	P.E.I. Senators	AHL	25	4	6	10	....	....	....	52	....	....	....	....	....	....	....	....	....	....	....	....	....	....	....	....	....	....
1994-95	P.E.I. Senators	AHL	45	4	14	18	....	....	....	137	....	....	....	....	....	....	....	....	....	....	....	....	....	....	....	....	....	....
	Pittsburgh Penguins	NHL	40	0	2	2	0	3	3	114	0	0	0	19	0.0	22	0	19	4	+7	12	0	2	2	14	0	0	0
1995-96	Pittsburgh Penguins	NHL	66	2	9	11	2	7	9	161	0	0	0	43	4.7	45	0	65	22	+2	18	1	1	2	20	0	0	1
1996-97	Pittsburgh Penguins	NHL	59	0	3	3	0	3	3	81	0	0	0	5	0.0	14	1	23	7	–3	3	0	0	0	0	0	0	0
1997-98	Colorado Avalanche	NHL	50	1	2	3	1	2	3	140	0	0	0	14	7.1	4	0	7	0	–3	....	....	....	....	....	....	....	....
	NHL Totals		249	3	20	23	3	19	22	577	0	0	0	90	3.3	97	2	134	37		33	1	3	4	34	0	0	1

Claimed on waivers by **Ottawa** from **Edmonton**, October 6, 1993. Claimed by **Pittsburgh** from **Ottawa** in Waiver Draft, January 18, 1995. Traded to **Colorado** by **Pittsburgh** for Colorado's 3rd round choice (David Cameron) in 1998 Entry Draft, September 28, 1997.

			REGULAR SEASON																		PLAYOFFS							
Season	**Club**	**League**	**GP**	**G**	**A**	**Pts**	**AG**	**AA**	**APts**	**PIM**	**PP**	**SH**	**GW**	**S**	**%**	**TGF**	**PGF**	**TGA**	**PGA**	**+/–**	**GP**	**G**	**A**	**Pts**	**PIM**	**PP**	**SH**	**GW**

• LEROUX, JEAN-YVES Jean-Yves Leroux LW – L. 6'2", 211 lbs. b: Montreal, Que., 6/24/1976. Chicago's 2nd choice, 40th overall, in 1994 Entry Draft.

Season	Club	League	GP	G	A	Pts	AG	AA	APts	PIM	PP	SH	GW	S	%	TGF	PGF	TGA	PGA	+/–	GP	G	A	Pts	PIM	PP	SH	GW
1992-93	Beauport Harfangs	QMJHL	62	20	25	45	....	....	....	33	....	....	....	....	....	....	....	....	....	....	....	....	....	....	....	....	....	....
1993-94	Beauport Harfangs	QMJHL	45	14	25	39	....	....	....	43	....	....	....	....	....	....	....	....	....	....	15	7	6	13	33	....	....	....
1994-95	Beauport Harfangs	QMJHL	59	19	33	52	....	....	....	125	....	....	....	....	....	....	....	....	....	....	17	4	6	10	39	....	....	....
1995-96	Beauport Harfangs	QMJHL	54	41	41	82	....	....	....	176	....	....	....	....	....	....	....	....	....	....	20	5	18	23	20	....	....	....
1996-97	**Chicago Blackhawks**	**NHL**	**1**	**0**	**1**	**1**	**0**	**1**	**1**	**5**	**0**	**0**	**0**	**0**	**0.0**	**1**	**0**	**0**	**0**	**+1**	....	....	....	....	....	....	....	....
	Indianapolis Ice	IHL	69	14	17	31	....	....	....	112	....	....	....	....	....	....	....	....	....	....	4	1	0	1	2	....	....	....
1997-98	**Chicago Blackhawks**	**NHL**	**66**	**6**	**7**	**13**	**7**	**7**	**14**	**55**	**0**	**0**	**0**	**57**	**10.5**	**25**	**2**	**25**	**0**	**–2**	....	....	....	....	....	....	....	....
	NHL Totals		**67**	**6**	**8**	**14**	**7**	**8**	**15**	**60**	**0**	**0**	**0**	**57**	**10.5**	**26**	**2**	**25**	**0**		....	....	....	....	....	....	....	....

QMJHL Second All-Star Team (1994)

• LESCHYSHYN, CURTIS Curtis Leschyshyn D – L. 6'1", 205 lbs. b: Thompson, Man., 9/21/1969. Quebec's 1st choice, 3rd overall, in 1988 Entry Draft.

Season	Club	League	GP	G	A	Pts	AG	AA	APts	PIM	PP	SH	GW	S	%	TGF	PGF	TGA	PGA	+/–	GP	G	A	Pts	PIM	PP	SH	GW
1986-87	Saskatoon Blades	WHL	70	14	26	40	....	....	....	107	....	....	....	....	....	....	....	....	....	....	11	1	5	6	14	....	....	....
1987-88	Saskatoon Blades	WHL	56	14	41	55	....	....	....	86	....	....	....	....	....	....	....	....	....	....	10	2	5	7	16	....	....	....
1988-89	**Quebec Nordiques**	**NHL**	**71**	**4**	**9**	**13**	**3**	**6**	**9**	**71**	**1**	**1**	**0**	**58**	**6.9**	**53**	**3**	**99**	**17**	**–32**	....	....	....	....	....	....	....	....
1989-90	**Quebec Nordiques**	**NHL**	**68**	**2**	**6**	**8**	**2**	**4**	**6**	**44**	**1**	**0**	**0**	**42**	**4.8**	**48**	**2**	**120**	**33**	**–41**	....	....	....	....	....	....	....	....
	Canada	WEC-A	9	0	0	0	....	....	....	4	....	....	....	....	....	....	....	....	....	....	....	....	....	....	....	....	....	....
1990-91	**Quebec Nordiques**	**NHL**	**55**	**3**	**7**	**10**	**3**	**5**	**8**	**49**	**2**	**0**	**1**	**57**	**5.3**	**41**	**6**	**70**	**16**	**–19**	....	....	....	....	....	....	....	....
1991-92	**Quebec Nordiques**	**NHL**	**42**	**5**	**12**	**17**	**5**	**9**	**14**	**42**	**3**	**0**	**1**	**61**	**8.2**	**43**	**22**	**61**	**12**	**–28**	....	....	....	....	....	....	....	....
	Halifax Citadels	AHL	6	0	2	2	....	....	....	4	....	....	....	....	....	....	....	....	....	....	....	....	....	....	....	....	....	....
1992-93	**Quebec Nordiques**	**NHL**	**82**	**9**	**23**	**32**	**7**	**16**	**23**	**61**	**4**	**0**	**2**	**73**	**12.3**	**110**	**23**	**100**	**38**	**+25**	**6**	**1**	**1**	**2**	**6**	**1**	**0**	**0**
1993-94	**Quebec Nordiques**	**NHL**	**72**	**5**	**17**	**22**	**5**	**13**	**18**	**65**	**3**	**0**	**2**	**97**	**5.2**	**90**	**24**	**103**	**35**	**–2**	....	....	....	....	....	....	....	....
1994-95	**Quebec Nordiques**	**NHL**	**44**	**2**	**13**	**15**	**4**	**19**	**23**	**20**	**0**	**0**	**0**	**43**	**4.7**	**67**	**9**	**45**	**16**	**+29**	**3**	**0**	**1**	**1**	**4**	**0**	**0**	**0**
1995-96	**Colorado Avalanche**	**NHL**	**77**	**4**	**15**	**19**	**4**	**12**	**16**	**73**	**0**	**0**	**1**	**76**	**5.3**	**86**	**9**	**62**	**17**	**+32**	**17**	**1**	**2**	**3**	**8**	**0**	**0**	**0**
1996-97	**Colorado Avalanche**	**NHL**	**11**	**0**	**5**	**5**	**0**	**4**	**4**	**6**	**0**	**0**	**0**	**8**	**0.0**	**6**	**0**	**5**	**0**	**+1**	....	....	....	....	....	....	....	....
	Washington Capitals	**NHL**	**2**	**0**	**0**	**0**	**0**	**0**	**0**	**2**	**0**	**0**	**0**	**0**	**0.0**	**1**	**0**	**1**	**0**	**0**	....	....	....	....	....	....	....	....
	Hartford Whalers	**NHL**	**64**	**4**	**13**	**17**	**4**	**11**	**15**	**30**	**1**	**1**	**1**	**94**	**4.3**	**49**	**13**	**74**	**19**	**–19**	....	....	....	....	....	....	....	....
1997-98	**Carolina Hurricanes**	**NHL**	**73**	**2**	**10**	**12**	**2**	**10**	**12**	**45**	**1**	**0**	**1**	**53**	**3.8**	**48**	**5**	**64**	**19**	**–2**	....	....	....	....	....	....	....	....
	NHL Totals		**661**	**40**	**130**	**170**	**39**	**109**	**148**	**508**	**16**	**2**	**9**	**662**	**6.0**	**642**	**116**	**804**	**222**		**26**	**2**	**4**	**6**	**18**	**1**	**0**	**0**

Transferred to **Colorado** after **Quebec** franchise relcoated, June 21, 1995. Traded to **Washington** by **Colorado** with Chris Simon for Keith Jones, Washington's 1st and 4th round choices in 1998 Entry Draft, November 2, 1996. Traded to **Hartford** by **Washington** for Andrei Nikolishin, November 9, 1996. Transferred to **Carolina** after **Hartford** franchise relocated, June 25, 1997.

• LESSARD, RICK Rick Lessard D – L. 6'2", 206 lbs. b: Timmins, Ont., 1/9/1968. Calgary's 6th choice, 142nd overall, in 1986 Entry Draft.

Season	Club	League	GP	G	A	Pts	AG	AA	APts	PIM	PP	SH	GW	S	%	TGF	PGF	TGA	PGA	+/–	GP	G	A	Pts	PIM	PP	SH	GW
1984-85	Ottawa 67's	OHL	60	2	13	15	....	....	....	128	....	....	....	....	....	....	....	....	....	....	5	1	4	5	10	....	....	....
1985-86	Ottawa 67's	OHL	64	1	20	21	....	....	....	231	....	....	....	....	....	....	....	....	....	....	....	....	....	....	....	....	....	....
1986-87	Ottawa 67's	OHL	66	5	36	41	....	....	....	188	....	....	....	....	....	....	....	....	....	....	11	1	7	8	30	....	....	....
1987-88	Ottawa 67's	OHL	58	5	34	39	....	....	....	210	....	....	....	....	....	....	....	....	....	....	16	1	0	1	31	....	....	....
1988-89	**Calgary Flames**	**NHL**	**6**	**0**	**1**	**1**	**0**	**1**	**1**	**2**	**0**	**0**	**0**	**0**	**0.0**	**2**	**0**	**4**	**0**	**–2**	....	....	....	....	....	....	....	....
	Salt Lake Golden Eagles	IHL	76	10	42	52	....	....	....	239	....	....	....	....	....	....	....	....	....	....	14	1	6	7	35	....	....	....
1989-90	Salt Lake Golden Eagles	IHL	66	3	18	21	....	....	....	169	....	....	....	....	....	....	....	....	....	....	10	1	2	3	64	....	....	....
1990-91	**Calgary Flames**	**NHL**	**1**	**0**	**1**	**1**	**0**	**1**	**1**	**0**	**0**	**0**	**0**	**0**	**0.0**	**1**	**0**	**2**	**0**	**–1**	....	....	....	....	....	....	....	....
	Salt Lake Golden Eagles	IHL	80	8	27	35	....	....	....	272	....	....	....	....	....	....	....	....	....	....	4	0	1	1	12	....	....	....
1991-92	**San Jose Sharks**	**NHL**	**8**	**0**	**2**	**2**	**0**	**1**	**1**	**16**	**0**	**0**	**0**	**4**	**0.0**	**4**	**0**	**10**	**2**	**–4**	....	....	....	....	....	....	....	....
	Kansas City Blades	IHL	46	3	16	19	....	....	....	117	....	....	....	....	....	....	....	....	....	....	3	0	0	0	2	....	....	....
1992-93	Kansas City Blades	IHL	1	0	0	0	....	....	....	0	....	....	....	....	....	....	....	....	....	....	....	....	....	....	....	....	....	....
	Providence Bruins	AHL	6	0	0	0	....	....	....	6	....	....	....	....	....	....	....	....	....	....	....	....	....	....	....	....	....	....
	Hamilton Canucks	AHL	52	0	17	17	....	....	....	151	....	....	....	....	....	....	....	....	....	....	....	....	....	....	....	....	....	....
1993-94	South Carolina Stingrays	ECHL	5	1	0	1	....	....	....	10	....	....	....	....	....	....	....	....	....	....	....	....	....	....	....	....	....	....
	Salt Lake Golden Eagles	IHL	31	1	2	3	....	....	....	110	....	....	....	....	....	....	....	....	....	....	....	....	....	....	....	....	....	....
	Rochester Americans	AHL	8	1	2	3	....	....	....	2	....	....	....	....	....	....	....	....	....	....	4	0	0	0	2	....	....	....
	NHL Totals		**15**	**0**	**4**	**4**	**0**	**3**	**3**	**18**	**0**	**0**	**0**	**4**	**0.0**	**7**	**0**	**16**	**2**		....	....	....	....	....	....	....	....

IHL First All-Star Team (1989)

Claimed by **San Jose** from **Calgary** in Expansion Draft, May 30, 1991. Traded to **Vancouver** by **San Jose** for Robin Bawa, December 15, 1992.

• LESUK, BILL Bill Lesuk LW – L. 5'9", 187 lbs. b: Moose Jaw, Sask., 11/1/1946.

Season	Club	League	GP	G	A	Pts	AG	AA	APts	PIM	PP	SH	GW	S	%	TGF	PGF	TGA	PGA	+/–	GP	G	A	Pts	PIM	PP	SH	GW
1963-64	Weyburn Red Wings	SJHL	62	12	18	30	....	....	....	78	....	....	....	....	....	....	....	....	....	....	8	4	2	6	18	....	....	....
1964-65	Weyburn Red Wings	SJHL	55	25	33	58	....	....	....	73	....	....	....	....	....	....	....	....	....	....	15	3	11	14	28	....	....	....
1965-66	Weyburn Red Wings	SJHL	60	36	40	76	....	....	....	111	....	....	....	....	....	....	....	....	....	....	18	6	10	16	40	....	....	....
1966-67	Weyburn Red Wings	SJHL	56	36	46	82	....	....	....	62	....	....	....	....	....	....	....	....	....	....	5	1	5	6	4	....	....	....
1967-68	Oklahoma City Blazers	CHL	67	14	10	24	....	....	....	53	....	....	....	....	....	....	....	....	....	....	7	3	3	6	0	....	....	....
1968-69	**Boston Bruins**	**NHL**	**5**	**0**	**1**	**1**	**0**	**1**	**1**	**0**	**0**	**0**	**0**	**2**	**0.0**	**2**	**0**	**0**	**0**	**+2**	**1**	**0**	**0**	**0**	**0**	**0**	**0**	**0**
	Oklahoma City Blazers	CHL	64	17	30	47	....	....	....	46	....	....	....	....	....	....	....	....	....	....	12	0	4	4	8	....	....	....
1969-70	**Boston Bruins**	**NHL**	**3**	**0**	**0**	**0**	**0**	**0**	**0**	**0**	**0**	**0**	**0**	**2**	**0.0**	**1**	**0**	**0**	**0**	**+1**	**2**	**0**	**0**	**0**	**0**	**0**	**0**	**0**
	Hershey Bears	AHL	70	20	20	40	....	....	....	82	....	....	....	....	....	....	....	....	....	....	7	5	4	9	10	....	....	....
1970-71	**Philadelphia Flyers**	**NHL**	**78**	**17**	**19**	**36**	**18**	**17**	**35**	**81**	**2**	**0**	**2**	**149**	**11.4**	**67**	**9**	**74**	**11**	**–5**	**4**	**1**	**0**	**1**	**8**	**1**	**0**	**0**
1971-72	**Philadelphia Flyers**	**NHL**	**45**	**7**	**6**	**13**	**7**	**5**	**12**	**31**	**2**	**0**	**1**	**116**	**6.0**	**29**	**7**	**48**	**12**	**–14**	....	....	....	....	....	....	....	....
	Los Angeles Kings	**NHL**	**27**	**4**	**10**	**14**	**4**	**9**	**13**	**14**	**1**	**0**	**1**	**47**	**8.5**	**27**	**6**	**19**	**0**	**+2**	....	....	....	....	....	....	....	....
1972-73	**Los Angeles Kings**	**NHL**	**67**	**6**	**14**	**20**	**6**	**12**	**18**	**90**	**0**	**0**	**0**	**129**	**4.7**	**35**	**4**	**35**	**2**	**–2**	....	....	....	....	....	....	....	....
1973-74	**Los Angeles Kings**	**NHL**	**35**	**2**	**1**	**3**	**2**	**1**	**3**	**32**	**0**	**0**	**0**	**25**	**8.0**	**7**	**0**	**12**	**1**	**–4**	**2**	**0**	**0**	**0**	**4**	**0**	**0**	**0**
1974-75	**Washington Capitals**	**NHL**	**79**	**8**	**11**	**19**	**7**	**9**	**16**	**77**	**1**	**2**	**0**	**119**	**6.7**	**34**	**6**	**107**	**45**	**–34**	....	....	....	....	....	....	....	....
1975-76	Winnipeg Jets	WHA	81	15	21	36	....	....	....	92	....	....	....	....	....	....	....	....	....	....	13	2	2	4	8	....	....	....
1976-77	Winnipeg Jets	WHA	78	14	27	41	....	....	....	85	....	....	....	....	....	....	....	....	....	....	18	2	1	3	22	....	....	....
1977-78	Winnipeg Jets	WHA	80	9	18	27	....	....	....	48	....	....	....	....	....	....	....	....	....	....	9	2	5	7	12	....	....	....
1978-79	Winnipeg Jets	WHA	79	17	15	32	....	....	....	44	....	....	....	....	....	....	....	....	....	....	10	1	3	4	6	....	....	....
1979-80	**Winnipeg Jets**	**NHL**	**49**	**0**	**1**	**1**	**0**	**1**	**1**	**43**	**0**	**0**	**0**	**37**	**0.0**	**4**	**0**	**27**	**8**	**–15**	....	....	....	....	....	....	....	....
	Tulsa Oilers	CHL	9	1	2	3	....	....	....	0	....	....	....	....	....	....	....	....	....	....	....	....	....	....	....	....	....	....
	NHL Totals		**388**	**44**	**63**	**107**	**44**	**55**	**99**	**368**	**6**	**2**	**4**	**626**	**7.0**	**206**	**32**	**322**	**79**		**9**	**1**	**0**	**1**	**12**	**1**	**0**	**0**
	Other Major League Totals		318	55	81	136	....	....	....	269	....	....	....	....	....	....	....	....	....	....	50	7	11	18	48	....	....	....

Traded to **Boston** by **Detroit** with Gary Doak and future considerations (Steve Atkinson, May 16, 1966) for Leo Boivin, February 18, 1966. Claimed by **Philadelphia** from **Boston** in Intra-League Draft, June 9, 1970. Traded to **LA Kings** by **Philadelphia** with Jim Johnson and Serge Bernier for Bill Flett, Jean Potvin, and Ross Lonsberry, January 28, 1972. Selected by **Alberta** (WHA) in 1972 WHA General Player Draft, February 12, 1972. Traded to **Washington** by **LA Kings** for cash, July 28, 1974. WHA rights traded to **Winnipeg** (WHA) by **Edmonton** (WHA) for future considerations, July, 1975.

• LEVEILLE, NORMAND Normand Leveille LW – L. 5'10", 175 lbs. b: Montreal, Que., 1/10/1963. Boston's 1st choice, 14th overall, in 1981 Entry Draft.

Season	Club	League	GP	G	A	Pts	AG	AA	APts	PIM	PP	SH	GW	S	%	TGF	PGF	TGA	PGA	+/–	GP	G	A	Pts	PIM	PP	SH	GW
1979-80	Chicoutimi Sagueneens	QMJHL	60	24	12	36	....	....	....	39	....	....	....	....	....	....	....	....	....	....	12	4	6	10	2	....	....	....
1980-81	Chicoutimi Sagueneens	QMJHL	72	55	46	101	....	....	....	46	....	....	....	....	....	....	....	....	....	....	12	11	15	26	8	....	....	....
1981-82	**Boston Bruins**	**NHL**	**66**	**14**	**19**	**33**	**11**	**13**	**24**	**49**	**1**	**0**	**4**	**148**	**9.5**	**58**	**4**	**38**	**0**	**+16**	....	....	....	....	....	....	....	....
1982-83	**Boston Bruins**	**NHL**	**9**	**3**	**6**	**9**	**2**	**4**	**6**	**0**	**2**	**0**	**2**	**31**	**9.7**	**12**	**4**	**7**	**0**	**+1**	....	....	....	....	....	....	....	....
	NHL Totals		**75**	**17**	**25**	**42**	**13**	**17**	**30**	**49**	**3**	**0**	**6**	**179**	**9.5**	**70**	**8**	**45**	**0**		....	....	....	....	....	....	....	....

QMJHL Second All-Star Team (1981)

• Suffered career-ending brain aneurysm during game vs. Vancouver, October 23, 1982.

• LEVEQUE, GUY Guy Leveque C – R. 5'11", 180 lbs. b: Kingston, Ont., 12/28/1972. Los Angeles' 1st choice, 42nd overall, in 1991 Entry Draft.

Season	Club	League	GP	G	A	Pts	AG	AA	APts	PIM	PP	SH	GW	S	%	TGF	PGF	TGA	PGA	+/–	GP	G	A	Pts	PIM	PP	SH	GW
1989-90	Cornwall Royals	OHL	62	10	15	25	....	....	....	30	....	....	....	....	....	....	....	....	....	....	3	0	0	0	4	....	....	....
1990-91	Cornwall Royals	OHL	66	41	56	97	....	....	....	34	....	....	....	....	....	....	....	....	....	....	....	....	....	....	....	....	....	....
1991-92	Cornwall Royals	OHL	37	23	36	59	....	....	....	40	....	....	....	....	....	....	....	....	....	....	6	3	5	8	2	....	....	....
1992-93	**Los Angeles Kings**	**NHL**	**12**	**2**	**1**	**3**	**2**	**1**	**3**	**19**	**0**	**0**	**0**	**12**	**16.7**	**4**	**1**	**7**	**0**	**–4**	....	....	....	....	....	....	....	....
	Phoenix Roadrunners	IHL	56	27	30	57	....	....	....	71	....	....	....	....	....	....	....	....	....	....	....	....	....	....	....	....	....	....

Season	Club	League	REGULAR SEASON																		PLAYOFFS							
			GP	G	A	Pts	AG	AA	APts	PIM	PP	SH	GW	S	%	TGF	PGF	TGA	PGA	+/–	GP	G	A	Pts	PIM	PP	SH	GW
1993-94	**Los Angeles Kings**	**NHL**	**5**	**0**	**1**	**1**	**0**	**1**	**1**	**2**	**0**	**0**	**0**	**3**	**0.0**	**1**	**0**	**0**	**0**	**+1**	....	....	....	....	....	....	....	....
	Phoenix Roadrunners	IHL	39	10	16	26	....	....	....	47	....	....	....	....	....	....	....	....	....	....	....	....	....	....	....	....	....	....
1994-95	Canada	Nat-Team	31	17	17	34	....	....	....	14	....	....	....	....	....	....	....	....	....	....	....	....	....	....	....	....	....	....
	Phoenix Roadrunners	IHL	2	0	0	0	....	....	....	15	....	....	....	....	....	....	....	....	....	....	....	....	....	....	....	....	....	....
	St. John's Maple Leafs	AHL	37	8	14	22	....	....	....	31	....	....	....	....	....	....	....	....	....	....	3	0	0	0	0	....	....	....
1995-96	Minnesota Moose	IHL	12	1	4	5	....	....	....	2	....	....	....	....	....	....	....	....	....	....	....	....	....	....	....	....	....	....
1996-97	San Antonio Dragons	IHL	3	0	1	1	....	....	....	0	....	....	....	....	....	....	....	....	....	....	....	....	....	....	....	....	....	....
1997-98	Phoenix Mustangs	WCHL	48	24	32	56	....	....	....	41	....	....	....	....	....	....	....	....	....	....	6	2	3	5	2	....	....	....
	NHL Totals		**17**	**2**	**2**	**4**	**2**	**2**	**4**	**21**	**0**	**0**	**0**	**15**	**13.3**	**5**	**1**	**7**	**0**		....	....	....	....	....	....	....	....

Traded to **Toronto** by **LA Kings** with Dixon Ward, Kelly Fairchild and Shayne Toporowski for Eric Lacroix, Chris Snell and Toronto's 4th round choice (Eric Belanger) in 1996 Entry Draft, October 3, 1994.

• LEVER, DON

Don "Cleaver" Lever LW – L. 5'11", 185 lbs. b: South Porcupine, Ont., 11/14/1952. Vancouver's 1st choice, 3rd overall, in 1972 Amateur Draft.

Season	Club	League	GP	G	A	Pts	AG	AA	APts	PIM	PP	SH	GW	S	%	TGF	PGF	TGA	PGA	+/–	GP	G	A	Pts	PIM	PP	SH	GW
1970-71	Niagara Falls Flyers	OHA	59	35	36	71	....	....	....	112	....	....	....	....	....	....	....	....	....	....	....	....	....	....	....	....	....	....
1971-72	Niagara Falls Flyers	OHA	63	61	65	126	....	....	....	69	....	....	....	....	....	....	....	....	....	....	....	....	....	....	....	....	....	....
1972-73	**Vancouver Canucks**	**NHL**	**78**	**12**	**26**	**38**	**12**	**22**	**34**	**49**	**3**	**1**	**1**	**138**	**8.7**	**62**	**12**	**85**	**8**	**–27**	....	....	....	....	....	....	....	....
1973-74	**Vancouver Canucks**	**NHL**	**78**	**23**	**25**	**48**	**23**	**22**	**45**	**28**	**4**	**1**	**1**	**175**	**13.1**	**70**	**20**	**96**	**30**	**–16**	....	....	....	....	....	....	....	....
1974-75	**Vancouver Canucks**	**NHL**	**80**	**38**	**30**	**68**	**35**	**24**	**59**	**49**	**11**	**0**	**3**	**214**	**17.8**	**92**	**34**	**73**	**2**	**–13**	**5**	**0**	**1**	**1**	**4**	**0**	**0**	**0**
1975-76	**Vancouver Canucks**	**NHL**	**80**	**25**	**40**	**65**	**23**	**31**	**54**	**93**	**8**	**0**	**1**	**166**	**15.1**	**89**	**28**	**72**	**9**	**–2**	**2**	**0**	**0**	**0**	**0**	**0**	**0**	**0**
1976-77	**Vancouver Canucks**	**NHL**	**80**	**27**	**30**	**57**	**26**	**24**	**50**	**28**	**8**	**1**	**2**	**198**	**13.6**	**90**	**24**	**95**	**21**	**–8**	....	....	....	....	....	....	....	....
1977-78	**Vancouver Canucks**	**NHL**	**75**	**17**	**32**	**49**	**16**	**26**	**42**	**58**	**6**	**0**	**1**	**168**	**10.1**	**74**	**21**	**100**	**18**	**–29**	....	....	....	....	....	....	....	....
	Canada	WEC-A	10	4	3	7	....	....	....	4	....	....	....	....	....	....	....	....	....	....	....	....	....	....	....	....	....	....
1978-79	**Vancouver Canucks**	**NHL**	**71**	**23**	**21**	**44**	**21**	**16**	**37**	**17**	**8**	**0**	**2**	**170**	**13.5**	**64**	**23**	**104**	**22**	**–41**	**3**	**2**	**1**	**3**	**2**	**1**	**0**	**1**
1979-80	**Vancouver Canucks**	**NHL**	**51**	**21**	**17**	**38**	**19**	**13**	**32**	**32**	**5**	**0**	**0**	**134**	**15.7**	**55**	**17**	**65**	**14**	**–13**	....	....	....	....	....	....	....	....
	Atlanta Flames	**NHL**	**28**	**14**	**16**	**30**	**13**	**12**	**25**	**4**	**1**	**1**	**1**	**74**	**18.9**	**41**	**6**	**32**	**2**	**+5**	**4**	**1**	**1**	**2**	**0**	**1**	**0**	**0**
1980-81	**Calgary Flames**	**NHL**	**62**	**26**	**31**	**57**	**21**	**22**	**43**	**56**	**4**	**1**	**4**	**157**	**16.6**	**99**	**24**	**74**	**20**	**+21**	**16**	**4**	**7**	**11**	**20**	**0**	**0**	**0**
1981-82	**Calgary Flames**	**NHL**	**23**	**8**	**11**	**19**	**6**	**7**	**13**	**6**	**1**	**0**	**0**	**55**	**14.5**	**24**	**8**	**35**	**5**	**–14**	....	....	....	....	....	....	....	....
	Colorado Rockies	**NHL**	**59**	**22**	**28**	**50**	**17**	**19**	**36**	**20**	**3**	**0**	**1**	**136**	**16.2**	**68**	**16**	**78**	**16**	**–10**	....	....	....	....	....	....	....	....
1982-83	**New Jersey Devils**	**NHL**	**79**	**23**	**30**	**53**	**19**	**21**	**40**	**68**	**9**	**3**	**0**	**143**	**16.1**	**80**	**35**	**126**	**46**	**–35**	....	....	....	....	....	....	....	....
1983-84	**New Jersey Devils**	**NHL**	**70**	**14**	**19**	**33**	**11**	**13**	**24**	**44**	**3**	**0**	**2**	**111**	**12.6**	**54**	**12**	**82**	**19**	**–21**	....	....	....	....	....	....	....	....
1984-85	**New Jersey Devils**	**NHL**	**67**	**10**	**8**	**18**	**8**	**5**	**13**	**31**	**0**	**1**	**1**	**83**	**12.0**	**30**	**5**	**68**	**14**	**–29**	....	....	....	....	....	....	....	....
1985-86	**Buffalo Sabres**	**NHL**	**29**	**7**	**1**	**8**	**6**	**1**	**7**	**6**	**0**	**1**	**1**	**31**	**22.6**	**14**	**0**	**30**	**11**	**–5**	....	....	....	....	....	....	....	....
	Rochester Americans	AHL	29	6	11	17	....	....	....	16	....	....	....	....	....	....	....	....	....	....	....	....	....	....	....	....	....	....
1986-87	**Buffalo Sabres**	**NHL**	**10**	**3**	**2**	**5**	**3**	**1**	**4**	**4**	**3**	**0**	**1**	**8**	**37.5**	**8**	**4**	**8**	**1**	**–3**	....	....	....	....	....	....	....	....
	Rochester Americans	AHL	57	29	25	54	....	....	....	69	....	....	....	....	....	....	....	....	....	....	18	4	3	7	14	....	....	....
	NHL Totals		**1020**	**313**	**367**	**680**	**279**	**279**	**558**	**593**	**77**	**10**	**22**	**2161**	**14.5**	**1014**	**289**	**1223**	**258**		**30**	**7**	**10**	**17**	**26**	**2**	**0**	**1**

OHA First All-Star Team (1972)

Played in NHL All-Star Game (1982)

Traded to **Atlanta** by **Vancouver** with Brad Smith for Ivan Boldirev and Darcy Rota, February 8, 1980. Transferred to **Calgary** after **Colorado** franchise relocated, June 24, 1980. Traded to **Colorado** by **Calgary** with Bob MacMillan for Lanny McDonald and Colorado's 4th round choice (later traded to NY Islanders — NY Islanders selected Mikko Makela) in 1983 Entry Draft, November 25, 1981. Transferred to **New Jersey** after **Colorado** franchise relocated, June 30, 1982. Rights traded to **Buffalo** by **New Jersey**, September 9, 1985.

• LEVIE, CRAIG

Craig Levie D – R. 5'11", 190 lbs. b: Calgary, Alta., 8/17/1959. Montreal's 3rd choice, 43rd overall, in 1979 Entry Draft.

Season	Club	League	GP	G	A	Pts	AG	AA	APts	PIM	PP	SH	GW	S	%	TGF	PGF	TGA	PGA	+/–	GP	G	A	Pts	PIM	PP	SH	GW
1976-77	Pincher Creek Panthers	AJHL	27	8	10	18	....	....	....	32	....	....	....	....	....	....	....	....	....	....	....	....	....	....	....	....	....	....
	Calgary Wranglers	WCJHL	2	0	1	1	....	....	....	0	....	....	....	....	....	....	....	....	....	....	....	....	....	....	....	....	....	....
1977-78	Flin Flon Bombers	WCJHL	72	25	64	89	....	....	....	167	....	....	....	....	....	....	....	....	....	....	16	3	7	10	58	....	....	....
1978-79	Edmonton Oil Kings	WHL	69	29	63	92	....	....	....	200	....	....	....	....	....	....	....	....	....	....	7	4	6	10	11	....	....	....
1979-80	Nova Scotia Voyageurs	AHL	72	6	21	27	....	....	....	74	....	....	....	....	....	....	....	....	....	....	6	0	2	2	17	....	....	....
1980-81	Nova Scotia Voyageurs	AHL	80	20	*62	82	....	....	....	162	....	....	....	....	....	....	....	....	....	....	6	5	2	7	10	....	....	....
1981-82	**Winnipeg Jets**	**NHL**	**40**	**4**	**9**	**13**	**3**	**6**	**9**	**48**	**0**	**0**	**1**	**56**	**7.1**	**40**	**4**	**33**	**1**	**+4**	....	....	....	....	....	....	....	....
	Tulsa Oilers	CHL	14	7	7	11	....	....	....	17	....	....	....	....	....	....	....	....	....	....	....	....	....	....	....	....	....	....
1982-83	**Winnipeg Jets**	**NHL**	**22**	**4**	**5**	**9**	**3**	**3**	**6**	**31**	**0**	**0**	**1**	**31**	**12.9**	**24**	**8**	**21**	**2**	**–3**	....	....	....	....	....	....	....	....
	Sherbrooke Jets	AHL	44	3	27	30	....	....	....	62	....	....	....	....	....	....	....	....	....	....	....	....	....	....	....	....	....	....
1983-84	**Minnesota North Stars**	**NHL**	**37**	**6**	**13**	**19**	**5**	**9**	**14**	**44**	**0**	**0**	**1**	**55**	**10.9**	**53**	**4**	**55**	**15**	**+9**	**15**	**2**	**3**	**5**	**32**	**0**	**0**	**0**
	Salt Lake Golden Eagles	CHL	37	8	20	28	....	....	....	101	....	....	....	....	....	....	....	....	....	....	....	....	....	....	....	....	....	....
1984-85	**St. Louis Blues**	**NHL**	**61**	**6**	**23**	**29**	**5**	**16**	**21**	**33**	**2**	**0**	**1**	**94**	**6.4**	**72**	**33**	**41**	**4**	**+2**	**1**	**0**	**0**	**0**	**0**	**0**	**0**	**0**
1985-86	**Minnesota North Stars**	**NHL**	**14**	**2**	**2**	**4**	**2**	**1**	**3**	**8**	**0**	**0**	**0**	**22**	**9.1**	**9**	**4**	**10**	**0**	**–5**	....	....	....	....	....	....	....	....
	Springfield Indians	AHL	36	5	23	28	....	....	....	82	....	....	....	....	....	....	....	....	....	....	....	....	....	....	....	....	....	....
1986-87	HC Davos	Switz.	STATISTICS NOT AVAILABLE																									
	Vancouver Canucks	**NHL**	**9**	**0**	**1**	**1**	**0**	**1**	**1**	**13**	**0**	**0**	**0**	**8**	**0.0**	**10**	**1**	**6**	**0**	**+3**	....	....	....	....	....	....	....	....
1987-88	HC Davos	Switz.	....	5	13	18	....	....	....	....	....	....	....	....	....	....	....	....	....	....	....	....	....	....	....	....	....	....
1988-89	Milano Devils	Italy	41	17	38	55	....	....	....	59	....	....	....	....	....	....	....	....	....	....	....	....	....	....	....	....	....	....
1989-90	Milano Devils	Italy	40	21	32	53	....	....	....	22	....	....	....	....	....	....	....	....	....	....	....	....	....	....	....	....	....	....
1990-91	Milano Devils	Italy	36	12	29	41	....	....	....	27	....	....	....	....	....	....	....	....	....	....	....	....	....	....	....	....	....	....
1991-92	Fort Wayne Komets	IHL	1	0	0	0	....	....	....	0	....	....	....	....	....	....	....	....	....	....	....	....	....	....	....	....	....	....
	NHL Totals		**183**	**22**	**53**	**75**	**18**	**36**	**54**	**177**	**2**	**0**	**4**	**266**	**8.3**	**208**	**54**	**166**	**22**		**16**	**2**	**3**	**5**	**32**	**0**	**0**	**0**

AHL First All-Star Team (1981) • Won Eddie Shore Award (Outstanding Defenseman - AHL) (1981)

Claimed by **Winnipeg** from **Montreal** in Waiver Draft, October 5, 1981. Traded to **Minnesota** by **Winnipeg** with the rights to Tom Ward for Tim Young, August 3, 1983. Claimed by **St. Louis** from **Minnesota** in Waiver Draft, October 9, 1984. Claimed by **Calgary** from **St. Louis** in Waiver Draft, October 7, 1985. Claimed on waivers by **Minnesota** from **Calgary**, October 7, 1985. Signed as a free agent by **Vancouver**, March 1, 1987.

• LEVINS, SCOTT

Scott Levins C/RW – R. 6'4", 210 lbs. b: Spokane, WA, 1/30/1970. Winnipeg's 4th choice, 75th overall, in 1990 Entry Draft.

Season	Club	League	GP	G	A	Pts	AG	AA	APts	PIM	PP	SH	GW	S	%	TGF	PGF	TGA	PGA	+/–	GP	G	A	Pts	PIM	PP	SH	GW
1988-89	Penticton Knights	BCJHL	50	27	58	85	....	....	....	154	....	....	....	....	....	....	....	....	....	....	....	....	....	....	....	....	....	....
1989-90	Tri-Cities Americans	WHL	71	25	37	62	....	....	....	132	....	....	....	....	....	....	....	....	....	....	6	2	3	5	18	....	....	....
1990-91	Moncton Hawks	AHL	74	12	26	38	....	....	....	133	....	....	....	....	....	....	....	....	....	....	4	0	0	0	4	....	....	....
1991-92	Moncton Hawks	AHL	69	15	18	33	....	....	....	271	....	....	....	....	....	....	....	....	....	....	11	3	4	7	30	....	....	....
1992-93	**Winnipeg Jets**	**NHL**	**9**	**0**	**1**	**1**	**0**	**1**	**1**	**18**	**0**	**0**	**0**	**8**	**0.0**	**1**	**0**	**3**	**0**	**–2**	....	....	....	....	....	....	....	....
	Moncton Hawks	AHL	54	22	26	48	....	....	....	158	....	....	....	....	....	....	....	....	....	....	5	1	3	4	14	....	....	....
1993-94	**Florida Panthers**	**NHL**	**29**	**5**	**6**	**11**	**5**	**5**	**10**	**69**	**2**	**0**	**1**	**38**	**13.2**	**16**	**6**	**10**	**0**	**0**	....	....	....	....	....	....	....	....
	Ottawa Senators	**NHL**	**33**	**3**	**5**	**8**	**3**	**4**	**7**	**93**	**2**	**0**	**0**	**39**	**7.7**	**13**	**7**	**33**	**1**	**–26**	....	....	....	....	....	....	....	....
1994-95	**Ottawa Senators**	**NHL**	**24**	**5**	**6**	**11**	**9**	**9**	**18**	**51**	**0**	**0**	**0**	**34**	**14.7**	**16**	**2**	**10**	**0**	**+4**	....	....	....	....	....	....	....	....
	P.E.I. Senators	AHL	6	0	4	4	....	....	....	14	....	....	....	....	....	....	....	....	....	....	....	....	....	....	....	....	....	....
1995-96	**Ottawa Senators**	**NHL**	**27**	**0**	**2**	**2**	**0**	**2**	**2**	**80**	**0**	**0**	**0**	**6**	**0.0**	**4**	**0**	**8**	**1**	**–3**	....	....	....	....	....	....	....	....
	Detroit Vipers	IHL	9	0	0	0	....	....	....	9	....	....	....	....	....	....	....	....	....	....	....	....	....	....	....	....	....	....
1996-97	Springfield Falcons	AHL	68	24	23	47	....	....	....	267	....	....	....	....	....	....	....	....	....	....	11	5	4	9	37	....	....	....
1997-98	**Phoenix Coyotes**	**NHL**	**2**	**0**	**0**	**0**	**0**	**0**	**0**	**5**	**0**	**0**	**0**	**2**	**0.0**	**0**	**0**	**1**	**0**	**–1**	....	....	....	....	....	....	....	....
	Springfield Falcons	AHL	79	28	39	67	....	....	....	177	....	....	....	....	....	....	....	....	....	....	4	2	0	2	24	....	....	....
	NHL Totals		**124**	**13**	**20**	**33**	**17**	**21**	**38**	**316**	**4**	**0**	**1**	**127**	**10.2**	**50**	**15**	**65**	**2**		....	....	....	....	....	....	....	....

WHL West Second All-Star Team (1990)

Claimed by **Florida** from **Winnipeg** in Expansion Draft, June 24, 1993. Traded to **Ottawa** by **Florida** with Evgeny Davydov, Florida's 6th round choice (Mike Gaffney) in 1994 Entry Draft and Dallas' 4th round choice (previously acquired, Ottawa selected Kevin Bolibruck) in 1995 Entry Draft for Bob Kudelski, January 6, 1994. Signed as a free agent by **Phoenix**, October 3, 1996.

• LEVO, TAPIO

Tapio Levo D – L. 6'2", 200 lbs. b: Pori, Finland, 9/24/1956. Pittsburgh's 8th choice, 139th overall, in 1975 Amateur Draft.

Season	Club	League	GP	G	A	Pts	AG	AA	APts	PIM	PP	SH	GW	S	%	TGF	PGF	TGA	PGA	+/–	GP	G	A	Pts	PIM	PP	SH	GW
1972-73	Assat Pori	Finland	1	0	0	0	....	....	....	0	....	....	....	....	....	....	....	....	....	....	....	....	....	....	....	....	....	....
1973-74	Assat Pori	Finland	10	0	0	0	....	....	....	4	....	....	....	....	....	....	....	....	....	....	....	....	....	....	....	....	....	....
1974-75	Assat Pori	Finland	36	5	2	7	....	....	....	48	....	....	....	....	....	....	....	....	....	....	....	....	....	....	....	....	....	....
	Finland	WJC-A	5	1	2	3	....	....	....	7	....	....	....	....	....	....	....	....	....	....	....	....	....	....	....	....	....	....
1975-76	Assat Pori	Finland	36	12	8	20	....	....	....	47	....	....	....	....	....	....	....	....	....	....	4	0	1	1	6	....	....	....
	Finland	WEC-A	10	1	0	1	....	....	....	6	....	....	....	....	....	....	....	....	....	....	....	....	....	....	....	....	....	....

			REGULAR SEASON																		PLAYOFFS							
Season	Club	League	GP	G	A	Pts	AG	AA	APts	PIM	PP	SH	GW	S	%	TGF	PGF	TGA	PGA	+/-	GP	G	A	Pts	PIM	PP	SH	GW
1976-77	Finland	C Cup	4	1	2	3	....	....	....	2	....	....	....	....	....	....	....	....	....	....	....	....	....	....	....	....	....	....
	Assat Pori	Finland	36	12	7	19	....	....	....	34	....	....	....	....	....	....	....	....	....	....	....	....	....	....	....	....	....	....
1977-78	Assat Pori	Finland	36	8	11	19	....	....	....	32	....	....	....	....	....	....	....	....	....	....	9	2	1	3	12	....	....	....
	Finland	WEC-A	10	2	0	2	....	....	....	2	....	....	....	....	....	....	....	....	....	....	....	....	....	....	....	....	....	....
1978-79	Assat Pori	Finland	36	15	6	21	....	....	....	34	....	....	....	....	....	....	....	....	....	....	8	7	2	9	20	....	....	....
1979-80	Assat Pori	Finland	30	11	8	19	....	....	....	55	....	....	....	....	....	....	....	....	....	....	7	6	3	9	4	....	....	....
	Finland	Olympics	4	1	4	5	....	....	....	2	....	....	....	....	....	....	....	....	....	....	....	....	....	....	....	....	....	....
1980-81	Assat Pori	Finland	36	16	7	23	....	....	....	38	....	....	....	....	....	....	....	....	....	....	2	1	1	2	4	....	....	....
	Finland	WEC-A	8	4	4	8	....	....	....	10	....	....	....	....	....	....	....	....	....	....	....	....	....	....	....	....	....	....
1981-82	Finland	C Cup	5	0	1	1	....	....	....	2	....	....	....	....	....	....	....	....	....	....	....	....	....	....	....	....	....	....
	Colorado Rockies	**NHL**	**34**	**9**	**13**	**22**	**7**	**9**	**16**	**14**	**3**	**0**	**0**	**70**	**12.9**	**47**	**14**	**55**	**9**	**–13**	....	....	....	....	....	....	....	....
	Finland	WEC-A	7	2	1	3	....	....	....	4	....	....	....	....	....	....	....	....	....	....	....	....	....	....	....	....	....	....
1982-83	**New Jersey Devils**	**NHL**	**73**	**7**	**40**	**47**	**6**	**28**	**34**	**22**	**5**	**0**	**0**	**187**	**3.7**	**102**	**56**	**89**	**2**	**–41**	....	....	....	....	....	....	....	....
	Finland	WEC-A	10	4	1	5	....	....	....	6	....	....	....	....	....	....	....	....	....	....	....	....	....	....	....	....	....	....
1983-84	Assat Pori	Finland	34	9	20	29	....	....	....	52	....	....	....	....	....	....	....	....	....	....	9	4	7	11	16	....	....	....
1984-85	Assat Pori	Finland	36	20	22	42	....	....	....	26	....	....	....	....	....	....	....	....	....	....	8	1	3	4	16	....	....	....
1985-86	Assat Pori	Finland	35	15	20	35	....	....	....	34	....	....	....	....	....	....	....	....	....	....	....	....	....	....	....	....	....	....
1986-87	Assat Pori	Finland	44	22	17	39	....	....	....	26	....	....	....	....	....	....	....	....	....	....	....	....	....	....	....	....	....	....
1987-88	Assat Pori	Finland	44	15	23	38	....	....	....	38	....	....	....	....	....	....	....	....	....	....	....	....	....	....	....	....	....	....
1988-89	Assat Pori	Finland	43	21	21	42	....	....	....	28	....	....	....	....	....	....	....	....	....	....	....	....	....	....	....	....	....	....
	NHL Totals		**107**	**16**	**53**	**69**	**13**	**37**	**50**	**36**	**8**	**0**	**0**	**257**	**6.2**	**149**	**70**	**144**	**11**		....	....	....	....	....	....	....	....

Finnish First All-Star Team (1984, 1985)

Signed as a free agent by **New Jersey**, July 8, 1981. Transferred to **New Jersey** after **Colorado** franchise relocated, June 30, 1982.

● LEWIS, DALE
Dale Lewis LW – L. 6', 190 lbs. b: Edmonton, Alta., 7/28/1952.

Season	Club	League	GP	G	A	Pts	AG	AA	APts	PIM	PP	SH	GW	S	%	TGF	PGF	TGA	PGA	+/-	GP	G	A	Pts	PIM	PP	SH	GW
1971-72	Red Deer Ramblers	AJHL	48	36	42	78	....	....	....	99	....	....	....	....	....	....	....	....	....	....	....	....	....	....	....	....	....	....
	Vancouver Nats	WCJHL	2	0	1	1	....	....	....	2	....	....	....	....	....	....	....	....	....	....	....	....	....	....	....	....	....	....
1972-73	Sun Coast Suns	EHL	76	32	43	75	....	....	....	51	....	....	....	....	....	....	....	....	....	....	5	4	3	7	2	....	....	....
1973-74	Portland Buckaroos	WHL	72	18	18	36	....	....	....	38	....	....	....	....	....	....	....	....	....	....	10	2	*7	9	8	....	....	....
1974-75	Springfield Indians	AHL	74	28	43	71	....	....	....	43	....	....	....	....	....	....	....	....	....	....	17	9	12	21	8	....	....	....
1975-76	**New York Rangers**	**NHL**	**8**	**0**	**0**	**0**	**0**	**0**	**0**	**0**	**0**	**0**	**0**	**3**	**0.0**	**0**	**0**	**2**	**0**	**–2**	....	....	....	....	....	....	....	....
	Providence Reds	AHL	65	14	27	41	....	....	....	37	....	....	....	....	....	....	....	....	....	....	3	1	1	2	0	....	....	....
1976-77	New Haven Nighthawks	AHL	80	25	45	70	....	....	....	10	....	....	....	....	....	....	....	....	....	....	6	4	1	5	2	....	....	....
1977-78	New Haven Nighthawks	AHL	80	19	29	48	....	....	....	20	....	....	....	....	....	....	....	....	....	....	15	6	4	10	2	....	....	....
1978-79	New Haven Nighthawks	AHL	76	29	51	80	....	....	....	20	....	....	....	....	....	....	....	....	....	....	10	2	2	4	2	....	....	....
1979-80	Birmingham Bulls	CHL	78	28	33	61	....	....	....	30	....	....	....	....	....	....	....	....	....	....	4	2	5	7	0	....	....	....
1980-81	Birmingham Bulls	CHL	12	5	9	14	....	....	....	13	....	....	....	....	....	....	....	....	....	....	....	....	....	....	....	....	....	....
	New Haven Nighthawks	AHL	63	13	26	39	....	....	....	14	....	....	....	....	....	....	....	....	....	....	4	2	1	3	0	....	....	....
	NHL Totals		**8**	**0**	**0**	**0**	**0**	**0**	**0**	**0**	**0**	**0**	**0**	**3**	**0.0**	**0**	**0**	**2**	**0**		....	....	....	....	....	....	....	....

Signed as a free agent by **LA Kings**, September, 1973. Claimed by **NY Rangers** from **LA Kings** (Springfield - AHL) in Intra-League Draft, June 17, 1975. Signed as a free agent by **Atlanta**, September 11, 1979.

● LEWIS, DAVE
Dave Lewis D – L. 6'2", 205 lbs. b: Kindersley, Sask., 7/3/1953. NY Islanders' 2nd choice, 33rd overall, in 1973 Amateur Draft.

Season	Club	League	GP	G	A	Pts	AG	AA	APts	PIM	PP	SH	GW	S	%	TGF	PGF	TGA	PGA	+/-	GP	G	A	Pts	PIM	PP	SH	GW
1971-72	Saskatoon Blades	WCJHL	52	2	9	11	....	....	....	68	....	....	....	....	....	....	....	....	....	....	8	2	3	5	4	....	....	....
1972-73	Saskatoon Blades	WCJHL	67	10	35	45	....	....	....	89	....	....	....	....	....	....	....	....	....	....	16	3	12	15	44	....	....	....
1973-74	**New York Islanders**	**NHL**	**66**	**2**	**15**	**17**	**2**	**13**	**15**	**58**	**1**	**1**	**1**	**63**	**3.2**	**55**	**3**	**78**	**19**	**–7**	....	....	....	....	....	....	....	....
1974-75	**New York Islanders**	**NHL**	**78**	**5**	**14**	**19**	**5**	**11**	**16**	**98**	**0**	**0**	**1**	**95**	**5.3**	**64**	**2**	**69**	**15**	**+8**	**17**	**0**	**1**	**1**	**28**	**0**	**0**	**0**
1975-76	**New York Islanders**	**NHL**	**73**	**0**	**19**	**19**	**0**	**15**	**15**	**54**	**0**	**0**	**0**	**91**	**0.0**	**75**	**1**	**58**	**13**	**+29**	**13**	**0**	**1**	**1**	**44**	**0**	**0**	**0**
1976-77	**New York Islanders**	**NHL**	**79**	**4**	**24**	**28**	**4**	**19**	**23**	**44**	**0**	**1**	**1**	**102**	**3.9**	**77**	**0**	**72**	**24**	**+29**	**12**	**1**	**6**	**7**	**4**	**0**	**0**	**0**
1977-78	**New York Islanders**	**NHL**	**77**	**3**	**11**	**14**	**3**	**9**	**12**	**58**	**0**	**1**	**1**	**111**	**2.7**	**93**	**0**	**82**	**21**	**+32**	**7**	**0**	**1**	**1**	**11**	**0**	**0**	**0**
1978-79	**New York Islanders**	**NHL**	**79**	**5**	**18**	**23**	**5**	**14**	**19**	**43**	**0**	**0**	**0**	**95**	**5.3**	**98**	**0**	**83**	**28**	**+43**	**10**	**0**	**0**	**0**	**4**	**0**	**0**	**0**
1979-80	**New York Islanders**	**NHL**	**62**	**5**	**16**	**21**	**5**	**12**	**17**	**54**	**0**	**0**	**0**	**66**	**7.6**	**65**	**2**	**90**	**37**	**+10**	....	....	....	....	....	....	....	....
	Los Angeles Kings	**NHL**	**11**	**1**	**1**	**2**	**1**	**1**	**2**	**12**	**0**	**0**	**0**	**11**	**9.1**	**11**	**1**	**9**	**2**	**+3**	**4**	**0**	**1**	**1**	**2**	**0**	**0**	**0**
1980-81	**Los Angeles Kings**	**NHL**	**67**	**1**	**12**	**13**	**1**	**8**	**9**	**98**	**0**	**0**	**0**	**46**	**2.2**	**73**	**1**	**73**	**26**	**+25**	**4**	**0**	**2**	**2**	**4**	**0**	**0**	**0**
1981-82	**Los Angeles Kings**	**NHL**	**64**	**1**	**13**	**14**	**1**	**9**	**10**	**75**	**0**	**0**	**0**	**50**	**2.0**	**54**	**2**	**99**	**28**	**–19**	**10**	**0**	**4**	**4**	**36**	**0**	**0**	**0**
1982-83	**Los Angeles Kings**	**NHL**	**79**	**2**	**10**	**12**	**2**	**7**	**9**	**53**	**0**	**0**	**0**	**64**	**3.1**	**67**	**4**	**111**	**26**	**–22**	....	....	....	....	....	....	....	....
1983-84	**New Jersey Devils**	**NHL**	**66**	**2**	**5**	**7**	**2**	**3**	**5**	**63**	**0**	**0**	**0**	**38**	**5.3**	**49**	**0**	**94**	**26**	**–19**	....	....	....	....	....	....	....	....
1984-85	**New Jersey Devils**	**NHL**	**74**	**3**	**9**	**12**	**2**	**6**	**8**	**78**	**0**	**0**	**2**	**51**	**5.9**	**57**	**0**	**120**	**34**	**–29**	....	....	....	....	....	....	....	....
1985-86	**New Jersey Devils**	**NHL**	**69**	**0**	**15**	**15**	**0**	**10**	**10**	**81**	**0**	**0**	**0**	**38**	**0.0**	**69**	**3**	**109**	**43**	**0**	....	....	....	....	....	....	....	....
1986-87	**Detroit Red Wings**	**NHL**	**58**	**2**	**5**	**7**	**2**	**4**	**6**	**66**	**0**	**0**	**0**	**37**	**5.4**	**42**	**0**	**46**	**16**	**+12**	**14**	**0**	**4**	**4**	**10**	**0**	**0**	**0**
1987-88	**Detroit Red Wings**	**NHL**	**6**	**0**	**0**	**0**	**0**	**0**	**0**	**18**	**0**	**0**	**0**	**3**	**0.0**	**2**	**1**	**7**	**3**	**–3**	....	....	....	....	....	....	....	....
	NHL Totals		**1008**	**36**	**187**	**223**	**35**	**141**	**176**	**953**	**1**	**3**	**6**	**961**	**3.7**	**951**	**20**	**1200**	**361**		**91**	**1**	**20**	**21**	**143**	**0**	**0**	**0**

Traded to **LA Kings** by **NY Islanders** with Billy Harris for Butch Goring, March 10, 1980. Traded to **Minnesoto** by **LA Kings** with LA Kings' 3rd round choice (Stephane Roy) in 1985 Entry Draft for Minnesota's 5th round choice (Petr Prasler) in 1985 Entry Draft, October 3, 1983. Traded to **New Jersey** by **Minnesota** for Brent Ashton, October 3, 1983. Signed as a free agent by **Detroit**, July 27, 1986.

● LEY, RICK
Rick Ley D – L. 5'9", 190 lbs. b: Orillia, Ont., 11/2/1948. Toronto's 3rd choice, 16th overall, in 1966 Amateur Draft.

Season	Club	League	GP	G	A	Pts	AG	AA	APts	PIM	PP	SH	GW	S	%	TGF	PGF	TGA	PGA	+/-	GP	G	A	Pts	PIM	PP	SH	GW
1964-65	Niagara Falls Flyers	OHA	50	0	11	11	....	....	....	58	....	....	....	....	....	....	....	....	....	....	11	0	3	3	28	....	....	....
1965-66	Niagara Falls Flyers	OHA	46	3	13	16	....	....	....	180	....	....	....	....	....	....	....	....	....	....	6	0	6	6	18	....	....	....
1966-67	Niagara Falls Flyers	OHA	48	10	27	37	....	....	....	128	....	....	....	....	....	....	....	....	....	....	12	2	4	6	24	....	....	....
1967-68	Niagara Falls Flyers	OHA	53	16	48	64	....	....	....	81	....	....	....	....	....	....	....	....	....	....	19	1	15	16	38	....	....	....
1968-69	**Toronto Maple Leafs**	**NHL**	**38**	**1**	**11**	**12**	**1**	**10**	**11**	**39**	**0**	**0**	**0**	**37**	**2.7**	**38**	**10**	**34**	**8**	**+2**	**3**	**0**	**0**	**0**	**9**	**0**	**0**	**0**
	Tulsa Oilers	CHL	19	0	5	5	....	....	....	23	....	....	....	....	....	....	....	....	....	....	....	....	....	....	....	....	....	....
1969-70	**Toronto Maple Leafs**	**NHL**	**48**	**2**	**13**	**15**	**2**	**13**	**15**	**102**	**1**	**0**	**0**	**52**	**3.8**	**52**	**10**	**78**	**20**	**–16**	....	....	....	....	....	....	....	....
1970-71	**Toronto Maple Leafs**	**NHL**	**76**	**4**	**16**	**20**	**4**	**14**	**18**	**151**	**0**	**0**	**0**	**78**	**5.1**	**90**	**13**	**87**	**21**	**+11**	**6**	**0**	**2**	**2**	**4**	**0**	**0**	**0**
1971-72	**Toronto Maple Leafs**	**NHL**	**67**	**1**	**14**	**15**	**1**	**13**	**14**	**124**	**0**	**0**	**0**	**65**	**1.5**	**49**	**7**	**70**	**31**	**+3**	**5**	**0**	**0**	**0**	**7**	**0**	**0**	**0**
1972-73	New England Whalers	WHA	76	3	27	30	....	....	....	108	....	....	....	....	....	....	....	....	....	....	15	3	7	10	24	....	....	....
1973-74	New England Whalers	WHA	72	6	35	41	....	....	....	148	....	....	....	....	....	....	....	....	....	....	7	1	5	6	18	....	....	....
1974-75	Canada	Summit	7	0	0	0	....	....	....	16	....	....	....	....	....	....	....	....	....	....	....	....	....	....	....	....	....	....
	New England Whalers	WHA	62	6	36	42	....	....	....	50	....	....	....	....	....	....	....	....	....	....	6	1	1	2	32	....	....	....
1975-76	New England Whalers	WHA	67	8	30	38	....	....	....	78	....	....	....	....	....	....	....	....	....	....	17	1	4	5	49	....	....	....
1976-77	New England Whalers	WHA	55	2	21	23	....	....	....	102	....	....	....	....	....	....	....	....	....	....	5	0	4	4	4	....	....	....
1977-78	New England Whalers	WHA	73	3	41	44	....	....	....	95	....	....	....	....	....	....	....	....	....	....	14	1	8	9	4	....	....	....
1978-79	New England Whalers	WHA	73	7	20	27	....	....	....	135	....	....	....	....	....	....	....	....	....	....	9	0	4	4	11	....	....	....
1979-80	**Hartford Whalers**	**NHL**	**65**	**4**	**16**	**20**	**4**	**12**	**16**	**92**	**0**	**0**	**1**	**78**	**5.1**	**104**	**13**	**120**	**31**	**+2**	....	....	....	....	....	....	....	....
1980-81	**Hartford Whalers**	**NHL**	**16**	**0**	**2**	**2**	**0**	**1**	**1**	**20**	**0**	**0**	**0**	**19**	**0.0**	**14**	**1**	**33**	**7**	**–13**	....	....	....	....	....	....	....	....
	NHL Totals		**310**	**12**	**72**	**84**	**12**	**63**	**75**	**528**	**1**	**0**	**1**	**329**	**3.6**	**347**	**54**	**422**	**118**		**14**	**0**	**2**	**2**	**20**	**0**	**0**	**0**
	Other Major League Totals		478	35	210	245				716											73	7	33	40	142			

OHA First All-Star Team (1968) • WHA Second All-Star Team (1978) • WHA First All-Star Team (1979) • Won Dennis A. Murphy Trophy (WHA Top Defenseman) (1979)

Selected by **New England** (WHA) in 1972 WHA General Player Draft, February 12, 1972. Reclaimed by **Toronto** from **Hartford** prior to Expansion Draft, June 9, 1979. Claimed by **Hartford** from **Toronto** in Expansion Draft, June 13, 1979.

● LIBA, IGOR
Igor Liba LW – R. 6', 192 lbs. b: Kosice, Czech., 11/4/1960. Calgary's 7th choice, 94th overall, in 1983 Entry Draft.

Season	Club	League	GP	G	A	Pts	AG	AA	APts	PIM	PP	SH	GW	S	%	TGF	PGF	TGA	PGA	+/-	GP	G	A	Pts	PIM	PP	SH	GW
1978-79	Czechoslovakia	WJC-A	5	0	0	0	....	....	....	0	....	....	....	....	....	....	....	....	....	....	....	....	....	....	....	....	....	....
1979-80	VSZ Kosice	Czech.	42	16	10	26	....	....	....	16	....	....	....	....	....	....	....	....	....	....	....	....	....	....	....	....	....	....
	Czechoslovakia	WJC-A	5	4	1	5	....	....	....	4	....	....	....	....	....	....	....	....	....	....	....	....	....	....	....	....	....	....
1980-81	VSZ Kosice	Czech.	43	17	24	41	....	....	....	....	....	....	....	....	....	....	....	....	....	....	....	....	....	....	....	....	....	....
1981-82	VSZ Kosice	Czech.	44	*35	18	53	....	....	....	34	....	....	....	....	....	....	....	....	....	....	....	....	....	....	....	....	....	....
	Czechoslovakia	WEC-A	10	3	2	5	....	....	....	6	....	....	....	....	....	....	....	....	....	....	....	....	....	....	....	....	....	....
1982-83	Dukla Jihlava	Czech.	43	27	18	45	....	....	....	24	....	....	....	....	....	....	....	....	....	....	....	....	....	....	....	....	....	....
	Czechoslovakia	WEC-A	10	2	8	10	....	....	....	0	....	....	....	....	....	....	....	....	....	....	....	....	....	....	....	....	....	....

			REGULAR SEASON																		PLAYOFFS							
Season	Club	League	GP	G	A	Pts	AG	AA	APts	PIM	PP	SH	GW	S	%	TGF	PGF	TGA	PGA	+/-	GP	G	A	Pts	PIM	PP	SH	GW
1983-84	Dukla Jihlava	Czech.	41	14	18	32				16																		
	Czechoslovakia	Olympics	7	4	3	7				6																		
1984-85	Czechoslovakia	C Cup	5	2	3	5				6																		
	VSZ Kosice	Czech.	44	28	26	54				22																		
	Czechoslovakia	WEC-A	10	2	5	7				16																		
1985-86	VSZ Kosice	Czech.	40	31	*36	67																						
	Czechoslovakia	WEC-A	10	2	4	6				18																		
1986-87	VSZ Kosice	Czech.	36	17	20	37				38																		
	Czechoslovakia	WEC-A	10	2	3	5				12																		
1987-88	Czechoslovakia	C Cup	6	0	4	4				6																		
	VSZ Kosice	Czech.	31	13	16	29																						
	Czechoslovakia	Olympics	8	4	6	10				8																		
1988-89	**New York Rangers**	**NHL**	**10**	**2**	**5**	**7**	**2**	**4**	**6**	**15**	**1**	**0**	**0**	**14**	**14.3**	**9**	**4**	**4**	**0**	**+1**								
	Los Angeles Kings	**NHL**	**27**	**5**	**13**	**18**	**4**	**9**	**13**	**21**	**1**	**0**	**0**	**28**	**17.9**	**25**	**9**	**20**	**0**	**–4**	**2**	**0**	**0**	**0**	**2**	**0**	**0**	**0**
1989-90	VSZ Kosice	Czech.	44	17	20	37																						
1990-91	VSZ Kosice	Czech.	2	0	1	1				0																		
	EHC Biel	Switz.	21	13	10	23																						
1991-92	Fiemme Abbasciano	Italy	22	13	41	54				8																		
	VSZ Kosice	Czech.	16	7	8	15																						
	Czechoslovakia	Olympics	4	1	2	3				4																		
	Czechoslovakia	WC-A	8	2	1	3				10																		
1992-93	TuTo Turku	Finland	44	22	34	56				111											4	2	2	4	4			
1993-94			DID NOT PLAY																									
1994-95	Zeltweg	Austria	31	30	23	53																						
1995-96	Zeltweg	Austria	33	15	19	34																						
1996-97	Spisska Nova Ves	Slovakia	46	26	25	51																						
1997-98	HC Kosice	Slovakia	32	10	24	34				36											10	3	4	7	24			
	NHL Totals		**37**	**7**	**18**	**25**	**6**	**13**	**19**	**36**	**2**	**0**	**0**	**42**	**16.7**	**34**	**13**	**24**	**0**		**2**	**0**	**0**	**0**	**2**	**0**	**0**	**0**

Czechoslovakian Player of the Year (1984) • Czechoslovakian First All-Star Team (1988)

Rights traded to **Minnesota** by **Calgary** for Minnesota's 5th round choice (Thomas Forslund) in 1988 Entry Draft, May 20, 1988. Traded to **NY Rangers** by **Minnesota** with Brian Lawton and the rights to Rick Bennett for Paul Jerrard, Mark Tinordi, Bret Barnett, Mike Sullivan and LA Kings' 3rd round choice (acquired earlier, Minnesota selected Murray Garbutt) in 1989 Entry Draft, October 11, 1988. Traded to **LA Kings** by **NY Rangers** for Dean Kennedy and Denis Larocque, December 12, 1988.

• LIBBY, JEFF

Jeff Libby D – L. 6'3", 215 lbs. b: Waterville, ME, 3/1/1974.

Season	Club	League	GP	G	A	Pts	AG	AA	APts	PIM	PP	SH	GW	S	%	TGF	PGF	TGA	PGA	+/-	GP	G	A	Pts	PIM	PP	SH	GW
1994-95	University of Maine	H.E.	22	2	4	6				6																		
1995-96	University of Maine	H.E.	39	0	9	9				42																		
1996-97	University of Maine	H.E.	34	6	25	31				41																		
1997-98	**New York Islanders**	**NHL**	**1**	**0**	**0**	**0**	**0**	**0**	**0**	**0**	**0**	**0**	**0**	**0**	**0.0**	**0**	**0**	**0**	**0**	**0**								
	Kentucky Thoroughblades	AHL	8	0	3	3				4											3	0	0	0	4			
	Utah Grizzlies	IHL	47	1	5	6				25											1	0	0	0	0			
	NHL Totals		**1**	**0**	**0**	**0**	**0**	**0**	**0**	**0**	**0**	**0**	**0**	**0**	**0.0**	**0**	**0**	**0**	**0**									

Signed as a free agent by **NY Islanders**, May 12, 1997.

• LIBETT, NICK

Nick Libett LW – L. 6'1", 195 lbs. b: Stratford, Ont., 12/9/1945.

Season	Club	League	GP	G	A	Pts	AG	AA	APts	PIM	PP	SH	GW	S	%	TGF	PGF	TGA	PGA	+/-	GP	G	A	Pts	PIM	PP	SH	GW
1962-63	Hamilton Red Wings	OHA	32	1	4	5				21																		
1963-64	Hamilton Red Wings	OHA	49	23	19	42				58																		
	Cincinnati Wings	CHL	3	0	2	2				0																		
1964-65	Hamilton Red Wings	OHA	51	24	37	61				60																		
1965-66	Hamilton Red Wings	OHA	42	22	22	44				39											5	2	1	3	6			
	Memphis Wings	CHL	4	1	0	1				2																		
1966-67	Memphis Wings	CHL	62	12	18	30				30											7	2	2	4	4			
1967-68	**Detroit Red Wings**	**NHL**	**22**	**2**	**1**	**3**	**2**	**1**	**3**	**12**	**1**	**0**	**0**	**29**	**6.9**	**10**	**3**	**20**	**0**	**–13**								
	Fort Worth Wings	CHL	40	11	28	39				22																		
	San Diego Gulls	WHL	10	4	2	6				0																		
1968-69	**Detroit Red Wings**	**NHL**	**75**	**10**	**14**	**24**	**11**	**13**	**24**	**34**	**1**	**0**	**2**	**98**	**10.2**	**33**	**3**	**64**	**18**	**–16**								
1969-70	**Detroit Red Wings**	**NHL**	**76**	**20**	**20**	**40**	**23**	**20**	**43**	**39**	**3**	**1**	**2**	**148**	**13.5**	**65**	**10**	**57**	**11**	**+9**	**4**	**2**	**0**	**2**	**2**	**1**	**0**	**0**
1970-71	**Detroit Red Wings**	**NHL**	**78**	**16**	**13**	**29**	**17**	**11**	**28**	**25**	**2**	**0**	**1**	**156**	**10.3**	**50**	**7**	**95**	**14**	**–38**								
1971-72	**Detroit Red Wings**	**NHL**	**77**	**31**	**22**	**53**	**33**	**20**	**53**	**50**	**6**	**3**	**5**	**219**	**14.2**	**83**	**13**	**81**	**18**	**+7**								
1972-73	**Detroit Red Wings**	**NHL**	**78**	**19**	**34**	**53**	**19**	**28**	**47**	**56**	**4**	**1**	**3**	**202**	**9.4**	**84**	**22**	**72**	**11**	**+1**								
1973-74	**Detroit Red Wings**	**NHL**	**67**	**24**	**24**	**48**	**25**	**21**	**46**	**37**	**3**	**1**	**5**	**177**	**13.6**	**68**	**13**	**90**	**9**	**–26**								
1974-75	**Detroit Red Wings**	**NHL**	**80**	**23**	**28**	**51**	**21**	**22**	**43**	**39**	**8**	**1**	**2**	**194**	**11.9**	**77**	**28**	**113**	**23**	**–41**								
1975-76	**Detroit Red Wings**	**NHL**	**80**	**20**	**26**	**46**	**19**	**20**	**39**	**71**	**3**	**1**	**3**	**224**	**8.9**	**72**	**16**	**85**	**20**	**–9**								
1976-77	**Detroit Red Wings**	**NHL**	**80**	**14**	**27**	**41**	**13**	**22**	**35**	**25**	**3**	**1**	**0**	**210**	**6.7**	**63**	**14**	**99**	**25**	**–25**								
1977-78	**Detroit Red Wings**	**NHL**	**80**	**23**	**22**	**45**	**22**	**18**	**40**	**46**	**1**	**1**	**1**	**155**	**14.8**	**63**	**10**	**77**	**21**	**–3**	**7**	**3**	**1**	**4**	**0**	**1**	**0**	**0**
1978-79	**Detroit Red Wings**	**NHL**	**68**	**15**	**19**	**34**	**14**	**14**	**28**	**20**	**3**	**1**	**0**	**130**	**11.5**	**60**	**13**	**58**	**15**	**+4**								
	Canada	WEC-A	8	1	0	1				4																		
1979-80	**Pittsburgh Penguins**	**NHL**	**78**	**14**	**12**	**26**	**13**	**9**	**22**	**14**	**1**	**1**	**2**	**118**	**11.9**	**44**	**3**	**72**	**12**	**–19**	**5**	**1**	**1**	**2**	**0**	**1**	**0**	**0**
1980-81	**Pittsburgh Penguins**	**NHL**	**43**	**6**	**6**	**12**	**5**	**4**	**9**	**4**	**1**	**0**	**1**	**47**	**12.8**	**19**	**2**	**18**	**3**	**+2**								
	NHL Totals		**982**	**237**	**268**	**505**	**237**	**223**	**460**	**472**	**40**	**12**	**27**	**2107**	**11.2**	**791**	**157**	**1001**	**200**		**16**	**6**	**2**	**8**	**2**	**3**	**0**	**0**

Played in NHL All-Star Game (1977)

Traded to **Pittsburgh** by **Detroit** for Pete Mahovlich, August 3, 1979.

• LIDDINGTON, BOB

Bob Liddington LW – L. 6', 175 lbs. b: Calgary, Alta., 9/15/1948.

Season	Club	League	GP	G	A	Pts	AG	AA	APts	PIM	PP	SH	GW	S	%	TGF	PGF	TGA	PGA	+/-	GP	G	A	Pts	PIM	PP	SH	GW
1966-67	Calgary Buffaloes	WCJHL	22	6	5	11				15																		
	Calgary Spurs	WCSHL																			1	0	0	0	0			
1967-68	Calgary Centennials	WCJHL	59	36	32	68				24																		
1968-69	Calgary Centennials	WCJHL	60	*58	33	91				26																		
1969-70	Tulsa Oilers	CHL	68	22	17	39				33											3	0	0	0	0			
1970-71	**Toronto Maple Leafs**	**NHL**	**11**	**0**	**1**	**1**	**0**	**1**	**1**	**2**	**0**	**0**	**0**	**2**	**0.0**	**4**	**1**	**5**	**0**	**–2**								
	Tulsa Oilers	CHL	61	18	21	39				55																		
1971-72	Phoenix Roadrunners	WHL	72	22	19	41				50											6	2	4	6	4			
1972-73	Chicago Cougars	WHA	78	20	11	31				24																		
1973-74	Chicago Cougars	WHA	73	26	21	47				20											18	6	5	11	11			
1974-75	Chicago Cougars	WHA	78	23	18	41				27																		
1975-76	Denver-Ottawa	WHA	35	7	8	15				14																		
	Houston Aeros	WHA	2	0	0	0				2																		
	Tucson Mavericks	CHL	23	12	12	24				20																		
1976-77	Phoenix Roadrunners	WHA	80	20	24	44				28																		
1977-78	Binghamton Dusters	AHL	11	3	2	5				2																		
	Long Beach Sharks-Rockets	PHL	33	15	24	39				6																		
1978-79	Phoenix Roadrunners	PHL	60	34	20	54				10																		
	NHL Totals		**11**	**0**	**1**	**1**	**0**	**1**	**1**	**2**	**0**	**0**	**0**	**2**	**0.0**	**4**	**1**	**5**	**0**									
	Other Major League Totals		346	96	82	178				115											18	6	5	11	11			

Signed as a free agent by **Toronto**, October, 1969. Selected by **LA Sharks** (WHA) in 1972 WHA General Player Draft, February 12, 1972. Traded to **Chicago** (WHA) by **LA Sharks** (WHA) with Bob Whitlock and the rights to Larry Cahan for Bill Young and future considerations, July, 1972. Selected by **Denver** (WHA) from **Chicago** (WHA) in WHA Expansion Draft, May, 1975. Signed as a free agent by **Houston** (WHA) after **Denver-Ottawa** (WHA) franchise folded, February, 1976. Traded to **Phoenix** (WHA) by **Houston** (WHA) for Cam Connor, October, 1976.

• LIDSTER, DOUG

Doug Lidster D – R. 6'1", 190 lbs. b: Kamloops, B.C., 10/18/1960. Vancouver's 6th choice, 133rd overall, in 1980 Entry Draft.

Season	Club	League	GP	G	A	Pts	AG	AA	APts	PIM	PP	SH	GW	S	%	TGF	PGF	TGA	PGA	+/-	GP	G	A	Pts	PIM	PP	SH	GW
1977-78	Seattle Breakers	WCJHL	2	0	0	0				0																		
1978-79	Kamloops Rockets	BCJHL	59	36	47	83				50																		
1979-80	Colorado College	WCHA	39	18	25	43				52																		

			REGULAR SEASON																		PLAYOFFS							
Season	Club	League	GP	G	A	Pts	AG	AA	APts	PIM	PP	SH	GW	S	%	TGF	PGF	TGA	PGA	+/–	GP	G	A	Pts	PIM	PP	SH	GW
1980-81	Colorado College	WCHA	36	10	30	40	....	....	....	54	....	....	....	....	....	....	....	....	....	....	....	....	....	....	....	....	....	....
1981-82	Colorado College	WCHA	36	13	22	35	....	....	....	32	....	....	....	....	....	....	....	....	....	....	....	....	....	....	....	....	....	....
1982-83	Colorado College	WCHA	34	15	41	56	....	....	....	30	....	....	....	....	....	....	....	....	....	....	....	....	....	....	....	....	....	....
1983-84	Canada	Nat-Team	59	6	20	26	....	....	....	28	....	....	....	....	....	....	....	....	....	....	....	....	....	....	....	....	....	....
	Canada	Olympics	7	0	2	2	....	....	....	2	....	....	....	....	....	....	....	....	....	....	....	....	....	....	....	....	....	....
	Vancouver Canucks	**NHL**	8	0	0	0	0	0	0	4	0	0	0	7	0.0	3	1	9	0	–7	2	0	1	1	0	0	0	0
1984-85	**Vancouver Canucks**	**NHL**	78	6	24	30	5	16	21	55	2	0	0	125	4.8	96	12	115	20	–11	....	....	....	....	....	....	....	....
	Canada	WEC-A	10	3	1	4	....	....	....	4	....	....	....	....	....	....	....	....	....	....	....	....	....	....	....	....	....	....
1985-86	**Vancouver Canucks**	**NHL**	78	12	16	28	10	11	21	56	1	1	0	151	7.9	95	8	131	32	–12	3	0	1	1	2	0	0	0
1986-87	**Vancouver Canucks**	**NHL**	80	12	51	63	10	37	47	40	3	0	0	176	6.8	154	61	172	44	–35	....	....	....	....	....	....	....	....
1987-88	**Vancouver Canucks**	**NHL**	64	4	32	36	3	23	26	105	2	1	0	133	3.0	97	42	110	36	–19	....	....	....	....	....	....	....	....
1988-89	**Vancouver Canucks**	**NHL**	63	5	17	22	4	12	16	78	3	0	0	116	4.3	62	17	82	33	–4	7	1	1	2	9	0	0	0
1989-90	**Vancouver Canucks**	**NHL**	80	8	28	36	7	20	27	36	1	0	0	143	5.6	85	19	136	54	–16	....	....	....	....	....	....	....	....
	Canada	WEC-A	10	1	0	1	....	....	....	6	....	....	....	....	....	....	....	....	....	....	....	....	....	....	....	....	....	....
1990-91	**Vancouver Canucks**	**NHL**	78	6	32	38	5	24	29	77	4	0	1	157	3.8	115	37	133	49	–6	6	0	2	2	6	0	0	0
	Canada	WEC-A	10	1	4	5	....	....	....	8	....	....	....	....	....	....	....	....	....	....	....	....	....	....	....	....	....	....
1991-92	**Vancouver Canucks**	**NHL**	66	6	23	29	5	17	22	39	3	0	2	89	6.7	77	20	79	31	+9	11	1	2	3	11	0	0	0
1992-93	**Vancouver Canucks**	**NHL**	71	6	19	25	5	13	18	36	3	0	0	76	7.9	80	10	93	32	+9	12	0	3	3	8	0	0	0
1993-94	**New York Rangers**	**NHL**	34	0	2	2	0	2	2	33	0	0	0	25	0.0	18	4	33	7	–12	9	2	0	2	10	0	0	0
1994-95	**St. Louis Blues**	**NHL**	37	2	7	9	4	10	14	12	1	0	0	37	5.4	33	3	30	9	+9	4	0	0	0	2	0	0	0
1995-96	**New York Rangers**	**NHL**	59	5	9	14	5	7	12	50	0	0	0	73	6.8	50	7	48	16	+11	7	1	0	1	6	1	0	0
1996-97	**New York Rangers**	**NHL**	48	3	4	7	3	4	7	24	0	0	0	42	7.1	31	0	27	6	+10	15	1	5	6	8	0	0	0
1997-98	**New York Rangers**	**NHL**	36	0	4	4	0	4	4	24	0	0	0	25	0.0	19	0	22	5	+2	....	....	....	....	....	....	....	....
	NHL Totals		880	75	268	343	66	200	266	669	23	2	3	1375	5.5	1015	241	1220	374		76	6	15	21	62	1	0	0

WCHA First All-Star Team (1982, 1983) • NCAA West First All-American Team (1983)

Traded to **NY Rangers** by **Vancouver** to complete transaction that sent John Vanbiesbrouck to Vancouver (June 30, 1993), June 25, 1993. Traded to **St. Louis** by **NY Rangers** with Esa Tikkanen for Petr Nedved, July 24, 1994. Traded to **NY Rangers** by **St. Louis** for Jay Wells, July 28, 1995.

• LIDSTROM, NICKLAS

Nicklas Lidstrom D – L. 6′2″, 185 lbs. b: Vasteras, Sweden, 4/28/1970. Detroit's 3rd choice, 53rd overall, in 1989 Entry Draft.

Season	Club	League	GP	G	A	Pts	AG	AA	APts	PIM	PP	SH	GW	S	%	TGF	PGF	TGA	PGA	+/–	GP	G	A	Pts	PIM	PP	SH	GW
1987-88	Vasteras IK	Sweden 2	3	....	....	....	....	....	....	....	....	....	....	....	....	....	....	....	....	....	....	....	....	....	....	....	....	....
1988-89	Vasteras IK	Sweden	19	0	2	2	....	....	....	4	....	....	....	....	....	....	....	....	....	....	....	....	....	....	....	....	....	....
1989-90	Vasteras IK	Sweden	39	8	8	16	....	....	....	14	....	....	....	....	....	....	....	....	....	....	2	0	1	1	2	....	....	....
	Sweden	WJC-A	7	3	3	6	....	....	....	2	....	....	....	....	....	....	....	....	....	....	....	....	....	....	....	....	....	....
1990-91	Vasteras IK	Sweden	38	4	19	23	....	....	....	2	....	....	....	....	....	....	....	....	....	....	4	0	0	0	4	....	....	....
	Sweden	WEC-A	10	3	3	6	....	....	....	4	....	....	....	....	....	....	....	....	....	....	....	....	....	....	....	....	....	....
1991-92	Sweden	C Cup	6	1	1	2	....	....	....	4	....	....	....	....	....	....	....	....	....	....	....	....	....	....	....	....	....	....
	Detroit Red Wings	**NHL**	80	11	49	60	10	37	47	22	5	0	1	168	6.5	141	50	80	25	+36	11	1	2	3	0	1	0	0
1992-93	**Detroit Red Wings**	**NHL**	84	7	34	41	6	23	29	28	3	0	2	156	4.5	136	51	100	22	+7	7	1	0	1	0	1	0	0
1993-94	**Detroit Red Wings**	**NHL**	84	10	46	56	9	36	45	26	4	0	3	200	5.0	174	45	111	25	+43	7	3	2	5	0	1	1	0
	Sweden	WC-A	4	1	0	1	....	....	....	2	....	....	....	....	....	....	....	....	....	....	....	....	....	....	....	....	....	....
1994-95	Vasteras IK	Sweden	13	2	10	12	....	....	....	4	....	....	....	....	....	....	....	....	....	....	....	....	....	....	....	....	....	....
	Detroit Red Wings	**NHL**	43	10	16	26	18	24	42	6	7	0	0	90	11.1	73	26	41	9	+15	18	4	12	16	8	3	0	2
1995-96	**Detroit Red Wings**	**NHL**	81	17	50	67	17	41	58	20	8	1	1	211	8.1	150	67	73	19	+29	19	5	9	14	10	1	0	0
1996-97	Sweden	W Cup	4	2	1	3	....	....	....	0	....	....	....	....	....	....	....	....	....	....	....	....	....	....	....	....	....	....
	Detroit Red Wings	**NHL**	79	15	42	57	16	37	53	30	8	0	1	214	7.0	117	48	87	29	+11	20	2	6	8	2	0	0	0
1997-98	**Detroit Red Wings**	**NHL**	80	17	42	59	20	41	61	18	7	1	1	205	8.3	126	48	75	19	+22	22	6	13	19	8	2	0	2
	NHL Totals		531	87	279	366	96	239	335	150	42	2	9	1244	7.0	917	335	567	148		104	22	44	66	28	9	1	4

NHL/Upper Deck All-Rookie Team (1992) • NHL First All-Star Team (1998)

Played in NHL All-Star Game (1996, 1998)

• LILLEY, JOHN

John Lilley RW – R. 5′9″, 170 lbs. b: Wakefield, MA, 8/3/1972. Winnipeg's 8th choice, 140th overall, in 1990 Entry Draft.

Season	Club	League	GP	G	A	Pts	AG	AA	APts	PIM	PP	SH	GW	S	%	TGF	PGF	TGA	PGA	+/–	GP	G	A	Pts	PIM	PP	SH	GW
1989-90	Cushing-Mass Academy	H.S.	20	22	30	52	....	....	....	....	....	....	....	....	....	....	....	....	....	....	....	....	....	....	....	....	....	....
1990-91	Cushing-Mass Academy	H.S.	25	29	42	71	....	....	....	....	....	....	....	....	....	....	....	....	....	....	....	....	....	....	....	....	....	....
1991-92	Boston University	H.E.	23	9	9	18	....	....	....	43	....	....	....	....	....	....	....	....	....	....	....	....	....	....	....	....	....	....
	United States	WJC-A	7	3	4	7	....	....	....	10	....	....	....	....	....	....	....	....	....	....	....	....	....	....	....	....	....	....
1992-93	Boston University	H.E.	4	0	1	1	....	....	....	13	....	....	....	....	....	....	....	....	....	....	....	....	....	....	....	....	....	....
	Seattle Thunderbirds	WHL	45	22	28	50	....	....	....	55	....	....	....	....	....	....	....	....	....	....	5	1	3	4	9	....	....	....
1993-94	United States	Nat-Team	58	27	23	50	....	....	....	117	....	....	....	....	....	....	....	....	....	....	....	....	....	....	....	....	....	....
	United States	Olympics	8	3	1	4	....	....	....	16	....	....	....	....	....	....	....	....	....	....	....	....	....	....	....	....	....	....
	Anaheim Mighty Ducks	**NHL**	13	1	6	7	1	5	6	8	0	0	1	20	5.0	7	0	6	0	+1	....	....	....	....	....	....	....	....
	San Diego Gulls	IHL	2	2	1	3	....	....	....	0	....	....	....	....	....	....	....	....	....	....	....	....	....	....	....	....	....	....
	United States	WC-A	8	1	0	1	....	....	....	29	....	....	....	....	....	....	....	....	....	....	....	....	....	....	....	....	....	....
1994-95	San Diego Gulls	IHL	45	9	15	24	....	....	....	71	....	....	....	....	....	....	....	....	....	....	2	0	0	0	2	....	....	....
	Anaheim Mighty Ducks	**NHL**	9	2	2	4	4	3	7	5	1	0	0	10	20.0	7	1	4	0	+2	....	....	....	....	....	....	....	....
1995-96	**Anaheim Mighty Ducks**	**NHL**	1	0	0	0	0	0	0	0	0	0	0	0	0.0	0	0	1	0	–1	....	....	....	....	....	....	....	....
	Baltimore Bandits	AHL	12	2	4	6	....	....	....	34	....	....	....	....	....	....	....	....	....	....	....	....	....	....	....	....	....	....
	Los Angeles Ice Dogs	IHL	64	12	20	32	....	....	....	112	....	....	....	....	....	....	....	....	....	....	....	....	....	....	....	....	....	....
1996-97	Rochester Americans	AHL	1	0	2	2	....	....	....	15	....	....	....	....	....	....	....	....	....	....	....	....	....	....	....	....	....	....
	Providence Bruins	AHL	63	12	23	35	....	....	....	130	....	....	....	....	....	....	....	....	....	....	10	3	0	3	24	....	....	....
	Detroit Vipers	IHL	1	0	0	0	....	....	....	2	....	....	....	....	....	....	....	....	....	....	....	....	....	....	....	....	....	....
1997-98	Dusseldorfer EG	Germany	44	9	14	23	....	....	....	120	....	....	....	....	....	....	....	....	....	....	3	0	0	0	4	....	....	....
	NHL Totals		23	3	8	11	5	8	13	13	1	0	1	30	10.0	14	1	11	0		....	....	....	....	....	....	....	....

Signed as a free agent by **Anaheim**, March 9, 1994.

• LIND, JUHA

Juha Lind C – L. 5′11″, 178 lbs. b: Helsinki, Finland, 1/2/1974. Minnesota's 6th choice, 178th overall, in 1992 Entry Draft.

Season	Club	League	GP	G	A	Pts	AG	AA	APts	PIM	PP	SH	GW	S	%	TGF	PGF	TGA	PGA	+/–	GP	G	A	Pts	PIM	PP	SH	GW
1991-92	Jokerit Helsinki	Finland	28	16	24	40	....	....	....	10	....	....	....	....	....	....	....	....	....	....	....	....	....	....	....	....	....	....
1992-93	Vantaa	Finland 2	25	8	12	20	....	....	....	8	....	....	....	....	....	....	....	....	....	....	....	....	....	....	....	....	....	....
	Jokerit Helsinki	Finland	6	0	0	0	....	....	....	2	....	....	....	....	....	....	....	....	....	....	1	0	0	0	0	....	....	....
1993-94	Jokerit Helsinki	Finland	47	17	11	28	....	....	....	37	....	....	....	....	....	....	....	....	....	....	11	2	5	7	4	....	....	....
	Finland	WJC-A	7	5	2	7	....	....	....	2	....	....	....	....	....	....	....	....	....	....	....	....	....	....	....	....	....	....
1994-95	Jokerit Helsinki	Finland	50	10	8	18	....	....	....	12	....	....	....	....	....	....	....	....	....	....	11	1	2	3	6	....	....	....
1995-96	Jokerit Helsinki	Finland	50	15	22	37	....	....	....	32	....	....	....	....	....	....	....	....	....	....	11	4	5	9	4	....	....	....
1996-97	Jokerit Helsinki	Finland	50	16	22	38	....	....	....	28	....	....	....	....	....	....	....	....	....	....	9	5	3	8	0	....	....	....
	Finland	WC-A	8	1	0	1	....	....	....	8	....	....	....	....	....	....	....	....	....	....	....	....	....	....	....	....	....	....
1997-98	**Dallas Stars**	**NHL**	39	2	3	5	2	3	5	6	0	0	0	27	7.4	9	0	7	2	+4	15	2	2	4	8	0	0	1
	Michigan K-Wings	IHL	8	2	2	4	....	....	....	2	....	....	....	....	....	....	....	....	....	....	....	....	....	....	....	....	....	....
	Finland	Olympics	6	0	1	1	....	....	....	6	....	....	....	....	....	....	....	....	....	....	....	....	....	....	....	....	....	....
	NHL Totals		39	2	3	5	2	3	5	6	0	0	0	27	7.4	9	0	7	2		15	2	2	4	8	0	0	1

Rights transferred to **Dallas** after **Minnesota** franchise relocated, June 9, 1993.

• LINDBERG, CHRIS

Chris Lindberg LW – L. 6′1″, 190 lbs. b: Fort Frances, Ont., 4/16/1967.

Season	Club	League	GP	G	A	Pts	AG	AA	APts	PIM	PP	SH	GW	S	%	TGF	PGF	TGA	PGA	+/–	GP	G	A	Pts	PIM	PP	SH	GW
1985-86	Estevan Bruins	SJHL	60	30	38	68	....	....	....	110	....	....	....	....	....	....	....	....	....	....	15	5	14	19	6	....	....	....
1986-87	University of Minnesota-Duluth	WCHA	DID NOT PLAY – FRESHMAN																									
1987-88	University of Minnesota-Duluth	WCHA	35	12	10	22	....	....	....	36	....	....	....	....	....	....	....	....	....	....	....	....	....	....	....	....	....	....
1988-89	University of Minnesota-Duluth	WCHA	36	15	18	33	....	....	....	51	....	....	....	....	....	....	....	....	....	....	....	....	....	....	....	....	....	....
1989-90	Binghamton Whalers	AHL	32	4	4	8	....	....	....	36	....	....	....	....	....	....	....	....	....	....	....	....	....	....	....	....	....	....
	Virginia Lancers	ECHL	26	11	23	34	....	....	....	27	....	....	....	....	....	....	....	....	....	....	4	0	3	3	2	....	....	....
1990-91	Canada	Nat-Team	55	25	31	56	....	....	....	53	....	....	....	....	....	....	....	....	....	....	....	....	....	....	....	....	....	....
	Springfield Indians	AHL	1	0	0	0	....	....	....	2	....	....	....	....	....	....	....	....	....	....	1	0	0	0	0	....	....	....

			REGULAR SEASON																		PLAYOFFS							
Season	Club	League	GP	G	A	Pts	AG	AA	APts	PIM	PP	SH	GW	S	%	TGF	PGF	TGA	PGA	+/–	GP	G	A	Pts	PIM	PP	SH	GW
1991-92	Canada	Nat-Team	56	33	35	68	....	....	....	63	....	....	....	....	....	....	....	....	....	....	....	....	....	....	....	....	....	....
	Canada	Olympics	8	1	4	5	....	....	....	4	....	....	....	....	....	....	....	....	....	....	....	....	....	....	....	....	....	....
	Calgary Flames	**NHL**	**17**	**2**	**5**	**7**	**2**	**4**	**6**	**17**	**0**	**0**	**0**	**19**	**10.5**	**9**	**0**	**16**	**10**	**+3**	....	....	....	....	....	....	....	....
	Canada	WC-A	5	1	0	1	....	....	....	8	....	....	....	....	....	....	....	....	....	....	....	....	....	....	....	....	....	....
1992-93	**Calgary Flames**	**NHL**	**62**	**9**	**12**	**21**	**7**	**8**	**15**	**18**	**1**	**0**	**1**	**74**	**12.2**	**35**	**2**	**54**	**18**	**–3**	**2**	**0**	**1**	**1**	**2**	**0**	**0**	**0**
1993-94	**Quebec Nordiques**	**NHL**	**37**	**6**	**8**	**14**	**6**	**6**	**12**	**12**	**0**	**0**	**0**	**42**	**14.3**	**19**	**1**	**20**	**1**	**–1**	....	....	....	....	....	....	....	....
	Cornwall Aces	AHL	23	14	13	27	....	....	....	28	....	....	....	....	....	....	....	....	....	....	13	11	3	14	10	....	....	....
1994-95	Krefeld Pinguine	Germany	42	25	41	66	....	....	....	103	....	....	....	....	....	....	....	....	....	....	15	4	10	14	20	....	....	....
1995-96	Krefeld Pinguine	Germany	49	21	35	56	....	....	....	96	....	....	....	....	....	....	....	....	....	....	6	4	7	11	8	....	....	....
1996-97	Krefeld Pinguine	Germany	47	*37	35	72	....	....	....	129	....	....	....	....	....	....	....	....	....	....	3	0	1	1	6	....	....	....
1997-98	Grand Rapids Griffins	IHL	18	8	14	22	....	....	....	25	....	....	....	....	....	....	....	....	....	....	....	....	....	....	....	....	....	....
	Krefeld Pinguine	Germany	15	2	7	9	....	....	....	33	....	....	....	....	....	....	....	....	....	....	....	....	....	....	....	....	....	....
	EV Zug	Switz.	2	1	1	2	....	....	....	0	....	....	....	....	....	....	....	....	....	....	17	6	15	21	22	....	....	....
	NHL Totals		**116**	**17**	**25**	**42**	**15**	**18**	**33**	**47**	**1**	**0**	**1**	**135**	**12.6**	**63**	**3**	**90**	**29**		**2**	**0**	**1**	**1**	**2**	**0**	**0**	**0**

Signed as a free agent by **Hartford**, March 17, 1989. Signed as a free agent by **Calgary**, August 2, 1991. Claimed by **Ottawa** from **Calgary** in Expansion Draft, June 18, 1992. Traded to **Calgary** by **Ottawa** for Mark Osiecki, June 22, 1992. Signed as a free agent by **Quebec**, September 9, 1993.

• LINDBOM, JOHAN

Johan Lindbom LW – L. 6'2", 216 lbs. b: Alvesta, Sweden, 7/8/1971. NY Rangers' 6th choice, 134th overall, in 1997 Entry Draft.

Season	Club	League	GP	G	A	Pts	AG	AA	APts	PIM	PP	SH	GW	S	%	TGF	PGF	TGA	PGA	+/–	GP	G	A	Pts	PIM	PP	SH	GW
1991-92	Tyringe	Sweden 2	30	10	11	21	....	....	....	68	....	....	....	....	....	....	....	....	....	....	....	....	....	....	....	....	....	....
1992-93	Troja-Ljungby	Sweden 2	30	10	16	26	....	....	....	20	....	....	....	....	....	....	....	....	....	....	10	6	3	9	18	....	....	....
1993-94	Troja-Ljungby	Sweden 2	33	16	11	27	....	....	....	30	....	....	....	....	....	....	....	....	....	....	11	6	6	12	2	....	....	....
1994-95	HV 71 Jonkoping	Sweden	39	9	7	16	....	....	....	30	....	....	....	....	....	....	....	....	....	....	13	2	5	7	12	....	....	....
1995-96	HV 71 Jonkoping	Sweden	37	12	14	26	....	....	....	30	....	....	....	....	....	....	....	....	....	....	4	0	0	0	4	....	....	....
1996-97	HV 71 Jonkoping	Sweden	49	20	14	34	....	....	....	26	....	....	....	....	....	....	....	....	....	....	5	1	0	1	6	....	....	....
	Sweden	WC-A	8	0	1	1	....	....	....	6	....	....	....	....	....	....	....	....	....	....	....	....	....	....	....	....	....	....
1997-98	**New York Rangers**	**NHL**	**38**	**1**	**3**	**4**	**1**	**3**	**4**	**28**	**0**	**0**	**0**	**38**	**2.6**	**13**	**0**	**10**	**1**	**+4**	....	....	....	....	....	....	....	....
	Hartford Wolf Pack	AHL	7	1	5	6	....	....	....	6	....	....	....	....	....	....	....	....	....	....	....	....	....	....	....	....	....	....
	NHL Totals		**38**	**1**	**3**	**4**	**1**	**3**	**4**	**20**	**0**	**0**	**0**	**38**	**2.6**	**13**	**0**	**10**	**1**		....	....	....	....	....	....	....	....

• LINDEN, JAMIE

Jamie Linden RW – R. 6'3", 185 lbs. b: Medicine Hat, Alta., 7/19/1972.

Season	Club	League	GP	G	A	Pts	AG	AA	APts	PIM	PP	SH	GW	S	%	TGF	PGF	TGA	PGA	+/–	GP	G	A	Pts	PIM	PP	SH	GW
1988-89	Portland Winter Hawks	WHL	1	0	1	1	....	....	....	0	....	....	....	....	....	....	....	....	....	....	....	....	....	....	....	....	....	....
1989-90	Portland Winter Hawks	WHL	67	5	7	12	....	....	....	124	....	....	....	....	....	....	....	....	....	....	....	....	....	....	....	....	....	....
1990-91	Portland Winter Hawks	WHL	2	0	1	1	....	....	....	6	....	....	....	....	....	....	....	....	....	....	....	....	....	....	....	....	....	....
	Prince Albert Raiders	WHL	64	9	12	21	....	....	....	114	....	....	....	....	....	....	....	....	....	....	3	0	0	0	0	....	....	....
1992-93	Spokane Chiefs	WHL	15	3	1	4	....	....	....	58	....	....	....	....	....	....	....	....	....	....	....	....	....	....	....	....	....	....
	Medicine Hat Tigers	WHL	50	9	9	18	....	....	....	147	....	....	....	....	....	....	....	....	....	....	10	1	6	7	15	....	....	....
1993-94	Cincinnati Cyclones	IHL	47	1	5	6	....	....	....	55	....	....	....	....	....	....	....	....	....	....	2	0	0	0	2	....	....	....
	Birmingham Bulls	ECHL	16	3	7	10	....	....	....	38	....	....	....	....	....	....	....	....	....	....	....	....	....	....	....	....	....	....
1994-95	Cincinnati Cyclones	IHL	51	3	6	9	....	....	....	173	....	....	....	....	....	....	....	....	....	....	....	....	....	....	....	....	....	....
	Florida Panthers	**NHL**	**4**	**0**	**0**	**0**	**0**	**0**	**0**	**17**	**0**	**0**	**0**	**0**	**0.0**	**0**	**0**	**1**	**0**	**–1**	....	....	....	....	....	....	....	....
1995-96	Carolina Monarchs	AHL	50	4	8	12	....	....	....	92	....	....	....	....	....	....	....	....	....	....	....	....	....	....	....	....	....	....
1996-97	Carolina Monarchs	AHL	3	0	0	0	....	....	....	5	....	....	....	....	....	....	....	....	....	....	....	....	....	....	....	....	....	....
	Grand Rapids Griffins	IHL	48	8	8	16	....	....	....	100	....	....	....	....	....	....	....	....	....	....	5	1	1	2	4	....	....	....
1997-98	Las Vegas Thunder	IHL	28	1	1	2	....	....	....	62	....	....	....	....	....	....	....	....	....	....	....	....	....	....	....	....	....	....
	Grand Rapids Griffins	IHL	2	0	1	1	....	....	....	5	....	....	....	....	....	....	....	....	....	....	1	0	0	0	0	....	....	....
	NHL Totals		**4**	**0**	**0**	**0**	**0**	**0**	**0**	**17**	**0**	**0**	**0**	**0**	**0.0**	**0**	**0**	**1**	**0**		....	....	....	....	....	....	....	....

Signed as a free agent by **Florida**, October 4, 1993.

• LINDEN, TREVOR

Trevor Linden C/RW – R. 6'4", 210 lbs. b: Medicine Hat, Alta., 4/11/1970. Vancouver's 1st choice, 2nd overall, in 1988 Entry Draft.

Season	Club	League	GP	G	A	Pts	AG	AA	APts	PIM	PP	SH	GW	S	%	TGF	PGF	TGA	PGA	+/–	GP	G	A	Pts	PIM	PP	SH	GW
1986-87	Medicine Hat Tigers	WHL	72	14	22	36			....	59	....	....	....	....	....	....	....	....	....	....	20	5	4	9	17	....	....	....
1987-88	Medicine Hat Tigers	WHL	67	46	64	110	....	....	....	76	....	....	....	....	....	....	....	....	....	....	16	*13	12	25	19	....	....	....
	Canada	WJC-A	7	1	0	1	....	....	....	0	....	....	....	....	....	....	....	....	....	....	....	....	....	....	....	....	....	....
1988-89	**Vancouver Canucks**	**NHL**	**80**	**30**	**29**	**59**	**25**	**20**	**45**	**41**	**10**	**1**	**2**	**186**	**16.1**	**99**	**41**	**74**	**6**	**–10**	**7**	**3**	**4**	**7**	**8**	**2**	**1**	**0**
1989-90	**Vancouver Canucks**	**NHL**	**73**	**21**	**30**	**51**	**18**	**21**	**39**	**43**	**6**	**2**	**3**	**171**	**12.3**	**83**	**34**	**85**	**19**	**–17**	....	....	....	....	....	....	....	....
1990-91	**Vancouver Canucks**	**NHL**	**80**	**33**	**37**	**70**	**30**	**28**	**58**	**65**	**16**	**2**	**4**	**229**	**14.4**	**103**	**47**	**109**	**28**	**–25**	**6**	**0**	**7**	**7**	**2**	**0**	**0**	**0**
	Canada	WEC-A	10	1	4	5	....	....	....	4	....	....	....	....	....	....	....	....	....	....	....	....	....	....	....	....	....	....
1991-92	**Vancouver Canucks**	**NHL**	**80**	**31**	**44**	**75**	**28**	**33**	**61**	**101**	**6**	**1**	**6**	**201**	**15.4**	**109**	**47**	**74**	**15**	**+3**	**13**	**4**	**8**	**12**	**6**	**2**	**0**	**1**
1992-93	**Vancouver Canucks**	**NHL**	**84**	**33**	**39**	**72**	**28**	**27**	**55**	**64**	**8**	**0**	**3**	**209**	**15.8**	**112**	**33**	**93**	**33**	**+19**	**12**	**5**	**8**	**13**	**16**	**2**	**0**	**1**
1993-94	**Vancouver Canucks**	**NHL**	**84**	**32**	**29**	**61**	**30**	**22**	**52**	**73**	**10**	**2**	**3**	**234**	**13.7**	**114**	**52**	**86**	**30**	**+6**	**24**	**12**	**13**	**25**	**18**	**5**	**1**	**1**
1994-95	**Vancouver Canucks**	**NHL**	**48**	**18**	**22**	**40**	**32**	**32**	**64**	**40**	**9**	**0**	**1**	**129**	**14.0**	**58**	**31**	**39**	**7**	**–5**	**11**	**2**	**6**	**8**	**12**	**1**	**0**	**0**
1995-96	**Vancouver Canucks**	**NHL**	**82**	**33**	**47**	**80**	**33**	**38**	**71**	**42**	**12**	**1**	**2**	**202**	**16.3**	**125**	**48**	**99**	**28**	**+6**	**6**	**4**	**4**	**8**	**6**	**2**	**0**	**0**
1996-97	Canada	W Cup	8	1	1	2	....	....	....	0	....	....	....	....	....	....	....	....	....	....	....	....	....	....	....	....	....	....
	Vancouver Canucks	**NHL**	**49**	**9**	**31**	**40**	**10**	**27**	**37**	**27**	**2**	**2**	**2**	**84**	**10.7**	**62**	**14**	**57**	**14**	**+5**	....	....	....	....	....	....	....	....
	Canada	WC-A	6	1	4	5	....	....	....	4	....	....	....	....	....	....	....	....	....	....	....	....	....	....	....	....	....	....
1997-98	**Vancouver Canucks**	**NHL**	**42**	**7**	**14**	**21**	**8**	**14**	**22**	**49**	**2**	**0**	**1**	**74**	**9.5**	**40**	**15**	**57**	**19**	**–13**	....	....	....	....	....	....	....	....
	New York Islanders	**NHL**	**25**	**10**	**7**	**17**	**12**	**7**	**19**	**33**	**3**	**2**	**1**	**59**	**16.9**	**34**	**14**	**27**	**6**	**–1**	....	....	....	....	....	....	....	....
	Canada	Olympics	6	1	0	1	....	....	....	10	....	....	....	....	....	....	....	....	....	....	....	....	....	....	....	....	....	....
	NHL Totals		**727**	**257**	**329**	**586**	**254**	**269**	**523**	**578**	**84**	**13**	**28**	**1778**	**14.5**	**939**	**376**	**800**	**205**		**79**	**30**	**50**	**80**	**68**	**14**	**2**	**3**

WHL East Second All-Star Team (1988) • NHL All-Rookie Team (1989) • Won King Clancy Memorial Trophy (1997)

Played in NHL All-Star Game (1991, 1992)

Traded to **NY Islanders** by **Vancouver** for Todd Bertuzzi, Bryan McCabe and NY Islanders' 3rd round choice (Jakko Ruutu) in 1998 Entry Draft, February 6, 1998.

• LINDGREN, LARS

Lars Lindgren D – L. 6'1", 200 lbs. b: Pitea, Sweden, 10/12/1952.

Season	Club	League	GP	G	A	Pts	AG	AA	APts	PIM	PP	SH	GW	S	%	TGF	PGF	TGA	PGA	+/–	GP	G	A	Pts	PIM	PP	SH	GW
1973-74	Skelleftea	Sweden	13	0	3	3	....	....	....	10	....	....	....	....	....	....	....	....	....	....	6	1	2	3	8	....	....	....
1974-75	MoDo AIK	Sweden	43	4	11	15	....	....	....	30	....	....	....	....	....	....	....	....	....	....	....	....	....	....	....	....	....	....
1975-76	MoDo AIK	Sweden	36	2	4	6	....	....	....	22	....	....	....	....	....	....	....	....	....	....	....	....	....	....	....	....	....	....
1976-77	MoDo AIK	Sweden	35	6	6	12	....	....	....	36	....	....	....	....	....	....	....	....	....	....	....	....	....	....	....	....	....	....
	Sweden	WEC-A	10	1	1	2	....	....	....	8	....	....	....	....	....	....	....	....	....	....	....	....	....	....	....	....	....	....
1977-78	MoDo AIK	Sweden	33	3	12	15	....	....	....	55	....	....	....	....	....	....	....	....	....	....	....	....	....	....	....	....	....	....
	Sweden	WEC-A	10	2	3	5	....	....	....	8	....	....	....	....	....	....	....	....	....	....	....	....	....	....	....	....	....	....
1978-79	**Vancouver Canucks**	**NHL**	**64**	**2**	**19**	**21**	**2**	**14**	**16**	**68**	**1**	**0**	**0**	**109**	**1.8**	**72**	**20**	**108**	**24**	**–32**	**3**	**0**	**0**	**0**	**6**	**0**	**0**	**0**
1979-80	**Vancouver Canucks**	**NHL**	**73**	**5**	**30**	**35**	**5**	**23**	**28**	**66**	**2**	**0**	**0**	**181**	**2.8**	**99**	**29**	**109**	**31**	**–8**	**2**	**0**	**1**	**1**	**0**	**0**	**0**	**0**
1980-81	**Vancouver Canucks**	**NHL**	**52**	**4**	**18**	**22**	**3**	**13**	**16**	**32**	**1**	**0**	**0**	**76**	**5.3**	**65**	**7**	**60**	**18**	**+16**	....	....	....	....	....	....	....	....
1981-82	Sweden	C Cup	5	0	1	1	....	....	....	6	....	....	....	....	....	....	....	....	....	....	....	....	....	....	....	....	....	....
	Vancouver Canucks	**NHL**	**75**	**5**	**16**	**21**	**4**	**11**	**15**	**74**	**0**	**0**	**1**	**95**	**5.3**	**78**	**7**	**105**	**36**	**+2**	**16**	**2**	**4**	**6**	**6**	**0**	**0**	**0**
1982-83	**Vancouver Canucks**	**NHL**	**64**	**6**	**14**	**20**	**5**	**10**	**15**	**48**	**1**	**0**	**1**	**72**	**8.3**	**68**	**4**	**97**	**36**	**+3**	**4**	**1**	**1**	**2**	**2**	**0**	**0**	**0**
1983-84	**Vancouver Canucks**	**NHL**	**7**	**1**	**2**	**3**	**1**	**1**	**2**	**4**	**0**	**0**	**0**	**4**	**25.0**	**12**	**2**	**19**	**9**	**0**	....	....	....	....	....	....	....	....
	Minnesota North Stars	**NHL**	**59**	**2**	**14**	**16**	**2**	**9**	**11**	**33**	**0**	**0**	**0**	**66**	**3.0**	**66**	**3**	**90**	**24**	**–3**	**15**	**2**	**0**	**2**	**6**	**0**	**0**	**0**
1984-85	Lulea HF	Sweden	33	8	3	11	....	....	....	46	....	....	....	....	....	....	....	....	....	....	....	....	....	....	....	....	....	....
1985-86	Lulea HF	Sweden	35	2	7	9	....	....	....	32	....	....	....	....	....	....	....	....	....	....	....	....	....	....	....	....	....	....
1986-87	Lulea HF	Sweden	35	4	9	13	....	....	....	42	....	....	....	....	....	....	....	....	....	....	3	0	0	0	2	....	....	....
1987-88	Lulea HF	Sweden	40	2	7	9	....	....	....	52	....	....	....	....	....	....	....	....	....	....	....	....	....	....	....	....	....	....
	NHL Totals		**394**	**25**	**113**	**138**	**22**	**81**	**103**	**325**	**5**	**0**	**2**	**603**	**4.1**	**460**	**72**	**588**	**178**		**40**	**5**	**6**	**11**	**20**	**0**	**0**	**0**

Played in NHL All-Star Game (1980)

Signed as a free agent by **Vancouver**, June 5, 1978. Traded to **Minnesota** by **Vancouver** for Minnesota's 3rd round choice (Landis Chaulk) in 1984 Entry Draft, October 20, 1983.

			REGULAR SEASON																		PLAYOFFS							
Season	Club	League	GP	G	A	Pts	AG	AA	APts	PIM	PP	SH	GW	S	%	TGF	PGF	TGA	PGA	+/–	GP	G	A	Pts	PIM	PP	SH	GW

• LINDGREN, MATS

Mats Lindgren C – L. 6'2", 200 lbs. b: Skelleftea, Sweden, 10/1/1974. Winnipeg's 1st choice, 15th overall, in 1993 Entry Draft.

Season	Club	League	GP	G	A	Pts	AG	AA	APts	PIM	PP	SH	GW	S	%	TGF	PGF	TGA	PGA	+/–	GP	G	A	Pts	PIM	PP	SH	GW
1991-92	Skelleftea AIK	Sweden 2	29	14	8	22	....	....	....	14	....	....	....	....	....	....	....	....	....	....	....	....	....	....	....	....	....	....
1992-93	Skelleftea AIK	Sweden 2	32	20	14	34	....	....	....	18	....	....	....	....	....	....	....	....	....	....	....	....	....	....	....	....	....	....
	Sweden	WJC-A	7	1	2	3	....	....	....	8	....	....	....	....	....	....	....	....	....	....	....	....	....	....	....	....	....	....
1993-94	Farjestad BK Stockholm	Sweden	22	11	6	17	....	....	....	26	....	....	....	....	....	....	....	....	....	....	....	....	....	....	....	....	....	....
	Sweden	WJC-A	7	5	4	9	....	....	....	2	....	....	....	....	....	....	....	....	....	....	....	....	....	....	....	....	....	....
1994-95	Farjestad BK Stockholm	Sweden	37	17	15	32	....	....	....	20	....	....	....	....	....	....	....	....	....	....	3	0	0	0	4	....	....	....
1995-96	Cape Breton Oilers	AHL	13	7	5	12	....	....	....	6	....	....	....	....	....	....	....	....	....	....	....	....	....	....	....	....	....	....
1996-97	**Edmonton Oilers**	**NHL**	**69**	**11**	**14**	**25**	**12**	**12**	**24**	**12**	**2**	**3**	**1**	**71**	**15.5**	**35**	**4**	**52**	**14**	**–7**	**12**	**0**	**4**	**4**	**0**	**0**	**0**	**0**
	Hamilton Bulldogs	AHL	9	6	7	13	....	....	....	6	....	....	....	....	....	....	....	....	....	....	....	....	....	....	....	....	....	....
1997-98	**Edmonton Oilers**	**NHL**	**82**	**13**	**13**	**26**	**15**	**13**	**28**	**42**	**1**	**3**	**3**	**131**	**9.9**	**41**	**6**	**59**	**24**	**0**	**12**	**1**	**1**	**2**	**10**	**0**	**0**	**0**
	Sweden	Olympics	4	0	0	0	....	....	....	2	....	....	....	....	....	....	....	....	....	....	....	....	....	....	....	....	....	....
	NHL Totals		**151**	**24**	**27**	**51**	**27**	**25**	**52**	**54**	**3**	**6**	**4**	**202**	**11.9**	**76**	**10**	**111**	**38**		**24**	**1**	**5**	**6**	**10**	**0**	**0**	**0**

Swedish Rookie of the Year (1994)

Traded to **Edmonton** by **Winnipeg** with Boris Mironov, Winnipeg's 1st round choice (Jason Bonsignore) in 1994 Entry Draft and Florida's 4th round choice (previously acquired by Winnipeg — Edmonton selected Adam Copeland) in 1994 Entry Draft for Dave Manson and St. Louis' 6th round choice (previously acquired, Winnipeg selected Chris Kibermanis) in 1994 Entry Draft, March 15, 1994.

• LINDHOLM, MIKAEL

Mikael Lindholm C – L. 6'1", 194 lbs. b: Gavle, Sweden, 12/19/1964. Los Angeles' 10th choice, 237th overall, in 1987 Entry Draft.

Season	Club	League	GP	G	A	Pts	AG	AA	APts	PIM	PP	SH	GW	S	%	TGF	PGF	TGA	PGA	+/–	GP	G	A	Pts	PIM	PP	SH	GW
1981-82	Gavle EIK	Sweden 2	18	3	3	6	....	....	....	8	....	....	....	....	....	....	....	....	....	....	....	....	....	....	....	....	....	....
1982-83	Gavle EIK	Sweden 2	27	6	7	13	....	....	....	44	....	....	....	....	....	....	....	....	....	....	....	....	....	....	....	....	....	....
1983-84	Stromsbro	Sweden 2	20	9	10	19	....	....	....	4	....	....	....	....	....	....	....	....	....	....	....	....	....	....	....	....	....	....
1984-85	Stromsbro	Sweden 2	30	14	17	31	....	....	....	29	....	....	....	....	....	....	....	....	....	....	....	....	....	....	....	....	....	....
1985-86	Stromsbro	Sweden 2	32	15	20	35	....	....	....	26	....	....	....	....	....	....	....	....	....	....	5	2	4	6	6	....	....	....
1986-87	Brynas IF Gavle	Sweden	36	8	9	17	....	....	....	46	....	....	....	....	....	....	....	....	....	....	....	....	....	....	....	....	....	....
1987-88	Brynas IF Gavle	Sweden	38	9	8	17	....	....	....	56	....	....	....	....	....	....	....	....	....	....	....	....	....	....	....	....	....	....
1988-89	Brynas IF Gavle	Sweden	40	9	17	26	....	....	....	*98	....	....	....	....	....	....	....	....	....	....	4	0	0	0	4	....	....	....
1989-90	**Los Angeles Kings**	**NHL**	**18**	**2**	**2**	**4**	**2**	**1**	**3**	**2**	**0**	**0**	**0**	**10**	**20.0**	**8**	**0**	**6**	**0**	**+2**	....	....	....	....	....	....	....	....
	New Haven Nighthawks	AHL	28	4	6	10	....	....	....	24	....	....	....	....	....	....	....	....	....	....	....	....	....	....	....	....	....	....
1990-91	Phoenix Roadrunners	IHL	70	16	45	61	....	....	....	92	....	....	....	....	....	....	....	....	....	....	11	0	12	12	14	....	....	....
1991-92	Brynas IF Gavle	Sweden	36	7	11	18	....	....	....	24	....	....	....	....	....	....	....	....	....	....	5	0	1	1	2	....	....	....
1992-93	Brynas IF Gavle	Sweden	15	2	3	5	....	....	....	16	....	....	....	....	....	....	....	....	....	....	....	....	....	....	....	....	....	....
1993-94	Boden	Sweden	36	19	22	41	....	....	....	44	....	....	....	....	....	....	....	....	....	....	9	0	7	7	20	....	....	....
1994-95	Boden	Sweden	36	10	19	29	....	....	....	48	....	....	....	....	....	....	....	....	....	....	10	5	6	11	10	....	....	....
1995-96	Lulea HF	Sweden	39	8	12	20	....	....	....	38	....	....	....	....	....	....	....	....	....	....	13	3	3	6	16	....	....	....
1996-97	Lulea HF	Sweden	46	6	14	20	....	....	....	75	....	....	....	....	....	....	....	....	....	....	10	1	4	5	31	....	....	....
1997-98	Hannover Scorpions	Germany	47	7	9	16	....	....	....	16	....	....	....	....	....	....	....	....	....	....	4	0	1	1	16	....	....	....
	NHL Totals		**18**	**2**	**2**	**4**	**2**	**1**	**3**	**2**	**0**	**0**	**0**	**10**	**20.0**	**8**	**0**	**6**	**0**		....	....	....	....	....	....	....	....

• LINDROS, BRETT

Brett Lindros RW – R. 6'4", 215 lbs. b: London, Ont., 12/2/1975. NY Islanders' 1st choice, 9th overall, in 1994 Entry Draft.

Season	Club	League	GP	G	A	Pts	AG	AA	APts	PIM	PP	SH	GW	S	%	TGF	PGF	TGA	PGA	+/–	GP	G	A	Pts	PIM	PP	SH	GW
1991-92	St. Michael's Buzzers	Jr. B	34	21	21	42	....	....	....	210	....	....	....	....	....	....	....	....	....	....	6	5	5	10	63	....	....	....
1992-93	Kingston Frontenacs	OHL	31	11	11	22	....	....	....	162	....	....	....	....	....	....	....	....	....	....	....	....	....	....	....	....	....	....
	Canada	Nat-Team	11	1	6	7	....	....	....	33	....	....	....	....	....	....	....	....	....	....	....	....	....	....	....	....	....	....
1993-94	Canada	Nat-Team	44	7	7	14	....	....	....	118	....	....	....	....	....	....	....	....	....	....	....	....	....	....	....	....	....	....
	Kingston Frontenacs	OHL	15	4	6	10	....	....	....	94	....	....	....	....	....	....	....	....	....	....	3	0	0	0	18	....	....	....
1994-95	**New York Islanders**	**NHL**	**33**	**1**	**3**	**4**	**2**	**4**	**6**	**100**	**0**	**0**	**1**	**35**	**2.9**	**13**	**3**	**18**	**0**	**–8**	....	....	....	....	....	....	....	....
	Kingston Frontenacs	OHL	26	24	23	47	....	....	....	63	....	....	....	....	....	....	....	....	....	....	....	....	....	....	....	....	....	....
1995-96	**New York Islanders**	**NHL**	**18**	**1**	**2**	**3**	**1**	**2**	**3**	**47**	**0**	**0**	**0**	**10**	**10.0**	**5**	**0**	**11**	**0**	**–6**	....	....	....	....	....	....	....	....
	NHL Totals		**51**	**2**	**5**	**7**	**3**	**6**	**9**	**147**	**0**	**0**	**1**	**45**	**4.4**	**18**	**3**	**29**	**0**		....	....	....	....	....	....	....	....

• LINDROS, ERIC

Eric Lindros C – R. 6'4", 236 lbs. b: London, Ont., 2/28/1973. Quebec's 1st choice, 1st overall, in 1991 Entry Draft.

Season	Club	League	GP	G	A	Pts	AG	AA	APts	PIM	PP	SH	GW	S	%	TGF	PGF	TGA	PGA	+/–	GP	G	A	Pts	PIM	PP	SH	GW
1988-89	St. Michael's Buzzers	Jr. B	37	24	43	67	....	....	....	193	....	....	....	....	....	....	....	....	....	....	27	23	25	48	155	....	....	....
	Canada	Nat-Team	2	1	0	1	....	....	....	0	....	....	....	....	....	....	....	....	....	....	....	....	....	....	....	....	....	....
1989-90	Detroit Compuware	USHL	14	23	29	52	....	....	....	123	....	....	....	....	....	....	....	....	....	....	....	....	....	....	....	....	....	....
	Canada	Nat-Team	3	1	0	1	....	....	....	4	....	....	....	....	....	....	....	....	....	....	....	....	....	....	....	....	....	....
	Canada	WJC-A	7	4	0	4	....	....	....	14	....	....	....	....	....	....	....	....	....	....	....	....	....	....	....	....	....	....
	Oshawa Generals	OHL	25	17	19	36	....	....	....	61	....	....	....	....	....	....	....	....	....	....	17	18	18	36	76	....	....	....
1990-91	Oshawa Generals	OHL	57	*71	78	*149	....	....	....	189	....	....	....	....	....	....	....	....	....	....	16	*18	20	*38	*93	....	....	....
	Canada	WJC-A	7	6	11	17	....	....	....	6	....	....	....	....	....	....	....	....	....	....	....	....	....	....	....	....	....	....
1991-92	Canada	C Cup	8	3	2	5	....	....	....	8	....	....	....	....	....	....	....	....	....	....	....	....	....	....	....	....	....	....
	Oshawa Generals	OHL	13	9	22	31	....	....	....	54	....	....	....	....	....	....	....	....	....	....	....	....	....	....	....	....	....	....
	Canada	Nat-Team	24	19	16	35	....	....	....	34	....	....	....	....	....	....	....	....	....	....	....	....	....	....	....	....	....	....
	Canada	WJC-A	7	2	8	10	....	....	....	12	....	....	....	....	....	....	....	....	....	....	....	....	....	....	....	....	....	....
	Canada	Olympics	8	5	6	11	....	....	....	5	....	....	....	....	....	....	....	....	....	....	....	....	....	....	....	....	....	....
1992-93	**Philadelphia Flyers**	**NHL**	**61**	**41**	**34**	**75**	**34**	**23**	**57**	**147**	**8**	**1**	**5**	**180**	**22.8**	**119**	**34**	**63**	**6**	**+28**	....	....	....	....	....	....	....	....
	Canada	WC-A	8	11	6	17	....	....	....	10	....	....	....	....	....	....	....	....	....	....	....	....	....	....	....	....	....	....
1993-94	**Philadelphia Flyers**	**NHL**	**65**	**44**	**53**	**97**	**41**	**41**	**82**	**103**	**13**	**2**	**9**	**197**	**22.3**	**134**	**47**	**82**	**11**	**+16**	....	....	....	....	....	....	....	....
1994-95	**Philadelphia Flyers**	**NHL**	**46**	**29**	**41**	***70**	**52**	**60**	**112**	**60**	**7**	**0**	**4**	**144**	**20.1**	**94**	**30**	**40**	**3**	**+27**	**12**	**4**	**11**	**15**	**18**	**0**	**0**	**1**
1995-96	**Philadelphia Flyers**	**NHL**	**73**	**47**	**68**	**115**	**46**	**56**	**102**	**163**	**15**	**0**	**4**	**294**	**16.0**	**148**	**57**	**78**	**13**	**+26**	**12**	**6**	**6**	**12**	**43**	**3**	**0**	**2**
1996-97	Canada	W Cup	8	3	3	6	....	....	....	10	....	....	....	....	....	....	....	....	....	....	....	....	....	....	....	....	....	....
	Philadelphia Flyers	**NHL**	**52**	**32**	**47**	**79**	**34**	**42**	**76**	**136**	**9**	**0**	**7**	**198**	**16.2**	**105**	**29**	**49**	**4**	**+31**	**19**	**12**	**14**	***26**	**40**	**4**	**0**	**1**
1997-98	**Philadelphia Flyers**	**NHL**	**63**	**30**	**41**	**71**	**35**	**40**	**75**	**134**	**10**	**1**	**4**	**202**	**14.9**	**92**	**35**	**47**	**4**	**+14**	**5**	**1**	**2**	**3**	**17**	**0**	**0**	**0**
	Canada	Olympics	6	2	3	5	....	....	....	2	....	....	....	....	....	....	....	....	....	....	....	....	....	....	....	....	....	....
	NHL Totals		**360**	**223**	**284**	**507**	**242**	**262**	**504**	**743**	**62**	**4**	**33**	**1215**	**18.4**	**692**	**232**	**359**	**41**		**48**	**23**	**33**	**56**	**118**	**7**	**0**	**4**

Memorial Cup All-Star Team (1990) • WJC-A All-Star Team (1991) • Named Best Forward at WJC-A (1991) • OHL First All-Star Team (1991) • Canadian Major Junior Player of the Year (1991) • NHL/Upper Deck All-Rookie Team (1993) • WC-A All-Star Team (1993) • Named Best Forward at WC-A (1993) • NHL First All-Star Team (1995) • Won Lester B. Pearson Award (1995) • Won Hart Trophy (1995) • NHL Second All-Star Team (1996)

Played in NHL All-Star Game (1994, 1996, 1997, 1998)

Traded to **Philadelphia** by **Quebec** for Peter Forsberg, Steve Duchesne, Kerry Huffman, Mike Ricci, Ron Hextall, Chris Simon, Philadelphia's 1st round choice in the 1993 (Jocelyn Thibault) and 1994 (later traded to Toronto — later traded to Washington — Washington selected Nolan Baumgartner) Entry Drafts and cash, June 30, 1992.

• LINDSAY, BILL

Bill Lindsay LW – L. 5'11", 190 lbs. b: Big Fork, MT, 5/17/1971. Quebec's 6th choice, 103rd overall, in 1991 Entry Draft.

Season	Club	League	GP	G	A	Pts	AG	AA	APts	PIM	PP	SH	GW	S	%	TGF	PGF	TGA	PGA	+/–	GP	G	A	Pts	PIM	PP	SH	GW
1989-90	Tri-City Americans	WHL	72	40	45	85	....	....	....	84	....	....	....	....	....	....	....	....	....	....	7	3	0	3	17	....	....	....
1990-91	Tri-City Americans	WHL	63	46	47	93	....	....	....	151	....	....	....	....	....	....	....	....	....	....	5	3	6	9	10	....	....	....
1991-92	Tri-City Americans	WHL	42	34	59	93	....	....	....	111	....	....	....	....	....	....	....	....	....	....	3	2	3	5	16	....	....	....
	Quebec Nordiques	**NHL**	**23**	**2**	**4**	**6**	**2**	**3**	**5**	**14**	**0**	**0**	**1**	**35**	**5.7**	**11**	**1**	**16**	**0**	**–6**	....	....	....	....	....	....	....	....
1992-93	**Quebec Nordiques**	**NHL**	**44**	**4**	**9**	**13**	**3**	**6**	**9**	**16**	**0**	**0**	**0**	**58**	**6.9**	**24**	**0**	**36**	**12**	**0**	....	....	....	....	....	....	....	....
	Halifax Citadels	AHL	20	11	13	24	....	....	....	18	....	....	....	....	....	....	....	....	....	....	....	....	....	....	....	....	....	....
1993-94	**Florida Panthers**	**NHL**	**84**	**6**	**6**	**12**	**6**	**5**	**11**	**97**	**0**	**0**	**0**	**90**	**6.7**	**26**	**0**	**38**	**10**	**–2**	....	....	....	....	....	....	....	....
	United States	WC-A	5	3	1	4	....	....	....	2	....	....	....	....	....	....	....	....	....	....	....	....	....	....	....	....	....	....
1994-95	**Florida Panthers**	**NHL**	**48**	**10**	**9**	**19**	**18**	**13**	**31**	**46**	**0**	**1**	**0**	**63**	**15.9**	**25**	**1**	**31**	**8**	**+1**	....	....	....	....	....	....	....	....
1995-96	**Florida Panthers**	**NHL**	**73**	**12**	**22**	**34**	**12**	**18**	**30**	**57**	**0**	**3**	**2**	**118**	**10.2**	**46**	**3**	**48**	**18**	**+13**	**22**	**5**	**5**	**10**	**18**	**0**	**1**	**1**
1996-97	**Florida Panthers**	**NHL**	**81**	**11**	**23**	**34**	**12**	**20**	**32**	**120**	**0**	**1**	**3**	**168**	**6.5**	**42**	**1**	**63**	**23**	**+1**	**3**	**0**	**1**	**1**	**8**	**0**	**0**	**0**
1997-98	**Florida Panthers**	**NHL**	**82**	**12**	**16**	**28**	**14**	**16**	**30**	**80**	**0**	**2**	**5**	**150**	**8.0**	**31**	**0**	**66**	**33**	**–2**	....	....	....	....	....	....	....	....
	NHL Totals		**435**	**57**	**89**	**146**	**67**	**81**	**148**	**430**	**0**	**7**	**11**	**682**	**8.4**	**205**	**6**	**298**	**104**		**25**	**5**	**6**	**11**	**26**	**0**	**1**	**1**

WHL West Second All-Star Team (1992)

WHL West Second All-Star Team (1992)

Claimed by **Florida** from **Quebec** in Expansion Draft, June 24, 1993.

• LINDSTROM, WILLY

Willy "The Wisp" Lindstrom RW – L. 6', 180 lbs. b: Grums, Sweden, 5/5/1951.

			REGULAR SEASON																		PLAYOFFS							
Season	Club	League	GP	G	A	Pts	AG	AA	APts	PIM	PP	SH	GW	S	%	TGF	PGF	TGA	PGA	+/–	GP	G	A	Pts	PIM	PP	SH	GW
1970-71	Vastra Frolunda	Sweden	14	7	4	11	....	....	....	10	....	....	....	....	....	....	....	....	....	....	8	3	0	3	2	....	....	....
1971-72	Vastra Frolunda	Sweden	27	12	11	23	....	....	....	18	....	....	....	....	....	....	....	....	....	....	....	....	....	....	....	....	....	....
1972-73	Vastra Frolunda	Sweden	14	7	5	12	....	....	....	14	....	....	....	....	....	....	....	....	....	....	14	6	1	7	4	....	....	....
1973-74	Vastra Frolunda	Sweden	27	19	11	30	....	....	....	22	....	....	....	....	....	....	....	....	....	....	....	....	....	....	....	....	....	....
	Sweden	Nat-Team	15	8	6	14	....	....	....	8	....	....	....	....	....	....	....	....	....	....	....	....	....	....	....	....	....	....
	Sweden	WEC-A	9	7	5	12	....	....	....	6	....	....	....	....	....	....	....	....	....	....	....	....	....	....	....	....	....	....
1974-75	Vastra Frolunda	Sweden	29	18	15	33	....	....	....	24	....	....	....	....	....	....	....	....	....	....	....	....	....	....	....	....	....	....
	Sweden	Nat-Team	27	7	5	12	....	....	....	10	....	....	....	....	....	....	....	....	....	....	....	....	....	....	....	....	....	....
	Sweden	WEC-A	7	2	1	3	....	....	....	4	....	....	....	....	....	....	....	....	....	....	....	....	....	....	....	....	....	....
1975-76	Winnipeg Jets	WHA	81	23	36	59	....	....	....	32	....	....	....	....	....	....	....	....	....	....	13	4	7	11	2	....	....	....
1976-77	Sweden	C Cup	1	0	0	0	....	....	....	5	....	....	....	....	....	....	....	....	....	....	....	....	....	....	....	....	....	....
	Winnipeg Jets	WHA	79	44	36	80	....	....	....	37	....	....	....	....	....	....	....	....	....	....	20	9	6	15	22	....	....	....
1977-78	Winnipeg Jets	WHA	77	30	30	60	....	....	....	42	....	....	....	....	....	....	....	....	....	....	8	3	4	7	17	....	....	....
1978-79	Winnipeg Jets	WHA	79	26	36	62	....	....	....	22	....	....	....	....	....	....	....	....	....	....	10	*10	5	15	9	....	....	....
1979-80	**Winnipeg Jets**	**NHL**	**79**	**23**	**26**	**49**	**21**	**20**	**41**	**20**	**5**	**0**	**4**	**243**	**9.5**	**91**	**36**	**79**	**5**	**–19**	....	....	....	....	....	....	....	....
1980-81	**Winnipeg Jets**	**NHL**	**72**	**22**	**13**	**35**	**18**	**9**	**27**	**45**	**7**	**0**	**1**	**163**	**13.5**	**60**	**22**	**72**	**6**	**–28**	....	....	....	....	....	....	....	....
1981-82	**Winnipeg Jets**	**NHL**	**74**	**32**	**27**	**59**	**25**	**18**	**43**	**33**	**5**	**0**	**5**	**236**	**13.6**	**87**	**17**	**59**	**0**	**+11**	**4**	**2**	**1**	**3**	**2**	**0**	**0**	**0**
1982-83	**Winnipeg Jets**	**NHL**	**63**	**20**	**25**	**45**	**16**	**17**	**33**	**8**	**5**	**0**	**3**	**204**	**9.8**	**67**	**14**	**58**	**0**	**–5**	....	....	....	....	....	....	....	....
	Edmonton Oilers	**NHL**	**10**	**6**	**5**	**11**	**5**	**3**	**8**	**2**	**0**	**0**	**0**	**21**	**28.6**	**14**	**1**	**8**	**0**	**+5**	**16**	**2**	**11**	**13**	**4**	**1**	**0**	**0**
1983-84	**Edmonton Oilers**	**NHL**	**73**	**22**	**16**	**38**	**18**	**11**	**29**	**38**	**2**	**0**	**3**	**116**	**19.0**	**68**	**13**	**38**	**0**	**+17**	**19**	**5**	**5**	**10**	**10**	**3**	**0**	**0**
1984-85	**Edmonton Oilers**	**NHL**	**80**	**12**	**20**	**32**	**10**	**14**	**24**	**18**	**1**	**0**	**1**	**98**	**12.2**	**53**	**11**	**38**	**1**	**+5**	**18**	**5**	**1**	**6**	**8**	**0**	**0**	**1**
1985-86	**Pittsburgh Penguins**	**NHL**	**71**	**14**	**17**	**31**	**11**	**11**	**22**	**30**	**0**	**0**	**1**	**87**	**16.1**	**43**	**1**	**44**	**2**	**0**	....	....	....	....	....	....	....	....
1986-87	**Pittsburgh Penguins**	**NHL**	**60**	**10**	**13**	**23**	**9**	**9**	**18**	**6**	**1**	**0**	**1**	**93**	**10.8**	**38**	**2**	**30**	**3**	**+9**	....	....	....	....	....	....	....	....
1987-88			DID NOT PLAY																									
1988-89	Brynas IF Gavle	Sweden	29	12	5	17	....	....	....	26	....	....	....	....	....	....	....	....	....	....	5	3	1	4	4	....	....	....
1989-90	Brynas IF Gavle	Sweden	29	8	5	13	....	....	....	12	....	....	....	....	....	....	....	....	....	....	3	0	0	0	0	....	....	....
	NHL Totals		**582**	**161**	**162**	**323**	**133**	**112**	**245**	**200**	**26**	**0**	**19**	**1261**	**12.8**	**521**	**117**	**426**	**17**		**57**	**14**	**18**	**32**	**24**	**4**	**0**	**1**
	Other Major League Totals		316	123	138	261	....	....	....	133	....	....	....	....	....	....	....	....	....	....	51	26	22	48	50	....	....	....

Signed as a free agent by **Winnipeg** (WHA), July, 1975. Signed as a free agent by **Winnipeg**, July 25, 1979. Traded to **Edmonton** by **Winnipeg** for Laurie Boschman, March 8, 1983. Claimed by **Pittsburgh** from **Edmonton** in Waiver Draft, October 7, 1985.

• LING, DAVID

David Ling RW – R. 5'9", 185 lbs. b: Halifax, N.S., 1/9/1975. Quebec's 9th choice, 179th overall, in 1993 Entry Draft.

Season	Club	League	GP	G	A	Pts	AG	AA	APts	PIM	PP	SH	GW	S	%	TGF	PGF	TGA	PGA	+/–	GP	G	A	Pts	PIM	PP	SH	GW
1992-93	Kingston Frontenacs	OHL	64	17	46	63	....	....	....	275	....	....	....	....	....	....	....	....	....	....	16	3	12	15	*72	....	....	....
1993-94	Kingston Frontenacs	OHL	61	37	40	77	....	....	....	*254	....	....	....	....	....	....	....	....	....	....	6	4	2	6	16	....	....	....
1994-95	Kingston Frontenacs	OHL	62	*61	74	135	....	....	....	136	....	....	....	....	....	....	....	....	....	....	6	7	8	15	12	....	....	....
1995-96	Saint John Flames	AHL	75	24	32	56	....	....	....	179	....	....	....	....	....	....	....	....	....	....	9	0	5	5	12	....	....	....
1996-97	Saint John Flames	AHL	5	0	2	2	....	....	....	19	....	....	....	....	....	....	....	....	....	....	....	....	....	....	....	....	....	....
	Montreal Canadiens	**NHL**	**2**	**0**	**0**	**0**	**0**	**0**	**0**	**0**	**0**	**0**	**0**	**0**	**0.0**	**0**	**0**	**0**	**0**	**0**	....	....	....	....	....	....	....	....
	Fredericton Canadiens	AHL	48	22	36	58	....	....	....	229	....	....	....	....	....	....	....	....	....	....	....	....	....	....	....	....	....	....
1997-98	**Montreal Canadiens**	**NHL**	**1**	**0**	**0**	**0**	**0**	**0**	**0**	**0**	**0**	**0**	**0**	**1**	**0.0**	**0**	**0**	**1**	**0**	**–1**	....	....	....	....	....	....	....	....
	Fredericton Canadiens	AHL	67	25	41	66	....	....	....	148	....	....	....	....	....	....	....	....	....	....	....	....	....	....	....	....	....	....
	Indianapolis Ice	IHL	12	8	6	14	....	....	....	30	....	....	....	....	....	....	....	....	....	....	5	4	1	5	31	....	....	....
	NHL Totals		**3**	**0**	**0**	**0**	**0**	**0**	**0**	**0**	**0**	**0**	**0**	**1**	**0.0**	**0**	**0**	**1**	**0**		....	....	....	....	....	....	....	....

OHL First All-Star Team (1995) • Canadian Major Junior First All-Star Team (1995) • Canadian Junior Player of the Year (1995)

Rights transferred to **Colorado** after **Quebec** franchise relocated, June 21, 1995. Traded to **Calgary** by **Colorado** with Colorado's 9th round choice (Steve Shirreffs) in 1995 Entry Draft for Calgary's 9th round choice (Chris George) in 1995 Entry Draft, July 7, 1995. Traded to **Montreal** by **Calgary** with Calgary's 6th round choice (Gordie Dwyer) in 1998 Entry Draft for Scott Fraser, October 24, 1996. Traded to **Chicago** by **Montreal** for Martin Gendron, March 14, 1998.

• LINSEMAN, KEN

Ken "The Rat" Linseman C – L. 5'11", 180 lbs. b: Kingston, Ont., 8/11/1958. Philadelphia's 2nd choice, 7th overall, in 1978 Amateur Draft.

Season	Club	League	GP	G	A	Pts	AG	AA	APts	PIM	PP	SH	GW	S	%	TGF	PGF	TGA	PGA	+/–	GP	G	A	Pts	PIM	PP	SH	GW
1974-75	Kingston Canadians	OHA	59	19	28	47	....	....	....	70	....	....	....	....	....	....	....	....	....	....	....	....	....	....	....	....	....	....
1975-76	Kingston Canadians	OHA	65	61	51	112	....	....	....	92	....	....	....	....	....	....	....	....	....	....	7	5	0	5	10	....	....	....
1976-77	Kingston Canadians	OHA	63	53	74	127	....	....	....	210	....	....	....	....	....	....	....	....	....	....	10	9	12	21	54	....	....	....
1977-78	Birmingham Bulls	WHA	71	38	38	76	....	....	....	126	....	....	....	....	....	....	....	....	....	....	5	2	2	4	15	....	....	....
1978-79	**Philadelphia Flyers**	**NHL**	**30**	**5**	**20**	**25**	**5**	**15**	**20**	**23**	**1**	**0**	**1**	**57**	**8.8**	**36**	**8**	**14**	**2**	**+16**	**8**	**2**	**6**	**8**	**22**	**0**	**0**	**1**
	Maine Mariners	AHL	38	17	22	39	....	....	....	106	....	....	....	....	....	....	....	....	....	....	....	....	....	....	....	....	....	....
1979-80	**Philadelphia Flyers**	**NHL**	**80**	**22**	**57**	**79**	**20**	**44**	**64**	**107**	**2**	**0**	**4**	**168**	**13.1**	**100**	**20**	**56**	**2**	**+26**	**17**	**4**	***18**	**22**	**40**	**0**	**0**	**1**
1980-81	**Philadelphia Flyers**	**NHL**	**51**	**17**	**30**	**47**	**14**	**21**	**35**	**150**	**1**	**1**	**1**	**126**	**13.5**	**61**	**15**	**45**	**8**	**+9**	**12**	**4**	**16**	**20**	**67**	**0**	**0**	**3**
1981-82	Canada	C Cup	4	0	1	1	....	....	....	4	....	....	....	....	....	....	....	....	....	....	....	....	....	....	....	....	....	....
	Philadelphia Flyers	**NHL**	**79**	**24**	**68**	**92**	**19**	**45**	**64**	**275**	**2**	**3**	**0**	**212**	**11.3**	**109**	**29**	**95**	**21**	**+6**	**4**	**1**	**2**	**3**	**6**	**1**	**0**	**0**
1982-83	**Edmonton Oilers**	**NHL**	**72**	**33**	**42**	**75**	**27**	**29**	**56**	**181**	**10**	**4**	**3**	**141**	**23.4**	**121**	**34**	**87**	**16**	**+16**	**16**	**6**	**8**	**14**	**22**	**1**	**0**	**1**
1983-84	**Edmonton Oilers**	**NHL**	**72**	**18**	**49**	**67**	**14**	**33**	**47**	**119**	**5**	**1**	**2**	**105**	**17.1**	**101**	**22**	**62**	**13**	**+30**	**19**	**10**	**4**	**14**	**65**	**3**	**1**	**4**
1984-85	**Boston Bruins**	**NHL**	**74**	**25**	**49**	**74**	**20**	**33**	**53**	**126**	**5**	**1**	**5**	**162**	**16.4**	**110**	**39**	**56**	**7**	**+22**	**5**	**4**	**6**	**10**	**8**	**0**	**0**	**1**
1985-86	**Boston Bruins**	**NHL**	**64**	**23**	**58**	**81**	**18**	**39**	**57**	**97**	**8**	**0**	**3**	**132**	**17.4**	**119**	**54**	**62**	**12**	**+15**	**3**	**0**	**1**	**1**	**17**	**0**	**0**	**0**
1986-87	**Boston Bruins**	**NHL**	**64**	**15**	**34**	**49**	**13**	**25**	**38**	**126**	**3**	**0**	**3**	**94**	**16.0**	**78**	**14**	**49**	**0**	**+15**	**4**	**1**	**1**	**2**	**22**	**0**	**0**	**0**
1987-88	**Boston Bruins**	**NHL**	**77**	**29**	**45**	**74**	**25**	**32**	**57**	**167**	**7**	**0**	**5**	**150**	**19.3**	**120**	**36**	**65**	**17**	**+36**	**23**	**11**	**14**	**25**	**56**	**4**	**1**	**0**
1988-89	**Boston Bruins**	**NHL**	**78**	**27**	**45**	**72**	**23**	**32**	**55**	**164**	**13**	**1**	**2**	**159**	**17.0**	**107**	**44**	**67**	**19**	**+15**	....	....	....	....	....	....	....	....
1989-90	**Boston Bruins**	**NHL**	**32**	**6**	**16**	**22**	**5**	**11**	**16**	**66**	**1**	**0**	**0**	**47**	**12.8**	**40**	**11**	**20**	**3**	**+12**	....	....	....	....	....	....	....	....
	Philadelphia Flyers	**NHL**	**29**	**5**	**9**	**14**	**4**	**6**	**10**	**30**	**1**	**0**	**0**	**32**	**15.6**	**22**	**8**	**26**	**5**	**–7**	....	....	....	....	....	....	....	....
1990-91	**Edmonton Oilers**	**NHL**	**56**	**7**	**29**	**36**	**6**	**22**	**28**	**94**	**2**	**1**	**0**	**49**	**14.3**	**53**	**7**	**36**	**5**	**+15**	**2**	**0**	**1**	**1**	**0**	**0**	**0**	**0**
1991-92	**Toronto Maple Leafs**	**NHL**	**2**	**0**	**0**	**0**	**0**	**0**	**0**	**2**	**0**	**0**	**0**	**0**	**0.0**	**0**	**0**	**2**	**0**	**–2**	....	....	....	....	....	....	....	....
	HC Asiago	Italy	5	3	3	6	....	....	....	4	....	....	....	....	....	....	....	....	....	....	7	3	4	7	47	....	....	....
	NHL Totals		**860**	**256**	**551**	**807**	**213**	**387**	**600**	**1727**	**61**	**12**	**29**	**1634**	**15.7**	**1177**	**341**	**742**	**130**		**113**	**43**	**77**	**120**	**325**	**9**	**2**	**11**
	Other Major League Totals		71	38	38	76	....	....	....	126	....	....	....	....	....	....	....	....	....	....	5	2	2	4	15	....	....	....

OHA Second All-Star Team (1977)

Traded to **Hartford** by **Philadelphia** with Greg C. Adams and Philadelphia's 1st round choice (David Jensen) and 3rd round choice (Leif Karlsson) in 1982 Entry Draft fror Mark Howe and Hartford's 3rd round choice (Derrick Smith), August 19, 1982. Traded to **Edmonton** by **Harford** with Dan Nachbaur for Risto Siltanen and Brent Loney, August 19, 1982. Traded to **Boston** by **Edmonton** for Mike Krushelnyski, June 21, 1984. Traded to **Philadelphia** by **Boston** for Dave Poulin, January 16, 1990. Signed as a free agent by **Edmonton**, August 31, 1990. Traded to **Toronto** by **Edmonton** for cash, October 7, 1991.

• LIPUMA, CHRIS

Chris Lipuma D – L. 6', 183 lbs. b: Bridgeview, IL, 3/23/1971.

Season	Club	League	GP	G	A	Pts	AG	AA	APts	PIM	PP	SH	GW	S	%	TGF	PGF	TGA	PGA	+/–	GP	G	A	Pts	PIM	PP	SH	GW
1988-89	Kitchener Rangers	OHL	59	7	13	20	....	....	....	101	....	....	....	....	....	....	....	....	....	....	....	....	....	....	....	....	....	....
1989-90	Kitchener Rangers	OHL	63	11	26	37	....	....	....	125	....	....	....	....	....	....	....	....	....	....	17	1	4	5	6	....	....	....
1990-91	Kitchener Rangers	OHL	61	6	30	36	....	....	....	145	....	....	....	....	....	....	....	....	....	....	4	0	1	1	4	....	....	....
1991-92	Kitchener Rangers	OHL	61	13	59	72	....	....	....	115	....	....	....	....	....	....	....	....	....	....	14	4	9	13	34	....	....	....
1992-93	**Tampa Bay Lightning**	**NHL**	**15**	**0**	**5**	**5**	**0**	**3**	**3**	**34**	**0**	**0**	**0**	**17**	**0.0**	**11**	**0**	**16**	**6**	**+1**	....	....	....	....	....	....	....	....
	Atlanta Knights	IHL	66	4	14	18	....	....	....	379	....	....	....	....	....	....	....	....	....	....	9	1	1	2	35	....	....	....
1993-94	**Tampa Bay Lightning**	**NHL**	**27**	**0**	**4**	**4**	**0**	**3**	**3**	**77**	**0**	**0**	**0**	**20**	**0.0**	**21**	**0**	**22**	**2**	**+1**	....	....	....	....	....	....	....	....
	Atlanta Knights	IHL	42	2	10	12	....	....	....	254	....	....	....	....	....	....	....	....	....	....	11	1	1	2	28	....	....	....
1994-95	Atlanta Knights	IHL	41	5	12	17	....	....	....	191	....	....	....	....	....	....	....	....	....	....	....	....	....	....	....	....	....	....
	Tampa Bay Lightning	**NHL**	**1**	**0**	**0**	**0**	**0**	**0**	**0**	**0**	**0**	**0**	**0**	**1**	**0.0**	**2**	**0**	**0**	**0**	**+2**	....	....	....	....	....	....	....	....
	Nashville Knights	ECHL	1	0	0	0	....	....	....	0	....	....	....	....	....	....	....	....	....	....	....	....	....	....	....	....	....	....
1995-96	**Tampa Bay Lightning**	**NHL**	**21**	**0**	**0**	**0**	**0**	**0**	**0**	**13**	**0**	**0**	**0**	**8**	**0.0**	**3**	**0**	**11**	**1**	**–7**	....	....	....	....	....	....	....	....
	Atlanta Knights	IHL	48	5	11	16	....	....	....	146	....	....	....	....	....	....	....	....	....	....	....	....	....	....	....	....	....	....
1996-97	**San Jose Sharks**	**NHL**	**8**	**0**	**0**	**0**	**0**	**0**	**0**	**22**	**0**	**0**	**0**	**4**	**0.0**	**3**	**0**	**6**	**1**	**–2**	....	....	....	....	....	....	....	....
	Kentucky Thoroughblades	AHL	48	6	17	23	....	....	....	93	....	....	....	....	....	....	....	....	....	....	4	0	3	3	6	....	....	....
1997-98	Orlando Solar Bears	IHL	13	1	4	5	....	....	....	63	....	....	....	....	....	....	....	....	....	....	....	....	....	....	....	....	....	....
	San Antonio Dragons	IHL	60	1	10	11	....	....	....	116	....	....	....	....	....	....	....	....	....	....	....	....	....	....	....	....	....	....
	NHL Totals		**72**	**0**	**9**	**9**	**0**	**6**	**0**	**140**	**0**	**0**	**0**	**50**	**0.0**	**40**	**0**	**55**	**10**		....	....	....	....	....	....	....	....

Signed as a free agent by **Tampa Bay**, June 29, 1992. Signed as a free agent by **San Jose**, August 23, 1996. Claimed on waivers by **New Jersey** from **San Jose**, March 18, 1997.

			REGULAR SEASON																		PLAYOFFS							
Season	Club	League	GP	G	A	Pts	AG	AA	APts	PIM	PP	SH	GW	S	%	TGF	PGF	TGA	PGA	+/–	GP	G	A	Pts	PIM	PP	SH	GW

• LOACH, LONNIE

Lonnie Loach LW – L. 5'10", 181 lbs. b: New Liskeard, Ont., 4/14/1968. Chicago's 4th choice, 98th overall, in 1986 Entry Draft.

Season	Club	League	GP	G	A	Pts	AG	AA	APts	PIM	PP	SH	GW	S	%	TGF	PGF	TGA	PGA	+/–	GP	G	A	Pts	PIM	PP	SH	GW
1985-86	Guelph Platers	OHL	65	41	42	83	....	....	....	63	....	....	....	....	....	....	....	....	....	....	20	7	8	15	16	....	....	....
1986-87	Guelph Platers	OHL	56	31	24	55	....	....	....	42	....	....	....	....	....	....	....	....	....	....	5	2	1	3	2	....	....	....
1987-88	Guelph Platers	OHL	66	43	49	92	....	....	....	75	....	....	....	....	....	....	....	....	....	....	....	....	....	....	....	....	....	....
1988-89	Flint Spirits	IHL	41	22	26	48	....	....	....	30	....	....	....	....	....	....	....	....	....	....	....	....	....	....	....	....	....	....
	Saginaw Hawks	IHL	32	7	6	13	....	....	....	27	....	....	....	....	....	....	....	....	....	....	....	....	....	....	....	....	....	....
1989-90	Canada	Nat-Team	9	3	1	4	....	....	....	2	....	....	....	....	....	....	....	....	....	....	....	....	....	....	....	....	....	....
	Indianapolis Ice	IHL	3	0	0	0	....	....	....	0	....	....	....	....	....	....	....	....	....	....	....	....	....	....	....	....	....	....
	Fort Wayne Komets	IHL	54	15	33	48	....	....	....	40	....	....	....	....	....	....	....	....	....	....	5	4	2	6	15	....	....	....
1990-91	Fort Wayne Komets	IHL	81	55	76	*131	....	....	....	45	....	....	....	....	....	....	....	....	....	....	19	5	11	16	13	....	....	....
1991-92	Adirondack Red Wings	AHL	67	37	49	86	....	....	....	69	....	....	....	....	....	....	....	....	....	....	19	*13	4	17	10	....	....	....
1992-93	**Ottawa Senators**	**NHL**	**3**	**0**	**0**	**0**	**0**	**0**	**0**	**0**	**0**	**0**	**0**	**3**	**0.0**	**1**	**1**	**0**	**0**	**0**	....	....	....	....	....	....	....	....
	Los Angeles Kings	**NHL**	**50**	**10**	**13**	**23**	**8**	**9**	**17**	**27**	**1**	**0**	**0**	**55**	**18.2**	**31**	**7**	**21**	**0**	**+3**	**1**	**0**	**0**	**0**	**0**	**0**	**0**	**0**
	Phoenix Roadrunners	IHL	4	2	3	5	....	....	....	10	....	....	....	....	....	....	....	....	....	....	....	....	....	....	....	....	....	....
1993-94	**Anaheim Mighty Ducks**	**NHL**	**3**	**0**	**0**	**0**	**0**	**0**	**0**	**2**	**0**	**0**	**0**	**8**	**0.0**	**0**	**0**	**2**	**0**	**–2**	....	....	....	....	....	....	....	....
	San Diego Gulls	IHL	74	42	49	91	....	....	....	65	....	....	....	....	....	....	....	....	....	....	9	4	10	14	6	....	....	....
1994-95	San Diego Gulls	IHL	13	3	10	13	....	....	....	21	....	....	....	....	....	....	....	....	....	....	....	....	....	....	....	....	....	....
	Detroit Vipers	IHL	64	32	43	75	....	....	....	45	....	....	....	....	....	....	....	....	....	....	3	2	1	3	2	....	....	....
1995-96	Detroit Vipers	IHL	79	35	51	86	....	....	....	75	....	....	....	....	....	....	....	....	....	....	11	1	5	6	8	....	....	....
1996-97	San Antonio Dragons	IHL	70	24	37	61	....	....	....	45	....	....	....	....	....	....	....	....	....	....	9	1	3	4	10	....	....	....
1997-98	Zurich SC	Switz.	15	2	5	7	....	....	....	6	....	....	....	....	....	....	....	....	....	....	....	....	....	....	....	....	....	....
	San Antonio Dragons	IHL	52	7	29	36	....	....	....	22	....	....	....	....	....	....	....	....	....	....	....	....	....	....	....	....	....	....
	NHL Totals		**56**	**10**	**13**	**23**	**8**	**9**	**17**	**29**	**1**	**0**	**0**	**66**	**15.2**	**32**	**8**	**23**	**0**		**1**	**0**	**0**	**0**	**0**	**0**	**0**	**0**

IHL Second All-Star Team (1991) • Won Leo P. Lamoureux Memorial Trophy (Leading Scorer - IHL) (1991)

Signed as a free agent by **Detroit**, June 7, 1991. Claimed by **Ottawa** from **Detroit** in Expansion Draft, June 18, 1992. Claimed on waivers by **LA Kings** from **Ottawa**, October 21, 1992. Claimed by **Anaheim** from **LA Kings** in Expansion Draft, June 24, 1993.

• LOCHEAD, BILL

Bill "Whip" Lochead LW – R. 6'1", 195 lbs. b: Forest, Ont., 10/13/1954. Detroit's 1st choice, 9th overall, in 1974 Amateur Draft.

Season	Club	League	GP	G	A	Pts	AG	AA	APts	PIM	PP	SH	GW	S	%	TGF	PGF	TGA	PGA	+/–	GP	G	A	Pts	PIM	PP	SH	GW
1971-72	Oshawa Generals	OHA	37	27	20	47	....	....	....	62	....	....	....	....	....	....	....	....	....	....	....	....	....	....	....	....	....	....
1972-73	Oshawa Generals	OHA	59	56	54	110	....	....	....	89	....	....	....	....	....	....	....	....	....	....	....	....	....	....	....	....	....	....
1973-74	Oshawa Generals	OHA	62	57	64	121	....	....	....	108	....	....	....	....	....	....	....	....	....	....	....	....	....	....	....	....	....	....
1974-75	**Detroit Red Wings**	**NHL**	**65**	**16**	**12**	**28**	**15**	**9**	**24**	**34**	**3**	**0**	**2**	**116**	**13.8**	**46**	**16**	**60**	**0**	**–30**	....	....	....	....	....	....	....	....
1975-76	**Detroit Red Wings**	**NHL**	**53**	**9**	**11**	**20**	**8**	**9**	**17**	**22**	**0**	**0**	**3**	**81**	**11.1**	**28**	**6**	**37**	**0**	**–15**	....	....	....	....	....	....	....	....
	New Haven Nighthawks	AHL	24	17	13	30	....	....	....	24	....	....	....	....	....	....	....	....	....	....	....	....	....	....	....	....	....	....
1976-77	**Detroit Red Wings**	**NHL**	**61**	**16**	**14**	**30**	**15**	**11**	**26**	**39**	**4**	**0**	**3**	**127**	**12.6**	**46**	**12**	**45**	**0**	**–11**	....	....	....	....	....	....	....	....
	Kansas City Blues	CHL	10	8	8	16	....	....	....	0	....	....	....	....	....	....	....	....	....	....	....	....	....	....	....	....	....	....
1977-78	**Detroit Red Wings**	**NHL**	**77**	**20**	**16**	**36**	**19**	**13**	**32**	**47**	**2**	**0**	**4**	**124**	**16.1**	**55**	**8**	**41**	**0**	**+6**	**7**	**3**	**0**	**3**	**6**	**0**	**0**	**1**
1978-79	**Detroit Red Wings**	**NHL**	**40**	**4**	**7**	**11**	**4**	**5**	**9**	**20**	**0**	**0**	**0**	**33**	**12.1**	**16**	**1**	**19**	**0**	**–4**	....	....	....	....	....	....	....	....
	Colorado Rockies	**NHL**	**27**	**4**	**2**	**6**	**4**	**2**	**6**	**14**	**1**	**1**	**0**	**64**	**6.3**	**12**	**6**	**21**	**0**	**–15**	....	....	....	....	....	....	....	....
1979-80	**New York Rangers**	**NHL**	**7**	**0**	**0**	**0**	**0**	**0**	**0**	**4**	**0**	**0**	**0**	**3**	**0.0**	**0**	**0**	**5**	**0**	**–5**	....	....	....	....	....	....	....	....
	New Haven Nighthawks	AHL	68	46	43	89	....	....	....	90	....	....	....	....	....	....	....	....	....	....	10	6	5	11	8	....	....	....
1980-81	Bad Nauheim	Germany	21	27	25	52	....	....	....	59	....	....	....	....	....	....	....	....	....	....	....	....	....	....	....	....	....	....
	Kolner Haie	Germany	14	12	7	19	....	....	....	48	....	....	....	....	....	....	....	....	....	....	3	4	1	5	13	....	....	....
1981-82	Bad Nauheim	Germany	42	*66	34	100	....	....	....	*195	....	....	....	....	....	....	....	....	....	....	....	....	....	....	....	....	....	....
1982-83	Mannheim	Germany	34	36	24	60	....	....	....	117	....	....	....	....	....	....	....	....	....	....	....	....	....	....	....	....	....	....
1983-84	Mannheim	Germany	47	36	27	63	....	....	....	77	....	....	....	....	....	....	....	....	....	....	....	....	....	....	....	....	....	....
1984-85	EHC Chur	Switz.	5	1	3	4	....	....	....	....	....	....	....	....	....	....	....	....	....	....	....	....	....	....	....	....	....	....
	Bad Nauheim	Germany	16	28	20	48	....	....	....	61	....	....	....	....	....	....	....	....	....	....	....	....	....	....	....	....	....	....
1985-86	Bad Nauheim	German 2	STATISTICS NOT AVAILABLE																									
1986-87	WEV Wiener	Austria	19	12	8	20	....	....	....	24	....	....	....	....	....	....	....	....	....	....	....	....	....	....	....	....	....	....
	NHL Totals		**330**	**69**	**62**	**131**	**65**	**49**	**114**	**180**	**10**	**1**	**12**	**548**	**12.6**	**203**	**49**	**228**	**0**		**7**	**3**	**0**	**3**	**6**	**0**	**0**	**1**

OHA Second All-Star Team (1973) • OHA First All-Star Team (1974) • AHL First All-Star Team (1980)

Claimed on waivers by **Colorado** from **Detroit**, February 9, 1979. Traded to **NY Rangers** by **Colorado** for the rights to Hardy Astrom, July 2, 1979.

• LOEWEN, DARCY

Darcy Loewen LW – L. 5'10", 185 lbs. b: Calgary, Alta., 2/26/1969. Buffalo's 2nd choice, 55th overall, in 1988 Entry Draft.

Season	Club	League	GP	G	A	Pts	AG	AA	APts	PIM	PP	SH	GW	S	%	TGF	PGF	TGA	PGA	+/–	GP	G	A	Pts	PIM	PP	SH	GW
1986-87	Spokane Chiefs	WHL	68	15	25	40	....	....	....	129	....	....	....	....	....	....	....	....	....	....	5	0	0	0	16	....	....	....
1987-88	Spokane Chiefs	WHL	72	30	44	74	....	....	....	231	....	....	....	....	....	....	....	....	....	....	15	7	5	12	54	....	....	....
1988-89	Spokane Chiefs	WHL	60	31	27	58	....	....	....	194	....	....	....	....	....	....	....	....	....	....	....	....	....	....	....	....	....	....
	Canada	Nat-Team	2	0	0	0	....	....	....	0	....	....	....	....	....	....	....	....	....	....	....	....	....	....	....	....	....	....
	Canada	WJC-A	7	1	1	2	....	....	....	12	....	....	....	....	....	....	....	....	....	....	....	....	....	....	....	....	....	....
1989-90	**Buffalo Sabres**	**NHL**	**4**	**0**	**0**	**0**	**0**	**0**	**0**	**4**	**0**	**0**	**0**	**1**	**0.0**	**1**	**0**	**4**	**0**	**–3**	....	....	....	....	....	....	....	....
	Rochester Americans	AHL	50	7	11	18	....	....	....	193	....	....	....	....	....	....	....	....	....	....	5	1	0	1	6	....	....	....
1990-91	**Buffalo Sabres**	**NHL**	**6**	**0**	**0**	**0**	**0**	**0**	**0**	**8**	**0**	**0**	**0**	**2**	**0.0**	**2**	**0**	**7**	**1**	**–4**	....	....	....	....	....	....	....	....
	Rochester Americans	AHL	71	13	15	28	....	....	....	130	....	....	....	....	....	....	....	....	....	....	15	1	5	6	14	....	....	....
1991-92	**Buffalo Sabres**	**NHL**	**2**	**0**	**0**	**0**	**0**	**0**	**0**	**2**	**0**	**0**	**0**	**1**	**0.0**	**0**	**0**	**0**	**0**	**0**	....	....	....	....	....	....	....	....
	Rochester Americans	AHL	73	11	20	31	....	....	....	193	....	....	....	....	....	....	....	....	....	....	4	0	1	1	8	....	....	....
1992-93	**Ottawa Senators**	**NHL**	**79**	**4**	**5**	**9**	**3**	**3**	**6**	**145**	**0**	**0**	**0**	**42**	**9.5**	**17**	**0**	**65**	**22**	**–26**	....	....	....	....	....	....	....	....
1993-94	**Ottawa Senators**	**NHL**	**44**	**0**	**3**	**3**	**0**	**2**	**2**	**52**	**0**	**0**	**0**	**39**	**0.0**	**10**	**0**	**27**	**6**	**–11**	....	....	....	....	....	....	....	....
1994-95	Las Vegas Thunder	IHL	64	9	21	30	....	....	....	183	....	....	....	....	....	....	....	....	....	....	7	1	1	2	16	....	....	....
1995-96	Las Vegas Thunder	IHL	72	14	23	37	....	....	....	198	....	....	....	....	....	....	....	....	....	....	....	....	....	....	....	....	....	....
1996-97	Las Vegas Thunder	IHL	76	14	19	33	....	....	....	177	....	....	....	....	....	....	....	....	....	....	3	0	0	0	0	....	....	....
1997-98	Las Vegas Thunder	IHL	42	4	6	10	....	....	....	117	....	....	....	....	....	....	....	....	....	....	....	....	....	....	....	....	....	....
	Utah Grizzlies	IHL	34	1	7	8	....	....	....	99	....	....	....	....	....	....	....	....	....	....	4	0	1	1	15	....	....	....
	NHL Totals		**135**	**4**	**8**	**12**	**3**	**5**	**8**	**211**	**0**	**0**	**0**	**85**	**4.7**	**30**	**0**	**103**	**29**		....	....	....	....	....	....	....	....

Claimed by **Ottawa** from **Buffalo** in Expansion Draft, June 18, 1992.

• LOFTHOUSE, MARK

Mark Lofthouse RW/C – R. 6'2", 195 lbs. b: New Westminster, B.C., 4/21/1957. Washington's 2nd choice, 21st overall, in 1977 Amateur Draft.

Season	Club	League	GP	G	A	Pts	AG	AA	APts	PIM	PP	SH	GW	S	%	TGF	PGF	TGA	PGA	+/–	GP	G	A	Pts	PIM	PP	SH	GW
1973-74	Kelowna Buckeroos	BCJHL	62	44	42	86	....	....	....	59	....	....	....	....	....	....	....	....	....	....	....	....	....	....	....	....	....	....
1974-75	New Westminster Bruins	WCJHL	61	36	28	64	....	....	....	53	....	....	....	....	....	....	....	....	....	....	....	....	....	....	....	....	....	....
1975-76	New Westminster Bruins	WCJHL	72	68	48	116	....	....	....	55	....	....	....	....	....	....	....	....	....	....	17	9	12	21	22	....	....	....
1976-77	New Westminster Bruins	WCJHL	70	54	58	112	....	....	....	59	....	....	....	....	....	....	....	....	....	....	14	10	8	18	19	....	....	....
1977-78	**Washington Capitals**	**NHL**	**18**	**2**	**1**	**3**	**2**	**1**	**3**	**8**	**0**	**0**	**0**	**21**	**9.5**	**6**	**2**	**9**	**0**	**–5**	....	....	....	....	....	....	....	....
	Hershey Bears	AHL	35	8	6	14	....	....	....	39	....	....	....	....	....	....	....	....	....	....	....	....	....	....	....	....	....	....
	Salt Lake Golden Eagles	CHL	13	0	1	1	....	....	....	4	....	....	....	....	....	....	....	....	....	....	5	0	1	1	6	....	....	....
1978-79	**Washington Capitals**	**NHL**	**52**	**13**	**10**	**23**	**12**	**8**	**20**	**10**	**1**	**0**	**0**	**75**	**17.3**	**29**	**4**	**36**	**0**	**–11**	....	....	....	....	....	....	....	....
	Hershey Bears	AHL	16	7	7	14	....	....	....	6	....	....	....	....	....	....	....	....	....	....	4	0	1	1	2	....	....	....
1979-80	**Washington Capitals**	**NHL**	**68**	**15**	**18**	**33**	**14**	**14**	**28**	**20**	**1**	**0**	**1**	**138**	**10.9**	**51**	**8**	**56**	**4**	**–9**	....	....	....	....	....	....	....	....
	Hershey Bears	AHL	9	7	3	10	....	....	....	6	....	....	....	....	....	....	....	....	....	....	....	....	....	....	....	....	....	....
1980-81	**Washington Capitals**	**NHL**	**3**	**1**	**1**	**2**	**1**	**1**	**2**	**4**	**0**	**0**	**0**	**3**	**33.3**	**2**	**0**	**2**	**0**	**0**	....	....	....	....	....	....	....	....
	Hershey Bears	AHL	72	*48	55	*103	....	....	....	131	....	....	....	....	....	....	....	....	....	....	10	6	9	15	24	....	....	....
1981-82	**Detroit Red Wings**	**NHL**	**12**	**3**	**4**	**7**	**2**	**3**	**5**	**13**	**0**	**0**	**0**	**21**	**14.3**	**8**	**1**	**14**	**0**	**–7**	....	....	....	....	....	....	....	....
	Adirondack Red Wings	AHL	69	33	38	71	....	....	....	75	....	....	....	....	....	....	....	....	....	....	5	2	3	5	2	....	....	....
1982-83	**Detroit Red Wings**	**NHL**	**28**	**8**	**4**	**12**	**7**	**3**	**10**	**18**	**0**	**0**	**0**	**37**	**21.6**	**22**	**4**	**10**	**0**	**+8**	....	....	....	....	....	....	....	....
	Adirondack Red Wings	AHL	39	27	18	45	....	....	....	20	....	....	....	....	....	....	....	....	....	....	....	....	....	....	....	....	....	....
1983-84	New Haven Nighthawks	AHL	79	37	64	101	....	....	....	45	....	....	....	....	....	....	....	....	....	....	....	....	....	....	....	....	....	....
1984-85	New Haven Nighthawks	AHL	12	11	4	15	....	....	....	4	....	....	....	....	....	....	....	....	....	....	....	....	....	....	....	....	....	....
1985-86	New Haven Nighthawks	AHL	70	32	35	67	....	....	....	56	....	....	....	....	....	....	....	....	....	....	5	2	1	3	0	....	....	....

			REGULAR SEASON																		PLAYOFFS							
Season	**Club**	**League**	**GP**	**G**	**A**	**Pts**	**AG**	**AA**	**APts**	**PIM**	**PP**	**SH**	**GW**	**S**	**%**	**TGF**	**PGF**	**TGA**	**PGA**	**+/–**	**GP**	**G**	**A**	**Pts**	**PIM**	**PP**	**SH**	**GW**
1986-87	New Haven Nighthawks	AHL	47	18	27	45	....	....	....	34	....	....	....	....	....	....	....	....	....	....	4	0	1	1	2	....	....	....
1987-88	Hershey Bears	AHL	51	21	21	42	....	....	....	64	....	....	....	....	....	....	....	....	....	....	10	6	5	11	6	....	....	....
1988-89	Hershey Bears	AHL	74	32	47	79	....	....	....	71	....	....	....	....	....	....	....	....	....	....	12	3	4	7	20	....	....	....
	NHL Totals		**181**	**42**	**38**	**80**	**38**	**30**	**68**	**73**	**2**	**0**	**1**	**295**	**14.2**	**118**	**19**	**127**	**4**		....	....	....	....	....	....	....	....

Memorial Cup All-Star Team (1977) • AHL First All Star Team (1981) • Won John B. Sollenberger Trophy (Top Scorer - AHL) (1981) • AHL Second All-Star Team (1984)

Traded to **Detroit** by **Washington** for Al Jensen, July 31, 1981. Signed as a free agent by **LA Kings**, August 10, 1983. Signed as a free agent by **Philadelphia**, August 15, 1987.

• LOGAN, DAVE

Dave Logan D – L. 5′10″, 190 lbs. b: Montreal, Que., 7/2/1954. Chicago's 5th choice, 88th overall, in 1974 Amateur Draft.

Season	Club	League	GP	G	A	Pts	AG	AA	APts	PIM	PP	SH	GW	S	%	TGF	PGF	TGA	PGA	+/–	GP	G	A	Pts	PIM	PP	SH	GW
1972-73	Montreal Jr. Canadiens	QMJHL	5	1	6	7	....	....	....	2	....	....	....	....	....	....	....	....	....	....	....	....	....	....	....	....	....	....
1973-74	Laval Nationale	QMJHL	65	21	41	62	....	....	....	156	....	....	....	....	....	....	....	....	....	....	11	2	2	4	36	....	....	....
1974-75	Dallas Black Hawks	CHL	74	7	18	25	....	....	....	239	....	....	....	....	....	....	....	....	....	....	10	0	3	3	48	....	....	....
1975-76	**Chicago Black Hawks**	**NHL**	**2**	**0**	**0**	**0**	**0**	**0**	**0**	**0**	**0**	**0**	**0**	**0**	**0.0**	**0**	**0**	**1**	**0**	**–1**	....	....	....	....	....	....	....	....
	Dallas Black Hawks	CHL	40	3	11	14	....	....	....	131	....	....	....	....	....	....	....	....	....	....	10	0	3	3	*68	....	....	....
1976-77	**Chicago Black Hawks**	**NHL**	**34**	**0**	**2**	**2**	**0**	**2**	**2**	**61**	**0**	**0**	**0**	**36**	**0.0**	**12**	**0**	**42**	**8**	**–22**	....	....	....	....	....	....	....	....
	Dallas Black Hawks	CHL	32	4	10	14	....	....	....	83	....	....	....	....	....	....	....	....	....	....	5	0	1	1	16	....	....	....
	Flint Generals	IHL	1	0	0	0	....	....	....	2	....	....	....	....	....	....	....	....	....	....	....	....	....	....	....	....	....	....
1977-78	**Chicago Black Hawks**	**NHL**	**54**	**1**	**5**	**6**	**1**	**4**	**5**	**77**	**1**	**0**	**0**	**51**	**2.0**	**30**	**2**	**51**	**9**	**–14**	**4**	**0**	**0**	**0**	**8**	**0**	**0**	**0**
1978-79	**Chicago Black Hawks**	**NHL**	**76**	**1**	**14**	**15**	**1**	**11**	**12**	**176**	**0**	**0**	**0**	**77**	**1.3**	**62**	**1**	**105**	**35**	**–9**	**4**	**0**	**0**	**0**	**2**	**0**	**0**	**0**
1979-80	**Chicago Black Hawks**	**NHL**	**12**	**2**	**3**	**5**	**2**	**2**	**4**	**34**	**0**	**0**	**1**	**13**	**15.4**	**10**	**0**	**6**	**1**	**+5**	....	....	....	....	....	....	....	....
	Vancouver Canucks	**NHL**	**33**	**1**	**5**	**6**	**1**	**4**	**5**	**109**	**0**	**0**	**0**	**31**	**3.2**	**27**	**1**	**43**	**8**	**–9**	**4**	**0**	**0**	**0**	**0**	**0**	**0**	**0**
1980-81	**Vancouver Canucks**	**NHL**	**7**	**0**	**0**	**0**	**0**	**0**	**0**	**13**	**0**	**0**	**0**	**3**	**0.0**	**4**	**0**	**3**	**0**	**+1**	....	....	....	....	....	....	....	....
	Dallas Black Hawks	CHL	23	1	8	9	....	....	....	28	....	....	....	....	....	....	....	....	....	....	....	....	....	....	....	....	....	....
	Maine Mariners	AHL	13	2	1	3	....	....	....	27	....	....	....	....	....	....	....	....	....	....	18	0	3	3	*129	....	....	....
1981-82	Cincinnati Tigers	CHL	53	4	12	16	....	....	....	199	....	....	....	....	....	....	....	....	....	....	4	0	0	0	36	....	....	....
1982-83	Birmingham South Stars	CHL	63	1	7	8	....	....	....	176	....	....	....	....	....	....	....	....	....	....	10	0	1	1	20	....	....	....
	St. Catharines Saints	AHL	12	2	2	4	....	....	....	2	....	....	....	....	....	....	....	....	....	....	....	....	....	....	....	....	....	....
	NHL Totals		**218**	**5**	**29**	**34**	**5**	**23**	**28**	**470**	**1**	**0**	**1**	**211**	**2.4**	**145**	**4**	**251**	**61**		**12**	**0**	**0**	**0**	**10**	**0**	**0**	**0**

Traded to **Vancouver** by **Chicago** with Harold Phillipoff for Ron Sedlbauer, December 21, 1979. Signed as a free agent by **Philadelphia**, March 6, 1981. Signed as a free agent by **Toronto**, August 11, 1981. Traded to **Minnesota** by **Toronto** for cash, January 10, 1983.

• LOGAN, ROBERT

Robert Logan RW – L. 6′, 190 lbs. b: Montreal, Que., 2/22/1964. Buffalo's 8th choice, 100th overall, in 1982 Entry Draft.

Season	Club	League	GP	G	A	Pts	AG	AA	APts	PIM	PP	SH	GW	S	%	TGF	PGF	TGA	PGA	+/–	GP	G	A	Pts	PIM	PP	SH	GW
1982-83	Yale University	ECAC	28	13	12	25	....	....	....	8	....	....	....	....	....	....	....	....	....	....	....	....	....	....	....	....	....	....
1983-84	Yale University	ECAC	22	9	13	22	....	....	....	25	....	....	....	....	....	....	....	....	....	....	....	....	....	....	....	....	....	....
1984-85	Yale University	ECAC	32	19	12	31	....	....	....	18	....	....	....	....	....	....	....	....	....	....	....	....	....	....	....	....	....	....
1985-86	Yale University	ECAC	27	19	21	40	....	....	....	22	....	....	....	....	....	....	....	....	....	....	....	....	....	....	....	....	....	....
1986-87	**Buffalo Sabres**	**NHL**	**22**	**7**	**3**	**10**	**6**	**2**	**8**	**0**	**1**	**0**	**0**	**22**	**31.8**	**13**	**1**	**7**	**0**	**+5**	....	....	....	....	....	....	....	....
	Rochester Americans	AHL	56	30	14	44	....	....	....	27	....	....	....	....	....	....	....	....	....	....	18	5	10	15	4	....	....	....
1987-88	**Buffalo Sabres**	**NHL**	**16**	**3**	**2**	**5**	**3**	**1**	**4**	**0**	**1**	**0**	**1**	**15**	**20.0**	**8**	**2**	**5**	**0**	**+1**	....	....	....	....	....	....	....	....
	Rochester Americans	AHL	45	23	15	38	....	....	....	35	....	....	....	....	....	....	....	....	....	....	....	....	....	....	....	....	....	....
1988-89	Rochester Americans	AHL	5	2	2	4	....	....	....	2	....	....	....	....	....	....	....	....	....	....	....	....	....	....	....	....	....	....
	Los Angeles Kings	**NHL**	**4**	**0**	**0**	**0**	**0**	**0**	**0**	**0**	**0**	**0**	**0**	**0**	**0.0**	**0**	**0**	**0**	**0**	**0**	....	....	....	....	....	....	....	....
	New Haven Nighthawks	AHL	66	21	32	53	....			27	....	....	....	....	....	....	....	....	....	....	13	2	3	5	9	....	....	....
1989-90	New Haven Nighthawks	AHL	11	2	4	6	....	....	....	4	....	....	....	....	....	....	....	....	....	....	....	....	....	....	....	....	....	....
	NHL Totals		**42**	**10**	**5**	**15**	**9**	**3**	**12**	**0**	**2**	**0**	**1**	**37**	**27.0**	**21**	**3**	**12**	**0**		....	....	....	....	....	....	....	....

ECAC Second All-Star Team (1986)

Traded to **LA Kings** by **Buffalo** with Bufalo's 9th round choice (Jim Glacin) in 1989 Entry Draft, October 21, 1988.

• LOISELLE, CLAUDE

Claude Loiselle C – L. 5′11″, 195 lbs. b: Ottawa, Ont., 5/29/1963. Detroit's 1st choice, 23rd overall, in 1981 Entry Draft.

Season	Club	League	GP	G	A	Pts	AG	AA	APts	PIM	PP	SH	GW	S	%	TGF	PGF	TGA	PGA	+/–	GP	G	A	Pts	PIM	PP	SH	GW
1979-80	Gloucester Rangers	OJHL	50	21	38	59	....	....	....	26	....	....	....	....	....	....	....	....	....	....	....	....	....	....	....	....	....	....
1980-81	Windsor Spitfires	OHA	68	38	56	94	....	....	....	103	....	....	....	....	....	....	....	....	....	....	11	3	3	6	40	....	....	....
1981-82	Windsor Spitfires	OHL	68	36	73	109	....	....	....	192	....	....	....	....	....	....	....	....	....	....	9	2	10	12	42	....	....	....
	Detroit Red Wings	**NHL**	**4**	**1**	**0**	**1**	**1**	**0**	**1**	**2**	**1**	**0**	**0**	**2**	**50.0**	**2**	**2**	**2**	**0**	**–2**	....	....	....	....	....	....	....	....
1982-83	Windsor Spitfires	OHL	46	39	49	88	....	....	....	75	....	....	....	....	....	....	....	....	....	....	....	....	....	....	....	....	....	....
	Detroit Red Wings	**NHL**	**18**	**2**	**0**	**2**	**2**	**0**	**2**	**15**	**0**	**0**	**0**	**24**	**8.3**	**7**	**0**	**27**	**6**	**–14**	....	....	....	....	....	....	....	....
	Adirondack Red Wings	AHL	6	1	7	8	....	....	....	0	....	....	....	....	....	....	....	....	....	....	6	2	4	6	0	....	....	....
1983-84	**Detroit Red Wings**	**NHL**	**28**	**4**	**6**	**10**	**3**	**4**	**7**	**32**	**0**	**0**	**0**	**20**	**20.0**	**13**	**0**	**13**	**4**	**+4**	....	....	....	....	....	....	....	....
	Adirondack Red Wings	AHL	29	13	16	29	....	....	....	59	....	....	....	....	....	....	....	....	....	....	....	....	....	....	....	....	....	....
1984-85	**Detroit Red Wings**	**NHL**	**30**	**8**	**1**	**9**	**7**	**1**	**8**	**45**	**0**	**0**	**0**	**30**	**26.7**	**15**	**0**	**22**	**2**	**–5**	**3**	**0**	**2**	**2**	**0**	**0**	**0**	**0**
	Adirondack Red Wings	AHL	47	22	29	51	....	....	....	24	....	....	....	....	....	....	....	....	....	....	....	....	....	....	....	....	....	....
1985-86	**Detroit Red Wings**	**NHL**	**48**	**7**	**15**	**22**	**6**	**10**	**16**	**142**	**2**	**0**	**1**	**83**	**8.4**	**29**	**8**	**71**	**23**	**–27**	....	....	....	....	....	....	....	....
	Adirondack Red Wings	AHL	21	15	11	26	....	....	....	32	....	....	....	....	....	....	....	....	....	....	16	5	10	15	38	....	....	....
1986-87	**New Jersey Devils**	**NHL**	**75**	**16**	**24**	**40**	**14**	**17**	**31**	**137**	**2**	**1**	**3**	**145**	**11.0**	**65**	**10**	**92**	**30**	**–7**	....	....	....	....	....	....	....	....
1987-88	**New Jersey Devils**	**NHL**	**68**	**17**	**18**	**35**	**15**	**13**	**28**	**121**	**3**	**2**	**2**	**117**	**14.5**	**47**	**8**	**67**	**35**	**+7**	**20**	**4**	**6**	**10**	**50**	**0**	**2**	**0**
1988-89	**New Jersey Devils**	**NHL**	**74**	**7**	**14**	**21**	**6**	**10**	**16**	**209**	**0**	**1**	**1**	**92**	**7.6**	**34**	**0**	**91**	**47**	**–10**	....	....	....	....	....	....	....	....
1989-90	**Quebec Nordiques**	**NHL**	**72**	**11**	**14**	**25**	**9**	**10**	**19**	**104**	**0**	**3**	**0**	**128**	**8.6**	**34**	**3**	**100**	**42**	**–27**	....	....	....	....	....	....	....	....
1990-91	**Quebec Nordiques**	**NHL**	**59**	**5**	**10**	**15**	**5**	**8**	**13**	**86**	**0**	**2**	**0**	**79**	**6.3**	**21**	**1**	**68**	**28**	**–20**	....	....	....	....	....	....	....	....
	Toronto Maple Leafs	**NHL**	**7**	**1**	**1**	**2**	**1**	**1**	**2**	**2**	**0**	**0**	**0**	**10**	**10.0**	**5**	**0**	**7**	**2**	**0**	....	....	....	....	....	....	....	....
1991-92	**Toronto Maple Leafs**	**NHL**	**64**	**6**	**9**	**15**	**5**	**7**	**12**	**102**	**1**	**0**	**1**	**91**	**6.6**	**24**	**2**	**63**	**20**	**–21**	....	....	....	....	....	....	....	....
	New York Islanders	**NHL**	**11**	**1**	**1**	**2**	**1**	**1**	**2**	**13**	**0**	**0**	**0**	**10**	**10.0**	**3**	**0**	**12**	**6**	**–3**	....	....	....	....	....	....	....	....
1992-93	**New York Islanders**	**NHL**	**41**	**5**	**3**	**8**	**4**	**2**	**6**	**90**	**0**	**0**	**0**	**41**	**12.2**	**11**	**0**	**23**	**7**	**5**	**10**	**0**	**3**	**3**	**10**	**0**	**0**	**0**
1993-94	**New York Islanders**	**NHL**	**17**	**1**	**1**	**2**	**1**	**1**	**2**	**49**	**0**	**0**	**0**	**14**	**7.1**	**6**	**0**	**15**	**7**	**–2**	....	....	....	....	....	....	....	....
	NHL Totals		**616**	**92**	**117**	**209**	**80**	**85**	**165**	**1149**	**9**	**9**	**8**	**886**	**10.4**	**316**	**34**	**673**	**259**		**41**	**4**	**11**	**15**	**60**	**0**	**2**	**0**

Traded to **New Jersey** by **Detroit** for Tim Higgins, June 25, 1986. Traded to **Quebec** by **New Jersey** with Joe Cirella and New Jersey's 8th round choice (Alexander Karpotsev) in 1990 Entry Draft for Walt Poddubny and Quebec's 4th round choice (Mike Bodnarchuk) in 1990 Entry Draft, June 17, 1989. Claimed on waivers by **Toronto** from **Quebec**, March 5, 1991. Traded to **NY Islanders** by **Toronto** with Daniel Marois for Ken Baumgartner and Dave McLlwain, March 10, 1992.

• LOMAKIN, ANDREI

Andrei Lomakin RW – L. 5′10″, 175 lbs. b: Voskresensk, USSR, 4/3/1964. Philadelphia's 7th choice, 138th overall, in 1991 Entry Draft.

Season	Club	League	GP	G	A	Pts	AG	AA	APts	PIM	PP	SH	GW	S	%	TGF	PGF	TGA	PGA	+/–	GP	G	A	Pts	PIM	PP	SH	GW
1981-82	Khimik	USSR	8	1	1	2	....	....		2	....	....	....	....	....	....	....	....	....	....	....	....	....	....	....	....	....	....
1982-83	Khimik	USSR	56	15	8	23	....	....	....	32	....	....	....	....	....	....	....	....	....	....	....	....	....	....	....	....	....	....
1983-84	Khimik	USSR	44	10	8	18	....	....	....	26	....	....	....	....	....	....	....	....	....	....	....	....	....	....	....	....	....	....
	Soviet Union	WJC-A	7	5	5	10	....	....	....	2	....	....	....	....	....	....	....	....	....	....	....	....	....	....	....	....	....	....
1984-85	Khimik	USSR	52	13	10	23	....	....	....	24	....	....	....	....	....	....	....	....	....	....	....	....	....	....	....	....	....	....
1985-86	Khimik	USSR		DID NOT PLAY																								
1986-87	Moscow Dynamo	USSR	40	15	14	29	....	....	....	30	....	....	....	....	....	....	....	....	....	....	....	....	....	....	....	....	....	....
1987-88	Soviet Union	C Cup	9	2	4	6	....	....	....	10	....	....	....	....	....	....	....	....	....	....	....	....	....	....	....	....	....	....
	Moscow Dynamo	USSR	45	10	15	25	....	....	....	24	....	....	....	....	....	....	....	....	....	....	....	....	....	....	....	....	....	....
	Soviet Union	Olympics	8	1	3	4	....	....	....	2	....	....	....	....	....	....	....	....	....	....	....	....	....	....	....	....	....	....
1988-89	Moscow Dynamo	USSR	44	9	16	25	....	....	....	22	....	....	....	....	....	....	....	....	....	....	....	....	....	....	....	....	....	....
	Dynamo Riga	SuperS	6	1	3	4	....	....	....	8	....	....	....	....	....	....	....	....	....	....	....	....	....	....	....	....	....	....
1989-90	Moscow Dynamo	FrTour	1	1	1	2	....	....	....	4	....	....	....	....	....	....	....	....	....	....	....	....	....	....	....	....	....	....
	Moscow Dynamo	USSR	48	11	15	26	....	....	....	36	....	....	....	....	....	....	....	....	....	....	....	....	....	....	....	....	....	....
	Moscow Dynamo	SuperS	4	3	1	4	....	....	....	0	....	....	....	....	....	....	....	....	....	....	....	....	....	....	....	....	....	....
1990-91	Moscow Dynamo	FrTour	1	0	0	0	....	....	....	0	....	....	....	....	....	....	....	....	....	....	....	....	....	....	....	....	....	....
	Moscow Dynamo	USSR	45	16	17	33	....	....	....	22	....	....	....	....	....	....	....	....	....	....	....	....	....	....	....	....	....	....
	Moscow Dynamo	SuperS	7	1	3	4	....	....	....	0	....	....	....	....	....	....	....	....	....	....	....	....	....	....	....	....	....	....
	Soviet Union	WEC-A	10	3	3	6	....	....	....	4	....	....	....	....	....	....	....	....	....	....	....	....	....	....	....	....	....	....
1991-92	Soviet Union	C Cup	5	0	2	2	....	....	....	0	....	....	....	....	....	....	....	....	....	....	....	....	....	....	....	....	....	....
	Moscow Dynamo	CIS	2	1	3	4	....	....	....	2	....	....	....	....	....	....	....	....	....	....	....	....	....	....	....	....	....	....
	Philadelphia Flyers	**NHL**	**57**	**14**	**16**	**30**	**13**	**12**	**25**	**26**	**2**	**0**	**0**	**82**	**17.1**	**43**	**8**	**51**	**10**	**–6**	....	....	....	....	....	....	....	....
1992-93	**Philadelphia Flyers**	**NHL**	**51**	**8**	**12**	**20**	**7**	**8**	**15**	**34**	**0**	**0**	**0**	**64**	**12.5**	**27**	**3**	**9**	**0**	**+15**	....	....	....	....	....	....	....	....
1993-94	**Florida Panthers**	**NHL**	**76**	**19**	**28**	**47**	**18**	**22**	**40**	**26**	**3**	**0**	**2**	**139**	**13.7**	**71**	**26**	**44**	**0**	**+1**	....	....	....	....	....	....	....	....

			REGULAR SEASON																		PLAYOFFS							
Season	Club	League	GP	G	A	Pts	AG	AA	APts	PIM	PP	SH	GW	S	%	TGF	PGF	TGA	PGA	+/–	GP	G	A	Pts	PIM	PP	SH	GW
1994-95	**Florida Panthers**	**NHL**	**31**	**1**	**6**	**7**	**2**	**9**	**11**	**6**	**1**	**0**	**0**	**25**	**4.0**	**13**	**5**	**13**	**0**	**–5**	....	....	....	....	....	....	....	....
1995-96	HC Fribourg-Gotteron	Switz.	8	3	3	6	....	....	....	10	....	....	....	....	....	....	....	....	....	....	....	....	....	....	....	....	....	....
	Eisbaren Berlin	Germany	26	21	14	35	....	....	....	30	....	....	....	....	....	....	....	....	....	....	....	....	....	....	....	....	....	....
1996-97	Eisbaren Berlin	Germany	30	7	8	15	....	....	....	10	....	....	....	....	....	....	....	....	....	....	....	....	....	....	....	....	....	....
	Frankfurt Lions	Germany	12	3	4	7	....	....	....	10	....	....	....	....	....	....	....	....	....	....	2	0	0	0	0	....	....	....
	NHL Totals		**215**	**42**	**62**	**104**	**40**	**51**	**91**	**92**	**6**	**0**	**2**	**310**	**13.5**	**154**	**42**	**117**	**10**		....	....	....	....	....	....	....	....

Claimed by **Florida** from **Philadelphia** in Expansion Draft, June 24, 1993.

• LONEY, BRIAN

Brian Loney RW – R. 6'2", 200 lbs. b: Winnipeg, Man., 8/9/1972. Vancouver's 6th choice, 110th overall, in 1992 Entry Draft.

Season	Club	League	GP	G	A	Pts	AG	AA	APts	PIM	PP	SH	GW	S	%	TGF	PGF	TGA	PGA	+/–	GP	G	A	Pts	PIM	PP	SH	GW
1991-92	Ohio State University	CCHA	37	21	34	55	....	....	....	109	....	....	....	....	....	....	....	....	....	....	....	....	....	....	....	....	....	....
1992-93	Red Deer Rebels	WHL	66	39	36	75	....	....	....	147	....	....	....	....	....	....	....	....	....	....	4	1	1	2	19	....	....	....
	Canada	Nat-Team	1	0	1	1	....	....	....	0	....	....	....	....	....	....	....	....	....	....	....	....	....	....	....	....	....	....
	Hamilton Canucks	AHL	3	0	2	2	....	....	....	0	....	....	....	....	....	....	....	....	....	....	....	....	....	....	....	....	....	....
1993-94	Hamilton Canucks	AHL	67	18	16	34	....	....	....	76	....	....	....	....	....	....	....	....	....	....	4	0	0	0	8	....	....	....
1994-95	Syracuse Crunch	AHL	67	23	17	40	....	....	....	98	....	....	....	....	....	....	....	....	....	....	....	....	....	....	....	....	....	....
1995-96	**Vancouver Canucks**	**NHL**	**12**	**2**	**3**	**5**	**2**	**2**	**4**	**6**	**0**	**0**	**0**	**19**	**10.5**	**5**	**0**	**3**	**0**	**+2**	....	....	....	....	....	....	....	....
	Syracuse Crunch	AHL	48	34	17	51	....	....	....	157	....	....	....	....	....	....	....	....	....	....	14	3	8	11	20	....	....	....
1996-97	Syracuse Crunch	AHL	76	19	39	58	....	....	....	123	....	....	....	....	....	....	....	....	....	....	3	0	0	0	0	....	....	....
1997-98	Lukko Rauma	Finland	12	5	2	7	....	....	....	45	....	....	....	....	....	....	....	....	....	....	....	....	....	....	....	....	....	....
	Kassel Huskies	EuroHL	2	0	1	1	....	....	....	0	....	....	....	....	....	....	....	....	....	....	....	....	....	....	....	....	....	....
	Kassel Huskies	Germany	19	6	7	13	....	....	....	24	....	....	....	....	....	....	....	....	....	....	....	....	....	....	....	....	....	....
	NHL Totals		**12**	**2**	**3**	**5**	**2**	**2**	**4**	**6**	**0**	**0**	**0**	**19**	**10.5**	**5**	**0**	**3**	**0**		....	....	....	....	....	....	....	....

• LONEY, TROY

Troy Loney LW – L. 6'3", 209 lbs. b: Bow Island, Alta., 9/21/1963. Pittsburgh's 3rd choice, 52nd overall, in 1982 Entry Draft.

Season	Club	League	GP	G	A	Pts	AG	AA	APts	PIM	PP	SH	GW	S	%	TGF	PGF	TGA	PGA	+/–	GP	G	A	Pts	PIM	PP	SH	GW
1980-81	Lethbridge Broncos	WHL	71	18	13	31	....	....	....	100	....	....	....	....	....	....	....	....	....	....	9	2	2	5	14	....	....	....
1981-82	Lethbridge Broncos	WHL	71	26	33	59	....	....	....	152	....	....	....	....	....	....	....	....	....	....	12	3	3	6	10	....	....	....
1982-83	Lethbridge Broncos	WHL	72	33	34	67	....	....	....	156	....	....	....	....	....	....	....	....	....	....	20	10	7	17	43	....	....	....
1983-84	**Pittsburgh Penguins**	**NHL**	**13**	**0**	**0**	**0**	**0**	**0**	**0**	**9**	**0**	**0**	**0**	**5**	**0.0**	**0**	**0**	**7**	**0**	**–7**	....	....	....	....	....	....	....	....
	Baltimore Skipjacks	AHL	63	18	13	31	....	....	....	147	....	....	....	....	....	....	....	....	....	....	10	0	2	2	19	....	....	....
1984-85	**Pittsburgh Penguins**	**NHL**	**46**	**10**	**8**	**18**	**8**	**5**	**13**	**59**	**1**	**0**	**1**	**79**	**12.7**	**32**	**2**	**57**	**16**	**–11**	....	....	....	....	....	....	....	....
	Baltimore Skipjacks	AHL	15	4	2	6	....	....	....	25	....	....	....	....	....	....	....	....	....	....	....	....	....	....	....	....	....	....
1985-86	**Pittsburgh Penguins**	**NHL**	**47**	**3**	**9**	**12**	**2**	**6**	**8**	**95**	**0**	**0**	**1**	**50**	**6.0**	**24**	**1**	**37**	**6**	**–8**	....	....	....	....	....	....	....	....
	Baltimore Skipjacks	AHL	33	12	11	23	....	....	....	84	....	....	....	....	....	....	....	....	....	....	....	....	....	....	....	....	....	....
1986-87	**Pittsburgh Penguins**	**NHL**	**23**	**8**	**7**	**15**	**7**	**5**	**12**	**22**	**1**	**0**	**1**	**48**	**16.7**	**19**	**3**	**17**	**1**	**0**	....	....	....	....	....	....	....	....
	Baltimore Skipjacks	AHL	40	13	14	27	....	....	....	134	....	....	....	....	....	....	....	....	....	....	....	....	....	....	....	....	....	....
1987-88	**Pittsburgh Penguins**	**NHL**	**65**	**5**	**13**	**18**	**4**	**9**	**13**	**151**	**1**	**0**	**0**	**87**	**5.7**	**38**	**4**	**56**	**19**	**–3**	....	....	....	....	....	....	....	....
1988-89	**Pittsburgh Penguins**	**NHL**	**69**	**10**	**6**	**16**	**8**	**4**	**12**	**165**	**0**	**0**	**1**	**90**	**11.1**	**38**	**0**	**73**	**30**	**–5**	**11**	**1**	**3**	**4**	**24**	**0**	**0**	**0**
1989-90	**Pittsburgh Penguins**	**NHL**	**67**	**11**	**16**	**27**	**9**	**11**	**20**	**168**	**0**	**0**	**1**	**78**	**14.1**	**37**	**0**	**52**	**6**	**–9**	....	....	....	....	....	....	....	....
1990-91	**Pittsburgh Penguins**	**NHL**	**44**	**7**	**9**	**16**	**6**	**7**	**13**	**85**	**0**	**0**	**2**	**51**	**13.7**	**27**	**0**	**17**	**0**	**+10**	**24**	**2**	**2**	**4**	**41**	**0**	**0**	**0**
	Muskegon Lumberjacks	IHL	2	0	0	0	....	....	....	5	....	....	....	....	....	....	....	....	....	....	....	....	....	....	....	....	....	....
1991-92	**Pittsburgh Penguins**	**NHL**	**76**	**10**	**16**	**26**	**9**	**12**	**21**	**127**	**0**	**0**	**1**	**94**	**10.6**	**32**	**0**	**44**	**7**	**–5**	**21**	**4**	**5**	**9**	**32**	**0**	**0**	**0**
1992-93	**Pittsburgh Penguins**	**NHL**	**82**	**5**	**16**	**21**	**4**	**11**	**15**	**99**	**0**	**0**	**1**	**83**	**6.0**	**32**	**2**	**34**	**5**	**+1**	**10**	**1**	**4**	**5**	**0**	**0**	**0**	**0**
1993-94	**Anaheim Mighty Ducks**	**NHL**	**62**	**13**	**6**	**19**	**12**	**5**	**17**	**88**	**6**	**0**	**1**	**93**	**14.0**	**45**	**13**	**38**	**1**	**–5**	....	....	....	....	....	....	....	....
1994-95	**New York Islanders**	**NHL**	**26**	**5**	**4**	**9**	**9**	**6**	**15**	**23**	**2**	**0**	**1**	**45**	**11.1**	**12**	**3**	**9**	**0**	**0**	....	....	....	....	....	....	....	....
	New York Rangers	**NHL**	**4**	**0**	**0**	**0**	**0**	**0**	**0**	**0**	**0**	**0**	**0**	**2**	**0.0**	**0**	**0**	**2**	**0**	**–2**	**1**	**0**	**0**	**0**	**0**	**0**	**0**	**0**
	NHL Totals		**624**	**87**	**110**	**197**	**78**	**81**	**159**	**1091**	**11**	**0**	**11**	**805**	**10.8**	**336**	**28**	**443**	**91**		**67**	**8**	**14**	**22**	**97**	**0**	**0**	**0**

Claimed by **Anaheim** from **Pittsburgh** in Expansion Draft, June 24, 1993. Traded to **NY Islanders** by **Anaheim** for Tom Kurvers, June 29, 1994. Claimed on waivers by **NY Rangers** from **NY Islanders**, April 10, 1995.

• LONG, BARRY

Barry "Marathon Man" Long D – L. 6'2", 210 lbs. b: Brantford, Ont., 1/3/1949.

Season	Club	League	GP	G	A	Pts	AG	AA	APts	PIM	PP	SH	GW	S	%	TGF	PGF	TGA	PGA	+/–	GP	G	A	Pts	PIM	PP	SH	GW
1966-67	Moose Jaw Canucks	WCJHL	56	8	11	19	....	....	....	148	....	....	....	....	....	....	....	....	....	....	14	3	9	12	16	....	....	....
1967-68	Moose Jaw Canucks	WCJHL	52	11	33	44	....	....	....	202	....	....	....	....	....	....	....	....	....	....	....	....	....	....	....	....	....	....
1968-69	Dallas Black Hawks	CHL	46	4	11	15	....	....	....	85	....	....	....	....	....	....	....	....	....	....	....	....	....	....	....	....	....	....
1969-70	Dallas Black Hawks	CHL	71	11	22	33	....	....	....	127	....	....	....	....	....	....	....	....	....	....	....	....	....	....	....	....	....	....
1970-71	Dallas Black Hawks	CHL	72	9	24	33	....	....	....	90	....	....	....	....	....	....	....	....	....	....	10	1	0	1	10	....	....	....
1971-72	Portland Buckaroos	WHL	66	14	33	47	....	....	....	52	....	....	....	....	....	....	....	....	....	....	11	3	7	10	8	....	....	....
1972-73	**Los Angeles Kings**	**NHL**	**70**	**2**	**13**	**15**	**2**	**11**	**13**	**48**	**0**	**0**	**0**	**110**	**1.8**	**57**	**2**	**65**	**3**	**–7**	....	....	....	....	....	....	....	....
1973-74	**Los Angeles Kings**	**NHL**	**60**	**3**	**19**	**22**	**3**	**16**	**19**	**118**	**1**	**0**	**0**	**111**	**2.7**	**84**	**7**	**70**	**18**	**+25**	**5**	**0**	**1**	**1**	**18**	**0**	**0**	**0**
1974-75	Canada	Summit	DID NOT PLAY																									
	Edmonton Oilers	WHA	78	20	40	60	....	....	....	116	....	....	....	....	....	....	....	....	....	....	....	....	....	....	....	....	....	....
1975-76	Edmonton Oilers	WHA	78	10	32	42	....	....	....	66	....	....	....	....	....	....	....	....	....	....	4	0	0	0	4	....	....	....
1976-77	Edmonton Oilers	WHA	2	0	1	1	....	....	....	2	....	....	....	....	....	....	....	....	....	....	....	....	....	....	....	....	....	....
	Winnipeg Jets	WHA	71	9	38	47	....	....	....	54	....	....	....	....	....	....	....	....	....	....	20	1	5	6	10	....	....	....
1977-78	Winnipeg Jets	WHA	78	7	24	31	....	....	....	42	....	....	....	....	....	....	....	....	....	....	9	0	5	5	6	....	....	....
1978-79	Winnipeg Jets	WHA	79	5	36	41	....	....	....	42	....	....	....	....	....	....	....	....	....	....	10	2	3	5	0	....	....	....
1979-80	**Detroit Red Wings**	**NHL**	**80**	**0**	**17**	**17**	**0**	**13**	**13**	**38**	**0**	**0**	**0**	**87**	**0.0**	**74**	**0**	**157**	**55**	**–28**	....	....	....	....	....	....	....	....
1980-81	**Winnipeg Jets**	**NHL**	**65**	**6**	**17**	**23**	**5**	**12**	**17**	**42**	**0**	**0**	**0**	**88**	**6.8**	**71**	**4**	**142**	**28**	**–47**	....	....	....	....	....	....	....	....
	Canada	WEC-A	7	1	0	1	....	....	....	8	....	....	....	....	....	....	....	....	....	....	....	....	....	....	....	....	....	....
1981-82	**Winnipeg Jets**	**NHL**	**5**	**0**	**2**	**2**	**0**	**1**	**1**	**4**	**0**	**0**	**0**	**8**	**0.0**	**9**	**1**	**11**	**2**	**–1**	....	....	....	....	....	....	....	....
	NHL Totals		**280**	**11**	**68**	**79**	**10**	**53**	**63**	**250**	**1**	**0**	**0**	**404**	**2.7**	**295**	**14**	**445**	**106**		**5**	**0**	**1**	**1**	**18**	**0**	**0**	**0**
	Other Major League Totals		386	51	171	222	....	....	....	322	....	....	....	....	....	....	....	....	....	....	43	3	13	16	20	....	....	....

WHA Second All-Star Team (1975, 1978)

Selected by **Edmonton** (WHA) in 1972 WHA General Player Draft, February 12, 1972. Claimed by **LA Kings** from **Chicago** in Intra-League Draft, June 5, 1972. Traded to **Winnipeg** (WHA) by **Edmonton** (WHA) for future considerations, October, 1976. Rights traded to **Detroit** by **LA Kings** with Montreal's 3rd round choice (acquired earlier, Detroit selected Doug Derkson) in 1978 Amateur Draft for Danny Grant, January 9, 1978. Reclaimed by **Detroit** from **Winnipeg** prior to Expansion Draft, June 9, 1979. Traded to **Winnipeg** by **Detroit** for cash, October 31, 1980.

• LONSBERRY, ROSS

Ross Lonsberry LW – L. 5'11", 195 lbs. b: Humboldt, Sask., 2/7/1947.

Season	Club	League	GP	G	A	Pts	AG	AA	APts	PIM	PP	SH	GW	S	%	TGF	PGF	TGA	PGA	+/–	GP	G	A	Pts	PIM	PP	SH	GW
1962-63	Estevan Bruins	SJHL	1	0	1	1	....	....	....	0	....	....	....	....	....	....	....	....	....	....	....	....	....	....	....	....	....	....
1963-64	Estevan Bruins	SJHL	61	18	26	44	....	....	....	55	....	....	....	....	....	....	....	....	....	....	11	6	9	15	23	....	....	....
1964-65	Estevan Bruins	SJHL	56	40	56	96	....	....	....	130	....	....	....	....	....	....	....	....	....	....	6	3	5	8	18	....	....	....
	Minneapolis Bruins	CHL	2	0	0	0	....	....	....	0	....	....	....	....	....	....	....	....	....	....	5	1	0	1	4	....	....	....
1965-66	Estevan Bruins	SJHL	60	*67	77	*144	....	....	....	109	....	....	....	....	....	....	....	....	....	....	12	*13	6	19	26	....	....	....
1966-67	**Boston Bruins**	**NHL**	**8**	**0**	**1**	**1**	**0**	**1**	**1**	**2**	....	....	....	....	....	....	....	....	....	....	....	....	....	....	....	....	....	....
	Buffalo Bisons	AHL	7	1	1	2	....	....	....	4	....	....	....	....	....	....	....	....	....	....	....	....	....	....	....	....	....	....
	Oklahoma City Blazers	CHL	46	12	10	22	....	....	....	83	....	....	....	....	....	....	....	....	....	....	11	3	2	5	31	....	....	....
1967-68	**Boston Bruins**	**NHL**	**19**	**2**	**2**	**4**	**2**	**2**	**4**	**12**	**0**	**0**	**0**	**39**	**5.1**	**13**	**2**	**9**	**0**	**+2**	....	....	....	....	....	....	....	....
	Oklahoma City Blazers	CHL	41	16	18	34	....	....	....	116	....	....	....	....	....	....	....	....	....	....	7	3	3	6	22	....	....	....
1968-69	**Boston Bruins**	**NHL**	**6**	**0**	**0**	**0**	**0**	**0**	**0**	**2**	**0**	**0**	**0**	**4**	**0.0**	**0**	**0**	**0**	**0**	**0**	....	....	....	....	....	....	....	....
	Oklahoma City Blazers	CHL	65	28	39	67	....	....	....	169	....	....	....	....	....	....	....	....	....	....	12	4	8	12	21	....	....	....
1969-70	**Los Angeles Kings**	**NHL**	**76**	**20**	**22**	**42**	**23**	**22**	**45**	**118**	**3**	**1**	**4**	**226**	**8.8**	**66**	**21**	**84**	**21**	**–18**	....	....	....	....	....	....	....	....
1970-71	**Los Angeles Kings**	**NHL**	**76**	**25**	**28**	**53**	**26**	**25**	**51**	**80**	**5**	**2**	**0**	**238**	**10.5**	**81**	**22**	**118**	**24**	**–35**	....	....	....	....	....	....	....	....
1971-72	**Los Angeles Kings**	**NHL**	**50**	**9**	**14**	**23**	**10**	**13**	**23**	**39**	**1**	**0**	**0**	**112**	**8.0**	**33**	**3**	**52**	**4**	**–18**	....	....	....	....	....	....	....	....
	Philadelphia Flyers	**NHL**	**32**	**7**	**7**	**14**	**7**	**6**	**13**	**22**	**0**	**0**	**0**	**88**	**8.0**	**25**	**5**	**30**	**1**	**–9**	....	....	....	....	....	....	....	....
1972-73	**Philadelphia Flyers**	**NHL**	**77**	**21**	**29**	**50**	**21**	**24**	**45**	**59**	**6**	**0**	**3**	**205**	**10.2**	**94**	**28**	**74**	**14**	**+6**	**11**	**4**	**3**	**7**	**9**	**0**	**0**	**1**
1973-74	**Philadelphia Flyers**	**NHL**	**75**	**32**	**19**	**51**	**33**	**16**	**49**	**48**	**6**	**1**	**5**	**213**	**15.0**	**75**	**22**	**49**	**12**	**+16**	**17**	**4**	**9**	**13**	**18**	**1**	**1**	**1**
1974-75	**Philadelphia Flyers**	**NHL**	**80**	**24**	**25**	**49**	**22**	**20**	**42**	**99**	**9**	**0**	**3**	**180**	**13.3**	**77**	**19**	**43**	**13**	**+28**	**17**	**4**	**3**	**7**	**10**	**1**	**0**	**1**
1975-76	**Philadelphia Flyers**	**NHL**	**80**	**19**	**28**	**47**	**18**	**22**	**40**	**87**	**4**	**0**	**0**	**209**	**9.1**	**88**	**26**	**56**	**23**	**+29**	**16**	**4**	**3**	**7**	**2**	**1**	**0**	**1**
1976-77	**Philadelphia Flyers**	**NHL**	**75**	**23**	**32**	**55**	**22**	**26**	**48**	**43**	**3**	**1**	**3**	**173**	**13.3**	**91**	**12**	**49**	**12**	**+42**	**10**	**1**	**2**	**3**	**29**	**0**	**0**	**0**
1977-78	**Philadelphia Flyers**	**NHL**	**78**	**18**	**30**	**48**	**17**	**24**	**41**	**45**	**2**	**1**	**5**	**172**	**10.5**	**82**	**11**	**47**	**17**	**+41**	**12**	**2**	**2**	**4**	**6**	**1**	**0**	**1**

Season	Club	League	REGULAR SEASON																		PLAYOFFS							
			GP	G	A	Pts	AG	AA	APts	PIM	PP	SH	GW	S	%	TGF	PGF	TGA	PGA	+/–	GP	G	A	Pts	PIM	PP	SH	GW
1978-79	**Pittsburgh Penguins**	NHL	80	24	22	46	22	17	39	38	4	0	1	179	13.4	86	20	72	13	+7	7	0	2	2	9	0	0	0
1979-80	**Pittsburgh Penguins**	NHL	76	15	18	33	14	14	28	36	2	0	0	135	11.1	71	10	81	16	–4	5	2	1	3	2	0	0	1
1980-81	**Pittsburgh Penguins**	NHL	80	17	33	50	14	23	37	76	7	1	2	161	10.6	111	45	92	23	–3	5	0	0	0	2	0	0	0
	NHL Totals		968	256	310	566	251	255	506	806	52	7	26	2334	11.0	993	246	856	193		100	21	25	46	87	4	1	6

CHL Second All-Star Team (1969)

Played in NHL All-Star Game (1972)

Traded to **LA Kings** by **Boston** with Eddie Shack for LA Kings' 1st round choices in 1971 (Ron Jones) and 1973 (Andre Savard) Amateur Drafts, May 14, 1969. Traded to **Philadelphia** by **LA Kings** with Bill Flett, Ed Joyal and Jean Potvin for Bil Lesuk, Jim Johnson and Serge Bernier, January 28, 1972. Traded to **Pittsburgh** by **Philadelphia** for Pittsburgh's 1st round choice (Behn Wilson) in 1978 Amateur Draft, June 14, 1978.

• LOOB, HAKAN

Hakan Loob RW – R. 5'9", 170 lbs. b: Karlstad, Sweden, 7/3/1960. Calgary's 10th choice, 181st overall, in 1980 Entry Draft.

1978-79	Sweden	WJC-A	6	0	2	2	....	....	....	0	....	....	....	....	....	....	....	....	....	....	....	....	....	....	....	....	....	....
1979-80	Farjestad BK Karlstad	Sweden	36	15	4	19	....	....	....	20	....	....	....	....	....	....	....	....	....	....	....	....	....	....	....	....	....	....
	Sweden	WJC-A	5	7	2	9	....	....	....	2	....	....	....	....	....	....	....	....	....	....	....	....	....	....	....	....	....	....
1980-81	Farjestad BK Karlstad	Sweden	36	23	6	29	....	....	....	14	....	....	....	....	....	....	....	....	....	....	7	*5	3	*8	6	....	....	....
1981-82	Farjestad BK Karlstad	Sweden	36	26	15	41	....	....	....	28	....	....	....	....	....	....	....	....	....	....	2	1	0	1	0	....	....	....
	Sweden	Nat-Team	21	8	3	11	....	....	....	8	....	....	....	....	....	....	....	....	....	....	....	....	....	....	....	....	....	....
	Sweden	WEC-A	8	3	1	4	....	....	....	6	....	....	....	....	....	....	....	....	....	....	....	....	....	....	....	....	....	....
1982-83	Farjestad BK Karlstad	Sweden	36	*42	*34	*76	....	....	....	29	....	....	....	....	....	....	....	....	....	....	8	*10	4	*14	6	....	....	....
	Sweden	Nat-Team	11	2	2	4	....	....	....	8	....	....	....	....	....	....	....	....	....	....	....	....	....	....	....	....	....	....
1983-84	**Calgary Flames**	NHL	77	30	25	55	24	17	41	22	3	0	2	178	16.9	88	16	65	4	+11	11	2	3	5	2	1	0	2
1984-85	Sweden	C Cup	8	6	4	10	....	....	....	2	....	....	....	....	....	....	....	....	....	....	....	....	....	....	....	....	....	....
	Calgary Flames	NHL	78	37	35	72	30	24	54	14	8	1	5	224	16.5	110	37	70	11	+14	4	3	3	6	0	0	1	0
1985-86	**Calgary Flames**	NHL	68	31	36	67	25	24	49	36	10	0	1	174	17.8	95	30	58	15	+22	22	4	10	14	6	1	2	0
1986-87	**Calgary Flames**	NHL	68	18	26	44	16	19	35	26	7	0	1	129	14.0	62	25	66	16	–13	5	1	2	3	0	0	1	0
	Sweden	WEC-A	8	5	4	9	....	....	....	4	....	....	....	....	....	....	....	....	....	....	....	....	....	....	....	....	....	....
1987-88	**Calgary Flames**	NHL	80	50	56	106	43	40	83	47	9	8	4	198	25.3	158	63	93	39	+41	9	8	1	9	4	2	2	0
1988-89	**Calgary Flames**	NHL	79	27	58	85	23	41	64	44	5	0	4	223	12.1	113	40	56	11	+28	22	8	9	17	4	2	2	1
1989-90	Farjestad BK Karlstad	Sweden	40	22	*31	53	....	....	....	24	....	....	....	....	....	....	....	....	....	....	10	*9	5	*14	2	....	....	....
	Sweden	WEC-A	10	4	7	11	....	....	....	10	....	....	....	....	....	....	....	....	....	....	....	....	....	....	....	....	....	....
1990-91	Farjestad BK Karlstad	Sweden	40	*33	25	*58	....	....	....	16	....	....	....	....	....	....	....	....	....	....	8	*6	4	10	8	....	....	....
	Sweden	WEC-A	10	2	7	9	....	....	....	6	....	....	....	....	....	....	....	....	....	....	....	....	....	....	....	....	....	....
1991-92	Farjestad BK Karlstad	Sweden	40	*37	29	*66	....	....	....	14	....	....	....	....	....	....	....	....	....	....	6	2	2	4	2	....	....	....
	Sweden	Olympics	8	4	4	8	....	....	....	0	....	....	....	....	....	....	....	....	....	....	....	....	....	....	....	....	....	....
1992-93	Farjestad BK Karlstad	Sweden	40	*25	26	*51	....	....	....	28	....	....	....	....	....	....	....	....	....	....	3	4	1	5	0	....	....	....
1993-94	Farjestad BK Karlstad	Sweden	22	9	11	20	....	....	....	12	....	....	....	....	....	....	....	....	....	....	....	....	....	....	....	....	....	....
	Sweden	Olympics	8	4	5	9	....	....	....	2	....	....	....	....	....	....	....	....	....	....	....	....	....	....	....	....	....	....
1994-95	Farjestad BK Karlstad	Sweden	39	13	25	38	....	....	....	58	....	....	....	....	....	....	....	....	....	....	4	2	0	2	2	....	....	....
1995-96	Farjestad BK Karlstad	Sweden	40	17	31	48	....	....	....	37	....	....	....	....	....	....	....	....	....	....	....	....	....	....	....	....	....	....
	NHL Totals		450	193	236	429	161	165	326	189	42	9	17	1126	17.1	626	211	408	96		73	26	28	54	16	6	8	3

WJC-A All-Star Team (1980) • Swedish World All-Star Team (1983, 1985, 1990, 1991, 1992) • Swedish Player of the Year (1983) • NHL All-Rookie Team (1984) • NHL First All-Star Team (1988)

• LOOB, PETER

Peter Loob D – R. 6'3", 190 lbs. b: Karlstad, Sweden, 7/23/1957. Quebec's 10th choice, 244th overall, in 1984 Entry Draft.

1980-81	Farjestad BK Karlstad	Sweden	16	1	3	4	....	....	....	15	....	....	....	....	....	....	....	....	....	....	....	....	....	....	....	....	....	....
1981-82	Farjestad BK Karlstad	Sweden	25	8	8	16	....	....	....	24	....	....	....	....	....	....	....	....	....	....	2	0	0	0	0	....	....	....
1982-83	Farjestad BK Karlstad	Sweden	36	16	23	39	....	....	....	32	....	....	....	....	....	....	....	....	....	....	8	0	7	7	18	....	....	....
	Sweden	WEC-A	3	1	2	3	....	....	....	8	....	....	....	....	....	....	....	....	....	....	....	....	....	....	....	....	....	....
1983-84	Sodertalje	Sweden	36	12	15	27	....	....	....	36	....	....	....	....	....	....	....	....	....	....	....	....	....	....	....	....	....	....
1984-85	**Quebec Nordiques**	NHL	8	1	2	3	1	1	2	0	0	0	0	10	10.0	10	1	5	1	+5	....	....	....	....	....	....	....	....
	Fredericton Express	AHL	35	4	10	14	....	....	....	12	....	....	....	....	....	....	....	....	....	....	....	....	....	....	....	....	....	....
	Muskegon Mohawks	IHL	10	0	4	4	....	....	....	0	....	....	....	....	....	....	....	....	....	....	....	....	....	....	....	....	....	....
1985-86	Sodertalje	Sweden	34	15	5	20	....	....	....	20	....	....	....	....	....	....	....	....	....	....	7	4	2	0	4	....	....	....
1986-87	Sodertalje	Sweden	33	6	11	17	....	....	....	22	....	....	....	....	....	....	....	....	....	....	....	....	....	....	....	....	....	....
	NHL Totals		8	1	2	3	1	1	2	0	0	0	0	10	10.0	10	1	5	1		....	....	....	....	....	....	....	....

• LORENTZ, JIM

Jim Lorentz C/RW – L. 6', 190 lbs. b: Waterloo, Ont., 5/1/1947.

1963-64	Waterloo Siskins	OJHL	STATISTICS NOT AVAILABLE																									
1964-65	Niagara Falls Flyers	OHA	43	7	14	21	....	....	....	20	....	....	....	....	....	....	....	....	....	....	11	5	6	11	16	....	....	....
1965-66	Niagara Falls Flyers	OHA	38	11	22	33	....	....	....	47	....	....	....	....	....	....	....	....	....	....	4	1	2	3	4	....	....	....
1966-67	Niagara Falls Flyers	OHA	48	33	59	92	....	....	....	79	....	....	....	....	....	....	....	....	....	....	13	4	*17	21	10	....	....	....
1967-68	Oklahoma City Blazers	CHL	70	33	50	83	....	....	....	105	....	....	....	....	....	....	....	....	....	....	7	1	1	2	10	....	....	....
1968-69	**Boston Bruins**	NHL	11	1	3	4	1	3	4	6	0	0	1	16	6.3	5	0	8	0	–3	....	....	....	....	....	....	....	....
	Oklahoma City Blazers	CHL	56	33	*68	*101	....	....	....	67	....	....	....	....	....	....	....	....	....	....	12	9	*16	*25	17	....	....	....
1969-70	**Boston Bruins**	NHL	68	7	16	23	8	16	24	30	2	0	0	92	7.6	42	7	21	0	+14	11	1	0	1	4	0	0	0
1970-71	**St. Louis Blues**	NHL	76	19	21	40	20	18	38	34	6	0	2	160	11.9	72	21	49	0	+2	6	0	1	1	4	0	0	0
1971-72	**St. Louis Blues**	NHL	12	0	1	1	0	1	1	12	0	0	0	16	0.0	2	0	10	0	–8	....	....	....	....	....	....	....	....
	New York Rangers	NHL	7	0	0	0	0	0	0	0	0	0	0	1	0.0	0	0	2	1	–1	....	....	....	....	....	....	....	....
	Buffalo Sabres	NHL	33	10	14	24	11	13	24	12	2	0	1	85	11.8	36	11	38	2	–11	....	....	....	....	....	....	....	....
1972-73	**Buffalo Sabres**	NHL	78	27	35	62	27	29	56	30	11	0	5	175	15.4	105	35	68	4	+6	6	0	3	3	2	0	0	0
1973-74	**Buffalo Sabres**	NHL	78	23	31	54	23	27	50	28	12	0	4	145	15.9	83	40	63	1	–19	....	....	....	....	....	....	....	....
1974-75	**Buffalo Sabres**	NHL	72	25	45	70	23	35	58	18	6	0	0	140	17.9	114	44	59	6	+17	16	6	4	10	6	0	0	2
1975-76	**Buffalo Sabres**	NHL	75	17	24	41	16	19	35	18	2	1	4	116	14.7	63	14	54	8	+3	9	1	2	3	6	0	0	0
1976-77	**Buffalo Sabres**	NHL	79	23	33	56	22	27	49	8	7	0	3	156	14.7	81	16	62	0	+3	6	4	0	4	8	0	0	0
1977-78	**Buffalo Sabres**	NHL	70	9	15	24	9	12	21	12	6	0	2	85	10.6	40	14	34	4	–4	....	....	....	....	....	....	....	....
	NHL Totals		659	161	238	399	160	200	360	208	64	1	20	1187	13.6	643	202	468	26		54	12	10	22	30	0	0	2

CHL First All-Star Team (1968, 1969) • Won Ken McKenzie Trophy (CHL's Rookie of the Year) (1968) • Won Tommy Ivan Trophy (CHL's MVP) (1969)

Traded to **St. Louis** by **Boston** for St. Louis' 1st round choice (Ron Plumb) in 1970 Amateur Draft, May, 1970. Traded to **NY Rangers** by **St. Louis** with Gene Carr and Wayne Connelly for Jack Egars, Andre Dupont and Mike Murphy, November 15, 1971. Traded to **Buffalo** by **NY Rangers** for Buffalo's 2nd round choice (Lawrence Sacharuk) in 1972 Amateur Draft, January 14, 1972.

• LORIMER, BOB

Bob Lorimer D – R. 6'1", 200 lbs. b: Toronto, Ont., 8/25/1953. NY Islanders' 10th choice, 129th overall, in 1973 Amateur Draft.

1970-71	Aurora Tigers	OJHL	STATISTICS NOT AVAILABLE																									
1971-72	Michigan Tech Huskies	WCHA	32	1	7	8	....	....	....	63	....	....	....	....	....	....	....	....	....	....	....	....	....	....	....	....	....	....
1972-73	Michigan Tech Huskies	WCHA	38	2	9	11	....	....	....	74	....	....	....	....	....	....	....	....	....	....	....	....	....	....	....	....	....	....
1973-74	Michigan Tech Huskies	WCHA	39	3	18	21	....	....	....	46	....	....	....	....	....	....	....	....	....	....	....	....	....	....	....	....	....	....
1974-75	Michigan Tech Huskies	WCHA	38	10	21	31	....	....	....	68	....	....	....	....	....	....	....	....	....	....	....	....	....	....	....	....	....	....
1975-76	Fort Worth Texans	CHL	2	0	0	0	....	....	....	2	....	....	....	....	....	....	....	....	....	....	3	0	0	0	2	....	....	....
	Muskegon Mohawks	IHL	78	6	21	27	....	....	....	94	....	....	....	....	....	....	....	....	....	....	....	....	....	....	....	....	....	....
1976-77	**New York Islanders**	NHL	1	0	1	1	0	1	1	0	0	0	0	0	0.0	1	0	0	0	+1	....	....	....	....	....	....	....	....
	Fort Worth Texans	CHL	28	4	6	10	....	....	....	38	....	....	....	....	....	....	....	....	....	....	6	0	0	0	17	....	....	....
1977-78	**New York Islanders**	NHL	5	1	0	1	1	0	1	0	0	0	0	3	33.3	5	0	5	0	0	....	....	....	....	....	....	....	....
	Fort Worth Texans	CHL	71	6	13	19	....	....	....	81	....	....	....	....	....	....	....	....	....	....	14	1	7	8	25	....	....	....
1978-79	**New York Islanders**	NHL	67	3	18	21	3	14	17	42	0	0	0	64	4.7	78	1	68	18	+27	10	1	3	4	15	0	0	0
1979-80	**New York Islanders**	NHL	74	3	16	19	3	12	15	53	0	0	1	98	3.1	91	3	92	36	+32	21	1	3	4	41	0	0	1
1980-81	**New York Islanders**	NHL	73	1	12	13	1	8	9	77	0	0	0	65	1.5	98	1	81	29	+45	18	1	4	5	27	0	0	0
1981-82	**Colorado Rockies**	NHL	79	5	15	20	4	10	14	68	1	0	0	69	7.2	74	2	128	37	–19	....	....	....	....	....	....	....	....
1982-83	**New Jersey Devils**	NHL	66	3	10	13	2	7	9	42	0	0	0	53	5.7	49	0	104	35	–20	....	....	....	....	....	....	....	....

Season	Club	League	REGULAR SEASON GP	G	A	Pts	AG	AA	APts	PIM	PP	SH	GW	S	%	TGF	PGF	TGA	PGA	+/-	PLAYOFFS GP	G	A	Pts	PIM	PP	SH	GW
1983-84	**New Jersey Devils**	**NHL**	**72**	**2**	**10**	**12**	**2**	**7**	**9**	**62**	**1**	**0**	**0**	**65**	**3.1**	**51**	**6**	**99**	**26**	**–28**	....	....	....	....	....	....	....	....
1984-85	**New Jersey Devils**	**NHL**	**46**	**2**	**6**	**8**	**2**	**4**	**6**	**35**	**0**	**0**	**0**	**40**	**5.0**	**47**	**1**	**56**	**16**	**+6**	....	....	....	....	....	....	....	....
1985-86	**New Jersey Devils**	**NHL**	**46**	**2**	**2**	**4**	**2**	**1**	**3**	**52**	**0**	**0**	**0**	**28**	**7.1**	**37**	**2**	**77**	**29**	**–13**	....	....	....	....	....	....	....	....
	NHL Totals		**529**	**22**	**90**	**112**	**20**	**64**	**84**	**431**	**2**	**0**	**1**	**485**	**4.5**	**531**	**16**	**710**	**226**		**49**	**3**	**10**	**13**	**83**	**0**	**0**	**1**

WCHA Second All-Star Team (1975) • NCAA Championship All-Tournament Team (1975)

Traded to **Colorado** by **NY Islanders** with Dave Cameron for Colorado's 1st round choice (Pat LaFontaine) in 1983 Entry Draft, October 1, 1981. Transferred to **New Jersey** after **Colorado** franchise relocated, June 30, 1982.

• LOVSIN, KEN
Ken Lovsin D – R. 6', 195 lbs. b: Peace River, Alta., 12/3/1966. Hartford's 1st choice, 22nd overall, in 1987 Supplemental Draft.

Season	Club	League	GP	G	A	Pts	AG	AA	APts	PIM	PP	SH	GW	S	%	TGF	PGF	TGA	PGA	+/-	GP	G	A	Pts	PIM	PP	SH	GW
1986-87	University of Saskatchewan	CWUAA	28	3	13	16	....	....	....	14	....	....	....	....	....	....	....	....	....	....	9	3	1	4	6	....	....	....
1987-88	University of Saskatchewan	CWUAA	29	11	31	32	....	....	....	29	....	....	....	....	....	....	....	....	....	....	....	....	....	....	....	....	....	....
1988-89	Canada	Nat-Team	59	0	10	10	....	....	....	59	....	....	....	....	....	....	....	....	....	....	....	....	....	....	....	....	....	....
1989-90	Canada	Nat-Team	66	7	15	22	....	....	....	80	....	....	....	....	....	....	....	....	....	....	....	....	....	....	....	....	....	....
1990-91	**Washington Capitals**	**NHL**	**1**	**0**	**0**	**0**	**0**	**0**	**0**	**0**	**0**	**0**	**0**	**2**	**0.0**	**1**	**1**	**2**	**0**	**–2**	....	....	....	....	....	....	....	....
	Baltimore Skipjacks	AHL	79	8	28	36	....	....	....	54	....	....	....	....	....	....	....	....	....	....	6	1	1	2	2	....	....	....
1991-92	Baltimore Skipjacks	AHL	77	11	24	35	....	....	....	60	....	....	....	....	....	....	....	....	....	....	....	....	....	....	....	....	....	....
1992-93	Mora	Sweden	36	7	13	20	....	....	....	50	....	....	....	....	....	....	....	....	....	....	....	....	....	....	....	....	....	....
	Canada	Nat-Team	9	0	3	3	....	....	....	0	....	....	....	....	....	....	....	....	....	....	....	....	....	....	....	....	....	....
	Canada	Olympics	8	0	0	0	....	....	....	8	....	....	....	....	....	....	....	....	....	....	....	....	....	....	....	....	....	....
	NHL Totals		**1**	**0**	**0**	**0**	**0**	**0**	**0**	**0**	**0**	**0**	**0**	**2**	**0.0**	**1**	**1**	**2**	**0**		....	....	....	....	....	....	....	....

Signed as a free agent by **Washington**, July 3, 1990.

• LOWDERMILK, DWAYNE
Dwayne Lowdermilk D – R. 6', 201 lbs. b: Burnaby, B.C., 1/9/1958. NY Islanders' 3rd choice, 51st overall, in 1978 Amateur Draft.

Season	Club	League	GP	G	A	Pts	AG	AA	APts	PIM	PP	SH	GW	S	%	TGF	PGF	TGA	PGA	+/-	GP	G	A	Pts	PIM	PP	SH	GW
1975-76	Langley Lords	BCJHL	STATISTICS NOT AVAILABLE																									
	Kamloops Chiefs	WCJHL	35	5	7	12	....	....	....	10	....	....	....	....	....	....	....	....	....	....	12	0	2	2	2	....	....	....
1976-77	Kamloops Chiefs	WCJHL	72	13	46	59	....	....	....	79	....	....	....	....	....	....	....	....	....	....	....	....	....	....	....	....	....	....
1977-78	Seattle Breakers	WCJHL	71	28	58	86	....	....	....	106	....	....	....	....	....	....	....	....	....	....	....	....	....	....	....	....	....	....
1978-79	Fort Worth Texans	CHL	75	13	37	50	....	....	....	63	....	....	....	....	....	....	....	....	....	....	4	0	0	0	2	....	....	....
1979-80	Indianapolis Checkers	CHL	79	7	29	36	....	....	....	38	....	....	....	....	....	....	....	....	....	....	7	2	2	4	0	....	....	....
1980-81	Indianapolis Checkers	CHL	5	0	4	4	....	....	....	8	....	....	....	....	....	....	....	....	....	....	....	....	....	....	....	....	....	....
	Washington Capitals	**NHL**	**2**	**0**	**1**	**1**	**0**	**1**	**1**	**2**	**0**	**0**	**0**	**2**	**0.0**	**3**	**2**	**2**	**0**	**–1**	....	....	....	....	....	....	....	....
	Hershey Bears	AHL	46	6	17	23	....	....	....	28	....	....	....	....	....	....	....	....	....	....	5	2	1	3	2	....	....	....
	Fort Wayne Komets	IHL	21	7	10	17	....	....	....	19	....	....	....	....	....	....	....	....	....	....	....	....	....	....	....	....	....	....
1981-82	Hershey Bears	AHL	70	4	34	38	....	....	....	44	....	....	....	....	....	....	....	....	....	....	5	1	3	4	2	....	....	....
	NHL Totals		**2**	**0**	**1**	**1**	**0**	**1**	**1**	**2**	**0**	**0**	**0**	**2**	**0.0**	**3**	**2**	**2**	**0**		....	....	....	....	....	....	....	....

Traded to **Washington** by **NY Islanders** for future considerations, December, 1980.

• LOWE, DARREN
Darren Lowe RW – R. 5'10", 185 lbs. b: Toronto, Ont., 10/13/1960.

Season	Club	League	GP	G	A	Pts	AG	AA	APts	PIM	PP	SH	GW	S	%	TGF	PGF	TGA	PGA	+/-	GP	G	A	Pts	PIM	PP	SH	GW
1980-81	University of Toronto	OUAA	28	28	23	51	....	....	....	26	....	....	....	....	....	....	....	....	....	....	....	....	....	....	....	....	....	....
1981-82	University of Toronto	OUAA	29	36	26	62	....	....	....	....	....	....	....	....	....	....	....	....	....	....	....	....	....	....	....	....	....	....
1982-83	University of Toronto	OUAA	24	23	32	55	....	....	....	....	....	....	....	....	....	....	....	....	....	....	....	....	....	....	....	....	....	....
1983-84	Canada	Nat-Team	60	16	13	29	....	....	....	22	....	....	....	....	....	....	....	....	....	....	....	....	....	....	....	....	....	....
	Canada	Olympics	7	2	1	3	....	....	....	0	....	....	....	....	....	....	....	....	....	....	....	....	....	....	....	....	....	....
	Pittsburgh Penguins	**NHL**	**8**	**1**	**2**	**3**	**1**	**1**	**2**	**0**	**0**	**0**	**0**	**14**	**7.1**	**4**	**0**	**9**	**0**	**–5**	....	....	....	....	....	....	....	....
1985-86	WEV Wien	Austria	STATISTICS NOT AVAILABLE																									
1986-87	WEV Wien	Austria	22	18	11	29	....	....	....	6	....	....	....	....	....	....	....	....	....	....	....	....	....	....	....	....	....	....
	Jokerit Helsinki	Finland	18	7	2	9	....	....	....	16	....	....	....	....	....	....	....	....	....	....	....	....	....	....	....	....	....	....
1987-88	Flint Spirits	IHL	82	53	64	117	....	....	....	24	....	....	....	....	....	....	....	....	....	....	16	10	*15	25	34	....	....	....
1988-89			DID NOT PLAY																									
1989-90	Flint Spirits	IHL	67	31	35	66	....	....	....	44	....	....	....	....	....	....	....	....	....	....	4	1	4	5	2	....	....	....
1990-91	San Diego Gulls	IHL	79	21	37	58	....	....	....	60	....	....	....	....	....	....	....	....	....	....	....	....	....	....	....	....	....	....
	NHL Totals		**8**	**1**	**2**	**3**	**1**	**1**	**2**	**0**	**0**	**0**	**0**	**14**	**7.1**	**4**	**0**	**9**	**0**		....	....	....	....	....	....	....	....

Signed as a free agent by **Pittsburgh**, February, 1983.

• LOWE, KEVIN
Kevin Lowe D – L. 6'2", 200 lbs. b: Lachute, Que., 4/15/1959. Edmonton's 1st choice, 21st overall, in 1979 Entry Draft.

Season	Club	League	GP	G	A	Pts	AG	AA	APts	PIM	PP	SH	GW	S	%	TGF	PGF	TGA	PGA	+/-	GP	G	A	Pts	PIM	PP	SH	GW
1976-77	Quebec Remparts	QMJHL	69	3	19	22	....	....	....	39	....	....	....	....	....	....	....	....	....	....	....	....	....	....	....	....	....	....
1977-78	Quebec Remparts	QMJHL	64	13	52	65	....	....	....	86	....	....	....	....	....	....	....	....	....	....	4	1	2	3	6	....	....	....
1978-79	Quebec Remparts	QMJHL	68	26	60	86	....	....	....	120	....	....	....	....	....	....	....	....	....	....	6	1	7	8	36	....	....	....
1979-80	**Edmonton Oilers**	**NHL**	**64**	**2**	**19**	**21**	**2**	**15**	**17**	**70**	**2**	**0**	**0**	**86**	**2.3**	**73**	**13**	**64**	**5**	**+1**	**3**	**0**	**1**	**1**	**0**	**0**	**0**	**0**
1980-81	**Edmonton Oilers**	**NHL**	**79**	**10**	**24**	**34**	**8**	**17**	**25**	**94**	**4**	**0**	**2**	**115**	**8.7**	**90**	**15**	**109**	**24**	**–10**	**9**	**0**	**2**	**2**	**11**	**0**	**0**	**0**
1981-82	**Edmonton Oilers**	**NHL**	**80**	**9**	**31**	**40**	**7**	**20**	**27**	**63**	**1**	**1**	**2**	**110**	**8.2**	**129**	**16**	**104**	**37**	**+46**	**5**	**0**	**3**	**3**	**0**	**0**	**0**	**0**
	Canada	WEC-A	9	1	1	2	....	....	....	2	....	....	....	....	....	....	....	....	....	....	....	....	....	....	....	....	....	....
1982-83	**Edmonton Oilers**	**NHL**	**80**	**6**	**34**	**40**	**5**	**23**	**28**	**43**	**1**	**0**	**0**	**92**	**6.5**	**122**	**15**	**111**	**43**	**+39**	**16**	**1**	**8**	**9**	**10**	**0**	**0**	**0**
1983-84	**Edmonton Oilers**	**NHL**	**80**	**4**	**42**	**46**	**3**	**28**	**31**	**59**	**1**	**0**	**1**	**81**	**4.9**	**122**	**15**	**106**	**36**	**+37**	**19**	**3**	**7**	**10**	**16**	**0**	**0**	**0**
1984-85	Canada	C Cup	7	0	4	4	....	....	....	8	....	....	....	....	....	....	....	....	....	....	....	....	....	....	....	....	....	....
	Edmonton Oilers	**NHL**	**80**	**4**	**21**	**25**	**3**	**14**	**17**	**104**	**1**	**0**	**1**	**83**	**4.8**	**93**	**15**	**106**	**37**	**+9**	**16**	**0**	**5**	**5**	**8**	**0**	**0**	**0**
1985-86	**Edmonton Oilers**	**NHL**	**74**	**2**	**16**	**18**	**2**	**11**	**13**	**90**	**0**	**0**	**0**	**57**	**3.5**	**88**	**8**	**77**	**21**	**+24**	**10**	**1**	**3**	**4**	**15**	**0**	**0**	**0**
1986-87	**Edmonton Oilers**	**NHL**	**77**	**8**	**29**	**37**	**7**	**21**	**28**	**94**	**2**	**2**	**1**	**99**	**8.1**	**112**	**11**	**85**	**25**	**+41**	**21**	**2**	**4**	**6**	**22**	**0**	**2**	**1**
1987-88	**Edmonton Oilers**	**NHL**	**70**	**9**	**15**	**24**	**8**	**11**	**19**	**89**	**2**	**1**	**2**	**82**	**11.0**	**104**	**19**	**102**	**35**	**+18**	**19**	**0**	**2**	**2**	**26**	**0**	**0**	**0**
1988-89	**Edmonton Oilers**	**NHL**	**76**	**7**	**18**	**25**	**6**	**13**	**19**	**98**	**0**	**0**	**1**	**85**	**8.2**	**113**	**12**	**112**	**37**	**+26**	**7**	**1**	**2**	**3**	**4**	**0**	**0**	**0**
1989-90	**Edmonton Oilers**	**NHL**	**78**	**7**	**26**	**33**	**6**	**19**	**25**	**140**	**2**	**1**	**0**	**74**	**9.5**	**98**	**9**	**108**	**37**	**+18**	**20**	**0**	**2**	**2**	**10**	**0**	**0**	**0**
1990-91	**Edmonton Oilers**	**NHL**	**73**	**3**	**13**	**16**	**3**	**10**	**13**	**113**	**0**	**0**	**0**	**51**	**5.9**	**51**	**2**	**81**	**23**	**–9**	**14**	**1**	**1**	**2**	**14**	**0**	**0**	**0**
1991-92	**Edmonton Oilers**	**NHL**	**55**	**2**	**8**	**10**	**2**	**6**	**8**	**107**	**0**	**0**	**0**	**33**	**6.1**	**38**	**0**	**64**	**22**	**–4**	**11**	**0**	**3**	**3**	**16**	**0**	**0**	**0**
1992-93	**New York Rangers**	**NHL**	**49**	**3**	**12**	**15**	**2**	**8**	**10**	**58**	**0**	**0**	**0**	**52**	**5.8**	**43**	**1**	**66**	**22**	**–2**	....	....	....	....	....	....	....	....
1993-94	**New York Rangers**	**NHL**	**71**	**5**	**14**	**19**	**5**	**11**	**16**	**70**	**0**	**0**	**1**	**50**	**10.0**	**59**	**3**	**64**	**12**	**+4**	**22**	**1**	**0**	**1**	**20**	**0**	**0**	**0**
1994-95	**New York Rangers**	**NHL**	**44**	**1**	**7**	**8**	**2**	**10**	**12**	**58**	**1**	**0**	**0**	**35**	**2.9**	**26**	**1**	**30**	**3**	**–2**	**10**	**0**	**1**	**1**	**12**	**0**	**0**	**0**
1995-96	**New York Rangers**	**NHL**	**53**	**1**	**5**	**6**	**1**	**4**	**5**	**76**	**0**	**0**	**0**	**30**	**3.3**	**37**	**0**	**31**	**14**	**+20**	**10**	**0**	**4**	**4**	**4**	**0**	**0**	**0**
1996-97	**Edmonton Oilers**	**NHL**	**64**	**1**	**13**	**14**	**1**	**11**	**12**	**50**	**0**	**0**	**0**	**46**	**2.2**	**43**	**3**	**59**	**18**	**–1**	**1**	**0**	**0**	**0**	**0**	**0**	**0**	**0**
1997-98	**Edmonton Oilers**	**NHL**	**7**	**0**	**0**	**0**	**0**	**0**	**0**	**22**	**0**	**0**	**0**	**5**	**0.0**	**2**	**0**	**5**	**0**	**–3**	**1**	**0**	**0**	**0**	**4**	**0**	**0**	**0**
	NHL Totals		**1254**	**84**	**347**	**431**	**73**	**252**	**325**	**1498**	**17**	**5**	**11**	**1266**	**6.6**	**1443**	**158**	**1484**	**451**		**214**	**10**	**48**	**58**	**192**	**0**	**2**	**1**

QMJHL Second All-Star Team (1978, 1979) • Won Bud Man of the Year Award (1990) • Won King Clancy Memorial Trophy (1990)

Played in NHL All-Star Game (1984, 1985, 1986, 1988, 1989, 1990, 1993)

Traded to **NY Rangers** by **Edmonton** for Roman Oksiuta and NY Rangers' 3rd round choice (Alexander Kerch) in 1993 Entry Draft, December 11, 1992. Signed as a free agent by **Edmonton**, September 28, 1996.

• LOWRY, DAVE
Dave "Pie" Lowry LW – L. 6'1", 200 lbs. b: Sudbury, Ont., 2/14/1965. Vancouver's 6th choice, 114th overall, in 1983 Entry Draft.

Season	Club	League	GP	G	A	Pts	AG	AA	APts	PIM	PP	SH	GW	S	%	TGF	PGF	TGA	PGA	+/-	GP	G	A	Pts	PIM	PP	SH	GW
1982-83	London Knights	OHL	42	11	16	27	....	....	....	48	....	....	....	....	....	....	....	....	....	....	3	0	0	0	14	....	....	....
1983-84	London Knights	OHL	66	29	47	76	....	....	....	125	....	....	....	....	....	....	....	....	....	....	8	6	6	12	41	....	....	....
1984-85	London Knights	OHL	61	60	60	120	....	....	....	94	....	....	....	....	....	....	....	....	....	....	8	6	5	11	10	....	....	....
1985-86	**Vancouver Canucks**	**NHL**	**73**	**10**	**8**	**18**	**8**	**5**	**13**	**143**	**1**	**0**	**1**	**66**	**15.2**	**25**	**3**	**43**	**0**	**–21**	**3**	**0**	**0**	**0**	**0**	**0**	**0**	**0**
1986-87	**Vancouver Canucks**	**NHL**	**70**	**8**	**10**	**18**	**7**	**7**	**14**	**176**	**0**	**0**	**1**	**74**	**10.8**	**25**	**0**	**48**	**0**	**–23**	....	....	....	....	....	....	....	....
1987-88	**Vancouver Canucks**	**NHL**	**22**	**1**	**3**	**4**	**1**	**2**	**3**	**38**	**0**	**0**	**0**	**14**	**7.1**	**12**	**6**	**9**	**1**	**–2**	....	....	....	....	....	....	....	....
	Fredericton Express	AHL	46	18	27	45	....	....	....	59	....	....	....	....	....	....	....	....	....	....	14	7	3	10	72	....	....	....
1988-89	**St. Louis Blues**	**NHL**	**21**	**3**	**3**	**6**	**3**	**2**	**5**	**11**	**0**	**1**	**0**	**22**	**13.6**	**13**	**0**	**21**	**9**	**+1**	**10**	**0**	**5**	**5**	**4**	**0**	**0**	**0**
	Peoria Rivermen	IHL	58	31	35	66	....	....	....	45	....	....	....	....	....	....	....	....	....	....	....	....	....	....	....	....	....	....
1989-90	**St. Louis Blues**	**NHL**	**78**	**19**	**6**	**25**	**16**	**4**	**20**	**75**	**0**	**2**	**1**	**98**	**19.4**	**35**	**0**	**73**	**39**	**+1**	**12**	**2**	**1**	**3**	**39**	**0**	**0**	**0**
1990-91	**St. Louis Blues**	**NHL**	**79**	**19**	**21**	**40**	**17**	**16**	**33**	**168**	**0**	**2**	**5**	**123**	**15.4**	**64**	**2**	**66**	**23**	**+19**	**13**	**1**	**4**	**5**	**35**	**0**	**0**	**0**
1991-92	**St. Louis Blues**	**NHL**	**75**	**7**	**13**	**20**	**6**	**10**	**16**	**77**	**0**	**0**	**1**	**85**	**8.2**	**27**	**0**	**56**	**18**	**–11**	**6**	**0**	**1**	**1**	**20**	**0**	**0**	**0**
1992-93	**St. Louis Blues**	**NHL**	**58**	**5**	**8**	**13**	**4**	**5**	**9**	**101**	**0**	**0**	**0**	**59**	**8.5**	**16**	**0**	**44**	**10**	**–18**	**11**	**2**	**0**	**2**	**14**	**0**	**1**	**0**

Season	Club	League	REGULAR SEASON GP	G	A	Pts	AG	AA	APts	PIM	PP	SH	GW	S	%	TGF	PGF	TGA	PGA	+/–	PLAYOFFS GP	G	A	Pts	PIM	PP	SH	GW
1993-94	**Florida Panthers**	**NHL**	**80**	**15**	**22**	**37**	**14**	**17**	**31**	**64**	**3**	**0**	**3**	**122**	**12.3**	**67**	**27**	**50**	**6**	**–4**	....	....	....	....	....	....	....	....
1994-95	**Florida Panthers**	**NHL**	**45**	**10**	**10**	**20**	**18**	**15**	**33**	**25**	**2**	**0**	**3**	**70**	**14.3**	**33**	**11**	**25**	**0**	**–3**	....	....	....	....	....	....	....	....
1995-96	**Florida Panthers**	**NHL**	**63**	**10**	**14**	**24**	**10**	**11**	**21**	**36**	**0**	**0**	**1**	**83**	**12.0**	**41**	**13**	**31**	**1**	**–2**	**22**	**10**	**7**	**17**	**39**	**4**	**0**	**2**
1996-97	**Florida Panthers**	**NHL**	**77**	**15**	**14**	**29**	**16**	**12**	**28**	**51**	**2**	**0**	**2**	**96**	**15.6**	**48**	**11**	**39**	**4**	**+2**	**5**	**0**	**0**	**0**	**0**	**0**	**0**	**0**
1997-98	**Florida Panthers**	**NHL**	**7**	**0**	**0**	**0**	**0**	**0**	**0**	**2**	**0**	**0**	**0**	**4**	**0.0**	**4**	**0**	**6**	**1**	**–1**	....	....	....	....	....	....	....	....
	San Jose Sharks	**NHL**	**50**	**4**	**4**	**8**	**5**	**4**	**9**	**51**	**0**	**0**	**1**	**47**	**8.5**	**12**	**0**	**13**	**1**	**0**	**6**	**0**	**0**	**0**	**18**	**0**	**0**	**0**
	NHL Totals		**798**	**126**	**136**	**262**	**125**	**110**	**235**	**1018**	**8**	**5**	**19**	**963**	**13.1**	**422**	**73**	**524**	**113**		**88**	**15**	**18**	**33**	**169**	**4**	**1**	**2**

OHL First All-Star Team (1985)

Traded to **St. Louis** by **Vancouver** for Ernie Vargas, September 29, 1988. Claimed by **Florida** from **St. Louis** in Expansion Draft, June 24, 1993. Traded to **San Jose** by **Florida** with Florida's 1st round choice (later traded to Tampa Bay - Tampa Bay selected Vincent Lecavalier) for Viktor Kozlov and Florida's 5th round choice (previously acquired, Florida selected Jaroslav Spacek) in 1998 Entry Draft, November 13, 1997.

• LUCAS, DANNY

Danny Lucas　RW – L. 6'1", 197 lbs.　b: Powell River, B.C., 2/28/1958.　Philadelphia's 3rd choice, 14th overall, in 1978 Amateur Draft.

Season	Club	League	GP	G	A	Pts	AG	AA	APts	PIM	PP	SH	GW	S	%	TGF	PGF	TGA	PGA	+/–	GP	G	A	Pts	PIM	PP	SH	GW
1973-74	Humboldt Indians	SJHL	18	11	11	22	....	....	....	14	....	....	....	....	....	....	....	....	....	....	....	....	....	....	....	....	....	....
	Victoria Cougars	WCJHL	29	6	10	16	....	....	....	38	....	....	....	....	....	....	....	....	....	....	....	....	....	....	....	....	....	....
1974-75	Victoria Cougars	WCJHL	70	57	56	113	....	....	....	74	....	....	....	....	....	....	....	....	....	....	12	3	2	5	22	....	....	....
1975-76	Victoria Cougars	WCJHL	32	20	24	44	....	....	....	63	....	....	....	....	....	....	....	....	....	....	....	....	....	....	....	....	....	....
1976-77	University of British Columbia	CWUAA	26	12	17	29	....	....	....	44	....	....	....	....	....	....	....	....	....	....	....	....	....	....	....	....	....	....
1977-78	Sault Ste. Marie Greyhounds	OHA	61	50	67	117	....	....	....	90	....	....	....	....	....	....	....	....	....	....	....	....	....	....	....	....	....	....
1978-79	**Philadelphia Flyers**	**NHL**	**6**	**1**	**0**	**1**	**1**	**0**	**1**	**0**	**0**	**0**	**0**	**8**	**12.5**	**2**	**1**	**3**	**0**	**–2**	....	....	....	....	....	....	....	....
	Maine Mariners	AHL	70	21	19	40	....	....	....	54	....	....	....	....	....	....	....	....	....	....	10	3	6	9	4	....	....	....
1979-80	Maine Mariners	AHL	80	25	27	52	....	....	....	33	....	....	....	....	....	....	....	....	....	....	12	2	9	11	6	....	....	....
1980-81	Fort Worth Texans	CHL	38	5	8	13	....	....	....	23	....	....	....	....	....	....	....	....	....	....	....	....	....	....	....	....	....	....
	Maine Mariners	AHL	2	0	0	0	....	....	....	2	....	....	....	....	....	....	....	....	....	....	....	....	....	....	....	....	....	....
	NHL Totals		**6**	**1**	**0**	**1**	**1**	**0**	**1**	**0**	**0**	**0**	**0**	**8**	**12.5**	**2**	**1**	**3**	**0**		....	....	....	....	....	....	....	....

Signed as a free agent by **Colorado**, October, 1980.

• LUCE, DON

Don Luce　C – L. 6'2", 185 lbs.　b: London, Ont., 10/2/1948.　NY Rangers' 3rd choice, 14th overall, in 1966 Amateur Draft.

Season	Club	League	GP	G	A	Pts	AG	AA	APts	PIM	PP	SH	GW	S	%	TGF	PGF	TGA	PGA	+/–	GP	G	A	Pts	PIM	PP	SH	GW
1965-66	Kitchener Rangers	OHA	47	16	19	35	....	....	....	71	....	....	....	....	....	....	....	....	....	....	19	4	12	16	20	....	....	....
1966-67	Kitchener Rangers	OHA	48	19	42	61	....	....	....	94	....	....	....	....	....	....	....	....	....	....	13	7	9	16	35	....	....	....
1967-68	Kitchener Rangers	OHA	54	24	*70	94	....	....	....	88	....	....	....	....	....	....	....	....	....	....	19	4	8	12	42	....	....	....
1968-69	Omaha Knights	CHL	72	22	34	56	....	....	....	56	....	....	....	....	....	....	....	....	....	....	7	3	4	7	11	....	....	....
1969-70	Omaha Knights	CHL	64	22	35	57	....	....	....	82	....	....	....	....	....	....	....	....	....	....	2	1	2	3	4	....	....	....
	New York Rangers	**NHL**	**12**	**1**	**2**	**3**	**1**	**2**	**3**	**8**	**0**	**0**	**0**	**20**	**5.0**	**3**	**0**	**5**	**0**	**–2**	**5**	**0**	**1**	**1**	**4**	**0**	**0**	**0**
1970-71	**New York Rangers**	**NHL**	**9**	**0**	**1**	**1**	**0**	**1**	**1**	**0**	**0**	**0**	**0**	**3**	**0.0**	**1**	**0**	**1**	**0**	**0**	....	....	....	....	....	....	....	....
	Detroit Red Wings	**NHL**	**58**	**3**	**11**	**14**	**3**	**10**	**13**	**18**	**0**	**0**	**0**	**71**	**4.2**	**25**	**1**	**39**	**9**	**–6**	....	....	....	....	....	....	....	....
1971-72	**Buffalo Sabres**	**NHL**	**78**	**11**	**8**	**19**	**12**	**7**	**19**	**38**	**0**	**0**	**1**	**126**	**8.7**	**26**	**0**	**84**	**40**	**–18**	....	....	....	....	....	....	....	....
1972-73	**Buffalo Sabres**	**NHL**	**78**	**18**	**25**	**43**	**18**	**21**	**39**	**32**	**0**	**3**	**2**	**198**	**9.1**	**51**	**0**	**69**	**25**	**+7**	**6**	**1**	**1**	**2**	**2**	**0**	**0**	**0**
1973-74	**Buffalo Sabres**	**NHL**	**75**	**26**	**31**	**57**	**27**	**27**	**54**	**44**	**2**	**3**	**1**	**237**	**11.0**	**67**	**4**	**93**	**33**	**+3**	....	....	....	....	....	....	....	....
1974-75	**Buffalo Sabres**	**NHL**	**80**	**33**	**43**	**76**	**31**	**34**	**65**	**45**	**1**	**8**	**6**	**245**	**13.5**	**105**	**7**	**79**	**42**	**+61**	**16**	**5**	**8**	**13**	**19**	**0**	**1**	**0**
1975-76	**Buffalo Sabres**	**NHL**	**77**	**21**	**49**	**70**	**20**	**39**	**59**	**42**	**2**	**2**	**2**	**214**	**9.8**	**95**	**8**	**85**	**35**	**+37**	**9**	**4**	**3**	**7**	**6**	**0**	**0**	**1**
1976-77	**Buffalo Sabres**	**NHL**	**80**	**26**	**43**	**69**	**25**	**35**	**60**	**16**	**6**	**1**	**6**	**206**	**12.6**	**97**	**14**	**69**	**24**	**+38**	**6**	**3**	**1**	**4**	**2**	**2**	**0**	**0**
1977-78	**Buffalo Sabres**	**NHL**	**78**	**26**	**35**	**61**	**25**	**29**	**54**	**24**	**5**	**2**	**3**	**170**	**15.3**	**103**	**17**	**79**	**25**	**+32**	**8**	**0**	**2**	**2**	**6**	**0**	**0**	**0**
1978-79	**Buffalo Sabres**	**NHL**	**79**	**26**	**35**	**61**	**24**	**27**	**51**	**14**	**6**	**2**	**7**	**149**	**17.4**	**86**	**18**	**87**	**39**	**+20**	**3**	**1**	**1**	**2**	**0**	**0**	**0**	**0**
1979-80	**Buffalo Sabres**	**NHL**	**80**	**14**	**29**	**43**	**13**	**22**	**35**	**30**	**0**	**0**	**0**	**137**	**10.2**	**65**	**4**	**69**	**30**	**+22**	**14**	**3**	**3**	**6**	**11**	**0**	**1**	**1**
1980-81	**Buffalo Sabres**	**NHL**	**61**	**15**	**13**	**28**	**12**	**9**	**21**	**19**	**0**	**4**	**2**	**94**	**16.0**	**38**	**0**	**47**	**23**	**+14**	....	....	....	....	....	....	....	....
	Los Angeles Kings	**NHL**	**10**	**1**	**0**	**1**	**1**	**0**	**1**	**2**	**0**	**0**	**0**	**8**	**12.5**	**1**	**0**	**10**	**5**	**–4**	**4**	**0**	**2**	**2**	**2**	**0**	**0**	**0**
1981-82	**Toronto Maple Leafs**	**NHL**	**39**	**4**	**4**	**8**	**3**	**3**	**6**	**32**	**0**	**1**	**0**	**36**	**11.1**	**12**	**0**	**37**	**18**	**–7**	....	....	....	....	....	....	....	....
	Salt Lake Golden Eagles	CHL	2	1	0	1	....	....	....	4				....	....	....	....	....	....	....	10	2	5	7	8	....	....	....
	NHL Totals		**894**	**225**	**329**	**554**	**215**	**266**	**481**	**364**	**22**	**26**	**30**	**1914**	**11.8**	**775**	**73**	**853**	**348**		**71**	**17**	**22**	**39**	**52**	**2**	**2**	**2**

CHL First All-Star Team (1970) • Won Bill Masterton Trophy (1975)

Played in NHL All-Star Game (1975)

Traded to **Detroit** by **NY Rangers** for Steve Andrascik, November 2, 1970. Traded to **Buffalo** by **Detroit** with Mike Robitaille for Joe Daly, May 25, 1971. Traded to **LA Kings** by **Buffalo** for LA Kings' 6th round choice (Jacob Gustavsson) in 1982 Entry Draft, March 10, 1981. Traded to **Toronto** by **LA Kings** for Bob Gladney and Toronto's 6th round choice (Joel Baillargeon) in 1983 Entry Draft, August 10, 1981.

• LUDVIG, JAN

Jan Ludvig　RW – R. 5'10", 190 lbs.　b: Liberec, Czech., 9/17/1961.

Season	Club	League	GP	G	A	Pts	AG	AA	APts	PIM	PP	SH	GW	S	%	TGF	PGF	TGA	PGA	+/–	GP	G	A	Pts	PIM	PP	SH	GW
1980-81	CHZ Litvinov	Czech.	3	0	0	0	....	....	....	0	....	....	....	....	....	....	....	....	....	....	....	....	....	....	....	....	....	....
1981-82	St. Albert Saints	AJHL	4	2	4	6	....	....	....	20	....	....	....	....	....	....	....	....	....	....	....	....	....	....	....	....	....	....
	Kamloops Jr. Oilers	WHL	37	31	34	65	....	....	....	36	....	....	....	....	....	....	....	....	....	....	4	2	0	2	7	....	....	....
	Wichita Wind	CHL	....	....	....	....	....	....	....	....	....	....	....	....	....	....	....	....	....	....	3	2	0	2	0	....	....	....
1982-83	**New Jersey Devils**	**NHL**	**51**	**7**	**10**	**17**	**6**	**7**	**13**	**30**	**2**	**0**	**0**	**103**	**6.8**	**33**	**11**	**49**	**0**	**–27**	....	....	....	....	....	....	....	....
	Wichita Wind	CHL	9	3	0	3	....	....	....	19	....	....	....	....	....	....	....	....	....	....	....	....	....	....	....	....	....	....
1983-84	**New Jersey Devils**	**NHL**	**74**	**22**	**32**	**54**	**18**	**22**	**40**	**70**	**7**	**0**	**2**	**176**	**12.5**	**76**	**31**	**65**	**2**	**–18**	....	....	....	....	....	....	....	....
1984-85	**New Jersey Devils**	**NHL**	**74**	**12**	**19**	**31**	**10**	**13**	**23**	**53**	**3**	**0**	**1**	**134**	**9.0**	**63**	**20**	**62**	**0**	**–19**	....	....	....	....	....	....	....	....
1985-86	**New Jersey Devils**	**NHL**	**42**	**5**	**9**	**14**	**4**	**6**	**10**	**63**	**0**	**0**	**0**	**72**	**6.9**	**22**	**7**	**31**	**0**	**–16**	....	....	....	....	....	....	....	....
1986-87	**New Jersey Devils**	**NHL**	**47**	**7**	**9**	**16**	**6**	**6**	**12**	**98**	**1**	**0**	**0**	**56**	**12.5**	**29**	**4**	**30**	**0**	**–5**	....	....	....	....	....	....	....	....
	Maine Mariners	AHL	14	6	4	10	....	....	....	46	....	....	....	....	....	....	....	....	....	....	....	....	....	....	....	....	....	....
1987-88	**Buffalo Sabres**	**NHL**	**13**	**1**	**6**	**7**	**1**	**4**	**5**	**65**	**0**	**0**	**0**	**13**	**7.7**	**11**	**2**	**8**	**0**	**+1**	....	....	....	....	....	....	....	....
1988-89	**Buffalo Sabres**	**NHL**	**13**	**0**	**2**	**2**	**0**	**1**	**1**	**39**	**0**	**0**	**0**	**11**	**0.0**	**6**	**0**	**7**	**0**	**–1**	....	....	....	....	....	....	....	....
	NHL Totals		**314**	**54**	**87**	**141**	**45**	**59**	**104**	**418**	**13**	**0**	**3**	**565**	**9.6**	**240**	**75**	**252**	**2**		....	....	....	....	....	....	....	....

EJC-A All-Star Team (1979) • Named Best Forward at EJC-A (1979)

Signed as a free agent by **New Jersey**, October 28, 1982. Traded to **Buffalo** by **New Jersey** for Jim Korn, May 22, 1987.

• LUDWIG, CRAIG

Craig Ludwig　D – L. 6'3", 220 lbs.　b: Rhinelander, WI, 3/15/1961.　Montreal's 5th choice, 61st overall, in 1980 Entry Draft.

Season	Club	League	GP	G	A	Pts	AG	AA	APts	PIM	PP	SH	GW	S	%	TGF	PGF	TGA	PGA	+/–	GP	G	A	Pts	PIM	PP	SH	GW
1979-80	University of North Dakota	WCHA	33	1	8	9	....	....	....	32	....	....	....	....	....	....	....	....	....	....	....	....	....	....	....	....	....	....
1980-81	University of North Dakota	WCHA	34	4	8	12	....	....	....	48	....	....	....	....	....	....	....	....	....	....	....	....	....	....	....	....	....	....
	United States	WJC-A	5	0	0	0	....	....	....	12	....	....	....	....	....	....	....	....	....	....	....	....	....	....	....	....	....	....
1981-82	University of North Dakota	WCHA	37	4	17	21	....	....	....	42	....	....	....	....	....	....	....	....	....	....	....	....	....	....	....	....	....	....
1982-83	**Montreal Canadiens**	**NHL**	**80**	**0**	**25**	**25**	**0**	**17**	**17**	**59**	**0**	**0**	**0**	**81**	**0.0**	**92**	**8**	**105**	**25**	**+4**	**3**	**0**	**0**	**0**	**2**	**0**	**0**	**0**
1983-84	**Montreal Canadiens**	**NHL**	**80**	**7**	**18**	**25**	**6**	**12**	**18**	**52**	**0**	**0**	**1**	**116**	**6.0**	**103**	**6**	**147**	**40**	**–10**	**15**	**0**	**3**	**3**	**23**	**0**	**0**	**0**
1984-85	**Montreal Canadiens**	**NHL**	**72**	**5**	**14**	**19**	**4**	**9**	**13**	**90**	**1**	**0**	**0**	**73**	**6.8**	**76**	**3**	**101**	**33**	**+5**	**12**	**0**	**2**	**2**	**6**	**0**	**0**	**0**
1985-86	**Montreal Canadiens**	**NHL**	**69**	**2**	**4**	**6**	**2**	**3**	**5**	**63**	**0**	**0**	**0**	**58**	**3.4**	**67**	**0**	**103**	**43**	**+7**	**20**	**0**	**1**	**1**	**48**	**0**	**0**	**0**
1986-87	**Montreal Canadiens**	**NHL**	**75**	**4**	**12**	**16**	**3**	**9**	**12**	**105**	**0**	**0**	**0**	**55**	**7.3**	**63**	**0**	**72**	**12**	**+3**	**17**	**2**	**3**	**5**	**30**	**0**	**0**	**1**
1987-88	**Montreal Canadiens**	**NHL**	**74**	**4**	**10**	**14**	**3**	**7**	**10**	**69**	**0**	**0**	**0**	**82**	**4.9**	**66**	**1**	**83**	**35**	**+17**	**11**	**1**	**1**	**2**	**6**	**0**	**0**	**0**
1988-89	**Montreal Canadiens**	**NHL**	**74**	**3**	**13**	**16**	**3**	**9**	**12**	**73**	**0**	**1**	**1**	**83**	**3.6**	**94**	**3**	**97**	**39**	**+33**	**21**	**0**	**2**	**2**	**24**	**0**	**0**	**0**
1989-90	**Montreal Canadiens**	**NHL**	**73**	**1**	**15**	**16**	**1**	**11**	**12**	**108**	**0**	**0**	**0**	**49**	**2.0**	**73**	**0**	**81**	**32**	**+24**	**11**	**0**	**1**	**1**	**16**	**0**	**0**	**0**
1990-91	**New York Islanders**	**NHL**	**75**	**1**	**8**	**9**	**1**	**6**	**7**	**77**	**0**	**0**	**0**	**46**	**2.2**	**46**	**0**	**108**	**38**	**–24**	....	....	....	....	....	....	....	....
1991-92	**Minnesota North Stars**	**NHL**	**73**	**2**	**0**	**11**	**2**	**7**	**9**	**54**	**0**	**0**	**0**	**51**	**3.9**	**45**	**0**	**85**	**40**	**0**	**7**	**0**	**1**	**1**	**19**	**0**	**0**	**0**
1992-93	**Minnesota North Stars**	**NHL**	**78**	**1**	**10**	**11**	**1**	**7**	**8**	**153**	**0**	**0**	**0**	**66**	**1.5**	**68**	**1**	**95**	**29**	**+1**	....	....	....	....	....	....	....	....
1993-94	**Dallas Stars**	**NHL**	**84**	**1**	**13**	**14**	**1**	**10**	**11**	**123**	**1**	**0**	**0**	**65**	**1.5**	**65**	**1**	**100**	**36**	**–1**	**9**	**0**	**3**	**3**	**8**	**0**	**0**	**0**
1994-95	**Dallas Stars**	**NHL**	**47**	**2**	**7**	**9**	**4**	**10**	**14**	**61**	**0**	**0**	**0**	**55**	**3.6**	**34**	**0**	**60**	**20**	**–6**	**4**	**0**	**1**	**1**	**2**	**0**	**0**	**0**

			REGULAR SEASON																		PLAYOFFS							
Season	Club	League	GP	G	A	Pts	AG	AA	APts	PIM	PP	SH	GW	S	%	TGF	PGF	TGA	PGA	+/–	GP	G	A	Pts	PIM	PP	SH	GW
1995-96	Dallas Stars	NHL	65	1	2	3	1	2	3	70	0	0	0	47	2.1	28	0	72	27	–17	....	....	....	....	....	....	....	....
1996-97	Dallas Stars	NHL	77	2	11	13	2	10	12	62	0	0	1	59	3.4	60	0	60	17	+17	7	0	2	2	18	0	0	0
1997-98	Dallas Stars	NHL	80	0	7	7	0	7	7	131	0	0	0	46	0.0	45	0	39	15	+21	17	0	1	1	22	0	0	0
	NHL Totals		1176	36	178	214	34	136	170	1350	2	1	3	1032	3.5	1025	23	1408	480		154	3	21	24	224	0	0	1

WCHA Second All-Star Team (1982)

Traded to **NY Islanders** by **Montreal** for Gerald Diduck, September 4, 1990. Traded to **Minnesota** by **NY Islanders** for Tom Kurvers, June 22, 1991. Transferred to **Dallas** after **Minnesota** franchise relocated, June 9, 1993.

● LUDZIK, STEVE

Steve Ludzik C – L. 5′11″, 185 lbs. b: Toronto, Ont., 4/3/1962. Chicago's 3rd choice, 28th overall, in 1980 Entry Draft.

Season	Club	League	GP	G	A	Pts	AG	AA	APts	PIM	PP	SH	GW	S	%	TGF	PGF	TGA	PGA	+/–	GP	G	A	Pts	PIM	PP	SH	GW
1977-78	Markham Waxers	OJHL	34	15	24	39	....	....	....	20	....	....	....	....	....	....	....	....	....	....	....	....	....	....	....	....	....	....
1978-79	Niagara Falls Flyers	OHA	68	32	65	97	....	....	....	138	....	....	....	....	....	....	....	....	....	....	....	....	....	....	....	....	....	....
1979-80	Niagara Falls Flyers	OHA	67	43	76	119	....	....	....	102	....	....	....	....	....	....	....	....	....	....	10	6	6	12	16	....	....	....
1980-81	Niagara Falls Flyers	OHA	58	50	92	142	....	....	....	108	....	....	....	....	....	....	....	....	....	....	12	5	9	14	40	....	....	....
1981-82	Chicago Black Hawks	NHL	8	2	1	3	2	1	3	2	0	0	0	9	22.2	4	0	3	0	+1	....	....	....	....	....	....	....	....
	New Brunswick Hawks	AHL	73	21	41	62	....	....	....	142	....	....	....	....	....	....	....	....	....	....	15	3	7	10	6	....	....	....
1982-83	Chicago Black Hawks	NHL	66	6	19	25	5	13	18	63	0	0	0	56	10.7	34	1	27	1	+7	13	3	5	8	20	0	0	0
1983-84	Chicago Black Hawks	NHL	80	9	20	29	7	14	21	73	0	0	0	102	8.8	44	4	49	4	–5	4	0	1	1	9	0	0	0
1984-85	Chicago Black Hawks	NHL	79	11	20	31	9	14	23	86	0	1	1	100	11.0	44	0	63	24	+5	15	1	1	2	16	0	0	0
1985-86	Chicago Black Hawks	NHL	49	6	5	11	5	3	8	21	0	1	0	41	14.6	19	0	39	18	–2	3	0	0	0	12	0	0	0
1986-87	Chicago Blackhawks	NHL	52	5	12	17	4	9	13	34	0	0	1	56	8.9	23	0	51	25	–3	4	0	0	0	0	0	0	0
1987-88	Chicago Blackhawks	NHL	73	6	15	21	5	11	16	40	1	0	1	55	10.9	28	4	58	20	–14	5	0	1	1	13	0	0	0
1988-89	Chicago Blackhawks	NHL	6	1	0	1	1	0	1	8	0	0	0	7	14.3	2	0	3	1	0	....	....	....	....	....	....	....	....
	Saginaw Hawks	IHL	65	21	57	78	....	....	....	129	....	....	....	....	....	....	....	....	....	....	6	0	1	1	17	....	....	....
1989-90	Buffalo Sabres	NHL	11	0	1	1	0	1	1	6	0	0	0	15	0.0	1	0	3	0	–2	....	....	....	....	....	....	....	....
	Rochester Americans	AHL	54	25	29	54	....	....	....	71	....	....	....	....	....	....	....	....	....	....	16	5	6	11	57	....	....	....
1990-91	Rochester Americans	AHL	65	22	29	51	....	....	....	137	....	....	....	....	....	....	....	....	....	....	8	3	5	8	6	....	....	....
1991-92	Rochester Americans	AHL	45	6	22	28	....	....	....	88	....	....	....	....	....	....	....	....	....	....	14	2	1	3	8	....	....	....
	NHL Totals		424	46	93	139	38	66	104	333	1	2	3	441	10.4	199	9	296	93		44	4	8	12	70	0	0	0

Traded to **Buffalo** by **Chicago** with Buffalo's 6th round choice (Derek Edgerly) in 1990 Entry Draft for Jacques Cloutier and Chicago's 5th round choice (Todd Bojcun) in 1990 Entry Draft, September 28, 1989.

● LUHNING, WARREN

Warren Luhning RW – R. 6′2″, 185 lbs. b: Edmonton, Alta., 7/3/1975. NY Islanders' 4th choice, 92nd overall, in 1993 Entry Draft.

Season	Club	League	GP	G	A	Pts	AG	AA	APts	PIM	PP	SH	GW	S	%	TGF	PGF	TGA	PGA	+/–	GP	G	A	Pts	PIM	PP	SH	GW
1992-93	Calgary Royals	AJHL	46	18	25	43	....	....	....	287	....	....	....	....	....	....	....	....	....	....	....	....	....	....	....	....	....	....
1993-94	University of Michigan	CCHA	38	13	6	19	....	....	....	83	....	....	....	....	....	....	....	....	....	....	....	....	....	....	....	....	....	....
1994-95	University of Michigan	CCHA	36	17	23	40	....	....	....	80	....	....	....	....	....	....	....	....	....	....	....	....	....	....	....	....	....	....
1995-96	University of Michigan	CCHA	40	20	32	52	....	....	....	123	....	....	....	....	....	....	....	....	....	....	....	....	....	....	....	....	....	....
1996-97	University of Michigan	CCHA	43	22	23	45	....	....	....	106	....	....	....	....	....	....	....	....	....	....	....	....	....	....	....	....	....	....
1997-98	New York Islanders	NHL	8	0	0	0	0	0	0	0	0	0	0	6	0.0	0	0	4	0	–4	....	....	....	....	....	....	....	....
	Kentucky Thoroughblades	AHL	51	6	7	13	....	....	....	82	....	....	....	....	....	....	....	....	....	....	....	....	....	....	....	....	....	....
	NHL Totals		8	0	0	0	0	0	0	0	0	0	0	6	0.0	0	0	4	0		....	....	....	....	....	....	....	....

● LUKOWICH, BERNIE

Bernie Lukowich RW – R. 6′, 190 lbs. b: North Battleford, Sask., 3/18/1952. Pittsburgh's 2nd choice, 30th overall, in 1972 Amateur Draft.

Season	Club	League	GP	G	A	Pts	AG	AA	APts	PIM	PP	SH	GW	S	%	TGF	PGF	TGA	PGA	+/–	GP	G	A	Pts	PIM	PP	SH	GW
1968-69	Estevan Bruins	WCJHL	3	0	0	0	....	....	....	0	....	....	....	....	....	....	....	....	....	....	....	....	....	....	....	....	....	....
1969-70	Estevan Bruins	WCJHL	60	23	31	54	....	....	....	47	....	....	....	....	....	....	....	....	....	....	5	0	0	0	6	....	....	....
1970-71	Estevan Bruins	WCJHL	65	36	38	74	....	....	....	75	....	....	....	....	....	....	....	....	....	....	7	5	3	8	2	....	....	....
1971-72	New Westminster Bruins	WCJHL	68	37	39	76	....	....	....	107	....	....	....	....	....	....	....	....	....	....	5	3	0	3	4	....	....	....
1972-73	Hershey Bears	AHL	69	22	23	45	....	....	....	64	....	....	....	....	....	....	....	....	....	....	7	0	2	2	26	....	....	....
1973-74	Pittsburgh Penguins	NHL	53	9	10	19	9	9	18	32	1	0	2	60	15.0	26	2	28	0	–4	....	....	....	....	....	....	....	....
	Hershey Bears	AHL	17	4	5	9	....	....	....	12	....	....	....	....	....	....	....	....	....	....	....	....	....	....	....	....	....	....
1974-75	Hershey Bears	AHL	27	9	14	23	....	....	....	53	....	....	....	....	....	....	....	....	....	....	....	....	....	....	....	....	....	....
	St. Louis Blues	NHL	26	4	5	9	4	4	8	2	2	0	2	19	21.1	14	3	8	1	+4	2	0	0	0	0	0	0	0
	Denver Spurs	CHL	7	6	6	12	....	....	....	8	....	....	....	....	....	....	....	....	....	....	....	....	....	....	....	....	....	....
1975-76	Providence Reds	AHL	64	21	17	38	....	....	....	62	....	....	....	....	....	....	....	....	....	....	....	....	....	....	....	....	....	....
	Calgary Cowboys	WHA	15	5	2	7	....	....	....	18	....	....	....	....	....	....	....	....	....	....	10	3	4	7	8	....	....	....
1976-77	Hershey Bears	AHL	37	15	18	33	....	....	....	19	....	....	....	....	....	....	....	....	....	....	6	1	1	2	4	....	....	....
	Tidewater Sharks	SHL	29	13	15	28	....	....	....	4	....	....	....	....	....	....	....	....	....	....	....	....	....	....	....	....	....	....
	Calgary Cowboys	WHA	6	0	1	1	....	....	....	0	....	....	....	....	....	....	....	....	....	....	....	....	....	....	....	....	....	....
1977-78	Cranbrook Royals	WIHL	....	10	25	35	....	....	....	30	....	....	....	....	....	....	....	....	....	....	....	....	....	....	....	....	....	....
1978-79			DID NOT PLAY – RETIRED																									
1979-80			DID NOT PLAY – RETIRED																									
1980-81	Cranbrook Royals	WIHL	34	15	12	27	....	....	....	29	....	....	....	....	....	....	....	....	....	....	....	....	....	....	....	....	....	....
1981-82	Cranbrook Royals	WIHL	32	10	22	32	....	....	....	35	....	....	....	....	....	....	....	....	....	....	....	....	....	....	....	....	....	....
	NHL Totals		79	13	15	28	13	13	26	34	3	0	4	79	16.5	40	5	36	1		2	0	0	0	0	0	0	0
	Other Major League Totals		6	0	1	1	....	....	....	0	....	....	....	....	....	....	....	....	....		....	....	....	....	....	....	....	....

Selected by **Calgary-Cleveland** (WHA) in 1972 WHA General Player Draft, February 12, 1972. Traded to **St. Louis** by **Pittsburgh** for Bob Stumpf, January 20, 1975. Signed as a free agent by **Calgary** (WHA), March, 1977.

● LUKOWICH, BRAD

Brad Lukowich D – L. 6′1″, 170 lbs. b: Cranbrook, B.C., 8/12/1976. NY Islanders' 4th choice, 90th overall, in 1994 Entry Draft.

Season	Club	League	GP	G	A	Pts	AG	AA	APts	PIM	PP	SH	GW	S	%	TGF	PGF	TGA	PGA	+/–	GP	G	A	Pts	PIM	PP	SH	GW
1992-93	Kamloops Blazers	WHL	1	0	0	0	....	....	....	0	....	....	....	....	....	....	....	....	....	....	....	....	....	....	....	....	....	....
1993-94	Kamloops Blazers	WHL	42	5	11	16	....	....	....	166	....	....	....	....	....	....	....	....	....	....	16	0	1	1	35	....	....	....
1994-95	Kamloops Blazers	WHL	63	10	35	45	....	....	....	125	....	....	....	....	....	....	....	....	....	....	18	0	7	7	21	....	....	....
1995-96	Kamloops Blazers	WHL	65	14	55	69	....	....	....	114	....	....	....	....	....	....	....	....	....	....	13	2	10	12	29	....	....	....
1996-97	Michigan K-Wings	IHL	69	2	6	8	....	....	....	77	....	....	....	....	....	....	....	....	....	....	4	0	1	1	2	....	....	....
1997-98	Dallas Stars	NHL	4	0	1	1	0	1	1	2	0	0	0	2	0.0	1	0	3	0	–2	....	....	....	....	....	....	....	....
	Michigan K-Wings	IHL	60	6	27	33	....	....	....	104	....	....	....	....	....	....	....	....	....	....	4	0	4	4	14	....	....	....
	NHL Totals		4	0	1	1	0	1	1	2	0	0	0	2	0.0	1	0	3	0		....	....	....	....	....	....	....	....

Traded to **Dallas** by **NY Islanders** for Dallas' 3rd round choice (Robert Schnabel) in 1997 Entry Draft, June 1, 1996.

● LUKOWICH, MORRIS

Morris Lukowich LW – L. 5′9″, 170 lbs. b: Speers, Sask., 6/1/1956. Pittsburgh's 4th choice, 47th overall, in 1976 Amateur Draft.

Season	Club	League	GP	G	A	Pts	AG	AA	APts	PIM	PP	SH	GW	S	%	TGF	PGF	TGA	PGA	+/–	GP	G	A	Pts	PIM	PP	SH	GW
1973-74	Medicine Hat Tigers	WCJHL	65	13	14	27	....	....	....	55	....	....	....	....	....	....	....	....	....	....	....	....	....	....	....	....	....	....
1974-75	Medicine Hat Tigers	WCJHL	70	40	54	94	....	....	....	111	....	....	....	....	....	....	....	....	....	....	5	4	1	5	2	....	....	....
1975-76	Medicine Hat Tigers	WCJHL	72	65	77	142	....	....	....	195	....	....	....	....	....	....	....	....	....	....	9	5	8	13	20	....	....	....
1976-77	Houston Aeros	WHA	62	27	18	45	....	....	....	67	....	....	....	....	....	....	....	....	....	....	11	6	4	10	19	....	....	....
1977-78	Houston Aeros	WHA	80	40	35	75	....	....	....	131	....	....	....	....	....	....	....	....	....	....	6	1	2	3	17	....	....	....
1978-79	Winnipeg Jets	WHA	80	65	34	99	....	....	....	119	....	....	....	....	....	....	....	....	....	....	10	8	7	15	21	....	....	....
1979-80	Winnipeg Jets	NHL	78	35	39	74	32	30	62	77	13	1	2	201	17.4	105	42	93	14	–16	....	....	....	....	....	....	....	....
1980-81	Winnipeg Jets	NHL	80	33	34	67	27	24	51	90	9	2	2	175	18.9	104	35	136	28	–39	....	....	....	....	....	....	....	....
	Canada	WEC-A	8	2	1	3	....	....	....	4	....	....	....	....	....	....	....	....	....	....	....	....	....	....	....	....	....	....
1981-82	Winnipeg Jets	NHL	77	43	49	92	34	32	66	102	13	0	6	229	18.8	121	39	94	8	–4	4	0	2	2	16	0	0	0
1982-83	Winnipeg Jets	NHL	69	22	21	43	18	14	32	67	6	0	2	162	13.6	62	23	67	0	–28	....	....	....	....	....	....	....	....
1983-84	Winnipeg Jets	NHL	80	30	25	55	24	17	41	71	4	0	1	155	19.4	94	23	61	0	+10	3	0	0	0	0	0	0	0
1984-85	Winnipeg Jets	NHL	47	5	9	14	4	6	10	31	1	0	2	37	13.5	25	8	32	2	–13	....	....	....	....	....	....	....	....
	Boston Bruins	NHL	22	5	8	13	4	5	9	21	0	0	1	29	17.2	20	2	12	1	+7	1	0	0	0	0	0	0	0

			REGULAR SEASON																		PLAYOFFS							
Season	Club	League	GP	G	A	Pts	AG	AA	APts	PIM	PP	SH	GW	S	%	TGF	PGF	TGA	PGA	+/-	GP	G	A	Pts	PIM	PP	SH	GW
1985-86	**Boston Bruins**	**NHL**	**14**	**1**	**4**	**5**	**1**	**3**	**4**	**10**	**0**	**0**	**0**	**25**	**4.0**	**10**	**1**	**7**	**0**	**+2**								
	Los Angeles Kings	**NHL**	**55**	**11**	**9**	**20**	**9**	**6**	**15**	**51**	**0**	**0**	**0**	**85**	**12.9**	**41**	**10**	**51**	**1**	**–19**								
1986-87	**Los Angeles Kings**	**NHL**	**60**	**14**	**21**	**35**	**12**	**15**	**27**	**64**	**4**	**0**	**2**	**105**	**13.3**	**69**	**32**	**37**	**0**	**0**	**3**	**0**	**0**	**0**	**8**	**0**	**0**	**0**
	NHL Totals		**582**	**199**	**219**	**418**	**165**	**152**	**317**	**584**	**50**	**3**	**18**	**1203**	**16.5**	**651**	**215**	**590**	**54**		**11**	**0**	**2**	**2**	**24**	**0**	**0**	**0**
	Other Major League Totals		222	132	87	219				317											27	15	13	28	57			

WCJHL All Star Team (1976) • WHA Second All-Star Team (1979)

Played in NHL All-Star Game (1980, 1981)

Selected by **Houston** (WHA) in 1976 WHA Amateur Draft, May, 1976. Traded to **Winnipeg** (WHA) by **Houston** (WHA) for cash, July, 1978. Reclaimed by **Pittsburgh** from **Winnipeg** prior to Expansion Draft, June 9, 1979. Claimed as a priority selection by **Winnipeg**, June 9, 1979. Traded to **Boston** by **Winnipeg** for Jim Nill, February 4, 1985. Claimed on waivers by **LA Kings** from **Boston**, November 15, 1985.

• LUKSA, CHARLIE

Charlie "Chuck" Luksa D – L. 6'1", 190 lbs. b: Toronto, Ont., 2/19/1954. Montreal's 15th choice, 172nd overall, in 1974 Amateur Draft.

Season	Club	League	GP	G	A	Pts	AG	AA	APts	PIM	PP	SH	GW	S	%	TGF	PGF	TGA	PGA	+/-	GP	G	A	Pts	PIM	PP	SH	GW
1971-72	Oshawa Generals	OHA	1	0	0	0				0																		
1972-73	Kenora Huskies	MJHL	47	7	37	44				119																		
1973-74	University of Toronto	OUAA	22	3	19	22				50																		
	Kitchener Rangers	OHA		2	7	9																						
1974-75	Nova Scotia Voyageurs	AHL	32	0	4	4				54											6	1	0	1	5			
1975-76	Nova Scotia Voyageurs	AHL	73	5	13	18				75											9	0	2	2	6			
1976-77	Nova Scotia Voyageurs	AHL	80	9	31	40				72											12	1	5	6	7			
1977-78	Nova Scotia Voyageurs	AHL	66	3	23	26				89											11	1	4	5	25			
1978-79	Cincinnati Stingers	WHA	78	8	12	20				116											3	0	0	0	7			
1979-80	**Hartford Whalers**	**NHL**	**8**	**0**	**1**	**1**	**0**	**1**	**1**	**4**	**0**	**0**	**0**	**3**	**0.0**	**6**	**0**	**8**	**2**	**0**								
	Springfield Indians	AHL	72	10	39	49				83																		
1980-81	Binghamton Whalers	AHL	63	3	18	21				104											6	0	2	2	12			
1981-82	Rochester Americans	AHL	33	2	8	10				33											6	0	2	2	4			
	NHL Totals		**8**	**0**	**1**	**1**	**0**	**1**	**1**	**4**	**0**	**0**	**0**	**3**	**0.0**	**6**	**0**	**8**	**2**									
	Other Major League Totals		78	8	12	20				116											3	0	0	0	7			

AHL Second All-Star Team (1978)

Selected by **Phoenix** (WHA) in 1974 WHA Amateur Draft, May, 1974. Signed as a free agent by **Cincinnati** (WHA) after **Phoenix** (WHA) franchise folded, July, 1978. Claimed by **Hartford** from **Cincinnati** (WHA) in WHA Dispersal Draft, June 9, 1979.

• LUMLEY, DAVE

Dave Lumley RW – R. 6', 185 lbs. b: Toronto, Ont., 9/1/1954. Montreal's 17th choice, 199th overall, in 1974 Amateur Draft.

Season	Club	League	GP	G	A	Pts	AG	AA	APts	PIM	PP	SH	GW	S	%	TGF	PGF	TGA	PGA	+/-	GP	G	A	Pts	PIM	PP	SH	GW
1973-74	University of New Hampshire	ECAC	31	12	19	31				38																		
1974-75	University of New Hampshire	ECAC	26	12	26	38				56																		
1975-76	University of New Hampshire	ECAC	30	9	32	41				55																		
1976-77	University of New Hampshire	ECAC	39	22	38	60				42																		
1977-78	Nova Scotia Voyageurs	AHL	58	22	21	43				58											2	0	1	1	5			
1978-79	**Montreal Canadiens**	**NHL**	**3**	**0**	**0**	**0**	**0**	**0**	**0**	**0**	**0**	**0**	**0**	**2**	**0.0**	**0**	**0**	**0**	**0**	**0**								
	Nova Scotia Voyageurs	AHL	61	22	58	80				160											10	6	8	14	35			
1979-80	**Edmonton Oilers**	**NHL**	**80**	**20**	**38**	**58**	**18**	**29**	**47**	**138**	**1**	**0**	**6**	**145**	**13.8**	**88**	**13**	**62**	**2**	**+15**	**3**	**1**	**0**	**1**	**12**	**1**	**0**	**0**
1980-81	**Edmonton Oilers**	**NHL**	**53**	**7**	**9**	**16**	**6**	**6**	**12**	**74**	**0**	**0**	**1**	**54**	**13.0**	**30**	**4**	**43**	**2**	**–15**	**7**	**1**	**0**	**1**	**4**	**0**	**0**	**0**
1981-82	**Edmonton Oilers**	**NHL**	**66**	**32**	**42**	**74**	**25**	**28**	**53**	**96**	**4**	**1**	**6**	**148**	**21.6**	**109**	**21**	**87**	**11**	**+12**	**5**	**2**	**1**	**3**	**21**	**0**	**0**	**0**
1982-83	**Edmonton Oilers**	**NHL**	**72**	**13**	**24**	**37**	**11**	**17**	**28**	**158**	**2**	**0**	**1**	**96**	**13.5**	**68**	**8**	**41**	**0**	**+19**	**16**	**0**	**0**	**0**	**19**	**0**	**0**	**0**
1983-84	**Edmonton Oilers**	**NHL**	**56**	**6**	**15**	**21**	**5**	**10**	**15**	**68**	**0**	**0**	**0**	**44**	**13.6**	**47**	**2**	**31**	**0**	**+14**	**19**	**2**	**5**	**7**	**44**	**0**	**0**	**0**
1984-85	**Hartford Whalers**	**NHL**	**48**	**8**	**20**	**28**	**7**	**14**	**21**	**98**	**1**	**0**	**0**	**77**	**10.4**	**41**	**6**	**62**	**10**	**–17**								
	Edmonton Oilers	**NHL**	**12**	**1**	**3**	**4**	**1**	**2**	**3**	**13**	**0**	**0**	**0**	**10**	**10.0**	**5**	**2**	**4**	**0**	**–1**	**8**	**0**	**0**	**0**	**29**	**0**	**0**	**0**
1985-86	**Edmonton Oilers**	**NHL**	**46**	**11**	**9**	**20**	**9**	**6**	**15**	**35**	**1**	**0**	**1**	**33**	**33.3**	**31**	**1**	**17**	**0**	**+13**	**3**	**0**	**2**	**2**	**2**	**0**	**0**	**0**
1986-87	**Edmonton Oilers**	**NHL**	**1**	**0**	**0**	**0**	**0**	**0**	**0**	**0**	**0**	**0**	**0**	**0**	**0.0**	**1**	**0**	**1**	**0**	**0**								
	NHL Totals		**437**	**98**	**160**	**258**	**82**	**112**	**194**	**680**	**9**	**1**	**15**	**609**	**16.1**	**420**	**57**	**348**	**25**		**61**	**6**	**8**	**14**	**131**	**1**	**0**	**0**

AHL Second All-Star Team (1978)

Traded to **Edmonton** by **Montreal** with Dan Newman for Edmonton's 2nd round choice (Ric Nattress) in 1980 Entry Draft, June 13, 1979. Claimed by **Hartford** from **Edmonton** in Waiver Draft, October 9, 1984. Claimed on waivers by **Edmonton** from **Hartford**, February 6, 1985.

• LUMME, JYRKI

Jyrki Lumme D – L. 6'1", 205 lbs. b: Tampere, Finland, 7/16/1966. Montreal's 3rd choice, 57th overall, in 1986 Entry Draft.

Season	Club	League	GP	G	A	Pts	AG	AA	APts	PIM	PP	SH	GW	S	%	TGF	PGF	TGA	PGA	+/-	GP	G	A	Pts	PIM	PP	SH	GW
1984-85	KooVee	Finland	30	6	4	10				44																		
1985-86	Ilves Tampere	Finland	31	1	4	5				4																		
	Finland	WJC-A	7	1	4	5				2																		
1986-87	Ilves Tampere	Finland	43	12	12	24				52											4	0	1	1	2			
1987-88	Ilves Tampere	Finland	43	8	22	30				75																		
	Finland	Olympics	6	0	1	1				2																		
1988-89	**Montreal Canadiens**	**NHL**	**21**	**1**	**3**	**4**	**1**	**2**	**3**	**10**	**1**	**0**	**0**	**18**	**5.6**	**21**	**8**	**12**	**2**	**+3**								
	Sherbrooke Canadiens	AHL	26	4	11	15				10											6	1	3	4	4			
1989-90	**Montreal Canadiens**	**NHL**	**54**	**1**	**19**	**20**	**1**	**14**	**15**	**41**	**0**	**0**	**0**	**79**	**1.3**	**64**	**13**	**39**	**5**	**+17**								
	Vancouver Canucks	**NHL**	**11**	**3**	**7**	**10**	**3**	**5**	**8**	**8**	**0**	**0**	**1**	**30**	**10.0**	**21**	**10**	**11**	**0**	**0**								
	Finland	WEC-A	10	3	4	7				6																		
1990-91	**Vancouver Canucks**	**NHL**	**80**	**5**	**27**	**32**	**5**	**20**	**25**	**59**	**1**	**0**	**0**	**157**	**3.2**	**91**	**25**	**96**	**15**	**–15**	**6**	**2**	**3**	**5**	**0**	**1**	**1**	**0**
	Finland	WEC-A	10	0	7	7				12																		
1991-92	Finland	C Cup	6	0	2	2				8																		
	Vancouver Canucks	**NHL**	**75**	**12**	**32**	**44**	**11**	**24**	**35**	**65**	**3**	**1**	**1**	**106**	**11.3**	**125**	**45**	**77**	**22**	**+25**	**13**	**2**	**3**	**5**	**4**	**1**	**0**	**1**
1992-93	**Vancouver Canucks**	**NHL**	**74**	**8**	**36**	**44**	**7**	**25**	**32**	**66**	**3**	**2**	**1**	**123**	**6.5**	**110**	**29**	**80**	**29**	**+30**	**12**	**0**	**5**	**5**	**6**	**0**	**0**	**0**
1993-94	**Vancouver Canucks**	**NHL**	**83**	**13**	**42**	**55**	**12**	**32**	**44**	**50**	**1**	**3**	**3**	**161**	**8.1**	**107**	**34**	**117**	**47**	**+3**	**24**	**2**	**11**	**13**	**16**	**2**	**0**	**1**
1994-95	Ilves	Finland	12	4	4	8				24																		
	Vancouver Canucks	**NHL**	**36**	**5**	**12**	**17**	**9**	**18**	**27**	**26**	**3**	**0**	**1**	**78**	**6.4**	**47**	**13**	**41**	**11**	**+4**	**11**	**2**	**6**	**8**	**8**	**1**	**0**	**0**
1995-96	**Vancouver Canucks**	**NHL**	**80**	**17**	**37**	**54**	**17**	**30**	**47**	**50**	**8**	**0**	**2**	**192**	**8.9**	**109**	**43**	**119**	**44**	**–9**	**6**	**1**	**3**	**4**	**2**	**1**	**0**	**0**
	Finland	WC-A	1	0	0	0				0																		
1996-97	Finland	W Cup	4	2	1	3				4																		
	Vancouver Canucks	**NHL**	**66**	**11**	**24**	**35**	**12**	**21**	**33**	**32**	**5**	**0**	**2**	**107**	**10.3**	**82**	**25**	**75**	**26**	**+8**								
	Finland	WC-A	8	0	3	3				4																		
1997-98	**Vancouver Canucks**	**NHL**	**74**	**9**	**21**	**30**	**11**	**20**	**31**	**34**	**4**	**0**	**1**	**117**	**7.7**	**66**	**20**	**117**	**34**	**–25**								
	Finland	Olympics	6	1	0	1				16																		
	NHL Totals		**654**	**85**	**260**	**345**	**89**	**211**	**300**	**430**	**29**	**6**	**12**	**1168**	**7.3**	**863**	**273**	**784**	**235**		**72**	**9**	**31**	**40**	**36**	**6**	**1**	**2**

Traded to **Vancouver** by **Montreal** for St. Louis' 2nd round choice (previously acquired, Montreal selected Craig Darby) in 1991 Entry Draft, March 6, 1990. Signed as a free agent by **Phoenix**, July 3, 1998.

• LUNDBERG, BRIAN

Brian Lundberg D – R. 5'10", 190 lbs. b: Burnaby, B.C., 6/5/1960. Pittsburgh's 7th choice, 177th overall, in 1980 Entry Draft.

Season	Club	League	GP	G	A	Pts	AG	AA	APts	PIM	PP	SH	GW	S	%	TGF	PGF	TGA	PGA	+/-	GP	G	A	Pts	PIM	PP	SH	GW
1977-78	Seattle Breakers	WCJHL	1	0	0	0				0																		
1978-79	University of Michigan	CCHA	DID NOT PLAY – FRESHMAN																									
1979-80	University of Michigan	CCHA	37	2	14	16				94																		
1980-81	University of Michigan	CCHA	40	1	6	7				42																		
1981-82	University of Michigan	CCHA	32	3	16	19				42																		
	Erie Blades	AHL	10	0	4	4				6																		
1982-83	**Pittsburgh Penguins**	**NHL**	**1**	**0**	**0**	**0**	**0**	**0**	**0**	**2**	**0**	**0**	**0**	**0**	**0.0**	**0**	**0**	**1**	**0**	**–1**								
	Baltimore Skipjacks	AHL	79	4	15	19				103																		
1983-84	Muskegon Mohawks	IHL	34	3	12	15				46																		
	Baltimore Skipjacks	AHL	47	1	5	6				97											10	0	3	3	8			
	NHL Totals		**1**	**0**	**0**	**0**	**0**	**0**	**0**	**2**	**0**	**0**	**0**	**0**	**0.0**	**0**	**0**	**1**	**0**									

• LUNDE, LEN

Len Lunde C – R. 6'1", 194 lbs. b: Campbell River, B.C., 11/13/1936.

			REGULAR SEASON																		PLAYOFFS							
Season	Club	League	GP	G	A	Pts	AG	AA	APts	PIM	PP	SH	GW	S	%	TGF	PGF	TGA	PGA	+/–	GP	G	A	Pts	PIM	PP	SH	GW
1953-54	Edmonton Oil Kings	WCJHL	3	0	0	0	....	....	....	0	....	....	....	....	....	....	....	....	....	....	....	....	....	....	....	....	....	....
1954-55	Edmonton Oil Kings	WCJHL	35	28	18	46	....	....	....	37	....	....	....	....	....	....	....	....	....	....	4	3	2	5	0	....	....	....
1955-56	Edmonton Oil Kings	WCJHL	35	37	30	67	....	....	....	27	....	....	....	....	....	....	....	....	....	....	6	2	2	4	2	....	....	....
	Edmonton Flyers	WHL	4	0	2	2	....	....	....	2	....	....	....	....	....	....	....	....	....	....	2	0	1	1	0	....	....	....
1956-57	Edmonton Flyers	WHL	70	20	41	61	....	....	....	22	....	....	....	....	....	....	....	....	....	....	8	3	5	8	2	....	....	....
1957-58	Edmonton Flyers	WHL	67	39	43	82	....	....	....	17	....	....	....	....	....	....	....	....	....	....	5	1	4	5	2	....	....	....
1958-59	**Detroit Red Wings**	**NHL**	**68**	**14**	**12**	**26**	**18**	**13**	**31**	**15**	....	....	....	....	....	....	....	....	....	....	....	....	....	....	....	....	....	....
1959-60	**Detroit Red Wings**	**NHL**	**66**	**6**	**17**	**23**	**7**	**17**	**24**	**10**	....	....	....	....	....	....	....	....	....	....	**6**	**1**	**2**	**3**	**0**	....	....	....
1960-61	**Detroit Red Wings**	**NHL**	**53**	**6**	**12**	**18**	**7**	**12**	**19**	**10**	....	....	....	....	....	....	....	....	....	....	**10**	**2**	**0**	**2**	**0**	....	....	....
1961-62	**Detroit Red Wings**	**NHL**	**23**	**2**	**9**	**11**	**2**	**9**	**11**	**4**	....	....	....	....	....	....	....	....	....	....	....	....	....	....	....	....	....	....
	Edmonton Flyers	WHL	41	26	37	63	....	....	....	21	....	....	....	....	....	....	....	....	....	....	12	9	9	18	2	....	....	....
1962-63	**Chicago Black Hawks**	**NHL**	**60**	**6**	**22**	**28**	**7**	**23**	**30**	**30**	....	....	....	....	....	....	....	....	....	....	**4**	**0**	**0**	**0**	**2**	....	....	....
1963-64	Buffalo Bisons	AHL	72	30	43	73	....	....	....	38	....	....	....	....	....	....	....	....	....	....	....	....	....	....	....	....	....	....
1964-65	Buffalo Bisons	AHL	72	*50	46	96	....	....	....	40	....	....	....	....	....	....	....	....	....	....	9	4	4	8	4	....	....	....
1965-66	**Chicago Black Hawks**	**NHL**	**24**	**4**	**7**	**11**	**5**	**7**	**12**	**4**	....	....	....	....	....	....	....	....	....	....	....	....	....	....	....	....	....	....
	St. Louis Braves	CHL	11	3	5	8	....	....	....	6	....	....	....	....	....	....	....	....	....	....	....	....	....	....	....	....	....	....
1966-67	Portland Buckaroos	WHL	72	26	33	59	....	....	....	16	....	....	....	....	....	....	....	....	....	....	4	0	0	0	7	....	....	....
1967-68	Rochester Americans	AHL	37	19	33	52	....	....	....	13	....	....	....	....	....	....	....	....	....	....	11	2	4	6	0	....	....	....
	Minnesota North Stars	**NHL**	**7**	**0**	**1**	**1**	**0**	**1**	**1**	**0**	**0**	**0**	**0**	**21**	**0.0**	**2**	**0**	**9**	**0**	**–7**	....	....	....	....	....	....	....	....
1968-69	Vancouver Canucks	WHL	65	26	27	53	....	....	....	0	....	....	....	....	....	....	....	....	....	....	8	3	3	6	0	....	....	....
1969-70	Vancouver Canucks	WHL	68	29	34	63	....	....	....	4	....	....	....	....	....	....	....	....	....	....	11	*10	5	15	8	....	....	....
1970-71	**Vancouver Canucks**	**NHL**	**20**	**1**	**3**	**4**	**1**	**3**	**4**	**2**	**0**	**1**	**0**	**20**	**5.0**	**5**	**1**	**17**	**10**	**–3**	....	....	....	....	....	....	....	....
1971-72	Ilves Tampere	Finland	31	28	21	49	....	....	....	40	....	....	....	....	....	....	....	....	....	....	....	....	....	....	....	....	....	....
1972-73	Ilves Tampere	Finland	DID NOT PLAY – COACHING																									
1973-74	Edmonton Oilers	WHA	71	26	22	48	....	....	....	8	....	....	....	....	....	....	....	....	....	....	5	0	1	1	0	....	....	....
	NHL Totals		**321**	**39**	**83**	**122**	**47**	**85**	**132**	**75**	**0**	**1**	**0**	**41**	**95.1**	**7**	**1**	**26**	**10**		**20**	**3**	**2**	**5**	**2**	**0**	**0**	**0**
	Other Major League Totals		71	26	22	48	....	....	....	8	....	....	....	....	....	....	....	....	....		5	0	1	1	0	....	....	....

AHL First All-Star Team (1965)

Traded to **Chicago** by **Detroit** with John McKenzie for Doug Barkley, June 5, 1962. Claimed by **Minnesota** from **Chicago** in Expansion Draft, June 6, 1967. Traded to **Toronto** by **Minnesota** with Duke Harris, Don Johns, Ted Taylor, Murray Hall and the loan of Carl Wetzel for Jean-Paul Parise and Milan Marcetta, December 26, 1967. Selected by **Edmonton** (WHA) in 1972 WHA General Player Draft, February 12, 1972.

• LUNDHOLM, BENGT

Bengt Lundholm LW – L. 6', 180 lbs. b: Falun, Sweden, 8/4/1955.

Season	Club	League	GP	G	A	Pts	AG	AA	APts	PIM	PP	SH	GW	S	%	TGF	PGF	TGA	PGA	+/–	GP	G	A	Pts	PIM	PP	SH	GW
1973-74	Sweden	WJC-A	1	0	1	1	....	....	....	0	....	....	....	....	....	....	....	....	....	....	....	....	....	....	....	....	....	....
1974-75	Leksands IF	Sweden	18	4	7	11	....	....	....	6	....	....	....	....	....	....	....	....	....	....	4	1	3	4	4	....	....	....
	Sweden	WJC-A	....	0	3	3	....	....	....	....	....	....	....	....	....	....	....	....	....	....	....	....	....	....	....	....	....	....
1975-76	Leksands IF	Sweden	36	15	22	37	....	....	....	23	....	....	....	....	....	....	....	....	....	....	7	3	4	7	2	....	....	....
	Sweden	WEC-A	8	0	2	2	....	....	....	6	....	....	....	....	....	....	....	....	....	....	....	....	....	....	....	....	....	....
1976-77	Leksands IF	Sweden	34	8	23	31	....	....	....	28	....	....	....	....	....	....	....	....	....	....	5	4	3	7	*16	....	....	....
	Sweden	WEC-A	8	5	3	8	....	....	....	4	....	....	....	....	....	....	....	....	....	....	....	....	....	....	....	....	....	....
1977-78	AIK Solna	Sweden	36	16	15	31	....	....	....	22	....	....	....	....	....	....	....	....	....	....	6	1	4	5	4	....	....	....
	Sweden	WEC-A	10	6	5	11	....	....	....	4	....	....	....	....	....	....	....	....	....	....	....	....	....	....	....	....	....	....
1978-79	AIK Solna	Sweden	34	10	10	20	....	....	....	24	....	....	....	....	....	....	....	....	....	....	....	....	....	....	....	....	....	....
	Sweden	Nat-Team	17	2	6	8	....	....	....	8	....	....	....	....	....	....	....	....	....	....	....	....	....	....	....	....	....	....
	Sweden	WEC-A	7	1	3	4	....	....	....	4	....	....	....	....	....	....	....	....	....	....	....	....	....	....	....	....	....	....
1979-80	AIK Solna	Sweden	36	16	16	32	....	....	....	34	....	....	....	....	....	....	....	....	....	....	....	....	....	....	....	....	....	....
	Sweden	Nat-Team	6	1	0	1	....	....	....	0	....	....	....	....	....	....	....	....	....	....	....	....	....	....	....	....	....	....
	Sweden	Olympics	7	1	0	1	....	....	....	2	....	....	....	....	....	....	....	....	....	....	....	....	....	....	....	....	....	....
1980-81	AIK Solna	Sweden	24	6	8	14	....	....	....	40	....	....	....	....	....	....	....	....	....	....	5	1	0	1	2	....	....	....
	Sweden	Nat-Team	4	1	1	2	....	....	....	0	....	....	....	....	....	....	....	....	....	....	....	....	....	....	....	....	....	....
1981-82	Sweden	C Cup	5	1	0	1	....	....	....	2	....	....	....	....	....	....	....	....	....	....	....	....	....	....	....	....	....	....
	Winnipeg Jets	**NHL**	**66**	**14**	**30**	**44**	**11**	**20**	**31**	**10**	**3**	**0**	**3**	**99**	**14.1**	**57**	**11**	**41**	**0**	**+5**	**4**	**1**	**1**	**2**	**2**	**0**	**0**	**0**
1982-83	**Winnipeg Jets**	**NHL**	**58**	**14**	**28**	**42**	**11**	**19**	**30**	**16**	**1**	**0**	**0**	**66**	**21.2**	**68**	**9**	**50**	**1**	**+10**	**3**	**0**	**1**	**1**	**2**	**0**	**0**	**0**
1983-84	**Winnipeg Jets**	**NHL**	**57**	**5**	**14**	**19**	**4**	**9**	**13**	**20**	**1**	**0**	**0**	**48**	**10.4**	**31**	**5**	**36**	**3**	**–7**	....	....	....	....	....	....	....	....
1984-85	**Winnipeg Jets**	**NHL**	**78**	**12**	**18**	**30**	**10**	**12**	**22**	**20**	**1**	**0**	**1**	**58**	**20.7**	**50**	**3**	**45**	**6**	**+8**	**5**	**2**	**2**	**4**	**8**	**0**	**2**	**0**
1985-86	**Winnipeg Jets**	**NHL**	**16**	**3**	**5**	**8**	**2**	**3**	**5**	**6**	**0**	**1**	**0**	**14**	**21.4**	**11**	**1**	**16**	**2**	**–4**	**2**	**0**	**0**	**0**	**2**	**0**	**0**	**0**
	Stockholm	Sweden	13	1	1	2	....	....	....	4	....	....	....	....	....	....	....	....	....	....	....	....	....	....	....	....	....	....
	NHL Totals		**275**	**48**	**95**	**143**	**38**	**63**	**101**	**72**	**6**	**1**	**4**	**285**	**16.8**	**217**	**29**	**188**	**12**		**14**	**3**	**4**	**7**	**14**	**0**	**2**	**0**

Signed as a free agent by **Winnipeg**, June 19, 1981.

• LUNDRIGAN, JOE

Joe Lundrigan D – L. 5'11", 180 lbs. b: Corner Brook, Nfld., 9/12/1948.

Season	Club	League	GP	G	A	Pts	AG	AA	APts	PIM	PP	SH	GW	S	%	TGF	PGF	TGA	PGA	+/–	GP	G	A	Pts	PIM	PP	SH	GW
1968-69	St. Francis Xavier X-Men	AUAA	....	14	11	25	....	....	....	50	....	....	....	....	....	....	....	....	....	....	....	....	....	....	....	....	....	....
1969-70	St. Francis Xavier X-Men	AUAA	....	10	6	16	....	....	....	73	....	....	....	....	....	....	....	....	....	....	....	....	....	....	....	....	....	....
1970-71	St. Francis Xavier X-Men	AUAA	....	6	13	19	....	....	....	56	....	....	....	....	....	....	....	....	....	....	....	....	....	....	....	....	....	....
	Tulsa Oilers	CHL	67	3	34	37	....	....	....	110	....	....	....	....	....	....	....	....	....	....	13	2	9	11	24	....	....	....
1972-73	Tulsa Oilers	CHL	8	3	2	5	....	....	....	10	....	....	....	....	....	....	....	....	....	....	....	....	....	....	....	....	....	....
1972-73	**Toronto Maple Leafs**	**NHL**	**49**	**2**	**8**	**10**	**2**	**7**	**9**	**20**	**1**	**0**	**1**	**53**	**3.8**	**44**	**3**	**47**	**10**	**+4**	....	....	....	....	....	....	....	....
1973-74	Oklahoma City Blazers	CHL	62	7	34	41	....	....	....	143	....	....	....	....	....	....	....	....	....	....	10	0	3	3	10	....	....	....
1974-75	**Washington Capitals**	**NHL**	**3**	**0**	**0**	**0**	**0**	**0**	**0**	**2**	**0**	**0**	**0**	**2**	**0.0**	**1**	**1**	**3**	**0**	**–3**	....	....	....	....	....	....	....	....
	Richmond Robins	AHL	28	3	3	6	....	....	....	49	....	....	....	....	....	....	....	....	....	....	....	....	....	....	....	....	....	....
	Hershey Bears	AHL	33	6	13	19	....	....	....	60	....	....	....	....	....	....	....	....	....	....	12	2	4	6	8	....	....	....
	NHL Totals		**52**	**2**	**8**	**10**	**2**	**7**	**9**	**22**	**1**	**0**	**1**	**55**	**3.6**	**45**	**4**	**50**	**10**		....	....	....	....	....	....	....	....

CHL Second All-Star Team (1972)

Signed as a free agent by **Toronto**, October 1, 1971. Claimed by **Washington** from **Toronto** in Expansion Draft, June 12, 1974.

• LUNDSTROM, TORD

Tord Lundstrom LW – L. 5'11", 176 lbs. b: Kiruna, Sweden, 3/4/1945.

Season	Club	League	GP	G	A	Pts	AG	AA	APts	PIM	PP	SH	GW	S	%	TGF	PGF	TGA	PGA	+/–	GP	G	A	Pts	PIM	PP	SH	GW
1963-64	Brynas IF Gavle	Sweden	14	10	6	16	....	....	....	8	....	....	....	....	....	....	....	....	....	....	7	7	7	14	11	....	....	....
1964-65	Brynas IF Gavle	Sweden	14	14	10	24	....	....	....	4	....	....	....	....	....	....	....	....	....	....	14	*17	12	29	4	....	....	....
	Sweden	WEC-A	7	6	3	9	....	....	....	4	....	....	....	....	....	....	....	....	....	....	....	....	....	....	....	....	....	....
1965-66	Brynas IF Gavle	Sweden	14	10	9	19	....	....	....	4	....	....	....	....	....	....	....	....	....	....	7	7	5	12	6	....	....	....
	Sweden	WEC-A	7	0	1	1	....	....	....	4	....	....	....	....	....	....	....	....	....	....	....	....	....	....	....	....	....	....
1966-67	Brynas IF Gavle	Sweden	14	18	6	24	....	....	....	12	....	....	....	....	....	....	....	....	....	....	6	5	6	11	0	....	....	....
1967-68	Brynas IF Gavle	Sweden	14	15	14	29	....	....	....	4	....	....	....	....	....	....	....	....	....	....	7	6	7	13	2	....	....	....
	Sweden	Olympics	7	2	3	5	....	....	....	6	....	....	....	....	....	....	....	....	....	....	....	....	....	....	....	....	....	....
1968-69	Brynas IF Gavle	Sweden	14	7	8	15	....	....	....	2	....	....	....	....	....	....	....	....	....	....	7	6	6	12	6	....	....	....
	Sweden	WEC-A	10	5	2	7	....	....	....	12	....	....	....	....	....	....	....	....	....	....	....	....	....	....	....	....	....	....
1969-70	Brynas IF Gavle	Sweden	14	*17	10	*27	....	....	....	8	....	....	....	....	....	....	....	....	....	....	14	10	6	16	6	....	....	....
	Sweden	WEC-A	10	5	5	10	....	....	....	0	....	....	....	....	....	....	....	....	....	....	....	....	....	....	....	....	....	....
1970-71	Brynas IF Gavle	Sweden	14	17	13	30	....	....	....	2	....	....	....	....	....	....	....	....	....	....	14	9	*16	*25	14	....	....	....
1970-71	Sweden	WEC-A	10	6	4	10	....	....	....	4	....	....	....	....	....	....	....	....	....	....	....	....	....	....	....	....	....	....
1971-72	Brynas IF Gavle	Sweden	14	8	6	14	....	....	....	4	....	....	....	....	....	....	....	....	....	....	14	9	10	19	4	....	....	....
	Sweden	Olympics	6	3	2	5	....	....	....	2	....	....	....	....	....	....	....	....	....	....	....	....	....	....	....	....	....	....
	Sweden	WEC-A	10	4	5	9	....	....	....	8	....	....	....	....	....	....	....	....	....	....	....	....	....	....	....	....	....	....
1972-73	Brynas IF Gavle	Sweden	14	16	11	27	....	....	....	4	....	....	....	....	....	....	....	....	....	....	14	10	4	14	6	....	....	....
	Sweden	WEC-A	10	3	2	5	....	....	....	0	....	....	....	....	....	....	....	....	....	....	....	....	....	....	....	....	....	....
1973-74	**Detroit Red Wings**	**NHL**	**11**	**1**	**1**	**2**	**1**	**1**	**2**	**0**	**0**	**0**	**0**	**7**	**14.3**	**2**	**0**	**4**	**0**	**–2**	....	....	....	....	....	....	....	....
	London Lions	Britain	45	38	31	69	....	....	....	24	....	....	....	....	....	....	....	....	....	....	....	....	....	....	....	....	....	....
1974-75	Brynas IF Gavle	Sweden	21	15	17	32	....	....	....	32	....	....	....	....	....	....	....	....	....	....	6	0	3	3	2	....	....	....
	Sweden	WEC-A	10	11	4	15	....	....	....	2	....	....	....	....	....	....	....	....	....	....	....	....	....	....	....	....	....	....
1975-76	Brynas IF Gavle	Sweden	35	21	*27	48	....	....	....	16	....	....	....	....	....	....	....	....	....	....	7	4	1	5	0	....	....	....

			REGULAR SEASON																		PLAYOFFS							
Season	Club	League	GP	G	A	Pts	AG	AA	APts	PIM	PP	SH	GW	S	%	TGF	PGF	TGA	PGA	+/–	GP	G	A	Pts	PIM	PP	SH	GW
1976-77	Sweden	C Cup	5	1	3	4	....	....	....	6	....	....	....	....	....	....	....	....	....	....	....	....	....	....	....	....	....	....
	Brynas IF Gavle	Sweden	36	16	19	35	....	....	....	37	....	....	....	....	....	....	....	....	....	....	4	1	*7	8	0	....	....	....
1977-78	Brynas IF Gavle	Sweden	36	20	15	35	....	....	....	28	....	....	....	....	....	....	....	....	....	....	3	0	1	1	0	....	....	....
1978-79	Brynas IF Gavle	Sweden	36	12	13	25	....	....	....	29	....	....	....	....	....	....	....	....	....	....	....	....	....	....	....	....	....	....
	NHL Totals		**11**	**1**	**1**	**2**	**1**	**1**	**2**	**0**	**0**	**0**	**0**	**7**	**14.3**	**2**	**0**	**4**	**0**		....	....	....	....	....	....	....	....

Signed as a free agent by **Detroit**, June, 1973.

• LUONGO, CHRIS

Chris Luongo D – R. 5'10", 206 lbs. b: Detroit, MI, 3/17/1967. Detroit's 5th choice, 92nd overall, in 1985 Entry Draft.

Season	Club	League	GP	G	A	Pts	AG	AA	APts	PIM	PP	SH	GW	S	%	TGF	PGF	TGA	PGA	+/–	GP	G	A	Pts	PIM	PP	SH	GW
1984-85	Detroit Falcons	NAJHL	41	2	27	29	....	....	....	....	....	....	....	....	....	....	....	....	....	....	....	....	....	....	....	....	....	....
1985-86	Michigan State Spartans	CCHA	38	1	5	6	....	....	....	29	....	....	....	....	....	....	....	....	....	....	....	....	....	....	....	....	....	....
1986-87	Michigan State Spartans	CCHA	27	4	16	20	....	....	....	38	....	....	....	....	....	....	....	....	....	....	....	....	....	....	....	....	....	....
1987-88	Michigan State Spartans	CCHA	45	3	15	18	....	....	....	49	....	....	....	....	....	....	....	....	....	....	....	....	....	....	....	....	....	....
1988-89	Michigan State Spartans	CCHA	47	4	21	25	....	....	....	42	....	....	....	....	....	....	....	....	....	....	....	....	....	....	....	....	....	....
1989-90	Adirondack Red Wings	AHL	53	9	14	23	....	....	....	37	....	....	....	....	....	....	....	....	....	....	3	0	0	0	0	....	....	....
	Phoenix Roadrunners	IHL	23	5	9	14	....	....	....	41	....	....	....	....	....	....	....	....	....	....	....	....	....	....	....	....	....	....
1990-91	**Detroit Red Wings**	**NHL**	**4**	**0**	**1**	**1**	**0**	**1**	**1**	**4**	**0**	**0**	**0**	**4**	**0.0**	**2**	**0**	**4**	**2**	**0**	....	....	....	....	....	....	....	....
	Adirondack Red Wings	AHL	76	14	25	39	....	....	....	71	....	....	....	....	....	....	....	....	....	....	2	0	0	0	7	....	....	....
1991-92	Adirondack Red Wings	AHL	80	6	20	26	....	....	....	60	....	....	....	....	....	....	....	....	....	....	19	3	5	8	10	....	....	....
1992-93	**Ottawa Senators**	**NHL**	**76**	**3**	**9**	**12**	**2**	**6**	**8**	**68**	**1**	**0**	**0**	**76**	**3.9**	**37**	**5**	**109**	**30**	**–47**	....	....	....	....	....	....	....	....
	New Haven Nighthawks	AHL	7	0	2	2	....	....	....	2	....	....	....	....	....	....	....	....	....	....	....	....	....	....	....	....	....	....
1993-94	**New York Islanders**	**NHL**	**17**	**1**	**3**	**4**	**1**	**2**	**3**	**13**	**0**	**0**	**0**	**16**	**6.3**	**11**	**0**	**19**	**7**	**–1**	....	....	....	....	....	....	....	....
	Salt Lake Golden Eagles	IHL	51	9	31	40	....	....	....	54	....	....	....	....	....	....	....	....	....	....	....	....	....	....	....	....	....	....
1994-95	Denver Grizzlies	IHL	41	1	14	15	....	....	....	26	....	....	....	....	....	....	....	....	....	....	....	....	....	....	....	....	....	....
	New York Islanders	**NHL**	**47**	**1**	**3**	**4**	**2**	**4**	**6**	**36**	**0**	**0**	**0**	**44**	**2.3**	**34**	**0**	**53**	**17**	**–2**	....	....	....	....	....	....	....	....
1995-96	**New York Islanders**	**NHL**	**74**	**3**	**7**	**10**	**3**	**6**	**9**	**55**	**1**	**0**	**0**	**46**	**6.5**	**42**	**4**	**83**	**22**	**–23**	....	....	....	....	....	....	....	....
	United States	WC-A	8	1	0	1	....	....	....	6	....	....	....	....	....	....	....	....	....	....	....	....	....	....	....	....	....	....
1996-97	Milwaukee Admirals	IHL	81	10	35	45	....	....	....	69	....	....	....	....	....	....	....	....	....	....	2	0	0	0	0	....	....	....
1997-98	EV Landshut	Germany	48	5	13	18	....	....	....	54	....	....	....	....	....	....	....	....	....	....	6	0	2	2	18	....	....	....
	United States	WC-A	6	0	0	0	....	....	....	2	....	....	....	....	....	....	....	....	....	....	....	....	....	....	....	....	....	....
	NHL Totals		**218**	**8**	**23**	**31**	**8**	**19**	**27**	**176**	**2**	**0**	**0**	**186**	**4.3**	**126**	**9**	**268**	**78**		....	....	....	....	....	....	....	....

NCAA Championship All-Tournament Team (1987) • CCHA Second All-Star Team (1989)

Signed as a free agent by **Ottawa**, September 9, 1992. Traded to **NY Islanders** by **Ottawa** for Jeff Finley, June 30, 1993.

• LUPIEN, GILLES

Gilles "Loopy" Lupien D – L. 6'6", 210 lbs. b: Lachute, Que., 4/20/1954. Montreal's 7th choice, 33rd overall, in 1974 Amateur Draft.

Season	Club	League	GP	G	A	Pts	AG	AA	APts	PIM	PP	SH	GW	S	%	TGF	PGF	TGA	PGA	+/–	GP	G	A	Pts	PIM	PP	SH	GW
1971-72	Quebec Remparts	QMJHL	36	0	5	5	....	....	....	54	....	....	....	....	....	....	....	....	....	....	15	0	3	3	17	....	....	....
1972-73	Montreal Jr. Canadiens	QMJHL	26	4	4	8	....	....	....	66	....	....	....	....	....	....	....	....	....	....	....	....	....	....	....	....	....	....
	Sherbrooke Castors	QMJHL	26	0	5	5	....	....	....	71	....	....	....	....	....	....	....	....	....	....	....	....	....	....	....	....	....	....
1973-74	Montreal Jr. Canadiens	QMJHL	44	3	29	32	....	....	....	168	....	....	....	....	....	....	....	....	....	....	....	....	....	....	....	....	....	....
1974-75	Nova Scotia Voyageurs	AHL	73	6	9	15	....	....	....	*316	....	....	....	....	....	....	....	....	....	....	6	0	0	0	61	....	....	....
1975-76	Nova Scotia Voyageurs	AHL	56	2	6	8	....	....	....	134	....	....	....	....	....	....	....	....	....	....	9	0	4	4	29	....	....	....
1976-77	Nova Scotia Voyageurs	AHL	69	6	16	22	....	....	....	*215	....	....	....	....	....	....	....	....	....	....	12	0	2	2	*35	....	....	....
1977-78	**Montreal Canadiens**	**NHL**	**46**	**1**	**3**	**4**	**1**	**2**	**3**	**108**	**0**	**0**	**0**	**20**	**5.0**	**28**	**1**	**8**	**0**	**+19**	**8**	**0**	**0**	**0**	**17**	**0**	**0**	**0**
	Nova Scotia Voyageurs	AHL	7	1	2	3	....	....	....	10	....	....	....	....	....	....	....	....	....	....	....	....	....	....	....	....	....	....
1978-79	**Montreal Canadiens**	**NHL**	**72**	**1**	**9**	**10**	**1**	**7**	**8**	**124**	**0**	**0**	**0**	**58**	**1.7**	**57**	**0**	**26**	**2**	**+33**	**13**	**0**	**0**	**0**	**2**	**0**	**0**	**0**
1979-80	**Montreal Canadiens**	**NHL**	**56**	**1**	**7**	**8**	**1**	**5**	**6**	**109**	**0**	**0**	**1**	**42**	**2.4**	**46**	**0**	**33**	**0**	**+13**	**4**	**0**	**0**	**0**	**2**	**0**	**0**	**0**
1980-81	**Pittsburgh Penguins**	**NHL**	**31**	**0**	**1**	**1**	**0**	**1**	**1**	**34**	**0**	**0**	**0**	**11**	**0.0**	**7**	**0**	**27**	**5**	**–15**	....	....	....	....	....	....	....	....
	Hartford Whalers	**NHL**	**20**	**2**	**4**	**6**	**2**	**3**	**5**	**39**	**0**	**0**	**0**	**16**	**12.5**	**16**	**1**	**22**	**1**	**–6**	....	....	....	....	....	....	....	....
	Binghamton Whalers	AHL	11	1	4	5	....	....	....	71	....	....	....	....	....	....	....	....	....	....	....	....	....	....	....	....	....	....
1981-82	**Hartford Whalers**	**NHL**	**1**	**0**	**1**	**1**	**0**	**1**	**1**	**2**	**0**	**0**	**0**	**0**	**0.0**	**1**	**0**	**2**	**1**	**0**	....	....	....	....	....	....	....	....
	Binghamton Whalers	AHL	53	8	10	[illegible]	....	....	....	280	....	....	....	....	....	....	....	....	....	....	13	2	5	7	58	....	....	....
	NHL Totals		**226**	**5**	**25**	**30**	**5**	**19**	**24**	**410**	**0**	**0**	**1**	**147**	**3.4**	**155**	**2**	**118**	**9**		**25**	**0**	**0**	**0**	**21**	**0**	**0**	**0**

Claimed by **Montreal** as a fill-in during Expansion Draft, June 13, 1979. Traded to **Pittsburgh** by **Montreal** for Pittsburgh's 3rd round choice (later traded to Winnipeg — Winnipeg selected Peter Taglianetti) in 1983 Entry Draft, September 26, 1980. Traded to **Hartford** by **Pittsburgh** for Hartford's 6th round choice (Paul Edwards) in 1981 Entry Draft, February 20, 1981.

• LUPUL, GARY

Gary Lupul C/LW – L. 5'9", 172 lbs. b: Powell River, B.C., 4/4/1959.

Season	Club	League	GP	G	A	Pts	AG	AA	APts	PIM	PP	SH	GW	S	%	TGF	PGF	TGA	PGA	+/–	GP	G	A	Pts	PIM	PP	SH	GW
1975-76	Nanaimo Clippers	BCJHL	66	49	68	117	....	....	....	....	....	....	....	....	....	....	....	....	....	....	....	....	....	....	....	....	....	....
	Victoria Cougars	WHL	4	1	1	2	....	....	....	2	....	....	....	....	....	....	....	....	....	....	1	0	0	0	0	....	....	....
1976-77	Victoria Cougars	WCJHL	71	38	63	101	....	....	....	116	....	....	....	....	....	....	....	....	....	....	4	1	0	1	2	....	....	....
1977-78	Victoria Cougars	WCJHL	59	37	49	86	....	....	....	79	....	....	....	....	....	....	....	....	....	....	13	6	15	21	2	....	....	....
1978-79	Victoria Cougars	WHL	71	53	54	107	....	....	....	85	....	....	....	....	....	....	....	....	....	....	15	10	14	24	19	....	....	....
	Canada	WJC-A	5	2	1	3	....	....	....	0	....	....	....	....	....	....	....	....	....	....	....	....	....	....	....	....	....	....
1979-80	**Vancouver Canucks**	**NHL**	**51**	**9**	**11**	**20**	**8**	**8**	**16**	**24**	**3**	**0**	**0**	**71**	**12.7**	**29**	**5**	**39**	**3**	**–12**	**4**	**1**	**0**	**1**	**0**	**1**	**0**	**0**
	Dallas Black Hawks	CHL	26	9	15	24	....	....	....	4	....	....	....	....	....	....	....	....	....	....	....	....	....	....	....	....	....	....
1980-81	**Vancouver Canucks**	**NHL**	**7**	**0**	**2**	**2**	**0**	**1**	**1**	**2**	**0**	**0**	**0**	**5**	**0.0**	**2**	**0**	**3**	**0**	**–1**	....	....	....	....	....	....	....	....
	Dallas Black Hawks	CHL	53	25	32	57	....	....	....	27	....	....	....	....	....	....	....	....	....	....	6	4	1	5	5	....	....	....
1981-82	**Vancouver Canucks**	**NHL**	**41**	**10**	**7**	**17**	**8**	**5**	**13**	**26**	**0**	**1**	**0**	**45**	**22.2**	**23**	**1**	**30**	**6**	**–2**	**10**	**2**	**3**	**5**	**4**	**0**	**0**	**1**
	Dallas Black Hawks	CHL	31	22	17	39	....	....	....	76	....	....	....	....	....	....	....	....	....	....	....	....	....	....	....	....	....	....
1982-83	**Vancouver Canucks**	**NHL**	**40**	**18**	**10**	**28**	**15**	**7**	**22**	**46**	**3**	**0**	**2**	**64**	**28.1**	**35**	**7**	**32**	**5**	**+1**	**4**	**1**	**3**	**4**	**0**	**0**	**0**	**0**
	Fredericton Express	AHL	35	16	26	42	....	....	....	48	....	....	....	....	....	....	....	....	....	....	....	....	....	....	....	....	....	....
1983-84	**Vancouver Canucks**	**NHL**	**69**	**17**	**27**	**44**	**14**	**18**	**32**	**51**	**6**	**0**	**2**	**128**	**13.3**	**62**	**21**	**72**	**15**	**–16**	**4**	**0**	**1**	**1**	**7**	**0**	**0**	**0**
1984-85	**Vancouver Canucks**	**NHL**	**66**	**12**	**17**	**29**	**10**	**11**	**21**	**82**	**2**	**0**	**2**	**107**	**11.2**	**46**	**6**	**65**	**11**	**–15**	....	....	....	....	....	....	....	....
1985-86	**Vancouver Canucks**	**NHL**	**19**	**4**	**1**	**5**	**3**	**1**	**4**	**12**	**0**	**0**	**0**	**17**	**23.5**	**10**	**2**	**9**	**1**	**0**	**3**	**0**	**0**	**0**	**0**	**0**	**0**	**0**
	Fredericton Express	AHL	43	13	22	35	....	....	....	76	....	....	....	....	....	....	....	....	....	....	3	2	0	2	4	....	....	....
1986-87	SG Brunico	Italy	42	28	38	66	....	....	....	24	....	....	....	....	....	....	....	....	....	....	....	....	....	....	....	....	....	....
1987-88	SC Preussen Berlin	Germany	27	17	12	29	....	....	....	20	....	....	....	....	....	....	....	....	....	....	....	....	....	....	....	....	....	....
	NHL Totals		**293**	**70**	**75**	**145**	**58**	**51**	**109**	**243**	**14**	**1**	**6**	**437**	**16.0**	**206**	**42**	**250**	**41**		**25**	**4**	**7**	**11**	**11**	**1**	**0**	**1**

Signed as a free agent by **Vancouver**, September 14, 1979.

• LYLE, GEORGE

George "Sparky" Lyle LW – L. 6'2", 205 lbs. b: North Vancouver, B.C., 11/24/1953. Detroit's 9th choice, 123rd overall, in 1973 Amateur Draft.

Season	Club	League	GP	G	A	Pts	AG	AA	APts	PIM	PP	SH	GW	S	%	TGF	PGF	TGA	PGA	+/–	GP	G	A	Pts	PIM	PP	SH	GW
1972-73	Calumet Miners	USHL	33	23	16	39	....	....	....	42	....	....	....	....	....	....	....	....	....	....	....	....	....	....	....	....	....	....
1973-74	Michigan Tech Huskies	WCHA	19	9	13	22	....	....	....	20	....	....	....	....	....	....	....	....	....	....	....	....	....	....	....	....	....	....
1974-75	Michigan Tech Huskies	WCHA	38	37	19	56	....	....	....	76	....	....	....	....	....	....	....	....	....	....	....	....	....	....	....	....	....	....
1975-76	Michigan Tech Huskies	WCHA	43	47	41	88	....	....	....	42	....	....	....	....	....	....	....	....	....	....	....	....	....	....	....	....	....	....
1976-77	New England Whalers	WHA	75	39	33	72	....	....	....	62	....	....	....	....	....	....	....	....	....	....	5	1	0	1	4	....	....	....
1977-78	New England Whalers	WHA	68	30	24	54	....	....	....	74	....	....	....	....	....	....	....	....	....	....	12	2	1	3	13	....	....	....
1978-79	Springfield Indians	AHL	4	2	4	6	....	....	....	6	....	....	....	....	....	....	....	....	....	....	....	....	....	....	....	....	....	....
	New England Whalers	WHA	59	17	18	35	....	....	....	54	....	....	....	....	....	....	....	....	....	....	9	3	5	8	25	....	....	....
1979-80	**Detroit Red Wings**	**NHL**	**27**	**7**	**4**	**11**	**6**	**3**	**9**	**2**	**0**	**0**	**2**	**41**	**17.1**	**20**	**1**	**21**	**0**	**–2**	....	....	....	....	....	....	....	....
	Adirondack Red Wings	AHL	33	23	9	32	....	....	....	40	....	....	....	....	....	....	....	....	....	....	....	....	....	....	....	....	....	....
1980-81	**Detroit Red Wings**	**NHL**	**31**	**10**	**14**	**24**	**8**	**10**	**18**	**28**	**3**	**0**	**0**	**49**	**20.4**	**35**	**10**	**28**	**3**	**0**	....	....	....	....	....	....	....	....
	Adirondack Red Wings	AHL	40	20	16	36	....	....	....	84	....	....	....	....	....	....	....	....	....	....	18	9	9	18	34	....	....	....

			REGULAR SEASON																		PLAYOFFS							
Season	Club	League	GP	G	A	Pts	AG	AA	APts	PIM	PP	SH	GW	S	%	TGF	PGF	TGA	PGA	+/–	GP	G	A	Pts	PIM	PP	SH	GW
1981-82	Detroit Red Wings	NHL	11	1	2	3	1	1	2	4	0	0	0	9	11.1	4	1	5	0	–2	....	....	....	....	....	....	....	....
	Hartford Whalers	NHL	14	2	12	14	2	8	10	9	1	0	0	33	6.1	21	9	15	0	–3	....	....	....	....	....	....	....	....
1982-83	Hartford Whalers	NHL	16	4	6	10	3	4	7	8	0	1	0	33	12.1	18	2	11	0	+5	....	....	....	....	....	....	....	....
	Binghamton Whalers	AHL	56	19	24	43	....	....	....	63	....	....	....	....	....	....	....	....	....	....	4	1	2	3	8	....	....	....
	NHL Totals		99	24	38	62	20	26	46	51	4	1	2	165	14.5	98	23	80	3		....	....	....	....	....	....	....	....
	Other Major League Totals		202	86	75	161	....	....	....	190	....	....	....	....	....	....	....	....	....	....	26	6	6	12	42	....	....	....

WCHA First All-Star Team (1976) • NCAA West First All-American Team (1976) • Won Lou Kaplan Trophy (WHA Rookie of the Year) (1977)

Signed as a free agent by **New England** (WHA), July, 1976. Reclaimed by **Detroit** from **Hartford** prior to Expansion Draft, June 9, 1979. Claimed on waivers by **Hartford** from **Detroit**, November 13, 1981.

• LYNCH, JACK

Jack Lynch D – R. 6′2″, 180 lbs. b: Toronto, Ont., 5/28/1952. Pittsburgh's 1st choice, 24th overall, in 1972 Amateur Draft.

Season	Club	League	GP	G	A	Pts	AG	AA	APts	PIM	PP	SH	GW	S	%	TGF	PGF	TGA	PGA	+/–	GP	G	A	Pts	PIM	PP	SH	GW
1970-71	Oshawa Generals	OHA	60	18	29	47	....	....	....	86	....	....	....	....	....	....	....	....	....	....	....	....	....	....	....	....	....	....
1971-72	Oshawa Generals	OHA	59	18	38	56	....	....	....	55	....	....	....	....	....	....	....	....	....	....	....	....	....	....	....	....	....	....
1972-73	Pittsburgh Penguins	NHL	47	1	18	19	1	15	16	40	0	0	0	78	1.3	53	21	63	10	–21	....	....	....	....	....	....	....	....
	Hershey Bears	AHL	26	4	17	21	....	....	....	26	....	....	....	....	....	....	....	....	....	....	7	0	1	1	28	....	....	....
1973-74	Pittsburgh Penguins	NHL	17	0	7	7	0	6	6	21	0	0	0	23	0.0	17	10	26	4	–15	....	....	....	....	....	....	....	....
	Hershey Bears	AHL	20	3	10	13	....	....	....	24	....	....	....	....	....	....	....	....	....	....	....	....	....	....	....	....	....	....
	Detroit Red Wings	NHL	35	3	9	12	3	8	11	27	1	0	1	64	4.7	49	8	64	9	–14	....	....	....	....	....	....	....	....
1974-75	Detroit Red Wings	NHL	50	2	15	17	2	12	14	46	0	0	0	52	3.8	51	8	74	16	–15	....	....	....	....	....	....	....	....
	Washington Capitals	NHL	20	1	5	6	1	4	5	16	0	0	0	28	3.6	18	12	78	18	–54	....	....	....	....	....	....	....	....
1975-76	Washington Capitals	NHL	79	9	13	22	8	10	18	78	5	0	1	126	7.1	90	24	151	33	–52	....	....	....	....	....	....	....	....
1976-77	Washington Capitals	NHL	75	5	25	30	5	20	25	90	0	0	0	132	3.8	87	19	99	16	–15	....	....	....	....	....	....	....	....
1977-78	Washington Capitals	NHL	29	1	8	9	1	7	8	4	0	0	0	58	1.7	25	5	39	6	–13	....	....	....	....	....	....	....	....
1978-79	Washington Capitals	NHL	30	2	6	8	2	5	7	14	1	0	0	37	5.4	26	6	21	3	+2	....	....	....	....	....	....	....	....
	Hershey Bears	AHL	20	7	6	13	....	....	....	8	....	....	....	....	....	....	....	....	....	....	....	....	....	....	....	....	....	....
	NHL Totals		382	24	106	130	23	87	110	336	7	0	2	598	4.0	416	113	615	115		....	....	....	....	....	....	....	....

Traded to **Detroit** by **Pittsburgh** with Jim Rutherford for Ron Stackhouse, January 12, 1974. Traded to **Washington** by **Detroit** for Dave Kryskow, February 8, 1975.

• LYON, STEVE

Steve Lyon D/RW – R. 5′10″, 169 lbs. b: Toronto, Ont., 5/16/1952. Minnesota's 10th choice, 145th overall, in 1972 Amateur Draft.

Season	Club	League	GP	G	A	Pts	AG	AA	APts	PIM	PP	SH	GW	S	%	TGF	PGF	TGA	PGA	+/–	GP	G	A	Pts	PIM	PP	SH	GW
1971-72	Peterborough Petes	OHA	36	7	21	28	....	....	....	118	....	....	....	....	....	....	....	....	....	....	....	....	....	....	....	....	....	....
1972-73	Saginaw Gears	IHL	65	3	30	33	....	....	....	105	....	....	....	....	....	....	....	....	....	....	....	....	....	....	....	....	....	....
1973-74	Columbus Owls	IHL	76	10	60	70	....	....	....	169	....	....	....	....	....	....	....	....	....	....	6	4	2	6	4	....	....	....
1974-75	Columbus Owls	IHL	76	15	51	66	....	....	....	130	....	....	....	....	....	....	....	....	....	....	5	0	1	1	22	....	....	....
	Rochester Americans	AHL	....	....	....	....	....	....	....	....	....	....	....	....	....	....	....	....	....	....	3	0	0	0	5	....	....	....
1975-76	Columbus Owls	IHL	76	25	43	68	....	....	....	165	....	....	....	....	....	....	....	....	....	....	....	....	....	....	....	....	....	....
1976-77	Pittsburgh Penguins	NHL	3	0	0	0	0	0	0	2	0	0	0	2	0.0	0	0	0	0	0	....	....	....	....	....	....	....	....
	Columbus Owls	IHL	77	33	58	91	....	....	....	123	....	....	....	....	....	....	....	....	....	....	7	1	1	2	17	....	....	....
1977-78	Grand Rapids Owls	IHL	3	0	3	3	....	....	....	2	....	....	....	....	....	....	....	....	....	....	....	....	....	....	....	....	....	....
	Whitby Warriors	OHA Sr.	28	2	21	23	....	....	....	20	....	....	....	....	....	....	....	....	....	....	....	....	....	....	....	....	....	....
1978-79			DID NOT PLAY																									
1979-80			DID NOT PLAY																									
1980-81	Georgetown Aces	Inter-Sr.	....	9	50	59	....	....	....	....	....	....	....	....	....	....	....	....	....	....	....	....	....	....	....	....	....	....
1981-82	Georgetown Aces	Inter-Sr.	....	11	*60	71	....	....	....	....	....	....	....	....	....	....	....	....	....	....	....	....	....	....	....	....	....	....
1982-83	Georgetown Aces	Inter-Sr.	STATISTICS NOT AVAILABLE																									
1983-84	Mohawk Valley–Virginia	ACHL	72	34	50	84	....	....	....	32	....	....	....	....	....	....	....	....	....	....	3	0	0	0	5	....	....	....
	NHL Totals		3	0	0	0	0	0	0	2	0	0	0	2	0.0	0	0	0	0		....	....	....	....	....	....	....	....

IHL First All-Star Team (1974, 1975)

Signed as a free agent by **Pittsburgh**, November, 1976.

• LYSIAK, TOM

Tom "The Bomb" Lysiak C – L. 6′1″, 185 lbs. b: High Prairie, Alta., 4/22/1953. Atlanta's 1st choice, 2nd overall, in 1973 Amateur Draft.

Season	Club	League	GP	G	A	Pts	AG	AA	APts	PIM	PP	SH	GW	S	%	TGF	PGF	TGA	PGA	+/–	GP	G	A	Pts	PIM	PP	SH	GW
1970-71	Medicine Hat Tigers	WCJHL	60	14	16	30	....	....	....	112	....	....	....	....	....	....	....	....	....	....	....	....	....	....	....	....	....	....
1971-72	Medicine Hat Tigers	WCJHL	68	46	*97	*143	....	....	....	96	....	....	....	....	....	....	....	....	....	....	7	7	5	12	18	....	....	....
1972-73	Medicine Hat Tigers	WCJHL	67	58	*96	*154	....	....	....	104	....	....	....	....	....	....	....	....	....	....	17	12	*27	*39	48	....	....	....
1973-74	Atlanta Flames	NHL	77	19	45	64	19	39	58	54	4	0	2	216	8.8	96	42	70	1	–15	4	0	2	2	0	0	0	0
1974-75	Atlanta Flames	NHL	77	25	52	77	23	41	64	73	9	0	2	206	12.1	122	49	68	18	+23	....	....	....	....	....	....	....	....
1975-76	Atlanta Flames	NHL	80	31	51	82	29	40	69	60	9	1	5	233	13.3	108	44	74	12	+2	2	0	0	0	2	0	0	0
1976-77	Atlanta Flames	NHL	79	30	51	81	29	41	70	52	5	1	3	277	10.8	120	30	93	6	+3	3	1	3	4	8	1	0	0
1977-78	Atlanta Flames	NHL	80	27	42	69	26	34	60	54	3	0	5	215	12.6	93	19	81	4	–3	2	1	0	1	2	0	0	0
	Canada	WEC-A	7	1	1	2	....	....	....	4	....	....	....	....	....	....	....	....	....	....	....	....	....	....	....	....	....	....
1978-79	Atlanta Flames	NHL	52	23	35	58	21	27	48	36	7	1	2	137	16.8	86	25	52	7	+16	....	....	....	....	....	....	....	....
	Chicago Black Hawks	NHL	14	0	10	10	0	8	8	14	0	0	0	27	0.0	18	4	11	0	+3	4	0	0	0	2	0	0	0
1979-80	Chicago Black Hawks	NHL	77	26	43	69	24	33	57	31	10	0	7	160	16.3	93	36	75	11	–7	7	4	4	8	0	4	0	0
1980-81	Chicago Black Hawks	NHL	72	21	55	76	17	39	56	20	5	2	3	167	12.6	105	31	103	36	+7	3	0	3	3	0	0	0	0
1981-82	Chicago Black Hawks	NHL	71	32	50	82	25	33	58	84	10	2	4	170	18.8	108	34	105	23	–8	15	6	9	15	13	3	0	0
1982-83	Chicago Black Hawks	NHL	61	23	38	61	19	26	45	27	6	0	4	122	18.9	82	25	52	8	+13	13	6	7	13	8	2	0	2
1983-84	Chicago Black Hawks	NHL	54	17	30	47	14	20	34	35	5	1	2	103	16.5	65	17	68	7	–13	5	1	1	2	2	0	0	0
1984-85	Chicago Black Hawks	NHL	74	16	30	46	13	20	33	13	2	0	4	100	16.0	72	20	76	8	–16	15	4	8	12	10	0	0	0
1985-86	Chicago Black Hawks	NHL	51	2	19	21	2	13	15	14	0	0	0	77	2.6	33	4	50	2	–19	3	2	1	3	2	0	0	0
	NHL Totals		919	292	551	843	261	414	675	567	75	8	43	2210	13.2	1201	380	978	143		76	25	38	63	49	10	0	2

WCJHL All-Star Team (1972, 1973)

Played in NHL All-Star Game (1975, 1976, 1977)

Traded to **Chicago** by **Atlanta** with Pat Ribble, Greg Fox, Harold Phillipoff and Miles Zaharko for Ivan Boldirev, Phil Russell and Darcy Rota, March 13, 1979.

• MACADAM, AL

Al MacAdam RW – L. 6′, 180 lbs. b: Charlottetown, P.E.I., 3/16/1952. Philadelphia's 4th choice, 55th overall, in 1972 Amateur Draft.

Season	Club	League	GP	G	A	Pts	AG	AA	APts	PIM	PP	SH	GW	S	%	TGF	PGF	TGA	PGA	+/–	GP	G	A	Pts	PIM	PP	SH	GW
1969-70	Charlottetown Islanders	PEI Jr.	42	27	31	58	....	....	....	55	....	....	....	....	....	....	....	....	....	....	....	....	....	....	....	....	....	....
1970-71	Charlottetown Islanders	PEI Jr.	43	51	43	94	....	....	....	58	....	....	....	....	....	....	....	....	....	....	....	....	....	....	....	....	....	....
1971-72	University of P.E.I.	AUAA	....	14	17	31	....	....	....	8	....	....	....	....	....	....	....	....	....	....	....	....	....	....	....	....	....	....
1972-73	Richmond Robins	AHL	68	19	32	51	....	....	....	42	....	....	....	....	....	....	....	....	....	....	4	0	2	2	0	....	....	....
1973-74	Philadelphia Flyers	NHL	5	0	0	0	0	0	0	0	0	0	0	2	0.0	0	0	2	0	–2	1	0	0	0	0	0	0	0
	Richmond Robins	AHL	62	23	22	45	....	....	....	36	....	....	....	....	....	....	....	....	....	....	5	1	4	5	4	....	....	....
1974-75	California Golden Seals	NHL	80	18	25	43	17	20	37	55	2	0	1	160	11.3	70	14	85	6	–23	....	....	....	....	....	....	....	....
1975-76	California Golden Seals	NHL	80	32	31	63	30	24	54	49	8	4	5	177	18.1	89	27	89	18	–9	....	....	....	....	....	....	....	....
1976-77	Cleveland Barons	NHL	80	22	41	63	21	33	54	68	6	0	3	194	11.3	97	27	85	13	–2	....	....	....	....	....	....	....	....
	Canada	WEC-A	10	4	4	8	....	....	....	0	....	....	....	....	....	....	....	....	....	....	....	....	....	....	....	....	....	....
1977-78	Cleveland Barons	NHL	80	16	32	48	15	26	41	42	3	0	1	149	10.7	76	17	110	32	–19	....	....	....	....	....	....	....	....
1978-79	Minnesota North Stars	NHL	69	24	34	58	22	26	48	30	6	0	4	135	17.8	89	27	66	4	0	....	....	....	....	....	....	....	....
	Canada	WEC-A	8	4	4	8	....	....	....	0	....	....	....	....	....	....	....	....	....	....	....	....	....	....	....	....	....	....
1979-80	Minnesota North Stars	NHL	80	42	51	93	38	39	77	24	13	0	2	170	24.7	139	47	60	4	+36	15	7	9	16	4	1	0	2
1980-81	Minnesota North Stars	NHL	78	21	39	60	17	27	44	94	6	0	7	145	14.5	103	47	64	2	–6	19	9	10	19	4	1	1	1
1981-82	Minnesota North Stars	NHL	79	18	43	61	14	28	42	37	5	2	4	141	12.8	100	28	82	19	+9	4	1	0	1	4	0	0	0
1982-83	Minnesota North Stars	NHL	73	11	22	33	9	15	24	60	0	3	2	93	11.8	51	5	68	25	+3	9	2	1	3	2	0	0	0
1983-84	Minnesota North Stars	NHL	80	22	13	35	18	9	27	23	1	4	1	104	21.2	52	1	92	36	–5	16	1	4	5	7	0	0	0
1984-85	Vancouver Canucks	NHL	80	14	20	34	11	14	25	27	0	2	2	80	17.5	48	4	108	35	–29	....	....	....	....	....	....	....	....

Season	Club	League	REGULAR SEASON																		PLAYOFFS							
			GP	G	A	Pts	AG	AA	APts	PIM	PP	SH	GW	S	%	TGF	PGF	TGA	PGA	+/–	GP	G	A	Pts	PIM	PP	SH	GW
1985-86	Fredericton Express	AHL	11	0	4	4	....	....	....	5	....	....	....	....	....	....	....	....	....	....	....	....	....	....	....	....	....	....
1986-87	Charlottetown Islanders	PEI Sr.	11	11	11	22	....	....	....	2	....	....	....	....	....	....	....	....	....	....	....	....	....	....	....	....	....	....
1987-88	St. Thomas University	AUAA	DID NOT PLAY – COACHING																									
	NHL Totals		**864**	**240**	**351**	**591**	**212**	**261**	**473**	**509**	**50**	**15**	**32**	**1550**	**15.5**	**914**	**244**	**911**	**194**		**64**	**20**	**24**	**44**	**21**	**2**	**1**	**3**

Won Bill Masterton Trophy (1980)

Played in NHL All-Star Game (1976, 1977)

Traded to **California** by **Philadelphia** with Larry Wright, Philadelphia's 1st round choice (Rob Chipperfield) and future considerations (George Pesut, December 11, 1974) in 1974 Amateur Draft for Reggie Leach, May 24, 1974. Transferred to **Cleveland** after **California** franchise relocated, August 26, 1976. Protected by **Minnesota** prior to **Minnesota-Cleveland** Dispersal Draft, June 15, 1978. Traded to **Vancouver** by **Minnesota** for Harold Snepsts, June 21, 1984.

• MacDERMID, PAUL

Paul MacDermid RW – R. 6'1", 205 lbs. b: Chesley, Ont., 4/14/1963. Hartford's 2nd choice, 61st overall, in 1981 Entry Draft.

Season	Club	League	GP	G	A	Pts	AG	AA	APts	PIM	PP	SH	GW	S	%	TGF	PGF	TGA	PGA	+/–	GP	G	A	Pts	PIM	PP	SH	GW
1979-80	Port Elgin Bears	Jr. C	30	23	20	43	....	....	....	87	....	....	....	....	....	....	....	....	....	....	....	....	....	....	....	....	....	....
1980-81	Windsor Spitfires	OHA	68	15	17	32	....	....	....	106	....	....	....	....	....	....	....	....	....	....	....	....	....	....	....	....	....	....
1981-82	Windsor Spitfires	OHL	65	26	45	71	....	....	....	179	....	....	....	....	....	....	....	....	....	....	9	6	4	10	17	....	....	....
	Hartford Whalers	**NHL**	**3**	**1**	**0**	**1**	**1**	**0**	**1**	**2**	**0**	**0**	**0**	**4**	**25.0**	**2**	**0**	**2**	**0**	**0**	....	....	....	....	....	....	....	....
1982-83	Windsor Spitfires	OHL	42	35	45	80	....	....	....	9	....	....	....	....	....	....	....	....	....	....	....	....	....	....	....	....	....	....
	Hartford Whalers	**NHL**	**7**	**0**	**0**	**0**	**0**	**0**	**0**	**2**	**0**	**0**	**0**	**7**	**0.0**	**0**	**0**	**6**	**0**	**–6**	....	....	....	....	....	....	....	....
1983-84	**Hartford Whalers**	**NHL**	**3**	**0**	**1**	**1**	**0**	**1**	**1**	**0**	**0**	**0**	**0**	**2**	**0.0**	**1**	**0**	**0**	**0**	**+1**	....	....	....	....	....	....	....	....
	Binghamton Whalers	AHL	70	31	30	61	....	....	....	130	....	....	....	....	....	....	....	....	....	....	....	....	....	....	....	....	....	....
1984-85	**Hartford Whalers**	**NHL**	**31**	**4**	**7**	**11**	**3**	**5**	**8**	**29**	**0**	**0**	**0**	**27**	**14.8**	**18**	**0**	**15**	**0**	**+3**	....	....	....	....	....	....	....	....
	Binghamton Whalers	AHL	48	9	31	40	....	....	....	87	....	....	....	....	....	....	....	....	....	....	....	....	....	....	....	....	....	....
1985-86	**Hartford Whalers**	**NHL**	**74**	**13**	**10**	**23**	**10**	**7**	**17**	**160**	**0**	**0**	**2**	**88**	**14.8**	**32**	**0**	**33**	**2**	**+1**	**10**	**2**	**1**	**3**	**20**	**0**	**0**	**1**
1986-87	**Hartford Whalers**	**NHL**	**72**	**7**	**11**	**18**	**6**	**8**	**14**	**202**	**0**	**0**	**1**	**72**	**9.7**	**28**	**1**	**24**	**0**	**+3**	**6**	**2**	**1**	**3**	**34**	**0**	**0**	**1**
1987-88	**Hartford Whalers**	**NHL**	**80**	**20**	**15**	**35**	**17**	**11**	**28**	**139**	**4**	**0**	**2**	**96**	**20.8**	**63**	**15**	**45**	**0**	**+3**	**6**	**0**	**5**	**5**	**14**	**0**	**0**	**0**
1988-89	**Hartford Whalers**	**NHL**	**74**	**17**	**27**	**44**	**14**	**19**	**33**	**141**	**5**	**0**	**3**	**113**	**15.0**	**83**	**28**	**54**	**0**	**+1**	**4**	**1**	**1**	**2**	**16**	**0**	**0**	**0**
1989-90	**Hartford Whalers**	**NHL**	**29**	**6**	**12**	**18**	**5**	**9**	**14**	**69**	**3**	**0**	**2**	**37**	**16.2**	**22**	**8**	**13**	**0**	**+1**	....	....	....	....	....	....	....	....
	Winnipeg Jets	**NHL**	**44**	**7**	**10**	**17**	**6**	**7**	**13**	**100**	**1**	**0**	**1**	**48**	**14.6**	**36**	**6**	**26**	**0**	**+4**	**7**	**0**	**2**	**2**	**8**	**0**	**0**	**0**
1990-91	**Winnipeg Jets**	**NHL**	**69**	**15**	**21**	**36**	**14**	**16**	**30**	**128**	**3**	**0**	**1**	**94**	**16.0**	**63**	**16**	**53**	**0**	**–6**	....	....	....	....	....	....	....	....
1991-92	**Winnipeg Jets**	**NHL**	**59**	**10**	**11**	**21**	**9**	**8**	**17**	**151**	**2**	**0**	**2**	**71**	**14.1**	**36**	**10**	**34**	**0**	**–8**	....	....	....	....	....	....	....	....
	Washington Capitals	**NHL**	**15**	**2**	**5**	**7**	**2**	**4**	**6**	**43**	**0**	**0**	**0**	**21**	**9.5**	**11**	**0**	**9**	**0**	**+2**	**7**	**0**	**1**	**1**	**22**	**0**	**0**	**0**
1992-93	**Washington Capitals**	**NHL**	**72**	**9**	**8**	**17**	**7**	**5**	**12**	**80**	**1**	**0**	**3**	**45**	**20.0**	**22**	**4**	**31**	**0**	**–13**	....	....	....	....	....	....	....	....
1993-94	**Quebec Nordiques**	**NHL**	**44**	**2**	**3**	**5**	**2**	**2**	**4**	**35**	**0**	**0**	**0**	**16**	**12.5**	**12**	**0**	**15**	**0**	**–3**	....	....	....	....	....	....	....	....
1994-95	**Quebec Nordiques**	**NHL**	**14**	**3**	**1**	**4**	**5**	**1**	**6**	**22**	**0**	**0**	**1**	**13**	**23.1**	**8**	**0**	**5**	**0**	**+3**	**3**	**0**	**0**	**0**	**2**	**0**	**0**	**0**
	NHL Totals		**690**	**116**	**142**	**258**	**101**	**103**	**204**	**1303**	**19**	**0**	**18**	**754**	**15.4**	**437**	**88**	**365**	**2**		**43**	**5**	**11**	**16**	**116**	**0**	**0**	**2**

Traded to **Winnipeg** by **Hartford** for Randy Cunneyworth, December 13, 1989. Traded to **Washington** by **Winnipeg** for Mike Lalor, March 2, 1992. Traded to **Quebec** by **Washington** with Reggie Savage for Mike Hough, June 20, 1993.

• MacDONALD, BLAIR

Blair MacDonald RW – R. 5'10", 180 lbs. b: Cornwall, Ont., 11/17/1953. Los Angeles' 4th choice, 86th overall, in 1973 Amateur Draft.

Season	Club	League	GP	G	A	Pts	AG	AA	APts	PIM	PP	SH	GW	S	%	TGF	PGF	TGA	PGA	+/–	GP	G	A	Pts	PIM	PP	SH	GW
1970-71	Cornwall Royals	QJHL	51	24	14	38	....	....	....	6	....	....	....	....	....	....	....	....	....	....	....	....	....	....	....	....	....	....
1971-72	Cornwall Royals	QMJHL	61	45	45	90	....	....	....	36	....	....	....	....	....	....	....	....	....	....	16	10	5	15	10	....	....	....
1972-73	Cornwall Royals	QMJHL	64	63	39	102	....	....	....	44	....	....	....	....	....	....	....	....	....	....	16	14	14	28	10	....	....	....
1973-74	Edmonton Oilers	WHA	78	21	24	45	....	....	....	34	....	....	....	....	....	....	....	....	....	....	5	4	2	6	2	....	....	....
1974-75	Edmonton Oilers	WHA	72	22	24	46	....	....	....	14	....	....	....	....	....	....	....	....	....	....	....	....	....	....	....	....	....	....
1975-76	Edmonton Oilers	WHA	29	7	5	12	....	....	....	8	....	....	....	....	....	....	....	....	....	....	....	....	....	....	....	....	....	....
	Indianapolis Racers	WHA	56	20	11	31	....	....	....	14	....	....	....	....	....	....	....	....	....	....	7	0	0	0	0	....	....	....
1976-77	Indianapolis Racers	WHA	81	34	30	64	....	....	....	28	....	....	....	....	....	....	....	....	....	....	13	7	8	15	4	....	....	....
1977-78	Edmonton Oilers	WHA	80	34	34	68	....	....	....	11	....	....	....	....	....	....	....	....	....	....	5	1	1	2	0	....	....	....
1978-79	Edmonton Oilers	WHA	80	34	37	71	....	....	....	44	....	....	....	....	....	....	....	....	....	....	13	8	10	18	6	....	....	....
1979-80	**Edmonton Oilers**	**NHL**	**80**	**46**	**48**	**94**	**42**	**37**	**79**	**6**	**13**	**2**	**6**	**266**	**17.3**	**144**	**45**	**139**	**41**	**+1**	**3**	**0**	**3**	**3**	**0**	**0**	**0**	**0**
1980-81	**Edmonton Oilers**	**NHL**	**51**	**19**	**24**	**43**	**16**	**17**	**33**	**27**	**5**	**0**	**1**	**134**	**14.2**	**67**	**23**	**70**	**18**	**–8**	....	....	....	....	....	....	....	....
	Vancouver Canucks	**NHL**	**12**	**5**	**9**	**14**	**4**	**6**	**10**	**10**	**2**	**0**	**2**	**38**	**13.2**	**19**	**4**	**14**	**0**	**+1**	**3**	**0**	**1**	**1**	**2**	**0**	**0**	**0**
1981-82	Dallas Black Hawks	CHL	3	1	1	2	....	....	....	0	....	....	....	....	....	....	....	....	....	....	....	....	....	....	....	....	....	....
	Vancouver Canucks	**NHL**	**59**	**18**	**15**	**33**	**14**	**10**	**24**	**20**	**4**	**0**	**2**	**116**	**15.5**	**54**	**18**	**37**	**1**	**0**	**3**	**0**	**0**	**0**	**0**	**0**	**0**	**0**
1982-83	**Vancouver Canucks**	**NHL**	**17**	**3**	**4**	**7**	**2**	**3**	**5**	**2**	**2**	**0**	**0**	**29**	**10.3**	**15**	**6**	**11**	**1**	**–1**	**2**	**0**	**2**	**2**	**0**	**0**	**0**	**0**
	Fredericton Express	AHL	60	29	37	66	....	....	....	20	....	....	....	....	....	....	....	....	....	....	7	2	3	5	2	....	....	....
1983-84			DID NOT PLAY																									
1984-85	WAT Stadlau	Austria	34	37	29	66	....	....	....	30	....	....	....	....	....	....	....	....	....	....	....	....	....	....	....	....	....	....
1985-86	FCS Innsbruck	Austria	23	20	18	38	....	....	....	8	....	....	....	....	....	....	....	....	....	....	....	....	....	....	....	....	....	....
	NHL Totals		**219**	**91**	**100**	**191**	**78**	**73**	**151**	**65**	**26**	**2**	**11**	**583**	**15.6**	**299**	**96**	**271**	**61**		**11**	**0**	**6**	**6**	**2**	**0**	**0**	**0**
	Other Major League Totals		476	172	165	337	....	....	....	153	....	....	....	....	....	....	....	....	....		43	20	21	41	12	....	....	....

QMJHL Second All-Star Team (1973) • WHA Second All-Star Team (1979)

Played in NHL All-Star Game (1980)

Selected by **Edmonton** (WHA) in 1972 WHA General Player Draft, February 12, 1972. Traded to **Indianapolis** (WHA) by **Edmonton** (WHA) for future considerations, December, 1976. Traded to **Edmonton** (WHA) by **Indianapolis** (WHA) with Dave Inkpen and Mike Zuke for Kevin Devine, Barry Wilkins, Rusty Patenaude and Claude St. Sauveur, September, 1977. Rights retained by **Edmonton** prior to Expansion Draft, June 9, 1979. Traded to **Vancouver** by **Edmonton** with the rights to Ken Berry for Garry Lariviere and the rights to Lars Gunnar Petterson, March 10, 1981.

• MacDONALD, BRETT

Brett MacDonald D – L. 6'1", 205 lbs. b: Bothwell, Ont., 1/5/1966. Vancouver's 7th choice, 94th overall, in 1984 Entry Draft.

Season	Club	League	GP	G	A	Pts	AG	AA	APts	PIM	PP	SH	GW	S	%	TGF	PGF	TGA	PGA	+/–	GP	G	A	Pts	PIM	PP	SH	GW
1982-83	Dixie Beehives	OJHL	44	5	18	23	....	....	....	28	....	....	....	....	....	....	....	....	....	....	....	....	....	....	....	....	....	....
1983-84	North Bay Centennials	OHL	70	8	18	26	....	....	....	83	....	....	....	....	....	....	....	....	....	....	4	0	1	1	0	....	....	....
1984-85	North Bay Centennials	OHL	58	6	27	33	....	....	....	72	....	....	....	....	....	....	....	....	....	....	8	1	1	2	11	....	....	....
1985-86	North Bay Centennials	OHL	15	0	6	6	....	....	....	42	....	....	....	....	....	....	....	....	....	....	....	....	....	....	....	....	....	....
	Kitchener Rangers	OHL	53	10	27	37	....	....	....	52	....	....	....	....	....	....	....	....	....	....	5	3	7	10	6	....	....	....
1986-87	Fredericton Express	AHL	49	0	9	9	....	....	....	29	....	....	....	....	....	....	....	....	....	....	....	....	....	....	....	....	....	....
1987-88	**Vancouver Canucks**	**NHL**	**1**	**0**	**0**	**0**	**0**	**0**	**0**	**0**	**0**	**0**	**0**	**0**	**0.0**	**1**	**0**	**2**	**0**	**–1**	....	....	....	....	....	....	....	....
	Fredericton Express	AHL	15	1	5	6	....	....	....	23	....	....	....	....	....	....	....	....	....	....	....	....	....	....	....	....	....	....
	Flint Spirits	IHL	49	2	21	23	....	....	....	43	....	....	....	....	....	....	....	....	....	....	15	2	2	4	12	....	....	....
1988-89	New Haven Nighthawks	AHL	15	2	4	6	....	....	....	6	....	....	....	....	....	....	....	....	....	....	....	....	....	....	....	....	....	....
	Flint Spirits	IHL	57	3	24	27	....	....	....	53	....	....	....	....	....	....	....	....	....	....	....	....	....	....	....	....	....	....
1989-90			DID NOT PLAY																									
1990-91	Nashville Knights	ECHL	64	19	62	81	....	....	....	56	....	....	....	....	....	....	....	....	....	....	....	....	....	....	....	....	....	....
	San Diego Gulls	IHL	3	0	1	1	....	....	....	0	....	....	....	....	....	....	....	....	....	....	....	....	....	....	....	....	....	....
	Moncton Hawks	AHL	2	0	0	0	....	....	....	0	....	....	....	....	....	....	....	....	....	....	7	1	3	4	4	....	....	....
1991-92	Flint Bulldogs	ColHL	46	12	33	45	....	....	....	23	....	....	....	....	....	....	....	....	....	....	....	....	....	....	....	....	....	....
	Moncton Hawks	AHL	3	0	0	0	....	....	....	2	....	....	....	....	....	....	....	....	....	....	....	....	....	....	....	....	....	....
1992-93	Flint Bulldogs	ColHL	60	12	39	51	....	....	....	60	....	....	....	....	....	....	....	....	....	....	6	0	5	5	21	....	....	....
1993-94	Chatham Wheels	ColHL	42	8	31	39	....	....	....	29	....	....	....	....	....	....	....	....	....	....	14	6	9	15	4	....	....	....
1994-95	Saginaw Wheels	ColHL	62	17	42	59	....	....	....	42	....	....	....	....	....	....	....	....	....	....	....	....	....	....	....	....	....	....
	Muskegon Fury	ColHL	11	3	8	11	....	....	....	14	....	....	....	....	....	....	....	....	....	....	16	2	5	7	12	....	....	....
1995-96	Orlando Solar Bears	IHL	1	0	0	0	....	....	....	2	....	....	....	....	....	....	....	....	....	....	....	....	....	....	....	....	....	....
	Flint Generals	ColHL	62	16	39	55	....	....	....	55	....	....	....	....	....	....	....	....	....	....	15	1	8	9	2	....	....	....
1996-97	Flint Generals	ColHL	74	8	64	72	....	....	....	44	....	....	....	....	....	....	....	....	....	....	14	1	11	12	12	....	....	....
1997-98	Flint Generals	UHL	56	7	37	44	....	....	....	32	....	....	....	....	....	....	....	....	....	....	17	1	6	7	14	....	....	....
	NHL Totals		**1**	**0**	**0**	**0**	**0**	**0**	**0**	**0**	**0**	**0**	**0**	**0**	**0.0**	**1**	**0**	**2**	**0**		....	....	....	....	....	....	....	....

Defenseman of the Year - ECHL (1991)

• MacDONALD, DOUG

Doug MacDonald LW – L. 6', 192 lbs. b: Assiniboia, Sask., 2/8/1969. Buffalo's 3rd choice, 77th overall, in 1989 Entry Draft.

Season	Club	League	GP	G	A	Pts	AG	AA	APts	PIM	PP	SH	GW	S	%	TGF	PGF	TGA	PGA	+/–	GP	G	A	Pts	PIM	PP	SH	GW
1988-89	University of Wisconsin	WCHA	44	23	25	48	....	....	....	50	....	....	....	....	....	....	....	....	....	....	....	....	....	....	....	....	....	....
1989-90	University of Wisconsin	WCHA	44	16	35	51	....	....	....	52	....	....	....	....	....	....	....	....	....	....	....	....	....	....	....	....	....	....
1990-91	University of Wisconsin	WCHA	31	20	26	46	....	....	....	50	....	....	....	....	....	....	....	....	....	....	....	....	....	....	....	....	....	....
1991-92	University of Wisconsin	WCHA	29	14	25	39	....	....	....	58	....	....	....	....	....	....	....	....	....	....	....	....	....	....	....	....	....	....

			REGULAR SEASON																		PLAYOFFS							
Season	Club	League	GP	G	A	Pts	AG	AA	APts	PIM	PP	SH	GW	S	%	TGF	PGF	TGA	PGA	+/–	GP	G	A	Pts	PIM	PP	SH	GW
1992-93	**Buffalo Sabres**	**NHL**	**5**	**1**	**0**	**1**	**1**	**0**	**1**	**2**	**0**	**0**	**0**	**1**	**100.0**	**3**	**0**	**3**	**0**	**0**	....	....	....	....	....	....	....	....
	Rochester Americans	AHL	64	25	33	58	....	....	....	58	....	....	....	....	....	....	....	....	....	....	7	0	2	2	4	....	....	....
1993-94	**Buffalo Sabres**	**NHL**	**4**	**0**	**0**	**0**	**0**	**0**	**0**	**0**	**0**	**0**	**0**	**3**	**0.0**	**1**	**0**	**3**	**0**	**–2**	....	....	....	....	....	....	....	....
	Rochester Americans	AHL	63	25	19	44	....	....	....	46	....	....	....	....	....	....	....	....	....	....	4	1	1	2	8	....	....	....
1994-95	Rochester Americans	AHL	58	21	25	46	....	....	....	73	....	....	....	....	....	....	....	....	....	....	5	0	1	1	0	....	....	....
	Buffalo Sabres	**NHL**	**2**	**0**	**0**	**0**	**0**	**0**	**0**	**0**	**0**	**0**	**0**	**0**	**0.0**	**0**	**0**	**1**	**0**	**–1**	....	....	....	....	....	....	....	....
1995-96	Cincinnati Cyclones	IHL	71	19	40	59	....	....	....	66	....	....	....	....	....	....	....	....	....	....	15	1	3	4	14	....	....	....
1996-97	Cincinnati Cyclones	IHL	65	20	34	54	....	....	....	36	....	....	....	....	....	....	....	....	....	....	3	0	0	0	0	....	....	....
1997-98	Cincinnati Cyclones	IHL	70	17	19	36	....	....	....	64	....	....	....	....	....	....	....	....	....	....	4	0	4	4	0	....	....	....
	NHL Totals		**11**	**1**	**0**	**1**	**1**	**0**	**1**	**2**	**0**	**0**	**0**	**4**	**25.0**	**4**	**0**	**7**	**0**		....	....	....	....	....	....	....	....

• MacDONALD, KEVIN

Kevin MacDonald D – L. 6′, 200 lbs. b: Prescott, Ont., 2/24/1966.

1983-84	Peterborough Petes	OHL	32	3	3	6	....	....	....	78	....	....	....	....	....	....	....	....	....	....	8	0	1	1	16	....	....	....
	Sudbury Wolves	OHL	1	0	0	0	....	....	....	0	....	....	....	....	....	....	....	....	....	....	....	....	....	....	....	....	....	....
1984-85	Peterborough Petes	OHL	63	3	13	16	....	....	....	162	....	....	....	....	....	....	....	....	....	....	15	1	1	2	6	....	....	....
1985-86	Peterborough Petes	OHL	51	4	15	19	....	....	....	132	....	....	....	....	....	....	....	....	....	....	16	0	5	5	24	....	....	....
1986-87	Peterborough Petes	OHL	48	4	4	8	....	....	....	183	....	....	....	....	....	....	....	....	....	....	10	0	1	1	16	....	....	....
1987-88	St. Thomas University	AUAA	24	7	14	21	....	....	....	140	....	....	....	....	....	....	....	....	....	....	....	....	....	....	....	....	....	....
1988-89	Muskegon Lumberjacks	IHL	64	2	13	15	....	....	....	190	....	....	....	....	....	....	....	....	....	....	11	2	3	5	22	....	....	....
1989-90	New Haven Nighthawks	AHL	27	0	1	1	....	....	....	111	....	....	....	....	....	....	....	....	....	....	....	....	....	....	....	....	....	....
	Phoenix Roadrunners	IHL	30	1	5	6	....	....	....	201	....	....	....	....	....	....	....	....	....	....	....	....	....	....	....	....	....	....
1990-91	Phoenix Roadrunners	IHL	74	1	9	10	....	....	....	327	....	....	....	....	....	....	....	....	....	....	11	0	1	1	22	....	....	....
1991-92	Phoenix Roadrunners	IHL	76	7	14	21	....	....	....	304	....	....	....	....	....	....	....	....	....	....	....	....	....	....	....	....	....	....
1992-93	Phoenix Roadrunners	IHL	6	0	1	1	....	....	....	23	....	....	....	....	....	....	....	....	....	....	....	....	....	....	....	....	....	....
	Fort Wayne Komets	IHL	65	4	9	13	....	....	....	283	....	....	....	....	....	....	....	....	....	....	11	0	0	0	21	....	....	....
1993-94	Fort Wayne Komets	IHL	29	0	3	3	....	....	....	140	....	....	....	....	....	....	....	....	....	....	15	0	4	4	76	....	....	....
	Ottawa Senators	**NHL**	**1**	**0**	**0**	**0**	**0**	**0**	**0**	**2**	**0**	**0**	**0**	**0**	**0.0**	**0**	**0**	**0**	**0**	**0**	....	....	....	....	....	....	....	....
	P.E.I. Senators	AHL	40	2	4	6	....	....	....	245	....	....	....	....	....	....	....	....	....	....	....	....	....	....	....	....	....	....
1994-95	Chicago Wolves	IHL	75	1	12	13	....	....	....	*390	....	....	....	....	....	....	....	....	....	....	3	0	0	0	17	....	....	....
1995-96	Chicago Wolves	IHL	75	2	6	8	....	....	....	274	....	....	....	....	....	....	....	....	....	....	9	0	3	3	23	....	....	....
1996-97	Fort Wayne Komets	IHL	53	1	2	3	....	....	....	251	....	....	....	....	....	....	....	....	....	....	....	....	....	....	....	....	....	....
	Hershey Bears	AHL	16	1	1	2	....	....	....	74	....	....	....	....	....	....	....	....	....	....	10	1	0	1	13	....	....	....
1997-98	Hershey Bears	AHL	5	0	0	0	....	....	....	37	....	....	....	....	....	....	....	....	....	....	....	....	....	....	....	....	....	....
	Baton Rouge Kingfish	ECHL	58	2	17	19	....	....	....	222	....	....	....	....	....	....	....	....	....	....	....	....	....	....	....	....	....	....
	NHL Totals		**1**	**0**	**0**	**0**	**0**	**0**	**0**	**2**	**0**	**0**	**0**	**0**	**0.0**	**0**	**0**	**0**	**0**		....	....	....	....	....	....	....	....

Signed as a free agent by **Edmonton**, July, 1990. Signed as a free agent by **Ottawa**, December 22, 1993.

• MacDONALD, LOWELL

Lowell MacDonald LW – R. 5′11″, 185 lbs. b: New Glasgow, N.S., 8/30/1941.

1959-60	Hamilton Tiger Cubs	OHA	48	17	19	36	....	....	....	7	....	....	....	....	....	....	....	....	....	....	....	....	....	....	....	....	....	....
1960-61	Hamilton Red Wings	OHA	48	26	28	54	....	....	....	15	....	....	....	....	....	....	....	....	....	....	11	6	9	15	4	....	....	....
1961-62	Hamilton Red Wings	OHA	50	*46	39	85	....	....	....	10	....	....	....	....	....	....	....	....	....	....	10	*7	5	*12	8	....	....	....
	Detroit Red Wings	**NHL**	**1**	**0**	**0**	**0**	**0**	**0**	**0**	**2**	....	....	....	....	....	....	....	....	....	....	....	....	....	....	....	....	....	....
1962-63	**Detroit Red Wings**	**NHL**	**26**	**2**	**1**	**3**	**2**	**1**	**3**	**8**	....	....	....	....	....	....	....	....	....	....	**1**	**0**	**0**	**0**	**2**	....	....	....
	Pittsburgh Hornets	AHL	41	20	19	39	....	....	....	4	....	....	....	....	....	....	....	....	....	....	....	....	....	....	....	....	....	....
1963-64	**Detroit Red Wings**	**NHL**	**10**	**1**	**4**	**5**	**1**	**4**	**5**	**0**	....	....	....	....	....	....	....	....	....	....	....	....	....	....	....	....	....	....
	Pittsburgh Hornets	AHL	59	31	29	60	....	....	....	6	....	....	....	....	....	....	....	....	....	....	5	3	1	4	2	....	....	....
1964-65	**Detroit Red Wings**	**NHL**	**9**	**2**	**1**	**3**	**3**	**1**	**4**	**0**	....	....	....	....	....	....	....	....	....	....	....	....	....	....	....	....	....	....
	Pittsburgh Hornets	AHL	59	16	20	36	....	....	....	10	....	....	....	....	....	....	....	....	....	....	2	0	0	0	0	....	....	....
1965-66	Rochester Americans	AHL	1	0	0	0	....	....	....	0	....	....	....	....	....	....	....	....	....	....	....	....	....	....	....	....	....	....
	Tulsa Oilers	CHL	57	33	25	58	....	....	....	4	....	....	....	....	....	....	....	....	....	....	11	5	4	9	0	....	....	....
1966-67	Tulsa Oilers	CHL	33	14	17	31	....	....	....	8	....	....	....	....	....	....	....	....	....	....	....	....	....	....	....	....	....	....
1967-68	**Los Angeles Kings**	**NHL**	**74**	**21**	**24**	**45**	**26**	**25**	**51**	**12**	**2**	**1**	**2**	**232**	**9.1**	**63**	**6**	**75**	**7**	**–11**	**7**	**3**	**4**	**7**	**2**	**1**	**0**	**1**
1968-69	**Los Angeles Kings**	**NHL**	**58**	**14**	**14**	**28**	**16**	**13**	**29**	**10**	**1**	**1**	**0**	**181**	**7.7**	**43**	**4**	**53**	**3**	**–11**	**7**	**2**	**3**	**5**	**0**	**0**	**1**	**0**
	Springfield Kings	AHL	9	6	9	15	....	....	....	0	....	....	....	....	....	....	....	....	....	....	....	....	....	....	....	....	....	....
1969-70	Springfield Kings	AHL	14	4	3	7	....	....	....	0	....	....	....	....	....	....	....	....	....	....	3	0	0	0	0	....	....	....
1970-71	**Pittsburgh Penguins**	**NHL**	**10**	**0**	**1**	**1**	**0**	**1**	**1**	**0**	**0**	**0**	**0**	**11**	**0.0**	**2**	**0**	**8**	**0**	**–6**	....	....	....	....	....	....	....	....
1971-72			DID NOT PLAY – RETIRED																									
1972-73	**Pittsburgh Penguins**	**NHL**	**78**	**34**	**41**	**75**	**34**	**34**	**68**	**8**	**6**	**0**	**3**	**244**	**13.9**	**115**	**22**	**68**	**12**	**+37**	....	....	....	....	....	....	....	....
1973-74	**Pittsburgh Penguins**	**NHL**	**78**	**43**	**39**	**82**	**44**	**34**	**78**	**14**	**9**	**0**	**2**	**260**	**16.5**	**120**	**36**	**75**	**8**	**+17**	....	....	....	....	....	....	....	....
1974-75	**Pittsburgh Penguins**	**NHL**	**71**	**27**	**33**	**60**	**25**	**26**	**51**	**24**	**6**	**0**	**5**	**220**	**12.3**	**101**	**26**	**59**	**0**	**+16**	**9**	**4**	**2**	**6**	**4**	**1**	**0**	**1**
1975-76	**Pittsburgh Penguins**	**NHL**	**69**	**30**	**43**	**73**	**28**	**34**	**62**	**12**	**12**	**0**	**3**	**181**	**16.6**	**106**	**40**	**56**	**4**	**+14**	**3**	**1**	**0**	**1**	**0**	**1**	**0**	**1**
1976-77	**Pittsburgh Penguins**	**NHL**	**3**	**1**	**1**	**2**	**1**	**1**	**2**	**0**	**1**	**0**	**0**	**9**	**11.1**	**2**	**1**	**2**	**0**	**–1**	**3**	**1**	**2**	**3**	**4**	**0**	**0**	**0**
1977-78	**Pittsburgh Penguins**	**NHL**	**19**	**5**	**8**	**13**	**5**	**7**	**12**	**2**	**2**	**0**	**0**	**31**	**16.1**	**18**	**8**	**10**	**0**	**0**	....	....	....	....	....	....	....	....
	NHL Totals		**506**	**180**	**210**	**390**	**185**	**181**	**366**	**92**	**39**	**2**	**15**	**1369**	**13.1**	**570**	**143**	**406**	**34**		**30**	**11**	**11**	**22**	**12**	**3**	**1**	**3**

Won Bill Masterton Trophy (1973)

Played in NHL All-Star Game (1973, 1974)

Traded to **Toronto** by **Detroit** with Marcel Pronovost, Ed Joyal, Larry Jeffrey and Aut Erickson for Andy Bathgate, Bily Harris and Gary Jarrett, May 20, 1965. Claimed by **LA Kings** from **Toronto** in Expansion Draft, June 6, 1967. Claimed by **Pittsburgh** from **LA Kings** in Intra-League Draft, June 9, 1970.

• MacDONALD, PARKER

Parker MacDonald C – L. 5′11″, 160 lbs. b: Sydney, N.S., 6/14/1933.

1949-50	Sydney Millionaires	MSHL	1	1	0	1	....	....	....	0	....	....	....	....	....	....	....	....	....	....	1	1	0	1	0	....	....	....
1950-51	Toronto Marlboros	OHA	51	31	22	53	....	....	....	50	....	....	....	....	....	....	....	....	....	....	13	9	5	14	6	....	....	....
1951-52	Toronto Marlboros	OHA	52	39	51	90	....	....	....	58	....	....	....	....	....	....	....	....	....	....	6	2	3	5	4	....	....	....
1952-53	Toronto Marlboros	OHA	55	39	20	59	....	....	....	48	....	....	....	....	....	....	....	....	....	....	7	3	2	5	4	....	....	....
	Toronto Maple Leafs	**NHL**	**1**	**0**	**0**	**0**	**0**	**0**	**0**	**0**	....	....	....	....	....	....	....	....	....	....	....	....	....	....	....	....	....	....
	Pittsburgh Hornets	AHL	....	....	....	....	....	....	....	....	....	....	....	....	....	....	....	....	....	....	1	0	0	0	0	....	....	....
1953-54	Pittsburgh Hornets	AHL	70	29	24	53	....	....	....	22	....	....	....	....	....	....	....	....	....	....	5	0	2	2	0	....	....	....
1954-55	**Toronto Maple Leafs**	**NHL**	**62**	**8**	**3**	**11**	**12**	**4**	**16**	**36**	....	....	....	....	....	....	....	....	....	....	**4**	**0**	**0**	**0**	**4**	....	....	....
	Pittsburgh Hornets	AHL	8	3	4	7	....	....	....	2	....	....	....	....	....	....	....	....	....	....	....	....	....	....	....	....	....	....
1955-56	Pittsburgh Hornets	AHL	58	35	32	67	....	....	....	60	....	....	....	....	....	....	....	....	....	....	3	0	3	3	2	....	....	....
1956-57	**New York Rangers**	**NHL**	**45**	**7**	**8**	**15**	**9**	**9**	**18**	**24**	....	....	....	....	....	....	....	....	....	....	**1**	**1**	**1**	**2**	**0**	....	....	....
	Providence Reds	AHL	2	4	1	5	....	....	....	0	....	....	....	....	....	....	....	....	....	....	....	....	....	....	....	....	....	....
1957-58	**New York Rangers**	**NHL**	**70**	**8**	**10**	**18**	**10**	**11**	**21**	**30**	....	....	....	....	....	....	....	....	....	....	**6**	**1**	**2**	**3**	**2**	....	....	....
1958-59	Buffalo Bisons	AHL	67	17	21	38	....	....	....	58	....	....	....	....	....	....	....	....	....	....	11	2	7	9	8	....	....	....
1959-60	**New York Rangers**	**NHL**	**4**	**0**	**0**	**0**	**0**	**0**	**0**	**0**	....	....	....	....	....	....	....	....	....	....	....	....	....	....	....	....	....	....
	Springfield Indians	AHL	65	37	36	73	....	....	....	16	....	....	....	....	....	....	....	....	....	....	10	3	7	10	4	....	....	....
1960-61	**Detroit Red Wings**	**NHL**	**70**	**14**	**12**	**26**	**17**	**12**	**29**	**6**	....	....	....	....	....	....	....	....	....	....	**9**	**1**	**0**	**1**	**0**	....	....	....
1961-62	**Detroit Red Wings**	**NHL**	**32**	**5**	**7**	**12**	**6**	**7**	**13**	**8**	....	....	....	....	....	....	....	....	....	....	....	....	....	....	....	....	....	....
	Hershey Bears	AHL	20	10	4	14	....	....	....	8	....	....	....	....	....	....	....	....	....	....	....	....	....	....	....	....	....	....
1962-63	**Detroit Red Wings**	**NHL**	**69**	**33**	**28**	**61**	**41**	**29**	**70**	**32**	....	....	....	....	....	....	....	....	....	....	**11**	**3**	**2**	**5**	**2**	....	....	....
1963-64	**Detroit Red Wings**	**NHL**	**68**	**21**	**25**	**46**	**28**	**28**	**56**	**25**	....	....	....	....	....	....	....	....	....	....	**14**	**3**	**3**	**6**	**2**	....	....	....
1964-65	**Detroit Red Wings**	**NHL**	**69**	**13**	**33**	**46**	**17**	**36**	**53**	**38**	....	....	....	....	....	....	....	....	....	....	**7**	**1**	**1**	**2**	**6**	....	....	....
1965-66	**Boston Bruins**	**NHL**	**29**	**6**	**4**	**10**	**7**	**4**	**11**	**6**	....	....	....	....	....	....	....	....	....	....	....	....	....	....	....	....	....	....
	Detroit Red Wings	**NHL**	**37**	**5**	**12**	**17**	**6**	**12**	**18**	**24**	....	....	....	....	....	....	....	....	....	....	**9**	**0**	**0**	**0**	**2**	....	....	....
1966-67	**Detroit Red Wings**	**NHL**	**16**	**3**	**5**	**8**	**4**	**5**	**9**	**2**	....	....	....	....	....	....	....	....	....	....	....	....	....	....	....	....	....	....
	Pittsburgh Hornets	AHL	59	16	30	46	....	....	....	18	....	....	....	....	....	....	....	....	....	....	9	1	3	4	4	....	....	....
1967-68	**Minnesota North Stars**	**NHL**	**69**	**19**	**23**	**42**	**23**	**24**	**47**	**22**	**9**	**0**	**3**	**183**	**10.4**	**67**	**28**	**57**	**0**	**–18**	**14**	**4**	**5**	**9**	**2**	**0**	**0**	**2**
	Memphis South Stars	CHL	5	2	3	5	....	....	....	2	....	....	....	....	....	....	....	....	....	....	....	....	....	....	....	....	....	....

Season	Club	League	GP	G	A	Pts	AG	AA	APts	PIM	PP	SH	GW	S	%	TGF	PGF	TGA	PGA	+/-	GP	G	A	Pts	PIM	PP	SH	GW
							REGULAR SEASON														PLAYOFFS							
1968-69	**Minnesota North Stars**	**NHL**	**35**	**2**	**9**	**11**	**2**	**8**	**10**	**0**	**0**	**0**	**0**	**50**	**4.0**	**20**	**9**	**25**	**0**	**–14**								
	Memphis South Stars	CHL	28	6	11	17				0																		
1969-70	Iowa Stars	CHL	DID NOT PLAY – COACHING																									
	NHL Totals		**676**	**144**	**179**	**323**	**182**	**189**	**371**	**253**	**9**	**0**	**3**	**233**	**61.8**	**87**	**37**	**82**	**0**		**75**	**14**	**14**	**28**	**20**	**0**	**0**	**2**

AHL Second All-Star Team (1956, 1960)

Claimed by **NY Rangers** from **Toronto** in Intra-League Draft, June 5, 1956. Claimed by **Detroit** from **NY Rangers** in Intra-League Draft, June 7, 1960. Traded to **Boston** by **Detroit** with Albert Langlois, Ron Harris and Bob Dillabough for Ab MacDonald, Bob McCord and Ken Stephanson, May 31, 1965. Traded to **Detroit** by **Boston** for Pit Martin, December 30, 1965. Claimed by **Minnesota** from **Detroit** in Expansion Draft, June 6, 1967.

• MacDOUGALL, KIM

Kim MacDougall D – L. 5'11", 180 lbs. b: Regina, Sask., 8/29/1954. Minnesota's 4th choice, 60th overall, in 1974 Amateur Draft.

Season	Club	League	GP	G	A	Pts	AG	AA	APts	PIM	PP	SH	GW	S	%	TGF	PGF	TGA	PGA	+/-	GP	G	A	Pts	PIM	PP	SH	GW
1971-72	Regina Pats	WCJHL	9	0	1	1				0																		
1972-73	Regina Pats	WJCHL	68	3	15	18				37																		
1973-74	Regina Pats	WCJHL	68	5	51	56				96																		
1974-75	**Minnesota North Stars**	**NHL**	**1**	**0**	**0**	**0**	**0**	**0**	**0**	**0**	**0**	**0**	**0**	**0**	**0.0**	**0**	**0**	**1**	**0**	**–1**								
	New Haven Nighthawks	AHL	57	3	12	15				24											16	0	2	2	21			
1975-76	Fort Wayne Komets	IHL	52	8	16	24				38																		
	Columbus Owls	IHL	8	0	2	2				2																		
	NHL Totals		**1**	**0**	**0**	**0**	**0**	**0**	**0**	**0**	**0**	**0**	**0**	**0**	**0.0**	**0**	**0**	**1**	**0**									

• MacEACHERN, SHANE

Shane MacEachern C – L. 5'11", 180 lbs. b: Charlottetown, P.E.I., 12/14/1967.

Season	Club	League	GP	G	A	Pts	AG	AA	APts	PIM	PP	SH	GW	S	%	TGF	PGF	TGA	PGA	+/-	GP	G	A	Pts	PIM	PP	SH	GW
1983-84	Verdun Jr. Canadiens	QMJHL	65	13	27	40				62											10	3	5	8	30			
1984-85	Verdun Jr. Canadiens	QMJHL	57	14	21	35				109											13	1	3	4	27			
1985-86	Hull Olympiques	QMJHL	70	20	45	65				128											15	11	11	22	17			
1986-87	Hull Olympiques	QMJHL	69	44	58	102				126											8	6	7	13	8			
1987-88	**St. Louis Blues**	**NHL**	**1**	**0**	**0**	**0**	**0**	**0**	**0**	**0**	**0**	**0**	**0**	**0**	**0.0**	**0**	**0**	**0**	**0**	**0**								
	Peoria Rivermen	IHL	68	18	30	48				67											7	1	6	7	8			
1988-89	Peoria Rivermen	IHL	73	17	37	54				83											4	0	1	1	2			
1989-90	Swindon Wildcats	Britain	9	17	17	34				10																		
	Charlottetown Wildcats	PEI Sr.	11	7	12	19				10																		
1990-91	Charlottetown Wildcats	PEI Sr.	10	8	7	15				2																		
1991-92			DID NOT PLAY																									
1992-93	Peterborough Pirates	Britain	29	33	44	77				48											6	9	5	14	8			
1993-94	Brantford Smoke	ColHL	71	30	52	82				58																		
	NHL Totals		**1**	**0**	**0**	**0**	**0**	**0**	**0**	**0**	**0**	**0**	**0**	**0**	**0.0**	**0**	**0**	**0**	**0**									

Signed as a free agent by **St. Louis**, September 22, 1986.

• MacGREGOR, BRUCE

Bruce "The Redheaded Rocket" MacGregor C – R. 5'10", 180 lbs. b: Edmonton, Alta., 4/26/1941.

Season	Club	League	GP	G	A	Pts	AG	AA	APts	PIM	PP	SH	GW	S	%	TGF	PGF	TGA	PGA	+/-	GP	G	A	Pts	PIM	PP	SH	GW
1958-59	Edmonton Jr. Oil Kings	WCJHL	37	33	39	72				22																		
1959-60	Edmonton Jr. Oil Kings	WCJHL	24	24	18	42				15																		
1960-61	Edmonton Flyers	WHL	54	20	26	46				33																		
	Detroit Red Wings	**NHL**	**12**	**0**	**1**	**1**	**0**	**1**	**1**	**0**											**8**	**1**	**2**	**3**	**6**			
1961-62	**Detroit Red Wings**	**NHL**	**65**	**6**	**12**	**18**	**7**	**12**	**19**	**10**																		
1962-63	**Detroit Red Wings**	**NHL**	**67**	**11**	**11**	**22**	**13**	**11**	**24**	**12**											**10**	**1**	**4**	**5**	**10**			
1963-64	**Detroit Red Wings**	**NHL**	**63**	**11**	**21**	**32**	**14**	**23**	**37**	**15**											**14**	**5**	**2**	**7**	**12**			
1964-65	**Detroit Red Wings**	**NHL**	**66**	**21**	**20**	**41**	**27**	**22**	**49**	**19**											**7**	**0**	**2**	**2**	**2**			
1965-66	**Detroit Red Wings**	**NHL**	**70**	**20**	**14**	**34**	**24**	**14**	**38**	**28**											**12**	**1**	**4**	**5**	**2**			
1966-67	**Detroit Red Wings**	**NHL**	**70**	**28**	**19**	**47**	**35**	**20**	**55**	**14**																		
1967-68	**Detroit Red Wings**	**NHL**	**71**	**15**	**24**	**39**	**19**	**25**	**44**	**13**	**1**	**0**	**0**	**165**	**9.1**	**67**	**12**	**95**	**21**	**–19**								
1968-69	**Detroit Red Wings**	**NHL**	**69**	**18**	**23**	**41**	**20**	**22**	**42**	**14**	**2**	**3**	**3**	**168**	**10.7**	**60**	**5**	**63**	**14**	**+6**								
1969-70	**Detroit Red Wings**	**NHL**	**73**	**15**	**23**	**38**	**17**	**23**	**40**	**24**	**3**	**1**	**4**	**153**	**9.8**	**55**	**12**	**60**	**16**	**–1**	**4**	**1**	**0**	**1**	**2**	**0**	**0**	**0**
1970-71	**Detroit Red Wings**	**NHL**	**47**	**6**	**16**	**22**	**6**	**14**	**20**	**18**	**0**	**0**	**0**	**68**	**8.8**	**34**	**3**	**55**	**13**	**–11**								
	New York Rangers	**NHL**	**27**	**12**	**13**	**25**	**13**	**11**	**24**	**4**	**2**	**1**	**3**	**60**	**20.0**	**30**	**6**	**16**	**4**	**+12**	**13**	**0**	**4**	**4**	**2**	**0**	**0**	**0**
1971-72	**New York Rangers**	**NHL**	**75**	**19**	**21**	**40**	**20**	**10**	**30**	**22**	**1**	**0**	**5**	**137**	**13.9**	**64**	**4**	**53**	**16**	**+23**	**16**	**2**	**6**	**8**	**4**	**0**	**1**	**0**
1972-73	**New York Rangers**	**NHL**	**52**	**14**	**12**	**26**	**14**	**10**	**24**	**12**	**0**	**0**	**4**	**85**	**16.5**	**44**	**3**	**34**	**7**	**+14**	**10**	**2**	**2**	**4**	**2**	**0**	**0**	**0**
1973-74	**New York Rangers**	**NHL**	**66**	**17**	**27**	**44**	**17**	**23**	**40**	**6**	**0**	**2**	**1**	**91**	**18.7**	**56**	**2**	**67**	**12**	**–1**	**13**	**6**	**2**	**8**	**2**	**0**	**0**	**2**
1974-75	Canada	Summit	5	0	1	1				5																		
	Edmonton Oilers	WHA	72	24	28	52				10																		
1975-76	Edmonton Oilers	WHA	63	13	10	23				13											4	0	1	1	0			
	NHL Totals		**893**	**213**	**257**	**470**	**246**	**250**	**496**	**217**	**9**	**10**	**20**	**927**	**23.0**	**410**	**47**	**443**	**103**		**107**	**19**	**28**	**47**	**44**	**0**	**1**	**2**
	Other Major League Totals		135	37	38	75				23											4	0	1	1	0			

Traded to **NY Rangers** by **Detroit** with Larry Brown for Arnie Brown, Mike Robitaille and Tom Miller, February 2, 1971 Selected by **Edmonton** (WHA) in 1973 WHA Professional Player Draft, June, 1973.

• MacGREGOR, RANDY

Randy MacGregor RW – L. 5'9", 175 lbs. b: Cobourg, Ont., 7/9/1953.

Season	Club	League	GP	G	A	Pts	AG	AA	APts	PIM	PP	SH	GW	S	%	TGF	PGF	TGA	PGA	+/-	GP	G	A	Pts	PIM	PP	SH	GW
1971-72	Chatham Maroons	SOJHL	56	18	25	53				*216																		
1972-73	Chatham Maroons	SOJHL	58	36	20	56				176																		
1973-74	Broome Dusters	NAHL	71	17	28	45				139																		
1974-75	Binghamton Dusters	NAHL	73	23	48	71				154																		
1975-76	Binghamton Dusters	NAHL	43	9	10	19				84																		
1976-77	Binghamton Dusters	NAHL	71	21	26	47				128											6	2	4	6	31			
	Muskegon Mohawks	IHL	....	....	....	....				....											3	0	0	0	5			
1977-78	Binghamton Dusters	AHL	78	20	29	49				117																		
1978-79	Binghamton Dusters	AHL	64	29	46	75				113																		
1979-80	Binghamton Dusters	AHL	71	21	23	44				164																		
1980-81	Binghamton Whalers	AHL	28	14	9	23				49											5	2	0	2	20			
1981-82	**Hartford Whalers**	**NHL**	**2**	**1**	**1**	**2**	**1**	**1**	**2**	**2**	**0**	**0**	**0**	**1**	**100.0**	**2**	**0**	**0**	**0**	**+2**								
	Binghamton Whalers	AHL	71	23	50	73				115											15	6	7	13	49			
1982-83	Binghamton Whalers	AHL	62	13	17	30				112											5	1	1	2	20			
1983-84	Adirondack Red Wings	AHL	45	6	15	21				60											2	0	0	0	2			
	NHL Totals		**2**	**1**	**1**	**2**	**1**	**1**	**2**	**2**	**0**	**0**	**0**	**1**	**100.0**	**2**	**0**	**0**	**0**									

Signed as a free agent by **Hartford**, February, 1981.

• MacGUIGAN, GARTH

Garth MacGuigan C – L. 6', 190 lbs. b: Charlottetown, P.E.I., 2/16/1956. NY Islanders' 3rd choice, 50th overall, in 1976 Amateur Draft.

Season	Club	League	GP	G	A	Pts	AG	AA	APts	PIM	PP	SH	GW	S	%	TGF	PGF	TGA	PGA	+/-	GP	G	A	Pts	PIM	PP	SH	GW
1974-75	Montreal Jr. Canadiens	QMJHL	63	30	38	68				97											9	2	4	6	14			
1975-76	Montreal Jr. Canadiens	QMJHL	69	47	46	93				94											6	5	2	7	33			
1976-77	Muskegon Mohawks	IHL	78	54	40	94				156											7	5	3	8	0			
	Fort Worth Texans	CHL	1	0	0	0				0											2	0	0	0	0			
1977-78	Fort Worth Texans	CHL	70	17	24	41				54											14	3	4	7	18			
1978-79	Fort Worth Texans	CHL	75	28	21	49				120											5	1	2	3	9			
1979-80	**New York Islanders**	**NHL**	**2**	**0**	**0**	**0**	**0**	**0**	**0**	**2**	**0**	**0**	**0**	**1**	**0.0**	**1**	**0**	**0**	**0**	**+1**								
	Indianapolis Checkers	CHL	77	28	34	62				94											7	2	3	5	14			
1980-81	Indianapolis Checkers	CHL	38	37	38	75				96											5	1	2	3	20			
1981-82	Indianapolis Checkers	CHL	80	24	51	75				112											13	4	7	11	54			
1982-83	Indianapolis Checkers	CHL	80	37	35	72				70											13	4	7	11	21			
1983-84	**New York Islanders**	**NHL**	**3**	**0**	**1**	**1**	**0**	**1**	**1**	**0**	**0**	**0**	**0**	**2**	**0.0**	**2**	**0**	**2**	**0**	**0**								
	Indianapolis Checkers	CHL	68	25	41	66				109											10	3	3	6	2			
1984-85	Indianapolis Checkers	IHL	67	21	29	50				52											7	0	5	5	4			
	NHL Totals		**5**	**0**	**1**	**1**	**0**	**1**	**1**	**2**	**0**	**0**	**0**	**3**	**0.0**	**3**	**0**	**2**	**0**									

QMJHL West Division Second All-Star Team (1976) • Won Garry F. Longman Memorial Trophy (Top Rookie - IHL) (1977) • CHL Second All-Star Team (1981)

• MacINNIS, AL

Al "Chopper" MacInnis D – R. 6'2", 196 lbs. b: Inverness, N.S., 7/11/1963. Calgary's 1st choice, 15th overall, in 1981 Entry Draft.

Season	Club	League	REGULAR SEASON GP	G	A	Pts	AG	AA	APts	PIM	PP	SH	GW	S	%	TGF	PGF	TGA	PGA	+/–	PLAYOFFS GP	G	A	Pts	PIM	PP	SH	GW
1979-80	Regina Blues	SJHL	59	20	28	48	....	....	....	110	....	....	....	....	....	....	....	....	....	....	....	....	....	....	....	....	....	....
1980-81	Kitchener Rangers	OHA	47	11	28	39	....	....	....	59	....	....	....	....	....	....	....	....	....	....	18	4	12	16	20	....	....	....
1981-82	Kitchener Rangers	OHL	59	25	50	75	....	....	....	145	....	....	....	....	....	....	....	....	....	....	15	5	10	15	44	....	....	....
	Calgary Flames	**NHL**	**2**	**0**	**0**	**0**	**0**	**0**	**0**	**0**	**0**	**0**	**0**	**2**	**0.0**	**1**	**0**	**1**	**0**	**0**	....	....	....	....	....	....	....	....
1982-83	Kitchener Rangers	OHL	51	38	46	84	....	....	....	67	....	....	....	....	....	....	....	....	....	....	8	3	8	11	9	....	....	....
	Calgary Flames	**NHL**	**14**	**1**	**3**	**4**	**1**	**2**	**3**	**9**	**0**	**0**	**0**	**7**	**14.3**	**13**	**0**	**14**	**1**	**0**	....	....	....	....	....	....	....	....
1983-84	**Calgary Flames**	**NHL**	**51**	**11**	**34**	**45**	**9**	**23**	**32**	**42**	**7**	**0**	**2**	**160**	**6.9**	**84**	**47**	**38**	**1**	**0**	**11**	**2**	**12**	**14**	**13**	**2**	**0**	**1**
	Colorado Flames	CHL	19	5	14	19	....	....	....	22	....	....	....	....	....	....	....	....	....	....	....	....	....	....	....	....	....	....
1984-85	**Calgary Flames**	**NHL**	**67**	**14**	**52**	**66**	**11**	**35**	**46**	**75**	**8**	**0**	**0**	**259**	**5.4**	**137**	**61**	**70**	**1**	**+7**	**4**	**1**	**2**	**3**	**8**	**1**	**0**	**0**
1985-86	**Calgary Flames**	**NHL**	**77**	**11**	**57**	**68**	**9**	**38**	**47**	**76**	**4**	**0**	**0**	**241**	**4.6**	**165**	**76**	**80**	**29**	**+38**	**21**	**4**	***15**	**19**	**30**	**2**	**0**	**0**
1986-87	**Calgary Flames**	**NHL**	**79**	**20**	**56**	**76**	**17**	**41**	**58**	**97**	**7**	**0**	**2**	**262**	**7.6**	**154**	**59**	**116**	**41**	**+20**	**4**	**1**	**0**	**1**	**0**	**1**	**0**	**0**
1987-88	**Calgary Flames**	**NHL**	**80**	**25**	**58**	**83**	**21**	**41**	**62**	**114**	**7**	**2**	**2**	**245**	**10.2**	**166**	**76**	**108**	**31**	**+13**	**7**	**3**	**6**	**9**	**18**	**2**	**0**	**0**
1988-89	**Calgary Flames**	**NHL**	**79**	**16**	**58**	**74**	**14**	**41**	**55**	**126**	**8**	**0**	**3**	**277**	**5.8**	**189**	**84**	**102**	**35**	**+38**	**22**	**7**	***24**	***31**	**46**	**5**	**0**	**4**
1989-90	Calgary Flames	FrTour	4	1	1	2	....	....	....	2	....	....	....	....	....	....	....	....	....	....	....	....	....	....	....	....	....	....
	Calgary Flames	**NHL**	**79**	**28**	**62**	**90**	**24**	**44**	**68**	**82**	**14**	**1**	**3**	**304**	**9.2**	**192**	**94**	**102**	**24**	**+20**	**6**	**2**	**3**	**5**	**8**	**1**	**0**	**0**
	Canada	WEC-A	9	1	3	4	....	....	....	10	....	....	....	....	....	....	....	....	....	....	....	....	....	....	....	....	....	....
1990-91	**Calgary Flames**	**NHL**	**78**	**28**	**75**	**103**	**26**	**57**	**83**	**90**	**17**	**0**	**1**	**305**	**9.2**	**185**	**83**	**90**	**30**	**+42**	**7**	**2**	**3**	**5**	**8**	**2**	**0**	**0**
1991-92	Canada	C Cup	8	2	4	6	....	....	....	23	....	....	....	....	....	....	....	....	....	....	....	....	....	....	....	....	....	....
	Calgary Flames	**NHL**	**72**	**20**	**57**	**77**	**18**	**43**	**61**	**83**	**11**	**0**	**0**	**304**	**6.6**	**146**	**71**	**112**	**50**	**+13**	....	....	....	....	....	....	....	....
1992-93	**Calgary Flames**	**NHL**	**50**	**11**	**43**	**54**	**9**	**29**	**38**	**61**	**7**	**0**	**4**	**201**	**5.5**	**106**	**49**	**57**	**15**	**+15**	**6**	**1**	**6**	**7**	**10**	**1**	**0**	**0**
1993-94	**Calgary Flames**	**NHL**	**75**	**28**	**54**	**82**	**26**	**42**	**68**	**95**	**12**	**1**	**5**	**324**	**8.6**	**154**	**67**	**77**	**25**	**+35**	**7**	**2**	**6**	**8**	**12**	**1**	**0**	**0**
1994-95	**St. Louis Blues**	**NHL**	**32**	**8**	**20**	**28**	**14**	**29**	**43**	**43**	**2**	**0**	**0**	**110**	**7.3**	**59**	**20**	**33**	**13**	**+19**	**7**	**1**	**5**	**6**	**10**	**0**	**0**	**0**
1995-96	**St. Louis Blues**	**NHL**	**82**	**17**	**44**	**61**	**17**	**36**	**53**	**88**	**9**	**1**	**1**	**317**	**5.4**	**128**	**60**	**105**	**42**	**+5**	**13**	**3**	**4**	**7**	**20**	**1**	**0**	**0**
1996-97	**St. Louis Blues**	**NHL**	**72**	**13**	**30**	**43**	**14**	**27**	**41**	**65**	**6**	**1**	**1**	**296**	**4.4**	**116**	**36**	**96**	**18**	**+2**	**6**	**1**	**2**	**3**	**4**	**1**	**0**	**0**
1997-98	**St. Louis Blues**	**NHL**	**71**	**19**	**30**	**49**	**22**	**29**	**51**	**80**	**9**	**1**	**2**	**227**	**8.4**	**113**	**46**	**78**	**17**	**+6**	**8**	**2**	**6**	**8**	**12**	**1**	**0**	**0**
	Canada	Olympics	6	2	0	2	....	....	....	2	....	....	....	....	....	....	....	....	....	....	....	....	....	....	....	....	....	....
	NHL Totals		**1060**	**270**	**733**	**1003**	**252**	**557**	**809**	**1226**	**128**	**7**	**26**	**3841**	**7.0**	**2108**	**929**	**1279**	**373**		**129**	**32**	**94**	**126**	**199**	**21**	**0**	**5**

OHL First All-Star Team (1982, 1983) • NHL Second All-Star Team (1987, 1989, 1994) • Won Conn Smythe Trophy (1989) • NHL First All-Star Team (1990, 1991) • Canada Cup All-Star Team (1991)

Played in NHL All-Star Game (1985, 1988, 1990, 1991, 1992, 1994, 1996, 1997, 1998)

Traded to **St. Louis** by **Calgary** with Calgary's 4th round choice (Didier Tremblay) in 1997 Entry Draft for Phil Housley, St. Louis' 2nd round choice (Steve Begin) in 1996 Entry Draft and 2nd round choice (John Tripp) in 1997 Entry Draft, July 4, 1994.

• MACIVER, DON

Don MacIver D – L. 6', 200 lbs. b: Montreal, Que., 5/3/1955.

Season	Club	League	GP	G	A	Pts	AG	AA	APts	PIM	PP	SH	GW	S	%	TGF	PGF	TGA	PGA	+/–	GP	G	A	Pts	PIM	PP	SH	GW
1976-77	St. Mary's University	AUAA	7	0	3	3	....	....	....	6	....	....	....	....	....	....	....	....	....	....	....	....	....	....	....	....	....	....
1977-78	St. Mary's University	AUAA	16	1	9	10	....	....	....	19	....	....	....	....	....	....	....	....	....	....	....	....	....	....	....	....	....	....
1978-79	St. Mary's University	AUAA	20	3	11	14	....	....	....	43	....	....	....	....	....	....	....	....	....	....	....	....	....	....	....	....	....	....
1979-80	**Winnipeg Jets**	**NHL**	**6**	**0**	**0**	**0**	**0**	**0**	**0**	**2**	**0**	**0**	**0**	**2**	**0.0**	**0**	**0**	**5**	**0**	**–5**	....	....	....	....	....	....	....	....
	Tulsa Oilers	CHL	56	3	12	15	....	....	....	98	....	....	....	....	....	....	....	....	....	....	3	0	0	0	6	....	....	....
1980-81	Tulsa Oilers	CHL	72	3	9	12	....	....	....	155	....	....	....	....	....	....	....	....	....	....	8	0	1	1	16	....	....	....
1981-82	Tulsa Oilers	CHL	66	2	22	24	....	....	....	166	....	....	....	....	....	....	....	....	....	....	2	0	0	0	0	....	....	....
1982-83	Tulsa Oilers	CHL	77	3	9	12	....	....	....	113	....	....	....	....	....	....	....	....	....	....	....	....	....	....	....	....	....	....
	NHL Totals		**6**	**0**	**0**	**0**	**0**	**0**	**0**	**2**	**0**	**0**	**0**	**2**	**0.0**	**0**	**0**	**5**	**0**		....	....	....	....	....	....	....	....

Signed as a free agent by **Winnipeg**, October 16, 1979.

• MACIVER, NORM

Norm Maciver D – L. 5'11", 180 lbs. b: Thunder Bay, Ont., 9/8/1964.

Season	Club	League	GP	G	A	Pts	AG	AA	APts	PIM	PP	SH	GW	S	%	TGF	PGF	TGA	PGA	+/–	GP	G	A	Pts	PIM	PP	SH	GW
1982-83	University of Minnesota-Duluth	WCHA	45	1	26	27	....	....	....	40	....	....	....	....	....	....	....	....	....	....	6	0	2	2	2	....	....	....
1983-84	University of Minnesota-Duluth	WCHA	31	13	28	41	....	....	....	28	....	....	....	....	....	....	....	....	....	....	8	1	10	11	8	....	....	....
1984-85	University of Minnesota-Duluth	WCHA	47	14	47	61	....	....	....	63	....	....	....	....	....	....	....	....	....	....	10	3	3	6	6	....	....	....
1985-86	University of Minnesota-Duluth	WCHA	42	11	51	62	....	....	....	36	....	....	....	....	....	....	....	....	....	....	4	2	3	5	2	....	....	....
1986-87	**New York Rangers**	**NHL**	**3**	**0**	**1**	**1**	**0**	**1**	**1**	**0**	**0**	**0**	**0**	**2**	**0.0**	**1**	**1**	**5**	**0**	**–5**	....	....	....	....	....	....	....	....
	New Haven Nighthawks	AHL	71	6	30	36	....	....	....	73	....	....	....	....	....	....	....	....	....	....	7	0	0	0	9	....	....	....
1987-88	**New York Rangers**	**NHL**	**37**	**9**	**15**	**24**	**8**	**11**	**19**	**14**	**1**	**0**	**2**	**65**	**13.8**	**66**	**30**	**26**	**0**	**+10**	....	....	....	....	....	....	....	....
	Colorado Rangers	IHL	27	6	20	26	....	....	....	22	....	....	....	....	....	....	....	....	....	....	....	....	....	....	....	....	....	....
1988-89	**New York Rangers**	**NHL**	**26**	**0**	**10**	**10**	**0**	**7**	**7**	**14**	**0**	**0**	**0**	**36**	**0.0**	**27**	**9**	**22**	**1**	**–3**	....	....	....	....	....	....	....	....
	Hartford Whalers	**NHL**	**37**	**1**	**22**	**23**	**1**	**15**	**16**	**24**	**1**	**0**	**0**	**51**	**2.0**	**51**	**25**	**26**	**0**	**0**	**1**	**0**	**0**	**0**	**2**	**0**	**0**	**0**
1989-90	Binghamton Whalers	AHL	2	0	0	0	....	....	....	0	....	....	....	....	....	....	....	....	....	....	....	....	....	....	....	....	....	....
	Edmonton Oilers	**NHL**	**1**	**0**	**0**	**0**	**0**	**0**	**0**	**0**	**0**	**0**	**0**	**0**	**0.0**	**1**	**0**	**2**	**0**	**–1**	....	....	....	....	....	....	....	....
	Cape Breton Oilers	AHL	68	13	37	50	....	....	....	55	....	....	....	....	....	....	....	....	....	....	6	0	7	7	10	....	....	....
1990-91	**Edmonton Oilers**	**NHL**	**21**	**2**	**5**	**7**	**2**	**4**	**6**	**14**	**1**	**0**	**0**	**25**	**8.0**	**21**	**6**	**21**	**7**	**+1**	**18**	**0**	**4**	**4**	**8**	**0**	**0**	**0**
	Cape Breton Oilers	AHL	56	13	46	59	....	....	....	60	....	....	....	....	....	....	....	....	....	....	....	....	....	....	....	....	....	....
1991-92	**Edmonton Oilers**	**NHL**	**57**	**6**	**34**	**40**	**5**	**26**	**31**	**38**	**2**	**0**	**3**	**69**	**8.7**	**98**	**27**	**63**	**12**	**+20**	**13**	**1**	**2**	**3**	**10**	**0**	**0**	**0**
1992-93	**Ottawa Senators**	**NHL**	**80**	**17**	**46**	**63**	**14**	**32**	**46**	**84**	**7**	**1**	**2**	**184**	**9.2**	**121**	**60**	**146**	**39**	**–46**	....	....	....	....	....	....	....	....
	Canada	WC-A	8	0	5	5	....	....	....	4	....	....	....	....	....	....	....	....	....	....	....	....	....	....	....	....	....	....
1993-94	**Ottawa Senators**	**NHL**	**53**	**3**	**20**	**23**	**3**	**15**	**18**	**26**	**0**	**0**	**0**	**88**	**3.4**	**60**	**27**	**66**	**7**	**–26**	....	....	....	....	....	....	....	....
1994-95	**Ottawa Senators**	**NHL**	**28**	**4**	**7**	**11**	**7**	**10**	**17**	**10**	**0**	**0**	**0**	**30**	**13.3**	**35**	**14**	**31**	**1**	**–9**	....	....	....	....	....	....	....	....
	Pittsburgh Penguins	**NHL**	**13**	**0**	**9**	**9**	**0**	**13**	**13**	**6**	**2**	**0**	**0**	**20**	**0.0**	**21**	**5**	**10**	**1**	**+7**	**12**	**1**	**4**	**5**	**8**	**0**	**0**	**1**
1995-96	**Pittsburgh Penguins**	**NHL**	**32**	**2**	**21**	**23**	**2**	**17**	**19**	**32**	**1**	**0**	**0**	**30**	**6.7**	**68**	**29**	**36**	**9**	**+12**	....	....	....	....	....	....	....	....
	Winnipeg Jets	**NHL**	**39**	**5**	**25**	**30**	**5**	**20**	**25**	**26**	**2**	**0**	**0**	**49**	**10.2**	**62**	**30**	**41**	**3**	**–6**	**6**	**1**	**0**	**1**	**2**	**0**	**0**	**0**
1996-97	**Phoenix Coyotes**	**NHL**	**32**	**4**	**9**	**13**	**4**	**8**	**12**	**24**	**1**	**0**	**1**	**40**	**10.0**	**36**	**21**	**27**	**1**	**–11**	....	....	....	....	....	....	....	....
1997-98	**Phoenix Coyotes**	**NHL**	**41**	**2**	**6**	**8**	**2**	**6**	**8**	**38**	**0**	**1**	**0**	**37**	**5.4**	**24**	**6**	**34**	**5**	**–11**	**6**	**0**	**1**	**1**	**2**	**0**	**0**	**0**
	NHL Totals		**500**	**55**	**230**	**285**	**53**	**185**	**238**	**350**	**18**	**2**	**8**	**726**	**7.6**	**692**	**290**	**556**	**86**		**56**	**3**	**11**	**14**	**32**	**0**	**0**	**1**

WCHA First All-Star Team (1985, 1986) • NCAA West First All-American Team (1985, 1986) • AHL First All-Star Team (1991) • Won Eddie Shore Plaque (Top Defenseman - AHL) (1991)

Signed as a free agent by **NY Rangers**, September 8, 1986. Traded to **Hartford** by **NY Rangers** with Brian Lawton and Don Maloney for Carey Wilson and Hartford's 5th round choice (Lubos Rob) in 1990 Entry Draft, December 26, 1988. Traded to **Edmonton** by **Hartford** for Jim Ennis, October 10, 1989. Claimed by **Ottawa** from **Edmonton** in NHL Waiver Draft, October 4, 1992. Traded to **Pittsburgh** by **Ottawa** with Troy Murray for Martin Straka, April 7, 1995. Traded to **Winnipeg** by **Pittsburgh** for Neil Wilkinson, December 28, 1995. Transferred to **Phoenix** after **Winnipeg** franchise relocated, July 1, 1996.

• MacKASEY, BLAIR

Blair MacKasey D – R. 6'2", 200 lbs. b: Hamilton, Ont., 12/13/1955. Washington's 3rd choice, 55th overall, in 1975 Amateur Draft.

Season	Club	League	GP	G	A	Pts	AG	AA	APts	PIM	PP	SH	GW	S	%	TGF	PGF	TGA	PGA	+/–	GP	G	A	Pts	PIM	PP	SH	GW
1971-72	Montreal Jr. Canadiens	OHA	59	2	25	27	....	....	....	85	....	....	....	....	....	....	....	....	....	....	....	....	....	....	....	....	....	....
1972-73	Montreal Jr. Canadiens	QMJHL	52	1	23	24	....	....	....	108	....	....	....	....	....	....	....	....	....	....	....	....	....	....	....	....	....	....
1973-74	Montreal Jr. Canadiens	QMJHL	60	13	41	54	....	....	....	70	....	....	....	....	....	....	....	....	....	....	....	....	....	....	....	....	....	....
1974-75	Montreal Jr. Canadiens	QMJHL	62	12	40	52	....	....	....	100	....	....	....	....	....	....	....	....	....	....	....	....	....	....	....	....	....	....
1975-76	Richmond Robins	AHL	9	1	0	1	....	....	....	4	....	....	....	....	....	....	....	....	....	....	....	....	....	....	....	....	....	....
	Dayton Gems	IHL	50	6	21	27	....	....	....	69	....	....	....	....	....	....	....	....	....	....	12	1	2	3	9	....	....	....
1976-77	**Toronto Maple Leafs**	**NHL**	**1**	**0**	**0**	**0**	**0**	**0**	**0**	**2**	....	....	....	....	....	....	....	....	....	....	....	....	....	....	....	....	....	....
	Dallas Black Hawks	CHL	24	1	11	12	....	....	....	51	....	....	....	....	....	....	....	....	....	....	....	....	....	....	....	....	....	....
1977-78	Dallas Black Hawks	CHL	54	1	8	9	....	....	....	58	....	....	....	....	....	....	....	....	....	....	11	0	0	0	8	....	....	....
	NHL Totals		**1**	**0**	**0**	**0**	**0**	**0**	**0**	**2**	**0**	**0**	**0**	**0**	**0.0**	**0**	**0**	**0**	**0**		....	....	....	....	....	....	....	....

Traded to **Toronto** by **Washington**, September 27, 1976.

• MacKENZIE, BARRY

Barry MacKenzie D – L. 6', 190 lbs. b: Toronto, Ont., 8/16/1941.

Season	Club	League	GP	G	A	Pts	AG	AA	APts	PIM	PP	SH	GW	S	%	TGF	PGF	TGA	PGA	+/–	GP	G	A	Pts	PIM	PP	SH	GW
1960-61	St. Michael's Majors	OHA	9	1	4	5	....	....	....	8	....	....	....	....	....	....	....	....	....	....	14	0	4	4	8	....	....	....
1961-62	St. Michael's Majors	MTHL	18	5	9	14	....	....	....	58	....	....	....	....	....	....	....	....	....	....	11	0	4	4	14	....	....	....
1962-63	University of British Columbia	WUAA	STATISTICS NOT AVAILABLE																									
1963-64	Canada	Nat-Team	....	....	....	....	....	....	....	....	....	....	....	....	....	....	....	....	....	....	....	....	....	....	....	....	....	....
	Canada	Olympics	7	0	2	2	....	....	....	4	....	....	....	....	....	....	....	....	....	....	....	....	....	....	....	....	....	....
1964-65	Canada	Nat-Team	STATISTICS NOT AVAILABLE																									
	Canada	WEC-A	7	2	1	3	....	....	....	8	....	....	....	....	....	....	....	....	....	....	....	....	....	....	....	....	....	....

			REGULAR SEASON																		PLAYOFFS							
Season	Club	League	GP	G	A	Pts	AG	AA	APts	PIM	PP	SH	GW	S	%	TGF	PGF	TGA	PGA	+/–	GP	G	A	Pts	PIM	PP	SH	GW
1965-66	Canada	Nat-Team	STATISTICS NOT AVAILABLE																									
	Canada	WEC-A	7	0	4	4				6																		
1966-67	Canada	Nat-Team	STATISTICS NOT AVAILABLE																									
	Canada	WEC-A	7	0	0	0				12																		
1967-68	Ottawa Nats	OHA Sr.	23	2	9	11				40																		
	Canada	Olympics	7	0	2	2				8																		
1968-69	Minnesota North Stars	NHL	6	0	1	1	0	1	1	6	0	0	0	3	0.0	2	0	4	0	–2								
	Memphis South Stars	CHL	57	5	16	21				54																		
	NHL Totals		6	0	1	1	0	1	1	6	0	0	0	3	0.0	2	0	4	0									

Traded to **Minnesota** by **Toronto** for cash, June 6, 1967.

• MACKEY, DAVID

David Mackey LW – L. 6'4", 205 lbs. b: Richmond, B.C., 7/24/1966. Chicago's 12th choice, 224th overall, in 1984 Entry Draft.

Season	Club	League	GP	G	A	Pts	AG	AA	APts	PIM	PP	SH	GW	S	%	TGF	PGF	TGA	PGA	+/–	GP	G	A	Pts	PIM	PP	SH	GW
1981-82	Seafair Midgets	BCJHL	60	48	62	110				99																		
1982-83	Victoria Cougars	WHL	69	16	16	32				53											12	11	1	2	4			
1983-84	Victoria Cougars	WHL	69	15	15	30				97																		
1984-85	Victoria Cougars	WHL	16	5	6	11				45																		
	Portland Winter Hawks	WHL	56	28	32	60				122											6	2	1	3	13			
1985-86	Kamloops Blazers	WHL	9	3	4	7				13																		
	Medicine Hat Tigers	WHL	60	25	32	57				167											25	6	3	9	72			
1986-87	Saginaw Generals	IHL	81	26	49	75				173											10	5	6	11	22			
1987-88	Chicago Blackhawks	NHL	23	1	3	4	1	2	3	71	0	0	1	23	4.3	7	0	22	1	–14								
	Saginaw Hawks	IHL	62	29	22	51				211											10	3	7	10	44			
1988-89	Chicago Blackhawks	NHL	23	1	2	3	1	1	2	78	0	0	0	15	6.7	7	0	8	0	–1								
	Saginaw Hawks	IHL	57	22	23	45				223																		
1989-90	Minnesota North Stars	NHL	16	2	0	2	2	0	2	28	0	0	1	8	25.0	2	0	5	0	–3								
1990-91	Milwaukee Admirals	IHL	82	28	30	58				226											6	7	2	9	6			
1991-92	St. Louis Blues	NHL	19	1	0	1	1	0	1	49	0	0	1	12	8.3	3	0	7	0	–4	1	0	0	0	0	0	0	0
	Peoria Rivermen	IHL	35	20	17	37				90																		
1992-93	St. Louis Blues	NHL	15	1	4	5	1	3	4	23	0	0	0	17	5.9	6	0	9	0	–3								
	Peoria Rivermen	IHL	42	24	22	46				112											4	1	0	1	22			
1993-94	St. Louis Blues	NHL	30	2	3	5	2	2	4	56	0	0	0	21	9.5	7	0	11	0	–4	2	0	0	0	2	0	0	0
	Peoria Rivermen	IHL	49	14	21	35				132																		
1994-95	Milwaukee Admirals	IHL	74	19	18	37				261											15	6	4	10	34			
1995-96	Milwaukee Admirals	IHL	77	15	16	31				235											4	2	1	3	10			
1996-97	Milwaukee Admirals	IHL	79	15	15	30				223											3	0	0	0	19			
1997-98	Milwaukee Admirals	IHL	36	3	6	9				134																		
	Orlando Solar Bears	IHL	31	5	6	11				68											14	4	3	7	92			
	NHL Totals		126	8	12	20	8	8	16	305	0	0	3	96	8.3	32	0	62	1		3	0	0	0	2	0	0	0

Claimed by **Minnesota** from **Chicago** in Waiver Draft, October 2, 1989. Traded to **Vancouver** by **Minnesota** for future considerations, September 7, 1990. Signed as a free agent by **St. Louis**, August 7, 1991.

• MacKINNON, PAUL

Paul MacKinnon D – R. 6', 195 lbs. b: Brantford, Ont., 11/6/1958. Washington's 4th choice, 23rd overall, in 1978 Amateur Draft.

Season	Club	League	GP	G	A	Pts	AG	AA	APts	PIM	PP	SH	GW	S	%	TGF	PGF	TGA	PGA	+/–	GP	G	A	Pts	PIM	PP	SH	GW
1975-76	Peterborough Petes	OHA	48	1	10	11				42																		
1976-77	Peterborough Petes	OHA	65	2	38	40				96											4	0	2	2	2			
1977-78	Peterborough Petes	OHA	60	1	25	26				77											21	0	7	7	28			
1978-79	Winnipeg Jets	WHA	73	2	15	17				70											10	2	5	7	4			
1979-80	Washington Capitals	NHL	63	1	11	12	1	8	9	22	0	0	0	68	1.5	67	0	91	23	–1								
1980-81	Washington Capitals	NHL	14	0	0	0	0	0	0	22	0	0	0	7	0.0	12	0	12	5	+5								
1981-82	Washington Capitals	NHL	39	2	9	11	2	6	8	35	0	0	0	28	7.1	34	2	61	19	–10								
	Hershey Bears	AHL	26	4	17	21				30											5	0	0	0	2			
1982-83	Washington Capitals	NHL	19	2	2	4	2	1	3	8	1	0	0	10	20.0	17	6	10	0	+1								
	Hershey Bears	AHL	59	2	14	16				32											5	1	0	1	0			
1983-84	Washington Capitals	NHL	12	0	1	1	0	1	1	4	0	0	0	3	0.0	3	0	11	1	–7								
	Hershey Bears	AHL	63	3	19	22				29																		
	NHL Totals		147	5	23	28	5	16	21	91	1	0	0	116	4.3	133	8	185	48									
	Other Major League Totals		73	2	15	17				70											10	2	5	7	4			

Memorial Cup All-Star Team (1978)

Signed as an underage free agent by **Winnipeg** (WHA), June, 1978. Reclaimed by **Washington** from **Winnipeg** prior to Expansion Draft, June 9, 1979.

• MacLEAN, DONALD

Donald MacLean C – L. 6'2", 174 lbs. b: Sydney, N.S., 1/14/1977. Los Angeles' 2nd choice, 33rd overall, in 1995 Entry Draft.

Season	Club	League	GP	G	A	Pts	AG	AA	APts	PIM	PP	SH	GW	S	%	TGF	PGF	TGA	PGA	+/–	GP	G	A	Pts	PIM	PP	SH	GW
1994-95	Beauport Harfangs	QMJHL	64	15	27	42				37											17	4	4	8	6			
1995-96	Beauport Harfangs	QMJHL	1	0	1	1				0																		
	Laval Titan	QMJHL	21	17	11	28				29																		
	Hull Olympiques	QMJHL	39	26	34	60				44											17	6	7	13	14			
1996-97	Hull Olympiques	QMJHL	69	34	47	81				67											14	11	10	21	39			
1997-98	Los Angeles Kings	NHL	22	5	2	7	6	2	8	4	2	0	0	25	20.0	9	2	8	0	–1								
	Fredericton Canadiens	AHL	39	9	5	14				32											4	1	3	4	2			
	NHL Totals		22	5	2	7	6	2	8	4	2	0	0	25	20.0	9	2	8	0									

• MacLEAN, JOHN

John MacLean RW – R. 6', 210 lbs. b: Oshawa, Ont., 11/20/1964. New Jersey's 1st choice, 6th overall, in 1983 Entry Draft.

Season	Club	League	GP	G	A	Pts	AG	AA	APts	PIM	PP	SH	GW	S	%	TGF	PGF	TGA	PGA	+/–	GP	G	A	Pts	PIM	PP	SH	GW
1981-82	Oshawa Generals	OHL	67	17	22	39				197											12	3	6	9	63			
1982-83	Oshawa Generals	OHL	66	47	51	98				138											17	*18	20	*38	35			
1983-84	Oshawa Generals	OHL	30	23	36	59				58											7	2	5	7	18			
	Canada	WJC-A	7	7	1	8				4																		
	New Jersey Devils	NHL	23	1	0	1	1	0	1	10	0	0	0	22	4.5	12	3	18	2	–7								
1984-85	New Jersey Devils	NHL	61	13	20	33	11	14	25	44	1	0	4	92	14.1	58	19	51	1	–11								
1985-86	New Jersey Devils	NHL	74	21	36	57	17	24	41	112	1	0	4	139	15.1	77	14	66	0	–3								
1986-87	New Jersey Devils	NHL	80	31	36	67	27	26	53	120	9	0	4	197	15.7	85	26	83	1	–23								
1987-88	New Jersey Devils	NHL	76	23	16	39	20	11	31	147	12	0	4	204	11.3	67	32	40	1	–10	20	7	11	18	60	2	0	2
1988-89	New Jersey Devils	NHL	74	42	45	87	36	32	68	122	14	0	4	266	15.8	125	47	57	5	+26								
	Canada	WEC-A	10	3	6	9				4																		
1989-90	New Jersey Devils	NHL	80	41	38	79	35	27	62	80	10	3	11	322	12.7	122	33	93	21	+17	6	4	1	5	12	2	1	0
1990-91	New Jersey Devils	NHL	78	45	33	78	42	25	67	150	19	2	7	292	15.4	108	37	79	16	+8	7	5	3	8	20	1	0	0
1991-92			DID NOT PLAY – INJURED																									
1992-93	New Jersey Devils	NHL	80	24	24	48	20	16	36	102	7	1	3	195	12.3	75	23	75	17	–6	5	0	1	1	10	0	0	0
1993-94	New Jersey Devils	NHL	80	37	33	70	35	25	60	95	8	0	4	277	13.4	105	29	69	23	+30	20	6	10	16	22	2	0	1
1994-95	New Jersey Devils	NHL	46	17	12	29	30	18	48	32	2	1	0	139	12.2	46	11	29	7	+13	20	5	13	18	14	2	0	0
1995-96	New Jersey Devils	NHL	76	20	28	48	20	23	43	91	3	3	3	237	8.4	58	19	57	21	+3								
1996-97	New Jersey Devils	NHL	80	29	25	54	31	22	53	49	5	0	6	264	11.4	71	13	65	18	+11	10	4	5	9	4	2	1	1
1997-98	New Jersey Devils	NHL	26	3	8	11	4	8	12	14	1	0	1	74	4.1	15	7	19	5	–6								
	San Jose Sharks	NHL	51	13	19	32	15	19	34	28	5	0	2	139	9.4	46	19	34	7	0	6	2	3	5	4	1	0	0
	NHL Totals		985	360	373	733	344	290	634	1196	97	10	57	2849	12.6	1070	332	841	145		94	33	47	80	146	12	2	4

Memorial Cup All-Star Team (1983)

Played in NHL All-Star Game (1989, 1991)

• Missed entire 1991-92 season with torn ligament in right knee. Traded to **San Jose** by **New Jersey** with Ken Sutton for Doug Bodger and Dody Wood, December 7, 1997. Signed as a free agent by **NY Rangers**, July 9, 1998.

			REGULAR SEASON																		PLAYOFFS							
Season	Club	League	GP	G	A	Pts	AG	AA	APts	PIM	PP	SH	GW	S	%	TGF	PGF	TGA	PGA	+/–	GP	G	A	Pts	PIM	PP	SH	GW

• MacLEAN, PAUL

Paul MacLean RW – R. 6'2", 218 lbs. b: Grostenquin, France, 3/9/1958. St. Louis' 6th choice, 109th overall, in 1978 Amateur Draft.

Season	Club	League	GP	G	A	Pts	AG	AA	APts	PIM	PP	SH	GW	S	%	TGF	PGF	TGA	PGA	+/–	GP	G	A	Pts	PIM	PP	SH	GW
1977-78	Hull Festivals	QMJHL	66	38	33	71	....	....	....	125	....	....	....	....	....	....	....	....	....	....	....	....	....	....	....	....	....	....
1978-79	Dalhousie University	AUAA	18	12	17	29	....	....	....	71	....	....	....	....	....	....	....	....	....	....	....	....	....	....	....	....	....	....
1979-80	Canada	Nat-Team	50	21	11	32	....	....	....	90	....	....	....	....	....	....	....	....	....	....	....	....	....	....	....	....	....	....
	Canada	Olympics	6	2	3	5	....	....	....	6	....	....	....	....	....	....	....	....	....	....	....	....	....	....	....	....	....	....
1980-81	**St. Louis Blues**	**NHL**	**1**	**0**	**0**	**0**	**0**	**0**	**0**	**0**	**0**	**0**	**0**	**1**	**0.0**	**1**	**0**	**1**	**1**	**+1**	**1**	**0**	**0**	**0**	**0**	**0**	**0**	**0**
	Salt Lake Golden Eagles	CHL	80	36	42	78	....	....	....	160	....	....	....	....	....	....	....	....	....	....	17	11	5	16	47	....	....	....
1981-82	**Winnipeg Jets**	**NHL**	**74**	**36**	**25**	**61**	**29**	**17**	**46**	**106**	**12**	**0**	**1**	**164**	**22.0**	**100**	**39**	**71**	**1**	**–9**	**4**	**3**	**2**	**5**	**26**	**2**	**0**	**1**
1982-83	**Winnipeg Jets**	**NHL**	**80**	**32**	**44**	**76**	**26**	**30**	**56**	**121**	**15**	**0**	**2**	**163**	**19.6**	**114**	**53**	**66**	**0**	**–5**	**3**	**1**	**2**	**3**	**6**	**1**	**0**	**0**
1983-84	**Winnipeg Jets**	**NHL**	**76**	**40**	**31**	**71**	**32**	**21**	**53**	**155**	**13**	**0**	**5**	**158**	**25.3**	**103**	**31**	**87**	**0**	**–15**	**3**	**1**	**0**	**1**	**0**	**0**	**0**	**0**
1984-85	**Winnipeg Jets**	**NHL**	**79**	**41**	**60**	**101**	**34**	**41**	**75**	**119**	**4**	**0**	**6**	**186**	**22.0**	**142**	**47**	**91**	**1**	**+5**	**8**	**3**	**4**	**7**	**4**	**2**	**0**	**0**
1985-86	**Winnipeg Jets**	**NHL**	**69**	**27**	**29**	**56**	**22**	**19**	**41**	**74**	**11**	**0**	**2**	**168**	**16.1**	**85**	**31**	**68**	**0**	**–14**	**2**	**1**	**0**	**1**	**7**	**0**	**0**	**0**
1986-87	**Winnipeg Jets**	**NHL**	**72**	**32**	**42**	**74**	**28**	**30**	**58**	**75**	**10**	**0**	**6**	**155**	**20.6**	**115**	**32**	**71**	**0**	**+12**	**10**	**5**	**2**	**7**	**16**	**2**	**0**	**0**
1987-88	**Winnipeg Jets**	**NHL**	**77**	**40**	**39**	**79**	**34**	**28**	**62**	**76**	**22**	**0**	**2**	**176**	**22.7**	**132**	**70**	**79**	**0**	**–17**	**5**	**2**	**0**	**2**	**23**	**2**	**0**	**0**
1988-89	**Detroit Red Wings**	**NHL**	**76**	**36**	**35**	**71**	**31**	**25**	**56**	**118**	**16**	**0**	**5**	**148**	**24.3**	**125**	**46**	**73**	**1**	**+7**	**5**	**1**	**1**	**2**	**8**	**0**	**0**	**0**
1989-90	**St. Louis Blues**	**NHL**	**78**	**34**	**33**	**67**	**29**	**24**	**53**	**100**	**12**	**0**	**6**	**141**	**24.1**	**85**	**25**	**58**	**0**	**+2**	**12**	**4**	**3**	**7**	**20**	**3**	**0**	**0**
1990-91	**St. Louis Blues**	**NHL**	**37**	**6**	**11**	**17**	**5**	**8**	**13**	**24**	**0**	**0**	**2**	**53**	**11.3**	**26**	**6**	**22**	**0**	**–2**	....	....	....	....	....	....	....	....
	NHL Totals		**719**	**324**	**349**	**673**	**270**	**243**	**513**	**968**	**115**	**0**	**37**	**1513**	**21.4**	**1028**	**380**	**687**	**4**		**53**	**21**	**14**	**35**	**110**	**12**	**0**	**1**

Played in NHL All-Star Game (1985)

Traded to **Winnipeg** by **St. Louis** with Bryan Maxwell and Ed Staniowski for Scott Campbell and John Markell, July 3, 1981. Traded to **Detroit** by **Winnipeg** for Brent Ashton, June 13, 1988. Traded to **St. Louis** by **Detroit** with Tony McKegney for Bernie Federko and Adam Oates, June 15, 1989.

• MacLEISH, RICK

Rick MacLeish C – L. 5'11", 185 lbs. b: Lindsay, Ont., 1/3/1950. Boston's 1st choice, 4th overall, in 1970 Amateur Draft.

Season	Club	League	GP	G	A	Pts	AG	AA	APts	PIM	PP	SH	GW	S	%	TGF	PGF	TGA	PGA	+/–	GP	G	A	Pts	PIM	PP	SH	GW
1966-67	London Knights	OHA	2	0	0	0	....	....	....	0	....	....	....	....	....	....	....	....	....	....	....	....	....	....	....	....	....	....
	Peterborough Petes	OHA	8	0	0	0	....	....	....	0	....	....	....	....	....	....	....	....	....	....	....	....	....	....	....	....	....	....
1967-68	Peterborough Petes	OHA	54	24	25	49	....	....	....	16	....	....	....	....	....	....	....	....	....	....	5	2	1	3	0	....	....	....
1968-69	Peterborough Petes	OHA	54	50	42	92	....	....	....	29	....	....	....	....	....	....	....	....	....	....	10	7	14	21	8	....	....	....
1969-70	Peterborough Petes	OHA	54	45	56	101	....	....	....	135	....	....	....	....	....	....	....	....	....	....	....	....	....	....	....	....	....	....
1970-71	**Philadelphia Flyers**	**NHL**	**26**	**2**	**4**	**6**	**2**	**4**	**6**	**19**	**0**	**0**	**0**	**54**	**3.7**	**13**	**2**	**18**	**3**	**–4**	**4**	**1**	**0**	**1**	**0**	**0**	**0**	**0**
	Oklahoma City Blazers	CHL	46	13	15	28	....	....	....	93	....	....	....	....	....	....	....	....	....	....	....	....	....	....	....	....	....	....
1971-72	**Philadelphia Flyers**	**NHL**	**17**	**1**	**2**	**3**	**1**	**2**	**3**	**9**	**0**	**0**	**0**	**37**	**2.7**	**5**	**2**	**13**	**1**	**–9**	....	....	....	....	....	....	....	....
	Richmond Robins	AHL	42	24	11	35	....	....	....	33	....	....	....	....	....	....	....	....	....	....	....	....	....	....	....	....	....	....
1972-73	**Philadelphia Flyers**	**NHL**	**78**	**50**	**50**	**100**	**50**	**42**	**92**	**69**	**21**	**2**	**6**	**279**	**17.9**	**124**	**46**	**83**	**20**	**+15**	**10**	**3**	**4**	**7**	**2**	**2**	**0**	**1**
1973-74	**Philadelphia Flyers**	**NHL**	**78**	**32**	**45**	**77**	**33**	**39**	**72**	**42**	**13**	**4**	**5**	**270**	**11.9**	**101**	**37**	**54**	**11**	**+21**	**17**	***13**	**9**	***22**	**20**	**5**	**0**	**4**
1974-75	**Philadelphia Flyers**	**NHL**	**80**	**38**	**41**	**79**	**35**	**32**	**67**	**50**	**11**	**3**	**8**	**309**	**12.3**	**110**	**44**	**52**	**15**	**+29**	**17**	**11**	**9**	***20**	**8**	**4**	**0**	**1**
1975-76	**Philadelphia Flyers**	**NHL**	**51**	**22**	**23**	**45**	**20**	**18**	**38**	**16**	**6**	**1**	**4**	**222**	**9.9**	**70**	**27**	**49**	**12**	**+6**	....	....	....	....	....	....	....	....
1976-77	**Philadelphia Flyers**	**NHL**	**79**	**49**	**48**	**97**	**47**	**39**	**86**	**42**	**10**	**1**	**8**	**252**	**19.4**	**126**	**33**	**58**	**11**	**+46**	**10**	**4**	**9**	**13**	**2**	**2**	**0**	**1**
1977-78	**Philadelphia Flyers**	**NHL**	**76**	**31**	**39**	**70**	**30**	**32**	**62**	**33**	**7**	**2**	**7**	**253**	**12.3**	**98**	**29**	**54**	**9**	**+24**	**12**	**7**	**9**	**16**	**4**	**3**	**0**	**3**
1978-79	**Philadelphia Flyers**	**NHL**	**71**	**26**	**32**	**58**	**24**	**24**	**48**	**47**	**7**	**5**	**4**	**211**	**12.3**	**83**	**26**	**73**	**20**	**+4**	**7**	**0**	**1**	**1**	**0**	**0**	**0**	**0**
1979-80	**Philadelphia Flyers**	**NHL**	**78**	**31**	**35**	**66**	**28**	**27**	**55**	**28**	**6**	**3**	**4**	**234**	**13.2**	**91**	**18**	**74**	**24**	**+23**	**19**	**9**	**6**	**15**	**2**	**1**	**0**	**1**
1980-81	**Philadelphia Flyers**	**NHL**	**78**	**38**	**36**	**74**	**31**	**25**	**56**	**25**	**14**	**0**	**3**	**214**	**17.8**	**102**	**33**	**60**	**13**	**+22**	**12**	**5**	**5**	**10**	**0**	**4**	**0**	**0**
1981-82	**Hartford Whalers**	**NHL**	**34**	**6**	**16**	**22**	**5**	**11**	**16**	**16**	**4**	**0**	**0**	**68**	**8.8**	**30**	**13**	**31**	**1**	**–13**	....	....	....	....	....	....	....	....
	Pittsburgh Penguins	**NHL**	**40**	**13**	**12**	**25**	**10**	**8**	**18**	**28**	**2**	**2**	**1**	**101**	**12.9**	**43**	**15**	**45**	**10**	**–7**	**5**	**1**	**1**	**2**	**0**	**0**	**0**	**0**
1982-83	**Pittsburgh Penguins**	**NHL**	**6**	**0**	**5**	**5**	**0**	**3**	**3**	**2**	**0**	**0**	**0**	**8**	**0.0**	**5**	**3**	**10**	**3**	**–5**	....	....	....	....	....	....	....	....
1983-84	**Philadelphia Flyers**	**NHL**	**29**	**8**	**14**	**22**	**6**	**9**	**15**	**4**	**3**	**0**	**2**	**70**	**11.4**	**31**	**11**	**18**	**2**	**+4**	....	....	....	....	....	....	....	....
	Detroit Red Wings	**NHL**	**25**	**2**	**8**	**10**	**2**	**5**	**7**	**4**	**0**	**0**	**0**	**26**	**7.7**	**16**	**1**	**19**	**0**	**–4**	**1**	**0**	**0**	**0**	**0**	**0**	**0**	**0**
	NHL Totals		**846**	**349**	**410**	**759**	**324**	**320**	**644**	**434**	**104**	**23**	**52**	**2608**	**13.4**	**1048**	**340**	**711**	**155**		**114**	**54**	**53**	**107**	**38**	**21**	**0**	**11**

OHA First All-Star Team (1970)

Played in NHL All-Star Game (1976, 1977, 1980)

Traded to **Philadelphia** by **Boston** with Danny Schock for Mike Walton, February 1, 1971. Traded to **Hartford** by **Philadelphia** with Blake Wesley, Don Gillen and Philadelphia's 1st (Paul Lawless) 2nd (Mark Patterson) and 3rd (Kevin Dineen) choices in 1982 Entry Draft for Ray Allison, Fred Arthur and Hartford's 1st (Ron Sutter), and 3rd (Miroslav Dvorak) choices in 1983 Entry Draft, July 3, 1981. Traded to **Pittsburgh** by **Hartford** for Pittsburgh 8th round choice (Chris Duperron) in 1983 Entry Draft and Russ Anderson, December 29, 1991 Signed as a free agent by **Philadelphia**, October 6, 1983. Traded to **Detroit** by **Philadelphia** for future considerations, January 8, 1984.

• MacLELLAN, BRIAN

Brian MacLellan LW – L. 6'3", 220 lbs. b: Guelph, Ont., 10/27/1958.

Season	Club	League	GP	G	A	Pts	AG	AA	APts	PIM	PP	SH	GW	S	%	TGF	PGF	TGA	PGA	+/–	GP	G	A	Pts	PIM	PP	SH	GW
1978-79	Bowling Green University	CCHA	44	34	29	63	....	....	....	94	....	....	....	....	....	....	....	....	....	....	....	....	....	....	....	....	....	....
1979-80	Bowling Green University	CCHA	38	8	15	23	....	....	....	46	....	....	....	....	....	....	....	....	....	....	....	....	....	....	....	....	....	....
1980-81	Bowling Green University	CCHA	37	11	14	25	....	....	....	96	....	....	....	....	....	....	....	....	....	....	....	....	....	....	....	....	....	....
1981-82	Bowling Green University	CCHA	41	11	21	32	....	....	....	109	....	....	....	....	....	....	....	....	....	....	....	....	....	....	....	....	....	....
1982-83	**Los Angeles Kings**	**NHL**	**8**	**0**	**3**	**3**	**0**	**2**	**2**	**7**	**0**	**0**	**0**	**5**	**0.0**	**3**	**0**	**8**	**0**	**–5**	....	....	....	....	....	....	....	....
	New Haven Nighthawks	AHL	71	11	15	26	....	....	....	40	....	....	....	....	....	....	....	....	....	....	12	5	3	8	4	....	....	....
1983-84	**Los Angeles Kings**	**NHL**	**72**	**25**	**29**	**54**	**20**	**20**	**40**	**45**	**3**	**1**	**1**	**106**	**23.6**	**91**	**25**	**109**	**22**	**–21**	....	....	....	....	....	....	....	....
	New Haven Nighthawks	AHL	2	0	2	2	....	....	....	0	....	....	....	....	....	....	....	....	....	....	....	....	....	....	....	....	....	....
1984-85	**Los Angeles Kings**	**NHL**	**80**	**31**	**54**	**85**	**25**	**37**	**62**	**53**	**14**	**0**	**3**	**170**	**18.2**	**133**	**56**	**75**	**0**	**+2**	**3**	**0**	**1**	**1**	**0**	**0**	**0**	**0**
	Canada	WEC-A	4	0	0	0	....	....	....	0	....	....	....	....	....	....	....	....	....	....	....	....	....	....	....	....	....	....
1985-86	**Los Angeles Kings**	**NHL**	**27**	**5**	**8**	**13**	**4**	**5**	**9**	**19**	**4**	**0**	**0**	**53**	**9.4**	**28**	**9**	**32**	**0**	**–13**	....	....	....	....	....	....	....	....
	New York Rangers	**NHL**	**51**	**11**	**21**	**32**	**9**	**14**	**23**	**47**	**8**	**0**	**1**	**112**	**9.8**	**46**	**22**	**44**	**0**	**–20**	**16**	**2**	**4**	**6**	**15**	**0**	**0**	**1**
1986-87	**Minnesota North Stars**	**NHL**	**76**	**32**	**31**	**63**	**28**	**22**	**50**	**69**	**13**	**0**	**5**	**146**	**21.9**	**93**	**42**	**64**	**1**	**–12**	....	....	....	....	....	....	....	....
1987-88	**Minnesota North Stars**	**NHL**	**75**	**16**	**32**	**48**	**14**	**23**	**37**	**74**	**7**	**0**	**4**	**194**	**8.2**	**78**	**42**	**86**	**6**	**–44**	....	....	....	....	....	....	....	....
1988-89	**Minnesota North Stars**	**NHL**	**60**	**16**	**23**	**39**	**14**	**16**	**30**	**104**	**7**	**0**	**0**	**114**	**14.0**	**51**	**17**	**34**	**0**	**0**	....	....	....	....	....	....	....	....
	Calgary Flames	**NHL**	**12**	**2**	**3**	**5**	**2**	**2**	**4**	**14**	**0**	**0**	**0**	**23**	**8.7**	**12**	**3**	**6**	**0**	**+3**	**21**	**3**	**2**	**5**	**19**	**0**	**0**	**1**
1989-90	Calgary Flames	FrTour	3	0	1	1	....	....	....	6	....	....	....	....	....	....	....	....	....	....	....	....	....	....	....	....	....	....
	Calgary Flames	**NHL**	**65**	**20**	**18**	**38**	**17**	**13**	**30**	**26**	**10**	**0**	**3**	**127**	**15.7**	**57**	**20**	**40**	**0**	**–3**	**6**	**0**	**2**	**2**	**8**	**0**	**0**	**0**
1990-91	**Calgary Flames**	**NHL**	**57**	**13**	**14**	**27**	**12**	**11**	**23**	**55**	**5**	**0**	**2**	**74**	**17.6**	**50**	**9**	**27**	**1**	**+15**	**1**	**0**	**0**	**0**	**0**	**0**	**0**	**0**
1991-92	**Detroit Red Wings**	**NHL**	**23**	**1**	**5**	**6**	**1**	**4**	**5**	**38**	**0**	**0**	**0**	**17**	**5.9**	**10**	**2**	**4**	**0**	**+4**	....	....	....	....	....	....	....	....
	NHL Totals		**606**	**172**	**241**	**413**	**146**	**169**	**315**	**551**	**71**	**1**	**19**	**1141**	**15.1**	**652**	**247**	**529**	**30**		**47**	**5**	**9**	**14**	**42**	**0**	**0**	**2**

CCHA First All-Star Team (1982) • NCAA West First All-American Team (1982)

Signed as a free agent by **LA Kings**, May 12, 1982. Traded to **NY Rangers** by **LA Kings** with LA Kings' 4th round choice (Mike Sullivan) in 1987 Entry Darft for Rollie Melanson and Grant Ledyard, December 9, 1985. Traded to **Minnesota** by **NY Rangers** for Minnesota's 3rd round choice (Simon Gagne) in 1987 Entry Draft, September 8, 1986. Traded to **Calgary** by **Minnesota** with Minnesota's 4th round choice (Robert Reichel) in 1989 Entry Draft for Shane Churla and Perry Berezan, March 4, 1989. Traded to **Detroit** by **Calgary** for Marc Habscheid, June 11, 1991.

• MacLEOD, PAT

Pat MacLeod D – L. 5'11", 190 lbs. b: Melfort, Sask., 6/15/1969. Minnesota's 5th choice, 87th overall, in 1989 Entry Draft.

Season	Club	League	GP	G	A	Pts	AG	AA	APts	PIM	PP	SH	GW	S	%	TGF	PGF	TGA	PGA	+/–	GP	G	A	Pts	PIM	PP	SH	GW
1987-88	Kamloops Chiefs	WHL	50	13	33	46	....	....	....	27	....	....	....	....	....	....	....	....	....	....	18	2	7	9	6	....	....	....
1988-89	Kamloops Chiefs	WHL	37	11	34	45	....	....	....	14	....	....	....	....	....	....	....	....	....	....	15	7	18	25	24	....	....	....
1989-90	Kalamazoo Wings	IHL	82	9	38	47	....	....	....	27	....	....	....	....	....	....	....	....	....	....	10	1	6	7	2	....	....	....
1990-91	**Minnesota North Stars**	**NHL**	**1**	**0**	**1**	**1**	**0**	**1**	**1**	**0**	**0**	**0**	**0**	**1**	**0.0**	**2**	**1**	**0**	**0**	**+1**	....	....	....	....	....	....	....	....
	Kalamazoo Wings	IHL	59	10	30	40	....	....	....	16	....	....	....	....	....	....	....	....	....	....	11	1	2	3	5	....	....	....
1991-92	**San Jose Sharks**	**NHL**	**37**	**5**	**11**	**16**	**5**	**8**	**13**	**4**	**3**	**0**	**0**	**77**	**6.5**	**34**	**19**	**59**	**12**	**–32**	....	....	....	....	....	....	....	....
	Kansas City Blades	IHL	45	9	21	30	....	....	....	19	....	....	....	....	....	....	....	....	....	....	11	1	4	5	4	....	....	....
1992-93	**San Jose Sharks**	**NHL**	**13**	**0**	**1**	**1**	**0**	**1**	**1**	**10**	**0**	**0**	**0**	**20**	**0.0**	**6**	**1**	**31**	**7**	**–19**	....	....	....	....	....	....	....	....
	Kansas City Blades	IHL	18	8	8	16	....	....	....	14	....	....	....	....	....	....	....	....	....	....	10	2	4	6	7	....	....	....
1993-94	Milwaukee Admirals	IHL	73	21	52	73	....	....	....	18	....	....	....	....	....	....	....	....	....	....	3	1	2	3	0	....	....	....
1994-95	Milwaukee Admirals	IHL	69	11	36	47	....	....	....	16	....	....	....	....	....	....	....	....	....	....	15	3	6	9	8	....	....	....
1995-96	**Dallas Stars**	**NHL**	**2**	**0**	**0**	**0**	**0**	**0**	**0**	**0**	**0**	**0**	**0**	**2**	**0.0**	**1**	**1**	**0**	**0**	**0**	....	....	....	....	....	....	....	....
	Michigan K-Wings	IHL	50	3	23	26	....	....	....	18	....	....	....	....	....	....	....	....	....	....	7	0	3	3	0	....	....	....

Season	Club	League	GP	G	A	Pts	AG	AA	APts	PIM	PP	SH	GW	S	%	TGF	PGF	TGA	PGA	+/-	GP	G	A	Pts	PIM	PP	SH	GW
			REGULAR SEASON																		PLAYOFFS							
1996-97	Farjestad BK Karlstad	Sweden	12	1	2	3	....	....	....	4	....	....	....	....	....	....	....	....	....	....	....	....	....	....	....	....	....	....
	Cincinnati Cyclones	IHL	41	5	8	13	....	....	....	8	....	....	....	....	....	....	....	....	....	....	3	2	0	2	0	....	....	....
1997-98	Cincinnati Cyclones	IHL	78	16	39	55	....	....	....	51	....	....	....	....	....	....	....	....	....	....	9	0	6	6	8	....	....	....
	NHL Totals		**53**	**5**	**13**	**18**	**5**	**10**	**15**	**14**	**3**	**0**	**0**	**100**	**5.0**	**43**	**22**	**90**	**19**		....	....	....	....	....	....	....	....

WHL West Second All-Star Team (1989) • IHL Second All-Star Team (1992) • IHL First All-Star Team (1994)

Claimed by **San Jose** from **Minnesota** in Dispersal Draft, May 30, 1991. Signed as a free agent by **Dallas**, July 31, 1995.

• MacMILLAN, BILLY

Billy MacMillan RW – L. 5'10", 185 lbs. b: Charlottetown, P.E.I., 3/7/1943.

Season	Club	League	GP	G	A	Pts	AG	AA	APts	PIM	PP	SH	GW	S	%	TGF	PGF	TGA	PGA	+/-	GP	G	A	Pts	PIM	PP	SH	GW
1959-60	St. Michael's Majors	OHA	2	0	0	0	....	....	....	0	....	....	....	....	....	....	....	....	....	....	5	0	1	1	0	....	....	....
1960-61	St. Michael's Majors	OHA	46	7	12	19	....	....	....	31	....	....	....	....	....	....	....	....	....	....	7	1	1	2	4	....	....	....
1961-62	St. Michael's Majors	MTHL	32	14	15	29	....	....	....	11	....	....	....	....	....	....	....	....	....	....	9	12	2	14	41	....	....	....
1962-63	Neil McNeil Maroons	OHA	32	25	12	37	....	....	....	11	....	....	....	....	....	....	....	....	....	....	16	10	15	25	27	....	....	....
	Sudbury Wolves	EPHL	1	0	0	0	....	....	....	0	....	....	....	....	....	....	....	....	....	....	....	....	....	....	....	....	....	....
1963-64	St. Dunstan's University	MIAU	11	*25	11	*36	....	....	....	17	....	....	....	....	....	....	....	....	....	....	....	....	....	....	....	....	....	....
1964-65	St. Dunstan's University	MIAU	STATISTICS NOT AVAILABLE																									
1965-66	Canada	Nat-Team	STATISTICS NOT AVAILABLE																									
1966-67	Canada	Nat-Team	STATISTICS NOT AVAILABLE																									
1967-68	Ottawa Nats	OHA Sr.	20	13	8	21	....	....	....	20	....	....	....	....	....	....	....	....	....	....	....	....	....	....	....	....	....	....
1968-69	Canada	Nat-Team	STATISTICS NOT AVAILABLE																									
1969-70	Canada	Nat-Team	STATISTICS NOT AVAILABLE																									
	Tulsa Oilers	CHL	3	1	6	7	....	....	....	0	....	....	....	....	....	....	....	....	....	....	....	....	....	....	....	....	....	....
1970-71	**Toronto Maple Leafs**	**NHL**	**76**	**22**	**19**	**41**	**23**	**17**	**40**	**42**	**3**	**1**	**4**	**156**	**14.1**	**67**	**9**	**61**	**13**	**+10**	**6**	**0**	**3**	**3**	**2**	**0**	**0**	**0**
1971-72	**Toronto Maple Leafs**	**NHL**	**61**	**10**	**7**	**17**	**11**	**6**	**17**	**39**	**2**	**0**	**2**	**95**	**10.5**	**30**	**5**	**26**	**0**	**–1**	**5**	**0**	**0**	**0**	**0**	**0**	**0**	**0**
1972-73	**Atlanta Flames**	**NHL**	**78**	**10**	**15**	**25**	**10**	**13**	**23**	**52**	**3**	**0**	**2**	**101**	**9.9**	**54**	**8**	**61**	**5**	**–10**	....	....	....	....	....	....	....	....
1973-74	**New York Islanders**	**NHL**	**55**	**4**	**9**	**13**	**4**	**8**	**12**	**16**	**0**	**0**	**0**	**65**	**6.2**	**23**	**0**	**34**	**5**	**–6**	....	....	....	....	....	....	....	....
1974-75	**New York Islanders**	**NHL**	**69**	**13**	**12**	**25**	**12**	**9**	**21**	**12**	**2**	**1**	**1**	**74**	**17.6**	**41**	**5**	**55**	**19**	**0**	**17**	**0**	**1**	**1**	**23**	**0**	**0**	**0**
1975-76	**New York Islanders**	**NHL**	**64**	**9**	**7**	**16**	**8**	**5**	**13**	**10**	**0**	**0**	**2**	**75**	**12.0**	**27**	**0**	**25**	**3**	**+5**	**13**	**4**	**2**	**6**	**8**	**0**	**0**	**2**
1976-77	**New York Islanders**	**NHL**	**43**	**6**	**8**	**14**	**6**	**6**	**12**	**13**	**0**	**1**	**1**	**34**	**17.6**	**21**	**0**	**22**	**5**	**+4**	**12**	**2**	**0**	**2**	**7**	**0**	**0**	**2**
	Rhode Island Reds	AHL	2	1	1	2	....	....	....	4	....	....	....	....	....	....	....	....	....	....	....	....	....	....	....	....	....	....
	Fort Worth Texans	CHL	12	1	7	8	....	....	....	2	....	....	....	....	....	....	....	....	....	....	....	....	....	....	....	....	....	....
1977-78	Fort Worth Texans	CHL	59	5	13	18	....	....	....	26	....	....	....	....	....	....	....	....	....	....	14	2	2	4	2	....	....	....
	NHL Totals		**446**	**74**	**77**	**151**	**74**	**64**	**138**	**184**	**10**	**3**	**12**	**600**	**12.3**	**263**	**27**	**284**	**50**		**53**	**6**	**6**	**12**	**40**	**0**	**0**	**4**

Claimed by **Atlanta** from **Toronto** in Expansion Draft, June 6, 1972. Traded to **NY Islanders** by **Atlanta** to complete transaction that sent Arnie Brown to Atlanta (February 13, 1972), May 29, 1973.

• MacMILLAN, BOB

Bob MacMillan RW – L. 5'11", 185 lbs. b: Charlottetown, P.E.I., 12/3/1952. NY Rangers' 2nd choice, 15th overall, in 1972 Amateur Draft.

Season	Club	League	GP	G	A	Pts	AG	AA	APts	PIM	PP	SH	GW	S	%	TGF	PGF	TGA	PGA	+/-	GP	G	A	Pts	PIM	PP	SH	GW
1970-71	St. Catharines Black Hawks	OHA	59	41	62	103	....	....	....	93	....	....	....	....	....	....	....	....	....	....	....	....	....	....	....	....	....	....
1971-72	St. Catharines Black Hawks	OHA	39	12	41	53	....	....	....	41	....	....	....	....	....	....	....	....	....	....	....	....	....	....	....	....	....	....
1972-73	Minnesota Fighting Saints	WHA	75	13	27	40	....	....	....	48	....	....	....	....	....	....	....	....	....	....	5	0	3	3	0	....	....	....
1973-74	Minnesota Fighting Saints	WHA	78	14	34	48	....	....	....	81	....	....	....	....	....	....	....	....	....	....	11	2	3	5	4	....	....	....
1974-75	**New York Rangers**	**NHL**	**22**	**1**	**2**	**3**	**1**	**2**	**3**	**4**	**0**	**0**	**0**	**16**	**6.3**	**7**	**0**	**5**	**1**	**+3**	....	....	....	....	....	....	....	....
	Providence Reds	AHL	46	18	29	47	....	....	....	58	....	....	....	....	....	....	....	....	....	....	6	3	2	5	17	....	....	....
1975-76	**St. Louis Blues**	**NHL**	**80**	**20**	**32**	**52**	**19**	**25**	**44**	**41**	**2**	**1**	**2**	**151**	**13.2**	**88**	**20**	**83**	**28**	**+13**	**3**	**0**	**1**	**1**	**0**	**0**	**0**	**0**
1976-77	**St. Louis Blues**	**NHL**	**80**	**19**	**39**	**58**	**18**	**32**	**50**	**11**	**10**	**0**	**1**	**168**	**11.3**	**86**	**31**	**57**	**3**	**+1**	**4**	**0**	**1**	**1**	**0**	**0**	**0**	**0**
1977-78	**St. Louis Blues**	**NHL**	**28**	**7**	**12**	**19**	**7**	**10**	**17**	**23**	**3**	**0**	**0**	**77**	**9.1**	**26**	**9**	**34**	**6**	**–11**	....	....	....	....	....	....	....	....
	Atlanta Flames	**NHL**	**52**	**31**	**21**	**52**	**30**	**17**	**47**	**26**	**5**	**0**	**3**	**148**	**20.9**	**84**	**22**	**40**	**6**	**+28**	**2**	**0**	**2**	**2**	**0**	**0**	**0**	**0**
	Canada	WEC-A	10	0	3	3	....	....	....	6	....	....	....	....	....	....	....	....	....	....	....	....	....	....	....	....	....	....
1978-79	**Atlanta Flames**	**NHL**	**79**	**37**	**71**	**108**	**34**	**55**	**89**	**14**	**8**	**1**	**4**	**194**	**19.1**	**143**	**35**	**78**	**4**	**+34**	**2**	**0**	**1**	**1**	**0**	**0**	**0**	**0**
1979-80	**Atlanta Flames**	**NHL**	**77**	**22**	**39**	**61**	**20**	**30**	**50**	**10**	**2**	**3**	**4**	**164**	**13.4**	**92**	**23**	**81**	**15**	**+3**	**4**	**0**	**0**	**0**	**0**	**0**	**0**	**0**
1980-81	**Calgary Flames**	**NHL**	**77**	**28**	**35**	**63**	**23**	**24**	**47**	**47**	**2**	**4**	**2**	**162**	**17.3**	**97**	**17**	**95**	**33**	**+18**	**16**	**8**	**6**	**14**	**7**	**2**	**0**	**1**
1981-82	**Calgary Flames**	**NHL**	**23**	**4**	**7**	**11**	**3**	**5**	**8**	**14**	**1**	**0**	**0**	**26**	**15.4**	**16**	**4**	**28**	**5**	**–11**	....	....	....	....	....	....	....	....
	Colorado Rockies	**NHL**	**57**	**18**	**32**	**50**	**14**	**21**	**35**	**27**	**3**	**0**	**1**	**106**	**17.0**	**69**	**18**	**74**	**14**	**–9**	....	....	....	....	....	....	....	....
1982-83	**New Jersey Devils**	**NHL**	**71**	**19**	**29**	**48**	**16**	**20**	**36**	**8**	**6**	**0**	**3**	**120**	**15.8**	**71**	**28**	**113**	**35**	**–35**	....	....	....	....	....	....	....	....
1983-84	**New Jersey Devils**	**NHL**	**71**	**17**	**23**	**40**	**14**	**16**	**30**	**23**	**2**	**0**	**2**	**114**	**14.9**	**58**	**13**	**83**	**17**	**–21**	....	....	....	....	....	....	....	....
1984-85	**Chicago Black Hawks**	**NHL**	**36**	**5**	**7**	**12**	**4**	**5**	**9**	**12**	**0**	**0**	**1**	[illegible]	**12.0**	**22**	**0**	**38**	**0**	**–16**	....	....	....	....	....	....	....	....
	Milwaukee Admirals	IHL	8	2	2	4	....	....	....	2	....	....	....	....	....	....	....	....	....	....	....	....	....	....	....	....	....	....
1985-86	Charlottetown Islanders	PEI Sr.	DID NOT PLAY – COACHING																									
1986-87	Charlottetown Islanders	PEI Sr.	DID NOT PLAY – COACHING																									
1987-88	Charlottetown Islanders	PEI Sr.	2	2	2	4	....	....	....	0	....	....	....	....	....	....	....	....	....	....	....	....	....	....	....	....	....	....
	NHL Totals		**753**	**228**	**349**	**577**	**203**	**262**	**465**	**260**	**44**	**9**	**23**	**1485**	**15.4**	**859**	**220**	**809**	**167**		**31**	**8**	**11**	**19**	**16**	**2**	**0**	**1**
	Other Major League Totals		153	27	61	88	....	....	....	129	....	....	....	....	....	....	....	....	....		16	2	6	8	4	....	....	....

Won Lady Byng Trophy (1979)

Selected by **Minnesota** (WHA) in 1972 WHA General Player Draft, February 12, 1972. Traded to **St. Louis** by **NY Rangers** with future considerations for Larry Sacharuk, September 21, 1975. Traded to **Atlanta** by **St. Louis** with Yves Belanger, Dick Redmond, Barry Gibbs and St. Louis' 2nd round choice (Mike Perovich) in 1979 Entry Draft for Phil Myre and Curt Bennett, December 12, 1977. Tansferred to **Calgary** after **Atlanta** franchise relocated, June 24, 1980. Traded to **Colorado** by **Calgary** with Don Lever for Lanny McDonald and Colorado's 4th round choice (later traded to NY Islanders — NY Islanders selected Mikko Makela) in 1983 Entry Draft, November 25, 1981. Transferred to **New Jersey** after **Colorado** franchise relocated, June 30, 1982. Traded to **Chicago** by **New Jersey** for Don Dietrich and Rich Preston, June 19, 1984.

• MacNEIL, BERNIE

Bernie MacNeil LW – L. 5'11", 190 lbs. b: Sudbury, Ont., 3/7/1950. Detroit's 6th choice, 82nd overall, in 1970 Amateur Draft.

Season	Club	League	GP	G	A	Pts	AG	AA	APts	PIM	PP	SH	GW	S	%	TGF	PGF	TGA	PGA	+/-	GP	G	A	Pts	PIM	PP	SH	GW
1969-70	Espanola Miners	NOHA	....	34	47	81	....	....	....	276	....	....	....	....	....	....	....	....	....	....	....	....	....	....	....	....	....	....
1970-71	Fort Wayne Komets	IHL	60	24	21	45	....	....	....	121	....	....	....	....	....	....	....	....	....	....	5	2	0	2	18	....	....	....
1971-72	Fort Wayne Komets	IHL	67	19	13	32	....	....	....	140	....	....	....	....	....	....	....	....	....	....	8	0	0	0	2	....	....	....
1972-73	Greensboro Generals	EHL	10	6	12	18	....	....	....	72	....	....	....	....	....	....	....	....	....	....	....	....	....	....	....	....	....	....
	Los Angeles Sharks	WHA	42	4	7	11	....	....	....	48	....	....	....	....	....	....	....	....	....	....	3	0	0	0	4	....	....	....
1973-74	**St. Louis Blues**	**NHL**	**4**	**0**	**0**	**0**	**0**	**0**	**0**	**0**	**0**	**0**	**0**	**5**	**0.0**	**1**	**0**	**0**	**0**	**+1**	....	....	....	....	....	....	....	....
	Denver Spurs	WHL	33	8	15	23	....	....	....	151	....	....	....	....	....	....	....	....	....	....	....	....	....	....	....	....	....	....
	San Diego Gulls	WHL	35	5	10	15	....	....	....	86	....	....	....	....	....	....	....	....	....	....	4	0	3	3	10	....	....	....
1974-75	Rochester Americans	AHL	9	0	1	1	....	....	....	12	....	....	....	....	....	....	....	....	....	....	....	....	....	....	....	....	....	....
	Binghamton Dusters	NAHL	53	12	20	32	....	....	....	145	....	....	....	....	....	....	....	....	....	....	14	5	4	9	*55	....	....	....
1975-76	Cincinnati Stingers	WHA	77	15	12	27	....	....	....	83	....	....	....	....	....	....	....	....	....	....	....	....	....	....	....	....	....	....
	NHL Totals		**4**	**0**	**0**	**0**	**0**	**0**	**0**	**0**	**0**	**0**	**0**	**5**	**0.0**	**1**	**0**	**0**	**0**		....	....	....	....	....	....	....	....
	Other Major League Totals		119	19	19	38	....	....	....	131	....	....	....	....	....	....	....	....	....		3	0	0	0	4	....	....	....

Selected by **LA Sharks** (WHA) in 1972 WHA General Player Draft, February 12, 1972. Signed as a free agent by **St. Louis**, September, 1975. Signed as a free agent by **Cincinnati** (WHA), May, 1975.

• MacNEIL, AL

Al MacNeil D – L. 5'10", 183 lbs. b: Sydney, N.S., 9/27/1935.

Season	Club	League	GP	G	A	Pts	AG	AA	APts	PIM	PP	SH	GW	S	%	TGF	PGF	TGA	PGA	+/-	GP	G	A	Pts	PIM	PP	SH	GW
1953-54	Toronto Marlboros	OHA	59	3	12	15	....	....	....	112	....	....	....	....	....	....	....	....	....	....	15	2	3	5	18	....	....	....
1954-55	Toronto Marlboros	OHA	47	3	16	19	....	....	....	141	....	....	....	....	....	....	....	....	....	....	13	0	4	4	*37	....	....	....
1955-56	Toronto Marlboros	OHA	48	9	12	21	....	....	....	58	....	....	....	....	....	....	....	....	....	....	11	0	5	5	*63	....	....	....
	Toronto Maple Leafs	**NHL**	**1**	**0**	**0**	**0**	**0**	**0**	**0**	**2**	....	....	....	....	....	....	....	....	....	....	....	....	....	....	....	....	....	....
1956-57	**Toronto Maple Leafs**	**NHL**	**53**	**4**	**8**	**12**	**5**	**9**	**14**	**84**	....	....	....	....	....	....	....	....	....	....	....	....	....	....	....	....	....	....
	Rochester Americans	AHL	13	0	4	4	....	....	....	35	....	....	....	....	....	....	....	....	....	....	....	....	....	....	....	....	....	....
1957-58	**Toronto Maple Leafs**	**NHL**	**13**	**0**	**0**	**0**	**0**	**0**	**0**	**9**	....	....	....	....	....	....	....	....	....	....	....	....	....	....	....	....	....	....
	Rochester Americans	AHL	54	3	18	21	....	....	....	91	....	....	....	....	....	....	....	....	....	....	....	....	....	....	....	....	....	....
1958-59	Rochester Americans	AHL	69	4	13	17	....	....	....	119	....	....	....	....	....	....	....	....	....	....	5	1	1	2	17	....	....	....
1959-60	**Toronto Maple Leafs**	**NHL**	**4**	**0**	**0**	**0**	**0**	**0**	**0**	**2**	....	....	....	....	....	....	....	....	....	....	....	....	....	....	....	....	....	....
	Rochester Americans	AHL	49	4	16	20	....	....	....	44	....	....	....	....	....	....	....	....	....	....	12	1	2	3	12	....	....	....
1960-61	Hull-Ottawa Canadiens	EPHL	60	6	20	26	....	....	....	101	....	....	....	....	....	....	....	....	....	....	14	2	4	6	21	....	....	....
1961-62	**Montreal Canadiens**	**NHL**	**61**	**1**	**7**	**8**	**1**	**7**	**8**	**74**	....	....	....	....	....	....	....	....	....	....	**5**	**0**	**0**	**0**	**2**	....	....	....
1962-63	**Chicago Black Hawks**	**NHL**	**70**	**2**	**19**	**21**	**2**	**20**	**22**	**100**	....	....	....	....	....	....	....	....	....	....	**4**	**0**	**1**	**1**	**4**	....	....	....
1963-64	**Chicago Black Hawks**	**NHL**	**70**	**5**	**19**	**24**	**7**	**21**	**28**	**91**	....	....	....	....	....	....	....	....	....	....	**7**	**0**	**2**	**2**	**25**	....	....	....

			REGULAR SEASON																		PLAYOFFS							
Season	Club	League	GP	G	A	Pts	AG	AA	APts	PIM	PP	SH	GW	S	%	TGF	PGF	TGA	PGA	+/–	GP	G	A	Pts	PIM	PP	SH	GW
1964-65	**Chicago Black Hawks**	**NHL**	**69**	**3**	**7**	**10**	**4**	**8**	**12**	**119**	....	....	....	....	....	....	....	....	....	....	**14**	**0**	**1**	**1**	**34**	....	....	....
1965-66	**Chicago Black Hawks**	**NHL**	**51**	**0**	**1**	**1**	**0**	**1**	**1**	**34**	....	....	....	....	....	....	....	....	....	....	**3**	**0**	**0**	**0**	**0**	....	....	....
1966-67	**New York Rangers**	**NHL**	**58**	**0**	**4**	**4**	**0**	**4**	**4**	**44**	....	....	....	....	....	....	....	....	....	....	**4**	**0**	**0**	**0**	**2**	....	....	....
1967-68	**Pittsburgh Penguins**	**NHL**	**74**	**2**	**10**	**12**	**2**	**10**	**12**	**58**	**0**	**0**	**0**	**76**	**2.6**	**61**	**1**	**75**	**9**	**–6**	....	....	....	....	....	....	....	....
1968-69	Houston Apollos	CHL	70	1	11	12	....	....	....	79	....	....	....	....	....	....	....	....	....	....	3	0	1	1	0	....	....	....
1969-70	Montreal Voyageurs	AHL	66	0	10	10	....	....	....	14	....	....	....	....	....	....	....	....	....	....	8	0	1	1	0	....	....	....
1970-71	**Montreal Canadiens**	**NHL**	DID NOT PLAY – COACHING																									
	NHL Totals		**524**	**17**	**75**	**92**	**21**	**80**	**101**	**617**	**0**	**0**	**0**	**76**	**22.4**	**61**	**1**	**75**	**9**		**37**	**0**	**4**	**4**	**67**	**0**	**0**	**0**

Traded to **Montreal** by **Toronto** for Stan Smrke, June 7, 1960. Traded to **Chicago** by **Montreal** for Wayne Hicks, May, 1962. Claimed by **Montreal** from **Chicago** in Intra-League Draft, June 15, 1966. Claimed by **NY Rangers** from **Montreal** in Intra-League Draft, June 15, 1966. Claimed by **Pittsburgh** from **NY Rangers** in Expansion Draft, June 6, 1967. Traded to **Montreal** by **Pittsburgh** for Wally Boyer, June 12, 1968.

• MACOUN, JAMIE

Jamie Macoun D – L. 6′2″, 200 lbs. b: Newmarket, Ont., 8/17/1961.

Season	Club	League	GP	G	A	Pts	AG	AA	APts	PIM	PP	SH	GW	S	%	TGF	PGF	TGA	PGA	+/–	GP	G	A	Pts	PIM	PP	SH	GW
1980-81	Ohio State University	CCHA	38	9	20	29	....	....	....	83	....	....	....	....	....	....	....	....	....	....	....	....	....	....	....	....	....	....
1981-82	Ohio State University	CCHA	25	2	18	20	....	....	....	89	....	....	....	....	....	....	....	....	....	....	....	....	....	....	....	....	....	....
1982-83	Ohio State University	CCHA	19	6	21	27	....	....	....	54	....	....	....	....	....	....	....	....	....	....	....	....	....	....	....	....	....	....
	Calgary Flames	**NHL**	**22**	**1**	**4**	**5**	**1**	**3**	**4**	**25**	**0**	**0**	**0**	**18**	**5.6**	**16**	**0**	**13**	**0**	**+3**	**9**	**0**	**2**	**2**	**8**	**0**	**0**	**0**
1983-84	**Calgary Flames**	**NHL**	**72**	**9**	**23**	**32**	**7**	**16**	**23**	**97**	**0**	**1**	**0**	**165**	**5.5**	**95**	**2**	**121**	**31**	**+3**	**11**	**1**	**0**	**1**	**0**	**1**	**0**	**0**
1984-85	**Calgary Flames**	**NHL**	**70**	**9**	**30**	**39**	**7**	**20**	**27**	**67**	**0**	**0**	**2**	**129**	**7.0**	**110**	**1**	**105**	**40**	**+44**	**4**	**1**	**0**	**1**	**4**	**0**	**0**	**0**
	Canada	WEC-A	9	0	0	0	....	....	....	10	....	....	....	....	....	....	....	....	....	....	....	....	....	....	....	....	....	....
1985-86	**Calgary Flames**	**NHL**	**77**	**11**	**21**	**32**	**9**	**14**	**23**	**81**	**0**	**2**	**1**	**133**	**8.3**	**91**	**2**	**120**	**45**	**+14**	**22**	**1**	**6**	**7**	**23**	**0**	**0**	**0**
1986-87	**Calgary Flames**	**NHL**	**79**	**7**	**33**	**40**	**6**	**24**	**30**	**111**	**1**	**0**	**0**	**137**	**5.1**	**118**	**14**	**114**	**43**	**+33**	**3**	**0**	**1**	**1**	**8**	**0**	**0**	**0**
1987-88			DID NOT PLAY – INJURED																									
1988-89	**Calgary Flames**	**NHL**	**72**	**8**	**19**	**27**	**7**	**13**	**20**	**76**	**0**	**0**	**2**	**89**	**9.0**	**92**	**3**	**73**	**24**	**+40**	**22**	**3**	**6**	**9**	**30**	**0**	**0**	**1**
1989-90	Calgary Flames	FrTour	1	0	0	0	....	....	....	0	....	....	....	....	....	....	....	....	....	....	....	....	....	....	....	....	....	....
	Calgary Flames	**NHL**	**78**	**8**	**27**	**35**	**7**	**19**	**26**	**70**	**1**	**0**	**1**	**120**	**6.7**	**97**	**10**	**95**	**42**	**+34**	**6**	**0**	**3**	**3**	**10**	**0**	**0**	**0**
	Canada	WEC-A	8	1	1	2	....	....	....	6	....	....	....	....	....	....	....	....	....	....	....	....	....	....	....	....	....	....
1990-91	**Calgary Flames**	**NHL**	**79**	**7**	**15**	**22**	**6**	**11**	**17**	**84**	**1**	**1**	**0**	**117**	**6.0**	**111**	**7**	**112**	**37**	**+29**	**7**	**0**	**1**	**1**	**4**	**0**	**0**	**0**
	Canada	WEC-A	8	4	1	5	....	....	....	10	....	....	....	....	....	....	....	....	....	....	....	....	....	....	....	....	....	....
1991-92	**Calgary Flames**	**NHL**	**37**	**2**	**12**	**14**	**2**	**9**	**11**	**53**	**1**	**0**	**0**	**58**	**3.4**	**45**	**4**	**45**	**14**	**+10**	....	....	....	....	....	....	....	....
	Toronto Maple Leafs	**NHL**	**39**	**3**	**13**	**16**	**3**	**10**	**13**	**18**	**2**	**0**	**0**	**71**	**4.2**	**70**	**24**	**65**	**19**	**0**	....	....	....	....	....	....	....	....
1992-93	**Toronto Maple Leafs**	**NHL**	**77**	**4**	**15**	**19**	**3**	**10**	**13**	**55**	**2**	**0**	**1**	**114**	**3.5**	**86**	**16**	**105**	**38**	**+3**	**21**	**0**	**6**	**6**	**36**	**0**	**0**	**0**
1993-94	**Toronto Maple Leafs**	**NHL**	**82**	**3**	**27**	**30**	**3**	**21**	**24**	**115**	**1**	**0**	**1**	**122**	**2.5**	**83**	**14**	**114**	**40**	**–5**	**18**	**1**	**1**	**2**	**12**	**0**	**0**	**0**
1994-95	**Toronto Maple Leafs**	**NHL**	**46**	**2**	**8**	**10**	**4**	**12**	**16**	**75**	**1**	**0**	**0**	**84**	**2.4**	**43**	**4**	**60**	**15**	**–6**	**7**	**1**	**2**	**3**	**8**	**0**	**0**	**0**
1995-96	**Toronto Maple Leafs**	**NHL**	**82**	**0**	**8**	**8**	**0**	**7**	**7**	**87**	**0**	**0**	**0**	**74**	**0.0**	**62**	**1**	**105**	**46**	**+2**	**6**	**0**	**2**	**2**	**8**	**0**	**0**	**0**
1996-97	**Toronto Maple Leafs**	**NHL**	**73**	**1**	**10**	**11**	**1**	**9**	**10**	**93**	**0**	**0**	**1**	**64**	**1.6**	**61**	**0**	**103**	**28**	**–14**	....	....	....	....	....	....	....	....
1997-98	**Toronto Maple Leafs**	**NHL**	**67**	**0**	**7**	**7**	**0**	**7**	**7**	**63**	**0**	**0**	**0**	**67**	**0.0**	**45**	**0**	**83**	**21**	**–17**	....	....	....	....	....	....	....	....
	Detroit Red Wings	**NHL**	**7**	**0**	**0**	**0**	**0**	**0**	**0**	**2**	**0**	**0**	**0**	**11**	**0.0**	**4**	**0**	**7**	**3**	**0**	**22**	**2**	**2**	**4**	**18**	**0**	**0**	**2**
	NHL Totals		**1059**	**75**	**272**	**347**	**66**	**205**	**271**	**1172**	**10**	**4**	**9**	**1573**	**4.8**	**1229**	**102**	**1440**	**486**		**158**	**10**	**32**	**42**	**169**	**1**	**0**	**3**

NHL All-Rookie Team (1984) • Named Best Defenseman at WEC-A (1991)

Signed as a free agent by **Calgary**, January 30, 1983. • Missed entire 1987-88 season recovering from nerve damage to arm after automobile accident, May, 1987. Traded to **Toronto** by **Calgary** with Doug Gilmour, Ric Natress, Kent Manderville and Rick Wamsley for Gary Leeman, Alexander Godynyuk, Jeff Reese, Michel Petit and Craig Berube, January 2, 1992. Traded to **Detroit** by **Toronto** for Tampa Bay's 4th round choice (previously acquired, Toronto selected Alexei Ponikarovsky) in 1998 Entry Draft, March 24, 1998.

• MacSWEYN, RALPH

Ralph MacSweyn D – R. 5′11″, 190 lbs. b: Hawkesbury, Ont., 9/8/1942. Deceased.

Season	Club	League	GP	G	A	Pts	AG	AA	APts	PIM	PP	SH	GW	S	%	TGF	PGF	TGA	PGA	+/–	GP	G	A	Pts	PIM	PP	SH	GW
1963-64	Lancaster Dodgers	OHA Sr.	STATISTICS NOT AVAILABLE																									
1964-65	Johnstown Jets	EHL	51	2	17	19	....	....	....	19	....	....	....	....	....	....	....	....	....	....	5	0	1	1	6	....	....	....
1965-66	Johnstown Jets	EHL	71	6	26	32	....	....	....	38	....	....	....	....	....	....	....	....	....	....	3	0	0	0	0	....	....	....
1966-67	Portland Buckaroos	WHL	1	0	0	0	....	....	....	0	....	....	....	....	....	....	....	....	....	....	....	....	....	....	....	....	....	....
	Johnstown Jets	EHL	72	6	28	34	....	....	....	82	....	....	....	....	....	....	....	....	....	....	5	0	3	3	6	....	....	....
1967-68	**Philadelphia Flyers**	**NHL**	**4**	**0**	**0**	**0**	**0**	**0**	**0**	**0**	**0**	**0**	**0**	**2**	**0.0**	**2**	**0**	**1**	**0**	**+1**	....	....	....	....	....	....	....	....
	Quebec Aces	AHL	51	2	11	13	....	....	....	56	....	....	....	....	....	....	....	....	....	....	15	0	8	8	37	....	....	....
1968-69	**Philadelphia Flyers**	**NHL**	**24**	**0**	**4**	**4**	**0**	**4**	**4**	**6**	**0**	**0**	**0**	**12**	**0.0**	**26**	**0**	**31**	**9**	**+4**	**4**	**0**	**0**	**0**	**4**	**0**	**0**	**0**
	Quebec Aces	AHL	41	1	12	13	....	....	....	30	....	....	....	....	....	....	....	....	....	....	....	....	....	....	....	....	....	....
1969-70	**Philadelphia Flyers**	**NHL**	**17**	**0**	**0**	**0**	**0**	**0**	**0**	**4**	**0**	**0**	**0**	**8**	**0.0**	**9**	**0**	**19**	**3**	**–7**	....	....	....	....	....	....	....	....
	Quebec Aces	AHL	54	2	19	21	....	....	....	31	....	....	....	....	....	....	....	....	....	....	6	0	3	3	9	....	....	....
1970-71	Quebec Aces	AHL	72	2	24	26	....	....	....	50	....	....	....	....	....	....	....	....	....	....	1	0	0	0	2	....	....	....
	Philadelphia Flyers	**NHL**	....	....	....	....	....	....	....	....	....	....	....	....	....	....	....	....	....	....	**4**	**0**	**0**	**0**	**2**	....	....	....
1971-72	**Philadelphia Flyers**	**NHL**	**2**	**0**	**1**	**1**	**0**	**1**	**1**	**0**	**0**	**0**	**0**	**2**	**0.0**	**3**	**1**	**2**	**0**	**0**	....	....	....	....	....	....	....	....
	Richmond Robins	AHL	60	0	15	15	....	....	....	52	....	....	....	....	....	....	....	....	....	....	....	....	....	....	....	....	....	....
1972-73	Los Angeles Sharks	WHA	78	0	23	23	....	....	....	39	....	....	....	....	....	....	....	....	....	....	6	1	2	3	4	....	....	....
1973-74	Los Angeles Sharks	WHA	13	0	3	3	....	....	....	6	....	....	....	....	....	....	....	....	....	....	....	....	....	....	....	....	....	....
	Vancouver Blazers	WHA	56	2	18	20	....	....	....	52	....	....	....	....	....	....	....	....	....	....	....	....	....	....	....	....	....	....
1974-75	Richmond Robins	AHL	54	1	6	7	....	....	....	32	....	....	....	....	....	....	....	....	....	....	6	0	3	3	6	....	....	....
1975-76	Baltimore Clippers	AHL	74	4	8	12	....	....	....	42	....	....	....	....	....	....	....	....	....	....	....	....	....	....	....	....	....	....
1976-77	Richmond Wildcats	SHL	37	1	6	7	....	....	....	10	....	....	....	....	....	....	....	....	....	....	....	....	....	....	....	....	....	....
	Johnstown Jets	NAHL	26	0	7	7	....	....	....	8	....	....	....	....	....	....	....	....	....	....	3	0	2	2	0	....	....	....
	NHL Totals		**47**	**0**	**5**	**5**	**0**	**5**	**5**	**10**	**0**	**0**	**0**	**24**	**0.0**	**40**	**1**	**53**	**12**		**8**	**0**	**0**	**0**	**6**	**0**	**0**	**0**
	Other Major League Totals		147	2	44	46	....	....	....	97	....	....	....	....	....	....	....	....	....		6	1	2	3	4	....	....	....

EHL North First All-Star Team (1967) • AHL First All-Star Team (1971) • AHL Second All-Star Team (1972)

NHL rights transferred to **Philadelphia** after NHL club purchased **Quebec** (AHL) franchise, May 8, 1967. Selected by **LA Sharks** (WHA) in 1972 WHA General Player Draft, February 12, 1972. Traded to **Vancouver** (WHA) by **LA Sharks** (WHA) to complete transaction that sent Ron Ward to LA Sharks (October, 1973), November 5, 1973.

• MacTAVISH, CRAIG

Craig MacTavish C – L. 6′1″, 195 lbs. b: London, Ont., 8/15/1958. Boston's 8th choice, 153rd overall, in 1978 Amateur Draft.

Season	Club	League	GP	G	A	Pts	AG	AA	APts	PIM	PP	SH	GW	S	%	TGF	PGF	TGA	PGA	+/–	GP	G	A	Pts	PIM	PP	SH	GW
1977-78	University of Lowell	ECAC 2	21	26	19	45	....	....	....	0	....	....	....	....	....	....	....	....	....	....	....	....	....	....	....	....	....	....
1978-79	University of Lowell	ECAC 2	31	36	52	*88	....	....	....	....	....	....	....	....	....	....	....	....	....	....	....	....	....	....	....	....	....	....
1979-80	**Boston Bruins**	**NHL**	**46**	**11**	**17**	**28**	**10**	**13**	**23**	**8**	**0**	**0**	**2**	**61**	**18.0**	**44**	**6**	**22**	**0**	**+16**	**10**	**2**	**3**	**5**	**7**	**0**	**0**	**0**
	Binghamton Whalers	AHL	34	17	15	32	....	....	....	29	....	....	....	....	....	....	....	....	....	....	....	....	....	....	....	....	....	....
1980-81	**Boston Bruins**	**NHL**	**24**	**3**	**5**	**8**	**2**	**3**	**5**	**13**	**0**	**0**	**0**	**44**	**6.8**	**16**	**5**	**12**	**0**	**–1**	....	....	....	....	....	....	....	....
	Springfield Indians	AHL	53	19	24	43	....	....	....	81	....	....	....	....	....	....	....	....	....	....	7	5	4	9	8	....	....	....
1981-82	**Boston Bruins**	**NHL**	**2**	**0**	**1**	**1**	**0**	**1**	**1**	**0**	**0**	**0**	**0**	**1**	**0.0**	**1**	**0**	**1**	**0**	**0**	....	....	....	....	....	....	....	....
	Erie Blades	AHL	72	23	32	55	....	....	....	37	....	....	....	....	....	....	....	....	....	....	....	....	....	....	....	....	....	....
1982-83	**Boston Bruins**	**NHL**	**75**	**10**	**20**	**30**	**8**	**14**	**22**	**18**	**0**	**0**	**1**	**120**	**8.3**	**51**	**2**	**34**	**0**	**+15**	**17**	**3**	**1**	**4**	**18**	**0**	**0**	**0**
1983-84	**Boston Bruins**	**NHL**	**70**	**20**	**23**	**43**	**16**	**16**	**32**	**35**	**7**	**0**	**4**	**135**	**14.8**	**61**	**11**	**42**	**1**	**+9**	**1**	**0**	**0**	**0**	**0**	**0**	**0**	**0**
1984-85			DID NOT PLAY																									
1985-86	**Edmonton Oilers**	**NHL**	**74**	**23**	**24**	**47**	**18**	**16**	**34**	**70**	**4**	**1**	**5**	**121**	**19.0**	**70**	**8**	**63**	**18**	**+17**	**10**	**4**	**4**	**8**	**11**	**1**	**0**	**0**
1986-87	**Edmonton Oilers**	**NHL**	**79**	**20**	**19**	**39**	**17**	**14**	**31**	**55**	**1**	**4**	**2**	**140**	**14.3**	**57**	**4**	**70**	**26**	**+9**	**21**	**1**	**9**	**10**	**16**	**0**	**0**	**0**
1987-88	**Edmonton Oilers**	**NHL**	**80**	**15**	**17**	**32**	**13**	**12**	**25**	**47**	**0**	**3**	**5**	**90**	**16.7**	**51**	**6**	**75**	**27**	**–3**	**19**	**0**	**1**	**1**	**31**	**0**	**0**	**0**
1988-89	**Edmonton Oilers**	**NHL**	**80**	**21**	**31**	**52**	**18**	**22**	**40**	**55**	**2**	**4**	**2**	**120**	**17.5**	**64**	**4**	**84**	**34**	**+10**	**7**	**0**	**1**	**1**	**8**	**0**	**0**	**0**
1989-90	**Edmonton Oilers**	**NHL**	**80**	**21**	**22**	**43**	**18**	**16**	**34**	**89**	**1**	**6**	**5**	**109**	**19.3**	**62**	**2**	**87**	**40**	**+13**	**22**	**2**	**6**	**8**	**29**	**0**	**0**	**0**
1990-91	**Edmonton Oilers**	**NHL**	**80**	**17**	**15**	**32**	**16**	**11**	**27**	**76**	**2**	**6**	**1**	**113**	**15.0**	**44**	**4**	**82**	**41**	**–1**	**18**	**3**	**3**	**6**	**20**	**0**	**0**	**1**
1991-92	**Edmonton Oilers**	**NHL**	**80**	**12**	**18**	**30**	**11**	**14**	**25**	**98**	**0**	**2**	**1**	**86**	**14.0**	**46**	**2**	**93**	**48**	**–1**	**16**	**3**	**0**	**3**	**28**	**0**	**1**	**1**
1992-93	**Edmonton Oilers**	**NHL**	**82**	**10**	**20**	**30**	**8**	**14**	**22**	**110**	**0**	**3**	**3**	**101**	**9.9**	**40**	**2**	**102**	**48**	**–16**	....	....	....	....	....	....	....	....
1993-94	**Edmonton Oilers**	**NHL**	**66**	**16**	**10**	**26**	**15**	**8**	**23**	**80**	**0**	**0**	**1**	**97**	**16.5**	**27**	**2**	**72**	**27**	**–20**	....	....	....	....	....	....	....	....
	New York Rangers	**NHL**	**12**	**4**	**2**	**6**	**4**	**2**	**6**	**11**	**1**	**0**	**1**	**25**	**16.0**	**10**	**1**	**5**	**2**	**+6**	**23**	**1**	**4**	**5**	**22**	**0**	**0**	**0**
1994-95	**Philadelphia Flyers**	**NHL**	**45**	**3**	**9**	**12**	**5**	**13**	**18**	**23**	**0**	**0**	**0**	**38**	**7.9**	**19**	**0**	**47**	**30**	**+2**	**15**	**1**	**4**	**5**	**20**	**0**	**0**	**0**

Season	Club	League	GP	G	A	Pts	AG	AA	APts	PIM	PP	SH	GW	S	%	TGF	PGF	TGA	PGA	+/-	GP	G	A	Pts	PIM	PP	SH	GW
1995-96	Philadelphia Flyers	NHL	55	5	8	13	5	7	12	62	0	0	1	42	11.9	18	0	32	11	-3	....	....	....	....	....			
	St. Louis Blues	NHL	13	0	1	1	0	1	1	8	0	0	0	16	0.0	3	0	13	4	-6	13	0	2	2	6	0	0	0
1996-97	St. Louis Blues	NHL	50	2	5	7	2	4	6	33	0	0	0	26	7.7	10	0	31	9	-12	1	0	0	0	2	0	0	0
	NHL Totals		1093	213	267	480	186	201	387	891	18	29	34	1485	14.3	694	59	967	366		193	20	38	58	218	1	1	2

NCAA (College Div.) East All-American Team (1979)

Played in NHL All-Star Game (1996)

Signed as a free agent by **Edmonton**, February 1, 1985. Traded to **NY Rangers** by Edmonton for Todd Marchant, March 21, 1994. Signed as a free agent by **Philadelphia**, July 6, 1994. Traded to **St. Louis** by Philadelphia for Dale Hawerchuk, March 15, 1996.

● MacWILLIAM, MIKE   Mike MacWilliam   LW – L. 6'4", 230 lbs.   b: Burnaby, B.C., 2/14/1967.

Season	Club	League	GP	G	A	Pts	AG	AA	APts	PIM	PP	SH	GW	S	%	TGF	PGF	TGA	PGA	+/-	GP	G	A	Pts	PIM	PP	SH	GW
1984-85	Langley Eagles	BCJHL	13	2	1	3				63											....	....	....	....	....			
1985-86	New Westminster Bruins	WHL	52	8	6	14				98											....	....	....	....	....			
1986-87	Medicine Hat Tigers	WHL	44	7	17	24				134											19	1	0	1	35			
1987-88			DID NOT PLAY – INJURED																									
1988-89	Milwaukee Admirals	IHL	6	1	1	2				28											1	0	0	0	0			
	Flint Spirits	IHL	18	0	0	0				92											....							
1989-90			DID NOT PLAY – INJURED																									
1990-91	Adirondack Red Wings	AHL	8	0	0	0				32											....							
	Greensboro Monarchs	ECHL	15	2	7	9				94											9	3	1	4	*118			
1991-92	St. John's Maple Leafs	AHL	44	7	8	15				301											2	0	0	0	8			
1992-93	Greensboro Monarchs	ECHL	12	5	5	10				137											....							
1993-94	Tulsa Oilers	CHL	39	16	12	28				*326											8	4	0	4	88			
1994-95	Denver Grizzlies	IHL	30	5	6	11				218											12	2	2	4	56			
1995-96	**New York Islanders**	**NHL**	6	0	0	0	0	0	0	14	0	0	0	4	0.0	0	0	1	0	-1	....							
	Utah Grizzlies	IHL	53	8	16	24				317											6	0	2	2	53			
1996-97	Phoenix Roadrunners	IHL	29	1	3	4				169											....							
1997-98	Cardiff Devils	Britain	36	5	26	31				10											9	4	2	6	0			
	NHL Totals		6	0	0	0	0	0	0	14	0	0	0	4	0.0	0	0	1	0		....							

Signed as a free agent by **Philadelphia**, October 7, 1986. Signed as a free agent by **Toronto**, July 30, 1991. Signed as a free agent by **NY Islanders**, July 25, 1995.

● MADIGAN, CONNIE   Connie Madigan   D – L. 5'10", 185 lbs.   b: Port Arthur, Ont., 10/4/1934.

Season	Club	League	GP	G	A	Pts	AG	AA	APts	PIM	PP	SH	GW	S	%	TGF	PGF	TGA	PGA	+/-	GP	G	A	Pts	PIM	PP	SH	GW
1952-53	Port Arthur Bruins	TBJHL	27	4	3	7				67											....	....	....	....	....			
1953-54	Port Arthur Bruins	TBJHL	26	2	11	13				124											9	1	2	3	*18			
1954-55	Humboldt Indians	MJHL	5	0	0	0				0											....							
1955-56	Penticton Vees	OSHL	53	8	15	23				240											....							
1956-57	Penticton Vees	OSHL	STATISTICS NOT AVAILABLE																									
1957-58	Vernon Canadians	WIHL	8	0	3	3				34											....							
1958-59	Nelson Maple Leafs	WIHL	....	4	24	28				*145											11	2	4	6	*24			
	Spokane Comets	WHL	3	1	1	2				2											....							
1959-60	Fort Wayne Komets	IHL	66	7	50	57				*272											13	0	3	3	44			
1960-61	Cleveland Barons	AHL	8	0	2	2				13											....							
	Fort Wayne Komets	IHL	67	9	20	37				231											8	2	3	5	26			
1961-62	Fort Wayne Komets	IHL	2	0	0	0				9											....							
	Spokane Comets	WHL	63	9	28	37				*171											16	0	4	4	28			
1962-63	Spokane Comets	WHL	48	7	15	22				115											....							
1963-64	Los Angeles Blades	WHL	68	10	27	37				120											12	2	4	6	*49			
1964-65	Providence Reds	AHL	10	1	2	3				34											....							
	Portland Buckaroos	WHL	60	11	20	31				158											10	1	4	5	18			
1965-66	Portland Buckaroos	WHL	72	13	31	44				159											14	1	6	7	15			
1966-67	Portland Buckaroos	WHL	72	9	42	51				147											4	2	1	3	6			
1967-68	Portland Buckaroos	WHL	59	7	25	32				105											12	1	5	6	16			
1968-69	Portland Buckaroos	WIHL	71	3	25	28				175											10	1	8	9	22			
1969-70	Dallas Black Hawks	CHL	10	1	4	5				26											....							
	Portland Buckaroos	WHL	60	5	28	33				101											11	0	6	6	59			
1970-71	Portland Buckaroos	WHL	72	8	59	67				175											3	0	3	3	38			
1971-72	Portland Buckaroos	WHL	61	8	48	56				170											11	0	7	7	*44			
1972-73	Portland Buckaroos	WHL	42	3	26	29				146											....							
	St. Louis Blues	**NHL**	20	0	3	3	0	2	2	25	0	0	0	11	0.0	0	16	0	16	1	+1	5	0	0	0	4	0	0	0
1973-74	San Diego Gulls	WHL	39	3	19	22				80											....							
	Portland Buckaroos	WHL	16	0	12	12				22											9	0	2	2	*40			
1974-75	Portland Buckaroos	WIHL	10	2	11	13				20											....							
	NHL Totals		20	0	3	3	0	2	2	25	0	0	0	11	0.0	16	0	16	1			5	0	0	0	4	0	0	0

IHL Second All-Star Team (1960) ● WHL Second All-Star Team (1965, 1971, 1972) ● WHL First All-Star Team (1966, 1967, 1968, 1969) ● Won Hal Laycoe Cup (WHL Top Defenseman) (1966)

Traded to **St. Louis** by **Portland** (WHL) for the loan of Andre Aubry for remainder of 1972-73 season, January, 1973. Traded to **Portland** (WHL) by **St. Louis** for cash, September, 1973.

● MADILL, JEFF   Jeff Madill   RW – L. 5'11", 195 lbs.   b: Oshawa, Ont., 6/21/1965.   New Jersey's 2nd choice, 7th overall, in 1987 Supplemental Draft.

Season	Club	League	GP	G	A	Pts	AG	AA	APts	PIM	PP	SH	GW	S	%	TGF	PGF	TGA	PGA	+/-	GP	G	A	Pts	PIM	PP	SH	GW
1984-85	Ohio State University	CCHA	12	5	6	11				18											....	....	....	....	....			
1985-86	Ohio State University	CCHA	41	32	25	57				65											....							
1986-87	Ohio State University	CCHA	43	38	32	70				139											....							
1987-88	Utica Devils	AHL	58	18	15	33				127											....							
1988-89	Utica Devils	AHL	69	23	25	48				225											4	1	0	1	35			
1989-90	Utica Devils	AHL	74	43	26	69				233											4	1	2	3	33			
1990-91	**New Jersey Devils**	**NHL**	14	4	0	4	4	0	4	46	0	0	0	24	16.7	6	2	7	2	-1	7	0	2	2	8	0	0	0
	Utica Devils	AHL	54	42	35	77				151											....							
1991-92	Kansas City Blades	IHL	62	32	20	52				167											6	2	2	4	30			
1992-93	Cincinnati Cyclones	IHL	58	36	17	53				175											....							
	Milwaukee Admirals	IHL	23	13	6	19				53											4	3	0	3	9			
1993-94	Atlanta Knights	IHL	80	42	44	86				186											14	4	2	6	9			
1994-95	Denver Grizzlies	IHL	73	35	30	65				207											17	8	6	14	53			
1995-96	San Francisco Spiders	IHL	27	16	13	29				73											....							
	Kansas City Blades	IHL	41	17	16	33				169											5	4	2	6	21			
	NHL Totals		14	4	0	4	4	0	4	46	0	0	0	24	16.7	6	2	7	2			7	0	2	2	8	0	0	0

AHL Second All-Star Team (1991) ● IHL Second All-Star Team (1993)

Claimed by **San Jose** from **New Jersey** in Expansion Draft, May 30, 1991.

● MAGEE, DEAN   Dean Magee   LW – L. 6'2", 210 lbs.   b: Rockey Mountain House, Alta., 4/29/1955.   Minnesota's 8th choice, 130th overall, in 1975 Amateur Draft.

Season	Club	League	GP	G	A	Pts	AG	AA	APts	PIM	PP	SH	GW	S	%	TGF	PGF	TGA	PGA	+/-	GP	G	A	Pts	PIM	PP	SH	GW
1972-73	Calgary Canucks	AJHL	....	22	51	79				127											....	....	....	....	....			
1973-74	Calgary Canucks	AJHL	56	36	30	66				142											....							
1974-75	Colorado College	WCHA	36	15	13	28				130											....							
1975-76	Colorado College	WCHA	33	9	7	16				104											....							
1976-77	Colorado College	WCHA	39	23	18	41				144											....							
1977-78	Colorado College	WCHA	25	13	15	28				60											....							
	Minnesota North Stars	**NHL**	7	0	0	0	0	0	0	4	0	0	0	4	0.0	0	0	3	0	-3	....							
	Fort Worth Texans	CHL	3	0	0	0				0											....							

			REGULAR SEASON																		PLAYOFFS							
Season	Club	League	GP	G	A	Pts	AG	AA	APts	PIM	PP	SH	GW	S	%	TGF	PGF	TGA	PGA	+/–	GP	G	A	Pts	PIM	PP	SH	GW
1978-79	Indianapolis Racers	WHA	5	0	1	1	....	....	....	10	....	....	....	....	....	....	....	....	....	....	....	....	....	....	....	....	....	....
	Grand Rapids Owls	IHL	68	35	37	72	....	....	....	148	....	....	....	....	....	....	....	....	....	....	21	*15	11	26	45	....	....	....
1979-80	Houston Apollos	CHL	70	24	34	58	....	....	....	73	....	....	....	....	....	....	....	....	....	....	6	2	4	6	6	....	....	....
	NHL Totals		**7**	**0**	**0**	**0**	**0**	**0**	**0**	**4**	**0**	**0**	**0**	**4**	**0.0**	**0**	**0**	**3**	**0**		....	....	....	....	....	....	....	....
	Other Major League Totals		5	0	1	1	....	....	....	10	....	....	....	....	....	....	....	....	....	....	....	....	....	....	....	....	....	....

Signed as a free agent by **Indianapolis** (WHA), November 15, 1978.

• MAGGS, DARYL

Daryl Maggs D – R. 6'2", 195 lbs. b: Victoria, B.C., 4/6/1949. Chicago's 4th choice, 48th overall, in 1969 Amateur Draft.

Season	Club	League	GP	G	A	Pts	AG	AA	APts	PIM	PP	SH	GW	S	%	TGF	PGF	TGA	PGA	+/–	GP	G	A	Pts	PIM	PP	SH	GW
1967-68	Red Deer Rustlers	AJHL	60	6	20	26	....	....	....	50	....	....	....	....	....	....	....	....	....	....	....	....	....	....	....	....	....	....
1968-69	Calgary Centennials	WCJHL	35	9	20	29	....	....	....	55	....	....	....	....	....	....	....	....	....	....	....	....	....	....	....	....	....	....
1969-70	University of Calgary	CWUAA	14	10	15	25	....	....	....	43	....	....	....	....	....	....	....	....	....	....	4	3	3	6	13	....	....	....
1970-71	Dallas Black Hawks	CHL	71	14	36	50	....	....	....	144	....	....	....	....	....	....	....	....	....	....	10	5	1	6	23	....	....	....
1971-72	**Chicago Black Hawks**	**NHL**	**59**	**7**	**4**	**11**	**7**	**4**	**11**	**4**	**0**	**0**	**0**	**47**	**14.9**	**17**	**0**	**18**	**0**	**–1**	**4**	**0**	**0**	**0**	**0**	**0**	**0**	**0**
1972-73	**Chicago Black Hawks**	**NHL**	**17**	**0**	**0**	**0**	**0**	**0**	**0**	**4**	**0**	**0**	**0**	**10**	**0.0**	**3**	**0**	**5**	**1**	**–1**	....	....	....	....	....	....	....	....
	California Golden Seals	**NHL**	**54**	**7**	**15**	**22**	**7**	**13**	**20**	**46**	**0**	**0**	**1**	**95**	**7.4**	**65**	**8**	**90**	**11**	**–22**	....	....	....	....	....	....	....	....
1973-74	Chicago Cougars	WHA	78	8	22	30	....	....	....	148	....	....	....	....	....	....	....	....	....	....	18	3	5	8	*71	....	....	....
1974-75	Chicago Cougars	WHA	77	6	27	33	....	....	....	137	....	....	....	....	....	....	....	....	....	....	....	....	....	....	....	....	....	....
1975-76	Denver-Ottawa	WHA	41	4	23	27	....	....	....	42	....	....	....	....	....	....	....	....	....	....	....	....	....	....	....	....	....	....
	Indianapolis Racers	WHA	36	5	16	21	....	....	....	40	....	....	....	....	....	....	....	....	....	....	7	1	0	1	20	....	....	....
1976-77	Indianapolis Racers	WHA	81	16	55	71	....	....	....	114	....	....	....	....	....	....	....	....	....	....	9	1	4	5	4	....	....	....
1977-78	Indianapolis Racers	WHA	51	6	15	21	....	....	....	30	....	....	....	....	....	....	....	....	....	....	....	....	....	....	....	....	....	....
	Cincinnati Stingers	WHA	11	2	5	7	....	....	....	7	....	....	....	....	....	....	....	....	....	....	....	....	....	....	....	....	....	....
1978-79	Cincinnati Stingers	WHA	27	4	14	18	....	....	....	63	....	....	....	....	....	....	....	....	....	....	....	....	....	....	....	....	....	....
	Mannheim	Germany	11	6	4	10	....	....	....	34	....	....	....	....	....	....	....	....	....	....	....	....	....	....	....	....	....	....
1979-80	**Toronto Maple Leafs**	**NHL**	**5**	**0**	**0**	**0**	**0**	**0**	**0**	**0**	**0**	**0**	**0**	**7**	**0.0**	**2**	**0**	**6**	**0**	**–4**	....	....	....	....	....	....	....	....
	NHL Totals		**135**	**14**	**19**	**33**	**14**	**17**	**31**	**54**	**0**	**0**	**1**	**159**	**8.8**	**87**	**8**	**119**	**12**		**4**	**0**	**0**	**0**	**0**	**0**	**0**	**0**
	Other Major League Totals		402	51	177	228	....	....	....	581	....	....	....	....	....	....	....	....	....	....	34	5	9	14	95	....	....	....

Selected by **Chicago** (WHA) in 1972 WHA General Player Draft, February 12, 1972. Traded to **California** by **Chicago** for Dick Redmond and the rights to Bobby Sheehan, December 5, 1972. Selected by **Denver** (WHA) from **Chicago** (WHA) in WHA Expansion Draft, May, 1975. Traded to **Indianapolis** (WHA) by **Denver-Ottawa** (WHA) with Byron Baltimore, Francois Rochon and Mark Lomenda for cash, January 20, 1976. Traded to **Cincinnati** (WHA) by **Indianapolis** (WHA) with Rich Leduc for Claude Andre Larose and Reg Thomas, February, 1978. Signed as a free agent by **Toronto**, December, 1979.

• MAGNAN, MARC

Marc Magnan LW – L. 5'11", 195 lbs. b: Beaumont, Alta., 2/17/1962. Toronto's 9th choice, 195th overall, in 1981 Entry Draft.

Season	Club	League	GP	G	A	Pts	AG	AA	APts	PIM	PP	SH	GW	S	%	TGF	PGF	TGA	PGA	+/–	GP	G	A	Pts	PIM	PP	SH	GW
1979-80	St. Albert Saints	AJHL	42	14	23	37	....	....	....	178	....	....	....	....	....	....	....	....	....	....	....	....	....	....	....	....	....	....
	Lethbridge Broncos	WHL	1	0	1	1	....	....	....	0	....	....	....	....	....	....	....	....	....	....	....	....	....	....	....	....	....	....
1980-81	Lethbridge Broncos	WHL	66	16	30	46	....	....	....	284	....	....	....	....	....	....	....	....	....	....	9	4	1	5	78	....	....	....
1981-82	Lethbridge Broncos	WHL	64	33	38	71	....	....	....	406	....	....	....	....	....	....	....	....	....	....	12	10	5	15	60	....	....	....
1982-83	**Toronto Maple Leafs**	**NHL**	**4**	**0**	**1**	**1**	**0**	**1**	**1**	**5**	**0**	**0**	**0**	**1**	**0.0**	**1**	**1**	**0**	**0**	**0**	....	....	....	....	....	....	....	....
	St. Catharines Saints	AHL	67	6	10	16	....	....	....	229	....	....	....	....	....	....	....	....	....	....	....	....	....	....	....	....	....	....
1983-84	St. Catharines Saints	AHL	54	3	6	9	....	....	....	170	....	....	....	....	....	....	....	....	....	....	....	....	....	....	....	....	....	....
	Muskegon Mohawks	IHL	19	3	10	13	....	....	....	30	....	....	....	....	....	....	....	....	....	....	....	....	....	....	....	....	....	....
1984-85	Indianapolis Checkers	IHL	72	9	24	33	....	....	....	244	....	....	....	....	....	....	....	....	....	....	7	1	3	4	13	....	....	....
1985-86	Indianapolis Checkers	IHL	69	15	22	37	....	....	....	279	....	....	....	....	....	....	....	....	....	....	5	0	1	1	48	....	....	....
1986-87	Indianapolis Checkers	IHL	77	11	21	32	....	....	....	353	....	....	....	....	....	....	....	....	....	....	6	0	0	0	22	....	....	....
1987-88	Flint Spirits	IHL	11	0	2	2	....	....	....	50	....	....	....	....	....	....	....	....	....	....	....	....	....	....	....	....	....	....
	NHL Totals		**4**	**0**	**1**	**1**	**0**	**1**	**1**	**5**	**0**	**0**	**0**	**1**	**0.0**	**1**	**1**	**0**	**0**		....	....	....	....	....	....	....	....

• MAGNUSON, KEITH

Keith Magnuson D – R. 6', 185 lbs. b: Saskatoon, Sask., 4/27/1947.

Season	Club	League	GP	G	A	Pts	AG	AA	APts	PIM	PP	SH	GW	S	%	TGF	PGF	TGA	PGA	+/–	GP	G	A	Pts	PIM	PP	SH	GW
1964-65	Saskatoon Blades	SJHL	54	2	9	11	....	....	....	77	....	....	....	....	....	....	....	....	....	....	5	0	2	2	6	....	....	....
1965-66	University of Denver	WCHA	DID NOT PLAY – FRESHMAN																									
1966-67	University of Denver	WCHA	30	4	17	21	....	....	....	56	....	....	....	....	....	....	....	....	....	....	....	....	....	....	....	....	....	....
1967-68	University of Denver	WCHA	34	5	15	20	....	....	....	59	....	....	....	....	....	....	....	....	....	....	....	....	....	....	....	....	....	....
1968-69	University of Denver	WCHA	32	7	27	34	....	....	....	48	....	....	....	....	....	....	....	....	....	....	....	....	....	....	....	....	....	....
1969-70	**Chicago Black Hawks**	**NHL**	**76**	**0**	**24**	**24**	**0**	**24**	**24**	***213**	**0**	**0**	**0**	**77**	**0.0**	**92**	**2**	**65**	**13**	**+38**	**8**	**1**	**2**	**3**	**17**	**0**	**0**	**0**
1970-71	**Chicago Black Hawks**	**NHL**	**76**	**3**	**20**	**23**	**3**	**18**	**21**	***291**	**0**	**0**	**1**	**66**	**4.5**	**91**	**1**	**85**	**27**	**+32**	**18**	**0**	**2**	**2**	***63**	**0**	**0**	**0**
1971-72	**Chicago Black Hawks**	**NHL**	**74**	**2**	**19**	**21**	**2**	**17**	**19**	**201**	**0**	**0**	**0**	**83**	**2.4**	**101**	**3**	**53**	**7**	**+52**	**8**	**0**	**1**	**1**	**29**	**0**	**0**	**0**
1972-73	**Chicago Black Hawks**	**NHL**	**77**	**0**	**19**	**19**	**0**	**16**	**16**	**140**	**0**	**0**	**0**	**64**	**0.0**	**94**	**1**	**88**	**19**	**+24**	**7**	**0**	**2**	**2**	**4**	**0**	**0**	**0**
1973-74	**Chicago Black Hawks**	**NHL**	**57**	**2**	**11**	**13**	**2**	**9**	**11**	**105**	**0**	**0**	**0**	**29**	**6.9**	**61**	**1**	**56**	**12**	**+16**	**11**	**1**	**0**	**1**	**17**	**0**	**0**	**0**
1974-75	**Chicago Black Hawks**	**NHL**	**48**	**2**	**12**	**14**	**2**	**9**	**11**	**117**	**0**	**0**	**0**	**31**	**6.5**	**43**	**1**	**45**	**13**	**+10**	**8**	**1**	**2**	**3**	**15**	**0**	**0**	**0**
1975-76	**Chicago Black Hawks**	**NHL**	**48**	**1**	**6**	**7**	**1**	**5**	**6**	**99**	**0**	**0**	**0**	**27**	**3.7**	**49**	**0**	**52**	**16**	**+13**	**4**	**0**	**0**	**0**	**12**	**0**	**0**	**0**
1976-77	**Chicago Black Hawks**	**NHL**	**37**	**1**	**6**	**7**	**1**	**5**	**6**	**86**	**0**	**0**	**0**	**30**	**3.3**	**25**	**0**	**48**	**12**	**–11**	....	....	....	....	....	....	....	....
1977-78	**Chicago Black Hawks**	**NHL**	**67**	**2**	**4**	**6**	**2**	**3**	**5**	**145**	**0**	**0**	**0**	**46**	**4.3**	**46**	**1**	**61**	**16**	**0**	**4**	**0**	**0**	**0**	**7**	**0**	**0**	**0**
1978-79	**Chicago Black Hawks**	**NHL**	**26**	**1**	**4**	**5**	**1**	**3**	**4**	**41**	**0**	**0**	**0**	**8**	**12.5**	**10**	**0**	**21**	**7**	**–4**	....	....	....	....	....	....	....	....
1979-80	**Chicago Black Hawks**	**NHL**	**3**	**0**	**0**	**0**	**0**	**0**	**0**	**4**	**0**	**0**	**0**	**0**	**0.0**	**2**	**0**	**2**	**0**	**0**	....	....	....	....	....	....	....	....
	NHL Totals		**589**	**14**	**125**	**139**	**14**	**109**	**123**	**1442**	**0**	**0**	**1**	**461**	**3.0**	**614**	**10**	**576**	**142**		**68**	**3**	**9**	**12**	**164**	**0**	**0**	**0**

WCHA First All-Star Team (1967, 1968, 1969) • NCAA West First All-American Team (1968, 1969) • NCAA Championship All-Tournament Team (1968, 1969) • NCAA Championship Tournament MVP (1969)

Played in NHL All-Star Game (1971, 1972)

Signed as a free agent by **Chicago**, September, 1969. Claimed by **Chicago** as a fill-in during Expansion Draft, June 13, 1979.

• MAGUIRE, KEVIN

Kevin Maguire RW – R. 6'2", 200 lbs. b: Toronto, Ont., 1/5/1963.

Season	Club	League	GP	G	A	Pts	AG	AA	APts	PIM	PP	SH	GW	S	%	TGF	PGF	TGA	PGA	+/–	GP	G	A	Pts	PIM	PP	SH	GW
1983-84	Orillia Travelways	OJHL	....	35	42	77	....	....	....	....	....	....	....	....	....	....	....	....	....	....	....	....	....	....	....	....	....	....
1984-85	St. Catharines Saints	AHL	76	10	15	25	....	....	....	112	....	....	....	....	....	....	....	....	....	....	....	....	....	....	....	....	....	....
1985-86	St. Catharines Saints	AHL	61	6	9	15	....	....	....	161	....	....	....	....	....	....	....	....	....	....	1	0	0	0	0	....	....	....
1986-87	**Toronto Maple Leafs**	**NHL**	**17**	**0**	**0**	**0**	**0**	**0**	**0**	**74**	**0**	**0**	**0**	**2**	**0.0**	**0**	**0**	**6**	**0**	**–6**	**1**	**0**	**0**	**0**	**0**	**0**	**0**	**0**
	Newmarket Saints	AHL	51	4	2	6	....	....	....	131	....	....	....	....	....	....	....	....	....	....	....	....	....	....	....	....	....	....
1987-88	**Buffalo Sabres**	**NHL**	**46**	**4**	**6**	**10**	**3**	**4**	**7**	**162**	**0**	**0**	**0**	**25**	**16.0**	**17**	**0**	**18**	**0**	**–1**	**5**	**0**	**0**	**0**	**50**	**0**	**0**	**0**
1988-89	**Buffalo Sabres**	**NHL**	**60**	**8**	**10**	**18**	**7**	**7**	**14**	**241**	**0**	**0**	**2**	**35**	**22.9**	**29**	**1**	**20**	**1**	**+9**	**5**	**0**	**0**	**0**	**36**	**0**	**0**	**0**
1989-90	**Buffalo Sabres**	**NHL**	**61**	**6**	**9**	**15**	**5**	**6**	**11**	**115**	**0**	**0**	**1**	**62**	**9.7**	**24**	**0**	**27**	**0**	**–3**	....	....	....	....	....	....	....	....
	Philadelphia Flyers	**NHL**	**5**	**1**	**0**	**1**	**1**	**0**	**1**	**6**	**0**	**0**	**0**	**7**	**14.3**	**1**	**0**	**2**	**0**	**–1**	....	....	....	....	....	....	....	....
1990-91	**Toronto Maple Leafs**	**NHL**	**63**	**9**	**5**	**14**	**8**	**4**	**12**	**180**	**1**	**0**	**0**	**52**	**17.3**	**24**	**2**	**32**	**0**	**–10**	....	....	....	....	....	....	....	....
1991-92	**Toronto Maple Leafs**	**NHL**	**8**	**1**	**0**	**1**	**1**	**0**	**1**	**4**	**0**	**0**	**0**	**8**	**12.5**	**2**	**1**	**5**	**0**	**–4**	....	....	....	....	....	....	....	....
	St. John's Maple Leafs	AHL	30	11	15	26	....	....	....	112	....	....	....	....	....	....	....	....	....	....	11	3	7	10	43	....	....	....
	NHL Totals		**260**	**29**	**30**	**59**	**25**	**21**	**46**	**782**	**1**	**0**	**3**	**191**	**15.2**	**97**	**4**	**110**	**1**		**11**	**0**	**0**	**0**	**86**	**0**	**0**	**0**

Signed as a free agent by **Toronto**, October 10, 1984. Claimed by **Buffalo** from **Toronto** in Waiver Draft, October 5, 1987. Traded to **Philadelphia** by **Buffalo** with Buffalo's 2nd round choice (Mikael Renberg) in 1990 Entry Draft for Jay Wells and Philadelphia's 4th round choice (Peter Ambroziak) in 1991 Entry Draft, March 5, 1990. Traded to **Toronto** by **Philadelphia** with Philadelphia's 8th round choice (Dimitri Mironov) in 1991 Entry Draft for Toronto's 3rd round choice (Al Kinsky) in 1990 Entry Draft, June 16, 1990.

• MAHOVLICH, FRANK

Frank "The Big M" Mahovlich LW – L. 6', 205 lbs. b: Timmins, Ont., 1/10/1938. HHOF

Season	Club	League	GP	G	A	Pts	AG	AA	APts	PIM	PP	SH	GW	S	%	TGF	PGF	TGA	PGA	+/–	GP	G	A	Pts	PIM	PP	SH	GW
1953-54	St. Michael's Majors	OHA	1	0	1	1	....	....	....	2	....	....	....	....	....	....	....	....	....	....	....	....	....	....	....	....	....	....
1954-55	St. Michael's Majors	OHA	25	12	11	23	....	....	....	18	....	....	....	....	....	....	....	....	....	....	....	....	....	....	....	....	....	....
1955-56	St. Michael's Majors	OHA	30	24	26	50	....	....	....	55	....	....	....	....	....	....	....	....	....	....	8	5	5	10	24	....	....	....
1956-57	St. Michael's Majors	OHA	49	*52	36	88	....	....	....	122	....	....	....	....	....	....	....	....	....	....	4	2	7	9	14	....	....	....
	Toronto Maple Leafs	**NHL**	**3**	**1**	**0**	**1**	**1**	**0**	**1**	**2**	....	....	....	....	....	....	....	....	....	....	....	....	....	....	....	....	....	....
1957-58	**Toronto Maple Leafs**	**NHL**	**67**	**20**	**16**	**36**	**26**	**17**	**43**	**67**	....	....	....	....	....	....	....	....	....	....	....	....	....	....	....	....	....	....
1958-59	**Toronto Maple Leafs**	**NHL**	**63**	**22**	**27**	**49**	**28**	**29**	**57**	**94**	....	....	....	....	....	....	....	....	....	....	**12**	**6**	**5**	**11**	**18**	....	....	....
1959-60	**Toronto Maple Leafs**	**NHL**	**70**	**18**	**21**	**39**	**22**	**21**	**43**	**61**	....	....	....	....	....	....	....	....	....	....	**10**	**3**	**1**	**4**	**27**	....	....	....
1960-61	**Toronto Maple Leafs**	**NHL**	**70**	**48**	**36**	**84**	**60**	**37**	**97**	**131**	....	....	....	....	....	....	....	....	....	....	**5**	**1**	**1**	**2**	**6**	....	....	....
1961-62	**Toronto Maple Leafs**	**NHL**	**70**	**33**	**38**	**71**	**41**	**39**	**80**	**87**	....	....	....	....	....	....	....	....	....	....	**12**	**6**	**6**	**12**	***29**	....	....	....
1962-63	**Toronto Maple Leafs**	**NHL**	**67**	**36**	**37**	**73**	**45**	**39**	**84**	**56**	....	....	....	....	....	....	....	....	....	....	**9**	**0**	**2**	**2**	**8**	....	....	....

			Regular Season																		Playoffs							
Season	Club	League	GP	G	A	Pts	AG	AA	APts	PIM	PP	SH	GW	S	%	TGF	PGF	TGA	PGA	+/–	GP	G	A	Pts	PIM	PP	SH	GW
1963-64	**Toronto Maple Leafs**	**NHL**	**70**	**26**	**29**	**55**	**35**	**32**	**67**	**66**	....	....	....	....	....	....	....	....	....	....	**14**	**4**	***11**	**15**	**20**	....	....	....
1964-65	**Toronto Maple Leafs**	**NHL**	**59**	**23**	**28**	**51**	**29**	**30**	**59**	**76**	....	....	....	....	....	....	....	....	....	....	**6**	**0**	**3**	**3**	**9**	....	....	....
1965-66	**Toronto Maple Leafs**	**NHL**	**68**	**32**	**24**	**56**	**39**	**24**	**63**	**68**	....	....	....	....	....	....	....	....	....	....	**4**	**1**	**0**	**1**	**10**	....	....	....
1966-67	**Toronto Maple Leafs**	**NHL**	**63**	**18**	**28**	**46**	**22**	**29**	**51**	**44**	....	....	....	....	....	....	....	....	....	....	**12**	**3**	**7**	**10**	**8**	....	....	....
1967-68	**Toronto Maple Leafs**	**NHL**	**50**	**19**	**17**	**36**	**23**	**18**	**41**	**30**	**2**	**0**	**4**	**151**	**12.6**	**48**	**11**	**36**	**0**	**+1**	....	....	....	....	....	....	....	....
	Detroit Red Wings	**NHL**	**13**	**7**	**9**	**16**	**9**	**9**	**18**	**2**	**0**	**0**	**1**	**39**	**17.9**	**25**	**5**	**19**	**2**	**+3**	....	....	....	....	....	....	....	....
1968-69	**Detroit Red Wings**	**NHL**	**76**	**49**	**29**	**78**	**56**	**27**	**83**	**38**	**7**	**0**	**5**	**293**	**16.7**	**124**	**27**	**53**	**2**	**+46**	....	....	....	....	....	....	....	....
1969-70	**Detroit Red Wings**	**NHL**	**74**	**38**	**32**	**70**	**44**	**32**	**76**	**59**	**15**	**1**	**5**	**251**	**15.1**	**98**	**35**	**55**	**8**	**+16**	**4**	**0**	**0**	**0**	**2**	**0**	**0**	**0**
1970-71	**Detroit Red Wings**	**NHL**	**35**	**14**	**18**	**32**	**15**	**16**	**31**	**30**	**6**	**1**	**2**	**104**	**13.5**	**51**	**19**	**35**	**6**	**+3**	....	....	....	....	....	....	....	....
	Montreal Canadiens	**NHL**	**38**	**17**	**24**	**41**	**18**	**21**	**39**	**11**	**4**	**1**	**2**	**100**	**17.0**	**59**	**22**	**42**	**9**	**+4**	**20**	***14**	**13**	***27**	**18**	**1**	**0**	**0**
1971-72	**Montreal Canadiens**	**NHL**	**76**	**43**	**53**	**96**	**46**	**49**	**95**	**36**	**14**	**4**	**4**	**261**	**16.5**	**149**	**54**	**70**	**17**	**+42**	**6**	**3**	**2**	**5**	**2**	**0**	**0**	**1**
1972-73	Canada	Summit	6	1	1	2	....	....	....	0	....	....	....	....	....	....	....	....	....	....	....	....	....	....	....	....	....	....
	Montreal Canadiens	**NHL**	**78**	**38**	**55**	**93**	**38**	**46**	**84**	**51**	**8**	**2**	**5**	**242**	**15.7**	**134**	**39**	**72**	**19**	**+42**	**17**	**9**	**14**	**23**	**6**	**1**	**0**	**0**
1973-74	**Montreal Canadiens**	**NHL**	**71**	**31**	**49**	**80**	**32**	**43**	**75**	**47**	**8**	**2**	**3**	**221**	**14.0**	**116**	**36**	**79**	**15**	**+16**	**6**	**1**	**2**	**3**	**0**	**0**	**0**	**0**
1974-75	Canada	Summit	6	1	1	2	....	....	....	6	....	....	....	....	....	....	....	....	....	....	....	....	....	....	....	....	....	....
	Toronto Toros	WHA	73	38	44	82	....	....	....	27	....	....	....	....	....	....	....	....	....	....	6	3	0	3	2	....	....	....
1975-76	Toronto Toros	WHA	75	34	55	89	....	....	....	14	....	....	....	....	....	....	....	....	....	....	....	....	....	....	....	....	....	....
1976-77	Birmingham Bulls	WHA	17	3	20	23	....	....	....	12	....	....	....	....	....	....	....	....	....	....	....	....	....	....	....	....	....	....
1977-78	Birmingham Bulls	WHA	72	14	24	38	....	....	....	22	....	....	....	....	....	....	....	....	....	....	3	1	1	2	0	....	....	....
	NHL Totals		**1181**	**533**	**570**	**1103**	**629**	**558**	**1187**	**1056**	**64**	**11**	**31**	**1662**	**32.1**	**804**	**248**	**461**	**78**		**137**	**51**	**67**	**118**	**163**	**2**	**0**	**1**
	Other Major League Totals		237	89	143	232	....	....	....	75	....	....	....	....	....	....	....	....	....	....	9	4	1	5	2	....	....	....

Won Calder Memorial Trophy (1958) • NHL First All-Star Team (1961, 1963, 1973) • NHL Second All-Star Team (1962, 1964, 1965, 1966, 1969, 1970)

Played in NHL All-Star Game (1959, 1960, 1961, 1962, 1963, 1964, 1965, 1967, 1968, 1969, 1970, 1971, 1972, 1973, 1974)

Traded to **Detroit** by **Toronto** with Pete Stemkowski, Garry Unger and the rights to Carl Brewer for Norm Ullman, Paul Henderson and Floyd Smith, March 3, 1968. Traded to **Montreal** by **Detroit** for Guy Charron, Bill Collins and Mickey Redmond, January 13, 1971. Selected by **Dayton-Houston** (WHA) in 1972 WHA General Player Draft, February 12, 1972. WHA rights traded to **Toronto** (WHA) by **Houston** (WHA) for future considerations, June, 1974. Transferred to **Birmingham** (WHA) after **Toronto** (WHA) franchise relocated, June 30, 1976.

• MAHOVLICH, PETE

Pete "The Little M" Mahovlich C – L. 6'5", 210 lbs. b: Timmins, Ont., 10/10/1946. Detroit's 1st choice, 2nd overall, in 1963 Amateur Draft.

Season	Club	League	GP	G	A	Pts	AG	AA	APts	PIM	PP	SH	GW	S	%	TGF	PGF	TGA	PGA	+/–	GP	G	A	Pts	PIM	PP	SH	GW
1963-64	Hamilton Red Wings	OHA	54	20	27	47	....	....	....	67	....	....	....	....	....	....	....	....	....	....	....	....	....	....	....	....	....	....
1964-65	Hamilton Red Wings	OHA	55	20	35	55	....	....	....	88	....	....	....	....	....	....	....	....	....	....	....	....	....	....	....	....	....	....
1965-66	Hamilton Red Wings	OHA	46	14	22	36	....	....	....	121	....	....	....	....	....	....	....	....	....	....	4	0	0	0	2	....	....	....
	Detroit Red Wings	**NHL**	**3**	**0**	**1**	**1**	**0**	**1**	**1**	**0**	....	....	....	....	....	....	....	....	....	....	....	....	....	....	....	....	....	....
1966-67	**Detroit Red Wings**	**NHL**	**34**	**1**	**3**	**4**	**1**	**3**	**4**	**16**	....	....	....	....	....	....	....	....	....	....	....	....	....	....	....	....	....	....
	Pittsburgh Hornets	AHL	18	4	7	11	....	....	....	37	....	....	....	....	....	....	....	....	....	....	9	0	0	0	2	....	....	....
1967-68	**Detroit Red Wings**	**NHL**	**15**	**6**	**4**	**10**	**7**	**4**	**11**	**13**	**0**	**0**	**0**	**35**	**17.1**	**17**	**4**	**19**	**0**	**–6**	....	....	....	....	....	....	....	....
	Fort Worth Wings	CHL	42	20	14	34	....	....	....	103	....	....	....	....	....	....	....	....	....	....	....	....	....	....	....	....	....	....
1968-69	**Detroit Red Wings**	**NHL**	**30**	**2**	**2**	**4**	**2**	**2**	**4**	**21**	**0**	**0**	**0**	**37**	**5.4**	**6**	**0**	**24**	**3**	**–15**	....	....	....	....	....	....	....	....
	Fort Worth Wings	CHL	34	19	17	36	....	....	....	54	....	....	....	....	....	....	....	....	....	....	....	....	....	....	....	....	....	....
1969-70	**Montreal Canadiens**	**NHL**	**36**	**9**	**8**	**17**	**10**	**8**	**18**	**51**	**0**	**0**	**2**	**75**	**12.0**	**29**	**6**	**14**	**0**	**+9**	....	....	....	....	....	....	....	....
	Montreal Voyageurs	AHL	31	21	19	40	....	....	....	77	....	....	....	....	....	....	....	....	....	....	....	....	....	....	....	....	....	....
1970-71	**Montreal Canadiens**	**NHL**	**78**	**35**	**26**	**61**	**37**	**23**	**60**	**181**	**12**	**3**	**5**	**189**	**18.5**	**108**	**41**	**55**	**13**	**+25**	**20**	**10**	**6**	**16**	**43**	**1**	**1**	**1**
1971-72	**Montreal Canadiens**	**NHL**	**75**	**35**	**32**	**67**	**37**	**29**	**66**	**103**	**7**	**4**	**6**	**207**	**16.9**	**107**	**31**	**80**	**20**	**+16**	**6**	**0**	**2**	**2**	**12**	**0**	**0**	**0**
1972-73	Canada	Summit	7	1	1	2	....	....	....	4	....	....	....	....	....	....	....	....	....	....	....	....	....	....	....	....	....	....
	Montreal Canadiens	**NHL**	**61**	**21**	**38**	**59**	**21**	**32**	**53**	**49**	**3**	**4**	**3**	**173**	**12.1**	**82**	**21**	**58**	**18**	**+21**	**17**	**4**	**9**	**13**	**22**	**2**	**1**	**0**
1973-74	**Montreal Canadiens**	**NHL**	**78**	**36**	**37**	**73**	**37**	**32**	**69**	**122**	**7**	**4**	**7**	**178**	**20.2**	**115**	**27**	**77**	**31**	**+42**	**6**	**2**	**1**	**3**	**4**	**1**	**0**	**0**
1974-75	**Montreal Canadiens**	**NHL**	**80**	**35**	**82**	**117**	**33**	**65**	**98**	**64**	**13**	**1**	**3**	**240**	**14.6**	**163**	**62**	**85**	**25**	**+41**	**11**	**6**	**10**	**16**	**10**	**1**	**0**	**1**
1975-76	**Montreal Canadiens**	**NHL**	**80**	**34**	**71**	**105**	**32**	**56**	**88**	**76**	**8**	**1**	**7**	**200**	**17.0**	**149**	**40**	**42**	**4**	**+71**	**13**	**4**	**8**	**12**	**24**	**2**	**0**	**1**
1976-77	**Montreal Canadiens**	**NHL**	**76**	**15**	**47**	**62**	**14**	**38**	**52**	**45**	**3**	**0**	**1**	**161**	**9.3**	**106**	**24**	**47**	**1**	**+36**	**13**	**4**	**5**	**9**	**19**	**2**	**0**	**1**
1977-78	**Montreal Canadiens**	**NHL**	**17**	**3**	**5**	**8**	**3**	**4**	**7**	**4**	**0**	**0**	**1**	**28**	**10.7**	**15**	**3**	**7**	**1**	**+6**	....	....	....	....	....	....	....	....
	Pittsburgh Penguins	**NHL**	**57**	**25**	**36**	**61**	**24**	**29**	**53**	**37**	**9**	**2**	**1**	**201**	**12.4**	**91**	**34**	**82**	**29**	**+4**	....	....	....	....	....	....	....	....
1978-79	**Pittsburgh Penguins**	**NHL**	**60**	**14**	**39**	**53**	**13**	**30**	**43**	**39**	**5**	**0**	**0**	**153**	**9.2**	**69**	**17**	**65**	**2**	**–11**	**2**	**0**	**1**	**1**	**0**	**0**	**0**	**0**
1979-80	**Detroit Red Wings**	**NHL**	**80**	**16**	**50**	**66**	**14**	**38**	**52**	**69**	**3**	**0**	**1**	**143**	**11.2**	**109**	**40**	**88**	**22**	**+3**	....	....	....	....	....	....	....	....
1980-81	**Detroit Red Wings**	**NHL**	**24**	**1**	**4**	**5**	**1**	**3**	**4**	**26**	**0**	**0**	**1**	**25**	**4.0**	**7**	**1**	**22**	**6**	**–8**	....	....	....	....	....	....	....	....
	Adirondack Red Wings	AHL	37	10	18	36	....	....	....	49	....	....	....	....	....	....	....	....	....	....	18	1	*18	19	23	....	....	....
1981-82	Adirondack Red Wings	AHL	80	22	45	67	....	....	....	71	....	....	....	....	....	....	....	....	....	....	4	2	1	3	2	....	....	....
1982-1985			DID NOT PLAY																									
1985-86	Toledo Goaldiggers	IHL	23	4	10	14	....	....	....	50	....	....	....	....	....	....	....	....	....	....	....	....	....	....	....	....	....	....
	NHL Totals		**884**	**288**	**485**	**773**	**286**	**397**	**683**	**916**	**70**	**19**	**38**	**2045**	**14.1**	**1173**	**351**	**765**	**177**		**88**	**30**	**42**	**72**	**134**	**9**	**2**	**4**

Played in NHL All-Star Game (1971, 1976)

Traded to **Montreal** by **Detroit** with Bart Crashley for Garry Monahan and Doug Piper, June 6, 1969. Traded to **Pittsburgh** by **Montreal** with Peter Lee for Pierre Larouche and future considerations (Peter Marsh, December 5, 1977), November 29, 1977. Traded to **Detroit** by **Pittsburgh** for Nick Libett, August 3, 1979.

• MAILHOT, JACQUES

Jacques Mailhot LW – L. 6'2", 208 lbs. b: Shawinigan, Que., 12/5/1961.

Season	Club	League	GP	G	A	Pts	AG	AA	APts	PIM	PP	SH	GW	S	%	TGF	PGF	TGA	PGA	+/–	GP	G	A	Pts	PIM	PP	SH	GW
1985-86	Rimouski Mariners	QSHL	36	13	17	30	....	....	....	*262	....	....	....	....	....	....	....	....	....	....	....	....	....	....	....	....	....	....
1986-87	Rimouski Mariners	QSHL	19	9	12	21	....	....	....	164	....	....	....	....	....	....	....	....	....	....	7	1	2	3	....	....	....	....
1987-88	Baltimore Skipjacks	AHL	15	2	0	2	....	....	....	167	....	....	....	....	....	....	....	....	....	....	....	....	....	....	....	....	....	....
	Fredericton Express	AHL	28	2	6	8	....	....	....	137	....	....	....	....	....	....	....	....	....	....	8	0	0	0	18	....	....	....
1988-89	**Quebec Nordiques**	**NHL**	**5**	**0**	**0**	**0**	**0**	**0**	**0**	**33**	**0**	**0**	**0**	**0**	**0.0**	**0**	**0**	**0**	**0**	**0**	....	....	....	....	....	....	....	....
	Halifax Citadels	AHL	35	4	1	5	....	....	....	259	....	....	....	....	....	....	....	....	....	....	1	0	0	0	5	....	....	....
1989-90	Moncton Hawks	AHL	6	0	0	0	....	....	....	20	....	....	....	....	....	....	....	....	....	....	....	....	....	....	....	....	....	....
	Cape Breton Oilers	AHL	6	0	1	1	....	....	....	12	....	....	....	....	....	....	....	....	....	....	....	....	....	....	....	....	....	....
	Hampton Roads Admirals	ECHL	5	0	2	2	....	....	....	62	....	....	....	....	....	....	....	....	....	....	....	....	....	....	....	....	....	....
	Phoenix Roadrunners	IHL	28	0	2	2	....	....	....	78	....	....	....	....	....	....	....	....	....	....	....	....	....	....	....	....	....	....
1990-91	Moncton Hawks	AHL	13	0	0	0	....	....	....	43	....	....	....	....	....	....	....	....	....	....	....	....	....	....	....	....	....	....
	San Diego Gulls	IHL	1	0	0	0	....	....	....	2	....	....	....	....	....	....	....	....	....	....	....	....	....	....	....	....	....	....
	Johnstown Chiefs	ECHL	2	0	0	0	....	....	....	21	....	....	....	....	....	....	....	....	....	....	9	1	3	4	46	....	....	....
	Miramichi Packers	NBSHL	....	10	6	16	....	....	....	117	....	....	....	....	....	....	....	....	....	....	....	....	....	....	....	....	....	....
1991-92	Flint Bulldogs	ColHL	29	15	12	27	....	....	....	237	....	....	....	....	....	....	....	....	....	....	....	....	....	....	....	....	....	....
	Detroit Falcons	ColHL	5	2	2	4	....	....	....	44	....	....	....	....	....	....	....	....	....	....	....	....	....	....	....	....	....	....
1992-93	Detroit Falcons	ColHL	48	14	21	35	....	....	....	273	....	....	....	....	....	....	....	....	....	....	4	2	4	0	12	....	....	....
1993-94	Detroit Falcons	ColHL	29	1	9	10	....	....	....	122	....	....	....	....	....	....	....	....	....	....	3	0	1	1	49	....	....	....
1994-95	Rochester Americans	AHL	15	0	1	1	....	....	....	52	....	....	....	....	....	....	....	....	....	....	....	....	....	....	....	....	....	....
	Utica Blizzard	ColHL	59	11	17	28	....	....	....	302	....	....	....	....	....	....	....	....	....	....	....	....	....	....	....	....	....	....
1995-96	Utica Blizzard	ColHL	8	1	0	1	....	....	....	71	....	....	....	....	....	....	....	....	....	....	....	....	....	....	....	....	....	....
	Quad City Mallards	ColHL	50	14	8	22	....	....	....	253	....	....	....	....	....	....	....	....	....	....	3	0	0	0	52	....	....	....
1996-97	Central Texas Stampede	WPHL	34	5	8	13	....	....	....	247	....	....	....	....	....	....	....	....	....	....	....	....	....	....	....	....	....	....
	Utah Grizzlies	IHL	4	0	1	1	....	....	....	32	....	....	....	....	....	....	....	....	....	....	....	....	....	....	....	....	....	....
1997-98	Central Texas Stampede	WPHL	50	14	18	32	....	....	....	277	....	....	....	....	....	....	....	....	....	....	4	2	1	3	44	....	....	....
	NHL Totals		**5**	**0**	**0**	**0**	**0**	**0**	**0**	**33**	**0**	**0**	**0**	**0**	**0.0**	**0**	**0**	**0**	**0**		....	....	....	....	....	....	....	....

Signed as a free agent by **Quebec**, August 15, 1988.

• MAIR, JIM

Jim Mair D – R. 5'9", 170 lbs. b: Schumacher, Ont., 5/15/1946.

Season	Club	League	GP	G	A	Pts	AG	AA	APts	PIM	PP	SH	GW	S	%	TGF	PGF	TGA	PGA	+/–	GP	G	A	Pts	PIM	PP	SH	GW
1963-64	Hamilton Red Wings	OHA	4	2	1	3	....	....	....	2	....	....	....	....	....	....	....	....	....	....	....	....	....	....	....	....	....	....
1964-65	Hamilton Red Wings	OHA	39	7	14	21	....	....	....	76	....	....	....	....	....	....	....	....	....	....	....	....	....	....	....	....	....	....
1965-66	St. Jerome Alouettes	QJHL	STATISTICS NOT AVAILABLE																									
1966-67	Johnstown Jets	EHL	62	10	25	35	....	....	....	247	....	....	....	....	....	....	....	....	....	....	5	2	3	5	0	....	....	....
1967-68	Johnstown Jets	EHL	71	20	45	65	....	....	....	247	....	....	....	....	....	....	....	....	....	....	3	0	0	0	0	....	....	....
1968-69	Johnstown Jets	EHL	61	27	31	58	....	....	....	158	....	....	....	....	....	....	....	....	....	....	3	0	2	2	0	....	....	....
1969-70	Quebec Aces	AHL	47	5	7	12	....	....	....	50	....	....	....	....	....	....	....	....	....	....	6	2	0	2	12	....	....	....
1970-71	**Philadelphia Flyers**	**NHL**	**2**	**0**	**0**	**0**	**0**	**0**	**0**	**0**	**0**	**0**	**0**	**6**	**0.0**	**2**	**2**	**1**	**0**	**–1**	**3**	**1**	**2**	**3**	**4**	**1**	**0**	**0**
	Quebec Aces	AHL	62	11	16	27	....	....	....	52	....	....	....	....	....	....	....	....	....	....	1	0	0	0	4	....	....	....

			REGULAR SEASON																		PLAYOFFS							
Season	Club	League	GP	G	A	Pts	AG	AA	APts	PIM	PP	SH	GW	S	%	TGF	PGF	TGA	PGA	+/–	GP	G	A	Pts	PIM	PP	SH	GW
1971-72	**Philadelphia Flyers**	**NHL**	**2**	**0**	**0**	**0**	**0**	**0**	**0**	**0**	**0**	**0**	**0**	**3**	**0.0**	**2**	**2**	**2**	**0**	**–2**	....	....	....	....	....	....	....	....
	Richmond Robins	AHL	69	10	25	35	....	....	....	75	....	....	....	....	....	....	....	....	....	....	....	....	....	....	....	....	....	....
1972-73	**New York Islanders**	**NHL**	**49**	**2**	**11**	**13**	**2**	**9**	**11**	**41**	**0**	**0**	**0**	**134**	**1.5**	**43**	**9**	**88**	**16**	**–38**	....	....	....	....	....	....	....	....
	Vancouver Canucks	**NHL**	**15**	**1**	**0**	**1**	**1**	**0**	**1**	**8**	**0**	**0**	**0**	**23**	**4.3**	**8**	**0**	**12**	**0**	**–4**	....	....	....	....	....	....	....	....
1973-74	**Vancouver Canucks**	**NHL**	**6**	**1**	**3**	**4**	**1**	**3**	**4**	**0**	**1**	**0**	**1**	**32**	**3.1**	**15**	**6**	**7**	**1**	**+3**	....	....	....	....	....	....	....	....
	Seattle Totems	WHL	65	8	30	38	....	....	....	115	....	....	....	....	....	....	....	....	....	....	....	....	....	....	....	....	....	....
1974-75	**Vancouver Canucks**	**NHL**	**2**	**0**	**1**	**1**	**0**	**1**	**1**	**0**	**0**	**0**	**0**	**8**	**0.0**	**1**	**1**	**2**	**0**	**–2**	....	....	....	....	....	....	....	....
	Seattle Totems	CHL	63	12	17	29	....	....	....	96	....	....	....	....	....	....	....	....	....	....	....	....	....	....	....	....	....	....
	NHL Totals		**76**	**4**	**15**	**19**	**4**	**13**	**17**	**49**	**1**	**0**	**1**	**206**	**1.9**	**71**	**20**	**112**	**17**		**3**	**1**	**2**	**3**	**4**	**1**	**0**	**0**

Signed as a free agent by **Philadelphia**, September 29, 1969. Claimed by **NY Islanders** from **Philadelphia** in Expansion Draft, June 6, 1972. Claimed by **Vancouver** from **NY Islanders** in Waiver Draft, February 19, 1973.

• MAJOR, BRUCE

Bruce Major C – L. 6'3", 180 lbs. b: Vernon, B.C., 1/3/1967. Quebec's 6th choice, 99th overall, in 1985 Entry Draft.

1984-85	Richmond Sockeyes	BCJHL	48	43	56	99	....	....	....	56	....	....	....	....	....	....	....	....	....	....	....	....	....	....	....	....	....	....
1985-86	University of Maine	H.E.	38	14	14	28	....	....	....	39	....	....	....	....	....	....	....	....	....	....	....	....	....	....	....	....	....	....
1986-87	University of Maine	H.E.	37	14	10	24	....	....	....	12	....	....	....	....	....	....	....	....	....	....	....	....	....	....	....	....	....	....
1987-88	University of Maine	H.E.	26	0	5	5	....	....	....	14	....	....	....	....	....	....	....	....	....	....	....	....	....	....	....	....	....	....
1988-89	University of Maine	H.E.	42	13	11	24	....	....	....	22	....	....	....	....	....	....	....	....	....	....	....	....	....	....	....	....	....	....
1989-90	Halifax Citadels	AHL	32	5	6	11	....	....	....	23	....	....	....	....	....	....	....	....	....	....	....	....	....	....	....	....	....	....
	Greensboro Monarchs	ECHL	12	4	3	7	....	....	....	6	....	....	....	....	....	....	....	....	....	....	10	2	2	4	12	....	....	....
1990-91	**Quebec Nordiques**	**NHL**	**4**	**0**	**0**	**0**	**0**	**0**	**0**	**0**	**0**	**0**	**0**	**0**	**0.0**	**0**	**0**	**1**	**0**	**–1**	....	....	....	....	....	....	....	....
	Halifax Citadels	AHL	9	2	0	2	....	....	....	9	....	....	....	....	....	....	....	....	....	....	....	....	....	....	....	....	....	....
	Fort Wayne Komets	IHL	62	11	25	36	....	....	....	48	....	....	....	....	....	....	....	....	....	....	18	1	3	4	6	....	....	....
1991-92	Halifax Citadels	AHL	16	1	3	4	....	....	....	11	....	....	....	....	....	....	....	....	....	....	....	....	....	....	....	....	....	....
	NHL Totals		**4**	**0**	**0**	**0**	**0**	**0**	**0**	**0**	**0**	**0**	**0**	**0**	**0.0**	**0**	**0**	**1**	**0**		....	....	....	....	....	....	....	....

• MAJOR, MARK

Mark Major LW – L. 6'3", 223 lbs. b: Toronto, Ont., 3/20/1970. Pittsburgh's 2nd choice, 25th overall, in 1988 Entry Draft.

1987-88	North Bay Centennials	OHL	57	16	17	33	....	....	....	272	....	....	....	....	....	....	....	....	....	....	4	0	2	2	8	....	....	....
1988-89	North Bay Centennials	OHL	11	3	2	5	....	....	....	58	....	....	....	....	....	....	....	....	....	....	....	....	....	....	....	....	....	....
	Kingston Frontenacs	OHL	53	22	29	51	....	....	....	193	....	....	....	....	....	....	....	....	....	....	....	....	....	....	....	....	....	....
1989-90	Kingston Frontenacs	OHL	62	29	32	61	....	....	....	168	....	....	....	....	....	....	....	....	....	....	6	3	3	6	12	....	....	....
1990-91	Muskegon Lumberjacks	IHL	60	8	10	18	....	....	....	160	....	....	....	....	....	....	....	....	....	....	5	0	0	0	0	....	....	....
1991-92	Muskegon Lumberjacks	IHL	80	13	18	31	....	....	....	302	....	....	....	....	....	....	....	....	....	....	12	1	3	4	29	....	....	....
1992-93	Cleveland Lumberjacks	IHL	82	13	15	28	....	....	....	155	....	....	....	....	....	....	....	....	....	....	3	0	0	0	0	....	....	....
1993-94	Providence Bruins	AHL	61	17	9	26	....	....	....	176	....	....	....	....	....	....	....	....	....	....	....	....	....	....	....	....	....	....
1994-95	Detroit Vipers	IHL	78	17	19	36	....	....	....	229	....	....	....	....	....	....	....	....	....	....	5	0	1	1	23	....	....	....
1995-96	Adirondack Red Wings	AHL	78	10	19	29	....	....	....	234	....	....	....	....	....	....	....	....	....	....	3	0	0	0	21	....	....	....
1996-97	**Detroit Red Wings**	**NHL**	**2**	**0**	**0**	**0**	**0**	**0**	**0**	**5**	**0**	**0**	**0**	**0**	**0.0**	**0**	**0**	**0**	**0**	**0**	....	....	....	....	....	....	....	....
	Adirondack Red Wings	AHL	78	17	18	35	....	....	....	213	....	....	....	....	....	....	....	....	....	....	4	0	0	0	13	....	....	....
1997-98	Portland Pirates	AHL	79	13	2	15	....	....	....	355	....	....	....	....	....	....	....	....	....	....	10	2	1	3	52	....	....	....
	NHL Totals		**2**	**0**	**0**	**0**	**0**	**0**	**0**	**5**	**0**	**0**	**0**	**0**	**0.0**	**0**	**0**	**0**	**0**		....	....	....	....	....	....	....	....

Signed as a free agent by **Boston**, July 22, 1993. Signed as a free agent by **Detroit**, June 26, 1995. Signed as a free agent by **Washington**, August 20, 1997.

• MAKAROV, SERGEI

Sergei Makarov RW – L. 5'11", 185 lbs. b: Chelyabinsk, USSR, 6/19/1958. Calgary's 14th choice, 241st overall, in 1983 Entry Draft.

1976-77	Chelyabinsk	USSR	11	1	0	1	....	....	....	4	....	....	....	....	....	....	....	....	....	....	....	....	....	....	....	....	....	....
	Soviet Union	WJC-A	7	4	4	8	....	....	....	4	....	....	....	....	....	....	....	....	....	....	....	....	....	....	....	....	....	....
1977-78	Chelyabinsk	USSR	36	18	13	31	....	....	....	10	....	....	....	....	....	....	....	....	....	....	....	....	....	....	....	....	....	....
	Soviet Union	WJC-A	7	8	7	15	....	....	....	4	....	....	....	....	....	....	....	....	....	....	....	....	....	....	....	....	....	....
	Soviet Union	WEC-A	10	3	2	5	....	....	....	5	....	....	....	....	....	....	....	....	....	....	....	....	....	....	....	....	....	....
1978-79	CSKA Moscow	USSR	44	18	21	39	....	....	....	12	....	....	....	....	....	....	....	....	....	....	....	....	....	....	....	....	....	....
	USSR	Chal Cup	3	1	2	3	....	....	....	0	....	....	....	....	....	....	....	....	....	....	....	....	....	....	....	....	....	....
	Soviet Union	WEC-A	8	8	4	12	....	....	....	6	....	....	....	....	....	....	....	....	....	....	....	....	....	....	....	....	....	....
1979-80	CSKA Moscow	USSR	44	29	39	68	....	....	....	16	....	....	....	....	....	....	....	....	....	....	....	....	....	....	....	....	....	....
	CSKA Moscow	SuperS	5	1	3	4	....	....	....	0	....	....	....	....	....	....	....	....	....	....	....	....	....	....	....	....	....	....
	Soviet Union	Olympics	7	5	6	11	....	....	....	2	....	....	....	....	....	....	....	....	....	....	....	....	....	....	....	....	....	....
1980-81	CSKA Moscow	USSR	49	42	37	79	....	....	....	22	....	....	....	....	....	....	....	....	....	....	....	....	....	....	....	....	....	....
	Soviet Union	WEC-A	8	3	5	8	....	....	....	12	....	....	....	....	....	....	....	....	....	....	....	....	....	....	....	....	....	....
1981-82	Soviet Union	C Cup	7	3	6	9	....	....	....	0	....	....	....	....	....	....	....	....	....	....	....	....	....	....	....	....	....	....
	CSKA Moscow	USSR	46	32	43	75	....	....	....	18	....	....	....	....	....	....	....	....	....	....	....	....	....	....	....	....	....	....
	Soviet Union	WEC-A	10	6	7	13	....	....	....	8	....	....	....	....	....	....	....	....	....	....	....	....	....	....	....	....	....	....
1982-83	CSKA Moscow	USSR	30	25	17	42	....	....	....	6	....	....	....	....	....	....	....	....	....	....	....	....	....	....	....	....	....	....
	Soviet Union	WEC-A	10	9	9	18	....	....	....	4	....	....	....	....	....	....	....	....	....	....	....	....	....	....	....	....	....	....
1983-84	CSKA Moscow	USSR	44	36	37	73	....	....	....	28	....	....	....	....	....	....	....	....	....	....	....	....	....	....	....	....	....	....
	Soviet Union	Olympics	7	3	3	6	....	....	....	6	....	....	....	....	....	....	....	....	....	....	....	....	....	....	....	....	....	....
1984-85	Soviet Union	C Cup	6	6	1	7	....	....	....	4	....	....	....	....	....	....	....	....	....	....	....	....	....	....	....	....	....	....
	CSKA Moscow	USSR	40	26	39	65	....	....	....	28	....	....	....	....	....	....	....	....	....	....	....	....	....	....	....	....	....	....
	Soviet Union	WEC-A	10	9	5	14	....	....	....	8	....	....	....	....	....	....	....	....	....	....	....	....	....	....	....	....	....	....
1985-86	CSKA Moscow	USSR	40	30	32	62	....	....	....	28	....	....	....	....	....	....	....	....	....	....	....	....	....	....	....	....	....	....
	CSKA Moscow	SuperS	6	5	1	6	....	....	....	0	....	....	....	....	....	....	....	....	....	....	....	....	....	....	....	....	....	....
	Soviet Union	WEC-A	10	4	14	18	....	....	....	12	....	....	....	....	....	....	....	....	....	....	....	....	....	....	....	....	....	....
1986-87	CSKA Moscow	USSR	40	21	32	53	....	....	....	26	....	....	....	....	....	....	....	....	....	....	....	....	....	....	....	....	....	....
	USSR	RV'87	2	0	1	1	....	....	....	0	....	....	....	....	....	....	....	....	....	....	....	....	....	....	....	....	....	....
	Soviet Union	WEC-A	10	4	10	14	....	....	....	8	....	....	....	....	....	....	....	....	....	....	....	....	....	....	....	....	....	....
1987-88	CSKA Moscow	USSR	51	23	45	68	....	....	....	50	....	....	....	....	....	....	....	....	....	....	....	....	....	....	....	....	....	....
	Soviet Union	C Cup	9	7	8	15	....	....	....	8	....	....	....	....	....	....	....	....	....	....	....	....	....	....	....	....	....	....
	Soviet Union	Olympics	8	3	8	11	....	....	....	10	....	....	....	....	....	....	....	....	....	....	....	....	....	....	....	....	....	....
1988-89	CSKA Moscow	USSR	44	21	33	54	....	....	....	42	....	....	....	....	....	....	....	....	....	....	....	....	....	....	....	....	....	....
	CSKA Moscow	SuperS	7	3	6	9	....	....	....	0	....	....	....	....	....	....	....	....	....	....	....	....	....	....	....	....	....	....
	Soviet Union	WEC-A	10	5	3	8	....	....	....	8	....	....	....	....	....	....	....	....	....	....	....	....	....	....	....	....	....	....
1989-90	Calgary Flames	FrTour	4	0	1	1	....	....	....	0	....	....	....	....	....	....	....	....	....	....	....	....	....	....	....	....	....	....
	Calgary Flames	**NHL**	**80**	**24**	**62**	**86**	**21**	**44**	**65**	**55**	**6**	**0**	**4**	**118**	**20.3**	**144**	**53**	**58**	**0**	**+33**	**6**	**0**	**6**	**6**	**0**	**0**	**0**	**0**
	Soviet Wings	SuperS	5	2	2	4	....	....	....	4	....	....	....	....	....	....	....	....	....	....	....	....	....	....	....	....	....	....
	Soviet Union	WEC-A	7	2	1	3	....	....	....	8	....	....	....	....	....	....	....	....	....	....	....	....	....	....	....	....	....	....
1990-91	Soviet Wings	FrTour	1	0	0	0	....	....	....	0	....	....	....	....	....	....	....	....	....	....	....	....	....	....	....	....	....	....
	Calgary Flames	**NHL**	**78**	**30**	**49**	**79**	**28**	**37**	**65**	**44**	**9**	**0**	**5**	**93**	**32.3**	**122**	**51**	**58**	**2**	**+15**	**3**	**1**	**0**	**1**	**0**	**0**	**0**	**0**
	Soviet Union	WEC-A	8	3	7	10	....	....	....	6	....	....	....	....	....	....	....	....	....	....	....	....	....	....	....	....	....	....
1991-92	**Calgary Flames**	**NHL**	**68**	**22**	**48**	**70**	**20**	**36**	**56**	**60**	**6**	**0**	**2**	**83**	**26.5**	**95**	**31**	**51**	**1**	**+14**	....	....	....	....	....	....	....	....
1992-93	**Calgary Flames**	**NHL**	**71**	**18**	**39**	**57**	**15**	**27**	**42**	**40**	**5**	**0**	**3**	**105**	**17.1**	**95**	**32**	**64**	**1**	**0**	....	....	....	....	....	....	....	....
1993-94	**San Jose Sharks**	**NHL**	**80**	**30**	**38**	**68**	**28**	**29**	**57**	**78**	**10**	**0**	**5**	**155**	**19.4**	**103**	**31**	**61**	**0**	**+11**	**14**	**8**	**2**	**10**	**4**	**3**	**0**	**2**
1994-95	**San Jose Sharks**	**NHL**	**43**	**10**	**14**	**24**	**18**	**21**	**39**	**40**	**1**	**0**	**1**	**56**	**17.9**	**33**	**5**	**32**	**0**	**–4**	**11**	**3**	**3**	**6**	**4**	**0**	**0**	**0**
1995-96			DID NOT PLAY																									
1996-97	**Dallas Stars**	**NHL**	**4**	**0**	**0**	**0**	**0**	**0**	**0**	**0**	**0**	**0**	**0**	**0**	**0.0**	**2**	**2**	**2**	**0**	**–2**	....	....	....	....	....	....	....	....
	HC Fribourg-Gotteron	Switz.	5	3	2	5	....	....	....	2	....	....	....	....	....	....	....	....	....	....	1	0	0	0	0	....	....	....
1997-98	CSKA Moscow	CIS	40	10	10	20	....	....	....	18	....	....	....	....	....	....	....	....	....	....	....	....	....	....	....	....	....	....
	Spartak	CIS	18	0	1	1	....	....	....	4	....	....	....	....	....	....	....	....	....	....	....	....	....	....	....	....	....	....
	NHL Totals		**424**	**134**	**250**	**384**	**130**	**194**	**324**	**317**	**37**	**0**	**20**	**610**	**22.0**	**594**	**205**	**326**	**4**		**34**	**12**	**11**	**23**	**8**	**3**	**0**	**2**

USSR First All-Star Team (1981, 1982, 1983, 1984, bAB1985, 1986, 1987, 1988) • Won Izvestia Trophy (USSR's leading scorer (1980, 1981, 1982, 1984, 1985, 1986, 1987, 1988, 1989) • USSR Player of the Year (1980, 1985, 1989) • Canada Cup All-Star Team (1984) • Named Best Forward at WEC-A (1985) • NHL All-Rookie Team (1990) • Won Calder Memorial Trophy (1990)

Traded to **Hartford** by **Calgary** for future considerations (Washington's 4th round choice — previously acquired, Calgary selected Jason Smith — in 1993 Entry Draft, June 26, 1993), June 20, 1993. Traded to **San Jose** by **Hartford** with Hartford's 1st (Viktor Kozlov) and 3rd (Ville Peltonen) round choices in 1993 Entry Draft and Toronto's 2nd round choice (previously acquired, San Jose selected Vlastimil Kroupa) in 1993 Entry Draft for San Jose's 1st round choice (Chris Pronger) in 1993 Entry Draft, June 26, 1993. Signed as a free agent by **Dallas**, November 1, 1996.

			REGULAR SEASON																		PLAYOFFS							
Season	Club	League	GP	G	A	Pts	AG	AA	APts	PIM	PP	SH	GW	S	%	TGF	PGF	TGA	PGA	+/–	GP	G	A	Pts	PIM	PP	SH	GW

● MAKELA, MIKKO Mikko Makela LW – L. 6'1", 194 lbs. b: Tampere, Finland, 2/28/1965. NY Islanders' 5th choice, 66th overall, in 1983 Entry Draft.

1983-84	Ilves Tampere	Finland	35	17	11	28				26											2	0	1	1	0			
	Finland	WJC-A	5	1	0	1				0																		
1984-85	Ilves Tampere	Finland	36	*34	25	59				24											9	4	7	11	10			
	Finland	WJC-A	7	11	2	13				6																		
	Finland	WEC-A	8	2	2	4				2																		
1985-86	New York Islanders	NHL	58	16	20	36	13	13	26	28	2	0	3	68	23.5	61	16	34	1	+12								
	Springfield Indians	AHL	2	1	1	2				0																		
1986-87	New York Islanders	NHL	80	24	33	57	21	24	45	24	11	0	3	142	16.9	89	29	57	0	+3	11	2	4	6	8	1	0	1
1987-88	Finland	C Cup	5	1	1	2				12																		
	New York Islanders	NHL	73	36	40	76	31	28	59	22	13	2	4	142	25.4	109	50	51	6	+14	6	1	4	5	6	1	0	0
1988-89	New York Islanders	NHL	76	17	28	45	14	20	34	22	4	0	0	123	13.8	72	24	68	4	–16								
1989-90	New York Islanders	NHL	20	2	3	5	2	2	4	2	1	0	0	24	8.3	11	4	17	0	–10								
	Los Angeles Kings	NHL	45	7	14	21	6	10	16	16	0	0	0	58	12.1	27	0	31	0	–4	1	0	0	0	0	0	0	0
1990-91	Buffalo Sabres	NHL	60	15	7	22	14	5	19	25	2	2	1	62	24.2	37	3	48	12	–2								
1991-92	TPS Turku	Finland	44	25	45	*70				38											3	2	3	5	0			
	Finland	Olympics	5	3	3	6				0																		
	Finland	WC-A	8	2	8	10				0																		
1992-93	TPS Turku	Finland	38	17	27	44				22											11	4	8	12	0			
1993-94	Malmo IF	Sweden	37	15	21	36				20											11	4	7	11	2			
	Finland	Olympics	8	2	3	5				4																		
	Finland	WC-A	8	5	4	9				6																		
1994-95	Ilves Tampere	Finland	18	3	11	14				4																		
	Boston Bruins	NHL	11	1	2	3	2	3	5	0	1	0	0	10	10.0	4	3	1	0	0								
	Providence Bruins	AHL																			7	2	4	6	2			
1995-96	Dusseldorfer EG	Germany	47	16	37	53				16											13	0	14	*14	12			
1996-97	Dusseldorfer EG	Germany	39	4	14	18				0											4	1	1	2	0			
1997-98	Sodertalje SK	Sweden	25	2	11	13				14																		
	NHL Totals		**423**	**118**	**147**	**265**	**103**	**105**	**208**	**139**	**34**	**4**	**11**	**629**	**18.8**	**410**	**129**	**307**	**23**		**18**	**3**	**8**	**11**	**14**	**2**	**0**	**1**

WJC-A All-Star Team (1985) • Finnish First All-Star Team (1985, 1992) • Finnish Player of the Year (1992)

Traded to **LA Kings** by **NY Islanders** for Ken Baumgartner and Hubie McDonough, November 29, 1989. Traded to **Buffalo** by **LA Kings** for Mike Donnelly, September 30, 1990. Signed as a free agent by **Boston**, July 18, 1994.

● MAKI, CHICO Chico (Ronald) Maki RW – R. 5'10", 170 lbs. b: Sault Ste. Marie, Ont., 8/17/1939.

1956-57	St. Catharines Teepees	OHA	47	6	6	12				32											14	2	1	3	32			
1957-58	St. Catharines Teepees	OHA	49	21	19	40				72											8	3	5	8	10			
1958-59	St. Catharines Teepees	OHA	54	*41	53	94				64											7	2	1	3	10			
	Buffalo Bisons	AHL	1	0	0	0				2																		
	Trois-Rivieres Lions	QHL																			1	0	0	0	0			
1959-60	St. Catharines Teepees	OHA	47	39	*53	*92				75											17	11	*18	29	40			
	Sault Ste. Marie Thunderbirds	EPHL	1	0	1	1				0																		
	Buffalo Bisons	AHL	3	1	4	5				0																		
1960-61	Buffalo Bisons	AHL	60	30	42	72				20											4	0	0	0	2			
	Chicago Black Hawks	NHL																			1	0	0	0	0			
1961-62	Chicago Black Hawks	NHL	16	4	6	10	5	6	11	2																		
	Buffalo Bisons	AHL	51	21	28	49				65											11	3	5	8	15			
1962-63	Chicago Black Hawks	NHL	65	7	17	24	9	18	27	35											6	0	1	1	2			
1963-64	Chicago Black Hawks	NHL	68	8	14	22	10	15	25	70											7	0	0	0	15			
1964-65	Chicago Black Hawks	NHL	65	18	24	40	20	26	46	58											14	3	9	12	8			
1965-66	Chicago Black Hawks	NHL	68	17	31	48	20	31	51	41											3	1	1	2	0			
1966-67	Chicago Black Hawks	NHL	56	9	29	38	11	30	41	14											6	0	0	0	0			
1967-68	Chicago Black Hawks	NHL	60	8	16	24	10	17	27	4	0	0	1	102	7.8	42	3	52	3	–10	11	2	5	7	4	0	0	1
1968-69	Chicago Black Hawks	NHL	66	7	21	28	8	20	28	30	0	1	0	127	5.5	40	1	57	17	–1								
1969-70	Chicago Black Hawks	NHL	75	10	24	34	12	24	36	27	0	1	2	93	10.8	51	9	45	12	+9	8	2	2	4	2	1	1	0
1970-71	Chicago Black Hawks	NHL	72	22	26	48	23	23	46	18	2	2	0	110	20.0	74	12	40	9	+31	18	6	5	11	6	1	0	0
1971-72	Chicago Black Hawks	NHL	62	13	34	47	14	31	45	22	3	1	2	136	9.6	81	17	25	5	+44	8	1	4	5	4	0	0	1
1972-73	Chicago Black Hawks	NHL	77	13	19	32	13	16	29	10	1	2	1	118	11.0	58	10	62	19	+5	16	2	8	10	0	0	0	0
1973-74	Chicago Black Hawks	NHL	69	9	25	34	9	22	31	12	2	0	0	89	10.1	51	6	42	10	+13	11	0	1	1	2	0	0	0
1974-75			DID NOT PLAY – RETIRED																									
1975-76	Chicago Black Hawks	NHL	22	0	6	6	0	5	5	2	0	0	0	13	0.0	11	6	15	1	–9	4	0	0	0	0	0	0	0
	NHL Totals		**841**	**143**	**292**	**435**	**164**	**284**	**448**	**345**	**8**	**7**	**9**	**788**	**18.1**	**408**	**64**	**338**	**76**		**113**	**17**	**36**	**53**	**43**	**2**	**1**	**2**

Won Dudley "Red" Garrett Memorial Award (Top Rookie - AHL) (1961)

Played in NHL All-Star Game (1961, 1971, 1972)

● MAKI, WAYNE Wayne Maki LW – L. 6', 185 lbs. b: Sault Ste. Marie, Ont., 11/10/1944. Deceased.

1963-64	Sault Ste. Marie Greyhounds	NOHA	36	43	31	74				44																		
1964-65	St. Catharines Black Hawks	OHA	56	29	48	77				43											4	3	4	7	10			
	St. Louis Braves	CHL	3	0	0	0				4																		
1965-66	St. Louis Braves	CHL	69	25	26	51				46											2	0	1	1	13			
1966-67	St. Louis Braves	CHL	67	31	28	59				69																		
1967-68	Dallas Black Hawks	CHL	12	5	7	12				14											5	2	1	3	17			
	Chicago Black Hawks	NHL	49	5	5	10	6	5	11	32	1	0	1	54	9.3	22	5	23	2	–4	2	1	0	1	2	0	0	0
1968-69	Chicago Black Hawks	NHL	1	0	0	0	0	0	0	0	0	0	0	1	0.0	0	0	0	0	0								
	Dallas Black Hawks	CHL	50	25	24	49				74											11	7	7	14	37			
1969-70	St. Louis Blues	NHL	16	2	1	3	2	1	3	4	0	0	1	35	5.7	6	0	10	0	–4								
	Buffalo Bisons	AHL	40	13	20	33				72											14	4	4	8	*61			
1970-71	Vancouver Canucks	NHL	78	25	38	63	26	34	60	99	8	0	2	184	13.6	86	27	72	0	–13								
1971-72	Vancouver Canucks	NHL	76	22	25	47	23	23	46	43	5	0	3	160	13.8	67	17	55	1	–4								
1972-73	Vancouver Canucks	NHL	26	3	10	13	3	8	11	6	0	0	0	56	5.4	17	1	27	0	–11								
	NHL Totals		**246**	**57**	**79**	**136**	**60**	**71**	**131**	**184**	**14**	**0**	**7**	**490**	**11.6**	**198**	**50**	**187**	**3**		**2**	**1**	**0**	**1**	**2**	**0**	**0**	**0**

CHL Second All-Star Team (1967)

Claimed by **St. Louis** from **Chicago** in Intra-League Draft, June 11, 1969. Claimed by **Vancouver** from **St. Louis** in Expansion Draft, June 10, 1970.

● MAKKONEN, KARI Kari Makkonen RW – R. 6', 190 lbs. b: Pori, Finland, 1/20/1955. NY Islanders' 12th choice, 194th overall, in 1975 Amateur Draft.

1974-75	Assat Pori	Finland	36	5	5	10				8																		
	Finland	WJC-A	5	2	2	4				4																		
1975-76	Assat Pori	Finland	36	24	15	39				25											4	1	2	3	2			
	Finland	WEC-A	10	3	3	6				6																		
1976-77	Finland	C Cup	5	3	1	4				2																		
	Assat Pori	Finland	36	17	20	37				18																		
	Finland	WEC-A	10	4	4	8				2																		
1977-78	Assat Pori	Finland	39	19	25	44				28											9	4	5	9	9			
	Finland	WEC-A	10	1	0	1				4																		
1978-79	Assat Pori	Finland	36	*36	18	54				55											1	0	0	0	0			
1979-80	Edmonton Oilers	NHL	9	2	2	4	2	2	4	0	0	0	0	11	18.2	8	2	8	0	–2								
	Houston Apollos	CHL	16	5	5	10				2																		
1980-81	Assat Pori	Finland	36	19	21	40				20											1	0	0	0	0			
	Finland	Nat-Team	18	3	3	6				14																		
1981-82	Finland	C Cup	3	0	0	0				0																		
	Assat Pori	Finland	36	24	20	44				12											9	5	4	9	0			
	Finland	WEC-A	7	2	2	4				2																		

			REGULAR SEASON																		PLAYOFFS							
Season	Club	League	GP	G	A	Pts	AG	AA	APts	PIM	PP	SH	GW	S	%	TGF	PGF	TGA	PGA	+/–	GP	G	A	Pts	PIM	PP	SH	GW
1982-83	Assat Pori	Finland	35	14	18	32	....	....	....	22	....	....	....	....	....	....	....	....	....	....	....	....	....	....	....	....	....	....
	Finland	WEC-A	10	1	1	2	....	....	....	8	....	....	....	....	....	....	....	....	....	....	....	....	....	....	....	....	....	....
1983-84	Assat Pori	Finland	37	27	15	42	....	....	....	28	....	....	....	....	....	....	....	....	....	....	9	3	4	7	19	....	....	....
1984-85	Assat Pori	Finland	36	18	20	38	....	....	....	32	....	....	....	....	....	....	....	....	....	....	8	6	4	10	6	....	....	....
	Finland	WEC-A	10	1	0	1	....	....	....	4	....	....	....	....	....	....	....	....	....	....	....	....	....	....	....	....	....	....
1985-86	Assat Pori	Finland	34	23	26	49	....	....	....	24	....	....	....	....	....	....	....	....	....	....	....	....	....	....	....	....	....	....
	Finland	WEC-A	10	4	2	6	....	....	....	10	....	....	....	....	....	....	....	....	....	....	....	....	....	....	....	....	....	....
1986-87	Assat Pori	Finland	43	14	22	36	....	....	....	20	....	....	....	....	....	....	....	....	....	....	....	....	....	....	....	....	....	....
1987-88	Assat Pori	Finland	43	21	16	37	....	....	....	36	....	....	....	....	....	....	....	....	....	....	....	....	....	....	....	....	....	....
1988-89	Assat Pori	Finland	42	16	24	40	....	....	....	20	....	....	....	....	....	....	....	....	....	....	....	....	....	....	....	....	....	....
	NHL Totals		**9**	**2**	**2**	**4**	**2**	**2**	**4**	**0**	**0**	**0**	**0**	**11**	**18.2**	**8**	**2**	**8**	**0**		....	....	....	....	....	....	....	....

Finnish Rookie of the Year (1976) • Finnish First All-Star Team (1978, 1979)

Signed as a free agent by **Edmonton**, July 22, 1979.

• MALAKHOV, VLADIMIR

Vladimir Malakhov D – L. 6'3", 220 lbs. b: Sverdlovsk, USSR, 8/30/1968. NY Islanders' 12th choice, 191st overall, in 1989 Entry Draft.

1986-87	Spartak Moscow	USSR	22	0	1	1	....	....	....	12	....	....	....	....	....	....	....	....	....	....	....	....	....	....	....	....	....	....
1987-88	Spartak Moscow	USSR	28	2	2	4	....	....	....	26	....	....	....	....	....	....	....	....	....	....	....	....	....	....	....	....	....	....
1988-89	CSKA Moscow	USSR	34	6	2	8	....	....	....	16	....	....	....	....	....	....	....	....	....	....	....	....	....	....	....	....	....	....
	CSKA Moscow	SuperS	7	0	1	1	....	....	....	6	....	....	....	....	....	....	....	....	....	....	....	....	....	....	....	....	....	....
1989-90	CSKA Moscow	FrTour	1	0	0	0	....	....	....	0	....	....	....	....	....	....	....	....	....	....	....	....	....	....	....	....	....	....
	CSKA Moscow	USSR	48	2	10	12	....	....	....	34	....	....	....	....	....	....	....	....	....	....	....	....	....	....	....	....	....	....
	CSKA Moscow	SuperS	5	0	1	1	....	....	....	8	....	....	....	....	....	....	....	....	....	....	....	....	....	....	....	....	....	....
	Soviet Union	WEC-A	10	0	1	1	....	....	....	10	....	....	....	....	....	....	....	....	....	....	....	....	....	....	....	....	....	....
1990-91	CSKA Moscow	FrTour	1	0	0	0	....	....	....	25	....	....	....	....	....	....	....	....	....	....	....	....	....	....	....	....	....	....
	CSKA Moscow	USSR	46	5	13	18	....	....	....	22	....	....	....	....	....	....	....	....	....	....	....	....	....	....	....	....	....	....
	CSKA Moscow	SuperS	3	1	0	1	....	....	....	0	....	....	....	....	....	....	....	....	....	....	....	....	....	....	....	....	....	....
	Soviet Union	WEC-A	10	0	0	0	....	....	....	4	....	....	....	....	....	....	....	....	....	....	....	....	....	....	....	....	....	....
1991-92	Soviet Union	C Cup	5	0	0	0	....	....	....	4	....	....	....	....	....	....	....	....	....	....	....	....	....	....	....	....	....	....
	CSKA Moscow	CIS	40	1	9	10	....	....	....	12	....	....	....	....	....	....	....	....	....	....	....	....	....	....	....	....	....	....
	Russia	Olympics	8	3	0	3	....	....	....	4	....	....	....	....	....	....	....	....	....	....	....	....	....	....	....	....	....	....
	Russia	WC-A	6	2	1	3	....	....	....	4	....	....	....	....	....	....	....	....	....	....	....	....	....	....	....	....	....	....
1992-93	**New York Islanders**	**NHL**	**64**	**14**	**38**	**52**	**12**	**26**	**38**	**59**	**7**	**0**	**0**	**178**	**7.9**	**117**	**44**	**72**	**13**	**+14**	**17**	**3**	**6**	**9**	**12**	**0**	**0**	**0**
	Capital District Islanders	AHL	3	2	1	3	....	....	....	11	....	....	....	....	....	....	....	....	....	....	....	....	....	....	....	....	....	....
1993-94	**New York Islanders**	**NHL**	**76**	**10**	**47**	**57**	**9**	**36**	**45**	**80**	**4**	**0**	**2**	**235**	**4.3**	**139**	**54**	**83**	**27**	**+29**	**4**	**0**	**0**	**0**	**6**	**0**	**0**	**0**
1994-95	**New York Islanders**	**NHL**	**26**	**3**	**13**	**16**	**5**	**19**	**24**	**32**	**1**	**0**	**0**	**61**	**4.9**	**31**	**12**	**27**	**7**	**–1**	....	....	....	....	....	....	....	....
	Montreal Canadiens	**NHL**	**14**	**1**	**4**	**5**	**2**	**6**	**8**	**14**	**0**	**0**	**0**	**30**	**3.3**	**14**	**4**	**19**	**7**	**–2**	....	....	....	....	....	....	....	....
1995-96	**Montreal Canadiens**	**NHL**	**61**	**5**	**23**	**28**	**5**	**19**	**24**	**79**	**2**	**0**	**0**	**122**	**4.1**	**82**	**30**	**57**	**12**	**+7**	....	....	....	....	....	....	....	....
1996-97	Russia	W Cup	4	1	0	1	....	....	....	8	....	....	....	....	....	....	....	....	....	....	....	....	....	....	....	....	....	....
	Montreal Canadiens	**NHL**	**65**	**10**	**20**	**30**	**11**	**18**	**29**	**43**	**5**	**0**	**1**	**177**	**5.6**	**81**	**29**	**71**	**22**	**+3**	**5**	**0**	**0**	**0**	**6**	**0**	**0**	**0**
1997-98	**Montreal Canadiens**	**NHL**	**74**	**13**	**31**	**44**	**15**	**30**	**45**	**70**	**8**	**0**	**2**	**166**	**7.8**	**110**	**47**	**68**	**21**	**+16**	**9**	**3**	**4**	**7**	**10**	**2**	**0**	**0**
	NHL Totals		**380**	**56**	**176**	**232**	**59**	**154**	**213**	**377**	**27**	**0**	**5**	**969**	**5.8**	**574**	**220**	**397**	**109**		**35**	**6**	**10**	**16**	**34**	**2**	**0**	**0**

NHL/Upper Deck All-Rookie Team (1993)

Traded to **Montreal** by **NY Islanders** with Pierre Turgeon for Kirk Muller, Mathieu Schneider and Craig Darby, April 5, 1995.

• MALEY, DAVID

David Maley LW – L. 6'2", 195 lbs. b: Beaver Dam, WI, 4/24/1963. Montreal's 4th choice, 33rd overall, in 1982 Entry Draft.

1981-82	Edina High School	H.S.	26	22	28	50	....	....	....	26	....	....	....	....	....	....	....	....	....	....	....	....	....	....	....	....	....	....
1982-83	University of Wisconsin	WCHA	47	17	23	40	....	....	....	24	....	....	....	....	....	....	....	....	....	....	....	....	....	....	....	....	....	....
1983-84	University of Wisconsin	WCHA	38	10	28	38	....	....	....	56	....	....	....	....	....	....	....	....	....	....	....	....	....	....	....	....	....	....
1984-85	University of Wisconsin	WCHA	38	19	9	28	....	....	....	86	....	....	....	....	....	....	....	....	....	....	....	....	....	....	....	....	....	....
1985-86	University of Wisconsin	WCHA	42	20	40	60	....	....	....	135	....	....	....	....	....	....	....	....	....	....	....	....	....	....	....	....	....	....
	Montreal Canadiens	**NHL**	**3**	**0**	**0**	**0**	**0**	**0**	**0**	**0**	**0**	**0**	**0**	**0**	**0.0**	**1**	**0**	**1**	**0**	**0**	**7**	**1**	**3**	**4**	**2**	**0**	**0**	**0**
1986-87	**Montreal Canadiens**	**NHL**	**48**	**6**	**12**	**18**	**5**	**9**	**14**	**55**	**0**	**0**	**0**	**45**	**13.3**	**20**	**3**	**18**	**0**	**–1**	....	....	....	....	....	....	....	....
	Sherbrooke Canadiens	AHL	11	1	5	6	....	....	....	25	....	....	....	....	....	....	....	....	....	....	12	7	7	14	10	....	....	....
1987-88	**New Jersey Devils**	**NHL**	**44**	**4**	**2**	**6**	**3**	**1**	**4**	**65**	**1**	**0**	**1**	**44**	**9.1**	**20**	**9**	**24**	**0**	**–13**	**20**	**3**	**1**	**4**	**80**	**0**	**0**	**0**
	Utica Devils	AHL	9	5	3	8	....	....	....	40	....	....	....	....	....	....	....	....	....	....	....	....	....	....	....	....	....	....
1988-89	**New Jersey Devils**	**NHL**	**68**	**5**	**6**	**11**	**4**	**4**	**8**	**249**	**0**	**0**	**0**	**63**	**7.9**	**23**	**7**	**43**	**0**	**–27**	....	....	....	....	....	....	....	....
1989-90	**New Jersey Devils**	**NHL**	**67**	**8**	**17**	**25**	**7**	**12**	**19**	**160**	**0**	**0**	**2**	**82**	**9.8**	**37**	**1**	**39**	**1**	**–2**	**6**	**0**	**0**	**0**	**25**	**0**	**0**	**0**
1990-91	**New Jersey Devils**	**NHL**	**64**	**8**	**14**	**22**	**7**	**11**	**18**	**151**	**1**	**0**	**3**	**67**	**11.9**	**34**	**3**	**25**	**3**	**+9**	....	....	....	....	....	....	....	....
	United States	WEC-A	8	0	1	1	....	....	....	2	....	....	....	....	....	....	....	....	....	....	....	....	....	....	....	....	....	....
1991-92	**New Jersey Devils**	**NHL**	**37**	**7**	**11**	**18**	**6**	**8**	**14**	**58**	**1**	**0**	**0**	**42**	**16.7**	**29**	**6**	**24**	**1**	**0**	....	....	....	....	....	....	....	....
	Edmonton Oilers	**NHL**	**23**	**3**	**6**	**9**	**3**	**4**	**7**	**46**	**0**	**0**	**1**	**31**	**9.7**	**20**	**1**	**12**	**1**	**+8**	**10**	**1**	**1**	**2**	**4**	**0**	**0**	**0**
1992-93	**Edmonton Oilers**	**NHL**	**13**	**1**	**1**	**2**	**1**	**1**	**2**	**29**	**0**	**0**	**0**	**9**	**11.1**	**3**	**0**	**6**	**0**	**–3**	....	....	....	....	....	....	....	....
	San Jose Sharks	**NHL**	**43**	**1**	**6**	**7**	**1**	**4**	**5**	**126**	**1**	**0**	**0**	**48**	**2.1**	**11**	**3**	**38**	**5**	**–25**	....	....	....	....	....	....	....	....
1993-94	**San Jose Sharks**	**NHL**	**19**	**0**	**0**	**0**	**0**	**0**	**0**	**30**	**0**	**0**	**0**	**4**	**0.0**	**2**	**0**	**3**	**0**	**–1**	....	....	....	....	....	....	....	....
	New York Islanders	**NHL**	**37**	**0**	**6**	**6**	**0**	**5**	**5**	**74**	**0**	**0**	**0**	**19**	**0.0**	**10**	**4**	**12**	**0**	**–6**	**3**	**0**	**0**	**0**	**0**	**0**	**0**	**0**
1994-95				DID NOT PLAY																								
1995-96	San Francisco Spiders	IHL	71	16	13	29	....	....	....	248	....	....	....	....	....	....	....	....	....	....	4	0	0	0	2	....	....	....
	NHL Totals		**466**	**43**	**81**	**124**	**37**	**59**	**96**	**1043**	**4**	**0**	**7**	**454**	**9.5**	**210**	**37**	**245**	**11**		**46**	**5**	**5**	**10**	**111**	**0**	**0**	**0**

Traded to **New Jersey** by **Montreal** for New Jersey's 3rd round choice (Mathieu Schnider) in 1987 Entry Draft, June 13, 1987. Traded to **Edmonton** by **New Jersey** for Troy Mallette, January 12, 1992. Claimed on waivers by **San Jose** from **Edmonton**, January 1, 1993. Traded to **NY Islanders** by **San Jose** for cash, January 23, 1994.

• MALGUNAS, STEWART

Stewart Malgunas D – L. 6', 200 lbs. b: Prince George, B.C., 4/21/1970. Detroit's 3rd choice, 66th overall, in 1990 Entry Draft.

1987-88	New Westminster Bruins	WHL	6	0	0	0	....	....	....	0	....	....	....	....	....	....	....	....	....	....	....	....	....	....	....	....	....	....
1988-89	Seattle Thunderbirds	WHL	72	11	41	52	....	....	....	51	....	....	....	....	....	....	....	....	....	....	....	....	....	....	....	....	....	....
1989-90	Seattle Thunderbirds	WHL	63	15	48	63	....	....	....	116	....	....	....	....	....	....	....	....	....	....	13	2	9	11	32	....	....	....
	Canada	WJC-A	7	0	1	1	....	....	....	0	....	....	....	....	....	....	....	....	....	....	....	....	....	....	....	....	....	....
1990-91	Adirondack Red Wings	AHL	78	5	19	24	....	....	....	70	....	....	....	....	....	....	....	....	....	....	2	0	0	0	4	....	....	....
1991-92	Adirondack Red Wings	AHL	69	4	28	32	....	....	....	82	....	....	....	....	....	....	....	....	....	....	18	2	6	8	28	....	....	....
1992-93	Adirondack Red Wings	AHL	45	3	12	15	....	....	....	39	....	....	....	....	....	....	....	....	....	....	11	3	3	6	8	....	....	....
1993-94	**Philadelphia Flyers**	**NHL**	**67**	**1**	**3**	**4**	**1**	**2**	**3**	**86**	**0**	**0**	**0**	**54**	**1.9**	**55**	**2**	**65**	**14**	**+2**	....	....	....	....	....	....	....	....
1994-95	**Philadelphia Flyers**	**NHL**	**4**	**0**	**0**	**0**	**0**	**0**	**0**	**4**	**0**	**0**	**0**	**1**	**0.0**	**3**	**0**	**4**	**0**	**–1**	....	....	....	....	....	....	....	....
	Hershey Bears	AHL	32	3	5	8	....	....	....	28	....	....	....	....	....	....	....	....	....	....	6	2	1	3	31	....	....	....
1995-96	**Winnipeg Jets**	**NHL**	**29**	**0**	**1**	**1**	**0**	**1**	**1**	**32**	**0**	**0**	**0**	**13**	**0.0**	**8**	**0**	**25**	**7**	**–10**	....	....	....	....	....	....	....	....
	Washington Capitals	**NHL**	**1**	**0**	**0**	**0**	**0**	**0**	**0**	**0**	**0**	**0**	**0**	**0**	**0.0**	**0**	**0**	**0**	**0**	**0**	....	....	....	....	....	....	....	....
	Portland Pirates	AHL	16	2	5	7	....	....	....	18	....	....	....	....	....	....	....	....	....	....	13	1	3	4	19	....	....	....
1996-97	**Washington Capitals**	**NHL**	**6**	**0**	**0**	**0**	**0**	**0**	**0**	**2**	**0**	**0**	**0**	**3**	**0.0**	**2**	**0**	**0**	**0**	**+2**	....	....	....	....	....	....	....	....
	Portland Pirates	AHL	68	6	12	18	....	....	....	59	....	....	....	....	....	....	....	....	....	....	5	0	0	0	8	....	....	....
1997-98	**Washington Capitals**	**NHL**	**8**	**0**	**0**	**0**	**0**	**0**	**0**	**12**	**0**	**0**	**0**	**5**	**0.0**	**6**	**0**	**6**	**1**	**+1**	....	....	....	....	....	....	....	....
	Portland Pirates	AHL	69	14	25	39	....	....	....	73	....	....	....	....	....	....	....	....	....	....	9	1	1	2	19	....	....	....
	NHL Totals		**115**	**1**	**4**	**5**	**1**	**3**	**4**	**136**	**0**	**0**	**0**	**76**	**1.3**	**74**	**2**	**100**	**22**		....	....	....	....	....	....	....	....

WHL West First All-Star Team (1990)

Traded to **Philadelphia** by **Detroit** for Philadelphia's 5th round choice (David Arsenault) in 1995 Entry Draft, September 9, 1993. Signed as a free agent by **Winnipeg**, August 9, 1995. Traded to **Washington** by **Winnipeg** for Denis Chasse, February 15, 1996.

• MALIK, MAREK

Marek Malik D – L. 6'5", 190 lbs. b: Ostrava, Czech., 6/24/1975. Hartford's 2nd choice, 72nd overall, in 1993 Entry Draft.

1992-93	TJ Vitkovice Jr.	Czech.	20	5	10	15	....	....	....	16	....	....	....	....	....	....	....	....	....	....	....	....	....	....	....	....	....	....
1993-94	TJ Vitkovice	Czech.	38	3	3	6	....	....	....	0	....	....	....	....	....	....	....	....	....	....	3	0	1	1	0	....	....	....
	Czech Republic	WJC-A	7	2	4	6	....	....	....	20	....	....	....	....	....	....	....	....	....	....	....	....	....	....	....	....	....	....

			REGULAR SEASON																		PLAYOFFS							
Season	Club	League	GP	G	A	Pts	AG	AA	APts	PIM	PP	SH	GW	S	%	TGF	PGF	TGA	PGA	+/–	GP	G	A	Pts	PIM	PP	SH	GW
1994-95	Springfield Falcons	AHL	58	11	30	41	....	....	....	91	....	....	....	....	....	....	....	....	....	....	....	....	....	....	....	....	....	....
	Czech Republic	WJC-A	7	2	5	7	....	....	....	12	....	....	....	....	....	....	....	....	....	....	....	....	....	....	....	....	....	....
	Hartford Whalers	**NHL**	**1**	**0**	**1**	**1**	**0**	**1**	**1**	**0**	**0**	**0**	**0**	**0**	**0.0**	**1**	**0**	**0**	**0**	**+1**	....	....	....	....	....	....	....	....
1995-96	**Hartford Whalers**	**NHL**	**7**	**0**	**0**	**0**	**0**	**0**	**0**	**4**	**0**	**0**	**0**	**2**	**0.0**	**4**	**0**	**9**	**2**	**–3**	....	....	....	....	....	....	....	....
	Springfield Falcons	AHL	68	8	14	22	....	....	....	135	....	....	....	....	....	....	....	....	....	....	8	1	3	4	20	....	....	....
1996-97	**Hartford Whalers**	**NHL**	**47**	**1**	**5**	**6**	**1**	**4**	**5**	**50**	**0**	**0**	**1**	**33**	**3.0**	**37**	**2**	**31**	**1**	**+5**	....	....	....	....	....	....	....	....
	Springfield Falcons	AHL	3	0	3	3	....	....	....	4	....	....	....	....	....	....	....	....	....	....	....	....	....	....	....	....	....	....
1997-98	Malmo IF	Sweden	37	1	5	6	....	....	....	21	....	....	....	....	....	....	....	....	....	....	....	....	....	....	....	....	....	....
	NHL Totals		**55**	**1**	**6**	**7**	**1**	**5**	**6**	**54**	**0**	**0**	**1**	**35**	**2.9**	**42**	**2**	**40**	**3**		....	....	....	....	....	....	....	....

• MALINOWSKI, MERLIN

Merlin Malinowski C – L. 6′, 190 lbs. b: North Battleford, Sask., 9/27/1958. Colorado's 2nd choice, 27th overall, in 1978 Amateur Draft.

Season	Club	League	GP	G	A	Pts	AG	AA	APts	PIM	PP	SH	GW	S	%	TGF	PGF	TGA	PGA	+/–	GP	G	A	Pts	PIM	PP	SH	GW
1973-74	Drumheller Falcons	AJHL	2	0	0	0	....	....	....	0	....	....	....	....	....	....	....	....	....	....	....	....	....	....	....	....	....	....
1974-75	Drumheller Falcons	AJHL	59	23	44	67	....	....	....	58	....	....	....	....	....	....	....	....	....	....	....	....	....	....	....	....	....	....
1975-76	Drumheller Falcons	AJHL	59	60	86	146	....	....	....	79	....	....	....	....	....	....	....	....	....	....	....	....	....	....	....	....	....	....
1976-77	Medicine Hat Tigers	WCJHL	70	22	48	70	....	....	....	40	....	....	....	....	....	....	....	....	....	....	4	1	5	6	4	....	....	....
1977-78	Medicine Hat Tigers	WCJHL	72	48	78	126	....	....	....	131	....	....	....	....	....	....	....	....	....	....	11	9	11	20	16	....	....	....
1978-79	Philadelphia Firebirds	AHL	25	3	9	12	....	....	....	12	....	....	....	....	....	....	....	....	....	....	....	....	....	....	....	....	....	....
	Colorado Rockies	**NHL**	**54**	**6**	**17**	**23**	**5**	**13**	**18**	**10**	**0**	**0**	**1**	**76**	**7.9**	**33**	**3**	**50**	**3**	**–17**	....	....	....	....	....	....	....	....
1979-80	**Colorado Rockies**	**NHL**	**10**	**2**	**4**	**6**	**2**	**3**	**5**	**2**	**0**	**0**	**0**	**16**	**12.5**	**8**	**2**	**8**	**1**	**–1**	....	....	....	....	....	....	....	....
	Fort Worth Texans	CHL	66	34	42	76	....	....	....	58	....	....	....	....	....	....	....	....	....	....	15	8	*16	*24	34	....	....	....
1980-81	**Colorado Rockies**	**NHL**	**69**	**25**	**37**	**62**	**21**	**26**	**47**	**61**	**4**	**0**	**1**	**152**	**16.4**	**84**	**33**	**77**	**2**	**–24**	....	....	....	....	....	....	....	....
1981-82	**Colorado Rockies**	**NHL**	**69**	**13**	**28**	**41**	**10**	**19**	**29**	**32**	**0**	**1**	**0**	**95**	**13.7**	**60**	**8**	**80**	**6**	**–22**	....	....	....	....	....	....	....	....
1982-83	**New Jersey Devils**	**NHL**	**5**	**3**	**2**	**5**	**2**	**1**	**3**	**0**	**1**	**0**	**1**	**8**	**37.5**	**6**	**3**	**2**	**0**	**+1**	....	....	....	....	....	....	....	....
	Hartford Whalers	**NHL**	**75**	**5**	**23**	**28**	**4**	**16**	**20**	**16**	**1**	**0**	**0**	**94**	**5.3**	**34**	**6**	**71**	**2**	**–41**	....	....	....	....	....	....	....	....
1983-84	EC Arosa	Switz.	32	37	26	63	....	....	....	....	....	....	....	....	....	....	....	....	....	....	....	....	....	....	....	....	....	....
1984-85	EC Arosa	Switz.	38	48	36	84	....	....	....	35	....	....	....	....	....	....	....	....	....	....	....	....	....	....	....	....	....	....
1985-86	EC Arosa	Switz.	36	26	28	54	....	....	....	30	....	....	....	....	....	....	....	....	....	....	....	....	....	....	....	....	....	....
1986-87	SC Langnau	Switz.	36	32	*45	77	....	....	....	42	....	....	....	....	....	....	....	....	....	....	....	....	....	....	....	....	....	....
1987-88	SC Langnau	Switz.	30	23	22	45	....	....	....	26	....	....	....	....	....	....	....	....	....	....	....	....	....	....	....	....	....	....
	Canada	Nat-Team	2	0	0	0	....	....	....	0	....	....	....	....	....	....	....	....	....	....	....	....	....	....	....	....	....	....
	Canada	Olympics	8	3	2	5	....	....	....	0	....	....	....	....	....	....	....	....	....	....	....	....	....	....	....	....	....	....
1988-89	SC Langnau	Switz.	32	28	34	62	....	....	....	....	....	....	....	....	....	....	....	....	....	....	8	7	8	15	....	....	....	....
	NHL Totals		**282**	**54**	**111**	**165**	**44**	**78**	**122**	**121**	**6**	**1**	**3**	**441**	**12.2**	**225**	**55**	**288**	**14**		....	....	....	....	....	....	....	....

CHL Second All-Star Team (1980)

Transferred to **New Jersey** after **Colorado** franchise relocated, June 30, 1982. Traded to **Hartford** by **New Jersey** with the rights to Scott Fusco for Garry Howatt and Rick Meagher, October 15, 1982.

• MALKOC, DEAN

Dean Malkoc D – L. 6′3″, 215 lbs. b: Vancouver, B.C., 1/26/1970. New Jersey's 7th choice, 95th overall, in 1990 Entry Draft.

Season	Club	League	GP	G	A	Pts	AG	AA	APts	PIM	PP	SH	GW	S	%	TGF	PGF	TGA	PGA	+/–	GP	G	A	Pts	PIM	PP	SH	GW
1989-90	Kamloops Blazers	WHL	48	3	18	21	....	....	....	209	....	....	....	....	....	....	....	....	....	....	17	0	3	3	56	....	....	....
1990-91	Kamloops Blazers	WHL	8	1	4	5	....	....	....	47	....	....	....	....	....	....	....	....	....	....	....	....	....	....	....	....	....	....
	Swift Current Broncos	WHL	56	10	23	33	....	....	....	248	....	....	....	....	....	....	....	....	....	....	3	0	2	2	5	....	....	....
	Utica Devils	AHL	1	0	0	0	....	....	....	0	....	....	....	....	....	....	....	....	....	....	....	....	....	....	....	....	....	....
1991-92	Utica Devils	AHL	66	1	11	12	....	....	....	274	....	....	....	....	....	....	....	....	....	....	4	0	2	2	6	....	....	....
1992-93	Utica Devils	AHL	73	5	19	24	....	....	....	255	....	....	....	....	....	....	....	....	....	....	5	0	1	1	8	....	....	....
1993-94	Albany River Rats	AHL	79	0	9	9	....	....	....	296	....	....	....	....	....	....	....	....	....	....	5	0	0	0	21	....	....	....
1994-95	Albany River Rats	AHL	9	0	1	1	....	....	....	52	....	....	....	....	....	....	....	....	....	....	....	....	....	....	....	....	....	....
	Indianapolis Ice	IHL	62	1	3	4	....	....	....	193	....	....	....	....	....	....	....	....	....	....	....	....	....	....	....	....	....	....
1995-96	**Vancouver Canucks**	**NHL**	**41**	**0**	**2**	**2**	**0**	**2**	**2**	**136**	**0**	**0**	**0**	**8**	**0.0**	**17**	**0**	**33**	**6**	**–10**	....	....	....	....	....	....	....	....
1996-97	**Boston Bruins**	**NHL**	**33**	**0**	**0**	**0**	**0**	**0**	**0**	**70**	**0**	**0**	**0**	**7**	**0.0**	**7**	**0**	**23**	**2**	**–14**	....	....	....	....	....	....	....	....
	Providence Bruins	AHL	4	0	2	2	....	....	....	28	....	....	....	....	....	....	....	....	....	....	....	....	....	....	....	....	....	....
1997-98	**Boston Bruins**	**NHL**	**40**	**1**	**0**	**1**	**1**	**0**	**1**	**86**	**0**	**0**	**0**	**15**	**6.7**	**7**	**0**	**19**	**0**	**–12**	....	....	....	....	....	....	....	....
	NHL Totals		**114**	**1**	**2**	**3**	**1**	**2**	**3**	**292**	**0**	**0**	**0**	**30**	**3.3**	**31**	**0**	**75**	**8**		....	....	....	....	....	....	....	....

Traded to **Chicago** by **New Jersey** for Rob Conn, January 30, 1995. Signed as a free agent by **Vancouver**, September 8, 1995. Claimed by **Boston** from **Vancouver** in NHL Waiver Draft, September 30, 1996.

• MALLETTE, TROY

Troy Mallette LW – L. 6′2″, 210 lbs. b: Sudbury, Ont., 2/25/1970. NY Rangers' 1st choice, 22nd overall, in 1988 Entry Draft.

Season	Club	League	GP	G	A	Pts	AG	AA	APts	PIM	PP	SH	GW	S	%	TGF	PGF	TGA	PGA	+/–	GP	G	A	Pts	PIM	PP	SH	GW
1986-87	Sault Ste. Marie Greyhounds	OHL	65	20	25	45	....	....	....	157	....	....	....	....	....	....	....	....	....	....	4	0	2	2	12	....	....	....
1987-88	Sault Ste. Marie Greyhounds	OHL	62	18	30	48	....	....	....	186	....	....	....	....	....	....	....	....	....	....	6	1	3	4	12	....	....	....
1988-89	Sault Ste. Marie Greyhounds	OHL	64	39	37	76	....	....	....	172	....	....	....	....	....	....	....	....	....	....	....	....	....	....	....	....	....	....
1989-90	**New York Rangers**	**NHL**	**79**	**13**	**16**	**29**	**11**	**11**	**22**	**305**	**4**	**0**	**1**	**107**	**12.1**	**54**	**16**	**46**	**0**	**–8**	**10**	**2**	**2**	**4**	**81**	**0**	**0**	**0**
1990-91	**New York Rangers**	**NHL**	**71**	**12**	**10**	**22**	**11**	**8**	**19**	**252**	**0**	**0**	**2**	**91**	**13.2**	**33**	**1**	**41**	**1**	**–8**	**5**	**0**	**0**	**0**	**18**	**0**	**0**	**0**
1991-92	**Edmonton Oilers**	**NHL**	**15**	**1**	**3**	**4**	**1**	**2**	**3**	**36**	**0**	**0**	**0**	**9**	**11.1**	**7**	**0**	**8**	**0**	**–1**	....	....	....	....	....	....	....	....
	New Jersey Devils	**NHL**	**17**	**3**	**4**	**7**	**3**	**3**	**6**	**43**	**0**	**0**	**0**	**19**	**15.8**	**9**	**0**	**2**	**0**	**+7**	....	....	....	....	....	....	....	....
1992-93	**New Jersey Devils**	**NHL**	**34**	**4**	**3**	**7**	**3**	**2**	**5**	**56**	**0**	**0**	**0**	**19**	**21.1**	**14**	**0**	**11**	**0**	**+3**	....	....	....	....	....	....	....	....
	Utica Devils	AHL	5	3	3	6	....	....	....	17	....	....	....	....	....	....	....	....	....	....	....	....	....	....	....	....	....	....
1993-94	**Ottawa Senators**	**NHL**	**82**	**7**	**16**	**23**	**7**	**12**	**19**	**166**	**0**	**0**	**0**	**100**	**7.0**	**32**	**4**	**72**	**11**	**–33**	....	....	....	....	....	....	....	....
1994-95	**Ottawa Senators**	**NHL**	**23**	**3**	**5**	**8**	**5**	**7**	**12**	**35**	**0**	**0**	**1**	**21**	**14.3**	**16**	**0**	**10**	**0**	**+6**	....	....	....	....	....	....	....	....
	P.E.I. Senators	AHL	5	1	5	6	....	....	....	9	....	....	....	....	....	....	....	....	....	....	....	....	....	....	....	....	....	....
1995-96	**Ottawa Senators**	**NHL**	**64**	**2**	**3**	**5**	**2**	**2**	**4**	**171**	**0**	**0**	**0**	**51**	**3.9**	**11**	**0**	**18**	**0**	**–7**	....	....	....	....	....	....	....	....
1996-97	**Boston Bruins**	**NHL**	**68**	**6**	**8**	**14**	**6**	**7**	**13**	**155**	**0**	**0**	**2**	**61**	**9.8**	**25**	**1**	**32**	**0**	**–8**	....	....	....	....	....	....	....	....
1997-98	**Tampa Bay Lightning**	**NHL**	**3**	**0**	**0**	**0**	**0**	**0**	**0**	**7**	**0**	**0**	**0**	**0**	**0.0**	**0**	**0**	**0**	**0**	**0**	....	....	....	....	....	....	....	....
	NHL Totals		**456**	**51**	**68**	**119**	**49**	**54**	**103**	**1226**	**4**	**0**	**6**	**478**	**10.7**	**201**	**22**	**240**	**12**		**15**	**2**	**2**	**4**	**99**	**0**	**0**	**0**

Transferred to **Edmonton** by **NY Rangers** as compensation for NY Rangers' signing of free agent Adam Graves, September 12, 1991. Traded to **New Jersey** by **Edmonton** for David Maley, January 12, 1992. Traded to **Ottawa** by **New Jersey** with Craig Billington and New Jersey's 4th round choice (Cosmo Dupaul) in 1993 Entry Draft for Peter Sidorkiewicz and future considerations (Mike Peluso, June 26, 1993), June 20, 1993. Signed as a free agent by **Boston**, July 24, 1996. Signed as a free agent by **Tampa Bay**, October 2, 1997.

• MALONE, GREG

Greg Malone C – L. 6′, 190 lbs. b: Fredericton, N.B., 3/8/1956. Pittsburgh's 2nd choice, 19th overall, in 1976 Amateur Draft.

Season	Club	League	GP	G	A	Pts	AG	AA	APts	PIM	PP	SH	GW	S	%	TGF	PGF	TGA	PGA	+/–	GP	G	A	Pts	PIM	PP	SH	GW
1971-72	Fredericton Black Kats	H.S.	21	26	21	47	....	....	....	28	....	....	....	....	....	....	....	....	....	....	4	6	7	13	4	....	....	....
1972-73	Fredericton Black Kats	H.S.	23	*35	*41	*76	....	....	....	79	....	....	....	....	....	....	....	....	....	....	8	*17	*10	*27	*37	....	....	....
1973-74	Oshawa Generals	OHA	62	11	45	56	....	....	....	63	....	....	....	....	....	....	....	....	....	....	....	....	....	....	....	....	....	....
1974-75	Oshawa Generals	OHA	68	37	41	78	....	....	....	86	....	....	....	....	....	....	....	....	....	....	5	1	3	4	9	....	....	....
1975-76	Oshawa Generals	OHA	61	36	36	72	....	....	....	75	....	....	....	....	....	....	....	....	....	....	5	3	2	5	2	....	....	....
1976-77	**Pittsburgh Penguins**	**NHL**	**66**	**18**	**19**	**37**	**17**	**15**	**32**	**43**	**4**	**0**	**1**	**121**	**14.9**	**46**	**7**	**40**	**4**	**+3**	**3**	**1**	**1**	**2**	**2**	**0**	**0**	**1**
1977-78	**Pittsburgh Penguins**	**NHL**	**78**	**18**	**43**	**61**	**17**	**35**	**52**	**80**	**2**	**0**	**1**	**179**	**10.1**	**88**	**13**	**118**	**27**	**–16**	....	....	....	....	....	....	....	....
1978-79	**Pittsburgh Penguins**	**NHL**	**80**	**35**	**30**	**65**	**32**	**23**	**55**	**52**	**8**	**0**	**5**	**198**	**17.7**	**94**	**13**	**87**	**12**	**+6**	**7**	**0**	**1**	**1**	**10**	**0**	**0**	**0**
1979-80	**Pittsburgh Penguins**	**NHL**	**51**	**19**	**32**	**51**	**17**	**25**	**42**	**46**	**5**	**0**	**2**	**103**	**18.4**	**71**	**16**	**65**	**14**	**+4**	....	....	....	....	....	....	....	....
1980-81	**Pittsburgh Penguins**	**NHL**	**62**	**21**	**29**	**50**	**17**	**20**	**37**	**68**	**5**	**0**	**2**	**144**	**14.6**	**77**	**22**	**76**	**7**	**–14**	**5**	**2**	**3**	**5**	**16**	**0**	**0**	**0**
1981-82	**Pittsburgh Penguins**	**NHL**	**78**	**15**	**24**	**39**	**12**	**16**	**28**	**125**	**3**	**0**	**2**	**120**	**12.5**	**62**	**13**	**79**	**6**	**–24**	**3**	**0**	**0**	**0**	**4**	**0**	**0**	**0**
1982-83	**Pittsburgh Penguins**	**NHL**	**80**	**17**	**44**	**61**	**14**	**30**	**44**	**82**	**3**	**0**	**0**	**158**	**10.8**	**91**	**26**	**145**	**51**	**–29**	....	....	....	....	....	....	....	....
1983-84	**Hartford Whalers**	**NHL**	**78**	**17**	**37**	**54**	**14**	**25**	**39**	**56**	**3**	**0**	**2**	**124**	**13.7**	**74**	**19**	**80**	**15**	**–10**	....	....	....	....	....	....	....	....
1984-85	**Hartford Whalers**	**NHL**	**76**	**22**	**39**	**61**	**18**	**26**	**44**	**67**	**6**	**0**	**4**	**131**	**16.8**	**73**	**18**	**75**	**4**	**–16**	....	....	....	....	....	....	....	....
1985-86	**Hartford Whalers**	**NHL**	**22**	**6**	**7**	**13**	**5**	**5**	**10**	**24**	**1**	**0**	**0**	**35**	**17.1**	**19**	**6**	**19**	**1**	**–5**	....	....	....	....	....	....	....	....
	Quebec Nordiques	**NHL**	**27**	**3**	**5**	**8**	**2**	**3**	**5**	**18**	**0**	**0**	**0**	**26**	**11.5**	**10**	**0**	**15**	**2**	**–3**	**1**	**0**	**0**	**0**	**0**	**0**	**0**	**0**
1986-87	**Quebec Nordiques**	**NHL**	**6**	**0**	**1**	**1**	**0**	**1**	**1**	**0**	**0**	**0**	**0**	**6**	**0.0**	**1**	**0**	**1**	**0**	**0**	**1**	**0**	**0**	**0**	**0**	**0**	**0**	**0**
	Fredericton Express	AHL	49	13	22	35	....	....	....	50	....	....	....	....	....	....	....	....	....	....	....	....	....	....	....	....	....	....
	NHL Totals		**704**	**191**	**310**	**501**	**165**	**224**	**389**	**661**	**40**	**0**	**19**	**1345**	**14.2**	**706**	**153**	**800**	**143**		**20**	**3**	**5**	**8**	**32**	**0**	**0**	**1**

Traded to **Hartford** by **Pittsburgh** for Hartford's 5th round choice (Bruce Racine) in 1985 Entry Draft, September 30, 1983. Traded to **Quebec** by **Hartford** for Wayne Babych, January 17, 1986.

● MALONEY, DAN

Dan Maloney LW – L. 6'2", 195 lbs. b: Barrie, Ont., 9/24/1950. Chicago's 1st choice, 14th overall, in 1970 Amateur Draft.

			REGULAR SEASON																		PLAYOFFS							
Season	Club	League	GP	G	A	Pts	AG	AA	APts	PIM	PP	SH	GW	S	%	TGF	PGF	TGA	PGA	+/–	GP	G	A	Pts	PIM	PP	SH	GW
1968-69	London Knights	OHA	53	12	28	40	....	....	....	62	....	....	....	....	....	....	....	....	....	....	6	2	1	3	16	....	....	....
1969-70	London Knights	OHA	54	31	35	66	....	....	....	232	....	....	....	....	....	....	....	....	....	....	....	....	....	....	....	....	....	....
1970-71	**Chicago Black Hawks**	**NHL**	**74**	**12**	**14**	**26**	**13**	**12**	**25**	**174**	**2**	**0**	**1**	**98**	**12.2**	**39**	**5**	**27**	**0**	**+7**	**10**	**0**	**1**	**1**	**8**	**0**	**0**	**0**
1971-72	Dallas Black Hawks	CHL	72	25	45	70	....	....	....	161	....	....	....	....	....	....	....	....	....	....	12	4	5	9	44	....	....	....
1972-73	**Chicago Black Hawks**	**NHL**	**57**	**13**	**17**	**30**	**13**	**14**	**27**	**63**	**5**	**0**	**4**	**104**	**12.5**	**45**	**10**	**25**	**1**	**+11**	....	....	....	....	....	....	....	....
	Los Angeles Kings	**NHL**	**14**	**4**	**7**	**11**	**4**	**6**	**10**	**18**	**0**	**0**	**1**	**35**	**11.4**	**18**	**4**	**8**	**0**	**+6**	....	....	....	....	....	....	....	....
1973-74	**Los Angeles Kings**	**NHL**	**65**	**15**	**17**	**32**	**15**	**15**	**30**	**113**	**5**	**0**	**5**	**157**	**9.6**	**55**	**11**	**38**	**0**	**+6**	**5**	**0**	**0**	**0**	**2**	**0**	**0**	**0**
1974-75	**Los Angeles Kings**	**NHL**	**80**	**27**	**39**	**66**	**25**	**31**	**56**	**165**	**3**	**0**	**2**	**227**	**11.9**	**91**	**11**	**53**	**2**	**+29**	**3**	**0**	**0**	**0**	**2**	**0**	**0**	**0**
1975-76	**Detroit Red Wings**	**NHL**	**77**	**27**	**39**	**66**	**25**	**31**	**56**	**203**	**6**	**2**	**3**	**254**	**10.6**	**94**	**28**	**84**	**18**	**0**	....	....	....	....	....	....	....	....
1976-77	**Detroit Red Wings**	**NHL**	**34**	**13**	**13**	**26**	**12**	**11**	**23**	**64**	**3**	**1**	**0**	**107**	**12.1**	**43**	**14**	**36**	**10**	**+3**	....	....	....	....	....	....	....	....
1977-78	**Detroit Red Wings**	**NHL**	**66**	**16**	**29**	**45**	**15**	**24**	**39**	**151**	**3**	**0**	**1**	**165**	**9.7**	**74**	**23**	**48**	**1**	**+4**	....	....	....	....	....	....	....	....
	Toronto Maple Leafs	**NHL**	**13**	**3**	**4**	**7**	**3**	**3**	**6**	**25**	**0**	**0**	**1**	**27**	**11.1**	**15**	**4**	**16**	**0**	**–5**	**13**	**1**	**3**	**4**	**17**	**1**	**0**	**0**
1978-79	**Toronto Maple Leafs**	**NHL**	**77**	**17**	**36**	**53**	**15**	**28**	**43**	**157**	**0**	**0**	**5**	**141**	**12.1**	**82**	**17**	**47**	**1**	**+19**	**6**	**3**	**3**	**6**	**2**	**1**	**0**	**1**
1979-80	**Toronto Maple Leafs**	**NHL**	**71**	**17**	**16**	**33**	**15**	**12**	**27**	**102**	**1**	**0**	**1**	**108**	**15.7**	**50**	**5**	**58**	**0**	**–13**	....	....	....	....	....	....	....	....
1980-81	**Toronto Maple Leafs**	**NHL**	**65**	**20**	**21**	**41**	**16**	**15**	**31**	**183**	**13**	**0**	**2**	**80**	**25.0**	**70**	**41**	**39**	**0**	**–10**	**3**	**0**	**0**	**0**	**4**	**0**	**0**	**0**
1981-82	**Toronto Maple Leafs**	**NHL**	**44**	**8**	**7**	**15**	**6**	**5**	**11**	**71**	**1**	**0**	**0**	**60**	**13.3**	**35**	**5**	**41**	**0**	**–11**	....	....	....	....	....	....	....	....
	NHL Totals		**737**	**192**	**259**	**451**	**177**	**207**	**384**	**1489**	**42**	**3**	**26**	**1563**	**12.3**	**711**	**178**	**520**	**33**		**40**	**4**	**7**	**11**	**35**	**2**	**0**	**1**

CHL First All-Star Team (1972)

Played in NHL All-Star Game (1976)

Traded to **LA Kings** by **Chicago** for Ralph Backstrom, February 26, 1973. Traded to **Detroit** by **LA Kings** with Terry Harper and LA Kings' 2nd round choice (later traded to Minnesota — Minnesota selected Jim Roberts) in 1976 Amateur Draft for Bart Crashley and the rights to Marcel Dionne, June 23, 1975. Traded to **Toronto** by **Detroit** with Detroit's 2nd round choice (Craig Muni) in 1980 Entry Draft for Errol Thompson and Toronto's 1st (Brent Peterson) and 2nd (Al Jenson) round choices in 1978 Amateur Draft and Toronto's 1st round choice (Mike Blaisdell) in 1980 Entry Draft, March 13, 1978.

● MALONEY, DAVE

Dave Maloney D – L. 6'1", 195 lbs. b: Kitchener, Ont., 7/31/1956. NY Rangers' 1st choice, 14th overall, in 1974 Amateur Draft.

Season	Club	League	GP	G	A	Pts	AG	AA	APts	PIM	PP	SH	GW	S	%	TGF	PGF	TGA	PGA	+/–	GP	G	A	Pts	PIM	PP	SH	GW
1971-72	St. Michael's Buzzers	Jr. B	STATISTICS NOT AVAILABLE																									
	Kitchener Rangers	OHA	1	0	0	0	....	....	....	0	....	....	....	....	....	....	....	....	....	....	....	....	....	....	....	....	....	....
1972-73	Kitchener Rangers	OHA	49	8	21	29	....	....	....	101	....	....	....	....	....	....	....	....	....	....	....	....	....	....	....	....	....	....
1973-74	Kitchener Rangers	OHA	69	15	53	68	....	....	....	109	....	....	....	....	....	....	....	....	....	....	....	....	....	....	....	....	....	....
1974-75	**New York Rangers**	**NHL**	**4**	**0**	**2**	**2**	**0**	**2**	**2**	**0**	**0**	**0**	**0**	**2**	**0.0**	**5**	**0**	**3**	**0**	**+2**	....	....	....	....	....	....	....	....
	Providence Reds	AHL	58	5	28	33	....	....	....	122	....	....	....	....	....	....	....	....	....	....	6	0	6	6	6	....	....	....
1975-76	**New York Rangers**	**NHL**	**21**	**1**	**3**	**4**	**1**	**2**	**3**	**66**	**0**	**0**	**0**	**40**	**2.5**	**18**	**3**	**29**	**7**	**–7**	....	....	....	....	....	....	....	....
	Providence Reds	AHL	26	5	17	22	....	....	....	81	....	....	....	....	....	....	....	....	....	....	....	....	....	....	....	....	....	....
1976-77	**New York Rangers**	**NHL**	**66**	**3**	**18**	**21**	**3**	**15**	**18**	**100**	**0**	**0**	**1**	**126**	**2.4**	**79**	**3**	**108**	**24**	**–8**	....	....	....	....	....	....	....	....
1977-78	**New York Rangers**	**NHL**	**56**	**2**	**19**	**21**	**2**	**15**	**17**	**63**	**0**	**0**	**0**	**71**	**2.8**	**68**	**3**	**65**	**18**	**+18**	**3**	**0**	**0**	**0**	**11**	**0**	**0**	**0**
1978-79	**New York Rangers**	**NHL**	**76**	**11**	**17**	**28**	**10**	**13**	**23**	**151**	**1**	**2**	**1**	**83**	**13.3**	**83**	**1**	**108**	**43**	**+17**	**17**	**3**	**4**	**7**	**45**	**0**	**1**	**0**
1979-80	**New York Rangers**	**NHL**	**77**	**12**	**25**	**37**	**11**	**19**	**30**	**186**	**3**	**0**	**0**	**102**	**11.8**	**97**	**15**	**91**	**19**	**+10**	**8**	**2**	**1**	**3**	**8**	**0**	**1**	**0**
1980-81	**New York Rangers**	**NHL**	**79**	**11**	**36**	**47**	**9**	**25**	**34**	**132**	**3**	**0**	**1**	**140**	**7.9**	**121**	**26**	**101**	**30**	**+24**	**2**	**0**	**2**	**2**	**9**	**0**	**0**	**0**
1981-82	**New York Rangers**	**NHL**	**64**	**13**	**36**	**49**	**10**	**24**	**34**	**105**	**6**	**1**	**3**	**107**	**12.1**	**101**	**22**	**106**	**29**	**+2**	**10**	**1**	**4**	**5**	**6**	**1**	**0**	**1**
1982-83	**New York Rangers**	**NHL**	**78**	**8**	**42**	**50**	**7**	**29**	**36**	**132**	**3**	**1**	**0**	**136**	**5.9**	**107**	**31**	**117**	**38**	**–3**	**7**	**1**	**6**	**7**	**10**	**0**	**0**	**0**
1983-84	**New York Rangers**	**NHL**	**68**	**7**	**26**	**33**	**6**	**18**	**24**	**168**	**2**	**0**	**1**	**76**	**9.2**	**90**	**20**	**75**	**16**	**+11**	**1**	**0**	**0**	**0**	**2**	**0**	**0**	**0**
1984-85	**New York Rangers**	**NHL**	**16**	**2**	**1**	**3**	**2**	**1**	**3**	**10**	**0**	**0**	**0**	**16**	**12.5**	**14**	**0**	**12**	**1**	**+3**	....	....	....	....	....	....	....	....
	Buffalo Sabres	**NHL**	**52**	**1**	**21**	**22**	**1**	**14**	**15**	**41**	**0**	**0**	**0**	**37**	**2.7**	**56**	**4**	**37**	**5**	**+20**	**1**	**0**	**0**	**0**	**0**	**0**	**0**	**0**
	NHL Totals		**657**	**71**	**246**	**317**	**62**	**177**	**239**	**1154**	**18**	**4**	**7**	**936**	**7.6**	**839**	**128**	**852**	**230**		**49**	**7**	**17**	**24**	**91**	**1**	**2**	**1**

OHA Second All-Star Team (1974)

Traded to **Buffalo** by **NY Rangers** with Chris Renaud for Steve Patrick and Jim Wiemer, December 8, 1984.

● MALONEY, DON

Don "Big Frame" Maloney LW – L. 6'1", 190 lbs. b: Lindsay, Ont., 9/5/1958. NY Rangers' 1st choice, 26th overall, in 1978 Amateur Draft.

Season	Club	League	GP	G	A	Pts	AG	AA	APts	PIM	PP	SH	GW	S	%	TGF	PGF	TGA	PGA	+/–	GP	G	A	Pts	PIM	PP	SH	GW
1974-75	Kitchener Rangers	OHA	5	1	3	4	....	....	....	0	....	....	....	....	....	....	....	....	....	....	....	....	....	....	....	....	....	....
1975-76	Kitchener Rangers	OHA	61	27	41	68	....	....	....	132	....	....	....	....	....	....	....	....	....	....	....	....	....	....	....	....	....	....
1976-77	Kitchener Rangers	OHA	38	22	34	56	....	....	....	126	....	....	....	....	....	....	....	....	....	....	....	....	....	....	....	....	....	....
1977-78	Kitchener Rangers	OHA	62	30	74	104	....	....	....	143	....	....	....	....	....	....	....	....	....	....	9	4	9	13	40	....	....	....
1978-79	**New York Rangers**	**NHL**	**28**	**9**	**17**	**26**	**8**	**13**	**21**	**39**	**3**	**0**	**0**	**39**	**23.1**	**36**	**11**	**22**	**1**	**+4**	**18**	**7**	***13**	**20**	**19**	**0**	**0**	**1**
	New Haven Nighthawks	AHL	38	18	26	44	....	....	....	62	....	....	....	....	....	....	....	....	....	....	....	....	....	....	....	....	....	....
1979-80	**New York Rangers**	**NHL**	**79**	**25**	**48**	**73**	**23**	**37**	**60**	**97**	**6**	**1**	**3**	**123**	**20.3**	**97**	**33**	**84**	**5**	**–15**	**9**	**0**	**4**	**4**	**10**	**0**	**0**	**0**
1980-81	**New York Rangers**	**NHL**	**61**	**29**	**23**	**52**	**24**	**16**	**40**	**99**	**7**	**5**	**9**	**124**	**23.4**	**89**	**23**	**60**	**11**	**+17**	**13**	**1**	**6**	**7**	**13**	**1**	**0**	**0**
1981-82	**New York Rangers**	**NHL**	**54**	**22**	**36**	**58**	**17**	**24**	**41**	**73**	**6**	**1**	**5**	**99**	**22.2**	**88**	**20**	**71**	**12**	**+9**	**10**	**5**	**5**	**10**	**10**	**2**	**0**	**0**
1982-83	**New York Rangers**	**NHL**	**78**	**29**	**40**	**69**	**24**	**28**	**52**	**88**	**14**	**1**	**2**	**133**	**21.8**	**105**	**39**	**83**	**12**	**–5**	**5**	**0**	**1**	**1**	**0**	**0**	**0**	**0**
1983-84	**New York Rangers**	**NHL**	**79**	**24**	**42**	**66**	**19**	**28**	**47**	**62**	**5**	**3**	**5**	**129**	**18.6**	**90**	**30**	**87**	**22**	**–5**	**5**	**1**	**4**	**5**	**0**	**0**	**0**	**0**
1984-85	**New York Rangers**	**NHL**	**37**	**11**	**16**	**27**	**9**	**11**	**20**	**32**	**5**	**0**	**0**	**56**	**19.6**	**41**	**13**	**45**	**8**	**–9**	**3**	**4**	**0**	**4**	**2**	**2**	**0**	**0**
	Canada	WEC-A	8	1	1	2	....	....	....	....	....	....	....	....	....	....	....	....	....	....	....	....	....	....	....	....	....	....
1985-86	**New York Rangers**	**NHL**	**68**	**11**	**17**	**28**	**9**	**11**	**20**	**56**	**0**	**0**	**1**	**89**	**12.4**	**55**	**10**	**50**	**23**	**+18**	**16**	**2**	**1**	**3**	**31**	**0**	**0**	**0**
1986-87	**New York Rangers**	**NHL**	**72**	**19**	**38**	**57**	**16**	**28**	**44**	**117**	**3**	**3**	**0**	**130**	**14.6**	**83**	**13**	**88**	**25**	**+7**	**6**	**2**	**1**	**3**	**6**	**0**	**0**	**0**
1987-88	**New York Rangers**	**NHL**	**66**	**12**	**21**	**33**	**10**	**15**	**25**	**60**	**1**	**0**	**2**	**88**	**13.6**	**46**	**1**	**59**	**26**	**+12**	....	....	....	....	....	....	....	....
1988-89	**New York Rangers**	**NHL**	**31**	**4**	**9**	**13**	**3**	**6**	**9**	**16**	**0**	**0**	**0**	**38**	**10.5**	**22**	**0**	**36**	**16**	**+2**	....	....	....	....	....	....	....	....
	Hartford Whalers	**NHL**	**21**	**3**	**11**	**14**	**3**	**8**	**11**	**23**	**1**	**0**	**1**	**34**	**8.8**	**18**	**5**	**13**	**1**	**+1**	**4**	**0**	**0**	**0**	**8**	**0**	**0**	**0**
1989-90	**New York Islanders**	**NHL**	**79**	**16**	**27**	**43**	**14**	**19**	**33**	**47**	**0**	**1**	**2**	**113**	**14.2**	**61**	**4**	**73**	**22**	**+6**	**5**	**0**	**0**	**0**	**2**	**0**	**0**	**0**
1990-91	**New York Islanders**	**NHL**	**12**	**0**	**5**	**5**	**0**	**4**	**4**	**6**	**0**	**0**	**0**	**10**	**0.0**	**5**	**0**	**10**	**2**	**–3**	....	....	....	....	....	....	....	....
	NHL Totals		**765**	**214**	**350**	**564**	**179**	**248**	**427**	**815**	**51**	**15**	**30**	**1205**	**17.8**	**836**	**202**	**781**	**186**		**94**	**22**	**35**	**57**	**101**	**5**	**0**	**1**

Played in NHL All-Star Game (1983, 1984)

Traded to **Hartford** by **NY Rangers** with Brian Lawton and Norm MacIver for Carey Wilson and Hartford's 5th round choice (Lubos Rob) in 1990 Entry Draft, December 26, 1988. Signed as a free agent by **NY Islanders**, August 25, 1989.

● MALTAIS, STEVE

Steve Maltais LW – L. 6'2", 205 lbs. b: Arvida, Que., 1/25/1969. Washington's 2nd choice, 57th overall, in 1987 Entry Draft.

Season	Club	League	GP	G	A	Pts	AG	AA	APts	PIM	PP	SH	GW	S	%	TGF	PGF	TGA	PGA	+/–	GP	G	A	Pts	PIM	PP	SH	GW
1986-87	Cornwall Royals	OHL	65	32	12	44	....	....	....	29	....	....	....	....	....	....	....	....	....	....	5	0	0	0	2	....	....	....
1987-88	Cornwall Royals	OHL	59	39	46	85	....	....	....	30	....	....	....	....	....	....	....	....	....	....	11	9	6	15	33	....	....	....
1988-89	Cornwall Royals	OHL	58	53	70	123	....	....	....	67	....	....	....	....	....	....	....	....	....	....	18	14	16	30	16	....	....	....
	Fort Wayne Komets	IHL	....	....	....	....	....	....	....	....	....	....	....	....	....	....	....	....	....	....	4	2	1	3	0	....	....	....
1989-90	**Washington Capitals**	**NHL**	**8**	**0**	**0**	**0**	**0**	**0**	**0**	**2**	**0**	**0**	**0**	**11**	**0.0**	**3**	**0**	**5**	**0**	**–2**	**1**	**0**	**0**	**0**	**0**	**0**	**0**	**0**
	Baltimore Skipjacks	AHL	67	29	37	66	....	....	....	54	....	....	....	....	....	....	....	....	....	....	12	6	10	16	6	....	....	....
1990-91	**Washington Capitals**	**NHL**	**7**	**0**	**0**	**0**	**0**	**0**	**0**	**2**	**0**	**0**	**0**	**3**	**0.0**	**1**	**0**	**2**	**0**	**–1**	....	....	....	....	....	....	....	....
	Baltimore Skipjacks	AHL	73	36	43	79	....	....	....	97	....	....	....	....	....	....	....	....	....	....	6	1	4	5	10	....	....	....
1991-92	**Minnesota North Stars**	**NHL**	**12**	**2**	**1**	**3**	**2**	**1**	**3**	**2**	**0**	**0**	**0**	**6**	**33.3**	**5**	**0**	**7**	**1**	**–1**	....	....	....	....	....	....	....	....
	Kalamazoo Wings	IHL	48	25	31	56	....	....	....	51	....	....	....	....	....	....	....	....	....	....	....	....	....	....	....	....	....	....
	Halifax Citadels	AHL	10	3	3	6	....	....	....	0	....	....	....	....	....	....	....	....	....	....	....	....	....	....	....	....	....	....
1992-93	**Tampa Bay Lightning**	**NHL**	**63**	**7**	**13**	**20**	**6**	**9**	**15**	**35**	**4**	**0**	**1**	**96**	**7.3**	**46**	**14**	**59**	**7**	**–20**	....	....	....	....	....	....	....	....
	Atlanta Knights	IHL	16	14	10	24	....	....	....	22	....	....	....	....	....	....	....	....	....	....	....	....	....	....	....	....	....	....
1993-94	**Detroit Red Wings**	**NHL**	**4**	**0**	**1**	**1**	**0**	**1**	**1**	**0**	**0**	**0**	**0**	**2**	**0.0**	**1**	**0**	**2**	**0**	**–1**	....	....	....	....	....	....	....	....
	Adirondack Red Wings	AHL	73	35	49	84	....	....	....	79	....	....	....	....	....	....	....	....	....	....	12	5	11	16	14	....	....	....
1994-95	Chicago Wolves	IHL	79	*57	40	97	....	....	....	145	....	....	....	....	....	....	....	....	....	....	3	1	1	2	0	....	....	....
1995-96	Chicago Wolves	IHL	81	56	66	122	....	....	....	161	....	....	....	....	....	....	....	....	....	....	9	7	7	14	20	....	....	....
1996-97	Chicago Wolves	IHL	81	*60	54	114	....	....	....	62	....	....	....	....	....	....	....	....	....	....	4	2	0	2	4	....	....	....
1997-98	Chicago Wolves	IHL	82	46	57	103	....	....	....	120	....	....	....	....	....	....	....	....	....	....	22	8	11	19	28	....	....	....
	NHL Totals		**94**	**9**	**15**	**24**	**8**	**11**	**19**	**41**	**4**	**0**	**1**	**118**	**7.6**	**56**	**14**	**75**	**8**		**1**	**0**	**0**	**0**	**0**	**0**	**0**	**0**

OHL Second All-Star Team (1989) • IHL First All-Star Team (1995) • IHL Second All-Star Team (1996, 1997)

Traded to **Minnesota** by **Washington** with Trent Klatt for Shawn Chambers, June 21, 1991. Traded to **Quebec** by **Minnesota** for Kip Miller, March 8, 1992. Claimed by **Tampa Bay** from **Quebec** in Expansion Draft, June 18, 1992. Traded to **Detroit** by **Tampa Bay** for Dennis Vial, June 8, 1993.

• MALTBY, KIRK

Kirk Maltby RW – R. 6', 180 lbs. b: Guelph, Ont., 12/22/1972. Edmonton's 4th choice, 65th overall, in 1992 Entry Draft.

Season	Club	League	GP	G	A	Pts	AG	AA	APts	PIM	PP	SH	GW	S	%	TGF	PGF	TGA	PGA	+/-	Playoffs GP	G	A	Pts	PIM	PP	SH	GW
1989-90	Owen Sound Platers	OHL	61	12	15	27	....	....	....	90	....	....	....	....	....	....	....	....	....	....	12	1	6	7	15	....	....	....
1990-91	Owen Sound Platers	OHL	66	34	32	66	....	....	....	100	....	....	....	....	....	....	....	....	....	....	....	....	....	....	....	....	....	....
1991-92	Owen Sound Platers	OHL	66	50	41	91	....	....	....	99	....	....	....	....	....	....	....	....	....	....	5	3	3	6	18	....	....	....
1992-93	Cape Breton Oilers	AHL	73	22	23	45	....	....	....	130	....	....	....	....	....	....	....	....	....	....	16	3	3	6	45	....	....	....
1993-94	**Edmonton Oilers**	**NHL**	**68**	**11**	**8**	**19**	**10**	**6**	**16**	**74**	**0**	**1**	**1**	**89**	**12.4**	**37**	**2**	**55**	**18**	**–2**	....	....	....	....	....	....	....	....
1994-95	**Edmonton Oilers**	**NHL**	**47**	**8**	**3**	**11**	**14**	**4**	**18**	**49**	**0**	**2**	**1**	**73**	**11.0**	**24**	**6**	**44**	**15**	**–11**	....	....	....	....	....	....	....	....
1995-96	**Edmonton Oilers**	**NHL**	**49**	**2**	**6**	**8**	**2**	**5**	**7**	**61**	**0**	**0**	**1**	**51**	**3.9**	**14**	**4**	**43**	**17**	**–16**	....	....	....	....	....	....	....	....
	Cape Breton Oilers	AHL	4	1	2	3	....	....	....	6	....	....	....	....	....	....	....	....	....	....	....	....	....	....	....	....	....	....
	Detroit Red Wings	**NHL**	**6**	**1**	**0**	**1**	**1**	**0**	**1**	**6**	**0**	**0**	**0**	**4**	**25.0**	**4**	**1**	**3**	**0**	**0**	**8**	**0**	**1**	**1**	**4**	**0**	**0**	**0**
1996-97	**Detroit Red Wings**	**NHL**	**66**	**3**	**5**	**8**	**3**	**4**	**7**	**75**	**0**	**0**	**0**	**62**	**4.8**	**18**	**2**	**21**	**8**	**+3**	**20**	**5**	**2**	**7**	**24**	**0**	**1**	**1**
1997-98	**Detroit Red Wings**	**NHL**	**65**	**14**	**9**	**23**	**16**	**9**	**25**	**89**	**2**	**1**	**3**	**106**	**13.2**	**37**	**2**	**37**	**13**	**+11**	**22**	**3**	**1**	**4**	**30**	**0**	**1**	**0**
	NHL Totals		**301**	**39**	**31**	**70**	**46**	**28**	**74**	**354**	**2**	**4**	**6**	**385**	**10.1**	**134**	**17**	**203**	**71**		**50**	**8**	**4**	**12**	**58**	**0**	**2**	**1**

Traded to **Detroit** by **Edmonton** for Dan McGillis, March 20, 1996.

• MALUTA, RAY

Ray Maluta D. 5'8", 173 lbs. b: Flin Flon, Man., 7/24/1954. Boston's 8th choice, 126th overall, in 1974 Amateur Draft.

Season	Club	League	GP	G	A	Pts	AG	AA	APts	PIM	PP	SH	GW	S	%	TGF	PGF	TGA	PGA	+/-	Playoffs GP	G	A	Pts	PIM	PP	SH	GW
1970-71	Flin Flon Bombers	WCJHL	9	0	2	2	....	....	....	6	....	....	....	....	....	....	....	....	....	....	....	....	....	....	....	....	....	....
1971-72	Flin Flon Bombers	WCJHL	64	8	32	40	....	....	....	142	....	....	....	....	....	....	....	....	....	....	....	....	....	....	....	....	....	....
1972-73	Flin Flon Bombers	WCJHL	65	11	18	29	....	....	....	43	....	....	....	....	....	....	....	....	....	....	....	....	....	....	....	....	....	....
1973-74	Flin Flon Bombers	WCJHL	68	40	57	97	....	....	....	151	....	....	....	....	....	....	....	....	....	....	....	....	....	....	....	....	....	....
1974-75	Rochester Americans	AHL	75	7	12	19	....	....	....	117	....	....	....	....	....	....	....	....	....	....	12	3	0	3	42	....	....	....
1975-76	**Boston Bruins**	**NHL**	**2**	**0**	**0**	**0**	**0**	**0**	**0**	**2**	**0**	**0**	**0**	**2**	**0.0**	**1**	**0**	**4**	**0**	**–3**	**2**	**0**	**0**	**0**	**0**	**0**	**0**	**0**
	Rochester Americans	AHL	74	3	43	46	....	....	....	170	....	....	....	....	....	....	....	....	....	....	7	0	2	2	6	....	....	....
1976-77	**Boston Bruins**	**NHL**	**23**	**2**	**3**	**5**	**2**	**2**	**4**	**4**	**0**	**0**	**0**	**24**	**8.3**	**17**	**3**	**10**	**0**	**+4**	....	....	....	....	....	....	....	....
	Rochester Americans	AHL	51	2	24	26	....	....	....	138	....	....	....	....	....	....	....	....	....	....	12	0	5	5	16	....	....	....
1977-78	Rochester Americans	AHL	79	9	32	41	....	....	....	125	....	....	....	....	....	....	....	....	....	....	6	1	3	4	16	....	....	....
1978-79	Rochester Americans	AHL	35	4	14	18	....	....	....	58	....	....	....	....	....	....	....	....	....	....	....	....	....	....	....	....	....	....
1979-80	Hasalzburg	Austria	33	15	55	60	....	....	....	60	....	....	....	....	....	....	....	....	....	....	....	....	....	....	....	....	....	....
	NHL Totals		**25**	**2**	**3**	**5**	**2**	**2**	**4**	**6**	**0**	**0**	**0**	**26**	**7.7**	**18**	**3**	**14**	**0**		**2**	**0**	**0**	**0**	**0**	**0**	**0**	**0**

• MANDERVILLE, KENT

Kent Manderville LW – L. 6'3", 210 lbs. b: Edmonton, Alta., 4/12/1971. Calgary's 1st choice, 24th overall, in 1989 Entry Draft.

Season	Club	League	GP	G	A	Pts	AG	AA	APts	PIM	PP	SH	GW	S	%	TGF	PGF	TGA	PGA	+/-	Playoffs GP	G	A	Pts	PIM	PP	SH	GW
1988-89	Notre Dame Hounds	SJHL	58	39	36	75	....	....	....	165	....	....	....	....	....	....	....	....	....	....	....	....	....	....	....	....	....	....
1989-90	Cornell University	ECAC	26	11	15	26	....	....	....	28	....	....	....	....	....	....	....	....	....	....	....	....	....	....	....	....	....	....
	Canada	WJC-A	7	1	2	3	....	....	....	0	....	....	....	....	....	....	....	....	....	....	....	....	....	....	....	....	....	....
1990-91	Cornell University	ECAC	28	17	14	31	....	....	....	60	....	....	....	....	....	....	....	....	....	....	....	....	....	....	....	....	....	....
	Canada	Nat-Team	3	1	2	3	....	....	....	0	....	....	....	....	....	....	....	....	....	....	....	....	....	....	....	....	....	....
	Canada	WJC-A	7	1	6	7	....	....	....	0	....	....	....	....	....	....	....	....	....	....	....	....	....	....	....	....	....	....
1991-92	Canada	Nat-Team	63	16	24	40	....	....	....	78	....	....	....	....	....	....	....	....	....	....	....	....	....	....	....	....	....	....
	Canada	Olympics	8	1	2	3	....	....	....	0	....	....	....	....	....	....	....	....	....	....	....	....	....	....	....	....	....	....
	Toronto Maple Leafs	**NHL**	**15**	**0**	**4**	**4**	**0**	**3**	**3**	**0**	**0**	**0**	**0**	**14**	**0.0**	**5**	**0**	**5**	**1**	**+1**	....	....	....	....	....	....	....	....
	St. John's Maple Leafs	AHL	....	....	....	....	....	....	....	....	....	....	....	....	....	....	....	....	....	....	12	5	9	14	14	....	....	....
1992-93	**Toronto Maple Leafs**	**NHL**	**18**	**1**	**1**	**2**	**1**	**1**	**2**	**17**	**0**	**0**	**1**	**15**	**6.7**	**2**	**0**	**19**	**8**	**–9**	**18**	**1**	**0**	**1**	**8**	**0**	**0**	**0**
	St. John's Maple Leafs	AHL	56	19	28	47	....	....	....	86	....	....	....	....	....	....	....	....	....	....	2	0	2	2	0	....	....	....
1993-94	**Toronto Maple Leafs**	**NHL**	**67**	**7**	**9**	**16**	**7**	**7**	**14**	**63**	**0**	**0**	**1**	**81**	**8.6**	**20**	**0**	**29**	**14**	**+5**	**12**	**1**	**0**	**1**	**4**	**0**	**1**	**0**
1994-95	**Toronto Maple Leafs**	**NHL**	**36**	**0**	**1**	**1**	**0**	**1**	**1**	**22**	**0**	**0**	**0**	**43**	**0.0**	**7**	**0**	**15**	**6**	**–2**	**7**	**0**	**0**	**0**	**6**	**0**	**0**	**0**
1995-96	**Edmonton Oilers**	**NHL**	**37**	**3**	**5**	**8**	**3**	**4**	**7**	**38**	**0**	**2**	**0**	**63**	**4.8**	**11**	**1**	**22**	**7**	**–5**	....	....	....	....	....	....	....	....
	St. John's Maple Leafs	AHL	27	16	12	28	....	....	....	26	....	....	....	....	....	....	....	....	....	....	....	....	....	....	....	....	....	....
1996-97	**Hartford Whalers**	**NHL**	**44**	**6**	**5**	**11**	**6**	**4**	**10**	**18**	**0**	**0**	**1**	**51**	**11.8**	**19**	**1**	**21**	**6**	**+3**	....	....	....	....	....	....	....	....
	Springfield Falcons	AHL	23	5	20	25	....	....	....	18	....	....	....	....	....	....	....	....	....	....	....	....	....	....	....	....	....	....
1997-98	**Carolina Hurricanes**	**NHL**	**77**	**4**	**4**	**8**	**5**	**4**	**9**	**31**	**0**	**0**	**0**	**80**	**5.0**	**13**	**0**	**35**	**16**	**6**	....	....	....	....	....	....	....	....
	NHL Totals		**294**	**21**	**29**	**50**	**22**	**24**	**46**	**189**	**0**	**2**	**3**	**347**	**6.1**	**77**	**2**	**146**	**58**		**37**	**2**	**0**	**2**	**18**	**0**	**1**	**0**

Traded to **Toronto** by **Calgary** with Doug Gilmour, Jamie Macoun, Rick Wamsley and Ric Nattress for Gary Leeman, Alexander Godynyuk, Jeff Reese, Michel Petit and Craig Berube, January 2, 1992. Traded to **Edmonton** by **Toronto** for Peter White and Edmonton's 4th round choice (Jason Sessa) in 1996 Entry Draft, December 4, 1995. Signed as a free agent by **Hartford**, October 2, 1996. Transferred to **Carolina** after **Hartford** franchise relocated, June 25, 1997.

• MANDICH, DAN

Dan Mandich D – R. 6'3", 205 lbs. b: Brantford, Ont., 6/12/1960.

Season	Club	League	GP	G	A	Pts	AG	AA	APts	PIM	PP	SH	GW	S	%	TGF	PGF	TGA	PGA	+/-	Playoffs GP	G	A	Pts	PIM	PP	SH	GW
1978-79	Ohio State University	CCHA	38	7	18	25	....	....	....	126	....	....	....	....	....	....	....	....	....	....	....	....	....	....	....	....	....	....
1979-80	Ohio State University	CCHA	35	10	17	27	....	....	....	146	....	....	....	....	....	....	....	....	....	....	....	....	....	....	....	....	....	....
1980-81	Ohio State University	CCHA	39	20	26	46	....	....	....	188	....	....	....	....	....	....	....	....	....	....	....	....	....	....	....	....	....	....
1981-82	Ohio State University	CCHA	33	14	26	40	....	....	....	157	....	....	....	....	....	....	....	....	....	....	....	....	....	....	....	....	....	....
	Nashville South Stars	CHL	16	2	5	7	....	....	....	24	....	....	....	....	....	....	....	....	....	....	3	0	0	0	26	....	....	....
1982-83	**Minnesota North Stars**	**NHL**	**67**	**3**	**4**	**7**	**2**	**3**	**5**	**169**	**0**	**0**	**1**	**49**	**6.1**	**48**	**1**	**57**	**10**	**0**	**7**	**0**	**0**	**0**	**2**	**0**	**0**	**0**
	Birmingham South Stars	CHL	6	0	4	4	....	....	....	18	....	....	....	....	....	....	....	....	....	....	....	....	....	....	....	....	....	....
1983-84	**Minnesota North Stars**	**NHL**	**31**	**2**	**7**	**9**	**2**	**5**	**7**	**77**	**0**	**0**	**0**	**29**	**6.9**	**23**	**1**	**33**	**5**	**–6**	....	....	....	....	....	....	....	....
	Salt Lake Golden Eagles	CHL	3	2	2	4	....	....	....	13	....	....	....	....	....	....	....	....	....	....	....	....	....	....	....	....	....	....
1984-85	**Minnesota North Stars**	**NHL**	**10**	**0**	**0**	**0**	**0**	**0**	**0**	**32**	**0**	**0**	**0**	**4**	**0.0**	**1**	**0**	**7**	**3**	**–3**	....	....	....	....	....	....	....	....
1985-86	**Minnesota North Stars**	**NHL**	**3**	**0**	**0**	**0**	**0**	**0**	**0**	**25**	**0**	**0**	**0**	**0**	**0.0**	**0**	**0**	**0**	**0**	**0**	....	....	....	....	....	....	....	....
	Springfield Indians	AHL	3	0	0	0	....	....	....	4	....	....	....	....	....	....	....	....	....	....	....	....	....	....	....	....	....	....
	NHL Totals		**111**	**5**	**11**	**16**	**4**	**8**	**12**	**303**	**0**	**0**	**1**	**82**	**6.1**	**72**	**2**	**97**	**18**		**7**	**0**	**0**	**0**	**2**	**0**	**0**	**0**

CCHA First All-Star Team (1981)

Signed as a free agent by **Minnesota**, July 19, 1982.

• MANERY, KRIS

Kris Manery C/RW – R. 6', 185 lbs. b: Leamington, Ont., 9/24/1954.

Season	Club	League	GP	G	A	Pts	AG	AA	APts	PIM	PP	SH	GW	S	%	TGF	PGF	TGA	PGA	+/-	Playoffs GP	G	A	Pts	PIM	PP	SH	GW
1973-74	University of Michigan	WCHA	36	14	14	28	....	....	....	36	....	....	....	....	....	....	....	....	....	....	....	....	....	....	....	....	....	....
1974-75	University of Michigan	WCHA	40	22	24	46	....	....	....	44	....	....	....	....	....	....	....	....	....	....	....	....	....	....	....	....	....	....
1975-76	University of Michigan	WCHA	42	37	24	61	....	....	....	42	....	....	....	....	....	....	....	....	....	....	....	....	....	....	....	....	....	....
1976-77	University of Michigan	WCHA	45	38	45	73	....	....	....	51	....	....	....	....	....	....	....	....	....	....	....	....	....	....	....	....	....	....
1977-78	**Cleveland Barons**	**NHL**	**78**	**22**	**27**	**49**	**21**	**22**	**43**	**14**	**7**	**0**	**1**	**188**	**11.7**	**80**	**16**	**87**	**8**	**–15**	....	....	....	....	....	....	....	....
1978-79	**Minnesota North Stars**	**NHL**	**60**	**17**	**19**	**36**	**15**	**14**	**29**	**16**	**3**	**0**	**1**	**126**	**13.5**	**58**	**17**	**59**	**5**	**–13**	....	....	....	....	....	....	....	....
	Oklahoma City Stars	CHL	13	4	4	8	....	....	....	6	....	....	....	....	....	....	....	....	....	....	....	....	....	....	....	....	....	....
1979-80	**Minnesota North Stars**	**NHL**	**28**	**3**	**4**	**7**	**3**	**3**	**6**	**16**	**0**	**0**	**0**	**40**	**7.5**	**17**	**1**	**22**	**1**	**–5**	....	....	....	....	....	....	....	....
	Vancouver Canucks	**NHL**	**21**	**2**	**1**	**3**	**2**	**1**	**3**	**15**	**0**	**0**	**0**	**34**	**5.9**	**8**	**0**	**16**	**2**	**–6**	....	....	....	....	....	....	....	....
	Winnipeg Jets	**NHL**	**16**	**6**	**4**	**10**	**5**	**3**	**8**	**6**	**4**	**0**	**0**	**36**	**16.7**	**18**	**10**	**16**	**0**	**–8**	....	....	....	....	....	....	....	....
1980-81	**Winnipeg Jets**	**NHL**	**47**	**13**	**9**	**22**	**11**	**6**	**17**	**24**	**4**	**1**	**0**	**82**	**15.9**	**35**	**13**	**41**	**4**	**–15**	....	....	....	....	....	....	....	....
	Tulsa Oilers	CHL	22	19	13	32	....	....	....	12	....	....	....	....	....	....	....	....	....	....	8	5	3	8	14	....	....	....
1981-82	Tulsa Oilers	CHL	80	54	35	89	....	....	....	60	....	....	....	....	....	....	....	....	....	....	3	0	0	0	2	....	....	....
	NHL Totals		**250**	**63**	**64**	**127**	**57**	**49**	**106**	**91**	**18**	**1**	**2**	**506**	**12.5**	**216**	**57**	**241**	**20**		....	....	....	....	....	....	....	....

WCHA First All-Star Team (1977) • CHL Second All-Star Team (1982)

Signed as a free agent by **Cleveland**, October, 1977. Placed on **Minnesota** Reserve List after **Minnesota-Cleveland** Dispersal Draft, June 15, 1978. Traded to **Vancouver** by **Minnesota** for Vancouver's 2nd round choice (later traded to Montreal — Montreal selected Kent Carlson) in 1982 Entry Draft, January 4, 1980. Claimed on waivers by **Winnipeg** from **Vancouver**, February 27, 1980.

• MANERY, RANDY

Randy Manery D – R. 6', 185 lbs. b: Leamington, Ont., 1/10/1949.

Season	Club	League	GP	G	A	Pts	AG	AA	APts	PIM	PP	SH	GW	S	%	TGF	PGF	TGA	PGA	+/-	Playoffs GP	G	A	Pts	PIM	PP	SH	GW
1966-67	Hamilton Red Wings	OHA	47	2	3	5	....	....	....	28	....	....	....	....	....	....	....	....	....	....	17	2	2	4	18	....	....	....
1967-68	Hamilton Red Wings	OHA	53	3	20	23	....	....	....	65	....	....	....	....	....	....	....	....	....	....	11	0	7	7	28	....	....	....
1968-69	Hamilton Red Wings	OHA	54	4	25	29	....	....	....	100	....	....	....	....	....	....	....	....	....	....	5	1	1	2	6	....	....	....
1969-70	Fort Worth Wings	CHL	67	1	15	16	....	....	....	46	....	....	....	....	....	....	....	....	....	....	7	0	0	0	2	....	....	....
1970-71	**Detroit Red Wings**	**NHL**	**2**	**0**	**0**	**0**	**0**	**0**	**0**	**0**	**0**	**0**	**0**	**3**	**0.0**	**0**	**0**	**1**	**0**	**–1**	....	....	....	....	....	....	....	....
	Fort Worth Wings	CHL	72	16	32	48	....	....	....	53	....	....	....	....	....	....	....	....	....	....	4	0	1	1	4	....	....	....

Season	Club	League	GP	G	A	Pts	AG	AA	APts	PIM	PP	SH	GW	S	%	TGF	PGF	TGA	PGA	+/–	GP	G	A	Pts	PIM	PP	SH	GW
			REGULAR SEASON																		PLAYOFFS							
1971-72	**Detroit Red Wings**	**NHL**	**1**	**0**	**0**	**0**	**0**	**0**	**0**	**0**	**0**	**0**	**0**	**0**	**0.0**	**0**	**0**	**0**	**0**	**0**	....	....	....	....	....	....	....	....
	Fort Worth Wings	CHL	72	6	35	41	....	....	....	89	....	....	....	....	....	....	....	....	....	....	7	1	3	4	6	....	....	....
1972-73	**Atlanta Flames**	**NHL**	**78**	**5**	**30**	**35**	**5**	**25**	**30**	**44**	**2**	**1**	**0**	**159**	**3.1**	**95**	**30**	**96**	**29**	**–2**	....	....	....	....	....	....	....	....
1973-74	**Atlanta Flames**	**NHL**	**78**	**8**	**29**	**37**	**8**	**25**	**33**	**75**	**2**	**0**	**1**	**189**	**4.2**	**121**	**30**	**105**	**29**	**+15**	**4**	**0**	**2**	**2**	**4**	**0**	**0**	**0**
1974-75	**Atlanta Flames**	**NHL**	**68**	**5**	**27**	**32**	**5**	**21**	**26**	**48**	**3**	**0**	**0**	**118**	**4.2**	**80**	**17**	**66**	**21**	**+18**	....	....	....	....	....	....	....	....
1975-76	**Atlanta Flames**	**NHL**	**80**	**7**	**32**	**39**	**7**	**25**	**32**	**42**	**3**	**0**	**3**	**139**	**5.0**	**95**	**27**	**71**	**5**	**+2**	**2**	**0**	**0**	**0**	**0**	**0**	**0**	**0**
1976-77	**Atlanta Flames**	**NHL**	**73**	**5**	**24**	**29**	**5**	**19**	**24**	**33**	**0**	**0**	**2**	**108**	**4.6**	**84**	**14**	**82**	**10**	**–2**	**3**	**0**	**0**	**0**	**0**	**0**	**0**	**0**
1977-78	**Los Angeles Kings**	**NHL**	**79**	**6**	**27**	**33**	**6**	**22**	**28**	**61**	**3**	**0**	**0**	**173**	**3.5**	**100**	**21**	**107**	**16**	**–12**	**2**	**0**	**0**	**0**	**2**	**0**	**0**	**0**
1978-79	**Los Angeles Kings**	**NHL**	**71**	**8**	**27**	**35**	**7**	**21**	**28**	**64**	**2**	**0**	**2**	**116**	**6.9**	**118**	**36**	**100**	**24**	**+6**	**2**	**0**	**0**	**0**	**6**	**0**	**0**	**0**
1979-80	**Los Angeles Kings**	**NHL**	**52**	**6**	**10**	**16**	**5**	**8**	**13**	**48**	**3**	**0**	**0**	**73**	**8.2**	**54**	**20**	**62**	**15**	**–13**	....	....	....	....	....	....	....	....
	NHL Totals		**582**	**50**	**206**	**256**	**48**	**166**	**214**	**415**	**18**	**1**	**8**	**1078**	**4.6**	**747**	**195**	**690**	**149**		**13**	**0**	**2**	**2**	**12**	**0**	**0**	**0**

OHA First All-Star Team (1969) • CHL Second All-Star Team (1972)

Played in NHL All-Star Game (1973)

Claimed by **Atlanta** from **Detroit** in Expansion Draft, June 6, 1972. Traded to **LA Kings** by **Atlanta** for Ab DeMarco, May 23, 1977.

• MANN, CAMERON

Cameron Mann RW – R. 6′, 194 lbs. b: Thompson, Man., 4/20/1977. Boston's 5th choice, 99th overall, in 1995 Entry Draft.

Season	Club	League	GP	G	A	Pts	AG	AA	APts	PIM	PP	SH	GW	S	%	TGF	PGF	TGA	PGA	+/–	GP	G	A	Pts	PIM	PP	SH	GW
1993-94	Peterborough Petes	OHL	49	8	17	25	....	....	....	18	....	....	....	....	....	....	....	....	....	....	7	1	1	2	2	....	....	....
1994-95	Peterborough Petes	OHL	64	19	24	43	....	....	....	40	....	....	....	....	....	....	....	....	....	....	11	3	8	11	4	....	....	....
1995-96	Peterborough Petes	OHL	66	42	60	102	....	....	....	108	....	....	....	....	....	....	....	....	....	....	24	*27	16	*43	33	....	....	....
1996-97	Peterborough Petes	OHL	51	33	50	83	....	....	....	91	....	....	....	....	....	....	....	....	....	....	11	10	18	28	16	....	....	....
	Canada	WJC-A	7	3	4	7	....	....	....	10	....	....	....	....	....	....	....	....	....	....	....	....	....	....	....	....	....	....
1997-98	**Boston Bruins**	**NHL**	**9**	**0**	**1**	**1**	**0**	**1**	**1**	**4**	**0**	**0**	**0**	**6**	**0.0**	**3**	**1**	**1**	**0**	**+1**	....	....	....	....	....	....	....	....
	Providence Bruins	AHL	71	21	26	47	....	....	....	99	....	....	....	....	....	....	....	....	....	....	....	....	....	....	....	....	....	....
	NHL Totals		**9**	**0**	**1**	**1**	**0**	**1**	**1**	**4**	**0**	**0**	**0**	**6**	**0.0**	**3**	**1**	**1**	**0**		....	....	....	....	....	....	....	....

OHL First All-Star Team (1996, 1997) • Memorial Cup All-Star Team (1996) • Won Stafford Smythe Memorial Trophy (Memorial Cup Tournament MVP) (1996)

• MANN, JIMMY

Jimmy Mann RW – R. 6′, 205 lbs. b: Montreal, Que., 4/17/1959. Winnipeg's 1st choice, 19th overall, in 1979 Entry Draft.

Season	Club	League	GP	G	A	Pts	AG	AA	APts	PIM	PP	SH	GW	S	%	TGF	PGF	TGA	PGA	+/–	GP	G	A	Pts	PIM	PP	SH	GW
1975-76	Laval National	QMJHL	65	8	9	17	....	....	....	107	....	....	....	....	....	....	....	....	....	....	....	....	....	....	....	....	....	....
1976-77	Sherbrooke Beavers	QMJHL	69	12	14	26	....	....	....	200	....	....	....	....	....	....	....	....	....	....	....	....	....	....	....	....	....	....
1977-78	Sherbrooke Beavers	QMJHL	67	27	54	81	....	....	....	277	....	....	....	....	....	....	....	....	....	....	7	3	9	12	14	....	....	....
1978-79	Sherbrooke Beavers	QMJHL	65	35	47	82	....	....	....	260	....	....	....	....	....	....	....	....	....	....	12	14	12	26	83	....	....	....
1979-80	**Winnipeg Jets**	**NHL**	**72**	**3**	**5**	**8**	**3**	**4**	**7**	***287**	**1**	**0**	**1**	**60**	**5.0**	**15**	**4**	**31**	**0**	**–20**	....	....	....	....	....	....	....	....
1980-81	**Winnipeg Jets**	**NHL**	**37**	**3**	**3**	**6**	**2**	**2**	**4**	**105**	**0**	**0**	**0**	**30**	**10.0**	**9**	**0**	**27**	**0**	**–18**	....	....	....	....	....	....	....	....
	Tulsa Oilers	CHL	26	4	7	11	....	....	....	175	....	....	....	....	....	....	....	....	....	....	5	0	0	0	21	....	....	....
1981-82	**Winnipeg Jets**	**NHL**	**37**	**3**	**2**	**5**	**2**	**1**	**3**	**79**	**0**	**0**	**0**	**22**	**13.6**	**9**	**0**	**17**	**0**	**–8**	**3**	**0**	**0**	**0**	**7**	**0**	**0**	**0**
1982-83	**Winnipeg Jets**	**NHL**	**40**	**0**	**1**	**1**	**0**	**1**	**1**	**73**	**0**	**0**	**0**	**20**	**0.0**	**2**	**0**	**9**	**0**	**–7**	**1**	**0**	**0**	**0**	**0**	**0**	**0**	**0**
1983-84	**Winnipeg Jets**	**NHL**	**16**	**0**	**1**	**1**	**0**	**1**	**1**	**54**	**0**	**0**	**0**	**5**	**0.0**	**2**	**0**	**2**	**0**	**0**	....	....	....	....	....	....	....	....
	Sherbrooke Jets	AHL	20	6	3	9	....	....	....	94	....	....	....	....	....	....	....	....	....	....	....	....	....	....	....	....	....	....
	Quebec Nordiques	**NHL**	**22**	**1**	**1**	**2**	**1**	**1**	**2**	**42**	**0**	**0**	**0**	**15**	**6.7**	**4**	**0**	**7**	**0**	**–3**	**3**	**0**	**0**	**0**	**22**	**0**	**0**	**0**
1984-85	**Quebec Nordiques**	**NHL**	**25**	**0**	**4**	**4**	**0**	**3**	**3**	**54**	**0**	**0**	**0**	**12**	**0.0**	**6**	**0**	**3**	**0**	**+3**	**13**	**0**	**0**	**0**	**41**	**0**	**0**	**0**
	Fredericton Express	AHL	13	4	4	8	....	....	....	97	....	....	....	....	....	....	....	....	....	....	....	....	....	....	....	....	....	....
1985-86	**Quebec Nordiques**	**NHL**	**35**	**0**	**3**	**3**	**0**	**2**	**2**	**148**	**0**	**0**	**0**	**4**	**0.0**	**2**	**0**	**4**	**0**	**–2**	**2**	**0**	**0**	**0**	**19**	**0**	**0**	**0**
1986-87			DID NOT PLAY – INJURED																									
1987-88	**Pittsburgh Penguins**	**NHL**	**9**	**0**	**0**	**0**	**0**	**0**	**0**	**53**	**0**	**0**	**0**	**1**	**0.0**	**0**	**0**	**0**	**0**	**0**	....	....	....	....	....	....	....	....
	Muskegon Lumberjacks	IHL	10	0	2	2	....	....	....	61	....	....	....	....	....	....	....	....	....	....	....	....	....	....	....	....	....	....
1988-89	Indianapolis Ice	IHL	38	5	10	15	....	....	....	275	....	....	....	....	....	....	....	....	....	....	....	....	....	....	....	....	....	....
	NHL Totals		**293**	**10**	**20**	**30**	**8**	**15**	**23**	**895**	**1**	**0**	**1**	**169**	**5.9**	**49**	**4**	**100**	**0**		**22**	**0**	**0**	**0**	**89**	**0**	**0**	**0**

QMJHL First All-Star Team (1979)

Traded to **Quebec** by **Winnipeg** for Quebec's 5th round choice (Brent Severyn) in 1984 Entry Draft, February 6, 1984. Signed as a free agent by **Pittsburgh**, June 16, 1987.

• MANN, KEN

Ken Mann RW – R. 5′11″, 200 lbs. b: Hamilton, Ont., 9/5/1953.

Season	Club	League	GP	G	A	Pts	AG	AA	APts	PIM	PP	SH	GW	S	%	TGF	PGF	TGA	PGA	+/–	GP	G	A	Pts	PIM	PP	SH	GW
1971-72	Hamilton Red Wings	OHA	36	1	11	12	....	....	....	40	....	....	....	....	....	....	....	....	....	....	....	....	....	....	....	....	....	....
1972-73	Windsor Spitfires	SOJHL	58	44	35	79	....	....	....	214	....	....	....	....	....	....	....	....	....	....	....	....	....	....	....	....	....	....
1973-74	Flint–Port Huron	IHL	68	32	26	58	....	....	....	46	....	....	....	....	....	....	....	....	....	....	....	....	....	....	....	....	....	....
1974-75	Virginia Wings	AHL	68	14	19	33	....	....	....	82	....	....	....	....	....	....	....	....	....	....	5	1	1	2	28	....	....	....
1975-76	**Detroit Red Wings**	**NHL**	**1**	**0**	**0**	**0**	**0**	**0**	**0**	**0**	**0**	**0**	**0**	**1**	**0.0**	**0**	**0**	**1**	**0**	**–1**	....	....	....	....	....	....	....	....
	Kalamazoo Wings	IHL	75	39	35	74	....	....	....	100	....	....	....	....	....	....	....	....	....	....	6	3	2	5	4	....	....	....
1976-77	Kansas City Blues	CHL	31	7	9	16	....	....	....	14	....	....	....	....	....	....	....	....	....	....	....	....	....	....	....	....	....	....
	Kalamazoo Wings	IHL	45	23	23	46	....	....	....	46	....	....	....	....	....	....	....	....	....	....	....	....	....	....	....	....	....	....
1977-78	Brantford Alexanders	OHA Sr.	34	6	10	16	....	....	....	49	....	....	....	....	....	....	....	....	....	....	....	....	....	....	....	....	....	....
	NHL Totals		**1**	**0**	**0**	**0**	**0**	**0**	**0**	**0**	**0**	**0**	**0**	**1**	**0.0**	**0**	**0**	**1**	**0**		....	....	....	....	....	....	....	....

Signed as a free agent by **Detroit**, October 2, 1974.

• MANNO, BOB

Bob Manno D – L. 6′, 185 lbs. b: Niagara Falls, Ont., 10/31/1956. Vancouver's 1st choice, 26th overall, in 1976 Amateur Draft.

Season	Club	League	GP	G	A	Pts	AG	AA	APts	PIM	PP	SH	GW	S	%	TGF	PGF	TGA	PGA	+/–	GP	G	A	Pts	PIM	PP	SH	GW
1972-73	Niagara Falls Flyers	SOJHL	36	1	14	15	....	....	....	78	....	....	....	....	....	....	....	....	....	....	....	....	....	....	....	....	....	....
1973-74	Hamilton Red Wings	OHA	63	3	19	22	....	....	....	105	....	....	....	....	....	....	....	....	....	....	....	....	....	....	....	....	....	....
1974-75	St. Catharines Black Hawks	OHA	70	9	38	47	....	....	....	171	....	....	....	....	....	....	....	....	....	....	4	0	1	1	23	....	....	....
1975-76	St. Catharines Black Hawks	OHA	55	9	54	63	....	....	....	187	....	....	....	....	....	....	....	....	....	....	4	1	0	4	14	....	....	....
1976-77	**Vancouver Canucks**	**NHL**	**2**	**0**	**0**	**0**	**0**	**0**	**0**	**0**	**0**	**0**	**0**	**0**	**0.0**	**0**	**0**	**3**	**1**	**–2**	....	....	....	....	....	....	....	....
	Tulsa Oilers	CHL	73	18	36	54	....	....	....	109	....	....	....	....	....	....	....	....	....	....	9	1	7	8	19	....	....	....
1977-78	**Vancouver Canucks**	**NHL**	**49**	**5**	**14**	**19**	**5**	**11**	**16**	**29**	**4**	**0**	**1**	**50**	**10.0**	**47**	**13**	**62**	**5**	**–23**	....	....	....	....	....	....	....	....
	Tulsa Oilers	CHL	20	5	15	20	....	....	....	21	....	....	....	....	....	....	....	....	....	....	....	....	....	....	....	....	....	....
1978-79	**Vancouver Canucks**	**NHL**	**52**	**5**	**16**	**21**	**5**	**12**	**17**	**42**	**0**	**0**	**1**	**71**	**7.0**	**52**	**14**	**62**	**7**	**–17**	**3**	**0**	**1**	**1**	**4**	**0**	**0**	**0**
	Dallas Black Hawks	CHL	23	8	9	17	....	....	....	18	....	....	....	....	....	....	....	....	....	....	....	....	....	....	....	....	....	....
1979-80	**Vancouver Canucks**	**NHL**	**40**	**3**	**14**	**17**	**3**	**11**	**14**	**14**	**1**	**0**	**0**	**73**	**4.1**	**46**	**11**	**45**	**15**	**+5**	**4**	**1**	**0**	**1**	**6**	**0**	**0**	**0**
1980-81	Dallas Black Hawks	CHL	40	7	36	43	....	....	....	65	....	....	....	....	....	....	....	....	....	....	....	....	....	....	....	....	....	....
	Vancouver Canucks	**NHL**	**20**	**0**	**11**	**11**	**0**	**8**	**8**	**30**	**0**	**0**	**0**	**29**	**0.0**	**23**	**4**	**33**	**8**	**–6**	**3**	**0**	**0**	**0**	**2**	**0**	**0**	**0**
1981-82	**Toronto Maple Leafs**	**NHL**	**72**	**9**	**41**	**50**	**7**	**27**	**34**	**67**	**3**	**1**	**0**	**108**	**8.3**	**129**	**28**	**142**	**46**	**+5**	....	....	....	....	....	....	....	....
	Italy	WEC-A	7	1	1	2	....	....	....	12	....	....	....	....	....	....	....	....	....	....	....	....	....	....	....	....	....	....
1982-83	HC Merano	Italy	28	15	32	47	....	....	....	40	....	....	....	....	....	....	....	....	....	....	10	4	12	16	17	....	....	....
	Italy	WEC-A	10	0	4	4	....	....	....	16	....	....	....	....	....	....	....	....	....	....	....	....	....	....	....	....	....	....
1983-84	**Detroit Red Wings**	**NHL**	**62**	**9**	**13**	**22**	**7**	**9**	**16**	**60**	**0**	**1**	**4**	**70**	**12.9**	**42**	**4**	**60**	**21**	**–1**	**4**	**0**	**3**	**3**	**0**	**0**	**0**	**0**
	Adirondack Red Wings	AHL	12	5	11	16	....	....	....	18	....	....	....	....	....	....	....	....	....	....	....	....	....	....	....	....	....	....
1984-85	**Detroit Red Wings**	**NHL**	**74**	**10**	**22**	**32**	**8**	**15**	**23**	**32**	**0**	**3**	**1**	**62**	**16.1**	**45**	**3**	**97**	**55**	**0**	**3**	**1**	**0**	**1**	**0**	**0**	**0**	**0**
1985-86	HC Merano	Italy	36	28	78	106	....	....	....	68	....	....	....	....	....	....	....	....	....	....	6	1	8	9	12	....	....	....
	Italy	WEC-B	7	2	1	3	....	....	....	10	....	....	....	....	....	....	....	....	....	....	....	....	....	....	....	....	....	....
1986-87	HC Merano	Italy	28	14	42	56	....	....	....	54	....	....	....	....	....	....	....	....	....	....	....	....	....	....	....	....	....	....
	Italy	WEC-B	4	0	2	2	....	....	....	8	....	....	....	....	....	....	....	....	....	....	....	....	....	....	....	....	....	....
1987-88	HC Fassa	Italy	43	14	61	75	....	....	....	97	....	....	....	....	....	....	....	....	....	....	....	....	....	....	....	....	....	....
1988-89	HC Fassa	Italy	38	12	52	64	....	....	....	61	....	....	....	....	....	....	....	....	....	....	....	....	....	....	....	....	....	....
	Italy	WEC-B	7	0	5	5	....	....	....	5	....	....	....	....	....	....	....	....	....	....	....	....	....	....	....	....	....	....
1989-90	HC Milan	Italy	40	14	42	56	....	....	....	74	....	....	....	....	....	....	....	....	....	....	....	....	....	....	....	....	....	....
	Italy	WEC-B	7	1	4	5	....	....	....	10	....	....	....	....	....	....	....	....	....	....	....	....	....	....	....	....	....	....
1990-91	HC Milan	Italy	32	7	43	50	....	....	....	61	....	....	....	....	....	....	....	....	....	....	....	....	....	....	....	....	....	....
	Italy	WEC-B	7	0	7	7	....	....	....	4	....	....	....	....	....	....	....	....	....	....	....	....	....	....	....	....	....	....
1991-92	HC Milano	Italy	23	7	19	26	....	....	....	23	....	....	....	....	....	....	....	....	....	....	....	....	....	....	....	....	....	....
	Italy	Olympics	7	1	2	3	....	....	....	22	....	....	....	....	....	....	....	....	....	....	....	....	....	....	....	....	....	....

			REGULAR SEASON																		PLAYOFFS							
Season	**Club**	**League**	**GP**	**G**	**A**	**Pts**	**AG**	**AA**	**APts**	**PIM**	**PP**	**SH**	**GW**	**S**	**%**	**TGF**	**PGF**	**TGA**	**PGA**	**+/–**	**GP**	**G**	**A**	**Pts**	**PIM**	**PP**	**SH**	**GW**
1992-93	HC Bolzano	Italy	26	4	21	25	....	....	....	29	....	....	....	....	....	....	....	....	....	....	....	....	....	....	....	....	....	....
	HC Bolzano	Alpenliga	26	5	17	22	....	....	....	73	....	....	....	....	....	....	....	....	....	....	....	....	....	....	....	....	....	....
1993-94	HC Bolzano	Italy	19	4	14	18	....	....	....	32	....	....	....	....	....	....	....	....	....	....	....	....	....	....	....	....	....	....
	HC Bolzano	Alpenliga	24	5	29	34	....	....	....	69	....	....	....	....	....	....	....	....	....	....	....	....	....	....	....	....	....	....
	NHL Totals		**371**	**41**	**131**	**172**	**35**	**93**	**128**	**274**	**8**	**5**	**7**	**463**	**8.9**	**384**	**77**	**504**	**158**		**17**	**2**	**4**	**6**	**12**	**0**	**0**	**0**

WEC-B All-Star Team (1986, 1989, 1991) • Named Best Defenseman at WEC-B (1989)

Played in NHL All-Star Game (1982)

Signed as a free agent by **Toronto**, September 30, 1981. Signed as a free agent by **Detroit**, August 2, 1983.

• MANSON, DAVE

Dave "Charlie" Manson D – L. 6'2", 202 lbs. b: Prince Albert, Sask., 1/27/1967. Chicago's 1st choice, 11th overall, in 1985 Entry Draft.

Season	Club	League	GP	G	A	Pts	AG	AA	APts	PIM	PP	SH	GW	S	%	TGF	PGF	TGA	PGA	+/–	GP	G	A	Pts	PIM	PP	SH	GW
1983-84	Prince Albert Raiders	WHL	70	2	7	9	....	....	....	233	....	....	....	....	....	....	....	....	....	....	5	0	0	0	4	....	....	....
1984-85	Prince Albert Raiders	WHL	72	8	30	38	....	....	....	247	....	....	....	....	....	....	....	....	....	....	13	1	0	1	34	....	....	....
1985-86	Prince Albert Raiders	WHL	70	14	34	48	....	....	....	177	....	....	....	....	....	....	....	....	....	....	20	1	8	9	63	....	....	....
1986-87	**Chicago Blackhawks**	**NHL**	**63**	**1**	**8**	**9**	**1**	**6**	**7**	**146**	**0**	**0**	**0**	**42**	**2.4**	**49**	**0**	**57**	**6**	**–2**	**3**	**0**	**0**	**0**	**10**	**0**	**0**	**0**
1987-88	**Chicago Blackhawks**	**NHL**	**54**	**1**	**6**	**7**	**1**	**4**	**5**	**185**	**0**	**0**	**0**	**47**	**2.1**	**38**	**1**	**62**	**13**	**–12**	**5**	**0**	**0**	**0**	**27**	**0**	**0**	**0**
	Saginaw Hawks	IHL	6	0	3	3	....	....	....	37	....	....	....	....	....	....	....	....	....	....	....	....	....	....	....	....	....	....
1988-89	**Chicago Blackhawks**	**NHL**	**79**	**18**	**36**	**54**	**15**	**25**	**40**	**352**	**8**	**1**	**0**	**224**	**8.0**	**151**	**50**	**159**	**63**	**+5**	**16**	**0**	**8**	**8**	**84**	**0**	**0**	**0**
1989-90	**Chicago Blackhawks**	**NHL**	**59**	**5**	**23**	**28**	**4**	**16**	**20**	**301**	**1**	**0**	**1**	**126**	**4.0**	**88**	**20**	**85**	**21**	**+4**	**20**	**2**	**4**	**6**	**46**	**1**	**0**	**0**
1990-91	**Chicago Blackhawks**	**NHL**	**75**	**14**	**15**	**29**	**13**	**11**	**24**	**191**	**6**	**1**	**2**	**154**	**9.1**	**93**	**18**	**77**	**22**	**+20**	**6**	**0**	**1**	**1**	**36**	**0**	**0**	**0**
1991-92	**Edmonton Oilers**	**NHL**	**79**	**15**	**32**	**47**	**14**	**24**	**38**	**220**	**7**	**0**	**2**	**206**	**7.3**	**130**	**39**	**110**	**28**	**+9**	**16**	**3**	**9**	**12**	**44**	**1**	**0**	**0**
1992-93	**Edmonton Oilers**	**NHL**	**83**	**15**	**30**	**45**	**12**	**21**	**33**	**210**	**9**	**1**	**1**	**244**	**6.1**	**118**	**46**	**137**	**37**	**–28**	....	....	....	....	....	....	....	....
	Canada	WC-A	8	3	7	10	....	....	....	22	....	....	....	....	....	....	....	....	....	....	....	....	....	....	....	....	....	....
1993-94	**Edmonton Oilers**	**NHL**	**57**	**3**	**13**	**16**	**3**	**10**	**13**	**140**	**0**	**0**	**0**	**144**	**2.1**	**67**	**18**	**75**	**22**	**–4**	....	....	....	....	....	....	....	....
	Winnipeg Jets	**NHL**	**13**	**1**	**4**	**5**	**1**	**3**	**4**	**51**	**1**	**0**	**0**	**36**	**2.8**	**18**	**7**	**29**	**8**	**–10**	....	....	....	....	....	....	....	....
1994-95	**Winnipeg Jets**	**NHL**	**44**	**3**	**15**	**18**	**5**	**22**	**27**	**139**	**2**	**0**	**1**	**104**	**2.9**	**48**	**13**	**79**	**24**	**–20**	....	....	....	....	....	....	....	....
1995-96	**Winnipeg Jets**	**NHL**	**82**	**7**	**23**	**30**	**7**	**19**	**26**	**205**	**3**	**0**	**0**	**189**	**3.7**	**112**	**18**	**130**	**44**	**+8**	**6**	**2**	**1**	**3**	**30**	**0**	**0**	**1**
1996-97	**Phoenix Coyotes**	**NHL**	**66**	**3**	**17**	**20**	**3**	**15**	**18**	**164**	**2**	**0**	**0**	**153**	**2.0**	**50**	**13**	**75**	**13**	**–25**	....	....	....	....	....	....	....	....
	Montreal Canadiens	**NHL**	**9**	**1**	**1**	**2**	**1**	**1**	**2**	**23**	**0**	**0**	**0**	**22**	**4.5**	**9**	**2**	**8**	**0**	**–1**	**5**	**0**	**0**	**0**	**17**	**0**	**0**	**0**
1997-98	**Montreal Canadiens**	**NHL**	**81**	**4**	**30**	**34**	**5**	**29**	**34**	**122**	**2**	**0**	**0**	**148**	**2.7**	**88**	**21**	**65**	**20**	**+22**	**10**	**0**	**1**	**1**	**14**	**0**	**0**	**0**
	NHL Totals		**844**	**91**	**253**	**344**	**85**	**206**	**291**	**2449**	**41**	**3**	**7**	**1839**	**4.9**	**1059**	**266**	**1148**	**321**		**87**	**7**	**24**	**31**	**308**	**2**	**0**	**1**

WHL East Second All-Star Team (1986) • WC-A All-Star Team (1993)

Played in NHL All-Star Game (1989, 1993)

Traded to **Edmonton** by **Chicago** with Chicago's 3rd round choice (Kirk Maltby) in 1992 Entry Draft for Steve Smith, October 2, 1991. Traded to **Winnipeg** by **Edmonton** with St. Louis' 6th round choice (previously acquired, Winnipeg selected Chris Kibermanis) in 1994 Entry Draft for Boris Mironov, Mats Lindgren, Winnipeg's 1st round choice (Jason Bonsignore) in 1994 Entry Draft and Florida's 4th round choice (previously acquired, Edmonton selected Adam Copeland) in 1994 Entry Draft, March 15, 1994. Transferred to **Phoenix** after **Winnipeg** franchise relocated, July 1, 1996. Traded to **Montreal** by **Phoenix** for Murray Baron and Chris Murray, March 18, 1997.

• MANTHA, MOE

Moe Mantha D – R. 6'2", 210 lbs. b: Lakewood, OH, 1/21/1961. Winnipeg's 2nd choice, 23rd overall, in 1980 Entry Draft.

Season	Club	League	GP	G	A	Pts	AG	AA	APts	PIM	PP	SH	GW	S	%	TGF	PGF	TGA	PGA	+/–	GP	G	A	Pts	PIM	PP	SH	GW
1978-79	Toronto Marlboros	OHA	68	10	38	48	....	....	....	57	....	....	....	....	....	....	....	....	....	....	4	0	2	2	11	....	....	....
1979-80	Toronto Marlboros	OHA	58	8	38	46	....	....	....	86	....	....	....	....	....	....	....	....	....	....	....	....	....	....	....	....	....	....
1980-81	**Winnipeg Jets**	**NHL**	**58**	**2**	**23**	**25**	**2**	**16**	**18**	**35**	**1**	**0**	**0**	**94**	**2.1**	**65**	**22**	**79**	**3**	**–33**	....	....	....	....	....	....	....	....
1981-82	**Winnipeg Jets**	**NHL**	**25**	**0**	**12**	**12**	**0**	**8**	**8**	**28**	**0**	**0**	**0**	**39**	**0.0**	**23**	**4**	**31**	**2**	**–10**	**4**	**1**	**3**	**4**	**16**	**0**	**0**	**0**
	Tulsa Oilers	CHL	33	8	15	23	....	....	....	56	....	....	....	....	....	....	....	....	....	....	....	....	....	....	....	....	....	....
	United States	WEC-A	7	1	1	2	....	....	....	6	....	....	....	....	....	....	....	....	....	....	....	....	....	....	....	....	....	....
1982-83	**Winnipeg Jets**	**NHL**	**21**	**2**	**7**	**9**	**2**	**5**	**7**	**6**	**1**	**0**	**1**	**27**	**7.4**	**17**	**9**	**8**	**0**	**0**	**2**	**2**	**2**	**4**	**0**	**2**	**0**	**0**
	Sherbrooke Jets	AHL	13	1	4	5	....	....	....	13	....	....	....	....	....	....	....	....	....	....	....	....	....	....	....	....	....	....
1983-84	**Winnipeg Jets**	**NHL**	**72**	**16**	**38**	**54**	**13**	**26**	**39**	**67**	**3**	**0**	**1**	**228**	**7.0**	**128**	**42**	**120**	**20**	**–14**	**3**	**1**	**0**	**1**	**0**	**0**	**1**	**0**
	Sherbrooke Jets	AHL	7	1	1	2	....	....	....	10	....	....	....	....	....	....	....	....	....	....	....	....	....	....	....	....	....	....
1984-85	**Pittsburgh Penguins**	**NHL**	**71**	**11**	**40**	**51**	**9**	**27**	**36**	**54**	**3**	**0**	**1**	**204**	**5.4**	**117**	**40**	**148**	**36**	**–35**	....	....	....	....	....	....	....	....
	United States	WEC-A	10	2	1	3	....	....	....	10	....	....	....	....	....	....	....	....	....	....	....	....	....	....	....	....	....	....
1985-86	**Pittsburgh Penguins**	**NHL**	**78**	**15**	**52**	**67**	**12**	**35**	**47**	**102**	**11**	**2**	**0**	**224**	**6.7**	**152**	**63**	**127**	**34**	**–4**	....	....	....	....	....	....	....	....
1986-87	**Pittsburgh Penguins**	**NHL**	**62**	**9**	**31**	**40**	**8**	**22**	**30**	**44**	**8**	**0**	**0**	**167**	**5.4**	**102**	**44**	**96**	**32**	**–6**	....	....	....	....	....	....	....	....
1987-88	**Pittsburgh Penguins**	**NHL**	**21**	**2**	**8**	**10**	**2**	**6**	**8**	**23**	**1**	**0**	**1**	**66**	**3.0**	**31**	**8**	**26**	**9**	**+6**	....	....	....	....	....	....	....	....
	Edmonton Oilers	**NHL**	**25**	**0**	**6**	**6**	**0**	**4**	**4**	**26**	**0**	**0**	**0**	**50**	**0.0**	**36**	**11**	**27**	**9**	**+7**	....	....	....	....	....	....	....	....
	Minnesota North Stars	**NHL**	**30**	**9**	**13**	**22**	**8**	**9**	**17**	**4**	**2**	**0**	**0**	**107**	**8.4**	**45**	**16**	**56**	**13**	**–14**	....	....	....	....	....	....	....	....
1988-89	**Minnesota North Stars**	**NHL**	**16**	**1**	**6**	**7**	**1**	**4**	**5**	**10**	**1**	**0**	**0**	**32**	**3.1**	**17**	**7**	**13**	**4**	**+1**	....	....	....	....	....	....	....	....
	Philadelphia Flyers	**NHL**	**30**	**3**	**8**	**11**	**3**	**6**	**9**	**33**	**2**	**0**	**0**	**71**	**4.2**	**35**	**14**	**28**	**2**	**–5**	....	....	....	....	....	....	....	....
1989-90	**Winnipeg Jets**	**NHL**	**73**	**2**	**26**	**28**	**2**	**19**	**21**	**28**	**0**	**1**	**0**	**114**	**1.8**	**91**	**10**	**82**	**9**	**+8**	**1**	**0**	**0**	**0**	**0**	**0**	**0**	**0**
1990-91	**Winnipeg Jets**	**NHL**	**57**	**9**	**15**	**24**	**8**	**11**	**19**	**33**	**4**	**1**	**2**	**102**	**8.8**	**53**	**11**	**76**	**14**	**–20**	**7**	**1**	**5**	**6**	**2**	**0**	**0**	**0**
	United States	WEC-A	9	0	0	0	....	....	....	2	....	....	....	....	....	....	....	....	....	....	....	....	....	....	....	....	....	....
1991-92	**Winnipeg Jets**	**NHL**	**12**	**0**	**4**	**4**	**0**	**3**	**3**	**6**	**0**	**0**	**0**	**10**	**0.0**	**8**	**1**	**9**	**2**	**0**	....	....	....	....	....	....	....	....
	United States	Nat-Team	13	0	2	2	....	....	....	29	....	....	....	....	....	....	....	....	....	....	....	....	....	....	....	....	....	....
	United States	Olympics	8	1	1	2	....	....	....	4	....	....	....	....	....	....	....	....	....	....	....	....	....	....	....	....	....	....
	Philadelphia Flyers	**NHL**	**5**	**0**	**0**	**0**	**0**	**0**	**0**	**2**	**0**	**0**	**0**	**7**	**0.0**	**1**	**0**	**3**	**2**	**0**	....	....	....	....	....	....	....	....
1992-93	Hershey Bears	AHL	1	0	0	0	....	....	....	0	....	....	....	....	....	....	....	....	....	....	....	....	....	....	....	....	....	....
	NHL Totals		**656**	**81**	**289**	**370**	**70**	**201**	**271**	**501**	**37**	**4**	**6**	**1542**	**5.3**	**921**	**302**	**929**	**191**		**17**	**5**	**10**	**15**	**18**	**2**	**1**	**0**

Traded to **Pittsburgh** by **Winnipeg** to complete transaction that sent Randy Carlyle to Winnipeg (March 5, 1984), May 1, 1984. Traded to **Edmonton** by **Pittsburgh** with Craig Simpson, Dave Hanna and Chris Joseph for Paul Coffey, Dave Hunter and Wayne Van Dorp, November 24, 1987. Traded to **Minnesota** by **Edmonton** for Keith Acton, January 22, 1988. Traded to **Philadelphia** by **Minnesota** for Toronto's 5th round choice (acquired earlier, Philadelphia chose Pat McLeod) in 1989 Entry Draft, December 8, 1988. Claimed by **Winnipeg** from **Philadelphia** in Waiver Draft, October 2, 1989. Traded to **Philadelphia** by **Winnipeg** for future considerations, February 27, 1992.

• MARCETTA, MILAN

Milan "Millie" Marcetta C – L. 6', 195 lbs. b: Cadomin, Alta., 9/19/1936.

Season	Club	League	GP	G	A	Pts	AG	AA	APts	PIM	PP	SH	GW	S	%	TGF	PGF	TGA	PGA	+/–	GP	G	A	Pts	PIM	PP	SH	GW
1953-54	Medicine Hat Tigers	WCJHL	13	5	3	8	....	....	....	2	....	....	....	....	....	....	....	....	....	....	10	2	3	5	0	....	....	....
1954-55	Medicine Hat Tigers	WCJHL	40	23	23	46	....	....	....	4	....	....	....	....	....	....	....	....	....	....	8	7	4	11	2	....	....	....
1955-56	Yorkton Terriers	SJHL	47	34	38	72	....	....	....	37	....	....	....	....	....	....	....	....	....	....	3	0	0	0	2	....	....	....
1956-57	Calgary Stampeders	WHL	67	27	22	49	....	....	....	20	....	....	....	....	....	....	....	....	....	....	1	0	0	0	0	....	....	....
1957-58	Buffalo Bisons	AHL	17	1	0	1	....	....	....	8	....	....	....	....	....	....	....	....	....	....	....	....	....	....	....	....	....	....
	Calgary Stampeders	WHL	41	11	6	17	....	....	....	14	....	....	....	....	....	....	....	....	....	....	14	4	0	4	2	....	....	....
1958-59	Saskatoon Quakers	WHL	20	4	5	9	....	....	....	2	....	....	....	....	....	....	....	....	....	....	....	....	....	....	....	....	....	....
	Springfield Indians	AHL	28	3	6	9	....	....	....	10	....	....	....	....	....	....	....	....	....	....	....	....	....	....	....	....	....	....
1959-60	Sault Ste. Marie Thunderbirds	EPHL	70	28	55	83	....	....	....	19	....	....	....	....	....	....	....	....	....	....	....	....	....	....	....	....	....	....
	Buffalo Bisons	AHL	1	0	1	1	....	....	....	0	....	....	....	....	....	....	....	....	....	....	....	....	....	....	....	....	....	....
1960-61	Sault Ste. Marie Thunderbirds	EPHL	50	8	18	26	....	....	....	59	....	....	....	....	....	....	....	....	....	....	6	0	0	0	0	....	....	....
1961-62	Sault Ste. Marie Thunderbirds	EPHL	69	32	45	77	....	....	....	11	....	....	....	....	....	....	....	....	....	....	....	....	....	....	....	....	....	....
1962-63	St. Louis Braves	EPHL	20	9	4	13	....	....	....	27	....	....	....	....	....	....	....	....	....	....	....	....	....	....	....	....	....	....
	Calgary Stampeders	WHL	44	18	23	41	....	....	....	40	....	....	....	....	....	....	....	....	....	....	....	....	....	....	....	....	....	....
1963-64	Denver Invaders	WHL	58	23	23	46	....	....	....	19	....	....	....	....	....	....	....	....	....	....	6	5	1	6	12	....	....	....
1964-65	Victoria Cougars	WHL	70	34	46	80	....	....	....	21	....	....	....	....	....	....	....	....	....	....	10	2	2	4	6	....	....	....
1965-66	Tulsa Oilers	CHL	8	8	7	15	....	....	....	2	....	....	....	....	....	....	....	....	....	....	....	....	....	....	....	....	....	....
	Victoria Cougars	WHL	61	28	54	82	....	....	....	22	....	....	....	....	....	....	....	....	....	....	14	7	*13	*20	6	....	....	....
1966-67	Victoria Cougars	WHL	70	40	35	75	....	....	....	2	....	....	....	....	....	....	....	....	....	....	....	....	....	....	....	....	....	....
	Toronto Maple Leafs	**NHL**			....	....	....	....	....	....	....	....	....	....	....	....	....	....	....	....	**3**	**0**	**0**	**0**	**0**	....	....	....
1967-68	Rochester Americans	AHL	29	18	21	39	....	....	....	4	....	....	....	....	....	....	....	....	....	....	....	....	....	....	....	....	....	....
	Minnesota North Stars	**NHL**	**36**	**4**	**13**	**17**	**5**	**14**	**19**	**6**	**0**	**0**	**0**	**41**	**9.8**	**20**	**4**	**26**	**0**	**–10**	**14**	**7**	**7**	**14**	**4**	**1**	**0**	**1**
1968-69	**Minnesota North Stars**	**NHL**	**18**	**3**	**2**	**5**	**3**	**2**	**5**	**4**	**2**	**0**	**0**	**18**	**16.7**	**5**	**3**	**6**	**0**	**–4**	....	....	....	....	....	....	....	....
	Memphis South Stars	CHL	22	6	9	15	....	....	....	22	....	....	....	....	....	....	....	....	....	....	....	....	....	....	....	....	....	....
	Phoenix Roadrunners	WHL	20	6	8	14	....	....	....	6	....	....	....	....	....	....	....	....	....	....	....	....	....	....	....	....	....	....
1969-70	Phoenix Roadrunners	WHL	73	34	32	66	....	....	....	14	....	....	....	....	....	....	....	....	....	....	....	....	....	....	....	....	....	....

			REGULAR SEASON																		PLAYOFFS							
Season	Club	League	GP	G	A	Pts	AG	AA	APts	PIM	PP	SH	GW	S	%	TGF	PGF	TGA	PGA	+/–	GP	G	A	Pts	PIM	PP	SH	GW
1970-71	Phoenix Roadrunners	WHL	12	2	4	6	....	....	....	0	....	....	....	....	....	....	....	....	....	....	....	....	....	....	....	....	....	....
	Denver Spurs	WHL	30	6	17	23	....	....	....	2	....	....	....	....	....	....	....	....	....	....	5	2	6	8	0	....	....	....
1971-72	Denver Spurs	WHL	72	22	45	67	....	....	....	19	....	....	....	....	....	....	....	....	....	....	9	2	2	4	6	....	....	....
1972-73	Denver Spurs	WHL	52	18	22	40	....	....	....	14	....	....	....	....	....	....	....	....	....	....	5	2	2	4	2	....	....	....
	NHL Totals		**54**	**7**	**15**	**22**	**8**	**16**	**24**	**10**	**2**	**0**	**0**	**59**	**11.9**	**25**	**7**	**32**	**0**		**17**	**7**	**7**	**14**	**4**	**1**	**0**	**1**

Traded to **Minnesota** by **Toronto** with Jean-Paul Parise for Murray Hall, Ted Taylor, Duke Harris, Len Lunde, Don Johns and the loan of Carl Wetzel, December 26, 1967. Traded to **Phoenix** (WHL) by **Minnesota** with Brian D. Smith for Tom Polanic, February 11, 1969.

• MARCHANT, TODD

Todd Marchant C – L. 5'10", 175 lbs. b: Buffalo, NY, 8/12/1973. NY Rangers' 8th choice, 164th overall, in 1993 Entry Draft.

Season	Club	League	GP	G	A	Pts	AG	AA	APts	PIM	PP	SH	GW	S	%	TGF	PGF	TGA	PGA	+/–	GP	G	A	Pts	PIM	PP	SH	GW
1991-92	Clarkson University	ECAC	32	20	12	32	....	....	....	32	....	....	....	....	....	....	....	....	....	....	....	....	....	....	....	....	....	....
1992-93	Clarkson University	ECAC	33	18	28	46	....	....	....	38	....	....	....	....	....	....	....	....	....	....	....	....	....	....	....	....	....	....
	United States	WJC-A	7	2	3	5	....	....	....	2	....	....	....	....	....	....	....	....	....	....	....	....	....	....	....	....	....	....
1993-94	United States	Nat-Team	59	28	39	67	....	....	....	48	....	....	....	....	....	....	....	....	....	....	....	....	....	....	....	....	....	....
	United States	Olympics	8	1	1	2	....	....	....	6	....	....	....	....	....	....	....	....	....	....	....	....	....	....	....	....	....	....
	New York Rangers	**NHL**	**1**	**0**	**0**	**0**	**0**	**0**	**0**	**0**	**0**	**0**	**0**	**1**	**0.0**	**1**	**0**	**2**	**0**	**–1**	....	....	....	....	....	....	....	....
	Binghamton Rangers	AHL	8	2	7	9	....	....	....	6	....	....	....	....	....	....	....	....	....	....	....	....	....	....	....	....	....	....
	Edmonton Oilers	**NHL**	**3**	**0**	**1**	**1**	**0**	**1**	**1**	**2**	**0**	**0**	**0**	**5**	**0.0**	**1**	**0**	**3**	**1**	**–1**	....	....	....	....	....	....	....	....
	Cape Breton Oilers	AHL	3	1	4	5	....	....	....	2	....	....	....	....	....	....	....	....	....	....	5	1	1	2	0	....	....	....
1994-95	Cape Breton Oilers	AHL	38	22	25	47	....	....	....	25	....	....	....	....	....	....	....	....	....	....	....	....	....	....	....	....	....	....
	Edmonton Oilers	**NHL**	**45**	**13**	**14**	**27**	**23**	**21**	**44**	**32**	**3**	**2**	**2**	**95**	**13.7**	**38**	**10**	**53**	**22**	**–3**	....	....	....	....	....	....	....	....
1995-96	**Edmonton Oilers**	**NHL**	**81**	**19**	**19**	**38**	**19**	**15**	**34**	**66**	**2**	**3**	**2**	**221**	**8.6**	**46**	**4**	**92**	**31**	**–19**	....	....	....	....	....	....	....	....
1996-97	**Edmonton Oilers**	**NHL**	**79**	**14**	**19**	**33**	**15**	**17**	**32**	**44**	**0**	**4**	**3**	**202**	**6.9**	**44**	**3**	**60**	**30**	**+11**	**12**	**4**	**2**	**6**	**12**	**0**	**3**	**1**
1997-98	**Edmonton Oilers**	**NHL**	**76**	**14**	**21**	**35**	**16**	**20**	**36**	**71**	**2**	**1**	**3**	**194**	**7.2**	**56**	**10**	**57**	**20**	**+9**	**12**	**1**	**1**	**2**	**10**	**0**	**0**	**0**
	NHL Totals		**285**	**60**	**74**	**134**	**73**	**74**	**147**	**215**	**7**	**10**	**10**	**718**	**8.4**	**186**	**27**	**267**	**104**		**24**	**5**	**3**	**8**	**22**	**0**	**3**	**1**

ECAC Second All-Star Team (1993)

Traded to **Edmonton** by **NY Rangers** for Craig MacTavish, March 21, 1994.

• MARCHINKO, BRIAN

Brian Marchinko C – R. 6', 180 lbs. b: Weyburn, Sask., 8/2/1948.

Season	Club	League	GP	G	A	Pts	AG	AA	APts	PIM	PP	SH	GW	S	%	TGF	PGF	TGA	PGA	+/–	GP	G	A	Pts	PIM	PP	SH	GW
1967-68	Flin Flon Bombers	WCJHL	43	9	16	25	....	....	....	19	....	....	....	....	....	....	....	....	....	....	....	....	....	....	....	....	....	....
	London Nationals	OHA	25	0	1	1	....	....	....	0	....	....	....	....	....	....	....	....	....	....	....	....	....	....	....	....	....	....
1968-69	Flin Flon Bombers	WCJHL	60	41	45	86	....	....	....	96	....	....	....	....	....	....	....	....	....	....	....	....	....	....	....	....	....	....
1969-70	Tulsa Oilers	CHL	59	8	14	22	....	....	....	30	....	....	....	....	....	....	....	....	....	....	6	1	0	1	0	....	....	....
1970-71	**Toronto Maple Leafs**	**NHL**	**2**	**0**	**0**	**0**	**0**	**0**	**0**	**0**	**0**	**0**	**0**	**0**	**0.0**	**0**	**0**	**0**	**0**	**0**	....	....	....	....	....	....	....	....
	Tulsa Oilers	CHL	67	15	24	39	....	....	....	47	....	....	....	....	....	....	....	....	....	....	....	....	....	....	....	....	....	....
1971-72	**Toronto Maple Leafs**	**NHL**	**3**	**0**	**0**	**0**	**0**	**0**	**0**	**0**	**0**	**0**	**0**	**1**	**0.0**	**0**	**0**	**0**	**0**	**0**	....	....	....	....	....	....	....	....
	Tulsa Oilers	CHL	68	10	24	34	....	....	....	29	....	....	....	....	....	....	....	....	....	....	13	3	3	6	7	....	....	....
1972-73	**New York Islanders**	**NHL**	**36**	**2**	**6**	**8**	**2**	**5**	**7**	**0**	**0**	**0**	**1**	**19**	**10.5**	**10**	**0**	**25**	**5**	**–10**	....	....	....	....	....	....	....	....
	New Haven Nighthawks	AHL	7	0	0	0	....	....	....	0	....	....	....	....	....	....	....	....	....	....	....	....	....	....	....	....	....	....
1973-74	**New York Islanders**	**NHL**	**6**	**0**	**0**	**0**	**0**	**0**	**0**	**0**	**0**	**0**	**0**	**7**	**0.0**	**0**	**0**	**0**	**0**	**0**	....	....	....	....	....	....	....	....
	Fort Worth Wings	CHL	54	7	19	26	....	....	....	24	....	....	....	....	....	....	....	....	....	....	....	....	....	....	....	....	....	....
	Providence Reds	AHL	10	3	0	3	....	....	....	8	....	....	....	....	....	....	....	....	....	....	15	7	2	9	9	....	....	....
1974-75	Fort Worth Texans	CHL	78	23	20	43	....	....	....	32	....	....	....	....	....	....	....	....	....	....	....	....	....	....	....	....	....	....
1975-76	Erie Blades	NAHL	63	27	34	61	....	....	....	29	....	....	....	....	....	....	....	....	....	....	5	1	2	3	0	....	....	....
1976-77	Erie Blades	NAHL	47	16	21	37	....	....	....	4	....	....	....	....	....	....	....	....	....	....	....	....	....	....	....	....	....	....
	Johnstown Jets	NAHL	21	8	9	17	....	....	....	4	....	....	....	....	....	....	....	....	....	....	3	2	0	2	0	....	....	....
	NHL Totals		**47**	**2**	**6**	**8**	**2**	**5**	**7**	**0**	**0**	**0**	**1**	**27**	**7.4**	**10**	**0**	**25**	**5**		....	....	....	....	....	....	....	....

Signed as a free agent by **Toronto**, October 1, 1969. Claimed by **NY Islanders** from **Toronto** in Expansion Draft, June 6, 1972.

• MARCHMENT, BRYAN

Bryan Marchment D – L. 6'1", 205 lbs. b: Scarborough, Ont., 5/1/1969. Winnipeg's 1st choice, 16th overall, in 1987 Entry Draft.

Season	Club	League	GP	G	A	Pts	AG	AA	APts	PIM	PP	SH	GW	S	%	TGF	PGF	TGA	PGA	+/–	GP	G	A	Pts	PIM	PP	SH	GW
1985-86	Belleville Bulls	OHL	57	5	15	20	....	....	....	225	....	....	....	....	....	....	....	....	....	....	21	0	7	7	83	....	....	....
1986-87	Belleville Bulls	OHL	52	6	38	44	....	....	....	238	....	....	....	....	....	....	....	....	....	....	6	0	4	4	17	....	....	....
1987-88	Belleville Bulls	OHL	56	7	51	58	....	....	....	200	....	....	....	....	....	....	....	....	....	....	6	1	3	4	19	....	....	....
1988-89	Belleville Bulls	OHL	43	14	36	50	....	....	....	118	....	....	....	....	....	....	....	....	....	....	5	0	1	1	12	....	....	....
	Winnipeg Jets	**NHL**	**2**	**0**	**0**	**0**	**0**	**0**	**0**	**2**	**0**	**0**	**0**	**1**	**0.0**	**0**	**0**	**0**	**0**	**0**	....	....	....	....	....	....	....	....
1989-90	**Winnipeg Jets**	**NHL**	**7**	**0**	**2**	**2**	**0**	**1**	**1**	**28**	**0**	**0**	**0**	**5**	**0.0**	**6**	**0**	**6**	**0**	**0**	....	....	....	....	....	....	....	....
	Moncton Hawks	AHL	56	4	19	23	....	....	....	217	....	....	....	....	....	....	....	....	....	....	....	....	....	....	....	....	....	....
1990-91	**Winnipeg Jets**	**NHL**	**28**	**2**	**2**	**4**	**2**	**2**	**4**	**91**	**0**	**0**	**0**	**24**	**8.3**	**24**	**3**	**30**	**4**	**–5**	....	....	....	....	....	....	....	....
	Moncton Hawks	AHL	33	2	11	13	....	....	....	101	....	....	....	....	....	....	....	....	....	....	....	....	....	....	....	....	....	....
1991-92	**Chicago Blackhawks**	**NHL**	**58**	**5**	**10**	**15**	**5**	**7**	**12**	**168**	**2**	**0**	**0**	**55**	**9.1**	**38**	**6**	**42**	**6**	**–4**	**16**	**1**	**0**	**1**	**36**	**0**	**0**	**0**
1992-93	**Chicago Blackhawks**	**NHL**	**78**	**5**	**15**	**20**	**4**	**10**	**14**	**313**	**1**	**0**	**1**	**75**	**6.7**	**61**	**5**	**51**	**10**	**+15**	**4**	**0**	**0**	**0**	**12**	**0**	**0**	**0**
1993-94	**Chicago Blackhawks**	**NHL**	**13**	**1**	**4**	**5**	**1**	**3**	**4**	**42**	**0**	**0**	**0**	**18**	**5.6**	**9**	**0**	**15**	**4**	**–2**	....	....	....	....	....	....	....	....
	Hartford Whalers	**NHL**	**42**	**3**	**7**	**10**	**3**	**5**	**8**	**124**	**0**	**1**	**1**	**74**	**4.1**	**30**	**1**	**55**	**14**	**–12**	....	....	....	....	....	....	....	....
1994-95	**Edmonton Oilers**	**NHL**	**40**	**1**	**5**	**6**	**2**	**7**	**9**	**184**	**0**	**0**	**0**	**57**	**1.8**	**25**	**1**	**47**	**12**	**–11**	....	....	....	....	....	....	....	....
1995-96	**Edmonton Oilers**	**NHL**	**78**	**3**	**15**	**18**	**3**	**12**	**15**	**202**	**0**	**0**	**0**	**96**	**3.1**	**82**	**9**	**121**	**41**	**–7**	....	....	....	....	....	....	....	....
1996-97	**Edmonton Oilers**	**NHL**	**71**	**3**	**13**	**16**	**3**	**11**	**14**	**132**	**1**	**0**	**0**	**89**	**3.4**	**64**	**2**	**67**	**18**	**+13**	**3**	**0**	**0**	**0**	**4**	**0**	**0**	**0**
1997-98	**Edmonton Oilers**	**NHL**	**27**	**0**	**4**	**4**	**0**	**4**	**4**	**58**	**0**	**0**	**0**	**23**	**0.0**	**17**	**2**	**26**	**9**	**–2**	....	....	....	....	....	....	....	....
	Tampa Bay Lightning	**NHL**	**22**	**2**	**4**	**6**	**2**	**4**	**6**	**43**	**0**	**0**	**0**	**20**	**10.0**	**20**	**1**	**30**	**8**	**–3**	....	....	....	....	....	....	....	....
	San Jose Sharks	**NHL**	**12**	**0**	**3**	**3**	**0**	**3**	**3**	**43**	**0**	**0**	**0**	**13**	**0.0**	**12**	**1**	**10**	**1**	**+2**	**6**	**0**	**0**	**0**	**10**	**0**	**0**	**0**
	NHL Totals		**478**	**25**	**84**	**109**	**25**	**69**	**94**	**1430**	**4**	**1**	**2**	**550**	**4.5**	**388**	**31**	**500**	**127**		**29**	**1**	**0**	**1**	**62**	**0**	**0**	**0**

OHL Second All-Star Team (1989)

Traded to **Chicago** by **Winnipeg** with Chris Norton for Troy Murray and Warren Rychel, July 22, 1991. Traded to **Hartford** by **Chicago** with Steve Larmer for Eric Weinrich and Patrick Poulin, November 2, 1993. Transferred to **Edmonton** from **Hartford** as compensation for Hartford's signing of free agent Steven Rice, August 30, 1994. Traded to **Tampa Bay** by **Edmonton** with Steve Kelly and Jason Bonsignore for Roman Hamrlik and Paul Comrie, December 30, 1997. Traded to **San Jose** by **Tampa Bay** with David Shaw and Tampa Bay's 1st round choice (later traded to Nashville - Nashville selected David Legwand) in 1998 Entry Draft for Andrei Nazarov and Florida's 1st round choice (previously acquired, Tampa Bay selected Vincent Lecavallier) in 1998 Entry Draft, March 24, 1998.

• MARCINYSHYN, DAVID

David Marcinyshyn D – L. 6'3", 210 lbs. b: Edmonton, Alta., 2/4/1967.

Season	Club	League	GP	G	A	Pts	AG	AA	APts	PIM	PP	SH	GW	S	%	TGF	PGF	TGA	PGA	+/–	GP	G	A	Pts	PIM	PP	SH	GW
1984-85	Fort Saskatchewan Traders	AJHL	55	11	41	52	....	....	....	311	....	....	....	....	....	....	....	....	....	....	....	....	....	....	....	....	....	....
1985-86	Kamloops Blazers	WHL	57	2	7	9	....	....	....	111	....	....	....	....	....	....	....	....	....	....	16	1	3	4	12	....	....	....
1986-87	Kamloops Blazers	WHL	68	5	27	32	....	....	....	106	....	....	....	....	....	....	....	....	....	....	13	0	3	3	35	....	....	....
1987-88	Utica Devils	AHL	73	2	7	9	....	....	....	179	....	....	....	....	....	....	....	....	....	....	....	....	....	....	....	....	....	....
	Flint Spirits	IHL	3	0	0	0	....	....	....	4	....	....	....	....	....	....	....	....	....	....	16	0	2	2	31	....	....	....
1988-89	Utica Devils	AHL	74	4	14	18	....	....	....	101	....	....	....	....	....	....	....	....	....	....	5	0	0	0	13	....	....	....
1989-90	Utica Devils	AHL	74	6	18	24	....	....	....	164	....	....	....	....	....	....	....	....	....	....	5	0	2	2	21	....	....	....
1990-91	**New Jersey Devils**	**NHL**	**9**	**0**	**1**	**1**	**0**	**1**	**1**	**21**	**0**	**0**	**0**	**4**	**0.0**	**5**	**0**	**7**	**1**	**–1**	....	....	....	....	....	....	....	....
	Utica Devils	AHL	52	4	9	13	....	....	....	81	....	....	....	....	....	....	....	....	....	....	....	....	....	....	....	....	....	....
1991-92	**Quebec Nordiques**	**NHL**	**5**	**0**	**0**	**0**	**0**	**0**	**0**	**26**	**0**	**0**	**0**	**3**	**0.0**	**2**	**0**	**3**	**0**	**–1**	....	....	....	....	....	....	....	....
	Halifax Citadels	AHL	74	10	42	52	....	....	....	138	....	....	....	....	....	....	....	....	....	....	....	....	....	....	....	....	....	....
1992-93	**New York Rangers**	**NHL**	**2**	**0**	**0**	**0**	**0**	**0**	**0**	**2**	**0**	**0**	**0**	**1**	**0.0**	**0**	**0**	**1**	**0**	**–1**	....	....	....	....	....	....	....	....
	Binghamton Rangers	AHL	67	5	25	30	....	....	....	184	....	....	....	....	....	....	....	....	....	....	6	0	3	3	14	....	....	....
1993-94	Milwaukee Admirals	IHL	1	0	0	0	....	....	....	0	....	....	....	....	....	....	....	....	....	....	....	....	....	....	....	....	....	....
1994-95	Milwaukee Admirals	IHL	3	0	0	0	....	....	....	6	....	....	....	....	....	....	....	....	....	....	....	....	....	....	....	....	....	....
	Kalamazoo K-Wings	IHL	63	2	14	16	....	....	....	176	....	....	....	....	....	....	....	....	....	....	16	0	1	1	16	....	....	....
	NHL Totals		**16**	**0**	**1**	**1**	**0**	**1**	**1**	**49**	**0**	**0**	**0**	**8**	**0.0**	**7**	**0**	**11**	**1**		....	....	....	....	....	....	....	....

Signed as a free agent by **New Jersey**, September 26, 1986. Traded to **Quebec** by **New Jersey** for Brent Severyn, June 3, 1991. Signed as a free agent by **NY Rangers**, August 5, 1992.

• MARCOTTE, DON Don Marcotte LW – L. 5'11", 183 lbs. b: Asbestos, Que., 4/15/1947.

			REGULAR SEASON																		PLAYOFFS							
Season	Club	League	GP	G	A	Pts	AG	AA	APts	PIM	PP	SH	GW	S	%	TGF	PGF	TGA	PGA	+/–	GP	G	A	Pts	PIM	PP	SH	GW
1964-65	Niagara Falls Flyers	OHA	56	28	23	51	....	....	....	94	....	....	....	....	....	....	....	....	....	....	11	7	5	12	30	....	....	....
1965-66	Niagara Falls Flyers	OHA	45	28	22	50	....	....	....	76	....	....	....	....	....	....	....	....	....	....	6	3	3	6	11	....	....	....
	Boston Bruins	**NHL**	**1**	**0**	**0**	**0**	**0**	**0**	**0**	**0**	....	....	....	....	....	....	....	....	....	....	....	....	....	....	....	....	....	....
	Oklahoma City Blazers	CHL	2	1	0	1	....	....	....	2	....	....	....	....	....	....	....	....	....	....	5	2	0	2	0	....	....	....
1966-67	Niagara Falls Flyers	OHA	35	21	21	42	....	....	....	38	....	....	....	....	....	....	....	....	....	....	13	8	8	16	28	....	....	....
1967-68	Hershey Bears	AHL	72	31	22	53	....	....	....	35	....	....	....	....	....	....	....	....	....	....	5	0	1	1	16	....	....	....
1968-69	**Boston Bruins**	**NHL**	**7**	**1**	**0**	**1**	**1**	**0**	**1**	**2**	**0**	**0**	**0**	**7**	**14.3**	**3**	**0**	**4**	**1**	**0**	....	....	....	....	....	....	....	....
	Hershey Bears	AHL	67	35	21	56	....	....	....	65	....	....	....	....	....	....	....	....	....	....	11	7	2	9	25	....	....	....
1969-70	**Boston Bruins**	**NHL**	**35**	**9**	**3**	**12**	**10**	**3**	**13**	**14**	**0**	**0**	**1**	**73**	**12.3**	**17**	**0**	**29**	**9**	**–3**	**14**	**2**	**0**	**2**	**11**	**0**	**0**	**1**
	Hershey Bears	AHL	35	28	15	43	....	....	....	23	....	....	....	....	....	....	....	....	....	....	....	....	....	....	....	....	....	....
1970-71	**Boston Bruins**	**NHL**	**75**	**15**	**13**	**28**	**16**	**11**	**27**	**30**	**0**	**6**	**2**	**87**	**17.2**	**40**	**0**	**46**	**26**	**+20**	**4**	**0**	**0**	**0**	**0**	**0**	**0**	**0**
1971-72	**Boston Bruins**	**NHL**	**47**	**6**	**4**	**10**	**6**	**4**	**10**	**12**	**0**	**0**	**1**	**51**	**11.8**	**16**	**0**	**26**	**10**	**0**	**14**	**3**	**0**	**3**	**6**	**0**	**1**	**1**
	Boston Braves	AHL	8	4	7	11	....	....	....	2	....	....	....	....	....	....	....	....	....	....	....	....	....	....	....	....	....	....
1972-73	**Boston Bruins**	**NHL**	**78**	**24**	**31**	**55**	**24**	**26**	**50**	**49**	**1**	**2**	**3**	**175**	**13.7**	**82**	**1**	**68**	**19**	**+32**	**5**	**1**	**1**	**2**	**0**	**0**	**0**	**0**
1973-74	**Boston Bruins**	**NHL**	**78**	**24**	**26**	**50**	**25**	**22**	**47**	**18**	**0**	**3**	**3**	**150**	**16.0**	**81**	**1**	**62**	**26**	**+44**	**16**	**4**	**2**	**6**	**8**	**0**	**0**	**1**
1974-75	**Boston Bruins**	**NHL**	**80**	**31**	**33**	**64**	**29**	**26**	**55**	**76**	**1**	**0**	**2**	**165**	**18.8**	**99**	**6**	**92**	**23**	**+24**	**3**	**1**	**0**	**1**	**0**	**0**	**0**	**0**
1975-76	**Boston Bruins**	**NHL**	**58**	**16**	**20**	**36**	**15**	**16**	**31**	**24**	**1**	**0**	**2**	**96**	**16.7**	**58**	**6**	**49**	**12**	**+15**	**12**	**4**	**2**	**6**	**8**	**1**	**0**	**0**
1976-77	**Boston Bruins**	**NHL**	**80**	**27**	**18**	**45**	**26**	**15**	**41**	**20**	**3**	**1**	**5**	**176**	**15.3**	**89**	**9**	**67**	**15**	**+28**	**14**	**5**	**6**	**11**	**10**	**0**	**1**	**0**
1977-78	**Boston Bruins**	**NHL**	**77**	**20**	**34**	**54**	**19**	**28**	**47**	**16**	**4**	**2**	**0**	**159**	**12.6**	**96**	**14**	**94**	**44**	**+32**	**15**	**5**	**4**	**9**	**8**	**1**	**0**	**1**
1978-79	**Boston Bruins**	**NHL**	**79**	**20**	**27**	**47**	**18**	**21**	**39**	**10**	**2**	**4**	**5**	**156**	**12.8**	**71**	**4**	**113**	**52**	**+6**	**11**	**5**	**3**	**8**	**10**	**0**	**0**	**0**
	NHL All-Stars	Chal Cup	1	0	0	0	....	....	....	2	....	....	....	....	....	....	....	....	....	....	....	....	....	....	....	....	....	....
1979-80	**Boston Bruins**	**NHL**	**32**	**4**	**11**	**15**	**4**	**8**	**12**	**0**	**0**	**1**	**1**	**39**	**10.3**	**22**	**0**	**29**	**11**	**+4**	**10**	**2**	**3**	**5**	**4**	**0**	**0**	**1**
1980-81	**Boston Bruins**	**NHL**	**72**	**20**	**13**	**33**	**16**	**9**	**25**	**32**	**4**	**1**	**2**	**128**	**15.6**	**58**	**5**	**87**	**37**	**+3**	**3**	**2**	**2**	**4**	**6**	**0**	**0**	**0**
1981-82	**Boston Bruins**	**NHL**	**69**	**13**	**21**	**34**	**10**	**14**	**24**	**14**	**0**	**0**	**3**	**86**	**15.1**	**62**	**2**	**84**	**22**	**–2**	**11**	**0**	**4**	**4**	**10**	**0**	**0**	**0**
	NHL Totals		**868**	**230**	**254**	**484**	**219**	**203**	**422**	**317**	**16**	**20**	**30**	**1548**	**14.9**	**794**	**48**	**850**	**307**		**132**	**34**	**27**	**61**	**81**	**2**	**2**	**5**

• MARHA, JOSEF Josef Marha C – L. 6', 176 lbs. b: Havlickuv Brod, Czech., 6/2/1976. Quebec's 3rd choice, 35th overall, in 1994 Entry Draft.

			REGULAR SEASON																		PLAYOFFS							
Season	Club	League	GP	G	A	Pts	AG	AA	APts	PIM	PP	SH	GW	S	%	TGF	PGF	TGA	PGA	+/–	GP	G	A	Pts	PIM	PP	SH	GW
1992-93	Dukla Jihlava	Czech.	7	2	2	4	....	....	....	....	....	....	....	....	....	....	....	....	....	....	....	....	....	....	....	....	....	....
1993-94	Dukla Jihlava	Czech.	41	7	2	9	....	....	....	....	....	....	....	....	....	....	....	....	....	....	3	0	1	1	....	....	....	....
	Czech Republic	WJC-A	5	4	0	4	....	....	....	2	....	....	....	....	....	....	....	....	....	....	....	....	....	....	....	....	....	....
1994-95	Dukla Jihlava	Czech.	35	3	7	10	....	....	....	6	....	....	....	....	....	....	....	....	....	....	....	....	....	....	....	....	....	....
	Czech Republic	WJC-A	7	5	5	10	....	....	....	0	....	....	....	....	....	....	....	....	....	....	....	....	....	....	....	....	....	....
1995-96	**Colorado Avalanche**	**NHL**	**2**	**0**	**1**	**1**	**0**	**1**	**1**	**0**	**0**	**0**	**0**	**2**	**0.0**	**1**	**0**	**0**	**0**	**+1**	....	....	....	....	....	....	....	....
	Cornwall Aces	AHL	74	18	30	48	....	....	....	30	....	....	....	....	....	....	....	....	....	....	8	1	2	3	10	....	....	....
1996-97	**Colorado Avalanche**	**NHL**	**6**	**0**	**1**	**1**	**0**	**1**	**1**	**0**	**0**	**0**	**0**	**6**	**0.0**	**2**	**0**	**2**	**0**	**0**	....	....	....	....	....	....	....	....
	Hershey Bears	AHL	67	23	49	72	....	....	....	44	....	....	....	....	....	....	....	....	....	....	19	6	*16	*22	10	....	....	....
1997-98	**Colorado Avalanche**	**NHL**	**11**	**2**	**5**	**7**	**2**	**5**	**7**	**4**	**0**	**0**	**0**	**10**	**20.0**	**8**	**4**	**4**	**0**	**0**	....	....	....	....	....	....	....	....
	Anaheim Mighty Ducks	**NHL**	**12**	**7**	**4**	**11**	**8**	**4**	**12**	**0**	**3**	**0**	**0**	**21**	**33.3**	**13**	**6**	**6**	**3**	**+4**	....	....	....	....	....	....	....	....
	Hershey Bears	AHL	55	6	46	52	....	....	....	30	....	....	....	....	....	....	....	....	....	....	....	....	....	....	....	....	....	....
	NHL Totals		**31**	**9**	**11**	**20**	**10**	**11**	**21**	**4**	**3**	**0**	**0**	**39**	**23.1**	**24**	**10**	**12**	**3**		....	....	....	....	....	....	....	....

Rights transferred to **Colorado** after **Quebec** franchise relocated, June 21, 1995. Traded to **Anaheim** by **Colorado** for Warren Rychel and future considerations, March 24, 1998.

• MARINI, HECTOR Hector "The Wreaker" Marini RW – R. 6'1", 204 lbs. b: Timmins, Ont., 1/27/1957. NY Islanders' 3rd choice, 50th overall, in 1977 Amateur Draft.

			REGULAR SEASON																		PLAYOFFS							
Season	Club	League	GP	G	A	Pts	AG	AA	APts	PIM	PP	SH	GW	S	%	TGF	PGF	TGA	PGA	+/–	GP	G	A	Pts	PIM	PP	SH	GW
1974-75	Sudbury Wolves	OHA	69	12	19	31	....	....	....	70	....	....	....	....	....	....	....	....	....	....	....	....	....	....	....	....	....	....
1975-76	Sudbury Wolves	OHA	66	32	45	77	....	....	....	102	....	....	....	....	....	....	....	....	....	....	17	7	5	12	32	....	....	....
1976-77	Sudbury Wolves	OHA	64	32	58	90	....	....	....	89	....	....	....	....	....	....	....	....	....	....	6	1	3	4	9	....	....	....
1977-78	Fort Worth Texans	CHL	2	0	0	0	....	....	....	4	....	....	....	....	....	....	....	....	....	....	....	....	....	....	....	....	....	....
	Muskegon Mohawks	IHL	80	33	60	93	....	....	....	107	....	....	....	....	....	....	....	....	....	....	6	7	4	11	5	....	....	....
1978-79	**New York Islanders**	**NHL**	**1**	**0**	**0**	**0**	**0**	**0**	**0**	**2**	**0**	**0**	**0**	**1**	**0.0**	**0**	**0**	**2**	**0**	**–2**	**1**	**0**	**0**	**0**	**0**	**0**	**0**	**0**
	Fort Worth Texans	CHL	74	21	27	48	....	....	....	172	....	....	....	....	....	....	....	....	....	....	5	1	4	5	7	....	....	....
1979-80	Indianapolis Checkers	CHL	76	29	34	63	....	....	....	144	....	....	....	....	....	....	....	....	....	....	7	1	4	5	20	....	....	....
1980-81	**New York Islanders**	**NHL**	**14**	**4**	**7**	**11**	**3**	**5**	**8**	**39**	**1**	**0**	**0**	**9**	**44.4**	**16**	**2**	**5**	**0**	**+9**	**9**	**3**	**6**	**9**	**14**	**0**	**0**	**0**
	Indianapolis Checkers	CHL	54	15	37	52	....	....	....	85	....	....	....	....	....	....	....	....	....	....	....	....	....	....	....	....	....	....
1981-82	**New York Islanders**	**NHL**	**30**	**4**	**9**	**13**	**3**	**6**	**9**	**53**	**1**	**0**	**1**	**14**	**28.6**	**16**	**2**	**11**	**0**	**+3**	....	....	....	....	....	....	....	....
1982-83	**New Jersey Devils**	**NHL**	**77**	**17**	**28**	**45**	**14**	**19**	**33**	**105**	**5**	**0**	**3**	**109**	**15.6**	**70**	**24**	**62**	**1**	**–15**	....	....	....	....	....	....	....	....
1983-84	**New Jersey Devils**	**NHL**	**32**	**2**	**2**	**4**	**2**	**1**	**3**	**47**	**0**	**0**	**0**	**33**	**6.1**	**14**	**2**	**14**	**0**	**–7**	....	....	....	....	....	....	....	....
	Maine Mariners	AHL	17	7	4	11	....	....	....	20	....	....	....	....	....	....	....	....	....	....	....	....	....	....	....	....	....	....
1984-85	Maine Mariners	AHL	30	1	5	6	....	....	....	67	....	....	....	....	....	....	....	....	....	....	....	....	....	....	....	....	....	....
1985-86	Maine Mariners	AHL	6	0	5	5	....	....	....	17	....	....	....	....	....	....	....	....	....	....	....	....	....	....	....	....	....	....
	Fort Wayne Komets	IHL	7	1	1	2	....	....	....	5	....	....	....	....	....	....	....	....	....	....	....	....	....	....	....	....	....	....
	NHL Totals		**154**	**27**	**46**	**73**	**22**	**31**	**53**	**246**	**7**	**0**	**4**	**166**	**16.3**	**116**	**30**	**94**	**1**		**10**	**3**	**6**	**9**	**14**	**0**	**0**	**0**

Played in NHL All-Star Game (1983)

Traded to **New Jersey** by **NY Islanders** with NY Islanders' 4th round choice (later traded to Calgary — Calgary selected Bill Claviter) in 1983 Entry Draft for New Jersey's 4th round choice (Mikko Makela) in 1983 Entry Draft, October 1, 1982. • Suffered career-ending eye injury in game vs. Indianapolis (IHL), December 5, 1985.

• MARINUCCI, CHRIS Chris Marinucci C – L. 6', 188 lbs. b: Grand Rapids, MN, 12/29/1971. NY Islanders' 4th choice, 90th overall, in 1990 Entry Draft.

			REGULAR SEASON																		PLAYOFFS							
Season	Club	League	GP	G	A	Pts	AG	AA	APts	PIM	PP	SH	GW	S	%	TGF	PGF	TGA	PGA	+/–	GP	G	A	Pts	PIM	PP	SH	GW
1989-90	Grand Rapids High School	H.S.	28	24	39	63	....	....	....	12	....	....	....	....	....	....	....	....	....	....	....	....	....	....	....	....	....	....
1990-91	University of Minnesota-Duluth	WCHA	36	6	10	16	....	....	....	20	....	....	....	....	....	....	....	....	....	....	....	....	....	....	....	....	....	....
1991-92	University of Minnesota-Duluth	WCHA	37	6	13	19	....	....	....	41	....	....	....	....	....	....	....	....	....	....	....	....	....	....	....	....	....	....
1992-93	University of Minnesota-Duluth	WCHA	40	35	42	77	....	....	....	52	....	....	....	....	....	....	....	....	....	....	....	....	....	....	....	....	....	....
1993-94	University of Minnesota-Duluth	WCHA	38	*30	31	61	....	....	....	65	....	....	....	....	....	....	....	....	....	....	....	....	....	....	....	....	....	....
1994-95	**New York Islanders**	**NHL**	**12**	**1**	**4**	**5**	**2**	**6**	**8**	**2**	**0**	**0**	**0**	**11**	**9.1**	**7**	**1**	**7**	**0**	**–1**	....	....	....	....	....	....	....	....
	Denver Grizzlies	IHL	74	29	40	69	....	....	....	42	....	....	....	....	....	....	....	....	....	....	14	3	4	7	12	....	....	....
1995-96	Utah Grizzlies	IHL	8	3	5	8	....	....	....	8	....	....	....	....	....	....	....	....	....	....	....	....	....	....	....	....	....	....
1996-97	Utah Grizzlies	IHL	21	3	13	16	....	....	....	6	....	....	....	....	....	....	....	....	....	....	....	....	....	....	....	....	....	....
	Los Angeles Kings	**NHL**	**1**	**0**	**0**	**0**	**0**	**0**	**0**	**0**	**0**	**0**	**0**	**1**	**0.0**	**0**	**0**	**2**	**0**	**–2**	....	....	....	....	....	....	....	....
	Phoenix Roadrunners	IHL	62	23	29	52	....	....	....	26	....	....	....	....	....	....	....	....	....	....	....	....	....	....	....	....	....	....
	United States	WC-A	8	1	0	1	....	....	....	2	....	....	....	....	....	....	....	....	....	....	....	....	....	....	....	....	....	....
1997-98	Chicago Wolves	IHL	78	27	48	75	....	....	....	35	....	....	....	....	....	....	....	....	....	....	22	7	6	13	12	....	....	....
	NHL Totals		**13**	**1**	**4**	**5**	**2**	**6**	**8**	**2**	**0**	**0**	**0**	**12**	**8.3**	**7**	**1**	**9**	**0**		....	....	....	....	....	....	....	....

WCHA Second All-Star Team (1993) • WCHA First All-Star Team (1994) • NCAA West First All-American Team (1994) • Won Hobey Baker Memorial Award (Top U.S. Collegiate Player) (1994)
Traded to **LA Kings** by **NY Islanders** for Nick Vachon, November 19, 1996.

• MARK, GORDON Gordon Mark D – R. 6'4", 218 lbs. b: Edmonton, Alta., 9/10/1964. New Jersey's 4th choice, 108th overall, in 1983 Entry Draft.

			REGULAR SEASON																		PLAYOFFS							
Season	Club	League	GP	G	A	Pts	AG	AA	APts	PIM	PP	SH	GW	S	%	TGF	PGF	TGA	PGA	+/–	GP	G	A	Pts	PIM	PP	SH	GW
1982-83	Kamloops Jr. Oilers	WHL	71	12	20	32	....	....	....	135	....	....	....	....	....	....	....	....	....	....	7	1	1	2	8	....	....	....
1983-84	Kamloops Jr. Oilers	WHL	67	12	30	42	....	....	....	202	....	....	....	....	....	....	....	....	....	....	17	2	6	8	27	....	....	....
1984-85	Kamloops Blazers	WHL	32	11	23	34	....	....	....	68	....	....	....	....	....	....	....	....	....	....	7	1	2	3	10	....	....	....
1985-86	Maine Mariners	AHL	77	9	13	22	....	....	....	134	....	....	....	....	....	....	....	....	....	....	5	0	1	1	9	....	....	....
1986-87	**New Jersey Devils**	**NHL**	**36**	**3**	**5**	**8**	**3**	**4**	**7**	**82**	**0**	**0**	**0**	**21**	**0.7**	**00**	**1**	**43**	**10**	**–4**	....	....	....	....	....	....	....	....
	Maine Mariners	AHL	29	4	10	14	....	....	....	66	....	....	....	....	....	....	....	....	....	....	....	....	....	....	....	....	....	....
1987-88	**New Jersey Devils**	**NHL**	**19**	**0**	**2**	**2**	**0**	**1**	**1**	**27**	**0**	**0**	**0**	**11**	**0.0**	**4**	**0**	**20**	**3**	**–13**	....	....	....	....	....	....	....	....
	Utica Devils	AHL	50	5	21	26	....	....	....	96	....	....	....	....	....	....	....	....	....	....	....	....	....	....	....	....	....	....
1988-1992	Stony Plain Eagles	ASHL	STATISTICS NOT AVAILABLE																		....	....	....	....	....	....	....	....
1992-93	Cape Breton Oilers	AHL	60	3	21	24	....	....	....	78	....	....	....	....	....	....	....	....	....	....	16	1	7	8	20	....	....	....
1993-94	**Edmonton Oilers**	**NHL**	**12**	**0**	**1**	**1**	**0**	**1**	**1**	**43**	**0**	**0**	**0**	**8**	**0.0**	**8**	**0**	**11**	**1**	**–2**	....	....	....	....	....	....	....	....
	Cape Breton Oilers	AHL	49	11	20	31	....	....	....	116	....	....	....	....	....	....	....	....	....	....	5	0	2	2	26	....	....	....

Season	Club	League	GP	G	A	Pts	AG	AA	APts	PIM	PP	SH	GW	S	%	TGF	PGF	TGA	PGA	+/–	GP	G	A	Pts	PIM	PP	SH	GW
			REGULAR SEASON																		PLAYOFFS							
1994-95	**Edmonton Oilers**	**NHL**	**18**	**0**	**2**	**2**	**0**	**3**	**3**	**35**	**0**	**0**	**0**	**21**	**0.0**	**8**	**0**	**20**	**3**	**–9**	....	....	....	....	....	....	....	....
1995-96	Las Vegas Thunder	IHL	60	2	7	9	....	....	....	98	....	....	....	....	....	....	....	....	....	....	1	0	0	0	0	....	....	....
1996-97	Providence Bruins	AHL	7	0	1	1	....	....	....	36	....	....	....	....	....	....	....	....	....	....	....	....	....	....	....	....	....	....
	Utah Grizzlies	IHL	12	1	2	3	....	....	....	11	....	....	....	....	....	....	....	....	....	....	....	....	....	....	....	....	....	....
	NHL Totals		**85**	**3**	**10**	**13**	**3**	**9**	**12**	**187**	**0**	**0**	**0**	**71**	**4.2**	**50**	**1**	**94**	**17**		....	....	....	....	....	....	....	....

Signed as a free agent by **Edmonton**, February 1, 1994.

• MARKELL, JOHN

John Markell LW – L. 5'11", 185 lbs. b: Cornwall, Ont., 3/10/1956.

Season	Club	League	GP	G	A	Pts	AG	AA	APts	PIM	PP	SH	GW	S	%	TGF	PGF	TGA	PGA	+/–	GP	G	A	Pts	PIM	PP	SH	GW
1973-74	Cornwall Royals	QMJHL	18	4	1	5	....	....	....	0	....	....	....	....	....	....	....	....	....	....	....	....	....	....	....	....	....	....
1974-75	Cornwall Royals	QMJHL	42	9	19	28	....	....	....	22	....	....	....	....	....	....	....	....	....	....	....	....	....	....	....	....	....	....
1975-76	Bowling Green University	CCHA	30	12	25	37	....	....	....	24	....	....	....	....	....	....	....	....	....	....	....	....	....	....	....	....	....	....
1976-77	Bowling Green University	CCHA	39	26	32	58	....	....	....	48	....	....	....	....	....	....	....	....	....	....	....	....	....	....	....	....	....	....
1977-78	Bowling Green University	CCHA	39	33	28	61	....	....	....	81	....	....	....	....	....	....	....	....	....	....	....	....	....	....	....	....	....	....
1978-79	Bowling Green University	CCHA	42	31	49	80	....	....	....	96	....	....	....	....	....	....	....	....	....	....	....	....	....	....	....	....	....	....
1979-80	**Winnipeg Jets**	**NHL**	**38**	**10**	**7**	**17**	**9**	**5**	**14**	**21**	**2**	**0**	**1**	**46**	**21.7**	**27**	**9**	**31**	**1**	**–12**	....	....	....	....	....	....	....	....
	Tulsa Oilers	CHL	35	15	14	29	....	....	....	45	....	....	....	....	....	....	....	....	....	....	....	....	....	....	....	....	....	....
1980-81	**Winnipeg Jets**	**NHL**	**14**	**1**	**3**	**4**	**1**	**2**	**3**	**15**	**1**	**0**	**0**	**11**	**9.1**	**7**	**4**	**15**	**1**	**–11**	....	....	....	....	....	....	....	....
	Tulsa Oilers	CHL	48	24	18	42	....	....	....	34	....	....	....	....	....	....	....	....	....	....	8	5	1	6	28	....	....	....
1981-82	Salt Lake Golden Eagles	CHL	69	19	53	72	....	....	....	33	....	....	....	....	....	....	....	....	....	....	10	4	11	15	2	....	....	....
1982-83	Salt Lake Golden Eagles	CHL	77	33	27	60	....	....	....	35	....	....	....	....	....	....	....	....	....	....	6	3	2	5	6	....	....	....
1983-84	**St. Louis Blues**	**NHL**	**2**	**0**	**0**	**0**	**0**	**0**	**0**	**0**	**0**	**0**	**0**	**0**	**0.0**	**0**	**0**	**4**	**0**	**–4**	....	....	....	....	....	....	....	....
	Montana Magic	CHL	69	*44	40	84	....	....	....	61	....	....	....	....	....	....	....	....	....	....	....	....	....	....	....	....	....	....
1984-85	**Minnesota North Stars**	**NHL**	**1**	**0**	**0**	**0**	**0**	**0**	**0**	....	**0**	**0**	**0**	**0**	**0.0**	**0**	**0**	**0**	**0**	**0**	....	....	....	....	....	....	....	....
	Springfield Indians	AHL	46	16	25	41	....	....	....	23	....	....	....	....	....	....	....	....	....	....	....	....	....	....	....	....	....	....
1985-86	ERC Schwenningen	Germany	23	13	15	28	....	....	....	65	....	....	....	....	....	....	....	....	....	....	....	....	....	....	....	....	....	....
	NHL Totals		**55**	**11**	**10**	**21**	**10**	**7**	**17**	**36**	**3**	**0**	**1**	**57**	**19.3**	**34**	**13**	**50**	**2**		....	....	....	....	....	....	....	....

CCHA First All-Star Team (1977, 1978, 1979) • CHL First All-Star Team (1984)

Signed as a free agent by **Winnipeg**, April 16, 1979. Traded to **St. Louis** by **Winnipeg** with Scott Campbell for Ed Staniowski, Bryan Maxwell and Paul MacLean, July 3, 1981. Signed as a free agent by **Minnesota**, December 17, 1984.

• MARKHAM, RAY

Ray Markham C – R. 6'3", 220 lbs. b: Windsor, Ont., 1/23/1958. NY Rangers' 2nd choice, 43rd overall, in 1978 Amateur Draft.

Season	Club	League	GP	G	A	Pts	AG	AA	APts	PIM	PP	SH	GW	S	%	TGF	PGF	TGA	PGA	+/–	GP	G	A	Pts	PIM	PP	SH	GW
1975-76	Notre Dame Hounds	SJHL	45	15	19	34	....	....	....	245	....	....	....	....	....	....	....	....	....	....	....	....	....	....	....	....	....	....
1976-77	Flin Flon Bombers	WCJHL	68	33	41	74	....	....	....	318	....	....	....	....	....	....	....	....	....	....	....	....	....	....	....	....	....	....
1977-78	Flin Flon Bombers	WCJHL	68	35	65	100	....	....	....	323	....	....	....	....	....	....	....	....	....	....	17	10	13	23	96	....	....	....
1978-79	New Haven Nighthawks	AHL	77	13	15	28	....	....	....	151	....	....	....	....	....	....	....	....	....	....	8	2	3	5	10	....	....	....
1979-80	**New York Rangers**	**NHL**	**14**	**1**	**1**	**2**	**1**	**1**	**2**	**21**	**0**	**0**	**0**	**6**	**16.7**	**3**	**0**	**6**	**0**	**–3**	**7**	**1**	**0**	**1**	**24**	**0**	**0**	**0**
	New Haven Nighthawks	AHL	57	9	20	29	....	....	....	198	....	....	....	....	....	....	....	....	....	....	....	....	....	....	....	....	....	....
1980-81	New Haven Nighthawks	AHL	42	10	9	19	....	....	....	122	....	....	....	....	....	....	....	....	....	....	....	....	....	....	....	....	....	....
	Wichita Wind	CHL	7	1	1	2	....	....	....	18	....	....	....	....	....	....	....	....	....	....	....	....	....	....	....	....	....	....
1981-82	Wichita Wind	CHL	48	15	12	27	....	....	....	110	....	....	....	....	....	....	....	....	....	....	....	....	....	....	....	....	....	....
1982-83	Flint Generals	IHL	42	16	30	46	....	....	....	176	....	....	....	....	....	....	....	....	....	....	5	2	4	6	52	....	....	....
1983-84	Flint Generals	IHL	12	2	3	5	....	....	....	39	....	....	....	....	....	....	....	....	....	....	....	....	....	....	....	....	....	....
	Kalamazoo Wings	IHL	69	23	28	51	....	....	....	172	....	....	....	....	....	....	....	....	....	....	3	1	2	3	9	....	....	....
	NHL Totals		**14**	**1**	**1**	**2**	**1**	**1**	**2**	**21**	**0**	**0**	**0**	**6**	**16.7**	**3**	**0**	**6**	**0**		**7**	**1**	**0**	**1**	**24**	**0**	**0**	**0**

• MARKOV, DANIIL

Daniil Markov D – L. 5'11", 176 lbs. b: Moscow, USSR, 7/11/1976. Toronto's 7th choice, 223rd overall, in 1995 Entry Draft.

Season	Club	League	GP	G	A	Pts	AG	AA	APts	PIM	PP	SH	GW	S	%	TGF	PGF	TGA	PGA	+/–	GP	G	A	Pts	PIM	PP	SH	GW
1993-94	Spartak Moscow	CIS	13	1	0	1	....	....	....	6	....	....	....	....	....	....	....	....	....	....	1	0	0	0	0	....	....	....
1994-95	Spartak Moscow	CIS	39	0	1	1	....	....	....	36	....	....	....	....	....	....	....	....	....	....	....	....	....	....	....	....	....	....
1995-96	Spartak Moscow	CIS	38	2	0	2	....	....	....	12	....	....	....	....	....	....	....	....	....	....	2	0	0	0	2	....	....	....
1996-97	Spartak Moscow	Russia	39	3	6	9	....	....	....	41	....	....	....	....	....	....	....	....	....	....	....	....	....	....	....	....	....	....
	St. John's Maple Leafs	AHL	10	2	4	6	....	....	....	18	....	....	....	....	....	....	....	....	....	....	11	2	6	8	14	....	....	....
1997-98	**Toronto Maple Leafs**	**NHL**	**25**	**2**	**5**	**7**	**2**	**5**	**7**	**28**	**1**	**0**	**0**	**15**	**13.3**	**18**	**3**	**16**	**1**	**0**	....	....	....	....	....	....	....	....
	St. John's Maple Leafs	AHL	52	3	23	26	....	....	....	124	....	....	....	....	....	....	....	....	....	....	2	0	1	1	0	....	....	....
	Russia	WC-A	4	0	0	0	....	....	....	0	....	....	....	....	....	....	....	....	....	....	....	....	....	....	....	....	....	....
	NHL Totals		**25**	**2**	**5**	**7**	**2**	**5**	**7**	**28**	**1**	**0**	**0**	**15**	**13.3**	**18**	**3**	**16**	**1**		....	....	....	....	....	....	....	....

• MARKS, JOHN

John Marks LW – L. 6'2", 200 lbs. b: Hamiota, Man., 3/22/1948. Chicago's 1st choice, 9th overall, in 1968 Amateur Draft.

Season	Club	League	GP	G	A	Pts	AG	AA	APts	PIM	PP	SH	GW	S	%	TGF	PGF	TGA	PGA	+/–	GP	G	A	Pts	PIM	PP	SH	GW
1967-68	University of North Dakota	WCHA	33	3	6	9	....	....	....	16	....	....	....	....	....	....	....	....	....	....	....	....	....	....	....	....	....	....
1968-69	University of North Dakota	WCHA	29	6	26	32	....	....	....	38	....	....	....	....	....	....	....	....	....	....	....	....	....	....	....	....	....	....
1969-70	University of North Dakota	WCHA	30	5	14	19	....	....	....	34	....	....	....	....	....	....	....	....	....	....	....	....	....	....	....	....	....	....
1970-71	Dallas Black Hawks	CHL	66	3	16	19	....	....	....	49	....	....	....	....	....	....	....	....	....	....	10	0	4	4	14	....	....	....
1971-72	Dallas Black Hawks	CHL	72	8	35	43	....	....	....	105	....	....	....	....	....	....	....	....	....	....	12	1	2	3	8	....	....	....
1972-73	**Chicago Black Hawks**	**NHL**	**55**	**3**	**10**	**13**	**3**	**8**	**11**	**21**	**1**	**0**	**0**	**45**	**6.7**	**33**	**4**	**28**	**4**	**+5**	**16**	**1**	**2**	**3**	**2**	**1**	**0**	**1**
1973-74	**Chicago Black Hawks**	**NHL**	**76**	**13**	**18**	**31**	**13**	**16**	**29**	**22**	**3**	**0**	**1**	**139**	**9.4**	**62**	**16**	**25**	**1**	**+22**	**11**	**2**	**0**	**2**	**8**	**0**	**0**	**1**
1974-75	**Chicago Black Hawks**	**NHL**	**80**	**17**	**30**	**47**	**16**	**24**	**40**	**56**	**4**	**0**	**3**	**163**	**10.4**	**86**	**19**	**49**	**9**	**+27**	**8**	**2**	**6**	**8**	**34**	**0**	**0**	**1**
1975-76	**Chicago Black Hawks**	**NHL**	**80**	**21**	**23**	**44**	**20**	**18**	**38**	**43**	**6**	**1**	**4**	**152**	**13.8**	**79**	**29**	**68**	**14**	**–4**	**4**	**0**	**0**	**0**	**10**	**0**	**0**	**0**
1976-77	**Chicago Black Hawks**	**NHL**	**80**	**7**	**15**	**22**	**7**	**12**	**19**	**41**	**0**	**0**	**0**	**156**	**4.5**	**54**	**7**	**84**	**16**	**–21**	**2**	**0**	**0**	**0**	**4**	**0**	**0**	**0**
1977-78	**Chicago Black Hawks**	**NHL**	**80**	**15**	**22**	**37**	**14**	**18**	**32**	**26**	**0**	**0**	**1**	**118**	**12.7**	**71**	**1**	**72**	**29**	**+27**	**4**	**0**	**1**	**1**	**0**	**0**	**0**	**0**
1978-79	**Chicago Black Hawks**	**NHL**	**80**	**21**	**24**	**45**	**19**	**18**	**37**	**35**	**4**	**0**	**2**	**152**	**13.8**	**69**	**11**	**91**	**35**	**+2**	**4**	**0**	**0**	**0**	**2**	**0**	**0**	**0**
1979-80	**Chicago Black Hawks**	**NHL**	**74**	**6**	**15**	**21**	**5**	**11**	**16**	**51**	**1**	**0**	**1**	**111**	**5.4**	**30**	**5**	**56**	**15**	**–16**	**4**	**0**	**0**	**0**	**0**	**0**	**0**	**0**
1980-81	**Chicago Black Hawks**	**NHL**	**39**	**8**	**6**	**14**	**7**	**4**	**11**	**28**	**1**	**1**	**0**	**41**	**19.5**	**21**	**1**	**36**	**13**	**–3**	**3**	**0**	**0**	**0**	**0**	**0**	**0**	**0**
1981-82	**Chicago Black Hawks**	**NHL**	**13**	**1**	**0**	**1**	**1**	**0**	**1**	**7**	**0**	**0**	**0**	**8**	**12.5**	**8**	**0**	**11**	**3**	**0**	**1**	**0**	**0**	**0**	**0**	**0**	**0**	**0**
	Indianapolis Checkers	CHL	53	6	20	26	....	....	....	73	....	....	....	....	....	....	....	....	....	....	....	....	....	....	....	....	....	....
1982-83	Kalamazoo K-Wings	IHL	DID NOT PLAY – COACHING																									
	NHL Totals		**657**	**112**	**163**	**275**	**105**	**129**	**234**	**330**	**20**	**2**	**12**	**1085**	**10.3**	**513**	**93**	**520**	**139**		**57**	**5**	**9**	**14**	**60**	**1**	**0**	**3**

WCHA Second All-Star Team (1969) • NCAA West First All-American Team (1969, 1970) • WCHA First All-Star Team (1970)

Played in NHL All-Star Game (1976)

• MARKWART, NEVIN

Nevin Markwart LW – L. 5'10", 180 lbs. b: Toronto, Ont., 12/9/1964. Boston's 1st choice, 21st overall, in 1983 Entry Draft.

Season	Club	League	GP	G	A	Pts	AG	AA	APts	PIM	PP	SH	GW	S	%	TGF	PGF	TGA	PGA	+/–	GP	G	A	Pts	PIM	PP	SH	GW
1981-82	Regina Pats	WHL	25	2	12	14	....	....	....	56	....	....	....	....	....	....	....	....	....	....	20	2	2	4	82	....	....	....
1982-83	Regina Pats	WHL	43	27	39	66	....	....	....	91	....	....	....	....	....	....	....	....	....	....	1	0	0	0	0	....	....	....
1983-84	**Boston Bruins**	**NHL**	**70**	**14**	**16**	**30**	**11**	**11**	**22**	**121**	**0**	**0**	**3**	**66**	**21.2**	**57**	**2**	**63**	**10**	**+2**	....	....	....	....	....	....	....	....
1984-85	**Boston Bruins**	**NHL**	**26**	**0**	**4**	**4**	**0**	**3**	**3**	**36**	**0**	**0**	**0**	**5**	**0.0**	**5**	**0**	**7**	**1**	**–1**	**1**	**0**	**0**	**0**	**0**	**0**	**0**	**0**
	Hershey Bears	AHL	38	13	18	31	....	....	....	79	....	....	....	....	....	....	....	....	....	....	....	....	....	....	....	....	....	....
1985-86	**Boston Bruins**	**NHL**	**65**	**7**	**15**	**22**	**6**	**10**	**16**	**207**	**0**	**0**	**1**	**42**	**16.7**	**34**	**1**	**54**	**19**	**–2**	....	....	....	....	....	....	....	....
1986-87	**Boston Bruins**	**NHL**	**64**	**10**	**9**	**19**	**9**	**6**	**15**	**225**	**0**	**0**	**2**	**65**	**15.4**	**33**	**0**	**39**	**0**	**–6**	**4**	**0**	**0**	**0**	**9**	**0**	**0**	**0**
	Moncton Golden Flames	AHL	3	3	3	6	....	....	....	11	....	....	....	....	....	....	....	....	....	....	....	....	....	....	....	....	....	....
1987-88	**Boston Bruins**	**NHL**	**25**	**1**	**12**	**13**	**1**	**9**	**10**	**85**	**0**	**0**	**0**	**24**	**4.2**	**19**	**1**	**17**	**3**	**+4**	**2**	**0**	**0**	**0**	**2**	**0**	**0**	**0**
1988-89	Maine Mariners	AHL	1	0	1	1	....	....	....	0	....	....	....	....	....	....	....	....	....	....	....	....	....	....	....	....	....	....
1989-90	**Boston Bruins**	**NHL**	**8**	**1**	**2**	**3**	**1**	**1**	**2**	**15**	**1**	**0**	**0**	**6**	**16.7**	**3**	**1**	**6**	**2**	**–2**	....	....	....	....	....	....	....	....
1990-91	**Boston Bruins**	**NHL**	**23**	**3**	**3**	**6**	**3**	**2**	**5**	**36**	**0**	**0**	**0**	**13**	**23.1**	**13**	**1**	**15**	**3**	**0**	**12**	**1**	**0**	**1**	**22**	**0**	**0**	**0**
	Maine Mariners	AHL	21	5	5	10	....	....	....	22	....	....	....	....	....	....	....	....	....	....	....	....	....	....	....	....	....	....
1991-92	**Boston Bruins**	**NHL**	**18**	**3**	**6**	**9**	**3**	**4**	**7**	**44**	**0**	**0**	**0**	**12**	**25.0**	**14**	**0**	**16**	**4**	**+2**	....	....	....	....	....	....	....	....
	Maine Mariners	AHL	17	4	7	11	....	....	....	32	....	....	....	....	....	....	....	....	....	....	....	....	....	....	....	....	....	....
	Calgary Flames	**NHL**	**10**	**2**	**1**	**3**	**2**	**1**	**3**	**25**	**0**	**0**	**0**	**4**	**50.0**	**5**	**0**	**10**	**3**	**–2**	....	....	....	....	....	....	....	....
	EHC Biel	Switz.	4	2	2	4	....	....	....	2	....	....	....	....	....	....	....	....	....	....	....	....	....	....	....	....	....	....
1992-93	Springfield Indians	AHL	7	2	0	2	....	....	....	24	....	....	....	....	....	....	....	....	....	....	....	....	....	....	....	....	....	....
	NHL Totals		**309**	**41**	**68**	**109**	**36**	**47**	**83**	**794**	**1**	**0**	**6**	**237**	**17.3**	**183**	**6**	**227**	**45**		**19**	**1**	**0**	**1**	**33**	**0**	**0**	**0**

Claimed on waivers by **Calgary** from **Boston**, February 14, 1992.

			REGULAR SEASON																		PLAYOFFS							
Season	Club	League	GP	G	A	Pts	AG	AA	APts	PIM	PP	SH	GW	S	%	TGF	PGF	TGA	PGA	+/–	GP	G	A	Pts	PIM	PP	SH	GW

• MARLEAU, PATRICK Patrick Marleau C – L. 6'2", 190 lbs. b: Swift Current, Sask., 9/15/1979. San Jose's 1st choice, 2nd overall, in 1997 Entry Draft.

Season	Club	League	GP	G	A	Pts	AG	AA	APts	PIM	PP	SH	GW	S	%	TGF	PGF	TGA	PGA	+/–	GP	G	A	Pts	PIM	PP	SH	GW
1995-96	Seattle Thunderbirds	WHL	72	32	42	74	....	....	....	22	....	....	....	....	....	....	....	....	....	....	5	3	4	7	4	....	....	....
1996-97	Seattle Thunderbirds	WHL	71	51	74	125	....	....	....	37	....	....	....	....	....	....	....	....	....	....	15	7	16	23	12	....	....	....
1997-98	**San Jose Sharks**	**NHL**	**74**	**13**	**19**	**32**	**15**	**19**	**34**	**14**	**1**	**0**	**2**	**90**	**14.4**	**50**	**13**	**32**	**0**	**+5**	**5**	**0**	**1**	**1**	**0**	**0**	**0**	**0**
	NHL Totals		**74**	**13**	**19**	**32**	**15**	**19**	**34**	**14**	**1**	**0**	**2**	**90**	**14.4**	**50**	**13**	**32**	**0**		**5**	**0**	**1**	**1**	**0**	**0**	**0**	**0**

WHL West First All-Star Team (1997)

• MAROIS, DANIEL Daniel Marois RW – R. 6', 190 lbs. b: Montreal, Que., 10/3/1968. Toronto's 2nd choice, 28th overall, in 1987 Entry Draft.

Season	Club	League	GP	G	A	Pts	AG	AA	APts	PIM	PP	SH	GW	S	%	TGF	PGF	TGA	PGA	+/–	GP	G	A	Pts	PIM	PP	SH	GW
1985-86	Verdun Jr. Canadiens	QMJHL	58	42	35	77	....	....	....	110	....	....	....	....	....	....	....	....	....	....	5	4	2	6	6	....	....	....
1986-87	Chicoutimi Sagueneens	QMJHL	40	22	26	48	....	....	....	143	....	....	....	....	....	....	....	....	....	....	16	7	14	21	25	....	....	....
1987-88	Verdun Jr. Canadiens	QMJHL	67	52	36	88	....	....	....	153	....	....	....	....	....	....	....	....	....	....	....	....	....	....	....	....	....	....
	Newmarket Saints	AHL	8	4	4	8	....	....	....	4	....	....	....	....	....	....	....	....	....	....	....	....	....	....	....	....	....	....
	Toronto Maple Leafs	**NHL**	....	....	....	....	....	....	....	....	....	....	....	....	....	....	....	....	....	....	**3**	**1**	**0**	**1**	**0**	....	....	....
1988-89	**Toronto Maple Leafs**	**NHL**	**76**	**31**	**23**	**54**	**26**	**16**	**42**	**76**	**7**	**0**	**4**	**146**	**21.2**	**77**	**17**	**64**	**0**	**–4**	....	....	....	....	....	....	....	....
1989-90	**Toronto Maple Leafs**	**NHL**	**68**	**39**	**37**	**76**	**34**	**26**	**60**	**82**	**14**	**0**	**3**	**183**	**21.3**	**111**	**40**	**70**	**0**	**+1**	**5**	**2**	**2**	**4**	**12**	**2**	**0**	**0**
1990-91	**Toronto Maple Leafs**	**NHL**	**78**	**21**	**9**	**30**	**19**	**7**	**26**	**112**	**6**	**0**	**1**	**152**	**13.8**	**70**	**25**	**61**	**0**	**–16**	....	....	....	....	....	....	....	....
1991-92	**Toronto Maple Leafs**	**NHL**	**63**	**15**	**11**	**26**	**14**	**8**	**22**	**76**	**4**	**0**	**0**	**140**	**10.7**	**51**	**18**	**69**	**0**	**–36**	....	....	....	....	....	....	....	....
	New York Islanders	**NHL**	**12**	**2**	**5**	**7**	**2**	**4**	**6**	**18**	**0**	**0**	**0**	**19**	**10.5**	**10**	**0**	**8**	**0**	**+2**	....	....	....	....	....	....	....	....
1992-93	**New York Islanders**	**NHL**	**28**	**2**	**5**	**7**	**2**	**3**	**5**	**35**	**0**	**0**	**0**	**41**	**4.9**	**14**	**1**	**18**	**2**	**–3**	....	....	....	....	....	....	....	....
	Capital District Islanders	AHL	4	2	0	2	....	....	....	0	....	....	....	....	....	....	....	....	....	....	....	....	....	....	....	....	....	....
1993-94	**Boston Bruins**	**NHL**	**22**	**7**	**3**	**10**	**7**	**2**	**9**	**18**	**3**	**0**	**0**	**32**	**21.9**	**18**	**8**	**15**	**1**	**–4**	**11**	**0**	**1**	**1**	**16**	**0**	**0**	**0**
	Providence Bruins	AHL	6	1	2	3	....	....	....	6	....	....	....	....	....	....	....	....	....	....	....	....	....	....	....	....	....	....
1994-95			DID NOT PLAY – INJURED																									
1995-96	Michigan K-Wings	IHL	61	28	28	56	....	....	....	105	....	....	....	....	....	....	....	....	....	....	....	....	....	....	....	....	....	....
	Dallas Stars	**NHL**	**3**	**0**	**0**	**0**	**0**	**0**	**0**	**2**	**0**	**0**	**0**	**1**	**0.0**	**2**	**2**	**0**	**0**	**0**	....	....	....	....	....	....	....	....
	Minnesota Moose	IHL	13	4	3	7	....	....	....	20	....	....	....	....	....	....	....	....	....	....	....	....	....	....	....	....	....	....
1996-97	Quebec Rafales	IHL	7	1	1	2	....	....	....	12	....	....	....	....	....	....	....	....	....	....	....	....	....	....	....	....	....	....
	Utah Grizzlies	IHL	29	7	9	16	....	....	....	58	....	....	....	....	....	....	....	....	....	....	....	....	....	....	....	....	....	....
	SC Bern	Switz.	8	7	7	14	....	....	....	10	....	....	....	....	....	....	....	....	....	....	11	4	8	12	26	....	....	....
1997-98	Adler Mannheim	EuroHL	4	1	1	2	....	....	....	52	....	....	....	....	....	....	....	....	....	....	....	....	....	....	....	....	....	....
	Adler Mannheim	Germany	19	3	6	9	....	....	....	38	....	....	....	....	....	....	....	....	....	....	....	....	....	....	....	....	....	....
	SC Bern	EuroHL	1	1	0	1	....	....	....	0	....	....	....	....	....	....	....	....	....	....	....	....	....	....	....	....	....	....
	SC Bern	Switz.	21	16	4	20	....	....	....	72	....	....	....	....	....	....	....	....	....	....	7	1	5	6	16	....	....	....
	NHL Totals		**350**	**117**	**93**	**210**	**104**	**66**	**170**	**419**	**34**	**0**	**8**	**714**	**16.4**	**353**	**111**	**305**	**3**		**19**	**3**	**3**	**6**	**28**	**2**	**0**	**0**

Traded to **NY Islanders** by **Toronto** with Claude Loiselle for Ken Baumgartner and Dave McLlwain, March 10, 1992. Traded to **Boston** by **NY Islanders** for Boston's 8th round choice (Peter Hogardh) in 1994 Entry Draft, March 18, 1993. • Missed entire 1994-95 season after undergoing back surgery, December, 1994. Signed as a free agent by **Dallas**, January 26, 1995. Signed as a free agent by **Toronto**, August 22, 1996.

• MAROIS, MARIO Mario Marois D – R. 5'11", 190 lbs. b: Quebec City, Que., 12/15/1957. NY Rangers' 5th choice, 62nd overall, in 1977 Amateur Draft.

Season	Club	League	GP	G	A	Pts	AG	AA	APts	PIM	PP	SH	GW	S	%	TGF	PGF	TGA	PGA	+/–	GP	G	A	Pts	PIM	PP	SH	GW
1975-76	Quebec Remparts	QMJHL	67	11	42	53	....	....	....	270	....	....	....	....	....	....	....	....	....	....	15	2	3	5	86	....	....	....
1976-77	Quebec Remparts	QMJHL	72	17	67	84	....	....	....	239	....	....	....	....	....	....	....	....	....	....	14	1	17	18	75	....	....	....
1977-78	**New York Rangers**	**NHL**	**8**	**1**	**1**	**2**	**1**	**1**	**2**	**15**	**0**	**0**	**0**	**13**	**7.7**	**6**	**2**	**7**	**0**	**–3**	**1**	**0**	**0**	**0**	**5**	**0**	**0**	**0**
	New Haven Nighthawks	AHL	52	8	23	31	....	....	....	147	....	....	....	....	....	....	....	....	....	....	12	5	3	8	31	....	....	....
1978-79	**New York Rangers**	**NHL**	**71**	**5**	**26**	**31**	**5**	**20**	**25**	**153**	**1**	**0**	**0**	**115**	**4.3**	**106**	**25**	**72**	**9**	**+18**	**18**	**0**	**6**	**6**	**29**	**0**	**0**	**0**
1979-80	**New York Rangers**	**NHL**	**79**	**8**	**23**	**31**	**7**	**18**	**25**	**142**	**1**	**0**	**1**	**158**	**5.1**	**96**	**13**	**102**	**19**	**0**	**9**	**0**	**2**	**2**	**8**	**0**	**0**	**0**
1980-81	**New York Rangers**	**NHL**	**8**	**1**	**2**	**3**	**1**	**1**	**2**	**46**	**0**	**0**	**0**	**11**	**9.1**	**8**	**2**	**12**	**1**	**–5**	....	....	....	....	....	....	....	....
	Vancouver Canucks	**NHL**	**50**	**4**	**12**	**16**	**3**	**8**	**11**	**115**	**1**	**0**	**0**	**79**	**5.1**	**50**	**3**	**52**	**5**	**0**	....	....	....	....	....	....	....	....
	Quebec Nordiques	**NHL**	**11**	**0**	**7**	**7**	**0**	**5**	**5**	**20**	**0**	**0**	**0**	**17**	**0.0**	**23**	**1**	**13**	**2**	**+11**	**5**	**0**	**1**	**1**	**6**	**0**	**0**	**0**
1981-82	**Quebec Nordiques**	**NHL**	**71**	**11**	**32**	**43**	**9**	**21**	**30**	**161**	**2**	**0**	**0**	**124**	**8.9**	**122**	**9**	**136**	**42**	**+19**	**13**	**1**	**2**	**3**	**44**	**0**	**0**	**0**
1982-83	**Quebec Nordiques**	**NHL**	**36**	**2**	**12**	**14**	**2**	**8**	**10**	**100**	**0**	**0**	**0**	**83**	**2.4**	**57**	**5**	**74**	**27**	**+5**	....	....	....	....	....	....	....	....
1983-84	**Quebec Nordiques**	**NHL**	**80**	**13**	**36**	**49**	**10**	**24**	**34**	**151**	**4**	**0**	**0**	**186**	**7.0**	**154**	**28**	**118**	**43**	**+51**	**9**	**1**	**4**	**5**	**6**	**0**	**0**	**0**
1984-85	**Quebec Nordiques**	**NHL**	**76**	**6**	**37**	**43**	**5**	**25**	**30**	**91**	**2**	**0**	**0**	**152**	**3.9**	**109**	**28**	**117**	**38**	**+2**	**18**	**0**	**8**	**8**	**12**	**0**	**0**	**0**
1985-86	**Quebec Nordiques**	**NHL**	**20**	**1**	**12**	**13**	**1**	**8**	**9**	**42**	**1**	**0**	**1**	**52**	**1.9**	**24**	**9**	**33**	**8**	**–10**	....	....	....	....	....	....	....	....
	Winnipeg Jets	**NHL**	**56**	**4**	**28**	**32**	**3**	**10**	**22**	**110**	**0**	**0**	**0**	**121**	**3.3**	**89**	**28**	**108**	**25**	**–22**	**3**	**1**	**4**	**5**	**6**	**1**	**0**	**0**
1986-87	**Winnipeg Jets**	**NHL**	**79**	**4**	**40**	**44**	**3**	**29**	**32**	**106**	**1**	**0**	**0**	**193**	**2.1**	**100**	**26**	**103**	**28**	**–1**	**10**	**1**	**3**	**4**	**23**	**0**	**0**	**1**
1987-88	**Winnipeg Jets**	**NHL**	**79**	**7**	**44**	**51**	**6**	**31**	**37**	**111**	**3**	**0**	**1**	**170**	**4.1**	**106**	**30**	**129**	**58**	**+5**	**5**	**0**	**4**	**4**	**6**	**0**	**0**	**0**
1988-89	**Winnipeg Jets**	**NHL**	**7**	**1**	**1**	**2**	**1**	**1**	**2**	**17**	**1**	**0**	**0**	**10**	**10.0**	**5**	**3**	**16**	**8**	**–6**	....	....	....	....	....	....	....	....
	Quebec Nordiques	**NHL**	**42**	**2**	**11**	**13**	**2**	**8**	**10**	**101**	**0**	**0**	**0**	**61**	**3.3**	**38**	**7**	**66**	**20**	**–15**	....	....	....	....	....	....	....	....
	Canada	WEC-A	10	0	4	4	....	....	....	6	....	....	....	....	....	....	....	....	....	....	....	....	....	....	....	....	....	....
1989-90	**Quebec Nordiques**	**NHL**	**67**	**3**	**15**	**18**	**3**	**11**	**14**	**104**	**2**	**0**	**0**	**108**	**2.8**	**54**	**10**	**124**	**35**	**–45**	....	....	....	....	....	....	....	....
1990-91	**St. Louis Blues**	**NHL**	**64**	**2**	**14**	**16**	**2**	**11**	**13**	**81**	**0**	**0**	**0**	**59**	**3.4**	**62**	**3**	**61**	**19**	**+17**	**9**	**0**	**0**	**0**	**37**	**0**	**0**	**0**
1991-92	**St. Louis Blues**	**NHL**	**17**	**0**	**1**	**1**	**0**	**1**	**1**	**38**	**0**	**0**	**0**	**11**	**0.0**	**6**	**0**	**12**	**3**	**–3**	....	....	....	....	....	....	....	....
	Winnipeg Jets	**NHL**	**34**	**1**	**3**	**4**	**1**	**2**	**3**	**34**	**0**	**1**	**0**	**32**	**3.1**	**15**	**0**	**32**	**9**	**–8**	....	....	....	....	....	....	....	....
1992-93	Hamilton Canucks	AHL	68	5	27	32	....	....	....	86	....	....	....	....	....	....	....	....	....	....	....	....	....	....	....	....	....	....
	NHL Totals		**955**	**76**	**357**	**433**	**65**	**252**	**317**	**1746**	**19**	**1**	**3**	**1755**	**4.3**	**1230**	**232**	**1387**	**399**		**100**	**4**	**34**	**38**	**182**	**1**	**0**	**1**

QMJHL Second All-Star Team (1977)

Traded to **Vancouver** by **NY Rangers** with Jim Mayer for Jere Gillis and Jeff Bandura, November 11, 1980. Traded to **Quebec** by **Vancouver** for Gerry Lariviere, March 10, 1981. Traded to **Winnipeg** by **Quebec** for Robert Picard, November 27, 1985. Traded to **Quebec** by **Winnipeg** for Gord Donnelly, December 6, 1988. Claimed by **St. Louis** from **Winnipeg** in Waiver Draft, October 1, 1990. Traded to **Winnipeg** by **Quebec** for future considerations, November 26, 1991.

• MAROTTE, GILLES Gilles "Captain Crunch" Marotte D – L. 5'9", 205 lbs. b: Montreal, Que., 6/7/1945.

Season	Club	League	GP	G	A	Pts	AG	AA	APts	PIM	PP	SH	GW	S	%	TGF	PGF	TGA	PGA	+/–	GP	G	A	Pts	PIM	PP	SH	GW
1962-63	Victoriaville Bruins	QJHL	52	12	25	37	....	....	....	....	....	....	....	....	....	....	....	....	....	....	....	....	....	....	....	....	....	....
1963-64	Niagara Falls Flyers	OHA	56	12	34	46	....	....	....	160	....	....	....	....	....	....	....	....	....	....	4	0	0	0	9	....	....	....
1964-65	Niagara Falls Flyers	OHA	52	12	25	37	....	....	....	122	....	....	....	....	....	....	....	....	....	....	11	2	0	2	50	....	....	....
1965-66	Niagara Falls Flyers	OHA	13	2	20	22	....	....	....	52	....	....	....	....	....	....	....	....	....	....	....	....	....	....	....	....	....	....
	Boston Bruins	**NHL**	**51**	**3**	**17**	**20**	**4**	**17**	**21**	**52**	....	....	....	....	....	....	....	....	....	....	....	....	....	....	....	....	....	....
1966-67	**Boston Bruins**	**NHL**	**67**	**7**	**8**	**15**	**9**	**8**	**17**	**112**	....	....	....	....	....	....	....	....	....	....	....	....	....	....	....	....	....	....
1967-68	**Chicago Black Hawks**	**NHL**	**73**	**0**	**21**	**21**	**0**	**22**	**22**	**122**	**0**	**0**	**0**	**153**	**0.0**	**92**	**2**	**97**	**11**	**+4**	**11**	**3**	**1**	**4**	**14**	**0**	**0**	**1**
1968-69	**Chicago Black Hawks**	**NHL**	**68**	**5**	**29**	**34**	**0**	**27**	**33**	**120**	**1**	**0**	**1**	**131**	**3.8**	**105**	**5**	**95**	**18**	**+23**	....	....	....	....	....	....	....	....
1969-70	**Chicago Black Hawks**	**NHL**	**51**	**5**	**13**	**18**	**6**	**13**	**19**	**52**	**0**	**0**	**1**	**101**	**5.0**	**57**	**7**	**68**	**5**	**–3**	....	....	....	....	....	....	....	....
	Los Angeles Kings	**NHL**	**21**	**0**	**6**	**6**	**0**	**6**	**6**	**32**	**0**	**0**	**0**	**57**	**0.0**	**24**	**2**	**40**	**10**	**–8**	....	....	....	....	....	....	....	....
1970-71	**Los Angeles Kings**	**NHL**	**78**	**6**	**27**	**33**	**6**	**24**	**30**	**96**	**0**	**0**	**0**	**218**	**2.8**	**116**	**24**	**131**	**30**	**–9**	....	....	....	....	....	....	....	....
1971-72	**Los Angeles Kings**	**NHL**	**72**	**10**	**24**	**34**	**11**	**22**	**33**	**83**	**4**	**0**	**1**	**203**	**4.9**	**111**	**26**	**152**	**34**	**–33**	....	....	....	....	....	....	....	....
1972-73	**Los Angeles Kings**	**NHL**	**78**	**6**	**39**	**45**	**6**	**33**	**39**	**70**	**3**	**0**	**0**	**207**	**2.9**	**120**	**50**	**121**	**24**	**–21**	....	....	....	....	....	....	....	....
1973-74	**Los Angeles Kings**	**NHL**	**22**	**1**	**11**	**12**	**1**	**9**	**10**	**23**	**1**	**0**	**0**	**48**	**2.1**	**24**	**11**	**39**	**7**	**–19**	....	....	....	....	....	....	....	....
	New York Rangers	**NHL**	**46**	**2**	**17**	**19**	**2**	**15**	**17**	**28**	**0**	**0**	**1**	**87**	**2.3**	**68**	**3**	**69**	**11**	**+7**	**12**	**0**	**1**	**1**	**6**	**0**	**0**	**0**
1974-75	**New York Rangers**	**NHL**	**77**	**4**	**32**	**36**	**4**	**25**	**29**	**69**	**0**	**0**	**1**	**148**	**2.7**	**117**	**7**	**140**	**30**	**0**	**3**	**0**	**1**	**1**	**4**	**0**	**0**	**0**
1975-76	**New York Rangers**	**NHL**	**57**	**4**	**17**	**21**	**4**	**13**	**17**	**34**	**1**	**0**	**0**	**113**	**3.5**	**75**	**8**	**98**	**28**	**–3**	....	....	....	....	....	....	....	....
1976-77	**St. Louis Blues**	**NHL**	**47**	**3**	**4**	**7**	**3**	**3**	**6**	**26**	**0**	**0**	**1**	**59**	**5.1**	**46**	**2**	**73**	**16**	**–13**	**3**	**0**	**0**	**0**	**2**	**0**	**0**	**0**
	Kansas City Blues	CHL	26	1	10	11	....	....	....	46	....	....	....	....	....	....	....	....	....	....	7	2	0	2	2	....	....	....
1977-78	Cincinnati Stingers	WHA	29	1	7	8	....	....	....	58	....	....	....	....	....	....	....	....	....	....	....	....	....	....	....	....	....	....
	Indianapolis Racers	WHA	44	2	13	15	....	....	....	18	....	....	....	....	....	....	....	....	....	....	....	....	....	....	....	....	....	....
	NHL Totals		**808**	**56**	**265**	**321**	**62**	**237**	**299**	**919**	**10**	**0**	**6**	**1525**	**3.7**	**961**	**147**	**1113**	**224**		**29**	**3**	**3**	**6**	**26**	**0**	**0**	**1**
	Other Major League Totals		73	3	20	23	....	....	....	76	....	....	....	....	....	....	....	....	....	....	....	....	....	....	....	....	....	....

Played in NHL All-Star Game (1973)

Traded to **Chicago** by **Boston** with Jack Norris and Pit Martin for Phil Esposito, Ken Hodge and Fred Stanfield, May 15, 1967. Traded to **LA Kings** by **Chicago** with Jim Stanfield and Denis DeJordy for Bryan Campbell, Bill White and Gerry Desjardins, February 10, 1970. Selected by **Edmonton** (WHA) in 1972 WHA General Player Draft, February 12, 1972. Traded to **NY Rangers** by **LA Kings** with Real Lemieux for Sheldon Kannegiesser, Mike Murphy and Tom Williams, November 30, 1973. Claimed on waivers by **St. Louis** from **NY Rangers**, October, 1976. WHA rights traded to **Cincinnati** (WHA) by **Edmonton** (WHA) for cash, July, 1976. Traded to **Indianapolis** (WHA) by **Cincinnati** (WHA) with Blaine Stoughton for Bryon Baltimore and Hugh Harris, January, 1978.

• MARSH, BRAD

Brad Marsh D – L. 6'3", 220 lbs. b: London, Ont., 3/31/1958. Atlanta's 1st choice, 11th overall, in 1978 Amateur Draft.

			REGULAR SEASON																		PLAYOFFS							
Season	Club	League	GP	G	A	Pts	AG	AA	APts	PIM	PP	SH	GW	S	%	TGF	PGF	TGA	PGA	+/–	GP	G	A	Pts	PIM	PP	SH	GW
1974-75	London Knights	OHA	70	4	17	21	....	....	....	160	....	....	....	....	....	....	....	....	....	....	....	....	....	....	....	....	....	....
1975-76	London Knights	OHA	61	3	26	29	....	....	....	184	....	....	....	....	....	....	....	....	....	....	....	....	....	....	....	....	....	....
1976-77	London Knights	OHA	63	7	33	40	....	....	....	121	....	....	....	....	....	....	....	....	....	....	20	3	5	8	47	....	....	....
	Canada	WJC-A	7	1	3	4	....	....	....	14	....	....	....	....	....	....	....	....	....	....	....	....	....	....	....	....	....	....
1977-78	London Knights	OHA	62	8	55	63	....	....	....	192	....	....	....	....	....	....	....	....	....	....	11	2	10	12	21	....	....	....
	Canada	WJC-A	6	0	4	4	....	....	....	2	....	....	....	....	....	....	....	....	....	....	....	....	....	....	....	....	....	....
1978-79	**Atlanta Flames**	**NHL**	**80**	**0**	**19**	**19**	**0**	**14**	**14**	**101**	**0**	**0**	**0**	**80**	**0.0**	**98**	**2**	**97**	**24**	**+23**	**2**	**0**	**0**	**0**	**17**	**0**	**0**	**0**
	Canada	WEC-A	6	1	0	1	....	....	....	4	....	....	....	....	....	....	....	....	....	....	....	....	....	....	....	....	....	....
1979-80	**Atlanta Flames**	**NHL**	**80**	**2**	**9**	**11**	**2**	**7**	**9**	**119**	**0**	**0**	**0**	**73**	**2.7**	**66**	**1**	**120**	**40**	**–15**	**4**	**0**	**1**	**1**	**2**	**0**	**0**	**0**
1980-81	**Calgary Flames**	**NHL**	**80**	**1**	**12**	**13**	**1**	**8**	**9**	**87**	**0**	**0**	**0**	**58**	**1.7**	**79**	**0**	**135**	**54**	**–2**	**16**	**0**	**5**	**5**	**8**	**0**	**0**	**0**
1981-82	**Calgary Flames**	**NHL**	**17**	**0**	**1**	**1**	**0**	**1**	**1**	**10**	**0**	**0**	**0**	**17**	**0.0**	**11**	**0**	**43**	**16**	**–16**	....	....	....	....	....	....	....	....
	Philadelphia Flyers	**NHL**	**66**	**2**	**22**	**24**	**2**	**15**	**17**	**106**	**0**	**0**	**1**	**58**	**3.4**	**81**	**0**	**98**	**34**	**+17**	**4**	**0**	**0**	**0**	**2**	**0**	**0**	**0**
1982-83	**Philadelphia Flyers**	**NHL**	**68**	**2**	**11**	**13**	**2**	**8**	**10**	**52**	**0**	**0**	**0**	**76**	**2.6**	**66**	**0**	**72**	**26**	**+20**	**2**	**0**	**1**	**1**	**0**	**0**	**0**	**0**
1983-84	**Philadelphia Flyers**	**NHL**	**77**	**3**	**14**	**17**	**2**	**9**	**11**	**83**	**0**	**0**	**0**	**90**	**3.3**	**89**	**1**	**95**	**31**	**+24**	**3**	**1**	**1**	**2**	**2**	**0**	**0**	**0**
1984-85	**Philadelphia Flyers**	**NHL**	**77**	**2**	**18**	**20**	**2**	**12**	**14**	**91**	**0**	**0**	**0**	**65**	**3.1**	**100**	**0**	**87**	**29**	**+42**	**19**	**0**	**6**	**6**	**65**	**0**	**0**	**0**
1985-86	**Philadelphia Flyers**	**NHL**	**79**	**0**	**13**	**13**	**0**	**9**	**9**	**123**	**0**	**0**	**0**	**104**	**0.0**	**77**	**2**	**108**	**33**	**0**	**5**	**0**	**0**	**0**	**2**	**0**	**0**	**0**
1986-87	**Philadelphia Flyers**	**NHL**	**77**	**2**	**9**	**11**	**2**	**6**	**8**	**124**	**0**	**0**	**1**	**81**	**2.5**	**62**	**1**	**81**	**29**	**+9**	**26**	**3**	**4**	**7**	**16**	**0**	**1**	**0**
1987-88	**Philadelphia Flyers**	**NHL**	**70**	**3**	**9**	**12**	**3**	**6**	**9**	**57**	**0**	**1**	**1**	**57**	**5.3**	**47**	**1**	**87**	**28**	**–13**	**7**	**1**	**0**	**1**	**8**	**0**	**0**	**0**
1988-89	**Toronto Maple Leafs**	**NHL**	**80**	**1**	**15**	**16**	**1**	**11**	**12**	**79**	**0**	**0**	**0**	**69**	**1.4**	**79**	**1**	**147**	**53**	**–16**	....	....	....	....	....	....	....	....
1989-90	**Toronto Maple Leafs**	**NHL**	**79**	**1**	**13**	**14**	**1**	**9**	**10**	**95**	**0**	**0**	**0**	**50**	**2.0**	**100**	**1**	**125**	**40**	**+14**	**5**	**1**	**0**	**1**	**2**	**0**	**0**	**0**
1990-91	**Toronto Maple Leafs**	**NHL**	**22**	**0**	**0**	**0**	**0**	**0**	**0**	**15**	**0**	**0**	**0**	**18**	**0.0**	**13**	**0**	**32**	**13**	**–6**	....	....	....	....	....	....	....	....
	Detroit Red Wings	**NHL**	**20**	**1**	**3**	**4**	**1**	**2**	**3**	**16**	**0**	**0**	**0**	**16**	**6.3**	**17**	**0**	**33**	**13**	**–3**	**1**	**0**	**0**	**0**	**0**	**0**	**0**	**0**
1991-92	**Detroit Red Wings**	**NHL**	**55**	**3**	**4**	**7**	**3**	**3**	**6**	**53**	**0**	**0**	**1**	**29**	**10.3**	**47**	**0**	**55**	**16**	**+8**	**3**	**0**	**0**	**0**	**0**	**0**	**0**	**0**
1992-93	**Ottawa Senators**	**NHL**	**59**	**0**	**3**	**3**	**0**	**2**	**2**	**30**	**0**	**0**	**0**	**35**	**0.0**	**16**	**0**	**66**	**21**	**–29**	....	....	....	....	....	....	....	....
	NHL Totals		**1086**	**23**	**175**	**198**	**22**	**122**	**144**	**1241**	**0**	**1**	**4**	**976**	**2.4**	**1048**	**10**	**1481**	**500**		**97**	**6**	**18**	**24**	**124**	**0**	**1**	**0**

OHA First All-Star Team (1978)

Played in NHL All-Star Game (1993)

Claimed by **Atlanta** as a fill-in during Expansion Draft, June 13, 1979. Transferred to **Calgary** after **Atlanta** franchise relocated, June 21, 1982. Traded to **Philadelphia** by **Calgary** for Mel Bridgman, November 11, 1981. Claimed by **Toronto** from **Philadelphia** in Waiver Draft, October 3, 1988. Traded to **Detroit** by **Toronto** for Detroit's 8th round choice (Robb McIntyre) in 1991 Entry Draft, February 4, 1991. Traded to **Toronto** by **Detroit** for cash, June 10, 1992. Traded to **Ottawa** by **Toronto** for future considerations, July 20, 1992.

• MARSH, GARY

Gary Marsh LW – L. 5'10", 172 lbs. b: Toronto, Ont., 3/9/1946.

Season	Club	League	GP	G	A	Pts	AG	AA	APts	PIM	PP	SH	GW	S	%	TGF	PGF	TGA	PGA	+/–	GP	G	A	Pts	PIM	PP	SH	GW
1962-63	Hamilton Red Wings	OHA	50	4	4	8	....	....	....	43	....	....	....	....	....	....	....	....	....	....	5	0	0	0	15	....	....	....
1963-64	Hamilton Red Wings	OHA	56	17	25	42	....	....	....	76	....	....	....	....	....	....	....	....	....	....	....	....	....	....	....	....	....	....
1964-65	Hamilton Red Wings	OHA	14	3	2	5	....	....	....	26	....	....	....	....	....	....	....	....	....	....	....	....	....	....	....	....	....	....
	Etobicoke Indians	Jr. B	STATISTICS NOT AVAILABLE																									
1965-66	Hamilton Red Wings	OHA	42	25	25	50	....	....	....	60	....	....	....	....	....	....	....	....	....	....	5	3	3	6	6	....	....	....
	Memphis Wings	CHL	4	1	1	2	....	....	....	4	....	....	....	....	....	....	....	....	....	....	....	....	....	....	....	....	....	....
1966-67	Memphis Wings	CHL	63	16	15	31	....	....	....	85	....	....	....	....	....	....	....	....	....	....	7	2	3	5	2	....	....	....
1967-68	**Detroit Red Wings**	**NHL**	**6**	**1**	**3**	**4**	**1**	**3**	**4**	**4**	**0**	**0**	**1**	**7**	**14.3**	**6**	**0**	**4**	**0**	**+2**	....	....	....	....	....	....	....	....
	Fort Worth Wings	CHL	64	25	28	53	....	....	....	77	....	....	....	....	....	....	....	....	....	....	13	*6	4	10	6	....	....	....
1968-69	**Toronto Maple Leafs**	**NHL**	**1**	**0**	**0**	**0**	**0**	**0**	**0**	**0**	**0**	**0**	**0**	**0**	**0.0**	**0**	**0**	**0**	**0**	**0**	....	....	....	....	....	....	....	....
	Phoenix Roadrunners	WHL	2	0	0	0	....	....	....	0	....	....	....	....	....	....	....	....	....	....	....	....	....	....	....	....	....	....
	Rochester Americans	AHL	7	1	2	3	....	....	....	4	....	....	....	....	....	....	....	....	....	....	....	....	....	....	....	....	....	....
	Tulsa Oilers	CHL	51	22	37	59	....	....	....	65	....	....	....	....	....	....	....	....	....	....	7	2	2	4	22	....	....	....
1969-70	Springfield Kings	AHL	22	2	1	3	....	....	....	0	....	....	....	....	....	....	....	....	....	....	14	0	0	0	2	....	....	....
	Phoenix Roadrunners	WHL	45	8	16	24	....	....	....	17	....	....	....	....	....	....	....	....	....	....	....	....	....	....	....	....	....	....
1970-71	Kansas City Blues	CHL	19	2	8	10	....	....	....	4	....	....	....	....	....	....	....	....	....	....	....	....	....	....	....	....	....	....
	Springfield Kings	AHL	26	2	4	6	....	....	....	6	....	....	....	....	....	....	....	....	....	....	....	....	....	....	....	....	....	....
1971-72	Orillia Terriers	OHA Sr.	38	15	26	41	....	....	....	37	....	....	....	....	....	....	....	....	....	....	....	....	....	....	....	....	....	....
1972-73	Orillia Terriers	OHA Sr.	39	12	15	27	....	....	....	33	....	....	....	....	....	....	....	....	....	....	....	....	....	....	....	....	....	....
1973-74	Orillia Terriers	OHA Sr.	34	11	35	46	....	....	....	32	....	....	....	....	....	....	....	....	....	....	....	....	....	....	....	....	....	....
	NHL Totals		**7**	**1**	**3**	**4**	**1**	**3**	**4**	**4**	**0**	**0**	**1**	**7**	**14.3**	**6**	**0**	**4**	**0**		....	....	....	....	....	....	....	....

Claimed by **Toronto** from **Detroit** in Intra-League Draft, June 12, 1968. Traded to **LA Kings** by **Toronto** for Jacques Lemieux, February, 1970.

• MARSH, PETER

Peter Marsh RW – L. 6'1", 180 lbs. b: Halifax, N.S., 12/21/1956. Pittsburgh's 3rd choice, 29th overall, in 1976 Amateur Draft.

Season	Club	League	GP	G	A	Pts	AG	AA	APts	PIM	PP	SH	GW	S	%	TGF	PGF	TGA	PGA	+/–	GP	G	A	Pts	PIM	PP	SH	GW
1973-74	Sherbrooke Castors	QMJHL	43	7	9	16	....	....	....	45	....	....	....	....	....	....	....	....	....	....	....	....	....	....	....	....	....	....
1974-75	Sherbrooke Castors	QMJHL	65	36	34	70	....	....	....	133	....	....	....	....	....	....	....	....	....	....	12	10	10	20	32	....	....	....
1975-76	Sherbrooke Castors	QMJHL	70	75	81	156	....	....	....	103	....	....	....	....	....	....	....	....	....	....	16	9	10	19	19	....	....	....
1976-77	Cincinnati Stingers	WHA	76	23	28	51	....	....	....	52	....	....	....	....	....	....	....	....	....	....	4	2	0	2	0	....	....	....
1977-78	Cincinnati Stingers	WHA	74	25	25	50	....	....	....	123	....	....	....	....	....	....	....	....	....	....	....	....	....	....	....	....	....	....
1978-79	Cincinnati Stingers	WHA	80	43	23	66	....	....	....	95	....	....	....	....	....	....	....	....	....	....	3	1	0	1	0	....	....	....
1979-80	**Winnipeg Jets**	**NHL**	**57**	**18**	**20**	**38**	**16**	**15**	**31**	**59**	**9**	**0**	**0**	**187**	**9.6**	**55**	**22**	**72**	**1**	**–38**	....	....	....	....	....	....	....	....
1980-81	**Winnipeg Jets**	**NHL**	**24**	**6**	**7**	**13**	**5**	**5**	**10**	**9**	**3**	**0**	**0**	**63**	**9.5**	**15**	**6**	**28**	**2**	**–17**	....	....	....	....	....	....	....	....
	Chicago Black Hawks	**NHL**	**29**	**4**	**6**	**10**	**3**	**4**	**7**	**10**	**0**	**0**	**0**	**48**	**8.3**	**16**	**2**	**15**	**1**	**0**	**2**	**1**	**1**	**2**	**2**	**0**	**0**	**0**
1981-82	**Chicago Black Hawks**	**NHL**	**57**	**10**	**18**	**28**	**8**	**12**	**20**	**47**	**0**	**0**	**0**	**122**	**8.2**	**45**	**2**	**49**	**9**	**+3**	**12**	**0**	**2**	**2**	**31**	**0**	**0**	**0**
1982-83	**Chicago Black Hawks**	**NHL**	**68**	**6**	**14**	**20**	**5**	**10**	**15**	**55**	**0**	**0**	**2**	**121**	**5.0**	**32**	**0**	**61**	**21**	**–8**	**12**	**0**	**2**	**2**	**0**	**0**	**0**	**0**
1983-84	**Chicago Black Hawks**	**NHL**	**43**	**4**	**6**	**10**	**3**	**4**	**7**	**44**	**0**	**0**	**0**	**86**	**4.7**	**18**	**0**	**40**	**11**	**–11**	....	....	....	....	....	....	....	....
	Springfield Indians	AHL	23	8	13	21	....	....	....	32	....	....	....	....	....	....	....	....	....	....	4	2	0	2	0	....	....	....
	NHL Totals		**278**	**48**	**71**	**119**	**40**	**50**	**90**	**224**	**12**	**0**	**2**	**627**	**7.7**	**181**	**32**	**265**	**45**		**26**	**1**	**5**	**6**	**33**	**0**	**0**	**0**
	Other Major League Totals		230	91	76	167	....	....	....	270	....	....	....	....	....	....	....	....	....		7	3	0	3	0	....	....	....

WJC-A All-Star Team (1976) • QMJHL West Division First All-Star Team (1976)

Selected by **Cincinnati** (WHA) in 1976 WHA Amateur Draft, May, 1976. Rights transferred to **Montreal** by **Pittsburgh** to complete transaction that sent Pierre Larouche to Pittsburgh (November 29, 1977), December 15, 1977. Reclaimed by **Montreal** from **Cincinnati** (WHA) prior to Expansion Draft, June 9, 1979. Claimed by **Winnipeg** from **Montreal** in Expansion Draft, June 13, 1979. Traded to **Chicago** by **Winnipeg** for Doug Lecuyer and Tim Trimper, December 1, 1980.

• MARSHALL, BERT

Bert Marshall D – L. 6'3", 205 lbs. b: Kamloops, B.C., 11/22/1943.

Season	Club	League	GP	G	A	Pts	AG	AA	APts	PIM	PP	SH	GW	S	%	TGF	PGF	TGA	PGA	+/–	GP	G	A	Pts	PIM	PP	SH	GW
1963-64	Edmonton Oil Kings	SJHL	14	2	11	13	....	....	....	14	....	....	....	....	....	....	....	....	....	....	....	....	....	....	....	....	....	....
	Cincinnati Wings	CHL	1	0	0	0	....	....	....	0	....	....	....	....	....	....	....	....	....	....	....	....	....	....	....	....	....	....
1964-65	Memphis Wings	CHL	51	3	11	14	....	....	....	43	....	....	....	....	....	....	....	....	....	....	....	....	....	....	....	....	....	....
1965-66	**Detroit Red Wings**	**NHL**	**61**	**0**	**19**	**19**	**0**	**19**	**19**	**45**	....	....	....	....	....	....	....	....	....	....	**12**	**1**	**3**	**4**	**16**	....	....	....
	Pittsburgh Hornets	AHL	12	2	0	2	....	....	....	8	....	....	....	....	....	....	....	....	....	....	....	....	....	....	....	....	....	....
1966-67	**Detroit Red Wings**	**NHL**	**57**	**0**	**10**	**10**	**0**	**10**	**10**	**68**	....	....	....	....	....	....	....	....	....	....	....	....	....	....	....	....	....	....
1967-68	**Detroit Red Wings**	**NHL**	**37**	**1**	**5**	**6**	**1**	**5**	**6**	**56**	**0**	**0**	**0**	**50**	**2.0**	**44**	**2**	**53**	**17**	**+6**	....	....	....	....	....	....	....	....
	Oakland Seals	**NHL**	**20**	**0**	**4**	**4**	**0**	**4**	**4**	**18**	**0**	**0**	**0**	**44**	**0.0**	**26**	**8**	**30**	**10**	**–2**	....	....	....	....	....	....	....	....
1968-69	**Oakland Seals**	**NHL**	**68**	**3**	**15**	**18**	**3**	**14**	**17**	**81**	**0**	**0**	**0**	**118**	**2.5**	**81**	**19**	**105**	**19**	**–24**	**7**	**0**	**7**	**7**	**20**	**0**	**0**	**0**
1969-70	**Oakland Seals**	**NHL**	**72**	**1**	**15**	**16**	**1**	**15**	**16**	**109**	**0**	**0**	**0**	**130**	**0.8**	**64**	**16**	**92**	**23**	**–21**	**4**	**0**	**1**	**1**	**12**	**0**	**0**	**0**
1970-71	**California Golden Seals**	**NHL**	**32**	**2**	**6**	**8**	**2**	**5**	**7**	**48**	**1**	**0**	**0**	**54**	**3.7**	**34**	**6**	**63**	**15**	**–20**	....	....	....	....	....	....	....	....
1971-72	**California Golden Seals**	**NHL**	**66**	**0**	**14**	**14**	**0**	**13**	**13**	**68**	**0**	**0**	**0**	**35**	**0.0**	**54**	**0**	**81**	**22**	**–5**	....	....	....	....	....	....	....	....
1972-73	**California Golden Seals**	**NHL**	**55**	**2**	**6**	**8**	**2**	**5**	**7**	**71**	**1**	**0**	**0**	**55**	**3.6**	**46**	**3**	**98**	**19**	**–36**	....	....	....	....	....	....	....	....
	New York Rangers	**NHL**	**8**	**0**	**0**	**0**	**0**	**0**	**0**	**14**	**0**	**0**	**0**	**4**	**0.0**	**1**	**0**	**4**	**0**	**–3**	**6**	**0**	**1**	**1**	**8**	**0**	**0**	**0**
1973-74	**New York Islanders**	**NHL**	**69**	**1**	**7**	**8**	**1**	**6**	**7**	**84**	**0**	**0**	**0**	**51**	**2.0**	**66**	**1**	**103**	**43**	**+5**	....	....	....	....	....	....	....	....
1974-75	**New York Islanders**	**NHL**	**77**	**2**	**28**	**30**	**2**	**22**	**24**	**58**	**0**	**0**	**0**	**69**	**2.9**	**80**	**1**	**95**	**34**	**+18**	**17**	**2**	**5**	**7**	**16**	**0**	**0**	**0**
1975-76	**New York Islanders**	**NHL**	**71**	**0**	**16**	**16**	**0**	**13**	**13**	**72**	**0**	**0**	**0**	**70**	**0.0**	**82**	**2**	**72**	**29**	**+37**	**13**	**1**	**3**	**4**	**12**	**0**	**0**	**1**
1976-77	**New York Islanders**	**NHL**	**72**	**4**	**21**	**25**	**4**	**17**	**21**	**61**	**0**	**0**	**1**	**62**	**6.5**	**93**	**0**	**74**	**29**	**+48**	**6**	**0**	**0**	**0**	**6**	**0**	**0**	**0**

			REGULAR SEASON																		PLAYOFFS							
Season	Club	League	GP	G	A	Pts	AG	AA	APts	PIM	PP	SH	GW	S	%	TGF	PGF	TGA	PGA	+/–	GP	G	A	Pts	PIM	PP	SH	GW
1977-78	New York Islanders	NHL	58	0	7	7	0	6	6	44	0	0	0	32	0.0	43	0	38	5	+10	7	0	2	2	9	0	0	0
1978-79	New York Islanders	NHL	45	1	8	9	1	6	7	29	0	0	0	26	3.8	43	0	42	8	+9	....	....	....	....	....	....	....	....
1979-80	Indianapolis Checkers	CHL	6	0	0	0	....	....	....	6	....	....	....	....	....	....	....	....	....	....	....	....	....	....	....	....	....	....
	NHL Totals		868	17	181	198	17	160	177	926	2	0	1	800	2.1	757	58	950	273		72	4	22	26	99	0	0	1

Traded to **Oakland** by **Detroit** with John Brenneman and Ted Hampson for Kent Douglas, January 9, 1968. Traded to **NY Rangers** by **California** for cash and future considerations (Dave Hrechosky and Gary Coalter, May 17, 1973), March 4, 1973. Claimed by **NY Islanders** from **NY Rangers** in Intra-League Draft, June 12, 1973.

• MARSHALL, DON

Don Marshall LW – L. 5'10", 160 lbs. b: Montreal, Que., 3/23/1932.

Season	Club	League	GP	G	A	Pts	AG	AA	APts	PIM	PP	SH	GW	S	%	TGF	PGF	TGA	PGA	+/–	GP	G	A	Pts	PIM	PP	SH	GW
1949-50	Montreal Jr. Canadiens	QJHL	35	8	7	15	....	....	....	10	....	....	....	....	....	....	....	....	....	....	29	9	10	19	6	....	....	....
1950-51	Montreal Jr. Canadiens	QJHL	37	19	32	51	....	....	....	6	....	....	....	....	....	....	....	....	....	....	9	5	8	13	0	....	....	....
1951-52	Montreal Jr. Canadiens	QJHL	43	32	46	78	....	....	....	6	....	....	....	....	....	....	....	....	....	....	19	10	10	20	14	....	....	....
	Montreal Canadiens	**NHL**	**1**	**0**	**0**	**0**	**0**	**0**	**0**	**0**	....	....	....	....	....	....	....	....	....	....	....	....	....	....	....	....	....	....
1952-53	Cincinnati Mohawks	IHL	60	46	51	97	....	....	....	24	....	....	....	....	....	....	....	....	....	....	....	....	....	....	....	....	....	....
	Montreal Royals	QSHL	2	0	0	0	....	....	....	2	....	....	....	....	....	....	....	....	....	....	9	5	5	10	0	....	....	....
1953-54	Buffalo Bisons	AHL	70	39	55	94	....	....	....	8	....	....	....	....	....	....	....	....	....	....	3	1	4	5	0	....	....	....
1954-55	**Montreal Canadiens**	**NHL**	**39**	**5**	**3**	**8**	**7**	**4**	**11**	**9**	....	....	....	....	....	....	....	....	....	....	**12**	**1**	**1**	**2**	**2**	....	....	....
	Montreal Royals	QHL	10	5	3	8	....	....	....	2	....	....	....	....	....	....	....	....	....	....	....	....	....	....	....	....	....	....
1955-56	**Montreal Canadiens**	**NHL**	**66**	**4**	**1**	**5**	**6**	**1**	**7**	**10**	....	....	....	....	....	....	....	....	....	....	**10**	**1**	**0**	**1**	**0**	....	....	....
1956-57	**Montreal Canadiens**	**NHL**	**70**	**12**	**8**	**20**	**16**	**9**	**25**	**6**	....	....	....	....	....	....	....	....	....	....	**10**	**1**	**3**	**4**	**2**	....	....	....
1957-58	**Montreal Canadiens**	**NHL**	**68**	**22**	**19**	**41**	**29**	**21**	**50**	**14**	....	....	....	....	....	....	....	....	....	....	**10**	**0**	**2**	**2**	**4**	....	....	....
1958-59	**Montreal Canadiens**	**NHL**	**70**	**10**	**22**	**32**	**13**	**23**	**36**	**12**	....	....	....	....	....	....	....	....	....	....	**11**	**0**	**2**	**2**	**2**	....	....	....
1959-60	**Montreal Canadiens**	**NHL**	**70**	**16**	**22**	**38**	**20**	**23**	**43**	**4**	....	....	....	....	....	....	....	....	....	....	**8**	**2**	**2**	**4**	**0**	....	....	....
1960-61	**Montreal Canadiens**	**NHL**	**70**	**14**	**17**	**31**	**17**	**17**	**34**	**8**	....	....	....	....	....	....	....	....	....	....	**6**	**0**	**2**	**2**	**0**	....	....	....
1961-62	**Montreal Canadiens**	**NHL**	**66**	**18**	**28**	**46**	**22**	**28**	**50**	**12**	....	....	....	....	....	....	....	....	....	....	**6**	**0**	**1**	**1**	**2**	....	....	....
1962-63	**Montreal Canadiens**	**NHL**	**65**	**13**	**20**	**33**	**16**	**21**	**37**	**6**	....	....	....	....	....	....	....	....	....	....	**5**	**0**	**0**	**0**	**0**	....	....	....
1963-64	**New York Rangers**	**NHL**	**70**	**11**	**12**	**23**	**14**	**13**	**27**	**8**	....	....	....	....	....	....	....	....	....	....	....	....	....	....	....	....	....	....
1964-65	**New York Rangers**	**NHL**	**69**	**20**	**15**	**35**	**26**	**16**	**42**	**2**	....	....	....	....	....	....	....	....	....	....	....	....	....	....	....	....	....	....
1965-66	**New York Rangers**	**NHL**	**69**	**26**	**28**	**54**	**32**	**28**	**60**	**6**	....	....	....	....	....	....	....	....	....	....	....	....	....	....	....	....	....	....
1966-67	**New York Rangers**	**NHL**	**70**	**24**	**22**	**46**	**30**	**23**	**53**	**4**	....	....	....	....	....	....	....	....	....	....	**4**	**0**	**1**	**1**	**2**	....	....	....
1967-68	**New York Rangers**	**NHL**	**70**	**19**	**30**	**49**	**23**	**31**	**54**	**2**	**4**	**0**	**3**	**146**	**13.0**	**81**	**19**	**61**	**18**	**+19**	**6**	**2**	**1**	**3**	**0**	**0**	**0**	**1**
1968-69	**New York Rangers**	**NHL**	**74**	**20**	**19**	**39**	**23**	**18**	**41**	**12**	**7**	**0**	**4**	**149**	**13.4**	**68**	**14**	**41**	**2**	**+15**	**4**	**1**	**0**	**1**	**0**	**0**	**0**	**0**
1969-70	**New York Rangers**	**NHL**	**57**	**9**	**15**	**24**	**10**	**15**	**25**	**6**	**2**	**0**	**3**	**81**	**11.1**	**32**	**4**	**38**	**16**	**+6**	**1**	**0**	**0**	**0**	**0**	**0**	**0**	**0**
1970-71	**Buffalo Sabres**	**NHL**	**62**	**20**	**29**	**49**	**21**	**26**	**47**	**6**	**9**	**0**	**1**	**112**	**17.9**	**77**	**39**	**53**	**2**	**–13**	....	....	....	....	....	....	....	....
1971-72	**Toronto Maple Leafs**	**NHL**	**50**	**2**	**14**	**16**	**2**	**13**	**15**	**0**	**1**	**0**	**0**	**48**	**4.2**	**26**	**8**	**30**	**14**	**+2**	**1**	**0**	**0**	**0**	**0**	**0**	**0**	**0**
	NHL Totals		**1176**	**265**	**324**	**589**	**327**	**330**	**657**	**127**	**23**	**0**	**11**	**536**	**49.4**	**284**	**84**	**223**	**52**		**94**	**8**	**15**	**23**	**14**	**0**	**0**	**1**

IHL First All-Star Team (1953) • Won James Gatschene Memorial Trophy (MVP - IHL) (1953) • Won Dudley "Red" Garrett Memorial Award (Top Rookie - AHL) (1954) • NHL Second All-Star Team (1967)

Played in NHL All-Star Game (1956, 1957, 1958, 1959, 1960, 1961, 1968)

Traded to **NY Rangers** by **Montreal** with Jacques Plante and Phil Goyette for Dave Balon, Leon Rochefort, Len Ronson and Gump Worsley, June 4, 1963. Claimed by **Buffalo** from **NY Rangers** in Expansion Draft, June 10, 1970. Claimed by **Toronto** from **Buffalo** in Intra-League Draft, June 8, 1971.

• MARSHALL, GRANT

Grant Marshall RW – R. 6'1", 193 lbs. b: Mississauga, Ont., 6/9/1973. Toronto's 2nd choice, 23rd overall, in 1992 Entry Draft.

Season	Club	League	GP	G	A	Pts	AG	AA	APts	PIM	PP	SH	GW	S	%	TGF	PGF	TGA	PGA	+/–	GP	G	A	Pts	PIM	PP	SH	GW
1990-91	Ottawa 67's	OHL	26	0	11	11	....	....	....	25	....	....	....	....	....	....	....	....	....	....	1	0	0	0	0	....	....	....
1991-92	Ottawa 67's	OHL	61	32	51	83	....	....	....	132	....	....	....	....	....	....	....	....	....	....	11	6	11	17	11	....	....	....
1992-93	Ottawa 67's	OHL	30	14	29	43	....	....	....	83	....	....	....	....	....	....	....	....	....	....	....	....	....	....	....	....	....	....
	Newmarket Royals	OHL	31	11	25	36	....	....	....	89	....	....	....	....	....	....	....	....	....	....	7	4	7	11	20	....	....	....
	St. John's Maple Leafs	AHL	2	0	0	0	....	....	....	0	....	....	....	....	....	....	....	....	....	....	2	0	0	0	2	....	....	....
1993-94	St. John's Maple Leafs	AHL	67	11	29	40	....	....	....	155	....	....	....	....	....	....	....	....	....	....	11	1	5	6	17	....	....	....
1994-95	**Dallas Stars**	**NHL**	**2**	**0**	**1**	**1**	**0**	**1**	**1**	**0**	**0**	**0**	**0**	**0**	**0.0**	**1**	**0**	**0**	**0**	**+1**	....	....	....	....	....	....	....	....
	Kalamazoo Wings	IHL	61	17	29	46	....	....	....	96	....	....	....	....	....	....	....	....	....	....	16	9	3	12	27	....	....	....
1995-96	**Dallas Stars**	**NHL**	**70**	**9**	**19**	**28**	**9**	**15**	**24**	**111**	**0**	**0**	**0**	**62**	**14.5**	**33**	**2**	**31**	**0**	**0**	....	....	....	....	....	....	....	....
1996-97	**Dallas Stars**	**NHL**	**56**	**6**	**4**	**10**	**6**	**4**	**10**	**98**	**0**	**0**	**0**	**0**	**0.0**	**23**	**1**	**17**	**0**	**+6**	**5**	**0**	**2**	**2**	**8**	**0**	**0**	**0**
1997-98	**Dallas Stars**	**NHL**	**72**	**9**	**10**	**19**	**11**	**10**	**21**	**96**	**3**	**0**	**1**	**91**	**9.9**	**23**	**7**	**18**	**0**	**–2**	**17**	**0**	**2**	**2**	**47**	**0**	**0**	**0**
	NHL Totals		**200**	**24**	**34**	**58**	**26**	**30**	**56**	**305**	**3**	**0**	**1**	**153**	**15.7**	**80**	**10**	**66**	**0**		**22**	**0**	**4**	**4**	**55**	**0**	**0**	**0**

Transferred to **Dallas** from **Toronto** with Peter Zezel as compensation for Toronto's signing of free agent Mike Craig, August 10, 1994.

• MARSHALL, JASON

Jason Marshall D – R. 6'2", 200 lbs. b: Cranbrook, B.C., 2/22/1971. St. Louis' 1st choice, 9th overall, in 1989 Entry Draft.

Season	Club	League	GP	G	A	Pts	AG	AA	APts	PIM	PP	SH	GW	S	%	TGF	PGF	TGA	PGA	+/–	GP	G	A	Pts	PIM	PP	SH	GW
1988-89	Vernon Lakers	BCJHL	48	10	30	40	....	....	....	197	....	....	....	....	....	....	....	....	....	....	31	6	6	12	14	....	....	....
	Canada	Nat-Team	2	0	1	1	....	....	....	0	....	....	....	....	....	....	....	....	....	....	....	....	....	....	....	....	....	....
1989-90	Canada	Nat-Team	73	1	11	12	....	....	....	57	....	....	....	....	....	....	....	....	....	....	....	....	....	....	....	....	....	....
1990-91	Tri-City Americans	WHL	59	10	34	44	....	....	....	236	....	....	....	....	....	....	....	....	....	....	7	1	2	3	20	....	....	....
	Canada	WJC-A	7	0	4	4	....	....	....	6	....	....	....	....	....	....	....	....	....	....	....	....	....	....	....	....	....	....
	Peoria Rivermen	IHL	....	....	....	....	....	....	....	....	....	....	....	....	....	....	....	....	....	....	18	0	1	1	48	....	....	....
1991-92	**St. Louis Blues**	**NHL**	**2**	**1**	**0**	**1**	**1**	**0**	**1**	**4**	**0**	**0**	**0**	**2**	**50.0**	**1**	**0**	**1**	**0**	**0**	....	....	....	....	....	....	....	....
	Peoria Rivermen	IHL	78	4	18	22	....	....	....	178	....	....	....	....	....	....	....	....	....	....	10	0	1	1	16	....	....	....
1992-93	Peoria Rivermen	IHL	77	4	16	20	....	....	....	229	....	....	....	....	....	....	....	....	....	....	4	0	0	0	20	....	....	....
1993-94	Canada	Nat-Team	41	3	10	13	....	....	....	60	....	....	....	....	....	....	....	....	....	....	....	....	....	....	....	....	....	....
	Peoria Rivermen	IHL	20	1	1	2	....	....	....	72	....	....	....	....	....	....	....	....	....	....	3	2	0	2	2	....	....	....
1994-95	**Anaheim Mighty Ducks**	**NHL**	**1**	**0**	**0**	**0**	**0**	**0**	**0**	**0**	**0**	**0**	**0**	**1**	**0.0**	**1**	**0**	**3**	**0**	**–2**	....	....	....	....	....	....	....	....
	San Diego Gulls	IHL	80	7	18	25	....	....	....	218	....	....	....	....	....	....	....	....	....	....	5	0	1	1	8	....	....	....
1995-96	**Anaheim Mighty Ducks**	**NHL**	**24**	**0**	**1**	**1**	**0**	**1**	**1**	**42**	**0**	**0**	**0**	**9**	**0.0**	**11**	**0**	**14**	**6**	**+3**	....	....	....	....	....	....	....	....
	Baltimore Bandits	AHL	57	1	13	14	....	....	....	150	....	....	....	....	....	....	....	....	....	....	....	....	....	....	....	....	....	....
1996-97	**Anaheim Mighty Ducks**	**NHL**	**73**	**1**	**9**	**10**	**1**	**8**	**9**	**140**	**0**	**0**	**0**	**34**	**2.9**	**44**	**1**	**60**	**23**	**+6**	**7**	**0**	**1**	**1**	**4**	**0**	**0**	**0**
1997-98	**Anaheim Mighty Ducks**	**NHL**	**72**	**3**	**6**	**9**	**4**	**6**	**10**	**189**	**1**	**0**	**0**	**68**	**4.4**	**47**	**7**	**71**	**23**	**–8**	....	....	....	....	....	....	....	....
	NHL Totals		**172**	**5**	**16**	**21**	**6**	**15**	**21**	**375**	**1**	**0**	**0**	**114**	**4.4**	**104**	**8**	**149**	**52**		**7**	**0**	**1**	**1**	**4**	**0**	**0**	**0**

Traded to **Anaheim** by **St. Louis** for Bill Houlder, August 29, 1994.

• MARSHALL, PAUL

Paul Marshall LW – L. 6'2", 180 lbs. b: Toronto, Ont., 9/7/1960. Pittsburgh's 1st choice, 31st overall, in 1979 Entry Draft.

Season	Club	League	GP	G	A	Pts	AG	AA	APts	PIM	PP	SH	GW	S	%	TGF	PGF	TGA	PGA	+/–	GP	G	A	Pts	PIM	PP	SH	GW
1976-77	Don Mills Flyers	Midget	58	42	56	98	....	....	....	....	....	....	....	....	....	....	....	....	....	....	....	....	....	....	....	....	....	....
1977-78	Hamilton Fincups	OHA	58	36	34	70	....	....	....	54	....	....	....	....	....	....	....	....	....	....	20	5	2	7	34	....	....	....
1978-79	Brantford Alexanders	OHA	67	42	72	114	....	....	....	59	....	....	....	....	....	....	....	....	....	....	....	....	....	....	....	....	....	....
1979-80	Brantford Alexanders	OHA	4	2	2	4	....	....	....	0	....	....	....	....	....	....	....	....	....	....	....	....	....	....	....	....	....	....
	Pittsburgh Penguins	**NHL**	**46**	**9**	**12**	**21**	**8**	**9**	**17**	**9**	**1**	**0**	**5**	**68**	**13.2**	**35**	**13**	**24**	**0**	**–2**	**1**	**0**	**0**	**0**	**0**	**0**	**0**	**0**
1980-81	**Pittsburgh Penguins**	**NHL**	**13**	**3**	**0**	**3**	**2**	**0**	**2**	**4**	**1**	**0**	**0**	**8**	**37.5**	**4**	**2**	**9**	**0**	**–7**	....	....	....	....	....	....	....	....
	Binghamton Whalers	AHL	2	2	1	3	....	....	....	0	....	....	....	....	....	....	....	....	....	....	....	....	....	....	....	....	....	....
	Toronto Maple Leafs	**NHL**	**13**	**0**	**2**	**2**	**0**	**1**	**1**	**2**	**0**	**0**	**0**	**8**	**0.0**	**4**	**2**	**4**	**0**	**–2**	....	....	....	....	....	....	....	....
	New Brunswick Hawks	AHL	47	25	28	53	....	....	....	41	....	....	....	....	....	....	....	....	....	....	13	6	7	13	10	....	....	....
1981-82	**Toronto Maple Leafs**	**NHL**	**10**	**2**	**2**	**4**	**2**	**1**	**3**	**2**	**1**	**0**	**0**	**14**	**14.3**	**7**	**2**	**9**	**0**	**–4**	....	....	....	....	....	....	....	....
	Cincinnati Tigers	CHL	54	23	29	52	....	....	....	61	....	....	....	....	....	....	....	....	....	....	4	2	1	3	0	....	....	....
1982-83	**Hartford Whalers**	**NHL**	**13**	**1**	**2**	**3**	**1**	**1**	**2**	**0**	**0**	**0**	**0**	**10**	**10.0**	**9**	**1**	**10**	**0**	**–2**	....	....	....	....	....	....	....	....
	Binghamton Whalers	AHL	61	25	26	51	....	....	....	21	....	....	....	....	....	....	....	....	....	....	5	3	2	5	0	....	....	....
	NHL Totals		**95**	**15**	**18**	**33**	**13**	**12**	**25**	**17**	**3**	**0**	**5**	**108**	**13.9**	**59**	**20**	**56**	**0**		**1**	**0**	**0**	**0**	**0**	**0**	**0**	**0**

Traded to **Toronto** by **Pittsburgh** with Kim Davis for Dave Burrows and Paul Gardner, November 18, 1980. Traded to **Hartford** by **Toronto** for Hartfrord's 10th round choice (Greg Rolston) in 1983 Entry Draft, October 5, 1982.

• MARSON, MIKE

Mike Marson LW – L. 5'9", 200 lbs. b: Scarborough, Ont., 7/24/1955. Washington's 2nd choice, 19th overall, in 1974 Amateur Draft.

Season	Club	League	GP	G	A	Pts	AG	AA	APts	PIM	PP	SH	GW	S	%	TGF	PGF	TGA	PGA	+/–	GP	G	A	Pts	PIM	PP	SH	GW
1972-73	Sudbury Wolves	OHA	57	12	21	33	....	....	....	117	....	....	....	....	....	....	....	....	....	....	....	....	....	....	....	....	....	....
1973-74	Sudbury Wolves	OHA	69	35	59	94	....	....	....	146	....	....	....	....	....	....	....	....	....	....	....	....	....	....	....	....	....	....
1974-75	**Washington Capitals**	**NHL**	**76**	**16**	**12**	**28**	**15**	**9**	**24**	**59**	**5**	**0**	**2**	**89**	**18.0**	**44**	**9**	**100**	**0**	**–65**	....	....	....	....	....	....	....	....

			REGULAR SEASON																		PLAYOFFS							
Season	Club	League	GP	G	A	Pts	AG	AA	APts	PIM	PP	SH	GW	S	%	TGF	PGF	TGA	PGA	+/–	GP	G	A	Pts	PIM	PP	SH	GW
1975-76	**Washington Capitals**	**NHL**	**57**	**4**	**7**	**11**	**4**	**5**	**9**	**50**	**0**	**0**	**0**	**35**	**11.4**	**16**	**2**	**34**	**1**	**–19**	....	....	....	....	....	....	....	....
	Baltimore Clippers	AHL	12	1	3	4	....	....	....	16	....	....	....	....	....	....	....	....	....	....	....	....	....	....	....	....	....	....
1976-77	**Washington Capitals**	**NHL**	**10**	**0**	**1**	**1**	**0**	**1**	**1**	**18**	**0**	**0**	**0**	**5**	**0.0**	**1**	**0**	**2**	**0**	**–1**	....	....	....	....	....	....	....	....
	Springfield Indians	AHL	66	15	17	32	....	....	....	81	....	....	....	....	....	....	....	....	....	....	....	....	....	....	....	....	....	....
1977-78	**Washington Capitals**	**NHL**	**46**	**4**	**4**	**8**	**4**	**3**	**7**	**101**	**0**	**0**	**0**	**30**	**13.3**	**16**	**0**	**15**	**0**	**+1**	....	....	....	....	....	....	....	....
	Hershey Bears	AHL	20	5	3	8	....	....	....	35	....	....	....	....	....	....	....	....	....	....	....	....	....	....	....	....	....	....
1978-79	**Washington Capitals**	**NHL**	**4**	**0**	**0**	**0**	**0**	**0**	**0**	**0**	**0**	**0**	**0**	**1**	**0.0**	**0**	**0**	**3**	**0**	**–3**	....	....	....	....	....	....	....	....
	Philadelphia Firebirds	AHL	6	3	2	5	....	....	....	19	....	....	....	....	....	....	....	....	....	....	....	....	....	....	....	....	....	....
	Binghamton Dusters	AHL	68	12	11	23	....	....	....	132	....	....	....	....	....	....	....	....	....	....	10	4	3	7	20	....	....	....
1979-80	**Los Angeles Kings**	**NHL**	**3**	**0**	**0**	**0**	**0**	**0**	**0**	**5**	**0**	**0**	**0**	**1**	**0.0**	**0**	**0**	**2**	**0**	**–2**	....	....	....	....	....	....	....	....
	Binghamton Dusters	AHL	58	7	8	15	....	....	....	85	....	....	....	....	....	....	....	....	....	....	....	....	....	....	....	....	....	....
	NHL Totals		**196**	**24**	**24**	**48**	**23**	**18**	**41**	**233**	**5**	**0**	**2**	**161**	**14.9**	**77**	**11**	**156**	**1**		....	....	....	....	....	....	....	....

OHA Second All-Star Team (1974)

Traded to **LA Kings** by **Washington** for Steve Clippingdale, June 11, 1979.

• MARTIN, CRAIG

Craig Martin RW – R. 6'2", 215 lbs. b: Amherst, N.S., 1/21/1971. Winnipeg's 6th choice, 98th overall, in 1990 Entry Draft.

Season	Club	League	GP	G	A	Pts	AG	AA	APts	PIM	PP	SH	GW	S	%	TGF	PGF	TGA	PGA	+/–	GP	G	A	Pts	PIM	PP	SH	GW
1989-90	Hull Olympiques	QMJHL	66	14	31	45	....	....	....	299	....	....	....	....	....	....	....	....	....	....	11	2	1	3	65	....	....	....
1990-91	Hull Olympiques	QMJHL	18	5	6	11	....	....	....	87	....	....	....	....	....	....	....	....	....	....	....	....	....	....	....	....	....	....
	St-Hyacinthe Laser	QMJHL	36	8	9	17	....	....	....	166	....	....	....	....	....	....	....	....	....	....	....	....	....	....	....	....	....	....
1991-92	Moncton Hawks	AHL	11	1	1	2	....	....	....	70	....	....	....	....	....	....	....	....	....	....	....	....	....	....	....	....	....	....
	Fort Wayne Komets	IHL	24	0	0	0	....	....	....	115	....	....	....	....	....	....	....	....	....	....	....	....	....	....	....	....	....	....
1992-93	Moncton Hawks	AHL	64	5	13	18	....	....	....	198	....	....	....	....	....	....	....	....	....	....	5	0	1	1	22	....	....	....
1993-94	Adirondack Red Wings	AHL	76	15	24	39	....	....	....	297	....	....	....	....	....	....	....	....	....	....	12	2	2	4	63	....	....	....
1994-95	**Winnipeg Jets**	**NHL**	**20**	**0**	**1**	**1**	**0**	**1**	**1**	**19**	**0**	**0**	**0**	**3**	**0.0**	**3**	**0**	**7**	**0**	**–4**	....	....	....	....	....	....	....	....
	Springfield Falcons	AHL	6	0	1	1	....	....	....	21	....	....	....	....	....	....	....	....	....	....	....	....	....	....	....	....	....	....
1995-96	Springfield Falcons	AHL	48	6	5	11	....	....	....	245	....	....	....	....	....	....	....	....	....	....	8	0	1	1	34	....	....	....
1996-97	**Florida Panthers**	**NHL**	**1**	**0**	**0**	**0**	**0**	**0**	**0**	**5**	**0**	**0**	**0**	**1**	**0.0**	**0**	**0**	**0**	**0**	**0**	....	....	....	....	....	....	....	....
	Carolina Monarchs	AHL	44	1	2	3	....	....	....	239	....	....	....	....	....	....	....	....	....	....	....	....	....	....	....	....	....	....
	San Antonio Dragons	IHL	15	3	3	6	....	....	....	99	....	....	....	....	....	....	....	....	....	....	6	0	1	1	25	....	....	....
1997-98	Quebec Rafales	IHL	24	1	3	4	....	....	....	115	....	....	....	....	....	....	....	....	....	....	....	....	....	....	....	....	....	....
	San Antonio Dragons	IHL	6	1	1	2	....	....	....	21	....	....	....	....	....	....	....	....	....	....	....	....	....	....	....	....	....	....
	Manitoba Moose	IHL	30	4	3	7	....	....	....	202	....	....	....	....	....	....	....	....	....	....	1	0	0	0	10	....	....	....
	NHL Totals		**21**	**0**	**1**	**1**	**0**	**1**	**1**	**24**	**0**	**0**	**0**	**4**	**0.0**	**3**	**0**	**7**	**0**		....	....	....	....	....	....	....	....

Signed as a free agent by **Detroit**, July 28, 1993. Claimed on waivers by **Winnipeg** from **Detroit**, January 20, 1995. Signed as a free agent by **Florida**, August 1, 1996.

• MARTIN, GRANT

Grant Martin LW – L. 5'10", 190 lbs. b: Smooth Rock Falls, Ont., 3/13/1962. Vancouver's 9th choice, 196th overall, in 1980 Entry Draft.

Season	Club	League	GP	G	A	Pts	AG	AA	APts	PIM	PP	SH	GW	S	%	TGF	PGF	TGA	PGA	+/–	GP	G	A	Pts	PIM	PP	SH	GW
1977-78	Hespeler Shamrocks	Jr. B	40	18	25	43	....	....	....	32	....	....	....	....	....	....	....	....	....	....	....	....	....	....	....	....	....	....
1978-79	Guelph Platers	OJHL	49	21	29	50	....	....	....	70	....	....	....	....	....	....	....	....	....	....	....	....	....	....	....	....	....	....
1979-80	Kitchener Rangers	OHA	65	31	21	52	....	....	....	62	....	....	....	....	....	....	....	....	....	....	....	....	....	....	....	....	....	....
1980-81	Kitchener Rangers	OHA	66	41	57	98	....	....	....	77	....	....	....	....	....	....	....	....	....	....	18	9	20	29	42	....	....	....
1981-82	Kitchener Rangers	OHL	54	33	63	96	....	....	....	97	....	....	....	....	....	....	....	....	....	....	12	3	15	18	33	....	....	....
1982-83	Fredericton Express	AHL	80	19	27	46	....	....	....	73	....	....	....	....	....	....	....	....	....	....	12	4	1	5	14	....	....	....
1983-84	**Vancouver Canucks**	**NHL**	**12**	**0**	**2**	**2**	**0**	**1**	**1**	**6**	**0**	**0**	**0**	**7**	**0.0**	**4**	**0**	**6**	**0**	**–2**	....	....	....	....	....	....	....	....
	Fredericton Express	AHL	57	36	24	60	....	....	....	46	....	....	....	....	....	....	....	....	....	....	7	4	5	9	16	....	....	....
1984-85	**Vancouver Canucks**	**NHL**	**12**	**0**	**1**	**1**	**0**	**1**	**1**	**39**	**0**	**0**	**0**	**1**	**0.0**	**3**	**0**	**14**	**3**	**–8**	....	....	....	....	....	....	....	....
	Fredericton Express	AHL	65	31	47	78	....	....	....	78	....	....	....	....	....	....	....	....	....	....	6	1	4	5	8	....	....	....
	Salt Lake Golden Eagles	IHL	2	0	0	0	....	....	....	0	....	....	....	....	....	....	....	....	....	....	....	....	....	....	....	....	....	....
1985-86	**Washington Capitals**	**NHL**	**11**	**0**	**1**	**1**	**0**	**1**	**1**	**6**	**0**	**0**	**0**	**5**	**0.0**	**2**	**0**	**7**	**0**	**–5**	....	....	....	....	....	....	....	....
	Baltimore Skipjacks	AHL	54	27	49	76	....	....	....	97	....	....	....	....	....	....	....	....	....	....	6	1	3	4	14	....	....	....
1986-87	**Washington Capitals**	**NHL**	**9**	**0**	**0**	**0**	**0**	**0**	**0**	**4**	**0**	**0**	**0**	**5**	**0.0**	**1**	**0**	**3**	**1**	**–1**	**1**	**1**	**0**	**1**	**2**	**0**	**0**	**0**
	Binghamton Whalers	AHL	63	30	23	53	....	....	....	86	....	....	....	....	....	....	....	....	....	....	12	3	1	4	16	....	....	....
1987-88	Rochester Americans	AHL	22	11	15	26	....	....	....	18	....	....	....	....	....	....	....	....	....	....	7	4	5	9	17	....	....	....
1988-89	Rochester Americans	AHL	6	7	5	12	....	....	....	6	....	....	....	....	....	....	....	....	....	....	....	....	....	....	....	....	....	....
	JyP-Jyvaskyla	Finland	43	20	29	49	....	....	....	48	....	....	....	....	....	....	....	....	....	....	11	1	5	6	11	....	....	....
1989-90	Schwenningen ERC	Germany	41	27	29	56	....	....	....	67	....	....	....	....	....	....	....	....	....	....	....	....	....	....	....	....	....	....
	Canada	Nat-Team	5	1	0	1	....	....	....	8	....	....	....	....	....	....	....	....	....	....	....	....	....	....	....	....	....	....
1990-91	Schwenningen ERC	Germany	44	33	33	66	....	....	....	93	....	....	....	....	....	....	....	....	....	....	....	....	....	....	....	....	....	....
	Villach	Austria	1	1	1	2	....	....	....	....	....	....	....	....	....	....	....	....	....	....	....	....	....	....	....	....	....	....
1991-92	Schwennigen ERC	Germany	43	26	35	61	....	....	....	32	....	....	....	....	....	....	....	....	....	....	....	....	....	....	....	....	....	....
1992-93	Schwennigen ERC	Germany	41	21	30	51	....	....	....	52	....	....	....	....	....	....	....	....	....	....	....	....	....	....	....	....	....	....
1993-94	Schwennigen ERC	Germany	41	14	27	41	....	....	....	52	....	....	....	....	....	....	....	....	....	....	....	....	....	....	....	....	....	....
1994-95	Schwennigen Wild Wings	German 2	STATISTICS NOT AVAILABLE																									
1995-96	Schwennigen Wild Wings	Germany	48	19	19	38	....	....	....	52	....	....	....	....	....	....	....	....	....	....	4	2	0	2	8	....	....	....
1996-97	Schwennigen Wild Wings	Germany	48	16	23	39	....	....	....	42	....	....	....	....	....	....	....	....	....	....	5	3	4	7	10	....	....	....
1997-98	Schwennigen Wild Wings	Germany	22	7	13	20	....	....	....	22	....	....	....	....	....	....	....	....	....	....	....	....	....	....	....	....	....	....
	NHL Totals		**44**	**0**	**4**	**4**	**0**	**3**	**3**	**55**	**0**	**0**	**0**	**18**	**0.0**	**10**	**0**	**30**	**4**		**1**	**1**	**0**	**1**	**2**	**0**	**0**	**0**

Signed as a free agent by **Washington**, August 6, 1985.

• MARTIN, MATT

Matt Martin D – L. 6'3", 205 lbs. b: Hamden, CT, 4/30/1971. Toronto's 4th choice, 66th overall, in 1989 Entry Draft.

Season	Club	League	GP	G	A	Pts	AG	AA	APts	PIM	PP	SH	GW	S	%	TGF	PGF	TGA	PGA	+/–	GP	G	A	Pts	PIM	PP	SH	GW
1988-89	Avon Old Farms	H.S.	25	9	23	32	....	....	....	....	....	....	....	....	....	....	....	....	....	....	....	....	....	....	....	....	....	....
1989-90			DID NOT PLAY																									
1990-91	University of Maine	H.E.	35	3	12	15	....	....	....	48	....	....	....	....	....	....	....	....	....	....	....	....	....	....	....	....	....	....
1991-92	University of Maine	H.E.	30	4	14	18	....	....	....	46	....	....	....	....	....	....	....	....	....	....	....	....	....	....	....	....	....	....
1992-93	University of Maine	H.E.	44	6	26	32	....	....	....	88	....	....	....	....	....	....	....	....	....	....	....	....	....	....	....	....	....	....
	St. John's Maple Leafs	AHL	2	0	0	0	....	....	....	2	....	....	....	....	....	....	....	....	....	....	9	1	5	6	4	....	....	....
1993-94	United States	Nat-Team	39	7	8	15	....	....	....	127	....	....	....	....	....	....	....	....	....	....	....	....	....	....	....	....	....	....
	United States	Olympics	8	0	2	2	....	....	....	8	....	....	....	....	....	....	....	....	....	....	....	....	....	....	....	....	....	....
	Toronto Maple Leafs	**NHL**	**12**	**0**	**1**	**1**	**0**	**1**	**1**	**6**	**0**	**0**	**0**	**6**	**0.0**	**4**	**0**	**5**	**1**	**0**	....	....	....	....	....	....	....	....
	St. John's Maple Leafs	AHL	12	1	5	6	....	....	....	9	....	....	....	....	....	....	....	....	....	....	11	1	5	6	33	....	....	....
1994-95	**Toronto Maple Leafs**	**NHL**	**15**	**0**	**0**	**0**	**0**	**0**	**0**	**13**	**0**	**0**	**0**	**14**	**0.0**	**10**	**0**	**9**	**1**	**+2**	....	....	....	....	....	....	....	....
	St. John's Maple Leafs	AHL	49	2	16	18	....	....	....	54	....	....	....	....	....	....	....	....	....	....	....	....	....	....	....	....	....	....
1995-96	**Toronto Maple Leafs**	**NHL**	**13**	**0**	**0**	**0**	**0**	**0**	**0**	**14**	**0**	**0**	**0**	**3**	**0.0**	**5**	**0**	**6**	**0**	**–1**	....	....	....	....	....	....	....	....
1996-97	**Toronto Maple Leafs**	**NHL**	**36**	**0**	**4**	**4**	**0**	**4**	**4**	**38**	**0**	**0**	**0**	**30**	**0.0**	**19**	**0**	**38**	**7**	**–12**	....	....	....	....	....	....	....	....
	St. John's Maple Leafs	AHL	12	1	3	4	....	....	....	4	....	....	....	....	....	....	....	....	....	....	....	....	....	....	....	....	....	....
	United States	WC-A	8	0	0	0	....	....	....	0	....	....	....	....	....	....	....	....	....	....	....	....	....	....	....	....	....	....
1997-98	Chicago Wolves	IHL	78	7	22	29	....	....	....	95	....	....	....	....	....	....	....	....	....	....	19	0	5	5	24	....	....	....
	NHL Totals		**76**	**0**	**5**	**5**	**0**	**5**	**5**	**71**	**0**	**0**	**0**	**53**	**0.0**	**38**	**0**	**58**	**9**		....	....	....	....	....	....	....	....

• MARTIN, PIT

Pit (Hubert Jacques) Martin C – R. 5'9", 170 lbs. b: Noranda, Que., 12/9/1943.

Season	Club	League	GP	G	A	Pts	AG	AA	APts	PIM	PP	SH	GW	S	%	TGF	PGF	TGA	PGA	+/–	GP	G	A	Pts	PIM	PP	SH	GW
1959-60	Hamilton Tiger-Cubs	OHA	29	13	12	25	....	....	....	14	....	....	....	....	....	....	....	....	....	....	....	....	....	....	....	....	....	....
1960-61	Hamilton Red Wings	OHA	48	20	21	41	....	....	....	17	....	....	....	....	....	....	....	....	....	....	10	7	2	9	8	....	....	....
1961-62	Hamilton Red Wings	OHA	48	42	46	88	....	....	....	46	....	....	....	....	....	....	....	....	....	....	10	3	*9	*12	0	....	....	....
	Detroit Red Wings	**NHL**	**1**	**0**	**1**	**1**	**0**	**1**	**1**	**0**	....	....	....	....	....	....	....	....	....	....	....	....	....	....	....	....	....	....
1962-63	Hamilton Red Wings	OHA	49	36	49	85	....	....	....	67	....	....	....	....	....	....	....	....	....	....	5	1	1	2	10	....	....	....
	Pittsburgh Hornets	AHL	5	1	2	3	....	....	....	0	....	....	....	....	....	....	....	....	....	....	....	....	....	....	....	....	....	....
1963-64	**Detroit Red Wings**	**NHL**	**50**	**9**	**12**	**21**	**12**	**13**	**25**	**28**	....	....	....	....	....	....	....	....	....	....	**14**	**1**	**4**	**5**	**14**	....	....	....
	Pittsburgh Hornets	AHL	21	3	7	10	....	....	....	2	....	....	....	....	....	....	....	....	....	....	....	....	....	....	....	....	....	....
1964-65	**Detroit Red Wings**	**NHL**	**58**	**8**	**9**	**17**	**10**	**10**	**20**	**32**	....	....	....	....	....	....	....	....	....	....	**3**	**0**	**1**	**1**	**2**	....	....	....
1965-66	Pittsburgh Hornets	AHL	16	6	6	12	....	....	....	26	....	....	....	....	....	....	....	....	....	....	....	....	....	....	....	....	....	....
	Detroit Red Wings	**NHL**	**10**	**1**	**1**	**2**	**1**	**1**	**2**	**0**	....	....	....	....	....	....	....	....	....	....	....	....	....	....	....	....	....	....
	Boston Bruins	**NHL**	**41**	**16**	**11**	**27**	**19**	**11**	**30**	**10**	....	....	....	....	....	....	....	....	....	....	....	....	....	....	....	....	....	....

			REGULAR SEASON																		PLAYOFFS							
Season	Club	League	GP	G	A	Pts	AG	AA	APts	PIM	PP	SH	GW	S	%	TGF	PGF	TGA	PGA	+/–	GP	G	A	Pts	PIM	PP	SH	GW
1966-67	Boston Bruins	NHL	70	20	22	42	25	23	48	40	....	....	....	....	....	....	....	....	....	....	....	....	....	....	....	....	....	....
1967-68	Chicago Black Hawks	NHL	63	16	19	35	20	20	40	36	0	0	2	118	13.6	57	6	42	0	+9	11	3	6	9	2	0	0	0
1968-69	Chicago Black Hawks	NHL	76	23	38	61	26	36	62	73	5	0	4	173	13.3	92	20	63	0	+9	....	....	....	....	....	....	....	....
1969-70	Chicago Black Hawks	NHL	73	30	33	63	35	33	68	61	5	0	1	160	18.8	86	26	38	0	+22	8	3	3	6	4	2	1	0
1970-71	Chicago Black Hawks	NHL	62	22	33	55	23	29	52	40	6	0	5	126	17.5	69	18	34	1	+18	17	2	7	9	12	0	0	1
1971-72	Chicago Black Hawks	NHL	78	24	51	75	26	47	73	56	5	1	7	170	14.1	101	16	42	1	+44	8	4	2	6	4	0	0	1
1972-73	Chicago Black Hawks	NHL	78	29	61	90	29	51	80	30	4	0	3	185	15.7	118	21	77	7	+27	15	10	6	16	6	4	0	1
1973-74	Chicago Black Hawks	NHL	78	30	47	77	31	41	72	43	8	2	4	175	17.1	103	27	62	15	+29	7	2	0	2	4	1	0	0
1974-75	Chicago Black Hawks	NHL	70	19	26	45	18	20	38	34	4	1	2	136	14.0	70	22	73	22	–3	8	1	1	2	2	0	0	0
1975-76	Chicago Black Hawks	NHL	80	32	39	71	30	31	61	44	8	2	4	188	17.0	109	43	95	35	+6	4	1	0	1	4	0	0	0
1976-77	Chicago Black Hawks	NHL	75	17	36	53	16	29	45	22	6	1	2	117	14.5	78	24	82	24	–4	2	0	0	0	0	0	0	0
1977-78	Chicago Black Hawks	NHL	7	1	1	2	1	1	2	0	0	0	0	7	14.3	2	0	3	0	–1	....	....	....	....	....	....	....	....
	Vancouver Canucks	NHL	67	15	31	46	14	25	39	36	4	0	0	104	14.4	70	25	80	9	–26	....	....	....	....	....	....	....	....
1978-79	Vancouver Canucks	NHL	64	12	14	26	11	11	22	24	1	0	1	80	15.0	37	6	43	9	–3	3	0	1	1	2	0	0	0
	NHL Totals		1101	324	485	809	347	433	780	609	56	7	35	1739	18.6	992	254	734	123		100	27	31	58	56	7	1	3

Won Bill Masterton Trophy (1970)

Played in NHL All-Star Game (1971, 1972, 1973, 1974)

Traded to **Boston** by **Detroit** for Parker MacDonald, December 30, 1965. Traded to **Chicago** by **Boston** with Jack Norris and Gilles Marotte for Phil Esposito, Ken Hodge and Fred Stanfield, May 15, 1967. Traded to **Vancouver** by **Chicago** for future considerations (Murray Bannerman, May 27, 1978), November 4, 1977.

• MARTIN, RICK

Rick Martin LW – L. 5'11", 179 lbs. b: Verdun, Que., 7/26/1951. Buffalo's 1st choice, 5th overall, in 1971 Amateur Draft.

Season	Club	League	GP	G	A	Pts	AG	AA	APts	PIM	PP	SH	GW	S	%	TGF	PGF	TGA	PGA	+/–	GP	G	A	Pts	PIM	PP	SH	GW
1967-68	Thetford Canadiens	QJHL	40	38	35	73	....	....	....	....	....	....	....	....	....	....	....	....	....	....	....	....	....	....	....	....	....	....
1968-69	Montreal Jr. Canadiens	OHA	52	22	21	43	....	....	....	27	....	....	....	....	....	....	....	....	....	....	14	3	0	3	2	....	....	....
1969-70	Montreal Jr. Canadiens	OHA	34	23	32	55	....	....	....	10	....	....	....	....	....	....	....	....	....	....	....	....	....	....	....	....	....	....
1970-71	Montreal Jr. Canadiens	OHA	60	*71	50	121	....	....	....	106	....	....	....	....	....	....	....	....	....	....	....	....	....	....	....	....	....	....
1971-72	Buffalo Sabres	NHL	73	44	30	74	47	27	74	36	19	0	5	266	16.5	109	49	98	0	–38	....	....	....	....	....	....	....	....
1972-73	Canada	Summit	DID NOT PLAY																									
	Buffalo Sabres	NHL	75	37	36	73	37	30	67	79	11	0	4	299	12.4	120	45	72	1	+4	6	3	2	5	12	2	0	0
1973-74	Buffalo Sabres	NHL	78	52	34	86	53	29	82	38	8	0	6	320	16.3	121	41	102	0	–22	....	....	....	....	....	....	....	....
1974-75	Buffalo Sabres	NHL	68	52	43	95	49	34	83	72	21	0	6	301	17.3	143	61	77	0	+5	17	7	8	15	20	5	0	1
1975-76	Buffalo Sabres	NHL	80	49	37	86	46	29	75	67	18	0	7	327	15.0	147	56	68	0	+23	9	4	7	11	12	2	0	1
1976-77	Canada	C Cup	4	3	2	5	....	....	....	0	....	....	....	....	....	....	....	....	....	....	....	....	....	....	....	....	....	....
	Buffalo Sabres	NHL	66	36	29	65	35	24	59	58	12	0	6	221	16.3	99	32	57	0	+10	6	2	1	3	9	1	0	1
1977-78	Buffalo Sabres	NHL	65	28	35	63	27	29	56	16	7	0	6	221	12.7	87	21	50	0	+16	7	2	4	6	13	1	0	1
1978-79	Buffalo Sabres	NHL	73	32	21	53	29	16	45	35	8	0	3	250	12.8	85	26	66	0	–7	3	0	3	3	0	0	0	0
1979-80	Buffalo Sabres	NHL	80	45	34	79	41	26	67	54	8	0	3	257	17.5	115	30	67	0	+18	14	6	4	10	8	1	0	0
1980-81	Buffalo Sabres	NHL	23	7	14	21	6	10	16	20	2	0	1	57	12.3	29	7	18	0	+4	....	....	....	....	....	....	....	....
	Los Angeles Kings	NHL	1	1	1	2	1	1	2	0	0	0	0	2	50.0	4	2	1	0	+1	1	0	0	0	0	0	0	0
1981-82	Los Angeles Kings	NHL	3	1	3	4	1	2	3	2	1	0	0	9	11.1	4	2	1	0	+1	....	....	....	....	....	....	....	....
	NHL Totals		685	384	317	701	372	257	629	477	115	0	47	2530	15.2	1063	372	677	1		63	24	29	53	74	12	0	4

OHA First All-Star Team (1971) • NHL First All-Star Team (1974, 1975) • NHL Second All-Star Team (1976, 1977)

Played in NHL All-Star Game (1972, 1973, 1974, 1975, 1976, 1977, 1978)

Traded to **LA Kings** by **Buffalo** for LA Kings' 3rd round choice (Colin Chisholm) in 1981 Entry Draft and 1st round choice (Tom Barrasso) in 1983 Entry Draft, March 10, 1981.

• MARTIN, TERRY

Terry Martin LW – L. 5'11", 195 lbs. b: Barrie, Ont., 10/25/1955. Buffalo's 3rd choice, 44th overall, in 1975 Amateur Draft.

Season	Club	League	GP	G	A	Pts	AG	AA	APts	PIM	PP	SH	GW	S	%	TGF	PGF	TGA	PGA	+/–	GP	G	A	Pts	PIM	PP	SH	GW
1972-73	London Knights	OHA	59	17	22	39	....	....	....	25	....	....	....	....	....	....	....	....	....	....	....	....	....	....	....	....	....	....
1973-74	London Knights	OHA	63	33	24	57	....	....	....	38	....	....	....	....	....	....	....	....	....	....	....	....	....	....	....	....	....	....
1974-75	London Knights	OHA	70	43	57	100	....	....	....	118	....	....	....	....	....	....	....	....	....	....	....	....	....	....	....	....	....	....
1975-76	Buffalo Sabres	NHL	1	0	0	0	0	0	0	0	0	0	0	0	0.0	0	0	0	0	0	....	....	....	....	....	....	....	....
	Charlotte Checkers	SHL	25	12	10	22				30	....	....	....	....	....	....	....	....	....	....	9	2	3	5	2	....	....	....
	Hershey Bears	AHL	19	3	6	9	....	....	....	18	....	....	....	....	....	....	....	....	....	....	....	....	....	....	....	....	....	....
1976-77	Buffalo Sabres	NHL	62	11	12	23	11	10	21	8	1	0	0	72	15.3	40	1	33	0	+6	3	0	2	2	5	0	0	0
	Hershey Bears	AHL	12	1	4	5	....	....	....	12	....	....	....	....	....	....	....	....	....	....	....	....	....	....	....	....	....	....
1977-78	Buffalo Sabres	NHL	21	3	2	5	3	2	5	9	0	0	2	17	17.6	6	0	7	0	1	0	2	0	2	5	0	0	0
	Hershey Bears	AHL	4	2	1	3	....	....	....	2	....	....	....	....	....	....	....	....	....	....	....	....	....	....	....	....	....	....
1978-79	Buffalo Sabres	NHL	64	6	8	14	5	6	11	33	1	0	0	38	15.8	29	4	50	8	–17	....	....	....	....	....	....	....	....
1979-80	Quebec Nordiques	NHL	3	0	0	0	0	0	0	0	0	0	0	4	0.0	0	0	5	0	–5	....	....	....	....	....	....	....	....
	Syracuse Firebirds	AHL	18	0	9	10	....	....	....	6	....	....	....	....	....	....	....	....	....	....	....	....	....	....	....	....	....	....
	Toronto Maple Leafs	NHL	37	6	15	21	5	11	16	2	1	0	2	40	15.0	41	2	34	1	+6	3	2	0	2	7	0	0	0
	New Brunswick Hawks	AHL	3	0	1	1	....	....	....	0	....	....	....	....	....	....	....	....	....	....	....	....	....	....	....	....	....	....
1980-81	Toronto Maple Leafs	NHL	69	23	14	37	19	10	29	32	1	0	4	111	20.7	71	3	69	16	+15	3	0	0	0	0	0	0	0
1981-82	Toronto Maple Leafs	NHL	72	25	24	49	20	16	36	39	4	0	1	133	18.8	74	17	89	14	–18	....	....	....	....	....	....	....	....
1982-83	Toronto Maple Leafs	NHL	76	14	13	27	11	9	20	28	3	1	0	95	14.7	48	9	92	24	–29	4	0	0	0	9	0	0	0
1983-84	Toronto Maple Leafs	NHL	63	15	10	25	12	7	19	51	2	2	1	62	24.2	43	8	66	23	–8	....	....	....	....	....	....	....	....
1984-85	Edmonton Oilers	NHL	4	0	2	2	0	1	1	0	0	0	0	6	0.0	3	0	0	0	+3	....	....	....	....	....	....	....	....
	Nova Scotia Oilers	AHL	28	17	11	28	....	....	....	4	....	....	....	....	....	....	....	....	....	....	....	....	....	....	....	....	....	....
	Minnesota North Stars	NHL	7	1	1	2	1	1	2	0	0	0	0	5	20.0	3	1	2	0	0	....	....	....	....	....	....	....	....
1985-86	Springfield Indians	AHL	72	19	22	41	....	....	....	17	....	....	....	....	....	....	....	....	....	....	....	....	....	....	....	....	....	....
1986-87	Newmarket Saints	AHL	72	8	7	15	....	....	....	8	....	....	....	....	....	....	....	....	....	....	....	....	....	....	....	....	....	....
	NHL Totals		479	104	101	205	87	73	160	202	13	3	10	583	17.8	358	45	447	86		21	4	2	6	26	0	0	0

Claimed by **Quebec** from **Buffalo** in Expansion Draft, June 13, 1979. Traded to **Toronto** by **Quebec** with Dave Farrish for Reggie Thomas, December 13, 1979. Claimed by **Edmonton** from **Toronto** in Waiver Draft, October 9, 1984. Traded to **Minnesota** by **Edmonton** with Gord Sherven for Mark Napier, January 24, 1985.

• MARTIN, THOMAS

Thomas "Tom" Martin RW – R. 5'9", 170 lbs. b: Toronto, Ont., 10/16/1947. Toronto's 1st choice, 5th overall, in 1964 Amateur Draft.

Season	Club	League	GP	G	A	Pts	AG	AA	APts	PIM	PP	SH	GW	S	%	TGF	PGF	TGA	PGA	+/–	GP	G	A	Pts	PIM	PP	SH	GW
1965-66	Toronto Marlboros	OHA	40	19	21	40	....	....	....	23	....	....	....	....	....	....	....	....	....	....	11	2	2	4	2	....	....	....
1966-67	Toronto Marlboros	OHA	42	18	28	46	....	....	....	29	....	....	....	....	....	....	....	....	....	....	17	12	12	24	4	....	....	....
1967-68	Toronto Marlboros	OHA	54	37	48	85	....	....	....	43	....	....	....	....	....	....	....	....	....	....	5	3	3	6	16	....	....	....
	Toronto Maple Leafs	NHL	3	1	0	1	1	0	1	0	1	0	0	2	50.0	1	1	0	0	0	....	....	....	....	....	....	....	....
	Tulsa Oilers	CHL	....	....	....	....	....	....	....	....	....	....	....	....	....	....	....	....	....	....	1	0	0	0	0	....	....	....
1968-69	Tulsa Oilers	CHL	4	2	0	2	....	....	....	4	....	....	....	....	....	....	....	....	....	....	....	....	....	....	....	....	....	....
	Ottawa Nats	OHA Sr.	6	3	8	11	....	....	....	8	....	....	....	....	....	....	....	....	....	....	....	....	....	....	....	....	....	....
1969-70	Tulsa Oilers	CHL	65	21	35	56	....	....	....	26	....	....	....	....	....	....	....	....	....	....	6	5	3	8	4	....	....	....
1970-71	Fort Worth Wings	CHL	59	23	33	56	....	....	....	31	....	....	....	....	....	....	....	....	....	....	....	....	....	....	....	....	....	....
1971-72	Fort Worth Wings	CHL	31	14	21	35	....	....	....	17	....	....	....	....	....	....	....	....	....	....	....	....	....	....	....	....	....	....
	Tidewater Wings	AHL	42	16	13	29	....	....	....	23	....	....	....	....	....	....	....	....	....	....	....	....	....	....	....	....	....	....
1972-73	Ottawa Nationals	WHA	75	19	27	46	....	....	....	27	....	....	....	....	....	....	....	....	....	....	5	0	5	5	2	....	....	....
1973-74	Toronto Toros	WHA	74	25	32	57	....	....	....	14	....	....	....	....	....	....	....	....	....	....	12	7	3	10	2	....	....	....
1974-75	Toronto Toros	WHA	64	14	17	31	....	....	....	18	....	....	....	....	....	....	....	....	....	....	5	1	5	6	0	....	....	....
1975-76			DID NOT PLAY																									
1976-77	MoDo AIK	Sweden	33	9	8	17	....	....	....	46	....	....	....	....	....	....	....	....	....	....	2	0	1	1	4	....	....	....
	NHL Totals		3	1	0	1	1	0	1	0	1	0	0	2	50.0	1	1	0	0		....	....	....	....	....	....	....	....
	Other Major League Totals		213	58	76	134	....	....	....	59	....	....	....	....	....	....	....	....	....	....	22	8	13	21	4	....	....	....

Claimed by **Detroit** from **Toronto** (Tulsa-CHL) in Intra-League Draft, June 9, 1970. Selected by **Ontario-Ottawa** (WHA) in 1972 WHA General Player Draft, February 12, 1972. Transferred to **Toronto** (WHA) after **Ottawa** (WHA) franchise relocated, May, 1973. Traded to **San Diego** (WHA) by **Toronto** (WHA) for the rights to Angelo Moretta, July, 1975.

• MARTIN, TOM

Tom Martin LW – L. 6'2", 200 lbs. b: Kelowna, B.C., 5/11/1965. Winnipeg's 2nd choice, 74th overall, in 1982 Entry Draft.

Season	Club	League	GP	G	A	Pts	AG	AA	APts	PIM	PP	SH	GW	S	%	TGF	PGF	TGA	PGA	+/–	GP	G	A	Pts	PIM	PP	SH	GW
1981-82	Kelowna Packers	BCJHL	43	32	34	66	....	....	....	194	....	....	....	....	....	....	....	....	....	....	....	....	....	....	....	....	....	....
1982-83	University of Denver	WCHA	37	8	18	26	....	....	....	128	....	....	....	....	....	....	....	....	....	....	....	....	....	....	....	....	....	....
1983-84	Victoria Cougars	WHL	60	30	45	75	....	....	....	261	....	....	....	....	....	....	....	....	....	....	....	....	....	....	....	....	....	....
	Sherbrooke Jets	AHL	5	0	0	0	....	....	....	16	....	....	....	....	....	....	....	....	....	....	....	....	....	....	....	....	....	....

Season	Club	League	GP	G	A	Pts	AG	AA	APts	PIM	PP	SH	GW	S	%	TGF	PGF	TGA	PGA	+/-	GP	G	A	Pts	PIM	PP	SH	GW
			REGULAR SEASON																		PLAYOFFS							
1984-85	**Winnipeg Jets**	**NHL**	**8**	**1**	**0**	**1**	**1**	**0**	**1**	**42**	**0**	**0**	**0**	**5**	**20.0**	**1**	**0**	**0**	**0**	**+1**	**3**	**0**	**0**	**0**	**2**	**0**	**0**	**0**
	Sherbrooke Canadiens	AHL	58	4	15	19	....	....	....	212	....	....	....	....	....	....	....	....	....	....	12	1	1	2	72	....	....	....
1985-86	**Winnipeg Jets**	**NHL**	**5**	**0**	**0**	**0**	**0**	**0**	**0**	**0**	**0**	**0**	**0**	**1**	**0.0**	**0**	**0**	**0**	**0**	**0**	....	....	....	....	....	....	....	....
	Sherbrooke Canadiens	AHL	69	11	18	29	....	....	....	227	....	....	....	....	....	....	....	....	....	....	....	....	....	....	....	....	....	....
1986-87	**Winnipeg Jets**	**NHL**	**11**	**1**	**0**	**1**	**1**	**0**	**1**	**49**	**0**	**0**	**0**	**2**	**50.0**	**1**	**0**	**0**	**0**	**+1**	....	....	....	....	....	....	....	....
	Adirondack Red Wings	AHL	18	5	6	11	....	....	....	57	....	....	....	....	....	....	....	....	....	....	....	....	....	....	....	....	....	....
1987-88	**Hartford Whalers**	**NHL**	**5**	**1**	**2**	**3**	**1**	**1**	**2**	**14**	**0**	**0**	**0**	**8**	**12.5**	**3**	**0**	**4**	**0**	**–1**	....	....	....	....	....	....	....	....
	Binghamton Whalers	AHL	71	28	61	89	....	....	....	344	....	....	....	....	....	....	....	....	....	....	3	0	0	0	18	....	....	....
1988-89	**Minnesota North Stars**	**NHL**	**4**	**1**	**1**	**2**	**1**	**1**	**2**	**4**	**0**	**0**	**0**	**6**	**16.7**	**2**	**0**	**1**	**0**	**+1**	....	....	....	....	....	....	....	....
	Hartford Whalers	**NHL**	**38**	**7**	**6**	**13**	**6**	**4**	**10**	**113**	**0**	**0**	**1**	**40**	**17.5**	**21**	**0**	**13**	**0**	**+8**	**1**	**0**	**0**	**0**	**4**	**0**	**0**	**0**
1989-90	**Hartford Whalers**	**NHL**	**21**	**1**	**2**	**3**	**1**	**1**	**2**	**27**	**0**	**0**	**0**	**13**	**7.7**	**6**	**0**	**6**	**0**	**0**	....	....	....	....	....	....	....	....
	Binghamton Whalers	AHL	24	4	10	14	....	....	....	113	....	....	....	....	....	....	....	....	....	....	....	....	....	....	....	....	....	....
1990-91	New Haven Nighthawks	AHL	22	11	7	18	....	....	....	88	....	....	....	....	....	....	....	....	....	....	....	....	....	....	....	....	....	....
	NHL Totals		**92**	**12**	**11**	**23**	**11**	**7**	**18**	**249**	**0**	**0**	**1**	**75**	**16.0**	**34**	**0**	**24**	**0**		**4**	**0**	**0**	**0**	**6**	**0**	**0**	**0**

AHL First All-Star Team (1988)

Rights traded to **Victoria** (WHL) by **Seattle** (WHL) for used bus and future considerations, January, 1983. Signed as a free agent by **Hartford**, July 29, 1987. Claimed by **Minnesota** from **Hartford** in Waiver Draft, October 3, 1988. Claimed on waivers by **Hartford** from **Minnesota**, December, 1988. Signed as a free agent by **LA Kings**, July, 1990.

• MARTINEAU, DON

Don Martineau RW – R. 6', 190 lbs. b: Kimberley, B.C., 4/25/1952. Atlanta's 4th choice, 50th overall, in 1972 Amateur Draft.

Season	Club	League	GP	G	A	Pts	AG	AA	APts	PIM	PP	SH	GW	S	%	TGF	PGF	TGA	PGA	+/-	GP	G	A	Pts	PIM	PP	SH	GW
1969-70	Estevan Bruins	WCJHL	56	4	3	7	....	....	....	106	....	....	....	....	....	....	....	....	....	....	3	0	0	0	16	....	....	....
1970-71	Estevan Bruins	WCJHL	66	18	32	50	....	....	....	126	....	....	....	....	....	....	....	....	....	....	7	0	3	3	8	....	....	....
1971-72	New Westminster Royals	WCJHL	67	25	35	60	....	....	....	221	....	....	....	....	....	....	....	....	....	....	5	1	2	3	15	....	....	....
1972-73	Omaha Knights	CHL	72	22	28	50	....	....	....	170	....	....	....	....	....	....	....	....	....	....	11	1	2	3	*36	....	....	....
1973-74	**Atlanta Flames**	**NHL**	**4**	**0**	**0**	**0**	**0**	**0**	**0**	**2**	**0**	**0**	**0**	**3**	**0.0**	**0**	**0**	**3**	**0**	**–3**	....	....	....	....	....	....	....	....
	Omaha Knights	CHL	48	12	26	38	....	....	....	122	....	....	....	....	....	....	....	....	....	....	5	2	2	4	18	....	....	....
1974-75	**Minnesota North Stars**	**NHL**	**76**	**6**	**9**	**15**	**6**	**7**	**13**	**61**	**0**	**0**	**0**	**54**	**11.1**	**21**	**0**	**34**	**0**	**–13**	....	....	....	....	....	....	....	....
1975-76	**Detroit Red Wings**	**NHL**	**9**	**0**	**1**	**1**	**0**	**1**	**1**	**0**	**0**	**0**	**0**	**1**	**0.0**	**1**	**0**	**2**	**0**	**–1**	....	....	....	....	....	....	....	....
	New Haven Nighthawks	AHL	64	15	20	35	....	....	....	129	....	....	....	....	....	....	....	....	....	....	3	0	1	1	2	....	....	....
1976-77	**Detroit Red Wings**	**NHL**	**1**	**0**	**0**	**0**	**0**	**0**	**0**	**0**	**0**	**0**	**0**	**0**	**0.0**	**0**	**0**	**0**	**0**	**0**	....	....	....	....	....	....	....	....
	Kansas City Blues	CHL	76	27	38	65	....	....	....	57	....	....	....	....	....	....	....	....	....	....	10	2	1	3	2	....	....	....
1977-78	Kansas City Red Wings	CHL	61	16	15	31	....	....	....	31	....	....	....	....	....	....	....	....	....	....	....	....	....	....	....	....	....	....
	NHL Totals		**90**	**6**	**10**	**16**	**6**	**8**	**14**	**63**	**0**	**0**	**0**	**58**	**10.3**	**22**	**0**	**39**	**0**		....	....	....	....	....	....	....	....

CHL First All-Star Team (1977)

Traded to **Minnesota** by **Atlanta** with John Flesch for Buster Harvey and Jerry Myers, May 28, 1974. Traded to **Detroit** by **Minnesota** for Pierre Jarry, November 25, 1975.

• MARTINI, DARCY

Darcy Martini D – L. 6'4", 220 lbs. b: Castlegar, B.C., 1/30/1969. Edmonton's 8th choice, 162nd overall, in 1989 Entry Draft.

Season	Club	League	GP	G	A	Pts	AG	AA	APts	PIM	PP	SH	GW	S	%	TGF	PGF	TGA	PGA	+/-	GP	G	A	Pts	PIM	PP	SH	GW
1988-89	Michigan Tech Huskies	WCHA	35	1	2	3	....	....	....	103	....	....	....	....	....	....	....	....	....	....	....	....	....	....	....	....	....	....
1989-90	Michigan Tech Huskies	WCHA	36	3	6	9	....	....	....	151	....	....	....	....	....	....	....	....	....	....	....	....	....	....	....	....	....	....
1990-91	Michigan Tech Huskies	WCHA	34	10	13	23	....	....	....	*184	....	....	....	....	....	....	....	....	....	....	....	....	....	....	....	....	....	....
1991-92	Michigan Tech Huskies	WCHA	17	5	13	18	....	....	....	58	....	....	....	....	....	....	....	....	....	....	....	....	....	....	....	....	....	....
1992-93	Cape Breton Oilers	AHL	47	1	6	7	....	....	....	36	....	....	....	....	....	....	....	....	....	....	2	0	1	1	0	....	....	....
	Wheeling Thunderbirds	ECHL	6	0	2	2	....	....	....	2	....	....	....	....	....	....	....	....	....	....	....	....	....	....	....	....	....	....
1993-94	**Edmonton Oilers**	**NHL**	**2**	**0**	**0**	**0**	**0**	**0**	**0**	**0**	**0**	**0**	**0**	**0**	**0.0**	**0**	**0**	**1**	**0**	**–1**	....	....	....	....	....	....	....	....
	Cape Breton Oilers	AHL	65	18	38	56	....	....	....	131	....	....	....	....	....	....	....	....	....	....	5	1	3	4	26	....	....	....
1994-95	Cape Breton Oilers	AHL	31	2	13	15	....	....	....	75	....	....	....	....	....	....	....	....	....	....	....	....	....	....	....	....	....	....
	Portland Pirates	AHL	22	3	6	9	....	....	....	28	....	....	....	....	....	....	....	....	....	....	....	....	....	....	....	....	....	....
	Minnesota Moose	IHL	10	3	1	4	....	....	....	10	....	....	....	....	....	....	....	....	....	....	1	0	0	0	2	....	....	....
1995-96	Los Angeles Ice Dogs	IHL	49	15	31	46	....	....	....	50	....	....	....	....	....	....	....	....	....	....	....	....	....	....	....	....	....	....
	San Francisco Spiders	IHL	17	3	4	7	....	....	....	10	....	....	....	....	....	....	....	....	....	....	4	0	2	2	2	....	....	....
1996-97	Klagenfurter AC	Austria	54	22	22	44	....	....	....	129	....	....	....	....	....	....	....	....	....	....	....	....	....	....	....	....	....	....
	NHL Totals		**2**	**0**	**0**	**0**	**0**	**0**	**0**	**0**	**0**	**0**	**0**	**0**	**0.0**	**0**	**0**	**1**	**0**		....	....	....	....	....	....	....	....

• MARTINS, STEVE

Steve Martins C – L. 5'9", 175 lbs. b: Gatineau, Que., 4/13/1972. Hartford's 1st choice, 5th overall, in 1994 Supplemental Draft.

Season	Club	League	GP	G	A	Pts	AG	AA	APts	PIM	PP	SH	GW	S	%	TGF	PGF	TGA	PGA	+/-	GP	G	A	Pts	PIM	PP	SH	GW
1991-92	Harvard University	ECAC	20	13	14	27	....	....	....	26	....	....	....	....	....	....	....	....	....	....	....	....	....	....	....	....	....	....
1992-93	Harvard University	ECAC	18	6	8	14	....	....	....	40	....	....	....	....	....	....	....	....	....	....	....	....	....	....	....	....	....	....
1993-94	Harvard University	ECAC	32	25	35	60	....	....	....	*93	....	....	....	....	....	....	....	....	....	....	....	....	....	....	....	....	....	....
1994-95	Harvard University	ECAC	28	15	23	38	....	....	....	93	....	....	....	....	....	....	....	....	....	....	....	....	....	....	....	....	....	....
1995-96	**Hartford Whalers**	**NHL**	**23**	**1**	**3**	**4**	**1**	**2**	**3**	**8**	**0**	**0**	**0**	**27**	**3.7**	**7**	**0**	**12**	**2**	**–3**	....	....	....	....	....	....	....	....
	Springfield Falcons	AHL	30	9	20	29	....	....	....	10	....	....	....	....	....	....	....	....	....	....	....	....	....	....	....	....	....	....
1996-97	**Hartford Whalers**	**NHL**	**2**	**0**	**1**	**1**	**0**	**1**	**1**	**0**	**0**	**0**	**0**	**2**	**0.0**	**1**	**0**	**1**	**0**	**0**	....	....	....	....	....	....	....	....
	Springfield Falcons	AHL	63	12	31	43	....	....	....	78	....	....	....	....	....	....	....	....	....	....	17	1	3	4	26	....	....	....
1997-98	**Carolina Hurricanes**	**NHL**	**3**	**0**	**0**	**0**	**0**	**0**	**0**	**0**	**0**	**0**	**0**	**0**	**0.0**	**0**	**0**	**0**	**0**	**0**	....	....	....	....	....	....	....	....
	Chicago Wolves	IHL	78	20	41	61	....	....	....	122	....	....	....	....	....	....	....	....	....	....	21	6	14	20	28	....	....	....
	NHL Totals		**28**	**1**	**4**	**5**	**1**	**3**	**4**	**8**	**0**	**0**	**0**	**29**	**3.4**	**8**	**0**	**13**	**2**		....	....	....	....	....	....	....	....

ECAC First All-Star Team (1994) • NCAA East First All-American Team (1994) • NCAA Final Four All-Tournament Team (1994)

Transferred to **Carolina** after **Hartford** franchise relocated, June 25, 1997.

• MARTINSON, STEVEN

Steven Martinson LW – L. 6'1", 205 lbs. b: Minnetonka, MN, 6/21/1959.

Season	Club	League	GP	G	A	Pts	AG	AA	APts	PIM	PP	SH	GW	S	%	TGF	PGF	TGA	PGA	+/-	GP	G	A	Pts	PIM	PP	SH	GW
1980-81	St. Cloud State	NCAA	....	19	21	40	....	....	....	57	....	....	....	....	....	....	....	....	....	....	....	....	....	....	....	....	....	....
1981-82	Toledo Goaldiggers	IHL	35	12	18	30	....	....	....	128	....	....	....	....	....	....	....	....	....	....	....	....	....	....	....	....	....	....
1982-83	Toledo Goaldiggers	IHL	32	9	10	19	....	....	....	111	....	....	....	....	....	....	....	....	....	....	....	....	....	....	....	....	....	....
	Birmingham South Stars	CHL	43	4	5	9	....	....	....	184	....	....	....	....	....	....	....	....	....	....	13	1	2	3	*80	....	....	....
1983-84	Tulsa Oilers	CHL	42	3	6	9	....	....	....	240	....	....	....	....	....	....	....	....	....	....	6	0	0	0	43	....	....	....
1984-85	Toledo Goaldiggers	IHL	54	4	10	14	....	....	....	300	....	....	....	....	....	....	....	....	....	....	2	0	0	0	21	....	....	....
1985-86	Hershey Bears	AHL	69	3	6	9	....	....	....	*432	....	....	....	....	....	....	....	....	....	....	3	0	0	0	56	....	....	....
1986-87	Hershey Bears	AHL	17	0	3	3	....	....	....	85	....	....	....	....	....	....	....	....	....	....	....	....	....	....	....	....	....	....
	Adirondack Red Wings	AHL	14	1	1	2	....	....	....	78	....	....	....	....	....	....	....	....	....	....	11	2	0	2	108	....	....	....
1987-88	**Detroit Red Wings**	**NHL**	**10**	**1**	**1**	**2**	**1**	**1**	**2**	**84**	**0**	**0**	**1**	**3**	**33.3**	**3**	**0**	**0**	**0**	**+3**	....	....	....	....	....	....	....	....
	Adirondack Red Wings	AHL	32	6	8	14	....	....	....	146	....	....	....	....	....	....	....	....	....	....	6	1	2	3	66	....	....	....
1988-89	**Montreal Canadiens**	**NHL**	**25**	**1**	**0**	**1**	**1**	**0**	**1**	**87**	**0**	**0**	**1**	**8**	**12.5**	**1**	**0**	**2**	**0**	**–1**	**1**	**0**	**0**	**0**	**10**	**0**	**0**	**0**
	Sherbrooke Canadiens	AHL	10	5	7	12	....	....	....	61	....	....	....	....	....	....	....	....	....	....	....	....	....	....	....	....	....	....
1989-90	**Montreal Canadiens**	**NHL**	**13**	**0**	**0**	**0**	**0**	**0**	**0**	**64**	**0**	**0**	**0**	**2**	**0.0**	**0**	**0**	**2**	**0**	**–2**	....	....	....	....	....	....	....	....
	Sherbrooke Canadiens	AHL	37	6	20	26	....	....	....	113	....	....	....	....	....	....	....	....	....	....	....	....	....	....	....	....	....	....
1990-91	San Diego Gulls	IHL	53	16	24	40	....	....	....	268	....	....	....	....	....	....	....	....	....	....	....	....	....	....	....	....	....	....
1991-92	**Minnesota North Stars**	**NHL**	**1**	**0**	**0**	**0**	**0**	**0**	**0**	**9**	**0**	**0**	**0**	**0**	**0.0**	**0**	**0**	**0**	**0**	**0**	....	....	....	....	....	....	....	....
	San Diego Gulls	IHL	70	18	15	33	....	....	....	279	....	....	....	....	....	....	....	....	....	....	4	1	1	2	15	....	....	....
1992-93	San Diego Gulls	IHL	10	0	4	4	....	....	....	55	....	....	....	....	....	....	....	....	....	....	....	....	....	....	....	....	....	....
1993-94			DID NOT PLAY																									
1994-95	Houston Aeros	IHL	6	0	1	1	....	....	....	30	....	....	....	....	....	....	....	....	....	....	....	....	....	....	....	....	....	....
	NHL Totals		**49**	**2**	**1**	**3**	**2**	**1**	**3**	**244**	**0**	**0**	**2**	**13**	**15.4**	**4**	**0**	**4**	**0**		**1**	**0**	**0**	**0**	**10**	**0**	**0**	**0**

Signed as a free agent by **Philadelphia**, September 30, 1985. Signed as a free agent by **Detroit**, October 3, 1987. Signed as a free agent by **Montreal**, August 2, 1988. Signed as a free agent by **Winnipeg**, August 28, 1990. Signed as a free agent by **Minnesota**, October 1, 1991.

• MARUK, DENNIS

Dennis Maruk C – L. 5'8", 175 lbs. b: Toronto, Ont., 11/17/1955. California's 2nd choice, 21st overall, in 1975 Amateur Draft.

Season	Club	League	GP	G	A	Pts	AG	AA	APts	PIM	PP	SH	GW	S	%	TGF	PGF	TGA	PGA	+/-	GP	G	A	Pts	PIM	PP	SH	GW
1971-72	Toronto Marlboros	OHA	8	2	1	3	....	....	....	4	....	....	....	....	....	....	....	....	....	....	....	....	....	....	....	....	....	....
1972-73	London Knights	OHA	59	46	67	113	....	....	....	54	....	....	....	....	....	....	....	....	....	....	....	....	....	....	....	....	....	....
1973-74	London Knights	OHA	67	47	65	112	....	....	....	61	....	....	....	....	....	....	....	....	....	....	....	....	....	....	....	....	....	....
1974-75	London Knights	OHA	65	66	79	145	....	....	....	53	....	....	....	....	....	....	....	....	....	....	....	....	....	....	....	....	....	....
1975-76	**California Golden Seals**	**NHL**	**80**	**30**	**32**	**62**	**28**	**25**	**53**	**44**	**7**	**5**	**3**	**233**	**12.9**	**88**	**26**	**93**	**25**	**–6**	....	....	....	....	....	....	....	....

Season	Club	League	REGULAR SEASON GP	G	A	Pts	AG	AA	APts	PIM	PP	SH	GW	S	%	TGF	PGF	TGA	PGA	+/–	PLAYOFFS GP	G	A	Pts	PIM	PP	SH	GW
1976-77	**Cleveland Barons**	**NHL**	**80**	**28**	**50**	**78**	**27**	**41**	**68**	**68**	**4**	**0**	**1**	**268**	**10.4**	**104**	**27**	**87**	**14**	**+4**	....	....	....	....	....	....	....	....
1977-78	**Cleveland Barons**	**NHL**	**76**	**36**	**35**	**71**	**35**	**29**	**64**	**50**	**4**	**2**	**4**	**198**	**18.2**	**85**	**17**	**107**	**13**	**–26**	....	....	....	....	....	....	....	....
	Canada	WEC-A	10	6	1	7	....	....	....	2	....	....	....	....	....	....	....	....	....	....	....	....	....	....	....	....	....	....
1978-79	**Minnesota North Stars**	**NHL**	**2**	**0**	**0**	**0**	**0**	**0**	**0**	**0**	**0**	**0**	**0**	**2**	**0.0**	**0**	**0**	**1**	**0**	**–1**	....	....	....	....	....	....	....	....
	Washington Capitals	**NHL**	**76**	**31**	**59**	**90**	**28**	**45**	**73**	**71**	**6**	**2**	**3**	**189**	**16.4**	**115**	**38**	**136**	**45**	**–14**	....	....	....	....	....	....	....	....
	Canada	WEC-A	7	1	1	2	....	....	....	2	....	....	....	....	....	....	....	....	....	....	....	....	....	....	....	....	....	....
1979-80	**Washington Capitals**	**NHL**	**27**	**10**	**17**	**27**	**9**	**13**	**22**	**8**	**1**	**1**	**0**	**58**	**17.2**	**35**	**12**	**27**	**4**	**0**	....	....	....	....	....	....	....	....
1980-81	**Washington Capitals**	**NHL**	**80**	**50**	**47**	**97**	**41**	**33**	**74**	**87**	**16**	**2**	**5**	**242**	**20.7**	**119**	**42**	**93**	**9**	**–7**	....	....	....	....	....	....	....	....
	Canada	WEC-A	8	5	3	8	....	....	....	6	....	....	....	....	....	....	....	....	....	....	....	....	....	....	....	....	....	....
1981-82	**Washington Capitals**	**NHL**	**80**	**60**	**76**	**136**	**48**	**50**	**98**	**128**	**20**	**2**	**1**	**268**	**22.4**	**168**	**73**	**104**	**5**	**–4**	....	....	....	....	....	....	....	....
1982-83	**Washington Capitals**	**NHL**	**80**	**31**	**50**	**81**	**25**	**35**	**60**	**71**	**12**	**0**	**2**	**185**	**16.8**	**113**	**43**	**91**	**0**	**–21**	**4**	**1**	**1**	**2**	**2**	**0**	**0**	**0**
	Canada	WEC-A	10	4	3	7	....	....	....	4	....	....	....	....	....	....	....	....	....	....	....	....	....	....	....	....	....	....
1983-84	**Minnesota North Stars**	**NHL**	**71**	**17**	**43**	**60**	**14**	**29**	**43**	**42**	**7**	**0**	**2**	**130**	**13.1**	**82**	**30**	**74**	**5**	**–17**	**16**	**5**	**5**	**10**	**8**	**1**	**1**	**0**
1984-85	**Minnesota North Stars**	**NHL**	**71**	**19**	**41**	**60**	**16**	**28**	**44**	**56**	**5**	**0**	**3**	**126**	**15.1**	**86**	**31**	**68**	**11**	**–2**	**9**	**4**	**7**	**11**	**12**	**3**	**0**	**1**
1985-86	**Minnesota North Stars**	**NHL**	**70**	**21**	**37**	**58**	**17**	**25**	**42**	**67**	**1**	**0**	**2**	**135**	**15.6**	**76**	**12**	**51**	**0**	**+13**	**5**	**4**	**9**	**13**	**4**	**1**	**0**	**0**
1986-87	**Minnesota North Stars**	**NHL**	**67**	**16**	**30**	**46**	**14**	**22**	**36**	**52**	**4**	**0**	**0**	**144**	**11.1**	**71**	**17**	**54**	**5**	**+5**	....	....	....	....	....	....	....	....
1987-88	**Minnesota North Stars**	**NHL**	**22**	**7**	**4**	**11**	**6**	**3**	**9**	**15**	**2**	**0**	**0**	**45**	**15.6**	**18**	**5**	**22**	**10**	**+1**	....	....	....	....	....	....	....	....
1988-89	**Minnesota North Stars**	**NHL**	**6**	**0**	**1**	**1**	**0**	**1**	**1**	**2**	**0**	**0**	**0**	**6**	**0.0**	**3**	**0**	**3**	**0**	**0**	....	....	....	....	....	....	....	....
	Kalamazoo Wings	IHL	5	1	5	6	....	....	....	4	....	....	....	....	....	....	....	....	....	....	....	....	....	....	....	....	....	....
	NHL Totals		**888**	**356**	**522**	**878**	**308**	**379**	**687**	**761**	**89**	**14**	**26**	**2229**	**16.0**	**1163**	**373**	**1011**	**146**		**34**	**14**	**22**	**36**	**26**	**5**	**1**	**1**

Played in NHL All-Star Game (1978, 1982)

Transferred to **Cleveland** after **California** franchise relocated, August 26, 1976. Protected by **Minnesota** prior to **Minnesota-Cleveland** Dispersal Draft, June 15, 1978. Traded to **Washington** by **Minnesota** for Pittsburgh's 1st round choice (acquired earlier, Minnesota chose Tom McCarthy) in 1979 Entry Draft, October 18, 1978. Traded to **Minnesota** by **Washington** for Minnesota's 2nd round choice (Stephen Leach) in 1984 Entry Draft, July 5, 1983.

• MASTERS, JAMIE

Jamie Masters D – R. 6'1", 190 lbs. b: Toronto, Ont., 4/14/1955. St. Louis' 2nd choice, 36th overall, in 1975 Amateur Draft.

Season	Club	League	GP	G	A	Pts	AG	AA	APts	PIM	PP	SH	GW	S	%	TGF	PGF	TGA	PGA	+/–	GP	G	A	Pts	PIM	PP	SH	GW
1972-73	Ottawa 67's	OHA	59	9	19	28	....	....	....	44	....	....	....	....	....	....	....	....	....	....	....	....	....	....	....	....	....	....
1973-74	Ottawa 67's	OHA	61	6	29	35	....	....	....	28	....	....	....	....	....	....	....	....	....	....	....	....	....	....	....	....	....	....
1974-75	Ottawa 67's	OHA	69	26	69	95	....	....	....	80	....	....	....	....	....	....	....	....	....	....	....	....	....	....	....	....	....	....
1975-76	**St. Louis Blues**	**NHL**	**7**	**0**	**0**	**0**	**0**	**0**	**0**	**0**	**0**	**0**	**0**	**1**	**0.0**	**4**	**0**	**1**	**1**	**+4**	**1**	**0**	**0**	**0**	**0**	**0**	**0**	**0**
	Providence Reds	AHL	62	7	27	34	....	....	....	86	....	....	....	....	....	....	....	....	....	....	1	1	0	1	2	....	....	....
1976-77	**St. Louis Blues**	**NHL**	**16**	**1**	**7**	**8**	**1**	**6**	**7**	**2**	**1**	**0**	**0**	**22**	**4.5**	**11**	**8**	**12**	**2**	**–7**	**1**	**0**	**0**	**0**	**0**	**0**	**0**	**0**
	Kansas City Blues	CHL	58	7	21	28	....	....	....	46	....	....	....	....	....	....	....	....	....	....	....	....	....	....	....	....	....	....
1977-78	Salt Lake Golden Eagles	CHL	76	4	20	24	....	....	....	73	....	....	....	....	....	....	....	....	....	....	6	0	3	3	0	....	....	....
1978-79	**St. Louis Blues**	**NHL**	**10**	**0**	**6**	**6**	**0**	**5**	**5**	**0**	**0**	**0**	**0**	**10**	**0.0**	**14**	**4**	**17**	**1**	**–6**	....	....	....	....	....	....	....	....
	Salt Lake Golden Eagles	CHL	62	2	24	26	....	....	....	98	....	....	....	....	....	....	....	....	....	....	10	0	1	1	13	....	....	....
1979-80	Cincinnati Stingers	CHL	33	9	13	22	....	....	....	24	....	....	....	....	....	....	....	....	....	....	....	....	....	....	....	....	....	....
	Syracuse Firebirds	AHL	46	6	17	23	....	....	....	26	....	....	....	....	....	....	....	....	....	....	4	0	3	3	0	....	....	....
1980-81	SB Rosenheim	Germany	44	15	14	29	....	....	....	61	....	....	....	....	....	....	....	....	....	....	6	2	1	3	20	....	....	....
1981-82	SB Rosenheim	Germany	44	11	29	40	....	....	....	51	....	....	....	....	....	....	....	....	....	....	....	....	....	....	....	....	....	....
1982-83	SB Rosenheim	Germany	35	5	16	21	....	....	....	22	....	....	....	....	....	....	....	....	....	....	....	....	....	....	....	....	....	....
1983-84	SB Rosenheim	Germany	46	29	24	53	....	....	....	38	....	....	....	....	....	....	....	....	....	....	....	....	....	....	....	....	....	....
1984-85	SB Rosenheim	Germany	45	7	18	25	....	....	....	31	....	....	....	....	....	....	....	....	....	....	....	....	....	....	....	....	....	....
1985-86	EC Villach	Austria	40	19	46	65	....	....	....	66	....	....	....	....	....	....	....	....	....	....	....	....	....	....	....	....	....	....
1986-87	EC Villach	Austria	23	8	31	39	....	....	....	12	....	....	....	....	....	....	....	....	....	....	....	....	....	....	....	....	....	....
	NHL Totals		**33**	**1**	**13**	**14**	**1**	**11**	**12**	**2**	**1**	**0**	**0**	**33**	**3.0**	**29**	**12**	**30**	**4**		**2**	**0**	**0**	**0**	**0**	**0**	**0**	**0**

Claimed by **Quebec** from **St. Louis** in Expansion Draft, June 13, 1979.

• MASTERTON, BILL

Bill "Bat" Masterton C – R. 6', 189 lbs. b: Winnipeg, Man., 8/16/1938. d. 1/15/1968.

Season	Club	League	GP	G	A	Pts	AG	AA	APts	PIM	PP	SH	GW	S	%	TGF	PGF	TGA	PGA	+/–	GP	G	A	Pts	PIM	PP	SH	GW
1955-56	St. Boniface Canadians	MJHL	22	23	26	49	....	....	....	16	....	....	....	....	....	....	....	....	....	....	10	7	7	14	4	....	....	....
1956-57	St. Boniface Canadians	MJHL	30	23	30	53	....	....	....	16	....	....	....	....	....	....	....	....	....	....	7	8	*10	18	2	....	....	....
1957-58	University of Denver	WCHA	DID NOT PLAY – FRESHMAN																									
1958-59	University of Denver	WCHA	23	21	28	49	....	....	....	6	....	....	....	....	....	....	....	....	....	....	....	....	....	....	....	....	....	....
1959-60	University of Denver	WCHA	34	21	46	67	....	....	....	2	....	....	....	....	....	....	....	....	....	....	....	....	....	....	....	....	....	....
1960-61	University of Denver	WCHA	32	24	56	80	....	....	....	4	....	....	....	....	....	....	....	....	....	....	....	....	....	....	....	....	....	....
1961-62	Hull-Ottawa Canadiens	EPHL	65	31	35	66	....	....	....	18	....	....	....	....	....	....	....	....	....	....	12	0	4	4	0	....	....	....
1962-63	Cleveland Barons	AHL	72	27	55	82	....	....	....	12	....	....	....	....	....	....	....	....	....	....	7	4	5	9	2	....	....	....
1963-64			DID NOT PLAY																									
1964-65	Rochester Mustangs	USHL	STATISTICS NOT AVAILABLE																									
1965-66	St. Paul Steers	USHL	30	27	*40	67	....	....	....	6	....	....	....	....	....	....	....	....	....	....	....	....	....	....	....	....	....	....
1966-67	United States	Nat-Team	21	10	*29	39	....	....	....	4	....	....	....	....	....	....	....	....	....	....	....	....	....	....	....	....	....	....
1967-68	**Minnesota North Stars**	**NHL**	**38**	**4**	**8**	**12**	**5**	**8**	**13**	**4**	**2**	**0**	**0**	**83**	**4.8**	**21**	**8**	**20**	**3**	**–4**	....	....	....	....	....	....	....	....
	NHL Totals		**38**	**4**	**8**	**12**	**5**	**8**	**13**	**4**	**2**	**0**	**0**	**83**	**4.8**	**21**	**8**	**20**	**3**		....	....	....	....	....	....	....	....

WCHA First All-Star Team (1960, 1961) • NCAA West First All-American Team (1960, 1961) • NCAA Championship All-Tournament Team (1961) • NCAA Championship Tournament MVP (1961)

Rights traded to **Minnesota** by **Montreal** for cash, June 14, 1967. • Suffered career-ending head injury in game vs. California, January 13, 1968. He died 48 hours later.

• MATHIASEN, DWIGHT

Dwight Mathiasen RW – R. 6'1", 190 lbs. b: Brandon, Man., 5/12/1963.

Season	Club	League	GP	G	A	Pts	AG	AA	APts	PIM	PP	SH	GW	S	%	TGF	PGF	TGA	PGA	+/–	GP	G	A	Pts	PIM	PP	SH	GW
1982-83	Abbotsford Pilots	BCJHL	48	50	73	123	....	....	....	113	....	....	....	....	....	....	....	....	....	....	....	....	....	....	....	....	....	....
1983-84	University of Denver	CCHA	36	24	27	51	....	....	....	48	....	....	....	....	....	....	....	....	....	....	....	....	....	....	....	....	....	....
1984-85	University of Denver	CCHA	39	26	32	58	....	....	....	64	....	....	....	....	....	....	....	....	....	....	....	....	....	....	....	....	....	....
1985-86	University of Denver	CCHA	48	40	49	89	....	....	....	48	....	....	....	....	....	....	....	....	....	....	....	....	....	....	....	....	....	....
	Pittsburgh Penguins	**NHL**	**4**	**1**	**0**	**1**	**1**	**0**	**1**	**2**	**0**	**0**	**0**	**4**	**25.0**	**2**	**1**	**5**	**0**	**–4**	....	....	....	....	....	....	....	....
1986-87	**Pittsburgh Penguins**	**NHL**	**6**	**0**	**1**	**1**	**0**	**1**	**1**	**2**	**0**	**0**	**0**	**4**	**0.0**	**1**	**0**	**2**	**0**	**–1**	....	....	....	....	....	....	....	....
	Baltimore Skipjacks	AHL	61	23	22	45	....	....	....	49	....	....	....	....	....	....	....	....	....	....	....	....	....	....	....	....	....	....
1987-88	**Pittsburgh Penguins**	**NHL**	**23**	**0**	**6**	**6**	**0**	**4**	**4**	**14**	**0**	**0**	**0**	**29**	**0.0**	**13**	**1**	**19**	**0**	**–7**	....	....	....	....	....	....	....	....
	Muskegon Lumberjacks	IHL	46	19	42	61	....	....	....	35	....	....	....	....	....	....	....	....	....	....	4	1	2	3	9	....	....	....
	NHL Totals		**33**	**1**	**7**	**8**	**1**	**5**	**6**	**18**	**0**	**0**	**0**	**37**	**2.7**	**16**	**2**	**26**	**0**		....	....	....	....	....	....	....	....

Signed as a free agent by **Pittsburgh**, March 31, 1986.

• MATHIESON, JIM

Jim Mathieson D – L. 6'1", 209 lbs. b: Kindersley, Sask., 1/24/1970. Washington's 3rd choice, 59th overall, in 1989 Entry Draft.

Season	Club	League	GP	G	A	Pts	AG	AA	APts	PIM	PP	SH	GW	S	%	TGF	PGF	TGA	PGA	+/–	GP	G	A	Pts	PIM	PP	SH	GW
1986-87	Regina Pats	WHL	40	0	9	9	....	....	....	40	....	....	....	....	....	....	....	....	....	....	3	0	1	1	2	....	....	....
1987-88	Regina Pats	WHL	72	3	12	15	....	....	....	115	....	....	....	....	....	....	....	....	....	....	4	0	2	2	4	....	....	....
1988-89	Regina Pats	WHL	62	5	22	27	....	....	....	151	....	....	....	....	....	....	....	....	....	....	....	....	....	....	....	....	....	....
1989-90	Regina Pats	WHL	67	1	26	27	....	....	....	158	....	....	....	....	....	....	....	....	....	....	11	0	7	7	16	....	....	....
	Washington Capitals	**NHL**	**2**	**0**	**0**	**0**	**0**	**0**	**0**	**4**	**0**	**0**	**0**	**0**	**0.0**	**0**	**0**	**0**	**0**	**0**	....	....	....	....	....	....	....	....
	Baltimore Skipjacks	AHL	....	....	....	....	....	....	....	....	....	....	....	....	....	....	....	....	....	....	3	0	0	0	4	....	....	....
1990-91	Baltimore Skipjacks	AHL	65	3	5	8	....	....	....	168	....	....	....	....	....	....	....	....	....	....	4	1	0	1	6	....	....	....
1991-92	Baltimore Skipjacks	AHL	74	2	9	11	....	....	....	206	....	....	....	....	....	....	....	....	....	....	....	....	....	....	....	....	....	....
1992-93	Baltimore Skipjacks	AHL	46	3	5	8	....	....	....	88	....	....	....	....	....	....	....	....	....	....	3	0	1	1	23	....	....	....
1993-94	Portland Pirates	AHL	43	0	7	7	....	....	....	89	....	....	....	....	....	....	....	....	....	....	12	0	1	1	36	....	....	....
1994-95	Portland Pirates	AHL	35	5	5	10	....	....	....	119	....	....	....	....	....	....	....	....	....	....	7	1	0	1	4	....	....	....
1995-96	Portland Pirates	AHL	35	3	4	7	....	....	....	110	....	....	....	....	....	....	....	....	....	....	....	....	....	....	....	....	....	....
1996-97	Newcastle Cobras	Britain	35	1	0	1	....	....	....	36	....	....	....	....	....	....	....	....	....	....	5	0	0	0	29	....	....	....
1997-98	Nottingham Panthers	Britain	40	2	7	9	....	....	....	64	....	....	....	....	....	....	....	....	....	....	6	0	0	0	4	....	....	....
	NHL Totals		**2**	**0**	**0**	**0**	**0**	**0**	**0**	**4**	**0**	**0**	**0**	**0**	**0.0**	**0**	**0**	**0**	**0**		....	....	....	....	....	....	....	....

• MATTE, CHRISTIAN

Christian Matte RW – R. 5'11", 166 lbs. b: Hull, Que., 1/20/1975. Quebec's 8th choice, 153rd overall, in 1993 Entry Draft.

			REGULAR SEASON																		PLAYOFFS							
Season	**Club**	**League**	**GP**	**G**	**A**	**Pts**	**AG**	**AA**	**APts**	**PIM**	**PP**	**SH**	**GW**	**S**	**%**	**TGF**	**PGF**	**TGA**	**PGA**	**+/–**	**GP**	**G**	**A**	**Pts**	**PIM**	**PP**	**SH**	**GW**
1992-93	Granby Bisons	QMJHL	68	17	36	53	....	....	....	59	....	....	....	....	....	....	....	....	....	....	....	....	....	....	....	....	....	....
1993-94	Granby Bisons	QMJHL	59	50	47	97	....	....	....	103	....	....	....	....	....	....	....	....	....	....	7	5	5	10	12	....	....	....
	Cornwall Aces	AHL	1	0	0	0	....	....	....	0	....	....	....	....	....	....	....	....	....	....	....	....	....	....	....	....	....	....
1994-95	Granby Bisons	QMJHL	66	50	66	116	....	....	....	86	....	....	....	....	....	....	....	....	....	....	13	11	7	18	12	....	....	....
	Cornwall Aces	AHL	....	....	....	....	....	....	....	....	....	....	....	....	....	....	....	....	....	....	3	0	1	1	2	....	....	....
1995-96	Cornwall Aces	AHL	64	20	32	52	....	....	....	51	....	....	....	....	....	....	....	....	....	....	7	1	1	2	6	....	....	....
1996-97	**Colorado Avalanche**	**NHL**	**5**	**1**	**1**	**2**	**1**	**1**	**2**	**0**	**0**	**0**	**0**	**6**	**16.7**	**2**	**0**	**1**	**0**	**+1**	....	....	....	....	....	....	....	....
	Hershey Bears	AHL	49	18	18	36	....	....	....	78	....	....	....	....	....	....	....	....	....	....	22	8	3	11	25	....	....	....
1997-98	**Colorado Avalanche**	**NHL**	**5**	**0**	**0**	**0**	**0**	**0**	**0**	**6**	**0**	**0**	**0**	**5**	**0.0**	**1**	**0**	**1**	**0**	**0**	....	....	....	....	....	....	....	....
	Hershey Bears	AHL	71	33	40	73	....	....	....	109	....	....	....	....	....	....	....	....	....	....	7	3	2	5	4	....	....	....
	NHL Totals		**10**	**1**	**1**	**2**	**1**	**1**	**2**	**6**	**0**	**0**	**0**	**11**	**9.1**	**3**	**0**	**2**	**0**		....	....	....	....	....	....	....	....

QMJHL Second All-Star Team (1994)

Rights transferred to **Colorado** after **Quebec** franchise relocated, June 21, 1995.

• MATTEAU, STEPHANE

Stephane Matteau LW – L. 6'3", 215 lbs. b: Rouyn-Noranda, Que., 9/2/1969. Calgary's 2nd choice, 25th overall, in 1987 Entry Draft.

			REGULAR SEASON																		PLAYOFFS							
Season	**Club**	**League**	**GP**	**G**	**A**	**Pts**	**AG**	**AA**	**APts**	**PIM**	**PP**	**SH**	**GW**	**S**	**%**	**TGF**	**PGF**	**TGA**	**PGA**	**+/–**	**GP**	**G**	**A**	**Pts**	**PIM**	**PP**	**SH**	**GW**
1985-86	Hull Olympiques	QMJHL	60	6	8	14	....	....	....	19	....	....	....	....	....	....	....	....	....	....	4	0	0	0	0	....	....	....
1986-87	Hull Olympiques	QMJHL	69	27	48	75	....	....	....	113	....	....	....	....	....	....	....	....	....	....	8	3	7	10	8	....	....	....
1987-88	Hull Olympiques	QMJHL	57	17	40	57	....	....	....	179	....	....	....	....	....	....	....	....	....	....	18	5	14	19	94	....	....	....
1988-89	Hull Olympiques	QMJHL	59	44	45	89	....	....	....	202	....	....	....	....	....	....	....	....	....	....	9	8	6	14	30	....	....	....
	Salt Lake Golden Eagles	IHL	....	....	....	....	....	....	....	....	....	....	....	....	....	....	....	....	....	....	9	0	4	4	13	....	....	....
1989-90	Salt Lake Golden Eagles	IHL	81	23	35	58	....	....	....	130	....	....	....	....	....	....	....	....	....	....	10	6	3	9	38	....	....	....
1990-91	**Calgary Flames**	**NHL**	**78**	**15**	**19**	**34**	**14**	**14**	**28**	**93**	**0**	**1**	**1**	**114**	**13.2**	**61**	**1**	**53**	**10**	**+17**	**5**	**0**	**1**	**1**	**0**	**0**	**0**	**0**
1991-92	**Calgary Flames**	**NHL**	**4**	**1**	**0**	**1**	**1**	**0**	**1**	**19**	**0**	**0**	**0**	**7**	**14.3**	**2**	**0**	**2**	**2**	**+2**	....	....	....	....	....	....	....	....
	Chicago Blackhawks	**NHL**	**20**	**5**	**8**	**13**	**5**	**6**	**11**	**45**	**1**	**0**	**0**	**31**	**16.1**	**15**	**2**	**10**	**0**	**+3**	**18**	**4**	**6**	**10**	**24**	**1**	**1**	**0**
1992-93	**Chicago Blackhawks**	**NHL**	**79**	**15**	**18**	**33**	**12**	**12**	**24**	**98**	**2**	**0**	**4**	**95**	**15.8**	**55**	**11**	**43**	**5**	**+6**	**3**	**0**	**1**	**1**	**2**	**0**	**0**	**0**
1993-94	**Chicago Blackhawks**	**NHL**	**65**	**15**	**16**	**31**	**14**	**12**	**26**	**55**	**2**	**0**	**2**	**113**	**13.3**	**47**	**6**	**45**	**14**	**+10**	....	....	....	....	....	....	....	....
	New York Rangers	**NHL**	**12**	**4**	**3**	**7**	**4**	**2**	**6**	**2**	**1**	**0**	**0**	**22**	**18.2**	**15**	**5**	**6**	**1**	**+5**	**23**	**6**	**3**	**9**	**20**	**1**	**0**	**2**
1994-95	**New York Rangers**	**NHL**	**41**	**3**	**5**	**8**	**5**	**7**	**12**	**25**	**0**	**0**	**0**	**37**	**8.1**	**13**	**0**	**21**	**0**	**–8**	**9**	**0**	**1**	**1**	**10**	**0**	**0**	**0**
1995-96	**New York Rangers**	**NHL**	**32**	**4**	**2**	**6**	**4**	**2**	**6**	**22**	**1**	**0**	**0**	**39**	**10.3**	**8**	**1**	**12**	**1**	**–4**	....	....	....	....	....	....	....	....
	St. Louis Blues	**NHL**	**46**	**7**	**13**	**20**	**7**	**11**	**18**	**65**	**3**	**0**	**2**	**70**	**10.0**	**33**	**8**	**36**	**7**	**–4**	**11**	**0**	**2**	**2**	**8**	**0**	**0**	**0**
1996-97	**St. Louis Blues**	**NHL**	**74**	**16**	**20**	**36**	**17**	**18**	**35**	**50**	**1**	**2**	**2**	**98**	**16.3**	**56**	**2**	**49**	**6**	**+11**	**5**	**0**	**0**	**0**	**0**	**0**	**0**	**0**
1997-98	**San Jose Sharks**	**NHL**	**73**	**15**	**14**	**29**	**18**	**14**	**32**	**60**	**1**	**0**	**2**	**79**	**19.0**	**45**	**3**	**46**	**8**	**+4**	**4**	**0**	**1**	**1**	**0**	**0**	**0**	**0**
	NHL Totals		**524**	**100**	**118**	**218**	**101**	**98**	**199**	**534**	**12**	**3**	**13**	**705**	**14.2**	**350**	**39**	**323**	**54**		**78**	**10**	**15**	**25**	**64**	**2**	**1**	**2**

Traded to **Chicago** by **Calgary** for Trent Yawney, December 16, 1991. Traded to **NY Rangers** by **Chicago** with Brian Noonan for Tony Amonte and the rights to Matt Oates, March 21, 1994. Traded to **St. Louis** by **NY Rangers** for Ian Laperriere, December 28, 1995. Traded to **San Jose** by **St. Louis** for Darren Turcotte, July 24, 1997.

• MATTIUSSI, DICK

Dick Mattiussi LW – L. 5'10", 185 lbs. b: Smooth Rock Falls, Ont., 5/1/1938.

			REGULAR SEASON																		PLAYOFFS							
Season	**Club**	**League**	**GP**	**G**	**A**	**Pts**	**AG**	**AA**	**APts**	**PIM**	**PP**	**SH**	**GW**	**S**	**%**	**TGF**	**PGF**	**TGA**	**PGA**	**+/–**	**GP**	**G**	**A**	**Pts**	**PIM**	**PP**	**SH**	**GW**
1955-56	St. Michael's Majors	OHA	48	10	7	17	....	....	....	68	....	....	....	....	....	....	....	....	....	....	8	0	2	2	11	....	....	....
1956-57	St. Michael's Majors	OHA	52	12	18	30	....	....	....	80	....	....	....	....	....	....	....	....	....	....	4	0	0	0	19	....	....	....
1957-58	St. Michael's Majors	OHA	51	9	15	24	....	....	....	98	....	....	....	....	....	....	....	....	....	....	9	0	6	6	26	....	....	....
1958-59	Kitchener-Waterloo Dutchmen	OHA Sr.	51	6	21	27	....	....	....	89	....	....	....	....	....	....	....	....	....	....	11	1	4	5	21	....	....	....
1959-60	Rochester Americans	AHL	72	2	20	22	....	....	....	76	....	....	....	....	....	....	....	....	....	....	12	0	0	0	14	....	....	....
1960-61	Rochester Americans	AHL	61	3	23	26	....	....	....	141	....	....	....	....	....	....	....	....	....	....	....	....	....	....	....	....	....	....
1961-62	Pittsburgh Hornets	AHL	65	9	19	28	....	....	....	164	....	....	....	....	....	....	....	....	....	....	....	....	....	....	....	....	....	....
1962-63	Cleveland Barons	AHL	70	6	28	34	....	....	....	124	....	....	....	....	....	....	....	....	....	....	4	2	2	4	6	....	....	....
1963-64	Cleveland Barons	AHL	72	6	17	23	....	....	....	110	....	....	....	....	....	....	....	....	....	....	9	1	5	6	20	....	....	....
1964-65	Cleveland Barons	AHL	67	8	18	26	....	....	....	98	....	....	....	....	....	....	....	....	....	....	....	....	....	....	....	....	....	....
1965-66	Cleveland Barons	AHL	72	8	35	43	....	....	....	138	....	....	....	....	....	....	....	....	....	....	12	0	5	5	10	....	....	....
1966-67	Cleveland Barons	AHL	71	10	44	54	....	....	....	78	....	....	....	....	....	....	....	....	....	....	5	1	2	3	2	....	....	....
1967-68	**Pittsburgh Penguins**	**NHL**	**32**	**0**	**2**	**2**	**0**	**2**	**2**	**18**	**0**	**0**	**0**	**31**	**0.0**	**15**	**1**	**26**	**3**	**–9**	....	....	....	....	....	....	....	....
	Baltimore Clippers	AHL	3	0	0	0	....	....	....	0	....	....	....	....	....	....	....	....	....	....	....	....	....	....	....	....	....	....
1968-69	**Pittsburgh Penguins**	**NHL**	**12**	**0**	**2**	**2**	**0**	**2**	**2**	**14**	**0**	**0**	**0**	**10**	**0.0**	**11**	**2**	**11**	**0**	**–2**	....	....	....	....	....	....	....	....
	Amarillo Wranglers	CHL	8	0	2	2	....	....	....	8	....	....	....	....	....	....	....	....	....	....	....	....	....	....	....	....	....	....
	Oakland Seals	**NHL**	**24**	**1**	**9**	**10**	**1**	**8**	**9**	**16**	**0**	**0**	**0**	**17**	**5.9**	**34**	**5**	**31**	**5**	**+3**	**7**	**0**	**1**	**1**	**6**	**0**	**0**	**0**
1969-70	**Oakland Seals**	**NHL**	**65**	**4**	**10**	**14**	**5**	**10**	**15**	**38**	**0**	**0**	**0**	**55**	**7.3**	**34**	**8**	**49**	**2**	**–21**	**1**	**0**	**0**	**0**	**0**	**0**	**0**	**0**
1970-71	**California Golden Seals**	**NHL**	**67**	**3**	**8**	**11**	**3**	**7**	**10**	**38**	**1**	**0**	**1**	**72**	**4.2**	**38**	**7**	**70**	**5**	**–34**	....	....	....	....	....	....	....	....
1971-72	Baltimore Clippers	AHL	67	3	8	11	....	....	....	103	....	....	....	....	....	....	....	....	....	....	18	0	0	0	10	....	....	....
1972-73	Providence Reds	AHL	23	2	6	8	....	....	....	30	....	....	....	....	....	....	....	....	....	....	....	....	....	....	....	....	....	....
1973-74	Rochester Americans	AHL	76	12	26	38	....	....	....	84	....	....	....	....	....	....	....	....	....	....	5	0	2	2	8	....	....	....
1974-75			DID NOT PLAY																									
1975-76	Rochester Americans	AHL	3	0	0	0	....	....	....	0	....	....	....	....	....	....	....	....	....	....	....	....	....	....	....	....	....	....
	NHL Totals		**200**	**8**	**31**	**39**	**9**	**29**	**38**	**124**	**1**	**0**	**1**	**185**	**4.3**	**132**	**23**	**187**	**15**		**8**	**0**	**1**	**1**	**6**	**0**	**0**	**0**

Traded to **Springfield** (AHL) by **Toronto** with Jim Wilcox, Wally Boyer, Bill White and Roger Cote for Kent Douglas, June, 1962. Traded to **Cleveland** (AHL) by **Springfield** (AHL) for Wayne Larkin and Murray Davison, October 16, 1962. Traded to **Pittsburgh** by **Cleveland** (AHL) for cash, August, 1967. Traded to **Oakland** by **Pittsburgh** with Earl Ingarfield and Gene Ubriaco for Bryan Watson, George Swarbrick and Tracy Pratt, January 30, 1969.

• MATVICHUK, RICHARD

Richard Matvichuk D – L. 6'2", 200 lbs. b: Edmonton, Alta., 2/5/1973. Minnesota's 1st choice, 8th overall, in 1991 Entry Draft.

			REGULAR SEASON																		PLAYOFFS							
Season	**Club**	**League**	**GP**	**G**	**A**	**Pts**	**AG**	**AA**	**APts**	**PIM**	**PP**	**SH**	**GW**	**S**	**%**	**TGF**	**PGF**	**TGA**	**PGA**	**+/–**	**GP**	**G**	**A**	**Pts**	**PIM**	**PP**	**SH**	**GW**
1989-90	Saskatoon Blades	WHL	56	8	24	32	....	....	....	126	....	....	....	....	....	....	....	....	....	....	10	2	8	10	16	....	....	....
1990-91	Saskatoon Blades	WHL	68	13	36	49	....	....	....	117	....	....	....	....	....	....	....	....	....	....	....	....	....	....	....	....	....	....
1991-92	Saskatoon Blades	WHL	58	14	40	54	....	....	....	126	....	....	....	....	....	....	....	....	....	....	22	1	9	10	61	....	....	....
	Canada	WJC-A	4	0	0	0	....	....	....	2	....	....	....	....	....	....	....	....	....	....	....	....	....	....	....	....	....	....
1992-93	**Minnesota North Stars**	**NHL**	**53**	**2**	**3**	**5**	**2**	**2**	**4**	**26**	**1**	**0**	**0**	**51**	**3.9**	**33**	**6**	**39**	**4**	**–8**	....	....	....	....	....	....	....	....
	Kalamazoo Wings	IHL	3	0	1	1	....	....	....	6	....	....	....	....	....	....	....	....	....	....	....	....	....	....	....	....	....	....
1993-94	**Dallas Stars**	**NHL**	**25**	**0**	**3**	**3**	**0**	**2**	**2**	**22**	**0**	**0**	**0**	**18**	**0.0**	**15**	**5**	**11**	**2**	**+1**	**7**	**1**	**1**	**2**	**12**	**1**	**0**	**0**
	Kalamazoo Wings	IHL	43	8	17	25	....	....	....	84	....	....	....	....	....	....	....	....	....	....	....	....	....	....	....	....	....	....
1994-95	**Dallas Stars**	**NHL**	**14**	**0**	**2**	**2**	**0**	**3**	**3**	**14**	**0**	**0**	**0**	**21**	**0.0**	**10**	**3**	**14**	**0**	**–7**	**5**	**0**	**2**	**2**	**4**	**0**	**0**	**0**
	Kalamazoo Wings	IHL	17	0	6	6	....	....	....	16	....	....	....	....	....	....	....	....	....	....	....	....	....	....	....	....	....	....
1995-96	**Dallas Stars**	**NHL**	**73**	**6**	**16**	**22**	**6**	**13**	**19**	**71**	**0**	**0**	**1**	**81**	**7.4**	**54**	**9**	**50**	**9**	**+4**	....	....	....	....	....	....	....	....
1996-97	**Dallas Stars**	**NHL**	**57**	**5**	**7**	**12**	**5**	**6**	**11**	**87**	**0**	**2**	**0**	**83**	**6.0**	**49**	**1**	**67**	**20**	**+1**	**7**	**0**	**1**	**1**	**20**	**0**	**0**	**0**
1997-98	**Dallas Stars**	**NHL**	**74**	**3**	**15**	**18**	**4**	**15**	**19**	**63**	**0**	**0**	**0**	**71**	**4.2**	**58**	**6**	**69**	**24**	**+7**	**16**	**1**	**1**	**2**	**14**	**0**	**0**	**0**
	NHL Totals		**296**	**16**	**46**	**62**	**17**	**41**	**58**	**283**	**1**	**2**	**1**	**325**	**4.9**	**219**	**30**	**250**	**59**		**35**	**2**	**5**	**7**	**50**	**1**	**0**	**0**

WHL East First All-Star Team (1992)

Transferred to **Dallas** after **Minnesota** franchise relocated, June 9, 1993.

• MAXWELL, BRAD

Brad Maxwell D – R. 6'2", 195 lbs. b: Brandon, Man., 7/8/1957. Minnesota's 1st choice, 7th overall, in 1977 Amateur Draft.

			REGULAR SEASON																		PLAYOFFS							
Season	**Club**	**League**	**GP**	**G**	**A**	**Pts**	**AG**	**AA**	**APts**	**PIM**	**PP**	**SH**	**GW**	**S**	**%**	**TGF**	**PGF**	**TGA**	**PGA**	**+/–**	**GP**	**G**	**A**	**Pts**	**PIM**	**PP**	**SH**	**GW**
1973-74	Bellingham Blazers	BCJHL	61	20	37	57	....	....	....	132	....	....	....	....	....	....	....	....	....	....	....	....	....	....	....	....	....	....
1974-75	New Westminster Bruins	WCJHL	69	13	47	60	....	....	....	124	....	....	....	....	....	....	....	....	....	....	....	....	....	....	....	....	....	....
1975-76	New Westminster Bruins	WCJHL	72	19	80	99	....	....	....	239	....	....	....	....	....	....	....	....	....	....	17	3	12	15	86	....	....	....
1976-77	New Westminster Bruins	WCJHL	70	21	58	79	....	....	....	205	....	....	....	....	....	....	....	....	....	....	14	7	15	22	39	....	....	....
1977-78	**Minnesota North Stars**	**NHL**	**75**	**18**	**29**	**47**	**17**	**24**	**41**	**100**	**12**	**0**	**0**	**209**	**8.6**	**110**	**42**	**131**	**6**	**–57**	....	....	....	....	....	....	....	....
	Canada	WEC-A	10	2	1	3	....	....	....	12	....	....	....	....	....	....	....	....	....	....	....	....	....	....	....	....	....	....
1978-79	**Minnesota North Stars**	**NHL**	**70**	**9**	**28**	**37**	**8**	**21**	**29**	**145**	**5**	**0**	**0**	**200**	**4.5**	**88**	**25**	**89**	**13**	**–13**	....	....	....	....	....	....	....	....
	Oklahoma City Stars	CHL	2	0	1	1	....	....	....	21	....	....	....	....	....	....	....	....	....	....	....	....	....	....	....	....	....	....
	Canada	WEC-A	4	1	0	1	....	....	....	8	....	....	....	....	....	....	....	....	....	....	....	....	....	....	....	....	....	....
1979-80	**Minnesota North Stars**	**NHL**	**58**	**7**	**30**	**37**	**6**	**23**	**29**	**126**	**0**	**0**	**0**	**135**	**5.2**	**109**	**27**	**82**	**9**	**+9**	**11**	**0**	**8**	**8**	**20**	**0**	**0**	**0**
1980-81	**Minnesota North Stars**	**NHL**	**27**	**3**	**13**	**16**	**2**	**9**	**11**	**98**	**3**	**0**	**1**	**71**	**4.2**	**43**	**15**	**35**	**6**	**–1**	**18**	**3**	**11**	**14**	**35**	**1**	**0**	**0**
1981-82	**Minnesota North Stars**	**NHL**	**51**	**10**	**21**	**31**	**8**	**14**	**22**	**96**	**0**	**1**	**1**	**109**	**9.2**	**85**	**30**	**57**	**8**	**+6**	**4**	**0**	**3**	**3**	**13**	**0**	**0**	**0**
	Canada	WEC-A	7	0	0	0	....	....	....	10	....	....	....	....	....	....	....	....	....	....	....	....	....	....	....	....	....	....
1982-83	**Minnesota North Stars**	**NHL**	**77**	**11**	**28**	**39**	**9**	**19**	**28**	**157**	**2**	**0**	**3**	**162**	**6.8**	**113**	**31**	**108**	**25**	**–1**	**9**	**5**	**6**	**11**	**23**	**2**	**0**	**0**

			REGULAR SEASON																		PLAYOFFS							
Season	Club	League	GP	G	A	Pts	AG	AA	APts	PIM	PP	SH	GW	S	%	TGF	PGF	TGA	PGA	+/–	GP	G	A	Pts	PIM	PP	SH	GW
1983-84	**Minnesota North Stars**	**NHL**	**78**	**19**	**54**	**73**	**15**	**37**	**52**	**225**	**8**	**0**	**2**	**228**	**8.3**	**179**	**72**	**142**	**28**	**–7**	**16**	**2**	**11**	**13**	**40**	**1**	**0**	**0**
1984-85	**Minnesota North Stars**	**NHL**	**18**	**3**	**7**	**10**	**2**	**5**	**7**	**53**	**1**	**0**	**0**	**29**	**10.3**	**19**	**8**	**25**	**6**	**–8**	....	....	....	....	....	....	....	....
	Quebec Nordiques	**NHL**	**50**	**7**	**24**	**31**	**6**	**16**	**22**	**119**	**1**	**0**	**1**	**109**	**6.4**	**87**	**24**	**45**	**4**	**+22**	**18**	**2**	**9**	**11**	**35**	**1**	**0**	**0**
1985-86	**Toronto Maple Leafs**	**NHL**	**52**	**8**	**18**	**26**	**6**	**12**	**18**	**108**	**4**	**0**	**0**	**93**	**8.6**	**79**	**29**	**87**	**10**	**–27**	**3**	**0**	**1**	**1**	**12**	**0**	**0**	**0**
1986-87	**Vancouver Canucks**	**NHL**	**30**	**1**	**7**	**8**	**1**	**5**	**6**	**28**	**1**	**0**	**0**	**43**	**2.3**	**25**	**11**	**26**	**3**	**–9**	....	....	....	....	....	....	....	....
	New York Rangers	**NHL**	**9**	**0**	**4**	**4**	**0**	**3**	**3**	**6**	**0**	**0**	**0**	**10**	**0.0**	**11**	**3**	**9**	**0**	**–1**	....	....	....	....	....	....	....	....
	Minnesota North Stars	**NHL**	**17**	**2**	**7**	**9**	**2**	**5**	**7**	**31**	**0**	**0**	**1**	**33**	**6.1**	**30**	**7**	**24**	**4**	**+3**	....	....	....	....	....	....	....	....
	NHL Totals		**612**	**98**	**270**	**368**	**82**	**193**	**275**	**1292**	**37**	**1**	**9**	**1431**	**6.8**	**978**	**324**	**860**	**122**		**79**	**12**	**49**	**61**	**178**	**5**	**0**	**0**

Memorial Cup All-Star Team (1975, 1977)

Played in NHL All-Star Game (1984)

Traded to **Quebec** by **Minnesota** with Brent Ashton for Tony McKegney and Bo Berglund, December 14, 1984. Traded to **Toronto** by **Quebec** for John Anderson, August 22, 1986. Traded to **Vancouver** by **Toronto** for Vancouver's 5th round choice (Len Esau) in 1988 Entry Draft, October 3, 1986. Claimed on waivers by **NY Rangers** from **Vancouver**, January 20, 1987. Traded to **Minnesota** by **NY Rangers** for future considerations, February 21, 1987.

• MAXWELL, BRYAN

Bryan Maxwell D – L. 6'2", 200 lbs. b: North Bay, Ont., 9/7/1955. Minnesota's 1st choice, 4th overall, in 1975 Amateur Draft.

1972-73	Drumheller Miners	AJHL	STATISTICS NOT AVAILABLE																									
	Medicine Hat Tigers	WCJHL	37	1	11	12	....	....	....	25	....	....	....	....	....	....	....	....	....	....	....	....	....	....	....	....	....	....
1973-74	Medicine Hat Tigers	WCJHL	63	11	56	67	....	....	....	229	....	....	....	....	....	....	....	....	....	....	6	0	4	4	18	....	....	....
1974-75	Medicine Hat Tigers	WCJHL	63	14	50	64	....	....	....	288	....	....	....	....	....	....	....	....	....	....	5	3	4	7	19	....	....	....
	Canada	WJC-A	5	0	0	0	....	....	....	10	....	....	....	....	....	....	....	....	....	....	....	....	....	....	....	....	....	....
1975-76	Cleveland Crusaders	WHA	73	3	14	17	....	....	....	177	....	....	....	....	....	....	....	....	....	....	2	0	0	0	4	....	....	....
1976-77	Cincinnati Stingers	WHA	34	1	8	9	....	....	....	29	....	....	....	....	....	....	....	....	....	....	4	0	0	0	29	....	....	....
	Springfield Indians	AHL	13	2	3	5	....	....	....	67	....	....	....	....	....	....	....	....	....	....	....	....	....	....	....	....	....	....
1977-78	New England Whalers	WHA	17	2	1	3	....	....	....	11	....	....	....	....	....	....	....	....	....	....	....	....	....	....	....	....	....	....
	Binghamton Whalers	AHL	24	2	8	10	....	....	....	69	....	....	....	....	....	....	....	....	....	....	....	....	....	....	....	....	....	....
	Minnesota North Stars	**NHL**	**18**	**2**	**5**	**7**	**2**	**4**	**6**	**41**	**1**	**0**	**0**	**33**	**6.1**	**20**	**1**	**23**	**6**	**+2**	....	....	....	....	....	....	....	....
1978-79	**Minnesota North Stars**	**NHL**	**25**	**1**	**6**	**7**	**1**	**5**	**6**	**46**	**0**	**0**	**0**	**32**	**3.1**	**15**	**0**	**32**	**4**	**–13**	....	....	....	....	....	....	....	....
	Oklahoma City Stars	CHL	15	1	4	5	....	....	....	35	....	....	....	....	....	....	....	....	....	....	....	....	....	....	....	....	....	....
1979-80	**St. Louis Blues**	**NHL**	**57**	**1**	**11**	**12**	**1**	**8**	**9**	**112**	**0**	**0**	**0**	**34**	**2.9**	**39**	**1**	**53**	**2**	**–13**	**1**	**0**	**0**	**0**	**9**	**0**	**0**	**0**
	Salt Lake Golden Eagles	CHL	3	0	1	1	....	....	....	10	....	....	....	....	....	....	....	....	....	....	....	....	....	....	....	....	....	....
1980-81	**St. Louis Blues**	**NHL**	**40**	**3**	**10**	**13**	**2**	**7**	**9**	**137**	**0**	**0**	**0**	**35**	**8.6**	**39**	**0**	**34**	**2**	**+7**	**11**	**0**	**1**	**1**	**54**	**0**	**0**	**0**
	Salt Lake Golden Eagles	CHL	5	0	1	1	....	....	....	7	....	....	....	....	....	....	....	....	....	....	....	....	....	....	....	....	....	....
1981-82	**Winnipeg Jets**	**NHL**	**45**	**1**	**9**	**10**	**1**	**6**	**7**	**110**	**0**	**0**	**0**	**45**	**2.2**	**50**	**4**	**73**	**16**	**–11**	....	....	....	....	....	....	....	....
1982-83	**Winnipeg Jets**	**NHL**	**54**	**7**	**13**	**20**	**6**	**9**	**15**	**131**	**1**	**0**	**0**	**78**	**9.0**	**65**	**12**	**55**	**8**	**+6**	**3**	**1**	**0**	**1**	**23**	**1**	**0**	**0**
1983-84	**Winnipeg Jets**	**NHL**	**3**	**0**	**3**	**3**	**0**	**2**	**2**	**27**	**0**	**0**	**0**	**6**	**0.0**	**5**	**0**	**4**	**0**	**+1**	....	....	....	....	....	....	....	....
	Pittsburgh Penguins	**NHL**	**45**	**3**	**12**	**15**	**2**	**8**	**10**	**84**	**0**	**0**	**0**	**55**	**5.5**	**58**	**10**	**64**	**18**	**+2**	....	....	....	....	....	....	....	....
1984-85	**Pittsburgh Penguins**	**NHL**	**44**	**0**	**8**	**8**	**0**	**5**	**5**	**57**	**0**	**0**	**0**	**27**	**0.0**	**30**	**1**	**73**	**21**	**–23**	....	....	....	....	....	....	....	....
	Baltimore Skipjacks	AHL	4	0	0	0	....	....	....	2	....	....	....	....	....	....	....	....	....	....	14	3	2	5	40	....	....	....
	NHL Totals		**331**	**18**	**77**	**95**	**15**	**54**	**69**	**745**	**2**	**0**	**0**	**345**	**5.2**	**321**	**29**	**411**	**77**		**15**	**1**	**1**	**2**	**86**	**1**	**0**	**0**
	Other Major League Totals		124	6	23	29	....	....	....	217	....	....	....	....	....	....	....	....	....		6	0	0	0	33	....	....	....

Selected by **Cleveland** (WHA) in 1975 WHA Amateur Draft, June, 1975. Transferred to **Minnesota** (WHA) after **Cleveland** (WHA) franchise relocated, June, 1976. Traded to **Cincinnati** (WHA) by **Minnesota** (WHA) for John McKenzie and the rights to Ivan Hlinka, September, 1976. Traded to **New England** (WHA) by **Cincinnati** (WHA) with Greg Carroll for the rights to Mike Liut and future considerations, May, 1977. Signed as a free agent by **Minnesota** after securing release from **New England** (WHA), February, 1978. Traded to **St. Louis** by **Minnesota** with Ritchie Hansen for St. Louis' 2nd round choice (later traded to Calgary — Calgary selected Dave Reierson) in 1982 Entry Draft, June 10, 1979. Traded to **Winnipeg** by **St. Louis** with Paul MacLean and Ed Staniowski for Scott Campbell and John Markell, July 3, 1981. Claimed on waivers by **Pittsburgh** from **Winnipeg**, October 13, 1983.

• MAXWELL, KEVIN

Kevin Maxwell C – R. 5'9", 165 lbs. b: Edmonton, Alta., 3/30/1960. Minnesota's 4th choice, 63rd overall, in 1979 Entry Draft.

1978-79	University of North Dakota	WCHA	42	31	51	82	....	....	....	79	....	....	....	....	....	....	....	....	....	....	....	....	....	....	....	....	....	....
1979-80	Canada	Nat-Team	57	25	46	71	....	....	....	28	....	....	....	....	....	....	....	....	....	....	....	....	....	....	....	....	....	....
	Canada	Olympics	6	0	5	5	....	....	....	4	....	....	....	....	....	....	....	....	....	....	....	....	....	....	....	....	....	....
1980-81	**Minnesota North Stars**	**NHL**	**6**	**0**	**3**	**3**	**0**	**2**	**2**	**7**	**0**	**0**	**0**	**9**	**0.0**	**4**	**0**	**5**	**0**	**–1**	**16**	**3**	**4**	**7**	**24**	**0**	**1**	**0**
	Oklahoma City Stars	CHL	31	8	13	21	....	....	....	38	....	....	....	....	....	....	....	....	....	....	....	....	....	....	....	....	....	....
1981-82	**Minnesota North Stars**	**NHL**	**12**	**1**	**4**	**5**	**1**	**3**	**4**	**8**	**0**	**0**	**0**	**20**	**5.0**	**9**	**1**	**9**	**0**	**–1**	....	....	....	....	....	....	....	....
	Nashville South Stars	CHL	5	4	2	6	....	....	....	6	....	....	....	....	....	....	....	....	....	....	....	....	....	....	....	....	....	....
	Colorado Rockies	**NHL**	**34**	**5**	**5**	**10**	**4**	**3**	**7**	**44**	**0**	**0**	**1**	**52**	**9.6**	**19**	**0**	**38**	**3**	**–16**	....	....	....	....	....	....	....	....
1982-83	Wichita Wind	CHL	68	24	41	65	....	....	....	47	....	....	....	....	....	....	....	....	....	....	....	....	....	....	....	....	....	....
1983-84	**New Jersey Devils**	**NHL**	**14**	**0**	**3**	**3**	**0**	**2**	**2**	**2**	**0**	**0**	**0**	**8**	**0.0**	**3**	**0**	**13**	**1**	**–9**	....	....	....	....	....	....	....	....
	Maine Mariners	AHL	50	21	27	48	....	....	....	59	....	....	....	....	....	....	....	....	....	....	17	5	11	16	36	....	....	....
1984-85	Maine Mariners	AHL	52	25	21	46	....	....	....	70	....	....	....	....	....	....	....	....	....	....	11	7	7	14	4	....	....	....
1985-86	Maine Mariners	AHL	49	14	17	31	....	....	....	77	....	....	....	....	....	....	....	....	....	....	5	2	1	3	9	....	....	....
1986-87	Hershey Bears	AHL	56	12	20	32	....	....	....	139	....	....	....	....	....	....	....	....	....	....	3	1	0	1	30	....	....	....
1987-88	Hershey Bears	AHL	77	36	49	85	....	....	....	55	....	....	....	....	....	....	....	....	....	....	12	3	5	8	20	....	....	....
	NHL Totals		**66**	**6**	**15**	**21**	**5**	**10**	**15**	**61**	**0**	**0**	**1**	**89**	**6.7**	**35**	**1**	**65**	**4**		**16**	**3**	**4**	**7**	**24**	**0**	**1**	**0**

WCHA First All-Star Team (1979) • NCAA West First All-American Team (1979)

Traded to **Colorado** by **Minnesota** for cash, December 31, 1981. Transferred to **New Jersey** after **Colorado** franchise relocated, June 30, 1982.

• MAY, ALAN

Alan May RW – R. 6'1", 200 lbs. b: Swan Hills, Alta., 1/14/1965.

1985-86	Medicine Hat Tigers	WHL	6	1	0	1	....	....	....	25	....	....	....	....	....	....	....	....	....	....	....	....	....	....	....	....	....	....
	New Westminster Bruins	WHL	32	8	9	17	....	....	....	81	....	....	....	....	....	....	....	....	....	....	....	....	....	....	....	....	....	....
1986-87	Springfield Indians	AHL	4	0	2	2	....	....	....	11	....	....	....	....	....	....	....	....	....	....	....	....	....	....	....	....	....	....
	Carolina Thunderbirds	ACHL	42	23	14	37	....	....	....	310	....	....	....	....	....	....	....	....	....	....	5	2	2	4	57	....	....	....
1987-88	**Boston Bruins**	**NHL**	**3**	**0**	**0**	**0**	**0**	**0**	**0**	**15**	**0**	**0**	**0**	**3**	**0.0**	**0**	**0**	**1**	**0**	**–1**	....	....	....	....	....	....	....	....
	Maine Mariners	AHL	61	14	11	25	....	....	....	257	....	....	....	....	....	....	....	....	....	....	....	....	....	....	....	....	....	....
	Nova Scotia Oilers	AHL	13	4	1	5	....	....	....	54	....	....	....	....	....	....	....	....	....	....	4	0	0	0	51	....	....	....
1988-89	**Edmonton Oilers**	**NHL**	**3**	**1**	**0**	**1**	**1**	**0**	**1**	**7**	**0**	**0**	**1**	**3**	**33.3**	**1**	**0**	**1**	**0**	**0**	....	....	....	....	....	....	....	....
	Cape Breton Oilers	AHL	50	12	13	25	....	....	....	214	....	....	....	....	....	....	....	....	....	....	....	....	....	....	....	....	....	....
	New Haven Nighthawks	AHL	12	2	8	10	....	....	....	99	....	....	....	....	....	....	....	....	....	....	16	6	3	9	*105	....	....	....
1989-90	Washington Capitals	FrTour	3	1	0	1	....	....	....	4	....	....	....	....	....	....	....	....	....	....	....	....	....	....	....	....	....	....
	Washington Capitals	**NHL**	**77**	**7**	**10**	**17**	**6**	**7**	**13**	**339**	**1**	**0**	**2**	**67**	**10.4**	**32**	**5**	**29**	**1**	**–1**	**15**	**0**	**0**	**0**	**37**	**0**	**0**	**0**
1990-91	**Washington Capitals**	**NHL**	**67**	**4**	**6**	**10**	**4**	**5**	**9**	**264**	**0**	**0**	**0**	**66**	**6.1**	**19**	**0**	**29**	**0**	**–10**	**11**	**1**	**1**	**2**	**37**	**0**	**0**	**1**
1991-92	**Washington Capitals**	**NHL**	**75**	**6**	**9**	**15**	**5**	**7**	**12**	**221**	**0**	**0**	**1**	**43**	**14.0**	**22**	**1**	**28**	**0**	**–7**	**7**	**0**	**0**	**0**	**0**	**0**	**0**	**0**
1992-93	**Washington Capitals**	**NHL**	**83**	**6**	**10**	**16**	**5**	**7**	**12**	**268**	**0**	**0**	**1**	**75**	**8.0**	**26**	**0**	**25**	**0**	**+1**	**6**	**0**	**1**	**1**	**6**	**0**	**0**	**0**
1993-94	**Washington Capitals**	**NHL**	**43**	**4**	**7**	**11**	**4**	**5**	**9**	**97**	**0**	**0**	**0**	**33**	**12.1**	**15**	**0**	**17**	**0**	**–2**	....	....	....	....	....	....	....	....
	Dallas Stars	**NHL**	**8**	**1**	**0**	**1**	**1**	**0**	**1**	**18**	**0**	**0**	**1**	**7**	**14.3**	**1**	**0**	**3**	**1**	**–1**	**1**	**0**	**0**	**0**	**0**	**0**	**0**	**0**
1994-95	**Dallas Stars**	**NHL**	**27**	**1**	**1**	**2**	**2**	**1**	**3**	**106**	**0**	**0**	**0**	**23**	**4.3**	**8**	**0**	**7**	**0**	**+1**	....	....	....	....	....	....	....	....
	Calgary Flames	**NHL**	**7**	**1**	**2**	**3**	**2**	**3**	**5**	**13**	**0**	**0**	**0**	**5**	**20.0**	**5**	**0**	**3**	**0**	**+2**	....	....	....	....	....	....	....	....
1995-96	Orlando Solar Bears	IHL	4	0	0	0	....	....	....	11	....	....	....	....	....	....	....	....	....	....	....	....	....	....	....	....	....	....
	Detroit Vipers	IHL	17	2	5	7	....	....	....	49	....	....	....	....	....	....	....	....	....	....	....	....	....	....	....	....	....	....
	Utah Grizzlies	IHL	53	13	12	25	....	....	....	108	....	....	....	....	....	....	....	....	....	....	14	1	2	3	14	....	....	....
1996-97	Houston Aeros	IHL	82	7	11	18	....	....	....	270	....	....	....	....	....	....	....	....	....	....	13	1	2	3	28	....	....	....
	NHL Totals		**393**	**31**	**45**	**76**	**30**	**35**	**65**	**1348**	**1**	**0**	**6**	**325**	**9.5**	**129**	**6**	**143**	**2**		**40**	**1**	**2**	**3**	**80**	**0**	**0**	**1**

Signed as a free agent by **Boston**, October 30, 1987. Traded to **Edmonton** by **Boston** for Moe Lemay, March 8, 1988. Traded to **LA Kings** by **Edmonton** with Jim Wiemer for Brian Wilks and John English, March 7, 1989. Traded to **Washington** by **LA Kings** for Washington's 5th round choice (Thomas Newman) in 1989 Entry Draft, June 17, 1989. Traded to **Dallas** by **Washington** with Washington's 7th round choice (Jeff Dewar) in 1995 Entry Draft for Jim Johnson, March 21, 1994. Traded to **Calgary** by **Dallas** for Calgary's 8th round choice (Sergei Luchinkin) in 1995 Entry Draft, April 7, 1995.

• MAY, BRAD

Brad May LW – L. 6'1", 206 lbs. b: Toronto, Ont., 11/29/1971. Buffalo's 1st choice, 14th overall, in 1990 Entry Draft.

Season	Club	League	GP	G	A	Pts	AG	AA	APts	PIM	PP	SH	GW	S	%	TGF	PGF	TGA	PGA	+/–	GP	G	A	Pts	PIM	PP	SH	GW
			REGULAR SEASON																		PLAYOFFS							
1988-89	Niagara Falls Thunder	OHL	65	8	14	22	....	....	....	304	....	....	....	....	....	....	....	....	....	....	17	0	1	1	55	....	....	....
1989-90	Niagara Falls Thunder	OHL	61	32	58	90	....	....	....	223	....	....	....	....	....	....	....	....	....	....	16	9	13	22	64	....	....	....
1990-91	Niagara Falls Thunder	OHL	34	37	32	69	....	....	....	93	....	....	....	....	....	....	....	....	....	....	14	11	14	25	53	....	....	....
	Canada	WJC-A	7	1	0	1	....	....	....	2	....	....	....	....	....	....	....	....	....	....	....	....	....	....	....	....	....	....
1991-92	**Buffalo Sabres**	**NHL**	**69**	**11**	**6**	**17**	**10**	**4**	**14**	**309**	**1**	**0**	**3**	**82**	**13.4**	**25**	**1**	**36**	**0**	**–12**	**7**	**1**	**4**	**5**	**2**	**0**	**0**	**1**
1992-93	**Buffalo Sabres**	**NHL**	**82**	**13**	**13**	**26**	**11**	**9**	**20**	**242**	**0**	**0**	**1**	**114**	**11.4**	**55**	**2**	**50**	**0**	**+3**	**8**	**1**	**1**	**2**	**14**	**0**	**0**	**1**
1993-94	**Buffalo Sabres**	**NHL**	**84**	**18**	**27**	**45**	**17**	**21**	**38**	**171**	**3**	**0**	**3**	**166**	**10.8**	**72**	**24**	**54**	**0**	**–6**	**7**	**0**	**2**	**2**	**9**	**0**	**0**	**0**
1994-95	**Buffalo Sabres**	**NHL**	**33**	**3**	**3**	**6**	**5**	**4**	**9**	**87**	**1**	**0**	**0**	**42**	**7.1**	**16**	**1**	**10**	**0**	**+5**	**4**	**0**	**0**	**0**	**2**	**0**	**0**	**0**
1995-96	**Buffalo Sabres**	**NHL**	**79**	**15**	**29**	**44**	**15**	**24**	**39**	**295**	**3**	**0**	**4**	**168**	**8.9**	**70**	**17**	**48**	**1**	**+6**	....	....	....	....	....	....	....	....
	Canada	WC-A	8	0	0	0	....	....	....	6	....	....	....	....	....	....	....	....	....	....	....	....	....	....	....	....	....	....
1996-97	**Buffalo Sabres**	**NHL**	**42**	**3**	**4**	**7**	**3**	**4**	**7**	**106**	**1**	**0**	**1**	**75**	**4.0**	**14**	**6**	**16**	**0**	**–8**	**10**	**1**	**1**	**2**	**32**	**0**	**0**	**0**
1997-98	**Buffalo Sabres**	**NHL**	**36**	**4**	**7**	**11**	**5**	**7**	**12**	**113**	**0**	**0**	**0**	**41**	**9.8**	**12**	**0**	**10**	**0**	**+2**	....	....	....	....	....	....	....	....
	Vancouver Canucks	**NHL**	**27**	**9**	**3**	**12**	**11**	**3**	**14**	**41**	**4**	**0**	**2**	**56**	**16.1**	**23**	**8**	**16**	**1**	**0**	....	....	....	....	....	....	....	....
	NHL Totals		**452**	**76**	**92**	**168**	**77**	**76**	**153**	**1364**	**13**	**0**	**14**	**744**	**10.2**	**287**	**59**	**240**	**2**		**36**	**3**	**8**	**11**	**59**	**0**	**0**	**2**

OHL Second All-Star Team (1990, 1991)

Traded to **Vancouver** by **Buffalo** with future considerations for Geoff Sanderson, February 4, 1998.

• MAYER, DEREK

Derek Mayer D – R. 6', 200 lbs. b: Rossland, B.C., 5/21/1967. Detroit's 3rd choice, 43rd overall, in 1986 Entry Draft.

Season	Club	League	GP	G	A	Pts	AG	AA	APts	PIM	PP	SH	GW	S	%	TGF	PGF	TGA	PGA	+/–	GP	G	A	Pts	PIM	PP	SH	GW
1984-85	Penticton Knights	BCJHL	42	6	30	36	....	....	....	137	....	....	....	....	....	....	....	....	....	....	....	....	....	....	....	....	....	....
1985-86	University of Denver	WCHA	44	2	7	9	....	....	....	42	....	....	....	....	....	....	....	....	....	....	....	....	....	....	....	....	....	....
1986-87	University of Denver	WCHA	38	5	17	22	....	....	....	87	....	....	....	....	....	....	....	....	....	....	....	....	....	....	....	....	....	....
1987-88	University of Denver	WCHA	34	5	16	21	....	....	....	82	....	....	....	....	....	....	....	....	....	....	....	....	....	....	....	....	....	....
1988-89	Canada	Nat-Team	58	3	13	16	....	....	....	81	....	....	....	....	....	....	....	....	....	....	....	....	....	....	....	....	....	....
1989-90	Adirondack Red Wings	AHL	62	4	26	30	....	....	....	56	....	....	....	....	....	....	....	....	....	....	5	0	6	6	4	....	....	....
1990-91	San Diego Gulls	IHL	31	9	24	33	....	....	....	31	....	....	....	....	....	....	....	....	....	....	....	....	....	....	....	....	....	....
	Adirondack Red Wings	AHL	21	4	9	13	....	....	....	20	....	....	....	....	....	....	....	....	....	....	2	0	1	1	0	....	....	....
1991-92	Adirondack Red Wings	AHL	25	4	11	15	....	....	....	31	....	....	....	....	....	....	....	....	....	....	....	....	....	....	....	....	....	....
	San Diego Gulls	IHL	30	7	16	23	....	....	....	47	....	....	....	....	....	....	....	....	....	....	4	0	0	0	20	....	....	....
1992-93	Canada	Nat-Team	64	12	28	40	....	....	....	108	....	....	....	....	....	....	....	....	....	....	....	....	....	....	....	....	....	....
	Canada	WC-A	8	0	0	0	....	....	....	2	....	....	....	....	....	....	....	....	....	....	....	....	....	....	....	....	....	....
1993-94	Canada	Nat-Team	49	4	15	19	....	....	....	61	....	....	....	....	....	....	....	....	....	....	....	....	....	....	....	....	....	....
	Canada	Olympics	8	1	2	3	....	....	....	18	....	....	....	....	....	....	....	....	....	....	....	....	....	....	....	....	....	....
	Ottawa Senators	**NHL**	**17**	**2**	**2**	**4**	**2**	**2**	**4**	**8**	**1**	**0**	**0**	**29**	**6.9**	**14**	**8**	**27**	**5**	**–16**	....	....	....	....	....	....	....	....
1994-95	Atlanta Knights	IHL	55	7	17	24	....	....	....	77	....	....	....	....	....	....	....	....	....	....	5	1	1	2	10	....	....	....
1995-96	Tappara Tampere	Finland	50	17	8	25	....	....	....	96	....	....	....	....	....	....	....	....	....	....	4	3	4	7	18	....	....	....
	Canada	Nat-Team	12	1	4	5	....	....	....	25	....	....	....	....	....	....	....	....	....	....	....	....	....	....	....	....	....	....
	Canada	WC-A	8	1	1	2	....	....	....	2	....	....	....	....	....	....	....	....	....	....	....	....	....	....	....	....	....	....
1996-97	EHC Eisbaren Berlin	Germany	47	7	14	21	....	....	....	134	....	....	....	....	....	....	....	....	....	....	8	0	3	3	16	....	....	....
1997-98	EHC Eisbaren Berlin	Germany	47	7	11	18	....	....	....	77	....	....	....	....	....	....	....	....	....	....	10	2	2	4	2	....	....	....
	NHL Totals		**17**	**2**	**2**	**4**	**2**	**2**	**4**	**8**	**1**	**0**	**0**	**29**	**6.9**	**14**	**8**	**27**	**5**		....	....	....	....	....	....	....	....

Signed as a free agent by **Ottawa**, March 4, 1994.

• MAYER, JIM

Jim Mayer RW – R. 6', 190 lbs. b: Capreol, Ont., 10/30/1954. NY Rangers' 20th choice, 239th overall, in 1974 Amateur Draft.

Season	Club	League	GP	G	A	Pts	AG	AA	APts	PIM	PP	SH	GW	S	%	TGF	PGF	TGA	PGA	+/–	GP	G	A	Pts	PIM	PP	SH	GW
1971-72	Chelmsford Cougars	NOHA	52	31	42	73	....	....	....	39	....	....	....	....	....	....	....	....	....	....	....	....	....	....	....	....	....	....
1972-73	Michigan Tech Huskies	WCHA	32	6	10	16	....	....	....	10	....	....	....	....	....	....	....	....	....	....	....	....	....	....	....	....	....	....
1973-74	Michigan Tech Huskies	WCHA	30	3	9	12	....	....	....	24	....	....	....	....	....	....	....	....	....	....	....	....	....	....	....	....	....	....
1974-75	Michigan Tech Huskies	WCHA	26	9	7	16	....	....	....	12	....	....	....	....	....	....	....	....	....	....	....	....	....	....	....	....	....	....
1975-76	Michigan Tech Huskies	WCHA	43	29	42	71	....	....	....	58	....	....	....	....	....	....	....	....	....	....	....	....	....	....	....	....	....	....
1976-77	Calgary Cowboys	WHA	21	2	3	5	....	....	....	0	....	....	....	....	....	....	....	....	....	....	....	....	....	....	....	....	....	....
	Erie Blades	NAHL	14	5	4	9	....	....	....	15	....	....	....	....	....	....	....	....	....	....	....	....	....	....	....	....	....	....
	Tidewater Sharks	SHL	23	11	12	23	....	....	....	8	....	....	....	....	....	....	....	....	....	....	....	....	....	....	....	....	....	....
1977-78	New England Whalers	WHA	51	11	9	20	....	....	....	21	....	....	....	....	....	....	....	....	....	....	....	....	....	....	....	....	....	....
	Springfield Indians	AHL	19	6	7	13	....	....	....	31	....	....	....	....	....	....	....	....	....	....	4	0	2	2	6	....	....	....
1978-79	Edmonton Oilers	WHA	2	0	0	0	....	....	....	0	....	....	....	....	....	....	....	....	....	....	....	....	....	....	....	....	....	....
	Dallas Black Hawks	CHL	64	33	43	76	....	....	....	78	....	....	....	....	....	....	....	....	....	....	9	4	6	10	14	....	....	....
1979-80	**New York Rangers**	**NHL**	**4**	**0**	**0**	**0**	**0**	**0**	**0**	**0**	**0**	**0**	**0**	**2**	**0.0**	**2**	**1**	**0**	**0**	**+1**	....	....	....	....	....	....	....	....
	New Haven Nighthawks	AHL	62	32	35	67	....	....	....	91	....	....	....	....	....	....	....	....	....	....	10	7	2	9	25	....	....	....
1980-81	New Haven Nighthawks	AHL	10	1	4	5	....	....	....	6	....	....	....	....	....	....	....	....	....	....	....	....	....	....	....	....	....	....
	Dallas Black Hawks	CHL	13	1	5	6	....	....	....	2	....	....	....	....	....	....	....	....	....	....	....	....	....	....	....	....	....	....
	Fort Worth Texans	CHL	50	13	9	22	....	....	....	36	....	....	....	....	....	....	....	....	....	....	5	0	2	2	2	....	....	....
1981-82	New Haven Nighthawks	AHL	75	11	23	34	....	....	....	33	....	....	....	....	....	....	....	....	....	....	4	2	3	5	0	....	....	....
	NHL Totals		**4**	**0**	**0**	**0**	**0**	**0**	**0**	**0**	**0**	**0**	**0**	**2**	**0.0**	**2**	**1**	**0**	**0**		....	....	....	....	....	....	....	....
	Other Major League Totals		74	13	12	25	....	....	....	21	....	....	....	....	....	....	....	....	....	....	....	....	....	....	....	....	....	....

CHL Second All-Star Team (1979)

Signed as a free agent by **Calgary** (WHA), September, 1976. Signed as a free agent by **New England** (WHA) after **Calgary** (WHA) franchise folded, July 11, 1977. Claimed on waivers by **Edmonton** (WHA) from **New England** (WHA), May, 1978. Reclaimed by **NY Rangers** from **Edmonton** prior to Expansion Draft, June 9, 1979. Traded to **Vancouver** by **NY Rangers** with Mario Marois for Jeff Bandura and Jere Gillis, November 11, 1980. Traded to **Colorado** by **Vancouver** for Mike Christie, December, 1980.

• MAYER, PAT

Pat Mayer D – L. 6'3", 225 lbs. b: Royal Oak, MI, 7/24/1961.

Season	Club	League	GP	G	A	Pts	AG	AA	APts	PIM	PP	SH	GW	S	%	TGF	PGF	TGA	PGA	+/–	GP	G	A	Pts	PIM	PP	SH	GW
1982-83	U.S. International University	GWHC	30	3	6	9	....	....	....	68	....	....	....	....	....	....	....	....	....	....	....	....	....	....	....	....	....	....
1983-84	U.S. International University	GWHC	35	1	15	16	....	....	....	89	....	....	....	....	....	....	....	....	....	....	....	....	....	....	....	....	....	....
1984-85	U.S. International University	GWHC	28	3	14	17	....	....	....	94	....	....	....	....	....	....	....	....	....	....	....	....	....	....	....	....	....	....
1985-86	Toledo Goaldiggers	IHL	61	1	13	14	....	....	....	216	....	....	....	....	....	....	....	....	....	....	....	....	....	....	....	....	....	....
	Muskegon Lumberjacks	IHL	13	1	2	3	....	....	....	17	....	....	....	....	....	....	....	....	....	....	13	0	2	2	37	....	....	....
1986-87	Muskegon Lumberjacks	IHL	71	4	14	18	....	....	....	387	....	....	....	....	....	....	....	....	....	....	13	1	0	1	53	....	....	....
1987-88	**Pittsburgh Penguins**	**NHL**	**1**	**0**	**0**	**0**	**0**	**0**	**0**	**4**	**0**	**0**	**0**	**0**	**0.0**	**0**	**0**	**0**	**0**	**0**	....	....	....	....	....	....	....	....
	Muskegon Lumberjacks	IHL	73	3	10	13	....	....	....	*450	....	....	....	....	....	....	....	....	....	....	5	0	0	0	47	....	....	....
1988-89	New Haven Nighthawks	AHL	6	0	0	0	....	....	....	35	....	....	....	....	....	....	....	....	....	....	....	....	....	....	....	....	....	....
	Muskegon Lumberjacks	IHL	56	0	13	13	....	....	....	314	....	....	....	....	....	....	....	....	....	....	....	....	....	....	....	....	....	....
	NHL Totals		**1**	**0**	**0**	**0**	**0**	**0**	**0**	**4**	**0**	**0**	**0**	**0**	**0.0**	**0**	**0**	**0**	**0**		....	....	....	....	....	....	....	....

Signed as a free agent by **Pittsburgh**, July 10, 1987. Traded to **LA Kings** by **Pittsburgh** for Tim Tookey, March 7, 1989.

• MAYERS, JAMAL

Jamal Mayers C – R. 6', 190 lbs. b: Toronto, Ont., 10/24/1974. St. Louis' 3rd choice, 89th overall, in 1993 Entry Draft.

Season	Club	League	GP	G	A	Pts	AG	AA	APts	PIM	PP	SH	GW	S	%	TGF	PGF	TGA	PGA	+/–	GP	G	A	Pts	PIM	PP	SH	GW
1992-93	Western Michigan University	CCHA	38	8	17	25	....	....	....	26	....	....	....	....	....	....	....	....	....	....	....	....	....	....	....	....	....	....
1993-94	Western Michigan University	CCHA	40	17	32	49	....	....	....	40	....	....	....	....	....	....	....	....	....	....	....	....	....	....	....	....	....	....
1994-95	Western Michigan University	CCHA	39	13	32	45	....	....	....	40	....	....	....	....	....	....	....	....	....	....	....	....	....	....	....	....	....	....
1995-96	Western Michigan University	CCHA	38	17	22	39	....	....	....	75	....	....	....	....	....	....	....	....	....	....	....	....	....	....	....	....	....	....
1996-97	**St. Louis Blues**	**NHL**	**6**	**0**	**1**	**1**	**0**	**1**	**1**	**2**	**0**	**0**	**0**	**7**	**0.0**	**1**	**1**	**4**	**1**	**–3**	....	....	....	....	....	....	....	....
	Worcester IceCats	AHL	62	12	14	26	....	....	....	104	....	....	....	....	....	....	....	....	....	....	5	4	5	9	4	....	....	....
1997-98	Worcester IceCats	AHL	61	19	24	43	....	....	....	117	....	....	....	....	....	....	....	....	....	....	11	3	4	7	10	....	....	....
	NHL Totals		**6**	**0**	**1**	**1**	**0**	**1**	**1**	**2**	**0**	**0**	**0**	**7**	**0.0**	**1**	**1**	**4**	**1**		....	....	....	....	....	....	....	....

• MAZUR, JAY

Jay Mazur C/RW – R. 6'2", 205 lbs. b: Hamilton, Ont., 1/22/1965. Vancouver's 12th choice, 240th overall, in 1983 Entry Draft.

Season	Club	League	GP	G	A	Pts	AG	AA	APts	PIM	PP	SH	GW	S	%	TGF	PGF	TGA	PGA	+/–	GP	G	A	Pts	PIM	PP	SH	GW
1982-83	Breck Minnesota High School	H.S.	STATISTICS NOT AVAILABLE																									
1983-84	University of Maine	H.E.	34	14	9	23	....	....	....	14	....	....	....	....	....	....	....	....	....	....	....	....	....	....	....	....	....	....
1984-85	University of Maine	H.E.	31	0	6	6	....	....	....	20	....	....	....	....	....	....	....	....	....	....	....	....	....	....	....	....	....	....
1985-86	University of Maine	H.E.	34	5	7	12	....	....	....	18	....	....	....	....	....	....	....	....	....	....	....	....	....	....	....	....	....	....
1986-87	University of Maine	H.E.	39	16	10	26	....	....	....	61	....	....	....	....	....	....	....	....	....	....	....	....	....	....	....	....	....	....

Season	Club	League	REGULAR SEASON																		PLAYOFFS							
			GP	G	A	Pts	AG	AA	APts	PIM	PP	SH	GW	S	%	TGF	PGF	TGA	PGA	+/–	GP	G	A	Pts	PIM	PP	SH	GW
1987-88	Flint Spirits	IHL	39	17	11	28	....	....	....	28	....	....	....	....	....	....	....	....	....	....	....	....	....	....	....	....	....	....
	Fredericton Express	AHL	31	14	6	20	....	....	....	28	....	....	....	....	....	....	....	....	....	....	15	4	2	6	38	....	....	....
1988-89	**Vancouver Canucks**	**NHL**	**1**	**0**	**0**	**0**	**0**	**0**	**0**	**0**	**0**	**0**	**0**	**0**	**0.0**	**0**	**0**	**0**	**0**	**0**	....	....	....	....	....	....	....	....
	Milwaukee Admirals	IHL	73	33	31	64	....	....	....	86	....	....	....	....	....	....	....	....	....	....	11	6	5	11	2	....	....	....
1989-90	**Vancouver Canucks**	**NHL**	**5**	**0**	**0**	**0**	**0**	**0**	**0**	**4**	**0**	**0**	**0**	**4**	**0.0**	**0**	**0**	**3**	**1**	**–2**	....	....	....	....	....	....	....	....
	Milwaukee Admirals	IHL	70	20	27	47	....	....	....	63	....	....	....	....	....	....	....	....	....	....	6	3	0	3	6	....	....	....
1990-91	**Vancouver Canucks**	**NHL**	**36**	**11**	**7**	**18**	**10**	**5**	**15**	**14**	**1**	**1**	**2**	**59**	**18.6**	**29**	**2**	**40**	**16**	**+3**	**6**	**0**	**1**	**1**	**8**	**0**	**0**	**0**
	Milwaukee Admirals	IHL	7	2	3	5	....	....	....	21	....	....	....	....	....	....	....	....	....	....	....	....	....	....	....	....	....	....
1991-92	**Vancouver Canucks**	**NHL**	**5**	**0**	**0**	**0**	**0**	**0**	**0**	**2**	**0**	**0**	**0**	**3**	**0.0**	**1**	**0**	**6**	**3**	**–2**	....	....	....	....	....	....	....	....
	Milwaukee Admirals	IHL	56	17	20	37	....	....	....	49	....	....	....	....	....	....	....	....	....	....	5	2	3	5	0	....	....	....
1992-93	Hamilton Canucks	AHL	59	21	17	38	....	....	....	30	....	....	....	....	....	....	....	....	....	....	....	....	....	....	....	....	....	....
1993-94	Hamilton Canucks	AHL	78	40	55	95	....	....	....	40	....	....	....	....	....	....	....	....	....	....	4	2	2	4	4	....	....	....
1994-95	Detroit Vipers	IHL	64	23	27	50	....	....	....	64	....	....	....	....	....	....	....	....	....	....	1	0	1	1	2	....	....	....
1995-96	Rochester Americans	AHL	16	5	2	7	....	....	....	16	....	....	....	....	....	....	....	....	....	....	....	....	....	....	....	....	....	....
	Portland Pirates	AHL	38	11	7	18	....	....	....	39	....	....	....	....	....	....	....	....	....	....	....	....	....	....	....	....	....	....
	Tallahassee Tiger Sharks	ECHL	10	7	8	15	....	....	....	6	....	....	....	....	....	....	....	....	....	....	....	....	....	....	....	....	....	....
1996-97	Milano 24	Italy	13	2	4	6	....	....	....	23	....	....	....	....	....	....	....	....	....	....	....	....	....	....	....	....	....	....
1997-98	Pee Dee Pride	ECHL	69	25	33	58	....	....	....	55	....	....	....	....	....	....	....	....	....	....	8	2	6	8	2	....	....	....
	NHL Totals		**47**	**11**	**7**	**18**	**10**	**5**	**15**	**20**	**1**	**1**	**2**	**66**	**16.7**	**30**	**2**	**49**	**20**		**6**	**0**	**1**	**1**	**8**	**0**	**0**	**0**

• McADAM, GARY

Gary McAdam LW – L. 5'11", 175 lbs. b: Smiths Falls, Ont., 12/31/1955. Buffalo's 4th choice, 53rd overall, in 1975 Amateur Draft.

Season	Club	League	GP	G	A	Pts	AG	AA	APts	PIM	PP	SH	GW	S	%	TGF	PGF	TGA	PGA	+/–	GP	G	A	Pts	PIM	PP	SH	GW
1972-73	Ottawa 67's	OHA	61	14	8	22	....	....	....	23	....	....	....	....	....	....	....	....	....	....	....	....	....	....	....	....	....	....
1973-74			DID NOT PLAY – INJURED																									
1974-75	St. Catherines Blackhawks	OHA	65	24	53	77	....	....	....	111	....	....	....	....	....	....	....	....	....	....	4	4	0	4	4	....	....	....
1975-76	**Buffalo Sabres**	**NHL**	**31**	**1**	**2**	**3**	**1**	**2**	**3**	**2**	**0**	**0**	**0**	**12**	**8.3**	**3**	**0**	**4**	**1**	**0**	**1**	**0**	**0**	**0**	**0**	**0**	**0**	**0**
	Hershey Bears	AHL	24	14	13	27	....	....	....	45	....	....	....	....	....	....	....	....	....	....	10	3	2	5	9	....	....	....
1976-77	**Buffalo Sabres**	**NHL**	**73**	**13**	**16**	**29**	**12**	**13**	**25**	**17**	**1**	**0**	**2**	**86**	**15.1**	**42**	**1**	**24**	**0**	**+17**	**6**	**1**	**0**	**1**	**0**	**0**	**0**	**0**
1977-78	**Buffalo Sabres**	**NHL**	**79**	**19**	**22**	**41**	**18**	**18**	**36**	**44**	**2**	**0**	**5**	**160**	**11.9**	**62**	**8**	**51**	**0**	**+3**	**8**	**2**	**2**	**4**	**7**	**0**	**0**	**0**
1978-79	**Buffalo Sabres**	**NHL**	**40**	**6**	**5**	**11**	**5**	**4**	**9**	**13**	**1**	**0**	**1**	**39**	**15.4**	**17**	**3**	**21**	**1**	**–6**	....	....	....	....	....	....	....	....
	Pittsburgh Penguins	**NHL**	**28**	**5**	**9**	**14**	**5**	**7**	**12**	**2**	**0**	**0**	**1**	**52**	**9.6**	**28**	**1**	**23**	**0**	**+4**	**7**	**2**	**1**	**3**	**0**	**0**	**0**	**0**
1979-80	**Pittsburgh Penguins**	**NHL**	**78**	**19**	**22**	**41**	**17**	**17**	**34**	**63**	**3**	**0**	**2**	**195**	**9.7**	**61**	**11**	**69**	**2**	**–17**	**5**	**1**	**2**	**3**	**9**	**0**	**0**	**0**
1980-81	**Pittsburgh Penguins**	**NHL**	**34**	**3**	**9**	**12**	**2**	**6**	**8**	**30**	**0**	**0**	**0**	**52**	**5.8**	**15**	**0**	**41**	**10**	**–16**	....	....	....	....	....	....	....	....
	Detroit Red Wings	**NHL**	**40**	**5**	**14**	**19**	**4**	**10**	**14**	**27**	**1**	**0**	**0**	**92**	**5.4**	**28**	**5**	**39**	**2**	**–14**	....	....	....	....	....	....	....	....
1981-82	**Calgary Flames**	**NHL**	**46**	**12**	**15**	**27**	**9**	**10**	**19**	**18**	**0**	**0**	**1**	**72**	**16.7**	**39**	**1**	**52**	**8**	**–6**	**3**	**0**	**0**	**0**	**0**	**0**	**0**	**0**
	Dallas Black Hawks	CHL	12	10	10	20	....	....	....	14	....	....	....	....	....	....	....	....	....	....	....	....	....	....	....	....	....	....
1982-83	**Buffalo Sabres**	**NHL**	**4**	**1**	**0**	**1**	**1**	**0**	**1**	**0**	**0**	**0**	**0**	**3**	**33.3**	**2**	**0**	**9**	**3**	**–4**	....	....	....	....	....	....	....	....
	Rochester Americans	AHL	73	40	29	69	....	....	....	58	....	....	....	....	....	....	....	....	....	....	16	3	4	7	4	....	....	....
1983-84	Maine Mariners	AHL	10	3	4	7	....	....	....	18	....	....	....	....	....	....	....	....	....	....	....	....	....	....	....	....	....	....
	Washington Capitals	**NHL**	**24**	**1**	**5**	**6**	**1**	**3**	**4**	**12**	**0**	**0**	**1**	**23**	**4.3**	**9**	**0**	**9**	**0**	**0**	....	....	....	....	....	....	....	....
	New Jersey Devils	**NHL**	**38**	**9**	**6**	**15**	**7**	**4**	**11**	**15**	**0**	**2**	**1**	**60**	**15.0**	**19**	**0**	**32**	**9**	**–4**	....	....	....	....	....	....	....	....
1984-85	**New Jersey Devils**	**NHL**	**4**	**1**	**1**	**2**	**1**	**1**	**2**	**0**	**0**	**0**	**0**	**1**	**100.0**	**2**	**0**	**4**	**2**	**0**	....	....	....	....	....	....	....	....
	Maine Mariners	AHL	70	32	20	52	....	....	....	39	....	....	....	....	....	....	....	....	....	....	10	4	6	10	0	....	....	....
1985-86	**Toronto Maple Leafs**	**NHL**	**15**	**1**	**6**	**7**	**1**	**4**	**5**	**0**	**0**	**0**	**0**	**9**	**11.1**	**9**	**0**	**25**	**5**	**–11**	....	....	....	....	....	....	....	....
	St. Catharines Saints	AHL	27	15	18	33	....	....	....	16	....	....	....	....	....	....	....	....	....	....	....	....	....	....	....	....	....	....
	NHL Totals		**534**	**96**	**132**	**228**	**84**	**99**	**183**	**243**	**8**	**2**	**14**	**856**	**11.2**	**336**	**30**	**403**	**43**		**30**	**6**	**5**	**11**	**16**	**0**	**0**	**0**

Traded to **Pittsburgh** by **Buffalo** for Dave Schultz, February 6, 1979. Traded to **Detroit** by **Pittsburgh** for Errol Thompson, January 8, 1981. Traded to **Calgary** by **Detroit** with Detroit's 4th round choice (previously acquired, Detroit selected John Bekkers) in 1983 Entry Draft for Eric Vail, November 10, 1981. Signed as a free agent by **Buffalo**, September 17, 1982. Signed as a free agent by **New Jersey**, August 4, 1983. Claimed on waivers by **Washington** from **New Jersey**, November 17, 1983. Rights traded to **New Jersey** by **Washington** for cash, January 18, 1984. Signed as a free agent by **Toronto**, July 31, 1985.

• McALLISTER, CHRIS

Chris McAllister D – L. 6'7", 225 lbs. b: Saskatoon, Sask., 6/16/1975. Vancouver's 1st choice, 40th overall, in 1995 Entry Draft.

Season	Club	League	GP	G	A	Pts	AG	AA	APts	PIM	PP	SH	GW	S	%	TGF	PGF	TGA	PGA	+/–	GP	G	A	Pts	PIM	PP	SH	GW
1993-94	Saskatoon Blades	WHL	2	0	0	0				5	....	....	....	....	....	....	....	....	....	....	....	....	....	....	....	....	....	....
1994-95	Saskatoon Blades	WHL	65	2	8	10	....	....	....	134	....	....	....	....	....	....	....	....	....	....	10	0	0	0	28	....	....	....
1995-96	Syracuse Crunch	AHL	68	0	2	2	....	....	....	142	....	....	....	....	....	....	....	....	....	....	16	0	0	0	34	....	....	....
1996-97	Syracuse Crunch	AHL	43	3	1	4	....	....	....	108	....	....	....	....	....	....	....	....	....	....	3	0	0	0	6	....	....	....
1997-98	**Vancouver Canucks**	**NHL**	**36**	**1**	**2**	**3**	**1**	**2**	**3**	**106**	**0**	**0**	**0**	**15**	**6.7**	**10**	**0**	**24**	**2**	**–12**	....	....	....	....	....	....	....	....
	Syracuse Crunch	AHL	23	0	1	1	....	....	....	71	....	....	....	....	....	....	....	....	....	....	5	0	0	0	21	....	....	....
	NHL Totals		**36**	**1**	**2**	**3**	**1**	**2**	**3**	**106**	**0**	**0**	**0**	**15**	**6.7**	**10**	**0**	**24**	**2**		....	....	....	....	....	....	....	....

• McALPINE, CHRIS

Chris McAlpine D – R. 6', 210 lbs. b: Roseville, MN, 12/1/1971. New Jersey's 10th choice, 137th overall, in 1990 Entry Draft.

Season	Club	League	GP	G	A	Pts	AG	AA	APts	PIM	PP	SH	GW	S	%	TGF	PGF	TGA	PGA	+/–	GP	G	A	Pts	PIM	PP	SH	GW
1989-90	Roseville High School	H.S.	25	15	13	28	....	....	....	....	....	....	....	....	....	....	....	....	....	....	....	....	....	....	....	....	....	....
1990-91	University of Minnesota	WCHA	38	7	9	16	....	....	....	112	....	....	....	....	....	....	....	....	....	....	....	....	....	....	....	....	....	....
1991-92	University of Minnesota	WCHA	39	3	9	12	....	....	....	126	....	....	....	....	....	....	....	....	....	....	....	....	....	....	....	....	....	....
1992-93	University of Minnesota	WCHA	41	14	9	23	....	....	....	82	....	....	....	....	....	....	....	....	....	....	....	....	....	....	....	....	....	....
1993-94	University of Minnesota	WCHA	36	12	18	30	....	....	....	121	....	....	....	....	....	....	....	....	....	....	....	....	....	....	....	....	....	....
1994-95	**New Jersey Devils**	**NHL**	**24**	**0**	**3**	**3**	**0**	**4**	**4**	**17**	**0**	**0**	**0**	**19**	**0.0**	**21**	**1**	**18**	**2**	**+4**	....	....	....	....	....	....	....	....
	Albany River Rats	AHL	48	4	18	22	....	....	....	49	....	....	....	....	....	....	....	....	....	....	....	....	....	....	....	....	....	....
1995-96	Albany River Rats	AHL	57	5	14	19	....	....	....	72	....	....	....	....	....	....	....	....	....	....	4	0	0	0	13	....	....	....
1996-97	**St. Louis Blues**	**NHL**	**15**	**0**	**0**	**0**	**0**	**0**	**0**	**24**	**0**	**0**	**0**	**3**	**0.0**	**4**	**0**	**6**	**0**	**–2**	**4**	**0**	**1**	**1**	**0**	**0**	**0**	**0**
	Albany River Rats	AHL	44	1	9	10	....	....	....	48	....	....	....	....	....	....	....	....	....	....	....	....	....	....	....	....	....	....
1997-98	**St. Louis Blues**	**NHL**	**54**	**3**	**7**	**10**	**4**	**7**	**11**	**36**	**0**	**0**	**0**	**35**	**8.6**	**29**	**0**	**17**	**2**	**+14**	**10**	**0**	**0**	**0**	**16**	**0**	**0**	**0**
	NHL Totals		**93**	**3**	**10**	**13**	**4**	**11**	**15**	**77**	**0**	**0**	**0**	**57**	**5.3**	**64**	**1**	**41**	**4**		**14**	**0**	**1**	**1**	**16**	**0**	**0**	**0**

WCHA First All-Star Team (1994) • NCAA West Second All-American Team (1994)

Traded to **St. Louis** by **New Jersey** with New Jersey's 9th round choice in 1999 Entry Draft for Peter Zezel, February 11, 1997.

• McAMMOND, DEAN

Dean McAmmond C – L. 5'11", 185 lbs. b: Grand Cache, Alta., 6/15/1973. Chicago's 1st choice, 22nd overall, in 1991 Entry Draft.

Season	Club	League	GP	G	A	Pts	AG	AA	APts	PIM	PP	SH	GW	S	%	TGF	PGF	TGA	PGA	+/–	GP	G	A	Pts	PIM	PP	SH	GW
1989-90	Prince Albert Raiders	WHL	53	11	11	22	....	....	....	49	....	....	....	....	....	....	....	....	....	....	14	2	3	5	18	....	....	....
1990-91	Prince Albert Raiders	WHL	71	33	35	68	....	....	....	108	....	....	....	....	....	....	....	....	....	....	2	0	1	1	6	....	....	....
1991-92	Prince Albert Raiders	WHL	63	37	54	91	....	....	....	189	....	....	....	....	....	....	....	....	....	....	10	12	11	23	26	....	....	....
	Chicago Blackhawks	**NHL**	**5**	**0**	**2**	**2**	**0**	**1**	**1**	**0**	**0**	**0**	**0**	**4**	**0.0**	**2**	**2**	**2**	**0**	**–2**	**3**	**0**	**0**	**0**	**2**	**0**	**0**	**0**
1992-93	Prince Albert Raiders	WHL	30	19	29	48	....	....	....	44	....	....	....	....	....	....	....	....	....	....	....	....	....	....	....	....	....	....
	Canada	WJC-A	7	0	1	1	....	....	....	12	....	....	....	....	....	....	....	....	....	....	....	....	....	....	....	....	....	....
	Swift Current Broncos	WHL	18	10	13	23	....	....	....	24	....	....	....	....	....	....	....	....	....	....	17	*16	19	35	20	....	....	....
1993-94	**Edmonton Oilers**	**NHL**	**45**	**6**	**21**	**27**	**6**	**16**	**22**	**16**	**2**	**0**	**0**	**52**	**11.5**	**42**	**9**	**26**	**5**	**+12**	....	....	....	....	....	....	....	....
	Cape Breton Oilers	AHL	28	9	12	21	....	....	....	38	....	....	....	....	....	....	....	....	....	....	....	....	....	....	....	....	....	....
1994-95	**Edmonton Oilers**	**NHL**	**6**	**0**	**0**	**0**	**0**	**0**	**0**	**0**	**0**	**0**	**0**	**3**	**0.0**	**0**	**0**	**2**	**1**	**–1**	....	....	....	....	....	....	....	....
1995-96	**Edmonton Oilers**	**NHL**	**53**	**15**	**15**	**30**	**15**	**12**	**27**	**23**	**4**	**0**	**0**	**79**	**19.0**	**42**	**12**	**28**	**4**	**+6**	....	....	....	....	....	....	....	....
	Cape Breton Oilers	AHL	22	9	15	24	....	....	....	55	....	....	....	....	....	....	....	....	....	....	....	....	....	....	....	....	....	....
	Canada	WC-A	8	0	2	2	....	....	....	2	....	....	....	....	....	....	....	....	....	....	....	....	....	....	....	....	....	....
1996-97	**Edmonton Oilers**	**NHL**	**57**	**12**	**17**	**29**	**13**	**15**	**28**	**28**	**4**	**0**	**6**	**106**	**11.3**	**40**	**13**	**47**	**5**	**–15**	....	....	....	....	....	....	....	....
1997-98	**Edmonton Oilers**	**NHL**	**77**	**19**	**31**	**50**	**22**	**30**	**52**	**46**	**8**	**0**	**3**	**128**	**14.8**	**78**	**36**	**33**	**0**	**+9**	**12**	**1**	**4**	**5**	**12**	**0**	**0**	**0**
	NHL Totals		**243**	**52**	**86**	**138**	**56**	**74**	**130**	**113**	**18**	**0**	**9**	**372**	**14.0**	**204**	**72**	**138**	**15**		**15**	**1**	**4**	**5**	**14**	**0**	**0**	**0**

Traded to **Edmonton** by **Chicago** with Igor Kravchuk for Joe Murphy, February 24, 1993.

• McANEELEY, TED

Ted McAneeley D – L. 5'9", 185 lbs. b: Cranbrook, B.C., 11/7/1950. California's 4th choice, 47th overall, in 1970 Amateur Draft.

Season	Club	League	GP	G	A	Pts	AG	AA	APts	PIM	PP	SH	GW	S	%	TGF	PGF	TGA	PGA	+/–	GP	G	A	Pts	PIM	PP	SH	GW
1966-67	Calgary Buffalos	WCJHL	53	3	10	13	....	....	....	102	....	....	....	....	....	....	....	....	....	....	....	....	....	....	....	....	....	....
1967-68	Edmonton Oil Kings	WCJHL	46	2	5	7	....	....	....	114	....	....	....	....	....	....	....	....	....	....	10	0	0	0	0	....	....	....
1968-69	Edmonton Oil Kings	WCJHL	52	8	19	27			....	171	....	....	....	....	....	....	....	....	....	....	17	1	7	8	10	....	....	....
1969-70	Edmonton Oil Kings	WCJHL	60	29	25	54	....	....	....	92	....	....	....	....	....	....	....	....	....	....	16	3	9	12	79	....	....	....
1970-71	Providence Reds	AHL	60	4	3	7	....	....	....	71	....	....	....	....	....	....	....	....	....	....	10	0	0	0	2	....	....	....

			REGULAR SEASON																		PLAYOFFS							
Season	Club	League	GP	G	A	Pts	AG	AA	APts	PIM	PP	SH	GW	S	%	TGF	PGF	TGA	PGA	+/–	GP	G	A	Pts	PIM	PP	SH	GW
1971-72	Baltimore Clippers	AHL	61	3	14	17	....	....	....	61	....	....	....	....	....	....	....	....	....	....	18	1	1	2	61	....	....	....
1972-73	**California Golden Seals**	**NHL**	**77**	**4**	**13**	**17**	**4**	**11**	**15**	**75**	**1**	**0**	**0**	**74**	**5.4**	**57**	**5**	**85**	**4**	**–29**	....	....	....	....	....	....	....	....
1973-74	**California Golden Seals**	**NHL**	**72**	**4**	**20**	**24**	**4**	**17**	**21**	**62**	**0**	**1**	**0**	**80**	**5.0**	**78**	**11**	**105**	**14**	**–24**	....	....	....	....	....	....	....	....
1974-75	**California Golden Seals**	**NHL**	**9**	**0**	**2**	**2**	**0**	**2**	**2**	**4**	**0**	**0**	**0**	**7**	**0.0**	**2**	**0**	**10**	**2**	**–6**	....	....	....	....	....	....	....	....
	Salt Lake Golden Eagles	CHL	63	9	41	50	....	....	....	147	....	....	....	....	....	....	....	....	....	....	11	1	4	5	18	....	....	....
1975-76	Edmonton Oilers	WHA	79	2	17	19	....	....	....	71	....	....	....	....	....	....	....	....	....	....	4	0	0	0	4	....	....	....
1976-77	Spokane Jets	WIHL	....	4	21	25	....	....	....	42	....	....	....	....	....	....	....	....	....	....	....	....	....	....	....	....	....	....
1977-78	Spokane Jets	WIHL	....	6	17	23	....	....	....	160	....	....	....	....	....	....	....	....	....	....	....	....	....	....	....	....	....	....
1978-79	Spokane Jets	WIHL	55	10	28	38	....	....	....	95	....	....	....	....	....	....	....	....	....	....	....	....	....	....	....	....	....	....
	NHL Totals		**158**	**8**	**35**	**43**	**8**	**30**	**38**	**141**	**1**	**1**	**0**	**161**	**5.0**	**137**	**16**	**200**	**20**		....	....	....	....	....	....	....	....
	Other Major League Totals		79	2	17	19	....	....	....	71	....	....	....	....	....	....	....	....	....	....	4	0	0	0	4	....	....	....

CHL Second All-Star Team (1975)

Selected by **Dayton-Houston** (WHA) in 1972 WHA General Player Draft, February 12, 1972. WHA rights traded to **Edmonton** (WHA) by **Houston** (WHA) for future considerations, June, 1975.

• McBAIN, ANDREW

Andrew McBain RW – R. 6'1", 205 lbs. b: Scarborough, Ont., 1/18/1965. Winnipeg's 1st choice, 8th overall, in 1983 Entry Draft.

Season	Club	League	GP	G	A	Pts	AG	AA	APts	PIM	PP	SH	GW	S	%	TGF	PGF	TGA	PGA	+/–	GP	G	A	Pts	PIM	PP	SH	GW
1981-82	Niagara Falls Flyers	OHL	68	19	25	44	....	....	....	35	....	....	....	....	....	....	....	....	....	....	5	0	3	3	4	....	....	....
1982-83	North Bay Centennials	OHL	67	33	87	120	....	....	....	61	....	....	....	....	....	....	....	....	....	....	8	2	6	8	17	....	....	....
1983-84	**Winnipeg Jets**	**NHL**	**78**	**11**	**19**	**30**	**9**	**13**	**22**	**37**	**0**	**0**	**0**	**93**	**11.8**	**41**	**1**	**46**	**0**	**–6**	**3**	**2**	**0**	**2**	**0**	**0**	**0**	**0**
1984-85	**Winnipeg Jets**	**NHL**	**77**	**7**	**15**	**22**	**6**	**10**	**16**	**45**	**0**	**0**	**0**	**63**	**11.1**	**39**	**3**	**39**	**1**	**–2**	**7**	**1**	**0**	**1**	**0**	**0**	**0**	**0**
1985-86	**Winnipeg Jets**	**NHL**	**28**	**3**	**3**	**6**	**2**	**2**	**4**	**17**	**0**	**0**	**0**	**24**	**12.5**	**8**	**0**	**19**	**0**	**–11**	....	....	....	....	....	....	....	....
1986-87	**Winnipeg Jets**	**NHL**	**71**	**11**	**21**	**32**	**10**	**15**	**25**	**106**	**1**	**1**	**0**	**85**	**12.9**	**53**	**5**	**51**	**9**	**+6**	**9**	**0**	**2**	**2**	**10**	**0**	**0**	**0**
1987-88	**Winnipeg Jets**	**NHL**	**74**	**32**	**31**	**63**	**27**	**22**	**49**	**145**	**20**	**0**	**5**	**146**	**21.9**	**102**	**60**	**72**	**20**	**–10**	**5**	**2**	**5**	**7**	**29**	**0**	**1**	**0**
1988-89	**Winnipeg Jets**	**NHL**	**80**	**37**	**40**	**77**	**31**	**28**	**59**	**71**	**20**	**1**	**3**	**180**	**20.6**	**113**	**52**	**120**	**24**	**–35**	....	....	....	....	....	....	....	....
	Canada	WEC-A	10	6	2	8	....	....	....	8	....	....	....	....	....	....	....	....	....	....	....	....	....	....	....	....	....	....
1989-90	**Pittsburgh Penguins**	**NHL**	**41**	**5**	**9**	**14**	**4**	**6**	**10**	**51**	**1**	**0**	**0**	**56**	**8.9**	**25**	**4**	**48**	**19**	**–8**	....	....	....	....	....	....	....	....
	Vancouver Canucks	**NHL**	**26**	**4**	**5**	**9**	**3**	**4**	**7**	**22**	**3**	**0**	**0**	**50**	**8.0**	**22**	**7**	**28**	**10**	**–3**	....	....	....	....	....	....	....	....
1990-91	**Vancouver Canucks**	**NHL**	**13**	**0**	**5**	**5**	**0**	**4**	**4**	**32**	**0**	**0**	**0**	**8**	**0.0**	**9**	**2**	**10**	**0**	**–3**	....	....	....	....	....	....	....	....
	Milwaukee Admirals	IHL	47	27	24	51	....	....	....	69	....	....	....	....	....	....	....	....	....	....	6	2	5	7	12	....	....	....
1991-92	**Vancouver Canucks**	**NHL**	**6**	**1**	**0**	**1**	**1**	**0**	**1**	**0**	**0**	**0**	**0**	**11**	**9.1**	**4**	**3**	**2**	**0**	**–1**	....	....	....	....	....	....	....	....
	Milwaukee Admirals	IHL	65	24	54	78	....	....	....	132	....	....	....	....	....	....	....	....	....	....	5	1	2	3	10	....	....	....
1992-93	**Ottawa Senators**	**NHL**	**59**	**7**	**16**	**23**	**6**	**11**	**17**	**43**	**1**	**0**	**0**	**71**	**9.9**	**29**	**7**	**63**	**4**	**–37**	....	....	....	....	....	....	....	....
	New Haven Nighthawks	AHL	1	0	1	1	....	....	....	4	....	....	....	....	....	....	....	....	....	....	....	....	....	....	....	....	....	....
1993-94	**Ottawa Senators**	**NHL**	**55**	**11**	**8**	**19**	**10**	**6**	**16**	**64**	**8**	**0**	**0**	**91**	**12.1**	**33**	**19**	**69**	**14**	**–41**	....	....	....	....	....	....	....	....
	P.E.I. Senators	AHL	26	6	10	16	....	....	....	102	....	....	....	....	....	....	....	....	....	....	....	....	....	....	....	....	....	....
1994-95	Las Vegas Thunder	IHL	62	15	27	42	....	....	....	111	....	....	....	....	....	....	....	....	....	....	8	0	3	3	33	....	....	....
1995-96	Fort Wayne Komets	IHL	77	15	15	30	....	....	....	85	....	....	....	....	....	....	....	....	....	....	5	0	2	2	10	....	....	....
	NHL Totals		**608**	**129**	**172**	**301**	**109**	**121**	**230**	**633**	**54**	**2**	**8**	**878**	**14.7**	**478**	**163**	**567**	**101**		**24**	**5**	**7**	**12**	**39**	**0**	**1**	**0**

OHL Second All-Star Team (1983)

Traded to **Pittsburgh** by **Winnipeg** with Jim Kyte and Randy Gilhen for Randy Cunneyworth, Rick Tabaracci and Dave McLlwain, June 17, 1989. Traded to **Vancouver** by **Pittsburgh** with Dave Capuano and Dan Quinn for Rod Buskas, Barry Pederson and Tony Tanti, January 8, 1990. Signed as a free agent by **Ottawa**, July 30, 1992.

• McBAIN, JASON

Jason McBain D – L. 6'2", 180 lbs. b: Ilion, NY, 4/12/1974. Hartford's 5th choice, 81st overall, in 1992 Entry Draft.

Season	Club	League	GP	G	A	Pts	AG	AA	APts	PIM	PP	SH	GW	S	%	TGF	PGF	TGA	PGA	+/–	GP	G	A	Pts	PIM	PP	SH	GW
1990-91	Lethbridge Hurricanes	WHL	52	2	7	9	....	....	....	39	....	....	....	....	....	....	....	....	....	....	1	0	0	0	0	....	....	....
1991-92	Lethbridge Hurricanes	WHL	13	0	1	1	....	....	....	12	....	....	....	....	....	....	....	....	....	....	....	....	....	....	....	....	....	....
	Portland Winter Hawks	WHL	54	9	23	32	....	....	....	95	....	....	....	....	....	....	....	....	....	....	6	1	0	1	13	....	....	....
1992-93	Portland Winter Hawks	WHL	71	9	35	44	....	....	....	76	....	....	....	....	....	....	....	....	....	....	16	2	12	14	14	....	....	....
1993-94	Portland Winter Hawks	WHL	63	15	51	66	....	....	....	86	....	....	....	....	....	....	....	....	....	....	10	2	7	9	14	....	....	....
	United States	WJC-A	7	1	1	2	....	....	....	10	....	....	....	....	....	....	....	....	....	....	....	....	....	....	....	....	....	....
1994-95	Springfield Falcons	AHL	77	16	28	44	....	....	....	92	....	....	....	....	....	....	....	....	....	....	....	....	....	....	....	....	....	....
	United States	WC-A	6	0	1	1	....	....	....	4	....	....	....	....	....	....	....	....	....	....	....	....	....	....	....	....	....	....
1995-96	**Hartford Whalers**	**NHL**	**3**	**0**	**0**	**0**	**0**	**0**	**0**	**0**	**0**	**0**	**0**	**0**	**0.0**	**1**	**0**	**2**	**0**	**–1**	....	....	....	....	....	....	....	....
	Springfield Falcons	AHL	73	11	33	44	....	....	....	43	....	....	....	....	....	....	....	....	....	....	8	1	1	2	2	....	....	....
1996-97	**Hartford Whalers**	**NHL**	**6**	**0**	**0**	**0**	**0**	**0**	**0**	**0**	**0**	**0**	**0**	**1**	**0.0**	**0**	**0**	**4**	**0**	**–4**	....	....	....	....	....	....	....	....
	Springfield Falcons	AHL	58	8	26	34	....	....	....	40	....	....	....	....	....	....	....	....	....	....	16	0	8	8	12	....	....	....
1997-98	Cleveland Lumberjacks	IHL	65	8	22	30	....	....	....	62	....	....	....	....	....	....	....	....	....	....	3	0	2	2	2	....	....	....
	NHL Totals		**9**	**0**	**0**	**0**	**0**	**0**	**0**	**0**	**0**	**0**	**0**	**1**	**0.0**	**1**	**0**	**6**	**0**		....	....	....	....	....	....	....	....

• McBAIN, MIKE

Mike McBain D – L. 6'2", 195 lbs. b: Kimberley, B.C., 1/12/1977. Tampa Bay's 2nd choice, 30th overall, in 1995 Entry Draft.

Season	Club	League	GP	G	A	Pts	AG	AA	APts	PIM	PP	SH	GW	S	%	TGF	PGF	TGA	PGA	+/–	GP	G	A	Pts	PIM	PP	SH	GW
1993-94	Red Deer Rebels	WHL	58	4	13	17	....	....	....	41	....	....	....	....	....	....	....	....	....	....	4	0	0	0	0	....	....	....
1994-95	Red Deer Rebels	WHL	68	6	28	34	....	....	....	55	....	....	....	....	....	....	....	....	....	....	....	....	....	....	....	....	....	....
1995-96	Red Deer Rebels	WHL	68	7	34	41	....	....	....	68	....	....	....	....	....	....	....	....	....	....	10	1	7	8	10	....	....	....
1996-97	Red Deer Rebels	WHL	59	14	35	49	....	....	....	55	....	....	....	....	....	....	....	....	....	....	15	1	6	7	9	....	....	....
1997-98	**Tampa Bay Lightning**	**NHL**	**27**	**0**	**1**	**1**	**0**	**1**	**1**	**8**	**0**	**0**	**0**	**17**	**0.0**	**8**	**0**	**28**	**10**	**–10**	....	....	....	....	....	....	....	....
	Adirondack Red Wings	AHL	42	2	13	15	....	....	....	28	....	....	....	....	....	....	....	....	....	....	....	....	....	....	....	....	....	....
	NHL Totals		**27**	**0**	**1**	**1**	**0**	**1**	**1**	**8**	**0**	**0**	**0**	**17**	**0.0**	**8**	**0**	**28**	**10**		....	....	....	....	....	....	....	....

• McBEAN, WAYNE

Wayne McBean D – L. 6'2", 185 lbs. b: Calgary, Alta., 2/21/1969. Los Angeles' 1st choice, 4th overall, in 1987 Entry Draft.

Season	Club	League	GP	G	A	Pts	AG	AA	APts	PIM	PP	SH	GW	S	%	TGF	PGF	TGA	PGA	+/–	GP	G	A	Pts	PIM	PP	SH	GW
1985-86	Medicine Hat Tigers	WHL	67	1	14	15	....	....	....	73	....	....	....	....	....	....	....	....	....	....	25	1	5	6	36	....	....	....
1986-87	Medicine Hat Tigers	WHL	71	12	41	53	....	....	....	163	....	....	....	....	....	....	....	....	....	....	20	2	8	10	40	....	....	....
1987-88	Medicine Hat Tigers	WHL	30	15	30	45	....	....	....	48	....	....	....	....	....	....	....	....	....	....	16	6	17	23	50	....	....	....
	Canada	WJC-A	7	1	0	1	....	....	....	2	....	....	....	....	....	....	....	....	....	....	....	....	....	....	....	....	....	....
	Los Angeles Kings	**NHL**	**27**	**0**	**1**	**1**	**0**	**1**	**1**	**26**	**0**	**0**	**0**	**21**	**0.0**	**17**	**2**	**46**	**17**	**–14**	....	....	....	....	....	....	....	....
1988-89	**Los Angeles Kings**	**NHL**	**33**	**0**	**5**	**5**	**0**	**4**	**4**	**23**	**0**	**0**	**0**	**19**	**0.0**	**12**	**0**	**22**	**1**	**–9**	....	....	....	....	....	....	....	....
	New Haven Nighthawks	AHL	7	1	1	2	....	....	....	2	....	....	....	....	....	....	....	....	....	....	....	....	....	....	....	....	....	....
	New York Islanders	**NHL**	**19**	**0**	**1**	**1**	**0**	**1**	**1**	**12**	**0**	**0**	**0**	**17**	**0.0**	**12**	**1**	**19**	**4**	**–4**	....	....	....	....	....	....	....	....
1989-90	**New York Islanders**	**NHL**	**5**	**0**	**1**	**1**	**0**	**1**	**1**	**2**	**0**	**0**	**0**	**3**	**0.0**	**4**	**1**	**4**	**0**	**–1**	**2**	**1**	**1**	**2**	**0**	**0**	**0**	**0**
	Springfield Indians	AHL	58	6	33	39	....	....	....	48	....	....	....	....	....	....	....	....	....	....	17	4	11	15	31	....	....	....
1990-91	**New York Islanders**	**NHL**	**52**	**5**	**14**	**19**	**5**	**11**	**16**	**47**	**2**	**0**	**0**	**93**	**5.4**	**43**	**16**	**62**	**14**	**–21**	....	....	....	....	....	....	....	....
	Capital District Islanders	AHL	22	9	9	18	....	....	....	19	....	....	....	....	....	....	....	....	....	....	....	....	....	....	....	....	....	....
1991-92	**New York Islanders**	**NHL**	**25**	**2**	**4**	**6**	**2**	**3**	**5**	**18**	**0**	**1**	**1**	**51**	**3.9**	**36**	**4**	**27**	**6**	**+11**	....	....	....	....	....	....	....	....
1992-93	Capital District Islanders	AHL	20	1	9	10	....	....	....	35	....	....	....	....	....	....	....	....	....	....	3	0	1	1	9	....	....	....
1993-94	**New York Islanders**	**NHL**	**19**	**1**	**4**	**5**	**1**	**3**	**4**	**16**	**0**	**0**	**0**	**33**	**3.0**	**13**	**5**	**22**	**1**	**–13**	....	....	....	....	....	....	....	....
	Salt Lake Golden Eagles	IHL	5	0	6	6	....	....	....	2	....	....	....	....	....	....	....	....	....	....	....	....	....	....	....	....	....	....
	Winnipeg Jets	**NHL**	**31**	**2**	**9**	**11**	**2**	**7**	**9**	**24**	**2**	**0**	**0**	**81**	**2.5**	**30**	**18**	**34**	**1**	**–21**	....	....	....	....	....	....	....	....
1994-95	**Pittsburgh Penguins**	**NHL**	DID NOT PLAY – INJURED																									
	NHL Totals		**211**	**10**	**39**	**49**	**10**	**31**	**41**	**168**	**4**	**1**	**1**	**318**	**3.1**	**167**	**47**	**236**	**44**		**2**	**1**	**1**	**2**	**0**	**0**	**0**	**0**

WHL East First All-Star Team (1987) • Memorial Cup All-Star Team (1987) • Won Stafford Smythe Memorial Trophy (Memorial Cup Tournament MVP) (1987)

Traded to **NY Islanders** by **LA Kings** with Mark Fitzpatrick and future considerations (Doug Crossman, May 23, 1989) for Kelly Hrudey, February 22, 1989. Traded to **Winnipeg** by **NY Islanders** for Yan Kaminsky, February 1, 1994. Claimed by **Pittsburgh** from **Winnipeg** in Waiver Draft, January 18, 1995. • Missed entire 1994-95 season after undergoing wrist surgery, October, 1994.

• McCABE, BRYAN

Bryan McCabe D – L. 6'1", 204 lbs. b: St. Catharines, Ont., 6/8/1975. NY Islanders' 2nd choice, 40th overall, in 1993 Entry Draft.

Season	Club	League	GP	G	A	Pts	AG	AA	APts	PIM	PP	SH	GW	S	%	TGF	PGF	TGA	PGA	+/–	GP	G	A	Pts	PIM	PP	SH	GW
1991-92	Medicine Hat Tigers	WHL	68	6	24	30	....	....	....	157	....	....	....	....	....	....	....	....	....	....	4	0	0	0	6	....	....	....
1992-93	Medicine Hat Tigers	WHL	14	0	13	13	....	....	....	83	....	....	....	....	....	....	....	....	....	....	....	....	....	....	....	....	....	....
	Spokane Chiefs	WHL	46	3	44	47	....	....	....	134	....	....	....	....	....	....	....	....	....	....	6	1	5	6	28	....	....	....
1993-94	Spokane Chiefs	WHL	64	22	62	84	....	....	....	218	....	....	....	....	....	....	....	....	....	....	3	0	4	4	4	....	....	....
	Canada	WJC-A	7	0	0	0	....	....	....	6	....	....	....	....	....	....	....	....	....	....	....	....	....	....	....	....	....	....
1994-95	Spokane Chiefs	WHL	42	14	39	53	....	....	....	115	....	....	....	....	....	....	....	....	....	....	....	....	....	....	....	....	....	....
	Canada	WJC-A	7	3	9	12	....	....	....	4	....	....	....	....	....	....	....	....	....	....	....	....	....	....	....	....	....	....
	Brandon Wheat Kings	WHL	20	6	10	16	....	....	....	38	....	....	....	....	....	....	....	....	....	....	18	4	13	17	59	....	....	....
1995-96	**New York Islanders**	**NHL**	**82**	**7**	**16**	**23**	**7**	**13**	**20**	**156**	**3**	**0**	**1**	**130**	**5.4**	**82**	**22**	**121**	**37**	**–24**	....	....	....	....	....	....	....	....

Season	Club	League	GP	G	A	Pts	AG	AA	APts	PIM	PP	SH	GW	S	%	TGF	PGF	TGA	PGA	+/–	GP	G	A	Pts	PIM	PP	SH	GW
			REGULAR SEASON																		PLAYOFFS							
1996-97	**New York Islanders**	**NHL**	**82**	**8**	**20**	**28**	**8**	**18**	**26**	**165**	**2**	**1**	**2**	**117**	**6.8**	**89**	**17**	**99**	**25**	**–2**	....	....	....	....	....	....	....	....
	Canada	WC-A	11	0	2	2	....	....	....	10	....	....	....	....	....	....	....	....	....	....	....	....	....	....	....	....	....	....
1997-98	**New York Islanders**	**NHL**	**56**	**3**	**9**	**12**	**4**	**9**	**13**	**145**	**1**	**0**	**0**	**81**	**3.7**	**57**	**7**	**57**	**16**	**+9**	....	....	....	....	....	....	....	....
	Vancouver Canucks	**NHL**	**26**	**1**	**11**	**12**	**1**	**11**	**12**	**64**	**0**	**1**	**0**	**42**	**2.4**	**32**	**7**	**26**	**11**	**+10**	....	....	....	....	....	....	....	....
	Canada	WC-A	6	1	2	3	....	....	....	4	....	....	....	....	....	....	....	....	....	....	....	....	....	....	....	....	....	....
	NHL Totals		**246**	**19**	**56**	**75**	**20**	**51**	**71**	**530**	**6**	**2**	**3**	**370**	**5.1**	**260**	**53**	**303**	**89**		....	....	....	....	....	....	....	....

WHL West Second All-Star Team (1993) • WHL West First All-Star Team (1994) • WJC-A All-Star Team (1995) • Named Best Defenseman at WJC-A (1995) • WHL East First All-Star Team (1996) • Memorial Cup All-Star Team (1995)

Traded to **Vancouver** by **NY Islanders** with Todd Bertuzzi and NY Islanders' 3rd round choice (Jakko Ruutu) in 1998 Entry Draft for Trevor Linden, February 6, 1998.

• McCAHILL, JOHN

John McCahill D – R. 6'1", 215 lbs. b: Sarnia, Ont., 12/2/1955.

Season	Club	League	GP	G	A	Pts	AG	AA	APts	PIM	PP	SH	GW	S	%	TGF	PGF	TGA	PGA	+/–	GP	G	A	Pts	PIM	PP	SH	GW
1974-75	University of Michigan	WCHA	21	0	7	7	....	....	....	18	....	....	....	....	....	....	....	....	....	....	....	....	....	....	....	....	....	....
1975-76	University of Michigan	WCHA	42	3	23	26	....	....	....	28	....	....	....	....	....	....	....	....	....	....	....	....	....	....	....	....	....	....
1976-77	University of Michigan	CCHA	45	0	27	27	....	....	....	54	....	....	....	....	....	....	....	....	....	....	....	....	....	....	....	....	....	....
1977-78	University of Michigan	CCHA	35	5	23	28	....	....	....	32	....	....	....	....	....	....	....	....	....	....	....	....	....	....	....	....	....	....
	Colorado Rockies	**NHL**	**1**	**0**	**0**	**0**	**0**	**0**	**0**	**0**	**0**	**0**	**0**	**0**	**0.0**	**0**	**0**	**0**	**0**	**0**	....	....	....	....	....	....	....	....
	Tulsa Oilers	CHL	9	1	0	1	....	....	....	0	....	....	....	....	....	....	....	....	....	....	7	0	0	0	7	....	....	....
1978-79	Philadelphia Firebirds	AHL	77	5	12	17	....	....	....	36	....	....	....	....	....	....	....	....	....	....	....	....	....	....	....	....	....	....
1979-80	Fort Worth Texans	CHL	31	4	14	18	....	....	....	10	....	....	....	....	....	....	....	....	....	....	....	....	....	....	....	....	....	....
	Oklahoma City Stars	CHL	51	4	19	23	....	....	....	14	....	....	....	....	....	....	....	....	....	....	....	....	....	....	....	....	....	....
1980-81	Fort Worth Texans	CHL	8	1	2	3	....	....	....	11	....	....	....	....	....	....	....	....	....	....	....	....	....	....	....	....	....	....
	Muskegon Mohawks	IHL	48	7	20	27	....	....	....	29	....	....	....	....	....	....	....	....	....	....	....	....	....	....	....	....	....	....
	NHL Totals		**1**	**0**	**0**	**0**	**0**	**0**	**0**	**0**	**0**	**0**	**0**	**0**	**0.0**	**0**	**0**	**0**	**0**		....	....	....	....	....	....	....	....

Signed as a free agent by **Colorado**, May 17, 1978.

• McCALLUM, DUNC

Dunc McCallum D – R. 6'1", 193 lbs. b: Flin Flon, Man., 3/29/1940. d: 3/31/1983.

Season	Club	League	GP	G	A	Pts	AG	AA	APts	PIM	PP	SH	GW	S	%	TGF	PGF	TGA	PGA	+/–	GP	G	A	Pts	PIM	PP	SH	GW
1958-59	Brandon Wheat Kings	MJHL	28	10	11	21	....	....	....	48	....	....	....	....	....	....	....	....	....	....	....	....	....	....	....	....	....	....
1959-60	Brandon Wheat Kings	MJHL	32	8	9	17	....	....	....	84	....	....	....	....	....	....	....	....	....	....	22	8	6	14	31	....	....	....
1960-61	Fort Wayne Komets	IHL	65	6	18	24	....	....	....	74	....	....	....	....	....	....	....	....	....	....	8	0	3	3	6	....	....	....
1961-62	Seattle Totems	WHL	69	1	12	13	....	....	....	82	....	....	....	....	....	....	....	....	....	....	2	1	0	1	2	....	....	....
1962-63	Sudbury Wolves	EPHL	62	5	20	25	....	....	....	153	....	....	....	....	....	....	....	....	....	....	8	1	2	3	8	....	....	....
1963-64	Vancouver Canucks	WHL	62	6	13	19	....	....	....	78	....	....	....	....	....	....	....	....	....	....	....	....	....	....	....	....	....	....
1964-65	Vancouver Canucks	WHL	68	8	11	19	....	....	....	104	....	....	....	....	....	....	....	....	....	....	5	1	0	1	10	....	....	....
1965-66	**New York Rangers**	**NHL**	**2**	**0**	**0**	**0**	**0**	**0**	**0**	**2**	....	....	....	....	....	....	....	....	....	....	....	....	....	....	....	....	....	....
	Vancouver Canucks	WHL	68	5	19	24	....	....	....	104	....	....	....	....	....	....	....	....	....	....	7	1	1	2	16	....	....	....
1966-67	Omaha Knights	CHL	38	3	16	19	....	....	....	91	....	....	....	....	....	....	....	....	....	....	10	0	3	3	23	....	....	....
1967-68	**Pittsburgh Penguins**	**NHL**	**32**	**0**	**2**	**2**	**0**	**2**	**2**	**36**	**0**	**0**	**0**	**34**	**0.0**	**28**	**2**	**29**	**1**	**–2**	....	....	....	....	....	....	....	....
	Baltimore Clippers	AHL	19	3	7	10	....	....	....	37	....	....	....	....	....	....	....	....	....	....	....	....	....	....	....	....	....	....
1968-69	**Pittsburgh Penguins**	**NHL**	**62**	**5**	**13**	**18**	**6**	**12**	**18**	**81**	**2**	**1**	**1**	**99**	**5.1**	**59**	**12**	**95**	**13**	**–35**	....	....	....	....	....	....	....	....
1969-70	**Pittsburgh Penguins**	**NHL**	**14**	**0**	**0**	**0**	**0**	**0**	**0**	**16**	**0**	**0**	**0**	**11**	**0.0**	**6**	**2**	**11**	**3**	**–4**	**10**	**1**	**2**	**3**	**12**	**0**	**0**	**0**
	Baltimore Clippers	AHL	4	2	0	2	....	....	....	6	....	....	....	....	....	....	....	....	....	....	....	....	....	....	....	....	....	....
1970-71	**Pittsburgh Penguins**	**NHL**	**77**	**9**	**20**	**29**	**9**	**18**	**27**	**95**	**1**	**0**	**1**	**104**	**8.7**	**70**	**4**	**93**	**14**	**–13**	....	....	....	....	....	....	....	....
1971-72	San Diego Gulls	WHL	61	10	30	40	....	....	....	99	....	....	....	....	....	....	....	....	....	....	4	1	1	2	2	....	....	....
1972-73	Houston Aeros	WHA	69	9	20	29	....	....	....	112	....	....	....	....	....	....	....	....	....	....	10	2	3	5	6	....	....	....
1973-74			DID NOT PLAY – INJURED																									
1974-75	Chicago Cougars	WHA	31	0	10	10	....	....	....	24	....	....	....	....	....	....	....	....	....	....	....	....	....	....	....	....	....	....
	Long Island Cougars	NAHL	10	1	6	7	....	....	....	30	....	....	....	....	....	....	....	....	....	....	....	....	....	....	....	....	....	....
	NHL Totals		**187**	**14**	**35**	**49**	**15**	**32**	**47**	**230**	**3**	**1**	**2**	**248**	**5.6**	**163**	**20**	**228**	**31**		**10**	**1**	**2**	**3**	**12**	**0**	**0**	**0**
	Other Major League Totals		100	9	30	39	....	....	....	136	....	....	....	....	....	....	....	....	....	....	10	2	3	5	6	....	....	....

Traded to **NY Rangers** by **Detroit** (Vancouver-WHL) for Bob Cunningham, June, 1965. Traded to **Pittsburgh** by **NY Rangers** with George Konik, Paul Andrea and Frank Francis for Larry Jeffrey, June 6, 1967. Selected by **Dayton-Houston** (WHA) in 1972 WHA General Player Draft, February 12, 1972. • Missed entire 1973-73 season after suffering broken leg in exhibition game vs. LA Sharks (WHA), September 27, 1973. Signed as a free agent by **Chicago** (WHA) November 4, 1974.

• McCANN, RICK

Rick McCann C – L. 5'9", 178 lbs. b: Hamilton, Ont., 5/27/1944.

Season	Club	League	GP	G	A	Pts	AG	AA	APts	PIM	PP	SH	GW	S	%	TGF	PGF	TGA	PGA	+/–	GP	G	A	Pts	PIM	PP	SH	GW
1963-64	St. Mary's Lincolns	Jr. B	STATISTICS NOT AVAILABLE																									
1964-65	Michigan Tech Huskies	WCHA	STATISTICS NOT AVAILABLE																									
1965-66	Canada	Nat-Team	STATISTICS NOT AVAILABLE																									
	Canada	WEC-A	1	0	0	0	....	....	....	2	....	....	....	....	....	....	....	....	....	....	....	....	....	....	....	....	....	....
1966-67	Memphis Wings	CHL	61	15	26	41	....	....	....	23	....	....	....	....	....	....	....	....	....	....	1	0	0	0	0	....	....	....
1967-68	**Detroit Red Wings**	**NHL**	**3**	**0**	**0**	**0**	**0**	**0**	**0**	**0**	**0**	**0**	**0**	**0**	**0.0**	**0**	**0**	**0**	**0**	**0**	....	....	....	....	....	....	....	....
	Fort Worth Wings	CHL	68	20	51	71	....	....	....	98	....	....	....	....	....	....	....	....	....	....	13	5	*11	*16	13	....	....	....
1968-69	**Detroit Red Wings**	**NHL**	**3**	**0**	**0**	**0**	**0**	**0**	**0**	**0**	**0**	**0**	**0**	**2**	**0.0**	**0**	**0**	**2**	**1**	**–1**	....	....	....	....	....	....	....	....
	Fort Worth Wings	CHL	67	22	49	71	....	....	....	63	....	....	....	....	....	....	....	....	....	....	....	....	....	....	....	....	....	....
1969-70	**Detroit Red Wings**	**NHL**	**18**	**0**	**1**	**1**	**0**	**1**	**1**	**4**	**0**	**0**	**0**	**10**	**0.0**	**2**	**0**	**6**	**2**	**–2**	....	....	....	....	....	....	....	....
	Fort Worth Wings	CHL	47	15	24	39	....	....	....	29	....	....	....	....	....	....	....	....	....	....	7	2	4	6	4	....	....	....
1970-71	**Detroit Red Wings**	**NHL**	**5**	**0**	**0**	**0**	**0**	**0**	**0**	**0**	**0**	**0**	**0**	**8**	**0.0**	**1**	**1**	**3**	**1**	**–2**	....	....	....	....	....	....	....	....
	Baltimore Clippers	AHL	62	18	20	38	....	....	....	21	....	....	....	....	....	....	....	....	....	....	6	3	1	4	13	....	....	....
1971-72	**Detroit Red Wings**	**NHL**	**1**	**0**	**0**	**0**	**0**	**0**	**0**	**0**	**0**	**0**	**0**	**0**	**0.0**	**0**	**0**	**0**	**0**	**0**	....	....	....	....	....	....	....	....
	Tidewater Wings	AHL	69	13	38	51	....	....	....	39	....	....	....	....	....	....	....	....	....	....	....	....	....	....	....	....	....	....
1972-73	Virginia Wings	AHL	66	12	44	56	....	....	....	75	....	....	....	....	....	....	....	....	....	....	11	1	9	10	4	....	....	....
1973-74	London Lions	Britain	70	25	55	80	....	....	....	28	....	....	....	....	....	....	....	....	....	....	....	....	....	....	....	....	....	....
1974-75	**Detroit Red Wings**	**NHL**	**13**	**1**	**3**	**4**	**1**	**2**	**3**	**2**	**0**	**0**	**0**	**10**	**10.0**	**5**	**0**	**12**	**3**	**–4**	....	....	....	....	....	....	....	....
	Virginia Wings	AHL	65	19	48	67	....	....	....	60	....	....	....	....	....	....	....	....	....	....	5	1	4	5	0	....	....	....
1975-76	New Haven Nighthawks	AHL	73	15	42	57	....	....	....	47	....	....	....	....	....	....	....	....	....	....	3	0	0	0	0	....	....	....
	NHL Totals		**43**	**1**	**4**	**5**	**1**	**3**	**4**	**6**	**0**	**0**	**0**	**30**	**3.3**	**8**	**1**	**23**	**7**		....	....	....	....	....	....	....	....

Signed as a free agent by **Detroit** (Memphis-CHL), September, 1967.

• McCARTHY, DAN

Dan McCarthy C – L. 5'9", 185 lbs. b: St. Mary's, Ont., 4/7/1958. NY Rangers' 16th choice, 223rd overall, in 1978 Amateur Draft.

Season	Club	League	GP	G	A	Pts	AG	AA	APts	PIM	PP	SH	GW	S	%	TGF	PGF	TGA	PGA	+/–	GP	G	A	Pts	PIM	PP	SH	GW
1975-76	Sudbury Wolves	OHA	65	17	30	47	....	....	....	23	....	....	....	....	....	....	....	....	....	....	....	....	....	....	....	....	....	....
1976-77	Sudbury Wolves	OHA	54	23	32	55	....	....	....	76	....	....	....	....	....	....	....	....	....	....	....	....	....	....	....	....	....	....
1977-78	Sudbury Wolves	OHA	68	30	51	81	....	....	....	96	....	....	....	....	....	....	....	....	....	....	....	....	....	....	....	....	....	....
	Toledo Goaldiggers	IHL	9	2	4	6	....	....	....	9	....	....	....	....	....	....	....	....	....	....	....	....	....	....	....	....	....	....
1978-79	Flint Generals	IHL	75	38	42	80	....	....	....	80	....	....	....	....	....	....	....	....	....	....	....	....	....	....	....	....	....	....
1979-80	New Haven Nighthawks	AHL	26	6	3	9	....	....	....	8	....	....	....	....	....	....	....	....	....	....	....	....	....	....	....	....	....	....
	Richmond Rifles	EHL	8	6	4	10	....	....	....	7	....	....	....	....	....	....	....	....	....	....	5	3	1	4	22	....	....	....
1980-81	**New York Rangers**	**NHL**	**5**	**4**	**0**	**4**	**3**	**0**	**3**	**4**	**2**	**0**	**0**	**7**	**57.1**	**7**	**2**	**2**	**0**	**+3**	....	....	....	....	....	....	....	....
	New Haven Nighthawks	AHL	71	28	17	45	....	....	....	54	....	....	....	....	....	....	....	....	....	....	4	0	0	0	4	....	....	....
1981-82	Springfield Indians	AHL	78	26	32	58	....	....	....	57	....	....	....	....	....	....	....	....	....	....	....	....	....	....	....	....	....	....
1982-83	Birmingham South Stars	CHL	76	30	35	65	....	....	....	67	....	....	....	....	....	....	....	....	....	....	13	4	5	9	15	....	....	....
1983-84	Baltimore Skipjacks	AHL	27	8	11	19	....	....	....	8	....	....	....	....	....	....	....	....	....	....	....	....	....	....	....	....	....	....
1984-85	Baltimore Skipjacks	AHL	32	3	11	14	....	....	....	15	....	....	....	....	....	....	....	....	....	....	15	3	4	7	18	....		
1985-86	Springfield Indians	AHL	33	7	9	16	....	....	....	46	....	....	....	....	....	....	....	....	....	....	....	....	....	....	....	....	....	....
	NHL Totals		**5**	**4**	**0**	**4**	**3**	**0**	**3**	**4**	**2**	**0**	**0**	**7**	**57.1**	**7**	**2**	**2**	**0**		....	....	....	....	....	....	....	....

Traded to **Minnesota** by **NY Rangers** for Shawn Dineen, August 23, 1982.

• McCARTHY, KEVIN

Kevin McCarthy D – R. 5'11", 195 lbs. b: Winnipeg, Man., 7/14/1957. Philadelphia's 1st choice, 17th overall, in 1977 Amateur Draft.

Season	Club	League	GP	G	A	Pts	AG	AA	APts	PIM	PP	SH	GW	S	%	TGF	PGF	TGA	PGA	+/–	GP	G	A	Pts	PIM	PP	SH	GW
1973-74	Winnipeg Clubs	WCJHL	66	5	22	27	....	....	....	65	....	....	....	....	....	....	....	....	....	....	....	....	....	....	....	....	....	....
1974-75	Winnipeg Clubs	WCJHL	66	20	61	81	....	....	....	102	....	....	....	....	....	....	....	....	....	....	....	....	....	....	....	....	....	....
	Canada	WJC-A	5	1	4	5	....	....	....	6	....	....	....	....	....	....	....	....	....	....	....	....	....	....	....	....	....	....
1975-76	Winnipeg Clubs	WCJHL	72	33	88	121	....	....	....	160	....	....	....	....	....	....	....	....	....	....	6	2	9	11	8	....	....	....

			REGULAR SEASON																		PLAYOFFS							
Season	Club	League	GP	G	A	Pts	AG	AA	APts	PIM	PP	SH	GW	S	%	TGF	PGF	TGA	PGA	+/–	GP	G	A	Pts	PIM	PP	SH	GW
1976-77	Winnipeg Monarchs	WCJHL	72	22	*105	127	....	....	....	110	....	....	....	....	....	....	....	....	....	....	7	0	4	4	27	....	....	....
1977-78	**Philadelphia Flyers**	**NHL**	**62**	**2**	**15**	**17**	**2**	**12**	**14**	**32**	**0**	**0**	**0**	**91**	**2.2**	**56**	**0**	**35**	**8**	**+29**	**10**	**0**	**1**	**1**	**8**	**0**	**0**	**0**
1978-79	**Philadelphia Flyers**	**NHL**	**22**	**1**	**2**	**3**	**1**	**2**	**3**	**21**	**0**	**0**	**0**	**16**	**6.3**	**14**	**2**	**16**	**6**	**+2**	....	....	....	....	....	....	....	....
	Vancouver Canucks	**NHL**	**1**	**0**	**0**	**0**	**0**	**0**	**0**	**0**	**0**	**0**	**0**	**0**	**0.0**	**0**	**0**	**2**	**0**	**–2**	....	....	....	....	....	....	....	....
1979-80	**Vancouver Canucks**	**NHL**	**79**	**15**	**30**	**45**	**14**	**23**	**37**	**70**	**4**	**0**	**3**	**161**	**9.3**	**106**	**28**	**113**	**30**	**–5**	**4**	**1**	**0**	**1**	**0**	**0**	**0**	**0**
1980-81	**Vancouver Canucks**	**NHL**	**80**	**16**	**37**	**53**	**13**	**26**	**39**	**85**	**4**	**1**	**1**	**140**	**11.4**	**119**	**42**	**145**	**57**	**–11**	**3**	**0**	**1**	**1**	**0**	**0**	**0**	**0**
1981-82	**Vancouver Canucks**	**NHL**	**71**	**6**	**39**	**45**	**5**	**26**	**31**	**84**	**1**	**0**	**0**	**152**	**3.9**	**119**	**34**	**104**	**31**	**+12**	....	....	....	....	....	....	....	....
1982-83	**Vancouver Canucks**	**NHL**	**74**	**12**	**28**	**40**	**10**	**19**	**29**	**88**	**3**	**0**	**0**	**99**	**12.1**	**85**	**13**	**94**	**21**	**–1**	**4**	**1**	**1**	**2**	**12**	**0**	**0**	**0**
1983-84	**Vancouver Canucks**	**NHL**	**47**	**2**	**14**	**16**	**2**	**9**	**11**	**61**	**0**	**0**	**0**	**44**	**4.5**	**42**	**9**	**52**	**11**	**–8**	....	....	....	....	....	....	....	....
	Pittsburgh Penguins	**NHL**	**31**	**4**	**16**	**20**	**3**	**11**	**14**	**52**	**1**	**0**	**0**	**57**	**7.0**	**36**	**11**	**76**	**19**	**–32**	....	....	....	....	....	....	....	....
1984-85	**Pittsburgh Penguins**	**NHL**	**64**	**9**	**10**	**19**	**7**	**7**	**14**	**30**	**0**	**1**	**0**	**46**	**19.6**	**35**	**3**	**74**	**22**	**–20**	....	....	....	....	....	....	....	....
1985-86	**Philadelphia Flyers**	**NHL**	**4**	**0**	**0**	**0**	**0**	**0**	**0**	**4**	**0**	**0**	**0**	**0**	**0.0**	**1**	**0**	**1**	**0**	**0**	....	....	....	....	....	....	....	....
	Hershey Bears	AHL	64	15	40	55	....	....	....	157	....	....	....	....	....	....	....	....	....	....	17	1	10	11	12	....	....	....
1986-87	**Philadelphia Flyers**	**NHL**	**2**	**0**	**0**	**0**	**0**	**0**	**0**	**0**	**0**	**0**	**0**	**0**	**0.0**	**0**	**0**	**1**	**0**	**–1**	....	....	....	....	....	....	....	....
	Hershey Bears	AHL	74	6	44	50	....	....	....	86	....	....	....	....	....	....	....	....	....	....	5	0	4	4	4	....	....	....
1987-88	Hershey Bears	AHL	61	9	30	39	....	....	....	83	....	....	....	....	....	....	....	....	....	....	12	2	6	8	17	....	....	....
	NHL Totals		**537**	**67**	**191**	**258**	**57**	**135**	**192**	**527**	**13**	**2**	**4**	**806**	**8.3**	**613**	**142**	**713**	**205**		**21**	**2**	**3**	**5**	**20**	**0**	**0**	**0**

WCJHL All-Star Team (1976, 1977) • AHL First All-Star Team (1986)

Played in NHL All-Star Game (1981)

Traded to **Vancouver** by **Philadelphia** with Drew Callander for Dennis Ververgaert, December 29, 1978. Traded to **Pittsburgh** by **Vancouver** for Philadelphia's 3rd round choice (acquired earlier and later returned to Philadelphia — Philadelphia chose David McClay) in 1985 Entry Draft, January 26, 1984. Signed as a free agent by **Philadelphia**, July 19, 1985.

• McCARTHY, SANDY

Sandy McCarthy RW – R. 6'3", 225 lbs. b: Toronto, Ont., 6/15/1972. Calgary's 3rd choice, 52nd overall, in 1991 Entry Draft.

Season	Club	League	GP	G	A	Pts	AG	AA	APts	PIM	PP	SH	GW	S	%	TGF	PGF	TGA	PGA	+/–	GP	G	A	Pts	PIM	PP	SH	GW
1989-90	Laval Titan	QMJHL	65	10	11	21	....	....	....	269	....	....	....	....	....	....	....	....	....	....	14	3	3	6	60	....	....	....
1990-91	Laval Titan	QMJHL	68	21	19	40	....	....	....	297	....	....	....	....	....	....	....	....	....	....	13	6	5	11	67	....	....	....
1991-92	Laval Titan	QMJHL	62	39	51	90	....	....	....	326	....	....	....	....	....	....	....	....	....	....	8	4	5	9	81	....	....	....
1992-93	Salt Lake Golden Eagles	IHL	77	18	20	38	....	....	....	220	....	....	....	....	....	....	....	....	....	....	....	....	....	....	....	....	....	....
1993-94	**Calgary Flames**	**NHL**	**79**	**5**	**5**	**10**	**5**	**4**	**9**	**173**	**0**	**0**	**0**	**39**	**12.8**	**18**	**0**	**22**	**1**	**–3**	**7**	**0**	**0**	**0**	**34**	**0**	**0**	**0**
1994-95	**Calgary Flames**	**NHL**	**37**	**5**	**3**	**8**	**9**	**4**	**13**	**101**	**0**	**0**	**2**	**29**	**17.2**	**21**	**6**	**14**	**0**	**+1**	**6**	**0**	**1**	**1**	**17**	**0**	**0**	**0**
1995-96	**Calgary Flames**	**NHL**	**75**	**9**	**7**	**16**	**9**	**6**	**15**	**173**	**3**	**0**	**1**	**98**	**9.2**	**36**	**16**	**28**	**0**	**–8**	**4**	**0**	**0**	**0**	**10**	**0**	**0**	**0**
1996-97	**Calgary Flames**	**NHL**	**33**	**3**	**5**	**8**	**3**	**4**	**7**	**113**	**1**	**0**	**1**	**38**	**7.9**	**12**	**4**	**16**	**0**	**–8**	....	....	....	....	....	....	....	....
1997-98	**Calgary Flames**	**NHL**	**52**	**8**	**5**	**13**	**9**	**5**	**14**	**170**	**1**	**0**	**1**	**68**	**11.8**	**19**	**7**	**30**	**0**	**–18**	....	....	....	....	....	....	....	....
	Tampa Bay Lightning	**NHL**	**14**	**0**	**5**	**5**	**0**	**5**	**5**	**71**	**0**	**0**	**0**	**26**	**0.0**	**6**	**1**	**6**	**0**	**–1**	....	....	....	....	....	....	....	....
	NHL Totals		**290**	**30**	**30**	**60**	**35**	**28**	**63**	**801**	**5**	**0**	**5**	**298**	**10.1**	**112**	**34**	**116**	**1**		**17**	**0**	**1**	**1**	**61**	**0**	**0**	**0**

Traded to **Tampa Bay** by **Calgary** with Calgary's 3rd (Brad Richards) and 5th (Curtis Rich) round choices in 1998 Entry Draft for Jason Wiemer, March 24, 1998.

• McCARTHY, TOM

Tom "Jug" McCarthy LW – L. 6'2", 200 lbs. b: Toronto, Ont., 7/31/1960. Minnesota's 2nd choice, 10th overall, in 1979 Entry Draft.

Season	Club	League	GP	G	A	Pts	AG	AA	APts	PIM	PP	SH	GW	S	%	TGF	PGF	TGA	PGA	+/–	GP	G	A	Pts	PIM	PP	SH	GW
1976-77	North York Rangers	OJHL	43	49	47	96	....	....	....	12	....	....	....	....	....	....	....	....	....	....	....	....	....	....	....	....	....	....
	Kingston Canadians	OHA	2	1	0	1	....	....	....	0	....	....	....	....	....	....	....	....	....	....	....	....	....	....	....	....	....	....
1977-78	Oshawa Generals	OHA	62	47	46	93	....	....	....	72	....	....	....	....	....	....	....	....	....	....	6	3	5	8	4	....	....	....
1978-79	Oshawa Generals	OHA	63	69	75	141	....	....	....	98	....	....	....	....	....	....	....	....	....	....	3	1	0	1	9	....	....	....
1979-80	**Minnesota North Stars**	**NHL**	**68**	**16**	**20**	**36**	**14**	**15**	**29**	**39**	**1**	**0**	**5**	**101**	**15.8**	**64**	**15**	**56**	**0**	**–7**	**15**	**5**	**6**	**11**	**20**	**3**	**0**	**0**
1980-81	**Minnesota North Stars**	**NHL**	**62**	**23**	**25**	**48**	**19**	**17**	**36**	**62**	**4**	**0**	**2**	**147**	**15.6**	**75**	**24**	**51**	**3**	**+3**	**8**	**0**	**3**	**3**	**6**	**0**	**0**	**0**
1981-82	**Minnesota North Stars**	**NHL**	**40**	**12**	**30**	**42**	**9**	**20**	**29**	**36**	**3**	**0**	**1**	**89**	**13.5**	**68**	**17**	**45**	**4**	**+10**	**4**	**0**	**2**	**2**	**4**	**0**	**0**	**0**
1982-83	**Minnesota North Stars**	**NHL**	**80**	**28**	**48**	**76**	**23**	**33**	**56**	**59**	**4**	**1**	**4**	**171**	**16.4**	**109**	**37**	**60**	**6**	**+18**	**9**	**2**	**4**	**6**	**9**	**0**	**0**	**0**
1983-84	**Minnesota North Stars**	**NHL**	**66**	**39**	**31**	**70**	**31**	**21**	**52**	**49**	**16**	**2**	**7**	**165**	**23.6**	**109**	**42**	**62**	**12**	**+17**	**8**	**1**	**4**	**5**	**6**	**1**	**0**	**1**
1984-85	**Minnesota North Stars**	**NHL**	**44**	**16**	**21**	**37**	**13**	**14**	**27**	**36**	**6**	**0**	**1**	**80**	**20.0**	**48**	**14**	**41**	**10**	**+3**	**7**	**0**	**2**	**2**	**0**	**0**	**0**	**0**
1985-86	**Minnesota North Stars**	**NHL**	**25**	**12**	**12**	**24**	**10**	**8**	**18**	**12**	**4**	**0**	**2**	**45**	**26.7**	**35**	**16**	**22**	**0**	**–3**	....	....	....	....	....	....	....	....
1986-87	**Boston Bruins**	**NHL**	**68**	**30**	**29**	**59**	**26**	**21**	**47**	**31**	**7**	**0**	**6**	**121**	**24.8**	**84**	**35**	**39**	**0**	**+10**	**4**	**1**	**1**	**2**	**4**	**1**	**0**	**0**
	Moncton Golden Flames	AHL	2	1	0	1	....	....	....	0	....	....	....	....	....	....	....	....	....	....	....	....	....	....	....	....	....	....
1987-88	Maine Mariners	AHL	17	7	6	13	....	....	....	14	....	....	....	....	....	....	....	....	....	....	....	....	....	....	....	....	....	....
	Boston Bruins	**NHL**	**7**	**2**	**5**	**7**	**2**	**4**	**6**	**6**	**1**	**0**	**0**	**10**	**20.0**	**7**	**2**	**2**	**0**	**+3**	**13**	**3**	**4**	**7**	**18**	**0**	**0**	**0**
1988-89	EC Asiago	Italy	19	9	26	35	....	....	....	8	....	....	....	....	....	....	....	....	....	....	....	....	....	....	....	....	....	....
	NHL Totals		**460**	**178**	**221**	**399**	**147**	**153**	**300**	**330**	**46**	**3**	**28**	**929**	**19.2**	**599**	**202**	**378**	**35**		**68**	**12**	**26**	**38**	**67**	**5**	**0**	**1**

OHA First All-Star Team (1979)

Played in NHL All-Star Game (1983)

Traded to **Boston** by **Minnesota** for Boston's 3rd round choice (Rob Zettler) in 1986 Entry Draft and 2nd round choice (Scott McGrady) in 1987 Entry Draft, May 16, 1986.

• McCARTY, DARREN

Darren McCarty RW – R. 6'1", 210 lbs. b: Burnaby, B.C., 4/1/1972. Detroit's 2nd choice, 46th overall, in 1992 Entry Draft.

Season	Club	League	GP	G	A	Pts	AG	AA	APts	PIM	PP	SH	GW	S	%	TGF	PGF	TGA	PGA	+/–	GP	G	A	Pts	PIM	PP	SH	GW
1989-90	Belleville Bulls	OHL	63	12	15	27	....	....	....	142	....	....	....	....	....	....	....	....	....	....	11	1	1	2	21	....	....	....
1990-91	Belleville Bulls	OHL	60	30	37	67	....	....	....	151	....	....	....	....	....	....	....	....	....	....	6	2	2	4	13	....	....	....
1991-92	Belleville Bulls	OHL	65	*55	72	127	....	....	....	177	....	....	....	....	....	....	....	....	....	....	5	1	4	5	13	....	....	....
1992-93	Adirondack Red Wings	AHL	73	17	19	36	....	....	....	278	....	....	....	....	....	....	....	....	....	....	11	0	1	1	33	....	....	....
1993-94	**Detroit Red Wings**	**NHL**	**67**	**9**	**17**	**26**	**8**	**13**	**21**	**181**	**0**	**0**	**2**	**81**	**11.1**	**47**	**3**	**32**	**0**	**+12**	**7**	**2**	**2**	**4**	**8**	**0**	**0**	**0**
1994-95	**Detroit Red Wings**	**NHL**	**31**	**5**	**8**	**13**	**9**	**12**	**21**	**88**	**1**	**0**	**2**	**27**	**18.5**	**19**	**3**	**12**	**1**	**+5**	**18**	**3**	**2**	**5**	**14**	**0**	**0**	**0**
1995-96	**Detroit Red Wings**	**NHL**	**63**	**15**	**14**	**29**	**15**	**11**	**26**	**158**	**8**	**0**	**1**	**102**	**14.7**	**56**	**16**	**27**	**1**	**+14**	**19**	**3**	**2**	**5**	**20**	**0**	**0**	**1**
1996-97	**Detroit Red Wings**	**NHL**	**68**	**19**	**30**	**49**	**20**	**27**	**47**	**126**	**5**	**0**	**6**	**171**	**11.1**	**77**	**26**	**37**	**0**	**+14**	**20**	**3**	**4**	**7**	**34**	**0**	**0**	**2**
1997-98	**Detroit Red Wings**	**NHL**	**71**	**15**	**22**	**37**	**18**	**21**	**39**	**157**	**5**	**1**	**2**	**166**	**9.0**	**66**	**27**	**47**	**8**	**0**	**22**	**3**	**8**	**11**	**34**	**0**	**0**	**1**
	NHL Totals		**300**	**63**	**91**	**154**	**70**	**84**	**154**	**710**	**19**	**1**	**13**	**547**	**11.5**	**265**	**75**	**155**	**10**		**86**	**14**	**18**	**32**	**110**	**0**	**0**	**4**

OHL First All-Star Team (1992)

• McCASKILL, TED

Ted McCaskill C – L. 6'1", 195 lbs. b: Kapuskasing, Ont., 10/29/1936.

Season	Club	League	GP	G	A	Pts	AG	AA	APts	PIM	PP	SH	GW	S	%	TGF	PGF	TGA	PGA	+/–	GP	G	A	Pts	PIM	PP	SH	GW
1954-55	Kitchener Canucks	OHA	39	7	7	14	....	....	....	59	....	....	....	....	....	....	....	....	....	....	....	....	....	....	....	....	....	....
1955-56	Kitchener Canucks	OHA	16	2	2	4	....	....	....	8	....	....	....	....	....	....	....	....	....	....	....	....	....	....	....	....	....	....
1956-57	Kapuskasing Huskies	NOHA	STATISTICS NOT AVAILABLE																									
1957-58	Kapuskasing Huskies	NOHA	STATISTICS NOT AVAILABLE																									
1958-59	Edinborough Royals	Scotland	25	27	18	45	....	....	....	21	....	....	....	....	....	....	....	....	....	....	....	....	....	....	....	....	....	....
1959-60	Paisley Pirates	Britain	54	53	44	97	....	....	....	85	....	....	....	....	....	....	....	....	....	....	....	....	....	....	....	....	....	....
1960-61	Kapuskasing Huskies	NOHA	STATISTICS NOT AVAILABLE																									
1961-62	Kapuskasing Huskies	NOHA	STATISTICS NOT AVAILABLE																									
1962-63	Nashville Dixie Flyers	EHL	65	21	43	64	....	....	....	62	....	....	....	....	....	....	....	....	....	....	3	1	1	2	6	....	....	....
1963-64	Nashville Dixie Flyers	EHL	70	36	50	86	....	....	....	107	....	....	....	....	....	....	....	....	....	....	3	1	1	2	2	....	....	....
1964-65	Nashville Dixie Flyers	EHL	72	60	65	125	....	....	....	....	....	....	....	....	....	....	....	....	....	....	13	8	14	22	26	....	....	....
1965-66	Nashville Dixie Flyers	EHL	70	39	61	100	....	....	....	151	....	....	....	....	....	....	....	....	....	....	11	3	*13	*16	18	....	....	....
1966-67	Nashville Dixie Flyers	EHL	72	53	65	118	....	....	....	188	....	....	....	....	....	....	....	....	....	....	14	8	13	21	46	....	....	....
1967-68	**Minnesota North Stars**	**NHL**	**4**	**0**	**2**	**2**	**0**	**2**	**2**	**0**	**0**	**0**	**0**	**2**	**0.0**	**3**	**1**	**4**	**0**	**–2**	....	....	....	....	....	....	....	....
	Memphis South Stars	CHL	62	17	29	46	....	....	....	136	....	....	....	....	....	....	....	....	....	....	3	2	0	2	0	....	....	....
1968-69	Memphis South Stars	CHL	5	0	0	0	....	....	....	6	....	....	....	....	....	....	....	....	....	....	....	....	....	....	....	....	....	....
	Vancouver Canucks	WHL	45	11	13	24	....	....	....	83	....	....	....	....	....	....	....	....	....	....	8	0	6	6	6	....	....	....
1969-70	Vancouver Canucks	WHL	72	24	18	42	....	....	....	110	....	....	....	....	....	....	....	....	....	....	11	0	2	2	47	....	....	....
1970-71	Phoenix Roadrunners	WHL	70	23	24	47	....	....	....	169	....	....	....	....	....	....	....	....	....	....	10	3	4	7	8	....	....	....
1971-72	Phoenix Roadrunners	WHL	71	18	37	55	....	....	....	*237	....	....	....	....	....	....	....	....	....	....	6	1	2	3	18	....	....	....

			REGULAR SEASON																		PLAYOFFS							
Season	Club	League	GP	G	A	Pts	AG	AA	APts	PIM	PP	SH	GW	S	%	TGF	PGF	TGA	PGA	+/–	GP	G	A	Pts	PIM	PP	SH	GW
1972-73	Los Angeles Sharks	WHA	73	11	11	22	....	....	....	150	....	....	....	....	....	....	....	....	....	....	6	2	3	5	12	....	....	....
1973-74	Los Angeles Sharks	WHA	18	2	2	4	....	....	....	63	....	....	....	....	....	....	....	....	....	....	....	....	....	....	....	....	....	....
1974-75	Binghamton Dusters	NAHL	40	14	20	34	....	....	....	77	....	....	....	....	....	....	....	....	....	....	15	3	10	13	....	....	....	....
	NHL Totals		**4**	**0**	**2**	**2**	**0**	**2**	**2**	**0**	**0**	**0**	**0**	**2**	**0.0**	**3**	**1**	**4**	**0**		....	....	....	....	....	....	....	....
	Other Major League Totals		91	13	13	26	....	....	....	213	....	....	....	....	....	....	....	....	....	....	6	2	3	5	12	....	....	....

EHL South First All-Star Team (1965, 1966, 1967)

Signed as a free agent by **Minnesota** (Memphis-CHL), September, 1967. Traded to **Vancouver** (WHL) by **Minnesota** for cash, November, 1968. Selected by **LA Sharks** (WHA) in 1972 WHA General Player Draft, February 12, 1972.

• McCAULEY, ALYN

Alyn McCauley C – L. 5'11", 185 lbs. b: Brockville, Ont., 5/29/1977. New Jersey's 5th choice, 79th overall, in 1995 Entry Draft.

Season	Club	League	GP	G	A	Pts	AG	AA	APts	PIM	PP	SH	GW	S	%	TGF	PGF	TGA	PGA	+/–	GP	G	A	Pts	PIM	PP	SH	GW
1993-94	Ottawa 67's	OHL	38	13	23	36	....	....	....	10	....	....	....	....	....	....	....	....	....	....	13	5	14	19	4	....	....	....
1994-95	Ottawa 67's	OHL	65	16	38	54	....	....	....	20	....	....	....	....	....	....	....	....	....	....	....	....	....	....	....	....	....	....
1995-96	Ottawa 67's	OHL	55	34	48	82	....	....	....	24	....	....	....	....	....	....	....	....	....	....	2	0	0	0	0	....	....	....
	Canada	WJC-A	6	2	3	5	....	....	....	2	....	....	....	....	....	....	....	....	....	....	....	....	....	....	....	....	....	....
1996-97	Ottawa 67's	OHL	50	*56	56	112	....	....	....	16	....	....	....	....	....	....	....	....	....	....	22	14	22	36	14	....	....	....
	Canada	WJC-A	7	0	5	5	....	....	....	2	....	....	....	....	....	....	....	....	....	....	....	....	....	....	....	....	....	....
	St. John's Maple Leafs	AHL	....	....	....	....	....	....	....	....	....	....	....	....	....	....	....	....	....	....	3	0	1	1	0	....	....	....
1997-98	**Toronto Maple Leafs**	**NHL**	**60**	**6**	**10**	**16**	**7**	**10**	**17**	**6**	**0**	**0**	**1**	**77**	**7.8**	**23**	**2**	**34**	**6**	**–7**	....	....	....	....	....	....	....	....
	NHL Totals		**60**	**6**	**10**	**16**	**7**	**10**	**17**	**6**	**0**	**0**	**1**	**77**	**7.8**	**23**	**2**	**34**	**6**		....	....	....	....	....	....	....	....

OHL First All-Star Team (1996, 1997) • Canadian Major Junior First All-Star Team (1997) • Canadian Major Junior Player of the Year (1997)

Rights traded to **Toronto** by **New Jersey** with Jason Smith and Steve Sullivan for Doug Gilmour, Dave Ellett and future considerations, February 25, 1997.

• McCLANAHAN, ROB

Rob McClanahan C – R. 5'10", 180 lbs. b: St. Paul, MN, 1/9/1958. Buffalo's 3rd choice, 49th overall, in 1978 Amateur Draft.

Season	Club	League	GP	G	A	Pts	AG	AA	APts	PIM	PP	SH	GW	S	%	TGF	PGF	TGA	PGA	+/–	GP	G	A	Pts	PIM	PP	SH	GW
1976-77	University of Minnesota	WCHA	40	11	6	17	....	....	....	24	....	....	....	....	....	....	....	....	....	....	....	....	....	....	....	....	....	....
1977-78	University of Minnesota	WCHA	38	17	25	42	....	....	....	10	....	....	....	....	....	....	....	....	....	....	....	....	....	....	....	....	....	....
1978-79	University of Minnesota	WCHA	43	17	32	49	....	....	....	34	....	....	....	....	....	....	....	....	....	....	....	....	....	....	....	....	....	....
	United States	WEC-A	8	1	3	4	....	....	....	6	....	....	....	....	....	....	....	....	....	....	....	....	....	....	....	....	....	....
1979-80	United States	Nat-Team	63	34	36	70	....	....	....	38	....	....	....	....	....	....	....	....	....	....	....	....	....	....	....	....	....	....
	United States	Olympics	7	5	3	8	....	....	....	2	....	....	....	....	....	....	....	....	....	....	....	....	....	....	....	....	....	....
	Buffalo Sabres	**NHL**	**13**	**2**	**5**	**7**	**2**	**4**	**6**	**0**	**0**	**0**	**0**	**13**	**15.4**	**12**	**1**	**4**	**1**	**+8**	**10**	**0**	**1**	**1**	**4**	**0**	**0**	**0**
1980-81	**Buffalo Sabres**	**NHL**	**53**	**3**	**12**	**15**	**2**	**8**	**10**	**38**	**1**	**0**	**1**	**67**	**4.5**	**26**	**7**	**42**	**4**	**–19**	**5**	**0**	**1**	**1**	**13**	**0**	**0**	**0**
	Rochester Americans	AHL	18	9	13	22	....	....	....	10	....	....	....	....	....	....	....	....	....	....	....	....	....	....	....	....	....	....
1981-82	United States	C Cup	6	0	0	0	....	....	....	2	....	....	....	....	....	....	....	....	....	....	....	....	....	....	....	....	....	....
	Hartford Whalers	**NHL**	**17**	**0**	**3**	**3**	**0**	**2**	**2**	**11**	**0**	**0**	**0**	**9**	**0.0**	**4**	**0**	**15**	**4**	**–7**	....	....	....	....	....	....	....	....
	Binghamton Whalers	AHL	27	11	18	29	....	....	....	21	....	....	....	....	....	....	....	....	....	....	....	....	....	....	....	....	....	....
	New York Rangers	**NHL**	**22**	**5**	**9**	**14**	**4**	**6**	**10**	**10**	**0**	**0**	**1**	**36**	**13.9**	**23**	**1**	**20**	**5**	**+7**	**10**	**2**	**5**	**7**	**2**	**0**	**0**	**0**
	Springfield Indians	AHL	7	4	5	9	....	....	....	0	....	....	....	....	....	....	....	....	....	....	....	....	....	....	....	....	....	....
1982-83	**New York Rangers**	**NHL**	**78**	**22**	**26**	**48**	**18**	**18**	**36**	**46**	**0**	**2**	**0**	**118**	**18.6**	**61**	**0**	**64**	**15**	**+12**	**9**	**2**	**5**	**7**	**12**	**0**	**0**	**1**
1983-84	**New York Rangers**	**NHL**	**41**	**6**	**8**	**14**	**5**	**5**	**10**	**21**	**0**	**0**	**2**	**52**	**11.5**	**21**	**0**	**24**	**3**	**0**	....	....	....	....	....	....	....	....
	Tulsa Oilers	CHL	10	4	10	14	....	....	....	10	....	....	....	....	....	....	....	....	....	....	....	....	....	....	....	....	....	....
	NHL Totals		**224**	**38**	**63**	**101**	**31**	**43**	**74**	**126**	**1**	**2**	**4**	**295**	**12.9**	**147**	**9**	**169**	**32**		**34**	**4**	**12**	**16**	**31**	**0**	**0**	**1**

Claimed by **Hartford** from **Buffalo** in Waiver Draft, October 0, 1981. Traded to **NY Rangers** by **Hartford** for NY Rangers' 10th round choice (Reine Karlsson) in 1983 Entry Draft, February 2, 1982. Traded to **Detroit** by **NY Rangers** for future considerations, May 23, 1984. Traded to **Vancouver** by **Detroit** for Tiger Williams, August 8, 1984.

• McCLEARY, TRENT

Trent McCleary RW – R. 6', 180 lbs. b: Swift Current, Sask., 9/8/1972.

Season	Club	League	GP	G	A	Pts	AG	AA	APts	PIM	PP	SH	GW	S	%	TGF	PGF	TGA	PGA	+/–	GP	G	A	Pts	PIM	PP	SH	GW
1989-90	Swift Current Broncos	WHL	70	3	15	18	....	....	....	43	....	....	....	....	....	....	....	....	....	....	4	1	0	1	0	....	....	....
1990-91	Swift Current Broncos	WHL	70	16	24	40	....	....	....	53	....	....	....	....	....	....	....	....	....	....	3	0	0	0	2	....	....	....
1991-92	Swift Current Broncos	WHL	72	23	22	45	....	....	....	240	....	....	....	....	....	....	....	....	....	....	8	1	2	3	16	....	....	....
1992-93	Swift Current Broncos	WHL	63	17	33	50	....	....	....	138	....	....	....	....	....	....	....	....	....	....	17	5	4	9	16	....	....	....
	New Haven Nighthawks	AHL	2	1	0	1	....	....	....	6	....	....	....	....	....	....	....	....	....	....	....	....	....	....	....	....	....	....
1993-94	P.E.I. Senators	AHL	4	0	0	0	....	....	....	6	....	....	....	....	....	....	....	....	....	....	....	....	....	....	....	....	....	....
	Thunder Bay Senators	ColHL	51	23	17	40	....	....	....	123	....	....	....	....	....	....	....	....	....	....	9	2	11	13	15	....	....	....
1994-95	P.E.I. Senators	AHL	51	9	20	29	....	....	....	60	....	....	....	....	....	....	....	....	....	....	9	2	3	5	26	....	....	....
1995-96	**Ottawa Senators**	**NHL**	**75**	**4**	**10**	**14**	**4**	**8**	**12**	**68**	**0**	**1**	**0**	**58**	**6.9**	**23**	**0**	**55**	**17**	**–15**	....	....	....	....	....	....	....	....
1996-97	**Boston Bruins**	**NHL**	**59**	**3**	**5**	**8**	**3**	**4**	**7**	**33**	**0**	**0**	**1**	**41**	**7.3**	**12**	**0**	**34**	**6**	**–16**	....	....	....	....	....	....	....	....
1997-98	Detroit Vipers	IHL	21	1	1	2	....	....	....	45	....	....	....	....	....	....	....	....	....	....	....	....	....	....	....	....	....	....
	Las Vegas Thunder	IHL	54	7	6	13	....	....	....	120	....	....	....	....	....	....	....	....	....	....	3	1	0	1	2	....	....	....
	NHL Totals		**134**	**7**	**15**	**22**	**7**	**12**	**19**	**101**	**0**	**1**	**1**	**99**	**7.1**	**35**	**0**	**89**	**23**		....	....	....	....	....	....	....	....

Signed as a free agent by **Ottawa**, October 9, 1992. Traded to **Boston** by **Ottawa** with Ottawa's 3rd round choice (Eric Naud) in 1996 Entry Draft for Shawn McEachern, June 22, 1996.

• McCLELLAND, KEVIN

Kevin McClelland RW – R. 6'2", 205 lbs. b: Oshawa, Ont., 7/4/1962. Hartford's 4th choice, 71st overall, in 1980 Entry Draft.

Season	Club	League	GP	G	A	Pts	AG	AA	APts	PIM	PP	SH	GW	S	%	TGF	PGF	TGA	PGA	+/–	GP	G	A	Pts	PIM	PP	SH	GW
1979-80	Niagara Falls Flyers	OHA	67	14	14	28	....	....	....	71	....	....	....	....	....	....	....	....	....	....	....	....	....	....	....	....	....	....
1980-81	Niagara Falls Flyers	OHA	68	36	72	108	....	....	....	186	....	....	....	....	....	....	....	....	....	....	12	8	13	21	42	....	....	....
1981-82	Niagara Falls Flyers	OHL	46	36	47	83	....	....	....	184	....	....	....	....	....	....	....	....	....	....	....	....	....	....	....	....	....	....
	Pittsburgh Penguins	**NHL**	**10**	**1**	**4**	**5**	**1**	**3**	**4**	**4**	**0**	**0**	**0**	**18**	**5.6**	**9**	**1**	**4**	**2**	**+6**	**5**	**1**	**1**	**2**	**5**	**0**	**0**	**0**
1982-83	**Pittsburgh Penguins**	**NHL**	**38**	**5**	**4**	**9**	**4**	**3**	**7**	**73**	**0**	**0**	**0**	**70**	**7.1**	**11**	**0**	**31**	**2**	**–18**	....	....	....	....	....	....	....	....
1983-84	**Pittsburgh Penguins**	**NHL**	**24**	**2**	**4**	**6**	**2**	**3**	**5**	**62**	**0**	**2**	**0**	**40**	**5.0**	**9**	**0**	**24**	**8**	**–7**	....	....	....	....	....	....	....	....
	Baltimore Skipjacks	AHL	3	1	1	2	....	....	....	0	....	....	....	....	....	....	....	....	....	....	....	....	....	....	....	....	....	....
	Edmonton Oilers	**NHL**	**52**	**8**	**20**	**28**	**6**	**14**	**20**	**127**	**0**	**2**	**2**	**65**	**12.3**	**43**	**1**	**33**	**0**	**+9**	**18**	**4**	**6**	**10**	**42**	**0**	**0**	**1**
1984-85	**Edmonton Oilers**	**NHL**	**62**	**8**	**15**	**23**	**7**	**10**	**17**	**205**	**0**	**0**	**3**	**96**	**8.3**	**36**	**1**	**49**	**3**	**–11**	**18**	**1**	**3**	**4**	**75**	**0**	**0**	**0**
1985-86	**Edmonton Oilers**	**NHL**	**79**	**11**	**25**	**36**	**9**	**17**	**26**	**266**	**0**	**0**	**1**	**104**	**10.6**	**45**	**1**	**37**	**2**	**+9**	**10**	**1**	**0**	**1**	**32**	**0**	**0**	**0**
1986-87	**Edmonton Oilers**	**NHL**	**72**	**12**	**13**	**25**	**10**	**9**	**19**	**238**	**0**	**0**	**1**	**76**	**15.8**	**38**	**0**	**42**	**0**	**–4**	**21**	**2**	**3**	**5**	**43**	**0**	**0**	**0**
1987-88	**Edmonton Oilers**	**NHL**	**74**	**10**	**6**	**16**	**9**	**4**	**13**	**281**	**0**	**0**	**0**	**61**	**16.4**	**28**	**0**	**28**	**1**	**+1**	**19**	**2**	**3**	**5**	**68**	**0**	**0**	**0**
1988-89	**Edmonton Oilers**	**NHL**	**79**	**6**	**14**	**20**	**5**	**10**	**15**	**161**	**0**	**0**	**0**	**43**	**14.0**	**25**	**2**	**33**	**0**	**–10**	**7**	**0**	**2**	**2**	**16**	**0**	**0**	**0**
1989-90	**Edmonton Oilers**	**NHL**	**10**	**1**	**1**	**2**	**1**	**1**	**2**	**13**	**0**	**0**	**0**	**7**	**14.3**	**3**	**0**	**4**	**0**	**–1**	....	....	....	....	....	....	....	....
	Detroit Red Wings	**NHL**	**61**	**4**	**5**	**9**	**3**	**4**	**7**	**183**	**0**	**0**	**0**	**24**	**16.7**	**13**	**0**	**19**	**1**	**–5**	....	....	....	....	....	....	....	....
1990-91	**Detroit Red Wings**	**NHL**	**3**	**0**	**0**	**0**	**0**	**0**	**0**	**7**	**0**	**0**	**0**	**1**	**0.0**	**0**	**0**	**4**	**0**	**–4**	....	....	....	....	....	....	....	....
	Adirondack Red Wings	AHL	27	5	14	19	....	....	....	125	....	....	....	....	....	....	....	....	....	....	....	....	....	....	....	....	....	....
1991-92	**Toronto Maple Leafs**	**NHL**	**10**	**0**	**1**	**1**	**0**	**1**	**1**	**33**	**0**	**0**	**0**	**5**	**0.0**	**1**	**0**	**4**	**0**	**–3**	....	....	....	....	....	....	....	....
	St. John's Maple Leafs	AHL	34	7	15	22	....	....	....	199	....	....	....	....	....	....	....	....	....	....	5	0	1	1	9	....	....	....
1992-93	St. John's Maple Leafs	AHL	55	7	20	27	....	....	....	221	....	....	....	....	....	....	....	....	....	....	1	0	0	0	7	....	....	....
1993-94	**Winnipeg Jets**	**NHL**	**6**	**0**	**0**	**0**	**0**	**0**	**0**	**19**	**0**	**0**	**0**	**1**	**0.0**	**0**	**0**	**0**	**0**	**0**	....	....	....	....	....	....	....	....
	Moncton Hawks	AHL	39	3	5	8	....	....	....	233	....	....	....	....	....	....	....	....	....	....	1	0	0	0	2	....	....	....
1994-95	Rochester Americans	AHL	22	0	2	2	....	....	....	93	....	....	....	....	....	....	....	....	....	....	....	....	....	....	....	....	....	....
	NHL Totals		**588**	**68**	**112**	**180**	**57**	**79**	**136**	**1672**	**0**	**4**	**7**	**611**	**11.1**	**261**	**6**	**312**	**19**		**98**	**11**	**18**	**29**	**281**	**0**	**0**	**1**

Transferred to **Pittsburgh** by **Hartford** with Pat Boutette as compensation for Hartford's signing of free agent Greg Malone, June 29, 1981 Traded to **Edmonton** by **Pittsburgh** with Pittsburgh's 2nd round choice (Emanuel Viveiros) in 1984 Entry Draft for Tom Roulston, December 5, 1983. Traded to **Detroit** by **Edmonton** with Jimmy Carson and Edmonton's 5th round choice (later traded to Montreal — Montreal selected Brad Layzell) in 1991 Entry Draft for Petr Klima, Joe Murphy, Adam Graves and Jeff Sharples, November 2, 1989. Signed as a free agent by **Toronto**, September 2, 1991. Traded to **Winnipeg** by **Toronto** for cash, August 12, 1993. Traded to **Buffalo** by **Winnipeg** for future considerations, July 8, 1994.

• McCORD, BOB

Bob McCord D – R. 6'1", 202 lbs. b: Matheson, Ont., 3/30/1934.

Season	Club	League	GP	G	A	Pts	AG	AA	APts	PIM	PP	SH	GW	S	%	TGF	PGF	TGA	PGA	+/–	GP	G	A	Pts	PIM	PP	SH	GW
1951-52	Porcupine Combines	Jr. B	STATISTICS NOT AVAILABLE																									
1952-53	Kitchener Greenshirts	OHA	23	3	7	10	....	....	....	14	....	....	....	....	....	....	....	....	....	....	....	....	....	....	....	....	....	....
	Montreal Jr. Canadiens	QJHL	21	0	4	4	....	....	....	10	....	....	....	....	....	....	....	....	....	....	7	2	3	5	6	....	....	....
1953-54	Montreal Jr. Canadiens	QJHL	49	11	20	31	....	....	....	84	....	....	....	....	....	....	....	....	....	....	8	5	4	9	20	....	....	....
	Montreal Royals	QHL	3	0	0	0	....	....	....	2	....	....	....	....	....	....	....	....	....	....	....	....	....	....	....	....	....	....
1954-55	Springfield Indians	AHL	62	5	18	23	....	....	....	32	....	....	....	....	....	....	....	....	....	....	4	1	1	2	4	....	....	....
1955-56	Springfield Indians	AHL	57	6	21	27	....	....	....	45	....	....	....	....	....	....	....	....	....	....	....	....	....	....	....	....	....	....
1956-57	Springfield Indians	AHL	59	10	21	31	....	....	....	53	....	....	....	....	....	....	....	....	....	....	....	....	....	....	....	....	....	....

			REGULAR SEASON																		PLAYOFFS							
Season	Club	League	GP	G	A	Pts	AG	AA	APts	PIM	PP	SH	GW	S	%	TGF	PGF	TGA	PGA	+/–	GP	G	A	Pts	PIM	PP	SH	GW
1957-58	Trois-Rivieres Lions	QHL	19	2	4	6	....	....	....	19	....	....	....	....	....	....	....	....	....	....	....	....	....	....	....	....	....	....
	Springfield Indians	AHL	41	0	5	5	....	....	....	38	....	....	....	....	....	....	....	....	....	....	....	....	....	....	....	....	....	....
1958-59	Springfield Indians	AHL	5	0	0	0	....	....	....	4	....	....	....	....	....	....	....	....	....	....	....	....	....	....	....	....	....	....
	Trois-Rivieres Lions	QHL	56	8	21	29	....	....	....	75	....	....	....	....	....	....	....	....	....	....	8	2	2	4	4	....	....	....
1959-60	Springfield Indians	AHL	70	11	28	39	....	....	....	114	....	....	....	....	....	....	....	....	....	....	9	0	2	2	8	....	....	....
1960-61	Springfield Indians	AHL	69	12	36	48	....	....	....	51	....	....	....	....	....	....	....	....	....	....	8	0	4	4	8	....	....	....
1961-62	Springfield Indians	AHL	66	8	29	37	....	....	....	62	....	....	....	....	....	....	....	....	....	....	11	0	5	5	16	....	....	....
1962-63	Springfield Indians	AHL	69	11	35	46	....	....	....	42	....	....	....	....	....	....	....	....	....	....	....	....	....	....	....	....	....	....
1963-64	**Boston Bruins**	**NHL**	**65**	**1**	**9**	**10**	**1**	**10**	**11**	**49**	....	....	....	....	....	....	....	....	....	....	....	....	....	....	....	....	....	....
1964-65	**Boston Bruins**	**NHL**	**43**	**0**	**6**	**6**	**0**	**6**	**6**	**26**	....	....	....	....	....	....	....	....	....	....	....	....	....	....	....	....	....	....
	Hershey Bears	AHL	24	3	7	10	....	....	....	16	....	....	....	....	....	....	....	....	....	....	15	1	6	7	44	....	....	....
1965-66	**Detroit Red Wings**	**NHL**	**9**	**0**	**2**	**2**	**0**	**2**	**2**	**16**	....	....	....	....	....	....	....	....	....	....	....	....	....	....	....	....	....	....
	Pittsburgh Hornets	AHL	62	7	26	33	....	....	....	54	....	....	....	....	....	....	....	....	....	....	3	0	0	0	7	....	....	....
1966-67	**Detroit Red Wings**	**NHL**	**14**	**1**	**2**	**3**	**1**	**2**	**3**	**27**	....	....	....	....	....	....	....	....	....	....	....	....	....	....	....	....	....	....
	Pittsburgh Hornets	AHL	61	8	26	34	....	....	....	40	....	....	....	....	....	....	....	....	....	....	9	2	4	6	2	....	....	....
1967-68	**Detroit Red Wings**	**NHL**	**3**	**0**	**0**	**0**	**0**	**0**	**0**	**2**	**0**	**0**	**0**	**1**	**0.0**	**2**	**0**	**6**	**1**	**–3**	....	....	....	....	....	....	....	....
	Minnesota North Stars	**NHL**	**70**	**3**	**9**	**12**	**4**	**9**	**13**	**39**	**0**	**0**	**0**	**97**	**3.1**	**68**	**1**	**98**	**21**	**–10**	**14**	**2**	**5**	**7**	**10**	**0**	**0**	**0**
1968-69	**Minnesota North Stars**	**NHL**	**69**	**4**	**17**	**21**	**4**	**16**	**20**	**70**	**1**	**0**	**0**	**85**	**4.7**	**55**	**4**	**99**	**15**	**–33**	....	....	....	....	....	....	....	....
1969-70	Phoenix Roadrunners	WHL	63	11	23	34	....	....	....	41	....	....	....	....	....	....	....	....	....	....	....	....	....	....	....	....	....	....
1970-71	Denver Spurs	WHL	71	7	38	45	....	....	....	54	....	....	....	....	....	....	....	....	....	....	5	1	1	2	2	....	....	....
1971-72	Denver Spurs	WHL	69	4	29	33	....	....	....	33	....	....	....	....	....	....	....	....	....	....	9	3	3	6	6	....	....	....
1972-73	**St. Louis Blues**	**NHL**	**43**	**1**	**13**	**14**	**1**	**11**	**12**	**33**	**0**	**0**	**0**	**41**	**2.4**	**41**	**2**	**51**	**7**	**–5**	....	....	....	....	....	....	....	....
	Denver Spurs	WHL	6	0	1	1	....	....	....	2	....	....	....	....	....	....	....	....	....	....	....	....	....	....	....	....	....	....
1973-74	Denver Spurs	WHL	32	6	12	18	....	....	....	8	....	....	....	....	....	....	....	....	....	....	....	....	....	....	....	....	....	....
1974-75	Denver Spurs	CHL	70	8	24	32	....	....	....	39	....	....	....	....	....	....	....	....	....	....	2	0	0	0	0	....	....	....
	NHL Totals		**316**	**10**	**58**	**68**	**11**	**56**	**67**	**262**	**1**	**0**	**0**	**224**	**4.5**	**166**	**7**	**254**	**44**		**14**	**2**	**5**	**7**	**10**	**0**	**0**	**0**

QHL Second All-Star Team (1959) • AHL Second All-Star Team (1960, 1962, 1963) • AHL First All-Star Team (1961, 1967) • Won Eddie Shore Award (Outstanding Defenseman - AHL) (1961, 1967) • WHL First All-Star Team (1972)

Traded to **Springfield** (AHL) by **Montreal** for Kelly Burnett, August, 1954. Traded to **Boston** by **Springfield** (AHL) for Bruce Gamble, Dale Rolfe, Terry Gray and Randy Miller, June, 1963. Traded to **Detroit** by **Boston** with Ab McDonald and Ken Stephanson for Albert Langlois, Ron Harris, Parker MacDonald and Bob Dillabough, May 31, 1965. Traded to **Minnesota** by **Detroit** with Duke Harris for Jean-Guy Talbot and Dave Richardson, October 19, 1967. Claimed by **Montreal** from **Minnesota** in Intra-League Draft, June 9, 1970. Traded to **Minnesota** by **Montreal** for cash, August, 1970. Traded to **St. Louis** (Denver-WHL) by **Minnesota** for cash, August, 1970.

• McCORD, DENNIS

Dennis McCord D – L. 5′10″, 190 lbs. b: Chatham, Ont., 7/28/1951. Vancouver's 8th choice, 115th overall, in 1972 Amateur Draft.

Season	Club	League	GP	G	A	Pts	AG	AA	APts	PIM	PP	SH	GW	S	%	TGF	PGF	TGA	PGA	+/–	GP	G	A	Pts	PIM	PP	SH	GW
1969-70	Kitchener Rangers	OHA	23	1	1	2	....	....	....	50	....	....	....	....	....	....	....	....	....	....	....	....	....	....	....	....	....	....
	Toronto Marlboros	OHA	14	1	2	3	....	....	....	34	....	....	....	....	....	....	....	....	....	....	....	....	....	....	....	....	....	....
1970-71	Chatham Maroons	SOJHL	STATISTICS NOT AVAILABLE																									
1971-72	London Knights	OHA	59	9	31	40	....	....	....	123	....	....	....	....	....	....	....	....	....	....	....	....	....	....	....	....	....	....
1972-73	Seattle Totems	WHL	71	5	23	28	....	....	....	100	....	....	....	....	....	....	....	....	....	....	....	....	....	....	....	....	....	....
1973-74	**Vancouver Canucks**	**NHL**	**3**	**0**	**0**	**0**	**0**	**0**	**0**	**6**	**0**	**0**	**0**	**2**	**0.0**	**1**	**0**	**1**	**0**	**0**	....	....	....	....	....	....	....	....
	Seattle Totems	WHL	74	4	33	37	....	....	....	57	....	....	....	....	....	....	....	....	....	....	....	....	....	....	....	....	....	....
1974-75	Seattle Totems	CHL	26	0	8	8	....	....	....	38	....	....	....	....	....	....	....	....	....	....	....	....	....	....	....	....	....	....
1975-76	Tulsa Oilers	CHL	9	2	5	7	....	....	....	6	....	....	....	....	....	....	....	....	....	....	....	....	....	....	....	....	....	....
	Fort Wayne Komets	IHL	59	6	17	23	....	....	....	57	....	....	....	....	....	....	....	....	....	....	9	1	4	5	26	....	....	....
	NHL Totals		**3**	**0**	**0**	**0**	**0**	**0**	**0**	**6**	**0**	**0**	**0**	**2**	**0.0**	**1**	**0**	**1**	**0**		....	....	....	....	....	....	....	....

• McCOSH, SHAWN

Shawn McCosh C – R. 6′, 197 lbs. b: Oshawa, Ont., 6/5/1969. Detroit's 5th choice, 95th overall, in 1989 Entry Draft.

Season	Club	League	GP	G	A	Pts	AG	AA	APts	PIM	PP	SH	GW	S	%	TGF	PGF	TGA	PGA	+/–	GP	G	A	Pts	PIM	PP	SH	GW
1986-87	Hamilton Steelhawks	OHL	50	11	17	28	....	....	....	49	....	....	....	....	....	....	....	....	....	....	6	1	0	1	2	....	....	....
1987-88	Hamilton Steelhawks	OHL	64	17	36	53	....	....	....	96	....	....	....	....	....	....	....	....	....	....	14	6	8	14	14	....	....	....
1988-89	Niagara Falls Thunder	OHL	56	41	62	103	....	....	....	75	....	....	....	....	....	....	....	....	....	....	14	4	13	17	23	....	....	....
1989-90	Niagara Falls Thunder	OHL	9	6	10	16	....	....	....	24	....	....	....	....	....	....	....	....	....	....	....	....	....	....	....	....	....	....
	Hamilton Steelhawks	OHL	39	24	28	52	....	....	....	65	....	....	....	....	....	....	....	....	....	....	....	....	....	....	....	....	....	....
1990-91	New Haven Nighthawks	AHL	66	16	21	37	....	....	....	104	....	....	....	....	....	....	....	....	....	....	....	....	....	....	....	....	....	....
1991-92	**Los Angeles Kings**	**NHL**	**4**	**0**	**0**	**0**	**0**	**0**	**0**	**4**	**0**	**0**	**0**	**2**	**0.0**	**0**	**0**	**0**	**0**	**0**	....	....	....	....	....	....	....	....
	Phoenix Roadrunners	IHL	71	21	32	53	....	....	....	118	....	....	....	....	....	....	....	....	....	....	....	....	....	....	....	....	....	....
	New Haven Nighthawks	AHL	....	....	....	....	....	....	....	....	....	....	....	....	....	....	....	....	....	....	5	0	1	1	0	....	....	....
1992-93	Phoenix Roadrunners	IHL	22	9	8	17	....	....	....	36	....	....	....	....	....	....	....	....	....	....	....	....	....	....	....	....	....	....
	New Haven Nighthawks	AHL	46	22	32	54	....	....	....	54	....	....	....	....	....	....	....	....	....	....	....	....	....	....	....	....	....	....
1993-94	Binghamton Rangers	AHL	75	31	44	75	....	....	....	68	....	....	....	....	....	....	....	....	....	....	....	....	....	....	....	....	....	....
1994-95	**New York Rangers**	**NHL**	**5**	**1**	**0**	**1**	**2**	**0**	**2**	**2**	**0**	**0**	**0**	**2**	**50.0**	**1**	**0**	**0**	**0**	**+1**	....	....	....	....	....	....	....	....
	Binghamton Rangers	AHL	67	23	60	83	....	....	....	73	....	....	....	....	....	....	....	....	....	....	8	3	9	12	6	....	....	....
1995-96	Hershey Bears	AHL	71	31	52	83	....	....	....	82	....	....	....	....	....	....	....	....	....	....	5	1	5	6	8	....	....	....
1996-97	Philadelphia Phantoms	AHL	79	30	51	81	....	....	....	110	....	....	....	....	....	....	....	....	....	....	10	3	9	12	23	....	....	....
1997-98	Philadelphia Phantoms	AHL	80	24	54	78	....	....	....	102	....	....	....	....	....	....	....	....	....	....	20	6	13	19	14	....	....	....
	NHL Totals		**9**	**1**	**0**	**1**	**2**	**0**	**2**	**6**	**0**	**0**	**0**	**4**	**25.0**	**1**	**0**	**0**	**0**		....	....	....	....	....	....	....	....

Traded to **LA Kings** by **Detroit** for LA Kings' 8th round choice (Justin Krall) in 1992 Entry Draft, August 15, 1990. Traded to **Ottawa** by **LA Kings** with Bob Kudelski for Marc Fortier and Jim Thomson, December 19, 1992. Signed as a free agent by **NY Rangers**, July 30, 1993. Signed as a free agent by **Philadelphia**, July 31, 1995.

• McCOURT, DALE

Dale "Chief" McCourt C – R. 5′10″, 180 lbs. b: Falconbridge, Ont., 1/26/1957. Detroit's 1st choice, 1st overall, in 1977 Amateur Draft.

Season	Club	League	GP	G	A	Pts	AG	AA	APts	PIM	PP	SH	GW	S	%	TGF	PGF	TGA	PGA	+/–	GP	G	A	Pts	PIM	PP	SH	GW
1972-73	Sudbury Wolves	OHA	26	6	11	17	....	....	....	0	....	....	....	....	....	....	....	....	....	....	....	....	....	....	....	....	....	....
1973-74	Hamilton Red Wings	OHA	69	20	38	58	....	....	....	45	....	....	....	....	....	....	....	....	....	....	....	....	....	....	....	....	....	....
1974-75	Hamilton Fincups	OHA	69	52	74	126	....	....	....	57	....	....	....	....	....	....	....	....	....	....	....	....	....	....	....	....	....	....
1975-76	Hamilton Fincups	OHA	66	55	84	139	....	....	....	19	....	....	....	....	....	....	....	....	....	....	14	20	8	28	12	....	....	....
1976-77	St. Catharines Fincups	OHA	66	60	79	139	....	....	....	26	....	....	....	....	....	....	....	....	....	....	14	7	13	20	6	....	....	....
	Canada	WJC-A	7	10	8	18	....	....	....	14	....	....	....	....	....	....	....	....	....	....	....	....	....	....	....	....	....	....
1977-78	**Detroit Red Wings**	**NHL**	**76**	**33**	**39**	**72**	**32**	**32**	**64**	**10**	**10**	**3**	**5**	**219**	**15.1**	**108**	**42**	**71**	**15**	**+10**	**7**	**4**	**2**	**6**	**2**	**2**	**0**	**0**
1978-79	**Detroit Red Wings**	**NHL**	**79**	**28**	**43**	**71**	**25**	**33**	**58**	**14**	**14**	**2**	**3**	**222**	**12.6**	**119**	**59**	**123**	**36**	**–27**	....	....	....	....	....	....	....	....
	Canada	WEC-A	7	0	1	1	....	....	....	6	....	....	....	....	....	....	....	....	....	....	....	....	....	....	....	....	....	....
1979-80	**Detroit Red Wings**	**NHL**	**80**	**30**	**51**	**81**	**27**	**39**	**66**	**12**	**7**	**2**	**3**	**200**	**15.0**	**122**	**34**	**120**	**33**	**+1**	....	....	....	....	....	....	....	....
1980-81	**Detroit Red Wings**	**NHL**	**80**	**30**	**56**	**86**	**25**	**39**	**64**	**50**	**11**	**2**	**2**	**286**	**10.5**	**128**	**46**	**140**	**41**	**–17**	....	....	....	....	....	....	....	....
	Canada	WEC-A	4	1	0	1	....	....	....	2	....	....	....	....	....	....	....	....	....	....	....	....	....	....	....	....	....	....
1981-82	**Detroit Red Wings**	**NHL**	**26**	**13**	**14**	**27**	**10**	**9**	**19**	**6**	**6**	**0**	**0**	**84**	**15.5**	**40**	**12**	**50**	**19**	**–3**	....	....	....	....	....	....	....	....
	Buffalo Sabres	**NHL**	**52**	**20**	**22**	**42**	**16**	**15**	**31**	**12**	**4**	**1**	**2**	**122**	**16.4**	**71**	**19**	**62**	**9**	**–1**	**4**	**2**	**3**	**5**	**0**	**1**	**0**	**0**
1982-83	**Buffalo Sabres**	**NHL**	**62**	**20**	**32**	**52**	**16**	**22**	**38**	**10**	**3**	**1**	**3**	**117**	**17.1**	**70**	**18**	**70**	**6**	**–12**	**10**	**3**	**2**	**5**	**4**	**2**	**0**	**1**
1983-84	**Buffalo Sabres**	**NHL**	**5**	**1**	**3**	**4**	**1**	**2**	**3**	**0**	**0**	**0**	**0**	**5**	**20.0**	**5**	**1**	**7**	**1**	**–2**	....	....	....	....	....	....	....	....
	Toronto Maple Leafs	**NHL**	**72**	**19**	**24**	**43**	**15**	**16**	**31**	**10**	**8**	**2**	**1**	**98**	**19.4**	**69**	**28**	**83**	**26**	**–16**	....	....	....	....	....	....	....	....
1984-85	Ambri Piotta	Switz. B	....	12	12	24	....	....	....	....	....	....	....	....	....	....	....	....	....	....	....	0	1	1	....	....	....	....
1985-86	Ambri Piotta	Switz. B	....	41	18	59	....	....	....	....	....	....	....	....	....	....	....	....	....	....	....	....	....	....	....	....	....	....
1986-87	Ambri Piotta	Switz. B	....	23	33	56	....	....	....	....	....	....	....	....	....	....	....	....	....	....	3	5	4	9	....	....	....	....
1987-88	Ambri Piotta	Switz.	....	32	20	52	....	....	....	....	....	....	....	....	....	....	....	....	....	....	4	6	5	11	....	....	....	....
1988-89	Ambri Piotta	Switz.	....	42	24	6	....	....	....	....	....	....	....	....	....	....	....	....	....	....	....	1	4	5	....	....	....	....
1989-90	Ambri Piotta	Switz.	....	18	26	44	....	....	....	....	....	....	....	....	....	....	....	....	....	....	2	0	0	0	0	....	....	....
1990-91	Ambri Piotta	Switz.	35	10	12	32	....	....	....	....	....	....	....	....	....	....	....	....	....	....	....	....	....	....	....	....	....	....
	NHL Totals		**532**	**194**	**284**	**478**	**167**	**207**	**374**	**124**	**63**	**13**	**19**	**1353**	**14.3**	**732**	**259**	**726**	**186**		**21**	**9**	**7**	**16**	**6**	**5**	**0**	**1**

OHA First All-Star Team (1976, 1977) • Memorial Cup All-Star Team (1976) • Won Stafford Smythe Memorial Trophy (Memorial Cup Tournament MVP) (1976) • WJC-A All-Star Team (1977) • Canadian Major Junior Player of the Year (1977)

Rights transferred to **LA Kings** by **Detroit** as compensation for Detroit's signing of free agent Rogie Vachon, August 8, 1978. McCourt remained property of Detroit pending result of litigation hearing. Rights traded to **Detroit** by **LA Kings** for Andre St. Laurent and Detroit's 1st round choices in 1980 (Larry Murphy) and 1981 (Doug Smith) Entry Drafts, August 22, 1979. Traded to **Buffalo** by **Detroit** with Mike Foligno and Brent Peterson for Danny Gare, Jim Schoenfeld and Derek Smith, December 2, 1981. Signed as a free agent by **Toronto**, October 22, 1983.

● McCREARY, BILL JR. Bill Jr. McCreary RW – R. 6', 190 lbs. b: Springfield, MA, 4/15/1960. Toronto's 5th choice, 114th overall, in 1979 Entry Draft.

			REGULAR SEASON																		PLAYOFFS							
Season	Club	League	GP	G	A	Pts	AG	AA	APts	PIM	PP	SH	GW	S	%	TGF	PGF	TGA	PGA	+/–	GP	G	A	Pts	PIM	PP	SH	GW
1978-79	Colgate University	ECAC	24	19	25	44				70																		
1979-80	Colgate University	ECAC	12	7	13	20				44																		
1980-81	**Toronto Maple Leafs**	**NHL**	**12**	**1**	**0**	**1**	**1**	**0**	**1**	**4**	**0**	**0**	**0**	**7**	**14.3**	**3**	**0**	**9**	**0**	**–6**								
	New Brunswick Hawks	AHL	61	19	24	43				120											12	2	0	2	13			
1981-82	Cincinnati Tigers	CHL	69	8	27	35				61											4	0	4	4	2			
1982-83	Saginaw Gears	IHL	60	19	28	47				17																		
	Peoria Prancers	IHL	16	4	6	10				11																		
	St. Catharines Saints	AHL	4	0	1	1				2																		
1983-84	Milwaukee Admirals	IHL	81	28	35	63				44											4	0	2	2	2			
1984-85	Milwaukee Admirals	IHL	10	1	0	1				4																		
1985-86	Milwaukee Admirals	IHL	80	30	31	61				83											5	3	0	3	6			
1986-87	Milwaukee Admirals	IHL	74	30	35	65				64											6	2	2	4	10			
1987-88	Milwaukee Admirals	IHL	67	23	30	53				51																		
	NHL Totals		**12**	**1**	**0**	**1**	**1**	**0**	**1**	**4**	**0**	**0**	**0**	**7**	**14.3**	**3**	**0**	**9**	**0**									

● McCREARY, BILL SR. Bill Sr. McCreary LW – L. 5'10", 172 lbs. b: Sundridge, Ont., 12/2/1934.

			REGULAR SEASON																		PLAYOFFS							
Season	Club	League	GP	G	A	Pts	AG	AA	APts	PIM	PP	SH	GW	S	%	TGF	PGF	TGA	PGA	+/–	GP	G	A	Pts	PIM	PP	SH	GW
1951-52	Guelph Biltmores	OHA	52	30	28	58				12											23	9	14	23	10			
1952-53	Guelph Biltmores	OHA	50	32	25	57				31																		
	Toronto Marlboros	OHA																			7	2	3	5	2			
1953-54	Guelph Biltmores	OHA	59	35	49	84				57											3	0	3	3	4			
	New York Rangers	**NHL**	**2**	**0**	**0**	**0**	**0**	**0**	**0**	**2**																		
1954-55	Guelph Biltmores	OHA	48	46	37	83				38											6	4	3	7	2			
	New York Rangers	**NHL**	**8**	**0**	**2**	**2**	**0**	**3**	**3**	**0**																		
1955-56	Providence Reds	AHL	37	8	13	21				18																		
	Saskatoon Quakers	WHL	25	12	20	32				45											3	0	0	0	0			
1956-57	Edmonton Flyers	WHL	69	33	26	59				37											8	2	7	9	4			
1957-58	**Detroit Red Wings**	**NHL**	**3**	**1**	**0**	**1**	**1**	**0**	**1**	**2**																		
	Edmonton Flyers	WHL	21	7	7	14				10											5	2	1	3	2			
	Hershey Bears	AHL	31	4	9	13				6																		
1958-59	Springfield Indians	AHL	65	14	34	48				22																		
1959-60	Springfield Indians	AHL	69	19	31	50				16											10	6	4	10	6			
1960-61	Springfield Indians	AHL	72	33	54	87				26											8	*5	4	9	6			
1961-62	Springfield Indians	AHL	69	27	49	76				49											2	0	2	2	0			
1962-63	**Montreal Canadiens**	**NHL**	**14**	**2**	**3**	**5**	**2**	**3**	**5**	**0**																		
	Hull-Ottawa Canadiens	EPHL	46	15	32	47				22																		
1963-64	Omaha Knights	CHL	72	24	51	75				56											3	1	0	1	2			
1964-65	Omaha Knights	CHL	70	24	44	68				48											6	0	3	3	0			
1965-66	Houston Apollos	CHL	70	26	26	52				44																		
1966-67	Houston Apollos	CHL	56	22	34	56				34											6	1	2	3	0			
1967-68	**St. Louis Blues**	**NHL**	**70**	**13**	**13**	**26**	**16**	**14**	**30**	**22**	**2**	**4**	**2**	**154**	**8.4**	**42**	**9**	**41**	**10**	**+2**	**15**	**3**	**2**	**5**	**0**	**0**	**2**	**2**
1968-69	**St. Louis Blues**	**NHL**	**71**	**13**	**17**	**30**	**15**	**16**	**31**	**50**	**3**	**1**	**4**	**130**	**10.0**	**41**	**6**	**46**	**15**	**+4**	**12**	**1**	**5**	**6**	**14**	**1**	**1**	**0**
1969-70	**St. Louis Blues**	**NHL**	**73**	**15**	**17**	**32**	**17**	**17**	**34**	**16**	**2**	**1**	**1**	**174**	**8.6**	**5**	**15**	**56**	**23**	**–13**	**16**	**1**	**7**	**8**	**0**	**0**	**0**	**0**
1970-71	**St. Louis Blues**	**NHL**	**68**	**9**	**10**	**19**	**9**	**9**	**18**	**16**	**0**	**3**	**0**	**90**	**10.0**	**30**	**4**	**39**	**20**	**+7**	**6**	**1**	**2**	**3**	**0**	**0**	**0**	**0**
	NHL Totals		**309**	**53**	**62**	**115**	**60**	**62**	**122**	**108**	**7**	**9**	**7**	**548**	**9.7**	**118**	**34**	**182**	**68**		**48**	**6**	**16**	**22**	**14**	**1**	**3**	**2**

WHL Prairie Division Second All-Star Team (1957) • CHL First All-Star Team (1964, 1966)

Claimed by **Detroit** from **NY Rangers** in Intra-League Draft, June 5, 1956. Traded to **Springfield** (AHL) by **Detroit** with Denis Olson and Hank Bassen for Gerry Ehman, April, 1958. Traded to **Montreal** by **Springfield** (AHL) for Bob McCammon, Andre Tardiff and Norm Waslowski, October 25, 1962. Traded to **St. Louis** by **Montreal** for Claude Cardin and Phil Obendorf, June 14, 1967.

● McCREARY, KEITH Keith McCreary RW – L. 5'10", 180 lbs. b: Sundridge, Ont., 6/19/1940.

			REGULAR SEASON																		PLAYOFFS							
Season	Club	League	GP	G	A	Pts	AG	AA	APts	PIM	PP	SH	GW	S	%	TGF	PGF	TGA	PGA	+/–	GP	G	A	Pts	PIM	PP	SH	GW
1956-57	Peterborough Petes	OHA	22	0	1	1				0																		
1957-58	Sundridge Beavers	Jr. B	STATISTICS NOT AVAILABLE																									
1958-59	Hull-Ottawa Jr. Canadiens	Ott-Jr.	STATISTICS NOT AVAILABLE																									
	Hull-Ottawa Jr. Canadiens	EOHL	3	1	0	1				0																		
1959-60	Hull-Ottawa Jr. Canadiens	Ott-Jr.																										
	Hull-Ottawa Jr. Canadiens	EPHL	5	0	0	0				0																		
1960-61	Hull-Ottawa Canadiens	EPHL	61	19	21	40				35											14	4	2	6	15			
1961-62	Hull-Ottawa Canadiens	EPHL	64	30	36	66				48											12	5	8	13	2			
	Montreal Canadiens	**NHL**																			**1**	**0**	**0**	**0**	**0**			
1962-63	Hull-Ottawa Canadiens	EPHL	69	27	34	61				44											3	1	1	2	0			
1963-64	Hershey Bears	AHL	66	25	19	44				21											6	2	4	6	2			
1964-65	**Montreal Canadiens**	**NHL**	**9**	**0**	**3**	**3**	**0**	**3**	**3**	**4**																		
	Hershey Bears	AHL	46	16	18	34				36											14	0	7	7	24			
1965-66	Cleveland Barons	AHL	66	18	24	42				42											12	5	4	9	8			
1966-67	Cleveland Barons	AHL	70	28	29	57				50											5	1	2	3	0			
1967-68	**Pittsburgh Penguins**	**NHL**	**70**	**14**	**12**	**26**	**17**	**13**	**30**	**44**	**0**	**0**	**1**	**133**	**10.5**	**45**	**3**	**50**	**5**	**–3**								
1968-69	**Pittsburgh Penguins**	**NHL**	**70**	**25**	**23**	**48**	**28**	**22**	**50**	**42**	**7**	**0**	**4**	**208**	**12.0**	**67**	**23**	**68**	**1**	**–23**								
1969-70	**Pittsburgh Penguins**	**NHL**	**60**	**18**	**8**	**26**	**21**	**8**	**29**	**67**	**4**	**0**	**2**	**134**	**13.4**	**35**	**8**	**33**	**0**	**–6**	**10**	**0**	**4**	**4**	**4**	**0**	**0**	**0**
1970-71	**Pittsburgh Penguins**	**NHL**	**59**	**21**	**12**	**33**	**22**	**11**	**33**	**24**	**3**	**0**	**3**	**116**	**18.1**	**56**	**9**	**41**	**1**	**+7**								
1971-72	**Pittsburgh Penguins**	**NHL**	**33**	**4**	**4**	**8**	**4**	**4**	**8**	**22**	**0**	**0**	**0**	**68**	**5.9**	**13**	**2**	**21**	**0**	**–10**	**1**	**0**	**0**	**0**	**2**	**0**	**0**	**0**
1972-73	**Atlanta Flames**	**NHL**	**77**	**20**	**21**	**41**	**20**	**18**	**38**	**21**	**9**	**0**	**3**	**157**	**12.7**	**53**	**13**	**69**	**7**	**–22**								
1973-74	**Atlanta Flames**	**NHL**	**76**	**18**	**19**	**37**	**18**	**16**	**34**	**62**	**2**	**0**	**4**	**109**	**16.5**	**53**	**3**	**58**	**2**	**–6**	**4**	**0**	**0**	**0**	**0**	**0**	**0**	**0**
1974-75	**Atlanta Flames**	**NHL**	**78**	**11**	**10**	**21**	**10**	**8**	**18**	**8**	**2**	**2**	**2**	**79**	**13.9**	**43**	**5**	**55**	**29**	**+12**								
	NHL Totals		**532**	**131**	**112**	**243**	**140**	**103**	**243**	**294**	**27**	**2**	**19**	**1004**	**13.0**	**365**	**66**	**395**	**45**		**16**	**0**	**4**	**4**	**6**	**0**	**0**	**0**

Claimed by **Pittsburgh** from **Montreal** in Expansion Draft, June 6, 1967. Claimed by **Atlanta** from **Pittsburgh** in Expansion Draft, June 6, 1972.

● McCRIMMON, BRAD Brad McCrimmon D – L. 5'11", 197 lbs. b: Dodsland, Sask., 3/29/1959. Boston's 2nd choice, 15th overall, in 1979 Entry Draft.

			REGULAR SEASON																		PLAYOFFS							
Season	Club	League	GP	G	A	Pts	AG	AA	APts	PIM	PP	SH	GW	S	%	TGF	PGF	TGA	PGA	+/–	GP	G	A	Pts	PIM	PP	SH	GW
1977-78	Brandon Wheat Kings	WCJHL	65	19	78	97				245											8	2	11	13	20			
	Canada	WJC-A	6	0	2	2				4																		
1978-79	Brandon Wheat Kings	WHL	66	24	74	98				139											22	9	19	28	34			
	Canada	WJC-A	5	1	2	3				2																		
1979-80	**Boston Bruins**	**NHL**	**72**	**5**	**11**	**16**	**5**	**8**	**13**	**94**	**1**	**0**	**1**	**89**	**5.6**	**67**	**1**	**80**	**11**	**–3**	**10**	**1**	**1**	**2**	**28**	**0**	**0**	**0**
1980-81	**Boston Bruins**	**NHL**	**78**	**11**	**18**	**29**	**9**	**13**	**22**	**148**	**1**	**0**	**1**	**113**	**9.7**	**91**	**4**	**94**	**34**	**+27**	**3**	**0**	**1**	**1**	**2**	**0**	**0**	**0**
1981-82	**Boston Bruins**	**NHL**	**70**	**1**	**8**	**9**	**1**	**5**	**6**	**83**	**0**	**0**	**0**	**136**	**0.7**	**89**	**1**	**95**	**11**	**+4**	**2**	**0**	**0**	**0**	**2**	**0**	**0**	**0**
1982-83	**Philadelphia Flyers**	**NHL**	**79**	**4**	**21**	**25**	**3**	**14**	**17**	**61**	**1**	**0**	**1**	**107**	**3.7**	**86**	**9**	**77**	**24**	**+24**	**3**	**0**	**0**	**0**	**4**	**0**	**0**	**0**
1983-84	**Philadelphia Flyers**	**NHL**	**71**	**0**	**24**	**24**	**0**	**16**	**16**	**76**	**0**	**0**	**0**	**106**	**0.0**	**89**	**10**	**93**	**33**	**+19**	**1**	**0**	**0**	**0**	**4**	**0**	**0**	**0**
1984-85	**Philadelphia Flyers**	**NHL**	**66**	**8**	**35**	**43**	**7**	**24**	**31**	**81**	**1**	**0**	**1**	**141**	**5.7**	**137**	**27**	**84**	**26**	**+52**	**11**	**2**	**1**	**3**	**15**	**0**	**0**	**0**
1985-86	**Philadelphia Flyers**	**NHL**	**80**	**13**	**43**	**56**	**10**	**29**	**39**	**85**	**2**	**0**	**2**	**162**	**8.0**	**176**	**34**	**93**	**34**	**+83**	**5**	**2**	**0**	**2**	**2**	**0**	**0**	**1**
1986-87	**Philadelphia Flyers**	**NHL**	**71**	**10**	**29**	**39**	**9**	**21**	**30**	**52**	**3**	**2**	**4**	**110**	**9.1**	**123**	**25**	**82**	**30**	**+46**	**26**	**3**	**5**	**8**	**30**	**1**	**0**	**1**
1987-88	**Calgary Flames**	**NHL**	**80**	**7**	**35**	**42**	**6**	**25**	**31**	**98**	**1**	**3**	**2**	**102**	**6.9**	**130**	**16**	**100**	**34**	**+48**	**9**	**2**	**3**	**5**	**22**	**2**	**0**	**0**
1988-89	**Calgary Flames**	**NHL**	**72**	**5**	**17**	**22**	**4**	**12**	**16**	**96**	**2**	**1**	**2**	**78**	**6.4**	**88**	**8**	**60**	**31**	**+43**	**22**	**0**	**3**	**3**	**30**	**0**	**0**	**0**
1989-90	Calgary Flames	FrTour	4	0	1	1				2																		
	Calgary Flames	**NHL**	**79**	**4**	**15**	**19**	**3**	**11**	**14**	**78**	**0**	**0**	**0**	**97**	**4.1**	**83**	**4**	**75**	**14**	**+18**	**6**	**0**	**2**	**2**	**8**	**0**	**0**	**0**
1990-91	**Detroit Red Wings**	**NHL**	**64**	**0**	**13**	**13**	**0**	**10**	**10**	**81**	**0**	**0**	**0**	**43**	**0.0**	**62**	**4**	**81**	**30**	**+7**	**7**	**1**	**1**	**2**	**21**	**0**	**0**	**0**
1991-92	**Detroit Red Wings**	**NHL**	**79**	**7**	**22**	**29**	**6**	**17**	**23**	**118**	**2**	**1**	**1**	**94**	**7.4**	**97**	**15**	**78**	**35**	**+39**	**11**	**0**	**1**	**1**	**8**	**0**	**0**	**0**
1992-93	**Detroit Red Wings**	**NHL**	**60**	**1**	**14**	**15**	**1**	**10**	**11**	**71**	**1**	**0**	**0**	**53**	**1.9**	**65**	**11**	**50**	**17**	**+21**								
1993-94	**Hartford Whalers**	**NHL**	**65**	**1**	**5**	**6**	**1**	**4**	**5**	**72**	**0**	**0**	**0**	**39**	**2.6**	**30**	**2**	**60**	**25**	**–7**								

			REGULAR SEASON																		PLAYOFFS							
Season	Club	League	GP	G	A	Pts	AG	AA	APts	PIM	PP	SH	GW	S	%	TGF	PGF	TGA	PGA	+/–	GP	G	A	Pts	PIM	PP	SH	GW
1994-95	**Hartford Whalers**	**NHL**	**33**	**0**	**1**	**1**	**0**	**1**	**1**	**42**	**0**	**0**	**0**	**13**	**0.0**	**17**	**1**	**18**	**9**	**+7**	....	....	....	....	....	....	....	....
1995-96	**Hartford Whalers**	**NHL**	**58**	**3**	**6**	**9**	**3**	**5**	**8**	**62**	**0**	**1**	**0**	**39**	**7.7**	**45**	**1**	**43**	**14**	**+15**	....	....	....	....	....	....	....	....
1996-97	**Phoenix Coyotes**	**NHL**	**37**	**1**	**5**	**6**	**1**	**4**	**5**	**18**	**0**	**0**	**0**	**28**	**3.6**	**21**	**0**	**23**	**4**	**+2**	....	....	....	....	....	....	....	....
	NHL Totals		**1222**	**81**	**322**	**403**	**69**	**229**	**298**	**1416**	**15**	**8**	**15**	**1550**	**5.2**	**1496**	**173**	**1294**	**415**		**116**	**11**	**18**	**29**	**176**	**3**	**0**	**2**

WHL First All-Star Team (1978, 1979) • NHL Second All-Star Team (1988) • NHL Plus/Minus Leader (1988)

Played in NHL All-Star Game (1988)

Traded to **Philadelphia** by **Boston** for Pete Peeters, June 9, 1982. Traded to **Calgary** by **Philadelphia** for Calgary's 3rd round choice (Dominic Roussel) in 1988 Entry Draft and 1st round choice (later traded to Toronto — Toronto selected Steve Bancroft) in 1989 Entry Draft, August 26, 1987. Traded to **Detroit** by **Calgary** for Detroit's 2nd round choice (later traded to New Jersey — New Jersey selected David Harlock) in 1990 Entry Draft, June 15, 1990. Traded to **Hartford** by **Detroit** for Detroit's 6th round choice (previously acquired, Detroit selected Tim Spitzig) in 1993 Entry Draft, June 1, 1993. Signed as a free agent by **Phoenix**, July 16, 1996.

• McCRIMMON, JIM

Jim McCrimmon D – R. 6'1", 210 lbs. b: Ponska, Ont., 5/29/1953. Los Angeles' 2nd choice, 54th overall, in 1973 Amateur Draft.

Season	Club	League	GP	G	A	Pts	AG	AA	APts	PIM	PP	SH	GW	S	%	TGF	PGF	TGA	PGA	+/–	GP	G	A	Pts	PIM	PP	SH	GW
1969-70	Ponoka Stampeders	AJHL	41	3	12	15	....	....	....	91	....	....	....	....	....	....	....	....	....	....	....	....	....	....	....	....	....	....
1970-71	Ponoka Stampeders	AJHL	10	0	3	3	....	....	....	8	....	....	....	....	....	....	....	....	....	....	....	....	....	....	....	....	....	....
	Medicine Hat Tigers	WCJHL	52	1	4	5	....	....	....	89	....	....	....	....	....	....	....	....	....	....	....	....	....	....	....	....	....	....
1971-72	Medicine Hat Tigers	WCJHL	53	3	20	23	....	....	....	270	....	....	....	....	....	....	....	....	....	....	....	....	....	....	....	....	....	....
1972-73	Medicine Hat Tigers	WCJHL	54	7	30	37	....	....	....	179	....	....	....	....	....	....	....	....	....	....	....	....	....	....	....	....	....	....
1973-74	Edmonton Oilers	WHA	75	2	3	5	....	....	....	106	....	....	....	....	....	....	....	....	....	....	....	....	....	....	....	....	....	....
1974-75	Edmonton Oilers	WHA	34	1	5	6	....	....	....	50	....	....	....	....	....	....	....	....	....	....	....	....	....	....	....	....	....	....
	Winston-Salem Polar Bears	SHL	21	8	13	21	....	....	....	64	....	....	....	....	....	....	....	....	....	....	....	....	....	....	....	....	....	....
	St. Louis Blues	**NHL**	**2**	**0**	**0**	**0**	**0**	**0**	**0**	**0**	**0**	**0**	**0**	**0**	**0.0**	**0**	**0**	**0**	**0**	**0**	....	....	....	....	....	....	....	....
1975-76	Providence Reds	AHL	47	1	9	10	....	....	....	94	....	....	....	....	....	....	....	....	....	....	....	....	....	....	....	....	....	....
	Calgary Cowboys	WHA	5	0	0	0	....	....	....	0	....	....	....	....	....	....	....	....	....	....	....	....	....	....	....	....	....	....
	Baltimore Clippers	AHL	9	1	0	1	....	....	....	6	....	....	....	....	....	....	....	....	....	....	....	....	....	....	....	....	....	....
1976-77	Richmond Wildcats	SHL	33	6	18	24	....	....	....	58	....	....	....	....	....	....	....	....	....	....	....	....	....	....	....	....	....	....
	Mohawk Valley Comets	NAHL	13	0	5	5	....	....	....	14	....	....	....	....	....	....	....	....	....	....	....	....	....	....	....	....	....	....
1977-78	Kimberly Dynamiters	WIHL	40	9	28	37	....	....	....	68	....	....	....	....	....	....	....	....	....	....	....	....	....	....	....	....	....	....
	NHL Totals		**2**	**0**	**0**	**0**	**0**	**0**	**0**	**0**	**0**	**0**	**0**	**0**	**0.0**	**0**	**0**	**0**	**0**		....	....	....	....	....	....	....	....
	Other Major League Totals		109	3	8	11	....	....	....	156	....	....	....	....	....	....	....	....	....		....	....	....	....	....	....	....	....

Selected by **Edmonton** (WHA) in 1973 WHA Amateur Draft, May, 1973. Traded to **St. Louis** by **LA Kings** for cash, March, 1975. Signed as a free agent by **Calgary** (WHA) after being released by **St. Louis**, March 5, 1975.

• McCUTCHEON, BRIAN

Brian "Boom-Boom" McCutcheon LW – L. 5'10", 180 lbs. b: Toronto, Ont., 8/3/1949.

Season	Club	League	GP	G	A	Pts	AG	AA	APts	PIM	PP	SH	GW	S	%	TGF	PGF	TGA	PGA	+/–	GP	G	A	Pts	PIM	PP	SH	GW
1968-69	Cornell University	ECAC	28	17	22	39	....	....	....	....	....	....	....	....	....	....	....	....	....	....	....	....	....	....	....	....	....	....
1969-70	Cornell University	ECAC	29	25	21	46	....	....	....	....	....	....	....	....	....	....	....	....	....	....	....	....	....	....	....	....	....	....
1970-71	Cornell University	ECAC	27	17	24	41	....	....	....	50	....	....	....	....	....	....	....	....	....	....	....	....	....	....	....	....	....	....
1971-72	Fort Worth Wings	CHL	13	0	1	1	....	....	....	9	....	....	....	....	....	....	....	....	....	....	....	....	....	....	....	....	....	....
	Tidewater Wings	AHL	18	1	1	2	....	....	....	2	....	....	....	....	....	....	....	....	....	....	....	....	....	....	....	....	....	....
	Port Huron Wings	IHL	14	2	2	4	....	....	....	0	....	....	....	....	....	....	....	....	....	....	....	....	....	....	....	....	....	....
1972-73	Tidewater Lions	AHL	68	23	19	42	....	....	....	64	....	....	....	....	....	....	....	....	....	....	13	3	1	4	7	....	....	....
1973-74	London Lions	Britain	71	47	28	75	....	....	....	75	....	....	....	....	....	....	....	....	....	....	....	....	....	....	....	....	....	....
1974-75	Virginia Wings	AHL	30	12	9	21	....	....	....	24	....	....	....	....	....	....	....	....	....	....	....	....	....	....	....	....	....	....
	Detroit Red Wings	**NHL**	**17**	**3**	**1**	**4**	**3**	**1**	**4**	**2**	**0**	**0**	**0**	**15**	**20.0**	**5**	**0**	**8**	**0**	**–3**	....	....	....	....	....	....	....	....
1975-76	**Detroit Red Wings**	**NHL**	**8**	**0**	**0**	**0**	**0**	**0**	**0**	**5**	**0**	**0**	**0**	**4**	**0.0**	**0**	**0**	**5**	**3**	**–2**	....	....	....	....	....	....	....	....
	New Haven Nighthawks	AHL	58	27	19	46	....	....	....	22	....	....	....	....	....	....	....	....	....	....	....	....	....	....	....	....	....	....
1976-77	**Detroit Red Wings**	**NHL**	**12**	**0**	**0**	**0**	**0**	**0**	**0**	**0**	**0**	**0**	**0**	**1**	**0.0**	**0**	**0**	**1**	**1**	**0**	....	....	....	....	....	....	....	....
	Kansas City Blues	CHL	27	11	8	19	....	....	....	12	....	....	....	....	....	....	....	....	....	....	....	....	....	....	....	....	....	....
1977-78	Kansas City Red Wings	CHL	60	17	16	33	....	....	....	27	....	....	....	....	....	....	....	....	....	....	....	....	....	....	....	....	....	....
	NHL Totals		**37**	**3**	**1**	**4**	**3**	**1**	**4**	**7**	**0**	**0**	**0**	**20**	**15.0**	**5**	**0**	**14**	**4**		....	....	....	....	....	....	....	....

ECAC Second All-Star Team (1971)

Signed as a free agent by **Detroit**, September 29, 1971.

• McCUTCHEON, DARWIN

Darwin McCutcheon D – L. 6'4", 190 lbs. b: Listowel, Ont., 4/19/1962. Toronto's 9th choice, 179th overall, in 1980 Entry Draft.

Season	Club	League	GP	G	A	Pts	AG	AA	APts	PIM	PP	SH	GW	S	%	TGF	PGF	TGA	PGA	+/–	GP	G	A	Pts	PIM	PP	SH	GW
1979-80	Kitchener Rangers	OHA	28	0	3	3	....	....	....	30	....	....	....	....	....	....	....	....	....	....	....	....	....	....	....	....	....	....
	Toronto Marlboros	OHA	18	0	1	1	....	....	....	2	....	....	....	....	....	....	....	....	....	....	....	....	....	....	....	....	....	....
1980-81	Windsor Spitfires	OHA	26	1	7	8	....	....	....	36	....	....	....	....	....	....	....	....	....	....	....	....	....	....	....	....	....	....
	Toronto Marlboros	OHA	38	1	3	4	....	....	....	50	....	....	....	....	....	....	....	....	....	....	....	....	....	....	....	....	....	....
1981-82	Windsor Spitfires	OHA	67	5	24	29	....	....	....	141	....	....	....	....	....	....	....	....	....	....	9	1	3	4	24	....	....	....
	Toronto Maple Leafs	**NHL**	**1**	**0**	**0**	**0**	**0**	**0**	**0**	**2**	**0**	**0**	**0**	**0**	**0.0**	**0**	**0**	**1**	**0**	**–1**	....	....	....	....	....	....	....	....
1982-83	Kitchener Rangers	OHL	11	4	7	11	....	....	....	25	....	....	....	....	....	....	....	....	....	....	....	....	....	....	....	....	....	....
	University of P.E.I.	AUAA	9	1	6	7	....	....	....	26	....	....	....	....	....	....	....	....	....	....	....	....	....	....	....	....	....	....
1983-84	University of P.E.I.	AUAA	24	4	13	17	....	....	....	25	....	....	....	....	....	....	....	....	....	....	....	....	....	....	....	....	....	....
1984-85	University of P.E.I.	AUAA	24	5	30	35	....	....	....	73	....	....	....	....	....	....	....	....	....	....	7	0	0	0	4	....	....	....
1985-86	University of P.E.I.	AUAA	24	4	21	25	....	....	....	55	....	....	....	....	....	....	....	....	....	....	....	....	....	....	....	....	....	....
	Moncton Golden Flames	AHL	12	0	2	2	....	....	....	30	....	....	....	....	....	....	....	....	....	....	9	0	0	0	9	....	....	....
1986-87	Moncton Golden Flames	AHL	69	1	10	11	....	....	....	187	....	....	....	....	....	....	....	....	....	....	4	0	1	1	51	....	....	....
1987-88	Salt Lake Golden Eagles	IHL	64	2	8	10	....	....	....	150	....	....	....	....	....	....	....	....	....	....	13	0	2	2	94	....	....	....
1988-89	Flint Spirits	IHL	37	2	4	6	....	....	....	89	....	....	....	....	....	....	....	....	....	....	....	....	....	....	....	....	....	....
	Indianapolis Ice	IHL	34	2	6	8	....	....	....	99	....	....	....	....	....	....	....	....	....	....	....	....	....	....	....	....	....	....
1989-90	Charlottetown Islanders	PEI Sr.	10	0	1	1	....	....	....	4	....	....	....	....	....	....	....	....	....	....	....	....	....	....	....	....	....	....
1990-91	Charlottetown Islanders	PEI Sr.	20	5	20	25	....	....	....	85	....	....	....	....	....	....	....	....	....	....	....	....	....	....	....	....	....	....
	NHL Totals		**1**	**0**	**0**	**0**	**0**	**0**	**0**	**2**	**0**	**0**	**0**	**0**	**0.0**	**0**	**0**	**1**	**0**		....	....	....	....	....	....	....	....

Signed as a free agent by **Calgary**, March 10, 1986.

• McDILL, JEFF

Jeff McDill RW – R. 5'11", 190 lbs. b: Thunder Bay, Ont., 3/16/1956. Chicago's 2nd choice, 27th overall, in 1976 Amateur Draft.

Season	Club	League	GP	G	A	Pts	AG	AA	APts	PIM	PP	SH	GW	S	%	TGF	PGF	TGA	PGA	+/–	GP	G	A	Pts	PIM	PP	SH	GW
1972-73	Dauphin Kings	MJHL	48	16	17	33	....	....	....	143	....	....	....	....	....	....	....	....	....	....	....	....	....	....	....	....	....	....
1973-74	Flin Flon Bombers	WCJHL	66	22	14	36	....	....	....	86	....	....	....	....	....	....	....	....	....	....	....	....	....	....	....	....	....	....
1974-75	Flin Flon Bombers	WCJHL	46	24	44	68	....	....	....	75	....	....	....	....	....	....	....	....	....	....	....	....	....	....	....	....	....	....
1975-76	Victoria Cougars	WHL	72	55	66	121	....	....	....	197	....	....	....	....	....	....	....	....	....	....	....	....	....	....	....	....	....	....
1976-77	**Chicago Black Hawks**	**NHL**	**1**	**0**	**0**	**0**	**0**	**0**	**0**	**0**	**0**	**0**	**0**	**0**	**0.0**	**0**	**0**	**0**	**0**	**0**	....	....	....	....	....	....	....	....
	Flint Generals	IHL	74	31	39	70	....	....	....	42	....	....	....	....	....	....	....	....	....	....	5	0	1	1	5	....	....	....
	Dallas Black Hawks	CHL	1	0	0	0	....	....	....	0	....	....	....	....	....	....	....	....	....	....	....	....	....	....	....	....	....	....
1977-78	Kalamazoo Wings	IHL	14	1	5	6	....	....	....	20	....	....	....	....	....	....	....	....	....	....	....	....	....	....	....	....	....	....
	Muskegon Mohawks	IHL	47	18	25	43	....	....	....	28	....	....	....	....	....	....	....	....	....	....	6	1	4	5	0	....	....	....
	Maine Mariners	AHL	4	1	1	2	....	....	....	5	....	....	....	....	....	....	....	....	....	....	....	....	....	....	....	....	....	....
1978-79	New Haven Nighthawks	AHL	71	24	26	50	....	....	....	75	....	....	....	....	....	....	....	....	....	....	10	5	7	12	12	....	....	....
1979-80	New Haven Nighthawks	AHL	75	27	36	63	....	....	....	61	....	....	....	....	....	....	....	....	....	....	10	5	0	5	20	....	....	....
	NHL Totals		**1**	**0**	**0**	**0**	**0**	**0**	**0**	**0**	**0**	**0**	**0**	**0**	**0.0**	**0**	**0**	**0**	**0**		....	....	....	....	....	....	....	....

Signed as a free agent by **NY Rangers**, October 13, 1978.

• McDONALD, AB

Ab (Alvin) McDonald LW – L. 6'3", 192 lbs. b: Winnipeg, Man., 2/18/1936.

Season	Club	League	GP	G	A	Pts	AG	AA	APts	PIM	PP	SH	GW	S	%	TGF	PGF	TGA	PGA	+/–	GP	G	A	Pts	PIM	PP	SH	GW
1951-52	St. Boniface Canadians	MJHL	20	*20	15	*35	....	....	....	....	....	....	....	....	....	....	....	....	....	....	17	11	12	23	6	....	....	....
1952-53	St. Boniface Canadians	MJHL	35	26	24	50	....	....	....	0	....	....	....	....	....	....	....	....	....	....	25	16	*19	*35	6	....	....	....
1953-54	St. Boniface Canadians	MJHL	35	33	25	*58	....	....	....	14	....	....	....	....	....	....	....	....	....	....	18	14	8	22	10	....	....	....
1954-55	St. Catharines Teepees	OHA	49	33	37	70	....	....	....	20	....	....	....	....	....	....	....	....	....	....	10	2	6	8	25	....	....	....
1955-56	St. Catharines Teepees	OHA	48	49	34	83	....	....	....	24	....	....	....	....	....	....	....	....	....	....	6	4	2	6	9	....	....	....
1956-57	Rochester Americans	AHL	64	21	31	52	....	....	....	8	....	....	....	....	....	....	....	....	....	....	9	3	1	4	0	....	....	....
1957-58	Rochester Americans	AHL	70	30	33	63	....	....	....	18	....	....	....	....	....	....	....	....	....	....	....	....	....	....	....	....	....	....
	Montreal Canadiens	**NHL**	....	....	....	....	....	....	....	....	....	....	....	....	....	....	....	....	....	....	**2**	**0**	**0**	**0**	**2**	....	....	....

Season	Club	League	GP	G	A	Pts	AG	AA	APts	PIM	PP	SH	GW	S	%	TGF	PGF	TGA	PGA	+/–	GP	G	A	Pts	PIM	PP	SH	GW
			REGULAR SEASON																		PLAYOFFS							
1958-59	**Montreal Canadiens**	**NHL**	**69**	**13**	**23**	**36**	**16**	**24**	**40**	**35**	....	....	....	....	....	....	....	....	....	....	**11**	**1**	**1**	**2**	**6**	....	....	....
1959-60	**Montreal Canadiens**	**NHL**	**68**	**9**	**13**	**22**	**11**	**13**	**24**	**26**	....	....	....	....	....	....	....	....	....	....	....	....	....	....	....	....	....	....
1960-61	**Chicago Black Hawks**	**NHL**	**61**	**17**	**16**	**33**	**21**	**16**	**37**	**22**	....	....	....	....	....	....	....	....	....	....	**8**	**2**	**2**	**4**	**0**	....	....	....
1961-62	**Chicago Black Hawks**	**NHL**	**65**	**22**	**18**	**40**	**27**	**18**	**45**	**8**	....	....	....	....	....	....	....	....	....	....	**12**	**6**	**6**	**12**	**0**	....	....	....
1962-63	**Chicago Black Hawks**	**NHL**	**69**	**20**	**41**	**61**	**25**	**43**	**68**	**12**	....	....	....	....	....	....	....	....	....	....	**6**	**2**	**3**	**5**	**9**	....	....	....
1963-64	**Chicago Black Hawks**	**NHL**	**70**	**14**	**32**	**46**	**18**	**36**	**54**	**19**	....	....	....	....	....	....	....	....	....	....	**7**	**2**	**2**	**4**	**0**	....	....	....
1964-65	**Boston Bruins**	**NHL**	**60**	**9**	**9**	**18**	**11**	**10**	**21**	**6**	....	....	....	....	....	....	....	....	....	....	....	....	....	....	....	....	....	....
	Providence Reds	AHL	6	2	1	3	....	....	....	2	....	....	....	....	....	....	....	....	....	....	....	....	....	....	....	....	....	....
1965-66	**Detroit Red Wings**	**NHL**	**43**	**6**	**16**	**22**	**7**	**16**	**23**	**6**	....	....	....	....	....	....	....	....	....	....	**10**	**1**	**4**	**5**	**2**	....	....	....
	Memphis Wings	CHL	20	9	6	15	....	....	....	4	....	....	....	....	....	....	....	....	....	....	....	....	....	....	....	....	....	....
1966-67	**Detroit Red Wings**	**NHL**	**12**	**2**	**0**	**2**	**2**	**0**	**2**	**2**	....	....	....	....	....	....	....	....	....	....	....	....	....	....	....	....	....	....
	Pittsburgh Hornets	AHL	61	25	31	56	....	....	....	22	....	....	....	....	....	....	....	....	....	....	9	5	2	7	4	....	....	....
1967-68	**Pittsburgh Penguins**	**NHL**	**74**	**22**	**21**	**43**	**27**	**22**	**49**	**38**	**6**	**1**	**2**	**185**	**11.9**	**68**	**14**	**64**	**6**	**–4**	....	....	....	....	....	....	....	....
1968-69	**St. Louis Blues**	**NHL**	**68**	**21**	**21**	**42**	**24**	**20**	**44**	**12**	**2**	**0**	**4**	**138**	**15.2**	**76**	**19**	**38**	**0**	**+19**	**12**	**2**	**1**	**3**	**10**	**0**	**0**	**0**
1969-70	**St. Louis Blues**	**NHL**	**64**	**25**	**30**	**55**	**29**	**30**	**59**	**8**	**11**	**0**	**4**	**170**	**14.7**	**88**	**42**	**35**	**0**	**+11**	**16**	**5**	**10**	**15**	**13**	**3**	**0**	**0**
1970-71	**St. Louis Blues**	**NHL**	**20**	**0**	**5**	**5**	**0**	**4**	**4**	**6**	**0**	**0**	**0**	**31**	**0.0**	**9**	**4**	**8**	**0**	**–3**	....	....	....	....	....	....	....	....
1971-72	**Detroit Red Wings**	**NHL**	**19**	**2**	**3**	**5**	**2**	**3**	**5**	**0**	**1**	**0**	**0**	**29**	**6.9**	**7**	**1**	**14**	**0**	**–8**	....	....	....	....	....	....	....	....
	Tidewater Wings	AHL	41	5	7	12	....	....	....	4	....	....	....	....	....	....	....	....	....	....	....	....	....	....	....	....	....	....
1972-73	Winnipeg Jets	WHA	77	17	24	41	....	....	....	14	....	....	....	....	....	....	....	....	....	....	14	2	5	7	2	....	....	....
1973-74	Winnipeg Jets	WHA	70	12	17	29	....	....	....	8	....	....	....	....	....	....	....	....	....	....	4	0	1	1	2	....	....	....
	NHL Totals		**762**	**182**	**248**	**430**	**220**	**255**	**475**	**200**	**20**	**1**	**10**	**553**	**32.9**	**248**	**80**	**159**	**6**		**84**	**21**	**29**	**50**	**42**	**3**	**0**	**0**
	Other Major League Totals		147	29	41	70	....	....	....	22	....	....	....	....	....	....	....	....	....	....	18	2	6	8	4	....	....	....

Played in NHL All-Star Game (1958, 1959, 1961, 1969, 1970)

Traded to **Chicago** by **Montreal** with Reggie Fleming, Bob Courcy and Cec Hoekstra for Terry Gray, Glen Skov, the rights to Danny Lewicki, Lorne Ferguson and Bob Bailey, June 7, 1960. Traded to **Boston** by **Chicago** with Reg Fleming for Doug Mohns, June 8, 1964. Traded to **Detroit** by **Boston** with Bob McCord and Ken Stephanson for Albert Langlois, Ron Harris, Parker MacDonald and Bob Dillabough, May 31, 1965. Claimed by **Pittsburgh** from **Detroit** in Expansion Draft, June 6, 1967. Traded to **St. Louis** by **Pittsburgh** for Lou Angotti, June 11, 1968. Traded to **Detroit** by **St. Louis** with Bob Wall and Mike Lowe to complete transaction that sent Carl Brewer to St. Louis (February 22, 1971), May 12, 1971. Selected by **Winnipeg** (WHA) in 1972 WHA General Player Draft, February 12, 1972.

• McDONALD, BRIAN

Brian "Butch" McDonald C – R. 5'11", 190 lbs. b: Toronto, Ont., 3/23/1945.

Season	Club	League	GP	G	A	Pts	AG	AA	APts	PIM	PP	SH	GW	S	%	TGF	PGF	TGA	PGA	+/–	GP	G	A	Pts	PIM	PP	SH	GW
1963-64	St. Catharines Black Hawks	OHA	56	31	44	75	....	....	....	98	....	....	....	....	....	....	....	....	....	....	13	7	11	18	24	....	....	....
1964-65	St. Catharines Black Hawks	OHA	56	47	61	108	....	....	....	100	....	....	....	....	....	....	....	....	....	....	5	4	2	6	34	....	....	....
	St. Louis Braves	CHL	3	0	1	1	....	....	....	0	....	....	....	....	....	....	....	....	....	....	....	....	....	....	....	....	....	....
1965-66	St. Louis Braves	CHL	70	13	33	46	....	....	....	45	....	....	....	....	....	....	....	....	....	....	5	1	2	3	2	....	....	....
1966-67	St. Louis Braves	CHL	67	10	33	43	....	....	....	59	....	....	....	....	....	....	....	....	....	....	....	....	....	....	....	....	....	....
1967-68	Dallas Black Hawks	CHL	67	24	45	69	....	....	....	104	....	....	....	....	....	....	....	....	....	....	5	0	4	4	21	....	....	....
	Chicago Black Hawks	**NHL**	....	....	....	....	....	....	....	....	....	....	....	....	....	....	....	....	....	....	**8**	**0**	**0**	**0**	**2**	....	....	....
1968-69	Dallas Black Hawks	CHL	67	19	41	60	....	....	....	65	....	....	....	....	....	....	....	....	....	....	11	7	6	13	28	....	....	....
1969-70	Denver Spurs	WHL	70	34	34	68	....	....	....	54	....	....	....	....	....	....	....	....	....	....	....	....	....	....	....	....	....	....
1970-71	**Buffalo Sabres**	**NHL**	**12**	**0**	**0**	**0**	**0**	**0**	**0**	**29**	**0**	**0**	**0**	**15**	**0.0**	**0**	**0**	**8**	**0**	**–8**	....	....	....	....	....	....	....	....
	Salt Lake Golden Eagles	WHL	56	29	18	47	....	....	....	70	....	....	....	....	....	....	....	....	....	....	....	....	....	....	....	....	....	....
1971-72	San Diego Gulls	WHL	63	24	22	46	....	....	....	88	....	....	....	....	....	....	....	....	....	....	4	0	1	1	24	....	....	....
1972-73	Houston Aeros	WHA	71	20	20	40	....	....	....	78	....	....	....	....	....	....	....	....	....	....	10	3	0	3	16	....	....	....
1973-74	Los Angeles Sharks	WHA	50	22	30	52	....	....	....	54	....	....	....	....	....	....	....	....	....	....	....	....	....	....	....	....	....	....
1974-75	Michigan Stags	WHA	18	3	5	8	....	....	....	15	....	....	....	....	....	....	....	....	....	....	....	....	....	....	....	....	....	....
	Indianapolis Racers	WHA	47	14	15	29	....	....	....	19	....	....	....	....	....	....	....	....	....	....	....	....	....	....	....	....	....	....
	Mohawk Valley Comets	NAHL	10	5	9	14	....	....	....	17	....	....	....	....	....	....	....	....	....	....	....	....	....	....	....	....	....	....
1975-76	Indianapolis Racers	WHA	62	15	18	33	....	....	....	54	....	....	....	....	....	....	....	....	....	....	7	0	1	1	12	....	....	....
1976-77	Indianapolis Racers	WHA	50	15	13	28	....	....	....	48	....	....	....	....	....	....	....	....	....	....	9	3	4	7	33	....	....	....
	NHL Totals		**12**	**0**	**0**	**0**	**0**	**0**	**0**	**29**	**0**	**0**	**0**	**15**	**0.0**	**0**	**0**	**8**	**0**		**8**	**0**	**0**	**0**	**2**	**0**	**0**	**0**
	Other Major League Totals		304	89	101	190	....	....	....	268	....	....	....	....	....	....	....	....	....	....	26	6	5	11	61	....	....	....

Claimed by **Buffalo** from **Chicago** (Denver-WHL) in Inter-League Draft, June 9, 1970. Claimed by **San Diego** (WHL) from **Buffalo** (Salt Lake-CHL) in Reverse Draft, June, 1971. Selected by **Dayton-Houston** (WHA) in 1972 WHA General Player Draft, February 12, 1972. Traded to **LA Sharks** (WHA) by **Houston** (WHA) for Jon Szura, September, 1973. Transferred to **Michigan** (WHA) after **LA Sharks** (WHA) franchise relocated, April 11, 1974. Traded to **Indianapolis** (WHA) by **Michigan** (WHA) with Jacques Locas for Steve Andrascik and Steve Richardson, November, 1974.

• McDONALD, GERRY

Gerry McDonald D – R. 6'3", 190 lbs. b: Weymouth, MA, 3/18/1958.

Season	Club	League	GP	G	A	Pts	AG	AA	APts	PIM	PP	SH	GW	S	%	TGF	PGF	TGA	PGA	+/–	GP	G	A	Pts	PIM	PP	SH	GW
1979-80	North Adams State College	ECAC II	STATISTICS NOT AVAILABLE																									
1980-81	Tulsa Oilers	CHL	5	0	1	1	....	....	....	2	....	....	....	....	....	....	....	....	....	....	....	....	....	....	....	....	....	....
	New Haven Nighthawks	AHL	70	6	23	29	....	....	....	67	....	....	....	....	....	....	....	....	....	....	4	0	0	0	0	....	....	....
1981-82	**Hartford Whalers**	**NHL**	**3**	**0**	**0**	**0**	**0**	**0**	**0**	**0**	**0**	**0**	**0**	**1**	**0.0**	**2**	**0**	**4**	**0**	**–2**	....	....	....	....	....	....	....	....
	Binghamton Whalers	AHL	57	3	11	14	....	....	....	42	....	....	....	....	....	....	....	....	....	....	....	....	....	....	....	....	....	....
1982-83	Binghamton Whalers	AHL	74	8	33	49	....	....	....	62	....	....	....	....	....	....	....	....	....	....	5	0	4	4	23	....	....	....
1983-84	**Hartford Whalers**	**NHL**	**5**	**0**	**0**	**0**	**0**	**0**	**0**	**4**	**0**	**0**	**0**	**7**	**0.0**	**4**	**1**	**7**	**1**	**–3**	....	....	....	....	....	....	....	....
	Binghamton Whalers	AHL	72	4	39	43	....	....	....	34	....	....	....	....	....	....	....	....	....	....	....	....	....	....	....	....	....	....
	NHL Totals		**8**	**0**	**0**	**0**	**0**	**0**	**0**	**4**	**0**	**0**	**0**	**8**	**0.0**	**6**	**1**	**11**	**1**		....	....	....	....	....	....	....	....

Signed as a free agent by **NY Rangers**, December 12, 1980. Traded to **Hartford** by **NY Rangers** with Doug Sulliman and Chris Kotsopoulous for Mike Rogers and Hartford's 10th round choice (Simo Saarinen) in 1982 Entry Draft, October 2, 1981.

• McDONALD, LANNY

Lanny McDonald RW – R. 6', 185 lbs. b: Hanna, Alta., 2/16/1953. Toronto's 1st choice, 4th overall, in 1973 Amateur Draft. **HHOF**

Season	Club	League	GP	G	A	Pts	AG	AA	APts	PIM	PP	SH	GW	S	%	TGF	PGF	TGA	PGA	+/–	GP	G	A	Pts	PIM	PP	SH	GW
1969-70	Lethbridge Hurricanes	AJHL	34	2	9	11	....	....	....	19	....	....	....	....	....	....	....	....	....	....	....	....	....	....	....	....	....	....
1970-71	Lethbridge Hurricanes	AJHL	45	37	45	82	....	....	....	56	....	....	....	....	....	....	....	....	....	....	....	....	....	....	....	....	....	....
	Calgary Centennials	WCJHL	6	0	2	2	....	....	....	6	....	....	....	....	....	....	....	....	....	....	....	....	....	....	....	....	....	....
1971-72	Medicine Hat Tigers	WCJHL	68	50	64	114	....	....	....	54	....	....	....	....	....	....	....	....	....	....	7	2	2	4	6	....	....	....
1972-73	Medicine Hat Tigers	WCJHL	68	62	77	139	....	....	....	84	....	....	....	....	....	....	....	....	....	....	17	*18	19	37	6	....	....	....
1973-74	**Toronto Maple Leafs**	**NHL**	**70**	**14**	**16**	**30**	**14**	**14**	**28**	**43**	**2**	**0**	**3**	**142**	**9.9**	**58**	**12**	**47**	**4**	**+3**	....	....	....	....	....	....	....	....
1974-75	**Toronto Maple Leafs**	**NHL**	**64**	**17**	**27**	**44**	**16**	**21**	**37**	**86**	**2**	**1**	**1**	**168**	**10.1**	**70**	**12**	**69**	**16**	**+5**	**7**	**0**	**0**	**0**	**2**	**0**	**0**	**0**
1975-76	**Toronto Maple Leafs**	**NHL**	**75**	**37**	**56**	**93**	**35**	**44**	**79**	**70**	**6**	**5**	**4**	**270**	**13.7**	**126**	**37**	**95**	**30**	**+24**	**10**	**4**	**4**	**8**	**4**	**2**	**0**	**1**
1976-77	Canada	C Cup	5	0	2	2	....	....	....	0	....	....	....	....	....	....	....	....	....	....	....	....	....	....	....	....	....	....
	Toronto Maple Leafs	**NHL**	**80**	**46**	**44**	**90**	**44**	**36**	**80**	**77**	**16**	**4**	**5**	**293**	**15.7**	**136**	**44**	**105**	**25**	**+12**	**9**	**10**	**7**	**17**	**6**	**3**	**0**	**1**
1977-78	**Toronto Maple Leafs**	**NHL**	**74**	**47**	**40**	**87**	**46**	**33**	**79**	**54**	**11**	**0**	**5**	**243**	**19.3**	**126**	**39**	**54**	**1**	**+34**	**13**	**3**	**4**	**7**	**10**	**1**	**0**	**2**
1978-79	**Toronto Maple Leafs**	**NHL**	**79**	**43**	**42**	**85**	**39**	**32**	**71**	**32**	**16**	**0**	**2**	**314**	**13.7**	**130**	**46**	**72**	**0**	**+12**	**6**	**3**	**2**	**5**	**0**	**0**	**0**	**0**
	NHL All-Stars	Chal Cup	3	0	0	0	....	....	....	2	....	....	....	....	....	....	....	....	....	....	....	....	....	....	....	....	....	....
1979-80	**Toronto Maple Leafs**	**NHL**	**35**	**15**	**15**	**30**	**14**	**11**	**25**	**10**	**6**	**0**	**2**	**140**	**10.7**	**51**	**17**	**36**	**1**	**–1**	....	....	....	....	....	....	....	....
	Colorado Rockies	**NHL**	**46**	**25**	**20**	**45**	**23**	**15**	**38**	**43**	**8**	**0**	**3**	**194**	**12.9**	**64**	**25**	**64**	**10**	**–15**	....	....	....	....	....	....	....	....
1980-81	**Colorado Rockies**	**NHL**	**80**	**35**	**46**	**81**	**29**	**32**	**61**	**56**	**11**	**0**	**2**	**298**	**11.7**	**116**	**45**	**117**	**19**	**–27**	....	....	....	....	....	....	....	....
	Canada	WEC-A	8	3	0	3	....	....	....	4	....	....	....	....	....	....	....	....	....	....	....	....	....	....	....	....	....	....
1981-82	**Colorado Rockies**	**NHL**	**16**	**6**	**9**	**15**	**5**	**6**	**11**	**20**	**0**	**0**	**1**	**65**	**9.2**	**25**	**8**	**20**	**0**	**–3**	....	....	....	....	....	....	....	....
	Calgary Flames	**NHL**	**55**	**34**	**33**	**67**	**27**	**22**	**49**	**37**	**10**	**1**	**3**	**178**	**19.1**	**99**	**34**	**57**	**14**	**+22**	**3**	**0**	**1**	**1**	**6**	**0**	**0**	**0**
1982-83	**Calgary Flames**	**NHL**	**80**	**66**	**32**	**98**	**55**	**22**	**77**	**90**	**17**	**0**	**8**	**272**	**24.3**	**151**	**61**	**98**	**6**	**–2**	**7**	**3**	**4**	**7**	**19**	**1**	**0**	**0**
1983-84	**Calgary Flames**	**NHL**	**65**	**33**	**33**	**66**	**27**	**22**	**49**	**64**	**10**	**0**	**1**	**248**	**13.5**	**101**	**41**	**76**	**1**	**–15**	**11**	**6**	**7**	**13**	**6**	**3**	**0**	**1**
1984-85	**Calgary Flames**	**NHL**	**43**	**19**	**18**	**37**	**16**	**12**	**28**	**36**	**9**	**0**	**2**	**117**	**16.2**	**60**	**21**	**43**	**0**	**–4**	**1**	**0**	**0**	**0**	**0**	**0**	**0**	**0**
1985-86	**Calgary Flames**	**NHL**	**80**	**28**	**43**	**71**	**22**	**29**	**51**	**44**	**11**	**0**	**3**	**227**	**12.3**	**102**	**42**	**64**	**2**	**–2**	**22**	**11**	**7**	**18**	**30**	**4**	**0**	**2**

			REGULAR SEASON																		PLAYOFFS							
Season	**Club**	**League**	**GP**	**G**	**A**	**Pts**	**AG**	**AA**	**APts**	**PIM**	**PP**	**SH**	**GW**	**S**	**%**	**TGF**	**PGF**	**TGA**	**PGA**	**+/–**	**GP**	**G**	**A**	**Pts**	**PIM**	**PP**	**SH**	**GW**
1986-87	**Calgary Flames**	**NHL**	**58**	**14**	**12**	**26**	**12**	**9**	**21**	**54**	**4**	**0**	**3**	**127**	**11.0**	**49**	**12**	**44**	**4**	**–3**	**5**	**0**	**0**	**0**	**2**	**0**	**0**	**0**
1987-88	**Calgary Flames**	**NHL**	**60**	**10**	**13**	**23**	**9**	**9**	**18**	**57**	**0**	**0**	**2**	**79**	**12.7**	**34**	**2**	**31**	**1**	**+2**	**9**	**3**	**1**	**4**	**6**	**0**	**0**	**0**
1988-89	**Calgary Flames**	**NHL**	**51**	**11**	**7**	**18**	**9**	**5**	**14**	**26**	**0**	**0**	**3**	**72**	**15.3**	**23**	**2**	**22**	**0**	**–1**	**14**	**1**	**3**	**4**	**29**	**0**	**0**	**0**
	NHL Totals		**1111**	**500**	**506**	**1006**	**442**	**374**	**816**	**899**	**139**	**11**	**53**	**3444**	**14.5**	**1521**	**500**	**1114**	**134**		**117**	**44**	**40**	**84**	**120**	**14**	**0**	**7**

WCJHL First All-Star Team (1973) • NHL Second All-Star Team (1977, 1983) • Won Bill Masterton Trophy (1983) • Won King Clancy Memorial Trophy (1988) • Won Bud Man of the Year Award (1989)

Played in NHL All-Star Game (1977, 1978, 1983, 1984)

Traded to **Colorado** by **Toronto** with Joel Quenneville for Pat Hickey and Wilf Paiement, December 29, 1979. Traded to **Calgary** by **Colorado** with Colorado's 4th round choice (later traded to NY Islanders — NY Islanders selected Mikko Makela) in 1983 Entry Draft for Bob MacMIllan and Don Lever, November 25, 1981.

• McDONALD, TERRY

Terry McDonald D – L. 6'1", 180 lbs. b: Coquitlam, B.C., 1/1/1956. Kansas City's 5th choice, 74th overall, in 1975 Amateur Draft.

Season	Club	League	GP	G	A	Pts	AG	AA	APts	PIM	PP	SH	GW	S	%	TGF	PGF	TGA	PGA	+/–	GP	G	A	Pts	PIM	PP	SH	GW
1971-72	Coquitlam Midgets	BCJHL	STATISTICS NOT AVAILABLE																									
1972-73	Vancouver Nats	WCJHL	49	9	18	27	....	....	....	81	....	....	....	....	....	....	....	....	....	....	....	....	....	....	....	....	....	....
1973-74	Kamloops Chiefs	WCJHL	68	10	22	32	....	....	....	102	....	....	....	....	....	....	....	....	....	....	....	....	....	....	....	....	....	....
1974-75	Kamloops Chiefs	WCJHL	66	32	37	69	....	....	....	89	....	....	....	....	....	....	....	....	....	....	6	3	1	4	2	....	....	....
1975-76	**Kansas City Scouts**	**NHL**	**8**	**0**	**1**	**1**	**0**	**1**	**1**	**6**	**0**	**0**	**0**	**4**	**0.0**	**4**	**1**	**9**	**1**	**–5**	....	....	....	....	....	....	....	....
	Springfield Indians	AHL	24	0	0	0	....	....	....	13	....	....	....	....	....	....	....	....	....	....	....	....	....	....	....	....	....	....
	Port Huron Flags	IHL	43	6	25	31	....	....	....	75	....	....	....	....	....	....	....	....	....	....	15	5	2	7	23	....	....	....
1976-77	Rhode Island Reds	AHL	76	20	18	38	....	....	....	18	....	....	....	....	....	....	....	....	....	....	....	....	....	....	....	....	....	....
	Flint Generals	IHL	2	0	0	0	....	....	....	0	....	....	....	....	....	....	....	....	....	....	....	....	....	....	....	....	....	....
1977-78	Phoenix Roadrunners	CHL	27	12	10	22	....	....	....	11	....	....	....	....	....	....	....	....	....	....	....	....	....	....	....	....	....	....
	Flint Generals	IHL	42	19	32	51	....	....	....	29	....	....	....	....	....	....	....	....	....	....	5	3	0	3	0	....	....	....
1978-79	Phoenix Roadrunners	PHL	60	26	31	57	....	....	....	20	....	....	....	....	....	....	....	....	....	....	....	....	....	....	....	....	....	....
	NHL Totals		**8**	**0**	**1**	**1**	**0**	**1**	**1**	**6**	**0**	**0**	**0**	**4**	**0.0**	**4**	**1**	**9**	**1**		....	....	....	....	....	....	....	....

• McDONNELL, JOE

Joe McDonnell D – R. 6'2", 200 lbs. b: Kitchener, Ont., 5/11/1961.

Season	Club	League	GP	G	A	Pts	AG	AA	APts	PIM	PP	SH	GW	S	%	TGF	PGF	TGA	PGA	+/–	GP	G	A	Pts	PIM	PP	SH	GW
1976-77	Kitchener Dutchmen	Jr. B	21	8	20	28	....	....	....	28	....	....	....	....	....	....	....	....	....	....	....	....	....	....	....	....	....	....
	Kitchener Rangers	OHA	29	0	4	4	....	....	....	8	....	....	....	....	....	....	....	....	....	....	....	....	....	....	....	....	....	....
1977-78	Kitchener Rangers	OHA	55	0	4	4	....	....	....	14	....	....	....	....	....	....	....	....	....	....	....	....	....	....	....	....	....	....
1978-79	Kitchener Rangers	OHA	60	1	6	7	....	....	....	43	....	....	....	....	....	....	....	....	....	....	....	....	....	....	....	....	....	....
1979-80	Kitchener Rangers	OHA	62	6	21	27	....	....	....	81	....	....	....	....	....	....	....	....	....	....	....	....	....	....	....	....	....	....
1980-81	Kitchener Rangers	OHA	66	15	50	65	....	....	....	103	....	....	....	....	....	....	....	....	....	....	16	4	9	13	8	....	....	....
1981-82	**Vancouver Canucks**	**NHL**	**7**	**0**	**1**	**1**	**0**	**1**	**1**	**12**	**0**	**0**	**0**	**6**	**0.0**	**4**	**0**	**6**	**0**	**–2**	....	....	....	....	....	....	....	....
	Dallas Black Hawks	CHL	60	13	24	37	....	....	....	46	....	....	....	....	....	....	....	....	....	....	9	2	1	3	12	....	....	....
1982-83	Moncton Alpines	AHL	79	14	21	35	....	....	....	44	....	....	....	....	....	....	....	....	....	....	....	....	....	....	....	....	....	....
1983-84	Moncton Alpines	AHL	78	12	33	45	....	....	....	44	....	....	....	....	....	....	....	....	....	....	....	....	....	....	....	....	....	....
1984-85	**Pittsburgh Penguins**	**NHL**	**40**	**2**	**9**	**11**	**2**	**6**	**8**	**20**	**2**	**0**	**0**	**75**	**2.7**	**46**	**10**	**64**	**9**	**–19**	....	....	....	....	....	....	....	....
	Baltimore Skipjacks	AHL	41	7	27	34	....	....	....	22	....	....	....	....	....	....	....	....	....	....	....	....	....	....	....	....	....	....
1985-86	**Pittsburgh Penguins**	**NHL**	**3**	**0**	**0**	**0**	**0**	**0**	**0**	**2**	**0**	**0**	**0**	**1**	**0.0**	**1**	**0**	**4**	**0**	**–3**	....	....	....	....	....	....	....	....
	Baltimore Skipjacks	AHL	31	1	13	14	....	....	....	20	....	....	....	....	....	....	....	....	....	....	....	....	....	....	....	....	....	....
	NHL Totals		**50**	**2**	**10**	**12**	**2**	**7**	**9**	**34**	**2**	**0**	**0**	**82**	**2.4**	**51**	**10**	**74**	**9**		....	....	....	....	....	....	....	....

Memorial Cup All-Star Team (1981)

Signed as a free agent by **Vancouver**, September 22, 1980. Signed as a free agent by **Edmonton**, August 16, 1982. Signed as a free agent by **Pittsburgh**, December 30, 1984.

• McDONOUGH, AL

Al McDonough RW – R. 6'1", 175 lbs. b: Hamilton, Ont., 6/6/1950. Los Angeles' 1st choice, 24th overall, in 1970 Amateur Draft.

Season	Club	League	GP	G	A	Pts	AG	AA	APts	PIM	PP	SH	GW	S	%	TGF	PGF	TGA	PGA	+/–	GP	G	A	Pts	PIM	PP	SH	GW
1967-68	St. Catharines Black Hawks	OHA	49	12	8	20	....	....	....	13	....	....	....	....	....	....	....	....	....	....	4	1	0	1	0	....	....	....
1968-69	St. Catharines Black Hawks	OHA	54	26	20	46	....	....	....	34	....	....	....	....	....	....	....	....	....	....	17	5	7	12	12	....	....	....
1969-70	St. Catharines Black Hawks	OHA	53	47	56	103	....	....	....	57	....	....	....	....	....	....	....	....	....	....	....	....	....	....	....	....	....	....
1970-71	**Los Angeles Kings**	**NHL**	**6**	**2**	**1**	**3**	**2**	**1**	**3**	**0**	**0**	**0**	**1**	**13**	**15.4**	**7**	**0**	**5**	**0**	**+2**	....	....	....	....	....	....	....	....
	Springfield Kings	AHL	65	33	16	49	....	....	....	27	....	....	....	....	....	....	....	....	....	....	12	1	2	3	9	....	....	....
1971-72	**Los Angeles Kings**	**NHL**	**31**	**3**	**2**	**5**	**3**	**2**	**5**	**8**	**1**	**0**	**0**	**28**	**10.7**	**9**	**5**	**12**	**0**	**–8**	....	....	....	....	....	....	....	....
	Pittsburgh Penguins	**NHL**	**37**	**7**	**11**	**18**	**7**	**10**	**17**	**8**	**1**	**0**	**1**	**113**	**6.2**	**35**	**17**	**24**	**0**	**–6**	**4**	**0**	**1**	**1**	**0**	**0**	**0**	**0**
1972-73	**Pittsburgh Penguins**	**NHL**	**78**	**35**	**41**	**76**	**35**	**34**	**69**	**26**	**7**	**0**	**4**	**285**	**12.3**	**118**	**38**	**60**	**0**	**+20**	....	....	....	....	....	....	....	....
1973-74	**Pittsburgh Penguins**	**NHL**	**37**	**14**	**22**	**36**	**14**	**19**	**33**	**12**	**3**	**0**	**4**	**142**	**9.9**	**50**	**18**	**35**	**0**	**–3**	....	....	....	....	....	....	....	....
	Atlanta Flames	**NHL**	**35**	**10**	**9**	**19**	**10**	**8**	**18**	**15**	**3**	**0**	**1**	**108**	**9.3**	**37**	**13**	**29**	**1**	**–4**	**4**	**0**	**0**	**0**	**2**	**0**	**0**	**0**
1974-75	Cleveland Crusaders	WHA	78	34	30	64	....	....	....	27	....	....	....	....	....	....	....	....	....	....	5	2	1	3	2	....	....	....
1975-76	Cleveland Crusaders	WHA	80	23	22	45	....	....	....	19	....	....	....	....	....	....	....	....	....	....	3	1	0	1	0	....	....	....
1976-77	Minnesota Fighting Saints	WHA	42	9	21	30	....	....	....	6	....	....	....	....	....	....	....	....	....	....	....	....	....	....	....	....	....	....
1977-78	**Detroit Red Wings**	**NHL**	**13**	**2**	**2**	**4**	**2**	**2**	**4**	**4**	**0**	**0**	**0**	**18**	**11.1**	**6**	**1**	**3**	**0**	**+2**	....	....	....	....	....	....	....	....
	Kansas City Red Wings	CHL	52	18	24	42	....	....	....	14	....	....	....	....	....	....	....	....	....	....	....	....	....	....	....	....	....	....
	NHL Totals		**237**	**73**	**88**	**161**	**73**	**76**	**149**	**73**	**15**	**0**	**11**	**707**	**10.3**	**262**	**92**	**168**	**1**		**8**	**0**	**1**	**1**	**2**	**0**	**0**	**0**
	Other Major League Totals		200	66	73	139	....	....	....	52	....	....	....	....	....	....	....	....	....		8	3	1	4	2	....	....	....

OHA First All-Star Team (1970)

Played in NHL All-Star Game (1974)

Traded to **Pittsburgh** by **LA Kings** for Bob Woytowich, January 11, 1972. Selected by **Calgary-Cleveland** (WHA) in 1972 WHA General Player Draft, February 12, 1972. Traded to **Atlanta** by **Pittsburgh** for Chuck Arnason and Bob Paradise, January 4, 1974. Transferred to **Minnesota** (WHA) after **Cleveland** (WHA) franchise relocated, July, 1976. Traded to **Detroit** by **Atlanta** for future considerations, August, 1977.

• McDONOUGH, HUBIE

Hubie McDonough C – L. 5'9", 180 lbs. b: Manchester, NH, 7/8/1963.

Season	Club	League	GP	G	A	Pts	AG	AA	APts	PIM	PP	SH	GW	S	%	TGF	PGF	TGA	PGA	+/–	GP	G	A	Pts	PIM	PP	SH	GW
1982-83	St. Anselm College	ECAC II	27	24	21	45	....	....	....	12	....	....	....	....	....	....	....	....	....	....	....	....	....	....	....	....	....	....
1983-84	St. Anselm College	ECAC II	26	37	15	52	....	....	....	20	....	....	....	....	....	....	....	....	....	....	....	....	....	....	....	....	....	....
1984-85	St. Anselm College	ECAC II	26	41	30	71	....	....	....	48	....	....	....	....	....	....	....	....	....	....	....	....	....	....	....	....	....	....
1985-86	St. Anselm College	ECAC II	25	22	20	42	....	....	....	16	....	....	....	....	....	....	....	....	....	....	....	....	....	....	....	....	....	....
1986-87	Flint Spirits	IHL	82	27	52	79	....	....	....	59	....	....	....	....	....	....	....	....	....	....	6	3	2	5	0	....	....	....
1987-88	New Haven Nighthawks	AHL	78	30	29	59	....	....	....	43	....	....	....	....	....	....	....	....	....	....	....	....	....	....	....	....	....	....
1988-89	**Los Angeles Kings**	**NHL**	**4**	**0**	**1**	**1**	**0**	**1**	**1**	**0**	**0**	**0**	**0**	**3**	**0.0**	**2**	**0**	**0**	**0**	**+2**	....	....	....	....	....	....	....	....
	New Haven Nighthawks	AHL	74	37	55	92	....	....	....	41	....	....	....	....	....	....	....	....	....	....	17	10	*21	*31	6	....	....	....
1989-90	**Los Angeles Kings**	**NHL**	**22**	**3**	**4**	**7**	**3**	**3**	**6**	**10**	**0**	**0**	**1**	**13**	**23.1**	**11**	**0**	**20**	**13**	**+4**	....	....	....	....	....	....	....	....
	New York Islanders	**NHL**	**54**	**18**	**11**	**29**	**16**	**8**	**24**	**26**	**0**	**3**	**3**	**92**	**19.6**	**36**	**1**	**44**	**19**	**+10**	**5**	**1**	**0**	**1**	**4**	**0**	**0**	**0**
1990-91	**New York Islanders**	**NHL**	**52**	**6**	**6**	**12**	**5**	**5**	**10**	**10**	**0**	**1**	**0**	**47**	**12.8**	**13**	**1**	**49**	**23**	**–14**	....	....	....	....	....	....	....	....
	Capital District Islanders	AHL	17	9	9	18	....	....	....	4	....	....	....	....	....	....	....	....	....	....	....	....	....	....	....	....	....	....
1991-92	**New York Islanders**	**NHL**	**33**	**7**	**2**	**9**	**6**	**1**	**7**	**15**	**1**	**1**	**0**	**31**	**22.6**	**11**	**1**	**26**	**12**	**–4**	....	....	....	....	....	....	....	....
	Capital District Islanders	AHL	21	11	18	29	....	....	....	14	....	....	....	....	....	....	....	....	....	....	....	....	....	....	....	....	....	....
1992-93	**San Jose Sharks**	**NHL**	**30**	**6**	**2**	**8**	**5**	**1**	**6**	**6**	**2**	**0**	**0**	**41**	**14.6**	**14**	**5**	**36**	**6**	**–21**	....	....	....	....	....	....	....	....
	San Diego Gulls	IHL	48	26	49	75	....	....	....	26	....	....	....	....	....	....	....	....	....	....	14	4	7	11	6	....	....	....
1993-94	San Diego Gulls	IHL	69	31	48	79	....	....	....	61	....	....	....	....	....	....	....	....	....	....	8	0	7	7	6	....	....	....
1994-95	San Diego Gulls	IHL	80	43	55	98	....	....	....	10	....	....	....	....	....	....	....	....	....	....	5	0	1	1	4	....	....	....
1995-96	Los Angeles Ice Dogs	IHL	11	11	9	20	....	....	....	10	....	....	....	....	....	....	....	....	....	....	....	....	....	....	....	....	....	....
	Orlando Solar Bears	IHL	58	26	32	58	....	....	....	40	....	....	....	....	....	....	....	....	....	....	23	7	11	18	10	....	....	....
1996-97	Orlando Solar Bears	IHL	68	30	25	55	....	....	....	60	....	....	....	....	....	....	....	....	....	....	10	5	8	13	6	....	....	....
1997-98	Orlando Solar Bears	IHL	80	32	33	65	....	....	....	62	....	....	....	....	....	....	....	....	....	....	17	11	10	21	2	....	....	....
	NHL Totals		**195**	**40**	**26**	**66**	**35**	**19**	**54**	**67**	**3**	**5**	**4**	**227**	**17.6**	**87**	**8**	**175**	**73**		**5**	**1**	**0**	**1**	**4**	**0**	**0**	**0**

NCAA (College Div.) East All-American Team (1986) • IHL Second All-Star Team (1993, 1995)

Signed as a free agent by **LA Kings**, April 18, 1988. Traded to **NY Islanders** by **LA Kings** with Ken Baumgartner for Mikko Makela, November 29, 1989. Traded to **San Jose** by **NY Islanders** for cash, August 28, 1992.

			REGULAR SEASON																		PLAYOFFS							
Season	Club	League	GP	G	A	Pts	AG	AA	APts	PIM	PP	SH	GW	S	%	TGF	PGF	TGA	PGA	+/–	GP	G	A	Pts	PIM	PP	SH	GW

• McDOUGAL, MIKE

Mike McDougal RW – L. 6′2″, 200 lbs. b: Port Huron, MI, 4/30/1958. NY Rangers' 6th choice, 76th overall, in 1978 Amateur Draft.

Season	Club	League	GP	G	A	Pts	AG	AA	APts	PIM	PP	SH	GW	S	%	TGF	PGF	TGA	PGA	+/–	GP	G	A	Pts	PIM	PP	SH	GW
1973-74	Port Huron Jr. Flags	MWJHL	40	27	33	60	....	....	....	....	....	....	....	....	....	....	....	....	....	....	....	....	....	....	....	....	....	....
1974-75	Montreal Jr. Canadiens	QMJHL	70	21	27	48	....	....	....	121	....	....	....	....	....	....	....	....	....	....	....	....	....	....	....	....	....	....
1975-76	Montreal Jr. Canadiens	QJMHL	71	31	44	75	....	....	....	71	....	....	....	....	....	....	....	....	....	....	....	....	....	....	....	....	....	....
1976-77	Port Huron Flags	IHL	59	25	29	54	....	....	....	46	....	....	....	....	....	....	....	....	....	....	....	....	....	....	....	....	....	....
	United States	WJC-A	....	....	....	....	....	....	....	....	....	....	....	....	....	....	....	....	....	....	....	....	....	....	....	....	....	....
1977-78	Port Huron Flags	IHL	44	15	16	31	....	....	....	65	....	....	....	....	....	....	....	....	....	....	....	....	....	....	....	....	....	....
	United States	WJC-A	6	3	5	8	....	....	....	10	....	....	....	....	....	....	....	....	....	....	....	....	....	....	....	....	....	....
1978-79	New York Rangers	NHL	1	0	0	0	0	0	0	0	0	0	0	0	0.0	0	0	0	0	0	....	....	....	....	....	....	....	....
	New Haven Nighthawks	AHL	78	24	26	50	....	....	....	60	....	....	....	....	....	....	....	....	....	....	10	1	5	6	8	....	....	....
1979-80	New Haven Nighthawks	AHL	68	17	25	42	....	....	....	43	....	....	....	....	....	....	....	....	....	....	3	0	3	3	0	....	....	....
1980-81	New York Rangers	NHL	2	0	0	0	0	0	0	0	0	0	0	1	0.0	1	0	0	0	+1	....	....	....	....	....	....	....	....
	New Haven Nighthawks	AHL	66	21	23	44	....	....	....	20	....	....	....	....	....	....	....	....	....	....	4	0	0	0	2	....	....	....
1981-82	Hartford Whalers	NHL	3	0	0	0	0	0	0	0	0	0	0	2	0.0	1	0	1	0	0	....	....	....	....	....	....	....	....
	Binghamton Whalers	AHL	58	10	18	28	....	....	....	56	....	....	....	....	....	....	....	....	....	....	14	1	8	9	12	....	....	....
1982-83	Hartford Whalers	NHL	55	8	10	18	7	7	14	43	0	0	0	61	13.1	32	1	68	4	–33	....	....	....	....	....	....	....	....
	Binghamton Whalers	AHL	14	7	5	12	....	....	....	20	....	....	....	....	....	....	....	....	....	....	....	....	....	....	....	....	....	....
1983-84	Binghamton Whalers	AHL	59	11	14	25	....	....	....	56	....	....	....	....	....	....	....	....	....	....	....	....	....	....	....	....	....	....
	NHL Totals		61	8	10	18	7	7	14	43	0	0	0	64	12.5	34	1	69	4		....	....	....	....	....	....	....	....

Claimed by **Hartford** from **NY Rangers** in Waiver Draft, October 6, 1981.

• McDOUGALL, BILL

Bill McDougall C – R. 6′, 185 lbs. b: Mississauga, Ont., 8/10/1966.

Season	Club	League	GP	G	A	Pts	AG	AA	APts	PIM	PP	SH	GW	S	%	TGF	PGF	TGA	PGA	+/–	GP	G	A	Pts	PIM	PP	SH	GW
1987-88	St. John's Capitals	Nfld.	42	66	71	137	....	....	....	47	....	....	....	....	....	....	....	....	....	....	....	....	....	....	....	....	....	....
1988-89	Port aux Basques Mariners	Nfld.	26	20	41	61	....	....	....	129	....	....	....	....	....	....	....	....	....	....	....	....	....	....	....	....	....	....
1989-90	Erie Panthers	ECHL	57	*80	*68	*148	....	....	....	226	....	....	....	....	....	....	....	....	....	....	7	5	5	10	20	....	....	....
	Adirondack Red Wings	AHL	11	10	7	17	....	....	....	4	....	....	....	....	....	....	....	....	....	....	2	1	1	2	2	....	....	....
1990-91	Detroit Red Wings	NHL	2	0	1	1	0	1	1	0	0	0	0	3	0.0	2	0	2	0	0	1	0	0	0	0	0	0	0
	Adirondack Red Wings	AHL	71	47	52	99	....	....	....	192	....	....	....	....	....	....	....	....	....	....	2	1	2	3	2	....	....	....
1991-92	Adirondack Red Wings	AHL	45	28	24	52	....	....	....	112	....	....	....	....	....	....	....	....	....	....	....	....	....	....	....	....	....	....
	Cape Breton Oilers	AHL	22	8	18	26	....	....	....	36	....	....	....	....	....	....	....	....	....	....	4	0	1	1	8	....	....	....
1992-93	Edmonton Oilers	NHL	4	2	1	3	2	1	3	4	0	0	0	8	25.0	6	2	2	0	+2	....	....	....	....	....	....	....	....
	Cape Breton Oilers	AHL	71	42	46	88	....	....	....	16	....	....	....	....	....	....	....	....	....	....	16	*26	*26	*52	30	....	....	....
1993-94	Tampa Bay Lightning	NHL	22	3	3	6	3	2	5	8	1	0	0	26	11.5	10	3	11	0	–4	....	....	....	....	....	....	....	....
	Atlanta Knights	IHL	48	17	30	47	....	....	....	141	....	....	....	....	....	....	....	....	....	....	14	12	7	19	30	....	....	....
1994-95	Courmaostar	Italy	30	30	34	64	....	....	....	107	....	....	....	....	....	....	....	....	....	....	....	....	....	....	....	....	....	....
1995-96	EV Zug	Switz.	15	15	14	29	....	....	....	69	....	....	....	....	....	....	....	....	....	....	9	7	4	11	37	....	....	....
1996-97	EV Zug	Switz.	45	*41	30	71	....	....	....	110	....	....	....	....	....	....	....	....	....	....	6	1	2	3	6	....	....	....
1997-98	EV Zug	EuroHL	5	2	6	8	....	....	....	20	....	....	....	....	....	....	....	....	....	....	....	....	....	....	....	....	....	....
	EV Zug	Switz.	40	25	25	50	....	....	....	50	....	....	....	....	....	....	....	....	....	....	19	16	11	27	51	....	....	....
	NHL Totals		28	5	5	10	5	4	9	12	1	0	0	37	13.5	18	5	15	0		1	0	0	0	0	0	0	0

ECHL First All-Star Team (1990) • Rookie of the Year - ECHL (1990) • MVP - ECHL (1990) • Won Jack A. Butterfield Trophy (Playoff MVP - AHL) (1993)

Signed as a free agent by **Detroit**, January 9, 1990. Traded to **Edmonton** by **Detroit** for Max Middendorf, February 22, 1992. Signed as a free agent by **Tampa Bay**, August 13, 1993

• McEACHERN, SHAWN

Shawn McEachern LW – L. 5′11″, 195 lbs. b: Waltham, MA, 2/28/1969. Pittsburgh's 6th choice, 110th overall, in 1987 Entry Draft.

Season	Club	League	GP	G	A	Pts	AG	AA	APts	PIM	PP	SH	GW	S	%	TGF	PGF	TGA	PGA	+/–	GP	G	A	Pts	PIM	PP	SH	GW
1986-87	Matignon-Mass High School	H.S.	16	29	28	57	....	....	....	....	....	....	....	....	....	....	....	....	....	....	....	....	....	....	....	....	....	....
1987-88	Matignon-Mass High School	H.S.	22	52	40	92	....	....	....	....	....	....	....	....	....	....	....	....	....	....	....	....	....	....	....	....	....	....
1988-89	Boston University	H.E.	36	20	28	48	....	....	....	32	....	....	....	....	....	....	....	....	....	....	....	....	....	....	....	....	....	....
1989-90	Boston University	H.E.	43	25	31	56	....	....	....	78	....	....	....	....	....	....	....	....	....	....	....	....	....	....	....	....	....	....
1990-91	Boston University	H.E.	41	34	48	82	....	....	....	43	....	....	....	....	....	....	....	....	....	....	....	....	....	....	....	....	....	....
	United States	WEC-A	10	3	2	5	....	....	....	6	....	....	....	....	....	....	....	....	....	....	....	....	....	....	....	....	....	....
1991-92	United States	Nat-Team	57	26	23	49	....	....	....	38	....	....	....	....	....	....	....	....	....	....	....	....	....	....	....	....	....	....
	United States	Olympics	8	1	0	1	....	....	....	10	....	....	....	....	....	....	....	....	....	....	....	....	....	....	....	....	....	....
	Pittsburgh Penguins	NHL	15	0	4	4	0	3	3	0	0	0	0	14	0.0	6	1	4	0	+1	19	2	7	9	4	0	0	0
1992-93	Pittsburgh Penguins	NHL	84	28	33	61	23	23	46	46	7	0	6	196	14.3	82	17	54	10	+21	12	3	2	5	10	0	0	1
1993-94	Los Angeles Kings	NHL	49	8	13	21	7	10	17	24	0	3	0	81	9.9	30	2	35	8	+1	....	....	....	....	....	....	....	....
	Pittsburgh Penguins	NHL	27	12	9	21	11	7	18	10	0	2	1	78	15.4	27	2	22	10	+13	6	1	0	1	2	0	0	0
1994-95	Kiekko-Espoo	Finland	8	1	3	4	....	....	....	6	....	....	....	....	....	....	....	....	....	....	....	....	....	....	....	....	....	....
	Pittsburgh Penguins	NHL	44	13	13	26	23	19	42	22	1	2	1	97	13.4	37	4	46	17	+4	11	0	2	2	8	0	0	0
1995-96	Boston Bruins	NHL	82	24	29	53	24	24	48	34	3	2	3	238	10.1	84	18	82	11	–5	5	2	1	3	8	0	0	0
1996-97	United States	W Cup	1	0	1	1	....	....	....	0	....	....	....	....	....	....	....	....	....	....	....	....	....	....	....	....	....	....
	Ottawa Senators	NHL	65	11	20	31	12	18	30	18	0	1	2	150	7.3	56	12	61	12	–5	7	2	0	2	8	1	0	0
1997-98	Ottawa Senators	NHL	81	24	24	48	28	23	51	42	8	2	4	229	10.5	74	22	65	14	+1	11	0	4	4	8	0	0	0
	NHL Totals		447	120	145	265	128	127	255	196	19	12	17	1083	11.1	396	78	369	82		71	10	16	26	48	1	0	1

Hockey East Second All-Star Team (1990) • Hockey East First All-Star Team (1991) • NCAA East First All-American Team (1991)

Traded to **LA Kings** by **Pittsburgh** for Marty McSorley, August 27, 1993. Traded to **Pittsburgh** by **LA Kings** with Tomas Sandstrom for Marty McSorley and Jim Paek, February 16, 1994. Traded to **Boston** by **Pittsburgh** with Kevin Stevens for Glen Murray, Bryan Smolinski and Boston's 3rd round choice (Boyd Kane) in 1996 Entry Draft, August 2, 1995. Traded to **Ottawa** by **Boston** for Trent McCleary and Ottawa's 3rd round choice (Eric Naud) in 1996 Entry Draft, June 22, 1996.

• McELMURY, JIM

Jim McElmury D – L. 6′1″, 190 lbs. b: St. Paul, MN, 10/3/1949.

Season	Club	League	GP	G	A	Pts	AG	AA	APts	PIM	PP	SH	GW	S	%	TGF	PGF	TGA	PGA	+/–	GP	G	A	Pts	PIM	PP	SH	GW
1970-71	Bemidji State University	NCAA	17	5	5	10	....	....	....	20	....	....	....	....	....	....	....	....	....	....	....	....	....	....	....	....	....	....
	United States	WEC-A	10	2	0	2	....	....	....	2	....	....	....	....	....	....	....	....	....	....	....	....	....	....	....	....	....	....
1971-72	United States	Nat-Team	10	2	0	2	....	....	....	2	....	....	....	....	....	....	....	....	....	....	....	....	....	....	....	....	....	....
	United States	Olympics	6	0	1	1	....	....	....	6	....	....	....	....	....	....	....	....	....	....	....	....	....	....	....	....	....	....
	Cleveland Barons	AHL	15	2	2	4	....	....	....	4	....	....	....	....	....	....	....	....	....	....	6	0	3	3	10	....	....	....
1972-73	Minnesota North Stars	NHL	7	0	1	1	0	1	1	2	0	0	0	0	0.0	2	0	2	1	+1	....	....	....	....	....	....	....	....
	Cleveland-Jacksonville Barons	AHL	69	4	23	27	....	....	....	20	....	....	....	....	....	....	....	....	....	....	....	....	....	....	....	....	....	....
1973-74	Portland Buckaroos	WHL	76	8	23	31	....	....	....	46	....	....	....	....	....	....	....	....	....	....	10	1	6	7	2	....	....	....
1974-75	Kansas City Scouts	NHL	78	5	17	22	5	13	18	25	1	0	1	137	3.6	64	24	110	22	–48	....	....	....	....	....	....	....	....
1975-76	Kansas City Scouts	NHL	38	2	6	8	2	5	7	6	1	0	0	43	4.7	28	4	49	12	–13	....	....	....	....	....	....	....	....
	Springfield Indians	AHL	36	4	12	16	....	....	....	10	....	....	....	....	....	....	....	....	....	....	....	....	....	....	....	....	....	....
1976-77	Colorado Rockies	NHL	55	7	23	30	7	19	26	16	1	0	1	81	8.6	75	26	77	13	–15	....	....	....	....	....	....	....	....
	Rhode Island Reds	AHL	24	3	13	16	....	....	....	16	....	....	....	....	....	....	....	....	....	....	....	....	....	....	....	....	....	....
	United States	WEC-A	10	2	3	5	....	....	....	10	....	....	....	....	....	....	....	....	....	....	....	....	....	....	....	....	....	....
1977-78	Colorado Rockies	NHL	2	0	0	0	0	0	0	0	0	0	0	0	0.0	1	0	0	0	+1	....	....	....	....	....	....	....	....
	Phoenix Roadrunners	CHL	12	0	3	3	....	....	....	8	....	....	....	....	....	....	....	....	....	....	....	....	....	....	....	....	....	....
	Hampton Gulls	AHL	11	1	7	8	....	....	....	4	....	....	....	....	....	....	....	....	....	....	....	....	....	....	....	....	....	....
	NHL Totals		180	14	47	61	14	38	52	49	3	0	2	261	5.4	170	54	238	48		....	....	....	....	....	....	....	....

Signed as a free agent by **Minnesota**, March, 1972. Traded to **LA Kings** by **Minnesota** for cash, March 1, 1974. Signed as a free agent by **Kansas City**, June 27, 1974. Transferred to **Colorado** after **Kansas City** franchise relocated, July 15, 1976.

• McEWEN, MIKE

Mike "Q" McEwen D – L. 6′1″, 185 lbs. b: Hornepayne, Ont., 8/10/1956. NY Rangers' 3rd choice, 42nd overall, in 1976 Amateur Draft.

Season	Club	League	GP	G	A	Pts	AG	AA	APts	PIM	PP	SH	GW	S	%	TGF	PGF	TGA	PGA	+/–	GP	G	A	Pts	PIM	PP	SH	GW
1973-74	Toronto Marlboros	OHA	68	5	32	37	....	....	....	81	....	....	....	....	....	....	....	....	....	....	....	....	....	....	....	....	....	....
1974-75	Toronto Marlboros	OHA	68	18	63	81	....	....	....	52	....	....	....	....	....	....	....	....	....	....	23	5	14	19	33	....	....	....
1975-76	Toronto Marlboros	OHA	65	23	40	63	....	....	....	63	....	....	....	....	....	....	....	....	....	....	10	3	9	12	20	....	....	....
1976-77	New York Rangers	NHL	80	14	29	43	13	24	37	38	5	0	0	204	6.9	107	35	102	6	–24	....	....	....	....	....	....	....	....
1977-78	New York Rangers	NHL	57	5	13	18	5	11	16	52	2	0	0	65	7.7	43	19	35	0	–11	....	....	....	....	....	....	....	....
1978-79	New York Rangers	NHL	80	20	38	58	18	29	47	35	7	0	4	204	9.8	121	38	91	18	+10	18	2	11	13	8	2	0	1
1979-80	New York Rangers	NHL	9	1	7	8	1	5	6	0	1	0	0	16	6.3	19	4	14	2	+3	....	....	....	....	....	....	....	....
	Colorado Rockies	NHL	67	11	40	51	10	31	41	33	5	1	1	178	6.2	99	31	86	5	–13	....	....	....	....	....	....	....	....

			REGULAR SEASON																		PLAYOFFS							
Season	Club	League	GP	G	A	Pts	AG	AA	APts	PIM	PP	SH	GW	S	%	TGF	PGF	TGA	PGA	+/–	GP	G	A	Pts	PIM	PP	SH	GW
1980-81	Colorado Rockies	NHL	65	11	35	46	9	24	33	84	5	0	1	229	4.8	105	35	128	25	–33	....	....	....	....	....	....	....	....
	New York Islanders	NHL	13	0	3	3	0	2	2	10	0	0	0	27	0.0	15	2	10	0	+3	17	6	8	14	6	4	0	0
1981-82	New York Islanders	NHL	73	10	39	49	8	26	34	50	1	0	1	161	6.2	114	22	77	15	+30	15	3	7	10	18	2	0	0
1982-83	New York Islanders	NHL	42	2	11	13	2	8	10	16	1	0	0	82	2.4	51	13	34	7	+11	12	0	2	2	4	0	0	0
1983-84	New York Islanders	NHL	15	0	2	2	0	1	1	6	0	0	0	27	0.0	12	0	18	1	–5	....	....	....	....	....	....	....	....
	Los Angeles Kings	NHL	47	10	24	34	8	16	24	14	7	0	0	133	7.5	74	35	54	3	–12	....	....	....	....	....	....	....	....
	New Haven Nighthawks	AHL	9	3	7	10	....	....	....	26	....	....	....	....	....	....	....	....	....	....	....	....	....	....	....	....	....	....
1984-85	Washington Capitals	NHL	56	11	27	38	9	18	27	42	4	0	3	151	7.3	97	40	37	2	+22	5	0	1	1	4	0	0	0
	Binghamton Whalers	AHL	14	2	10	12	....	....	....	14	....	....	....	....	....	....	....	....	....	....	....	....	....	....	....	....	....	....
1985-86	Detroit Red Wings	NHL	29	0	10	10	0	7	7	16	0	0	0	82	0.0	36	15	36	7	–8	....	....	....	....	....	....	....	....
	New York Rangers	NHL	16	2	5	7	2	3	5	8	0	0	1	36	5.6	17	4	17	0	–4	....	....	....	....	....	....	....	....
	New Haven Nighthawks	AHL	2	0	3	3	....	....	....	2	....	....	....	....	....	....	....	....	....	....	....	....	....	....	....	....	....	....
	Hartford Whalers	NHL	10	3	2	5	2	1	3	6	0	0	0	18	16.7	13	2	6	0	+5	8	0	4	4	6	0	0	0
1986-87	Hartford Whalers	NHL	48	8	8	16	7	6	13	32	5	0	2	86	9.3	40	19	30	0	–9	1	1	1	2	0	1	0	0
1987-88	Sierre	Switz.	....	18	19	37	....	....	....	....	....	....	....	....	....	....	....	....	....	....	....	....	....	....	....	....	....	....
	Hartford Whalers	NHL	9	0	3	3	0	2	2	10	0	0	0	22	0.0	11	2	10	0	–1	2	0	2	2	2	0	0	0
	NHL Totals		716	108	296	404	94	214	308	460	43	1	13	1721	6.3	974	316	785	91		78	12	36	48	48	9	0	1

Played in NHL All-Star Game (1980)

Traded to **Colorado** by **NY Rangers** with Lucien DeBlois, Pat Hickey, Dean Turner and future considerations (Bobby Sheehan) for Barry Beck, November 2, 1979. Traded to **NY Islanders** by **Colorado** with Jari Kaarela for Chico Resch and Steve Tambellini, March 10, 1981. Traded to **LA Kings** by **NY Islanders** for Detroit's 4th round choice (acquired earlier, NY Islanders selected Doug Wieck) in 1984 Entry Draft, November 17, 1983. Signed as a free agent by **Washington**, August 7, 1984. Signed as a free agent by **Detroit**, August 12, 1985. Traded to **NY Rangers** by **Detroit** for Steve Richmond, December 26, 1985. Traded to **Hartford** by **NY Rangers** for Bob Crawford, March 11, 1986.

• McFALL, DAN

Dan McFall D – R. 6', 180 lbs. b: Kenmore, NY, 4/8/1963. Winnipeg's 8th choice, 148th overall, in 1981 Entry Draft.

1980-81	Buffalo Jr. Sabres	NYJHL	STATISTICS NOT AVAILABLE																									
1981-82	Michigan State Spartans	CCHA	42	3	17	20	....	....	....	28	....	....	....	....	....	....	....	....	....	....	....	....	....	....	....	....	....	....
	United States	WJC-A	7	2	0	2	....	....	....	4	....	....	....	....	....	....	....	....	....	....	....	....	....	....	....	....	....	....
1982-83	Michigan State Spartans	CCHA	36	12	14	26	....	....	....	22	....	....	....	....	....	....	....	....	....	....	....	....	....	....	....	....	....	....
	United States	WJC-A	7	0	0	0	....	....	....	6	....	....	....	....	....	....	....	....	....	....	....	....	....	....	....	....	....	....
1983-84	Michigan State Spartans	CCHA	46	14	20	34	....	....	....	56	....	....	....	....	....	....	....	....	....	....	....	....	....	....	....	....	....	....
1984-85	Michigan State Spartans	CCHA	44	7	25	32	....	....	....	32	....	....	....	....	....	....	....	....	....	....	....	....	....	....	....	....	....	....
	Winnipeg Jets	NHL	2	0	0	0	0	0	0	0	0	0	0	2	0.0	1	0	4	0	–3	....	....	....	....	....	....	....	....
1985-86	Winnipeg Jets	NHL	7	0	1	1	0	1	1	0	0	0	0	2	0.0	3	0	7	1	–3	....	....	....	....	....	....	....	....
	Sherbrooke Canadiens	AHL	50	2	10	12	....	....	....	16	....	....	....	....	....	....	....	....	....	....	....	....	....	....	....	....	....	....
1986-87	Fort Wayne Komets	IHL	11	0	5	5	....	....	....	0	....	....	....	....	....	....	....	....	....	....	....	....	....	....	....	....	....	....
	NHL Totals		9	0	1	1	0	1	1	0	0	0	0	4	0.0	4	0	11	1		....	....	....	....	....	....	....	....

CCHA First All-Star Team (1984) • NCAA West Second All-American Team (1984) • CCHA Second All-Star Team (1985) • NCAA West First All-American Team (1985)

• McGEOUGH, JIM

Jim McGeough C – L. 5'8", 170 lbs. b: Regina, Sask., 4/13/1963. Washington's 6th choice, 110th overall, in 1981 Entry Draft.

1979-80	Regina Capitals	SJHL	57	56	77	133	....	....	....	94	....	....	....	....	....	....	....	....	....	....	....	....	....	....	....	....	....	....
	Regina Pats	WHL	10	1	4	5	....	....	....	2	....	....	....	....	....	....	....	....	....	....	....	....	....	....	....	....	....	....
1980-81	Regina Pats	WHL	4	1	2	3	....	....	....	2	....	....	....	....	....	....	....	....	....	....	....	....	....	....	....	....	....	....
	Billings Bighorns	WHL	67	49	42	91	....	....	....	139	....	....	....	....	....	....	....	....	....	....	5	2	5	7	15	....	....	....
1981-82	Billings Bighorns	WHL	71	93	66	159	....	....	....	142	....	....	....	....	....	....	....	....	....	....	5	2	1	3	4	....	....	....
	Washington Capitals	NHL	4	0	0	0	0	0	0	0	0	0	0	7	0.0	0	0	2	0	–2	....	....	....	....	....	....	....	....
1982-83	Nanaimo Islanders	WHL	72	76	56	132	....	....	....	126	....	....	....	....	....	....	....	....	....	....	....	....	....	....	....	....	....	....
	Hershey Bears	AHL	5	1	1	2	....	....	....	10	....	....	....	....	....	....	....	....	....	....	5	0	2	2	25	....	....	....
1983-84	Hershey Bears	AHL	79	40	36	76	....	....	....	108	....	....	....	....	....	....	....	....	....	....	....	....	....	....	....	....	....	....
1984-85	Washington Capitals	NHL	11	3	0	3	2	0	2	12	0	0	0	22	13.6	4	0	4	0	0	....	....	....	....	....	....	....	....
	Pittsburgh Penguins	NHL	14	0	4	4	0	3	3	4	0	0	0	34	0.0	8	0	12	0	–4	....	....	....	....	....	....	....	....
	Binghamton Whalers	AHL	57	32	21	53	....	....	....	26	....	....	....	....	....	....	....	....	....	....	....	....	....	....	....	....	....	....
1985-86	Pittsburgh Penguins	NHL	17	3	2	5	2	1	3	8	0	0	1	29	10.3	8	0	18	6	–4	....	....	....	....	....	....	....	....
	Baltimore Skipjacks	AHL	38	14	13	27	....	....	....	20	....	....	....	....	....	....	....	....	....	....	....	....	....	....	....	....	....	....
1986-87	Pittsburgh Penguins	NHL	11	1	4	5	1	3	4	8	0	0	0	24	4.2	8	0	13	0	–5	....	....	....	....	....	....	....	....
	Baltimore Skipjacks	AHL	45	18	19	37	....	....	....	37	....	....	....	....	....	....	....	....	....	....	....	....	....	....	....	....	....	....
	Muskegon Lumberjacks	IHL	18	13	15	28	....	....	....	6	....	....	....	....	....	....	....	....	....	....	15	*14	8	22	10	....	....	....
1987-88	Springfield Indians	AHL	30	11	13	24	....	....	....	28	....	....	....	....	....	....	....	....	....	....	....	....	....	....	....	....	....	....
1988-89	Klagenfurter	Germany	44	28	24	52	....	....	....	....	....	....	....	....	....	....	....	....	....	....	....	....	....	....	....	....	....	....
1989-90	Klagenfurter	German 2	STATISTICS NOT AVAILABLE																									
1990-91	Albany River Rats	IHL	12	9	3	12	....	....	....	4	....	....	....	....	....	....	....	....	....	....	....	....	....	....	....	....	....	....
	Kalamazoo Wings	IHL	7	0	0	0	....	....	....	2	....	....	....	....	....	....	....	....	....	....	....	....	....	....	....	....	....	....
	San Diego Gulls	IHL	10	2	4	6	....	....	....	4	....	....	....	....	....	....	....	....	....	....	....	....	....	....	....	....	....	....
1991-92	Bracknell Bees	Britain	12	15	9	24	....	....	....	20	....	....	....	....	....	....	....	....	....	....	....	....	....	....	....	....	....	....
	Richmond Renegades	ECHL	24	16	12	28	....	....	....	34	....	....	....	....	....	....	....	....	....	....	7	0	2	2	8	....	....	....
1992-93	Richmond Renegades	ECHL	39	14	27	41	....	....	....	66	....	....	....	....	....	....	....	....	....	....	....	....	....	....	....	....	....	....
1993-94	Richmond Renegades	ECHL	26	10	8	18	....	....	....	10	....	....	....	....	....	....	....	....	....	....	....	....	....	....	....	....	....	....
	Dallas Freeze	CHL	28	21	16	37	....	....	....	24	....	....	....	....	....	....	....	....	....	....	7	3	5	8	8	....	....	....
1994-95	Dallas Freeze	CHL	66	50	50	100	....	....	....	38	....	....	....	....	....	....	....	....	....	....	....	....	....	....	....	....	....	....
1995-96	Wichita Thunder	CHL	31	11	20	31	....	....	....	16	....	....	....	....	....	....	....	....	....	....	....	....	....	....	....	....	....	....
1996-97	Wichita Thunder	CHL	21	6	20	26	....	....	....	4	....	....	....	....	....	....	....	....	....	....	9	9	2	11	8	....	....	....
1997-98	Wichita Thunder	CHL	68	38	39	77	....	....	....	78	....	....	....	....	....	....	....	....	....	....	15	10	9	19	10	....	....	....
	NHL Totals		57	7	10	17	5	7	12	32	0	0	1	116	6.0	28	0	49	6		....	....	....	....	....	....	....	....

Traded to **Pittsburgh** by **Washington** for Mark Taylor, March 12, 1985.

• McGILL, BOB

Bob "Big Daddy" McGill D – R. 6'1", 193 lbs. b: Edmonton, Alta., 4/27/1962. Toronto's 2nd choice, 26th overall, in 1980 Entry Draft.

1978-79	Abbotsford Pilots	BCJHL	46	3	20	23	....	....	....	242	....	....	....	....	....	....	....	....	....	....	....	....	....	....	....	....	....	....
1979-80	Victoria Cougars	WHL	70	3	18	21	....	....	....	230	....	....	....	....	....	....	....	....	....	....	15	0	5	5	64	....	....	....
1980-81	Victoria Cougars	WHL	66	5	36	41	....	....	....	295	....	....	....	....	....	....	....	....	....	....	11	1	5	6	67	....	....	....
1981-82	Toronto Maple Leafs	NHL	68	1	10	11	1	7	8	263	0	0	0	34	2.9	59	1	83	16	–9	....	....	....	....	....	....	....	....
1982-83	Toronto Maple Leafs	NHL	30	0	0	0	0	0	0	146	0	0	0	13	0.0	11	1	37	3	–24	....	....	....	....	....	....	....	....
	St. Catharines Saints	AHL	32	2	5	7	....	....	....	95	....	....	....	....	....	....	....	....	....	....	....	....	....	....	....	....	....	....
1983-84	Toronto Maple Leafs	NHL	11	0	2	2	0	1	1	51	0	0	0	3	0.0	5	0	5	1	+1	....	....	....	....	....	....	....	....
	St. Catharines Saints	AHL	55	1	15	16	....	....	....	217	....	....	....	....	....	....	....	....	....	....	6	0	0	0	26	....	....	....
1984-85	Toronto Maple Leafs	NHL	72	0	5	5	0	3	3	250	0	0	0	22	0.0	31	0	54	23	0	....	....	....	....	....	....	....	....
1985-86	Toronto Maple Leafs	NHL	61	1	4	5	1	3	4	141	0	0	0	28	3.6	45	0	82	20	–17	9	0	0	0	35	0	0	0
1986-87	Toronto Maple Leafs	NHL	56	1	4	5	1	3	4	103	0	0	0	27	3.7	33	0	40	5	–2	3	0	0	0	0	0	0	0
1987-88	Chicago Blackhawks	NHL	67	4	7	11	3	5	8	131	0	0	1	56	7.1	45	1	100	37	–19	3	0	0	0	2	0	0	0
1988-89	Chicago Blackhawks	NHL	68	0	4	4	0	3	3	155	0	0	0	38	0.0	30	0	26	5	+9	16	0	0	0	33	0	0	0
1989-90	Chicago Blackhawks	NHL	69	2	10	12	2	7	9	204	0	1	0	53	3.8	42	0	55	6	–7	5	0	0	0	2	0	0	0
1990-91	Chicago Blackhawks	NHL	77	4	5	9	4	4	8	151	0	0	0	69	5.8	40	2	32	2	+8	5	0	0	0	2	0	0	0
1991-92	San Jose Sharks	NHL	62	3	1	4	3	1	4	70	0	1	1	56	5.4	35	2	96	29	–34	....	....	....	....	....	....	....	....
	Detroit Red Wings	NHL	12	0	0	0	0	0	0	21	0	0	0	6	0.0	5	0	9	1	–3	8	0	0	0	14	0	0	0
1992-93	Toronto Maple Leafs	NHL	19	1	0	1	1	0	1	34	0	0	0	8	12.5	10	0	6	1	+5	....	....	....	....	....	....	....	....

			REGULAR SEASON																		PLAYOFFS							
Season	Club	League	GP	G	A	Pts	AG	AA	APts	PIM	PP	SH	GW	S	%	TGF	PGF	TGA	PGA	+/–	GP	G	A	Pts	PIM	PP	SH	GW
1993-94	New York Islanders	NHL	3	0	0	0	0	0	0	5	0	0	0	0	0.0	2	0	2	0	0								
	Hartford Whalers	NHL	30	0	3	3	0	2	2	41	0	0	0	14	0.0	16	0	30	7	–7								
	Springfield Indians	AHL	5	0	0	0				24																		
1994-95			DID NOT PLAY																									
1995-96	Chicago Wolves	IHL	8	0	0	0				6																		
	NHL Totals		705	17	55	72	16	39	55	1766	0	2	2	427	4.0	409	7	657	156		49	0	0	0	88	0	0	0

Traded to **Chicago** by **Toronto** with Steve Thomas and Rick Vaive for Ed Olczyk and Al Secord, September 3, 1987. Claimed by **San Jose** from **Chicago** in Expansion Draft, May 30, 1991. Traded to **Detroit** by **San Jose** with Vancouver's 8th round choice (acquired earlier, Detroit selected C.J. Denomme) in 1992 Entry Draft for Johan Garpenlov, March 10, 1992. Claimed by **Tampa Bay** from **Detroit** in Expansion Draft, June 18, 1992. Claimed on waivers by **Toronto** from **Tampa Bay**, September 9, 1992. Signed as a free agent by **NY Islanders**, September 7, 1993. Claimed on waivers by **Hartford** from **NY Islanders**, November 3, 1993.

• McGILL, RYAN

Ryan McGill D – R. 6'2", 210 lbs. b: Prince Albert, Sask., 2/28/1969. Chicago's 2nd choice, 29th overall, in 1987 Entry Draft.

Season	Club	League	GP	G	A	Pts	AG	AA	APts	PIM	PP	SH	GW	S	%	TGF	PGF	TGA	PGA	+/–	GP	G	A	Pts	PIM	PP	SH	GW
1985-86	Lethbridge Broncos	WHL	64	5	10	15				171											10	0	1	1	9			
1986-87	Swift Current Broncos	WHL	72	12	36	48				226											4	1	0	1	9			
1987-88	Medicine Hat Tigers	WHL	67	5	30	35				224											15	7	3	10	47			
1988-89	Medicine Hat Tigers	WHL	57	26	45	71				172											3	0	2	2	15			
	Saginaw Hawks	IHL	8	2	0	2				12											6	0	0	0	42			
1989-90	Indianapolis Ice	IHL	77	11	17	28				215											14	2	2	4	29			
1990-91	Halifax Citadels	AHL	7	0	4	4				6																		
	Indianapolis Ice	IHL	63	11	40	51				200																		
1991-92	Chicago Blackhawks	NHL	9	0	2	2	0	1	1	20	0	0	0	15	0.0	8	0	9	2	+1								
	Indianapolis Ice	IHL	40	7	19	26				170																		
	Hershey Bears	AHL	17	3	5	8				67											6	1	1	2	4			
1992-93	Philadelphia Flyers	NHL	72	3	10	13	2	7	9	238	0	0	0	68	4.4	57	0	56	8	+9								
	Hershey Bears	AHL	4	0	2	2				26																		
1993-94	Philadelphia Flyers	NHL	50	1	3	4	1	2	3	112	0	0	0	53	1.9	34	0	54	15	–5								
1994-95	Philadelphia Flyers	NHL	12	0	0	0	0	0	0	13	0	0	0	2	0.0	3	0	3	0	0								
	Edmonton Oilers	NHL	8	0	0	0	0	0	0	8	0	0	0	6	0.0	5	0	10	1	–4								
	NHL Totals		151	4	15	19	3	10	13	391	0	0	0	144	2.8	107	0	132	26									

IHL Second All-Star Team (1991)

Traded to **Quebec** by **Chicago** with Mike McNeil for Paul Gillis and Dan Vincelette, March 5, 1991. Traded to **Chicago** by **Quebec** for Mike Dagenais, September 27, 1991. Traded to **Philadelphia** by **Chicago** for Tony Horcek, February 7, 1992. Traded to **Edmonton** by **Philadelphia** for Brad Zavisha and Edmonton's 6th round choice (Jamie Sokolosky) in 1995 Entry Draft, March 13, 1995.

• McGILLIS, DANIEL

Daniel McGillis D – L. 6'2", 225 lbs. b: Hawkesbury, Ont., 7/1/1972. Detroit's 10th choice, 238th overall, in 1992 Entry Draft.

Season	Club	League	GP	G	A	Pts	AG	AA	APts	PIM	PP	SH	GW	S	%	TGF	PGF	TGA	PGA	+/–	GP	G	A	Pts	PIM	PP	SH	GW
1991-92	Hawkesbury Hawks	OJHL	36	5	19	24				106																		
1992-93	Northeastern University	H.E.	35	5	12	17				42																		
1993-94	Northeastern University	H.E.	38	4	25	29				82																		
1994-95	Northeastern University	H.E.	34	9	22	31				70																		
1995-96	Northeastern University	H.E.	34	12	24	36				50																		
1996-97	Edmonton Oilers	NHL	73	6	16	22	6	14	20	52	2	1	2	139	4.3	85	27	69	13	+2	12	0	5	5	24	0	0	0
1997-98	Edmonton Oilers	NHL	67	10	15	25	12	15	27	74	5	0	3	119	8.4	58	23	75	23	–17								
	Philadelphia Flyers	NHL	13	1	5	6	1	5	6	35	1	0	0	18	5.6	15	7	15	3	–4	5	1	2	3	10	1	0	0
	NHL Totals		153	17	36	53	19	34	53	161	8	1	5	276	6.2	158	57	159	39		17	1	7	8	34	1	0	0

Hockey East First All-Star Team (1995, 1996) • NCAA East First All-American Team (1996)

Traded to **Edmonton** by **Detroit** for Kirk Maltby, March 20, 1996. Traded to **Philadelphia** by **Edmonton** with Edmonton's 2nd round choice (Jason Beckett) in 1998 Entry Draft for Janne Niinimaa, March 24, 1998.

• McHUGH, MIKE

Mike McHugh LW – L. 5'10", 190 lbs. b: Bowdoin, MA, 8/16/1965. Minnesota's 1st choice, 1st overall, in 1988 Supplemental Draft.

Season	Club	League	GP	G	A	Pts	AG	AA	APts	PIM	PP	SH	GW	S	%	TGF	PGF	TGA	PGA	+/–	GP	G	A	Pts	PIM	PP	SH	GW
1983-84	New Hampton Prep School	H.S.		24	22	46																						
1984-85	University of Maine	H.E.	25	9	8	17				9																		
1985-86	University of Maine	H.E.	38	9	10	19				24																		
1986-87	University of Maine	H.E.	42	21	29	50				40																		
1987-88	University of Maine	H.E.	44	29	37	66				90																		
1988-89	Minnesota North Stars	NHL	3	0	0	0	0	0	0	2	0	0	0	1	0.0	0	0	2	1	–1								
	Kalamazoo Wings	IHL	70	17	29	46				89											6	3	1	4	17			
1989-90	Minnesota North Stars	NHL	3	0	0	0	0	0	0	0	0	0	0	2	0.0	0	0	1	0	–1								
	Kalamazoo Wings	IHL	73	14	17	31				96											10	0	6	6	16			
1990-91	Minnesota North Stars	NHL	6	0	0	0	0	0	0	0	0	0	0	4	0.0	0	0	3	0	–3								
	Kalamazoo Wings	IHL	69	27	38	65				82											11	3	8	11	6			
1991-92	San Jose Sharks	NHL	8	1	0	1	1	0	1	14	0	0	0	5	20.0	4	0	8	1	–3								
	Springfield Indians	AHL	70	23	31	54				51											11	4	7	11	25			
1992-93	Springfield Indians	AHL	67	19	27	46				111											11	5	2	7	12			
1993-94	Hershey Bears	AHL	80	27	43	70				58											11	9	3	12	14			
1994-95	Hershey Bears	AHL	68	24	26	50				102											6	3	2	5	6			
1995-96	Hershey Bears	AHL	75	15	42	57				118											5	2	2	4	2			
1996-97	Hershey Bears	AHL	77	23	45	68				135											19	5	7	12	29			
1997-98	Hershey Bears	AHL	66	12	25	37				143											7	1	1	2	16			
	NHL Totals		20	1	0	1	1	0	1	16	0	0	0	12	8.3	4	0	14	2									

Hockey East First All-Star Team (1988) • Won Jack A. Butterfield Trophy (Playoff MVP - AHL) (1997)

Claimed by **San Jose** from **Minnesota** in Dispersal Draft, May 30, 1991. Traded to **Hartford** by **San Jose** for Paul Fenton, October 18, 1991.

• McILHARGEY, JACK

Jack McIlhargey D – L. 6', 190 lbs. b: Edmonton, Alta., 3/7/1952.

Season	Club	League	GP	G	A	Pts	AG	AA	APts	PIM	PP	SH	GW	S	%	TGF	PGF	TGA	PGA	+/–	GP	G	A	Pts	PIM	PP	SH	GW
1971-72	Victoria Cougars	WCJHL	24	1	1	2				137																		
	Flin Flon Bombers	WCJHL	33	1	4	5				142																		
1972-73	Jersey Devils	EHL	72	2	7	9				229																		
	Richmond Robins	AHL	9	0	1	1				4											4	0	0	0	7			
1973-74	Des Moines Capitols	IHL	16	1	2	3				52																		
	Richmond Robins	AHL	54	2	10	12				163											5	0	0	0	12			
1974-75	Philadelphia Flyers	NHL	2	0	0	0	0	0	0	11	0	0	0	1	0.0	0	0	1	0	–1								
	Richmond Robins	AHL	72	4	3	7				*316											7	0	3	3	45			
1975-76	Philadelphia Flyers	NHL	57	1	2	3	1	2	3	205	0	0	0	23	4.3	31	1	20	1	+11	15	0	3	3	41	0	0	0
	Richmond Robins	AHL	4	0	0	0				17																		
1976-77	Philadelphia Flyers	NHL	40	2	1	3	2	1	3	164	0	0	0	27	7.4	26	0	21	1	+6								
	Vancouver Canucks	NHL	21	1	7	8	1	6	7	61	0	0	0	18	5.6	25	1	29	8	+3								
1977-78	Vancouver Canucks	NHL	69	3	5	8	3	4	7	172	0	0	0	36	8.3	42	1	103	17	–45								
1978-79	Vancouver Canucks	NHL	53	2	4	6	2	3	5	129	0	0	0	26	7.7	41	1	66	10	–16	3	0	0	0	2	0	0	0
1979-80	Vancouver Canucks	NHL	24	0	2	2	0	2	2	41	0	0	0	6	0.0	9	0	14	0	–5								
	Philadelphia Flyers	NHL	26	0	4	4	0	3	3	95	0	0	0	15	0.0	22	0	26	11	+17	0	0	0	0	25	0	0	0
1980-81	Philadelphia Flyers	NHL	3	0	0	0	0	0	0	22	0	0	0	0	0.0	3	0	1	0	+2								
	Maine Mariners	AHL	3	0	1	1				7																		
	Hartford Whalers	NHL	48	1	6	7	1	4	5	142	0	0	0	14	7.1	37	0	53	13	–3								
1981-82	Hartford Whalers	NHL	50	1	5	6	1	3	4	60	0	0	0	23	4.3	21	0	33	4	–8								
	NHL Totals		393	11	36	47	11	28	39	1102	0	0	0	189	5.8	257	4	367	65		27	0	3	3	68	0	0	0

Signed as a free agent by **Philadelphia** (Jersey-EHL), September, 1972. Traded to **Vancouver** by **Philadelphia** with Larry Goodenough for Bob Dailey, January 20, 1977. Traded to **Philadelphia** by **Vancouver** for cash, January 2, 1980. Traded to **Hartford** by **Philadelphia** with Norm Barnes for Hartford's 2nd round choice (later traded to Toronto — Toronto selected Gary Leeman) in 1982 Entry Draft, November 21, 1980.

• McINNIS, MARTY

Marty McInnis C – R. 5'11", 183 lbs. b: Hingham, MA., 6/2/1970. NY Islanders' 10th choice, 163rd overall, in 1988 Entry Draft.

			REGULAR SEASON																		PLAYOFFS							
Season	Club	League	GP	G	A	Pts	AG	AA	APts	PIM	PP	SH	GW	S	%	TGF	PGF	TGA	PGA	+/-	GP	G	A	Pts	PIM	PP	SH	GW
1987-88	Milton-Mass Academy	H.S.	25	26	25	51	....	....	....	....	....	....	....	....	....	....	....	....	....	....	....	....	....	....	....	....	....	....
1988-89	Boston College	H.E.	39	13	19	32	....	....	....	8	....	....	....	....	....	....	....	....	....	....	....	....	....	....	....	....	....	....
1989-90	Boston College	H.E.	41	24	29	53	....	....	....	43	....	....	....	....	....	....	....	....	....	....	....	....	....	....	....	....	....	....
1990-91	Boston College	H.E.	38	21	36	57	....	....	....	40	....	....	....	....	....	....	....	....	....	....	....	....	....	....	....	....	....	....
1991-92	United States	Nat-Team	54	15	19	34	....	....	....	20	....	....	....	....	....	....	....	....	....	....	....	....	....	....	....	....	....	....
	United States	Olympics	8	5	2	7	....	....	....	4	....	....	....	....	....	....	....	....	....	....	....	....	....	....	....	....	....	....
	New York Islanders	**NHL**	**15**	**3**	**5**	**8**	**3**	**4**	**7**	**0**	**0**	**0**	**0**	**24**	**12.5**	**14**	**3**	**8**	**3**	**+6**	....	....	....	....	....	....	....	....
1992-93	**New York Islanders**	**NHL**	**56**	**10**	**20**	**30**	**8**	**14**	**22**	**24**	**0**	**1**	**0**	**60**	**16.7**	**46**	**4**	**47**	**12**	**+7**	**3**	**0**	**1**	**1**	**0**	**0**	**0**	**0**
	Capital District Islanders	AHL	10	4	12	16	....	....	....	2	....	....	....	....	....	....	....	....	....	....	....	....	....	....	....	....	....	....
1993-94	**New York Islanders**	**NHL**	**81**	**25**	**31**	**56**	**23**	**24**	**47**	**24**	**3**	**5**	**3**	**136**	**18.4**	**78**	**10**	**71**	**34**	**+31**	**4**	**0**	**0**	**0**	**0**	**0**	**0**	**0**
1994-95	**New York Islanders**	**NHL**	**41**	**9**	**7**	**16**	**16**	**10**	**26**	**8**	**0**	**0**	**1**	**68**	**13.2**	**23**	**4**	**33**	**13**	**–1**	....	....	....	....	....	....	....	....
1995-96	**New York Islanders**	**NHL**	**74**	**12**	**34**	**46**	**12**	**28**	**40**	**39**	**2**	**0**	**1**	**167**	**7.2**	**72**	**23**	**92**	**32**	**–11**	....	....	....	....	....	....	....	....
	United States	WC-A	7	0	2	2	....	....	....	4	....	....	....	....	....	....	....	....	....	....	....	....	....	....	....	....	....	....
1996-97	United States	WC-A	8	2	2	4	....	....	....	2	....	....	....	....	....	....	....	....	....	....	....	....	....	....	....	....	....	....
	New York Islanders	**NHL**	**70**	**20**	**22**	**42**	**21**	**19**	**40**	**20**	**4**	**1**	**4**	**163**	**12.3**	**71**	**19**	**78**	**19**	**–7**	....	....	....	....	....	....	....	....
	Calgary Flames	**NHL**	**10**	**3**	**4**	**7**	**3**	**4**	**7**	**2**	**1**	**0**	**0**	**19**	**15.8**	**7**	**2**	**9**	**3**	**–1**	....	....	....	....	....	....	....	....
1997-98	**Calgary Flames**	**NHL**	**75**	**19**	**25**	**44**	**22**	**24**	**46**	**34**	**5**	**4**	**0**	**128**	**14.8**	**63**	**14**	**74**	**26**	**+1**	....	....	....	....	....	....	....	....
	NHL Totals		**422**	**101**	**148**	**249**	**108**	**127**	**235**	**151**	**15**	**11**	**9**	**765**	**13.2**	**374**	**79**	**412**	**142**		**7**	**0**	**1**	**1**	**0**	**0**	**0**	**0**

Traded to **Calgary** by **NY Islanders** with Tyrone Garner and Calgary's 6th round choice (previously acquired, Calgary selected Ilja Demidov) in 1997 Entry Draft for Robert Reichel, March 18, 1997.

• McINTOSH, BRUCE

Bruce McIntosh D – L. 6', 178 lbs. b: Minneapolis, MN, 3/17/1949.

Season	Club	League	GP	G	A	Pts	AG	AA	APts	PIM	PP	SH	GW	S	%	TGF	PGF	TGA	PGA	+/-	GP	G	A	Pts	PIM	PP	SH	GW
1968-69	University of Minnesota	WCHA	7	0	0	0	....	....	....	0	....	....	....	....	....	....	....	....	....	....	....	....	....	....	....	....	....	....
1969-70	University of Minnesota	WCHA	33	3	12	15	....	....	....	26	....	....	....	....	....	....	....	....	....	....	....	....	....	....	....	....	....	....
1970-71	University of Minnesota	WCHA	33	8	13	21	....	....	....	29	....	....	....	....	....	....	....	....	....	....	....	....	....	....	....	....	....	....
1971-72	United States	Nat-Team	STATISTICS NOT AVAILABLE																									
1972-73	**Minnesota North Stars**	**NHL**	**2**	**0**	**0**	**0**	**0**	**0**	**0**	**0**	**0**	**0**	**0**	**0**	**0.0**	**0**	**0**	**0**	**0**	**0**	....	....	....	....	....	....	....	....
	Cleveland-Jacksonville Barons	AHL	23	1	5	6	....	....	....	4	....	....	....	....	....	....	....	....	....	....	....	....	....	....	....	....	....	....
	Saginaw Gears	IHL	30	5	16	21	....	....	....	23	....	....	....	....	....	....	....	....	....	....	....	....	....	....	....	....	....	....
	NHL Totals		**2**	**0**	**0**	**0**	**0**	**0**	**0**	**0**	**0**	**0**	**0**	**0**	**0.0**	**0**	**0**	**0**	**0**		....	....	....	....	....	....	....	....

NCAA Championship All-Tournament Team (1971)

Signed as a free agent by **Minnesota**, September 30, 1972.

• McINTOSH, PAUL

Paul McIntosh D – R. 5'10", 177 lbs. b: Listowel, Ont., 3/13/1954. Buffalo's 4th choice, 65th overall, in 1974 Amateur Draft.

Season	Club	League	GP	G	A	Pts	AG	AA	APts	PIM	PP	SH	GW	S	%	TGF	PGF	TGA	PGA	+/-	GP	G	A	Pts	PIM	PP	SH	GW
1972-73	Peterborough Petes	OHA	63	7	32	39	....	....	....	67	....	....	....	....	....	....	....	....	....	....	....	....	....	....	....	....	....	....
1973-74	Peterborough Petes	OHA	62	16	34	50	....	....	....	153	....	....	....	....	....	....	....	....	....	....	15	0	13	13	....	....	....	....
	Canada	WJC-A	5	3	2	5	....	....	....	6	....	....	....	....	....	....	....	....	....	....	....	....	....	....	....	....	....	....
1974-75	**Buffalo Sabres**	**NHL**	**6**	**0**	**1**	**1**	**0**	**1**	**1**	**5**	**0**	**0**	**0**	**1**	**0.0**	**4**	**0**	**3**	**1**	**+2**	**1**	**0**	**0**	**0**	**0**	**0**	**0**	**0**
	Hershey Bears	AHL	68	2	11	13	....	....	....	195	....	....	....	....	....	....	....	....	....	....	12	1	1	2	43	....	....	....
1975-76	**Buffalo Sabres**	**NHL**	**42**	**0**	**1**	**1**	**0**	**1**	**1**	**61**	**0**	**0**	**0**	**9**	**0.0**	**13**	**0**	**19**	**1**	**–5**	**1**	**0**	**0**	**0**	**7**	**0**	**0**	**0**
	Hershey Bears	AHL	12	0	2	2	....	....	....	63	....	....	....	....	....	....	....	....	....	....	....	....	....	....	....	....	....	....
1976-77	Hershey Bears	AHL	62	6	10	16	....	....	....	171	....	....	....	....	....	....	....	....	....	....	3	0	0	0	6	....	....	....
1977-78	Springfield Indians	AHL	77	5	22	27	....	....	....	189	....	....	....	....	....	....	....	....	....	....	4	0	0	0	18	....	....	....
1978-79	Saginaw Gears	IHL	78	11	34	45	....	....	....	147	....	....	....	....	....	....	....	....	....	....	4	0	1	1	6	....	....	....
1979-80	Saginaw Gears	IHL	10	0	3	3	....	....	....	62	....	....	....	....	....	....	....	....	....	....	....	....	....	....	....	....	....	....
	NHL Totals		**48**	**0**	**2**	**2**	**0**	**2**	**2**	**66**	**0**	**0**	**0**	**10**	**0.0**	**17**	**0**	**22**	**2**		**2**	**0**	**0**	**0**	**7**	**0**	**0**	**0**

WJC-A All-Star Team (1974) • OHA Second All-Star Team (1974)

• McINTYRE, JOHN

John McIntyre C – L. 6'1", 190 lbs. b: Ravenswood, Ont., 4/29/1969. Toronto's 3rd choice, 49th overall, in 1987 Entry Draft.

Season	Club	League	GP	G	A	Pts	AG	AA	APts	PIM	PP	SH	GW	S	%	TGF	PGF	TGA	PGA	+/-	GP	G	A	Pts	PIM	PP	SH	GW
1984-85	Strathroy Rockets	Jr. B	48	21	23	44	....	....	....	49	....	....	....	....	....	....	....	....	....	....	....	....	....	....	....	....	....	....
1985-86	Guelph Platers	OHL	30	4	6	10	....	....	....	25	....	....	....	....	....	....	....	....	....	....	20	1	5	6	31	....	....	....
1986-87	Guelph Platers	OHL	47	8	22	30	....	....	....	95	....	....	....	....	....	....	....	....	....	....	....	....	....	....	....	....	....	....
1987-88	Guelph Platers	OHL	39	24	18	42	....	....	....	109	....	....	....	....	....	....	....	....	....	....	....	....	....	....	....	....	....	....
1988-89	Guelph Platers	OHL	52	30	26	56	....	....	....	129	....	....	....	....	....	....	....	....	....	....	7	5	4	9	25	....	....	....
	Canada	WJC-A	7	1	0	1	....	....	....	4	....	....	....	....	....	....	....	....	....	....	....	....	....	....	....	....	....	....
	Newmarket Saints	AHL	3	0	2	2	....	....	....	7	....	....	....	....	....	....	....	....	....	....	5	1	1	2	20	....	....	....
1989-90	**Toronto Maple Leafs**	**NHL**	**59**	**5**	**12**	**17**	**4**	**9**	**13**	**117**	**0**	**1**	**1**	**44**	**11.4**	**26**	**5**	**46**	**13**	**–12**	**2**	**0**	**0**	**0**	**2**	**0**	**0**	**0**
	Newmarket Saints	AHL	6	2	2	4	....	....	....	12	....	....	....	....	....	....	....	....	....	....	....	....	....	....	....	....	....	....
1990-91	**Toronto Maple Leafs**	**NHL**	**13**	**0**	**3**	**3**	**0**	**2**	**2**	**25**	**0**	**0**	**0**	**7**	**0.0**	**4**	**0**	**11**	**7**	**0**	....	....	....	....	....	....	....	....
	Los Angeles Kings	**NHL**	**56**	**8**	**5**	**13**	**7**	**4**	**11**	**115**	**0**	**1**	**0**	**26**	**30.8**	**18**	**0**	**21**	**9**	**+6**	**12**	**0**	**1**	**1**	**24**	**0**	**0**	**0**
1991-92	**Los Angeles Kings**	**NHL**	**73**	**5**	**19**	**24**	**5**	**14**	**19**	**100**	**0**	**0**	**1**	**40**	**12.5**	**31**	**0**	**51**	**20**	**0**	**6**	**0**	**4**	**4**	**12**	**0**	**0**	**0**
1992-93	**Los Angeles Kings**	**NHL**	**49**	**2**	**5**	**7**	**2**	**3**	**5**	**80**	**0**	**0**	**0**	**31**	**6.5**	**16**	**0**	**39**	**10**	**–13**	....	....	....	....	....	....	....	....
	New York Rangers	**NHL**	**11**	**1**	**0**	**1**	**1**	**0**	**1**	**4**	**0**	**0**	**0**	**5**	**20.0**	**2**	**0**	**4**	**1**	**–1**	....	....	....	....	....	....	....	....
1993-94	**Vancouver Canucks**	**NHL**	**62**	**3**	**6**	**9**	**3**	**5**	**8**	**38**	**0**	**0**	**0**	**30**	**10.0**	**15**	**0**	**49**	**25**	**–9**	**24**	**0**	**1**	**1**	**16**	**0**	**0**	**0**
1994-95	**Vancouver Canucks**	**NHL**	**28**	**0**	**4**	**4**	**0**	**6**	**6**	**37**	**0**	**0**	**0**	**6**	**0.0**	**5**	**0**	**13**	**5**	**–3**	....	....	....	....	....	....	....	....
1995-96	Syracuse Crunch	AHL	53	13	14	27	....	....	....	78	....	....	....	....	....	....	....	....	....	....	....	....	....	....	....	....	....	....
	NHL Totals		**351**	**24**	**54**	**78**	**22**	**43**	**65**	**516**	**0**	**2**	**2**	**189**	**12.7**	**117**	**5**	**234**	**90**		**44**	**0**	**6**	**6**	**54**	**0**	**0**	**0**

Traded to **LA Kings** by **Toronto** for Mike Krushelnyski, November 9, 1990. Traded to **NY Rangers** by **LA Kings** for Mark Hardy and Ottawa's 5th round choice (previously acquired, LA Kings selected Frederick Beaubien) in 1993 Entry Draft, March 22, 1993. Claimed by **Vancouver** from **NY Rangers** in Waiver Draft, October 3, 1993.

• McINTYRE, LARRY

Larry McIntyre D – L. 6'1", 190 lbs. b: Moose Jaw, Sask., 7/13/1949. Toronto's 3rd choice, 31st overall, in 1969 Amateur Draft.

Season	Club	League	GP	G	A	Pts	AG	AA	APts	PIM	PP	SH	GW	S	%	TGF	PGF	TGA	PGA	+/-	GP	G	A	Pts	PIM	PP	SH	GW
1966-67	Moose Jaw Canucks	WCJHL	32	0	3	3	....	....	....	9	....	....	....	....	....	....	....	....	....	....	10	0	0	0	2	....	....	....
1967-68	Moose Jaw Canucks	WCJHL	60	7	13	20	....	....	....	66	....	....	....	....	....	....	....	....	....	....	....	....	....	....	....	....	....	....
1968-69	Moose Jaw Canucks	WCJHL	4	1	6	7	....	....	....	4	....	....	....	....	....	....	....	....	....	....	....	....	....	....	....	....	....	....
1969-70	Tulsa Oilers	CHL	60	2	12	14	....	....	....	41	....	....	....	....	....	....	....	....	....	....	6	0	0	0	4	....	....	....
	Toronto Maple Leafs	**NHL**	**1**	**0**	**0**	**0**	**0**	**0**	**0**	**0**	**0**	**0**	**0**	**1**	**0.0**	**3**	**0**	**0**	**0**	**+3**	....	....	....	....	....	....	....	....
	Buffalo Bisons	AHL	....	....	....	....	....	....	....	....	....	....	....	....	....	....	....	....	....	....	1	0	0	0	0	....	....	....
1970-71	Tulsa Oilers	CHL	41	0	4	4	....	....	....	18	....	....	....	....	....	....	....	....	....	....	....	....	....	....	....	....	....	....
1971-72	Tulsa Oilers	CHL	72	1	11	12	....	....	....	55	....	....	....	....	....	....	....	....	....	....	13	0	9	9	10	....	....	....
1972-73	**Toronto Maple Leafs**	**NHL**	**40**	**0**	**3**	**3**	**0**	**2**	**2**	**26**	**0**	**0**	**0**	**22**	**0.0**	**31**	**0**	**32**	**7**	**+6**	....	....	....	....	....	....	....	....
	Tulsa Oilers	CHL	14	0	8	8	....	....	....	20	....	....	....	....	....	....	....	....	....	....	....	....	....	....	....	....	....	....
1973-74	Seattle Totems	WHL	52	2	14	16	....	....	....	32	....	....	....	....	....	....	....	....	....	....	....	....	....	....	....	....	....	....
1974-75	Seattle Totems	CHL	68	2	13	15	....	....	....	50	....	....	....	....	....	....	....	....	....	....	....	....	....	....	....	....	....	....
1975-76	Tulsa Oilers	CHL	76	7	29	36	....	....	....	36	....	....	....	....	....	....	....	....	....	....	9	1	3	4	6	....	....	....
	NHL Totals		**41**	**0**	**3**	**3**	**0**	**2**	**2**	**26**	**0**	**0**	**0**	**23**	**0.0**	**34**	**0**	**32**	**7**		....	....	....	....	....	....	....	....

CHL Second All-Star Team (1976)

Traded to **Vancouver** by **Toronto** with Murray Heatley for Dunc Wilson, May 29, 1973.

• McKAY, RANDY

Randy McKay RW – R. 6'1", 210 lbs. b: Montreal, Que., 1/25/1967. Detroit's 6th choice, 113th overall, in 1985 Entry Draft.

Season	Club	League	GP	G	A	Pts	AG	AA	APts	PIM	PP	SH	GW	S	%	TGF	PGF	TGA	PGA	+/-	GP	G	A	Pts	PIM	PP	SH	GW
1984-85	Michigan Tech Huskies	WCHA	25	4	5	9	....	....	....	32	....	....	....	....	....	....	....	....	....	....	....	....	....	....	....	....	....	....
1985-86	Michigan Tech Huskies	WCHA	40	12	22	34	....	....	....	46	....	....	....	....	....	....	....	....	....	....	....	....	....	....	....	....	....	....
1986-87	Michigan Tech Huskies	WCHA	39	5	11	16	....	....	....	46	....	....	....	....	....	....	....	....	....	....	....	....	....	....	....	....	....	....
1987-88	Michigan Tech Huskies	WCHA	41	17	24	41	....	....	....	70	....	....	....	....	....	....	....	....	....	....	....	....	....	....	....	....	....	....
	Adirondack Red Wings	AHL	10	0	3	3	....	....	....	12	....	....	....	....	....	....	....	....	....	....	6	0	4	4	0	....	....	....
1988-89	**Detroit Red Wings**	**NHL**	**3**	**0**	**0**	**0**	**0**	**0**	**0**	**0**	**0**	**0**	**0**	**2**	**0.0**	**1**	**0**	**2**	**0**	**–1**	**2**	**0**	**0**	**0**	**2**	**0**	**0**	**0**
	Adirondack Red Wings	AHL	58	29	34	63	....	....	....	170	....	....	....	....	....	....	....	....	....	....	14	4	7	11	60	....	....	....
1989-90	**Detroit Red Wings**	**NHL**	**33**	**3**	**6**	**9**	**3**	**4**	**7**	**51**	**0**	**0**	**0**	**33**	**9.1**	**17**	**0**	**16**	**0**	**+1**	....	....	....	....	....	....	....	....
	Adirondack Red Wings	AHL	36	16	23	39	....	....	....	99	....	....	....	....	....	....	....	....	....	....	6	3	0	3	35	....	....	....

			REGULAR SEASON																	PLAYOFFS							
Season	Club	League	GP	G	A	Pts	AG	AA	APts	PIM	PP	SH	GW	S	%	TGF	PGF	TGA	PGA	+/–	GP	G	A	Pts	PIM	PP	SH	GW
1990-91	**Detroit Red Wings**	**NHL**	**47**	**1**	**7**	**8**	**1**	**5**	**6**	**183**	**0**	**0**	**0**	**22**	**4.5**	**12**	**0**	**27**	**0**	**–15**	**5**	**0**	**1**	**1**	**41**	**0**	**0**	**0**
1991-92	**New Jersey Devils**	**NHL**	**80**	**17**	**16**	**33**	**16**	**12**	**28**	**246**	**2**	**0**	**1**	**111**	**15.3**	**47**	**4**	**43**	**6**	**+6**	**7**	**1**	**3**	**4**	**10**	**1**	**0**	**0**
1992-93	**New Jersey Devils**	**NHL**	**73**	**11**	**11**	**22**	**9**	**8**	**17**	**206**	**1**	**0**	**2**	**94**	**11.7**	**31**	**1**	**40**	**10**	**0**	**5**	**0**	**0**	**0**	**16**	**0**	**0**	**0**
1993-94	**New Jersey Devils**	**NHL**	**78**	**12**	**15**	**27**	**11**	**12**	**23**	**244**	**0**	**0**	**1**	**77**	**15.6**	**41**	**0**	**17**	**0**	**+24**	**20**	**1**	**2**	**3**	**24**	**0**	**0**	**0**
1994-95	**New Jersey Devils**	**NHL**	**33**	**5**	**7**	**12**	**9**	**10**	**19**	**44**	**0**	**0**	**0**	**44**	**11.4**	**20**	**3**	**7**	**0**	**+10**	**19**	**8**	**4**	**12**	**11**	**2**	**0**	**2**
1995-96	**New Jersey Devils**	**NHL**	**76**	**11**	**10**	**21**	**11**	**8**	**19**	**145**	**3**	**0**	**3**	**97**	**11.3**	**39**	**9**	**23**	**0**	**+7**	....	....	....	....	....	....	....	....
1996-97	**New Jersey Devils**	**NHL**	**77**	**9**	**18**	**27**	**10**	**16**	**26**	**109**	**0**	**0**	**2**	**92**	**9.8**	**42**	**5**	**22**	**0**	**+15**	**10**	**1**	**1**	**2**	**0**	**0**	**0**	**0**
1997-98	**New Jersey Devils**	**NHL**	**74**	**24**	**24**	**48**	**28**	**23**	**51**	**86**	**8**	**0**	**5**	**141**	**17.0**	**70**	**19**	**21**	**0**	**+30**	**6**	**0**	**1**	**1**	**0**	**0**	**0**	**0**
	NHL Totals		**574**	**93**	**114**	**207**	**98**	**98**	**196**	**1314**	**14**	**0**	**14**	**713**	**13.0**	**320**	**41**	**218**	**16**		**74**	**11**	**12**	**23**	**104**	**3**	**0**	**2**

Transferred to **New Jersey** by **Detroit** with Dave Barr as compensation for Detroit's signing of free agent Troy Crowder, September 9, 1991.

• McKAY, RAY

Ray McKay   D – L. 6'4", 183 lbs.   b: Edmonton, Alta., 8/22/1946.

Season	Club	League	GP	G	A	Pts	AG	AA	APts	PIM	PP	SH	GW	S	%	TGF	PGF	TGA	PGA	+/–	GP	G	A	Pts	PIM	PP	SH	GW
1965-66	Moose Jaw Canucks	WCJHL	57	3	20	23	....	....	....	103	....	....	....	....	....	....	....	....	....	....	5	0	2	2	8	....	....	....
1966-67	Moose Jaw Canucks	WCJHL	56	6	22	28	....	....	....	104	....	....	....	....	....	....	....	....	....	....	14	0	6	6	34	....	....	....
1967-68	Dallas Black Hawks	CHL	58	2	5	7	....	....	....	68	....	....	....	....	....	....	....	....	....	....	5	0	0	0	9	....	....	....
1968-69	**Chicago Black Hawks**	**NHL**	**9**	**0**	**1**	**1**	**0**	**1**	**1**	**12**	**0**	**0**	**0**	**4**	**0.0**	**8**	**0**	**5**	**0**	**+3**	....	....	....	....	....	....	....	....
	Dallas Black Hawks	CHL	61	4	13	17	....	....	....	164	....	....	....	....	....	....	....	....	....	....	....	....	....	....	....	....	....	....
1969-70	**Chicago Black Hawks**	**NHL**	**17**	**0**	**0**	**0**	**0**	**0**	**0**	**23**	**0**	**0**	**0**	**7**	**0.0**	**2**	**0**	**12**	**2**	**–8**	....	....	....	....	....	....	....	....
	Dallas Black Hawks	CHL	12	0	3	3	....	....	....	18	....	....	....	....	....	....	....	....	....	....	....	....	....	....	....	....	....	....
	Portland Buckaroos	WHL	....	....	....	....	....	....	....	....	....	....	....	....	....	....	....	....	....	....	2	0	0	0	25	....	....	....
1970-71	**Chicago Black Hawks**	**NHL**	**2**	**0**	**0**	**0**	**0**	**0**	**0**	**0**	**0**	**0**	**0**	**1**	**0.0**	**0**	**0**	**0**	**0**	**0**	....	....	....	....	....	....	....	....
	Portland Buckaroos	WHL	55	1	25	26	....	....	....	111	....	....	....	....	....	....	....	....	....	....	11	0	7	7	10	....	....	....
1971-72	**Buffalo Sabres**	**NHL**	**39**	**0**	**3**	**3**	**0**	**3**	**3**	**18**	**0**	**0**	**0**	**18**	**0.0**	**9**	**0**	**32**	**11**	**–12**	....	....	....	....	....	....	....	....
	Cincinnati Swords	AHL	14	1	4	5	....	....	....	39	....	....	....	....	....	....	....	....	....	....	10	0	4	4	36	....	....	....
1972-73	**Buffalo Sabres**	**NHL**	**1**	**0**	**0**	**0**	**0**	**0**	**0**	**0**	**0**	**0**	**0**	**0**	**0.0**	**0**	**0**	**0**	**0**	**0**	....	....	....	....	....	....	....	....
	Cincinnati Swords	AHL	70	5	32	37	....	....	....	123	....	....	....	....	....	....	....	....	....	....	15	0	8	8	49	....	....	....
1973-74	**California Golden Seals**	**NHL**	**72**	**2**	**12**	**14**	**2**	**10**	**12**	**49**	**1**	**0**	**0**	**101**	**2.0**	**71**	**7**	**106**	**11**	**–31**	....	....	....	....	....	....	....	....
1974-75	Edmonton Oilers	WHA	69	8	20	28	....	....	....	47	....	....	....	....	....	....	....	....	....	....	....	....	....	....	....	....	....	....
1975-76	Cleveland Crusaders	WHA	68	3	10	13	....	....	....	44	....	....	....	....	....	....	....	....	....	....	3	0	0	0	4	....	....	....
	Syracuse Blazers	NAHL	3	1	1	2	....	....	....	0	....	....	....	....	....	....	....	....	....	....	....	....	....	....	....	....	....	....
1976-77	Minnesota Fighting Saints	WHA	42	2	9	11	....	....	....	28	....	....	....	....	....	....	....	....	....	....	....	....	....	....	....	....	....	....
	Birmingham Bulls	WHA	19	0	1	1	....	....	....	11	....	....	....	....	....	....	....	....	....	....	....	....	....	....	....	....	....	....
1977-78	Edmonton Oilers	WHA	14	1	4	5	....	....	....	4	....	....	....	....	....	....	....	....	....	....	4	0	1	1	4	....	....	....
1978-79	Springfield Indians	AHL	69	2	27	29	....	....	....	42	....	....	....	....	....	....	....	....	....	....	....	....	....	....	....	....	....	....
1979-80	Adirondack Red Wings	AHL	5	0	0	0	....	....	....	27	....	....	....	....	....	....	....	....	....	....	....	....	....	....	....	....	....	....
	Hershey Bears	AHL	67	2	28	30	....	....	....	37	....	....	....	....	....	....	....	....	....	....	16	4	10	14	11	....	....	....
	NHL Totals		**140**	**2**	**16**	**18**	**2**	**14**	**16**	**102**	**1**	**0**	**0**	**131**	**1.5**	**90**	**7**	**155**	**24**		....	....	....	....	....	....	....	....
	Other Major League Totals		212	14	44	58	....	....	....	134	....	....	....	....	....	....	....	....	....	....	7	0	1	1	8	....	....	....

AHL First All-Star Team (1973) • Won Eddie Shore Award (Outstanding Defenseman - AHL) (1973)

Claimed by **Buffalo** from **Chicago** in Intra-League Draft, June 8, 1971. Selected by **Calgary-Cleveland** (WHA) in 1972 WHA General Player Draft, February 12, 1972. Claimed by **California** from **Buffalo** in Intra-League Draft, June 12, 1973. WHA rights traded to **Edmonton** (WHA) by **Cleveland** (WHA) for future considerations, June, 1974. Traded to **Cleveland** (WHA) by **Edmonton** (WHA) for Skip Krake, August, 1975. Transferred to **Minnesota** (WHA) after **Cleveland** (WHA) franchise relocated, July, 1976. Signed as a free agent by **Birmingham** (WHA) after **Minnesota** (WHA) franchise folded, January 27, 1977. Signed as a free agent by **Edmonton** (WHA), March, 1978.

• McKAY, SCOTT

Scott McKay   C – R. 5'11", 200 lbs.   b: Burlington, Ont., 1/26/1972.

Season	Club	League	GP	G	A	Pts	AG	AA	APts	PIM	PP	SH	GW	S	%	TGF	PGF	TGA	PGA	+/–	GP	G	A	Pts	PIM	PP	SH	GW
1989-90	London Knights	OHL	59	20	29	49	....	....	....	37	....	....	....	....	....	....	....	....	....	....	5	1	1	2	12	....	....	....
1990-91	London Knights	OHL	62	29	40	69	....	....	....	29	....	....	....	....	....	....	....	....	....	....	7	4	2	6	6	....	....	....
1991-92	London Knights	OHL	64	30	45	75	....	....	....	97	....	....	....	....	....	....	....	....	....	....	10	3	8	11	8	....	....	....
1992-93	London Knights	OHL	63	38	57	95	....	....	....	49	....	....	....	....	....	....	....	....	....	....	12	1	14	15	6	....	....	....
1993-94	**Anaheim Mighty Ducks**	**NHL**	**1**	**0**	**0**	**0**	**0**	**0**	**0**	**0**	**0**	**0**	**0**	**1**	**0.0**	**0**	**0**	**0**	**0**	**0**	....	....	....	....	....	....	....	....
	San Diego Gulls	IHL	58	10	6	16	....	....	....	35	....	....	....	....	....	....	....	....	....	....	9	2	5	7	6	....	....	....
1994-95	Greensboro Monarchs	ECHL	17	7	7	14	....	....	....	54	....	....	....	....	....	....	....	....	....	....	....	....	....	....	....	....	....	....
	San Diego Gulls	IHL	1	0	0	0	....	....	....	2	....	....	....	....	....	....	....	....	....	....	....	....	....	....	....	....	....	....
1995-96	Baltimore Bandits	AHL	16	1	0	1	....	....	....	6	....	....	....	....	....	....	....	....	....	....	....	....	....	....	....	....	....	....
	Raleigh IceCaps	ECHL	2	1	0	1	....	....	....	0	....	....	....	....	....	....	....	....	....	....	....	....	....	....	....	....	....	....
1996-97	EC Graz	Austria	17	6	7	13	....	....	....	16	....	....	....	....	....	....	....	....	....	....	....	....	....	....	....	....	....	....
1997-98	Louisiana IceGators	ECHL	48	20	16	36	....	....	....	55	....	....	....	....	....	....	....	....	....	....	9	2	3	5	4	....	....	....
	NHL Totals		**1**	**0**	**0**	**0**	**0**	**0**	**0**	**0**	**0**	**0**	**0**	**1**	**0.0**	**0**	**0**	**0**	**0**		....	....	....	....	....	....	....	....

Signed as a free agent by **Anaheim**, August 2, 1993.

• McKECHNIE, WALT

Walt "McKetch" McKechnie   C – L. 6'2", 195 lbs.   b: London, Ont., 6/19/1947.   Toronto's 1st choice, 6th overall, in 1963 Amateur Draft.

Season	Club	League	GP	G	A	Pts	AG	AA	APts	PIM	PP	SH	GW	S	%	TGF	PGF	TGA	PGA	+/–	GP	G	A	Pts	PIM	PP	SH	GW
1965-66	London Nationals	OHA	46	13	28	41	....	....	....	68	....	....	....	....	....	....	....	....	....	....	....	....	....	....	....	....	....	....
1966-67	London Nationals	OHA	48	13	46	59	....	....	....	125	....	....	....	....	....	....	....	....	....	....	6	7	10	17	2	....	....	....
1967-68	London Nationals	OHA	1	0	0	0	....	....	....	2	....	....	....	....	....	....	....	....	....	....	....	....	....	....	....	....	....	....
	Phoenix Roadrunners	WHL	67	24	30	54	....	....	....	24	....	....	....	....	....	....	....	....	....	....	4	1	1	2	2	....	....	....
	Minnesota North Stars	**NHL**	**4**	**0**	**0**	**0**	**0**	**0**	**0**	**0**	**0**	**0**	**0**	**9**	**0.0**	**1**	**1**	**3**	**0**	**–3**	**9**	**3**	**2**	**5**	**0**	**0**	**0**	**0**
1968-69	**Minnesota North Stars**	**NHL**	**58**	**5**	**9**	**14**	**6**	**8**	**14**	**22**	**1**	**0**	**1**	**81**	**6.2**	**19**	**3**	**27**	**1**	**–10**	....	....	....	....	....	....	....	....
	Phoenix Roadrunners	WHL	10	3	11	14	....	....	....	6	....	....	....	....	....	....	....	....	....	....	....	....	....	....	....	....	....	....
1969-70	**Minnesota North Stars**	**NHL**	**20**	**1**	**3**	**4**	**1**	**3**	**4**	**21**	**0**	**0**	**0**	**16**	**6.3**	**4**	**0**	**10**	**1**	**–5**	....	....	....	....	....	....	....	....
	Iowa Stars	CHL	42	17	24	41	....	....	....	82	....	....	....	....	....	....	....	....	....	....	11	1	9	10	18	....	....	....
1970-71	**Minnesota North Stars**	**NHL**	**30**	**3**	**1**	**4**	**3**	**1**	**4**	**34**	**0**	**0**	**0**	**39**	**7.7**	**7**	**2**	**13**	**1**	**–7**	....	....	....	....	....	....	....	....
	Cleveland Barons	AHL	35	16	31	47	....	....	....	28	....	....	....	....	....	....	....	....	....	....	8	2	4	6	10	....	....	....
1971-72	**California Golden Seals**	**NHL**	**56**	**11**	**20**	**31**	**12**	**18**	**30**	**40**	**2**	**1**	**1**	**111**	**9.9**	**50**	**11**	**44**	**7**	**+2**	....	....	....	....	....	....	....	....
1972-73	**California Golden Seals**	**NHL**	**78**	**16**	**38**	**54**	**16**	**32**	**48**	**58**	**4**	**1**	**0**	**182**	**8.8**	**86**	**20**	**123**	**31**	**–26**	....	....	....	....	....	....	....	....
1973-74	**California Golden Seals**	**NHL**	**63**	**23**	**29**	**52**	**23**	**25**	**48**	**14**	**4**	**2**	**1**	**135**	**17.0**	**65**	**18**	**69**	**8**	**–14**	....	....	....	....	....	....	....	....
1974-75	**Boston Bruins**	**NHL**	**53**	**3**	**3**	**6**	**3**	**2**	**5**	**8**	**0**	**1**	**0**	**36**	**8.3**	**15**	**2**	**33**	**14**	**–6**	....	....	....	....	....	....	....	....
	Detroit Red Wings	**NHL**	**23**	**6**	**11**	**17**	**6**	**9**	**15**	**6**	**1**	**0**	**2**	**41**	**14.6**	**26**	**6**	**24**	**1**	**–3**	....	....	....	....	....	....	....	....
1975-76	**Detroit Red Wings**	**NHL**	**80**	**26**	**56**	**82**	**24**	**44**	**68**	**85**	**2**	**3**	**7**	**186**	**14.0**	**110**	**30**	**112**	**41**	**+9**	....	....	....	....	....	....	....	....
1976-77	**Detroit Red Wings**	**NHL**	**80**	**25**	**34**	**59**	**24**	**28**	**52**	**50**	**3**	**3**	**1**	**189**	**13.2**	**78**	**24**	**110**	**32**	**–24**	....	....	....	....	....	....	....	....
	Canada	WEC-A	10	1	6	7	....	....	....	28	....	....	....	....	....	....	....	....	....	....	....	....	....	....	....	....	....	....
1977-78	**Washington Capitals**	**NHL**	**16**	**4**	**1**	**5**	**4**	**1**	**5**	**0**	**1**	**0**	**0**	**24**	**16.7**	**7**	**2**	**20**	**1**	**–14**	....	....	....	....	....	....	....	....
	Cleveland Barons	**NHL**	**53**	**12**	**22**	**34**	**12**	**18**	**30**	**12**	**2**	**0**	**0**	**97**	**12.4**	**45**	**11**	**67**	**25**	**–8**	....	....	....	....	....	....	....	....
1978-79	**Toronto Maple Leafs**	**NHL**	**79**	**25**	**36**	**61**	**23**	**28**	**51**	**18**	**7**	**1**	**6**	**123**	**20.3**	**80**	**14**	**49**	**4**	**+21**	**6**	**4**	**3**	**7**	**7**	**0**	**1**	**1**
1979-80	**Toronto Maple Leafs**	**NHL**	**54**	**7**	**36**	**43**	**6**	**28**	**34**	**4**	**1**	**0**	**0**	**77**	**9.1**	**71**	**32**	**73**	**28**	**–6**	....	....	....	....	....	....	....	....
	Colorado Rockies	**NHL**	**17**	**0**	**4**	**4**	**0**	**3**	**3**	**2**	**0**	**0**	**0**	**35**	**0.0**	**7**	**4**	**23**	**6**	**–14**	....	....	....	....	....	....	....	....
1980-81	**Colorado Rockies**	**NHL**	**53**	**15**	**23**	**38**	**12**	**16**	**28**	**18**	**2**	**2**	**2**	**92**	**16.3**	**68**	**22**	**82**	**29**	**–7**	....	....	....	....	....	....	....	....
1981-82	**Detroit Red Wings**	**NHL**	**74**	**18**	**37**	**55**	**14**	**24**	**38**	**35**	**2**	**0**	**3**	**87**	**20.7**	**86**	**16**	**80**	**9**	**–1**	....	....	....	....	....	....	....	....
1982-83	**Detroit Red Wings**	**NHL**	**64**	**14**	**29**	**43**	**11**	**20**	**31**	**42**	**3**	**3**	**0**	**73**	**19.2**	**57**	**12**	**80**	**36**	**+1**	....	....	....	....	....	....	....	....
1983-84	Salt Lake Golden Eagles	CHL	69	9	32	41	....	....	....	36	....	....	....	....	....	....	....	....	....	....	....	....	....	....	....	....	....	....
	NHL Totals		**955**	**214**	**392**	**606**	**200**	**308**	**508**	**469**	**35**	**17**	**24**	**1633**	**13.1**	**882**	**230**	**1042**	**275**		**15**	**7**	**5**	**12**	**7**	**0**	**1**	**1**

Won WHL Rookie of the Year Award (1968)

Traded to **Phoenix** (WHL) by **Toronto** for Steve Witiuk, October 15, 1967. Traded to **Minnesota** by **Phoenix** (WHL) for Leo Thiffault and Bob Charlebois, February 17, 1968. Traded to **California** by **Minnesota** with Joey Johnson for Dennis Hextall, May 20, 1971. Claimed by **NY Rangers** from **California** in Intra-League Draft, June 10, 1974. Traded to **Boston** by **NY Rangers** for Derek Sanderson, June 12, 1974. Traded to **Detroit** by **Boston** with Boston's 3rd round choice (Clarke Hamilton) in 1975 Amateur Draft for Hank Nowak and Earl Anderson, February 18, 1975. Traded to **Washington** by **Detroit** with Detroit's 3rd round choice (Jay Johnston) in 1978 Amateur Draft and 2nd round choice (Errol Rousse) in 1979 Amateur Draft for the rights to Ron Low and Washington's 3rd round choice (Borris Fistric) in 1979 Amateur Draft, August 17, 1977. Traded to **Cleveland** by **Washington** for Bob Girard and Cleveland's 2nd round choice (Paul McKinnon) in 1978 Amateur Draft, December 9, 1977. Placed on **Minnesota** Reserve List after **Cleveland-Minnesota** Dispersal Draft, June 15, 1978. Traded to **Toronto** by **Minnesota** for Toronto's 3rd round choice (Randy Velishek) in 1980 Entry Draft, October 5, 1978. Traded to **Colorado** by **Toronto** for Colorado's 3rd round choice (Fred Boimistruck) in 1980 Entry Draft, March 3, 1980. Signed as a free agent by **Detroit**, October 1, 1981.

			REGULAR SEASON																		PLAYOFFS							
Season	Club	League	GP	G	A	Pts	AG	AA	APts	PIM	PP	SH	GW	S	%	TGF	PGF	TGA	PGA	+/–	GP	G	A	Pts	PIM	PP	SH	GW

• McKEE, JAY Jay McKee D – L. 6'3", 195 lbs. b: Kingston, Ont., 9/8/1977. Buffalo's 1st choice, 14th overall, in 1995 Entry Draft.

Season	Club	League	GP	G	A	Pts	AG	AA	APts	PIM	PP	SH	GW	S	%	TGF	PGF	TGA	PGA	+/–	GP	G	A	Pts	PIM	PP	SH	GW
1993-94	Sudbury Wolves	OHL	51	0	1	1	....	....	....	51	....	....	....	....	....	....	....	....	....	....	3	0	0	0	0	....	....	....
1994-95	Sudbury Wolves	OHL	39	6	6	12	....	....	....	91	....	....	....	....	....	....	....	....	....	....	....	....	....	....	....	....	....	....
	Niagara Falls Thunder	OHL	26	3	13	16	....	....	....	60	....	....	....	....	....	....	....	....	....	....	6	2	3	5	10	....	....	....
1995-96	Niagara Falls Thunder	OHL	64	5	41	46	....	....	....	129	....	....	....	....	....	....	....	....	....	....	10	1	5	6	16	....	....	....
	Buffalo Sabres	NHL	1	0	1	1	0	1	1	2	0	0	0	2	0.0	2	0	1	0	+1	....	....	....	....	....	....	....	....
	Rochester Americans	AHL	4	0	1	1	....	....	....	15	....	....	....	....	....	....	....	....	....	....	....	....	....	....	....	....	....	....
1996-97	Buffalo Sabres	NHL	43	1	9	10	1	8	9	35	0	0	0	29	3.4	35	7	28	3	+3	3	0	0	0	0	0	0	0
	Rochester Americans	AHL	7	2	5	7	....	....	....	4	....	....	....	....	....	....	....	....	....	....	....	....	....	....	....	....	....	....
1997-98	Buffalo Sabres	NHL	56	1	13	14	1	13	14	42	0	0	0	55	1.8	38	8	46	15	–1	1	0	0	0	0	0	0	0
	Rochester Americans	AHL	13	1	7	8	....	....	....	11	....	....	....	....	....	....	....	....	....	....	....	....	....	....	....	....	....	....
	NHL Totals		100	2	23	25	2	22	24	79	0	0	0	86	2.3	75	15	75	18		4	0	0	0	0	0	0	0

OHL Second All-Star Team (1996)

• McKEE, MIKE Mike McKee LW – R. 6'3", 203 lbs. b: Toronto, Ont., 6/18/1969. Quebec's 1st choice, 1st overall, in 1990 Supplemental Draft.

Season	Club	League	GP	G	A	Pts	AG	AA	APts	PIM	PP	SH	GW	S	%	TGF	PGF	TGA	PGA	+/–	GP	G	A	Pts	PIM	PP	SH	GW
1988-89	Princeton University	ECAC	16	2	1	3	....	....	....	14	....	....	....	....	....	....	....	....	....	....	....	....	....	....	....	....	....	....
1989-90	Princeton University	ECAC	26	7	18	25	....	....	....	18	....	....	....	....	....	....	....	....	....	....	....	....	....	....	....	....	....	....
1990-91	Princeton University	ECAC	15	1	4	5	....	....	....	16	....	....	....	....	....	....	....	....	....	....	....	....	....	....	....	....	....	....
1991-92	Princeton University	ECAC	27	12	17	29	....	....	....	34	....	....	....	....	....	....	....	....	....	....	....	....	....	....	....	....	....	....
1992-93	Halifax Citadels	AHL	32	6	7	13	....	....	....	25	....	....	....	....	....	....	....	....	....	....	....	....	....	....	....	....	....	....
	Greensboro Monarchs	ECHL	7	1	3	4	....	....	....	6	....	....	....	....	....	....	....	....	....	....	....	....	....	....	....	....	....	....
1993-94	Quebec Nordiques	NHL	48	3	12	15	3	9	12	41	2	0	0	60	5.0	50	13	35	3	+5	....	....	....	....	....	....	....	....
	Cornwall Aces	AHL	24	6	14	20	....	....	....	18	....	....	....	....	....	....	....	....	....	....	10	0	3	3	4	....	....	....
1994-95	Cornwall Aces	AHL	36	2	11	13	....	....	....	24	....	....	....	....	....	....	....	....	....	....	....	....	....	....	....	....	....	....
	NHL Totals		48	3	12	15	3	9	12	41	2	0	0	60	5.0	50	13	35	3		....	....	....	....	....	....	....	....

ECAC Second All-Star Team (1990)

• McKEGNEY, IAN Ian McKegney D – L. 5'11", 165 lbs. b: Sarnia, Ont., 5/7/1947.

Season	Club	League	GP	G	A	Pts	AG	AA	APts	PIM	PP	SH	GW	S	%	TGF	PGF	TGA	PGA	+/–	GP	G	A	Pts	PIM	PP	SH	GW
1970-71	University of Waterloo	QUAA	....	2	12	14	....	....	....	15	....	....	....	....	....	....	....	....	....	....	....	....	....	....	....	....	....	....
1971-72	IFL Lulea	Sweden 2	STATISTICS NOT AVAILABLE																									
1972-73	Dallas Black Hawks	CHL	72	10	24	34	....	....	....	20	....	....	....	....	....	....	....	....	....	....	7	1	2	3	0	....	....	....
1973-74	Dallas Black Hawks	CHL	65	1	27	28	....	....	....	18	....	....	....	....	....	....	....	....	....	....	10	2	4	6	4	....	....	....
1974-75	Dallas Black Hawks	CHL	76	10	31	41	....	....	....	21	....	....	....	....	....	....	....	....	....	....	10	2	5	7	2	....	....	....
1975-76	Dallas Black Hawks	CHL	76	3	29	32	....	....	....	20	....	....	....	....	....	....	....	....	....	....	10	3	2	5	0	....	....	....
1976-77	Chicago Black Hawks	NHL	3	0	0	0	0	0	0	2	0	0	0	1	0.0	5	0	13	0	–8	....	....	....	....	....	....	....	....
	Dallas Black Hawks	CHL	61	6	22	28	....	....	....	18	....	....	....	....	....	....	....	....	....	....	5	1	1	2	0	....	....	....
1977-78	Nova Scotia Voyageurs	AHL	12	0	5	5	....	....	....	0	....	....	....	....	....	....	....	....	....	....	11	1	4	5	7	....	....	....
	NHL Totals		3	0	0	0	0	0	0	2	0	0	0	1	0.0	5	0	13	0		....	....	....	....	....	....	....	....

CHL Second All-Star Team (1973) • CHL First All-Star Team (1975, 1976) • Named CHL's Top Defenseman (1975, 1976) • Won Tommy Ivan Trophy (CHL's MVP) (1976)

Signed as a free agent by **Chicago**, September 30, 1972.

• McKEGNEY, TONY Tony McKegney LW – L. 6'1", 200 lbs. b: Montreal, Que., 2/15/1958. Buffalo's 2nd choice, 32nd overall, in 1978 Amateur Draft.

Season	Club	League	GP	G	A	Pts	AG	AA	APts	PIM	PP	SH	GW	S	%	TGF	PGF	TGA	PGA	+/–	GP	G	A	Pts	PIM	PP	SH	GW
1974-75	Kingston Canadians	OHA	52	27	48	75	....	....	....	36	....	....	....	....	....	....	....	....	....	....	....	....	....	....	....	....	....	....
1975-76	Kingston Canadians	OHA	65	24	56	80	....	....	....	20	....	....	....	....	....	....	....	....	....	....	....	....	....	....	....	....	....	....
1976-77	Kingston Canadians	OHA	66	58	77	135	....	....	....	30	....	....	....	....	....	....	....	....	....	....	14	13	10	23	14	....	....	....
1977-78	Kingston Canadians	OHA	55	43	49	92	....	....	....	19	....	....	....	....	....	....	....	....	....	....	5	3	3	6	0	....	....	....
	Canada	WJC-A	6	2	6	8	....	....	....	0	....	....	....	....	....	....	....	....	....	....	....	....	....	....	....	....	....	....
1978-79	Buffalo Sabres	NHL	52	8	14	22	7	11	18	10	0	0	1	67	11.9	32	4	30	0	–2	2	0	1	1	0	0	0	0
	Hershey Bears	AHL	24	21	18	39	....	....	....	4	....	....	....	....	....	....	....	....	....	....	1	0	0	0	0	....	....	....
1979-80	Buffalo Sabres	NHL	80	23	29	52	21	22	43	24	1	0	6	140	16.4	77	4	33	0	+40	14	3	4	7	2	0	0	0
1980-81	Buffalo Sabres	NHL	80	37	32	69	31	22	53	24	9	0	4	236	15.7	97	24	63	1	+11	8	5	3	8	2	1	0	0
1981-82	Buffalo Sabres	NHL	73	23	29	52	18	19	37	41	8	0	0	187	12.3	71	21	62	0	–12	4	0	0	0	2	0	0	0
1982-83	Buffalo Sabres	NHL	78	36	37	73	30	26	56	18	10	0	2	180	20.0	96	23	76	5	+2	10	3	1	4	4	1	0	2
1983-84	Quebec Nordiques	NHL	75	24	27	51	19	18	37	23	4	0	2	171	14.0	85	21	63	3	+4	7	0	0	0	0	0	0	0
1984-85	Quebec Nordiques	NHL	30	12	9	21	10	6	16	12	1	3	1	85	14.1	30	4	33	9	+2	....	....	....	....	....	....	....	....
	Minnesota North Stars	NHL	27	11	13	24	9	9	18	4	2	0	1	81	13.6	36	8	29	10	+9	9	8	6	14	0	2	0	1
1985-86	Minnesota North Stars	NHL	70	15	25	40	12	17	29	48	3	1	0	141	10.6	57	11	71	20	–5	5	2	1	3	22	0	0	0
1986-87	Minnesota North Stars	NHL	11	2	3	5	2	2	4	16	0	0	0	15	13.3	7	1	4	0	+2	....	....	....	....	....	....	....	....
	New York Rangers	NHL	64	29	17	46	25	12	37	56	7	2	6	166	17.5	68	16	55	2	–1	6	0	0	0	12	0	0	0
1987-88	St. Louis Blues	NHL	80	40	38	78	34	27	61	82	13	3	1	241	16.6	111	39	84	22	+10	9	3	6	9	8	1	0	1
1988-89	St. Louis Blues	NHL	71	25	17	42	21	12	33	58	7	0	2	154	16.2	71	25	52	5	–1	3	0	1	1	0	0	0	0
1989-90	Detroit Red Wings	NHL	14	2	1	3	2	1	3	8	0	0	0	18	11.1	10	1	7	0	+2	....	....	....	....	....	....	....	....
	Quebec Nordiques	NHL	48	16	11	27	14	8	22	45	5	0	0	89	18.0	39	16	63	9	–31	....	....	....	....	....	....	....	....
1990-91	Quebec Nordiques	NHL	50	17	16	33	16	12	28	44	7	0	2	111	15.3	58	28	55	0	–25	....	....	....	....	....	....	....	....
	Chicago Blackhawks	NHL	9	0	1	1	0	1	1	4	0	0	0	10	0.0	3	1	5	1	–2	2	0	0	0	4	0	0	0
1991-92	Varese	Italy	16	15	13	28	....	....	....	70	....	....	....	....	....	....	....	....	....	....	6	8	2	10	12	....	....	....
1992-93	San Diego Gulls	IHL	23	8	5	13	....	....	....	38	....	....	....	....	....	....	....	....	....	....	3	0	1	1	4	....	....	....
	NHL Totals		912	320	319	639	271	225	496	517	77	9	28	2092	15.3	948	247	785	87		79	24	23	47	56	5	0	4

OHA First All-Star Team (1977) • OHA Second All-Star Team (1978)

Traded to **Quebec** by **Buffalo** with Andre Savard, Jean Sauve and Buffalo's 3rd round choice (Liro Jarvi) in 1983 Entry Draft for Real Cloutier and Quebec's 1st round choice (Adam Creighton) in 1983 Entry Draft, June 8, 1983. Traded to **Minnesota** by **Quebec** with Bo Berlund for Brad Maxwell and Brent Ashton, December 14, 1984 Traded to **NY Rangers** by **Minnesota** with Curt Giles and Minnesota's 2nd round choice (Troy Mallette) in 1988 Entry Draft for Bob Brooke, Minnesota's 4th round choice (previously acquired, Minnesota selected Jeffrey Stolp) in 1988 Entry Draft, November 13, 1986. Traded to **St. Louis** by **NY Rangers** with Rob Whistle for Bruce Bell and future considerations, May 28, 1987. Traded to **Detroit** by **St. Louis** with Bernie Federko for Adam Oates and Paul MacLean, June 15, 1989. Traded to **Quebec** by **Detroit** for Robert Picard and Greg C. Adams, December 4, 1989. Traded to **Chicago** by **Quebec** for Jacques Cloutier, January 29, 1991.

• McKENDRY, ALEX Alex McKendry LW/RW – L. 6'4", 200 lbs. b: Midland, Ont., 11/21/1956. NY Islanders' 1st choice, 14th overall, in 1976 Amateur Draft.

Season	Club	League	GP	G	A	Pts	AG	AA	APts	PIM	PP	SH	GW	S	%	TGF	PGF	TGA	PGA	+/–	GP	G	A	Pts	PIM	PP	SH	GW
1973-74	Sudbury Wolves	OHA	61	4	8	12	....	....	....	173	....	....	....	....	....	....	....	....	....	....	....	....	....	....	....	....	....	....
1974-75	Sudbury Wolves	OHA	57	19	34	53	....	....	....	181	....	....	....	....	....	....	....	....	....	....	15	5	8	13	29	....	....	....
1975-76	Sudbury Wolves	OHA	65	43	59	102	....	....	....	121	....	....	....	....	....	....	....	....	....	....	....	....	....	....	....	....	....	....
1976-77	Fort Worth Texans	CHL	65	7	14	21	....	....	....	80	....	....	....	....	....	....	....	....	....	....	6	0	2	2	4	....	....	....
1977-78	New York Islanders	NHL	4	0	0	0	0	0	0	2	0	0	0	7	0.0	1	0	1	0	0	....	....	....	....	....	....	....	....
	Fort Worth Texans	CHL	72	22	22	44	....	....	....	148	....	....	....	....	....	....	....	....	....	....	10	1	3	4	30	....	....	....
1978-79	New York Islanders	NHL	4	0	0	0	0	0	0	0	0	0	0	0	0.0	0	0	1	0	–1	....	....	....	....	....	....	....	....
	Fort Worth Texans	CHL	59	12	26	38	....	....	....	202	....	....	....	....	....	....	....	....	....	....	5	0	2	2	4	....	....	....
1979-80	New York Islanders	NHL	2	0	0	0	0	0	0	0	0	0	0	0	0.0	0	0	1	0	–1	6	2	2	4	0	0	0	0
	Indianapolis Checkers	CHL	76	40	37	77	....	....	....	64	....	....	....	....	....	....	....	....	....	....	4	2	4	6	7	....	....	....
1980-81	Calgary Flames	NHL	36	3	6	9	2	4	6	19	0	0	0	30	10.0	17	1	22	0	–6	....	....	....	....	....	....	....	....
	Birmingham Bulls	CHL	10	1	5	6	....	....	....	23	....	....	....	....	....	....	....	....	....	....	....	....	....	....	....	....	....	....
	Fort Worth Texans	CHL	19	3	3	6	....	....	....	25	....	....	....	....	....	....	....	....	....	....	5	0	0	0	13	....	....	....
1981-82	Oklahoma City Stars	CHL	80	27	39	86	....	....	....	163	....	....	....	....	....	....	....	....	....	....	4	1	1	2	9	....	....	....
1982-83	Colorado Flames	CHL	72	25	42	67	....	....	....	44	....	....	....	....	....	....	....	....	....	....	5	0	2	2	4	....	....	....
	NHL Totals		46	3	6	9	2	4	6	21	0	0	0	37	8.1	18	1	25	0		6	2	2	4	0	0	0	0

CHL First All-Star Team (1980)

Traded to **Calgary** by **NY Islanders** for Calgary's 3rd round choice (Ron Handy) in 1981 Entry Draft, October 9, 1980.

			REGULAR SEASON																		PLAYOFFS							
Season	Club	League	GP	G	A	Pts	AG	AA	APts	PIM	PP	SH	GW	S	%	TGF	PGF	TGA	PGA	+/-	GP	G	A	Pts	PIM	PP	SH	GW

• McKENNA, SEAN

Sean McKenna RW – R. 6', 190 lbs. b: Asbestos, Que., 3/7/1962. Buffalo's 3rd choice, 56th overall, in 1980 Entry Draft.

Season	Club	League	GP	G	A	Pts	AG	AA	APts	PIM	PP	SH	GW	S	%	TGF	PGF	TGA	PGA	+/-	GP	G	A	Pts	PIM	PP	SH	GW
1978-79	Montreal Jr. Canadiens	QMJHL	66	9	14	23	....	....	....	14	....	....	....	....	....	....	....	....	....	....	....	....	....	....	....	....	....	....
1979-80	Montreal Jr. Canadiens	QMJHL	16	1	3	4	....	....	....	5	....	....	....	....	....	....	....	....	....	....	....	....	....	....	....	....	....	....
	Sherbrooke Beavers	QMJHL	43	19	16	35	....	....	....	19	....	....	....	....	....	....	....	....	....	....	15	7	7	14	9	....	....	....
1980-81	Sherbrooke Beavers	QMJHL	71	57	47	104	....	....	....	122	....	....	....	....	....	....	....	....	....	....	14	9	9	18	12	....	....	....
1981-82	Sherbrooke Beavers	QMJHL	59	57	33	90	....	....	....	29	....	....	....	....	....	....	....	....	....	....	22	*26	18	44	28	....	....	....
	Buffalo Sabres	**NHL**	**3**	**0**	**1**	**1**	**0**	**1**	**1**	**2**	**0**	**0**	**0**	**6**	**0.0**	**4**	**0**	**1**	**0**	**+3**	....	....	....	....	....	....	....	....
1982-83	**Buffalo Sabres**	**NHL**	**46**	**10**	**14**	**24**	**8**	**10**	**18**	**4**	**1**	**0**	**1**	**69**	**14.5**	**35**	**4**	**35**	**0**	**–4**	....	....	....	....	....	....	....	....
	Rochester Americans	AHL	26	16	10	26	....	....	....	14	....	....	....	....	....	....	....	....	....	....	16	*14	8	22	18	....	....	....
1983-84	**Buffalo Sabres**	**NHL**	**78**	**20**	**10**	**30**	**16**	**7**	**23**	**45**	**0**	**0**	**2**	**107**	**18.7**	**47**	**0**	**49**	**2**	**0**	**3**	**1**	**0**	**1**	**2**	**0**	**0**	**0**
1984-85	**Buffalo Sabres**	**NHL**	**65**	**20**	**16**	**36**	**16**	**11**	**27**	**41**	**2**	**0**	**0**	**109**	**18.3**	**49**	**6**	**49**	**0**	**–6**	**5**	**0**	**1**	**1**	**0**	**0**	**0**	**0**
1985-86	**Buffalo Sabres**	**NHL**	**45**	**6**	**12**	**18**	**5**	**8**	**13**	**28**	**1**	**0**	**2**	**83**	**7.2**	**32**	**5**	**41**	**6**	**–8**	....	....	....	....	....	....	....	....
	Los Angeles Kings	**NHL**	**30**	**4**	**0**	**4**	**3**	**0**	**3**	**7**	**0**	**1**	**0**	**47**	**8.5**	**10**	**0**	**35**	**10**	**–15**	....	....	....	....	....	....	....	....
1986-87	**Los Angeles Kings**	**NHL**	**69**	**14**	**19**	**33**	**12**	**14**	**26**	**10**	**0**	**1**	**0**	**102**	**13.7**	**52**	**3**	**69**	**31**	**+11**	**5**	**0**	**1**	**1**	**0**	**0**	**0**	**0**
1987-88	**Los Angeles Kings**	**NHL**	**30**	**3**	**2**	**5**	**3**	**1**	**4**	**12**	**0**	**0**	**0**	**34**	**8.8**	**9**	**1**	**26**	**4**	**–14**	....	....	....	....	....	....	....	....
	Toronto Maple Leafs	**NHL**	**40**	**5**	**5**	**10**	**4**	**4**	**8**	**12**	**0**	**0**	**1**	**46**	**10.9**	**18**	**0**	**30**	**1**	**–11**	**2**	**0**	**0**	**0**	**0**	**0**	**0**	**0**
1988-89	**Toronto Maple Leafs**	**NHL**	**3**	**0**	**1**	**1**	**0**	**1**	**1**	**0**	**0**	**0**	**0**	**1**	**0.0**	**1**	**0**	**3**	**1**	**–1**	....	....	....	....	....	....	....	....
	Newmarket Saints	AHL	61	14	27	41	....	....	....	35	....	....	....	....	....	....	....	....	....	....	5	1	1	2	4	....	....	....
1989-90	**Toronto Maple Leafs**	**NHL**	**5**	**0**	**0**	**0**	**0**	**0**	**0**	**20**	**0**	**0**	**0**	**6**	**0.0**	**0**	**0**	**3**	**0**	**–3**	....	....	....	....	....	....	....	....
	Newmarket Saints	AHL	73	17	17	34	....	....	....	30	....	....	....	....	....	....	....	....	....	....	....	....	....	....	....	....	....	....
	NHL Totals		**414**	**82**	**80**	**162**	**67**	**57**	**124**	**181**	**4**	**2**	**6**	**610**	**13.4**	**257**	**19**	**341**	**55**		**15**	**1**	**2**	**3**	**2**	**0**	**0**	**0**

QMJHL First All-Star Team (1981) • QMJHL Second All-Star Team (1982) • Memorial Cup All-Star Team (1982) • Won Stafford Smythe Memorial Trophy (Memorial Cup Tournament MVP) (1982)

Traded to **LA Kings** by **Buffalo** with Larry Playfair and Ken Baumgartner for Brian Engblom and Doug Smith, Januray 30, 1986. Traded to **Toronto** by **LA Kings** for Mike Allison, December 14, 1987.

• McKENNA, STEVE

Steve "Stretch" McKenna LW – L. 6'8", 247 lbs. b: Toronto, Ont., 8/21/1973.

Season	Club	League	GP	G	A	Pts	AG	AA	APts	PIM	PP	SH	GW	S	%	TGF	PGF	TGA	PGA	+/-	GP	G	A	Pts	PIM	PP	SH	GW
1993-94	Merrimack College	H.E.	37	1	2	3	....	....	....	74	....	....	....	....	....	....	....	....	....	....	....	....	....	....	....	....	....	....
1994-95	Merrimack College	H.E.	37	1	9	10	....	....	....	74	....	....	....	....	....	....	....	....	....	....	....	....	....	....	....	....	....	....
1995-96	Merrimack College	H.E.	33	3	11	14	....	....	....	67	....	....	....	....	....	....	....	....	....	....	....	....	....	....	....	....	....	....
1996-97	**Los Angeles Kings**	**NHL**	**9**	**0**	**0**	**0**	**0**	**0**	**0**	**37**	**0**	**0**	**0**	**6**	**0.0**	**2**	**0**	**1**	**0**	**+1**	....	....	....	....	....	....	....	....
	Phoenix Roadrunners	IHL	66	6	5	11	....	....	....	187	....	....	....	....	....	....	....	....	....	....	....	....	....	....	....	....	....	....
1997-98	**Los Angeles Kings**	**NHL**	**62**	**4**	**4**	**8**	**5**	**4**	**9**	**150**	**1**	**0**	**0**	**42**	**9.5**	**14**	**1**	**25**	**3**	**–9**	**3**	**0**	**1**	**1**	**8**	**0**	**0**	**0**
	Fredericton Canadiens	AHL	6	2	1	3	....	....	....	48	....	....	....	....	....	....	....	....	....	....	....	....	....	....	....	....	....	....
	NHL Totals		**71**	**4**	**4**	**8**	**5**	**4**	**9**	**187**	**1**	**0**	**0**	**48**	**8.3**	**16**	**1**	**26**	**3**		**3**	**0**	**1**	**1**	**8**	**0**	**0**	**0**

Signed as a free agent by **LA Kings**, May 23, 1996.

• McKENNEY, DON

Don "Slip" McKenney C – L. 5'11", 160 lbs. b: Smith Falls, Ont., 4/30/1934.

Season	Club	League	GP	G	A	Pts	AG	AA	APts	PIM	PP	SH	GW	S	%	TGF	PGF	TGA	PGA	+/-	GP	G	A	Pts	PIM	PP	SH	GW
1950-51	Barrie Flyers	OHA	4	0	2	2	....	....	....	6	....	....	....	....	....	....	....	....	....	....	....	....	....	....	....	....	....	....
1951-52	Barrie Flyers	OHA	52	32	39	71	....	....	....	24	....	....	....	....	....	....	....	....	....	....	....	....	....	....	....	....	....	....
1952-53	Barrie Flyers	OHA	50	33	33	66	....	....	....	24	....	....	....	....	....	....	....	....	....	....	15	6	8	14	2	....	....	....
1953-54	Hershey Bears	AHL	54	13	21	34	....	....	....	4	....	....	....	....	....	....	....	....	....	....	11	3	5	8	4	....	....	....
1954-55	**Boston Bruins**	**NHL**	**60**	**22**	**20**	**42**	**32**	**20**	**58**	**34**	....	....	....	....	....	....	....	....	....	....	**5**	**1**	**2**	**3**	**4**	....	....	....
1955-56	**Boston Bruins**	**NHL**	**65**	**10**	**24**	**34**	**14**	**30**	**44**	**20**	....	....	....	....	....	....	....	....	....	....	....	....	....	....	....	....	....	....
1956-57	**Boston Bruins**	**NHL**	**69**	**21**	**39**	**60**	**29**	**46**	**75**	**31**	....	....	....	....	....	....	....	....	....	....	**10**	**1**	**5**	**6**	**4**	....	....	....
1957-58	**Boston Bruins**	**NHL**	**70**	**28**	**30**	**58**	**37**	**33**	**70**	**22**	....	....	....	....	....	....	....	....	....	....	**12**	**9**	**8**	**17**	**0**	....	....	....
1958-59	**Boston Bruins**	**NHL**	**70**	**32**	**30**	**62**	**41**	**32**	**73**	**20**	....	....	....	....	....	....	....	....	....	....	**7**	**2**	**5**	**7**	**0**	....	....	....
1959-60	**Boston Bruins**	**NHL**	**70**	**20**	***49**	**69**	**25**	**51**	**76**	**28**	....	....	....	....	....	....	....	....	....	....	....	....	....	....	....	....	....	....
1960-61	**Boston Bruins**	**NHL**	**68**	**26**	**23**	**49**	**32**	**23**	**55**	**22**	....	....	....	....	....	....	....	....	....	....	....	....	....	....	....	....	....	....
1961-62	**Boston Bruins**	**NHL**	**70**	**22**	**33**	**55**	**27**	**33**	**60**	**10**	....	....	....	....	....	....	....	....	....	....	....	....	....	....	....	....	....	....
1962-63	**Boston Bruins**	**NHL**	**41**	**14**	**19**	**33**	**17**	**20**	**37**	**2**	....	....	....	....	....	....	....	....	....	....	....	....	....	....	....	....	....	....
	New York Rangers	**NHL**	**21**	**8**	**16**	**24**	**10**	**17**	**27**	**4**	....	....	....	....	....	....	....	....	....	....	....	....	....	....	....	....	....	....
1963-64	**New York Rangers**	**NHL**	**55**	**9**	**17**	**26**	**12**	**19**	**31**	**6**	....	....	....	....	....	....	....	....	....	....	....	....	....	....	....	....	....	....
	Toronto Maple Leafs	**NHL**	**15**	**9**	**6**	**15**	**12**	**7**	**19**	**2**	....	....	....	....	....	....	....	....	....	....	**12**	**4**	**8**	**12**	**0**	....	....	....
1964-65	**Toronto Maple Leafs**	**NHL**	**52**	**6**	**13**	**19**	**0**	**14**	**22**	**0**	....	....	....	....	....	....	....	....	....	....	**6**	**0**	**0**	**0**	**0**	....	....	....
	Rochester Americans	AHL	18	7	9	16	....	....	....	4	....	....	....	....	....	....	....	....	....	....	....	....	....	....	....	....	....	....
1965-66	**Detroit Red Wings**	**NHL**	**24**	**1**	**6**	**7**	**1**	**6**	**7**	**0**	....	....	....	....	....	....	....	....	....	....	....	....	....	....	....	....	....	....
	Pittsburgh Hornets	AHL	37	11	19	30	....	....	....	8	....	....	....	....	....	....	....	....	....	....	3	0	1	1	0	....	....	....
1966-67	Pittsburgh Hornets	AHL	67	26	36	62	....	....	....	16	....	....	....	....	....	....	....	....	....	....	9	2	7	9	2	....	....	....
1967-68	**St. Louis Blues**	**NHL**	**39**	**9**	**20**	**29**	**11**	**21**	**32**	**4**	**1**	**0**	**1**	**93**	**9.7**	**45**	**15**	**29**	**0**	**+1**	**6**	**1**	**1**	**2**	**2**	**0**	**0**	**0**
	Kansas City Blues	CHL	11	9	6	15	....	....	....	5	....	....	....	....	....	....	....	....	....	....	1	0	0	0	0	....	....	....
1968-69	Providence Reds	AHL	74	26	48	74	....	....	....	12	....	....	....	....	....	....	....	....	....	....	9	4	7	11	0	....	....	....
1969-70	Providence Reds	AHL	31	3	12	15	....	....	....	2	....	....	....	....	....	....	....	....	....	....	....	....	....	....	....	....	....	....
	NHL Totals		**798**	**237**	**345**	**582**	**308**	**378**	**686**	**211**	**1**	**0**	**1**	**93**	**254.8**	**45**	**15**	**29**	**0**		**58**	**18**	**29**	**47**	**10**	**0**	**0**	**0**

Won Lady Byng Trophy (1960)

Played in NHL All-Star Game (1957, 1958, 1959, 1960, 1961, 1962, 1964)

Traded to **NY Rangers** by **Boston** for Dean Prentice, February 4, 1963. Traded to **Toronto** by **NY Rangers** with Andy Bathgate for Dick Duff, Rod Seiling, Bill Collins, Bob Nevin and Arnie Brown, February 22, 1964. Claimed on waivers by **Detroit** from **Toronto**, June 8, 1965. Claimed by **St. Louis** from **Detroit** in Expansion Draft, June 6, 1967.

• McKENNY, JIM

Jim "Howie" McKenny D – R. 5'11", 192 lbs. b: Ottawa, Ont., 12/1/1946. Toronto's 3rd choice, 17th overall, in 1963 Amateur Draft.

Season	Club	League	GP	G	A	Pts	AG	AA	APts	PIM	PP	SH	GW	S	%	TGF	PGF	TGA	PGA	+/-	GP	G	A	Pts	PIM	PP	SH	GW
1962-63	Neil McNeil Maroons	City Jr.	37	5	12	17	....	....	....	43	....	....	....	....	....	....	....	....	....	....	16	4	4	8	18	....	....	....
1963-64	Toronto Marlboros	OHA	56	7	31	38	....	....	....	102	....	....	....	....	....	....	....	....	....	....	9	2	0	2	22	....	....	....
1964-65	Toronto Marlboros	OHA	52	7	41	48	....	....	....	117	....	....	....	....	....	....	....	....	....	....	19	4	15	19	43	....	....	....
1965-66	Toronto Marlboros	OHA	42	14	26	40	....	....	....	78	....	....	....	....	....	....	....	....	....	....	14	3	10	13	38	....	....	....
	Toronto Maple Leafs	**NHL**	**2**	**0**	**0**	**0**	**0**	**0**	**0**	**2**	....	....	....	....	....	....	....	....	....	....	....	....	....	....	....	....	....	....
	Rochester Americans	AHL	1	0	1	1	....	....	....	0	....	....	....	....	....	....	....	....	....	....	....	....	....	....	....	....	....	....
	Tulsa Oilers	CHL	....	....	....	....	....	....	....	....	....	....	....	....	....	....	....	....	....	....	4	2	2	4	2	....	....	....
1966-67	**Toronto Maple Leafs**	**NHL**	**6**	**1**	**0**	**1**	**1**	**0**	**1**	**0**	....	....	....	....	....	....	....	....	....	....	....	....	....	....	....	....	....	....
	Tulsa Oilers	CHL	45	9	19	28	....	....	....	29	....	....	....	....	....	....	....	....	....	....	....	....	....	....	....	....	....	....
	Rochester Americans	AHL	19	3	6	9	....	....	....	10	....	....	....	....	....	....	....	....	....	....	7	0	0	0	2	....	....	....
1967-68	**Toronto Maple Leafs**	**NHL**	**5**	**1**	**0**	**1**	**1**	**0**	**1**	**0**	**1**	**0**	**1**	**2**	**50.0**	**1**	**1**	**2**	**0**	**–2**	....	....	....	....	....	....	....	....
	Rochester Americans	AHL	46	10	22	32	....	....	....	33	....	....	....	....	....	....	....	....	....	....	11	2	2	4	4	....	....	....
1968-69	**Toronto Maple Leafs**	**NHL**	**7**	**0**	**0**	**0**	**0**	**0**	**0**	**2**	**0**	**0**	**0**	**5**	**0.0**	**5**	**2**	**3**	**1**	**+1**	....	....	....	....	....	....	....	....
	Rochester Americans	AHL	47	19	31	50	....	....	....	22	....	....	....	....	....	....	....	....	....	....	....	....	....	....	....	....	....	....
	Vancouver Canucks	WHL	18	7	14	21	....	....	....	4	....	....	....	....	....	....	....	....	....	....	8	5	5	10	6	....	....	....
1969-70	**Toronto Maple Leafs**	**NHL**	**73**	**11**	**33**	**44**	**13**	**33**	**46**	**34**	**3**	**0**	**0**	**170**	**6.5**	**104**	**29**	**95**	**18**	**–2**	....	....	....	....	....	....	....	....
1970-71	**Toronto Maple Leafs**	**NHL**	**68**	**4**	**26**	**30**	**4**	**23**	**27**	**42**	**2**	**1**	**1**	**131**	**3.1**	**85**	**21**	**68**	**15**	**+11**	**6**	**2**	**1**	**3**	**2**	**1**	**0**	**0**
1971-72	**Toronto Maple Leafs**	**NHL**	**76**	**5**	**31**	**36**	**5**	**28**	**33**	**27**	**2**	**0**	**0**	**156**	**3.2**	**86**	**27**	**73**	**15**	**+1**	**5**	**3**	**0**	**3**	**2**	**2**	**1**	**0**
1972-73	**Toronto Maple Leafs**	**NHL**	**77**	**11**	**41**	**52**	**11**	**34**	**45**	**55**	**5**	**0**	**0**	**208**	**5.3**	**148**	**31**	**145**	**34**	**+6**	....	....	....	....	....	....	....	....
1973-74	**Toronto Maple Leafs**	**NHL**	**77**	**14**	**28**	**42**	**14**	**24**	**38**	**38**	**3**	**0**	**1**	**129**	**10.9**	**111**	**21**	**99**	**25**	**+16**	**4**	**0**	**2**	**2**	**0**	**0**	**0**	**0**
1974-75	**Toronto Maple Leafs**	**NHL**	**66**	**8**	**35**	**43**	**7**	**28**	**35**	**31**	**0**	**1**	**1**	**105**	**7.6**	**106**	**30**	**98**	**18**	**–4**	**7**	**0**	**1**	**1**	**2**	**0**	**0**	**0**
1975-76	**Toronto Maple Leafs**	**NHL**	**46**	**10**	**19**	**29**	**9**	**15**	**24**	**19**	**4**	**0**	**0**	**76**	**13.2**	**44**	**14**	**42**	**5**	**–7**	**6**	**2**	**3**	**5**	**2**	**1**	**0**	**1**
1976-77	**Toronto Maple Leafs**	**NHL**	**76**	**14**	**31**	**45**	**13**	**25**	**38**	**36**	**3**	**0**	**3**	**115**	**12.2**	**80**	**13**	**111**	**18**	**–26**	**9**	**0**	**2**	**2**	**2**	**0**	**0**	**0**

			REGULAR SEASON																		PLAYOFFS							
Season	Club	League	GP	G	A	Pts	AG	AA	APts	PIM	PP	SH	GW	S	%	TGF	PGF	TGA	PGA	+/–	GP	G	A	Pts	PIM	PP	SH	GW
1977-78	**Toronto Maple Leafs**	**NHL**	**15**	**2**	**2**	**4**	**2**	**2**	**4**	**8**	**0**	**0**	**0**	**12**	**16.7**	**9**	**2**	**3**	**0**	**+4**	....	....	....	....	....	....	....	....
	Dallas Black Hawks	CHL	55	21	31	52	....	....	....	45	....	....	....	....	....	....	....	....	....	....	13	1	6	7	8	....	....	....
1978-79	**Minnesota North Stars**	**NHL**	**10**	**1**	**1**	**2**	**1**	**1**	**2**	**2**	**1**	**0**	**0**	**8**	**12.5**	**5**	**2**	**7**	**1**	**–3**	....	....	....	....	....	....	....	....
	Oklahoma City Stars	CHL	33	11	23	34	....	....	....	10	....	....	....	....	....	....	....	....	....	....	....	....	....	....	....	....	....	....
	NHL Totals		**604**	**82**	**247**	**329**	**81**	**213**	**294**	**294**	**24**	**2**	**7**	**1117**	**7.3**	**784**	**193**	**746**	**150**		**37**	**7**	**9**	**16**	**10**	**4**	**1**	**1**

CHL Second All-Star Team (1978)

Played in NHL All-Star Game (1974)

Traded to **Minnesota** by **Toronto** for cash and future considerations (the rights to Owen Lloyd, October 25, 1978), May 15, 1978.

• McKENZIE, BRIAN

Brian McKenzie LW – L. 5'10", 165 lbs. b: St. Catharines, Ont., 3/16/1951. Pittsburgh's 1st choice, 18th overall, in 1971 Amateur Draft.

Season	Club	League	GP	G	A	Pts	AG	AA	APts	PIM	PP	SH	GW	S	%	TGF	PGF	TGA	PGA	+/–	GP	G	A	Pts	PIM	PP	SH	GW
1967-68	Stamford Steamers	Jr. B	STATISTICS NOT AVAILABLE																									
1968-69	St. Catharines Black Hawks	OHA	54	10	21	31	....	....	....	70	....	....	....	....	....	....	....	....	....	....	18	5	5	10	29	....	....	....
1969-70	St. Catharines Black Hawks	OHA	53	17	41	58	....	....	....	128	....	....	....	....	....	....	....	....	....	....	....	....	....	....	....	....	....	....
1970-71	St. Catharines Black Hawks	OHA	60	39	*85	124	....	....	....	108	....	....	....	....	....	....	....	....	....	....	....	....	....	....	....	....	....	....
1971-72	**Pittsburgh Penguins**	**NHL**	**6**	**1**	**1**	**2**	**1**	**1**	**2**	**4**	**0**	**0**	**0**	**8**	**12.5**	**3**	**1**	**4**	**0**	**–2**	....	....	....	....	....	....	....	....
	Hershey Bears	AHL	66	15	13	28	....	....	....	92	....	....	....	....	....	....	....	....	....	....	4	0	0	0	0	....	....	....
1972-73	Hershey Bears	AHL	3	0	2	2	....	....	....	16	....	....	....	....	....	....	....	....	....	....	....	....	....	....	....	....	....	....
	Omaha Knights	CHL	64	16	36	52	....	....	....	71	....	....	....	....	....	....	....	....	....	....	9	5	4	9	28	....	....	....
1973-74	Edmonton Oilers	WHA	78	18	20	38	....	....	....	66	....	....	....	....	....	....	....	....	....	....	5	0	1	1	0	....	....	....
1974-75	Mohawk Valley Comets	NAHL	55	28	37	65	....	....	....	37	....	....	....	....	....	....	....	....	....	....	....	....	....	....	....	....	....	....
	Indianapolis Racers	WHA	9	1	0	1	....	....	....	6	....	....	....	....	....	....	....	....	....	....	....	....	....	....	....	....	....	....
1975-76	Mohawk Valley Comets	NAHL	20	10	14	24	....	....	....	24	....	....	....	....	....	....	....	....	....	....	....	....	....	....	....	....	....	....
	Toledo Goaldiggers	IHL	42	12	19	31	....	....	....	64	....	....	....	....	....	....	....	....	....	....	4	2	3	5	2	....	....	....
1976-77	Toledo Goaldiggers	IHL	77	32	58	90	....	....	....	85	....	....	....	....	....	....	....	....	....	....	15	9	5	14	10	....	....	....
1977-78	Toledo Goaldiggers	IHL	2	0	0	0	....	....	....	0	....	....	....	....	....	....	....	....	....	....	....	....	....	....	....	....	....	....
	Milwaukee Admirals	IHL	15	2	9	11	....	....	....	18	....	....	....	....	....	....	....	....	....	....	....	....	....	....	....	....	....	....
	NHL Totals		**6**	**1**	**1**	**2**	**1**	**1**	**2**	**4**	**0**	**0**	**0**	**8**	**12.5**	**3**	**1**	**4**	**0**		....	....	....	....	....	....	....	....
	Other Major League Totals		87	19	20	39	....	....	....	72	....	....	....	....	....	....	....	....	....	....	5	0	1	1	0	....	....	....

Selected by **Ontario-Ottawa** (WHA) in 1972 WHA General Player Draft, February 12, 1972. Traded to **Atlanta** by **Pittsburgh** for cash, October, 1972. Selected by **Edmonton** (WHA) in 1973 WHA Professional Player Draft, May, 1973. Claimed by **Indianapolis** (WHA) from **Edmonton** (WHA) in 1974 WHA Expansion Draft, May, 1974. Signed as a free agent by **Toledo** (IHL), December, 1975.

• McKENZIE, JIM

Jim McKenzie LW – L. 6'3", 205 lbs. b: Gull Lake, Sask., 11/3/1969. Hartford's 3rd choice, 73rd overall, in 1989 Entry Draft.

Season	Club	League	GP	G	A	Pts	AG	AA	APts	PIM	PP	SH	GW	S	%	TGF	PGF	TGA	PGA	+/–	GP	G	A	Pts	PIM	PP	SH	GW
1985-86	Moose Jaw Warriors	WHL	3	0	2	2	....	....	....	0	....	....	....	....	....	....	....	....	....	....	....	....	....	....	....	....	....	....
1986-87	Moose Jaw Warriors	WHL	65	5	3	8	....	....	....	125	....	....	....	....	....	....	....	....	....	....	9	0	0	0	7	....	....	....
1987-88	Moose Jaw Warriors	WHL	62	1	17	18	....	....	....	134	....	....	....	....	....	....	....	....	....	....	....	....	....	....	....	....	....	....
1988-89	Victoria Cougars	WHL	67	15	27	42	....	....	....	176	....	....	....	....	....	....	....	....	....	....	8	1	4	5	30	....	....	....
1989-90	**Hartford Whalers**	**NHL**	**5**	**0**	**0**	**0**	**0**	**0**	**0**	**4**	**0**	**0**	**0**	**0**	**0.0**	**0**	**0**	**0**	**0**	**0**	....	....	....	....	....	....	....	....
	Binghamton Whalers	AHL	56	4	12	16	....	....	....	149	....	....	....	....	....	....	....	....	....	....	....	....	....	....	....	....	....	....
1990-91	**Hartford Whalers**	**NHL**	**41**	**4**	**3**	**7**	**4**	**2**	**6**	**108**	**0**	**0**	**0**	**16**	**25.0**	**9**	**0**	**16**	**0**	**–7**	**6**	**0**	**0**	**0**	**8**	**0**	**0**	**0**
	Springfield Indians	AHL	24	3	4	7	....	....	....	102	....	....	....	....	....	....	....	....	....	....	....	....	....	....	....	....	....	....
1991-92	**Hartford Whalers**	**NHL**	**67**	**5**	**1**	**6**	**5**	**1**	**6**	**87**	**0**	**0**	**0**	**34**	**14.7**	**11**	**0**	**17**	**0**	**–6**	....	....	....	....	....	....	....	....
1992-93	**Hartford Whalers**	**NHL**	**64**	**3**	**6**	**9**	**2**	**4**	**6**	**202**	**0**	**0**	**0**	**36**	**8.3**	**19**	**0**	**29**	**0**	**–10**	....	....	....	....	....	....	....	....
1993-94	**Hartford Whalers**	**NHL**	**26**	**1**	**2**	**3**	**1**	**2**	**3**	**67**	**0**	**0**	**0**	**9**	**11.1**	**5**	**2**	**10**	**1**	**–6**	....	....	....	....	....	....	....	....
	Dallas Stars	**NHL**	**34**	**2**	**3**	**5**	**2**	**2**	**4**	**63**	**0**	**0**	**1**	**18**	**11.1**	**10**	**0**	**6**	**0**	**+4**	....	....	....	....	....	....	....	....
	Pittsburgh Penguins	**NHL**	**11**	**0**	**0**	**0**	**0**	**0**	**0**	**16**	**0**	**0**	**0**	**6**	**0.0**	**0**	**0**	**5**	**0**	**–5**	**3**	**0**	**0**	**0**	**0**	**0**	**0**	**0**
1994-95	**Pittsburgh Penguins**	**NHL**	**39**	**2**	**1**	**3**	**4**	**1**	**5**	**63**	**0**	**0**	**1**	**16**	**12.5**	**8**	**1**	**14**	**0**	**–7**	**5**	**0**	**0**	**0**	**4**	**0**	**0**	**0**
1995-96	**Winnipeg Jets**	**NHL**	**73**	**4**	**2**	**6**	**4**	**2**	**6**	**202**	**0**	**0**	**0**	**28**	**14.3**	**9**	**0**	**13**	**0**	**–4**	**1**	**0**	**0**	**0**	**2**	**0**	**0**	**0**
1996-97	**Phoenix Coyotes**	**NHL**	**65**	**5**	**3**	**8**	**5**	**3**	**8**	**200**	**0**	**0**	**1**	**38**	**13.2**	**12**	**0**	**17**	**0**	**–5**	**7**	**0**	**0**	**0**	**2**	**0**	**0**	**0**
1997-98	**Phoenix Coyotes**	**NHL**	**64**	**3**	**4**	**7**	**4**	**4**	**8**	**146**	**0**	**0**	**0**	**35**	**8.6**	**17**	**0**	**24**	**0**	**–7**	**1**	**0**	**0**	**0**	**0**	**0**	**0**	**0**
	NHL Totals		**489**	**29**	**25**	**54**	**31**	**21**	**52**	**1158**	**0**	**0**	**3**	**236**	**12.3**	**100**	**3**	**151**	**1**		**23**	**0**	**0**	**0**	**16**	**0**	**0**	**0**

Traded to **Florida** by **Hartford** for Alexander Godynyuk, December 16, 1993. Traded to **Dallas** by **Florida** for Dallas' 4th round choice (later traded to Ottawa — Ottawa selected Kevin Bolibruck) in 1995 Entry Draft, December 16, 1993. Traded to **Pittsburgh** by **Dallas** for Mike Needham, March 21, 1994. Signed as a free agent by **NY Islanders**, August 2, 1995. Claimed by **Winnipeg** from **NY Islanders** in NHL Waiver Draft, October 2, 1995. Transferred to **Phoenix** after **Winnipeg** franchise relocated, July 1, 1996. Traded to **Anaheim** by **Phoenix** for J.F. Jomphe, June 18, 1998.

• McKENZIE, JOHN

John "Pie" McKenzie RW – R. 5'9", 175 lbs. b: High River, Alta., 12/12/1937.

Season	Club	League	GP	G	A	Pts	AG	AA	APts	PIM	PP	SH	GW	S	%	TGF	PGF	TGA	PGA	+/–	GP	G	A	Pts	PIM	PP	SH	GW
1953-54	Calgary Buffalos	WCJHL	34	6	8	14	....	....	....	12	....	....	....	....	....	....	....	....	....	....	5	0	0	0	2	....	....	....
1954-55	Medicine Hat Tigers	WCJHL	39	14	4	18	....	....	....	33	....	....	....	....	....	....	....	....	....	....	5	0	0	0	4	....	....	....
1955-56	Medicine Hat Tigers	WCJHL	DID NOT PLAY – INJURED																									
	Calgary Stampeders	WHL	1	0	0	0	....	....	....	0	....	....	....	....	....	....	....	....	....	....	2	0	1	1	2	....	....	....
1956-57	St. Catharines Teepees	OHA	52	32	38	70	....	....	....	143	....	....	....	....	....	....	....	....	....	....	14	9	11	20	50	....	....	....
1957-58	St. Catharines Teepees	OHA	52	*48	51	*99	....	....	....	*227	....	....	....	....	....	....	....	....	....	....	8	8	4	12	19	....	....	....
1958-59	**Chicago Black Hawks**	**NHL**	**32**	**3**	**4**	**7**	**4**	**4**	**8**	**22**	....	....	....	....	....	....	....	....	....	....	**2**	**0**	**0**	**0**	**2**	....	....	....
	Calgary Stampeders	WHL	13	2	5	7	....	....	....	18	....	....	....	....	....	....	....	....	....	....	....	....	....	....	....	....	....	....
1959-60	**Detroit Red Wings**	**NHL**	**59**	**8**	**12**	**20**	**10**	**12**	**22**	**50**	....	....	....	....	....	....	....	....	....	....	**2**	**0**	**0**	**0**	**0**	....	....	....
1960-61	**Detroit Red Wings**	**NHL**	**16**	**3**	**1**	**4**	**4**	**1**	**5**	**13**	....	....	....	....	....	....	....	....	....	....	....	....	....	....	....	....	....	....
	Hershey Bears	AHL	47	19	23	42	....	....	....	84	....	....	....	....	....	....	....	....	....	....	8	3	6	9	10	....	....	....
1961-62	Hershey Bears	AHL	58	30	29	59	....	....	....	149	....	....	....	....	....	....	....	....	....	....	7	1	2	3	19	....	....	....
1962-63	Buffalo Bisons	AHL	71	35	46	81	....	....	....	122	....	....	....	....	....	....	....	....	....	....	13	8	12	*20	28	....	....	....
1963-64	**Chicago Black Hawks**	**NHL**	**45**	**9**	**9**	**18**	**12**	**10**	**22**	**50**	....	....	....	....	....	....	....	....	....	....	**4**	**0**	**1**	**1**	**6**	....	....	....
1964-65	**Chicago Black Hawks**	**NHL**	**51**	**8**	**10**	**18**	**10**	**11**	**21**	**46**	....	....	....	....	....	....	....	....	....	....	**11**	**0**	**1**	**1**	**6**	....	....	....
	St. Louis Braves	CHL	5	5	4	9	....	....	....	17	....	....	....	....	....	....	....	....	....	....	....	....	....	....	....	....	....	....
1965-66	**New York Rangers**	**NHL**	**35**	**6**	**5**	**11**	**7**	**5**	**12**	**36**	....	....	....	....	....	....	....	....	....	....	....	....	....	....	....	....	....	....
	Boston Bruins	**NHL**	**36**	**13**	**9**	**22**	**16**	**9**	**25**	**36**	....	....	....	....	....	....	....	....	....	....	....	....	....	....	....	....	....	....
1966-67	**Boston Bruins**	**NHL**	**69**	**17**	**19**	**36**	**21**	**20**	**41**	**98**	....	....	....	....	....	....	....	....	....	....	....	....	....	....	....	....	....	....
1967-68	**Boston Bruins**	**NHL**	**74**	**28**	**38**	**66**	**35**	**40**	**75**	**107**	**7**	**0**	**4**	**184**	**15.2**	**93**	**21**	**62**	**4**	**+14**	**4**	**1**	**1**	**2**	**8**	**0**	**0**	**0**
1968-69	**Boston Bruins**	**NHL**	**60**	**29**	**27**	**56**	**33**	**25**	**58**	**99**	**8**	**1**	**7**	**123**	**23.6**	**82**	**27**	**48**	**6**	**+13**	**10**	**2**	**2**	**4**	**17**	**1**	**0**	**0**
1969-70	**Boston Bruins**	**NHL**	**72**	**29**	**41**	**70**	**34**	**41**	**75**	**114**	**9**	**1**	**6**	**196**	**14.8**	**109**	**55**	**48**	**14**	**+20**	**14**	**5**	**12**	**17**	**35**	**0**	**3**	**0**
1970-71	**Boston Bruins**	**NHL**	**65**	**31**	**46**	**77**	**33**	**41**	**74**	**120**	**11**	**0**	**3**	**151**	**20.5**	**120**	**52**	**42**	**1**	**+27**	**7**	**2**	**3**	**5**	**22**	**1**	**0**	**1**
1971-72	**Boston Bruins**	**NHL**	**77**	**22**	**47**	**69**	**23**	**43**	**66**	**126**	**10**	**0**	**3**	**133**	**16.5**	**121**	**61**	**41**	**0**	**+19**	**15**	**5**	**12**	**17**	**37**	**3**	**0**	**0**
1972-73	Philadelphia Blazers	WHA	60	28	50	78	....	....	....	157	....	....	....	....	....	....	....	....	....	....	4	3	1	4	8	....	....	....
1973-74	Vancouver Blazers	WHA	45	14	38	52	....	....	....	71	....	....	....	....	....	....	....	....	....	....	....	....	....	....	....	....	....	....
1974-75	Canada	Summit	7	2	3	5	....	....	....	14	....	....	....	....	....	....	....	....	....	....	....	....	....	....	....	....	....	....
	Vancouver Blazers	WHA	74	23	37	60	....	....	....	84	....	....	....	....	....	....	....	....	....	....	....	....	....	....	....	....	....	....
1975-76	Minnesota Fighting Saints	WHA	57	21	26	47	....	....	....	48	....	....	....	....	....	....	....	....	....	....	....	....	....	....	....	....	....	....
	Cincinnati Stingers	WHA	12	3	10	13	....	....	....	6	....	....	....	....	....	....	....	....	....	....	....	....	....	....	....	....	....	....

			REGULAR SEASON																		PLAYOFFS							
Season	Club	League	GP	G	A	Pts	AG	AA	APts	PIM	PP	SH	GW	S	%	TGF	PGF	TGA	PGA	+/-	GP	G	A	Pts	PIM	PP	SH	GW
1976-77	Minnesota Fighting Saints	WHA	40	17	13	30				77																		
	New England Whalers	WHA	34	11	19	30				25											5	2	1	3	8			
1977-78	New England Whalers	WHA	79	27	29	56				61											14	6	6	12	16			
1978-79	New England Whalers	WHA	76	19	28	47				115											10	3	7	10	10			
	NHL Totals		**691**	**206**	**268**	**474**	**242**	**262**	**504**	**917**	**45**	**2**	**23**	**787**	**26.2**	**525**	**216**	**241**	**25**		**69**	**15**	**32**	**47**	**133**	**5**	**3**	**1**
	Other Major League Totals		477	163	250	413				644											33	14	15	29	42			

AHL First All-Star Team (1963) • NHL Second All-Star Team (1970)

Played in NHL All-Star Game (1970, 1972)

Claimed by **Detroit** from **Chicago** in Intra-League Draft, June 10, 1959. Traded to **Chicago** by **Detroit** with Len Lunde for Doug Barkley, June 6, 1962. Traded to **NY Rangers** by **Chicago** with Ray Cullen for Tracy Pratt, Dick Meissner, Dave Richardson and Mel Pearson, June 4, 1965. Traded to **Boston** by **NY Rangers** for Reggie Fleming, January 10, 1966. Selected by **Quebec** (WHA) in 1972 WHA General Player Draft, February 12, 1972. WHA rights traded to **Philadelphia** (WHA) by **Quebec** (WHA) for future considerations, May, 1972. Traded to **Philadelphia** by **Boston** for cash, August 3, 1972. Transferred to **Vancouver** (WHA) after **Philadelphia** (WHA) franchise relocated, May, 1973. Traded to **Minnesota** (WHA) by **Vancouver** (WHA) with cash for George Morrison, Dan Tannahill and the rights to Joe Micheletti and Wally Olds, September, 1975. Signed as a free agent by **Cincinnati** (WHA) after **Minnesota** (WHA) franchise folded, February 27, 1976. Traded to **Minnesota** (WHA) by **Cincinnati** (WHA) with the rights to Ivan Hlinka for Bryan Maxwell, September, 1976. Traded to **Edmonton** (WHA) by **Minnesota** (WHA) with Jean-Louis Lavasseur, Bill Butters, Mike Antonovich, Dave Keon, Steve Carlson and Jack Carlson for cash, December, 1977. Traded to **New England** (WHA) by **Edmonton** (WHA) with Dave Keon, Steve Carlson, Dave Dryden and Jack Carlson for future considerations (Dave Debol, June, 1977), Dan Arndt and cash, January, 1977.

• McKIM, ANDREW

Andrew McKim C – R. 5'8", 175 lbs. b: St. John, N.B., 7/6/1970.

1985-86	Moncton Flyers	Midget	....	6	8	14				....																		
1986-87	Verdun Jr. Canadiens	QJMHL	70	28	59	87				12																		
1987-88	Verdun Jr. Canadiens	QMJHL	62	27	32	59				27																		
1988-89	Verdun Jr. Canadiens	QMJHL	68	50	56	106				36																		
1989-90	Hull Olympiques	QMJHL	70	66	84	130				44											11	8	10	18	8			
1990-91	Salt Lake Golden Eagles	IHL	74	30	30	60				48											4	0	2	2	6			
1991-92	St. John's Maple Leafs	AHL	79	43	50	93				79											16	11	12	23	4			
1992-93	**Boston Bruins**	**NHL**	**7**	**1**	**3**	**4**	**1**	**2**	**3**	**0**	**0**	**0**	**0**	**12**	**8.3**	**7**	**2**	**3**	**0**	**+2**								
	Providence Bruins	AHL	61	23	46	69				64											6	2	2	4	0			
1993-94	**Boston Bruins**	**NHL**	**29**	**0**	**1**	**1**	**0**	**1**	**1**	**4**	**0**	**0**	**0**	**22**	**0.0**	**2**	**0**	**12**	**0**	**–10**								
	Providence Bruins	AHL	46	13	24	37				49																		
1994-95	**Detroit Red Wings**	**NHL**	**2**	**0**	**0**	**0**	**0**	**0**	**0**	**2**	**0**	**0**	**0**	**0**	**0.0**	**0**	**0**	**0**	**0**	**0**								
	Adirondack Red Wings	AHL	77	39	55	94				22											4	3	3	6	0			
	Canada	Nat-Team	8	6	*9	*15				....																		
	Canada	WC-A	8	6	7	13				4																		
1995-96	Geneva	Switz.	27	3	5	8				18											1	0	0	0	0			
	Canada	Nat-Team	10	7	7	14				6																		
1996-97	EHC Eisbaren Berlin	Germany	47	23	22	45				12											8	3	7	10	29			
1997-98	EHC Eisbaren Berlin	Germany	48	16	29	45				10											10	6	5	11	6			
	NHL Totals		**38**	**1**	**4**	**5**	**1**	**3**	**4**	**6**	**0**	**0**	**0**	**34**	**2.9**	**9**	**2**	**15**	**0**									

QMJHL First All-Star Team (1990) • Canadian Major Junior Most Sportsmanlike Player of the Year (1990)

Signed as a free agent by **Calgary**, October 5, 1990. Signed as a free agent by **Boston**, July 23, 1992. Signed as a free agent by **Detroit**, August 31, 1994.

• McLAREN, KYLE

Kyle McLaren D – L. 6'4", 219 lbs. b: Humbolt, Sask., 6/18/1977. Boston's 1st choice, 9th overall, in 1995 Entry Draft.

1993-94	Tacoma Rockets	WHL	62	1	9	10				53											6	1	4	5	6			
1994-95	Tacoma Rockets	WHL	47	13	19	32				68											4	1	1	2	4			
1995-96	**Boston Bruins**	**NHL**	**74**	**5**	**12**	**17**	**5**	**10**	**15**	**73**	**0**	**0**	**0**	**74**	**6.8**	**83**	**3**	**93**	**29**	**+16**	**5**	**0**	**0**	**0**	**14**	**0**	**0**	**0**
1996-97	**Boston Bruins**	**NHL**	**58**	**5**	**9**	**14**	**5**	**8**	**13**	**54**	**0**	**0**	**1**	**68**	**7.4**	**53**	**2**	**80**	**20**	**–9**								
1997-98	**Boston Bruins**	**NHL**	**66**	**5**	**20**	**25**	**6**	**19**	**25**	**56**	**2**	**0**	**0**	**101**	**5.0**	**78**	**23**	**54**	**12**	**+13**	**6**	**1**	**0**	**1**	**4**	**1**	**0**	**0**
	NHL Totals		**198**	**15**	**41**	**56**	**16**	**37**	**53**	**183**	**2**	**0**	**1**	**243**	**6.2**	**214**	**28**	**227**	**61**		**11**	**1**	**0**	**1**	**18**	**1**	**0**	**0**

NHL All-Rookie Team (1996)

• McLEAN, DON

Don McLean D – R. 6'1", 200 lbs. b: Niagara Falls, Ont., 1/19/1954. Philadelphia's 1st choice, 35th overall, in 1974 Amateur Draft.

1968-69	Niagara Falls Flyers	OHA	1	0	1	1				2																		
1969-70	Niagara Falls Flyers	OHA	29	0	0	0				58																		
1970-71	Niagara Falls Flyers	OHA	54	1	6	7				72																		
1971-72	Niagara Falls Flyers	OHA	34	0	5	5				10																		
1972-73	Sudbury Wolves	OHA	46	5	12	17				124																		
1973-74	Sudbury Wolves	OHA	57	6	17	23				*305																		
1974-75	Richmond Robins	AHL	58	1	8	9				188											4	0	1	1	2			
1975-76	**Washington Capitals**	**NHL**	**9**	**0**	**0**	**0**	**0**	**0**	**0**	**6**	**0**	**0**	**0**	**4**	**0.0**	**5**	**0**	**10**	**2**	**–3**								
	Richmond Robins	AHL	20	0	0	0				16																		
	Salt Lake City Golden Eagles	CHL	34	1	12	13				77											3	0	0	0	2			
1976-77	Johnstown Jets	NAHL	5	0	3	3				4																		
	NHL Totals		**9**	**0**	**0**	**0**	**0**	**0**	**0**	**6**	**0**	**0**	**0**	**4**	**0.0**	**5**	**0**	**10**	**2**									

Traded to **Washington** by **Philadelphia** with Bill Clement and Washington's 1st round choice (Alex Forsythe) in 1975 Amateur Draft for Washington's 1st round choice (Mel Bridgman) in 1975 Amateur Draft, June 4, 1975.

• McLEAN, JEFF

Jeff McLean C – L. 5'10", 190 lbs. b: Port Moody, B.C., 10/6/1969. San Jose's 1st choice, 1st overall, in 1991 Supplemental Draft.

1987-88	New Westminster Bruins	BCJHL	60	70	91	161				128																		
1988-89	University of North Dakota	WCHA	37	0	3	3				14																		
1989-90	University of North Dakota	WCHA	45	10	16	26				42																		
1990-91	University of North Dakota	WCHA	42	19	26	45				22																		
1991-92	University of North Dakota	WCHA	38	27	43	70				40																		
1992-93	Kansas City Blades	IHL	60	21	23	44				45											10	3	1	4	2			
1993-94	**San Jose Sharks**	**NHL**	**6**	**1**	**0**	**1**	**1**	**0**	**1**	**0**	**0**	**0**	**0**	**5**	**20.0**	**2**	**0**	**1**	**0**	**+1**								
	Kansas City Blades	IHL	69	27	30	57				44																		
1994-95	Kalamazoo Wings	IHL	41	16	18	34				22											4	1	4	5	0			
1995-96	Kansas City Blades	IHL	71	17	27	44				34											3	0	3	3	2			
1996-97	Kansas City Blades	IHL	39	8	15	23				14																		
	Cincinnati Cyclones	IHL	9	1	3	4				2																		
	Fort Wayne Komets	IHL	6	1	1	2				2																		
1997-98	Kassel Huskies	EuroHL	2	1	0	1				0																		
	Kassel Huskies	Germany	12	3	5	8				12																		
	NHL Totals		**6**	**1**	**0**	**1**	**1**	**0**	**1**	**0**	**0**	**0**	**0**	**5**	**20.0**	**2**	**0**	**1**	**0**									

• McLELLAN, SCOTT

Scott McLellan RW – R. 6'1", 175 lbs. b: Toronto, Ont., 2/10/1963. Boston's 3rd choice, 77th overall, in 1981 Entry Draft.

1979-80	St. Michael's Buzzers	Midget	41	43	48	91				....																		
1980-81	Niagara Falls Flyers	OHA	33	7	4	11				39											12	1	0	1	2			
1981-82	Niagara Falls Flyers	OHL	12	1	6	7				33																		
	Peterborough Petes	OHL	46	20	31	51				42											6	1	2	3	10			
1982-83	Peterborough Petes	OHL	65	43	58	101				38											4	2	2	4	2			
	Boston Bruins	**NHL**	**2**	**0**	**0**	**0**	**0**	**0**	**0**	**0**	**0**	**0**	**0**	**0**	**0.0**	**0**	**0**	**0**	**0**	**0**								
1983-84	Toledo Goaldiggers	IHL	5	1	2	3				0																		
	Hershey Bears	AHL	73	9	12	21				14																		
1984-85	Hershey Bears	AHL	47	12	12	24				32																		
	NHL Totals		**2**	**0**	**0**	**0**	**0**	**0**	**0**	**0**	**0**	**0**	**0**	**0**	**0.0**	**0**	**0**	**0**	**0**									

			REGULAR SEASON																		PLAYOFFS							
Season	Club	League	GP	G	A	Pts	AG	AA	APts	PIM	PP	SH	GW	S	%	TGF	PGF	TGA	PGA	+/–	GP	G	A	Pts	PIM	PP	SH	GW

• McLELLAN, TODD

Todd McLellan C – L. 5'11", 185 lbs. b: Melville, Sask., 10/3/1967. NY Islanders' 6th choice, 104th overall, in 1986 Entry Draft.

Season	Club	League	GP	G	A	Pts	AG	AA	APts	PIM	PP	SH	GW	S	%	TGF	PGF	TGA	PGA	+/–	GP	G	A	Pts	PIM	PP	SH	GW
1982-83	Saskatoon Blazers	SJHL	25	6	9	15	....	....	....	6	....	....	....	....	....	....	....	....	....	....	....	....	....	....	....	....	....	....
1983-84	Saskatoon Blades	WHL	50	8	14	22	....	....	....	15	....	....	....	....	....	....	....	....	....	....	....	....	....	....	....	....	....	....
1984-85	Saskatoon Blades	WHL	41	15	35	50	....	....	....	33	....	....	....	....	....	....	....	....	....	....	3	1	0	1	0	....	....	....
1985-86	Saskatoon Blades	WHL	27	9	10	19	....	....	....	13	....	....	....	....	....	....	....	....	....	....	13	9	3	12	8	....	....	....
1986-87	Saskatoon Blades	WHL	60	34	39	73	....	....	....	66	....	....	....	....	....	....	....	....	....	....	6	1	1	2	2	....	....	....
1987-88	**New York Islanders**	**NHL**	**5**	**1**	**1**	**2**	**1**	**1**	**2**	**0**	**0**	**0**	**0**	**4**	**25.0**	**2**	**0**	**4**	**1**	**–1**	....	....	....	....	....	....	....	....
	Springfield Indians	AHL	70	18	26	44	....	....	....	32	....	....	....	....	....	....	....	....	....	....	....	....	....	....	....	....	....	....
1988-89	Springfield Indians	AHL	37	7	19	26	....	....	....	17	....	....	....	....	....	....	....	....	....	....	....	....	....	....	....	....	....	....
	NHL Totals		**5**	**1**	**1**	**2**	**1**	**1**	**2**	**0**	**0**	**0**	**0**	**4**	**25.0**	**2**	**0**	**4**	**1**		....	....	....	....	....	....	....	....

• McLEOD, AL

Al "Moose" McLeod D – L. 5'11", 200 lbs. b: Medicine Hat, Alta., 6/17/1949.

Season	Club	League	GP	G	A	Pts	AG	AA	APts	PIM	PP	SH	GW	S	%	TGF	PGF	TGA	PGA	+/–	GP	G	A	Pts	PIM	PP	SH	GW
1966-67	Calgary Buffaloes	WCJHL	10	2	3	5	....	....	....	0	....	....	....	....	....	....	....	....	....	....	....	....	....	....	....	....	....	....
1967-68	Michigan Tech Huskies	WCHA	DID NOT PLAY – FRESHMAN																									
1968-69	Michigan Tech Huskies	WCHA	23	2	3	5	....	....	....	10	....	....	....	....	....	....	....	....	....	....	....	....	....	....	....	....	....	....
1969-70	Michigan Tech Huskies	WCHA	34	14	17	31	....	....	....	32	....	....	....	....	....	....	....	....	....	....	....	....	....	....	....	....	....	....
1970-71	Michigan Tech Huskies	WCHA	32	13	26	39	....	....	....	14	....	....	....	....	....	....	....	....	....	....	....	....	....	....	....	....	....	....
1971-72	Fort Worth Wings	CHL	22	1	6	7	....	....	....	4	....	....	....	....	....	....	....	....	....	....	....	....	....	....	....	....	....	....
	Port Huron Wings	IHL	35	1	12	13	....	....	....	15	....	....	....	....	....	....	....	....	....	....	15	0	3	3	13	....	....	....
1972-73	Virginia Wings	AHL	76	4	15	19	....	....	....	105	....	....	....	....	....	....	....	....	....	....	13	0	1	1	22	....	....	....
1973-74	**Detroit Red Wings**	**NHL**	**26**	**2**	**2**	**4**	**2**	**2**	**4**	**24**	**0**	**0**	**0**	**23**	**8.7**	**24**	**2**	**35**	**6**	**–7**	....	....	....	....	....	....	....	....
	Virginia Wings	AHL	54	1	13	14	....	....	....	52	....	....	....	....	....	....	....	....	....	....	....	....	....	....	....	....	....	....
1974-75	Phoenix Roadrunners	WHA	77	3	16	19	....	....	....	98	....	....	....	....	....	....	....	....	....	....	5	0	4	4	4	....	....	....
1975-76	Phoenix Roadrunners	WHA	80	2	18	20	....	....	....	82	....	....	....	....	....	....	....	....	....	....	5	0	2	2	4	....	....	....
1976-77	Phoenix Roadrunners	WHA	29	1	5	6	....	....	....	35	....	....	....	....	....	....	....	....	....	....	....	....	....	....	....	....	....	....
	Houston Aeros	WHA	51	7	21	28	....	....	....	20	....	....	....	....	....	....	....	....	....	....	10	1	3	4	9	....	....	....
1977-78	Houston Aeros	WHA	80	2	22	24	....	....	....	54	....	....	....	....	....	....	....	....	....	....	6	1	0	1	2	....	....	....
1978-79	Indianapolis Racers	WHA	25	0	11	11	....	....	....	22	....	....	....	....	....	....	....	....	....	....	....	....	....	....	....	....	....	....
	NHL Totals		**26**	**2**	**2**	**4**	**2**	**2**	**4**	**24**	**0**	**0**	**0**	**23**	**8.7**	**24**	**2**	**35**	**6**		....	....	....	....	....	....	....	....
	Other Major League Totals		342	15	93	108				311											26	2	9	11	19	....	....	....

Signed as a free agent by **Detroit** (Fort Worth-CHL), October 1, 1971. Signed as a free agent by **Phoenix** (WHA), August, 1974. Traded to **Houston** (WHA) by **Phoenix** (WHA) with John Gray for Andre Hinse and Frank Hughes, Decemeber, 1976. Traded to **Winnipeg** (WHA) by **Houston** (WHA) for cash, July 6, 1978. Traded to **Indianapolis** (WHA) by **Winnipeg** (WHA) for cash, July 15, 1978.

• McLLWAIN, DAVE

Dave McLlwain C/RW – L. 6', 185 lbs. b: Seaforth, Ont., 1/9/1967. Pittsburgh's 9th choice, 172nd overall, in 1986 Entry Draft.

Season	Club	League	GP	G	A	Pts	AG	AA	APts	PIM	PP	SH	GW	S	%	TGF	PGF	TGA	PGA	+/–	GP	G	A	Pts	PIM	PP	SH	GW
1984-85	Kitchener Rangers	OHL	61	13	21	34	....	....	....	29	....	....	....	....	....	....	....	....	....	....	....	....	....	....	....	....	....	....
1985-86	Kitchener Rangers	OHL	13	7	7	14	....	....	....	12	....	....	....	....	....	....	....	....	....	....	....	....	....	....	....	....	....	....
	North Bay Centennials	OHL	51	30	28	58	....	....	....	25	....	....	....	....	....	....	....	....	....	....	10	4	4	8	2	....	....	....
1986-87	North Bay Centennials	OHL	60	46	73	119	....	....	....	35	....	....	....	....	....	....	....	....	....	....	24	7	18	25	40	....	....	....
	Canada	WJC-A	6	4	3	7	....	....	....	2	....	....	....	....	....	....	....	....	....	....	....	....	....	....	....	....	....	....
1987-88	**Pittsburgh Penguins**	**NHL**	**66**	**11**	**8**	**19**	**9**	**6**	**15**	**40**	**1**	**0**	**0**	**65**	**16.9**	**28**	**2**	**35**	**8**	**–1**	....	....	....	....	....	....	....	....
	Muskegon Lumberjacks	IHL	9	4	6	10	....	....	....	23	....	....	....	....	....	....	....	....	....	....	6	2	3	5	8	....	....	....
1988-89	**Pittsburgh Penguins**	**NHL**	**24**	**1**	**2**	**3**	**1**	**1**	**2**	**4**	**0**	**0**	**0**	**14**	**7.1**	**5**	**1**	**15**	**0**	**–11**	**3**	**0**	**1**	**1**	**0**	**0**	**0**	**0**
	Muskegon Lumberjacks	IHL	46	37	35	72	....	....	....	51	....	....	....	....	....	....	....	....	....	....	7	8	2	10	6	....	....	....
1989-90	**Winnipeg Jets**	**NHL**	**80**	**25**	**26**	**51**	**22**	**19**	**41**	**60**	**1**	**7**	**2**	**180**	**13.9**	**64**	**9**	**70**	**14**	**–1**	**7**	**0**	**1**	**1**	**2**	**0**	**0**	**0**
1990-91	**Winnipeg Jets**	**NHL**	**60**	**14**	**11**	**25**	**13**	**8**	**21**	**46**	**2**	**2**	**2**	**104**	**13.5**	**40**	**2**	**75**	**24**	**–13**	....	....	....	....	....	....	....	....
1991-92	**Winnipeg Jets**	**NHL**	**3**	**1**	**1**	**2**	**1**	**1**	**2**	**2**	**0**	**0**	**0**	**3**	**33.3**	**2**	**0**	**3**	**2**	**+1**	....	....	....	....	....	....	....	....
	Buffalo Sabres	**NHL**	**5**	**0**	**0**	**0**	**0**	**0**	**0**	**2**	**0**	**0**	**0**	**5**	**0.0**	**1**	**0**	**8**	**4**	**–3**	....	....	....	....	....	....	....	....
	New York Islanders	**NHL**	**54**	**8**	**15**	**23**	**7**	**11**	**18**	**28**	**1**	**1**	**1**	**71**	**11.3**	**30**	**2**	**65**	**29**	**–8**	....	....	....	....	....	....	....	....
	Toronto Maple Leafs	**NHL**	**11**	**1**	**2**	**3**	**1**	**1**	**2**	**4**	**0**	**0**	**1**	**12**	**8.3**	**5**	**0**	**8**	**4**	**+1**	....	....	....	....	....	....	....	....
1992-93	**Toronto Maple Leafs**	**NHL**	**66**	**14**	**4**	**18**	**12**	**3**	**15**	**30**	**1**	**1**	**3**	**85**	**16.5**	**23**	**3**	**63**	**25**	**–18**	**4**	**0**	**0**	**0**	**0**	**0**	**0**	**0**
1993-94	**Ottawa Senators**	**NHL**	**66**	**17**	**26**	**43**	**16**	**20**	**36**	**48**	**1**	**1**	**1**	**115**	**14.8**	**62**	**13**	**123**	**34**	**–40**	....	....	....	....	....	....	....	....
1994-95	**Ottawa Senators**	**NHL**	**43**	**5**	**6**	**11**	**9**	**9**	**18**	**22**	**1**	**0**	**0**	**48**	**10.4**	**17**	**3**	**59**	**19**	**–26**	....	....	....	....	....	....	....	....
1995-96	**Ottawa Senators**	**NHL**	**1**	**0**	**1**	**1**	**0**	**1**	**1**	**2**	**0**	**0**	**0**	**1**	**0.0**	**1**	**1**	**0**	**0**	**0**	....	....	....	....	....	....	....	....
	Cleveland Lumberjacks	IHL	60	30	45	75	....	....	....	80	....	....	....	....	....	....	....	....	....	....	....	....	....	....	....	....	....	....
	Pittsburgh Penguins	**NHL**	**18**	**2**	**4**	**6**	**2**	**3**	**5**	**4**	**0**	**0**	**1**	**19**	**10.5**	**8**	**0**	**15**	**2**	**–5**	**6**	**0**	**0**	**0**	**0**	**0**	**0**	**0**
1996-97	**New York Islanders**	**NHL**	**4**	**1**	**1**	**2**	**1**	**1**	**2**	**0**	**1**	**0**	**0**	**3**	**33.3**	**3**	**1**	**4**	**0**	**–2**	....	....	....	....	....	....	....	....
	Cleveland Lumberjacks	IHL	63	29	46	75	....	....	....	85	....	....	....	....	....	....	....	....	....	....	14	8	15	23	6	....	....	....
	NHL Totals		**501**	**100**	**107**	**207**	**94**	**84**	**178**	**292**	**9**	**12**	**11**	**725**	**13.8**	**289**	**37**	**543**	**165**		**20**	**0**	**2**	**2**	**2**	**0**	**0**	**0**

OHL Second All-Star Team (1987)

Traded to **Winnipeg** by **Pittsburgh** with Randy Cunneyworth and Rick Tabaracci for Jim Kyte, Andrew McBain and Randy Gilhen, June 17, 1989. Traded to **Buffalo** by **Winnipeg** with Gord Donnelly, Winnipeg's 5th round choice (Yuri Khmylev) in 1992 Entry Draft and future considerations for Darrin Shannon, Mike Hartman and Dean Kennedy, October 11, 1991. Traded to **NY Islanders** by **Buffalo** with Pierre Turgeon, Uwe Krupp and Benoit Hogue for Pat Lafontaine, Randy Hillier, Randy Wood and NY Islanders' 4th round choice (Dean Melanson) in 1992 Entry Draft, October 25, 1991. Traded to **Toronto** by **NY Islanders** with Ken Baumgartner for Daniel Marois and Claude Loiselle, March 10, 1992. Claimed by **Ottawa** from **Toronto** in NHL Waiver Draft, October 3, 1993. Traded to **Pittsburgh** by **Ottawa** for Pittsburgh's 8th round choice (Erich Goldmann) in 1996 Entry Draft, March 1, 1996. Signed as a free agent by **NY Islanders**, July 29, 1996.

• McMAHON, MIKE JR.

Mike Jr. McMahon D – L. 5'11", 180 lbs. b: Quebec City, Que., 8/30/1941.

Season	Club	League	GP	G	A	Pts	AG	AA	APts	PIM	PP	SH	GW	S	%	TGF	PGF	TGA	PGA	+/–	GP	G	A	Pts	PIM	PP	SH	GW
1959-60	Guelph Biltmores	OHA	48	7	16	23	....	....	....	94	....	....	....	....	....	....	....	....	....	....	5	0	0	0	15	....	....	....
1960-61	Guelph Biltmores	OHA	46	10	36	46	....	....	....	114	....	....	....	....	....	....	....	....	....	....	9	3	6	9	8	....	....	....
1961-62	Guelph Biltmores	OHA	45	9	28	37	....	....	....	94	....	....	....	....	....	....	....	....	....	....	....	....	....	....	....	....	....	....
	Kitchener-Waterloo Beavers	EPHL	5	0	1	1	....	....	....	0	....	....	....	....	....	....	....	....	....	....	3	0	0	0	0	....	....	....
1962-63	Sudbury Wolves	EPHL	71	12	39	51	....	....	....	107	....	....	....	....	....	....	....	....	....	....	8	3	3	6	8	....	....	....
1963-64	**New York Rangers**	**NHL**	**18**	**0**	**1**	**1**	**0**	**1**	**1**	**16**	....	....	....	....	....	....	....	....	....	....	....	....	....	....	....	....	....	....
	Baltimore Clippers	AHL	40	7	10	17	....	....	....	66	....	....	....	....	....	....	....	....	....	....	....	....	....	....	....	....	....	....
	St. Paul Rangers	CHL	13	3	9	12	....	....	....	30	....	....	....	....	....	....	....	....	....	....	....	....	....	....	....	....	....	....
1964-65	**New York Rangers**	**NHL**	**1**	**0**	**0**	**0**	**0**	**0**	**0**	**0**	....	....	....	....	....	....	....	....	....	....	....	....	....	....	....	....	....	....
	Baltimore Clippers	AHL	8	0	0	0	....	....	....	6	....	....	....	....	....	....	....	....	....	....	....	....	....	....	....	....	....	....
	St. Paul Rangers	CHL	63	20	41	61	....	....	....	204	....	....	....	....	....	....	....	....	....	....	11	4	5	9	23	....	....	....
1965-66	**New York Rangers**	**NHL**	**41**	**0**	**12**	**12**	**0**	**12**	**12**	**34**	....	....	....	....	....	....	....	....	....	....	....	....	....	....	....	....	....	....
	Minnesota Rangers	CHL	25	3	13	16	....	....	....	45	....	....	....	....	....	....	....	....	....	....	4	1	3	4	0	....	....	....
1966-67	Houston Apollos	CHL	64	13	37	50	....	....	....	129	....	....	....	....	....	....	....	....	....	....	6	0	3	3	6	....	....	....
	Quebec Aces	AHL	....	....	....	....	....	....	....	....	....	....	....	....	....	....	....	....	....	....	1	0	1	1	2	....	....	....
1967-68	**Minnesota North Stars**	**NHL**	**74**	**14**	**33**	**47**	**17**	**35**	**52**	**71**	**4**	**0**	**1**	**150**	**9.3**	**119**	**48**	**98**	**14**	**–13**	**14**	**3**	**7**	**10**	**4**	**0**	**2**	**0**
1968-69	**Minnesota North Stars**	**NHL**	**43**	**0**	**11**	**11**	**0**	**10**	**10**	**21**	**0**	**0**	**0**	**113**	**0.0**	**52**	**25**	**55**	**2**	**–26**	....	....	....	....	....	....	....	....
	Cleveland Barons	AHL	6	1	4	5	....	....	....	4	....	....	....	....	....	....	....	....	....	....	....	....	....	....	....	....	....	....
	Chicago Black Hawks	**NHL**	**20**	**0**	**8**	**8**	**0**	**7**	**7**	**6**	**0**	**0**	**0**	**31**	**0.0**	**29**	**2**	**18**	**6**	**+15**	....	....	....	....	....	....	....	....
1969-70	**Detroit Red Wings**	**NHL**	**2**	**0**	**0**	**0**	**0**	**0**	**0**	**0**	**0**	**0**	**0**	**0**	**0.0**	**1**	**0**	**2**	**1**	**0**	....	....	....	....	....	....	....	....
	Pittsburgh Penguins	**NHL**	**12**	**1**	**3**	**4**	**1**	**3**	**4**	**19**	**0**	**0**	**0**	**12**	**8.3**	**11**	**6**	**9**	**6**	**+2**	....	....	....	....	....	....	....	....
	Baltimore Clippers	AHL	48	13	25	38	....	....	....	29	....	....	....	....	....	....	....	....	....	....	5	0	0	0	2	....	....	....
1970-71	**Buffalo Sabres**	**NHL**	**12**	**0**	**0**	**0**	**0**	**0**	**0**	**4**	**0**	**0**	**0**	**20**	**0.0**	**5**	**3**	**14**	**4**	**–8**	....	....	....	....	....	....	....	....
	Springfield Kings	AHL	36	5	14	19	....	....	....	43	....	....	....	....	....	....	....	....	....	....	12	3	10	13	57	....	....	....
1971-72	**New York Rangers**	**NHL**	**1**	**0**	**0**	**0**	**0**	**0**	**0**	**0**	**0**	**0**	**0**	**0**	**0.0**	**1**	**0**	**0**	**0**	**+1**	....	....	....	....	....	....	....	....
	Providence Reds	AHL	39	3	19	22	....	....	....	74	....	....	....	....	....	....	....	....	....	....	....	....	....	....	....	....	....	....
	Rochester Americans	AHL	9	0	10	10	....	....	....	4	....	....	....	....	....	....	....	....	....	....	....	....	....	....	....	....	....	....
1972-73	Minnesota Fighting Saints	WHA	75	12	39	51	....	....	....	87	....	....	....	....	....	....	....	....	....	....	5	0	5	5	2	....	....	....
1973-74	Minnesota Fighting Saints	WHA	71	10	35	45	....	....	....	82	....	....	....	....	....	....	....	....	....	....	11	1	7	8	9	....	....	....

			REGULAR SEASON																		PLAYOFFS							
Season	Club	League	GP	G	A	Pts	AG	AA	APts	PIM	PP	SH	GW	S	%	TGF	PGF	TGA	PGA	+/–	GP	G	A	Pts	PIM	PP	SH	GW
1974-75	Minnesota Fighting Saints	WHA	64	5	15	20	....	....	....	42	....	....	....	....	....	....	....	....	....	....	7	0	1	1	0	....	....	....
1975-76	San Diego Mariners	WHA	69	2	12	14	....	....	....	38	....	....	....	....	....	....	....	....	....	....	9	0	1	1	2	....	....	....
1976-77	Springfield Indians	AHL	59	6	25	31	....	....	....	64	....	....	....	....	....	....	....	....	....	....	....	....	....	....	....	....	....	....
	NHL Totals		**224**	**15**	**68**	**83**	**18**	**68**	**86**	**171**	**4**	**0**	**1**	**326**	**4.6**	**218**	**84**	**196**	**33**		**14**	**3**	**7**	**10**	**4**	**0**	**2**	**0**
	Other Major League Totals		279	29	101	130	....	....	....	249	....	....	....	....	....	....	....	....	....		32	1	14	15	13	....	....	....

CHL First All-Star Team (1965) • Named CHL's Top Defenseman (1965, 1967) • CHL First All-Star Team (1967) • AHL Second All-Star Team (1970)

Claimed by **Montreal** from **NY Rangers** in Intra-League Draft, June 15, 1966. Traded to **Minnesota** by **Montreal** for cash, June 14, 1967. Traded to **Chicago** by **Minnesota** with Andre Boudrias for Tom Reid and Bill Orban, February 14, 1969. Claimed on waivers by **Detroit** from **Chicago**, October 14, 1969. Traded to **Pittsburgh** by **Detroit** for Billy Dea, October 28, 1969. Claimed by **Buffalo** from **Pittsburgh** in Expansion Draft, June 10, 1970. Traded to **LA Kings** by **Buffalo** for Eddie Shack and Dick Duff, November 25, 1970. Traded to **NY Rangers** by **LA Kings** for Wayne Rivers, May, 1971. Selected by **Minnesota** (WHA) in 1972 WHA General Player Draft, February 12, 1972. Loaned to **Rochester** (AHL) by **NY Rangers** (Providence - AHL) for Ron Stewart, March, 1972. Claimed by **San Diego** (WHA) from **Minnesota** (WHA) in WHA Intra-League Draft, June, 1975.

• McMANAMA, BOB

Bob McManama C – L. 6', 180 lbs. b: Belmont, MA, 10/7/1951.

Season	Club	League	GP	G	A	Pts	AG	AA	APts	PIM	PP	SH	GW	S	%	TGF	PGF	TGA	PGA	+/–	GP	G	A	Pts	PIM	PP	SH	GW
1970-71	Harvard University	ECAC	27	13	32	45	....	....	....	36	....	....	....	....	....	....	....	....	....	....	....	....	....	....	....	....	....	....
1971-72	Hrvard University	ECAC	26	24	30	54	....	....	....	34	....	....	....	....	....	....	....	....	....	....	....	....	....	....	....	....	....	....
1972-73	Harvard University	ECAC	22	27	25	52	....	....	....	33	....	....	....	....	....	....	....	....	....	....	....	....	....	....	....	....	....	....
	United States	Nat-Team	7	4	10	14	....	....	....	....	....	....	....	....	....	....	....	....	....	....	....	....	....	....	....	....	....	....
1973-74	**Pittsburgh Penguins**	**NHL**	**47**	**5**	**14**	**19**	**5**	**12**	**17**	**18**	**0**	**0**	**1**	**70**	**7.1**	**27**	**2**	**38**	**1**	**–12**	....	....	....	....	....	....	....	....
	Hershey Bears	AHL	26	10	18	28	....	....	....	12	....	....	....	....	....	....	....	....	....	....	....	....	....	....	....	....	....	....
1974-75	**Pittsburgh Penguins**	**NHL**	**40**	**5**	**9**	**14**	**5**	**7**	**12**	**6**	**0**	**0**	**0**	**33**	**15.2**	**17**	**1**	**17**	**7**	**+6**	**8**	**0**	**1**	**1**	**6**	**0**	**0**	**0**
	Hershey Bears	AHL	21	9	13	22	....	....	....	19	....	....	....	....	....	....	....	....	....	....	....	....	....	....	....	....	....	....
1975-76	**Pittsburgh Penguins**	**NHL**	**12**	**1**	**2**	**3**	**1**	**2**	**3**	**4**	**0**	**1**	**0**	**4**	**25.0**	**3**	**0**	**11**	**8**	**0**	....	....	....	....	....	....	....	....
	Hershey Bears	AHL	8	3	3	6	....	....	....	6	....	....	....	....	....	....	....	....	....	....	....	....	....	....	....	....	....	....
	New England Whalers	WHA	37	3	10	13	....	....	....	28	....	....	....	....	....	....	....	....	....	....	12	4	3	7	4	....	....	....
	Binghamton Dusters	NAHL	5	3	5	8	....	....	....	0	....	....	....	....	....	....	....	....	....	....	....	....	....	....	....	....	....	....
	NHL Totals		**99**	**11**	**25**	**36**	**11**	**21**	**32**	**28**	**0**	**1**	**1**	**107**	**10.3**	**47**	**3**	**66**	**16**		**8**	**0**	**1**	**1**	**6**	**0**	**0**	**0**
	Other Major League Totals		37	3	10	13	....	....	....	28	....	....	....	....	....	....	....	....	....		12	4	3	7	4	....	....	....

ECAC Second All-Star Team (1972) • ECAC First All-Star Team (1973) • NCAA East First All-American Team (1973)

Selected by **New England** (WHA) in 1972 WHA General Player Draft, February 12, 1972. Signed as a free agent by **Pittsburgh**, August, 1973. Traded to **Minnesota** (WHA) by **New England** (WHA) with Fred O'Donnell for Wayne Connelly, June, 1976.

• McMURCHY, TOM

Tom McMurchy RW – L. 5'9", 165 lbs. b: New Westminster, B.C., 12/2/1963. Chicago's 3rd choice, 49th overall, in 1982 Entry Draft.

Season	Club	League	GP	G	A	Pts	AG	AA	APts	PIM	PP	SH	GW	S	%	TGF	PGF	TGA	PGA	+/–	GP	G	A	Pts	PIM	PP	SH	GW
1980-81	Medicine Hat Tigers	WHL	14	5	0	5	....	....	....	46	....	....	....	....	....	....	....	....	....	....	....	....	....	....	....	....	....	....
	Brandon Wheat Kings	WHL	46	20	33	53	....	....	....	101	....	....	....	....	....	....	....	....	....	....	5	2	2	4	4	....	....	....
1981-82	Brandon Wheat Kings	WHL	68	59	63	122	....	....	....	179	....	....	....	....	....	....	....	....	....	....	4	7	3	10	4	....	....	....
1982-83	Brandon Wheat Kings	WHL	42	43	38	81	....	....	....	48	....	....	....	....	....	....	....	....	....	....	....	....	....	....	....	....	....	....
	Springfield Indians	AHL	8	2	2	4	....	....	....	0	....	....	....	....	....	....	....	....	....	....	....	....	....	....	....	....	....	....
1983-84	**Chicago Black Hawks**	**NHL**	**27**	**3**	**1**	**4**	**2**	**1**	**3**	**42**	**0**	**0**	**0**	**21**	**14.3**	**7**	**0**	**15**	**1**	**–7**	....	....	....	....	....	....	....	....
	Springfield Indians	AHL	43	16	14	30	....	....	....	54	....	....	....	....	....	....	....	....	....	....	4	4	0	4	0	....	....	....
1984-85	**Chicago Black Hawks**	**NHL**	**15**	**1**	**2**	**3**	**1**	**1**	**2**	**13**	**0**	**0**	**0**	**8**	**12.5**	**4**	**0**	**5**	**0**	**–1**	....	....	....	....	....	....	....	....
	Milwaukee Admirals	IHL	69	30	26	56	....	....	....	61	....	....	....	....	....	....	....	....	....	....	....	....	....	....	....	....	....	....
1985-86	**Chicago Black Hawks**	**NHL**	**4**	**0**	**0**	**0**	**0**	**0**	**0**	**2**	**0**	**0**	**0**	**2**	**0.0**	**2**	**0**	**3**	**0**	**–1**	....	....	....	....	....	....	....	....
	Nova Scotia Oilers	AHL	49	26	21	47	....	....	....	73	....	....	....	....	....	....	....	....	....	....	....	....	....	....	....	....	....	....
	Moncton Golden Flames	AHL	16	7	3	10	....	....	....	27	....	....	....	....	....	....	....	....	....	....	2	0	1	1	6	....	....	....
1986-87	Nova Scotia Oilers	AHL	67	21	35	56	....	....	....	99	....	....	....	....	....	....	....	....	....	....	4	3	2	5	4	....	....	....
1987-88	**Edmonton Oilers**	**NHL**	**9**	**4**	**1**	**5**	**3**	**1**	**4**	**8**	**0**	**0**	**1**	**11**	**36.4**	**6**	**0**	**4**	**0**	**+2**	....	....	....	....	....	....	....	....
	Nova Scotia Oilers	AHL	61	40	21	61	....	....	....	132	....	....	....	....	....	....	....	....	....	....	3	2	1	3	4	....	....	....
1988-89	Halifax Citadels	AHL	11	10	3	13	....	....	....	18	....	....	....	....	....	....	....	....	....	....	3	0	2	2	2	....	....	....
1989-90	HC Fiemme	Italy	43	72	76	148	....	....	....	80	....	....	....	....	....	....	....	....	....	....	....	....	....	....	....	....	....	....
1990-91	HC Fiemme	Italy	29	22	26	48	....	....	....	56	....	....	....	....	....	....	....	....	....	....	....	....	....	....	....	....	....	....
	NHL Totals		**55**	**8**	**4**	**12**	**6**	**3**	**9**	**65**	**0**	**0**	**1**	**42**	**19.0**	**19**	**0**	**27**	**1**		....	....	....			....	....	....

Traded to **Calgary** by **Chicago** for Rik Wilson, March 11, 1986. Signed as a free agent by **Edmonton**, August 18, 1986.

• McNAB, PETER

Peter McNab C – L. 6'3", 210 lbs. b: Vancouver, B.C., 5/8/1952. Buffalo's 6th choice, 85th overall, in 1972 Amateur Draft.

Season	Club	League	GP	G	A	Pts	AG	AA	APts	PIM	PP	SH	GW	S	%	TGF	PGF	TGA	PGA	+/–	GP	G	A	Pts	PIM	PP	SH	GW
1970-71	University of Denver	WCHA	28	19	14	33	....	....	....	6	....	....	....	....	....	....	....	....	....	....	....	....	....	....	....	....	....	....
1971-72	University of Denver	WCHA	38	27	38	65	....	....	....	16	....	....	....	....	....	....	....	....	....	....	....	....	....	....	....	....	....	....
1972-73	University of Denver	WCHA	28	23	29	52	....	....	....	12	....	....	....	....	....	....	....	....	....	....	....	....	....	....	....	....	....	....
1973-74	**Buffalo Sabres**	**NHL**	**22**	**3**	**6**	**9**	**3**	**5**	**8**	**2**	**0**	**0**	**0**	**24**	**12.5**	**14**	**1**	**16**	**0**	**–3**	....	....	....	....	....	....	....	....
	Cincinnati Swords	AHL	49	34	39	73	....	....	....	16	....	....	....	....	....	....	....	....	....	....	5	2	6	8	0	....	....	....
1974-75	**Buffalo Sabres**	**NHL**	**53**	**22**	**21**	**43**	**20**	**17**	**37**	**8**	**1**	**0**	**1**	**90**	**24.4**	**48**	**5**	**30**	**0**	**+13**	**17**	**2**	**6**	**8**	**4**	**0**	**0**	**0**
1975-76	**Buffalo Sabres**	**NHL**	**79**	**24**	**32**	**56**	**22**	**25**	**47**	**16**	**3**	**0**	**3**	**125**	**19.2**	**69**	**8**	**43**	**0**	**+18**	**8**	**0**	**0**	**0**	**0**	**0**	**0**	**0**
1976-77	**Boston Bruins**	**NHL**	**80**	**38**	**48**	**86**	**36**	**39**	**75**	**11**	**6**	**0**	**8**	**207**	**18.4**	**101**	**17**	**58**	**0**	**+26**	**14**	**5**	**3**	**8**	**2**	**2**	**0**	**0**
1977-78	**Boston Bruins**	**NHL**	**79**	**41**	**39**	**80**	**40**	**32**	**72**	**4**	**5**	**0**	**5**	**227**	**18.1**	**104**	**16**	**53**	**0**	**+35**	**15**	**8**	**11**	**19**	**2**	**0**	**0**	**2**
1978-79	**Boston Bruins**	**NHL**	**76**	**35**	**45**	**80**	**32**	**34**	**66**	**10**	**4**	**0**	**4**	**200**	**17.5**	**119**	**20**	**71**	**1**	**+29**	**11**	**5**	**3**	**8**	**0**	**0**	**0**	**0**
1979-80	**Boston Bruins**	**NHL**	**74**	**40**	**38**	**78**	**36**	**29**	**65**	**10**	**11**	**0**	**9**	**193**	**20.7**	**100**	**19**	**59**	**2**	**+24**	**10**	**8**	**6**	**14**	**2**	**3**	**0**	**1**
1980-81	**Boston Bruins**	**NHL**	**80**	**37**	**46**	**83**	**31**	**32**	**63**	**24**	**16**	**0**	**4**	**201**	**18.4**	**113**	**50**	**52**	**1**	**+12**	**3**	**3**	**0**	**3**	**0**	**1**	**0**	**0**
1981-82	**Boston Bruins**	**NHL**	**80**	**36**	**40**	**76**	**29**	**26**	**55**	**19**	**11**	**1**	**5**	**172**	**20.9**	**105**	**41**	**72**	**8**	**0**	**11**	**6**	**8**	**14**	**6**	**2**	**0**	**1**
1982-83	**Boston Bruins**	**NHL**	**74**	**22**	**52**	**74**	**18**	**36**	**54**	**23**	**5**	**0**	**2**	**160**	**13.8**	**97**	**40**	**42**	**1**	**+16**	**15**	**3**	**5**	**8**	**4**	**0**	**0**	**0**
1983-84	**Boston Bruins**	**NHL**	**52**	**14**	**16**	**30**	**11**	**11**	**22**	**10**	**2**	**0**	**3**	**81**	**17.3**	**53**	**15**	**31**	**0**	**+7**	....	....	....	....	....	....	....	....
	Vancouver Canucks	**NHL**	**13**	**1**	**6**	**7**	**1**	**4**	**5**	**10**	**1**	**0**	**0**	**20**	**5.0**	**11**	**6**	**7**	**0**	**–2**	**3**	**0**	**0**	**0**	**0**	**0**	**0**	**0**
1984-85	**Vancouver Canucks**	**NHL**	**75**	**23**	**25**	**48**	**19**	**17**	**36**	**10**	**9**	**0**	**1**	**114**	**20.2**	**63**	**17**	**67**	**1**	**–20**	....	....	....	....	....	....	....	....
1985-86	**New Jersey Devils**	**NHL**	**71**	**19**	**24**	**43**	**15**	**16**	**31**	**14**	**6**	**0**	**0**	**93**	**20.4**	**57**	**15**	**54**	**1**	**–11**	....	....	....	....	....	....	....	....
	United States	WEC-A	10	0	1	1	....	....	....	4	....	....	....	....	....	....	....	....	....	....	....	....	....	....	....	....	....	....
1986-87	**New Jersey Devils**	**NHL**	**46**	**8**	**12**	**20**	**7**	**9**	**16**	**8**	**2**	**0**	**2**	**49**	**16.3**	**24**	**3**	**35**	**0**	**–14**	....	....	....	....	....	....	....	....
	NHL Totals		**954**	**363**	**450**	**813**	**320**	**332**	**652**	**179**	**82**	**1**	**47**	**1956**	**18.6**	**1078**	**273**	**690**	**15**		**107**	**40**	**42**	**82**	**20**	**8**	**0**	**4**

WCHA First All-Star Team (1973) • NCAA Championship All-Tournament Team (1973)

Played in NHL All-Star Game (1977)

Transferred to **Boston** by **Buffalo** as compensation for Buffalo's signing of free agent Andre Savard, June 11, 1976. Traded to **Vancouver** by **Boston** for Jim Nill, February 3, 1984. Signed as a free agent by **New Jersey**, August 20, 1985.

• McNEILL, MIKE

Mike McNeill RW – L. 6'1", 195 lbs. b: Winona, MN, 7/22/1966. St. Louis' 1st choice, 14th overall, in 1988 Supplemental Draft.

Season	Club	League	GP	G	A	Pts	AG	AA	APts	PIM	PP	SH	GW	S	%	TGF	PGF	TGA	PGA	+/–	GP	G	A	Pts	PIM	PP	SH	GW
1984-85	University of Notre Dame	NCAA	28	16	26	42	....	....	....	12	....	....	....	....	....	....	....	....	....	....	....	....	....	....	....	....	....	....
1985-86	University of Notre Dame	NCAA	34	18	29	47	....	....	....	32	....	....	....	....	....	....	....	....	....	....	....	....	....	....	....	....	....	....
1986-87	University of Notre Dame	NCAA	30	21	16	37	....	....	....	24	....	....	....	....	....	....	....	....	....	....	....	....	....	....	....	....	....	....
1987-88	University of Notre Dame	NCAA	32	28	44	72	....	....	....	12	....	....	....	....	....	....	....	....	....	....	....	....	....	....	....	....	....	....
1988-89	Moncton Hawks	AHL	1	0	0	0	....	....	....	0	....	....	....	....	....	....	....	....	....	....	....	....	....	....	....	....	....	....
	Fort Wayne Komets	IHL	75	27	35	62	....	....	....	12	....	....	....	....	....	....	....	....	....	....	11	1	5	6	2	....	....	....
1989-90	Indianapolis Ice	IHL	74	17	24	41	....	....	....	10	....	....	....	....	....	....	....	....	....	....	14	0	4	10	21	....	....	....
1990-91	**Chicago Blackhawks**	**NHL**	**23**	**2**	**2**	**4**	**2**	**2**	**4**	**6**	**0**	**1**	**0**	**20**	**10.0**	**6**	**0**	**11**	**4**	**–1**	....	....	....	....	....	....	....	....
	Indianapolis Ice	IHL	33	16	9	25	....	....	....	19	....	....	....	....	....	....	....	....	....	....	....	....	....	....	....	....	....	....
	Quebec Nordiques	**NHL**	**14**	**2**	**5**	**7**	**2**	**4**	**6**	**4**	**1**	**0**	**0**	**11**	**18.2**	**9**	**1**	**10**	**7**	**+5**	....	....	....	....	....	....	....	....
	United States	WEC-A	10	1	0	1	....	....	....	4	....	....	....	....	....	....	....	....	....	....	....	....	....	....	....	....	....	....
1991-92	**Quebec Nordiques**	**NHL**	**26**	**1**	**4**	**5**	**1**	**3**	**4**	**8**	**1**	**0**	**0**	**15**	**6.7**	**10**	**6**	**23**	**11**	**–8**	....	....	....	....	....	....	....	....
	Halifax Citadels	AHL	30	10	8	18	....	....	....	20	....	....	....	....	....	....	....	....	....	....	....	....	....	....	....	....	....	....
1992-93	Milwaukee Admirals	IHL	75	17	17	34	....	....	....	34	....	....	....	....	....	....	....	....	....	....	6	2	0	2	0	....	....	....
1993-94	Milwaukee Admirals	IHL	78	21	25	46	....	....	....	40	....	....	....	....	....	....	....	....	....	....	4	0	1	1	6	....	....	....
1994-95	Milwaukee Admirals	IHL	80	23	15	38	....	....	....	30	....	....	....	....	....	....	....	....	....	....	15	2	2	4	14	....	....	....

			REGULAR SEASON																		PLAYOFFS							
Season	Club	League	GP	G	A	Pts	AG	AA	APts	PIM	PP	SH	GW	S	%	TGF	PGF	TGA	PGA	+/–	GP	G	A	Pts	PIM	PP	SH	GW
1995-96	Milwaukee Admirals	IHL	64	8	9	17	....	....	....	32	....	....	....	....	....	....	....	....	....	....	5	2	0	2	2	....	....	....
1996-97	Milwaukee Admirals	IHL	74	18	26	44	....	....	....	24	....	....	....	....	....	....	....	....	....	....	3	0	1	1	0	....	....	....
1997-98	Milwaukee Admirals	IHL	81	10	18	28	....	....	....	58	....	....	....	....	....	....	....	....	....	....	10	2	1	3	12	....	....	....
	NHL Totals		**63**	**5**	**11**	**16**	**5**	**9**	**14**	**18**	**2**	**1**	**0**	**46**	**10.9**	**25**	**7**	**44**	**22**		....	....	....	....	....	....	....	....

Won "Bud" Poile Trophy (Playoff MVP - IHL) (1990)

Signed as a free agent by **Chicago**, September, 1989. Traded to **Quebec** by **Chicago** with Ryan McGill and Dan Vincelette, March 5, 1991.

• McPHEE, GEORGE

George "Fenster" McPhee LW – L. 5'9", 170 lbs. b: Guelph, Ont., 7/2/1958.

Season	Club	League	GP	G	A	Pts	AG	AA	APts	PIM	PP	SH	GW	S	%	TGF	PGF	TGA	PGA	+/–	GP	G	A	Pts	PIM	PP	SH	GW
1977-78	Guelph Platers	OJHL	48	53	57	110	....	....	....	150	....	....	....	....	....	....	....	....	....	....	....	....	....	....	....	....	....	....
1978-79	Bowling Green University	CCHA	43	*40	48	*88	....	....	....	58	....	....	....	....	....	....	....	....	....	....	....	....	....	....	....	....	....	....
1979-80	Bowling Green University	CCHA	34	21	24	45	....	....	....	51	....	....	....	....	....	....	....	....	....	....	....	....	....	....	....	....	....	....
1980-81	Bowling Green University	CCHA	36	25	29	54	....	....	....	68	....	....	....	....	....	....	....	....	....	....	....	....	....	....	....	....	....	....
1981-82	Bowling Green University	CCHA	40	28	52	80	....	....	....	57	....	....	....	....	....	....	....	....	....	....	....	....	....	....	....	....	....	....
1982-83	Tulsa Oilers	CHL	61	17	43	60	....	....	....	145	....	....	....	....	....	....	....	....	....	....	7	1	1	2	14	....	....	....
	New York Rangers	**NHL**	....	....	....	....	....	....	....	....	**0**	**0**	**0**	**0**	**0.0**	**0**	**0**	**0**	**0**	**0**	**9**	**3**	**3**	**6**	**2**	**1**	**0**	**0**
1983-84	**New York Rangers**	**NHL**	**9**	**1**	**1**	**2**	**1**	**1**	**2**	**11**	**0**	**0**	**0**	**1**	**100.0**	**2**	**0**	**2**	**0**	**0**	....	....	....	....	....	....	....	....
	Tulsa Oilers	CHL	49	20	28	48	....	....	....	133	....	....	....	....	....	....	....	....	....	....	....	....	....	....	....	....	....	....
1984-85	**New York Rangers**	**NHL**	**49**	**12**	**15**	**27**	**10**	**10**	**20**	**139**	**1**	**0**	**1**	**54**	**22.2**	**36**	**2**	**43**	**0**	**–9**	**3**	**1**	**0**	**1**	**7**	**0**	**0**	**0**
	New Haven Nighthawks	AHL	3	2	2	4	....	....	....	13	....	....	....	....	....	....	....	....	....	....	....	....	....	....	....	....	....	....
1985-86	**New York Rangers**	**NHL**	**30**	**4**	**4**	**8**	**3**	**3**	**6**	**63**	**0**	**0**	**1**	**31**	**12.9**	**15**	**0**	**10**	**0**	**+5**	**11**	**0**	**0**	**0**	**32**	**0**	**0**	**0**
1986-87	**New York Rangers**	**NHL**	**21**	**4**	**4**	**8**	**3**	**3**	**6**	**34**	**0**	**0**	**2**	**31**	**12.9**	**14**	**0**	**16**	**0**	**–2**	**6**	**1**	**0**	**1**	**28**	**1**	**0**	**0**
1987-88	**New Jersey Devils**	**NHL**	**5**	**3**	**0**	**3**	**3**	**0**	**3**	**8**	**0**	**0**	**1**	**5**	**60.0**	**4**	**0**	**2**	**0**	**+2**	....	....	....	....	....	....	....	....
1988-89	**New Jersey Devils**	**NHL**	**1**	**0**	**1**	**1**	**0**	**1**	**1**	**2**	**0**	**0**	**0**	**0**	**0.0**	**1**	**0**	**0**	**0**	**+1**	....	....	....	....	....	....	....	....
	Utica Devils	AHL	8	3	2	5	....	....	....	31	....	....	....	....	....	....	....	....	....	....	3	1	0	1	26	....	....	....
	NHL Totals		**115**	**24**	**25**	**49**	**20**	**18**	**38**	**257**	**1**	**0**	**5**	**122**	**19.7**	**72**	**2**	**73**	**0**		**29**	**5**	**3**	**8**	**69**	**2**	**0**	**0**

CCHA Second All-Star Team (1979, 1981) • CCHA First All-Star Team (1982) • NCAA West First All-American Team (1982) • Won Hobey Baker Memorial Award (Top U.S. Collegiate Player) (1982)

Signed as a free agent by **NY Rangers**, July 1, 1982. Traded to **Winnipeg** by **NY Rangers** for Winnipeg's 4th round choice (Jim Cummins) in 1989 Entry Draft, September 30, 1987. Traded to **New Jersey** by **Winnipeg** for New Jersey's 7th round choice (Doug Evans) in 1989 Entry Draft, October 7, 1987.

• McPHEE, MIKE

Mike McPhee LW – L. 6'1", 203 lbs. b: Sydney, N.S., 7/14/1960. Montreal's 8th choice, 124th overall, in 1980 Entry Draft.

Season	Club	League	GP	G	A	Pts	AG	AA	APts	PIM	PP	SH	GW	S	%	TGF	PGF	TGA	PGA	+/–	GP	G	A	Pts	PIM	PP	SH	GW
1978-79	RPI Engineers	ECAC	26	14	19	33	....	....	....	16	....	....	....	....	....	....	....	....	....	....	....	....	....	....	....	....	....	....
1979-80	RPI Engineers	ECAC	27	15	21	36	....	....	....	22	....	....	....	....	....	....	....	....	....	....	....	....	....	....	....	....	....	....
1980-81	RPI Engineers	ECAC	29	28	18	46	....	....	....	22	....	....	....	....	....	....	....	....	....	....	....	....	....	....	....	....	....	....
1981-82	RPI Engineers	ECAC	6	0	3	3	....	....	....	4	....	....	....	....	....	....	....	....	....	....	....	....	....	....	....	....	....	....
1982-83	Nova Scotia Voyageurs	AHL	42	10	15	25	....	....	....	29	....	....	....	....	....	....	....	....	....	....	7	1	1	2	14	....	....	....
1983-84	**Montreal Canadiens**	**NHL**	**14**	**5**	**2**	**7**	**4**	**1**	**5**	**41**	**0**	**0**	**0**	**22**	**22.7**	**10**	**0**	**6**	**0**	**+4**	**15**	**1**	**0**	**1**	**31**	**0**	**0**	**0**
	Nova Scotia Voyageurs	AHL	67	22	33	55	....	....	....	101	....	....	....	....	....	....	....	....	....	....	....	....	....	....	....	....	....	....
1984-85	**Montreal Canadiens**	**NHL**	**70**	**17**	**22**	**39**	**14**	**15**	**29**	**120**	**0**	**0**	**2**	**135**	**12.6**	**54**	**3**	**59**	**9**	**+1**	**12**	**4**	**1**	**5**	**32**	**0**	**0**	**0**
1985-86	**Montreal Canadiens**	**NHL**	**70**	**19**	**21**	**40**	**15**	**14**	**29**	**69**	**0**	**2**	**3**	**103**	**18.4**	**53**	**1**	**54**	**10**	**+8**	**20**	**3**	**4**	**7**	**45**	**0**	**1**	**1**
1986-87	**Montreal Canadiens**	**NHL**	**79**	**18**	**21**	**39**	**16**	**15**	**31**	**58**	**0**	**2**	**2**	**150**	**12.0**	**53**	**2**	**57**	**13**	**+7**	**17**	**7**	**2**	**9**	**13**	**1**	**0**	**2**
1987-88	**Montreal Canadiens**	**NHL**	**77**	**23**	**20**	**43**	**20**	**14**	**34**	**53**	**0**	**2**	**4**	**151**	**15.2**	**61**	**2**	**58**	**18**	**+19**	**11**	**4**	**3**	**7**	**8**	**0**	**1**	**0**
1988-89	**Montreal Canadiens**	**NHL**	**73**	**19**	**22**	**41**	**16**	**15**	**31**	**74**	**1**	**1**	**1**	**154**	**12.3**	**59**	**7**	**52**	**14**	**+14**	**20**	**4**	**7**	**11**	**30**	**0**	**0**	**1**
1989-90	**Montreal Canadiens**	**NHL**	**56**	**23**	**18**	**41**	**20**	**13**	**33**	**47**	**-3**	**1**	**1**	**118**	**19.5**	**63**	**2**	**42**	**9**	**+28**	**9**	**1**	**1**	**2**	**16**	**0**	**0**	**0**
1990-91	Montreal Canadiens	FrTour	2	0	0	0	....	....	....	27	....	....	....	....	....	....	....	....	....	....	....	....	....	....	....	....	....	....
	Montreal Canadiens	**NHL**	**64**	**22**	**21**	**43**	**20**	**16**	**36**	**56**	**2**	**0**	**4**	**123**	**17.9**	**66**	**12**	**53**	**5**	**+6**	**13**	**1**	**7**	**8**	**12**	**1**	**0**	**0**
1991-92	**Montreal Canadiens**	**NHL**	**78**	**16**	**15**	**31**	**15**	**11**	**26**	**63**	**0**	**0**	**1**	**146**	**11.0**	**47**	**1**	**47**	**7**	**+6**	**8**	**1**	**1**	**2**	**4**	**0**	**0**	**0**
1992-93	**Minnesota North Stars**	**NHL**	**84**	**18**	**22**	**40**	**15**	**15**	**30**	**44**	**1**	**2**	**2**	**161**	**11.2**	**59**	**6**	**72**	**17**	**–2**	....	....	....	....	....	....	....	....
1993-94	**Dallas Stars**	**NHL**	**79**	**20**	**15**	**35**	**19**	**12**	**31**	**36**	**1**	**3**	**1**	**115**	**17.4**	**56**	**1**	**65**	**18**	**+8**	**9**	**2**	**1**	**3**	**2**	**0**	**0**	**0**
	NHL Totals		**744**	**200**	**199**	**399**	**174**	**141**	**315**	**661**	**2**	**13**	**21**	**1378**	**14.5**	**581**	**37**	**565**	**120**		**134**	**28**	**27**	**55**	**193**	**2**	**2**	**4**

Played in NHL All-Star Game (1989)

Traded to **Minnesota** by **Montreal** for Minnesota's 5th round choice (Jeff Lank) in 1993 Entry Draft, August 14, 1992. Transferred to **Dallas** after **Minnesota** franchise relocated, June 9, 1993.

• McRAE, BASIL

Basil McRae LW – L. 6'2", 210 lbs. b: Beaverton, Ont., 1/5/1961. Quebec's 3rd choice, 87th overall, in 1980 Entry Draft.

Season	Club	League	GP	G	A	Pts	AG	AA	APts	PIM	PP	SH	GW	S	%	TGF	PGF	TGA	PGA	+/–	GP	G	A	Pts	PIM	PP	SH	GW
1979-80	London Knights	OHA	67	24	36	60	....	....	....	116	....	....	....	....	....	....	....	....	....	....	5	0	0	0	18	....	....	....
1980-81	London Knights	OHA	65	29	23	52	....	....	....	266	....	....	....	....	....	....	....	....	....	....	....	....	....	....	....	....	....	....
1981-82	**Quebec Nordiques**	**NHL**	**20**	**4**	**3**	**7**	**3**	**2**	**5**	**69**	**0**	**0**	**0**	**20**	**20.0**	**10**	**1**	**12**	**0**	**–3**	**9**	**1**	**0**	**1**	**34**	**0**	**0**	**0**
	Fredericton Express	AHL	47	11	15	26	....	....	....	175	....	....	....	....	....	....	....	....	....	....	....	....	....	....	....	....	....	....
1982-83	**Quebec Nordiques**	**NHL**	**22**	**1**	**1**	**2**	**1**	**1**	**2**	**59**	**0**	**0**	**0**	**6**	**16.7**	**4**	**0**	**5**	**0**	**–1**	....	....	....	....	....	....	....	....
	Fredericton Express	AHL	53	22	19	41	....	....	....	146	....	....	....	....	....	....	....	....	....	....	12	1	5	6	75	....	....	....
1983-84	**Toronto Maple Leafs**	**NHL**	**3**	**0**	**0**	**0**	**0**	**0**	**0**	**19**	**0**	**0**	**0**	**7**	**0.0**	**0**	**0**	**3**	**0**	**–3**	....	....	....	....	....	....	....	....
	St. Catharines Saints	AHL	78	14	25	39	....	....	....	187	....	....	....	....	....	....	....	....	....	....	6	0	0	0	40	....	....	....
1984-85	**Toronto Maple Leafs**	**NHL**	**1**	**0**	**0**	**0**	**0**	**0**	**0**	**0**	**0**	**0**	**0**	**0**	**0.0**	**0**	**0**	**0**	**0**	**0**	....	....	....	....	....	....	....	....
	St. Catharines Saints	AHL	72	30	25	55	....	....	....	186	....	....	....	....	....	....	....	....	....	....	....	....	....	....	....	....	....	....
1985-86	**Detroit Red Wings**	**NHL**	**4**	**0**	**0**	**0**	**0**	**0**	**0**	**5**	**0**	**0**	**0**	**3**	**0.0**	**0**	**0**	**4**	**0**	**–4**	....	....	....	....	....	....	....	....
	Adirondack Red Wings	AHL	69	22	30	52	....	....	....	259	....	....	....	....	....	....	....	....	....	....	17	5	4	9	101	....	....	....
1986-87	**Detroit Red Wings**	**NHL**	**36**	**2**	**2**	**4**	**2**	**1**	**3**	**193**	**1**	**0**	**1**	**21**	**9.5**	**12**	**2**	**13**	**0**	**–3**	....	....	....	....	....	....	....	....
	Quebec Nordiques	**NHL**	**33**	**9**	**5**	**14**	**8**	**4**	**12**	**149**	**3**	**0**	**1**	**36**	**25.0**	**21**	**5**	**15**	**0**	**+1**	**13**	**3**	**1**	**4**	***99**	**0**	**0**	**1**
1987-88	**Minnesota North Stars**	**NHL**	**80**	**5**	**11**	**16**	**4**	**8**	**12**	**382**	**0**	**0**	**0**	**107**	**4.7**	**26**	**1**	**53**	**0**	**–28**	....	....	....	....	....	....	....	....
1988-89	**Minnesota North Stars**	**NHL**	**78**	**12**	**19**	**31**	**10**	**13**	**23**	**365**	**4**	**0**	**0**	**122**	**9.8**	**54**	**15**	**47**	**0**	**–8**	**5**	**0**	**0**	**0**	**58**	**0**	**0**	**0**
1989-90	**Minnesota North Stars**	**NHL**	**66**	**9**	**17**	**26**	**8**	**12**	**20**	***351**	**2**	**0**	**2**	**95**	**9.5**	**36**	**8**	**33**	**0**	**–5**	**7**	**1**	**0**	**1**	**24**	**0**	**0**	**0**
1990-91	Minnesota North Stars	FrTour	3	1	0	1	....	....	....	26	....	....	....	....	....	....	....	....	....	....	....	....	....	....	....	....	....	....
	Minnesota North Stars	**NHL**	**40**	**1**	**3**	**4**	**1**	**2**	**3**	**224**	**0**	**0**	**0**	**44**	**2.3**	**9**	**2**	**15**	**0**	**–8**	**22**	**1**	**1**	**2**	***94**	**0**	**0**	**0**
1991-92	**Minnesota North Stars**	**NHL**	**59**	**5**	**8**	**13**	**5**	**6**	**11**	**245**	**0**	**0**	**0**	**64**	**7.8**	**17**	**1**	**30**	**0**	**–14**	....	....	....	....	....	....	....	....
1992-93	**Tampa Bay Lightning**	**NHL**	**14**	**2**	**3**	**5**	**2**	**2**	**4**	**71**	**1**	**0**	**0**	**23**	**8.7**	**11**	**5**	**9**	**0**	**–3**	....	....	....	....	....	....	....	....
	St. Louis Blues	**NHL**	**33**	**1**	**3**	**4**	**1**	**2**	**3**	**98**	**1**	**0**	**0**	**22**	**4.5**	**6**	**1**	**18**	**0**	**–13**	**11**	**0**	**1**	**1**	**24**	**0**	**0**	**0**
1993-94	**St. Louis Blues**	**NHL**	**40**	**1**	**2**	**3**	**1**	**2**	**3**	**103**	**0**	**0**	**0**	**23**	**4.3**	**8**	**0**	**16**	**1**	**–7**	**2**	**0**	**0**	**0**	**12**	**0**	**0**	**0**
1994-95	**St. Louis Blues**	**NHL**	**21**	**0**	**5**	**5**	**0**	**7**	**7**	**72**	**0**	**0**	**0**	**14**	**0.0**	**7**	**0**	**3**	**0**	**+4**	**7**	**2**	**1**	**3**	**4**	**0**	**0**	**0**
	Peoria Rivermen	IHL	2	0	0	0	....	....	....	12	....	....	....	....	....	....	....	....	....	....	....	....	....	....	....	....	....	....
1995-96	**St. Louis Blues**	**NHL**	**18**	**1**	**1**	**2**	**1**	**1**	**2**	**40**	**0**	**0**	**0**	**5**	**20.0**	**2**	**0**	**7**	**0**	**–5**	**2**	**0**	**0**	**0**	**0**	**0**	**0**	**0**
1996-97	**Chicago Blackhawks**	**NHL**	**8**	**0**	**0**	**0**	**0**	**0**	**0**	**12**	**0**	**0**	**0**	**1**	**0.0**	**1**	**0**	**3**	**0**	**–2**	....	....	....	....	....	....	....	....
	NHL Totals		**576**	**53**	**83**	**136**	**47**	**63**	**110**	**2457**	**12**	**0**	**4**	**613**	**8.6**	**224**	**41**	**286**	**1**		**78**	**8**	**4**	**12**	**349**	**0**	**0**	**1**

Traded to **Toronto** by **Quebec** for Richard Turmel, August 12, 1983. Signed as a free agent by **Detroit**, July 17, 1985. Traded to **Quebec** by **Detroit** with John Ogrodnick and Doug Shedden for Brent Ashton, Gilbert Delorme and Mark Kumpel, January 17, 1987. Signed as a free agent by **Minnesota**, June 29, 1987. Claimed by **Tampa Bay** from **Minnesota** in Expansion Draft, June 18, 1992. Traded to **St. Louis** by **Tampa Bay** with Doug Crossman and Tampa Bay's 4th round choice (Andrei Petrakov) in 1996 Entry Draft for Jason Ruff and future considerations, January 28, 1993. Signed as a free agent by **Chicago**, October 9, 1996.

• McRAE, CHRIS

Chris McRae LW – L. 6', 200 lbs. b: Beaverton, Ont., 8/26/1965.

Season	Club	League	GP	G	A	Pts	AG	AA	APts	PIM	PP	SH	GW	S	%	TGF	PGF	TGA	PGA	+/–	GP	G	A	Pts	PIM	PP	SH	GW
1982-83	Newmarket Saints	Jr. A	42	11	22	33	....	....	....	207	....	....	....	....	....	....	....	....	....	....	....	....	....	....	....	....	....	....
1983-84	Belleville Bulls	OHL	9	0	0	0	....	....	....	19	....	....	....	....	....	....	....	....	....	....	....	....	....	....	....	....	....	....
	Sudbury Wolves	OHL	53	14	31	45	....	....	....	120	....	....	....	....	....	....	....	....	....	....	....	....	....	....	....	....	....	....
1984-85	Sudbury Wolves	OHL	6	0	2	2	....	....	....	10	....	....	....	....	....	....	....	....	....	....	....	....	....	....	....	....	....	....
	Oshawa Generals	OHL	43	8	7	15	....	....	....	118	....	....	....	....	....	....	....	....	....	....	5	0	1	1	2	....	....	....
	St. Catharines Saints	AHL	6	4	3	7	....	....	....	24	....	....	....	....	....	....	....	....	....	....	....	....	....	....	....	....	....	....
1985-86	St. Catharines Saints	AHL	59	1	1	2	....	....	....	233	....	....	....	....	....	....	....	....	....	....	11	0	1	1	65	....	....	....
1986-87	Newmarket Saints	AHL	51	3	6	9	....	....	....	193	....	....	....	....	....	....	....	....	....	....	....	....	....	....	....	....	....	....
1987-88	**Toronto Maple Leafs**	**NHL**	**11**	**0**	**0**	**0**	**0**	**0**	**0**	**65**	**0**	**0**	**0**	**0**	**0.0**	**0**	**0**	**0**	**0**	**0**	....	....	....	....	....	....	....	....
	Newmarket Saints	AHL	34	7	6	13	....	....	....	165	....	....	....	....	....	....	....	....	....	....	....	....	....	....	....	....	....	....

			REGULAR SEASON																		PLAYOFFS							
Season	Club	League	GP	G	A	Pts	AG	AA	APts	PIM	PP	SH	GW	S	%	TGF	PGF	TGA	PGA	+/-	GP	G	A	Pts	PIM	PP	SH	GW
1988-89	**Toronto Maple Leafs**	**NHL**	**3**	**0**	**0**	**0**	**0**	**0**	**0**	**12**	**0**	**0**	**0**	**0**	**0.0**	**0**	**0**	**0**	**0**	**0**	....	....	....	....	....	....	....	....
	Newmarket Saints	AHL	18	3	1	4	....	....	....	85	....	....	....	....	....	....	....	....	....	....	....	....	....	....	....	....	....	....
	Denver Rangers	IHL	23	1	4	5	....	....	....	121	....	....	....	....	....	....	....	....	....	....	2	0	0	0	20	....	....	....
1989-90	**Detroit Red Wings**	**NHL**	**7**	**1**	**0**	**1**	**1**	**0**	**1**	**45**	**0**	**0**	**0**	**1**	**100.0**	**1**	**0**	**1**	**0**	**0**	....	....	....	....	....	....	....	....
	Adirondack Red Wings	AHL	46	9	10	19	....	....	....	290	....	....	....	....	....	....	....	....	....	....	....	....	....	....	....	....	....	....
1990-91	Adirondack Red Wings	AHL	23	2	3	5	....	....	....	109	....	....	....	....	....	....	....	....	....	....	2	0	0	0	11	....	....	....
1991-92	Fort Wayne Komets	IHL	60	20	14	34	....	....	....	*413	....	....	....	....	....	....	....	....	....	....	5	1	0	1	44	....	....	....
	NHL Totals		**21**	**1**	**0**	**1**	**1**	**0**	**1**	**122**	**0**	**0**	**0**	**1**	**100.0**	**1**	**0**	**1**	**0**		....	....	....	....	....	....	....	....

Signed as a free agent by **Toronto**, October 16, 1985. Traded to **NY Rangers** by **Toronto** for Ken Hammond, February 21, 1988. Traded to **Detroit** by **NY Rangers** with Detroit's 5th round choice (acquired earlier, Detroit selected Tony Burns) in 1990 Entry Draft for Kris King, September 7, 1989.

• McRAE, KEN

Ken McRae C – R. 6'1", 195 lbs. b: Winchester, Ont., 4/23/1968. Quebec's 1st choice, 18th overall, in 1986 Entry Draft.

1984-85	Hawkesbury Hawks	Jr. A	51	38	50	88	....	....	....	77	....	....	....	....	....	....	....	....	....	....	....	....	....	....	....	....	....	....
1985-86	Sudbury Wolves	OHL	66	25	49	74	....	....	....	127	....	....	....	....	....	....	....	....	....	....	4	2	1	3	12	....	....	....
1986-87	Sudbury Wolves	OHL	21	12	15	27	....	....	....	40	....	....	....	....	....	....	....	....	....	....	....	....	....	....	....	....	....	....
	Hamilton Steelhawks	OHL	20	7	12	19	....	....	....	25	....	....	....	....	....	....	....	....	....	....	7	1	1	2	12	....	....	....
1987-88	Hamilton Steelhawks	OHL	62	30	55	85	....	....	....	158	....	....	....	....	....	....	....	....	....	....	14	13	9	22	35	....	....	....
	Quebec Nordiques	**NHL**	**1**	**0**	**0**	**0**	**0**	**0**	**0**	**0**	**0**	**0**	**0**	**1**	**0.0**	**0**	**0**	**0**	**0**	**0**	....	....	....	....	....	....	....	....
	Fredericton Express	AHL	....	....	....	....	....	....	....	....	....	....	....	....	....	....	....	....	....	....	3	0	0	0	8	....	....	....
1988-89	**Quebec Nordiques**	**NHL**	**37**	**6**	**11**	**17**	**5**	**8**	**13**	**68**	**1**	**0**	**2**	**47**	**12.8**	**22**	**4**	**31**	**4**	**–9**	....	....	....	....	....	....	....	....
	Halifax Citadels	AHL	41	20	21	41	....	....	....	87	....	....	....	....	....	....	....	....	....	....	....	....	....	....	....	....	....	....
1989-90	**Quebec Nordiques**	**NHL**	**66**	**7**	**8**	**15**	**6**	**6**	**12**	**191**	**0**	**0**	**1**	**83**	**8.4**	**28**	**0**	**76**	**10**	**–38**	....	....	....	....	....	....	....	....
1990-91	**Quebec Nordiques**	**NHL**	**12**	**0**	**0**	**0**	**0**	**0**	**0**	**36**	**0**	**0**	**0**	**6**	**0.0**	**0**	**0**	**7**	**0**	**–7**	....	....	....	....	....	....	....	....
	Halifax Citadels	AHL	60	10	36	46	....	....	....	193	....	....	....	....	....	....	....	....	....	....	....	....	....	....	....	....	....	....
1991-92	**Quebec Nordiques**	**NHL**	**10**	**0**	**1**	**1**	**0**	**1**	**1**	**31**	**0**	**0**	**0**	**10**	**0.0**	**1**	**0**	**6**	**0**	**–5**	....	....	....	....	....	....	....	....
	Halifax Citadels	AHL	52	30	41	71	....	....	....	184	....	....	....	....	....	....	....	....	....	....	....	....	....	....	....	....	....	....
1992-93	**Toronto Maple Leafs**	**NHL**	**2**	**0**	**0**	**0**	**0**	**0**	**0**	**2**	**0**	**0**	**0**	**3**	**0.0**	**0**	**0**	**1**	**0**	**–1**	....	....	....	....	....	....	....	....
	St. John's Maple Leafs	AHL	64	30	44	74	....	....	....	135	....	....	....	....	....	....	....	....	....	....	9	6	6	12	27	....	....	....
1993-94	**Toronto Maple Leafs**	**NHL**	**9**	**1**	**1**	**2**	**1**	**1**	**2**	**36**	**0**	**0**	**0**	**11**	**9.1**	**5**	**0**	**4**	**0**	**+1**	**6**	**0**	**0**	**0**	**4**	**0**	**0**	**0**
	St. John's Maple Leafs	AHL	65	23	41	64	....	....	....	200	....	....	....	....	....	....	....	....	....	....	....	....	....	....	....	....	....	....
1994-95	Detroit Vipers	IHL	24	4	9	13	....	....	....	38	....	....	....	....	....	....	....	....	....	....	....	....	....	....	....	....	....	....
	Phoenix Roadrunners	IHL	2	2	0	2	....	....	....	0	....	....	....	....	....	....	....	....	....	....	9	3	8	11	21	....	....	....
1995-96	Phoenix Roadrunners	IHL	45	11	14	25	....	....	....	102	....	....	....	....	....	....	....	....	....	....	4	1	1	2	24	....	....	....
1996-97	Phoenix Roadrunners	IHL	72	25	28	53	....	....	....	190	....	....	....	....	....	....	....	....	....	....	....	....	....	....	....	....	....	....
	Providence Bruins	AHL	9	5	5	10	....	....	....	26	....	....	....	....	....	....	....	....	....	....	10	1	3	4	17	....	....	....
1997-98	Houston Aeros	IHL	78	22	32	54	....	....	....	192	....	....	....	....	....	....	....	....	....	....	1	0	0	0	0	....	....	....
	NHL Totals		**137**	**14**	**21**	**35**	**12**	**16**	**28**	**364**	**1**	**0**	**3**	**161**	**8.7**	**56**	**4**	**125**	**14**		**6**	**0**	**0**	**0**	**4**	**0**	**0**	**0**

Traded to **Toronto** by **Quebec** for Len Esau, July 21, 1992.

• McREYNOLDS, BRIAN

Brian McReynolds C – L. 6'1", 192 lbs. b: Penetanguishene, Ont., 1/5/1965. NY Rangers' 6th choice, 112th overall, in 1985 Entry Draft.

1984-85	Orillia Travelways	OJHL	48	40	54	94	....	....	....	....	....	....	....	....	....	....	....	....	....	....	....	....	....	....	....	....	....	....
1985-86	Michigan State Spartans	CCHA	45	14	24	38	....	....	....	78	....	....	....	....	....	....	....	....	....	....	....	....	....	....	....	....	....	....
1986-87	Michigan State Spartans	CCHA	45	16	24	40	....	....	....	68	....	....	....	....	....	....	....	....	....	....	....	....	....	....	....	....	....	....
1987-88	Michigan State Spartans	CCHA	43	10	24	34	....	....	....	50	....	....	....	....	....	....	....	....	....	....	....	....	....	....	....	....	....	....
1988-89	Canada	Nat-Team	58	5	25	30	....	....	....	59	....	....	....	....	....	....	....	....	....	....	....	....	....	....	....	....	....	....
1989-90	**Winnipeg Jets**	**NHL**	**9**	**0**	**2**	**2**	**0**	**1**	**1**	**4**	**0**	**0**	**0**	**11**	**0.0**	**3**	**0**	**8**	**1**	**–4**	....	....	....	....	....	....	....	....
	Moncton Hawks	AHL	72	18	41	59	....	....	....	87	....	....	....	....	....	....	....	....	....	....	....	....	....	....	....	....	....	....
1990-91	**New York Rangers**	**NHL**	**1**	**0**	**0**	**0**	**0**	**0**	**0**	**0**	**0**	**0**	**0**	**0**	**0.0**	**0**	**0**	**1**	**0**	**–1**	....	....	....	....	....	....	....	....
	Binghamton Rangers	AHL	77	30	42	72	....	....	....	74	....	....	....	....	....	....	....	....	....	....	10	0	1	1	6	....	....	....
1991-92	Binghamton Rangers	AHL	48	19	28	47	....	....	....	22	....	....	....	....	....	....	....	....	....	....	7	2	2	4	12	....	....	....
1992-93	Binghamton Rangers	AHL	79	30	70	100	....	....	....	88	....	....	....	....	....	....	....	....	....	....	14	3	10	13	18	....	....	....
1993-94	**Los Angeles Kings**	**NHL**	**20**	**1**	**3**	**4**	**1**	**2**	**3**	**4**	**0**	**0**	**0**	**10**	**10.0**	**6**	**0**	**14**	**6**	**–2**	....	....	....	....	....	....	....	....
	Phoenix Roadrunners	IHL	51	14	33	47	....	....	....	65	....	....	....	....	....	....	....	....	....	....	....	....	....	....	....	....	....	....
1994-95	Phoenix Roadrunners	IHL	55	5	27	32	....	....	....	60	....	....	....	....	....	....	....	....	....	....	....	....	....	....	....	....	....	....
	Atlanta Knights	IHL	11	5	7	12	....	....	....	14	....	....	....	....	....	....	....	....	....	....	5	4	5	9	4	....	....	....
1995-96	Ratingen Lowen	Germany	6	2	4	6	....	....	....	29	....	....	....	....	....	....	....	....	....	....	....	....	....	....	....	....	....	....
	Malmo IF	Sweden	16	1	4	5	....	....	....	12	....	....	....	....	....	....	....	....	....	....	....	....	....	....	....	....	....	....
1996-97	Ratinger Lowen	Germany	35	9	20	29	....	....	....	53	....	....	....	....	....	....	....	....	....	....	7	1	2	3	20	....	....	....
1997-98	Star Bulls Rosenheim	Germany	31	2	12	14	....	....	....	28	....	....	....	....	....	....	....	....	....	....	....	....	....	....	....	....	....	....
	Kolner Haie	Germany	16	2	6	8	....	....	....	10	....	....	....	....	....	....	....	....	....	....	3	0	0	0	4	....	....	....
	NHL Totals		**30**	**1**	**5**	**6**	**1**	**3**	**4**	**8**	**0**	**0**	**0**	**21**	**4.8**	**9**	**0**	**23**	**7**		....	....	....	....	....	....	....	....

Signed as a free agent by **Winnipeg**, June 20, 1989. Traded to **NY Rangers** by **Winnipeg** for Simon Wheeldon, July 10, 1990. Signed as a free agent by **LA Kings**, July 29, 1993.

• McSHEFFREY, BRYAN

Bryan McSheffrey RW – R. 6'2", 205 lbs. b: Ottawa, Ont., 9/25/1952. Vancouver's 2nd choice, 19th overall, in 1972 Amateur Draft.

1967-68	Oshawa Generals	OHA	1	0	1	1	....	....	....	0	....	....	....	....	....	....	....	....	....	....	....	....	....	....	....	....	....	....
1968-69	Ottawa 67's	OHA	53	10	7	17	....	....	....	12	....	....	....	....	....	....	....	....	....	....	7	1	1	2	2	....	....	....
1969-70	Ottawa 67's	OHA	54	35	32	67	....	....	....	51	....	....	....	....	....	....	....	....	....	....	....	....	....	....	....	....	....	....
1970-71	Ottawa 67's	OHA	57	38	41	79	....	....	....	86	....	....	....	....	....	....	....	....	....	....	....	....	....	....	....	....	....	....
1971-72	Ottawa 67's	OHA	61	52	44	96	....	....	....	63	....	....	....	....	....	....	....	....	....	....	....	....	....	....	....	....	....	....
1972-73	**Vancouver Canucks**	**NHL**	**33**	**4**	**4**	**8**	**4**	**3**	**7**	**10**	**0**	**0**	**0**	**45**	**8.9**	**10**	**2**	**41**	**1**	**–32**	....	....	....	....	....	....	....	....
	Seattle Totems	WHL	39	27	22	49	....	....	....	24	....	....	....	....	....	....	....	....	....	....	....	....	....	....	....	....	....	....
1973-74	**Vancouver Canucks**	**NHL**	**54**	**9**	**3**	**12**	**9**	**3**	**12**	**34**	**3**	**0**	**0**	**71**	**12.7**	**17**	**5**	**26**	**0**	**–14**	....	....	....	....	....	....	....	....
1974-75	**Buffalo Sabres**	**NHL**	**3**	**0**	**0**	**0**	**0**	**0**	**0**	**0**	**0**	**0**	**0**	**1**	**0.0**	**2**	**1**	**0**	**0**	**+1**	....	....	....	....	....	....	....	....
	Hershey Bears	AHL	47	12	8	20	....	....	....	20	....	....	....	....	....	....	....	....	....	....	11	1	0	1	0	....	....	....
1975-76	Mohawk Valley Comets	NAHL	12	4	3	7	....	....	....	0	....	....	....	....	....	....	....	....	....	....	4	0	2	2	6	....	....	....
	Cape Cod Codders	NAHL	3	1	0	1	....	....	....	0	....	....	....	....	....	....	....	....	....	....	....	....	....	....	....	....	....	....
	Buffalo Norsemen	NAHL	46	27	31	58	....	....	....	26	....	....	....	....	....	....	....	....	....	....	....	....	....	....	....	....	....	....
1976-77	Mohawk Valley Comets	NAHL	63	29	43	72	....	....	....	28	....	....	....	....	....	....	....	....	....	....	3	0	1	1	0	....	....	....
1977-78	Long Beach Sharks-Rockets	PHL	18	7	8	15	....	....	....	11	....	....	....	....	....	....	....	....	....	....	....	....	....	....	....	....	....	....
1978-79	HYS	Holland	18	*32	32	*64	....	....	....	18	....	....	....	....	....	....	....	....	....	....	18	*29	22	51	19	....	....	....
1979-80	HYS	Holland	22	26	34	50	....	....	....	....	....	....	....	....	....	....	....	....	....	....	....	....	....	....	....	....	....	....
	NHL Totals		**90**	**13**	**7**	**20**	**13**	**6**	**19**	**44**	**3**	**0**	**0**	**117**	**11.1**	**29**	**8**	**67**	**1**		....	....	....	....	....	....	....	....

Traded to **Buffalo** by **Vancouver** with Jocelyn Guevremont for Gerry Meehan and Mike Robitaille, October 14, 1974.

• McSORLEY, MARTY

Marty McSorley D – R. 6'1", 235 lbs. b: Hamilton, Ont., 5/18/1963.

1981-82	Belleville Bulls	OHL	58	6	13	19	....	....	....	234	....	....	....	....	....	....	....	....	....	....	....	....	....	....	....	....	....	....
1982-83	Belleville Bulls	OHL	70	10	41	51	....	....	....	183	....	....	....	....	....	....	....	....	....	....	4	0	0	0	7	....	....	....
	Baltimore Skipjacks	AHL	2	0	0	0	....	....	....	22	....	....	....	....	....	....	....	....	....	....	....	....	....	....	....	....	....	....
1983-84	**Pittsburgh Penguins**	**NHL**	**72**	**2**	**7**	**9**	**2**	**5**	**7**	**224**	**0**	**0**	**0**	**75**	**2.7**	**39**	**0**	**83**	**5**	**–39**	....	....	....	....	....	....	....	....
1984-85	**Pittsburgh Penguins**	**NHL**	**15**	**0**	**0**	**0**	**0**	**0**	**0**	**15**	**0**	**0**	**0**	**11**	**0.0**	**1**	**0**	**4**	**0**	**–3**	....	....	....	....	....	....	....	....
	Baltimore Skipjacks	AHL	58	6	24	30	....	....	....	154	....	....	....	....	....	....	....	....	....	....	14	0	7	7	47	....	....	....
1985-86	**Edmonton Oilers**	**NHL**	**59**	**11**	**12**	**23**	**9**	**8**	**17**	**265**	**0**	**0**	**2**	**72**	**15.3**	**39**	**1**	**30**	**1**	**+9**	**8**	**0**	**2**	**2**	**50**	**0**	**0**	**0**
	Nova Scotia Oilers	AHL	9	2	4	6	....	....	....	34	....	....	....	....	....	....	....	....	....	....	....	....	....	....	....	....	....	....
1986-87	**Edmonton Oilers**	**NHL**	**41**	**2**	**4**	**6**	**2**	**3**	**5**	**159**	**0**	**0**	**0**	**32**	**6.3**	**14**	**0**	**18**	**0**	**–4**	**21**	**4**	**3**	**7**	**65**	**0**	**0**	**1**
	Nova Scotia Oilers	AHL	7	2	2	4	....	....	....	48	....	....	....	....	....	....	....	....	....	....	....	....	....	....	....	....	....	....
1987-88	**Edmonton Oilers**	**NHL**	**60**	**9**	**17**	**26**	**8**	**12**	**20**	**223**	**0**	**0**	**1**	**66**	**13.6**	**40**	**1**	**17**	**1**	**+23**	**16**	**0**	**3**	**3**	**67**	**0**	**0**	**0**
1988-89	**Los Angeles Kings**	**NHL**	**66**	**10**	**17**	**27**	**8**	**12**	**20**	**350**	**2**	**0**	**1**	**87**	**11.5**	**56**	**5**	**49**	**1**	**+3**	**11**	**0**	**2**	**2**	**33**	**0**	**0**	**0**
1989-90	**Los Angeles Kings**	**NHL**	**75**	**15**	**21**	**36**	**13**	**15**	**28**	**322**	**2**	**1**	**0**	**127**	**11.8**	**98**	**15**	**98**	**17**	**+2**	**10**	**1**	**3**	**4**	**18**	**1**	**0**	**0**
1990-91	**Los Angeles Kings**	**NHL**	**61**	**7**	**32**	**39**	**6**	**24**	**30**	**221**	**1**	**1**	**1**	**100**	**7.0**	**106**	**15**	**64**	**21**	**+48**	**12**	**0**	**0**	**0**	**58**	**0**	**0**	**0**
1991-92	**Los Angeles Kings**	**NHL**	**71**	**7**	**22**	**29**	**6**	**17**	**23**	**268**	**2**	**1**	**0**	**119**	**5.9**	**80**	**24**	**93**	**24**	**–13**	**6**	**1**	**0**	**1**	**21**	**0**	**0**	**0**

			REGULAR SEASON																		PLAYOFFS							
Season	Club	League	GP	G	A	Pts	AG	AA	APts	PIM	PP	SH	GW	S	%	TGF	PGF	TGA	PGA	+/–	GP	G	A	Pts	PIM	PP	SH	GW
1992-93	**Los Angeles Kings**	**NHL**	**81**	**15**	**26**	**41**	**12**	**18**	**30**	***399**	**3**	**3**	**0**	**197**	**7.6**	**101**	**26**	**127**	**53**	**+1**	**24**	**4**	**6**	**10**	***60**	**2**	**0**	**1**
1993-94	**Pittsburgh Penguins**	**NHL**	**47**	**3**	**18**	**21**	**3**	**14**	**17**	**139**	**0**	**0**	**0**	**122**	**2.5**	**53**	**15**	**61**	**14**	**–9**	....	....	....	....	....	....	....	....
	Los Angeles Kings	**NHL**	**18**	**4**	**6**	**10**	**4**	**5**	**9**	**55**	**1**	**0**	**1**	**38**	**10.5**	**20**	**7**	**31**	**15**	**–3**	....	....	....	....	....	....	....	....
1994-95	**Los Angeles Kings**	**NHL**	**41**	**3**	**18**	**21**	**5**	**26**	**31**	**83**	**1**	**0**	**0**	**75**	**4.0**	**51**	**19**	**59**	**13**	**–14**	....	....	....	....	....	....	....	....
1995-96	**Los Angeles Kings**	**NHL**	**59**	**10**	**21**	**31**	**10**	**17**	**27**	**148**	**1**	**1**	**1**	**118**	**8.5**	**68**	**20**	**91**	**29**	**–14**	....	....	....	....	....	....	....	....
	New York Rangers	**NHL**	**9**	**0**	**2**	**2**	**0**	**2**	**2**	**21**	**0**	**0**	**0**	**12**	**0.0**	**3**	**1**	**10**	**2**	**–6**	**4**	**0**	**0**	**0**	**0**	**0**	**0**	**0**
1996-97	**San Jose Sharks**	**NHL**	**57**	**4**	**12**	**16**	**4**	**11**	**15**	**186**	**0**	**1**	**1**	**74**	**5.4**	**62**	**13**	**65**	**10**	**–6**	....	....	....	....	....	....	....	....
1997-98	**San Jose Sharks**	**NHL**	**56**	**2**	**10**	**12**	**2**	**10**	**12**	**140**	**0**	**0**	**0**	**46**	**4.3**	**33**	**2**	**23**	**2**	**+10**	....	....	....	....	....	....	....	....
	NHL Totals		**888**	**104**	**245**	**349**	**94**	**199**	**293**	**3218**	**13**	**8**	**8**	**1371**	**7.6**	**864**	**164**	**923**	**208**		**112**	**10**	**19**	**29**	**372**	**3**	**0**	**2**

Co-winner of Alka-Seltzer Plus Award with Theoren Fleury (1991)

Signed as a free agent by **Pittsburgh**, July 30, 1982. Traded to **Edmonton** by **Pittsburgh** with Tim Hrynewich and future considerations (Craig Muni, October 6, 1986) for Gilles Meloche, September 12, 1985. Traded to **LA Kings** by **Edmonton** with Wayne Gretzky and Mike Krushelnyski for Jimmy Carson, Martin Gelinas, LA Kings' 1st round choices in 1989 (previously acquired, New Jersey selected Jason Miller), 1991 (Martin Rucinsky) and 1993 (Nick Stajduhar) Entry Drafts and cash, August 9, 1988. Traded to **Pittsburgh** by **LA Kings**, for Shawn McEachern, August 27, 1993. Traded to **LA Kings** by **Pittsburgh** with Jim Paek for Tomas Sandstrom and Shawn McEachern, February 16, 1994. Traded to **NY Rangers** by **LA Kings** with Jari Kurri and Shane Churla for Ray Ferraro, Ian Laperriere, Mattias Norstrom, Nathan Lafayette and NY Rangers' 4th round choice (Sean Blanchard) in 1997 Entry Draft, March 14, 1996. Traded to **San Jose** by **NY Rangers** for Jayson More, Brian Swanson and future considerations, August 20, 1996.

• McSWEEN, DON

Don McSween D – L. 5'11", 197 lbs. b: Detroit, MI, 6/9/1964. Buffalo's 10th choice, 160th overall, in 1983 Entry Draft.

1982-83	Redford Royals	NAJHL	STATISTICS NOT AVAILABLE																									
1983-84	Michigan State Spartans	CCHA	46	10	26	36	....	....	....	30	....	....	....	....	....	....	....	....	....	....	....	....	....	....	....	....	....	....
1984-85	Michigan State Spartans	CCHA	44	2	23	25	....	....	....	52	....	....	....	....	....	....	....	....	....	....	....	....	....	....	....	....	....	....
1985-86	Michigan State Spartans	CCHA	45	9	29	38	....	....	....	18	....	....	....	....	....	....	....	....	....	....	....	....	....	....	....	....	....	....
1986-87	Michigan State Spartans	CCHA	45	7	23	30	....	....	....	34	....	....	....	....	....	....	....	....	....	....	....	....	....	....	....	....	....	....
1987-88	**Buffalo Sabres**	**NHL**	**5**	**0**	**1**	**1**	**0**	**1**	**1**	**6**	**0**	**0**	**0**	**4**	**0.0**	**4**	**0**	**3**	**0**	**+1**	....	....	....	....	....	....	....	....
	Rochester Americans	AHL	63	9	29	38	....	....	....	108	....	....	....	....	....	....	....	....	....	....	6	0	1	1	15	....	....	....
1988-89	Rochester Americans	AHL	66	7	22	29	....	....	....	45	....	....	....	....	....	....	....	....	....	....	....	....	....	....	....	....	....	....
1989-90	**Buffalo Sabres**	**NHL**	**4**	**0**	**0**	**0**	**0**	**0**	**0**	**6**	**0**	**0**	**0**	**4**	**0.0**	**2**	**1**	**4**	**0**	**–3**	....	....	....	....	....	....	....	....
	Rochester Americans	AHL	70	16	43	59	....	....	....	43	....	....	....	....	....	....	....	....	....	....	17	3	10	13	12	....	....	....
1990-91	Rochester Americans	AHL	74	7	44	51	....	....	....	57	....	....	....	....	....	....	....	....	....	....	15	2	5	7	8	....	....	....
1991-92	Rochester Americans	AHL	75	6	32	38	....	....	....	60	....	....	....	....	....	....	....	....	....	....	16	5	6	11	18	....	....	....
1992-93	San Diego Gulls	IHL	80	15	40	55	....	....	....	85	....	....	....	....	....	....	....	....	....	....	14	1	2	3	10	....	....	....
1993-94	San Diego Gulls	IHL	38	5	13	18	....	....	....	36	....	....	....	....	....	....	....	....	....	....	....	....	....	....	....	....	....	....
	Anaheim Mighty Ducks	**NHL**	**32**	**3**	**9**	**12**	**3**	**7**	**10**	**39**	**1**	**0**	**2**	**43**	**7.0**	**30**	**8**	**24**	**6**	**+4**	....	....	....	....	....	....	....	....
	United States	WC-A	8	1	1	2	....	....	....	0	....	....	....	....	....	....	....	....	....	....	....	....	....	....	....	....	....	....
1994-95	**Anaheim Mighty Ducks**	**NHL**	**2**	**0**	**0**	**0**	**0**	**0**	**0**	**0**	**0**	**0**	**0**	**1**	**0.0**	**0**	**0**	**1**	**1**	**0**	....	....	....	....	....	....	....	....
1995-96	**Anaheim Mighty Ducks**	**NHL**	**4**	**0**	**0**	**0**	**0**	**0**	**0**	**4**	**0**	**0**	**0**	**1**	**0.0**	**2**	**0**	**3**	**1**	**0**	....	....	....	....	....	....	....	....
	Baltimore Bandits	AHL	12	1	9	10	....	....	....	2	....	....	....	....	....	....	....	....	....	....	....	....	....	....	....	....	....	....
1996-97	Grand Rapids Griffins	IHL	75	7	20	27	....	....	....	66	....	....	....	....	....	....	....	....	....	....	3	0	1	1	8	....	....	....
1997-98	Grand Rapids Griffins	IHL	2	0	0	0	....	....	....	4	....	....	....	....	....	....	....	....	....	....	....	....	....	....	....	....	....	....
	Milwaukee Admirals	IHL	76	4	21	25	....	....	....	128	....	....	....	....	....	....	....	....	....	....	10	0	0	0	14	....	....	....
	NHL Totals		**47**	**3**	**10**	**13**	**3**	**8**	**11**	**55**	**1**	**0**	**2**	**53**	**5.7**	**38**	**9**	**35**	**8**		....	....	....	....	....	....	....	....

CCHA First All-Star Team (1985, 1986, 1987) • NCAA West Second All-American Team (1986, 1987) • NCAA Championship All-Tournament Team (1986, 1987) • AHL First All-Star Team (1990)

Signed as a free agent by **Anaheim**, January 12, 1994.

• McTAGGART, JIM

Jim McTaggart D – L. 5'11", 200 lbs. b: Weyburn, Sask., 3/31/1960.

1976-77	Swift Current Broncos	SJHL	47	5	29	34	....	....	....	97	....	....	....	....	....	....	....	....	....	....	....	....	....	....	....	....	....	....
1977-78	Saskatoon Blades	WCJHL	65	7	20	27	....	....	....	221	....	....	....	....	....	....	....	....	....	....	....	....	....	....	....	....	....	....
1978-79	Saskatoon Blades	WHL	37	6	19	25	....	....	....	86	....	....	....	....	....	....	....	....	....	....	....	....	....	....	....	....	....	....
	Billings Bighorns	WHL	30	1	12	13	....	....	....	93	....	....	....	....	....	....	....	....	....	....	....	....	....	....	....	....	....	....
1979-80	Billings Bighorns	WHL	65	16	37	53	....	....	....	204	....	....	....	....	....	....	....	....	....	....	....	....	....	....	....	....	....	....
	Hershey Bears	AHL	....	....	....	....	....	....	....	....	....	....	....	....	....	....	....	....	....	....	9	0	0	0	23	....	....	....
1980-81	**Washington Capitals**	**NHL**	**52**	**1**	**6**	**7**	**1**	**4**	**5**	**185**	**0**	**0**	**0**	**40**	**2.5**	**42**	**2**	**65**	**20**	**–5**	....	....	....	....	....	....	....	....
	Hershey Bears	AHL	23	2	1	3	....	....	....	81	....	....	....	....	....	....	....	....	....	....	....	....	....	....	....	....	....	....
1981-82	**Washington Capitals**	**NHL**	**19**	**2**	**4**	**6**	**2**	**3**	**5**	**20**	**0**	**1**	**1**	**24**	**8.3**	**17**	**1**	**25**	**7**	**–2**	....	....	....	....	....	....	....	....
	Hershey Bears	AHL	57	3	12	15	....	....	....	190	....	....	....	....	....	....	....	....	....	....	5	0	3	3	2	....	....	....
1982-83	Wichita Wind	CHL	21	3	9	12	....	....	....	38	....	....	....	....	....	....	....	....	....	....	....	....	....	....	....	....	....	....
	Moncton Alpines	AHL	49	0	7	7	....	....	....	63	....	....	....	....	....	....	....	....	....	....	....	....	....	....	....	....	....	....
1983-84	Montana Majic	CHL	70	5	13	18	....	....	....	104	....	....	....	....	....	....	....	....	....	....	....	....	....	....	....	....	....	....
1984-85	Peterborough Pirates	Britain	28	9	24	33	....	....	....	92	....	....	....	....	....	....	....	....	....	....	....	....	....	....	....	....	....	....
1985-86			DID NOT PLAY																									
1986-87			DID NOT PLAY																									
1987-88	Peterborough Pirates	Britain	28	9	24	33	....	....	....	92	....	....	....	....	....	....	....	....	....	....	2	0	5	5	6	....	....	....
	NHL Totals		**71**	**3**	**10**	**13**	**3**	**7**	**10**	**205**	**0**	**1**	**1**	**64**	**4.7**	**59**	**3**	**90**	**27**		....	....	....	....	....	....	....	....

Signed as a free agent by **Washington**, November 9, 1979. Signed as a free agent by **Edmonton**, October 27, 1982. Traded to **New Jersey** by **Edmonton** with Ron Low for Lindsay Middlebrook and Paul Miller, February 23, 1989.

• McTAVISH, DALE

Dale McTavish C – L. 6'1", 200 lbs. b: Eganville, Ont., 2/28/1972.

1989-90	Peterborough Petes	OHL	66	26	35	61	....	....	....	34	....	....	....	....	....	....	....	....	....	....	12	1	5	6	2	....	....	....
1990-91	Peterborough Petes	OHL	66	21	27	48	....	....	....	44	....	....	....	....	....	....	....	....	....	....	4	1	0	1	0	....	....	....
1991-92	Peterborough Petes	OHL	60	25	31	56	....	....	....	59	....	....	....	....	....	....	....	....	....	....	10	2	5	7	11	....	....	....
1992-93	Peterborough Petes	OHL	66	31	50	81	....	....	....	98	....	....	....	....	....	....	....	....	....	....	21	9	8	17	22	....	....	....
1993-94	St. Francis Xavier X-Men	AUAA	27	30	24	54	....	....	....	71	....	....	....	....	....	....	....	....	....	....	....	....	....	....	....	....	....	....
1994-95	St. Francis Xavier X-Men	AUAA	27	25	27	52	....	....	....	59	....	....	....	....	....	....	....	....	....	....	....	....	....	....	....	....	....	....
1995-96	Canada	Nat-Team	53	24	32	56	....	....	....	91	....	....	....	....	....	....	....	....	....	....	....	....	....	....	....	....	....	....
	Saint John Flames	AHL	4	2	3	5	....	....	....	5	....	....	....	....	....	....	....	....	....	....	15	5	4	9	15	....	....	....
1996-97	**Calgary Flames**	**NHL**	**9**	**1**	**2**	**3**	**1**	**2**	**3**	**2**	**0**	**0**	**0**	**14**	**7.1**	**3**	**0**	**7**	**0**	**–4**	....	....	....	....	....	....	....	....
	Saint John Flames	AHL	53	16	21	37	....	....	....	65	....	....	....	....	....	....	....	....	....	....	3	0	1	1	0	....	....	....
1997-98	SaiPa Lapeenranta	Finland	47	25	18	43	....	....	....	73	....	....	....	....	....	....	....	....	....	....	3	0	3	3	4	....	....	....
	NHL Totals		**9**	**1**	**2**	**3**	**1**	**2**	**3**	**2**	**0**	**0**	**0**	**14**	**7.1**	**3**	**0**	**7**	**0**		....	....	....	....	....	....	....	....

Signed as a free agent by **Calgary**, August 1, 1996.

• McTAVISH, GORDON

Gordon McTavish C – R. 6'4", 200 lbs. b: Guelph, Ont., 6/3/1954. Montreal's 5th choice, 15th overall, in 1974 Amateur Draft.

1973-74	Sudbury Wolves	OHA	68	34	49	83	....	....	....	155	....	....	....	....	....	....	....	....	....	....	....	....	....	....	....	....	....	....
1974-75	Nova Scotia Voyageurs	AHL	63	14	19	33	....	....	....	125	....	....	....	....	....	....	....	....	....	....	4	0	1	1	5	....	....	....
1975-76	Nova Scotia Voyageurs	AHL	44	12	17	29	....	....	....	69	....	....	....	....	....	....	....	....	....	....	9	3	2	5	18	....	....	....
1976-77	Nova Scotia Voyageurs	AHL	78	30	28	58	....	....	....	84	....	....	....	....	....	....	....	....	....	....	12	4	8	12	12	....	....	....
1977-78	Nova Scotia Voyageurs	AHL	76	26	41	67	....	....	....	108	....	....	....	....	....	....	....	....	....	....	11	4	5	9	6	....	....	....
1978-79	**St. Louis Blues**	**NHL**	**1**	**0**	**0**	**0**	**0**	**0**	**0**	**0**	**0**	**0**	**0**	**1**	**0.0**	**0**	**0**	**2**	**0**	**–2**	....	....	....	....	....	....	....	....
	Salt Lake Golden Eagles	CHL	68	36	22	58	....	....	....	64	....	....	....	....	....	....	....	....	....	....	10	*6	6	12	27	....	....	....
1979-80	**Winnipeg Jets**	**NHL**	**10**	**1**	**3**	**4**	**1**	**2**	**3**	**2**	**0**	**0**	**0**	**9**	**11.1**	**8**	**0**	**4**	**0**	**+4**	....	....	....	....	....	....	....	....
	Tulsa Oilers	CHL	26	6	12	18	....	....	....	6	....	....	....	....	....	....	....	....	....	....	....	....	....	....	....	....	....	....
	NHL Totals		**11**	**1**	**3**	**4**	**1**	**2**	**3**	**2**	**0**	**0**	**0**	**10**	**10.0**	**8**	**0**	**6**	**0**		....	....	....	....	....	....	....	....

Traded to **St. Louis** by **Montreal** for Mike Korney, October 7, 1978. Selected by **Winnipeg** from **St. Louis** in Expansion Draft, June 13, 1979.

• MEAGHER, RICK

Rick Meagher C – L. 5'9", 192 lbs. b: Belleville, Ont., 11/2/1953.

1973-74	Boston University	ECAC	30	19	21	40	....	....	....	26	....	....	....	....	....	....	....	....	....	....	....	....	....	....	....	....	....	....
1974-75	Boston University	ECAC	32	25	28	53	....	....	....	80	....	....	....	....	....	....	....	....	....	....	....	....	....	....	....	....	....	....
1975-76	Boston University	ECAC	28	12	25	37	....	....	....	22	....	....	....	....	....	....	....	....	....	....	....	....	....	....	....	....	....	....
1976-77	Boston University	ECAC	34	34	46	80	....	....	....	42	....	....	....	....	....	....	....	....	....	....	....	....	....	....	....	....	....	....

Season	Club	League	GP	G	A	Pts	AG	AA	APts	PIM	PP	SH	GW	S	%	TGF	PGF	TGA	PGA	+/–	GP	G	A	Pts	PIM	PP	SH	GW
			REGULAR SEASON																		PLAYOFFS							
1977-78	Nova Scotia Voyageurs	AHL	57	20	27	47	....	....	....	33	....	....	....	....	....	....	....	....	....	....	11	5	3	8	11	....	....	....
1978-79	Nova Scotia Voyageurs	AHL	79	35	46	81	....	....	....	57	....	....	....	....	....	....	....	....	....	....	10	1	6	7	11	....	....	....
1979-80	**Montreal Canadiens**	**NHL**	**2**	**0**	**0**	**0**	0	0	0	0	0	0	0	0	0.0	0	0	0	0	0	....	....	....	....	....	....	....	....
	Nova Scotia Voyageurs	AHL	64	32	44	76	....	....	....	53	....	....	....	....	....	....	....	....	....	....	6	3	4	7	2	....	....	....
1980-81	**Hartford Whalers**	**NHL**	**27**	**7**	**10**	**17**	6	7	13	19	0	0	0	73	9.6	25	3	25	5	+2	....	....	....	....	....	....	....	....
	Binghamton Whalers	AHL	50	23	35	58	....	....	....	54	....	....	....	....	....	....	....	....	....	....	....	....	....	....	....	....	....	....
1981-82	**Hartford Whalers**	**NHL**	**65**	**24**	**19**	**43**	19	13	32	51	2	1	2	171	14.0	63	9	75	17	–4	....	....	....	....	....	....	....	....
1982-83	**Hartford Whalers**	**NHL**	**4**	**0**	**0**	**0**	0	0	0	0	0	0	0	3	0.0	0	0	3	0	–3	....	....	....	....	....	....	....	....
	New Jersey Devils	**NHL**	**57**	**15**	**14**	**29**	12	10	22	11	7	0	1	135	11.1	41	18	54	10	–21	....	....	....	....	....	....	....	....
1983-84	**New Jersey Devils**	**NHL**	**52**	**14**	**14**	**28**	11	9	20	16	2	0	2	125	11.2	39	10	41	3	–9	....	....	....	....	....	....	....	....
	Maine Mariners	AHL	10	6	4	10	....	....	....	2	....	....	....	....	....	....	....	....	....	....	....	....	....	....	....	....	....	....
1984-85	**New Jersey Devils**	**NHL**	**71**	**11**	**20**	**31**	9	14	23	22	1	1	1	139	7.9	43	3	76	23	–13	....	....	....	....	....	....	....	....
1985-86	**St. Louis Blues**	**NHL**	**79**	**11**	**19**	**30**	9	13	22	28	0	3	3	109	10.1	37	1	78	41	–1	19	4	4	8	12	0	1	0
1986-87	**St. Louis Blues**	**NHL**	**80**	**18**	**21**	**39**	16	15	31	54	2	2	1	170	10.6	50	5	80	26	–9	6	0	0	0	11	0	0	0
1987-88	**St. Louis Blues**	**NHL**	**76**	**18**	**16**	**34**	15	11	26	76	0	5	3	113	15.9	47	2	79	34	0	10	0	0	0	8	0	0	0
1988-89	**St. Louis Blues**	**NHL**	**78**	**15**	**14**	**29**	13	10	23	53	0	1	1	109	13.8	45	0	74	38	+9	10	3	2	5	6	0	0	1
1989-90	**St. Louis Blues**	**NHL**	**76**	**8**	**17**	**25**	7	12	19	47	0	2	1	99	8.1	36	0	68	36	+4	8	1	0	1	2	0	0	0
1990-91	**St. Louis Blues**	**NHL**	**24**	**3**	**1**	**4**	3	1	4	6	0	0	0	21	14.3	10	1	11	2	0	9	0	1	1	2	0	0	0
	NHL Totals		**691**	**144**	**165**	**309**	120	115	235	383	14	15	15	1267	11.4	436	52	664	235		62	8	7	15	41	0	1	1

ECAC Second All-Star Team (1974, 1975) • NCAA East First All-American Team (1975, 1976, 1977) • ECAC First All-Star Team (1976, 1977) • NCAA Championship All-Tournament Team (1977) • Won Frank J. Selke Trophy (1990)

Signed as a free agent by **Montreal**, June 27, 1977. Traded to **Hartford** by **Montreal** with Montreal's 3rd (Paul MacDermid) and 5th (Dan Bourbonnais) round choices in 1981 Entry Draft for Hartford's 3rd (Dieter Hegen) and 5th (Steve Rooney) round choices in 1981 Entry Draft, June 5, 1980. Traded to **New Jersey** by **Hartford** with the rights to Garry Howatt for Merlin Malinowski and the rights to Scott Fusco, October 15, 1982. Traded to **St. Louis** by **New Jersey** with New Jersey's 12th round choice (Bill Butler) in 1986 Entry Draft for Perry Anderson, August 29, 1985.

• MEEHAN, GERRY

Gerry Meehan C – L. 6'2", 200 lbs. b: Toronto, Ont., 9/3/1946. Toronto's 4th choice, 21st overall, in 1963 Amateur Draft.

Season	Club	League	GP	G	A	Pts	AG	AA	APts	PIM	PP	SH	GW	S	%	TGF	PGF	TGA	PGA	+/–	GP	G	A	Pts	PIM	PP	SH	GW
1962-63	Neil McNeil Maroons	Tor-Jr.	7	1	0	1	....	....	....	0	....	....	....	....	....	....	....	....	....	....	5	0	0	0	0	....	....	....
1963-64	Toronto Marlboros	OHA	12	2	3	5	....	....	....	0	....	....	....	....	....	....	....	....	....	....	....	....	....	....	....	....	....	....
1964-65	Toronto Marlboros	OHA	56	14	30	44	....	....	....	24	....	....	....	....	....	....	....	....	....	....	19	7	4	11	12	....	....	....
1965-66	Toronto Marlboros	OHA	47	25	26	51	....	....	....	47	....	....	....	....	....	....	....	....	....	....	14	6	10	16	9	....	....	....
	Rochester Americans	AHL	1	0	0	0	....	....	....	0	....	....	....	....	....	....	....	....	....	....	....	....	....	....	....	....	....	....
1966-67	Toronto Marlboros	OHA	48	26	42	68	....	....	....	27	....	....	....	....	....	....	....	....	....	....	17	8	8	16	8	....	....	....
1967-68	Tulsa Oilers	CHL	70	31	41	72	....	....	....	17	....	....	....	....	....	....	....	....	....	....	11	3	8	11	0	....	....	....
1968-69	**Toronto Maple Leafs**	**NHL**	**25**	**0**	**2**	**2**	0	2	2	2	0	0	0	28	0.0	7	2	6	0	–1	....	....	....	....	....	....	....	....
	Phoenix Roadrunners	WHL	17	6	6	12	....	....	....	2	....	....	....	....	....	....	....	....	....	....	....	....	....	....	....	....	....	....
	Philadelphia Flyers	**NHL**	**12**	**0**	**3**	**3**	0	3	3	4	0	0	0	25	0.0	6	1	6	0	–1	4	0	0	0	0	0	0	0
1969-70	Seattle Totems	WHL	67	23	30	53	....	....	....	23	....	....	....	....	....	....	....	....	....	....	4	0	1	1	0	....	....	....
1970-71	**Buffalo Sabres**	**NHL**	**77**	**24**	**31**	**55**	25	27	52	8	5	0	1	163	14.7	67	12	67	0	–12	....	....	....	....	....	....	....	....
1971-72	**Buffalo Sabres**	**NHL**	**77**	**19**	**27**	**46**	20	25	45	12	4	0	2	164	11.6	56	12	72	0	–28	....	....	....	....	....	....	....	....
1972-73	**Buffalo Sabres**	**NHL**	**77**	**31**	**29**	**60**	31	24	55	21	3	1	6	208	14.9	70	8	61	3	+4	6	0	1	1	0	0	0	0
1973-74	**Buffalo Sabres**	**NHL**	**72**	**20**	**26**	**46**	20	22	42	17	6	0	1	160	12.5	57	20	44	0	–7	....	....	....	....	....	....	....	....
1974-75	**Buffalo Sabres**	**NHL**	**3**	**0**	**1**	**1**	0	1	1	2	0	0	0	4	0.0	1	0	4	0	–3	....	....	....	....	....	....	....	....
	Vancouver Canucks	**NHL**	**57**	**10**	**15**	**25**	9	12	21	4	0	0	2	121	8.3	33	3	37	0	–7	....	....	....	....	....	....	....	....
	Atlanta Flames	**NHL**	**14**	**4**	**10**	**14**	4	8	12	0	2	0	1	29	13.8	20	7	13	2	+2	....	....	....	....	....	....	....	....
1975-76	**Atlanta Flames**	**NHL**	**48**	**7**	**20**	**27**	7	16	23	8	2	0	1	71	9.9	37	9	30	1	–1	....	....	....	....	....	....	....	....
	Washington Capitals	**NHL**	**32**	**16**	**15**	**31**	15	12	27	10	3	0	0	80	20.0	42	12	47	10	–7	....	....	....	....	....	....	....	....
1976-77	**Washington Capitals**	**NHL**	**80**	**28**	**36**	**64**	27	29	56	13	9	1	6	193	14.5	83	31	70	7	–11	....	....	....	....	....	....	....	....
1977-78	**Washington Capitals**	**NHL**	**78**	**19**	**24**	**43**	18	20	38	10	7	0	2	172	11.0	60	20	87	6	–41	....	....	....	....	....	....	....	....
1978-79	**Washington Capitals**	**NHL**	**18**	**2**	**4**	**6**	2	3	5	0	1	0	1	32	6.3	8	2	13	4	–3	....	....	....	....	....	....	....	....
	Cincinnati Stingers	WHA	2	0	0	0	....	....	....	0	....	....	....	....	....	....	....	....	....	....	....	....	....	....	....	....	....	....
	NHL Totals		**670**	**180**	**243**	**423**	178	204	382	111	42	2	23	1450	12.4	547	139	557	33		10	0	1	1	0	0	0	0
	Other Major League Totals		2	0	0	0	....	....	....	0	....	....	....	....	....	....	....	....	....	....	....	....	....	....	....	....	....	....

Traded to **Philadelphia** by **Toronto** with Mike Byers and Bill Sutherland for Brit Selby and Forbes Kennedy, March 2, 1969. Claimed by **Buffalo** from **Philadelphia** in Expansion Draft, June 10, 1970. Selected by **LA Sharks** (WHA) in 1972 WHA General Player Draft, February 12, 1972. Traded to **Vancouver** by **Buffalo** with Mike Robitaille for Jocelyn Guevremont and Bryan McSherry, October 14, 1974. Traded to **Atlanta** by **Vancouver** for Bob J. Murray, March 9, 1975. Traded to **Washington** by **Atlanta** with Jean Lemieux and Buffalo's 1st round choice (acquired earlier, Washington selected Greg Carrol) in 1976 Amateur Draft for Bill Clement, January 22, 1976. Signed as a free agent **Cincinnati** (WHA) after being released by **Washington**, December 4, 1978.

• MEEKE, BRENT

Brent Meeke D – L. 5'11", 175 lbs. b: Toronto, Ont., 4/10/1952. California's 8th choice, 118th overall, in 1972 Amateur Draft.

Season	Club	League	GP	G	A	Pts	AG	AA	APts	PIM	PP	SH	GW	S	%	TGF	PGF	TGA	PGA	+/–	GP	G	A	Pts	PIM	PP	SH	GW
1969-70	Niagara Falls Flyers	OHA	53	5	11	16	....	....	....	26	....	....	....	....	....	....	....	....	....	....	....	....	....	....	....	....	....	....
1970-71	Niagara Falls Flyers	OHA	59	3	27	30	....	....	....	69	....	....	....	....	....	....	....	....	....	....	....	....	....	....	....	....	....	....
1971-72	Niagara Falls Flyers	OHA	30	2	12	14	....	....	....	35	....	....	....	....	....	....	....	....	....	....	....	....	....	....	....	....	....	....
1972-73	**California Golden Seals**	**NHL**	**3**	**0**	**0**	**0**	0	0	0	0	0	0	0	1	0.0	1	1	0	0	0	....	....	....	....	....	....	....	....
	Phoenix Roadrunners	WHL	62	14	22	36	....	....	....	36	....	....	....	....	....	....	....	....	....	....	6	1	1	2	4	....	....	....
1973-74	**California Golden Seals**	**NHL**	**18**	**1**	**9**	**10**	1	8	9	4	0	0	0	40	2.5	26	4	34	1	–11	....	....	....	....	....	....	....	....
	Salt Lake Golden Eagles	WHL	65	15	37	52	....	....	....	44	....	....	....	....	....	....	....	....	....	....	5	1	0	1	4	....	....	....
1974-75	**California Golden Seals**	**NHL**	**4**	**0**	**0**	**0**	0	0	0	0	0	0	0	6	0.0	3	0	2	0	+1	....	....	....	....	....	....	....	....
	Salt Lake Golden Eagles	CHL	75	18	39	57	....	....	....	72	....	....	....	....	....	....	....	....	....	....	11	1	8	9	14	....	....	....
1975-76	**California Golden Seals**	**NHL**	**1**	**0**	**0**	**0**	0	0	0	0	0	0	0	2	0.0	0	0	0	0	0	....	....	....	....	....	....	....	....
	Salt Lake City Golden Eagles	CHL	76	23	39	62	....	....	....	71	....	....	....	....	....	....	....	....	....	....	5	1	3	4	0	....	....	....
1976-77	**Cleveland Barons**	**NHL**	**49**	**8**	**13**	**21**	8	11	19	4	1	0	0	74	10.8	47	19	43	0	–15	....	....	....	....	....	....	....	....
	Salt Lake Golden Eagles	CHL	26	5	16	21	....	....	....	24	....	....	....	....	....	....	....	....	....	....	....	....	....	....	....	....	....	....
1977-78			DID NOT PLAY																									
1978-79	ERC Mannheim	Germany	51	18	23	41	....	....	....	118	....	....	....	....	....	....	....	....	....	....	....	....	....	....	....	....	....	....
1979-80	ERC Mannheim	Germany	48	13	31	44	....	....	....	135	....	....	....	....	....	....	....	....	....	....	....	....	....	....	....	....	....	....
1980-81	ERC Mannheim	Germany	53	11	35	46	....	....	....	122	....	....	....	....	....	....	....	....	....	....	10	0	4	4	12	....	....	....
	NHL Totals		**75**	**9**	**22**	**31**	9	19	28	8	1	0	0	123	7.3	77	24	79	1		....	....	....	....	....	....	....	....

CHL Second All-Star Team (1975, 1976)

Transferred to **Cleveland** after **California** franchise relocated, August 26, 1976.

• MEEKER, MIKE

Mike Meeker RW – R. 5'11", 195 lbs. b: Kingston, Ont., 2/23/1958. Pittsburgh's 1st choice, 25th overall, in 1978 Amateur Draft.

Season	Club	League	GP	G	A	Pts	AG	AA	APts	PIM	PP	SH	GW	S	%	TGF	PGF	TGA	PGA	+/–	GP	G	A	Pts	PIM	PP	SH	GW
1975-76	University of Wisconsin	WCHA	31	12	9	21	....	....	....	21	....	....	....	....	....	....	....	....	....	....	....	....	....	....	....	....	....	....
1976-77	University of Wisconsin	WCHA	41	26	27	53	....	....	....	50	....	....	....	....	....	....	....	....	....	....	....	....	....	....	....	....	....	....
1977-78	University of Wisconsin	WCHA	4	6	2	8	....	....	....	4	....	....	....	....	....	....	....	....	....	....	....	....	....	....	....	....	....	....
	Peterborough Petes	OHA	44	33	36	69	....	....	....	21	....	....	....	....	....	....	....	....	....	....	....	....	....	....	....	....	....	....
1978-79	**Pittsburgh Penguins**	**NHL**	**4**	**0**	**0**	**0**	0	0	0	5	0	0	0	2	0.0	0	0	1	0	–1	....	....	....	....	....	....	....	....
	Binghamton Dusters	AHL	75	30	35	65	....	....	....	70	....	....	....	....	....	....	....	....	....	....	....	....	....	....	....	....	....	....
	NHL Totals		**4**	**0**	**0**	**0**	0	0	0	5	0	0	0	2	0.0	0	0	1	0		....	....	....	....	....	....	....	....

Won Dudley "Red" Garrett Memorial Award (Top Rookie - AHL) (1979)

• MEIGHAN, RON

Ron Meighan D – R. 6'3", 195 lbs. b: Montreal, Que., 5/26/1963. Minnesota's 1st choice, 13th overall, in 1981 Entry Draft.

Season	Club	League	GP	G	A	Pts	AG	AA	APts	PIM	PP	SH	GW	S	%	TGF	PGF	TGA	PGA	+/–	GP	G	A	Pts	PIM	PP	SH	GW
			REGULAR SEASON																		PLAYOFFS							
1979-80	Niagara Falls Flyers	OHA	61	3	10	13	....	....	....	20	....	....	....	....	....	....	....	....	....	....	....	....	....	....	....	....	....	....
1980-81	Niagara Falls Flyers	OHA	63	8	27	35	....	....	....	92	....	....	....	....	....	....	....	....	....	....	12	0	0	0	14	....	....	....
1981-82	Niagara Falls Flyers	OHL	58	27	41	68	....	....	....	85	....	....	....	....	....	....	....	....	....	....	4	0	4	4	9	....	....	....
	Minnesota North Stars	**NHL**	**7**	**1**	**1**	**2**	**1**	**1**	**2**	**2**	**0**	**0**	**0**	**4**	**25.0**	**8**	**0**	**11**	**1**	**–2**	....	....	....	....	....	....	....	....
1982-83	North Bay Centennials	OHL	29	19	22	41	....	....	....	30	....	....	....	....	....	....	....	....	....	....	....	....	....	....	....	....	....	....
	Pittsburgh Penguins	**NHL**	**41**	**2**	**6**	**8**	**2**	**4**	**6**	**16**	**1**	**0**	**0**	**48**	**4.2**	**36**	**5**	**47**	**6**	**–10**	....	....	....	....	....	....	....	....
1983-84	Baltimore Skipjacks	AHL	75	4	16	20	....	....	....	36	....	....	....	....	....	....	....	....	....	....	....	....	....	....	....	....	....	....
	NHL Totals		**48**	**3**	**7**	**10**	**3**	**5**	**8**	**18**	**1**	**0**	**0**	**52**	**5.8**	**44**	**5**	**58**	**7**		....	....	....	....	....	....	....	....

OHL First All-Star Team (1982)

Traded to **Pittsburgh** by **Minnesota** with Anders Hakansson and Minnesota's 1st round choice (Bob Errey) in 1983 Entry Draft for George Ferguson and Pittsburgh's 1st round choice (Brain Lawton) in 1983 Entry Draft, October 28, 1982.

• MEISSNER, BARRIE

Barrie Meissner LW – L. 5'9", 165 lbs. b: Kindersley, Sask., 7/26/1946.

Season	Club	League	GP	G	A	Pts	AG	AA	APts	PIM	PP	SH	GW	S	%	TGF	PGF	TGA	PGA	+/–	GP	G	A	Pts	PIM	PP	SH	GW
1963-64	Regina Pats	SJHL	6	0	0	0	....	....	....	4	....	....	....	....	....	....	....	....	....	....	1	0	0	0	2	....	....	....
1964-65	Regina Pats	SJHL	52	27	31	58	....	....	....	91	....	....	....	....	....	....	....	....	....	....	12	4	4	8	32	....	....	....
1965-66	Regina Pats	SJHL	60	47	56	103	....	....	....	148	....	....	....	....	....	....	....	....	....	....	5	1	5	6	8	....	....	....
1966-67	Regina Pats	WCJHL	53	35	44	79	....	....	....	78	....	....	....	....	....	....	....	....	....	....	15	12	17	29	34	....	....	....
1967-68	**Minnesota North Stars**	**NHL**	**1**	**0**	**0**	**0**	**0**	**0**	**0**	**2**	**0**	**0**	**0**	**2**	**0.0**	**1**	**1**	**1**	**0**	**–1**	....	....	....	....	....	....	....	....
	Memphis South Stars	CHL	64	15	24	39	....	....	....	66	....	....	....	....	....	....	....	....	....	....	....	....	....	....	....	....	....	....
1968-69	**Minnesota North Stars**	**NHL**	**5**	**0**	**1**	**1**	**0**	**1**	**1**	**2**	**0**	**0**	**0**	**1**	**0.0**	**1**	**0**	**0**	**0**	**+1**	....	....	....	....	....	....	....	....
	Memphis South Stars	CHL	67	27	26	53	....	....	....	80	....	....	....	....	....	....	....	....	....	....	....	....	....	....	....	....	....	....
1969-70	Iowa Stars	CHL	49	7	10	17	....	....	....	62	....	....	....	....	....	....	....	....	....	....	11	0	2	2	4	....	....	....
1970-71	Cleveland Barons	AHL	61	22	16	38	....	....	....	39	....	....	....	....	....	....	....	....	....	....	4	1	4	5	14	....	....	....
1971-72	Cleveland Barons	AHL	9	2	1	3	....	....	....	6	....	....	....	....	....	....	....	....	....	....	....	....	....	....	....	....	....	....
	Seattle Totems	WHL	7	0	2	2	....	....	....	6	....	....	....	....	....	....	....	....	....	....	....	....	....	....	....	....	....	....
	Omaha Knights	CHL	37	6	9	15	....	....	....	18	....	....	....	....	....	....	....	....	....	....	....	....	....	....	....	....	....	....
1972-73	Cleveland-Jacksonville Barons	AHL	68	20	25	45	....	....	....	71	....	....	....	....	....	....	....	....	....	....	....	....	....	....	....	....	....	....
	NHL Totals		**6**	**0**	**1**	**1**	**0**	**1**	**1**	**4**	**0**	**0**	**0**	**3**	**0.0**	**2**	**1**	**1**	**0**		....	....	....	....	....	....	....	....

Rights traded to **Minnesota** by **Montreal** with Bill Plager and the rights to Leo Thiffault for Bryan Watson, June 6, 1967.

• MELAMETSA, ANSSI

Anssi Melametsa LW – L. 6', 190 lbs. b: Jyvaskyla, Fin., 6/21/1961. Winnipeg's 12th choice, 249th overall, in 1985 Entry Draft.

Season	Club	League	GP	G	A	Pts	AG	AA	APts	PIM	PP	SH	GW	S	%	TGF	PGF	TGA	PGA	+/–	GP	G	A	Pts	PIM	PP	SH	GW
1978-79	Peterborough Petes	OHL	64	9	21	30	....	....	....	27	....	....	....	....	....	....	....	....	....	....	....	....	....	....	....	....	....	....
1979-80	Jokerit Helsinki	Finland	36	6	13	19	....	....	....	55	....	....	....	....	....	....	....	....	....	....	....	....	....	....	....	....	....	....
	Finland	WJC-A	5	0	4	4	....	....	....	4	....	....	....	....	....	....	....	....	....	....	....	....	....	....	....	....	....	....
1980-81	Jokerit Helsinki	Finland	36	14	22	36	....	....	....	46	....	....	....	....	....	....	....	....	....	....	....	....	....	....	....	....	....	....
	Finland	WJC-A	5	1	3	4	....	....	....	2	....	....	....	....	....	....	....	....	....	....	....	....	....	....	....	....	....	....
1981-82	HIFK Helsinki	Finland	28	16	12	38	....	....	....	30	....	....	....	....	....	....	....	....	....	....	7	2	5	7	8	....	....	....
1982-83	HIFK Helsinki	Finland	36	13	20	33	....	....	....	59	....	....	....	....	....	....	....	....	....	....	9	2	6	8	6	....	....	....
	Finland	WEC-A	10	6	3	9	....	....	....	20	....	....	....	....	....	....	....	....	....	....	....	....	....	....	....	....	....	....
1983-84	HIFK Helsinki	Finland	37	16	17	33	....	....	....	44	....	....	....	....	....	....	....	....	....	....	2	0	0	0	0	....	....	....
	Finland	Nat-Team	10	2	2	4	....	....	....	10	....	....	....	....	....	....	....	....	....	....	....	....	....	....	....	....	....	....
	Finland	Olympics	6	4	3	7	....	....	....	10	....	....	....	....	....	....	....	....	....	....	....	....	....	....	....	....	....	....
1984-85	HIFK Helsinki	Finland	36	16	15	31	....	....	....	18	....	....	....	....	....	....	....	....	....	....	....	....	....	....	....	....	....	....
	Finland	WEC-A	10	2	2	4	....	....	....	10	....	....	....	....	....	....	....	....	....	....	....	....	....	....	....	....	....	....
1985-86	**Winnipeg Jets**	**NHL**	**27**	**0**	**3**	**3**	**0**	**2**	**2**	**2**	**0**	**0**	**0**	**20**	**0.0**	**5**	**0**	**10**	**0**	**–5**	....	....	....	....	....	....	....	....
	Sherbrooke Canadiens	AHL	14	7	5	12	....	....	....	16	....	....	....	....	....	....	....	....	....	....	....	....	....	....	....	....	....	....
1986-87	HIFK Helsinki	Finland	35	13	12	25	....	....	....	44	....	....	....	....	....	....	....	....	....	....	4	0	0	0	0	....	....	....
1987-88	HIFK Helsinki	Finland	35	13	12	25	....	....	....	44	....	....	....	....	....	....	....	....	....	....	4	0	0	0	0	....	....	....
1988-89	HIFK Helsinki	Finland	41	8	8	16	....	....	....	42	....	....	....	....	....	....	....	....	....	....	6	2	0	2	12	....	....	....
1989-90	Jokerit Helsinki	Finland	44	24	27	51	....	....	....	28	....	....	....	....	....	....	....	....	....	....	....	....	....	....	....	....	....	....
1990-91	Jokerit Helsinki	Finland	44	10	21	31	....	....	....	20	....	....	....	....	....	....	....	....	....	....	....	....	....	....	....	....	....	....
	NHL Totals		**27**	**0**	**3**	**3**	**0**	**2**	**2**	**2**	**0**	**0**	**0**	**20**	**0.0**	**5**	**0**	**10**	**0**		....	....	....	....	....	....	....	....

• MELANSON, DEAN

Dean Melanson D – R. 5'11", 211 lbs. b: Antigonish, N.S., 11/19/1973. Buffalo's 4th choice, 80th overall, in 1992 Entry Draft.

Season	Club	League	GP	G	A	Pts	AG	AA	APts	PIM	PP	SH	GW	S	%	TGF	PGF	TGA	PGA	+/–	GP	G	A	Pts	PIM	PP	SH	GW
1990-91	St-Hyacinthe Laser	QMJHL	69	10	17	27	....	....	....	110	....	....	....	....	....	....	....	....	....	....	4	0	1	1	2	....	....	....
1991-92	St-Hyacinthe Laser	QMJHL	42	8	19	27	....	....	....	158	....	....	....	....	....	....	....	....	....	....	6	1	2	3	25	....	....	....
1992-93	St-Hyacinthe Laser	QMJHL	57	13	29	42	....	....	....	253	....	....	....	....	....	....	....	....	....	....	....	....	....	....	....	....	....	....
	Rochester Americans	AHL	8	0	1	1	....	....	....	6	....	....	....	....	....	....	....	....	....	....	14	1	6	7	18	....	....	....
1993-94	Rochester Americans	AHL	80	1	21	22	....	....	....	138	....	....	....	....	....	....	....	....	....	....	4	0	1	1	2	....	....	....
1994-95	**Buffalo Sabres**	**NHL**	**5**	**0**	**0**	**0**	**0**	**0**	**0**	**4**	**0**	**0**	**0**	**1**	**0.0**	**1**	**0**	**2**	**0**	**–1**	....	....	....	....	....	....	....	....
	Rochester Americans	AHL	43	4	7	11	....	....	....	84	....	....	....	....	....	....	....	....	....	....	....	....	....	....	....	....	....	....
1995-96	Rochester Americans	AHL	70	3	13	16	....	....	....	204	....	....	....	....	....	....	....	....	....	....	14	3	3	6	22	....	....	....
1996-97	Quebec Rafales	IHL	72	3	21	24	....	....	....	95	....	....	....	....	....	....	....	....	....	....	7	0	2	2	12	....	....	....
1997-98	Rochester Americans	AHL	73	7	9	16	....	....	....	228	....	....	....	....	....	....	....	....	....	....	4	0	2	2	0	....	....	....
	NHL Totals		**5**	**0**	**0**	**0**	**0**	**0**	**0**	**4**	**0**	**0**	**0**	**1**	**0.0**	**1**	**0**	**2**	**0**		....	....	....	....	....	....	....	....

• MELIN, ROGER

Roger Melin LW – L. 6'4", 195 lbs. b: Enkoping, Sweden, 4/25/1956.

Season	Club	League	GP	G	A	Pts	AG	AA	APts	PIM	PP	SH	GW	S	%	TGF	PGF	TGA	PGA	+/–	GP	G	A	Pts	PIM	PP	SH	GW
1976-77	Orebro	Sweden	21	3	3	6	....	....	....	2	....	....	....	....	....	....	....	....	....	....	....	....	....	....	....	....	....	....
1977-78	Orebro	Sweden 2	STATISTICS NOT AVAILABLE																									
1978-79	Orebro	Sweden	23	2	1	3	....	....	....	6	....	....	....	....	....	....	....	....	....	....	....	....	....	....	....	....	....	....
1979-80	Vasby	Sweden	STATISTICS NOT AVAILABLE																									
1980-81	**Minnesota North Stars**	**NHL**	**1**	**0**	**0**	**0**	**0**	**0**	**0**	**0**	**0**	**0**	**0**	**1**	**0.0**	**0**	**0**	**1**	**0**	**–1**	....	....	....	....	....	....	....	....
	Oklahoma City Stars	CHL	9	1	1	2	....	....	....	4	....	....	....	....	....	....	....	....	....	....	....	....	....	....	....	....	....	....
1981-82	**Minnesota North Stars**	**NHL**	**2**	**0**	**0**	**0**	**0**	**0**	**0**	**0**	**0**	**0**	**0**	**0**	**0.0**	**0**	**0**	**0**	**0**	**0**	....	....	....	....	....	....	....	....
	Nashville South Stars	CHL	77	18	27	45	....	....	....	7	....	....	....	....	....	....	....	....	....	....	3	0	2	2	0	....	....	....
1982-83	Hammarby	Sweden	26	9	8	17	....	....	....	14	....	....	....	....	....	....	....	....	....	....	....	....	....	....	....	....	....	....
1983-84	Hammarby	Sweden	32	6	9	15	....	....	....	8	....	....	....	....	....	....	....	....	....	....	....	....	....	....	....	....	....	....
	NHL Totals		**3**	**0**	**0**	**0**	**0**	**0**	**0**	**0**	**0**	**0**	**0**	**1**	**0.0**	**0**	**0**	**1**	**0**		....	....	....	....	....	....	....	....

Signed as a free agent by **Minnesota**, March 23, 1981.

• MELLANBY, SCOTT

Scott Mellanby RW – R. 6'1", 199 lbs. b: Montreal, Que., 6/11/1966. Philadelphia's 2nd choice, 27th overall, in 1984 Entry Draft.

Season	Club	League	GP	G	A	Pts	AG	AA	APts	PIM	PP	SH	GW	S	%	TGF	PGF	TGA	PGA	+/–	GP	G	A	Pts	PIM	PP	SH	GW
1983-84	Henry Carr High School	MTHL	39	37	37	74	....	....	....	97	....	....	....	....	....	....	....	....	....	....	....	....	....	....	....	....	....	....
1984-85	University of Wisconsin	WCHA	40	14	24	38	....	....	....	60	....	....	....	....	....	....	....	....	....	....	....	....	....	....	....	....	....	....
1985-86	University of Wisconsin	WCHA	32	21	23	44	....	....	....	89	....	....	....	....	....	....	....	....	....	....	....	....	....	....	....	....	....	....
	Canada	WJC-A	7	5	4	9	....	....	....	6	....	....	....	....	....	....	....	....	....	....	....	....	....	....	....	....	....	....
	Philadelphia Flyers	**NHL**	**2**	**0**	**0**	**0**	**0**	**0**	**0**	**0**	**0**	**0**	**0**	**0**	**0.0**	**0**	**0**	**1**	**0**	**–1**	....	....	....	....	....	....	....	....
1986-87	**Philadelphia Flyers**	**NHL**	**71**	**11**	**21**	**32**	**10**	**15**	**25**	**94**	**1**	**0**	**0**	**118**	**9.3**	**54**	**10**	**38**	**2**	**+8**	**24**	**5**	**5**	**10**	**46**	**0**	**0**	**1**
1987-88	**Philadelphia Flyers**	**NHL**	**75**	**25**	**26**	**51**	**21**	**18**	**39**	**185**	**7**	**0**	**2**	**190**	**13.2**	**81**	**31**	**65**	**8**	**–7**	**7**	**0**	**1**	**1**	**16**	**0**	**0**	**0**
1988-89	**Philadelphia Flyers**	**NHL**	**76**	**21**	**29**	**50**	**18**	**20**	**38**	**183**	**11**	**0**	**3**	**202**	**10.4**	**73**	**31**	**56**	**1**	**–13**	**19**	**4**	**5**	**9**	**28**	**0**	**0**	**0**
1989-90	**Philadelphia Flyers**	**NHL**	**57**	**6**	**17**	**23**	**5**	**12**	**17**	**77**	**0**	**0**	**1**	**104**	**5.8**	**41**	**6**	**39**	**0**	**–4**	....	....	....	....	....	....	....	....
1990-91	**Philadelphia Flyers**	**NHL**	**74**	**20**	**21**	**41**	**18**	**16**	**34**	**155**	**5**	**0**	**6**	**165**	**12.1**	**62**	**15**	**39**	**0**	**+8**	....	....	....	....	....	....	....	....
1991-92	**Edmonton Oilers**	**NHL**	**80**	**23**	**27**	**50**	**21**	**20**	**41**	**197**	**7**	**0**	**5**	**159**	**14.5**	**79**	**23**	**51**	**0**	**+5**	**16**	**2**	**1**	**3**	**29**	**1**	**0**	**1**
1992-93	**Edmonton Oilers**	**NHL**	**69**	**15**	**17**	**32**	**12**	**12**	**24**	**147**	**6**	**0**	**3**	**114**	**13.2**	**55**	**16**	**43**	**0**	**–4**	....	....	....	....	....	....	....	....
1993-94	**Florida Panthers**	**NHL**	**80**	**30**	**30**	**60**	**28**	**23**	**51**	**149**	**17**	**0**	**4**	**204**	**14.7**	**87**	**40**	**47**	**0**	**0**	....	....	....	....	....	....	....	....
1994-95	**Florida Panthers**	**NHL**	**48**	**13**	**12**	**25**	**23**	**18**	**41**	**90**	**4**	**0**	**5**	**130**	**10.0**	**40**	**16**	**40**	**0**	**–16**	....	....	....	....	....	....	....	....

Season	Club	League	REGULAR SEASON GP	G	A	Pts	AG	AA	APts	PIM	PP	SH	GW	S	%	TGF	PGF	TGA	PGA	+/-	PLAYOFFS GP	G	A	Pts	PIM	PP	SH	GW
1995-96	Florida Panthers	NHL	79	32	38	70	32	31	63	160	19	0	3	225	14.2	106	55	47	0	+4	22	3	6	9	44	2	0	0
1996-97	Florida Panthers	NHL	82	27	29	56	29	26	55	170	9	1	4	221	12.2	81	28	46	0	+7	5	0	2	2	4	0	0	0
1997-98	Florida Panthers	NHL	79	15	24	39	18	23	41	127	6	0	1	188	8.0	67	29	54	2	–14	....	....	....	....	....	....	....	....
	NHL Totals		872	238	291	529	235	234	469	1734	92	1	37	2020	11.8	826	300	566	13		93	14	20	34	167	3	0	2

Played in NHL All-Star Game (1996)

Traded to **Edmonton** by **Philadelphia** with Craig Fisher and Craig Berube for Dave Brown, Corey Foster and Jari Kurri, May 30, 1991. Claimed by **Florida** from **Edmonton** in Expansion Draft, June 24, 1993.

• MELLOR, TOM

Tom Mellor D – R. 6'1", 185 lbs. b: Cranston, RI, 1/27/1950. Detroit's 5th choice, 68th overall, in 1970 Amateur Draft.

Season	Club	League	GP	G	A	Pts	AG	AA	APts	PIM	PP	SH	GW	S	%	TGF	PGF	TGA	PGA	+/-	GP	G	A	Pts	PIM	PP	SH	GW
1968-69	Boston College	ECAC	17	9	10	19	....	....	....	12	....	....	....	....	....	....	....	....	....	....	....	....	....	....	....	....	....	....
1969-70	Boston College	ECAC	26	21	23	44	....	....	....	40	....	....	....	....	....	....	....	....	....	....	....	....	....	....	....	....	....	....
1970-71	Boston College	ECAC	25	10	30	40	....	....	....	43	....	....	....	....	....	....	....	....	....	....	....	....	....	....	....	....	....	....
1971-72	United States	Nat-Team	7	4	8	12	....	....	....	6	....	....	....	....	....	....	....	....	....	....	....	....	....	....	....	....	....	....
	United States	Olympics	6	0	0	0	....	....	....	4	....	....	....	....	....	....	....	....	....	....	....	....	....	....	....	....	....	....
	United States	WEC-A	10	1	3	4	....	....	....	2	....	....	....	....	....	....	....	....	....	....	....	....	....	....	....	....	....	....
1972-73	Boston College	ECAC	30	6	*45	51	....	....	....	50	....	....	....	....	....	....	....	....	....	....	....	....	....	....	....	....	....	....
1973-74	Detroit Red Wings	NHL	25	2	4	6	2	3	5	25	0	0	0	24	8.3	18	1	30	4	–9	....	....	....	....	....	....	....	....
	Virginia Wings	AHL	23	5	18	23	....	....	....	40	....	....	....	....	....	....	....	....	....	....	....	....	....	....	....	....	....	....
	London Lions	Britain	6	2	5	7	....	....	....	20	....	....	....	....	....	....	....	....	....	....	....	....	....	....	....	....	....	....
1974-75	Detroit Red Wings	NHL	1	0	0	0	0	0	0	0	0	0	0	1	0.0	0	0	0	0	0	....	....	....	....	....	....	....	....
	Virginia Wings	AHL	73	17	35	52	....	....	....	147	....	....	....	....	....	....	....	....	....	....	5	0	2	2	17	....	....	....
1975-76	Vastra Frolunda	Sweden	34	8	8	16	....	....	....	41	....	....	....	....	....	....	....	....	....	....	....	....	....	....	....	....	....	....
	Toledo Goaldiggers	IHL	13	3	12	15	....	....	....	19	....	....	....	....	....	....	....	....	....	....	4	0	2	2	7	....	....	....
1976-77	Toledo Goaldiggers	IHL	75	13	62	75	....	....	....	118	....	....	....	....	....	....	....	....	....	....	19	4	*17	21	16	....	....	....
	NHL Totals		26	2	4	6	2	3	5	25	0	0	0	25	8.0	18	1	30	4		....	....	....	....	....	....	....	....

ECAC Second All-Star Team (1970, 1971) • ECAC First All-Star Team (1973) • NCAA East First All-American Team (1973) • IHL First All-Star Team (1977) • Won Governors' Trophy (Top Defenseman - IHL) (1977) • Won James Gatschene Memorial Trophy (MVP - IHL) (1977)

• MELNYK, GERRY

Gerry Melnyk C – R. 5'10", 165 lbs. b: Edmonton, Alta., 9/16/1934.

Season	Club	League	GP	G	A	Pts	AG	AA	APts	PIM	PP	SH	GW	S	%	TGF	PGF	TGA	PGA	+/-	GP	G	A	Pts	PIM	PP	SH	GW
1951-52	Edmonton Oil Kings	WCJHL	42	29	29	58	....	....	....	24	....	....	....	....	....	....	....	....	....	....	9	*9	4	13	2	....	....	....
1952-53	Edmonton Oil Kings	WCJHL	36	27	28	55	....	....	....	22	....	....	....	....	....	....	....	....	....	....	9	5	8	13	6	....	....	....
	Edmonton Flyers	WHL	....	....	....	....	....	....	....	....	....	....	....	....	....	....	....	....	....	....	2	0	1	1	0	....	....	....
1953-54	Edmonton Oil Kings	WCJHL	36	39	*49	88	....	....	....	25	....	....	....	....	....	....	....	....	....	....	10	10	15	25	10	....	....	....
	Edmonton Flyers	WHL	3	1	1	2	....	....	....	0	....	....	....	....	....	....	....	....	....	....	....	....	....	....	....	....	....	....
1954-55	Edmonton Flyers	WHL	69	14	29	43	....	....	....	24	....	....	....	....	....	....	....	....	....	....	9	2	*8	10	0	....	....	....
1955-56	Edmonton Flyers	WHL	70	37	50	87	....	....	....	37	....	....	....	....	....	....	....	....	....	....	3	1	3	4	2	....	....	....
	Detroit Red Wings	NHL	....	....	....	....	....	....	....	....	....	....	....	....	....	....	....	....	....	....	6	0	0	0	0	....	....	....
1956-57	Edmonton Flyers	WHL	60	21	44	65	....	....	....	26	....	....	....	....	....	....	....	....	....	....	8	5	3	8	2	....	....	....
1957-58	Edmonton Flyers	WHL	50	22	40	62	....	....	....	19	....	....	....	....	....	....	....	....	....	....	....	....	....	....	....	....	....	....
1958-59	Edmonton Flyers	WHL	64	30	37	67	....	....	....	8	....	....	....	....	....	....	....	....	....	....	3	0	1	1	2	....	....	....
1959-60	Detroit Red Wings	NHL	63	10	10	20	12	10	22	12	....	....	....	....	....	....	....	....	....	....	6	3	0	3	0	....	....	....
1960-61	Detroit Red Wings	NHL	70	9	16	25	11	16	27	2	....	....	....	....	....	....	....	....	....	....	11	1	0	1	2	....	....	....
1961-62	Chicago Black Hawks	NHL	63	5	16	21	6	16	22	6	....	....	....	....	....	....	....	....	....	....	7	0	0	0	2	....	....	....
1962-63	Buffalo Bisons	AHL	72	14	36	50	....	....	....	20	....	....	....	....	....	....	....	....	....	....	13	6	7	13	4	....	....	....
1963-64	Buffalo Bisons	AHL	70	11	34	45	....	....	....	0	....	....	....	....	....	....	....	....	....	....	....	....	....	....	....	....	....	....
	St. Louis Braves	CHL	....	....	....	....	....	....	....	....	....	....	....	....	....	....	....	....	....	....	6	1	4	5	2	....	....	....
1964-65	Buffalo Bisons	AHL	72	22	47	69	....	....	....	12	....	....	....	....	....	....	....	....	....	....	9	1	4	5	2	....	....	....
	Chicago Black Hawks	NHL	....	....	....	....	....	....	....	....	....	....	....	....	....	....	....	....	....	....	6	0	0	0	0	....	....	....
1965-66	Buffalo Bisons	AHL	69	18	61	79	....	....	....	10	....	....	....	....	....	....	....	....	....	....	....	....	....	....	....	....	....	....
1966-67	St. Louis Braves	CHL	67	24	47	71	....	....	....	12	....	....	....	....	....	....	....	....	....	....	....	....	....	....	....	....	....	....
1967-68	St. Louis Blues	NHL	73	15	35	50	19	37	56	14	3	1	3	144	10.4	71	26	71	15	–11	17	2	6	8	2	1	1	0
	NHL Totals		269	39	77	116	48	79	127	34	3	1	3	144	27.1	71	26	71	15		53	6	6	12	6	1	1	0

CHL Second All-Star Team (1967)

Played in NHL All-Star Game (1961)

Traded to **Chicago** by **Detroit** with Brian Smith for Eddie Litzenberger, June 13, 1961. Claimed by **St. Louis** from **Chicago** in Expansion Draft, June 6, 1967.

• MELNYK, LARRY

Larry Melnyk D – L. 6', 195 lbs. b: Saskatoon, Sask., 2/21/1960. Boston's 5th choice, 78th overall, in 1979 Entry Draft.

Season	Club	League	GP	G	A	Pts	AG	AA	APts	PIM	PP	SH	GW	S	%	TGF	PGF	TGA	PGA	+/-	GP	G	A	Pts	PIM	PP	SH	GW
1977-78	Abbotsford Pilots	BCJHL	39	10	9	19	....	....	....	100	....	....	....	....	....	....	....	....	....	....	....	....	....	....	....	....	....	....
	New Westminster Royals	WCJHL	44	3	22	25	....	....	....	71	....	....	....	....	....	....	....	....	....	....	....	....	....	....	....	....	....	....
1978-79	New Westminster Royals	WHL	71	7	33	40	....	....	....	142	....	....	....	....	....	....	....	....	....	....	8	1	4	5	14	....	....	....
	Canada	WJC-A	5	1	1	2	....	....	....	2	....	....	....	....	....	....	....	....	....	....	....	....	....	....	....	....	....	....
1979-80	New Westminster Royals	WHL	67	13	38	51	....	....	....	236	....	....	....	....	....	....	....	....	....	....	....	....	....	....	....	....	....	....
1980-81	Boston Bruins	NHL	26	0	4	4	0	3	3	39	0	0	0	30	0.0	13	1	21	2	–7	....	....	....	....	....	....	....	....
	Springfield Indians	AHL	47	1	10	11	....	....	....	109	....	....	....	....	....	....	....	....	....	....	1	0	0	0	0	....	....	....
1981-82	Boston Bruins	NHL	48	0	8	8	0	5	5	84	0	0	0	40	0.0	37	2	32	0	+3	11	0	3	3	40	0	0	0
	Erie Blades	AHL	10	0	3	3	....	....	....	36	....	....	....	....	....	....	....	....	....	....	....	....	....	....	....	....	....	....
1982-83	Boston Bruins	NHL	1	0	0	0	0	0	0	0	0	0	0	2	0.0	0	0	2	0	–2	11	0	0	0	9	0	0	0
	Baltimore Skipjacks	AHL	72	2	24	26	....	....	....	215	....	....	....	....	....	....	....	....	....	....	....	....	....	....	....	....	....	....
1983-84	Hershey Bears	AHL	50	0	18	18	....	....	....	156	....	....	....	....	....	....	....	....	....	....	....	....	....	....	....	....	....	....
	Moncton Alpines	AHL	14	0	3	3	....	....	....	17	....	....	....	....	....	....	....	....	....	....	....	....	....	....	....	....	....	....
	Edmonton Oilers	NHL	....	....	....	....	....	....	....	....	....	....	....	....	....	....	....	....	....	....	6	0	1	1	0	....	....	....
1984-85	Edmonton Oilers	NHL	28	0	11	11	0	7	7	25	0	0	0	8	0.0	33	3	21	3	+12	12	1	3	4	26	0	0	0
	Nova Scotia Voyageurs	AHL	37	2	10	12	....	....	....	97	....	....	....	....	....	....	....	....	....	....	....	....	....	....	....	....	....	....
1985-86	Edmonton Oilers	NHL	6	2	3	5	2	2	4	11	0	0	0	4	50.0	11	0	5	2	+8	....	....	....	....	....	....	....	....
	Nova Scotia Oilers	AHL	19	2	8	10	....	....	....	72	....	....	....	....	....	....	....	....	....	....	....	....	....	....	....	....	....	....
	New York Rangers	NHL	46	1	8	9	1	5	6	65	0	0	0	33	3.0	45	1	58	16	+2	16	1	2	3	46	0	0	0
1986-87	New York Rangers	NHL	73	3	12	15	3	9	12	182	0	0	1	53	5.7	62	3	110	38	–13	6	0	0	0	4	0	0	0
1987-88	New York Rangers	NHL	14	0	1	1	0	1	1	34	0	0	0	8	0.0	9	0	21	5	–7	....	....	....	....	....	....	....	....
	Vancouver Canucks	NHL	49	2	3	5	2	2	4	73	0	0	0	32	6.3	41	0	73	20	–12	....	....	....	....	....	....	....	....
1988-89	Vancouver Canucks	NHL	74	3	11	14	3	8	11	82	0	1	1	59	5.1	50	1	62	16	+3	4	0	0	0	2	0	0	0
1989-90	Vancouver Canucks	NHL	67	0	2	2	0	1	1	91	0	0	0	45	0.0	37	0	84	20	–27	....	....	....	....	....	....	....	....
	NHL Totals		432	11	63	74	11	43	54	686	0	1	2	314	3.5	338	11	489	122		66	2	9	11	127	0	0	0

Traded to **Edmonton** by **Boston** for John Blum, March 6, 1984. Traded to **NY Rangers** by **Edmonton** with Todd Strueby for Mike Rogers, December 20, 1985. Traded to **Vancouver** by **NY Rangers** with Willie Huber for Michel Petit, November 4, 1987.

• MELROSE, BARRY

Barry Melrose D – R. 6', 205 lbs. b: Kelvington, Sask., 7/15/1956. Montreal's 4th choice, 36th overall, in 1976 Amateur Draft.

Season	Club	League	GP	G	A	Pts	AG	AA	APts	PIM	PP	SH	GW	S	%	TGF	PGF	TGA	PGA	+/-	GP	G	A	Pts	PIM	PP	SH	GW
1973-74	Weyburn Red Wings	SJHL	50	2	19	21	....	....	....	162	....	....	....	....	....	....	....	....	....	....	....	....	....	....	....	....	....	....
1974-75	Kamloops Chiefs	WCJHL	70	6	18	24	....	....	....	95	....	....	....	....	....	....	....	....	....	....	6	1	1	2	21	....	....	....
1975-76	Kamloops Chiefs	WHL	72	12	49	61	....	....	....	112	....	....	....	....	....	....	....	....	....	....	12	4	6	10	14	....	....	....
1976-77	Cincinnati Stingers	WHA	29	1	4	5	....	....	....	8	....	....	....	....	....	....	....	....	....	....	2	0	0	0	0	....	....	....
	Springfield Indians	AHL	23	0	3	3	....	....	....	17	....	....	....	....	....	....	....	....	....	....	....	....	....	....	....	....	....	....
1977-78	Cincinnati Stingers	WHA	69	2	9	11	....	....	....	113	....	....	....	....	....	....	....	....	....	....	....	....	....	....	....	....	....	....
1978-79	Cincinnati Stingers	WHA	80	2	14	16	....	....	....	222	....	....	....	....	....	....	....	....	....	....	3	0	1	1	8	....	....	....
1979-80	Winnipeg Jets	NHL	74	4	6	10	4	5	9	124	0	0	1	101	4.0	42	3	109	29	–41	....	....	....	....	....	....	....	....
1980-81	Winnipeg Jets	NHL	18	1	1	2	1	1	2	40	0	0	0	16	6.3	9	0	28	7	–12	....	....	....	....	....	....	....	....
	Toronto Maple Leafs	NHL	57	2	5	7	2	3	5	166	0	1	0	39	5.1	58	1	104	29	–18	3	0	1	1	15	0	0	0
1981-82	Toronto Maple Leafs	NHL	64	1	5	6	1	3	4	186	0	0	0	45	2.2	34	0	78	18	–26	....	....	....	....	....	....	....	....
1982-83	Toronto Maple Leafs	NHL	52	2	5	7	2	3	5	68	0	0	0	25	8.0	36	0	68	16	–16	4	0	1	1	23	0	0	0
	St. Catharines Saints	AHL	25	1	10	11	....	....	....	106	....	....	....	....	....	....	....	....	....	....	....	....	....	....	....	....	....	....

			REGULAR SEASON																		PLAYOFFS							
Season	Club	League	GP	G	A	Pts	AG	AA	APts	PIM	PP	SH	GW	S	%	TGF	PGF	TGA	PGA	+/–	GP	G	A	Pts	PIM	PP	SH	GW
1983-84	Detroit Red Wings	NHL	21	0	1	1	0	1	1	74	0	0	0	8	0.0	6	0	10	4	0	....	....	....	....	....	....	....	....
	Adirondack Red Wings	AHL	16	2	1	3	....	....	....	37	....	....	....	....	....	....	....	....	....	....	....	....	....	....	....	....	....	....
1984-85	Adirondack Red Wings	AHL	72	3	13	16	....	....	....	226	....	....	....	....	....	....	....	....	....	....	....	....	....	....	....	....	....	....
1985-86	Detroit Red Wings	NHL	14	0	0	0	0	0	0	70	0	0	0	2	0.0	6	0	13	1	–6	....	....	....	....	....	....	....	....
	Adirondack Red Wings	AHL	57	4	4	8	....	....	....	204	....	....	....	....	....	....	....	....	....	....	....	....	....	....	....	....	....	....
1986-87	Adirondack Red Wings	AHL	55	4	9	13	....	....	....	170	....	....	....	....	....	....	....	....	....	....	11	1	2	3	107	....	....	....
	NHL Totals		300	10	23	33	10	16	26	728	0	1	1	236	4.2	191	4	410	104		7	0	2	2	38	0	0	0
	Other Major League Totals		178	5	27	32	....	....	....	343	....	....	....	....	....	....	....	....	....		5	0	1	1	8	....	....	....

Selected by **Cincinnati** (WHA) in 1976 WHA Amateur Draft, May, 1976. Claimed by **Quebec** from **Cincinnati** (WHA) in WHA Dispersal Draft, June 8, 1979. Traded to **Winnipeg** by **Quebec** for Jamie Hislop and Barry Legge, June 28, 1979. Claimed on waivers by **Toronto** from **Winnipeg**, November 30, 1980. Signed as a free agent by **Detroit**, July 5, 1983.

• MENARD, HOWIE

Howie Menard C – R. 5′8″, 160 lbs. b: Timmins, Ont., 4/28/1942.

Season	Club	League	GP	G	A	Pts	AG	AA	APts	PIM	PP	SH	GW	S	%	TGF	PGF	TGA	PGA	+/–	GP	G	A	Pts	PIM	PP	SH	GW
1959-60	Toronto Marlboros	OHA	48	21	29	50	....	....	....	63	....	....	....	....	....	....	....	....	....	....	4	1	1	2	2	....	....	....
1960-61	Toronto Marlboros	OHA	21	11	9	20	....	....	....	34	....	....	....	....	....	....	....	....	....	....	....	....	....	....	....	....	....	....
	Hamilton Red Wings	OHA	24	7	7	14	....	....	....	29	....	....	....	....	....	....	....	....	....	....	12	4	6	10	35	....	....	....
1961-62	Hamilton Red Wings	OHA	48	12	32	44	....	....	....	87	....	....	....	....	....	....	....	....	....	....	10	6	4	10	*30	....	....	....
1962-63	Pittsburgh Hornets	AHL	69	16	29	45	....	....	....	62	....	....	....	....	....	....	....	....	....	....	....	....	....	....	....	....	....	....
1963-64	Detroit Red Wings	NHL	3	0	0	0	0	0	0	0	....	....	....	....	....	....	....	....	....	....	....	....	....	....	....	....	....	....
	Cincinnati Wings	CHL	69	25	37	62	....	....	....	75	....	....	....	....	....	....	....	....	....	....	....	....	....	....	....	....	....	....
1964-65	Memphis Wings	CHL	61	9	33	42	....	....	....	66	....	....	....	....	....	....	....	....	....	....	....	....	....	....	....	....	....	....
1965-66	Springfield Indians	AHL	71	15	42	57	....	....	....	42	....	....	....	....	....	....	....	....	....	....	6	3	2	5	10	....	....	....
1966-67	Springfield Indians	AHL	68	25	39	64	....	....	....	52	....	....	....	....	....	....	....	....	....	....	....	....	....	....	....	....	....	....
1967-68	Los Angeles Kings	NHL	35	9	15	24	11	16	27	32	1	0	5	86	10.5	28	3	21	0	+4	7	0	5	5	24	0	0	0
	Springfield Kings	AHL	37	18	33	51	....	....	....	33	....	....	....	....	....	....	....	....	....	....	....	....	....	....	....	....	....	....
1968-69	Los Angeles Kings	NHL	56	10	17	27	11	16	27	31	1	0	1	94	10.6	38	3	35	0	0	11	3	2	5	12	1	0	0
	Springfield Kings	AHL	20	3	15	18	....	....	....	18	....	....	....	....	....	....	....	....	....	....	....	....	....	....	....	....	....	....
1969-70	Chicago Black Hawks	NHL	19	2	3	5	2	3	5	8	1	0	0	10	20.0	7	1	1	0	+5	....	....	....	....	....	....	....	....
	Oakland Seals	NHL	38	2	7	9	2	7	9	16	0	0	0	52	3.8	14	2	31	14	–5	1	0	0	0	0	0	0	0
1970-71	Providence Reds	AHL	59	10	21	31	....	....	....	75	....	....	....	....	....	....	....	....	....	....	1	0	0	0	2	....	....	....
1971-72	Baltimore Clippers	AHL	73	26	30	56	....	....	....	79	....	....	....	....	....	....	....	....	....	....	18	5	13	18	28	....	....	....
1972-73	Salt Lake Golden Eagles	WHL	59	12	38	50	....	....	....	46	....	....	....	....	....	....	....	....	....	....	9	4	3	7	12	....	....	....
1973-74	Baltimore Clippers	AHL	73	42	39	81	....	....	....	66	....	....	....	....	....	....	....	....	....	....	9	3	3	6	13	....	....	....
1974-75	Baltimore Clippers	AHL	43	14	18	32	....	....	....	44	....	....	....	....	....	....	....	....	....	....	....	....	....	....	....	....	....	....
	Providence Reds	AHL	10	1	2	3	....	....	....	20	....	....	....	....	....	....	....	....	....	....	3	0	0	0	0	....	....	....
1975-76	Baltimore Clippers	AHL	38	7	11	18	....	....	....	30	....	....	....	....	....	....	....	....	....	....	....	....	....	....	....	....	....	....
	Whitby Warriors	OHA Sr.	23	11	8	19	....	....	....	14	....	....	....	....	....	....	....	....	....	....	....	....	....	....	....	....	....	....
1976-77	Whitby Warriors	OHA Sr.	2	0	1	1	....	....	....	0	....	....	....	....	....	....	....	....	....	....	....	....	....	....	....	....	....	....
	NHL Totals		151	23	42	65	26	42	68	87	3	0	6	242	9.5	87	9	88	14		19	3	7	10	36	1	0	0

Claimed by **Springfield** (AHL) from **Detroit** in Reverse Draft, June, 1965. NHL rights transferred to **LA Kings** after NHL club purchased **Springfield** (AHL) franchise, May, 1967. Claimed by **Chicago** from **LA Kings** in Intra-League Draft, June 11, 1969. Traded to **Oakland** by **Chicago** for Gene Ubriaco, December 15, 1969. Claimed by **Buffalo** from **Oakland** in Expansion Draft, June 10, 1970. Traded to **California** by **Buffalo** for cash, October, 1970.

• MERCREDI, VIC

Vic Mercredi C – R. 5′11″, 185 lbs. b: Yellowknife, NWT, 3/31/1953. Atlanta's 2nd choice, 16th overall, in 1973 Amateur Draft.

Season	Club	League	GP	G	A	Pts	AG	AA	APts	PIM	PP	SH	GW	S	%	TGF	PGF	TGA	PGA	+/–	GP	G	A	Pts	PIM	PP	SH	GW
1969-70	Penticton Panthers	BCJHL	48	16	18	34	....	....	....	....	....	....	....	....	....	....	....	....	....	....	....	....	....	....	....	....	....	....
1970-71	Penticton Panthers	BCJHL	51	50	56	106	....	....	....	38	....	....	....	....	....	....	....	....	....	....	....	....	....	....	....	....	....	....
1971-72	New Westminster Bruins	WCJHL	68	24	30	54	....	....	....	87	....	....	....	....	....	....	....	....	....	....	....	....	....	....	....	....	....	....
1972-73	New Westminster Bruins	WCJHL	67	52	61	113	....	....	....	135	....	....	....	....	....	....	....	....	....	....	....	....	....	....	....	....	....	....
1973-74	Omaha Knights	CHL	68	21	36	57	....	....	....	34	....	....	....	....	....	....	....	....	....	....	5	1	2	3	2	....	....	....
1974-75	Atlanta Flames	NHL	2	0	0	0	0	0	0	0	0	0	0	0	0.0	0	0	0	0	0	....	....	....	....	....	....	....	....
	Omaha Knights	CHL	64	10	16	26	....	....	....	16	....	....	....	....	....	....	....	....	....	....	6	0	0	0	0	....	....	....
1975-76	Calgary Cowboys	WHA	3	0	0	0	....	....	....	29	....	....	....	....	....	....	....	....	....	....	....	....	....	....	....	....	....	....
	Baltimore Clippers	AHL	52	6	9	15	....	....	....	15	....	....	....	....	....	....	....	....	....	....	....	....	....	....	....	....	....	....
1976-77	DID NOT PLAY – INJURED																											
1977-78	Springfield Indians	AHL	1	0	0	0	....	....	....	0	....	....	....	....	....	....	....	....	....	....	....	....	....	....	....	....	....	....
	Phoenix Roadrunners	PHL	42	16	24	40	....	....	....	48	....	....	....	....	....	....	....	....	....	....	....	....	....	....	....	....	....	....
1978-79	Tucson Rustlers	PHL	29	8	20	28	....	....	....	4	....	....	....	....	....	....	....	....	....	....	....	....	....	....	....	....	....	....
	NHL Totals		2	0	0	0	0	0	0	0	0	0	0	0	0.0	0	0	0	0		....	....	....	....	....	....	....	....
	Other Major League Totals		3	0	0	0	....	....	....	29	....	....	....	....	....	....	....	....	....		....	....	....	....	....	....	....	....

Selected by **Houston** (WHA) in 1973 WHA Amateur Player Draft, May, 1973. WHA rights traded to **Calgary** (WHA) by **Houston** (WHA) for future considerations, March, 1976.

• MEREDITH, GREG

Greg Meredith RW – R. 6′1″, 210 lbs. b: Toronto, Ont., 2/23/1958. Atlanta's 5th choice, 97th overall, in 1978 Amateur Draft.

Season	Club	League	GP	G	A	Pts	AG	AA	APts	PIM	PP	SH	GW	S	%	TGF	PGF	TGA	PGA	+/–	GP	G	A	Pts	PIM	PP	SH	GW
1976-77	University of Notre Dame	WCHA	34	21	20	41	....	....	....	18	....	....	....	....	....	....	....	....	....	....	....	....	....	....	....	....	....	....
1977-78	University of Notre Dame	WCHA	38	13	13	26	....	....	....	24	....	....	....	....	....	....	....	....	....	....	....	....	....	....	....	....	....	....
1978-79	University of Notre Dame	WCHA	35	28	22	50	....	....	....	14	....	....	....	....	....	....	....	....	....	....	....	....	....	....	....	....	....	....
1979-80	University of Notre Dame	WCHA	40	42	31	71	....	....	....	80	....	....	....	....	....	....	....	....	....	....	....	....	....	....	....	....	....	....
1980-81	Calgary Flames	NHL	3	1	0	1	1	0	1	0	0	0	0	5	20.0	1	0	0	0	+1	....	....	....	....	....	....	....	....
	Birmingham Bulls	CHL	39	17	10	27	....	....	....	36	....	....	....	....	....	....	....	....	....	....	....	....	....	....	....	....	....	....
	Tulsa Oilers	CHL	10	6	4	10	....	....	....	12	....	....	....	....	....	....	....	....	....	....	....	....	....	....	....	....	....	....
1981-82	Oklahoma City Stars	CHL	80	10	23	33	....	....	....	64	....	....	....	....	....	....	....	....	....	....	4	2	0	2	6	....	....	....
1982-83	Calgary Flames	NHL	35	5	4	9	4	3	7	8	2	1	0	39	12.8	24	8	23	2	–5	5	3	1	4	4	0	1	2
	Colorado Flames	CHL	36	16	10	26	....	....	....	14	....	....	....	....	....	....	....	....	....	....	....	....	....	....	....	....	....	....
1983-84	Colorado Flames	CHL	54	23	20	43	....	....	....	39	....	....	....	....	....	....	....	....	....	....	6	1	2	3	9	....	....	....
	NHL Totals		38	6	4	10	5	3	8	8	2	1	0	44	13.6	25	8	23	2		5	3	1	4	4	0	1	2

WCHA First All-Star Team (1980) • NCAA West First All-American Team (1980)

Transferred to **Calgary** after **Atlanta** franchise relocated, June 24, 1980.

• MERKOSKY, GLENN

Glenn Merkosky C – L. 5′10″, 185 lbs. b: Edmonton, Alta., 4/8/1959.

Season	Club	League	GP	G	A	Pts	AG	AA	APts	PIM	PP	SH	GW	S	%	TGF	PGF	TGA	PGA	+/–	GP	G	A	Pts	PIM	PP	SH	GW
1977-78	Kelowna Packers	BCJHL	....	52	90	142	....	....	....	....	....	....	....	....	....	....	....	....	....	....	....	....	....	....	....	....	....	....
	Seattle Breakers	WCJHL	6	5	2	7	....	....	....	2	....	....	....	....	....	....	....	....	....	....	....	....	....	....	....	....	....	....
1978-79	Michigan Tech Huskies	WCHA	38	14	29	43	....	....	....	22	....	....	....	....	....	....	....	....	....	....	....	....	....	....	....	....	....	....
1979-80	Calgary Wranglers	WHL	72	49	40	89	....	....	....	95	....	....	....	....	....	....	....	....	....	....	7	4	6	10	14	....	....	....
1980-81	Binghamton Whalers	AHL	80	26	35	61	....	....	....	61	....	....	....	....	....	....	....	....	....	....	5	0	2	2	2	....	....	....
1981-82	Hartford Whalers	NHL	7	0	0	0	0	0	0	2	0	0	0	2	0.0	2	0	3	0	–1	....	....	....	....	....	....	....	....
	Binghamton Whalers	AHL	72	29	40	69	....	....	....	83	....	....	....	....	....	....	....	....	....	....	10	0	2	2	2	....	....	....
1982-83	New Jersey Devils	NHL	34	4	10	14	3	7	10	20	1	0	0	43	9.3	17	1	42	16	–10	....	....	....	....	....	....	....	....
	Wichita Wind	CHL	45	26	23	49	....	....	....	15	....	....	....	....	....	....	....	....	....	....	....	....	....	....	....	....	....	....
1983-84	New Jersey Devils	NHL	5	1	0	1	1	0	1	0	0	0	0	6	16.7	1	0	2	1	0	....	....	....	....	....	....	....	....
	Maine Mariners	AHL	75	28	28	56	....	....	....	56	....	....	....	....	....	....	....	....	....	....	17	11	10	21	20	....	....	....
1984-85	Maine Mariners	AHL	80	38	38	76	....	....	....	19	....	....	....	....	....	....	....	....	....	....	11	2	3	5	13	....	....	....
1985-86	Detroit Red Wings	NHL	17	0	2	2	0	1	1	0	0	0	0	18	0.0	5	0	28	11	–12	....	....	....	....	....	....	....	....
	Adirondack Red Wings	AHL	59	24	33	57	....	....	....	22	....	....	....	....	....	....	....	....	....	....	17	5	7	12	15	....	....	....
1986-87	Adirondack Red Wings	AHL	77	*54	31	85	....	....	....	66	....	....	....	....	....	....	....	....	....	....	11	6	8	14	7	....	....	....
1987-88	Adirondack Red Wings	AHL	66	34	42	76	....	....	....	34	....	....	....	....	....	....	....	....	....	....	11	4	6	10	4	....	....	....
	SB Rosenheim	Germany	6	2	3	5	....	....	....	17	....	....	....	....	....	....	....	....	....	....	....	....	....	....	....	....	....	....
1988-89	Adirondack Red Wings	AHL	76	31	46	77	....	....	....	13	....	....	....	....	....	....	....	....	....	....	17	8	11	19	10	....	....	....

			REGULAR SEASON																		PLAYOFFS							
Season	Club	League	GP	G	A	Pts	AG	AA	APts	PIM	PP	SH	GW	S	%	TGF	PGF	TGA	PGA	+/–	GP	G	A	Pts	PIM	PP	SH	GW
1989-90	Detroit Red Wings	NHL	3	0	0	0	0	0	0	0	0	0	0	0	0.0	0	0	0	0	0	....	....	....	....	....	....	....	....
	Adirondack Red Wings	AHL	75	33	31	64	....	....	....	29	....	....	....	....	....	....	....	....	....	....	6	2	1	3	6	....	....	....
1990-91	Adirondack Red Wings	AHL	77	28	39	57	....	....	....	37	....	....	....	....	....	....	....	....	....	....	2	1	1	2	0	....	....	....
	NHL Totals		66	5	12	17	4	8	12	22	1	0	0	69	7.2	25	1	75	28		....	....	....	....	....	....	....	....

AHL Second All-Star Team (1985) • AHL First All-Star Team (1987) • Won Fred T. Hunt Memorial Trophy (Sportsmanship - AHL) (1987, 1991)

Signed as a free agent by **Hartford**, August 10, 1980. Signed as a free agent by **New Jersey**, September 14, 1982. Signed as a free agent by **Detroit**, July 15, 1985.

• MERRICK, WAYNE

Wayne "Bones" Merrick C – L. 6'1", 195 lbs. b: Sarnia, Ont., 4/23/1952. St. Louis' 1st choice, 9th overall, in 1972 Amateur Draft.

Season	Club	League	GP	G	A	Pts	AG	AA	APts	PIM	PP	SH	GW	S	%	TGF	PGF	TGA	PGA	+/–	GP	G	A	Pts	PIM	PP	SH	GW
1969-70	Ottawa 67's	OHA	51	10	17	27	....	....	....	10	....	....	....	....	....	....	....	....	....	....	....	....	....	....	....	....	....	....
1970-71	Ottawa 67's	OHA	62	34	42	76	....	....	....	41	....	....	....	....	....	....	....	....	....	....	....	....	....	....	....	....	....	....
1971-72	Ottawa 67's	OHA	62	39	56	95	....	....	....	21	....	....	....	....	....	....	....	....	....	....	....	....	....	....	....	....	....	....
1972-73	St. Louis Blues	NHL	50	10	11	21	10	9	19	10	3	0	0	81	12.3	26	3	27	2	–2	5	0	1	1	2	0	0	0
	Denver Spurs	WHL	22	6	13	19	....	....	....	6	....	....	....	....	....	....	....	....	....	....	....	....	....	....	....	....	....	....
1973-74	St. Louis Blues	NHL	64	20	23	43	20	20	40	32	2	0	4	147	13.6	55	7	73	14	–11	....	....	....	....	....	....	....	....
1974-75	St. Louis Blues	NHL	76	28	37	65	26	29	55	57	2	0	3	205	13.7	95	20	48	2	+29	2	1	1	2	0	1	0	0
1975-76	St. Louis Blues	NHL	19	7	8	15	7	6	13	0	1	0	0	56	12.5	17	4	15	2	0	....	....	....	....	....	....	....	....
	California Golden Seals	NHL	56	25	27	52	23	21	44	36	7	0	4	190	13.2	66	25	44	0	–3	....	....	....	....	....	....	....	....
1976-77	Cleveland Barons	NHL	80	18	38	56	17	31	48	25	4	0	2	201	9.0	76	26	71	0	–21	....	....	....	....	....	....	....	....
	Canada	WEC-A	10	4	3	7	....	....	....	10	....	....	....	....	....	....	....	....	....	....	....	....	....	....	....	....	....	....
1977-78	Cleveland Barons	NHL	18	2	5	7	2	4	6	8	0	0	0	42	4.8	13	7	17	1	–10	....	....	....	....	....	....	....	....
	New York Islanders	NHL	37	10	14	24	10	11	21	8	2	0	2	60	16.7	31	5	24	0	+2	7	1	0	1	0	0	0	0
1978-79	New York Islanders	NHL	75	20	21	41	18	16	34	24	2	0	0	128	15.6	58	4	41	0	+13	10	2	3	5	2	0	0	0
1979-80	New York Islanders	NHL	70	13	22	35	12	17	29	16	2	0	4	111	11.7	49	5	32	0	+12	21	2	4	6	2	0	0	1
1980-81	New York Islanders	NHL	71	16	15	31	13	10	23	30	1	0	2	89	18.0	43	5	28	2	+12	18	6	12	18	8	0	0	1
1981-82	New York Islanders	NHL	68	12	27	39	9	18	27	20	1	0	3	112	10.7	56	5	47	0	+4	19	6	6	12	6	0	0	1
1982-83	New York Islanders	NHL	59	4	12	16	3	8	11	27	1	0	2	46	8.7	20	3	20	0	–3	19	1	3	4	10	0	0	0
1983-84	New York Islanders	NHL	31	6	5	11	5	3	8	10	0	0	0	32	18.8	14	0	12	0	+2	1	0	0	0	0	0	0	0
	NHL Totals		774	191	265	456	175	203	378	303	28	0	26	1500	12.7	619	119	499	23		102	19	30	49	30	1	0	3

Traded to **California** by **St. Louis** for Larry Patey and California's 3rd round choice (traded back to California — California/Cleveland selected Reg Kerr) in 1977 Amateur Draft, November 24, 1975. Transferred to **Cleveland** after **California** franchise relocated, August 26, 1976. Traded to **NY Islanders** by **Cleveland** with Darcy Regier and Cleveland's 4th round choice - draft choice cancelled by the Cleveland-Minnesota merger - in 1978 Amateur Draft for Jean-Paul Parise and Jean Potvin, January 10, 1978.

• MESSIER, ERIC

Eric Messier D – L. 6'2", 200 lbs. b: Drummondville, Que., 10/29/1973.

Season	Club	League	GP	G	A	Pts	AG	AA	APts	PIM	PP	SH	GW	S	%	TGF	PGF	TGA	PGA	+/–	GP	G	A	Pts	PIM	PP	SH	GW
1991-92	Trois-Rivieres Draveurs	QMJHL	58	2	10	12	....	....	....	28	....	....	....	....	....	....	....	....	....	....	15	2	2	4	13	....	....	....
1992-93	Sherbrooke Faucons	QMJHL	51	4	17	21	....	....	....	82	....	....	....	....	....	....	....	....	....	....	15	0	4	4	18	....	....	....
1993-94	Sherbrooke Faucons	QMJHL	67	4	24	28	....	....	....	69	....	....	....	....	....	....	....	....	....	....	12	1	7	8	14	....	....	....
1994-95	Univ. of Quebec at Trois-Rivieres	OUAA	13	8	5	13	....	....	....	20	....	....	....	....	....	....	....	....	....	....	4	0	3	3	8	....	....	....
1995-96	Cornwall Aces	AHL	72	5	9	14	....	....	....	111	....	....	....	....	....	....	....	....	....	....	8	1	1	2	20	....	....	....
1996-97	Colorado Avalanche	NHL	21	0	0	0	0	0	0	4	0	0	0	11	0.0	17	0	13	3	+7	6	0	0	0	4	0	0	0
	Hershey Bears	AHL	55	16	26	42	....	....	....	69	....	....	....	....	....	....	....	....	....	....	5	2	4	6	12	....	....	....
1997-98	Colorado Avalanche	NHL	62	4	12	16	5	12	17	20	0	0	0	66	6.1	56	16	43	7	+4	....	....	....	....	....	....		
	NHL Totals		83	4	12	16	5	12	17	24	0	0	0	77	5.2	73	16	56	10		6	0	0	0	4	0	0	0

QMJHL Second All-Star Team (1994)

Signed as a free agent by **Colorado**, June 14, 1995.

• MESSIER, JOBY

Joby Messier D – R. 6', 200 lbs. b: Regina, Sask., 3/2/1970. NY Rangers' 7th choice, 118th overall, in 1989 Entry Draft.

Season	Club	League	GP	G	A	Pts	AG	AA	APts	PIM	PP	SH	GW	S	%	TGF	PGF	TGA	PGA	+/–	GP	G	A	Pts	PIM	PP	SH	GW
1988-89	Michigan State Spartans	CCHA	39	2	10	12	....	....	....	66	....	....	....	....	....	....	....	....	....	....	....	....	....	....	....	....	....	....
1989-90	Michigan State Spartans	CCHA	42	1	11	12	....	....	....	58	....	....	....	....	....	....	....	....	....	....	....	....	....	....	....	....	....	....
1990-91	Michigan State Spartans	CCHA	39	5	11	16	....	....	....	71	....	....	....	....	....	....	....	....	....	....	....	....	....	....	....	....	....	....
1991-92	Michigan State Spartans	CCHA	41	13	15	28	....	....	....	81	....	....	....	....	....	....	....	....	....	....	....	....	....	....	....	....	....	....
1992-93	New York Rangers	NHL	11	0	0	0	0	0	0	6	0	0	0	11	0.0	5	0	7	2	0	....	....	....	....	....	....	....	....
	Binghamton Rangers	AHL	60	5	16	21	....	....	....	63	....	....	....	....	....	....	....	....	....	....	14	1	1	2	6	....	....	....
1993-94	New York Rangers	NHL	4	0	2	2	0	2	2	0	0	0	0	7	0.0	3	1	4	1	–1	....	....	....	....	....	....	....	....
	Binghamton Rangers	AHL	42	6	14	20	....	....	....	58	....	....	....	....	....	....	....	....	....	....	....	....	....	....	....	....	....	....
1994-95	New York Rangers	NHL	10	0	2	2	0	3	3	18	0	0	0	4	0.0	5	0	4	1	+2	....	....	....	....	....	....	....	....
	Binghamton Rangers	AHL	25	2	9	11	....	....	....	36	....	....	....	....	....	....	....	....	....		1	0	0	0	0	....	....	....
1995-96			DID NOT PLAY – INJURED																									
1996-97	Utah Grizzlies	IHL	44	6	20	26	....	....	....	41	....	....	....	....	....	....	....	....	....	....	7	0	1	1	10	....	....	....
1997-98	Long Beach Ice Dogs	IHL	24	0	3	3	....	....	....	45	....	....	....	....	....	....	....	....	....	....	....	....	....	....	....	....	....	....
	NHL Totals		25	0	4	4	0	5	5	24	0	0	0	22	0.0	13	1	15	4		....	....	....	....	....	....	....	

CCHA First All-Star Team (1992) • NCAA West First All-American Team (1992)

Signed as a free agent by **NY Islanders**, September 26, 1995.

• MESSIER, MARK

Mark Messier C – L. 6'1", 205 lbs. b: Edmonton, Alta., 1/18/1961. Edmonton's 2nd choice, 48th overall, in 1979 Entry Draft.

Season	Club	League	GP	G	A	Pts	AG	AA	APts	PIM	PP	SH	GW	S	%	TGF	PGF	TGA	PGA	+/–	GP	G	A	Pts	PIM	PP	SH	GW
1976-77	Spruce Grove Mets	AJHL	57	27	39	55	....	....	....	91	....	....	....	....	....	....	....	....	....	....	....	....	....	....	....	....	....	....
1977-78	St. Albert Saints	AJHL	STATISTICS NOT AVAILABLE																									
	Portland Winter Hawks	WCJHL	....	....	....	....	....	....	....	....	....	....	....	....	....	....	....	....	....	....	7	4	1	5	2	....		
1978-79	Indianapolis Racers	WHA	5	0	0	0	....	....	....	0	....	....	....	....	....	....	....	....	....		....	....	....	....	....	....	....	....
	Cincinnati Stingers	WHA	47	1	10	11	....	....	....	58	....	....	....	....	....	....	....	....	....	....	....	....	....	....	....	....	....	....
1979-80	Edmonton Oilers	NHL	75	12	21	33	11	16	27	120	1	1	1	113	10.6	50	6	62	8	–10	3	1	2	3	2	0	1	0
	Houston Apollos	CHL	4	0	3	3	....	....	....	4	....	....	....	....	....	....	....	....	....	....	....	....	....	....	....	....	....	....
1980-81	Edmonton Oilers	NHL	72	23	40	63	19	28	47	102	4	0	1	179	12.8	82	17	107	30	–12	9	2	5	7	13	0	0	0
1981-82	Edmonton Oilers	NHL	78	50	38	88	40	25	65	119	10	0	3	235	21.3	135	32	95	13	+21	5	1	2	3	8	0	0	0
1982-83	Edmonton Oilers	NHL	77	48	58	106	40	40	80	72	12	1	2	237	20.3	150	47	118	34	+19	15	15	6	21	14	4	2	0
1983-84	Edmonton Oilers	NHL	73	37	64	101	30	43	73	165	7	4	7	219	16.9	140	40	85	25	+40	19	8	18	26	19	1	1	2
1984-85	Canada	C Cup	8	2	4	6	....	....	....	8	....	....	....	....	....	....	....	....	....	....	....	....	....	....	....	....	....	....
	Edmonton Oilers	NHL	55	23	31	54	19	21	40	57	4	5	1	136	16.9	74	20	71	25	+8	18	12	13	25	12	1	1	1
1985-86	Edmonton Oilers	NHL	63	35	49	84	28	33	61	68	10	5	7	201	17.4	116	33	71	24	+36	10	4	6	10	18	0	2	0
1986-87	Edmonton Oilers	NHL	77	37	70	107	32	51	83	73	7	4	5	208	17.8	130	39	108	38	+21	21	12	16	28	16	1	2	1
	NHL All-Stars	RV'87	2	1	0	1	....	....	....	0	....	....	....	....	....	....	....	....	....	....	....	....	....	....	....	....	....	....
1987-88	Canada	C Cup	9	1	6	7	....	....	....	6	....	....	....	....	....	....	....	....	....	....	....	....	....	....	....	....	....	....
	Edmonton Oilers	NHL	77	37	74	111	32	53	85	103	12	3	7	182	20.3	149	54	114	40	+21	19	11	23	34	29	7	1	0
1988-89	Edmonton Oilers	NHL	72	33	61	94	28	43	71	130	6	6	4	164	20.1	117	46	107	31	–5	7	1	11	12	8	0	0	0
	Canada	WEC-A	6	3	3	6	....	....	....	8	....	....	....	....	....	....	....	....	....	....	....	....	....	....	....	....	....	....
1989-90	Edmonton Oilers	NHL	79	45	84	129	39	60	99	79	13	6	3	211	21.3	159	60	117	37	+19	22	9	*22	31	20	1	1	1
1990-91	Edmonton Oilers	NHL	53	12	52	64	11	39	50	34	3	1	2	109	11.0	86	30	63	22	+15	18	4	11	15	16	1	0	0
1991-92	Canada	C Cup	8	2	6	8	....	....	....	10	....	....	....	....	....	....	....	....	....	....	....	....	....	....	....	....	....	....
	New York Rangers	NHL	79	35	72	107	32	54	86	76	12	4	6	212	16.5	150	48	92	21	+31	11	7	7	14	6	2	2	0
1992-93	New York Rangers	NHL	75	25	66	91	21	45	66	72	7	2	2	215	11.6	118	44	106	26	–6	....	....	....	....	....	....	....	....
1993-94	New York Rangers	NHL	76	26	58	84	24	45	69	76	6	2	5	216	12.0	127	56	81	35	+25	23	12	10	30	33	2	1	4
1994-95	New York Rangers	NHL	40	14	39	53	25	58	83	40	3	3	2	126	11.1	71	30	50	17	+8	10	3	10	13	8	2	0	1

			REGULAR SEASON																		PLAYOFFS							
Season	Club	League	GP	G	A	Pts	AG	AA	APts	PIM	PP	SH	GW	S	%	TGF	PGF	TGA	PGA	+/–	GP	G	A	Pts	PIM	PP	SH	GW
1995-96	**New York Rangers**	**NHL**	**74**	**47**	**52**	**99**	**46**	**43**	**89**	**122**	**14**	**1**	**5**	**241**	**19.5**	**129**	**48**	**98**	**46**	**+29**	**11**	**4**	**7**	**11**	**16**	**2**	**0**	**1**
1996-97	Canada	W Cup	7	1	4	5	....	....	....	12	....	....	....	....	....	....	....	....	....	....	....	....	....	....	....	....	....	....
	New York Rangers	**NHL**	**71**	**36**	**48**	**84**	**38**	**43**	**81**	**88**	**7**	**5**	**9**	**227**	**15.9**	**105**	**30**	**95**	**32**	**+12**	**15**	**3**	**9**	**12**	**6**	**0**	**0**	**1**
1997-98	**Vancouver Canucks**	**NHL**	**82**	**22**	**38**	**60**	**26**	**37**	**63**	**58**	**8**	**2**	**2**	**139**	**15.8**	**100**	**36**	**113**	**39**	**–10**	....	....	....	....	....	....	....	....
	NHL Totals		**1354**	**597**	**1015**	**1612**	**541**	**777**	**1318**	**1654**	**146**	**55**	**74**	**3570**	**16.7**	**2188**	**716**	**1753**	**543**		***236**	**109**	**186**	**295**	**244**	**24**	**14**	**12**
	Other Major League Totals		52	1	10	11	....	....	....	58	....	....	....	....	....	....	....	....	....		....	....	....	....	....	....	....	....

NHL First All-Star Team (1982, 1983, 1990, 1992) • NHL Second All-Star Team (1984) • Won Conn Smythe Trophy (1984) • Won Hart Trophy (1990, 1992) • Won Lester B. Pearson Award (1990, 1992)

Played in NHL All-Star Game (1982, 1983, 1984, 1985, 1986, 1988, 1989, 1990, 1991, 1992, 1994, 1996, 1997, 1998)

Signed as an underage free agent by **Indianapolis** (WHA) to 10-game tryout contract, November 5, 1978. Signed as a free agent by **Cincinnati** (WHA) after **Indianapolis** (WHA) franchise folded, December, 1978. Traded to **NY Rangers** by **Edmonton** with future considerations for Bernie Nicholls, Steven Rice and Louie DeBrusk, October 4, 1991. Signed as a free agent by **Vancouver**, July 30, 1997.

• MESSIER, MITCH

Mitch Messier C – R. 6'2", 200 lbs. b: Regina, Sask., 8/21/1965. Minnesota's 4th choice, 57th overall, in 1983 Entry Draft.

Season	Club	League	GP	G	A	Pts	AG	AA	APts	PIM	PP	SH	GW	S	%	TGF	PGF	TGA	PGA	+/–	GP	G	A	Pts	PIM	PP	SH	GW
1981-82	Notre Dame Hounds	SJHL	26	8	20	28	....	....	....	....	....	....	....	....	....	....	....	....	....	....	....	....	....	....	....	....	....	....
1982-83	Notre Dame Hounds	SJHL	60	*108	73	*181	....	....	....	160	....	....	....	....	....	....	....	....	....	....	....	....	....	....	....	....	....	....
1983-84	Michigan State Spartans	CCHA	37	6	15	21	....	....	....	22	....	....	....	....	....	....	....	....	....	....	....	....	....	....	....	....	....	....
1984-85	Michigan State Spartans	CCHA	42	12	21	33	....	....	....	46	....	....	....	....	....	....	....	....	....	....	....	....	....	....	....	....	....	....
1985-86	Michigan State Spartans	CCHA	38	24	40	64	....	....	....	36	....	....	....	....	....	....	....	....	....	....	....	....	....	....	....	....	....	....
1986-87	Michigan State Spartans	CCHA	45	44	48	92	....	....	....	89	....	....	....	....	....	....	....	....	....	....	....	....	....	....	....	....	....	....
1987-88	**Minnesota North Stars**	**NHL**	**13**	**0**	**1**	**1**	**0**	**1**	**1**	**11**	**0**	**0**	**0**	**5**	**0.0**	**2**	**0**	**7**	**0**	**–5**	....	....	....	....	....	....	....	....
	Kalamazoo Wings	IHL	69	29	37	66	....	....	....	42	....	....	....	....	....	....	....	....	....	....	4	2	1	3	0	....	....	....
1988-89	**Minnesota North Stars**	**NHL**	**3**	**0**	**1**	**1**	**0**	**1**	**1**	**0**	**0**	**0**	**0**	**3**	**0.0**	**3**	**0**	**4**	**0**	**–1**	....	....	....	....	....	....	....	....
	Kalamazoo Wings	IHL	67	34	46	80	....	....	....	71	....	....	....	....	....	....	....	....	....	....	6	4	3	7	0	....	....	....
1989-90	**Minnesota North Stars**	**NHL**	**2**	**0**	**0**	**0**	**0**	**0**	**0**	**0**	**0**	**0**	**0**	**1**	**0.0**	**0**	**0**	**2**	**0**	**–2**	....	....	....	....	....	....	....	....
	Kalamazoo Wings	IHL	65	26	58	84	....	....	....	56	....	....	....	....	....	....	....	....	....	....	8	4	3	7	25	....	....	....
1990-91	**Minnesota North Stars**	**NHL**	**2**	**0**	**0**	**0**	**0**	**0**	**0**	**0**	**0**	**0**	**0**	**0**	**0.0**	**0**	**0**	**2**	**0**	**–2**	....	....	....	....	....	....	....	....
	Kalamazoo Wings	IHL	73	30	46	76	....	....	....	34	....	....	....	....	....	....	....	....	....	....	11	4	8	12	2	....	....	....
1991-92	Kalamazoo Wings	IHL	77	43	33	76	....	....	....	42	....	....	....	....	....	....	....	....	....	....	12	3	3	6	25	....	....	....
1992-93	Milwaukee Admirals	IHL	62	18	23	41	....	....	....	84	....	....	....	....	....	....	....	....	....	....	6	0	1	1	0	....	....	....
1993-94	Fort Wayne Komets	IHL	69	33	27	60	....	....	....	77	....	....	....	....	....	....	....	....	....	....	14	8	6	14	14	....	....	....
	NHL Totals		**20**	**0**	**2**	**2**	**0**	**2**	**2**	**11**	**0**	**0**	**0**	**9**	**0.0**	**5**	**0**	**15**	**0**		....	....	....	....	....	....	....	....

CCHA First All-Star Team (1987) • NCAA West First All-American Team (1987)

• MESSIER, PAUL

Paul Messier C – R. 6'1", 185 lbs. b: Nottingham, England, 1/27/1958. Colorado's 3rd choice, 41st overall, in 1978 Amateur Draft.

Season	Club	League	GP	G	A	Pts	AG	AA	APts	PIM	PP	SH	GW	S	%	TGF	PGF	TGA	PGA	+/–	GP	G	A	Pts	PIM	PP	SH	GW
1973-74	Edmonton Mets	AJHL	59	37	39	76	....	....	....	43	....	....	....	....	....	....	....	....	....	....	....	....	....	....	....	....	....	....
1974-75	Spruce Grove Mets	AJHL	57	45	56	101	....	....	....	48	....	....	....	....	....	....	....	....	....	....	11	7	*13	20	10	....	....	....
1975-76	Spruce Grove Mets	AJHL	44	32	45	77	....	....	....	46	....	....	....	....	....	....	....	....	....	....	10	4	12	16	11	....	....	....
1976-77	University of Denver	WCHA	30	15	12	27	....	....	....	47	....	....	....	....	....	....	....	....	....	....	....	....	....	....	....	....	....	....
1977-78	University of Denver	WCHA	38	20	31	51	....	....	....	53	....	....	....	....	....	....	....	....	....	....	....	....	....	....	....	....	....	....
1978-79	**Colorado Rockies**	**NHL**	**9**	**0**	**0**	**0**	**0**	**0**	**0**	**4**	**0**	**0**	**0**	**9**	**0.0**	**2**	**0**	**8**	**0**	**–6**	....	....	....	....	....	....	....	....
	Philadelphia Firebirds	AHL	16	2	3	5	....	....	....	18	....	....	....	....	....	....	....	....	....	....	....	....	....	....	....	....	....	....
	Tulsa Oilers	CHL	27	3	4	7	....	....	....	11	....	....	....	....	....	....	....	....	....	....	....	....	....	....	....	....	....	....
1979-80	Fort Worth Texans	CHL	7	0	1	1	....	....	....	2	....	....	....	....	....	....	....	....	....	....	....	....	....	....	....	....	....	....
	Birmingham Bulls	CHL	50	6	14	20	....	....	....	14	....	....	....	....	....	....	....	....	....	....	2	2	1	3	0	....	....	....
1980-81	Wichita Wind	CHL	45	13	13	26	....	....	....	26	....	....	....	....	....	....	....	....	....	....	....	....	....	....	....	....	....	....
1981-82	Binghamton Whalers	AHL	62	26	37	63	....	....	....	74	....	....	....	....	....	....	....	....	....	....	15	5	6	11	2	....	....	....
1982-83	Moncton Alpines	AHL	77	27	50	77	....	....	....	30	....	....	....	....	....	....	....	....	....	....	....	....	....	....	....	....	....	....
1983-84	Isserlohn	Germany	46	24	26	50	....	....	....	40	....	....	....	....	....	....	....	....	....	....	....	....	....	....	....	....	....	....
1984-85	ERC Mannheim	Germany	36	32	31	63	....	....	....	35	....	....	....	....	....	....	....	....	....	....	9	5	8	13	14	....	....	....
1985-86	ERC Mannheim	Germany	38	32	35	67	....	....	....	66	....	....	....	....	....	....	....	....	....	....	....	....	....	....	....	....	....	....
1986-87	ERC Mannheim	Germany	46	42	29	71	....	....	....	60	....	....	....	....	....	....	....	....	....	....	7	*10	3	13	....	....	....	....
1987-88	ERC Mannheim	Germany	43	25	38	63	....	....	....	46	....	....	....	....	....	....	....	....	....	....	....	....	....	....	....	....	....	....
1988-89	ERC Mannheim	Germany	36	32	17	49	....	....	....	30	....	....	....	....	....	....	....	....	....	....	9	3	11	14	6	....	....	....
1989-90	ERC Mannheim	Germany	36	11	23	34	....	....	....	22	....	....	....	....	....	....	....	....	....	....	3	2	2	4	2	....	....	....
1990-91	HC Bolzano	Italy	2	1	1	2	....	....	....	0	....	....	....	....	....	....	....	....	....	....	....	....	....	....	....	....	....	....
	NHL Totals		**9**	**0**	**0**	**0**	**0**	**0**	**0**	**4**	**0**	**0**	**0**	**9**	**0.0**	**2**	**0**	**8**	**0**		....	....	....	....	....	....	....	....

• METCALFE, SCOTT

Scott Metcalfe LW – L. 6', 195 lbs. b: Toronto, Ont., 1/6/1967. Edmonton's 1st choice, 20th overall, in 1985 Entry Draft.

Season	Club	League	GP	G	A	Pts	AG	AA	APts	PIM	PP	SH	GW	S	%	TGF	PGF	TGA	PGA	+/–	GP	G	A	Pts	PIM	PP	SH	GW
1982-83	Toronto Young Nats	Jr. B	39	22	43	65	....	....	....	74	....	....	....	....	....	....	....	....	....	....	....	....	....	....	....	....	....	....
1983-84	Kingston Canadians	OHL	68	25	49	74	....	....	....	154	....	....	....	....	....	....	....	....	....	....	....	....	....	....	....	....	....	....
1984-85	Kingston Canadians	OHL	58	27	33	60	....	....	....	100	....	....	....	....	....	....	....	....	....	....	....	....	....	....	....	....	....	....
1985-86	Kingston Canadians	OHL	66	36	43	79	....	....	....	213	....	....	....	....	....	....	....	....	....	....	10	3	6	9	21	....	....	....
1986-87	Windsor Spitfires	OHL	57	25	57	82	....	....	....	156	....	....	....	....	....	....	....	....	....	....	13	5	5	10	27	....	....	....
	Canada	WJC-A	6	2	5	7	....	....	....	12	....	....	....	....	....	....	....	....	....	....	....	....	....	....	....	....	....	....
1987-88	**Edmonton Oilers**	**NHL**	**2**	**0**	**0**	**0**	**0**	**0**	**0**	**0**	**0**	**0**	**0**	**0**	**0.0**	**0**	**0**	**1**	**0**	**–1**	....	....	....	....	....	....	....	....
	Nova Scotia Oilers	AHL	43	9	19	28	....	....	....	87	....	....	....	....	....	....	....	....	....	....	....	....	....	....	....	....	....	....
	Buffalo Sabres	**NHL**	**1**	**0**	**1**	**1**	**0**	**1**	**1**	**0**	**0**	**0**	**0**	**1**	**0.0**	**1**	**0**	**2**	**0**	**–1**	....	....	....	....	....	....	....	....
	Rochester Americans	AHL	22	2	13	15	....	....	....	56	....	....	....	....	....	....	....	....	....	....	7	1	3	4	24	....	....	....
1988-89	**Buffalo Sabres**	**NHL**	**9**	**1**	**1**	**2**	**1**	**1**	**2**	**13**	**0**	**0**	**0**	**11**	**9.1**	**3**	**0**	**4**	**0**	**–1**	....	....	....	....	....	....	....	....
	Rochester Americans	AHL	60	20	31	51	....	....	....	241	....	....	....	....	....	....	....	....	....	....	....	....	....	....	....	....	....	....
1989-90	**Buffalo Sabres**	**NHL**	**7**	**0**	**0**	**0**	**0**	**0**	**0**	**5**	**0**	**0**	**0**	**5**	**0.0**	**2**	**0**	**2**	**0**	**0**	....	....	....	....	....	....	....	....
	Rochester Americans	AHL	43	12	17	29	....	....	....	93	....	....	....	....	....	....	....	....	....	....	2	0	1	1	0	....	....	....
1990-91	Rochester Americans	AHL	69	17	22	39	....	....	....	177	....	....	....	....	....	....	....	....	....	....	14	4	1	5	27	....	....	....
	NHL Totals		**19**	**1**	**2**	**3**	**1**	**2**	**3**	**18**	**0**	**0**	**0**	**17**	**5.9**	**6**	**0**	**9**	**0**		....	....	....	....	....	....	....	....

Traded to **Buffalo** by **Edmonton** with Edmonton's 9th round choice (Donald Audette) in 1989 Entry Draft for Steve Dykstra and Buffalo's 7th round choice (David Payne) in 1989 Entry Draft, February 11, 1988.

• MICHAYLUK, DAVE

Dave Michayluk LW – L. 5'10", 189 lbs. b: Wakaw, Sask., 5/18/1962. Philadelphia's 5th choice, 65th overall, in 1981 Entry Draft.

Season	Club	League	GP	G	A	Pts	AG	AA	APts	PIM	PP	SH	GW	S	%	TGF	PGF	TGA	PGA	+/–	GP	G	A	Pts	PIM	PP	SH	GW
1979-80	Prince Albert Saints	AJHL	60	46	67	113	....	....	....	49	....	....	....	....	....	....	....	....	....	....	....	....	....	....	....	....	....	....
1980-81	Regina Pats	WHL	72	62	71	133	....	....	....	39	....	....	....	....	....	....	....	....	....	....	11	5	12	17	8	....	....	....
1981-82	Regina Pats	WHL	72	62	111	172	....	....	....	128	....	....	....	....	....	....	....	....	....	....	12	16	24	*40	23	....	....	....
	Philadelphia Flyers	**NHL**	**1**	**0**	**0**	**0**	**0**	**0**	**0**	**0**	**0**	**0**	**0**	**0**	**0.0**	**0**	**0**	**2**	**0**	**–2**	....	....	....	....	....	....	....	....
1982-83	**Philadelphia Flyers**	**NHL**	**13**	**2**	**6**	**8**	**2**	**4**	**6**	**8**	**0**	**0**	**0**	**18**	**11.1**	**12**	**3**	**12**	**4**	**+1**	....	....	....	....	....	....	....	....
	Maine Mariners	AHL	69	32	40	72	....	....	....	16	....	....	....	....	....	....	....	....	....	....	8	0	2	2	0	....	....	....
1983-84	Springfield Indians	AHL	79	18	44	62	....	....	....	37	....	....	....	....	....	....	....	....	....	....	4	0	0	0	2	....	....	....
1984-85	Hershey Bears	AHL	3	0	2	2	....	....	....	2	....	....	....	....	....	....	....	....	....	....	....	....	....	....	....	....	....	....
	Kalamazoo Wings	IHL	82	*66	33	99	....	....	....	49	....	....	....	....	....	....	....	....	....	....	11	7	7	14	0	....	....	....
1985-86	Nova Scotia Oilers	AHL	3	0	1	1	....	....	....	0	....	....	....	....	....	....	....	....	....	....	....	....	....	....	....	....	....	....
	Muskegon Lumberjacks	IHL	77	52	52	104	....	....	....	73	....	....	....	....	....	....	....	....	....	....	14	6	9	15	12	....	....	....
1986-87	Muskegon Lumberjacks	IHL	82	47	53	100	....	....	....	29	....	....	....	....	....	....	....	....	....	....	15	2	14	16	8	....	....	....
1987-88	Muskegon Lumberjacks	IHL	81	*56	81	137	....	....	....	46	....	....	....	....	....	....	....	....	....	....	6	2	0	2	18	....	....	....
1988-89	Muskegon Lumberjacks	IHL	80	50	72	*122	....	....	....	84	....	....	....	....	....	....	....	....	....	....	13	*9	12	*21	24	....	....	....
1989-90	Muskegon Lumberjacks	IHL	79	*51	51	102	....	....	....	80	....	....	....	....	....	....	....	....	....	....	15	8	*14	*22	10	....	....	....
1990-91	Muskegon Lumberjacks	IHL	83	40	62	102	....	....	....	16	....	....	....	....	....	....	....	....	....	....	5	2	2	4	4	....	....	....
1991-92	Muskegon Lumberjacks	IHL	82	39	63	102	....	....	....	154	....	....	....	....	....	....	....	....	....	....	13	9	8	17	4	....	....	....
	Pittsburgh Penguins	**NHL**	....	....	....	....	....	....	....	....	....	....	....	....	....	....	....	....	....	....	**7**	**1**	**1**	**2**	**0**	....	....	....
1992-93	Cleveland Lumberjacks	IHL	82	47	65	112	....	....	....	104	....	....	....	....	....	....	....	....	....	....	4	1	2	3	4	....	....	....
1993-94	Cleveland Lumberjacks	IHL	81	48	51	99	....	....	....	92	....	....	....	....	....	....	....	....	....	....	....	....	....	....	....	....	....	....

Season	Club	League	REGULAR SEASON																		PLAYOFFS							
			GP	G	A	Pts	AG	AA	APts	PIM	PP	SH	GW	S	%	TGF	PGF	TGA	PGA	+/–	GP	G	A	Pts	PIM	PP	SH	GW
1994-95	Cleveland Lumberjacks	IHL	60	19	17	36				22											1	0	0	0	0			
1995-96	Cleveland Lumberjacks	IHL	53	22	21	43				27											3	1	0	1	4			
1996-97	Cleveland Lumberjacks	IHL	46	10	15	25				18																		
	NHL Totals		**14**	**2**	**6**	**8**	**2**	**4**	**6**	**8**	**0**	**0**	**0**	**18**	**11.1**	**12**	**3**	**14**	**4**		**7**	**1**	**1**	**2**	**0**	**0**	**0**	**0**

WHL Second All-Star Team (1982) • IHL Second All-Star Team (1985, 1992, 1993) • IHL First All-Star Team (1987, 1988, 1989, 1990) • Won Leo P. Lamoureux Memorial Trophy (Top Scorer - IHL) (1989) • Won James Gatschene Memorial Trophy (MVP - IHL) (1989) • Won "Bud" Poile Trophy (Playoff MVP - IHL) (1989)

Signed as a free agent by **Pittsburgh**, May 24, 1989.

• MICHELETTI, JOE

Joe Micheletti D – L. 6′, 185 lbs. b: Hibbing, MN, 10/24/1954. Montreal's 12th choice, 123rd overall, in 1974 Amateur Draft.

Season	Club	League	GP	G	A	Pts	AG	AA	APts	PIM	PP	SH	GW	S	%	TGF	PGF	TGA	PGA	+/–	GP	G	A	Pts	PIM	PP	SH	GW
1973-74	University of Minnesota	WCHA	21	2	5	7				10																		
1974-75	University of Minnesota	WCHA	42	7	13	20				44																		
1975-76	University of Minnesota	WCHA	33	7	24	31				46																		
1976-77	University of Minnesota	WCHA	39	9	39	48				53																		
	Calgary Cowboys	WHA	14	3	3	6				10																		
	United States	WEC-A	10	0	5	5				8																		
1977-78	Edmonton Oilers	WHA	56	14	34	48				56											5	0	2	2	4			
1978-79	Edmonton Oilers	WHA	72	14	33	47				85											13	0	9	9	2			
1979-80	**St. Louis Blues**	**NHL**	**54**	**2**	**16**	**18**	**2**	**12**	**14**	**29**	**2**	**0**	**0**	**68**	**2.9**	**72**	**12**	**74**	**9**	**–5**								
1980-81	**St. Louis Blues**	**NHL**	**63**	**4**	**27**	**31**	**3**	**19**	**22**	**53**	**3**	**0**	**1**	**102**	**3.9**	**95**	**42**	**50**	**9**	**+12**	**11**	**1**	**11**	**12**	**10**	**1**	**0**	**0**
1981-82	**St. Louis Blues**	**NHL**	**20**	**3**	**11**	**14**	**2**	**7**	**9**	**28**	**2**	**0**	**0**	**30**	**10.0**	**33**	**12**	**27**	**4**	**–2**								
	Colorado Rockies	**NHL**	**21**	**2**	**6**	**8**	**2**	**4**	**6**	**4**	**0**	**0**	**0**	**41**	**4.9**	**27**	**7**	**26**	**2**	**–4**								
	Fort Worth Texans	CHL	17	3	14	17				26																		
	United States	WEC-A	5	0	0	0				2																		
	NHL Totals		**158**	**11**	**60**	**71**	**9**	**42**	**51**	**114**	**7**	**0**	**1**	**241**	**4.6**	**227**	**73**	**177**	**24**		**11**	**1**	**11**	**12**	**10**	**1**	**0**	**0**
	Other Major League Totals		142	31	70	101				151											18	0	11	11	6			

Selected by **Cincinnati** (WHA) in 1974 WHA Amateur Draft, May, 1974. WHA rights traded to **Minnesota** (WHA) by **Cincinnati** (WHA) for future considerations, July, 1975. WHA rights traded to **Calgary** (WHA) by **Minnesota** (WHA) with Don Tannahill, George Morrison and the rights to Wally Olds for John McKenzie and cash, September, 1975. Traded to **Winnipeg** (WHA) by **Calgary** (WHA) for future considerations, August, 1977. Traded to **Edmonton** (WHA) by **Winnipeg** (WHA) for future considerations, September, 1977. Rights retained by **Edmonton** prior to Expansion Draft, June 9, 1979. Traded to **St. Louis** by **Edmonton** for Tom Roulston and Risto Siltanen, August 7, 1979. Traded to **Colorado** by **St. Louis** with Dick Lamby for Bill Baker, December 4, 1981.

• MICHELETTI, PAT

Pat Micheletti C – L. 5′10″, 175 lbs. b: Hibbing, MN, 12/11/1963. Minnesota's 9th choice, 185th overall, in 1982 Entry Draft.

Season	Club	League	GP	G	A	Pts	AG	AA	APts	PIM	PP	SH	GW	S	%	TGF	PGF	TGA	PGA	+/–	GP	G	A	Pts	PIM	PP	SH	GW
1981-82	Hibbing High School	H.S.	22	26	39	65				50																		
1982-83	University of Minnesota	WCHA	20	11	11	22				52																		
1983-84	University of Minnesota	WCHA	39	26	34	60				62																		
1984-85	University of Minnesota	WCHA	44	48	48	96				154																		
1985-86	University of Minnesota	WCHA	48	32	48	80				113																		
	Springfield Indians	AHL	2	1	0	1				0																		
1986-87	Springfield Indians	AHL	67	17	26	43				39																		
1987-88	**Minnesota North Stars**	**NHL**	**12**	**2**	**0**	**2**	**2**	**0**	**2**	**8**	**0**	**0**	**0**	**18**	**11.1**	**4**	**0**	**2**	**0**	**+2**								
	Kalamazoo Wings	IHL	19	12	6	18				12											7	2	2	4	0			
1988-89	Varese HC	Italy	46	48	50	98				105																		
1989-90	Varese HC	Italy 2	STATISTICS NOT AVAILABLE																									
1990-91	Varese HC	Italy	36	24	58	92				22																		
1991-92	HC Asagio	Italy	19	6	15	21				42																		
	NHL Totals		**12**	**2**	**0**	**2**	**2**	**0**	**2**	**8**	**0**	**0**	**0**	**18**	**11.1**	**4**	**0**	**2**	**0**									

WCHA First All-Star Team (1985) • NCAA West First All-American Team (1985) • WCHA Second All-Star Team (1986)

• MICKEY, LARRY

Larry Mickey RW – R. 5′11″, 175 lbs. b: Lacombe, Alta., 10/21/1943. Deceased.

Season	Club	League	GP	G	A	Pts	AG	AA	APts	PIM	PP	SH	GW	S	%	TGF	PGF	TGA	PGA	+/–	GP	G	A	Pts	PIM	PP	SH	GW
1962-63	Moose Jaw Canucks	SJHL	54	32	38	70				85											6	1	5	6	23			
	Calgary Stampeders	WHL	2	0	1	1				0																		
1963-64	Moose Jaw Canucks	SJHL	62	69	73	142				139											5	7	2	9	6			
	St. Louis Braves	CHL	1	0	0	0				0											5	1	2	3	2			
1964-65	**Chicago Black Hawks**	**NHL**	**1**	**0**	**0**	**0**	**0**	**0**	**0**	**0**																		
	St. Louis Braves	CHL	52	16	21	37				85																		
	Buffalo Bisons	AHL	1	0	1	1				2																		
1965-66	**New York Rangers**	**NHL**	**7**	**0**	**0**	**0**	**0**	**0**	**0**	**2**																		
	Minnesota Rangers	CHL	38	14	25	39				50											7	5	5	10	2			
1966-67	**New York Rangers**	**NHL**	**8**	**0**	**0**	**0**	**0**	**0**	**0**	**0**																		
	Omaha Knights	CHL	63	33	41	74				86											9	5	*10	*15	4			
1967-68	**New York Rangers**	**NHL**	**4**	**0**	**2**	**2**	**0**	**2**	**2**	**0**	**0**	**0**	**0**	**2**	**0.0**	**2**	**0**	**0**	**0**	**+2**								
	Buffalo Bisons	AHL	30	9	17	26				48																		
1968-69	**Toronto Maple Leafs**	**NHL**	**55**	**8**	**19**	**27**	**9**	**18**	**27**	**43**	**0**	**0**	**3**	**80**	**10.0**	**36**	**10**	**28**	**2**	**0**	**3**	**0**	**0**	**0**	**5**	**0**	**0**	**0**
1969-70	**Montreal Canadiens**	**NHL**	**21**	**4**	**4**	**8**	**5**	**4**	**9**	**4**	**3**	**0**	**2**	**38**	**10.5**	**15**	**9**	**16**	**0**	**–10**								
	Montreal Voyageurs	AHL	50	24	38	62				90																		
1970-71	**Los Angeles Kings**	**NHL**	**65**	**6**	**12**	**18**	**6**	**11**	**17**	**46**	**0**	**1**	**2**	**101**	**5.9**	**37**	**13**	**49**	**10**	**–15**								
1971-72	**Philadelphia Flyers**	**NHL**	**14**	**1**	**2**	**3**	**1**	**2**	**3**	**8**	**1**	**0**	**0**	**22**	**4.5**	**8**	**4**	**9**	**0**	**–5**								
	Buffalo Sabres	**NHL**	**4**	**0**	**1**	**1**	**0**	**1**	**1**	**0**	**0**	**0**	**0**	**5**	**0.0**	**5**	**4**	**3**	**1**	**–1**								
	Salt Lake Golden Eagles	WHL	53	19	30	49				92																		
1972-73	**Buffalo Sabres**	**NHL**	**77**	**15**	**9**	**24**	**15**	**8**	**23**	**47**	**1**	**0**	**2**	**160**	**9.4**	**40**	**1**	**47**	**2**	**–6**	**6**	**1**	**0**	**1**	**5**	**0**	**0**	**0**
1973-74	**Buffalo Sabres**	**NHL**	**13**	**3**	**4**	**7**	**3**	**3**	**6**	**8**	**0**	**0**	**0**	**18**	**16.7**	**10**	**0**	**0**	**1**	**+5**								
	Cincinnati Swords	AHL	9	2	3	5				5																		
1974-75	**Buffalo Sabres**	**NHL**	**23**	**2**	**0**	**2**	**2**	**0**	**2**	**2**	**0**	**0**	**0**	**6**	**33.3**	**2**	**0**	**2**	**1**	**+1**								
1975-76			DID NOT PLAY																									
1976-77	Dayton Gems	IHL	DID NOT PLAY – COACHING																									
1977-78	Dayton Gems	IHL	DID NOT PLAY – COACHING																									
1978-79	Utica Mohawks	NEHL	12	5	4	9				21																		
1979-80	Utica Mohawks	EHL	4	0	4	4				14																		
1980-81	Hampton Aces	EHL	38	5	14	19				50																		
	NHL Totals		**292**	**39**	**53**	**92**	**41**	**40**	**90**	**160**	**5**	**1**	**9**	**432**	**9.0**	**155**	**41**	**180**	**17**		**9**	**1**	**0**	**1**	**10**	**0**	**0**	**0**

CHL First All-Star Team (1967)

Claimed by **NY Rangers** from **Chicago** (St. Louis-CHL) in Inter-League Draft, June 8, 1965. Claimed by **Toronto** from **NY Rangers** in Intra-League Draft, June 12, 1968. Claimed by **Montreal** from **Toronto** in Intra-League Draft, June 11, 1969. Traded to **LA Kings** by **Montreal** with Lucien Grenier and Jack Norris for Leon Rochefort, Wayne Thomas and Greg Boddy, May 22, 1970. Traded to **Philadelphia** by **LA Kings** for Larry Hillman, June 13, 1971. Traded to **Buffalo** by **Philadelphia** for Larry Keenan, November 16, 1971.

• MIDDENDORF, MAX

Max Middendorf RW – R. 6′4″, 210 lbs. b: Syracuse, NY, 8/18/1967. Quebec's 3rd choice, 57th overall, in 1985 Entry Draft.

Season	Club	League	GP	G	A	Pts	AG	AA	APts	PIM	PP	SH	GW	S	%	TGF	PGF	TGA	PGA	+/–	GP	G	A	Pts	PIM	PP	SH	GW
1983-84	New Jersey Rockets	NYJHL	58	94	74	168																						
1984-85	Sudbury Wolves	OHL	63	16	28	44				106																		
1985-86	Sudbury Wolves	OHL	61	40	42	82				71											4	4	2	6	11			
	United States	WJC-A	7	2	2	4				4																		
1986-87	Sudbury Wolves	OHL	31	31	29	60				7																		
	Kitchener Rangers	OHL	17	7	15	22				6											4	2	5	7	5			
	Quebec Nordiques	**NHL**	**6**	**1**	**4**	**5**	**1**	**3**	**4**	**4**	**0**	**0**	**0**	**4**	**25.0**	**7**	**4**	**5**	**0**	**–2**								
1987-88	**Quebec Nordiques**	**NHL**	**1**	**0**	**0**	**0**	**0**	**0**	**0**	**0**	**0**	**0**	**0**	**0**	**0.0**	**0**	**0**	**0**	**0**	**0**								
	Fredericton Express	AHL	38	11	13	24				57											12	4	4	8	18			
1988-89	Halifax Citadels	AHL	72	41	39	80				85											4	1	2	3	6			
1989-90	**Quebec Nordiques**	**NHL**	**3**	**0**	**0**	**0**	**0**	**0**	**0**	**0**	**0**	**0**	**0**	**5**	**0.0**	**0**	**0**	**9**	**0**	**–9**								
	Halifax Citadels	AHL	48	20	17	37				60																		
1990-91	**Edmonton Oilers**	**NHL**	**3**	**1**	**0**	**1**	**1**	**0**	**1**	**2**	**0**	**0**	**0**	**1**	**100.0**	**1**	**0**	**1**	**0**	**0**								
	Fort Wayne Komets	IHL	15	9	11	20				12																		
	Cape Breton Oilers	AHL	44	14	21	35				82											4	0	1	1	6			

Season	Club	League	GP	G	A	Pts	AG	AA	APts	PIM	PP	SH	GW	S	%	TGF	PGF	TGA	PGA	+/–	GP	G	A	Pts	PIM	PP	SH	GW
			REGULAR SEASON																		PLAYOFFS							
1991-92	Cape Breton Oilers	AHL	51	20	19	39	....	....	....	108	....	....	....	....	....	....	....	....	....	....	....	....	....	....	....	....	....	....
	Adirondack Red Wings	AHL	6	3	5	8	....	....	....	12	....	....	....	....	....	....	....	....	....	....	5	0	1	1	16	....	....	....
1992-93	Fort Wayne Komets	IHL	24	9	13	22	....	....	....	58	....	....	....	....	....	....	....	....	....	....	....	....	....	....	....	....	....	....
	San Diego Gulls	IHL	30	15	11	26	....	....	....	25	....	....	....	....	....	....	....	....	....	....	8	1	2	3	8	....	....	....
1993-94	Fort Wayne Komets	IHL	36	16	20	36	....	....	....	43	....	....	....	....	....	....	....	....	....	....	9	1	2	3	24	....	....	....
1994-95	Fort Wayne Komets	IHL	15	1	4	5	....	....	....	34	....	....	....	....	....	....	....	....	....	....	....	....	....	....	....	....	....	....
1995-96	Klagenfurt	Austria	9	1	6	7	....	....	....	86	....	....	....	....	....	....	....	....	....	....	....	....	....	....	....	....	....	....
	Winston-Salem Mammoths	SHL	4	1	5	6	....	....	....	27	....	....	....	....	....	....	....	....	....	....	....	....	....	....	....	....	....	....
	Bakersfield Fog	WCHL	23	4	12	16	....	....	....	80	....	....	....	....	....	....	....	....	....	....	....	....	....	....	....	....	....	....
1996-97	Huntsville Channel Cats	CHL	42	14	32	46	....	....	....	79	....	....	....	....	....	....	....	....	....	....	....	....	....	....	....	....	....	....
1997-98	Fort Worth Bulls	WPHL	18	4	10	14	....	....	....	56	....	....	....	....	....	....	....	....	....	....	....	....	....	....	....	....	....	....
	NHL Totals		**13**	**2**	**4**	**6**	**2**	**3**	**5**	**6**	**0**	**0**	**0**	**10**	**20.0**	**8**	**4**	**15**	**0**		....	....	....	....	....	....	....	....

Traded to **Edmonton** by **Quebec** for Edmonton's 9th round choice (Brent Brekke) in 1991 Entry Draft, November 10, 1990. Traded to **Detroit** by **Edmonton** for Bill McDougall, February 22, 1992.

• MIDDLETON, RICK

Rick "Slick" Middleton RW – R. 5'11", 170 lbs. b: Toronto, Ont., 12/4/1953. NY Rangers' 1st choice, 14th overall, in 1973 Amateur Draft.

Season	Club	League	GP	G	A	Pts	AG	AA	APts	PIM	PP	SH	GW	S	%	TGF	PGF	TGA	PGA	+/–	GP	G	A	Pts	PIM	PP	SH	GW
1971-72	Oshawa Generals	OHA	53	36	34	70	....	....	....	24	....	....	....	....	....	....	....	....	....	....	....	....	....	....	....	....	....	....
1972-73	Oshawa Generals	OHA	62	*67	70	137	....	....	....	14	....	....	....	....	....	....	....	....	....	....	....	....	....	....	....	....	....	....
1973-74	Providence Reds	AHL	63	36	48	84	....	....	....	14	....	....	....	....	....	....	....	....	....	....	15	9	6	15	2	....	....	....
1974-75	**New York Rangers**	**NHL**	**47**	**22**	**18**	**40**	**20**	**14**	**34**	**19**	**6**	**0**	**2**	**106**	**20.8**	**57**	**24**	**39**	**0**	**–6**	**3**	**0**	**0**	**0**	**2**	**0**	**0**	**0**
1975-76	**New York Rangers**	**NHL**	**77**	**24**	**26**	**50**	**22**	**20**	**42**	**14**	**7**	**0**	**5**	**159**	**15.1**	**85**	**38**	**86**	**1**	**–38**	....	....	....	....	....	....	....	....
1976-77	**Boston Bruins**	**NHL**	**72**	**20**	**22**	**42**	**19**	**18**	**37**	**2**	**0**	**0**	**1**	**128**	**15.6**	**70**	**8**	**60**	**0**	**+2**	**13**	**5**	**4**	**9**	**0**	**0**	**0**	**1**
1977-78	**Boston Bruins**	**NHL**	**79**	**25**	**35**	**60**	**24**	**29**	**53**	**8**	**2**	**0**	**6**	**171**	**14.6**	**101**	**10**	**52**	**1**	**+40**	**15**	**5**	**2**	**7**	**0**	**0**	**0**	**2**
1978-79	**Boston Bruins**	**NHL**	**71**	**38**	**48**	**86**	**35**	**37**	**72**	**7**	**12**	**1**	**5**	**152**	**25.0**	**117**	**29**	**69**	**14**	**+33**	**11**	**4**	**8**	**12**	**0**	**2**	**0**	**1**
1979-80	**Boston Bruins**	**NHL**	**80**	**40**	**52**	**92**	**36**	**40**	**76**	**24**	**9**	**0**	**4**	**223**	**17.9**	**135**	**50**	**56**	**2**	**+31**	**10**	**4**	**2**	**6**	**5**	**0**	**0**	**0**
1980-81	**Boston Bruins**	**NHL**	**80**	**44**	**59**	**103**	**36**	**41**	**77**	**16**	**16**	**4**	**7**	**222**	**19.8**	**138**	**64**	**68**	**9**	**+15**	**3**	**0**	**1**	**1**	**2**	**0**	**0**	**0**
1981-82	Canada	C Cup	7	1	2	3	....	....	....	0	....	....	....	....	....	....	....	....	....	....	....	....	....	....	....	....	....	....
	Boston Bruins	**NHL**	**75**	**51**	**43**	**94**	**41**	**28**	**69**	**12**	**19**	**1**	**9**	**202**	**25.2**	**140**	**52**	**92**	**19**	**+15**	**11**	**6**	**9**	**15**	**0**	**2**	**0**	**0**
1982-83	**Boston Bruins**	**NHL**	**80**	**49**	**47**	**96**	**40**	**32**	**72**	**8**	**6**	**3**	**7**	**214**	**22.9**	**134**	**29**	**102**	**30**	**+33**	**17**	**11**	**22**	**33**	**6**	**4**	**1**	**1**
1983-84	**Boston Bruins**	**NHL**	**80**	**47**	**58**	**105**	**38**	**39**	**77**	**14**	**16**	**4**	**6**	**209**	**22.5**	**155**	**56**	**91**	**18**	**+26**	**3**	**0**	**0**	**0**	**0**	**0**	**0**	**0**
1984-85	Canada	C Cup	7	4	4	8	....	....	....	0	....	....	....	....	....	....	....	....	....	....	....	....	....	....	....	....	....	....
	Boston Bruins	**NHL**	**80**	**30**	**46**	**76**	**25**	**31**	**56**	**6**	**12**	**3**	**3**	**169**	**17.8**	**107**	**32**	**102**	**29**	**+2**	**5**	**3**	**0**	**3**	**0**	**0**	**0**	**0**
1985-86	**Boston Bruins**	**NHL**	**49**	**14**	**30**	**44**	**11**	**20**	**31**	**10**	**4**	**2**	**0**	**100**	**14.0**	**68**	**18**	**60**	**27**	**+17**	....	....	....	....	....	....	....	....
1986-87	**Boston Bruins**	**NHL**	**76**	**31**	**37**	**68**	**27**	**27**	**54**	**6**	**4**	**4**	**3**	**141**	**22.0**	**105**	**32**	**89**	**23**	**+7**	**4**	**2**	**2**	**4**	**0**	**1**	**1**	**0**
1987-88	**Boston Bruins**	**NHL**	**59**	**13**	**19**	**32**	**11**	**14**	**25**	**11**	**2**	**3**	**1**	**79**	**16.5**	**49**	**11**	**62**	**27**	**+3**	**19**	**5**	**5**	**10**	**4**	**0**	**1**	**3**
	NHL Totals		**1005**	**448**	**540**	**988**	**385**	**390**	**775**	**157**	**115**	**25**	**59**	**2275**	**19.7**	**1461**	**453**	**1028**	**200**		**114**	**45**	**55**	**100**	**19**	**9**	**3**	**8**

OHA Second All-Star Team (1973) • AHL First All-Star Team (1974) • Won Dudley "Red" Garrett Memorial Award (Top Rookie - AHL) (1974) • NHL Second All-Star Team (1982) • Won Lady Byng Trophy (1982)

Played in NHL All-Star Game (1981, 1982, 1984)

Traded to **Boston** by **NY Rangers** for Ken Hodge, May 26, 1976.

• MIEHM, KEVIN

Kevin Miehm C – L. 6'2", 200 lbs. b: Kitchener, Ont., 9/10/1969. St. Louis' 2nd choice, 54th overall, in 1987 Entry Draft.

Season	Club	League	GP	G	A	Pts	AG	AA	APts	PIM	PP	SH	GW	S	%	TGF	PGF	TGA	PGA	+/–	GP	G	A	Pts	PIM	PP	SH	GW
1985-86	Kitchener Dutchmen	Tier II	20	20	37	57	....	....	....	65	....	....	....	....	....	....	....	....	....	....	....	....	....	....	....	....	....	....
1986-87	Oshawa Generals	OHL	61	12	27	39	....	....	....	19	....	....	....	....	....	....	....	....	....	....	26	1	8	9	12	....	....	....
1987-88	Oshawa Generals	OHL	52	16	36	52	....	....	....	30	....	....	....	....	....	....	....	....	....	....	7	2	5	7	0	....	....	....
1988-89	Oshawa Generals	OHL	63	43	79	122	....	....	....	19	....	....	....	....	....	....	....	....	....	....	6	6	6	12	0	....	....	....
	Peoria Rivermen	IHL	3	1	1	2	....	....	....	0	....	....	....	....	....	....	....	....	....	....	4	0	2	2	0	....	....	....
1989-90	Peoria Rivermen	IHL	76	23	38	61	....	....	....	20	....	....	....	....	....	....	....	....	....	....	3	0	0	0	4	....	....	....
1990-91	Peoria Rivermen	IHL	73	25	39	64	....	....	....	14	....	....	....	....	....	....	....	....	....	....	16	5	7	12	2	....	....	....
1991-92	Peoria Rivermen	IHL	66	21	53	74	....	....	....	22	....	....	....	....	....	....	....	....	....	....	10	3	4	7	2	....	....	....
1992-93	**St. Louis Blues**	**NHL**	**8**	**1**	**3**	**4**	**1**	**2**	**3**	**4**	**0**	**0**	**0**	**5**	**20.0**	**4**	**0**	**3**	**0**	**+1**	**2**	**0**	**1**	**1**	**0**	**0**	**0**	**0**
	Peoria Rivermen	IHL	30	12	33	45	....	....	....	13	....	....	....	....	....	....	....	....	....	....	4	0	1	1	2	....	....	....
1993-94	**St. Louis Blues**	**NHL**	**14**	**0**	**1**	**1**	**0**	**1**	**1**	**4**	**0**	**0**	**0**	**5**	**0.0**	**1**	**0**	**4**	**0**	**–3**	....	....	....	....	....	....	....	....
	Peoria Rivermen	IHL	11	2	3	5	....	....	....	0	....	....	....	....	....	....	....	....	....	....	4	1	0	1	0	....	....	....
1994-95	Peoria Rivermen	IHL	5	1	5	6	....	....	....	2	....	....	....	....	....	....	....	....	....	....	....	....	....	....	....	....	....	....
	Fort Wayne Komets	IHL	30	10	25	35	....	....	....	18	....	....	....	....	....	....	....	....	....	....	4	1	4	5	0	....	....	....
1995-96	Fort Wayne Komets	IHL	12	2	5	7	....	....	....	2	....	....	....	....	....	....	....	....	....	....	....	....	....	....	....	....	....	....
	Michigan K-Wings	IHL	44	13	20	33	....	....	....	12	....	....	....	....	....	....	....	....	....	....	10	1	1	2	4	....	....	....
1996-97	VSV Villach	Austria	45	32	*68	*100	....	....	....	14	....	....	....	....	....	....	....	....	....	....	....	....	....	....	....	....	....	....
	NHL Totals		**22**	**1**	**4**	**5**	**1**	**3**	**4**	**8**	**0**	**0**	**0**	**10**	**10.0**	**5**	**0**	**7**	**0**		**2**	**0**	**1**	**1**	**0**	**0**	**0**	**0**

• MIKITA, STAN

Stan (Stanislaus Guoth) "Stosh" Mikita RW – R. 5'9", 169 lbs. b: Sokolce, Czech., 5/20/1940. **HHOF**

Season	Club	League	GP	G	A	Pts	AG	AA	APts	PIM	PP	SH	GW	S	%	TGF	PGF	TGA	PGA	+/–	GP	G	A	Pts	PIM	PP	SH	GW
1956-57	St. Catharines Teepees	OHA	52	16	31	47	....	....	....	129	....	....	....	....	....	....	....	....	....	....	14	8	9	17	44	....	....	....
1957-58	St. Catharines Teepees	OHA	52	31	47	78	....	....	....	146	....	....	....	....	....	....	....	....	....	....	8	4	5	9	46	....	....	....
1958-59	St. Catharines Teepees	OHA	45	38	*59	*97	....	....	....	197	....	....	....	....	....	....	....	....	....	....	....	....	....	....	....	....	....	....
	Chicago Black Hawks	**NHL**	**3**	**0**	**1**	**1**	**0**	**1**	**1**	**4**	....	....	....	....	....	....	....	....	....	....	....	....	....	....	....	....	....	....
1959-60	**Chicago Black Hawks**	**NHL**	**67**	**8**	**18**	**26**	**10**	**18**	**28**	**119**	....	....	....	....	....	....	....	....	....	....	**3**	**0**	**1**	**1**	**2**	....	....	....
1960-61	**Chicago Black Hawks**	**NHL**	**66**	**19**	**34**	**53**	**23**	**35**	**58**	**100**	....	....	....	....	....	....	....	....	....	....	**12**	***6**	**5**	**11**	**21**	....	....	....
1961-62	**Chicago Black Hawks**	**NHL**	**70**	**25**	**52**	**77**	**31**	**53**	**84**	**97**	....	....	....	....	....	....	....	....	....	....	**12**	**6**	***15**	***21**	**19**	....	....	....
1962-63	**Chicago Black Hawks**	**NHL**	**65**	**31**	**45**	**76**	**39**	**48**	**87**	**69**	....	....	....	....	....	....	....	....	....	....	**6**	**3**	**2**	**5**	**2**	....	....	....
1963-64	**Chicago Black Hawks**	**NHL**	**70**	**39**	**50**	***89**	**53**	**56**	**109**	**146**	....	....	....	....	....	....	....	....	....	....	**7**	**3**	**6**	**9**	**8**	....	....	....
1964-65	**Chicago Black Hawks**	**NHL**	**70**	**28**	***59**	***87**	**36**	**65**	**101**	**154**	....	....	....	....	....	....	....	....	....	....	**14**	**3**	**7**	**10**	***53**	....	....	....
1965-66	**Chicago Black Hawks**	**NHL**	**68**	**30**	***48**	**78**	**37**	**49**	**86**	**58**	....	....	....	....	....	....	....	....	....	....	**6**	**1**	**2**	**3**	**2**	....	....	....
1966-67	**Chicago Black Hawks**	**NHL**	**70**	**35**	***62**	***97**	**44**	**65**	**109**	**12**	....	....	....	....	....	....	....	....	....	....	**6**	**2**	**2**	**4**	**2**	....	....	....
1967-68	**Chicago Black Hawks**	**NHL**	**72**	**40**	**47**	***87**	**50**	**49**	**99**	**14**	**13**	**2**	**8**	**303**	**13.2**	**110**	**37**	**86**	**10**	**–3**	**11**	**5**	**7**	**12**	**6**	**2**	**1**	**0**
1968-69	**Chicago Black Hawks**	**NHL**	**74**	**30**	**67**	**97**	**34**	**64**	**98**	**52**	**7**	**3**	**2**	**299**	**10.0**	**126**	**39**	**83**	**13**	**+17**	....	....	....	....	....	....	....	....
1969-70	**Chicago Black Hawks**	**NHL**	**76**	**39**	**47**	**86**	**45**	**47**	**92**	**50**	**7**	**0**	**8**	**352**	**11.1**	**120**	**44**	**60**	**13**	**+29**	**8**	**4**	**6**	**10**	**2**	**3**	**1**	**0**
1970-71	**Chicago Black Hawks**	**NHL**	**74**	**24**	**48**	**72**	**25**	**42**	**67**	**85**	**7**	**0**	**4**	**220**	**10.9**	**103**	**43**	**46**	**7**	**+21**	**18**	**5**	**13**	**18**	**16**	**1**	**0**	**1**
1971-72	**Chicago Black Hawks**	**NHL**	**74**	**26**	**39**	**65**	**28**	**36**	**64**	**46**	**5**	**0**	**6**	**185**	**14.1**	**86**	**24**	**55**	**9**	**+16**	**8**	**3**	**1**	**4**	**4**	**0**	**0**	**0**
1972-73	Canada	Summit	2	0	1	1	....	....	....	0	....	....	....	....	....	....	....	....	....	....	....	....	....	....	....	....	....	....
	Chicago Black Hawks	**NHL**	**57**	**27**	**56**	**83**	**27**	**47**	**74**	**32**	**7**	**1**	**5**	**177**	**15.3**	**90**	**24**	**45**	**10**	**+31**	**15**	**7**	**13**	**20**	**8**	**1**	**0**	**2**
1973-74	**Chicago Black Hawks**	**NHL**	**76**	**30**	**50**	**80**	**31**	**43**	**74**	**46**	**6**	**2**	**1**	**171**	**17.5**	**105**	**35**	**49**	**3**	**+24**	**11**	**5**	**6**	**11**	**8**	**1**	**0**	**1**
1974-75	**Chicago Black Hawks**	**NHL**	**79**	**36**	**50**	**86**	**33**	**39**	**72**	**48**	**12**	**0**	**6**	**253**	**14.2**	**113**	**49**	**77**	**27**	**+14**	**8**	**3**	**4**	**7**	**12**	**1**	**0**	**1**
1975-76	**Chicago Black Hawks**	**NHL**	**48**	**16**	**41**	**57**	**15**	**32**	**47**	**37**	**6**	**0**	**1**	**159**	**10.1**	**72**	**37**	**47**	**8**	**–4**	**4**	**0**	**0**	**0**	**4**	**0**	**0**	**0**
1976-77	**Chicago Black Hawks**	**NHL**	**57**	**19**	**30**	**49**	**18**	**24**	**42**	**20**	**6**	**1**	**4**	**128**	**14.8**	**64**	**25**	**62**	**14**	**–9**	**2**	**0**	**1**	**1**	**0**	**0**	**0**	**0**
1977-78	**Chicago Black Hawks**	**NHL**	**76**	**18**	**41**	**59**	**17**	**33**	**50**	**35**	**6**	**0**	**2**	**202**	**8.9**	**92**	**31**	**51**	**8**	**+18**	**4**	**3**	**0**	**3**	**0**	**2**	**0**	**0**
1978-79	**Chicago Black Hawks**	**NHL**	**65**	**19**	**36**	**55**	**17**	**28**	**45**	**34**	**4**	**0**	**1**	**147**	**12.9**	**70**	**18**	**57**	**8**	**+3**	....	....	....	....	....	....	....	....
1979-80	**Chicago Black Hawks**	**NHL**	**17**	**2**	**5**	**7**	**2**	**4**	**6**	**12**	**0**	**0**	**0**	**28**	**7.1**	**12**	**2**	**8**	**0**	**+2**	....	....	....	....	....	....	....	....
	NHL Totals		**1394**	**541**	**926**	**1467**	**615**	**878**	**1493**	**1270**	**86**	**9**	**48**	**2624**	**20.6**	**1163**	**408**	**726**	**130**		**155**	**59**	**91**	**150**	**169**	**11**	**2**	**5**

NHL First All-Star Team (1962, 1963, 1964, 1966, 1967, 1968) • Won Art Ross Trophy (1964, 1965, 1967, 1968) • NHL Second All-Star Team (1965, 1970) • Won Lady Byng Trophy (1967, 1968) • Won Hart Trophy (1967, 1968) • Won Lester Patrick Trophy (1976)

Played in NHL All-Star Game (1964, 1967, 1968, 1969, 1971, 1972, 1973, 1974, 1975)

• MIKKELSON, BILL

Bill Mikkelson D – L. 6', 185 lbs. b: Neepouna, Man., 5/21/1948.

Season	Club	League	GP	G	A	Pts	AG	AA	APts	PIM	PP	SH	GW	S	%	TGF	PGF	TGA	PGA	+/–	GP	G	A	Pts	PIM	PP	SH	GW
1964-65	Brandon Wheat Kings	SJHL	1	0	1	1	....	....	....	0	....	....	....	....	....	....	....	....	....	....	1	0	1	1	0	....	....	....
1965-66	Brandon Wheat Kings	SJHL	60	9	14	23	....	....	....	92	....	....	....	....	....	....	....	....	....	....	11	1	3	4	12	....	....	....
1966-67	Brandon Wheat Kings	CMJHL	STATISTICS NOT AVAILABLE																									
1967-68	Brandon Wheat Kings	WCJHL	56	14	27	41	....	....	....	119	....	....	....	....	....	....	....	....	....	....	....	....	....	....	....	....	....	....
1968-69	Winnipeg Jets	WCJHL	53	5	26	31	....	....	....	43	....	....	....	....	....	....	....	....	....	....	....	....	....	....	....	....	....	....
1969-70	Winnipeg Jets	WCJHL	59	5	34	39	....	....	....	76	....	....	....	....	....	....	....	....	....	....	....	....	....	....	....	....	....	....
1970-71	Springfield Kings	AHL	69	2	9	11	....	....	....	50	....	....	....	....	....	....	....	....	....	....	12	1	2	3	14	....	....	....

Season	Club	League	GP	G	A	Pts	AG	AA	APts	PIM	PP	SH	GW	S	%	TGF	PGF	TGA	PGA	+/-	GP	G	A	Pts	PIM	PP	SH	GW
			REGULAR SEASON																		PLAYOFFS							
1971-72	**Los Angeles Kings**	**NHL**	**15**	**0**	**1**	**1**	**0**	**1**	**1**	**6**	**0**	**0**	**0**	**8**	**0.0**	**3**	**0**	**15**	**1**	**–11**								
	Springfield Kings	AHL	32	2	3	5				36																		
1972-73	**New York Islanders**	**NHL**	**72**	**1**	**10**	**11**	**1**	**8**	**9**	**45**	**0**	**0**	**0**	**39**	**2.6**	**55**	**0**	**137**	**28**	**–54**								
1973-74	Baltimore Clippers	AHL	75	1	21	22				77											7	0	1	1	6			
1974-75	**Washington Capitals**	**NHL**	**59**	**3**	**7**	**10**	**3**	**5**	**8**	**52**	**3**	**0**	**0**	**49**	**6.1**	**45**	**11**	**156**	**40**	**–82**								
	Richmond Robins	AHL	10	0	0	0				16											3	0	0	0	4			
1975-76	Baltimore Clippers	AHL	76	3	18	21				52																		
1976-77	**Washington Capitals**	**NHL**	**1**	**0**	**0**	**0**	**0**	**0**	**0**	**2**	**0**	**0**	**0**	**0**	**0.0**	**1**	**0**	**1**	**0**	**0**								
	Hershey Bears	AHL	22	1	2	3				18											6	0	1	1	4			
	Rhode Island Reds	AHL	51	3	7	10				28																		
	NHL Totals		**147**	**4**	**18**	**22**	**4**	**14**	**18**	**105**	**3**	**0**	**0**	**96**	**4.2**	**104**	**11**	**309**	**69**									

Signed as a free agent by **LA Kings** (Springfield - AHL), September, 1970. Claimed by **NY Islanders** from **LA Kings** in Expansion Draft, June 6, 1972. Claimed by **Washington** from **NY Islanders** in Expansion Draft, June 12, 1974. Traded to **LA Kings** by **Washington** for cash, March 3, 1975.

• MIKULCHIK, OLEG

Oleg Mikulchik D – R. 6'2", 200 lbs. b: Minsk, USSR, 6/27/1964.

Season	Club	League	GP	G	A	Pts	AG	AA	APts	PIM	PP	SH	GW	S	%	TGF	PGF	TGA	PGA	+/-	GP	G	A	Pts	PIM	PP	SH	GW
1983-84	Moscow Dynamo	USSR	17	0	0	0				6																		
	Soviet Union	WJC-A	7	0	3	3				2																		
1984-85	Moscow Dynamo	USSR	30	1	3	4				26																		
1985-86	Moscow Dynamo	USSR	40	0	1	1				36																		
	Moscow Dynamo	SuperS	2	0	0	0				2																		
1986-87	Moscow Dynamo	USSR	39	5	3	8				34																		
1987-88	Moscow Dynamo	USSR	48	7	8	15				63																		
1988-89	Moscow Dynamo	USSR	43	4	7	11				52																		
1989-90	Moscow Dynamo	FrTour	1	0	0	0				15																		
	Moscow Dynamo	USSR	32	1	3	4				31																		
	Moscow Dynamo	SuperS	5	0	2	2				0																		
1990-91	Moscow Dynamo	FrTour	1	0	0	0				20																		
	Moscow Dynamo	USSR	36	2	6	8				40																		
1991-92	Khimik Voskresensk	CIS	15	3	2	5				20																		
	New Haven Nighthawks	AHL	30	3	3	6				63											4	1	3	4	6			
1992-93	Moncton Hawks	AHL	75	6	20	26				159											5	0	0	0	4			
1993-94	**Winnipeg Jets**	**NHL**	**4**	**0**	**1**	**1**	**0**	**1**	**1**	**17**	**0**	**0**	**0**	**3**	**0.0**	**2**	**0**	**4**	**0**	**–2**								
	Moncton Hawks	AHL	67	9	38	47				121											21	2	10	12	18			
1994-95	**Winnipeg Jets**	**NHL**	**25**	**0**	**2**	**2**	**0**	**3**	**3**	**12**	**0**	**0**	**0**	**5**	**0.0**	**28**	**0**	**19**	**1**	**+10**								
	Springfield Falcons	AHL	50	5	16	21				59																		
1995-96	**Anaheim Mighty Ducks**	**NHL**	**8**	**0**	**0**	**0**	**0**	**0**	**0**	**4**	**0**	**0**	**0**	**0**	**0.0**	**3**	**1**	**5**	**1**	**–2**								
	Baltimore Bandits	AHL	19	1	7	8				46											12	2	3	5	22			
1996-97	Long Beach Ice Dogs	IHL	16	0	5	5				29																		
	Fort Wayne Komets	IHL	51	5	13	18				75																		
1997-98	Nurnberg Ice Tigers	Germany	41	4	15	19				174																		
	Belarus	WC A	6	0	1	1				12																		
	NHL Totals		**37**	**0**	**3**	**3**	**0**	**4**	**4**	**33**	**0**	**0**	**0**	**8**	**0.0**	**33**	**1**	**28**	**2**									

Signed as a free agent by **Winnipeg**, July 26, 1993. Signed as a free agent by **Anaheim**, August 8, 1995.

• MILBURY, MIKE

Mike Milbury D – L. 6'1", 200 lbs. b: Brighton, MA, 6/17/1952.

Season	Club	League	GP	G	A	Pts	AG	AA	APts	PIM	PP	SH	GW	S	%	TGF	PGF	TGA	PGA	+/-	GP	G	A	Pts	PIM	PP	SH	GW
1972-73	Colgate University	ECAC	23	2	19	21				68																		
1973-74	Boston Braves	AHL	5	0	0	0				7																		
1974-75	Rochester Americans	AHL	71	2	15	17				246											8	0	3	3	24			
1975-76	**Boston Bruins**	**NHL**	**3**	**0**	**0**	**0**	**0**	**0**	**0**	**9**	**0**	**0**	**0**	**2**	**0.0**	**2**	**0**	**2**	**1**	**+1**	**11**	**0**	**0**	**0**	**[illegible]**	**0**	**0**	**0**
	Rochester Americans	AHL	70	0	15	15				199											3	0	1	1	13			
1976-77	United States	C Cup	5	1	3	4				16																		
	Boston Bruins	**NHL**	**77**	**6**	**18**	**24**	**6**	**15**	**21**	**166**	**0**	**0**	**2**	**89**	**6.7**	**102**	**4**	**89**	**16**	**+25**	**13**	**2**	**2**	**4**	***47**	**0**	**0**	**1**
1977-78	**Boston Bruins**	**NHL**	**80**	**8**	**30**	**38**	**8**	**24**	**32**	**151**	**0**	**0**	**0**	**82**	**9.8**	**135**	**4**	**108**	**27**	**+52**	**15**	**1**	**8**	**9**	**27**	**0**	**0**	**0**
1978-79	**Boston Bruins**	**NHL**	**74**	**1**	**34**	**35**	**1**	**26**	**27**	**149**	**0**	**0**	**0**	**76**	**1.3**	**113**	**9**	**120**	**39**	**+23**	**11**	**1**	**7**	**8**	**7**	**0**	**0**	**1**
1979-80	**Boston Bruins**	**NHL**	**72**	**10**	**13**	**23**	**9**	**10**	**19**	**59**	**1**	**0**	**0**	**101**	**9.9**	**79**	**4**	**94**	**36**	**+17**	**10**	**0**	**2**	**2**	**80**	**0**	**0**	**0**
1980-81	**Boston Bruins**	**NHL**	**77**	**0**	**18**	**18**	**0**	**13**	**13**	**222**	**0**	**0**	**0**	**77**	**0.0**	**78**	**3**	**86**	**25**	**+14**	**2**	**0**	**1**	**1**	**10**	**0**	**0**	**0**
1981-82	**Boston Bruins**	**NHL**	**51**	**2**	**10**	**12**	**2**	**7**	**9**	**71**	**0**	**0**	**1**	**42**	**4.8**	**66**	**1**	**64**	**9**	**+10**	**11**	**0**	**4**	**4**	**6**	**0**	**0**	**0**
1982-83	**Boston Bruins**	**NHL**	**78**	**9**	**15**	**24**	**7**	**10**	**17**	**216**	**1**	**0**	**2**	**95**	**9.5**	**88**	**2**	**91**	**27**	**+22**								
1983-84	**Boston Bruins**	**NHL**	**74**	**2**	**17**	**19**	**2**	**12**	**14**	**169**	**0**	**0**	**1**	**66**	**3.0**	**85**	**4**	**109**	**30**	**+2**	**3**	**0**	**0**	**0**	**12**	**0**	**0**	**0**
1984-85	**Boston Bruins**	**NHL**	**78**	**3**	**13**	**16**	**2**	**9**	**11**	**152**	**0**	**1**	**0**	**84**	**3.6**	**81**	**3**	**119**	**35**	**–6**	**5**	**0**	**0**	**0**	**10**	**0**	**0**	**0**
1985-86	**Boston Bruins**	**NHL**	**22**	**2**	**5**	**7**	**2**	**3**	**5**	**102**	**0**	**0**	**0**	**12**	**16.7**	**20**	**1**	**27**	**9**	**+1**	**1**	**0**	**0**	**0**	**17**	**0**	**0**	**0**
1986-87	**Boston Bruins**	**NHL**	**68**	**6**	**16**	**22**	**5**	**12**	**17**	**96**	**0**	**1**	**1**	**59**	**10.2**	**86**	**4**	**93**	**33**	**+22**	**4**	**0**	**0**	**0**	**4**	**0**	**0**	**0**
1987-88	Maine Mariners	AHL	DID NOT PLAY – COACHING																									
	NHL Totals		**754**	**49**	**189**	**238**	**44**	**141**	**185**	**1552**	**2**	**2**	**7**	**785**	**6.2**	**935**	**39**	**1000**	**277**		**86**	**4**	**24**	**28**	**219**	**0**	**0**	**2**

Signed as a free agent by **Boston**, November 5, 1974.

• MILLAR, CRAIG

Craig Millar D – L. 6'2", 200 lbs. b: Winnipeg, Man., 5/10/1977. Buffalo's 10th choice, 225th overall, in 1994 Entry Draft.

Season	Club	League	GP	G	A	Pts	AG	AA	APts	PIM	PP	SH	GW	S	%	TGF	PGF	TGA	PGA	+/-	GP	G	A	Pts	PIM	PP	SH	GW
1992-93	Swift Current Broncos	WHL	43	2	1	3				8																		
1993-94	Swift Current Broncos	WHL	66	2	9	11				53											7	0	3	3	4			
1994-95	Swift Current Broncos	WHL	72	8	42	50				80											6	1	1	2	10			
1995-96	Swift Current Broncos	WHL	72	31	46	77				151											6	1	0	1	22			
1996-97	Rochester Americans	AHL	64	7	18	25				65																		
	Edmonton Oilers	**NHL**	**1**	**0**	**0**	**0**	**0**	**0**	**0**	**2**	**0**	**0**	**0**	**1**	**0.0**	**0**	**0**	**0**	**0**	**0**								
	Hamilton Bulldogs	AHL	10	1	3	4				10											22	4	4	8	21			
1997-98	**Edmonton Oilers**	**NHL**	**11**	**4**	**0**	**4**	**5**	**0**	**5**	**8**	**1**	**0**	**0**	**10**	**40.0**	**10**	**3**	**14**	**4**	**–3**								
	Hamilton Bulldogs	AHL	60	10	22	32				113											9	3	1	4	22			
	NHL Totals		**12**	**4**	**0**	**4**	**5**	**0**	**5**	**10**	**1**	**0**	**0**	**11**	**36.4**	**10**	**3**	**14**	**4**									

WHL East First All-Star Team (1996)

Traded to **Edmonton** by **Buffalo** with Barrie Moore for Miroslav Satan, March 18, 1997.

• MILLAR, MIKE

Mike Millar RW – L. 5'10", 170 lbs. b: St. Catharines, Ont., 4/28/1965. Hartford's 2nd choice, 110th overall, in 1984 Entry Draft.

Season	Club	League	GP	G	A	Pts	AG	AA	APts	PIM	PP	SH	GW	S	%	TGF	PGF	TGA	PGA	+/-	GP	G	A	Pts	PIM	PP	SH	GW
1981-82	St. Catharines Midgets	Midget	30	32	32	64				24																		
1982-83	Brantford Alexanders	OHL	53	20	29	49				10											8	0	5	5	2			
1983-84	Brantford Alexanders	OHL	69	50	45	95				48											6	4	0	4	2			
1984-85	Hamilton Steelhawks	OHL	63	*66	60	126				54											17	9	10	19	14			
1985-86	Canada	Nat-Team	69	50	38	88				74																		
1986-87	**Hartford Whalers**	**NHL**	**10**	**2**	**2**	**4**	**2**	**1**	**3**	**0**	**1**	**0**	**0**	**13**	**15.4**	**6**	**2**	**1**	**0**	**+3**								
	Binghamton Whalers	AHL	61	45	32	77				38											13	7	4	11	27			
1987-88	**Hartford Whalers**	**NHL**	**28**	**7**	**7**	**14**	**6**	**5**	**11**	**6**	**4**	**0**	**2**	**58**	**12.1**	**24**	**15**	**14**	**0**	**–5**								
	Binghamton Whalers	AHL	31	32	17	49				42																		
1988-89	**Washington Capitals**	**NHL**	**18**	**6**	**3**	**9**	**5**	**2**	**7**	**4**	**3**	**0**	**1**	**37**	**16.2**	**11**	**6**	**9**	**0**	**–4**								
	Baltimore Skipjacks	AHL	53	47	35	82				58																		
1989-90	Washington Capitals	FrTour	1	0	0	0				2																		
	Boston Bruins	**NHL**	**15**	**1**	**4**	**5**	**1**	**3**	**4**	**0**	**0**	**0**	**0**	**18**	**5.6**	**6**	**1**	**7**	**0**	**–2**								
	Maine Mariners	AHL	60	40	33	73				77																		
1990-91	**Toronto Maple Leafs**	**NHL**	**7**	**2**	**2**	**4**	**2**	**2**	**4**	**2**	**0**	**0**	**0**	**11**	**18.2**	**8**	**2**	**7**	**0**	**–1**								
	Newmarket Saints	AHL	62	33	29	62				63																		
1991-92	ESV Kaufbeuren	Germany	42	34	21	55				86																		
1992-93	EHC Chur	Switz.	35	31	21	52				70																		
1993-94	Kassel Huskies	German 2	62	66	44	110				170																		
1994-95	Kassel Huskies	Germany	43	39	21	60				76											9	6	5	11	24			

			REGULAR SEASON																		PLAYOFFS							
Season	Club	League	GP	G	A	Pts	AG	AA	APts	PIM	PP	SH	GW	S	%	TGF	PGF	TGA	PGA	+/–	GP	G	A	Pts	PIM	PP	SH	GW
1995-96	Kassel Huskies	Germany	50	31	23	54	....	....	....	96	....	....	....	....	....	....	....	....	....	....	8	3	5	8	8	....	....	....
1996-97	Kassel Huskies	Germany	42	23	35	58	....	....	....	48	....	....	....	....	....	....	....	....	....	....	10	2	1	3	6	....	....	....
1997-98	Kassel Huskies	EuroHL	2	1	0	1	....	....	....	0	....	....	....	....	....	....	....	....	....	....	....	....	....	....	....	....	....	....
	Kassel Huskies	Germany	6	1	3	4	....	....	....	6	....	....	....	....	....	....	....	....	....	....	....	....	....	....	....	....	....	....
	Frankfurt Lions	Germany	39	13	21	34	....	....	....	20	....	....	....	....	....	....	....	....	....	....	7	2	3	5	2	....	....	....
	NHL Totals		**78**	**18**	**18**	**36**	**16**	**13**	**29**	**12**	**8**	**0**	**3**	**137**	**13.1**	**55**	**26**	**38**	**0**		....	....	....	....	....	....	....	....

AHL Second All-Star Team (1989)

Traded to **Washington** by **Hartford** with Neil Sheehy for Grant Jennings and Ed Kastelic, July 6, 1988. Traded to **Boston** by **Washington** for Alfie Turcotte, October 2, 1989. Signed as a free agent by **Toronto**, July 19, 1990.

• MILLEN, COREY

Corey Millen C – R. 5'7", 170 lbs. b: Cloquet, MN, 3/30/1964. NY Rangers' 3rd choice, 57th overall, in 1982 Entry Draft.

Season	Club	League	GP	G	A	Pts	AG	AA	APts	PIM	PP	SH	GW	S	%	TGF	PGF	TGA	PGA	+/–	GP	G	A	Pts	PIM	PP	SH	GW
1981-82	Cloquet High School	H.S.	18	46	35	81	....	....	....	....	....	....	....	....	....	....	....	....	....	....	....	....	....	....	....	....	....	....
1982-83	University of Minnesota	WCHA	21	14	15	29	....	....	....	18	....	....	....	....	....	....	....	....	....	....	....	....	....	....	....	....	....	....
1983-84	United States	Nat-Team	45	15	11	26	....	....	....	10	....	....	....	....	....	....	....	....	....	....	....	....	....	....	....	....	....	....
	United States	Olympics	6	0	0	0	....	....	....	2	....	....	....	....	....	....	....	....	....	....	....	....	....	....	....	....	....	....
1984-85	University of Minnesota	WCHA	38	28	36	64	....	....	....	60	....	....	....	....	....	....	....	....	....	....	....	....	....	....	....	....	....	....
	United States	WEC-A	10	3	1	4	....	....	....	10	....	....	....	....	....	....	....	....	....	....	....	....	....	....	....	....	....	....
1985-86	University of Minnesota	WCHA	48	41	42	83	....	....	....	64	....	....	....	....	....	....	....	....	....	....	....	....	....	....	....	....	....	....
1986-87	University of Minnesota	WCHA	42	36	29	65	....	....	....	62	....	....	....	....	....	....	....	....	....	....	....	....	....	....	....	....	....	....
1987-88	United States	C Cup	1	1	0	1	....	....	....	0	....	....	....	....	....	....	....	....	....	....	....	....	....	....	....	....	....	....
	United States	Nat-Team	47	41	43	84	....	....	....	26	....	....	....	....	....	....	....	....	....	....	....	....	....	....	....	....	....	....
	United States	Olympics	6	6	5	11	....	....	....	4	....	....	....	....	....	....	....	....	....	....	....	....	....	....	....	....	....	....
1988-89	Ambri-Piotta	Switz.	36	32	22	54	....	....	....	18	....	....	....	....	....	....	....	....	....	....	6	4	3	7	0	....	....	....
	United States	WEC-A	4	0	1	1	....	....	....	0	....	....	....	....	....	....	....	....	....	....	....	....	....	....	....	....	....	....
1989-90	**New York Rangers**	**NHL**	**4**	**0**	**0**	**0**	**0**	**0**	**0**	**2**	**0**	**0**	**0**	**4**	**0.0**	**1**	**1**	**2**	**0**	**–2**	....	....	....	....	....	....	....	....
	Flint Spirits	IHL	11	4	5	9	....	....	....	2	....	....	....	....	....	....	....	....	....	....	....	....	....	....	....	....	....	....
1990-91	**New York Rangers**	**NHL**	**4**	**3**	**1**	**4**	**3**	**1**	**4**	**0**	**2**	**0**	**0**	**8**	**37.5**	**4**	**2**	**1**	**0**	**+1**	**6**	**1**	**2**	**3**	**0**	**1**	**0**	**0**
	Binghamton Rangers	AHL	40	19	37	56	....	....	....	68	....	....	....	....	....	....	....	....	....	....	6	0	7	7	6	....	....	....
1991-92	**New York Rangers**	**NHL**	**11**	**1**	**4**	**5**	**1**	**3**	**4**	**10**	**0**	**0**	**0**	**20**	**5.0**	**7**	**4**	**4**	**0**	**–1**	....	....	....	....	....	....	....	....
	Binghamton Rangers	AHL	15	8	7	15	....	....	....	44	....	....	....	....	....	....	....	....	....	....	....	....	....	....	....	....	....	....
	Los Angeles Kings	**NHL**	**46**	**20**	**21**	**41**	**18**	**16**	**34**	**44**	**8**	**1**	**3**	**89**	**22.5**	**61**	**27**	**41**	**10**	**+3**	**6**	**0**	**1**	**1**	**6**	**0**	**0**	**0**
1992-93	**Los Angeles Kings**	**NHL**	**42**	**23**	**16**	**39**	**19**	**11**	**30**	**42**	**9**	**2**	**1**	**100**	**23.0**	**58**	**20**	**32**	**10**	**+16**	**23**	**2**	**4**	**6**	**12**	**0**	**0**	**0**
1993-94	**New Jersey Devils**	**NHL**	**78**	**20**	**30**	**50**	**19**	**23**	**42**	**52**	**4**	**0**	**3**	**132**	**15.2**	**80**	**17**	**40**	**1**	**+24**	**7**	**1**	**0**	**1**	**2**	**0**	**0**	**1**
1994-95	**New Jersey Devils**	**NHL**	**17**	**2**	**3**	**5**	**4**	**4**	**8**	**8**	**0**	**0**	**0**	**30**	**6.7**	**7**	**0**	**6**	**1**	**+2**	....	....	....	....	....	....	....	....
	Dallas Stars	**NHL**	**28**	**3**	**15**	**18**	**5**	**22**	**27**	**28**	**1**	**0**	**0**	**44**	**6.8**	**25**	**7**	**14**	**0**	**+4**	**5**	**1**	**0**	**1**	**2**	**0**	**0**	**0**
1995-96	**Dallas Stars**	**NHL**	**13**	**3**	**4**	**7**	**3**	**3**	**6**	**8**	**1**	**0**	**0**	**25**	**12.0**	**8**	**2**	**6**	**0**	**0**	....	....	....	....	....	....	....	....
	Michigan K-Wings	IHL	11	8	11	19	....	....	....	14	....	....	....	....	....	....	....	....	....	....	....	....	....	....	....	....	....	....
	Calgary Flames	**NHL**	**31**	**4**	**10**	**14**	**4**	**8**	**12**	**10**	**1**	**0**	**1**	**48**	**8.3**	**26**	**7**	**21**	**10**	**+8**	....	....	....	....	....	....	....	....
1996-97	**Calgary Flames**	**NHL**	**61**	**11**	**15**	**26**	**12**	**13**	**25**	**32**	**1**	**0**	**0**	**82**	**13.4**	**33**	**11**	**44**	**3**	**–19**	....	....	....	....	....	....	....	....
1997-98	Kolner Haie	EuroHL	5	1	5	6	....	....	....	10	....	....	....	....	....	....	....	....	....	....	....	....	....	....	....	....	....	....
	Kolner Haie	Germany	30	17	17	34	....	....	....	52	....	....	....	....	....	....	....	....	....	....	3	2	1	3	6	....	....	....
	NHL Totals		**335**	**90**	**119**	**209**	**88**	**104**	**192**	**236**	**27**	**3**	**8**	**582**	**15.5**	**310**	**98**	**211**	**35**		**47**	**5**	**7**	**12**	**22**	**1**	**0**	**1**

WCHA Second All-Star Team (1985, 1986, 1987) • NCAA West Second All-American Team (1986) • NCAA Championship All-Tournament Team (1987)

Traded to **LA Kings** by **NY Rangers** for Randy Gilhen, December 23, 1991. Traded to **New Jersey** by **LA Kings** for New Jersey's 5th round choice (Jason Saal) in 1993 Entry Draft, June 26, 1993. Traded to **Dallas** by **New Jersey** for Neal Broten, February 27, 1995. Traded to **Calgary** by **Dallas** with Jarome Iginla for Joe Nieuwendyk, December 19, 1995.

• MILLER, AARON

Aaron Miller D – R. 6'3", 197 lbs. b: Buffalo, NY, 8/11/1971. NY Rangers' 6th choice, 88th overall, in 1989 Entry Draft.

Season	Club	League	GP	G	A	Pts	AG	AA	APts	PIM	PP	SH	GW	S	%	TGF	PGF	TGA	PGA	+/–	GP	G	A	Pts	PIM	PP	SH	GW
1988-89	Niagara Scenics	NAJHL	59	24	38	62	....	....	....	60	....	....	....	....	....	....	....	....	....	....	....	....	....	....	....	....	....	....
1989-90	University of Vermont	ECAC	31	1	15	16	....	....	....	24	....	....	....	....	....	....	....	....	....	....	....	....	....	....	....	....	....	....
1990-91	University of Vermont	ECAC	30	3	7	10	....	....	....	22	....	....	....	....	....	....	....	....	....	....	....	....	....	....	....	....	....	....
1991-92	University of Vermont	ECAC	31	3	16	19	....	....	....	28	....	....	....	....	....	....	....	....	....	....	....	....	....	....	....	....	....	....
1992-93	University of Vermont	ECAC	30	4	13	17	....	....	....	16	....	....	....	....	....	....	....	....	....	....	....	....	....	....	....	....	....	....
1993-94	**Quebec Nordiques**	**NHL**	**1**	**0**	**0**	**0**	**0**	**0**	**0**	**0**	**0**	**0**	**0**	**0**	**0.0**	**0**	**0**	**1**	**0**	**–1**	....	....	....	....	....	....	....	....
	Cornwall Aces	AHL	64	4	10	14	....	....	....	49	....	....	....	....	....	....	....	....	....	....	13	0	2	2	10	....	....	....
1994-95	**Quebec Nordiques**	**NHL**	**9**	**0**	**3**	**3**	**0**	**4**	**4**	**6**	**0**	**0**	**0**	**12**	**0.0**	**9**	**1**	**6**	**0**	**+2**	....	....	....	....	....	....	....	....
	Cornwall Aces	AHL	76	4	18	22	....	....	....	69	....	....	....	....	....	....	....	....	....	....	....	....	....	....	....	....	....	....
1995-96	**Colorado Avalanche**	**NHL**	**5**	**0**	**0**	**0**	**0**	**0**	**0**	**0**	**0**	**0**	**0**	**2**	**0.0**	**1**	**0**	**1**	**0**	**0**	....	....	....	....	....	....	....	....
	Cornwall Aces	AHL	62	4	23	27	....	....	....	77	....	....	....	....	....	....	....	....	....	....	8	0	1	1	6	....	....	....
1996-97	**Colorado Avalanche**	**NHL**	**56**	**5**	**12**	**17**	**5**	**11**	**16**	**15**	**0**	**0**	**3**	**47**	**10.6**	**38**	**2**	**22**	**1**	**+15**	**17**	**1**	**2**	**3**	**10**	**0**	**0**	**0**
1997-98	**Colorado Avalanche**	**NHL**	**55**	**2**	**2**	**4**	**2**	**2**	**4**	**51**	**0**	**0**	**0**	**29**	**6.9**	**19**	**1**	**22**	**4**	**0**	**7**	**0**	**0**	**0**	**8**	**0**	**0**	**0**
	NHL Totals		**126**	**7**	**17**	**24**	**7**	**17**	**24**	**72**	**0**	**0**	**3**	**90**	**7.8**	**67**	**4**	**52**	**5**		**24**	**1**	**2**	**3**	**18**	**0**	**0**	**0**

ECAC First All-Star Team (1993) • NCAA East Second All-American Team (1993)

Traded to **Quebec** by **NY Rangers** with NY Rangers' 5th round choice (Bill Lindsay) in 1991 Entry Draft for Joe Cirella, January 17, 1991. Transferred to **Colorado** after **Quebec** franchise relocated, June 21, 1996.

• MILLER, BOB

Bob Miller C – L. 5'11", 180 lbs. b: Medford, MA, 9/28/1956. Boston's 9th choice, 70th overall, in 1976 Amateur Draft.

Season	Club	League	GP	G	A	Pts	AG	AA	APts	PIM	PP	SH	GW	S	%	TGF	PGF	TGA	PGA	+/–	GP	G	A	Pts	PIM	PP	SH	GW
1974-75	University of New Hampshire	ECAC	27	21	38	59	....	....	....	26	....	....	....	....	....	....	....	....	....	....	....	....	....	....	....	....	....	....
1975-76	United States	Nat-Team	63	33	61	94	....	....	....	83	....	....	....	....	....	....	....	....	....	....	....	....	....	....	....	....	....	....
	United States	Olympics	6	0	3	3	....	....	....	0	....	....	....	....	....	....	....	....	....	....	....	....	....	....	....	....	....	....
	Ottawa 67's	OHA	6	5	5	10	....	....	....	5	....	....	....	....	....	....	....	....	....	....	12	2	4	6	9	....	....	....
1976-77	University of New Hampshire	ECAC	38	30	59	89	....	....	....	45	....	....	....	....	....	....	....	....	....	....	....	....	....	....	....	....	....	....
	United States	WEC-A	10	5	3	8	....	....	....	4	....	....	....	....	....	....	....	....	....	....	....	....	....	....	....	....	....	....
1977-78	**Boston Bruins**	**NHL**	**76**	**20**	**20**	**40**	**19**	**16**	**35**	**41**	**1**	**1**	**4**	**134**	**14.9**	**52**	**2**	**38**	**4**	**+16**	**13**	**0**	**3**	**3**	**15**	**0**	**0**	**0**
	Rochester Americans	AHL	3	1	3	4	....	....	....	7	....	....	....	....	....	....	....	....	....	....	....	....	....	....	....	....	....	....
1978-79	**Boston Bruins**	**NHL**	**77**	**15**	**33**	**48**	**14**	**25**	**39**	**30**	**0**	**0**	**1**	**149**	**10.1**	**67**	**2**	**51**	**6**	**+20**	**11**	**1**	**1**	**2**	**8**	**0**	**0**	**0**
1979-80	**Boston Bruins**	**NHL**	**80**	**16**	**25**	**41**	**14**	**19**	**33**	**53**	**0**	**1**	**2**	**137**	**11.7**	**57**	**1**	**86**	**39**	**+9**	**10**	**3**	**2**	**5**	**4**	**0**	**1**	**0**
1980-81	**Boston Bruins**	**NHL**	**30**	**4**	**4**	**8**	**3**	**3**	**6**	**19**	**0**	**1**	**1**	**23**	**17.4**	**9**	**0**	**31**	**17**	**–5**	....	....	....	....	....	....	....	....
	Springfield Indians	AHL	3	1	2	3	....	....	....	0	....	....	....	....	....	....	....	....	....	....	....	....	....	....	....	....	....	....
	Colorado Rockies	**NHL**	**22**	**5**	**1**	**6**	**4**	**1**	**5**	**15**	**2**	**0**	**0**	**41**	**12.2**	**13**	**8**	**40**	**16**	**–19**	....	....	....	....	....	....	....	....
	United States	WEC-A	8	5	4	9	....	....	....	4	....	....	....	....	....	....	....	....	....	....	....	....	....	....	....	....	....	....
1981-82	United States	C Cup	6	0	1	1	....	....	....	6	....	....	....	....	....	....	....	....	....	....	....	....	....	....	....	....	....	....
	Colorado Rockies	**NHL**	**56**	**11**	**20**	**31**	**9**	**13**	**22**	**27**	**1**	**0**	**2**	**94**	**11.7**	**43**	**4**	**87**	**24**	**–24**	....	....	....	....	....	....	....	....
	United States	WEC-A	7	3	1	4	....	....	....	4	....	....	....	....	....	....	....	....	....	....	....	....	....	....	....	....	....	....
1982-83	Springfield Indians	AHL	59	17	31	48	....	....	....	60	....	....	....	....	....	....	....	....	....	....	....	....	....	....	....	....	....	....
1983-84	Karpat Oulu	Finland	37	17	31	48	....	....	....	66	....	....	....	....	....	....	....	....	....	....	9	5	4	9	20	....	....	....
1984-85	**Los Angeles Kings**	**NHL**	**63**	**4**	**16**	**20**	**3**	**11**	**14**	**35**	**0**	**0**	**0**	**64**	**6.3**	**24**	**0**	**59**	**18**	**–17**	**2**	**0**	**1**	**1**	**0**	**0**	**0**	**0**
	United States	WEC-A	10	1	6	7	....	....	....	2	....	....	....	....	....	....	....	....	....	....	....	....	....	....	....	....	....	....
1985-86	HC Sierre	Switz.	....	35	34	69	....	....	....	....	....	....	....	....	....	....	....	....	....	....	4	2	0	2	0	....	....	....
1986-87	HC Sierre	Switz.	....	2	6	8	....	....	....	....	....	....	....	....	....	....	....	....	....	....	....	....	....	....	....	....	....	....
	NHL Totals		**404**	**75**	**119**	**194**	**66**	**88**	**154**	**220**	**4**	**3**	**10**	**642**	**11.7**	**265**	**17**	**392**	**124**		**36**	**4**	**7**	**11**	**27**	**0**	**1**	**0**

ECAC First All-Star Team (1977) • NCAA East First All-American Team (1977)

Traded to **Colorado** by **Boston** for Mike Gillis, February 18, 1981. Signed as a free agent by **LA Kings**, October 9, 1984.

• MILLER, BRAD

Brad Miller D – L. 6'4", 220 lbs. b: Edmonton, Alta., 7/23/1969. Buffalo's 2nd choice, 22nd overall, in 1987 Entry Draft.

Season	Club	League	GP	G	A	Pts	AG	AA	APts	PIM	PP	SH	GW	S	%	TGF	PGF	TGA	PGA	+/–	GP	G	A	Pts	PIM	PP	SH	GW
1984-85	Edmonton K. of C.	Midget	42	7	26	33	....	....	....	154	....	....	....	....	....	....	....	....	....	....	....	....	....	....	....	....	....	....
1985-86	Regina Pats	WHL	71	2	14	16	....	....	....	99	....	....	....	....	....	....	....	....	....	....	10	1	1	2	4	....	....	....
1986-87	Regina Pats	WHL	67	10	38	48	....	....	....	154	....	....	....	....	....	....	....	....	....	....	3	0	0	0	6	....	....	....
1987-88	Regina Pats	WHL	61	9	34	43	....	....	....	148	....	....	....	....	....	....	....	....	....	....	4	1	1	2	12	....	....	....
	Rochester Americans	AHL	3	0	0	0	....	....	....	4	....	....	....	....	....	....	....	....	....	....	2	0	0	0	2	....	....	....

Season	Club	League	REGULAR SEASON																		PLAYOFFS							
			GP	G	A	Pts	AG	AA	APts	PIM	PP	SH	GW	S	%	TGF	PGF	TGA	PGA	+/–	GP	G	A	Pts	PIM	PP	SH	GW
1988-89	Regina Pats	WHL	34	8	18	26	....	....	....	95	....	....	....	....	....	....	....	....	....	....	....	....	....	....	....	....	....	....
	Buffalo Sabres	NHL	7	0	0	0	0	0	0	6	0	0	0	0	0.0	5	0	6	0	–1	....	....	....	....	....	....	....	....
	Rochester Americans	AHL	3	0	0	0	....	....	....	4	....	....	....	....	....	....	....	....	....	....	....	....	....	....	....	....	....	....
1989-90	Buffalo Sabres	NHL	1	0	0	0	0	0	0	0	0	0	0	0	0.0	1	0	0	0	+1	....	....	....	....	....	....	....	....
	Rochester Americans	AHL	60	2	10	12	....	....	....	273	....	....	....	....	....	....	....	....	....	....	8	1	0	1	52	....	....	....
1990-91	Buffalo Sabres	NHL	13	0	0	0	0	0	0	67	0	0	0	4	0.0	1	0	2	0	–1	....	....	....	....	....	....	....	....
	Rochester Americans	AHL	49	0	9	9	....	....	....	248	....	....	....	....	....	....	....	....	....	....	12	0	4	4	*67	....	....	....
1991-92	Buffalo Sabres	NHL	42	1	4	5	1	3	4	192	0	0	0	30	3.3	26	0	32	1	–5	....	....	....	....	....	....	....	....
	Rochester Americans	AHL	27	0	4	4	....	....	....	113	....	....	....	....	....	....	....	....	....	....	11	0	0	0	61	....	....	....
1992-93	Ottawa Senators	NHL	11	0	0	0	0	0	0	42	0	0	0	2	0.0	1	0	6	0	–5	....	....	....	....	....	....	....	....
	New Haven Nighthawks	AHL	41	1	9	10	....	....	....	138	....	....	....	....	....	....	....	....	....	....	....	....	....	....	....	....	....	....
	St. John's Maple Leafs	AHL	20	0	3	3	....	....	....	61	....	....	....	....	....	....	....	....	....	....	8	0	2	2	10	....	....	....
1993-94	Calgary Flames	NHL	8	0	1	1	0	1	1	14	0	0	0	2	0.0	3	0	5	0	–2	....	....	....	....	....	....	....	....
	Saint John Flames	AHL	36	3	12	15	....	....	....	174	....	....	....	....	....	....	....	....	....	....	6	1	0	1	21	....	....	....
1994-95	Minnesota Moose	IHL	55	1	13	14	....	....	....	181	....	....	....	....	....	....	....	....	....	....	3	0	0	0	12	....	....	....
1995-96	Minnesota Moose	IHL	33	0	5	5	....	....	....	170	....	....	....	....	....	....	....	....	....	....	....	....	....	....	....	....	....	....
	Atlanta Knights	IHL	5	0	0	0	....	....	....	8	....	....	....	....	....	....	....	....	....	....	....	....	....	....	....	....	....	....
1996-97	Quebec Rafales	IHL	57	1	7	8	....	....	....	132	....	....	....	....	....	....	....	....	....	....	4	0	0	0	2	....	....	....
1997-98	San Antonio Dragons	IHL	58	3	6	9	....	....	....	228	....	....	....	....	....	....	....	....	....	....	....	....	....	....	....	....	....	....
	Utah Grizzlies	IHL	9	0	1	1	....	....	....	46	....	....	....	....	....	....	....	....	....	....	4	0	0	0	8	....	....	....
	NHL Totals		82	1	5	6	1	4	5	321	0	0	0	38	2.6	37	0	51	1		....	....	....	....	....	....	....	....

Claimed by **Ottawa** from **Buffalo** in Expansion Draft, June 18, 1992. Traded to **Toronto** by **Ottawa** for Toronto's 9th round choice (Pavol Demitra) in 1993 Entry Draft, February 25, 1993. Traded to **Calgary** by **Toronto** with Jeff Perry for Todd Gillingham and Paul Holden, September 2, 1993.

• MILLER, JASON

Jason Miller   LW – L. 6′1″, 190 lbs.   b: Edmonton, Alta., 3/1/1971.   New Jersey's 5th choice, 18th overall, in 1989 Entry Draft.

Season	Club	League	GP	G	A	Pts	AG	AA	APts	PIM	PP	SH	GW	S	%	TGF	PGF	TGA	PGA	+/–	GP	G	A	Pts	PIM	PP	SH	GW
1987-88	Medicine Hat Tigers	WHL	71	11	18	29	....	....	....	28	....	....	....	....	....	....	....	....	....	....	15	0	1	1	2	....	....	....
1988-89	Medicine Hat Tigers	WHL	72	51	55	106	....	....	....	44	....	....	....	....	....	....	....	....	....	....	3	1	2	3	2	....	....	....
1989-90	Medicine Hat Tigers	WHL	66	43	56	99	....	....	....	40	....	....	....	....	....	....	....	....	....	....	3	3	2	5	0	....	....	....
1990-91	Medicine Hat Tigers	WHL	66	60	76	136	....	....	....	31	....	....	....	....	....	....	....	....	....	....	12	9	10	19	8	....	....	....
	New Jersey Devils	NHL	1	0	0	0	0	0	0	0	0	0	0	0	0.0	1	0	0	0	+1	....	....	....	....	....	....	....	....
1991-92	New Jersey Devils	NHL	3	0	0	0	0	0	0	0	0	0	0	1	0.0	1	0	1	0	0	....	....	....	....	....	....	....	....
	Utica Devils	AHL	71	23	32	55	....	....	....	31	....	....	....	....	....	....	....	....	....	....	4	1	3	4	0	....	....	....
1992-93	New Jersey Devils	NHL	2	0	0	0	0	0	0	0	0	0	0	1	0.0	0	0	1	0	–1	....	....	....	....	....	....	....	....
	Utica Devils	AHL	72	28	42	70	....	....	....	43	....	....	....	....	....	....	....	....	....	....	5	4	4	8	2	....	....	....
1993-94	Albany River Rats	AHL	77	22	53	75	....	....	....	65	....	....	....	....	....	....	....	....	....	....	5	1	1	2	4	....	....	....
1994-95	Adirondack Red Wings	AHL	77	32	33	65	....	....	....	39	....	....	....	....	....	....	....	....	....	....	4	1	0	1	0	....	....	....
1995-96	HPK Hameenlina	Finland	22	4	6	10	....	....	....	10	....	....	....	....	....	....	....	....	....	....	....	....	....	....	....	....	....	....
	Kaufbeuren Eagles	Germany	3	1	1	2	....	....	....	0	....	....	....	....	....	....	....	....	....	....	....	....	....	....	....	....	....	....
	Peoria Rivermen	IHL	39	16	22	38	....	....	....	6	....	....	....	....	....	....	....	....	....	....	11	1	2	3	4	....	....	....
1996-97	San Antonio Dragons	IHL	76	26	43	69	....	....	....	43	....	....	....	....	....	....	....	....	....	....	9	1	4	5	6	....	....	....
1997-98	Dusseldorfer EG	Germany	46	15	19	34	....	....	....	26	....	....	....	....	....	....	....	....	....	....	3	1	2	3	0	....	....	....
	NHL Totals		6	0	0	0	0	0	0	0	0	0	0	2	0.0	2	0	2	0		....	....	....	....	....	....	....	....

WHL East Second All-Star Team (1991)

Signed as a free agent by **Detroit**, August 26, 1994.

• MILLER, JAY

Jay Miller   LW – L. 6′2″, 210 lbs.   b: Wellesley, MA, 7/16/1960.   Quebec's 2nd choice, 66th overall, in 1980 Entry Draft.

Season	Club	League	GP	G	A	Pts	AG	AA	APts	PIM	PP	SH	GW	S	%	TGF	PGF	TGA	PGA	+/–	GP	G	A	Pts	PIM	PP	SH	GW
1979-80	University of New Hampshire	ECAC	28	7	12	19	....	....	....	53	....	....	....	....	....	....	....	....	....	....	....	....	....	....	....	....	....	....
1980-81	University of New Hampshire	ECAC	10	4	8	12	....	....	....	14	....	....	....	....	....	....	....	....	....	....	....	....	....	....	....	....	....	....
1981-82	University of New Hampshire	ECAC	24	6	4	10	....	....	....	34	....	....	....	....	....	....	....	....	....	....	....	....	....	....	....	....	....	....
1982-83	University of New Hampshire	ECAC	28	6	4	10	....	....	....	20	....	....	....	....	....	....	....	....	....	....	....	....	....	....	....	....	....	....
	Fredericton Express	AHL	3	1	2	3	....	....	....	0	....	....	....	....	....	....	....	....	....	....	....	....	....	....	....	....	....	....
1983-84	Toledo Goaldiggers	IHL	2	0	0	0	....	....	....	2	....	....	....	....	....	....	....	....	....	....	....	....	....	....	....	....	....	....
	Maine Mariners	AHL	15	1	1	2	....	....	....	27	....	....	....	....	....	....	....	....	....	....	....	....	....	....	....	....	....	....
	Mohawk Valley Suns	ACHL	48	15	36	51	....	....	....	167	....	....	....	....	....	....	....	....	....	....	....	....	....	....	....	....	....	....
1984-85	Muskegon Mohawks	IHL	56	5	29	34	....	....	....	177	....	....	....	....	....	....	....	....	....	....	17	1	1	2	56	....	....	....
1985-86	Boston Bruins	NHL	46	3	0	3	2	0	2	178	0	0	0	21	14.3	6	0	9	0	–3	2	0	0	0	17	0	0	0
	Moncton Golden Flames	AHL	18	4	6	10	....	....	....	113	....	....	....	....	....	....	....	....	....	....	....	....	....	....	....	....	....	....
1986-87	Boston Bruins	NHL	55	1	4	5	1	3	4	208	0	0	0	27	3.7	13	0	24	0	–11	....	....	....	....	....	....	....	....
1987-88	Boston Bruins	NHL	78	7	12	19	6	9	15	304	0	0	1	44	15.9	24	0	29	0	–5	12	0	0	0	*124	0	0	0
1988-89	Boston Bruins	NHL	37	2	4	6	2	3	5	168	0	0	0	14	14.3	8	0	14	0	–6	....	....	....	....	....	....	....	....
	Los Angeles Kings	NHL	29	5	3	8	4	2	6	133	0	0	0	16	31.3	11	0	14	0	–3	11	0	1	1	63	0	0	0
1989-90	Los Angeles Kings	NHL	68	10	2	12	9	1	10	224	0	0	1	44	22.7	19	0	25	0	–6	10	1	1	2	10	0	0	0
1990-91	Los Angeles Kings	NHL	66	8	12	20	7	9	16	259	1	0	0	35	22.9	34	7	19	1	+9	8	0	0	0	17	0	0	0
1991-92	Los Angeles Kings	NHL	67	4	7	11	4	5	9	249	0	0	0	32	12.5	17	2	23	0	–8	5	1	1	2	12	0	0	0
	NHL Totals		446	40	44	84	35	32	67	1723	1	0	2	233	17.2	132	9	157	1		48	2	3	5	243	0	0	0

Signed as a free agent by **Boston**, October 1, 1985. Traded to **LA Kings** by **Boston** for future considerations, January 22, 1989.

• MILLER, KELLY

Kelly Miller   LW – L. 5′11″, 197 lbs.   b: Lansing, MI, 3/3/1963.   NY Rangers' 9th choice, 183rd overall, in 1982 Entry Draft.

Season	Club	League	GP	G	A	Pts	AG	AA	APts	PIM	PP	SH	GW	S	%	TGF	PGF	TGA	PGA	+/–	GP	G	A	Pts	PIM	PP	SH	GW
1981-82	Michigan State Spartans	CCHA	38	11	18	29	....	....	....	17	....	....	....	....	....	....	....	....	....	....	....	....	....	....	....	....	....	....
	United States	WJC-A	7	2	4	6	....	....	....	0	....	....	....	....	....	....	....	....	....	....	....	....	....	....	....	....	....	....
1982-83	Michigan State Spartans	CCHA	36	16	19	35	....	....	....	12	....	....	....	....	....	....	....	....	....	....	....	....	....	....	....	....	....	....
	United States	WJC-A	7	0	1	1	....	....	....	0	....	....	....	....	....	....	....	....	....	....	....	....	....	....	....	....	....	....
1983-84	Michigan State Spartans	CCHA	46	28	21	49	....	....	....	12	....	....	....	....	....	....	....	....	....	....	....	....	....	....	....	....	....	....
1984-85	Michigan State Spartans	CCHA	43	27	23	50	....	....	....	21	....	....	....	....	....	....	....	....	....	....	....	....	....	....	....	....	....	....
	New York Rangers	NHL	5	0	2	2	0	1	1	2	0	0	0	5	0.0	3	1	5	1	–2	3	0	0	0	2	0	0	0
	United States	WEC-A	10	2	3	5	....	....	....	2	....	....	....	....	....	....	....	....	....	....	....	....	....	....	....	....	....	....
1985-86	New York Rangers	NHL	74	13	20	33	10	13	23	52	0	1	3	112	11.6	53	1	75	26	+3	16	3	4	7	4	0	1	0
1986-87	New York Rangers	NHL	38	6	14	20	5	10	15	22	2	0	1	58	10.3	30	8	39	12	–5	....	....	....	....	....	....	....	....
	Washington Capitals	NHL	39	10	12	22	9	9	18	26	3	1	0	50	20.0	38	9	23	4	+10	7	2	2	4	0	0	0	0
1987-88	United States	C Cup	5	0	0	0	....	....	....	0	....	....	....	....	....	....	....	....	....	....	....	....	....	....	....	....	....	....
	Washington Capitals	NHL	80	9	23	32	8	16	24	35	0	1	3	96	9.4	52	1	65	23	+9	14	4	4	8	10	0	1	1
1988-89	Washington Capitals	NHL	78	19	21	40	16	15	31	45	2	1	3	121	15.7	62	6	74	31	+13	6	1	0	1	2	0	0	1
	United States	WEC-A	9	2	4	6	....	....	....	2	....	....	....	....	....	....	....	....	....	....	....	....	....	....	....	....	....	....
1989-90	Washington Capitals	NHL	80	18	22	40	16	16	32	49	3	2	2	107	16.8	67	12	98	41	–2	15	3	5	8	23	0	1	0
1990-91	Washington Capitals	NHL	80	24	26	50	22	20	42	29	4	2	3	155	15.5	79	13	84	28	+10	11	4	2	6	6	0	1	0
1991-92	Washington Capitals	NHL	78	14	38	52	13	29	42	49	0	1	3	144	9.7	78	6	88	36	+20	7	1	2	3	4	0	0	0
1992-93	Washington Capitals	NHL	84	18	27	45	15	18	33	32	3	0	3	144	12.5	63	6	110	51	–2	6	0	3	3	2	0	0	0
1993-94	Washington Capitals	NHL	84	14	25	39	13	19	32	32	0	1	3	138	10.1	59	2	79	30	+8	11	2	7	9	0	1	1	0
1994-95	Washington Capitals	NHL	48	10	13	23	18	19	37	6	2	0	1	70	14.3	32	8	36	15	+5	7	0	3	3	4	0	0	0
1995-96	Washington Capitals	NHL	74	7	13	20	7	11	18	30	0	2	1	93	7.5	33	4	57	35	+7	6	0	1	1	4	0	0	0
1996-97	Washington Capitals	NHL	77	10	14	24	11	12	23	33	0	1	3	95	10.5	39	2	60	27	+4	....	....	....	....	....	....	....	....
1997-98	Washington Capitals	NHL	76	7	7	14	8	7	15	41	0	3	3	68	10.3	22	0	35	11	–2	10	0	1	1	4	0	0	0
	NHL Totals		995	179	277	456	171	215	386	483	19	16	32	1456	12.3	710	77	928	371		119	20	34	54	65	1	5	2

CCHA First All-Star Team (1985) • NCAA West First All-American Team (1985)

Traded to **Washington** by **NY Rangers** with Bob Crawford and Mike Ridley for Bob Carpenter and Washington's 2nd round choice (Jason Prosofsky) in 1989 Entry Draft, January 1, 1987.

• MILLER, KEVIN

Kevin Miller   C – R. 5′11″, 190 lbs.   b: Lansing, MI, 9/2/1965   NY Rangers' 10th choice, 202nd overall, in 1984 Entry Draft.

Season	Club	League	GP	G	A	Pts	AG	AA	APts	PIM	PP	SH	GW	S	%	TGF	PGF	TGA	PGA	+/–	GP	G	A	Pts	PIM	PP	SH	GW
1984-85	Michigan State Spartans	CCHA	44	11	29	40	....	....	....	84	....	....	....	....	....	....	....	....	....	....	....	....	....	....	....	....	....	....
1985-86	Michigan State Spartans	CCHA	45	19	52	71	....	....	....	112	....	....	....	....	....	....	....	....	....	....	....	....	....	....	....	....	....	....
1986-87	Michigan State Spartans	CCHA	42	25	56	81	....	....	....	63	....	....	....	....	....	....	....	....	....	....	....	....	....	....	....	....	....	....

			REGULAR SEASON																		PLAYOFFS							
Season	Club	League	GP	G	A	Pts	AG	AA	APts	PIM	PP	SH	GW	S	%	TGF	PGF	TGA	PGA	+/–	GP	G	A	Pts	PIM	PP	SH	GW
1987-88	Michigan State Spartans	CCHA	9	6	3	9	....	....	....	18	....	....	....	....	....	....	....	....	....	....	....	....	....	....	....	....	....	....
	United States	Nat-Team	48	31	32	63	....	....	....	33	....	....	....	....	....	....	....	....	....	....	....	....	....	....	....	....	....	....
	United States	Olympics	5	1	3	4	....	....	....	4	....	....	....	....	....	....	....	....	....	....	....	....	....	....	....	....	....	....
1988-89	**New York Rangers**	**NHL**	**24**	**3**	**5**	**8**	**3**	**4**	**7**	**2**	**0**	**0**	**1**	**40**	**7.5**	**12**	**0**	**13**	**0**	**–1**	....	....	....	....	....	....	....	....
	Denver Rangers	IHL	55	29	47	76	....	....	....	19	....	....	....	....	....	....	....	....	....	....	4	2	1	3	2	....	....	....
1989-90	**New York Rangers**	**NHL**	**16**	**0**	**5**	**5**	**0**	**4**	**4**	**2**	**0**	**0**	**0**	**9**	**0.0**	**6**	**1**	**6**	**0**	**–1**	**1**	**0**	**0**	**0**	**0**	**0**	**0**	**0**
	Flint Spirits	IHL	48	19	23	42	....	....	....	41	....	....	....	....	....	....	....	....	....	....	....	....	....	....	....	....	....	....
1990-91	**New York Rangers**	**NHL**	**63**	**17**	**27**	**44**	**16**	**20**	**36**	**63**	**1**	**2**	**3**	**113**	**15.0**	**56**	**7**	**60**	**12**	**+1**	....	....	....	....	....	....	....	....
	Detroit Red Wings	**NHL**	**11**	**5**	**2**	**7**	**5**	**2**	**7**	**4**	**0**	**1**	**0**	**23**	**21.7**	**9**	**2**	**15**	**4**	**–4**	**7**	**3**	**2**	**5**	**20**	**0**	**1**	**0**
	United States	WEC-A	9	3	5	8	....	....	....	10	....	....	....	....	....	....	....	....	....	....	....	....	....	....	....	....	....	....
1991-92	United States	C Cup	8	2	3	5	....	....	....	16	....	....	....	....	....	....	....	....	....	....	....	....	....	....	....	....	....	....
	Detroit Red Wings	**NHL**	**80**	**20**	**26**	**46**	**18**	**20**	**38**	**53**	**3**	**1**	**4**	**130**	**15.4**	**73**	**13**	**91**	**37**	**+6**	**9**	**0**	**2**	**2**	**4**	**0**	**0**	**0**
1992-93	**Washington Capitals**	**NHL**	**10**	**0**	**3**	**3**	**0**	**2**	**2**	**35**	**0**	**0**	**0**	**10**	**0.0**	**3**	**0**	**7**	**0**	**–4**	....	....	....	....	....	....	....	....
	St. Louis Blues	**NHL**	**72**	**24**	**22**	**46**	**20**	**15**	**35**	**65**	**8**	**3**	**4**	**153**	**15.7**	**75**	**24**	**56**	**11**	**+6**	**10**	**0**	**3**	**3**	**11**	**0**	**0**	**0**
1993-94	**St. Louis Blues**	**NHL**	**75**	**23**	**25**	**48**	**21**	**19**	**40**	**83**	**6**	**3**	**5**	**154**	**14.9**	**84**	**30**	**72**	**24**	**+6**	**3**	**1**	**0**	**1**	**4**	**0**	**1**	**0**
1994-95	**St. Louis Blues**	**NHL**	**15**	**2**	**5**	**7**	**4**	**7**	**11**	**0**	**0**	**0**	**0**	**19**	**10.5**	**10**	**0**	**8**	**2**	**+4**	....	....	....	....	....	....	....	....
	San Jose Sharks	**NHL**	**21**	**6**	**7**	**13**	**11**	**10**	**21**	**13**	**1**	**1**	**2**	**41**	**14.6**	**16**	**2**	**20**	**6**	**0**	**6**	**0**	**0**	**0**	**2**	**0**	**0**	**0**
1995-96	**San Jose Sharks**	**NHL**	**68**	**22**	**20**	**42**	**22**	**16**	**38**	**41**	**2**	**2**	**2**	**146**	**15.1**	**75**	**25**	**89**	**31**	**–8**	....	....	....	....	....	....	....	....
	Pittsburgh Penguins	**NHL**	**13**	**6**	**5**	**11**	**6**	**4**	**10**	**4**	**1**	**0**	**0**	**33**	**18.2**	**16**	**3**	**14**	**5**	**+4**	**18**	**3**	**2**	**5**	**8**	**0**	**0**	**0**
1996-97	**Chicago Blackhawks**	**NHL**	**69**	**14**	**17**	**31**	**15**	**15**	**30**	**41**	**5**	**1**	**2**	**139**	**10.1**	**40**	**11**	**57**	**18**	**–10**	**6**	**0**	**1**	**1**	**0**	**0**	**0**	**0**
	United States	WC-A	5	0	1	1	....	....	....	29	....	....	....	....	....	....	....	....	....	....	....	....	....	....	....	....	....	....
1997-98	**Chicago Blackhawks**	**NHL**	**37**	**4**	**7**	**11**	**5**	**7**	**12**	**8**	**0**	**0**	**1**	**37**	**10.8**	**15**	**0**	**22**	**3**	**–4**	....	....	....	....	....	....	....	....
	Indianapolis Ice	IHL	26	11	11	22	....	....	....	41	....	....	....	....	....	....	....	....	....	....	2	1	1	2	0	....	....	....
	NHL Totals		**574**	**146**	**176**	**322**	**146**	**145**	**291**	**414**	**27**	**14**	**24**	**1047**	**13.9**	**490**	**118**	**530**	**153**		**60**	**7**	**10**	**17**	**49**	**0**	**2**	**0**

Traded to **Detroit** by **NY Rangers** with Jim Cummins and Dennis Vial for Joey Kocur and Per Djoos, March 5, 1991. Traded to **Washington** by **Detroit** for Dino Ciccarelli, June 20, 1992. Traded to **St. Louis** by **Washington** for Paul Cavallini, November 2, 1992. Traded to **San Jose** by **St. Louis** for Todd Elik, March 23, 1995. Traded to **Pittsburgh** by **San Jose** for Pittsburgh's 5th round choice (later traded to Boston — Boston selected Elias Abrahamsson) in 1996 Entry Draft and future considerations, March 20, 1996. Signed as a free agent by **Chicago**, July 18, 1996.

• MILLER, KIP

Kip Miller C – L. 5'10", 190 lbs. b: Lansing, MI, 6/11/1969. Quebec's 9th choice, 72nd overall, in 1987 Entry Draft.

Season	Club	League	GP	G	A	Pts	AG	AA	APts	PIM	PP	SH	GW	S	%	TGF	PGF	TGA	PGA	+/–	GP	G	A	Pts	PIM	PP	SH	GW
1986-87	Michigan State Spartans	CCHA	41	20	19	39	....	....	....	92	....	....	....	....	....	....	....	....	....	....	....	....	....	....	....	....	....	....
1987-88	Michigan State Spartans	CCHA	39	16	25	41	....	....	....	51	....	....	....	....	....	....	....	....	....	....	....	....	....	....	....	....	....	....
	United States	WJC-A	7	2	2	4	....	....	....	2	....	....	....	....	....	....	....	....	....	....	....	....	....	....	....	....	....	....
1988-89	Michigan State Spartans	CCHA	47	32	45	77	....	....	....	94	....	....	....	....	....	....	....	....	....	....	....	....	....	....	....	....	....	....
1989-90	Michigan State Spartans	CCHA	45	*48	53	*101	....	....	....	60	....	....	....	....	....	....	....	....	....	....	....	....	....	....	....	....	....	....
	United States	WEC-A	9	1	1	2	....	....	....	10	....	....	....	....	....	....	....	....	....	....	....	....	....	....	....	....	....	....
1990-91	**Quebec Nordiques**	**NHL**	**13**	**4**	**3**	**7**	**4**	**2**	**6**	**7**	**0**	**0**	**0**	**16**	**25.0**	**10**	**0**	**11**	**0**	**–1**	....	....	....	....	....	....	....	....
	Halifax Citadels	AHL	66	36	33	69	....	....	....	40	....	....	....	....	....	....	....	....	....	....	....	....	....	....	....	....	....	....
1991-92	**Quebec Nordiques**	**NHL**	**36**	**5**	**10**	**15**	**5**	**7**	**12**	**12**	**1**	**0**	**2**	**46**	**10.9**	**19**	**3**	**38**	**1**	**–21**	....	....	....	....	....	....	....	....
	Halifax Citadels	AHL	24	9	17	26	....	....	....	8	....	....	....	....	....	....	....	....	....	....	....	....	....	....	....	....	....	....
	Minnesota North Stars	**NHL**	**3**	**1**	**2**	**3**	**1**	**1**	**2**	**2**	**1**	**0**	**0**	**3**	**33.3**	**3**	**2**	**2**	**0**	**–1**	....	....	....	....	....	....	....	....
	Kalamazoo Wings	IHL	6	1	8	9	....	....	....	4	....	....	....	....	....	....	....	....	....	....	12	3	9	12	12	....	....	....
1992-93	Kalamazoo Wings	IHL	61	17	39	56	....	....	....	59	....	....	....	....	....	....	....	....	....	....	....	....	....	....	....	....	....	....
1993-94	**San Jose Sharks**	**NHL**	**11**	**2**	**2**	**4**	**2**	**2**	**4**	**6**	**0**	**0**	**0**	**21**	**9.5**	**9**	**2**	**8**	**0**	**–1**	....	....	....	....	....	....	....	....
	Kansas City Blades	IHL	71	38	54	92	....	....	....	51	....	....	....	....	....	....	....	....	....	....	....	....	....	....	....	....	....	....
1994-95	Denver Grizzlies	IHL	71	46	60	106	....	....	....	54	....	....	....	....	....	....	....	....	....	....	17	*15	14	29	8	....	....	....
	New York Islanders	**NHL**	**8**	**0**	**1**	**1**	**0**	**1**	**1**	**0**	**0**	**0**	**0**	**11**	**0.0**	**3**	**1**	**1**	**0**	**+1**	....	....	....	....	....	....	....	....
1995-96	**Chicago Blackhawks**	**NHL**	**10**	**1**	**4**	**5**	**1**	**3**	**4**	**2**	**0**	**0**	**0**	**12**	**8.3**	**8**	**3**	**4**	**0**	**+1**	....	....	....	....	....	....	....	....
	Indianapolis Ice	IHL	73	32	59	91	....	....	....	46	....	....	....	....	....	....	....	....	....	....	5	2	6	8	2	....	....	....
1996-97	Chicago Wolves	IHL	43	11	41	52	....	....	....	32	....	....	....	....	....	....	....	....	....	....	....	....	....	....	....	....	....	....
	Indianapolis Ice	IHL	37	17	24	41	....	....	....	18	....	....	....	....	....	....	....	....	....	....	4	2	2	4	2	....	....	....
1997-98	**New York Islanders**	**NHL**	**9**	**1**	**3**	**4**	**1**	**3**	**4**	**2**	**0**	**0**	**0**	**11**	**9.1**	**6**	**1**	**7**	**0**	**–2**	....	....	....	....	....	....	....	....
	Utah Grizzlies	IHL	72	38	59	97	....	....	....	30	....	....	....	....	....	....	....	....	....	....	4	3	2	5	10	....	....	....
	NHL Totals		**90**	**14**	**25**	**39**	**14**	**19**	**33**	**31**	**2**	**0**	**2**	**120**	**11.7**	**58**	**12**	**71**	**1**		....	....	....	....	....	....	....	....

CCHA First All-Star Team (1989, 1990) • NCAA West First All-American Team (1989, 1990) • Won Hobey Baker Memorial Award (Top U.S. Collegiate Player) (1990)

Traded to **Minnesota** by **Quebec** for Steve Maltais, March 8, 1992. Signed as a free agent by **San Jose**, August 10, 1993. Signed as a free agent by **NY Islanders**, July 7, 1994. Signed as a free agent by **Chicago**, July 21, 1995.

• MILLER, PAUL

Paul Miller C – L. 5'10", 170 lbs. b: Billerica, MA, 8/21/1959. Minnesota's 8th choice, 164th overall, in 1982 Entry Draft.

Season	Club	League	GP	G	A	Pts	AG	AA	APts	PIM	PP	SH	GW	S	%	TGF	PGF	TGA	PGA	+/–	GP	G	A	Pts	PIM	PP	SH	GW
1977-78	Boston University	ECAC	31	10	14	24	....	....	....	28	....	....	....	....	....	....	....	....	....	....	....	....	....	....	....	....	....	....
1978-79	Boston University	ECAC	29	15	20	35	....	....	....	10	....	....	....	....	....	....	....	....	....	....	....	....	....	....	....	....	....	....
1979-80	Boston University	ECAC	20	4	10	14	....	....	....	13	....	....	....	....	....	....	....	....	....	....	....	....	....	....	....	....	....	....
	Flint Generals	IHL	13	3	2	5	....	....	....	31	....	....	....	....	....	....	....	....	....	....	5	1	1	2	6	....	....	....
1980-81	Syracuse Hornets	EHL	10	3	5	8	....	....	....	9	....	....	....	....	....	....	....	....	....	....	....	....	....	....	....	....	....	....
	Richmond Rifles	EHL	21	9	16	25	....	....	....	20	....	....	....	....	....	....	....	....	....	....	10	1	2	3	19	....	....	....
1981-82	**Colorado Rockies**	**NHL**	**3**	**0**	**3**	**3**	**0**	**2**	**2**	**0**	**0**	**0**	**0**	**0**	**0.0**	**3**	**0**	**2**	**1**	**+2**	....	....	....	....	....	....	....	....
	Fort Worth Texans	CHL	65	25	38	63	....	....	....	44	....	....	....	....	....	....	....	....	....	....	....	....	....	....	....	....	....	....
	United States	WEC-A	4	0	0	0	....	....	....	0	....	....	....	....	....	....	....	....	....	....	....	....	....	....	....	....	....	....
1982-83	Wichita Wind	CHL	55	17	18	35	....	....	....	44	....	....	....	....	....	....	....	....	....	....	....	....	....	....	....	....	....	....
	Moncton Alpines	AHL	19	2	8	10	....	....	....	7	....	....	....	....	....	....	....	....	....	....	....	....	....	....	....	....	....	....
1983-84	Muskegon Mohawks	IHL	4	0	1	1	....	....	....	0	....	....	....	....	....	....	....	....	....	....	....	....	....	....	....	....	....	....
	Moncton Alpines	AHL	46	9	2	11	....	....	....	68	....	....	....	....	....	....	....	....	....	....	....	....	....	....	....	....	....	....
	Milwaukee Admirals	IHL	3	1	3	4	....	....	....	2	....	....	....	....	....	....	....	....	....	....	....	....	....	....	....	....	....	....
	NHL Totals		**3**	**0**	**3**	**3**	**0**	**2**	**2**	**0**	**0**	**0**	**0**	**0**	**0.0**	**3**	**0**	**2**	**1**		....	....	....	....	....	....	....	....

Signed as a free agent by **Colorado**, November 20, 1981. Transfrerred to **New Jersey** after **Colorado** franchise relocated, June 30, 1982. Traded to **Edmonton** by **New Jersey** with Lindsay Middlebrook for Ron Low and Jim McTaggart, February 23, 1983.

• MILLER, PERRY

Perry Miller D – L. 6'1", 194 lbs. b: Winnipeg, Man., 6/24/1952.

Season	Club	League	GP	G	A	Pts	AG	AA	APts	PIM	PP	SH	GW	S	%	TGF	PGF	TGA	PGA	+/–	GP	G	A	Pts	PIM	PP	SH	GW
1970-71	West Kildanan North Stars	MJHL	40	3	11	14	....	....	....	179	....	....	....	....	....	....	....	....	....	....	....	....	....	....	....	....	....	....
1971-72	West Kildanan North Stars	MJHL	39	15	23	38	....	....	....	187	....	....	....	....	....	....	....	....	....	....	....	....	....	....	....	....	....	....
1972-73	Charlotte Checkers	EHL	65	3	20	23	....	....	....	126	....	....	....	....	....	....	....	....	....	....	....	....	....	....	....	....	....	....
1973-74	Charlotte Checkers	SHL	66	12	31	43	....	....	....	203	....	....	....	....	....	....	....	....	....	....	....	....	....	....	....	....	....	....
1974-75	Winnipeg Jets	WHA	67	9	19	28	....	....	....	133	....	....	....	....	....	....	....	....	....	....	....	....	....	....	....	....	....	....
1975-76	Winnipeg Jets	WHA	47	7	6	13	....	....	....	41	....	....	....	....	....	....	....	....	....	....	....	....	....	....	....	....	....	....
	Minnesota Fighting Saints	WHA	13	1	4	5	....	....	....	11	....	....	....	....	....	....	....	....	....	....	....	....	....	....	....	....	....	....
1976-77	Winnipeg Jets	WHA	74	14	30	44	....	....	....	124	....	....	....	....	....	....	....	....	....	....	20	4	6	10	27	....	....	....
1977-78	**Detroit Red Wings**	**NHL**	**62**	**4**	**17**	**21**	**4**	**14**	**18**	**120**	**0**	**1**	**1**	**122**	**3.3**	**77**	**11**	**95**	**24**	**–5**	....	....	....	....	....	....	....	....
1978-79	**Detroit Red Wings**	**NHL**	**75**	**5**	**23**	**28**	**5**	**18**	**23**	**156**	**3**	**0**	**1**	**122**	**4.1**	**81**	**18**	**110**	**34**	**–13**	....	....	....	....	....	....	....	....
1979-80	**Detroit Red Wings**	**NHL**	**16**	**0**	**3**	**3**	**0**	**2**	**2**	**41**	**0**	**0**	**0**	**13**	**0.0**	**14**	**1**	**17**	**0**	**–4**	....	....	....	....	....	....	....	....
	Adirondack Red Wings	AHL	55	9	27	36	....	....	....	155	....	....	....	....	....	....	....	....	....	....	5	3	0	3	6	....	....	....
1980-81	**Detroit Red Wings**	**NHL**	**64**	**1**	**8**	**9**	**1**	**6**	**7**	**70**	**0**	**0**	**0**	**54**	**1.9**	**36**	**2**	**54**	**2**	**–18**	....	....	....	....	....	....	....	....
	Adirondack Red Wings	AHL	4	1	1	2	....	....	....	47	....	....	....	....	....	....	....	....	....	....	....	....	....	....	....	....	....	....
1981-82	Adirondack Red Wings	AHL	58	12	31	43	....	....	....	118	....	....	....	....	....	....	....	....	....	....	2	0	0	0	10	....	....	....
	NHL Totals		**217**	**10**	**51**	**61**	**10**	**40**	**50**	**387**	**3**	**1**	**2**	**311**	**3.2**	**208**	**32**	**276**	**60**		....	....	....	....	....	....	....	....
	Other Major League Totals		201	31	59	90	....	....	....	309	....	....	....	....	....	....	....	....	....		20	4	6	10	27	....	....	....

SHL Second All-Star Team (1974)

Signed as a free agent by **Winnipeg** (WHA), September, 1974. Traded to **Minnesota** (WHA) by **Winnipeg** (WHA) for Gerry Odrowski, January, 1976. Signed as a free agent by **Winnipeg** (WHA) after **Minnesota** (WHA) franchise folded, March, 1976. Signed as a free agent by **Detroit**, July 8, 1977.

● **MILLER, TOM** Tom Miller C – L. 6', 187 lbs. b: Kitchener, Ont., 3/31/1947.

Season	Club	League	GP	G	A	Pts	AG	AA	APts	PIM	PP	SH	GW	S	%	TGF	PGF	TGA	PGA	+/-	GP	G	A	Pts	PIM	PP	SH	GW
			REGULAR SEASON																		PLAYOFFS							
1962-63	Guelph Royals	Jr. B	1	0	0	0	....	....	....	0	....	....	....	....	....	....	....	....	....	....	....	....	....	....	....	....	....	....
1963-64	Kitchener Rangers	OHA	56	9	18	27	....	....	....	21	....	....	....	....	....	....	....	....	....	....	....	....	....	....	....	....	....	....
1964-65	Kitchener Rangers	OHA	55	14	13	27	....	....	....	23	....	....	....	....	....	....	....	....	....	....	....	....	....	....	....	....	....	....
1965-66	University of Denver	WCHA	DID NOT PLAY – FRESHMAN																									
1966-67	University of Denver	WCHA	30	24	17	41	....	....	....	16	....	....	....	....	....	....	....	....	....	....	....	....	....	....	....	....	....	....
1967-68	University of Denver	WCHA	34	20	27	47	....	....	....	16	....	....	....	....	....	....	....	....	....	....	....	....	....	....	....	....	....	....
1968-69	University of Denver	WCHA	24	7	16	23	....	....	....	14	....	....	....	....	....	....	....	....	....	....	....	....	....	....	....	....	....	....
1969-70	Omaha Knights	CHL	63	19	20	39	....	....	....	23	....	....	....	....	....	....	....	....	....	....	12	3	5	8	4	....	....	....
1970-71	**Detroit Red Wings**	**NHL**	**29**	**1**	**7**	**8**	**1**	**6**	**7**	**9**	**1**	**0**	**0**	**30**	**3.3**	**14**	**1**	**31**	**0**	**–18**	....	....	....	....	....	....	....	....
	Omaha Knights	CHL	47	19	33	52	....	....	....	7	....	....	....	....	....	....	....	....	....	....	....	....	....	....	....	....	....	....
1971-72	Cincinnati Swords	AHL	62	18	27	45	....	....	....	41	....	....	....	....	....	....	....	....	....	....	3	0	0	0	0	....	....	....
1972-73	**New York Islanders**	**NHL**	**69**	**13**	**17**	**30**	**13**	**14**	**27**	**21**	**2**	**0**	**1**	**92**	**14.1**	**43**	**10**	**86**	**24**	**–29**	....	....	....	....	....	....	....	....
1973-74	**New York Islanders**	**NHL**	**19**	**2**	**1**	**3**	**2**	**1**	**3**	**4**	**0**	**1**	**0**	**19**	**10.5**	**4**	**0**	**14**	**7**	**–3**	....	....	....	....	....	....	....	....
	Fort Worth Wings	CHL	11	3	7	10	....	....	....	0	....	....	....	....	....	....	....	....	....	....	....	....	....	....	....	....	....	....
1974-75	**New York Islanders**	**NHL**	**1**	**0**	**0**	**0**	**0**	**0**	**0**	**0**	**0**	**0**	**0**	**1**	**0.0**	**0**	**0**	**0**	**0**	**0**	....	....	....	....	....	....	....	....
	New Haven Nighthawks	AHL	73	13	30	43	....	....	....	28	....	....	....	....	....	....	....	....	....	....	16	1	7	8	19	....	....	....
	NHL Totals		**118**	**16**	**25**	**41**	**16**	**21**	**37**	**34**	**3**	**1**	**1**	**142**	**11.3**	**61**	**11**	**131**	**31**		....	....	....	....	....	....	....	....

WCHA Second All-Star Team (1969) • NCAA Championship All-Tournament Team (1969)

Traded to **Detroit** by **NY Rangers** with Arnie Brown and Mike Robitaille for Bruce MacGregor and Larry Brown, February 2, 1971. Clamed by **Buffalo** from **Detroit** in Intra-League Draft, June 8, 1971. Claimed by **NY Islanders** from **Buffalo** in Expansion Draft, June 6, 1972.

● **MILLER, WARREN** Warren Miller RW – R. 6', 180 lbs. b: South St. Paul, MN, 1/1/1954. NY Rangers' 21st choice, 241st overall, in 1974 Amateur Draft.

Season	Club	League	GP	G	A	Pts	AG	AA	APts	PIM	PP	SH	GW	S	%	TGF	PGF	TGA	PGA	+/-	GP	G	A	Pts	PIM	PP	SH	GW
1972-73	University of Minnesota	WCHA	32	5	3	8	....	....	....	22	....	....	....	....	....	....	....	....	....	....	....	....	....	....	....	....	....	....
1973-74	University of Minnesota	WCHA	40	11	16	27	....	....	....	34	....	....	....	....	....	....	....	....	....	....	....	....	....	....	....	....	....	....
1974-75	University of Minnesota	WCHA	41	16	21	37	....	....	....	40	....	....	....	....	....	....	....	....	....	....	....	....	....	....	....	....	....	....
1975-76	University of Minnesota	WCHA	44	26	31	57	....	....	....	50	....	....	....	....	....	....	....	....	....	....	....	....	....	....	....	....	....	....
	Calgary Cowboys	WHA	3	0	0	0	....	....	....	0	....	....	....	....	....	....	....	....	....	....	10	1	0	1	28	....	....	....
1976-77	Calgary Cowboys	WHA	80	23	32	55	....	....	....	51	....	....	....	....	....	....	....	....	....	....	3	0	0	0	0	....	....	....
	United States	WEC-A	10	2	2	4	....	....	....	4	....	....	....	....	....	....	....	....	....	....	....	....	....	....	....	....	....	....
1977-78	Edmonton Oilers	WHA	18	2	4	6	....	....	....	18	....	....	....	....	....	....	....	....	....	....	....	....	....	....	....	....	....	....
	Quebec Nordiques	WHA	60	14	24	38	....	....	....	50	....	....	....	....	....	....	....	....	....	....	11	0	2	2	0	....	....	....
1978-79	New England Whalers	WHA	77	26	23	49	....	....	....	44	....	....	....	....	....	....	....	....	....	....	10	0	8	8	28	....	....	....
1979-80	**New York Rangers**	**NHL**	**55**	**7**	**6**	**13**	**6**	**5**	**11**	**17**	**0**	**0**	**3**	**51**	**13.7**	**32**	**1**	**53**	**16**	**–6**	**6**	**1**	**0**	**1**	**0**	**0**	**0**	**0**
1980-81	**Hartford Whalers**	**NHL**	**77**	**22**	**22**	**44**	**18**	**15**	**33**	**37**	**3**	**3**	**1**	**160**	**13.8**	**64**	**15**	**107**	**27**	**–31**	....	....	....	....	....	....	....	....
	United States	WEC-A	7	3	2	5	....	....	....	4	....	....	....	....	....	....	....	....	....	....	....	....	....	....	....	....	....	....
1981-82	United States	C Cup	6	2	0	2	....	....	....	2	....	....	....	....	....	....	....	....	....	....	....	....	....	....	....	....	....	....
	Hartford Whalers	**NHL**	**74**	**10**	**12**	**22**	**8**	**8**	**16**	**68**	**1**	**1**	**0**	**152**	**6.6**	**41**	**6**	**67**	**18**	**–14**	....	....	....	....	....	....	....	....
1982-83	**Hartford Whalers**	**NHL**	**56**	**1**	**10**	**11**	**1**	**7**	**8**	**15**	**0**	**0**	**0**	**75**	**1.3**	**18**	**1**	**41**	**11**	**–13**	....	....	....	....	....	....	....	....
	NHL Totals		**262**	**40**	**50**	**90**	**33**	**35**	**68**	**137**	**4**	**4**	**4**	**438**	**9.1**	**155**	**23**	**268**	**72**		**6**	**1**	**0**	**1**	**0**	**0**	**0**	**0**
	Other Major League Totals		238	65	83	148	....	....	....	163	....	....	....	....	....	....	....	....	....	....	34	1	10	11	56	....	....	....

NCAA Championship All-Tournament Team (1975)

Selected by **Vancouver** (WHA) in 1974 WHA Amateur Draft, May, 1974. WHA rights transferred to **Calagry** (WHA) after **Vancouver** (WHA) franchise relocated, May 7, 1975. Signed as a free agent by **Edmonton** (WHA) after Calgary (WHA) franchise folded, May 31, 1977. Traded to **Quebec** (WHA) by **Edmonton** (WHA) with Rick Morris, Ken Broderick and Dave Inkpen for Don McLeod and Pierre Guite, November, 1977. Traded to **New England** (WHA) by **Quebec** (WHA) for Jean-Louis Levasseur, September, 1977. Reclaimed by **NY Rangers** from **Hartford** prior to Expansion Draft, June 9, 1979. Traded to **Hartford** by **NY Rangers** for cash, August 7, 1980.

● **MILLS, CRAIG** Craig Mills RW – R. 6', 190 lbs. b: Toronto, Ont., 8/27/1976. Winnipeg's 5th choice, 108th overall, in 1994 Entry Draft.

Season	Club	League	GP	G	A	Pts	AG	AA	APts	PIM	PP	SH	GW	S	%	TGF	PGF	TGA	PGA	+/-	GP	G	A	Pts	PIM	PP	SH	GW
1993-94	Belleville Bulls	OHL	63	15	18	33	....	....	....	88	....	....	....	....	....	....	....	....	....	....	12	2	1	3	11	....	....	....
1994-95	Belleville Bulls	OHL	62	39	41	80	....	....	....	104	....	....	....	....	....	....	....	....	....	....	13	7	9	16	8	....	....	....
1995-96	Belleville Bulls	OHL	48	10	19	29	....	....	....	113	....	....	....	....	....	....	....	....	....	....	14	4	5	9	32	....	....	....
	Canada	WJC-A	6	0	0	0	....	....	....	4	....	....	....	....	....	....	....	....	....	....	....	....	....	....	....	....	....	....
	Winnipeg Jets	**NHL**	**4**	**0**	**2**	**2**	**0**	**2**	**2**	**0**	**0**	**0**	**0**	**0**	**0.0**	**3**	**0**	**3**	**0**	**0**	**1**	**0**	**0**	**0**	**0**	**0**	**0**	**0**
	Springfield Falcons	AHL	....	....	....	....	....	....	....	....	....	....	....	....	....	....	....	....	....	....	2	0	0	0	0	....	....	....
1996-97	Indianapolis Ice	IHL	80	12	7	19	....	....	....	199	....	....	....	....	....	....	....	....	....	....	4	0	0	0	4	....	....	....
1997-98	**Chicago Blackhawks**	**NHL**	**20**	**0**	**3**	**3**	**0**	**3**	**3**	**34**	**0**	**0**	**0**	**5**	**0.0**	**4**	**0**	**3**	**0**	**+1**	....	....	....	....	....	....	....	....
	Indianapolis Ice	IHL	42	8	11	19	....	....	....	110	....	....	....	....	....	....	....	....	....	....	5	0	0	0	27	....	....	....
	NHL Totals		**24**	**0**	**5**	**5**	**0**	**5**	**5**	**34**	**0**	**0**	**0**	**5**	**0.0**	**7**	**0**	**6**	**0**		**1**	**0**	**0**	**0**	**0**	**0**	**0**	**0**

Canadian Major Junior Humanitarian Player of the Year (1996)

Rights transferred to **Phoenix** after **Winnipeg** franchise relocated, July 1, 1996. Traded to **Chicago** by **Phoenix** with Alexei Zhamnov and Phoenix's 1st round choice (Ty Jones) in 1997 Entry Draft for Jeremy Roenick, August 16, 1996.

● **MINER, JOHN** John Miner D – R. 5'10", 180 lbs. b: Moose Jaw, Sask., 8/28/1965. Edmonton's 10th choice, 229th overall, in 1983 Entry Draft.

Season	Club	League	GP	G	A	Pts	AG	AA	APts	PIM	PP	SH	GW	S	%	TGF	PGF	TGA	PGA	+/-	GP	G	A	Pts	PIM	PP	SH	GW
1982-83	Regina Pats	WHL	71	11	23	34	....	....	....	126	....	....	....	....	....	....	....	....	....	....	5	1	1	2	20	....	....	....
1983-84	Regina Pats	WHL	70	27	42	69	....	....	....	132	....	....	....	....	....	....	....	....	....	....	23	9	25	34	54	....	....	....
1984-85	Regina Pats	WHL	66	30	54	84	....	....	....	128	....	....	....	....	....	....	....	....	....	....	8	4	10	14	12	....	....	....
	Canada	WJC-A	7	0	2	2	....	....	....	12	....	....	....	....	....	....	....	....	....	....	....	....	....	....	....	....	....	....
1985-86	Nova Scotia Oilers	AHL	79	10	33	43	....	....	....	90	....	....	....	....	....	....	....	....	....	....	....	....	....	....	....	....	....	....
1986-87	Nova Scotia Oilers	AHL	45	5	28	33	....	....	....	38	....	....	....	....	....	....	....	....	....	....	5	0	3	3	4	....	....	....
1987-88	**Edmonton Oilers**	**NHL**	**14**	**2**	**3**	**5**	**2**	**2**	**4**	**16**	**0**	**0**	**0**	**16**	**12.5**	**21**	**4**	**21**	**0**	**–4**	....	....	....	....	....	....	....	....
	Nova Scotia Oilers	AHL	61	8	26	34	....	....	....	61	....	....	....	....	....	....	....	....	....	....	....	....	....	....	....	....	....	....
1988-89	New Haven Nighthawks	AHL	7	2	3	5	....	....	....	4	....	....	....	....	....	....	....	....	....	....	17	3	12	15	40	....	....	....
	WEV Wien	Austria	37	19	33	52	....	....	....	....	....	....	....	....	....	....	....	....	....	....	....	....	....	....	....	....	....	....
1989-90	Lausanne HC	Switz.	36	19	32	51	....	....	....	....	....	....	....	....	....	....	....	....	....	....	....	....	....	....	....	....	....	....
	New Haven Nighthawks	AHL	7	1	6	7	....	....	....	2	....	....	....	....	....	....	....	....	....	....	....	....	....	....	....	....	....	....
1990-91	Lausanne HC	Switz.	36	12	24	36	....	....	....	....	....	....	....	....	....	....	....	....	....	....	....	....	....	....	....	....	....	....
1991-92	Zell-A-See	Switz.	42	16	37	53	....	....	....	....	....	....	....	....	....	....	....	....	....	....	....	....	....	....	....	....	....	....
1992-93	Zell-A-See	Switz.	52	19	52	71	....	....	....	....	....	....	....	....	....	....	....	....	....	....	....	....	....	....	....	....	....	....
1993-94	HC Ajoie	Switz.	34	10	22	38	....	....	....	42	....	....	....	....	....	....	....	....	....	....	4	3	3	6	18	....	....	....
1994-95	Martigny	Switz.	36	15	28	43	....	....	....	67	....	....	....	....	....	....	....	....	....	....	4	1	2	3	2	....	....	....
1995-96	EV Zug	Switz.	29	12	20	32	....	....	....	36	....	....	....	....	....	....	....	....	....	....	4	0	5	5	4	....	....	....
1996-97	EV Zug	Switz.	45	15	32	47	....	....	....	50	....	....	....	....	....	....	....	....	....	....	10	2	7	9	4	....	....	....
1997-98	EV Zug	Switz.	35	5	17	22	....	....	....	28	....	....	....	....	....	....	....	....	....	....	4	0	2	2	0	....	....	....
	NHL Totals		**14**	**2**	**3**	**5**	**2**	**2**	**4**	**16**	**0**	**0**	**0**	**16**	**12.5**	**21**	**4**	**21**	**0**		....	....	....	....	....	....	....	....

WHL East First All-Star Team (1985)

Traded to **LA Kings** by **Edmonton** for Craig Redmond, August 10, 1989.

● **MINOR, GERRY** Gerry "Bucky" Minor C – L. 5'8", 178 lbs. b: Regina, Sask., 10/27/1958. Vancouver's 6th choice, 90th overall, in 1978 Amateur Draft.

Season	Club	League	GP	G	A	Pts	AG	AA	APts	PIM	PP	SH	GW	S	%	TGF	PGF	TGA	PGA	+/-	GP	G	A	Pts	PIM	PP	SH	GW
1974-75	Regina Capitals	SJHL	38	28	19	47	....	....	....	56	....	....	....	....	....	....	....	....	....	....	....	....	....	....	....	....	....	....
	Regina Pats	WCJHL	16	2	6	8	....	....	....	6	....	....	....	....	....	....	....	....	....	....	....	....	....	....	....	....	....	....
1975-76	Regina Pats	WHL	71	24	41	65	....	....	....	124	....	....	....	....	....	....	....	....	....	....	....	....	....	....	....	....	....	....
1976-77	Regina Pats	WCJHL	48	22	32	54	....	....	....	120	....	....	....	....	....	....	....	....	....	....	....	....	....	....	....	....	....	....
1977-78	Regina Pats	WCJHL	66	54	75	129	....	....	....	238	....	....	....	....	....	....	....	....	....	....	13	5	22	*37	31	....	....	....
1978-79	Fort Wayne Komets	IHL	42	18	28	46	....	....	....	67	....	....	....	....	....	....	....	....	....	....	....	....	....	....	....	....	....	....
	Dallas Black Hawks	CHL	37	14	25	39	....	....	....	76	....	....	....	....	....	....	....	....	....	....	9	3	4	7	31	....	....	....
1979-80	**Vancouver Canucks**	**NHL**	**5**	**0**	**1**	**1**	**0**	**1**	**1**	**2**	**0**	**0**	**0**	**4**	**0.0**	**1**	**0**	**2**	**1**	**0**	....	....	....	....	....	....	....	....
	Dallas Black Hawks	CHL	73	31	52	83	....	....	....	162	....	....	....	....	....	....	....	....	....	....	....	....	....	....	....	....	....	....
1980-81	**Vancouver Canucks**	**NHL**	**74**	**10**	**14**	**24**	**8**	**10**	**18**	**108**	**1**	**6**	**0**	**93**	**10.8**	**35**	**4**	**69**	**42**	**+4**	**3**	**0**	**0**	**0**	**8**	**0**	**0**	**0**

			REGULAR SEASON																		PLAYOFFS							
Season	Club	League	GP	G	A	Pts	AG	AA	APts	PIM	PP	SH	GW	S	%	TGF	PGF	TGA	PGA	+/–	GP	G	A	Pts	PIM	PP	SH	GW
1981-82	Vancouver Canucks	NHL	13	0	1	1	0	1	1	6	0	0	0	18	0.0	1	0	18	11	–6	9	1	3	4	17	0	0	0
	Dallas Black Hawks	CHL	12	5	8	13	....	....	....	92	....	....	....	....	....	....	....	....	....	....	....	....	....	....	....	....	....	....
1982-83	Vancouver Canucks	NHL	39	1	5	6	1	3	4	57	0	0	0	24	4.2	8	0	35	21	–6	....	....	....	....	....	....	....	....
	Fredericton Express	AHL	17	4	17	21	....	....	....	14	....	....	....	....	....	....	....	....	....	....	....	....	....	....	....	....	....	....
1983-84	Vancouver Canucks	NHL	9	0	0	0	0	0	0	0	0	0	0	2	0.0	0	0	5	5	0	....	....	....	....	....	....	....	....
	Fredericton Express	AHL	66	16	42	58	....	....	....	85	....	....	....	....	....	....	....	....	....	....	7	1	4	5	20	....	....	....
1984-85	Nova Scotia Voyageurs	AHL	21	4	10	14	....	....	....	8	....	....	....	....	....	....	....	....	....	....	....	....	....	....	....	....	....	....
	New Haven Nighthawks	AHL	52	11	29	40	....	....	....	65	....	....	....	....	....	....	....	....	....	....	....	....	....	....	....	....	....	....
1985-86	Indianapolis Checkers	IHL	72	28	46	74	....	....	....	108	....	....	....	....	....	....	....	....	....	....	5	3	4	7	8	....	....	....
1986-87	Indianapolis Checkers	IHL	68	17	22	39	....	....	....	93	....	....	....	....	....	....	....	....	....	....	15	3	9	12	32	....	....	....
	NHL Totals		140	11	21	32	9	15	24	173	1	6	0	141	7.8	45	4	129	80		12	1	3	4	25	0	0	0

• MIRONOV, BORIS

Boris Mironov D – R. 6'3", 220 lbs. b: Moscow, USSR, 3/21/1972. Winnipeg's 2nd choice, 27th overall, in 1992 Entry Draft.

1988-89	CSKA Moscow	USSR	1	0	0	0	....	....	....	0	....	....	....	....	....	....	....	....	....	....	....	....	....	....	....	....	....	....
1989-90	CSKA Moscow	USSR	7	0	0	0	....	....	....	0	....	....	....	....	....	....	....	....	....	....	....	....	....	....	....	....	....	....
1990-91	CSKA Moscow	USSR	36	1	5	6	....	....	....	16	....	....	....	....	....	....	....	....	....	....	....	....	....	....	....	....	....	....
1991-92	CSKA Moscow	CIS	36	2	1	3	....	....	....	22	....	....	....	....	....	....	....	....	....	....	....	....	....	....	....	....	....	....
	Russia	WJC-A	7	2	2	4	....	....	....	29	....	....	....	....	....	....	....	....	....	....	....	....	....	....	....	....	....	....
1992-93	CSKA Moscow	CIS	19	0	5	5	....	....	....	20	....	....	....	....	....	....	....	....	....	....	....	....	....	....	....	....	....	....
1993-94	Winnipeg Jets	NHL	65	7	22	29	7	17	24	96	5	0	0	122	5.7	70	29	76	6	–29	....	....	....	....	....	....	....	....
	Edmonton Oilers	NHL	14	0	2	2	0	2	2	14	0	0	0	23	0.0	11	2	15	2	–4	....	....	....	....	....	....	....	....
1994-95	Edmonton Oilers	NHL	29	1	7	8	2	10	12	40	0	0	0	48	2.1	22	8	27	4	–9	....	....	....	....	....	....	....	....
	Cape Breton Oilers	AHL	4	2	5	7	....	....	....	23	....	....	....	....	....	....	....	....	....	....	....	....	....	....	....	....	....	....
1995-96	Edmonton Oilers	NHL	78	8	24	32	8	20	28	101	7	0	1	158	5.1	72	30	81	16	–23	....	....	....	....	....	....	....	....
	Russia	WC-A	8	0	3	3	....	....	....	12	....	....	....	....	....	....	....	....	....	....	....	....	....	....	....	....	....	....
1996-97	Edmonton Oilers	NHL	55	6	26	32	6	23	29	85	2	0	1	147	4.1	79	33	60	16	+2	12	2	8	10	16	2	0	0
1997-98	Edmonton Oilers	NHL	81	16	30	46	19	29	48	100	10	1	1	203	7.9	108	51	93	28	–8	12	3	3	6	27	1	0	1
	Russia	Olympics	6	0	2	2	....	....	....	2	....	....	....	....	....	....	....	....	....	....	....	....	....	....	....	....	....	....
	NHL Totals		322	38	111	149	42	101	143	436	24	1	3	701	5.4	362	153	352	72		24	5	11	16	43	3	0	1

NHL/Upper Deck All-Rookie Team (1994)

Traded to **Edmonton** by **Winnipeg** with Mats Lindgren, Winnipeg's 1st round choice (Jason Bonsignore) in 1994 Entry Draft and Florida's 4th round choice (previously acquired, Edmonton selected Adam Copeland) in 1994 Entry Draft for Dave Manson and St. Louis' 6th round choice (previously acquired, Winnipeg selected Chris Kibermanis) in 1994 Entry Draft, March 15, 1994.

• MIRONOV, DMITRI

Dmitri "Tree" Mironov D – R. 6'3", 215 lbs. b: Moscow, USSR, 12/25/1965. Toronto's 7th choice, 160th overall, in 1991 Entry Draft.

1985-86	CSKA Moscow	USSR	9	0	1	1	....	....	....	8	....	....	....	....	....	....	....	....	....	....	....	....	....	....	....	....	....	....
1986-87	CSKA Moscow	USSR	20	1	3	4	....	....	....	10	....	....	....	....	....	....	....	....	....	....	....	....	....	....	....	....	....	....
1987-88	Soviet Wings	USSR	44	12	6	18	....	....	....	30	....	....	....	....	....	....	....	....	....	....	....	....	....	....	....	....	....	....
1988-89	Soviet Wings	USSR	44	5	6	11	....	....	....	44	....	....	....	....	....	....	....	....	....	....	....	....	....	....	....	....	....	....
1989-90	Soviet Wings	FrTour	1	0	0	0	....	....	....	0	....	....	....	....	....	....	....	....	....	....	....	....	....	....	....	....	....	....
	Soviet Wings	USSR	45	4	11	15	....	....	....	34	....	....	....	....	....	....	....	....	....	....	....	....	....	....	....	....	....	....
	Soviet Wings	SuperS	5	0	1	1	....	....	....	4	....	....	....	....	....	....	....	....	....	....	....	....	....	....	....	....	....	....
1990-91	Soviet Wings	FrTour	1	0	1	1	....	....	....	0	....	....	....	....	....	....	....	....	....	....	....	....	....	....	....	....	....	....
	Soviet Wings	USSR	45	16	12	28	....	....	....	22	....	....	....	....	....	....	....	....	....	....	....	....	....	....	....	....	....	....
	CSKA Moscow	SuperS	6	0	1	1	....	....	....	6	....	....	....	....	....	....	....	....	....	....	....	....	....	....	....	....	....	....
	Soviet Union	WEC-A	10	4	2	6	....	....	....	6	....	....	....	....	....	....	....	....	....	....	....	....	....	....	....	....	....	....
1991-92	Soviet Union	C Cup	5	0	1	1	....	....	....	4	....	....	....	....	....	....	....	....	....	....	....	....	....	....	....	....	....	....
	Soviet Wings	CIS	35	15	16	31	....	....	....	62	....	....	....	....	....	....	....	....	....	....	....	....	....	....	....	....	....	....
	Toronto Maple Leafs	NHL	7	1	0	1	1	0	1	0	0	0	1	7	14.3	3	0	8	1	–4	....	....	....	....	....	....	....	....
	Russia	Olympics	8	3	1	4	....	....	....	6	....	....	....	....	....	....	....	....	....	....	....	....	....	....	....	....	....	....
	Russia	WC-A	6	1	1	2	....	....	....	2	....	....	....	....	....	....	....	....	....	....	....	....	....	....	....	....	....	....
1992-93	Toronto Maple Leafs	NHL	59	7	24	31	6	16	22	40	4	0	1	105	6.7	73	32	44	2	–1	14	1	2	3	2	1	0	0
1993-94	Toronto Maple Leafs	NHL	76	9	27	36	8	21	29	78	3	0	0	147	6.1	94	44	55	10	+5	18	6	9	15	6	6	0	0
1994-95	Toronto Maple Leafs	NHL	33	5	12	17	9	18	27	28	2	0	0	68	7.4	44	20	20	2	+6	6	2	1	3	2	1	0	0
1995-96	Pittsburgh Penguins	NHL	72	3	31	34	3	25	28	88	1	0	1	86	3.5	110	21	98	28	+19	15	0	1	1	10	0	0	0
1996-97	Pittsburgh Penguins	NHL	15	1	5	6	1	4	5	24	0	0	1	19	5.3	12	3	14	1	–4	....	....	....	....	....	....	....	....
	Anaheim Mighty Ducks	NHL	62	12	34	46	13	30	43	77	3	1	1	158	7.6	116	39	76	19	+20	11	1	10	11	10	1	0	0
1997-98	Anaheim Mighty Ducks	NHL	66	6	30	36	7	29	36	115	2	0	1	142	4.2	82	24	93	28	–7	....	....	....	....	....	....	....	....
	Russia	Olympics	6	0	3	3	....	....	....	0	....	....	....	....	....	....	....	....	....	....	....	....	....	....	....	....	....	....
	Detroit Red Wings	NHL	11	2	5	7	2	5	7	4	1	0	0	28	7.1	15	7	12	4	0	7	0	3	3	14	0	0	0
	NHL Totals		401	46	168	214	50	148	198	454	16	1	6	760	6.1	549	190	420	95		71	10	26	36	44	9	0	0

Played in NHL All-Star Game (1998)

Traded to **Pittsburgh** by **Toronto** with Toronto's 2nd round choice (later traded to New Jersey — New Jersey selected Joshua Dewolf) in 1996 Entry Draft for Larry Murphy, July 8, 1995. Traded to **Anaheim** by **Pittsburgh** with Shawn Antoski for Alex Hicks and Fredrik Olausson, November 19, 1996. Traded to **Detroit** by **Anaheim** for Jamie Pushor and Detroit's 4th round choice (Viktor Wallin) in 1998 Entry Draft, March 24, 1998. Signed as a free agent by **Washington**, July 14, 1998.

• MISZUK, JOHN

John Miszuk D – L. 6'1", 192 lbs. b: Naliboki, Poland, 9/29/1940.

1957-58	Hamilton Tiger Cubs	OHA	....	....	....	....	....	....	....	....	....	....	....	....	....	....	....	....	....	....	1	0	0	0	0	....	....	....
1958-59	Hamilton Tiger Cubs	OHA	2	0	0	0	....	....	....	0	....	....	....	....	....	....	....	....	....	....	....	....	....	....	....	....	....	....
1959-60	Hamilton Tiger Cubs	OHA	6	1	3	4	....	....	....	0	....	....	....	....	....	....	....	....	....	....	....	....	....	....	....	....	....	....
1960-61	Hamilton Tiger Cubs	OHA	48	6	19	25	....	....	....	89	....	....	....	....	....	....	....	....	....	....	12	1	8	9	28	....	....	....
1961-62	Edmonton Flyers	WHL	65	4	30	34	....	....	....	88	....	....	....	....	....	....	....	....	....	....	12	1	6	7	20	....	....	....
1962-63	Edmonton Flyers	WHL	59	8	25	33	....	....	....	99	....	....	....	....	....	....	....	....	....	....	3	0	0	0	8	....	....	....
	Pittsburgh Hornets	AHL	10	0	3	3	....	....	....	16	....	....	....	....	....	....	....	....	....	....	....	....	....	....	....	....	....	....
1963-64	Detroit Red Wings	NHL	42	0	2	2	0	2	2	30	....	....	....	....	....	....	....	....	....	....	3	0	0	0	2	....	....	....
	Pittsburgh Hornets	AHL	25	1	7	8	....	....	....	34	....	....	....	....	....	....	....	....	....	....	....	....	....	....	....	....	....	....
1964-65	Buffalo Bisons	AHL	71	9	46	55	....	....	....	100	....	....	....	....	....	....	....	....	....	....	9	0	3	3	12	....	....	....
1965-66	Chicago Black Hawks	NHL	2	1	1	2	1	1	2	2	....	....	....	....	....	....	....	....	....	....	3	0	0	0	4	....	....	....
	St. Louis Braves	CHL	69	7	29	36	....	....	....	116	....	....	....	....	....	....	....	....	....	....	5	0	2	2	4	....	....	....
1966-67	Chicago Black Hawks	NHL	3	0	0	0	0	0	0	0	....	....	....	....	....	....	....	....	....	....	2	0	0	0	2	....	....	....
	St. Louis Braves	CHL	68	3	28	31	....	....	....	104	....	....	....	....	....	....	....	....	....	....	....	....	....	....	....	....	....	....
1967-68	Philadelphia Flyers	NHL	74	5	17	22	6	18	24	79	1	1	1	78	6.4	77	13	80	17	+1	7	0	3	3	11	0	0	0
1968-69	Philadelphia Flyers	NHL	66	1	13	14	1	12	13	70	1	0	0	70	1.4	50	3	69	16	–6	4	0	0	0	0	0	0	0
1969-70	Minnesota North Stars	NHL	50	0	6	6	0	6	6	51	0	0	0	34	0.0	37	3	62	25	–3	....	....	....	....	....	....	....	....
	Iowa Stars	CHL	16	1	6	7	....	....	....	37	....	....	....	....	....	....	....	....	....	....	9	0	3	3	10	....	....	....
1970-71	San Diego Gulls	WHL	72	5	30	35	....	....	....	98	....	....	....	....	....	....	....	....	....	....	6	0	1	1	4	....	....	....
1971-72	San Diego Gulls	WHL	72	5	33	38	....	....	....	118	....	....	....	....	....	....	....	....	....	....	4	0	1	1	6	....	....	....
1972-73	San Diego Gulls	WHL	72	2	39	41	....	....	....	85	....	....	....	....	....	....	....	....	....	....	6	0	4	4	13	....	....	....
1973-74	San Diego Gulls	WHL	77	8	49	57	....	....	....	103	....	....	....	....	....	....	....	....	....	....	4	0	0	0	2	....	....	....
1974-75	Michigan-Baltimore	WHA	66	2	19	21	....	....	....	56	....	....	....	....	....	....	....	....	....	....	....	....	....	....	....	....	....	....
1975-76	Calgary Cowboys	WHA	69	2	21	23	....	....	....	66	....	....	....	....	....	....	....	....	....	....	10	1	0	1	28	....	....	....
1976-77	Calgary Cowboys	WHA	79	2	26	28	....	....	....	57	....	....	....	....	....	....	....	....	....	....	....	....	....	....	....	....	....	....
1977-78	San Francisco Shamrocks	PHL	10	0	15	15	....	....	....	12	....	....	....	....	....	....	....	....	....	....	....	....	....	....	....	....	....	....
1978-79	San Diego Hawks	PHL	25	2	11	13	....	....	....	24	....	....	....	....	....	....	....	....	....	....	....	....	....	....	....	....	....	....
	NHL Totals		237	7	39	46	8	39	47	232	2	1	1	182	3.8	164	19	211	58		19	0	3	3	19	0	0	0
	Other Major League Totals		214	6	66	72	....	....	....	179	....	....	....	....	....	....	....	....	....	....	10	1	0	1	28	....	....	....

AHL Second All-Star Team (1965) • CHL First All-Star Team (1967) • WHL First All-Star Team (1973, 1974)

Traded to **Chicago** by **Detroit** with Art Stratton and Ian Cushenan for Ron Murphy and Aut Erickson, June 9, 1964. Claimed by **Philadelphia** from **Chicago** in Expansion Draft, June 6, 1967. Traded to **Minnesota** by **Philadelphia** for Wayne Hillman, May 14, 1969. Traded to **San Diego** (WHL) by **Minnesota** for cash, July, 1970. Selected by **LA Sharks** (WHA) in 1972 WHA General Player Draft, February 12, 1972. WHA rights transferred to **Michigan** (WHA) after **LA Sharks** (WHA) franchise relocated, April 30, 1974. Claimed by **Calgary** (WHA) from **Michigan-Baltimore** (WHA) in 1975 WHA Dispersal Draft, June, 1975.

			REGULAR SEASON																		PLAYOFFS							
Season	Club	League	GP	G	A	Pts	AG	AA	APts	PIM	PP	SH	GW	S	%	TGF	PGF	TGA	PGA	+/–	GP	G	A	Pts	PIM	PP	SH	GW

• MITCHELL, JEFF

Jeff Mitchell C/RW – R. 6'1", 190 lbs. b: Wayne, MI, 5/16/1975. Los Angeles' 2nd choice, 68th overall, in 1993 Entry Draft.

1992-93	Detroit Jr. Red Wings	OHL	62	10	15	25	....	....	....	100	....	....	....	....	....	....	....	....	....	....	15	3	3	6	16	....	....	....
1993-94	Detroit Jr. Red Wings	OHL	59	25	18	43	....	....	....	99	....	....	....	....	....	....	....	....	....	....	17	3	5	8	22	....	....	....
1994-95	Detroit Jr. Red Wings	OHL	61	30	30	60	....	....	....	121	....	....	....	....	....	....	....	....	....	....	21	9	12	21	48	....	....	....
1995-96	Michigan K Wings	IHL	50	5	4	9	....	....	....	119	....	....	....	....	....	....	....	....	....	....	....	....	....	....	....	....	....	....
1996-97	Michigan K-Wings	IHL	24	0	3	3	....	....	....	40	....	....	....	....	....	....	....	....	....	....	....	....	....	....	....	....	....	....
	Philadelphia Phantoms	AHL	31	7	5	12	....	....	....	103	....	....	....	....	....	....	....	....	....	....	10	1	1	2	20	....	....	....
1997-98	**Dallas Stars**	**NHL**	**7**	**0**	**0**	**0**	**0**	**0**	**0**	**7**	....	....	....	....	....	....	....	....	....	....	....	....	....	....	....	....	....	....
	Michigan K-Wings	IHL	62	9	8	17	....	....	....	206	....	....	....	....	....	....	....	....	....	....	4	0	0	0	30	....	....	....
	NHL Totals		**7**	**0**	**0**	**0**	**0**	**0**	**0**	**7**	**0**	**0**	**0**	**0**	**0.0**	**0**	**0**	**0**	**0**		....	....	....	....	....	....	....	....

Rights traded to **Dallas** by **LA Kings** for Vancouver's fifth round choice (previously acquired, LA Kings selected Jason Morgan) in 1995 Entry Draft, June 7, 1995.

• MITCHELL, ROY

Roy Mitchell D – R. 6'1", 199 lbs. b: Edmonton, Alta., 3/14/1969. Montreal's 10th choice, 188th overall, in 1989 Entry Draft.

1985-86	St. Albert Saints	AJHL	39	2	18	20	....	....	....	32	....	....	....	....	....	....	....	....	....	....	....	....	....	....	....	....	....	....
1986-87	Portland Winter Hawks	WHL	68	7	32	39	....	....	....	103	....	....	....	....	....	....	....	....	....	....	20	0	3	3	23	....	....	....
1987-88	Portland Winter Hawks	WHL	72	5	42	47	....	....	....	219	....	....	....	....	....	....	....	....	....	....	....	....	....	....	....	....	....	....
1988-89	Portland Winter Hawks	WHL	72	9	34	43	....	....	....	177	....	....	....	....	....	....	....	....	....	....	19	1	8	9	38	....	....	....
1989-90	Sherbrooke Canadiens	AHL	77	5	12	17	....	....	....	98	....	....	....	....	....	....	....	....	....	....	12	0	2	2	31	....	....	....
1990-91	Fredericton Canadiens	AHL	71	2	15	17	....	....	....	137	....	....	....	....	....	....	....	....	....	....	9	0	1	1	11	....	....	....
1991-92	Kalamazoo Wings	IHL	69	3	26	29	....	....	....	102	....	....	....	....	....	....	....	....	....	....	11	1	4	5	18	....	....	....
1992-93	**Minnesota North Stars**	**NHL**	**3**	**0**	**0**	**0**	**0**	**0**	**0**	**0**	**0**	**0**	**0**	**0**	**0.0**	**0**	**0**	**0**	**0**	**0**	....	....	....	....	....	....	....	....
	Kalamazoo Wings	IHL	79	7	25	32	....	....	....	119	....	....	....	....	....	....	....	....	....	....	....	....	....	....	....	....	....	....
1993-94	Kalamazoo Wings	IHL	13	0	4	4	....	....	....	21	....	....	....	....	....	....	....	....	....	....	....	....	....	....	....	....	....	....
	Binghamton Rangers	AHL	11	1	3	4	....	....	....	18	....	....	....	....	....	....	....	....	....	....	....	....	....	....	....	....	....	....
	Albany River Rats	AHL	42	3	12	15	....	....	....	43	....	....	....	....	....	....	....	....	....	....	3	0	0	0	0	....	....	....
1994-95	Worcester IceCats	AHL	80	5	25	30	....	....	....	97	....	....	....	....	....	....	....	....	....	....	....	....	....	....	....	....	....	....
1995-96	Worcester IceCats	AHL	52	1	3	4	....	....	....	62	....	....	....	....	....	....	....	....	....	....	4	0	0	0	2	....	....	....
1996-97	Central Texas Stampede	WPHL	20	1	8	9	....	....	....	12	....	....	....	....	....	....	....	....	....	....	11	2	7	9	10	....	....	....
	NHL Totals		**3**	**0**	**0**	**0**	**0**	**0**	**0**	**0**	**0**	**0**	**0**	**0**	**0.0**	**0**	**0**	**0**	**0**		....	....	....	....	....	....	....	....

Signed as a free agent by **Minnesota**, July 25, 1991. Transferred to **Dallas** after **Minnesota** franchise relocated, June 9, 1993. Traded to **New Jersey** by **Dallas** with Reid Simpson for future considerations, March 21, 1994.

• MODANO, MIKE

Mike Modano C – L. 6'3", 200 lbs. b: Livonia, MI, 6/7/1970. Minnesota's 1st choice, 1st overall, in 1988 Entry Draft.

1986-87	Prince Albert Raiders	WHL	70	32	30	62	....	....	....	96	....	....	....	....	....	....	....	....	....	....	8	1	4	5	4	....	....	....
1987-88	Prince Albert Raiders	WHL	65	47	80	127	....	....	....	80	....	....	....	....	....	....	....	....	....	....	9	7	11	18	18	....	....	....
	United States	WJC-A	7	4	1	5	....	....	....	8	....	....	....	....	....	....	....	....	....	....	....	....	....	....	....	....	....	....
1988-89	Prince Albert Raiders	WHL	41	39	66	105	....	....	....	74	....	....	....	....	....	....	....	....	....	....	....	....	....	....	....	....	....	....
	United States	WJC-A	7	6	9	15	....	....	....	12	....	....	....	....	....	....	....	....	....	....	....	....	....	....	....	....	....	....
	Minnesota North Stars	**NHL**	....	....	....	....	....	....	....	....	....	....	....	....	....	....	....	....	....	....	**2**	**0**	**0**	**0**	**0**	....	....	....
1989-90	**Minnesota North Stars**	**NHL**	**80**	**29**	**46**	**75**	**25**	**33**	**58**	**63**	**12**	**0**	**2**	**172**	**16.9**	**109**	**49**	**67**	**0**	**–7**	**7**	**1**	**1**	**2**	**12**	**0**	**0**	**0**
	United States	WEC-A	8	3	3	6	....	....	....	2	....	....	....	....	....	....	....	....	....	....	....	....	....	....	....	....	....	....
1990-91	Minnesota North Stars	FrTour	4	3	0	3	....	....	....	2	....	....	....	....	....	....	....	....	....	....	....	....	....	....	....	....	....	....
	Minnesota North Stars	**NHL**	**79**	**28**	**36**	**64**	**26**	**27**	**53**	**65**	**9**	**0**	**2**	**232**	**12.1**	**95**	**38**	**59**	**4**	**+2**	**23**	**8**	**12**	**20**	**16**	**3**	**0**	**1**
1991-92	United States	C Cup	8	2	7	9	....	....	....	2	....	....	....	....	....	....	....	....	....	....	....	....	....	....	....	....	....	....
	Minnesota North Stars	**NHL**	**76**	**33**	**44**	**77**	**30**	**33**	**63**	**46**	**5**	**0**	**8**	**256**	**12.9**	**102**	**38**	**75**	**2**	**–9**	**7**	**3**	**2**	**5**	**4**	**1**	**0**	**0**
1992-93	**Minnesota North Stars**	**NHL**	**82**	**33**	**60**	**93**	**28**	**41**	**69**	**83**	**9**	**0**	**7**	**307**	**10.7**	**130**	**59**	**90**	**12**	**–7**	....	....	....	....	....	....	....	....
	United States	WC-A	6	0	0	0	....	....	....	2	....	....	....	....	....	....	....	....	....	....	....	....	....	....	....	....	....	....
1993-94	**Dallas Stars**	**NHL**	**76**	**50**	**43**	**93**	**47**	**33**	**80**	**54**	**18**	**0**	**4**	**281**	**17.8**	**111**	**53**	**69**	**3**	**–8**	**9**	**7**	**3**	**10**	**16**	**2**	**0**	**2**
1994-95	**Dallas Stars**	**NHL**	**30**	**12**	**17**	**29**	**21**	**25**	**46**	**8**	**4**	**1**	**0**	**100**	**12.0**	**38**	**16**	**19**	**4**	**+7**	....	....	....	....	....	....	....	....
1995-96	**Dallas Stars**	**NHL**	**78**	**36**	**45**	**81**	**36**	**37**	**73**	**63**	**8**	**4**	**4**	**320**	**11.3**	**112**	**49**	**99**	**24**	**–12**	....	....	....	....	....	....	....	....
1996-97	United States	W Cup	7	2	4	6	....	....	....	4	....	....	....	....	....	....	....	....	....	....	....	....	....	....	....	....	....	....
	Dallas Stars	**NHL**	**80**	**35**	**48**	**83**	**37**	**43**	**80**	**42**	**9**	**5**	**9**	**291**	**12.0**	**113**	**31**	**65**	**26**	**+43**	**7**	**4**	**1**	**5**	**0**	**1**	**1**	**2**
1997-98	**Dallas Stars**	**NHL**	**52**	**21**	**38**	**59**	**25**	**37**	**62**	**32**	**7**	**5**	**2**	**191**	**11.0**	**76**	**28**	**30**	**7**	**+25**	**17**	**4**	**10**	**14**	**12**	**1**	**0**	**1**
	United States	Olympics	4	2	0	2	....	....	....	0	....	....	....	....	....	....	....	....	....	....	....	....	....	....	....	....	....	....
	NHL Totals		**633**	**277**	**377**	**654**	**275**	**309**	**584**	**456**	**81**	**15**	**38**	**2150**	**12.9**	**886**	**361**	**573**	**82**		**72**	**27**	**29**	**56**	**60**	**8**	**1**	**6**

WHL East All-Star Team (1989) • NHL All-Rookie Team (1990)

Played in NHL All-Star Game (1993, 1998)

Transferred to **Dallas** after **Minnesota** franchise relocated, June 9, 1993.

• MODIN, FREDRIK

Fredrik Modin LW – L. 6'3", 222 lbs. b: Sundsvall, Sweden, 10/8/1974. Toronto's 3rd choice, 64th overall, in 1994 Entry Draft.

1991-92	Sundsvall	Sweden 2	11	1	0	1	....	....	....	0	....	....	....	....	....	....	....	....	....	....	....	....	....	....	....	....	....	....
1992-93	Sundsvall	Sweden 2	30	5	7	12	....	....	....	12	....	....	....	....	....	....	....	....	....	....	....	....	....	....	....	....	....	....
1993-94	Sundsvall	Sweden 2	30	16	15	31	....	....	....	36	....	....	....	....	....	....	....	....	....	....	....	....	....	....	....	....	....	....
	Sweden	WJC-A	7	2	2	4	....	....	....	2	....	....	....	....	....	....	....	....	....	....	....	....	....	....	....	....	....	....
1994-95	Brynas IF Gavle	Sweden	38	9	10	19	....	....	....	33	....	....	....	....	....	....	....	....	....	....	14	4	4	8	6	....	....	....
1995-96	Brynas IF Gavle	Sweden	22	4	8	12	....	....	....	22	....	....	....	....	....	....	....	....	....	....	....	....	....	....	....	....	....	....
	Sweden	WC-A	6	1	1	2	....	....	....	4	....	....	....	....	....	....	....	....	....	....	....	....	....	....	....	....	....	....
1996-97	**Toronto Maple Leafs**	**NHL**	**76**	**6**	**7**	**13**	**6**	**6**	**12**	**24**	**0**	**0**	**0**	**85**	**7.1**	**32**	**6**	**40**	**0**	**–14**	....	....	....	....	....	....	....	....
1997-98	**Toronto Maple Leafs**	**NHL**	**74**	**16**	**16**	**32**	**19**	**16**	**35**	**32**	**1**	**0**	**4**	**137**	**11.7**	**44**	**5**	**44**	**0**	**–5**	....	....	....	....	....	....	....	....
	Sweden	WC-A	5	3	3	6	....	....	....	2	....	....	....	....	....	....	....	....	....	....	....	....	....	....	....	....	....	....
	NHL Totals		**150**	**22**	**23**	**45**	**25**	**22**	**47**	**56**	**1**	**0**	**4**	**222**	**9.9**	**76**	**11**	**84**	**0**		....	....	....	....	....	....	....	....

• MODRY, JAROSLAV

Jaroslav Modry D – L. 6'2", 195 lbs. b: Ceske-Budejovice, Czech., 2/27/1971. New Jersey's 11th choice, 179th overall, in 1990 Entry Draft.

1987-88	Motor Ceske Budejovice	Czech.	3	0	0	0	....	....	....	0	....	....	....	....	....	....	....	....	....	....	....	....	....	....	....	....	....	....
1988-89	Motor Ceske Budejovice	Czech.	28	0	1	1	....	....	....	8	....	....	....	....	....	....	....	....	....	....	....	....	....	....	....	....	....	....
1989-90	Motor Ceske Budejovice	Czech.	41	2	2	4	....	....	....	....	....	....	....	....	....	....	....	....	....	....	....	....	....	....	....	....	....	....
1990-91	Dukla Trencin	Czech.	33	1	9	10	....	....	....	6	....	....	....	....	....	....	....	....	....	....	....	....	....	....	....	....	....	....
	Czechoslovakia	WJC-A	6	0	1	1	....	....	....	2	....	....	....	....	....	....	....	....	....	....	....	....	....	....	....	....	....	....
1991-92	Dukla Trencin	Czech.	18	0	4	4	....	....	....	6	....	....	....	....	....	....	....	....	....	....	....	....	....	....	....	....	....	....
	Motor Ceske Budejovice	Czech. 2	14	4	10	14	....	....	....	....	....	....	....	....	....	....	....	....	....	....	....	....	....	....	....	....	....	....
1992-93	Utica Devils	AHL	80	7	35	42	....	....	....	62	....	....	....	....	....	....	....	....	....	....	5	0	2	2	2	....	....	....
1993-94	**New Jersey Devils**	**NHL**	**41**	**2**	**15**	**17**	**2**	**12**	**14**	**18**	**2**	**0**	**0**	**35**	**5.7**	**48**	**8**	**35**	**5**	**+10**	....	....	....	....	....	....	....	....
	Albany River Rats	AHL	19	1	5	6	....	....	....	25	....	....	....	....	....	....	....	....	....	....	....	....	....	....	....	....	....	....
1994-95	Motor Ceske Budejovice	Czech.	19	1	3	4	....	....	....	30	....	....	....	....	....	....	....	....	....	....	....	....	....	....	....	....	....	....
	New Jersey Devils	**NHL**	**11**	**0**	**0**	**0**	**0**	**0**	**0**	**0**	**0**	**0**	**0**	**10**	**0.0**	**3**	**0**	**4**	**0**	**–1**	....	....	....	....	....	....	....	....
	Albany River Rats	AHL	18	5	6	11	....	....	....	14	....	....	....	....	....	....	....	....	....	....	14	3	3	6	4	....	....	....
1995-96	**Ottawa Senators**	**NHL**	**64**	**4**	**14**	**18**	**4**	**11**	**15**	**38**	**1**	**0**	**1**	**89**	**4.5**	**48**	**11**	**67**	**13**	**–17**	....	....	....	....	....	....	....	....
	Los Angeles Kings	**NHL**	**9**	**0**	**3**	**3**	**0**	**2**	**2**	**6**	**0**	**0**	**0**	**17**	**0.0**	**12**	**1**	**18**	**3**	**–4**	....	....	....	....	....	....	....	....
1996-97	**Los Angeles Kings**	**NHL**	**30**	**3**	**3**	**6**	**3**	**3**	**6**	**25**	**1**	**1**	**0**	**32**	**9.4**	**16**	**2**	**31**	**4**	**–13**	....	....	....	....	....	....	....	....
	Phoenix Roadrunners	IHL	23	3	12	15	....	....	....	17	....	....	....	....	....	....	....	....	....	....	....	....	....	....	....	....	....	....
	Utah Grizzlies	IHL	11	1	4	5	....	....	....	20	....	....	....	....	....	....	....	....	....	....	7	0	1	1	6	....	....	....
1997-98	Utah Grizzlies	IHL	74	12	21	33	....	....	....	72	....	....	....	....	....	....	....	....	....	....	4	0	2	2	6	....	....	....
	NHL Totals		**155**	**9**	**35**	**44**	**9**	**28**	**37**	**87**	**4**	**1**	**1**	**183**	**4.9**	**127**	**22**	**155**	**25**		....	....	....	....	....	....	....	....

Traded to **Ottawa** by **New Jersey** for Ottawa's 4th round choice (Alyn McCauley) in 1995 Entry Draft, July 8, 1995. Traded to **LA Kings** by **Ottawa** with Ottawa's 8th round choice (Stephen Valiquette) in 1996 Entry Draft for Kevin Brown, March 20, 1996.

• MOFFAT, LYLE

Lyle Moffat LW. 5'10", 180 lbs. b: Calgary, Alta., 3/19/1948.

Season	Club	League	REGULAR SEASON GP	G	A	Pts	AG	AA	APts	PIM	PP	SH	GW	S	%	TGF	PGF	TGA	PGA	+/-	PLAYOFFS GP	G	A	Pts	PIM	PP	SH	GW
1966-67	Calgary Buffalos	WCJHL	56	30	33	63	....	....	....	64	....	....	....	....	....	....	....	....	....	....	....	....	....	....	....	....	....	....
1967-68	Michigan Tech Huskies	WCHA	DID NOT PLAY – FRESHMAN																									
1968-69	Michigan Tech Huskies	WCHA	28	10	19	29	....	....	....	36	....	....	....	....	....	....	....	....	....	....	....	....	....	....	....	....	....	....
1969-70	Michigan Tech Huskies	WCHA	29	12	11	23	....	....	....	44	....	....	....	....	....	....	....	....	....	....	....	....	....	....	....	....	....	....
1970-71	Michigan Tech Huskies	WCHA	DID NOT PLAY – INJURED																									
1971-72	Tulsa Oilers	CHL	70	15	16	31	....	....	....	82	....	....	....	....	....	....	....	....	....	....	13	2	4	6	25	....	....	....
1972-73	**Toronto Maple Leafs**	**NHL**	**1**	**0**	**0**	**0**	**0**	**0**	**0**	**0**	**0**	**0**	**0**	**0**	**0.0**	**0**	**0**	**1**	**0**	**–1**	....	....	....	....	....	....	....	....
	Tulsa Oilers	CHL	71	*40	40	*80	....	....	....	108	....	....	....	....	....	....	....	....	....	....	....	....	....	....	....	....	....	....
1973-74	Oklahoma City Blazers	CHL	50	19	30	49	....	....	....	70	....	....	....	....	....	....	....	....	....	....	....	....	....	....	....	....	....	....
1974-75	**Toronto Maple Leafs**	**NHL**	**22**	**2**	**7**	**9**	**2**	**5**	**7**	**13**	**0**	**0**	**0**	**18**	**11.1**	**15**	**3**	**14**	**0**	**–2**	....	....	....	....	....	....	....	....
	Oklahoma City Blazers	CHL	39	17	19	36	....	....	....	87	....	....	....	....	....	....	....	....	....	....	5	3	3	6	18	....	....	....
1975-76	Cleveland Crusaders	WHA	33	4	7	11	....	....	....	33	....	....	....	....	....	....	....	....	....	....	....	....	....	....	....	....	....	....
	Winnipeg Jets	WHA	42	13	9	22	....	....	....	44	....	....	....	....	....	....	....	....	....	....	13	3	3	6	9	....	....	....
1976-77	Winnipeg Jets	WHA	74	13	11	24	....	....	....	90	....	....	....	....	....	....	....	....	....	....	17	2	0	2	6	....	....	....
1977-78	Winnipeg Jets	WHA	57	9	16	25	....	....	....	39	....	....	....	....	....	....	....	....	....	....	9	5	7	12	9	....	....	....
1978-79	Winnipeg Jets	WHA	70	14	18	32	....	....	....	38	....	....	....	....	....	....	....	....	....	....	10	3	1	4	22	....	....	....
1979-80	**Winnipeg Jets**	**NHL**	**74**	**10**	**9**	**19**	**9**	**7**	**16**	**38**	**0**	**0**	**1**	**86**	**11.6**	**25**	**1**	**71**	**23**	**–24**	....	....	....	....	....	....	....	....
1980-81	Tulsa Oilers	CHL	66	17	31	48	....	....	....	58	....	....	....	....	....	....	....	....	....	....	8	4	8	12	8	....	....	....
	NHL Totals		**97**	**12**	**16**	**28**	**11**	**12**	**23**	**51**	**0**	**0**	**1**	**104**	**11.5**	**40**	**4**	**86**	**23**		....	....	....	....	....	....	....	....
	Other Major League Totals		276	53	61	114	....	....	....	244	....	....	....	....	....	....	....	....	....	....	49	13	11	24	46	....	....	....

Signed as a free agent by **Toronto**, September, 1971. Signed as a free agent by **Cleveland** (WHA), July, 1975. Traded to **Winnipeg** (WHA) by **Cleveland** (WHA) for Randy Legge and future considerations, January, 1976. Rights retained by **Winnipeg** prior to Expansion Draft, June 9, 1979.

• MOGER, SANDY

Sandy Moger C – R. 6'3", 214 lbs. b: 100 Mile House, B.C., 3/21/1969. Vancouver's 7th choice, 176th overall, in 1989 Entry Draft.

Season	Club	League	GP	G	A	Pts	AG	AA	APts	PIM	PP	SH	GW	S	%	TGF	PGF	TGA	PGA	+/-	GP	G	A	Pts	PIM	PP	SH	GW
1988-89	Lake Superior State	CCHA	21	3	5	8	....	....	....	26	....	....	....	....	....	....	....	....	....	....	....	....	....	....	....	....	....	....
1989-90	Lake Superior State	CCHA	46	17	15	32	....	....	....	76	....	....	....	....	....	....	....	....	....	....	....	....	....	....	....	....	....	....
1990-91	Lake Superior State	CCHA	45	27	21	48	....	....	....	*172	....	....	....	....	....	....	....	....	....	....	....	....	....	....	....	....	....	....
1991-92	Lake Superior State	CCHA	38	24	24	48	....	....	....	93	....	....	....	....	....	....	....	....	....	....	....	....	....	....	....	....	....	....
1992-93	Hamilton Canucks	AHL	78	23	26	49	....	....	....	57	....	....	....	....	....	....	....	....	....	....	....	....	....	....	....	....	....	....
1993-94	Hamilton Canucks	AHL	29	9	8	17	....	....	....	41	....	....	....	....	....	....	....	....	....	....	....	....	....	....	....	....	....	....
1994-95	**Boston Bruins**	**NHL**	**18**	**2**	**6**	**8**	**4**	**9**	**13**	**6**	**2**	**0**	**0**	**32**	**6.3**	**19**	**11**	**9**	**0**	**–1**	....	....	....	....	....	....	....	....
	Providence Bruins	AHL	63	32	29	61	....	....	....	105	....	....	....	....	....	....	....	....	....	....	....	....	....	....	....	....	....	....
1995-96	**Boston Bruins**	**NHL**	**80**	**15**	**14**	**29**	**15**	**11**	**26**	**65**	**4**	**0**	**6**	**103**	**14.6**	**42**	**7**	**44**	**0**	**–9**	**5**	**2**	**2**	**4**	**12**	**1**	**0**	**0**
1996-97	**Boston Bruins**	**NHL**	**34**	**10**	**3**	**13**	**11**	**3**	**14**	**45**	**3**	**0**	**0**	**54**	**18.5**	**21**	**5**	**29**	**1**	**–12**	....	....	....	....	....	....	....	....
	Providence Bruins	AHL	3	0	2	2	....	....	....	19	....	....	....	....	....	....	....	....	....	....	....	....	....	....	....	....	....	....
1997-98	**Los Angeles Kings**	**NHL**	**62**	**11**	**13**	**24**	**13**	**13**	**26**	**70**	**1**	**0**	**2**	**89**	**12.4**	**43**	**11**	**28**	**0**	**+4**	....	....	....	....	....	....	....	....
	NHL Totals		**194**	**38**	**36**	**74**	**43**	**36**	**79**	**186**	**10**	**0**	**8**	**278**	**13.7**	**125**	**34**	**110**	**1**		**5**	**2**	**2**	**4**	**12**	**1**	**0**	**0**

CCHA Second All-Star Team (1992)

Signed as a free agent by **Boston**, June 22, 1994. Traded to **Los Angeles** by **Boston** with Jozef Stumpel and Boston's 4th round choice (later traded to New Jersey — New Jersey selected Pierre Dagenais) in 1998 Entry Draft for Dimitri Khristich and Byron Dafoe, August 29, 1997.

• MOGILNY, ALEXANDER

Alexander Mogilny RW – L. 5'11", 187 lbs. b: Khabarovsk, USSR, 2/18/1969. Buffalo's 4th choice, 89th overall, in 1988 Entry Draft.

Season	Club	League	GP	G	A	Pts	AG	AA	APts	PIM	PP	SH	GW	S	%	TGF	PGF	TGA	PGA	+/-	GP	G	A	Pts	PIM	PP	SH	GW
1986-87	CSKA Moscow	USSR	28	15	1	16	....	....	....	4	....	....	....	....	....	....	....	....	....	....	....	....	....	....	....	....	....	....
1987-88	CSKA Moscow	USSR	39	12	8	20	....	....	....	14	....	....	....	....	....	....	....	....	....	....	....	....	....	....	....	....	....	....
	Soviet Union	WJC-A	7	9	9	18	....	....	....	2	....	....	....	....	....	....	....	....	....	....	....	....	....	....	....	....	....	....
	Soviet Union	Olympics	6	3	2	5	....	....	....	2	....	....	....	....	....	....	....	....	....	....	....	....	....	....	....	....	....	....
1988-89	CSKA Moscow	USSR	31	11	11	22	....	....	....	24	....	....	....	....	....	....	....	....	....	....	....	....	....	....	....	....	....	....
	Soviet Union	WJC-A	7	7	5	12	....	....	....	4	....	....	....	....	....	....	....	....	....	....	....	....	....	....	....	....	....	....
	Soviet Union	WEC-A	10	0	3	3	....	....	....	2	....	....	....	....	....	....	....	....	....	....	....	....	....	....	....	....	....	....
1989-90	**Buffalo Sabres**	**NHL**	**65**	**15**	**28**	**43**	**13**	**20**	**33**	**16**	**4**	**0**	**2**	**130**	**11.5**	**57**	**14**	**35**	**0**	**+8**	**4**	**0**	**1**	**1**	**2**	**0**	**0**	**0**
1990-91	**Buffalo Sabres**	**NHL**	**62**	**30**	**34**	**64**	**28**	**26**	**54**	**16**	**3**	**3**	**5**	**201**	**14.9**	**81**	**14**	**63**	**10**	**+14**	**6**	**0**	**6**	**6**	**2**	**0**	**0**	**0**
1991-92	**Buffalo Sabres**	**NHL**	**67**	**39**	**45**	**84**	**36**	**34**	**70**	**73**	**15**	**0**	**2**	**236**	**16.5**	**133**	**67**	**71**	**12**	**+7**	**2**	**0**	**2**	**2**	**0**	**0**	**0**	**0**
1992-93	**Buffalo Sabres**	**NHL**	**77**	***76**	**51**	**127**	**64**	**35**	**99**	**40**	**27**	**0**	**11**	**360**	**21.1**	**172**	**77**	**89**	**1**	**+7**	**7**	**7**	**3**	**10**	**6**	**2**	**0**	**0**
1993-94	**Buffalo Sabres**	**NHL**	**66**	**32**	**47**	**79**	**30**	**36**	**66**	**22**	**17**	**0**	**7**	**258**	**12.4**	**106**	**56**	**42**	**0**	**+8**	**7**	**4**	**2**	**6**	**6**	**1**	**0**	**0**
1994-95	Spartak	CIS	1	0	1	1	....	....	....	0	....	....	....	....	....	....	....	....	....	....	....	....	....	....	....	....	....	....
	Buffalo Sabres	**NHL**	**44**	**19**	**28**	**47**	**34**	**41**	**75**	**36**	**12**	**0**	**2**	**148**	**12.8**	**62**	**35**	**27**	**0**	**0**	**5**	**3**	**2**	**5**	**2**	**0**	**0**	**0**
1995-96	**Vancouver Canucks**	**NHL**	**79**	**55**	**52**	**107**	**54**	**43**	**97**	**16**	**10**	**5**	**6**	**292**	**18.8**	**135**	**44**	**101**	**24**	**+14**	**6**	**1**	**8**	**9**	**8**	**0**	**0**	**0**
1996-97	Russia	W Cup	5	2	4	6	....	....	....	0	....	....	....	....	....	....	....	....	....	....	....	....	....	....	....	....	....	....
	Vancouver Canucks	**NHL**	**76**	**31**	**42**	**73**	**33**	**37**	**70**	**18**	**7**	**1**	**4**	**174**	**17.8**	**97**	**22**	**73**	**7**	**+9**	....	....	....	....	....	....	....	....
1997-98	**Vancouver Canucks**	**NHL**	**51**	**18**	**27**	**45**	**21**	**26**	**47**	**36**	**5**	**4**	**1**	**118**	**15.3**	**62**	**23**	**55**	**10**	**–6**	....	....	....	....	....	....	....	....
	NHL Totals		**587**	**315**	**354**	**669**	**313**	**298**	**611**	**273**	**100**	**13**	**40**	**1917**	**16.4**	**905**	**352**	**556**	**64**		**37**	**15**	**24**	**39**	**26**	**3**	**0**	**0**

WJC-A All-Star Team (1988)

Named Best Forward at WJC-A (1988) • NHL Second All-Star Team (1993, 1996)

Played in NHL All-Star Game (1992, 1993, 1994, 1996)

Traded to **Vancouver** by **Buffalo** with Buffalo's 5th round choice (Todd Norman) in 1995 Entry Draft for Mike Peca, Mike Wilson and Vancouver's 1st round choice (Jay McKee) in 1995 Entry Draft, July 8, 1995.

• MOHER, MIKE

Mike Moher RW – R. 5'10", 180 lbs. b: Manitouwadge, Ont., 3/26/1962. New Jersey's 6th choice, 106th overall, in 1982 Entry Draft.

Season	Club	League	GP	G	A	Pts	AG	AA	APts	PIM	PP	SH	GW	S	%	TGF	PGF	TGA	PGA	+/-	GP	G	A	Pts	PIM	PP	SH	GW
1977-78	Schreiber North Stars	Jr. B	20	35	30	65	....	....	....	121	....	....	....	....	....	....	....	....	....	....	....	....	....	....	....	....	....	....
1978-79	Garson Native Sons	Jr. A	40	28	35	63	....	....	....	*248	....	....	....	....	....	....	....	....	....	....	....	....	....	....	....	....	....	....
1979-80	Sudbury Wolves	OHA	23	2	5	7	....	....	....	87	....	....	....	....	....	....	....	....	....	....	....	....	....	....	....	....	....	....
	Kitchener Rangers	OHA	45	11	21	32	....	....	....	271	....	....	....	....	....	....	....	....	....	....	....	....	....	....	....	....	....	....
1980-81	Kitchener Rangers	OHA	51	8	14	22	....	....	....	*372	....	....	....	....	....	....	....	....	....	....	18	3	3	6	*112	....	....	....
1981-82	Kitchener Rangers	OHL	43	13	14	27	....	....	....	*384	....	....	....	....	....	....	....	....	....	....	13	1	4	5	*120	....	....	....
1982-83	**New Jersey Devils**	**NHL**	**9**	**0**	**1**	**1**	**0**	**1**	**1**	**28**	**0**	**0**	**0**	**8**	**0.0**	**2**	**0**	**5**	**0**	**–3**	....	....	....	....	....	....	....	....
	Wichita Wind	CHL	48	19	7	26	....	....	....	238	....	....	....	....	....	....	....	....	....	....	....	....	....	....	....	....	....	....
1983-84	Maine Mariners	AHL	25	5	6	11	....	....	....	119	....	....	....	....	....	....	....	....	....	....	....	....	....	....	....	....	....	....
	NHL Totals		**9**	**0**	**1**	**1**	**0**	**1**	**1**	**28**	**0**	**0**	**0**	**8**	**0.0**	**2**	**0**	**5**	**0**		....	....	....	....	....	....	....	....

• MOHNS, DOUG

Doug "Diesel" Mohns LW/D – L. 6', 185 lbs. b: Capreol, Ont., 12/13/1933.

Season	Club	League	GP	G	A	Pts	AG	AA	APts	PIM	PP	SH	GW	S	%	TGF	PGF	TGA	PGA	+/-	GP	G	A	Pts	PIM	PP	SH	GW
1950-51	Barrie Flyers	OHA	....	....	....	....	....	....	....	....	....	....	....	....	....	....	....	....	....	....	1	0	0	0	0	....	....	....
1951-52	Barrie Flyers	OHA	53	40	36	76	....	....	....	46	....	....	....	....	....	....	....	....	....	....	....	....	....	....	....	....	....	....
1952-53	Barrie Flyers	OHA	56	34	42	76	....	....	....	28	....	....	....	....	....	....	....	....	....	....	15	5	4	9	8	....	....	....
1953-54	**Boston Bruins**	**NHL**	**70**	**13**	**14**	**27**	**20**	**19**	**39**	**27**	....	....	....	....	....	....	....	....	....	....	**4**	**1**	**0**	**1**	**4**	....	....	....
1954-55	**Boston Bruins**	**NHL**	**70**	**14**	**18**	**32**	**20**	**23**	**43**	**82**	....	....	....	....	....	....	....	....	....	....	**5**	**0**	**0**	**0**	**4**	....	....	....
1955-56	**Boston Bruins**	**NHL**	**64**	**10**	**8**	**18**	**14**	**10**	**24**	**48**	....	....	....	....	....	....	....	....	....	....	....	....	....	....	....	....	....	....
1956-57	**Boston Bruins**	**NHL**	**68**	**6**	**34**	**40**	**8**	**40**	**48**	**89**	....	....	....	....	....	....	....	....	....	....	**10**	**2**	**3**	**5**	**2**	....	....	....
1957-58	**Boston Bruins**	**NHL**	**54**	**5**	**16**	**21**	**6**	**17**	**23**	**28**	....	....	....	....	....	....	....	....	....	....	**12**	**3**	**10**	**13**	**18**	....	....	....
1958-59	**Boston Bruins**	**NHL**	**47**	**6**	**24**	**30**	**8**	**26**	**34**	**40**	....	....	....	....	....	....	....	....	....	....	**4**	**0**	**2**	**2**	**12**	....	....	....
1959-60	**Boston Bruins**	**NHL**	**65**	**20**	**25**	**45**	**25**	**26**	**51**	**62**	....	....	....	....	....	....	....	....	....	....	....	....	....	....	....	....	....	....
1960-61	**Boston Bruins**	**NHL**	**65**	**12**	**21**	**33**	**15**	**21**	**36**	**63**	....	....	....	....	....	....	....	....	....	....	....	....	....	....	....	....	....	....
1961-62	**Boston Bruins**	**NHL**	**69**	**16**	**29**	**45**	**19**	**29**	**48**	**74**	....	....	....	....	....	....	....	....	....	....	....	....	....	....	....	....	....	....
1962-63	**Boston Bruins**	**NHL**	**68**	**7**	**23**	**30**	**9**	**24**	**33**	**63**	....	....	....	....	....	....	....	....	....	....	....	....	....	....	....	....	....	....
1963-64	**Boston Bruins**	**NHL**	**70**	**9**	**17**	**26**	**12**	**19**	**31**	**95**	....	....	....	....	....	....	....	....	....	....	....	....	....	....	....	....	....	....
1964-65	**Chicago Black Hawks**	**NHL**	**49**	**13**	**20**	**33**	**17**	**22**	**39**	**84**	....	....	....	....	....	....	....	....	....	....	**14**	**3**	**4**	**7**	**21**	....	....	....
1965-66	**Chicago Black Hawks**	**NHL**	**70**	**22**	**27**	**49**	**27**	**27**	**54**	**63**	....	....	....	....	....	....	....	....	....	....	**5**	**1**	**0**	**1**	**4**	....	....	....
1966-67	**Chicago Black Hawks**	**NHL**	**61**	**25**	**35**	**60**	**31**	**36**	**67**	**58**	....	....	....	....	....	....	....	....	....	....	**5**	**0**	**5**	**5**	**8**	....	....	....
1967-68	**Chicago Black Hawks**	**NHL**	**65**	**24**	**29**	**53**	**30**	**30**	**60**	**53**	**5**	**1**	**4**	**161**	**14.9**	**90**	**29**	**61**	**7**	**+7**	**11**	**1**	**5**	**6**	**12**	**0**	**0**	**0**
1968-69	**Chicago Black Hawks**	**NHL**	**65**	**22**	**19**	**41**	**25**	**18**	**43**	**47**	**7**	**0**	**2**	**149**	**14.8**	**84**	**19**	**67**	**10**	**+8**	....	....	....	....	....	....	....	....

			REGULAR SEASON																		PLAYOFFS							
Season	Club	League	GP	G	A	Pts	AG	AA	APts	PIM	PP	SH	GW	S	%	TGF	PGF	TGA	PGA	+/–	GP	G	A	Pts	PIM	PP	SH	GW
1969-70	Chicago Black Hawks	NHL	66	6	27	33	7	27	34	46	3	1	1	118	5.1	100	22	61	12	+29	8	0	2	2	15	0	0	0
1970-71	Chicago Black Hawks	NHL	39	4	6	10	4	5	9	16	0	1	1	31	12.9	27	4	21	3	+5	....	....	....	....	....	....	....	....
	Minnesota North Stars	NHL	17	2	5	7	2	4	6	14	1	0	0	39	5.1	20	6	16	5	+3	6	2	2	4	10	1	0	0
1971-72	Minnesota North Stars	NHL	78	6	30	36	6	27	33	82	4	0	3	143	4.2	96	34	77	21	+6	4	1	2	3	10	1	0	0
1972-73	Minnesota North Stars	NHL	67	4	13	17	4	11	15	52	0	0	1	104	3.8	67	16	55	15	+11	6	0	1	1	2	0	0	0
1973-74	Atlanta Flames	NHL	28	0	3	3	0	3	3	10	0	0	0	25	0.0	12	2	24	7	–7	....	....	....	....	....	....	....	....
1974-75	Washington Capitals	NHL	75	2	19	21	2	15	17	54	1	0	0	83	2.4	74	17	146	37	–52	....	....	....	....	....	....	....	....
	NHL Totals		1390	248	462	710	311	479	790	1250	21	3	12	853	29.1	570	149	528	117		94	14	36	50	122	2	0	0

Played in NHL All-Star Game (1954, 1958, 1959, 1961, 1962, 1965, 1972)

Traded to **Chicago** by **Boston** for Reggie Fleming and Ab McDonald, June 8, 1964. Traded to **Minnesota** by **Chicago** with Terry Caffery for Danny O'Shea, February 22, 1971. Claimed by **Atlanta** from **Minnesota** in Intra-League Draft, June 12, 1973. Traded to **Washington** by **Atlanta** for cash, June 20, 1974.

• MOKOSAK, CARL

Carl Mokosak LW – L. 6'1", 180 lbs. b: Fort Saskatchewan, Alta., 9/22/1962.

Season	Club	League	GP	G	A	Pts	AG	AA	APts	PIM	PP	SH	GW	S	%	TGF	PGF	TGA	PGA	+/–	GP	G	A	Pts	PIM	PP	SH	GW
1978-79	Brandon Bobcats	MJHL	44	12	11	23	....	....	....	146	....	....	....	....	....	....	....	....	....	....	....	....	....	....	....	....	....	....
1979-80	Brandon Wheat Kings	WHL	61	12	21	33	....	....	....	226	....	....	....	....	....	....	....	....	....	....	11	0	4	4	66	....	....	....
1980-81	Brandon Wheat Kings	WHL	70	28	44	72	....	....	....	116	....	....	....	....	....	....	....	....	....	....	5	1	3	4	12	....	....	....
1981-82	Brandon Wheat Kings	WHL	69	46	61	107	....	....	....	363	....	....	....	....	....	....	....	....	....	....	4	0	1	1	11	....	....	....
	Calgary Flames	NHL	1	0	1	1	0	1	1	0	0	0	0	0	0.0	1	0	0	0	+1	....	....	....	....	....	....	....	....
	Oklahoma City Stars	CHL	2	1	1	2	....	....	....	2	....	....	....	....	....	....	....	....	....	....	4	1	1	2	0	....	....	....
1982-83	Calgary Flames	NHL	41	7	6	13	6	4	10	87	0	0	0	38	18.4	19	0	24	0	–5	....	....	....	....	....	....	....	....
	Colorado Flames	CHL	28	10	12	22	....	....	....	106	....	....	....	....	....	....	....	....	....	....	5	1	0	1	12	....	....	....
1983-84	New Haven Nighthawks	AHL	80	18	21	39	....	....	....	206	....	....	....	....	....	....	....	....	....	....	....	....	....	....	....	....	....	....
1984-85	Los Angeles Kings	NHL	30	4	8	12	3	5	8	43	0	0	0	29	13.8	14	0	23	1	–8	....	....	....	....	....	....	....	....
	New Haven Nighthawks	AHL	11	6	6	12	....	....	....	26	....	....	....	....	....	....	....	....	....	....	....	....	....	....	....	....	....	....
1985-86	Philadelphia Flyers	NHL	1	0	0	0	0	0	0	5	0	0	0	0	0.0	0	0	0	0	0	....	....	....	....	....	....	....	....
	Hershey Bears	AHL	79	30	42	72	....	....	....	312	....	....	....	....	....	....	....	....	....	....	16	0	4	4	111	....	....	....
1986-87	Pittsburgh Penguins	NHL	3	0	0	0	0	0	0	4	0	0	0	3	0.0	0	0	4	0	–4	....	....	....	....	....	....	....	....
	Baltimore Skipjacks	AHl	67	23	27	50	....	....	....	228	....	....	....	....	....	....	....	....	....	....	....	....	....	....	....	....	....	....
1987-88	Muskegon Lumberjacks	IHL	81	29	37	66	....	....	....	308	....	....	....	....	....	....	....	....	....	....	6	3	2	5	60	....	....	....
1988-89	Boston Bruins	NHL	7	0	0	0	0	0	0	31	0	0	0	3	0.0	0	0	2	0	–2	1	0	0	0	0	0	0	0
	Maine Mariners	AHL	53	20	18	38	....	....	....	337	....	....	....	....	....	....	....	....	....	....	....	....	....	....	....	....	....	....
1989-90	Fort Wayne Komets	IHL	55	12	21	33	....	....	....	315	....	....	....	....	....	....	....	....	....	....	....	....	....	....	....	....	....	....
	Phoenix Roadrunners	IHL	15	6	6	12	....	....	....	48	....	....	....	....	....	....	....	....	....	....	....	....	....	....	....	....	....	....
1990-91	Indianapolis Ice	IHL	70	12	26	38	....	....	....	205	....	....	....	....	....	....	....	....	....	....	5	0	0	0	2	....	....	....
	San Diego Gulls	IHL	5	0	0	0	....	....	....	30	....	....	....	....	....	....	....	....	....	....	....	....	....	....	....	....	....	....
	NHL Totals		83	11	15	26	9	10	19	170	0	0	0	73	15.1	34	0	53	1		1	0	0	0	0	0	0	0

Signed as a free agent by **Calgary**, July 21, 1981. Traded to **LA Kings** by **Calgary** with Kevin LaVallee for Steve Bozek, June 20, 1983. Signed as a free agent by **Philadelphia**, July 23, 1985. Signed as a free agent by **Pittsburgh**, July 23, 1986. Signed as a free agent by **Boston**, October 4, 1988.

• MOKOSAK, JOHN

John Mokosak D – L. 5'11", 200 lbs. b: Edmonton, Alta., 9/7/1963. Hartford's 6th choice, 130th overall, in 1981 Entry Draft.

Season	Club	League	GP	G	A	Pts	AG	AA	APts	PIM	PP	SH	GW	S	%	TGF	PGF	TGA	PGA	+/–	GP	G	A	Pts	PIM	PP	SH	GW
1979-80	Fort Saskatchewan Traders	SJHL	58	5	13	18	....	....	....	57	....	....	....	....	....	....	....	....	....	....	....	....	....	....	....	....	....	....
1980-81	Victoria Cougars	WHL	71	2	18	20	....	....	....	59	....	....	....	....	....	....	....	....	....	....	15	0	3	3	53	....	....	....
1981-82	Victoria Cougars	WHL	69	6	45	51	....	....	....	102	....	....	....	....	....	....	....	....	....	....	4	1	1	2	0	....	....	....
1982-83	Victoria Cougars	WHL	70	10	33	43	....	....	....	102	....	....	....	....	....	....	....	....	....	....	12	0	0	0	8	....	....	....
1983-84	Binghamton Whalers	AHL	79	3	21	24	....	....	....	80	....	....	....	....	....	....	....	....	....	....	....	....	....	....	....	....	....	....
1984-85	Binghamton Whalers	AHL	54	1	13	14	....	....	....	109	....	....	....	....	....	....	....	....	....	....	7	0	0	0	12	....	....	....
	Salt Lake Golden Eagles	IHL	22	1	10	11	....	....	....	41	....	....	....	....	....	....	....	....	....	....	....	....	....	....	....	....	....	....
1985-86	Binghamton Whalers	AHL	64	0	9	9	....	....	....	196	....	....	....	....	....	....	....	....	....	....	6	0	0	0	6	....	....	....
1986-87	Binghamton Whalers	AHL	72	2	15	17	....	....	....	187	....	....	....	....	....	....	....	....	....	....	9	0	2	2	42	....	....	....
1987-88	Springfield Indians	AHL	77	1	16	17	....	....	....	178	....	....	....	....	....	....	....	....	....	....	....	....	....	....	....	....	....	....
1988-89	Detroit Red Wings	NHL	8	0	1	1	0	1	1	14	0	0	0	0	0.0	6	0	6	0	0	....	....	....	....	....	....	....	....
	Adirondack Red Wings	AHL	65	4	31	35	....	....	....	195	....	....	....	....	....	....	....	....	....	....	17	0	5	5	49	....	....	....
1989-90	Detroit Red Wings	NHL	33	0	1	1	0	1	1	82	0	0	0	15	0.0	16	0	28	3	–9	....	....	....	....	....	....	....	....
	Adirondack Red Wings	AHL	29	2	6	8	....	....	....	80	....	....	....	....	....	....	....	....	....	....	6	1	0	4	10	....	....	....
1990-91	Maine Mariners	AHL	60	1	12	13	....	....	....	104	....	....	....	....	....	....	....	....	....	....	2	0	1	1	4	....	....	....
1991-92	Binghamton Rangers	AHL	28	0	2	2	....	....	....	123	....	....	....	....	....	....	....	....	....	....	9	0	1	1	14	....	....	....
1992-93	Phoenix Roadrunners	IHL	46	4	9	13	....	....	....	169	....	....	....	....	....	....	....	....	....	....	....	....	....	....	....	....	....	....
	NHL Totals		41	0	2	2	0	2	2	96	0	0	0	15	0.0	22	0	34	3		....	....	....	....	....	....	....	....

Signed as a free agent by **Detroit**, August 29, 1988. Signed as a free agent by **Boston**, July 16, 1990. Signed as a free agent by **NY Rangers**, August 28, 1991.

• MOLIN, LARS

Lars Molin LW – L. 6', 180 lbs. b: Ornskoldsvik, Sweden, 5/7/1956.

Season	Club	League	GP	G	A	Pts	AG	AA	APts	PIM	PP	SH	GW	S	%	TGF	PGF	TGA	PGA	+/–	GP	G	A	Pts	PIM	PP	SH	GW
1975-76	MoDo AIK	Sweden	33	12	7	19	....	....	....	22	....	....	....	....	....	....	....	....	....	....	....	....	....	....	....	....	....	....
	Sweden	WJC-A	4	2	0	2	....	....	....	2	....	....	....	....	....	....	....	....	....	....	....	....	....	....	....	....	....	....
1976-77	MoDo AIK	Sweden	36	18	11	29	....	....	....	20	....	....	....	....	....	....	....	....	....	....	4	1	1	2	2	....	....	....
1977-78	MoDo AIK	Sweden	36	15	10	25	....	....	....	24	....	....	....	....	....	....	....	....	....	....	2	1	0	1	0	....	....	....
1978-79	Sweden	Nat-Team	11	4	11	15	....	....	....	14	....	....	....	....	....	....	....	....	....	....	....	....	....	....	....	....	....	....
1979-80	MoDo AIK	Sweden	36	12	8	20	....	....	....	34	....	....	....	....	....	....	....	....	....	....	....	....	....	....	....	....	....	....
	Sweden	Olympics	7	2	5	7	....	....	....	2	....	....	....	....	....	....	....	....	....	....	....	....	....	....	....	....	....	....
1980-81	MoDo AIK	Sweden	30	17	13	30	....	....	....	30	....	....	....	....	....	....	....	....	....	....	....	....	....	....	....	....	....	....
	Sweden	WEC-A	8	2	2	4	....	....	....	4	....	....	....	....	....	....	....	....	....	....	....	....	....	....	....	....	....	....
1981-82	Sweden	C Cup	5	2	2	4	....	....	....	0	....	....	....	....	....	....	....	....	....	....	....	....	....	....	....	....	....	....
	Vancouver Canucks	NHL	72	15	31	46	12	20	32	10	1	1	4	150	10.0	63	16	64	17	0	17	2	9	11	7	0	0	2
1982-83	Vancouver Canucks	NHL	58	12	27	39	10	19	29	23	2	0	1	128	9.4	66	29	79	22	–20	....	....	....	....	....	....	....	....
1983-84	Vancouver Canucks	NHL	42	6	7	13	5	5	10	4	0	1	0	47	12.8	19	2	38	12	–9	2	0	0	0	0	0	0	0
1984-85	MoDo AIK	Sweden	....	....	....	....	....	....	....	....	....	....	....	....	....	....	....	....	....	....	....	....	....	....	....	....	....	....
	Sweden	WEC-A	5	1	2	3	....	....	....	2	....	....	....	....	....	....	....	....	....	....	....	....	....	....	....	....	....	....
1985-86	MoDo AIK	Sweden	34	19	19	38	....	....	....	24	....	....	....	....	....	....	....	....	....	....	....	....	....	....	....	....	....	....
1986-87	MoDo AIK	Sweden	34	8	16	24	....	....	....	42	....	....	....	....	....	....	....	....	....	....	....	....	....	....	....	....	....	....
	Sweden	WEC-A	9	1	1	2	....	....	....	8	....	....	....	....	....	....	....	....	....	....	....	....	....	....	....	....	....	....
1987-88	MoDo AIK	Sweden	24	7	7	14	....	....	....	54	....	....	....	....	....	....	....	....	....	....	4	1	0	1	2	....	....	....
	Sweden	Olympics	7	0	2	2	....	....	....	2	....	....	....	....	....	....	....	....	....	....	....	....	....	....	....	....	....	....
	NHL Totals		172	33	65	98	27	44	71	37	3	2	5	325	10.2	148	47	181	51		19	2	9	11	7	0	0	2

Swedish World All-Star Team (1980)

Signed as a free agent by **Vancouver**, May 18, 1981.

• MOLLER, MIKE

Mike Moller RW – R. 6', 194 lbs. b: Calgary, Alta., 6/16/1962. Buffalo's 2nd choice, 41st overall, in 1980 Entry Draft.

Season	Club	League	GP	G	A	Pts	AG	AA	APts	PIM	PP	SH	GW	S	%	TGF	PGF	TGA	PGA	+/–	GP	G	A	Pts	PIM	PP	SH	GW
1979-80	Lethbridge Broncos	WHL	72	30	41	71	....	....	....	55	....	....	....	....	....	....	....	....	....	....	4	0	6	6	0	....	....	....
1980-81	Lethbridge Broncos	WHL	70	39	69	108	....	....	....	71	....	....	....	....	....	....	....	....	....	....	9	6	10	16	12	....	....	....
	Buffalo Sabres	NHL	5	2	2	4	2	1	3	0	0	0	0	7	28.6	6	0	3	0	+3	3	0	1	1	0	0	0	0
1981-82	Lethbridge Broncos	WHL	49	41	81	122	....	....	....	38	....	....	....	....	....	....	....	....	....	....	12	5	12	17	9	....	....	....
	Canada	WJC-A	7	5	9	14	....	....	....	4	....	....	....	....	....	....	....	....	....	....	....	....	....	....	....	....	....	....
	Buffalo Sabres	NHL	9	0	0	0	0	0	0	0	0	0	0	2	0.0	2	0	9	0	–7	....	....	....	....	....	....	....	....
1982-83	Buffalo Sabres	NHL	49	6	12	18	5	8	13	14	1	0	3	43	14.0	28	1	25	0	+2	....	....	....	....	....	....	....	....
	Rochester Americans	AHL	10	1	6	7	....	....	....	2	....	....	....	....	....	....	....	....	....	....	11	2	4	6	4	....	....	....
1983-84	Buffalo Sabres	NHL	59	5	11	16	4	7	11	27	0	0	1	43	11.6	31	3	29	3	+2	....	....	....	....	....	....	....	....
1984-85	Buffalo Sabres	NHL	5	0	2	2	0	1	1	0	0	0	0	5	0.0	2	0	3	1	0	....	....	....	....	....	....	....	....
	Rochester Americans	AHL	73	19	46	65	....	....	....	27	....	....	....	....	....	....	....	....	....	....	5	1	1	2	0	....	....	....
1985-86	Edmonton Oilers	NHL	1	0	0	0	0	0	0	0	0	0	0	2	0.0	0	0	0	0	0	....	....	....	....	....	....	....	....
	Nova Scotia Oilers	AHL	62	16	15	31	....	....	....	24	....	....	....	....	....	....	....	....	....	....	....	....	....	....	....	....	....	....
1986-87	Edmonton Oilers	NHL	6	2	1	3	2	1	3	0	0	0	0	10	20.0	3	0	2	1	+2	....	....	....	....	....	....	....	....
	Nova Scotia Oilers	AHL	70	14	33	47	....	....	....	28	....	....	....	....	....	....	....	....	....	....	1	0	0	0	0	....	....	....

Season	Club	League	GP	G	A	Pts	AG	AA	APts	PIM	PP	SH	GW	S	%	TGF	PGF	TGA	PGA	+/-	GP	G	A	Pts	PIM	PP	SH	GW
			REGULAR SEASON																		PLAYOFFS							
1987-88	Nova Scotia Oilers	AHL	60	12	31	43	....	....	....	14	....	....	....	....	....	....	....	....	....	....	5	3	0	3	0	....	....	....
1988-89	Canada	Nat-Team	58	18	16	34	....	....	....	18	....	....	....	....	....	....	....	....	....	....	....	....	....	....	....	....	....	....
1989-90	Binghamton Whalers	AHL	12	1	2	3	....	....	....	6	....	....	....	....	....	....	....	....	....	....	....	....	....	....	....	....	....	....
	NHL Totals		**134**	**15**	**28**	**43**	**13**	**18**	**31**	**41**	**1**	**0**	**4**	**112**	**13.4**	**72**	**4**	**71**	**5**		**3**	**0**	**1**	**1**	**0**	**0**	**0**	**0**

WHL All-Star Team (1981) • WJC-A All-Star Team (1982) • WHL First All-Star Team (1982)

Traded to **Pittsburgh** by **Buffalo** with Randy Cunneyworth for Pat Hughes, October 4, 1985. Traded to **Edmonton** by **Pittsburgh** for Pat Hughes, October 4, 1985.

• MOLLER, RANDY

Randy Moller D – R. 6'2", 210 lbs. b: Red Deer, Alta., 8/23/1963. Quebec's 2nd choice, 11th overall, in 1981 Entry Draft.

Season	Club	League	GP	G	A	Pts	AG	AA	APts	PIM	PP	SH	GW	S	%	TGF	PGF	TGA	PGA	+/-	GP	G	A	Pts	PIM	PP	SH	GW
1979-80	Red Deer Rustlers	AJHL	56	3	34	37	....	....	....	253	....	....	....	....	....	....	....	....	....	....	....	....	....	....	....	....	....	....
1980-81	Lethbridge Broncos	WHL	46	4	21	25	....	....	....	176	....	....	....	....	....	....	....	....	....	....	9	0	4	4	24	....	....	....
1981-82	Lethbridge Broncos	WHL	60	20	55	75	....	....	....	249	....	....	....	....	....	....	....	....	....	....	12	4	6	10	65	....	....	....
	Canada	WJC-A	7	0	3	3	....	....	....	4	....	....	....	....	....	....	....	....	....	....	....	....	....	....	....	....	....	....
	Quebec Nordiques	**NHL**	....	....	....	....	....	....	....	....	....	....	....	....	....	....	....	....	....	....	1	0	0	0	0	....	....	....
1982-83	**Quebec Nordiques**	**NHL**	75	2	12	14	2	8	10	145	0	0	1	72	2.8	74	1	88	26	+11	4	1	0	1	4	1	0	1
1983-84	**Quebec Nordiques**	**NHL**	74	4	14	18	3	9	12	147	0	0	1	78	5.1	93	3	82	18	+26	9	1	0	1	45	0	0	0
1984-85	**Quebec Nordiques**	**NHL**	79	7	22	29	6	15	21	120	0	0	0	126	5.6	101	5	94	27	+29	18	2	2	4	40	1	0	0
1985-86	**Quebec Nordiques**	**NHL**	69	5	18	23	4	12	16	141	0	0	1	105	4.8	78	7	98	36	+9	3	0	0	0	26	0	0	0
1986-87	**Quebec Nordiques**	**NHL**	71	5	9	14	4	6	10	144	1	0	1	106	4.7	70	1	102	22	–11	13	1	4	5	23	0	0	0
1987-88	**Quebec Nordiques**	**NHL**	66	3	22	25	3	16	19	169	0	0	2	116	2.6	66	8	106	37	–11	....	....	....	....	....	....	....	....
1988-89	**Quebec Nordiques**	**NHL**	74	7	22	29	6	15	21	136	2	0	0	117	6.0	85	15	98	30	+2	....	....	....	....	....	....	....	....
1989-90	**New York Rangers**	**NHL**	60	1	12	13	1	9	10	139	0	0	0	47	2.1	46	1	63	17	–1	10	1	6	7	32	0	0	0
1990-91	**New York Rangers**	**NHL**	61	4	19	23	4	14	18	161	1	0	0	75	5.3	85	21	64	13	+13	6	0	2	2	11	0	0	0
1991-92	**New York Rangers**	**NHL**	43	2	7	9	2	5	7	78	0	0	1	44	4.5	33	3	55	10	–15	....	....	....	....	....	....	....	....
	Binghamton Rangers	AHL	3	0	1	1	....	....	....	0	....	....	....	....	....	....	....	....	....	....	....	....	....	....	....	....	....	....
	Buffalo Sabres	**NHL**	13	1	2	3	1	1	2	59	0	0	0	19	5.3	6	0	11	6	+1	7	0	0	0	8	0	0	0
1992-93	**Buffalo Sabres**	**NHL**	35	2	7	9	2	5	7	83	0	0	0	25	8.0	30	1	33	10	+6	....	....	....	....	....	....	....	....
	Rochester Americans	AHL	3	1	0	1	....	....	....	10	....	....	....	....	....	....	....	....	....	....	....	....	....	....	....	....	....	....
1993-94	**Buffalo Sabres**	**NHL**	78	2	11	13	2	8	10	154	0	0	0	77	2.6	56	4	68	11	–5	7	0	2	2	8	0	0	0
1994-95	**Florida Panthers**	**NHL**	17	0	3	3	0	4	4	16	0	0	0	12	0.0	7	0	14	2	–5	....	....	....	....	....	....	....	....
	NHL Totals		**815**	**45**	**180**	**225**	**40**	**127**	**167**	**1692**	**4**	**0**	**7**	**1019**	**4.4**	**830**	**70**	**976**	**265**		**78**	**6**	**16**	**22**	**197**	**2**	**0**	**1**

WHL Second All-Star Team (1982)

Traded to **NY Rangers** by **Quebec** for Michel Petit, October 5, 1989. Traded to **Buffalo** by **NY Rangers** for Jay Wells, March 9, 1992. Signed as a free agent by **Florida**, July 11, 1994.

• MOLLOY, MITCH

Mitch Molloy LW – L. 6'3", 212 lbs. b: Red Lake, Ont., 10/10/1966.

Season	Club	League	GP	G	A	Pts	AG	AA	APts	PIM	PP	SH	GW	S	%	TGF	PGF	TGA	PGA	+/-	GP	G	A	Pts	PIM	PP	SH	GW
1986-87	Camrose Lutheran College	CCAA	STATISTICS NOT AVAILABLE																									
1987-88	Virginia Lancers	ACHL	43	26	45	71	....	....	....	196	....	....	....	....	....	....	....	....	....	....	8	5	4	9	63	....	....	....
1988-89	Maine Mariners	AHL	47	1	8	9	....	....	....	177	....	....	....	....	....	....	....	....	....	....	....	....	....	....	....	....	....	....
	Flint Spirits	IHL	5	1	1	2	....	....	....	21	....	....	....	....	....	....	....	....	....	....	....	....	....	....	....	....	....	....
1989-90	Johnstown Chiefs	ECHL	18	10	10	20	....	....	....	102	....	....	....	....	....	....	....	....	....	....	....	....	....	....	....	....	....	....
	Buffalo Sabres	**NHL**	2	0	0	0	0	0	0	10	0	0	0	0	0.0	0	0	0	0	0	....	....	....	....	....	....	....	....
	Rochester Americans	AHL	15	1	1	2	....	....	....	43	....	....	....	....	....	....	....	....	....	....	....	....	....	....	....	....	....	....
1990-91	Rochester Americans	AHL	25	1	0	1	....	....	....	127	....	....	....	....	....	....	....	....	....	....	....	....	....	....	....	....	....	....
1991-92	St. Thomas Wildcats	ColHL	52	26	33	59	....	....	....	149	....	....	....	....	....	....	....	....	....	....	....	....	....	....	....	....	....	....
1992-93	San Diego Gulls	IHL	8	0	0	0	....	....	....	8	....	....	....	....	....	....	....	....	....	....	....	....	....	....	....	....	....	....
	St. Thomas Wildcats	ColHL	9	2	6	8	....	....	....	14	....	....	....	....	....	....	....	....	....	....	12	6	3	9	39	....	....	....
	NHL Totals		**2**	**0**	**0**	**0**	**0**	**0**	**0**	**10**	**0**	**0**	**0**	**0**	**0.0**	**0**	**0**	**0**	**0**		....	....	....	....	....	....	....	....

Signed as a free agent by **Buffalo**, Februrary, 1990.

• MOMESSO, SERGIO

Sergio Momesso LW – L. 6'3", 215 lbs. b: Montreal, Que., 9/4/1965. Montreal's 3rd choice, 27th overall, in 1983 Entry Draft.

Season	Club	League	GP	G	A	Pts	AG	AA	APts	PIM	PP	SH	GW	S	%	TGF	PGF	TGA	PGA	+/-	GP	G	A	Pts	PIM	PP	SH	GW
1982-83	Shawinigan Cataractes	QMJHL	70	27	42	69	....	....	....	93	....	....	....	....	....	....	....	....	....	....	10	5	4	9	55	....	....	....
1983-84	Shawinigan Cataractes	QMJHL	68	42	88	130	....	....	....	235	....	....	....	....	....	....	....	....	....	....	6	4	4	8	13	....	....	....
	Montreal Canadiens	**NHL**	1	0	0	0	0	0	0	0	0	0	0	0	0.0	1	0	0	0	+1	....	....	....	....	....	....	....	....
	Nova Scotia Voyageurs	AHL	....	....	....	....	....	....	....	....	....	....	....	....	....	....	....	....	....	....	8	0	2	2	4	....	....	....
1984-85	Shawinigan Cataractes	QMJHL	64	56	90	146	....	....	....	216	....	....	....	....	....	....	....	....	....	....	8	7	8	15	17	....	....	....
1985-86	**Montreal Canadiens**	**NHL**	24	8	7	15	6	5	11	46	3	0	3	37	21.6	25	10	19	0	–4	....	....	....	....	....	....	....	....
1986-87	**Montreal Canadiens**	**NHL**	59	14	17	31	12	12	24	96	2	0	1	28	50.0	18	3	14	0	+1	11	1	3	4	31	0	0	0
	Sherbrooke Canadiens	AHL	6	1	6	7	....	....	....	10	....	....	....	....	....	....	....	....	....	....	....	....	....	....	....	....	....	....
1987-88	**Montreal Canadiens**	**NHL**	53	7	14	21	6	10	16	101	1	0	0	72	9.7	33	4	20	0	+9	6	0	2	2	16	0	0	0
1988-89	**St. Louis Blues**	**NHL**	53	9	17	26	8	12	20	139	0	0	0	81	11.1	41	3	39	0	–1	10	2	5	7	24	0	0	0
1989-90	**St. Louis Blues**	**NHL**	79	24	32	56	21	23	44	199	4	0	4	182	13.2	94	31	79	1	–15	12	3	2	5	63	0	0	1
1990-91	**St. Louis Blues**	**NHL**	59	10	18	28	9	14	23	131	0	0	1	86	11.6	42	2	28	0	+12	....	....	....	....	....	....	....	....
	Vancouver Canucks	**NHL**	11	6	2	8	5	2	7	43	3	0	2	33	18.2	9	3	5	0	+1	6	0	3	3	25	0	0	0
1991-92	**Vancouver Canucks**	**NHL**	58	20	23	43	18	17	35	198	2	0	3	153	13.1	62	15	32	1	+16	13	0	5	5	30	0	0	0
1992-93	**Vancouver Canucks**	**NHL**	84	18	20	38	15	14	29	200	4	0	1	146	12.3	70	16	44	1	+11	12	3	0	3	30	0	0	1
1993-94	**Vancouver Canucks**	**NHL**	68	14	13	27	13	10	23	149	4	0	1	112	12.5	51	11	42	0	–2	24	3	4	7	56	0	0	1
1994-95	Milano Devils	Italy	2	1	4	5	....	....	....	2	....	....	....	....	....	....	....	....	....	....	....	....	....	....	....	....	....	....
	Milano Devils	EuroHL	2	2	3	5	....	....	....	0	....	....	....	....	....	....	....	....	....	....	....	....	....	....	....	....	....	....
	Vancouver Canucks	**NHL**	48	10	15	25	18	22	40	65	6	0	1	82	12.2	40	13	29	0	–2	11	3	1	4	16	1	0	0
1995-96	**Toronto Maple Leafs**	**NHL**	54	7	8	15	7	7	14	112	4	0	1	91	7.7	30	12	29	0	–11	....	....	....	....	....	....	....	....
	New York Rangers	**NHL**	19	4	4	8	4	3	7	30	2	0	0	35	11.4	12	6	8	0	–2	11	3	1	4	14	0	0	0
1996-97	**New York Rangers**	**NHL**	9	0	0	0	0	0	0	11	0	0	0	11	0.0	0	0	2	0	–2	....	....	....	....	....	....	....	....
	St. Louis Blues	**NHL**	31	1	3	4	1	3	4	37	0	0	0	32	3.1	8	0	12	0	–4	3	0	0	0	6	0	0	0
1997-98	Kolner Haie	Germany	42	14	18	32	....	....	....	193	....	....	....	....	....	....	....	....	....	....	3	1	2	3	4	....	....	....
	Kolner Haie	EuroHL	6	4	4	8	....	....	....	29	....	....	....	....	....	....	....	....	....	....	....	....	....	....	....	....	....	....
	NHL Totals		**710**	**152**	**193**	**345**	**143**	**154**	**297**	**1557**	**35**	**0**	**18**	**1181**	**12.9**	**536**	**129**	**402**	**3**		**119**	**18**	**26**	**44**	**311**	**1**	**0**	**3**

QMJHL First All-Star Team (1985)

Traded to **St. Louis** by **Montreal** with Vincent Riendeau for Jocelyn Lemieux, Darrell May and St. Louis' 2nd round choice (Patrice Brisebois) in the 1989 Entry Draft, August 9, 1988. Traded to **Vancouver** by **St. Louis** with Geoff Courtnall, Robert Dirk, Cliff Ronning and St. Louis' 5th round choice (Brian Loney) in 1992 Entry Draft for Dan Quinn and Garth Butcher, March 5, 1991. Traded to **Toronto** by **Vancouver** for Mike Ridley, July 8, 1995. Traded by **NY Rangers** by **Toronto** for Wayne Presley, February 29, 1996. Traded to **St. Louis** by **NY Rangers** for Brian Noonan, November 13, 1996.

• MONAHAN, GARRY

Garry Monahan LW – L. 6', 199 lbs. b: Barrie, Ont., 10/20/1946. Montreal's 1st choice, 1st overall, in 1963 Amateur Draft.

Season	Club	League	GP	G	A	Pts	AG	AA	APts	PIM	PP	SH	GW	S	%	TGF	PGF	TGA	PGA	+/-	GP	G	A	Pts	PIM	PP	SH	GW
1964-65	Peterborough Petes	OHA	55	12	16	28	....	....	....	28	....	....	....	....	....	....	....	....	....	....	12	1	2	3	11	....	....	....
1965-66	Peterborough Petes	OHA	46	6	10	16	....	....	....	43	....	....	....	....	....	....	....	....	....	....	6	0	3	3	9	....	....	....
1966-67	Peterborough Petes	OHA	47	30	54	84	....	....	....	79	....	....	....	....	....	....	....	....	....	....	6	2	2	4	20	....	....	....
	Houston Apollos	CHL	....	....	....	....	....	....	....	....	....	....	....	....	....	....	....	....	....	....	3	1	0	1	0	....	....	....
1967-68	**Montreal Canadiens**	**NHL**	11	0	0	0	0	0	0	8	0	0	0	3	0.0	1	0	3	0	–2	....	....	....	....	....	....	....	....
	Houston Apollos	CHL	56	17	31	48	....	....	....	86	....	....	....	....	....	....	....	....	....	....	....	....	....	....	....	....	....	....
1968-69	**Montreal Canadiens**	**NHL**	3	0	0	0	0	0	0	0	0	0	0	0	0.0	0	0	0	0	0	....	....	....	....	....	....	....	....
	Cleveland Barons	AHL	70	18	26	44	....	....	....	81	....	....	....	....	....	....	....	....	....	....	5	2	0	2	10	....	....	....
1969-70	**Detroit Red Wings**	**NHL**	51	3	4	7	3	4	7	24	0	0	1	44	6.8	13	2	18	1	–6	....	....	....	....	....	....	....	....
	Los Angeles Kings	**NHL**	21	0	3	3	0	3	3	12	0	0	0	15	0.0	6	1	15	4	–6	....	....	....	....	....	....	....	....
1970-71	**Toronto Maple Leafs**	**NHL**	78	15	22	37	16	19	35	79	4	1	4	173	8.7	75	11	60	7	+11	6	2	0	2	2	0	0	0
1971-72	**Toronto Maple Leafs**	**NHL**	78	14	17	31	15	15	30	47	2	1	2	186	7.5	48	6	57	17	+2	5	0	0	0	0	0	0	0
1972-73	**Toronto Maple Leafs**	**NHL**	78	13	18	31	13	15	28	53	0	0	3	135	9.6	56	3	72	16	–3	....	....	....	....	....	....	....	....
1973-74	**Toronto Maple Leafs**	**NHL**	78	9	16	25	9	14	23	70	0	0	1	139	6.5	37	3	58	28	+4	4	0	1	1	7	0	0	0
1974-75	**Toronto Maple Leafs**	**NHL**	1	0	0	0	0	0	0	0	0	0	0	0	0.0	0	0	0	0	0	....	....	....	....	....	....	....	....
	Vancouver Canucks	**NHL**	78	14	20	34	13	16	29	51	3	1	2	154	9.1	55	6	82	23	–10	5	1	0	1	2	0	0	1
1975-76	**Vancouver Canucks**	**NHL**	66	16	17	33	15	13	28	39	3	1	2	126	12.7	51	6	69	25	+1	2	0	0	0	2	0	0	0
1976-77	**Vancouver Canucks**	**NHL**	76	18	26	44	17	21	38	48	3	0	1	169	10.7	62	10	75	22	–1	....	....	....	....	....	....	....	....

			REGULAR SEASON																		PLAYOFFS							
Season	**Club**	**League**	**GP**	**G**	**A**	**Pts**	**AG**	**AA**	**APts**	**PIM**	**PP**	**SH**	**GW**	**S**	**%**	**TGF**	**PGF**	**TGA**	**PGA**	**+/–**	**GP**	**G**	**A**	**Pts**	**PIM**	**PP**	**SH**	**GW**
1977-78	**Vancouver Canucks**	**NHL**	**67**	**10**	**19**	**29**	**10**	**15**	**25**	**28**	**0**	**0**	**1**	**105**	**9.5**	**40**	**5**	**56**	**23**	**+2**	....	....	....	....	....	....	....	....
	Tulsa Oilers	CHL	7	3	2	5	....	....	....	0	....	....	....	....	....	....	....	....	....	....	....	....	....	....	....	....	....	....
1978-79	**Toronto Maple Leafs**	**NHL**	**62**	**4**	**7**	**11**	**4**	**5**	**9**	**25**	**0**	**2**	**0**	**55**	**7.3**	**25**	**3**	**41**	**23**	**+4**	....	....	....	....	....	....	....	....
1979-80	Seibu-Tetsudo	Japan	20	13	17	30	....	....	....	....	....	....	....	....	....	....	....	....	....	....	....	....	....	....	....	....	....	....
1980-81	Seibu-Tetsudo	Japan	20	12	14	26	....	....	....	....	....	....	....	....	....	....	....	....	....	....	....	....	....	....	....	....	....	....
1981-82	Seibu-Tetsudo	Japan	20	17	19	36	....	....	....	....	....	....	....	....	....	....	....	....	....	....	....	....	....	....	....	....	....	....
	NHL Totals		**748**	**116**	**169**	**285**	**115**	**140**	**255**	**484**	**15**	**6**	**17**	**1304**	**8.9**	**469**	**56**	**606**	**189**		**22**	**3**	**1**	**4**	**13**	**0**	**0**	**1**

Traded to **Detroit** by **Montreal** with Doug Piper for Pete Mahovlich and Bart Crashley, June 6, 1969. Traded to **LA Kings** by **Detroit** with Brian Gibbons for Dale Rolfe, Gary Croteau and Larry Johnson, February 20, 1970. Traded to **Toronto** by **LA Kings** with Brian Murphy for Bob Pulford, September 3, 1970. Traded to **Vancouver** by **Toronto** with John Grisdale for Dave Dunn, September 3, 1970. Traded to **Toronto** by **Vancouver** for cash, September 13, 1978.

• MONAHAN, HARTLAND

Hartland Monahan RW – R. 5'11", 197 lbs. b: Montreal, Que., 3/29/1951. California's 3rd choice, 43rd overall, in 1971 Amateur Draft.

Season	Club	League	GP	G	A	Pts	AG	AA	APts	PIM	PP	SH	GW	S	%	TGF	PGF	TGA	PGA	+/–	GP	G	A	Pts	PIM	PP	SH	GW
1968-69	Laval Saints	QJHL	STATISTICS NOT AVAILABLE																									
1969-70	Montreal Jr. Canadiens	OHA	54	10	14	24	....	....	....	72	....	....	....	....	....	....	....	....	....	....	....	....	....	....	....	....	....	....
1970-71	Montreal Jr. Canadiens	OHA	43	14	29	43	....	....	....	135	....	....	....	....	....	....	....	....	....	....	....	....	....	....	....	....	....	....
1971-72	Baltimore Clippers	AHL	20	1	1	2	....	....	....	4	....	....	....	....	....	....	....	....	....	....	....	....	....	....	....	....	....	....
	Columbus Seals	IHL	36	8	19	27	....	....	....	55	....	....	....	....	....	....	....	....	....	....	....	....	....	....	....	....	....	....
1972-73	Salt Lake Golden Eagles	WHL	61	18	34	52	....	....	....	60	....	....	....	....	....	....	....	....	....	....	9	5	2	7	6	....	....	....
1973-74	**California Golden Seals**	**NHL**	**1**	**0**	**0**	**0**	**0**	**0**	**0**	**0**	**0**	**0**	**0**	**1**	**0.0**	**0**	**0**	**0**	**0**	**0**	....	....	....	....	....	....	....	....
	Salt Lake Golden Eagles	WHL	66	14	28	42	....	....	....	76	....	....	....	....	....	....	....	....	....	....	5	1	2	3	2	....	....	....
1974-75	**New York Rangers**	**NHL**	**6**	**0**	**1**	**1**	**0**	**1**	**1**	**4**	**0**	**0**	**0**	**5**	**0.0**	**2**	**0**	**4**	**0**	**–2**	....	....	....	....	....	....	....	....
	Providence Reds	AHL	70	28	42	70	....	....	....	96	....	....	....	....	....	....	....	....	....	....	6	2	2	4	14	....	....	....
1975-76	**Washington Capitals**	**NHL**	**80**	**17**	**29**	**46**	**16**	**23**	**39**	**35**	**2**	**0**	**2**	**142**	**12.0**	**76**	**17**	**122**	**14**	**–49**	....	....	....	....	....	....	....	....
1976-77	**Washington Capitals**	**NHL**	**79**	**23**	**27**	**50**	**22**	**22**	**44**	**37**	**7**	**1**	**4**	**137**	**16.8**	**80**	**20**	**92**	**4**	**–28**	....	....	....	....	....	....	....	....
1977-78	**Pittsburgh Penguins**	**NHL**	**7**	**2**	**0**	**2**	**2**	**0**	**2**	**2**	**1**	**0**	**0**	**13**	**15.4**	**5**	**2**	**10**	**0**	**–7**	....	....	....	....	....	....	....	....
	Los Angeles Kings	**NHL**	**64**	**10**	**9**	**19**	**10**	**7**	**17**	**45**	**0**	**0**	**1**	**97**	**10.3**	**35**	**2**	**46**	**0**	**–13**	**2**	**0**	**0**	**0**	**0**	**0**	**0**	**0**
1978-79	Springfield Indians	AHL	76	30	36	66	....	....	....	71	....	....	....	....	....	....	....	....	....	....	....	....	....	....	....	....	....	....
1979-80	**St. Louis Blues**	**NHL**	**72**	**5**	**12**	**17**	**5**	**9**	**14**	**36**	**1**	**1**	**0**	**93**	**5.4**	**32**	**1**	**67**	**14**	**–22**	**3**	**0**	**0**	**0**	**0**	**0**	**0**	**0**
1980-81	**St. Louis Blues**	**NHL**	**25**	**4**	**2**	**6**	**3**	**1**	**4**	**4**	**0**	**2**	**0**	**32**	**12.5**	**15**	**0**	**19**	**6**	**+2**	**1**	**0**	**0**	**0**	**4**	**0**	**0**	**0**
	NHL Totals		**334**	**61**	**80**	**141**	**58**	**63**	**121**	**163**	**11**	**4**	**7**	**520**	**11.7**	**245**	**42**	**360**	**38**		**6**	**0**	**0**	**0**	**4**	**0**	**0**	**0**

AHL Second All-Star Team (1975)

Traded to **NY Rangers** by **California** for Brian Lavender, September 23, 1974. Claimed by **Washington** from **NY Rangers** in Intra-League Draft, June 17, 1975. Traded to **Pittsburgh** by **Washington** for Pittsburgh's 1st round choice (later traded to Minnesota — Minnesota selected Tom McCarthy) in 1979 Entry Draft, October 17, 1977. Traded to **LA Kings** by **Pittsburgh** with Syl Apps Jr. for Dave Schultz, Gene Carr and LA Kings' 4th round choice (Shane Pearsall) in 1978 Amateur Draft, November 2, 1977. Claimed by **Quebec** from **LA Kings** in Expansion Draft, June 13, 1979. Traded to **St. Louis** by **Quebec** for cash, June 13, 1979.

• MONDOU, PIERRE

Pierre Mondou C – R. 5'10", 185 lbs. b: Sorel, Que., 11/27/1955. Montreal's 2nd choice, 15th overall, in 1975 Amateur Draft.

Season	Club	League	GP	G	A	Pts	AG	AA	APts	PIM	PP	SH	GW	S	%	TGF	PGF	TGA	PGA	+/–	GP	G	A	Pts	PIM	PP	SH	GW
1972-73	Sorel Eperviers	QMJHL	64	37	43	80	....	....	....	57	....	....	....	....	....	....	....	....	....	....	10	6	4	10	12	....	....	....
1973-74	Sorel Eperviers	QMJHL	60	62	57	119	....	....	....	104	....	....	....	....	....	....	....	....	....	....	2	0	0	0	0	....	....	....
1974-75	Sorel Eperviers	QMJHL	28	16	23	39	....	....	....	13	....	....	....	....	....	....	....	....	....	....	....	....	....	....	....	....	....	....
	Montreal Juniors	QMJHL	40	40	47	87	....	....	....	23	....	....	....	....	....	....	....	....	....	....	9	8	7	15	13	....	....	....
1975-76	Nova Scotia Voyageurs	AHL	74	34	43	77	....	....	....	30	....	....	....	....	....	....	....	....	....	....	9	1	5	6	4	....	....	....
1976-77	Nova Scotia Voyageurs	AHL	71	*44	45	89	....	....	....	21	....	....	....	....	....	....	....	....	....	....	12	*8	*11	*19	6	....	....	....
	Montreal Canadiens	**NHL**	....	....	....	....	....	....	....	....	....	....	....	....	....	....	....	....	....	....	**4**	**0**	**0**	**0**	**0**	....	....	....
1977-78	**Montreal Canadiens**	**NHL**	**71**	**19**	**30**	**49**	**18**	**24**	**42**	**8**	**4**	**0**	**3**	**132**	**14.4**	**71**	**15**	**24**	**0**	**+32**	**15**	**3**	**7**	**10**	**4**	**2**	**0**	**1**
1978-79	**Montreal Canadiens**	**NHL**	**77**	**31**	**41**	**72**	**28**	**31**	**59**	**26**	**6**	**1**	**7**	**163**	**19.0**	**114**	**26**	**29**	**0**	**+59**	**16**	**3**	**6**	**9**	**4**	**1**	**0**	**0**
1979-80	**Montreal Canadiens**	**NHL**	**75**	**30**	**36**	**66**	**27**	**28**	**55**	**12**	**8**	**0**	**3**	**152**	**19.7**	**92**	**28**	**38**	**0**	**+26**	**4**	**1**	**4**	**5**	**4**	**0**	**0**	**0**
1980-81	**Montreal Canadiens**	**NHL**	**57**	**17**	**24**	**41**	**14**	**17**	**31**	**16**	**5**	**0**	**2**	**106**	**16.0**	**70**	**22**	**24**	**0**	**+24**	**3**	**0**	**1**	**1**	**0**	**0**	**0**	**0**
1981-82	**Montreal Canadiens**	**NHL**	**73**	**35**	**33**	**68**	**28**	**22**	**50**	**57**	**8**	**2**	**4**	**146**	**24.0**	**92**	**20**	**69**	**15**	**+18**	**5**	**2**	**5**	**7**	**8**	**1**	**1**	**0**
1982-83	**Montreal Canadiens**	**NHL**	**76**	**29**	**37**	**66**	**24**	**26**	**50**	**31**	**8**	**1**	**3**	**178**	**16.3**	**100**	**20**	**77**	**29**	**+32**	**3**	**0**	**1**	**1**	**2**	**0**	**0**	**0**
1983-84	**Montreal Canadiens**	**NHL**	**52**	**15**	**22**	**37**	**12**	**15**	**27**	**8**	**3**	**1**	**1**	**105**	**14.3**	**51**	**7**	**46**	**11**	**+9**	**14**	**6**	**3**	**9**	**2**	**1**	**0**	**1**
1984-85	**Montreal Canadiens**	**NHL**	**67**	**18**	**39**	**57**	**15**	**26**	**41**	**21**	**2**	**0**	**2**	**128**	**14.1**	**81**	**23**	**57**	**14**	**+15**	**5**	**2**	**1**	**3**	**2**	**0**	**0**	**0**
	NHL Totals		**548**	**194**	**262**	**456**	**166**	**189**	**355**	**179**	**44**	**5**	**25**	**1110**	**17.5**	**671**	**161**	**364**	**69**		**69**	**17**	**28**	**45**	**26**	**5**	**1**	**2**

QMJHL Second All-Star Team (1975) • Won Dudley "Red" Garrett Memorial Award (Top Rookie - AHL) (1976) • AHL Second All-Star Team (1977)

• Suffered career-ending eye injury in game vs. Hartford, March 9, 1985.

• MONGEAU, MICHEL

Michel Mongeau C – L. 5'9", 190 lbs. b: Montreal, Que., 2/9/1965.

Season	Club	League	GP	G	A	Pts	AG	AA	APts	PIM	PP	SH	GW	S	%	TGF	PGF	TGA	PGA	+/–	GP	G	A	Pts	PIM	PP	SH	GW
1983-84	Laval Titan	QMJHL	60	45	49	94	....	....	....	30	....	....	....	....	....	....	....	....	....	....	....	....	....	....	....	....	....	....
1984-85	Laval Titan	QMJHL	67	60	84	144	....	....	....	56	....	....	....	....	....	....	....	....	....	....	....	....	....	....	....	....	....	....
1985-86	Laval Titan	QMJHL	72	71	109	180	....	....	....	45	....	....	....	....	....	....	....	....	....	....	....	....	....	....	....	....	....	....
1986-87	Saginaw Generals	IHL	76	42	53	95	....	....	....	34	....	....	....	....	....	....	....	....	....	....	10	3	6	9	6	....	....	....
1987-88	France	Nat-Team	30	31	21	52	....	....	....	....	....	....	....	....	....	....	....	....	....	....	....	....	....	....	....	....	....	....
1988-89	Flint Spirits	IHL	82	41	*76	117	....	....	....	57	....	....	....	....	....	....	....	....	....	....	....	....	....	....	....	....	....	....
1989-90	**St. Louis Blues**	**NHL**	**7**	**1**	**5**	**6**	**1**	**4**	**5**	**2**	**0**	**0**	**0**	**2**	**50.0**	**8**	**3**	**1**	**0**	**+4**	**2**	**0**	**1**	**1**	**0**	**0**	**0**	**0**
	Peoria Rivermen	IHL	73	39	*78	*117	....	....	....	53	....	....	....	....	....	....	....	....	....	....	5	3	4	7	6	....	....	....
1990-91	**St. Louis Blues**	**NHL**	**7**	**1**	**1**	**2**	**1**	**1**	**2**	**0**	**1**	**0**	**0**	**13**	**7.7**	**4**	**2**	**1**	**0**	**+1**	....	....	....	....	....	....	....	....
	Peoria Rivermen	IHL	73	41	65	106	....	....	....	114	....	....	....	....	....	....	....	....	....	....	19	10	*16	26	32	....	....	....
1991-92	**St. Louis Blues**	**NHL**	**36**	**3**	**12**	**15**	**3**	**9**	**12**	**6**	**2**	**0**	**0**	**23**	**13.0**	**25**	**17**	**10**	**0**	**–2**	....	....	....	....	....	....	....	....
	Peoria Rivermen	IHL	32	21	34	55	....	....	....	77	....	....	....	....	....	....	....	....	....	....	10	5	14	19	8	....	....	....
1992-93	**Tampa Bay Lightning**	**NHL**	**4**	**1**	**1**	**2**	**1**	**1**	**2**	**2**	**0**	**0**	**0**	**2**	**50.0**	**3**	**2**	**3**	**0**	**–2**	....	....	....	....	....	....	....	....
	Milwaukee Admirals	IHL	45	24	41	65	....	....	....	69	....	....	....	....	....	....	....	....	....	....	4	1	4	5	4	....	....	....
	Halifax Citadels	AHL	22	13	18	31	....	....	....	10	....	....	....	....	....	....	....	....	....	....	....	....	....	....	....	....	....	....
1993-94	Cornwall Aces	AHL	7	3	11	14	....	....	....	4	....	....	....	....	....	....	....	....	....	....	....	....	....	....	....	....	....	....
	Peoria Rivermen	IHL	52	29	36	65	....	....	....	50	....	....	....	....	....	....	....	....	....	....	....	....	....	....	....	....	....	....
1994-95	Peoria Rivermen	IHL	74	30	52	82	....	....	....	72	....	....	....	....	....	....	....	....	....	....	....	....	....	....	....	....	....	....
1995-96	Peoria Rivermen	IHL	24	5	17	22	....	....	....	24	....	....	....	....	....	....	....	....	....	....	12	4	11	15	8	....	....	....
	NHL Totals		**54**	**6**	**19**	**25**	**6**	**15**	**21**	**10**	**3**	**0**	**0**	**40**	**15.0**	**40**	**24**	**15**	**0**		**2**	**0**	**1**	**1**	**0**	**0**	**0**	**0**

QMJHL Second All-Star Team (1986) • Won Garry F. Longman Memorial Trophy (Top Rookie - IHL) (1987) • IHL First All-Star Team (1990) • Won Leo P. Lamoureux Memorial Trophy (Top Scorer - IHL) (1990) • Won James Gatschene Memorial Trophy (MVP - IHL) (1990) • IHL Second All-Star Team (1991) • Won "Bud" Poile Trophy (Playoff MVP - IHL) (1991)

Signed as a free agent by **St. Louis**, August 21, 1989. Claimed by **Tampa Bay** from **St. Louis** in Expansion Draft, June 18, 1992. Traded to **Quebec** by **Tampa Bay** with Martin Simard and Steve Tuttle and Herb Raglan, February 12, 1993.

• MONGRAIN, BOB

Bob Mongrain C – L. 5'10", 165 lbs. b: La Sarre, Que., 8/31/1959.

Season	Club	League	GP	G	A	Pts	AG	AA	APts	PIM	PP	SH	GW	S	%	TGF	PGF	TGA	PGA	+/–	GP	G	A	Pts	PIM	PP	SH	GW
1975-76	Trois-Rivieres Draveurs	QMJHL	1	0	0	0	....	....	....	0	....	....	....	....	....	....	....	....	....	....	....	....	....	....	....	....	....	....
1976-77	Cap-de-Madelaine	Tier II	....	53	79	132	....	....	....	....	....	....	....	....	....	....	....	....	....	....	....	....	....	....	....	....	....	....
	Trois-Rivieres Draveurs	QMJHL	12	0	2	2	....	....	....	0	....	....	....	....	....	....	....	....	....	....	....	....	....	....	....	....	....	....
1977-78	Trois-Rivieres Draveurs	QMJHL	72	35	43	78	....	....	....	77	....	....	....	....	....	....	....	....	....	....	13	2	4	6	7	....	....	....
1978-79	Trois Rivieres Draveurs	QMJHL	72	66	76	142	....	....	....	55	....	....	....	....	....	....	....	....	....	....	13	4	14	18	13	....	....	....
1979-80	**Buffalo Sabres**	**NHL**	**34**	**4**	**6**	**10**	**4**	**5**	**9**	**4**	**0**	**0**	**1**	**33**	**12.1**	**14**	**0**	**11**	**3**	**+6**	**9**	**1**	**2**	**3**	**2**	**0**	**0**	**0**
	Rochester Americans	AHL	39	25	24	49	....	....	....	58	....	....	....	....	....	....	....	....	....	....	....	....	....	....	....	....	....	....
1980-81	**Buffalo Sabres**	**NHL**	**4**	**0**	**0**	**0**	**0**	**0**	**0**	**2**	**0**	**0**	**0**	**2**	**0.0**	**1**	**1**	**3**	**1**	**–2**	....	....	....	....	....	....	....	....
	Rochester Americans	AHL	69	21	29	50	....	....	....	101	....	....	....	....	....	....	....	....	....	....	....	....	....	....	....	....	....	....
1981-82	**Buffalo Sabres**	**NHL**	**24**	**6**	**4**	**10**	**5**	**3**	**8**	**6**	**0**	**0**	**2**	**29**	**20.7**	**16**	**2**	**23**	**6**	**–3**	**1**	**0**	**0**	**0**	**0**	**0**	**0**	**0**
	Rochester Americans	AHL	56	37	37	74	....	....	....	45	....	....	....	....	....	....	....	....	....	....	....	....	....	....	....	....	....	....
1982-83	Rochester Americans	AHL	80	29	52	81	....	....	....	72	....	....	....	....	....	....	....	....	....	....	16	3	5	8	24	....	....	....
1983-84	Rochester Americans	AHL	78	41	44	85	....	....	....	154	....	....	....	....	....	....	....	....	....	....	18	11	9	20	46	....	....	....
	Buffalo Sabres	**NHL**	....	....	....	....	....	....	....	....	....	....	....	....	....	....	....	....	....	....	**1**	**0**	**0**	**0**	**0**	....	....	....
1984-85	**Buffalo Sabres**	**NHL**	**8**	**1**	**1**	**2**	**1**	**1**	**2**	**0**	**0**	**0**	**0**	**10**	**10.0**	**3**	**0**	**5**	**3**	**+1**	....	....	....	....	....	....	....	....
	EC Kloten	Switz.	38	42	30	72	....	....	....	....	....	....	....	....	....	....	....	....	....	....	....	....	....	....	....	....	....	....

			REGULAR SEASON																		PLAYOFFS							
Season	Club	League	GP	G	A	Pts	AG	AA	APts	PIM	PP	SH	GW	S	%	TGF	PGF	TGA	PGA	+/-	GP	G	A	Pts	PIM	PP	SH	GW
1985-86	EC Kloten	Switz.	38	*46	32	78	....	....	....	....	....	....	....	....	....	....	....	....	....	....	5	*9	1	10	....	....	....	....
	Los Angeles Kings	**NHL**	**11**	**2**	**3**	**5**	**2**	**2**	**4**	**2**	**0**	**0**	**0**	**10**	**20.0**	**6**	**0**	**20**	**11**	**–3**	....	....	....	....	....	....	....	....
1986-87	EC Kloten	Switz.	....	24	17	41	....	....	....	....	....	....	....	....	....	....	....	....	....	....	3	0	0	0	0	....	....	....
1987-88	EC Kloten	Switz. 2	....	28	16	44	....	....	....	....	....	....	....	....	....	....	....	....	....	....	7	8	3	11	....	....	....	....
1988-89	Martigny	Switz. 2	....	36	31	67	....	....	....	....	....	....	....	....	....	....	....	....	....	....	7	6	4	10	....	....	....	....
1989-90	HC Sierre	Switz. 2	....	27	39	66	....	....	....	....	....	....	....	....	....	....	....	....	....	....	....	....	....	....	....	....	....	....
1990-91	HC Sierre	Switz.	29	19	24	43	....	....	....	....	....	....	....	....	....	....	....	....	....	....	10	11	11	22	....	....	....	....
	NHL Totals		**81**	**13**	**14**	**27**	**12**	**11**	**23**	**14**	**0**	**0**	**3**	**84**	**15.5**	**40**	**3**	**62**	**24**		**11**	**1**	**2**	**3**	**2**	**0**	**0**	**0**

Signed as a free agent by **Buffalo**, September 16, 1979. Signed as a free agent by **LA Kings**, Macrch 6, 1986.

• MONTEITH, HANK

Hank Monteith LW – L. 5'10", 170 lbs. b: Stratford, Ont., 10/2/1945.

Season	Club	League	GP	G	A	Pts	AG	AA	APts	PIM	PP	SH	GW	S	%	TGF	PGF	TGA	PGA	+/-	GP	G	A	Pts	PIM	PP	SH	GW
1965-66	University of Toronto	OUAA	16	*23	20	*43	....	....	....	30	....	....	....	....	....	....	....	....	....	....	....	....	....	....	....	....	....	....
1966-67	University of Toronto	OUAA	16	21	24	45	....	....	....	....	....	....	....	....	....	....	....	....	....	....	....	....	....	....	....	....	....	....
1967-68	Fort Worth Wings	CHL	66	19	31	50	....	....	....	36	....	....	....	....	....	....	....	....	....	....	11	1	3	4	0	....	....	....
1968-69	**Detroit Red Wings**	**NHL**	**34**	**1**	**9**	**10**	**1**	**8**	**9**	**6**	**0**	**0**	**0**	**20**	**5.0**	**14**	**3**	**7**	**0**	**+4**	....	....	....	....	....	....	....	....
	Fort Worth Wings	CHL	33	17	13	30	....	....	....	14	....	....	....	....	....	....	....	....	....	....	....	....	....	....	....	....	....	....
1969-70	**Detroit Red Wings**	**NHL**	**9**	**0**	**0**	**0**	**0**	**0**	**0**	**0**	**0**	**0**	**0**	**4**	**0.0**	**0**	**0**	**1**	**0**	**–1**	**4**	**0**	**0**	**0**	**0**	**0**	**0**	**0**
	Fort Worth Wings	CHL	52	20	28	48	....	....	....	38	....	....	....	....	....	....	....	....	....	....	....	....	....	....	....	....	....	....
1970-71	**Detroit Red Wings**	**NHL**	**34**	**4**	**3**	**7**	**4**	**3**	**7**	**0**	**0**	**0**	**0**	**37**	**10.8**	**14**	**0**	**19**	**0**	**–5**	....	....	....	....	....	....	....	....
	Fort Worth Wings	CHL	21	11	15	26	....	....	....	4	....	....	....	....	....	....	....	....	....	....	4	1	2	3	4	....	....	....
1971-72	Oakville Oaks	OHA Sr.	27	16	24	40	....	....	....	14	....	....	....	....	....	....	....	....	....	....	....	....	....	....	....	....	....	....
1972-73	Oakville Oaks	OHA Sr.	20	17	26	43	....	....	....	10	....	....	....	....	....	....	....	....	....	....	....	....	....	....	....	....	....	....
	Orillia Terriers	OHA Sr.	16	4	15	19	....	....	....	4	....	....	....	....	....	....	....	....	....	....	....	....	....	....	....	....	....	....
1973-74	Orillia Terriers	OHA Sr.	31	15	34	49	....	....	....	19	....	....	....	....	....	....	....	....	....	....	....	....	....	....	....	....	....	....
1974-75	Orillia Terriers	OHA Sr.	29	20	14	34	....	....	....	6	....	....	....	....	....	....	....	....	....	....	....	....	....	....	....	....	....	....
	NHL Totals		**77**	**5**	**12**	**17**	**5**	**11**	**16**	**6**	**0**	**0**	**0**	**61**	**8.2**	**28**	**3**	**27**	**0**		**4**	**0**	**0**	**0**	**0**	**0**	**0**	**0**

Signed as a free agent by **Detroit**, September, 1967.

• MONTGOMERY, JIM

Jim Montgomery C – R. 5'10", 185 lbs. b: Montreal, Que., 6/30/1969.

Season	Club	League	GP	G	A	Pts	AG	AA	APts	PIM	PP	SH	GW	S	%	TGF	PGF	TGA	PGA	+/-	GP	G	A	Pts	PIM	PP	SH	GW
1989-90	University of Maine	H.E.	45	26	34	60	....	....	....	35	....	....	....	....	....	....	....	....	....	....	....	....	....	....	....	....	....	....
1990-91	University of Maine	H.E.	43	24	*57	81	....	....	....	44	....	....	....	....	....	....	....	....	....	....	....	....	....	....	....	....	....	....
1991-92	University of Maine	H.E.	37	21	44	65	....	....	....	46	....	....	....	....	....	....	....	....	....	....	....	....	....	....	....	....	....	....
1992-93	University of Maine	H.E.	45	32	63	95	....	....	....	40	....	....	....	....	....	....	....	....	....	....	....	....	....	....	....	....	....	....
1993-94	**St. Louis Blues**	**NHL**	**67**	**6**	**14**	**20**	**6**	**11**	**17**	**44**	**0**	**0**	**1**	**67**	**9.0**	**34**	**2**	**48**	**15**	**–1**	....	....	....	....	....	....	....	....
	Peoria Rivermen	IHL	12	7	8	15	....	....	....	10	....	....	....	....	....	....	....	....	....	....	....	....	....	....	....	....	....	....
1994-95	**Montreal Canadiens**	**NHL**	**5**	**0**	**0**	**0**	**0**	**0**	**0**	**2**	**0**	**0**	**0**	**3**	**0.0**	**0**	**0**	**2**	**0**	**–2**	....	....	....	....	....	....	....	....
	Philadelphia Flyers	**NHL**	**8**	**1**	**1**	**2**	**2**	**1**	**3**	**6**	**0**	**0**	**0**	**10**	**10.0**	**2**	**1**	**4**	**1**	**–2**	**7**	**1**	**0**	**1**	**2**	**0**	**0**	**0**
	Hershey Bears	AHL	16	8	6	14	....	....	....	14	....	....	....	....	....	....	....	....	....	....	6	3	2	5	25	....	....	....
1995-96	**Philadelphia Flyers**	**NHL**	**5**	**1**	**2**	**3**	**1**	**2**	**3**	**9**	**0**	**0**	**0**	**4**	**25.0**	**4**	**0**	**3**	**0**	**+1**	**1**	**0**	**0**	**0**	**0**	**0**	**0**	**0**
	Hershey Bears	AHL	78	34	*71	105	....	....	....	95	....	....	....	....	....	....	....	....	....	....	4	3	2	5	6	....	....	....
1996-97	Kolner Haie	Germany	50	12	35	47	....	....	....	111	....	....	....	....	....	....	....	....	....	....	4	0	1	1	6	....	....	....
1997-98	Philadelphia Phantoms	AHL	68	19	43	62	....	....	....	75	....	....	....	....	....	....	....	....	....	....	20	13	16	29	55	....	....	....
	NHL Totals		**85**	**8**	**17**	**25**	**9**	**14**	**23**	**61**	**0**	**0**	**1**	**84**	**9.5**	**40**	**3**	**57**	**16**		**8**	**1**	**0**	**1**	**2**	**0**	**0**	**0**

Hockey East Second All-Star Team (1991, 1992) • Hockey East First All-Star Team (1993) • NCAA East Second All-American Team (1993) • NCAA Championship All-Tournament Team (1993) • NCAA Championship Tournament MVP (1993) • AHL Second All-Star Team (1996)

Signed as a free agent by **St. Louis**, June 2, 1993. Traded to **Montreal** by **St. Louis** for Guy Carbonneau, August 19, 1994. Claimed on waivers by **Philadelphia** from **Montreal**, February 10, 1995.

• MOORE, BARRIE

Barrie Moore LW – L. 5'11", 175 lbs. b: London, Ont., 5/22/1975. Buffalo's 7th choice, 220th overall, in 1993 Entry Draft.

Season	Club	League	GP	G	A	Pts	AG	AA	APts	PIM	PP	SH	GW	S	%	TGF	PGF	TGA	PGA	+/-	GP	G	A	Pts	PIM	PP	SH	GW
1991-92	Sudbury Wolves	OHL	62	15	38	53	....	....	....	57	....	....	....	....	....	....	....	....	....	....	11	0	7	7	12	....	....	....
1992-93	Sudbury Wolves	OHL	57	13	26	39	....	....	....	71	....	....	....	....	....	....	....	....	....	....	14	4	3	7	19	....	....	....
1993-94	Sudbury Wolves	OHL	65	36	49	85	....	....	....	69	....	....	....	....	....	....	....	....	....	....	10	3	5	8	14	....	....	....
1994-95	Sudbury Wolves	OHL	60	47	42	89	....	....	....	67	....	....	....	....	....	....	....	....	....	....	18	*15	14	29	24	....	....	....
1995-96	**Buffalo Sabres**	**NHL**	**3**	**0**	**0**	**0**	**0**	**0**	**0**	**0**	**0**	**0**	**0**	**3**	**0.0**	**1**	**0**	**1**	**0**	**0**	....	....	....	....	....	....	....	....
	Rochester Americans	AHL	64	26	30	56	....	....	....	40	....	....	....	....	....	....	....	....	....	....	18	3	6	9	18	....	....	....
1996-97	**Buffalo Sabres**	**NHL**	**31**	**2**	**6**	**8**	**2**	**5**	**7**	**18**	**1**	**0**	**0**	**42**	**4.8**	**11**	**1**	**12**	**3**	**+1**	....	....	....	....	....	....	....	....
	Rochester Americans	AHL	32	14	15	29	....	....	....	14	....	....	....	....	....	....	....	....	....	....	....	....	....	....	....	....	....	....
	Edmonton Oilers	**NHL**	**4**	**0**	**0**	**0**	**0**	**0**	**0**	**0**	**0**	**0**	**0**	**1**	**0.0**	**0**	**0**	**0**	**0**	**0**	....	....	....	....	....	....	....	....
	Hamilton Bulldogs	AHL	9	5	2	7	....	....	....	0	....	....	....	....	....	....	....	....	....	....	22	2	6	8	15	....	....	....
1997-98	Hamilton Bulldogs	AHL	70	22	29	51	....	....	....	64	....	....	....	....	....	....	....	....	....	....	8	0	1	1	4	....	....	....
	NHL Totals		**38**	**2**	**6**	**8**	**2**	**5**	**7**	**18**	**1**	**0**	**0**	**46**	**4.3**	**12**	**1**	**13**	**3**		....	....	....	....	....	....	....	....

Traded to **Edmonton** by **Buffalo** with Craig Millar for Miroslav Satan, March 18, 1997.

• MOORE, DICKIE

Dickie "Digging Dicker" Moore LW – L. 5'10", 168 lbs. b: Montreal, Que., 1/6/1931. **HHOF**

Season	Club	League	GP	G	A	Pts	AG	AA	APts	PIM	PP	SH	GW	S	%	TGF	PGF	TGA	PGA	+/-	GP	G	A	Pts	PIM	PP	SH	GW
1947-48	Montreal Jr. Royals	QJHL	29	10	11	22	....	....	....	20	....	....	....	....	....	....	....	....	....	....	13	6	5	11	14	....	....	....
1948-49	Montreal Jr. Royals	QJHL	47	22	34	56	....	....	....	71	....	....	....	....	....	....	....	....	....	....	25	12	13	25	37	....	....	....
	Montreal Royals	QSHL	2	0	0	0	....	....	....	0	....	....	....	....	....	....	....	....	....	....	....	....	....	....	....	....	....	....
1949-50	Montreal Jr. Royals	QJHL	1	0	1	1	....	....	....	5	....	....	....	....	....	....	....	....	....	....	....	....	....	....	....	....	....	....
	Montreal Jr. Canadiens	QJHL	35	24	19	43	....	....	....	110	....	....	....	....	....	....	....	....	....	....	29	18	*27	45	*92	....	....	....
1950-51	Montreal Jr. Canadiens	QJHL	33	12	22	34	....	....	....	58	....	....	....	....	....	....	....	....	....	....	9	5	4	9	34	....	....	....
1951-52	**Montreal Canadiens**	**NHL**	**33**	**18**	**15**	**33**	**25**	**19**	**44**	**44**	....	....	....	....	....	....	....	....	....	....	**11**	**1**	**1**	**2**	**12**	....	....	....
	Montreal Royals	QSHL	26	15	20	35	....	....	....	32	....	....	....	....	....	....	....	....	....	....	....	....	....	....	....	....	....	....
1952-53	**Montreal Canadiens**	**NHL**	**18**	**2**	**6**	**8**	**3**	**8**	**11**	**19**	....	....	....	....	....	....	....	....	....	....	**12**	**3**	**2**	**5**	**13**	....	....	....
	Buffalo Bisons	AHL	6	2	3	5	....	....	....	10	....	....	....	....	....	....	....	....	....	....	....	....	....	....	....	....	....	....
1953-54	**Montreal Canadiens**	**NHL**	**13**	**1**	**4**	**5**	**2**	**5**	**7**	**12**	....	....	....	....	....	....	....	....	....	....	**11**	**5**	***8**	***13**	**8**	....	....	....
	Montreal Royals	QHL	2	0	1	1	....	....	....	4	....	....	....	....	....	....	....	....	....	....	....	....	....	....	....	....	....	....
1954-55	**Montreal Canadiens**	**NHL**	**67**	**16**	**20**	**36**	**23**	**26**	**49**	**32**	....	....	....	....	....	....	....	....	....	....	**12**	**1**	**5**	**6**	**22**	....	....	....
1955-56	**Montreal Canadiens**	**NHL**	**70**	**11**	**39**	**50**	**16**	**49**	**65**	**55**	....	....	....	....	....	....	....	....	....	....	**10**	**3**	**6**	**9**	**12**	....	....	....
1956-57	**Montreal Canadiens**	**NHL**	**70**	**29**	**29**	**58**	**40**	**34**	**74**	**56**	....	....	....	....	....	....	....	....	....	....	**10**	**3**	**7**	**10**	**4**	....	....	....
1957-58	**Montreal Canadiens**	**NHL**	**70**	***36**	**48**	***84**	**48**	**53**	**101**	**65**	....	....	....	....	....	....	....	....	....	....	**10**	**4**	**7**	**11**	**4**	....	....	....
1958-59	**Montreal Canadiens**	**NHL**	**70**	**41**	***55**	***96**	**53**	**59**	**112**	**61**	....	....	....	....	....	....	....	....	....	....	**11**	**5**	***12**	***17**	**8**	....	....	....
1959-60	**Montreal Canadiens**	**NHL**	**62**	**22**	**42**	**64**	**27**	**43**	**70**	**54**	....	....	....	....	....	....	....	....	....	....	**8**	***6**	**4**	**10**	**4**	....	....	....
1960-61	**Montreal Canadiens**	**NHL**	**57**	**35**	**34**	**69**	**43**	**35**	**78**	**62**	....	....	....	....	....	....	....	....	....	....	**6**	**3**	**1**	**4**	**4**	....	....	....
1961-62	**Montreal Canadiens**	**NHL**	**57**	**19**	**22**	**41**	**23**	**22**	**45**	**54**	....	....	....	....	....	....	....	....	....	....	**6**	**4**	**2**	**6**	**8**	....	....	....
1962-63	**Montreal Canadiens**	**NHL**	**67**	**24**	**26**	**50**	**30**	**27**	**57**	**61**	....	....	....	....	....	....	....	....	....	....	**5**	**0**	**1**	**1**	**2**	....	....	....
1963-64				DID NOT PLAY																								
1964-65	**Toronto Maple Leafs**	**NHL**	**38**	**2**	**4**	**6**	**3**	**4**	**7**	**68**	....	....	....	....	....	....	....	....	....	....	**5**	**1**	**1**	**2**	**6**	....	....	....
1965-66				DID NOT PLAY																								
1966-67				DID NOT PLAY																								
1967-68	**St. Louis Blues**	**NHL**	**27**	**5**	**3**	**8**	**6**	**3**	**9**	**9**	**1**	**0**	**1**	**37**	**13.5**	**13**	**4**	**17**	**0**	**–8**	**18**	**7**	**7**	**14**	**15**	**2**	**0**	**1**
	NHL Totals		**719**	**261**	**347**	**608**	**342**	**387**	**729**	**652**	**1**	**0**	**1**	**37**	**705.4**	**13**	**4**	**17**	**0**		**135**	**46**	**64**	**110**	**122**	**2**	**0**	**1**

NHL First All-Star Team (1958, 1959) • Won Art Ross Trophy (1958, 1959) • NHL Second All-Star Team (1961)

Played in NHL All-Star Game (1953, 1956, 1957, 1958, 1959, 1960)

Claimed by **Toronto** from **Montreal** in Intra-League Draft, June 10, 1964. Signed as a free agent by **St. Louis**, November 29, 1968.

• MORAN, IAN

Ian Moran D – R. 5'11", 195 lbs. b: Cleveland, OH, 8/24/1972. Pittsburgh's 5th choice, 107th overall, in 1990 Entry Draft.

Season	Club	League	GP	G	A	Pts	AG	AA	APts	PIM	PP	SH	GW	S	%	TGF	PGF	TGA	PGA	+/-	GP	G	A	Pts	PIM	PP	SH	GW
1989-90	Belmont Hill High School	H.S.	23	10	36	46	....	....	....	....	....	....	....	....	....	....	....	....	....	....	....	....	....	....	....	....	....	....
1990-91	Belmont Hill High School	H.S.	23	7	44	51	....	....	....	12	....	....	....	....	....	....	....	....	....	....	....	....	....	....	....	....	....	....
1991-92	Boston College	H.E.	30	2	16	18	....	....	....	44	....	....	....	....	....	....	....	....	....	....	....	....	....	....	....	....	....	....

Season	Club	League	GP	G	A	Pts	AG	AA	APts	PIM	PP	SH	GW	S	%	TGF	PGF	TGA	PGA	+/–	GP	G	A	Pts	PIM	PP	SH	GW
			REGULAR SEASON																		PLAYOFFS							
1992-93	Boston College	H.E.	31	8	12	20				32																		
	United States	WC-A	6	0	0	0				0																		
1993-94	United States	Nat-Team	50	8	15	23				69																		
	Cleveland Lumberjacks	IHL	33	5	13	18				39																		
1994-95	Cleveland Lumberjacks	IHL	64	7	31	38				94											4	0	1	1	2			
	Pittsburgh Penguins	**NHL**					-2	-1	-3												8	0	0	0	0			
1995-96	**Pittsburgh Penguins**	**NHL**	51	1	1	2	1	1	2	47	0	0	0	44	2.3	28	0	43	14	–1								
1996-97	**Pittsburgh Penguins**	**NHL**	36	4	5	9	4	4	8	22	0	0	0	50	8.0	33	7	47	10	–11	5	1	2	3	4	0	0	0
	Cleveland Lumberjacks	IHL	36	6	23	29				26																		
1997-98	**Pittsburgh Penguins**	**NHL**	37	1	6	7	1	6	7	19	0	0	1	33	3.0	12	2	14	4	0	6	0	0	0	2	0	0	0
	NHL Totals		124	6	12	18	4	10	14	88	0	0	1	127	4.7	73	9	104	28		19	1	2	3	6	0	0	0

• MORE, JAYSON

Jayson More D – R. 6'2", 210 lbs. b: Souris, Man., 1/12/1969. NY Rangers' 1st choice, 10th overall, in 1987 Entry Draft.

Season	Club	League	GP	G	A	Pts	AG	AA	APts	PIM	PP	SH	GW	S	%	TGF	PGF	TGA	PGA	+/–	GP	G	A	Pts	PIM	PP	SH	GW
1984-85	Lethbridge Broncos	WHL	71	3	9	12				101											4	1	0	1	7			
1985-86	Lethbridge Broncos	WHL	61	7	18	25				155											9	0	2	2	36			
1986-87	Brandon Wheat Kings	WHL	21	4	6	10				62																		
	New Westminster Bruins	WHL	43	4	23	27				155																		
1987-88	New Westminster Bruins	WHL	70	13	47	60				270											5	0	2	2	26			
1988-89	**New York Rangers**	**NHL**	1	0	0	0	0	0	0	0	0	0	0	0	0.0	1	0	2	0	–1								
	Denver Rangers	IHL	62	7	15	22				138											3	0	1	1	26			
1989-90	Flint Spirits	IHL	9	1	5	6				41																		
	Minnesota North Stars	**NHL**	5	0	0	0	0	0	0	16	0	0	0	4	0.0	2	0	1	0	+1								
	Kalamazoo Wings	IHL	64	9	25	34				316											10	0	3	3	13			
1990-91	Kalamazoo Wings	IHL	10	0	5	5				46																		
	Fredericton Canadiens	AHL	57	7	17	24				152											9	1	1	2	34			
1991-92	**San Jose Sharks**	**NHL**	46	4	13	17	4	10	14	85	1	0	1	60	6.7	41	14	79	20	–32								
	Kansas City Blades	IHL	2	0	2	2				4																		
1992-93	**San Jose Sharks**	**NHL**	73	5	6	11	4	4	8	179	0	1	0	107	4.7	51	2	129	45	–35								
1993-94	**San Jose Sharks**	**NHL**	49	1	6	7	1	5	6	63	0	0	0	38	2.6	32	2	56	21	–5	13	0	2	2	32	0	0	0
	Kansas City Blades	IHL	2	1	0	1				25																		
1994-95	**San Jose Sharks**	**NHL**	45	0	6	6	0	9	9	71	0	0	0	25	0.0	32	2	36	13	+7	11	0	4	4	6	0	0	0
1995-96	**San Jose Sharks**	**NHL**	74	2	7	9	2	6	8	147	0	0	0	67	3.0	51	1	122	40	–32								
1996-97	**New York Rangers**	**NHL**	14	0	1	1	0	1	1	25	0	0	0	10	0.0	4	0	6	2	0								
	Phoenix Coyotes	**NHL**	23	1	6	7	1	5	6	37	0	0	1	18	5.6	22	0	15	3	+10	7	0	0	0	7	0	0	0
1997-98	**Phoenix Coyotes**	**NHL**	41	5	5	10	6	5	11	53	0	1	0	40	12.5	27	2	34	9	0								
	Chicago Blackhawks	**NHL**	17	0	2	2	0	2	2	8	0	0	0	17	0.0	10	0	3	0	+7								
	NHL Totals		388	18	52	70	18	47	65	684	1	2	2	386	4.7	273	23	483	153		31	0	6	6	45	0	0	0

WHL All-Star Team (1988)

Traded to **Minnesota** by **NY Rangers** for Dave Archibald, November 1, 1989. Traded to **Montreal** by **Minnesota** for Brian Hayward, November 7, 1990. Claimed by **San Jose** from **Montreal** in Expansion Draft, May 30, 1991. Traded to **NY Rangers** by **San Jose** with Brian Swanson and future considerations for Marty McSorley, August 20, 1996. Traded to **Phoenix** by **NY Rangers** for Mike Eastwood and Dallas Eakins, February 6, 1997. Traded to **Chicago** by **Phoenix** with Chad Kilger for Keith Carney and Jim Cummins, March 4, 1998. Signed as a free agent by **Nashville**, June 4, 1998.

• MOREAU, ETHAN

Ethan Moreau LW – L. 6'2", 205 lbs. b: Huntsville, Ont., 9/22/1975. Chicago's 1st choice, 14th overall, in 1994 Entry Draft.

Season	Club	League	GP	G	A	Pts	AG	AA	APts	PIM	PP	SH	GW	S	%	TGF	PGF	TGA	PGA	+/–	GP	G	A	Pts	PIM	PP	SH	GW
1991-92	Niagara Falls Thunder	OHL	62	20	35	55				39											17	4	6	10	4			
1992-93	Niagara Falls Thunder	OHL	65	32	41	73				69											4	0	3	3	4			
1993-94	Niagara Falls Thunder	OHL	59	44	54	98				100																		
1994-95	Niagara Falls Thunder	OHL	39	25	41	66				69																		
	Sudbury Wolves	OHL	23	13	17	30				22											18	6	12	18	26			
1995-96	**Chicago Blackhawks**	**NHL**	8	0	1	1	0	1	1	4	0	0	0	1	0.0	1	0	0	0	+1								
	Indianapolis Ice	IHL	71	21	20	41				126											5	4	0	4	0			
1996-97	**Chicago Blackhawks**	**NHL**	82	15	16	31	16	14	30	123	0	0	1	114	13.2	52	1	39	1	+13	6	1	0	1	9	0	0	0
1997-98	**Chicago Blackhawks**	**NHL**	54	9	9	18	11	9	20	73	2	0	0	87	10.3	32	7	30	5	0								
	NHL Totals		144	24	26	50	27	24	51	200	2	0	1	202	11.9	85	8	69	6		6	1	0	1	9	0	0	0

• MORETTO, ANGELO

Angelo Moretto C – L. 6'3", 212 lbs. b: Toronto, Ont., 9/18/1953. California's 9th choice, 160th overall, in 1973 Amateur Draft.

Season	Club	League	GP	G	A	Pts	AG	AA	APts	PIM	PP	SH	GW	S	%	TGF	PGF	TGA	PGA	+/–	GP	G	A	Pts	PIM	PP	SH	GW
1972-73	University of Michigan	WCHA	30	10	17	27				36																		
1973-74	University of Michigan	WCHA	34	25	22	47				20																		
1974-75	University of Michigan	WCHA	38	39	28	67				43																		
1975-76	University of Michigan	CCHA	27	24	18	42				50																		
1976-77	**Cleveland Barons**	**NHL**	5	1	2	3	1	2	3	2	0	0	0	13	7.7	5	1	4	0	0								
	Salt Lake Golden Eagles	CHL	71	19	13	32				19																		
1977-78	Phoenix Roadrunners	CHL	14	1	6	7				22																		
1978-79	Oklahoma City Stars	CHL	47	17	21	38				28																		
	Indianapolis Racers	WHA	18	3	1	4				2																		
	NHL Totals		5	1	2	3	1	2	3	2	0	0	0	13	7.7	5	1	4	0									
	Other Major League Totals		18	3	1	4				2																		

Transferred to **Cleveland** after **California** franchise relocated, August 26, 1976. Signed as a free agent by **Indianapolis**, September 30, 1978.

• MORGAN, JASON

Jason Morgan C – L. 6'1", 185 lbs. b: St. John's, Nfld., 10/9/1976. Los Angeles' 5th choice, 118th overall, in 1995 Entry Draft.

Season	Club	League	GP	G	A	Pts	AG	AA	APts	PIM	PP	SH	GW	S	%	TGF	PGF	TGA	PGA	+/–	GP	G	A	Pts	PIM	PP	SH	GW
1993-94	Kitchener Rangers	OHL	65	6	15	21				16											5	1	0	1	0			
1994-95	Kitchener Rangers	OHL	35	3	15	18				25																		
	Kingston Frontenacs	OHL	20	0	3	3				14											6	0	2	2	0			
1995-96	Kingston Frontenacs	OHL	66	16	38	54				50											6	1	2	3	0			
1996-97	**Los Angeles Kings**	**NHL**	3	0	0	0	0	0	0	0	0	0	0	4	0.0	0	0	3	0	–3								
	Phoenix Roadrunners	IHL	57	3	6	9				29																		
	Mississippi Sea Wolves	ECHL	6	3	0	3				0											3	1	1	2	6			
1997-98	**Los Angeles Kings**	**NHL**	11	1	0	1	1	0	1	4	0	0	0	5	20.0	1	0	9	1	–7								
	Springfield Falcons	AHL	58	13	22	35				66											3	1	0	1	18			
	NHL Totals		14	1	0	1	1	0	1	4	0	0	0	9	11.1	1	0	12	1									

• MORIN, STEPHANE

Stephane Morin C – L. 6', 174 lbs. b: Montreal, Que., 3/27/1969. Quebec's 3rd choice, 43rd overall, in 1989 Entry Draft.

Season	Club	League	GP	G	A	Pts	AG	AA	APts	PIM	PP	SH	GW	S	%	TGF	PGF	TGA	PGA	+/–	GP	G	A	Pts	PIM	PP	SH	GW
1986-87	Shawinigan Cataractes	QMJHL	65	9	14	23				28																		
1987-88	Chicoutimi Sagueneens	QMJHL	68	38	45	83				18											6	3	8	11	2			
1988-89	Chicoutimi Sagueneens	QMJHL	70	77	*109	*186				71																		
1989-90	**Quebec Nordiques**	**NHL**	6	0	2	2	0	1	1	2	0	0	0	11	0.0	2	0	1	0	+1								
	Halifax Citadels	AHL	65	28	32	60				60											6	3	4	7	6			
1990-91	**Quebec Nordiques**	**NHL**	48	13	27	40	12	20	32	30	3	1	2	63	20.6	53	11	42	6	+6								
	Halifax Citadels	AHL	17	8	14	22				18																		
1991-92	**Quebec Nordiques**	**NHL**	30	2	8	10	2	6	8	14	0	0	0	41	4.9	19	4	17	0	–2								
	Halifax Citadels	AHL	30	17	13	30				20																		
1992-93	**Vancouver Canucks**	**NHL**	1	0	1	1	0	1	1	0	0	0	0	3	0.0	1	0	2	0	–1								
	Hamilton Canucks	AHL	70	31	54	85				49																		
1993-94	**Vancouver Canucks**	**NHL**	5	1	1	2	1	1	2	6	0	0	0	6	16.7	2	0	2	0	0								
	Hamilton Canucks	AHL	69	38	71	109				48											4	3	2	5	4			
1994-95	Minnesota Moose	IHL	81	33	*81	*114				53											2	0	1	1	0			
1995-96	Minnesota Moose	IHL	80	27	51	78				75																		

Season	Club	League	GP	G	A	Pts	AG	AA	APts	PIM	PP	SH	GW	S	%	TGF	PGF	TGA	PGA	+/–	GP	G	A	Pts	PIM	PP	SH	GW
			REGULAR SEASON																		PLAYOFFS							
1996-97	Manitoba Moose	IHL	12	3	6	9	....	....	....	4	....	....	....	....	....	....	....	....	....	....	....	....	....	....	....	....	....	....
	Long Beach Ice Dogs	IHL	65	25	57	82	....	....	....	73	....	....	....	....	....	....	....	....	....	....	18	6	13	19	14	....	....	....
1997-98	Long Beach Ice Dogs	IHL	27	10	17	27	....	....	....	30	....	....	....	....	....	....	....	....	....	....	13	1	10	11	18	....	....	....
	NHL Totals		**90**	**16**	**39**	**55**	**15**	**29**	**44**	**52**	**3**	**1**	**2**	**124**	**12.9**	**77**	**15**	**64**	**6**		....	....	....	....	....	....	....	....

QMJHL First All-Star Team (1989) • IHL First All-Star Team (1995) • Won Leo P. Lamoureux Memorial Trophy (Top Scorer - IHL) (1995)
Signed as a free agent by **Vancouver**, October 5, 1992.

• MORO, MARC

Marc Moro D – L. 6'1", 220 lbs. b: Toronto, Ont., 7/17/1977. Ottawa's 2nd choice, 27th overall, in 1995 Entry Draft.

Season	Club	League	GP	G	A	Pts	AG	AA	APts	PIM	PP	SH	GW	S	%	TGF	PGF	TGA	PGA	+/–	GP	G	A	Pts	PIM	PP	SH	GW
1993-94	Kingston Frontenacs	OHL	43	0	3	3	....	....	....	81	....	....	....	....	....	....	....	....	....	....	....	....	....	....	....	....	....	....
1994-95	Kingston Frontenacs	OHL	64	4	12	16	....	....	....	255	....	....	....	....	....	....	....	....	....	....	6	0	0	0	23	....	....	....
1995-96	Kingston Frontenacs	OHL	66	4	17	21	....	....	....	261	....	....	....	....	....	....	....	....	....	....	6	0	0	0	12	....	....	....
	P.E.I. Senators	AHL	2	0	0	0	....	....	....	7	....	....	....	....	....	....	....	....	....	....	2	0	0	0	4	....	....	....
1996-97	Kingsto Frontenacs	OHL	37	4	8	12	....	....	....	97	....	....	....	....	....	....	....	....	....	....	....	....	....	....	....	....	....	....
	Sault Ste. Marie Greyhounds	OHL	26	....	5	5	....	....	....	74	....	....	....	....	....	....	....	....	....	....	11	1	6	7	38	....	....	....
1997-98	**Anaheim Mighty Ducks**	**NHL**	**1**	**0**	**0**	**0**	**0**	**0**	**0**	**0**	**0**	**0**	**0**	**0**	**0.0**	**0**	**0**	**0**	**0**	**0**	....	....	....	....	....	....	....	....
	Cincinnati Mighty Ducks	AHL	74	1	6	7	....	....	....	181	....	....	....	....	....	....	....	....	....	....	....	....	....	....	....	....	....	....
	NHL Totals		**1**	**0**	**0**	**0**	**0**	**0**	**0**	**0**	**0**	**0**	**0**	**0**	**0.0**	**0**	**0**	**0**	**0**		....	....	....	....	....	....	....	....

Rights traded to **Anaheim** by **Ottawa** with Ted Drury for Jason York and Shaun Van Allen, October 1, 1996.

• MOROZOV, ALEXEI

Alexei Morozov RW – L. 6'1", 180 lbs. b: Moscow, USSR, 2/16/1977. Pittsburgh's 1st choice, 24th overall, in 1995 Entry Draft.

Season	Club	League	GP	G	A	Pts	AG	AA	APts	PIM	PP	SH	GW	S	%	TGF	PGF	TGA	PGA	+/–	GP	G	A	Pts	PIM	PP	SH	GW
1993-94	Soviet Wings	CIS	7	0	0	0	....	....	....	0	....	....	....	....	....	....	....	....	....	....	3	0	0	0	2	....	....	....
1994-95	Soviet Wings	CIS	48	15	12	27	....	....	....	53	....	....	....	....	....	....	....	....	....	....	4	0	3	3	0	....	....	....
1995-96	Soviet Wings	CIS	47	13	9	22	....	....	....	26	....	....	....	....	....	....	....	....	....	....	....	....	....	....	....	....	....	....
	Russia	WJC-A	7	5	3	8	....	....	....	2	....	....	....	....	....	....	....	....	....	....	....	....	....	....	....	....	....	....
1996-97	Soviet Wings	Russia	44	21	11	32	....	....	....	32	....	....	....	....	....	....	....	....	....	....	2	0	1	1	2	....	....	....
	Russia	WJC-A	6	5	3	8	....	....	....	6	....	....	....	....	....	....	....	....	....	....	....	....	....	....	....	....	....	....
	Russia	WC-A	9	3	3	6	....	....	....	2	....	....	....	....	....	....	....	....	....	....	....	....	....	....	....	....	....	....
1997-98	Soviet Wings	CIS	6	2	1	3	....	....	....	4	....	....	....	....	....	....	....	....	....	....	....	....	....	....	....	....	....	....
	Pittsburgh Penguins	**NHL**	**76**	**13**	**13**	**26**	**15**	**13**	**28**	**8**	**2**	**0**	**3**	**80**	**16.3**	**32**	**4**	**32**	**0**	**–4**	**6**	**0**	**1**	**1**	**2**	**0**	**0**	**0**
	Russia	Olympics	6	2	2	4	....	....	....	0	....	....	....	....	....	....	....	....	....	....	....	....	....	....	....	....	....	....
	Russia	WC-A	4	0	3	3	....	....	....	2	....	....	....	....	....	....	....	....	....	....	....	....	....	....	....	....	....	....
	NHL Totals		**76**	**13**	**13**	**26**	**15**	**13**	**28**	**8**	**2**	**0**	**3**	**80**	**16.3**	**32**	**4**	**32**	**0**		**6**	**0**	**1**	**1**	**2**	**0**	**0**	**0**

EJC-A All-Star Team (1995) • CIS Rookie of the Year (1995) • WJC-A All-Star Team (1996) • Named Best Forward at WJC-A (1997)

• MORRIS, DEREK

Derek Morris D – R. 5'11", 180 lbs. b: Edmonton, Alta., 8/24/1978. Calgary's 1st choice, 13th overall, in 1996 Entry Draft.

Season	Club	League	GP	G	A	Pts	AG	AA	APts	PIM	PP	SH	GW	S	%	TGF	PGF	TGA	PGA	+/–	GP	G	A	Pts	PIM	PP	SH	GW
1995-96	Regina Pats	WHL	67	8	44	52	....	....	....	70	....	....	....	....	....	....	....	....	....	....	11	1	7	8	26	....	....	....
1996-97	Regina Pats	WHL	67	18	57	75	....	....	....	180	....	....	....	....	....	....	....	....	....	....	5	0	3	3	9	....	....	....
	Saint John Flames	AHL	7	0	3	3	....	....	....	7	....	....	....	....	....	....	....	....	....	....	5	0	3	3	7	....	....	....
1997-98	**Calgary Flames**	**NHL**	**82**	**9**	**20**	**29**	**11**	**19**	**30**	**88**	**5**	**1**	**1**	**120**	**7.5**	**80**	**18**	**76**	**15**	**+1**	....	....	....	....	....	....	....	....
	NHL Totals		**82**	**9**	**20**	**29**	**11**	**19**	**30**	**88**	**5**	**1**	**1**	**120**	**7.5**	**80**	**18**	**76**	**15**		....	....	....	....	....	....	....	....

WHL East First All-Star Team (1997) • NHL All-Rookie Team (1998)

• MORRIS, JON

Jon Morris C – R. 6', 175 lbs. b: Lowell, MA, 5/6/1966. New Jersey's 5th choice, 86th overall, in 1984 Entry Draft.

Season	Club	League	GP	G	A	Pts	AG	AA	APts	PIM	PP	SH	GW	S	%	TGF	PGF	TGA	PGA	+/–	GP	G	A	Pts	PIM	PP	SH	GW
1983-84	Chelmsford High	H.S.	24	31	50	81	....	....	....	....	....	....	....	....	....	....	....	....	....	....	....	....	....	....	....	....	....	....
1984-85	University of Lowell	H.E.	42	29	31	60	....	....	....	16	....	....	....	....	....	....	....	....	....	....	....	....	....	....	....	....	....	....
1985-86	University of Lowell	H.E.	39	25	31	56	....	....	....	52	....	....	....	....	....	....	....	....	....	....	....	....	....	....	....	....	....	....
1986-87	University of Lowell	H.E.	35	28	33	61	....	....	....	48	....	....	....	....	....	....	....	....	....	....	....	....	....	....	....	....	....	....
1987-88	University of Lowell	H.E.	37	15	39	54	....	....	....	39	....	....	....	....	....	....	....	....	....	....	....	....	....	....	....	....	....	....
1988-89	**New Jersey Devils**	**NHL**	**4**	**0**	**2**	**2**	**0**	**1**	**1**	**0**	**0**	**0**	**0**	**1**	**0.0**	**4**	**2**	**2**	**0**	**0**	....	....	....	....	....	....	....	....
1989-90	**New Jersey Devils**	**NHL**	**20**	**6**	**7**	**13**	**5**	**5**	**10**	**8**	**2**	**0**	**1**	**17**	**35.3**	**23**	**5**	**6**	**0**	**+12**	**6**	**1**	**3**	**4**	**23**	**1**	**0**	**0**
	Utica Devils	AHL	49	27	37	64	....	....	....	6	....	....	....	....	....	....	....	....	....	....	....	....	....	....	....	....	....	....
1990-91	**New Jersey Devils**	**NHL**	**53**	**9**	**19**	**28**	**8**	**14**	**22**	**27**	**1**	**0**	**1**	**44**	**20.5**	**47**	**6**	**34**	**2**	**+9**	**5**	**0**	**4**	**4**	**2**	**0**	**0**	**0**
	Utica Devils	AHL	6	4	2	6	....	....	....	5	....	....	....	....	....	....	....	....	....	....	....	....	....	....	....	....	....	....
1991-92	**New Jersey Devils**	**NHL**	**7**	**1**	**2**	**3**	**1**	**1**	**2**	**6**	**1**	**0**	**0**	**5**	**20.0**	**4**	**4**	**6**	**0**	**–6**	....	....	....	....	....	....	....	....
	Utica Devils	AHL	7	1	4	5	....	....	....	0	....	....	....	....	....	....	....	....	....	....	....	....	....	....	....	....	....	....
1992-93	**New Jersey Devils**	**NHL**	**2**	**0**	**0**	**0**	**0**	**0**	**0**	**0**	**0**	**0**	**0**	**1**	**0.0**	**0**	**0**	**1**	**0**	**–1**	....	....	....	....	....	....	....	....
	Utica Devils	AHL	31	16	24	40	....	....	....	28	....	....	....	....	....	....	....	....	....	....	....	....	....	....	....	....	....	....
	Cincinnati Cyclones	IHL	18	7	19	26	....	....	....	24	....	....	....	....	....	....	....	....	....	....	....	....	....	....	....	....	....	....
	San Jose Sharks	**NHL**	**13**	**0**	**3**	**3**	**0**	**2**	**2**	**6**	**0**	**0**	**0**	**11**	**0.0**	**3**	**1**	**12**	**0**	**–10**	....	....	....	....	....	....	....	....
1993-94	Kansas City Blades	IHL	3	0	3	3	....	....	....	2	....	....	....	....	....	....	....	....	....	....	....	....	....	....	....	....	....	....
	Boston Bruins	**NHL**	**4**	**0**	**0**	**0**	**0**	**0**	**0**	**0**	**0**	**0**	**0**	**3**	**0.0**	**0**	**0**	**2**	**0**	**–2**	....	....	....	....	....	....	....	....
	Providence Bruins	AHL	67	22	44	66	....	....	....	20	....	....	....	....	....	....	....	....	....	....	....	....	....	....	....	....	....	....
1994-95	Val Gardena	Italy	38	29	44	73	....	....	....	36	....	....	....	....	....	....	....	....	....	....	....	....	....	....	....	....	....	....
	United States	WC-A	6	3	5	8	....	....	....	4	....	....	....	....	....	....	....	....	....	....	....	....	....	....	....	....	....	....
1995-96	Rattingen Lions	Germany	4	2	4	6	....	....	....	4	....	....	....	....	....	....	....	....	....	....	....	....	....	....	....	....	....	....
	NHL Totals		**103**	**16**	**33**	**49**	**14**	**23**	**37**	**47**	**4**	**0**	**2**	**82**	**19.5**	**81**	**18**	**63**	**2**		**11**	**1**	**7**	**8**	**25**	**1**	**0**	**0**

Hockey East First All-Star Team (1987)
Claimed on waivers by **San Jose** from **New Jersey**, March 13, 1993. Traded to **Boston** by **San Jose** for cash, October 28, 1993.

• MORRISON, BRENDAN

Brendan Morrison C – L. 5'11", 175 lbs. b: N. Vancouver, B.C., 8/12/1975. New Jersey's 3rd choice, 39th overall, in 1993 Entry Draft.

Season	Club	League	GP	G	A	Pts	AG	AA	APts	PIM	PP	SH	GW	S	%	TGF	PGF	TGA	PGA	+/–	GP	G	A	Pts	PIM	PP	SH	GW
1992-93	Penticton Panthers	BCJHL	56	35	59	94	....	....	....	45	....	....	....	....	....	....	....	....	....	....	....	....	....	....	....	....	....	....
1993-94	University of Michigan	CCHA	38	20	28	48	....	....	....	24	....	....	....	....	....	....	....	....	....	....	....	....	....	....	....	....	....	....
1994-95	University of Michigan	CCHA	39	23	*53	*76	....	....	....	42	....	....	....	....	....	....	....	....	....	....	....	....	....	....	....	....	....	....
1995-96	University of Michigan	CCHA	35	28	44	*72	....	....	....	41	....	....	....	....	....	....	....	....	....	....	....	....	....	....	....	....	....	....
1996-97	University of Michigan	CCHA	43	31	*57	*88	....	....	....	52	....	....	....	....	....	....	....	....	....	....	....	....	....	....	....	....	....	....
1997-98	**New Jersey Devils**	**NHL**	**11**	**5**	**4**	**9**	**6**	**4**	**10**	**0**	**0**	**0**	**1**	**19**	**26.3**	**13**	**4**	**6**	**0**	**+3**	**3**	**0**	**1**	**1**	**0**	**0**	**0**	**0**
	Albany River Rats	AHL	72	35	49	84	....	....	....	44	....	....	....	....	....	....	....	....	....	....	8	3	4	7	19	....	....	....
	NHL Totals		**11**	**5**	**4**	**9**	**6**	**4**	**10**	**0**	**0**	**0**	**1**	**19**	**26.3**	**13**	**4**	**6**	**0**		**3**	**0**	**1**	**1**	**0**	**0**	**0**	**0**

CCHA First All-Star Team (1995, 1996, 1997) • NCAA West First All-American Team (1995, 1996, 1997) • NCAA Championship All-Tournament Team (1996) • NCAA Championship Tournament MVP (1996) • Won Hobey Baker Memorial Award (Top U.S. Collegiate Player) (1997)

• MORRISON, DAVE

Dave Morrison RW – R. 6', 190 lbs. b: Toronto, Ont., 6/12/1962. Los Angeles' 4th choice, 34th overall, in 1980 Entry Draft.

Season	Club	League	GP	G	A	Pts	AG	AA	APts	PIM	PP	SH	GW	S	%	TGF	PGF	TGA	PGA	+/–	GP	G	A	Pts	PIM	PP	SH	GW
1979-80	Peterborough Petes	OHA	48	18	19	37	....	....	....	35	....	....	....	....	....	....	....	....	....	....	....	....	....	....	....	....	....	....
1980-81	Peterborough Petes	OHA	62	44	53	97	....	....	....	71	....	....	....	....	....	....	....	....	....	....	5	0	3	3	11	....	....	....
	Los Angeles Kings	**NHL**	**3**	**0**	**0**	**0**	**0**	**0**	**0**	**0**	**0**	**0**	**0**	**2**	**0.0**	**0**	**0**	**1**	**0**	**–1**	....	....	....	....	....	....	....	....
1981-82	Peterborough Petes	OHL	53	33	31	64	....	....	....	38	....	....	....	....	....	....	....	....	....	....	9	6	6	12	27	....	....	....
	Canada	WJC-A	7	1	2	3	....	....	....	0	....	....	....	....	....	....	....	....	....	....	....	....	....	....	....	....	....	....
	Los Angeles Kings	**NHL**	**4**	**0**	**0**	**0**	**0**	**0**	**0**	**0**	**0**	**0**	**0**	**6**	**0.0**	**1**	**0**	**2**	**0**	**–1**	....	....	....	....	....	....	....	....
	New Haven Nighthawks	AHL	2	0	0	0	....	....	....	2	....	....	....	....	....	....	....	....	....	....	3	1	1	2	0	....	....	....
1982-83	**Los Angeles Kings**	**NHL**	**24**	**3**	**3**	**6**	**2**	**2**	**4**	**4**	**0**	**0**	**1**	**16**	**18.8**	**13**	**2**	**19**	**1**	**–7**	....	....	....	....	....	....	....	....
	New Haven Nighthawks	AHL	59	23	17	40	....	....	....	36	....	....	....	....	....	....	....	....	....	....	11	3	1	4	23	....	....	....
1983-84	New Haven Nighthawks	AHL	8	0	4	4	....	....	....	2	....	....	....	....	....	....	....	....	....	....	....	....	....	....	....	....	....	....
	Fredericton Express	AHL	68	14	19	33	....	....	....	51	....	....	....	....	....	....	....	....	....	....	7	2	4	6	0	....	....	....
1984-85	**Vancouver Canucks**	**NHL**	**8**	**0**	**0**	**0**	**0**	**0**	**0**	**0**	**0**	**0**	**0**	**8**	**0.0**	**0**	**0**	**12**	**6**	**–6**	....	....	....	....	....	....	....	....
1985-86	Stuttgart	German3	29	66	53	119	....	....	....	28	....	....	....	....	....	....	....	....	....	....	....	....	....	....	....	....	....	....
1986-87	Pandas-Rotterdam	Holland	40	20	30	50	....	....	....	....	....	....	....	....	....	....	....	....	....	....	....	....	....	....	....	....	....	....
1987-88	Pandas-Rotterdam	Holland	46	16	33	49	....	....	....	....	....	....	....	....	....	....	....	....	....	....	....	....	....	....	....	....	....	....
1988-89	Pandas-Rotterdam	Holland	40	20	30	50	....	....	....	....	....	....	....	....	....	....	....	....	....	....	....	....	....	....	....	....	....	....

			REGULAR SEASON																		PLAYOFFS							
Season	Club	League	GP	G	A	Pts	AG	AA	APts	PIM	PP	SH	GW	S	%	TGF	PGF	TGA	PGA	+/–	GP	G	A	Pts	PIM	PP	SH	GW
1989-90	Ratingen Lions	German 2	52	67	98	165	....	....	....	37	....	....	....	....	....	....	....	....	....	....	....	....	....	....	....	....	....	....
	Holland	WEC-B	7	1	3	4	....	....	....	0	....	....	....	....	....	....	....	....	....	....	....	....	....	....	....	....	....	....
1990-91	Ratingen Lions	German 2	34	28	51	79	....	....	....	28	....	....	....	....	....	....	....	....	....	....	....	....	....	....	....	....	....	....
	Holland	WEC-B	7	0	0	0	....	....	....	2	....	....	....	....	....	....	....	....	....	....	....	....	....	....	....	....	....	....
1991-92	Kassel Huskies	German 2	43	59	45	104	....	....	....	48	....	....	....	....	....	....	....	....	....	....	....	....	....	....	....	....	....	....
1992-93	Eisbaren Berlin	Germany	13	8	9	17	....	....	....	6	....	....	....	....	....	....	....	....	....	....	....	....	....	....	....	....	....	....
1993-94	Eisbaren Berlin	Germany	44	13	15	28	....	....	....	32	....	....	....	....	....	....	....	....	....	....	....	....	....	....	....	....	....	....
1994-95	Kassel Huskies	Germany	29	4	13	17	....	....	....	14	....	....	....	....	....	....	....	....	....	....	9	1	6	7	4	....	....	....
1995-96	Kassel Huskies	Germany	50	9	26	35	....	....	....	16	....	....	....	....	....	....	....	....	....	....	8	1	4	5	0	....	....	....
1996-97	Kassel Huskies	Germany	49	6	21	27	....	....	....	32	....	....	....	....	....	....	....	....	....	....	10	0	5	5	2	....	....	....
1997-98	Manchester Storm	Britain	36	5	26	31	....	....	....	10	....	....	....	....	....	....	....	....	....	....	9	4	2	6	0	....	....	....
	NHL Totals		**39**	**3**	**3**	**6**	**2**	**2**	**4**	**4**	**0**	**0**	**1**	**32**	**9.4**	**14**	**2**	**34**	**7**		....	....	....	....	....	....	....	....

Signed as a free agent by **Vancouver**, October 28, 1983.

• MORRISON, DOUG

Doug Morrison RW – R. 5'11", 184 lbs. b: Vancouver, B.C., 2/1/1960. Boston's 3rd choice, 36th overall, in 1979 Entry Draft.

Season	Club	League	GP	G	A	Pts	AG	AA	APts	PIM	PP	SH	GW	S	%	TGF	PGF	TGA	PGA	+/–	GP	G	A	Pts	PIM	PP	SH	GW
1976-77	Lethbridge Broncos	WCJHL	70	24	35	59	....	....	....	80	....	....	....	....	....	....	....	....	....	....	....	....	....	....	....	....	....	....
1977-78	Lethbridge Broncos	WCJHL	66	25	45	70	....	....	....	116	....	....	....	....	....	....	....	....	....	....	....	....	....	....	....	....	....	....
1978-79	Lethbridge Broncos	WHL	64	56	67	123	....	....	....	159	....	....	....	....	....	....	....	....	....	....	19	20	15	35	7	....	....	....
1979-80	Lethbridge Broncos	WHL	68	58	59	117	....	....	....	188	....	....	....	....	....	....	....	....	....	....	4	5	3	8	15	....	....	....
	Boston Bruins	**NHL**	**1**	**0**	**0**	**0**	**0**	**0**	**0**	**0**	**0**	**0**	**0**	**1**	**0.0**	**0**	**0**	**0**	**0**	**0**	....	....	....	....	....	....	....	....
1980-81	**Boston Bruins**	**NHL**	**18**	**7**	**3**	**10**	**6**	**2**	**8**	**13**	**2**	**0**	**0**	**30**	**23.3**	**17**	**5**	**7**	**0**	**+5**	....	....	....	....	....	....	....	....
	Springfield Indians	AHL	42	19	30	49	....	....	....	28	....	....	....	....	....	....	....	....	....	....	7	4	5	9	2	....	....	....
1981-82	**Boston Bruins**	**NHL**	**3**	**0**	**0**	**0**	**0**	**0**	**0**	**0**	**0**	**0**	**0**	**1**	**0.0**	**1**	**0**	**3**	**0**	**–2**	....	....	....	....	....	....	....	....
	Erie Blades	AHL	75	23	35	58	....	....	....	31	....	....	....	....	....	....	....	....	....	....	....	....	....	....	....	....	....	....
1982-83	Maine Mariners	AHL	61	38	29	67	....	....	....	44	....	....	....	....	....	....	....	....	....	....	14	5	1	6	4	....	....	....
1983-84	Hershey Bears	AHL	72	38	40	78	....	....	....	42	....	....	....	....	....	....	....	....	....	....	....	....	....	....	....	....	....	....
1984-85	**Boston Bruins**	**NHL**	**1**	**0**	**0**	**0**	**0**	**0**	**0**	**2**	**0**	**0**	**0**	**1**	**0.0**	**0**	**0**	**0**	**0**	**0**	....	....	....	....	....	....	....	....
	Hershey Bears	AHL	65	28	25	53	....	....	....	25	....	....	....	....	....	....	....	....	....	....	....	....	....	....	....	....	....	....
1985-86	Salt Lake Golden Eagles	IHL	80	27	34	61	....	....	....	30	....	....	....	....	....	....	....	....	....	....	5	7	3	10	14	....	....	....
1986-87	Salt Lake Golden Eagles	IHL	73	48	39	87	....	....	....	24	....	....	....	....	....	....	....	....	....	....	17	9	8	17	26	....	....	....
1987-88	Hedos Munchen	Germany	18	20	16	36	....	....	....	25	....	....	....	....	....	....	....	....	....	....	....	....	....	....	....	....	....	....
	NHL Totals		**23**	**7**	**3**	**10**	**6**	**2**	**8**	**15**	**2**	**0**	**0**	**33**	**21.2**	**18**	**5**	**10**	**0**		....	....	....	....	....	....	....	....

• MORRISON, GARY

Gary Morrison RW – R. 6'2", 200 lbs. b: Detroit, MI, 11/8/1955. Philadelphia's 4th choice, 90th overall, in 1975 Amateur Draft.

Season	Club	League	GP	G	A	Pts	AG	AA	APts	PIM	PP	SH	GW	S	%	TGF	PGF	TGA	PGA	+/–	GP	G	A	Pts	PIM	PP	SH	GW
1973-74	University of Michigan	WCHA	15	7	0	7	....	....	....	25	....	....	....	....	....	....	....	....	....	....	....	....	....	....	....	....	....	....
1974-75	University of Michigan	WCHA	34	8	6	14	....	....	....	31	....	....	....	....	....	....	....	....	....	....	....	....	....	....	....	....	....	....
1975-76	University of Michigan	WCHA	25	5	5	10	....	....	....	27	....	....	....	....	....	....	....	....	....	....	....	....	....	....	....	....	....	....
1976-77	University of Michigan	WCHA	38	6	5	11	....	....	....	25	....	....	....	....	....	....	....	....	....	....	....	....	....	....	....	....	....	....
1977-78	Milwaukee Admirals	IHL	76	21	21	42	....	....	....	203	....	....	....	....	....	....	....	....	....	....	4	0	3	3	7	....	....	....
1978-79	Maine Mariners	AHL	62	14	15	29	....	....	....	73	....	....	....	....	....	....	....	....	....	....	10	0	8	8	35	....	....	....
1979-80	**Philadelphia Flyers**	**NHL**	**3**	**0**	**2**	**2**	**0**	**2**	**2**	**0**	**0**	**0**	**0**	**1**	**0.0**	**3**	**0**	**3**	**0**	**0**	**5**	**0**	**1**	**1**	**2**	**0**	**0**	**0**
	Maine Mariners	AHL	75	29	23	52	....	....	....	151	....	....	....	....	....	....	....	....	....	....	2	1	0	1	4	....	....	....
1980-81	**Philadelphia Flyers**	**NHL**	**33**	**1**	**13**	**14**	**1**	**9**	**10**	**68**	**0**	**0**	**1**	**21**	**4.8**	**24**	**2**	**12**	**0**	**+10**	....	....	....	....	....	....	....	....
	Maine Mariners	AHL	34	9	6	15	....	....	....	53	....	....	....	....	....	....	....	....	....	....	17	4	5	9	80	....	....	....
1981-82	**Philadelphia Flyers**	**NHL**	**7**	**0**	**0**	**0**	**0**	**0**	**0**	**2**	**0**	**0**	**0**	**5**	**0.0**	**1**	**0**	**7**	**0**	**–6**	....	....	....	....	....	....	....	....
	Maine Mariners	AHL	46	13	10	23	....	....	....	52	....	....	....	....	....	....	....	....	....	....	3	1	0	1	4	....	....	....
	NHL Totals		**43**	**1**	**15**	**16**	**1**	**11**	**12**	**70**	**0**	**0**	**1**	**27**	**3.7**	**28**	**2**	**22**	**0**		**5**	**0**	**1**	**1**	**2**	**0**	**0**	**0**

• MORRISON, GEORGE

George Morrison LW – L. 6'1", 170 lbs. b: Toronto, Ont., 12/24/1948.

Season	Club	League	GP	G	A	Pts	AG	AA	APts	PIM	PP	SH	GW	S	%	TGF	PGF	TGA	PGA	+/–	GP	G	A	Pts	PIM	PP	SH	GW
1968-69	University of Denver	WCHA	32	40	18	58	....	....	....	12	....	....	....	....	....	....	....	....	....	....	....	....	....	....	....	....	....	....
1969-70	University of Denver	WCHA	32	30	27	57	....	....	....	12	....	....	....	....	....	....	....	....	....	....	....	....	....	....	....	....	....	....
1970-71	**St. Louis Blues**	**NHL**	**73**	**15**	**10**	**25**	**16**	**9**	**25**	**6**	**3**	**0**	**1**	**122**	**12.3**	**42**	**12**	**32**	**0**	**–2**	**3**	**0**	**0**	**0**	**0**	**0**	**0**	**0**
1971-72	**St. Louis Blues**	**NHL**	**42**	**2**	**11**	**13**	**2**	**10**	**12**	**7**	**2**	**0**	**1**	**34**	**5.9**	**21**	**9**	**23**	**0**	**–11**	....	....	....	....	....	....	....	....
1972-73	Minnesota Fighting Saints	WHA	70	16	24	40	....	....	....	20	....	....	....	....	....	....	....	....	....	....	5	1	1	2	2	....	....	....
1973-74	Minnesota Fighting Saints	WHA	73	40	38	78	....	....	....	37	....	....	....	....	....	....	....	....	....	....	11	5	5	10	12	....	....	....
1974-75	Minnesota Fighting Saints	WHA	76	31	29	60	....	....	....	30	....	....	....	....	....	....	....	....	....	....	12	5	9	14	0	....	....	....
1975-76	Calgary Cowboys	WHA	79	25	32	57	....	....	....	13	....	....	....	....	....	....	....	....	....	....	10	3	2	5	0	....	....	....
1976-77	Calgary Cowboys	WHA	63	11	19	30	....	....	....	10	....	....	....	....	....	....	....	....	....	....	....	....	....	....	....	....	....	....
	NHL Totals		**115**	**17**	**21**	**38**	**18**	**19**	**37**	**13**	**5**	**0**	**2**	**156**	**10.9**	**63**	**21**	**55**	**0**		**3**	**0**	**0**	**0**	**0**	**0**	**0**	**0**
	Other Major League Totals		361	123	142	265	....	....	....	110	....	....	....	....	....	....	....	....	....	....	38	14	17	31	14	....	....	....

WCHA First All-Star Team (1969, 1970) • NCAA West First All-American Team (1969, 1970)

Signed as a free agent by **St. Louis**, September 30, 1970. Selected by **Minnesota** (WHA) in 1972 WHA General Player Draft, February 12, 1972. Traded to **Buffalo** by **St. Louis** with St. Louis' 2nd round choice (Larry Carriere) in 1972 Amateur Draft for Chris Evans, March 5, 1972. • Suspended by **Buffalo** for refusing to report to **Rochester** (AHL), March 8, 1972. Traded to **Calgary** (WHA) by **Minnesota** (WHA) with Don Tannahill, Joe Micheletti and the rights to Wally Olds for John McKenzie and cash, September, 1975.

• MORRISON, JIM

Jim Morrison D – L. 5'10", 183 lbs. b: Montreal, Que., 10/11/1931.

Season	Club	League	GP	G	A	Pts	AG	AA	APts	PIM	PP	SH	GW	S	%	TGF	PGF	TGA	PGA	+/–	GP	G	A	Pts	PIM	PP	SH	GW
1949-50	Verdun Jr Maple Leafs	QJHL	36	15	15	30	....	....	....	16	....	....	....	....	....	....	....	....	....	....	4	3	1	4	0	....	....	....
1950-51	Barrie Flyers	OHA	53	14	42	61	....	....	....	63	....	....	....	....	....	....	....	....	....	....	12	3	10	13	14	....	....	....
1951-52	**Boston Bruins**	**NHL**	**14**	**0**	**2**	**2**	**0**	**3**	**3**	**2**	....	....	....	....	....	....	....	....	....	....	....	....	....	....	....	....	....	....
	Hershey–Pittsburgh	AHL	39	8	25	33	....	....	....	18	....	....	....	....	....	....	....	....	....	....	....	....	....	....	....	....	....	....
	Toronto Maple Leafs	**NHL**	**17**	**0**	**1**	**1**	**0**	**1**	**1**	**4**	....	....	....	....	....	....	....	....	....	....	**2**	**0**	**0**	**0**	**0**	....	....	....
1952-53	**Toronto Maple Leafs**	**NHL**	**56**	**1**	**8**	**9**	**2**	**11**	**13**	**36**	....	....	....	....	....	....	....	....	....	....	....	....	....	....	....	....	....	....
1953-54	**Toronto Maple Leafs**	**NHL**	**60**	**9**	**11**	**20**	**14**	**15**	**29**	**51**	....	....	....	....	....	....	....	....	....	....	**5**	**0**	**0**	**0**	**4**	....	....	....
1954-55	**Toronto Maple Leafs**	**NHL**	**70**	**5**	**12**	**17**	**7**	**15**	**22**	**84**	....	....	....	....	....	....	....	....	....	....	**4**	**0**	**1**	**1**	**4**	....	....	....
1955-56	**Toronto Maple Leafs**	**NHL**	**63**	**2**	**17**	**19**	**3**	**21**	**24**	**77**	....	....	....	....	....	....	....	....	....	....	**5**	**0**	**0**	**0**	**4**	....	....	....
1956-57	**Toronto Maple Leafs**	**NHL**	**63**	**3**	**17**	**20**	**4**	**20**	**24**	**44**	....	....	....	....	....	....	....	....	....	....	....	....	....	....	....	....	....	....
1957-58	**Toronto Maple Leafs**	**NHL**	**70**	**3**	**21**	**24**	**4**	**23**	**27**	**62**	....	....	....	....	....	....	....	....	....	....	....	....	....	....	....	....	....	....
1958-59	**Boston Bruins**	**NHL**	**70**	**8**	**17**	**25**	**10**	**18**	**28**	**42**	....	....	....	....	....	....	....	....	....	....	**6**	**0**	**6**	**6**	**16**	....	....	....
1959-60	**Detroit Red Wings**	**NHL**	**70**	**3**	**23**	**26**	**4**	**24**	**28**	**62**	....	....	....	....	....	....	....	....	....	....	**6**	**0**	**2**	**2**	**0**	....	....	....
1960-61	**New York Rangers**	**NHL**	**19**	**1**	**6**	**7**	**1**	**6**	**7**	**6**	....	....	....	....	....	....	....	....	....	....	....	....	....	....	....	....	....	....
	Quebec Aces	AHL	45	9	24	33	....	....	....	61	....	....	....	....	....	....	....	....	....	....	....	....	....	....	....	....	....	....
1961-62	Quebec Aces	AHL	68	8	28	36	....	....	....	55	....	....	....	....	....	....	....	....	....	....	....	....	....	....	....	....	....	....
1962-63	Quebec Aces	AHL	51	5	22	27	....	....	....	26	....	....	....	....	....	....	....	....	....	....	....	....	....	....	....	....	....	....
1963-64	Quebec Aces	AHL	69	11	28	39	....	....	....	42	....	....	....	....	....	....	....	....	....	....	9	1	0	1	8	....	....	....
1964-65	Quebec Aces	AHL	52	6	21	27	....	....	....	66	....	....	....	....	....	....	....	....	....	....	4	0	0	0	0	....	....	....
1965-66	Quebec Aces	AHL	71	11	48	59	....	....	....	78	....	....	....	....	....	....	....	....	....	....	6	2	3	5	8	....	....	....
1966-67	Quebec Aces	AHL	70	5	45	50	....	....	....	37	....	....	....	....	....	....	....	....	....	....	5	1	4	5	12	....	....	....
1967-68	Quebec Aces	AHL	58	4	35	39	....	....	....	30	....	....	....	....	....	....	....	....	....	....	15	4	12	16	14	....	....	....
1968-69	Baltimore Clippers	AHL	65	5	32	37	....	....	....	35	....	....	....	....	....	....	....	....	....	....	4	2	1	3	10	....	....	....
1969-70	**Pittsburgh Penguins**	**NHL**	**59**	**5**	**15**	**20**	**6**	**15**	**21**	**40**	**2**	**0**	**0**	**135**	**3.7**	**64**	**28**	**78**	**22**	**–20**	**8**	**0**	**3**	**3**	**10**	**0**	**0**	**0**
1970-71	**Pittsburgh Penguins**	**NHL**	**73**	**0**	**10**	**10**	**0**	**9**	**9**	**32**	**0**	**0**	**0**	**134**	**0.0**	**52**	**4**	**82**	**22**	**–12**	....	....	....	....	....	....	....	....
1971-72	Baltimore Clippers	AHL	68	8	22	30	....	....	....	62	....	....	....	....	....	....	....	....	....	....	18	2	7	9	14	....	....	....
1972-73	Baltimore Clippers	AHL	65	5	11	16	....	....	....	46	....	....	....	....	....	....	....	....	....	....	....	....	....	....	....	....	....	....
	NHL Totals		**704**	**40**	**160**	**200**	**55**	**181**	**236**	**542**	**2**	**0**	**0**	**269**	**14.9**	**116**	**32**	**160**	**44**		**36**	**0**	**12**	**12**	**38**	**0**	**0**	**0**

AHL Second All-Star Team (1962, 1964, 1965, 1967, 1968, 1969, 1972) • AHL First All-Star Team (1966) • Won Eddie Shore Award (Outstanding Defenseman - AHL) (1966)

Played in NHL All-Star Game (1955, 1956, 1957)

Traded to **Toronto** by **Boston** for Fleming MacKell, January 9, 1952. Traded to **Boston** by **Toronto** for Allan Stanley, October 8, 1958. Traded to **Detroit** by **Boston** for Nick Mickoski, August 25, 1959. Traded to **Chicago** by **Detroit** for Howie Glover, June 5, 1960. Claimed by **NY Rangers** from **Chicago** in Intra League Draft, June 6, 1960. Traded to **Quebec** (AHL) by **NY Rangers** for cash, December 1, 1960. NHL rights transferred to **Philadelphia** after NHL club purchased **Quebec** (AHL) franchise, May 8, 1967. Claimed by **Baltimore** (AHL) from **Philadelphia** (Quebec - AHL) in Reverse Draft, June 13, 1968. Traded to **Pittsburgh** by **Baltimore** (AHL) for cash and Bobby Rivard, November, 1969.

• MORRISON, KEVIN

Kevin Morrison D – L. 6', 202 lbs. b: Sydney, N.S., 10/28/1949. NY Rangers' 4th choice, 35th overall, in 1969 Amateur Draft.

			REGULAR SEASON																		PLAYOFFS							
Season	Club	League	GP	G	A	Pts	AG	AA	APts	PIM	PP	SH	GW	S	%	TGF	PGF	TGA	PGA	+/–	GP	G	A	Pts	PIM	PP	SH	GW
1968-69	St. Jerome Alouettes	QJHL	STATISTICS NOT AVAILABLE																									
1969-70	New Haven Blades	EHL	48	24	18	42	....	....	....	136	....	....	....	....	....	....	....	....	....	....	11	4	7	11	53	....	....	....
	Omaha Knights	CHL	....	....	....	....	....	....	....	....	....	....	....	....	....	....	....	....	....	....	5	2	0	2	20	....	....	....
1970-71	New Haven Blades	EHL	64	11	44	55	....	....	....	*348	....	....	....	....	....	....	....	....	....	....	14	3	6	9	67	....	....	....
	Fort Worth Wings	CHL	3	0	0	0	....	....	....	0	....	....	....	....	....	....	....	....	....	....	....	....	....	....	....	....	....	....
1971-72	Tidewater Wings	AHL	11	0	2	2	....	....	....	18	....	....	....	....	....	....	....	....	....	....	....	....	....	....	....	....	....	....
	Fort Worth Wings	CHL	26	2	1	3	....	....	....	56	....	....	....	....	....	....	....	....	....	....	....	....	....	....	....	....	....	....
	Rochester Americans	AHL	29	2	0	2	....	....	....	49	....	....	....	....	....	....	....	....	....	....	....	....	....	....	....	....	....	....
1972-73	New Haven Nighthawks	AHL	74	7	28	35	....	....	....	154	....	....	....	....	....	....	....	....	....	....	....	....	....	....	....	....	....	....
1973-74	New York-New Jersey	WHA	78	24	43	67	....	....	....	132	....	....	....	....	....	....	....	....	....	....	....	....	....	....	....	....	....	....
1974-75	San Diego Mariners	WHA	78	20	61	81	....	....	....	143	....	....	....	....	....	....	....	....	....	....	10	0	7	7	2	....	....	....
1975-76	San Diego Mariners	WHA	80	22	43	65	....	....	....	56	....	....	....	....	....	....	....	....	....	....	11	1	5	6	12	....	....	....
1976-77	San Diego Mariners	WHA	75	8	30	38	....	....	....	68	....	....	....	....	....	....	....	....	....	....	7	1	3	4	8	....	....	....
1977-78	Indianapolis Racers	WHA	75	17	40	57	....	....	....	49	....	....	....	....	....	....	....	....	....	....	....	....	....	....	....	....	....	....
1978-79	Indianapolis Racers	WHA	5	0	2	2	....	....	....	0	....	....	....	....	....	....	....	....	....	....	....	....	....	....	....	....	....	....
	Quebec Nordiques	WHA	27	2	5	7	....	....	....	14	....	....	....	....	....	....	....	....	....	....	....	....	....	....	....	....	....	....
	Philadelphia Firebirds	AHL	23	1	13	14	....	....	....	15	....	....	....	....	....	....	....	....	....	....	....	....	....	....	....	....	....	....
1979-80	**Colorado Rockies**	**NHL**	**41**	**4**	**11**	**15**	**4**	**8**	**12**	**23**	**2**	**0**	**1**	**64**	**6.3**	**40**	**11**	**39**	**4**	**–6**	....	....	....	....	....	....	....	....
	Fort Worth Texans	CHL	33	5	16	21	....	....	....	45	....	....	....	....	....	....	....	....	....	....	....	....	....	....	....	....	....	....
	NHL Totals		**41**	**4**	**11**	**15**	**4**	**8**	**12**	**23**	**2**	**0**	**1**	**64**	**6.3**	**40**	**11**	**39**	**4**		....	....	....	....	....	....	....	....
	Other Major League Totals		418	93	224	317	....	....	....	462	....	....	....	....	....	....	....	....	....		28	2	15	17	22	....	....	....

EHL North First All-Star Team (1971) • WHA First All-Star Team (1975) • WHA Second All-Star Team (1976)

Claimed by **Detroit** from **NY Rangers** in Intra-League Draft, June, 1970. Selected by **LA Sharks** (WHA) in 1972 WHA General Player Draft, February 12, 1972. WHA rights traded to **NY Raiders** by **LA Sharks** for future considerations, June, 1973. Transferred to **San Diego** (WHA) after **New York-New Jersey** (WHA) franchise relocated, April 30, 1974. Signed as a free agent by **Indianapolis** (WHA) after **San Diego** (WHA) franchise folded, July, 1977. Traded to **Quebec** (WHA) by **Indianapolis** (WHA) with Rich LeDuc for future considerations, November, 1978. Signed as a free agent by **Colorado**, June, 1979.

• MORRISON, LEW

Lew Morrison RW – R. 6', 185 lbs. b: Gainsborough, Sask., 2/11/1948. Philadelphia's 1st choice, 8th overall, in 1968 Amateur Draft.

			REGULAR SEASON																		PLAYOFFS							
Season	Club	League	GP	G	A	Pts	AG	AA	APts	PIM	PP	SH	GW	S	%	TGF	PGF	TGA	PGA	+/–	GP	G	A	Pts	PIM	PP	SH	GW
1967-68	Flin Flon Bombers	WCJHL	56	26	23	49	....	....	....	31	....	....	....	....	....	....	....	....	....	....	....	....	....	....	....	....	....	....
1968-69	Quebec Aces	AHL	70	12	13	25	....	....	....	24	....	....	....	....	....	....	....	....	....	....	15	4	5	9	6	....	....	....
1969-70	**Philadelphia Flyers**	**NHL**	**66**	**9**	**10**	**19**	**10**	**10**	**20**	**19**	**3**	**0**	**3**	**130**	**6.9**	**41**	**8**	**52**	**16**	**–3**	....	....	....	....	....	....	....	....
1970-71	**Philadelphia Flyers**	**NHL**	**78**	**5**	**7**	**12**	**5**	**6**	**11**	**25**	**0**	**0**	**0**	**129**	**3.9**	**30**	**1**	**69**	**28**	**–12**	**4**	**0**	**0**	**0**	**2**	**0**	**0**	**0**
1971-72	**Philadelphia Flyers**	**NHL**	**58**	**5**	**5**	**10**	**5**	**5**	**10**	**26**	**1**	**0**	**0**	**57**	**8.8**	**15**	**1**	**49**	**17**	**–18**	....	....	....	....	....	....	....	....
	Richmond Robins	AHL	12	4	5	9	....	....	....	2	....	....	....	....	....	....	....	....	....	....	....	....	....	....	....	....	....	....
1972-73	**Atlanta Flames**	**NHL**	**78**	**6**	**9**	**15**	**6**	**8**	**14**	**19**	**0**	**1**	**2**	**52**	**11.5**	**23**	**5**	**70**	**41**	**–11**	....	....	....	....	....	....	....	....
1973-74	**Atlanta Flames**	**NHL**	**52**	**1**	**4**	**5**	**1**	**3**	**4**	**0**	**0**	**0**	**0**	**31**	**3.2**	**10**	**0**	**32**	**21**	**–1**	....	....	....	....	....	....	....	....
1974-75	Richmond Robins	AHL	9	7	4	11	....	....	....	8	....	....	....	....	....	....	....	....	....	....	....	....	....	....	....	....	....	....
	Washington Capitals	**NHL**	**18**	**0**	**4**	**4**	**0**	**3**	**3**	**6**	**0**	**0**	**0**	**21**	**0.0**	**9**	**2**	**30**	**9**	**–14**	....	....	....	....	....	....	....	....
	Pittsburgh Penguins	**NHL**	**52**	**7**	**5**	**12**	**6**	**4**	**10**	**4**	**1**	**1**	**1**	**41**	**17.1**	**19**	**2**	**40**	**18**	**–5**	**9**	**0**	**0**	**0**	**0**	**0**	**0**	**0**
1975-76	**Pittsburgh Penguins**	**NHL**	**78**	**4**	**5**	**9**	**4**	**4**	**8**	**8**	**0**	**2**	**0**	**24**	**16.7**	**15**	**0**	**51**	**43**	**+7**	**3**	**0**	**0**	**0**	**0**	**0**	**0**	**0**
1976-77	**Pittsburgh Penguins**	**NHL**	**76**	**2**	**1**	**3**	**2**	**1**	**3**	**0**	**0**	**0**	**0**	**25**	**8.0**	**4**	**0**	**31**	**21**	**–6**	**1**	**0**	**0**	**0**	**0**	**0**	**0**	**0**
1977-78	**Pittsburgh Penguins**	**NHL**	**8**	**0**	**2**	**2**	**0**	**2**	**2**	**0**	**0**	**0**	**0**	**3**	**0.0**	**3**	**0**	**0**	**0**	**+3**	....	....	....	....	....	....	....	....
	Binghamton Dusters	AHL	65	6	14	20	....	....	....	6	....	....	....	....	....	....	....	....	....	....	....	....	....	....	....	....	....	....
	NHL Totals		**564**	**39**	**52**	**91**	**39**	**46**	**85**	**107**	**5**	**4**	**6**	**513**	**7.6**	**169**	**19**	**424**	**214**		**17**	**0**	**0**	**0**	**2**	**0**	**0**	**0**

Claimed by **Atlanta** from **Philadelphia** in Expansion Draft, June 6, 1972. Claimed by **Washington** from **Atlanta** in Expansion Draft, June 12, 1974. Traded to **Pittsburgh** by **Washington** for Ron Lablonde, December 14, 1974.

• MORRISON, MARK

Mark Morrison C – R. 5'8", 150 lbs. b: Prince George, B.C., 3/11/1963. NY Rangers' 6th choice, 51st overall, in 1981 Entry Draft.

			REGULAR SEASON																		PLAYOFFS							
Season	Club	League	GP	G	A	Pts	AG	AA	APts	PIM	PP	SH	GW	S	%	TGF	PGF	TGA	PGA	+/–	GP	G	A	Pts	PIM	PP	SH	GW
1979-80	Victoria Cougars	WHL	72	25	33	58	....	....	....	26	....	....	....	....	....	....	....	....	....	....	16	3	5	8	20	....	....	....
1980-81	Victoria Cougars	WHL	58	31	61	92	....	....	....	66	....	....	....	....	....	....	....	....	....	....	15	6	13	19	9	....	....	....
1981-82	Victoria Cougars	WHL	56	48	66	114	....	....	....	83	....	....	....	....	....	....	....	....	....	....	4	0	0	0	12	....	....	....
	Canada	WJC-A	7	3	7	10	....	....	....	0	....	....	....	....	....	....	....	....	....	....	....	....	....	....	....	....	....	....
	New York Rangers	**NHL**	**9**	**1**	**1**	**2**	**1**	**1**	**2**	**0**	**0**	**0**	**1**	**6**	**16.7**	**2**	**0**	**7**	**0**	**–5**	....	....	....	....	....	....	....	....
1982-83	Victoria Cougars	WHL	58	55	75	13	....	....	....	54	....	....	....	....	....	....	....	....	....	....	12	10	17	27	8	....	....	....
	Canada	WJC-A	7	3	2	5	....	....	....	0	....	....	....	....	....	....	....	....	....	....	....	....	....	....	....	....	....	....
1983-84	Canada	Nat-Team	43	15	22	37	....	....	....	34	....	....	....	....	....	....	....	....	....	....	....	....	....	....	....	....	....	....
	New York Rangers	**NHL**	**1**	**0**	**0**	**0**	**0**	**0**	**0**	**0**	**0**	**0**	**0**	**5**	**0.0**	**0**	**0**	**0**	**0**	**0**	....	....	....	....	....	....	....	....
	Tulsa Oilers	CHL	11	4	4	8	....	....	....	2	....	....	....	....	....	....	....	....	....	....	7	4	4	8	2	....	....	....
1984-85	New Haven Nighthawks	AHL	20	5	4	9	....	....	....	0	....	....	....	....	....	....	....	....	....	....	....	....	....	....	....	....	....	....
	Nova Scotia Voyageurs	AHL	11	0	1	1	....	....	....	4	....	....	....	....	....	....	....	....	....	....	....	....	....	....	....	....	....	....
1985-86	HC Meran	Italy	36	59	*88	*147	....	....	....	30	....	....	....	....	....	....	....	....	....	....	6	8	10	18	6	....	....	....
1986-87	Fribourg	Switz.	....	18	19	37	....	....	....	....	....	....	....	....	....	....	....	....	....	....	....	....	....	....	....	....	....	....
1987-88	HC Meran	Italy	STATISTICS NOT AVAILABLE																									
1988-89	Canada	Nat-Team	4	1	2	3	....	....	....	0	....	....	....	....	....	....	....	....	....	....	....	....	....	....	....	....	....	....
	HC Meran	Italy	41	38	76	114	....	....	....	25	....	....	....	....	....	....	....	....	....	....	....	....	....	....	....	....	....	....
1989-90	HC Meran	Italy	STATISTICS NOT AVAILABLE																									
1990-91	Milano Devils	Italy	33	29	41	70	....	....	....	18	....	....	....	....	....	....	....	....	....	....	....	....	....	....	....	....	....	....
1991-92	HC Meran	Italy	41	38	76	114	....	....	....	25	....	....	....	....	....	....	....	....	....	....	....	....	....	....	....	....	....	....
1992-93	Milano Devils	Italy	45	46	67	113	....	....	....	48	....	....	....	....	....	....	....	....	....	....	....	....	....	....	....	....	....	....
1993-94	Fife Flyers	Britain	44	78	77	155	....	....	....	73	....	....	....	....	....	....	....	....	....	....	9	7	11	18	20	....	....	....
1994-95	Fife Flyers	Britain	36	52	63	115	....	....	....	24	....	....	....	....	....	....	....	....	....	....	2	2	4	6	2	....	....	....
1995-96	Fife Flyers	Britain	31	34	36	70	....	....	....	64	....	....	....	....	....	....	....	....	....	....	1	1	0	1	2	....	....	....
1996-97	Fife Flyers	Britain	35	68	58	126	....	....	....	60	....	....	....	....	....	....	....	....	....	....	12	11	22	33	22	....	....	....
1997-98	Fife Flyers	Britain	40	49	54	103	....	....	....	74	....	....	....	....	....	....	....	....	....	....	9	7	11	18	2	....	....	....
	NHL Totals		**10**	**1**	**1**	**2**	**1**	**1**	**2**	**0**	**0**	**0**	**1**	**11**	**9.1**	**2**	**0**	**7**	**0**		....	....	....	....	....	....	....	....

Won George Parsons Trophy (Memorial Cup Tournament Most Sportsmanlike Player) (1981)

Traded to **Edmonton** by **NY Rangers** for cash, November 27, 1984.

• MORROW, KEN

Ken Morrow D – R. 6'4", 210 lbs. b: Flint, MI, 10/17/1956. NY Islanders' 4th choice, 68th overall, in 1976 Amateur Draft. **USHOF**

			REGULAR SEASON																		PLAYOFFS							
Season	Club	League	GP	G	A	Pts	AG	AA	APts	PIM	PP	SH	GW	S	%	TGF	PGF	TGA	PGA	+/–	GP	G	A	Pts	PIM	PP	SH	GW
1975-76	Bowling Green University	CCHA	31	4	15	19	....	....	....	34	....	....	....	....	....	....	....	....	....	....	....	....	....	....	....	....	....	....
1976-77	Bowling Green University	CCHA	39	7	22	29	....	....	....	22	....	....	....	....	....	....	....	....	....	....	....	....	....	....	....	....	....	....
1977-78	Bowling Green University	CCHA	39	8	18	26	....	....	....	26	....	....	....	....	....	....	....	....	....	....	....	....	....	....	....	....	....	....
	United States	WEC-A	6	0	0	0	....	....	....	0	....	....	....	....	....	....	....	....	....	....	....	....	....	....	....	....	....	....
1978-79	Bowling Green University	CCHA	45	15	37	52	....	....	....	22	....	....	....	....	....	....	....	....	....	....	....	....	....	....	....	....	....	....
1979-80	United States	Nat-Team	56	4	18	22	....	....	....	6	....	....	....	....	....	....	....	....	....	....	....	....	....	....	....	....	....	....
	United States	Olympics	7	1	2	3	....	....	....	6	....	....	....	....	....	....	....	....	....	....	....	....	....	....	....	....	....	....
	New York Islanders	**NHL**	**18**	**0**	**3**	**3**	**0**	**2**	**2**	**4**	**0**	**0**	**0**	**19**	**0.0**	**20**	**0**	**22**	**6**	**+4**	**20**	**1**	**2**	**3**	**12**	**0**	**0**	**1**
1980-81	**New York Islanders**	**NHL**	**80**	**2**	**11**	**13**	**2**	**8**	**10**	**20**	**0**	**0**	**0**	**69**	**2.9**	**89**	**1**	**98**	**29**	**+19**	**18**	**3**	**4**	**7**	**8**	**0**	**0**	**1**
1981-82	United States	C Cup	6	0	0	0	....	....	....	6	....	....	....	....	....	....	....	....	....	....	....	....	....	....	....	....	....	....
	New York Islanders	**NHL**	**75**	**1**	**18**	**19**	**1**	**12**	**13**	**56**	**0**	**0**	**0**	**91**	**1.1**	**116**	**1**	**92**	**30**	**+53**	**19**	**0**	**4**	**4**	**8**	**0**	**0**	**0**
1982-83	**New York Islanders**	**NHL**	**79**	**5**	**11**	**16**	**4**	**8**	**12**	**44**	**0**	**0**	**1**	**135**	**3.7**	**79**	**1**	**92**	**32**	**+18**	**19**	**5**	**7**	**12**	**18**	**0**	**0**	**0**
1983-84	**New York Islanders**	**NHL**	**63**	**3**	**11**	**14**	**2**	**7**	**9**	**45**	**0**	**0**	**1**	**71**	**4.2**	**85**	**0**	**88**	**29**	**+26**	**20**	**1**	**2**	**3**	**20**	**0**	**0**	**1**
1984-85	**New York Islanders**	**NHL**	**15**	**1**	**7**	**8**	**1**	**5**	**6**	**14**	**0**	**0**	**0**	**14**	**7.1**	**19**	**0**	**21**	**7**	**+5**	**10**	**0**	**0**	**0**	**17**	**0**	**0**	**0**
1985-86	**New York Islanders**	**NHL**	**69**	**0**	**12**	**12**	**0**	**8**	**8**	**22**	**0**	**0**	**0**	**55**	**0.0**	**78**	**1**	**87**	**34**	**+24**	**2**	**0**	**0**	**0**	**4**	**0**	**0**	**0**
1986-87	**New York Islanders**	**NHL**	**64**	**3**	**8**	**11**	**3**	**6**	**9**	**32**	**0**	**0**	**0**	**52**	**5.8**	**44**	**0**	**63**	**26**	**+7**	**13**	**1**	**3**	**4**	**2**	**0**	**0**	**0**
1987-88	**New York Islanders**	**NHL**	**53**	**1**	**4**	**5**	**1**	**3**	**4**	**40**	**0**	**0**	**0**	**50**	**2.0**	**41**	**1**	**64**	**24**	**0**	**6**	**0**	**0**	**0**	**8**	**0**	**0**	**0**
1988-89	**New York Islanders**	**NHL**	**34**	**1**	**3**	**4**	**1**	**2**	**3**	**32**	**0**	**0**	**0**	**27**	**3.7**	**25**	**0**	**56**	**24**	**–7**	....	....	....	....	....	....	....	....
	NHL Totals		**550**	**17**	**88**	**105**	**15**	**61**	**76**	**309**	**0**	**0**	**2**	**583**	**2.9**	**596**	**5**	**683**	**241**		**127**	**11**	**22**	**33**	**97**	**0**	**0**	**3**

CCHA First All-Star Team (1976, 1978, 1979) • CCHA Second All-Star Team (1977) • NCAA West First All-American Team (1978) • Won Lester Patrick Trophy (1996)

● **MORROW, SCOTT** Scott Morrow LW – L. 6'1", 185 lbs. b: Chicago, IL, 6/18/1969. Hartford's 4th choice, 95th overall, in 1988 Entry Draft.

			REGULAR SEASON																		PLAYOFFS							
Season	Club	League	GP	G	A	Pts	AG	AA	APts	PIM	PP	SH	GW	S	%	TGF	PGF	TGA	PGA	+/–	GP	G	A	Pts	PIM	PP	SH	GW
1987-88	Northwood Prep School	H.S.	24	10	18	28	....	....	....	30	....	....	....	....	....	....	....	....	....	....	....	....	....	....	....	....	....	....
1988-89	University of New Hampshire	H.E.	19	6	7	13	....	....	....	14	....	....	....	....	....	....	....	....	....	....	....	....	....	....	....	....	....	....
1989-90	University of New Hampshire	H.E.	29	10	11	21	....	....	....	35	....	....	....	....	....	....	....	....	....	....	....	....	....	....	....	....	....	....
1990-91	University of New Hampshire	H.E.	31	11	11	22	....	....	....	52	....	....	....	....	....	....	....	....	....	....	....	....	....	....	....	....	....	....
1991-92	University of New Hampshire	H.E.	35	30	23	53	....	....	....	65	....	....	....	....	....	....	....	....	....	....	....	....	....	....	....	....	....	....
	Springfield Indians	AHL	2	0	1	1	....	....	....	0	....	....	....	....	....	....	....	....	....	....	5	0	0	0	9	....	....	....
1992-93	Springfield Indians	AHL	70	22	29	51	....	....	....	80	....	....	....	....	....	....	....	....	....	....	15	6	9	15	21	....	....	....
1993-94	Springfield Indians	AHL	30	12	15	27	....	....	....	28	....	....	....	....	....	....	....	....	....	....	....	....	....	....	....	....	....	....
	Saint John Flames	AHL	8	2	2	4	....	....	....	0	....	....	....	....	....	....	....	....	....	....	7	2	1	3	10	....	....	....
1994-95	**Calgary Flames**	**NHL**	**4**	**0**	**0**	**0**	**0**	**0**	**0**	**0**	**0**	**0**	**0**	**1**	**0.0**	**1**	**0**	**1**	**0**	**0**	....	....	....	....	....	....	....	....
	Saint John Flames	AHL	64	18	21	39	....	....	....	105	....	....	....	....	....	....	....	....	....	....	5	2	0	2	4	....	....	....
1995-96	Hershey Bears	AHL	79	48	45	93	....	....	....	110	....	....	....	....	....	....	....	....	....	....	5	2	2	4	6	....	....	....
1996-97	Cincinnati Cyclones	IHL	67	14	23	37	....	....	....	50	....	....	....	....	....	....	....	....	....	....	....	....	....	....	....	....	....	....
	Providence Bruins	AHL	11	3	4	7	....	....	....	15	....	....	....	....	....	....	....	....	....	....	7	2	1	3	0	....	....	....
1997-98	Binghamton	UHL	8	3	2	5	....	....	....	14	....	....	....	....	....	....	....	....	....	....	....	....	....	....	....	....	....	....
	Providence Bruins	AHL	5	1	4	5	....	....	....	7	....	....	....	....	....	....	....	....	....	....	....	....	....	....	....	....	....	....
	Cincinnati Cyclones	IHL	55	15	12	27	....	....	....	44	....	....	....	....	....	....	....	....	....	....	9	3	1	4	23	....	....	....
	NHL Totals		**4**	**0**	**0**	**0**	**0**	**0**	**0**	**0**	**0**	**0**	**0**	**1**	**0.0**	**1**	**0**	**1**	**0**		....	....	....	....	....	....	....	....

Hockey East Second All-Star Team (1992)

Traded to **Calgary** by **Hartford** for Todd Harkins, January 24, 1994. Signed as a free agent by **Philadelphia**, July 31, 1995.

● **MORTON, DEAN** Dean Morton D – R. 6'1", 196 lbs. b: Peterborough, Ont., 2/27/1968. Detroit's 8th choice, 148th overall, in 1986 Entry Draft.

1984-85	Peterborough Bees	Midget	47	9	38	47	....	....	....	158	....	....	....	....	....	....	....	....	....	....	....	....	....	....	....	....	....	....
1985-86	Ottawa 67's	OHL	16	3	1	4	....	....	....	32	....	....	....	....	....	....	....	....	....	....	....	....	....	....	....	....	....	....
	Oshawa Generals	OHL	48	2	6	8	....	....	....	92	....	....	....	....	....	....	....	....	....	....	5	0	0	0	9	....	....	....
1986-87	Oshawa Generals	OHL	62	1	11	12	....	....	....	165	....	....	....	....	....	....	....	....	....	....	23	3	6	9	112	....	....	....
1987-88	Oshawa Generals	OHL	57	6	19	25	....	....	....	187	....	....	....	....	....	....	....	....	....	....	7	0	0	0	18	....	....	....
1988-89	Adirondack Red Wings	AHL	66	2	15	17	....	....	....	186	....	....	....	....	....	....	....	....	....	....	8	0	1	1	13	....	....	....
1989-90	**Detroit Red Wings**	**NHL**	**1**	**1**	**0**	**1**	**1**	**0**	**1**	**2**	**0**	**0**	**0**	**2**	**50.0**	**1**	**0**	**2**	**0**	**–1**	....	....	....	....	....	....	....	....
	Adirondack Red Wings	AHL	75	1	15	16	....	....	....	183	....	....	....	....	....	....	....	....	....	....	6	0	0	0	30	....	....	....
1990-91	Adirondack Red Wings	AHL	1	0	0	0	....	....	....	0	....	....	....	....	....	....	....	....	....	....	....	....	....	....	....	....	....	....
	San Diego Gulls	IHL	47	0	6	6	....	....	....	124	....	....	....	....	....	....	....	....	....	....	....	....	....	....	....	....	....	....
1991-92	Moncton Hawks	AHL	6	1	1	2	....	....	....	15	....	....	....	....	....	....	....	....	....	....	....	....	....	....	....	....	....	....
	Michigan Falcons	ColHL	38	4	19	23	....	....	....	96	....	....	....	....	....	....	....	....	....	....	....	....	....	....	....	....	....	....
1992-93	Cincinnati Cyclones	IHL	7	0	0	0	....	....	....	44	....	....	....	....	....	....	....	....	....	....	....	....	....	....	....	....	....	....
	Brantford Smoke	ColHL	37	2	17	19	....	....	....	217	....	....	....	....	....	....	....	....	....	....	15	1	3	4	38	....	....	....
	NHL Totals		**1**	**1**	**0**	**1**	**1**	**0**	**1**	**2**	**0**	**0**	**0**	**2**	**50.0**	**1**	**0**	**2**	**0**		....	....	....	....	....	....	....	....

• One of only two players (Rolly Huard) to score a goal in only NHL game.

● **MOTT, MORRIS** Morris Mott RW – L. 5'10", 165 lbs. b: Creelman, Sask., 5/25/1946.

1963-64	Weyburn Red Wings	SJHL	62	19	30	49	....	....	....	16	....	....	....	....	....	....	....	....	....	....	8	0	7	7	0	....	....	....
1964-65	Weyburn Red Wings	SJHL	34	21	*52	*73	....	....	....	12	....	....	....	....	....	....	....	....	....	....	15	11	21	33	10	....	....	....
1965-66	Canada	Nat-Team	STATISTICS NOT AVAILABLE																									
	Canada	WEC-A	7	3	0	3	....	....	....	0	....	....	....	....	....	....	....	....	....	....	....	....	....	....	....	....	....	....
1966-67	Canada	Nat-Team	STATISTICS NOT AVAILABLE																									
	Canada	WEC-A	7	4	1	5	....	....	....	4	....	....	....	....	....	....	....	....	....	....	....	....	....	....	....	....	....	....
1967-68	Winnipeg Nats	WCSHL	15	13	9	22	....	....	....	14	....	....	....	....	....	....	....	....	....	....	....	....	....	....	....	....	....	....
	Canada	Olympics	7	5	1	0	....	....	....	2	....	....	....	....	....	....	....	....	....	....	....	....	....	....	....	....	....	....
1968-69	Canada	Nat-Team	STATISTICS NOT AVAILABLE																									
	Canada	WEC-A	10	2	2	4	....	....	....	4	....	....	....	....	....	....	....	....	....	....	....	....	....	....	....	....	....	....
1969-70	Canada	Nat-Team	STATISTICS NOT AVAILABLE																									
1970-71	Queens University	OUAA	20	14	*30	*44	....	....	....	6	....	....	....	....	....	....	....	....	....	....	....	....	....	....	....	....	....	....
1971-72	Queens University	OUAA	20	12	22	34	....	....	....	6	....	....	....	....	....	....	....	....	....	....	....	....	....	....	....	....	....	....
1972-73	**California Golden Seals**	**NHL**	**70**	**6**	**7**	**13**	**6**	**6**	**12**	**8**	**1**	**0**	**1**	**71**	**8.5**	**27**	**4**	**55**	**15**	**–17**	....	....	....	....	....	....	....	....
	Salt Lake Golden Eagles	WHL	6	8	5	13	....	....	....	0	....	....	....	....	....	....	....	....	....	....	....	....	....	....	....	....	....	....
1973-74	**California Golden Seals**	**NHL**	**77**	**9**	**17**	**26**	**9**	**15**	**24**	**33**	**1**	**1**	**0**	**90**	**10.0**	**35**	**7**	**70**	**23**	**–19**	....	....	....	....	....	....	....	....
1974-75	**California Golden Seals**	**NHL**	**52**	**3**	**8**	**11**	**3**	**6**	**9**	**8**	**0**	**0**	**1**	**31**	**9.7**	**16**	**2**	**46**	**22**	**–10**	....	....	....	....	....	....	....	....
	Salt Lake Golden Eagles	CHL	11	6	2	8	....	....	....	12	....	....	....	....	....	....	....	....	....	....	11	2	7	9	8	....	....	....
1975-76	Vastra Frolunda	Sweden	36	16	14	30	....	....	....	62	....	....	....	....	....	....	....	....	....	....	....	....	....	....	....	....	....	....
	Winnipeg Jets	WHA	2	0	1	1	....	....	....	0	....	....	....	....	....	....	....	....	....	....	....	....	....	....	....	....	....	....
	NHL Totals		**199**	**18**	**32**	**50**	**18**	**27**	**45**	**49**	**2**	**1**	**2**	**192**	**9.4**	**78**	**13**	**171**	**60**		....	....	....	....	....	....	....	....
	Other Major League Totals		2	0	1	1	....	....	....	0	....	....	....	....	....	....	....	....	....		....	....	....	....	....	....	....	....

Selected by **Calgary-Cleveland** (WHA) in 1972 WHA General Player Draft, February 12, 1972. Signed as a free agent by **California**, October 1, 1972. Signed as a free agent by **Winnipeg** (WHA), March, 1976.

● **MOXEY, JIM** Jim Moxey RW – L. 6'1", 190 lbs. b: Toronto, Ont., 5/28/1953. California's 3rd choice, 66th overall, in 1973 Amateur Draft.

1970-71	Hamilton Red Wings	OHA	43	10	5	15	....	....	....	46	....	....	....	....	....	....	....	....	....	....	....	....	....	....	....	....	....	....
1971-72	Hamilton Red Wings	OHA	62	20	35	55	....	....	....	71	....	....	....	....	....	....	....	....	....	....	....	....	....	....	....	....	....	....
1972-73	Hamilton Red Wings	OHA	59	40	40	80	....	....	....	85	....	....	....	....	....	....	....	....	....	....	....	....	....	....	....	....	....	....
1973-74	Salt Lake Golden Eagles	WHL	76	26	23	49	....	....	....	83	....	....	....	....	....	....	....	....	....	....	5	0	0	0	0	....	....	....
1974-75	**California Golden Seals**	**NHL**	**47**	**5**	**4**	**9**	**5**	**3**	**8**	**4**	**1**	**0**	**0**	**77**	**6.5**	**18**	**4**	**33**	**15**	**–4**	....	....	....	....	....	....	....	....
	Salt Lake Golden Eagles	CHL	11	3	11	14	....	....	....	7	....	....	....	....	....	....	....	....	....	....	....	....	....	....	....	....	....	....
1975-76	**California Golden Seals**	**NHL**	**44**	**10**	**16**	**26**	**9**	**13**	**22**	**33**	**2**	**0**	**0**	**106**	**9.4**	**42**	**10**	**50**	**8**	**–10**	....	....	....	....	....	....	....	....
	Salt Lake City Golden Eagles	CHL	30	11	17	28	....	....	....	31	....	....	....	....	....	....	....	....	....	....	....	....	....	....	....	....	....	....
1976-77	**Cleveland Barons**	**NHL**	**35**	**7**	**7**	**14**	**7**	**6**	**13**	**20**	**1**	**0**	**0**	**62**	**11.3**	**25**	**5**	**49**	**14**	**–15**	....	....	....	....	....	....	....	....
	Salt Lake Golden Eagles	CHL	4	6	3	9	....	....	....	4	....	....	....	....	....	....	....	....	....	....	....	....	....	....	....	....	....	....
	Los Angeles Kings	**NHL**	**1**	**0**	**0**	**0**	**0**	**0**	**0**	**2**	**0**	**0**	**0**	**0**	**0.0**	**0**	**0**	**0**	**0**	**0**	....	....	....	....	....	....	....	....
	Fort Worth Texans	CHL	29	9	9	18	....	....	....	27	....	....	....	....	....	....	....	....	....	....	6	1	1	2	2	....	....	....
1977-78	Springfield Indians	AHL	71	22	34	56	....	....	....	24	....	....	....	....	....	....	....	....	....	....	4	0	0	0	5	....	....	....
	NHL Totals		**127**	**22**	**27**	**49**	**21**	**22**	**43**	**59**	**4**	**0**	**0**	**245**	**9.0**	**85**	**19**	**132**	**37**		....	....	....	....	....	....	....	....

Transferred to **Cleveland** after **California** franchise relocated, August 26, 1976. Traded to **LA Kings** by **Cleveland** with Gary Simmons for Juha Widing and Gary Edwards, January 22, 1977.

● **MUIR, BRYAN** Bryan Muir D – L. 6'4", 220 lbs. b: Winnipeg, Man., 6/8/1973.

1992-93	University of New Hampshire	H.E.	26	1	2	3	....	....	....	24	....	....	....	....	....	....	....	....	....	....	....	....	....	....	....	....	....	....
1993-94	University of New Hampshire	H.E.	40	0	4	4	....	....	....	48	....	....	....	....	....	....	....	....	....	....	....	....	....	....	....	....	....	....
1994-95	University of New Hampshire	H.E.	28	9	9	18	....	....	....	46	....	....	....	....	....	....	....	....	....	....	....	....	....	....	....	....	....	....
1995-96	Canada	Nat-Team	42	6	12	18	....	....	....	38	....	....	....	....	....	....	....	....	....	....	....	....	....	....	....	....	....	....
	Edmonton Oilers	**NHL**	**5**	**0**	**0**	**0**	**0**	**0**	**0**	**6**	**0**	**0**	**0**	**4**	**0.0**	**1**	**0**	**5**	**0**	**–4**	....	....	....	....	....	....	....	....
1996-97	Hamilton Bulldogs	AHL	75	8	16	24	....	....	....	80	....	....	....	....	....	....	....	....	....	....	14	0	5	5	12	....	....	....
	Edmonton Oilers	**NHL**	....	....	....	....	....	....	....	....	....	....	....	....	....	....	....	....	....	....	**5**	**0**	**0**	**0**	**4**	....	....	....
1997-98	**Edmonton Oilers**	**NHL**	**7**	**0**	**0**	**0**	**0**	**0**	**0**	**17**	**0**	**0**	**0**	**6**	**0.0**	**2**	**0**	**3**	**1**	**0**	....	....	....	....	....	....	....	....
	Hamilton Bulldogs	AHL	28	3	10	13	....	....	....	62	....	....	....	....	....	....	....	....	....	....	....	....	....	....	....	....	....	....
	Albany River Rats	AHL	41	3	10	13	....	....	....	67	....	....	....	....	....	....	....	....	....	....	13	3	0	3	12	....	....	....
	NHL Totals		**12**	**0**	**0**	**0**	**0**	**0**	**0**	**23**	**0**	**0**	**0**	**10**	**0.0**	**3**	**0**	**8**	**1**		**5**	**0**	**0**	**0**	**4**	**0**	**0**	**0**

Signed as a free agent by **Edmonton**, April 30, 1996.

Traded to **New Jersey** by **Edmonton** with Jason Arnott for Valeri Zelepukin and Bill Guerin, January 4, 1998.

• MULHERN, RICHARD

Richard Mulhern D – L. 6'1", 188 lbs. b: Edmonton, Alta., 3/1/1955. Atlanta's 1st choice, 8th overall, in 1975 Amateur Draft.

			REGULAR SEASON																		PLAYOFFS							
Season	Club	League	GP	G	A	Pts	AG	AA	APts	PIM	PP	SH	GW	S	%	TGF	PGF	TGA	PGA	+/–	GP	G	A	Pts	PIM	PP	SH	GW
1973-74	Sherbrooke Beavers	QMJHL	40	8	37	45	....	....	....	96	....	....	....	....	....	....	....	....	....	....	....	....	....	....	....	....	....	....
1974-75	Sherbrooke Beavers	QMJHL	70	26	64	90	....	....	....	152	....	....	....	....	....	....	....	....	....	....	....	....	....	....	....	....	....	....
1975-76	**Atlanta Flames**	**NHL**	**12**	**1**	**0**	**1**	**1**	**0**	**1**	**4**	**1**	**0**	**0**	**17**	**5.9**	**3**	**2**	**9**	**0**	**–8**	....	....	....	....	....	....	....	....
	Tulsa Oilers	CHL	56	7	26	33	....	....	....	84	....	....	....	....	....	....	....	....	....	....	9	1	6	7	6	....	....	....
1976-77	**Atlanta Flames**	**NHL**	**79**	**12**	**32**	**44**	**11**	**26**	**37**	**80**	**2**	**1**	**1**	**156**	**7.7**	**104**	**19**	**93**	**14**	**+6**	**3**	**0**	**2**	**2**	**5**	**0**	**0**	**0**
1977-78	**Atlanta Flames**	**NHL**	**79**	**9**	**23**	**32**	**9**	**19**	**28**	**47**	**0**	**0**	**1**	**125**	**7.2**	**88**	**6**	**82**	**11**	**+11**	**2**	**0**	**1**	**1**	**0**	**0**	**0**	**0**
1978-79	**Atlanta Flames**	**NHL**	**37**	**3**	**12**	**15**	**3**	**9**	**12**	**22**	**0**	**0**	**0**	**58**	**5.2**	**50**	**2**	**43**	**1**	**+6**	....	....	....	....	....	....	....	....
	Los Angeles Kings	**NHL**	**36**	**2**	**9**	**11**	**2**	**7**	**9**	**23**	**1**	**0**	**0**	**57**	**3.5**	**48**	**2**	**63**	**14**	**–3**	**1**	**0**	**0**	**0**	**0**	**0**	**0**	**0**
1979-80	**Los Angeles Kings**	**NHL**	**15**	**0**	**3**	**3**	**0**	**2**	**2**	**16**	**0**	**0**	**0**	**8**	**0.0**	**16**	**1**	**22**	**8**	**+1**	....	....	....	....	....	....	....	....
	Toronto Maple Leafs	**NHL**	**26**	**0**	**10**	**10**	**0**	**8**	**8**	**11**	**0**	**0**	**0**	**30**	**0.0**	**31**	**5**	**30**	**3**	**–1**	**1**	**0**	**0**	**0**	**0**	**0**	**0**	**0**
1980-81	**Winnipeg Jets**	**NHL**	**19**	**0**	**4**	**4**	**0**	**3**	**3**	**14**	**0**	**0**	**0**	**24**	**0.0**	**19**	**2**	**27**	**1**	**–9**	....	....	....	....	....	....	....	....
	Tulsa Oilers	CHL	5	2	3	5	....	....	....	0	....	....	....	....	....	....	....	....	....	....	....	....	....	....	....	....	....	....
	Dallas Black Hawks	CHL	20	7	11	18	....	....	....	16	....	....	....	....	....	....	....	....	....	....	....	....	....	....	....	....	....	....
	NHL Totals		**303**	**27**	**93**	**120**	**26**	**74**	**100**	**217**	**4**	**1**	**2**	**475**	**5.7**	**359**	**39**	**369**	**52**		**7**	**0**	**3**	**3**	**5**	**0**	**0**	**0**

QMJHL Second All-Star Team (1974) • QMJHL First All-Star Team (1975)

Traded to **LA Kings** by **Atlanta** with Atlanta's 2nd round choice (Dave Morrison) in 1980 Entry Draft for Bob Murdoch and LA Kings' 2nd round choice (Tony Curtale) in 1980 Entry Draft, January 16, 1979. Claimed on waivers by **Toronto** from **LA Kings**, February 10, 1980. Traded to **Winnipeg** by **Toronto** for cash, December 2, 1980.

• MULHERN, RYAN

Ryan Mulhern C – R. 6'1", 180 lbs. b: Philadelphia, PA, 1/11/1973. Calgary's 9th choice, 174th overall, in 1992 Entry Draft.

Season	Club	League	GP	G	A	Pts	AG	AA	APts	PIM	PP	SH	GW	S	%	TGF	PGF	TGA	PGA	+/–	GP	G	A	Pts	PIM	PP	SH	GW
1991-92	Canterbury High School	H.S.	37	51	27	78	....	....	....	50	....	....	....	....	....	....	....	....	....	....	....	....	....	....	....	....	....	....
1992-93	Brown University	ECAC	31	15	9	24	....	....	....	46	....	....	....	....	....	....	....	....	....	....	....	....	....	....	....	....	....	....
1993-94	Brown University	ECAC	27	18	17	35	....	....	....	48	....	....	....	....	....	....	....	....	....	....	....	....	....	....	....	....	....	....
1994-95	Brown University	ECAC	30	18	16	34	....	....	....	*108	....	....	....	....	....	....	....	....	....	....	....	....	....	....	....	....	....	....
1995-96	Brown University	ECAC	32	10	16	26	....	....	....	78	....	....	....	....	....	....	....	....	....	....	....	....	....	....	....	....	....	....
1996-97	Hampton Rds.	ECHL	40	22	16	38	....	....	....	52	....	....	....	....	....	....	....	....	....	....	....	....	....	....	....	....	....	....
	Portland Pirates	AHL	38	19	15	34	....	....	....	16	....	....	....	....	....	....	....	....	....	....	5	1	1	2	2	....	....	....
1997-98	**Washington Capitals**	**NHL**	**3**	**0**	**0**	**0**	**0**	**0**	**0**	**0**	**0**	**0**	**0**	**1**	**0.0**	**1**	**0**	**1**	**0**	**0**	....	....	....	....	....	....	....	....
	Portland Pirates	AHL	71	25	40	65	....	....	....	85	....	....	....	....	....	....	....	....	....	....	6	1	0	1	12	....	....	....
	NHL Totals		**3**	**0**	**0**	**0**	**0**	**0**	**0**	**0**	**0**	**0**	**0**	**1**	**0.0**	**1**	**0**	**1**	**0**		....	....	....	....	....	....	....	....

AHL First All-Star Team (1998)

Signed as a free agent by **Washington**, March 17, 1997.

• MULLEN, BRIAN

Brian Mullen RW – L. 5'10", 180 lbs. b: New York, NY, 3/16/1962. Winnipeg's 7th choice, 128th overall, in 1980 Entry Draft.

Season	Club	League	GP	G	A	Pts	AG	AA	APts	PIM	PP	SH	GW	S	%	TGF	PGF	TGA	PGA	+/–	GP	G	A	Pts	PIM	PP	SH	GW
1977-78	New York Westsiders	NYMJHL	33	21	36	57	....	....	....	38	....	....	....	....	....	....	....	....	....	....	....	....	....	....	....	....	....	....
1978-79	New York Westsiders	NYMJHL	STATISTICS NOT AVAILABLE																									
1979-80	New York Westsiders	NYMJHL	STATISTICS NOT AVAILABLE																									
	United States	WJC-A	5	2	3	5	....	....	....	0	....	....	....	....	....	....	....	....	....	....	....	....	....	....	....	....	....	....
1980-81	University of Wisconsin	WCHA	38	11	13	24	....	....	....	28	....	....	....	....	....	....	....	....	....	....	....	....	....	....	....	....	....	....
	United States	WJC-A	5	0	2	2	....	....	....	6	....	....	....	....	....	....	....	....	....	....	....	....	....	....	....	....	....	....
1981-82	University of Wisconsin	WCHA	33	20	17	37	....	....	....	10	....	....	....	....	....	....	....	....	....	....	....	....	....	....	....	....	....	....
1982-83	**Winnipeg Jets**	**NHL**	**80**	**24**	**26**	**50**	**20**	**18**	**38**	**14**	**7**	**0**	**1**	**194**	**12.4**	**90**	**27**	**52**	**0**	**+11**	**3**	**1**	**0**	**1**	**0**	**0**	**0**	**0**
1983-84	**Winnipeg Jets**	**NHL**	**75**	**21**	**41**	**62**	**17**	**28**	**45**	**28**	**4**	**4**	**1**	**164**	**12.8**	**91**	**27**	**101**	**25**	**–12**	**3**	**0**	**3**	**3**	**6**	**0**	**0**	**0**
1984-85	United States	C Cup	4	0	0	0	....	....	....	0	....	....	....	....	....	....	....	....	....	....	....	....	....	....	....	....	....	....
	Winnipeg Jets	**NHL**	**69**	**32**	**39**	**71**	**26**	**26**	**52**	**32**	**8**	**0**	**4**	**191**	**16.8**	**123**	**40**	**72**	**4**	**+15**	**8**	**1**	**2**	**3**	**4**	**0**	**0**	**1**
1985-86	**Winnipeg Jets**	**NHL**	**79**	**28**	**34**	**62**	**22**	**23**	**45**	**38**	**13**	**0**	**3**	**211**	**13.3**	**100**	**42**	**76**	**1**	**–17**	**3**	**1**	**2**	**3**	**6**	**1**	**0**	**0**
1986-87	**Winnipeg Jets**	**NHL**	**69**	**19**	**32**	**51**	**16**	**23**	**39**	**20**	**7**	**0**	**4**	**185**	**10.3**	**82**	**26**	**58**	**0**	**–2**	**9**	**4**	**2**	**6**	**0**	**2**	**0**	**0**
1987-88	**New York Rangers**	**NHL**	**74**	**25**	**29**	**54**	**21**	**21**	**42**	**42**	**10**	**0**	**4**	**147**	**17.0**	**75**	**25**	**55**	**3**	**–2**	....	....	....	....	....	....	....	....
1988-89	**New York Rangers**	**NHL**	**78**	**29**	**35**	**64**	**25**	**25**	**50**	**60**	**8**	**3**	**5**	**217**	**13.4**	**93**	**30**	**76**	**20**	**+7**	**3**	**0**	**1**	**1**	**4**	**0**	**0**	**0**
	United States	WEC-A	10	2	3	5	....	....	....	4	....	....	....	....	....	....	....	....	....	....	....	....	....	....	....	....	....	....
1989-90	**New York Rangers**	**NHL**	**76**	**27**	**41**	**68**	**23**	**29**	**52**	**42**	**7**	**3**	**3**	**186**	**14.5**	**102**	**38**	**86**	**29**	**+7**	**10**	**2**	**2**	**4**	**8**	**2**	**0**	**0**
1990-91	**New York Rangers**	**NHL**	**79**	**19**	**43**	**62**	**17**	**33**	**50**	**44**	**4**	**0**	**3**	**188**	**10.1**	**98**	**35**	**69**	**18**	**+12**	**5**	**0**	**2**	**2**	**0**	**0**	**0**	**0**
	United States	WEC-A	10	4	4	8	....	....	....	6	....	....	....	....	....	....	....	....	....	....	....	....	....	....	....	....	....	....
1991-92	**San Jose Sharks**	**NHL**	**72**	**18**	**28**	**46**	**16**	**21**	**37**	**66**	**5**	**3**	**1**	**168**	**10.7**	**70**	**22**	**79**	**17**	**–14**	....	....	....	....	....	....	....	....
1992-93	**New York Islanders**	**NHL**	**81**	**18**	**14**	**32**	**15**	**10**	**25**	**28**	**1**	**0**	**1**	**126**	**14.3**	**49**	**3**	**62**	**21**	**+5**	**18**	**3**	**4**	**7**	**2**	**0**	**0**	**0**
	NHL Totals		**832**	**260**	**362**	**622**	**218**	**257**	**475**	**414**	**74**	**13**	**30**	**1977**	**13.2**	**973**	**315**	**786**	**138**		**62**	**12**	**18**	**30**	**30**	**5**	**0**	**1**

Won Lester Patrick Trophy (1995)

Played in NHL All-Star Game (1989)

Traded to **NY Rangers** by **Winnipeg** with Winnipeg's 10th round choice (Brett Barnett) in 1987 Entry Draft for NY Rangers' 5th round choice (previously acquired, Winnipeg selected Benoit Lebeau) in 1988 Entry Draft and NY Rangers' 3rd round choice (later traded to St. Louis — St. Louis selected Danny Felsner) in 1989 Entry Draft, June 8, 1987. Traded to **NY Islanders** by **San Jose** for the rights to Marcus Thuresson, August 24, 1992. • Suffered career-ending heart attack during training camp, September, 13, 1993.

• MULLEN, JOE

Joe Mullen RW – R. 5'9", 180 lbs. b: New York, NY, 2/26/1957.

Season	Club	League	GP	G	A	Pts	AG	AA	APts	PIM	PP	SH	GW	S	%	TGF	PGF	TGA	PGA	+/–	GP	G	A	Pts	PIM	PP	SH	GW
1971-72	New York 14th Precinct	NYMJHL	30	13	11	24	....	....	....	2	....	....	....	....	....	....	....	....	....	....	....	....	....	....	....	....	....	....
1972-73	New York Westsiders	NYMJHL	40	14	28	42	....	....	....	8	....	....	....	....	....	....	....	....	....	....	....	....	....	....	....	....	....	....
1973-74	New York Westsiders	NYMJHL	42	71	49	120	....	....	....	41	....	....	....	....	....	....	....	....	....	....	....	....	....	....	....	....	....	....
1974-75	New York Westsiders	NYMJHL	40	110	72	*182	....	....	....	20	....	....	....	....	....	....	....	....	....	....	....	....	....	....	....	....	....	....
1975-76	Boston College	ECAC	24	16	18	34	....	....	....	4	....	....	....	....	....	....	....	....	....	....	....	....	....	....	....	....	....	....
1976-77	Boston College	ECAC	28	28	26	54	....	....	....	8	....	....	....	....	....	....	....	....	....	....	....	....	....	....	....	....	....	....
1977-78	Boston College	ECAC	34	34	34	68	....	....	....	12	....	....	....	....	....	....	....	....	....	....	....	....	....	....	....	....	....	....
1978-79	Boston College	ECAC	25	32	24	56	....	....	....	8	....	....	....	....	....	....	....	....	....	....	....	....	....	....	....	....	....	....
	United States	WEC-A	8	7	1	8	....	....	....	2	....	....	....	....	....	....	....	....	....	....	....	....	....	....	....	....	....	....
1979-80	Salt Lake Golden Eagles	CHL	75	40	32	72	....	....	....	21	....	....	....	....	....	....	....	....	....	....	13	*9	11	20	0	....	....	....
	St. Louis Blues	**NHL**	....	....	....	....	....	....	....	....	....	....	....	....	....	....	....	....	....	....	**1**	**0**	**0**	**0**	**0**	....	....	....
1980-81	Salt Lake Golden Eagles	CHL	80	59	58	*117	....	....	....	8	....	....	....	....	....	....	....	....	....	....	17	11	9	20	0	....	....	....
1981-82	**St. Louis Blues**	**NHL**	**45**	**25**	**34**	**59**	**20**	**22**	**42**	**4**	**10**	**0**	**3**	**141**	**17.7**	**82**	**27**	**44**	**0**	**+11**	**10**	**7**	**11**	**18**	**4**	**1**	**0**	**0**
	Salt Lake Golden Eagles	CHL	27	21	27	48	....	....	....	12	....	....	....	....	....	....	....	....	....	....	....	....	....	....	....	....	....	....
1982-83	**St. Louis Blues**	**NHL**	**49**	**17**	**30**	**47**	**14**	**21**	**35**	**6**	**5**	**0**	**0**	**128**	**13.3**	**63**	**21**	**48**	**1**	**–5**	....	....	....	....	....	....	....	....
1983-84	**St. Louis Blues**	**NHL**	**80**	**41**	**44**	**85**	**33**	**30**	**63**	**19**	**13**	**0**	**6**	**228**	**18.0**	**124**	**51**	**81**	**0**	**–8**	**6**	**2**	**0**	**2**	**0**	**0**	**0**	**0**
1984-85	United States	C Cup	6	1	3	4	....	....	....	2	....	....	....	....	....	....	....	....	....	....	....	....	....	....	....	....	....	....
	St. Louis Blues	**NHL**	**79**	**40**	**52**	**92**	**33**	**35**	**68**	**6**	**13**	**0**	**4**	**252**	**15.9**	**123**	**43**	**75**	**0**	**+5**	**3**	**0**	**0**	**0**	**0**	**0**	**0**	**0**
1985-86	**St. Louis Blues**	**NHL**	**48**	**28**	**24**	**52**	**22**	**16**	**38**	**10**	**9**	**0**	**4**	**142**	**19.7**	**71**	**32**	**46**	**0**	**–7**	....	....	....	....	....	....	....	....
	Calgary Flames	**NHL**	**29**	**16**	**22**	**38**	**13**	**15**	**28**	**11**	**5**	**0**	**4**	**61**	**26.2**	**58**	**28**	**28**	**0**	**+2**	**21**	***12**	**7**	**19**	**4**	**4**	**0**	**2**
1986-87	**Calgary Flames**	**NHL**	**79**	**47**	**40**	**87**	**41**	**29**	**70**	**14**	**15**	**0**	**12**	**206**	**22.8**	**123**	**45**	**60**	**0**	**+18**	**6**	**2**	**1**	**3**	**0**	**1**	**0**	**1**
1987-88	United States	C Cup	4	3	0	3	....	....	....	0	....	....	....	....	....	....	....	....	....	....	....	....	....	....	....	....	....	....
	Calgary Flames	**NHL**	**80**	**40**	**44**	**84**	**34**	**31**	**65**	**30**	**12**	**0**	**5**	**205**	**19.5**	**133**	**42**	**63**	**0**	**+28**	**7**	**2**	**4**	**6**	**10**	**0**	**0**	**0**
1988-89	**Calgary Flames**	**NHL**	**79**	**51**	**59**	**110**	**43**	**42**	**85**	**16**	**13**	**1**	**7**	**270**	**18.9**	**155**	**62**	**57**	**15**	**+51**	**21**	***16**	**8**	**24**	**4**	**6**	**0**	**1**
1989-90	**Calgary Flames**	**NHL**	**78**	**36**	**33**	**69**	**31**	**24**	**55**	**24**	**8**	**3**	**5**	**236**	**15.3**	**118**	**47**	**83**	**18**	**+6**	**6**	**3**	**0**	**3**	**0**	**0**	**1**	**0**
1990-91	**Pittsburgh Penguins**	**NHL**	**47**	**17**	**22**	**39**	**16**	**17**	**33**	**6**	**8**	**0**	**2**	**85**	**20.0**	**63**	**24**	**35**	**5**	**+9**	**22**	**8**	**9**	**17**	**4**	**1**	**0**	**1**
1991-92	United States	C Cup	8	2	3	5	....	....	....	0	....	....	....	....	....	....	....	....	....	....	....	....	....	....	....	....	....	....
	Pittsburgh Penguins	**NHL**	**77**	**42**	**45**	**87**	**38**	**34**	**72**	**30**	**14**	**0**	**4**	**226**	**18.6**	**119**	**40**	**86**	**19**	**+12**	**9**	**3**	**1**	**4**	**4**	**1**	**0**	**0**
1992-93	**Pittsburgh Penguins**	**NHL**	**72**	**33**	**37**	**70**	**28**	**25**	**53**	**14**	**9**	**3**	**3**	**175**	**18.9**	**97**	**26**	**64**	**12**	**+19**	**12**	**4**	**2**	**6**	**6**	**0**	**1**	**1**
1993-94	**Pittsburgh Penguins**	**NHL**	**84**	**38**	**32**	**70**	**36**	**25**	**61**	**41**	**6**	**2**	**9**	**231**	**16.5**	**96**	**19**	**91**	**23**	**+9**	**6**	**1**	**0**	**1**	**2**	**0**	**0**	**0**

Season	Club	League	REGULAR SEASON																		PLAYOFFS							
			GP	G	A	Pts	AG	AA	APts	PIM	PP	SH	GW	S	%	TGF	PGF	TGA	PGA	+/–	GP	G	A	Pts	PIM	PP	SH	GW
1994-95	Pittsburgh Penguins	NHL	45	16	21	37	28	31	59	6	5	2	3	78	20.5	56	14	33	6	+15	12	0	3	3	4	0	0	0
1995-96	Boston Bruins	NHL	37	8	7	15	8	6	14	0	4	0	1	60	13.3	23	8	17	0	–2	....	....	....	....	....	....	....	....
1996-97	Pittsburgh Penguins	NHL	54	7	15	22	7	13	20	4	1	0	1	63	11.1	30	6	24	0	0	1	0	0	0	0	0	0	0
	NHL Totals		1062	502	561	1063	445	416	861	241	150	11	73	2787	18.0	1534	535	935	99		143	60	46	106	42	14	2	6

ECAC First All-Star Team (1978, 1979) • NCAA East First All-American Team (1978, 1979) • CHL Second All-Star Team (1980) • Won Ken McKenzie Trophy (CHL's Top Rookie) (1980) • CHL First All-Star Team (1981) • Won Tommy Ivan Trophy (CHL's MVP) (1981) • Won Lady Byng Trophy (1987, 1989) • NHL First All-Star Team (1989) • NHL Plus/Minus Leader (1989) • Won Lester Patrick Trophy (1995)

Played in NHL All-Star Game (1989, 1990, 1994)

Signed as a free agent by **St. Louis,** August 16, 1979. Traded to **Calgary** by **St. Louis** with Terry Johnson and Rik Wilson for Ed Beers, Charles Bourgeois and Gino Cavallini, February 1, 1986. Traded to **Pittsburgh** by **Calgary** for Pittsburgh's 2nd round choice (Nicolas Perreault) in 1990 Entry Draft, June 16, 1990. Signed as a free agent by **Boston**, September 13, 1995. Signed as a free agent by **Pittsburgh**, September 5, 1996.

• MULLER, KIRK

Kirk "Captain Kirk" Muller LW – L. 6', 205 lbs. b: Kingston, Ont., 2/8/1966. New Jersey's 1st choice, 2nd overall, in 1984 Entry Draft.

Season	Club	League	GP	G	A	Pts	AG	AA	APts	PIM	PP	SH	GW	S	%	TGF	PGF	TGA	PGA	+/–	GP	G	A	Pts	PIM	PP	SH	GW
1981-82	Kingston Canadians	OHL	67	12	39	51	....	....	....	27	....	....	....	....	....	....	....	....	....	....	4	5	1	6	4	....	....	....
1982-83	Guelph Platers	OHL	66	52	60	112	....	....	....	41	....	....	....	....	....	....	....	....	....	....	....	....	....	....	....	....	....	....
1983-84	Guelph Platers	OHL	49	31	63	94	....	....	....	27	....	....	....	....	....	....	....	....	....	....	....	....	....	....	....	....	....	....
	Canada	Nat-Team	15	2	2	4	....	....	....	6	....	....	....	....	....	....	....	....	....	....	....	....	....	....	....	....	....	....
	Canada	WJC-A	7	2	1	3	....	....	....	16	....	....	....	....	....	....	....	....	....	....	....	....	....	....	....	....	....	....
	Canada	Olympics	7	2	1	3	....	....	....	0	....	....	....	....	....	....	....	....	....	....	....	....	....	....	....	....	....	....
1984-85	New Jersey Devils	NHL	80	17	37	54	14	25	39	69	9	1	0	157	10.8	79	29	109	28	–31	....	....	....	....	....	....	....	....
	Canada	WEC-A	10	2	2	4	....	....	....	12	....	....	....	....	....	....	....	....	....	....	....	....	....	....	....	....	....	....
1985-86	New Jersey Devils	NHL	77	25	41	66	20	27	47	45	5	1	1	168	14.9	90	23	122	35	–20	....	....	....	....	....	....	....	....
	Canada	WEC-A	9	4	3	7	....	....	....	12	....	....	....	....	....	....	....	....	....	....	....	....	....	....	....	....	....	....
1986-87	New Jersey Devils	NHL	79	26	50	76	23	36	59	75	10	1	4	193	13.5	110	48	96	27	–7	....	....	....	....	....	....	....	....
	NHL All-Stars	RV'87	2	0	0	0	....	....	....	0	....	....	....	....	....	....	....	....	....	....	....	....	....	....	....	....	....	....
	Canada	WEC-A	10	2	0	2	....	....	....	8	....	....	....	....	....	....	....	....	....	....	....	....	....	....	....	....	....	....
1987-88	New Jersey Devils	NHL	80	37	57	94	32	41	73	114	6	1	1	215	17.2	134	52	82	19	+19	20	4	8	12	37	0	0	0
1988-89	New Jersey Devils	NHL	80	31	43	74	26	30	56	119	12	1	4	182	17.0	97	33	101	14	–23	....	....	....	....	....	....	....	....
	Canada	WEC-A	9	6	4	10	....	....	....	6	....	....	....	....	....	....	....	....	....	....	....	....	....	....	....	....	....	....
1989-90	New Jersey Devils	NHL	80	30	56	86	26	40	66	74	9	0	6	200	15.0	109	31	92	13	–1	6	1	3	4	11	0	0	0
1990-91	New Jersey Devils	NHL	80	19	51	70	17	39	56	76	7	0	3	221	8.6	110	43	88	22	+1	7	0	2	2	10	0	0	0
1991-92	Montreal Canadiens	NHL	78	36	41	77	33	31	64	86	15	1	7	191	18.8	101	43	59	16	+15	11	4	3	7	31	2	1	1
1992-93	Montreal Canadiens	NHL	80	37	57	94	31	39	70	77	12	0	4	231	16.0	131	47	103	27	+8	20	10	7	17	18	3	0	3
1993-94	Montreal Canadiens	NHL	76	23	34	57	21	26	47	96	9	2	3	168	13.7	95	45	79	28	–1	7	6	2	8	4	3	0	2
1994-95	Montreal Canadiens	NHL	33	8	11	19	14	16	30	33	3	0	1	81	9.9	32	14	54	15	–21	....	....	....	....	....	....	....	....
	New York Islanders	NHL	12	3	5	8	5	7	12	14	1	1	1	16	18.8	15	4	14	6	+3	....	....	....	....	....	....	....	....
1995-96	New York Islanders	NHL	15	4	3	7	4	2	6	15	0	0	0	23	17.4	10	2	28	10	–10	....	....	....	....	....	....	....	....
	Toronto Maple Leafs	NHL	36	9	16	25	9	13	22	42	7	0	1	79	11.4	39	15	46	19	–3	6	3	2	5	0	2	0	0
1996-97	Toronto Maple Leafs	NHL	66	20	17	37	21	15	36	85	9	1	3	153	13.1	57	19	80	19	–23	....	....	....	....	....	....	....	....
	Florida Panthers	NHL	10	1	2	3	1	2	3	4	1	0	1	21	4.8	8	4	8	2	–2	5	1	2	3	4	1	0	0
1997-98	Florida Panthers	NHL	70	8	21	29	9	20	29	54	1	0	3	115	7.0	44	13	61	16	–14	....	....	....	....	....	....	....	....
	NHL Totals		1032	334	542	876	306	409	715	1078	118	10	43	2414	13.8	1261	465	1222	316		82	29	29	58	115	11	1	6

Played in NHL All-Star Game (1985, 1986, 1988, 1990, 1992, 1993)

Traded to **Montreal** by **New Jersey** with Roland Melanson for Stephane Richer and Tom Chorske, September 20, 1991. Traded to **NY Islanders** by **Montreal** with Mathieu Schneider and Craig Darby for Pierre Turgeon and Vladimir Malakhov, April 5, 1995. Traded to **Toronto** by **NY Islanders** with Don Beaupre for future considerations, January 23, 1996. Traded to **Florida** by **Toronto** for Jason Podollan, March 18, 1997.

• MULOIN, WAYNE

Wayne Muloin D – L. 5'8", 175 lbs. b: Dryden, Ont., 12/24/1941.

Season	Club	League	GP	G	A	Pts	AG	AA	APts	PIM	PP	SH	GW	S	%	TGF	PGF	TGA	PGA	+/–	GP	G	A	Pts	PIM	PP	SH	GW
1961-62	Edmonton Oil Kings	WCJHL	STATISTICS NOT AVAILABLE																									
	Edmonton Flyers	WHL	4	0	0	0	....	....	....	0	....	....	....	....	....	....	....	....	....	....	....							
1962-63	Edmonton Flyers	WHL	61	2	6	8	....	....	....	52	....	....	....	....	....	....	....	....	....	....	3	0	2	2	2	....	....	....
1963-64	Detroit Red Wings	NHL	3	0	1	1	0	1	1	2	....	....	....	....	....	....	....	....	....	....	....	....	....	....	....	....	....	....
	Cincinnati Wings	CHL	69	4	11	15	....	....	....	169	....	....	....	....	....	....	....	....	....	....	....	....	....	....	....	....	....	....
1964-65	St. Paul Rangers	CHL	67	0	10	10	....	....	....	95	....	....	....	....	....	....	....	....	....	....	5	0	2	2	6	....	....	....
1965-66	Vancouver Canucks	WHL	15	1	0	1	....	....	....	8	....	....	....	....	....	....	....	....	....	....	....	....	....	....	....	....	....	....
	Providence Reds	AHL	45	3	11	14	....	....	....	70	....	....	....	....	....	....	....	....	....	....	....	....	....	....	....	....	....	....
1966-67	Providence Reds	AHL	68	0	10	10	....	....	....	99	....	....	....	....	....	....	....	....	....	....	....	....	....	....	....	....	....	....
1967-68	Providence Reds	AHL	66	1	16	17	....	....	....	78	....	....	....	....	....	....	....	....	....	....	8	0	3	3	10	....	....	....
1968-69	Providence Reds	AHL	72	6	18	24	....	....	....	77	....	....	....	....	....	....	....	....	....	....	9	0	2	2	10	....	....	....
1969-70	Oakland Seals	NHL	71	3	6	9	3	6	9	53	0	1	0	64	4.7	54	12	72	9	–21	4	0	0	0	0	0	0	0
1970-71	California Golden Seals	NHL	66	0	14	14	0	12	12	32	0	0	0	68	0.0	47	3	96	18	–34	....	....	....	....	....	....	....	....
	Minnesota North Stars	NHL	7	0	0	0	0	0	0	6	0	0	0	4	0.0	2	0	4	0	–2	7	0	0	0	2	0	0	0
1971-72	Cleveland Barons	AHL	71	1	14	15	....	....	....	82	....	....	....	....	....	....	....	....	....	....	3	0	0	0	6	....	....	....
1972-73	Cleveland Crusaders	WHA	67	2	13	15	....	....	....	64	....	....	....	....	....	....	....	....	....	....	9	1	3	4	14	....	....	....
1973-74	Cleveland Crusaders	WHA	76	3	7	10	....	....	....	39	....	....	....	....	....	....	....	....	....	....	5	1	0	1	0	....	....	....
1974-75	Cleveland Crusaders	WHA	78	4	17	21	....	....	....	65	....	....	....	....	....	....	....	....	....	....	5	0	1	1	4	....	....	....
1975-76	Cleveland Crusaders	WHA	27	0	5	5	....	....	....	12	....	....	....	....	....	....	....	....	....	....	....	....	....	....	....	....	....	....
	Syracuse Blazers	NAHL	3	0	0	0	....	....	....	4	....	....	....	....	....	....	....	....	....	....	....	....	....	....	....	....	....	....
	Edmonton Oilers	WHA	10	1	1	2	....	....	....	0	....	....	....	....	....	....	....	....	....	....	1	0	0	0	0	....	....	....
1976-77	Rhode Island Reds	AHL	52	1	3	4	....	....	....	20	....	....	....	....	....	....	....	....	....	....	....	....	....	....	....	....	....	....
	NHL Totals		147	3	21	24	3	19	22	93	0	1	0	136	2.2	103	15	172	27		11	0	0	0	2	0	0	0
	Other Major League Totals		258	10	43	53	....	....	....	180	....	....	....	....	....	....	....	....	....		20	2	4	6	18	....	....	....

Claimed by **NY Rangers** from **Detroit** in Intra-League Draft, June, 1964. Traded to **Providence** (AHL) by **NY Rangers** (Vancouver-WHL) for cash, December, 1965. NHL rights transferred to **Oakland** when NHL club signed affiliation agreement with **Providence** (AHL), June, 1968. Traded to **Minnesota** by **Oakland** with Ted Hampson for Tom Williams and Dick Redmond, March 7, 1971. Selected by **Calgary-Cleveland** (WHA) in 1972 WHA General Player Draft, February 12, 1972. Traded to **Edmonton** (WHA) by **Cleveland** (WHA) for Bill Evo, January, 1976.

• MULVENNA, GLENN

Glenn Mulvenna C – L. 5'11", 187 lbs. b: Calgary, Alta., 2/18/1967.

Season	Club	League	GP	G	A	Pts	AG	AA	APts	PIM	PP	SH	GW	S	%	TGF	PGF	TGA	PGA	+/–	GP	G	A	Pts	PIM	PP	SH	GW
1984-85	New Westminster Royals	WHL	66	16	15	31	....	....	....	34	....	....	....	....	....	....	....	....	....	....	11	2	3	5	2	....	....	....
1985-86	New Westminster Royals	WHL	65	24	31	55	....	....	....	55	....	....	....	....	....	....	....	....	....	....	....	....	....	....	....	....	....	....
1986-87	New Westminster Bruins	WHL	53	24	44	68	....	....	....	43	....	....	....	....	....	....	....	....	....	....	....	....	....	....	....	....	....	....
	Kamloops Chiefs	WHL	18	13	8	21	....	....	....	18	....	....	....	....	....	....	....	....	....	....	13	4	6	10	10	....	....	....
1987-88	Kamloops Chiefs	WHL	38	21	38	59	....	....	....	35	....	....	....	....	....	....	....	....	....	....	15	6	11	17	14	....	....	....
1988-89	Flint Spirits	IHL	32	9	14	23	....	....	....	12	....	....	....	....	....	....	....	....	....	....	....	....	....	....	....	....	....	....
	Muskegon Lumberjacks	IHL	11	3	2	5	....	....	....	0	....	....	....	....	....	....	....	....	....	....	....	....	....	....	....	....	....	....
	Knoxville Cherokees	ECHL	2	0	0	0	....	....	....	0	....	....	....	....	....	....	....	....	....	....	....	....	....	....	....	....	....	....
1989-90	Muskegon Lumberjacks	IHL	52	14	21	35	....	....	....	17	....	....	....	....	....	....	....	....	....	....	11	2	3	5	0	....	....	....
	Fort Wayne Komets	IHL	6	2	5	7	....	....	....	2	....	....	....	....	....	....	....	....	....	....	....	....	....	....	....	....	....	....
1990-91	Muskegon Lumberjacks	IHL	48	9	27	36	....	....	....	25	....	....	....	....	....	....	....	....	....	....	5	1	1	2	0	....	....	....
1991-92	Pittsburgh Penguins	NHL	1	0	0	0	0	0	0	2	0	0	0	0	0.0	0	0	1	0	–1	....	....	....	....	....	....	....	....
	Muskegon Lumberjacks	IHL	70	15	27	42	....	....	....	24	....	....	....	....	....	....	....	....	....	....	14	5	6	11	11	....	....	....
1992-93	Philadelphia Flyers	NHL	1	0	0	0	0	0	0	2	0	0	0	1	0.0	0	0	0	0	0	....	....	....	....	....	....	....	....
	Hershey Bears	AHL	35	5	17	22	....	....	....	8	....	....	....	....	....	....	....	....	....	....	....	....	....	....	....	....	....	....
1993-94	Kalamazoo Wings	IHL	55	13	9	22	....	....	....	18	....	....	....	....	....	....	....	....	....	....	4	0	0	0	0	....	....	....
1994-95	Peoria Rivermen	IHL	48	7	9	16	....	....	....	20	....	....	....	....	....	....	....	....	....	....	7	3	0	3	2	....	....	....
1995-96			DID NOT PLAY																									
1996-97	Sheffield Steelers	Britain	36	7	16	23	....	....	....	28	....	....	....	....	....	....	....	....	....	....	8	1	5	6	6	....	....	....
	VEU Feldkirch	EuroHL	1	0	0	0	....	....	....	0	....	....	....	....	....	....	....	....	....	....	....	....	....	....	....	....	....	....
	NHL Totals		2	0	0	0	0	0	0	4	0	0	0	1	0.0	0	0	1	0		....	....	....	....	....	....	....	....

Signed as a free agent by **Pittsburgh**, December 3, 1987. Signed as a free agent by **Philadelphia**, July 11, 1992.

			REGULAR SEASON																		PLAYOFFS							
Season	Club	League	GP	G	A	Pts	AG	AA	APts	PIM	PP	SH	GW	S	%	TGF	PGF	TGA	PGA	+/–	GP	G	A	Pts	PIM	PP	SH	GW

• MULVEY, GRANT

Grant Mulvey RW – R. 6′4″, 200 lbs. b: Sudbury, Ont., 9/17/1956. Chicago's 1st choice, 16th overall, in 1974 Amateur Draft.

Season	Club	League	GP	G	A	Pts	AG	AA	APts	PIM	PP	SH	GW	S	%	TGF	PGF	TGA	PGA	+/–	GP	G	A	Pts	PIM	PP	SH	GW
1972-73	Penticton Panthers	BCJHL	55	42	43	85	....	....	....	120	....	....	....	....	....	....	....	....	....	....	....	....	....	....	....	....	....	....
1973-74	Calgary Centennials	WHL	68	31	31	62	....	....	....	192	....	....	....	....	....	....	....	....	....	....	14	4	6	10	55	....	....	....
1974-75	**Chicago Black Hawks**	**NHL**	74	7	4	11	6	3	9	36	0	0	2	59	11.9	20	2	22	1	–3	6	2	0	2	6	0	0	0
1975-76	**Chicago Black Hawks**	**NHL**	64	11	17	28	10	13	23	72	1	0	1	90	12.2	48	4	50	1	–5	4	0	0	0	2	0	0	0
1976-77	**Chicago Black Hawks**	**NHL**	80	10	14	24	10	11	21	111	0	0	1	90	11.1	52	9	61	1	–17	2	1	0	1	2	1	0	0
1977-78	**Chicago Black Hawks**	**NHL**	78	14	24	38	13	20	33	135	3	0	0	157	8.9	66	20	48	1	–1	4	2	2	4	0	1	0	0
1978-79	**Chicago Black Hawks**	**NHL**	80	19	15	34	17	11	28	99	5	0	1	136	14.0	53	7	60	0	–14	1	0	0	0	2	0	0	0
1979-80	**Chicago Black Hawks**	**NHL**	80	39	26	65	35	20	55	122	14	0	7	228	17.1	94	28	63	0	+3	7	1	1	2	8	0	0	0
1980-81	**Chicago Black Hawks**	**NHL**	42	18	14	32	15	10	25	81	6	1	4	168	10.7	49	13	56	2	–18	3	0	0	0	0	0	0	0
1981-82	**Chicago Black Hawks**	**NHL**	73	30	19	49	24	13	37	141	3	0	3	184	16.3	75	15	69	0	–9	15	4	2	6	50	1	0	0
1982-83	**Chicago Black Hawks**	**NHL**	3	0	0	0	0	0	0	0	0	0	0	4	0.0	2	0	2	0	0	....	....	....	....	....	....	....	....
	Springfield Indians	AHL	5	0	2	2	....	....	....	4	....	....	....	....	....	....	....	....	....	....	....	....	....	....	....	....	....	....
1983-84	**New Jersey Devils**	**NHL**	12	1	2	3	1	1	2	19	0	0	0	15	6.7	4	1	8	0	–5	....	....	....	....	....	....	....	....
	Maine Mariners	AHL	29	6	8	14	....	....	....	49	....	....	....	....	....	....	....	....	....	....	16	5	2	7	39	....	....	....
	NHL Totals		**586**	**149**	**135**	**284**	**131**	**102**	**233**	**816**	**32**	**1**	**19**	**1131**	**13.2**	**463**	**99**	**439**	**6**		**42**	**10**	**5**	**15**	**70**	**3**	**0**	**0**

Claimed by **Pittsburgh** from **Chicago** in Waiver Draft, October 3, 1983. Claimed on waivers by **New Jersey** from **Pittsburgh**, October 8, 1983.

• MULVEY, PAUL

Paul Mulvey LW – L. 6′4″, 220 lbs. b: Sudbury, Ont., 9/27/1958. Washington's 3rd choice, 20th overall, in 1978 Amateur Draft.

Season	Club	League	GP	G	A	Pts	AG	AA	APts	PIM	PP	SH	GW	S	%	TGF	PGF	TGA	PGA	+/–	GP	G	A	Pts	PIM	PP	SH	GW
1973-74	Merritt Centennials	BCJHL	60	27	31	58	....	....	....	200	....	....	....	....	....	....	....	....	....	....	....	....	....	....	....	....	....	....
1974-75	Edmonton Oil Kings	WCJHL	49	18	19	37	....	....	....	179	....	....	....	....	....	....	....	....	....	....	....	....	....	....	....	....	....	....
1975-76	Edmonton Oil Kings	WCJHL	69	29	38	67	....	....	....	331	....	....	....	....	....	....	....	....	....	....	5	1	3	4	13	....	....	....
1976-77	Portland Winter Hawks	WCJHL	63	43	25	68	....	....	....	251	....	....	....	....	....	....	....	....	....	....	3	2	1	3	11	....	....	....
1977-78	Portland Winter Hawks	WCJHL	64	43	33	76	....	....	....	262	....	....	....	....	....	....	....	....	....	....	8	0	3	3	60	....	....	....
1978-79	**Washington Capitals**	**NHL**	55	7	4	11	6	3	9	81	1	0	1	60	11.7	22	2	39	1	–18	....	....	....	....	....	....	....	....
	Hershey Bears	AHL	24	10	3	13	....	....	....	113	....	....	....	....	....	....	....	....	....	....	....	....	....	....	....	....	....	....
1979-80	**Washington Capitals**	**NHL**	77	15	19	34	14	15	29	240	2	0	3	140	10.7	57	5	60	0	–8	....	....	....	....	....	....	....	....
1980-81	**Washington Capitals**	**NHL**	55	7	14	21	6	10	16	166	1	0	0	96	7.3	33	4	38	0	–9	....	....	....	....	....	....	....	....
	Hershey Bears	AHL	19	4	8	12	....	....	....	21	....	....	....	....	....	....	....	....	....	....	10	2	3	5	54	....	....	....
1981-82	**Pittsburgh Penguins**	**NHL**	27	1	7	8	1	5	6	76	0	0	0	44	2.3	16	3	20	0	–7	....	....	....	....	....	....	....	....
	Los Angeles Kings	**NHL**	11	0	7	7	0	5	5	50	0	0	0	8	0.0	10	0	10	0	0	....	....	....	....	....	....	....	....
	New Haven Nighthawks	AHL	19	3	3	6	....	....	....	65	....	....	....	....	....	....	....	....	....	....	3	0	0	0	14	....	....	....
1982-83	Moncton Alpines	AHL	58	11	11	22	....	....	....	270	....	....	....	....	....	....	....	....	....	....	....	....	....	....	....	....	....	....
	NHL Totals		**225**	**30**	**51**	**81**	**27**	**38**	**65**	**613**	**4**	**0**	**4**	**348**	**8.6**	**138**	**14**	**167**	**1**		....	....	....	....	....	....	....	....

Transferred to **Pittsburgh** by **Washington** as compensation for Washington's signing of free agent Orest Kindrachuk, September 4, 1981. Claimed on waivers by **LA Kings** from **Pittsburgh**, December 30, 1981. Traded to **Edmonton** by **LA Kings** for Blair Barnes, June 22, 1982.

• MUNI, CRAIG

Craig Muni D – L. 6′3″, 208 lbs. b: Toronto, Ont., 7/19/1962. Toronto's 1st choice, 25th overall, in 1980 Entry Draft.

Season	Club	League	GP	G	A	Pts	AG	AA	APts	PIM	PP	SH	GW	S	%	TGF	PGF	TGA	PGA	+/–	GP	G	A	Pts	PIM	PP	SH	GW
1979-80	Kingston Canadians	OHA	66	6	28	34	....	....	....	114	....	....	....	....	....	....	....	....	....	....	....	....	....	....	....	....	....	....
1980-81	Kingston Canadians	OHA	38	2	14	16	....	....	....	65	....	....	....	....	....	....	....	....	....	....	....	....	....	....	....	....	....	....
	Windsor Spitfires	OHA	25	5	11	16	....	....	....	41	....	....	....	....	....	....	....	....	....	....	11	1	4	5	14	....	....	....
	New Brunswick Hawks	AHL	....	....	....	....	....	....	....	....	....	....	....	....	....	....	....	....	....	....	2	0	1	1	10	....	....	....
1981-82	Windsor Spitfires	OHL	49	5	32	37	....	....	....	92	....	....	....	....	....	....	....	....	....	....	9	2	3	5	16	....	....	....
	Toronto Maple Leafs	**NHL**	3	0	0	0	0	0	0	2	0	0	0	0	0.0	0	0	5	1	–4	....	....	....	....	....	....	....	....
	Cincinnati Tigers	CHL	....	....	....	....	....	....	....	....	....	....	....	....	....	....	....	....	....	....	3	0	2	2	2	....	....	....
1982-83	**Toronto Maple Leafs**	**NHL**	2	0	1	1	0	1	1	0	0	0	0	2	0.0	0	0	3	0	–3	....	....	....	....	....	....	....	....
	St. Catharines Saints	AHL	64	6	32	38	....	....	....	52	....	....	....	....	....	....	....	....	....	....	....	....	....	....	....	....	....	....
1983-84	St. Catharines Saints	AHL	64	4	16	20	....	....	....	79	....	....	....	....	....	....	....	....	....	....	7	0	1	1	0	....	....	....
1984-85	**Toronto Maple Leafs**	**NHL**	8	0	0	0	0	0	0	0	0	0	0	1	0.0	2	0	5	3	0	....	....	....	....	....	....	....	....
	St. Catharines Saints	AHL	68	7	17	24	....	....	....	54	....	....	....	....	....	....	....	....	....	....	....	....	....	....	....	....	....	....
1985-86	**Toronto Maple Leafs**	**NHL**	6	0	1	1	0	1	1	4	0	0	0	2	0.0	5	0	15	7	–3	....	....	....	....	....	....	....	....
	St. Catharines Saints	AHL	73	3	34	37	....	....	....	91	....	....	....	....	....	....	....	....	....	....	13	0	5	5	16	....	....	....
1986-87	**Edmonton Oilers**	**NHL**	79	7	22	29	6	16	22	85	0	0	2	69	10.1	110	3	87	25	+45	14	0	2	2	17	0	0	0
1987-88	**Edmonton Oilers**	**NHL**	72	4	15	19	3	11	14	77	0	1	0	56	7.1	90	1	86	29	+32	19	0	4	4	31	0	0	0
1988-89	**Edmonton Oilers**	**NHL**	69	5	13	18	4	9	13	71	0	0	1	40	12.5	92	1	84	36	+43	7	0	3	3	8	0	0	0
1989-90	**Edmonton Oilers**	**NHL**	71	5	12	17	4	9	13	81	0	2	0	42	11.9	77	0	83	28	+22	22	0	3	3	16	0	0	0
1990-91	**Edmonton Oilers**	**NHL**	76	1	9	10	1	7	8	77	0	0	0	47	2.1	64	1	87	34	+10	18	0	3	3	20	0	0	0
1991-92	**Edmonton Oilers**	**NHL**	54	2	5	7	2	4	6	34	0	0	0	38	5.3	52	1	59	19	+11	3	0	0	0	2	0	0	0
1992-93	**Edmonton Oilers**	**NHL**	72	0	11	11	0	8	8	67	0	0	0	51	0.0	48	0	104	41	–15	....	....	....	....	....	....	....	....
	Chicago Blackhawks	**NHL**	9	0	0	0	0	0	0	8	0	0	0	9	0.0	5	1	5	2	+1	4	0	0	0	2	0	0	0
1993-94	**Chicago Blackhawks**	**NHL**	9	0	4	4	0	3	3	4	0	0	0	6	0.0	6	0	5	2	+3	....	....	....	....	....	....	....	....
	Buffalo Sabres	**NHL**	73	2	8	10	2	6	8	62	0	1	2	39	5.1	59	0	63	32	+28	7	0	0	0	4	0	0	0
1994-95	**Buffalo Sabres**	**NHL**	40	0	6	6	0	9	9	36	0	0	0	32	0.0	25	1	39	11	–4	5	0	1	1	2	0	0	0
1995-96	**Buffalo Sabres**	**NHL**	47	0	4	4	0	3	3	69	0	0	0	25	0.0	22	0	61	27	–12	....	....	....	....	....	....	....	....
	Winnipeg Jets	**NHL**	25	1	3	4	1	2	3	37	0	0	0	16	6.3	19	0	21	8	+6	6	0	1	1	2	0	0	0
1996-97	**Pittsburgh Penguins**	**NHL**	64	0	4	4	0	4	4	36	0	0	0	19	0.0	32	0	59	21	–6	3	0	0	0	0	0	0	0
1997-98	**Dallas Stars**	**NHL**	40	1	1	2	1	1	2	25	0	0	1	12	8.3	15	0	21	6	0	5	0	0	0	4	0	0	0
	NHL Totals		**819**	**28**	**119**	**147**	**24**	**94**	**118**	**775**	**0**	**4**	**6**	**506**	**5.5**	**723**	**9**	**892**	**332**		**113**	**0**	**17**	**17**	**108**	**0**	**0**	**0**

Signed as a free agent by **Edmonton,** August 18, 1986. Sold to **Buffalo** by **Edmonton**, October 2, 1986. Traded to **Pittsburgh** by **Buffalo** for future considerations, October 3, 1986. Traded to **Edmonton** by **Pittsburgh** to complete September 11, 1985 trade which sent Gilles Meloche to Pittsburgh for Tim Hrynewich, Marty McSorley and future considerations, October 6, 1986. Traded to **Chicago** by **Edmonton** for Mike Hudson, March 22, 1993. Traded to **Buffalo** by **Chicago** with Chicago's 5th round choice (Daniel Bienvenue) in 1995 Entry Draft for Keith Carney and Buffalo's 6th round choice (Marc Magliarditi) in 1995 Entry Draft, October 26, 1993. Traded to **Winnipeg** by **Buffalo** for Darryl Shannon and Michael Grosek, February 15, 1996. Signed as a free agent by **Pittsburgh**, October 2, 1996.

• MURDOCH, BOB

Bob (L.) Murdoch RW – R. 5′11″, 191 lbs. b: Cranbrook, B.C., 1/29/1954.

Season	Club	League	GP	G	A	Pts	AG	AA	APts	PIM	PP	SH	GW	S	%	TGF	PGF	TGA	PGA	+/–	GP	G	A	Pts	PIM	PP	SH	GW
1972-73	Cranbrook Colts	BCJHL	STATISTICS NOT AVAILABLE																									
	Edmonton Oil Kings	WCJHL	1	0	0	0	....	....	....	0	....	....	....	....	....	....	....	....	....	....	....	....	....	....	....	....	....	....
1973-74	Cranbrook Royals	WIHL	48	37	24	61	....	....	....	....	....	....	....	....	....	....	....	....	....	....	....	....	....	....	....	....	....	....
1974-75	Salt Lake Golden Eagles	CHL	76	33	30	63	....	....	....	66	....	....	....	....	....	....	....	....	....	....	11	6	6	12	8	....	....	....
1975-76	**California Golden Seals**	**NHL**	78	22	27	49	20	21	41	53	9	0	3	166	13.3	75	26	63	1	–13	....	....	....	....	....	....	....	....
1976-77	**Cleveland Barons**	**NHL**	57	23	19	42	22	15	37	30	6	0	3	141	16.3	60	18	47	0	–5	....	....	....	....	....	....	....	....
1977-78	**Cleveland Barons**	**NHL**	71	14	26	40	13	21	34	27	5	0	4	131	10.7	57	16	59	0	–18	....	....	....	....	....	....	....	....
1978-79	**St. Louis Blues**	**NHL**	54	13	13	26	12	10	22	17	1	0	3	92	14.1	43	8	41	0	–6	....	....	....	....	....	....	....	....
	Salt Lake Golden Eagles	CHL	6	1	1	2	....	....	....	9	....	....	....	....	....	....	....	....	....	....	....	....	....	....	....	....	....	....
1979-80	Salt Lake Golden Eagles	CHL	29	8	14	22	....	....	....	23	....	....	....	....	....	....	....	....	....	....	....	....	....	....	....	....	....	....
	Adirondack Red Wings	AHL	21	5	9	14	....	....	....	19	....	....	....	....	....	....	....	....	....	....	....	....	....	....	....	....	....	....
	NHL Totals		**260**	**72**	**85**	**157**	**67**	**67**	**134**	**127**	**21**	**0**	**13**	**530**	**13.6**	**235**	**68**	**210**	**1**		....	....	....	....	....	....	....	....

CHL Second All-Star Team (1975)

Played in NHL All-Star Game (1975)

Signed as a free agent by **California**, October, 1974. Transferred to **Cleveland** after **California** franchise relocated, August 26, 1976. Placed on **Minnesota** Reserve List after **Cleveland-Minnesota** Dispersal Draft, June 15, 1978. Traded to **St. Louis** by **Minnesota** for cash, August 8, 1978. Claimed by **St. Louis** as a fill-in during Expansion Draft, June 13, 1979.

• MURDOCH, BOB

Bob (J.) Murdoch D – R. 6′, 200 lbs. b: Kirkland Lake, Ont., 11/20/1946.

Season	Club	League	GP	G	A	Pts	AG	AA	APts	PIM	PP	SH	GW	S	%	TGF	PGF	TGA	PGA	+/–	GP	G	A	Pts	PIM	PP	SH	GW
1968-69	Winnipeg Nats	MHL Sr.	6	0	1	1	....	....	....	2	....	....	....	....	....	....	....	....	....	....	....	....	....	....	....	....	....	....
1969-70	Canada	Nat-Team	STATISTICS NOT AVAILABLE																									
	Montreal Voyageurs	AHL	6	0	2	2	....	....	....	6	....	....	....	....	....	....	....	....	....	....	....	....	....	....	....	....	....	....
1970-71	**Montreal Canadiens**	**NHL**	1	0	2	2	0	2	2	2	0	0	0	2	0.0	2	1	1	0	0	2	0	0	0	0	0	0	0
	Montreal Voyageurs	AHL	66	8	20	28	....	....	....	69	....	....	....	....	....	....	....	....	....	....	3	1	2	3	4	....	....	....
1971-72	**Montreal Canadiens**	**NHL**	11	1	1	2	1	1	2	8	0	0	0	16	6.3	15	0	10	3	+8	1	0	0	0	0	0	0	0
	Nova Scotia Voyageurs	AHL	53	7	32	39	....	....	....	53	....	....	....	....	....	....	....	....	....	....	....	....	....	....	....	....	....	....

			REGULAR SEASON																		PLAYOFFS							
Season	Club	League	GP	G	A	Pts	AG	AA	APts	PIM	PP	SH	GW	S	%	TGF	PGF	TGA	PGA	+/–	GP	G	A	Pts	PIM	PP	SH	GW
1972-73	Montreal Canadiens	NHL	69	2	22	24	2	18	20	55	0	0	2	54	3.7	77	2	54	18	+39	13	0	3	3	10	0	0	0
1973-74	Los Angeles Kings	NHL	76	8	20	28	8	17	25	85	1	0	1	160	5.0	87	11	107	20	–11	5	0	0	0	2	0	0	0
1974-75	Los Angeles Kings	NHL	80	13	29	42	12	23	35	116	2	1	0	201	6.5	126	26	80	19	+39	3	0	1	1	4	0	0	0
1975-76	Los Angeles Kings	NHL	80	6	29	35	6	23	29	103	2	0	1	172	3.5	128	35	113	33	+13	9	0	5	5	15	0	0	0
1976-77	Los Angeles Kings	NHL	70	9	23	32	9	19	28	79	0	0	1	125	7.2	113	9	91	23	+36	9	2	3	5	14	1	0	1
1977-78	Los Angeles Kings	NHL	76	2	17	19	2	14	16	68	0	0	0	144	1.4	80	2	101	25	+2	2	0	1	1	5	0	0	0
1978-79	Los Angeles Kings	NHL	32	3	12	15	3	9	12	46	0	0	1	63	4.8	52	11	49	8	0	....	....	....	....	....	....	....	....
	Atlanta Flames	NHL	35	5	11	16	5	8	13	24	2	0	0	53	9.4	51	8	53	12	+2	2	0	0	0	4	0	0	0
1979-80	Atlanta Flames	NHL	80	5	16	21	5	12	17	48	0	0	1	68	7.4	75	0	105	32	+2	4	1	1	2	2	0	0	0
1980-81	Calgary Flames	NHL	74	3	19	22	2	13	15	54	0	0	0	90	3.3	100	4	91	17	+22	16	1	4	5	36	0	0	0
1981-82	Calgary Flames	NHL	73	3	17	20	2	11	13	76	0	0	0	81	3.7	86	0	108	27	+5	3	0	0	0	0	0	0	0
	NHL Totals		757	60	218	278	57	170	227	764	7	1	7	1229	4.9	992	109	963	237		69	4	18	22	92	1	0	1

Won Jack Adams Award (1990)

Signed as a free agent by **Montreal**, March 2, 1970. Traded to **Minnesota** by **Montreal** to complete transaction that sent Danny Grant to Montreal (June 10, 1968), May 25, 1971. Montreal also received the rights to Marshall Johnston. Claimed by **Montreal** from **Minnesota** in Intra-League Draft, June 8, 1971. Traded to **LA Kings** by **Montreal** with Randy Rota for LA Kings' 1st round choice (Mario Tremblay) in 1974 Amateur Draft and cash, May 29, 1973. Traded to **Atlanta** by **LA Kings** with LA Kings' 2nd round choice (Tony Curtale) in 1980 Entry Draft for Richard Mulhern and Atlanta's 2nd round choice (Dave Morrison) in 1980 Entry Draft, January 16, 1979. Transferred to **Calgary** after **Atlanta** franchise relocated, June 24, 1980.

• MURDOCH, DON

Don "Murder" Murdoch RW – R. 5'11", 180 lbs. b: Cranbrook, B.C., 10/25/1956. NY Rangers' 1st choice, 6th overall, in 1976 Amateur Draft.

1973-74	Vernon Vipers	BCJHL	45	50	32	82	....	....	....	69	....	....	....	....	....	....	....	....	....	....	....	....	....	....	....	....	....	....
	Kamloops Chiefs	WCJHL	4	1	0	1	....	....	....	9	....	....	....	....	....	....	....	....	....	....	....	....	....	....	....	....	....	....
1974-75	Medicine Hat Tigers	WCJHL	70	*82	59	141	....	....	....	83	....	....	....	....	....	....	....	....	....	....	5	1	5	6	15	....	....	....
1975-76	Medicine Hat Tigers	WHL	70	*88	77	165	....	....	....	202	....	....	....	....	....	....	....	....	....	....	7	4	3	7	23	....	....	....
1976-77	New York Rangers	NHL	59	32	24	56	31	19	50	47	11	0	6	223	14.3	79	25	58	9	+5	....	....	....	....	....	....	....	....
1977-78	New York Rangers	NHL	66	27	28	55	26	23	49	41	10	0	1	188	14.4	89	37	57	0	–5	3	1	3	4	4	0	0	1
1978-79	New York Rangers	NHL	40	15	22	37	14	17	31	6	4	0	2	133	11.3	54	19	41	0	–6	18	7	5	12	12	3	0	1
1979-80	New York Rangers	NHL	56	23	19	42	21	15	36	16	5	1	2	143	16.1	68	23	56	0	–11	....	....	....	....	....	....	....	....
	Edmonton Oilers	NHL	10	5	2	7	5	2	7	4	1	0	0	35	14.3	12	2	10	0	0	3	2	0	2	0	0	0	0
1980-81	Edmonton Oilers	NHL	40	10	9	19	8	6	14	18	4	0	2	102	9.8	33	11	38	0	–16	....	....	....	....	....	....	....	....
	Wichita Wind	CHL	22	15	10	25	....	....	....	48	....	....	....	....	....	....	....	....	....	....	18	*17	7	24	24	....	....	....
1981-82	Detroit Red Wings	NHL	49	9	13	22	7	9	16	23	1	0	1	97	9.3	38	8	29	0	+1	....	....	....	....	....	....	....	....
	Adirondack Red Wings	AHL	24	11	13	24	....	....	....	24	....	....	....	....	....	....	....	....	....	....	4	5	0	5	14	....	....	....
1982-83	Adirondack Red Wings	AHL	35	10	12	22	....	....	....	19	....	....	....	....	....	....	....	....	....	....	....	....	....	....	....	....	....	....
1983-84	Adirondack Red Wings	AHL	59	26	20	46	....	....	....	19	....	....	....	....	....	....	....	....	....	....	....	....	....	....	....	....	....	....
	Montana Magic	CHL	17	10	10	20	....	....	....	2	....	....	....	....	....	....	....	....	....	....	....	....	....	....	....	....	....	....
1984-85	Muskegon Mohawks	IHL	32	18	13	31	....	....	....	4	....	....	....	....	....	....	....	....	....	....	16	6	3	9	26	....	....	....
1985-86	Indianapolis Checkers	IHL	11	4	3	7	....	....	....	4	....	....	....	....	....	....	....	....	....	....	....	....	....	....	....	....	....	....
	Toledo Goaldiggers	IHL	37	15	23	38	....	....	....	8	....	....	....	....	....	....	....	....	....	....	....	....	....	....	....	....	....	....
	Muskegon Lumberjacks	IHL	12	4	4	8	....	....	....	0	....	....	....	....	....	....	....	....	....	....	....	....	....	....	....	....	....	....
	NHL Totals		320	121	117	238	112	91	203	155	36	1	14	921	13.1	373	125	289	9		24	10	8	18	16	3	0	2

WCJHL First All-Star Team (1975, 1976)

Played in NHL All-Star Game (1977)

Traded to **Edmonton** by **NY Rangers** for Cam Connor and Edmonton's 3rd round choice (Peter Sundstrum) in 1981 Entry Draft, March 11, 1980. Rights traded to **Minnesota** by **Edmonton** for Don Jackson, August 21, 1981. Rights traded to **Detroit** by **Minnesota** with Greg Smith and Minnesota's 1st round choice (Murray Craven) in 1982 Entry Draft for Detroit's 1st round choice (Brian Bellows) in 1982 Entry Draft, August 21, 1981.

• MURPHY, BRIAN

Brian Murphy C/LW – L. 6'3", 200 lbs. b: Toronto, Ont., 8/20/1947.

1964-65	Toronto Marlboros	OHA	4	0	0	0	....	....	....	0	....	....	....	....	....	....	....	....	....	....	....	....	....	....	....	....	....	....
1965-66	Markham Waxers	Jr. B	....	24	16	40	....	....	....	....	....	....	....	....	....	....	....	....	....	....	....	....	....	....	....	....	....	....
	London Knights	OHA	2	0	1	1	....	....	....	2	....	....	....	....	....	....	....	....	....	....	....	....	....	....	....	....	....	....
1966-67	London Knights	OHA	42	10	29	39	....	....	....	9	....	....	....	....	....	....	....	....	....	....	6	1	3	4	2	....	....	....
1967-68	London Knights	OHA	54	25	31	56	....	....	....	41	....	....	....	....	....	....	....	....	....	....	5	5	2	7	0	....	....	....
1968-69	Springfield Kings	AHL	72	7	8	15	....	....	....	15	....	....	....	....	....	....	....	....	....	....	....	....	....	....	....	....	....	....
1969-70	Springfield Kings	AHL	72	8	23	31	....	....	....	31	....	....	....	....	....	....	....	....	....	....	14	4	3	7	16	....	....	....
1970-71	Springfield Kings	AHL	51	11	8	19	....	....	....	27	....	....	....	....	....	....	....	....	....	....	8	2	0	2	0	....	....	....
1971-72	Baltimore Clippers	AHL	57	7	16	23	....	....	....	22	....	....	....	....	....	....	....	....	....	....	18	2	8	10	20	....	....	....
1972-73	Baltimore Clippers	AHL	73	23	36	59	....	....	....	53	....	....	....	....	....	....	....	....	....	....	....	....	....	....	....	....	....	....
1973-74	Baltimore Clippers	AHL	76	30	48	78	....	....	....	74	....	....	....	....	....	....	....	....	....	....	9	1	3	4	6	....	....	....
1974-75	Baltimore Clippers	AHL	16	1	2	3	....	....	....	13	....	....	....	....	....	....	....	....	....	....	....	....	....	....	....	....	....	....
	Detroit Red Wings	NHL	1	0	0	0	0	0	0	0	0	0	0	1	0.0	1	0	1	0	0	....	....	....	....	....	....	....	....
	Virginia Wings	AHL	45	10	20	30	....	....	....	33	....	....	....	....	....	....	....	....	....	....	5	2	1	3	14	....	....	....
1975-76	Rochester Americans	AHL	66	14	22	36	....	....	....	37	....	....	....	....	....	....	....	....	....	....	2	0	0	0	0	....	....	....
1976-77			DID NOT PLAY																									
1977-78	Lancaster Lancers	OHA Sr.	21	14	19	33	....	....	....	31	....	....	....	....	....	....	....	....	....	....	....	....	....	....	....	....	....	....
	NHL Totals		1	0	0	0	0	0	0	0	0	0	0	1	0.0	1	0	1	0		....	....	....	....	....	....	....	....

Traded to **LA Kings** by **Toronto** with Gary Croteau and Wayne Thomas for Grant Moore and Lou Deveault, September, 1968. Traded to **Toronto** by **LA Kings** with Garry Monahan for Bob Pulford, September 3, 1970. Signed as a free agent by **Springfield** (AHL), November, 1970. Traded to **Baltimore** (AHL) by **Springfield** (AHL) for cash, June, 1971. Traded to **Detroit** by **Baltimore** (AHL) for cash, November, 1974.

• MURPHY, GORD

Gord Murphy D – R. 6'2", 191 lbs. b: Willowdale, Ont., 3/23/1967. Philadelphia's 10th choice, 189th overall, in 1985 Entry Draft.

1984-85	Oshawa Generals	OHL	59	3	12	15	....	....	....	25	....	....	....	....	....	....	....	....	....	....	....	....	....	....	....	....	....	....
1985-86	Oshawa Generals	OHL	64	7	15	22	....	....	....	56	....	....	....	....	....	....	....	....	....	....	6	1	1	2	6	....	....	....
1986-87	Oshawa Generals	OHL	56	7	30	37	....	....	....	95	....	....	....	....	....	....	....	....	....	....	24	6	16	22	22	....	....	....
1987-88	Hershey Bears	AHL	62	8	20	28	....	....	....	44	....	....	....	....	....	....	....	....	....	....	12	0	8	8	12	....	....	....
1988-89	Philadelphia Flyers	NHL	75	4	31	35	3	22	25	68	3	0	1	116	3.4	122	60	86	11	–3	19	2	7	9	13	1	0	1
1989-90	Philadelphia Flyers	NHL	75	14	27	41	12	19	31	95	4	0	1	160	8.8	106	37	100	24	–7	....	....	....	....	....	....	....	....
1990-91	Philadelphia Flyers	NHL	80	11	31	42	10	23	33	58	6	0	2	203	5.4	111	45	98	25	–7	....	....	....	....	....	....	....	....
1991-92	Philadelphia Flyers	NHL	31	2	8	10	2	6	8	33	0	0	0	50	4.0	32	10	32	6	–4	....	....	....	....	....	....	....	....
	Boston Bruins	NHL	42	3	6	9	3	4	7	51	0	0	0	82	3.7	41	5	48	14	+2	15	1	0	1	12	0	0	0
1992-93	Boston Bruins	NHL	49	5	12	17	4	8	12	62	3	0	2	68	7.4	39	13	42	3	–13	....	....	....	....	....	....	....	....
	Providence Bruins	AHL	2	1	3	4	....	....	....	2	....	....	....	....	....	....	....	....	....	....	....	....	....	....	....	....	....	....
1993-94	Florida Panthers	NHL	84	14	29	43	13	22	35	71	9	0	2	172	8.1	106	44	101	28	–11	....	....	....	....	....	....	....	....
1994-95	Florida Panthers	NHL	46	6	16	22	11	24	35	24	5	0	0	94	6.4	50	20	63	19	–14	....	....	....	....	....	....	....	....
1995-96	Florida Panthers	NHL	70	8	22	30	8	18	26	30	4	0	0	125	6.4	82	28	90	41	+5	14	0	4	4	6	0	0	0
1996-97	Florida Panthers	NHL	80	8	15	23	8	13	21	51	2	0	0	137	5.8	73	15	86	31	+3	5	0	5	5	4	0	0	0
1997-98	Florida Panthers	NHL	79	6	11	17	7	11	18	46	3	0	0	123	4.9	65	8	102	42	–3	....	....	....	....	....	....	....	....
	Canada	WC-A	6	1	0	1	....	....	....	2	....	....	....	....	....	....	....	....	....	....	....	....	....	....	....	....	....	....
	NHL Totals		711	81	208	289	81	170	251	589	39	0	8	1330	6.1	827	275	848	244		53	3	16	19	35	1	0	1

Traded to **Boston** by **Philadelphia** with Brian Dobbin, Philadelphia's 3rd round choice (Sergei Zholtok) in 1992 Entry Draft and Philadelphia's 4th round choice (Charles Paquette) in 1993 Entry Draft, for Garry Galley, Wes Walz and Boston's 3rd round choice (Milos Holan) in 1993 Entry Draft, January 2, 1992. Traded to **Dallas** by **Boston** for future considerations (Jon Casey, June 25, 1993), June 20, 1993. Claimed by **Florida** from **Dallas** in Expansion Draft, June 24, 1993.

• MURPHY, JOE

Joe Murphy RW – L. 6'1", 190 lbs. b: London, Ont., 10/16/1967. Detroit's 1st choice, 1st overall, in 1986 Entry Draft.

1985-86	Michigan State Spartans	CCHA	35	24	37	61	....	....	....	50	....	....	....	....	....	....	....	....	....	....	....	....	....	....	....	....	....	....
	Canada	Nat-Team	8	3	3	6	....	....	....	2	....	....	....	....	....	....	....	....	....	....	....	....	....	....	....	....	....	....
	Canada	WJC-A	7	4	10	14	....	....	....	2	....	....	....	....	....	....	....	....	....	....	....	....	....	....	....	....	....	....
1986-87	Detroit Red Wings	NHL	5	0	1	1	0	1	1	2	0	0	0	3	0.0	1	0	1	0	0	....	....	....	....	....	....	....	....
	Adirondack Red Wings	AHL	71	21	38	59	....	....	....	61	....	....	....	....	....	....	....	....	....	....	10	2	1	3	33	....	....	....
1987-88	Detroit Red Wings	NHL	50	10	9	19	9	6	15	37	1	0	2	82	12.2	28	6	26	0	–4	8	0	1	1	6	0	0	0
	Adirondack Red Wings	AHL	6	5	6	11	....	....	....	4	....	....	....	....	....	....	....	....	....	....	....	....	....	....	....	....	....	....

			REGULAR SEASON																		PLAYOFFS							
Season	**Club**	**League**	**GP**	**G**	**A**	**Pts**	**AG**	**AA**	**APts**	**PIM**	**PP**	**SH**	**GW**	**S**	**%**	**TGF**	**PGF**	**TGA**	**PGA**	**+/–**	**GP**	**G**	**A**	**Pts**	**PIM**	**PP**	**SH**	**GW**
1988-89	**Detroit Red Wings**	**NHL**	**26**	**1**	**7**	**8**	**1**	**5**	**6**	**28**	**0**	**0**	**0**	**29**	**3.4**	**14**	**5**	**16**	**0**	**–7**	....	....	....	....	....	....	....	....
	Adirondack Red Wings	AHL	47	31	35	66	....	....	....	66	....	....	....	....	....	....	....	....	....	....	16	6	11	17	17	....	....	....
1989-90	**Detroit Red Wings**	**NHL**	**9**	**3**	**1**	**4**	**3**	**1**	**4**	**4**	**0**	**0**	**1**	**16**	**18.8**	**8**	**1**	**3**	**0**	**+4**	....	....	....	....	....	....	....	....
	Edmonton Oilers	**NHL**	**62**	**7**	**18**	**25**	**6**	**13**	**19**	**56**	**2**	**0**	**0**	**101**	**6.9**	**43**	**4**	**38**	**0**	**+1**	**22**	**6**	**8**	**14**	**16**	**0**	**0**	**2**
1990-91	**Edmonton Oilers**	**NHL**	**80**	**27**	**35**	**62**	**25**	**27**	**52**	**35**	**4**	**1**	**4**	**141**	**19.1**	**82**	**21**	**69**	**10**	**+2**	**15**	**2**	**5**	**7**	**14**	**1**	**0**	**1**
1991-92	**Edmonton Oilers**	**NHL**	**80**	**35**	**47**	**82**	**32**	**35**	**67**	**52**	**10**	**2**	**2**	**193**	**18.1**	**122**	**36**	**86**	**17**	**+17**	**16**	**8**	**16**	**24**	**12**	**4**	**0**	**2**
1992-93	**Chicago Blackhawks**	**NHL**	**19**	**7**	**10**	**17**	**6**	**7**	**13**	**18**	**5**	**0**	**1**	**43**	**16.3**	**27**	**18**	**12**	**0**	**–3**	**4**	**0**	**0**	**0**	**8**	**0**	**0**	**0**
1993-94	**Chicago Blackhawks**	**NHL**	**81**	**31**	**39**	**70**	**29**	**30**	**59**	**111**	**7**	**4**	**4**	**222**	**14.0**	**100**	**42**	**69**	**12**	**+1**	**6**	**1**	**3**	**4**	**25**	**0**	**0**	**0**
1994-95	**Chicago Blackhawks**	**NHL**	**40**	**23**	**18**	**41**	**41**	**26**	**67**	**89**	**7**	**0**	**3**	**120**	**19.2**	**50**	**21**	**28**	**6**	**+7**	**16**	**9**	**3**	**12**	**29**	**3**	**0**	**3**
1995-96	**Chicago Blackhawks**	**NHL**	**70**	**22**	**29**	**51**	**22**	**24**	**46**	**86**	**8**	**0**	**3**	**212**	**10.4**	**72**	**26**	**52**	**3**	**–3**	**10**	**6**	**2**	**8**	**33**	**0**	**0**	**2**
1996-97	**St. Louis Blues**	**NHL**	**75**	**20**	**25**	**45**	**21**	**22**	**43**	**69**	**4**	**1**	**2**	**151**	**13.2**	**65**	**18**	**56**	**8**	**–1**	**6**	**1**	**1**	**2**	**10**	**1**	**0**	**0**
1997-98	**St. Louis Blues**	**NHL**	**27**	**4**	**9**	**13**	**5**	**9**	**14**	**22**	**2**	**0**	**0**	**52**	**7.7**	**25**	**8**	**9**	**0**	**+8**	....	....	....	....	....	....	....	....
	San Jose Sharks	**NHL**	**10**	**5**	**4**	**9**	**6**	**4**	**10**	**14**	**2**	**0**	**0**	**29**	**17.2**	**12**	**6**	**5**	**0**	**+1**	**6**	**1**	**1**	**2**	**20**	**1**	**0**	**0**
	NHL Totals		**634**	**195**	**252**	**447**	**206**	**210**	**416**	**623**	**52**	**8**	**22**	**1394**	**14.0**	**649**	**212**	**470**	**56**		**109**	**34**	**40**	**74**	**173**	**10**	**0**	**10**

Traded to **Edmonton** by **Detroit** with Petr Klima, Adam Graves and Jeff Sharples for Jimmy Carson, Kevin McClelland and Edmonton's 5th round choice (later traded to Montreal — Montreal selected Brad Layzell) in 1991 Entry Draft, November 2, 1989. Traded to **Chicago** by **Edmonton** for Igor Kravchuk and Dean McAmmond, February 24, 1993. Signed as a free agent by **St. Louis**, July 8, 1996. Traded to **San Jose** by **St. Louis** for Todd Gill, March 24, 1998.

• MURPHY, LARRY

Larry Murphy D – R. 6'2", 210 lbs. b: Scarborough, Ont., 3/8/1961. Los Angeles' 1st choice, 4th overall, in 1980 Entry Draft.

1978-79	Peterborough Petes	OHA	66	6	21	27	....	....	....	82	....	....	....	....	....	....	....	....	....	....	19	1	9	10	42	....	....	....
1979-80	Peterborough Petes	OHA	68	21	68	89	....	....	....	88	....	....	....	....	....	....	....	....	....	....	14	4	13	17	20	....	....	....
	Canada	WJC-A	5	1	0	1	....	....	....	4	....	....	....	....	....	....	....	....	....	....	....	....	....	....	....	....	....	....
1980-81	**Los Angeles Kings**	**NHL**	**80**	**16**	**60**	**76**	**13**	**42**	**55**	**79**	**5**	**1**	**1**	**153**	**10.5**	**161**	**63**	**115**	**34**	**+17**	**4**	**3**	**0**	**3**	**2**	**1**	**0**	**0**
1981-82	**Los Angeles Kings**	**NHL**	**79**	**22**	**44**	**66**	**17**	**29**	**46**	**95**	**8**	**1**	**2**	**191**	**11.5**	**134**	**43**	**133**	**29**	**–13**	**10**	**2**	**8**	**10**	**12**	**1**	**0**	**0**
1982-83	**Los Angeles Kings**	**NHL**	**77**	**14**	**48**	**62**	**11**	**33**	**44**	**81**	**9**	**0**	**2**	**172**	**8.1**	**133**	**51**	**108**	**28**	**+2**	....	....	....	....	....	....	....	....
1983-84	**Los Angeles Kings**	**NHL**	**6**	**0**	**3**	**3**	**0**	**2**	**2**	**0**	**0**	**0**	**0**	**11**	**0.0**	**9**	**4**	**11**	**2**	**–4**	....	....	....	....	....	....	....	....
	Washington Capitals	**NHL**	**72**	**13**	**33**	**46**	**10**	**22**	**32**	**50**	**2**	**0**	**2**	**138**	**9.4**	**115**	**41**	**75**	**13**	**+12**	**8**	**0**	**3**	**3**	**6**	**0**	**0**	**0**
1984-85	**Washington Capitals**	**NHL**	**79**	**13**	**42**	**55**	**11**	**28**	**39**	**51**	**3**	**0**	**0**	**153**	**8.5**	**125**	**43**	**79**	**18**	**+21**	**5**	**2**	**3**	**5**	**0**	**2**	**0**	**0**
	Canada	WEC-A	8	2	6	8	....	....	....	4	....	....	....	....	....	....	....	....	....	....	....	....	....	....	....	....	....	....
1985-86	**Washington Capitals**	**NHL**	**78**	**21**	**44**	**65**	**17**	**29**	**46**	**50**	**8**	**1**	**2**	**180**	**11.7**	**131**	**50**	**100**	**21**	**+2**	**9**	**1**	**5**	**6**	**6**	**1**	**0**	**0**
1986-87	**Washington Capitals**	**NHL**	**80**	**23**	**58**	**81**	**20**	**42**	**62**	**39**	**8**	**0**	**4**	**226**	**10.2**	**163**	**48**	**104**	**14**	**+25**	**7**	**2**	**2**	**4**	**6**	**0**	**0**	**1**
	Canada	WEC-A	6	0	3	3	....	....	....	4	....	....	....	....	....	....	....	....	....	....	....	....	....	....	....	....	....	....
1987-88	Canada	C Cup	8	1	6	7	....	....	....	4	....	....	....	....	....	....	....	....	....	....	....	....	....	....	....	....	....	....
	Washington Capitals	**NHL**	**79**	**8**	**53**	**61**	**7**	**38**	**45**	**72**	**7**	**0**	**1**	**201**	**4.0**	**132**	**58**	**89**	**17**	**+2**	**13**	**4**	**4**	**8**	**33**	**2**	**0**	**1**
1988-89	**Washington Capitals**	**NHL**	**65**	**7**	**29**	**36**	**6**	**20**	**26**	**70**	**3**	**0**	**0**	**129**	**5.4**	**95**	**39**	**67**	**6**	**–5**	....	....	....	....	....	....	....	....
	Minnesota North Stars	**NHL**	**13**	**4**	**6**	**10**	**3**	**4**	**7**	**12**	**3**	**0**	**1**	**31**	**12.9**	**20**	**11**	**5**	**1**	**+5**	**5**	**0**	**2**	**2**	**8**	**0**	**0**	**0**
1989-90	**Minnesota North Stars**	**NHL**	**77**	**10**	**58**	**68**	**9**	**41**	**50**	**44**	**4**	**0**	**1**	**173**	**5.8**	**141**	**66**	**89**	**1**	**–13**	**7**	**1**	**2**	**3**	**31**	**0**	**0**	**1**
1990-91	Minnesota North Stars	FrTour	3	0	0	0	....	....	....	0	....	....	....	....	....	....	....	....	....	....	....	....	....	....	....	....	....	....
	Pittsburgh Penguins	**NHL**	**44**	**5**	**23**	**28**	**5**	**17**	**22**	**30**	**2**	**0**	**0**	**85**	**5.9**	**86**	**36**	**53**	**5**	**+2**	**23**	**5**	**18**	**23**	**44**	**4**	**0**	**0**
	Minnesota North Stars	**NHL**	**31**	**4**	**11**	**15**	**4**	**8**	**12**	**38**	**1**	**0**	**2**	**103**	**3.9**	**39**	**17**	**39**	**9**	**–8**	....	....	....	....	....	....	....	....
1991-92	Canada	C Cup	8	0	1	1	....	....	....	0	....	....	....	....	....	....	....	....	....	....	....	....	....	....	....	....	....	....
	Pittsburgh Penguins	**NHL**	**77**	**21**	**56**	**77**	**19**	**42**	**61**	**48**	**7**	**2**	**3**	**206**	**10.2**	**180**	**67**	**110**	**30**	**+33**	**21**	**6**	**10**	**16**	**19**	**3**	**0**	**1**
1992-93	**Pittsburgh Penguins**	**NHL**	**83**	**22**	**63**	**85**	**18**	**43**	**61**	**73**	**6**	**2**	**2**	**230**	**9.6**	**225**	**82**	**137**	**39**	**+45**	**12**	**2**	**11**	**13**	**10**	**2**	**0**	**1**
1993-94	**Pittsburgh Penguins**	**NHL**	**84**	**17**	**56**	**73**	**16**	**43**	**59**	**44**	**7**	**0**	**4**	**236**	**7.2**	**165**	**65**	**122**	**32**	**+10**	**6**	**0**	**5**	**5**	**0**	**0**	**0**	**0**
1994-95	**Pittsburgh Penguins**	**NHL**	**48**	**13**	**25**	**38**	**23**	**37**	**60**	**18**	**4**	**0**	**3**	**124**	**10.5**	**97**	**33**	**71**	**19**	**+12**	**12**	**2**	**13**	**15**	**0**	**1**	**0**	**0**
1995-96	**Toronto Maple Leafs**	**NHL**	**82**	**12**	**49**	**61**	**12**	**40**	**52**	**34**	**8**	**0**	**1**	**182**	**6.6**	**129**	**67**	**75**	**11**	**–2**	**6**	**0**	**2**	**2**	**4**	**0**	**0**	**0**
1996-97	**Toronto Maple Leafs**	**NHL**	**69**	**7**	**32**	**39**	**7**	**28**	**35**	**20**	**4**	**0**	**0**	**137**	**5.1**	**99**	**37**	**77**	**16**	**+1**	....	....	....	....	....	....	....	....
	Detroit Red Wings	**NHL**	**12**	**2**	**4**	**6**	**2**	**4**	**6**	**0**	**1**	**0**	**1**	**21**	**9.5**	**12**	**3**	**8**	**1**	**+2**	**20**	**2**	**9**	**11**	**8**	**1**	**0**	**1**
1997-98	**Detroit Red Wings**	**NHL**	**82**	**11**	**41**	**52**	**13**	**40**	**53**	**37**	**2**	**1**	**2**	**129**	**8.5**	**121**	**37**	**73**	**24**	**+35**	**22**	**3**	**12**	**15**	**2**	**1**	**2**	**1**
	NHL Totals		**1397**	**265**	**838**	**1103**	**243**	**632**	**875**	**985**	**102**	**8**	**34**	**3211**	**8.3**	**2512**	**961**	**1740**	**370**		**190**	**35**	**109**	**144**	**191**	**19**	**2**	**7**

OHA First All-Star Team (1980) • NHL Second All-Star Team (1987, 1993, 1995)

Played in NHL All-Star Game (1994, 1996)

Traded to **Washington** by **LA Kings** for Ken Houston and Brian Engblom, October 18, 1983. Traded to **Minnesota** by **Washington** with Mike Gartner for Dino Ciccarelli and Bob Rouse, March 7, 1989. Traded to **Pittsburgh** by **Minnesota** with Peter Taglianetti for Chris Dahlquist and Jim Johnson, December 11, 1990. Traded to **Toronto** by **Pittsburgh** for Dmitri Mironov and Toronto's 2nd round choice (later traded to New Jersey — New Jersey selected Joshua Dewolf) in 1996 Entry Draft, July 8, 1995. Traded to **Detroit** by **Toronto** for future considerations, March 18, 1997.

• MURPHY, MIKE

Mike "Murph" Murphy RW – R. 6', 190 lbs. b: Toronto, Ont., 9/12/1950. NY Rangers' 2nd choice, 25th overall, in 1970 Amateur Draft.

1967-68	York Steel	Jr. B	30	19	19	38	....	....	....	....	....	....	....	....	....	....	....	....	....	....	....	....	....	....	....	....	....	....
1968-69	Toronto Marlboros	OHA	44	16	23	39	....	....	....	53	....	....	....	....	....	....	....	....	....	....	6	1	4	5	6	....	....	....
1969-70	Toronto Marlboros	OHA	54	23	27	50	....	....	....	68	....	....	....	....	....	....	....	....	....	....	....	....	....	....	....	....	....	....
1970-71	Omaha Knights	CHL	59	24	47	71	....	....	....	37	....	....	....	....	....	....	....	....	....	....	11	4	8	12	17	....	....	....
1971-72	**St. Louis Blues**	**NHL**	**63**	**20**	**23**	**43**	**21**	**21**	**42**	**19**	**5**	**0**	**3**	**176**	**11.4**	**74**	**20**	**59**	**1**	**–4**	**11**	**2**	**3**	**5**	**6**	**1**	**0**	**0**
	Omaha Knights	CHL	8	1	4	5	....	....	....	12	....	....	....	....	....	....	....	....	....	....	....	....	....	....	....	....	....	....
1972-73	**St. Louis Blues**	**NHL**	**64**	**18**	**27**	**45**	**18**	**23**	**41**	**48**	**3**	**0**	**3**	**182**	**9.9**	**72**	**12**	**48**	**1**	**+13**	....	....	....	....	....	....	....	....
	New York Rangers	**NHL**	**15**	**4**	**4**	**8**	**4**	**3**	**7**	**5**	**0**	**0**	**1**	**35**	**11.4**	**9**	**0**	**15**	**1**	**–5**	**10**	**0**	**0**	**0**	**0**	**0**	**0**	**0**
1973-74	**New York Rangers**	**NHL**	**16**	**2**	**1**	**3**	**2**	**1**	**3**	**0**	**0**	**0**	**0**	**28**	**7.1**	**7**	**1**	**8**	**0**	**–2**	....	....	....	....	....	....	....	....
	Los Angeles Kings	**NHL**	**53**	**13**	**16**	**29**	**13**	**14**	**27**	**38**	**1**	**0**	**2**	**142**	**9.2**	**45**	**9**	**39**	**5**	**+2**	**5**	**0**	**4**	**4**	**0**	**0**	**0**	**0**
1974-75	**Los Angeles Kings**	**NHL**	**78**	**30**	**38**	**68**	**28**	**30**	**58**	**44**	**3**	**3**	**6**	**175**	**17.1**	**98**	**23**	**57**	**14**	**+32**	**3**	**3**	**0**	**3**	**4**	**2**	**0**	**1**
1975-76	**Los Angeles Kings**	**NHL**	**80**	**26**	**42**	**68**	**24**	**33**	**57**	**61**	**7**	**1**	**5**	**205**	**12.7**	**99**	**28**	**90**	**16**	**–3**	**9**	**1**	**4**	**5**	**6**	**1**	**0**	**0**
1976-77	**Los Angeles Kings**	**NHL**	**76**	**25**	**36**	**61**	**24**	**29**	**53**	**58**	**9**	**3**	**3**	**165**	**15.2**	**121**	**51**	**82**	**27**	**+15**	**9**	**4**	**9**	**13**	**4**	**1**	**0**	**0**
1977-78	**Los Angeles Kings**	**NHL**	**72**	**20**	**36**	**56**	**19**	**29**	**48**	**48**	**7**	**0**	**6**	**207**	**9.7**	**83**	**28**	**79**	**23**	**–1**	**2**	**0**	**0**	**0**	**0**	**0**	**0**	**0**
	Canada	WEC-A	10	1	4	5	....	....	....	16	....	....	....	....	....	....	....	....	....	....	....	....	....	....	....	....	....	....
1978-79	**Los Angeles Kings**	**NHL**	**64**	**16**	**29**	**45**	**15**	**22**	**37**	**38**	**4**	**1**	**2**	**150**	**10.7**	**74**	**20**	**93**	**27**	**–12**	**2**	**0**	**1**	**1**	**0**	**0**	**0**	**0**
1979-80	**Los Angeles Kings**	**NHL**	**80**	**27**	**22**	**49**	**24**	**17**	**41**	**29**	**7**	**3**	**1**	**176**	**15.3**	**83**	**24**	**131**	**60**	**–12**	**4**	**1**	**0**	**1**	**2**	**0**	**1**	**0**
1980-81	**Los Angeles Kings**	**NHL**	**68**	**16**	**23**	**39**	**13**	**16**	**29**	**54**	**2**	**1**	**1**	**131**	**12.2**	**51**	**7**	**88**	**37**	**–7**	**1**	**0**	**1**	**1**	**0**	**0**	**0**	**0**
1981-82	**Los Angeles Kings**	**NHL**	**28**	**5**	**10**	**15**	**4**	**7**	**11**	**20**	**0**	**2**	**0**	**36**	**13.9**	**21**	**1**	**30**	**10**	**0**	**10**	**2**	**1**	**3**	**32**	**0**	**0**	**0**
1982-83	**Los Angeles Kings**	**NHL**	**74**	**16**	**11**	**27**	**13**	**8**	**21**	**52**	**0**	**5**	**2**	**135**	**11.9**	**42**	**3**	**79**	**29**	**–11**	....	....	....	....	....	....	....	....
	NHL Totals		**831**	**238**	**318**	**556**	**222**	**253**	**475**	**514**	**48**	**19**	**35**	**1943**	**12.2**	**879**	**227**	**898**	**251**		**66**	**13**	**23**	**36**	**54**	**5**	**1**	**1**

CHL Second All-Star Team (1971) • Won Ken McKenzie Trophy (CHL's Rookie of the Year) (1971)

Played in NHL All-Star Game (1980)

Traded to **St. Louis** by **NY Rangers** with Jack Egars and Andre Dupont for Gene Carr, Jim Lorentz and Wayne Connelly, November 15, 1971. Traded to **NY Rangers** by **St. Louis** for Ab DeMarco, March 2, 1973. Traded to **LA Kings** by **NY Rangers** with Sheldon Kannegiesser and Tom Williams for Gilles Marcotte and Real Lemieux, November 30, 1973.

• MURPHY, ROB

Rob Murphy C – L. 6'3", 205 lbs. b: Hull, Que., 4/7/1969. Vancouver's 1st choice, 24th overall, in 1987 Entry Draft.

1985-86	Outaouais Midgets	Midget	41	17	33	50	....	....	....	47	....	....	....	....	....	....	....	....	....	....	....	....	....	....	....	....	....	....
1986-87	Laval Titan	QMJHL	70	35	54	89	....	....	....	86	....	....	....	....	....	....	....	....	....	....	14	3	4	7	15	....	....	....
1987-88	Laval Titan	QMJHL	26	11	25	36	....	....	....	82	....	....	....	....	....	....	....	....	....	....	....	....	....	....	....	....	....	....
	Drummondville Voltigeurs	QMJHL	33	16	28	44	....	....	....	41	....	....	....	....	....	....	....	....	....	....	17	4	15	19	45	....	....	....
	Vancouver Canucks	**NHL**	**5**	**0**	**0**	**0**	**0**	**0**	**0**	**2**	**0**	**0**	**0**	**4**	**0.0**	**1**	**0**	**2**	**0**	**–1**	....	....	....	....	....	....	....	....
1988-89	Drummondville Voltigeurs	QMJHL	26	13	25	38	....	....	....	16	....	....	....	....	....	....	....	....	....	....	4	1	3	4	20	....	....	....
	Canada	WJC-A	7	1	0	1	....	....	....	8	....	....	....	....	....	....	....	....	....	....	....	....	....	....	....	....	....	....
	Vancouver Canucks	**NHL**	**8**	**0**	**1**	**1**	**0**	**1**	**1**	**2**	**0**	**0**	**0**	**10**	**0.0**	**3**	**0**	**4**	**0**	**–1**	....	....	....	....	....	....	....	....
	Milwaukee Admirals	IHL	8	4	2	6	....	....	....	4	....	....	....	....	....	....	....	....	....	....	11	3	5	8	34	....	....	....
1989-90	**Vancouver Canucks**	**NHL**	**12**	**1**	**1**	**2**	**1**	**1**	**2**	**0**	**0**	**0**	**1**	**6**	**16.7**	**6**	**0**	**19**	**0**	**–13**	....	....	....	....	....	....	....	....
	Milwaukee Admirals	IHL	64	24	47	71	....	....	....	87	....	....	....	....	....	....	....	....	....	....	6	2	6	8	12	....	....	....
1990-91	**Vancouver Canucks**	**NHL**	**42**	**5**	**1**	**6**	**5**	**1**	**6**	**90**	**0**	**0**	**0**	**19**	**26.3**	**7**	**0**	**19**	**1**	**–11**	**4**	**0**	**0**	**0**	**2**	**0**	**0**	**0**
	Milwaukee Admirals	IHL	23	1	7	8	....	....	....	48	....	....	....	....	....	....	....	....	....	....	....	....	....	....	....	....	....	....
1991-92	**Vancouver Canucks**	**NHL**	**6**	**0**	**1**	**1**	**0**	**1**	**1**	**6**	**0**	**0**	**0**	**2**	**0.0**	**1**	**0**	**3**	**0**	**–2**	....	....	....	....	....	....	....	....
	Milwaukee Admirals	IHL	73	26	38	64	....	....	....	141	....	....	....	....	....	....	....	....	....	....	5	0	3	3	2	....	....	....

			REGULAR SEASON																		PLAYOFFS							
Season	Club	League	GP	G	A	Pts	AG	AA	APts	PIM	PP	SH	GW	S	%	TGF	PGF	TGA	PGA	+/–	GP	G	A	Pts	PIM	PP	SH	GW
1992-93	**Ottawa Senators**	**NHL**	**44**	**3**	**7**	**10**	**2**	**5**	**7**	**30**	**0**	**0**	**0**	**55**	**5.5**	**13**	**0**	**36**	**0**	**–23**								
	New Haven Nighthawks	AHL	26	8	12	20				28																		
1993-94	**Los Angeles Kings**	**NHL**	**8**	**0**	**1**	**1**	**0**	**1**	**1**	**22**	**0**	**0**	**0**	**4**	**0.0**	**2**	**0**	**5**	**0**	**–3**								
	Phoenix Roadrunners	IHL	72	23	34	57				101																		
1994-95	Phoenix Roadrunners	IHL	2	0	0	0				10											2	0	1	1	0			
1995-96	Fort Wayne Komets	IHL	82	24	52	76				107											5	1	2	3	8			
1996-97	Fort Wayne Komets	IHL	35	9	16	25				40																		
1997-98	Star Bulls Rosenheim	Germany	44	9	24	33				68																		
	NHL Totals		**125**	**9**	**12**	**21**	**8**	**10**	**18**	**152**	**0**	**0**	**1**	**100**	**9.0**	**33**	**0**	**88**	**1**		**4**	**0**	**0**	**0**	**2**	**0**	**0**	**0**

Won Garry F. Longman Memorial Trophy (Top Rookie - IHL) (1990)

Claimed by **Ottawa** from **Vancouver** in Expansion Draft, June 18, 1992. Signed as a free agent by **LA Kings**, August 2, 1993.

• MURPHY, RON

Ron Murphy LW – L. 5'11", 185 lbs. b: Hamilton, Ont., 4/10/1933.

Season	Club	League	GP	G	A	Pts	AG	AA	APts	PIM	PP	SH	GW	S	%	TGF	PGF	TGA	PGA	+/–	GP	G	A	Pts	PIM	PP	SH	GW
1949-50	Guelph Biltmores	OHA	1	0	0	0				2																		
1950-51	Guelph Biltmores	OHA	54	44	44	88				38											4	2	1	3	2			
1951-52	Guelph Biltmores	OHA	51	58	58	116				36											22	*21	22	43	6			
	Cincinnati Mohawks	AHL	1	0	0	0				0																		
1952-53	Guelph Biltmores	OHA	45	39	42	81				52																		
	New York Rangers	**NHL**	**15**	**3**	**1**	**4**	**5**	**1**	**6**	**0**																		
1953-54	**New York Rangers**	**NHL**	**27**	**1**	**3**	**4**	**2**	**4**	**6**	**20**																		
	Saskatoon Quakers	WHL	24	7	5	12				2											6	1	2	3	2			
1954-55	**New York Rangers**	**NHL**	**66**	**14**	**16**	**30**	**20**	**20**	**40**	**36**																		
1955-56	**New York Rangers**	**NHL**	**66**	**16**	**28**	**44**	**23**	**35**	**58**	**71**											**5**	**0**	**1**	**1**	**2**			
1956-57	**New York Rangers**	**NHL**	**33**	**7**	**12**	**19**	**9**	**14**	**23**	**14**											**5**	**0**	**0**	**0**	**0**			
	Providence Reds	AHL	21	12	11	23				14																		
1957-58	**Chicago Black Hawks**	**NHL**	**69**	**11**	**17**	**28**	**14**	**18**	**32**	**32**																		
1958-59	**Chicago Black Hawks**	**NHL**	**59**	**17**	**30**	**47**	**22**	**32**	**54**	**52**																		
1959-60	**Chicago Black Hawks**	**NHL**	**63**	**15**	**21**	**36**	**19**	**21**	**40**	**18**											**4**	**1**	**0**	**1**	**0**			
1960-61	**Chicago Black Hawks**	**NHL**	**70**	**21**	**19**	**40**	**26**	**19**	**45**	**30**											**12**	**2**	**1**	**3**	**0**			
1961-62	**Chicago Black Hawks**	**NHL**	**60**	**12**	**16**	**28**	**15**	**16**	**31**	**41**																		
1962-63	**Chicago Black Hawks**	**NHL**	**68**	**18**	**16**	**34**	**22**	**17**	**39**	**28**											**1**	**0**	**0**	**0**	**0**			
1963-64	**Chicago Black Hawks**	**NHL**	**70**	**11**	**8**	**19**	**14**	**9**	**23**	**32**											**7**	**0**	**1**	**1**	**8**			
1964-65	**Detroit Red Wings**	**NHL**	**58**	**20**	**19**	**39**	**26**	**20**	**46**	**32**											**5**	**0**	**1**	**1**	**4**			
1965-66	**Detroit Red Wings**	**NHL**	**32**	**10**	**7**	**17**	**12**	**7**	**19**	**10**																		
	Boston Bruins	**NHL**	**2**	**0**	**1**	**1**	**0**	**1**	**1**	**0**																		
1966-67	**Boston Bruins**	**NHL**	**39**	**11**	**16**	**27**	**13**	**16**	**29**	**6**																		
1967-68	**Boston Bruins**	**NHL**	**12**	**0**	**1**	**1**	**0**	**1**	**1**	**4**	**0**	**0**	**0**	**17**	**0.0**	**2**	**1**	**3**	**0**	**–2**	**4**	**0**	**0**	**0**	**0**	**0**	**0**	**0**
	Oklahoma City Blazers	CHL	6	2	2	4				2																		
1968-69	**Boston Bruins**	**NHL**	**60**	**16**	**38**	**54**	**18**	**36**	**54**	**26**	**5**	**0**	**0**	**113**	**14.2**	**76**	**15**	**38**	**0**	**+23**	**10**	**4**	**4**	**8**	**12**	**0**	**0**	**0**
1969-70	**Boston Bruins**	**NHL**	**20**	**2**	**5**	**7**	**2**	**5**	**7**	**8**	**0**	**0**	**2**	**35**	**5.7**	**11**	**1**	**12**	**3**	**+1**								
	NHL Totals		**889**	**205**	**274**	**479**	**262**	**292**	**554**	**460**	**5**	**0**	**2**	**165**	**124.2**	**89**	**17**	**53**	**3**		**53**	**7**	**8**	**15**	**26**	**0**	**0**	**0**

Played in NHL All-Star Game (1961)

Traded to **Chicago** by **NY Rangers** for Hank Ciesla, June, 1957. Traded to **Detroit** by **Chicago** with Aut Erickson for Art Stratton, John Mizuk and Ian Cushenan, June 9, 1964. Traded to **Boston** by **Detroit** for Dean Prentice, February 18, 1966.

• MURRAY, BOB

Bob (Robert F.) Murray D. 5'10", 183 lbs. b: Kingston, Ont., 11/26/1954. Chicago's 3rd choice, 52nd overall, in 1974 Amateur Draft.

Season	Club	League	GP	G	A	Pts	AG	AA	APts	PIM	PP	SH	GW	S	%	TGF	PGF	TGA	PGA	+/–	GP	G	A	Pts	PIM	PP	SH	GW
1971-72	Cornwall Royals	QMJHL	62	14	49	63				88											16	2	6	8	18			
1972-73	Cornwall Royals	QMJHL	32	9	26	35				34											12	1	21	22	43			
1973-74	Cornwall Royals	QMJHL	63	23	76	99				88											5	0	6	6	6			
1974-75	Dallas Black Hawks	CHL	75	14	43	57				130											10	2	6	8	13			
1975-76	**Chicago Black Hawks**	**NHL**	**64**	**1**	**2**	**3**	**1**	**2**	**3**	**44**	**0**	**0**	**0**	**61**	**1.6**	**34**	**2**	**41**	**3**	**–6**								
1976-77	**Chicago Black Hawks**	**NHL**	**77**	**10**	**11**	**21**	**10**	**9**	**19**	**71**	**0**	**0**	**0**	**84**	**11.9**	**70**	**9**	**87**	**19**	**–7**	**2**	**0**	**1**	**1**	**2**	**0**	**0**	**0**
1977-78	**Chicago Black Hawks**	**NHL**	**70**	**14**	**17**	**31**	**13**	**14**	**27**	**41**	**2**	**0**	**3**	**124**	**11.3**	**87**	**9**	**81**	**14**	**+11**	**4**	**1**	**4**	**5**	**2**	**0**	**0**	**0**
1978-79	**Chicago Black Hawks**	**NHL**	**70**	**19**	**32**	**51**	**17**	**24**	**41**	**38**	**4**	**1**	**0**	**220**	**8.6**	**125**	**23**	**134**	**36**	**+4**	**4**	**1**	**0**	**1**	**6**	**0**	**0**	**0**
1979-80	**Chicago Black Hawks**	**NHL**	**74**	**16**	**34**	**50**	**14**	**26**	**40**	**60**	**8**	**0**	**1**	**224**	**7.1**	**116**	**56**	**96**	**20**	**–16**	**7**	**2**	**4**	**6**	**6**	**0**	**0**	**0**
1980-81	**Chicago Black Hawks**	**NHL**	**77**	**13**	**47**	**60**	**11**	**33**	**44**	**93**	**6**	**0**	**1**	**206**	**6.3**	**128**	**46**	**114**	**38**	**+6**	**3**	**0**	**0**	**0**	**2**	**0**	**0**	**0**
1981-82	**Chicago Black Hawks**	**NHL**	**45**	**8**	**22**	**30**	**6**	**15**	**21**	**48**	**3**	**1**	**0**	**109**	**7.3**	**76**	**26**	**76**	**27**	**+1**	**15**	**1**	**6**	**7**	**16**	**0**	**0**	**0**
1982-83	**Chicago Black Hawks**	**NHL**	**79**	**7**	**32**	**39**	**6**	**22**	**28**	**73**	**5**	**0**	**1**	**186**	**3.8**	**128**	**37**	**98**	**31**	**+24**	**13**	**2**	**3**	**5**	**10**	**1**	**0**	**0**
1983-84	**Chicago Black Hawks**	**NHL**	**78**	**11**	**37**	**48**	**9**	**25**	**34**	**78**	**3**	**1**	**1**	**190**	**5.8**	**134**	**45**	**129**	**41**	**+1**	**5**	**3**	**1**	**4**	**6**	**1**	**0**	**0**
1984-85	**Chicago Black Hawks**	**NHL**	**80**	**5**	**38**	**43**	**4**	**26**	**30**	**56**	**4**	**0**	**1**	**156**	**3.2**	**132**	**35**	**119**	**35**	**+13**	**15**	**3**	**6**	**9**	**20**	**1**	**0**	**0**
1985-86	**Chicago Black Hawks**	**NHL**	**80**	**9**	**29**	**38**	**7**	**19**	**26**	**75**	**3**	**0**	**1**	**139**	**6.5**	**131**	**42**	**116**	**33**	**+6**	**3**	**0**	**2**	**2**	**0**	**0**	**0**	**0**
1986-87	**Chicago Blackhawks**	**NHL**	**79**	**6**	**38**	**44**	**5**	**28**	**33**	**80**	**4**	**0**	**1**	**177**	**3.4**	**110**	**41**	**113**	**35**	**–9**	**4**	**1**	**0**	**1**	**4**	**0**	**0**	**0**
1987-88	**Chicago Blackhawks**	**NHL**	**62**	**6**	**20**	**26**	**5**	**14**	**19**	**44**	**1**	**0**	**0**	**97**	**6.2**	**72**	**29**	**71**	**21**	**–7**	**5**	**1**	**3**	**4**	**2**	**1**	**0**	**0**
1988-89	**Chicago Blackhawks**	**NHL**	**15**	**2**	**4**	**6**	**2**	**3**	**5**	**27**	**2**	**0**	**0**	**19**	**10.5**	**11**	**7**	**9**	**1**	**–4**	**16**	**2**	**3**	**5**	**22**	**1**	**0**	**0**
	Saginaw Hawks	IHL	18	3	7	10				14																		
1989-90	**Chicago Blackhawks**	**NHL**	**49**	**5**	**19**	**24**	**4**	**14**	**18**	**45**	**3**	**0**	**1**	**84**	**6.0**	**76**	**37**	**50**	**14**	**+3**	**16**	**2**	**4**	**6**	**8**	**0**	**0**	**0**
	NHL Totals		**1008**	**132**	**382**	**514**	**114**	**274**	**388**	**873**	**48**	**3**	**11**	**2076**	**6.4**	**1430**	**444**	**1334**	**368**		**112**	**19**	**37**	**56**	**106**	**5**	**0**	**0**

QMJHL First All-Star Team (1974)

Played in NHL All-Star Game (1981, 1983)

• MURRAY, BOB

Bob (Robert J.) Murray D – R. 6'1", 195 lbs. b: Peterborough, Ont., 7/16/1948.

Season	Club	League	GP	G	A	Pts	AG	AA	APts	PIM	PP	SH	GW	S	%	TGF	PGF	TGA	PGA	+/–	GP	G	A	Pts	PIM	PP	SH	GW
1966-67	Peterborough Petes	OHA	48	3	9	12				32											6	0	0	0	0			
1967-68	Michigan Tech Huskies	WCHA	DID NOT PLAY – FRESHMAN																									
1968-69	Michigan Tech Huskies	WCHA	31	2	13	15				43																		
1969-70	Michigan Tech Huskies	WCHA	32	3	12	15				61																		
1970-71	Michigan Tech Huskies	WCHA	32	6	19	25				67																		
1971-72	Nova Scotia Voyageurs	AHL	73	1	12	13				62											15	3	0	3	10			
1972-73	Nova Scotia Voyageurs	AHL	60	4	22	26				61											13	1	5	6	29			
1973-74	**Atlanta Flames**	**NHL**	**62**	**0**	**3**	**3**	**0**	**3**	**3**	**34**	**0**	**0**	**0**	**67**	**0.0**	**31**	**1**	**57**	**7**	**–20**	**4**	**1**	**0**	**1**	**2**	**0**	**0**	**0**
1974-75	**Atlanta Flames**	**NHL**	**42**	**3**	**3**	**6**	**3**	**2**	**5**	**22**	**0**	**0**	**1**	**34**	**8.8**	**24**	**0**	**28**	**9**	**+5**								
	Vancouver Canucks	**NHL**	**13**	**1**	**5**	**6**	**1**	**4**	**5**	**8**	**0**	**0**	**0**	**13**	**7.7**	**13**	**0**	**9**	**2**	**+6**	**5**	**0**	**1**	**1**	**13**	**0**	**0**	**0**
1975-76	**Vancouver Canucks**	**NHL**	**65**	**2**	**5**	**7**	**2**	**4**	**6**	**28**	**0**	**1**	**0**	**48**	**4.2**	**30**	**0**	**45**	**18**	**+3**	**1**	**0**	**0**	**0**	**0**	**0**	**0**	**0**
1976-77	**Vancouver Canucks**	**NHL**	**12**	**0**	**0**	**0**	**0**	**0**	**0**	**6**	**0**	**0**	**0**	**10**	**0.0**	**2**	**0**	**4**	**1**	**–1**								
	Tulsa Oilers	CHL	58	5	16	21				49											9	1	0	1	14			
1977-78	SC Riessersee	Germany	43	10	28	38				39																		
1978-79	SC Riessersee	Germany	33	10	29	39				26																		
1979-80	SC Riessersee	Germany	41	10	16	26				48																		
1980-81	Frieburg	German 2	STATISTICS NOT AVAILABLE																									
1981-82	Mannheimer ERC	Germany	31	8	14	22				44																		
1982-83	Dusseldorfer EG	Germany	24	1	3	4				20																		
	SC Riessersee	Germany	11	2	1	3				14																		
1983-84	SC Riessersee	Germany	46	7	15	22				35																		
1984-85	Bad Nauheim	Germany	35	5	29	34				40																		
1985-86	Bad Nauheim	German 2	STATISTICS NOT AVAILABLE																									
1986-87	Bad Nauheim	German 2	STATISTICS NOT AVAILABLE																									
1987-88	EV Landshut	Germany	23	0	1	1				2																		
	NHL Totals		**194**	**6**	**16**	**22**	**6**	**13**	**19**	**98**	**0**	**1**	**1**	**172**	**3.5**	**100**	**1**	**143**	**37**		**10**	**1**	**1**	**2**	**15**	**0**	**0**	**0**

WCHA First All-Star Team (1971) • NCAA West First All-American Team (1971) • AHL First All-Star Team (1973)

Signed as a territoral exemption by **Montreal** from **Peterborough** (OHA), September, 1971. Traded to **Atlanta** by **Montreal** for Atlanta's 3rd round choice (Pierre Lagace) in 1977 Amateur Draft, May 29, 1973. Traded to **Vancouver** by **Atlanta** for Gerry Meehan, March 9, 1975.

• MURRAY, CHRIS

Chris Murray RW – R. 6'2", 209 lbs. b: Port Hardy, B.C., 10/25/1974. Montreal's 3rd choice, 54th overall, in 1994 Entry Draft.

Season	Club	League	GP	G	A	Pts	AG	AA	APts	PIM	PP	SH	GW	S	%	TGF	PGF	TGA	PGA	+/–	Playoffs GP	G	A	Pts	PIM	PP	SH	GW
1991-92	Kamloops Blazers	WHL	33	1	1	2				218											5	0	0	0	10			
1992-93	Kamloops Blazers	WHL	62	6	10	16				217											13	0	4	4	34			
1993-94	Kamloops Blazers	WHL	59	14	16	30				260											15	4	2	6	*107			
1994-95	**Montreal Canadiens**	**NHL**	**3**	**0**	**0**	**0**	**0**	**0**	**0**	**4**	**0**	**0**	**0**	**0**	**0.0**	**0**	**0**	**0**	**0**	**0**								
	Fredericton Canadiens	AHL	55	6	12	18				234											12	1	1	2	50			
1995-96	**Montreal Canadiens**	**NHL**	**48**	**3**	**4**	**7**	**3**	**3**	**6**	**163**	**0**	**0**	**1**	**32**	**9.4**	**13**	**0**	**9**	**1**	**+5**	**4**	**0**	**0**	**0**	**4**	**0**	**0**	**0**
	Fredericton Canadiens	AHL	30	13	13	26				217																		
1996-97	**Montreal Canadiens**	**NHL**	**56**	**4**	**2**	**6**	**4**	**2**	**6**	**114**	**0**	**0**	**0**	**32**	**12.5**	**8**	**0**	**16**	**0**	**–8**								
	Hartford Whalers	**NHL**	**8**	**1**	**1**	**2**	**1**	**1**	**2**	**10**	**0**	**0**	**0**	**9**	**11.1**	**3**	**0**	**2**	**0**	**+1**								
1997-98	**Carolina Hurricanes**	**NHL**	**7**	**0**	**1**	**1**	**0**	**1**	**1**	**22**	**0**	**0**	**0**	**3**	**0.0**	**2**	**0**	**0**	**0**	**+2**								
	Ottawa Senators	**NHL**	**46**	**5**	**3**	**8**	**6**	**3**	**9**	**96**	**0**	**0**	**2**	**48**	**10.4**	**12**	**0**	**11**	**0**	**+1**	**11**	**1**	**0**	**1**	**8**	**0**	**0**	**0**
	NHL Totals		**168**	**13**	**11**	**24**	**14**	**10**	**24**	**409**	**0**	**0**	**3**	**124**	**10.5**	**38**	**0**	**38**	**1**		**15**	**1**	**0**	**1**	**12**	**0**	**0**	**0**

Traded to **Phoenix** by **Montreal** with Murray Baron for Dave Manson, March 18, 1997. Traded to **Hartford** by **Phoenix** for Gerald Diduck, March 18, 1997. Transferred to **Carolina** after **Hartford** franchise relocated, June 25, 1997. Traded to **Ottawa** by **Carolina** for Sean Hill, November 18, 1997.

• MURRAY, GLEN

Glen "Muzz" Murray RW – R. 6'2", 220 lbs. b: Halifax, N.S., 11/1/1972. Boston's 1st choice, 18th overall, in 1991 Entry Draft.

Season	Club	League	GP	G	A	Pts	AG	AA	APts	PIM	PP	SH	GW	S	%	TGF	PGF	TGA	PGA	+/–	Playoffs GP	G	A	Pts	PIM	PP	SH	GW
1989-90	Sudbury Wolves	OHL	62	8	28	36				17											7	0	0	0	4			
1990-91	Sudbury Wolves	OHL	66	27	38	65				82											5	8	4	12	10			
1991-92	Sudbury Wolves	OHL	54	37	47	84				93											11	7	4	11	18			
	Boston Bruins	**NHL**	**5**	**3**	**1**	**4**	**3**	**1**	**4**	**0**	**1**	**0**	**0**	**20**	**15.0**	**8**	**3**	**3**	**0**	**+2**	**15**	**4**	**2**	**6**	**10**	**1**	**0**	**0**
1992-93	**Boston Bruins**	**NHL**	**27**	**3**	**4**	**7**	**2**	**3**	**5**	**8**	**2**	**0**	**1**	**28**	**10.7**	**13**	**3**	**16**	**0**	**–6**								
	Providence Bruins	AHL	48	30	26	56				42											6	1	4	5	4			
1993-94	**Boston Bruins**	**NHL**	**81**	**18**	**13**	**31**	**17**	**10**	**27**	**48**	**0**	**0**	**4**	**114**	**15.8**	**42**	**1**	**43**	**1**	**–1**	**13**	**4**	**5**	**9**	**14**	**0**	**0**	**0**
1994-95	**Boston Bruins**	**NHL**	**35**	**5**	**2**	**7**	**9**	**3**	**12**	**46**	**0**	**0**	**2**	**64**	**7.8**	**18**	**1**	**28**	**0**	**–11**	**2**	**0**	**0**	**0**	**2**	**0**	**0**	**0**
1995-96	**Pittsburgh Penguins**	**NHL**	**69**	**14**	**15**	**29**	**14**	**12**	**26**	**57**	**0**	**0**	**2**	**100**	**14.0**	**40**	**0**	**37**	**1**	**+4**	**18**	**2**	**6**	**8**	**10**	**0**	**0**	**1**
1996-97	**Pittsburgh Penguins**	**NHL**	**66**	**11**	**11**	**22**	**12**	**10**	**22**	**24**	**3**	**0**	**1**	**127**	**8.7**	**33**	**5**	**47**	**0**	**–19**								
	Los Angeles Kings	**NHL**	**11**	**5**	**3**	**8**	**5**	**3**	**8**	**8**	**0**	**0**	**0**	**26**	**19.2**	**11**	**3**	**10**	**0**	**–2**								
1997-98	**Los Angeles Kings**	**NHL**	**81**	**29**	**31**	**60**	**34**	**30**	**64**	**54**	**7**	**3**	**7**	**193**	**15.0**	**95**	**25**	**73**	**9**	**+6**	**4**	**2**	**0**	**2**	**6**	**0**	**0**	**0**
	Canada	WC-A	5	1	2	3				4																		
	NHL Totals		**375**	**88**	**80**	**168**	**96**	**72**	**168**	**245**	**13**	**3**	**17**	**672**	**13.1**	**260**	**41**	**257**	**11**		**52**	**12**	**13**	**25**	**42**	**1**	**0**	**1**

Traded to **Pittsburgh** by **Boston** with Bryan Smolinski and Boston's 3rd round choice (Boyd Kane) in 1996 Entry Draft for Kevin Stevens and Shawn McEachern, August 2, 1995. Traded to **LA Kings** by **Pittsburgh** for Ed Olczyk, March 18, 1997.

• MURRAY, JIM

Jim Murray D – L. 6'1", 165 lbs. b: Virden, Man., 11/25/1943.

Season	Club	League	GP	G	A	Pts	AG	AA	APts	PIM	PP	SH	GW	S	%	TGF	PGF	TGA	PGA	+/–	Playoffs GP	G	A	Pts	PIM	PP	SH	GW
1961-62	Brandon Wheat Kings	MJHL	37	6	8	14				32											19	0	4	4	26			
1962-63	Brandon Wheat Kings	MJHL	39	11	21	34				51											19	5	9	14	18			
1963-64	Brandon Wheat Kings	MJHL	30	11	23	34				38											21	3	*12	15	38			
1964-65	New York Rovers	EHL	72	10	29	39				113																		
1965-66	Knoxville Knights	EHL	70	9	42	51				50											3	0	2	2	2			
1966-67	Knoxville Knights	EHL	72	17	35	52				79											4	0	1	1	4			
1967-68	**Los Angeles Kings**	**NHL**	**30**	**0**	**2**	**2**	**0**	**2**	**2**	**14**	**0**	**0**	**0**	**24**	**0.0**	**23**	**4**	**30**	**7**	**–4**								
	Springfield Kings	AHL	30	2	8	10				33																		
1968-69	Springfield Kings	AHL	72	7	26	33				83																		
1969-70	Phoenix Roadrunners	WHL	72	2	28	30				93																		
1970-71	Phoenix Roadrunners	WHL	72	4	18	22				58											10	0	1	1	14			
1971-72	Phoenix Roadrunners	WHL	72	7	30	37				136											6	0	4	4	10			
1972-73	Phoenix Roadrunners	WHL	72	10	53	63				138											10	1	6	7	8			
1973-74	Phoenix Roadrunners	WHL	76	10	39	49				113																		
1974-75	Johnstown Jets	NAHL	5	0	2	2				2																		
	Winston-Salem Polar Bears	SHL	37	7	33	40				74											7	1	5	6	6			
	NHL Totals		**30**	**0**	**2**	**2**	**0**	**2**	**2**	**14**	**0**	**0**	**0**	**24**	**0.0**	**23**	**4**	**30**	**7**									

WHL Second All-Star Team (1973) • SHL Second All-Star Team (1975)

Traded to **LA Kings** by **NY Rangers** with Trevor Fahey and Ken Turlik for Barclay Plager, June 16, 1967. Traded to **Phoenix** (WHL) by **LA Kings** for Roger Cote, September, 1969.

• MURRAY, KEN

Ken Murray D – R. 6', 180 lbs. b: Toronto, Ont., 1/22/1948.

Season	Club	League	GP	G	A	Pts	AG	AA	APts	PIM	PP	SH	GW	S	%	TGF	PGF	TGA	PGA	+/–	Playoffs GP	G	A	Pts	PIM	PP	SH	GW
1968-69	St. Thomas Barons	Jr. B	STATISTICS NOT AVAILABLE																									
1969-70	**Toronto Maple Leafs**	**NHL**	**1**	**0**	**1**	**1**	**0**	**1**	**1**	**2**	**0**	**0**	**0**	**1**	**0.0**	**1**	**0**	**0**	**0**	**+1**								
	Tulsa Oilers	CHL	62	3	13	16				136											6	0	0	0	6			
1970-71	**Toronto Maple Leafs**	**NHL**	**4**	**0**	**0**	**0**	**0**	**0**	**0**	**0**	**0**	**0**	**0**	**1**	**0.0**	**1**	**0**	**0**	**0**	**+1**								
	Tulsa Oilers	CHL	62	3	13	16				143																		
1971-72	Cincinnati Swords	AHL	68	0	7	7				167											10	0	0	0	14			
1972-73	**New York Islanders**	**NHL**	**39**	**0**	**4**	**4**	**0**	**3**	**3**	**59**	**0**	**0**	**0**	**20**	**0.0**	**22**	**0**	**53**	**10**	**–21**								
	Detroit Red Wings	**NHL**	**31**	**1**	**1**	**2**	**1**	**1**	**2**	**36**	**0**	**0**	**0**	**18**	**5.6**	**14**	**0**	**18**	**3**	**–1**								
1973-74	Virginia Wings	AHL	54	3	6	9				159																		
	Seattle Totems	WHL	18	0	9	9				34																		
1974-75	**Kansas City Scouts**	**NHL**	**8**	**0**	**2**	**2**	**0**	**2**	**2**	**14**	**0**	**0**	**0**	**5**	**0.0**	**9**	**0**	**6**	**0**	**+3**								
	Baltimore Clippers	AHL	31	2	3	5				52																		
	Springfield Indians	AHL	29	1	9	10				91											15	3	5	8	30			
1975-76	**Kansas City Scouts**	**NHL**	**23**	**0**	**2**	**2**	**0**	**2**	**2**	**24**	**0**	**0**	**0**	**12**	**0.0**	**9**	**0**	**16**	**6**	**–1**								
	Springfield Indians	AHL	42	5	16	21				72																		
1976-77	Rhode Island Reds	AHL	59	1	9	10				107																		
1977-78	New Haven Nighthawks	AHL	68	2	12	14				84											15	0	1	1	22			
1978-79	Philadelphia Firebirds	AHL	3	0	0	0				2																		
	NHL Totals		**106**	**1**	**10**	**11**	**1**	**9**	**10**	**135**	**0**	**0**	**0**	**57**	**1.8**	**56**	**0**	**93**	**19**									

Signed as a free agent by **Toronto**, April 5, 1971. Claimed by **Buffalo** from **Toronto** in Intra-League Draft, June 8, 1971. Claimed by **NY Islanders** from **Buffalo** in Expansion Draft, June 6, 1972. Traded to **Detroit** by **NY Islanders** with Brian Lavender for Ralph Stewart and Bob Cook, January 17, 1973. Traded to **Seattle** (WHL) by **Detroit** (Virginia - AHL) for Gene Sobchuk, February, 1974. Claimed by **Kansas City** from **Detroit** in Expansion Draft, June 12, 1974. Traded to **LA Kings** by **Kansas City** for cash, February 10, 1975.

• MURRAY, MARTY

Marty Murray C – L. 5'9", 175 lbs. b: Deloraine, Man., 2/16/1975. Calgary's 5th choice, 96th overall, in 1993 Entry Draft.

Season	Club	League	GP	G	A	Pts	AG	AA	APts	PIM	PP	SH	GW	S	%	TGF	PGF	TGA	PGA	+/–	Playoffs GP	G	A	Pts	PIM	PP	SH	GW
1991-92	Brandon Wheat Kings	WHL	68	20	36	56				22																		
1992-93	Brandon Wheat Kings	WHL	67	29	65	94				50											4	1	3	4	0			
1993-94	Brandon Wheat Kings	WHL	64	43	71	114				33											14	6	14	20	14			
	Canada	WJC-A	7	1	3	4				4																		
1994-95	Brandon Wheat Kings	WHL	65	40	*88	128				53											18	9	*20	29	16			
	Canada	WJC-A	7	6	9	15				0																		
1995-96	**Calgary Flames**	**NHL**	**15**	**3**	**3**	**6**	**3**	**2**	**5**	**0**	**2**	**0**	**0**	**22**	**13.6**	**9**	**5**	**12**	**4**	**–4**								
	Saint John Flames	AHL	58	25	31	56				20											14	2	4	6	4			
1996-97	**Calgary Flames**	**NHL**	**2**	**0**	**0**	**0**	**0**	**0**	**0**	**4**	**0**	**0**	**0**	**2**	**0.0**	**0**	**0**	**1**	**1**	**0**								
	Saint John Flames	AHL	67	19	39	58				40											5	2	3	5	4			
1997-98	**Calgary Flames**	**NHL**	**2**	**0**	**0**	**0**	**0**	**0**	**0**	**2**	**0**	**0**	**0**	**2**	**0.0**	**1**	**0**	**0**	**0**	**+1**								
	Saint John Flames	AHL	41	10	30	40				16											21	10	10	20	12			
	NHL Totals		**19**	**3**	**3**	**6**	**3**	**2**	**5**	**6**	**2**	**0**	**0**	**26**	**11.5**	**10**	**5**	**13**	**5**									

WHL East First All-Star Team (1994, 1995) • Canadian Major Junior Second All-Star Team (1994) • WJC-A All-Star Team (1995) • Named Best Forward at WJC-A (1995)

			REGULAR SEASON																		PLAYOFFS							
Season	Club	League	GP	G	A	Pts	AG	AA	APts	PIM	PP	SH	GW	S	%	TGF	PGF	TGA	PGA	+/–	GP	G	A	Pts	PIM	PP	SH	GW

● MURRAY, MIKE
Mike Murray C – L. 6', 195 lbs. b: Kingston, Ont., 8/29/1966. NY Islanders' 6th choice, 104th overall, in 1984 Entry Draft.

Season	Club	League	GP	G	A	Pts	AG	AA	APts	PIM	PP	SH	GW	S	%	TGF	PGF	TGA	PGA	+/–	GP	G	A	Pts	PIM	PP	SH	GW
1982-83	Sarnia Bees	Jr. B	57	61	39	100				48																		
1983-84	London Knights	OHL	70	8	24	32				14											8	1	4	5	2			
1984-85	London Knights	OHL	43	21	35	56				19																		
	Guelph Platers	OHL	23	10	9	19				8																		
1985-86	Guelph Platers	OHL	56	27	38	65				19											20	7	13	20	0			
1986-87	Hershey Bears	AHL	70	8	16	24				10											2	0	0	0	0			
1987-88	**Philadelphia Flyers**	**NHL**	**1**	**0**	**0**	**0**	**0**	**0**	**0**	**0**	**0**	**0**	**0**	**1**	**0.0**	**0**	**0**	**0**	**0**	**0**								
	Hershey Bears	AHL	57	14	14	28				34											2	0	0	0	0			
1988-89	Hershey Bears	AHL	19	1	2	3				8																		
	Indianapolis Ice	IHL	17	5	11	16				2																		
1989-90	Knoxville Cherokees	ECHL	21	11	17	28				4																		
1990-91	Kansas City Blades	IHL	2	0	0	0				0																		
	Knoxville Cherokees	ECHL	56	33	37	70				18											3	10	1	4				
1991-92			DID NOT PLAY																									
1992-93	Knoxville Cherokees	ECHL	64	23	42	65				40																		
1993-94	Knoxville Cherokees	ECHL	68	32	45	77				36											3	1	3	4	2			
1994-95	Knoxville Cherokees	ECHL	53	24	23	47				56																		
	NHL Totals		**1**	**0**	**0**	**0**	**0**	**0**	**0**	**0**	**0**	**0**	**0**	**1**	**0.0**	**0**	**0**	**0**	**0**									

Traded to **Philadelphia** by **NY Islanders** for Philadelphia's 5th round choice (Todd McLellan) in 1986 Entry Draft, June 21, 1986.

● MURRAY, PAT
Pat Murray LW – L. 6'2", 185 lbs. b: Stratford, Ont., 8/20/1969. Philadelphia's 2nd choice, 35th overall, in 1988 Entry Draft.

Season	Club	League	GP	G	A	Pts	AG	AA	APts	PIM	PP	SH	GW	S	%	TGF	PGF	TGA	PGA	+/–	GP	G	A	Pts	PIM	PP	SH	GW
1986-87	Stratford Cullitons	Jr. B	42	34	75	109				38																		
1987-88	Michigan State Spartans	CCHA	42	14	21	35				26																		
1988-89	Michigan State Spartans	CCHA	46	21	41	62				65																		
1989-90	Michigan State Spartans	CCHA	45	24	60	84				36																		
1990-91	**Philadelphia Flyers**	**NHL**	**16**	**2**	**1**	**3**	**2**	**1**	**3**	**15**	**1**	**0**	**0**	**16**	**12.5**	**5**	**2**	**8**	**0**	**–5**								
	Hershey Bears	AHL	57	15	38	53				8											7	5	2	7	0			
1991-92	**Philadelphia Flyers**	**NHL**	**9**	**1**	**0**	**1**	**1**	**0**	**1**	**0**	**0**	**0**	**0**	**8**	**12.5**	**4**	**0**	**1**	**0**	**+3**								
	Hershey Bears	AHL	69	19	43	62				25											6	1	2	3	0			
1992-93	Hershey Bears	AHL	69	21	32	53				63																		
1993-94	Kalamazoo Wings	IHL	17	2	3	5				6																		
	Phoenix Roadrunners	IHL	25	6	8	14				44																		
1994-95	Knoxville Cherokees	ECHL	11	7	9	16				4																		
	Kalamazoo Wings	IHL	33	11	10	21				16											6	3	0	3	2			
	NHL Totals		**25**	**3**	**1**	**4**	**3**	**1**	**4**	**15**	**1**	**0**	**0**	**24**	**12.5**	**9**	**2**	**9**	**0**									

CCHA Second All-Star Team (1990)

● MURRAY, RANDY
Randy Murray D – R. 6'1", 195 lbs. b: Chatham, Ont., 8/24/1945.

Season	Club	League	GP	G	A	Pts	AG	AA	APts	PIM	PP	SH	GW	S	%	TGF	PGF	TGA	PGA	+/–	GP	G	A	Pts	PIM	PP	SH	GW
1965-66	London Nationals	OHA	38	11	13	24				120																		
1966-67	Charlotte Checkers	EHL	65	10	25	35				148											8	1	4	5	19			
	Tulsa Oilers	CHL	5	0	0	0				17																		
1967-68	Tulsa Oilers	CHL	61	3	14	17				108											6	1	0	1	12			
1968-69	Tulsa Oilers	CHL	64	7	14	21				97											7	2	4	6	16			
1969-70	**Toronto Maple Leafs**	**NHL**	**3**	**0**	**0**	**0**	**0**	**0**	**0**	**2**	**0**	**0**	**0**	**3**	**0.0**	**2**	**0**	**2**	**0**	**0**								
	Tulsa Oilers	CHL	55	5	14	19				90											6	0	0	0	13			
1970-71	Tulsa Oilers	CHL	68	2	27	29				143																		
1971-72	Calgary Stampeders	PrSHL	24	6	5	11				47																		
1972-73	Tulsa Oilers	CHL	38	0	10	10				59																		
	NHL Totals		**3**	**0**	**0**	**0**	**0**	**0**	**0**	**2**	**0**	**0**	**0**	**3**	**0.0**	**2**	**0**	**2**	**0**									

● MURRAY, REM
Rem Murray LW – L. 6'2", 195 lbs. b: Stratford, Ont., 10/9/1972. Los Angeles' 2nd choice, 135th overall, in 1992 Entry Draft.

Season	Club	League	GP	G	A	Pts	AG	AA	APts	PIM	PP	SH	GW	S	%	TGF	PGF	TGA	PGA	+/–	GP	G	A	Pts	PIM	PP	SH	GW
1991-92	Michigan State Spartans	CCHA	41	12	36	48				16																		
1992-93	Michigan State Spartans	CCHA	40	22	35	57				24																		
1993-94	Michigan State Spartans	CCHA	41	16	38	54				18																		
1994-95	Michigan State Spartans	CCHA	40	20	36	56				21																		
1995-96	Cape Breton Oilers	AHL	79	31	59	90				40																		
1996-97	**Edmonton Oilers**	**NHL**	**82**	**11**	**20**	**31**	**12**	**18**	**30**	**16**	**1**	**0**	**2**	**85**	**12.9**	**51**	**8**	**50**	**16**	**+9**	**12**	**1**	**2**	**3**	**4**	**0**	**0**	**0**
1997-98	**Edmonton Oilers**	**NHL**	**61**	**9**	**9**	**18**	**11**	**9**	**20**	**39**	**2**	**2**	**0**	**59**	**15.3**	**27**	**7**	**46**	**17**	**–9**	**11**	**1**	**4**	**5**	**2**	**0**	**0**	**0**
	NHL Totals		**143**	**20**	**29**	**49**	**23**	**27**	**50**	**55**	**3**	**2**	**2**	**144**	**13.9**	**78**	**15**	**96**	**33**		**23**	**2**	**6**	**8**	**6**	**0**	**0**	**0**

CCHA Second All-Star Team (1995)

Signed as a free agent by **Edmonton**, September 19, 1995.

● MURRAY, ROB
Rob Murray C – R. 6'1", 180 lbs. b: Toronto, Ont., 4/4/1967. Washington's 3rd choice, 61st overall, in 1985 Entry Draft.

Season	Club	League	GP	G	A	Pts	AG	AA	APts	PIM	PP	SH	GW	S	%	TGF	PGF	TGA	PGA	+/–	GP	G	A	Pts	PIM	PP	SH	GW
1984-85	Peterborough Petes	OHL	63	12	9	21				155											17	2	7	9	45			
1985-86	Peterborough Petes	OHL	52	14	18	32				125											16	1	2	3	50			
1986-87	Peterborough Petes	OHL	62	17	37	54				204											3	1	4	5	8			
1987-88	Fort Wayne Komets	IHL	80	12	21	33				139											6	0	2	2	16			
1988-89	Baltimore Skipjacks	AHL	80	11	23	34				235																		
1989-90	**Washington Capitals**	**NHL**	**41**	**2**	**7**	**9**	**2**	**5**	**7**	**58**	**0**	**0**	**0**	**29**	**6.9**	**13**	**0**	**35**	**12**	**–10**	**9**	**0**	**0**	**0**	**18**	**0**	**0**	**0**
	Baltimore Skipjacks	AHL	23	5	4	9				63																		
1990-91	**Washington Capitals**	**NHL**	**17**	**0**	**3**	**3**	**0**	**2**	**2**	**19**	**0**	**0**	**0**	**8**	**0.0**	**6**	**0**	**6**	**0**	**0**								
	Baltimore Skipjacks	AHL	48	6	20	26				177											4	0	0	0	12			
1991-92	**Winnipeg Jets**	**NHL**	**9**	**0**	**1**	**1**	**0**	**1**	**1**	**18**	**0**	**0**	**0**	**2**	**0.0**	**1**	**0**	**4**	**1**	**–2**								
	Moncton Hawks	AHL	60	16	15	31				247											8	0	1	1	56			
1992-93	**Winnipeg Jets**	**NHL**	**10**	**1**	**0**	**1**	**1**	**0**	**1**	**6**	**0**	**0**	**1**	**4**	**25.0**	**1**	**0**	**8**	**7**	**0**								
	Moncton Hawks	AHL	56	16	21	37				147											3	0	0	0	6			
1993-94	**Winnipeg Jets**	**NHL**	**6**	**0**	**0**	**0**	**0**	**0**	**0**	**2**	**0**	**0**	**0**	**1**	**0.0**	**1**	**0**	**1**	**0**	**0**								
	Moncton Hawks	AHL	69	25	32	57				280											21	2	3	5	60			
1994-95	Springfield Falcons	AHL	78	16	38	54				373																		
	Winnipeg Jets	**NHL**	**10**	**0**	**2**	**2**	**0**	**3**	**3**	**2**	**0**	**0**	**0**	**5**	**0.0**	**2**	**0**	**1**	**0**	**+1**								
1995-96	**Winnipeg Jets**	**NHL**	**1**	**0**	**0**	**0**	**0**	**0**	**0**	**2**	**0**	**0**	**0**	**1**	**0.0**	**0**	**0**	**1**	**0**	**–1**								
	Springfield Falcons	AHL	74	10	28	38				263											10	1	6	7	32			
1996-97	Springfield Falcons	AHL	78	16	27	43				234											17	2	3	5	66			
1997-98	Springfield Falcons	AHL	80	7	30	37				255											4	0	2	2	2			
	NHL Totals		**94**	**3**	**13**	**16**	**3**	**11**	**14**	**107**	**0**	**0**	**1**	**50**	**6.0**	**24**	**0**	**56**	**20**		**9**	**0**	**0**	**0**	**18**	**0**	**0**	**0**

Claimed by **Minnesota** from **Washington** in Expansion Draft, May 30, 1991. Traded to **Winnipeg** by **Minnesota** with future considerations for Winnipeg's 7th round choice (Geoff Finch) in 1991 Entry Draft and future considerations, May 31, 1991.

● MURRAY, TERRY
Terry Murray D – R. 6'2", 190 lbs. b: Shawville, Que., 7/20/1950. Oakland's 3rd choice, 88th overall, in 1970 Amateur Draft.

Season	Club	League	GP	G	A	Pts	AG	AA	APts	PIM	PP	SH	GW	S	%	TGF	PGF	TGA	PGA	+/–	GP	G	A	Pts	PIM	PP	SH	GW
1967-68	Ottawa 67's	OHA	53	0	4	4				59																		
1968-69	Ottawa 67's	OHA	50	1	16	17				39											7	0	1	1	4			
1969-70	Ottawa 67's	OHA	50	4	24	28				43																		
1970-71	Providence Reds	AHL	57	1	22	23				47											10	0	1	1	5			
1971-72	Baltimore Clippers	AHL	30	0	5	5				13																		
	Boston Braves	AHL	9	0	0	0				0																		
	Oklahoma City Blazers	CHL	17	1	1	2				10											6	0	0	0	2			
1972-73	**California Golden Seals**	**NHL**	**23**	**0**	**3**	**3**	**0**	**2**	**2**	**4**	**0**	**0**	**0**	**9**	**0.0**	**12**	**0**	**34**	**8**	**–14**								
	Salt Lake Golden Eagles	WHL	39	3	8	11				30											9	0	6	6	14			

			REGULAR SEASON																		PLAYOFFS							
Season	Club	League	GP	G	A	Pts	AG	AA	APts	PIM	PP	SH	GW	S	%	TGF	PGF	TGA	PGA	+/–	GP	G	A	Pts	PIM	PP	SH	GW
1973-74	California Golden Seals	NHL	58	0	12	12	0	10	10	48	0	0	0	55	0.0	55	9	103	14	–43	....	....	....	....	....	....	....	....
1974-75	California Golden Seals	NHL	9	0	2	2	0	2	2	8	0	0	0	8	0.0	8	0	7	1	+2	....	....	....	....	....	....	....	....
	Salt Lake Golden Eagles	CHL	62	5	30	35	....	....	....	122	....	....	....	....	....	....	....	....	....	....	11	2	2	4	30	....	....	....
1975-76	Philadelphia Flyers	NHL	3	0	0	0	0	0	0	2	0	0	0	3	0.0	1	0	1	0	0	6	0	1	1	0	0	0	0
	Richmond Robins	AHL	67	8	48	56	....	....	....	95	....	....	....	....	....	....	....	....	....	....	6	1	4	5	2	....	....	....
1976-77	Philadelphia Flyers	NHL	36	0	13	13	0	11	11	14	0	0	0	32	0.0	46	5	24	4	+21	....	....	....	....	....	....	....	....
	Detroit Red Wings	NHL	23	0	7	7	0	6	6	10	0	0	0	24	0.0	16	3	46	15	–18	....	....	....	....	....	....	....	....
1977-78	Philadelphia Firebirds	AHL	7	2	1	3	....	....	....	13	....	....	....	....	....	....	....	....	....	....	....	....	....	....	....	....	....	....
	Maine Mariners	AHL	68	9	40	49	....	....	....	53	....	....	....	....	....	....	....	....	....	....	12	1	7	8	28	....	....	....
1978-79	Philadelphia Flyers	NHL	5	0	0	0	0	0	0	0	0	0	0	3	0.0	2	1	1	0	0	....	....	....	....	....	....	....	....
	Maine Mariners	AHL	55	14	23	37	....	....	....	14	....	....	....	....	....	....	....	....	....	....	10	1	5	6	6	....	....	....
1979-80	Maine Mariners	AHL	68	3	19	22	....	....	....	26	....	....	....	....	....	....	....	....	....	....	12	2	2	4	10	....	....	....
1980-81	Philadelphia Flyers	NHL	71	1	17	18	1	12	13	53	0	0	0	65	1.5	96	2	72	24	+46	12	2	1	3	10	0	0	0
	Maine Mariners	AHL	2	0	1	1	....	....	....	0	....	....	....	....	....	....	....	....	....	....	....	....	....	....	....	....	....	....
1981-82	Washington Capitals	NHL	74	3	22	25	2	15	17	60	0	0	0	75	4.0	85	6	126	33	–14	....	....	....	....	....	....	....	....
	NHL Totals		302	4	76	80	3	58	61	199	0	0	0	274	1.5	321	26	414	99		18	2	2	4	10	0	0	0

AHL First All-Star Team (1976, 1978, 1979) • Won Eddie Shore Award (Outstanding Defenseman - AHL) (1978, 1979)

Signed as a free agent by **Philadelphia**, September 23, 1975. Traded to **Detroit** by **Philadelphia** with Steve Coates, Bob Ritchie and Dave Kelly for Rick Lapointe and Mike Korney, February 17, 1977. Traded to **Philadelphia** by **Detroit** for cash, November 1, 1977. Claimed by **Washington** from **Philadelphia** in Waiver Draft, October 5, 1981.

• MURRAY, TROY

Troy Murray C – R. 6'1", 195 lbs. b: Calgary, Alta., 7/31/1962. Chicago's 6th choice, 57th overall, in 1980 Entry Draft.

Season	Club	League	GP	G	A	Pts	AG	AA	APts	PIM	PP	SH	GW	S	%	TGF	PGF	TGA	PGA	+/–	GP	G	A	Pts	PIM	PP	SH	GW
1979-80	St. Albert Saints	AJHL	60	53	47	100	....	....	....	101	....	....	....	....	....	....	....	....	....	....	....	....	....	....	....	....	....	....
1980-81	University of North Dakota	WCHA	38	33	45	78	....	....	....	28	....	....	....	....	....	....	....	....	....	....	....	....	....	....	....	....	....	....
1981-82	University of North Dakota	WCHA	26	13	17	30	....	....	....	62	....	....	....	....	....	....	....	....	....	....	....	....	....	....	....	....	....	....
	Canada	WJC-A	7	4	4	8	....	....	....	6	....	....	....	....	....	....	....	....	....	....	....	....	....	....	....	....	....	....
	Chicago Black Hawks	NHL	1	0	0	0	0	0	0	0	0	0	0	2	0.0	0	0	0	0	0	7	1	0	1	5	0	0	0
1982-83	Chicago Black Hawks	NHL	54	8	8	16	7	6	13	27	1	0	2	53	15.1	26	2	31	3	–4	2	0	0	0	0	0	0	0
1983-84	Chicago Black Hawks	NHL	61	15	15	30	12	10	22	45	0	1	2	119	12.6	45	3	42	10	+10	5	1	0	1	7	0	0	1
1984-85	Chicago Black Hawks	NHL	80	26	40	66	21	27	48	82	6	4	5	157	16.6	100	22	91	29	+16	15	5	14	19	24	1	0	0
1985-86	Chicago Black Hawks	NHL	80	45	54	99	36	36	72	94	9	5	7	197	22.8	139	38	109	40	+32	2	0	0	0	2	0	0	0
1986-87	Chicago Blackhawks	NHL	77	28	43	71	24	31	55	59	4	2	3	127	22.0	99	20	106	41	+14	4	0	0	0	5	0	0	0
	Canada	WEC-A	10	2	2	4	....	....	....	14	....	....	....	....	....	....	....	....	....	....	....	....	....	....	....	....	....	....
1987-88	Chicago Blackhawks	NHL	79	22	36	58	19	26	45	96	3	2	2	148	14.9	97	36	109	31	–17	5	1	0	1	8	1	0	0
1988-89	Chicago Blackhawks	NHL	79	21	30	51	18	21	39	113	5	2	2	156	13.5	89	31	98	40	0	16	3	6	9	25	1	0	0
1989-90	Chicago Blackhawks	NHL	68	17	38	55	15	27	42	86	3	1	4	111	15.3	89	31	86	26	–2	20	4	4	8	22	1	0	0
1990-91	Chicago Blackhawks	NHL	75	14	23	37	13	17	30	74	4	0	2	130	10.8	56	16	46	19	+13	6	0	1	1	12	0	0	0
1991-92	Winnipeg Jets	NHL	74	17	30	47	16	23	39	69	5	2	1	156	10.9	83	35	98	37	–13	7	0	0	0	2	0	0	0
1992-93	Winnipeg Jets	NHL	29	3	4	7	2	3	5	34	1	0	0	45	6.7	15	4	40	14	–15	....	....	....	....	....	....	....	....
	Chicago Blackhawks	NHL	22	1	3	4	1	2	3	25	1	0	0	32	3.1	6	1	9	4	0	4	0	0	0	2	0	0	0
1993-94	Chicago Blackhawks	NHL	12	0	1	1	0	1	1	6	0	0	0	7	0.0	2	0	2	1	+1	....	....	....	....	....	....	....	....
	Indianapolis Ice	IHL	8	3	3	6	....	....	....	12	....	....	....	....	....	....	....	....	....	....	....	....	....	....	....	....	....	....
	Ottawa Senators	NHL	15	2	3	5	2	2	4	4	0	1	0	14	14.3	8	0	13	6	+1	....	....	....	....	....	....	....	....
1994-95	Ottawa Senators	NHL	33	4	10	14	7	15	22	16	0	0	1	38	10.5	15	1	29	14	–1	....	....	....	....	....	....	....	....
	Pittsburgh Penguins	NHL	13	0	2	2	0	3	3	23	0	0	0	7	0.0	5	0	12	6	–1	12	2	1	3	12	0	0	0
1995-96	Colorado Avalanche	NHL	63	7	14	21	7	11	18	22	0	0	1	36	19.4	27	0	28	16	+15	8	0	0	0	19	0	0	0
1996-97	Chicago Wolves	IHL	81	21	29	50	....	....	....	63	....	....	....	....	....	....	....	....	....	....	4	0	2	2	2	....	....	....
	NHL Totals		915	230	354	584	200	261	461	875	42	20	32	1535	15.0	901	240	949	337		113	17	26	43	145	4	0	1

Won Frank J. Selke Trophy (1986)

WCHA Second All-Star Team (1981, 1982) • Won Frank J. Selke Memorial Trophy (1986)

Traded to **Winnipeg** by **Chicago** with Warren Rychel for Bryan Marchment and Chris Norton, July 22, 1991. Traded to **Chicago** by **Winnipeg** for Steve Bancroft and future considerations, February 21, 1993. Traded to **Ottawa** by **Chicago** with Chicago's 11th round choice (Antti Tormanen) in 1994 Entry Draft for Ottawa's 11th round choice (Rob Mara) in 1994 Entry Draft, March 11, 1994. Traded to **Pittsburgh** by **Ottawa** with Norm Maciver for Martin Straka, April 7, 1995. Signed as a free agent by **Colorado**, August 7, 1995.

• MURZYN, DANA

Dana Murzyn D – L. 6'2", 200 lbs. b: Calgary, Alta., 12/9/1966. Hartford's 1st choice, 5th overall, in 1985 Entry Draft.

Season	Club	League	GP	G	A	Pts	AG	AA	APts	PIM	PP	SH	GW	S	%	TGF	PGF	TGA	PGA	+/–	GP	G	A	Pts	PIM	PP	SH	GW
1983-84	Calgary Wranglers	WHL	65	11	20	31	....	....	....	135	....	....	....	....	....	....	....	....	....	....	2	0	0	0	10	....	....	....
1984-85	Calgary Wranglers	WHL	72	32	60	92	....	....	....	233	....	....	....	....	....	....	....	....	....	....	8	1	11	12	16	....	....	....
1985-86	Hartford Whalers	NHL	78	3	23	26	2	15	17	125	0	0	1	79	3.8	80	8	76	5	+1	4	0	0	0	10	0	0	0
1986-87	Hartford Whalers	NHL	74	9	19	28	8	14	22	95	1	0	0	135	6.7	88	4	70	3	+17	6	2	1	3	29	1	0	1
1987-88	Hartford Whalers	NHL	33	1	6	7	1	4	5	45	1	0	0	49	2.0	23	3	28	0	–8	....	....	....	....	....	....	....	....
	Calgary Flames	NHL	41	6	5	11	5	4	9	94	0	0	1	58	10.3	49	0	50	10	+9	5	2	0	2	13	0	0	0
1988-89	Calgary Flames	NHL	63	3	19	22	3	13	16	142	0	1	1	91	3.3	60	6	43	15	+26	21	0	3	3	20	0	0	0
1989-90	Calgary Flames	FrTour	4	1	0	1	....	....	....	6	....	....	....	....	....	....	....	....	....	....	....	....	....	....	....	....	....	....
	Calgary Flames	NHL	78	7	13	20	6	9	15	140	1	0	0	97	7.2	80	1	82	22	+19	6	2	2	4	2	0	0	0
1990-91	Calgary Flames	NHL	19	0	2	2	0	2	2	30	0	0	0	25	0.0	13	0	19	2	–4	....	....	....	....	....	....	....	....
	Vancouver Canucks	NHL	10	1	0	1	1	0	1	8	0	0	0	15	6.7	8	0	14	3	–3	6	0	1	1	8	0	0	0
1991-92	Vancouver Canucks	NHL	70	3	11	14	3	8	11	147	0	1	0	99	3.0	67	3	68	19	+15	1	0	0	0	15	0	0	0
1992-93	Vancouver Canucks	NHL	79	5	11	16	4	8	12	196	0	0	2	82	6.1	83	1	74	26	+34	12	3	2	5	18	0	0	0
1993-94	Vancouver Canucks	NHL	80	6	14	20	6	11	17	109	0	1	0	79	7.6	66	0	100	38	+4	7	0	0	0	4	0	0	0
1994-95	Vancouver Canucks	NHL	40	0	8	8	0	12	12	129	0	0	0	29	0.0	35	0	29	8	+14	8	0	1	1	22	0	0	0
1995-96	Vancouver Canucks	NHL	69	2	10	12	2	8	10	130	0	0	0	68	2.9	62	0	88	35	+9	6	0	0	0	25	0	0	0
1996-97	Vancouver Canucks	NHL	61	1	7	8	1	6	7	118	0	0	0	70	1.4	55	0	68	20	+7	....	....	....	....	....	....	....	....
1997-98	Vancouver Canucks	NHL	31	5	2	7	6	2	8	42	0	0	2	29	17.2	23	1	41	16	–3	....	....	....	....	....	....	....	....
	NHL Totals		826	52	150	202	48	116	164	1550	3	3	7	1005	5.2	792	27	850	222		82	9	10	19	166	1	0	1

WHL East First All-Star Team, (1985) • NHL All-Rookie Team (1986)

Traded to **Calgary** by **Hartford** with Shane Churla for Neil Sheehy, Carey Wilson and the rights to Lane MacDonald, January 3, 1988. Traded to **Vancouver** by **Calgary** for Ron Stern, Kevan Guy and future considerations, March 5, 1991.

• MUSIL, FRANTISEK

Frantisek Musil D – L. 6'3", 215 lbs. b: Pardubice, Czech., 12/17/1964. Minnesota's 3rd choice, 38th overall, in 1983 Entry Draft.

Season	Club	League	GP	G	A	Pts	AG	AA	APts	PIM	PP	SH	GW	S	%	TGF	PGF	TGA	PGA	+/–	GP	G	A	Pts	PIM	PP	SH	GW
1980-81	HC Pardubice	Czech.	2	0	0	0	....	....	....	0	....	....	....	....	....	....	....	....	....	....	....	....	....	....	....	....	....	....
1981-82	HC Pardubice	Czech.	35	1	3	4	....	....	....	34	....	....	....	....	....	....	....	....	....	....	....	....	....	....	....	....	....	....
	Czechoslovakia	WJC-A	7	1	1	2	....	....	....	8	....	....	....	....	....	....	....	....	....	....	....	....	....	....	....	....	....	....
1982-83	HC Pardubice	Czech.	33	1	2	3	....	....	....	44	....	....	....	....	....	....	....	....	....	....	....	....	....	....	....	....	....	....
	Czechoslovakia	WJC-A	6	0	2	2	....	....	....	8	....	....	....	....	....	....	....	....	....	....	....	....	....	....	....	....	....	....
	Czechoslovakia	WEC-A	4	0	1	1	....	....	....	6	....	....	....	....	....	....	....	....	....	....	....	....	....	....	....	....	....	....
1983-84	HC Pardubice	Czech.	37	4	8	12	....	....	....	72	....	....	....	....	....	....	....	....	....	....	....	....	....	....	....	....	....	....
	Czechoslovakia	WJC-A	7	0	2	2	....	....	....	10	....	....	....	....	....	....	....	....	....	....	....	....	....	....	....	....	....	....
1984-85	Czechoslovakia	C Cup	5	0	1	1	....	....	....	4	....	....	....	....	....	....	....	....	....	....	....	....	....	....	....	....	....	....
	Dukla Jihlava	Czech.	44	4	6	10	....	....	....	76	....	....	....	....	....	....	....	....	....	....	....	....	....	....	....	....	....	....
	Czechoslovakia	WEC-A	10	1	1	2	....	....	....	12	....	....	....	....	....	....	....	....	....	....	....	....	....	....	....	....	....	....
1985-86	Dukla Jihlava	Czech.	34	4	7	11	....	....	....	42	....	....	....	....	....	....	....	....	....	....	....	....	....	....	....	....	....	....
	Czechoslovakia	WEC-A	10	0	2	2	....	....	....	20	....	....	....	....	....	....	....	....	....	....	....	....	....	....	....	....	....	....
1986-87	Minnesota North Stars	NHL	72	2	9	11	2	6	8	148	0	0	0	83	2.4	62	8	87	33	0	....	....	....	....	....	....	....	....
1987-88	Minnesota North Stars	NHL	80	9	8	17	8	6	14	213	1	1	0	78	11.5	72	5	111	42	–2	....	....	....	....	....	....	....	....
1988-89	Minnesota North Stars	NHL	55	1	19	20	1	13	14	54	0	0	1	78	1.3	52	10	57	19	+4	5	1	1	2	4	0	0	0
1989-90	Minnesota North Stars	NHL	56	2	8	10	2	6	8	109	0	0	1	78	2.6	56	5	72	21	0	4	0	0	0	14	0	0	0
1990-91	Minnesota North Stars	NHL	8	0	2	2	0	2	2	23	0	0	0	5	0.0	4	1	6	3	0	....	....	....	....	....	....	....	....
	Calgary Flames	NHL	67	7	14	21	6	11	17	160	2	0	1	68	10.3	60	7	63	22	+12	7	0	0	0	10	0	0	0
	Czechoslovakia	WEC-A	10	2	0	2	....	....	....	40	....	....	....	....	....	....	....	....	....	....	....	....	....	....	....	....	....	....
1991-92	Czechoslovakia	C Cup	5	0	0	0	....	....	....	6	....	....	....	....	....	....	....	....	....	....	....	....	....	....	....	....	....	....
	Calgary Flames	NHL	78	4	8	12	4	6	10	103	1	1	0	71	5.6	61	2	89	42	+12	....	....	....	....	....	....	....	....
	Czechoslovakia	WC-A	7	3	1	4	....	....	....	26	....	....	....	....	....	....	....	....	....	....	....	....	....	....	....	....	....	....

Season	Club	League	GP	G	A	Pts	AG	AA	APts	PIM	PP	SH	GW	S	%	TGF	PGF	TGA	PGA	+/–	GP	G	A	Pts	PIM	PP	SH	GW
			REGULAR SEASON																		PLAYOFFS							
1992-93	**Calgary Flames**	**NHL**	**80**	**6**	**10**	**16**	**5**	**7**	**12**	**131**	**0**	**0**	**1**	**87**	**6.9**	**73**	**5**	**62**	**22**	**+28**	**6**	**1**	**1**	**2**	**7**	**0**	**0**	**0**
1993-94	**Calgary Flames**	**NHL**	**75**	**1**	**8**	**9**	**1**	**6**	**7**	**50**	**0**	**0**	**0**	**65**	**1.5**	**70**	**0**	**70**	**38**	**+38**	**7**	**0**	**1**	**1**	**4**	**0**	**0**	**0**
	Czech Republic	WC-A	2	0	0	0	....	....	....	2	....	....	....	....	....	....	....	....	....	....	....	....	....	....	....	....	....	....
1994-95	Sparta Praha	Czech.	19	1	4	5	....	....	....	50	....	....	....	....	....	....	....	....	....	....	....	....	....	....	....	....	....	....
	Saxonia	Germany	1	0	0	0	....	....	....	2	....	....	....	....	....	....	....	....	....	....	....	....	....	....	....	....	....	....
	Calgary Flames	**NHL**	**35**	**0**	**5**	**5**	**0**	**7**	**7**	**61**	**0**	**0**	**0**	**18**	**0.0**	**20**	**0**	**28**	**14**	**+6**	**5**	**0**	**1**	**1**	**0**	**0**	**0**	**0**
1995-96	Karlovy Vary	Czech. 2	16	7	4	11	....	....	....	16	....	....	....	....	....	....	....	....	....	....	....	....	....	....	....	....	....	....
	Ottawa Senators	**NHL**	**65**	**1**	**3**	**4**	**1**	**2**	**3**	**85**	**0**	**0**	**0**	**37**	**2.7**	**37**	**0**	**78**	**31**	**–10**	....	....	....	....	....	....	....	....
1996-97	**Ottawa Senators**	**NHL**	**57**	**0**	**5**	**5**	**0**	**4**	**4**	**58**	**0**	**0**	**0**	**24**	**0.0**	**37**	**0**	**42**	**11**	**+6**	....	....	....	....	....	....	....	....
1997-98	Indianapolis Ice	IHL	52	5	8	13	....	....	....	122	....	....	....	....	....	....	....	....	....	....	....	....	....	....	....	....	....	....
	Detroit Vipers	IHL	9	0	0	0	....	....	....	6	....	....	....	....	....	....	....	....	....	....	....	....	....	....	....	....	....	....
	Edmonton Oilers	**NHL**	**17**	**1**	**2**	**3**	**1**	**2**	**3**	**8**	**0**	**1**	**1**	**8**	**12.5**	**11**	**1**	**17**	**8**	**+1**	**7**	**0**	**0**	**0**	**6**	**0**	**0**	**0**
	NHL Totals		**745**	**34**	**101**	**135**	**31**	**78**	**109**	**1203**	**4**	**3**	**5**	**700**	**4.9**	**615**	**44**	**782**	**306**		**41**	**2**	**4**	**6**	**45**	**0**	**0**	**0**

WC-A All-Star Team (1992)

Traded to **Calgary** by **Minnesota** for Brian Glynn, October 26, 1990. Traded to **Ottawa** by **Calgary** for Ottawa's 4th round choice (Chris St. Croix) in 1997 Entry Draft, October 7, 1995. Traded to **Edmonton** by **Ottawa** for Scott Ferguson, March 9, 1998.

• MYERS, HAP

Hap (Harold) Myers D – L. 5'11", 195 lbs. b: Edmonton, Alta., 7/28/1947.

Season	Club	League	GP	G	A	Pts	AG	AA	APts	PIM	PP	SH	GW	S	%	TGF	PGF	TGA	PGA	+/–	GP	G	A	Pts	PIM	PP	SH	GW
1965-66	Edmonton Oil Kings	AJHL	....	0	3	3	....	....	....	18	....	....	....	....	....	....	....	....	....	....	....	....	....	....	....	....	....	....
1966-67	Edmonton Oil Kings	WCJHL	56	6	33	39	....	....	....	86	....	....	....	....	....	....	....	....	....	....	9	0	7	7	30	....	....	....
1967-68	Edmonton Oil Kings	WCJHL	55	13	37	50	....	....	....	98	....	....	....	....	....	....	....	....	....	....	....	....	....	....	....	....	....	....
1968-69	Fort Worth Wings	CHL	70	8	13	21	....	....	....	52	....	....	....	....	....	....	....	....	....	....	....	....	....	....	....	....	....	....
1969-70	Cleveland Barons	AHL	72	9	28	37	....	....	....	61	....	....	....	....	....	....	....	....	....	....	....	....	....	....	....	....	....	....
1970-71	**Buffalo Sabres**	**NHL**	**13**	**0**	**0**	**0**	**0**	**0**	**0**	**6**	**0**	**0**	**0**	**14**	**0.0**	**0**	**0**	**14**	**3**	**–11**	....	....	....	....	....	....	....	....
	Salt Lake Golden Eagles	WHL	43	1	4	5	....	....	....	14	....	....	....	....	....	....	....	....	....	....	....	....	....	....	....	....	....	....
1971-72	Cincinnati Swords	AHL	67	4	16	20	....	....	....	55	....	....	....	....	....	....	....	....	....	....	10	0	3	3	14	....	....	....
1972-73	Cincinnati Swords	AHL	37	0	9	9	....	....	....	2	....	....	....	....	....	....	....	....	....	....	15	0	4	4	12	....	....	....
1973-74	Cincinnati Swords	AHL	76	6	25	31	....	....	....	51	....	....	....	....	....	....	....	....	....	....	5	0	2	2	8	....	....	....
	NHL Totals		**13**	**0**	**0**	**0**	**0**	**0**	**0**	**6**	**0**	**0**	**0**	**14**	**0.0**	**0**	**0**	**14**	**3**		....	....	....	....	....	....	....	....

Claimed by **Buffalo** (Salt Lake-CHL) from **Detroit** in Reverse Draft, June, 1970.

• MYHRES, BRANTT

Brantt Myhres RW – R. 6'4", 222 lbs. b: Edmonton, Alta., 3/18/1974. Tampa Bay's 5th choice, 97th overall, in 1992 Entry Draft.

Season	Club	League	GP	G	A	Pts	AG	AA	APts	PIM	PP	SH	GW	S	%	TGF	PGF	TGA	PGA	+/–	GP	G	A	Pts	PIM	PP	SH	GW
1990-91	Portland Winter Hawks	WHL	59	2	7	9	....	....	....	125	....	....	....	....	....	....	....	....	....	....	....	....	....	....	....	....	....	....
1991-92	Portland Winter Hawks	WHL	4	0	2	2	....	....	....	22	....	....	....	....	....	....	....	....	....	....	....	....	....	....	....	....	....	....
	Lethbridge Huricanes	WHL	53	4	11	15	....	....	....	359	....	....	....	....	....	....	....	....	....	....	5	0	0	0	36	....	....	....
1992-93	Lethbridge Hurricanes	WHL	64	13	35	48	....	....	....	277	....	....	....	....	....	....	....	....	....	....	3	0	0	0	11	....	....	....
1993-94	Lethbridge Hurricanes	WHL	34	10	21	31	....	....	....	103	....	....	....	....	....	....	....	....	....	....	....	....	....	....	....	....	....	....
	Spokane Chiefs	WHL	27	10	22	32	....	....	....	139	....	....	....	....	....	....	....	....	....	....	3	1	4	5	7	....	....	....
	Atlanta Knights	IHL	2	0	0	0	....	....	....	17	....	....	....	....	....	....	....	....	....	....	....	....	....	....	....	....	....	....
1994-95	Atlanta Knights	IHL	40	5	5	10	....	....	....	213	....	....	....	....	....	....	....	....	....	....	....	....	....	....	....	....	....	....
	Tampa Bay Lightning	**NHL**	**15**	**2**	**0**	**2**	**4**	**0**	**4**	**81**	**0**	**0**	**1**	**4**	**50.0**	**2**	**0**	**4**	**0**	**–2**	....	....	....	....	....	....	....	....
1995-96	Atlanta Knights	IHL	12	0	2	2	....	....	....	58	....	....	....	....	....	....	....	....	....	....	....	....	....	....	....	....	....	....
1996-97	**Tampa Bay Lightning**	**NHL**	**47**	**3**	**1**	**4**	**3**	**1**	**4**	**136**	**0**	**0**	**1**	**13**	**23.1**	**7**	**0**	**6**	**0**	**+1**	....	....	....	....	....	....	....	....
	San Antonio Dragons	IHL	12	0	0	0	....	....	....	98	....	....	....	....	....	....	....	....	....	....	....	....	....	....	....	....	....	....
1997-98	**Philadelphia Flyers**	**NHL**	**23**	**0**	**0**	**0**	**0**	**0**	**0**	**169**	**0**	**0**	**0**	**0**	**0.0**	**1**	**0**	**2**	**0**	**–1**	....	....	....	....	....	....	....	....
	Philadelphia Phantoms	AHL	18	4	4	8	....	....	....	67	....	....	....	....	....	....	....	....	....	....	....	....	....	....	....	....	....	....
	NHL Totals		**85**	**5**	**1**	**6**	**7**	**1**	**8**	**386**	**0**	**0**	**2**	**17**	**29.4**	**10**	**0**	**12**	**0**		....	....	....	....	....	....	....	....

Traded to **Edmonton** by **Tampa Bay** with a conditional draft choice for Vladimir Vujtek and Edmonton's 3rd round choice in 1998 Entry Draft, July 16, 1997. Traded to **Philadelphia** by **Edmonton** for Jason Bowen, October 15, 1997.

• MYRVOLD, ANDERS

Anders Myrvold D – L. 6'2", 200 lbs. b: Lorenskog, Norway, 8/12/1975. Quebec's 6th choice, 127th overall, in 1993 Entry Draft.

Season	Club	League	GP	G	A	Pts	AG	AA	APts	PIM	PP	SH	GW	S	%	TGF	PGF	TGA	PGA	+/–	GP	G	A	Pts	PIM	PP	SH	GW
1992-93	Farjestads BK Karlstad	Sweden	2	0	0	0	....	....	....	0	....	....	....	....	....	....	....	....	....	....	....	....	....	....	....	....	....	....
	Norway	WJC-B	7	5	1	6	....	....	....	10	....	....	....	....	....	....	....	....	....	....	....	....	....	....	....	....	....	....
1993-94	Grum	Sweden 2	24	1	0	1	....	....	....	59	....	....	....	....	....	....	....	....	....	....	....	....	....	....	....	....	....	....
	Norway	WJC-B	7	0	2	2	....	....	....	14	....	....	....	....	....	....	....	....	....	....	....	....	....	....	....	....	....	....
	Norway	WC-A	6	1	0	1	....	....	....	6	....	....	....	....	....	....	....	....	....	....	....	....	....	....	....	....	....	....
1994-95	Laval Titan	QMJHL	64	14	50	64	....	....	....	173	....	....	....	....	....	....	....	....	....	....	20	4	10	14	68	....	....	....
	Norway	WJC-B	7	0	3	3	....	....	....	36	....	....	....	....	....	....	....	....	....	....	....	....	....	....	....	....	....	....
	Cornwall Aces	AHL	....	....	....	....	....	....	....	....	....	....	....	....	....	....	....	....	....	....	3	0	1	1	2	....	....	....
1995-96	**Colorado Avalanche**	**NHL**	**4**	**0**	**1**	**1**	**0**	**1**	**1**	**6**	**0**	**0**	**0**	**4**	**0.0**	**1**	**1**	**2**	**0**	**–2**	....	....	....	....	....	....	....	....
	Cornwall Aces	AHL	70	5	24	29	....	....	....	125	....	....	....	....	....	....	....	....	....	....	5	1	0	1	19	....	....	....
1996-97	Hershey Bears	AHL	20	0	3	3	....	....	....	16	....	....	....	....	....	....	....	....	....	....	....	....	....	....	....	....	....	....
	Boston Bruins	**NHL**	**9**	**0**	**2**	**2**	**0**	**2**	**2**	**4**	**0**	**0**	**0**	**8**	**0.0**	**9**	**1**	**9**	**0**	**–1**	....	....	....	....	....	....	....	....
	Providence Bruins	AHL	53	6	15	21	....	....	....	107	....	....	....	....	....	....	....	....	....	....	10	0	1	1	6	....	....	....
1997-98	Providence Bruins	AHL	75	4	21	25	....	....	....	91	....	....	....	....	....	....	....	....	....	....	....	....	....	....	....	....	....	....
	NHL Totals		**13**	**0**	**3**	**3**	**0**	**3**	**3**	**10**	**0**	**0**	**0**	**12**	**0.0**	**10**	**2**	**11**	**0**		....	....	....	....	....	....	....	....

WJC-B All-Star Team (1993) • Named Best Defenseman at WJC-B (1993, 1994, 1995)

Rights transferred to **Colorado** after **Quebec** franchise relocated, June 21, 1995. Traded to **Boston** by **Colorado** with Landon Wilson for Boston's 1st round choice in 1998 Entry Draft, November 22, 1996.

• NABOKOV, DMITRI

Dmitri Nabokov C – R. 6'2", 209 lbs. b: Novosibirsk, USSR, 1/4/1977. Chicago's 1st choice, 19th overall, in 1995 Entry Draft.

Season	Club	League	GP	G	A	Pts	AG	AA	APts	PIM	PP	SH	GW	S	%	TGF	PGF	TGA	PGA	+/–	GP	G	A	Pts	PIM	PP	SH	GW
1993-94	Soviet Wings	CIS	17	0	2	2	....	....	....	6	....	....	....	....	....	....	....	....	....	....	3	0	0	0	0	....	....	....
1994-95	Soviet Wings	CIS	49	15	12	27	....	....	....	32	....	....	....	....	....	....	....	....	....	....	4	5	0	5	6	....	....	....
1995-96	Soviet Wings	CIS	50	12	14	26	....	....	....	51	....	....	....	....	....	....	....	....	....	....	....	....	....	....	....	....	....	....
	Russia	WJC-A	7	3	5	8	....	....	....	4	....	....	....	....	....	....	....	....	....	....	....	....	....	....	....	....	....	....
1996-97	Soviet Wings	Rus.	1	0	0	0	....	....	....	0	....	....	....	....	....	....	....	....	....	....	....	....	....	....	....	....	....	....
	Regina Pats	WHL	50	39	56	95	....	....	....	61	....	....	....	....	....	....	....	....	....	....	5	2	3	5	2	....	....	....
	Indianapolis Ice	IHL	2	0	0	0	....	....	....	0	....	....	....	....	....	....	....	....	....	....	....	....	....	....	....	....	....	....
1997-98	**Chicago Blackhawks**	**NHL**	**25**	**7**	**4**	**11**	**8**	**4**	**12**	**10**	**3**	**0**	**2**	**34**	**20.6**	**19**	**9**	**11**	**0**	**–1**	....	....	....	....	....	....	....	....
	Indianapolis Ice	IHL	46	6	15	21	....	....	....	16	....	....	....	....	....	....	....	....	....	....	5	2	1	3	0	....	....	....
	NHL Totals		**25**	**7**	**4**	**11**	**8**	**4**	**12**	**10**	**3**	**0**	**2**	**34**	**20.6**	**19**	**9**	**11**	**0**		....	....	....	....	....	....	....	....

WHL East Second All-Star Team (1997)

Traded to **NY Islanders** by **Chicago** for Jean-Pierre Dumont and Chicago's 5th round choice (later traded to Philadelphia - Philadelphia selected Francis Belanger) in 1998 Entry Draft, June 1, 1998.

• NACHBAUR, DON

Don Nachbaur C – L. 6'2", 200 lbs. b: Kitimat, B.C., 1/30/1959. Hartford's 3rd choice, 60th overall, in 1979 Entry Draft.

Season	Club	League	GP	G	A	Pts	AG	AA	APts	PIM	PP	SH	GW	S	%	TGF	PGF	TGA	PGA	+/–	GP	G	A	Pts	PIM	PP	SH	GW
1976-77	Merritt Luckies	Jr. B	54	22	27	49	....	....	....	31	....	....	....	....	....	....	....	....	....	....	....	....	....	....	....	....	....	....
1977-78	Billings Bighorns	WCJHL	68	23	27	50	....	....	....	128	....	....	....	....	....	....	....	....	....	....	20	*18	7	25	37	....	....	....
1978-79	Billings Bighorns	WHL	69	44	52	96	....	....	....	175	....	....	....	....	....	....	....	....	....	....	8	2	3	5	10	....	....	....
1979-80	Springfield Indians	AHL	70	12	17	29	....	....	....	119	....	....	....	....	....	....	....	....	....	....	....	....	....	....	....	....	....	....
1980-81	**Hartford Whalers**	**NHL**	**77**	**16**	**17**	**33**	**13**	**12**	**25**	**139**	**2**	**0**	**1**	**70**	**22.9**	**44**	**2**	**43**	**0**	**–1**	....	....	....	....	....	....	....	....
1981-82	**Hartford Whalers**	**NHL**	**77**	**5**	**21**	**26**	**4**	**14**	**18**	**117**	**0**	**0**	**0**	**113**	**4.4**	**35**	**5**	**63**	**12**	**–21**	....	....	....	....	....	....	....	....
1982-83	**Edmonton Oilers**	**NHL**	**4**	**0**	**0**	**0**	**0**	**0**	**0**	**17**	**0**	**0**	**0**	**0**	**0.0**	**2**	**0**	**3**	**0**	**–1**	**2**	**0**	**0**	**0**	**7**	**0**	**0**	**0**
	Moncton Alpines	AHL	70	33	32	65	....	....	....	125	....	....	....	....	....	....	....	....	....	....	....	....	....	....	....	....	....	....
1983-84	New Haven Nighthawks	AHL	70	33	32	65	....	....	....	194	....	....	....	....	....	....	....	....	....	....	....	....	....	....	....	....	....	....
1984-85	Hershey Bears	AHL	7	2	3	5	....	....	....	21	....	....	....	....	....	....	....	....	....	....	....	....	....	....	....	....	....	....
1985-86	**Philadelphia Flyers**	**NHL**	**5**	**1**	**1**	**2**	**1**	**1**	**2**	**7**	**0**	**0**	**0**	**4**	**25.0**	**3**	**0**	**0**	**0**	**+3**	....	....	....	....	....	....	....	....
	Hershey Bears	AHL	74	23	24	47	....	....	....	301	....	....	....	....	....	....	....	....	....	....	18	5	4	9	70	....	....	....

Season	Club	League	REGULAR SEASON																		PLAYOFFS							
			GP	G	A	Pts	AG	AA	APts	PIM	PP	SH	GW	S	%	TGF	PGF	TGA	PGA	+/–	GP	G	A	Pts	PIM	PP	SH	GW
1986-87	**Philadelphia Flyers**	**NHL**	**23**	**0**	**2**	**2**	**0**	**1**	**1**	**87**	**0**	**0**	**0**	**12**	**0.0**	**4**	**0**	**3**	**0**	**+1**	**7**	**1**	**1**	**2**	**15**	**0**	**0**	**1**
	Hershey Bears	AHL	57	18	17	35	....	....	....	274	....	....	....	....	....	....	....	....	....	....	5	0	3	3	47	....	....	....
1987-88	**Philadelphia Flyers**	**NHL**	**20**	**0**	**4**	**4**	**0**	**3**	**3**	**61**	**0**	**0**	**0**	**11**	**0.0**	**5**	**0**	**3**	**0**	**+2**	**2**	**0**	**0**	**0**	**2**	**0**	**0**	**0**
	Hershey Bears	AHL	42	19	21	40	....	....	....	174	....	....	....	....	....	....	....	....	....	....	8	4	3	7	47	....	....	....
1988-89	**Philadelphia Flyers**	**NHL**	**15**	**1**	**0**	**1**	**1**	**0**	**1**	**37**	**0**	**0**	**0**	**10**	**10.0**	**2**	**0**	**3**	**0**	**–1**	....	....	....	....	....	....	....	....
	Hershey Bears	AHL	49	24	31	55	....	....	....	172	....	....	....	....	....	....	....	....	....	....	12	0	5	5	58	....	....	....
1989-90	**Philadelphia Flyers**	**NHL**	**2**	**0**	**1**	**1**	**0**	**1**	**1**	**0**	**0**	**0**	**0**	**0**	**0.0**	**1**	**0**	**0**	**0**	**+1**	....	....	....	....	....	....	....	....
	Hershey Bears	AHL	30	10	9	19	....	....	....	72	....	....	....	....	....	....	....	....	....	....	....	....	....	....	....	....	....	....
1990-91	EC Graz	Austria	33	18	25	43	....	....	....	....	....	....	....	....	....	....	....	....	....	....	....	....	....	....	....	....	....	....
1991-92	EC Graz	Austria	44	32	29	61	....	....	....	....	....	....	....	....	....	....	....	....	....	....	....	....	....	....	....	....	....	....
1992-93	EC Graz	Austria	53	35	29	64	....	....	....	....	....	....	....	....	....	....	....	....	....	....	....	....	....	....	....	....	....	....
1993-94	EC Graz	Austria	52	21	20	41	....	....	....	....	....	....	....	....	....	....	....	....	....	....	....	....	....	....	....	....	....	....
	NHL Totals		**223**	**23**	**46**	**69**	**19**	**32**	**51**	**465**	**2**	**0**	**1**	**220**	**10.5**	**96**	**7**	**118**	**12**		**11**	**1**	**1**	**2**	**24**	**0**	**0**	**1**

Traded to **Edmonton** by **Hartford** with Ken Linseman for Risto Siltanen and the rights to Brent Loney, August 19, 1982. Claimed by **LA Kings** from **Edmonton** in Waiver Draft, October 3, 1983. Signed as a free agent by **Philadelphia**, October 4, 1984.

• NAHRGANG, JIM

Jim Nahrgang D – R. 6', 185 lbs. b: Millbank, Ont., 4/17/1951. Detroit's 7th choice, 86th overall, in 1971 Amateur Draft.

Season	Club	League	GP	G	A	Pts	AG	AA	APts	PIM	PP	SH	GW	S	%	TGF	PGF	TGA	PGA	+/–	GP	G	A	Pts	PIM	PP	SH	GW
1967-68	Ottawa 67's	OHA	52	1	9	10	....	....	....	74	....	....	....	....	....	....	....	....	....	....	....	....	....	....	....	....	....	....
1968-69	Ottawa 67's	OHA	52	1	7	8	....	....	....	47	....	....	....	....	....	....	....	....	....	....	7	0	0	0	2	....	....	....
1969-70	Kitchener Rangers	OHA	51	10	23	33	....	....	....	119	....	....	....	....	....	....	....	....	....	....	....	....	....	....	....	....	....	....
1970-71	Michigan Tech Huskies	WCHA	31	6	13	19	....	....	....	70	....	....	....	....	....	....	....	....	....	....	....	....	....	....	....	....	....	....
1971-72	Michigan Tech Huskies	WCHA	31	8	18	26	....	....	....	66	....	....	....	....	....	....	....	....	....	....	....	....	....	....	....	....	....	....
1972-73	Michigan Tech Huskies	WCHA	36	11	16	27	....	....	....	85	....	....	....	....	....	....	....	....	....	....	....	....	....	....	....	....	....	....
1973-74	Michigan Tech Huskies	WCHA	39	8	24	32	....	....	....	95	....	....	....	....	....	....	....	....	....	....	....	....	....	....	....	....	....	....
1974-75	**Detroit Red Wings**	**NHL**	**1**	**0**	**0**	**0**	**0**	**0**	**0**	**0**	**0**	**0**	**0**	**2**	**0.0**	**0**	**0**	**0**	**0**	**0**	....	....	....	....	....	....	....	....
	Virginia Wings	AHL	71	4	19	23	....	....	....	73	....	....	....	....	....	....	....	....	....	....	5	0	3	3	2	....	....	....
1975-76	**Detroit Red Wings**	**NHL**	**3**	**0**	**1**	**1**	**0**	**1**	**1**	**0**	**0**	**0**	**0**	**2**	**0.0**	**1**	**0**	**7**	**1**	**–5**	....	....	....	....	....	....	....	....
	New Haven Nighthawks	AHL	49	4	11	15	....	....	....	74	....	....	....	....	....	....	....	....	....	....	....	....	....	....	....	....	....	....
1976-77	**Detroit Red Wings**	**NHL**	**53**	**5**	**11**	**16**	**5**	**9**	**14**	**34**	**3**	**1**	**1**	**96**	**5.2**	**40**	**8**	**52**	**8**	**–12**	....	....	....	....	....	....	....	....
	Kansas City Blues	CHL	16	2	6	8	....	....	....	38	....	....	....	....	....	....	....	....	....	....	10	0	4	4	26	....	....	....
1977-78	Kansas City Red Wings	CHL	9	0	3	3	....	....	....	13	....	....	....	....	....	....	....	....	....	....	....	....	....	....	....	....	....	....
	Philadelphia Firebirds	AHL	69	8	22	30	....	....	....	147	....	....	....	....	....	....	....	....	....	....	4	0	1	1	4	....	....	....
	NHL Totals		**57**	**5**	**12**	**17**	**5**	**10**	**15**	**34**	**3**	**1**	**1**	**100**	**5.0**	**41**	**8**	**59**	**9**		....	....	....	....	....	....	....	....

WCHA Second All-Star Team (1973) • WCHA First All-Star Team (1974) • NCAA West First All-American Team (1974) • NCAA Championship All-Tournament Team (1974)

• NAMESTNIKOV, YEVGENY

Yevgeny Namestnikov D – R. 5'11", 190 lbs. b: Arzamis-Ig, USSR, 10/9/1971. Vancouver's 5th choice, 117th overall, in 1991 Entry Draft.

Season	Club	League	GP	G	A	Pts	AG	AA	APts	PIM	PP	SH	GW	S	%	TGF	PGF	TGA	PGA	+/–	GP	G	A	Pts	PIM	PP	SH	GW
1988-89	Torpedo Gorky	USSR	2	0	0	0	....	....	....	2	....	....	....	....	....	....	....	....	....	....	....	....	....	....	....	....	....	....
1989-90	Torpedo Gorky	USSR	23	0	0	0	....	....	....	25	....	....	....	....	....	....	....	....	....	....	....	....	....	....	....	....	....	....
	Soviet Union	WJC-A	7	0	1	1	....	....	....	6	....	....	....	....	....	....	....	....	....	....	....	....	....	....	....	....	....	....
1990-91	Torpedo Niz	USSR	42	1	2	3	....	....	....	49	....	....	....	....	....	....	....	....	....	....	....	....	....	....	....	....	....	....
1991-92	CSKA Moscow	CIS	42	1	1	2	....	....	....	47	....	....	....	....	....	....	....	....	....	....	....	....	....	....	....	....	....	....
1992-93	CSKA Moscow	CIS	42	5	5	10	....	....	....	68	....	....	....	....	....	....	....	....	....	....	....	....	....	....	....	....	....	....
1993-94	**Vancouver Canucks**	**NHL**	**17**	**0**	**5**	**5**	**0**	**4**	**4**	**10**	**0**	**0**	**0**	**11**	**0.0**	**13**	**2**	**15**	**2**	**–2**	....	....	....	....	....	....	....	....
	Hamilton Canucks	AHL	59	7	27	34	....	....	....	97	....	....	....	....	....	....	....	....	....	....	4	0	2	2	19	....	....	....
1994-95	Syracuse Crunch	AHL	59	11	22	33	....	....	....	59	....	....	....	....	....	....	....	....	....	....	....	....	....	....	....	....	....	....
	Vancouver Canucks	**NHL**	**16**	**0**	**3**	**3**	**0**	**4**	**4**	**4**	**0**	**0**	**0**	**18**	**0.0**	**12**	**3**	**9**	**2**	**+2**	**1**	**0**	**0**	**0**	**2**	**0**	**0**	**0**
1995-96	Syracuse Crunch	AHL	59	13	34	47	....	....	....	85	....	....	....	....	....	....	....	....	....	....	15	1	8	9	16	....	....	....
	Vancouver Canucks	**NHL**	....	....	....	....	....	....	....	....	....	....	....	....	....	....	....	....	....	....	**1**	**0**	**0**	**0**	**0**	....	....	....
1996-97	**Vancouver Canucks**	**NHL**	**2**	**0**	**0**	**0**	**0**	**0**	**0**	**4**	**0**	**0**	**0**	**1**	**0.0**	**0**	**0**	**1**	**0**	**–1**	....	....	....	....	....	....	....	....
	Syracuse Crunch	AHL	55	9	37	46	....	....	....	73	....	....	....	....	....	....	....	....	....	....	3	2	0	2	0	....	....	....
1997-98	**New York Islanders**	**NHL**	**6**	**0**	**1**	**1**	**0**	**1**	**1**	**4**	**0**	**0**	**0**	**2**	**0.0**	**4**	**2**	**3**	**0**	**–1**	....	....	....	....	....	....	....	....
	NHL Totals		**41**	**0**	**9**	**9**	**0**	**9**	**9**	**22**	**0**	**0**	**0**	**32**	**0.0**	**29**	**7**	**28**	**4**		**2**	**0**	**0**	**0**	**2**	**0**	**0**	**0**

Signed as a free agent by **NY Islanders**, July 21, 1997.

• NANNE, LOU

Lou "Sweet Lou from the Soo" Nanne D/RW – R. 6'1", 185 lbs. b: Sault Ste. Marie, Ont., 6/2/1941.

Season	Club	League	GP	G	A	Pts	AG	AA	APts	PIM	PP	SH	GW	S	%	TGF	PGF	TGA	PGA	+/–	GP	G	A	Pts	PIM	PP	SH	GW
1960-61	University of Minnesota	WCHA	30	4	12	16	....	....	....	52	....	....	....	....	....	....	....	....	....	....	....	....	....	....	....	....	....	....
1961-62	University of Minnesota	WCHA	22	4	11	15	....	....	....	37	....	....	....	....	....	....	....	....	....	....	....	....	....	....	....	....	....	....
1962-63	University of Minnesota	WCHA	29	14	29	*43	....	....	....	30	....	....	....	....	....	....	....	....	....	....	....	....	....	....	....	....	....	....
1963-64	Rochester Mustangs	USHL	STATISTICS NOT AVAILABLE																									
1964-65	Rochester Mustangs	USHL	STATISTICS NOT AVAILABLE																									
1965-66	Rochester Mustangs	USHL	25	23	22	45	....	....	....	4	....	....	....	....	....	....	....	....	....	....	....	....	....	....	....	....	....	....
1966-67	Rochester Mustangs	USHL	24	11	12	23	....	....	....	8	....	....	....	....	....	....	....	....	....	....	....	....	....	....	....	....	....	....
1967-68	United States	Nat-Team	....	....	....	....	....	....	....	....	....	....	....	....	....	....	....	....	....	....	....	....	....	....	....	....	....	....
	United States	Olympics	7	2	2	4	....	....	....	12	....	....	....	....	....	....	....	....	....	....	....	....	....	....	....	....	....	....
	Minnesota North Stars	**NHL**	**2**	**0**	**1**	**1**	**0**	**1**	**1**	**0**	**0**	**0**	**0**	**0**	**0.0**	**1**	**0**	**1**	**0**	**0**	....	....	....	....	....	....	....	....
1968-69	**Minnesota North Stars**	**NHL**	**41**	**2**	**12**	**14**	**2**	**11**	**13**	**47**	**1**	**1**	**0**	**71**	**2.8**	**51**	**10**	**59**	**9**	**–9**	....	....	....	....	....	....	....	....
	Memphis South Stars	CHL	3	0	1	1	....	....	....	0	....	....	....	....	....	....	....	....	....	....	....	....	....	....	....	....	....	....
	Cleveland Barons	AHL	10	1	2	3	....	....	....	8	....	....	....	....	....	....	....	....	....	....	....	....	....	....	....	....	....	....
1969-70	**Minnesota North Stars**	**NHL**	**74**	**3**	**20**	**23**	**3**	**20**	**23**	**75**	**1**	**0**	**0**	**96**	**3.1**	**66**	**13**	**75**	**14**	**–8**	**5**	**0**	**2**	**2**	**2**	**0**	**0**	**0**
1970-71	**Minnesota North Stars**	**NHL**	**68**	**5**	**11**	**16**	**5**	**10**	**15**	**22**	**0**	**0**	**0**	**61**	**8.2**	**34**	**2**	**49**	**11**	**–6**	**12**	**3**	**6**	**9**	**4**	**0**	**0**	**2**
1971-72	**Minnesota North Stars**	**NHL**	**78**	**21**	**28**	**49**	**22**	**26**	**48**	**27**	**7**	**0**	**6**	**154**	**13.6**	**68**	**21**	**52**	**0**	**–5**	**7**	**0**	**0**	**0**	**0**	**0**	**0**	**0**
1972-73	**Minnesota North Stars**	**NHL**	**74**	**15**	**20**	**35**	**15**	**17**	**32**	**39**	**2**	**0**	**2**	**142**	**10.6**	**68**	**12**	**38**	**1**	**+19**	**6**	**1**	**2**	**3**	**0**	**0**	**0**	**0**
1973-74	**Minnesota North Stars**	**NHL**	**76**	**11**	**21**	**32**	**11**	**18**	**29**	**46**	**2**	**0**	**2**	**139**	**7.9**	**90**	**14**	**90**	**13**	**–1**	....	....	....	....	....	....	....	....
1974-75	**Minnesota North Stars**	**NHL**	**49**	**6**	**9**	**15**	**6**	**7**	**13**	**35**	**1**	**0**	**0**	**49**	**12.2**	**43**	**9**	**65**	**7**	**–24**	....	....	....	....	....	....	....	....
1975-76	**Minnesota North Stars**	**NHL**	**79**	**3**	**14**	**17**	**3**	**11**	**14**	**45**	**2**	**0**	**0**	**83**	**3.6**	**53**	**18**	**101**	**32**	**–34**	....	....	....	....	....	....	....	....
	United States	WEC-A	10	1	3	4	....	....	....	26	....	....	....	....	....	....	....	....	....	....	....	....	....	....	....	....	....	....
1976-77	United States	C Cup	5	0	2	2	....	....	....	6	....	....	....	....	....	....	....	....	....	....	....	....	....	....	....	....	....	....
	Minnesota North Stars	**NHL**	**68**	**2**	**20**	**22**	**2**	**16**	**18**	**12**	**2**	**0**	**0**	**69**	**2.9**	**74**	**27**	**82**	**11**	**–24**	**2**	**0**	**0**	**0**	**2**	**0**	**0**	**0**
	United States	WEC-A	10	2	2	4	....	....	....	19	....	....	....	....	....	....	....	....	....	....	....	....	....	....	....	....	....	....
1977-78	**Minnesota North Stars**	**NHL**	**26**	**0**	**1**	**1**	**0**	**1**	**1**	**8**	**0**	**0**	**0**	**22**	**0.0**	**14**	**3**	**32**	**7**	**–14**	....	....	....	....	....	....	....	....
	NHL Totals		**635**	**68**	**157**	**225**	**69**	**138**	**207**	**356**	**18**	**1**	**10**	**886**	**7.7**	**562**	**129**	**644**	**105**		**32**	**4**	**10**	**14**	**8**	**0**	**0**	**2**

WCHA First All-Star Team (1963) • NCAA West First All-American Team (1963) • Won Lester Patrick Trophy (1989)

Signed as a free agent by **Minnesota**, March, 1968.

• NANTAIS, RICHARD

Richard Nantais LW – L. 5'11", 188 lbs. b: Repentigny, Que., 10/27/1954. Minnesota's 2nd choice, 24th overall, in 1974 Amateur Draft.

Season	Club	League	GP	G	A	Pts	AG	AA	APts	PIM	PP	SH	GW	S	%	TGF	PGF	TGA	PGA	+/–	GP	G	A	Pts	PIM	PP	SH	GW
1970-71	Quebec Remaprts	QMJHL	....	....	....	....	....	....	....	....	....	....	....	....	....	....	....	....	....	....	7	0	0	0	2	....	....	....
1971-72	Quebec Remparts	QMJHL	62	25	46	71	....	....	....	*283	....	....	....	....	....	....	....	....	....	....	15	8	12	20	34	....	....	....
1972-73	Quebec Remparts	QMJHL	59	21	27	48	....	....	....	165	....	....	....	....	....	....	....	....	....	....	....	....	....	....	....	....	....	....
1973-74	Quebec Remparts	QMJHL	67	64	130	194	....	....	....	213	....	....	....	....	....	....	....	....	....	....	....	....	....	....	....	....	....	....
1974-75	**Minnesota North Stars**	**NHL**	**18**	**4**	**1**	**5**	**4**	**1**	**5**	**9**	**0**	**0**	**1**	**13**	**30.8**	**7**	**0**	**6**	**0**	**+1**	....	....	....	....	....	....	....	....
	New Haven Nighthawks	AHL	47	21	12	33	....	....	....	145	....	....	....	....	....	....	....	....	....	....	16	3	3	6	44	....	....	....
1975-76	**Minnesota North Stars**	**NHL**	**5**	**0**	**0**	**0**	**0**	**0**	**0**	**17**	**0**	**0**	**0**	**2**	**0.0**	**1**	**1**	**1**	**0**	**–1**	....	....	....	....	....	....	....	....
	New Haven Nighthawks	AHL	38	8	6	14	....	....	....	79	....	....	....	....	....	....	....	....	....	....	....	....	....	....	....	....	....	....
	Springfield Indians	AHL	3	0	1	1	....	....	....	4	....	....	....	....	....	....	....	....	....	....	....	....	....	....	....	....	....	....
	Richmond Robins	AHL	21	3	4	7	....	....	....	39	....	....	....	....	....	....	....	....	....	....	8	2	4	6	*33	....	....	....
1976-77	**Minnesota North Stars**	**NHL**	**40**	**1**	**3**	**4**	**1**	**2**	**3**	**53**	**0**	**0**	**0**	**23**	**4.3**	**9**	**1**	**16**	**0**	**–8**	....	....	....	....	....	....	....	....
1977-78	Fort Worth Texans	CHL	60	11	18	29	....	....	....	197	....	....	....	....	....	....	....	....	....	....	13	3	1	4	*49	....	....	....
	NHL Totals		**63**	**5**	**4**	**9**	**5**	**3**	**8**	**79**	**0**	**0**	**1**	**38**	**13.2**	**17**	**2**	**23**	**0**		....	....	....	....	....	....	....	....

● **NAPIER, MARK** Mark Napier RW – L. 5'10", 182 lbs. b: Toronto, Ont., 1/28/1957. Montreal's 1st choice, 10th overall, in 1977 Amateur Draft.

			REGULAR SEASON																		PLAYOFFS							
Season	Club	League	GP	G	A	Pts	AG	AA	APts	PIM	PP	SH	GW	S	%	TGF	PGF	TGA	PGA	+/-	GP	G	A	Pts	PIM	PP	SH	GW
1972-73	Wexford Raiders	OJHL	44	41	27	68	....	....	....	201	....	....	....	....	....	....	....	....	....	....	....	....	....	....	....	....	....	....
1973-74	Toronto Marlboros	OHA	70	47	46	93	....	....	....	63	....	....	....	....	....	....	....	....	....	....	....	....	....	....	....	....	....	....
1974-75	Toronto Marlboros	OHA	61	66	64	130	....	....	....	106	....	....	....	....	....	....	....	....	....	....	23	*24	24	*48	13	....	....	....
1975-76	Toronto Toros	WHA	78	43	50	93	....	....	....	20	....	....	....	....	....	....	....	....	....	....	....	....	....	....	....	....	....	....
1976-77	Birmingham Bulls	WHA	80	60	36	96	....	....	....	24	....	....	....	....	....	....	....	....	....	....	....	....	....	....	....	....	....	....
1977-78	Birmingham Bulls	WHA	79	33	32	65	....	....	....	9	....	....	....	....	....	....	....	....	....	....	5	0	2	2	14	....	....	....
1978-79	Montreal Canadiens	NHL	54	11	20	31	10	15	25	11	2	0	0	73	15.1	53	17	20	1	+17	12	3	2	5	2	0	0	0
1979-80	Montreal Canadiens	NHL	76	16	33	49	14	25	39	7	4	0	1	123	13.0	75	25	40	1	+11	10	2	6	8	0	1	0	0
1980-81	Montreal Canadiens	NHL	79	35	36	71	29	25	54	24	5	0	6	185	18.9	105	24	48	1	+34	3	0	0	0	2	0	0	0
1981-82	Montreal Canadiens	NHL	80	40	41	81	32	27	59	14	9	0	5	186	21.5	105	20	39	3	+49	5	3	2	5	0	1	1	1
	Canada	WEC-A	9	3	1	4	....	....	....	0	....	....	....	....	....	....	....	....	....	....	....	....	....	....	....	....	....	....
1982-83	Montreal Canadiens	NHL	73	40	27	67	33	19	52	6	3	0	6	171	23.4	82	11	51	0	+20	3	0	0	0	0	0	0	0
1983-84	Montreal Canadiens	NHL	5	3	2	5	2	1	3	0	0	0	1	11	27.3	7	1	6	0	0	....	....	....	....	....	....	....	....
	Minnesota North Stars	NHL	58	13	28	41	10	19	29	17	0	0	1	83	15.7	55	14	41	2	+2	12	3	2	5	0	3	0	0
1984-85	Minnesota North Stars	NHL	39	10	18	28	8	12	20	2	3	1	1	97	10.3	43	16	39	6	–6	....	....	....	....	....	....	....	....
	Edmonton Oilers	NHL	33	9	26	35	7	18	25	19	3	0	0	50	18.0	53	12	29	0	+12	18	5	5	10	7	1	0	0
1985-86	Edmonton Oilers	NHL	80	24	32	56	19	21	40	14	3	1	4	117	20.5	73	7	54	1	+13	10	1	4	5	0	0	0	0
1986-87	Edmonton Oilers	NHL	62	8	13	21	7	9	16	2	0	1	0	88	9.1	29	1	35	10	+3	....	....	....	....	....	....	....	....
	Buffalo Sabres	NHL	15	5	5	10	4	4	8	0	1	0	0	40	12.5	16	7	23	9	–5	....	....	....	....	....	....	....	....
1987-88	Buffalo Sabres	NHL	47	10	8	18	9	6	15	8	0	1	2	81	12.3	27	0	48	18	–3	6	0	3	3	0	0	0	0
1988-89	Buffalo Sabres	NHL	66	11	17	28	9	12	21	33	0	2	1	92	12.0	40	0	68	25	–3	3	1	0	1	0	0	0	0
1989-90	HC Bolzano	Italy	36	68	72	140	....	....	....	6	....	....	....	....	....	....	....	....	....	....	6	8	6	14	2	....	....	....
1990-91	Varese	Italy	36	*45	*73	*118	....	....	....	4	....	....	....	....	....	....	....	....	....	....	10	8	18	26	0	....	....	....
1991-92	Milano Devils	Italy	23	26	27	53	....	....	....	0	....	....	....	....	....	....	....	....	....	....	....	....	....	....	....	....	....	....
1992-93	Milano Lions	Italy	27	19	32	51	....	....	....	2	....	....	....	....	....	....	....	....	....	....	....	....	....	....	....	....	....	....
	NHL Totals		767	235	306	541	193	213	406	157	33	6	28	1397	16.8	763	155	541	77		82	18	24	42	11	6	1	1
	Other Major League Totals		237	136	118	254	....	....	....	53	....	....	....	....	....	....	....	....	....		5	0	2	2	14	....	....	....

OHA First All-Star Team (1975) • Won Lou Kaplan Trophy (WHA Rookie of the Year) (1976)

Signed as an underage free agent by **Toronto** (WHA), May, 1975. Transferred to **Birmingham** (WHA) after **Toronto** (WHA) franchise relocated, June 30, 1976. Traded to **Minnesota** by **Montreal** with Keith Acton and Toronto's 3rd round choice (previously acquired, Minnesota selected Ken Hodge Jr.) in 1984 Entry Draft for Bobby Smith, October 28, 1983. Traded to **Edmonton** by **Minnesota** for Gord Sherven and Terry Martin, January 24, 1985. Traded to **Buffalo** by **Edmonton** with Lee Fogolin for Normand Lacombe, Wayne Van Dorp and future considerations, March 6, 1987.

● **NASLUND, MARKUS** Markus Naslund RW – L. 6', 186 lbs. b: Ornskoldsvik, Sweden, 7/30/1973. Pittsburgh's 1st choice, 16th overall, in 1991 Entry Draft.

Season	Club	League	GP	G	A	Pts	AG	AA	APts	PIM	PP	SH	GW	S	%	TGF	PGF	TGA	PGA	+/-	GP	G	A	Pts	PIM	PP	SH	GW
1990-91	MoDo AIK	Sweden	32	10	9	19	....	....	....	14	....	....	....	....	....	....	....	....	....	....	....	....	....	....	....	....	....	....
1991-92	MoDo AIK	Sweden	39	22	18	40	....	....	....	54	....	....	....	....	....	....	....	....	....	....	....	....	....	....	....	....	....	....
	Sweden	WJC-A	7	8	2	10	....	....	....	12	....	....	....	....	....	....	....	....	....	....	....	....	....	....	....	....	....	....
1992-93	MoDo AIK	Sweden	39	22	17	39	....	....	....	67	....	....	....	....	....	....	....	....	....	....	3	3	2	5	0	....	....	....
	Sweden	WJC-A	7	13	11	24	....	....	....	33	....	....	....	....	....	....	....	....	....	....	....	....	....	....	....	....	....	....
	Sweden	WC-A	8	1	1	2	....	....	....	14	....	....	....	....	....	....	....	....	....	....	....	....	....	....	....	....	....	....
1993-94	Pittsburgh Penguins	NHL	71	4	7	11	4	5	9	27	1	0	0	80	5.0	23	1	25	0	–3	....	....	....	....	....	....	....	....
	Cleveland Lumberjacks	IHL	5	1	6	7	....	....	....	4	....	....	....	....	....	....	....	....	....	....	....	....	....	....	....	....	....	....
1994-95	Pittsburgh Penguins	NHL	14	2	2	4	4	3	7	2	0	0	0	13	15.4	4	1	3	0	0	....	....	....	....	....	....	....	....
	Cleveland Lumberjacks	IHL	7	3	4	7	....	....	....	6	....	....	....	....	....	....	....	....	....	....	4	1	3	4	8	....	....	....
1995-96	Pittsburgh Penguins	NHL	66	19	33	52	19	27	46	36	3	0	4	125	15.2	71	10	44	0	+17	....	....	....	....	....	....	....	....
	Vancouver Canucks	NHL	10	3	0	3	3	0	3	6	1	0	1	19	15.8	7	3	1	0	+3	6	1	2	3	8	1	0	0
	Sweden	WC-A	1	0	0	0	....	....	....	0	....	....	....	....	....	....	....	....	....	....	....	....	....	....	....	....	....	....
1996-97	Sweden	W-Cup	1	0	0	0	....	....	....	2	....	....	....	....	....	....	....	....	....	....	....	....	....	....	....	....	....	....
	Vancouver Canucks	NHL	78	21	20	41	22	18	40	30	4	0	4	120	17.5	54	15	64	0	–15	....	....	....	....	....	....	....	....
1997-98	Vancouver Canucks	NHL	76	14	20	34	16	19	35	56	2	1	0	106	13.2	50	9	40	4	+5	....	....	....	....	....	....	....	....
	NHL Totals		315	63	82	145	68	72	140	157	11	1	9	463	13.6	209	39	167	4		6	1	2	3	8	1	0	0

WJC-A All-Star Team (1993)

Traded to **Vancouver** by **Pittsburgh** for Alek Stojanov, March 20, 1996.

● **NASLUND, MATS** Mats Naslund LW – L. 5'7", 160 lbs. b: Timra, Sweden, 10/31/1959. Montreal's 2nd choice, 37th overall, in 1979 Entry Draft.

Season	Club	League	GP	G	A	Pts	AG	AA	APts	PIM	PP	SH	GW	S	%	TGF	PGF	TGA	PGA	+/-	GP	G	A	Pts	PIM	PP	SH	GW
1977-78	Timra	Sweden	35	13	6	19	....	....	....	14	....	....	....	....	....	....	....	....	....	....	....	....	....	....	....	....	....	....
	Sweden	WJC-A	7	2	8	10	....	....	....	6	....	....	....	....	....	....	....	....	....	....	....	....	....	....	....	....	....	....
1978-79	Brynas IF Gavle	Sweden	36	12	12	24	....	....	....	19	....	....	....	....	....	....	....	....	....	....	....	....	....	....	....	....	....	....
	Sweden	WJC-A	6	3	2	5	....	....	....	6	....	....	....	....	....	....	....	....	....	....	....	....	....	....	....	....	....	....
	Sweden	WEC-A	8	5	2	7	....	....	....	8	....	....	....	....	....	....	....	....	....	....	....	....	....	....	....	....	....	....
1979-80	Brynas IF Gavle	Sweden	36	18	19	37	....	....	....	34	....	....	....	....	....	....	....	....	....	....	7	2	2	4	4	....	....	....
	Sweden	Olympics	7	3	7	10	....	....	....	6	....	....	....	....	....	....	....	....	....	....	....	....	....	....	....	....	....	....
1980-81	Brynas IF Gavle	Sweden	36	17	*25	*42	....	....	....	34	....	....	....	....	....	....	....	....	....	....	....	....	....	....	....	....	....	....
	Sweden	WEC-A	8	0	3	3	....	....	....	6	....	....	....	....	....	....	....	....	....	....	....	....	....	....	....	....	....	....
1981-82	Brynas IF Gavle	Sweden	36	24	18	42	....	....	....	16	....	....	....	....	....	....	....	....	....	....	....	....	....	....	....	....	....	....
	Sweden	WEC-A	10	2	4	6	....	....	....	6	....	....	....	....	....	....	....	....	....	....	....	....	....	....	....	....	....	....
1982-83	Montreal Canadiens	NHL	74	26	45	71	21	31	52	10	1	0	6	122	21.3	102	22	46	0	+34	3	1	0	1	0	1	0	0
	Sweden	WEC-A	10	3	4	7	....	....	....	2	....	....	....	....	....	....	....	....	....	....	....	....	....	....	....	....	....	....
1983-84	Montreal Canadiens	NHL	77	29	35	64	23	24	47	4	3	0	1	146	19.9	91	24	71	9	+5	15	6	8	14	4	3	1	3
1984-85	Sweden	C-Cup	8	2	3	5	....	....	....	6	....	....	....	....	....	....	....	....	....	....	....	....	....	....	....	....	....	....
	Montreal Canadiens	NHL	80	42	37	79	34	25	59	14	9	2	8	179	23.5	110	38	69	16	+19	12	7	4	11	6	3	0	2
1985-86	Montreal Canadiens	NHL	80	43	67	110	35	45	80	16	19	0	7	223	19.3	155	71	76	3	+11	20	8	11	19	4	4	0	0
1986-87	Montreal Canadiens	NHL	79	25	55	80	22	40	62	16	10	0	3	173	14.5	114	57	60	0	–3	17	7	15	22	11	4	0	3
1987-88	Sweden	C-Cup	6	1	2	3	....	....	....	2	....	....	....	....	....	....	....	....	....	....	....	....	....	....	....	....	....	....
	Montreal Canadiens	NHL	78	24	59	83	21	42	63	14	4	0	2	167	14.4	125	49	61	2	+17	6	0	7	7	2	0	0	0
1988-89	Montreal Canadiens	NHL	77	33	51	84	28	36	64	14	14	0	4	165	20.0	117	43	40	0	+34	21	4	11	15	6	1	0	0
1989-90	Montreal Canadiens	NHL	72	21	20	41	18	14	32	19	6	0	3	136	15.4	58	14	43	2	+3	3	1	1	2	0	0	0	1
1990-91	HC Lugano	Switz.	31	27	29	56	....	....	....	....	....	....	....	....	....	....	....	....	....	....	11	4	8	12	....	....	....	....
	Sweden	WEC-A	10	3	5	8	....	....	....	0	....	....	....	....	....	....	....	....	....	....	....	....	....	....	....	....	....	....
1991-92	Sweden	C-Cup	6	1	3	4	....	....	....	0	....	....	....	....	....	....	....	....	....	....	....	....	....	....	....	....	....	....
	Malmo IF	Sweden	39	15	24	39	....	....	....	10	....	....	....	....	....	....	....	....	....	....	10	3	2	5	....	....	....	....
	Sweden	Olympics	8	1	5	6	....	....	....	27	....	....	....	....	....	....	....	....	....	....	....	....	....	....	....	....	....	....
1992-93	Malmo IF	Sweden	33	11	21	32	....	....	....	10	....	....	....	....	....	....	....	....	....	....	1	0	0	0	....	....	....	....
1993-94	Malmo IF	Sweden	40	14	30	44	....	....	....	8	....	....	....	....	....	....	....	....	....	....	11	2	4	6	4	....	....	....
	Sweden	Olympics	8	0	7	7	....	....	....	0	....	....	....	....	....	....	....	....	....	....	....	....	....	....	....	....	....	....
1994-95	Boston Bruins	NHL	34	8	14	22	14	21	35	4	2	0	1	48	16.7	34	16	23	1	–4	5	1	0	1	0	0	0	0
	NHL Totals		651	251	383	634	216	278	494	111	68	2	35	1359	18.5	906	334	489	33		102	35	57	92	33	16	1	9

WJC-A All-Star Team (1978) • Swedish World All-Star Team (1979, 1980, 1981, 1982, 1983) • Swedish Player of the Year (1980) • NHL All-Rookie Team (1983) • NHL Second All-Star Team (1986) • Won Lady Byng Trophy (1988)

Played in NHL All-Star Game (1984, 1986, 1988)

Signed as a free agent by **Boston**, February 21, 1994.

● **NATTRESS, RIC** Ric "Stash" Nattress D – R, 6'2", 210 lbs. b: Hamilton, Ont., 5/25/1962. Montreal's 2nd choice, 27th overall, in 1980 Entry Draft.

Season	Club	League	GP	G	A	Pts	AG	AA	APts	PIM	PP	SH	GW	S	%	TGF	PGF	TGA	PGA	+/-	GP	G	A	Pts	PIM	PP	SH	GW
1979-80	Brantford Alexanders	OHA	65	3	21	24	....	....	....	94	....	....	....	....	....	....	....	....	....	....	11	1	6	7	38	....	....	....
1980-81	Brantford Alexanders	OHA	51	8	34	42	....	....	....	106	....	....	....	....	....	....	....	....	....	....	6	1	4	5	19	....	....	....
1981-82	Brantford Alexanders	OHL	59	11	50	61	....	....	....	126	....	....	....	....	....	....	....	....	....	....	11	3	7	10	17	....	....	....
	Nova Scotia Voyageurs	AHL	....	....	....	....	....	....	....	....	....	....	....	....	....	....	....	....	....	....	5	0	1	1	7	....	....	....
1982-83	Montreal Canadiens	NHL	40	1	3	4	1	2	3	19	0	0	0	44	2.3	31	1	25	3	+8	3	0	0	0	10	0	0	0
	Nova Scotia Voyageurs	AHL	9	0	4	4	....	....	....	16	....	....	....	....	....	....	....	....	....	....	....	....	....	....	....	....	....	....
1983-84	Montreal Canadiens	NHL	34	0	12	12	0	8	8	15	0	0	0	33	0.0	32	10	34	1	–11	....	....	....	....	....	....	....	....

Season	Club	League	GP	G	A	Pts	AG	AA	APts	PIM	PP	SH	GW	S	%	TGF	PGF	TGA	PGA	+/–	GP	G	A	Pts	PIM	PP	SH	GW
			REGULAR SEASON																		PLAYOFFS							
1984-85	**Montreal Canadiens**	**NHL**	**5**	**0**	**1**	**1**	**0**	**1**	**1**	**2**	**0**	**0**	**0**	**3**	**0.0**	**3**	**0**	**5**	**0**	**–2**	**2**	**0**	**0**	**0**	**2**	**0**	**0**	**0**
	Sherbrooke Canadiens	AHL	72	8	40	48	....	....	....	37	....	....	....	....	....	....	....	....	....	....	16	4	13	17	20	....	....	....
1985-86	**St. Louis Blues**	**NHL**	**78**	**4**	**20**	**24**	**3**	**13**	**16**	**52**	**1**	**0**	**2**	**124**	**3.2**	**89**	**20**	**98**	**21**	**–8**	**18**	**1**	**4**	**5**	**24**	**0**	**0**	**0**
1986-87	**St. Louis Blues**	**NHL**	**73**	**6**	**22**	**28**	**5**	**16**	**21**	**24**	**2**	**0**	**0**	**133**	**4.5**	**99**	**31**	**132**	**30**	**–34**	**6**	**0**	**0**	**0**	**2**	**0**	**0**	**0**
1987-88	**Calgary Flames**	**NHL**	**63**	**2**	**13**	**15**	**2**	**9**	**11**	**37**	**0**	**0**	**0**	**48**	**4.2**	**67**	**0**	**77**	**24**	**+14**	**6**	**1**	**3**	**4**	**0**	**0**	**0**	**0**
1988-89	**Calgary Flames**	**NHL**	**38**	**1**	**8**	**9**	**1**	**6**	**7**	**47**	**0**	**0**	**0**	**28**	**3.6**	**34**	**0**	**28**	**6**	**+12**	**19**	**0**	**3**	**3**	**20**	**0**	**0**	**0**
1989-90	Calgary Flames	FrTour	4	0	0	0	....	....	....	0	....	....	....	....	....	....	....	....	....	....	....	....	....	....	....	....	....	....
	Calgary Flames	**NHL**	**49**	**1**	**14**	**15**	**1**	**10**	**11**	**26**	**0**	**0**	**0**	**65**	**1.5**	**52**	**2**	**67**	**31**	**+14**	**6**	**2**	**0**	**2**	**0**	**0**	**0**	**0**
1990-91	**Calgary Flames**	**NHL**	**58**	**5**	**13**	**18**	**5**	**10**	**15**	**63**	**0**	**0**	**1**	**81**	**6.2**	**57**	**0**	**75**	**17**	**–1**	**7**	**1**	**0**	**1**	**2**	**0**	**0**	**1**
	Canada	WEC-A	7	0	1	1	....	....	....	4	....	....	....	....	....	....	....	....	....	....	....	....	....	....	....	....	....	....
1991-92	**Calgary Flames**	**NHL**	**18**	**0**	**5**	**5**	**0**	**4**	**4**	**31**	**0**	**0**	**0**	**23**	**0.0**	**15**	**0**	**21**	**6**	**0**	....	....	....	....	....	....	....	....
	Toronto Maple Leafs	**NHL**	**36**	**2**	**14**	**16**	**2**	**11**	**13**	**32**	**0**	**0**	**1**	**43**	**4.7**	**41**	**1**	**57**	**16**	**–1**	....	....	....	....	....	....	....	....
1992-93	**Philadelphia Flyers**	**NHL**	**44**	**7**	**10**	**17**	**6**	**7**	**13**	**29**	**0**	**0**	**4**	**57**	**12.3**	**41**	**0**	**60**	**20**	**+1**	....	....	....	....	....	....	....	....
	NHL Totals		**536**	**29**	**135**	**164**	**26**	**97**	**123**	**377**	**3**	**0**	**8**	**682**	**4.3**	**561**	**65**	**679**	**175**		**67**	**5**	**10**	**15**	**60**	**0**	**0**	**1**

Rights traded to **St. Louis** by **Montreal** for cash, October 7, 1985. Traded to **Calgary** by **St. Louis** for Calgary's 4th round choice (Andy Rymsha) in 1987 Entry Draft and 5th round choice (Dave Lacouture) in 1988 Entry Draft, June 13, 1987. Traded to **Toronto** by **Calgary** with Doug Gilmour, Jamie Macoun, Kent Manderville and Rick Wamsley for Gary Leeman, Alexander Godynyuk, Jeff Resse, Michel Petit and Craig Berube, January 2, 1992. Signed as a free agent by **Philadelphia**, August 21, 1992.

• NATYSHAK, MIKE

Mike Natyshak RW – R. 6'2", 201 lbs. b: Belle River, Ont., 11/29/1963. Quebec's 1st choice, 23rd overall, in 1986 Supplemental Draft.

Season	Club	League	GP	G	A	Pts	AG	AA	APts	PIM	PP	SH	GW	S	%	TGF	PGF	TGA	PGA	+/–	GP	G	A	Pts	PIM	PP	SH	GW
1983-84	Bowling Green University	CCHA	19	0	0	0	....	....	....	0	....	....	....	....	....	....	....	....	....	....	....	....	....	....	....	....	....	....
1984-85	Bowling Green University	CCHA	38	4	9	13	....	....	....	79	....	....	....	....	....	....	....	....	....	....	....	....	....	....	....	....	....	....
1985-86	Bowling Green University	CCHA	40	3	5	8	....	....	....	62	....	....	....	....	....	....	....	....	....	....	....	....	....	....	....	....	....	....
1986-87	Bowling Green University	CCHA	45	5	10	15	....	....	....	101	....	....	....	....	....	....	....	....	....	....	....	....	....	....	....	....	....	....
1987-88	**Quebec Nordiques**	**NHL**	**4**	**0**	**0**	**0**	**0**	**0**	**0**	**0**	**0**	**0**	**0**	**0**	**0.0**	**0**	**0**	**1**	**0**	**–1**	....	....	....	....	....	....	....	....
	Fredericton Express	AHL	46	5	9	14	....	....	....	34	....	....	....	....	....	....	....	....	....	....	6	0	3	3	13	....	....	....
1988-89	Fort Wayne Komets	IHL	48	5	9	14	....	....	....	95	....	....	....	....	....	....	....	....	....	....	3	0	0	0	0	....	....	....
	NHL Totals		**4**	**0**	**0**	**0**	**0**	**0**	**0**	**0**	**0**	**0**	**0**	**0**	**0.0**	**0**	**0**	**1**	**0**		....	....	....	....	....	....	....	....

• NAZAROV, ANDREI

Andrei Nazarov LW – R. 6'5", 230 lbs. b: Chelyabinsk, USSR, 5/22/1974. San Jose's 2nd choice, 10th overall, in 1992 Entry Draft.

Season	Club	League	GP	G	A	Pts	AG	AA	APts	PIM	PP	SH	GW	S	%	TGF	PGF	TGA	PGA	+/–	GP	G	A	Pts	PIM	PP	SH	GW
1991-92	Moscow Dynamo	CIS	2	1	0	1	....	....	....	2	....	....	....	....	....	....	....	....	....	....	....	....	....	....	....	....	....	....
1992-93	Moscow Dynamo	CIS	42	8	2	10	....	....	....	79	....	....	....	....	....	....	....	....	....	....	10	1	1	2	8	....	....	....
1993-94	Moscow Dynamo	CIS	6	2	2	4	....	....	....	0	....	....	....	....	....	....	....	....	....	....	....	....	....	....	....	....	....	....
	San Jose Sharks	**NHL**	**1**	**0**	**0**	**0**	**0**	**0**	**0**	**0**	**0**	**0**	**0**	**0**	**0.0**	**0**	**0**	**0**	**0**	**0**	....	....	....	....	....	....	....	....
	Kansas City Blades	IHL	71	15	18	33	....	....	....	64	....	....	....	....	....	....	....	....	....	....	....	....	....	....	....	....	....	....
1994-95	Kansas City Blades	IHL	43	15	10	25	....	....	....	55	....	....	....	....	....	....	....	....	....	....	....	....	....	....	....	....	....	....
	San Jose Sharks	**NHL**	**26**	**3**	**5**	**8**	**5**	**7**	**12**	**94**	**0**	**0**	**0**	**19**	**15.8**	**13**	**2**	**12**	**0**	**–1**	**6**	**0**	**0**	**0**	**9**	**0**	**0**	**0**
1995-96	**San Jose Sharks**	**NHL**	**42**	**7**	**7**	**14**	**7**	**6**	**13**	**62**	**2**	**0**	**1**	**55**	**12.7**	**21**	**7**	**29**	**0**	**–15**	....	....	....	....	....	....	....	....
	Kansas City Blades	IHL	27	4	6	10	....	....	....	118	....	....	....	....	....	....	....	....	....	....	2	0	0	0	2	....	....	....
1996-97	**San Jose Sharks**	**NHL**	**60**	**12**	**15**	**27**	**13**	**13**	**26**	**222**	**1**	**0**	**1**	**116**	**10.3**	**39**	**5**	**38**	**0**	**–4**	....	....	....	....	....	....	....	....
	Kentucky Thoroughblades	AHL	3	1	2	3	....	....	....	4	....	....	....	....	....	....	....	....	....	....	....	....	....	....	....	....	....	....
1997-98	**San Jose Sharks**	**NHL**	**40**	**1**	**1**	**2**	**1**	**1**	**2**	**112**	**0**	**0**	**0**	**31**	**3.2**	**9**	**2**	**11**	**0**	**–4**	....	....	....	....	....	....	....	....
	Tampa Bay Lightning	**NHL**	**14**	**1**	**1**	**2**	**1**	**1**	**2**	**58**	**0**	**0**	**0**	**19**	**5.3**	**3**	**0**	**12**	**0**	**–9**	....	....	....	....	....	....	....	....
	Russia	WC-A	6	1	2	3	....	....	....	10	....	....	....	....	....	....	....	....	....	....	....	....	....	....	....	....	....	....
	NHL Totals		**183**	**24**	**29**	**53**	**27**	**28**	**55**	**548**	**3**	**0**	**2**	**240**	**10.0**	**85**	**16**	**102**	**0**		**6**	**0**	**0**	**0**	**9**	**0**	**0**	**0**

Traded to **Tampa Bay** by **San Jose** with Florida's 1st round choice (previously acquired, Tampa Bay selected Vincent Lecavalier) for Bryan Marchment, David Shaw and Tampa Bay's 1st round choice (later traded to Nashville — Nashville selected David Legwand) in 1998 Entry Draft, March 24, 1998.

• NDUR, RUMUN

Rumun Ndur D – L. 6'2", 200 lbs. b: Zaria, Nigeria, 7/7/1975. Buffalo's 3rd choice, 69th overall, in 1994 Entry Draft.

Season	Club	League	GP	G	A	Pts	AG	AA	APts	PIM	PP	SH	GW	S	%	TGF	PGF	TGA	PGA	+/–	GP	G	A	Pts	PIM	PP	SH	GW
1992-93	Guelph Platers	OHL	22	1	3	4	....	....	....	30	....	....	....	....	....	....	....	....	....	....	4	0	1	1	4	....	....	....
1993-94	Guelph Platers	OHL	61	6	33	39	....	....	....	176	....	....	....	....	....	....	....	....	....	....	9	4	1	5	24	....	....	....
1994-95	Guelph Platers	OHL	63	10	21	31	....	....	....	187	....	....	....	....	....	....	....	....	....	....	14	0	4	4	28	....	....	....
1995-96	Rochester Americans	AHL	73	2	12	14	....	....	....	306	....	....	....	....	....	....	....	....	....	....	17	1	2	3	33	....	....	....
1996-97	**Buffalo Sabres**	**NHL**	**2**	**0**	**0**	**0**	**0**	**0**	**0**	**2**	**0**	**0**	**0**	**0**	**0.0**	**1**	**0**	**0**	**0**	**+1**	....	....	....	....	....	....	....	....
	Rochester Americans	AHL	68	5	11	16	....	....	....	282	....	....	....	....	....	....	....	....	....	....	10	3	1	4	21	....	....	....
1997-98	**Buffalo Sabres**	**NHL**	**1**	**0**	**0**	**0**	**0**	**0**	**0**	**2**	**0**	**0**	**0**	**0**	**0.0**	**0**	**0**	**1**	**0**	**–1**	....	....	....	....	....	....	....	....
	Rochester Americans	AHL	50	1	12	13	....	....	....	207	....	....	....	....	....	....	....	....	....	....	4	0	2	2	16	....	....	....
	NHL Totals		**3**	**0**	**0**	**0**	**0**	**0**	**0**	**4**	**0**	**0**	**0**	**0**	**0.0**	**1**	**0**	**1**	**0**		....	....	....	....	....	....	....	....

• NEATON, PAT

Pat Neaton D – L. 6', 180 lbs. b: Redford, MI, 5/21/1971. Pittsburgh's 9th choice, 145th overall, in 1990 Entry Draft.

Season	Club	League	GP	G	A	Pts	AG	AA	APts	PIM	PP	SH	GW	S	%	TGF	PGF	TGA	PGA	+/–	GP	G	A	Pts	PIM	PP	SH	GW
1989-90	University of Michigan	CCHA	42	3	23	26	....	....	....	36	....	....	....	....	....	....	....	....	....	....	....	....	....	....	....	....	....	....
1990-91	University of Michigan	CCHA	44	15	28	43	....	....	....	78	....	....	....	....	....	....	....	....	....	....	....	....	....	....	....	....	....	....
1991-92	University of Michigan	CCHA	43	10	20	30	....	....	....	62	....	....	....	....	....	....	....	....	....	....	....	....	....	....	....	....	....	....
1992-93	University of Michigan	CCHA	38	10	18	28	....	....	....	37	....	....	....	....	....	....	....	....	....	....	....	....	....	....	....	....	....	....
1993-94	**Pittsburgh Penguins**	**NHL**	**9**	**1**	**1**	**2**	**1**	**1**	**2**	**12**	**1**	**0**	**0**	**11**	**9.1**	**9**	**5**	**2**	**1**	**+3**	....	....	....	....	....	....	....	....
	Cleveland Lumberjacks	IHL	71	8	24	32	....	....	....	78	....	....	....	....	....	....	....	....	....	....	....	....	....	....	....	....	....	....
	United States	WC-A	8	2	0	2	....	....	....	12	....	....	....	....	....	....	....	....	....	....	....	....	....	....	....	....	....	....
1994-95	Cleveland Lumberjacks	IHL	2	0	0	0	....	....	....	4	....	....	....	....	....	....	....	....	....	....	....	....	....	....	....	....	....	....
	San Diego Gulls	IHL	71	8	27	35	....	....	....	86	....	....	....	....	....	....	....	....	....	....	5	0	1	1	0	....	....	....
	United States	WC-A	4	1	0	1	....	....	....	8	....	....	....	....	....	....	....	....	....	....	....	....	....	....	....	....	....	....
1995-96	Orlando Solar Bears	IHL	77	8	27	35	....	....	....	148	....	....	....	....	....	....	....	....	....	....	21	3	5	8	34	....	....	....
1996-97	Orlando Solar Bears	IHL	81	17	35	52	....	....	....	68	....	....	....	....	....	....	....	....	....	....	10	0	1	1	13	....	....	....
1997-98	Orlando Solar Bears	IHL	78	11	24	35	....	....	....	114	....	....	....	....	....	....	....	....	....	....	17	3	11	14	12	....	....	....
	NHL Totals		**9**	**1**	**1**	**2**	**1**	**1**	**2**	**12**	**1**	**0**	**0**	**11**	**9.1**	**9**	**5**	**2**	**1**		....	....	....	....	....	....	....	....

CCHA Second All-Star Team (1991) • CCHA First All-Star Team (1993)

• NECHAYEV, VIKTOR

Viktor Nechayev C – L. 6'1", 183 lbs. b: Kuib-Vost, Siberia, 1/28/1955. Los Angeles' 7th choice, 132nd overall, in 1982 Entry Draft.

Season	Club	League	GP	G	A	Pts	AG	AA	APts	PIM	PP	SH	GW	S	%	TGF	PGF	TGA	PGA	+/–	GP	G	A	Pts	PIM	PP	SH	GW
1980-81	Binokar	USSR	20	10	7	17	....	....	....	....	....	....	....	....	....	....	....	....	....	....	....	....	....	....	....	....	....	....
1981-82	Izhorets	USSR	20	16	7	23	....	....	....	....	....	....	....	....	....	....	....	....	....	....	....	....	....	....	....	....	....	....
1982-83	**Los Angeles Kings**	**NHL**	**3**	**1**	**0**	**1**	**1**	**0**	**1**	**0**	**0**	**0**	**0**	**7**	**14.3**	**2**	**0**	**1**	**0**	**+1**	....	....	....	....	....	....	....	....
	New Haven Nighthawks	AHL	28	4	7	11	....	....	....	6	....	....	....	....	....	....	....	....	....	....	....	....	....	....	....	....	....	....
	Saginaw Gears	IHL	10	1	4	5	....	....	....	0	....	....	....	....	....	....	....	....	....	....	....	....	....	....	....	....	....	....
1983-84	Dusseldorfer EG	Germany	38	7	9	16	....	....	....	30	....	....	....	....	....	....	....	....	....	....	....	....	....	....	....	....	....	....
	NHL Totals		**3**	**1**	**0**	**1**	**1**	**0**	**1**	**0**	**0**	**0**	**0**	**7**	**14.3**	**2**	**0**	**1**	**0**		....	....	....	....	....	....	....	....

• NECKAR, STANISLAV

Stanislav Neckar D – L. 6'1", 212 lbs. b: Ceske Budejovice, Czech., 12/22/1975. Ottawa's 2nd choice, 29th overall, in 1994 Entry Draft.

Season	Club	League	GP	G	A	Pts	AG	AA	APts	PIM	PP	SH	GW	S	%	TGF	PGF	TGA	PGA	+/–	GP	G	A	Pts	PIM	PP	SH	GW
1992-93	Budejovice	Czech.	42	2	9	11	....	....	....	12	....	....	....	....	....	....	....	....	....	....	....	....	....	....	....	....	....	....
	Czech Republic	WJC-A	7	2	0	2	....	....	....	6	....	....	....	....	....	....	....	....	....	....	....	....	....	....	....	....	....	....
1993-94	Budejovice	Czech.	12	3	2	5	....	....	....	2	....	....	....	....	....	....	....	....	....	....	3	0	0	0	....	....	....	....
1994-95	Detroit Vipers	IHL	15	2	2	4	....	....	....	15	....	....	....	....	....	....	....	....	....	....	....	....	....	....	....	....	....	....
	Ottawa Senators	**NHL**	**48**	**1**	**3**	**4**	**2**	**4**	**6**	**37**	**0**	**0**	**0**	**34**	**2.9**	**38**	**7**	**64**	**13**	**–20**	....	....	....	....	....	....	....	....
1995-96	**Ottawa Senators**	**NHL**	**82**	**3**	**9**	**12**	**3**	**7**	**10**	**54**	**1**	**0**	**0**	**57**	**5.3**	**53**	**1**	**106**	**38**	**–16**	....	....	....	....	....	....	....	....
	Czech Republic	WC-A	8	1	3	4	....	....	....	2	....	....	....	....	....	....	....	....	....	....	....	....	....	....	....	....	....	....
1996-97	Czech Republic	W Cup	3	0	0	0	....	....	....	0	....	....	....	....	....	....	....	....	....	....	....	....	....	....	....	....	....	....
	Ottawa Senators	**NHL**	**5**	**0**	**0**	**0**	**0**	**0**	**0**	**2**	**0**	**0**	**0**	**3**	**0.0**	**5**	**0**	**6**	**3**	**+2**	....	....	....	....	....	....	....	....
1997-98	**Ottawa Senators**	**NHL**	**60**	**2**	**2**	**4**	**2**	**2**	**4**	**31**	**0**	**0**	**0**	**43**	**4.7**	**22**	**0**	**51**	**15**	**–14**	**9**	**0**	**0**	**0**	**2**	**0**	**0**	**0**
	NHL Totals		**195**	**6**	**14**	**20**	**7**	**13**	**20**	**124**	**1**	**0**	**0**	**137**	**4.4**	**118**	**8**	**227**	**69**		**9**	**0**	**0**	**0**	**2**	**0**	**0**	**0**

• NEDOMANSKY, VACLAV

Vaclav "Big Ned" Nedomansky RW – L. 6'2", 205 lbs. b: Hodonin, Czech., 3/14/1944.

Season	Club	League	GP	G	A	Pts	AG	AA	APts	PIM	PP	SH	GW	S	%	TGF	PGF	TGA	PGA	+/–	GP	G	A	Pts	PIM	PP	SH	GW
			REGULAR SEASON																		PLAYOFFS							
1964-65	Czechoslovakia	WEC-A	7	4	2	6	....	....	....	2	....	....	....	....	....	....	....	....	....	....	....	....	....	....	....	....	....	....
1965-66	Czechoslovakia	WEC-A	7	5	2	7	....	....	....	8	....	....	....	....	....	....	....	....	....	....	....	....	....	....	....	....	....	....
1966-67	Czechoslovakia	WEC-A	7	1	2	3	....	....	....	14	....	....	....	....	....	....	....	....	....	....	....	....	....	....	....	....	....	....
1967-68	Czechoslovakia	Olympics	7	5	2	7	....	....	....	4	....	....	....	....	....	....	....	....	....	....	....	....	....	....	....	....	....	....
1968-69	Czechoslovakia	WEC-A	10	9	2	11	....	....	....	10	....	....	....	....	....	....	....	....	....	....	....	....	....	....	....	....	....	....
1969-70	Czechoslovakia	WEC-A	10	10	7	17	....	....	....	11	....	....	....	....	....	....	....	....	....	....	....	....	....	....	....	....	....	....
1970-71	Czechoslovakia	WEC-A	10	10	7	17	....	....	....	....	....	....	....	....	....	....	....	....	....	....	....	....	....	....	....	....	....	....
1971-72	Czechoslovakia	Olympics	6	8	3	11	....	....	....	0	....	....	....	....	....	....	....	....	....	....	....	....	....	....	....	....	....	....
	Czechoslovakia	WEC-A	9	9	6	15	....	....	....	0	....	....	....	....	....	....	....	....	....	....	....	....	....	....	....	....	....	....
1972-73	Czechoslovakia	WEC-A	10	9	3	12	....	....	....	2	....	....	....	....	....	....	....	....	....	....	....	....	....	....	....	....	....	....
1973-74	Czechoslovakia	WEC-A	10	10	3	13	....	....	....	4	....	....	....	....	....	....	....	....	....	....	....	....	....	....	....	....	....	....
1974-75	Toronto Toros	WHA	78	41	40	81	....	....	....	19	....	....	....	....	....	....	....	....	....	....	6	3	1	4	9	....	....	....
1975-76	Toronto Toros	WHA	81	56	42	98	....	....	....	8	....	....	....	....	....	....	....	....	....	....	....	....	....	....	....	....	....	....
1976-77	Birmingham Bulls	WHA	81	36	33	69	....	....	....	10	....	....	....	....	....	....	....	....	....	....	....	....	....	....	....	....	....	....
1977-78	Birmingham Bulls	WHA	12	2	3	5	....	....	....	6	....	....	....	....	....	....	....	....	....	....	....	....	....	....	....	....	....	....
	Detroit Red Wings	**NHL**	**63**	**11**	**17**	**28**	**11**	**14**	**25**	**2**	**5**	**0**	**1**	**107**	**10.3**	**39**	**19**	**37**	**0**	**–17**	**7**	**3**	**5**	**8**	**0**	**1**	**0**	**0**
1978-79	**Detroit Red Wings**	**NHL**	**80**	**38**	**35**	**73**	**35**	**27**	**62**	**19**	**13**	**0**	**2**	**212**	**17.9**	**106**	**50**	**69**	**0**	**–13**	....	....	....	....	....	....	....	....
1979-80	**Detroit Red Wings**	**NHL**	**79**	**35**	**39**	**74**	**32**	**30**	**62**	**13**	**11**	**0**	**5**	**235**	**14.9**	**106**	**41**	**70**	**0**	**–5**	....	....	....	....	....	....	....	....
1980-81	**Detroit Red Wings**	**NHL**	**74**	**12**	**20**	**32**	**10**	**14**	**24**	**30**	**6**	**0**	**0**	**128**	**9.4**	**44**	**17**	**62**	**0**	**–35**	....	....	....	....	....	....	....	....
1981-82	**Detroit Red Wings**	**NHL**	**68**	**12**	**28**	**40**	**9**	**19**	**28**	**22**	**1**	**0**	**0**	**103**	**11.7**	**51**	**16**	**51**	**1**	**–15**	....	....	....	....	....	....	....	....
1982-83	**New York Rangers**	**NHL**	**1**	**1**	**0**	**1**	**1**	**0**	**1**	**0**	....	....	....	....	....	....	....	....	....	....	....	....	....	....	....	....	....	....
	St. Louis Blues	**NHL**	**22**	**2**	**9**	**11**	**2**	**6**	**8**	**2**	**1**	**0**	**0**	**35**	**5.7**	**21**	**15**	**14**	**0**	**–8**	....	....	....	....	....	....	....	....
	New York Rangers	**NHL**	**34**	**11**	**8**	**19**	**9**	**6**	**15**	**0**	**8**	**0**	**3**	**52**	**21.2**	**29**	**20**	**8**	**0**	**+1**	....	....	....	....	....	....	....	....
	NHL Totals		**421**	**122**	**156**	**278**	**109**	**116**	**225**	**88**	**45**	**0**	**11**	**872**	**14.0**	**396**	**178**	**311**	**1**		**7**	**3**	**5**	**8**	**0**	**1**	**0**	**0**
	Other Major League Totals		252	135	118	253	....	....	....	43	....	....	....	....	....	....	....	....	....	....	6	3	1	4	9	....	....	

WEC-A First All-Star Team (1969, 1970, 1974) • Named Best Forward at WEC-A (1974) • Won Paul Daneau Trophy (WHA Most Gentlemanly Player) (1976)

Signed as a free agent by **Toronto** (WHA), July, 1974. Transferred to **Birmingham** (WHA) after **Toronto** (WHA) franchise relocated, June 30, 1976. Signed as a free agent by **Detroit** after securing release from **Birmingham** (WHA), November 18, 1977. Signed as a free agent by **NY Rangers** on September 30, 1982. Claimed on waivers by **St. Louis** from **NY Rangers**, October 6, 1982. Traded to **NY Rangers** by **St. Louis** with Glen Hanlon for Andre Dore, January 4, 1983.

• NEDVED, PETR

Petr Nedved C – L. 6'3", 195 lbs. b: Liberec, Czech., 12/9/1971. Vancouver's 1st choice, 2nd overall, in 1990 Entry Draft.

Season	Club	League	GP	G	A	Pts	AG	AA	APts	PIM	PP	SH	GW	S	%	TGF	PGF	TGA	PGA	+/–	GP	G	A	Pts	PIM	PP	SH	GW
1989-90	Seattle Thunderbirds	WHL	71	65	80	145	....	....	....	80	....	....	....	....	....	....	....	....	....	....	11	4	9	13	2	....	....	....
1990-91	**Vancouver Canucks**	**NHL**	**61**	**10**	**6**	**16**	**9**	**5**	**14**	**20**	**1**	**0**	**0**	**97**	**10.3**	**25**	**3**	**45**	**2**	**–21**	**6**	**0**	**1**	**1**	**0**	**0**	**0**	**0**
1991-92	**Vancouver Canucks**	**NHL**	**77**	**15**	**22**	**37**	**14**	**17**	**31**	**36**	**5**	**0**	**1**	**99**	**15.2**	**49**	**11**	**44**	**3**	**–3**	**10**	**1**	**4**	**5**	**16**	**0**	**0**	**0**
1992-93	**Vancouver Canucks**	**NHL**	**84**	**38**	**33**	**71**	**32**	**23**	**55**	**96**	**2**	**1**	**3**	**149**	**25.5**	**106**	**28**	**75**	**17**	**+20**	**12**	**2**	**3**	**5**	**2**	**0**	**0**	**0**
1993-94	Canada	Nat-Team	17	19	12	31	....	....	....	16	....	....	....	....	....	....	....	....	....	....	....	....	....	....	....	....	....	....
	Canada	Olympics	8	5	1	6	....	....	....	6	....	....	....	....	....	....	....	....	....	....	....	....	....	....	....	....	....	....
	St. Louis Blues	**NHL**	**19**	**6**	**14**	**20**	**6**	**11**	**17**	**8**	**2**	**0**	**0**	**63**	**9.5**	**27**	**12**	**16**	**3**	**+2**	**4**	**0**	**1**	**1**	**4**	**0**	**0**	**0**
1994-95	**New York Rangers**	**NHL**	**46**	**11**	**12**	**23**	**19**	**18**	**37**	**26**	**1**	**0**	**3**	**123**	**8.9**	**35**	**6**	**30**	**0**	**–1**	**10**	**3**	**2**	**5**	**6**	**2**	**0**	**0**
1995-96	**Pittsburgh Penguins**	**NHL**	**80**	**45**	**54**	**99**	**44**	**44**	**88**	**68**	**8**	**1**	**5**	**204**	**22.1**	**129**	**31**	**86**	**25**	**+37**	**18**	**10**	**10**	**20**	**16**	**4**	**0**	**2**
1996-97	Czech Republic	W Cup	3	0	1	1	....	....	....	8	....	....	....	....	....	....	....	....	....	....	....	....	....	....	....	....	....	....
	Pittsburgh Penguins	**NHL**	**74**	**33**	**38**	**71**	**35**	**34**	**69**	**66**	**12**	**3**	**4**	**189**	**17.5**	**103**	**38**	**88**	**21**	**–2**	**5**	**1**	**2**	**3**	**12**	**0**	**1**	**0**
1997-98	Sparta Praha	Czech.	5	2	3	5	....	....	....	8	....	....	....	....	....	....	....	....	....	....	6	0	2	2	52	....	....	....
	Las Vegas Thunder	IHL	3	3	3	6	....	....	....	4	....	....	....	....	....	....	....	....	....	....	....	....	....	....	....	....	....	....
	NHL Totals		**441**	**158**	**179**	**337**	**159**	**152**	**311**	**320**	**31**	**5**	**16**	**924**	**17.1**	**474**	**129**	**384**	**71**		**65**	**17**	**23**	**40**	**56**	**6**	**1**	**2**

Canadian Major Junior Rookie of the Year (1990)

Signed as a free agent by **St. Louis**, March 5, 1994. Traded to **NY Rangers** by **St. Louis** for Esa Tikkanen and Doug Lidster, July 24, 1994. Traded to **Pittsburgh** by **NY Rangers** with Sergei Zubov for Luc Robitaille and Ulf Samuelsson, August 31, 1995.

• NEDVED, ZDENEK

Zdenek Nedved RW – L. 6', 180 lbs. b: Lany, Czech., 3/3/1975. Toronto's 3rd choice, 123rd overall, in 1993 Entry Draft.

Season	Club	League	GP	G	A	Pts	AG	AA	APts	PIM	PP	SH	GW	S	%	TGF	PGF	TGA	PGA	+/–	GP	G	A	Pts	PIM	PP	SH	GW
1991-92	Poldi Kladno	Czech.	19	15	12	27	....	....	....	22	....	....	....	....	....	....	....	....	....	....	....	....	....	....	....	....	....	....
1992-93	Sudbury Wolves	OHL	18	3	9	12	....	....	....	6	....	....	....	....	....	....	....	....	....	....	....	....	....	....	....	....	....	....
1993-94	Sudbury Wolves	OHL	60	50	50	100	....	....	....	42	....	....	....	....	....	....	....	....	....	....	10	7	8	15	10	....	....	....
	Czech Republic	WJC-A	7	4	3	7	....	....	....	10	....	....	....	....	....	....	....	....	....	....	....	....	....	....	....	....	....	....
1994-95	Sudbury Wolves	OHL	59	47	51	98	....	....	....	36	....	....	....	....	....	....	....	....	....	....	18	12	16	28	16	....	....	....
	Czech Republic	WJC-A	7	4	4	8	....	....	....	10	....	....	....	....	....	....	....	....	....	....	....	....	....	....	....	....	....	....
	Toronto Maple Leafs	**NHL**	**1**	**0**	**0**	**0**	**0**	**0**	**0**	**2**	**0**	**0**	**0**	**0**	**0.0**	**0**	**0**	**0**	**0**	**0**	....	....	....	....	....	....	....	....
1995-96	**Toronto Maple Leafs**	**NHL**	**7**	**1**	**1**	**2**	**1**	**1**	**2**	**6**	**0**	**0**	**0**	**7**	**14.3**	**2**	**1**	**2**	**0**	**–1**	....	....	....	....	....	....	....	....
	St. John's Maple Leafs	AHL	41	13	14	27	....	....	....	22	....	....	....	....	....	....	....	....	....	....	4	2	0	2	0	....	....	....
1996-97	**Toronto Maple Leafs**	**NHL**	**23**	**3**	**5**	**8**	**3**	**4**	**7**	**6**	**1**	**0**	**0**	**22**	**13.6**	**16**	**3**	**9**	**0**	**+4**	....	....	....	....	....	....	....	....
	St. John's Maple Leafs	AHL	51	9	25	34	....	....	....	34	....	....	....	....	....	....	....	....	....	....	7	2	2	4	6	....	....	....
1997-98	St. John's Maple Leafs	AHL	45	7	8	15	....	....	....	24	....	....	....	....	....	....	....	....	....	....	3	1	0	1	2	....	....	....
	Long Beach Ice Dogs	IHL	19	3	8	11	....	....	....	18	....	....	....	....	....	....	....	....	....	....	....	....	....	....	....	....	....	....
	NHL Totals		**31**	**4**	**6**	**10**	**4**	**5**	**9**	**14**	**1**	**0**	**0**	**29**	**13.8**	**18**	**4**	**11**	**0**		....	....	....	....	....	....	....	....

• NEEDHAM, MIKE

Mike Needham RW R. 5'10", 185 lbs. b: Calgary, Alta., 4/4/1970. Pittsburgh's 7th choice, 126th overall, in 1989 Entry Draft.

Season	Club	League	GP	G	A	Pts	AG	AA	APts	PIM	PP	SH	GW	S	%	TGF	PGF	TGA	PGA	+/–	GP	G	A	Pts	PIM	PP	SH	GW
1985-86	Fort Saskatchewan Traders	AJHL	49	19	26	45	....	....	....	97	....	....	....	....	....	....	....	....	....	....	....	....	....	....	....	....	....	....
1986-87	Kamloops Blazers	WHL	3	1	2	3	....	....	....	0	....	....	....	....	....	....	....	....	....	....	11	2	1	3	5	....	....	....
1987-88	Kamloops Blazers	WHL	64	31	33	64	....	....	....	93	....	....	....	....	....	....	....	....	....	....	5	0	1	1	5	....	....	....
1988-89	Kamloops Blazers	WHL	49	24	27	51	....	....	....	55	....	....	....	....	....	....	....	....	....	....	16	2	9	11	13	....	....	....
1989-90	Kamloops Blazers	WHL	60	59	66	125	....	....	....	75	....	....	....	....	....	....	....	....	....	....	17	11	13	24	10	....	....	....
	Canada	WJC-A	7	3	4	7	....	....	....	2	....	....	....	....	....	....	....	....	....	....	....	....	....	....	....	....	....	....
1990-91	Muskegon Lumberjacks	IHL	65	14	31	45	....	....	....	17	....	....	....	....	....	....	....	....	....	....	5	2	2	4	5	....	....	....
1991-92	Muskegon Lumberjacks	IHL	80	41	37	78	....	....	....	83	....	....	....	....	....	....	....	....	....	....	8	4	4	8	6	....	....	....
	Pittsburgh Penguins	**NHL**	....	....	....	....	....	....	....	....	....	....	....	....	....	....	....	....	....	....	**5**	**1**	**0**	**1**	**2**	....	....	....
1992-93	**Pittsburgh Penguins**	**NHL**	**56**	**8**	**5**	**13**	**7**	**3**	**10**	**14**	**0**	**0**	**2**	**49**	**16.3**	**21**	**3**	**20**	**1**	**–1**	**9**	**1**	**0**	**1**	**2**	**0**	**0**	**0**
	Cleveland Lumberjacks	IHL	1	2	0	2	....	....	....	0	....	....	....	....	....	....	....	....	....	....	....	....	....	....	....	....	....	....
1993-94	**Pittsburgh Penguins**	**NHL**	**25**	**1**	**0**	**1**	**1**	**0**	**1**	**2**	**0**	**0**	**1**	**6**	**16.7**	**2**	**0**	**2**	**0**	**0**	....	....	....	....	....	....	....	....
	Cleveland Lumberjacks	IHL	6	4	3	7	....	....	....	7	....	....	....	....	....	....	....	....	....	....	....	....	....	....	....	....	....	....
	Dallas Stars	**NHL**	**5**	**0**	**0**	**0**	**0**	**0**	**0**	**0**	**0**	**0**	**0**	**3**	**0.0**	**2**	**1**	**3**	**0**	**–2**	....	....	....	....	....	....	....	....
1994-95	Kalamazoo Wings	IHL	37	9	9	18	....	....	....	31	....	....	....	....	....	....	....	....	....	....	14	5	5	10	11	....	....	....
1995-96	Adirondack Red Wings	AHL	16	5	10	15	....	....	....	12	....	....	....	....	....	....	....	....	....	....	....	....	....	....	....	....	....	....
	NHL Totals		**86**	**9**	**5**	**14**	**8**	**3**	**11**	**16**	**0**	**0**	**3**	**58**	**15.5**	**25**	**4**	**25**	**1**		**14**	**2**	**0**	**2**	**4**	**0**	**0**	**0**

WHL West First All-Star Team (1990)

Traded to **Dallas** by **Pittsburgh** for Jim McKenzie, March 21, 1994.

• NEELY, BOB

Bob "Waldo" Neely LW – L. 6'1", 210 lbs. b: Sarnia, Ont., 11/9/1953. Toronto's 2nd choice, 10th overall, in 1973 Amateur Draft.

Season	Club	League	GP	G	A	Pts	AG	AA	APts	PIM	PP	SH	GW	S	%	TGF	PGF	TGA	PGA	+/–	GP	G	A	Pts	PIM	PP	SH	GW
1970-71	Hamilton Red Wings	OHA	34	4	11	15	....	....	....	129	....	....	....	....	....	....	....	....	....	....	....	....	....	....	....	....	....	....
1971-72	Hamilton Red Wings	OHA	17	3	8	11	....	....	....	109	....	....	....	....	....	....	....	....	....	....	....	....	....	....	....	....	....	....
	Peterborough Petes	OHA	32	8	22	30	....	....	....	90	....	....	....	....	....	....	....	....	....	....	....	....	....	....	....	....	....	....
1972-73	Peterborough Petes	OHA	55	24	52	76	....	....	....	304	....	....	....	....	....	....	....	....	....	....	17	3	17	20	44	....	....	....
1973-74	**Toronto Maple Leafs**	**NHL**	**54**	**5**	**7**	**12**	**5**	**6**	**11**	**98**	**2**	**0**	**0**	**77**	**6.5**	**45**	**9**	**52**	**2**	**–14**	**4**	**1**	**3**	**4**	**0**	**0**	**0**	**0**
1974-75	**Toronto Maple Leafs**	**NHL**	**57**	**5**	**16**	**21**	**5**	**13**	**18**	**61**	**2**	**0**	**1**	**103**	**4.9**	**64**	**12**	**86**	**16**	**–18**	**3**	**0**	**0**	**0**	**2**	**0**	**0**	**0**
	Oklahoma City Blazers	CHL	9	2	4	6	....	....	....	14	....	....	....	....	....	....	....	....	....	....	....	....	....	....	....	....	....	....
1975-76	**Toronto Maple Leafs**	**NHL**	**69**	**9**	**13**	**22**	**8**	**10**	**18**	**89**	**0**	**0**	**0**	**107**	**8.4**	**64**	**9**	**87**	**17**	**–15**	**10**	**3**	**1**	**4**	**7**	**2**	**0**	**0**
1976-77	**Toronto Maple Leafs**	**NHL**	**70**	**17**	**16**	**33**	**16**	**13**	**29**	**16**	**3**	**0**	**5**	**123**	**13.8**	**72**	**18**	**82**	**11**	**–17**	**9**	**1**	**3**	**4**	**6**	**1**	**0**	**0**

Season	Club	League	REGULAR SEASON GP	G	A	Pts	AG	AA	APts	PIM	PP	SH	GW	S	%	TGF	PGF	TGA	PGA	+/–	PLAYOFFS GP	G	A	Pts	PIM	PP	SH	GW
1977-78	Toronto Maple Leafs	NHL	11	0	1	1	0	1	1	0	0	0	0	7	0.0	3	0	6	0	–3	....	....	....	....	....	....	....	....
	Colorado Rockies	NHL	22	3	6	9	3	5	8	2	1	0	0	33	9.1	21	8	23	0	–10	....	....	....	....	....	....	....	....
	Philadelphia Firebirds	AHL	29	6	14	20	....	....	....	47	....	....	....	....	....	....	....	....	....	....	4	1	3	4	2	....	....	....
1978-79	New Brunswick Hawks	AHL	60	17	29	46	....	....	....	55	....	....	....	....	....	....	....	....	....	....	5	0	1	1	0	....	....	....
1979-80	New Brunswick Hawks	AHL	64	14	51	65	....	....	....	46	....	....	....	....	....	....	....	....	....	....	8	1	4	5	2	....	....	....
	NHL Totals		283	39	59	98	37	48	85	266	8	0	6	450	8.7	269	56	336	46		26	5	7	12	15	3	0	0

OHA First All-Star Team (1973) • AHL First All-Star Team (1980)

Traded to **Colorado** by **Toronto** for cash, January 9, 1978. Traded to **Toronto** by **Colordo** for cash, May 30, 1978.

• NEELY, CAM

Cam Neely RW – R. 6'1", 218 lbs. b: Comox, B.C., 6/6/1965. Vancouver's 1st choice, 9th overall, in 1983 Entry Draft.

Season	Club	League	GP	G	A	Pts	AG	AA	APts	PIM	PP	SH	GW	S	%	TGF	PGF	TGA	PGA	+/–	GP	G	A	Pts	PIM	PP	SH	GW
1982-83	Portland Winter Hawks	WHL	72	56	64	120	....	....	....	130	....	....	....	....	....	....	....	....	....	....	14	9	11	20	17	....	....	....
1983-84	Portland Winter Hawks	WHL	19	8	18	26	....	....	....	29	....	....	....	....	....	....	....	....	....	....	....	....	....	....	....	....	....	....
	Vancouver Canucks	NHL	56	16	15	31	13	10	23	57	3	0	1	87	18.4	55	17	39	1	0	4	2	0	2	2	1	0	0
1984-85	Vancouver Canucks	NHL	72	21	18	39	17	12	29	137	4	0	1	138	15.2	65	12	79	0	–26	....	....	....	....	....	....	....	....
1985-86	Vancouver Canucks	NHL	73	14	20	34	11	13	24	126	6	0	3	113	12.4	50	17	63	0	–30	3	0	0	0	6	0	0	0
1986-87	Boston Bruins	NHL	75	36	36	72	31	26	57	143	7	0	3	206	17.5	105	26	56	0	+23	4	5	1	6	8	3	0	0
1987-88	Boston Bruins	NHL	69	42	27	69	36	19	55	175	11	0	3	207	20.3	102	31	41	0	+30	23	9	8	17	51	2	0	2
1988-89	Boston Bruins	NHL	74	37	38	75	31	27	58	190	18	0	6	235	15.7	108	40	54	0	+14	10	7	2	9	8	4	0	2
1989-90	Boston Bruins	NHL	76	55	37	92	48	26	74	117	25	0	12	271	20.3	128	58	65	5	+10	21	12	16	28	51	4	1	2
1990-91	Boston Bruins	NHL	69	51	40	91	47	30	77	98	18	1	8	262	19.5	139	60	57	4	+26	19	16	4	20	36	9	0	4
1991-92	Boston Bruins	NHL	9	9	3	12	8	2	10	16	1	0	2	30	30.0	15	1	5	0	+9	....	....	....	....	....	....	....	....
1992-93	Boston Bruins	NHL	13	11	7	18	9	5	14	25	6	0	1	45	24.4	25	10	11	0	+4	4	4	1	5	4	1	0	0
1993-94	Boston Bruins	NHL	49	50	24	74	47	19	66	54	20	0	13	185	27.0	109	48	53	4	+12	....	....	....	....	....	....	....	....
1994-95	Boston Bruins	NHL	42	27	14	41	48	21	69	72	16	0	5	178	15.2	64	28	32	3	+7	5	2	0	2	2	1	0	1
1995-96	Boston Bruins	NHL	49	26	20	46	26	16	42	31	7	0	3	191	13.6	78	28	47	0	+3	....	....	....	....	....	....	....	....
	NHL Totals		726	395	299	694	372	226	598	1241	142	1	61	2148	18.4	1043	376	602	17		93	57	32	89	168	25	1	11

NHL Second All-Star Team (1988, 1990, 1991, 1994) • Won Bill Masterton Trophy (1994)

Played in NHL All-Star Game (1988, 1989, 1990, 1991, 1996)

Traded to **Boston** by **Vancouver** with Vancouver's 1st round choice (Glen Wesley) in 1987 Entry Draft for Barry Pederson, June 6, 1986.

• NEILSON, JIM

Jim "Chief" Neilson D – L. 6'2", 205 lbs. b: Big River, Sask., 11/28/1940.

Season	Club	League	GP	G	A	Pts	AG	AA	APts	PIM	PP	SH	GW	S	%	TGF	PGF	TGA	PGA	+/–	GP	G	A	Pts	PIM	PP	SH	GW
1958-59	Prince Albert Mintos	SJHL	10	1	2	3	....	....	....	6	....	....	....	....	....	....	....	....	....	....	....	....	....	....	....	....	....	....
1959-60	Prince Albert Mintos	SJHL	57	21	28	49	....	....	....	61	....	....	....	....	....	....	....	....	....	....	7	2	2	4	6	....	....	....
1960-61	Prince Albert Mintos	SJHL	59	20	26	46	....	....	....	59	....	....	....	....	....	....	....	....	....	....	....	....	....	....	....	....	....	....
1961-62	Kitchener-Waterloo Beavers	EPHL	70	9	33	42	....	....	....	78	....	....	....	....	....	....	....	....	....	....	7	2	3	5	2	....	....	....
1962-63	New York Rangers	NHL	69	5	11	16	6	11	17	38	....	....	....	....	....	....	....	....	....	....	....	....	....	....	....	....	....	....
1963-64	New York Rangers	NHL	69	5	24	29	7	27	34	93	....	....	....	....	....	....	....	....	....	....	....	....	....	....	....	....	....	....
1964-65	New York Rangers	NHL	62	0	13	13	0	14	14	58	....	....	....	....	....	....	....	....	....	....	....	....	....	....	....	....	....	....
1965-66	New York Rangers	NHL	65	4	19	23	5	19	24	84	....	....	....	....	....	....	....	....	....	....	....	....	....	....	....	....	....	....
1966-67	New York Rangers	NHL	61	4	11	15	5	11	16	65	....	....	....	....	....	....	....	....	....	....	4	1	0	1	0	....	....	....
1967-68	New York Rangers	NHL	67	6	29	35	7	30	37	60	2	0	1	172	3.5	108	26	71	18	+29	6	0	2	2	4	0	0	0
1968-69	New York Rangers	NHL	76	10	34	44	11	32	43	95	3	0	2	274	3.6	130	38	97	11	+6	4	0	3	3	5	0	0	0
1969-70	New York Rangers	NHL	62	3	20	23	3	20	23	75	0	0	0	204	1.5	94	16	66	12	+24	6	0	1	1	8	0	0	0
1970-71	New York Rangers	NHL	77	8	24	32	8	21	29	69	2	0	3	200	4.0	112	27	73	19	+31	13	0	3	3	30	0	0	0
1971-72	New York Rangers	NHL	78	7	30	37	7	27	34	56	2	0	0	183	3.8	131	18	97	22	+38	10	0	3	3	8	0	0	0
1972-73	New York Rangers	NHL	52	4	16	20	4	13	17	35	0	0	0	99	4.0	76	7	60	13	+22	10	0	4	4	2	0	0	0
1973-74	New York Rangers	NHL	72	4	7	11	4	6	10	38	2	0	1	103	3.9	62	4	77	15	–4	12	0	1	1	4	0	0	0
1974-75	California Golden Seals	NHL	72	3	17	20	3	13	16	56	0	0	0	112	2.7	77	18	130	25	–46	....	....	....	....	....	....	....	....
1975-76	California Golden Seals	NHL	26	1	6	7	1	5	6	20	1	0	0	41	2.4	28	7	34	7	–6	....	....	....	....	....	....	....	....
1976-77	Cleveland Barons	NHL	47	3	17	20	3	14	17	42	0	0	0	42	7.1	64	3	82	16	–5	....	....	....	....	....	....	....	....
1977-78	Cleveland Barons	NHL	68	2	21	23	2	17	19	20	0	0	0	51	3.9	65	4	109	23	–25	....	....	....	....	....	....	....	....
1978-79	Edmonton Oilers	WHA	35	0	5	5	....	....	....	18	....	....	....	....	....	....	....	....	....	....	....	....	....	....	....	....	....	....
	NHL Totals		1023	69	299	368	76	280	356	904	12	0	7	1481	4.7	947	168	896	181		65	1	17	18	61	0	0	0
	Other Major League Totals		35	0	5	5	....	....	....	18	....	....	....	....	....	....	....	....	....		....	....	....	....	....	....	....	....

NHL Second All-Star Team (1968)

Played in NHL All-Star Game (1967, 1971)

Selected by **LA Sharks** (WHA) in 1972 WHA General Player Draft, February 12, 1972. Claimed by **California** from **NY Rangers** in Intra-League Draft, June 10, 1974. Transferred to **Cleveland** after **California** franchise relocated, August 26, 1976. Placed on **Minnesota** Reserve List after **Cleveland-Minnesota** Dispersal Draft, June 15, 1978. Signed as a free agent by **Edmonton** (WHA), June, 1978.

• NELSON, GORDIE

Gordie Nelson D – L. 5'8", 180 lbs. b: Kinistino, Sask., 5/10/1947.

Season	Club	League	GP	G	A	Pts	AG	AA	APts	PIM	PP	SH	GW	S	%	TGF	PGF	TGA	PGA	+/–	GP	G	A	Pts	PIM	PP	SH	GW
1964-65	Melville Millionaires	SJHL	55	3	16	19	....	....	....	99	....	....	....	....	....	....	....	....	....	....	....	....	....	....	....	....	....	....
1965-66	Melville Millionaires	SJHL	60	11	24	35	....	....	....	91	....	....	....	....	....	....	....	....	....	....	....	....	....	....	....	....	....	....
1966-67	Trois-Rivieres Reds	QJHL	STATISTICS NOT AVAILABLE																									
1967-68	Tulsa Oilers	CHL	62	4	18	22	....	....	....	114	....	....	....	....	....	....	....	....	....	....	10	0	5	5	4	....	....	....
1968-69	Tulsa Oilers	CHL	71	8	22	30	....	....	....	136	....	....	....	....	....	....	....	....	....	....	7	2	3	5	25	....	....	....
1969-70	Toronto Maple Leafs	NHL	3	0	0	0	0	0	0	11	0	0	0	5	0.0	3	0	2	1	+2	....	....	....	....	....	....	....	....
	Tulsa Oilers	CHL	69	10	38	48	....	....	....	158	....	....	....	....	....	....	....	....	....	....	6	2	4	6	10	....	....	....
1970-71	Tulsa Oilers	CHL	57	4	26	30	....	....	....	23	....	....	....	....	....	....	....	....	....	....	....	....	....	....	....	....	....	....
1971-72	Phoenix Roadrunners	WHL	67	7	35	42	....	....	....	102	....	....	....	....	....	....	....	....	....	....	6	0	2	2	16	....	....	....
1972-73	Phoenix Roadrunners	WHL	9	1	3	4	....	....	....	28	....	....	....	....	....	....	....	....	....	....	....	....	....	....	....	....	....	....
	Portland Buckaroos	WHL	65	5	25	30	....	....	....	143	....	....	....	....	....	....	....	....	....	....	....	....	....	....	....	....	....	....
	NHL Totals		3	0	0	0	0	0	0	11	0	0	0	5	0.0	3	0	2	1		....	....	....	....	....	....	....	....

NCAA West First All-American Team (1971)

Signed as a free agent by **Toronto**, December 10, 1969.

• NELSON, JEFF

Jeff Nelson C – L. 6', 190 lbs. b: Prince Albert, Sask., 12/18/1972. Washington's 4th choice, 36th overall, in 1991 Entry Draft.

Season	Club	League	GP	G	A	Pts	AG	AA	APts	PIM	PP	SH	GW	S	%	TGF	PGF	TGA	PGA	+/–	GP	G	A	Pts	PIM	PP	SH	GW
1988-89	Prince Albert Raiders	WHL	71	30	57	87	....	....	....	74	....	....	....	....	....	....	....	....	....	....	4	0	3	3	39	....	....	....
1989-90	Prince Albert Raiders	WHL	72	28	69	97	....	....	....	79	....	....	....	....	....	....	....	....	....	....	14	2	11	13	10	....	....	....
1990-91	Prince Albert Raiders	WHL	72	46	74	120	....	....	....	58	....	....	....	....	....	....	....	....	....	....	3	1	1	2	4	....	....	....
1991-92	Prince Albert Raiders	WHL	64	48	65	113	....	....	....	84	....	....	....	....	....	....	....	....	....	....	9	7	14	21	18	....	....	....
	Canada	WJC-A	7	1	1	2	....	....	....	2	....	....	....	....	....	....	....	....	....	....	....	....	....	....	....	....	....	....
1992-93	Baltimore Skipjacks	AHL	72	14	38	52	....	....	....	12	....	....	....	....	....	....	....	....	....	....	7	1	3	4	2	....	....	....
1993-94	Portland Pirates	AHL	80	34	73	107	....	....	....	92	....	....	....	....	....	....	....	....	....	....	17	10	5	15	20	....	....	....
1994-95	Portland Pirates	AHL	64	33	50	83	....	....	....	57	....	....	....	....	....	....	....	....	....	....	7	1	4	5	8	....	....	....
	Washington Capitals	NHL	10	1	0	1	2	0	2	2	0	0	0	4	25.0	2	0	4	0	–2	....	....	....	....	....	....	....	....
1995-96	Washington Capitals	NHL	33	0	7	7	0	6	6	16	0	0	0	21	0.0	12	0	9	0	+3	3	0	0	0	4	0	0	0
	Portland Pirates	AHL	39	15	32	47	....	....	....	62	....	....	....	....	....	....	....	....	....	....	....	....	....	....	....	....	....	....
1996-97	Grand Rapids Griffins	IHL	82	34	55	89	....	....	....	85	....	....	....	....	....	....	....	....	....	....	5	0	4	4	4	....	....	....
1997-98	Milwaukee Admirals	IHL	52	20	34	54	....	....	....	30	....	....	....	....	....	....	....	....	....	....	10	2	7	9	15	....	....	....
	NHL Totals		43	1	7	8	2	6	8	18	0	0	0	25	4.0	14	0	13	0		3	0	0	0	4	0	0	0

Canadian Major Junior Scholastic Player of the Year (1989, 1990) • WHL East Second All-Star Team (1991, 1992)

• NELSON, TODD

Todd Nelson D – L. 6', 201 lbs. b: Prince Albert, Sask., 5/11/1969. Pittsburgh's 4th choice, 79th overall, in 1989 Entry Draft.

Season	Club	League	GP	G	A	Pts	AG	AA	APts	PIM	PP	SH	GW	S	%	TGF	PGF	TGA	PGA	+/–	GP	G	A	Pts	PIM	PP	SH	GW
1985-86	Prince Albert Raiders	WHL	4	0	0	0	....	....	....	0	....	....	....	....	....	....	....	....	....	....	....	....	....	....	....	....	....	....
1986-87	Prince Albert Raiders	WHL	35	1	6	7	....	....	....	10	....	....	....	....	....	....	....	....	....	....	4	0	0	0	0	....	....	....
1987-88	Prince Albert Raiders	WHL	72	3	21	24	....	....	....	59	....	....	....	....	....	....	....	....	....	....	10	3	2	5	4	....	....	....
1988-89	Prince Albert Raiders	WHL	72	14	45	59	....	....	....	72	....	....	....	....	....	....	....	....	....	....	4	1	3	4	4	....	....	....

			REGULAR SEASON																		PLAYOFFS							
Season	Club	League	GP	G	A	Pts	AG	AA	APts	PIM	PP	SH	GW	S	%	TGF	PGF	TGA	PGA	+/-	GP	G	A	Pts	PIM	PP	SH	GW
1989-90	Prince Albert Raiders	WHL	69	13	42	55	....	....	....	88	....	....	....	....	....	....	....	....	....	....	14	3	12	15	12	....	....	....
1990-91	Muskegon Lumberjacks	IHL	79	4	20	24	....	....	....	32	....	....	....	....	....	....	....	....	....	....	3	0	0	0	4	....	....	....
1991-92	**Pittsburgh Penguins**	**NHL**	**1**	**0**	**0**	**0**	**0**	**0**	**0**	**0**	**0**	**0**	**0**	**0**	**0.0**	**0**	**0**	**0**	**0**	**0**	....	....	....	....	....	....	....	....
	Muskegon Lumberjacks	IHL	80	6	35	41	....	....	....	46	....	....	....	....	....	....	....	....	....	....	14	1	11	12	4	....	....	....
1992-93	Cleveland Lumberjacks	IHL	76	7	35	42	....	....	....	115	....	....	....	....	....	....	....	....	....	....	4	0	2	2	4	....	....	....
1993-94	**Washington Capitals**	**NHL**	**2**	**1**	**0**	**1**	**1**	**0**	**1**	**2**	**1**	**0**	**1**	**1**	**100.0**	**3**	**1**	**1**	**0**	**+1**	**4**	**0**	**0**	**0**	**0**	**0**	**0**	**0**
	Portland Pirates	AHL	80	11	34	45	....	....	....	69	....	....	....	....	....	....	....	....	....	....	11	0	6	6	6	....	....	....
1994-95	Portland Pirates	AHL	75	10	35	45	....	....	....	76	....	....	....	....	....	....	....	....	....	....	7	0	4	4	6	....	....	....
1995-96	Hershey Bears	AHL	70	10	40	50	....	....	....	38	....	....	....	....	....	....	....	....	....	....	5	1	2	3	8	....	....	....
1996-97	Grand Rapids Griffins	IHL	81	3	18	21	....	....	....	32	....	....	....	....	....	....	....	....	....	....	5	1	0	1	0	....	....	....
1997-98	Grand Rapids Griffins	IHL	75	6	21	27	....	....	....	36	....	....	....	....	....	....	....	....	....	....	3	0	0	0	2	....	....	....
	NHL Totals		**3**	**1**	**0**	**1**	**1**	**0**	**1**	**2**	**1**	**0**	**1**	**1**	**100.0**	**3**	**1**	**1**	**0**		**4**	**0**	**0**	**0**	**0**	**0**	**0**	**0**

WHL East Second All-Star Team (1989, 1990)

Signed as a free agent by **Washington**, August 15, 1993.

• NEMCHINOV, SERGEI

Sergei Nemchinov C – L. 6', 200 lbs. b: Moscow, USSR, 1/14/1964. NY Rangers' 14th choice, 244th overall, in 1990 Entry Draft.

Season	Club	League	GP	G	A	Pts	AG	AA	APts	PIM	PP	SH	GW	S	%	TGF	PGF	TGA	PGA	+/-	GP	G	A	Pts	PIM	PP	SH	GW
1981-82	Soviet Wings	USSR	15	1	0	1	....	....	....	0	....	....	....	....	....	....	....	....	....	....	....	....	....	....	....	....	....	....
1982-83	CSKA Moscow	USSR	11	0	0	0	....	....	....	2	....	....	....	....	....	....	....	....	....	....	....	....	....	....	....	....	....	....
	Soviet Union	WJC-A	7	4	3	7	....	....	....	2	....	....	....	....	....	....	....	....	....	....	....	....	....	....	....	....	....	....
1983-84	CSKA Moscow	USSR	20	6	5	11	....	....	....	4	....	....	....	....	....	....	....	....	....	....	....	....	....	....	....	....	....	....
	Soviet Union	WJC-A	7	5	6	11	....	....	....	2	....	....	....	....	....	....	....	....	....	....	....	....	....	....	....	....	....	....
1984-85	CSKA Moscow	USSR	31	2	4	6	....	....	....	4	....	....	....	....	....	....	....	....	....	....	....	....	....	....	....	....	....	....
1985-86	Soviet Wings	USSR	39	7	12	19	....	....	....	28	....	....	....	....	....	....	....	....	....	....	....	....	....	....	....	....	....	....
1986-87	Soviet Wings	USSR	40	13	9	22	....	....	....	24	....	....	....	....	....	....	....	....	....	....	....	....	....	....	....	....	....	....
	USSR	RV'87	1	0	0	0	....	....	....	4	....	....	....	....	....	....	....	....	....	....	....	....	....	....	....	....	....	....
1987-88	Soviet Union	C Cup	5	0	0	0	....	....	....	6	....	....	....	....	....	....	....	....	....	....	....	....	....	....	....	....	....	....
	Soviet Wings	USSR	48	17	11	28	....	....	....	26	....	....	....	....	....	....	....	....	....	....	....	....	....	....	....	....	....	....
1988-89	Soviet Wings	USSR	43	15	14	29	....	....	....	28	....	....	....	....	....	....	....	....	....	....	....	....	....	....	....	....	....	....
	CSKA Moscow	SuperS	7	2	2	4	....	....	....	2	....	....	....	....	....	....	....	....	....	....	....	....	....	....	....	....	....	....
	Soviet Union	WEC-A	7	2	0	2	....	....	....	2	....	....	....	....	....	....	....	....	....	....	....	....	....	....	....	....	....	....
1989-90	Soviet Wings	FrTour	1	0	0	0	....	....	....	0	....	....	....	....	....	....	....	....	....	....	....	....	....	....	....	....	....	....
	Soviet Wings	USSR	48	17	16	33	....	....	....	34	....	....	....	....	....	....	....	....	....	....	....	....	....	....	....	....	....	....
	Soviet Wings	SuperS	5	0	2	2	....	....	....	2	....	....	....	....	....	....	....	....	....	....	....	....	....	....	....	....	....	....
	Soviet Union	WEC-A	10	5	2	7	....	....	....	4	....	....	....	....	....	....	....	....	....	....	....	....	....	....	....	....	....	....
1990-91	Soviet Wings	FrTour	1	1	0	1	....	....	....	0	....	....	....	....	....	....	....	....	....	....	....	....	....	....	....	....	....	....
	Soviet Wings	USSR	46	21	24	45	....	....	....	30	....	....	....	....	....	....	....	....	....	....	....	....	....	....	....	....	....	....
	CSKA Moscow	SuperS	7	1	6	7	....	....	....	0	....	....	....	....	....	....	....	....	....	....	....	....	....	....	....	....	....	....
	Soviet Union	WEC-A	10	2	3	5	....	....	....	2	....	....	....	....	....	....	....	....	....	....	....	....	....	....	....	....	....	....
1991-92	**New York Rangers**	**NHL**	**73**	**30**	**28**	**58**	**27**	**21**	**48**	**15**	**2**	**0**	**5**	**124**	**24.2**	**79**	**17**	**61**	**18**	**+19**	**13**	**1**	**4**	**5**	**8**	**0**	**0**	**0**
1992-93	**New York Rangers**	**NHL**	**81**	**23**	**31**	**54**	**19**	**21**	**40**	**34**	**0**	**1**	**3**	**144**	**16.0**	**74**	**5**	**74**	**20**	**+15**	....	....	....	....	....	....	....	....
1993-94	**New York Rangers**	**NHL**	**76**	**22**	**27**	**49**	**21**	**21**	**42**	**36**	**4**	**0**	**6**	**144**	**15.3**	**59**	**11**	**51**	**16**	**+13**	**23**	**2**	**5**	**7**	**6**	**0**	**0**	**0**
1994-95	**New York Rangers**	**NHL**	**47**	**7**	**6**	**13**	**12**	**9**	**21**	**16**	**0**	**0**	**3**	**67**	**10.4**	**21**	**1**	**32**	**6**	**–6**	**10**	**4**	**5**	**9**	**2**	**0**	**0**	**1**
1995-96	**New York Rangers**	**NHL**	**78**	**17**	**15**	**32**	**17**	**12**	**29**	**38**	**0**	**0**	**2**	**118**	**14.4**	**43**	**3**	**42**	**11**	**+9**	**6**	**0**	**1**	**1**	**2**	**0**	**0**	**0**
1996-97	Russia	W Cup	5	1	2	3	....	....	....	2	....	....	....	....	....	....	....	....	....	....	....	....	....	....	....	....	....	....
	New York Rangers	**NHL**	**63**	**6**	**13**	**19**	**6**	**11**	**17**	**12**	**1**	**0**	**1**	**90**	**6.7**	**29**	**3**	**23**	**2**	**+5**	....	....	....	....	....	....	....	....
	Vancouver Canucks	**NHL**	**6**	**2**	**3**	**5**	**2**	**3**	**5**	**4**	**0**	**0**	**1**	**7**	**28.6**	**6**	**1**	**1**	**0**	**+4**	....	....	....	....	....	....	....	....
1997-98	**New York Islanders**	**NHL**	**74**	**10**	**19**	**29**	**12**	**19**	**31**	**24**	**2**	**1**	**1**	**94**	**10.6**	**51**	**8**	**61**	**21**	**+3**	....	....	....	....	....	....	....	....
	Russia	Olympics	6	1	0	1	....	....	....	0	....	....	....	....	....	....	....	....	....	....	....	....	....	....	....	....	....	....
	Russia	WC-A	6	0	1	1	....	....	....	8	....	....	....	....	....	....	....	....	....	....	....	....	....	....	....	....	....	....
	NHL Totals		**498**	**117**	**142**	**259**	**110**	**117**	**233**	**179**	**9**	**2**	**22**	**788**	**14.8**	**362**	**49**	**345**	**94**		**52**	**7**	**16**	**23**	**18**	**0**	**0**	**1**

Traded to **Vancouver** by **NY Rangers** with Brian Noonan for Esa Tikkanen and Russ Courtnall, March 8, 1997. Signed as a free agent by **NY Islanders**, July 10, 1997.

• NEMETH, STEVE

Steve Nemeth C – L. 5'8", 170 lbs. b: Calgary, Alta., 2/11/1967. NY Rangers' 10th choice, 196th overall, in 1985 Entry Draft.

Season	Club	League	GP	G	A	Pts	AG	AA	APts	PIM	PP	SH	GW	S	%	TGF	PGF	TGA	PGA	+/-	GP	G	A	Pts	PIM	PP	SH	GW
1982-83	Lethbridge Broncos	WHL	2	0	1	1	....	....	....	0	....	....	....	....	....	....	....	....	....	....	....	....	....	....	....	....	....	....
1983-84	Lethbridge Broncos	WHL	68	22	20	42	....	....	....	33	....	....	....	....	....	....	....	....	....	....	5	1	1	2	2	....	....	....
1984-85	Lethbridge Broncos	WHL	67	39	55	94	....	....	....	39	....	....	....	....	....	....	....	....	....	....	4	2	3	5	13	....	....	....
1985-86	Lethbridge Broncos	WHL	70	42	69	111	....	....	....	47	....	....	....	....	....	....	....	....	....	....	10	5	5	10	6	....	....	....
1986-87	Canada	Nat-Team	43	14	7	21	....	....	....	12	....	....	....	....	....	....	....	....	....	....	....	....	....	....	....	....	....	....
	Canada	WJC-A	6	4	4	8	....	....	....	4	....	....	....	....	....	....	....	....	....	....	....	....	....	....	....	....	....	....
	Kamloops Blazers	WHL	10	10	4	14	....	....	....	0	....	....	....	....	....	....	....	....	....	....	13	11	9	20	12	....	....	....
1987-88	**New York Rangers**	**NHL**	**12**	**2**	**0**	**2**	**2**	**0**	**2**	**2**	**0**	**1**	**0**	**12**	**16.7**	**4**	**0**	**10**	**2**	**–4**	....	....	....	....	....	....	....	....
	Colorado Rangers	IHL	57	13	24	37	....	....	....	28	....	....	....	....	....	....	....	....	....	....	10	2	1	3	8	....	....	....
1988-89	Canada	Nat-Team	26	6	10	16	....	....	....	10	....	....	....	....	....	....	....	....	....	....	....	....	....	....	....	....	....	....
	Denver Rangers	IHL	11	5	2	7	....	....	....	8	....	....	....	....	....	....	....	....	....	....	....	....	....	....	....	....	....	....
1989-90	Canada	Nat-Team	73	24	42	66	....	....	....	40	....	....	....	....	....	....	....	....	....	....	....	....	....	....	....	....	....	....
1990-91			DID NOT PLAY – RETIRED																									
1991-92			DID NOT PLAY – RETIRED																									
1992-93	Shefield Steelers	Britain	32	67	64	131	....	....	....	67	....	....	....	....	....	....	....	....	....	....	....	....	....	....	....	....	....	....
1993-94	Sheffield Steelers	Britain	35	40	59	99	....	....	....	67	....	....	....	....	....	....	....	....	....	....	5	4	6	10	6	....	....	....
1994-95	Sheffield Steelers	Britain	41	54	51	105	....	....	....	39	....	....	....	....	....	....	....	....	....	....	7	1	3	4	0	....	....	....
1995-96	Sheffield Steelers	Britain	31	28	27	55	....	....	....	24	....	....	....	....	....	....	....	....	....	....	8	5	5	10	10	....	....	....
1996-97	Sheffield Steelers	Britain	9	0	5	5	....	....	....	4	....	....	....	....	....	....	....	....	....	....	....	....	....	....	....	....	....	....
	NHL Totals		**12**	**2**	**0**	**2**	**2**	**0**	**2**	**2**	**0**	**1**	**0**	**12**	**16.7**	**4**	**0**	**10**	**2**		....	....	....	....	....	....	....	....

• NEMIROVSKY, DAVID

David Nemirovsky RW – R. 6'1", 192 lbs. b: Toronto, Ont., 8/1/1976. Florida's 5th choice, 84th overall, in 1994 Entry Draft.

Season	Club	League	GP	G	A	Pts	AG	AA	APts	PIM	PP	SH	GW	S	%	TGF	PGF	TGA	PGA	+/-	GP	G	A	Pts	PIM	PP	SH	GW
1993-94	Ottawa 67's	OHL	64	21	31	52	....	....	....	18	....	....	....	....	....	....	....	....	....	....	17	10	10	20	2	....	....	....
1994-95	Ottawa 67's	OHL	59	27	29	56	....	....	....	25	....	....	....	....	....	....	....	....	....	....	....	....	....	....	....	....	....	....
1995-96	Sarnia Sting	OHL	26	18	27	45	....	....	....	14	....	....	....	....	....	....	....	....	....	....	10	8	8	16	6	....	....	....
	Florida Panthers	**NHL**	**9**	**0**	**2**	**2**	**0**	**2**	**2**	**2**	**0**	**0**	**0**	**6**	**0.0**	**2**	**0**	**3**	**0**	**–1**	....	....	....	....	....	....	....	....
	Carolina Monarchs	AHL	5	1	2	3	....	....	....	0	....	....	....	....	....	....	....	....	....	....	....	....	....	....	....	....	....	....
1996-97	**Florida Panthers**	**NHL**	**39**	**7**	**7**	**14**	**7**	**6**	**13**	**32**	**1**	**0**	**0**	**53**	**13.2**	**23**	**5**	**17**	**0**	**+1**	**3**	**1**	**0**	**1**	**0**	**0**	**0**	**0**
	Carolina Monarchs	AHL	34	21	21	42	....	....	....	18	....	....	....	....	....	....	....	....	....	....	....	....	....	....	....	....	....	....
1997-98	**Florida Panthers**	**NHL**	**41**	**9**	**12**	**21**	**11**	**12**	**23**	**8**	**2**	**0**	**1**	**62**	**14.5**	**30**	**12**	**21**	**0**	**–3**	....	....	....	....	....	....	....	....
	New Haven	AHL	29	10	15	25	....	....	....	10	....	....	....	....	....	....	....	....	....	....	1	1	0	1	0	....	....	....
	NHL Totals		**89**	**16**	**21**	**37**	**18**	**20**	**38**	**42**	**3**	**0**	**1**	**121**	**13.2**	**55**	**17**	**41**	**0**		**3**	**1**	**0**	**1**	**0**	**0**	**0**	**0**

• NESTERENKO, ERIC

Eric "Elbows" Nesterenko RW – R. 6'2", 197 lbs. b: Flin Flon, Man., 10/31/1933.

Season	Club	League	GP	G	A	Pts	AG	AA	APts	PIM	PP	SH	GW	S	%	TGF	PGF	TGA	PGA	+/-	GP	G	A	Pts	PIM	PP	SH	GW
1949-50	Toronto Marlboros	OHA	1	0	0	0	....	....	....	0	....	....	....	....	....	....	....	....	....	....	....	....	....	....	....	....	....	....
1950-51	Toronto Marlboros	OHA	46	28	22	50	....	....	....	90	....	....	....	....	....	....	....	....	....	....	13	7	9	16	27	....	....	....
1951-52	Toronto Marlboros	OHA	52	53	42	95	....	....	....	133	....	....	....	....	....	....	....	....	....	....	6	2	6	0	12	....	....	....
	Toronto Maple Leafs	**NHL**	**1**	**0**	**0**	**0**	**0**	**0**	**0**	**0**	....	....	....	....	....	....	....	....	....	....	....	....	....	....	....	....	....	....
1952-53	Toronto Marlboros	OHA	34	27	21	48	....	....	....	46	....	....	....	....	....	....	....	....	....	....	....	....	....	....	....	....	....	....
	Toronto Maple Leafs	**NHL**	**35**	**10**	**6**	**16**	**15**	**8**	**23**	**27**	....	....	....	....	....	....	....	....	....	....	....	....	....	....	....	....	....	....
1953-54	**Toronto Maple Leafs**	**NHL**	**68**	**14**	**9**	**23**	**21**	**12**	**33**	**70**	....	....	....	....	....	....	....	....	....	....	**5**	**0**	**1**	**1**	**9**	....	....	....
1954-55	**Toronto Maple Leafs**	**NHL**	**62**	**15**	**15**	**30**	**22**	**19**	**41**	**99**	....	....	....	....	....	....	....	....	....	....	**4**	**0**	**1**	**1**	**6**	....	....	....
1955-56	**Toronto Maple Leafs**	**NHL**	**40**	**4**	**6**	**10**	**6**	**7**	**13**	**65**	....	....	....	....	....	....	....	....	....	....	....	....	....	....	....	....	....	....
	Winnipeg Warriors	WHL	20	8	6	14	....	....	....	27	....	....	....	....	....	....	....	....	....	....	14	3	7	10	22	....	....	....
1956-57	**Chicago Black Hawks**	**NHL**	**24**	**8**	**15**	**23**	**11**	**17**	**28**	**32**	....	....	....	....	....	....	....	....	....	....	....	....	....	....	....	....	....	....
1957-58	**Chicago Black Hawks**	**NHL**	**70**	**20**	**18**	**38**	**26**	**20**	**46**	**104**	....	....	....	....	....	....	....	....	....	....	....	....	....	....	....	....	....	....
1958-59	**Chicago Black Hawks**	**NHL**	**70**	**16**	**18**	**34**	**20**	**19**	**39**	**81**	....	....	....	....	....	....	....	....	....	....	**6**	**2**	**2**	**4**	**8**	....	....	....
1959-60	**Chicago Black Hawks**	**NHL**	**61**	**13**	**23**	**36**	**16**	**24**	**40**	**71**	....	....	....	....	....	....	....	....	....	....	**4**	**0**	**0**	**0**	**2**	....	....	....
1960-61	**Chicago Black Hawks**	**NHL**	**68**	**19**	**19**	**38**	**23**	**19**	**42**	**125**	....	....	....	....	....	....	....	....	....	....	**11**	**2**	**3**	**5**	**6**	....	....	....

			REGULAR SEASON																		PLAYOFFS							
Season	Club	League	GP	G	A	Pts	AG	AA	APts	PIM	PP	SH	GW	S	%	TGF	PGF	TGA	PGA	+/–	GP	G	A	Pts	PIM	PP	SH	GW
1961-62	**Chicago Black Hawks**	**NHL**	**68**	**15**	**14**	**29**	**18**	**14**	**32**	**97**	....	....	....	....	....	....	....	....	....	....	**12**	**0**	**5**	**5**	**22**	....	....	....
1962-63	**Chicago Black Hawks**	**NHL**	**67**	**12**	**15**	**27**	**15**	**16**	**31**	**103**	....	....	....	....	....	....	....	....	....	....	**6**	**2**	**3**	**5**	**8**	....	....	....
1963-64	**Chicago Black Hawks**	**NHL**	**70**	**7**	**19**	**26**	**9**	**21**	**30**	**93**	....	....	....	....	....	....	....	....	....	....	**7**	**2**	**1**	**3**	**8**	....	....	....
1964-65	**Chicago Black Hawks**	**NHL**	**56**	**14**	**16**	**30**	**18**	**17**	**35**	**63**	....	....	....	....	....	....	....	....	....	....	**14**	**2**	**2**	**4**	**16**	....	....	....
1965-66	**Chicago Black Hawks**	**NHL**	**67**	**15**	**25**	**40**	**18**	**25**	**43**	**58**	....	....	....	....	....	....	....	....	....	....	**6**	**1**	**0**	**1**	**4**	....	....	....
1966-67	**Chicago Black Hawks**	**NHL**	**68**	**14**	**23**	**37**	**17**	**24**	**41**	**38**	....	....	....	....	....	....	....	....	....	....	**6**	**1**	**2**	**3**	**2**	....	....	....
1967-68	**Chicago Black Hawks**	**NHL**	**71**	**11**	**25**	**36**	**14**	**26**	**40**	**37**	**1**	**2**	**1**	**93**	**11.8**	**61**	**7**	**66**	**15**	**+3**	**10**	**0**	**1**	**1**	**2**	**0**	**0**	**0**
1968-69	**Chicago Black Hawks**	**NHL**	**72**	**15**	**17**	**32**	**17**	**16**	**33**	**29**	**1**	**3**	**1**	**90**	**16.7**	**60**	**6**	**79**	**30**	**+5**	....	....	....	....	....	....	....	....
1969-70	**Chicago Black Hawks**	**NHL**	**67**	**16**	**18**	**34**	**18**	**18**	**36**	**26**	**3**	**2**	**3**	**124**	**12.9**	**55**	**8**	**43**	**13**	**+17**	**7**	**1**	**2**	**3**	**4**	**0**	**0**	**0**
1970-71	**Chicago Black Hawks**	**NHL**	**76**	**8**	**15**	**23**	**8**	**13**	**21**	**28**	**1**	**0**	**2**	**72**	**11.1**	**40**	**5**	**50**	**28**	**+13**	**18**	**0**	**1**	**1**	**19**	**0**	**0**	**0**
1971-72	**Chicago Black Hawks**	**NHL**	**38**	**4**	**8**	**12**	**4**	**7**	**11**	**27**	**1**	**0**	**0**	**25**	**16.0**	**19**	**3**	**15**	**6**	**+7**	**8**	**0**	**0**	**0**	**11**	**0**	**0**	**0**
1972-73			DID NOT PLAY																									
1973-74	Chicago Cougars	WHA	29	2	5	7	....	....	....	8	....	....	....	....	....	....	....	....	....	....	....	....	....	....	....	....	....	....
1974-75			DID NOT PLAY																									
1975-76	Trail Smoke Eaters	WIHL	40	10	25	35	....	....	....	38	....	....	....	....	....	....	....	....	....	....	....	....	....	....	....	....	....	....
	NHL Totals		**1219**	**250**	**324**	**574**	**316**	**342**	**658**	**1273**	**7**	**7**	**7**	**404**	**61.9**	**235**	**29**	**253**	**92**		**124**	**13**	**24**	**37**	**127**	**0**	**0**	**0**
	Other Major League Totals		29	2	5	7	....	....	....	8	....	....	....	....	....	....	....	....	....		....	....	....	....	....	....	....	....

Played in NHL All-Star Game (1961, 1965)

Traded to **Chicago** by **Toronto** for $20,000, May 21, 1956. Selected by **Dayton-Houston** (WHA) in 1972 WHA General Player Draft, February 12, 1972. WHA rights traded to **Chicago** (WHA) by **Houston** (WHA) for future considerations, June, 1973.

• NETHERY, LANCE

Lance Nethery C – L. 6'1", 185 lbs. b: Toronto, Ont., 6/28/1957. NY Rangers' 9th choice, 131st overall, in 1977 Amateur Draft.

Season	Club	League	GP	G	A	Pts	AG	AA	APts	PIM	PP	SH	GW	S	%	TGF	PGF	TGA	PGA	+/–	GP	G	A	Pts	PIM	PP	SH	GW
1975-76	Cornell University	ECAC	29	18	27	45	....	....	....	16	....	....	....	....	....	....	....	....	....	....	....	....	....	....	....	....	....	....
1976-77	Cornell University	ECAC	29	32	46	78	....	....	....	18	....	....	....	....	....	....	....	....	....	....	....	....	....	....	....	....	....	....
1977-78	Cornell University	ECAC	26	23	*60	*83	....	....	....	12	....	....	....	....	....	....	....	....	....	....	....	....	....	....	....	....	....	....
1978-79	Cornell University	ECAC	27	18	47	65	....	....	....	30	....	....	....	....	....	....	....	....	....	....	....	....	....	....	....	....	....	....
	New Haven Nighthawks	AHL	1	0	0	0	....	....	....	0	....	....	....	....	....	....	....	....	....	....	....	....	....	....	....	....	....	....
1979-80	New Haven Nighthawks	AHL	74	23	39	62	....	....	....	20	....	....	....	....	....	....	....	....	....	....	10	3	12	15	2	....	....	....
1980-81	**New York Rangers**	**NHL**	**33**	**11**	**12**	**23**	**9**	**8**	**17**	**12**	**2**	**0**	**0**	**47**	**23.4**	**31**	**3**	**34**	**6**	**0**	**14**	**5**	**3**	**8**	**9**	**0**	**0**	**1**
	New Haven Nighthawks	AHL	36	18	30	48	....	....	....	8	....	....	....	....	....	....	....	....	....	....	....	....	....	....	....	....	....	....
1981-82	**New York Rangers**	**NHL**	**5**	**0**	**0**	**0**	**0**	**0**	**0**	**0**	**0**	**0**	**0**	**4**	**0.0**	**0**	**0**	**1**	**0**	**–1**	....	....	....	....	....	....	....	....
	Springfield Indians	AHL	9	5	5	10	....	....	....	0	....	....	....	....	....	....	....	....	....	....	....	....	....	....	....	....	....	....
	Edmonton Oilers	**NHL**	**3**	**0**	**2**	**2**	**0**	**1**	**1**	**2**	**0**	**0**	**0**	**1**	**0.0**	**2**	**0**	**1**	**0**	**+1**	....	....	....	....	....	....	....	....
	Wichita Wind	CHL	46	35	32	67	....	....	....	26	....	....	....	....	....	....	....	....	....	....	7	1	4	5	8	....	....	....
1982-83	Wichita Wind	CHL	10	7	5	12	....	....	....	0	....	....	....	....	....	....	....	....	....	....	....	....	....	....	....	....	....	....
1983-84	HC Davos	Switz.	....	39	43	82	....	....	....	....	....	....	....	....	....	....	....	....	....	....	....	....	....	....	....	....	....	....
1984-85	HC Davos	Switz.	38	42	36	78	....	....	....	....	....	....	....	....	....	....	....	....	....	....	4	2	1	3	....	....	....	....
1985-86	HC Davos	Switz.	38	*46	35	81	....	....	....	....	....	....	....	....	....	....	....	....	....	....	5	2	*7	9	....	....	....	....
	Hershey Bears	AHL	13	5	6	11	....	....	....	2	....	....	....	....	....	....	....	....	....	....	18	4	9	13	2	....	....	....
1986-87	HC Davos	Switz.	36	24	31	55	....	....	....	....	....	....	....	....	....	....	....	....	....	....	10	*8	7	*15	....	....	....	....
1987-88	HC Davos	Switz.	36	35	24	59	....	....	....	....	....	....	....	....	....	....	....	....	....	....	4	4	3	7	....	....	....	....
	NHL Totals		**41**	**11**	**14**	**25**	**9**	**9**	**18**	**14**	**2**	**0**	**0**	**52**	**21.2**	**33**	**3**	**36**	**6**		**14**	**5**	**3**	**8**	**9**	**0**	**0**	**1**

ECAC Second All-Star Team (1977) • ECAC First All-Star Team (1978, 1979) • NCAA East First All-American Team (1978, 1979)

Traded to **Edmonton** by **NY Rangers** for Ed Mio, December 11, 1981.

• NEUFELD, RAY

Ray Neufeld RW – R. 6'3", 210 lbs. b: St. Boniface, Man., 4/15/1959. Hartford's 4th choice, 81st overall, in 1979 Entry Draft.

Season	Club	League	GP	G	A	Pts	AG	AA	APts	PIM	PP	SH	GW	S	%	TGF	PGF	TGA	PGA	+/–	GP	G	A	Pts	PIM	PP	SH	GW
1976-77	Flin Flon Bombers	WCJHL	68	13	19	32	....	....	....	63	....	....	....	....	....	....	....	....	....	....	....	....	....	....	....	....	....	....
1977-78	Flin Flon Bombers	WCJHL	72	23	46	69	....	....	....	224	....	....	....	....	....	....	....	....	....	....	15	4	4	8	39	....	....	....
1978-79	Edmonton Oil Kings	WHL	57	54	48	102	....	....	....	138	....	....	....	....	....	....	....	....	....	....	8	5	1	6	2	....	....	....
1979-80	**Hartford Whalers**	**NHL**	**8**	**1**	**0**	**1**	**1**	**0**	**1**	**0**	**0**	**0**	**0**	**4**	**25.0**	**2**	**0**	**5**	**0**	**–3**	**2**	**1**	**0**	**1**	**0**	**0**	**0**	**0**
	Springfield Indians	AHL	73	23	29	52	....	....	....	51	....	....	....	....	....	....	....	....	....	....	....	....	....	....	....	....	....	....
1980-81	**Hartford Whalers**	**NHL**	**52**	**5**	**10**	**15**	**4**	**7**	**11**	**44**	**0**	**0**	**0**	**55**	**9.1**	**32**	**3**	**28**	**0**	**+1**	....	....	....	....	....	....	....	....
	Binghamton Whalers	AHL	25	7	7	14	....	....	....	43	....	....	....	....	....	....	....	....	....	....	6	2	0	2	0	....	....	....
1981-82	**Hartford Whalers**	**NHL**	**19**	**4**	**3**	**7**	**3**	**2**	**5**	**4**	**1**	**0**	**0**	**33**	**12.1**	**11**	**1**	**17**	**0**	**–7**	....	....	....	....	....	....	....	....
	Binghamton Whalers	AHL	61	28	31	59	....	....	....	81	....	....	....	....	....	....	....	....	....	....	15	*9	8	17	10	....	....	....
1982-83	**Hartford Whalers**	**NHL**	**80**	**26**	**31**	**57**	**21**	**21**	**42**	**86**	**4**	**0**	**1**	**165**	**15.8**	**77**	**16**	**125**	**30**	**–34**	....	....	....	....	....	....	....	....
1983-84	**Hartford Whalers**	**NHL**	**80**	**27**	**42**	**69**	**22**	**28**	**50**	**97**	**5**	**0**	**5**	**163**	**16.6**	**109**	**36**	**94**	**3**	**–18**	....	....	....	....	....	....	....	....
1984-85	**Hartford Whalers**	**NHL**	**76**	**27**	**35**	**62**	**22**	**24**	**46**	**129**	**12**	**0**	**2**	**176**	**15.3**	**95**	**45**	**81**	**2**	**–29**	....	....	....	....	....	....	....	....
1985-86	**Hartford Whalers**	**NHL**	**16**	**5**	**10**	**15**	**4**	**7**	**11**	**40**	**3**	**0**	**0**	**35**	**14.3**	**26**	**13**	**17**	**1**	**–3**	....	....	....	....	....	....	....	....
	Winnipeg Jets	**NHL**	**60**	**20**	**28**	**48**	**16**	**19**	**35**	**62**	**7**	**0**	**4**	**132**	**15.2**	**80**	**27**	**71**	**1**	**–17**	**3**	**2**	**0**	**2**	**10**	**1**	**0**	**0**
1986-87	**Winnipeg Jets**	**NHL**	**80**	**18**	**18**	**36**	**16**	**13**	**29**	**105**	**5**	**0**	**2**	**134**	**13.4**	**56**	**8**	**61**	**0**	**–13**	**8**	**1**	**1**	**2**	**30**	**0**	**0**	**0**
1987-88	**Winnipeg Jets**	**NHL**	**78**	**18**	**18**	**36**	**15**	**13**	**28**	**169**	**9**	**0**	**2**	**115**	**15.7**	**61**	**30**	**61**	**1**	**–29**	**5**	**2**	**2**	**4**	**6**	**1**	**0**	**0**
1988-89	**Winnipeg Jets**	**NHL**	**31**	**5**	**2**	**7**	**4**	**1**	**5**	**52**	**0**	**0**	**0**	**47**	**10.6**	**20**	**1**	**28**	**0**	**–9**	....	....	....	....	....	....	....	....
	Boston Bruins	**NHL**	**14**	**1**	**3**	**4**	**1**	**2**	**3**	**28**	**0**	**0**	**0**	**16**	**6.3**	**6**	**0**	**8**	**0**	**–2**	**10**	**2**	**3**	**5**	**9**	**0**	**0**	**1**
1989-90	**Boston Bruins**	**NHL**	**1**	**0**	**0**	**0**	**0**	**0**	**0**	**0**	**0**	**0**	**0**	**1**	**0.0**	**0**	**0**	**0**	**0**	**0**	....	....	....	....	....	....	....	....
	Maine Mariners	AHL	76	27	29	56	....	....	....	117	....	....	....	....	....	....	....	....	....	....	....	....	....	....	....	....	....	....
	NHL Totals		**595**	**157**	**200**	**357**	**129**	**137**	**266**	**816**	**46**	**0**	**16**	**1076**	**14.6**	**575**	**180**	**596**	**38**		**28**	**8**	**6**	**14**	**55**	**2**	**0**	**1**

Traded to **Winnipeg** by **Hartford** for Dave Babych, November 21, 1985. Traded to **Boston** by **Winnipeg** for Moe Lemay, December 30, 1988.

• NEVIN, BOB

Bob "Nevvy" Nevin RW – R. 6', 185 lbs. b: South Porcupine, Ont., 3/18/1938.

Season	Club	League	GP	G	A	Pts	AG	AA	APts	PIM	PP	SH	GW	S	%	TGF	PGF	TGA	PGA	+/–	GP	G	A	Pts	PIM	PP	SH	GW
1954-55	Toronto Marlboros	OHA	3	0	0	0	....	....	....	0	....	....	....	....	....	....	....	....	....	....	....	....	....	....	....	....	....	....
1955-56	Toronto Marlboros	OHA	48	34	31	65	....	....	....	34	....	....	....	....	....	....	....	....	....	....	11	7	4	11	7	....	....	....
1956-57	Toronto Marlboros	OHA	51	45	29	74	....	....	....	52	....	....	....	....	....	....	....	....	....	....	9	5	6	11	13	....	....	....
	Rochester Americans	AHL	1	0	0	0	....	....	....	0	....	....	....	....	....	....	....	....	....	....	....	....	....	....	....	....	....	....
1957-58	Toronto Marlboros	OHA	50	32	39	71	....	....	....	29	....	....	....	....	....	....	....	....	....	....	13	*13	10	*23	15	....	....	....
	Toronto Maple Leafs	**NHL**	**4**	**0**	**0**	**0**	**0**	**0**	**0**	**0**	....	....	....	....	....	....	....	....	....	....	....	....	....	....	....	....	....	....
	Rochester Americans	AHL	1	0	2	2	....	....	....	2	....	....	....	....	....	....	....	....	....	....	....	....	....	....	....	....	....	....
1958-59	**Toronto Maple Leafs**	**NHL**	**2**	**0**	**0**	**0**	**0**	**0**	**0**	**2**	....	....	....	....	....	....	....	....	....	....	....	....	....	....	....	....	....	....
	Chicoutimi Sagueneens	QHL	35	16	8	24	....	....	....	12	....	....	....	....	....	....	....	....	....	....	....	....	....	....	....	....	....	....
	Rochester Americans	AHL	21	3	3	6	....	....	....	6	....	....	....	....	....	....	....	....	....	....	....	....	....	....	....	....	....	....
1959-60	Rochester Americans	AHL	71	32	42	74	....	....	....	10	....	....	....	....	....	....	....	....	....	....	12	6	4	10	4	....	....	....
1960-61	**Toronto Maple Leafs**	**NHL**	**68**	**21**	**37**	**58**	**26**	**38**	**64**	**13**	....	....	....	....	....	....	....	....	....	....	**5**	**1**	**0**	**1**	**2**	....	....	....
1961-62	**Toronto Maple Leafs**	**NHL**	**69**	**15**	**30**	**45**	**18**	**30**	**48**	**10**	....	....	....	....	....	....	....	....	....	....	**12**	**2**	**4**	**6**	**6**	....	....	....
1962-63	**Toronto Maple Leafs**	**NHL**	**58**	**12**	**21**	**33**	**15**	**22**	**37**	**4**	....	....	....	....	....	....	....	....	....	....	**10**	**3**	**0**	**3**	**2**	....	....	....
1963-64	**Toronto Maple Leafs**	**NHL**	**49**	**7**	**12**	**19**	**9**	**13**	**22**	**26**	....	....	....	....	....	....	....	....	....	....	....	....	....	....	....	....	....	....
	New York Rangers	**NHL**	**14**	**5**	**4**	**9**	**7**	**4**	**11**	**9**	....	....	....	....	....	....	....	....	....	....	....	....	....	....	....	....	....	....
1964-65	**New York Rangers**	**NHL**	**64**	**16**	**14**	**30**	**20**	**15**	**35**	**28**	....	....	....	....	....	....	....	....	....	....	....	....	....	....	....	....	....	....
1965-66	**New York Rangers**	**NHL**	**69**	**29**	**33**	**62**	**35**	**33**	**68**	**10**	....	....	....	....	....	....	....	....	....	....	....	....	....	....	....	....	....	....
1966-67	**New York Rangers**	**NHL**	**67**	**20**	**24**	**44**	**25**	**25**	**50**	**6**	....	....	....	....	....	....	....	....	....	....	**4**	**0**	**3**	**3**	**2**	....	....	....
1967-68	**New York Rangers**	**NHL**	**74**	**28**	**30**	**58**	**35**	**31**	**66**	**20**	**3**	**0**	**4**	**217**	**12.9**	**82**	**17**	**69**	**19**	**+15**	**6**	**0**	**3**	**3**	**4**	**0**	**0**	**0**
1968-69	**New York Rangers**	**NHL**	**71**	**31**	**25**	**56**	**35**	**23**	**58**	**14**	**11**	**0**	**6**	**236**	**13.1**	**89**	**33**	**66**	**13**	**+3**	**4**	**0**	**2**	**2**	**0**	**0**	**0**	**0**
1969-70	**New York Rangers**	**NHL**	**68**	**18**	**19**	**37**	**21**	**19**	**40**	**8**	**3**	**1**	**4**	**126**	**14.3**	**61**	**18**	**58**	**16**	**+1**	**6**	**1**	**1**	**2**	**2**	**1**	**0**	**0**
1970-71	**New York Rangers**	**NHL**	**78**	**21**	**25**	**46**	**22**	**22**	**44**	**10**	**3**	**0**	**3**	**154**	**13.6**	**68**	**14**	**51**	**14**	**+17**	**13**	**5**	**3**	**8**	**0**	**1**	**0**	**1**
1971-72	**Minnesota North Stars**	**NHL**	**72**	**15**	**19**	**34**	**16**	**17**	**33**	**6**	**2**	**0**	**2**	**96**	**15.6**	**52**	**10**	**40**	**5**	**+7**	**7**	**1**	**1**	**2**	**0**	**0**	**0**	**0**
1972-73	**Minnesota North Stars**	**NHL**	**66**	**5**	**13**	**18**	**5**	**11**	**16**	**0**	**0**	**0**	**1**	**55**	**9.1**	**30**	**7**	**71**	**36**	**–12**	....	....	....	....	....	....	....	....
1973-74	**Los Angeles Kings**	**NHL**	**78**	**20**	**30**	**50**	**20**	**26**	**46**	**12**	**5**	**0**	**6**	**127**	**15.7**	**72**	**16**	**69**	**21**	**+8**	**5**	**1**	**0**	**1**	**2**	**0**	**0**	**0**

			REGULAR SEASON																		PLAYOFFS							
Season	Club	League	GP	G	A	Pts	AG	AA	APts	PIM	PP	SH	GW	S	%	TGF	PGF	TGA	PGA	+/-	GP	G	A	Pts	PIM	PP	SH	GW
1974-75	**Los Angeles Kings**	**NHL**	**80**	**31**	**41**	**72**	**29**	**32**	**61**	**19**	**7**	**2**	**3**	**157**	**19.7**	**98**	**18**	**70**	**26**	**+36**	**3**	**0**	**0**	**0**	**0**	**0**	**0**	**0**
1975-76	**Los Angeles Kings**	**NHL**	**77**	**13**	**42**	**55**	**12**	**33**	**45**	**14**	**2**	**1**	**0**	**121**	**10.7**	**87**	**25**	**85**	**33**	**+10**	**9**	**2**	**1**	**3**	**4**	**0**	**0**	**1**
1976-77	Edmonton Oilers	WHA	13	3	2	5				0																		
	NHL Totals		**1128**	**307**	**419**	**726**	**350**	**394**	**744**	**211**	**36**	**4**	**29**	**1289**	**23.8**	**639**	**158**	**579**	**183**		**84**	**16**	**18**	**34**	**24**	**2**	**0**	**2**
	Other Major League Totals		13	3	2	5				0																		

Played in NHL All-Star Game (1962, 1963, 1967, 1969)

Traded to **NY Rangers** by **Toronto** with Rod Seiling, Dick Duff, Arnie Brown and Bill Collins for Andy Bathgate and Don McKenney, February 22, 1964 Traded to **Minnesota** by **NY Rangers** for future considerations (Bobby Rousseau, June 8, 1971), May 25, 1971. Selected by **Ontario-Ottawa** (WHA) in 1972 WHA General Player Draft, February 12, 1972. Claimed by **LA Kings** (Springfield - AHL) from **Minnesota** in Reverse Draft, June 13, 1973. Signed as a free agent by **Edmonton** (WHA), October 25, 1976.

• NEWBERRY, JOHN

John Newberry C – L. 6′, 190 lbs. b: Port Alberni, B.C., 4/8/1962. Montreal's 4th choice, 45th overall, in 1980 Entry Draft.

Season	Club	League	GP	G	A	Pts	AG	AA	APts	PIM	PP	SH	GW	S	%	TGF	PGF	TGA	PGA	+/-	GP	G	A	Pts	PIM	PP	SH	GW
1979-80	Nanaimo Clippers	BCJHL	65	*84	*101	*185																						
1980-81	University of Wisconsin	WCHA	39	30	32	62				77																		
1981-82	University of Wisconsin	WCHA	39	38	27	65																						
1982-83	Nova Scotia Voyageurs	AHL	71	29	29	58				43											6	3	1	4	2			
	Montreal Canadiens	**NHL**																			**2**	**0**	**0**	**0**	**0**			
1983-84	**Montreal Canadiens**	**NHL**	**3**	**0**	**0**	**0**	**0**	**0**	**0**	**0**	**0**	**0**	**0**	**2**	**0.0**	**0**	**0**	**0**	**0**	**0**								
	Nova Scotia Voyageurs	AHL	78	25	37	52				116											12	7	12	19	22			
1984-85	**Montreal Canadiens**	**NHL**	**16**	**0**	**4**	**4**	**0**	**3**	**3**	**6**	**0**	**0**	**0**	**12**	**0.0**	**9**	**0**	**6**	**0**	**+3**								
	Sherbrooke Canadiens	AHL	58	23	40	63				30											17	6	*14	*20	18			
1985-86	**Hartford Whalers**	**NHL**	**3**	**0**	**0**	**0**	**0**	**0**	**0**	**0**	**0**	**0**	**0**	**4**	**0.0**	**1**	**0**	**5**	**0**	**–4**								
	Binghamton Whalers	AHL	21	6	11	17				38																		
	Moncton Golden Flames	AHL	44	10	24	34				31											9	1	4	5	2			
1986-87	Karpat Oulu	Finland	39	16	14	30				63											9	3	4	7	17			
	NHL Totals		**22**	**0**	**4**	**4**	**0**	**3**	**3**	**6**	**0**	**0**	**0**	**18**	**0.0**	**10**	**0**	**11**	**0**		**2**	**0**	**0**	**0**	**0**	**0**	**0**	**0**

NCAA Championship All-Tournament Team (1981, 1982) • WCHA First All-Star Team (1982) • NCAA West First All-American Team (1982)

Signed as a free agent by **Hartford**, September 19, 1985.

• NEWELL, RICK

Rick Newell D – L. 5′11″, 180 lbs. b: Winnipeg, Man., 2/18/1948.

Season	Club	League	GP	G	A	Pts	AG	AA	APts	PIM	PP	SH	GW	S	%	TGF	PGF	TGA	PGA	+/-	GP	G	A	Pts	PIM	PP	SH	GW
1964-65	Winnipeg Rangers	MJHL	35	5	13	18				74											5	1	*8	9	15			
1965-66	Winnipeg Rangers	MJHL	3	0	2	2				6																		
1966-67	University of Minnesota-Duluth	WCHA	22	6	13	19																						
1967-68	University of Minnesota-Duluth	WCHA	STATISTICS NOT AVAILABLE																									
1968-69	University of Minnesota-Duluth	WCHA	STATISTICS NOT AVAILABLE																									
1969-70	Omaha Knights	CHL	6	0	0	0				4																		
1970-71	Omaha Knights	CHL	69	6	17	23				110											11	1	4	5	4			
1971-72	Phoenix Roadrunners	WHL	1	0	0	0				0																		
	Providence Reds	AHL	19	1	6	7				15																		
	Omaha Knights	CHL	53	8	21	29				76																		
1972-73	**Detroit Red Wings**	**NHL**	**3**	**0**	**0**	**0**	**0**	**0**	**0**	**0**	**0**	**0**	**0**	**0**	**0.0**	**1**	**0**	**3**	**1**	**–1**								
	Virginia Wings	AHL	68	24	23	47				125											9	2	3	5	6			
1973-74	**Detroit Red Wings**	**NHL**	**3**	**0**	**0**	**0**	**0**	**0**	**0**	**0**	**0**	**0**	**0**	**1**	**0.0**	**2**	**0**	**3**	**0**	**–1**								
	Virginia Wings	AHL	50	9	22	31				44																		
	London Lions	Britain	17	12	11	23				63																		
1974-75	Phoenix Roadrunners	WHA	25	0	4	4				39											5	0	1	1	2			
	Tulsa Oilers	CHL	22	5	9	14				24																		
1975-76	Tucson Mavericks	CHL	57	9	23	32				104																		
	Syracuse Blazers	NAHL	6	1	3	4				0																		
1976-77			DID NOT PLAY																									
1977-78	Phoenix Roadrunners	PHL	35	10	32	42				28																		
	NHL Totals		**6**	**0**	**0**	**0**	**0**	**0**	**0**	**0**	**0**	**0**	**0**	**1**	**0.0**	**3**	**0**	**6**	**1**									
	Other Major League Totals		25	0	4	4				39											5	0	1	1	2			

Re-claimed as a territorial exemption by **NY Rangers** (Winnipeg Rangers MJHL), March, 1969. Traded to **Detroit** by **NY Rangers** with Gary Doak for Joe Zanussi and Detroit's 1st choice (Albert Bouchard) in 1972 Amateur Draft, May 24, 1972. Selected by **Chicago** (WHA) in 1973 WHA Professional Player Draft, June, 1973. WHA rights traded to **Phoenix** (WHA) by **Chicago** (WHA) for future considerations, June, 1974.

• NEWMAN, DAN

Dan Newman LW – L. 6′1″, 195 lbs. b: Windsor, Ont., 1/26/1952.

Season	Club	League	GP	G	A	Pts	AG	AA	APts	PIM	PP	SH	GW	S	%	TGF	PGF	TGA	PGA	+/-	GP	G	A	Pts	PIM	PP	SH	GW
1970-71	St. Clair College	NCAA	22	13	17	30				42																		
1971-72	St. Clair College	NCAA	20	28	13	41																						
1972-73	Virginia Wings	AHL	5	1	0	1				0																		
	Des Moines–Port Huron	IHL	61	8	14	22				27											3	0	0	0	0			
1973-74	Port Huron Wings	IHL	66	14	16	30				129																		
1974-75	Port Huron Flags	IHL	72	8	22	30				72											5	1	2	3	0			
1975-76	Port Huron Flags	IHL	75	39	45	84				114											15	6	9	15	35			
1976-77	**New York Rangers**	**NHL**	**41**	**9**	**8**	**17**	**9**	**6**	**15**	**37**	**0**	**0**	**1**	**67**	**13.4**	**30**	**3**	**31**	**0**	**–4**								
	New Haven Nighthawks	AHL	33	12	17	29				57																		
1977-78	**New York Rangers**	**NHL**	**59**	**5**	**13**	**18**	**5**	**11**	**16**	**22**	**0**	**0**	**1**	**81**	**6.2**	**27**	**2**	**36**	**0**	**–11**	**3**	**0**	**0**	**0**	**4**	**0**	**0**	**0**
	New Haven Nighthawks	AHL	8	2	4	6				7																		
1978-79	**Montreal Canadiens**	**NHL**	**16**	**0**	**2**	**2**	**0**	**2**	**2**	**4**	**0**	**0**	**0**	**9**	**0.0**	**4**	**0**	**5**	**0**	**–1**								
	Nova Scotia Voyageurs	AHL	54	24	22	46				54											9	3	1	4	2			
1979-80	**Edmonton Oilers**	**NHL**	**10**	**3**	**1**	**4**	**3**	**1**	**4**	**0**	**0**	**0**	**0**	**16**	**18.8**	**5**	**0**	**6**	**0**	**–1**								
	Binghamton Whalers	AHL	55	11	17	28				50																		
	Houston Apollos	CHL	14	5	9	14				4																		
	NHL Totals		**126**	**17**	**24**	**41**	**17**	**20**	**37**	**63**	**0**	**0**	**2**	**173**	**9.8**	**66**	**5**	**78**	**0**		**3**	**0**	**0**	**0**	**4**	**0**	**0**	**0**

Signed as a free agent by **Port Huron** (IHL), September, 1972. NHL rights transferred to **NY Rangers** after NHL club signed affiliation agreement with **Port Huron** (IHL), June, 1974. Claimed by **Montreal** from **NY Rangers** in Waiver Draft, October 9, 1978. Traded to **Edmonton** by **Montreal** with Dave Lumley for Edmonton's 2nd round choice (Ric Nattress) in 1980 Entry Draft, June 13, 1979. Traded to **Boston** by **Edmonton** for Bobby Schmautz, December 10, 1979.

• NICHOL, SCOTT

Scott Nichol C – R. 5′8″, 160 lbs. b: Edmonton, Alta., 12/31/1974. Buffalo's 9th choice, 272nd overall, in 1993 Entry Draft.

Season	Club	League	GP	G	A	Pts	AG	AA	APts	PIM	PP	SH	GW	S	%	TGF	PGF	TGA	PGA	+/-	GP	G	A	Pts	PIM	PP	SH	GW
1992-93	Portland Winter Hawks	WHL	67	31	33	64				146											16	8	8	16	41			
1993-94	Portland Winter Hawks	WHL	65	40	53	93				144											10	3	8	11	16			
1994-95	Rochester Americans	AHL	71	11	16	27				136											5	0	3	3	14			
1995-96	**Buffalo Sabres**	**NHL**	**2**	**0**	**0**	**0**	**0**	**0**	**0**	**10**	**0**	**0**	**0**	**4**	**0.0**	**0**	**0**	**0**	**0**	**0**								
	Rochester Americans	AHL	62	14	18	32				170											19	7	6	13	36			
1996-97	Rochester Americans	AHL	68	22	21	43				133											10	2	1	3	26			
1997-98	**Buffalo Sabres**	**NHL**	**3**	**0**	**0**	**0**	**0**	**0**	**0**	**4**	**0**	**0**	**0**	**5**	**0.0**	**0**	**0**	**0**	**0**	**0**								
	Rochester Americans	AHL	35	13	7	20				113																		
	NHL Totals		**5**	**0**	**0**	**0**	**0**	**0**	**0**	**14**	**0**	**0**	**0**	**9**	**0.0**	**0**	**0**	**0**	**0**									

• NICHOLLS, BERNIE

Bernie "The Pumper Nicholl Kid" Nicholls C – R. 6′, 185 lbs. b: Haliburton, Ont., 6/24/1961. Los Angeles' 6th choice, 73rd overall, in 1980 Entry Draft.

Season	Club	League	GP	G	A	Pts	AG	AA	APts	PIM	PP	SH	GW	S	%	TGF	PGF	TGA	PGA	+/-	GP	G	A	Pts	PIM	PP	SH	GW
1979-80	Kingston Canadians	OHA	68	36	43	79				85											3	1	0	1	10			
1980-81	Kingston Canadians	OHA	65	63	89	152				109											14	8	10	18	17			
1981-82	**Los Angeles Kings**	**NHL**	**22**	**14**	**18**	**32**	**11**	**12**	**23**	**27**	**8**	**1**	**1**	**63**	**22.2**	**38**	**14**	**29**	**7**	**+2**	**10**	**4**	**0**	**4**	**23**	**0**	**0**	**1**
	New Haven Nighthawks	AHL	55	41	30	71				31																		
1982-83	**Los Angeles Kings**	**NHL**	**71**	**28**	**22**	**50**	**23**	**15**	**38**	**124**	**12**	**0**	**3**	**171**	**16.4**	**68**	**24**	**83**	**16**	**–23**								
1983-84	**Los Angeles Kings**	**NHL**	**78**	**41**	**54**	**95**	**33**	**37**	**70**	**83**	**8**	**4**	**2**	**255**	**16.1**	**123**	**37**	**136**	**29**	**–21**								
1984-85	**Los Angeles Kings**	**NHL**	**80**	**46**	**54**	**100**	**38**	**37**	**75**	**76**	**15**	**0**	**6**	**329**	**14.0**	**153**	**68**	**89**	**0**	**–4**	**3**	**1**	**1**	**2**	**0**	**0**	**0**	**0**
	Canada	WEC-A	10	0	2	2				12																		
1985-86	**Los Angeles Kings**	**NHL**	**80**	**36**	**61**	**97**	**29**	**41**	**70**	**78**	**10**	**4**	**0**	**281**	**12.8**	**140**	**49**	**114**	**18**	**–5**								
1986-87	**Los Angeles Kings**	**NHL**	**80**	**33**	**48**	**81**	**29**	**35**	**64**	**101**	**10**	**1**	**2**	**227**	**14.5**	**115**	**47**	**86**	**2**	**–16**	**5**	**2**	**5**	**7**	**6**	**1**	**0**	**0**

			REGULAR SEASON																		PLAYOFFS							
Season	**Club**	**League**	**GP**	**G**	**A**	**Pts**	**AG**	**AA**	**APts**	**PIM**	**PP**	**SH**	**GW**	**S**	**%**	**TGF**	**PGF**	**TGA**	**PGA**	**+/–**	**GP**	**G**	**A**	**Pts**	**PIM**	**PP**	**SH**	**GW**
1987-88	**Los Angeles Kings**	**NHL**	**65**	**32**	**46**	**78**	**27**	**33**	**60**	**114**	**8**	**7**	**1**	**236**	**13.6**	**125**	**53**	**102**	**32**	**+2**	**5**	**2**	**6**	**8**	**11**	**1**	**0**	**0**
1988-89	**Los Angeles Kings**	**NHL**	**79**	**70**	**80**	**150**	**60**	**57**	**117**	**96**	**21**	**8**	**6**	**385**	**18.2**	**194**	**63**	**139**	**38**	**+30**	**11**	**7**	**9**	**16**	**12**	**3**	**0**	**1**
1989-90	**Los Angeles Kings**	**NHL**	**47**	**27**	**48**	**75**	**23**	**34**	**57**	**66**	**8**	**0**	**1**	**172**	**15.7**	**96**	**35**	**75**	**8**	**–6**	....	....	....	....	....	....	....	....
	New York Rangers	**NHL**	**32**	**12**	**25**	**37**	**10**	**18**	**28**	**20**	**7**	**0**	**0**	**115**	**10.4**	**56**	**35**	**29**	**5**	**–3**	**10**	**7**	**5**	**12**	**16**	**3**	**0**	**0**
1990-91	**New York Rangers**	**NHL**	**71**	**25**	**48**	**73**	**23**	**36**	**59**	**96**	**8**	**0**	**2**	**163**	**15.3**	**121**	**50**	**67**	**1**	**+5**	**5**	**4**	**3**	**7**	**8**	**0**	**0**	**1**
1991-92	**New York Rangers**	**NHL**	**1**	**0**	**0**	**0**	**0**	**0**	**0**	**0**	**0**	**0**	**0**	**2**	**0.0**	**1**	**0**	**2**	**0**	**–1**	....	....	....	....	....	....	....	....
	Edmonton Oilers	**NHL**	**49**	**20**	**29**	**49**	**18**	**22**	**40**	**60**	**7**	**0**	**2**	**115**	**17.4**	**69**	**25**	**40**	**1**	**+5**	**16**	**8**	**11**	**19**	**25**	**4**	**0**	**1**
1992-93	**Edmonton Oilers**	**NHL**	**46**	**8**	**32**	**40**	**7**	**22**	**29**	**40**	**4**	**0**	**1**	**86**	**9.3**	**56**	**28**	**46**	**2**	**–16**	....	....	....	....	....	....	....	....
	New Jersey Devils	**NHL**	**23**	**5**	**15**	**20**	**4**	**10**	**14**	**40**	**1**	**0**	**0**	**46**	**10.9**	**33**	**12**	**19**	**1**	**+3**	**5**	**0**	**0**	**0**	**6**	**0**	**0**	**0**
1993-94	**New Jersey Devils**	**NHL**	**61**	**19**	**27**	**46**	**18**	**21**	**39**	**86**	**3**	**0**	**1**	**142**	**13.4**	**66**	**17**	**45**	**20**	**+24**	**16**	**4**	**9**	**13**	**28**	**2**	**1**	**0**
1994-95	**Chicago Blackhawks**	**NHL**	**48**	**22**	**29**	**51**	**39**	**43**	**82**	**32**	**11**	**2**	**5**	**114**	**19.3**	**74**	**39**	**41**	**10**	**+4**	**16**	**1**	**11**	**12**	**8**	**1**	**0**	**0**
1995-96	**Chicago Blackhawks**	**NHL**	**59**	**19**	**41**	**60**	**19**	**33**	**52**	**60**	**6**	**0**	**2**	**100**	**19.0**	**88**	**36**	**50**	**9**	**+11**	**10**	**2**	**7**	**9**	**4**	**1**	**0**	**0**
1996-97	**San Jose Sharks**	**NHL**	**65**	**12**	**33**	**45**	**13**	**29**	**42**	**63**	**2**	**1**	**0**	**137**	**8.8**	**60**	**19**	**90**	**28**	**–21**	....	....	....	....	....	....	....	....
1997-98	**San Jose Sharks**	**NHL**	**60**	**6**	**22**	**28**	**7**	**21**	**28**	**26**	**3**	**0**	**0**	**81**	**7.4**	**42**	**12**	**43**	**9**	**–4**	**6**	**0**	**5**	**5**	**8**	**0**	**0**	**0**
	NHL Totals		**1117**	**475**	**732**	**1207**	**431**	**556**	**987**	**1288**	**152**	**28**	**35**	**3220**	**14.8**	**1718**	**663**	**1325**	**236**		**118**	**42**	**72**	**114**	**164**	**16**	**1**	**4**

Played in NHL All-Star Game (1984, 1989, 1990)

Traded to **NY Rangers** by **LA Kings** for Tomas Sandstrom and Tony Granato, January 20, 1990. Traded to **Edmonton** by **NY Rangers** with Steven Rice and Louie DeBrusk for Mark Messier and future considerations, October 4, 1991. Traded to **New Jersey** by **Edmonton** for Zdeno Ciger and Kevin Todd, January 13, 1993. Signed as a free agent by **Chicago**, July 14, 1994. Signed as a free agent by **San Jose**, August 5, 1996.

• NICHOLSON, NEIL

Neil Nicholson D – R. 5'11", 180 lbs. b: Saint John, N.B., 9/12/1949. Oakland's 6th choice, 65th overall, in 1969 Amateur Draft.

Season	Club	League	GP	G	A	Pts	AG	AA	APts	PIM	PP	SH	GW	S	%	TGF	PGF	TGA	PGA	+/–	GP	G	A	Pts	PIM	PP	SH	GW
1966-67	Fredericton Jr. Red Wings	NBJHL	....	9	11	20	....	....	....	39	....	....	....	....	....	....	....	....	....	....	....	....	....	....	....	....	....	....
	Halifax Jr. Canadiens	NSJHL	....	....	....	....	....	....	....	....	....	....	....	....	....	....	....	....	....	....	4	0	1	1	4	....	....	....
1967-68	Fredericton Jr. Red Wings	NBJHL	4	0	2	2	....	....	....	2	....	....	....	....	....	....	....	....	....	....	12	6	9	15	24	....	....	....
	Fredericton Red Wings	NBSHL	31	11	20	31	....	....	....	30	....	....	....	....	....	....	....	....	....	....	5	2	2	4	6	....	....	....
1968-69	London Knights	OHA	54	16	26	42	....	....	....	62	....	....	....	....	....	....	....	....	....	....	6	0	2	2	8	....	....	....
1969-70	Providence Reds	AHL	63	3	21	24	....	....	....	120	....	....	....	....	....	....	....	....	....	....	....	....	....	....	....	....	....	....
	Oakland Seals	**NHL**	....	....	....	....	....	....	....	....	....	....	....	....	....	....	....	....	....	....	**2**	**0**	**0**	**0**	**0**	....	....	....
1970-71	Providence Reds	AHL	56	8	16	24	....	....	....	41	....	....	....	....	....	....	....	....	....	....	10	4	1	5	6	....	....	....
1971-72	Providence Reds	AHL	73	18	18	36	....	....	....	21	....	....	....	....	....	....	....	....	....	....	5	2	2	4	4	....	....	....
1972-73	**New York Islanders**	**NHL**	**30**	**3**	**1**	**4**	**3**	**1**	**4**	**23**	**0**	**0**	**0**	**51**	**5.9**	**18**	**0**	**47**	**7**	**–22**	....	....	....	....	....	....	....	....
	New Haven Nighthawks	AHL	43	7	12	19	....	....	....	44	....	....	....	....	....	....	....	....	....	....	....	....	....	....	....	....	....	....
1973-74	**New York Islanders**	**NHL**	**8**	**0**	**0**	**0**	**0**	**0**	**0**	**0**	**0**	**0**	**0**	**2**	**0.0**	**2**	**0**	**0**	**0**	**+2**	....	....	....	....	....	....	....	....
	Fort Worth Wings	CHL	47	10	16	26	....	....	....	30	....	....	....	....	....	....	....	....	....	....	4	0	2	2	11	....	....	....
1974-75	Fort Worth Texans	CHL	74	14	47	61	....	....	....	99	....	....	....	....	....	....	....	....	....	....	....	....	....	....	....	....	....	....
1975-76	Fort Worth Texans	CHL	74	16	39	55	....	....	....	119	....	....	....	....	....	....	....	....	....	....	....	....	....	....	....	....	....	....
1976-77	Fort Worth Texans	CHL	65	6	43	49	....	....	....	78	....	....	....	....	....	....	....	....	....	....	6	1	5	6	9	....	....	....
1977-78	**New York Islanders**	**NHL**	**1**	**0**	**0**	**0**	**0**	**0**	**0**	**0**	**0**	**0**	**0**	**2**	**0.0**	**3**	**0**	**1**	**0**	**+2**	....	....	....	....	....	....	....	....
	Fort Worth Texans	CHL	69	16	36	52	....	....	....	73	....	....	....	....	....	....	....	....	....	....	14	2	6	8	8	....	....	....
1978-79	Fort Worth Texans	CHL	19	0	13	13	....	....	....	6	....	....	....	....	....	....	....	....	....	....	5	2	0	2	8	....	....	....
1979-80	SC Langnau	Switz.	....	11	8	19	....	....	....	....	....	....	....	....	....	....	....	....	....	....	....	....	....	....	....	....	....	....
1980-81	SC Langnau	Switz.	....	14	17	31	....	....	....	....	....	....	....	....	....	....	....	....	....	....	....	....	....	....	....	....	....	....
1981-82	Dallas Black Hawks	CHL	10	0	0	0	....	....	....	2	....	....	....	....	....	....	....	....	....	....	8	0	2	2	0	....	....	....
1982-83	Moncton Alpines	AHL	12	0	2	2	....	....	....	9	....	....	....	....	....	....	....	....	....	....	....	....	....	....	....	....	....	....
1983-84	SC Langnau	Switz.	26	6	13	19	....	....	....	0	....	....	....	....	....	....	....	....	....	....	....	....	....	....	....	....	....	....
1984-85	SC Langnau	Switz.	27	6	8	14	....	....	....	....	....	....	....	....	....	....	....	....	....	....	....	....	....	....	....	....	....	....
	NHL Totals		**39**	**3**	**1**	**4**	**3**	**1**	**4**	**23**	**0**	**0**	**0**	**55**	**5.5**	**23**	**0**	**48**	**7**		**2**	**0**	**0**	**0**	**0**	**0**	**0**	**0**

CHL First All-Star Team (1977)

Claimed by **NY Islanders** from **California** (Salt Lake-CHL) in Inter-League Draft, June 6, 1972.

• NICHOLSON, PAUL

Paul Nicholson LW – L. 6', 190 lbs. b: London, Ont., 2/16/1954. Washington's 6th choice, 55th overall, in 1974 Amateur Draft.

Season	Club	League	GP	G	A	Pts	AG	AA	APts	PIM	PP	SH	GW	S	%	TGF	PGF	TGA	PGA	+/–	GP	G	A	Pts	PIM	PP	SH	GW
1971-72	London Knights	OHA	62	18	16	34	....	....	....	50	....	....	....	....	....	....	....	....	....	....	....	....	....	....	....	....	....	....
1972-73	London Knights	OHA	60	16	18	34	....	....	....	42	....	....	....	....	....	....	....	....	....	....	....	....	....	....	....	....	....	....
1973-74	London Knights	OHA	67	36	33	69	....	....	....	60	....	....	....	....	....	....	....	....	....	....	....	....	....	....	....	....	....	....
1974-75	**Washington Capitals**	**NHL**	**39**	**4**	**5**	**9**	**4**	**4**	**8**	**7**	**0**	**0**	**1**	**46**	**8.7**	**14**	**1**	**42**	**0**	**–29**	....	....	....	....	....	....	....	....
	Richmond Robins	AHL	34	9	13	22	....	....	....	26	....	....	....	....	....	....	....	....	....	....	2	0	0	0	2	....	....	....
1975-76	**Washington Capitals**	**NHL**	**14**	**0**	**2**	**2**	**0**	**2**	**2**	**9**	**0**	**0**	**0**	**10**	**0.0**	**4**	**0**	**9**	**1**	**–4**	....	....	....	....	....	....	....	....
	Richmond Robins	AHL	4	0	0	0	....	....	....	0	....	....	....	....	....	....	....	....	....	....	....	....	....	....	....	....	....	....
	Dayton Gems	IHL	55	35	37	72	....	....	....	76	....	....	....	....	....	....	....	....	....	....	15	11	9	20	15	....	....	....
1976-77	**Washington Capitals**	**NHL**	**9**	**0**	**1**	**1**	**0**	**1**	**1**	**2**	**0**	**0**	**0**	**16**	**0.0**	**1**	**0**	**7**	**0**	**–6**	....	....	....	....	....	....	....	....
	Dayton Gems	IHL	67	28	39	67	....	....	....	50	....	....	....	....	....	....	....	....	....	....	4	1	4	5	2	....	....	....
	Springfield Indians	AHL	1	0	0	0	....	....	....	0	....	....	....	....	....	....	....	....	....	....	....	....	....	....	....	....	....	....
1977-78	Port Huron Flags	IHL	77	34	46	80	....	....	....	54	....	....	....	....	....	....	....	....	....	....	17	9	8	17	6	....	....	....
	NHL Totals		**62**	**4**	**8**	**12**	**4**	**7**	**11**	**18**	**0**	**0**	**1**	**72**	**5.6**	**19**	**1**	**58**	**1**		....	....	....	....	....	....	....	....

• NICOLSON, GRAEME

Graeme Nicolson D – R. 6', 185 lbs. b: North Bay, Ont., 1/13/1958. Boston's 2nd choice, 35th overall, in 1978 Amateur Draft.

Season	Club	League	GP	G	A	Pts	AG	AA	APts	PIM	PP	SH	GW	S	%	TGF	PGF	TGA	PGA	+/–	GP	G	A	Pts	PIM	PP	SH	GW
1975-76	Cornwall Royals	QMJHL	72	11	36	47	....	....	....	101	....	....	....	....	....	....	....	....	....	....	....	....	....	....	....	....	....	....
1976-77	Cornwall Royals	QMJHL	64	21	46	67	....	....	....	197	....	....	....	....	....	....	....	....	....	....	12	3	9	12	34	....	....	....
1977-78	Cornwall Royals	QMJHL	62	13	52	65	....	....	....	122	....	....	....	....	....	....	....	....	....	....	9	1	4	5	45	....	....	....
1978-79	**Boston Bruins**	**NHL**	**1**	**0**	**0**	**0**	**0**	**0**	**0**	**0**	**0**	**0**	**0**	**0**	**0.0**	**0**	**0**	**0**	**0**	**0**	....	....	....	....	....	....	....	....
	Rochester Americans	AHL	80	16	35	51	....	....	....	112	....	....	....	....	....	....	....	....	....	....	....	....	....	....	....	....	....	....
1979-80	Binghamton Whalers	AHL	79	7	36	43	....	....	....	151	....	....	....	....	....	....	....	....	....	....	....	....	....	....	....	....	....	....
1980-81			DID NOT PLAY																									
1981-82	**Colorado Rockies**	**NHL**	**41**	**2**	**7**	**9**	**2**	**5**	**7**	**51**	**0**	**0**	**0**	**39**	**5.1**	**30**	**0**	**49**	**3**	**–16**	....	....	....	....	....	....	....	....
	Fort Worth Texans	CHL	30	9	12	21	....	....	....	38	....	....	....	....	....	....	....	....	....	....	....	....	....	....	....	....	....	....
1982-83	**New York Rangers**	**NHL**	**10**	**0**	**0**	**0**	**0**	**0**	**0**	**9**	**0**	**0**	**0**	**3**	**0.0**	**3**	**0**	**9**	**1**	**–5**	....	....	....	....	....	....	....	....
	Tulsa Oilers	CHL	64	19	28	47	....	....	....	166	....	....	....	....	....	....	....	....	....	....	....	....	....	....	....	....	....	....
1983-84	Tulsa Oilers	CHL	62	7	24	31	....	....	....	61	....	....	....	....	....	....	....	....	....	....	9	1	6	7	12	....	....	....
1984-85	Binghamton Whalers	AHL	37	3	9	12	....	....	....	53	....	....	....	....	....	....	....	....	....	....	4	0	0	0	2	....	....	....
	NHL Totals		**52**	**2**	**7**	**9**	**2**	**5**	**7**	**60**	**0**	**0**	**0**	**42**	**4.8**	**33**	**0**	**58**	**4**		....	....	....	....	....	....	....	....

QMJHL First All-Star Team (1977) • QMJHL Second All-Star Team (1978) • CHL Second All-Star Team (1984)

Signed as a free agent by **Colorado**, September 2, 1981. Transferred to **New Jersey** after **Colorado** franchise relocated, June 30, 1982. Claimed by **NY Rangers** from **New Jersey** in Waiver Draft, October 4, 1982. Signed as a free agent by **Washington**, August 17, 1984.

• NIECKAR, BARRY

Barry Nieckar LW – L. 6'3", 205 lbs. b: Rama, Sask., 12/16/1967.

Season	Club	League	GP	G	A	Pts	AG	AA	APts	PIM	PP	SH	GW	S	%	TGF	PGF	TGA	PGA	+/–	GP	G	A	Pts	PIM	PP	SH	GW
1991-92	Phoenix Roadrunners	IHL	5	0	0	0	....	....	....	9	....	....	....	....	....	....	....	....	....	....	....	....	....	....	....	....	....	....
	Raleigh IceCaps	ECHL	46	10	18	28	....	....	....	229	....	....	....	....	....	....	....	....	....	....	4	4	0	4	22	....	....	....
1992-93	**Hartford Whalers**	**NHL**	**2**	**0**	**0**	**0**	**0**	**0**	**0**	**2**	**0**	**0**	**0**	**1**	**0.0**	**0**	**0**	**2**	**0**	**–2**	....	....	....	....	....	....	....	....
	Springfield Indians	AHL	21	2	4	6	....	....	....	65	....	....	....	....	....	....	....	....	....	....	6	1	0	1	14	....	....	....
1993-94	Springfield Indians	AHL	30	0	2	2	....	....	....	67	....	....	....	....	....	....	....	....	....	....	....	....	....	....	....	....	....	....
	Raleigh IceCaps	ECHL	18	4	6	10	....	....	....	126	....	....	....	....	....	....	....	....	....	....	15	5	7	12	51	....	....	....
1994-95	Saint John Flames	AHL	65	8	7	15	....	....	....	*491	....	....	....	....	....	....	....	....	....	....	4	0	0	0	22	....	....	....
	Calgary Flames	**NHL**	**3**	**0**	**0**	**0**	**0**	**0**	**0**	**12**	**0**	**0**	**0**	**0**	**0.0**	**0**	**0**	**0**	**0**	**0**	....	....	....	....	....	....	....	....
1995-96	Utah Grizzlies	IHL	53	9	15	24	....	....	....	194	....	....	....	....	....	....	....	....	....	....	....	....	....	....	....	....	....	....
	Peoria Rivermen	IHL	10	3	3	6	....	....	....	72	....	....	....	....	....	....	....	....	....	....	12	4	6	10	48	....	....	....

			REGULAR SEASON																		PLAYOFFS							
Season	Club	League	GP	G	A	Pts	AG	AA	APts	PIM	PP	SH	GW	S	%	TGF	PGF	TGA	PGA	+/-	GP	G	A	Pts	PIM	PP	SH	GW
1996-97	**Anaheim Mighty Ducks**	**NHL**	**2**	**0**	**0**	**0**	**0**	**0**	**0**	**5**	**0**	**0**	**0**	**0**	**0.0**	**0**	**0**	**0**	**0**	**0**	....	....	....	....	....	....	....	....
	Long Beach Ice Dogs	IHL	63	3	10	13	....	....	....	386	....	....	....	....	....	....	....	....	....	....	5	0	0	0	22	....	....	....
1997-98	**Anaheim Mighty Ducks**	**NHL**	**1**	**0**	**0**	**0**	**0**	**0**	**0**	**2**	**0**	**0**	**0**	**0**	**0.0**	**0**	**0**	**0**	**0**	**0**	....	....	....	....	....	....	....	....
	Cincinnati Mighty Ducks	AHL	75	10	14	24	....	....	....	295	....	....	....	....	....	....	....	....	....	....	....	....	....	....	....	....	....	....
	NHL Totals		**8**	**0**	**0**	**0**	**0**	**0**	**0**	**21**	**0**	**0**	**0**	**1**	**0.0**	**0**	**0**	**2**	**0**		....	....	....	....	....	....	....	....

Signed as a free agent by **Hartford**, September 25, 1992. Signed as a free agent by **Calgary**, February 11, 1995. Signed as a free agent by **NY Islanders**, August 8, 1995. Signed as a free agent by **Anaheim**, October 2, 1996.

• NIEDERMAYER, ROB

Rob Niedermayer C – L. 6'2", 201 lbs. b: Cassiar, B.C., 12/28/1974. Florida's 1st choice, 5th overall, in 1993 Entry Draft.

Season	Club	League	GP	G	A	Pts	AG	AA	APts	PIM	PP	SH	GW	S	%	TGF	PGF	TGA	PGA	+/-	GP	G	A	Pts	PIM	PP	SH	GW
1990-91	Medicine Hat Tigers	WHL	71	24	26	50	....	....	....	8	....	....	....	....	....	....	....	....	....	....	12	3	7	10	2	....	....	....
1991-92	Medicine Hat Tigers	WHL	71	32	46	78	....	....	....	77	....	....	....	....	....	....	....	....	....	....	4	2	3	5	2	....	....	....
1992-93	Medicine Hat Tigers	WHL	52	43	34	77	....	....	....	67	....	....	....	....	....	....	....	....	....	....	....	....	....	....	....	....	....	....
	Canada	WJC-A	7	0	2	2	....	....	....	2	....	....	....	....	....	....	....	....	....	....	....	....	....	....	....	....	....	....
1993-94	**Florida Panthers**	**NHL**	**65**	**9**	**17**	**26**	**8**	**13**	**21**	**51**	**3**	**0**	**2**	**67**	**13.4**	**38**	**18**	**31**	**0**	**–11**	....	....	....	....	....	....	....	....
1994-95	Medicine Hat Tigers	WHL	13	9	15	24	....	....	....	14	....	....	....	....	....	....	....	....	....	....	....	....	....	....	....	....	....	....
	Florida Panthers	**NHL**	**48**	**4**	**6**	**10**	**7**	**9**	**16**	**36**	**1**	**0**	**0**	**58**	**6.9**	**26**	**11**	**28**	**0**	**–13**	....	....	....	....	....	....	....	....
1995-96	**Florida Panthers**	**NHL**	**82**	**26**	**35**	**61**	**26**	**29**	**55**	**107**	**11**	**0**	**6**	**155**	**16.8**	**97**	**44**	**54**	**2**	**+1**	**22**	**5**	**3**	**8**	**12**	**2**	**0**	**2**
1996-97	**Florida Panthers**	**NHL**	**60**	**14**	**24**	**38**	**15**	**21**	**36**	**54**	**3**	**0**	**2**	**136**	**10.3**	**55**	**16**	**43**	**8**	**+4**	**5**	**2**	**1**	**3**	**6**	**1**	**0**	**0**
1997-98	**Florida Panthers**	**NHL**	**33**	**8**	**7**	**15**	**9**	**7**	**16**	**41**	**5**	**0**	**2**	**64**	**12.5**	**27**	**14**	**27**	**5**	**–9**	....	....	....	....	....	....	....	....
	NHL Totals		**288**	**61**	**89**	**150**	**65**	**79**	**144**	**289**	**23**	**0**	**12**	**480**	**12.7**	**243**	**103**	**183**	**15**		**27**	**7**	**4**	**11**	**18**	**3**	**0**	**2**

WHL East First All-Star Team (1993)

• NIEDERMAYER, SCOTT

Scott Niedermayer D – L. 6', 200 lbs. b: Edmonton, Alta., 8/31/1973. New Jersey's 1st choice, 3rd overall, in 1991 Entry Draft.

Season	Club	League	GP	G	A	Pts	AG	AA	APts	PIM	PP	SH	GW	S	%	TGF	PGF	TGA	PGA	+/-	GP	G	A	Pts	PIM	PP	SH	GW
1989-90	Kamloops Blazers	WHL	64	14	55	69	....	....	....	64	....	....	....	....	....	....	....	....	....	....	17	2	14	16	35	....	....	....
1990-91	Kamloops Blazers	WHL	57	26	56	82	....	....	....	52	....	....	....	....	....	....	....	....	....	....	....	....	....	....	....	....	....	....
	Canada	WJC-A	7	0	0	0	....	....	....	0	....	....	....	....	....	....	....	....	....	....	....	....	....	....	....	....	....	....
1991-92	Kamloops Blazers	WHL	35	7	32	39	....	....	....	61	....	....	....	....	....	....	....	....	....	....	17	9	14	23	28	....	....	....
	Canada	WJC-A	7	0	0	0	....	....	....	10	....	....	....	....	....	....	....	....	....	....	....	....	....	....	....	....	....	....
	New Jersey Devils	**NHL**	**4**	**0**	**1**	**1**	**0**	**1**	**1**	**2**	**0**	**0**	**0**	**4**	**0.0**	**5**	**0**	**4**	**0**	**+1**	....	....	....	....	....	....	....	....
1992-93	**New Jersey Devils**	**NHL**	**80**	**11**	**29**	**40**	**9**	**20**	**29**	**47**	**5**	**0**	**0**	**131**	**8.4**	**116**	**36**	**77**	**5**	**+8**	**5**	**0**	**3**	**3**	**2**	**0**	**0**	**0**
1993-94	**New Jersey Devils**	**NHL**	**81**	**10**	**36**	**46**	**9**	**28**	**37**	**42**	**5**	**0**	**2**	**135**	**7.4**	**121**	**29**	**77**	**19**	**+34**	**20**	**2**	**2**	**4**	**8**	**1**	**0**	**0**
1994-95	**New Jersey Devils**	**NHL**	**48**	**4**	**15**	**19**	**7**	**22**	**29**	**18**	**4**	**0**	**0**	**52**	**7.7**	**68**	**13**	**50**	**14**	**+19**	**20**	**4**	**7**	**11**	**10**	**2**	**0**	**1**
1995-96	**New Jersey Devils**	**NHL**	**79**	**8**	**25**	**33**	**8**	**20**	**28**	**46**	**6**	**0**	**0**	**179**	**4.5**	**102**	**34**	**83**	**20**	**+5**	....	....	....	....	....	....	....	....
1996-97	Canada	W Cup	8	1	3	4	....	....	....	6	....	....	....	....	....	....	....	....	....	....	....	....	....	....	....	....	....	....
	New Jersey Devils	**NHL**	**81**	**5**	**30**	**35**	**5**	**27**	**32**	**64**	**3**	**0**	**3**	**159**	**3.1**	**82**	**24**	**72**	**10**	**–4**	**10**	**2**	**4**	**6**	**6**	**2**	**0**	**1**
1997-98	**New Jersey Devils**	**NHL**	**81**	**14**	**43**	**57**	**16**	**42**	**58**	**27**	**11**	**0**	**1**	**175**	**8.0**	**115**	**53**	**71**	**14**	**+5**	**6**	**0**	**2**	**2**	**4**	**0**	**0**	**0**
	NHL Totals		**454**	**52**	**179**	**231**	**54**	**160**	**214**	**246**	**34**	**0**	**6**	**835**	**6.2**	**609**	**189**	**434**	**82**		**61**	**8**	**18**	**26**	**30**	**5**	**0**	**2**

WHL West First All-Star Team (1991, 1992) • Canadian Major Junior Scholastic Player of the Year (1991)
WJC-A All-Star Team (1992) • Memorial Cup All-Star Team (1992) • Won Stafford Smythe Memorial Trophy (Memorial Cup Tournament MVP) (1992) • NHL/Upper Deck All-Rookie Team (1993) • NHL Second All-Star Team (1998)

Played in NHL All-Star Game (1998)

• NIEKAMP, JIM

Jim Niekamp D – R. 6'1", 185 lbs. b: Detroit, MI, 3/11/1946.

Season	Club	League	GP	G	A	Pts	AG	AA	APts	PIM	PP	SH	GW	S	%	TGF	PGF	TGA	PGA	+/-	GP	G	A	Pts	PIM	PP	SH	GW
1965-66	St. Jerome Alouettes	QJHL	STATISTICS NOT AVAILABLE																									
	Hamilton Red Wings	OHA	11	1	6	7	....	....	....	55	....	....	....	....	....	....	....	....	....	....	....	....	....	....	....	....	....	....
1966-67	Toledo Blades	IHL	66	6	24	30	....	....	....	163	....	....	....	....	....	....	....	....	....	....	8	0	1	1	12	....	....	....
1967-68	Fort Worth Wings	CHL	40	6	9	15	....	....	....	76	....	....	....	....	....	....	....	....	....	....	7	0	2	2	24	....	....	....
1968-69	Fort Worth Wings	CHL	63	13	21	34	....	....	....	113	....	....	....	....	....	....	....	....	....	....	....	....	....	....	....	....	....	....
1969-70	Cleveland Barons	AHL	47	6	16	22	....	....	....	114	....	....	....	....	....	....	....	....	....	....	....	....	....	....	....	....	....	....
1970-71	**Detroit Red Wings**	**NHL**	**24**	**0**	**2**	**2**	**0**	**2**	**2**	**27**	**0**	**0**	**0**	**21**	**0.0**	**14**	**1**	**36**	**9**	**–14**	....	....	....	....	....	....	....	....
	Baltimore Clippers	AHL	46	9	29	38	....	....	....	93	....	....	....	....	....	....	....	....	....	....	....	....	....	....	....	....	....	....
1971-72	**Detroit Red Wings**	**NHL**	**5**	**0**	**0**	**0**	**0**	**0**	**0**	**10**	**0**	**0**	**0**	**2**	**0.0**	**3**	**0**	**11**	**5**	**–3**	....	....	....	....	....	....	....	....
	Tidewater Wings	AHL	65	6	11	17	....	....	....	216	....	....	....	....	....	....	....	....	....	....	....	....	....	....	....	....	....	....
1972-73	Los Angeles Sharks	WHA	78	7	22	29	....	....	....	155	....	....	....	....	....	....	....	....	....	....	6	2	1	3	10	....	....	....
1973-74	Los Angeles Sharks	WHA	76	2	19	21	....	....	....	95	....	....	....	....	....	....	....	....	....	....	....	....	....	....	....	....	....	....
1974-75	Phoenix Roadrunners	WHA	71	2	26	28	....	....	....	66	....	....	....	....	....	....	....	....	....	....	5	0	0	0	8	....	....	....
1975-76	Phoenix Roadrunners	WHA	79	4	14	18	....	....	....	77	....	....	....	....	....	....	....	....	....	....	5	1	0	1	0	....	....	....
1976-77	Phoenix Roadrunners	WHA	79	1	15	16	....	....	....	91	....	....	....	....	....	....	....	....	....	....	....	....	....	....	....	....	....	....
1977-78	Phoenix Roadrunners	PHL	23	1	11	12	....	....	....	12	....	....	....	....	....	....	....	....	....	....	....	....	....	....	....	....	....	....
	NHL Totals		**29**	**0**	**2**	**2**	**0**	**2**	**2**	**37**	**0**	**0**	**0**	**23**	**0.0**	**17**	**1**	**47**	**14**		....	....	....	....	....	....	....	....
	Other Major League Totals		383	16	96	112	....	....	....	484	....	....	....	....	....	....	....	....	....	....	16	3	1	4	18	....	....	....

Selected by **LA Sharks** (WHA) in 1972 WHA General Player Draft, February 12, 1972. Traded to **Vancouver** by **Detroit** for Ralph Stewart, March 6, 1972. Transferred to **Michigan** (WHA) after **LA Sharks** (WHA) franchise relocated, April 11, 1974. Traded to **Phoenix** (WHA) by **Michigan** (WHA) for the rights to Danny Gruen, May, 1974.

• NIELSEN, JEFF

Jeff Nielsen RW – R. 6', 200 lbs. b: Grand Rapids, MN, 9/20/1971. NY Rangers' 4th choice, 69th overall, in 1990 Entry Draft.

Season	Club	League	GP	G	A	Pts	AG	AA	APts	PIM	PP	SH	GW	S	%	TGF	PGF	TGA	PGA	+/-	GP	G	A	Pts	PIM	PP	SH	GW
1989-90	Grand Rapids High School	H.S.	28	32	25	57	....	....	....	....	....	....	....	....	....	....	....	....	....	....	....	....	....	....	....	....	....	....
1990-91	University of Minnesota	WCHA	45	11	14	25	....	....	....	50	....	....	....	....	....	....	....	....	....	....	....	....	....	....	....	....	....	....
1991-92	University of Minnesota	WCHA	41	14	14	28	....	....	....	70	....	....	....	....	....	....	....	....	....	....	....	....	....	....	....	....	....	....
1992-93	University of Minnesota	WCHA	42	21	20	41	....	....	....	80	....	....	....	....	....	....	....	....	....	....	....	....	....	....	....	....	....	....
1993-94	University of Minnesota	WCHA	41	20	16	45	....	....	....	94	....	....	....	....	....	....	....	....	....	....	....	....	....	....	....	....	....	....
1994-95	Binghamton Rangers	AHL	76	24	13	37	....	....	....	139	....	....	....	....	....	....	....	....	....	....	7	0	0	0	22	....	....	....
1995-96	Binghamton Rangers	AHL	64	22	20	42	....	....	....	56	....	....	....	....	....	....	....	....	....	....	4	1	1	2	4	....	....	....
1996-97	**New York Rangers**	**NHL**	**2**	**0**	**0**	**0**	**0**	**0**	**0**	**2**	**0**	**0**	**0**	**1**	**0.0**	**0**	**0**	**1**	**0**	**–1**	....	....	....	....	....	....	....	....
	Binghamton Rangers	AHL	76	27	26	53	....	....	....	71	....	....	....	....	....	....	....	....	....	....	4	0	0	0	7	....	....	....
1997-98	Leksands IF	Sweden	44	14	10	24	....	....	....	48	....	....	....	....	....	....	....	....	....	....	4	1	1	2	8	....	....	....
	Anaheim Mighty Ducks	**NHL**	**32**	**4**	**5**	**9**	**5**	**5**	**10**	**16**	**0**	**0**	**0**	**36**	**11.1**	**12**	**0**	**17**	**4**	**–1**	....	....	....	....	....	....	....	....
	Cincinnati Mighty Ducks	AHL	18	4	8	12	....	....	....	37	....	....	....	....	....	....	....	....	....	....	....	....	....	....	....	....	....	....
	NHL Totals		**34**	**4**	**5**	**9**	**5**	**5**	**10**	**18**	**0**	**0**	**0**	**37**	**10.8**	**12**	**0**	**18**	**4**		....	....	....	....	....	....	....	....

WCHA Second All-Star Team (1994)

Signed as a free agent by **Anaheim**, August 18, 1997.

• NIELSEN, KIRK

Kirk Nielsen RW – R. 6'1", 205 lbs. b: Grand Rapids, MN, 10/19/1973. Philadelphia's 1st choice, 10th overall, in 1994 Supplemental Draft.

Season	Club	League	GP	G	A	Pts	AG	AA	APts	PIM	PP	SH	GW	S	%	TGF	PGF	TGA	PGA	+/-	GP	G	A	Pts	PIM	PP	SH	GW
1992-93	Harvard University	ECAC	30	2	2	4	....	....	....	38	....	....	....	....	....	....	....	....	....	....	....	....	....	....	....	....	....	....
1993-94	Harvard University	ECAC	32	6	9	15	....	....	....	41	....	....	....	....	....	....	....	....	....	....	....	....	....	....	....	....	....	....
1994-95	Harvard University	ECAC	30	13	8	21	....	....	....	24	....	....	....	....	....	....	....	....	....	....	....	....	....	....	....	....	....	....
1995-96	Harvard University	ECAC	31	12	16	28	....	....	....	66	....	....	....	....	....	....	....	....	....	....	....	....	....	....	....	....	....	....
1996-97	Providence Bruins	AHL	68	12	23	35	....	....	....	30	....	....	....	....	....	....	....	....	....	....	9	2	1	3	2	....	....	....
1997-98	**Boston Bruins**	**NHL**	**6**	**0**	**0**	**0**	**0**	**0**	**0**	**0**	**0**	**0**	**0**	**1**	**0.0**	**0**	**0**	**1**	**0**	**–1**	....	....	....	....	....	....	....	....
	Providence Bruins	AHL	72	19	29	48	....	....	....	40	....	....	....	....	....	....	....	....	....	....	....	....	....	....	....	....	....	....
	NHL Totals		**6**	**0**	**0**	**0**	**0**	**0**	**0**	**0**	**0**	**0**	**0**	**1**	**0.0**	**0**	**0**	**1**	**0**		....	....	....	....	....	....	....	....

Signed as a free agent by **Boston**, June 7, 1996.

• NIENHUIS, KRAIG

Kraig Nienhuis LW – L. 6'2", 205 lbs. b: Sarnia, Ont., 5/9/1961.

Season	Club	League	GP	G	A	Pts	AG	AA	APts	PIM	PP	SH	GW	S	%	TGF	PGF	TGA	PGA	+/-	GP	G	A	Pts	PIM	PP	SH	GW
1982-83	RPI Engineers	ECAC	24	9	11	20	....	....	....	34	....	....	....	....	....	....	....	....	....	....	....	....	....	....	....	....	....	....
1983-84	RPI Engineers	ECAC	35	10	12	22	....	....	....	26	....	....	....	....	....	....	....	....	....	....	....	....	....	....	....	....	....	....
1984-85	RPI Engineers	ECAC	36	11	10	21	....	....	....	55	....	....	....	....	....	....	....	....	....	....	....	....	....	....	....	....	....	....
1985-86	**Boston Bruins**	**NHL**	**70**	**16**	**14**	**30**	**13**	**9**	**22**	**37**	**3**	**0**	**2**	**120**	**13.3**	**40**	**8**	**52**	**10**	**–10**	**2**	**0**	**0**	**0**	**14**	**0**	**0**	**0**

			REGULAR SEASON																		PLAYOFFS							
Season	Club	League	GP	G	A	Pts	AG	AA	APts	PIM	PP	SH	GW	S	%	TGF	PGF	TGA	PGA	+/-	GP	G	A	Pts	PIM	PP	SH	GW
1986-87	**Boston Bruins**	**NHL**	**16**	**4**	**2**	**6**	**3**	**1**	**4**	**2**	**2**	**0**	**0**	**25**	**16.0**	**9**	**4**	**11**	**1**	**–5**	....	....	....	....	....	....	....	....
	Moncton Golden Flames	AHL	54	10	17	27	....	....	....	44	....	....	....	....	....	....	....	....	....	....	....	....	....	....	....	....	....	....
1987-88	**Boston Bruins**	**NHL**	**1**	**0**	**0**	**0**	**0**	**0**	**0**	**0**	**0**	**0**	**0**	**4**	**0.0**	**0**	**0**	**1**	**0**	**–1**	....	....	....	....	....	....	....	....
	Maine Mariners	AHL	36	16	17	33	....	....	....	57	....	....	....	....	....	....	....	....	....	....	....	....	....	....	....	....	....	....
1988-89	Canada	Nat-Team	4	0	0	0	....	....	....	12	....	....	....	....	....	....	....	....	....	....	....	....	....	....	....	....	....	....
	ESC Kaufbeuren	Germany	35	23	28	51	....	....	....	60	....	....	....	....	....	....	....	....	....	....	12	15	18	33	30	....	....	....
1989-90	Mannheimer ERC	Germany	13	7	4	11	....	....	....	18	....	....	....	....	....	....	....	....	....	....	....	....	....	....	....	....	....	....
1990-91	Klagenfurter AC	Austria	30	31	22	53	....	....	....	....	....	....	....	....	....	....	....	....	....	....	....	....	....	....	....	....	....	....
	Albany Choppers	IHL	3	3	1	4	....	....	....	0	....	....	....	....	....	....	....	....	....	....	....	....	....	....	....	....	....	....
1991-92	Klagenfurter AC	Austria	43	35	28	63	....	....	....	....	....	....	....	....	....	....	....	....	....	....	....	....	....	....	....	....	....	....
1992-93	Klagenfurter AC	Austria	48	40	46	86	....	....	....	....	....	....	....	....	....	....	....	....	....	....	....	....	....	....	....	....	....	....
1993-94	Klagenfurter AC	Austria	33	19	27	46	....	....	....	....	....	....	....	....	....	....	....	....	....	....	....	....	....	....	....	....	....	....
1994-95	Olimpija Ljubljana	Slovenia	36	53	38	91	....	....	....	93	....	....	....	....	....	....	....	....	....	....	....	....	....	....	....	....	....	....
1995-96	Olimpija Ljubljana	Slovenia	43	40	35	75	....	....	....	40	....	....	....	....	....	....	....	....	....	....	....	....	....	....	....	....	....	....
	Austria	WC-A	6	0	0	0	....	....	....	12	....	....	....	....	....	....	....	....	....	....	....	....	....	....	....	....	....	....
1996-97	Eisbaren Berlin	Germany	48	12	22	34	....	....	....	79	....	....	....	....	....	....	....	....	....	....	8	0	0	0	10	....	....	....
1997-98	Nottingham Panthers	Britain	42	21	24	45	....	....	....	43	....	....	....	....	....	....	....	....	....	....	6	0	5	5	8	....	....	....
	NHL Totals		**87**	**20**	**16**	**36**	**16**	**10**	**26**	**39**	**5**	**0**	**2**	**149**	**13.4**	**49**	**12**	**64**	**11**		**2**	**0**	**0**	**0**	**14**	**0**	**0**	**0**

Signed as a free agent by **Boston**, May 28, 1985.

• NIEUWENDYK, JOE

Joe Nieuwendyk C – L. 6'1", 195 lbs. b: Oshawa, Ont., 9/10/1966. Calgary's 2nd choice, 27th overall, in 1985 Entry Draft.

Season	Club	League	GP	G	A	Pts	AG	AA	APts	PIM	PP	SH	GW	S	%	TGF	PGF	TGA	PGA	+/-	GP	G	A	Pts	PIM	PP	SH	GW
1984-85	Cornell University	ECAC	29	21	24	45	....	....	....	30	....	....	....	....	....	....	....	....	....	....	....	....	....	....	....	....	....	....
1985-86	Cornell University	ECAC	29	26	28	54	....	....	....	67	....	....	....	....	....	....	....	....	....	....	....	....	....	....	....	....	....	....
	Canada	WJC-A	7	5	7	12	....	....	....	6	....	....	....	....	....	....	....	....	....	....	....	....	....	....	....	....	....	....
1986-87	Cornell University	ECAC	23	26	26	52	....	....	....	26	....	....	....	....	....	....	....	....	....	....	....	....	....	....	....	....	....	....
	Canada	Nat-Team	5	2	0	2	....	....	....	0	....	....	....	....	....	....	....	....	....	....	....	....	....	....	....	....	....	....
	Calgary Flames	**NHL**	**9**	**5**	**1**	**6**	**4**	**1**	**5**	**0**	**2**	**0**	**1**	**16**	**31.3**	**8**	**2**	**6**	**0**	**0**	**6**	**2**	**2**	**4**	**0**	**0**	**0**	**0**
1987-88	**Calgary Flames**	**NHL**	**75**	**51**	**41**	**92**	**44**	**29**	**73**	**23**	**31**	**3**	**8**	**212**	**24.1**	**139**	**65**	**82**	**28**	**+20**	**8**	**3**	**4**	**7**	**2**	**1**	**0**	**0**
1988-89	**Calgary Flames**	**NHL**	**77**	**51**	**31**	**82**	**43**	**22**	**65**	**40**	**19**	**3**	**11**	**215**	**23.7**	**115**	**42**	**67**	**20**	**+26**	**22**	**10**	**4**	**14**	**10**	**6**	**0**	**1**
1989-90	Calgary Flames	FrTour	4	0	2	2	....	....	....	2	....	....	....	....	....	....	....	....	....	....	....	....	....	....	....	....	....	....
	Calgary Flames	**NHL**	**79**	**45**	**50**	**95**	**39**	**36**	**75**	**40**	**18**	**0**	**3**	**226**	**19.9**	**137**	**51**	**66**	**12**	**+32**	**6**	**4**	**6**	**10**	**4**	**1**	**0**	**0**
	Canada	WEC-A	1	0	0	0	....	....	....	0	....	....	....	....	....	....	....	....	....	....	....	....	....	....	....	....	....	....
1990-91	**Calgary Flames**	**NHL**	**79**	**45**	**40**	**85**	**42**	**30**	**72**	**36**	**22**	**4**	**1**	**222**	**20.3**	**127**	**57**	**71**	**20**	**+19**	**7**	**4**	**1**	**5**	**10**	**2**	**0**	**0**
1991-92	**Calgary Flames**	**NHL**	**69**	**22**	**34**	**56**	**20**	**26**	**46**	**55**	**7**	**0**	**2**	**137**	**16.1**	**88**	**33**	**76**	**20**	**–1**	....	....	....	....	....	....	....	....
1992-93	**Calgary Flames**	**NHL**	**79**	**38**	**37**	**75**	**32**	**25**	**57**	**52**	**14**	**0**	**6**	**208**	**18.3**	**113**	**43**	**62**	**1**	**+9**	**6**	**3**	**6**	**9**	**10**	**1**	**0**	**0**
1993-94	**Calgary Flames**	**NHL**	**64**	**36**	**39**	**75**	**34**	**30**	**64**	**51**	**14**	**1**	**7**	**191**	**18.8**	**102**	**42**	**43**	**2**	**+19**	**6**	**2**	**2**	**4**	**0**	**1**	**0**	**0**
1994-95	**Calgary Flames**	**NHL**	**46**	**21**	**29**	**50**	**37**	**43**	**80**	**33**	**3**	**0**	**4**	**122**	**17.2**	**71**	**27**	**33**	**0**	**+11**	**5**	**4**	**3**	**7**	**0**	**2**	**0**	**1**
1995-96	**Dallas Stars**	**NHL**	**52**	**14**	**18**	**32**	**14**	**15**	**29**	**41**	**8**	**0**	**3**	**138**	**10.1**	**50**	**25**	**49**	**7**	**–17**	....	....	....	....	....	....	....	....
1996-97	**Dallas Stars**	**NHL**	**66**	**30**	**21**	**51**	**32**	**19**	**51**	**32**	**8**	**0**	**2**	**173**	**17.3**	**63**	**22**	**47**	**1**	**–5**	**7**	**2**	**2**	**4**	**6**	**0**	**0**	**0**
1997-98	**Dallas Stars**	**NHL**	**73**	**39**	**30**	**69**	**46**	**29**	**75**	**30**	**14**	**0**	**11**	**203**	**19.2**	**88**	**38**	**34**	**0**	**+16**	**1**	**1**	**0**	**1**	**0**	**0**	**0**	**0**
	NHL Totals		**768**	**397**	**371**	**768**	**387**	**305**	**692**	**433**	**160**	**11**	**59**	**2063**	**19.2**	**1101**	**447**	**636**	**111**		**74**	**35**	**30**	**65**	**42**	**14**	**0**	**2**

NCAA East First All-American Team (1986, 1987) • ECAC First All-Star Team (1986, 1987) • Won Calder Memorial Trophy (1988) • NHL All-Rookie Team (1988) • Won Dodge Ram Tough Award (1988) • Won King Clancy Memorial Trophy (1995)

Played in NHL All-Star Game (1988, 1989, 1990, 1994)

Traded to **Dallas** by **Calgary** for Corey Millen and Jarome Iginla, December 19, 1995.

• NIGRO, FRANK

Frank Nigro C – R. 5'9", 182 lbs. b: Richmond Hill, Ont., 2/11/1960. Toronto's 4th choice, 93rd overall, in 1979 Entry Draft.

Season	Club	League	GP	G	A	Pts	AG	AA	APts	PIM	PP	SH	GW	S	%	TGF	PGF	TGA	PGA	+/-	GP	G	A	Pts	PIM	PP	SH	GW
1976-77	Richmond Hill Rams	OJHL	40	31	35	66	....	....	....	22	....	....	....	....	....	....	....	....	....	....	....	....	....	....	....	....	....	....
1977-78	London Knights	OHA	68	35	52	87	....	....	....	37	....	....	....	....	....	....	....	....	....	....	11	7	0	7	6	....	....	....
1978-79	London Knights	OHA	63	33	56	89	....	....	....	64	....	....	....	....	....	....	....	....	....	....	6	0	1	1	0	....	....	....
1979-80	London Knights	OHA	46	12	26	38	....	....	....	30	....	....	....	....	....	....	....	....	....	....	5	0	0	0	0	....	....	....
1980-81	London Knights	OHA	46	12	26	40	....	....	....	30	....	....	....	....	....	....	....	....	....	....	....	....	....	....	....	....	....	....
	New Brunswick Hawks	AHL	1	0	0	0	....	....	....	0	....	....	....	....	....	....	....	....	....	....	....	....	....	....	....	....	....	....
1981-82	Cincinnati Tigers	CHL	49	24	26	50	....	....	....	24	....	....	....	....	....	....	....	....	....	....	4	1	3	4	2	....	....	....
1982-83	**Toronto Maple Leafs**	**NHL**	**51**	**6**	**15**	**21**	**5**	**10**	**15**	**23**	**1**	**0**	**0**	**77**	**7.8**	**28**	**5**	**24**	**0**	**–1**	**3**	**0**	**0**	**0**	**2**	**0**	**0**	**0**
	St. Catharines Saints	AHL	30	20	13	33	....	....	....	8	....	....	....	....	....	....	....	....	....	....	....	....	....	....	....	....	....	....
1983-84	**Toronto Maple Leafs**	**NHL**	**17**	**2**	**3**	**5**	**2**	**2**	**4**	**16**	**0**	**0**	**0**	**18**	**11.1**	**8**	**1**	**11**	**0**	**–4**	....	....	....	....	....	....	....	....
	St. Catharines Saints	AHL	41	17	24	41	....	....	....	16	....	....	....	....	....	....	....	....	....	....	7	0	6	6	9	....	....	....
1984-85	HC Groden	Italy	26	37	43	80	....	....	....	16	....	....	....	....	....	....	....	....	....	....	4	7	7	14	6	....	....	....
1985-86	HC Merano	Italy	34	68	64	132	....	....	....	6	....	....	....	....	....	....	....	....	....	....	6	7	9	16	0	....	....	....
1986-87	HC Merano	Italy	33	36	51	87	....	....	....	14	....	....	....	....	....	....	....	....	....	....	....	....	....	....	....	....	....	....
1987-88	HC Merano	Italy	35	36	36	72	....	....	....	31	....	....	....	....	....	....	....	....	....	....	....	....	....	....	....	....	....	....
1988-89	Varese HC	Italy	43	39	52	91	....	....	....	12	....	....	....	....	....	....	....	....	....	....	....	....	....	....	....	....	....	....
	Italy	WEC-B	7	2	8	10	....	....	....	10	....	....	....	....	....	....	....	....	....	....	....	....	....	....	....	....	....	....
1989-90	Varese HC	Italy	39	26	55	81	....	....	....	10	....	....	....	....	....	....	....	....	....	....	....	....	....	....	....	....	....	....
	Italy	WEC-B	7	4	8	12	....	....	....	2	....	....	....	....	....	....	....	....	....	....	....	....	....	....	....	....	....	....
1990-91	Varese HC	Italy	35	39	45	84	....	....	....	7	....	....	....	....	....	....	....	....	....	....	....	....	....	....	....	....	....	....
	Italy	WEC-B	7	5	3	8	....	....	....	0	....	....	....	....	....	....	....	....	....	....	....	....	....	....	....	....	....	....
1991-92	HC Bolzano	Italy	25	13	32	45	....	....	....	8	....	....	....	....	....	....	....	....	....	....	....	....	....	....	....	....	....	....
	HC Bolzano	Alpenliga	20	12	22	34	....	....	....	2	....	....	....	....	....	....	....	....	....	....	....	....	....	....	....	....	....	....
	Italy	Olympics	7	0	3	3	....	....	....	6	....	....	....	....	....	....	....	....	....	....	....	....	....	....	....	....	....	....
	NHL Totals		**68**	**8**	**18**	**26**	**7**	**12**	**19**	**39**	**1**	**0**	**0**	**95**	**8.4**	**36**	**6**	**35**	**0**		**3**	**0**	**0**	**0**	**2**	**0**	**0**	**0**

• NIINIMAA, JANNE

Janne Niinimaa D – L. 6'1", 220 lbs. b: Raahe, Finland, 5/22/1975. Philadelphia's 1st choice, 36th overall, in 1993 Entry Draft.

Season	Club	League	GP	G	A	Pts	AG	AA	APts	PIM	PP	SH	GW	S	%	TGF	PGF	TGA	PGA	+/-	GP	G	A	Pts	PIM	PP	SH	GW
1991-92	Karpat Oulu	Finland 2	41	2	11	13	....	....	....	49	....	....	....	....	....	....	....	....	....	....	....	....	....	....	....	....	....	....
	Finland	WJC-A	5	0	0	0	....	....	....	2	....	....	....	....	....	....	....	....	....	....	....	....	....	....	....	....	....	....
1992-93	Karpat Oulu	Finland 2	29	2	3	5	....	....	....	14	....	....	....	....	....	....	....	....	....	....	....	....	....	....	....	....	....	....
1993-94	Jokerit Helsinki	Finland	45	3	8	11	....	....	....	24	....	....	....	....	....	....	....	....	....	....	12	1	1	2	4	....	....	....
	Finland	WJC-A	7	0	0	0	....	....	....	10	....	....	....	....	....	....	....	....	....	....	....	....	....	....	....	....	....	....
1994-95	Jokerit Helsinki	Finland	42	7	10	17	....	....	....	36	....	....	....	....	....	....	....	....	....	....	10	1	4	5	35	....	....	....
	Finland	WJC-A	7	2	3	5	....	....	....	6	....	....	....	....	....	....	....	....	....	....	....	....	....	....	....	....	....	....
	Finland	WC-A	8	1	2	3	....	....	....	10	....	....	....	....	....	....	....	....	....	....	....	....	....	....	....	....	....	....
1995-96	Jokerit Helsinki	Finland	49	5	15	20	....	....	....	79	....	....	....	....	....	....	....	....	....	....	11	0	2	2	12	....	....	....
	Finland	WC-A	5	1	0	1	....	....	....	10	....	....	....	....	....	....	....	....	....	....	....	....	....	....	....	....	....	....
1996-97	Finland	W Cup	2	0	0	0	....	....	....	2	....	....	....	....	....	....	....	....	....	....	....	....	....	....	....	....	....	....
	Philadelphia Flyers	**NHL**	**77**	**4**	**40**	**44**	**4**	**35**	**39**	**58**	**1**	**0**	**2**	**141**	**2.8**	**109**	**35**	**67**	**5**	**+12**	**19**	**1**	**12**	**13**	**16**	**1**	**0**	**1**
1997-98	**Philadelphia Flyers**	**NHL**	**66**	**3**	**31**	**34**	**4**	**30**	**34**	**56**	**2**	**0**	**1**	**115**	**2.6**	**84**	**34**	**48**	**4**	**+6**	....	....	....	....	....	....	....	....
	Finland	Olympics	6	0	3	3	....	....	....	8	....	....	....	....	....	....	....	....	....	....	....	....	....	....	....	....	....	....
	Edmonton Oilers	**NHL**	**11**	**1**	**8**	**9**	**1**	**8**	**9**	**6**	**1**	**0**	**0**	**19**	**5.3**	**19**	**9**	**7**	**4**	**+7**	**11**	**1**	**1**	**2**	**12**	**0**	**0**	**1**
	NHL Totals		**154**	**8**	**79**	**87**	**9**	**73**	**82**	**120**	**4**	**0**	**3**	**275**	**2.9**	**212**	**78**	**122**	**13**		**30**	**2**	**13**	**15**	**28**	**1**	**0**	**2**

EJC-A All-Star Team (1993) • Named Best Defenseman at EJC-A (1993) • NHL All-Rookie Team (1997)

Traded to **Edmonton** by **Philadelphia** for Dan McGillis and Edmonton's 2nd round choice (Jason Beckett) in 1998 Entry Draft, March 24, 1998.

• NIKOLISHIN, ANDREI

Andrei Nikolishin LW – L. 5'11", 180 lbs. b: Vorkuta, USSR, 3/25/1973. Hartford's 2nd choice, 47th overall, in 1992 Entry Draft.

Season	Club	League	GP	G	A	Pts	AG	AA	APts	PIM	PP	SH	GW	S	%	TGF	PGF	TGA	PGA	+/-	GP	G	A	Pts	PIM	PP	SH	GW
1990-91	Moscow Dynamo	USSR	2	0	0	0	....	....	....	0	....	....	....	....	....	....	....	....	....	....	....	....	....	....	....	....	....	....
1991-92	Moscow Dynamo	CIS	18	1	0	1	....	....	....	4	....	....	....	....	....	....	....	....	....	....	....	....	....	....	....	....	....	....
	Russia	WJC-A	7	1	2	3	....	....	....	2	....	....	....	....	....	....	....	....	....	....	....	....	....	....	....	....	....	....
1992-93	Moscow Dynamo	CIS	42	5	7	12	....	....	....	30	....	....	....	....	....	....	....	....	....	....	10	2	1	3	8	....	....	....
	Russia	WC-A	8	1	3	4	....	....	....	8	....	....	....	....	....	....	....	....	....	....	....	....	....	....	....	....	....	....

			REGULAR SEASON																		PLAYOFFS							
Season	Club	League	GP	G	A	Pts	AG	AA	APts	PIM	PP	SH	GW	S	%	TGF	PGF	TGA	PGA	+/-	GP	G	A	Pts	PIM	PP	SH	GW
1993-94	Moscow Dynamo	CIS	41	8	12	20				30											9	1	3	4	4			
	Russia	Olympics	8	2	5	7				6																		
	Russia	WC-A	6	0	0	0				4																		
1994-95	Moscow Dynamo	CIS	12	7	2	9				6																		
	Hartford Whalers	**NHL**	**39**	**8**	**10**	**18**	**14**	**15**	**29**	**10**	**1**	**1**	**0**	**57**	**14.0**	**28**	**7**	**17**	**3**	**+7**								
1995-96	**Hartford Whalers**	**NHL**	**61**	**14**	**37**	**51**	**14**	**30**	**44**	**34**	**4**	**1**	**3**	**83**	**16.9**	**63**	**22**	**55**	**12**	**–2**								
	Russia	WC-A	8	2	3	5				10																		
1996-97	Russia	W Cup	4	1	3	4				4																		
	Hartford Whalers	**NHL**	**12**	**2**	**5**	**7**	**2**	**4**	**6**	**2**	**0**	**0**	**0**	**25**	**8.0**	**10**	**2**	**10**	**0**	**–2**								
	Washington Capitals	**NHL**	**59**	**7**	**14**	**21**	**7**	**12**	**19**	**30**	**1**	**0**	**0**	**73**	**9.6**	**40**	**6**	**39**	**10**	**+5**								
	Russia	WC-A	5	0	1	1				6																		
1997-98	**Washington Capitals**	**NHL**	**38**	**6**	**10**	**16**	**7**	**10**	**17**	**14**	**1**	**0**	**1**	**40**	**15.0**	**21**	**4**	**20**	**4**	**+1**	**21**	**1**	**13**	**14**	**12**	**1**	**0**	**0**
	Portland Pirates	AHL	2	0	0	0				2																		
	NHL Totals		**209**	**37**	**76**	**113**	**44**	**71**	**115**	**90**	**7**	**2**	**4**	**278**	**13.3**	**162**	**41**	**141**	**29**		**21**	**1**	**13**	**14**	**12**	**1**	**0**	**0**

CIS First All-Star Team (1994) • CIS Player of the Year (1994)

Traded to **Washington** by **Hartford** for Curtis Leschyshyn, November 9, 1996.

• NIKULIN, IGOR

Igor Nikulin RW – L. 6'1", 200 lbs. b: Cherepovets, USSR, 8/26/1972. Anaheim's 4th choice, 107th overall, in 1995 Entry Draft.

Season	Club	League	GP	G	A	Pts	AG	AA	APts	PIM	PP	SH	GW	S	%	TGF	PGF	TGA	PGA	+/-	GP	G	A	Pts	PIM	PP	SH	GW
1992-93	Severstal Cherepovets	CIS	42	11	11	22				22																		
1993-94	Severstal Cherepovets	CIS	44	14	15	29				52											2	1	0	1	0			
1994-95	Severstal Cherepovets	CIS	52	14	12	26				28																		
1995-96	Severstal Cherepovets	CIS	47	20	13	33				28											4	1	0	1	0			
	Baltimore Bandits	AHL	4	2	2	4				2																		
1996-97	Baltimore Bandits	AHL	61	27	25	52				14											3	2	1	3	2			
	Fort Wayne Komets	IHL	10	1	2	3				4																		
	Anaheim Mighty Ducks	**NHL**																			**1**	**0**	**0**	**0**	**0**			
1997-98	Cincinnati Mighty Ducks	AHL	54	14	11	25				40																		
	NHL Totals		**0**	**0**	**0**	**0**	**0**	**0**	**0**	**0**	**0**	**0**	**0**	**0**	**0.0**	**0**	**0**	**0**	**0**		**1**	**0**	**0**	**0**	**0**	**0**	**0**	**0**

• NILAN, CHRIS

Chris Nilan RW – R. 6', 205 lbs. b: Boston, MA, 2/9/1958. Montreal's 22nd choice, 231st overall, in 1978 Amateur Draft.

Season	Club	League	GP	G	A	Pts	AG	AA	APts	PIM	PP	SH	GW	S	%	TGF	PGF	TGA	PGA	+/-	GP	G	A	Pts	PIM	PP	SH	GW
1977-78	Northeastern University	ECAC	STATISTICS NOT AVAILABLE																									
1978-79	Northeastern University	ECAC	32	9	17	26																						
1979-80	Nova Scotia Voyageurs	AHL	49	15	10	25				*304																		
	Montreal Canadiens	**NHL**	**15**	**0**	**2**	**2**	**0**	**2**	**2**	**50**	**0**	**0**	**0**	**8**	**0.0**	**2**	**0**	**3**	**0**	**–1**	**5**	**0**	**0**	**0**	**2**	**0**	**0**	**0**
1980-81	**Montreal Canadiens**	**NHL**	**57**	**7**	**8**	**15**	**6**	**6**	**12**	**262**	**0**	**0**	**1**	**69**	**10.1**	**21**	**1**	**13**	**0**	**+7**	**2**	**0**	**0**	**0**	**0**	**0**	**0**	**0**
1981-82	**Montreal Canadiens**	**NHL**	**49**	**7**	**4**	**11**	**6**	**3**	**9**	**204**	**0**	**0**	**1**	**45**	**15.6**	**19**	**1**	**12**	**0**	**+6**	**5**	**1**	**1**	**2**	**22**	**0**	**0**	**0**
1982-83	**Montreal Canadiens**	**NHL**	**66**	**6**	**8**	**14**	**5**	**6**	**11**	**213**	**0**	**0**	**0**	**67**	**9.0**	**25**	**0**	**35**	**0**	**–10**	**3**	**0**	**0**	**0**	**5**	**0**	**0**	**0**
1983-84	**Montreal Canadiens**	**NHL**	**76**	**16**	**10**	**26**	**13**	**7**	**20**	***338**	**4**	**0**	**1**	**98**	**16.3**	**46**	**12**	**38**	**0**	**–4**	**15**	**1**	**0**	**1**	***81**	**0**	**0**	**0**
1984-85	**Montreal Canadiens**	**NHL**	**77**	**21**	**16**	**37**	**17**	**11**	**28**	***358**	**1**	**0**	**2**	**98**	**21.4**	**52**	**3**	**46**	**0**	**+3**	**12**	**2**	**1**	**3**	**81**	**1**	**0**	**1**
1985-86	**Montreal Canadiens**	**NHL**	**72**	**19**	**15**	**34**	**15**	**10**	**25**	**274**	**2**	**0**	**1**	**120**	**15.8**	**63**	**12**	**41**	**0**	**+10**	**18**	**1**	**2**	**3**	***141**	**1**	**0**	**0**
1986-87	**Montreal Canadiens**	**NHL**	**44**	**4**	**16**	**20**	**3**	**12**	**15**	**266**	**0**	**0**	**1**	**68**	**5.9**	**31**	**2**	**27**	**0**	**+2**	**17**	**3**	**0**	**3**	**75**	**0**	**0**	**0**
1987-88	United States	C Cup	5	2	0	2				14																		
	New York Rangers	**NHL**	**22**	**3**	**5**	**8**	**3**	**4**	**7**	**96**	**0**	**0**	**0**	**20**	**15.0**	**14**	**1**	**13**	**0**	**0**								
	Montreal Canadiens	**NHL**	**50**	**7**	**5**	**12**	**6**	**4**	**10**	**209**	**0**	**0**	**1**	**68**	**10.3**	**21**	**2**	**21**	**0**	**–2**								
1988-89	**New York Rangers**	**NHL**	**38**	**7**	**7**	**14**	**6**	**5**	**11**	**177**	**0**	**0**	**1**	**39**	**17.9**	**23**	**0**	**32**	**1**	**–8**	**4**	**0**	**1**	**1**	**38**	**0**	**0**	**0**
1989-90	**New York Rangers**	**NHL**	**25**	**1**	**2**	**3**	**1**	**1**	**2**	**59**	**0**	**0**	**0**	**24**	**4.2**	**7**	**0**	**15**	**0**	**–8**	**4**	**0**	**1**	**1**	**19**	**0**	**0**	**0**
1990-91	**Boston Bruins**	**NHL**	**41**	**6**	**9**	**15**	**5**	**7**	**12**	**277**	**0**	**0**	**2**	**41**	**14.6**	**28**	**2**	**23**	**1**	**+4**	**19**	**0**	**2**	**2**	**62**	**0**	**0**	**0**
1991-92	**Boston Bruins**	**NHL**	**39**	**5**	**5**	**10**	**5**	**4**	**9**	**186**	**0**	**0**	**0**	**33**	**15.2**	**14**	**0**	**19**	**0**	**–5**								
	Montreal Canadiens	**NHL**	**17**	**1**	**3**	**4**	**1**	**2**	**3**	**74**	**0**	**0**	**0**	**22**	**4.5**	**6**	**0**	**7**	**0**	**–1**	**7**	**0**	**1**	**1**	**15**	**0**	**0**	**0**
	NHL Totals		**688**	**110**	**115**	**225**	**92**	**84**	**176**	**3043**	**7**	**0**	**11**	**820**	**13.4**	**372**	**36**	**345**	**2**		**111**	**8**	**9**	**17**	**541**	**2**	**0**	**1**

Traded to **NY Rangers** by **Montreal** with Montreal's 1st round choice (Steven Rice) in 1989 Entry Draft for NY Rangers' 1st round choice (Lindsay Vallis) in 1989 Entry Draft, January 27, 1988. Traded to **Boston** by **NY Rangers** for Greg Johnston and future considerations, June 28, 1990. Claimed on waivers by **Montreal** from **Boston**, February 12, 1992.

• NILL, JIM

Jim Nill RW – R. 6', 185 lbs. b: Hanna, Alta., 4/11/1958. St. Louis' 4th choice, 89th overall, in 1978 Amateur Draft.

Season	Club	League	GP	G	A	Pts	AG	AA	APts	PIM	PP	SH	GW	S	%	TGF	PGF	TGA	PGA	+/-	GP	G	A	Pts	PIM	PP	SH	GW
1974-75	Drumheller Falcons	AJHL	59	30	30	60				103											12	5	6	11	35			
1975-76	Medicine Hat Tigers	WHL	62	5	11	16				69											9	1	1	2	20			
1976-77	Medicine Hat Tigers	WCJHL	71	23	24	47				140											4	2	2	4	4			
1977-78	Medicine Hat Tigers	WCJHL	72	47	46	93				252											12	8	7	15	37			
1978-79	University of Calgary	CWUAA	17	8	7	15				36											3	1	2	3	4			
1979-80	Canada	Nat-Team	45	13	19	32				54																		
	Canada	Olympics	6	1	2	3				4																		
1980-81	Salt Lake Golden Eagles	CHL	79	28	34	62				222											16	9	8	17	38			
1981-82	**St. Louis Blues**	**NHL**	**61**	**9**	**12**	**21**	**7**	**8**	**15**	**127**	**1**	**2**	**0**	**65**	**13.8**	**40**	**2**	**68**	**17**	**–13**								
	Vancouver Canucks	**NHL**	**8**	**1**	**2**	**3**	**1**	**1**	**2**	**5**	**0**	**0**	**1**	**6**	**16.7**	**5**	**0**	**6**	**1**	**0**	**16**	**4**	**3**	**7**	**67**	**1**	**0**	**1**
1982-83	**Vancouver Canucks**	**NHL**	**65**	**7**	**15**	**22**	**6**	**10**	**16**	**136**	**1**	**1**	**0**	**53**	**13.2**	**39**	**7**	**62**	**12**	**–18**	**4**	**0**	**0**	**0**	**6**	**0**	**0**	**0**
1983-84	**Vancouver Canucks**	**NHL**	**51**	**9**	**6**	**15**	**7**	**4**	**11**	**78**	**0**	**0**	**0**	**53**	**17.0**	**25**	**0**	**56**	**24**	**–7**								
	Boston Bruins	**NHL**	**27**	**3**	**2**	**5**	**2**	**1**	**3**	**81**	**0**	**0**	**0**	**19**	**15.8**	**14**	**0**	**24**	**5**	**–5**	**3**	**0**	**0**	**0**	**4**	**0**	**0**	**0**
1984-85	**Boston Bruins**	**NHL**	**49**	**1**	**9**	**10**	**1**	**6**	**7**	**62**	**0**	**0**	**0**	**23**	**4.3**	**12**	**0**	**35**	**12**	**–11**								
	Winnipeg Jets	**NHL**	**20**	**8**	**8**	**16**	**7**	**5**	**12**	**38**	**1**	**0**	**1**	**22**	**36.4**	**22**	**3**	**22**	**5**	**+2**	**8**	**0**	**1**	**1**	**28**	**0**	**0**	**0**
1985-86	**Winnipeg Jets**	**NHL**	**61**	**6**	**8**	**14**	**5**	**5**	**10**	**75**	**0**	**0**	**1**	**35**	**17.1**	**26**	**1**	**45**	**14**	**–6**	**3**	**0**	**0**	**0**	**4**	**0**	**0**	**0**
1986-87	**Winnipeg Jets**	**NHL**	**36**	**3**	**4**	**7**	**3**	**3**	**6**	**52**	**1**	**0**	**2**	**12**	**25.0**	**13**	**1**	**16**	**4**	**+1**	**3**	**0**	**0**	**0**	**7**	**0**	**0**	**0**
1987-88	**Winnipeg Jets**	**NHL**	**24**	**0**	**1**	**1**	**0**	**1**	**1**	**44**	**0**	**0**	**0**	**13**	**0.0**	**4**	**1**	**12**	**2**	**–7**								
	Moncton Hawks	AHL	3	0	0	0				6																		
	Detroit Red Wings	**NHL**	**36**	**3**	**11**	**14**	**3**	**8**	**11**	**55**	**0**	**0**	**0**	**25**	**12.0**	**24**	**1**	**29**	**8**	**+2**	**16**	**6**	**1**	**7**	**62**	**0**	**1**	**0**
1988-89	**Detroit Red Wings**	**NHL**	**71**	**8**	**7**	**15**	**7**	**5**	**12**	**83**	**0**	**1**	**2**	**39**	**20.5**	**23**	**0**	**33**	**9**	**–1**	**6**	**0**	**0**	**0**	**25**	**0**	**0**	**0**
1989-90	**Detroit Red Wings**	**NHL**	**15**	**0**	**2**	**2**	**0**	**1**	**1**	**18**	**0**	**0**	**0**	**10**	**0.0**	**4**	**0**	**10**	**3**	**–3**								
	Adirondack Red Wings	AHL	20	10	8	18				24																		
1990-91	Adirondack Red Wings	AHL	32	3	10	13				74											2	0	0	0	2			
	NHL Totals		**524**	**58**	**87**	**145**	**49**	**58**	**107**	**854**	**4**	**4**	**7**	**375**	**15.5**	**251**	**16**	**417**	**116**		**59**	**10**	**5**	**15**	**203**	**1**	**1**	**1**

CHL Second All-Star Team (1981)

Traded to **Vancouver** by **St. Louis** with Tony Currie, Rick Heinz and St. Louis' 4th round choice (Shawn Kilroy) in 1982 Entry Draft for Glen Hanlon, March 9, 1982. Traded to **Boston** by **Vancouver** for Peter McNab, February 3, 1984. Traded to **Winnipeg** by **Boston** for Morris Lukowich, February 14, 1985. Traded to **Detroit** by **Winnipeg** for Mark Kumpel, January 11, 1988.

• NILSSON, KENT

Kent Nilsson C – L. 6'1", 195 lbs. b: Nynasham, Sweden, 8/31/1956. Atlanta's 5th choice, 64th overall, in 1976 Amateur Draft.

Season	Club	League	GP	G	A	Pts	AG	AA	APts	PIM	PP	SH	GW	S	%	TGF	PGF	TGA	PGA	+/-	GP	G	A	Pts	PIM	PP	SH	GW
1974-75	Djurgardens IF Stockholm	Sweden	28	13	12	25				14																		
	Sweden	WJC-A		3	3	6																						
1975-76	Djurgardens IF Stockholm	Sweden	36	28	26	*54				10																		
	Sweden	Nat-Team	6	0	0	0				0																		
	Sweden	WJC-A	4	1	3	4				2																		
1976-77	AIK Helsinki	Sweden	36	30	19	49				18																		
1977-78	Winnipeg Jets	WHA	80	42	65	107				8											9	2	8	10	10			
1978-79	Winnipeg Jets	WHA	78	39	68	107				8											10	3	11	14	4			
1979-80	**Atlanta Flames**	**NHL**	**80**	**40**	**53**	**93**	**36**	**41**	**77**	**10**	**14**	**0**	**3**	**217**	**18.4**	**118**	**44**	**77**	**0**	**–3**	**4**	**0**	**0**	**0**	**2**	**0**	**0**	**0**
1980-81	**Calgary Flames**	**NHL**	**80**	**49**	**82**	**131**	**41**	**58**	**99**	**26**	**20**	**0**	**8**	**217**	**22.6**	**164**	**68**	**81**	**0**	**+15**	**14**	**3**	**9**	**12**	**2**	**0**	**0**	**0**
1981-82	Sweden	C Cup	5	0	2	2				4																		
	Calgary Flames	**NHL**	**41**	**26**	**29**	**55**	**21**	**19**	**40**	**8**	**13**	**0**	**0**	**103**	**25.2**	**68**	**38**	**50**	**0**	**–20**	**3**	**0**	**3**	**3**	**2**	**0**	**0**	**0**
1982-83	**Calgary Flames**	**NHL**	**80**	**46**	**58**	**104**	**38**	**40**	**78**	**10**	**16**	**4**	**6**	**217**	**21.2**	**149**	**57**	**109**	**22**	**+5**	**9**	**1**	**11**	**12**	**2**	**1**	**0**	**0**
1983-84	**Calgary Flames**	**NHL**	**67**	**31**	**49**	**80**	**25**	**33**	**58**	**22**	**7**	**9**	**5**	**181**	**17.1**	**104**	**51**	**100**	**20**	**–24**								
1984-85	Sweden	C Cup	8	3	8	11				4																		
	Calgary Flames	**NHL**	**77**	**37**	**62**	**99**	**30**	**42**	**72**	**14**	**9**	**3**	**3**	**201**	**18.4**	**129**	**58**	**103**	**28**	**–4**	**3**	**0**	**1**	**1**	**0**	**0**	**0**	**0**
	Sweden	WEC-A	8	6	5	11				6																		

			REGULAR SEASON																		PLAYOFFS							
Season	Club	League	GP	G	A	Pts	AG	AA	APts	PIM	PP	SH	GW	S	%	TGF	PGF	TGA	PGA	+/–	GP	G	A	Pts	PIM	PP	SH	GW
1985-86	**Minnesota North Stars**	NHL	61	16	44	60	13	29	42	10	8	0	2	122	13.1	94	52	41	3	+4	5	1	4	5	0	0	0	0
1986-87	**Minnesota North Stars**	NHL	44	13	33	46	11	24	35	12	8	0	1	89	14.6	67	29	41	5	+2	....							
	Edmonton Oilers	NHL	17	5	12	17	4	9	13	4	1	0	0	25	20.0	26	4	13	1	+10	21	6	13	19	6	2	0	0
1987-88	Sweden	C Cup	6	0	4	4				0											....							
	HC Bolzano	Italy	35	60	72	132				48											8	14	14	28				
	SC Lugano	Switz.	2	2	0	2															....							
1988-89	Djurgarden IF Stockholm	Sweden	35	21	21	42				36											1	0	1	1	0			
	Sweden	WEC-A	10	3	11	14				0											....							
1989-90	EHC Kloten	Switz.	36	21	19	40															5	4	5	9				
	Sweden	WEC-A	10	10	2	12				6											....							
1990-91	EHC Kloten	Switz.	33	37	39	76															8	3	8	11				
1991-92	EHC Kloten	Switz.	17	11	14	25				8											2	0	0	2				
1992-93	Djurgarden IF Stockholm	Sweden	40	11	20	31				20											6	2	3	5	0			
1993-94	EC Graz	Alpenliga	30	15	33	48															....							
	EC Graz	Austria	27	8	9	17															....							
1994-95	Valerengen	Norway	6	1	1	2				8											....							
	Edmonton Oilers	NHL	6	1	0	1	2	0	2	0	1	0	0	2	50.0	1	1	5	0	–5	....							
	NHL Totals		553	264	422	686	221	295	516	116	97	16	28	1374	19.2	920	402	620	82		59	11	41	52	14	3	0	0
	Other Major League Totals		158	81	133	214				16											19	5	19	24	14			

Won Lou Kaplan Trophy (WHA Rookie of the Year) (1978) • Won Paul Daneau Trophy (WHA Most Gentlemanly Player) (1979) • Swedish World All-Star Team (1985, 1989, 1990) • Swedish Player of the Year (1989)

Played in NHL All-Star Game (1980, 1981)

Signed as a free agent by **Winnipeg** (WHA), July 29, 1977. Reclaimed by **Atlanta** from **Winnipeg** prior to Expansion Draft, June 9, 1979. Transferred to **Calgary** after **Atlanta** franchise relocated, June 24, 1980. Traded to **Minnesota** by **Calgary** with Calgary's 3rd round choice (Brad Turner) in 1986 Entry Draft for Minnesota's 2nd round choice (Joe Nieuwendyck) in 1985 Entry Draft and 2nd round choice (Stephane Matteau) in 1987 Entry Draft, June 15, 1985. Traded to **Edmonton** by **Minnesota** for future considerations, March 2, 1987. Signed as a free agent by **Edmonton**, January 26, 1995.

● NILSSON, ULF   Ulf Nilsson   C – R. 5'11", 175 lbs.   b: Nynasham, Sweden, 5/11/1950.   NY Rangers' 11th choice, 243rd overall, in 1983 Entry Draft.

			REGULAR SEASON																		PLAYOFFS							
Season	Club	League	GP	G	A	Pts	AG	AA	APts	PIM	PP	SH	GW	S	%	TGF	PGF	TGA	PGA	+/–	GP	G	A	Pts	PIM	PP	SH	GW
1969-70	AIK Solna	Sweden	14	6	6	12				10											14	5	3	8	2			
1970-71	AIK Solna	Sweden	14	10	3	13				6											14	2	4	6	8			
1971-72	AIK Solna	Sweden	14	5	6	11				2											8	5	1	6	2			
1972-73	AIK Solna	Sweden	14	11	7	18				4											14	10	8	18	23			
	Sweden	WEC-A	10	5	3	8				4											....							
1973-74	AIK Solna	Sweden			STATISTICS NOT AVAILABLE																							
	Sweden	WEC-A	2	0	0	0															....							
1974-75	Winnipeg Jets	WHA	78	26	94	120				79											....							
1975-76	Winnipeg Jets	WHA	78	38	76	114				84											13	7	*19	26	6			
1976-77	Sweden	C Cup	5	1	1	2				6											....							
	Winnipeg Jets	WHA	71	39	*85	124				89											20	6	21	27	33			
1977-78	Winnipeg Jets	WHA	73	37	*89	126				89											9	1	*13	14	12			
1978-79	**New York Rangers**	NHL	59	27	39	66	25	30	55	21	8	2	5	96	28.1	89	27	53	8	+17	2	0	0	0	2	0	0	0
	NHL All-Stars	Chal Cup	2	0	0	0				0											....							
1979-80	**New York Rangers**	NHL	50	14	44	58	13	34	47	20	5	0	1	72	19.4	69	22	36	4	+15	9	0	6	6	2	0	0	0
1980-81	**New York Rangers**	NHL	51	14	25	39	12	17	29	42	1	0	3	80	17.5	59	20	55	13	–3	14	8	8	16	23	3	0	1
1981-82	Sweden	C Cup	4	1	2	3				2											....							
	Springfield Indians	AHL	2	0	0	0				0											....							
1982-83	**New York Rangers**	NHL	10	2	4	6	2	3	5	2	0	0	1	9	22.2	7	0	8	0	–1	....							
	Tulsa Oilers	CHL	3	2	1	3				4											....							
	NHL Totals		170	57	112	169	52	84	136	85	14	2	10	257	22.2	224	69	152	25		25	8	14	22	27	3	0	1
	Other Major League Totals		300	140	344	484				341											42	13	67	51				

WHA First All-Star Team (1976, 1978) • Won WHA Playoff MVP Trophy (1976) • WHA Second All-Star Team (1977)

Signed as a free agent by **Winnipeg** (WHA), May 3, 1974. Signed as a free agent by **NY Rangers**, June 5, 1978.

● NISTICO, LOU   Lou Nistico   C – L. 5'7", 170 lbs.   b: Thunder Bay, Ont., 1/25/1953.   Minnesota's 7th choice, 105th overall, in 1973 Amateur Draft.

			REGULAR SEASON																		PLAYOFFS							
Season	Club	League	GP	G	A	Pts	AG	AA	APts	PIM	PP	SH	GW	S	%	TGF	PGF	TGA	PGA	+/–	GP	G	A	Pts	PIM	PP	SH	GW
1970-71	London Knights	OHA	45	11	11	22				119											....							
1971-72	London Knights	OHA	62	22	30	52				193											....							
1972-73	London Knights	OHA	65	31	64	95				108											....							
1973-74	Toronto Toros	WHA	13	1	3	4				14											....							
	Jacksonville Barons	AHL	51	12	24	36				109											....							
1974-75	Toronto Toros	WHA	29	11	11	22				75											6	6	1	7	19			
	Mohawk Valley Comets	NAHL	42	21	27	48				103											....							
1975-76	Toronto Toros	WHA	65	12	22	34				120											....							
	Buffalo Norsemen	NAHL	10	9	5	14				49											....							
1976-77	Birmingham Bulls	WHA	79	20	36	56				166											....							
1977-78	**Colorado Rockies**	NHL	3	0	0	0	0	0	0	0	0	0	0	0	0.0	0	0	0	0		....							
	Phoenix Roadrunners	CHL	4	0	0	0				0											....							
	Brantford Alexanders	OHA Sr.	27	19	16	35				85											....							
	NHL Totals		3	0	0	0	0	0	0	0	0	0	0	0	0.0	0	0	0	0		....							
	Other Major League Totals		186	44	72	116				375											6	6	1	7	19			

NAHL Second All-Star Team (1975)

Selected by **Toronto** (WHA) in 1973 WHA Amateur Draft, June, 1973. Transferred to **Birmingham** after **Toronto** (WHA) franchise relocated, June 30, 1976. Traded to **Edmonton** (WHA) by **Birmingham** (WHA) with Jeff Jacques for Pete Laframboise, Dan Ardnt and Chris Evans, September, 1977. Signed as a free agent by **Colorado** to a five-game tryout contract, November 6, 1977.

● NOEL, CLAUDE   Claude Noel   C – L. 5'11", 165 lbs.   b: Kirkland Lake, Ont., 10/31/1955.

			REGULAR SEASON																		PLAYOFFS							
Season	Club	League	GP	G	A	Pts	AG	AA	APts	PIM	PP	SH	GW	S	%	TGF	PGF	TGA	PGA	+/–	GP	G	A	Pts	PIM	PP	SH	GW
1973-74	North Bay Trappers	OJHL	44	19	43	62				35											....							
1974-75	Kitchener Rangers	OHA	70	14	37	51				28											4	1	1	2	2			
1975-76	Buffalo Norsmen	NAHL	74	19	42	61				27											6	2	1	3	0			
1976-77	Hershey Bears	AHL	80	14	32	46				19											....							
1977-78	Hershey Bears	AHL	65	13	25	38				18											....							
1978-79	Hershey Bears	AHL	76	30	50	80				27											4	1	4	5				
1979-80	**Washington Capitals**	NHL	7	0	0	0	0	0	0	0	0	0	0	5	0.0	0	0	5	2	–3	....							
	Hershey Bears	AHL	68	24	38	62				18											16	9	10	19	6			
1980-81	Hershey Bears	AHL	64	14	44	58				50											10	2	2	4	14			
1981-82					DID NOT PLAY																							
1982-83	Toledo Goaldiggers	IHL	82	42	82	124				41											11	3	*15	18	4			
1983-84					DID NOT PLAY																							
1984-85	Toledo Goaldiggers	IHL	74	16	56	72				30											6	3	3	2				
1985-86	Toledo Goaldiggers	IHL	12	1	7	8				4											....							
	Kalamazoo Wings	IHL	71	15	38	53				18											6	2	4	6	2			
1986-87	Kalamazoo Wings	IHL	80	33	37	70				28											5	1	2	3	0			
1987-88	Milwaukee Admirals	IHL	56	8	34	42				18											....							
	NHL Totals		7	0	0	0	0	0	0	0	0	0	0	5	0.0	0	0	5	2		....							

IHL Second All-Star Team (1983) • Won James Gatschene Memorial Trophy (MVP - IHL) (1983)

Signed as a free agent by **Washington**, October 9, 1979.

			REGULAR SEASON																		PLAYOFFS							
Season	Club	League	GP	G	A	Pts	AG	AA	APts	PIM	PP	SH	GW	S	%	TGF	PGF	TGA	PGA	+/–	GP	G	A	Pts	PIM	PP	SH	GW

• NOLAN, OWEN Owen Nolan RW – R. 6'1", 201 lbs. b: Belfast, Ireland, 2/12/1972. Quebec's 1st choice, 1st overall, in 1990 Entry Draft.

Season	Club	League	GP	G	A	Pts	AG	AA	APts	PIM	PP	SH	GW	S	%	TGF	PGF	TGA	PGA	+/–	GP	G	A	Pts	PIM	PP	SH	GW
1988-89	Cornwall Royals	OHL	62	34	25	59	....	....	....	213	....	....	....	....	....	....	....	....	....	....	18	5	11	16	41	....	....	....
1989-90	Cornwall Royals	OHL	58	51	59	110	....	....	....	240	....	....	....	....	....	....	....	....	....	....	6	7	5	12	26	....	....	....
1990-91	**Quebec Nordiques**	**NHL**	**59**	**3**	**10**	**13**	**3**	**8**	**11**	**109**	**0**	**0**	**0**	**54**	**5.6**	**25**	**2**	**43**	**1**	**–19**	....	....	....	....	....	....	....	....
	Halifax Citadels	AHL	6	4	4	8	....	....	....	11	....	....	....	....	....	....	....	....	....	....	....	....	....	....	....	....	....	....
1991-92	**Quebec Nordiques**	**NHL**	**75**	**42**	**31**	**73**	**38**	**23**	**61**	**183**	**17**	**0**	**0**	**190**	**22.1**	**98**	**31**	**78**	**2**	**–9**	....	....	....	....	....	....	....	....
1992-93	**Quebec Nordiques**	**NHL**	**73**	**36**	**41**	**77**	**30**	**28**	**58**	**185**	**15**	**0**	**4**	**241**	**14.9**	**111**	**42**	**78**	**8**	**–1**	**5**	**1**	**0**	**1**	**2**	**0**	**0**	**0**
1993-94	**Quebec Nordiques**	**NHL**	**6**	**2**	**2**	**4**	**2**	**2**	**4**	**8**	**0**	**0**	**0**	**15**	**13.3**	**9**	**3**	**7**	**3**	**+2**	....	....	....	....	....	....	....	....
1994-95	**Quebec Nordiques**	**NHL**	**46**	**30**	**19**	**49**	**53**	**28**	**81**	**46**	**13**	**2**	**8**	**137**	**21.9**	**61**	**21**	**29**	**10**	**+21**	**6**	**2**	**3**	**5**	**6**	**0**	**0**	**0**
1995-96	**Colorado Avalanche**	**NHL**	**9**	**4**	**4**	**8**	**4**	**3**	**7**	**9**	**4**	**0**	**0**	**23**	**17.4**	**12**	**8**	**8**	**1**	**–3**	....	....	....	....	....	....	....	....
	San Jose Sharks	**NHL**	**72**	**29**	**32**	**61**	**29**	**26**	**55**	**137**	**12**	**1**	**2**	**184**	**15.8**	**81**	**32**	**97**	**18**	**–30**	....	....	....	....	....	....	....	....
1996-97	**San Jose Sharks**	**NHL**	**72**	**31**	**32**	**63**	**33**	**28**	**61**	**155**	**10**	**0**	**3**	**225**	**13.8**	**85**	**28**	**79**	**3**	**–19**	....	....	....	....	....	....	....	....
	Canada	WC-A	10	4	3	7	....	....	....	31	....	....	....	....	....	....	....	....	....	....	....	....	....	....	....	....	....	....
1997-98	**San Jose Sharks**	**NHL**	**75**	**14**	**27**	**41**	**16**	**26**	**42**	**144**	**3**	**1**	**1**	**192**	**7.3**	**52**	**15**	**58**	**19**	**–2**	**6**	**2**	**2**	**4**	**26**	**2**	**0**	**1**
	NHL Totals		**487**	**191**	**198**	**389**	**208**	**172**	**380**	**976**	**74**	**4**	**18**	**1261**	**15.1**	**534**	**182**	**477**	**65**		**17**	**5**	**5**	**10**	**34**	**2**	**0**	**1**

OHL First All-Star Team (1990)

Played in NHL All-Star Game (1992, 1996, 1997)

Transferred to **Colorado** after **Quebec** franchise relocated, June 21, 1995. Traded to **San Jose** by **Colorado** for Sandis Ozolinsh, October 26, 1995.

• NOLAN, TED Ted Nolan C – L. 6', 185 lbs. b: Sault Ste. Marie, Ont., 4/7/1958. Detroit's 7th choice, 78th overall, in 1978 Amateur Draft.

Season	Club	League	GP	G	A	Pts	AG	AA	APts	PIM	PP	SH	GW	S	%	TGF	PGF	TGA	PGA	+/–	GP	G	A	Pts	PIM	PP	SH	GW
1976-77	Sault Ste. Marie Greyhounds	OHA	60	8	16	24	....	....	....	109	....	....	....	....	....	....	....	....	....	....	9	1	2	3	19	....	....	....
1977-78	Sault Ste. Marie Greyhounds	OHA	66	14	30	44	....	....	....	106	....	....	....	....	....	....	....	....	....	....	13	1	3	4	20	....	....	....
1978-79	Kansas City Red Wings	CHL	73	12	38	50	....	....	....	66	....	....	....	....	....	....	....	....	....	....	4	1	2	3	0	....	....	....
1979-80	Adirondack Red Wings	AHL	75	16	24	40	....	....	....	106	....	....	....	....	....	....	....	....	....	....	5	0	1	1	0	....	....	....
1980-81	Adirondack Red Wings	AHL	76	22	28	50	....	....	....	86	....	....	....	....	....	....	....	....	....	....	18	6	10	16	11	....	....	....
1981-82	**Detroit Red Wings**	**NHL**	**41**	**4**	**13**	**17**	**3**	**9**	**12**	**45**	**0**	**2**	**0**	**67**	**6.0**	**25**	**2**	**37**	**8**	**–6**	....	....	....	....	....	....	....	....
	Adirondack Red Wings	AHL	39	12	18	30	....	....	....	81	....	....	....	....	....	....	....	....	....	....	....	....	....	....	....	....	....	....
1982-83	Adirondack Red Wings	AHL	78	24	40	64	....	....	....	103	....	....	....	....	....	....	....	....	....	....	6	2	5	7	14	....	....	....
1983-84	**Detroit Red Wings**	**NHL**	**19**	**1**	**2**	**3**	**1**	**1**	**2**	**26**	**0**	**0**	**1**	**15**	**6.7**	**5**	**1**	**16**	**1**	**–11**	....	....	....	....	....	....	....	....
	Adirondack Red Wings	AHL	31	10	16	26	....	....	....	76	....	....	....	....	....	....	....	....	....	....	7	2	3	5	18	....	....	....
1984-85	Rochester Americans	AHL	65	28	34	62	....	....	....	152	....	....	....	....	....	....	....	....	....	....	5	4	0	4	18	....	....	....
1985-86	**Pittsburgh Penguins**	**NHL**	**18**	**1**	**1**	**2**	**1**	**1**	**2**	**34**	**0**	**0**	**0**	**17**	**5.9**	**5**	**1**	**5**	**0**	**–1**	....	....	....	....	....	....	....	....
	Baltimore Skipjacks	AHL	10	4	4	8	....	....	....	19	....	....	....	....	....	....	....	....	....	....	....	....	....	....	....	....	....	....
	NHL Totals		**78**	**6**	**16**	**22**	**5**	**11**	**16**	**105**	**0**	**2**	**1**	**99**	**6.1**	**35**	**4**	**58**	**9**		....	....	....	....	....	....	....	....

Won Jack Adams Award (1997)

Signed as a free agent by **Buffalo**, March 7, 1985. Rights traded to **Pittsburgh** by **Buffalo** for cash, September 16, 1985.

• NOLET, SIMON Simon Nolet RW – R. 5'9", 185 lbs. b: St. Odilon, Que., 11/23/1941.

Season	Club	League	GP	G	A	Pts	AG	AA	APts	PIM	PP	SH	GW	S	%	TGF	PGF	TGA	PGA	+/–	GP	G	A	Pts	PIM	PP	SH	GW
1961-62	Quebec Citadelle	QJHL	STATISTICS NOT AVAILABLE																									
	Quebec Aces	AHL	1	0	0	0	....	....	....	2	....	....	....	....	....	....	....	....	....	....	....	....	....	....				....
1962-63	Windsor Maple Leafs	NSSHL		53	55	108	....	....	....	30	....	....	....	....	....	....	....	....	....	....	7	5	6	11	14			
	Moncton Hawks	NSSHL			....	....	....	....	....	....	....	....	....	....	....	....	....	....	....	....	12	4	5	9	2	....	....	....
1963-64	Windsor Maple Leafs	NSSHL	....	68	65	133	....	....	....	19	....	....	....	....	....	....	....	....	....	....	....	....	....	....	....	....	....	....
1964-65	Sherbrooke Castors	QPHL	STATISTICS NOT AVAILABLE																									
	Quebec Aces	AHL	2	2	1	3	....	....	....	2	....	....	....	....	....	....	....	....	....	....	....	....	....	....	....	....	....	....
1965-66	Quebec Aces	AHL	61	16	17	33	....	....	....	12	....	....	....	....	....	....	....	....	....	....	6	0	0	0	2	....	....	....
1966-67	Quebec Aces	AHL	66	32	24	56	....	....	....	28	....	....	....	....	....	....	....	....	....	....	5	1	4	5	4	....	....	....
1967-68	**Philadelphia Flyers**	**NHL**	**4**	**0**	**0**	**0**	**0**	**0**	**0**	**2**	**0**	**0**	**0**	**9**	**0.0**	**0**	**0**	**1**	**0**	**–1**	**1**	**0**	**0**	**0**	**0**	**0**	**0**	**0**
	Quebec Aces	AHL	70	44	52	96	....	....	....	45	....	....	....	....	....	....	....	....	....	....	10	5	10	15	10	....	....	....
1968-69	**Philadelphia Flyers**	**NHL**	**35**	**4**	**10**	**14**	**4**	**9**	**13**	**8**	**2**	**0**	**0**	**77**	**5.2**	**20**	**12**	**18**	**0**	**–10**	....	....	....	....	....	....	....	....
	Quebec Aces	AHL	33	11	21	32	....	....	....	28	....	....	....	....	....	....	....	....	....	....	15	5	3	8	28	....	....	....
1969-70	**Philadelphia Flyers**	**NHL**	**56**	**22**	**22**	**44**	**25**	**22**	**47**	**36**	**6**	**0**	**4**	**163**	**13.5**	**62**	**18**	**32**	**0**	**+12**	....	....	....	....	....	....	....	....
	Quebec Aces	AHL	22	13	18	31	....	....	....	14	....	....	....	....	....	....	....	....	....	....	....	....	....	....	....	....	....	....
1970-71	**Philadelphia Flyers**	**NHL**	**74**	**9**	**19**	**28**	**9**	**17**	**26**	**42**	**4**	**0**	**0**	**168**	**5.4**	**44**	**15**	**30**	**0**	**–1**	**4**	**2**	**1**	**3**	**0**	**1**	**0**	**0**
1971-72	**Philadelphia Flyers**	**NHL**	**67**	**23**	**20**	**43**	**25**	**18**	**43**	**22**	**6**	**0**	**5**	**201**	**11.4**	**70**	**27**	**40**	**3**	**+6**	....	....	....	....	....	....	....	....
1972-73	**Philadelphia Flyers**	**NHL**	**70**	**16**	**20**	**36**	**16**	**17**	**33**	**6**	**6**	**0**	**0**	**146**	**11.0**	**61**	**28**	**39**	**3**	**–3**	**11**	**3**	**1**	**4**	**4**	**0**	**0**	**0**
1973-74	**Philadelphia Flyers**	**NHL**	**52**	**19**	**17**	**36**	**19**	**15**	**34**	**13**	**1**	**0**	**1**	**97**	**10.6**	**51**	**8**	**15**	**0**	**+28**	**15**	**1**	**1**	**2**	**4**	**0**	**0**	**0**
1974-75	**Kansas City Scouts**	**NHL**	**72**	**26**	**32**	**58**	**24**	**25**	**49**	**30**	**11**	**2**	**2**	**197**	**13.2**	**76**	**39**	**95**	**6**	**–52**	....	....	....	....	....	....	....	....
1975-76	**Kansas City Scouts**	**NHL**	**41**	**10**	**15**	**25**	**9**	**12**	**21**	**16**	**2**	**0**	**1**	**123**	**8.1**	**35**	**12**	**33**	**1**	**–9**	....	....	....	....	....	....	....	....
	Pittsburgh Penguins	**NHL**	**39**	**9**	**8**	**17**	**8**	**6**	**14**	**2**	**1**	**0**	**1**	**74**	**12.2**	**34**	**6**	**21**	**0**	**+7**	**3**	**0**	**0**	**0**	**0**	**0**	**0**	**0**
1976-77	**Colorado Rockies**	**NHL**	**52**	**12**	**19**	**31**	**11**	**15**	**26**	**10**	**1**	**1**	**2**	**105**	**11.4**	**44**	**5**	**52**	**13**	**0**	....	....	....	....	....	....	....	....
	NHL Totals		**562**	**150**	**182**	**332**	**150**	**156**	**306**	**187**	**40**	**3**	**16**	**1360**	**11.0**	**497**	**170**	**376**	**26**		**34**	**6**	**3**	**9**	**8**	**1**	**0**	**0**

AHL Second All-Star Team (1968) • Won John B. Sollenberger Trophy (Top Scorer - AHL) (1968)

Played in NHL All-Star Game (1972, 1975)

NHL rights transferred to **Philadelphia** after NHL club purchased **Quebec** (AHL) franchise, May 8, 1967. Claimed by **Kansas City** from **Philadelphia** in Expansion Draft, June 12, 1974. Traded to **Pittsburgh** by **Kansas City** with Ed Gilbert and Kansas City's 1st round choice (Blair Chapman) in 1976 Amateur Draft for Steve Durbano, Chuck Arnason and Pittsburgh's 1st round choice (Greg Carroll) in 1976 Amateur Draft, January 9, 1976. Transferred to **Colorado** by **Pittsburgh** with Michel Plasse as compensation for Pittsburgh's signing of free agent Denis Herron, August 7, 1976.

• NOONAN, BRIAN Brian Noonan RW – R. 6'1", 200 lbs. b: Boston, MA, 5/29/1965. Chicago's 10th choice, 186th overall, in 1983 Entry Draft.

Season	Club	League	GP	G	A	Pts	AG	AA	APts	PIM	PP	SH	GW	S	%	TGF	PGF	TGA	PGA	+/–	GP	G	A	Pts	PIM	PP	SH	GW
1982-83	Archbishop Williams High	H.S.	21	26	17	43	....	....	....	....	....	....	....	....	....	....	....	....	....	....	....	....	....	....	....	....	....	....
1983-84	Archbishop Williams High	H.S.	17	14	23	32	....	....	....	....	....	....	....	....	....	....	....	....	....	....	....	....	....	....	....	....	....	....
1984-85	New Westminster Bruins	WHL	72	50	66	116	....	....	....	76	....	....	....	....	....	....	....	....	....	....	11	8	7	15	4	....	....	....
1985-86	Nova Scotia Oilers	AHL	2	0	0	0	....	....	....	0	....	....	....	....	....	....	....	....	....	....	....	....	....	....	....	....	....	....
	Saginaw Generals	IHL	76	39	39	78	....	....	....	69	....	....	....	....	....	....	....	....	....	....	11	6	3	9	6	....	....	....
1986-87	Nova Scotia Oilers	AHL	70	25	26	51	....	....	....	30	....	....	....	....	....	....	....	....	....	....	5	3	1	4	4	....	....	....
1987-88	**Chicago Blackhawks**	**NHL**	**77**	**10**	**20**	**30**	**9**	**14**	**23**	**44**	**3**	**0**	**2**	**87**	**11.5**	**64**	**31**	**66**	**6**	**–27**	**3**	**0**	**0**	**0**	**4**	**0**	**0**	**0**
1988-89	**Chicago Blackhawks**	**NHL**	**45**	**4**	**12**	**16**	**3**	**8**	**11**	**20**	**2**	**0**	**0**	**84**	**4.8**	**29**	**7**	**32**	**8**	**–2**	**1**	**0**	**0**	**0**	**0**	**0**	**0**	**0**
	Saginaw Hawks	IHL	19	18	13	31	....	....	....	36	....	....	....	....	....	....	....	....	....	....	1	0	0	0	0	....	....	....
1989-90	**Chicago Blackhawks**	**NHL**	**8**	**0**	**2**	**2**	**0**	**1**	**1**	**6**	**0**	**0**	**0**	**13**	**0.0**	**3**	**0**	**6**	**3**	**0**	....	....	....	....	....	....	....	....
	Indianapolis Ice	IHL	56	40	36	76	....	....	....	85	....	....	....	....	....	....	....	....	....	....	14	6	9	15	20	....	....	....
1990-91	**Chicago Blackhawks**	**NHL**	**7**	**0**	**4**	**4**	**0**	**3**	**3**	**2**	**0**	**0**	**0**	**12**	**0.0**	**4**	**1**	**4**	**0**	**–1**	....	....	....	....	....	....	....	....
	Indianapolis Ice	IHL	59	38	53	91	....	....	....	67	....	....	....	....	....	....	....	....	....	....	7	6	4	10	18	....	....	....
1991-92	**Chicago Blackhawks**	**NHL**	**65**	**19**	**12**	**31**	**17**	**9**	**26**	**81**	**4**	**0**	**0**	**154**	**12.3**	**57**	**15**	**38**	**5**	**+9**	**18**	**6**	**9**	**15**	**30**	**3**	**0**	**1**
1992-93	**Chicago Blackhawks**	**NHL**	**63**	**16**	**14**	**30**	**13**	**10**	**23**	**82**	**5**	**0**	**3**	**129**	**12.4**	**47**	**17**	**29**	**2**	**+3**	**4**	**3**	**0**	**3**	**4**	**1**	**0**	**0**
1993-94	**Chicago Blackhawks**	**NHL**	**64**	**14**	**21**	**35**	**13**	**16**	**29**	**57**	**8**	**0**	**3**	**134**	**10.4**	**63**	**33**	**28**	**0**	**+2**	....	....	....	....	....	....	....	....
	New York Rangers	**NHL**	**12**	**4**	**2**	**6**	**4**	**2**	**6**	**12**	**2**	**0**	**3**	**26**	**15.4**	**13**	**4**	**4**	**0**	**+5**	**22**	**4**	**7**	**11**	**17**	**2**	**0**	**1**
1994-95	**New York Rangers**	**NHL**	**45**	**14**	**13**	**27**	**25**	**19**	**44**	**26**	**7**	**0**	**1**	**95**	**14.7**	**48**	**16**	**46**	**11**	**–3**	**5**	**0**	**0**	**0**	**8**	**0**	**0**	**0**
1995-96	**St. Louis Blues**	**NHL**	**81**	**13**	**22**	**35**	**13**	**18**	**31**	**64**	**3**	**1**	**6**	**131**	**9.9**	**54**	**13**	**62**	**23**	**+2**	**13**	**4**	**1**	**5**	**10**	**0**	**0**	**0**
1996-97	**St. Louis Blues**	**NHL**	**13**	**2**	**5**	**7**	**2**	**4**	**6**	**0**	**0**	**0**	**0**	**13**	**15.4**	**8**	**0**	**7**	**1**	**+2**	....	....	....	....	....	....	....	....
	New York Rangers	**NHL**	**44**	**6**	**9**	**15**	**6**	**8**	**14**	**28**	**3**	**0**	**1**	**62**	**9.7**	**22**	**10**	**22**	**3**	**–7**	....	....	....	....	....	....	....	....
	Vancouver Canucks	**NHL**	**16**	**4**	**8**	**12**	**4**	**7**	**11**	**6**	**0**	**1**	**0**	**25**	**16.0**	**17**	**3**	**17**	**5**	**+2**	....	....	....	....	....	....	....	....
1997-98	**Vancouver Canucks**	**NHL**	**82**	**10**	**15**	**25**	**12**	**15**	**27**	**62**	**1**	**0**	**2**	**87**	**11.5**	**41**	**6**	**67**	**13**	**–19**	....	....	....	....	....	....	....	....
	NHL Totals		**622**	**116**	**159**	**275**	**121**	**134**	**255**	**518**	**38**	**2**	**21**	**1052**	**11.0**	**470**	**156**	**428**	**80**		**66**	**17**	**17**	**34**	**73**	**6**	**0**	**2**

IHL Second All-Star Team (1990) • IHL First All-Star Team (1991)

Traded to **NY Rangers** by **Chicago** with Stephane Matteau for Tony Amonte and the rights to Matt Oates, March 21, 1994. Signed as a free agent by **St. Louis**, July 24, 1995. Traded to **NY Rangers** by **St. Louis** for Sergio Momesso, November 13, 1996. Traded to **Vancouver** by **NY Rangers** with Sergei Nemchinov for Esa Tikkanen and Russ Courtnall, March 8, 1997.

• NORDMARK, ROBERT

Robert Nordmark D – R. 6', 209 lbs. b: Lulea, Sweden, 8/20/1962. St. Louis' 8th choice, 59th overall, in 1987 Entry Draft.

			REGULAR SEASON																		PLAYOFFS							
Season	Club	League	GP	G	A	Pts	AG	AA	APts	PIM	PP	SH	GW	S	%	TGF	PGF	TGA	PGA	+/–	GP	G	A	Pts	PIM	PP	SH	GW
1979-80	Lulea HF	Sweden 2	24	4	2	6	....	....	....	16	....	....	....	....	....	....	....	....	....	....	....	....	....	....	....	....	....	....
1980-81	Vastra Frolunda	Sweden	34	4	3	7	....	....	....	30	....	....	....	....	....	....	....	....	....	....	2	0	0	0	0	....	....	....
	Sweden	WJC-A	5	0	0	0	....	....	....	2	....	....	....	....	....	....	....	....	....	....	....	....	....	....	....	....	....	....
1981-82	Brynas IF Gavle	Sweden	34	5	5	10	....	....	....	16	....	....	....	....	....	....	....	....	....	....	....	....	....	....	....	....	....	....
	Sweden	WJC-A	7	2	1	3	....	....	....	0	....	....	....	....	....	....	....	....	....	....	....	....	....	....	....	....	....	....
1982-83	Brynas IF Gavle	Sweden	36	8	5	13	....	....	....	32	....	....	....	....	....	....	....	....	....	....	....	....	....	....	....	....	....	....
1983-84	Brynas IF Gavle	Sweden	32	10	15	25	....	....	....	44	....	....	....	....	....	....	....	....	....	....	....	....	....	....	....	....	....	....
1984-85	Lulea HF	Sweden	33	3	9	12	....	....	....	30	....	....	....	....	....	....	....	....	....	....	....	....	....	....	....	....	....	....
1985-86	Lulea HF	Sweden	35	9	15	24	....	....	....	48	....	....	....	....	....	....	....	....	....	....	....	....	....	....	....	....	....	....
	Sweden	WEC-A	8	3	2	5	....	....	....	10	....	....	....	....	....	....	....	....	....	....	....	....	....	....	....	....	....	....
1986-87	Lulea HF	Sweden	32	7	8	15	....	....	....	46	....	....	....	....	....	....	....	....	....	....	3	0	3	3	4	....	....	....
	Sweden	WEC-A	9	1	2	3	....	....	....	16	....	....	....	....	....	....	....	....	....	....	....	....	....	....	....	....	....	....
1987-88	**St. Louis Blues**	**NHL**	**67**	**3**	**18**	**21**	**3**	**13**	**16**	**60**	**2**	**0**	**0**	**78**	**3.8**	**58**	**23**	**50**	**9**	**–6**	....	....	....	....	....	....	....	....
1988-89	**Vancouver Canucks**	**NHL**	**80**	**6**	**35**	**41**	**5**	**25**	**30**	**97**	**5**	**0**	**1**	**156**	**3.8**	**113**	**62**	**62**	**7**	**–4**	**7**	**3**	**2**	**5**	**8**	**2**	**0**	**0**
1989-90	**Vancouver Canucks**	**NHL**	**44**	**2**	**11**	**13**	**2**	**8**	**10**	**34**	**1**	**0**	**0**	**86**	**2.3**	**42**	**20**	**38**	**0**	**–16**	....	....	....	....	....	....	....	....
1990-91	**Vancouver Canucks**	**NHL**	**45**	**2**	**6**	**8**	**2**	**5**	**7**	**63**	**1**	**0**	**0**	**65**	**3.1**	**40**	**13**	**46**	**9**	**–10**	....	....	....	....	....	....	....	....
1991-92	Vasteras IK	Sweden	36	11	6	17	....	....	....	72	....	....	....	....	....	....	....	....	....	....	....	....	....	....	....	....	....	....
1992-93	Vasteras IK	Sweden	24	11	4	15	....	....	....	52	....	....	....	....	....	....	....	....	....	....	3	1	0	1	10	....	....	....
1993-94	Djurgardens IF Stockholm	Sweden	35	5	9	14	....	....	....	62	....	....	....	....	....	....	....	....	....	....	....	....	....	....	....	....	....	....
1994-95	Djurgardens IF Stockholm	Sweden	34	7	11	18	....	....	....	50	....	....	....	....	....	....	....	....	....	....	3	1	0	1	2	....	....	....
	Sweden	WC-A	6	1	1	2	....	....	....	4	....	....	....	....	....	....	....	....	....	....	....	....	....	....	....	....	....	....
1995-96	Lukko Rauma	Finland	43	16	13	29	....	....	....	58	....	....	....	....	....	....	....	....	....	....	8	2	4	6	6	....	....	....
1996-97	Zurich SC	Switz.	41	9	17	26	....	....	....	59	....	....	....	....	....	....	....	....	....	....	5	0	2	2	4	....	....	....
1997-98	Djurgardens IF Stockholm	Sweden	11	3	5	8	....	....	....	10	....	....	....	....	....	....	....	....	....	....	6	0	0	0	4	....	....	....
	NHL Totals		**236**	**13**	**70**	**83**	**12**	**51**	**63**	**254**	**9**	**0**	**1**	**385**	**3.4**	**253**	**118**	**196**	**25**		**7**	**3**	**2**	**5**	**8**	**2**	**0**	**0**

Traded to **Vancouver** by **St. Louis** for Dave Richter and future considerations, September 6, 1988.

• NORIS, JOE

Joe Noris C/D – R. 6', 185 lbs. b: Denver, CO, 10/26/1951. Pittsburgh's 2nd choice, 32nd overall, in 1971 Amateur Draft.

Season	Club	League	GP	G	A	Pts	AG	AA	APts	PIM	PP	SH	GW	S	%	TGF	PGF	TGA	PGA	+/–	GP	G	A	Pts	PIM	PP	SH	GW
1968-69	Kitchener Rangers	OHA	18	5	9	14	....	....	....	21	....	....	....	....	....	....	....	....	....	....	....	....	....	....	....	....	....	....
1969-70	Kitchener Rangers	OHA	48	27	19	46	....	....	....	45	....	....	....	....	....	....	....	....	....	....	....	....	....	....	....	....	....	....
1970-71	Toronto Marlboros	OHA	42	12	24	36	....	....	....	22	....	....	....	....	....	....	....	....	....	....	....	....	....	....	....	....	....	....
1971-72	**Pittsburgh Penguins**	**NHL**	**35**	**2**	**5**	**7**	**2**	**5**	**7**	**20**	**0**	**0**	**0**	**48**	**4.2**	**22**	**1**	**31**	**2**	**–8**	....	....	....	....	....	....	....	....
	Hershey Bears	AHL	42	8	15	23	....	....	....	37	....	....	....	....	....	....	....	....	....	....	4	1	1	2	8	....	....	....
1972-73	Hershey Bears	AHL	8	2	5	7	....	....	....	9	....	....	....	....	....	....	....	....	....	....	....	....	....	....	....	....	....	....
	San Diego Gulls	WHL	25	3	13	16	....	....	....	14	....	....	....	....	....	....	....	....	....	....	....	....	....	....	....	....	....	....
	St. Louis Blues	**NHL**	**2**	**0**	**0**	**0**	**0**	**0**	**0**	**0**	**0**	**0**	**0**	**0**	**0.0**	**0**	**0**	**2**	**0**	**–2**	....	....	....	....	....	....	....	....
	Denver Spurs	WHL	35	10	18	28	....	....	....	14	....	....	....	....	....	....	....	....	....	....	5	1	2	3	7	....	....	....
1973-74	**Buffalo Sabres**	**NHL**	**18**	**0**	**0**	**0**	**0**	**0**	**0**	**2**	**0**	**0**	**0**	**9**	**0.0**	**7**	**2**	**9**	**0**	**–4**	....	....	....	....	....	....	....	....
	Cincinnati Swords	AHL	28	5	13	18	....	....	....	20	....	....	....	....	....	....	....	....	....	....	5	3	3	6	0	....	....	....
1974-75	Syracuse Eagles	AHL	73	26	36	62	....	....	....	41	....	....	....	....	....	....	....	....	....	....	1	1	1	2	0	....	....	....
1975-76	San Diego Mariners	WHA	80	28	40	68	....	....	....	24	....	....	....	....	....	....	....	....	....	....	11	2	4	6	6	....	....	....
1976-77	United States	C Cup	4	0	1	1	....	....	....	6	....	....	....	....	....	....	....	....	....	....	....	....	....	....	....	....	....	....
	San Diego Mariners	WHA	73	35	57	92	....	....	....	30	....	....	....	....	....	....	....	....	....	....	7	2	1	3	6	....	....	....
1977-78	Birmingham Bulls	WHA	45	9	19	28	....	....	....	4	....	....	....	....	....	....	....	....	....	....	....	....	....	....	....	....	....	....
1978-79	San Diego Hawks	PHL	58	27	*77	*104	....	....	....	8	....	....	....	....	....	....	....	....	....	....	....	....	....	....	....	....	....	....
1979-80	Atse Graz	Austria	6	2	2	4	....	....	....	2	....	....	....	....	....	....	....	....	....	....	....	....	....	....	....	....	....	....
	NHL Totals		**55**	**2**	**5**	**7**	**2**	**5**	**7**	**22**	**0**	**0**	**0**	**57**	**3.5**	**29**	**3**	**42**	**2**		....	....	....	....	....	....	....	....
	Other Major League Totals		198	72	116	188	....	....	....	58	....	....	....	....	....	....	....	....	....		18	4	5	9	12	....	....	....

Selected by **Ontario-Ottawa** (WHA) in 1972 WHA General Player Draft, February 12, 1972. Traded to **St. Louis** by **Pittsburgh** for Jim Shires, January 8, 1973. Claimed by **Buffalo** from **St. Louis** in Intra-League Draft, June 12, 1973. WHA rights claimed on waivers by **Calgary** (WHA) from **Toronto** (WHA), June, 1975. WHA rights traded to **San Diego** (WHA) by **Calgary** (WHA) for Richard Sentes, August, 1975. Signed as a free agent by **Birmingham** (WHA) after **San Diego** (WHA) franchise folded, June, 1977.

• NORRIS, DWAYNE

Dwayne Norris RW – R. 5'10", 175 lbs. b: St. John's, Nfld., 1/8/1970. Quebec's 5th choice, 127th overall, in 1990 Entry Draft.

Season	Club	League	GP	G	A	Pts	AG	AA	APts	PIM	PP	SH	GW	S	%	TGF	PGF	TGA	PGA	+/–	GP	G	A	Pts	PIM	PP	SH	GW
1988-89	Michigan State Spartans	CCHA	40	16	21	37	....	....	....	32	....	....	....	....	....	....	....	....	....	....	....	....	....	....	....	....	....	....
1989-90	Michigan State Spartans	CCHA	33	18	25	43	....	....	....	30	....	....	....	....	....	....	....	....	....	....	....	....	....	....	....	....	....	....
	Canada	WJC-A	7	2	4	6	....	....	....	2	....	....	....	....	....	....	....	....	....	....	....	....	....	....	....	....	....	....
1990-91	Michigan State Spartans	CCHA	40	26	25	51	....	....	....	60	....	....	....	....	....	....	....	....	....	....	....	....	....	....	....	....	....	....
1991-92	Michigan State Spartans	CCHA	41	40	38	78	....	....	....	58	....	....	....	....	....	....	....	....	....	....	....	....	....	....	....	....	....	....
1992-93	Halifax Citadels	AHL	50	25	28	53	....	....	....	62	....	....	....	....	....	....	....	....	....	....	....	....	....	....	....	....	....	....
1993-94	Canada	Nat-Team	48	18	14	32	....	....	....	22	....	....	....	....	....	....	....	....	....	....	....	....	....	....	....	....	....	....
	Canada	Olympics	8	2	2	4	....	....	....	4	....	....	....	....	....	....	....	....	....	....	....	....	....	....	....	....	....	....
	Quebec Nordiques	**NHL**	**4**	**1**	**1**	**2**	**1**	**1**	**2**	**4**	**0**	**0**	**0**	**7**	**14.3**	**4**	**2**	**1**	**0**	**+1**	....	....	....	....	....	....	....	....
	Cornwall Aces	AHL	9	2	9	11	....	....	....	0	....	....	....	....	....	....	....	....	....	....	13	7	4	11	17	....	....	....
1994-95	Cornwall Aces	AHL	60	30	43	73	....	....	....	61	....	....	....	....	....	....	....	....	....	....	12	7	8	15	4	....	....	....
	Quebec Nordiques	**NHL**	**13**	**1**	**2**	**3**	**2**	**3**	**5**	**2**	**0**	**0**	**1**	**7**	**14.3**	**4**	**0**	**3**	**0**	**+1**	....	....	....	....	....	....	....	....
1995-96	Los Angeles Ice Dogs	IHL	14	7	16	23	....	....	....	22	....	....	....	....	....	....	....	....	....	....	....	....	....	....	....	....	....	....
	Anaheim Mighty Ducks	**NHL**	**3**	**0**	**1**	**1**	**0**	**1**	**1**	**2**	**0**	**0**	**0**	**3**	**0.0**	**1**	**0**	**1**	**0**	**0**	....	....	....	....	....	....	....	....
	Baltimore Bandits	AHL	62	31	55	86	....	....	....	16	....	....	....	....	....	....	....	....	....	....	12	6	9	15	12	....	....	....
1996-97	Kolner Haie	Germany	49	16	28	44	....	....	....	24	....	....	....	....	....	....	....	....	....	....	4	3	0	3	0	....	....	....
1997-98	Kolner Haie	EuroHL	6	1	3	4	....	....	....	2	....	....	....	....	....	....	....	....	....	....	....	....	....	....	....	....	....	....
	Kolner Haie	Germany	42	13	14	27	....	....	....	34	....	....	....	....	....	....	....	....	....	....	3	0	0	0	0	....	....	....
	NHL Totals		**20**	**2**	**4**	**6**	**3**	**5**	**8**	**8**	**0**	**0**	**1**	**17**	**11.8**	**9**	**2**	**5**	**0**		....	....	....	....	....	....	....	....

CCHA First All-Star Team (1992) • NCAA West First All-American Team (1992) • AHL First All-Star Team (1995) • AHL Second All-Star Team (1996)

Signed as a free agent by **Anaheim**, November 3, 1995.

• NORRISH, ROD

Rod Norrish LW – L. 5'10", 185 lbs. b: Saskatoon, Sask., 11/27/1951. Minnesota's 1st choice, 21st overall, in 1971 Amateur Draft.

Season	Club	League	GP	G	A	Pts	AG	AA	APts	PIM	PP	SH	GW	S	%	TGF	PGF	TGA	PGA	+/–	GP	G	A	Pts	PIM	PP	SH	GW
1969-70	Regina Pats	SJHL	50	*37	19	56	....	....	....	11	....	....	....	....	....	....	....	....	....	....	....	....	....	....	....	....	....	....
1970-71	Regina Pats	WCJHL	65	49	32	81	....	....	....	49	....	....	....	....	....	....	....	....	....	....	....	....	....	....	....	....	....	....
1971-72	Cleveland Barons	AHL	39	0	1	1	....	....	....	0	....	....	....	....	....	....	....	....	....	....	6	0	0	0	0	....	....	....
1972-73	Cleveland-Jacksonville Barons	AHL	76	22	33	55	....	....	....	22	....	....	....	....	....	....	....	....	....	....	....	....	....	....	....	....	....	....
1973-74	**Minnesota North Stars**	**NHL**	**9**	**2**	**1**	**3**	**2**	**1**	**3**	**0**	**0**	**0**	**0**	**6**	**33.3**	**3**	**0**	**6**	**0**	**–3**	....	....	....	....	....	....	....	....
	New Haven Nighthawks	AHL	53	19	16	35	....	....	....	11	....	....	....	....	....	....	....	....	....	....	10	1	5	6	2	....	....	....
1974-75	**Minnesota North Stars**	**NHL**	**12**	**1**	**2**	**3**	**1**	**2**	**3**	**2**	**0**	**0**	**0**	**13**	**7.7**	**5**	**3**	**5**	**1**	**–2**	....	....	....	....	....	....	....	....
	New Haven Nighthawks	AHL	52	9	21	30	....	....	....	13	....	....	....	....	....	....	....	....	....	....	16	6	8	14	0	....	....	....
	NHL Totals		**21**	**3**	**3**	**6**	**3**	**3**	**6**	**2**	**0**	**0**	**0**	**19**	**15.8**	**8**	**3**	**11**	**1**		....	....	....	....	....	....	....	....

WCJHL All-Star Team (1971)

• NORSTROM, MATTIAS

Mattias Norstrom D – L. 6'1", 205 lbs. b: Stockholm, Sweden, 1/2/1972. NY Rangers' 2nd choice, 48th overall, in 1992 Entry Draft.

Season	Club	League	GP	G	A	Pts	AG	AA	APts	PIM	PP	SH	GW	S	%	TGF	PGF	TGA	PGA	+/–	GP	G	A	Pts	PIM	PP	SH	GW
1991-92	AIK Solna	Sweden	39	4	3	7	....	....	....	28	....	....	....	....	....	....	....	....	....	....	3	0	2	2	2	....	....	....
	Sweden	WJC-A	7	0	1	1	....	....	....	10	....	....	....	....	....	....	....	....	....	....	....	....	....	....	....	....	....	....
1992-93	AIK Solna	Sweden	22	0	1	1	....	....	....	16	....	....	....	....	....	....	....	....	....	....	....	....	....	....	....	....	....	....
1993-94	**New York Rangers**	**NHL**	**9**	**0**	**2**	**2**	**0**	**2**	**2**	**6**	**0**	**0**	**0**	**3**	**0.0**	**5**	**1**	**4**	**0**	**0**	....	....	....	....	....	....	....	....
	Binghamton Rangers	AHL	55	1	9	10	....	....	....	70	....	....	....	....	....	....	....	....	....	....	....	....	....	....	....	....	....	....
1994-95	Binghamton Rangers	AHL	63	9	10	19	....	....	....	91	....	....	....	....	....	....	....	....	....	....	....	....	....	....	....	....	....	....
	New York Rangers	**NHL**	**9**	**0**	**3**	**3**	**0**	**4**	**4**	**2**	**0**	**0**	**0**	**4**	**0.0**	**10**	**0**	**8**	**0**	**+2**	**3**	**0**	**0**	**0**	**0**	**0**	**0**	**0**
1995-96	**New York Rangers**	**NHL**	**25**	**2**	**1**	**3**	**2**	**1**	**3**	**22**	**0**	**0**	**0**	**17**	**11.8**	**14**	**1**	**10**	**2**	**+5**	....	....	....	....	....	....	....	....
	Los Angeles Kings	**NHL**	**11**	**0**	**1**	**1**	**0**	**1**	**1**	**18**	**0**	**0**	**0**	**17**	**0.0**	**8**	**3**	**14**	**1**	**–8**	....	....	....	....	....	....	....	....
	Sweden	WC-A	6	0	0	0	....	....	....	6	....	....	....	....	....	....	....	....	....	....	....	....	....	....	....	....	....	....

										REGULAR SEASON											PLAYOFFS							
Season	Club	League	GP	G	A	Pts	AG	AA	APts	PIM	PP	SH	GW	S	%	TGF	PGF	TGA	PGA	+/-	GP	G	A	Pts	PIM	PP	SH	GW
1996-97	Sweden	W Cup	4	0	1	1				0																		
	Los Angeles Kings	**NHL**	**80**	**1**	**21**	**22**	**1**	**19**	**20**	**84**	**0**	**0**	**0**	**106**	**0.9**	**76**	**12**	**76**	**8**	**–4**								
	Sweden	WC-A	11	0	2	2				14																		
1997-98	**Los Angeles Kings**	**NHL**	**73**	**1**	**12**	**13**	**1**	**12**	**13**	**90**	**0**	**0**	**0**	**61**	**1.6**	**76**	**13**	**73**	**24**	**+14**	**4**	**0**	**0**	**0**	**2**	**0**	**0**	**0**
	Sweden	Olympics	4	0	1	1				2																		
	Sweden	WC-A	1	0	0	0				0																		
	NHL Totals		**207**	**4**	**40**	**44**	**4**	**39**	**43**	**222**	**0**	**0**	**0**	**208**	**1.9**	**189**	**30**	**185**	**35**		**7**	**0**	**0**	**0**	**2**	**0**	**0**	**0**

Traded to **LA Kings** by **NY Rangers** with Ray Ferraro, Ian Laperriere, Nathan Lafayette and NY Rangers' 4th round choice (Sean Blanchard) in 1997 Entry Draft for Marty McSorley, Jari Kurri and Shane Churla, March 14, 1996.

• NORTON, JEFF

Jeff Norton D – L. 6'2", 200 lbs. b: Acton, MA, 11/25/1965. NY Islanders' 3rd choice, 62nd overall, in 1984 Entry Draft.

Season	Club	League	GP	G	A	Pts	AG	AA	APts	PIM	PP	SH	GW	S	%	TGF	PGF	TGA	PGA	+/-	GP	G	A	Pts	PIM	PP	SH	GW
1983-84	Cardinal Cushing Academy	H.S.	21	22	33	55																						
1984-85	University of Michigan	CCHA	37	8	16	24				103																		
1985-86	University of Michigan	CCHA	37	15	30	45				99																		
1986-87	University of Michigan	CCHA	39	12	36	48				92																		
1987-88	United States	Nat-Team	54	7	22	29				52																		
	United States	Olympics	6	0	4	4				4																		
	New York Islanders	**NHL**	**15**	**1**	**6**	**7**	**1**	**4**	**5**	**14**	**1**	**0**	**1**	**18**	**5.6**	**24**	**8**	**22**	**9**	**+3**	**3**	**0**	**2**	**2**	**13**	**0**	**0**	**0**
1988-89	**New York Islanders**	**NHL**	**69**	**1**	**30**	**31**	**1**	**21**	**22**	**74**	**1**	**0**	**0**	**126**	**0.8**	**87**	**36**	**104**	**29**	**–24**								
	United States	WEC-A	6	1	0	1				4																		
1989-90	**New York Islanders**	**NHL**	**60**	**4**	**49**	**53**	**3**	**35**	**38**	**65**	**4**	**0**	**0**	**104**	**3.8**	**108**	**56**	**73**	**12**	**–9**	**4**	**1**	**3**	**4**	**17**	**0**	**0**	**0**
	United States	WEC-A	10	4	1	5				14																		
1990-91	**New York Islanders**	**NHL**	**44**	**3**	**25**	**28**	**3**	**19**	**22**	**16**	**2**	**1**	**0**	**87**	**3.4**	**64**	**31**	**53**	**7**	**–13**								
1991-92	**New York Islanders**	**NHL**	**28**	**1**	**18**	**19**	**1**	**14**	**15**	**18**	**0**	**1**	**0**	**34**	**2.9**	**51**	**20**	**45**	**16**	**+2**								
1992-93	**New York Islanders**	**NHL**	**66**	**12**	**38**	**50**	**10**	**26**	**36**	**45**	**5**	**0**	**0**	**127**	**9.4**	**124**	**55**	**95**	**23**	**–3**	**10**	**1**	**1**	**2**	**4**	**0**	**0**	**0**
1993-94	**San Jose Sharks**	**NHL**	**64**	**7**	**33**	**40**	**7**	**25**	**32**	**36**	**1**	**0**	**0**	**92**	**7.6**	**85**	**20**	**59**	**10**	**+16**	**14**	**1**	**5**	**6**	**20**	**0**	**0**	**0**
1994-95	**San Jose Sharks**	**NHL**	**20**	**1**	**9**	**10**	**2**	**13**	**15**	**39**	**0**	**0**	**0**	**21**	**4.8**	**17**	**2**	**16**	**2**	**+1**								
	St. Louis Blues	**NHL**	**28**	**2**	**18**	**20**	**4**	**26**	**30**	**33**	**0**	**0**	**1**	**27**	**7.4**	**50**	**10**	**28**	**9**	**+21**	**7**	**1**	**1**	**2**	**11**	**0**	**0**	**0**
1995-96	**St. Louis Blues**	**NHL**	**36**	**4**	**7**	**11**	**4**	**6**	**10**	**26**	**0**	**0**	**1**	**33**	**12.1**	**44**	**16**	**33**	**9**	**+4**								
	Edmonton Oilers	**NHL**	**30**	**4**	**16**	**20**	**4**	**13**	**17**	**16**	**1**	**0**	**1**	**52**	**7.7**	**57**	**21**	**47**	**16**	**+5**								
1996-97	**Edmonton Oilers**	**NHL**	**62**	**2**	**11**	**13**	**2**	**10**	**12**	**42**	**0**	**0**	**0**	**68**	**2.9**	**57**	**14**	**62**	**12**	**–7**								
	Tampa Bay Lightning	**NHL**	**13**	**0**	**5**	**5**	**0**	**4**	**4**	**16**	**0**	**0**	**0**	**13**	**0.0**	**15**	**6**	**12**	**3**	**0**								
1997-98	**Tampa Bay Lightning**	**NHL**	**37**	**4**	**6**	**10**	**5**	**6**	**11**	**26**	**4**	**0**	**0**	**41**	**9.8**	**22**	**9**	**48**	**10**	**–25**								
	Florida Panthers	**NHL**	**19**	**0**	**7**	**7**	**0**	**7**	**7**	**18**	**0**	**0**	**0**	**20**	**0.0**	**12**	**6**	**18**	**5**	**–7**								
	NHL Totals		**591**	**46**	**278**	**324**	**47**	**229**	**276**	**484**	**19**	**2**	**4**	**863**	**5.3**	**817**	**310**	**715**	**172**		**38**	**4**	**12**	**16**	**65**	**0**	**0**	**0**

CCHA Second All-Star Team (1987)

Traded to **San Jose** by **NY Islanders** for San Jose's 3rd round choice (Jason Strudwick) in 1994 Entry Draft, June 20, 1993. Traded to **St. Louis** by **San Jose** with San Jose's 3rd round choice (later traded to Colorado — Colorado selected Rick Berry) in 1997 Entry Draft for Craig Janney and cash, March 6, 1995. Traded to **Edmonton** by **St. Louis** with Donald Dufresne for Igor Kravchuk and Ken Sutton, January 4, 1996. Traded to **Tampa Bay** by **Edmonton** for Drew Bannister and Tampa Bay's 6th round choice (Peter Sarno) in 1997 Entry Draft, March 18, 1997. Traded to **Florida** by **Tampa Bay** with Dino Ciccarelli for Mark Fitzpatrick and Jody Hull, January 15, 1998.

• NORWICH, CRAIG

Craig Norwich D – L. 5'11", 175 lbs. b: Edina, MN, 12/15/1955. Montreal's 11th choice, 142nd overall, in 1975 Amateur Draft.

Season	Club	League	GP	G	A	Pts	AG	AA	APts	PIM	PP	SH	GW	S	%	TGF	PGF	TGA	PGA	+/-	GP	G	A	Pts	PIM	PP	SH	GW
1974-75	University of Wisconsin	WCHA	38	11	34	45				24																		
1975-76	University of Wisconsin	WCHA	32	13	27	40				66																		
1976-77	University of Wisconsin	WCHA	44	18	65	83				70																		
1977-78	Cincinnati Stingers	WHA	65	7	23	30				48																		
	United States	WEC-A	10	1	2	3				2																		
1978-79	Cincinnati Stingers	WHA	80	6	51	57				73											3	0	1	1	4			
1979-80	**Winnipeg Jets**	**NHL**	**70**	**10**	**35**	**45**	**9**	**27**	**36**	**36**	**7**	**0**	**0**	**217**	**4.6**	**106**	**44**	**80**	**7**	**–11**								
1980-81	**St. Louis Blues**	**NHL**	**23**	**4**	**12**	**16**	**3**	**8**	**11**	**14**	**3**	**0**	**1**	**64**	**6.3**	**38**	**14**	**24**	**1**	**+1**								
	Colorado Rockies	**NHL**	**11**	**3**	**11**	**14**	**2**	**8**	**10**	**10**	**1**	**0**	**0**	**23**	**13.0**	**26**	**9**	**16**	**3**	**+4**								
	Fort Worth Texans	CHL	8	0	4	4				6																		
	United States	WEC-A	8	1	0	1				0																		
1981-82	Springfield Indians	AHL	28	5	9	14				26																		
1982-83	Gardenia Finstral	Italy	31	35	62	97				61																		
1983-84	Lausanne	Switz.	STATISTICS NOT AVAILABLE																									
1984-85	Groden	Italy	1	2	2	4				2																		
	Adirondack Red Wings	AHL	16	4	7	11				16																		
1985-86	HC Fassa	Italy	31	14	63	77				20																		
1986-87	HC Fassa	Italy	37	14	55	69				82											3	0	11	11	4			
	NHL Totals		**104**	**17**	**58**	**75**	**14**	**43**	**57**	**60**	**11**	**0**	**1**	**304**	**5.6**	**170**	**67**	**120**	**11**									
	Other Major League Totals		145	13	74	87				121											3	0	1	1	4			

WCHA Second All-Star Team (1976) • NCAA West First All-American Team (1976, 1977) • WCHA First All-Star Team (1977) • NCAA Championship All-Tournament Team (1977) • WEC-B All-Star Team (1983)

Selected by **Houston** (WHA) in 1974 WHA Amateur Draft, May, 1974. WHA rights traded to **Cincinnati** (WHA) by **Houston** (WHA) with the WHA rights to David Taylor for John Hughes, May, 1977. Claimed by **Winnipeg** from **Cincinnati** (WHA) in WHA Dispersal Draft, June 9, 1979. Traded to **St. Louis** by **Winnipeg** for Rick Bowness, June 19, 1980. Claimed on waivers by **Colorado** from **St. Louis**, February 2, 1981. Signed as a free agent by **NY Rangers**, December, 1981.

• NORWOOD, LEE

Lee Norwood D – L. 6'1", 198 lbs. b: Oakland, CA, 2/2/1960. Quebec's 3rd choice, 62nd overall, in 1979 Entry Draft.

Season	Club	League	GP	G	A	Pts	AG	AA	APts	PIM	PP	SH	GW	S	%	TGF	PGF	TGA	PGA	+/-	GP	G	A	Pts	PIM	PP	SH	GW
1977-78	Hull Olympiques	QMJHL	51	3	17	20				83																		
1978-79	Oshawa Generals	OHA	61	23	38	61				171											5	2	2	4	17			
1979-80	Oshawa Generals	OHA	60	13	39	52				143											6	2	7	9	15			
1980-81	**Quebec Nordiques**	**NHL**	**11**	**1**	**1**	**2**	**1**	**1**	**2**	**9**	**0**	**0**	**0**	**8**	**12.5**	**6**	**2**	**7**	**0**	**–3**	**3**	**0**	**0**	**0**	**2**	**0**	**0**	**0**
	Hershey Bears	AHL	52	11	32	43				78											8	0	4	4	14			
1981-82	**Quebec Nordiques**	**NHL**	**2**	**0**	**0**	**0**	**0**	**0**	**0**	**2**	**0**	**0**	**0**	**1**	**0.0**	**1**	**0**	**0**	**0**	**+1**								
	Fredericton Express	AHL	29	6	13	19				74																		
	Washington Capitals	**NHL**	**26**	**7**	**10**	**17**	**6**	**7**	**13**	**125**	**3**	**0**	**1**	**33**	**21.2**	**41**	**16**	**22**	**4**	**+7**								
1982-83	**Washington Capitals**	**NHL**	**8**	**0**	**1**	**1**	**0**	**1**	**1**	**14**	**0**	**0**	**0**	**6**	**0.0**	**3**	**1**	**8**	**3**	**–3**								
	Hershey Bears	AHL	67	12	36	48				90											5	0	1	1	2			
1983-84	St. Catharines Saints	AHL	75	13	46	59				91											7	0	5	5	31			
1984-85	Peoria Rivermen	IHL	80	17	60	77				229											18	1	11	12	62			
1985-86	**St. Louis Blues**	**NHL**	**71**	**5**	**24**	**29**	**4**	**16**	**20**	**134**	**2**	**0**	**1**	**111**	**4.5**	**91**	**28**	**81**	**25**	**+7**	**19**	**2**	**7**	**9**	**64**	**0**	**0**	**0**
1986-87	**Detroit Red Wings**	**NHL**	**57**	**6**	**21**	**27**	**5**	**15**	**20**	**163**	**4**	**0**	**2**	**101**	**5.9**	**74**	**28**	**95**	**26**	**–23**	**16**	**1**	**6**	**7**	**31**	**0**	**0**	**1**
	Adirondack Red Wings	AHL	3	0	3	3				0																		
1987-88	**Detroit Red Wings**	**NHL**	**51**	**9**	**22**	**31**	**8**	**16**	**24**	**131**	**3**	**0**	**2**	**106**	**8.5**	**80**	**21**	**74**	**19**	**+4**	**16**	**2**	**6**	**8**	**40**	**2**	**0**	**0**
1988-89	**Detroit Red Wings**	**NHL**	**66**	**10**	**32**	**42**	**8**	**22**	**30**	**100**	**4**	**1**	**0**	**97**	**10.3**	**109**	**31**	**103**	**31**	**+6**	**6**	**1**	**2**	**3**	**16**	**1**	**0**	**0**
1989-90	**Detroit Red Wings**	**NHL**	**64**	**8**	**14**	**22**	**7**	**10**	**17**	**95**	**1**	**0**	**1**	**60**	**13.3**	**76**	**5**	**97**	**40**	**+14**								
1990-91	**Detroit Red Wings**	**NHL**	**21**	**3**	**7**	**10**	**3**	**5**	**8**	**50**	**1**	**0**	**0**	**36**	**8.3**	**23**	**4**	**20**	**7**	**+6**								
	New Jersey Devils	**NHL**	**28**	**3**	**2**	**5**	**3**	**2**	**5**	**87**	**1**	**0**	**0**	**27**	**11.1**	**25**	**3**	**32**	**9**	**–1**	**4**	**0**	**0**	**0**	**18**	**0**	**0**	**0**
1991-92	**Hartford Whalers**	**NHL**	**6**	**0**	**0**	**0**	**0**	**0**	**0**	**16**	**0**	**0**	**0**	**1**	**0.0**	**2**	**0**	**3**	**1**	**0**								
	St. Louis Blues	**NHL**	**44**	**3**	**11**	**14**	**3**	**8**	**11**	**94**	**1**	**0**	**1**	**51**	**5.9**	**47**	**8**	**35**	**10**	**+14**	**1**	**0**	**1**	**1**	**0**	**0**	**0**	**0**
1992-93	**St. Louis Blues**	**NHL**	**32**	**3**	**7**	**10**	**2**	**5**	**7**	**63**	**2**	**0**	**0**	**36**	**8.3**	**36**	**16**	**36**	**11**	**–5**								
1993-94	**Calgary Flames**	**NHL**	**16**	**0**	**1**	**1**	**0**	**1**	**1**	**16**	**0**	**0**	**0**	**10**	**0.0**	**10**	**1**	**10**	**4**	**+3**								
	San Diego Gulls	IHL	4	0	0	0				0											8	0	1	1	11			
1994-95			DID NOT PLAY – RETIRED																									

			REGULAR SEASON																		PLAYOFFS							
Season	Club	League	GP	G	A	Pts	AG	AA	APts	PIM	PP	SH	GW	S	%	TGF	PGF	TGA	PGA	+/–	GP	G	A	Pts	PIM	PP	SH	GW
1995-96	Chicago Wolves	IHL	21	2	6	8	....	....	....	26	....	....	....	....	....	....	....	....	....	....	....	....	....	....	....	....	....	....
	Detroit Vipers	IHL	27	3	11	14	....	....	....	26	....	....	....	....	....	....	....	....	....	....	5	0	3	3	6	....	....	....
1996-97	Saginaw Wheels	ColHL	12	3	3	6	....	....	....	8	....	....	....	....	....	....	....	....	....	....	....	....	....	....	....	....	....	....
	San Antonio Dragons	IHL	12	0	6	6	....	....	....	10	....	....	....	....	....	....	....	....	....	....	3	0	0	0	2	....	....	....
	NHL Totals		**503**	**58**	**153**	**211**	**50**	**109**	**159**	**1099**	**22**	**1**	**8**	**684**	**8.5**	**624**	**164**	**623**	**190**		**65**	**6**	**22**	**28**	**171**	**3**	**0**	**1**

IHL First All-Star Team (1985) • Won Governors' Trophy (Top Defenseman - IHL) (1985)

Traded to **Washington** by **Quebec** for Tim Tookey and Washington's 7th round choice (Daniel Poudrier) in 1982 Entry Draft, February 1, 1982. Traded to **Toronto** by **Washington** for Dave Shand, October 6, 1983. Signed as a free agent by **St. Louis**, August 13, 1985. Traded to **Detroit** by **St. Louis** for Larry Trader, August 7, 1986. Traded to **New Jersey** by **Detroit** with Detroit's 4th round choice (Scott McCabe) in 1992 Entry Draft for Paul Ysebaert, November 27, 1990. Traded to **Hartford** by **New Jersey** for Hartford's 5th round choice (John Guirestante) in 1993 Entry Draft, October 3, 1991. Traded to **St. Louis** by **Hartford** for St. Louis' 5th round choice (Nolan Pratt) in 1993 Entry Draft, November 13, 1991. Signed as a free agent by **Calgary**, October 22, 1993.

• NOVY, MILAN

Milan Novy C – L. 5'10", 196 lbs. b: Kladno, Czech., 9/23/1951. Washington's 2nd choice, 58th overall, in 1982 Entry Draft.

			REGULAR SEASON																		PLAYOFFS							
Season	Club	League	GP	G	A	Pts	AG	AA	APts	PIM	PP	SH	GW	S	%	TGF	PGF	TGA	PGA	+/–	GP	G	A	Pts	PIM	PP	SH	GW
1974-75	SONP Kladno	Czech.	40	46	22	68	....	....	....	....	....	....	....	....	....	....	....	....	....	....	....	....	....	....	....	....	....	....
	Czechoslovakia	WEC-A	10	4	4	8	....	....	....	4	....	....	....	....	....	....	....	....	....	....	....	....	....	....	....	....	....	....
1975-76	SONP Kladno	Czech.	STATISTICS NOT AVAILABLE																									
	Czechoslovakia	Olympics	5	5	0	5	....	....	....	0	....	....	....	....	....	....	....	....	....	....	....	....	....	....	....	....	....	....
	Czechoslovakia	WEC-A	10	9	6	15	....	....	....	4	....	....	....	....	....	....	....	....	....	....	....	....	....	....	....	....	....	....
1976-77	Czechoslovakia	C Cup	7	5	3	8	....	....	....	2	....	....	....	....	....	....	....	....	....	....	....	....	....	....	....	....	....	....
	SONP Kladno	Czech.	44	59	31	90	....	....	....	....	....	....	....	....	....	....	....	....	....	....	....	....	....	....	....	....	....	....
	Czechoslovakia	WEC-A	10	7	9	16	....	....	....	2	....	....	....	....	....	....	....	....	....	....	....	....	....	....	....	....	....	....
1977-78	SONP Kladno	Czech.	44	40	35	75	....	....	....	64	....	....	....	....	....	....	....	....	....	....	....	....	....	....	....	....	....	....
	Czechoslovakia	WEC-A	9	4	1	5	....	....	....	2	....	....	....	....	....	....	....	....	....	....	....	....	....	....	....	....	....	....
1978-79	Poldi Kladno	Czech.	44	33	23	56	....	....	....	....	....	....	....	....	....	....	....	....	....	....	....	....	....	....	....	....	....	....
	Czechoslovakia	WEC-A	5	0	2	2	....	....	....	4	....	....	....	....	....	....	....	....	....	....	....	....	....	....	....	....	....	....
1979-80	Poldi Kladno	Czech.	44	36	30	66	....	....	....	....	....	....	....	....	....	....	....	....	....	....	....	....	....	....	....	....	....	....
	Czechoslovakia	Olympics	6	7	8	15	....	....	....	0	....	....	....	....	....	....	....	....	....	....	....	....	....	....	....	....	....	....
1980-81	Poldi Kladno	Czech.	44	32	*48	*80	....	....	....	....	....	....	....	....	....	....	....	....	....	....	....	....	....	....	....	....	....	....
	Czechoslovakia	WEC-A	8	6	2	8	....	....	....	2	....	....	....	....	....	....	....	....	....	....	....	....	....	....	....	....	....	....
1981-82	Czechoslovakia	C Cup	6	1	2	3	....	....	....	7	....	....	....	....	....	....	....	....	....	....	....	....	....	....	....	....	....	....
	Poldi Kladno	Czech.	44	29	*38	*67	....	....	....	40	....	....	....	....	....	....	....	....	....	....	....	....	....	....	....	....	....	....
	Czechoslovakia	WEC-A	10	3	1	4	....	....	....	6	....	....	....	....	....	....	....	....	....	....	....	....	....	....	....	....	....	....
1982-83	**Washington Capitals**	**NHL**	**73**	**18**	**30**	**48**	**15**	**21**	**36**	**16**	**3**	**0**	**3**	**131**	**13.7**	**62**	**16**	**45**	**0**	**+1**	**2**	**0**	**0**	**0**	**0**	**0**	**0**	**0**
1983-84	Czechoslovakia	Nat-Team	35	19	8	27	....	....	....	25	....	....	....	....	....	....	....	....	....	....	....	....	....	....	....	....	....	....
1984-85	Zurich	Switz. B	....	17	12	29	....	....	....	....	....	....	....	....	....	....	....	....	....	....	4	1	3	4	....	....	....	....
1985-86	WEV Wien	Austria	40	31	50	81	....	....	....	16	....	....	....	....	....	....	....	....	....	....	....	....	....	....	....	....	....	....
1986-87			DID NOT PLAY																									
1987-88	Poldi Kladno	Czech.	47	24	29	53	....	....	....	10	....	....	....	....	....	....	....	....	....	....	....	....	....	....	....	....	....	....
	NHL Totals		**73**	**18**	**30**	**48**	**15**	**21**	**36**	**16**	**3**	**0**	**3**	**131**	**13.7**	**62**	**16**	**45**	**0**		**2**	**0**	**0**	**0**	**0**	**0**	**0**	**0**

WEC-A All-Star Team (1976) • Canada Cup All-Star Team (1976) • Czechoslovakian Player of the Year (1977, 1981, 1982)

• NOWAK, HANK

Hank Nowak LW – L. 6'1", 195 lbs. b: Oshawa, Ont., 11/24/1950. Philadelphia's 5th choice, 87th overall, in 1970 Amateur Draft.

			REGULAR SEASON																		PLAYOFFS							
Season	Club	League	GP	G	A	Pts	AG	AA	APts	PIM	PP	SH	GW	S	%	TGF	PGF	TGA	PGA	+/–	GP	G	A	Pts	PIM	PP	SH	GW
1968-69	Oshawa Generals	OHA	26	2	3	5	....	....	....	37	....	....	....	....	....	....	....	....	....	....	....	....	....	....	....	....	....	....
1969-70	Oshawa Generals	OHA	53	17	22	39	....	....	....	37	....	....	....	....	....	....	....	....	....	....	....	....	....	....	....	....	....	....
1970-71	Quebec Aces	AHL	49	2	7	9	....	....	....	26	....	....	....	....	....	....	....	....	....	....	1	0	0	0	0	....	....	....
1971-72	Richmond Robins	AHL	62	2	3	5	....	....	....	8	....	....	....	....	....	....	....	....	....	....	....	....	....	....	....	....	....	....
1972-73	Hershey Bears	AHL	66	25	22	47	....	....	....	77	....	....	....	....	....	....	....	....	....	....	7	1	2	3	8	....	....	....
1973-74	**Pittsburgh Penguins**	**NHL**	**13**	**0**	**0**	**0**	**0**	**0**	**0**	**11**	**0**	**0**	**0**	**26**	**0.0**	**1**	**0**	**15**	**0**	**–14**	....	....	....	....	....	....	....	....
	Hershey Bears	AHL	56	32	37	69	....	....	....	90	....	....	....	....	....	....	....	....	....	....	14	3	12	15	14	....	....	....
1974-75	**Detroit Red Wings**	**NHL**	**56**	**8**	**14**	**22**	**7**	**11**	**18**	**69**	**1**	**0**	**0**	**110**	**7.3**	**27**	**2**	**69**	**10**	**–34**	....	....	....	....	....	....	....	....
	Boston Bruins	**NHL**	**21**	**4**	**7**	**11**	**4**	**5**	**9**	**26**	**0**	**0**	**1**	**38**	**10.5**	**13**	**0**	**10**	**5**	**+8**	**3**	**1**	**0**	**1**	**0**	**0**	**0**	**0**
1975-76	**Boston Bruins**	**NHL**	**66**	**7**	**3**	**10**	**7**	**2**	**9**	**41**	**0**	**0**	**1**	**60**	**11.7**	**24**	**1**	**26**	**2**	**–1**	**10**	**0**	**0**	**0**	**8**	**0**	**0**	**0**
1976-77	**Boston Bruins**	**NHL**	**24**	**7**	**5**	**12**	**7**	**4**	**11**	**14**	**0**	**0**	**1**	**36**	**19.4**	**19**	**1**	**14**	**0**	**+4**	....	....	....	....	....	....	....	....
	Rochester Americans	AHL	35	12	17	29	....	....	....	26	....	....	....	....	....	....	....	....	....	....	....	....	....	....	....	....	....	....
1977-78	Binghamton Dusters	AHL	77	20	24	44	....	....	....	50	....	....	....	....	....	....	....	....	....	....	....	....	....	....	....	....	....	....
1978-79	Philadelphia Firebirds	AHL	32	7	12	19	....	....	....	16	....	....	....	....	....	....	....	....	....	....	....	....	....	....	....	....	....	....
	Cape Cod Freedoms	NEHL	1	0	0	0	....	....	....	0	....	....	....	....	....	....	....	....	....	....	....	....	....	....	....	....	....	....
	Utica Mohawks	NEHL	43	27	43	70	....	....	....	49	....	....	....	....	....	....	....	....	....	....	....	....	....	....	....	....	....	....
1979-80	Saginaw–Toledo	IHL	77	20	25	45	....	....	....	103	....	....	....	....	....	....	....	....	....	....	4	0	0	0	2	....	....	....
	NHL Totals		**180**	**26**	**29**	**55**	**25**	**22**	**47**	**161**	**1**	**0**	**3**	**270**	**9.6**	**84**	**4**	**134**	**17**		**13**	**1**	**0**	**1**	**8**	**0**	**0**	**0**

Claimed by **Hershey** (AHL) from **Philadelphia** in Reverse Draft, June 8, 1972. Traded to **Pittsburgh** by **Hershey** (AHL) for cash, May 22, 1973. Traded to **Detroit** by **Pittsburgh** with Pittsburgh's 3rd round choice (Dan Mandryck) in 1974 Amateur Draft for Nelson Debenedet, May 27, 1974. Traded to **Boston** by **Detroit** with Earl Anderson for Walt McKechnie and Boston's 3rd choice (Claire Hamilton) in 1975 Amateur Draft, February 18, 1975.

• NUMMINEN, TEPPO

Teppo Numminen D – R. 6'1", 190 lbs. b: Tampere, Finland, 7/3/1968. Winnipeg's 2nd choice, 29th overall, in 1986 Entry Draft.

			REGULAR SEASON																		PLAYOFFS							
Season	Club	League	GP	G	A	Pts	AG	AA	APts	PIM	PP	SH	GW	S	%	TGF	PGF	TGA	PGA	+/–	GP	G	A	Pts	PIM	PP	SH	GW
1985-86	Tappara Tampere	Finland	31	2	4	6	....	....	....	6	....	....	....	....	....	....	....	....	....	....	8	0	0	0	0	....	....	....
1986-87	Tappara Tampere	Finland	44	9	9	18	....	....	....	16	....	....	....	....	....	....	....	....	....	....	9	4	1	5	4	....	....	....
	Finland	WEC-A	10	5	0	5	....	....	....	4	....	....	....	....	....	....	....	....	....	....	....	....	....	....	....	....	....	....
1987-88	Finland	C Cup	4	1	0	1	....	....	....	2	....	....	....	....	....	....	....	....	....	....	....	....	....	....	....	....	....	....
	Tappara Tampere	Finland	40	10	10	20	....	....	....	29	....	....	....	....	....	....	....	....	....	....	10	6	6	12	6	....	....	....
	Finland	WJC-A	7	5	2	7	....	....	....	4	....	....	....	....	....	....	....	....	....	....	....	....	....	....	....	....	....	....
	Finland	Olympics	6	1	4	5	....	....	....	0	....	....	....	....	....	....	....	....	....	....	....	....	....	....	....	....	....	....
1988-89	**Winnipeg Jets**	**NHL**	**69**	**1**	**14**	**15**	**1**	**10**	**11**	**36**	**0**	**1**	**0**	**85**	**1.2**	**65**	**13**	**73**	**10**	**–11**	....	....	....	....	....	....	....	....
1989-90	**Winnipeg Jets**	**NHL**	**79**	**11**	**32**	**43**	**9**	**23**	**32**	**20**	**1**	**0**	**1**	**105**	**10.5**	**88**	**22**	**92**	**22**	**–4**	**7**	**1**	**2**	**3**	**10**	**0**	**0**	**0**
1990-91	**Winnipeg Jets**	**NHL**	**80**	**8**	**25**	**33**	**7**	**19**	**26**	**28**	**3**	**0**	**0**	**151**	**5.3**	**88**	**31**	**99**	**27**	**–15**	....	....	....	....	....	....	....	....
	Finland	WEC-A	10	1	3	4	....	....	....	10	....	....	....	....	....	....	....	....	....	....	....	....	....	....	....	....	....	....
1991-92	Finland	C Cup	6	1	1	2	....	....	....	2	....	....	....	....	....	....	....	....	....	....	....	....	....	....	....	....	....	....
	Winnipeg Jets	**NHL**	**80**	**5**	**34**	**39**	**5**	**26**	**31**	**32**	**4**	**0**	**1**	**143**	**3.5**	**106**	**38**	**85**	**32**	**+15**	**7**	**0**	**0**	**0**	**0**	**0**	**0**	**0**
1992-93	**Winnipeg Jets**	**NHL**	**66**	**7**	**30**	**37**	**6**	**21**	**27**	**33**	**3**	**1**	**0**	**103**	**6.8**	**92**	**26**	**96**	**34**	**+4**	**6**	**1**	**1**	**2**	**2**	**1**	**0**	**0**
1993-94	**Winnipeg Jets**	**NHL**	**57**	**5**	**18**	**23**	**5**	**14**	**19**	**28**	**4**	**0**	**1**	**89**	**5.6**	**68**	**24**	**108**	**41**	**–23**	....	....	....	....	....	....	....	....
1994-95	TuTo	Finland	12	3	8	11	....	....	....	4	....	....	....	....	....	....	....	....	....	....	....	....	....	....	....	....	....	....
	Winnipeg Jets	**NHL**	**42**	**5**	**16**	**21**	**9**	**24**	**33**	**16**	**2**	**0**	**0**	**86**	**5.8**	**68**	**17**	**60**	**21**	**+12**	....	....	....	....	....	....	....	....
1995-96	**Winnipeg Jets**	**NHL**	**74**	**11**	**43**	**54**	**11**	**35**	**46**	**22**	**6**	**0**	**3**	**165**	**6.7**	**115**	**53**	**109**	**43**	**–4**	**6**	**0**	**0**	**0**	**2**	**0**	**0**	**0**
	Finland	WC-A	1	0	1	1	....	....	....	0	....	....	....	....	....	....	....	....	....	....	....	....	....	....	....	....	....	....
1996-97	Finland	W Cup	2	0	0	0	....	....	....	0	....	....	....	....	....	....	....	....	....	....	....	....	....	....	....	....	....	....
	Phoenix Coyotes	**NHL**	**82**	**2**	**25**	**27**	**2**	**22**	**24**	**28**	**0**	**0**	**0**	**135**	**1.5**	**93**	**20**	**102**	**26**	**–3**	**7**	**3**	**3**	**6**	**0**	**1**	**0**	**1**
	Finland	WC-A	5	2	2	4	....	....	....	6	....	....	....	....	....	....	....	....	....	....	....	....	....	....	....	....	....	....
1997-98	**Phoenix Coyotes**	**NHL**	**82**	**11**	**40**	**51**	**13**	**39**	**52**	**30**	**6**	**0**	**2**	**126**	**8.7**	**101**	**30**	**84**	**38**	**+25**	**1**	**0**	**0**	**0**	**0**	**0**	**0**	**0**
	Finland	Olympics	6	1	1	2	....	....	....	2	....	....	....	....	....	....	....	....	....	....	....	....	....	....	....	....	....	....
	NHL Totals		**711**	**66**	**277**	**343**	**68**	**233**	**301**	**273**	**29**	**2**	**8**	**1188**	**5.6**	**884**	**274**	**908**	**294**		**34**	**5**	**6**	**11**	**14**	**2**	**0**	**1**

WJC-A All-Star Team (1988) • Named Best Defenseman at WJC-A (1988) • WC-A All-Star Team (1997)

Transferred to **Phoenix** after **Winnipeg** franchise relocated, July 1, 1996.

• NURMINEN, KAI

Kai Nurminen LW – L. 6'1", 198 lbs. b: Turku, Finland, 3/29/1969. Los Angeles' 9th choice, 193rd overall, in 1996 Entry Draft.

			REGULAR SEASON																		PLAYOFFS							
Season	Club	League	GP	G	A	Pts	AG	AA	APts	PIM	PP	SH	GW	S	%	TGF	PGF	TGA	PGA	+/–	GP	G	A	Pts	PIM	PP	SH	GW
1990-91	TuTo	Finland 2	33	26	20	46	....	....	....	14	....	....	....	....	....	....	....	....	....	....	....	....	....	....	....	....	....	....
1991-92	Kiekko-67	Finland 2	44	44	19	63	....	....	....	34	....	....	....	....	....	....	....	....	....	....	....	....	....	....	....	....	....	....
1992-93	TPS Turku	Finland	31	4	6	10	....	....	....	13	....	....	....	....	....	....	....	....	....	....	7	1	2	3	0	....	....	....
	Kiekko-67	Finland 2	8	6	4	10	....	....	....	2	....	....	....	....	....	....	....	....	....	....	....	....	....	....	....	....	....	....
1993-94	TPS Turku	Finland	45	23	12	35	....	....	....	20	....	....	....	....	....	....	....	....	....	....	11	0	3	3	4	....	....	....
1994-95	HPK Hameenlinna	Finland	49	30	25	55	....	....	....	40	....	....	....	....	....	....	....	....	....	....	....	....	....	....	....	....	....	....

			REGULAR SEASON																		PLAYOFFS							
Season	Club	League	GP	G	A	Pts	AG	AA	APts	PIM	PP	SH	GW	S	%	TGF	PGF	TGA	PGA	+/–	GP	G	A	Pts	PIM	PP	SH	GW
1995-96	HV 71	Finland	40	31	24	55	....	....	....	30	....	....	....	....	....	....	....	....	....	....	4	3	1	4	8	....	....	....
	Finland	WC-A	6	4	2	6	....	....	....	6	....	....	....	....	....	....	....	....	....	....	....	....	....	....	....	....	....	....
1996-97	Finland	W Cup	2	0	1	1	....	....	....	0	....	....	....	....	....	....	....	....	....	....	....	....	....	....	....	....	....	....
	Los Angeles Kings	**NHL**	**67**	**16**	**11**	**27**	**17**	**10**	**27**	**22**	**4**	**0**	**1**	**112**	**14.3**	**50**	**13**	**41**	**1**	**–3**	....	....	....	....	....	....	....	....
	Finland	WC-A	6	3	0	3	....	....	....	0	....	....	....	....	....	....	....	....	....	....	....	....	....	....	....	....	....	....
1997-98	Vastra Frolunda	Sweden	23	9	7	16	....	....	....	24	....	....	....	....	....	....	....	....	....	....	....	....	....	....	....	....	....	....
	Jokerit Helsinki	Finland	20	7	9	16	....	....	....	30	....	....	....	....	....	....	....	....	....	....	8	5	3	8	4	....	....	....
	NHL Totals		**67**	**16**	**11**	**27**	**17**	**10**	**27**	**22**	**4**	**0**	**1**	**112**	**14.3**	**50**	**13**	**41**	**1**		....	....	....	....	....	....	....	....

Finnish First All-Star Team (1995)

• NYLANDER, MICHAEL

Michael Nylander C – L. 5′11″, 190 lbs. b: Stockholm, Sweden, 10/3/1972. Hartford's 4th choice, 59th overall, in 1991 Entry Draft.

Season	Club	League	GP	G	A	Pts	AG	AA	APts	PIM	PP	SH	GW	S	%	TGF	PGF	TGA	PGA	+/–	GP	G	A	Pts	PIM	PP	SH	GW
1989-90	Huddinge	Sweden 2	31	7	15	22	....	....	....	4	....	....	....	....	....	....	....	....	....	....	....	....	....	....	....	....	....	....
1990-91	Huddinge	Sweden 2	33	14	20	34	....	....	....	10	....	....	....	....	....	....	....	....	....	....	....	....	....	....	....	....	....	....
	Sweden	WJC-A	7	6	5	11	....	....	....	8	....	....	....	....	....	....	....	....	....	....	....	....	....	....	....	....	....	....
1991-92	AIK Solna	Sweden	40	11	17	28	....	....	....	30	....	....	....	....	....	....	....	....	....	....	3	1	4	5	4	....	....	....
	Sweden	WJC-A	7	8	9	17	....	....	....	6	....	....	....	....	....	....	....	....	....	....	....	....	....	....	....	....	....	....
	Sweden	WC-A	6	0	1	1	....	....	....	0	....	....	....	....	....	....	....	....	....	....	....	....	....	....	....	....	....	....
1992-93	**Hartford Whalers**	**NHL**	**59**	**11**	**22**	**33**	**9**	**15**	**24**	**36**	**3**	**0**	**1**	**85**	**12.9**	**48**	**13**	**47**	**5**	**–7**	....	....	....	....	....	....	....	....
	Springfield Indians	AHL	....	....	....	....	....	....	....	....	....	....	....	....	....	....	....	....	....	....	3	3	3	6	2	....	....	....
	Sweden	WC-A	7	1	7	8	....	....	....	4	....	....	....	....	....	....	....	....	....	....	....	....	....	....	....	....	....	....
1993-94	**Hartford Whalers**	**NHL**	**58**	**11**	**33**	**44**	**10**	**25**	**35**	**24**	**4**	**0**	**1**	**74**	**14.9**	**52**	**15**	**40**	**1**	**–2**	....	....	....	....	....	....	....	....
	Springfield Indians	AHL	4	0	9	9	....	....	....	0	....	....	....	....	....	....	....	....	....	....	....	....	....	....	....	....	....	....
	Calgary Flames	**NHL**	**15**	**2**	**9**	**11**	**2**	**7**	**9**	**6**	**0**	**0**	**0**	**21**	**9.5**	**18**	**2**	**6**	**0**	**+10**	**3**	**0**	**0**	**0**	**0**	**0**	**0**	**0**
1994-95	JyP HT Jyvaskyla	Finland	16	11	19	30	....	....	....	63	....	....	....	....	....	....	....	....	....	....	....	....	....	....	....	....	....	....
	Calgary Flames	**NHL**	**6**	**0**	**1**	**1**	**0**	**1**	**1**	**2**	**0**	**0**	**0**	**2**	**0.0**	**5**	**1**	**3**	**0**	**+1**	**6**	**0**	**6**	**6**	**2**	**0**	**0**	**0**
1995-96	**Calgary Flames**	**NHL**	**73**	**17**	**38**	**55**	**17**	**31**	**48**	**20**	**4**	**0**	**6**	**163**	**10.4**	**84**	**34**	**52**	**2**	**0**	**4**	**0**	**0**	**0**	**0**	**0**	**0**	**0**
	Sweden	WC-A	3	2	3	5	....	....	....	0	....	....	....	....	....	....	....	....	....	....	....	....	....	....	....	....	....	....
1996-97	Sweden	W Cup	4	2	1	3	....	....	....	0	....	....	....	....	....	....	....	....	....	....	....	....	....	....	....	....	....	....
	HC Lugano	Switz	36	12	43	55	....	....	....	28	....	....	....	....	....	....	....	....	....	....	8	3	8	11	8	....	....	....
	Sweden	WC-A	11	6	5	11	....	....	....	6	....	....	....	....	....	....	....	....	....	....	....	....	....	....	....	....	....	....
1997-98	**Calgary Flames**	**NHL**	**65**	**13**	**23**	**36**	**15**	**22**	**37**	**24**	**0**	**0**	**2**	**117**	**11.1**	**55**	**13**	**32**	**0**	**+10**	....	....	....	....	....	....	....	....
	Sweden	Olympics	4	0	0	0	....	....	....	6	....	....	....	....	....	....	....	....	....	....	....	....	....	....	....	....	....	....
	NHL Totals		**276**	**54**	**126**	**180**	**53**	**101**	**154**	**112**	**11**	**0**	**10**	**462**	**11.7**	**262**	**78**	**180**	**8**		**13**	**0**	**6**	**6**	**2**	**0**	**0**	**0**

WJC-A All-Star Team (1992) • Named Best Forward at WJC-A (1992) • Swedish Rookie of the Year (1992) • Swedish World All-Star Team (1996, 1997) • WC-A All-Star Team (1997) • Named Best Forward at WC-A (1997)

Traded to **Calgary** by **Hartford** with James Patrick and Zarley Zalapski for Gary Suter, Paul Ranheim and Ted Drury, March 10, 1994.

• NYLUND, GARY

Gary Nylund D – L. 6′4″, 210 lbs. b: Surrey, B.C., 10/28/1963. Toronto's 1st choice, 3rd overall, in 1982 Entry Draft.

Season	Club	League	GP	G	A	Pts	AG	AA	APts	PIM	PP	SH	GW	S	%	TGF	PGF	TGA	PGA	+/–	GP	G	A	Pts	PIM	PP	SH	GW
1978-79	Delta Islanders	BCJHL	57	6	29	35	....	....	....	107	....	....	....	....	....	....	....	....	....	....	....	....	....	....	....	....	....	....
	Portland Winter Hawks	WHL	2	0	0	0	....	....	....	0	....	....	....	....	....	....	....	....	....	....	....	....	....	....	....	....	....	....
1979-80	Portland Winter Hawks	WHL	72	5	21	26	....	....	....	59	....	....	....	....	....	....	....	....	....	....	8	0	1	1	2	....	....	....
1980-81	Portland Winter Hawks	WHL	70	6	40	46	....	....	....	186	....	....	....	....	....	....	....	....	....	....	9	1	7	8	17	....	....	....
1981-82	Portland Winter Hawks	WHL	65	7	59	66	....	....	....	267	....	....	....	....	....	....	....	....	....	....	15	3	16	19	74	....	....	....
	Canada	WJC-A	7	1	3	4	....	....	....	0	....	....	....	....	....	....	....	....	....	....	....	....	....	....	....	....	....	....
1982-83	**Toronto Maple Leafs**	**NHL**	**16**	**0**	**3**	**3**	**0**	**2**	**2**	**16**	**0**	**0**	**0**	**12**	**0.0**	**12**	**0**	**14**	**2**	**0**	....	....	....	....	....	....	....	....
1983-84	**Toronto Maple Leafs**	**NHL**	**47**	**2**	**14**	**16**	**2**	**9**	**11**	**103**	**0**	**0**	**0**	**71**	**2.8**	**57**	**3**	**109**	**28**	**–27**	....	....	....	....	....	....	....	....
1984-85	**Toronto Maple Leafs**	**NHL**	**76**	**3**	**17**	**20**	**2**	**11**	**13**	**99**	**0**	**0**	**0**	**61**	**4.9**	**64**	**1**	**138**	**38**	**–37**	....	....	....	....	....	....	....	....
1985-86	**Toronto Maple Leafs**	**NHL**	**79**	**2**	**16**	**18**	**2**	**11**	**13**	**180**	**0**	**0**	**0**	**84**	**2.4**	**108**	**1**	**182**	**46**	[illegible]	**10**	**0**	**2**	**2**	**25**	**0**	**0**	**0**
1986-87	**Chicago Blackhawks**	**NHL**	**80**	**7**	**20**	**27**	**6**	**14**	**20**	**190**	**2**	**0**	**0**	**123**	**5.7**	**97**	**11**	**128**	**33**	**–9**	**4**	**0**	**2**	**2**	**11**	**0**	**0**	**0**
1987-88	**Chicago Blackhawks**	**NHL**	**76**	**4**	**15**	**19**	**3**	**11**	**14**	**208**	**0**	**0**	**0**	**92**	**4.3**	**65**	**1**	**117**	**44**	**–9**	**5**	**0**	**0**	**0**	**10**	**0**	**0**	**0**
1988-89	**Chicago Blackhawks**	**NHL**	**23**	**3**	**2**	**5**	**3**	**1**	**4**	**63**	**0**	**0**	**0**	**26**	**11.5**	**12**	**2**	**28**	**14**	**–4**	....	....	....	....	....	....	....	....
	New York Islanders	**NHL**	**46**	**4**	**8**	**12**	**3**	**6**	**9**	**74**	**0**	**0**	**0**	**48**	**8.3**	**31**	**0**	**70**	**24**	**–15**	....	....	....	....	....	....	....	....
1989-90	**New York Islanders**	**NHL**	**64**	**4**	**21**	**25**	**3**	**15**	**18**	**144**	**2**	**0**	**0**	**65**	**6.2**	**69**	**7**	**80**	**26**	**+8**	**5**	**0**	**2**	**2**	**17**	**0**	**0**	**0**
1990-91	**New York Islanders**	**NHL**	**72**	**2**	**21**	**23**	**2**	**16**	**18**	**105**	**0**	**0**	**0**	**102**	**2.0**	**85**	**17**	**103**	**27**	**–8**	....	....	....	....	....	....	....	....
1991-92	**New York Islanders**	**NHL**	**7**	**0**	**1**	**1**	**0**	**1**	**1**	**10**	**0**	**0**	**0**	**5**	**0.0**	**7**	**2**	**10**	**2**	**–3**	....	....	....	....	....	....	....	....
	Capital District Islanders	AHL	4	0	0	0	....	....	....	0	....	....	....	....	....	....	....	....	....	....	....	....	....	....	....	....	....	....
1992-93	**New York Islanders**	**NHL**	**22**	**1**	**1**	**2**	**1**	**1**	**2**	**43**	**0**	**0**	**0**	**19**	**5.3**	**15**	**0**	**21**	**4**	**–2**	....	....	....	....	....	....	....	....
	Capital District Islanders	AHL	2	0	0	0	....	....	....	0	....	....	....	....	....	....	....	....	....	....	....	....	....	....	....	....	....	....
	NHL Totals		**608**	**32**	**139**	**171**	**27**	**98**	**125**	**1235**	**4**	**0**	**0**	**708**	**4.5**	**622**	**47**	**1000**	**287**		**24**	**0**	**6**	**6**	**63**	**0**	**0**	**0**

WHL First All-Star Team (1982) • Memorial Cup All-Star Team (1982)

Signed as a free agent by **Chicago**, August 27, 1986. Traded to **NY Islanders** by **Chicago** with Marc Bergevin for Steve Konroyd and Bob Bassen, November 25, 1988.

• NYROP, BILL

Bill Nyrop D – L. 6′2″, 205 lbs. b: Washington, DC, 7/23/1952. d: 1/1/1996. Montreal's 7th choice, 66th overall, in 1972 Amateur Draft. **USHOF**

Season	Club	League	GP	G	A	Pts	AG	AA	APts	PIM	PP	SH	GW	S	%	TGF	PGF	TGA	PGA	+/–	GP	G	A	Pts	PIM	PP	SH	GW
1970-71	University of Notre Dame	WCHA	30	2	4	6	....	....	....	40	....	....	....	....	....	....	....	....	....	....	....	....	....	....	....	....	....	....
1971-72	University of Notre Dame	WCHA	31	3	18	21	....	....	....	44	....	....	....	....	....	....	....	....	....	....	....	....	....	....	....	....	....	....
1972-73	University of Notre Dame	WCHA	38	3	21	24	....	....	....	46	....	....	....	....	....	....	....	....	....	....	....	....	....	....	....	....	....	....
1973-74	University of Notre Dame	WCHA	33	9	29	38	....	....	....	44	....	....	....	....	....	....	....	....	....	....	....	....	....	....	....	....	....	....
1974-75	Nova Scotia Voyageurs	AHL	75	2	22	24	....	....	....	76	....	....	....	....	....	....	....	....	....	....	6	0	5	5	0	....	....	....
1975-76	**Montreal Canadiens**	**NHL**	**19**	**0**	**3**	**3**	**0**	**2**	**2**	**8**	**0**	**0**	**0**	**23**	**0.0**	**28**	**1**	**9**	**3**	**+21**	**13**	**0**	**3**	**3**	**12**	**0**	**0**	**0**
	Nova Scotia Voyageurs	AHL	52	3	25	28	....	....	....	30	....	....	....	....	....	....	....	....	....	....	....	....	....	....	....	....	....	....
1976-77	United States	C Cup	5	1	1	2	....	....	....	0	....	....	....	....	....	....	....	....	....	....	....	....	....	....	....	....	....	....
	Montreal Canadiens	**NHL**	**74**	**3**	**19**	**22**	**3**	**15**	**18**	**21**	**0**	**0**	**1**	**47**	**6.4**	**85**	**0**	**46**	**3**	**+42**	**8**	**1**	**0**	**1**	**4**	**0**	**0**	**0**
1977-78	**Montreal Canadiens**	**NHL**	**72**	**5**	**21**	**26**	**5**	**17**	**22**	**37**	**1**	**2**	**1**	**69**	**7.2**	**108**	**1**	**62**	**11**	**+56**	**12**	**0**	**4**	**4**	**6**	**0**	**0**	**0**
1978-79			DID NOT PLAY – RETIRED																									
1979-80			DID NOT PLAY – RETIRED																									
1980-81	Minnesota North Stars	DN-Cup	3	2	1	3	....	....	....	0	....	....	....	....	....	....	....	....	....	....	....	....	....	....	....	....	....	....
1981-82	**Minnesota North Stars**	**NHL**	**42**	**4**	**8**	**12**	**3**	**5**	**8**	**35**	**0**	**1**	**1**	**25**	**16.0**	**59**	**1**	**52**	**8**	**+14**	**2**	**0**	**0**	**0**	**0**	**0**	**0**	**0**
1982-83	Kolner Haie	Germany	19	3	2	5	....	....	....	8	....	....	....	....	....	....	....	....	....	....	....	....	....	....	....	....	....	....
	NHL Totals		**207**	**12**	**51**	**63**	**11**	**39**	**50**	**101**	**1**	**3**	**3**	**164**	**7.3**	**280**	**3**	**169**	**25**		**35**	**1**	**7**	**8**	**22**	**0**	**0**	**0**

WCHA Second All-Star Team (1973) • NCAA West First All-American Team (1973) • WEC-B All-Star Team (1974)

Traded to **Minnesota** by **Montreal** for future considerations, September, 1980. Traded to **Calgary** by **Minnesota** with Steve Christoff and Minnesota's 2nd round choice (Dave Reierson) in 1982 Entry Draft for Willi Plett and Calgary's 4th round choice (Dusan Pasek) in 1982 Entry Draft, June 7, 1982

• NYSTROM, BOB

Bob Nystrom RW – R. 6′1″, 200 lbs. b: Stockholm, Sweden, 10/10/1952. NY Islanders' 3rd choice, 33rd overall, in 1972 Amateur Draft.

Season	Club	League	GP	G	A	Pts	AG	AA	APts	PIM	PP	SH	GW	S	%	TGF	PGF	TGA	PGA	+/–	GP	G	A	Pts	PIM	PP	SH	GW
1969-70	Kamloops Rockets	BCJHL	STATISTICS NOT AVAILABLE																									
1970-71	Calgary Centennials	WCJHL	66	15	16	31	....	....	....	153	....	....	....	....	....	....	....	....	....	....	10	2	3	5	32	....	....	....
1971-72	Calgary Centennials	WCJHL	64	27	25	52	....	....	....	178	....	....	....	....	....	....	....	....	....	....	11	3	6	9	27	....	....	....
1972-73	**New York Islanders**	**NHL**	**11**	**1**	**1**	**2**	**1**	**1**	**2**	**10**	**0**	**0**	**0**	**12**	**8.3**	**3**	**0**	**14**	**0**	**–11**	....	....	....	....	....	....	....	....
	New Haven Nighthawks	AHL	60	12	10	22	....	....	....	114	....	....	....	....	....	....	....	....	....	....	....	....	....	....	....	....	....	....
1973-74	**New York Islanders**	**NHL**	**77**	**21**	**20**	**41**	**21**	**17**	**38**	**118**	**3**	**0**	**5**	**176**	**11.9**	**57**	**7**	**67**	**0**	**–17**	....	....	....	....	....	....	....	....
1974-75	**New York Islanders**	**NHL**	**76**	**27**	**28**	**55**	**25**	**22**	**47**	**122**	**3**	**0**	**3**	**104**	**13.0**	**70**	**10**	**49**	**0**	**+17**	**17**	**1**	**3**	**4**	**27**	**0**	**0**	**0**
1975-76	**New York Islanders**	**NHL**	**80**	**23**	**25**	**48**	**21**	**20**	**41**	**106**	**2**	**0**	**4**	**185**	**12.4**	**72**	**6**	**42**	**0**	**+24**	**13**	**3**	**6**	**9**	**30**	**1**	**0**	**0**
1976-77	**New York Islanders**	**NHL**	**80**	**29**	**27**	**56**	**28**	**22**	**50**	**91**	**5**	**0**	**3**	**207**	**14.0**	**80**	**18**	**40**	**0**	**+22**	**12**	**0**	**2**	**2**	**7**	**0**	**0**	**0**
1977-78	**New York Islanders**	**NHL**	**80**	**30**	**29**	**59**	**29**	**24**	**53**	**94**	**3**	**0**	**6**	**178**	**16.9**	**85**	**6**	**60**	**0**	**+19**	**7**	**3**	**1**	**4**	**14**	**1**	**0**	**2**
1978-79	**New York Islanders**	**NHL**	**78**	**19**	**20**	**39**	**17**	**15**	**32**	**113**	**1**	**0**	**5**	**161**	**11.8**	**68**	**4**	**46**	**1**	**+19**	**10**	**3**	**2**	**5**	**4**	**0**	**0**	**1**
1979-80	**New York Islanders**	**NHL**	**67**	**21**	**18**	**39**	**19**	**14**	**33**	**94**	**2**	**0**	**4**	**146**	**14.4**	**52**	**6**	**42**	**0**	**+4**	**20**	**9**	**9**	**18**	**50**	**0**	**0**	**3**
1980-81	**New York Islanders**	**NHL**	**79**	**14**	**30**	**44**	**12**	**21**	**33**	**145**	**3**	**0**	**0**	**161**	**8.7**	**73**	**9**	**58**	**0**	**+6**	**18**	**6**	**6**	**12**	**20**	**0**	**0**	**1**
1981-82	**New York Islanders**	**NHL**	**74**	**22**	**25**	**47**	**17**	**17**	**34**	**103**	**0**	**0**	**4**	**136**	**16.2**	**69**	**3**	**53**	**0**	**+13**	**15**	**5**	**5**	**10**	**32**	**0**	**0**	**0**
1982-83	**New York Islanders**	**NHL**	**74**	**10**	**20**	**30**	**8**	**14**	**22**	**98**	**3**	**0**	**3**	**100**	**10.0**	**45**	**4**	**35**	**0**	**+6**	**20**	**7**	**6**	**13**	**15**	**0**	**0**	**0**

			REGULAR SEASON																		PLAYOFFS							
Season	Club	League	GP	G	A	Pts	AG	AA	APts	PIM	PP	SH	GW	S	%	TGF	PGF	TGA	PGA	+/–	GP	G	A	Pts	PIM	PP	SH	GW
1983-84	**New York Islanders**	**NHL**	**74**	**15**	**29**	**44**	**12**	**20**	**32**	**80**	**1**	**0**	**1**	**134**	**11.2**	**75**	**10**	**56**	**0**	**+9**	**15**	**0**	**2**	**2**	**8**	**0**	**0**	**0**
1984-85	**New York Islanders**	**NHL**	**36**	**2**	**5**	**7**	**2**	**3**	**5**	**58**	**0**	**0**	**0**	**18**	**11.1**	**18**	**1**	**11**	**0**	**+6**	**10**	**2**	**2**	**4**	**29**	**0**	**0**	**0**
1985-86	**New York Islanders**	**NHL**	**14**	**1**	**1**	**2**	**1**	**1**	**2**	**16**	**1**	**0**	**0**	**17**	**5.9**	**5**	**1**	**8**	**0**	**–4**	....	....	....	....	....	....	....	....
	NHL Totals		**900**	**235**	**278**	**513**	**213**	**211**	**424**	**1248**	**27**	**0**	**38**	**1825**	**12.9**	**778**	**85**	**581**	**1**		**157**	**39**	**44**	**83**	**236**	**2**	**0**	**7**

Played in NHL All-Star Game (1977)

● OATES, ADAM

Adam Oates C – R. 5'11", 185 lbs. b: Weston, Ont., 8/27/1962.

1982-83	RPI Engineers	ECAC	22	9	33	42	....	....	....	8	....	....	....	....	....	....	....	....	....	....	....	....	....	....	....	....	....	....
1983-84	RPI Engineers	ECAC	38	26	57	83	....	....	....	15	....	....	....	....	....	....	....	....	....	....	....	....	....	....	....	....	....	....
1984-85	RPI Engineers	ECAC	38	31	60	91	....	....	....	29	....	....	....	....	....	....	....	....	....	....	....	....	....	....	....	....	....	....
1985-86	**Detroit Red Wings**	**NHL**	**38**	**9**	**11**	**20**	**7**	**7**	**14**	**10**	**1**	**0**	**1**	**49**	**18.4**	**30**	**10**	**50**	**6**	**–24**	....	....	....	....	....	....	....	....
	Adirondack Red Wings	AHL	34	18	28	46	....	....	....	4	....	....	....	....	....	....	....	....	....	....	17	7	14	21	4	....	....	....
1986-87	**Detroit Red Wings**	**NHL**	**76**	**15**	**32**	**47**	**13**	**23**	**36**	**21**	**4**	**0**	**1**	**138**	**10.9**	**64**	**16**	**49**	**1**	**0**	**16**	**4**	**7**	**11**	**6**	**0**	**0**	**1**
1987-88	**Detroit Red Wings**	**NHL**	**63**	**14**	**40**	**54**	**12**	**28**	**40**	**20**	**3**	**0**	**3**	**111**	**12.6**	**75**	**19**	**41**	**1**	**+16**	**16**	**8**	**12**	**20**	**6**	**4**	**0**	**1**
1988-89	**Detroit Red Wings**	**NHL**	**69**	**16**	**62**	**78**	**14**	**44**	**58**	**14**	**2**	**0**	**1**	**127**	**12.6**	**106**	**43**	**64**	**0**	**–1**	**6**	**0**	**8**	**8**	**2**	**0**	**0**	**0**
1989-90	**St. Louis Blues**	**NHL**	**80**	**23**	**79**	**102**	**20**	**57**	**77**	**30**	**6**	**2**	**3**	**168**	**13.7**	**163**	**73**	**100**	**19**	**+9**	**12**	**2**	**12**	**14**	**4**	**1**	**0**	**0**
1990-91	**St. Louis Blues**	**NHL**	**61**	**25**	**90**	**115**	**23**	**69**	**92**	**29**	**3**	**1**	**3**	**139**	**18.0**	**144**	**55**	**78**	**4**	**+15**	**13**	**7**	**13**	**20**	**10**	**2**	**0**	**1**
1991-92	**St. Louis Blues**	**NHL**	**54**	**10**	**59**	**69**	**9**	**44**	**53**	**12**	**3**	**0**	**3**	**118**	**8.5**	**109**	**41**	**80**	**8**	**–4**	....	....	....	....	....	....	....	....
	Boston Bruins	**NHL**	**26**	**10**	**20**	**30**	**9**	**15**	**24**	**10**	**3**	**0**	**1**	**73**	**13.7**	**46**	**23**	**34**	**6**	**–5**	**15**	**5**	**14**	**19**	**4**	**3**	**0**	**2**
1992-93	**Boston Bruins**	**NHL**	**84**	**45**	***97**	**142**	**38**	**67**	**105**	**32**	**24**	**1**	**11**	**254**	**17.7**	**197**	**85**	**110**	**13**	**+15**	**4**	**0**	**9**	**9**	**4**	**0**	**0**	**0**
1993-94	**Boston Bruins**	**NHL**	**77**	**32**	**80**	**112**	**30**	**62**	**92**	**45**	**16**	**2**	**3**	**197**	**16.2**	**159**	**69**	**101**	**21**	**+10**	**13**	**3**	**9**	**12**	**8**	**2**	**0**	**0**
1994-95	**Boston Bruins**	**NHL**	**48**	**12**	**41**	**53**	**21**	**60**	**81**	**8**	**4**	**1**	**2**	**109**	**11.0**	**72**	**33**	**57**	**7**	**–11**	**5**	**1**	**0**	**1**	**2**	**1**	**0**	**0**
1995-96	**Boston Bruins**	**NHL**	**70**	**25**	**67**	**92**	**25**	**55**	**80**	**18**	**7**	**1**	**2**	**183**	**13.7**	**126**	**43**	**100**	**33**	**+16**	**5**	**2**	**5**	**7**	**2**	**0**	**1**	**0**
1996-97	**Boston Bruins**	**NHL**	**63**	**18**	**52**	**70**	**19**	**46**	**65**	**10**	**2**	**2**	**4**	**138**	**13.0**	**88**	**21**	**96**	**26**	**–3**	....	....	....	....	....	....	....	....
	Washington Capitals	**NHL**	**17**	**4**	**8**	**12**	**4**	**7**	**11**	**4**	**1**	**0**	**1**	**22**	**18.2**	**23**	**7**	**25**	**7**	**–2**	....	....	....	....	....	....	....	....
1997-98	**Washington Capitals**	**NHL**	**82**	**18**	**58**	**76**	**21**	**57**	**78**	**36**	**3**	**2**	**3**	**121**	**14.9**	**114**	**44**	**80**	**16**	**+6**	**21**	**6**	**11**	**17**	**8**	**1**	**1**	**1**
	NHL Totals		**908**	**276**	**796**	**1072**	**265**	**641**	**906**	**299**	**82**	**12**	**42**	**1947**	**14.2**	**1516**	**582**	**1065**	**168**		**126**	**38**	**100**	**138**	**56**	**14**	**2**	**6**

NCAA East First All-American Team (1984, 1985) • ECAC Second All-Star Team (1984) • ECAC First All-Star Team (1985) • NCAA Championship All-Tournament Team (1985) • NHL Second All-Star Team (1991)

Played in NHL All-Star Game (1991, 1992, 1993, 1994, 1997)

Signed as a free agent by **Detroit,** June 28, 1985. Traded to **St. Louis** by **Detroit** with Paul MacLean for Bernie Federko and Tony McKegney, June 15, 1989. Traded to **Boston** by **St. Louis** for Craig Janney and Stephane Quintal, February 7, 1992. Traded to **Washington** by **Boston** with Bill Ranford and Rick Tocchet for Jim Carey, Anson Carter, Jason Allison and Washington's 3rd round choice (Lee Goren) in 1997 Entry Draft, March 1, 1997.

● O'BRIEN, DENNIS

Dennis O'Brien D – L. 6', 195 lbs. b: Port Hope, Ont., 6/10/1949. Minnesota's 2nd choice, 14th overall, in 1969 Amateur Draft.

1967-68	Coborg Cougars	Jr. B	STATISTICS NOT AVAILABLE																									
1968-69	St. Catherines Black Hawks	OHA	52	1	19	20	....	....	....	*235	....	....	....	....	....	....	....	....	....	....	18	1	7	8	72	....	....	....
1969-70	Iowa Stars	CHL	72	2	18	20	....	....	....	*331	....	....	....	....	....	....	....	....	....	....	11	0	2	2	30	....	....	....
1970-71	**Minnesota North Stars**	**NHL**	**27**	**3**	**2**	**5**	**3**	**2**	**5**	**29**	**0**	**0**	**0**	**15**	**20.0**	**11**	**0**	**17**	**4**	**–2**	**9**	**0**	**0**	**0**	**20**	**0**	**0**	**0**
	Cleveland Barons	AHL	27	1	6	7	....	....	....	100	....	....	....	....	....	....	....	....	....	....	....	....	....	....	....	....	....	....
1971-72	**Minnesota North Stars**	**NHL**	**70**	**3**	**6**	**9**	**3**	**5**	**8**	**108**	**0**	**0**	**1**	**68**	**4.4**	**36**	**3**	**27**	**5**	**+11**	**3**	**0**	**1**	**1**	**11**	**0**	**0**	**0**
1972-73	**Minnesota North Stars**	**NHL**	**74**	**3**	**11**	**14**	**3**	**9**	**12**	**75**	**0**	**0**	**0**	**58**	**5.2**	**65**	**3**	**63**	**12**	**+11**	**6**	**1**	**0**	**1**	**38**	**0**	**0**	**0**
1973-74	**Minnesota North Stars**	**NHL**	**77**	**5**	**12**	**17**	**5**	**10**	**15**	**166**	**0**	**0**	**2**	**66**	**7.6**	**67**	**0**	**61**	**4**	**+10**	....	....	....	....	....	....	....	....
1974-75	**Minnesota North Stars**	**NHL**	**56**	**6**	**10**	**16**	**6**	**8**	**14**	**125**	**0**	**1**	**1**	**79**	**7.6**	**58**	**6**	**87**	**24**	**–11**	....	....	....	....	....	....	....	....
1975-76	**Minnesota North Stars**	**NHL**	**78**	**1**	**14**	**15**	**1**	**11**	**12**	**187**	**0**	**0**	**0**	**72**	**1.4**	**58**	**7**	**117**	**40**	**–26**	....	....	....	....	....	....	....	....
1976-77	**Minnesota North Stars**	**NHL**	**75**	**6**	**18**	**24**	**6**	**15**	**21**	**114**	**2**	**0**	**1**	**74**	**8.1**	**74**	**5**	**116**	**12**	**–35**	**2**	**0**	**0**	**0**	**4**	**0**	**0**	**0**
1977-78	**Minnesota North Stars**	**NHL**	**13**	**0**	**2**	**2**	**0**	**2**	**2**	**32**	**0**	**0**	**0**	**8**	**0.0**	**13**	**2**	**20**	**4**	**–5**	....	....	....	....	....	....	....	....
	Colorado Rockies	**NHL**	**16**	**0**	**2**	**2**	**0**	**2**	**2**	**12**	**0**	**0**	**0**	**9**	**0.0**	**8**	**0**	**19**	**1**	**–10**	....	....	....	....	....	....	....	....
	Cleveland Barons	**NHL**	**23**	**0**	**3**	**3**	**0**	**2**	**2**	**31**	**0**	**0**	**0**	**17**	**0.0**	**19**	**0**	**34**	**2**	**–13**	....	....	....	....	....	....	....	....
	Boston Bruins	**NHL**	**16**	**2**	**3**	**5**	**2**	**2**	**4**	**29**	**0**	**0**	**0**	**15**	**13.3**	**23**	**0**	**20**	**3**	**+6**	**14**	**0**	**1**	**1**	**28**	**0**	**0**	**0**
1978-79	**Boston Bruins**	**NHL**	**64**	**2**	**8**	**10**	**2**	**6**	**8**	**107**	**0**	**0**	**0**	**73**	**2.7**	**75**	**1**	**83**	**25**	**+16**	....	....	....	....	....	....	....	....
	Rochester Americans	AHL	2	0	0	0	....	....	....	2	....	....	....	....	....	....	....	....	....	....	....	....	....	....	....	....	....	....
1979-80	**Boston Bruins**	**NHL**	**3**	**0**	**0**	**0**	**0**	**0**	**0**	**2**	**0**	**0**	**0**	**2**	**0.0**	**0**	**0**	**4**	**0**	**–4**	....	....	....	....	....	....	....	....
	Binghamton Dusters	AHL	6	2	5	7	....	....	....	65	....	....	....	....	....	....	....	....	....	....	....	....	....	....	....	....	....	....
	NHL Totals		**592**	**31**	**91**	**122**	**31**	**74**	**105**	**1017**	**2**	**1**	**5**	**556**	**5.6**	**507**	**27**	**668**	**136**		**34**	**1**	**2**	**3**	**101**	**0**	**0**	**0**

Claimed on waivers by **Colorado** from **Minnesota**, December 2, 1977. Traded to **Cleveland** by **Colorado** for Mike Christie, January 12, 1978. Claimed on waivers by **Boston** from **Cleveland**, March 10, 1978.

● O'CALLAHAN, JACK

Jack O'Callahan D – R. 6'1", 190 lbs. b: Charleston, MA, 7/24/1957. Chicago's 5th choice, 96th overall, in 1977 Amateur Draft.

1976-77	Boston University	ECAC	31	1	23	24	....	....	....	90	....	....	....	....	....	....	....	....	....	....	....	....	....	....	....	....	....	....
1977-78	Boston University	ECAC	31	8	47	55	....	....	....	61	....	....	....	....	....	....	....	....	....	....	....	....	....	....	....	....	....	....
1978-79	Boston University	ECAC	29	6	16	22	....	....	....	72	....	....	....	....	....	....	....	....	....	....	....	....	....	....	....	....	....	....
	United States	WEC-A	8	0	1	1	....	....	....	12	....	....	....	....	....	....	....	....	....	....	....	....	....	....	....	....	....	....
1979-80	United States	Nat-Team	51	7	29	36	....	....	....	83	....	....	....	....	....	....	....	....	....	....	....	....	....	....	....	....	....	....
	United States	Olympics	4	0	1	1	....	....	....	2	....	....	....	....	....	....	....	....	....	....	....	....	....	....	....	....	....	....
1980-81	New Brunswick Hawks	AHL	78	9	25	34	....	....	....	167	....	....	....	....	....	....	....	....	....	....	13	1	6	7	36	....	....	....
1981-82	New Brunswick Hawks	AHL	79	15	33	48	....	....	....	130	....	....	....	....	....	....	....	....	....	....	15	2	6	8	24	....	....	....
1982-83	**Chicago Black Hawks**	**NHL**	**39**	**0**	**11**	**11**	**0**	**8**	**8**	**46**	**0**	**0**	**0**	**45**	**0.0**	**31**	**1**	**23**	**2**	**+9**	**5**	**0**	**2**	**2**	**2**	**0**	**0**	**0**
	Springfield Indians	AHL	35	2	24	26	....	....	....	25	....	....	....	....	....	....	....	....	....	....	....	....	....	....	....	....	....	....
1983-84	**Chicago Black Hawks**	**NHL**	**70**	**4**	**13**	**17**	**3**	**9**	**12**	**67**	**0**	**0**	**1**	**88**	**4.5**	**44**	**1**	**54**	**5**	**–6**	**2**	**0**	**0**	**0**	**2**	**0**	**0**	**0**
1984-85	**Chicago Black Hawks**	**NHL**	**66**	**6**	**8**	**14**	**5**	**5**	**10**	**105**	**0**	**0**	**1**	**70**	**8.6**	**58**	**2**	**64**	**14**	**+6**	**15**	**3**	**5**	**8**	**25**	**0**	**0**	**0**
1985-86	**Chicago Black Hawks**	**NHL**	**80**	**4**	**19**	**23**	**3**	**13**	**16**	**116**	**0**	**0**	**0**	**86**	**4.7**	**84**	**2**	**91**	**14**	**+5**	**3**	**0**	**1**	**1**	**4**	**0**	**0**	**0**
1986-87	**Chicago Blackhawks**	**NHL**	**48**	**1**	**13**	**14**	**1**	**9**	**10**	**59**	**1**	**0**	**0**	**65**	**1.5**	**59**	**2**	**53**	**6**	**+10**	**2**	**0**	**0**	**0**	**2**	**0**	**0**	**0**
1987-88	**New Jersey Devils**	**NHL**	**50**	**7**	**19**	**26**	**6**	**14**	**20**	**97**	**4**	**0**	**1**	**90**	**7.8**	**58**	**29**	**37**	**5**	**–3**	**5**	**1**	**3**	**4**	**6**	**0**	**0**	**0**
1988-89	**New Jersey Devils**	**NHL**	**36**	**5**	**21**	**26**	**4**	**15**	**19**	**51**	**5**	**0**	**0**	**96**	**5.2**	**49**	**33**	**16**	**0**	**0**	....	....	....	....	....	....	....	....
	United States	WEC-A	10	0	2	2	....	....	....	14	....	....	....	....	....	....	....	....	....	....	....	....	....	....	....	....	....	....
	NHL Totals		**389**	**27**	**104**	**131**	**22**	**73**	**95**	**541**	**10**	**0**	**3**	**540**	**5.0**	**383**	**70**	**338**	**46**		**32**	**4**	**11**	**15**	**41**	**0**	**0**	**0**

ECAC First All-Star Team (1978, 1979) • NCAA Championship All-Tournament Team (1978) • NCAA Championship Tournament MVP (1978) • NCAA East First All-American Team (1979)

Claimed by **New Jersey** from **Chicago** in Waiver Draft, October 5, 1987.

● O'CONNELL, MIKE

Mike O'Connell D – R. 5'9", 180 lbs. b: Chicago, IL, 11/25/1955. Chicago's 3rd choice, 43rd overall, in 1975 Amateur Draft.

1973-74	Kingston Canadians	OHA	70	16	43	59	....	....	....	81	....	....	....	....	....	....	....	....	....	....	....	....	....	....	....	....	....	....
1974-75	Kingston Canadians	OHA	50	18	55	73	....	....	....	47	....	....	....	....	....	....	....	....	....	....	8	1	3	4	8	....	....	....
1975-76	Dallas Black Hawks	CHL	70	6	37	43	....	....	....	50	....	....	....	....	....	....	....	....	....	....	10	2	*8	10	8	....	....	....
1976-77	Dallas Black Hawks	CHL	63	15	53	68	....	....	....	30	....	....	....	....	....	....	....	....	....	....	5	1	4	5	0	....	....	....
1977-78	**Chicago Black Hawks**	**NHL**	**6**	**1**	**1**	**2**	**1**	**1**	**2**	**2**	**0**	**0**	**0**	**7**	**14.3**	**4**	**0**	**4**	**0**	**0**	....	....	....	....	....	....	....	....
	Dallas Black Hawks	CHL	62	6	45	51	....	....	....	75	....	....	....	....	....	....	....	....	....	....	13	1	*11	12	8	....	....	....
1978-79	**Chicago Black Hawks**	**NHL**	**48**	**4**	**22**	**26**	**4**	**17**	**21**	**20**	**1**	**0**	**0**	**83**	**4.8**	**66**	**13**	**68**	**14**	**–1**	**4**	**0**	**0**	**0**	**4**	**0**	**0**	**0**
	New Brunswick Hawks	AHL	35	5	19	24	....	....	....	19	....	....	....	....	....	....	....	....	....	....	....	....	....	....	....	....	....	....
1979-80	**Chicago Black Hawks**	**NHL**	**78**	**8**	**22**	**30**	**7**	**17**	**24**	**52**	**2**	**0**	**2**	**158**	**5.1**	**85**	**17**	**93**	**23**	**–2**	**7**	**0**	**1**	**1**	**0**	**0**	**0**	**0**
1980-81	**Chicago Black Hawks**	**NHL**	**34**	**5**	**16**	**21**	**4**	**11**	**15**	**32**	**1**	**1**	**0**	**79**	**6.3**	**54**	**15**	**50**	**16**	**+5**	....	....	....	....	....	....	....	....
	Boston Bruins	**NHL**	**48**	**10**	**22**	**32**	**8**	**15**	**23**	**42**	**2**	**1**	**0**	**96**	**10.4**	**75**	**32**	**55**	**11**	**–1**	**3**	**1**	**3**	**4**	**2**	**0**	**1**	**0**
1981-82	United States	C Cup	4	1	3	4	....	....	....	2	....	....	....	....	....	....	....	....	....	....	....	....	....	....	....	....	....	....
	Boston Bruins	**NHL**	**80**	**5**	**34**	**39**	**4**	**22**	**26**	**75**	**1**	**0**	**0**	**170**	**2.9**	**142**	**33**	**130**	**29**	**+8**	**11**	**2**	**2**	**4**	**20**	**0**	**0**	**0**
1982-83	**Boston Bruins**	**NHL**	**80**	**14**	**39**	**53**	**11**	**27**	**38**	**42**	**7**	**1**	**5**	**168**	**8.3**	**153**	**46**	**90**	**27**	**+44**	**17**	**3**	**5**	**8**	**12**	**2**	**0**	**1**
1983-84	**Boston Bruins**	**NHL**	**75**	**18**	**42**	**60**	**14**	**28**	**42**	**42**	**9**	**0**	**1**	**194**	**9.3**	**151**	**52**	**116**	**35**	**+18**	**3**	**0**	**0**	**0**	**0**	**0**	**0**	**0**
1984-85	**Boston Bruins**	**NHL**	**78**	**15**	**40**	**55**	**12**	**27**	**39**	**64**	**8**	**0**	**2**	**257**	**5.8**	**149**	**55**	**119**	**28**	**+3**	**5**	**1**	**5**	**6**	**0**	**1**	**0**	**0**
	United States	WEC-A	8	1	0	1	....	....	....	2	....	....	....	....	....	....	....	....	....	....	....	....	....	....	....	....	....	....
1985-86	**Boston Bruins**	**NHL**	**63**	**8**	**21**	**29**	**6**	**14**	**20**	**47**	**4**	**1**	**0**	**174**	**4.6**	**99**	**39**	**94**	**26**	**–8**	....	....	....	....	....	....	....	....
	Detroit Red Wings	**NHL**	**13**	**1**	**7**	**8**	**1**	**5**	**6**	**16**	**0**	**1**	**0**	**38**	**2.6**	**23**	**10**	**23**	**4**	**–6**	....	....	....	....	....	....	....	....

			REGULAR SEASON																		PLAYOFFS							
Season	Club	League	GP	G	A	Pts	AG	AA	APts	PIM	PP	SH	GW	S	%	TGF	PGF	TGA	PGA	+/–	GP	G	A	Pts	PIM	PP	SH	GW
1986-87	**Detroit Red Wings**	**NHL**	77	5	26	31	4	19	23	70	3	1	0	141	3.5	104	37	117	25	–25	16	1	4	5	14	0	0	0
1987-88	**Detroit Red Wings**	**NHL**	48	6	13	19	5	9	14	38	0	0	0	68	8.8	71	15	53	21	+24	10	0	4	4	8	0	0	0
1988-89	**Detroit Red Wings**	**NHL**	66	1	15	16	1	11	12	41	0	0	0	49	2.0	79	15	104	32	–8	6	0	0	0	4	0	0	0
1989-90	**Detroit Red Wings**	**NHL**	66	4	14	18	3	10	13	22	0	0	0	57	7.0	68	6	109	35	–12	....	....	....	....	....	....	....	....
	NHL Totals		860	105	334	439	85	233	318	605	38	6	10	1739	6.0	1323	385	1225	326		82	8	24	32	64	3	1	1

OHA First All-Star Team (1975) • CHL First All-Star Team (1977) • Named CHL's Top Defenseman (1977)

Played in NHL All-Star Game (1984)

Traded to **Boston** by **Chicago** for Al Secord, December 18, 1980. Traded to **Detroit** by **Boston** for Reed Larson, March 10, 1986.

• O'CONNOR, MYLES

Myles O'Connor D – L. 5'11", 190 lbs. b: Calgary, Alta., 4/2/1967. St. Louis' 2nd choice, 44th overall, in 1985 Entry Draft.

Season	Club	League	GP	G	A	Pts	AG	AA	APts	PIM	PP	SH	GW	S	%	TGF	PGF	TGA	PGA	+/–	GP	G	A	Pts	PIM	PP	SH	GW
1984-85	Notre Dame Hounds	SJHL	40	20	35	55	....	....	....	40	....	....	....	....	....	....	....	....	....	....	....	....	....	....	....	....	....	....
1985-86	University of Michigan	CCHA	37	6	19	25	....	....	....	73	....	....	....	....	....	....	....	....	....	....	....	....	....	....	....	....	....	....
	Canada	Nat-Team	8	0	0	0	....	....	....	0	....	....	....	....	....	....	....	....	....	....	....	....	....	....	....	....	....	....
1986-87	University of Michigan	CCHA	39	15	39	54	....	....	....	111	....	....	....	....	....	....	....	....	....	....	....	....	....	....	....	....	....	....
1987-88	University of Michigan	CCHA	40	9	25	34	....	....	....	78	....	....	....	....	....	....	....	....	....	....	....	....	....	....	....	....	....	....
1988-89	University of Michigan	CCHA	40	3	31	34	....	....	....	91	....	....	....	....	....	....	....	....	....	....	....	....	....	....	....	....	....	....
	Utica Devils	AHL	1	0	0	0	....	....	....	0	....	....	....	....	....	....	....	....	....	....	....	....	....	....	....	....	....	....
1989-90	Utica Devils	AHL	76	14	33	47	....	....	....	124	....	....	....	....	....	....	....	....	....	....	5	1	2	3	26	....	....	....
1990-91	**New Jersey Devils**	**NHL**	22	3	1	4	3	1	4	41	0	0	0	14	21.4	16	1	15	3	+3	....	....	....	....	....	....	....	....
	Utica Devils	AHL	33	6	17	23	....	....	....	62	....	....	....	....	....	....	....	....	....	....	....	....	....	....	....	....	....	....
1991-92	**New Jersey Devils**	**NHL**	9	0	2	2	0	1	1	13	0	0	0	13	0.0	6	1	9	2	–2	....	....	....	....	....	....	....	....
	Utica Devils	AHL	66	9	39	48	....	....	....	184	....	....	....	....	....	....	....	....	....	....	....	....	....	....	....	....	....	....
1992-93	**New Jersey Devils**	**NHL**	7	0	0	0	0	0	0	9	0	0	0	4	0.0	3	0	10	3	–4	....	....	....	....	....	....	....	....
	Utica Devils	AHL	9	1	5	6	....	....	....	10	....	....	....	....	....	....	....	....	....	....	....	....	....	....	....	....	....	....
1993-94	**Anaheim Mighty Ducks**	**NHL**	5	0	1	1	0	1	1	6	0	0	0	7	0.0	3	0	3	0	0	....	....	....	....	....	....	....	....
	San Diego Gulls	IHL	39	1	13	14	....	....	....	117	....	....	....	....	....	....	....	....	....	....	9	1	4	5	83	....	....	....
1994-95	San Diego Gulls	IHL	16	1	4	5	....	....	....	50	....	....	....	....	....	....	....	....	....	....	5	0	1	1	0	....	....	....
1995-96	Houston Aeros	IHL	80	2	24	26	....	....	....	256	....	....	....	....	....	....	....	....	....	....	....	....	....	....	....	....	....	....
1996-97	Houston Aeros	IHL	3	0	0	0	....	....	....	6	....	....	....	....	....	....	....	....	....	....	....	....	....	....	....	....	....	....
	Cincinnati Cyclones	IHL	62	0	4	4	....	....	....	241	....	....	....	....	....	....	....	....	....	....	3	0	0	0	34	....	....	....
1997-98	Kushiro Cranes	Japan	31	4	11	15	....	....	....	107	....	....	....	....	....	....	....	....	....	....	....	....	....	....	....	....	....	....
	NHL Totals		43	3	4	7	3	3	6	69	0	0	0	38	7.9	28	2	37	8		....	....	....	....	....	....	....	....

CCHA First All-Star Team (1989) • NCAA West First All-American Team (1989)

Signed as a free agent by **Anaheim**, July 22, 1993.

• ODDLEIFSON, CHRIS

Chris Oddleifson C – R. 6'2", 185 lbs. b: Brandon, Man., 9/7/1950. California's 1st choice, 10th overall, in 1970 Amateur Draft.

Season	Club	League	GP	G	A	Pts	AG	AA	APts	PIM	PP	SH	GW	S	%	TGF	PGF	TGA	PGA	+/–	GP	G	A	Pts	PIM	PP	SH	GW
1968-69	Winnipeg Jets	WCJHL	46	14	30	44	....	....	....	118	....	....	....	....	....	....	....	....	....	....	....	....	....	....	....	....	....	....
1969-70	Winnipeg Jets	WCJHL	59	31	*64	95	....	....	....	243	....	....	....	....	....	....	....	....	....	....	....	....	....	....	....	....	....	....
1970-71	Providence Reds	AHL	66	15	42	57	....	....	....	95	....	....	....	....	....	....	....	....	....	....	10	1	4	5	25	....	....	....
1971-72	Oklahoma City Blazers	CHL	68	18	44	62	....	....	....	134	....	....	....	....	....	....	....	....	....	....	6	0	2	2	12	....	....	....
1972-73	**Boston Bruins**	**NHL**	6	0	0	0	0	0	0	0	0	0	0	1	0.0	0	0	1	0	–1	....	....	....	....	....	....	....	....
	Boston Braves	AHL	63	12	42	54	....	....	....	127	....	....	....	....	....	....	....	....	....	....	10	3	6	9	41	....	....	....
1973-74	**Boston Bruins**	**NHL**	49	10	11	21	10	9	19	25	0	0	1	63	15.9	32	0	18	2	+16	....	....	....	....	....	....	....	....
	Vancouver Canucks	**NHL**	21	3	5	8	3	4	7	19	1	0	1	22	13.6	14	2	20	8	0	....	....	....	....	....	....	....	....
1974-75	**Vancouver Canucks**	**NHL**	60	16	35	51	15	28	43	54	3	0	2	74	21.6	68	13	53	15	+17	5	0	3	3	2	0	0	0
1975-76	**Vancouver Canucks**	**NHL**	80	16	46	62	15	36	51	88	2	2	1	133	12.0	94	27	72	22	+17	2	1	2	3	0	0	0	0
1976-77	**Vancouver Canucks**	**NHL**	80	14	26	40	13	21	34	81	3	1	0	99	14.1	64	16	84	18	18	....	....	....	....	....	....	....	....
1977-78	**Vancouver Canucks**	**NHL**	78	17	22	39	16	18	34	64	2	1	2	91	18.7	60	9	91	22	–18	....	....	....	....	....	....	....	....
1978-79	**Vancouver Canucks**	**NHL**	67	11	26	37	10	20	30	51	4	0	1	83	13.3	54	10	80	21	–15	3	0	1	1	2	0	0	0
1979-80	**Vancouver Canucks**	**NHL**	75	8	20	28	7	15	22	76	1	1	0	62	12.9	45	4	90	40	–9	4	0	0	0	4	0	0	0
1980-81	**Vancouver Canucks**	**NHL**	8	0	0	0	0	0	0	6	0	0	0	3	0.0	0	0	3	2	–1	....	....	....	....	....	....	....	....
	Dallas Black Hawks	CHL	46	12	36	48	....	....		30	....	....	....	....	....	....	....	....	....	....	5	0	3	3	0	....	....	....
	NHL Totals		524	95	191	286	89	151	240	464	16	5	8	631	15.1	431	01	512	150		14	1	6	7	8	0	0	0

WCJHL First All-Star Team (1970)

Traded to **Boston** by **California** with Richard Leduc for Ivan Boldirev, November 17, 1971. Traded to **Vancouver** by **Boston** with Fred O'Donnell for Bobby Schmautz, February 7, 1974.

• ODELEIN, LYLE

Lyle Odelein D – R. 5'11", 210 lbs. b: Quill Lake, Sask., 7/21/1968. Montreal's 8th choice, 141st overall, in 1986 Entry Draft.

Season	Club	League	GP	G	A	Pts	AG	AA	APts	PIM	PP	SH	GW	S	%	TGF	PGF	TGA	PGA	+/–	GP	G	A	Pts	PIM	PP	SH	GW
1985-86	Moose Jaw Warriors	WHL	67	9	37	46	....	....	....	117	....	....	....	....	....	....	....	....	....	....	13	1	6	7	34	....	....	....
1986-87	Moose Jaw Warriors	WHL	59	9	50	59	....	....	....	70	....	....	....	....	....	....	....	....	....	....	9	2	5	7	26	....	....	....
1987-88	Moose Jaw Warriors	WHL	63	15	43	58	....	....	....	166	....	....	....	....	....	....	....	....	....	....	....	....	....	....	....	....	....	....
1988-89	Sherbrooke Canadiens	AHL	33	3	4	7	....	....	....	120	....	....	....	....	....	....	....	....	....	....	....	....	....	....	....	....	....	....
	Peoria Rivermen	IHL	36	2	8	10	....	....	....	116	....	....	....	....	....	....	....	....	....	....	3	0	2	2	5	....	....	....
1989-90	**Montreal Canadiens**	**NHL**	8	0	2	2	0	1	1	33	0	0	0	1	0.0	5	0	6	0	–1	....	....	....	....	....	....	....	....
	Sherbrooke Canadiens	AHL	68	7	24	31	....	....	....	265	....	....	....	....	....	....	....	....	....	....	12	6	5	11	79	....	....	....
1990-91	Montreal Canadiens	FrTour	2	0	0	0	....	....	....	2	....	....	....	....	....	....	....	....	....	....	....	....	....	....	....	....	....	....
	Montreal Canadiens	**NHL**	52	0	2	2	0	2	2	259	0	0	0	25	0.0	36	1	34	6	+7	12	0	0	0	54	0	0	0
1991-92	**Montreal Canadiens**	**NHL**	71	1	7	8	1	5	6	212	0	0	0	43	2.3	42	0	32	5	+15	7	0	0	0	11	0	0	0
1992-93	**Montreal Canadiens**	**NHL**	83	2	14	16	2	10	12	205	0	0	0	79	2.5	86	0	69	18	+35	20	1	5	6	30	0	0	0
1993-94	**Montreal Canadiens**	**NHL**	79	11	29	40	10	22	32	276	6	0	2	116	9.5	100	31	87	26	+8	7	0	0	0	17	0	0	0
1994-95	**Montreal Canadiens**	**NHL**	48	3	7	10	5	10	15	152	0	0	0	74	4.1	37	4	54	8	–13	....	....	....	....	....	....	....	....
1995-96	**Montreal Canadiens**	**NHL**	79	3	14	17	3	11	14	230	0	1	0	74	4.1	67	3	72	16	+8	6	1	1	2	6	0	1	0
1996-97	Canada	W Cup	2	0	0	0	....	....	....	0	....	....	....	....	....	....	....	....	....	....	....	....	....	....	....	....	....	....
	New Jersey Devils	**NHL**	79	3	13	16	3	11	14	110	1	0	2	93	3.2	75	10	54	5	+16	10	2	2	4	19	1	0	0
1997-98	**New Jersey Devils**	**NHL**	79	4	19	23	5	19	24	171	1	0	0	76	5.3	71	13	64	17	+11	6	1	1	2	21	1	0	1
	NHL Totals		578	27	107	134	29	91	120	1648	8	1	4	581	4.6	519	62	472	101		68	5	9	14	158	2	1	1

Traded to **New Jersey** by **Montreal** for Stephane Richer, August 22, 1996.

• ODELEIN, SELMAR

Selmar Odelein D – R. 6', 195 lbs. b: Quill Lake, Sask., 4/11/1966. Edmonton's 1st choice, 21st overall, in 1984 Entry Draft.

Season	Club	League	GP	G	A	Pts	AG	AA	APts	PIM	PP	SH	GW	S	%	TGF	PGF	TGA	PGA	+/–	GP	G	A	Pts	PIM	PP	SH	GW
1982-83	Regina Canadians	SJHL	70	30	84	114	....	....	....	38	....	....	....	....	....	....	....	....	....	....	....	....	....	....	....	....	....	....
1983-84	Regina Pats	WHL	71	9	42	51	....	....	....	45	....	....	....	....	....	....	....	....	....	....	23	4	11	15	45	....	....	....
1984-85	Regina Pats	WHL	64	24	35	59	....	....	....	121	....	....	....	....	....	....	....	....	....	....	8	2	2	4	13	....	....	....
	Canada	WJC-A	7	1	5	6	....	....	....	8	....	....	....	....	....	....	....	....	....	....	....	....	....	....	....	....	....	....
1985-86	Regina Pats	WHL	36	13	28	41	....	....	....	57	....	....	....	....	....	....	....	....	....	....	8	5	2	7	24	....	....	....
	Canada	WJC-A	7	0	1	1	....	....	....	6	....	....	....	....	....	....	....	....	....	....	....	....	....	....	....	....	....	....
	Edmonton Oilers	**NHL**	4	0	0	0	0	0	0	0	0	0	0	2	0.0	3	0	2	0	+1	....	....	....	....	....	....	....	....
1986-87	Nova Scotia Oilers	AHL	2	0	1	1	....	....	....	2	....	....	....	....	....	....	....	....	....	....	....	....	....	....	....	....	....	....
1987-88	**Edmonton Oilers**	**NHL**	12	0	2	2	0	1	1	33	0	0	0	17	0.0	11	2	12	1	–2	....	....	....	....	....	....	....	....
	Nova Scotia Oilers	AHL	43	9	14	23	....	....	....	75	....	....	....	....	....	....	....	....	....	....	5	0	1	1	31	....	....	....
1988-89	**Edmonton Oilers**	**NHL**	2	0	0	0	0	0	0	2	0	0	0	0	0.0	1	0	2	0	–1	....	....	....	....	....	....	....	....
	Cape Breton Oilers	AHL	63	8	21	29	....	....	....	150	....	....	....	....	....	....	....	....	....	....	....	....	....	....	....	....	....	....
1989-90	Canada	Nat-Team	73	7	30	37	....	....	....	69	....	....	....	....	....	....	....	....	....	....	....	....	....	....	....	....	....	....
1990-91	IEV Innsbruck	Austria	38	9	21	30	....	....	....	....	....	....	....	....	....	....	....	....	....	....	....	....	....	....	....	....	....	....
1991-92	VEU Feldkirch	Austria	29	9	18	27	....	....	....	....	....	....	....	....	....	....	....	....	....	....	....	....	....	....	....	....	....	....
1992-93	Nottingham Panthers	Britain	23	17	18	35	....	....	....	48	....	....	....	....	....	....	....	....	....	....	7	5	10	15	12	....	....	....
1993-94	Sheffield Steelers	Britain	25	5	21	26	....	....	....	28	....	....	....	....	....	....	....	....	....	....	4	0	4	4	6	....	....	....
	NHL Totals		18	0	2	2	0	1	1	35	0	0	0	19	0.0	15	2	16	1		....	....	....	....	....	....	....	....

• ODGERS, JEFF

Jeff Odgers RW – R. 6', 200 lbs. b: Spy Hill, Sask., 5/31/1969.

Season	Club	League	GP	G	A	Pts	AG	AA	APts	PIM	PP	SH	GW	S	%	TGF	PGF	TGA	PGA	+/–	GP	G	A	Pts	PIM	PP	SH	GW
			REGULAR SEASON																		PLAYOFFS							
1986-87	Brandon Wheat Kings	WHL	70	7	14	21	....	....	....	150	....	....	....	....	....	....	....	....	....	....	....	....	....	....	....	....	....	....
1987-88	Brandon Wheat Kings	WHL	70	17	18	35	....	....	....	202	....	....	....	....	....	....	....	....	....	....	4	1	1	2	14	....	....	....
1988-89	Brandon Wheat Kings	WHL	71	31	29	60	....	....	....	277	....	....	....	....	....	....	....	....	....	....	....	....	....	....	....	....	....	....
1989-90	Brandon Wheat Kings	WHL	64	37	28	65	....	....	....	209	....	....	....	....	....	....	....	....	....	....	....	....	....	....	....	....	....	....
1990-91	Kansas City Blades	IHL	77	12	19	31	....	....	....	318	....	....	....	....	....	....	....	....	....	....	....	....	....	....	....	....	....	....
1991-92	**San Jose Sharks**	**NHL**	**61**	**7**	**4**	**11**	**6**	**3**	**9**	**217**	**0**	**0**	**0**	**64**	**10.9**	**19**	**2**	**39**	**1**	**–21**	....	....	....	....	....	....	....	....
	Kansas City Blades	IHL	12	2	2	4	....	....	....	56	....	....	....	....	....	....	....	....	....	....	4	2	1	3	0	....	....	....
1992-93	**San Jose Sharks**	**NHL**	**66**	**12**	**15**	**27**	**10**	**10**	**20**	**253**	**6**	**0**	**0**	**100**	**12.0**	**47**	**16**	**57**	**0**	**–26**	....	....	....	....	....	....	....	....
1993-94	**San Jose Sharks**	**NHL**	**81**	**13**	**8**	**21**	**12**	**6**	**18**	**222**	**7**	**0**	**0**	**73**	**17.8**	**36**	**19**	**31**	**1**	**–13**	**11**	**0**	**0**	**0**	**11**	**0**	**0**	**0**
1994-95	**San Jose Sharks**	**NHL**	**48**	**4**	**3**	**7**	**7**	**4**	**11**	**117**	**0**	**0**	**1**	**47**	**8.5**	**11**	**0**	**19**	**0**	**–8**	**11**	**1**	**1**	**2**	**23**	**0**	**0**	**0**
1995-96	**San Jose Sharks**	**NHL**	**78**	**12**	**4**	**16**	**12**	**3**	**15**	**192**	**0**	**0**	**1**	**84**	**14.3**	**26**	**0**	**31**	**1**	**–4**	....	....	....	....	....	....	....	....
1996-97	**Boston Bruins**	**NHL**	**80**	**7**	**8**	**15**	**7**	**7**	**14**	**197**	**1**	**0**	**1**	**84**	**8.3**	**22**	**5**	**32**	**0**	**–15**	....	....	....	....	....	....	....	....
1997-98	**Colorado Avalanche**	**NHL**	**68**	**5**	**8**	**13**	**6**	**8**	**14**	**213**	**0**	**0**	**0**	**47**	**10.6**	**17**	**0**	**12**	**0**	**+5**	**6**	**0**	**0**	**0**	**25**	**0**	**0**	**0**
	Providence Bruins	AHL	4	0	0	0	....	....	....	31	....	....	....	....	....	....	....	....	....	....	....	....	....	....	....	....	....	....
	NHL Totals		**482**	**60**	**50**	**110**	**60**	**41**	**101**	**1411**	**14**	**0**	**3**	**499**	**12.0**	**178**	**42**	**221**	**3**		**28**	**1**	**1**	**2**	**59**	**0**	**0**	**0**

Signed as a free agent by **San Jose**, September 3, 1991. Traded to **Boston** by **San Jose** with Pittsburgh's 5th round choice (previously acquired by San Jose — Boston selected Elias Abrahamsson) in 1996 Entry Draft for Al Iafrate, June 21, 1996.

• ODJICK, GINO

Gino Odjick LW – L. 6'3", 210 lbs. b: Maniwaki, Que., 9/7/1970. Vancouver's 5th choice, 86th overall, in 1990 Entry Draft.

Season	Club	League	GP	G	A	Pts	AG	AA	APts	PIM	PP	SH	GW	S	%	TGF	PGF	TGA	PGA	+/–	GP	G	A	Pts	PIM	PP	SH	GW
1988-89	Laval Titan	QMJHL	50	9	15	24	....	....	....	278	....	....	....	....	....	....	....	....	....	....	16	0	9	9	129	....	....	....
1989-90	Laval Titan	QMJHL	51	12	26	38	....	....	....	280	....	....	....	....	....	....	....	....	....	....	....	....	....	....	....	....	....	....
1990-91	**Vancouver Canucks**	**NHL**	**45**	**7**	**1**	**8**	**6**	**1**	**7**	**296**	**0**	**0**	**0**	**39**	**17.9**	**12**	**0**	**18**	**0**	**–6**	**6**	**0**	**0**	**0**	**18**	**0**	**0**	**0**
	Milwaukee Admirals	IHL	17	7	3	10	....	....	....	102	....	....	....	....	....	....	....	....	....	....	....	....	....	....	....	....	....	....
1991-92	**Vancouver Canucks**	**NHL**	**65**	**4**	**6**	**10**	**4**	**4**	**8**	**348**	**0**	**0**	**0**	**68**	**5.9**	**16**	**1**	**16**	**0**	**–1**	**4**	**0**	**0**	**0**	**6**	**0**	**0**	**0**
1992-93	**Vancouver Canucks**	**NHL**	**75**	**4**	**13**	**17**	**3**	**9**	**12**	**370**	**0**	**0**	**1**	**79**	**5.1**	**28**	**2**	**23**	**0**	**+3**	**1**	**0**	**0**	**0**	**0**	**0**	**0**	**0**
1993-94	**Vancouver Canucks**	**NHL**	**76**	**16**	**13**	**29**	**15**	**10**	**25**	**271**	**4**	**0**	**5**	**121**	**13.2**	**48**	**8**	**28**	**1**	**+13**	**10**	**0**	**0**	**0**	**18**	**0**	**0**	**0**
1994-95	**Vancouver Canucks**	**NHL**	**23**	**4**	**5**	**9**	**7**	**7**	**14**	**109**	**0**	**0**	**0**	**35**	**11.4**	**12**	**2**	**13**	**0**	**–3**	**5**	**0**	**0**	**0**	**47**	**0**	**0**	**0**
1995-96	**Vancouver Canucks**	**NHL**	**55**	**3**	**4**	**7**	**3**	**3**	**6**	**181**	**0**	**0**	**0**	**59**	**5.1**	**11**	**0**	**27**	**0**	**–16**	**6**	**3**	**1**	**4**	**6**	**0**	**0**	**2**
1996-97	**Vancouver Canucks**	**NHL**	**70**	**5**	**8**	**13**	**5**	**7**	**12**	***371**	**1**	**0**	**0**	**85**	**5.9**	**22**	**3**	**24**	**0**	**–5**	....	....	....	....	....	....	....	....
1997-98	**Vancouver Canucks**	**NHL**	**35**	**3**	**2**	**5**	**4**	**2**	**6**	**181**	**0**	**0**	**1**	**36**	**8.3**	**9**	**0**	**12**	**0**	**–3**	....	....	....	....	....	....	....	....
	New York Islanders	**NHL**	**13**	**0**	**0**	**0**	**0**	**0**	**0**	**31**	**0**	**0**	**0**	**16**	**0.0**	**4**	**2**	**1**	**0**	**+1**	....	....	....	....	....	....	....	....
	NHL Totals		**457**	**46**	**52**	**98**	**47**	**43**	**90**	**2158**	**5**	**0**	**7**	**538**	**8.6**	**162**	**18**	**162**	**1**		**32**	**3**	**1**	**4**	**95**	**0**	**0**	**2**

Traded to **NY Islanders** by **Vancouver** for Jason Strudwick, March 23, 1998.

• O'DONNELL, FRED

Fred O'Donnell RW – R. 5'10", 175 lbs. b: Kingston, Ont., 12/6/1949. Minnesota's 4th choice, 37th overall, in 1969 Amateur Draft.

Season	Club	League	GP	G	A	Pts	AG	AA	APts	PIM	PP	SH	GW	S	%	TGF	PGF	TGA	PGA	+/–	GP	G	A	Pts	PIM	PP	SH	GW
1966-67	Oshawa Generals	OHA	36	6	9	15	....	....	....	44	....	....	....	....	....	....	....	....	....	....	....	....	....	....	....	....	....	....
1967-68	Oshawa Generals	OHA	44	24	14	38	....	....	....	72	....	....	....	....	....	....	....	....	....	....	....	....	....	....	....	....	....	....
1968-69	Oshawa Generals	OHA	54	31	27	58	....	....	....	124	....	....	....	....	....	....	....	....	....	....	....	....	....	....	....	....	....	....
1969-70	Kingston Aces	OHA Sr.	36	16	22	38	....	....	....	76	....	....	....	....	....	....	....	....	....	....	....	....	....	....	....	....	....	....
	Oklahoma City Blazers	CHL	2	2	2	4	....	....	....	0	....	....	....	....	....	....	....	....	....	....	....	....	....	....	....	....	....	....
1970-71	Oklahoma City Blazers	CHL	67	23	23	46	....	....	....	158	....	....	....	....	....	....	....	....	....	....	5	4	1	5	30	....	....	....
1971-72	Boston Braves	AHL	62	16	22	38	....	....	....	161	....	....	....	....	....	....	....	....	....	....	....	....	....	....	....	....	....	....
1972-73	**Boston Bruins**	**NHL**	**72**	**10**	**4**	**14**	**10**	**3**	**13**	**55**	**0**	**0**	**2**	**56**	**17.9**	**19**	**0**	**17**	**1**	**+3**	**5**	**0**	**1**	**1**	**5**	**0**	**0**	**0**
1973-74	**Boston Bruins**	**NHL**	**43**	**5**	**7**	**12**	**5**	**6**	**11**	**43**	**0**	**0**	**1**	**39**	**12.8**	**20**	**0**	**17**	**0**	**+3**	....	....	....	....	....	....	....	....
1974-75	New England Whalers	WHA	76	20	16	36	....	....	....	84	....	....	....	....	....	....	....	....	....	....	3	0	0	0	15	....	....	....
1975-76	New England Whalers	WHA	79	11	11	22	....	....	....	81	....	....	....	....	....	....	....	....	....	....	17	2	5	7	20	....	....	....
	NHL Totals		**115**	**15**	**11**	**26**	**15**	**9**	**24**	**98**	**0**	**0**	**3**	**95**	**15.8**	**39**	**0**	**34**	**1**		**5**	**0**	**1**	**1**	**5**	**0**	**0**	**0**
	Other Major League Totals		155	31	27	58	....	....	....	165	....	....	....	....	....	....	....	....	....		20	2	5	7	35	....	....	....

Rights traded to **Boston** by **Minnesota** to complete transaction that sent Barry Gibbs and Tommy Williams to Boston (June, 1969), May 7, 1971. Selected by **Winnipeg** (WHA) in 1972 WHA General Player Draft, February 1972. WHA rights traded to **New England** (WHA) by **Winnipeg** (WHA) for future considerations, June, 1972. Traded to **Vancouver** by **Boston** with Chris Oddleifson for Bobby Schmautz, February 7, 1974. • Suspended by **Vancouver** for refusing to report to NHL club after trade from Boston, February 9, 1974. Traded to **Cleveland** (WHA) by **New England** (WHA) with Bob McManama for Wayne Connelly, June, 1976.

• O'DONNELL, SEAN

Sean "O.D." O'Donnell D – L. 6'3", 225 lbs. b: Ottawa, Ont., 10/13/1971. Buffalo's 6th choice, 123rd overall, in 1991 Entry Draft.

Season	Club	League	GP	G	A	Pts	AG	AA	APts	PIM	PP	SH	GW	S	%	TGF	PGF	TGA	PGA	+/–	GP	G	A	Pts	PIM	PP	SH	GW
1990-91	Sudbury Wolves	OHL	66	8	23	31	....	....	....	114	....	....	....	....	....	....	....	....	....	....	5	1	4	5	10	....	....	....
1991-92	Rochester Americans	AHL	73	4	9	13	....	....	....	193	....	....	....	....	....	....	....	....	....	....	16	1	2	3	21	....	....	....
1992-93	Rochester Americans	AHL	74	3	18	21	....	....	....	203	....	....	....	....	....	....	....	....	....	....	17	1	6	7	38	....	....	....
1993-94	Rochester Americans	AHL	64	2	10	12	....	....	....	242	....	....	....	....	....	....	....	....	....	....	4	0	1	1	21	....	....	....
1994-95	Phoenix Roadrunners	IHL	61	2	18	20	....	....	....	132	....	....	....	....	....	....	....	....	....	....	9	0	1	1	21	....	....	....
	Los Angeles Kings	**NHL**	**15**	**0**	**2**	**2**	**0**	**3**	**3**	**49**	**0**	**0**	**0**	**12**	**0.0**	**7**	**0**	**14**	**5**	**–2**	....	....	....	....	....	....	....	....
1995-96	**Los Angeles Kings**	**NHL**	**71**	**2**	**5**	**7**	**2**	**4**	**6**	**127**	**0**	**0**	**0**	**65**	**3.1**	**58**	**3**	**79**	**27**	**+3**	....	....	....	....	....	....	....	....
1996-97	**Los Angeles Kings**	**NHL**	**55**	**5**	**12**	**17**	**5**	**11**	**16**	**144**	**2**	**0**	**0**	**68**	**7.4**	**44**	**7**	**61**	**11**	**–13**	....	....	....	....	....	....	....	....
1997-98	**Los Angeles Kings**	**NHL**	**80**	**2**	**15**	**17**	**2**	**15**	**17**	**179**	**0**	**0**	**1**	**71**	**2.8**	**63**	**7**	**70**	**21**	**+7**	**4**	**1**	**0**	**1**	**36**	**0**	**0**	**0**
	NHL Totals		**221**	**9**	**34**	**43**	**9**	**33**	**42**	**499**	**2**	**0**	**1**	**216**	**4.2**	**172**	**17**	**224**	**64**		**4**	**1**	**0**	**1**	**36**	**0**	**0**	**0**

Traded to **LA Kings** by **Buffalo** for Doug Houda, July 26, 1994.

• O'DONOGHUE, DON

Don O'Donoghue RW – R. 5'10", 180 lbs. b: Kingston, Ont., 8/27/1949. Oakland's 3rd choice, 29th overall, in 1969 Amateur Draft.

Season	Club	League	GP	G	A	Pts	AG	AA	APts	PIM	PP	SH	GW	S	%	TGF	PGF	TGA	PGA	+/–	GP	G	A	Pts	PIM	PP	SH	GW
1967-68	St. Catharines Black Hawks	OHA	54	5	15	20	....	....	....	12	....	....	....	....	....	....	....	....	....	....	5	0	1	1	2	....	....	....
1968-69	St. Catharines Black Hawks	OHA	45	9	12	21	....	....	....	61	....	....	....	....	....	....	....	....	....	....	18	4	3	7	32	....	....	....
1969-70	**Oakland Seals**	**NHL**	**68**	**5**	**6**	**11**	**6**	**6**	**12**	**21**	**0**	**0**	**1**	**55**	**9.1**	**16**	**2**	**47**	**7**	**–26**	**3**	**0**	**0**	**0**	**0**	**0**	**0**	**0**
1970-71	**California Golden Seals**	**NHL**	**43**	**11**	**9**	**20**	**11**	**8**	**19**	**10**	**3**	**1**	**0**	**63**	**17.5**	**28**	**7**	**64**	**23**	**–20**	....	....	....	....	....	....	....	....
	Providence Reds	AHL	25	9	8	17	....	....	....	20	....	....	....	....	....	....	....	....	....	....	....	....	....	....	....	....	....	....
1971-72	**California Golden Seals**	**NHL**	**14**	**2**	**2**	**4**	**2**	**2**	**4**	**4**	**0**	**0**	**0**	**11**	**18.2**	**6**	**0**	**11**	**1**	**–4**	....	....	....	....	....	....	....	....
	Baltimore Clippers	AHL	23	3	6	9	....	....	....	10	....	....	....	....	....	....	....	....	....	....	....	....	....	....	....	....	....	....
	Boston Braves	AHL	16	0	3	3	....	....	....	0	....	....	....	....	....	....	....	....	....	....	9	0	1	1	7	....	....	....
1972-73	Philadelphia Blazers	WHA	74	16	23	39	....	....	....	43	....	....	....	....	....	....	....	....	....	....	4	0	1	1	0	....	....	....
1973-74	Vancouver Blazers	WHA	49	8	6	14	....	....	....	20	....	....	....	....	....	....	....	....	....	....	....	....	....	....	....	....	....	....
1974-75	Vancouver Blazers	WHA	4	0	0	0	....	....	....	0	....	....	....	....	....	....	....	....	....	....	....	....	....	....	....	....	....	....
	Tulsa Oilers	CHL	46	8	22	30	....	....	....	60	....	....	....	....	....	....	....	....	....	....	2	1	0	1	2	....	....	....
1975-76	Cincinnati Stingers	WHA	20	1	8	9	....	....	....	0	....	....	....	....	....	....	....	....	....	....	....	....	....	....	....	....	....	....
	Hampton Gulls	SHL	45	15	26	41	....	....	....	59	....	....	....	....	....	....	....	....	....	....	9	2	6	8	4	....	....	....
1976-77	Hampton Gulls	SHL	50	16	26	42	....	....	....	46	....	....	....	....	....	....	....	....	....	....	....	....	....	....	....	....	....	....
1977-78	Hampton Gulls	AHL	43	4	8	12	....	....	....	84	....	....	....	....	....	....	....	....	....	....	....	....	....	....	....	....	....	....
	NHL Totals		**125**	**18**	**17**	**35**	**19**	**16**	**35**	**35**	**3**	**1**	**1**	**129**	**14.0**	**50**	**9**	**122**	**31**		**3**	**0**	**0**	**0**	**0**	**0**	**0**	**0**
	Other Major League Totals		147	25	37	62	....	....	....	63	....	....	....	....	....	....	....	....	....		4	0	1	1	0	....	....	....

Selected by **New England** (WHA) in 1972 WHA General Player Draft, February 12, 1972. Traded to **Boston** by **California** with Carol Vadnais for Reg Leach, Rick Smith and Bob Stewart, February 23, 1972. WHA rights traded to **Philadelphia** (WHA) by **New England** (WHA) for cash, June, 1972. Claimed by **Rochester** (AHL) from **Boston** in Reverse Draft, June 12, 1972. Transferred to **Vancouver** (WHA) after **Philadelphia** (WHA) franchise relocated, May, 1973. Selected by **Cincinnati** (WHA) from **Toronto** (WHA) in 1975 WHA Expansion Draft, June, 1975.

• ODROWSKI, GERRY

Gerry "Snowy / The Hook" Odrowski D – L. 5'10", 185 lbs. b: Trout Creek, Ont., 10/4/1938.

Season	Club	League	GP	G	A	Pts	AG	AA	APts	PIM	PP	SH	GW	S	%	TGF	PGF	TGA	PGA	+/–	GP	G	A	Pts	PIM	PP	SH	GW
1956-57	St. Michaels Majors	OHA	52	0	1	1	....	....	....	4	....	....	....	....	....	....	....	....	....	....	....	....	....	....	....	....	....	....
1957-58	Sault Ste. Marie Greyhounds	NOHA	48	4	7	11	....	....	....	20	....	....	....	....	....	....	....	....	....	....	1	0	0	0	0	....	....	....
1958-59	Sault Ste. Marie Greyhounds	NOHA	53	3	12	15	....	....	....	40	....	....	....	....	....	....	....	....	....	....	4	0	0	0	2	....	....	....
1959-60	Sudbury Wolves	EPHL	67	8	21	29	....	....	....	69	....	....	....	....	....	....	....	....	....	....	4	1	8	9	28	....	....	....
1960-61	**Detroit Red Wings**	**NHL**	**68**	**1**	**4**	**5**	**1**	**4**	**5**	**45**	....	....	....	....	....	....	....	....	....	....	**10**	**0**	**0**	**0**	**4**	....	....	....
1961-62	**Detroit Red Wings**	**NHL**	**69**	**1**	**6**	**7**	**1**	**6**	**7**	**24**	....	....	....	....	....	....	....	....	....	....	....	....	....	....	....	....	....	....
1962-63	**Detroit Red Wings**	**NHL**	**1**	**0**	**0**	**0**	**0**	**0**	**0**	**0**	....	....	....	....	....	....	....	....	....	....	**2**	**0**	**0**	**0**	**2**	....	....	....
	Pittsburgh Hornets	AHL	69	7	23	30	....	....	....	125	....	....	....	....	....	....	....	....	....	....	....	....	....	....	....	....	....	....

			REGULAR SEASON																		PLAYOFFS							
Season	Club	League	GP	G	A	Pts	AG	AA	APts	PIM	PP	SH	GW	S	%	TGF	PGF	TGA	PGA	+/–	GP	G	A	Pts	PIM	PP	SH	GW
1963-64	Quebec Aces	AHL	8	0	0	0	....	....	....	25	....	....	....	....	....	....	....	....	....	....	....	....	....	....	....	....	....	....
	San Francisco Seals	WHL	37	3	12	15	....	....	....	70	....	....	....	....	....	....	....	....	....	....	11	0	3	3	30	....	....	....
1964-65	San Francisco Seals	WHL	70	9	20	29	....	....	....	114	....	....	....	....	....	....	....	....	....	....	....	....	....	....	....	....	....	....
1965-66	San Francisco Seals	WHL	71	7	24	31	....	....	....	102	....	....	....	....	....	....	....	....	....	....	7	0	0	0	4	....	....	....
1966-67	California Seals	WHL	72	8	27	35	....	....	....	64	....	....	....	....	....	....	....	....	....	....	6	0	1	1	10	....	....	....
1967-68	**Oakland Seals**	**NHL**	**42**	**4**	**6**	**10**	**5**	**6**	**11**	**10**	**0**	**2**	**2**	**40**	**10.0**	**17**	**3**	**28**	**14**	**0**	....	....	....	....	....	....	....	....
	Vancouver Canucks	WHL	8	2	3	5	....	....	....	6	....	....	....	....	....	....	....	....	....	....	....	....	....	....	....	....	....	....
1968-69	**Oakland Seals**	**NHL**	**74**	**5**	**1**	**6**	**6**	**1**	**7**	**24**	**0**	**3**	**0**	**54**	**9.3**	**14**	**0**	**44**	**34**	**+4**	**7**	**0**	**1**	**1**	**2**	**0**	**0**	**0**
1969-70	San Diego Gulls	WHL	68	6	30	36	....	....	....	78	....	....	....	....	....	....	....	....	....	....	6	0	2	2	12	....	....	....
1970-71	Phoenix Roadrunners	WHL	70	7	28	35	....	....	....	56	....	....	....	....	....	....	....	....	....	....	10	0	5	5	13	....	....	....
1971-72	Phoenix Roadrunners	WHL	20	3	4	7	....	....	....	30	....	....	....	....	....	....	....	....	....	....	....	....	....	....	....	....	....	....
	St. Louis Blues	**NHL**	**55**	**1**	**2**	**3**	**1**	**2**	**3**	**8**	**0**	**1**	**0**	**30**	**3.3**	**7**	**0**	**33**	**25**	**–1**	**11**	**0**	**0**	**0**	**8**	**0**	**0**	**0**
1972-73	Los Angeles Sharks	WHA	78	6	31	37	....	....	....	89	....	....	....	....	....	....	....	....	....	....	6	1	2	3	6	....	....	....
1973-74	Los Angeles Sharks	WHA	77	4	32	36	....	....	....	48	....	....	....	....	....	....	....	....	....	....	....	....	....	....	....	....	....	....
1974-75	Phoenix Roadrunners	WHA	77	5	38	43	....	....	....	77	....	....	....	....	....	....	....	....	....	....	5	0	2	2	0	....	....	....
1975-76	Minnesota Fighting Saints	WHA	37	1	12	13	....	....	....	10	....	....	....	....	....	....	....	....	....	....	....	....	....	....	....	....	....	....
	Winnipeg Jets	WHA	13	0	1	1	....	....	....	6	....	....	....	....	....	....	....	....	....	....	....	....	....	....	....	....	....	....
	NHL Totals		**309**	**12**	**19**	**31**	**14**	**19**	**33**	**111**	**0**	**6**	**2**	**124**	**9.7**	**38**	**3**	**105**	**73**		**30**	**0**	**1**	**1**	**16**	**0**	**0**	**0**
	Other Major League Totals		282	16	114	130	....	....	....	230	....	....	....	....	....	....	....	....	....		11	1	4	5	6	....	....	....

WHL Second All-Star Team (1967)

Traded to **Boston** by **Detroit** for Warren Godfrey, October 10, 1963. NHL rights transferred to **California** after owners of **San Francisco** (WHL) franchise awarded NHL expansion franchise, April 5, 1966. Traded to **San Diego** (WHL) by **Oakland** for cash, Septmeber, 1969. Traded to **Oakland** by **San Diego** (WHL) for cash, October, 1970. Traded to **Phoenix** (WHL) by **Oakland** for cash, October, 1970. Traded to **St. Louis** by **Phoenix** (WHL) for cash, November, 1971. Selected by **LA Sharks** (WHA) in 1972 WHA General Player Draft, February 12, 1972. Transferred to **Michigan** (WHA) after **LA Sharks** (WHA) franchise relocated, April 11, 1974. Claimed by **Phoenix** (WHA) from **Michigan** (WHA) in 1974 WHA Expansion Draft, June, 1974. Claimed by **Minnesota** (WHA) from **Phoenix** (WHA) in 1975 WHA Intra-League Draft, June, 1975. Traded to **Winnipeg** (WHA) by **Minnesota** (WHA) for Perry Miller, January, 1976.

● O'DWYER, BILL

Bill O'Dwyer C – L. 6', 190 lbs. b: Boston, MA, 1/25/1960. Los Angeles' 10th choice, 157th overall, in 1980 Entry Draft.

Season	Club	League	GP	G	A	Pts	AG	AA	APts	PIM	PP	SH	GW	S	%	TGF	PGF	TGA	PGA	+/–	GP	G	A	Pts	PIM	PP	SH	GW
1978-79	Boston College	ECAC	30	9	30	39	....	....	....	14	....	....	....	....	....	....	....	....	....	....	....	....	....	....	....	....	....	....
1979-80	Boston College	ECAC	33	20	22	42	....	....	....	22	....	....	....	....	....	....	....	....	....	....	....	....	....	....	....	....	....	....
1980-81	Boston College	ECAC	31	20	20	40	....	....	....	6	....	....	....	....	....	....	....	....	....	....	....	....	....	....	....	....	....	....
1981-82	Boston College	ECAC	30	15	26	41	....	....	....	10	....	....	....	....	....	....	....	....	....	....	....	....	....	....	....	....	....	....
1982-83	New Haven Nighthawks	AHL	77	24	23	47	....	....	....	29	....	....	....	....	....	....	....	....	....	....	11	3	4	7	9	....	....	....
1983-84	**Los Angeles Kings**	**NHL**	**5**	**0**	**0**	**0**	**0**	**0**	**0**	**0**	**0**	**0**	**0**	**2**	**0.0**	**1**	**0**	**0**	**0**	**+1**	....	....	....	....	....	....	....	....
	New Haven Nighthawks	AHL	58	15	42	57	....	....	....	39	....	....	....	....	....	....	....	....	....	....	....	....	....	....	....	....	....	....
1984-85	**Los Angeles Kings**	**NHL**	**13**	**1**	**0**	**1**	**1**	**0**	**1**	**15**	**0**	**0**	**0**	**8**	**12.5**	**2**	**0**	**4**	**2**	**0**	....	....	....	....	....	....	....	....
	New Haven Nighthawks	AHL	46	19	24	43	....	....	....	27	....	....	....	....	....	....	....	....	....	....	....	....	....	....	....	....	....	....
1985-86	New Haven Nighthawks	AHL	41	10	15	25	....	....	....	41	....	....	....	....	....	....	....	....	....	....	5	0	1	1	2	....	....	....
1986 87	New Haven Nighthawks	AHL	65	22	42	64	....	....	....	74	....	....	....	....	....	....	....	....	....	....	3	0	0	0	14	....	....	....
1987-88	**Boston Bruins**	**NHL**	**77**	**7**	**10**	**17**	**6**	**7**	**13**	**83**	**1**	**0**	**1**	**98**	**7.1**	**33**	**1**	**53**	**18**	**–3**	**9**	**0**	**0**	**0**	**0**	**0**	**0**	**0**
1988-89	**Boston Bruins**	**NHL**	**19**	**1**	**2**	**3**	**1**	**1**	**2**	**8**	**0**	**0**	**0**	**18**	**5.6**	**4**	**0**	**11**	**3**	**–4**	....	....	....	....	....	....	....	....
1989-90	**Boston Bruins**	**NHL**	**6**	**0**	**1**	**1**	**0**	**1**	**1**	**7**	**0**	**0**	**0**	**7**	**0.0**	**1**	**0**	**3**	**0**	**–2**	**1**	**0**	**0**	**0**	**2**	**0**	**0**	**0**
	Maine Mariners	AHL	71	26	45	71	....	....	....	56	....	....	....	....	....	....	....	....	....	....	....	....	....	....	....	....	....	....
1990-91	New Haven Nighthawks	AHL	6	2	1	3	....	....	....	2	....	....	....	....	....	....	....	....	....	....	....	....	....	....	....	....	....	....
	Phoenix Roadrunners	IHL	25	3	9	12	....	....	....	12	....	....	....	....	....	....	....	....	....	....	11	7	6	13	0	....	....	....
1991-92	Phoenix Roadrunners	IHL	39	9	17	26	....	....	....	12	....	....	....	....	....	....	....	....	....	....	....	....	....	....	....	....	....	....
	NHL Totals		**120**	**9**	**13**	**22**	**8**	**9**	**17**	**113**	**1**	**0**	**1**	**133**	**6.8**	**41**	**1**	**71**	**23**		**10**	**0**	**0**	**0**	**2**	**0**	**0**	**0**

ECAC Second All-Star Team (1980, 1981, 1982)

Signed as a free agent by **NY Rangers**, July 13, 1985. Signed as a free agent by **Boston**, August 13, 1987. Signed as a free agent by **LA Kings**, July 11, 1990.

● O'FLAHERTY, GERRY

Gerry O'Flaherty LW – L. 5'10", 182 lbs. b: Pittsburgh, PA, 8/31/1950. Toronto's 3rd choice, 36th overall, in 1970 Amateur Draft.

Season	Club	League	GP	G	A	Pts	AG	AA	APts	PIM	PP	SH	GW	S	%	TGF	PGF	TGA	PGA	+/–	GP	G	A	Pts	PIM	PP	SH	GW
1967-68	North York Rangers	MTHL	36	19	24	43	....	....	....	13	....	....	....	....	....	....	....	....	....	....	....	....	....	....	....	....	....	....
1968-69	Kitchener Rangers	OHA	22	4	3	7	....	....	....	4	....	....	....	....	....	....	....	....	....	....	....	....	....	....	....	....	....	....
1969-70	Kitchener Rangers	OHA	54	40	38	78	....	....	....	30	....	....	....	....	....	....	....	....	....	....	....	....	....	....	....	....	....	....
1970-71	Tulsa Oilers	CHL	70	23	29	52	....	....	....	33	....	....	....	....	....	....	....	....	....	....	....	....	....	....	....	....	....	....
1971-72	**Toronto Maple Leafs**	**NHL**	**2**	**0**	**0**	**0**	**0**	**0**	**0**	**0**	**0**	**0**	**0**	**3**	**0.0**	**0**	**0**	**0**	**0**	**0**	....	....	....	....	....	....	....	....
	Tulsa Oilers	CHL	57	22	30	52	....	....	....	48	....	....	....	....	....	....	....	....	....	....	13	6	*9	15	28	....	....	....
1972-73	**Vancouver Canucks**	**NHL**	**78**	**13**	**17**	**30**	**13**	**14**	**27**	**29**	**0**	**0**	**0**	**135**	**9.6**	**46**	**1**	**84**	**22**	**–17**	....	....	....	....	....	....	....	....
1973-74	**Vancouver Canucks**	**NHL**	**78**	**22**	**20**	**42**	**22**	**17**	**39**	**18**	**2**	**0**	**2**	**142**	**15.5**	**61**	**10**	**76**	**20**	**–5**	....	....	....	....	....	....	....	....
1974-75	**Vancouver Canucks**	**NHL**	**80**	**25**	**17**	**42**	**23**	**13**	**36**	**37**	**3**	**2**	**2**	**164**	**15.2**	**62**	**12**	**70**	**26**	**+6**	**5**	**2**	**2**	**4**	**6**	**0**	**0**	**0**
1975-76	**Vancouver Canucks**	**NHL**	**68**	**20**	**18**	**38**	**19**	**14**	**33**	**47**	**0**	**1**	**3**	**129**	**15.5**	**56**	**2**	**71**	**28**	**+11**	**2**	**0**	**0**	**0**	**0**	**0**	**0**	**0**
1976-77	United States	C Cup	4	0	1	1	....	....	....	0	....	....	....	....	....	....	....	....	....	....	....	....	....	....	....	....	....	....
	Vancouver Canucks	**NHL**	**72**	**12**	**12**	**24**	**11**	**10**	**21**	**20**	**1**	**0**	**2**	**114**	**10.5**	**35**	**8**	**66**	**15**	**–24**	....	....	....	....	....	....	....	....
	Tulsa Oilers	CHL	5	2	3	5	....	....	....	2	....	....	....	....	....	....	....	....	....	....	....	....	....	....	....	....	....	....
1977-78	**Vancouver Canucks**	**NHL**	**59**	**6**	**11**	**17**	**6**	**9**	**15**	**15**	**0**	**1**	**0**	**90**	**6.7**	**27**	**2**	**44**	**14**	**–5**	....	....	....	....	....	....	....	....
	Tulsa Oilers	CHL	10	9	7	16	....	....	....	0	....	....	....	....	....	....	....	....	....	....	....	....	....	....	....	....	....	....
1978-79	**Atlanta Flames**	**NHL**	**1**	**1**	**0**	**1**	**1**	**0**	**1**	**2**	**0**	**0**	**0**	**2**	**50.0**	**1**	**0**	**1**	**0**	**0**	....	....	....	....	....	....	....	....
	Tulsa Oilers	CHL	38	18	24	42	....	....	....	18	....	....	....	....	....	....	....	....	....	....	....	....	....	....	....	....	....	....
	Nova Scotia Voyageurs	AHL	35	8	14	22	....	....	....	18	....	....	....	....	....	....	....	....	....	....	10	2	1	3	6	....	....	....
	NHL Totals		**438**	**99**	**95**	**194**	**95**	**77**	**172**	**168**	**6**	**4**	**9**	**779**	**12.7**	**288**	**35**	**412**	**125**		**7**	**2**	**2**	**4**	**6**	**0**	**0**	**0**

Claimed by **Vancouver** from **Toronto** in Intra-League Draft, June 5, 1972. Signed as a free agent by **Minnesota**, July 15, 1978. Traded to **Atlanta** by **Minnesota** for cash, October 10, 1978.

● OGILVIE, BRIAN

Brian Ogilvie C – R. 5'11", 180 lbs. b: Stettler, Alta., 1/30/1952. Chicago's 2nd choice, 29th overall, in 1972 Amateur Draft.

Season	Club	League	GP	G	A	Pts	AG	AA	APts	PIM	PP	SH	GW	S	%	TGF	PGF	TGA	PGA	+/–	GP	G	A	Pts	PIM	PP	SH	GW
1968-69	Red Deer Rustlers	AJHL	....	1	0	1	....	....	....	0	....	....	....	....	....	....	....	....	....	....	....	....	....	....	....	....	....	....
1969-70	Red Deer Rustlers	AJHL	40	24	17	41	....	....	....	52	....	....	....	....	....	....	....	....	....	....	....	....	....	....	....	....	....	....
1970-71	Red Deer Rustlers	AJHL	....	29	47	76	....	....	....	106	....	....	....	....	....	....	....	....	....	....	....	....	....	....	....	....	....	....
1971-72	Vancouver–Edmonton	WCJHL	54	34	49	83	....	....	....	61	....	....	....	....	....	....	....	....	....	....	....	....	....	....	....	....	....	....
1972-73	**Chicago Black Hawks**	**NHL**	**12**	**1**	**2**	**3**	**1**	**2**	**3**	**4**	**1**	**0**	**0**	**12**	**8.3**	**3**	**1**	**4**	**0**	**–2**	....	....	....	....	....	....	....	....
	Dallas Black Hawks	CHL	58	17	25	42	....	....	....	64	....	....	....	....	....	....	....	....	....	....	7	1	2	3	16	....	....	....
1973-74	Dallas Black Hawks	CHL	70	21	33	54	....	....	....	66	....	....	....	....	....	....	....	....	....	....	10	2	2	4	4	....	....	....
1974-75	**St. Louis Blues**	**NHL**	**20**	**5**	**5**	**10**	**5**	**4**	**9**	**4**	**0**	**0**	**2**	**36**	**13.9**	**18**	**7**	**25**	**10**	**–4**	....	....	....	....	....	....	....	....
	Denver Spurs	CHL	34	20	12	32	....	....	....	45	....	....	....	....	....	....	....	....	....	....	2	1	0	1	0	....	....	....
1975-76	**St. Louis Blues**	**NHL**	**9**	**2**	**1**	**3**	**2**	**1**	**3**	**2**	**0**	**0**	**0**	**14**	**14.3**	**3**	**0**	**4**	**0**	**–1**	....	....	....	....	....	....	....	....
	Providence Reds	AHL	47	16	18	34	....	....	....	61	....	....	....	....	....	....	....	....	....	....	3	0	2	2	9	....	....	....
1976-77	**St. Louis Blues**	**NHL**	**3**	**0**	**0**	**0**	**0**	**0**	**0**	**0**	**0**	**0**	**0**	**0**	**0.0**	**0**	**0**	**1**	**0**	**1**	....	....	....	....	....	....	....	....
	Kansas City Blues	CHL	66	26	28	54	....	....	....	91	....	....	....	....	....	....	....	....	....	....	10	2	4	6	17	....	....	....
1977-78	**St. Louis Blues**	**NHL**	**32**	**6**	**8**	**14**	**6**	**7**	**13**	**12**	**3**	**0**	**0**	**63**	**9.5**	**19**	**4**	**30**	**3**	**–12**	....	....	....	....	....	....	....	....
	Salt Lake Golden Eagles	CHL	15	7	7	14	....	....	....	22	....	....	....	....	....	....	....	....	....	....	....	....	....	....	....	....	....	....
1978-79	**St. Louis Blues**	**NHL**	**14**	**1**	**5**	**6**	**1**	**4**	**5**	**7**	**0**	**0**	**0**	**21**	**4.8**	**6**	**1**	**8**	**0**	**–3**	....	....	....	....	....	....	....	....
	Salt Lake Golden Eagles	CHL	59	26	28	54	....	....	....	72	....	....	....	....	....	....	....	....	....	....	5	0	5	5	8	....	....	....
1979-80	Salt Lake Golden Eagles	CHL	75	30	31	61	....	....	....	88	....	....	....	....	....	....	....	....	....	....	13	5	9	14	16	....	....	....
	NHL Totals		**90**	**15**	**21**	**36**	**15**	**18**	**33**	**29**	**4**	**0**	**2**	**146**	**10.3**	**49**	**13**	**72**	**13**		....	....	....	....	....	....	....	....

Claimed by **St. Louis** from **Chicago** in Intra-League Draft, June 10, 1974.

● OGRODNICK, JOHN

John Ogrodnick LW – L. 6', 204 lbs. b: Ottawa, Ont., 6/20/1959. Detroit's 4th choice, 66th overall, in 1979 Entry Draft.

Season	Club	League	GP	G	A	Pts	AG	AA	APts	PIM	PP	SH	GW	S	%	TGF	PGF	TGA	PGA	+/–	GP	G	A	Pts	PIM	PP	SH	GW
1976-77	Maple Ridge Bruins	BCJHL	67	54	56	110	....	....	....	63	....	....	....	....	....	....	....	....	....	....	....	....	....	....	....	....	....	....
	New Westminster Bruins	WCJHL	14	2	4	6	....	....	....	0	....	....	....	....	....	....	....	....	....	....	14	3	3	6	2	....	....	....
1977-78	New Westminster Bruins	WCJHL	72	59	29	88	....	....	....	47	....	....	....	....	....	....	....	....	....	....	21	14	7	21	14	....	....	....
1978-79	New Westminster Bruins	WHL	72	48	36	84	....	....	....	38	....	....	....	....	....	....	....	....	....	....	6	2	0	2	4	....	....	....
	Canada	WJC-A	5	3	0	3	....	....	....	4	....	....	....	....	....	....	....	....	....	....	....	....	....	....	....	....	....	....
1979-80	**Detroit Red Wings**	**NHL**	**41**	**8**	**24**	**32**	**7**	**18**	**25**	**8**	**3**	**0**	**1**	**121**	**6.6**	**55**	**13**	**46**	**0**	**–4**	....	....	....	....	....	....	....	....
	Adirondack Red Wings	AHL	39	13	20	33	....	....	....	21	....	....	....	....	....	....	....	....	....	....	....	....	....	....	....	....	....	....

			REGULAR SEASON																		PLAYOFFS							
Season	Club	League	GP	G	A	Pts	AG	AA	APts	PIM	PP	SH	GW	S	%	TGF	PGF	TGA	PGA	+/–	GP	G	A	Pts	PIM	PP	SH	GW
1980-81	Detroit Red Wings	NHL	80	35	35	70	29	24	53	14	9	2	2	276	12.7	114	37	102	8	–17	....	....	....	....	....	....	....	....
	Canada	WEC-A	8	3	2	5	....	....	....	0	....	....	....	....	....	....	....	....	....	....	....	....	....	....	....	....	....	....
1981-82	Detroit Red Wings	NHL	80	28	26	54	22	17	39	28	3	2	3	254	11.0	81	18	93	15	–15	....	....	....	....	....	....	....	....
1982-83	Detroit Red Wings	NHL	80	41	44	85	34	30	64	30	5	0	2	254	16.1	110	20	90	11	+11	....	....	....	....	....	....	....	....
1983-84	Detroit Red Wings	NHL	64	42	36	78	34	24	58	14	19	3	5	252	16.7	112	54	89	15	–16	4	0	0	0	0	0	0	0
1984-85	Detroit Red Wings	NHL	79	55	50	105	45	34	79	30	15	1	6	303	18.2	159	54	125	21	+1	3	1	1	2	0	0	0	0
1985-86	Detroit Red Wings	NHL	76	38	32	70	30	21	51	18	15	1	2	208	18.3	101	44	90	3	–30	....	....	....	....	....	....	....	....
1986-87	Detroit Red Wings	NHL	39	12	28	40	10	20	30	6	4	1	1	117	10.3	60	23	40	1	–2	....	....	....	....	....	....	....	....
	Quebec Nordiques	NHL	32	11	16	27	10	12	22	4	2	0	1	127	8.7	44	20	30	0	–6	13	9	4	13	6	3	0	2
1987-88	New York Rangers	NHL	64	22	32	54	19	23	42	16	7	0	5	152	14.5	85	40	48	0	–3	....	....	....	....	....	....	....	....
1988-89	New York Rangers	NHL	60	13	29	42	11	20	31	14	1	0	1	149	8.7	58	7	51	0	0	3	2	0	2	0	1	0	0
	Denver Rangers	IHL	3	2	0	2	....	....	....	0	....	....	....	....	....	....	....	....	....	....	....	....	....	....	....	....	....	....
1989-90	New York Rangers	NHL	80	43	31	74	37	22	59	44	19	0	8	215	20.0	120	55	54	0	+11	10	6	3	9	0	3	0	1
1990-91	New York Rangers	NHL	79	31	23	54	29	17	46	10	12	0	4	250	12.4	98	32	51	0	+15	4	0	0	0	0	0	0	0
1991-92	New York Rangers	NHL	55	17	13	30	16	10	26	22	3	0	4	110	15.5	55	18	32	1	+6	3	0	0	0	0	0	0	0
1992-93	Detroit Red Wings	NHL	19	6	6	12	5	4	9	2	4	0	0	25	24.0	17	11	8	0	–2	1	0	0	0	0	0	0	0
	Adirondack Red Wings	AHL	4	2	2	4	....	....	....	0	....	....	....	....	....	....	....	....	....	....	....	....	....	....	....	....	....	....
	NHL Totals		928	402	425	827	338	296	634	260	121	10	45	2813	14.3	1269	446	949	75		41	18	8	26	6	7	0	3

NHL First All-Star Team (1985)

Played in NHL All-Star Game (1981, 1982, 1984, 1985, 1986)

Traded to **Quebec** by **Detroit** with Basil McRae and Doug Shedden for Brent Ashton, Gilbert Delorme and Mark Kumpel, January 17, 1987. Traded to **NY Rangers** by **Quebec** with David Shaw for Jeff Jackson and Terry Carkner, September 30, 1987. Signed as a free agent by **Detroit**, September 29, 1992.

• OHLUND, MATTIAS

Mattias Ohlund D – L. 6'3", 209 lbs. b: Pitea, Sweden, 9/9/1976. Vancouver's 1st choice, 13th overall, in 1994 Entry Draft.

Season	Club	League	GP	G	A	Pts	AG	AA	APts	PIM	PP	SH	GW	S	%	TGF	PGF	TGA	PGA	+/–	GP	G	A	Pts	PIM	PP	SH	GW
1992-93	Pitea	Sweden 2	22	0	6	6	....	....	....	16	....	....	....	....	....	....	....	....	....	....	....	....	....	....	....	....	....	....
1993-94	Pitea	Sweden 2	28	7	10	17	....	....	....	62	....	....	....	....	....	....	....	....	....	....	....	....	....	....	....	....	....	....
	Sweden	WJC-A	7	0	2	2	....	....	....	2	....	....	....	....	....	....	....	....	....	....	....	....	....	....	....	....	....	....
1994-95	Lulea HF	Sweden	34	6	10	16	....	....	....	34	....	....	....	....	....	....	....	....	....	....	9	4	0	4	16	....	....	....
	Sweden	WJC-A	7	1	0	1	....	....	....	4	....	....	....	....	....	....	....	....	....	....	....	....	....	....	....	....	....	....
1995-96	Lulea HF	Sweden	38	4	10	14	....	....	....	26	....	....	....	....	....	....	....	....	....	....	13	1	0	1	47	....	....	....
	Sweden	WJC-A	7	0	5	5	....	....	....	32	....	....	....	....	....	....	....	....	....	....	....	....	....	....	....	....	....	....
1996-97	Lulea HF	Sweden	47	7	9	16	....	....	....	38	....	....	....	....	....	....	....	....	....	....	10	1	2	3	8	....	....	....
	Sweden	WC-A	11	2	1	3	....	....	....	12	....	....	....	....	....	....	....	....	....	....	....	....	....	....	....	....	....	....
1997-98	**Vancouver Canucks**	**NHL**	**77**	**7**	**23**	**30**	**8**	**22**	**30**	**76**	**1**	**0**	**0**	**172**	**4.1**	**84**	**19**	**81**	**19**	**+3**	....	....	....	....	....	....	....	....
	Sweden	Olympics	4	0	1	1	....	....	....	4	....	....	....	....	....	....	....	....	....	....	....	....	....	....	....	....	....	....
	NHL Totals		77	7	23	30	8	22	30	76	1	0	0	172	4.1	84	19	81	19		....	....	....	....	....	....	....	....

EJC-A All-Star Team (1994) • Named Best Defenseman at EJC-A (1994) • WJC-A All-Star Team (1996) • Named Best Defenseman at WJC-A (1996) • NHL All-Rookie Team (1998)

• OJANEN, JANNE

Janne Ojanen C – L. 6'2", 200 lbs. b: Tampere, Finland, 4/9/1968. New Jersey's 3rd choice, 45th overall, in 1986 Entry Draft.

Season	Club	League	GP	G	A	Pts	AG	AA	APts	PIM	PP	SH	GW	S	%	TGF	PGF	TGA	PGA	+/–	GP	G	A	Pts	PIM	PP	SH	GW
1985-86	Tappara Tampere	Finland Jr.	14	5	17	22	....	....	....	14	....	....	....	....	....	....	....	....	....	....	5	2	3	5	8	....	....	....
	Tappara Tampere	Finland	3	0	0	0	....	....	....	2	....	....	....	....	....	....	....	....	....	....	....	....	....	....	....	....	....	....
1986-87	Tappara Tampere	Finland	40	18	13	31	....	....	....	16	....	....	....	....	....	....	....	....	....	....	9	4	6	10	2	....	....	....
	Finland	WJC-A	7	2	10	12	....	....	....	6	....	....	....	....	....	....	....	....	....	....	....	....	....	....	....	....	....	....
	Finland	WEC-A	8	3	3	6	....	....	....	9	....	....	....	....	....	....	....	....	....	....	....	....	....	....	....	....	....	....
1987-88	Finland	C Cup	5	0	1	1	....	....	....	0	....	....	....	....	....	....	....	....	....	....	....	....	....	....	....	....	....	....
	Tappara Tampere	Finland	44	21	31	52	....	....	....	30	....	....	....	....	....	....	....	....	....	....	10	4	4	8	12	....	....	....
	Finland	WJC-A	7	6	5	11	....	....	....	16	....	....	....	....	....	....	....	....	....	....	....	....	....	....	....	....	....	....
	Finland	Olympics	8	2	1	3	....	....	....	4	....	....	....	....	....	....	....	....	....	....	....	....	....	....	....	....	....	....
1988-89	**New Jersey Devils**	**NHL**	**3**	**0**	**1**	**1**	**0**	**1**	**1**	**2**	**0**	**0**	**0**	**1**	**0.0**	**1**	**0**	**2**	**0**	**–1**	....	....	....	....	....	....	....	....
	Utica Devils	AHL	72	23	37	60	....	....	....	10	....	....	....	....	....	....	....	....	....	....	5	0	3	3	0	....	....	....
1989-90	**New Jersey Devils**	**NHL**	**64**	**17**	**13**	**30**	**15**	**9**	**24**	**12**	**1**	**0**	**1**	**76**	**22.4**	**38**	**7**	**37**	**1**	**–5**	....	....	....	....	....	....	....	....
1990-91	Tappara Tampere	Finland	44	15	33	48	....	....	....	36	....	....	....	....	....	....	....	....	....	....	3	1	2	3	6	....	....	....
1991-92	Finland	C Cup	6	2	2	4	....	....	....	2	....	....	....	....	....	....	....	....	....	....	....	....	....	....	....	....	....	....
	Tappara Tampere	Finland	44	21	27	48	....	....	....	24	....	....	....	....	....	....	....	....	....	....	....	....	....	....	....	....	....	....
	New Jersey Devils	**NHL**	....	....	....	....	....	....	....	....	....	....	....	....	....	....	....	....	....	....	**3**	**0**	**2**	**2**	**0**	....	....	....
1992-93	**New Jersey Devils**	**NHL**	**31**	**4**	**9**	**13**	**3**	**6**	**9**	**14**	**1**	**0**	**1**	**44**	**9.1**	**29**	**14**	**18**	**1**	**–2**	....	....	....	....	....	....	....	....
	Cincinnati Cyclones	IHL	7	1	8	9	....	....	....	0	....	....	....	....	....	....	....	....	....	....	....	....	....	....	....	....	....	....
1993-94	Tappara Tampere	Finland	39	22	24	46	....	....	....	24	....	....	....	....	....	....	....	....	....	....	....	....	....	....	....	....	....	....
	Finland	Olympics	8	4	2	6	....	....	....	8	....	....	....	....	....	....	....	....	....	....	....	....	....	....	....	....	....	....
	Finland	WC-A	8	2	2	4	....	....	....	6	....	....	....	....	....	....	....	....	....	....	....	....	....	....	....	....	....	....
1994-95	Tappara Tampere	Finland	50	22	33	55	....	....	....	74	....	....	....	....	....	....	....	....	....	....	....	....	....	....	....	....	....	....
	Finland	WC-A	8	0	4	4	....	....	....	4	....	....	....	....	....	....	....	....	....	....	....	....	....	....	....	....	....	....
1995-96	Tappara Tampere	Finland	45	20	*44	64	....	....	....	34	....	....	....	....	....	....	....	....	....	....	4	2	2	4	2	....	....	....
	Finland	WC-A	6	2	0	2	....	....	....	6	....	....	....	....	....	....	....	....	....	....	....	....	....	....	....	....	....	....
1996-97	Finland	W Cup	4	1	1	2	....	....	....	0	....	....	....	....	....	....	....	....	....	....	....	....	....	....	....	....	....	....
	Tappara Tampere	Finland	41	10	29	39	....	....	....	28	....	....	....	....	....	....	....	....	....	....	4	0	1	1	4	....	....	....
	Finland	WC-A	7	2	4	6	....	....	....	6	....	....	....	....	....	....	....	....	....	....	....	....	....	....	....	....	....	....
1997-98	Malmo IF	Sweden	45	11	22	33	....	....	....	25	....	....	....	....	....	....	....	....	....	....	....	....	....	....	....	....	....	....
	NHL Totals		98	21	23	44	18	16	34	28	2	0	2	121	17.4	68	21	57	2		3	0	2	2	0	0	0	0

EJC-A All-Star Team (1986) • Finnish Rookie of the Year (1987)

• OKERLUND, TODD

Todd Okerlund RW – R. 5'11", 200 lbs. b: Burnsville, MN, 9/6/1964. NY Islanders' 8th choice, 168th overall, in 1982 Entry Draft.

Season	Club	League	GP	G	A	Pts	AG	AA	APts	PIM	PP	SH	GW	S	%	TGF	PGF	TGA	PGA	+/–	GP	G	A	Pts	PIM	PP	SH	GW
1981-82	Burnsfield High School	H.S.	25	12	20	32	....	....	....	8	....	....	....	....	....	....	....	....	....	....	....	....	....	....	....	....	....	....
1982-83	Burnsfield High School	H.S.	DID NOT PLAY																									
1983-84	University of Minnesota	WCHA	34	11	20	31	....	....	....	18	....	....	....	....	....	....	....	....	....	....	....	....	....	....	....	....	....	....
	United States	WJC-A	7	2	3	5	....	....	....	4	....	....	....	....	....	....	....	....	....	....	....	....	....	....	....	....	....	....
1984-85	University of Minnesota	WCHA	47	16	27	43	....	....	....	80	....	....	....	....	....	....	....	....	....	....	....	....	....	....	....	....	....	....
1985-86	University of Minnesota	WCHA	48	17	32	49	....	....	....	58	....	....	....	....	....	....	....	....	....	....	....	....	....	....	....	....	....	....
1986-87	University of Minnesota	WCHA	4	0	7	7	....	....	....	0	....	....	....	....	....	....	....	....	....	....	....	....	....	....	....	....	....	....
1987-88	United States	Nat-Team	40	9	16	25	....	....	....	34	....	....	....	....	....	....	....	....	....	....	....	....	....	....	....	....	....	....
	United States	Olympics	3	1	0	1	....	....	....	4	....	....	....	....	....	....	....	....	....	....	....	....	....	....	....	....	....	....
	New York Islanders	**NHL**	**4**	**0**	**0**	**0**	**0**	**0**	**0**	**2**	**0**	**0**	**0**	**3**	**0.0**	**0**	**0**	**0**	**0**	**0**	....	....	....	....	....	....	....	....
	Springfield Indians	AHL	13	2	1	3	....	....	....	9	....	....	....	....	....	....	....	....	....	....	....	....	....	....	....	....	....	....
	NHL Totals		4	0	0	0	0	0	0	2	0	0	0	3	0.0	0	0	0	0		....	....	....	....	....	....	....	....

• OKSIUTA, ROMAN

Roman Oksiuta RW – L. 6'3", 230 lbs. b: Murmansk, USSR, 8/21/1970. NY Rangers' 11th choice, 202nd overall, in 1989 Entry Draft.

Season	Club	League	GP	G	A	Pts	AG	AA	APts	PIM	PP	SH	GW	S	%	TGF	PGF	TGA	PGA	+/–	GP	G	A	Pts	PIM	PP	SH	GW
1987-88	Khimik Voskresensk	USSR	11	1	0	1	....	....	....	4	....	....	....	....	....	....	....	....	....	....	....	....	....	....	....	....	....	....
1988-89	Khimik Voskresensk	USSR	34	13	3	16	....	....	....	14	....	....	....	....	....	....	....	....	....	....	....	....	....	....	....	....	....	....
	Soviet Union	WJC-A	7	6	3	9	....	....	....	4	....	....	....	....	....	....	....	....	....	....	....	....	....	....	....	....	....	....
1989-90	Khimik Voskresensk	FrTour	1	0	0	0	....	....	....	0	....	....	....	....	....	....	....	....	....	....	....	....	....	....	....	....	....	....
	Khimik Voskresensk	USSR	37	13	6	19	....	....	....	16	....	....	....	....	....	....	....	....	....	....	....	....	....	....	....	....	....	....
	Soviet Union	WJC-A	7	7	2	9	....	....	....	4	....	....	....	....	....	....	....	....	....	....	....	....	....	....	....	....	....	....
1990-91	Khimik Voskresensk	FrTour	1	0	0	0	....	....	....	0	....	....	....	....	....	....	....	....	....	....	....	....	....	....	....	....	....	....
	Khimik Voskresensk	USSR	41	12	8	20	....	....	....	24	....	....	....	....	....	....	....	....	....	....	....	....	....	....	....	....	....	....
	Khimik Voskresensk	SuperS	4	1	2	3	....	....	....	0	....	....	....	....	....	....	....	....	....	....	....	....	....	....	....	....	....	....
1991-92	Khimik Voskresensk	CIS	42	24	20	44	....	....	....	28	....	....	....	....	....	....	....	....	....	....	....	....	....	....	....	....	....	....
1992-93	Khimik Voskresensk	CIS	20	11	2	13	....	....	....	42	....	....	....	....	....	....	....	....	....	....	....	....	....	....	....	....	....	....
	Cape Breton Oilers	AHL	43	26	25	51	....	....	....	22	....	....	....	....	....	....	....	....	....	....	16	9	19	28	12	....	....	....
1993-94	**Edmonton Oilers**	**NHL**	**10**	**1**	**2**	**3**	**1**	**2**	**3**	**4**	**0**	**0**	**0**	**18**	**5.6**	**9**	**2**	**8**	**0**	**–1**	....	....	....	....	....	....	....	....
	Cape Breton Oilers	AHL	47	31	22	53	....	....	....	90	....	....	....	....	....	....	....	....	....	....	4	2	2	4	22	....	....	....

Season	Club	League	REGULAR SEASON GP	G	A	Pts	AG	AA	APts	PIM	PP	SH	GW	S	%	TGF	PGF	TGA	PGA	+/-	PLAYOFFS GP	G	A	Pts	PIM	PP	SH	GW
1994-95	Cape Breton Oilers	AHL	25	9	7	16	....	....	....	20	....	....	....	....	....	....	....	....	....	....	....	....	....	....	....	....	....	....
	Edmonton Oilers	NHL	26	11	2	13	19	3	22	8	5	0	0	52	21.2	20	9	25	0	–14	....	....	....	....	....	....	....	....
	Vancouver Canucks	NHL	12	5	2	7	9	3	12	2	1	0	1	15	33.3	11	3	6	0	+2	10	2	3	5	0	1	0	0
1995-96	Vancouver Canucks	NHL	56	16	23	39	16	19	35	42	5	0	1	92	17.4	70	20	50	2	+2	....	....	....	....	....	....	....	....
	Anaheim Mighty Ducks	NHL	14	7	5	12	7	4	11	18	6	0	0	27	25.9	19	12	5	0	+2	....	....	....	....	....	....	....	....
	Russia	WC-A	7	3	0	3	....	....	....	2	....	....	....	....	....	....	....	....	....	....	....	....	....	....	....	....	....	....
1996-97	Anaheim Mighty Ducks	NHL	28	6	7	13	6	6	12	22	2	0	0	48	12.5	18	6	24	0	–12	....	....	....	....	....	....	....	....
	Pittsburgh Penguins	NHL	7	0	0	0	0	0	0	4	0	0	0	10	0.0	2	0	6	0	–4	....	....	....	....	....	....	....	....
1997-98	Fort Wayne Komets	IHL	19	5	8	13	....	....	....	50	....	....	....	....	....	....	....	....	....	....	3	0	0	0	12	....	....	....
	NHL Totals		**153**	**46**	**41**	**87**	**58**	**37**	**95**	**100**	**19**	**0**	**2**	**262**	**17.6**	**149**	**52**	**124**	**2**		**10**	**2**	**3**	**5**	**0**	**1**	**0**	**0**

Won Izvestia Trophy (CIS Top Scorer) (1992)

Traded to **Edmonton** by **NY Rangers** with NY Rangers' 3rd round choice (Alexander Kerch) in 1993 Entry Draft for Kevin Lowe, December 11, 1992. Traded to **Vancouver** by **Edmonton** for Jiri Slegr, April 7, 1995. Traded to **Anaheim** by **Vancouver** for Mike Sillinger, March 15, 1996. Traded to **Pittsburgh** by **Anaheim** for Richard Park, March 18, 1997.

• OLAUSSON, FREDRIK

Fredrik Olausson D – R. 6'2", 195 lbs. b: Dadesjo, Sweden, 10/5/1966. Winnipeg's 4th choice, 81st overall, in 1985 Entry Draft.

Season	Club	League	GP	G	A	Pts	AG	AA	APts	PIM	PP	SH	GW	S	%	TGF	PGF	TGA	PGA	+/-	GP	G	A	Pts	PIM	PP	SH	GW
1982-83	Nybro	Sweden 2	31	4	4	8	....	....	....	12	....	....	....	....	....	....	....	....	....	....	....	....	....	....	....	....	....	....
1983-84	Nybro	Sweden 2	28	8	14	22	....	....	....	32	....	....	....	....	....	....	....	....	....	....	....	....	....	....	....	....	....	....
1984-85	Farjestad BK Stockholm	Sweden	29	5	12	17	....	....	....	22	....	....	....	....	....	....	....	....	....	....	3	1	0	1	0	....	....	....
	Sweden	WJC-A	7	1	1	2	....	....	....	4	....	....	....	....	....	....	....	....	....	....	....	....	....	....	....	....	....	....
1985-86	Farjestad BK Stockholm	Sweden	33	4	12	16	....	....	....	22	....	....	....	....	....	....	....	....	....	....	8	3	2	5	6	....	....	....
	Sweden	WJC-A	7	4	2	6	....	....	....	11	....	....	....	....	....	....	....	....	....	....	....	....	....	....	....	....	....	....
	Sweden	WEC-A	10	1	0	1	....	....	....	4	....	....	....	....	....	....	....	....	....	....	....	....	....	....	....	....	....	....
1986-87	Winnipeg Jets	NHL	72	7	29	36	6	21	27	24	1	0	2	119	5.9	82	21	70	6	–3	10	2	3	5	4	1	0	0
1987-88	Winnipeg Jets	NHL	38	5	10	15	4	7	11	18	2	0	2	65	7.7	47	15	32	3	+3	5	1	1	2	0	0	0	0
1988-89	Winnipeg Jets	NHL	75	15	47	62	13	33	46	32	4	0	1	178	8.4	148	41	129	28	+6	....	....	....	....	....	....	....	....
	Sweden	WEC-A	9	3	1	4	....	....	....	6	....	....	....	....	....	....	....	....	....	....	....	....	....	....	....	....	....	....
1989-90	Winnipeg Jets	NHL	77	9	46	55	8	33	41	32	3	0	0	147	6.1	116	36	106	25	–1	7	0	2	2	2	0	0	0
1990-91	Winnipeg Jets	NHL	71	12	29	41	11	22	33	24	5	0	0	168	7.1	95	40	91	14	–22	....	....	....	....	....	....	....	....
1991-92	Winnipeg Jets	NHL	77	20	42	62	18	32	50	34	13	1	2	227	8.8	108	65	94	20	–31	7	1	5	6	4	1	0	0
1992-93	Winnipeg Jets	NHL	68	16	41	57	13	28	41	22	11	0	3	165	9.7	110	65	57	8	–4	6	0	2	2	2	0	0	0
1993-94	Winnipeg Jets	NHL	18	2	5	7	2	4	6	10	1	0	0	41	4.9	20	10	13	0	–3	....	....	....	....	....	....	....	....
	Edmonton Oilers	NHL	55	9	19	28	8	15	23	20	6	0	1	85	10.6	72	31	67	22	–4	....	....	....	....	....	....	....	....
1994-95	Ehrwald	Austria	10	4	3	7	....	....	....	8	....	....	....	....	....	....	....	....	....	....	....	....	....	....	....	....	....	....
	Edmonton Oilers	NHL	33	0	10	10	0	15	15	20	0	0	0	52	0.0	35	10	42	13	–4	....	....	....	....	....	....	....	....
1995-96	Edmonton Oilers	NHL	20	0	6	6	0	5	5	14	0	0	0	20	0.0	19	11	28	6	–14	....	....	....	....	....	....	....	....
	Anaheim Mighty Ducks	NHL	36	2	16	18	2	13	15	24	1	0	0	63	3.2	50	27	20	4	+7	....	....	....	....	....	....	....	....
1996-97	Anaheim Mighty Ducks	NHL	20	2	9	11	2	8	10	8	1	0	0	35	5.7	28	9	29	5	–5	....	....	....	....	....	....	....	....
	Pittsburgh Penguins	NHL	51	7	20	27	7	18	25	24	2	0	3	75	9.3	83	25	44	7	+21	4	0	1	1	0	0	0	0
1997-98	Pittsburgh Penguins	NHL	76	6	27	33	7	26	33	42	2	0	1	89	6.7	96	39	54	10	+13	6	0	3	3	2	0	0	0
	NHL Totals		**787**	**112**	**356**	**468**	**101**	**280**	**381**	**348**	**52**	**1**	**15**	**1529**	**7.3**	**1109**	**445**	**876**	**171**		**45**	**4**	**17**	**21**	**14**	**2**	**0**	**0**

Swedish World All-Star Team (1986)

Traded to **Edmonton** by **Winnipeg** with Winnipeg's 7th round choice (Curtis Sheptak) in 1994 Entry Draft for Edmonton's 3rd round choice (Tavis Hansen) in 1994 Entry Draft, December 6, 1993. Claimed on waivers by **Anaheim** from **Edmonton**, January 16, 1996. Traded to **Pittsburgh** by **Anaheim** with Alex Hicks for Shawn Antoski and Dmitri Mironov, November 19, 1996.

• OLCZYK, ED

Ed Olczyk C – L. 6'1", 205 lbs. b: Chicago, IL, 8/16/1966. Chicago's 1st choice, 3rd overall, in 1984 Entry Draft.

Season	Club	League	GP	G	A	Pts	AG	AA	APts	PIM	PP	SH	GW	S	%	TGF	PGF	TGA	PGA	+/-	GP	G	A	Pts	PIM	PP	SH	GW
1983-84	United States	Nat-Team	62	21	47	68	....	....	....	36	....	....	....	....	....	....	....	....	....	....	....	....	....	....	....	....	....	....
	United States	Olympics	6	2	5	7	....	....	....	0	....	....	....	....	....	....	....	....	....	....	....	....	....	....	....	....	....	....
1984-85	Chicago Black Hawks	NHL	70	20	30	50	16	20	36	67	1	1	2	136	14.7	72	7	59	5	+11	15	6	5	11	11	1	1	0
	United States	WEC-A	6	1	6	7	....	....	....	6	....	....	....	....	....	....	....	....	....	....	....	....	....	....	....	....	....	....
1985-86	Chicago Black Hawks	NHL	79	29	50	79	23	33	56	47	8	1	2	218	13.3	124	37	108	23	+2	3	0	0	0	0	0	0	0
	United States	WEC-A	7	4	6	10	....	....	....	12	....	....	....	....	....	....	....	....	....	....	....	....	....	....	....	....	....	....
1986-87	Chicago Blackhawks	NHL	79	16	35	51	14	25	39	119	2	1	2	181	8.8	67	11	73	13	–4	4	1	1	2	4	0	0	0
	United States	WEC-A	10	4	3	7	....	....	....	10	....	....	....	....	....	....	....	....	....	....	....	....	....	....	....	....	....	....
1987-88	United States	C Cup	5	1	1	2	....	....	....	2	....	....	....	....	....	....	....	....	....	....	....	....	....	....	....	....	....	....
	Toronto Maple Leafs	NHL	80	42	33	75	36	23	59	55	14	4	3	243	17.3	100	34	132	44	–22	6	5	4	9	2	1	1	1
1988-89	Toronto Maple Leafs	NHL	80	38	52	90	32	37	69	75	11	2	4	249	15.3	119	39	111	31	0	....	....	....	....	....	....	....	....
	United States	WEC-A	10	4	3	7	....	....	....	10	....	....	....	....	....	....	....	....	....	....	....	....	....	....	....	....	....	....
1989-90	Toronto Maple Leafs	NHL	79	32	56	88	38	40	60	70	0	0	4	208	15.4	128	36	101	9	0	5	1	2	3	14	0	0	0
1990-91	Toronto Maple Leafs	NHL	18	4	10	14	4	8	12	13	0	0	0	45	8.9	17	7	21	4	–7	....	....	....	....	....	....	....	....
	Winnipeg Jets	NHL	61	26	31	57	24	23	47	69	14	0	2	181	14.4	77	36	61	0	–20	....	....	....	....	....	....	....	....
1991-92	United States	C Cup	8	0	3	3	....	....	....	4	....	....	....	....	....	....	....	....	....	....	....	....	....	....	....	....	....	....
	Winnipeg Jets	NHL	64	32	33	65	29	25	54	67	12	0	7	245	13.1	101	49	41	0	+11	6	2	1	3	4	0	0	1
1992-93	Winnipeg Jets	NHL	25	8	12	20	7	8	15	26	2	0	0	81	9.9	34	17	28	0	–11	....	....	....	....	....	....	....	....
	New York Rangers	NHL	46	13	16	29	11	11	22	26	0	0	1	109	11.9	49	15	25	0	+9	....	....	....	....	....	....	....	....
	United States	WC-A	6	1	1	2	....	....	....	18	....	....	....	....	....	....	....	....	....	....	....	....	....	....	....	....	....	....
1993-94	New York Rangers	NHL	37	3	5	8	3	4	7	28	0	0	1	40	7.5	12	2	11	0	–1	1	0	0	0	0	0	0	0
1994-95	New York Rangers	NHL	20	2	1	3	4	1	5	4	1	0	0	29	6.9	7	1	8	0	–2	....	....	....	....	....	....	....	....
	Winnipeg Jets	NHL	13	2	8	10	4	12	16	8	1	0	0	27	7.4	14	5	8	0	+1	....	....	....	....	....	....	....	....
1995-96	Winnipeg Jets	NHL	51	27	22	49	27	18	45	65	16	0	1	147	18.4	69	28	42	1	0	6	1	2	3	6	0	0	0
1996-97	Los Angeles Kings	NHL	67	21	23	44	22	20	42	45	0	0	5	166	12.7	66	22	75	9	–22	....	....	....	....	....	....	....	....
	Pittsburgh Penguins	NHL	12	4	7	11	4	6	10	6	5	1	1	29	13.8	16	4	4	0	+8	5	1	0	1	12	0	1	1
1997-98	Pittsburgh Penguins	NHL	56	11	11	22	13	11	24	35	5	1	1	123	8.9	39	17	38	7	–9	6	2	0	2	4	1	1	1
	NHL Totals		**937**	**330**	**435**	**765**	**301**	**325**	**626**	**833**	**98**	**11**	**36**	**2457**	**13.4**	**1111**	**367**	**946**	**146**		**57**	**19**	**15**	**34**	**57**	**3**	**4**	**4**

Traded to **Toronto** by **Chicago** with Al Secord for Rick Vaive, Steve Thomas and Bob McGill, September 3, 1987. Traded to **Winnipeg** by **Toronto** with Mark Osborne for Dave Ellett and Paul Fenton, November 10, 1990. Traded to **NY Rangers** by **Winnipeg** for Kris King and Tie Domi, December 28, 1992. Traded to **Winnipeg** by **NY Rangers** for Winnipeg's 5th round choice (Alexei Vasiliev) in 1995 Entry Draft, April 7, 1995. Signed as a free agent by **LA Kings**, July 8, 1996. Traded to **Pittsburgh** by **LA Kings** for Glen Murray, March 18, 1997.

• OLIVER, DAVID

David Oliver RW – R. 6', 190 lbs. b: Sechelt, B.C., 4/17/1971. Edmonton's 7th choice, 144th overall, in 1991 Entry Draft.

Season	Club	League	GP	G	A	Pts	AG	AA	APts	PIM	PP	SH	GW	S	%	TGF	PGF	TGA	PGA	+/-	GP	G	A	Pts	PIM	PP	SH	GW
1990-91	University of Michigan	CCHA	27	13	11	24	....	....	....	34	....	....	....	....	....	....	....	....	....	....	....	....	....	....	....	....	....	....
1991-92	University of Michigan	CCHA	44	31	27	58	....	....	....	32	....	....	....	....	....	....	....	....	....	....	....	....	....	....	....	....	....	....
1992-93	University of Michigan	CCHA	40	35	20	55	....	....	....	18	....	....	....	....	....	....	....	....	....	....	....	....	....	....	....	....	....	....
1993-94	University of Michigan	CCHA	41	28	40	68	....	....	....	16	....	....	....	....	....	....	....	....	....	....	....	....	....	....	....	....	....	....
1994-95	Cape Breton Oilers	AHL	32	11	18	29	....	....	....	8	....	....	....	....	....	....	....	....	....	....	....	....	....	....	....	....	....	....
	Edmonton Oilers	NHL	44	16	14	30	28	21	49	20	10	0	0	79	20.3	43	23	31	0	–11	....	....	....	....	....	....	....	....
1995-96	Edmonton Oilers	NHL	80	20	19	39	20	15	35	34	14	0	0	131	15.3	64	34	53	1	–22	....	....	....	....	....	....	....	....
1996-97	Edmonton Oilers	NHL	17	1	2	3	1	2	3	4	0	0	0	22	4.5	5	1	12	0	–8	....	....	....	....	....	....	....	....
	New York Rangers	NHL	14	2	1	3	2	1	3	4	0	0	0	13	15.4	5	0	3	1	+3	3	0	0	0	0	0	0	0
1997-98	Houston Aeros	IHL	78	38	27	65	....	....	....	60	....	....	....	....	....	....	....	....	....	....	4	3	0	3	4	....	....	....
	NHL Totals		**155**	**39**	**36**	**75**	**51**	**39**	**90**	**62**	**24**	**0**	**0**	**245**	**15.9**	**117**	**58**	**99**	**2**		**3**	**0**	**0**	**0**	**0**	**0**	**0**	**0**

CCHA Second All-Star Team (1993) • CCHA First All-Star Team (1994) • NCAA West First All-American Team (1994)

Claimed on waivers by **NY Rangers** from **Edmonton**, February 21, 1997. Signed as a free agent by **Ottawa**, July 2, 1998.

• OLIVER, MURRAY

Murray Oliver C – L. 5'10", 170 lbs. b: Hamilton, Ont., 11/14/1937.

Season	Club	League	GP	G	A	Pts	AG	AA	APts	PIM	PP	SH	GW	S	%	TGF	PGF	TGA	PGA	+/-	GP	G	A	Pts	PIM	PP	SH	GW
1953-54	Hamilton Tiger Cubs	OHA	2	0	2	2	....	....	....	0	....	....	....	....	....	....	....	....	....	....	5	1	0	1	0	....	....	....
1954-55	Hamilton Tiger Cubs	OHA	39	5	13	18	....	....	....	19	....	....	....	....	....	....	....	....	....	....	3	2	0	2	0	....	....	....
1955-56	Hamilton Tiger Cubs	OHA	5	1	1	2	....	....	....	2	....	....	....	....	....	....	....	....	....	....	....	....	....	....	....	....	....	....
1956-57	Hamilton Tiger Cubs	OHA	52	17	42	59	....	....	....	20	....	....	....	....	....	....	....	....	....	....	4	3	1	4	0	....	....	....
1957-58	Hamilton Tiger Cubs	OHA	52	34	56	90	....	....	....	37	....	....	....	....	....	....	....	....	....	....	4	2	5	7	8	....	....	....
	Detroit Red Wings	NHL	1	0	1	1	0	1	1	0	....	....	....	....	....	....	....	....	....	....	....	....	....	....	....	....	....	....
1958-59	Edmonton Flyers	WHL	64	33	34	67	....	....	....	35	....	....	....	....	....	....	....	....	....	....	3	1	1	2	0	....	....	....

Season	Club	League	GP	G	A	Pts	AG	AA	APts	PIM	PP	SH	GW	S	%	TGF	PGF	TGA	PGA	+/–	Playoffs GP	G	A	Pts	PIM	PP	SH	GW
			REGULAR SEASON																		PLAYOFFS							
1959-60	Detroit Red Wings	NHL	54	20	19	39	25	19	44	16	....	....	....	....	....	....	....	....	....	....	6	1	0	1	4	....	....	....
	Edmonton Flyers	WHL	16	8	12	20	....	....	....	6	....	....	....	....	....	....	....	....	....	....	....	....	....	....	....	....	....	....
1960-61	Detroit Red Wings	NHL	49	11	12	23	13	12	25	8	....	....	....	....	....	....	....	....	....	....	....	....	....	....	....	....	....	....
	Boston Bruins	NHL	21	6	10	16	7	10	17	8	....	....	....	....	....	....	....	....	....	....	....	....	....	....	....	....	....	....
1961-62	Boston Bruins	NHL	70	17	29	46	21	29	50	21	....	....	....	....	....	....	....	....	....	....	....	....	....	....	....	....	....	....
1962-63	Boston Bruins	NHL	65	22	40	62	27	42	69	38	....	....	....	....	....	....	....	....	....	....	....	....	....	....	....	....	....	....
1963-64	Boston Bruins	NHL	70	24	44	68	32	49	81	41	....	....	....	....	....	....	....	....	....	....	....	....	....	....	....	....	....	....
1964-65	Boston Bruins	NHL	65	20	23	43	26	25	51	30	....	....	....	....	....	....	....	....	....	....	....	....	....	....	....	....	....	....
1965-66	Boston Bruins	NHL	70	18	42	60	22	42	64	30	....	....	....	....	....	....	....	....	....	....	....	....	....	....	....	....	....	....
1966-67	Boston Bruins	NHL	65	9	26	35	11	27	38	16	....	....	....	....	....	....	....	....	....	....	....	....	....	....	....	....	....	....
1967-68	Toronto Maple Leafs	NHL	74	16	21	37	20	22	42	18	2	0	2	155	10.3	54	10	42	6	+8	....	....	....	....	....	....	....	....
1968-69	Toronto Maple Leafs	NHL	76	14	36	50	16	34	50	16	3	2	3	192	7.3	78	11	66	11	+12	4	1	2	3	0	0	0	0
1969-70	Toronto Maple Leafs	NHL	76	14	33	47	16	33	49	16	5	0	3	200	7.0	66	23	75	13	–19	....	....	....	....	....	....	....	....
1970-71	Minnesota North Stars	NHL	61	9	23	32	9	20	29	8	3	1	0	115	7.8	49	21	58	30	0	12	7	4	11	0	2	0	0
1971-72	Minnesota North Stars	NHL	77	27	29	56	29	26	55	16	7	0	4	191	14.1	88	37	50	8	+9	7	0	6	6	4	0	0	0
1972-73	Minnesota North Stars	NHL	75	11	31	42	11	26	37	10	2	0	2	174	6.3	55	7	68	24	+4	6	0	4	4	2	0	0	0
1973-74	Minnesota North Stars	NHL	78	17	20	37	17	17	34	4	3	1	0	146	11.6	53	7	95	36	–13	....	....	....	....	....	....	....	....
1974-75	Minnesota North Stars	NHL	80	19	15	34	18	12	30	24	3	1	1	137	13.9	48	11	109	53	–19	....	....	....	....	....	....	....	....
	NHL Totals		1127	274	454	728	320	446	766	320	28	5	15	1310	20.9	491	127	563	181		35	9	16	25	10	2	0	0

Played in NHL All-Star Game (1963, 1964, 1965, 1967, 1968)

Traded to **Boston** by **Detroit** with Gary Aldcorn and Tom McCarthy for Vic Stasiuk and Leo Labine, January, 1961. Traded to **Toronto** by **Boston** with cash for Eddie Shack, May 15, 1967. Traded to **Minnesota** by **Toronto** for Brian Conacher, Terry O'Malley and cash, May 22, 1970.

• OLIWA, KRZYSZTOF

Krzysztof Oliwa LW – L. 6'5", 235 lbs. b: Tychy, Poland, 4/12/1973. New Jersey's 4th choice, 65th overall, in 1993 Entry Draft.

Season	Club	League	GP	G	A	Pts	AG	AA	APts	PIM	PP	SH	GW	S	%	TGF	PGF	TGA	PGA	+/–	Playoffs GP	G	A	Pts	PIM	PP	SH	GW
1991-92	GKS Tychy	Poland	10	3	7	10	....	....	....	6	....	....	....	....	....	....	....	....	....	....	....	....	....	....	....	....	....	....
	Poland	WJC-B	6	1	1	2	....	....	....	14	....	....	....	....	....	....	....	....	....	....	....	....	....	....	....	....	....	....
1992-93	Welland Cougars	GHJHL	30	13	21	34	....	....	....	127	....	....	....	....	....	....	....	....	....	....	....	....	....	....	....	....	....	....
1993-94	Albany River Rats	AHL	33	2	4	6	....	....	....	151	....	....	....	....	....	....	....	....	....	....	....	....	....	....	....	....	....	....
	Raleigh IceCaps	ECHL	15	0	2	2	....	....	....	65	....	....	....	....	....	....	....	....	....	....	9	0	0	0	35	....	....	....
1994-95	Albany River Rats	AHL	20	1	1	2	....	....	....	77	....	....	....	....	....	....	....	....	....	....	....	....	....	....	....	....	....	....
	Saint John Flames	AHL	14	1	4	5	....	....	....	79	....	....	....	....	....	....	....	....	....	....	....	....	....	....	....	....	....	....
	Raleigh IceCaps	ECHL	5	0	2	2	....	....	....	32	....	....	....	....	....	....	....	....	....	....	....	....	....	....	....	....	....	....
	Detroit Vipers	IHL	4	0	1	1	....	....	....	24	....	....	....	....	....	....	....	....	....	....	....	....	....	....	....	....	....	....
1995-96	Albany River Rats	AHL	51	5	11	16	....	....	....	217	....	....	....	....	....	....	....	....	....	....	....	....	....	....	....	....	....	....
	Raleigh IceCaps	ECHL	9	1	0	1	....	....	....	53	....	....	....	....	....	....	....	....	....	....	....	....	....	....	....	....	....	....
1996-97	New Jersey Devils	NHL	1	0	0	0	0	0	0	5	0	0	0	0	0.0	0	0	1	0	–1	....	....	....	....	....	....	....	....
	Albany River Rats	AHL	60	13	14	27	....	....	....	322	....	....	....	....	....	....	....	....	....	....	15	7	1	8	49	....	....	....
1997-98	New Jersey Devils	NHL	73	2	3	5	2	3	5	295	0	0	2	53	3.8	10	0	7	0	+3	6	0	0	0	23	0	0	0
	NHL Totals		74	2	3	5	2	3	5	300	0	0	2	53	3.8	10	0	8	0		6	0	0	0	23	0	0	0

• OLSEN, DARRYL

Darryl Olsen D – L. 6', 180 lbs. b: Calgary, Alta., 10/7/1966. Calgary's 10th choice, 185th overall, in 1985 Entry Draft.

Season	Club	League	GP	G	A	Pts	AG	AA	APts	PIM	PP	SH	GW	S	%	TGF	PGF	TGA	PGA	+/–	Playoffs GP	G	A	Pts	PIM	PP	SH	GW
1984-85	St. Albert Saints	AJHL	57	19	48	67	....	....	....	77	....	....	....	....	....	....	....	....	....	....	....	....	....	....	....	....	....	....
1985-86	Northern Michigan University	WCHA	37	5	20	25	....	....	....	46	....	....	....	....	....	....	....	....	....	....	....	....	....	....	....	....	....	....
1986-87	Northern Michigan University	WCHA	37	5	20	25	....	....	....	96	....	....	....	....	....	....	....	....	....	....	....	....	....	....	....	....	....	....
1987-88	Northern Michigan University	WCHA	35	11	20	31	....	....	....	59	....	....	....	....	....	....	....	....	....	....	....	....	....	....	....	....	....	....
1988-89	Northern Michigan University	WCHA	45	16	26	42	....	....	....	88	....	....	....	....	....	....	....	....	....	....	....	....	....	....	....	....	....	....
	Canada	Nat-Team	3	1	0	1	....	....	....	4	....	....	....	....	....	....	....	....	....	....	....	....	....	....	....	....	....	....
1989-90	Salt Lake Golden Eagles	IHL	72	16	50	66	....	....	....	90	....	....	....	....	....	....	....	....	....	....	11	3	6	9	2	....	....	....
1990-91	Salt Lake Golden Eagles	IHL	76	15	40	55	....	....	....	89	....	....	....	....	....	....	....	....	....	....	4	1	5	6	2	....	....	....
1991-92	Calgary Flames	NHL	1	0	0	0	0	0	0	0	0	0	0	3	0.0	0	0	2	0	–2	....	....	....	....	....	....	....	....
	Salt Lake Golden Eagles	IHL	59	7	33	40	....	....	....	80	....	....	....	....	....	....	....	....	....	....	5	2	1	3	4	....	....	....
1992-93	Providence Bruins	AHL	50	7	27	34	....	....	....	38	....	....	....	....	....	....	....	....	....	....	....	....	....	....	....	....	....	....
	San Diego Gulls	IHL	21	2	8	10	....	....	....	26	....	....	....	....	....	....	....	....	....	....	10	1	3	4	30	....	....	....
1993-94	Salt Lake Golden Eagles	IHL	73	17	32	49	....	....	....	97	....	....	....	....	....	....	....	....	....	....	....	....	....	....	....	....	....	....
1994-95	Val Gardena	Italy	37	8	18	26	....	....	....	49	....	....	....	....	....	....	....	....	....	....	....	....	....	....	....	....	....	....
	Houston Aeros	IHL	4	0	1	1	....	....	....	12	....	....	....	....	....	....	....	....	....	....	....	....	....	....	....	....	....	....
1995-96	VSV Villach	Austria	33	10	31	41	....	....	....	92	....	....	....	....	....	....	....	....	....	....	....	....	....	....	....	....	....	....
1996-97	Nottingham Panthers	Britain	39	7	21	28	....	....	....	24	....	....	....	....	....	....	....	....	....	....	8	1	2	3	0	....	....	....
	NHL Totals		1	0	0	0	0	0	0	0	0	0	0	3	0.0	0	0	2	0		....	....	....	....	....	....	....	....

WCHA First All-Star Team (1989) • NCAA West First All-American Team (1991)

Signed as a free agent by **Boston**, July 23, 1992.

• OLSSON, CHRISTER

Christer Olsson D – L. 5'11", 190 lbs. b: Arboga, Sweden, 7/24/1970. St. Louis' 10th choice, 275th overall, in 1993 Entry Draft.

Season	Club	League	GP	G	A	Pts	AG	AA	APts	PIM	PP	SH	GW	S	%	TGF	PGF	TGA	PGA	+/–	Playoffs GP	G	A	Pts	PIM	PP	SH	GW
1991-92	Mora	Sweden 2	36	6	10	16	....	....	....	38	....	....	....	....	....	....	....	....	....	....	....	....	....	....	....	....	....	....
1992-93	Brynas IF Gavle	Sweden	22	4	4	8	....	....	....	18	....	....	....	....	....	....	....	....	....	....	....	....	....	....	....	....	....	....
1993-94	Brynas IF Gavle	Sweden	38	7	3	10	....	....	....	50	....	....	....	....	....	....	....	....	....	....	7	0	3	3	6	....	....	....
1994-95	Brynas IF Gavle	Sweden	39	6	5	11	....	....	....	18	....	....	....	....	....	....	....	....	....	....	14	1	3	4	8	....	....	....
	Sweden	WC-A	8	2	1	3	....	....	....	4	....	....	....	....	....	....	....	....	....	....	....	....	....	....	....	....	....	....
1995-96	St. Louis Blues	NHL	26	2	8	10	2	7	9	14	2	0	0	32	6.3	17	13	10	0	–6	3	0	0	0	0	0	0	0
	Worcester IceCats	AHL	39	7	7	14	....	....	....	22	....	....	....	....	....	....	....	....	....	....	....	....	....	....	....	....	....	....
1996-97	St. Louis Blues	NHL	5	0	1	1	0	1	1	0	0	0	0	2	0.0	3	0	3	1	+1	....	....	....	....	....	....	....	....
	Worcester IceCats	AHL	2	0	0	0	....	....	....	0	....	....	....	....	....	....	....	....	....	....	....	....	....	....	....	....	....	....
	Ottawa Senators	NHL	25	2	3	5	2	3	5	10	1	0	0	24	8.3	19	6	20	2	–5	....	....	....	....	....	....	....	....
1997-98	Vastra Frolunda	Sweden	45	13	8	21	....	....	....	54	....	....	....	....	....	....	....	....	....	....	7	0	1	1	18	....	....	....
	Sweden	WC-A	10	2	1	3	....	....	....	2	....	....	....	....	....	....	....	....	....	....	....	....	....	....	....	....	....	....
	NHL Totals		56	4	12	16	4	11	15	24	3	0	0	58	6.9	39	19	33	3		3	0	0	0	0	0	0	0

Named Best Defenseman at WC-A (1995)

Traded to **Ottawa** by **St. Louis** for Pavol Demitra, November 27, 1996.

• O'NEIL, PAUL

Paul O'Neil C/RW – R. 6'1", 185 lbs. b: Charlestown, Mass., 8/24/1953. Vancouver's 6th choice, 67th overall, in 1973 Amateur Draft.

Season	Club	League	GP	G	A	Pts	AG	AA	APts	PIM	PP	SH	GW	S	%	TGF	PGF	TGA	PGA	+/–	Playoffs GP	G	A	Pts	PIM	PP	SH	GW
1971-72	Boston University	ECAC	17	13	14	27	....	....	....	6	....	....	....	....	....	....	....	....	....	....	....	....	....	....	....	....	....	....
1972-73	Boston University	ECAC	28	35	19	54	....	....	....	8	....	....	....	....	....	....	....	....	....	....	....	....	....	....	....	....	....	....
1973-74	Vancouver Canucks	NHL	5	0	0	0	0	0	0	0	0	0	0	2	0.0	0	0	2	0	–2	....	....	....	....	....	....	....	....
	Seattle Totems	WHL	66	29	17	46	....	....	....	14	....	....	....	....	....	....	....	....	....	....	....	....	....	....	....	....	....	....
1974-75	Seattle Totems	CHL	49	16	19	51	....	....	....	17	....	....	....	....	....	....	....	....	....	....	....	....	....	....	....	....	....	....
1975-76	Boston Bruins	NHL	1	0	0	0	0	0	0	0	....	....	....	....	....	....	....	....	....	....	....	....	....	....	....	....	....	....
	Rochester Americans	AHL	49	35	16	51	....	....	....	17	....	....	....	....	....	....	....	....	....	....	6	4	3	7	4	....	....	....
1976-77	Hampton Gulls	SHL	48	21	34	55	....	....	....	0	....	....	....	....	....	....	....	....	....	....	....	....	....	....	....	....	....	....
1977-78	Hampton Gulls	AHL	36	17	27	44	....	....	....	9	....	....	....	....	....	....	....	....	....	....	....	....	....	....	....	....	....	....
	San Diego Mariners	PHL	17	11	9	20	....	....	....	0	....	....	....	....	....	....	....	....	....	....	....	....	....	....	....	....	....	....
1978-79	Birmingham Bulls	WHA	1	0	0	0	....	....	....	0	....	....	....	....	....	....	....	....	....	....	....	....	....	....	....	....	....	....
	Binghamton Dusters	AHL	5	0	3	3	....	....	....	0	....	....	....	....	....	....	....	....	....	....	....	....	....	....	....	....	....	....
	San Diego Hawks	PHL	39	30	14	44	....	....	....	14	....	....	....	....	....	....	....	....	....	....	....	....	....	....	....	....	....	....
1979-80	HC Salzburg	Austria	34	55	43	98	....	....	....	28	....	....	....	....	....	....	....	....	....	....	....	....	....	....	....	....	....	....
1980-81	Hampton Aces	EHL	33	21	16	37	....	....	....	9	....	....	....	....	....	....	....	....	....	....	....	....	....	....	....	....	....	....
	HC Salzburg	Austria	9	7	3	10	....	....	....	0	....	....	....	....	....	....	....	....	....	....	....	....	....	....	....	....	....	....
1981-82	HC Salzburg	Austria	STATISTICS NOT AVAILABLE																									
1982-83	Virginia Raiders	ACHL	55	38	41	69	....	....	....	20	....	....	....	....	....	....	....	....	....	....	1	0	1	1	0	....	....	....

Season	Club	League	GP	G	A	Pts	AG	AA	APts	PIM	PP	SH	GW	S	%	TGF	PGF	TGA	PGA	+/–	GP	G	A	Pts	PIM	PP	SH	GW
			REGULAR SEASON																		PLAYOFFS							
1983-84	Birmingham–Virginia	ACHL	70	51	72	123	....	....	....	8	....	....	....	....	....	....	....	....	....	....	4	1	0	1	0	....	....	....
1984-85	Virginia Lancers	ACHL	47	28	41	69	....	....	....	20	....	....	....	....	....	....	....	....	....	....	....	....	....	....	....	....	....	....
1985-86	Virginia Lancers	ACHL	57	34	38	72	....	....	....	18	....	....	....	....	....	....	....	....	....	....	5	2	2	4	2	....	....	....
	NHL Totals		**6**	**0**	**0**	**0**	**0**	**0**	**0**	**0**	**0**	**0**	**0**	**2**	**0.0**	**0**	**0**	**2**	**0**		....	....	....	....	....	....	....	....
	Other Major League Totals		1	0	0	0	....	....	....	0	....	....	....	....	....	....	....	....	....	....	....	....	....	....	....	....	....	....

Selected by **Houston** (WHA) in 1972 WHA General Player Draft, February 12, 1972. Signed as a free agent by **Boston**, October 10, 1975. Signed as a free agent by **Birmingham** (WHA) after **Houston** (WHA) franchise folded, July 6, 1978.

• O'NEILL, JEFF

Jeff O'Neill C – R. 6'1", 190 lbs. b: Richmond Hill, Ont., 2/23/1976. Hartford's 1st choice, 5th overall, in 1994 Entry Draft.

Season	Club	League	GP	G	A	Pts	AG	AA	APts	PIM	PP	SH	GW	S	%	TGF	PGF	TGA	PGA	+/–	GP	G	A	Pts	PIM	PP	SH	GW
1992-93	Guelph Storm	OHL	65	32	47	79	....	....	....	88	....	....	....	....	....	....	....	....	....	....	5	2	2	4	6	....	....	....
1993-94	Guelph Storm	OHL	66	45	81	126	....	....	....	95	....	....	....	....	....	....	....	....	....	....	9	2	11	13	31	....	....	....
1994-95	Guelph Storm	OHL	57	43	81	124	....	....	....	56	....	....	....	....	....	....	....	....	....	....	14	8	18	26	34	....	....	....
	Canada	WJC-A	7	2	4	6	....	....	....	2	....	....	....	....	....	....	....	....	....	....	....	....	....	....	....	....	....	....
1995-96	**Hartford Whalers**	**NHL**	**65**	**8**	**19**	**27**	**8**	**15**	**23**	**40**	**1**	**0**	**1**	**65**	**12.3**	**42**	**10**	**48**	**13**	**–3**	....	....	....	....	....	....	....	....
1996-97	**Hartford Whalers**	**NHL**	**72**	**14**	**16**	**30**	**15**	**14**	**29**	**40**	**2**	**1**	**2**	**101**	**13.9**	**38**	**9**	**58**	**5**	**–24**	....	....	....	....	....	....	....	....
	Springfield Falcons	AHL	1	0	0	0	....	....	....	0	....	....	....	....	....	....	....	....	....	....	....	....	....	....	....	....	....	....
1997-98	**Carolina Hurricanes**	**NHL**	**74**	**19**	**20**	**39**	**22**	**19**	**41**	**67**	**7**	**1**	**4**	**114**	**16.7**	**53**	**16**	**57**	**12**	**–8**	....	....	....	....	....	....	....	....
	NHL Totals		**211**	**41**	**55**	**96**	**45**	**48**	**93**	**147**	**10**	**2**	**7**	**280**	**14.6**	**133**	**35**	**163**	**30**		....	....	....	....	....	....	....	....

OHL First All-Star Team (1995)

Transferred to **Carolina** after **Hartford** franchise relocated, June 25, 1997.

• ORBAN, BILL

Bill Orban C/LW – L. 6', 185 lbs. b: Regina, Sask., 2/20/1944.

Season	Club	League	GP	G	A	Pts	AG	AA	APts	PIM	PP	SH	GW	S	%	TGF	PGF	TGA	PGA	+/–	GP	G	A	Pts	PIM	PP	SH	GW
1962-63	Saskatoon Jr. Quakers	SJHL	49	22	20	42	....	....	....	126	....	....	....	....	....	....	....	....	....	....	....	....	....	....	....	....	....	....
	Saskatoon Quakers	SSHL	....	....	....	....	....	....	....	....	....	....	....	....	....	....	....	....	....	....	3	2	2	4	0	....	....	....
1963-64	Saskatoon Jr. Quakers	SJHL	53	44	55	99	....	....	....	101	....	....	....	....	....	....	....	....	....	....	12	16	12	28	15	....	....	....
1964-65	Fort Wayne Komets	IHL	54	25	36	61	....	....	....	70	....	....	....	....	....	....	....	....	....	....	10	7	7	14	33	....	....	....
1965-66	Los Angeles Blades	WHL	72	11	20	31	....	....	....	55	....	....	....	....	....	....	....	....	....	....	....	....	....	....	....	....	....	....
1966-67	Los Angeles Blades	WHL	72	14	12	26	....	....	....	33	....	....	....	....	....	....	....	....	....	....	....	....	....	....	....	....	....	....
1967-68	**Chicago Black Hawks**	**NHL**	**39**	**3**	**2**	**5**	**4**	**2**	**6**	**17**	**0**	**0**	**0**	**21**	**14.3**	**7**	**1**	**20**	**3**	**–11**	**3**	**0**	**0**	**0**	**0**	**0**	**0**	**0**
1968-69	**Chicago Black Hawks**	**NHL**	**45**	**4**	**6**	**10**	**4**	**6**	**10**	**33**	**0**	**0**	**0**	**38**	**10.5**	**16**	**0**	**27**	**8**	**–3**	....	....	....	....	....	....	....	....
	Minnesota North Stars	**NHL**	**21**	**1**	**5**	**6**	**1**	**5**	**6**	**10**	**0**	**0**	**0**	**24**	**4.2**	**10**	**2**	**9**	**0**	**–1**	....	....	....	....	....	....	....	....
1969-70	**Minnesota North Stars**	**NHL**	**9**	**0**	**2**	**2**	**0**	**2**	**2**	**7**	**0**	**0**	**0**	**3**	**0.0**	**2**	**0**	**7**	**3**	**–2**	....	....	....	....	....	....	....	....
	Iowa Stars	CHL	65	31	44	75	....	....	....	78	....	....	....	....	....	....	....	....	....	....	10	4	2	6	27	....	....	....
1970-71	Cleveland Barons	AHL	27	6	9	15	....	....	....	34	....	....	....	....	....	....	....	....	....	....	....	....	....	....	....	....	....	....
	Springfield Kings	AHL	8	0	5	5	....	....	....	11	....	....	....	....	....	....	....	....	....	....	12	10	6	16	16	....	....	....
1971-72	Springfield Kings	AHL	42	13	18	31	....	....	....	55	....	....	....	....	....	....	....	....	....	....	5	0	0	0	9	....	....	....
1972-73	Portland Buckaroos	WHL	18	8	3	11	....	....	....	18	....	....	....	....	....	....	....	....	....	....	....	....	....	....	....	....	....	....
1973-74	Tulsa Oilers	CHL	62	16	20	36	....	....	....	38	....	....	....	....	....	....	....	....	....	....	....	....	....	....	....	....	....	....
1974-75	Dallas Black Hawks	CHL	72	15	24	39	....	....	....	46	....	....	....	....	....	....	....	....	....	....	10	5	3	8	2	....	....	....
	NHL Totals		**114**	**8**	**15**	**23**	**9**	**15**	**24**	**67**	**0**	**0**	**0**	**86**	**9.3**	**35**	**3**	**63**	**14**		**3**	**0**	**0**	**0**	**0**	**0**	**0**	**0**

Won WHL Rookie of the Year Award (1966) • CHL Second All-Star Team (1970)

Traded to **Minnesota** by **Chicago** with Tom Reid for André Boudrias and Mike McMahon, February 14, 1969. Traded to **Springfield** (AHL) by **Cleveland** (AHL) for Roger Cote, March, 1971. Claimed by **Chicago** from **LA Kings** in Intra-League Draft, June 5, 1972.

• O'REGAN, TOM

Tom O'Regan C/D – L. 5'10", 180 lbs. b: Cambridge, MA, 12/29/1961.

Season	Club	League	GP	G	A	Pts	AG	AA	APts	PIM	PP	SH	GW	S	%	TGF	PGF	TGA	PGA	+/–	GP	G	A	Pts	PIM	PP	SH	GW
1979-80	Boston University	ECAC	28	9	15	24	....	....	....	31	....	....	....	....	....	....	....	....	....	....	....	....	....	....	....	....	....	....
1980-81	Boston University	ECAC	20	10	10	20	....	....	....	41	....	....	....	....	....	....	....	....	....	....	....	....	....	....	....	....	....	....
1981-82	Boston University	ECAC	28	18	34	52	....	....	....	67	....	....	....	....	....	....	....	....	....	....	....	....	....	....	....	....	....	....
1982-83	Boston University	ECAC	27	15	17	32	....	....	....	43	....	....	....	....	....	....	....	....	....	....	....	....	....	....	....	....	....	....
1983-84	**Pittsburgh Penguins**	**NHL**	**51**	**4**	**10**	**14**	**3**	**7**	**10**	**8**	**0**	**0**	**0**	**44**	**9.1**	**16**	**1**	**63**	**26**	**–22**	....	....	....	....	....	....	....	....
	Baltimore Skipjacks	AHL	25	13	14	27	....	....	....	15	....	....	....	....	....	....	....	....	....	....	....	....	....	....	....	....	....	....
1984-85	**Pittsburgh Penguins**	**NHL**	**1**	**0**	**0**	**0**	**0**	**0**	**0**	**0**	**0**	**0**	**0**	**1**	**0.0**	**0**	**0**	**2**	**1**	**–1**	....	....	....	....	....	....	....	....
	Baltimore Skipjacks	AHL	62	28	28	56	....	....	....	62	....	....	....	....	....	....	....	....	....	....	10	4	5	9	0	....	....	....
1985-86	**Pittsburgh Penguins**	**NHL**	**9**	**1**	**2**	**3**	**1**	**1**	**2**	**2**	**0**	**0**	**0**	**7**	**14.3**	**3**	**0**	**8**	**6**	**+1**	....	....	....	....	....	....	....	....
	Baltimore Skipjacks	AHL	61	23	31	54	....	....	....	65	....	....	....	....	....	....	....	....	....	....	....	....	....	....	....	....	....	....
1986-87	Adirondack Red Wings	AHL	58	20	42	62	....	....	....	78	....	....	....	....	....	....	....	....	....	....	11	3	9	12	10	....	....	....
1987-88	EV Landshut	Germany	39	31	30	61	....	....	....	110	....	....	....	....	....	....	....	....	....	....	....	....	....	....	....	....	....	....
1988-89	EV Landshut	Germany	36	19	34	53	....	....	....	74	....	....	....	....	....	....	....	....	....	....	3	2	1	3	8	....	....	....
	United States	WEC-A	8	2	1	3	....	....	....	8	....	....	....	....	....	....	....	....	....	....	....	....	....	....	....	....	....	....
1989-90	Preussen Berlin Devils	Germany	34	27	32	59	....	....	....	71	....	....	....	....	....	....	....	....	....	....	6	1	5	6	14	....	....	....
	United States	WEC-A	10	1	1	2	....	....	....	6	....	....	....	....	....	....	....	....	....	....	....	....	....	....	....	....	....	....
1990-91	Preussen Berlin Devils	Germany	43	21	26	47	....	....	....	72	....	....	....	....	....	....	....	....	....	....	8	6	3	9	6	....	....	....
1991-92	Preussen Berlin Devils	Germany	42	20	30	50	....	....	....	93	....	....	....	....	....	....	....	....	....	....	....	....	....	....	....	....	....	....
1992-93	Preussen Berlin Devils	Germany	30	11	18	29	....	....	....	*98	....	....	....	....	....	....	....	....	....	....	....	....	....	....	....	....	....	....
1993-94	Preussen Berlin Devils	Germany	42	18	28	46	....	....	....	66	....	....	....	....	....	....	....	....	....	....	....	....	....	....	....	....	....	....
1994-95	Preussen Berlin Devils	Germany	43	7	43	50	....	....	....	66	....	....	....	....	....	....	....	....	....	....	12	4	9	13	12	....	....	....
	United States	WC-A	6	0	2	2	....	....	....	6	....	....	....	....	....	....	....	....	....	....	....	....	....	....	....	....	....	....
1995-96	Preussen Berlin Devils	Germany	45	14	34	48	....	....	....	20	....	....	....	....	....	....	....	....	....	....	13	4	10	14	22	....	....	....
	United States	WC-A	8	0	0	0	....	....	....	4	....	....	....	....	....	....	....	....	....	....	....	....	....	....	....	....	....	....
1996-97	Berlin Capitals	Germany	43	5	18	23	....	....	....	30	....	....	....	....	....	....	....	....	....	....	4	1	1	2	0	....	....	....
1997-98	Berlin Capitals	Germany	47	9	22	31	....	....	....	78	....	....	....	....	....	....	....	....	....	....	....	....	....	....	....	....	....	....
	NHL Totals		**61**	**5**	**12**	**17**	**4**	**8**	**12**	**10**	**0**	**0**	**0**	**52**	**9.6**	**19**	**1**	**73**	**33**		....	....	....	....	....	....	....	....

Signed as a free agent by **Pittsburgh**, September 4, 1983. Signed as a free agent by **Detroit**, September 29, 1986.

• O'REILLY, TERRY

Terry O'Reilly RW – R. 6'1", 200 lbs. b: Niagara Falls, Ont., 6/7/1951. Boston's 2nd choice, 14th overall, in 1971 Amateur Draft.

Season	Club	League	GP	G	A	Pts	AG	AA	APts	PIM	PP	SH	GW	S	%	TGF	PGF	TGA	PGA	+/–	GP	G	A	Pts	PIM	PP	SH	GW
1968-69	Oshawa Generals	OHA	46	5	15	20	....	....	....	87	....	....	....	....	....	....	....	....	....	....	....	....	....	....	....	....	....	....
1969-70	Oshawa Generals	OHA	54	13	36	49	....	....	....	60	....	....	....	....	....	....	....	....	....	....	....	....	....	....	....	....	....	....
1970-71	Oshawa Generals	OHA	54	23	42	65	....	....	....	151	....	....	....	....	....	....	....	....	....	....	....	....	....	....	....	....	....	....
1971-72	**Boston Bruins**	**NHL**	**1**	**1**	**0**	**1**	**1**	**0**	**1**	**0**	**0**	**0**	**0**	**2**	**50.0**	**3**	**0**	**0**	**0**	**+3**	....	....	....	....	....	....	....	....
	Boston Braves	AHL	60	9	8	17	....	....	....	134	....	....	....	....	....	....	....	....	....	....	9	2	2	4	31	....	....	....
1972-73	**Boston Bruins**	**NHL**	**72**	**5**	**22**	**27**	**5**	**18**	**23**	**109**	**0**	**0**	**1**	**80**	**6.3**	**54**	**0**	**27**	**0**	**+27**	**5**	**0**	**0**	**0**	**2**	**0**	**0**	**0**
1973-74	**Boston Bruins**	**NHL**	**76**	**11**	**24**	**35**	**11**	**21**	**32**	**94**	**0**	**0**	**1**	**86**	**12.8**	**55**	**0**	**25**	**0**	**+30**	**16**	**2**	**5**	**7**	**38**	**0**	**0**	**0**
1974-75	**Boston Bruins**	**NHL**	**68**	**15**	**20**	**35**	**14**	**16**	**30**	**146**	**2**	**0**	**2**	**93**	**16.1**	**60**	**3**	**42**	**0**	**+15**	**3**	**0**	**0**	**0**	**17**	**0**	**0**	**0**
1975-76	**Boston Bruins**	**NHL**	**80**	**23**	**27**	**50**	**21**	**21**	**42**	**150**	**2**	**0**	**2**	**135**	**17.0**	**60**	**4**	**53**	**0**	**+3**	**12**	**3**	**1**	**4**	**25**	**0**	**0**	**0**
1976-77	**Boston Bruins**	**NHL**	**79**	**14**	**41**	**55**	**13**	**33**	**46**	**147**	**1**	**1**	**4**	**137**	**10.2**	**85**	**4**	**43**	**0**	**+38**	**14**	**5**	**6**	**11**	**28**	**0**	**0**	**1**
1977-78	**Boston Bruins**	**NHL**	**77**	**29**	**61**	**90**	**28**	**50**	**78**	**211**	**5**	**0**	**4**	**166**	**17.5**	**120**	**28**	**52**	**0**	**+40**	**15**	**5**	**10**	**15**	**40**	**1**	**0**	**1**
1978-79	**Boston Bruins**	**NHL**	**80**	**26**	**51**	**77**	**24**	**39**	**63**	**205**	**3**	**0**	**5**	**120**	**21.7**	**106**	**23**	**76**	**0**	**+7**	**11**	**0**	**6**	**6**	**25**	**0**	**0**	**0**
1979-80	**Boston Bruins**	**NHL**	**71**	**19**	**42**	**61**	**17**	**32**	**49**	**265**	**3**	**0**	**5**	**105**	**18.1**	**87**	**14**	**58**	**2**	**+17**	**10**	**3**	**6**	**9**	**69**	**2**	**0**	**1**
1980-81	**Boston Bruins**	**NHL**	**77**	**8**	**35**	**43**	**7**	**24**	**31**	**223**	**0**	**0**	**0**	**84**	**9.5**	**69**	**11**	**63**	**7**	**+2**	**3**	**1**	**2**	**3**	**12**	**0**	**0**	**0**
1981-82	**Boston Bruins**	**NHL**	**70**	**22**	**30**	**52**	**17**	**20**	**37**	**213**	**0**	**1**	**3**	**114**	**19.3**	**72**	**4**	**55**	**10**	**+23**	**11**	**5**	**4**	**9**	**56**	**0**	**0**	**1**
1982-83	**Boston Bruins**	**NHL**	**19**	**6**	**14**	**20**	**5**	**10**	**15**	**40**	**0**	**1**	**1**	**23**	**26.1**	**28**	**1**	**13**	**2**	**+16**	....	....	....	....	....	....	....	....
1983-84	**Boston Bruins**	**NHL**	**58**	**12**	**18**	**30**	**10**	**12**	**22**	**124**	**2**	**0**	**2**	**48**	**25.0**	**44**	**3**	**43**	**11**	**+9**	**3**	**0**	**0**	**0**	**14**	**0**	**0**	**0**
1984-85	**Boston Bruins**	**NHL**	**63**	**13**	**17**	**30**	**11**	**11**	**22**	**168**	**0**	**1**	**2**	**61**	**21.3**	**43**	**3**	**66**	**8**	**–18**	**5**	**1**	**2**	**3**	**9**	**0**	**0**	**0**
	NHL Totals		**891**	**204**	**402**	**606**	**184**	**307**	**491**	**2095**	**18**	**4**	**32**	**1254**	**16.3**	**886**	**98**	**616**	**40**		**108**	**25**	**42**	**67**	**335**	**3**	**0**	**4**

Played in NHL All-Star Game (1975, 1978)

			REGULAR SEASON																		PLAYOFFS							
Season	Club	League	GP	G	A	Pts	AG	AA	APts	PIM	PP	SH	GW	S	%	TGF	PGF	TGA	PGA	+/–	GP	G	A	Pts	PIM	PP	SH	GW

● ORLANDO, GAETANO

Gaetano "Gates" Orlando C – R. 5'8", 180 lbs. b: Montreal, Que., 11/13/1962. Buffalo's 10th choice, 164th overall, in 1981 Entry Draft.

Season	Club	League	GP	G	A	Pts	AG	AA	APts	PIM	PP	SH	GW	S	%	TGF	PGF	TGA	PGA	+/–	GP	G	A	Pts	PIM	PP	SH	GW
1979-80	Montreal Jr. Canadiens	QMJHL	70	28	44	72	....	....	....	50	....	....	....	....	....	....	....	....	....	....	9	6	5	11	8	....	....	....
1980-81	Providence College	ECAC	31	24	32	56	....	....	....	45	....	....	....	....	....	....	....	....	....	....	....	....	....	....	....	....	....	....
1981-82	Providence College	ECAC	28	18	18	36	....	....	....	31	....	....	....	....	....	....	....	....	....	....	....	....	....	....	....	....	....	....
1982-83	Providence College	ECAC	40	30	39	69	....	....	....	32	....	....	....	....	....	....	....	....	....	....	....	....	....	....	....	....	....	....
1983-84	Providence College	ECAC	30	21	28	49	....	....	....	....	....	....	....	....	....	....	....	....	....	....	....	....	....	....	....	....	....	....
	Rochester Americans	AHL	11	8	7	15	....	....	....	2	....	....	....	....	....	....	....	....	....	....	18	4	10	14	6	....	....	....
1984-85	**Buffalo Sabres**	**NHL**	**11**	**3**	**6**	**9**	**2**	**4**	**6**	**6**	**1**	**0**	**0**	**22**	**13.6**	**12**	**3**	**6**	**0**	**+3**	**5**	**0**	**4**	**4**	**14**	**0**	**0**	**0**
	Rochester Americans	AHL	49	26	30	56	....	....	....	62	....	....	....	....	....	....	....	....	....	....	2	0	1	1	6	....	....	....
1985-86	**Buffalo Sabres**	**NHL**	**60**	**13**	**12**	**25**	**10**	**8**	**18**	**29**	**1**	**2**	**1**	**70**	**18.6**	**32**	**3**	**48**	**12**	**–7**	....	....	....	....	....	....	....	....
	Rochester Americans	AHL	3	4	0	4	....	....	....	10	....	....	....	....	....	....	....	....	....	....	....	....	....	....	....	....	....	....
1986-87	**Buffalo Sabres**	**NHL**	**27**	**2**	**8**	**10**	**2**	**6**	**8**	**16**	**0**	**0**	**0**	**24**	**8.3**	**14**	**0**	**31**	**11**	**–6**	....	....	....	....	....	....	....	....
	Rochester Americans	AHL	44	22	42	64	....	....	....	42	....	....	....	....	....	....	....	....	....	....	18	9	13	*22	14	....	....	....
1987-88	HC Meran	Italy	36	49	44	93	....	....	....	66	....	....	....	....	....	....	....	....	....	....	....	....	....	....	....	....	....	....
	Rochester Americans	AHL	13	4	13	17	....	....	....	18	....	....	....	....	....	....	....	....	....	....	7	2	6	8	6	....	....	....
1988-89	HC Bolzano	Italy	44	57	44	102	....	....	....	66	....	....	....	....	....	....	....	....	....	....	....	....	....	....	....	....	....	....
1989-90	HC Bolzano	Italy	42	72	72	144	....	....	....	24	....	....	....	....	....	....	....	....	....	....	....	....	....	....	....	....	....	....
	Italy	WEC-B	7	9	4	13	....	....	....	6	....	....	....	....	....	....	....	....	....	....	....	....	....	....	....	....	....	....
1990-91	HC Bolzano	Italy	27	39	33	72	....	....	....	29	....	....	....	....	....	....	....	....	....	....	....	....	....	....	....	....	....	....
	Italy	WEC-B	7	8	4	12	....	....	....	2	....	....	....	....	....	....	....	....	....	....	....	....	....	....	....	....	....	....
1991-92	Milano Devils	Italy	29	32	39	*71	....	....	....	54	....	....	....	....	....	....	....	....	....	....	....	....	....	....	....	....	....	....
	Italy	WC-A	5	0	3	3	....	....	....	4	....	....	....	....	....	....	....	....	....	....	....	....	....	....	....	....	....	....
1992-93	Milano Devils	Italy	27	14	27	41	....	....	....	37	....	....	....	....	....	....	....	....	....	....	....	....	....	....	....	....	....	....
	Italy	WC-A	6	1	0	1	....	....	....	2	....	....	....	....	....	....	....	....	....	....	....	....	....	....	....	....	....	....
1993-94	Milano Devils	Italy	28	24	*54	*78	....	....	....	37	....	....	....	....	....	....	....	....	....	....	....	....	....	....	....	....	....	....
	Italy	Olympics	7	3	6	9	....	....	....	4	....	....	....	....	....	....	....	....	....	....	....	....	....	....	....	....	....	....
	Italy	WC-A	6	3	4	7	....	....	....	6	....	....	....	....	....	....	....	....	....	....	....	....	....	....	....	....	....	....
1994-95	SC Bern	Switz.	36	24	31	55	....	....	....	58	....	....	....	....	....	....	....	....	....	....	6	3	7	10	8	....	....	....
	Italy	WC-A	6	1	2	3	....	....	....	12	....	....	....	....	....	....	....	....	....	....	....	....	....	....	....	....	....	....
1995-96	SC Bern	Switz.	34	15	26	41	....	....	....	62	....	....	....	....	....	....	....	....	....	....	11	*10	8	18	*45	....	....	....
	Italy	WC-A	6	2	5	7	....	....	....	6	....	....	....	....	....	....	....	....	....	....	....	....	....	....	....	....	....	....
1996-97	SC Bern	Switz.	46	26	*56	*82	....	....	....	34	....	....	....	....	....	....	....	....	....	....	13	7	*10	*17	12	....	....	....
	Italy	WC-A	8	5	4	9	....	....	....	14	....	....	....	....	....	....	....	....	....	....	....	....	....	....	....	....	....	....
1997-98	SC Bern	Switz.	38	16	32	48	....	....	....	73	....	....	....	....	....	....	....	....	....	....	7	6	3	9	18	....	....	....
	Italy	Olympics	4	1	2	3	....	....	....	4	....	....	....	....	....	....	....	....	....	....	....	....	....	....	....	....	....	....
	Italy	WC-A	6	3	2	5	....	....	....	2	....	....	....	....	....	....	....	....	....	....	....	....	....	....	....	....	....	....
	NHL Totals		**98**	**18**	**26**	**44**	**14**	**18**	**32**	**51**	**2**	**2**	**1**	**116**	**15.5**	**58**	**6**	**85**	**23**		**5**	**0**	**4**	**4**	**14**	**0**	**0**	**0**

ECAC First All-Star Team (1984) • Named Best Forward at WEC-B (1990) • WEC-B All-Star Team (1991)

● ORLESKI, DAVE

Dave Orleski LW – L. 6'4", 210 lbs. b: Edmonton, Alta., 12/26/1959. Montreal's 6th choice, 79th overall, in 1979 Entry Draft.

Season	Club	League	GP	G	A	Pts	AG	AA	APts	PIM	PP	SH	GW	S	%	TGF	PGF	TGA	PGA	+/–	GP	G	A	Pts	PIM	PP	SH	GW
1975-76	Edmonton Midgets	Midget	STATISTICS NOT AVAILABLE																									
1976-77	New Westminster Bruins	WCHL	62	8	14	22	....	....	....	29	....	....	....	....	....	....	....	....	....	....	14	3	4	7	8	....	....	....
1977-78	New Westminster Bruins	WCJHL	64	15	35	50	....	....	....	132	....	....	....	....	....	....	....	....	....	....	14	12	9	21	28	....	....	....
1978-79	New Westminster Bruins	WHL	71	27	39	66	....	....	....	128	....	....	....	....	....	....	....	....	....	....	8	3	4	7	2	....	....	....
	Canada	WJC-A	5	2	0	2	....	....	....	0	....	....	....	....	....	....	....	....	....	....	....	....	....	....	....	....	....	....
1979-80	Nova Scotia Voyageurs	AHL	70	24	24	48	....	....	....	32	....	....	....	....	....	....	....	....	....	....	6	0	2	2	0	....	....	....
1980-81	**Montreal Canadiens**	**NHL**	**1**	**0**	**0**	**0**	**0**	**0**	**0**	**0**	**0**	**0**	**0**	**0**	**0.0**	**0**	**0**	**0**	**0**	**0**	....	....	....	....	....	....	....	....
	Nova Scotia Voyageurs	AHL	37	8	13	21	....	....	....	44	....	....	....	....	....	....	....	....	....	....	6	2	1	3	7	....	....	....
1981-82	**Montreal Canadiens**	**NHL**	**1**	**0**	**0**	**0**	**0**	**0**	**0**	**0**	**0**	**0**	**0**	**0**	**0.0**	**0**	**0**	**0**	**0**	**0**	....	....	....	....	....	....	....	....
	Nova Scotia Voyageurs	AHL	64	14	23	37	....	....	....	15	....	....	....	....	....	....	....	....	....	....	9	1	2	3	6	....	....	....
1982-83	Nova Scotia Voyageurs	AHL	68	30	37	67	....	....	....	28	....	....	....	....	....	....	....	....	....	....	3	1	0	1	0	....	....	....
1983-84	Salt Lake Golden Eagles	CHL	3	0	1	1	....	....	....	4	....	....	....	....	....	....	....	....	....	....	....	....	....	....	....	....	....	....
	Nova Scotia Voyageurs	AHL	20	6	9	15	....	....	....	14	....	....	....	....	....	....	....	....	....	....	12	2	2	4	0	....	....	....
1984-85	Nova Scotia Voyageurs	AHL	2	0	1	1	....	....	....	0	....	....	....	....	....	....	....	....	....	....	....	....	....	....	....	....	....	....
	NHL Totals		**2**	**0**	**0**	**0**	**0**	**0**	**0**	**0**	**0**	**0**	**0**	**0**	**0.0**	**0**	**0**	**0**	**0**		....	....	....	....	....	....	....	....

● ORR, BOBBY

Bobby Orr D – L. 6', 197 lbs. b: Parry Sound, Ont., 3/20/1948. **HHOF**

Season	Club	League	GP	G	A	Pts	AG	AA	APts	PIM	PP	SH	GW	S	%	TGF	PGF	TGA	PGA	+/–	GP	G	A	Pts	PIM	PP	SH	GW
1962-63	Oshawa Generals	Tor-Jr.	34	6	15	21	....	....	....	45	....	....	....	....	....	....	....	....	....	....	....	....	....	....	....	....	....	....
1963-64	Oshawa Generals	OHA	56	29	43	72	....	....	....	142	....	....	....	....	....	....	....	....	....	....	6	0	7	7	21	....	....	....
1964-65	Oshawa Generals	OHA	56	34	59	93	....	....	....	112	....	....	....	....	....	....	....	....	....	....	6	0	6	6	10	....	....	....
1965-66	Oshawa Generals	OHA	47	38	56	94	....	....	....	92	....	....	....	....	....	....	....	....	....	....	17	9	19	28	14	....	....	....
1966-67	**Boston Bruins**	**NHL**	**61**	**13**	**28**	**41**	**16**	**29**	**45**	**102**	....	....	....	....	....	....	....	....	....	....	....	....	....	....	....	....	....	....
1967-68	**Boston Bruins**	**NHL**	**46**	**11**	**20**	**31**	**14**	**21**	**35**	**63**	**3**	**0**	**1**	**172**	**6.4**	**99**	**28**	**56**	**15**	**+30**	**4**	**0**	**2**	**2**	**2**	**0**	**0**	**0**
1968-69	**Boston Bruins**	**NHL**	**67**	**21**	**43**	**64**	**24**	**41**	**65**	**133**	**4**	**0**	**2**	**285**	**7.4**	**163**	**46**	**87**	**35**	**+65**	**10**	**1**	**7**	**8**	**10**	**0**	**0**	**0**
1969-70	**Boston Bruins**	**NHL**	**76**	**33**	***87**	***120**	**38**	**87**	**125**	**125**	**11**	**4**	**3**	**413**	**8.0**	**192**	**79**	**100**	**41**	**+54**	**14**	**9**	**11**	**20**	**14**	**3**	**2**	**1**
1970-71	**Boston Bruins**	**NHL**	**78**	**37**	***102**	**139**	**39**	**91**	**130**	**91**	**5**	**3**	**5**	**392**	**9.4**	**258**	**79**	**85**	**30**	**+124**	**7**	**5**	**7**	**12**	**25**	**1**	**1**	**1**
1971-72	**Boston Bruins**	**NHL**	**76**	**37**	**80**	**117**	**40**	**74**	**114**	**106**	**11**	**4**	**4**	**353**	**10.5**	**209**	**69**	**83**	**29**	**+86**	**15**	**5**	***19**	***24**	**19**	**4**	**0**	**1**
1972-73	Canada	Summit	DID NOT PLAY – INJURED																									
	Boston Bruins	**NHL**	**63**	**29**	**72**	**101**	**29**	**61**	**90**	**99**	**7**	**1**	**3**	**282**	**10.3**	**173**	**57**	**90**	**30**	**+56**	**5**	**1**	**1**	**2**	**7**	**0**	**0**	**0**
1973-74	**Boston Bruins**	**NHL**	**74**	**32**	***90**	**122**	**33**	**79**	**112**	**82**	**11**	**0**	**4**	**384**	**8.3**	**229**	**62**	**115**	**32**	**+84**	**16**	**4**	***14**	**18**	**28**	**1**	**0**	**2**
1974-75	**Boston Bruins**	**NHL**	**80**	**46**	***89**	***135**	**43**	**71**	**114**	**101**	**16**	**2**	**4**	**384**	**12.0**	**246**	**81**	**129**	**44**	**+80**	**3**	**1**	**5**	**6**	**2**	**0**	**1**	**0**
1975-76	**Boston Bruins**	**NHL**	**10**	**5**	**13**	**18**	**5**	**10**	**15**	**22**	**3**	**1**	**0**	**57**	**8.8**	**32**	**13**	**11**	**2**	**+10**	....	....	....	....	....	....	....	....
1976-77	Canada	C Cup	7	2	7	9	....	....	....	8	....	....	....	....	....	....	....	....	....	....	....	....	....	....	....	....	....	....
	Chicago Black Hawks	**NHL**	**20**	**4**	**19**	**23**	**4**	**15**	**19**	**25**	**2**	**0**	**0**	**55**	**7.3**	**42**	**20**	**20**	**4**	**+6**	....	....	....	....	....	....	....	....
1977-78			DID NOT PLAY – INJURED																									
1978-79	**Chicago Black Hawks**	**NHL**	**6**	**2**	**2**	**4**	**2**	**2**	**4**	**4**	**0**	**0**	**0**	**18**	**11.1**	**8**	**1**	**5**	**0**	**+2**	....	....	....	....	....	....	....	....
	NHL Totals		**657**	**270**	**645**	**915**	**287**	**581**	**868**	**953**	**73**	**15**	**26**	**2795**	**9.7**	**1651**	**535**	**781**	**262**		**74**	**26**	**66**	**92**	**107**	**9**	**4**	**5**

Canada Cup All-Star Team (1976) • Named Canada Cup MVP (1976) • Won Lester Patrick Trophy (1979) • NHL Second All-Star Team (1967) • Won Calder Memorial Trophy (1967) • NHL First All-Star Team (1968, 1969, 1970, 1971, 1972, 1973, 1974, 1975) • Won James Norris Trophy (1968, 1969, 1970, 1971, 1972, 1973, 1974,1975) • NHL Plus/Minus Leader (1969, 1970, 1971, 1972, 1974, 1975) • Won Art Ross Trophy (1970, 1975) • Won Hart Trophy (1970, 1971, 1972) • Won Conn Smythe Trophy (1970, 1972) • Won Lester B. Pearson Award (1975)

Played in NHL All-Star Game (1968, 1969, 1970, 1971, 1972, 1973, 1975)

Signed as a free agent by **Chicago**, June 24, 1976. • Missed entire 1977-78 season recovering from knee surgery, April 19, 1977.

● ORSZAGH, VLADIMIR

Vladimir Orszagh RW – L. 5'11", 173 lbs. b: Banska Bystrica, Czech., 5/24/1977. NY Islanders' 4th choice, 106th overall, in 1995 Entry Draft.

Season	Club	League	GP	G	A	Pts	AG	AA	APts	PIM	PP	SH	GW	S	%	TGF	PGF	TGA	PGA	+/–	GP	G	A	Pts	PIM	PP	SH	GW
1994-95	B. Bystrica	Slov. 2	38	18	12	30	....	....	....	....	....	....	....	....	....	....	....	....	....	....	....	....	....	....	....	....	....	....
	Slovakia	WJC-B	7	1	2	3	....	....	....	8	....	....	....	....	....	....	....	....	....	....	....	....	....	....	....	....	....	....
1995-96	B. Bystrica	Slovakia	31	9	5	14	....	....	....	22	....	....	....	....	....	....	....	....	....	....	....	....	....	....	....	....	....	....
	Slovakia	WJC-A	6	5	1	6	....	....	....	18	....	....	....	....	....	....	....	....	....	....	....	....	....	....	....	....	....	....
1996-97	Utah Grizzlies	IHL	68	12	15	27	....	....	....	30	....	....	....	....	....	....	....	....	....	....	3	0	1	1	4	....	....	....
1997-98	**New York Islanders**	**NHL**	**11**	**0**	**1**	**1**	**0**	**1**	**1**	**2**	**0**	**0**	**0**	**9**	**0.0**	**1**	**0**	**4**	**0**	**–3**	....	....	....	....	....	....	....	....
	Utah Grizzlies	IHL	62	13	10	23	....	....	....	60	....	....	....	....	....	....	....	....	....	....	4	2	0	2	0	....	....	....
	NHL Totals		**11**	**0**	**1**	**1**	**0**	**1**	**1**	**2**	**0**	**0**	**0**	**9**	**0.0**	**1**	**0**	**4**	**0**		....	....	....	....	....	....	....	....

● OSBORNE, KEITH

Keith Osborne RW – R. 6'1", 180 lbs. b: Toronto, Ont., 4/2/1969. St. Louis' 1st choice, 12th overall, in 1987 Entry Draft.

Season	Club	League	GP	G	A	Pts	AG	AA	APts	PIM	PP	SH	GW	S	%	TGF	PGF	TGA	PGA	+/–	GP	G	A	Pts	PIM	PP	SH	GW
1985-86	Toronto Red Wings	Midget	42	48	63	111	....	....	....	36	....	....	....	....	....	....	....	....	....	....	....	....	....	....	....	....	....	....
1986-87	North Bay Centennials	OHL	61	34	55	89	....	....	....	31	....	....	....	....	....	....	....	....	....	....	24	11	11	22	25	....	....	....
1987-88	North Bay Centennials	OHL	30	14	22	36	....	....	....	20	....	....	....	....	....	....	....	....	....	....	4	1	5	6	8	....	....	....
1988-89	North Bay Centennials	OHL	15	11	15	26	....	....	....	12	....	....	....	....	....	....	....	....	....	....	....	....	....	....	....	....	....	....
	Niagara Falls Thunder	OHL	50	34	49	83	....	....	....	45	....	....	....	....	....	....	....	....	....	....	17	12	12	24	36	....	....	....
1989-90	**St. Louis Blues**	**NHL**	**5**	**0**	**2**	**2**	**0**	**1**	**1**	**8**	**0**	**0**	**0**	**4**	**0.0**	**3**	**0**	**5**	**0**	**–2**	....	....	....	....	....	....	....	....
	Peoria Rivermen	IHL	56	23	24	47	....	....	....	58	....	....	....	....	....	....	....	....	....	....	5	1	1	2	4	....	....	....

Season	Club	League	REGULAR SEASON																		PLAYOFFS							
			GP	G	A	Pts	AG	AA	APts	PIM	PP	SH	GW	S	%	TGF	PGF	TGA	PGA	+/–	GP	G	A	Pts	PIM	PP	SH	GW
1990-91	Peoria Rivermen	IHL	54	10	20	30	....	....	....	79	....	....	....	....	....	....	....	....	....	....	....	....	....	....	....	....	....	....
	Newmarket Saints	AHL	12	0	3	3	....	....	....	6	....	....	....	....	....	....	....	....	....	....	....	....	....	....	....	....	....	....
1991-92	St. John's Maple Leafs	AHL	53	11	16	27	....	....	....	21	....	....	....	....	....	....	....	....	....	....	4	0	1	1	2	....	....	....
1992-93	**Tampa Bay Lightning**	**NHL**	**11**	**1**	**1**	**2**	**1**	**1**	**2**	**8**	**0**	**0**	**1**	**11**	**9.1**	**5**	**1**	**5**	**0**	**–1**	....	....	....	....	....	....	....	....
	Atlanta Knights	IHL	72	40	49	89	....	....	....	91	....	....	....	....	....	....	....	....	....	....	8	1	5	6	2	....	....	....
1993-94	Zurich Grasshoppers	Switz. B	36	26	31	57	....	....	....	....	....	....	....	....	....	....	....	....	....	....	....	....	....	....	....	....	....	....
	NHL Totals		**16**	**1**	**3**	**4**	**1**	**2**	**3**	**16**	**0**	**0**	**1**	**15**	**6.7**	**8**	**1**	**10**	**0**		....	....	....	....	....	....	....	....

Traded to **Toronto** by **St. Louis** for Darren Veitch and future considerations, March 5, 1991. Claimed by **Tampa Bay** from **Toronto** in Expansion Draft, June 18, 1992.

• OSBORNE, MARK

Mark "Ozzie" Osborne LW – L. 6'2", 205 lbs. b: Toronto, Ont., 8/13/1961. Detroit's 2nd choice, 46th overall, in 1980 Entry Draft.

Season	Club	League	GP	G	A	Pts	AG	AA	APts	PIM	PP	SH	GW	S	%	TGF	PGF	TGA	PGA	+/–	GP	G	A	Pts	PIM	PP	SH	GW
1978-79	Niagara Falls Flyers	OHA	62	17	25	42	....	....	....	53	....	....	....	....	....	....	....	....	....	....	....	....	....	....	....	....	....	....
1979-80	Niagara Falls Flyers	OHA	52	10	33	43	....	....	....	104	....	....	....	....	....	....	....	....	....	....	10	2	1	3	23	....	....	....
1980-81	Niagara Falls Flyers	OHA	54	39	41	80	....	....	....	140	....	....	....	....	....	....	....	....	....	....	12	11	10	21	20	....	....	....
	Adirondack Red Wings	AHL	....	....	....	....	....	....	....	....	....	....	....	....	....	....	....	....	....	....	13	2	3	5	2	....	....	....
1981-82	**Detroit Red Wings**	**NHL**	**80**	**26**	**41**	**67**	**21**	**27**	**48**	**61**	**5**	**0**	**3**	**181**	**14.4**	**97**	**19**	**88**	**3**	**–7**	....	....	....	....	....	....	....	....
1982-83	**Detroit Red Wings**	**NHL**	**80**	**19**	**24**	**43**	**16**	**17**	**33**	**83**	**3**	**0**	**3**	**159**	**11.9**	**76**	**17**	**104**	**4**	**–41**	....	....	....	....	....	....	....	....
1983-84	**New York Rangers**	**NHL**	**73**	**23**	**28**	**51**	**19**	**19**	**38**	**88**	**6**	**0**	**5**	**139**	**16.5**	**85**	**22**	**66**	**4**	**+1**	**5**	**0**	**1**	**1**	**7**	**0**	**0**	**0**
1984-85	**New York Rangers**	**NHL**	**23**	**4**	**4**	**8**	**3**	**3**	**6**	**33**	**0**	**0**	**0**	**29**	**13.8**	**20**	**2**	**22**	**2**	**–2**	**3**	**0**	**0**	**0**	**4**	**0**	**0**	**0**
1985-86	**New York Rangers**	**NHL**	**62**	**16**	**24**	**40**	**13**	**16**	**29**	**80**	**5**	**1**	**1**	**134**	**11.9**	**58**	**14**	**49**	**10**	**+5**	**15**	**2**	**3**	**5**	**26**	**0**	**1**	**1**
1986-87	**New York Rangers**	**NHL**	**58**	**17**	**15**	**32**	**15**	**11**	**26**	**101**	**5**	**0**	**2**	**129**	**13.2**	**51**	**15**	**69**	**18**	**–15**	....	....	....	....	....	....	....	....
	Toronto Maple Leafs	**NHL**	**16**	**5**	**10**	**15**	**4**	**7**	**11**	**12**	**1**	**0**	**0**	**31**	**16.1**	**17**	**5**	**13**	**0**	**–1**	**9**	**1**	**3**	**4**	**6**	**0**	**0**	**0**
1987-88	**Toronto Maple Leafs**	**NHL**	**79**	**23**	**37**	**60**	**20**	**26**	**46**	**102**	**4**	**2**	**0**	**155**	**14.8**	**102**	**24**	**102**	**21**	**–3**	**6**	**1**	**3**	**4**	**16**	**0**	**0**	**1**
1988-89	**Toronto Maple Leafs**	**NHL**	**75**	**16**	**30**	**46**	**14**	**21**	**35**	**112**	**5**	**0**	**1**	**118**	**13.6**	**88**	**24**	**86**	**17**	**–5**	....	....	....	....	....	....	....	....
1989-90	**Toronto Maple Leafs**	**NHL**	**78**	**23**	**50**	**73**	**20**	**36**	**56**	**91**	**3**	**1**	**6**	**137**	**16.8**	**116**	**32**	**104**	**22**	**+2**	**5**	**2**	**3**	**5**	**12**	**0**	**1**	**0**
1990-91	**Toronto Maple Leafs**	**NHL**	**18**	**3**	**3**	**6**	**3**	**2**	**5**	**4**	**1**	**1**	**0**	**32**	**9.4**	**8**	**1**	**24**	**7**	**–10**	....	....	....	....	....	....	....	....
	Winnipeg Jets	**NHL**	**37**	**8**	**8**	**16**	**7**	**6**	**13**	**59**	**0**	**0**	**2**	**55**	**14.5**	**26**	**0**	**31**	**4**	**–1**	....	....	....	....	....	....	....	....
1991-92	**Winnipeg Jets**	**NHL**	**43**	**4**	**12**	**16**	**4**	**9**	**13**	**65**	**0**	**0**	**0**	**50**	**8.0**	**22**	**1**	**30**	**1**	**–8**	....	....	....	....	....	....	....	....
	Toronto Maple Leafs	**NHL**	**11**	**3**	**1**	**4**	**3**	**1**	**4**	**8**	**0**	**2**	**0**	**16**	**18.8**	**6**	**0**	**10**	**2**	**–2**	....	....	....	....	....	....	....	....
1992-93	**Toronto Maple Leafs**	**NHL**	**76**	**12**	**14**	**26**	**10**	**10**	**20**	**89**	**0**	**2**	**2**	**110**	**10.9**	**36**	**2**	**71**	**30**	**–7**	**19**	**1**	**1**	**2**	**16**	**0**	**0**	**0**
1993-94	**Toronto Maple Leafs**	**NHL**	**73**	**9**	**15**	**24**	**8**	**12**	**20**	**145**	**1**	**1**	**2**	**103**	**8.7**	**31**	**1**	**41**	**13**	**+2**	**18**	**4**	**2**	**6**	**52**	**0**	**2**	**1**
1994-95	**New York Rangers**	**NHL**	**37**	**1**	**3**	**4**	**2**	**4**	**6**	**19**	**0**	**0**	**0**	**32**	**3.1**	**8**	**0**	**12**	**2**	**–2**	**7**	**1**	**0**	**1**	**2**	**0**	**0**	**0**
1995-96	Cleveland Lumberjacks	IHL	70	31	38	69	....	....	....	131	....	....	....	....	....	....	....	....	....	....	3	1	2	3	2	....	....	....
1996-97	Cleveland Lumberjacks	IHL	59	7	25	32	....	....	....	96	....	....	....	....	....	....	....	....	....	....	6	1	2	3	14	....	....	....
1997-98	Cleveland Lumberjacks	IHL	3	0	0	0	....	....	....	22	....	....	....	....	....	....	....	....	....	....	....	....	....	....	....	....	....	....
	NHL Totals		**919**	**212**	**319**	**531**	**182**	**227**	**409**	**1152**	**39**	**10**	**27**	**1610**	**13.2**	**847**	**179**	**922**	**160**		**87**	**12**	**16**	**28**	**141**	**0**	**4**	**3**

Traded to **NY Rangers** by **Detroit** with Mike Blaisdell and Willy Huber for Ron Duguay, Eddie Mio and Eddie Johnstone, June 13, 1983. Traded to **Toronto** by **NY Rangers** for Jeff Jackson and Toronto's 3rd round choice (Rod Zamaner) in 1989 Entry Draft, March 5, 1987. Traded to **Winnipeg** by **Toronto** with Ed Olczyk for Dave Ellett and Paul Fenton, November 10, 1989. Traded to **Toronto** by **Winnipeg** for Lucien DeBlois, March 10, 1992. Signed as a free agent by **NY Rangers**, January 25, 1995.

• OSBURN, RANDY

Randy Osburn LW – L. 6', 190 lbs. b: Collingwood, Ont., 11/26/1952. Toronto's 2nd choice, 27th overall, in 1972 Amateur Draft.

Season	Club	League	GP	G	A	Pts	AG	AA	APts	PIM	PP	SH	GW	S	%	TGF	PGF	TGA	PGA	+/–	GP	G	A	Pts	PIM	PP	SH	GW
1970-71	Hamilton Red Wings	OHA	12	1	4	5	....	....	....	7	....	....	....	....	....	....	....	....	....	....	....	....	....	....	....	....	....	....
	London Knights	OHA	42	18	29	47	....	....	....	8	....	....	....	....	....	....	....	....	....	....	....	....	....	....	....	....	....	....
1971-72	London Knights	OHA	63	43	57	100	....	....	....	29	....	....	....	....	....	....	....	....	....	....	....	....	....	....	....	....	....	....
1972-73	**Toronto Maple Leafs**	**NHL**	**26**	**0**	**2**	**2**	**0**	**2**	**2**	**0**	**0**	**0**	**0**	**15**	**0.0**	**5**	**1**	**9**	**0**	**–5**	....	....	....	....	....	....	....	....
	Tulsa Oilers	CHL	27	9	11	20	....	....	....	25	....	....	....	....	....	....	....	....	....	....	....	....	....	....	....	....	....	....
1973-74	Oklahoma City Blazers	CHL	72	*37	25	62	....	....	....	13	....	....	....	....	....	....	....	....	....	....	10	3	3	6	4	....	....	....
1974-75	**Philadelphia Flyers**	**NHL**	**1**	**0**	**0**	**0**	**0**	**0**	**0**	**0**	**0**	**0**	**0**	**0**	**0.0**	**0**	**0**	**0**	**0**	**0**	....	....	....	....	....	....	....	....
	Richmond Robins	AHL	13	1	3	4	....	....	....	0	....	....	....	....	....	....	....	....	....	....	....	....	....	....	....	....	....	....
	Philadelphia Firebirds	NAHL	26	12	11	23	....	....	....	10	....	....	....	....	....	....	....	....	....	....	4	1	1	2	5	....	....	....
1975-76	Philadelphia Firebirds	NAHL	69	29	39	68	....	....	....	46	....	....	....	....	....	....	....	....	....	....	16	11	8	19	10	....	....	....
1976-77	Philadelphia Firebirds	NAHL	40	32	26	58	....	....	....	10	....	....	....	....	....	....	....	....	....	....	....	....	....	....	....	....	....	....
1977-78	Philadelphia Firebirds	AHL	78	35	26	61	....	....	....	30	....	....	....	....	....	....	....	....	....	....	4	1	0	1	2	....	....	....
	NHL Totals		**27**	**0**	**2**	**2**	**0**	**2**	**2**	**0**	**0**	**0**	**0**	**15**	**0.0**	**5**	**1**	**9**	**0**		....	....	....	....	....	....	....	....

OHA Second All-Star Team (1972) • CHL First All-Star Team (1974)

Traded to **Philadelphia** by **Toronto** with Dave Fortier for Bill Flett, May 27, 1974.

• O'SHEA, DANNY

Danny O'Shea C – L. 6'1", 190 lbs. b: Toronto, Ont., 6/15/1945.

Season	Club	League	GP	G	A	Pts	AG	AA	APts	PIM	PP	SH	GW	S	%	TGF	PGF	TGA	PGA	+/–	GP	G	A	Pts	PIM	PP	SH	GW
1961-62	Peterborough Petes	OHA	47	5	4	9	....	....	....	21	....	....	....	....	....	....	....	....	....	....	....	....	....	....	....	....	....	....
1962-63	Peterborough Petes	OHA	30	7	7	14	....	....	....	16	....	....	....	....	....	....	....	....	....	....	....	....	....	....	....	....	....	....
1963-64	Oshawa Generals	OHA	55	30	49	79	....	....	....	92	....	....	....	....	....	....	....	....	....	....	6	6	3	9	16	....	....	....
1964-65	Oshawa Generals	OHA	24	16	19	35	....	....	....	60	....	....	....	....	....	....	....	....	....	....	6	0	5	5	17	....	....	....
1965-66	Oshawa Generals	OHA	48	36	45	81	....	....	....	132	....	....	....	....	....	....	....	....	....	....	17	*15	18	33	47	....	....	....
1966-67	Canada	Nat-Team	STATISTICS NOT AVAILABLE																									
1967-68	Winnipeg Nats	WCSHL	....	7	5	12	....	....	....	27	....	....	....	....	....	....	....	....	....	....	....	....	....	....	....	....	....	....
1968-69	**Minnesota North Stars**	**NHL**	**74**	**15**	**34**	**49**	**17**	**32**	**49**	**88**	**4**	**0**	**3**	**157**	**9.6**	**72**	**20**	**82**	**4**	**–26**	....	....	....	....	....	....	....	....
1969-70	**Minnesota North Stars**	**NHL**	**75**	**10**	**24**	**34**	**12**	**24**	**36**	**82**	**4**	**0**	**0**	**136**	**7.4**	**61**	**24**	**54**	**13**	**–4**	**6**	**1**	**0**	**1**	**8**	**0**	**0**	**0**
1970-71	**Minnesota North Stars**	**NHL**	**59**	**14**	**12**	**26**	**15**	**11**	**26**	**16**	**0**	**0**	**3**	**155**	**9.0**	**35**	**0**	**42**	**4**	**–3**	....	....	....	....	....	....	....	....
	Chicago Black Hawks	**NHL**	**18**	**4**	**7**	**11**	**4**	**6**	**10**	**10**	**0**	**0**	**1**	**31**	**12.9**	**15**	**2**	**11**	**3**	**+5**	**18**	**2**	**5**	**7**	**15**	**0**	**0**	**0**
1971-72	**Chicago Black Hawks**	**NHL**	**48**	**6**	**9**	**15**	**6**	**8**	**14**	**28**	**0**	**0**	**2**	**63**	**9.5**	**30**	**2**	**35**	**7**	**0**	....	....	....	....	....	....	....	....
	St. Louis Blues	**NHL**	**20**	**3**	**3**	**6**	**3**	**3**	**6**	**11**	**0**	**0**	**0**	**25**	**12.0**	**8**	**0**	**18**	**6**	**–4**	**10**	**0**	**2**	**2**	**36**	**0**	**0**	**0**
1972-73	**St. Louis Blues**	**NHL**	**75**	**12**	**26**	**38**	**12**	**22**	**34**	**30**	**0**	**2**	**2**	**110**	**10.9**	**52**	**2**	**86**	**31**	**–5**	**5**	**0**	**0**	**0**	**2**	**0**	**0**	**0**
1973-74			DID NOT PLAY																									
1974-75	Minnesota Fighting Saints	WHA	76	16	25	41	....	....	....	47	....	....	....	....	....	....	....	....	....	....	11	0	0	0	6	....	....	....
	NHL Totals		**369**	**64**	**115**	**179**	**69**	**106**	**175**	**265**	**8**	**2**	**11**	**677**	**9.5**	**273**	**50**	**328**	**68**		**39**	**3**	**7**	**10**	**61**	**0**	**0**	**0**
	Other Major League Totals		76	16	25	41	....	....	....	47	....	....	....	....	....	....	....	....	....		11	0	0	0	6	....	....	....

Played in NHL All-Star Game (1969, 1970)

Rights traded to **Minnesota** by **Montreal** for cash, June 6, 1967. Traded to **Chicago** by **Minnesota** for Doug Mohns and Terry Caffery, February 22, 1971. Traded to **St. Louis** by **Chicago** for Chris Bordeleau and future considerations (John Garrett, September, 1972), February 8, 1972. Selected by **Winnipeg** (WHA) in 1972 WHA General Player Draft, February 13, 1972. • Suffered minor heart attack that forced him to miss entire 1973-74 season. Could not receive medical clearance to play in NHL. WHA rights traded to **Minnesota** (WHA) by **Winnipeg** (WHA) for future considerations, June, 1974.

• O'SHEA, KEVIN

Kevin O'Shea RW – R. 6'2", 205 lbs. b: Toronto, Ont., 5/28/1947.

Season	Club	League	GP	G	A	Pts	AG	AA	APts	PIM	PP	SH	GW	S	%	TGF	PGF	TGA	PGA	+/–	GP	G	A	Pts	PIM	PP	SH	GW
1966-67	St. Lawrence University	ECAC	DID NOT PLAY – FRESHMAN																									
1967-68	St. Lawrence University	ECAC	STATISTICS NOT AVAILABLE																									
1968-69	Ottawa Nats	OHA Sr.	6	3	1	4	....	....	....	32	....	....	....	....	....	....	....	....	....	....	....	....	....	....	....	....	....	....
	Canada	WEC-A	7	0	0	0	....	....	....	23	....	....	....	....	....	....	....	....	....	....	....	....	....	....	....	....	....	....
1969-70	San Diego Gulls	WHL	71	12	22	34	....	....	....	49	....	....	....	....	....	....	....	....	....	....	6	1	2	3	9	....	....	....
1970-71	**Buffalo Sabres**	**NHL**	**41**	**4**	**4**	**8**	**4**	**4**	**8**	**8**	**0**	**1**	**1**	**33**	**12.1**	**13**	**1**	**23**	**0**	**–11**	....	....	....	....	....	....	....	....
1971-72	**Buffalo Sabres**	**NHL**	**52**	**6**	**9**	**15**	**6**	**8**	**14**	**44**	**0**	**0**	**0**	**56**	**10.7**	**21**	**1**	**43**	**4**	**–19**	....	....	....	....	....	....	....	....
	St. Louis Blues	**NHL**	**4**	**0**	**0**	**0**	**0**	**0**	**0**	**2**	**0**	**0**	**0**	**3**	**0.0**	**1**	**0**	**2**	**0**	**–1**	**11**	**2**	**1**	**3**	**10**	**0**	**0**	**1**
1972-73	**St. Louis Blues**	**NHL**	**37**	**3**	**5**	**8**	**3**	**4**	**7**	**31**	**0**	**0**	**0**	**39**	**7.7**	**11**	**1**	**26**	**3**	**–13**	**1**	**0**	**0**	**0**	**0**	**0**	**0**	**0**
	Denver Spurs	WHL	16	11	7	18	....	....	....	29	....	....	....	....	....	....	....	....	....	....	....	....	....	....	....	....	....	....
1973-74	Phoenix Roadrunners	WHL	54	24	21	45	....	....	....	40	....	....	....	....	....	....	....	....	....	....	9	6	5	*11	0	....	....	....
1974-75	Minnesota Fighting Saints	WHA	68	10	10	20	....	....	....	42	....	....	....	....	....	....	....	....	....	....	....	....	....	....	....	....	....	....
1975-76	Timra	Sweden	33	16	5	21	....	....	....	*72	....	....	....	....	....	....	....	....	....	....	....	....	....	....	....	....	....	....
	NHL Totals		**134**	**13**	**18**	**31**	**13**	**16**	**29**	**85**	**0**	**1**	**1**	**131**	**9.9**	**46**	**3**	**94**	**7**		**12**	**2**	**1**	**3**	**10**	**0**	**0**	**1**
	Other Major League Totals		68	10	10	20	....	....	....	42	....	....	....	....	....	....	....	....	....	....	....	....	....	....	....	....	....	....

Claimed by **San Diego** (WHL) from **NY Rangers** in Reverse Draft, June 6, 1969. Claimed by **Buffalo** from **San Diego** (WHL) in Inter-League Draft, June, 1970. Selected by **Minnesota** (WHA) in 1972 WHA General Player Draft, February 12, 1972.

● OSIECKI, MARK
Mark Osiecki D – R. 6'2", 200 lbs. b: St. Paul, MN, 7/23/1968. Calgary's 10th choice, 187th overall, in 1987 Entry Draft.

			REGULAR SEASON																		PLAYOFFS							
Season	Club	League	GP	G	A	Pts	AG	AA	APts	PIM	PP	SH	GW	S	%	TGF	PGF	TGA	PGA	+/–	GP	G	A	Pts	PIM	PP	SH	GW
1986-87	University of Wisconsin	WCHA	8	0	1	1	....	....	....	4	....	....	....	....	....	....	....	....	....	....	....	....	....	....	....	....	....	....
1987-88	University of Wisconsin	WCHA	18	0	1	1	....	....	....	22	....	....	....	....	....	....	....	....	....	....	....	....	....	....	....	....	....	....
1988-89	University of Wisconsin	WCHA	44	1	3	4	....	....	....	56	....	....	....	....	....	....	....	....	....	....	....	....	....	....	....	....	....	....
1989-90	University of Wisconsin	WCHA	46	5	38	43	....	....	....	78	....	....	....	....	....	....	....	....	....	....	....	....	....	....	....	....	....	....
1990-91	Salt Lake Golden Eagles	IHL	75	1	24	25	....	....	....	36	....	....	....	....	....	....	....	....	....	....	4	2	0	2	2	....	....	....
1991-92	**Calgary Flames**	**NHL**	**50**	**2**	**7**	**9**	**2**	**5**	**7**	**24**	**1**	**0**	**2**	**44**	**4.5**	**42**	**4**	**57**	**15**	**–4**	....	....	....	....	....	....	....	....
	Salt Lake Golden Eagles	IHL	1	0	0	0	....	....	....	0	....	....	....	....	....	....	....	....	....	....	....	....	....	....	....	....	....	....
	United States	WC-A	6	0	1	1	....	....	....	4	....	....	....	....	....	....	....	....	....	....	....	....	....	....	....	....	....	....
1992-93	**Ottawa Senators**	**NHL**	**34**	**0**	**4**	**4**	**0**	**3**	**3**	**12**	**0**	**0**	**0**	**20**	**0.0**	**18**	**0**	**54**	**15**	**–21**	....	....	....	....	....	....	....	....
	New Haven Nighthawks	AHL	4	0	1	1	....	....	....	0	....	....	....	....	....	....	....	....	....	....	....	....	....	....	....	....	....	....
	Winnipeg Jets	**NHL**	**4**	**1**	**0**	**1**	**1**	**0**	**1**	**2**	**1**	**0**	**0**	**5**	**20.0**	**5**	**2**	**2**	**0**	**+1**	....	....	....	....	....	....	....	....
	Minnesota North Stars	**NHL**	**5**	**0**	**0**	**0**	**0**	**0**	**0**	**5**	**0**	**0**	**0**	**1**	**0.0**	**1**	**0**	**2**	**1**	**0**	....	....	....	....	....	....	....	....
1993-94	Kalamazoo Wings	IHL	65	4	14	18	....	....	....	45	....	....	....	....	....	....	....	....	....	....	5	0	0	0	5	....	....	....
1994-95	Detroit Vipers	IHL	4	0	0	0	....	....	....	4	....	....	....	....	....	....	....	....	....	....	....	....	....	....	....	....	....	....
	Minnesota Moose	IHL	39	1	2	3	....	....	....	22	....	....	....	....	....	....	....	....	....	....	2	0	0	0	2	....	....	....
	NHL Totals		**93**	**3**	**11**	**14**	**3**	**8**	**11**	**43**	**2**	**0**	**2**	**70**	**4.3**	**66**	**6**	**115**	**31**		....	....	....	....	....	....	....	....

NCAA Championship All-Tournament Team (1990)

Traded to **Ottawa** by **Calgary** for Chris Lindberg, June 22, 1992. Claimed on waivers by **Winnipeg** from **Ottawa**, February 20, 1993. Traded to **Minnesota** by **Winnipeg** with Winnipeg's 10th round choice (Bill Lang) in 1993 Entry Draft for Minnesota's 9th round choice (Vladimir Potatov) in 1993 Entry Draft, March 20, 1993. Transferred to **Dallas** after **Minnesota** franchise relocated, June 9, 1993.

● O'SULLIVAN, CHRIS
Chris O'Sullivan D – L. 6'2", 185 lbs. b: Dorchester, MA, 5/15/1974. Calgary's 7th choice, 30th overall, in 1992 Entry Draft.

Season	Club	League	GP	G	A	Pts	AG	AA	APts	PIM	PP	SH	GW	S	%	TGF	PGF	TGA	PGA	+/–	GP	G	A	Pts	PIM	PP	SH	GW
1991-92	Catholic Memorial High	H.S.	26	26	23	49	....	....	....	65	....	....	....	....	....	....	....	....	....	....	....	....	....	....	....	....	....	....
1992-93	Boston University	H.E.	5	0	2	2	....	....	....	4	....	....	....	....	....	....	....	....	....	....	....	....	....	....	....	....	....	....
1993-94	Boston University	H.E.	32	5	18	23	....	....	....	25	....	....	....	....	....	....	....	....	....	....	....	....	....	....	....	....	....	....
	United States	WJC-A	7	0	3	3	....	....	....	4	....	....	....	....	....	....	....	....	....	....	....	....	....	....	....	....	....	....
1994-95	Boston University	H.E.	40	23	33	56	....	....	....	48	....	....	....	....	....	....	....	....	....	....	....	....	....	....	....	....	....	....
	United States	WC-A	6	0	0	0	....	....	....	10	....	....	....	....	....	....	....	....	....	....	....	....	....	....	....	....	....	....
1995-96	Boston University	H.E.	37	12	35	47	....	....	....	50	....	....	....	....	....	....	....	....	....	....	....	....	....	....	....	....	....	....
1996-97	**Calgary Flames**	**NHL**	**27**	**2**	**8**	**10**	**2**	**7**	**9**	**2**	**1**	**0**	**1**	**41**	**4.9**	**25**	**15**	**13**	**3**	**0**	....	....	....	....	....	....	....	....
	Saint John Flames	AHL	29	3	8	11	....	....	....	17	....	....	....	....	....	....	....	....	....	....	5	0	4	4	0	....	....	....
1997-98	**Calgary Flames**	**NHL**	**12**	**0**	**2**	**2**	**0**	**2**	**2**	**10**	**0**	**0**	**0**	**12**	**0.0**	**10**	**1**	**5**	**0**	**+4**	....	....	....	....	....	....	....	....
	Saint John Flames	AHL	32	4	10	14	....	....	....	2	....	....	....	....	....	....	....	....	....	....	21	2	17	19	18	....	....	....
	NHL Totals		**39**	**2**	**10**	**12**	**2**	**9**	**11**	**12**	**1**	**0**	**1**	**53**	**3.8**	**35**	**16**	**18**	**3**		....	....	....	....	....	....	....	....

Hockey East First All-Star Team (1995) • NCAA East Second All-American Team (1995) • NCAA Championship All-Tournament Team (1995) • NCAA Championship Tournament MVP (1995)

● OTEVREL, JAROSLAV
Jaroslav Otevrel LW – L. 6'3", 215 lbs. b: Gottwaldov, Czech., 9/16/1968. San Jose's 8th choice, 133rd overall, in 1991 Entry Draft.

Season	Club	League	GP	G	A	Pts	AG	AA	APts	PIM	PP	SH	GW	S	%	TGF	PGF	TGA	PGA	+/–	GP	G	A	Pts	PIM	PP	SH	GW
1987-88	TJ Gottwaldov	Czech.	32	4	7	11	....	....	....	18	....	....	....	....	....	....	....	....	....	....	....	....	....	....	....	....	....	....
1988-89	TJ Gottwaldov	Czech.	40	14	6	20	....	....	....	37	....	....	....	....	....	....	....	....	....	....	....	....	....	....	....	....	....	....
1989-90	Dukla Trencin	Czech.	43	7	10	17	....	....	....	20	....	....	....	....	....	....	....	....	....	....	....	....	....	....	....	....	....	....
1990-91	TJ Zlin	Czech.	49	24	26	50	....	....	....	105	....	....	....	....	....	....	....	....	....	....	....	....	....	....	....	....	....	....
1991-92	ZPS Zlin	Czech.	36	14	12	26	....	....	....	44	....	....	....	....	....	....	....	....	....	....	4	0	3	3	0	....	....	....
1992-93	**San Jose Sharks**	**NHL**	**7**	**0**	**2**	**2**	**0**	**1**	**1**	**0**	**0**	**0**	**0**	**4**	**0.0**	**2**	**1**	**7**	**0**	**–6**	....	....	....	....	....	....	....	....
	Kansas City Blades	IHL	62	17	27	44	....	....	....	58	....	....	....	....	....	....	....	....	....	....	6	1	4	5	4	....	....	....
1993-94	**San Jose Sharks**	**NHL**	**9**	**3**	**2**	**5**	**3**	**2**	**5**	**2**	**1**	**0**	**0**	**11**	**27.3**	**6**	**2**	**9**	**0**	**–5**	....	....	....	....	....	....	....	....
	Kansas City Blades	IHL	62	20	33	53	....	....	....	46	....	....	....	....	....	....	....	....	....	....	....	....	....	....	....	....	....	....
1994-95	Assat Pori	Finland	50	13	18	31	....	....	....	26	....	....	....	....	....	....	....	....	....	....	7	1	4	5	2	....	....	....
1995-96	Assat Pori	Finland	43	10	26	36	....	....	....	44	....	....	....	....	....	....	....	....	....	....	....	....	....	....	....	....	....	....
	NHL Totals		**16**	**3**	**4**	**7**	**3**	**3**	**6**	**2**	**1**	**0**	**0**	**15**	**20.0**	**8**	**3**	**16**	**0**		....	....	....	....	....	....	....	....

• Suffered career-ending neck injury resulting in paralysis below the waist during 1995-96 season.

● OTTO, JOEL
Joel Otto C – R. 6'4", 220 lbs. b: Elk River, MN, 10/29/1961.

Season	Club	League	GP	G	A	Pts	AG	AA	APts	PIM	PP	SH	GW	S	%	TGF	PGF	TGA	PGA	+/–	GP	G	A	Pts	PIM	PP	SH	GW
1980-81	Bemidji State	NCAA	23	5	11	16	....	....	....	10	....	....	....	....	....	....	....	....	....	....	....	....	....	....	....	....	....	....
1981-82	Bemidji State	NCAA	31	19	33	52	....	....	....	24	....	....	....	....	....	....	....	....	....	....	....	....	....	....	....	....	....	....
1982-83	Bemidji State	NCAA	37	33	28	61	....	....	....	68	....	....	....	....	....	....	....	....	....	....	....	....	....	....	....	....	....	....
1983-84	Bemidji State	NCAA	31	32	43	75	....	....	....	32	....	....	....	....	....	....	....	....	....	....	....	....	....	....	....	....	....	....
1984-85	**Calgary Flames**	**NHL**	**17**	**4**	**8**	**12**	**3**	**5**	**8**	**30**	**1**	**0**	**0**	**27**	**14.8**	**20**	**7**	**10**	**0**	**+3**	**3**	**2**	**1**	**3**	**10**	**1**	**0**	**1**
	Moncton Golden Flames	AHL	56	27	36	63	....	....	....	89	....	....	....	....	....	....	....	....	....	....	....	....	....	....	....	....	....	....
	United States	WEC-A	10	2	1	3	....	....	....	8	....	....	....	....	....	....	....	....	....	....	....	....	....	....	....	....	....	....
1985-86	**Calgary Flames**	**NHL**	**79**	**25**	**34**	**59**	**20**	**23**	**43**	**188**	**9**	**0**	**2**	**147**	**17.0**	**103**	**32**	**49**	**1**	**+23**	**22**	**5**	**10**	**15**	**80**	**3**	**0**	**1**
1986-87	**Calgary Flames**	**NHL**	**68**	**19**	**31**	**50**	**16**	**22**	**38**	**185**	**5**	**0**	**1**	**127**	**15.0**	**91**	**33**	**63**	**13**	**+8**	**2**	**0**	**2**	**2**	**6**	**0**	**0**	**0**
1987-88	United States	C Cup	5	0	2	2	....	....	....	4	....	....	....	....	....	....	....	....	....	....	....	....	....	....	....	....	....	....
	Calgary Flames	**NHL**	**62**	**13**	**39**	**52**	**11**	**28**	**39**	**194**	**4**	**1**	**4**	**105**	**12.4**	**87**	**26**	**70**	**25**	**+16**	**9**	**3**	**2**	**5**	**26**	**1**	**0**	**1**
1988-89	**Calgary Flames**	**NHL**	**72**	**23**	**30**	**53**	**20**	**21**	**41**	**213**	**10**	**2**	**2**	**123**	**18.7**	**82**	**35**	**73**	**38**	**+12**	**22**	**6**	**13**	**19**	**46**	**2**	**1**	**1**
1989-90	Calgary Flames	FrTour	4	0	0	0	....	....	....	2	....	....	....	....	....	....	....	....	....	....	....	....	....	....	....	....	....	....
	Calgary Flames	**NHL**	**75**	**13**	**20**	**33**	**11**	**14**	**25**	**116**	**7**	**0**	**0**	**96**	**13.5**	**55**	**16**	**70**	**35**	**+4**	**6**	**2**	**2**	**4**	**2**	**0**	**0**	**0**
	United States	WEC-A	9	2	4	6	....	....	....	2	....	....	....	....	....	....	....	....	....	....	....	....	....	....	....	....	....	....
1990-91	**Calgary Flames**	**NHL**	**76**	**19**	**20**	**39**	**17**	**15**	**32**	**183**	**7**	**1**	**4**	**109**	**17.4**	**62**	**20**	**79**	**33**	**–4**	**7**	**1**	**2**	**3**	**8**	**0**	**0**	**0**
1991-92	United States	C Cup	8	4	0	4	....	....	....	2	....	....	....	....	....	....	....	....	....	....	....	....	....	....	....	....	....	....
	Calgary Flames	**NHL**	**78**	**13**	**21**	**34**	**12**	**16**	**28**	**161**	**5**	**1**	**3**	**105**	**12.4**	**65**	**20**	**99**	**44**	**–10**	....	....	....	....	....	....	....	....
1992-93	**Calgary Flames**	**NHL**	**75**	**19**	**33**	**52**	**16**	**23**	**39**	**150**	**6**	**1**	**4**	**115**	**16.5**	**74**	**23**	**89**	**40**	**+2**	**6**	**4**	**2**	**6**	**4**	**0**	**1**	**1**
1993-94	**Calgary Flames**	**NHL**	**81**	**11**	**12**	**23**	**10**	**9**	**19**	**92**	**3**	**1**	**1**	**108**	**10.2**	**38**	**7**	**84**	**36**	**–17**	**3**	**0**	**1**	**1**	**4**	**0**	**0**	**0**
1994-95	**Calgary Flames**	**NHL**	**47**	**8**	**13**	**21**	**14**	**19**	**33**	**130**	**0**	**2**	**2**	**46**	**17.4**	**34**	**2**	**45**	**21**	**+8**	**7**	**0**	**3**	**3**	**2**	**0**	**0**	**0**
1995-96	**Philadelphia Flyers**	**NHL**	**67**	**12**	**29**	**41**	**12**	**24**	**36**	**115**	**6**	**1**	**1**	**91**	**13.2**	**64**	**24**	**47**	**18**	**+11**	**12**	**3**	**4**	**7**	**11**	**1**	**0**	**1**
1996-97	United States	W Cup	7	1	2	3	....	....	....	6	....	....	....	....	....	....	....	....	....	....	....	....	....	....	....	....	....	....
	Philadelphia Flyers	**NHL**	**78**	**13**	**19**	**32**	**14**	**17**	**31**	**99**	**0**	**1**	**2**	**105**	**12.4**	**44**	**1**	**49**	**18**	**+12**	**18**	**1**	**5**	**6**	**8**	**0**	**0**	**0**
1997-98	**Philadelphia Flyers**	**NHL**	**68**	**3**	**4**	**7**	**4**	**4**	**8**	**78**	**0**	**0**	**0**	**53**	**5.7**	**12**	**0**	**32**	**18**	**–2**	**5**	**0**	**0**	**0**	**0**	**0**	**0**	**0**
	United States	Olympics	4	0	0	0	....	....	....	0	....	....	....	....	....	....	....	....	....	....	....	....	....	....	....	....	....	....
	NHL Totals		**943**	**195**	**313**	**508**	**180**	**240**	**420**	**1934**	**63**	**11**	**26**	**1357**	**14.4**	**831**	**246**	**859**	**340**		**122**	**27**	**47**	**74**	**207**	**8**	**2**	**6**

NCAA (College Div.) West All-American Team (1983, 1984)

Signed as a free agent by **Calgary,** September 11, 1984. Signed as a free agent by **Philadelphia**, July 31, 1995.

● OWCHAR, DENNIS
Dennis Owchar D – R. 5'11", 190 lbs. b: Dryden, Ont., 3/28/1953. Pittsburgh's 4th choice, 55th overall, in 1973 Amateur Draft.

Season	Club	League	GP	G	A	Pts	AG	AA	APts	PIM	PP	SH	GW	S	%	TGF	PGF	TGA	PGA	+/–	GP	G	A	Pts	PIM	PP	SH	GW
1972-73	St. Catharines Black Hawks	OHA	19	3	13	16	....	....	....	13	....	....	....	....	....	....	....	....	....	....	....	....	....	....	....	....	....	....
	Toronto Marlboros	OHA	20	7	8	15	....	....	....	27	....	....	....	....	....	....	....	....	....	....	....	....	....	....	....	....	....	....
1973-74	Hershey Bears	AHL	74	16	17	33	....	....	....	51	....	....	....	....	....	....	....	....	....	....	14	1	5	6	14	....	....	....
1974-75	**Pittsburgh Penguins**	**NHL**	**46**	**6**	**11**	**17**	**6**	**9**	**15**	**67**	**0**	**0**	**0**	**62**	**9.7**	**54**	**0**	**56**	**14**	**+12**	**6**	**0**	**1**	**1**	**4**	**0**	**0**	**0**
	Hershey Bears	AHL	24	3	14	17	....	....	....	31	....	....	....	....	....	....	....	....	....	....	4	0	1	1	0	....	....	....
1975-76	**Pittsburgh Penguins**	**NHL**	**54**	**5**	**12**	**17**	**5**	**9**	**14**	**19**	**1**	**0**	**0**	**62**	**8.1**	**66**	**3**	**65**	**15**	**+13**	**2**	**0**	**0**	**0**	**2**	**0**	**0**	**0**
	Hershey Bears	AHL	7	5	1	6	....	....	....	13	....	....	....	....	....	....	....	....	....	....	....	....	....	....	....	....	....	....
1976-77	**Pittsburgh Penguins**	**NHL**	**46**	**5**	**18**	**23**	**5**	**15**	**20**	**37**	**1**	**0**	**0**	**86**	**5.8**	**57**	**6**	**68**	**10**	**–7**	....	....	....	....	....	....	....	....
1977-78	**Pittsburgh Penguins**	**NHL**	**22**	**2**	**8**	**10**	**2**	**7**	**9**	**23**	**0**	**0**	**0**	**51**	**3.9**	**25**	**0**	**44**	**7**	**–12**	....	....	....	....	....	....	....	....
	Colorado Rockies	**NHL**	**60**	**8**	**23**	**31**	**8**	**19**	**27**	**25**	**2**	**0**	**0**	**120**	**6.7**	**69**	**14**	**122**	**18**	**–49**	**2**	**1**	**0**	**1**	**2**	**0**	**0**	**0**
1978-79	**Colorado Rockies**	**NHL**	**50**	**3**	**13**	**16**	**3**	**10**	**13**	**27**	**1**	**0**	**0**	**77**	**3.9**	**48**	**18**	**78**	**15**	**–33**	....	....	....	....	....	....	....	....

			REGULAR SEASON																		PLAYOFFS							
Season	Club	League	GP	G	A	Pts	AG	AA	APts	PIM	PP	SH	GW	S	%	TGF	PGF	TGA	PGA	+/–	GP	G	A	Pts	PIM	PP	SH	GW
1979-80	**Colorado Rockies**	**NHL**	10	1	0	1	1	0	1	2	0	0	0	7	14.3	4	0	8	1	–3	....	....	....	....	....	....	....	....
	New Haven Nighthawks	AHL	40	6	27	33	....	....	....	26	....	....	....	....	....	....	....	....	....	....	....	....	....	....	....	....	....	....
1980-81	New Haven Nighthawks	AHL	57	2	16	18	....	....	....	67	....	....	....	....	....	....	....	....	....	....	4	0	0	0	5	....	....	....
	NHL Totals		288	30	85	115	30	69	99	200	5	0	0	465	6.5	323	41	441	80		10	1	1	2	8	0	0	0

Traded to **Colorado** by **Pittsburgh** for Tom Edur, December 2, 1977. Traded to **New Haven** (AHL) by **Colorado** with Larry Skinner for Bobby Sheehan, May 12, 1979.

• OZOLINSH, SANDIS

Sandis Ozolinsh D – L. 6'1", 195 lbs. b: Riga, Latvia, 8/3/1972. San Jose's 3rd choice, 30th overall, in 1991 Entry Draft.

Season	Club	League	GP	G	A	Pts	AG	AA	APts	PIM	PP	SH	GW	S	%	TGF	PGF	TGA	PGA	+/–	GP	G	A	Pts	PIM	PP	SH	GW
1990-91	Dynamo Riga	FrTour	1	0	0	0	....	....	....	0	....	....	....	....	....	....	....	....	....	....	....	....	....	....	....	....	....	....
	Dynamo Riga	USSR	44	0	3	3	....	....	....	51	....	....	....	....	....	....	....	....	....	....	....	....	....	....	....	....	....	....
1991-92	Dynamo Riga	CIS	30	6	0	6	....	....	....	42	....	....	....	....	....	....	....	....	....	....	....	....	....	....	....	....	....	....
	Russia	WJC-A	7	1	5	6	....	....	....	4	....	....	....	....	....	....	....	....	....	....	....	....	....	....	....	....	....	....
	Kansas City Blades	IHL	34	6	9	15	....	....	....	20	....	....	....	....	....	....	....	....	....	....	15	2	5	7	22	....	....	....
1992-93	**San Jose Sharks**	**NHL**	37	7	16	23	6	11	17	40	2	0	0	83	8.4	52	17	67	23	–9	....	....	....	....	....	....	....	....
1993-94	**San Jose Sharks**	**NHL**	81	26	38	64	24	29	53	24	4	0	3	157	16.6	118	36	87	21	+16	14	0	10	10	8	0	0	0
1994-95	**San Jose Sharks**	**NHL**	48	9	16	25	16	24	40	30	3	1	2	83	10.8	58	10	62	8	–6	11	3	2	5	6	1	0	0
1995-96	San Francisco Spiders	IHL	2	1	0	1	....	....	....	0	....	....	....	....	....	....	....	....	....	....	....	....	....	....	....	....	....	....
	San Jose Sharks	**NHL**	7	1	3	4	1	2	3	4	1	0	0	21	4.8	12	3	15	8	+2	....	....	....	....	....	....	....	....
	Colorado Avalanche	**NHL**	66	13	37	50	13	30	43	50	7	1	1	145	9.0	124	57	67	0	0	22	5	14	19	16	2	0	1
1996-97	**Colorado Avalanche**	**NHL**	80	23	45	68	24	40	64	88	13	0	4	232	9.9	132	69	60	1	+4	17	4	13	17	24	2	0	1
1997-98	**Colorado Avalanche**	**NHL**	66	13	38	51	15	37	52	65	9	0	2	135	9.6	92	54	51	1	–12	7	0	7	7	14	0	0	0
	NHL Totals		385	92	193	285	99	173	272	301	39	2	12	856	10.7	588	246	409	62		71	12	46	58	68	5	0	2

NHL First All-Star Team (1997)

Played in NHL All-Star Game (1994, 1997, 1998)

Traded to **Colorado** by **San Jose** for Owen Nolan, October 26, 1995.

• PACHAL, CLAYTON

Clayton Pachal C/LW – L. 5'10", 185 lbs. b: Yorkton, Sask., 4/21/1956. Boston's 7th choice, 16th overall, in 1976 Amateur Draft.

Season	Club	League	GP	G	A	Pts	AG	AA	APts	PIM	PP	SH	GW	S	%	TGF	PGF	TGA	PGA	+/–	GP	G	A	Pts	PIM	PP	SH	GW
1972-73	New Westminster Bruins	WCJHL	37	2	2	4	....	....	....	67	....	....	....	....	....	....	....	....	....	....	5	0	0	0	16	....	....	....
1973-74	New Westminster Bruins	WCJHL	67	8	11	19	....	....	....	278	....	....	....	....	....	....	....	....	....	....	11	1	1	2	39	....	....	....
1974-75	New Westminster Bruins	WCJHL	65	17	30	47	....	....	....	306	....	....	....	....	....	....	....	....	....	....	17	3	6	9	72	....	....	....
	Canada	WJC-A	3	0	0	0	....	....	....	2	....	....	....	....	....	....	....	....	....	....	....	....	....	....	....	....	....	....
1975-76	New Westminster Bruins	WHL	65	31	57	88	....	....	....	259	....	....	....	....	....	....	....	....	....	....	15	9	8	17	29	....	....	....
1976-77	**Boston Bruins**	**NHL**	1	0	0	0	0	0	0	12	0	0	0	0	0.0	0	0	0	0	0	....	....	....	....	....	....	....	....
	Rochester Americans	AHL	70	8	20	28	....	....	....	150	....	....	....	....	....	....	....	....	....	....	9	4	2	6	2	....	....	....
	Binghamton Dusters	NAHL	1	0	0	0	....	....	....	0	....	....	....	....	....	....	....	....	....	....	....	....	....	....	....	....	....	....
1977-78	**Boston Bruins**	**NHL**	10	0	0	0	0	0	0	14	0	0	0	4	0.0	0	0	1	0	–1	....	....	....	....	....	....	....	....
	Rochester Americans	AHL	61	10	10	20	....	....	....	105	....	....	....	....	....	....	....	....	....	....	6	1	2	3	7	....	....	....
1978-79	**Colorado Rockies**	**NHL**	24	2	3	5	2	2	4	69	1	0	0	19	10.5	13	5	21	2	–11	....	....	....	....	....	....	....	....
	Philadelphia Firebirds	AHL	26	1	4	5	....	....	....	75	....	....	....	....	....	....	....	....	....	....	....	....	....	....	....	....	....	....
1979-80	Cincinnati Stingers	CHL	18	0	2	2	....	....	....	31	....	....	....	....	....	....	....	....	....	....	....	....	....	....	....	....	....	....
	Grand Rapids Owls	IHL	34	8	17	25	....	....	....	64	....	....	....	....	....	....	....	....	....	....	....	....	....	....	....	....	....	....
	NHL Totals		35	2	3	5	2	2	4	95	1	0	0	23	8.7	13	5	22	2		....	....	....	....	....	....	....	....

Traded to **Colorado** by **Boston** for Mark Suzor, October 11, 1978. Signed as a free agent by **Edmonton**, July, 1979.

• PADDOCK, JOHN

John Paddock RW – R. 6'3", 190 lbs. b: Brandon, Man., 6/9/1954. Washington's 3rd choice, 37th overall, in 1974 Amateur Draft.

Season	Club	League	GP	G	A	Pts	AG	AA	APts	PIM	PP	SH	GW	S	%	TGF	PGF	TGA	PGA	+/–	GP	G	A	Pts	PIM	PP	SH	GW
1972-73	Brandon Wheat Kings	WCJHL	11	3	2	5	....	....	....	6	....	....	....	....	....	....	....	....	....	....	....	....	....	....	....	....	....	....
1973-74	Brandon Wheat Kings	WCJHL	68	34	49	83	....	....	....	228	....	....	....	....	....	....	....	....	....	....	....	....	....	....	....	....	....	....
1974-75	Richmond Robins	AHL	72	20	22	48	....	....	....	296	....	....	....	....	....	....	....	....	....	....	7	5	3	8	38	....	....	....
1975-76	**Washington Capitals**	**NHL**	8	1	1	2	1	1	2	12	0	0	0	5	20.0	3	0	8	0	–5	....	....	....	....	....	....	....	....
	Richmond Robins	AHL	42	11	14	25	....	....	....	98	....	....	....	....	....	....	....	....	....	....	8	0	3	3	5	....	....	....
1976-77	**Philadelphia Flyers**	**NHL**	5	0	0	0	0	0	0	9	0	0	0	3	0.0	1	0	1	0	0	....	....	....	....	....	....	....	....
	Springfield Indians	AHL	61	13	16	29	....	....	....	106	....	....	....	....	....	....	....	....	....	....	....	....	....	....	....	....	....	....
1977-78	Maine Mariners	AHL	61	0	12	20	....	....	....	152	....	....	....	....	....	....	....	....	....	....	6	1	2	3	7	....	....	....
1978-79	Maine Mariners	AHL	79	30	37	67	....	....	....	275	....	....	....	....	....	....	....	....	....	....	10	*9	1	10	13	....	....	....
1979-80	**Philadelphia Flyers**	**NHL**	32	3	7	10	3	5	8	36	0	0	0	29	10.3	16	1	19	0	–4	3	2	0	2	0	0	0	0
1980-81	**Quebec Nordiques**	**NHL**	32	2	5	7	2	3	5	25	0	0	0	32	6.3	13	0	25	5	–7	2	0	0	0	0	0	0	0
	Maine Mariners	AHL	22	8	7	15	....	....	....	53	....	....	....	....	....	....	....	....	....	....	8	10	6	16	48	....	....	....
1981-82	Maine Mariners	AHL	39	6	10	16	....	....	....	123	....	....	....	....	....	....	....	....	....	....	3	0	1	1	18	....	....	....
1982-83	**Philadelphia Flyers**	**NHL**	10	2	1	3	2	1	3	4	0	0	0	14	14.3	6	2	10	0	–6	....	....	....	....	....	....	....	....
	Maine Mariners	AHL	69	30	23	53	....	....	....	188	....	....	....	....	....	....	....	....	....	....	13	2	2	4	18	....	....	....
1983-84	Maine Mariners	AHL	17	3	6	9	....	....	....	20	....	....	....	....	....	....	....	....	....	....	....	....	....	....	....	....	....	....
	NHL Totals		87	8	14	22	8	10	18	86	0	0	0	83	9.6	39	3	63	5		5	2	0	2	0	0	0	0

Traded to **Philadelphia** by **Washington** to complete transaction that sent Bob Sirois to Washington (December 15, 1975), December 1, 1976. Traded to **Quebec** by **Philadelphia** for cash, August 11, 1980. Signed as a free agent by **Philadelphia**, January 4, 1983. Signed as a free agent by **New Jersey**, August 1, 1983.

• PAEK, JIM

Jim Paek D – L. 6'1", 195 lbs. b: Seoul, South Korea, 4/7/1967. Pittsburgh's 9th choice, 170th overall, in 1985 Entry Draft.

Season	Club	League	GP	G	A	Pts	AG	AA	APts	PIM	PP	SH	GW	S	%	TGF	PGF	TGA	PGA	+/–	GP	G	A	Pts	PIM	PP	SH	GW
1984-85	Oshawa Generals	OHL	54	2	13	15	....	....	....	57	....	....	....	....	....	....	....	....	....	....	5	1	0	1	9	....	....	....
1985-86	Oshawa Generals	OHL	64	5	21	26	....	....	....	122	....	....	....	....	....	....	....	....	....	....	6	0	1	1	9	....	....	....
1986-87	Oshawa Generals	OHL	57	5	17	22	....	....	....	75	....	....	....	....	....	....	....	....	....	....	26	1	14	15	43	....	....	....
1987-88	Muskegon Lumberjacks	IHL	82	7	52	59	....	....	....	141	....	....	....	....	....	....	....	....	....	....	6	0	0	0	29	....	....	....
1988-89	Muskegon Lumberjacks	IHL	80	3	54	57	....	....	....	96	....	....	....	....	....	....	....	....	....	....	14	1	10	11	24	....	....	....
1989-90	Muskegon Lumberjacks	IHL	81	9	41	50	....	....	....	115	....	....	....	....	....	....	....	....	....	....	15	1	10	11	41	....	....	....
1990-91	Canada	Nat-Team	48	2	12	14	....	....	....	24	....	....	....	....	....	....	....	....	....	....	....	....	....	....	....	....	....	....
	Pittsburgh Penguins	**NHL**	3	0	0	0	0	0	0	9	0	0	0	0	0.0	2	0	0	0	+2	8	1	0	1	2	0	0	0
1991-92	**Pittsburgh Penguins**	**NHL**	49	1	7	8	1	5	6	36	0	0	0	33	3.0	43	0	50	7	0	19	0	4	4	6	0	0	0
1992-93	**Pittsburgh Penguins**	**NHL**	77	3	15	18	2	10	12	64	0	0	0	57	5.3	72	3	71	15	+13	....	....	....	....	....	....	....	....
1993-94	**Pittsburgh Penguins**	**NHL**	41	0	4	4	0	3	3	8	0	0	0	24	0.0	22	0	30	1	–7	....	....	....	....	....	....	....	....
	Los Angeles Kings	**NHL**	18	1	1	2	1	1	2	10	0	0	0	11	9.1	9	0	11	1	–1	....	....	....	....	....	....	....	....
1994-95	**Ottawa Senators**	**NHL**	29	0	2	2	0	3	3	28	0	0	0	16	0.0	14	1	27	9	–5	....	....	....	....	....	....	....	....
1995-96	Houston Aeros	IHL	25	2	5	7	....	....	....	20	....	....	....	....	....	....	....	....	....	....	....	....	....	....	....	....	....	....
	Minnesota Moose	IHL	42	1	11	12	....	....	....	54	....	....	....	....	....	....	....	....	....	....	....	....	....	....	....	....	....	....
1996-97	Manitoba Moose	IHL	9	0	2	2	....	....	....	12	....	....	....	....	....	....	....	....	....	....	....	....	....	....	....	....	....	....
	Cleveland Lumberjacks	IHL	74	3	25	28	....	....	....	36	....	....	....	....	....	....	....	....	....	....	14	0	1	1	2	....	....	....
1997-98	Cleveland Lumberjacks	IHL	75	7	9	16	....	....	....	48	....	....	....	....	....	....	....	....	....	....	10	2	1	3	4	....	....	....
	NHL Totals		217	5	29	34	4	22	26	155	0	0	0	141	3.5	162	4	189	33		27	1	4	5	8	0	0	0

Traded to **LA Kings** by **Pittsburgh** with Marty McSorley for Tomas Sandstrom and Shawn McEachern, February 16, 1994. Traded to **Ottawa** by **LA Kings** for Ottawa's 7th round choice (Benoit Larose) in 1995 Entry Draft, June 26, 1994.

• PAIEMENT, ROSAIRE

Rosaire "Rosie" Paiement C – R. 5'11", 170 lbs. b: Earlton, Ont., 8/12/1945.

Season	Club	League	GP	G	A	Pts	AG	AA	APts	PIM	PP	SH	GW	S	%	TGF	PGF	TGA	PGA	+/–	GP	G	A	Pts	PIM	PP	SH	GW
1964-65	Niagara Falls Flyers	OHA	56	13	24	37	....	....	....	40	....	....	....	....	....	....	....	....	....	....	9	0	2	2	5	....	....	....
1965-66	Niagara Falls Flyers	OHA	47	14	25	39	....	....	....	38	....	....	....	....	....	....	....	....	....	....	6	0	1	1	10	....	....	....
1966-67	New Jersey Devils	EHL	72	*61	64	*125	....	....	....	175	....	....	....	....	....	....	....	....	....	....	16	3	11	14	53	....	....	....
1967-68	**Philadelphia Flyers**	**NHL**	7	1	0	1	1	0	1	11	0	0	0	11	9.1	3	1	1	0	+1	3	3	0	3	0	2	0	1
	Quebec Aces	AHL	64	18	30	48	....	....	....	189	....	....	....	....	....	....	....	....	....	....	12	4	6	10	*41	....	....	....
1968-69	**Philadelphia Flyers**	**NHL**	27	2	4	6	2	4	6	52	0	0	0	58	3.4	9	0	23	0	–14	....	....	....	....	....	....	....	....
	Quebec Aces	AHL	42	16	22	38	....	....	....	122	....	....	....	....	....	....	....	....	....	....	15	*9	5	14	35	....	....	....
1969-70	**Philadelphia Flyers**	**NHL**	9	1	1	2	1	1	2	11	0	0	0	29	3.4	1	0	5	0	–4	....	....	....	....	....	....	....	....
	Quebec Aces	AHL	67	28	40	68	....	....	....	*242	....	....	....	....	....	....	....	....	....	....	6	1	1	2	15	....	....	....
1970-71	**Vancouver Canucks**	**NHL**	78	34	28	62	36	25	61	152	4	1	4	249	13.7	84	17	79	24	+12	....	....	....	....	....	....	....	....
1971-72	**Vancouver Canucks**	**NHL**	69	10	19	29	11	17	28	117	1	0	1	177	5.6	46	3	84	4	–37	....	....	....	....	....	....	....	....

			REGULAR SEASON																		PLAYOFFS							
Season	Club	League	GP	G	A	Pts	AG	AA	APts	PIM	PP	SH	GW	S	%	TGF	PGF	TGA	PGA	+/–	GP	G	A	Pts	PIM	PP	SH	GW
1972-73	Chicago Cougars	WHA	78	33	36	69	....	....	....	137	....	....	....	....	....	....	....	....	....	....	....	....	....	....	....	....	....	....
1973-74	Chicago Cougars	WHA	78	30	43	73	....	....	....	87	....	....	....	....	....	....	....	....	....	....	18	9	6	15	16	....	....	....
1974-75	Chicago Cougars	WHA	78	26	48	74	....	....	....	97	....	....	....	....	....	....	....	....	....	....	....	....	....	....	....	....	....	....
1975-76	New England Whalers	WHA	80	28	43	71	....	....	....	89	....	....	....	....	....	....	....	....	....	....	17	4	11	15	41	....	....	....
1976-77	New England Whalers	WHA	13	5	2	7	....	....	....	12	....	....	....	....	....	....	....	....	....	....	....	....	....	....	....	....	....	....
	Indianapolis Racers	WHA	67	18	25	43	....	....	....	91	....	....	....	....	....	....	....	....	....	....	9	0	5	5	15	....	....	....
1977-78	Indianapolis Racers	WHA	61	6	24	30	....	....	....	81	....	....	....	....	....	....	....	....	....	....	....	....	....	....	....	....	....	....
	NHL Totals		**190**	**48**	**52**	**100**	**51**	**47**	**98**	**343**	**5**	**1**	**5**	**524**	**9.2**	**143**	**21**	**192**	**28**		**3**	**3**	**0**	**3**	**0**	**2**	**0**	**1**
	Other Major League Totals		455	146	221	367	....	....	....	594	....	....	....	....	....	....	....	....	....		44	13	22	35	72	....	....	....

EHL North First All-Star Team (1967) • EHL North Rookie of the Year (1967) • Won John Carlin Trophy (Top Scorer - EHL) (1967)

Traded to **Philadelphia** by **Boston** for cash, October, 1967. Claimed by **Vancouver** from **Philadelphia** in Expansion Draft, June 10, 1970. Selected by **Chicago** (WHA) in 1972 WHA General Player Draft, February 12, 1972. Selected by **Denver** (WHA) from **Chicago** (WHA) in WHA Expansion Draft, May, 1975. Traded to **New England** (WHA) by **Denver** (WHA) for New England's 1st round choice (later traded to Indianapolis — Indianapolis selected Bob Simpson) in 1976 WHA Amateur Draft, July, 1975. Traded to **Indianapolis** (WHA) by **New England** (WHA) for Gary MacGregor, November, 1976.

• PAIEMENT, WILF

Wilf Paiement RW – R. 6'1", 210 lbs. b: Earlton, Ont., 10/16/1955. Kansas City's 1st choice, 2nd overall, in 1974 Amateur Draft.

Season	Club	League	GP	G	A	Pts	AG	AA	APts	PIM	PP	SH	GW	S	%	TGF	PGF	TGA	PGA	+/–	GP	G	A	Pts	PIM	PP	SH	GW
1971-72	Niagara Falls Flyers	OHA	34	6	13	19	....	....	....	74	....	....	....	....	....	....	....	....	....	....	....	....	....	....	....	....	....	....
1972-73	St. Catharines Black Hawks	OHA	61	18	27	46	....	....	....	173	....	....	....	....	....	....	....	....	....	....	....	....	....	....	....	....	....	....
1973-74	St. Catherines Blackhawks	OHA	70	50	73	123	....	....	....	134	....	....	....	....	....	....	....	....	....	....	....	....	....	....	....	....	....	....
1974-75	**Kansas City Scouts**	**NHL**	**78**	**26**	**13**	**39**	**24**	**10**	**34**	**101**	**6**	**0**	**3**	**195**	**13.3**	**59**	**21**	**80**	**0**	**–42**	....	....	....	....	....	....	....	....
1975-76	**Kansas City Scouts**	**NHL**	**57**	**21**	**22**	**43**	**20**	**17**	**37**	**121**	**4**	**0**	**3**	**178**	**11.8**	**53**	**18**	**75**	**3**	**–37**	....	....	....	....	....	....	....	....
1976-77	**Colorado Rockies**	**NHL**	**78**	**41**	**40**	**81**	**39**	**32**	**71**	**101**	**9**	**5**	**2**	**287**	**14.3**	**109**	**35**	**102**	**15**	**–13**	....	....	....	....	....	....	....	....
	Canada	WEC-A	10	5	5	10	....	....	....	32	....	....	....	....	....	....	....	....	....	....	....	....	....	....	....	....	....	....
1977-78	**Colorado Rockies**	**NHL**	**80**	**31**	**56**	**87**	**30**	**46**	**76**	**114**	**7**	**2**	**1**	**287**	**10.8**	**126**	**43**	**115**	**18**	**–14**	**2**	**0**	**0**	**0**	**7**	**0**	**0**	**0**
	Canada	WEC-A	10	6	1	7	....	....	....	8	....	....	....	....	....	....	....	....	....	....	....	....	....	....	....	....	....	....
1978-79	**Colorado Rockies**	**NHL**	**65**	**24**	**36**	**60**	**22**	**28**	**50**	**80**	**5**	**0**	**1**	**206**	**11.7**	**79**	**27**	**93**	**11**	**–30**	....	....	....	....	....	....	....	....
	Canada	WEC-A	8	3	3	6	....	....	....	6	....	....	....	....	....	....	....	....	....	....	....	....	....	....	....	....	....	....
1979-80	**Colorado Rockies**	**NHL**	**34**	**10**	**16**	**26**	**9**	**12**	**21**	**41**	**2**	**2**	**1**	**111**	**9.0**	**37**	**11**	**35**	**3**	**–6**	....	....	....	....	....	....	....	....
	Toronto Maple Leafs	**NHL**	**41**	**20**	**28**	**48**	**18**	**21**	**39**	**72**	**8**	**0**	**2**	**159**	**12.6**	**72**	**29**	**48**	**6**	**+1**	**3**	**0**	**2**	**2**	**17**	**0**	**0**	**0**
1980-81	**Toronto Maple Leafs**	**NHL**	**77**	**40**	**57**	**97**	**33**	**40**	**73**	**145**	**13**	**3**	**2**	**302**	**13.2**	**133**	**48**	**134**	**42**	**–7**	**3**	**0**	**0**	**0**	**2**	**0**	**0**	**0**
1981-82	**Toronto Maple Leafs**	**NHL**	**69**	**18**	**40**	**58**	**14**	**26**	**40**	**203**	**6**	**1**	**1**	**186**	**9.7**	**80**	**22**	**96**	**17**	**–21**	....	....	....	....	....	....	....	....
	Quebec Nordiques	**NHL**	**8**	**7**	**6**	**13**	**6**	**4**	**10**	**18**	**3**	**2**	**1**	**24**	**29.2**	**16**	**5**	**14**	**2**	**–1**	**14**	**6**	**6**	**12**	**28**	**1**	**0**	**1**
1982-83	**Quebec Nordiques**	**NHL**	**80**	**26**	**38**	**64**	**21**	**26**	**47**	**170**	**6**	**0**	**2**	**191**	**13.6**	**97**	**25**	**93**	**11**	**–10**	**4**	**0**	**1**	**1**	**4**	**0**	**0**	**0**
1983-84	**Quebec Nordiques**	**NHL**	**80**	**39**	**37**	**76**	**31**	**25**	**56**	**121**	**8**	**3**	**3**	**207**	**18.8**	**103**	**19**	**71**	**15**	**+28**	**9**	**3**	**1**	**4**	**24**	**0**	**0**	**0**
1984-85	**Quebec Nordiques**	**NHL**	**68**	**23**	**28**	**51**	**19**	**19**	**38**	**165**	**2**	**1**	**4**	**156**	**14.7**	**71**	**9**	**57**	**7**	**+12**	**18**	**4**	**2**	**6**	**58**	**0**	**0**	**0**
1985-86	**Quebec Nordiques**	**NHL**	**44**	**7**	**12**	**19**	**6**	**8**	**14**	**145**	**2**	**0**	**0**	**75**	**9.3**	**34**	**5**	**29**	**0**	**0**	....	....	....	....	....	....	....	....
	New York Rangers	**NHL**	**8**	**1**	**6**	**7**	**1**	**4**	**5**	**13**	**0**	**0**	**0**	**14**	**7.1**	**8**	**1**	**5**	**0**	**+2**	**16**	**5**	**5**	**10**	**45**	**4**	**0**	**0**
1986-87	**Buffalo Sabres**	**NHL**	**56**	**20**	**17**	**37**	**17**	**12**	**29**	**108**	**2**	**0**	**3**	**117**	**17.1**	**57**	**10**	**46**	**1**	**+2**	....	....	....	....	....	....	....	....
1987-88	**Pittsburgh Penguins**	**NHL**	**23**	**2**	**6**	**8**	**2**	**4**	**6**	**39**	**0**	**0**	**0**	**25**	**8.0**	**11**	**0**	**15**	**0**	**–4**	....	....	....	....	....	....	....	....
	Muskegon Lumberjacks	IHL	28	17	18	35	....	....	....	52	....	....	....	....	....	....	....	....	....	....	5	0	2	2	15	....	....	....
	NHL Totals		**946**	**356**	**458**	**814**	**312**	**334**	**646**	**1757**	**83**	**19**	**29**	**2720**	**13.1**	**1145**	**328**	**1108**	**151**		**69**	**18**	**17**	**35**	**185**	**5**	**0**	**1**

OHA First All-Star Team (1974) • Named Best Forward (Tied with Sergei Makarov) at WEC-A (1979)

Played in NHL All-Star Game (1976, 1977, 1978)

Transferred to **Colorado** after **Kansas City** franchise relocated, July 15, 1976. Traded to **Toronto** by **Colorado** with Pat Hickey for Lanny McDonald and Joel Quenneville, December 29, 1979. Traded to **Quebec** by **Toronto** for Miroslav Frycer and Quebec's 7th round choice (Jeff Triano) in 1982 Entry Draft, March 9, 1982. Traded to **NY Rangers** by **Quebec** for Steve Patrick, February 6, 1986. Claimed by **Buffalo** from **NY Rangers** in Waiver Draft, October 6, 1986. Signed as a free agent by **Pittsburgh**, September 10, 1987.

• PALAZZARI, DOUG

Doug Palazzari C – L. 5'5", 170 lbs. b: Eveleth, MN, 11/3/1952.

Season	Club	League	GP	G	A	Pts	AG	AA	APts	PIM	PP	SH	GW	S	%	TGF	PGF	TGA	PGA	+/–	GP	G	A	Pts	PIM	PP	SH	GW
1970-71	Colorado College	WCHA	26	8	17	25	....	....	....	37	....	....	....	....	....	....	....	....	....	....	....	....	....	....	....	....	....	....
1971-72	Colorado College	WCHA	32	32	40	72	....	....	....	42	....	....	....	....	....	....	....	....	....	....	....	....	....	....	....	....	....	....
1972-73	Colorado College	WCHA	27	24	28	52	....	....	....	32	....	....	....	....	....	....	....	....	....	....	....	....	....	....	....	....	....	....
	United States	WEC-B	....	6	3	9	....	....	....	....	....	....	....	....	....	....	....	....	....	....	....	....	....	....	....	....	....	....
1973-74	Colorado College	WCHA	28	25	42	67	....	....	....	18	....	....	....	....	....	....	....	....	....	....	....	....	....	....	....	....	....	....
	United States	WEC-B	....	5	4	9	....	....	....	....	....	....	....	....	....	....	....	....	....	....	....	....	....	....	....	....	....	....
1974-75	**St. Louis Blues**	**NHL**	**73**	**14**	**17**	**31**	**13**	**13**	**26**	**19**	**0**	**1**	**1**	**110**	**12.7**	**45**	**8**	**45**	**16**	**+8**	**2**	**0**	**0**	**0**	**0**	**0**	**0**	**0**
1975-76	Providence Reds	AHL	55	19	32	51	....	....	....	72	....	....	....	....	....	....	....	....	....	....	3	1	1	2	2	....	....	....
1976-77	United States	C Cup	2	0	0	0	....	....	....	2	....	....	....	....	....	....	....	....	....	....	....	....	....	....	....	....	....	....
	St. Louis Blues	**NHL**	**12**	**1**	**0**	**1**	**1**	**0**	**1**	**0**	**0**	**0**	**0**	**11**	**9.1**	**1**	**0**	**5**	**1**	**–3**	....	....	....	....	....	....	....	....
	Kansas City Blues	CHL	41	18	34	52	....	....	....	31	....	....	....	....	....	....	....	....	....	....	....	....	....	....	....	....	....	....
1977-78	**St. Louis Blues**	**NHL**	**3**	**1**	**0**	**1**	**1**	**0**	**1**	**0**	**0**	**0**	**0**	**3**	**33.3**	**1**	**0**	**3**	**0**	**–2**	....	....	....	....	....	....	....	....
	Salt Lake Golden Eagles	CHL	70	*45	*56	*101	....	....	....	82	....	....	....	....	....	....	....	....	....	....	6	2	3	5	18	....	....	....
1978-79	**St. Louis Blues**	**NHL**	**20**	**2**	**3**	**5**	**2**	**2**	**4**	**4**	**0**	**0**	**0**	**16**	**12.5**	**8**	**0**	**17**	**4**	**–5**	....	....	....	....	....	....	....	....
	Salt Lake Golden Eagles	CHL	35	24	32	56	....	....	....	19	....	....	....	....	....	....	....	....	....	....	10	2	*14	*16	11	....	....	....
1979-80	Salt Lake Golden Eagles	CHL	74	*48	*61	*109	....	....	....	62	....	....	....	....	....	....	....	....	....	....	13	7	7	14	6	....	....	....
1980-81	Salt Lake Golden Eagles	CHL	27	16	21	37	....	....	....	57	....	....	....	....	....	....	....	....	....	....	17	7	11	18	15	....	....	....
1981-82	Salt Lake Golden Eagles	CHL	68	34	41	75	....	....	....	44	....	....	....	....	....	....	....	....	....	....	10	11	6	17	13	....	....	....
	NHL Totals		**108**	**18**	**20**	**38**	**17**	**15**	**32**	**23**	**0**	**1**	**1**	**140**	**12.9**	**55**	**8**	**70**	**21**		**2**	**0**	**0**	**0**	**0**	**0**	**0**	**0**

WCHA First All-Star Team (1972, 1974) • NCAA West First All-American Team (1972, 1974) • CHL First All-Star Team (1978, 1980) • Won Tommy Ivan Trophy (CHL's MVP) (1978, 1980)

Signed as a free agent by **St. Louis**, August, 1974.

• PALFFY, ZIGMUND

Zigmund Palffy LW – L. 5'10", 183 lbs. b: Skalica, Czech., 5/5/1972. NY Islanders' 2nd choice, 26th overall, in 1991 Entry Draft.

Season	Club	League	GP	G	A	Pts	AG	AA	APts	PIM	PP	SH	GW	S	%	TGF	PGF	TGA	PGA	+/–	GP	G	A	Pts	PIM	PP	SH	GW
1990-91	AC Nitra	Czech.	50	34	16	50	....	....	....	18	....	....	....	....	....	....	....	....	....	....	....	....	....	....	....	....	....	....
	Czechoslovakia	WJC-A	7	7	6	13	....	....	....	2	....	....	....	....	....	....	....	....	....	....	....	....	....	....	....	....	....	....
1991-92	Czechoslovakia	C Cup	5	1	0	1	....	....	....	2	....	....	....	....	....	....	....	....	....	....	....	....	....	....	....	....	....	....
	Dukla Trencin	Czech.	45	41	33	74	....	....	....	36	....	....	....	....	....	....	....	....	....	....	....	....	....	....	....	....	....	....
	Czechoslovakia	WJC-A	6	3	1	4	....	....	....	6	....	....	....	....	....	....	....	....	....	....	....	....	....	....	....	....	....	....
1992-93	Dukla Trencin	Czech.	43	38	41	79	....	....	....	....	....	....	....	....	....	....	....	....	....	....	....	....	....	....	....	....	....	....
1993-94	**New York Islanders**	**NHL**	**5**	**0**	**0**	**0**	**0**	**0**	**0**	**0**	**0**	**0**	**0**	**5**	**0.0**	**1**	**1**	**6**	**0**	**–6**	....	....	....	....	....	....	....	....
	Salt Lake Golden Eagles	IHL	57	25	32	57	....	....	....	83	....	....	....	....	....	....	....	....	....	....	....	....	....	....	....	....	....	....
	Slovakia	Olympics	8	3	7	10	....	....	....	8	....	....	....	....	....	....	....	....	....	....	....	....	....	....	....	....	....	....
1994-95	Denver Grizzlies	IHL	33	20	23	43	....	....	....	40	....	....	....	....	....	....	....	....	....	....	....	....	....	....	....	....	....	....
	New York Islanders	**NHL**	**33**	**10**	**7**	**17**	**18**	**10**	**28**	**6**	**1**	**0**	**1**	**75**	**13.3**	**25**	**5**	**17**	**0**	**+3**	....	....	....	....	....	....	....	....
1995-96	**New York Islanders**	**NHL**	**81**	**43**	**44**	**87**	**43**	**36**	**79**	**56**	**17**	**1**	**6**	**257**	**16.7**	**109**	**52**	**84**	**10**	**–17**	....	....	....	....	....	....	....	....
	Slovakia	WC-A	5	2	0	2	....	....	....	10	....	....	....	....	....	....	....	....	....	....	....	....	....	....	....	....	....	....
1996-97	Slovakia	W Cup	3	1	2	3	....	....	....	2	....	....	....	....	....	....	....	....	....	....	....	....	....	....	....	....	....	....
	Dukla Trencin	Slovakia	1	0	0	0	....	....	....	....	....	....	....	....	....	....	....	....	....	....	....	....	....	....	....	....	....	....
	New York Islanders	**NHL**	**80**	**48**	**42**	**90**	**51**	**37**	**88**	**43**	**6**	**4**	**6**	**292**	**16.4**	**119**	**32**	**77**	**11**	**+21**	....	....	....	....	....	....	....	....
1997-98	**New York Islanders**	**NHL**	**82**	**45**	**42**	**87**	**53**	**41**	**94**	**34**	**17**	**2**	**5**	**277**	**16.2**	**118**	**52**	**81**	**13**	**–2**	....	....	....	....	....	....	....	....
	NHL Totals		**281**	**146**	**135**	**281**	**165**	**124**	**289**	**139**	**41**	**7**	**18**	**906**	**16.1**	**372**	**142**	**265**	**34**		....	....	....	....	....	....	....	....

Czechoslovakian Rookie of the Year (1991) • Czechoslovakian First All-Star Team (1992)

Played in NHL All-Star Game (1998)

• PALMER, BRAD

Brad Palmer LW – L. 6', 185 lbs. b: Duncan, B.C., 9/14/1961. Minnesota's 1st choice, 16th overall, in 1980 Entry Draft.

Season	Club	League	GP	G	A	Pts	AG	AA	APts	PIM	PP	SH	GW	S	%	TGF	PGF	TGA	PGA	+/–	GP	G	A	Pts	PIM	PP	SH	GW
1977-78	Kelowna Rockets	BCJHL	46	20	21	41	....	....	....	32	....	....	....	....	....	....	....	....	....	....	....	....	....	....	....	....	....	....
1978-79	Victoria Cougars	WHL	69	18	15	33	....	....	....	53	....	....	....	....	....	....	....	....	....	....	15	2	7	9	2	....	....	....
1979-80	Victoria Cougars	WHL	72	45	49	94	....	....	....	61	....	....	....	....	....	....	....	....	....	....	17	11	8	19	6	....	....	....
1980-81	Victoria Cougars	WHL	44	34	53	87	....	....	....	72	....	....	....	....	....	....	....	....	....	....	....	....	....	....	....	....	....	....
	Minnesota North Stars	**NHL**	**23**	**4**	**4**	**8**	**3**	**3**	**6**	**22**	**0**	**0**	**0**	**59**	**6.8**	**17**	**2**	**22**	**1**	**–6**	**19**	**8**	**5**	**13**	**4**	**1**	**2**	**1**
1981-82	**Minnesota North Stars**	**NHL**	**72**	**22**	**23**	**45**	**17**	**15**	**32**	**18**	**7**	**0**	**3**	**180**	**12.2**	**73**	**23**	**64**	**1**	**–13**	**3**	**0**	**0**	**0**	**12**	**0**	**0**	**0**
1982-83	**Boston Bruins**	**NHL**	**73**	**6**	**11**	**17**	**5**	**8**	**13**	**18**	**0**	**0**	**0**	**123**	**4.9**	**25**	**0**	**44**	**12**	**–7**	**7**	**1**	**0**	**1**	**0**	**0**	**1**	**1**

			REGULAR SEASON																		PLAYOFFS							
Season	Club	League	GP	G	A	Pts	AG	AA	APts	PIM	PP	SH	GW	S	%	TGF	PGF	TGA	PGA	+/–	GP	G	A	Pts	PIM	PP	SH	GW
1983-84	Hershey Bears	AHL	62	25	32	57	....	....	....	16	....	....	....	....	....	....	....	....	....	....	....	....	....	....	....	....	....	....
1984-85	EHC Chur	Switz.	10	4	3	7	....	....	....	....	....	....	....	....	....	....	....	....	....	....	....	....	....	....	....	....	....	....
1985-86	Lukko Rauma	Finland	31	16	8	24	....	....	....	10	....	....	....	....	....	....	....	....	....	....	....	....	....	....	....	....	....	....
1986-87	Lukko Rauma	Finland	22	5	6	11	....	....	....	16	....	....	....	....	....	....	....	....	....	....	....	....	....	....	....	....	....	....
1987-88	Lukko Rauma	Finland 2	....	....	....	....	....	....	....	....	....	....	....	....	....	....	....	....	....	....	....	....	....	....	....	....	....	....
1988-89	Lukko Rauma	Finalnd 2	STATISTICS NOT AVAILABLE																									
1989-90	Lustenau	Austria	16	8	5	13	....	....	....	4	....	....	....	....	....	....	....	....	....	....	....	....	....	....	....	....	....	....
	NHL Totals		**168**	**32**	**38**	**70**	**25**	**26**	**51**	**58**	**7**	**0**	**3**	**362**	**8.8**	**115**	**25**	**130**	**14**		**29**	**9**	**5**	**14**	**16**	**1**	**3**	**2**

Traded to **Boston** by **Minnesota** with Dave Donnelly for future considerations, June 9, 1981.

• PALMER, ROB

Rob (H.) Palmer C – L. 6', 190 lbs. b: Detroit, MI, 10/2/1952. Chicago's 6th choice, 93rd overall, in 1972 Amateur Draft.

Season	Club	League	GP	G	A	Pts	AG	AA	APts	PIM	PP	SH	GW	S	%	TGF	PGF	TGA	PGA	+/–	GP	G	A	Pts	PIM	PP	SH	GW
1970-71	University of Denver	WCHA	36	14	23	37	....	....	....	14	....	....	....	....	....	....	....	....	....	....	....	....	....	....	....	....	....	....
1971-72	University of Denver	WCHA	36	14	25	39	....	....	....	20	....	....	....	....	....	....	....	....	....	....	....	....	....	....	....	....	....	....
1972-73	University of Denver	WCHA	26	18	27	45	....	....	....	8	....	....	....	....	....	....	....	....	....	....	....	....	....	....	....	....	....	....
1973-74	**Chicago Black Hawks**	**NHL**	**1**	**0**	**0**	**0**	**0**	**0**	**0**	**0**	**0**	**0**	**0**	**0**	**0.0**	**0**	**0**	**0**	**0**	**0**	....	....	....	....	....	....	....	....
	Dallas Black Hawks	CHL	49	11	16	27	....	....	....	44	....	....	....	....	....	....	....	....	....	....	10	3	0	3	4	....	....	....
1974-75	**Chicago Black Hawks**	**NHL**	**13**	**0**	**2**	**2**	**0**	**2**	**2**	**2**	**0**	**0**	**0**	**8**	**0.0**	**3**	**0**	**2**	**0**	**+1**	....	....	....	....	....	....	....	....
	Dallas Black Hawks	CHL	55	12	34	46	....	....	....	32	....	....	....	....	....	....	....	....	....	....	10	2	9	11	14	....	....	....
1975-76	**Chicago Black Hawks**	**NHL**	**2**	**0**	**1**	**1**	**0**	**1**	**1**	**0**	**0**	**0**	**0**	**0**	**0.0**	**1**	**0**	**0**	**0**	**+1**	....	....	....	....	....	....	....	....
	Dallas Black Hawks	CHL	62	14	17	31	....	....	....	56	....	....	....	....	....	....	....	....	....	....	10	4	3	7	2	....	....	....
	NHL Totals		**16**	**0**	**3**	**3**	**0**	**3**	**3**	**2**	**0**	**0**	**0**	**8**	**0.0**	**4**	**0**	**2**	**0**		....	....	....	....	....	....	....	....

WCHA First All-Star Team (1973) • NCAA West First All-American Team (1973)

• PALMER, ROBERT ROSS

Robert Ross Palmer D – R. 5'11", 190 lbs. b: Sarnia, Ont., 9/10/1956. Los Angeles' 4th choice, 85th overall, in 1976 Amateur Draft.

Season	Club	League	GP	G	A	Pts	AG	AA	APts	PIM	PP	SH	GW	S	%	TGF	PGF	TGA	PGA	+/–	GP	G	A	Pts	PIM	PP	SH	GW
1973-74	University of Michigan	WCHA	36	3	12	15	....	....	....	14	....	....	....	....	....	....	....	....	....	....	....	....	....	....	....	....	....	....
1974-75	University of Michigan	WCHA	40	5	15	20	....	....	....	26	....	....	....	....	....	....	....	....	....	....	....	....	....	....	....	....	....	....
1975-76	University of Michigan	WCHA	42	5	16	21	....	....	....	58	....	....	....	....	....	....	....	....	....	....	....	....	....	....	....	....	....	....
1976-77	University of Michigan	WCHA	45	5	37	42	....	....	....	32	....	....	....	....	....	....	....	....	....	....	....	....	....	....	....	....	....	....
	Fort Worth Texans	CHL	3	0	2	2	....	....	....	0	....	....	....	....	....	....	....	....	....	....	5	0	0	0	0	....	....	....
1977-78	**Los Angeles Kings**	**NHL**	**48**	**0**	**3**	**3**	**0**	**2**	**2**	**27**	**0**	**0**	**0**	**38**	**0.0**	**22**	**1**	**31**	**2**	**–8**	**2**	**0**	**0**	**0**	**0**	**0**	**0**	**0**
	Springfield Indians	AHL	19	1	7	8	....	....	....	18	....	....	....	....	....	....	....	....	....	....	....	....	....	....	....	....	....	....
1978-79	**Los Angeles Kings**	**NHL**	**78**	**4**	**41**	**45**	**4**	**31**	**35**	**26**	**2**	**1**	**0**	**130**	**3.1**	**123**	**16**	**154**	**34**	**–13**	**2**	**0**	**0**	**0**	**2**	**0**	**0**	**0**
1979-80	**Los Angeles Kings**	**NHL**	**78**	**4**	**36**	**40**	**4**	**28**	**32**	**18**	**1**	**0**	**0**	**110**	**3.6**	**122**	**9**	**134**	**50**	**+29**	**4**	**1**	**2**	**3**	**4**	**0**	**0**	**0**
1980-81	**Los Angeles Kings**	**NHL**	**13**	**0**	**4**	**4**	**0**	**3**	**3**	**13**	**0**	**0**	**0**	**11**	**0.0**	**12**	**0**	**10**	**3**	**+5**	....	....	....	....	....	....	....	....
	Houston Apollos	CHL	28	3	10	13	....	....	....	23	....	....	....	....	....	....	....	....	....	....	....	....	....	....	....	....	....	....
	Indianapolis Checkers	CHL	27	1	9	10	....	....	....	16	....	....	....	....	....	....	....	....	....	....	5	1	1	2	0	....	....	....
1981-82	**Los Angeles Kings**	**NHL**	**5**	**0**	**2**	**2**	**0**	**1**	**1**	**0**	**0**	**0**	**0**	**2**	**0.0**	**10**	**0**	**10**	**1**	**+1**	....	....	....	....	....	....	....	....
	New Haven Nighthawks	AHL	41	2	23	25	....	....	....	22	....	....	....	....	....	....	....	....	....	....	4	1	4	5	2	....	....	....
1982-83	**New Jersey Devils**	**NHL**	**60**	**1**	**10**	**11**	**1**	**7**	**8**	**21**	**0**	**0**	**0**	**81**	**1.2**	**48**	**6**	**69**	**21**	**–6**	....	....	....	....	....	....	....	....
1983-84	**New Jersey Devils**	**NHL**	**38**	**0**	**5**	**5**	**0**	**3**	**3**	**10**	**0**	**0**	**0**	**18**	**0.0**	**22**	**1**	**48**	**17**	**–10**	....	....	....	....	....	....	....	....
	Maine Mariners	AHL	33	5	10	15	....	....	....	10	....	....	....	....	....	....	....	....	....	....	17	3	10	13	8	....	....	....
1984-85	Maine Mariners	AHL	79	1	23	24	....	....	....	22	....	....	....	....	....	....	....	....	....	....	11	0	3	3	2	....	....	....
1985-86	Maine Mariners	AHL	73	2	10	12	....	....	....	18	....	....	....	....	....	....	....	....	....	....	5	0	0	0	0	....	....	....
	NHL Totals		**320**	**9**	**101**	**110**	**9**	**75**	**84**	**115**	**3**	**1**	**0**	**390**	**2.3**	**359**	**33**	**456**	**128**		**8**	**1**	**2**	**3**	**6**	**0**	**0**	**0**

Signed as a free agent by **New Jersey**, September 9, 1982.

• PANDOLFO, JAY

Jay Pandolfo LW – L. 6'1", 195 lbs. b: Winchester, MA, 12/27/1974. New Jersey's 2nd choice, 32nd overall, in 1993 Entry Draft.

Season	Club	League	GP	G	A	Pts	AG	AA	APts	PIM	PP	SH	GW	S	%	TGF	PGF	TGA	PGA	+/–	GP	G	A	Pts	PIM	PP	SH	GW
1992-93	Boston University	H.E.	37	16	22	38	....	....	....	16	....	....	....	....	....	....	....	....	....	....	....	....	....	....	....	....	....	....
1993-94	Boston University	H.E.	37	17	25	42	....	....	....	27	....	....	....	....	....	....	....	....	....	....	....	....	....	....	....	....	....	....
	United States	WJC-A	7	0	0	0	....	....	....	2	....	....	....	....	....	....	....	....	....	....	....	....	....	....	....	....	....	....
1994-95	Boston University	H.E.	20	7	13	20	....	....	....	6	....	....	....	....	....	....	....	....	....	....	....	....	....	....	....	....	....	....
1995-96	Boston University	H.E.	39	*38	29	67	....	....	....	6	....	....	....	....	....	....	....	....	....	....	....	....	....	....	....	....	....	....
	Albany River Rats	AHL	5	3	1	4	....	....	....	0	....	....	....	....	....	....	....	....	....	....	3	0	0	0	0	....	....	....
1996-97	**New Jersey Devils**	**NHL**	**46**	**6**	**8**	**14**	**6**	**7**	**13**	**6**	**0**	**0**	**1**	**61**	**9.8**	**22**	**2**	**22**	**1**	**–1**	**6**	**0**	**1**	**1**	**0**	**0**	**0**	**0**
	Albany River Rats	AHL	12	3	9	12	....	....	....	0	....	....	....	....	....	....	....	....	....	....	....	....	....	....	....	....	....	....
1997-98	**New Jersey Devils**	**NHL**	**23**	**1**	**3**	**4**	**1**	**3**	**4**	**4**	**0**	**0**	**0**	**23**	**4.3**	**6**	**0**	**10**	**0**	**–4**	**3**	**0**	**2**	**2**	**0**	**0**	**0**	**0**
	Albany River Rats	AHL	51	18	19	37	....	....	....	24	....	....	....	....	....	....	....	....	....	....	....	....	....	....	....	....	....	....
	NHL Totals		**69**	**7**	**11**	**18**	**7**	**10**	**17**	**10**	**0**	**0**	**1**	**84**	**8.3**	**28**	**2**	**32**	**1**		**9**	**0**	**3**	**3**	**0**	**0**	**0**	**0**

Hockey East First All-Star Team (1996) • NCAA East First All-American Team (1996)

• PANKEWICZ, GREG

Greg Pankowicz RW – R. 6', 185 lbs. b: Drayton Valley, Alta., 10/6/1970.

Season	Club	League	GP	G	A	Pts	AG	AA	APts	PIM	PP	SH	GW	S	%	TGF	PGF	TGA	PGA	+/–	GP	G	A	Pts	PIM	PP	SH	GW
1989-90	Regina Pats	WHL	63	14	24	38	....	....	....	136	....	....	....	....	....	....	....	....	....	....	10	1	3	4	19	....	....	....
1990-91	Regina Pats	WHL	72	39	41	80	....	....	....	134	....	....	....	....	....	....	....	....	....	....	8	4	7	11	12	....	....	....
1991-92	Knoxville Cherokees	ECHL	59	41	39	80	....	....	....	214	....	....	....	....	....	....	....	....	....	....	....	....	....	....	....	....	....	....
1992-93	New Haven Nighthawks	AHL	62	23	20	43	....	....	....	163	....	....	....	....	....	....	....	....	....	....	....	....	....	....	....	....	....	....
1993-94	**Ottawa Senators**	**NHL**	**3**	**0**	**0**	**0**	**0**	**0**	**0**	**2**	**0**	**0**	**0**	**3**	**0.0**	**2**	**0**	**3**	**0**	**–1**	....	....	....	....	....	....	....	....
	P.E.I. Senators	AHL	69	33	29	62	....	....	....	241	....	....	....	....	....	....	....	....	....	....	....	....	....	....	....	....	....	....
1994-95	P.E.I. Senators	AHL	75	37	30	67	....	....	....	161	....	....	....	....	....	....	....	....	....	....	6	1	1	2	24	....	....	....
1995-96	Portland Pirates	AHL	28	9	12	21	....	....	....	99	....	....	....	....	....	....	....	....	....	....	....	....	....	....	....	....	....	....
	Chicago Wolves	IHL	45	9	16	25	....	....	....	164	....	....	....	....	....	....	....	....	....	....	5	4	0	4	8	....	....	....
1996-97	Manitoba Moose	IHL	70	32	34	66	....	....	....	222	....	....	....	....	....	....	....	....	....	....	....	....	....	....	....	....	....	....
1997-98	Manitoba Moose	IHL	76	42	34	76	....	....	....	246	....	....	....	....	....	....	....	....	....	....	3	0	0	0	6	....	....	....
	NHL Totals		**3**	**0**	**0**	**0**	**0**	**0**	**0**	**2**	**0**	**0**	**0**	**3**	**0.0**	**2**	**0**	**3**	**0**		....	....	....	....	....	....	....	....

Signed as a free agent by **Ottawa**, May 27, 1993.

• PANTELEEV, GRIGORI

Grigori Panteleev LW – L. 5'9", 190 lbs. b: Gastello, USSR, 11/13/1972. Boston's 5th choice, 136th overall, in 1992 Entry Draft.

Season	Club	League	GP	G	A	Pts	AG	AA	APts	PIM	PP	SH	GW	S	%	TGF	PGF	TGA	PGA	+/–	GP	G	A	Pts	PIM	PP	SH	GW
1990-91	HC Riga	USSR	23	4	1	5	....	....	....	4	....	....	....	....	....	....	....	....	....	....	....	....	....	....	....	....	....	....
1991-92	HC Riga	CIS	26	4	8	12	....	....	....	4	....	....	....	....	....	....	....	....	....	....	....	....	....	....	....	....	....	....
1992-93	**Boston Bruins**	**NHL**	**39**	**8**	**6**	**14**	**7**	**4**	**11**	**12**	**2**	**0**	**1**	**45**	**17.8**	**24**	**6**	**24**	**0**	**–6**	....	....	....	....	....	....	....	....
	Providence Bruins	AHL	39	17	30	47	....	....	....	22	....	....	....	....	....	....	....	....	....	....	3	0	0	0	10	....	....	....
1993-94	**Boston Bruins**	**NHL**	**10**	**0**	**0**	**0**	**0**	**0**	**0**	**0**	**0**	**0**	**0**	**8**	**0.0**	**1**	**0**	**3**	**0**	**–2**	....	....	....	....	....	....	....	....
	Providence Bruins	AHL	55	24	26	50	....	....	....	20	....	....	....	....	....	....	....	....	....	....	....	....	....	....	....	....	....	....
1994-95	**Boston Bruins**	**NHL**	**1**	**0**	**0**	**0**	**0**	**0**	**0**	**0**	**0**	**0**	**0**	**0**	**0.0**	**0**	**0**	**0**	**0**	**0**	....	....	....	....	....	....	....	....
	Providence Bruins	AHL	70	20	23	43	....	....	....	36	....	....	....	....	....	....	....	....	....	....	13	8	11	19	6	....	....	....
1995-96	**New York Islanders**	**NHL**	**4**	**0**	**0**	**0**	**0**	**0**	**0**	**0**	**0**	**0**	**0**	**1**	**0.0**	**0**	**0**	**3**	**0**	**–3**	....	....	....	....	....	....	....	....
	Utah Grizzlies	IHL	33	11	25	36	....	....	....	18	....	....	....	....	....	....	....	....	....	....	....	....	....	....	....	....	....	....
	Las Vegas Thunder	IHL	29	15	21	36	....	....	....	14	....	....	....	....	....	....	....	....	....	....	15	4	7	11	2	....	....	....
1996-97	San Antonio Dragons	IHL	81	25	37	62	....	....	....	41	....	....	....	....	....	....	....	....	....	....	9	4	2	6	4	....	....	....
1997-98	San Antonio Dragons	IHL	19	2	13	15	....	....	....	8	....	....	....	....	....	....	....	....	....	....	....	....	....	....	....	....	....	....
	Orlando Solar Bears	IHL	63	27	29	56	....	....	....	44	....	....	....	....	....	....	....	....	....	....	17	8	9	15	2	....	....	....
	NHL Totals		**54**	**8**	**6**	**14**	**7**	**4**	**11**	**12**	**2**	**0**	**1**	**54**	**14.8**	**25**	**8**	**30**	**0**		....	....	....	....	....	....	....	....

Signed as a free agent by **NY Islanders**, September 20, 1995.

• PAPPIN, JIM

Jim "Pappy" Pappin RW – R. 6', 190 lbs. b: Sudbury, Ont., 9/10/1939.

Season	Club	League	GP	G	A	Pts	AG	AA	APts	PIM	PP	SH	GW	S	%	TGF	PGF	TGA	PGA	+/–	GP	G	A	Pts	PIM	PP	SH	GW
1958-59	Toronto Marlboros	OHA	54	17	18	35	....	....	....	86	....	....	....	....	....	....	....	....	....	....	5	2	3	5	4	....	....	....
1959-60	Toronto Marlboros	OHA	48	40	34	74	....	....	....	126	....	....	....	....	....	....	....	....	....	....	4	3	0	3	20	....	....	....
	Sudbury Wolves	EPHL	4	1	0	1	....	....	....	4	....	....	....	....	....	....	....	....	....	....	3	0	1	1	0	....	....	....
1960-61	Sudbury Wolves	EPHL	46	17	20	37	....	....	....	74	....	....	....	....	....	....	....	....	....	....	....	....	....	....	....	....	....	....
	Rochester Americans	AHL	22	7	4	11	....	....	....	4	....	....	....	....	....	....	....	....	....	....	....	....	....	....	....	....	....	....

			REGULAR SEASON																		PLAYOFFS							
Season	Club	League	GP	G	A	Pts	AG	AA	APts	PIM	PP	SH	GW	S	%	TGF	PGF	TGA	PGA	+/-	GP	G	A	Pts	PIM	PP	SH	GW
1961-62	Rochester Americans	AHL	69	28	21	49	....	....	....	105	....	....	....	....	....	....	....	....	....	....	2	1	0	1	2	....	....	....
1962-63	Rochester Americans	AHL	72	34	23	57	....	....	....	100	....	....	....	....	....	....	....	....	....	....	2	1	2	3	2	....	....	....
1963-64	**Toronto Maple Leafs**	**NHL**	**50**	**11**	**8**	**19**	**14**	**9**	**23**	**33**	....	....	....	....	....	....	....	....	....	....	**11**	**0**	**0**	**0**	**0**	....	....	....
	Rochester Americans	AHL	16	10	6	16	....	....	....	16	....	....	....	....	....	....	....	....	....	....	....	....	....	....	....	....	....	....
1964-65	**Toronto Maple Leafs**	**NHL**	**44**	**9**	**9**	**18**	**11**	**10**	**21**	**33**	....	....	....	....	....	....	....	....	....	....	....	....	....	....	....	....	....	....
	Rochester Americans	AHL	22	14	11	25	....	....	....	36	....	....	....	....	....	....	....	....	....	....	10	*11	5	16	32	....	....	....
1965-66	**Toronto Maple Leafs**	**NHL**	**7**	**0**	**3**	**3**	**0**	**3**	**3**	**8**	....	....	....	....	....	....	....	....	....	....	....	....	....	....	....	....	....	....
	Rochester Americans	AHL	63	36	51	87	....	....	....	116	....	....	....	....	....	....	....	....	....	....	12	*8	3	11	13	....	....	....
1966-67	**Toronto Maple Leafs**	**NHL**	**64**	**21**	**11**	**32**	**26**	**11**	**37**	**89**	....	....	....	....	....	....	....	....	....	....	**12**	***7**	**8**	***15**	**12**	....	....	....
	Rochester Americans	AHL	6	4	3	7	....	....	....	4	....	....	....	....	....	....	....	....	....	....	....	....	....	....	....	....	....	....
1967-68	**Toronto Maple Leafs**	**NHL**	**58**	**13**	**15**	**28**	**16**	**16**	**32**	**37**	**2**	**0**	**1**	**117**	**11.1**	**45**	**18**	**27**	**0**	**0**	....	....	....	....	....	....	....	....
	Rochester Americans	AHL	5	1	5	6	....	....	....	16	....	....	....	....	....	....	....	....	....	....	11	2	6	8	32	....	....	....
1968-69	**Chicago Black Hawks**	**NHL**	**75**	**30**	**40**	**70**	**34**	**38**	**72**	**49**	**3**	**0**	**4**	**208**	**14.4**	**98**	**27**	**72**	**8**	**+7**	....	....	....	....	....	....	....	....
1969-70	**Chicago Black Hawks**	**NHL**	**66**	**28**	**25**	**53**	**32**	**25**	**57**	**68**	**9**	**0**	**7**	**158**	**17.7**	**81**	**27**	**37**	**0**	**+17**	**8**	**3**	**2**	**5**	**6**	**1**	**0**	**0**
1970-71	**Chicago Black Hawks**	**NHL**	**58**	**22**	**23**	**45**	**23**	**20**	**43**	**40**	**7**	**0**	**2**	**113**	**19.5**	**62**	**22**	**33**	**2**	**+9**	**18**	**10**	**4**	**14**	**24**	**2**	**0**	**1**
1971-72	**Chicago Black Hawks**	**NHL**	**64**	**27**	**21**	**48**	**29**	**19**	**48**	**38**	**1**	**1**	**5**	**145**	**18.6**	**65**	**7**	**65**	**10**	**+3**	**8**	**2**	**5**	**7**	**4**	**0**	**1**	**1**
1972-73	**Chicago Black Hawks**	**NHL**	**76**	**41**	**51**	**92**	**41**	**43**	**84**	**82**	**7**	**2**	**4**	**182**	**22.5**	**126**	**27**	**82**	**8**	**+25**	**16**	**8**	**7**	**15**	**24**	**1**	**0**	**1**
1973-74	**Chicago Black Hawks**	**NHL**	**78**	**32**	**41**	**73**	**33**	**36**	**69**	**76**	**8**	**1**	**8**	**160**	**20.0**	**107**	**30**	**65**	**13**	**+25**	**11**	**3**	**6**	**9**	**29**	**0**	**0**	**2**
1974-75	**Chicago Black Hawks**	**NHL**	**71**	**36**	**27**	**63**	**33**	**21**	**54**	**94**	**7**	**2**	**5**	**158**	**22.8**	**94**	**25**	**84**	**14**	**–1**	**8**	**0**	**2**	**2**	**2**	**0**	**0**	**0**
1975-76	**California Golden Seals**	**NHL**	**32**	**6**	**13**	**19**	**6**	**10**	**16**	**12**	**2**	**0**	**0**	**72**	**8.3**	**30**	**15**	**31**	**0**	**–16**	....	....	....	....	....	....	....	....
1976-77	**Cleveland Barons**	**NHL**	**24**	**2**	**8**	**10**	**2**	**6**	**8**	**8**	**0**	**0**	**1**	**28**	**7.1**	**19**	**5**	**9**	**0**	**+5**	....	....	....	....	....	....	....	....
	NHL Totals		**767**	**278**	**295**	**573**	**300**	**267**	**567**	**667**	**46**	**6**	**37**	**1341**	**20.7**	**727**	**203**	**505**	**55**		**92**	**33**	**34**	**67**	**101**	**4**	**1**	**5**

AHL Second All-Star Team (1966)

Played in NHL All-Star Game (1964, 1968, 1973, 1974, 1975)

Traded to **Chicago** by **Toronto** for Pierre Pilote, May 23, 1968. Traded to **California** by **Chicago** with Chicago's 3rd round choice (Guy Lash) in 1977 Amateur Draft for Joey Johnston, June 1, 1975. Transferred to **Cleveland** after **California** franchise relocated, August 26, 1976.

• PARADISE, BOB

Bob Paradise D – L. 6'1", 205 lbs. b: St. Paul, MN, 4/22/1944. **USHOF**

1966-67	Muskegon Mohawks	IHL	42	5	6	11	....	....	....	47	....	....	....	....	....	....	....	....	....	....	....	....	....	....	....	....	....	....
1967-68	Minnesota Rangers	USHL	....	2	6	8	....	....	....	43	....	....	....	....	....	....	....	....	....	....	....	....	....	....	....	....	....	....
	United States	Olympics	6	0	0	0	....	....	....	0	....	....	....	....	....	....	....	....	....	....	....	....	....	....	....	....	....	....
1968-69	Michigan Tech Huskies	WCHA	STATISTICS NOT AVAILABLE																									
	United States	WEC-A	8	0	0	0	....	....	....	30	....	....	....	....	....	....	....	....	....	....	....	....	....	....	....	....	....	....
1969-70	Omaha Knights	CHL	61	3	14	17	....	....	....	98	....	....	....	....	....	....	....	....	....	....	12	0	2	2	27	....	....	....
1970-71	Montreal Voyageurs	AHL	72	0	9	9	....	....	....	107	....	....	....	....	....	....	....	....	....	....	3	0	0	0	0	....	....	....
1971-72	**Minnesota North Stars**	**NHL**	**6**	**0**	**0**	**0**	**0**	**0**	**0**	**6**	**0**	**0**	**0**	**1**	**0.0**	**1**	**0**	**0**	**0**	**+1**	**4**	**0**	**0**	**0**	**2**	**0**	**0**	**0**
	Seattle Totems	WHL	54	5	8	13	....	....	....	80	....	....	....	....	....	....	....	....	....	....	....	....	....	....	....	....	....	....
	Cleveland Barons	AHL	4	0	0	0	....	....	....	0	....	....	....	....	....	....	....	....	....	....	....	....	....	....	....	....	....	....
1972-73	**Atlanta Flames**	**NHL**	**71**	**1**	**7**	**8**	**1**	**6**	**7**	**103**	**0**	**0**	**1**	**53**	**1.9**	**42**	**0**	**76**	**14**	**–20**	....	....	....	....	....	....	....	....
1973-74	**Atlanta Flames**	**NHL**	**18**	**0**	**1**	**1**	**0**	**1**	**1**	**13**	**0**	**0**	**0**	**8**	**0.0**	**8**	**0**	**19**	**4**	**–7**	....	....	....	....	....	....	....	....
	Pittsburgh Penguins	**NHL**	**38**	**2**	**7**	**9**	**2**	**6**	**8**	**39**	**1**	**0**	**0**	**35**	**5.7**	**39**	**4**	**44**	**6**	**–3**	....	....	....	....	....	....	....	....
1974-75	**Pittsburgh Penguins**	**NHL**	**78**	**3**	**15**	**18**	**3**	**12**	**15**	**109**	**0**	**0**	**0**	**55**	**5.5**	**88**	**4**	**104**	**18**	**–2**	**6**	**0**	**1**	**1**	**17**	**0**	**0**	**0**
1975-76	**Pittsburgh Penguins**	**NHL**	**9**	**0**	**0**	**0**	**0**	**0**	**0**	**4**	**0**	**0**	**0**	**4**	**0.0**	**4**	**0**	**15**	**4**	**–7**	....	....	....	....	....	....	....	....
	Washington Capitals	**NHL**	**48**	**0**	**8**	**8**	**0**	**6**	**6**	**42**	**0**	**0**	**0**	**26**	**0.0**	**38**	**3**	**83**	**7**	**–41**	....	....	....	....	....	....	....	....
1976-77	**Washington Capitals**	**NHL**	**22**	**0**	**5**	**5**	**0**	**4**	**4**	**20**	**0**	**0**	**0**	**15**	**0.0**	**20**	**0**	**30**	**7**	**–3**	....	....	....	....	....	....	....	....
	Springfield Indians	AHL	14	0	4	4	....	....	....	18	....	....	....	....	....	....	....	....	....	....	....	....	....	....	....	....	....	....
	United States	WEC-A	9	0	0	0	....	....	....	8	....	....	....	....	....	....	....	....	....	....	....	....	....	....	....	....	....	....
1977-78	**Pittsburgh Penguins**	**NHL**	**64**	**2**	**10**	**12**	**2**	**8**	**10**	**53**	**0**	**0**	**0**	**34**	**5.9**	**54**	**0**	**107**	**23**	**–30**	....	....	....	....	....	....	....	....
1978-79	**Pittsburgh Penguins**	**NHL**	**14**	**0**	**1**	**1**	**0**	**1**	**1**	**4**	**0**	**0**	**0**	**4**	**0.0**	**9**	**0**	**13**	**0**	**–4**	**2**	**0**	**0**	**0**	**0**	**0**	**0**	**0**
	Binghamton Dusters	AHL	16	0	1	1	....	....	....	12	....	....	....	....	....	....	....	....	....	....	....	....	....	....	....	....	....	....
	NHL Totals		**368**	**8**	**54**	**62**	**8**	**44**	**52**	**393**	**1**	**0**	**1**	**235**	**3.4**	**303**	**11**	**491**	**83**		**12**	**0**	**1**	**1**	**19**	**0**	**0**	**0**

Signed as a free agent by **Montreal**, June, 1970. Traded to **Minnesota** by **Montreal** with the rights to Gary Gambucci for cash and future considerations, May, 1971. Traded to **Atlanta** by **Minnesota** for cash, June 6, 1972. Traded to **Pittsburgh** by **Atlanta** with Chuck Arnason for Al McDonough, January 4, 1972. Traded to **Washington** by **Pittsburgh** for Washington's 2nd round choice (Greg Malone) in 1976 Amateur Draft, November 26, 1975. Traded to **Pittsburgh** by **Washington** for Don Awrey, October 1, 1977.

• PARISE, JEAN-PAUL

Jean-Paul "J.P." Parise LW – L. 5'9", 175 lbs. b: Smooth Rock Falls, Ont., 12/11/1941.

1961-62	Niagara Falls Flyers	OHA	38	8	20	28	....	....	....	28	....	....	....	....	....	....	....	....	....	....	....	....	....	....	....	....	....	....
	Kingston Frontenacs	EPHL	1	0	0	0	....	....	....	0	....	....	....	....	....	....	....	....	....	....	....	....	....	....	....	....	....	....
1962-63	Kingston Frontenacs	EPHL	64	11	17	28	....	....	....	64	....	....	....	....	....	....	....	....	....	....	5	0	0	0	6	....	....	....
1963-64	Minneapolis Bruins	CHL	72	27	36	63	....	....	....	77	....	....	....	....	....	....	....	....	....	....	5	1	2	3	10	....	....	....
1964-65	Minneapolis Bruins	CHL	70	17	56	73	....	....	....	106	....	....	....	....	....	....	....	....	....	....	5	5	1	6	0	....	....	....
1965-66	**Boston Bruins**	**NHL**	**3**	**0**	**0**	**0**	**0**	**0**	**0**	**0**	....	....	....	....	....	....	....	....	....	....	....	....	....	....	....	....	....	....
	Oklahoma City Blazers	CHL	69	19	30	49	....	....	....	137	....	....	....	....	....	....	....	....	....	....	7	*6	3	9	2	....	....	....
1966-67	**Boston Bruins**	**NHL**	**18**	**2**	**2**	**4**	**2**	**2**	**4**	**10**	....	....	....	....	....	....	....	....	....	....	....	....	....	....	....	....	....	....
	Oklahoma City Blazers	CHL	42	11	22	33	....	....	....	98	....	....	....	....	....	....	....	....	....	....	11	1	9	10	32	....	....	....
1967-68	**Toronto Maple Leafs**	**NHL**	**1**	**0**	**1**	**1**	**0**	**1**	**1**	**0**	**0**	**0**	**0**	**1**	**0.0**	**1**	**0**	**1**	**0**	**0**	....	....	....	....	....	....	....	....
	Rochester Americans	AHL	30	10	18	28	....	....	....	37	....	....	....	....	....	....	....	....	....	....	....	....	....	....	....	....	....	....
	Minnesota North Stars	**NHL**	**43**	**11**	**16**	**27**	**14**	**17**	**31**	**27**	**1**	**0**	**3**	**110**	**10.0**	**46**	**8**	**53**	**5**	**–10**	**14**	**2**	**5**	**7**	**10**	**0**	**1**	**0**
1968-69	**Minnesota North Stars**	**NHL**	**76**	**22**	**27**	**49**	**25**	**25**	**50**	**57**	**7**	**1**	**3**	**196**	**11.2**	**71**	**18**	**108**	**11**	**–44**	....	....	....	....	....	....	....	....
1969-70	**Minnesota North Stars**	**NHL**	**74**	**24**	**48**	**72**	**28**	**48**	**76**	**72**	**6**	**1**	**1**	**168**	**14.3**	**104**	**31**	**82**	**6**	**–3**	**6**	**3**	**2**	**5**	**2**	**2**	**0**	**0**
1970-71	**Minnesota North Stars**	**NHL**	**73**	**11**	**23**	**34**	**11**	**20**	**31**	**60**	**1**	**1**	**3**	**191**	**5.8**	**52**	**11**	**57**	**1**	**–15**	**12**	**3**	**3**	**6**	**22**	**2**	**0**	**1**
1971-72	**Minnesota North Stars**	**NHL**	**71**	**19**	**18**	**37**	**20**	**16**	**36**	**70**	**6**	**0**	**3**	**183**	**10.4**	**60**	**15**	**35**	**0**	**+10**	**7**	**3**	**3**	**6**	**6**	**2**	**0**	**0**
1972-73	Canada	Summit	6	2	2	4	....	....	....	28	....	....	....	....	....	....	....	....	....	....	....	....	....	....	....	....	....	....
	Minnesota North Stars	**NHL**	**78**	**27**	**48**	**75**	**27**	**40**	**67**	**96**	**6**	**0**	**4**	**188**	**14.4**	**100**	**20**	**64**	**2**	**+18**	**6**	**0**	**0**	**0**	**9**	**0**	**0**	**0**
1973-74	**Minnesota North Stars**	**NHL**	**78**	**18**	**37**	**55**	**18**	**32**	**50**	**42**	**2**	**0**	**1**	**188**	**9.6**	**83**	**16**	**77**	**2**	**–8**	....	....	....	....	....	....	....	....
1974-75	**Minnesota North Stars**	**NHL**	**38**	**9**	**16**	**25**	**8**	**13**	**21**	**40**	**1**	**0**	**0**	**65**	**13.8**	**43**	**9**	**56**	**4**	**–18**	....	....	....	....	....	....	....	....
	New York Islanders	**NHL**	**41**	**14**	**16**	**30**	**13**	**13**	**26**	**22**	**4**	**0**	**1**	**88**	**15.9**	**46**	**11**	**25**	**0**	**+10**	**17**	**8**	**8**	**16**	**22**	**4**	**0**	**1**
1975-76	**New York Islanders**	**NHL**	**80**	**22**	**35**	**57**	**20**	**28**	**48**	**80**	**5**	**2**	**4**	**152**	**14.5**	**91**	**31**	**50**	**2**	**+12**	**13**	**4**	**6**	**10**	**10**	**1**	**0**	**0**
1976-77	**New York Islanders**	**NHL**	**80**	**25**	**31**	**56**	**24**	**25**	**49**	**46**	**5**	**0**	**7**	**147**	**17.0**	**91**	**25**	**41**	**1**	**+26**	**11**	**4**	**4**	**8**	**6**	**1**	**0**	**0**
1977-78	**New York Islanders**	**NHL**	**39**	**12**	**16**	**28**	**12**	**13**	**25**	**12**	**1**	**0**	**0**	**68**	**17.6**	**44**	**3**	**22**	**0**	**+19**	....	....	....	....	....	....	....	....
	Cleveland Barons	**NHL**	**40**	**9**	**13**	**22**	**9**	**11**	**20**	**27**	**1**	**0**	**0**	**61**	**14.8**	**33**	**3**	**46**	**1**	**–15**	....	....	....	....	....	....	....	....
1978-79	**Minnesota North Stars**	**NHL**	**57**	**13**	**9**	**22**	**12**	**7**	**19**	**45**	**1**	**0**	**0**	**73**	**17.8**	**47**	**21**	**39**	**1**	**–12**	....	....	....	....	....	....	....	....
	NHL Totals		**890**	**238**	**356**	**594**	**243**	**311**	**554**	**706**	**47**	**5**	**30**	**1879**	**12.7**	**912**	**222**	**756**	**36**		**86**	**27**	**31**	**58**	**87**	**12**	**1**	**2**

CHL Second All-Star Team (1966)

Played in NHL All-Star Game (1970, 1973)

Claimed by **Oakland** from **Boston** in Expansion Draft, June 6, 1967. Traded to **Toronto** by **Oakland** with Bryan Hextall for Gerry Ehman, October 3, 1967. Traded to **Minnesota** by **Toronto** with Milan Marcetta for Murray Hall, Ted Taylor, Len Lunde, Don Johns, Duke Harris and the loan of Carl Wetzel, December 26, 1967. Traded to **NY Islanders** by **Minnesota** for Doug Rombough and Ernie Hicke, January 5, 1975. Traded to **Cleveland** by **NY Islanders** with Jean Potvin and a 4th round choice in 1978 Entry Draft (later cancelled by Cleveland-California merger) for Wayne Merrick and Darcy Reiger, January 10, 1978. Placed on **Minnesota** Reserve List after **Cleveland-Minnesota** Dispersal Draft, June 5, 1978.

• PARIZEAU, MICHEL

Michel Parizeau C – L. 5'10", 165 lbs. b: Montreal, Que., 4/9/1948. NY Rangers' 3rd choice, 10th overall, in 1965 Amateur Draft.

1967-68	Drummondville Rangers	QJHL	STATISTICS NOT AVAILABLE																									
1968-69	Omaha Knights	CHL	71	22	39	61	....	....	....	20	....	....	....	....	....	....	....	....	....	....	7	1	3	4	0	....	....	....
1969-70	Omaha Knights	CHL	71	13	16	29	....	....	....	30	....	....	....	....	....	....	....	....	....	....	12	7	3	10	9	....	....	....
1970-71	Omaha Knights	CHL	72	35	49	84	....	....	....	43	....	....	....	....	....	....	....	....	....	....	11	4	7	11	11	....	....	....
1971-72	**St. Louis Blues**	**NHL**	**21**	**1**	**2**	**3**	**1**	**2**	**3**	**8**	**1**	**0**	**0**	**14**	**7.1**	**4**	**1**	**5**	**1**	**–1**	....	....	....	....	....	....	....	....
	Philadelphia Flyers	**NHL**	**37**	**2**	**12**	**14**	**2**	**11**	**13**	**10**	**1**	**0**	**1**	**39**	**5.1**	**21**	**9**	**21**	**3**	**–6**	....	....	....	....	....	....	....	....
1972-73	Quebec Nordiques	WHA	75	25	48	73	....	....	....	50	....	....	....	....	....	....	....	....	....	....	....	....	....	....	....	....	....	....
1973-74	Quebec Nordiques	WHA	78	26	34	60	....	....	....	39	....	....	....	....	....	....	....	....	....	....	....	....	....	....	....	....	....	....
1974-75	Quebec Nordiques	WHA	78	28	46	74	....	....	....	69	....	....	....	....	....	....	....	....	....	....	15	2	4	6	10	....	....	....

			REGULAR SEASON																		PLAYOFFS							
Season	Club	League	GP	G	A	Pts	AG	AA	APts	PIM	PP	SH	GW	S	%	TGF	PGF	TGA	PGA	+/–	GP	G	A	Pts	PIM	PP	SH	GW
1975-76	Quebec Nordiques	WHA	58	12	27	39	....	....	....	22	....	....	....	....	....	....	....	....	....	....	....	....	....	....	....	....	....	....
	Indianapolis Racers	WHA	23	13	15	28	....	....	....	20	....	....	....	....	....	....	....	....	....	....	7	4	4	8	6	....	....	....
1976-77	Indianapolis Racers	WHA	75	18	37	55	....	....	....	39	....	....	....	....	....	....	....	....	....	....	8	3	6	9	8	....	....	....
1977-78	Indianapolis Racers	WHA	70	13	27	40	....	....	....	47	....	....	....	....	....	....	....	....	....	....	....	....	....	....	....	....	....	....
1978-79	Indianapolis Racers	WHA	22	4	9	13	....	....	....	4	....	....	....	....	....	....	....	....	....	....	....	....	....	....	....	....	....	....
	Cincinnati Stingers	WHA	30	3	9	12	....	....	....	28	....	....	....	....	....	....	....	....	....	....	3	1	0	1	0	....	....	....
1979-80	Syracuse Firebirds	AHL	DID NOT PLAY – COACHING																									
	NHL Totals		**58**	**3**	**14**	**17**	**3**	**13**	**16**	**18**	**2**	**0**	**1**	**53**	**5.7**	**25**	**10**	**26**	**4**		....	....	....	....	....	....	....	....
	Other Major League Totals		509	142	252	394	....	....	....	318	....	....	....	....	....	....	....	....	....		33	10	14	24	24	....	....	....

CHL First All-Star Team (1971)

Claimed by **St. Louis** from **NY Rangers** in Intra-League Draft, June 8, 1971. Claimed on waivers by **Philadelphia** from **St. Louis**, December 8, 1971. Selected by **Quebec** (WHA) in 1972 WHA General Player Draft, February 12, 1972. Traded to **Indianapolis** (WHA) by **Quebec** (WHA) for Michel Dubois and Bob Fitchner, February, 1976. Signed as a free agent by **Cincinnati** (WHA) after **Indianapolis** (WHA) franchise folded, December 15, 1978.

• PARK, BRAD

Brad Park D – L. 6', 200 lbs. b: Toronto, Ont., 7/6/1948. NY Rangers' 1st choice, 2nd overall, in 1966 Amateur Draft. **HHOF**

Season	Club	League	GP	G	A	Pts	AG	AA	APts	PIM	PP	SH	GW	S	%	TGF	PGF	TGA	PGA	+/–	GP	G	A	Pts	PIM	PP	SH	GW
1965-66	Toronto Westclairs	Jr. B	STATISTICS NOT AVAILABLE																									
	Toronto Marlboros	OHA	33	0	14	14	....	....	....	48	....	....	....	....	....	....	....	....	....	....	14	1	0	1	38	....	....	....
1966-67	Toronto Marlboros	OHA	28	4	15	19	....	....	....	73	....	....	....	....	....	....	....	....	....	....	8	4	3	7	17	....	....	....
1967-68	Toronto Marlboros	OHA	50	10	33	43	....	....	....	120	....	....	....	....	....	....	....	....	....	....	5	0	6	6	37	....	....	....
	Toronto Marlboros	OHA Sr.	1	0	0	0	....	....	....	0	....	....	....	....	....	....	....	....	....	....	....	....	....	....	....	....	....	....
1968-69	**New York Rangers**	**NHL**	**54**	**3**	**23**	**26**	**3**	**22**	**25**	**70**	**2**	**0**	**0**	**103**	**2.9**	**71**	**14**	**48**	**3**	**+12**	**4**	**0**	**2**	**2**	**7**	**0**	**0**	**0**
	Buffalo Bisons	AHL	17	2	12	14	....	....	....	49	....	....	....	....	....	....	....	....	....	....	....	....	....	....	....	....	....	....
1969-70	**New York Rangers**	**NHL**	**60**	**11**	**26**	**37**	**13**	**26**	**39**	**98**	**6**	**1**	**2**	**161**	**6.8**	**105**	**32**	**62**	**12**	**+23**	**5**	**1**	**2**	**3**	**11**	**1**	**0**	**0**
1970-71	**New York Rangers**	**NHL**	**68**	**7**	**37**	**44**	**7**	**33**	**40**	**114**	**3**	**0**	**0**	**199**	**3.5**	**114**	**39**	**63**	**13**	**+25**	**13**	**0**	**4**	**4**	**42**	**0**	**0**	**0**
1971-72	**New York Rangers**	**NHL**	**75**	**24**	**49**	**73**	**26**	**45**	**71**	**130**	**8**	**2**	**4**	**263**	**9.1**	**159**	**42**	**70**	**15**	**+62**	**16**	**4**	**7**	**11**	**21**	**2**	**0**	**1**
1972-73	Canada	Summit	8	1	4	5	....	....	....	2	....	....	....	....	....	....	....	....	....	....	....	....	....	....	....	....	....	....
	New York Rangers	**NHL**	**52**	**10**	**43**	**53**	**10**	**36**	**46**	**51**	**4**	**0**	**1**	**142**	**7.0**	**99**	**24**	**56**	**12**	**+31**	**10**	**2**	**5**	**7**	**8**	**1**	**0**	**1**
1973-74	**New York Rangers**	**NHL**	**78**	**25**	**57**	**82**	**26**	**50**	**76**	**148**	**4**	**0**	**4**	**227**	**11.0**	**168**	**57**	**115**	**22**	**+18**	**13**	**4**	**8**	**12**	**38**	**1**	**0**	**1**
1974-75	**New York Rangers**	**NHL**	**65**	**13**	**44**	**57**	**12**	**35**	**47**	**104**	**8**	**0**	**2**	**189**	**6.9**	**166**	**63**	**111**	**25**	**+6**	**3**	**1**	**4**	**5**	**2**	**0**	**0**	**0**
1975-76	**New York Rangers**	**NHL**	**13**	**2**	**4**	**6**	**2**	**3**	**5**	**23**	**0**	**0**	**1**	**28**	**7.1**	**20**	**10**	**21**	**7**	**–4**	....	....	....	....	....	....	....	....
	Boston Bruins	**NHL**	**43**	**16**	**37**	**53**	**15**	**29**	**44**	**95**	**7**	**1**	**2**	**163**	**9.8**	**119**	**43**	**66**	**13**	**+23**	**11**	**3**	**8**	**11**	**14**	**1**	**1**	**0**
1976-77	**Boston Bruins**	**NHL**	**77**	**12**	**55**	**67**	**11**	**45**	**56**	**67**	**4**	**1**	**4**	**238**	**5.0**	**178**	**42**	**116**	**27**	**+47**	**14**	**2**	**10**	**12**	**4**	**0**	**0**	**0**
1977-78	**Boston Bruins**	**NHL**	**80**	**22**	**57**	**79**	**21**	**47**	**68**	**79**	**9**	**0**	**3**	**225**	**9.8**	**199**	**46**	**118**	**33**	**+68**	**15**	**9**	**11**	**20**	**14**	**4**	**0**	**0**
1978-79	**Boston Bruins**	**NHL**	**40**	**7**	**32**	**39**	**6**	**24**	**30**	**10**	**3**	**0**	**0**	**96**	**7.3**	**87**	**34**	**35**	**10**	**+28**	**11**	**1**	**4**	**5**	**8**	**0**	**0**	**1**
1979-80	**Boston Bruins**	**NHL**	**32**	**5**	**16**	**21**	**5**	**12**	**17**	**27**	**2**	**0**	**2**	**67**	**7.5**	**53**	**19**	**31**	**8**	**+11**	**10**	**3**	**6**	**9**	**4**	**0**	**0**	**0**
1980-81	**Boston Bruins**	**NHL**	**78**	**14**	**52**	**66**	**12**	**36**	**48**	**111**	**10**	**0**	**2**	**201**	**7.0**	**166**	**78**	**106**	**39**	**+21**	**3**	**1**	**3**	**4**	**11**	**1**	**0**	**0**
1981-82	**Boston Bruins**	**NHL**	**75**	**14**	**42**	**56**	**11**	**28**	**39**	**82**	**8**	**0**	**1**	**159**	**8.8**	**150**	**59**	**113**	**33**	**+11**	**11**	**1**	**4**	**5**	**4**	**0**	**0**	**1**
1982-83	**Boston Bruins**	**NHL**	**76**	**10**	**26**	**36**	**8**	**18**	**26**	**82**	**5**	**0**	**0**	**127**	**7.9**	**110**	**30**	**85**	**25**	**+20**	**16**	**3**	**9**	**12**	**18**	**1**	**0**	**1**
1983-84	**Detroit Red Wings**	**NHL**	**80**	**5**	**53**	**58**	**4**	**36**	**40**	**85**	**4**	**0**	**0**	**140**	**3.6**	**144**	**68**	**122**	**17**	**–29**	**3**	**0**	**3**	**3**	**0**	**0**	**0**	**0**
1984-85	**Detroit Red Wings**	**NHL**	**67**	**13**	**30**	**43**	**11**	**20**	**31**	**53**	**6**	**0**	**0**	**92**	**14.1**	**97**	**38**	**76**	**2**	**–15**	**3**	**0**	**0**	**0**	**11**	**0**	**0**	**0**
	NHL Totals		**1113**	**213**	**683**	**896**	**203**	**545**	**748**	**1429**	**93**	**5**	**28**	**2820**	**7.6**	**2194**	**738**	**1414**	**316**		**161**	**35**	**90**	**125**	**217**	**12**	**1**	**6**

OHA Second All-Star Team (1968) • NHL First All-Star Team (1970, 1972, 1974, 1976, 1978) • NHL Second All-Star Team (1971, 1973) • Won Bill Masterton Trophy (1984)

Played in NHL All-Star Game (1970, 1971, 1972, 1973, 1974, 1975, 1976, 1977, 1978)

Traded to **Boston** by **NY Rangers** with Jean Ratelle and Joe Zanussi for Phil Esposito and Carol Vadnais, November 7, 1975. Signed as a free agent by **Detroit**, August 9, 1983.

• PARK, RICHARD

Richard Park C – R. 5'11", 190 lbs. b: Seoul, S. Korea, 5/27/1976. Pittsburgh's 2nd choice, 50th overall, in 1994 Entry Draft.

Season	Club	League	GP	G	A	Pts	AG	AA	APts	PIM	PP	SH	GW	S	%	TGF	PGF	TGA	PGA	+/–	GP	G	A	Pts	PIM	PP	SH	GW
1992-93	Belleville Bulls	OHL	66	23	38	61	....	....	....	38	....	....	....	....	....	....	....	....	....	....	5	0	0	0	14	....	....	....
1993-94	Belleville Bulls	OHL	59	27	49	76	....	....	....	70	....	....	....	....	....	....	....	....	....	....	12	3	5	8	18	....	....	....
	United States	WJC-A	7	3	2	5	....	....	....	4	....	....	....	....	....	....	....	....	....	....	....	....	....	....	....	....	....	....
1994-95	Belleville Bulls	OHL	45	28	51	79	....	....	....	35	....	....	....	....	....	....	....	....	....	....	16	9	18	27	12	....	....	....
	United States	WJC-A	7	1	7	8	....	....	....	29	....	....	....	....	....	....	....	....	....	....	....	....	....	....	....	....	....	....
	Pittsburgh Penguins	**NHL**	**1**	**0**	**1**	**1**	**0**	**1**	**1**	**2**	**0**	**0**	**0**	**4**	**0.0**	**1**	**0**	**1**	**1**	**+1**	**3**	**0**	**0**	**0**	**2**	**0**	**0**	**0**
1995-96	Belleville Bulls	OHL	6	7	6	13	....	....	....	2	....	....	....	....	....	....	....	....	....	....	14	18	12	30	10	....	....	....
	Pittsburgh Penguins	**NHL**	**56**	**4**	**6**	**10**	**4**	**5**	**9**	**36**	**0**	**1**	**1**	**62**	**6.5**	**18**	**1**	**23**	**9**	**+3**	**1**	**0**	**0**	**0**	**0**	**0**	**0**	**0**
1996-97	**Pittsburgh Penguins**	**NHL**	**1**	**0**	**0**	**0**	**0**	**0**	**0**	**0**	**0**	**0**	**0**	**1**	**0.0**	**0**	**0**	**1**	**0**	**–1**	....	....	....	....	....	....	....	....
	Cleveland Lumberjacks	IHL	50	12	15	27	....	....	....	30	....	....	....	....	....	....	....	....	....	....	....	....	....	....	....	....	....	....
	Anaheim Mighty Ducks	**NHL**	**11**	**1**	**1**	**2**	**1**	**1**	**2**	**10**	**0**	**0**	**0**	**9**	**11.1**	**4**	**0**	**4**	**0**	**0**	**11**	**0**	**1**	**1**	**2**	**0**	**0**	**0**
1997-98	**Anaheim Mighty Ducks**	**NHL**	**15**	**0**	**2**	**2**	**0**	**2**	**2**	**8**	**0**	**0**	**0**	**14**	**0.0**	**5**	**0**	**8**	**0**	**–3**	....	....	....	....	....	....	....	....
	Cincinnati Mighty Ducks	AHL	56	17	26	43	....	....	....	36	....	....	....	....	....	....	....	....	....	....	....	....	....	....	....	....	....	....
	NHL Totals		**84**	**5**	**10**	**15**	**5**	**9**	**14**	**56**	**0**	**1**	**1**	**90**	**5.6**	**28**	**1**	**37**	**10**		**15**	**0**	**1**	**1**	**4**	**0**	**0**	**0**

Traded to **Anaheim** by **Pittsburgh** for Roman Oksiuta, March 18, 1997.

• PARKER, JEFF

Jeff Parker RW – R. 6'3", 194 lbs. b: St. Paul, MN, 9/7/1964. Buffalo's 9th choice, 111th overall, in 1982 Entry Draft.

Season	Club	League	GP	G	A	Pts	AG	AA	APts	PIM	PP	SH	GW	S	%	TGF	PGF	TGA	PGA	+/–	GP	G	A	Pts	PIM	PP	SH	GW
1983-84	Michigan State Spartans	CCHA	44	8	13	21	....	....	....	82	....	....	....	....	....	....	....	....	....	....	....	....	....	....	....	....	....	....
1984-85	Michigan State Spartans	CCHA	42	10	12	22	....	....	....	89	....	....	....	....	....	....	....	....	....	....	....	....	....	....	....	....	....	....
1985-86	Michigan State Spartans	CCHA	41	15	20	35	....	....	....	88	....	....	....	....	....	....	....	....	....	....	....	....	....	....	....	....	....	....
1986-87	**Buffalo Sabres**	**NHL**	**15**	**3**	**3**	**6**	**3**	**2**	**5**	**7**	**0**	**0**	**0**	**10**	**30.0**	**11**	**1**	**10**	**1**	**+1**	....	....	....	....	....	....	....	....
	Rochester Americans	AHL	54	14	8	22	....	....	....	75	....	....	....	....	....	....	....	....	....	....	14	1	3	4	19	....	....	....
1987-88	**Buffalo Sabres**	**NHL**	**4**	**0**	**2**	**2**	**0**	**1**	**1**	**2**	**0**	**0**	**0**	**0**	**0.0**	**2**	**0**	**4**	**1**	**–1**	....	....	....	....	....	....	....	....
	Rochester Americans	AHL	34	13	31	44	....	....	....	69	....	....	....	....	....	....	....	....	....	....	2	1	1	2	0	....	....	....
1988-89	**Buffalo Sabres**	**NHL**	**57**	**9**	**9**	**18**	**8**	**6**	**14**	**82**	**0**	**0**	**2**	**78**	**11.5**	**30**	**1**	**44**	**18**	**+3**	**5**	**0**	**0**	**0**	**26**	**0**	**0**	**0**
	Rochester Americans	AHL	6	2	4	6	....	....	....	9	....	....	....	....	....	....	....	....	....	....	....	....	....	....	....	....	....	....
1989-90	**Buffalo Sabres**	**NHL**	**61**	**4**	**5**	**9**	**3**	**4**	**7**	**70**	**0**	**0**	**0**	**61**	**6.6**	**23**	**2**	**35**	**5**	**–9**	....	....	....	....	....	....	....	....
1990-91	Muskegon Lumberjacks	IHL	11	1	7	8	....	....	....	13	....	....	....	....	....	....	....	....	....	....	....	....	....	....	....	....	....	....
	Hartford Whalers	**NHL**	**4**	**0**	**0**	**0**	**0**	**0**	**0**	**2**	**0**	**0**	**0**	**4**	**0.0**	**0**	**0**	**6**	**4**	**–2**	....	....	....	....	....	....	....	....
	NHL Totals		**141**	**16**	**19**	**35**	**14**	**13**	**27**	**163**	**0**	**0**	**2**	**153**	**10.5**	**66**	**4**	**99**	**29**		**5**	**0**	**0**	**0**	**26**	**0**	**0**	**0**

NCAA Championship All-Tournament Team (1986)

Traded to **Winnipeg** by **Buffalo** with Phil Housley, Scott Arneil and Buffalo's 1st round choice (Keith Tkachuk) in 1990 Entry Draft for Dale Hawerchuk, Winnipeg's 1st round choice (Brad May) in 1990 Entry Draft and future considerations, June 16, 1990. Signed as a free agent by **Pittsburgh**, February 5, 1991. Traded to **Harford** by **Pittsburgh** with John Cullen and Zarley Zalapski for Ron Francis, Grant Jennings and Ulf Samuelsson, March 4, 1991.

• PARKS, GREG

Greg Parks C – R. 5'9", 180 lbs. b: Edmonton, Alta., 3/25/1967.

Season	Club	League	GP	G	A	Pts	AG	AA	APts	PIM	PP	SH	GW	S	%	TGF	PGF	TGA	PGA	+/–	GP	G	A	Pts	PIM	PP	SH	GW
1984-85	St. Albert Saints	AJHL	48	36	74	110	....	....	....	....	....	....	....	....	....	....	....	....	....	....	....	....	....	....	....	....	....	....
1985-86	Bowling Green University	CCHA	41	16	26	42	....	....	....	43	....	....	....	....	....	....	....	....	....	....	....	....	....	....	....	....	....	....
1986-87	Bowling Green University	CCHA	45	23	27	50	....	....	....	52	....	....	....	....	....	....	....	....	....	....	....	....	....	....	....	....	....	....
1987-88	Bowling Green University	CCHA	45	30	44	74	....	....	....	84	....	....	....	....	....	....	....	....	....	....	....	....	....	....	....	....	....	....
1988-89	Bowling Green University	CCHA	47	32	42	74	....	....	....	98	....	....	....	....	....	....	....	....	....	....	....	....	....	....	....	....	....	....
1989-90	Springfield Indians	AHL	49	22	32	54	....	....	....	30	....	....	....	....	....	....	....	....	....	....	18	9	*13	*22	22	....	....	....
	Johnstown Chiefs	ECHL	8	5	9	14	....	....	....	7	....	....	....	....	....	....	....	....	....	....	....	....	....	....	....	....	....	....
1990-91	**New York Islanders**	**NHL**	**20**	**1**	**2**	**3**	**1**	**2**	**3**	**4**	**0**	**0**	**0**	**10**	**10.0**	**6**	**0**	**6**	**0**	**0**	....	....	....	....	....	....	....	....
	Capital District Islanders	AHL	48	32	43	75	....	....	....	67	....	....	....	....	....	....	....	....	....	....	....	....	....	....	....	....	....	....
1991-92	**New York Islanders**	**NHL**	**1**	**0**	**0**	**0**	**0**	**0**	**0**	**2**	**0**	**0**	**0**	**0**	**0.0**	**0**	**0**	**0**	**0**	**0**	....	....	....	....	....	....	....	....
	Capital District Islanders	AHL	70	36	57	93	....	....	....	84	....	....	....	....	....	....	....	....	....	....	7	5	8	13	4	....	....	....
1992-93	Leksands IF	Sweden	39	21	19	40	....	....	....	66	....	....	....	....	....	....	....	....	....	....	1	0	0	0	4	....	....	....
	Canada	Nat-Team	9	2	2	4	....	....	....	4	....	....	....	....	....	....	....	....	....	....	....	....	....	....	....	....	....	....
	New York Islanders	**NHL**	**2**	**0**	**0**	**0**	**0**	**0**	**0**	**0**	**0**	**0**	**0**	**3**	**0.0**	**0**	**0**	**0**	**0**	**0**	**2**	**0**	**0**	**0**	**0**	**0**	**0**	**0**
1993-94	Leksands IF	Sweden	39	21	18	39	....	....	....	44	....	....	....	....	....	....	....	....	....	....	4	3	1	4	....	....	....	....
	Canada	Nat-Team	13	1	1	2	....	....	....	112	....	....	....	....	....	....	....	....	....	....	....	....	....	....	....	....	....	....
	Canada	Olympics	8	1	2	3	....	....	....	10	....	....	....	....	....	....	....	....	....	....	....	....	....	....	....	....	....	....

			REGULAR SEASON																		PLAYOFFS							
Season	**Club**	**League**	**GP**	**G**	**A**	**Pts**	**AG**	**AA**	**APts**	**PIM**	**PP**	**SH**	**GW**	**S**	**%**	**TGF**	**PGF**	**TGA**	**PGA**	**+/–**	**GP**	**G**	**A**	**Pts**	**PIM**	**PP**	**SH**	**GW**
1994-95	Krefeld Pinguine	Germany	10	2	7	9				8											1	0	0	0	0			
1995-96	Brynas IF Gavle	Sweden	22	10	12	22				22																		
	Canada	Nat-Team	7	0	0	0				6																		
	NHL Totals		**23**	**1**	**2**	**3**	**1**	**2**	**3**	**6**	**0**	**0**	**0**	**13**	**7.7**	**6**	**0**	**6**	**0**		**2**	**0**	**0**	**0**	**0**	**0**	**0**	**0**

CCHA First All-Star Team (1989) • NCAA West First All-American Team (1989)

Signed as a free agent by **NY Islanders**, August 13, 1990.

• PASEK, DUSAN

Dusan Pasek C – L. 6'1", 200 lbs. b: Bratislava, Czech., 9/7/1960. Minnesota's 4th choice, 81st overall, in 1982 Entry Draft.

Season	**Club**	**League**	**GP**	**G**	**A**	**Pts**	**AG**	**AA**	**APts**	**PIM**	**PP**	**SH**	**GW**	**S**	**%**	**TGF**	**PGF**	**TGA**	**PGA**	**+/–**	**GP**	**G**	**A**	**Pts**	**PIM**	**PP**	**SH**	**GW**
1977-78	Slovan Bratislava	Czech.	5	0	1	1				0																		
1978-79	Slovan Bratislava	Czech.	36	9	12	21				18																		
	Czechoslovakia	WJC-A	6	2	0	2				2																		
1979-80	Slovan Bratislava	Czech.	40	18	1	19				22																		
	Czechoslovakia	WJC-A	5	6	1	7				4																		
1980-81			STATISTICS NOT AVAILABLE																									
1981-82	Czechoslovakia	C Cup	6	0	2	2				2																		
	Slovan Bratislava	Czech. 2	STATISTICS NOT AVAILABLE																									
	Czechoslovakia	WEC-A	10	1	2	3				4																		
1982-83	Czechoslovakia	WEC-A	10	3	2	5				6																		
1983-84	Czechoslovakia	Olympics	7	0	4	4				2																		
1984-85	Czechoslovakia	C Cup	5	0	0	0				4																		
	Slovan Bratislava	Czech.	40	23	14	37				60																		
	Czechoslovakia	WEC-A	10	3	3	6				6																		
1985-86	Dukla Islau	Czech.	45	13	11	24																						
	Czechoslovakia	WEC-A	10	4	3	7				16																		
1986-87	Slovan Bratislava	Czech.	38	21	*29	50				*81																		
	Czechoslovakia	WEC-A	10	6	2	8				2																		
1987-88	Czechoslovakia	C Cup	6	4	1	5				12																		
	Slovan Bratislava	Czech.	28	13	10	23																						
	Czechoslovakia	Olympics	8	6	5	11				8																		
1988-89	**Minnesota North Stars**	**NHL**	**48**	**4**	**10**	**14**	**3**	**7**	**10**	**30**	**1**	**0**	**0**	**86**	**4.7**	**29**	**8**	**29**	**0**	**–8**	**2**	**1**	**0**	**1**	**0**	**0**	**0**	**0**
1989-90	Kalamazoo Wings	IHL	20	10	14	24				6																		
1990-91	Slovan Bratislava	Czech.	11	11	5	16				20																		
	HC Asiago	Italy	34	35	41	76				22											3	5	1	6	0			
1991-92	Fassa Merloni	Italy	25	22	33	55				22																		
1992-93	Kalpal Kuopio	Finland	10	2	4	6				16																		
	NHL Totals		**48**	**4**	**10**	**14**	**3**	**7**	**10**	**30**	**1**	**0**	**0**	**86**	**4.7**	**29**	**8**	**29**	**0**		**2**	**1**	**0**	**1**	**0**	**0**	**0**	**0**

Czechoslovakian First All-Star Team (1988)

• PASIN, DAVE

Dave Pasin RW – R. 6'1", 205 lbs. b: Edmonton, Alta., 7/8/1966. Boston's 1st choice, 19th overall, in 1984 Entry Draft.

Season	**Club**	**League**	**GP**	**G**	**A**	**Pts**	**AG**	**AA**	**APts**	**PIM**	**PP**	**SH**	**GW**	**S**	**%**	**TGF**	**PGF**	**TGA**	**PGA**	**+/–**	**GP**	**G**	**A**	**Pts**	**PIM**	**PP**	**SH**	**GW**
1982-83	Prince Albert Raiders	WHL	62	40	42	82				48																		
1983-84	Prince Albert Raiders	WHL	71	68	54	122				68											5	1	4	5	0			
1984-85	Prince Albert Raiders	WHL	65	64	52	116				88											10	10	11	21	10			
1985-86	**Boston Bruins**	**NHL**	**71**	**18**	**19**	**37**	**14**	**13**	**27**	**50**	**4**	**0**	**3**	**116**	**15.5**	**57**	**12**	**47**	**1**	**–1**	**3**	**0**	**1**	**1**	**0**	**0**	**0**	**0**
1986-87	Moncton Golden Flames	AHL	66	27	25	52				47											6	1	1	2	14			
1987-88	Maine Mariners	AHL	30	8	14	22				39											8	4	3	7	13			
1988-89	Maine Mariners	AHL	11	2	5	7				6																		
	Los Angeles Kings	**NHL**	**5**	**0**	**0**	**0**	**0**	**0**	**0**	**0**	**0**	**0**	**0**	**2**	**0.0**	**1**	**0**	**2**	**0**	**–1**								
	New Haven Nighthawks	AHL	48	25	23	48				42											17	8	8	16	47			
1989-90	New Haven Nighthawks	AHL	7	7	4	11				14																		
	Springfield Indians	AHL	11	2	3	5				2											3	1	2	3	2			
1990-91	New Haven Nighthawks	AHL	39	13	25	38				57																		
	Phoenix Roadrunners	IHL	13	4	3	7				24											9	3	4	7	8			
1991-92			DID NOT PLAY																									
1992-93	HC Bolzano	Italy	18	15	19	34				13																		
1993-94	HC Bolzano	Italy	21	17	34	51				49																		
1994-95	HC Bolzono	Italy	42	43	*65	*108				80																		
1995-96	San Francisco Spiders	IHL	26	5	9	14				16																		
1996-97	HC Bolzano	Alpenliga	38	23	28	51				127																		
	HC Davos	Switz.	2	3	1	4				6											6	4	3	7	16			
	NHL Totals		**76**	**18**	**19**	**37**	**14**	**13**	**27**	**50**	**4**	**0**	**3**	**118**	**15.3**	**58**	**12**	**49**	**1**		**3**	**0**	**1**	**1**	**0**	**0**	**0**	**0**

WHL East Second All-Star Team (1985)

Rights traded to **LA Kings** by **Boston** for Paul Guay, November 3, 1988. Claimed on waivers by **NY Islanders** from **LA Kings**, March 6, 1990.

• PASLAWSKI, GREG

Greg Paslawski RW – R. 5'11", 190 lbs. b: Kindersley, Sask., 8/25/1961.

Season	**Club**	**League**	**GP**	**G**	**A**	**Pts**	**AG**	**AA**	**APts**	**PIM**	**PP**	**SH**	**GW**	**S**	**%**	**TGF**	**PGF**	**TGA**	**PGA**	**+/–**	**GP**	**G**	**A**	**Pts**	**PIM**	**PP**	**SH**	**GW**
1980-81	Prince Albert Raiders	SJHL	59	55	60	115				106																		
1981-82	Nova Scotia Voyageurs	AHL	43	15	11	26				31																		
1982-83	Nova Scotia Voyageurs	AHL	75	46	42	88				32											6	1	3	4	8			
1983-84	**Montreal Canadiens**	**NHL**	**26**	**1**	**4**	**5**	**1**	**3**	**4**	**4**	**0**	**0**	**0**	**27**	**3.7**	**10**	**0**	**15**	**0**	**–5**								
	St. Louis Blues	**NHL**	**34**	**8**	**6**	**14**	**6**	**4**	**10**	**17**	**1**	**0**	**0**	**36**	**22.2**	**20**	**3**	**15**	**2**	**+4**	**9**	**1**	**0**	**1**	**2**	**0**	**0**	**0**
1984-85	**St. Louis Blues**	**NHL**	**72**	**22**	**20**	**42**	**18**	**14**	**32**	**21**	**7**	**0**	**2**	**159**	**13.8**	**60**	**15**	**39**	**0**	**+6**	**3**	**0**	**0**	**0**	**2**	**0**	**0**	**0**
1985-86	**St. Louis Blues**	**NHL**	**56**	**22**	**11**	**33**	**18**	**7**	**25**	**18**	**1**	**1**	**2**	**150**	**14.7**	**47**	**10**	**56**	**7**	**–12**	**17**	**10**	**7**	**17**	**13**	**2**	**0**	**0**
1986-87	**St. Louis Blues**	**NHL**	**76**	**29**	**35**	**64**	**25**	**25**	**50**	**27**	**5**	**1**	**7**	**204**	**14.2**	**95**	**27**	**78**	**11**	**+1**	**6**	**1**	**1**	**2**	**4**	**0**	**0**	**0**
1987-88	**St. Louis Blues**	**NHL**	**17**	**2**	**1**	**3**	**2**	**1**	**3**	**4**	**0**	**0**	**1**	**30**	**6.7**	**6**	**2**	**20**	**2**	**–14**	**3**	**1**	**1**	**2**	**2**	**1**	**0**	**0**
1988-89	**St. Louis Blues**	**NHL**	**75**	**26**	**26**	**52**	**22**	**18**	**40**	**18**	**8**	**0**	**3**	**179**	**14.5**	**79**	**26**	**61**	**16**	**+8**	**9**	**2**	**1**	**3**	**2**	**1**	**0**	**0**
1989-90	**Winnipeg Jets**	**NHL**	**71**	**18**	**30**	**48**	**16**	**21**	**37**	**14**	**7**	**0**	**6**	**122**	**14.8**	**80**	**25**	**63**	**4**	**–4**	**7**	**1**	**3**	**4**	**0**	**0**	**0**	**0**
1990-91	**Winnipeg Jets**	**NHL**	**43**	**9**	**10**	**19**	**8**	**8**	**16**	**10**	**1**	**0**	**1**	**66**	**13.6**	**32**	**9**	**29**	**0**	**–6**								
	Buffalo Sabres	**NHL**	**12**	**2**	**1**	**3**	**2**	**1**	**3**	**4**	**0**	**0**	**1**	**9**	**22.2**	**6**	**0**	**6**	**0**	**0**								
1991-92	**Quebec Nordiques**	**NHL**	**80**	**28**	**17**	**45**	**26**	**13**	**39**	**18**	**5**	**1**	**4**	**134**	**20.9**	**68**	**20**	**82**	**22**	**–12**								
1992-93	**Philadelphia Flyers**	**NHL**	**60**	**14**	**19**	**33**	**12**	**13**	**25**	**12**	**4**	**0**	**0**	**90**	**15.6**	**56**	**10**	**46**	**0**	**0**								
	Calgary Flames	**NHL**	**13**	**4**	**5**	**9**	**3**	**3**	**6**	**0**	**0**	**0**	**1**	**19**	**21.1**	**13**	**4**	**6**	**0**	**+3**	**6**	**3**	**0**	**3**	**0**	**0**	**0**	**1**
1993-94	**Calgary Flames**	**NHL**	**15**	**2**	**0**	**2**	**2**	**0**	**2**	**2**	**0**	**0**	**1**	**13**	**15.4**	**7**	**2**	**9**	**0**	**–4**								
	Peoria Rivermen	IHL	29	16	16	32				12											6	3	3	6	0			
1994-95	Peoria Rivermen	IHL	69	26	43	69				15											9	9	1	10	4			
1995-96	Peoria Rivermen	IHL	60	16	27	43				22											1	0	0	0	0			
	NHL Totals		**650**	**187**	**185**	**372**	**161**	**131**	**292**	**169**	**39**	**3**	**29**	**1238**	**15.1**	**579**	**153**	**525**	**64**		**60**	**19**	**13**	**32**	**25**	**4**	**0**	**1**

Signed as a free agent by **Montreal**, October 5, 1981. Traded to **St. Louis** by **Montreal** with Gilbert Delorme and Doug Wickenheiser for Perry Turnbull, December 21, 1983. Traded to **Winnipeg** by **St. Louis** with St. Louis' 3rd round choice (Kris Draper) in 1989 Entry Draft for Winnipeg's 3rd round choice (Denny Felsner) in 1989 Entry Draft and 2nd round choice (Steve Staios) in 1991 Entry Draft, June 17, 1989. Traded to **Buffalo** by **Winnipeg** for future considerations, February 4, 1991. Claimed by **San Jose** from **Buffalo** in Expansion Draft, May 30, 1991. Traded to **Quebec** by **San Jose** for Tony Hrkac, May 31, 1991. Signed as a free agent by **Philadelphia**, August 25, 1992. Traded to **Calgary** by **Philadelphia** for Calgary's 9th round choice (E.J. Bradley) in 1993 Entry Draft, March 18, 1993.

• PATERSON, JOE

Joe Paterson LW – L. 6'2", 207 lbs. b: Toronto, Ont., 6/25/1960. Detroit's 5th choice, 87th overall, in 1979 Entry Draft.

Season	**Club**	**League**	**GP**	**G**	**A**	**Pts**	**AG**	**AA**	**APts**	**PIM**	**PP**	**SH**	**GW**	**S**	**%**	**TGF**	**PGF**	**TGA**	**PGA**	**+/–**	**GP**	**G**	**A**	**Pts**	**PIM**	**PP**	**SH**	**GW**
1977-78	London Knights	OHA	68	17	16	33				100																		
1978-79	London Knights	OHA	59	22	19	41				158											7	2	3	5	13			
1979-80	London Knights	OHA	62	21	50	71				156																		
	Kalamazoo Wings	IHL	4	1	2	3				2											3	2	1	3	11			
1980-81	**Detroit Red Wings**	**NHL**	**38**	**2**	**5**	**7**	**2**	**3**	**5**	**53**	**0**	**0**	**0**	**36**	**5.6**	**14**	**0**	**10**	**0**	**+4**								
	Adirondack Red Wings	AHL	39	9	16	25				68																		
1981-82	**Detroit Red Wings**	**NHL**	**3**	**0**	**0**	**0**	**0**	**0**	**0**	**0**	**0**	**0**	**0**	**1**	**0.0**	**1**	**0**	**0**	**0**	**+1**								
	Adirondack Red Wings	AHL	74	22	28	50				132											5	1	4	5	6			

Season	Club	League	GP	G	A	Pts	AG	AA	APts	PIM	PP	SH	GW	S	%	TGF	PGF	TGA	PGA	+/–	GP	G	A	Pts	PIM	PP	SH	GW
			REGULAR SEASON																		PLAYOFFS							
1982-83	Detroit Red Wings	NHL	33	2	1	3	2	1	3	14	0	0	1	18	11.1	5	0	14	1	–8	....	....	....	....	....	....	....	....
	Adirondack Red Wings	AHL	36	11	10	21	....	....	....	85	....	....	....	....	....	....	....	....	....	....	6	1	2	3	21	....	....	....
1983-84	Detroit Red Wings	NHL	41	2	5	7	2	3	5	148	0	0	0	26	7.7	13	0	13	0	0	3	0	0	0	7	0	0	0
	Adirondack Red Wings	AHL	20	10	15	25	....	....	....	43	....	....	....	....	....	....	....	....	....	....	....	....	....	....	....	....	....	....
1984-85	Philadelphia Flyers	NHL	6	0	0	0	0	0	0	31	0	0	0	4	0.0	0	0	1	0	–1	17	3	4	7	70	1	0	0
	Hershey Bears	AHL	67	26	27	53	....	....	....	173	....	....	....	....	....	....	....	....	....	....	....	....	....	....	....	....	....	....
1985-86	Philadelphia Flyers	NHL	5	0	0	0	0	0	0	12	0	0	0	4	0.0	2	0	1	0	+1	....	....	....	....	....	....	....	....
	Hershey Bears	AHL	20	5	10	15	....	....	....	68	....	....	....	....	....	....	....	....	....	....	....	....	....	....	....	....	....	....
	Los Angeles Kings	NHL	47	9	18	27	7	12	19	153	2	0	1	75	12.0	45	12	41	1	–7	....	....	....	....	....	....	....	....
1986-87	Los Angeles Kings	NHL	45	2	1	3	2	1	3	158	0	0	1	30	6.7	5	0	20	0	–15	2	0	0	0	0	0	0	0
1987-88	Los Angeles Kings	NHL	32	1	3	4	1	2	3	113	0	0	0	20	5.0	6	0	16	0	–10	....	....	....	....	....	....	....	....
	New York Rangers	NHL	21	1	3	4	1	2	3	63	0	0	0	9	11.1	7	0	12	1	–4	....	....	....	....	....	....	....	....
1988-89	New York Rangers	NHL	20	0	1	1	0	1	1	84	0	0	0	8	0.0	2	0	5	0	–3	....	....	....	....	....	....	....	....
	Denver Rangers	IHL	9	5	4	9	....	....	....	31	....	....	....	....	....	....	....	....	....	....	....	....	....	....	....	....	....	....
1989-90	Flint Spirits	IHL	69	21	26	47	....	....	....	198	....	....	....	....	....	....	....	....	....	....	4	0	1	1	2	....	....	....
1990-91	Binghamton Rangers	AHL	80	16	35	51	....	....	....	221	....	....	....	....	....	....	....	....	....	....	10	5	3	8	25	....	....	....
1991-92	Binghamton Rangers	AHL	49	7	10	17	....	....	....	115	....	....	....	....	....	....	....	....	....	....	5	0	0	0	4	....	....	....
	Phoenix Roadrunners	IHL	2	0	0	0	....	....	....	2	....	....	....	....	....	....	....	....	....	....	....	....	....	....	....	....	....	....
	NHL Totals		**291**	**19**	**37**	**56**	**17**	**25**	**42**	**829**	**2**	**0**	**3**	**231**	**8.2**	**100**	**12**	**133**	**3**		**22**	**3**	**4**	**7**	**77**	**1**	**0**	**0**

Traded to **Philadelphia** by **Detroit** with Murray Craven for Darryl Sittler, October 19, 1984. Trade to **LA Kings** by **Philadelphia** for Philadelphia's 4th round choice (previously acquired, Philadelphia selected Mark Bar) in 1986 Entry Draft, December 18, 1985. Traded to **NY Rangers** by **LA Kings** for Gord Walker and Mike Siltala, January 21, 1988.

• PATERSON, MARK

Mark Paterson D – L. 5'11", 180 lbs. b: Ottawa, Ont., 2/22/1964. Hartford's 2nd choice, 35th overall, in 1982 Entry Draft.

Season	Club	League	GP	G	A	Pts	AG	AA	APts	PIM	PP	SH	GW	S	%	TGF	PGF	TGA	PGA	+/–	GP	G	A	Pts	PIM	PP	SH	GW
1980-81	Nepean Raiders	OJHL	50	6	13	19	....	....	....	98	....	....	....	....	....	....	....	....	....	....	....	....	....	....	....	....	....	....
1981-82	Ottawa 67's	OHL	64	4	13	17	....	....	....	59	....	....	....	....	....	....	....	....	....	....	17	1	5	6	40	....	....	....
1982-83	Ottawa 67's	OHL	57	7	14	21	....	....	....	140	....	....	....	....	....	....	....	....	....	....	9	1	4	5	31	....	....	....
	Hartford Whalers	NHL	2	0	0	0	0	0	0	0	0	0	0	1	0.0	0	0	1	0	–1	....	....	....	....	....	....	....	....
1983-84	Ottawa 67's	OHL	45	8	16	24	....	....	....	114	....	....	....	....	....	....	....	....	....	....	13	2	7	9	16	....	....	....
	Hartford Whalers	NHL	9	2	0	2	2	0	2	4	0	0	0	10	20.0	13	0	9	0	+4	....	....	....	....	....	....	....	....
1984-85	Hartford Whalers	NHL	13	1	3	4	1	2	3	24	0	0	0	9	11.1	9	0	16	1	–6	....	....	....	....	....	....	....	....
	Binghamton Whalers	AHL	44	2	18	20	....	....	....	74	....	....	....	....	....	....	....	....	....	....	8	0	0	0	18	....	....	....
1985-86	Hartford Whalers	NHL	5	0	0	0	0	0	0	5	0	0	0	0	0.0	0	0	5	0	–5	....	....	....	....	....	....	....	....
	Binghamton Whalers	AHL	67	2	16	18	....	....	....	121	....	....	....	....	....	....	....	....	....	....	6	0	0	0	6	....	....	....
1986-87	Moncton Golden Flames	AHL	70	6	21	27	....	....	....	112	....	....	....	....	....	....	....	....	....	....	3	0	0	0	0	....	....	....
1987-88	Saginaw Hawks	IHL	23	1	5	6	....	....	....	55	....	....	....	....	....	....	....	....	....	....	8	0	4	4	15	....	....	....
1988-89	Saginaw Hawks	IHL	17	1	3	4	....	....	....	42	....	....	....	....	....	....	....	....	....	....	....	....	....	....	....	....	....	....
	NHL Totals		**29**	**3**	**3**	**6**	**3**	**2**	**5**	**33**	**0**	**0**	**0**	**20**	**15.0**	**22**	**0**	**31**	**1**		....	....	....	....	....	....	....	....

Traded to **Calgary** by **Hartford** for Yves Courteau, October 7, 1986.

• PATERSON, RICK

Rick Paterson C – R. 5'9", 187 lbs. b: Kingston, Ont., 2/10/1958. Chicago's 3rd choice, 46th overall, in 1978 Amateur Draft.

Season	Club	League	GP	G	A	Pts	AG	AA	APts	PIM	PP	SH	GW	S	%	TGF	PGF	TGA	PGA	+/–	GP	G	A	Pts	PIM	PP	SH	GW
1973-74	Cornwall Royals	QMJHL	60	1	14	15	....	....	....	5			....	....	....	....	....	....	....	....	....	....	....	....	....	....	....	....
1974-75	Cornwall Royals	QMJHL	68	18	20	38	....	....	....	50	....	....	....	....	....	....	....	....	....	....	....	....	....	....	....	....	....	....
1975-76	Cornwall Royals	QMJHL	71	20	60	80		....	....	59	....	....	....	....	....	....	....	....	....	....	....	....	....	....	....	....	....	....
1976-77	Cornwall Royals	QMJHL	72	31	63	94	....	....	....	90	....	....	....	....	....	....	....	....	....	....	12	6	9	15	22	....	....	....
1977-78	Cornwall Royals	QMJHL	71	58	80	138	....	....	....	105	....	....	....	....	....	....	....	....	....	....	9	3	7	10	27	....	....	....
	Canada	WJC-A	6	1	2	3	....	....	....	0	....	....	....	....	....	....	....	....	....	....	....	....	....	....	....	....	....	....
1978-79	New Brunswick Hawks	AHL	73	21	19	40	....	....	....	30	....	....	....	....	....	....	....	....	....	....	5	0	1	1	9	....	....	....
	Chicago Black Hawks	NHL	....	....	....	....	....	....	....	....	....	....	....	....	....	....	....	....	....	....	1	0	1	1	0	....	....	....
1979-80	Chicago Black Hawks	NHL	11	0	2	2	0	2	2	0	0	0	0	11	0.0	4	0	4	0	0	7	0	0	0	5	0	0	0
	New Brunswick Hawks	AHL	55	22	30	52				18	....	....	....	....	....	....	....	....	....	....	12	5	6	11	9	....	....	....
1980-81	Chicago Black Hawks	NHL	49	8	2	10	7	1	8	18	1	2	1	38	21.1	18	2	41	23	–2	2	1	0	1	0	0	1	0
	New Brunswick Hawks	AHL	21	7	8	15	....	....	....	6	....	....	....	....	....	....	....	....	....	....	....	....	....	....	....	....	....	....
1981-82	Chicago Black Hawks	NHL	48	4	7	11	3	5	8	8	0	0	1	45	8.9	17	0	60	41	–2	15	3	2	5	21	0	0	0
	New Brunswick Hawks	AHL	30	8	16	24	....	....	....	45	....	....	....	....	....	....	....	....	....	....	....	....	....	....	....	....	....	....
1982-83	Chicago Black Hawks	NHL	79	14	9	23	11	6	17	14	1	3	2	78	17.9	33	2	76	44	–1	13	1	1	2	4	0	1	1
1983-84	Chicago Black Hawks	NHL	72	7	6	13	6	4	10	41	0	0	0	64	10.9	33	0	83	37	–13	5	1	1	2	6	0	1	0
1984-85	Chicago Black Hawks	NHL	79	7	12	19	6	8	14	25	0	3	1	53	13.2	31	0	63	38	+6	15	1	5	6	15	0	0	0
1985-86	Chicago Black Hawks	NHL	70	9	3	12	7	2	9	24	0	5	0	36	25.0	17	0	50	32	–1	3	0	0	0	0	0	0	0
1986-87	Chicago Blackhawks	NHL	22	1	2	3	1	1	2	6	0	1	0	4	25.0	5	0	12	8	+1	....	....	....	....	....	....	....	....
	Nova Scotia Oilers	AHL	31	5	7	12	....	....	....	2	....	....	....	....	....	....	....	....	....	....	5	0	1	1	10	....	....	....
1987-88	Saginaw Hawks	IHL	82	19	26	45	....	....	....	83	....	....	....	....	....	....	....	....	....	....	10	2	4	6	16	....	....	....
	NHL Totals		**430**	**50**	**43**	**93**	**41**	**29**	**70**	**136**	**2**	**14**	**5**	**329**	**15.2**	**158**	**4**	**389**	**223**		**61**	**7**	**10**	**17**	**51**	**0**	**3**	**1**

• PATEY, DOUG

Doug Patey RW – R. 5'11", 180 lbs. b: Toronto, Ont., 12/28/1956. Washington's 5th choice, 73rd overall, in 1976 Amateur Draft.

Season	Club	League	GP	G	A	Pts	AG	AA	APts	PIM	PP	SH	GW	S	%	TGF	PGF	TGA	PGA	+/–	GP	G	A	Pts	PIM	PP	SH	GW
1973-74	Dixie Beehives	Jr. A	42	31	30	61	....	....	....	28	....	....	....	....	....	....	....	....	....	....	....	....	....	....	....	....	....	....
1974-75	Sault Ste. Marie Greyhounds	OHA	64	31	28	59	....	....	....	20	....	....	....	....	....	....	....	....	....	....	....	....	....	....	....	....	....	....
1975-76	Sault Ste. Marie Greyhounds	OHA	59	45	65	110	....	....	....	52	....	....	....	....	....	....	....	....	....	....	....	....	....	....	....	....	....	....
1976-77	Washington Capitals	NHL	37	3	1	4	3	1	4	6	0	0	0	43	7.0	9	0	24	0	–15	....	....	....	....	....	....	....	....
	Dayton Gems	IHL	38	11	16	27	....	....	....	23	....	....	....	....	....	....	....	....	....	....	4	1	1	2	2	....	....	....
1977-78	Washington Capitals	NHL	2	0	1	1	0	1	1	0	0	0	0	0	0.0	1	0	0	0	+1	....	....	....	....	....	....	....	....
	Hershey Bears	AHL	79	27	33	60	....	....	....	23	....	....	....	....	....	....	....	....	....	....	....	....	....	....	....	....	....	....
1978-79	Washington Capitals	NHL	6	1	0	1	1	0	1	2	0	0	0	6	16.7	1	0	3	0	–2	....	....	....	....	....	....	....	....
	Hershey Bears	AHL	74	22	24	46	....	....	....	16	....	....	....	....	....	....	....	....	....	....	4	1	0	1	0	....	....	....
1979-80	Cincinnati Stingers	CHL	14	5	9	14	....	....	....	2	....	....	....	....	....	....	....	....	....	....	....	....	....	....	....	....	....	....
	Houston Apollos	CHL	33	15	15	30	....	....	....	16	....	....	....	....	....	....	....	....	....	....	....	....	....	....	....	....	....	....
	NHL Totals		**45**	**4**	**2**	**6**	**4**	**2**	**6**	**8**	**0**	**0**	**0**	**49**	**8.2**	**11**	**0**	**27**	**0**		....	....	....	....	....	....	....	....

Claimed by **Edmonton** from **Washington** in Expansion Draft, June 13, 1979.

• PATEY, LARRY

Larry Patey C – L. 6'1", 185 lbs. b: Toronto, Ont., 3/19/1953. California's 7th choice, 130th overall, in 1973 Amateur Draft.

Season	Club	League	GP	G	A	Pts	AG	AA	APts	PIM	PP	SH	GW	S	%	TGF	PGF	TGA	PGA	+/–	GP	G	A	Pts	PIM	PP	SH	GW
1972-73	Braintree Bruins	NEHL	47	30	27	63	....	....	....	....	....	....	....	....	....	....	....	....	....	....	....	....	....	....	....	....	....	....
1973-74	California Golden Seals	NHL	1	0	0	0	0	0	0	0	0	0	0	0	0.0	0	0	0	0	0	....	....	....	....	....	....	....	....
	Salt Lake Golden Eagles	WHL	76	40	43	83	....	....	....	91	....	....	....	....	....	....	....	....	....	....	5	2	2	4	15	....	....	....
1974-75	California Golden Seals	NHL	79	25	20	45	23	16	39	68	8	1	4	156	16.0	62	20	73	11	–20	....	....	....	....	....	....	....	....
1975-76	California Golden Seals	NHL	18	4	4	8	4	3	7	23	1	0	0	25	16.0	11	4	15	0	–8	....	....	....	....	....	....	....	....
	St. Louis Blues	NHL	53	8	6	14	7	5	12	26	2	1	0	80	10.0	22	4	35	5	–12	3	1	1	2	2	1	0	1
1976-77	St. Louis Blues	NHL	80	21	29	50	20	24	44	41	1	2	2	134	15.7	62	3	70	22	+11	4	1	0	1	0	0	0	0
1977-78	St. Louis Blues	NHL	80	17	17	34	16	14	30	29	3	0	3	129	13.2	46	5	76	15	–20	....	....	....	....	....	....	....	....
1978-79	St. Louis Blues	NHL	78	15	19	34	14	14	28	60	0	2	2	124	12.1	42	1	100	32	–27	....	....	....	....	....	....	....	....
1979-80	St. Louis Blues	NHL	78	17	17	34	15	13	28	76	0	3	3	144	11.8	42	0	77	17	–18	3	1	0	1	2	0	0	0
1980-81	St. Louis Blues	NHL	80	22	23	45	18	16	34	107	0	8	3	125	17.6	54	0	82	30	+2	11	2	4	6	30	0	0	0
1981-82	St. Louis Blues	NHL	70	14	12	26	11	8	19	97	1	4	2	109	12.8	40	1	86	37	–10	10	2	4	6	13	0	1	0
1982-83	St. Louis Blues	NHL	67	9	12	21	7	8	15	80	0	3	0	72	12.5	28	0	71	37	–6	4	1	0	1	4	0	0	0
1983-84	St. Louis Blues	NHL	17	0	1	1	0	1	1	8	0	0	0	9	0.0	1	0	31	18	–12	....	....	....	....	....	....	....	....
	New York Rangers	NHL	9	1	2	3	1	1	2	4	0	1	0	6	16.7	6	0	9	3	0	4	0	1	1	6	0	0	0
1984-85	New York Rangers	NHL	7	0	1	1	0	1	1	12	0	0	0	2	0.0	1	0	7	0	–6	1	0	0	0	0	0	0	0
	New Haven Nighthawks	AHL	62	14	14	28	....	....	....	43	....	....	....	....	....	....	....	....	....	....	....	....	....	....	....	....	....	....
	NHL Totals		**717**	**153**	**163**	**316**	**136**	**124**	**260**	**631**	**16**	**25**	**19**	**1115**	**13.7**	**417**	**38**	**732**	**227**		**40**	**8**	**10**	**18**	**57**	**1**	**1**	**1**

Won WHL Rookie of the Year Award (1974)

Traded to **St. Louis** by **California** with California's 3rd round choice (Reg Kerr) in 1977 Amateur Draft for Wayne Merrick, November 24, 1975. Traded to **NY Rangers** by **St. Louis** with Bob Brooke for Dave Barr and NY Rangers' 3rd round choice (Alan Perry) in 1984 Entry Draft and cash, March 5, 1984.

			REGULAR SEASON																		PLAYOFFS							
Season	Club	League	GP	G	A	Pts	AG	AA	APts	PIM	PP	SH	GW	S	%	TGF	PGF	TGA	PGA	+/–	GP	G	A	Pts	PIM	PP	SH	GW

• PATRICK, CRAIG

Craig Patrick RW – L. 6', 190 lbs. b: Detroit, MI, 5/20/1946. USHOF

1963-64	Lachine Maroons	QJHL	43	12	31	43	....	....	....	12	....	....	....	....	....	....	....	....	....	....	....	....	....	....	....	....	....	....
1964-65	Montreal Jr. Canadiens	OHA	56	13	18	31	....	....	....	18	....	....	....	....	....	....	....	....	....	....	7	1	0	1	2	....	....	....
1965-66	Los Angeles Hechter Hawks	Calif-Sr.	9	15	8	23	....	....	....	4	....	....	....	....	....	....	....	....	....	....	....	....	....	....	....	....	....	....
1966-67	University of Denver	WCHA	30	18	16	34	....	....	....	6	....	....	....	....	....	....	....	....	....	....	....	....	....	....	....	....	....	....
1967-68	University of Denver	WCHA	34	23	26	49	....	....	....	12	....	....	....	....	....	....	....	....	....	....	....	....	....	....	....	....	....	....
1968-69	University of Denver	WCHA	17	7	8	15	....	....	....	6	....	....	....	....	....	....	....	....	....	....	....	....	....	....	....	....	....	....
1969-70	United States	Nat-Team	6	0	3	3	....	....	....	0	....	....	....	....	....	....	....	....	....	....	....	....	....	....	....	....	....	....
	United States	WEC-B	7	8	5	13	....	....	....	2	....	....	....	....	....	....	....	....	....	....	....	....	....	....	....	....	....	....
1970-71	United States	Nat-Team	STATISTICS NOT AVAILABLE																									
	Montreal Voyageurs	AHL	3	0	1	1	....	....	....	0	....	....	....	....	....	....	....	....	....	....	....	....	....	....	....	....	....	....
	United States	WEC-A	10	3	2	5	....	....	....	2	....	....	....	....	....	....	....	....	....	....	....	....	....	....	....	....	....	....
1971-72	**California Golden Seals**	**NHL**	**59**	**8**	**3**	**11**	**8**	**3**	**11**	**12**	**0**	**0**	**0**	**73**	**11.0**	**20**	**1**	**51**	**8**	**–24**	....	....	....	....	....	....	....	....
	Baltimore Clippers	AHL	12	3	0	3	....	....	....	0	....	....	....	....	....	....	....	....	....	....	....	....	....	....	....	....	....	....
1972-73	**California Golden Seals**	**NHL**	**71**	**20**	**22**	**42**	**20**	**18**	**38**	**6**	**2**	**1**	**0**	**152**	**13.2**	**69**	**15**	**108**	**22**	**–32**	....	....	....	....	....	....	....	....
1973-74	**California Golden Seals**	**NHL**	**59**	**10**	**20**	**30**	**10**	**17**	**27**	**17**	**2**	**0**	**1**	**95**	**10.5**	**48**	**11**	**72**	**5**	**–30**	....	....	....	....	....	....	....	....
1974-75	**California Golden Seals**	**NHL**	**14**	**2**	**1**	**3**	**2**	**1**	**3**	**0**	**0**	**0**	**0**	**15**	**13.3**	**4**	**0**	**13**	**1**	**–8**	....	....	....	....	....	....	....	....
	St. Louis Blues	**NHL**	**43**	**6**	**9**	**15**	**6**	**7**	**13**	**6**	**0**	**0**	**2**	**58**	**10.3**	**32**	**3**	**30**	**7**	**+6**	**2**	**0**	**1**	**1**	**0**	**0**	**0**	**0**
1975-76	**Kansas City Scouts**	**NHL**	**80**	**17**	**18**	**35**	**16**	**14**	**30**	**14**	**3**	**1**	**0**	**143**	**11.9**	**63**	**10**	**109**	**32**	**–24**	....	....	....	....	....	....	....	....
1976-77	United States	C Cup	5	2	2	4	....	....	....	0	....	....	....	....	....	....	....	....	....	....	....	....	....	....	....	....	....	....
	Washington Capitals	**NHL**	**28**	**7**	**10**	**17**	**7**	**8**	**15**	**2**	**1**	**0**	**0**	**47**	**14.9**	**25**	**10**	**29**	**4**	**–10**	....	....	....	....	....	....	....	....
	Minnesota Fighting Saints	WHA	30	6	11	17	....	....	....	6	....	....	....	....	....	....	....	....	....	....	....	....	....	....	....	....	....	....
1977-78	**Washington Capitals**	**NHL**	**44**	**1**	**7**	**8**	**1**	**6**	**7**	**4**	**1**	**0**	**0**	**43**	**2.3**	**19**	**2**	**26**	**1**	**–8**	....	....	....	....	....	....	....	....
	Hershey Bears	AHL	27	5	4	9	....	....	....	4	....	....	....	....	....	....	....	....	....	....	....	....	....	....	....	....	....	....
1978-79	**Washington Capitals**	**NHL**	**3**	**1**	**1**	**2**	**1**	**1**	**2**	**0**	**0**	**0**	**0**	**3**	**33.3**	**2**	**0**	**3**	**0**	**–1**	....	....	....	....	....	....	....	....
	Tulsa Oilers	CHL	69	22	23	45	....	....	....	12	....	....	....	....	....	....	....	....	....	....	....	....	....	....	....	....	....	....
	United States	WEC-A	8	0	3	3	....	....	....	2	....	....	....	....	....	....	....	....	....	....	....	....	....	....	....	....	....	....
1979-80	Los Angeles Blades	PHL	7	0	1	1	....	....	....	27	....	....	....	....	....	....	....	....	....	....	....	....	....	....	....	....	....	....
	NHL Totals		**401**	**72**	**91**	**163**	**71**	**75**	**146**	**61**	**9**	**2**	**3**	**629**	**11.4**	**282**	**52**	**441**	**80**		**2**	**0**	**1**	**1**	**0**	**0**	**0**	**0**
	Other Major League Totals		30	6	11	17	....	....	....	6	....	....	....	....	....	....	....	....	....	....	....	....	....	....	....	....	....	....

Signed as a free agent to five-game amateur tryout contract by **Montreal Voyageurs** (AHL), February 24, 1971. Signed as a free agent by **California**, October 6, 1971. Selected by **Miami-Philadelphia** (WHA) in 1972 WHA General Player Draft, February 12, 1972. Traded to **St. Louis** by **California** with Stan Gilbertson for Warren Williams and Dave Gardner, November 11, 1974. Traded to **Kansas City** by **St. Louis** with Denis Dupere and cash for Lynn Powis and Kansas City's 2nd choice (Brian Sutter) in 1976 Amateur Draft, June 18, 1975. WHA rights traded to **Minnesota** (WHA) by **Calgary** (WHA) for future considerations, June, 1976. Signed as a free agent by **Washington** after **Minnesota** (WHA) franchise folded, February 1, 1977.

• PATRICK, GLENN

Glenn Patrick D – L. 6'2", 190 lbs. b: New York, NY, 4/26/1950.

1970-71	Kansas City Blues	CHL	3	0	0	0	....	....	....	0	....	....	....	....	....	....	....	....	....	....	....	....	....	....	....	....	....	....
1971-72	Columbus Seals	IHL	52	1	8	9	....	....	....	89	....	....	....	....	....	....	....	....	....	....	....	....	....	....	....	....	....	....
	Denver Spurs	WHL	5	0	1	1	....	....	....	6	....	....	....	....	....	....	....	....	....	....	9	0	2	2	21	....	....	....
1972-73	Denver Spurs	WHL	72	5	21	26	....	....	....	125	....	....	....	....	....	....	....	....	....	....	5	0	1	1	0	....	....	....
1973-74	**St. Louis Blues**	**NHL**	**1**	**0**	**0**	**0**	**0**	**0**	**0**	**2**	**0**	**0**	**0**	**0**	**0.0**	**0**	**0**	**1**	**0**	**–1**	....	....	....	....	....	....	....	....
	Denver Spurs	WHL	68	7	24	31	....	....	....	163	....	....	....	....	....	....	....	....	....	....	....	....	....	....	....	....	....	....
1974-75	**California Golden Seals**	**NHL**	**2**	**0**	**0**	**0**	**0**	**0**	**0**	**0**	**0**	**0**	**0**	**2**	**0.0**	**0**	**0**	**3**	**1**	**–2**	....	....	....	....	....	....	....	....
	Salt Lake Golden Eagles	CHL	75	2	26	28	....	....	....	151	....	....	....	....	....	....	....	....	....	....	11	1	2	3	31	....	....	....
1975-76	Salt Lake Golden Eagles	CHL	63	7	18	25	....	....	....	140	....	....	....	....	....	....	....	....	....	....	5	0	0	0	0	....	....	....
1976-77	**Cleveland Barons**	**NHL**	**35**	**2**	**3**	**5**	**2**	**2**	**4**	**70**	**0**	**0**	**0**	**26**	**7.7**	**22**	**0**	**40**	**7**	**–11**	....	....	....	....	....	....	....	....
	Salt Lake Golden Eagles	CHL	14	0	7	7	....	....	....	46	....	....	....	....	....	....	....	....	....	....	....	....	....	....	....	....	....	....
	Edmonton Oilers	WHA	23	0	4	4	....	....	....	62	....	....	....	....	....	....	....	....	....	....	2	0	0	0	0	....	....	....
1977-78	Hampton Gulls	AHL	13	0	1	1	....	....	....	21	....	....	....	....	....	....	....	....	....	....	....	....	....	....	....	....	....	....
	Hershey Bears	AHL	13	1	8	9	....	....	....	15	....	....	....	....	....	....	....	....	....	....	....	....	....	....	....	....	....	....
	United States	Nat-Team	9	1	3	4	....	....	....	4	....	....	....	....	....	....	....	....	....	....	....	....	....	....	....	....	....	....
	United States	WEC-A	9	1	3	4	....	....	....	4	....	....	....	....	....	....	....	....	....	....	....	....	....	....	....	....	....	....
1978-79	Hampton Aces	NEHL	11	0	1	1	....	....	....	11	....	....	....	....	....	....	....	....	....	....	....	....	....	....	....	....	....	....
	NHL Totals		**38**	**2**	**3**	**5**	**2**	**2**	**4**	**72**	**0**	**0**	**0**	**28**	**7.1**	**22**	**0**	**44**	**8**		....	....	....	....	....	....	....	....
	Other Major League Totals		23	0	4	4	....	....	....	62	....	....	....	....	....	....	....	....	....	....	2	0	0	0	0	....	....	....

Signed as a free agent by **St. Louis**, March 10, 1970. Selected by **Miami-Philadelphia** (WHA) in 1972 WHA General Player Draft, February 12, 1972. Traded to **California** by **St. Louis** for Ron Serafini, July 18, 1974. Transferred to **Cleveland** after **California** franchise relocated, August 26, 1976. Signed as a free agent by **Edmonton** (WHA) after being released by Washington, February 10, 1977.

• PATRICK, JAMES

James "Jeep" Patrick D – R. 6'2", 198 lbs. b: Winnipeg, Man., 6/14/1963. NY Rangers' 1st choice, 9th overall, in 1981 Entry Draft.

1980-81	Prince Albert Raiders	SJHL	59	21	61	82	....	....	....	162	....	....	....	....	....	....	....	....	....	....	....	....	....	....	....	....	....	....
1981-82	University of North Dakota	WCHA	42	5	24	29	....	....	....	26	....	....	....	....	....	....	....	....	....	....	....	....	....	....	....	....	....	....
	Canada	WJC-A	7	0	2	2	....	....	....	6	....	....	....	....	....	....	....	....	....	....	....	....	....	....	....	....	....	....
1982-83	University of North Dakota	WCHA	36	12	36	48	....	....	....	29	....	....	....	....	....	....	....	....	....	....	....	....	....	....	....	....	....	....
	Canada	WJC-A	7	0	2	2	....	....	....	4	....	....	....	....	....	....	....	....	....	....	....	....	....	....	....	....	....	....
	Canada	WEC-A	9	1	1	2	....	....	....	10	....	....	....	....	....	....	....	....	....	....	....	....	....	....	....	....	....	....
1983-84	Canada	Nat-Team	63	7	24	31	....	....	....	52	....	....	....	....	....	....	....	....	....	....	....	....	....	....	....	....	....	....
	Canada	Olympics	7	0	3	3	....	....	....	4	....	....	....	....	....	....	....	....	....	....	....	....	....	....	....	....	....	....
	New York Rangers	**NHL**	**12**	**1**	**7**	**8**	**1**	**5**	**6**	**2**	**0**	**0**	**0**	**15**	**6.7**	**18**	**5**	**10**	**3**	**+6**	**5**	**0**	**3**	**3**	**2**	**0**	**0**	**0**
1984-85	**New York Rangers**	**NHL**	**75**	**8**	**28**	**36**	**7**	**19**	**26**	**71**	**4**	**1**	**1**	**101**	**7.9**	**94**	**25**	**105**	**19**	**–17**	**3**	**0**	**0**	**0**	**4**	**0**	**0**	**0**
1985-86	**New York Rangers**	**NHL**	**75**	**14**	**29**	**43**	**11**	**19**	**30**	**88**	**2**	**1**	**1**	**131**	**10.7**	**100**	**34**	**85**	**33**	**+14**	**16**	**1**	**5**	**6**	**34**	**0**	**0**	**0**
1986-87	**New York Rangers**	**NHL**	**78**	**10**	**45**	**55**	**9**	**33**	**42**	**62**	**5**	**0**	**0**	**143**	**7.0**	**125**	**37**	**95**	**20**	**+13**	**6**	**1**	**2**	**3**	**2**	**2**	**0**	**1**
	Canada	WEC-A	8	0	1	1	....	....	....	2	....	....	....	....	....	....	....	....	....	....	....	....	....	....	....	....	....	....
1987-88	Canada	C Cup	6	0	1	1	....	....	....	2	....	....	....	....	....	....	....	....	....	....	....	....	....	....	....	....	....	....
	New York Rangers	**NHL**	**70**	**17**	**45**	**62**	**15**	**32**	**47**	**52**	**9**	**0**	**1**	**187**	**9.1**	**120**	**52**	**78**	**26**	**+16**	....	....	....	....	....	....	....	....
1988-89	**New York Rangers**	**NHL**	**68**	**11**	**36**	**47**	**9**	**25**	**34**	**41**	**6**	**0**	**2**	**147**	**7.5**	**107**	**49**	**80**	**25**	**+3**	**4**	**0**	**1**	**1**	**2**	**0**	**0**	**0**
	Canada	WEC-A	10	2	2	4	....	....	....	8	....	....	....	....	....	....	....	....	....	....	....	....	....	....	....	....	....	....
1989-90	**New York Rangers**	**NHL**	**73**	**14**	**43**	**57**	**12**	**31**	**43**	**50**	**9**	**0**	**0**	**136**	**10.3**	**125**	**54**	**99**	**32**	**+4**	**10**	**3**	**8**	**11**	**0**	**2**	**0**	**1**
1990-91	**New York Rangers**	**NHL**	**74**	**10**	**49**	**59**	**9**	**37**	**46**	**58**	**6**	**0**	**2**	**138**	**7.2**	**115**	**60**	**83**	**23**	**–5**	**6**	**0**	**0**	**0**	**6**	**0**	**0**	**0**
1991-92	**New York Rangers**	**NHL**	**80**	**14**	**57**	**71**	**13**	**43**	**56**	**54**	**6**	**0**	**1**	**148**	**9.5**	**143**	**52**	**82**	**25**	**+34**	**13**	**0**	**7**	**7**	**12**	**0**	**0**	**0**
1992-93	**New York Rangers**	**NHL**	**60**	**5**	**21**	**26**	**4**	**14**	**18**	**61**	**3**	**0**	**0**	**99**	**5.1**	**82**	**28**	**80**	**27**	**+1**	....	....	....	....	....	....	....	....
1993-94	**New York Rangers**	**NHL**	**6**	**0**	**3**	**3**	**0**	**2**	**2**	**2**	**0**	**0**	**0**	**6**	**0.0**	**4**	**1**	**4**	**2**	**+1**	....	....	....	....	....	....	....	....
	Hartford Whalers	**NHL**	**47**	**8**	**20**	**28**	**7**	**15**	**22**	**32**	**4**	**1**	**2**	**65**	**12.3**	**54**	**24**	**57**	**15**	**–12**	....	....	....	....	....	....	....	....
	Calgary Flames	**NHL**	**15**	**2**	**2**	**4**	**2**	**2**	**4**	**6**	**1**	**0**	**0**	**20**	**10.0**	**14**	**2**	**9**	**3**	**+6**	**7**	**0**	**1**	**1**	**6**	**0**	**0**	**0**
1994-95	**Calgary Flames**	**NHL**	**43**	**0**	**10**	**10**	**0**	**15**	**15**	**14**	**0**	**0**	**0**	**43**	**0.0**	**34**	**3**	**44**	**10**	**–3**	**5**	**0**	**1**	**1**	**0**	**0**	**0**	**0**
1995-96	**Calgary Flames**	**NHL**	**80**	**3**	**32**	**35**	**3**	**26**	**29**	**30**	**1**	**0**	**0**	**116**	**2.6**	**81**	**31**	**79**	**32**	**+3**	**4**	**0**	**0**	**0**	**2**	**0**	**0**	**0**
1996-97	**Calgary Flames**	**NHL**	**19**	**3**	**1**	**4**	**3**	**1**	**4**	**6**	**1**	**0**	**0**	**22**	**13.6**	**15**	**2**	**16**	**5**	**+2**	....	....	....	....	....	....	....	....
1997-98	**Calgary Flames**	**NHL**	**60**	**6**	**11**	**17**	**7**	**11**	**18**	**26**	**1**	**0**	**1**	**57**	**10.5**	**54**	**8**	**64**	**16**	**–2**	....	....	....	....	....	....	....	....
	Canada	WC-A	6	0	1	1	....	....	....	0	....	....	....	....	....	....	....	....	....	....	....	....	....	....	....	....	....	....
	NHL Totals		**935**	**126**	**439**	**565**	**112**	**330**	**442**	**655**	**58**	**3**	**11**	**1574**	**8.0**	**1285**	**467**	**1070**	**316**		**79**	**5**	**28**	**33**	**70**	**4**	**0**	**2**

WCHA Second All-Star Team (1982) • NCAA Chamionship All-Tournament Team (1982) • WCHA First All-Star Team (1983) • NCAA West All American Team (1983)

Traded to **Hartford** by **NY Rangers** with Darren Turcotte for Steve Larmer, Nick Kypreos, Barry Richter and Hartford's 6th round choice (Yuri Litvinov) in 1994 Entry Draft, November 2, 1993. Traded to **Calgary** by **Hartford** with Zarley Zalapski and Michael Nylander for Gary Suter, Paul Ranheim and Ted Drury, March 10, 1994.

• PATRICK, STEVE

Steve "Steepashakis" Patrick RW – R. 6'4", 206 lbs. b: Winnipeg, Man., 2/4/1961. Buffalo's 1st choice, 20th overall, in 1980 Entry Draft.

1978-79	Brandon Wheat Kings	WHL	52	23	31	54	....	....	....	105	....	....	....	....	....	....	....	....	....	....	....	....	....	....	....	....	....	....
1979-80	Brandon Wheat Kings	WHL	71	28	38	66	....	....	....	185	....	....	....	....	....	....	....	....	....	....	11	6	6	12	19	....	....	....
1980-81	Brandon Wheat Kings	WHL	34	29	30	59	....	....	....	56	....	....	....	....	....	....	....	....	....	....	....	....	....	....	....	....	....	....
	Buffalo Sabres	**NHL**	**30**	**1**	**7**	**8**	**1**	**5**	**6**	**25**	**0**	**0**	**0**	**35**	**2.9**	**16**	**1**	**14**	**0**	**+1**	**5**	**0**	**1**	**1**	**6**	**0**	**0**	**0**
1981-82	**Buffalo Sabres**	**NHL**	**41**	**8**	**8**	**16**	**6**	**5**	**11**	**64**	**0**	**0**	**0**	**52**	**15.4**	**23**	**1**	**23**	**4**	**+3**	....	....	....	....	....	....	....	....
	Rochester Americans	AHL	38	11	9	20	....	....	....	15	....	....	....	....	....	....	....	....	....	....	5	3	2	5	12	....	....	....
1982-83	**Buffalo Sabres**	**NHL**	**56**	**9**	**13**	**22**	**7**	**9**	**16**	**26**	**0**	**0**	**1**	**63**	**14.3**	**37**	**2**	**37**	**6**	**+4**	**2**	**0**	**0**	**0**	**0**	**0**	**0**	**0**

			REGULAR SEASON																		PLAYOFFS							
Season	Club	League	GP	G	A	Pts	AG	AA	APts	PIM	PP	SH	GW	S	%	TGF	PGF	TGA	PGA	+/-	GP	G	A	Pts	PIM	PP	SH	GW
1983-84	Buffalo Sabres	NHL	11	1	4	5	1	3	4	6	0	0	0	11	9.1	7	0	9	0	–2	1	0	0	0	0	0	0	0
	Rochester Americans	AHL	30	8	14	22	....	....	....	33	....	....	....	....	....	....	....	....	....	....	13	2	1	3	18	....	....	....
1984-85	Buffalo Sabres	NHL	14	2	2	4	2	1	3	4	0	0	0	12	16.7	5	0	8	0	–3	....	....	....	....	....	....	....	....
	New York Rangers	NHL	43	11	18	29	9	12	21	63	4	0	0	63	17.5	48	14	40	1	–5	1	0	0	0	0	0	0	0
1985-86	New York Rangers	NHL	28	4	3	7	3	2	5	37	0	0	0	20	20.0	10	0	17	0	–7	....	....	....	....	....	....	....	....
	Quebec Nordiques	NHL	27	4	13	17	3	9	12	17	1	0	0	29	13.8	35	11	23	0	+1	3	0	0	0	6	0	0	0
	NHL Totals		250	40	68	108	32	46	78	242	5	0	1	285	14.0	181	29	171	11		12	0	1	1	12	0	0	0

Traded to **NY Rangers** by **Buffalo** with Jim Wiemer for Dave Maloney and Chris Renauld, December 6, 1984. Traded to **Quebec** by **NY Rangers** for Wilf Paiement, February 6, 1986.

• PATTERSON, COLIN

Colin Patterson RW/LW – R. 6'2", 195 lbs. b: Rexdale, Ont., 5/11/1960.

Season	Club	League	GP	G	A	Pts	AG	AA	APts	PIM	PP	SH	GW	S	%	TGF	PGF	TGA	PGA	+/-	GP	G	A	Pts	PIM	PP	SH	GW
1980-81	Clarkson College	ECAC	34	20	31	51	....	....	....	8	....	....	....	....	....	....	....	....	....	....	....	....	....	....	....	....	....	....
1981-82	Clarkson College	ECAC	34	21	31	52	....	....	....	32	....	....	....	....	....	....	....	....	....	....	....	....	....	....	....	....	....	....
1982-83	Clarkson College	ECAC	31	23	29	52	....	....	....	30	....	....	....	....	....	....	....	....	....	....	....	....	....	....	....	....	....	....
	Colorado Flames	CHL	7	1	1	2	....	....	....	0	....	....	....	....	....	....	....	....	....	....	3	0	0	0	15	....	....	....
1983-84	Calgary Flames	NHL	56	13	14	27	10	9	19	15	0	1	1	87	14.9	38	0	34	13	+17	11	1	1	2	6	0	0	0
	Colorado Flames	CHL	6	2	3	5	....	....	....	9	....	....	....	....	....	....	....	....	....	....	....	....	....	....	....	....	....	....
1984-85	Calgary Flames	NHL	57	22	21	43	18	14	32	5	3	0	2	104	21.2	67	10	54	17	+20	4	0	0	0	5	0	0	0
1985-86	Calgary Flames	NHL	61	14	13	27	11	9	20	22	0	0	1	84	16.7	47	1	67	29	+8	19	6	3	9	10	1	1	1
1986-87	Calgary Flames	NHL	68	13	13	26	11	9	20	41	0	1	3	78	16.7	51	2	62	20	+7	6	0	2	2	2	0	0	0
1987-88	Calgary Flames	NHL	39	7	11	18	6	8	14	28	0	0	0	37	18.9	35	1	47	20	+7	9	1	0	1	8	0	1	0
1988-89	Calgary Flames	NHL	74	14	24	38	12	17	29	56	0	0	1	103	13.6	68	1	63	40	+44	22	3	10	13	24	0	0	0
1989-90	Calgary Flames	FrTour	3	0	0	0	....	....	....	4	....	....	....	....	....	....	....	....	....	....	....	....	....	....	....	....	....	....
	Calgary Flames	NHL	61	5	3	8	4	2	6	20	0	0	0	56	8.9	20	0	44	20	–4	....	....	....	....	....	....	....	....
1990-91	Calgary Flames	NHL	DID NOT PLAY																									
1991-92	Buffalo Sabres	NHL	52	4	8	12	4	6	10	30	0	2	0	33	12.1	20	0	41	17	–4	5	1	0	1	0	0	0	0
1992-93	Buffalo Sabres	NHL	36	4	2	6	3	1	4	22	0	1	0	30	13.3	11	0	25	12	–2	8	0	1	1	2	0	0	0
	NHL Totals		504	96	109	205	79	75	154	239	3	5	8	612	15.7	357	15	437	188		85	12	17	29	57	1	2	1

ECAC Second All-Star Team (1983) • NCAA East First All-American Team (1983)

Signed as a free agent by **Calgary**, March 24, 1983. • Missed entire 1990-91 regular season after undergoing knee surgery, October 12, 1990. Traded to **Buffalo** by **Calgary** for future considerations, October 24, 1991.

• PATTERSON, DENNIS

Dennis Patterson D – L. 5'8", 175 lbs. b: Peterborough, Ont., 1/9/1950. Minnesota's 3rd choice, 34th overall, in 1970 Amateur Draft.

Season	Club	League	GP	G	A	Pts	AG	AA	APts	PIM	PP	SH	GW	S	%	TGF	PGF	TGA	PGA	+/-	GP	G	A	Pts	PIM	PP	SH	GW
1968-69	Peterborough Petes	OHA	54	5	17	22	....	....	....	56	....	....	....	....	....	....	....	....	....	....	10	0	2	2	12	....	....	....
1969-70	Peterborough Petes	OHA	54	8	29	37	....	....	....	84	....	....	....	....	....	....	....	....	....	....	....	....	....	....	....	....	....	....
1970-71	Clinton Comets	FHL	72	6	30	36	....	....	....	93	....	....	....	....	....	....	....	....	....	....	....	....	....	....	....	....	....	....
	Cleveland Barons	AHL	9	0	2	2	....	....	....	4	....	....	....	....	....	....	....	....	....	....	8	0	1	1	22	....	....	....
1971-72	Cleveland Barons	AHL	76	3	17	20	....	....	....	62	....	....	....	....	....	....	....	....	....	....	6	0	1	1	12	....	....	....
1972-73	Cleveland Barons	AHL	42	1	11	12	....	....	....	40	....	....	....	....	....	....	....	....	....	....	....	....	....	....	....	....	....	....
1973-74	New Haven Eagles	AHL	70	8	25	33	....	....	....	69	....	....	....	....	....	....	....	....	....	....	10	1	3	4	4	....	....	....
1974-75	Kansas City Scouts	NHL	66	1	5	6	1	4	5	39	0	0	0	53	1.9	41	2	113	17	–57	....	....	....	....	....	....	....	....
	Baltimore Clippers	AHL	12	1	3	4	....	....	....	6	....	....	....	....	....	....	....	....	....	....	....	....	....	....	....	....	....	....
1975-76	Kansas City Scouts	NHL	69	5	16	21	5	13	18	28	0	0	0	76	6.6	60	7	98	17	–28	....	....	....	....	....	....	....	....
	Springfield Indians	AHL	10	0	5	5	....	....	....	12	....	....	....	....	....	....	....	....	....	....	....	....	....	....	....	....	....	....
1976-77	Rhode Island Reds	AHL	51	3	18	21	....	....	....	22	....	....	....	....	....	....	....	....	....	....	....	....	....	....	....	....	....	....
	Edmonton Oilers	WHA	23	0	2	2	....	....	....	2	....	....	....	....	....	....	....	....	....	....	....	....	....	....	....	....	....	....
1977-78	Maine Mariners	AHL	78	3	24	27	....	....	....	26	....	....	....	....	....	....	....	....	....	....	12	0	3	3	22	....	....	....
1978-79	Maine Mariners	AHL	74	3	29	32	....	....	....	112	....	....	....	....	....	....	....	....	....	....	10	1	4	5	32	....	....	....
1979-80	Philadelphia Flyers	NHL	3	0	1	1	0	1	1	0	0	0	0	3	0.0	1	0	2	0	–1	....	....	....	....	....	....	....	....
	Maine Mariners	AHL	67	2	25	27	....	....	....	72	....	....	....	....	....	....	....	....	....	....	10	2	6	8	20	....	....	....
1980-81	Maine Mariners	AHL	70	3	26	29	....	....	....	74	....	....	....	....	....	....	....	....	....	....	....	....	....	....	....	....	....	....
1981-82	Maine Mariners	AHL	51	1	14	15	....	....	....	111	....	....	....	....	....	....	....	....	....	....	4	0	0	0	12	....	....	....
1982-83	Maine Mariners	AHL	76	1	19	20	....	....	....	71	....	....	....	....	....	....	....	....	....	....	17	0	4	4	9	....	....	....
	NHL Totals		138	6	22	28	6	18	24	67	0	0	0	132	4.5	102	9	213	34		....	....	....	....	....	....	....	....
	Other Major League Totals		23	0	2	2	....	....	....	2	....	....	....	....	....	....	....	....	....	....	....	....	....	....	....	....	....	....

AHL Second All-Star Team (1979, 1980, 1981)

Claimed by **Kansas City** from **Minnesota** in Expansion Draft, June 12, 1974. Signed as a free agent by **Edmonton** (WHA), September, 1976. Signed as a free agent by **Philadelphia**, August 8, 1979.

• PATTERSON, ED

Ed Patterson RW – R. 6'2", 210 lbs. b: Delta, B.C., 11/14/1972. Pittsburgh's 5th choice, 148th overall, in 1991 Entry Draft.

Season	Club	League	GP	G	A	Pts	AG	AA	APts	PIM	PP	SH	GW	S	%	TGF	PGF	TGA	PGA	+/-	GP	G	A	Pts	PIM	PP	SH	GW
1988-89	Seattle Thunderbirds	WHL	46	4	6	10	....	....	....	55	....	....	....	....	....	....	....	....	....	....	....	....	....	....	....	....	....	....
1989-90	Seattle Thunderbirds	WHL	18	9	2	11	....	....	....	19	....	....	....	....	....	....	....	....	....	....	....	....	....	....	....	....	....	....
	Swift Current Broncos	WHL	15	1	3	4	....	....	....	0	....	....	....	....	....	....	....	....	....	....	4	0	0	0	2	....	....	....
1990-91	Swift Current Broncos	WHL	7	2	7	9	....	....	....	0	....	....	....	....	....	....	....	....	....	....	....	....	....	....	....	....	....	....
	Kamloops Blazers	WHL	55	14	33	47	....	....	....	134	....	....	....	....	....	....	....	....	....	....	5	0	0	0	7	....	....	....
1991-92	Kamloops Blazers	WHL	38	19	25	44	....	....	....	120	....	....	....	....	....	....	....	....	....	....	1	0	0	0	0	....	....	....
1992-93	Cleveland Lumberjacks	IHL	63	4	16	20	....	....	....	131	....	....	....	....	....	....	....	....	....	....	3	1	1	2	2	....	....	....
1993-94	Pittsburgh Penguins	NHL	27	3	1	4	3	1	4	10	0	0	0	15	20.0	4	0	11	2	–5	....	....	....	....	....	....	....	....
	Cleveland Lumberjacks	IHL	55	21	32	53	....	....	....	73	....	....	....	....	....	....	....	....	....	....	....	....	....	....	....	....	....	....
1994-95	Cleveland Lumberjacks	IHL	58	13	17	30	....	....	....	93	....	....	....	....	....	....	....	....	....	....	4	1	2	3	6	....	....	....
1995-96	Pittsburgh Penguins	NHL	35	0	2	2	0	2	2	38	0	0	0	17	0.0	2	0	11	4	–5	....	....	....	....	....	....	....	....
1996-97	Pittsburgh Penguins	NHL	6	0	0	0	0	0	0	8	0	0	0	2	0.0	1	0	2	1	0	....	....	....	....	....	....	....	....
	Cleveland Lumberjacks	IHL	40	6	12	18	....	....	....	75	....	....	....	....	....	....	....	....	....	....	13	2	4	6	61	....	....	....
1997-98	Grand Rapids Griffins	IHL	61	12	31	43	....	....	....	226	....	....	....	....	....	....	....	....	....	....	3	2	1	3	8	....	....	....
	NHL Totals		68	3	3	6	3	3	6	56	0	0	0	34	8.8	7	0	24	7		....	....	....	....	....	....	....	....

• PAVELICH, MARK

Mark "Weber" Pavelich C – R. 5'8", 170 lbs. b: Eveleth, MN, 2/28/1958.

Season	Club	League	GP	G	A	Pts	AG	AA	APts	PIM	PP	SH	GW	S	%	TGF	PGF	TGA	PGA	+/-	GP	G	A	Pts	PIM	PP	SH	GW
1976-77	University of Minnesota-Duluth	WCHA	37	12	7	19	....	....	....	8	....	....	....	....	....	....	....	....	....	....	....	....	....	....	....	....	....	....
1977-78	University of Minnesota-Duluth	WCHA	36	14	30	44	....	....	....	44	....	....	....	....	....	....	....	....	....	....	....	....	....	....	....	....	....	....
1978-79	University of Minnesota-Duluth	WCHA	37	31	48	79	....	....	....	52	....	....	....	....	....	....	....	....	....	....	....	....	....	....	....	....	....	....
1979-80	United States	Nat-Team	53	15	30	45	....	....	....	12	....	....	....	....	....	....	....	....	....	....	....	....	....	....	....	....	....	....
	United States	Olympics	7	1	6	7	....	....	....	2	....	....	....	....	....	....	....	....	....	....	....	....	....	....	....	....	....	....
1980-81	HC Lugano	Switz.	60	24	49	73	....	....	....	....	....	....	....	....	....	....	....	....	....	....	....	....	....	....	....	....	....	....
	United States	WEC-A	8	2	3	5	....	....	....	4	....	....	....	....	....	....	....	....	....	....	....	....	....	....	....	....	....	....
1981-82	New York Rangers	NHL	79	33	43	76	26	28	54	67	12	3	3	180	18.3	113	34	83	25	+21	6	1	5	6	0	0	0	0
1982-83	New York Rangers	NHL	78	37	38	75	30	26	56	52	10	2	6	154	24.0	107	33	71	17	+20	9	4	5	9	12	2	0	2
1983-84	New York Rangers	NHL	77	29	53	82	23	36	59	96	12	1	2	164	17.7	118	41	92	26	+11	5	2	4	6	0	0	1	0
1984-85	New York Rangers	NHL	48	14	31	45	11	21	32	29	6	0	3	91	15.4	66	27	45	7	+1	3	0	3	3	2	0	0	0
1985-86	New York Rangers	NHL	59	20	20	40	16	13	29	82	8	0	3	104	19.2	59	23	40	1	–3	....	....	....	....	....	....	....	....
1986-87	Minnesota North Stars	NHL	12	4	6	10	3	4	7	10	0	0	0	25	16.0	19	4	9	1	+7	....	....	....	....	....	....	....	....
1987-88	HC Bolzano	Italy	36	31	44	73	....	....	....	19	....	....	....	....	....	....	....	....	....	....	8	9	13	22	8	....	....	....
1988-89	HC Bolzano	Italy	44	23	34	57	....	....	....	42	....	....	....	....	....	....	....	....	....	....	....	....	....	....	....	....	....	....
1989-90			DID NOT PLAY																									
1990-91			DID NOT PLAY																									
1991-92	San Jose Sharks	NHL	2	0	1	1	0	1	1	4	0	0	0	0	0.0	1	0	3	0	–2	....	....	....	....	....	....	....	....
	NHL Totals		355	137	192	329	109	129	238	340	48	6	17	718	19.1	483	162	343	77		23	7	17	24	14	2	1	2

WCHA First All-Star Team (1979) • NCAA West First All-American Team (1979)

Signed as a free agent by **NY Rangers**, June 5, 1981. Traded to **Minnesota** by **NY Rangers** for Minnesota's 2nd round choice (Troy Mallette) in 1988 Entry Draft, October 24, 1986. Signed as a free agent by **San Jose**, August 9, 1991.

• PAVESE, JIM

Jim Pavese D – L. 6'2", 205 lbs. b: New York, NY, 5/8/1962. St. Louis' 2nd choice, 54th overall, in 1980 Entry Draft.

			REGULAR SEASON																		PLAYOFFS							
Season	Club	League	GP	G	A	Pts	AG	AA	APts	PIM	PP	SH	GW	S	%	TGF	PGF	TGA	PGA	+/–	GP	G	A	Pts	PIM	PP	SH	GW
1976-77	Suffolk Royals	NYJHL	32	6	31	37	....	....	....	32	....	....	....	....	....	....	....	....	....	....	....	....	....	....	....	....	....	....
1977-78	Suffolk Royals	NYJHL	34	18	40	58	....	....	....	102	....	....	....	....	....	....	....	....	....	....	....	....	....	....	....	....	....	....
1978-79	Peterborough Petes	OHA	16	1	1	2	....	....	....	22	....	....	....	....	....	....	....	....	....	....	....	....	....	....	....	....	....	....
1979-80	Kitchener Rangers	OHA	68	10	26	36	....	....	....	206	....	....	....	....	....	....	....	....	....	....	....	....	....	....	....	....	....	....
1980-81	Kitchener Rangers	OHA	19	3	12	15	....	....	....	93	....	....	....	....	....	....	....	....	....	....	....	....	....	....	....	....	....	....
	Sault Ste. Marie Greyhounds	OHA	43	3	25	28	....	....	....	127	....	....	....	....	....	....	....	....	....	....	19	1	3	4	69	....	....	....
1981-82	Sault Ste. Marie Greyhounds	OHL	26	4	21	25	....	....	....	110	....	....	....	....	....	....	....	....	....	....	13	2	12	14	38	....	....	....
	St. Louis Blues	**NHL**	**42**	**2**	**9**	**11**	**2**	**6**	**8**	**101**	**0**	**0**	**1**	**29**	**6.9**	**40**	**1**	**66**	**13**	**–14**	**3**	**0**	**3**	**3**	**2**	**0**	**0**	**0**
	Salt Lake Golden Eagles	CHL	....	....	....	....	....	....	....	....	....	....	....	....	....	....	....	....	....	....	1	0	0	0	17	....	....	....
1982-83	**St. Louis Blues**	**NHL**	**24**	**0**	**2**	**2**	**0**	**1**	**1**	**45**	**0**	**0**	**0**	**9**	**0.0**	**19**	**0**	**30**	**0**	**–11**	**4**	**0**	**0**	**0**	**6**	**0**	**0**	**0**
	Salt Lake Golden Eagles	CHL	36	5	6	11	....	....	....	165	....	....	....	....	....	....	....	....	....	....	4	1	3	4	2	....	....	....
1983-84	**St. Louis Blues**	**NHL**	**4**	**0**	**1**	**1**	**0**	**1**	**1**	**19**	**0**	**0**	**0**	**1**	**0.0**	**3**	**0**	**4**	**0**	**–1**	....	....	....	....	....	....	....	....
	Montana Magic	CHL	47	1	19	20	....	....	....	147	....	....	....	....	....	....	....	....	....	....	....	....	....	....	....	....	....	....
1984-85	**St. Louis Blues**	**NHL**	**51**	**2**	**5**	**7**	**2**	**3**	**5**	**69**	**0**	**0**	**1**	**27**	**7.4**	**31**	**1**	**35**	**1**	**–4**	**1**	**0**	**0**	**0**	**5**	**0**	**0**	**0**
1985-86	**St. Louis Blues**	**NHL**	**69**	**4**	**7**	**11**	**3**	**5**	**8**	**116**	**1**	**0**	**0**	**51**	**7.8**	**61**	**3**	**80**	**19**	**–3**	**19**	**0**	**2**	**2**	**51**	**0**	**0**	**0**
1986-87	**St. Louis Blues**	**NHL**	**69**	**2**	**9**	**11**	**2**	**6**	**8**	**127**	**0**	**0**	**0**	**45**	**4.4**	**39**	**1**	**74**	**15**	**–21**	**2**	**0**	**0**	**0**	**2**	**0**	**0**	**0**
1987-88	**St. Louis Blues**	**NHL**	**4**	**0**	**1**	**1**	**0**	**1**	**1**	**8**	**0**	**0**	**0**	**3**	**0.0**	**1**	**0**	**4**	**2**	**–1**	....	....	....	....	....	....	....	....
	New York Rangers	**NHL**	**14**	**0**	**1**	**1**	**0**	**1**	**1**	**48**	**0**	**0**	**0**	**13**	**0.0**	**5**	**0**	**14**	**2**	**–7**	....	....	....	....	....	....	....	....
	Colorado Rangers	IHL	1	0	0	0	....	....	....	2	....	....	....	....	....	....	....	....	....	....	....	....	....	....	....	....	....	....
	Detroit Red Wings	**NHL**	**7**	**0**	**3**	**3**	**0**	**2**	**2**	**21**	**0**	**0**	**0**	**4**	**0.0**	**8**	**1**	**7**	**3**	**+3**	**4**	**0**	**1**	**1**	**15**	**0**	**0**	**0**
	New Haven Nighthawks	AHL	1	0	1	1	....	....	....	0	....	....	....	....	....	....	....	....	....	....	....	....	....	....	....	....	....	....
1988-89	**Detroit Red Wings**	**NHL**	**39**	**3**	**6**	**9**	**3**	**4**	**7**	**130**	**0**	**0**	**0**	**27**	**11.1**	**35**	**0**	**44**	**8**	**–1**	....	....	....	....	....	....	....	....
	Hartford Whalers	**NHL**	**5**	**0**	**0**	**0**	**0**	**0**	**0**	**5**	**0**	**0**	**0**	**6**	**0.0**	**1**	**0**	**2**	**0**	**–1**	**1**	**0**	**0**	**0**	**0**	**0**	**0**	**0**
	NHL Totals		**328**	**13**	**44**	**57**	**12**	**30**	**42**	**689**	**1**	**0**	**2**	**215**	**6.0**	**243**	**7**	**360**	**63**		**34**	**0**	**6**	**6**	**81**	**0**	**0**	**0**

Traded to **NY Rangers** by **St. Louis** for future considerations, October 23, 1987. Traded to **Detroit** by **NY Rangers** for future considerations, March 8, 1988. Traded to **Hartford** by **Detroit** for Torrie Robertson, March 7, 1989.

• PAYNE, DAVIS

Davis Payne LW – L. 6'2", 205 lbs. b: Port Alberni, B.C., 9/24/1970. Edmonton's 6th choice, 140th overall, in 1989 Entry Draft.

Season	Club	League	GP	G	A	Pts	AG	AA	APts	PIM	PP	SH	GW	S	%	TGF	PGF	TGA	PGA	+/–	GP	G	A	Pts	PIM	PP	SH	GW
1988-89	Michigan Tech Huskies	WCHA	35	5	3	8	....	....	....	39	....	....	....	....	....	....	....	....	....	....	....	....	....	....	....	....	....	....
1989-90	Michigan Tech Huskies	WCHA	30	11	10	21	....	....	....	81	....	....	....	....	....	....	....	....	....	....	....	....	....	....	....	....	....	....
1990-91	Michigan Tech Huskies	WCHA	41	15	20	35	....	....	....	82	....	....	....	....	....	....	....	....	....	....	....	....	....	....	....	....	....	....
1991-92	Michigan Tech Huskies	WCHA	24	6	1	7	....	....	....	71	....	....	....	....	....	....	....	....	....	....	....	....	....	....	....	....	....	....
1992-93	Greensboro Monarchs	ECHL	57	15	20	35	....	....	....	178	....	....	....	....	....	....	....	....	....	....	1	0	0	0	4	....	....	....
1993-94	Greensboro Monarchs	ECHL	36	17	17	34	....	....	....	139	....	....	....	....	....	....	....	....	....	....	8	2	1	3	27	....	....	....
	Phoenix Roadrunners	IHL	22	6	3	9	....	....	....	51	....	....	....	....	....	....	....	....	....	....	....	....	....	....	....	....	....	....
	Rochester Americans	AHL	2	0	0	0	....	....	....	5	....	....	....	....	....	....	....	....	....	....	3	0	2	2	0	....	....	....
1994-95	Greensboro Monarchs	ECHL	62	25	36	61	....	....	....	195	....	....	....	....	....	....	....	....	....	....	17	7	10	17	38	....	....	....
	Providence Bruins	AHL	2	1	0	1	....	....	....	0	....	....	....	....	....	....	....	....	....	....	....	....	....	....	....	....	....	....
1995-96	**Boston Bruins**	**NHL**	**7**	**0**	**0**	**0**	**0**	**0**	**0**	**7**	**0**	**0**	**0**	**2**	**0.0**	**0**	**0**	**0**	**0**	**0**	....	....	....	....	....	....	....	....
	Providence Bruins	AHL	51	17	22	39	....	....	....	72	....	....	....	....	....	....	....	....	....	....	4	1	4	5	2	....	....	....
1996-97	**Boston Bruins**	**NHL**	**15**	**0**	**1**	**1**	**0**	**1**	**1**	**7**	**0**	**0**	**0**	**8**	**0.0**	**2**	**1**	**7**	**2**	**–4**	....	....	....	....	....	....	....	....
	Providence Bruins	AHL	57	18	15	33	....	....	....	104	....	....	....	....	....	....	....	....	....	....	....	....	....	....	....	....	....	....
1997-98	Providence Bruins	AHL	3	0	0	0	....	....	....	0	....	....	....	....	....	....	....	....	....	....	....	....	....	....	....	....	....	....
	San Antonio Dragons	IHL	59	15	10	25	....	....	....	117	....	....	....	....	....	....	....	....	....	....	....	....	....	....	....	....	....	....
	NHL Totals		**22**	**0**	**1**	**1**	**0**	**1**	**1**	**14**	**0**	**0**	**0**	**10**	**0.0**	**2**	**1**	**7**	**2**		....	....	....	....	....	....	....	....

Signed as a free agent by **Boston**, September 6, 1995.

• PAYNE, STEVE

Steve Payne LW – L. 6'2", 210 lbs. b: Toronto, Ont., 8/16/1958. Minnesota's 2nd choice, 19th overall, in 1978 Amateur Draft.

Season	Club	League	GP	G	A	Pts	AG	AA	APts	PIM	PP	SH	GW	S	%	TGF	PGF	TGA	PGA	+/–	GP	G	A	Pts	PIM	PP	SH	GW
1976-77	Ottawa 67's	OHA	61	25	26	51	....	....	....	22	....	....	....	....	....	....	....	....	....	....	19	4	14	18	5	....	....	....
1977-78	Ottawa 67's	OHA	52	57	37	94	....	....	....	22	....	....	....	....	....	....	....	....	....	....	16	12	8	20	4	....	....	....
1978-79	**Minnesota North Stars**	**NHL**	**70**	**23**	**17**	**40**	**21**	**13**	**34**	**29**	**3**	**0**	**2**	**165**	**13.9**	**63**	**11**	**57**	**0**	**–5**	....	....	....	....	....	....	....	....
	Oklahoma City Stars	CHL	5	3	4	7	....	....	....	2	....	....	....	....	....	....	....	....	....	....	....	....	....	....	....	....	....	....
	Canada	WEC-A	7	2	0	2	....	....	....	2	....	....	....	....	....	....	....	....	....	....	....	....	....	....	....	....	....	....
1979-80	**Minnesota North Stars**	**NHL**	**80**	**42**	**43**	**85**	**38**	**33**	**71**	**40**	**16**	**0**	**2**	**233**	**18.0**	**138**	**47**	**55**	**1**	**+37**	**15**	**7**	**7**	**14**	**9**	**3**	**0**	**3**
1980-81	**Minnesota North Stars**	**NHL**	**76**	**30**	**28**	**58**	**25**	**20**	**45**	**88**	**11**	**0**	**2**	**243**	**12.3**	**105**	**49**	**42**	**0**	**+14**	**19**	**17**	**12**	**29**	**6**	**6**	**0**	**4**
1981-82	**Minnesota North Stars**	**NHL**	**74**	**33**	**45**	**78**	**26**	**30**	**56**	**76**	**11**	**0**	**3**	**239**	**13.8**	**115**	**40**	**56**	**1**	**+20**	**4**	**4**	**2**	**6**	**2**	**2**	**0**	**0**
1982-83	**Minnesota North Stars**	**NHL**	**80**	**30**	**39**	**69**	**25**	**27**	**52**	**53**	**14**	**1**	**2**	**199**	**15.1**	**112**	**48**	**75**	**2**	**–9**	**9**	**3**	**6**	**9**	**19**	**1**	**0**	**0**
1983-84	**Minnesota North Stars**	**NHL**	**78**	**28**	**31**	**59**	**23**	**21**	**44**	**49**	**7**	**0**	**2**	**174**	**16.1**	**94**	**27**	**71**	**2**	**–2**	**15**	**3**	**6**	**9**	**18**	**1**	**0**	**2**
1984-85	**Minnesota North Stars**	**NHL**	**76**	**29**	**22**	**51**	**24**	**15**	**39**	**61**	**14**	**0**	**4**	**224**	**12.9**	**75**	**31**	**59**	**1**	**–14**	**9**	**1**	**2**	**3**	**6**	**0**	**0**	**0**
1985-86	**Minnesota North Stars**	**NHL**	**22**	**8**	**4**	**12**	**6**	**3**	**9**	**8**	**3**	**0**	**2**	**60**	**13.3**	**19**	**7**	**12**	**0**	**0**	....	....	....	....	....	....	....	....
1986-87	**Minnesota North Stars**	**NHL**	**48**	**4**	**6**	**10**	**3**	**4**	**7**	**19**	**0**	**0**	**0**	**67**	**6.0**	**22**	**4**	**30**	**0**	**–12**	....	....	....	....	....	....	....	....
1987-88	**Minnesota North Stars**	**NHL**	**9**	**1**	**3**	**4**	**1**	**2**	**3**	**12**	**0**	**0**	**0**	**15**	**6.7**	**7**	**3**	**5**	**0**	**–1**	....	....	....	....	....	....	....	....
	Kalamazoo Wings	IHL	5	3	5	8	....	....	....	6	....	....	....	....	....	....	....	....	....	....	....	....	....	....	....	....	....	....
	NHL Totals		**613**	**228**	**238**	**466**	**192**	**168**	**360**	**435**	**79**	**1**	**19**	**1619**	**14.1**	**750**	**267**	**462**	**7**		**71**	**35**	**35**	**70**	**60**	**13**	**0**	**9**

Played in NHL All-Star Game (1980, 1985)

• PAYNTER, KENT

Kent Paynter D – L. 6', 183 lbs. b: Summerside, P.E.I., 4/17/1965. Chicago's 9th choice, 165th overall, in 1983 Entry Draft.

Season	Club	League	GP	G	A	Pts	AG	AA	APts	PIM	PP	SH	GW	S	%	TGF	PGF	TGA	PGA	+/–	GP	G	A	Pts	PIM	PP	SH	GW
1981-82	Summerside Capitals	PEI Jr.	35	7	23	30	....	....	....	65	....	....	....	....	....	....	....	....	....	....	....	....	....	....	....	....	....	....
1982-83	Kitchener Rangers	OHL	65	4	11	15	....	....	....	97	....	....	....	....	....	....	....	....	....	....	12	1	0	1	20	....	....	....
1983-84	Kitchener Rangers	OHL	65	9	27	36	....	....	....	94	....	....	....	....	....	....	....	....	....	....	16	4	9	13	18	....	....	....
1984-85	Kitchener Rangers	OHL	58	7	28	35	....	....	....	93	....	....	....	....	....	....	....	....	....	....	4	2	1	3	4	....	....	....
1985-86	Nova Scotia Oilers	AHL	23	1	2	3	....	....	....	36	....	....	....	....	....	....	....	....	....	....	....	....	....	....	....	....	....	....
	Saginaw Generals	IHL	4	0	1	1	....	....	....	2	....	....	....	....	....	....	....	....	....	....	....	....	....	....	....	....	....	....
1986-87	Nova Scotia Oilers	AHL	66	2	6	8	....	....	....	57	....	....	....	....	....	....	....	....	....	....	2	0	0	0	0	....	....	....
1987-88	**Chicago Blackhawks**	**NHL**	**2**	**0**	**0**	**0**	**0**	**0**	**0**	**2**	**0**	**0**	**0**	**0**	**0.0**	**0**	**0**	**0**	**0**	**0**	....	....	....	....	....	....	....	....
	Saginaw Hawks	IHL	74	8	20	28	....	....	....	141	....	....	....	....	....	....	....	....	....	....	10	0	1	1	30	....	....	....
1988-89	**Chicago Blackhawks**	**NHL**	**1**	**0**	**0**	**0**	**0**	**0**	**0**	**2**	**0**	**0**	**0**	**0**	**0.0**	**0**	**0**	**1**	**0**	**–1**	....	....	....	....	....	....	....	....
	Saginaw Hawks	IHL	69	12	14	26	....	....	....	148	....	....	....	....	....	....	....	....	....	....	6	2	2	4	17	....	....	....
1989-90	**Washington Capitals**	**NHL**	**13**	**1**	**2**	**3**	**1**	**1**	**2**	**18**	**0**	**0**	**0**	**15**	**6.7**	**11**	**1**	**19**	**2**	**–7**	**3**	**0**	**0**	**0**	**10**	**0**	**0**	**0**
	Baltimore Skipjacks	AHL	60	7	20	27	....	....	....	110	....	....	....	....	....	....	....	....	....	....	11	5	6	1	34	....	....	....
1990-91	**Washington Capitals**	**NHL**	**1**	**0**	**0**	**0**	**0**	**0**	**0**	**15**	**0**	**0**	**0**	**0**	**0.0**	**0**	**0**	**0**	**0**	**0**	**1**	**0**	**0**	**0**	**0**	**0**	**0**	**0**
	Baltimore Skipjacks	AHL	43	10	17	27	....	....	....	64	....	....	....	....	....	....	....	....	....	....	6	2	1	3	8	....	....	....
1991-92	**Winnipeg Jets**	**NHL**	**5**	**0**	**0**	**0**	**0**	**0**	**0**	**4**	**0**	**0**	**0**	**6**	**0.0**	**2**	**0**	**3**	**0**	**–1**	....	....	....	....	....	....	....	....
	Moncton Hawks	AHL	62	3	30	33	....	....	....	71	....	....	....	....	....	....	....	....	....	....	11	2	6	8	25	....	....	....
1992-93	**Ottawa Senators**	**NHL**	**6**	**0**	**0**	**0**	**0**	**0**	**0**	**20**	**0**	**0**	**0**	**3**	**0.0**	**2**	**0**	**13**	**4**	**–7**	....	....	....	....	....	....	....	....
	New Haven Nighthawks	AHL	48	7	17	24	....	....	....	81	....	....	....	....	....	....	....	....	....	....	....	....	....	....	....	....	....	....
1993-94	**Ottawa Senators**	**NHL**	**9**	**0**	**1**	**1**	**0**	**1**	**1**	**8**	**0**	**0**	**0**	**8**	**0.0**	**4**	**1**	**16**	**7**	**–6**	....	....	....	....	....	....	....	....
	P.E.I. Senators	AHL	63	6	20	26	....	....	....	125	....	....	....	....	....	....	....	....	....	....	....	....	....	....	....	....	....	....
1994-95	Milwaukee Admirals	IHL	73	3	22	25	....	....	....	104	....	....	....	....	....	....	....	....	....	....	5	2	3	5	8	....	....	....
1995-96	Milwaukee Admirals	IHL	79	9	19	28	....	....	....	147	....	....	....	....	....	....	....	....	....	....	5	0	2	2	10	....	....	....
1996-97	Milwaukee Admirals	IHL	77	10	28	38	....	....	....	97	....	....	....	....	....	....	....	....	....	....	3	1	1	2	4	....	....	....
1997-98	Milwaukee Admirals	IHL	15	0	6	6	....	....	....	14	....	....	....	....	....	....	....	....	....	....	....	....	....	....	....	....	....	....
	Indianapolis Ice	IHL	37	3	7	10	....	....	....	36	....	....	....	....	....	....	....	....	....	....	5	0	1	1	4	....	....	....
	NHL Totals		**37**	**1**	**3**	**4**	**1**	**2**	**3**	**69**	**0**	**0**	**0**	**32**	**3.1**	**19**	**2**	**52**	**13**		**4**	**0**	**0**	**0**	**10**	**0**	**0**	**0**

Signed as a free agent by **Washington**, August 21, 1989. Traded to **Winnipeg** by **Washington** with Tyler Larter and Bob Joyce for Craig Duncanson, Brent Hughes, and Simon Wheeldon, May 21, 1991. Claimed by **Ottawa** from **Winnipeg** in Expansion Draft, June 18, 1992.

• PEAKE, PAT
Pat Peake C – R. 6'1", 195 lbs. b: Rochester, MI, 5/28/1973. Washington's 1st choice, 14th overall, in 1991 Entry Draft.

			REGULAR SEASON																		PLAYOFFS							
Season	Club	League	GP	G	A	Pts	AG	AA	APts	PIM	PP	SH	GW	S	%	TGF	PGF	TGA	PGA	+/–	GP	G	A	Pts	PIM	PP	SH	GW
1990-91	Detroit Ambassadors	OHL	63	39	51	90	....	....	....	54	....	....	....	....	....	....	....	....	....	....	....	....	....	....	....	....	....	....
1991-92	Detroit Ambassadors	OHL	53	41	52	93	....	....	....	44	....	....	....	....	....	....	....	....	....	....	7	8	9	17	10	....	....	....
	United States	WJC-A	7	5	1	6	....	....	....	4	....	....	....	....	....	....	....	....	....	....	....	....	....	....	....	....	....	....
	Baltimore Skipjacks	AHL	3	1	0	1	....	....	....	4	....	....	....	....	....	....	....	....	....	....	....	....	....	....	....	....	....	....
1992-93	Detroit Jr. Red Wings	OHL	46	58	78	136	....	....	....	64	....	....	....	....	....	....	....	....	....	....	2	1	3	4	2	....	....	....
	United States	WJC-A	7	4	9	13	....	....	....	18	....	....	....	....	....	....	....	....	....	....	....	....	....	....	....	....	....	....
1993-94	**Washington Capitals**	**NHL**	**49**	**11**	**18**	**29**	**10**	**14**	**24**	**39**	**3**	**0**	**1**	**91**	**12.1**	**40**	**15**	**24**	**0**	**+1**	**8**	**0**	**1**	**1**	**8**	**0**	**0**	**0**
	Portland Pirates	AHL	4	0	5	5	....	....	....	2	....	....	....	....	....	....	....	....	....	....	....	....	....	....	....	....	....	....
1994-95	**Washington Capitals**	**NHL**	**18**	**0**	**4**	**4**	**0**	**6**	**6**	**12**	**0**	**0**	**0**	**30**	**0.0**	**5**	**3**	**8**	**0**	**–6**	....	....	....	....	....	....	....	....
	Portland Pirates	AHL	5	1	3	4	....	....	....	2	....	....	....	....	....	....	....	....	....	....	4	0	3	3	6	....	....	....
1995-96	**Washington Capitals**	**NHL**	**62**	**17**	**19**	**36**	**17**	**15**	**32**	**46**	**8**	**0**	**3**	**129**	**13.2**	**56**	**27**	**23**	**1**	**+7**	**5**	**2**	**1**	**3**	**12**	**2**	**0**	**0**
1996-97	**Washington Capitals**	**NHL**	**4**	**0**	**0**	**0**	**0**	**0**	**0**	**4**	**0**	**0**	**0**	**9**	**0.0**	**2**	**1**	**0**	**0**	**+1**	....	....	....	....	....	....	....	....
	Portland Pirates	AHL	3	0	2	2	....	....	....	0	....	....	....	....	....	....	....	....	....	....	....	....	....	....	....	....	....	....
1997-98	**Washington Capitals**	**NHL**	**1**	**0**	**0**	**0**	**0**	**0**	**0**	**4**	**0**	**0**	**0**	**0**	**0.0**	**0**	**0**	**0**	**0**	**0**	....	....	....	....	....	....	....	....
	NHL Totals		**134**	**28**	**41**	**69**	**27**	**35**	**62**	**105**	**11**	**0**	**4**	**259**	**10.8**	**103**	**46**	**55**	**1**		**13**	**2**	**2**	**4**	**20**	**2**	**0**	**0**

Canadian Major Junior Player of the Year (1993) • Canadian Major Junior First All-Star Team (1993) • OHL First All-Star Team (1993)

• PEARSON, MEL
Mel Pearson LW – L. 5'10", 175 lbs. b: Flin Flon, Man., 4/29/1938.

Season	Club	League	GP	G	A	Pts	AG	AA	APts	PIM	PP	SH	GW	S	%	TGF	PGF	TGA	PGA	+/–	GP	G	A	Pts	PIM	PP	SH	GW
1955-56	Flin Flon Bombers	SJHL	48	26	23	49	....	....	....	32	....	....	....	....	....	....	....	....	....	....	12	1	0	1	6	....	....	....
1956-57	Flin Flon Bombers	SJHL	56	*59	49	108	....	....	....	86	....	....	....	....	....	....	....	....	....	....	10	*13	9	*22	6	....	....	....
1957-58	Trois-Rivieres Lions	QHL	54	17	28	45	....	....	....	60	....	....	....	....	....	....	....	....	....	....	....	....	....	....	....	....	....	....
	Providence Reds	AHL	10	1	2	3	....	....	....	0	....	....	....	....	....	....	....	....	....	....	....	....	....	....	....	....	....	....
1958-59	Vancouver Canucks	WHL	70	16	33	49	....	....	....	35	....	....	....	....	....	....	....	....	....	....	8	1	2	3	11	....	....	....
1959-60	**New York Rangers**	**NHL**	**23**	**1**	**5**	**6**	**1**	**5**	**6**	**13**	....	....	....	....	....	....	....	....	....	....	....	....	....	....	....	....	....	....
	Trois-Rivieres Lions	EPHL	43	21	23	44	....	....	....	26	....	....	....	....	....	....	....	....	....	....	....	....	....	....	....	....	....	....
1960-61	Kitchener-Waterloo Beavers	EPHL	69	20	27	47	....	....	....	62	....	....	....	....	....	....	....	....	....	....	7	1	1	2	10	....	....	....
1961-62	**New York Rangers**	**NHL**	**3**	**0**	**0**	**0**	**0**	**0**	**0**	**2**	....	....	....	....	....	....	....	....	....	....	....	....	....	....	....	....	....	....
	Kitchener-Waterloo Beavers	EPHL	66	23	38	61	....	....	....	44	....	....	....	....	....	....	....	....	....	....	7	1	0	1	10	....	....	....
1962-63	**New York Rangers**	**NHL**	**5**	**1**	**0**	**1**	**1**	**0**	**1**	**6**	....	....	....	....	....	....	....	....	....	....	....	....	....	....	....	....	....	....
	Baltimore Clippers	AHL	67	13	29	42	....	....	....	40	....	....	....	....	....	....	....	....	....	....	3	1	1	2	4	....	....	....
1963-64	Baltimore Clippers	AHL	68	8	22	30	....	....	....	35	....	....	....	....	....	....	....	....	....	....	....	....	....	....	....	....	....	....
1964-65	**New York Rangers**	**NHL**	**5**	**0**	**0**	**0**	**0**	**0**	**0**	**4**	....	....	....	....	....	....	....	....	....	....	....	....	....	....	....	....	....	....
	St. Paul Rangers	CHL	61	24	46	70	....	....	....	30	....	....	....	....	....	....	....	....	....	....	11	5	7	12	20	....	....	....
1965-66	Buffalo Bisons	AHL	72	18	40	58	....	....	....	30	....	....	....	....	....	....	....	....	....	....	....	....	....	....	....	....	....	....
1966-67	Los Angeles Blades	WHL	68	17	45	62	....	....	....	24	....	....	....	....	....	....	....	....	....	....	....	....	....	....	....	....	....	....
1967-68	**Pittsburgh Penguins**	**NHL**	**2**	**0**	**1**	**1**	**0**	**1**	**1**	**0**	**0**	**0**	**0**	**2**	**0.0**	**1**	**0**	**2**	**0**	**–1**	....	....	....	....	....	....	....	....
	Portland Buckaroos	WHL	68	19	20	39	....	....	....	16	....	....	....	....	....	....	....	....	....	....	12	1	4	5	7	....	....	....
1968-69	Portland Buckaroos	WHL	74	19	26	45	....	....	....	44	....	....	....	....	....	....	....	....	....	....	11	0	1	1	10	....	....	....
1969-70	Portland Buckaroos	WHL	72	26	22	48	....	....	....	24	....	....	....	....	....	....	....	....	....	....	11	2	4	6	30	....	....	....
1970-71	Portland Buckaroos	WHL	72	23	19	42	....	....	....	52	....	....	....	....	....	....	....	....	....	....	11	1	6	7	10	....	....	....
1971-72	Portland Buckaroos	WHL	72	21	38	59	....	....	....	45	....	....	....	....	....	....	....	....	....	....	11	1	1	2	17	....	....	....
1972-73	Minnesota Fighting Saints	WHA	70	8	12	20	....	....	....	12	....	....	....	....	....	....	....	....	....	....	5	2	0	2	0	....	....	....
	NHL Totals		**38**	**2**	**6**	**8**	**2**	**6**	**8**	**25**	**0**	**0**	**0**	**2**	**100.0**	**1**	**0**	**2**	**0**		....	....	....	....	....	....	....	....
	Other Major League Totals		70	8	12	20	....	....	....	12	....	....	....	....	....	....	....	....	....	....	5	2	0	2	0	....	....	....

Traded to **Chicago** by **NY Rangers** with Dave Richardson, Tracy Pratt and Dick Meissner for John McKenzie and Ray Cullen, June, 1965. Claimed by **Pittsburgh** from **Chicago** in Expansion Draft, June 6, 1967. Traded to **Portland** (WHL) by **Pittsburgh**, July, 1968. Selected by **Dayton-Houston** (WHA) in 1972 WHA General Player Draft, February 12, 1972. Traded to **Minnesota** (WHA) by **Houston** (WHA) for future considerations and cash, September, 1972.

• PEARSON, ROB
Rob Pearson RW – R. 6'3", 198 lbs. b: Oshawa, Ont., 3/8/1971. Toronto's 2nd choice, 12th overall, in 1989 Entry Draft.

Season	Club	League	GP	G	A	Pts	AG	AA	APts	PIM	PP	SH	GW	S	%	TGF	PGF	TGA	PGA	+/–	GP	G	A	Pts	PIM	PP	SH	GW
1988-89	Belleville Bulls	OHL	26	8	12	20	....	....	....	51	....	....	....	....	....	....	....	....	....	....	....	....	....	....	....	....	....	....
1989-90	Belleville Bulls	OHL	58	48	40	88	....	....	....	174	....	....	....	....	....	....	....	....	....	....	11	5	5	10	26	....	....	....
1990-91	Belleville Bulls	OHL	10	6	3	9	....	....	....	27	....	....	....	....	....	....	....	....	....	....	....	....	....	....	....	....	....	....
	Oshawa Generals	OHL	41	57	52	109	....	....	....	76	....	....	....	....	....	....	....	....	....	....	16	16	17	33	39	....	....	....
	Newmarket Saints	AHL	3	0	0	0	....	....	....	29	....	....	....	....	....	....	....	....	....	....	....	....	....	....	....	....	....	....
1991-92	**Toronto Maple Leafs**	**NHL**	**47**	**14**	**10**	**24**	**13**	**7**	**20**	**58**	**6**	**0**	**0**	**79**	**17.7**	**30**	**14**	**32**	**0**	**–16**	....	....	....	....	....	....	....	....
	St. John's Maple Leafs	AHL	27	15	14	29	....	....	....	107	....	....	....	....	....	....	....	....	....	....	13	5	4	9	40	....	....	....
1992-93	**Toronto Maple Leafs**	**NHL**	**78**	**23**	**14**	**37**	**19**	**10**	**29**	**211**	**8**	**0**	**3**	**164**	**14.0**	**66**	**21**	**48**	**1**	**–2**	**14**	**2**	**2**	**4**	**31**	**0**	**0**	**0**
1993-94	**Toronto Maple Leafs**	**NHL**	**67**	**12**	**18**	**30**	**11**	**14**	**25**	**189**	**1**	**0**	**4**	**119**	**10.1**	**49**	**13**	**42**	**0**	**–6**	**14**	**1**	**0**	**1**	**32**	**0**	**0**	**0**
1994-95	**Washington Capitals**	**NHL**	**32**	**0**	**6**	**6**	**0**	**9**	**9**	**96**	**0**	**0**	**0**	**34**	**0.0**	**9**	**2**	**13**	**0**	**–6**	**3**	**1**	**0**	**1**	**17**	**0**	**0**	**1**
1995-96	Portland Pirates	AHL	44	18	24	42	....	....	....	143	....	....	....	....	....	....	....	....	....	....	....	....	....	....	....	....	....	....
	St. Louis Blues	**NHL**	**27**	**6**	**4**	**10**	**6**	**3**	**9**	**54**	**1**	**0**	**1**	**51**	**11.8**	**17**	**4**	**10**	**1**	**+4**	**2**	**0**	**0**	**0**	**14**	**0**	**0**	**0**
1996-97	**St. Louis Blues**	**NHL**	**18**	**1**	**2**	**3**	**1**	**2**	**3**	**37**	**0**	**0**	**0**	**14**	**7.1**	**5**	**2**	**8**	**0**	**–5**	....	....	....	....	....	....	....	....
	Worcester IceCats	AHL	46	11	16	27	....	....	....	199	....	....	....	....	....	....	....	....	....	....	5	3	0	3	16	....	....	....
1997-98	Cleveland Lumberjacks	IHL	46	17	14	31	....	....	....	118	....	....	....	....	....	....	....	....	....	....	10	6	4	10	43	....	....	....
	NHL Totals		**269**	**56**	**54**	**110**	**50**	**45**	**95**	**645**	**16**	**0**	**8**	**461**	**12.1**	**176**	**56**	**153**	**2**		**33**	**4**	**2**	**6**	**94**	**0**	**0**	**1**

OHL First All-Star Team (1991)

Traded to **Washington** by **Toronto** with Philadelphia's 1st round choice (previously acquired by Toronto — Washington selected Nolan Baumgartner) in 1994 Entry Draft for Mike Ridley and St. Louis' 1st round choice (previously acquired, Toronto selected Eric Fichaud) in 1994 Entry Draft, June 28, 1994. Traded to **St. Louis** by **Washington** for Denis Chasse, January 29, 1996.

• PEARSON, SCOTT
Scott Pearson LW – L. 6'1", 205 lbs. b: Cornwall, Ont., 12/19/1969. Toronto's 1st choice, 6th overall, in 1988 Entry Draft.

Season	Club	League	GP	G	A	Pts	AG	AA	APts	PIM	PP	SH	GW	S	%	TGF	PGF	TGA	PGA	+/–	GP	G	A	Pts	PIM	PP	SH	GW
1985-86	Kingston Canadians	OHL	63	16	23	39	....	....	....	56	....	....	....	....	....	....	....	....	....	....	....	....	....	....	....	....	....	....
1986-87	Kingston Canadians	OHL	62	30	24	54	....	....	....	101	....	....	....	....	....	....	....	....	....	....	9	3	3	6	42	....	....	....
1987-88	Kingston Canadians	OHL	46	26	32	58	....	....	....	117	....	....	....	....	....	....	....	....	....	....	....	....	....	....	....	....	....	....
1988-89	Kingston Canadians	OHL	13	9	8	17	....	....	....	34	....	....	....	....	....	....	....	....	....	....	....	....	....	....	....	....	....	....
	Niagara Falls Thunder	OHL	32	26	34	60	....	....	....	90	....	....	....	....	....	....	....	....	....	....	17	14	10	24	53	....	....	....
	Toronto Maple Leafs	**NHL**	**9**	**0**	**1**	**1**	**0**	**1**	**1**	**2**	**0**	**0**	**0**	**6**	**0.0**	**2**	**0**	**2**	**0**	**0**	....	....	....	....	....	....	....	....
1989-90	**Toronto Maple Leafs**	**NHL**	**41**	**5**	**10**	**15**	**4**	**7**	**11**	**90**	**0**	**0**	**1**	**66**	**7.6**	**24**	**4**	**27**	**0**	**–7**	**2**	**2**	**0**	**2**	**10**	**0**	**0**	**0**
	Newmarket Saints	AHL	18	12	11	23	....	....	....	64	....	....	....	....	....	....	....	....	....	....	....	....	....	....	....	....	....	....
1990-91	**Toronto Maple Leafs**	**NHL**	**12**	**0**	**0**	**0**	**0**	**0**	**0**	**20**	**0**	**0**	**0**	**13**	**0.0**	**1**	**0**	**6**	**0**	**–5**	....	....	....	....	....	....	....	....
	Quebec Nordiques	**NHL**	**35**	**11**	**4**	**15**	**10**	**3**	**13**	**86**	**0**	**0**	**0**	**61**	**18.0**	**25**	**2**	**27**	**0**	**–4**	....	....	....	....	....	....	....	....
	Halifax Citadels	AHL	24	12	15	27	....	....	....	44	....	....	....	....	....	....	....	....	....	....	....	....	....	....	....	....	....	....
1991-92	**Quebec Nordiques**	**NHL**	**10**	**1**	**2**	**3**	**1**	**1**	**2**	**14**	**0**	**0**	**0**	**14**	**7.1**	**4**	**1**	**8**	**0**	**–5**	....	....	....	....	....	....	....	....
	Halifax Citadels	AHL	5	2	1	3	....	....	....	4	....	....	....	....	....	....	....	....	....	....	....	....	....	....	....	....	....	....
1992-93	**Quebec Nordiques**	**NHL**	**41**	**13**	**1**	**14**	**11**	**1**	**12**	**95**	**0**	**0**	**1**	**45**	**28.9**	**20**	**0**	**17**	**0**	**+3**	**3**	**0**	**0**	**0**	**0**	**0**	**0**	**0**
	Halifax Citadels	AHL	5	3	1	4	....	....	....	25	....	....	....	....	....	....	....	....	....	....	....	....	....	....	....	....	....	....
1993-94	**Edmonton Oilers**	**NHL**	**72**	**19**	**18**	**37**	**18**	**14**	**32**	**165**	**3**	**0**	**7**	**160**	**11.9**	**54**	**10**	**48**	**0**	**–4**	....	....	....	....	....	....	....	....
1994-95	**Edmonton Oilers**	**NHL**	**28**	**1**	**4**	**5**	**2**	**6**	**8**	**54**	**0**	**0**	**0**	**21**	**4.8**	**6**	**0**	**17**	**0**	**–11**	....	....	....	....	....	....	....	....
	Buffalo Sabres	**NHL**	**14**	**2**	**1**	**3**	**4**	**1**	**5**	**20**	**0**	**0**	**0**	**19**	**10.5**	**6**	**0**	**9**	**0**	**–3**	**5**	**0**	**0**	**0**	**4**	**0**	**0**	**0**
1995-96	**Buffalo Sabres**	**NHL**	**27**	**4**	**0**	**4**	**4**	**0**	**4**	**67**	**0**	**0**	**1**	**26**	**15.4**	**4**	**0**	**8**	**0**	**–4**	....	....	....	....	....	....	....	....
	Rochester Americans	AHL	26	8	8	16	....	....	....	113	....	....	....	....	....	....	....	....	....	....	....	....	....	....	....	....	....	....
1996-97	**Toronto Maple Leafs**	**NHL**	**1**	**0**	**0**	**0**	**0**	**0**	**0**	**2**	**0**	**0**	**0**	**0**	**0.0**	**0**	**0**	**0**	**0**	**0**	....	....	....	....	....	....	....	....
	St. John's Maple Leafs	AHL	14	5	2	7	....	....	....	26	....	....	....	....	....	....	....	....	....	....	9	5	2	7	14	....	....	....
1997-98	Chicago Wolves	IHL	78	34	17	51	....	....	....	225	....	....	....	....	....	....	....	....	....	....	22	12	6	18	50	....	....	....
	NHL Totals		**290**	**56**	**41**	**97**	**54**	**34**	**88**	**615**	**3**	**0**	**10**	**431**	**13.0**	**146**	**17**	**169**	**0**		**10**	**2**	**0**	**2**	**14**	**0**	**0**	**0**

Traded to **Quebec** by **Toronto** with Toronto's 2nd round choices in 1991 (later traded to Washington — Washington selected Eric Lavigne) and 1992 (Tuomas Gronman) Entry Drafts for Aaron Broten, Lucien Deblois and Michel Petit, November 17, 1990. Traded to **Edmonton** by **Quebec** for Martin Gelinas and Edmonton's 6th round choice (Nicholas Checco) in 1993 Entry Draft, June 20, 1993. Traded to **Buffalo** by **Edmonton** for Ken Sutton, April 7, 1995. Signed as a free agent by **Toronto**, July 24, 1996.

• PECA, MICHAEL

Michael Peca C – R. 5'11", 181 lbs. b: Toronto, Ont., 3/26/1974. Vancouver's 2nd choice, 40th overall, in 1992 Entry Draft.

			REGULAR SEASON																		PLAYOFFS							
Season	Club	League	GP	G	A	Pts	AG	AA	APts	PIM	PP	SH	GW	S	%	TGF	PGF	TGA	PGA	+/–	GP	G	A	Pts	PIM	PP	SH	GW
1990-91	Sudbury Wolves	OHL	62	14	27	41	....	....	....	24	....	....	....	....	....	....	....	....	....	....	5	1	0	1	7	....	....	....
1991-92	Sudbury Wolves	OHL	39	16	34	50	....	....	....	61	....	....	....	....	....	....	....	....	....	....	....	....	....	....	....	....	....	....
	Ottawa 67's	OHL	27	8	17	25	....	....	....	32	....	....	....	....	....	....	....	....	....	....	11	6	10	16	6	....	....	....
1992-93	Ottawa 67's	OHL	55	38	64	102	....	....	....	80	....	....	....	....	....	....	....	....	....	....	....	....	....	....	....	....	....	....
	Hamilton Canucks	AHL	9	6	3	9	....	....	....	11	....	....	....	....	....	....	....	....	....	....	....	....	....	....	....	....	....	....
1993-94	Ottawa 67's	OHL	55	50	63	113	....	....	....	101	....	....	....	....	....	....	....	....	....	....	17	7	22	29	30	....	....	....
	Vancouver Canucks	NHL	4	0	0	0	0	0	0	2	0	0	0	5	0.0	0	0	1	0	–1	....	....	....	....	....	....	....	....
1994-95	Syracuse Crunch	AHL	35	10	24	34	....	....	....	75	....	....	....	....	....	....	....	....	....	....	....	....	....	....	....	....	....	....
	Vancouver Canucks	NHL	33	6	6	12	11	9	20	30	2	0	1	46	13.0	21	7	25	5	–6	5	0	1	1	8	0	0	0
1995-96	Buffalo Sabres	NHL	68	11	20	31	11	16	27	67	4	3	1	109	10.1	50	14	55	18	–1	....	....	....	....	....	....	....	....
1996-97	Buffalo Sabres	NHL	79	20	29	49	21	26	47	80	5	6	4	137	14.6	73	14	65	32	+26	10	0	2	2	8	0	0	0
1997-98	Buffalo Sabres	NHL	61	18	22	40	21	21	42	57	6	5	1	132	13.6	63	22	49	20	+12	13	3	2	5	8	0	0	1
	NHL Totals		245	55	77	132	64	72	136	236	17	14	7	429	12.8	207	57	195	75		28	3	5	8	24	0	0	1

Won Frank J. Selke Trophy (1997)

Traded to **Buffalo** by **Vancouver** with Mike Wilson and Vancouver's 1st round choice (Jay McKee) in 1995 Entry Draft for Alexander Mogilny and Buffalo's 5th round choice (Todd Norman) in 1995 Entry Draft, July 8, 1995.

• PEDERSEN, ALLEN

Allen Pedersen D – L. 6'3", 210 lbs. b: Fort Saskatchewan, Alta., 1/13/1965. Boston's 5th choice, 105th overall, in 1983 Entry Draft.

Season	Club	League	GP	G	A	Pts	AG	AA	APts	PIM	PP	SH	GW	S	%	TGF	PGF	TGA	PGA	+/–	GP	G	A	Pts	PIM	PP	SH	GW
1982-83	Medicine Hat Tigers	WHL	63	3	10	13	....	....	....	49	....	....	....	....	....	....	....	....	....	....	5	0	0	0	7	....	....	....
1983-84	Medicine Hat Tigers	WHL	44	0	11	11	....	....	....	47	....	....	....	....	....	....	....	....	....	....	14	0	2	2	24	....	....	....
1984-85	Medicine Hat Tigers	WHL	72	6	16	22	....	....	....	66	....	....	....	....	....	....	....	....	....	....	10	0	0	0	9	....	....	....
1985-86	Moncton Golden Flames	AHL	59	1	8	9	....	....	....	39	....	....	....	....	....	....	....	....	....	....	3	0	0	0	0	....	....	....
1986-87	Boston Bruins	NHL	79	1	11	12	1	8	9	71	0	0	0	56	1.8	63	0	99	21	–15	4	0	0	0	4	0	0	0
1987-88	Boston Bruins	NHL	78	0	6	6	0	4	4	90	0	0	0	43	0.0	45	0	57	18	+6	21	0	0	0	34	0	0	0
1988-89	Boston Bruins	NHL	51	0	6	6	0	4	4	69	0	0	0	24	0.0	37	0	63	23	–3	10	0	0	0	2	0	0	0
1989-90	Boston Bruins	NHL	68	1	2	3	1	1	2	71	0	0	0	32	3.1	50	1	69	15	–5	21	0	0	0	41	0	0	0
1990-91	Boston Bruins	NHL	57	2	6	8	2	5	7	107	0	0	0	34	5.9	42	0	42	15	+15	8	0	0	0	10	0	0	0
	Maine Mariners	AHL	15	0	6	6	....	....	....	18	....	....	....	....	....	....	....	....	....	....	2	0	1	1	2	....	....	....
1991-92	Minnesota North Stars	NHL	29	0	1	1	0	1	1	10	0	0	0	17	0.0	16	0	22	5	–1	....	....	....	....	....	....	....	....
1992-93	Hartford Whalers	NHL	59	1	4	5	1	3	4	60	0	0	0	16	6.3	43	0	81	38	0	....	....	....	....	....	....	....	....
1993-94	Hartford Whalers	NHL	7	0	0	0	0	0	0	9	0	0	0	1	0.0	3	0	4	0	–1	....	....	....	....	....	....	....	....
	Springfield Indians	AHL	45	2	4	6	....	....	....	28	....	....	....	....	....	....	....	....	....	....	3	0	1	1	6	....	....	....
1994-95	Atlanta Knights	IHL	71	0	5	5	....	....	....	61	....	....	....	....	....	....	....	....	....	....	5	0	0	0	2	....	....	....
	NHL Totals		428	5	36	41	5	26	31	487	0	0	0	223	2.2	299	1	437	135		64	0	0	0	91	0	0	0

Claimed by **Minnesota** from **Boston** in Expansion Draft, May 30, 1991. Traded to **Hartford** by **Minnesota** for Hartford's 6th round choice (Rick Mrozik) in 1993 Entry Draft, June 15, 1992.

• PEDERSON, BARRY

Barry Pederson C – R. 5'11", 185 lbs. b: Big River, Sask., 3/13/1961. Boston's 1st choice, 18th overall, in 1980 Entry Draft.

Season	Club	League	GP	G	A	Pts	AG	AA	APts	PIM	PP	SH	GW	S	%	TGF	PGF	TGA	PGA	+/–	GP	G	A	Pts	PIM	PP	SH	GW
1977-78	Nanaimo Clippers	BCJHL	63	49	99	148	....	....	....	68	....	....	....	....	....	....	....	....	....	....	....	....	....	....	....	....	....	....
	Victoria Cougars	WCJHL	3	1	4	5	....	....	....	2	....	....	....	....	....	....	....	....	....	....	....	....	....	....	....	....	....	....
1978-79	Victoria Cougars	WHL	72	31	53	84	....	....	....	41	....	....	....	....	....	....	....	....	....	....	....	....	....	....	....	....	....	....
1979-80	Victoria Cougars	WHL	72	52	88	140	....	....	....	50	....	....	....	....	....	....	....	....	....	....	16	13	14	27	31	....	....	....
1980-81	Victoria Cougars	WHL	55	65	82	147	....	....	....	65	....	....	....	....	....	....	....	....	....	....	15	15	21	36	10	....	....	....
	Boston Bruins	NHL	9	1	4	5	1	3	4	6	1	0	0	20	5.0	8	5	9	1	–5	....	....	....	....	....	....	....	....
1981-82	Boston Bruins	NHL	80	44	48	92	35	32	67	53	13	4	7	197	22.3	121	40	72	18	+27	11	7	11	18	2	1	0	2
1982-83	Boston Bruins	NHL	77	46	61	107	38	42	80	47	15	1	10	212	21.7	144	47	79	20	+38	17	14	18	32	21	1	1	2
1983-84	Boston Bruins	NHL	80	39	77	116	31	52	83	64	10	3	7	236	16.5	152	61	93	29	+27	3	0	1	1	2	0	0	0
1984-85	Boston Bruins	NHL	22	4	8	12	3	5	8	10	0	2	0	35	11.4	18	8	24	3	–11	....	....	....	....	....	....	....	....
1985-86	Boston Bruins	NHL	79	29	47	76	23	31	54	60	12	0	6	192	15.1	122	51	80	28	+19	3	1	0	1	0	0	0	0
1986-87	Vancouver Canucks	NHL	79	24	52	76	21	38	59	50	6	0	3	184	13.0	109	46	108	32	–13	....	....	....	....	....	....	....	....
	Canada	WEC-A	10	2	3	5	....	....	....	2	....	....	....	....	....	....	....	....	....	....	....	....	....	....	....	....	....	....
1987-88	Vancouver Canucks	NHL	76	19	52	71	16	37	53	92	4	1	1	163	11.7	100	40	89	31	+2	....	....	....	....	....	....	....	....
1988-89	Vancouver Canucks	NHL	62	15	26	41	13	18	31	22	7	1	0	98	15.3	60	20	56	21	+5	....	....	....	....	....	....	....	....
1989-90	Vancouver Canucks	NHL	16	2	7	9	2	5	7	10	0	0	0	22	9.1	12	3	18	6	–3	....	....	....	....	....	....	....	....
	Pittsburgh Penguins	NHL	38	4	18	22	3	13	16	29	1	0	1	58	6.9	45	18	46	9	–10	....	....	....	....	....	....	....	....
1990-91	Pittsburgh Penguins	NHL	46	6	8	14	5	6	11	21	1	0	1	26	23.1	22	2	27	9	+2	....	....	....	....	....	....	....	....
1991-92	Hartford Whalers	NHL	5	2	2	4	2	1	3	0	1	0	0	6	33.3	7	4	6	1	–2	....	....	....	....	....	....	....	....
	Boston Bruins	NHL	32	3	6	9	3	4	7	8	1	0	0	41	7.3	14	3	26	10	–5	....	....	....	....	....	....	....	....
	Maine Mariners	AHL	14	5	13	18	....	....	....	6	....	....	....	....	....	....	....	....	....	....	....	....	....	....	....	....	....	....
	NHL Totals		701	238	416	654	196	287	483	472	72	12	36	1490	16.0	934	348	733	218		34	22	30	52	25	2	1	4

WHL All-Star Team (1981)

Played in NHL All-Star Game (1983, 1984)

Traded to **Vancouver** by **Boston** for Cam Neely and Vancouver's 1st round choice (Glen Wesley) in 1987 Entry Draft, June 6, 1986. Traded to **Pittsburgh** by **Vancouver** with Rod Buskas and Tony Tanti for Dave Capuano, Andrew McBain and Dan Quinn, January 8, 1990. Signed as a free agent by **Hartford**, September 5, 1991. Traded to **Boston** by **Hartford** for future considerations, November 14, 1991.

• PEDERSON, DENIS

Denis Pederson C – R. 6'2", 190 lbs. b: Prince Albert, Sask., 9/10/1975. New Jersey's 1st choice, 13th overall, in 1993 Entry Draft.

Season	Club	League	GP	G	A	Pts	AG	AA	APts	PIM	PP	SH	GW	S	%	TGF	PGF	TGA	PGA	+/–	GP	G	A	Pts	PIM	PP	SH	GW
1991-92	Prince Albert Midget Raiders	Midget	21	33	25	58	....	....	....	40	....	....	....	....	....	....	....	....	....	....	....	....	....	....	....	....	....	....
	Prince Albert Raiders	WHL	10	0	0	0	....	....	....	6	....	....	....	....	....	....	....	....	....	....	7	0	1	1	13	....	....	....
1992-93	Prince Albert Raiders	WHL	72	33	40	73	....	....	....	134	....	....	....	....	....	....	....	....	....	....	....	....	....	....	....	....	....	....
1993-94	Prince Albert Raiders	WHL	71	53	45	98	....	....	....	157	....	....	....	....	....	....	....	....	....	....	....	....	....	....	....	....	....	....
1994-95	Prince Albert Raiders	WHL	63	30	38	68	....	....	....	122	....	....	....	....	....	....	....	....	....	....	15	11	14	25	14	....	....	....
	Canada	WJC-A	7	2	2	4	....	....	....	0	....	....	....	....	....	....	....	....	....	....	....	....	....	....	....	....	....	....
	Albany River Rats	AHL	....	....	....	....	....	....	....	....	....	....	....	....	....	....	....	....	....	....	3	0	0	0	2	....	....	....
1995-96	New Jersey Devils	NHL	10	3	1	4	3	1	4	0	1	0	2	6	50.0	5	1	5	0	–1	....	....	....	....	....	....	....	....
	Albany River Rats	AHL	68	28	43	71	....	....	....	104	....	....	....	....	....	....	....	....	....	....	4	1	2	3	0	....	....	....
1996-97	New Jersey Devils	NHL	70	12	20	32	13	18	31	62	3	0	3	106	11.3	43	6	30	0	+7	9	0	0	0	2	0	0	0
	Albany River Rats	AHL	3	1	3	4	....	....	....	7	....	....	....	....	....	....	....	....	....	....	....	....	....	....	....	....	....	....
1997-98	New Jersey Devils	NHL	80	15	13	28	18	13	31	97	7	0	1	135	11.1	44	17	40	7	–6	6	1	1	2	2	0	1	0
	NHL Totals		160	30	34	64	34	32	66	159	11	0	6	247	12.1	92	24	75	7		15	1	1	2	4	0	1	0

WHL East Second All-Star Team (1994)

• PEDERSON, MARK

Mark Pederson LW – L. 6'2", 196 lbs. b: Prelate, Sask., 1/14/1968. Montreal's 1st choice, 15th overall, in 1986 Entry Draft.

Season	Club	League	GP	G	A	Pts	AG	AA	APts	PIM	PP	SH	GW	S	%	TGF	PGF	TGA	PGA	+/–	GP	G	A	Pts	PIM	PP	SH	GW
1984-85	Medicine Hat Tigers	WHL	71	42	40	82	....	....	....	63	....	....	....	....	....	....	....	....	....	....	10	3	2	5	0	....	....	....
1985-86	Medicine Hat Tigers	WHL	72	46	60	106	....	....	....	46	....	....	....	....	....	....	....	....	....	....	25	12	6	18	25	....	....	....
1986-87	Medicine Hat Tigers	WHL	69	56	46	102	....	....	....	58	....	....	....	....	....	....	....	....	....	....	20	*19	7	26	14	....	....	....
1987-88	Medicine Hat Tigers	WHL	62	53	58	111	....	....	....	55	....	....	....	....	....	....	....	....	....	....	16	*13	6	19	16	....	....	....
	Canada	WJC-A	7	1	2	3	....	....	....	4	....	....	....	....	....	....	....	....	....	....	....	....	....	....	....	....	....	....
1988-89	Sherbrooke Canadiens	AHL	75	43	38	81	....	....	....	53	....	....	....	....	....	....	....	....	....	....	6	7	5	12	4	....	....	....
1989-90	Montreal Canadiens	NHL	9	0	2	2	0	1	1	2	0	0	0	10	0.0	3	0	3	0	0	2	0	0	0	0	0	0	0
	Sherbrooke Canadiens	AHL	72	53	42	95	....	....	....	60	....	....	....	....	....	....	....	....	....	....	11	10	8	18	19	....	....	....
1990-91	Montreal Canadiens	FrTour	4	2	0	2	....	....	....	2	....	....	....	....	....	....	....	....	....	....	....	....	....	....	....	....	....	....
	Philadelphia Flyers	NHL	12	2	1	3	2	1	3	5	1	0	0	14	14.3	6	2	12	0	–8	....	....	....	....	....	....	....	....
	Montreal Canadiens	NHL	47	8	15	23	7	11	18	18	4	0	2	62	12.9	32	14	15	0	+3	....	....	....	....	....	....	....	....
1991-92	Philadelphia Flyers	NHL	58	15	25	40	14	19	33	22	4	0	3	94	16.0	57	19	25	1	+14	....	....	....	....	....	....	....	....
1992-93	Philadelphia Flyers	NHL	14	3	4	7	2	3	5	6	1	0	0	21	14.3	8	4	6	0	–2	....	....	....	....	....	....	....	....
	San Jose Sharks	NHL	27	7	3	10	6	2	8	22	1	0	0	42	16.7	15	5	30	0	–20	....	....	....	....	....	....	....	....
1993-94	Detroit Red Wings	NHL	2	0	0	0	0	0	0	2	0	0	0	0	0.0	0	0	1	0	–1	....	....	....	....	....	....	....	....
	Adirondack Red Wings	AHL	62	52	45	97	....	....	....	37	....	....	....	....	....	....	....	....	....	....	12	4	7	11	10	....	....	....
1994-95	Kalamazoo Wings	IHL	75	31	32	63	....	....	....	47	....	....	....	....	....	....	....	....	....	....	16	8	4	12	2	....	....	....

Season	Club	League	GP	G	A	Pts	AG	AA	APts	PIM	PP	SH	GW	S	%	TGF	PGF	TGA	PGA	+/–	GP	G	A	Pts	PIM	PP	SH	GW
			REGULAR SEASON																		PLAYOFFS							
1995-96	VSV Villach	Austria	34	28	32	60	....	....	....	52	....	....	....	....	....	....	....	....	....	....	....	....	....	....	....	....	....	....
1996-97	Zurich SC	Switz.	9	7	3	10	....	....	....	4	....	....	....	....	....	....	....	....	....	....	5	1	3	4	30	....	....	....
1997-98	Hannover Scorpions	Germany	47	20	38	58	....	....	....	61	....	....	....	....	....	....	....	....	....	....	4	0	1	1	2	....	....	....
	NHL Totals		**169**	**35**	**50**	**85**	**31**	**37**	**68**	**77**	**11**	**0**	**5**	**243**	**14.4**	**121**	**44**	**92**	**1**		**2**	**0**	**0**	**0**	**0**	**0**	**0**	**0**

WHL East First All-Star Team (1987) • WHL East Second All-Star Team (1988) • AHL First All-Star Team (1990, 1994)

Traded to **Philadelphia** by **Montreal** for Philadelphia's 2nd round choice (Jim Campbell) in 1991 Entry Draft, March 15, 1991. Traded to **San Jose** by **Philadelphia** with future considerations for Dave Snuggerud, December 19, 1992. Signed as a free agent by **Detroit**, August 23, 1993.

• PEDERSON, TOM

Tom Pederson D – R. 5'9", 175 lbs. b: Bloomington, MN, 1/14/1970. Minnesota's 12th choice, 217th overall, in 1989 Entry Draft.

Season	Club	League	GP	G	A	Pts	AG	AA	APts	PIM	PP	SH	GW	S	%	TGF	PGF	TGA	PGA	+/–	GP	G	A	Pts	PIM	PP	SH	GW
1988-89	University of Minnesota	WCHA	36	4	20	24	....	....	....	40	....	....	....	....	....	....	....	....	....	....	....	....	....	....	....	....	....	....
	United States	WJC-A	7	2	8	10	....	....	....	4	....	....	....	....	....	....	....	....	....	....	....	....	....	....	....	....	....	....
1989-90	University of Minnesota	WCHA	43	8	30	38	....	....	....	58	....	....	....	....	....	....	....	....	....	....	....	....	....	....	....	....	....	....
1990-91	University of Minnesota	WCHA	36	12	20	32	....	....	....	46	....	....	....	....	....	....	....	....	....	....	....	....	....	....	....	....	....	....
	United States	WEC-A	9	0	4	4	....	....	....	10	....	....	....	....	....	....	....	....	....	....	....	....	....	....	....	....	....	....
1991-92	United States	Nat-Team	44	3	11	14	....	....	....	41	....	....	....	....	....	....	....	....	....	....	....	....	....	....	....	....	....	....
	Kansas City Blades	IHL	20	6	9	15	....	....	....	16	....	....	....	....	....	....	....	....	....	....	13	1	6	7	14	....	....	....
1992-93	**San Jose Sharks**	**NHL**	**44**	**7**	**13**	**20**	**6**	**9**	**15**	**31**	**2**	**0**	**2**	**102**	**6.9**	**45**	**21**	**56**	**16**	**–16**	....	....	....	....	....	....	....	....
	Kansas City Blades	IHL	26	6	15	21	....	....	....	10	....	....	....	....	....	....	....	....	....	....	12	1	6	7	2	....	....	....
1993-94	**San Jose Sharks**	**NHL**	**74**	**6**	**19**	**25**	**6**	**15**	**21**	**31**	**3**	**0**	**1**	**185**	**3.2**	**88**	**31**	**82**	**28**	**+3**	**14**	**1**	**6**	**7**	**2**	**0**	**1**	**0**
	Kansas City Blades	IHL	7	3	1	4	....	....	....	0	....	....	....	....	....	....	....	....	....	....	....	....	....	....	....	....	....	....
1994-95	**San Jose Sharks**	**NHL**	**47**	**5**	**11**	**16**	**9**	**16**	**25**	**31**	**0**	**0**	**0**	**59**	**8.5**	**45**	**13**	**62**	**16**	**–14**	**10**	**0**	**5**	**5**	**8**	**0**	**0**	**0**
1995-96	**San Jose Sharks**	**NHL**	**60**	**1**	**4**	**5**	**1**	**3**	**4**	**40**	**1**	**0**	**1**	**59**	**1.7**	**51**	**9**	**67**	**16**	**–9**	....	....	....	....	....	....	....	....
	United States	WC-A	8	1	0	1	....	....	....	2	....	....	....	....	....	....	....	....	....	....	....	....	....	....	....	....	....	....
1996-97	Seibu Tetsudo Tokyo	Japan	29	10	28	38	....	....	....	24	....	....	....	....	....	....	....	....	....	....	....	....	....	....	....	....	....	....
	Toronto Maple Leafs	**NHL**	**15**	**1**	**2**	**3**	**1**	**2**	**3**	**9**	**1**	**0**	**0**	**23**	**4.3**	**14**	**7**	**8**	**1**	**0**	....	....	....	....	....	....	....	....
	St. John's Maple Leafs	AHL	1	0	4	4	....	....	....	2	....	....	....	....	....	....	....	....	....	....	....	....	....	....	....	....	....	....
	Utah Grizzlies	IHL	10	1	2	3	....	....	....	8	....	....	....	....	....	....	....	....	....	....	7	1	3	4	4	....	....	....
1997-98	Fort Wayne Komets	IHL	78	12	24	36	....	....	....	87	....	....	....	....	....	....	....	....	....	....	4	2	0	2	4	....	....	....
	NHL Totals		**240**	**20**	**49**	**69**	**23**	**45**	**68**	**142**	**7**	**0**	**4**	**428**	**4.7**	**243**	**81**	**275**	**77**		**24**	**1**	**11**	**12**	**10**	**0**	**1**	**0**

Claimed by **San Jose** from **Minnesota** in Dispersal Draft, May 30, 1991. Signed as a free agent by **Toronto**, December 11, 1996.

• PELENSKY, PERRY

Perry Pelensky RW – R. 5'11", 180 lbs. b: Edmonton, Alta., 5/22/1962. Chicago's 4th choice, 75th overall, in 1981 Entry Draft.

Season	Club	League	GP	G	A	Pts	AG	AA	APts	PIM	PP	SH	GW	S	%	TGF	PGF	TGA	PGA	+/–	GP	G	A	Pts	PIM	PP	SH	GW
1979-80	Fort Saskatchewan Traders	SJHL	59	55	59	114	....	....	....	105	....	....	....	....	....	....	....	....	....	....	....	....	....	....	....	....	....	....
	Portland Winter Hawks	WHL	....	....	....	....	....	....	....	....	....	....	....	....	....	....	....	....	....	....	5	0	0	0	0	....	....	....
1980-81	Portland Winter Hawks	WHL	65	35	32	67	....	....	....	124	....	....	....	....	....	....	....	....	....	....	9	7	2	9	30	....	....	....
1981-82	Portland Winter Hawks	WHL	71	40	46	86	....	....	....	192	....	....	....	....	....	....	....	....	....	....	15	10	5	15	41	....	....	....
1982-83	Springfield Indians	AHL	80	15	25	40	....	....	....	89	....	....	....	....	....	....	....	....	....	....	....	....	....	....	....	....	....	....
1983-84	**Chicago Black Hawks**	**NHL**	**4**	**0**	**0**	**0**	**0**	**0**	**0**	**5**	**0**	**0**	**0**	**4**	**0.0**	**1**	**0**	**1**	**0**	**0**	....	....	....	....	....	....	....	....
	Springfield Indians	AHL	73	22	16	38	....	....	....	185	....	....	....	....	....	....	....	....	....	....	4	0	1	1	9	....	....	....
1984-85	Milwaukee Admirals	IHL	82	21	39	60	....	....	....	222	....	....	....	....	....	....	....	....	....	....	....	....	....	....	....	....	....	....
	NHL Totals		**4**	**0**	**0**	**0**	**0**	**0**	**0**	**5**	**0**	**0**	**0**	**4**	**0.0**	**1**	**0**	**1**	**0**		....	....	....	....	....	....	....	....

• PELLERIN, SCOTT

Scott Pellerin LW – L. 5'11", 180 lbs. b: Shediac, N.B., 1/9/1970. New Jersey's 4th choice, 47th overall, in 1989 Entry Draft.

Season	Club	League	GP	G	A	Pts	AG	AA	APts	PIM	PP	SH	GW	S	%	TGF	PGF	TGA	PGA	+/–	GP	G	A	Pts	PIM	PP	SH	GW
1988-89	University of Maine	H.E.	45	29	33	62	....	....	....	92	....	....	....	....	....	....	....	....	....	....	....	....	....	....	....	....	....	....
1989-90	University of Maine	H.E.	42	22	34	56	....	....	....	68	....	....	....	....	....	....	....	....	....	....	....	....	....	....	....	....	....	....
	Canada	WJC-A	7	2	0	2	....	....	....	2	....	....	....	....	....	....	....	....	....	....	....	....	....	....	....	....	....	....
1990-91	University of Maine	H.E.	43	23	25	48	....	....	....	60	....	....	....	....	....	....	....	....	....	....	....	....	....	....	....	....	....	....
1991-92	University of Maine	H.E.	37	*32	25	57	....	....	....	54	....	....	....	....	....	....	....	....	....	....	....	....	....	....	....	....	....	....
	Utica Devils	AHL	....	....	....	....	....	....	....	....	....	....	....	....	....	....	....	....	....	....	3	1	0	1	0	....	....	....
1992-93	**New Jersey Devils**	**NHL**	**45**	**10**	**11**	**21**	**8**	**8**	**16**	**41**	**1**	**2**	**0**	**60**	**16.7**	**29**	**1**	**45**	**16**	**–1**	....	....	....	....	....	....	....	....
	Utica Devils	AHL	27	15	18	33	....	....	....	33	....	....	....	....	....	....	....	....	....	....	2	0	1	1	0	....	....	....
1993-94	**New Jersey Devils**	**NHL**	**1**	**0**	**0**	**0**	**0**	**0**	**0**	**2**	**0**	**0**	**0**	**0**	**0.0**	**0**	**0**	**0**	**0**	**0**	....	....	....	....	....	....	....	....
	Albany River Rats	AHL	73	28	46	74	....	....	....	84	....	....	....	....	....	....	....	....	....	....	5	2	1	3	11	....	....	....
1994-95	Albany River Rats	AHL	74	23	33	56	....	....	....	95	....	....	....	....	....	....	....	....	....	....	14	6	4	10	8	....	....	....
1995-96	**New Jersey Devils**	**NHL**	**6**	**2**	**1**	**3**	**2**	**1**	**3**	**0**	**0**	**0**	**0**	**9**	**22.2**	**4**	**0**	**3**	**0**	**+1**	....	....	....	....	....	....	....	....
	Albany River Rats	AHL	75	35	47	82	....	....	....	142	....	....	....	....	....	....	....	....	....	....	4	0	3	3	10	....	....	....
1996-97	**St. Louis Blues**	**NHL**	**54**	**8**	**10**	**18**	**8**	**9**	**17**	**35**	**0**	**2**	**2**	**76**	**10.5**	**32**	**0**	**34**	**14**	**+12**	**6**	**0**	**0**	**0**	**6**	**0**	**0**	**0**
	Worcester IceCats	AHL	24	10	16	26	....	....	....	37	....	....	....	....	....	....	....	....	....	....	....	....	....	....	....	....	....	....
1997-98	**St. Louis Blues**	**NHL**	**80**	**8**	**21**	**29**	**9**	**20**	**29**	**62**	**1**	**1**	**0**	**96**	**8.3**	**47**	**1**	**58**	**26**	**+14**	**10**	**0**	**2**	**2**	**10**	**0**	**0**	**0**
	NHL Totals		**186**	**28**	**43**	**71**	**27**	**38**	**65**	**140**	**2**	**5**	**2**	**241**	**11.6**	**112**	**2**	**140**	**56**		**16**	**0**	**2**	**2**	**16**	**0**	**0**	**0**

Hockey East First All-Star Team (1992) • NCAA East First All-American Team (1992) • Won Hobey Baker Memorial Award (Top U.S. Collegiate Player) (1992)

Signed as a free agent by **St. Louis**, July 10, 1996.

• PELLETIER, ROGER

Roger Pelletier D – R. 5'11", 195 lbs. b: Montreal, Que., 6/22/1945.

Season	Club	League	GP	G	A	Pts	AG	AA	APts	PIM	PP	SH	GW	S	%	TGF	PGF	TGA	PGA	+/–	GP	G	A	Pts	PIM	PP	SH	GW
1965-66	Thetford Mines Aces	QJHL	STATISTICS NOT AVAILABLE																									
	Quebec Aces	AHL	1	0	1	1	....	....	....	0	....	....	....	....	....	....	....	....	....	....	....	....	....	....	....	....	....	....
1966-67	Quebec Aces	AHL	31	0	1	1	....	....	....	24	....	....	....	....	....	....	....	....	....	....	3	0	0	0	4	....	....	....
1967-68	**Philadelphia Flyers**	**NHL**	**1**	**0**	**0**	**0**	**0**	**0**	**0**	**0**	**0**	**0**	**0**	**0**	**0.0**	**0**	**0**	**0**	**0**	**0**	....	....	....	....	....	....	....	....
	Quebec Aces	AHL	56	5	8	13	....	....	....	42	....	....	....	....	....	....	....	....	....	....	15	0	0	0	8	....	....	....
1968-69	Quebec Aces	AHL	64	2	14	16	....	....	....	66	....	....	....	....	....	....	....	....	....	....	4	0	0	0	6	....	....	....
1969-70	Quebec Aces	AHL	44	3	4	7	....	....	....	26	....	....	....	....	....	....	....	....	....	....	6	0	0	0	2	....	....	....
1970-71	Quebec Aces	AHL	71	3	14	17	....	....	....	123	....	....	....	....	....	....	....	....	....	....	1	0	0	0	0	....	....	....
1971-72	Richmond Robins	AHL	58	5	11	16	....	....	....	62	....	....	....	....	....	....	....	....	....	....	....	....	....	....	....	....	....	....
1972-73	Richmond Robins	AHL	76	6	18	24	....	....	....	93	....	....	....	....	....	....	....	....	....	....	4	1	0	1	6	....	....	....
1973-74	Richmond Robins	AHL	41	1	7	8	....	....	....	49	....	....	....	....	....	....	....	....	....	....	....	....	....	....	....	....	....	....
	Springfield Kings	AHL	26	1	12	13	....	....	....	37	....	....	....	....	....	....	....	....	....	....	....	....	....	....	....	....	....	....
	NHL Totals		**1**	**0**	**0**	**0**	**0**	**0**	**0**	**0**	**0**	**0**	**0**	**0**	**0.0**	**0**	**0**	**0**	**0**		....	....	....	....	....	....	....	....

NHL rights transferred to **Philadelphia** after NHL club purchased **Quebec** (AHL) franchise, May 8, 1967. Claimed by **Quebec** (AHL) from **Philadelphia** in Reverse Draft, June, 1969. Traded to **Springfield** (AHL) by **Richmond** (AHL) for Doug Volmar, February, 1974.

• PELOFFY, ANDRE

Andre Peloffy C – L. 5'8", 160 lbs. b: Sote, France, 2/25/1951. NY Rangers' 12th choice, 111th overall, in 1971 Amateur Draft.

Season	Club	League	GP	G	A	Pts	AG	AA	APts	PIM	PP	SH	GW	S	%	TGF	PGF	TGA	PGA	+/–	GP	G	A	Pts	PIM	PP	SH	GW
1969-70	Laval Saints	QJHL	56	37	43	80	....	....	....	67	....	....	....	....	....	....	....	....	....	....	....	....	....	....	....	....	....	....
1970-71	Rosemount Nationals	QJHL	60	49	69	118	....	....	....	67	....	....	....	....	....	....	....	....	....	....	....	....	....	....	....	....	....	....
1971-72	New Haven Blades	EHL	42	32	44	76	....	....	....	31	....	....	....	....	....	....	....	....	....	....	7	2	5	7	0	....	....	....
	Providence Reds	AHL	2	1	2	3	....	....	....	0	....	....	....	....	....	....	....	....	....	....	....	....	....	....	....	....	....	....
1972-73	Providence Reds	AHL	62	16	23	39	....	....	....	24	....	....	....	....	....	....	....	....	....	....	3	2	1	3	2	....	....	....
1973-74	Providence Reds	AHL	72	26	45	71	....	....	....	52	....	....	....	....	....	....	....	....	....	....	14	7	5	12	12	....	....	....
1974-75	**Washington Capitals**	**NHL**	**9**	**0**	**0**	**0**	**0**	**0**	**0**	**0**	**0**	**0**	**0**	**7**	**0.0**	**2**	**1**	**9**	**0**	**–8**	....	....	....	....	....	....	....	....
	Richmond Robins	AHL	62	29	44	73	....	....	....	84	....	....	....	....	....	....	....	....	....	....	7	0	4	4	2	....	....	....
1975-76	Richmond Robins	AHL	67	29	30	59	....	....	....	78	....	....	....	....	....	....	....	....	....	....	8	2	1	3	8	....	....	....
1976-77	Springfield Indians	AHL	79	42	57	*99	....	....	....	106	....	....	....	....	....	....	....	....	....	....	....	....	....	....	....	....	....	....
1977-78	New England Whalers	WHA	10	2	0	2	....	....	....	2	....	....	....	....	....	....	....	....	....	....	2	0	0	0	0	....	....	....
	Springfield Indians	AHL	67	33	55	88	....	....	....	73	....	....	....	....	....	....	....	....	....	....	4	2	3	5	8	....	....	....
1978-79	Springfield Indians	AHL	77	28	48	76	....	....	....	138	....	....	....	....	....	....	....	....	....	....	....	....	....	....	....	....	....	....
1979-80	ASG Tours	France	....	42	24	66	....	....	....	....	....	....	....	....	....	....	....	....	....	....	....	....	....	....	....	....	....	....
1980-81	Heraklith	Austria	34	45	42	87	....	....	....	79	....	....	....	....	....	....	....	....	....	....	....	....	....	....	....	....	....	....
	Springfield Indians	AHL	7	2	0	2	....	....	....	6	....	....	....	....	....	....	....	....	....	....	6	2	5	7	2	....	....	....
	France	WEC-C	7	7	8	15	....	....	....	6	....	....	....	....	....	....	....	....	....	....	....	....	....	....	....	....	....	....
1981-82	Heraklith	Austria	....	29	45	74	....	....	....	....	....	....	....	....	....	....	....	....	....	....	....	15	13	28	....	....	....	....
	France	WEC-C	7	7	4	11	....	....	....	6	....	....	....	....	....	....	....	....	....	....	....	....	....	....	....	....	....	....

			REGULAR SEASON																		PLAYOFFS							
Season	Club	League	GP	G	A	Pts	AG	AA	APts	PIM	PP	SH	GW	S	%	TGF	PGF	TGA	PGA	+/–	GP	G	A	Pts	PIM	PP	SH	GW
1982-83	HC St-Gervais	France	....	42	45	87	....	....	....	....	....	....	....	....	....	....	....	....	....	....	....	....	....	....	....	....	....	....
	France	WEC-C	7	7	11	18	....	....	....	4	....	....	....	....	....	....	....	....	....	....	....	....	....	....	....	....	....	....
1983-84	HC St-Gervais	France	....	36	39	75	....	....	....	....	....	....	....	....	....	....	....	....	....	....	....	....	....	....	....	....	....	....
1984-85	HC St-Gervais	France	30	25	*44	69	....	....	....	....	....	....	....	....	....	....	....	....	....	....	....	....	....	....	....	....	....	....
	France	WEC-C	1	2	0	2	....	....	....	0	....	....	....	....	....	....	....	....	....	....	....	....	....	....	....	....	....	....
1985-86	HC St-Gervais	France	....	27	50	77	....	....	....	....	....	....	....	....	....	....	....	....	....	....	....	....	....	....	....	....	....	....
	France	WEC-B	7	3	0	3	....	....	....	0	....	....	....	....	....	....	....	....	....	....	....	....	....	....	....	....	....	....
1986-87	HC St-Gervais	France	STATISTICS NOT AVAILABLE																									
	France	WEC-B	7	2	2	4	....	....	....	4	....	....	....	....	....	....	....	....	....	....	....	....	....	....	....	....	....	....
1987-88	Paris Volants	France	29	30	34	64	....	....	....	20	....	....	....	....	....	....	....	....	....	....	....	....	....	....	....	....	....	....
	France	Olympics	6	0	2	2	....	....	....	0	....	....	....	....	....	....	....	....	....	....	....	....	....	....	....	....	....	....
1988-89	Paris Volants	France	38	14	19	33	....	....	....	20	....	....	....	....	....	....	....	....	....	....	....	....	....	....	....	....	....	....
	NHL Totals		**9**	**0**	**0**	**0**	**0**	**0**	**0**	**0**	**0**	**0**	**0**	**7**	**0.0**	**2**	**1**	**9**	**0**		....	....	....	....	....	....	....	....
	Other Major League Totals		10	2	0	2	....	....	....	2	....	....	....	....	....	....	....	....	....		2	0	0	0	0	....	....	....

EHL North Rookie of the Year (1972) • Won John B. Sollenberger Trophy (Top Scorer - AHL) (1977) • WEC-C All-Star Team (1981, 1983)

Selected by **Quebec** (WHA) in 1972 WHA General Player Draft, February 12, 1972. Traded to **Washington** by **NY Rangers** for cash, July 29, 1974. Signed as a free agent by **New England** (WHA), August, 1977.

• PELTONEN, VILLE

Ville Peltonen LW – L. 5'11", 180 lbs. b: Vantaa, Finland, 5/24/1973. San Jose's 4th choice, 58th overall, in 1993 Entry Draft.

Season	Club	League	GP	G	A	Pts	AG	AA	APts	PIM	PP	SH	GW	S	%	TGF	PGF	TGA	PGA	+/–	GP	G	A	Pts	PIM	PP	SH	GW
1991-92	HIFK Helsinki	Finland	6	0	0	0	....	....	....	0	....	....	....	....	....	....	....	....	....	....	....	....	....	....	....	....	....	....
1992-93	HIFK Helsinki	Finland	46	13	24	37	....	....	....	16	....	....	....	....	....	....	....	....	....	....	4	0	2	2	2	....	....	....
	Finland	WJC-A	7	5	6	11	....	....	....	20	....	....	....	....	....	....	....	....	....	....	....	....	....	....	....	....	....	....
1993-94	HIFK Helsinki	Finland	43	16	22	38	....	....	....	14	....	....	....	....	....	....	....	....	....	....	3	0	0	0	2	....	....	....
	Finland	Olympics	8	4	3	7	....	....	....	0	....	....	....	....	....	....	....	....	....	....	....	....	....	....	....	....	....	....
	Finland	WC-A	8	4	1	5	....	....	....	4	....	....	....	....	....	....	....	....	....	....	....	....	....	....	....	....	....	....
1994-95	HIFK Helsinki	Finland	45	20	16	36	....	....	....	16	....	....	....	....	....	....	....	....	....	....	3	0	0	0	0	....	....	....
	Finland	WC-A	8	6	5	11	....	....	....	4	....	....	....	....	....	....	....	....	....	....	....	....	....	....	....	....	....	....
1995-96	**San Jose Sharks**	**NHL**	**31**	**2**	**11**	**13**	**2**	**9**	**11**	**14**	**0**	**0**	**0**	**58**	**3.4**	**26**	**4**	**34**	**5**	**–7**	....	....	....	....	....	....	....	....
	Kansas City Blades	IHL	29	5	13	18	....	....	....	8	....	....	....	....	....	....	....	....	....	....	....	....	....	....	....	....	....	....
	Finland	WC-A	6	3	2	5	....	....	....	6	....	....	....	....	....	....	....	....	....	....	....	....	....	....	....	....	....	....
1996-97	Finland	W Cup	4	1	3	4	....	....	....	0	....	....	....	....	....	....	....	....	....	....	....	....	....	....	....	....	....	....
	San Jose Sharks	**NHL**	**28**	**2**	**3**	**5**	**2**	**3**	**5**	**0**	**1**	**0**	**0**	**35**	**5.7**	**13**	**1**	**22**	**2**	**–8**	....	....	....	....	....	....	....	....
	Kentucky Thoroughblades	AHL	40	22	30	52	....	....	....	21	....	....	....	....	....	....	....	....	....	....	....	....	....	....	....	....	....	....
	Finland	WC-A	7	2	2	4	....	....	....	0	....	....	....	....	....	....	....	....	....	....	....	....	....	....	....	....	....	....
1997-98	Vastra Frolunda	Sweden	45	22	29	51	....	....	....	44	....	....	....	....	....	....	....	....	....	....	7	4	2	6	0	....	....	....
	Finland	Olympics	6	2	1	3	....	....	....	6	....	....	....	....	....	....	....	....	....	....	....	....	....	....	....	....	....	....
	Finland	WC-A	10	4	6	10	....	....	....	8	....	....	....	....	....	....	....	....	....	....	....	....	....	....	....	....	....	....
	NHL Totals		**59**	**4**	**14**	**18**	**4**	**12**	**16**	**14**	**1**	**0**	**0**	**93**	**4.3**	**39**	**5**	**56**	**7**		....	....	....	....	....	....	....	....

Finnish Rookie of the Year (1993) • WC-A All-Star Team (1995)

Traded to **Nashville** by **San Jose** for Nashville's 5th round choice (later traded to Phoenix - Phoenix selected Josh Blackburn) in 1998 Entry Draft, June 26, 1998.

• PELUSO, MIKE

Mike Peluso LW – L. 6'4", 225 lbs. b: Pengilly, MN, 11/8/1965. New Jersey's 10th choice, 190th overall, in 1984 Entry Draft.

Season	Club	League	GP	G	A	Pts	AG	AA	APts	PIM	PP	SH	GW	S	%	TGF	PGF	TGA	PGA	+/–	GP	G	A	Pts	PIM	PP	SH	GW
1983-84	Greenway High School	H.S.	12	5	15	20	....	....	....	30	....	....	....	....	....	....	....	....	....	....	....	....	....	....	....	....	....	....
1984-85	Stratford Collitons	OJHL	52	11	45	56	....	....	....	114	....	....	....	....	....	....	....	....	....	....	....	....	....	....	....	....	....	....
1985-86	University of Alaska-Anchorage	G.N.	32	2	11	13	....	....	....	59	....	....	....	....	....	....	....	....	....	....	....	....	....	....	....	....	....	....
1986-87	University of Alaska-Anchorage	G.N.	30	5	21	26	....	....	....	68	....	....	....	....	....	....	....	....	....	....	....	....	....	....	....	....	....	....
1987-88	Universwity of Alaska-Anchorage	G.N.	35	4	33	37	....	....	....	76	....	....	....	....	....	....	....	....	....	....	....	....	....	....	....	....	....	....
1988-89	University of Alaska-Anchorage	G.N.	33	10	27	37	....	....	....	75	....	....	....	....	....	....	....	....	....	....	....	....	....	....	....	....	....	....
1989-90	**Chicago Blackhawks**	**NHL**	**2**	**0**	**0**	**0**	**0**	**0**	**0**	**15**	**0**	**0**	**0**	**0**	**0.0**	**0**	**0**	**0**	**0**	**0**	....	....	....	....	....	....	....	....
	Indianapolis Ice	IHL	75	7	10	17	....	....	....	279	....	....	....	....	....	....	....	....	....	....	14	0	1	1	58	....	....	....
1990-91	**Chicago Blackhawks**	**NHL**	**53**	**6**	**1**	**7**	**5**	**1**	**6**	**320**	**2**	**0**	**0**	**29**	**20.7**	**12**	**2**	**13**	**0**	**–3**	**3**	**0**	**0**	**0**	**2**	**0**	**0**	**0**
	Indianapolis Ice	IHL	6	2	1	3	....	....	....	21	....	....	....	....	....	....	....	....	....	....	5	0	2	2	40	....	....	....
1991-92	**Chicago Blackhawks**	**NHL**	**63**	**6**	**3**	**9**	**5**	**2**	**7**	***408**	**2**	**0**	**0**	**32**	**18.8**	**15**	**3**	**13**	**2**	**+1**	**17**	**1**	**2**	**3**	**8**	**0**	**0**	**1**
	Indianapolis Ice	IHL	4	0	1	1	....	....	....	15	....	....	....	....	....	....	....	....	....	....	....	....	....	....	....	....	....	....
1992-93	**Ottawa Senators**	**NHL**	**81**	**15**	**10**	**25**	**12**	**7**	**19**	**318**	**2**	**0**	**1**	**93**	**16.1**	**34**	**5**	**64**	**0**	**–35**	....	....	....	....	....	....	....	....
1993-94	**New Jersey Devils**	**NHL**	**69**	**4**	**16**	**20**	**4**	**12**	**16**	**238**	**0**	**0**	**0**	**44**	**9.1**	**33**	**0**	**15**	**1**	**+19**	**17**	**1**	**0**	**1**	***64**	**0**	**0**	**1**
1994-95	**New Jersey Devils**	**NHL**	**46**	**2**	**9**	**11**	**4**	**13**	**17**	**167**	**0**	**0**	**1**	**27**	**7.4**	**19**	**0**	**14**	**0**	**+5**	**20**	**1**	**2**	**3**	**8**	**0**	**0**	**0**
1995-96	**New Jersey Devils**	**NHL**	**57**	**3**	**8**	**11**	**3**	**7**	**10**	**146**	**0**	**0**	**0**	**41**	**7.3**	**17**	**1**	**12**	**0**	**+4**	....	....	....	....	....	....	....	....
1996-97	**New Jersey Devils**	**NHL**	**20**	**0**	**2**	**2**	**0**	**2**	**2**	**68**	**0**	**0**	**0**	**14**	**0.0**	**3**	**0**	**3**	**0**	**0**	....	....	....	....	....	....	....	....
	St. Louis Blues	**NHL**	**44**	**2**	**3**	**5**	**2**	**3**	**5**	**158**	**0**	**0**	**0**	**23**	**8.7**	**7**	**0**	**7**	**0**	**0**	**5**	**0**	**0**	**0**	**25**	**0**	**0**	**0**
	Calgary Flames	**NHL**	**23**	**0**	**0**	**0**	**0**	**0**	**0**	**113**	**0**	**0**	**0**	**8**	**0.0**	**0**	**0**	**6**	**0**	**–6**	....	....	....	....	....	....	....	....
	NHL Totals		**458**	**38**	**52**	**90**	**35**	**47**	**82**	**1951**	**6**	**0**	**2**	**311**	**12.2**	**140**	**11**	**147**	**3**		**62**	**3**	**4**	**7**	**107**	**0**	**0**	**2**

Signed as a free agent by **Chicago**, September 7, 1989. Claimed by **Ottawa** from **Chicago** in Expansion Draft, June 18, 1992. Traded to **New Jersey** by **Ottawa** to complete transaction that sent Craig Billington, Troy Mallette and New Jersey's 4th round choice (Cosmo Dupaul) in 1993 Entry Draft to Ottawa (June 20, 1993), June 26, 1993. Traded to **St. Louis** by **New Jersey** with Ricard Persson for Ken Sutton and St. Louis' 2nd round choice in 1999 Entry Draft, November 26, 1996. Transferred to **NY Rangers** from **St. Louis** as compensation for St. Louis' signing of Larry Pleau as head coach, June 21, 1997. Claimed by **Calgary** from **NY Rangers** in NHL Waiver Draft, September 28, 1997.

• PELYK, MIKE

Mike "Mike Mikita" Pelyk D – L. 6'1", 190 lbs. b: Toronto, Ont., 9/29/1947. Toronto's 3rd choice, 17th overall, in 1964 Amateur Draft.

Season	Club	League	GP	G	A	Pts	AG	AA	APts	PIM	PP	SH	GW	S	%	TGF	PGF	TGA	PGA	+/–	GP	G	A	Pts	PIM	PP	SH	GW
1964-65	Toronto York Steel	Jr. B	....	2	21	23	....	....	....	....	....	....	....	....	....	....	....	....	....	....	....	....	....	....	....	....	....	....
1965-66	Toronto Westclairs	Jr. B	STATISTICS NOT AVAILABLE																									
	Toronto Marlboros	OHA	17	0	3	3	....	....	....	20	....	....	....	....	....	....	....	....	....	....	....	....	....	....	....	....	....	....
1966-67	Toronto Marlboros	OHA	48	2	18	20	....	....	....	146	....	....	....	....	....	....	....	....	....	....	17	3	10	13	35	....	....	....
1967-68	**Toronto Maple Leafs**	**NHL**	**24**	**0**	**3**	**3**	**0**	**3**	**3**	**55**	**0**	**0**	**0**	**18**	**0.0**	**16**	**1**	**13**	**1**	**+3**	....	....	....	....	....	....	....	....
	Tulsa Oilers	CHL	47	0	16	16	....	....	....	131	....	....	....	....	....	....	....	....	....	....	....	....	....	....	....	....	....	....
1968-69	**Toronto Maple Leafs**	**NHL**	**65**	**3**	**9**	**12**	**3**	**8**	**11**	**146**	**0**	**0**	**0**	**67**	**4.5**	**59**	**2**	**71**	**12**	**–2**	**4**	**0**	**0**	**0**	**8**	**0**	**0**	**0**
1969-70	**Toronto Maple Leafs**	**NHL**	**36**	**1**	**3**	**4**	**1**	**3**	**4**	**37**	**0**	**0**	**0**	**47**	**2.1**	**16**	**0**	**36**	**10**	**–10**	....	....	....	....	....	....	....	....
1970-71	**Toronto Maple Leafs**	**NHL**	**73**	**5**	**21**	**26**	**5**	**18**	**23**	**54**	**0**	**0**	**1**	**78**	**6.4**	**71**	**7**	**64**	**17**	**+17**	**6**	**0**	**0**	**0**	**10**	**0**	**0**	**0**
1971-72	**Toronto Maple Leafs**	**NHL**	**46**	**1**	**4**	**5**	**1**	**4**	**5**	**44**	**0**	**0**	**0**	**58**	**1.7**	**28**	**3**	**49**	**22**	**–2**	**5**	**0**	**0**	**0**	**8**	**0**	**0**	**0**
1972-73	**Toronto Maple Leafs**	**NHL**	**72**	**3**	**16**	**19**	**3**	**13**	**16**	**118**	**0**	**0**	**1**	**113**	**2.7**	**89**	**9**	**118**	**18**	**–20**	....	....	....	....	....	....	....	....
1973-74	**Toronto Maple Leafs**	**NHL**	**71**	**12**	**19**	**31**	**12**	**16**	**28**	**94**	**0**	**0**	**1**	**115**	**10.4**	**77**	**8**	**83**	**19**	**+5**	**4**	**0**	**0**	**0**	**4**	**0**	**0**	**0**
1974-75	Vancouver Blazers	WHA	75	14	26	40	....	....	....	121	....	....	....	....	....	....	....	....	....	....	....	....	....	....	....	....	....	....
1975-76	Cincinnati Stingers	WHA	75	10	23	33	....	....	....	117	....	....	....	....	....	....	....	....	....	....	....	....	....	....	....	....	....	....
1976-77	**Toronto Maple Leafs**	**NHL**	**13**	**0**	**2**	**2**	**0**	**2**	**2**	**4**	**0**	**0**	**0**	**9**	**0.0**	**9**	**0**	**22**	**9**	**–4**	**9**	**0**	**2**	**2**	**4**	**0**	**0**	**0**
	Dallas Black Hawks	CHL	62	9	26	35	....	....	....	73	....	....	....	....	....	....	....	....	....	....	....	....	....	....	....	....	....	....
1977-78	**Toronto Maple Leafs**	**NHL**	**41**	**1**	**11**	**12**	**1**	**9**	**10**	**14**	**1**	**0**	**0**	**40**	**2.5**	**34**	**3**	**40**	**10**	**+1**	**12**	**0**	**1**	**1**	**7**	**0**	**0**	**0**
	Tulsa Oilers	CHL	32	2	12	14	....	....	....	35	....	....	....	....	....	....	....	....	....	....	....	....	....	....	....	....	....	....
	NHL Totals		**441**	**26**	**88**	**114**	**26**	**76**	**102**	**566**	**1**	**0**	**3**	**545**	**4.8**	**399**	**33**	**496**	**118**		**40**	**0**	**3**	**3**	**41**	**0**	**0**	**0**
	Other Major League Totals		150	24	49	73	....	....	....	238	....	....	....	....	....	....	....	....	....		....	....	....	....	....	....	....	....

Selected by **Minnesota** (WHA) in 1972 WHA General Player Draft, February 12, 1972. WHA rights traded to **Cincinnati** (WHA) by **Minnesota** (WHA) for future considerations, June, 1974. Loaned to **Vancouver** (WHA) by **Cincinnati** (WHA) for 1974-75 season, June, 1974. Rights traded to **Toronto** by **Cincinnati** (WHA) with the rights to Randy Carlyle for cash, June, 1976.

Season	Club	League	GP	G	A	Pts	AG	AA	APts	PIM	PP	SH	GW	S	%	TGF	PGF	TGA	PGA	+/–	GP	G	A	Pts	PIM	PP	SH	GW
			REGULAR SEASON																		PLAYOFFS							

● **PENNEY, CHAD** Chad Penney LW – L. 6', 195 lbs. b: Labrador City, Nfld., 9/18/1973. Ottawa's 2nd choice, 25th overall, in 1992 Entry Draft.

Season	Club	League	GP	G	A	Pts	AG	AA	APts	PIM	PP	SH	GW	S	%	TGF	PGF	TGA	PGA	+/–	GP	G	A	Pts	PIM	PP	SH	GW
1990-91	North Bay Centennials	OHL	66	33	34	67	....	....	....	56	....	....	....	....	....	....	....	....	....	....	10	2	6	8	12	....	....	....
1991-92	North Bay Centennials	OHL	57	25	27	52	....	....	....	90	....	....	....	....	....	....	....	....	....	....	21	13	17	30	9	....	....	....
	Canada	WJC-A	7	0	0	0	....	....	....	2	....	....	....	....	....	....	....	....	....	....	....	....	....	....	....	....	....	....
1992-93	North Bay Centennials	OHL	18	8	7	15	....	....	....	19	....	....	....	....	....	....	....	....	....	....	....	....	....	....	....	....	....	....
	Sault Ste. Marie Greyhounds	OHL	48	29	44	73	....	....	....	67	....	....	....	....	....	....	....	....	....	....	18	7	10	17	18	....	....	....
1993-94	**Ottawa Senators**	**NHL**	**3**	**0**	**0**	**0**	**0**	**0**	**0**	**2**	**0**	**0**	**0**	**2**	**0.0**	**1**	**0**	**3**	**0**	**–2**	....	....	....	....	....	....	....	....
	P.E.I. Senators	AHL	73	20	30	50	....	....	....	66	....	....	....	....	....	....	....	....	....	....	....	....	....	....	....	....	....	....
1994-95	P.E.I. Senators	AHL	66	16	16	32	....	....	....	19	....	....	....	....	....	....	....	....	....	....	11	2	2	4	2	....	....	....
1995-96	P.E.I. Senators	AHL	79	23	37	60	....	....	....	48	....	....	....	....	....	....	....	....	....	....	3	1	1	2	0	....	....	....
1996-97	Manchester Storm	Britain	39	9	16	25	....	....	....	48	....	....	....	....	....	....	....	....	....	....	6	1	1	2	6	....	....	....
	NHL Totals		**3**	**0**	**0**	**0**	**0**	**0**	**0**	**2**	**0**	**0**	**0**	**2**	**0.0**	**1**	**0**	**3**	**0**		....	....	....	....	....	....	....	....

Memorial Cup All-Star Team (1993)

● **PEPLINSKI, JIM** Jim Peplinski RW – R. 6'3", 210 lbs. b: Renfrew, Ont., 10/24/1960. Atlanta's 5th choice, 75th overall, in 1979 Entry Draft.

Season	Club	League	GP	G	A	Pts	AG	AA	APts	PIM	PP	SH	GW	S	%	TGF	PGF	TGA	PGA	+/–	GP	G	A	Pts	PIM	PP	SH	GW
1977-78	Toronto Marlboros	OHA	66	13	28	41	....	....	....	44	....	....	....	....	....	....	....	....	....	....	....	....	....	....	....	....	....	....
1978-79	Toronto Marlboros	OHA	66	23	32	55	....	....	....	88	....	....	....	....	....	....	....	....	....	....	3	0	1	1	0	....	....	....
1979-80	Toronto Marlboros	OHA	67	35	66	101	....	....	....	89	....	....	....	....	....	....	....	....	....	....	4	1	2	3	15	....	....	....
1980-81	**Calgary Flames**	**NHL**	**80**	**13**	**25**	**38**	**11**	**17**	**28**	**108**	**1**	**0**	**2**	**107**	**12.1**	**54**	**6**	**50**	**0**	**–2**	**16**	**2**	**3**	**5**	**41**	**0**	**0**	**0**
1981-82	**Calgary Flames**	**NHL**	**74**	**30**	**37**	**67**	**24**	**24**	**48**	**115**	**3**	**3**	**5**	**141**	**21.3**	**90**	**13**	**100**	**23**	**0**	**3**	**1**	**0**	**1**	**13**	**1**	**0**	**0**
1982-83	**Calgary Flames**	**NHL**	**80**	**15**	**26**	**41**	**12**	**18**	**30**	**134**	**1**	**0**	**1**	**147**	**10.2**	**73**	**5**	**77**	**4**	**–5**	**8**	**1**	**1**	**2**	**45**	**0**	**0**	**0**
1983-84	**Calgary Flames**	**NHL**	**74**	**11**	**22**	**33**	**9**	**15**	**24**	**114**	**0**	**0**	**1**	**149**	**7.4**	**54**	**6**	**70**	**1**	**–21**	**11**	**3**	**4**	**7**	**21**	**0**	**0**	**0**
1984-85	**Calgary Flames**	**NHL**	**80**	**16**	**29**	**45**	**13**	**20**	**33**	**111**	**0**	**0**	**1**	**174**	**9.2**	**67**	**0**	**77**	**22**	**+12**	**4**	**1**	**3**	**4**	**11**	**0**	**0**	**0**
1985-86	**Calgary Flames**	**NHL**	**77**	**24**	**35**	**59**	**19**	**23**	**42**	**214**	**0**	**1**	**3**	**161**	**14.9**	**84**	**0**	**71**	**18**	**+31**	**22**	**5**	**9**	**14**	**107**	**0**	**0**	**0**
1986-87	**Calgary Flames**	**NHL**	**80**	**18**	**32**	**50**	**16**	**23**	**39**	**181**	**0**	**2**	**3**	**145**	**12.4**	**72**	**0**	**77**	**18**	**+13**	**6**	**1**	**0**	**1**	**24**	**0**	**0**	**0**
1987-88	**Calgary Flames**	**NHL**	**75**	**20**	**31**	**51**	**17**	**22**	**39**	**234**	**0**	**2**	**4**	**128**	**15.6**	**70**	**0**	**68**	**18**	**+20**	**9**	**0**	**5**	**5**	**45**	**0**	**0**	**0**
	Canada	Olympics	7	0	1	1	....	....	....	6	....	....	....	....	....	....	....	....	....	....	....	....	....	....	....	....	....	....
1988-89	**Calgary Flames**	**NHL**	**79**	**13**	**25**	**38**	**11**	**18**	**29**	**241**	**0**	**0**	**2**	**103**	**12.6**	**48**	**0**	**42**	**0**	**+6**	**20**	**1**	**6**	**7**	**75**	**0**	**0**	**0**
1989-90	Calgary Flames	FrTour	4	0	1	1	....	....	....	0	....	....	....	....	....	....	....	....	....	....	....	....	....	....	....	....	....	....
	Calgary Flames	**NHL**	**6**	**1**	**0**	**1**	**1**	**0**	**1**	**4**	**0**	**0**	**0**	**12**	**8.3**	**3**	**0**	**4**	**0**	**–1**	....	....	....	....	....	....	....	....
1990-1994			DID NOT PLAY – RETIRED																									
1994-95	**Calgary Flames**	**NHL**	**6**	**0**	**1**	**1**	**0**	**1**	**1**	**11**	**0**	**0**	**0**	**5**	**0.0**	**3**	**0**	**5**	**0**	**–2**	....	....	....	....	....	....	....	....
	NHL Totals		**711**	**161**	**263**	**424**	**133**	**181**	**314**	**1467**	**5**	**8**	**22**	**1272**	**12.7**	**618**	**30**	**641**	**104**		**99**	**15**	**31**	**46**	**382**	**1**	**0**	**0**

Transferred to **Calgary** after **Atlanta** franchise relocated, June 24, 1980. Signed as a free agent by **Calgary**, April 6, 1995.

● **PERLINI, FRED** Fred Perlini C – L. 6'2", 175 lbs. b: Sault Ste. Marie, Ont., 4/12/1962. Toronto's 8th choice, 158th overall, in 1980 Entry Draft.

Season	Club	League	GP	G	A	Pts	AG	AA	APts	PIM	PP	SH	GW	S	%	TGF	PGF	TGA	PGA	+/–	GP	G	A	Pts	PIM	PP	SH	GW
1979-80	Toronto Marlboros	OHA	67	13	18	31	....	....	....	12	....	....	....	....	....	....	....	....	....	....	4	0	1	1	5	....	....	....
1980-81	Toronto Marlboros	OHA	35	37	29	66	....	....	....	48	....	....	....	....	....	....	....	....	....	....	5	0	0	0	4	....	....	....
1981-82	Toronto Marlboros	OHL	68	47	64	111	....	....	....	75	....	....	....	....	....	....	....	....	....	....	10	4	9	13	9	....	....	....
	Toronto Maple Leafs	**NHL**	**7**	**2**	**3**	**5**	**2**	**2**	**4**	**0**	**1**	**0**	**0**	**12**	**16.7**	**8**	**3**	**7**	**0**	**–2**	....	....	....	....	....	....	....	....
1982-83	St. Catharines Saints	AHL	76	8	22	30	....	....	....	24	....	....	....	....	....	....	....	....	....	....	....	....	....	....	....	....	....	....
1983-84	**Toronto Maple Leafs**	**NHL**	**1**	**0**	**0**	**0**	**0**	**0**	**0**	**0**	**0**	**0**	**0**	**3**	**0.0**	**0**	**0**	**0**	**0**	**0**				....	....	....	....	....
	St. Catharines Saints	AHL	79	21	31	52	....	....	....	67	....	....	....	....	....	....	....	....	....	....	7	1	1	2	17	....	....	....
1984-85	St. Catharines Saints	AHL	77	21	28	49	....	....	....	26	....	....	....	....	....	....	....	....	....	....	....	....	....	....	....	....	....	....
1985-86	Baltimore Skipjacks	AHL	25	6	4	10	....	....	....	6	....	....	....	....	....	....	....	....	....	....	....	....	....	....	....	....	....	....
1986-87	Nottingham Panthers	Britain	35	89	82	171	....	....	....	135	....	....	....	....	....	....	....	....	....	....	4	6	8	14	8	....	....	....
1987-88	Fife Flyers	Britain	35	103	73	176	....	....	....	34	....	....	....	....	....	....	....	....	....	....	8	*20	14	34	0	....	....	....
1988-89	Deeside Dragons	Britain	24	103	60	172	....	....	....	42	....	....	....	....	....	....	....	....	....	....	....	....	....	....	....	....	....	....
1989-90	Trafford Metros	Britain	25	81	59	140	....	....	....	14	....	....	....	....	....	....	....	....	....	....	....	....	....	....	....	....	....	....
1990-91	Blackburn Black Hawks	Britain	21	83	49	132	....	....	....	48	....	....	....	....	....	....	....	....	....	....	....	....	....	....	....	....	....	....
	Telford Tigers	Britain	5	9	8	17	....	....	....	2	....	....	....	....	....	....	....	....	....	....	....	....	....	....	....	....	....	....
1991-92	Streatham Redskins	Britain	23	93	53	146	....	....	....	42	....	....	....	....	....	....	....	....	....	....	6	12	4	16	8	....	....	....
1992-93	Streatham Redskin	Britain	31	135	91	226	....	....	....	20	....	....	....	....	....	....	....	....	....	....	6	17	9	26	4	....	....	....
1993-94	Basingstroke Beavers	Britain	1	0	0	0	....	....	....	0	....	....	....	....	....	....	....	....	....	....	....	....	....	....	....	....	....	....
	Lee Valley Lions	Britain	20	71	47	118	....	....	....	26	....	....	....	....	....	....	....	....	....	....	....	....	....	....	....	....	....	....
1994-95	Guildford Flames	Britain	44	78	57	135	....	....	....	40	....	....	....	....	....	....	....	....	....	....	....	....	....	....	....	....	....	....
1995-96	Guildford Flames	Britain	50	90	56	146	....	....	....	51	....	....	....	....	....	....	....	....	....	....	....	....	....	....	....	....	....	....
1996-97	Guildford Flames	Britain	27	32	18	50	....	....	....	14	....	....	....	....	....	....	....	....	....	....	10	8	6	14	0	....	....	....
	NHL Totals		**8**	**2**	**3**	**5**	**2**	**2**	**4**	**0**	**1**	**0**	**0**	**15**	**13.3**	**8**	**3**	**7**	**0**		....	....	....	....	....	....	....	....

● **PERREAULT, GILBERT** Gilbert Perreault C – L. 6'1", 180 lbs. b: Victoriaville, Que., 11/13/1950. Buffalo's 1st choice, 1st overall, in 1970 Amateur Draft. **HHOF**

Season	Club	League	GP	G	A	Pts	AG	AA	APts	PIM	PP	SH	GW	S	%	TGF	PGF	TGA	PGA	+/–	GP	G	A	Pts	PIM	PP	SH	GW
1966-67	Thetford Canadiens	QJHL	STATISTICS NOT AVAILABLE																									
1967-68	Montreal Jr. Canadiens	OHA	47	15	34	49	....	....	....	10	....	....	....	....	....	....	....	....	....	....	11	8	9	17	5	....	....	....
1968-69	Montreal Jr. Canadiens	OHA	54	37	60	97	....	....	....	29	....	....	....	....	....	....	....	....	....	....	14	5	10	15	10	....	....	....
1969-70	Montreal Jr. Canadiens	OHA	54	51	70	121	....	....	....	26	....	....	....	....	....	....	....	....	....	....	....	....	....	....	....	....	....	....
1970-71	**Buffalo Sabres**	**NHL**	**78**	**38**	**34**	**72**	**40**	**30**	**70**	**19**	**14**	**0**	**5**	**210**	**18.1**	**105**	**48**	**97**	**1**	**–39**	....	....	....	....	....	....	....	....
1971-72	**Buffalo Sabres**	**NHL**	**76**	**26**	**48**	**74**	**28**	**44**	**72**	**24**	**11**	**0**	**1**	**218**	**11.9**	**105**	**50**	**100**	**5**	**–40**	....	....	....	....	....	....	....	....
1972-73	Canada	Summit	2	1	1	2	....	....	....	0	....	....	....	....	....	....	....	....	....	....	....	....	....	....	....	....	....	....
	Buffalo Sabres	**NHL**	**78**	**28**	**60**	**88**	**28**	**50**	**78**	**10**	**8**	**0**	**7**	**234**	**12.0**	**126**	**43**	**74**	**2**	**+11**	**6**	**3**	**7**	**10**	**2**	**1**	**0**	**1**
1973-74	**Buffalo Sabres**	**NHL**	**55**	**18**	**33**	**51**	**18**	**29**	**47**	**10**	**6**	**0**	**7**	**163**	**11.0**	**84**	**29**	**66**	**3**	**–8**	....	....	....	....	....	....	....	....
1974-75	**Buffalo Sabres**	**NHL**	**68**	**39**	**57**	**96**	**36**	**45**	**81**	**36**	**12**	**0**	**8**	**245**	**15.9**	**139**	**60**	**78**	**0**	**+1**	**17**	**6**	**9**	**15**	**10**	**4**	**0**	**1**
1975-76	**Buffalo Sabres**	**NHL**	**80**	**44**	**69**	**113**	**41**	**54**	**95**	**36**	**14**	**0**	**4**	**237**	**18.6**	**142**	**57**	**68**	**0**	**+17**	**9**	**4**	**4**	**8**	**4**	**0**	**0**	**0**
1976-77	Canada	C Cup	7	4	4	8	....	....	....	2	....	....	....	....	....	....	....	....	....	....	....	....	....	....	....	....	....	....
	Buffalo Sabres	**NHL**	**80**	**39**	**56**	**95**	**37**	**46**	**83**	**30**	**7**	**2**	**9**	**196**	**20.0**	**120**	**42**	**75**	**7**	**+10**	**6**	**1**	**8**	**9**	**4**	**0**	**0**	**0**
1977-78	**Buffalo Sabres**	**NHL**	**79**	**41**	**48**	**89**	**40**	**39**	**79**	**20**	**7**	**0**	**7**	**192**	**21.4**	**122**	**36**	**68**	**0**	**+18**	**8**	**3**	**2**	**5**	**0**	**0**	**0**	**1**
1978-79	**Buffalo Sabres**	**NHL**	**79**	**27**	**58**	**85**	**25**	**44**	**69**	**20**	**6**	**0**	**4**	**172**	**15.7**	**116**	**39**	**65**	**0**	**+12**	**3**	**1**	**0**	**1**	**2**	**1**	**0**	**0**
	NHL All-Stars	Chal Cup	3	1	1	2	....	....	....	2	....	....	....	....	....	....	....	....	....	....	....	....	....	....	....	....	....	....
1979-80	**Buffalo Sabres**	**NHL**	**80**	**40**	**66**	**106**	**36**	**51**	**87**	**57**	**10**	**0**	**5**	**180**	**22.2**	**153**	**57**	**65**	**1**	**+32**	**14**	**10**	**11**	**21**	**8**	**3**	**0**	**2**
1980-81	**Buffalo Sabres**	**NHL**	**56**	**20**	**39**	**59**	**16**	**27**	**43**	**56**	**5**	**0**	**3**	**150**	**13.3**	**92**	**34**	**59**	**4**	**+3**	**8**	**2**	**10**	**12**	**2**	**0**	**0**	**0**
1981-82	Canada	C Cup	4	3	6	9	....	....	....	2	....	....	....	....	....	....	....	....	....	....	....	....	....	....	....	....	....	....
	Buffalo Sabres	**NHL**	**62**	**31**	**42**	**73**	**25**	**28**	**53**	**40**	**2**	**0**	**4**	**155**	**20.0**	**103**	**22**	**71**	**9**	**+19**	**4**	**0**	**7**	**7**	**0**	**0**	**0**	**0**
1982-83	**Buffalo Sabres**	**NHL**	**77**	**30**	**46**	**76**	**25**	**32**	**57**	**34**	**8**	**2**	**5**	**192**	**15.6**	**112**	**34**	**95**	**7**	**–10**	**10**	**0**	**7**	**7**	**8**	**0**	**0**	**0**
1983-84	**Buffalo Sabres**	**NHL**	**73**	**31**	**59**	**90**	**25**	**40**	**65**	**32**	**8**	**2**	**7**	**165**	**18.8**	**115**	**37**	**80**	**21**	**+19**	....	....	....	....	....	....	....	....
1984-85	**Buffalo Sabres**	**NHL**	**78**	**30**	**53**	**83**	**25**	**36**	**61**	**42**	**10**	**1**	**1**	**172**	**17.4**	**117**	**44**	**82**	**18**	**+9**	**5**	**3**	**5**	**8**	**4**	**1**	**0**	**0**
1985-86	**Buffalo Sabres**	**NHL**	**72**	**21**	**39**	**60**	**17**	**26**	**43**	**28**	**5**	**1**	**3**	**164**	**12.8**	**83**	**23**	**80**	**10**	**–10**	....	....	....	....	....	....	....	....
1986-87	**Buffalo Sabres**	**NHL**	**20**	**9**	**7**	**16**	**8**	**5**	**13**	**6**	**1**	**0**	**1**	**35**	**25.7**	**23**	**6**	**26**	**7**	**–2**	....	....	....	....	....	....	....	....
	NHL Totals		**1191**	**512**	**814**	**1326**	**470**	**626**	**1096**	**500**	**134**	**8**	**81**	**3079**	**16.6**	**1857**	**661**	**1249**	**95**		**90**	**33**	**70**	**103**	**44**	**10**	**0**	**5**

OHA First All-Star Team (1969, 1970) • Won Calder Memorial Trophy (1971) • Won Lady Byng Trophy (1973) • NHL Second All-Star Team (1976, 1977) • Canada Cup All-Star Team (1981)
Played in NHL All-Star Game (1971, 1977, 1978, 1980, 1984)

● **PERREAULT, YANIC** Yanic Perreault C – L. 5'11", 182 lbs. b: Sherbrooke, Que., 4/4/1971. Toronto's 1st choice, 47th overall, in 1991 Entry Draft.

Season	Club	League	GP	G	A	Pts	AG	AA	APts	PIM	PP	SH	GW	S	%	TGF	PGF	TGA	PGA	+/–	GP	G	A	Pts	PIM	PP	SH	GW
1988-89	Trois-Rivières Draveurs	QMJHL	70	53	55	108	....	....	....	48	....	....	....	....	....	....	....	....	....	....	....	....	....	....	....	....	....	....
1989-90	Trois-Rivières Draveurs	QMJHL	63	51	63	114	....	....	....	75	....	....	....	....	....	....	....	....	....	....	7	6	5	11	19	....	....	....
1990-91	Trois-Rivières Draveurs	QMJHL	67	*87	98	*185	....	....	....	103	....	....	....	....	....	....	....	....	....	....	6	4	7	11	6	....	....	....
1991-92	St. John's Maple Leafs	AHL	62	38	38	76	....	....	....	19	....	....	....	....	....	....	....	....	....	....	16	7	8	15	4	....	....	....
1992-93	St. John's Maple Leafs	AHL	79	49	46	95	....	....	....	56	....	....	....	....	....	....	....	....	....	....	9	4	5	9	2	....	....	....
1993-94	**Toronto Maple Leafs**	**NHL**	**13**	**3**	**3**	**6**	**3**	**2**	**5**	**0**	**2**	**0**	**0**	**24**	**12.5**	**7**	**2**	**4**	**0**	**+1**	....	....	....	....	....	....	....	....
	St. John's Maple Leafs	AHL	62	45	60	105				38	....	....	....	....	....	....	....	....	....	....	11	*12	6	10	14	....	....	....
1994-95	Phoenix Roadrunners	IHL	68	51	48	99	....	....	....	52	....	....	....	....	....	....	....	....	....	....	....	....	....	....	....	....	....	....
	Los Angeles Kings	**NHL**	**26**	**2**	**5**	**7**	**4**	**7**	**11**	**20**	**0**	**0**	**1**	**43**	**4.7**	**14**	**2**	**9**	**0**	**+3**	....	....	....	....	....	....	....	....

			REGULAR SEASON																		PLAYOFFS							
Season	Club	League	GP	G	A	Pts	AG	AA	APts	PIM	PP	SH	GW	S	%	TGF	PGF	TGA	PGA	+/-	GP	G	A	Pts	PIM	PP	SH	GW
1995-96	**Los Angeles Kings**	**NHL**	78	25	24	49	25	20	45	16	8	3	7	175	14.3	63	23	56	5	–11								
	Canada	WC-A	8	6	3	9				0																		
1996-97	**Los Angeles Kings**	**NHL**	41	11	14	25	12	12	24	20	1	1	0	98	11.2	33	6	38	11	0								
1997-98	**Los Angeles Kings**	**NHL**	79	28	20	48	33	19	52	32	3	2	3	206	13.6	73	12	77	22	+6	4	1	2	3	6	1	0	0
	NHL Totals		237	69	66	135	77	60	137	88	14	6	11	546	12.6	190	45	184	38		4	1	2	3	6	1	0	0

Canadian Major Junior Rookie of the Year (1989) • QMJHL First All-Star Team (1991)

Traded to **LA Kings** by **Toronto** for LA Kings' 4th round choice (later traded to Philadelphia — later traded to LA Kings — LA Kings selected Mikael Simons) in 1996 Entry Draft, July 11, 1994.

• PERRY, BRIAN

Brian Perry C – L. 5'11", 180 lbs. b: Aldershot, England, 4/6/1944.

Season	Club	League	GP	G	A	Pts	AG	AA	APts	PIM	PP	SH	GW	S	%	TGF	PGF	TGA	PGA	+/-	GP	G	A	Pts	PIM	PP	SH	GW
1963-64	Owen Sound Greys	Jr. B		44	41	*85																						
1964-65	New York Rovers	EHL	8	1	0	1				4																		
	New Glasgow Rangers	NSSHL		12	12	24				12																		
1965-66	New Haven Blades	EHL	71	39	49	88				28											3	0	2	2	0			
	Providence Reds	AHL	8	3	1	4				2																		
1966-67	Providence Reds	AHL	62	23	30	53				10																		
1967-68	Providence Reds	AHL	71	31	38	69				36											8	0	9	9	8			
1968-69	**Oakland Seals**	**NHL**	61	10	21	31	11	20	31	10	0	0	1	75	13.3	42	6	42	0	–6	6	1	1	2	4	0	0	0
1969-70	**Oakland Seals**	**NHL**	34	6	8	14	7	8	15	14	0	0	0	41	14.6	21	5	19	0	–3	2	0	0	0	0	0	0	0
	Providence Reds	AHL	24	10	17	27				4																		
1970-71	**Buffalo Sabres**	**NHL**	1	0	0	0	0	0	0	0	0	0	0	0	0.0	0	0	0	0	0								
	Seattle Totems	WHL	47	12	11	23				24																		
1971-72	Providence Reds	AHL	76	24	25	49				52											5	1	4	5	2			
1972-73	New York Raiders	WHA	74	13	20	33				30																		
1973-74	New York-New Jersey	WHA	71	20	11	31				19																		
1974-75	Syracuse Blazers	NAHL	73	32	56	88				102																		
	San Diego Mariners	WHA																			6	1	2	3	6			
	NHL Totals		96	16	29	45	18	28	46	24	0	0	1	116	13.8	63	11	61	0		8	1	1	2	4	0	0	0
	Other Major League Totals		145	33	31	64				49											6	1	2	3	6			

Claimed by **Oakland** from **Providence** (AHL) in Inter-League Draft, June 6, 1968. Claimed by **Buffalo** from **Oakland** in Expansion Draft, June 10, 1970. Claimed by **Providence** (AHL) from **Buffalo** in Reverse Draft, June, 1971. Selected by **NY Raiders** (WHA) in 1972 WHA General Player Draft, February 12, 1972. Transferred to **San Diego** (WHA) after **New York-New Jersey** (WHA) franchise relocated, April 30, 1974.

• PERSSON, RICARD

Ricard Persson D – L. 6'2", 205 lbs. b: Ostersund, Sweden, 8/24/1969. New Jersey's 2nd choice, 23rd overall, in 1987 Entry Draft.

Season	Club	League	GP	G	A	Pts	AG	AA	APts	PIM	PP	SH	GW	S	%	TGF	PGF	TGA	PGA	+/-	GP	G	A	Pts	PIM	PP	SH	GW
1985-86	Ostersund	Sweden 2	24	2	2	4				16																		
1986-87	Ostersund	Sweden 2	31	10	11	21				28																		
1987-88	Leksands IF	Sweden	31	2	0	2				8											2	0	1	1	2			
1988-89	Leksands IF	Sweden	33	2	4	6				28											9	0	1	1	6			
1989-90	Leksands IF	Sweden	43	9	10	19				62											3	0	0	0	6			
1990-91	Leksands IF	Sweden	37	6	9	15				42																		
1991-92	Leksands IF	Sweden	21	0	7	7				28																		
1992-93	Leksands IF	Sweden	36	7	15	22				63											2	0	2	2	0			
1993-94	Malmo IF	Sweden	40	11	9	20				38											11	2	0	2	12			
1994-95	Malmo IF	Sweden	31	3	13	16				38											9	0	2	2	8			
	Albany River Rats	AHL	3	0	0	0				0											9	3	5	8	7			
1995-96	**New Jersey Devils**	**NHL**	12	2	1	3	2	1	3	8	1	0	0	41	4.9	10	3	3	1	+5								
	Albany River Rats	AHL	67	15	31	46				59											4	0	0	0	7			
1996-97	**New Jersey Devils**	**NHL**	1	0	0	0	0	0	0	0	0	0	0	2	0.0	0	0	0	0	0								
	Albany River Rats	AHL	13	1	4	5				8																		
	St. Louis Blues	**NHL**	53	4	8	12	4	7	11	45	1	0	0	68	5.9	42	5	43	4	–2	6	0	0	0	27	0	0	0
1997-98	**St. Louis Blues**	**NHL**	1	0	0	0	0	0	0	0	0	0	0	0	0.0	0	0	0	0	0								
	Worcester IceCats	AHL	32	2	16	18				58											10	3	7	10	24			
	NHL Totals		67	6	9	15	6	8	14	53	2	0	0	111	5.4	52	8	46	5		6	0	0	0	27	0	0	0

Traded to **St. Louis** by **New Jersey** with Mike Peluso for Ken Sutton and St. Louis' 2nd round choice in 1999 Entry Draft, November 26, 1996.

• PERSSON, STEFAN

Stefan Persson D – L. 6'1", 189 lbs. b: Umea, Sweden, 12/22/1954. NY Islanders' 13th choice, 214th overall, in 1974 Amateur Draft.

Season	Club	League	GP	G	A	Pts	AG	AA	APts	PIM	PP	SH	GW	S	%	TGF	PGF	TGA	PGA	+/-	GP	G	A	Pts	PIM	PP	SH	GW
1974-75	Brynas IF Gavle	Sweden	30	5	7	12				34											6	1	0	1	2			
	Sweden	Nat-Team	11	0	1	1				0																		
1975-76	Brynas IF Gavle	Sweden	34	8	9	17				51											4	0	2	2	10			
1976-77	Brynas IF Gavle	Sweden	31	5	11	16				70											4	1	0	1	2			
	Sweden	Nat-Team	18	4	1	5				34																		
	Sweden	WEC-A	10	2	0	2				20																		
1977-78	**New York Islanders**	**NHL**	66	6	50	56	6	41	47	54	3	0	0	77	7.8	128	66	52	9	+19	7	0	2	2	6	0	0	0
1978-79	**New York Islanders**	**NHL**	78	10	56	66	9	43	52	57	6	0	1	113	8.8	162	78	62	16	+38	10	0	4	4	8	0	0	0
1979-80	**New York Islanders**	**NHL**	73	4	35	39	4	27	31	76	2	0	0	91	4.4	100	47	49	9	+13	21	5	10	15	16	4	0	0
1980-81	**New York Islanders**	**NHL**	80	9	52	61	7	36	43	82	6	0	2	120	7.5	166	86	75	19	+24	7	0	5	5	6	0	0	0
1981-82	Sweden	C Cup	5	0	0	0				2																		
	New York Islanders	**NHL**	70	6	37	43	5	24	29	99	3	0	2	107	5.6	135	55	73	28	+35	13	1	14	15	9	1	0	0
1982-83	**New York Islanders**	**NHL**	70	4	25	29	3	17	20	71	2	0	0	80	5.0	95	34	59	10	+12	18	1	5	6	18	1	0	0
1983-84	**New York Islanders**	**NHL**	75	9	24	33	7	16	23	65	4	0	2	95	9.5	127	36	89	28	+30	16	0	6	6	2	0	0	0
1984-85	**New York Islanders**	**NHL**	54	3	19	22	2	13	15	30	3	0	0	56	5.4	83	22	68	15	+8	10	0	4	4	4	0	0	0
1985-86	**New York Islanders**	**NHL**	56	1	19	20	1	13	14	40	1	0	0	46	2.2	75	28	69	19	–3								
	NHL Totals		622	52	317	369	44	230	274	574	30	0	7	785	6.6	1071	452	596	153		102	7	50	57	69	6	0	0

• PESUT, GEORGE

George Pesut D – L. 6'1", 205 lbs. b: Saskatoon, Sask., 6/17/1953. St. Louis' 2nd choice, 24th overall, in 1973 Amateur Draft.

Season	Club	League	GP	G	A	Pts	AG	AA	APts	PIM	PP	SH	GW	S	%	TGF	PGF	TGA	PGA	+/-	GP	G	A	Pts	PIM	PP	SH	GW
1971-72	Victoria Cougars	WCJHL	38	3	13	16				83																		
	Flin Flon Bombers	WCJHL	25	3	8	11				73																		
	Sakatoon Blades	WCJHL	2	0	0	0				4																		
1972-73	Saskatoon Blades	WCJHL	68	12	25	37				98																		
1973-74	Denver Spurs	WHL	7	0	2	2				19																		
	Richmond Robins	AHL	38	3	5	8				4																		
1974-75	**California Golden Seals**	**NHL**	47	0	13	13	0	10	10	73	0	0	0	33	0.0	48	7	65	8	–16								
	Richmond Robins	AHL	8	0	1	1				7																		
1975-76	**California Golden Seals**	**NHL**	45	3	9	12	3	7	10	57	2	0	0	35	8.6	31	14	29	4	–8								
1976-77	Calgary Cowboys	WHA	17	2	0	2				2																		
	Tidewater Sharks	SHL	14	4	6	10				19																		
	Erie Blades	NAHL	25	5	7	12				62											9	2	1	3	6			
	NHL Totals		92	3	22	25	3	17	20	130	2	0	0	68	4.4	79	21	94	12									
	Other Major League Totals		17	2	0	2				2																		

WCHA Second All-Star Team (1986) • WCJHL First All-Star Team (1973)

Selected by **Cleveland** (WHA) in 1973 WHA Amateur Draft, June, 1973. Traded to **Philadelphia** by **St. Louis** for Bob Stumpf, November, 1973. Traded to **California** by **Philadelphia** to complete transcation that sent Reggie Leach to Philadelphia (May 24, 1974), December 11, 1974. WHA rights traded to **Calgary** (WHA) by **Cleveland** (WHA) for future considerations, June, 1976.

• PETERS, GARRY

Garry Peters C – L. 5'10", 170 lbs. b: Regina, Sask., 10/9/1942.

Season	Club	League	GP	G	A	Pts	AG	AA	APts	PIM	PP	SH	GW	S	%	TGF	PGF	TGA	PGA	+/-	GP	G	A	Pts	PIM	PP	SH	GW
1959-60	Regina Caps	SJHL	37	9	6	15				39											11	4	4	8	12			
1960-61	Regina Caps	SJHL	57	36	46	82				94											10	*10	*12	*22	8			
1961-62	Regina Caps	SJHL	56	45	*69	*114				68																		
1962-63	Regina Pats	SJHL	50	37	39	76				100											4	1	0	1	5			
	Hull-Ottawa Canadiens	EPHL	4	0	1	1				2											1	0	0	0	0			
1963-64	Omaha Knights	CHL	72	32	49	81				82											10	5	9	14	17			

			REGULAR SEASON																		PLAYOFFS							
Season	Club	League	GP	G	A	Pts	AG	AA	APts	PIM	PP	SH	GW	S	%	TGF	PGF	TGA	PGA	+/–	GP	G	A	Pts	PIM	PP	SH	GW
1964-65	Montreal Canadiens	NHL	13	0	2	2	0	2	2	6																		
	Quebec Aces	AHL	4	1	2	3				4																		
	Omaha Knights	CHL	43	21	23	44				56																		
1965-66	New York Rangers	NHL	63	7	3	10	8	3	11	42																		
1966-67	Montreal Canadiens	NHL	4	0	1	1	0	1	1	2																		
	Houston Apollos	CHL	50	21	31	52				90																		
1967-68	Philadelphia Flyers	NHL	31	7	5	12	9	5	14	22	1	0	1	79	8.9	16	4	20	6	–2								
1968-69	Philadelphia Flyers	NHL	66	8	6	14	9	6	15	49	1	1	2	166	4.8	21	3	55	17	–20	4	1	1	2	16	0	0	1
1969-70	Philadelphia Flyers	NHL	59	6	10	16	7	10	17	69	1	0	0	102	5.9	20	3	43	17	–9								
1970-71	Philadelphia Flyers	NHL	73	6	7	13	6	6	12	69	0	2	2	135	4.4	17	0	47	16	–14	4	1	1	2	15	0	0	0
1971-72	Boston Bruins	NHL	2	0	0	0	0	0	0	2	0	0	0	1	0.0	0	0	0	0	0	1	0	0	0	0	0	0	0
	Boston Braves	AHL	58	39	34	73				118											8	1	2	3	4			
1972-73	New York Raiders	WHA	23	2	7	9				24																		
1973-74	New York-New Jersey	WHA	34	2	5	7				18																		
	NHL Totals		311	34	34	68	39	33	72	261	3	3	5	483	7.0	74	10	165	56		9	2	2	4	31	0	0	1
	Other Major League Totals		57	4	12	16				42																		

Shared Ken McKenzie Trophy (CHL's Rookie of the Year) with Poul Popiel (1964) • AHL First All-Star Team (1972) • Won Les Cunningham Award (MVP - AHL) (1972)

Traded to **NY Rangers** by **Montreal** with Cesare Maniago for Noel Price, Gord Labossiere and Dave McComb, June 8, 1965. Traded to **Montreal** by **NY Rangers** with Ted Taylor for Red Berenson, June 13, 1966. Claimed by **Philadelphia** from **Montreal** in Expansion Draft, June 6, 1967. Claimed by **Boston** from **Philadelphia** in Intra-League Draft, June 8, 1971. Selected by **NY Raiders** (WHA) in 1972 WHA General Player Draft, February 12, 1972. Claimed by **NY Islanders** from **Boston** in Expansion Draft, June 6, 1972.

• PETERS, JIMMY JR.

Jimmy Jr. Peters C – L. 6'2", 185 lbs. b: Montreal, Que., 6/20/1944.

Season	Club	League	GP	G	A	Pts	AG	AA	APts	PIM	PP	SH	GW	S	%	TGF	PGF	TGA	PGA	+/–	GP	G	A	Pts	PIM	PP	SH	GW
1961-62	Hamilton Red Wings	OHA	42	4	9	13				4											10	2	2	4	7			
1962-63	Hamilton Red Wings	OHA	50	9	24	33				12											5	3	3	6	4			
1963-64	Hamilton Red Wings	OHA	54	31	45	76				6																		
	Cincinnati Wings	CHL	5	3	0	3				0																		
1964-65	Hamilton Red Wings	OHA	51	36	65	101				12																		
	Detroit Red Wings	NHL	1	0	0	0	0	0	0	0																		
	Memphis Wings	CHL	8	0	1	1				2																		
1965-66	Detroit Red Wings	NHL	6	1	1	2	1	1	2	2																		
	Memphis Wings	CHL	64	15	28	43				2																		
1966-67	Detroit Red Wings	NHL	2	0	0	0	0	0	0	0																		
	Pittsburgh Hornets	AHL	16	2	5	7				0																		
	Memphis Wings	CHL	51	6	19	25				10											7	1	2	3	2			
1967-68	Detroit Red Wings	NHL	45	5	6	11	6	6	12	8	1	0	1	36	13.9	12	3	21	2	–10								
	Fort Worth Wings	CHL	20	10	18	28				13																		
1968-69	Los Angeles Kings	NHL	76	10	15	25	11	14	25	28	1	0	1	109	9.2	38	5	74	31	–10	11	0	2	2	2	0	0	0
1969-70	Los Angeles Kings	NHL	74	15	9	24	17	9	26	10	2	3	2	118	12.7	33	5	69	28	–13								
1970-71	Springfield Kings	AHL	26	5	14	19				9																		
	Denver Spurs	WHL	42	8	22	30				6											5	2	2	4	2			
1971-72	Seattle Totems	WHL	63	16	36	52				8																		
1972-73	Los Angeles Kings	NHL	77	4	5	9	4	4	8	0	1	1	0	40	10.0	10	2	35	24	–3								
1973-74	Los Angeles Kings	NHL	25	2	0	2	2	0	2	0	0	0	0	19	10.5	2	0	16	12	–2								
	Portland Buckaroos	WHL	42	7	15	22				15											10	4	3	7	0			
1974-75	Los Angeles Kings	NHL	3	0	0	0	0	0	0	0	0	0	0	1	0.0	0	0	1	1	0								
	Springfield Indians	AHL	69	24	37	61				10											15	6	0	6	4			
1975-76	Fort Worth Texans	CHL	76	16	30	46				17																		
	NHL Totals		309	37	36	73	41	34	75	48	5	4	4	323	11.5	95	15	216	98		11	0	2	2	2	0	0	0

Traded to **LA Kings** by **Detroit** for Terry Sawchuk, October 10, 1968. Traded to **Denver** (WHL) by **LA Kings** with LA Kings holding rights of recall for Ed Hoekstra, December, 1970.

• PETERS, STEVE

Steve Peters C – L. 5'11", 186 lbs. b: Peterborough, Ont., 1/23/1960. Colorado's 2nd choice, 64th overall, in 1979 Entry Draft.

Season	Club	League	GP	G	A	Pts	AG	AA	APts	PIM	PP	SH	GW	S	%	TGF	PGF	TGA	PGA	+/–	GP	G	A	Pts	PIM	PP	SH	GW
1976-77	Peterborough Petes	OHA	62	6	10	16				40																		
1977-78	Niagara Falls Flyers	OHA	67	18	38	56				49																		
1978-79	Oshawa 67's	OHA	64	36	56	92				70											5	1	7	8	0			
1979-80	Oshawa 67's	OHA	21	13	14	27				22																		
	Windsor Spitfires	OHA	39	24	30	54				22											16	4	15	19	14			
	Colorado Rockies	NHL	2	0	1	1	0	1	1	0	0	0	0	0	0.0	1	0	0	0	+1								
	Fort Worth Texans	CHL																			2	0	0	0	0			
1980-81	Fort Worth Texans	CHL	34	4	5	9				30																		
	Muskegon Mohawks	IHL	38	6	20	26				8											3	1	0	1	5			
1981-82	Fort Worth Texans	CHL	79	13	28	41				15																		
1982-83	Muskegon Mohawks	IHL	80	38	58	96				35											4	0	4	4	2			
1983-84	SC Riessersee	Germany	46	22	29	51				60																		
1984-85	EHC Chur	Switz.	33	13	10	23																						
1985-86	Saipa	Finland	32	6	8	14				58																		
1986-87	HIFK Helsinki	Finland	40	9	4	13				22											5	1	2	3	4			
1987-88	Miami Valley Sabres	AAHL	12	4	4	8				12																		
1988-89	Tappara Tempere	Finland	38	5	14	19				28											8	0	0	0	18			
1989-90	Saipa Lappeenranta	Finland	43	4	11	15				28																		
	NHL Totals		2	0	1	1	0	1	1	0	0	0	0	0	0.0	1	0	0	0									

• PETERSON, BRENT

Brent Peterson C – R. 6', 190 lbs. b: Calgary, Alta., 2/15/1958. Detroit's 2nd choice, 12th overall, in 1978 Amateur Draft.

Season	Club	League	GP	G	A	Pts	AG	AA	APts	PIM	PP	SH	GW	S	%	TGF	PGF	TGA	PGA	+/–	GP	G	A	Pts	PIM	PP	SH	GW
1974-75	Edmonton Oil Kings	WCJHL	66	17	26	43				44																		
1975-76	Edmonton Oil Kings	WCJHL	70	22	39	61				57											5	4	2	6	7			
1976-77	Portland Winter Hawks	WCJHL	69	34	78	112				98											10	3	8	11	8			
1977-78	Portland Winter Hawks	WCJHL	51	33	50	83				95											3	1	1	2	2			
1978-79	Detroit Red Wings	NHL	5	0	0	0	0	0	0	0	0	0	0	7	0.0	1	0	1	0	0								
1979-80	Detroit Red Wings	NHL	18	1	2	3	1	2	3	2	0	0	0	6	16.7	5	0	7	1	–1								
	Adirondack Red Wings	AHL	52	9	22	31				61											5	0	0	0	6			
1980-81	Detroit Red Wings	NHL	53	6	18	24	5	13	18	24	1	0	1	40	15.0	33	5	40	14	+2								
	Adirondack Red Wings	AHL	3	1	0	1				10																		
1981-82	Detroit Red Wings	NHL	15	1	0	1	1	0	1	6	0	0	0	10	10.0	2	0	16	8	–6								
	Buffalo Sabres	NHL	46	9	5	14	7	3	10	43	0	0	0	41	22.0	25	7	29	8	–3	4	1	0	1	12	1	0	0
1982-83	Buffalo Sabres	NHL	75	13	24	37	11	17	28	38	1	1	0	98	13.3	57	5	57	15	+10	10	1	2	3	28	0	0	1
1983-84	Buffalo Sabres	NHL	70	9	12	21	7	8	15	52	0	0	0	81	11.1	35	2	47	17	+3	3	0	1	1	4	0	0	0
1984-85	Buffalo Sabres	NHL	74	12	22	34	10	15	25	47	2	1	2	104	11.5	45	4	37	14	+18	5	0	0	0	6	0	0	0
1985-86	Vancouver Canucks	NHL	77	8	23	31	6	15	21	94	0	3	2	86	9.3	65	15	95	35	–10	3	2	0	2	9	1	0	0
1986-87	Vancouver Canucks	NHL	69	7	15	22	6	11	17	77	2	1	2	71	9.9	34	3	82	37	–14								
1987-88	Hartford Whalers	NHL	52	2	7	9	2	5	7	40	0	0	0	33	6.1	12	1	41	21	–9	4	0	0	0	2	0	0	0
1988-89	Hartford Whalers	NHL	66	4	13	17	3	9	12	61	0	0	2	56	7.1	22	0	60	40	+2	2	0	1	1	4	0	0	0
	NHL Totals		620	72	141	213	59	98	157	484	6	6	9	633	11.4	336	42	512	210		31	4	4	8	65	2	0	1

Traded to **Buffalo** by **Detroit** with Mike Foligno and Dale McCourt for Danny Gare, Jim Schoenfeld and Derek Smith, December 21, 1981. Claimed by **Vanouver** from **Buffalo** in Waiver Draft, October 7, 1985. Claimed by **Hartford** from **Vancouver** in Waiver Draft, October 5, 1987.

• PETERSON, BRENT

Brent Peterson LW – L. 6'3", 200 lbs. b: Calgary, Alta., 7/20/1972. Tampa Bay's 1st choice, 3rd overall, in 1993 Supplemental Draft.

			REGULAR SEASON																		PLAYOFFS							
Season	Club	League	GP	G	A	Pts	AG	AA	APts	PIM	PP	SH	GW	S	%	TGF	PGF	TGA	PGA	+/-	GP	G	A	Pts	PIM	PP	SH	GW
1991-92	Michigan Tech Huskies	WCHA	39	11	9	20				18																		
1992-93	Michigan Tech Huskies	WCHA	37	24	18	42				32																		
1993-94	Michigan Tech Huskies	WCHA	43	25	21	46				30																		
1994-95	Michigan Tech Huskies	WCHA	39	20	16	36				27																		
1995-96	Atlanta Knights	IHL	69	9	19	28				33											3	0	0	0	0			
1996-97	**Tampa Bay Lightning**	**NHL**	**17**	**2**	**0**	**2**	**2**	**0**	**2**	**4**	**0**	**0**	**0**	**11**	**18.2**	**2**	**0**	**7**	**1**	**–4**								
	Adirondack Red Wings	AHL	52	22	23	45				56											4	3	1	4	2			
1997-98	**Tampa Bay Lightning**	**NHL**	**19**	**5**	**0**	**5**	**6**	**0**	**6**	**2**	**0**	**0**	**0**	**15**	**33.3**	**7**	**0**	**10**	**1**	**–2**								
	Milwaukee Admirals	IHL	63	20	39	59				48											8	5	3	8	22			
	NHL Totals		**36**	**7**	**0**	**7**	**8**	**0**	**8**	**6**	**0**	**0**	**0**	**26**	**26.9**	**9**	**0**	**17**	**2**									

• PETIT, MICHEL

Michel Petit D – R. 6'1", 205 lbs. b: St. Malo, Que., 2/12/1964. Vancouver's 1st choice, 11th overall, in 1982 Entry Draft.

Season	Club	League	GP	G	A	Pts	AG	AA	APts	PIM	PP	SH	GW	S	%	TGF	PGF	TGA	PGA	+/-	GP	G	A	Pts	PIM	PP	SH	GW
1981-82	Sherbrooke Castors	QMJHL	63	10	39	49				106											22	5	20	25	24			
1982-83	St-Jean Castors	QMJHL	62	19	67	86				196											3	0	0	0	35			
	Vancouver Canucks	**NHL**	**2**	**0**	**0**	**0**	**0**	**0**	**0**	**0**	**0**	**0**	**0**	**1**	**0.0**	**0**	**0**	**4**	**0**	**–4**								
1983-84	Canada	Nat-Team	19	3	10	13				58																		
	Vancouver Canucks	**NHL**	**44**	**6**	**9**	**15**	**5**	**6**	**11**	**53**	**5**	**0**	**0**	**78**	**7.7**	**52**	**17**	**42**	**1**	**–6**	**1**	**0**	**0**	**0**	**0**	**0**	**0**	**0**
1984-85	**Vancouver Canucks**	**NHL**	**69**	**5**	**26**	**31**	**4**	**18**	**22**	**127**	**1**	**1**	**1**	**96**	**5.2**	**90**	**26**	**101**	**11**	**–26**								
1985-86	**Vancouver Canucks**	**NHL**	**32**	**1**	**6**	**7**	**1**	**4**	**5**	**27**	**1**	**0**	**0**	**43**	**2.3**	**24**	**7**	**28**	**5**	**–6**								
	Fredericton Express	AHL	25	0	13	13				79																		
1986-87	**Vancouver Canucks**	**NHL**	**69**	**12**	**13**	**25**	**10**	**9**	**19**	**131**	**4**	**0**	**1**	**116**	**10.3**	**85**	**18**	**100**	**28**	**–5**								
1987-88	**Vancouver Canucks**	**NHL**	**10**	**0**	**3**	**3**	**0**	**2**	**2**	**35**	**0**	**0**	**0**	**13**	**0.0**	**11**	**6**	**12**	**3**	**–4**								
	New York Rangers	**NHL**	**64**	**9**	**24**	**33**	**8**	**17**	**25**	**223**	**2**	**0**	**3**	**96**	**9.4**	**89**	**26**	**81**	**21**	**+3**								
1988-89	**New York Rangers**	**NHL**	**69**	**8**	**25**	**33**	**7**	**18**	**25**	**154**	**5**	**0**	**1**	**132**	**6.1**	**101**	**25**	**129**	**38**	**–15**	**4**	**0**	**2**	**2**	**27**	**0**	**0**	**0**
1989-90	**Quebec Nordiques**	**NHL**	**63**	**12**	**24**	**36**	**10**	**17**	**27**	**215**	**5**	**0**	**0**	**137**	**8.8**	**86**	**41**	**124**	**41**	**–38**								
	Canada	WEC-A	8	0	1	1				8																		
1990-91	**Quebec Nordiques**	**NHL**	**19**	**4**	**7**	**11**	**4**	**5**	**9**	**47**	**3**	**0**	**0**	**39**	**10.3**	**24**	**12**	**35**	**8**	**–15**								
	Toronto Maple Leafs	**NHL**	**54**	**9**	**19**	**28**	**8**	**14**	**22**	**132**	**3**	**1**	**2**	**95**	**9.5**	**70**	**26**	**93**	**30**	**–19**								
1991-92	**Toronto Maple Leafs**	**NHL**	**34**	**1**	**13**	**14**	**1**	**10**	**11**	**85**	**1**	**0**	**1**	**61**	**1.6**	**32**	**9**	**51**	**11**	**–17**								
	Calgary Flames	**NHL**	**36**	**3**	**10**	**13**	**3**	**7**	**10**	**79**	**3**	**0**	**0**	**68**	**4.4**	**33**	**6**	**37**	**12**	**+2**								
1992-93	**Calgary Flames**	**NHL**	**35**	**3**	**9**	**12**	**2**	**6**	**8**	**54**	**2**	**0**	**0**	**58**	**5.2**	**27**	**4**	**30**	**2**	**–5**								
1993-94	**Calgary Flames**	**NHL**	**63**	**2**	**21**	**23**	**2**	**16**	**18**	**110**	**0**	**0**	**0**	**103**	**1.9**	**62**	**12**	**64**	**19**	**+5**								
1994-95	**Los Angeles Kings**	**NHL**	**40**	**5**	**12**	**17**	**9**	**18**	**27**	**84**	**2**	**0**	**0**	**70**	**7.1**	**61**	**9**	**61**	**13**	**+4**								
1995-96	**Los Angeles Kings**	**NHL**	**9**	**0**	**1**	**1**	**0**	**1**	**1**	**27**	**0**	**0**	**0**	**12**	**0.0**	**7**	**1**	**7**	**0**	**–1**								
	Tampa Bay Lightning	**NHL**	**45**	**4**	**7**	**11**	**4**	**6**	**10**	**108**	**0**	**0**	**1**	**56**	**7.1**	**43**	**15**	**51**	**13**	**–10**	**6**	**0**	**0**	**0**	**20**	**0**	**0**	**0**
1996-97	**Edmonton Oilers**	**NHL**	**18**	**2**	**4**	**6**	**2**	**4**	**6**	**20**	**0**	**0**	**0**	**30**	**6.7**	**12**	**2**	**26**	**3**	**–13**								
	Philadelphia Flyers	**NHL**	**20**	**0**	**3**	**3**	**0**	**3**	**3**	**51**	**0**	**0**	**0**	**13**	**0.0**	**17**	**0**	**21**	**6**	**+2**	**3**	**0**	**0**	**0**	**6**	**0**	**0**	**0**
1997-98	Detroit Vipers	IHL	9	2	3	5				24																		
	Phoenix Coyotes	**NHL**	**32**	**4**	**2**	**6**	**5**	**2**	**7**	**77**	**1**	**0**	**0**	**34**	**11.8**	**21**	**2**	**28**	**5**	**–4**	**5**	**0**	**0**	**0**	**8**	**0**	**0**	**0**
	NHL Totals		**827**	**90**	**238**	**328**	**85**	**183**	**268**	**1839**	**38**	**2**	**10**	**1351**	**6.7**	**947**	**264**	**1125**	**270**		**19**	**0**	**2**	**2**	**61**	**0**	**0**	**0**

QMJHL First All-Star Team (1982, 1983)

Traded to **NY Rangers** by **Vancouver** for Willie Huber and Larry Melnyk, November 4, 1987. Traded to **Quebec** by **NY Rangers** for Randy Moller, October 5, 1989. Traded to **Toronto** by **Quebec** with Aaron Broten and Lucien Deblois for Scott Pearson and Toronto's 2nd round choices in 1991 (later traded to Washington — Washington selected Eric Lavigne) and 1992 (Tuomas Gronman) Entry Drafts, November 17, 1990. Traded to **Calgary** by **Toronto** with Craig Berube, Alexander Godynyuk, Gary Leeman and Jeff Reese for Doug Gilmour, Jamie Macoun, Ric Nattress, Rick Wamsley and Kent Manderville, January 2, 1992. Signed as a free agent by **LA Kings**, June 16, 1994. Traded to **Tampa Bay** by **LA Kings** for Steven Finn, November 13, 1995. Signed as a free agent by **Edmonton**, October 24, 1996. Claimed on waivers by **Philadelphia** from **Edmonton**, January 17, 1997. Signed as a free agent by **Phoenix**, November 25, 1997.

• PETRENKO, SERGEI

Sergei Petrenko LW – L. 6', 176 lbs. b: Kharkov, USSR, 9/10/1968. Buffalo's 5th choice, 168th overall, in 1993 Entry Draft.

Season	Club	League	GP	G	A	Pts	AG	AA	APts	PIM	PP	SH	GW	S	%	TGF	PGF	TGA	PGA	+/-	GP	G	A	Pts	PIM	PP	SH	GW
1987-88	Moscow Dynamo	USSR	31	2	5	7				4																		
1988-89	Moscow Dynamo	USSR	23	4	6	10				6																		
1989-90	Moscow Dynamo	FrTour	1	0	0	0				0																		
	Moscow Dynamo	USSR	33	5	4	9				8																		
	Moscow Dynamo	SuperS	5	1	1	2				2																		
1990-91	Moscow Dynamo	FrTour	1	0	0	0				0																		
	Moscow Dynamo	USSR	43	14	13	27				10																		
	Moscow Dynamo	SuperS	DID NOT PLAY																									
1991-92	Moscow Dynamo	CIS	31	9	10	19				10																		
	Russia	Olympics	8	3	2	5				0																		
	Russia	WC-A	6	1	0	1				2																		
1992-93	Moscow Dynamo	CIS	36	12	12	24				10											10	4	5	9	6			
	Russia	WC-A	4	0	1	1				2																		
1993-94	**Buffalo Sabres**	**NHL**	**14**	**0**	**4**	**4**	**0**	**3**	**3**	**0**	**0**	**0**	**0**	**7**	**0.0**	**6**	**2**	**7**	**0**	**–3**								
	Rochester Americans	AHL	38	16	15	31				8																		
1994-95	Rochester Americans	AHL	43	12	16	28				16																		
1995-96	Moscow Dynamo	CIS	22	8	7	15				14																		
1996-97	HC Davos	Switz.	41	19	23	42				20											1	0	0	0	0			
	Russia	WC-A	4	2	2	4				4																		
1997-98	Moscow Dynamo	EuroHL	10	7	2	9				4																		
	Moscow Dynamo	CIS	44	14	19	33				8																		
	Russia	WC-A	6	2	4	6				2																		
	NHL Totals		**14**	**0**	**4**	**4**	**0**	**3**	**3**	**0**	**0**	**0**	**0**	**7**	**0.0**	**6**	**2**	**7**	**0**									

• PETROV, OLEG

Oleg Petrov RW – L. 5'8", 175 lbs. b: Moscow, USSR, 4/18/1971. Montreal's 9th choice, 127th overall, in 1991 Entry Draft.

Season	Club	League	GP	G	A	Pts	AG	AA	APts	PIM	PP	SH	GW	S	%	TGF	PGF	TGA	PGA	+/-	GP	G	A	Pts	PIM	PP	SH	GW
1989-90	CSKA Moscow	USSR	30	4	7	11				4																		
	CSKA Moscow	SuperS	1	1	0	1				0																		
1990-91	CSKA Moscow	FrTour	1	0	0	0				0																		
	CSKA Moscow	USSR	43	7	4	11				8																		
1991-92	CSKA Moscow	CIS	42	10	16	26				8																		
1992-93	**Montreal Canadiens**	**NHL**	**9**	**2**	**1**	**3**	**2**	**1**	**3**	**10**	**0**	**0**	**1**	**20**	**10.0**	**6**	**1**	**4**	**1**	**+2**	**1**	**0**	**0**	**0**	**0**	**0**	**0**	**0**
	Fredericton Canadiens	AHL	55	26	29	55				36											5	4	1	5	0			
1993-94	**Montreal Canadiens**	**NHL**	**55**	**12**	**15**	**27**	**11**	**12**	**23**	**2**	**1**	**0**	**1**	**107**	**11.2**	**38**	**5**	**26**	**0**	**+7**	**2**	**0**	**0**	**0**	**0**	**0**	**0**	**0**
	Fredericton Canadiens	AHL	23	8	20	28				18																		
1994-95	**Montreal Canadiens**	**NHL**	**12**	**2**	**3**	**5**	**4**	**4**	**8**	**4**	**0**	**0**	**0**	**26**	**7.7**	**5**	**1**	**11**	**0**	**–7**								
	Fredericton Canadiens	AHL	17	7	11	18				12											17	5	6	11	10			
1995-96	**Montreal Canadiens**	**NHL**	**36**	**4**	**7**	**11**	**4**	**6**	**10**	**23**	**0**	**0**	**2**	**44**	**9.1**	**16**	**3**	**23**	**1**	**–9**	**5**	**0**	**1**	**1**	**0**	**0**	**0**	**0**
	Fredericton Canadiens	AHL	22	12	18	30				71											6	2	6	8	0			
1996-97	Ambri-Piotta	Switz.	45	24	28	52				44																		
	HC Meran	Italy	12	5	12	17				4																		
1997-98	Ambri-Piotta	Switz.	40	30	63	93				60											14	11	11	22	40			
	Russia	WC-A	6	3	3	6				4																		
	NHL Totals		**112**	**20**	**26**	**46**	**21**	**23**	**44**	**39**	**1**	**0**	**4**	**197**	**10.2**	**65**	**10**	**64**	**2**		**8**	**0**	**1**	**1**	**0**	**0**	**0**	**0**

NHL/Upper Deck All-Rookie Team (1994)

• PETROVICKY, ROBERT

Robert Petrovicky C – L. 5'11", 172 lbs. b: Kosice, Czech., 10/26/1973. Hartford's 1st choice, 9th overall, in 1992 Entry Draft.

Season	Club	League	GP	G	A	Pts	AG	AA	APts	PIM	PP	SH	GW	S	%	TGF	PGF	TGA	PGA	+/-	GP	G	A	Pts	PIM	PP	SH	GW
1990-91	Dukla Trencin	Czech.	33	9	14	23				12																		
1991-92	Dukla Trencin	Czech.	46	25	36	61				28																		
	Czechoslovakia	WJC-A	7	3	6	9				10																		
1992-93	**Hartford Whalers**	**NHL**	**42**	**3**	**6**	**9**	**2**	**4**	**6**	**45**	**0**	**0**	**0**	**41**	**7.3**	**18**	**4**	**24**	**0**	**–10**								
	Springfield Indians	AHL	16	5	3	8				39											15	5	6	11	14			

Season	Club	League	GP	G	A	Pts	AG	AA	APts	PIM	PP	SH	GW	S	%	TGF	PGF	TGA	PGA	+/–	GP	G	A	Pts	PIM	PP	SH	GW
1993-94	Dukla Trencin	Slovakia	1	0	0	0				0																		
	Hartford Whalers	**NHL**	**33**	**6**	**5**	**11**	**6**	**4**	**10**	**39**	**1**	**0**	**0**	**33**	**18.2**	**12**	**2**	**12**	**1**	**–1**								
	Springfield Indians	AHL	30	16	8	24				39											4	0	2	2	4			
	Slovakia	Olympics	8	1	6	7				18																		
1994-95	Springfield Falcons	AHL	74	30	52	82				121																		
	Hartford Whalers	**NHL**	**2**	**0**	**0**	**0**	**0**	**0**	**0**	**0**	**0**	**0**	**0**	**1**	**0.0**	**0**	**0**	**0**	**0**	**0**								
	Slovakia	WC-B	6	4	7	11				8																		
1995-96	Springfield Falcons	AHL	9	4	8	12				18																		
	Detroit Vipers	IHL	12	5	3	8				16																		
	Dallas Stars	**NHL**	**5**	**1**	**1**	**2**	**1**	**1**	**2**	**0**	**1**	**0**	**1**	**3**	**33.3**	**4**	**3**	**0**	**0**	**+1**								
	Michigan K-Wings	IHL	50	23	23	46				63											7	3	1	4	16			
	Slovakia	WC-A	5	0	1	1				0																		
1996-97	**St. Louis Blues**	**NHL**	**44**	**7**	**12**	**19**	**7**	**11**	**18**	**10**	**0**	**0**	**1**	**54**	**13.0**	**29**	**6**	**22**	**1**	**+2**	**2**	**0**	**0**	**0**	**0**	**0**	**0**	**0**
	Worcester IceCats	AHL	12	5	4	9				19																		
1997-98	Worcester IceCats	AHL	65	27	34	61				97											10	3	4	7	12			
	Slovakia	Olympics	4	2	1	3				0																		
	NHL Totals		**126**	**17**	**24**	**41**	**16**	**20**	**36**	**94**	**2**	**0**	**2**	**132**	**12.9**	**63**	**15**	**58**	**2**		**2**	**0**	**0**	**0**	**0**	**0**	**0**	**0**

Czechoslovakian First All-Star Team (1992) • WC-B All-Star Team (1995)

Traded to **Dallas** by **Hartford** for Dan Kesa and future considerations, November 29, 1995. Signed as a free agent by **St. Louis**, September 6, 1996.

• PETTERSSON, JORGEN

Jorgen Pettersson LW – L. 6′2″, 185 lbs. b: Gothenburg, Sweden, 7/11/1956.

Season	Club	League	GP	G	A	Pts	AG	AA	APts	PIM	PP	SH	GW	S	%	TGF	PGF	TGA	PGA	+/–	GP	G	A	Pts	PIM	PP	SH	GW
1974-75	Vastra Frolunda	Sweden	29	19	3	22				4																		
	Sweden	WJC-A	DID NOT PLAY																									
1975-76	Vastra Frolunda	Sweden	29	18	8	26				6																		
	Sweden	WJC-A	4	2	1	3				0																		
1976-77	Vastra Frolunda	Sweden	19	15	4	19				4																		
1977-78	Vastra Frolunda	Sweden	16	5	8	13				8																		
1978-79	Vastra Frolunda	Sweden	35	23	11	34				12																		
1979-80	Vastra Frolunda	Sweden	33	17	15	32				18											8	4	*4	*8	8			
1980-81	**St. Louis Blues**	**NHL**	**62**	**37**	**36**	**73**	**31**	**25**	**56**	**24**	**8**	**0**	**5**	**172**	**21.5**	**100**	**26**	**60**	**0**	**+14**	**11**	**4**	**3**	**7**	**0**	**1**	**0**	**2**
1981-82	Sweden	C Cup	5	0	0	0				0																		
	St. Louis Blues	**NHL**	**77**	**38**	**31**	**69**	**30**	**20**	**50**	**28**	**8**	**0**	**2**	**227**	**16.7**	**92**	**29**	**72**	**1**	**–8**	**7**	**1**	**2**	**3**	**0**	**1**	**0**	**0**
1982-83	**St. Louis Blues**	**NHL**	**74**	**35**	**38**	**73**	**29**	**26**	**55**	**4**	**7**	**3**	**4**	**201**	**17.4**	**93**	**29**	**87**	**13**	**–10**	**4**	**1**	**1**	**2**	**0**	**1**	**0**	**0**
	Sweden	WEC-A	10	2	0	2				4																		
1983-84	**St. Louis Blues**	**NHL**	**77**	**28**	**34**	**62**	**23**	**23**	**46**	**29**	**7**	**0**	**7**	**212**	**13.2**	**83**	**25**	**69**	**9**	**–2**	**11**	**7**	**3**	**10**	**2**	**2**	**0**	**1**
1984-85	**St. Louis Blues**	**NHL**	**75**	**23**	**32**	**55**	**19**	**22**	**41**	**20**	**8**	**0**	**3**	**180**	**12.8**	**90**	**34**	**50**	**2**	**+8**	**3**	**1**	**1**	**2**	**0**	**0**	**0**	**0**
1985-86	**Hartford Whalers**	**NHL**	**23**	**5**	**5**	**10**	**4**	**3**	**7**	**2**	**2**	**0**	**0**	**27**	**18.5**	**13**	**7**	**22**	**4**	**–12**								
	Washington Capitals	**NHL**	**47**	**8**	**16**	**24**	**6**	**11**	**17**	**10**	**2**	**0**	**3**	**74**	**10.8**	**35**	**10**	**32**	**3**	**–4**	**8**	**1**	**2**	**3**	**2**	**1**	**0**	**0**
1986-87	Vastra Frolunda	Sweden	STATISTICS NOT AVAILABLE																									
1987-88	Vastra Frolunda	Sweden 2	35	22	21	43				18											11	6	5	11	2			
1988-89	Vastra Frolunda	Sweden 2	STATISTICS NOT AVAILABLE																									
1989-90	Vastra Frolunda	Sweden	36	13	11	24				16																		
1990-91	Vastra Frolunda	Sweden	1	0	0	0				0																		
	NHL Totals		**435**	**174**	**192**	**366**	**142**	**130**	**272**	**117**	**42**	**3**	**24**	**1093**	**15.9**	**506**	**160**	**302**	**32**		**44**	**15**	**12**	**27**	**4**	**6**	**0**	**3**

Signed as a free agent by **St. Louis**, May 8, 1980. Traded to **Hartford** by **St. Louis** with Mike Luit for Mark Johnson and Greg Millen, February 21, 1985. Traded to **Washington** by **Hartford** for Doug Jarvis, December 8, 1985.

• PHAIR, LYLE

Lyle Phair LW – L. 6′1″, 190 lbs. b: Pilot Mound, Man., 8/31/1961.

Season	Club	League	GP	G	A	Pts	AG	AA	APts	PIM	PP	SH	GW	S	%	TGF	PGF	TGA	PGA	+/–	GP	G	A	Pts	PIM	PP	SH	GW
1981-82	Michigan State Spartans	CCHA	42	19	24	43				40																		
1982-83	Michigan State Spartans	CCHA	42	20	15	35				64																		
1983-84	Michigan State Spartans	CCHA	45	15	16	31				58																		
1984-85	Michigan State Spartans	CCHA	43	23	27	50				86																		
1985-86	**Los Angeles Kings**	**NHL**	**15**	**0**	**1**	**1**	**0**	**1**	**1**	**2**	**0**	**0**	**0**	**11**	**0.0**	**4**	**0**	**17**	**1**	**–12**								
	New Haven Nighthawks	AHL	35	9	9	18				15											2	0	1	1	0			
1986-87	**Los Angeles Kings**	**NHL**	**5**	**2**	**0**	**2**	**2**	**0**	**2**	**2**	**0**	**0**	**0**	**4**	**50.0**	**3**	**0**	**4**	**0**	**–1**								
	New Haven Nighthawks	AHL	65	19	27	46				77											7	0	3	3	13			
1987-88	**Los Angeles Kings**	**NHL**	**28**	**4**	**6**	**10**	**3**	**4**	**7**	**8**	**0**	**0**	**0**	**35**	**11.4**	**17**	**3**	**20**	**1**	**–6**	**1**	**0**	**0**	**0**	**0**	**0**	**0**	**0**
	New Haven Nighthawks	AHL	45	15	12	27				26																		
1988-89	New Haven Nighthawks	AHL	11	2	3	5				4																		
	Utica Devils	AHL	58	5	19	24				24											3	0	0	0	2			
	NHL Totals		**48**	**6**	**7**	**13**	**5**	**5**	**10**	**12**	**0**	**0**	**0**	**50**	**12.0**	**24**	**3**	**41**	**2**		**1**	**0**	**0**	**0**	**0**	**0**	**0**	**0**

NCAA Championship All-Tournament Team (1984)

Signed as a free agent by **LA Kings**, June 7, 1985. Traded to **New Jersey** by **LA Kings** for cash, December 13, 1988.

• PHILLIPOFF, HAROLD

Harold Phillipoff LW – L. 6′3″, 220 lbs. b: Kamsack, Sask., 7/14/1956. Atlanta's 2nd choice, 10th overall, in 1976 Amateur Draft.

Season	Club	League	GP	G	A	Pts	AG	AA	APts	PIM	PP	SH	GW	S	%	TGF	PGF	TGA	PGA	+/–	GP	G	A	Pts	PIM	PP	SH	GW
1973-74	Bellingham Bulls	BCHL	61	27	35	62				182																		
	New Westminster Bruins	WCJHL	2	1	0	1				0											11	0	1	1	45			
1974-75	New Westminster Bruins	WCJHL	70	26	32	58				280											18	6	12	18	94			
1975-76	New Westminster Bruins	WCJHL	67	38	51	89				146											15	9	7	16	28			
1976-77	Nova Scotia Voyageurs	AHL	67	6	16	22				155											12	1	2	3	8			
1977-78	**Atlanta Flames**	**NHL**	**67**	**17**	**36**	**53**	**16**	**29**	**45**	**128**	**2**	**0**	**2**	**132**	**12.9**	**85**	**12**	**46**	**0**	**+27**	**2**	**0**	**1**	**1**	**2**	**0**	**0**	**0**
1978-79	**Atlanta Flames**	**NHL**	**51**	**9**	**17**	**26**	**8**	**13**	**21**	**113**	**0**	**0**	**2**	**66**	**13.6**	**38**	**0**	**33**	**0**	**+5**								
	Chicago Black Hawks	**NHL**	**14**	**0**	**4**	**4**	**0**	**3**	**3**	**6**	**0**	**0**	**0**	**13**	**0.0**	**8**	**2**	**10**	**0**	**–4**	**4**	**0**	**1**	**1**	**7**	**0**	**0**	**0**
1979-80	**Chicago Black Hawks**	**NHL**	**9**	**0**	**0**	**0**	**0**	**0**	**0**	**20**	**0**	**0**	**0**	**2**	**0.0**	**1**	**0**	**4**	**0**	**–3**								
1980-81	Dallas Black Hawks	CHL	75	26	37	63				121											2	4	0	4	7			
1981-82	Oklahoma City Stars	CHL	13	1	5	6				44																		
	Fredericton Express	AHL	58	19	28	47				122																		
	NHL Totals		**141**	**26**	**57**	**83**	**24**	**45**	**69**	**267**	**2**	**0**	**4**	**213**	**12.2**	**132**	**14**	**93**	**0**		**6**	**0**	**2**	**2**	**9**	**0**	**0**	**0**

Memorial Cup All-Star Team (1976)

Traded to **Chicago** by **Atlanta** with Pat Ribble, Greg Fox, Tom Lysiak and Miles Zaharko for Ivan Boldirev, Phil Russell and Darcy Rota, March 13, 1979. Traded to **Vancouver** by **Chicago** with Dave Logan for Ron Sedlbauer, December 21, 1979.

• PHILLIPS, CHRIS

Chris Phillips D – L. 6′2″, 200 lbs. b: Fort McMurray, Alta., 3/9/1978. Ottawa's 1st choice, 1st overall, in 1996 Entry Draft.

Season	Club	League	GP	G	A	Pts	AG	AA	APts	PIM	PP	SH	GW	S	%	TGF	PGF	TGA	PGA	+/–	GP	G	A	Pts	PIM	PP	SH	GW
1995-96	Prince Albert Raiders	WHL	61	10	30	40				97											18	2	12	14	30			
	Canada	WJC-A	6	0	0	0				0																		
1996-97	Prince Albert Raiders	WHL	32	3	23	26				58																		
	Canada	WJC-A	7	0	1	1				4																		
	Lethbridge Hurricanes	WHL	26	4	18	22				28											19	4	*21	25	20			
1997-98	**Ottawa Senators**	**NHL**	**72**	**5**	**11**	**16**	**6**	**11**	**17**	**38**	**2**	**0**	**2**	**107**	**4.7**	**56**	**19**	**40**	**5**	**+2**	**11**	**0**	**2**	**2**	**2**	**0**	**0**	**0**
	NHL Totals		**72**	**5**	**11**	**16**	**6**	**11**	**17**	**38**	**2**	**0**	**2**	**107**	**4.7**	**56**	**19**	**40**	**5**		**11**	**0**	**2**	**2**	**2**	**0**	**0**	**0**

WJC-A All-Star Team (1997) • WHL East First All-Star Team (1997) • Canadian Major Junior First All-Star Team (1997)

• PICARD, MICHEL

Michel Picard LW – L. 5′11″, 190 lbs. b: Beauport, Que., 11/7/1969. Hartford's 8th choice, 178th overall, in 1989 Entry Draft.

Season	Club	League	GP	G	A	Pts	AG	AA	APts	PIM	PP	SH	GW	S	%	TGF	PGF	TGA	PGA	+/–	GP	G	A	Pts	PIM	PP	SH	GW
1986-87	Trois-Rivières Draveurs	QMJHL	66	33	35	68				53																		
1987-88	Trois-Rivières Draveurs	QMJHL	69	40	55	95				71																		
1988-89	Trois-Rivières Draveurs	QMJHL	66	59	81	140				170											4	1	3	4	2			
1989-90	Binghamton Whalers	AHL	67	16	24	40				98																		
1990-91	**Hartford Whalers**	**NHL**	**5**	**1**	**0**	**1**	**1**	**0**	**1**	**2**	**0**	**0**	**0**	**7**	**14.3**	**2**	**0**	**4**	**0**	**–2**								
	Springfield Indians	AHL	77	*56	40	96				61											18	8	13	21	18			

			REGULAR SEASON																		PLAYOFFS							
Season	Club	League	GP	G	A	Pts	AG	AA	APts	PIM	PP	SH	GW	S	%	TGF	PGF	TGA	PGA	+/–	GP	G	A	Pts	PIM	PP	SH	GW
1991-92	Hartford Whalers	NHL	25	3	5	8	3	4	7	6	1	0	0	41	7.3	13	3	12	0	–2	....	....	....	....	....	....	....	....
	Springfield Indians	AHL	40	21	17	38	....	....	....	44	....	....	....	....	....	....	....	....	....	....	11	2	0	2	34	....	....	....
1992-93	San Jose Sharks	NHL	25	4	0	4	3	0	3	24	2	0	0	32	12.5	9	2	24	0	–17	....	....	....	....	....	....	....	....
	Kansas City Blades	IHL	33	7	10	17	....	....	....	51	....	....	....	....	....	....	....	....	....	....	12	3	2	5	20	....	....	....
1993-94	Portland Pirates	AHL	61	41	44	85	....	....	....	99	....	....	....	....	....	....	....	....	....	....	17	11	10	21	22	....	....	....
1994-95	P.E.I. Senators	AHL	57	32	57	89	....	....	....	58	....	....	....	....	....	....	....	....	....	....	8	4	4	8	6	....	....	....
	Ottawa Senators	NHL	24	5	8	13	9	12	21	14	1	0	0	33	15.2	17	6	12	0	–1	....	....	....	....	....	....	....	....
1995-96	Ottawa Senators	NHL	17	2	6	8	2	5	7	10	0	0	1	21	9.5	13	5	9	0	–1	....	....	....	....	....	....	....	....
	P.E.I. Senators	AHL	55	37	45	82	....	....	....	79	....	....	....	....	....	....	....	....	....	....	5	5	1	6	2	....	....	....
1996-97	Vastra Frolunda	Sweden	3	0	1	1	....	....	....	0	....	....	....	....	....	....	....	....	....	....	....	....	....	....	....	....	....	....
	Grand Rapids Griffins	IHL	82	46	55	101	....	....	....	58	....	....	....	....	....	....	....	....	....	....	5	2	0	2	10	....	....	....
1997-98	Grand Rapids Griffins	IHL	58	28	41	69	....	....	....	42	....	....	....	....	....	....	....	....	....	....	....	....	....	....	....	....	....	....
	St. Louis Blues	NHL	16	1	8	9	1	8	9	29	0	0	0	19	5.3	11	1	7	0	+3	....	....	....	....	....	....	....	....
	NHL Totals		112	16	27	43	19	29	48	85	4	0	1	153	10.5	65	17	68	0		....	....	....	....	....	....	....	....

QMJHL Second All-Star Team (1989) • AHL First All-Star Team (1991, 1995) • AHL Second All-Star Team (1994) • IHL First All-Star Team (1997)

Traded to **San Jose** by **Hartford** for future considerations (Yvon Corriveau, January 21, 1993), October 9, 1992. Signed as a free agent by **Ottawa**, June 16, 1994. Traded to **Washington** by **Ottawa** for cash, May 21, 1996. Signed as a free agent by **St. Louis**, January 3, 1998.

• PICARD, NOEL

Noel Picard D – R. 6'1", 185 lbs. b: Montreal, Que., 12/25/1938.

Season	Club	League	GP	G	A	Pts	AG	AA	APts	PIM	PP	SH	GW	S	%	TGF	PGF	TGA	PGA	+/–	GP	G	A	Pts	PIM	PP	SH	GW
1960-61	Jersey Devils	EHL	55	2	6	8	....	....	....	55	....	....	....	....	....	....	....	....	....	....	....	....	....	....	....	....	....	....
1961-62	Montreal Olympics	QSHL	STATISTICS NOT AVAILABLE																									
1962-63	Montreal Olympics	QSHL	STATISTICS NOT AVAILABLE																									
	Sherbrooke Castors	QSHL	....	....	....	....	....	....	....	....	....	....	....	....	....	....	....	....	....	....	1	0	0	0	0	....	....	....
1963-64	Omaha Knights	CHL	59	4	25	29	....	....	....	147	....	....	....	....	....	....	....	....	....	....	9	1	2	3	12	....	....	....
1964-65	Montreal Canadiens	NHL	16	0	7	7	0	8	8	33	....	....	....	....	....	....	....	....	....	....	3	0	1	1	0	....	....	....
	Omaha Knights	CHL	50	13	23	36	....	....	....	142	....	....	....	....	....	....	....	....	....	....	....	....	....	....	....	....	....	....
1965-66	Houston Apollos	CHL	58	3	15	18	....	....	....	186	....	....	....	....	....	....	....	....	....	....	....	....	....	....	....	....	....	....
1966-67	Seattle Totems	WHL	63	3	24	27	....	....	....	135	....	....	....	....	....	....	....	....	....	....	10	2	5	7	16	....	....	....
	Providence Reds	AHL	9	0	3	3	....	....	....	17	....	....	....	....	....	....	....	....	....	....	....	....	....	....	....	....	....	....
1967-68	St. Louis Blues	NHL	66	1	10	11	1	10	11	142	0	0	1	120	0.8	54	7	65	14	–4	13	0	3	3	46	0	0	0
1968-69	St. Louis Blues	NHL	67	5	19	24	6	18	24	131	0	0	1	136	3.7	70	10	54	13	+19	12	1	4	5	30	0	0	0
1969-70	St. Louis Blues	NHL	39	1	4	5	1	4	5	88	1	0	0	31	3.2	27	3	28	4	0	16	0	2	2	65	0	0	0
1970-71	St. Louis Blues	NHL	75	3	8	11	3	7	10	119	0	0	1	128	2.3	73	0	91	20	+2	6	1	1	2	26	1	0	0
1971-72	St. Louis Blues	NHL	15	1	5	6	1	5	6	50	0	0	0	34	2.9	15	0	15	1	+1	....	....	....	....	....	....	....	....
1972-73	St. Louis Blues	NHL	16	1	0	1	1	0	1	10	0	0	0	19	5.3	7	0	9	0	–2	....	....	....	....	....	....	....	....
	Atlanta Flames	NHL	41	0	10	10	0	8	8	43	0	0	0	37	0.0	29	1	35	1	–6	....	....	....	....	....	....	....	....
	NHL Totals		335	12	63	75	13	60	73	616	1	0	3	505	2.4	275	21	297	53		50	2	11	13	167	1	0	0

Played in NHL All-Star Game (1969)

Claimed by **St. Louis** from **Montreal** in Expansion Draft, June 6, 1967. Claimed on waivers by **Atlanta** from **St. Louis**, November 25, 1972.

• PICARD, ROBERT

Robert Picard D – L. 6'2", 207 lbs. b: Montreal, Que., 5/25/1957. Washington's 1st choice, 3rd overall, in 1977 Amateur Draft.

Season	Club	League	GP	G	A	Pts	AG	AA	APts	PIM	PP	SH	GW	S	%	TGF	PGF	TGA	PGA	+/–	GP	G	A	Pts	PIM	PP	SH	GW
1973-74	Montreal Jr. Canadiens	QMJHL	70	7	46	53	....	....	....	*296	....	....	....	....	....	....	....	....	....	....	....	....	....	....	....	....	....	....
1974-75	Montreal Jr. Canadiens	QMJHL	70	13	74	87	....	....	....	339	....	....	....	....	....	....	....	....	....	....	....	....	....	....	....	....	....	....
1975-76	Montreal Jr. Canadiens	QMJHL	72	14	67	81	....	....	....	282	....	....	....	....	....	....	....	....	....	....	6	2	9	11	25	....	....	....
1976-77	Montreal Jr. Canadiens	QMJHL	70	32	60	92	....	....	....	267	....	....	....	....	....	....	....	....	....	....	13	2	10	12	20	....	....	....
1977-78	Washington Capitals	NHL	75	10	27	37	10	22	32	101	2	0	4	170	5.9	69	12	106	23	–26	....	....	....	....	....	....	....	....
	Canada	WEC-A	10	1	2	3	....	....	....	4	....	....	....	....	....	....	....	....	....	....	....	....	....	....	....	....	....	....
1978-79	Washington Capitals	NHL	77	21	44	65	19	34	53	85	8	0	2	243	8.6	153	48	138	36	+3	....	....	....	....	....	....	....	....
	NHL All-Stars	Chal Cup	DID NOT PLAY																									
	Canada	WEC-A	7	0	0	0	....	....	....	2	....	....	....	....	....	....	....	....	....	....	....	....	....	....	....	....	....	....
1979-80	Washington Capitals	NHL	78	11	43	54	10	33	43	122	5	0	1	212	5.2	141	48	135	21	–21	....	....	....	....	....	....	....	....
1980-81	Toronto Maple Leafs	NHL	59	6	19	25	5	13	18	68	2	0	0	160	3.8	81	28	112	27	–32	....	....	....	....	....	....	....	....
	Montreal Canadiens	NHL	8	2	2	4	2	1	3	6	1	0	0	12	16.7	7	3	5	0	–1	1	0	0	0	0	0	0	0
1981-82	Montreal Canadiens	NHL	62	2	26	28	2	17	19	106	2	0	0	132	1.5	82	24	47	6	+17	5	1	1	2	7	0	0	0
1982-83	Montreal Canadiens	NHL	64	7	31	38	6	21	27	60	1	0	1	117	6.0	105	18	83	27	+31	3	0	0	0	0	0	0	0
1983-84	Montreal Canadiens	NHL	7	0	2	2	0	1	1	0	0	0	0	7	0.0	7	2	6	0	–1	....	....	....	....	....	....	....	....
	Winnipeg Jets	NHL	62	6	16	22	5	11	16	34	1	1	1	126	4.8	87	7	106	35	+9	3	0	0	0	12	0	0	0
1984-85	Winnipeg Jets	NHL	78	12	22	34	10	15	25	107	0	0	3	151	7.9	123	10	123	41	+31	8	2	2	4	8	1	0	0
1985-86	Winnipeg Jets	NHL	20	2	5	7	2	3	5	17	0	0	1	40	5.0	26	2	34	8	–2	....	....	....	....	....	....	....	....
	Quebec Nordiques	NHL	48	7	27	34	6	18	24	36	1	1	0	131	5.3	101	43	79	19	–2	3	0	2	2	2	0	0	0
1986-87	Quebec Nordiques	NHL	78	8	20	28	7	14	21	71	1	1	3	163	4.9	73	16	101	27	–17	13	2	10	12	10	1	0	0
1987-88	Quebec Nordiques	NHL	65	3	13	16	3	9	12	103	0	1	1	110	2.7	64	7	103	45	–1	....	....	....	....	....	....	....	....
1988-89	Quebec Nordiques	NHL	74	7	14	21	6	10	16	61	2	1	1	102	6.9	71	12	119	32	–28	....	....	....	....	....	....	....	....
1989-90	Quebec Nordiques	NHL	24	0	5	5	0	4	4	28	0	0	0	25	0.0	24	2	36	9	–5	....	....	....	....	....	....	....	....
	Detroit Red Wings	NHL	20	0	3	3	0	2	2	20	0	0	0	14	0.0	17	2	20	7	+2	....	....	....	....	....	....	....	....
	NHL Totals		899	104	319	423	93	228	321	1025	26	5	18	1915	5.4	1231	284	1353	363		36	5	15	20	39	2	0	0

QMJHL Second All-Star Team (1975) • QMJHL West First All-Star Team (1976) • QMJHL First All-Star Team (1977)

Played in NHL All-Star Game (1980, 1981)

Traded to **Toronto** by **Washington** with Tim Coulis and Washington's 2nd round choice (Bob McGill) in 1980 Entry Draft for Mike Palmateer and Toronto's 3rd round choice (Torrie Robertson), June 11, 1980. Traded to **Montreal** by **Toronto** for Michel Larocque, March 10, 1981. Traded to **Winnipeg** by **Montreal** for Winnipeg's 3rd round choice (Patrick Roy) in 1984 Entry Draft, November 4, 1983. Traded to **Quebec** by **Winnipeg** with Mario Marois, November 27, 1985. Traded to **Detroit** by **Quebec** with Greg C. Adams for Tony McKegney, December 4, 1989.

• PICARD, ROGER

Roger Picard RW – R. 6', 200 lbs. b: Montreal, Que., 1/13/1935.

Season	Club	League	GP	G	A	Pts	AG	AA	APts	PIM	PP	SH	GW	S	%	TGF	PGF	TGA	PGA	+/–	GP	G	A	Pts	PIM	PP	SH	GW
1955-56	Montreal Lakeshore Royals	City Jr.	....	22	20	42	....	....	....	28	....	....	....	....	....	....	....	....	....	....	....	....	....	....	....	....	....	....
1956-57	Montreal Lakeshore Royals	QJHL	33	12	21	33	....	....	....	28	....	....	....	....	....	....	....	....	....	....	....	....	....	....	....	....	....	....
1957-58	Granby Victorias	QSHL	STATISTICS NOT AVAILABLE																									
1958-59	Granby Victorias	QSHL	STATISTICS NOT AVAILABLE																									
1959-60	Granby Victorias	QSHL	STATISTICS NOT AVAILABLE																									
1960-61	Granby Victorias	QSHL	STATISTICS NOT AVAILABLE																									
1961-62	Montreal Olympics	QSHL	STATISTICS NOT AVAILABLE																									
1962-63	Montreal Olympics	QSHL	STATISTICS NOT AVAILABLE																									
1963-64	Montreal Olympics	QSHL	STATISTICS NOT AVAILABLE																									
1964-65	Drummondville Eagles	QSHL	STATISTICS NOT AVAILABLE																									
1965-66	Drummondville Eagles	QSHL	37	20	32	52	....	....	....	30	....	....	....	....	....	....	....	....	....	....	....	....	....	....	....	....	....	....
1966-67	Drummondville Eagles	QSHL	35	21	33	54	....	....	....	47	....	....	....	....	....	....	....	....	....	....	....	....	....	....	....	....	....	....
1967-68	St. Louis Blues	NHL	15	2	2	4	2	2	4	21	0	0	0	45	4.4	5	0	9	0	–4	....	....	....	....	....	....	....	....
	Kansas City Blues	CHL	43	15	28	43	....	....	....	82	....	....	....	....	....	....	....	....	....	....	7	0	10	10	21	....	....	....
1968-69	Denver Spurs	WHL	26	6	3	9	....	....	....	8	....	....	....	....	....	....	....	....	....	....	....	....	....	....	....	....	....	....
	Buffalo Bisons	AHL	11	5	4	9	....	....	....	4	....	....	....	....	....	....	....	....	....	....	....	....	....	....	....	....	....	....
	Omaha Knights	CHL	31	9	11	20	....	....	....	41	....	....	....	....	....	....	....	....	....	....	1	0	0	0	0	....	....	....
	NHL Totals		15	2	2	4	2	2	4	21	0	0	0	45	4.4	5	0	9	0		....	....	....	....	....	....	....	....

Signed as a free agent by **St. Louis**, June 6, 1967.

● **PICHETTE, DAVE** Dave Pichette D – L. 6'3", 190 lbs. b: Grand Falls, Nfld., 2/4/1960.

Season	Club	League	GP	G	A	Pts	AG	AA	APts	PIM	PP	SH	GW	S	%	TGF	PGF	TGA	PGA	+/–	GP	G	A	Pts	PIM	PP	SH	GW
			REGULAR SEASON																		PLAYOFFS							
1978-79	Quebec Remparts	QMJHL	57	10	16	26	....	....	....	134	....	....	....	....	....	....	....	....	....	....	6	1	1	2	35	....	....	....
1979-80	Quebec Remparts	QMJHL	56	8	19	27	....	....	....	129	....	....	....	....	....	....	....	....	....	....	5	1	3	4	8	....	....	....
1980-81	**Quebec Nordiques**	**NHL**	**46**	**4**	**16**	**20**	**3**	**11**	**14**	**62**	**2**	**0**	**0**	**47**	**8.5**	**60**	**14**	**50**	**7**	**+3**	**1**	**0**	**0**	**0**	**14**	**0**	**0**	**0**
	Hershey Bears	AHL	20	2	3	5	....	....	....	37	....	....	....	....	....	....	....	....	....	....	....	....	....	....	....	....	....	....
1981-82	**Quebec Nordiques**	**NHL**	**67**	**7**	**30**	**37**	**6**	**20**	**26**	**152**	**3**	**0**	**0**	**84**	**8.3**	**131**	**51**	**94**	**13**	**–1**	**16**	**2**	**4**	**6**	**22**	**1**	**0**	**1**
1982-83	**Quebec Nordiques**	**NHL**	**53**	**3**	**21**	**24**	**2**	**14**	**16**	**49**	**0**	**0**	**0**	**62**	**4.8**	**92**	**27**	**62**	**6**	**+9**	**2**	**0**	**1**	**1**	**0**	**0**	**0**	**0**
	Fredericton Express	AHL	16	3	11	14	....	....	....	14	....	....	....	....	....	....	....	....	....	....	....	....	....	....	....	....	....	....
1983-84	**Quebec Nordiques**	**NHL**	**23**	**2**	**7**	**9**	**2**	**5**	**7**	**12**	**0**	**0**	**0**	**34**	**5.9**	**28**	**8**	**20**	**2**	**+2**	....	....	....	....	....	....	....	....
	Fredericton Express	AHL	10	2	1	3	....	....	....	13	....	....	....	....	....	....	....	....	....	....	....	....	....	....	....	....	....	....
	St. Louis Blues	**NHL**	**23**	**0**	**11**	**11**	**0**	**7**	**7**	**6**	**0**	**0**	**0**	**37**	**0.0**	**37**	**16**	**30**	**4**	**–5**	**9**	**1**	**2**	**3**	**18**	**0**	**0**	**0**
1984-85	**New Jersey Devils**	**NHL**	**71**	**17**	**40**	**57**	**14**	**27**	**41**	**41**	**8**	**0**	**2**	**140**	**12.1**	**101**	**43**	**86**	**8**	**–20**	....	....	....	....	....	....	....	....
1985-86	**New Jersey Devils**	**NHL**	**33**	**7**	**12**	**19**	**6**	**8**	**14**	**22**	**4**	**0**	**1**	**59**	**11.9**	**56**	**22**	**45**	**0**	**–11**	....	....	....	....	....	....	....	....
	Maine Mariners	AHL	25	4	15	19	....	....	....	28	....	....	....	....	....	....	....	....	....	....	....	....	....	....	....	....	....	....
1986-87	Maine Mariners	AHL	61	6	16	22	....	....	....	69	....	....	....	....	....	....	....	....	....	....	....	....	....	....	....	....	....	....
1987-88	**New York Rangers**	**NHL**	**6**	**1**	**3**	**4**	**1**	**2**	**3**	**4**	**0**	**0**	**0**	**7**	**14.3**	**6**	**4**	**5**	**0**	**–3**	....	....	....	....	....	....	....	....
	New Haven Nighthawks	AHL	46	10	21	31	....	....	....	37	....	....	....	....	....	....	....	....	....	....	....	....	....	....	....	....	....	....
1988-89	Cape Breton Oilers	AHL	39	5	21	26	....	....	....	20	....	....	....	....	....	....	....	....	....	....	....	....	....	....	....	....	....	....
1989-90	Halifax Citadels	AHL	58	3	18	21	....	....	....	65	....	....	....	....	....	....	....	....	....	....	....	....	....	....	....	....	....	....
	NHL Totals		**322**	**41**	**140**	**181**	**34**	**94**	**128**	**348**	**17**	**0**	**3**	**470**	**8.7**	**511**	**185**	**392**	**40**		**28**	**3**	**7**	**10**	**54**	**1**	**0**	**1**

Signed as a free agent by **Quebec**, October 31, 1979. Traded to **St. Louis** by **Quebec** for Andre Dore, February 10, 1984. Claimed by **New Jersey** from **St. Louis** in Waiver Draft, October 9, 1984.

● **PIERCE, RANDY** Randy Pierce RW – R. 5'11", 187 lbs. b: Arnprior, Ont., 11/23/1957. Colorado's 3rd choice, 47th overall, in 1977 Amateur Draft.

Season	Club	League	GP	G	A	Pts	AG	AA	APts	PIM	PP	SH	GW	S	%	TGF	PGF	TGA	PGA	+/–	GP	G	A	Pts	PIM	PP	SH	GW
1975-76	Sudbury Wolves	OHA	56	21	44	65	....	....	....	72	....	....	....	....	....	....	....	....	....	....	15	9	16	25	13	....	....	....
1976-77	Sudbury Wolves	OHA	60	38	60	98	....	....	....	67	....	....	....	....	....	....	....	....	....	....	6	2	3	5	7	....	....	....
1977-78	**Colorado Rockies**	**NHL**	**35**	**9**	**10**	**19**	**9**	**8**	**17**	**15**	**1**	**0**	**3**	**60**	**15.0**	**33**	**9**	**24**	**0**	**0**	**2**	**0**	**0**	**0**	**0**	**0**	**0**	**0**
	Hampton Gulls	AHL	3	0	1	1	....	....	....	2	....	....	....	....	....	....	....	....	....	....	....	....	....	....	....	....	....	....
	Phoenix Roadrunners	CHL	12	3	1	4	....	....	....	11	....	....	....	....	....	....	....	....	....	....	....	....	....	....	....	....	....	....
1978-79	**Colorado Rockies**	**NHL**	**70**	**19**	**17**	**36**	**17**	**13**	**30**	**35**	**4**	**1**	**3**	**145**	**13.1**	**58**	**18**	**68**	**7**	**–21**	....	....	....	....	....	....	....	....
	Philadelphia Firebirds	AHL	1	0	0	0	....	....	....	0	....	....	....	....	....	....	....	....	....	....	....	....	....	....	....	....	....	....
1979-80	**Colorado Rockies**	**NHL**	**75**	**16**	**23**	**39**	**14**	**18**	**32**	**100**	**0**	**0**	**1**	**171**	**9.4**	**59**	**9**	**62**	**1**	**–11**	....	....	....	....	....	....	....	....
1980-81	**Colorado Rockies**	**NHL**	**55**	**9**	**21**	**30**	**7**	**15**	**22**	**52**	**3**	**0**	**3**	**124**	**7.3**	**48**	**18**	**65**	**7**	**–28**	....	....	....	....	....	....	....	....
1981-82	**Colorado Rockies**	**NHL**	**5**	**0**	**0**	**0**	**0**	**0**	**0**	**4**	**0**	**0**	**0**	**7**	**0.0**	**0**	**0**	**1**	**0**	**–1**	....	....	....	....	....	....	....	....
	Fort Worth Texans	CHL	15	6	6	12	....	....	....	19	....	....	....	....	....	....	....	....	....	....	....	....	....	....	....	....	....	....
1982-83	**New Jersey Devils**	**NHL**	**3**	**0**	**0**	**0**	**0**	**0**	**0**	**0**	**0**	**0**	**0**	**2**	**0.0**	**2**	**0**	**2**	**0**	**0**	....	....	....	....	....	....	....	....
	Wichita Wind	CHL	14	4	8	12	....	....	....	4	....	....	....	....	....	....	....	....	....	....	....	....	....	....	....	....	....	....
	Binghamton Whalers	AHL	46	14	41	55	....	....	....	33	....	....	....	....	....	....	....	....	....	....	2	0	1	1	0	....	....	....
1983-84	**Hartford Whalers**	**NHL**	**17**	**6**	**3**	**9**	**5**	**2**	**7**	**9**	**0**	**1**	**0**	**25**	**24.0**	**14**	**0**	**16**	**7**	**+5**	....	....	....	....	....	....	....	....
	Binghamton Whalers	AHL	46	22	24	46	....	....	....	41	....	....	....	....	....	....	....	....	....	....	....	....	....	....	....	....	....	....
1984-85	**Hartford Whalers**	**NHL**	**17**	**3**	**2**	**5**	**2**	**1**	**3**	**8**	**0**	**0**	**0**	**24**	**12.5**	**9**	**0**	**21**	**8**	**–4**	....	....	....	....	....	....	....	....
	Binghamton Whalers	AHL	31	6	10	16	....	....	....	45	....	....	....	....	....	....	....	....	....	....	6	2	1	3	6	....	....	....
1985-86	Salt Lake Golden Eagles	IHL	20	5	5	10	....	....	....	25	....	....	....	....	....	....	....	....	....	....	....	....	....	....	....	....	....	....
	NHL Totals		**277**	**62**	**76**	**138**	**54**	**57**	**111**	**223**	**8**	**2**	**10**	**558**	**11.1**	**223**	**54**	**259**	**30**		**2**	**0**	**0**	**0**	**0**	**0**	**0**	**0**

Transferred to **New Jersey** after **Colorado** franchise relocated, June 30, 1982. Signed as a free agent by **Hartford**, October 6, 1983.

● **PILON, RICHARD** Richard Pilon D – L. 6', 205 lbs. b: Saskatoon, Sask., 4/30/1968. NY Islanders' 9th choice, 143rd overall, in 1986 Entry Draft.

Season	Club	League	GP	G	A	Pts	AG	AA	APts	PIM	PP	SH	GW	S	%	TGF	PGF	TGA	PGA	+/–	GP	G	A	Pts	PIM	PP	SH	GW
1985-86	Prince Albert Midget Raiders	Midget	35	3	28	31	....	....	....	142	....	....	....	....	....	....	....	....	....	....	....	....	....	....	....	....	....	....
1986-87	Prince Albert Raiders	WHL	68	4	21	25	....	....	....	192	....	....	....	....	....	....	....	....	....	....	7	1	6	7	17	....	....	....
1987-88	Prince Albert Raiders	WHL	65	13	34	47	....	....	....	177	....	....	....	....	....	....	....	....	....	....	9	0	6	6	38	....	....	....
1988-89	**New York Islanders**	**NHL**	**62**	**0**	**14**	**14**	**0**	**10**	**10**	**242**	**0**	**0**	**0**	**47**	**0.0**	**53**	**9**	**74**	**21**	**–9**	....	....	....	....	....	....	....	....
1989-90	**New York Islanders**	**NHL**	**14**	**0**	**2**	**2**	**0**	**1**	**1**	**31**	**0**	**0**	**0**	**5**	**0.0**	**8**	**0**	**17**	**11**	**+2**	....	....	....	....	....	....	....	....
1990-91	**New York Islanders**	**NHL**	**60**	**1**	**4**	**5**	**1**	**3**	**4**	**126**	**0**	**0**	**0**	**33**	**3.0**	**41**	**1**	**78**	**24**	**–12**	....	....	....	....	....	....	....	....
1991-92	**New York Islanders**	**NHL**	**65**	**1**	**6**	**7**	**1**	**4**	**5**	**183**	**0**	**0**	**0**	**27**	**3.7**	**57**	**2**	**85**	**29**	**–1**	....	....	....	....	....	....	....	....
1992-93	**New York Islanders**	**NHL**	**44**	**1**	**3**	**4**	**1**	**2**	**3**	**164**	**0**	**0**	**0**	**20**	**5.0**	**28**	**0**	**52**	**20**	**–4**	**15**	**0**	**0**	**0**	**50**	**0**	**0**	**0**
	Capital District Islanders	AHL	6	0	1	1	....	....	....	8	....	....	....	....	....	....	....	....	....	....	....	....	....	....	....	....	....	....
1993-94	**New York Islanders**	**NHL**	**28**	**1**	**4**	**5**	**1**	**3**	**4**	**75**	**0**	**0**	**0**	**20**	**5.0**	**17**	**0**	**31**	**10**	**–4**	....	....	....	....	....	....	....	....
	Salt Lake Golden Eagles	IHL	2	0	0	0	....	....	....	8	....	....	....	....	....	....	....	....	....	....	....	....	....	....	....	....	....	....
1994-95	**New York Islanders**	**NHL**	**20**	**1**	**1**	**2**	**2**	**1**	**3**	**40**	**0**	**0**	**0**	**11**	**9.1**	**8**	**1**	**14**	**4**	**–3**	....	....	....	....	....	....	....	....
1995-96	**New York Islanders**	**NHL**	**27**	**0**	**3**	**3**	**0**	**2**	**2**	**72**	**0**	**0**	**0**	**7**	**0.0**	**14**	**0**	**30**	**7**	**–9**	....	....	....	....	....	....	....	....
1996-97	**New York Islanders**	**NHL**	**52**	**1**	**4**	**5**	**1**	**4**	**5**	**179**	**0**	**0**	**0**	**17**	**5.9**	**37**	**0**	**42**	**9**	**+4**	....	....	....	....	....	....	....	....
1997-98	**New York Islanders**	**NHL**	**76**	**0**	**7**	**7**	**0**	**7**	**7**	**291**	**0**	**0**	**0**	**37**	**0.0**	**38**	**0**	**57**	**20**	**+1**	....	....	....	....	....	....	....	....
	NHL Totals		**448**	**6**	**48**	**54**	**7**	**37**	**44**	**1403**	**0**	**0**	**0**	**224**	**2.7**	**301**	**13**	**478**	**155**		**15**	**0**	**0**	**0**	**50**	**0**	**0**	**0**

WHL East Second All-Star Team (1988)

● **PILOTE, PIERRE** Pierre "Pete" Pilote D – L. 5'10", 178 lbs. b: Kenogami, Que., 12/11/1931. **HHOF**

Season	Club	League	GP	G	A	Pts	AG	AA	APts	PIM	PP	SH	GW	S	%	TGF	PGF	TGA	PGA	+/–	GP	G	A	Pts	PIM	PP	SH	GW
1950-51	St. Catharines Teepees	OHA	54	13	13	26	....	....	....	*230	....	....	....	....	....	....	....	....	....	....	9	2	2	4	23	....	....	....
1951-52	St. Catharines Teepees	OHA	52	21	32	53	....	....	....	139	....	....	....	....	....	....	....	....	....	....	14	3	12	15	*50	....	....	....
	Buffalo Bisons	AHL	2	0	1	1	....	....	....	4	....	....	....	....	....	....	....	....	....	....	....	....	....	....	....	....	....	....
1952-53	Buffalo Bisons	AHL	61	2	14	16	....	....	....	85	....	....	....	....	....	....	....	....	....	....	....	....	....	....	....	....	....	....
1953-54	Buffalo Bisons	AHL	67	2	28	30	....	....	....	108	....	....	....	....	....	....	....	....	....	....	3	0	0	0	6	....	....	....
1954-55	Buffalo Bisons	AHL	63	10	28	38	....	....	....	120	....	....	....	....	....	....	....	....	....	....	10	0	4	4	18	....	....	....
1955-56	**Chicago Black Hawks**	**NHL**	**20**	**3**	**5**	**8**	**4**	**6**	**10**	**34**	....	....	....	....	....	....	....	....	....	....	....	....	....	....	....	....	....	....
	Buffalo Bisons	AHL	43	0	11	11	....	....	....	118	....	....	....	....	....	....	....	....	....	....	5	0	2	2	4	....	....	....
1956-57	**Chicago Black Hawks**	**NHL**	**70**	**3**	**14**	**17**	**4**	**16**	**20**	**117**	....	....	....	....	....	....	....	....	....	....	....	....	....	....	....	....	....	....
1957-58	**Chicago Black Hawks**	**NHL**	**70**	**6**	**24**	**30**	**8**	**26**	**34**	**91**	....	....	....	....	....	....	....	....	....	....	....	....	....	....	....	....	....	....
1958-59	**Chicago Black Hawks**	**NHL**	**70**	**7**	**30**	**37**	**9**	**32**	**41**	**79**	....	....	....	....	....	....	....	....	....	....	**6**	**0**	**2**	**2**	**10**	....	....	....
1959-60	**Chicago Black Hawks**	**NHL**	**70**	**7**	**38**	**45**	**9**	**39**	**48**	**100**	....	....	....	....	....	....	....	....	....	....	**4**	**0**	**1**	**1**	**8**	....	....	....
1960-61	**Chicago Black Hawks**	**NHL**	**70**	**6**	**29**	**35**	**7**	**30**	**37**	***165**	....	....	....	....	....	....	....	....	....	....	**12**	**3**	***12**	***15**	**8**	....	....	....
1961-62	**Chicago Black Hawks**	**NHL**	**59**	**7**	**35**	**42**	**8**	**36**	**44**	**97**	....	....	....	....	....	....	....	....	....	....	**12**	**0**	**7**	**7**	**8**	....	....	....
1962-63	**Chicago Black Hawks**	**NHL**	**59**	**8**	**18**	**26**	**10**	**19**	**29**	**57**	....	....	....	....	....	....	....	....	....	....	**6**	**0**	**8**	**8**	**8**	....	....	....
1963-64	**Chicago Black Hawks**	**NHL**	**70**	**7**	**46**	**53**	**9**	**51**	**60**	**84**	....	....	....	....	....	....	....	....	....	....	**7**	**2**	**6**	**8**	**6**	....	....	....
1964-65	**Chicago Black Hawks**	**NHL**	**68**	**14**	**45**	**59**	**18**	**49**	**67**	**162**	....	....	....	....	....	....	....	....	....	....	**12**	**0**	**7**	**7**	**22**	....	....	....
1965-66	**Chicago Black Hawks**	**NHL**	**51**	**2**	**34**	**36**	**2**	**34**	**36**	**60**	....	....	....	....	....	....	....	....	....	....	**6**	**0**	**2**	**2**	**10**	....	....	....
1966-67	**Chicago Black Hawks**	**NHL**	**70**	**6**	**46**	**52**	**7**	**48**	**55**	**90**	....	....	....	....	....	....	....	....	....	....	**6**	**2**	**4**	**6**	**6**	....	....	....
1967-68	**Chicago Black Hawks**	**NHL**	**74**	**1**	**36**	**37**	**1**	**38**	**39**	**69**	**0**	**0**	**0**	**69**	**1.4**	**98**	**22**	**97**	**13**	**–8**	**11**	**1**	**3**	**4**	**12**	**1**	**0**	**0**
1968-69	**Toronto Maple Leafs**	**NHL**	**69**	**3**	**18**	**21**	**3**	**17**	**20**	**46**	**1**	**0**	**0**	**48**	**6.3**	**67**	**13**	**64**	**15**	**+5**	**4**	**0**	**1**	**1**	**4**	**0**	**0**	**0**
	NHL Totals		**890**	**80**	**418**	**498**	**99**	**441**	**540**	**1251**	**1**	**0**	**0**	**117**	**68.4**	**165**	**35**	**161**	**28**		**86**	**8**	**53**	**61**	**102**	**1**	**0**	**0**

NHL Second All-Star Team (1960, 1961, 1962) • NHL First All-Star Team (1963, 1964, 1965, 1966, 1967) • Won James Norris Trophy (1963, 1964, 1965)
Played in NHL All-Star Game (1960, 1961, 1962, 1963, 1964, 1965, 1967, 1968)
Traded to **Toronto** by **Chicago** for Jim Pappin, May 23, 1968.

● **PINDER, GERRY** Gerry Pinder LW – R. 5'8", 165 lbs. b: Saskatoon, Sask., 9/15/1948.

Season	Club	League	GP	G	A	Pts	AG	AA	APts	PIM	PP	SH	GW	S	%	TGF	PGF	TGA	PGA	+/–	GP	G	A	Pts	PIM	PP	SH	GW
1964-65	Saskatoon Quakers	SJHL	48	9	9	18	....	....	....	7	....	....	....	....	....	....	....	....	....	....	....	....	....	....	....	....	....	....
1965-66	Saskatoon Blades	SJHL	54	36	46	82	....	....	....	60	....	....	....	....	....	....	....	....	....	....	5	1	2	3	9	....	....	....
1966-67	Saskatoon Blades	SJHL	55	*78	62	*140	....	....	....	95	....	....	....	....	....	....	....	....	....	....	4	4	1	5	4	....	....	....
1967-68	Winnipeg Nats	WCSHL	25	11	14	25	....	....	....	12	....	....	....	....	....	....	....	....	....	....	....	....	....	....	....	....	....	....
	Canada	Olympics	7	1	0	1	....	....	....	2	....	....	....	....	....	....	....	....	....	....	....	....	....	....	....	....	....	....
1968-69	Canada	Nat-Team	STATISTICS NOT AVAILABLE																									
	Canada	WEC-A	10	3	1	4	....	....	....	14	....	....	....	....	....	....	....	....	....	....	....	....	....	....	....	....	....	....

			REGULAR SEASON																		PLAYOFFS							
Season	Club	League	GP	G	A	Pts	AG	AA	APts	PIM	PP	SH	GW	S	%	TGF	PGF	TGA	PGA	+/–	GP	G	A	Pts	PIM	PP	SH	GW
1969-70	**Chicago Black Hawks**	**NHL**	**75**	**19**	**20**	**39**	**22**	**20**	**42**	**41**	**4**	**1**	**3**	**169**	**11.2**	**71**	**16**	**36**	**4**	**+23**	**8**	**0**	**4**	**4**	**4**	**0**	**0**	**0**
1970-71	**Chicago Black Hawks**	**NHL**	**74**	**13**	**18**	**31**	**14**	**16**	**30**	**35**	**1**	**0**	**2**	**102**	**12.7**	**59**	**19**	**42**	**0**	**–2**	**9**	**0**	**0**	**0**	**2**	**0**	**0**	**0**
1971-72	**California Golden Seals**	**NHL**	**74**	**23**	**31**	**54**	**25**	**28**	**53**	**59**	**7**	**1**	**1**	**140**	**16.4**	**77**	**25**	**78**	**8**	**–18**	....	....	....	....	....	....	....	....
1972-73	Cleveland Crusaders	WHA	78	30	36	66	....	....	....	21	....	....	....	....	....	....	....	....	....	....	9	2	9	11	30	....	....	....
1973-74	Cleveland Crusaders	WHA	73	23	33	56	....	....	....	90	....	....	....	....	....	....	....	....	....	....	1	0	0	0	0	....	....	....
1974-75	Cleveland Crusaders	WHA	74	13	28	41	....	....	....	71	....	....	....	....	....	....	....	....	....	....	5	3	1	4	6	....	....	....
1975-76	Cleveland Crusaders	WHA	79	21	30	51	....	....	....	118	....	....	....	....	....	....	....	....	....	....	3	0	0	0	4	....	....	....
1976-77	San Diego Mariners	WHA	44	6	13	19	....	....	....	36	....	....	....	....	....	....	....	....	....	....	....	....	....	....	....	....	....	....
	Maine Nordiques	NAHL	11	6	3	9	....	....	....	4	....	....	....	....	....	....	....	....	....	....	10	8	2	10	12	....	....	....
1977-78	Edmonton Oilers	WHA	5	0	1	1	....	....	....	0	....	....	....	....	....	....	....	....	....	....	....	....	....	....	....	....	....	....
	NHL Totals		**223**	**55**	**69**	**124**	**61**	**64**	**125**	**135**	**12**	**2**	**6**	**411**	**13.4**	**207**	**60**	**156**	**12**		**17**	**0**	**4**	**4**	**6**	**0**	**0**	**0**
	Other Major League Totals		353	93	141	234	....	....	....	336	....	....	....	....	....	....	....	....	....		18	5	10	15	40	....	....	....

Traded to **California** by **Chicago** with Gerry Desjardins and Kerry Bond for Gary Smith, September 9, 1971. Selected by **Calgary-Cleveland** (WHA) in 1972 WHA General Player Draft, February 12, 1972. Traded to **San Diego** (WHA) by **Cleveland-Minnesota** (WHA) with Paul Shymr for Ray Adduano and Bob Wall, September, 1976. Signed as a free agent by **Edmonton** (WHA) after **San Diego** (WHA) franchise folded, June, 1977.

• PIRUS, ALEX

Alex Pirus RW – R. 6′1″, 205 lbs. b: Toronto, Ont., 1/12/1955. Minnesota's 3rd choice, 41st overall, in 1975 Amateur Draft.

Season	Club	League	GP	G	A	Pts	AG	AA	APts	PIM	PP	SH	GW	S	%	TGF	PGF	TGA	PGA	+/–	GP	G	A	Pts	PIM	PP	SH	GW
1972-73	Richmond Hill Ramblers	Jr. B	....	40	44	84	....	....	....	97	....	....	....	....	....	....	....	....	....	....	....	....	....	....	....	....	....	....
1973-74	University of Notre Dame	WCHA	28	8	16	24	....	....	....	22	....	....	....	....	....	....	....	....	....	....	....	....	....	....	....	....	....	....
1974-75	University of Notre Dame	WCHA	37	23	32	55	....	....	....	94	....	....	....	....	....	....	....	....	....	....	....	....	....	....	....	....	....	....
1975-76	University of Notre Dame	WCHA	38	26	18	44	....	....	....	65	....	....	....	....	....	....	....	....	....	....	....	....	....	....	....	....	....	....
1976-77	**Minnesota North Stars**	**NHL**	**79**	**20**	**17**	**37**	**19**	**14**	**33**	**47**	**1**	**0**	**1**	**128**	**15.6**	**45**	**4**	**61**	**0**	**–20**	**2**	**0**	**1**	**1**	**2**	**0**	**0**	**0**
1977-78	**Minnesota North Stars**	**NHL**	**61**	**9**	**6**	**15**	**9**	**5**	**14**	**38**	**1**	**0**	**1**	**89**	**10.1**	**28**	**3**	**50**	**0**	**–25**	....	....	....	....	....	....	....	....
	Fort Worth Texans	CHL	18	9	6	15	....	....	....	4	....	....	....	....	....	....	....	....	....	....	14	6	2	8	11	....	....	....
1978-79	**Minnesota North Stars**	**NHL**	**15**	**1**	**3**	**4**	**1**	**2**	**3**	**9**	**0**	**0**	**0**	**14**	**7.1**	**8**	**1**	**15**	**0**	**–8**	....	....	....	....	....	....	....	....
	Oklahoma City Stars	CHL	51	16	16	32	....	....	....	33	....	....	....	....	....	....	....	....	....	....	....	....	....	....	....	....	....	....
1979-80	**Detroit Red Wings**	**NHL**	**4**	**0**	**2**	**2**	**0**	**2**	**2**	**0**	**0**	**0**	**0**	**0**	**0.0**	**2**	**0**	**2**	**0**	**0**	....	....	....	....	....	....	....	....
	Oklahoma City Stars	CHL	62	23	23	46	....	....	....	49	....	....	....	....	....	....	....	....	....	....	....	....	....	....	....	....	....	....
1980-81	Indianapolis Checkers	CHL	79	25	46	71	....	....	....	78	....	....	....	....	....	....	....	....	....	....	5	3	2	5	4	....	....	....
	NHL Totals		**159**	**30**	**28**	**58**	**29**	**23**	**52**	**94**	**2**	**0**	**2**	**231**	**13.0**	**83**	**8**	**128**	**0**		**2**	**0**	**1**	**1**	**2**	**0**	**0**	**0**

Traded to **Detroit** by **Minnesota** for cash, January 3, 1980. Traded to **Minnesota** by **Detroit** for cash, June 6, 1980. Traded to **NY Islanders** by **Minnesota** for future considerations, July 4, 1980.

• PITLICK, LANCE

Lance Pitlick D – R. 6′, 203 lbs. b: Minneapolis, MN, 11/5/1967. Minnesota's 10th choice, 180th overall, in 1986 Entry Draft.

Season	Club	League	GP	G	A	Pts	AG	AA	APts	PIM	PP	SH	GW	S	%	TGF	PGF	TGA	PGA	+/–	GP	G	A	Pts	PIM	PP	SH	GW
1985-86	Cooper-Minnesota High	H.S.	21	17	8	25	....	....	....	....	....	....	....	....	....	....	....	....	....	....	....	....	....	....	....	....	....	....
1986-87	University of Minnesota	WCHA	45	0	9	9	....	....	....	88	....	....	....	....	....	....	....	....	....	....	....	....	....	....	....	....	....	....
1987-88	University of Minnesota	WCHA	38	3	9	12	....	....	....	76	....	....	....	....	....	....	....	....	....	....	....	....	....	....	....	....	....	....
1988-89	University of Minnesota	WCHA	47	4	9	13	....	....	....	95	....	....	....	....	....	....	....	....	....	....	....	....	....	....	....	....	....	....
1989-90	University of Minnestoa	WCHA	14	3	2	5	....	....	....	26	....	....	....	....	....	....	....	....	....	....	....	....	....	....	....	....	....	....
1990-91	Hershey Bears	AHL	64	6	15	21	....	....	....	75	....	....	....	....	....	....	....	....	....	....	3	0	0	0	9	....	....	....
1991-92	United States	Nat-Team	19	0	1	1	....	....	....	38	....	....	....	....	....	....	....	....	....	....	....	....	....	....	....	....	....	....
	Hershey Bears	AHL	4	0	0	0	....	....	....	6	....	....	....	....	....	....	....	....	....	....	3	0	0	0	4	....	....	....
1992-93	Hershey Bears	AHL	53	5	10	15	....	....	....	77	....	....	....	....	....	....	....	....	....	....	....	....	....	....	....	....	....	....
1993-94	Hershey Bears	AHL	58	4	13	17	....	....	....	93	....	....	....	....	....	....	....	....	....	....	11	1	0	1	11	....	....	....
1994-95	P.E.I. Senators	AHL	61	8	19	27	....	....	....	55	....	....	....	....	....	....	....	....	....	....	11	1	4	5	10	....	....	....
	Ottawa Senators	**NHL**	**15**	**0**	**1**	**1**	**0**	**1**	**1**	**6**	**0**	**0**	**0**	**11**	**0.0**	**5**	**1**	**12**	**3**	**–5**	....	....	....	....	....	....	....	....
1995-96	**Ottawa Senators**	**NHL**	**28**	**1**	**6**	**7**	**1**	**5**	**6**	**20**	**0**	**0**	**0**	**13**	**7.7**	**14**	**0**	**26**	**4**	**–8**	....	....	....	....	....	....	....	....
	P.E.I. Senators	AHL	29	4	10	14	....	....	....	39	....	....	....	....	....	....	....	....	....	....	5	0	0	0	0	....	....	....
1996-97	**Ottawa Senators**	**NHL**	**66**	**5**	**5**	**10**	**5**	**4**	**9**	**91**	**0**	**0**	**1**	**54**	**9.3**	**38**	**0**	**54**	**18**	**+2**	**7**	**0**	**0**	**0**	**4**	**0**	**0**	**0**
1997-98	**Ottawa Senators**	**NHL**	**69**	**2**	**7**	**9**	**2**	**7**	**9**	**50**	**0**	**0**	**0**	**66**	**3.0**	**43**	**0**	**45**	**10**	**+8**	**11**	**0**	**1**	**1**	**17**	**0**	**0**	**0**
	NHL Totals		**178**	**8**	**19**	**27**	**8**	**17**	**25**	**167**	**0**	**0**	**1**	**144**	**5.6**	**100**	**1**	**137**	**35**		**18**	**0**	**1**	**1**	**21**	**0**	**0**	**0**

Signed as a free agent by **Philadelphia**, September 5, 1990. Signed as a free agent by **Ottawa**, June 22, 1994.

• PITTIS, DOMENIC

Domenic Pittis C – L. 5′11″, 190 lbs. b: Calgary, Alta., 10/1/1974. Pittsburgh's 2nd choice, 52nd overall, in 1993 Entry Draft.

Season	Club	League	GP	G	A	Pts	AG	AA	APts	PIM	PP	SH	GW	S	%	TGF	PGF	TGA	PGA	+/–	GP	G	A	Pts	PIM	PP	SH	GW
1991-92	Lethbridge Hurricanes	WHL	65	6	17	23	....	....	....	48	....	....	....	....	....	....	....	....	....	....	5	0	2	2	4	....	....	....
1992-93	Lethbridge Hurricanes	WHL	66	46	73	119	....	....	....	69	....	....	....	....	....	....	....	....	....	....	4	3	3	6	8	....	....	....
1993-94	Lethbridge Hurricanes	WHL	72	58	69	127	....	....	....	93	....	....	....	....	....	....	....	....	....	....	8	4	11	15	16	....	....	....
1994-95	Cleveland Lumberjacks	IHL	62	18	32	50	....	....	....	66	....	....	....	....	....	....	....	....	....	....	3	0	2	2	2	....	....	....
1995-96	Cleveland Lumberjacks	IHL	74	10	28	38	....	....	....	100	....	....	....	....	....	....	....	....	....	....	3	0	0	0	2	....	....	....
1996-97	**Pittsburgh Penguins**	**NHL**	**1**	**0**	**0**	**0**	**0**	**0**	**0**	**0**	**0**	**0**	**0**	**0**	**0.0**	**0**	**0**	**1**	**0**	**–1**	....	....	....	....	....	....	....	....
	Long Beach Ice Dogs	IHL	65	23	43	66	....	....	....	91	....	....	....	....	....	....	....	....	....	....	18	5	9	14	26	....	....	....
1997-98	Syracuse Crunch	AHL	75	23	41	64	....	....	....	90	....	....	....	....	....	....	....	....	....	....	5	1	3	4	4	....	....	....
	NHL Totals		**1**	**0**	**0**	**0**	**0**	**0**	**0**	**0**	**0**	**0**	**0**	**0**	**0.0**	**0**	**0**	**1**	**0**		....	....	....	....	....	....	....	....

WHL East Second All-Star Team (1994)

• PIVONKA, MICHAL

Michal Pivonka C – L. 6′2″, 195 lbs. b: Kladno, Czech., 1/28/1966. Washington's 3rd choice, 59th overall, in 1984 Entry Draft.

Season	Club	League	GP	G	A	Pts	AG	AA	APts	PIM	PP	SH	GW	S	%	TGF	PGF	TGA	PGA	+/–	GP	G	A	Pts	PIM	PP	SH	GW
1983-84	Czechoslovakia	WJC-A	7	1	2	3	....	....	....	0	....	....	....	....	....	....	....	....	....	....	....	....	....	....	....	....	....	....
1984-85	Dukla Jihlava	Czech.	33	8	11	19	....	....	....	18	....	....	....	....	....	....	....	....	....	....	....	....	....	....	....	....	....	....
	Czechoslovakia	WJC-A	7	9	4	13	....	....	....	14	....	....	....	....	....	....	....	....	....	....	....	....	....	....	....	....	....	....
	Czechoslovakia	WEC-A	10	0	1	1	....	....	....	0	....	....	....	....	....	....	....	....	....	....	....	....	....	....	....	....	....	....
1985-86	Dukla Jihlava	Czech.	42	5	13	18	....	....	....	18	....	....	....	....	....	....	....	....	....	....	....	....	....	....	....	....	....	....
	Czechoslovakia	WJC-A	7	5	5	10	....	....	....	10	....	....	....	....	....	....	....	....	....	....	....	....	....	....	....	....	....	....
	Czechoslovakia	WEC-A	10	2	1	3	....	....	....	8	....	....	....	....	....	....	....	....	....	....	....	....	....	....	....	....	....	....
1986-87	**Washington Capitals**	**NHL**	**73**	**18**	**25**	**43**	**16**	**18**	**34**	**41**	**4**	**0**	**2**	**117**	**15.4**	**65**	**23**	**62**	**1**	**–19**	**7**	**1**	**1**	**2**	**2**	**0**	**0**	**0**
1987-88	**Washington Capitals**	**NHL**	**71**	**11**	**23**	**34**	**9**	**16**	**25**	**28**	**3**	**0**	**0**	**96**	**11.5**	**57**	**24**	**32**	**0**	**+1**	**14**	**4**	**9**	**13**	**4**	**2**	**0**	**0**
1988-89	**Washington Capitals**	**NHL**	**52**	**8**	**19**	**27**	**7**	**13**	**20**	**30**	**1**	**0**	**1**	**73**	**11.0**	**42**	**9**	**24**	**0**	**+9**	**6**	**3**	**1**	**4**	**10**	**0**	**1**	**0**
	Baltimore Skipjacks	AHL	31	12	24	36	....	....	....	19	....	....	....	....	....	....	....	....	....	....	....	....	....	....	....	....	....	....
1989-90	Washington Capitals	FrTour	4	0	0	0	....	....	....	2	....	....	....	....	....	....	....	....	....	....	....	....	....	....	....	....	....	....
	Washington Capitals	**NHL**	**77**	**25**	**39**	**64**	**22**	**28**	**50**	**54**	**10**	**3**	**0**	**149**	**16.8**	**80**	**27**	**79**	**19**	**–7**	**11**	**0**	**2**	**2**	**6**	**0**	**0**	**0**
1990-91	**Washington Capitals**	**NHL**	**79**	**20**	**50**	**70**	**18**	**38**	**56**	**34**	**6**	**0**	**4**	**172**	**11.6**	**94**	**31**	**65**	**5**	**+3**	**11**	**2**	**3**	**5**	**8**	**0**	**0**	**0**
1991-92	Czechoslovakia	C Cup	5	0	3	3	....	....	....	2	....	....	....	....	....	....	....	....	....	....	....	....	....	....	....	....	....	....
	Washington Capitals	**NHL**	**80**	**23**	**57**	**80**	**21**	**43**	**64**	**47**	**7**	**4**	**2**	**177**	**13.0**	**111**	**38**	**78**	**15**	**+10**	**7**	**1**	**5**	**6**	**13**	**1**	**0**	**1**
1992-93	**Washington Capitals**	**NHL**	**69**	**21**	**53**	**74**	**17**	**36**	**53**	**66**	**6**	**1**	**5**	**147**	**14.3**	**105**	**37**	**71**	**17**	**+14**	**6**	**0**	**2**	**2**	**0**	**0**	**0**	**0**
1993-94	**Washington Capitals**	**NHL**	**82**	**14**	**36**	**50**	**13**	**28**	**41**	**38**	**5**	**0**	**4**	**138**	**10.1**	**72**	**26**	**59**	**15**	**+2**	**7**	**4**	**4**	**8**	**4**	**1**	**0**	**0**
1994-95	Klagenfurt	Austria	7	2	4	6	....	....	....	4	....	....	....	....	....	....	....	....	....	....	....	....	....	....	....	....	....	....
	Washington Capitals	**NHL**	**46**	**10**	**23**	**33**	**18**	**34**	**52**	**50**	**4**	**2**	**2**	**80**	**12.5**	**53**	**26**	**36**	**12**	**+3**	**7**	**1**	**4**	**5**	**21**	**0**	**0**	**0**
1995-96	Detroit Vipers	IHL	7	1	9	10	....	....	....	19	....	....	....	....	....	....	....	....	....	....	....	....	....	....	....	....	....	....
	Washington Capitals	**NHL**	**73**	**16**	**65**	**81**	**16**	**53**	**69**	**36**	**6**	**2**	**5**	**168**	**9.5**	**100**	**33**	**66**	**17**	**+18**	**6**	**3**	**2**	**5**	**18**	**1**	**0**	**0**
1996-97	**Washington Capitals**	**NHL**	**54**	**7**	**16**	**23**	**7**	**14**	**21**	**22**	**2**	**0**	**1**	**83**	**8.4**	**47**	**11**	**58**	**7**	**–15**	....	....	....	....	....	....	....	....
1997-98	**Washington Capitals**	**NHL**	**33**	**3**	**6**	**9**	**4**	**6**	**10**	**20**	**0**	**0**	**1**	**38**	**7.9**	**16**	**5**	**10**	**4**	**+5**	**13**	**0**	**3**	**3**	**0**	**0**	**0**	**0**
	NHL Totals		**789**	**176**	**412**	**588**	**168**	**327**	**495**	**466**	**54**	**12**	**27**	**1438**	**12.2**	**842**	**290**	**640**	**112**		**95**	**19**	**36**	**55**	**86**	**5**	**1**	**1**

EJC-A All-Star Team (1983) • WJC-A All-Star Team (1985, 1986) • Named Best Forward at WJC-A (1985)

• PLAGER, BARCLAY

Barclay Plager D – L. 5′11″, 175 lbs. b: Kirkland Lake, Ont., 3/26/1941. d: 2/6/1988.

Season	Club	League	GP	G	A	Pts	AG	AA	APts	PIM	PP	SH	GW	S	%	TGF	PGF	TGA	PGA	+/–	GP	G	A	Pts	PIM	PP	SH	GW
1957-58	Quebec Baronets	QJHL	STATISTICS NOT AVAILABLE																									
	Peterborough Petes	OHA	4	0	0	0	....	....	....	2	....	....	....	....	....	....	....	....	....	....	....	....	....	....	....	....	....	....
1958-59	Peterborough Petes	OHA	54	4	16	20	....	....	....	252	....	....	....	....	....	....	....	....	....	....	19	6	6	12	*74	....	....	....
1959-60	Peterborough Petes	OHA	48	8	27	35	....	....	....	165	....	....	....	....	....	....	....	....	....	....	12	1	7	8	37	....	....	....
1960-61	Peterborough Petes	OHA	48	11	33	44	....	....	....	*155	....	....	....	....	....	....	....	....	....	....	3	0	0	0	23	....	....	....
	Hull-Ottawa Canadiens	EPHL	3	0	0	0	....	....	....	2	....	....	....	....	....	....	....	....	....	....	....	....	....	....	....	....	....	....

			REGULAR SEASON																		PLAYOFFS							
Season	Club	League	GP	G	A	Pts	AG	AA	APts	PIM	PP	SH	GW	S	%	TGF	PGF	TGA	PGA	+/–	GP	G	A	Pts	PIM	PP	SH	GW
1961-62	Quebec Aces	AHL	1	0	1	1	....	....	....	2	....	....	....	....	....	....	....	....	....	....	....	....	....	....	....	....	....	....
	Hull-Ottawa Canadiens	EPHL	60	8	16	24	....	....	....	102	....	....	....	....	....	....	....	....	....	....	10	1	1	2	22	....	....	....
1962-63	Pittsburgh Hornets	AHL	13	0	1	1	....	....	....	15	....	....	....	....	....	....	....	....	....	....	....	....	....	....	....	....	....	....
	Edmonton Flyers	WHL	52	2	18	20	....	....	....	67	....	....	....	....	....	....	....	....	....	....	....	....	....	....	....	....	....	....
1963-64	Omaha Knights	CHL	70	14	*61	75	....	....	....	*208	....	....	....	....	....	....	....	....	....	....	10	2	*11	13	29	....	....	....
1964-65	Springfield Indians	AHL	39	2	16	18	....	....	....	65	....	....	....	....	....	....	....	....	....	....	....	....	....	....	....	....	....	....
1965-66	Springfield Indians	AHL	58	11	20	31	....	....	....	54	....	....	....	....	....	....	....	....	....	....	6	1	0	1	0	....	....	....
1966-67	Springfield Indians	AHL	36	6	12	18	....	....	....	60	....	....	....	....	....	....	....	....	....	....	....	....	....	....	....	....	....	....
	Omaha Knights	CHL	11	1	10	11	....	....	....	39	....	....	....	....	....	....	....	....	....	....	12	3	8	11	*42	....	....	....
1967-68	**St. Louis Blues**	**NHL**	**49**	**5**	**15**	**20**	**6**	**16**	**22**	***153**	**2**	**0**	**1**	**61**	**8.2**	**50**	**10**	**38**	**2**	**+4**	**18**	**2**	**5**	**7**	***73**	**0**	**1**	**0**
	Buffalo Bisons	AHL	20	2	13	15	....	....	....	37	....	....	....	....	....	....	....	....	....	....	....	....	....	....	....	....	....	....
1968-69	**St. Louis Blues**	**NHL**	**61**	**4**	**26**	**30**	**4**	**24**	**28**	**120**	**0**	**0**	**1**	**88**	**4.5**	**73**	**14**	**36**	**8**	**+31**	**12**	**0**	**4**	**4**	**31**	**0**	**0**	**0**
1969-70	**St. Louis Blues**	**NHL**	**75**	**6**	**26**	**32**	**7**	**26**	**33**	**128**	**1**	**1**	**1**	**97**	**6.2**	**71**	**13**	**79**	**23**	**+2**	**13**	**0**	**2**	**2**	**20**	**0**	**0**	**0**
1970-71	**St. Louis Blues**	**NHL**	**69**	**4**	**20**	**24**	**4**	**18**	**22**	**172**	**1**	**0**	**0**	**87**	**4.6**	**82**	**15**	**75**	**19**	**+11**	**6**	**0**	**3**	**3**	**10**	**0**	**0**	**0**
1971-72	**St. Louis Blues**	**NHL**	**78**	**7**	**22**	**29**	**7**	**20**	**27**	**176**	**1**	**2**	**0**	**128**	**5.5**	**105**	**21**	**118**	**40**	**+6**	**11**	**1**	**4**	**5**	**21**	**1**	**0**	**1**
1972-73	**St. Louis Blues**	**NHL**	**68**	**8**	**25**	**33**	**8**	**21**	**29**	**102**	**3**	**0**	**2**	**131**	**6.1**	**83**	**14**	**98**	**29**	**0**	**5**	**0**	**1**	**1**	**0**	**0**	**0**	**0**
1973-74	**St. Louis Blues**	**NHL**	**72**	**6**	**20**	**26**	**6**	**17**	**23**	**99**	**1**	**0**	**0**	**104**	**5.8**	**71**	**12**	**107**	**37**	**–11**	....	....	....	....	....	....	....	....
1974-75	**St. Louis Blues**	**NHL**	**76**	**4**	**24**	**28**	**4**	**19**	**23**	**96**	**0**	**0**	**1**	**88**	**4.5**	**87**	**11**	**106**	**50**	**+20**	**2**	**0**	**1**	**1**	**14**	**0**	**0**	**0**
1975-76	**St. Louis Blues**	**NHL**	**64**	**0**	**8**	**8**	**0**	**6**	**6**	**67**	**0**	**0**	**0**	**32**	**0.0**	**42**	**3**	**78**	**33**	**–6**	**1**	**0**	**0**	**0**	**13**	**0**	**0**	**0**
1976-77	**St. Louis Blues**	**NHL**	**2**	**0**	**1**	**1**	**0**	**1**	**1**	**2**	**0**	**0**	**0**	**2**	**0.0**	**3**	**0**	**2**	**0**	**+1**	....	....	....	....	....	....	....	....
	Kansas City Blues	CHL	75	6	42	48	....	....	....	157	....	....	....	....	....	....	....	....	....	....	9	2	4	6	12	....	....	....
1977-78	Salt Lake Golden Eagles	CHL	46	2	19	21	....	....	....	80	....	....	....	....	....	....	....	....	....	....	....	....	....	....	....	....	....	....
	NHL Totals		**614**	**44**	**187**	**231**	**46**	**168**	**214**	**1115**	**9**	**3**	**6**	**818**	**5.4**	**667**	**113**	**737**	**241**		**68**	**3**	**20**	**23**	**182**	**1**	**1**	**1**

CHL First All-Star Team (1964) • Named CHL's Top Defenseman (1964) • CHL Second All-Star Team (1977) • Won Tommy Ivan Trophy (CHL's MVP) (1977)

Played in NHL All-Star Game (1970, 1971, 1973, 1974)

Claimed by **Detroit** from **Quebec** (AHL) in Inter-League Draft, June, 1962. Traded to **Springfield** (AHL) by **Detroit** for cash, August, 1964. NHL rights transferred to **LA Kings** after NHL club purchased **Springfield** (AHL) franchise, May, 1968. Traded to **NY Rangers** by **LA Kings** for Trevor Fahey, Ken Turlik and Jim Murray, June 16, 1967. Traded to **St. Louis** by **NY Rangers** with Red Bersenson for Ron Stewart and Ron Attwell, November 29, 1967.

• PLAGER, BILL

Bill Plager D – R. 5'9", 175 lbs. b: Kirkland Lake, Ont., 7/6/1945.

1962-63	Peterborough Petes	OHA	49	1	5	6	....	....	....	94	....	....	....	....	....	....	....	....	....	....	6	0	0	0	0	....	....	....
1963-64	Lachine Maroons	QJHL	40	6	34	40	....	....	....	*187	....	....	....	....	....	....	....	....	....	....	....	....	....	....	....	....	....	....
1964-65	Peterborough Petes	OHA	27	4	3	7	....	....	....	77	....	....	....	....	....	....	....	....	....	....	12	0	3	3	31	....	....	....
1965-66	Peterborough Petes	OHA	47	1	21	22	....	....	....	190	....	....	....	....	....	....	....	....	....	....	6	0	1	1	14	....	....	....
1966-67	Houston Apollos	CHL	51	4	13	17	....	....	....	130	....	....	....	....	....	....	....	....	....	....	6	0	1	1	14	....	....	....
1967-68	**Minnesota North Stars**	**NHL**	**32**	**0**	**2**	**2**	**0**	**2**	**2**	**30**	**0**	**0**	**0**	**12**	**0.0**	**9**	**1**	**25**	**1**	**–16**	**12**	**0**	**2**	**2**	**8**	**0**	**0**	**0**
	Memphis South Stars	CHL	30	0	7	7	....	....	....	51	....	....	....	....	....	....	....	....	....	....	....	....	....	....	....	....	....	....
1968-69	**St. Louis Blues**	**NHL**	**2**	**0**	**0**	**0**	**0**	**0**	**0**	**2**	**0**	**0**	**0**	**3**	**0.0**	**0**	**0**	**0**	**0**	**0**	**4**	**0**	**0**	**0**	**4**	**0**	**0**	**0**
	Kansas City Blues	CHL	35	1	4	5	....	....	....	66	....	....	....	....	....	....	....	....	....	....	4	0	1	1	6	....	....	....
1969-70	**St. Louis Blues**	**NHL**	**24**	**1**	**4**	**5**	**1**	**4**	**5**	**30**	**0**	**0**	**0**	**23**	**4.3**	**12**	**2**	**16**	**1**	**–5**	**3**	**0**	**0**	**0**	**0**	**0**	**0**	**0**
	Buffalo Bisons	AHL	48	2	28	30	....	....	....	91	....	....	....	....	....	....	....	....	....	....	....	....	....	....	....	....	....	....
1970-71	**St. Louis Blues**	**NHL**	**36**	**0**	**3**	**3**	**0**	**3**	**3**	**45**	**0**	**0**	**0**	**24**	**0.0**	**14**	**0**	**14**	**0**	**0**	**1**	**0**	**0**	**0**	**2**	**0**	**0**	**0**
	Kansas City Blues	CHL	7	0	0	0	....	....	....	31	....	....	....	....	....	....	....	....	....	....	....	....	....	....	....	....	....	....
1971-72	**St. Louis Blues**	**NHL**	**65**	**1**	**11**	**12**	**1**	**10**	**11**	**64**	**0**	**0**	**1**	**63**	**1.6**	**40**	**3**	**66**	**14**	**–16**	**11**	**0**	**0**	**0**	**12**	**0**	**0**	**0**
	Denver Spurs	WHL	8	0	5	5	....	....	....	18	....	....	....	....	....	....	....	....	....	....	....	....	....	....	....	....	....	....
1972-73	**Atlanta Flames**	**NHL**	**76**	**2**	**11**	**13**	**2**	**9**	**11**	**92**	**0**	**0**	**0**	**60**	**3.3**	**40**	**1**	**72**	**15**	**–18**	....	....	....	....	....	....	....	....
1973-74	**Minnesota North Stars**	**NHL**	**1**	**0**	**0**	**0**	**0**	**0**	**0**	**2**	**0**	**0**	**0**	**0**	**0.0**	**0**	**0**	**1**	**0**	**–1**	....	....	....	....	....	....	....	....
	New Haven Nighthawks	AHL	67	4	33	37	....	....	....	122	....	....	....	....	....	....	....	....	....	....	10	1	5	6	8	....	....	....
1974-75	**Minnesota North Stars**	**NHL**	**7**	**0**	**0**	**0**	**0**	**0**	**0**	**8**	**0**	**0**	**0**	**10**	**0.0**	**6**	**0**	**13**	**4**	**–3**	....	....	....	....	....	....	....	....
	New Haven Nighthawks	AHL	64	6	27	33	....	....	....	101	....	....	....	....	....	....	....	....	....	....	16	0	4	4	23	....	....	....
1975-76	**Minnesota North Stars**	**NHL**	**20**	**0**	**3**	**3**	**0**	**2**	**2**	**21**	**0**	**0**	**0**	**9**	**0.0**	**6**	**0**	**16**	**5**	**–5**	....	....	....	....	....	....	....	....
	New Haven Nighthawks	AHL	48	3	14	17	....	....	....	58	....	....	....	....	....	....	....	....	....	....	3	0	1	1	4	....	....	....
1976-77	Erie Blades	NAHL	64	5	25	30	....	....	....	65	....	....	....	....	....	....	....	....	....	....	....	....	....	....	....	....	....	....
	NHL Totals		**263**	**4**	**34**	**38**	**4**	**30**	**34**	**294**	**0**	**0**	**1**	**204**	**2.0**	**127**	**7**	**223**	**40**		**31**	**0**	**2**	**2**	**26**	**0**	**0**	**0**

AHL Second All-Star Team (1975)

Traded to **Minnesota** by **Montreal** with the rights to Barrie Meissner and Leo Thiffault for Bryan Watson, June 6, 1967. Claimed by **NY Rangers** from **Minnesota** in Intra-League Draft, June 12, 1968. Traded to **St. Louis** by **NY Rangers** with Camille Henry and Robbie Irons for Don Caley and Wayne Rivers, June 13, 1968. Claimed by **Atlanta** from **St. Louis** in Expansion Draft, June 6, 1972. Claimed by **Minnesota** from **Atlanta** in Intra-League Draft, June 12, 1973.

• PLAGER, BOB

Bob Plager D – L. 5'11", 195 lbs. b: Kirkland Lake, Ont., 3/11/1943.

1959-60	Guelph Biltmores	OHA	44	0	1	1	....	....	....	37	....	....	....	....	....	....	....	....	....	....	5	0	1	1	4	....	....	....
1960-61	Guelph Royals	OHA	43	3	12	15	....	....	....	99	....	....	....	....	....	....	....	....	....	....	14	3	8	11	73	....	....	....
1961-62	Guelph Royals	OHA	50	5	22	27	....	....	....	*161	....	....	....	....	....	....	....	....	....	....	....	....	....	....	....	....	....	....
	Kitchener Frontenacs	EPHL	3	0	0	0	....	....	....	2	....	....	....	....	....	....	....	....	....	....	....	....	....	....	....	....	....	....
1962-63	Guelph Royals	OHA	45	11	29	39	....	....	....	97	....	....	....	....	....	....	....	....	....	....	....	....	....	....	....	....	....	....
	Baltimore Clippers	AHL	4	0	0	0	....	....	....	6	....	....	....	....	....	....	....	....	....	....	2	0	0	0	10	....	....	....
1963-64	St. Paul Rangers	CHL	61	13	35	48	....	....	....	158	....	....	....	....	....	....	....	....	....	....	8	3	6	9	21	....	....	....
1964-65	**New York Rangers**	**NHL**	**10**	**0**	**0**	**0**	**0**	**0**	**0**	**18**	....	....	....	....	....	....	....	....	....	....	....	....	....	....	....	....	....	....
	Vancouver Canucks	WHL	31	5	12	17	....	....	....	103	....	....	....	....	....	....	....	....	....	....	....	....	....	....	....	....	....	....
	Baltimore Clippers	AHL	19	2	12	14	....	....	....	27	....	....	....	....	....	....	....	....	....	....	5	0	0	0	6	....	....	....
1965-66	**New York Rangers**	**NHL**	**18**	**0**	**5**	**5**	**0**	**5**	**5**	**22**	....	....	....	....	....	....	....	....	....	....	....	....	....	....	....	....	....	....
	Minnesota Rangers	CHL	44	7	12	19	....	....	....	145	....	....	....	....	....	....	....	....	....	....	....	....	....	....	....	....	....	....
1966-67	**New York Rangers**	**NHL**	**1**	**0**	**0**	**0**	**0**	**0**	**0**	**0**	....	....	....	....	....	....	....	....	....	....	....	....	....	....	....	....	....	....
	Baltimore Clippers	AHL	63	3	16	19	....	....	....	*169	....	....	....	....	....	....	....	....	....	....	9	0	5	5	15	....	....	....
1967-68	**St. Louis Blues**	**NHL**	**53**	**2**	**5**	**7**	**2**	**5**	**7**	**86**	**0**	**0**	**0**	**52**	**3.8**	**41**	**3**	**62**	**13**	**–11**	**18**	**1**	**2**	**3**	**69**	**0**	**0**	**0**
1968-69	**St. Louis Blues**	**NHL**	**32**	**0**	**7**	**7**	**0**	**7**	**7**	**43**	**0**	**0**	**0**	**46**	**0.0**	**28**	**0**	**25**	**7**	**+10**	**9**	**0**	**4**	**4**	**47**	**0**	**0**	**0**
	Kansas City Blues	CHL	5	1	3	4	....	....	....	16	....	....	....	....	....	....	....	....	....	....	....	....	....	....	....	....	....	....
1969-70	**St. Louis Blues**	**NHL**	**64**	**3**	**11**	**14**	**3**	**11**	**14**	**113**	**0**	**0**	**0**	**83**	**3.6**	**43**	**1**	**60**	**20**	**+2**	**16**	**0**	**3**	**3**	**46**	**0**	**0**	**0**
1970-71	**St. Louis Blues**	**NHL**	**70**	**1**	**19**	**20**	**1**	**17**	**18**	**114**	**0**	**0**	**1**	**70**	**1.4**	**66**	**2**	**87**	**32**	**+9**	**6**	**0**	**2**	**2**	**4**	**0**	**0**	**0**
1971-72	**St. Louis Blues**	**NHL**	**50**	**4**	**7**	**11**	**4**	**6**	**10**	**81**	**0**	**0**	**0**	**59**	**6.8**	**49**	**2**	**72**	**24**	**–1**	**11**	**1**	**4**	**5**	**5**	**0**	**0**	**0**
1972-73	**St. Louis Blues**	**NHL**	**77**	**2**	**31**	**33**	**2**	**26**	**28**	**107**	**0**	**0**	**1**	**117**	**1.7**	**94**	**7**	**128**	**40**	**–1**	**5**	**0**	**2**	**2**	**2**	**0**	**0**	**0**
1973-74	**St. Louis Blues**	**NHL**	**61**	**3**	**10**	**13**	**3**	**9**	**12**	**48**	**0**	**1**	**1**	**78**	**3.8**	**58**	**0**	**70**	**21**	**+9**	....	....	....	....	....	....	....	....
1974-75	**St. Louis Blues**	**NHL**	**73**	**1**	**14**	**15**	**1**	**11**	**12**	**53**	**0**	**0**	**0**	**85**	**1.2**	**74**	**1**	**106**	**43**	**+10**	**2**	**0**	**0**	**0**	**20**	**0**	**0**	**0**
1975-76	**St. Louis Blues**	**NHL**	**63**	**3**	**8**	**11**	**3**	**6**	**9**	**90**	**0**	**1**	**1**	**43**	**7.0**	**66**	**3**	**86**	**40**	**+17**	**3**	**0**	**0**	**0**	**2**	**0**	**0**	**0**
1976-77	**St. Louis Blues**	**NHL**	**54**	**1**	**9**	**10**	**1**	**7**	**8**	**23**	**0**	**0**	**0**	**64**	**1.6**	**36**	**3**	**50**	**8**	**–9**	**4**	**0**	**0**	**0**	**0**	**0**	**0**	**0**
	Kansas City Blues	CHL	4	0	2	2	....	....	....	15	....	....	....	....	....	....	....	....	....	....	....	....	....	....	....	....	....	....
1977-78	**St. Louis Blues**	**NHL**	**18**	**0**	**0**	**0**	**0**	**0**	**0**	**4**	**0**	**0**	**0**	**15**	**0.0**	**6**	**0**	**17**	**3**	**–8**	....	....	....	....	....	....	....	....
	Salt Lake Golden Eagles	CHL	11	0	3	3	....	....	....	52	....	....	....	....	....	....	....	....	....	....	6	0	3	3	6	....	....	....
	NHL Totals		**644**	**20**	**126**	**146**	**20**	**110**	**130**	**802**	**0**	**2**	**4**	**712**	**2.8**	**561**	**22**	**763**	**251**		**74**	**2**	**17**	**19**	**195**	**0**	**0**	**0**

Traded to **St. Louis** by **NY Rangers** with Gary Sabourin, Tim Ecclestone and Gord Kannegiesser for Rod Seiling, June 6, 1967.

• PLANTE, CAM

Cam Plante D – L. 6'1", 195 lbs. b: Brandon, Man., 3/12/1964. Toronto's 5th choice, 133rd overall, in 1983 Entry Draft.

1980-81	Brandon Wheat Kings	WHL	70	3	14	17	....	....	....	17	....	....	....	....	....	....	....	....	....	....	5	0	2	2	0	....	....	....
1981-82	Brandon Wheat Kings	WHL	36	4	12	16	....	....	....	22	....	....	....	....	....	....	....	....	....	....	4	0	6	6	4	....	....	....
1982-83	Brandon Wheat Kings	WHL	56	19	56	75	....	....	....	71	....	....	....	....	....	....	....	....	....	....	....	....	....	....	....	....	....	....
1983-84	Brandon Wheat Kings	WHL	72	22	118	140	....	....	....	96	....	....	....	....	....	....	....	....	....	....	11	4	16	20	14	....	....	....
1984-85	**Toronto Maple Leafs**	**NHL**	**2**	**0**	**0**	**0**	**0**	**0**	**0**	**0**	**0**	**0**	**0**	**0**	**0.0**	**0**	**0**	**0**	**0**	**0**	....	....	....	....	....	....	....	....
	St. Catharines Saints	AHL	54	5	31	36	....	....	....	42	....	....	....	....	....	....	....	....	....	....	....	....	....	....	....	....	....	....
1985-86	St. Catharines Saints	AHL	49	6	15	21	....	....	....	28	....	....	....	....	....	....	....	....	....	....	5	0	3	3	2	....	....	....
1986-87	Newmarket Saints	AHL	19	3	4	7	....	....	....	14	....	....	....	....	....	....	....	....	....	....	....	....	....	....	....	....	....	....
	Milwaukee Admirals	IHL	56	7	47	54	....	....	....	44	....	....	....	....	....	....	....	....	....	....	5	2	2	4	4	....	....	....

			REGULAR SEASON																		PLAYOFFS							
Season	Club	League	GP	G	A	Pts	AG	AA	APts	PIM	PP	SH	GW	S	%	TGF	PGF	TGA	PGA	+/–	GP	G	A	Pts	PIM	PP	SH	GW
1987-88	Newmarket Saints	AHL	18	2	8	10	....	....	....	14	....	....	....	....	....	....	....	....	....	....	....	....	....	....	....	....	....	....
	Villach HC	Austria	11	2	10	12	....	....	....	14	....	....	....	....	....	....	....	....	....	....	....	....	....	....	....	....	....	....
	Basel	Switz.	....	9	26	35	....	....	....	....	....	....	....	....	....	....	....	....	....	....	....	....	....	....	....	....	....	....
1988-89	HC Davos	Switz.	....	3	2	5	....	....	....	....	....	....	....	....	....	....	....	....	....	....	....	....	....	....	....	....	....	....
1989-90	HC Davos	Switz.	STATISTICS NOT AVAILABLE																									
1990-91	Kansas City Blades	IHL	43	6	14	20	....	....	....	34	....	....	....	....	....	....	....	....	....	....	....	....	....	....	....	....	....	....
1991-92	Thunder Bay Thunder Hawks	ColHL	54	16	57	73	....	....	....	32	....	....	....	....	....	....	....	....	....	....	....	....	....	....	....	....	....	....
1992-93	Peterborough Pirates	Britain	25	14	52	66	....	....	....	93	....	....	....	....	....	....	....	....	....	....	....	....	....	....	....	....	....	....
1993-94	Peterborough Pirates	Britain	37	13	55	68	....	....	....	56	....	....	....	....	....	....	....	....	....	....	....	....	....	....	....	....	....	....
1994-95	Peterborough Pirates	Britain	34	22	52	74	....	....	....	60	....	....	....	....	....	....	....	....	....	....	....	....	....	....	....	....	....	....
1995-96	Peterborough Pirates	Britain	16	4	32	36	....	....	....	93	....	....	....	....	....	....	....	....	....	....	....	....	....	....	....	....	....	....
	Chelmsford Chieftans	Britain	10	8	15	23	....	....	....	22	....	....	....	....	....	....	....	....	....	....	....	....	....	....	....	....	....	....
	Humberside Hawks	Britain	9	3	5	8	....	....	....	18	....	....	....	....	....	....	....	....	....	....	7	2	14	16	8	....	....	....
1996-97	Wichita Thunder	CHL	55	12	63	75	....	....	....	74	....	....	....	....	....	....	....	....	....	....	9	2	7	9	18	....	....	....
1997-98	Wichita Thunder	CHL	67	8	62	70	....	....	....	112	....	....	....	....	....	....	....	....	....	....	14	0	8	8	16	....	....	....
	NHL Totals		**2**	**0**	**0**	**0**	**0**	**0**	**0**	**0**	**0**	**0**	**0**	**0**	**0.0**	**0**	**0**	**0**	**0**		....	....	....	....	....	....	....	....

WHL East All-Star Team (1984)

• PLANTE, DAN

Dan Plante RW – R. 5'11", 202 lbs. b: Hayward, WI, 10/5/1971. NY Islanders' 3rd choice, 48th overall, in 1990 Entry Draft.

Season	Club	League	GP	G	A	Pts	AG	AA	APts	PIM	PP	SH	GW	S	%	TGF	PGF	TGA	PGA	+/–	GP	G	A	Pts	PIM	PP	SH	GW
1989-90	Edina-Minnesota High	H.S.	24	8	18	26	....	....	....	12	....	....	....	....	....	....	....	....	....	....	....	....	....	....	....	....	....	....
1990-91	University of Wisconsin	WCHA	33	1	2	3	....	....	....	54	....	....	....	....	....	....	....	....	....	....	....	....	....	....	....	....	....	....
1991-92	University of Wisconsin	WCHA	36	13	13	26	....	....	....	107	....	....	....	....	....	....	....	....	....	....	....	....	....	....	....	....	....	....
1992-93	University of Wisconsin	WCHA	42	26	31	57	....	....	....	142	....	....	....	....	....	....	....	....	....	....	....	....	....	....	....	....	....	....
1993-94	**New York Islanders**	**NHL**	**12**	**0**	**1**	**1**	**0**	**1**	**1**	**4**	**0**	**0**	**0**	**9**	**0.0**	**2**	**0**	**4**	**0**	**–2**	**1**	**1**	**0**	**1**	**2**	**0**	**0**	**0**
	Salt Lake Golden Eagles	IHL	66	7	17	24	....	....	....	148	....	....	....	....	....	....	....	....	....	....	....	....	....	....	....	....	....	....
1994-95	Denver Grizzlies	IHL	2	0	0	0	....	....	....	4	....	....	....	....	....	....	....	....	....	....	....	....	....	....	....	....	....	....
1995-96	**New York Islanders**	**NHL**	**73**	**5**	**3**	**8**	**5**	**2**	**7**	**50**	**0**	**2**	**0**	**103**	**4.9**	**16**	**1**	**64**	**27**	**–22**	....	....	....	....	....	....	....	....
	United States	WC-A	7	1	1	2	....	....	....	0	....	....	....	....	....	....	....	....	....	....	....	....	....	....	....	....	....	....
1996-97	**New York Islanders**	**NHL**	**67**	**4**	**9**	**13**	**4**	**8**	**12**	**75**	**0**	**2**	**0**	**61**	**6.6**	**21**	**0**	**36**	**9**	**–6**	....	....	....	....	....	....	....	....
	United States	WC-A	8	1	1	2	....	....	....	6	....	....	....	....	....	....	....	....	....	....	....	....	....	....	....	....	....	....
1997-98	**New York Islanders**	**NHL**	**7**	**0**	**1**	**1**	**0**	**1**	**1**	**6**	**0**	**0**	**0**	**7**	**0.0**	**1**	**0**	**2**	**0**	**–1**	....	....	....	....	....	....	....	....
	Utah Grizzlies	IHL	73	22	27	49	....	....	....	125	....	....	....	....	....	....	....	....	....	....	4	0	2	2	14	....	....	....
	NHL Totals		**159**	**9**	**14**	**23**	**9**	**12**	**21**	**135**	**0**	**4**	**0**	**180**	**5.0**	**40**	**1**	**106**	**36**		**1**	**1**	**0**	**1**	**2**	**0**	**0**	**0**

• PLANTE, DEREK

Derek Plante C – L. 5'11", 181 lbs. b: Cloquet, MN, 1/17/1971. Buffalo's 7th choice, 161st overall, in 1989 Entry Draft.

Season	Club	League	GP	G	A	Pts	AG	AA	APts	PIM	PP	SH	GW	S	%	TGF	PGF	TGA	PGA	+/–	GP	G	A	Pts	PIM	PP	SH	GW
1988-89	Cloquet-Minnesota High School	H.S.	24	30	33	63	....	....	....	....	....	....	....	....	....	....	....	....	....	....	....	....	....	....	....	....	....	....
1989-90	University of Minnesota-Duluth	WCHA	28	10	11	21	....	....	....	12	....	....	....	....	....	....	....	....	....	....	....	....	....	....	....	....	....	....
1990-91	University of Minnesota-Duluth	WCHA	36	23	20	43	....	....	....	6	....	....	....	....	....	....	....	....	....	....	....	....	....	....	....	....	....	....
1991-92	University of Minnesota-Duluth	WCHA	37	27	36	63	....	....	....	28	....	....	....	....	....	....	....	....	....	....	....	....	....	....	....	....	....	....
	United States	WC-A	6	0	1	1	....	....	....	0	....	....	....	....	....	....	....	....	....	....	....	....	....	....	....	....	....	....
1992-93	University of Minnesota-Duluth	WCHA	37	*36	*56	*92	....	....	....	30	....	....	....	....	....	....	....	....	....	....	....	....	....	....	....	....	....	....
	United States	WC-A	6	1	0	1	....	....	....	2	....	....	....	....	....	....	....	....	....	....	....	....	....	....	....	....	....	....
1993-94	**Buffalo Sabres**	**NHL**	**77**	**21**	**35**	**56**	**20**	**27**	**47**	**24**	**8**	**1**	**2**	**147**	**14.3**	**81**	**42**	**40**	**5**	**+4**	**7**	**1**	**0**	**1**	**0**	**0**	**0**	**0**
	United States	Nat-Team	2	0	1	1	....	....	....	0	....	....	....	....	....	....	....	....	....	....	....	....	....	....	....	....	....	....
1994-95	**Buffalo Sabres**	**NHL**	**47**	**3**	**19**	**22**	**5**	**28**	**33**	**12**	**2**	**0**	**0**	**94**	**3.2**	**29**	**13**	**29**	**9**	**–4**	....	....	....	....	....	....	....	....
1995-96	**Buffalo Sabres**	**NHL**	**76**	**23**	**33**	**56**	**23**	**27**	**50**	**28**	**4**	**0**	**5**	**203**	**11.3**	**78**	**22**	**78**	**18**	**–4**	....	....	....	....	....	....	....	....
	United States	WC-A	8	1	1	2	....	....	....	4	....	....	....	....	....	....	....	....	....	....	....	....	....	....	....	....	....	....
1996-97	**Buffalo Sabres**	**NHL**	**82**	**27**	**26**	**53**	**29**	**23**	**52**	**24**	**5**	**0**	**6**	**191**	**14.1**	**82**	**19**	**62**	**13**	**+14**	**12**	**4**	**6**	**10**	**4**	**0**	**0**	**0**
1997-98	**Buffalo Sabres**	**NHL**	**72**	**13**	**21**	**34**	**15**	**20**	**35**	**26**	**5**	**0**	**1**	**150**	**8.7**	**51**	**16**	**52**	**25**	**+8**	**11**	**0**	**3**	**3**	**10**	**0**	**0**	**0**
	NHL Totals		**354**	**87**	**134**	**221**	**92**	**125**	**217**	**114**	**24**	**1**	**14**	**785**	**11.1**	**321**	**112**	**261**	**70**		**30**	**5**	**9**	**14**	**14**	**0**	**0**	**0**

WCHA Second All-Star Team (1992) • WCHA First All-Star Team (1993) • NCAA West First All-American Team (1993)

• PLANTE, PIERRE

Pierre Plante RW – R. 6'1", 190 lbs. b: Valleyfield, Que., 5/14/1951. Philadelphia's 2nd choice, 9th overall, in 1971 Amateur Draft.

Season	Club	League	GP	G	A	Pts	AG	AA	APts	PIM	PP	SH	GW	S	%	TGF	PGF	TGA	PGA	+/–	GP	G	A	Pts	PIM	PP	SH	GW
1969-70	Drummondville Rangers	QJHL	51	51	51	102	....	....	....	186	....	....	....	....	....	....	....	....	....	....	1	1	0	1	7	....	....	....
1970-71	Drummondville Rangers	QJHL	58	38	50	88	....	....	....	251	....	....	....	....	....	....	....	....	....	....	6	1	9	10	14	....	....	....
1971-72	**Philadelphia Flyers**	**NHL**	**24**	**1**	**0**	**1**	**1**	**0**	**1**	**15**	**0**	**0**	**0**	**24**	**4.2**	**4**	**1**	**14**	**0**	**–11**	....	....	....	....	....	....	....	....
	Richmond Robins	AHL	47	10	17	27	....	....	....	51	....	....	....	....	....	....	....	....	....	....	....	....	....	....	....	....	....	....
1972-73	**Philadelphia Flyers**	**NHL**	**2**	**0**	**3**	**3**	**0**	**2**	**2**	**0**	**0**	**0**	**0**	**5**	**0.0**	**4**	**0**	**1**	**0**	**+3**	....	....	....	....	....	....	....	....
	Richmond Robins	AHL	30	9	11	20	....	....	....	56	....	....	....	....	....	....	....	....	....	....	....	....	....	....	....	....	....	....
	St. Louis Blues	**NHL**	**49**	**12**	**13**	**25**	**12**	**11**	**23**	**56**	**0**	**0**	**1**	**90**	**13.3**	**46**	**6**	**33**	**1**	**+8**	**5**	**2**	**0**	**2**	**15**	**0**	**0**	**0**
1973-74	**St. Louis Blues**	**NHL**	**78**	**26**	**28**	**54**	**27**	**24**	**51**	**85**	**8**	**0**	**3**	**151**	**17.2**	**77**	**24**	**68**	**1**	**–14**	....	....	....	....	....	....	....	....
1974-75	**St. Louis Blues**	**NHL**	**80**	**34**	**32**	**66**	**32**	**25**	**57**	**125**	**4**	**0**	**4**	**162**	**21.0**	**100**	**16**	**70**	**2**	**+16**	**2**	**0**	**0**	**0**	**8**	**0**	**0**	**0**
1975-76	**St. Louis Blues**	**NHL**	**74**	**14**	**19**	**33**	**13**	**15**	**28**	**77**	**5**	**0**	**2**	**125**	**11.2**	**53**	**14**	**61**	**0**	**–22**	**3**	**0**	**0**	**0**	**6**	**0**	**0**	**0**
1976-77	**St. Louis Blues**	**NHL**	**76**	**18**	**20**	**38**	**17**	**16**	**33**	**77**	**4**	**0**	**3**	**124**	**14.5**	**68**	**17**	**55**	**0**	**–4**	**4**	**0**	**0**	**0**	**2**	**0**	**0**	**0**
1977-78	**Chicago Black Hawks**	**NHL**	**77**	**10**	**18**	**28**	**10**	**15**	**25**	**59**	**0**	**0**	**2**	**104**	**9.6**	**44**	**2**	**63**	**19**	**–2**	**1**	**0**	**0**	**0**	**0**	**0**	**0**	**0**
1978-79	**New York Rangers**	**NHL**	**70**	**6**	**25**	**31**	**5**	**19**	**24**	**37**	**0**	**0**	**1**	**84**	**7.1**	**53**	**4**	**63**	**25**	**+11**	**18**	**0**	**6**	**6**	**20**	**0**	**0**	**0**
1979-80	**Quebec Nordiques**	**NHL**	**69**	**4**	**14**	**18**	**4**	**11**	**15**	**68**	**0**	**0**	**1**	**82**	**4.9**	**29**	**1**	**70**	**28**	**–14**	....	....	....	....	....	....	....	....
	Syracuse Firebirds	AHL	3	0	0	0	....	....	....	2	....	....	....	....	....	....	....	....	....	....	....	....	....	....	....	....	....	....
	NHL Totals		**599**	**125**	**172**	**297**	**121**	**138**	**259**	**599**	**21**	**0**	**17**	**951**	**13.1**	**478**	**85**	**498**	**76**		**33**	**2**	**6**	**8**	**51**	**0**	**0**	**0**

QJHL First All-Star Team (1970)

Traded to **St. Louis** by **Philadelphia** with Brent Hughes for Andre Dupont and St. Louis' 3rd round choice (Bob Stumpf) in 1973 Amateur Draft, December 14, 1972. Traded to **Chicago** by **St. Louis** for Dick Redmond, August 9, 1977. Traded to **Minnesota** by **Chicago** to complete transaction that sent Doug Hicks to Chicago (May 4, 1978), March 14, 1978. Claimed on waivers by **Detroit** from **Minnesota**, September 13, 1978. Claimed by **NY Rangers** from **Detroit** in Waiver Draft, October 2, 1978. Claimed by **Quebec** from **NY Rangers** in Expansion Draft, June 13, 1979.

• PLANTERY, MARK

Mark Plantery D – L. 6'1", 185 lbs. b: St. Catharines, Ont., 8/14/1959.

Season	Club	League	GP	G	A	Pts	AG	AA	APts	PIM	PP	SH	GW	S	%	TGF	PGF	TGA	PGA	+/–	GP	G	A	Pts	PIM	PP	SH	GW
1976-77	St.Catherines Fincups	OHL	54	1	23	24	....	....	....	112	....	....	....	....	....	....	....	....	....	....	....	....	....	....	....	....	....	....
	Canada	WJC-A	7	0	1	1	....	....	....	6	....	....	....	....	....	....	....	....	....	....	....	....	....	....	....	....	....	....
1977-78	Hamilton Fincups	OHA	51	0	6	6	....	....	....	91	....	....	....	....	....	....	....	....	....	....	20	1	2	3	29	....	....	....
1978-79	Brantford Alexanders	OHA	37	4	19	23	....	....	....	98	....	....	....	....	....	....	....	....	....	....	....	....	....	....	....	....	....	....
	Windsor Spitfires	OHA	27	3	15	18	....	....	....	43	....	....	....	....	....	....	....	....	....	....	7	0	2	2	17	....	....	....
1979-80	Tulsa Oilers	CHL	67	6	26	32	....	....	....	102	....	....	....	....	....	....	....	....	....	....	3	0	0	0	2	....	....	....
1980-81	**Winnipeg Jets**	**NHL**	**25**	**1**	**5**	**6**	**1**	**3**	**4**	**14**	**0**	**0**	**0**	**18**	**5.6**	**23**	**1**	**34**	**2**	**–10**	....	....	....	....	....	....	....	....
	Tulsa Oilers	CHL	50	3	15	18	....	....	....	77	....	....	....	....	....	....	....	....	....	....	....	....	....	....	....	....	....	....
1981-82	Tulsa Oilers	CHL	76	9	40	49	....	....	....	65	....	....	....	....	....	....	....	....	....	....	3	1	0	1	0	....	....	....
1982-83	Sherbrooke Jets	AHL	75	6	25	31	....	....	....	51	....	....	....	....	....	....	....	....	....	....	....	....	....	....	....	....	....	....
1983-84			DID NOT PLAY																									
1984-85	Toledo Goaldiggers	IHL	33	1	15	16	....	....	....	37	....	....	....	....	....	....	....	....	....	....	....	....	....	....	....	....	....	....
	Flint Generals	IHL	44	3	17	20	....	....	....	44	....	....	....	....	....	....	....	....	....	....	4	0	0	0	5	....	....	....
1985-86	Milwaukee Admirals	IHL	1	0	0	0	....	....	....	0	....	....	....	....	....	....	....	....	....	....	....	....	....	....	....	....	....	....
	NHL Totals		**25**	**1**	**5**	**6**	**1**	**3**	**4**	**14**	**0**	**0**	**0**	**18**	**5.6**	**23**	**1**	**34**	**2**		....	....	....	....	....	....	....	....

Signed as a free agent by **Winnipeg**, October 5, 1979.

			REGULAR SEASON																		PLAYOFFS							
Season	Club	League	GP	G	A	Pts	AG	AA	APts	PIM	PP	SH	GW	S	%	TGF	PGF	TGA	PGA	+/–	GP	G	A	Pts	PIM	PP	SH	GW

• PLAVSIC, ADRIEN

Adrien Plavsic D – L. 6'1", 200 lbs. b: Montreal, Que., 1/13/1970. St. Louis' 2nd choice, 30th overall, in 1988 Entry Draft.

Season	Club	League	GP	G	A	Pts	AG	AA	APts	PIM	PP	SH	GW	S	%	TGF	PGF	TGA	PGA	+/–	GP	G	A	Pts	PIM	PP	SH	GW
1987-88	University of New Hampshire	H.E.	30	5	6	11	....	....	....	45	....	....	....	....	....	....	....	....	....	....	....	....	....	....	....	....	....	....
1988-89	Canada	Nat-Team	62	5	10	15	....	....	....	25	....	....	....	....	....	....	....	....	....	....	....	....	....	....	....	....	....	....
1989-90	**St. Louis Blues**	**NHL**	**4**	**0**	**1**	**1**	**0**	**1**	**1**	**2**	**0**	**0**	**0**	**1**	**0.0**	**4**	**0**	**1**	**0**	**+3**	....	....	....	....	....	....	....	....
	Canada	WJC-A	7	0	1	1	....	....	....	8	....	....	....	....	....	....	....	....	....	....	....	....	....	....	....	....	....	....
	Peoria Rivermen	IHL	51	7	14	21	....	....	....	87	....	....	....	....	....	....	....	....	....	....	....	....	....	....	....	....	....	....
	Vancouver Canucks	**NHL**	**11**	**3**	**2**	**5**	**3**	**1**	**4**	**8**	**2**	**0**	**0**	**13**	**23.1**	**10**	**2**	**10**	**0**	**–2**	....	....	....	....	....	....	....	....
	Milwaukee Admirals	IHL	3	1	2	3	....	....	....	14	....	....	....	....	....	....	....	....	....	....	6	1	3	4	6	....	....	....
1990-91	**Vancouver Canucks**	**NHL**	**48**	**2**	**10**	**12**	**2**	**8**	**10**	**62**	**0**	**0**	**0**	**69**	**2.9**	**33**	**10**	**48**	**2**	**–23**	....	....	....	....	....	....	....	....
1991-92	Canada	Nat-Team	38	7	8	15	....	....	....	44	....	....	....	....	....	....	....	....	....	....	....	....	....	....	....	....	....	....
	Canada	Olympics	8	0	2	2	....	....	....	0	....	....	....	....	....	....	....	....	....	....	....	....	....	....	....	....	....	....
	Vancouver Canucks	**NHL**	**16**	**1**	**9**	**10**	**1**	**7**	**8**	**14**	**0**	**0**	**0**	**21**	**4.8**	**23**	**6**	**21**	**8**	**+4**	**13**	**1**	**7**	**8**	**4**	**0**	**0**	**0**
1992-93	**Vancouver Canucks**	**NHL**	**57**	**6**	**21**	**27**	**5**	**14**	**19**	**53**	**5**	**0**	**2**	**62**	**9.7**	**86**	**22**	**51**	**15**	**+28**	....	....	....	....	....	....	....	....
1993-94	**Vancouver Canucks**	**NHL**	**47**	**1**	**9**	**10**	**1**	**7**	**8**	**6**	**0**	**0**	**1**	**41**	**2.4**	**24**	**4**	**38**	**13**	**–5**	....	....	....	....	....	....	....	....
	Hamilton Canucks	AHL	2	0	0	0	....	....	....	0	....	....	....	....	....	....	....	....	....	....	....	....	....	....	....	....	....	....
1994-95	**Vancouver Canucks**	**NHL**	**3**	**0**	**1**	**1**	**0**	**1**	**1**	**4**	**0**	**0**	**0**	**11**	**0.0**	**4**	**0**	**1**	**0**	**+3**	....	....	....	....	....	....	....	....
	Tampa Bay Lightning	**NHL**	**15**	**2**	**1**	**3**	**4**	**1**	**5**	**4**	**0**	**0**	**0**	**24**	**8.3**	**14**	**2**	**7**	**0**	**+5**	....	....	....	....	....	....	....	....
1995-96	**Tampa Bay Lightning**	**NHL**	**7**	**1**	**2**	**3**	**1**	**2**	**3**	**6**	**0**	**0**	**0**	**4**	**25.0**	**7**	**0**	**2**	**0**	**+5**	....	....	....	....	....	....	....	....
	Atlanta Knights	IHL	68	5	34	39	....	....	....	32	....	....	....	....	....	....	....	....	....	....	3	0	1	1	4	....	....	....
1996-97	**Anaheim Mighty Ducks**	**NHL**	**6**	**0**	**0**	**0**	**0**	**0**	**0**	**2**	**0**	**0**	**0**	**3**	**0.0**	**4**	**4**	**6**	**1**	**–5**	....	....	....	....	....	....	....	....
	Long Beach Ice Dogs	IHL	69	7	28	35	....	....	....	86	....	....	....	....	....	....	....	....	....	....	18	0	9	9	10	....	....	....
1997-98	ECR Revier Lowen	Germany	36	4	15	19	....	....	....	28	....	....	....	....	....	....	....	....	....	....	....	....	....	....	....	....	....	....
	NHL Totals		**214**	**16**	**56**	**72**	**17**	**42**	**59**	**161**	**7**	**0**	**3**	**249**	**6.4**	**209**	**50**	**185**	**39**		**13**	**1**	**7**	**8**	**4**	**0**	**0**	**0**

Traded to **Vancouver** by **St. Louis** with Montreal's 1st round choice (previously acquired, Vancouver selected Shawn Antoski) in 1990 Entry Draft and St. Louis' 2nd round choice (later traded to Montreal — Montreal selected Craig Darby) in 1991 Entry Draft for Rich Sutter, Harold Snepsts and St. Louis' 2nd round choice (previously acquired, St. Louis selected Craig Johnson) in 1990 Entry Draft, March 6, 1990. Traded to **Tampa Bay** by **Vancouver** for Tampa Bay's 5th round choice (David Darguzas) in 1997 Entry Draft, March 23, 1995. Signed as a free agent by **Anaheim**, September 6, 1996.

• PLAYFAIR, JIM

Jim Playfair D – L. 6'4", 200 lbs. b: Fort St. James, B.C., 5/22/1964. Edmonton's 1st choice, 20th overall, in 1982 Entry Draft.

Season	Club	League	GP	G	A	Pts	AG	AA	APts	PIM	PP	SH	GW	S	%	TGF	PGF	TGA	PGA	+/–	GP	G	A	Pts	PIM	PP	SH	GW
1980-81	Fort Saskatchewan Traders	AJHL	31	2	17	19	....	....	....	105	....	....	....	....	....	....	....	....	....	....	....	....	....	....	....	....	....	....
1981-82	Portland Winter Hawks	WHL	70	4	13	17	....	....	....	121	....	....	....	....	....	....	....	....	....	....	15	1	2	3	21	....	....	....
1982-83	Portland Winter Hawks	WHL	63	8	27	35	....	....	....	218	....	....	....	....	....	....	....	....	....	....	14	0	5	5	16	....	....	....
1983-84	Portland Winter Hawks	WHL	16	5	6	11	....	....	....	38	....	....	....	....	....	....	....	....	....	....	....	....	....	....	....	....	....	....
	Calgary Wranglers	WHL	46	6	9	15	....	....	....	96	....	....	....	....	....	....	....	....	....	....	4	0	1	1	2	....	....	....
	Edmonton Oilers	**NHL**	**2**	**1**	**1**	**2**	**1**	**1**	**2**	**2**	**0**	**0**	**0**	**2**	**50.0**	**4**	**0**	**0**	**0**	**+4**	....	....	....	....	....	....	....	....
1984-85	Nova Scotia Voyageurs	AHL	41	0	4	4	....	....	....	107	....	....	....	....	....	....	....	....	....	....	....	....	....	....	....	....	....	....
1985-86	Nova Scotia Oilers	AHL	73	2	12	14	....	....	....	160	....	....	....	....	....	....	....	....	....	....	....	....	....	....	....	....	....	....
1986-87	Nova Scotia Oilers	AHL	60	1	21	22	....	....	....	82	....	....	....	....	....	....	....	....	....	....	....	....	....	....	....	....	....	....
1987-88	**Chicago Blackhawks**	**NHL**	**12**	**1**	**3**	**4**	**1**	**2**	**3**	**21**	**1**	**0**	**0**	**11**	**9.1**	**14**	**2**	**8**	**0**	**+4**	....	....	....	....	....	....	....	....
	Saginaw Hawks	IHL	50	5	21	26	....	....	....	133	....	....	....	....	....	....	....	....	....	....	....	....	....	....	....	....	....	....
1988-89	**Chicago Blackhawks**	**NHL**	**7**	**0**	**0**	**0**	**0**	**0**	**0**	**28**	**0**	**0**	**0**	**1**	**0.0**	**2**	**0**	**1**	**0**	**+1**	....	....	....	....	....	....	....	....
	Saginaw Hawks	IHL	23	3	6	9	....	....	....	73	....	....	....	....	....	....	....	....	....	....	6	0	2	2	20	....	....	....
1989-90	Indianapolis Ice	IHL	67	7	24	31	....	....	....	137	....	....	....	....	....	....	....	....	....	....	14	1	5	6	24	....	....	....
1990-91	Indianapolis Ice	IHL	23	3	4	7	....	....	....	31	....	....	....	....	....	....	....	....	....	....	....	....	....	....	....	....	....	....
1991-92	Indianapolis Ice	IHL	23	1	1	2	....	....	....	53	....	....	....	....	....	....	....	....	....	....	....	....	....	....	....	....	....	....
	NHL Totals		**21**	**2**	**4**	**6**	**2**	**3**	**5**	**51**	**1**	**0**	**0**	**14**	**14.3**	**20**	**2**	**9**	**0**		....	....	....	....	....	....	....	....

Signed as a free agent by **Chicago**, July 31, 1987.

• PLAYFAIR, LARRY

Larry Playfair D – L. 6'4", 205 lbs. b: Fort St. James, B.C., 6/23/1958. Buffalo's 1st choice, 13th overall, in 1978 Amateur Draft.

Season	Club	League	GP	G	A	Pts	AG	AA	APts	PIM	PP	SH	GW	S	%	TGF	PGF	TGA	PGA	+/–	GP	G	A	Pts	PIM	PP	SH	GW
1975-76	Langley Thunder Hawks	BCJHL	72	10	20	30	....	....	....	162	....	....	....	....	....	....	....	....	....	....	....	....	....	....	....	....	....	....
1976-77	Portland Winter Hawks	WCJHL	65	2	17	19	....	....	....	199	....	....	....	....	....	....	....	....	....	....	8	0	0	0	4	....	....	....
1977-78	Portland Winter Hawks	WCJHL	71	13	19	32	....	....	....	402	....	....	....	....	....	....	....	....	....	....	8	0	2	2	58	....	....	....
1978-79	**Buffalo Sabres**	**NHL**	**26**	**0**	**3**	**3**	**0**	**2**	**2**	**60**	**0**	**0**	**0**	**12**	**0.0**	**18**	**1**	**17**	**1**	**+1**	....	....	....	....	....	....	....	....
	Hershey Bears	AHL	45	0	12	12	....	....	....	148	....	....	....	....	....	....	....	....	....	....	....	....	....	....	....	....	....	....
1979-80	**Buffalo Sabres**	**NHL**	**79**	**2**	**10**	**12**	**2**	**8**	**10**	**145**	**0**	**0**	**0**	**32**	**6.3**	**50**	**0**	**38**	**1**	**+13**	**14**	**0**	**2**	**2**	**29**	**0**	**0**	**0**
1980-81	**Buffalo Sabres**	**NHL**	**75**	**3**	**9**	**12**	**2**	**6**	**8**	**169**	**0**	**0**	**1**	**54**	**5.6**	**59**	**0**	**56**	**1**	**+4**	**8**	**0**	**0**	**0**	**26**	**0**	**0**	**0**
1981-82	**Buffalo Sabres**	**NHL**	**77**	**6**	**10**	**16**	**5**	**7**	**12**	**258**	**0**	**0**	**0**	**68**	**8.8**	**62**	**0**	**79**	**12**	**–5**	**4**	**0**	**0**	**0**	**22**	**0**	**0**	**0**
1982-83	**Buffalo Sabres**	**NHL**	**79**	**4**	**13**	**17**	**3**	**9**	**12**	**180**	**0**	**0**	**0**	**75**	**5.3**	**79**	**2**	**91**	**19**	**+5**	**5**	**0**	**1**	**1**	**11**	**0**	**0**	**0**
1983-84	**Buffalo Sabres**	**NHL**	**76**	**5**	**11**	**16**	**4**	**7**	**11**	**211**	**0**	**0**	**0**	**67**	**7.5**	**67**	**5**	**72**	**14**	**+4**	**3**	**0**	**0**	**0**	**0**	**0**	**0**	**0**
1984-85	**Buffalo Sabres**	**NHL**	**72**	**3**	**14**	**17**	**2**	**9**	**11**	**157**	**0**	**0**	**1**	**64**	**4.7**	**48**	**0**	**59**	**8**	**–3**	**5**	**0**	**3**	**3**	**9**	**0**	**0**	**0**
1985-86	**Buffalo Sabres**	**NHL**	**47**	**1**	**2**	**3**	**1**	**1**	**2**	**100**	**0**	**0**	**0**	**35**	**2.9**	**29**	**0**	**49**	**12**	**–8**	....	....	....	....	....	....	....	....
	Los Angeles Kings	**NHL**	**14**	**0**	**1**	**1**	**0**	**1**	**1**	**26**	**0**	**0**	**0**	**6**	**0.0**	**10**	**1**	**30**	**7**	**–14**	....	....	....	....	....	....	....	....
1986-87	**Los Angeles Kings**	**NHL**	**37**	**2**	**7**	**9**	**2**	**5**	**7**	**181**	**0**	**0**	**0**	**20**	**10.0**	**33**	**0**	**39**	**5**	**–1**	....	....	....	....	....	....	....	....
1987-88	**Los Angeles Kings**	**NHL**	**54**	**0**	**7**	**7**	**0**	**5**	**5**	**197**	**0**	**0**	**0**	**20**	**0.0**	**34**	**0**	**52**	**5**	**–13**	**3**	**0**	**0**	**0**	**14**	**0**	**0**	**0**
1988-89	**Los Angeles Kings**	**NHL**	**6**	**0**	**3**	**3**	**0**	**2**	**2**	**16**	**0**	**0**	**0**	**4**	**0.0**	**5**	**0**	**2**	**0**	**+3**	....	....	....	....	....	....	....	....
	Buffalo Sabres	**NHL**	**42**	**0**	**3**	**3**	**0**	**2**	**2**	**110**	**0**	**0**	**0**	**6**	**0.0**	**17**	**0**	**32**	**5**	**–10**	**1**	**0**	**0**	**0**	**0**	**0**	**0**	**0**
1989-90	**Buffalo Sabres**	**NHL**	**4**	**0**	**1**	**1**	**0**	**1**	**1**	**2**	**0**	**0**	**0**	**0**	**0.0**	**1**	**0**	**3**	**0**	**–2**	....	....	....	....	....	....	....	....
	NHL Totals		**688**	**26**	**94**	**120**	**21**	**65**	**86**	**1812**	**0**	**0**	**2**	**463**	**5.6**	**512**	**9**	**619**	**90**		**43**	**0**	**6**	**6**	**111**	**0**	**0**	**0**

WCJHL All-Star Team (1978)

Traded to **LA Kings** by **Buffalo** with Sean McKenna and Ken Baumgartner for Brian Engblom and Doug Smith, Januray 30, 1986. Traded to **Buffalo** by **LA Kings** for Bob Logan and Buffalo's 9th round choice (Jim Glacin) in 1989 Entry Draft, Ocotber 21, 1988.

• PLEAU, LARRY

Larry Pleau C – L. 6'1", 190 lbs. b: Lynn, MA, 1/29/1947.

Season	Club	League	GP	G	A	Pts	AG	AA	APts	PIM	PP	SH	GW	S	%	TGF	PGF	TGA	PGA	+/–	GP	G	A	Pts	PIM	PP	SH	GW
1963-64	Notre Dame de Grace	QJHL	44	8	22	30	....	....	....	33	....	....	....	....	....	....	....	....	....	....	....	....	....	....	....	....	....	....
1964-65	Montreal Jr. Canadiens	OHA	55	9	17	26	....	....	....	24	....	....	....	....	....	....	....	....	....	....	7	0	0	0	10	....	....	....
1965-66	Montreal Jr. Canadiens	OHA	40	13	11	24	....	....	....	47	....	....	....	....	....	....	....	....	....	....	10	0	6	6	6	....	....	....
1966-67	Montreal Jr. Canadiens	OHA	45	20	32	52	....	....	....	34	....	....	....	....	....	....	....	....	....	....	4	0	2	2	2	....	....	....
1967-68	United States	Nat-Team	STATISTICS NOT AVAILABLE																									
	United States	Olympics	7	2	4	6	....	....	....	2	....	....	....	....	....	....	....	....	....	....	....	....	....	....	....	....	....	....
1968-69	Jersey Devils	EHL	66	37	44	81	....	....	....	53	....	....	....	....	....	....	....	....	....	....	....	....	....	....	....	....	....	....
	United States	WEC-A	10	5	0	5	....	....	....	8	....	....	....	....	....	....	....	....	....	....	....	....	....	....	....	....	....	....
1969-70	**Montreal Canadiens**	**NHL**	**20**	**1**	**0**	**1**	**1**	**0**	**1**	**0**	**0**	**1**	**0**	**19**	**5.3**	**3**	**0**	**12**	**8**	**–1**	....	....	....	....	....	....	....	....
	Montreal Voyageurs	AHL	50	15	16	31	....	....	....	19	....	....	....	....	....	....	....	....	....	....	....	....	....	....	....	....	....	....
1970-71	**Montreal Canadiens**	**NHL**	**19**	**1**	**5**	**6**	**1**	**4**	**5**	**8**	**0**	**0**	**1**	**24**	**4.2**	**7**	**0**	**24**	**9**	**–8**	....	....	....	....	....	....	....	....
1971-72	**Montreal Canadiens**	**NHL**	**55**	**7**	**10**	**17**	**7**	**9**	**16**	**19**	**0**	**0**	**2**	**67**	**10.4**	**25**	**0**	**25**	**4**	**+4**	**4**	**0**	**0**	**0**	**0**	**0**	**0**	**0**
	Nova Scotia Voyageurs	AHL	11	7	6	13	....	....	....	19	....	....	....	....	....	....	....	....	....	....	....	....	....	....	....	....	....	....
1972-73	New England Whalers	WHA	78	39	48	87	....	....	....	42	....	....	....	....	....	....	....	....	....	....	15	12	7	19	15	....	....	....
1973-74	New England Whalers	WHA	77	26	43	69	....	....	....	35	....	....	....	....	....	....	....	....	....	....	2	2	0	2	0	....	....	....
1974-75	New England Whalers	WHA	78	30	34	64	....	....	....	50	....	....	....	....	....	....	....	....	....	....	6	2	3	5	14	....	....	....
1975-76	New England Whalers	WHA	75	29	45	74	....	....	....	21	....	....	....	....	....	....	....	....	....	....	14	5	7	12	0	....	....	....
1976-77	New England Whalers	WHA	78	11	21	32	....	....	....	22	....	....	....	....	....	....	....	....	....	....	5	1	0	1	0	....	....	....
1977-78	New England Whalers	WHA	54	10	18	34	....	....	....	4	....	....	....	....	....	....	....	....	....	....	14	5	4	9	8	....		
1978-79	New England Whalers	WHA	28	6	6	12	....	....	....	6	....	....	....	....	....	....	....	....	....	....	10	2	1	3	0	....	....	....
	Springfield Indians	AHL	5	1	3	4	....	....	....	0	....	....	....	....	....	....	....	....	....	....	....	....	....	....	....	....	....	....
	NHL Totals		**94**	**9**	**15**	**24**	**9**	**13**	**22**	**27**	**0**	**1**	**3**	**110**	**8.2**	**35**	**0**	**61**	**21**		**4**	**0**	**0**	**0**	**0**	**0**	**0**	**0**
	Other Major League Totals		468	157	215	372	....	....	....	180	....	....	....	....	....	....	....	....	....		66	29	22	51	37	....	....	....

EHL North Rookie of the Year (1969)

Selected by **New England** (WHA) in 1972 WHA General Player Draft, February 12, 1972. Claimed by **Toronto** from **Montreal** in Intra-League Draft, June 5, 1972.

• PLETT, WILLI

Willi Plett RW – R. 6'3", 205 lbs. b: Paraguay, South America, 6/7/1955. Atlanta's 4th choice, 80th overall, in 1975 Amateur Draft.

			REGULAR SEASON																		PLAYOFFS							
Season	Club	League	GP	G	A	Pts	AG	AA	APts	PIM	PP	SH	GW	S	%	TGF	PGF	TGA	PGA	+/–	GP	G	A	Pts	PIM	PP	SH	GW
1974-75	Niagara Falls Flyers	SOJHL	STATISTICS NOT AVAILABLE																									
	St. Catharines Black Hawks	OHA	22	6	8	14	....	....	....	63	....	....	....	....	....	....	....	....	....	....	4	1	1	2	42	....	....	....
1975-76	**Atlanta Flames**	**NHL**	**4**	**0**	**0**	**0**	**0**	**0**	**0**	**0**	**0**	**0**	**0**	**5**	**0.0**	**1**	**0**	**1**	**0**	**0**	....	....	....	....	....	....	....	....
	Tulsa Oilers	CHL	73	30	20	50	....	....	....	163	....	....	....	....	....	....	....	....	....	....	9	*5	4	9	21	....	....	....
1976-77	**Atlanta Flames**	**NHL**	**64**	**33**	**23**	**56**	**32**	**19**	**51**	**123**	**5**	**0**	**6**	**156**	**21.2**	**91**	**22**	**54**	**0**	**+15**	**3**	**1**	**0**	**1**	**19**	**0**	**0**	**0**
	Tulsa Oilers	CHL	14	8	4	12	....	....	....	68	....	....	....	....	....	....	....	....	....	....	....	....	....	....	....	....	....	....
1977-78	**Atlanta Flames**	**NHL**	**78**	**22**	**21**	**43**	**21**	**17**	**38**	**171**	**2**	**0**	**3**	**191**	**11.5**	**82**	**14**	**74**	**0**	**–6**	....	....	....	....	....	....	....	....
1978-79	**Atlanta Flames**	**NHL**	**74**	**23**	**20**	**43**	**21**	**15**	**36**	**213**	**0**	**0**	**4**	**164**	**14.0**	**78**	**6**	**59**	**0**	**+13**	**2**	**1**	**0**	**1**	**29**	**0**	**0**	**0**
1979-80	**Atlanta Flames**	**NHL**	**76**	**13**	**19**	**32**	**12**	**15**	**27**	**231**	**0**	**0**	**2**	**119**	**10.9**	**56**	**1**	**59**	**0**	**–4**	**4**	**1**	**0**	**1**	**15**	**1**	**0**	**0**
1980-81	**Calgary Flames**	**NHL**	**78**	**38**	**30**	**68**	**31**	**21**	**52**	**239**	**8**	**0**	**4**	**159**	**23.9**	**121**	**44**	**72**	**0**	**+5**	**15**	**8**	**4**	**12**	**89**	**5**	**0**	**3**
1981-82	**Calgary Flames**	**NHL**	**78**	**21**	**36**	**57**	**17**	**24**	**41**	**288**	**5**	**0**	**2**	**152**	**13.8**	**112**	**37**	**97**	**0**	**–22**	**3**	**1**	**2**	**3**	**39**	**1**	**0**	**0**
1982-83	**Minnesota North Stars**	**NHL**	**71**	**25**	**14**	**39**	**21**	**10**	**31**	**170**	**8**	**0**	**3**	**125**	**20.0**	**72**	**27**	**57**	**0**	**–12**	**9**	**1**	**3**	**4**	**38**	**0**	**0**	**0**
1983-84	**Minnesota North Stars**	**NHL**	**73**	**15**	**23**	**38**	**12**	**16**	**28**	**316**	**1**	**0**	**1**	**103**	**14.6**	**65**	**4**	**68**	**1**	**–6**	**16**	**6**	**2**	**8**	**51**	**1**	**0**	**0**
1984-85	**Minnesota North Stars**	**NHL**	**47**	**14**	**14**	**28**	**11**	**9**	**20**	**157**	**1**	**0**	**1**	**83**	**16.9**	**43**	**11**	**28**	**0**	**+4**	**9**	**3**	**6**	**9**	**67**	**1**	**0**	**0**
1985-86	**Minnesota North Stars**	**NHL**	**59**	**10**	**7**	**17**	**8**	**5**	**13**	**231**	**4**	**0**	**0**	**72**	**13.9**	**28**	**8**	**41**	**1**	**–20**	**5**	**0**	**1**	**1**	**45**	**0**	**0**	**0**
1986-87	**Minnesota North Stars**	**NHL**	**67**	**6**	**5**	**11**	**5**	**4**	**9**	**263**	**0**	**0**	**1**	**50**	**12.0**	**22**	**2**	**20**	**1**	**+1**	....	....	....	....	....	....	....	....
1987-88	**Boston Bruins**	**NHL**	**65**	**2**	**3**	**5**	**2**	**2**	**4**	**170**	**1**	**0**	**0**	**29**	**6.9**	**14**	**2**	**22**	**0**	**–10**	**17**	**2**	**4**	**6**	**74**	**0**	**0**	**1**
	NHL Totals		**834**	**222**	**215**	**437**	**193**	**157**	**350**	**2572**	**35**	**0**	**27**	**1408**	**15.8**	**785**	**178**	**652**	**3**		**83**	**24**	**22**	**46**	**466**	**9**	**0**	**4**

Won Calder Memorial Trophy (1977)

Transferred to **Calgary** after **Atlanta** franchise relocated, June 24, 1980. Traded to **Minnesota** by **Calgary** with Calgary's 4th round choice (Dusan Pasek) in 1982 Entry Draft for Steve Christoff, Bill Nyrop and Minnesota's 2nd round choice (Dave Reierson) in 1982 Entry Draft, June 7, 1982. Traded to **NY Rangers** by **Minnesota** for Pat Price, September 8, 1987. Claimed by **Boston** from **NY Rangers** in Waiver Draft, October 5, 1987.

• PLUMB, ROB

Rob Plumb LW – L. 5'8", 166 lbs. b: Kingston, Ont., 8/29/1957. Detroit's 10th choice, 163rd overall, in 1977 Amateur Draft.

Season	Club	League	GP	G	A	Pts	AG	AA	APts	PIM	PP	SH	GW	S	%	TGF	PGF	TGA	PGA	+/–	GP	G	A	Pts	PIM	PP	SH	GW
1974-75	Kingston Canadians	OHA	58	9	16	25	....	....	....	41	....	....	....	....	....	....	....	....	....	....	....	....	....	....	....	....	....	....
1975-76	Kingston Canadians	OHA	26	6	5	11	....	....	....	20	....	....	....	....	....	....	....	....	....	....	....	....	....	....	....	....	....	....
1976-77	Kingston Canadians	OHA	64	20	31	51	....	....	....	73	....	....	....	....	....	....	....	....	....	....	....	....	....	....	....	....	....	....
1977-78	**Detroit Red Wings**	**NHL**	**7**	**2**	**1**	**3**	**2**	**1**	**3**	**0**	**1**	**0**	**0**	**7**	**28.6**	**4**	**2**	**7**	**1**	**–4**	....	....	....	....	....	....	....	....
	Kansas City Red Wings	CHL	55	18	11	29	....	....	....	34	....	....	....	....	....	....	....	....	....	....	....	....	....	....	....	....	....	....
1978-79	**Detroit Red Wings**	**NHL**	**7**	**1**	**1**	**2**	**1**	**1**	**2**	**2**	**0**	**0**	**0**	**4**	**25.0**	**4**	**1**	**4**	**0**	**–1**	....	....	....	....	....	....	....	....
	Kansas City Red Wings	CHL	44	17	20	37	....	....	....	16	....	....	....	....	....	....	....	....	....	....	4	0	0	0	0	....	....	....
1979-80	Adirondack Red Wings	AHL	18	1	2	3	....	....	....	8	....	....	....	....	....	....	....	....	....	....	....	....	....	....	....	....	....	....
	Kalamazoo Wings	IHL	56	24	44	68	....	....	....	39	....	....	....	....	....	....	....	....	....	....	13	4	4	8	24	....	....	....
1980-81	Kalamazoo Wings	IHL	82	54	55	109	....	....	....	70	....	....	....	....	....	....	....	....	....	....	8	3	1	4	4	....	....	....
1981-82			DID NOT PLAY																									
1982-83	Dubendorfer EG	Switz. 2	....	37	39	76	....	....	....	....	....	....	....	....	....	....	....	....	....	....	....	....	....	....	....	....	....	....
1983-84	Dubendorfer EG	Switz. 2	....	43	38	81	....	....	....	....	....	....	....	....	....	....	....	....	....	....	....	....	....	....	....	....	....	....
1984-85	Dubendorfer EG	Switz.	....	45	48	93	....	....	....	....	....	....	....	....	....	....	....	....	....	....	....	....	....	....	....	....	....	....
1985-86	Zurich SC	Switz.	....	19	20	39	....	....	....	....	....	....	....	....	....	....	....	....	....	....	....	....	....	....	....	....	....	....
	NHL Totals		**14**	**3**	**2**	**5**	**3**	**2**	**5**	**2**	**1**	**0**	**0**	**11**	**27.3**	**8**	**3**	**11**	**1**		....	....	....	....	....	....	....	....

IHL Second All-Star Team (1981)

• PLUMB, RON

Ron Plumb D – L. 5'10", 175 lbs. b: Kingston, Ont., 7/17/1950. Boston's 3rd choice, 9th overall, in 1970 Amateur Draft.

Season	Club	League	GP	G	A	Pts	AG	AA	APts	PIM	PP	SH	GW	S	%	TGF	PGF	TGA	PGA	+/–	GP	G	A	Pts	PIM	PP	SH	GW
1967-68	Peterborough Petes	OHA	47	3	19	22	....	....	....	38	....	....	....	....	....	....	....	....	....	....	5	0	2	2	7	....	....	....
1968-69	Peterborough Petes	OHA	53	4	10	14	....	....	....	57	....	....	....	....	....	....	....	....	....	....	10	2	1	3	19	....	....	....
1969-70	Peterborough Petes	OHA	54	16	29	45	....	....	....	77	....	....	....	....	....	....	....	....	....	....	....	....	....	....	....	....	....	....
1970-71	Oklahoma City Blazers	CHL	72	3	19	22	....	....	....	73	....	....	....	....	....	....	....	....	....	....	5	0	0	0	12	....	....	....
1971-72	Oklahoma City Blazers	CHL	72	10	42	52	....	....	....	90	....	....	....	....	....	....	....	....	....	....	6	1	2	3	8	....	....	....
1972-73	Philadelphia Blazers	WHA	78	10	41	51	....	....	....	66	....	....	....	....	....	....	....	....	....	....	4	0	2	2	13	....	....	....
1973-74	Vancouver Blazers	WHA	75	6	32	38	....	....	....	40	....	....	....	....	....	....	....	....	....	....	....	....	....	....	....	....	....	....
1974-75	San Diego Mariners	WHA	78	10	38	48	....	....	....	56	....	....	....	....	....	....	....	....	....	....	10	2	3	5	19	....	....	....
1975-76	Cincinnati Stingers	WHA	80	10	36	46	....	....	....	31	....	....	....	....	....	....	....	....	....	....	....	....	....	....	....	....	....	....
1976-77	Cincinnati Stingers	WHA	79	11	58	69	....	....	....	52	....	....	....	....	....	....	....	....	....	....	4	1	2	3	0	....	....	....
1977-78	Cincinnati Stingers	WHA	54	13	34	47	....	....	....	45	....	....	....	....	....	....	....	....	....	....	....	....	....	....	....	....	....	....
	New England Whalers	WHA	27	1	9	10	....	....	....	18	....	....	....	....	....	....	....	....	....	....	14	1	5	6	16	....	....	....
1978-79	New England Whalers	WHA	78	4	16	20	....	....	....	33	....	....	....	....	....	....	....	....	....	....	9	1	3	4	0	....	....	....
1979-80	**Hartford Whalers**	**NHL**	**26**	**3**	**4**	**7**	**3**	**3**	**6**	**14**	**0**	**0**	**0**	**38**	**7.9**	**35**	**1**	**26**	**2**	**+10**	....	....	....	....	....	....	....	....
	Springfield Indians	AHL	52	2	20	22	....	....	....	42	....	....	....	....	....	....	....	....	....	....	....	....	....	....	....	....	....	....
1980-81	Springfield Indians	AHL	79	11	51	52	....	....	....	150	....	....	....	....	....	....	....	....	....	....	7	3	6	9	8	....	....	....
1981-82	Springfield Indians	AHL	80	4	31	35	....	....	....	56	....	....	....	....	....	....	....	....	....	....	....	....	....	....	....	....	....	....
	NHL Totals		**26**	**3**	**4**	**7**	**3**	**3**	**6**	**14**	**0**	**0**	**0**	**38**	**7.9**	**35**	**1**	**26**	**2**		....	....	....	....	....	....	....	....
	Other Major League Totals		549	65	264	329	....	....	....	341	....	....	....	....	....	....	....	....	....		41	5	15	20	48	....	....	....

OHA First All-Star Team (1970) • CHL First All-Star Team (1972) • WHA First All-Star Team (1977) • Won Dennis A. Murphy Trophy (WHA Top Defenseman) (1977)

Selected by **Miami-Philadelphia** (WHA) in 1972 WHA General Player Draft, February 12, 1972. Transferred to **Vancouver** (WHA) after **Philadelphia** (WHA) franchise relocated, May, 1973. Traded to **Cincinnati** (WHA) by **Vancouver** (WHA) for future considerations, August, 1974. Loaned to **San Diego** (WHA) by **Cincinnati** (WHA) for 1974-75 season, August, 1974. Traded to **New England** (WHA) by **Cincinnati** (WHA) for Greg Carroll, February, 1978. Rights retained by **Hartford** prior to Expansion Draft, June 9, 1979.

• POAPST, STEVE

Steve Poapst D – L. 6', 200 lbs. b: Cornwall, Ont., 1/3/1969.

Season	Club	League	GP	G	A	Pts	AG	AA	APts	PIM	PP	SH	GW	S	%	TGF	PGF	TGA	PGA	+/–	GP	G	A	Pts	PIM	PP	SH	GW
1987-88	Colgate University	ECAC	32	3	13	16	....	....	....	22	....	....	....	....	....	....	....	....	....	....	....	....	....	....	....	....	....	....
1988-89	Colgate University	ECAC	30	0	5	5	....	....	....	38	....	....	....	....	....	....	....	....	....	....	....	....	....	....	....	....	....	....
1989-90	Colgate University	ECAC	38	4	15	19	....	....	....	54	....	....	....	....	....	....	....	....	....	....	....	....	....	....	....	....	....	....
1990-91	Colgate University	ECAC	32	6	15	21	....	....	....	43	....	....	....	....	....	....	....	....	....	....	....	....	....	....	....	....	....	....
1991-92	Hampton Rds.	ECHL	55	8	20	28	....	....	....	29	....	....	....	....	....	....	....	....	....	....	14	1	4	5	12	....	....	....
1992-93	Hampton Rds.	ECHL	63	10	35	45	....	....	....	57	....	....	....	....	....	....	....	....	....	....	4	0	1	1	4	....	....	....
	Baltimore Skipjacks	AHL	7	0	1	1	....	....	....	4	....	....	....	....	....	....	....	....	....	....	7	0	3	3	6	....	....	....
1993-94	Portland Pirates	AHL	78	14	21	35	....	....	....	47	....	....	....	....	....	....	....	....	....	....	12	0	3	3	8	....	....	....
1994-95	Portland Pirates	AHL	71	8	22	30	....	....	....	60	....	....	....	....	....	....	....	....	....	....	7	0	1	1	16	....	....	....
1995-96	**Washington Capitals**	**NHL**	**3**	**1**	**0**	**1**	**1**	**0**	**1**	**0**	**0**	**0**	**1**	**2**	**50.0**	**1**	**0**	**2**	**0**	**–1**	**6**	**0**	**0**	**0**	**0**	**0**	**0**	**0**
	Portland Pirates	AHL	70	10	24	34	....	....	....	79	....	....	....	....	....	....	....	....	....	....	20	2	6	8	16	....	....	....
1996-97	Portland Pirates	AHL	47	1	20	21	....	....	....	34	....	....	....	....	....	....	....	....	....	....	5	0	1	1	6	....	....	....
1997-98	Portland Pirates	AHL	76	8	29	37	....	....	....	46	....	....	....	....	....	....	....	....	....	....	10	2	3	5	8	....	....	....
	NHL Totals		**3**	**1**	**0**	**1**	**1**	**0**	**1**	**0**	**0**	**0**	**1**	**2**	**50.0**	**1**	**0**	**2**	**0**		**6**	**0**	**0**	**0**	**0**	**0**	**0**	**0**

ECHL First All-Star Team (1993)

Signed as a free agent by **Washington**, February 4, 1995.

• POCZA, HARVIE

Harvie Pocza LW – L. 6'2", 200 lbs. b: Lethbridge, Alta., 9/22/1959. Washington's 3rd choice, 67th overall, in 1979 Entry Draft.

Season	Club	League	GP	G	A	Pts	AG	AA	APts	PIM	PP	SH	GW	S	%	TGF	PGF	TGA	PGA	+/–	GP	G	A	Pts	PIM	PP	SH	GW
1975-76	The Pas Red Devils	MJHL	5	1	1	2	....	....	....	0	....	....	....	....	....	....	....	....	....	....	....	....	....	....	....	....	....	....
1976-77	Pincher Creek	AJHL	57	23	36	59	....	....	....	187	....	....	....	....	....	....	....	....	....	....	....	....	....	....	....	....	....	....
	Calgary Centennials	WCJHL	10	4	5	9	....	....	....	9	....	....	....	....	....	....	....	....	....	....	....	....	....	....	....	....	....	....
1977-78	Billings Bighorns	WCJHL	71	34	32	66	....	....	....	168	....	....	....	....	....	....	....	....	....	....	19	9	11	20	60	....	....	....
1978-79	Billings Bighorns	WHL	72	42	55	97	....	....	....	151	....	....	....	....	....	....	....	....	....	....	8	1	4	5	8	....	....	....
1979-80	**Washington Capitals**	**NHL**	**1**	**0**	**0**	**0**	**0**	**0**	**0**	**0**	**0**	**0**	**0**	**2**	**0.0**	**0**	**0**	**0**	**0**	**0**	....	....	....	....	....	....	....	....
	Port Huron Flags	IHL	13	9	7	16	....	....	....	11	....	....	....	....	....	....	....	....	....	....	....	....	....	....	....	....	....	....
	Hershey Bears	AHL	59	13	12	25	....	....	....	28	....	....	....	....	....	....	....	....	....	....	8	4	3	7	22	....	....	....
1980-81	Hershey Bears	AHL	78	27	18	45	....	....	....	108	....	....	....	....	....	....	....	....	....	....	10	10	2	12	21	....	....	....

			REGULAR SEASON																		PLAYOFFS							
Season	Club	League	GP	G	A	Pts	AG	AA	APts	PIM	PP	SH	GW	S	%	TGF	PGF	TGA	PGA	+/–	GP	G	A	Pts	PIM	PP	SH	GW
1981-82	**Washington Capitals**	**NHL**	**2**	**0**	**0**	**0**	**0**	**0**	**0**	**2**	**0**	**0**	**0**	**1**	**0.0**	**1**	**0**	**3**	**0**	**–2**	....	....	....	....	....	....	....	....
	Hershey Bears	AHL	61	29	23	52	....	....	....	116	....	....	....	....	....	....	....	....	....	....	5	1	1	2	0	....	....	....
1982-83	Hershey Bears	AHL	77	13	29	42	....	....	....	85	....	....	....	....	....	....	....	....	....	....	5	1	2	3	9	....	....	....
	NHL Totals		**3**	**0**	**0**	**0**	**0**	**0**	**0**	**2**	**0**	**0**	**0**	**3**	**0.0**	**1**	**0**	**3**	**0**		....	....	....	....	....	....	....	....

• PODDUBNY, WALT

Walt Poddubny LW – L. 6'1", 210 lbs. b: Thunder Bay, Ont., 2/14/1960. Edmonton's 4th choice, 90th overall, in 1980 Entry Draft.

Season	Club	League	GP	G	A	Pts	AG	AA	APts	PIM	PP	SH	GW	S	%	TGF	PGF	TGA	PGA	+/–	GP	G	A	Pts	PIM	PP	SH	GW
1978-79	Brandon Wheat Kings	WHL	20	11	11	22	....	....	....	12	....	....	....	....	....	....	....	....	....	....	....	....	....	....	....	....	....	....
1979-80	Kitchener Rangers	OHA	19	3	9	12	....	....	....	35	....	....	....	....	....	....	....	....	....	....	....	....	....	....	....	....	....	....
	Kingston Canadians	OHA	43	30	17	47	....	....	....	36	....	....	....	....	....	....	....	....	....	....	3	0	2	2	0	....	....	....
1980-81	Milwaukee Admirals	IHL	5	4	2	6	....	....	....	4	....	....	....	....	....	....	....	....	....	....	....	....	....	....	....	....	....	....
	Wichita Wind	CHL	70	21	29	50	....	....	....	207	....	....	....	....	....	....	....	....	....	....	11	1	6	7	26	....	....	....
1981-82	**Edmonton Oilers**	**NHL**	**4**	**0**	**0**	**0**	**0**	**0**	**0**	**0**	**0**	**0**	**0**	**2**	**0.0**	**0**	**0**	**1**	**0**	**–1**	....	....	....	....	....	....	....	....
	Wichita Wind	CHL	60	35	46	81	....	....	....	79	....	....	....	....	....	....	....	....	....	....	....	....	....	....	....	....	....	....
	Toronto Maple Leafs	**NHL**	**11**	**3**	**4**	**7**	**2**	**3**	**5**	**8**	**1**	**0**	**0**	**22**	**13.6**	**13**	**4**	**10**	**1**	**0**	....	....	....	....	....	....	....	....
1982-83	**Toronto Maple Leafs**	**NHL**	**72**	**28**	**31**	**59**	**23**	**21**	**44**	**71**	**9**	**0**	**3**	**163**	**17.2**	**76**	**16**	**52**	**0**	**+8**	**4**	**3**	**1**	**4**	**0**	**2**	**0**	**1**
1983-84	**Toronto Maple Leafs**	**NHL**	**38**	**11**	**14**	**25**	**9**	**9**	**18**	**48**	**4**	**0**	**0**	**77**	**14.3**	**32**	**10**	**35**	**0**	**–13**	....	....	....	....	....	....	....	....
1984-85	**Toronto Maple Leafs**	**NHL**	**32**	**5**	**15**	**20**	**4**	**10**	**14**	**26**	**1**	**0**	**0**	**51**	**9.8**	**26**	**5**	**20**	**0**	**+1**	....	....	....	....	....	....	....	....
	St. Catharines Saints	AHL	8	5	7	12	....	....	....	10	....	....	....	....	....	....	....	....	....	....	....	....	....	....	....	....	....	....
1985-86	**Toronto Maple Leafs**	**NHL**	**33**	**12**	**22**	**34**	**10**	**15**	**25**	**25**	**5**	**0**	**1**	**76**	**15.8**	**43**	**16**	**21**	**0**	**+6**	**9**	**4**	**1**	**5**	**4**	**0**	**0**	**3**
	St. Catharines Saints	AHL	37	28	27	55	....	....	....	52	....	....	....	....	....	....	....	....	....	....	....	....	....	....	....	....	....	....
1986-87	**New York Rangers**	**NHL**	**75**	**40**	**47**	**87**	**35**	**34**	**69**	**49**	**11**	**0**	**5**	**253**	**15.8**	**115**	**38**	**62**	**1**	**+16**	**6**	**0**	**0**	**0**	**8**	**0**	**0**	**0**
1987-88	**New York Rangers**	**NHL**	**77**	**38**	**50**	**88**	**33**	**36**	**69**	**76**	**13**	**0**	**4**	**202**	**18.8**	**121**	**65**	**54**	**0**	**+2**	....	....	....	....	....	....	....	....
1988-89	**Quebec Nordiques**	**NHL**	**72**	**38**	**37**	**75**	**32**	**26**	**58**	**107**	**14**	**0**	**2**	**197**	**19.3**	**102**	**52**	**69**	**1**	**–18**	....	....	....	....	....	....	....	....
1989-90	**New Jersey Devils**	**NHL**	**33**	**4**	**10**	**14**	**3**	**7**	**10**	**28**	**1**	**0**	**0**	**50**	**8.0**	**21**	**6**	**19**	**0**	**–4**	....	....	....	....	....	....	....	....
	Utica Devils	AHL	2	1	2	3	....	....	....	0	....	....	....	....	....	....	....	....	....	....	....	....	....	....	....	....	....	....
1990-91	**New Jersey Devils**	**NHL**	**14**	**4**	**6**	**10**	**4**	**5**	**9**	**10**	**0**	**0**	**0**	**22**	**18.2**	**14**	**2**	**4**	**0**	**+8**	....	....	....	....	....	....	....	....
1991-92	**New Jersey Devils**	**NHL**	**7**	**1**	**2**	**3**	**1**	**1**	**2**	**6**	**0**	**0**	**0**	**9**	**11.1**	**3**	**1**	**3**	**0**	**–1**	....	....	....	....	....	....	....	....
1992-93			DID NOT PLAY																									
1993-94			DID NOT PLAY																									
1994-95	Worcester IceCats	AHL	34	7	6	13	....	....	....	32	....	....	....	....	....	....	....	....	....	....	....	....	....	....	....	....	....	....
	NHL Totals		**468**	**184**	**238**	**422**	**156**	**167**	**323**	**454**	**59**	**0**	**15**	**1124**	**16.4**	**566**	**215**	**350**	**3**		**19**	**7**	**2**	**9**	**12**	**2**	**0**	**4**

Played in NHL All-Star Game (1989)

Traded to **Toronto** by **Edmonton** with Phil Drouilliard for Laurie Boschman, March 28, 1982. Traded to **NY Rangers** by **Toronto** for Mike Allison, August 18, 1986. Traded to **Quebec** by **NY Rangers** with Jari Gronstad, Bruce Bell and the NY Rangers' 4th round choice (Eric Dubois) in 1989 Entry Draft for Jason Lafrieniere and Normand Rochefort, August 1, 1988. Traded to **New Jersey** by **Quebec** with Quebec's 4th round choice (Mike Bodnarchuk) in 1990 Entry Draft for Joe Cirella, Claude Loiselle and New Jersey's 8th round choice (Alexander Karpotsev) in 1990 Entry Draft, June 17, 1989.

• PODEIN, SHJON

Shjon Podein LW – L. 6'2", 200 lbs. b: Rochester, MN, 3/5/1968. Edmonton's 9th choice, 166th overall, in 1988 Entry Draft.

Season	Club	League	GP	G	A	Pts	AG	AA	APts	PIM	PP	SH	GW	S	%	TGF	PGF	TGA	PGA	+/–	GP	G	A	Pts	PIM	PP	SH	GW
1987-88	University of Minnesota-Duluth	WCHA	30	4	4	8	....	....	....	48	....	....	....	....	....	....	....	....	....	....	....	....	....	....	....	....	....	....
1988-89	University of Minnesota-Duluth	WCHA	36	7	5	12	....	....	....	46	....	....	....	....	....	....	....	....	....	....	....	....	....	....	....	....	....	....
1989-90	University of Minnesota-Duluth	WCHA	35	21	18	39	....	....	....	36	....	....	....	....	....	....	....	....	....	....	....	....	....	....	....	....	....	....
1990-91	Cape Breton Oilers	AHL	63	14	15	29	....	....	....	65	....	....	....	....	....	....	....	....	....	....	4	0	0	0	5	....	....	....
1991-92	Cape Breton Oilers	AHL	80	30	24	54	....	....	....	46	....	....	....	....	....	....	....	....	....	....	5	3	1	4	2	....	....	....
1992-93	**Edmonton Oilers**	**NHL**	**40**	**13**	**6**	**19**	**11**	**4**	**15**	**25**	**2**	**1**	**1**	**64**	**20.3**	**26**	**4**	**25**	**1**	**–2**	....	....	....	....	....	....	....	....
	Cape Breton Oilers	AHL	38	18	21	39	....	....	....	32	....	....	....	....	....	....	....	....	....	....	9	2	2	4	29	....	....	....
	United States	WC-A	6	1	3	4	....	....	....	8	....	....	....	....	....	....	....	....	....	....	....	....	....	....	....	....	....	....
1993-94	**Edmonton Oilers**	**NHL**	**28**	**3**	**5**	**8**	**3**	**4**	**7**	**8**	**0**	**0**	**0**	**26**	**11.5**	**11**	**0**	**8**	**0**	**+3**	....	....	....	....	....	....	....	....
	Cape Breton Oilers	AHL	5	4	4	8	....	....	....	4	....	....	....	....	....	....	....	....	....	....	....	....	....	....	....	....	....	....
	United States	WC-A	8	3	1	4	....	....	....	14	....	....	....	....	....	....	....	....	....	....	....	....	....	....	....	....	....	....
1994-95	**Philadelphia Flyers**	**NHL**	**44**	**3**	**7**	**10**	**5**	**10**	**15**	**33**	**0**	**0**	**1**	**48**	**6.3**	**18**	**0**	**22**	**2**	**–2**	**15**	**1**	**3**	**4**	**10**	**0**	**0**	**0**
1995-96	**Philadelphia Flyers**	**NHL**	**79**	**15**	**10**	**25**	**15**	**8**	**23**	**89**	**0**	**4**	**4**	**115**	**13.0**	**41**	**2**	**27**	**13**	**+25**	**12**	**1**	**2**	**3**	**60**	**0**	**0**	**1**
1996-97	**Philadelphia Flyers**	**NHL**	**82**	**14**	**18**	**32**	**15**	**16**	**31**	**41**	**0**	**0**	**4**	**153**	**9.2**	**41**	**1**	**52**	**19**	**+7**	**19**	**4**	**3**	**7**	**16**	**0**	**0**	**1**
1997-98	**Philadelphia Flyers**	**NHL**	**82**	**11**	**13**	**24**	**13**	**13**	**26**	**53**	**1**	**1**	**2**	**126**	**8.7**	**34**	**3**	**41**	**18**	**+8**	**5**	**0**	**0**	**0**	**10**	**0**	**0**	**0**
	United States	WC-A	4	0	0	0	....	....	....	4	....	....	....	....	....	....	....	....	....	....	....	....	....	....	....	....	....	....
	NHL Totals		**355**	**59**	**59**	**118**	**62**	**55**	**117**	**249**	**3**	**6**	**12**	**532**	**11.1**	**171**	**10**	**175**	**53**		**51**	**6**	**8**	**14**	**86**	**0**	**0**	**2**

Signed as a free agent by **Philadelphia**, July 27, 1994.

• PODLOSKI, RAY

Ray Podloski C – L. 6'2", 210 lbs. b: Edmonton, Alta., 1/5/1966. Boston's 2nd choice, 40th overall, in 1984 Entry Draft.

Season	Club	League	GP	G	A	Pts	AG	AA	APts	PIM	PP	SH	GW	S	%	TGF	PGF	TGA	PGA	+/–	GP	G	A	Pts	PIM	PP	SH	GW
1982-83	Red Deer Rustlers	AJHL	59	49	49	98	....	....	....	47	....	....	....	....	....	....	....	....	....	....	....	....	....	....	....	....	....	....
	Portland Winter Hawks	WHL	2	0	1	1	....	....	....	0	....	....	....	....	....	....	....	....	....	....	....	....	....	....	....	....	....	....
1983-84	Portland Winter Hawks	WHL	66	46	50	96	....	....	....	44	....	....	....	....	....	....	....	....	....	....	14	8	14	22	14	....	....	....
1984-85	Portland Winter Hawks	WHL	67	63	75	138	....	....	....	41	....	....	....	....	....	....	....	....	....	....	6	3	1	4	7	....	....	....
1985-86	Portland Winter Hawks	WHL	66	59	75	134	....	....	....	68	....	....	....	....	....	....	....	....	....	....	7	1	9	10	8	....	....	....
1986-87	Moncton Golden Flames	AHL	70	23	27	50	....	....	....	12	....	....	....	....	....	....	....	....	....	....	3	0	0	0	15	....	....	....
1987-88	Maine Mariners	AHL	36	12	20	32	....	....	....	12	....	....	....	....	....	....	....	....	....	....	5	1	2	3	19	....	....	....
1988-89	**Boston Bruins**	**NHL**	**8**	**0**	**1**	**1**	**0**	**1**	**1**	**22**	**0**	**0**	**0**	**3**	**0.0**	**1**	**0**	**2**	**0**	**–1**	....	....	....	....	....	....	....	....
	Maine Mariners	AHL	71	20	34	54	....	....	....	70	....	....	....	....	....	....	....	....	....	....	....	....	....	....	....	....	....	....
1989-90	Canada	Nat-Team	58	18	16	34	....	....	....	38	....	....	....	....	....	....	....	....	....	....	....	....	....	....	....	....	....	....
1990-91	Numberg	Germany	52	59	65	124	....	....	....	58	....	....	....	....	....	....	....	....	....	....	....	....	....	....	....	....	....	....
1991-92	Numberg	Germany	STATISTICS NOT AVAILABLE																									
1992-93	Klagenfurt	Austria	49	35	50	85	....	....	....	....	....	....	....	....	....	....	....	....	....	....								
1993-94	HC Bolzano	Italy	25	14	25	39	....	....	....	47	....	....	....	....	....	....	....	....	....	....	....	....	....	....	....	....	....	....
1994-95	Lustenau	Austria	20	21	10	31	....	....	....	28	....	....	....	....	....	....	....	....	....	....	3	0	0	0	2	....	....	....
	HC Asiago	Italy	8	10	11	21	....	....	....	2	....	....	....	....	....	....	....	....	....	....	....	....	....	....	....	....	....	....
1995-96	Lustenau	Austria	33	25	38	63	....	....	....	20	....	....	....	....	....	....	....	....	....	....	....	....	....	....	....	....	....	....
	NHL Totals		**8**	**0**	**1**	**1**	**0**	**1**	**1**	**22**	**0**	**0**	**0**	**3**	**0.0**	**1**	**0**	**2**	**0**		....	....	....	....	....	....	....	....

• PODOLLAN, JASON

Jason Podollan RW – R. 6'1", 192 lbs. b: Vernon, B.C., 2/18/1976. Florida's 3rd choice, 31st overall, in 1994 Entry Draft.

Season	Club	League	GP	G	A	Pts	AG	AA	APts	PIM	PP	SH	GW	S	%	TGF	PGF	TGA	PGA	+/–	GP	G	A	Pts	PIM	PP	SH	GW
1991-92	Spokane Chiefs	WHL	2	0	0	0	....	....	....	2	....	....	....	....	....	....	....	....	....	....	10	3	1	4	16	....	....	....
1992-93	Spokane Chiefs	WHL	72	36	33	69	....	....	....	108	....	....	....	....	....	....	....	....	....	....	10	4	4	8	14	....	....	....
1993-94	Spokane Chiefs	WHL	69	29	37	66	....	....	....	108	....	....	....	....	....	....	....	....	....	....	3	3	0	3	2	....	....	....
1994-95	Spokane Chiefs	WHL	72	43	41	84	....	....	....	102	....	....	....	....	....	....	....	....	....	....	11	5	7	12	18	....	....	....
	Cincinnati Cyclones	IHL	....	....	....	....	....	....	....	....	....	....	....	....	....	....	....	....	....	....	3	0	0	0	2	....	....	....
1995-96	Spokane Chiefs	WHL	56	37	25	62	....	....	....	103	....	....	....	....	....	....	....	....	....	....	18	*21	12	33	28	....	....	....
	Canada	WJC-A	6	2	3	5	....	....	....	2	....	....	....	....	....	....	....	....	....	....	....	....	....	....	....	....	....	....
1996-97	**Florida Panthers**	**NHL**	**19**	**1**	**1**	**2**	**1**	**1**	**2**	**4**	**1**	**0**	**0**	**20**	**5.0**	**6**	**3**	**6**	**0**	**–3**	....	....	....	....	....	....	....	....
	Carolina Monarchs	AHL	39	21	25	46	....	....	....	36	....	....	....	....	....	....	....	....	....	....	....	....	....	....	....	....	....	....
	Toronto Maple Leafs	**NHL**	**10**	**0**	**3**	**3**	**0**	**3**	**3**	**6**	**0**	**0**	**0**	**10**	**0.0**	**6**	**0**	**8**	**0**	**–2**	....	....	....	....	....	....	....	....
	St. John's Maple Leafs	AHL	....	....	....	....	....	....	....	....	....	....	....	....	....	....	....	....	....	....	11	2	3	5	6	....	....	....
1997-98	St. John's Maple Leafs	AHL	70	30	31	61	....	....	....	116	....	....	....	....	....	....	....	....	....	....	4	1	0	1	10	....	....	....
	NHL Totals		**29**	**1**	**4**	**5**	**1**	**4**	**5**	**10**	**1**	**0**	**0**	**30**	**3.3**	**12**	**3**	**14**	**0**		....	....	....	....	....	....	....	....

WHL West Second All-Star Team (1996)

Traded to **Toronto** by **Florida** for Kirk Muller, March 18, 1997.

• POESCHEK, RUDY

Rudy Poeschek RW/D – R. 6'2", 218 lbs. b: Kamloops, B.C., 9/29/1966. NY Rangers' 12th choice, 238th overall, in 1985 Entry Draft.

Season	Club	League	GP	G	A	Pts	AG	AA	APts	PIM	PP	SH	GW	S	%	TGF	PGF	TGA	PGA	+/–	GP	G	A	Pts	PIM	PP	SH	GW
1983-84	Kamloops Blazers	WHL	47	3	9	12	....	....	....	93	....	....	....	....	....	....	....	....	....	....	8	0	2	2	7	....	....	....
1984-85	Kamloops Blazers	WHL	34	6	7	13	....	....	....	100	....	....	....	....	....	....	....	....	....	....	16	0	3	3	50	....	....	....
1985-86	Kamloops Blazers	WHL	32	3	13	16	....	....	....	92	....	....	....	....	....	....	....	....	....	....	16	3	7	10	40	....	....	....
1986-87	Kamloops Blazers	WHL	54	13	18	31	....	....	....	153	....	....	....	....	....	....	....	....	....	....	15	2	4	6	37	....	....	....

			REGULAR SEASON																		PLAYOFFS							
Season	Club	League	GP	G	A	Pts	AG	AA	APts	PIM	PP	SH	GW	S	%	TGF	PGF	TGA	PGA	+/-	GP	G	A	Pts	PIM	PP	SH	GW
1987-88	New York Rangers	NHL	1	0	0	0	0	0	0	2	0	0	0	1	0.0	0	0	0	0	0	....	....	....	....	....	....	....	....
	Colorado Rangers	IHL	82	7	31	38	....	....	....	210	....	....	....	....	....	....	....	....	....	....	12	2	2	4	31	....	....	....
1988-89	New York Rangers	NHL	52	0	2	2	0	1	1	199	0	0	0	17	0.0	7	0	15	0	–8	....	....	....	....	....	....	....	....
	Colorado Rangers	IHL	2	0	0	0	....	....	....	6	....	....	....	....	....	....	....	....	....	....	....	....	....	....	....	....	....	....
1989-90	New York Rangers	NHL	15	0	0	0	0	0	0	55	0	0	0	1	0.0	1	0	2	0	–1	....	....	....	....	....	....	....	....
	Flint Spirits	IHL	38	8	13	21	....	....	....	109	....	....	....	....	....	....	....	....	....	....	4	0	0	0	16	....	....	....
1990-91	Binghamton Rangers	AHL	38	1	3	4	....	....	....	162	....	....	....	....	....	....	....	....	....	....	....	....	....	....	....	....	....	....
	Winnipeg Jets	NHL	1	0	0	0	0	0	0	5	0	0	0	0	0.0	0	0	0	0	0	....	....	....	....	....	....	....	....
	Moncton Hawks	AHL	23	2	4	6	....	....	....	67	....	....	....	....	....	....	....	....	....	....	9	1	1	2	41	....	....	....
1991-92	Winnipeg Jets	NHL	4	0	0	0	0	0	0	17	0	0	0	1	0.0	0	0	5	0	–5	....	....	....	....	....	....	....	....
	Moncton Hawks	AHL	63	4	18	22	....	....	....	170	....	....	....	....	....	....	....	....	....	....	11	0	2	2	48	....	....	....
1992-93	St. John's Maple Leafs	AHL	78	7	24	31	....	....	....	189	....	....	....	....	....	....	....	....	....	....	9	0	4	4	13	....	....	....
1993-94	Tampa Bay Lightning	NHL	71	3	6	9	3	5	8	118	0	0	1	46	6.5	27	0	27	3	+3	....	....	....	....	....	....	....	....
1994-95	Tampa Bay Lightning	NHL	25	1	1	2	2	1	3	92	0	0	0	14	7.1	7	0	8	1	0	....	....	....	....	....	....	....	....
1995-96	Tampa Bay Lightning	NHL	57	1	3	4	1	2	3	88	0	0	0	36	2.8	16	1	24	7	–2	3	0	0	0	12	0	0	0
1996-97	Tampa Bay Lightning	NHL	60	0	6	6	0	5	5	120	0	0	0	30	0.0	25	0	47	19	–3	....	....	....	....	....	....	....	....
1997-98	St. Louis Blues	NHL	50	1	7	8	1	7	8	64	0	0	0	29	3.4	27	2	36	6	–5	2	0	0	0	6	0	0	0
	NHL Totals		336	6	25	31	7	21	28	760	0	0	1	175	3.4	110	3	164	36		5	0	0	0	18	0	0	0

Traded to **Winnipeg** by **NY Rangers** for Guy Larose, January 22, 1991. Signed as a free agent by **Toronto**, July 8, 1992. Signed as a free agent by **Tampa Bay**, August 10, 1993. Signed as a free agent by **St. Louis**, July 31, 1997.

• POLANIC, TOM

Tom Polanic D – L. 6'3", 205 lbs. b: Toronto, Ont., 4/2/1943.

Season	Club	League	GP	G	A	Pts	AG	AA	APts	PIM	PP	SH	GW	S	%	TGF	PGF	TGA	PGA	+/-	GP	G	A	Pts	PIM	PP	SH	GW
1960-61	St. Michael's Majors	OHA	11	0	0	0	....	....	....	8	....	....	....	....	....	....	....	....	....	....	1	0	0	0	0	....	....	....
1961-62	St. Michael's College	Tor-Jr.	23	9	10	19	....	....	....	24	....	....	....	....	....	....	....	....	....	....	12	0	11	11	23	....	....	....
1962-63	University of Michigan	WCHA	DID NOT PLAY – FRESHMAN																									
1963-64	University of Michigan	WCHA	....	8	38	46	....	....	....	92	....	....	....	....	....	....	....	....	....	....	....	....	....	....	....	....	....	....
1964-65	University of Michigan	WCHA	....	5	12	17	....	....	....	56	....	....	....	....	....	....	....	....	....	....	....	....	....	....	....	....	....	....
1965-66	Charlotte Checkers	EHL	64	7	24	31	....	....	....	101	....	....	....	....	....	....	....	....	....	....	9	1	4	5	23	....	....	....
	Tulsa Oilers	CHL	2	0	1	1	....	....	....	0	....	....	....	....	....	....	....	....	....	....	....	....	....	....	....	....	....	....
1966-67	Tulsa Oilers	CHL	19	0	1	1	....	....	....	25	....	....	....	....	....	....	....	....	....	....	....	....	....	....	....	....	....	....
1967-68	Phoenix Roadrunners	WHL	70	3	10	13	....	....	....	136	....	....	....	....	....	....	....	....	....	....	4	1	0	1	6	....	....	....
1968-69	Phoenix Roadrunners	WHL	74	5	17	22	....	....	....	*187	....	....	....	....	....	....	....	....	....	....	....	....	....	....	....	....	....	....
1969-70	Minnesota North Stars	NHL	16	0	2	2	0	2	2	53	0	0	0	4	0.0	5	0	10	0	–5	5	1	1	2	4	0	0	0
	Iowa Stars	CHL	44	1	8	9	....	....	....	88	....	....	....	....	....	....	....	....	....	....	8	0	1	1	8	....	....	....
1970-71	Minnesota North Stars	NHL	3	0	0	0	0	0	0	0	0	0	0	2	0.0	1	0	1	0	0	....	....	....	....	....	....	....	....
	Cleveland Barons	AHL	68	2	20	22	....	....	....	154	....	....	....	....	....	....	....	....	....	....	8	0	3	3	35	....	....	....
1971-72	Orillia Terriers	OHA Sr.	31	6	24	30	....	....	....	67	....	....	....	....	....	....	....	....	....	....	....	....	....	....	....	....	....	....
1972-73	Orillia Terriers	OHA Sr.	35	4	13	17	....	....	....	87	....	....	....	....	....	....	....	....	....	....	....	....	....	....	....	....	....	....
1973-74	Orillia Terriers	OHA Sr.	33	2	27	29	....	....	....	63	....	....	....	....	....	....	....	....	....	....	....	....	....	....	....	....	....	....
1974-75	Brantford Forresters	OHA Sr.	39	3	18	21	....	....	....	65	....	....	....	....	....	....	....	....	....	....	....	....	....	....	....	....	....	....
1975-76			DID NOT PLAY – RETIRED																									
1976-77	Barrie Flyers	OHA Sr.	30	1	14	15	....	....	....	31	....	....	....	....	....	....	....	....	....	....	....	....	....	....	....	....	....	....
	NHL Totals		19	0	2	2	0	2	2	53	0	0	0	6	0.0	6	0	11	0		5	1	1	2	4	0	0	0

WCHA First All-Star Team (1964) • NCAA West First All-American Team (1964) • NCAA Championship All-Tournament Team (1964) • WCHA Second All-Star Team (1965)

Traded to **Phoenix** (WHL) by **Toronto** for cash, September 12, 1967. Traded to **Minnesota** by **Phoenix** (WHL) for Brian D. Smith and Milan Marcetta, February 11, 1969.

• POLICH, MIKE

Mike Polich C/LW – L. 5'8", 170 lbs. b: Hibbing, MN, 12/19/1952.

Season	Club	League	GP	G	A	Pts	AG	AA	APts	PIM	PP	SH	GW	S	%	TGF	PGF	TGA	PGA	+/-	GP	G	A	Pts	PIM	PP	SH	GW
1971-72	University of Minnesota	WCHA	32	8	5	13	....	....	....	14	....	....	....	....	....	....	....	....	....	....	....	....	....	....	....	....	....	....
1972-73	University of Minnesota	WCHA	34	18	14	32	....	....	....	34	....	....	....	....	....	....	....	....	....	....	....	....	....	....	....	....	....	....
1973-74	University of Minnesota	WCHA	40	19	33	52	....	....	....	36	....	....	....	....	....	....	....	....	....	....	....	....	....	....	....	....	....	....
	United States	WEC-B	....	7	5	12	....	....	....	....	....	....	....	....	....	....	....	....	....	....	....	....	....	....	....	....	....	....
1974-75	University of Minnesota	WCHA	42	25	37	62	....	....	....	84	....	....	....	....	....	....	....	....	....	....	....	....	....	....	....	....	....	....
	United States	WEC-A	10	2	5	7	....	....	....	34	....	....	....	....	....	....	....	....	....	....	....	....	....	....	....	....	....	....
1975-76	Nova Scotia Voyageurs	AHL	75	24	19	43	....	....	....	66	....	....	....	....	....	....	....	....	....	....	9	4	5	9	6	....	....	....
1976-77	United States	C Cup	5	1	1	2	....	....	....	4	....	....	....	....	....	....	....	....	....	....	....	....	....	....	....	....	....	....
	Nova Scotia Voyageurs	AHL	69	19	41	60	....	....	....	48	....	....	....	....	....	....	....	....	....	....	11	4	4	8	6	....	....	....
	Montreal Canadiens	NHL	....	....	....	....	....	....	....	....	....	....	....	....	....	....	....	....	....	....	5	0	0	0	0	....	....	....
1977-78	Montreal Canadiens	NHL	1	0	0	0	0	0	0	0	0	0	0	0	0.0	0	0	0	0	0	....	....	....	....	....	....	....	....
	Nova Scotia Voyageurs	AHL	79	22	38	60	....	....	....	70	....	....	....	....	....	....	....	....	....	....	11	2	6	8	4	....	....	....
1978-79	Minnesota North Stars	NHL	73	6	10	16	5	8	13	18	0	0	0	66	9.1	28	1	59	19	–13	....	....	....	....	....	....	....	....
	Oklahoma City Stars	CHL	9	0	7	7	....	....	....	0	....	....	....	....	....	....	....	....	....	....	....	....	....	....	....	....	....	....
1979-80	Minnesota North Stars	NHL	78	10	14	24	9	11	20	20	0	0	1	94	10.6	34	0	61	27	0	15	2	1	3	2	0	0	0
1980-81	Minnesota North Stars	NHL	74	8	5	13	7	3	10	19	0	1	0	58	13.8	19	1	59	39	–2	3	0	0	0	0	0	0	0
	NHL Totals		226	24	29	53	21	22	43	57	0	1	1	218	11.0	81	2	179	85		23	2	1	3	2	0	0	0

NCAA Championship All-Tournament Team (1974) • WCHA First All-Star Team (1975) • NCAA West First All-American Team (1975)

Signed as a free agent by **Montreal**, September 27, 1975. Signed as a free agent by **Minnesota**, September 6, 1978.

• POLIS, GREG

Greg "Pole Cat" Polis LW – L. 6', 195 lbs. b: Westlock, Alta., 8/8/1950. Pittsburgh's 1st choice, 7th overall, in 1970 Amateur Draft.

Season	Club	League	GP	G	A	Pts	AG	AA	APts	PIM	PP	SH	GW	S	%	TGF	PGF	TGA	PGA	+/-	GP	G	A	Pts	PIM	PP	SH	GW
1966-67	Estevan Bruins	WCJHL	54	12	20	32	....	....	....	83	....	....	....	....	....	....	....	....	....	....	13	1	5	6	12	....	....	....
1967-68	Estevan Bruins	WCJHL	59	35	32	67	....	....	....	124	....	....	....	....	....	....	....	....	....	....	13	3	6	9	20	....	....	....
1968-69	Estevan Bruins	WCJHL	60	40	85	125	....	....	....	94	....	....	....	....	....	....	....	....	....	....	12	4	6	10	8	....	....	....
1969-70	Estevan Bruins	WCJHL	60	48	56	104	....	....	....	69	....	....	....	....	....	....	....	....	....	....	5	2	1	3	2	....	....	....
1970-71	Pittsburgh Penguins	NHL	61	18	15	33	19	13	32	40	5	0	2	157	11.5	56	17	45	0	–6	....	....	....	....	....	....	....	....
1971-72	Pittsburgh Penguins	NHL	76	30	19	49	32	17	49	38	8	0	0	208	14.4	74	20	58	0	–4	4	0	2	2	0	0	0	0
1972-73	Pittsburgh Penguins	NHL	78	26	23	49	26	19	45	36	8	0	2	221	11.8	73	23	82	0	–32	....	....	....	....	....	....	....	....
1973-74	Pittsburgh Penguins	NHL	41	14	13	27	14	11	25	32	5	0	1	163	8.6	35	13	40	0	–18	....	....	....	....	....	....	....	....
	St. Louis Blues	NHL	37	8	12	20	8	10	18	24	3	0	0	122	6.6	31	9	29	0	–7	....	....	....	....	....	....	....	....
1974-75	New York Rangers	NHL	76	26	15	41	24	12	36	55	4	0	4	213	12.2	63	13	48	1	+3	3	0	0	0	6	0	0	0
1975-76	New York Rangers	NHL	79	15	21	36	14	16	30	77	0	0	1	158	9.5	50	3	58	3	–8	....	....	....	....	....	....	....	....
1976-77	New York Rangers	NHL	77	16	23	39	15	19	34	44	3	0	2	187	8.6	58	4	66	12	0	....	....	....	....	....	....	....	....
1977-78	New York Rangers	NHL	37	7	16	23	7	13	20	12	0	4	1	72	9.7	32	1	44	10	–3	....	....	....	....	....	....	....	....
1978-79	New York Rangers	NHL	6	1	1	2	1	1	2	8	0	0	0	10	10.0	4	0	3	0	+1	....	....	....	....	....	....	....	....
	Washington Capitals	NHL	19	12	6	18	11	5	16	6	6	0	1	46	26.1	28	9	18	2	+3	....	....	....	....	....	....	....	....
	New Haven Nighthawks	AHL	10	3	3	6	....	....	....	0	....	....	....	....	....	....	....	....	....	....	....	....	....	....	....	....	....	....
1979-80	Washington Capitals	NHL	28	1	5	6	1	4	5	19	0	0	0	30	3.3	15	1	22	2	–6	....	....	....	....	....	....	....	....
	Hershey Bears	AHL	9	0	2	2	....	....	....	2	....	....	....	....	....	....	....	....	....	....	....	....	....	....	....	....	....	....
1980-81	Hershey Bears	AHL	2	1	0	1	....	....	....	5	....	....	....	....	....	....	....	....	....	....	....	....	....	....	....	....	....	....
	NHL Totals		615	174	169	343	172	140	312	391	42	4	14	1587	11.0	519	113	513	30		7	0	2	2	6	0	0	0

WCJHL All-Star Team (1969, 1970)

Played in NHL All-Star Game (1971, 1972, 1973)

Traded to **St. Louis** by **Pittsburgh** with Bryan Watson and Pittsburgh's 2nd round choice (Bob Hess) in 1974 Amateur Draft for Steve Durbano, Ab Demarco and Bob Kelly, January 17, 1974. Traded to **NY Rangers** by **St. Louis** for Larry Sacharuk, August 29, 1974. Claimed on waivers by **Washington** from **NY Rangers**, January 15, 1979.

• POLONICH, DENNIS

Dennis Polonich C/RW – R. 5'6", 166 lbs. b: Foam Lake, Sask., 12/4/1953. Detroit's 8th choice, 118th overall, in 1973 Amateur Draft.

Season	Club	League	GP	G	A	Pts	AG	AA	APts	PIM	PP	SH	GW	S	%	TGF	PGF	TGA	PGA	+/-	GP	G	A	Pts	PIM	PP	SH	GW
1971-72	Flin Flon Bombers	WCJHL	65	9	21	30	....	....	....	200	....	....	....	....	....	....	....	....	....	....	7	0	1	1	41	....	....	....
1972-73	Flin Flon Bombers	WCJHL	68	26	48	74	....	....	....	222	....	....	....	....	....	....	....	....	....	....	....	....	....	....	....	....	....	....
1973-74	London Lions	Britain	67	17	43	60	....	....	....	57	....	....	....	....	....	....	....	....	....	....	....	....	....	....	....	....	....	....
1974-75	Detroit Red Wings	NHL	4	0	0	0	0	0	0	0	0	0	0	4	0.0	0	0	1	0	–1	....	....	....	....	....	....	....	....
	Virginia Wings	AHL	60	14	20	34	....	....	....	194	....	....	....	....	....	....	....	....	....	....	5	0	2	2	30	....	....	....

			REGULAR SEASON																		PLAYOFFS							
Season	Club	League	GP	G	A	Pts	AG	AA	APts	PIM	PP	SH	GW	S	%	TGF	PGF	TGA	PGA	+/–	GP	G	A	Pts	PIM	PP	SH	GW
1975-76	**Detroit Red Wings**	**NHL**	**57**	**11**	**12**	**23**	**10**	**9**	**19**	**302**	**1**	**0**	**0**	**97**	**11.3**	**30**	**4**	**36**	**1**	**–9**	....	....	....	....	....	....	....	....
	Kalamazoo Wings	IHL	5	1	8	9	....	....	....	32	....	....	....	....	....	....	....	....	....	....	....	....	....	....	....	....	....	....
1976-77	**Detroit Red Wings**	**NHL**	**79**	**18**	**28**	**46**	**17**	**23**	**40**	**274**	**6**	**1**	**1**	**183**	**9.8**	**67**	**19**	**73**	**5**	**–20**	....	....	....	....	....	....	....	....
1977-78	**Detroit Red Wings**	**NHL**	**79**	**16**	**19**	**35**	**15**	**15**	**30**	**254**	**5**	**0**	**0**	**128**	**12.5**	**63**	**18**	**50**	**0**	**–5**	**7**	**1**	**0**	**1**	**19**	**0**	**0**	**0**
1978-79	**Detroit Red Wings**	**NHL**	**62**	**10**	**12**	**22**	**9**	**9**	**18**	**208**	**1**	**0**	**0**	**80**	**12.5**	**44**	**9**	**45**	**0**	**–10**	....	....	....	....	....	....	....	....
1979-80	**Detroit Red Wings**	**NHL**	**66**	**2**	**8**	**10**	**2**	**6**	**8**	**127**	**0**	**0**	**0**	**61**	**3.3**	**22**	**1**	**43**	**7**	**–15**	....	....	....	....	....	....	....	....
1980-81	**Detroit Red Wings**	**NHL**	**32**	**2**	**2**	**4**	**2**	**1**	**3**	**77**	**0**	**0**	**0**	**27**	**7.4**	**8**	**2**	**26**	**6**	**–14**	....	....	....	....	....	....	....	....
	Adirondack Red Wings	AHL	40	16	13	29	....	....	....	99	....	....	....	....	....	....	....	....	....	....	14	9	5	14	95	....	....	....
1981-82	Adirondack Red Wings	AHL	80	30	26	56	....	....	....	202	....	....	....	....	....	....	....	....	....	....	5	2	2	4	0	....	....	....
1982-83	**Detroit Red Wings**	**NHL**	**11**	**0**	**1**	**1**	**0**	**1**	**1**	**0**	**0**	**0**	**0**	**7**	**0.0**	**1**	**0**	**7**	**2**	**–4**	....	....	....	....	....	....	....	....
	Adirondack Red Wings	AHL	61	18	22	40	....	....	....	128	....	....	....	....	....	....	....	....	....	....	6	2	2	4	10	....	....	....
1983-84	Adirondack Red Wings	AHL	66	14	26	40	....	....	....	122	....	....	....	....	....	....	....	....	....	....	....	....	....	....	....	....	....	....
1984-85	Adirondack Red Wings	AHL	53	18	17	35	....	....	....	133	....	....	....	....	....	....	....	....	....	....	....	....	....	....	....	....	....	....
1985-86	Muskegon Lumberjacks	IHL	78	32	36	68	....	....	....	222	....	....	....	....	....	....	....	....	....	....	14	8	10	18	36	....	....	....
1986-87	Muskegon Lumberjacks	IHL	22	2	9	11	....	....	....	24	....	....	....	....	....	....	....	....	....	....	....	....	....	....	....	....	....	....
	NHL Totals		**390**	**59**	**82**	**141**	**55**	**64**	**119**	**1242**	**13**	**1**	**1**	**587**	**10.1**	**235**	**53**	**281**	**21**		**7**	**1**	**0**	**1**	**19**	**0**	**0**	**0**

• POOLEY, PAUL

Paul Pooley C – R. 6′, 175 lbs. b: Exeter, Ont., 8/2/1960.

Season	Club	League	GP	G	A	Pts	AG	AA	APts	PIM	PP	SH	GW	S	%	TGF	PGF	TGA	PGA	+/–	GP	G	A	Pts	PIM	PP	SH	GW
1980-81	Ohio State University	CCHA	38	28	30	58	....	....	....	41	....	....	....	....	....	....	....	....	....	....	....	....	....	....	....	....	....	....
1981-82	Ohio State University	CCHA	34	21	24	45	....	....	....	34	....	....	....	....	....	....	....	....	....	....	....	....	....	....	....	....	....	....
1982-83	Ohio State University	CCHA	30	24	29	53	....	....	....	48	....	....	....	....	....	....	....	....	....	....	....	....	....	....	....	....	....	....
1983-84	Ohio State University	CCHA	41	32	64	96	....	....	....	40	....	....	....	....	....	....	....	....	....	....	....	....	....	....	....	....	....	....
1984-85	**Winnipeg Jets**	**NHL**	**12**	**0**	**2**	**2**	**0**	**1**	**1**	**0**	**0**	**0**	**0**	**1**	**0.0**	**2**	**0**	**2**	**1**	**+1**	....	....	....	....	....	....	....	....
	Sherbrooke Canadiens	AHL	57	18	17	35	....	....	....	16	....	....	....	....	....	....	....	....	....	....	17	2	2	4	7	....	....	....
1985-86	**Winnipeg Jets**	**NHL**	**3**	**0**	**1**	**1**	**0**	**1**	**1**	**0**	**0**	**0**	**0**	**2**	**0.0**	**2**	**0**	**2**	**1**	**+1**	....	....	....	....	....	....	....	....
	Sherbrooke Canadiens	AHL	70	20	21	41	....	....	....	31	....	....	....	....	....	....	....	....	....	....	....	....	....	....	....	....	....	....
1986-87	Fort Wayne Komets	IHL	77	28	44	72	....	....	....	47	....	....	....	....	....	....	....	....	....	....	2	1	3	2	2	....	....	....
	NHL Totals		**15**	**0**	**3**	**3**	**0**	**2**	**2**	**0**	**0**	**0**	**0**	**3**	**0.0**	**4**	**0**	**4**	**2**		....	....	....	....	....	....	....	....

CCHA Second All-Star Team (1981) • CCHA First All-Star Team (1984) • NCAA West First All-American Team (1984)

Signed as a free agent by **Winnipeg**, May 24, 1984.

• POPEIN, LARRY

Larry "Pope" Popein C – L. 5′10″, 165 lbs. b: Yorkton, Sask., 8/11/1930.

Season	Club	League	GP	G	A	Pts	AG	AA	APts	PIM	PP	SH	GW	S	%	TGF	PGF	TGA	PGA	+/–	GP	G	A	Pts	PIM	PP	SH	GW
1947-48	Moose Jaw Canucks	MJHL	27	21	12	33	....	....	....	6	....	....	....	....	....	....	....	....	....	....	4	4	0	4	7	....	....	....
1948-49	Moose Jaw Canucks	MJHL	26	21	12	33	....	....	....	34	....	....	....	....	....	....	....	....	....	....	8	5	2	7	0	....	....	....
1949-50	Moose Jaw Canucks	WCJHL	38	31	22	53	....	....	....	4	....	....	....	....	....	....	....	....	....	....	4	5	2	7	0	....	....	....
1950-51	Regina Capitals	WCSHL	54	21	19	40	....	....	....	14	....	....	....	....	....	....	....	....	....	....	....	....	....	....	....	....	....	....
1951-52	Vancouver Canucks	PCHL	69	32	36	68	....	....	....	14	....	....	....	....	....	....	....	....	....	....	....	....	....	....	....	....	....	....
1952-53	Vancouver Canucks	WHL	70	25	44	69	....	....	....	23	....	....	....	....	....	....	....	....	....	....	9	5	10	15	0	....	....	....
1953-54	Vancouver Canucks	WHL	70	34	32	66	....	....	....	22	....	....	....	....	....	....	....	....	....	....	10	4	7	11	4	....	....	....
1954-55	**New York Rangers**	**NHL**	**70**	**11**	**17**	**28**	**16**	**22**	**38**	**27**	....	....	....	....	....	....	....	....	....	....	....	....	....	....	....	....	....	....
1955-56	**New York Rangers**	**NHL**	**64**	**14**	**25**	**39**	**20**	**31**	**51**	**37**	....	....	....	....	....	....	....	....	....	....	**5**	**0**	**1**	**1**	**2**	....	....	....
1956-57	**New York Rangers**	**NHL**	**67**	**11**	**19**	**30**	**15**	**22**	**37**	**20**	....	....	....	....	....	....	....	....	....	....	**5**	**0**	**3**	**3**	**0**	....	....	....
1957-58	**New York Rangers**	**NHL**	**70**	**12**	**22**	**34**	**16**	**24**	**40**	**22**	....	....	....	....	....	....	....	....	....	....	**6**	**1**	**0**	**1**	**4**	....	....	....
1958-59	**New York Rangers**	**NHL**	**61**	**13**	**21**	**34**	**16**	**22**	**38**	**28**	....	....	....	....	....	....	....	....	....	....	....	....	....	....	....	....	....	....
1959-60	**New York Rangers**	**NHL**	**66**	**14**	**22**	**36**	**17**	**23**	**40**	**16**	....	....	....	....	....	....	....	....	....	....	....	....	....	....	....	....	....	....
1960-61	**New York Rangers**	**NHL**	**4**	**0**	**1**	**1**	**0**	**1**	**1**	**0**	....	....	....	....	....	....	....	....	....	....	....	....	....	....	....	....	....	....
	Vancouver Canucks	WHL	69	19	48	67	....	....	....	12	....	....	....	....	....	....	....	....	....	....	9	1	3	4	0	....	....	....
1961-62	Vancouver Canucks	WHL	59	9	22	31	....	....	....	12	....	....	....	....	....	....	....	....	....	....	10	0	3	3	2	....	....	....
1962-63	Vancouver Canucks	WHL	65	15	21	36	....	....	....	24	....	....	....	....	....	....	....	....	....	....	7	0	1	1	4	....	....	....
1963-64	Vancouver Canucks	WHL	39	8	11	19	....	....	....	18	....	....	....	....	....	....	....	....	....	....	....	....	....	....	....	....	....	....
1964-65	Vancouver Canucks	WHL	59	7	9	16	....	....	....	12	....	....	....	....	....	....	....	....	....	....	5	0	1	1	2	....	....	....
1965-66	Vancouver Canucks	WHL	68	16	15	31	....	....	....	20	....	....	....	....	....	....	....	....	....	....	7	2	3	5	2	....	....	....
1966-67	Vancouver Canucks	WHL	71	22	26	48	....	....	....	18	....	....	....	....	....	....	....	....	....	....	3	1	1	2	2	....	....	....
1967-68	**Oakland Seals**	**NHL**	**47**	**5**	**14**	**19**	**6**	**15**	**21**	**12**	**0**	**1**	**0**	**51**	**9.8**	**23**	**3**	**53**	**16**	**–17**	....	....	....	....	....	....	....	....
	Vancouver Canucks	WHL	27	6	6	12	....	....	....	4	....	....	....	....	....	....	....	....	....	....	....	....	....	....	....	....	....	....
1968-69	Omaha Knights	CHL	57	1	4	5	....	....	....	16	....	....	....	....	....	....	....	....	....	....	7	1	0	1	0	....	....	....
1969-70	Omaha Knights	CHL	2	0	0	0	....	....	....	0	....	....	....	....	....	....	....	....	....	....	....	....	....	....	....	....	....	....
	NHL Totals		**449**	**80**	**141**	**221**	**106**	**160**	**266**	**162**	**0**	**1**	**0**	**51**	**156.9**	**23**	**3**	**53**	**16**		**16**	**1**	**4**	**5**	**6**	**0**	**0**	**0**

Traded to **Oakland** by **NY Rangers** for cash, December, 1967. Traded to **NY Rangers** by **Oakland** for cash, May, 1968.

• POPIEL, POUL

Poul "Paul" Popiel D – L. 5′10″, 175 lbs. b: Sollested, Denmark, 2/28/1943.

Season	Club	League	GP	G	A	Pts	AG	AA	APts	PIM	PP	SH	GW	S	%	TGF	PGF	TGA	PGA	+/–	GP	G	A	Pts	PIM	PP	SH	GW
1960-61	St. Catharines Teepees	OHA	38	2	9	11	....	....	....	74	....	....	....	....	....	....	....	....	....	....	3	0	1	1	2	....	....	....
1961-62	St. Catharines Teepees	OHA	49	3	16	19	....	....	....	128	....	....	....	....	....	....	....	....	....	....	6	0	0	0	11	....	....	....
1962-63	St. Catharines Black Hawks	OHA	50	11	34	45	....	....	....	131	....	....	....	....	....	....	....	....	....	....	....	....	....	....	....	....	....	....
	Buffalo Bisons	AHL	2	0	1	1	....	....	....	2	....	....	....	....	....	....	....	....	....	....	....	....	....	....	....	....	....	....
1963-64	Buffalo Bisons	AHL	4	0	0	0	....	....	....	4	....	....	....	....	....	....	....	....	....	....	....	....	....	....	....	....	....	....
	St. Louis Braves	CHL	54	9	14	23	....	....	....	78	....	....	....	....	....	....	....	....	....	....	6	0	1	1	17	....	....	....
1964-65	Buffalo Bisons	AHL	48	7	12	19	....	....	....	76	....	....	....	....	....	....	....	....	....	....	9	0	1	1	29	....	....	....
1965-66	**Boston Bruins**	**NHL**	**3**	**0**	**1**	**1**	**0**	**1**	**1**	**2**	....	....	....	....	....	....	....	....	....	....	....	....	....	....	....	....	....	....
	Hershey Bears	AHL	63	6	26	32	....	....	....	101	....	....	....	....	....	....	....	....	....	....	3	0	0	0	2	....	....	....
1966-67	Hershey Bears	AHL	63	5	27	32	....	....	....	134	....	....	....	....	....	....	....	....	....	....	5	1	0	1	10	....	....	....
1967-68	**Los Angeles Kings**	**NHL**	**1**	**0**	**0**	**0**	**0**	**0**	**0**	**0**	**0**	**0**	**0**	**3**	**0.0**	**0**	**0**	**2**	**1**	**–1**	**3**	**1**	**0**	**1**	**4**	**0**	**0**	**0**
	Springfield Kings	AHL	72	8	27	35	....	....	....	180	....	....	....	....	....	....	....	....	....	....	4	0	0	0	4	....	....	....
1968-69	Springfield Kings	AHL	13	0	10	10	....	....	....	19	....	....	....	....	....	....	....	....	....	....	....	....	....	....	....	....	....	....
	Detroit Red Wings	**NHL**	**62**	**2**	**13**	**15**	**2**	**12**	**14**	**82**	**0**	**0**	**2**	**99**	**2.0**	**58**	**1**	**53**	**6**	**+10**	....	....	....	....	....	....	....	....
1969-70	Cleveland Barons	AHL	22	3	15	18	....	....	....	14	....	....	....	....	....	....	....	....	....	....	....	....	....	....	....	....	....	....
	Detroit Red Wings	**NHL**	**32**	**0**	**4**	**4**	**0**	**4**	**4**	**29**	**0**	**0**	**0**	**22**	**0.0**	**16**	**2**	**9**	**0**	**+5**	**1**	**0**	**0**	**0**	**0**	**0**	**0**	**0**
1970-71	**Vancouver Canucks**	**NHL**	**78**	**10**	**22**	**32**	**10**	**19**	**29**	**61**	**2**	**0**	**2**	**136**	**7.4**	**70**	**12**	**60**	**11**	**+9**	....	....	....	....	....	....	....	....
1971-72	**Vancouver Canucks**	**NHL**	**38**	**1**	**1**	**2**	**1**	**1**	**2**	**36**	**0**	**0**	**0**	**32**	**3.1**	**5**	**0**	**37**	**21**	**–11**	....	....	....	....	....	....	....	....
	Rochester Americans	AHL	12	7	4	11	....	....	....	10	....	....	....	....	....	....	....	....	....	....	....	....	....	....	....	....	....	....
1972-73	Houston Aeros	WHA	74	16	48	64	....	....	....	158	....	....	....	....	....	....	....	....	....	....	10	2	9	11	23	....	....	....
1973-74	Houston Aeros	WHA	78	7	41	48	....	....	....	126	....	....	....	....	....	....	....	....	....	....	14	1	*14	15	22	....	....	....
1974-75	Houston Aeros	WHA	78	11	53	64	....	....	....	22	....	....	....	....	....	....	....	....	....	....	13	1	10	11	34	....	....	....
1975-76	Houston Aeros	WHA	78	10	36	46	....	....	....	71	....	....	....	....	....	....	....	....	....	....	17	3	5	8	16	....	....	....
1976-77	Houston Aeros	WHA	80	12	56	68	....	....	....	87	....	....	....	....	....	....	....	....	....	....	11	0	7	7	10	....	....	....
1977-78	Houston Aeros	WHA	80	6	31	37	....	....	....	53	....	....	....	....	....	....	....	....	....	....	6	0	2	2	13	....	....	....
1978-79	ECS Innsbruck	Austria	34	6	28	34	....	....	....	99	....	....	....	....	....	....	....	....	....	....	....	....	....	....	....	....	....	....
1979-80	**Edmonton Oilers**	**NHL**	**10**	**0**	**0**	**0**	**0**	**0**	**0**	**0**	**0**	**0**	**0**	**12**	**0.0**	**5**	**1**	**11**	**2**	**–5**	....	....	....	....	....	....	....	....
	Houston Apollos	CHL	57	2	27	29	....	....	....	28	....	....	....	....	....	....	....	....	....	....	6	0	1	1	10	....	....	....
1980-81			DID NOT PLAY																									
1981-82	Muskegon Mohawks	IHL	12	0	4	4	....	....	....	10	....	....	....	....	....	....	....	....	....	....	....	....	....	....	....	....	....	....
	NHL Totals		**224**	**13**	**41**	**54**	**13**	**37**	**50**	**210**	**2**	**0**	**4**	**304**	**4.3**	**154**	**16**	**172**	**41**		**4**	**1**	**0**	**1**	**4**	**0**	**0**	**0**
	Other Major League Totals		468	62	265	327	....	....	....	517	....	....	....	....	....	....	....	....	....		71	7	47	54	118	....	....	....

Shared Ken McKenzie Trophy (CHL's Rookie of the Year) with Garry Peters (1964) • WHA Second All-Star Team (1975, 1977)

Claimed by **Boston** from **Chicago** in Intra-League Draft, June 9, 1965. Claimed by **LA Kings** from **Boston** in Expansion Draft, June 6, 1967. Traded to **Detroit** by **LA Kings** for Ron Anderson, November 12, 1968. Claimed by **Vancouver** from **Detroit** in Expansion Draft, June 10, 1970. Selected by **Dayton-Houston** (WHA) in 1972 WHA General Player Draft, February 12, 1972. Signed as a free agent by **Edmonton**, November 2, 1979.

			REGULAR SEASON																		PLAYOFFS							
Season	Club	League	GP	G	A	Pts	AG	AA	APts	PIM	PP	SH	GW	S	%	TGF	PGF	TGA	PGA	+/–	GP	G	A	Pts	PIM	PP	SH	GW

• POPOVIC, PETER

Peter Popovic D – L. 6'6", 235 lbs. b: Koping, Sweden, 2/10/1968. Montreal's 5th choice, 93rd overall, in 1988 Entry Draft.

Season	Club	League	GP	G	A	Pts	AG	AA	APts	PIM	PP	SH	GW	S	%	TGF	PGF	TGA	PGA	+/–	GP	G	A	Pts	PIM	PP	SH	GW
1986-87	Vasteras IK	Sweden 2	24	1	2	3	....	....	....	10	....	....	....	....	....	....	....	....	....	....	....	....	....	....	....	....	....	....
1987-88	Vasteras IK	Sweden 2	28	3	17	20	....	....	....	16	....	....	....	....	....	....	....	....	....	....	....	....	....	....	....	....	....	....
1988-89	Vasteras IK	Sweden	22	1	4	5	....	....	....	32	....	....	....	....	....	....	....	....	....	....	....	....	....	....	....	....	....	....
1989-90	Vasteras IK	Sweden	30	2	10	12	....	....	....	24	....	....	....	....	....	....	....	....	....	....	2	0	1	1	2	....	....	....
1990-91	Vasteras IK	Sweden	40	3	2	5	....	....	....	62	....	....	....	....	....	....	....	....	....	....	4	0	0	0	4	....	....	....
1991-92	Vasteras IK	Sweden	34	7	10	17	....	....	....	30	....	....	....	....	....	....	....	....	....	....	....	....	....	....	....	....	....	....
1992-93	Vasteras IK	Sweden	39	6	12	18	....	....	....	46	....	....	....	....	....	....	....	....	....	....	3	0	1	1	2	....	....	....
	Sweden	WC-A	8	0	1	1	....	....	....	2	....	....	....	....	....	....	....	....	....	....	....	....	....	....	....	....	....	....
1993-94	**Montreal Canadiens**	**NHL**	**47**	**2**	**12**	**14**	**2**	**9**	**11**	**26**	**1**	**0**	**0**	**58**	**3.4**	**43**	**11**	**32**	**10**	**+10**	**6**	**0**	**1**	**1**	**0**	**0**	**0**	**0**
1994-95	Vasteras IK	Sweden	11	0	3	3	....	....	....	10	....	....	....	....	....	....	....	....	....	....	....	....	....	....	....	....	....	....
	Montreal Canadiens	**NHL**	**33**	**0**	**5**	**5**	**0**	**7**	**7**	**8**	**0**	**0**	**0**	**23**	**0.0**	**11**	**0**	**27**	**6**	**–10**	....	....	....	....	....	....	....	....
1995-96	**Montreal Canadiens**	**NHL**	**76**	**2**	**12**	**14**	**2**	**10**	**12**	**69**	**0**	**0**	**0**	**59**	**3.4**	**82**	**8**	**87**	**34**	**+21**	**6**	**0**	**2**	**2**	**4**	**0**	**0**	**0**
1996-97	Sweden	W Cup	3	0	0	0	....	....	....	2	....	....	....	....	....	....	....	....	....	....	....	....	....	....	....	....	....	....
	Montreal Canadiens	**NHL**	**78**	**1**	**13**	**14**	**1**	**11**	**12**	**32**	**0**	**0**	**0**	**82**	**1.2**	**71**	**2**	**87**	**27**	**+9**	**3**	**0**	**0**	**0**	**2**	**0**	**0**	**0**
1997-98	**Montreal Canadiens**	**NHL**	**69**	**2**	**6**	**8**	**2**	**6**	**8**	**38**	**0**	**0**	**0**	**40**	**5.0**	**37**	**0**	**63**	**20**	**–6**	**10**	**1**	**1**	**2**	**2**	**0**	**0**	**0**
	NHL Totals		**303**	**7**	**48**	**55**	**7**	**43**	**50**	**173**	**1**	**0**	**0**	**262**	**2.7**	**244**	**21**	**296**	**97**		**25**	**1**	**4**	**5**	**8**	**0**	**0**	**0**

Traded to **NY Rangers** by **Montreal** for Sylvain Blouin and NY Rangers' 6th round choice in 1999 Entry Draft, June 30, 1998.

• PORVARI, JUKKA

Jukka Porvari RW – L. 5'11", 175 lbs. b: Tampere, Finland, 1/19/1954.

Season	Club	League	GP	G	A	Pts	AG	AA	APts	PIM	PP	SH	GW	S	%	TGF	PGF	TGA	PGA	+/–	GP	G	A	Pts	PIM	PP	SH	GW
1973-74	Finland	WJC-A	5	1	1	2	....	....	....	0	....	....	....	....	....	....	....	....	....	....	....	....	....	....	....	....	....	....
1974-75	Tappara Tampere	Finland	36	7	9	16	....	....	....	2	....	....	....	....	....	....	....	....	....	....	....	....	....	....	....	....	....	....
1975-76	Tappara Tampere	Finland	36	10	10	20	....	....	....	4	....	....	....	....	....	....	....	....	....	....	4	0	2	2	4	....	....	....
1976-77	Tappara Tampere	Finland	36	17	16	33	....	....	....	20	....	....	....	....	....	....	....	....	....	....	6	3	5	8	5	....	....	....
	Finland	WEC-A	10	3	3	6	....	....	....	2	....	....	....	....	....	....	....	....	....	....	....	....	....	....	....	....	....	....
1977-78	Tappara Tampere	Finland	26	11	7	18	....	....	....	18	....	....	....	....	....	....	....	....	....	....	8	1	1	2	16	....	....	....
	Finland	WEC-A	10	3	1	4	....	....	....	8	....	....	....	....	....	....	....	....	....	....	....	....	....	....	....	....	....	....
1978-79	Tappara Tampere	Finland	35	20	22	42	....	....	....	38	....	....	....	....	....	....	....	....	....	....	10	*9	4	13	0	....	....	....
	Finland	WEC-A	8	4	2	6	....	....	....	8	....	....	....	....	....	....	....	....	....	....	....	....	....	....	....	....	....	....
1979-80	Tappara Tampere	Finland	31	19	15	34	....	....	....	36	....	....	....	....	....	....	....	....	....	....	7	4	0	4	0	....	....	....
	Finland	Nat-Team	19	9	6	15	....	....	....	10	....	....	....	....	....	....	....	....	....	....	....	....	....	....	....	....	....	....
	Finland	Olympics	7	7	4	11	....	....	....	4	....	....	....	....	....	....	....	....	....	....	....	....	....	....	....	....	....	....
1980-81	Tappara Tampere	Finland	36	14	18	32	....	....	....	22	....	....	....	....	....	....	....	....	....	....	8	4	6	10	6	....	....	....
	Finland	WEC-A	8	3	0	3	....	....	....	8	....	....	....	....	....	....	....	....	....	....	....	....	....	....	....	....	....	....
1981-82	Finland	C Cup	5	1	0	1	....	....	....	0	....	....	....	....	....	....	....	....	....	....	....	....	....	....	....	....	....	....
	Colorado Rockies	**NHL**	**31**	**2**	**6**	**8**	**2**	**4**	**6**	**0**	**0**	**0**	**0**	**45**	**4.4**	**16**	**1**	**42**	**5**	**–22**	....	....	....	....	....	....	....	....
	Fort Worth Texans	CHL	2	0	0	0	....	....	....	0	....	....	....	....	....	....	....	....	....	....	....	....	....	....	....	....	....	....
1982-83	**New Jersey Devils**	**NHL**	**8**	**1**	**3**	**4**	**1**	**2**	**3**	**4**	**0**	**0**	**0**	**10**	**10.0**	**4**	**1**	**4**	**0**	**–1**	....	....	....	....	....	....	....	....
	Wichita Wind	CHL	11	2	3	5	....	....	....	0	....	....	....	....	....	....	....	....	....	....	....	....	....	....	....	....	....	....
1983-84	TPS Turku	Finland	37	18	8	26	....	....	....	16	....	....	....	....	....	....	....	....	....	....	10	5	1	6	4	....	....	....
1984-85	TPS Turku	Finland	36	27	16	43	....	....	....	26	....	....	....	....	....	....	....	....	....	....	10	*7	2	9	12	....	....	....
1985-86	TPS Turku	Finland	36	9	9	18	....	....	....	12	....	....	....	....	....	....	....	....	....	....	7	0	3	3	0	....	....	....
	NHL Totals		**39**	**3**	**9**	**12**	**3**	**6**	**9**	**4**	**0**	**0**	**0**	**55**	**5.5**	**20**	**2**	**46**	**5**		....	....	....	....	....	....	....	....

Finnish First All-Star Team (1978, 1980, 1981)

Signed as a free agent by **Colorado**, July 8, 1981. Transferred to **New Jersey** after **Colorado** franchise relocated, June 30, 1982.

• POSA, VICTOR

Victor Posa LW/D – L. 6', 195 lbs. b: Bari, Italy, 11/5/1966. Chicago's 7th choice, 137th overall, in 1985 Entry Draft.

Season	Club	League	GP	G	A	Pts	AG	AA	APts	PIM	PP	SH	GW	S	%	TGF	PGF	TGA	PGA	+/–	GP	G	A	Pts	PIM	PP	SH	GW
1983-84	Henry Carr Crusaders	MTHL	25	16	21	37	....	....	....	139	....	....	....	....	....	....	....	....	....	....	....	....	....	....	....	....	....	....
1984-85	University of Wisconsin	WCHA	33	1	5	6	....	....	....	47	....	....	....	....	....	....	....	....	....	....	....	....	....	....	....	....	....	....
1985-86	Toronto Marlboros	OHL	48	28	39	62	....	....	....	116	....	....	....	....	....	....	....	....	....	....	....	....	....	....	....	....	....	....
	Chicago Black Hawks	**NHL**	**2**	**0**	**0**	**0**	**0**	**0**	**0**	**2**	**0**	**0**	**0**	**1**	**0.0**	**0**	**0**	**0**	**0**	**0**	....	....	....	....	....	....	....	....
1986-87	Nova Scotia Oilers	AHL	2	1	0	1	....	....	....	2	....	....	....	....	....	....	....	....	....	....	....	....	....	....	....	....	....	....
	Saginaw Generals	IHL	61	13	27	40	....	....	....	203	....	....	....	....	....	....	....	....	....	....	7	1	0	1	34	....	....	....
1987-88	Saginaw Hawks	IHL	2	0	0	0	....	....	....	0	....	....	....	....	....	....	....	....	....	....	....	....	....	....	....	....	....	....
	Flint Spirits	IHL	9	1	0	1	....	....	....	36	....	....	....	....	....	....	....	....	....	....	....	....	....	....	....	....	....	....
	Peoria Rivermen	IHL	10	0	2	2	....	....	....	106	....	....	....	....	....	....	....	....	....	....	....	....	....	....	....	....	....	....
1988-89	Flint Spirits	IHL	3	0	0	0	....	....	....	21	....	....	....	....	....	....	....	....	....	....	....	....	....	....	....	....	....	....
	Carolina Thunderbirds	EHL	10	4	4	8	....	....	....	41	....	....	....	....	....	....	....	....	....	....	....	....	....	....	....	....	....	....
1989-90			DID NOT PLAY – RETIRED																									
1990-91	Winston-Salem Thunderbirds	ECHL	9	1	4	5	....	....	....	41	....	....	....	....	....	....	....	....	....	....	....	....	....	....	....	....	....	....
	Richmond Renegades	ECHL	20	4	9	13	....	....	....	102	....	....	....	....	....	....	....	....	....	....	....	....	....	....	....	....	....	....
1991-92			DID NOT PLAY – RETIRED																									
1992-93	Detroit Falcons	ColHL	39	15	16	31	....	....	....	102	....	....	....	....	....	....	....	....	....	....	6	0	1	1	30	....	....	....
1993-94	Huntsville Blast	ECHL	9	1	3	4	....	....	....	33	....	....	....	....	....	....	....	....	....	....	....	....	....	....	....	....	....	....
	NHL Totals		**2**	**0**	**0**	**0**	**0**	**0**	**0**	**2**	**0**	**0**	**0**	**1**	**0.0**	**0**	**0**	**0**	**0**		....	....	....	....	....	....	....	....

• POSAVAD, MIKE

Mike Posavad D – R. 5'11", 195 lbs. b: Brantford, Ont., 1/3/1964. St. Louis' 1st choice, 50th overall, in 1982 Entry Draft.

Season	Club	League	GP	G	A	Pts	AG	AA	APts	PIM	PP	SH	GW	S	%	TGF	PGF	TGA	PGA	+/–	GP	G	A	Pts	PIM	PP	SH	GW
1979-80	Brantford Midgets	Jr. B	43	11	22	33	....	....	....	18	....	....	....	....	....	....	....	....	....	....	....	....	....	....	....	....	....	....
1980-81	Peterborough Petes	OHL	58	3	12	15	....	....	....	55	....	....	....	....	....	....	....	....	....	....	....	....	....	....	....	....	....	....
1981-82	Peterborough Petes	OHL	64	7	23	30	....	....	....	110	....	....	....	....	....	....	....	....	....	....	9	3	4	7	15	....	....	....
1982-83	Peterborough Petes	OHL	70	1	36	37	....	....	....	68	....	....	....	....	....	....	....	....	....	....	4	0	2	2	2	....	....	....
	Salt Lake Golden Eagles	CHL	1	0	0	0	....	....	....	0	....	....	....	....	....	....	....	....	....	....	....	....	....	....	....	....	....	....
1983-84	Peterborough Petes	OHL	63	3	25	28	....	....	....	78	....	....	....	....	....	....	....	....	....	....	8	3	2	5	8	....	....	....
1984-85	Peoria Rivermen	IHL	67	2	19	21	....	....	....	58	....	....	....	....	....	....	....	....	....	....	19	1	5	6	42	....	....	....
1985-86	**St. Louis Blues**	**NHL**	**6**	**0**	**0**	**0**	**0**	**0**	**0**	**0**	**0**	**0**	**0**	**2**	**0.0**	**0**	**0**	**1**	**0**	**–1**	....	....	....	....	....	....	....	....
	Peoria Rivermen	IHL	72	1	17	18	....	....	....	75	....	....	....	....	....	....	....	....	....	....	11	0	1	1	13	....	....	....
1986-87	**St. Louis Blues**	**NHL**	**2**	**0**	**0**	**0**	**0**	**0**	**0**	**0**	**0**	**0**	**0**	**0**	**0.0**	**2**	**0**	**1**	**0**	**+1**	....	....	....	....	....	....	....	....
	Peoria Rivermen	IHL	77	2	15	17	....	....	....	77	....	....	....	....	....	....	....	....	....	....	....	....	....	....	....	....	....	....
1987-88	Peoria Rivermen	IHL	27	0	4	4	....	....	....	23	....	....	....	....	....	....	....	....	....	....	....	....	....	....	....	....	....	....
	NHL Totals		**8**	**0**	**0**	**0**	**0**	**0**	**0**	**0**	**0**	**0**	**0**	**2**	**0.0**	**2**	**0**	**2**	**0**		....	....	....	....	....	....	....	....

OHL Second All-Star Team (1982)

• POTOMSKI, BARRY

Barry Potomski LW – L. 6'2", 215 lbs. b: Windsor, Ont., 11/24/1972.

Season	Club	League	GP	G	A	Pts	AG	AA	APts	PIM	PP	SH	GW	S	%	TGF	PGF	TGA	PGA	+/–	GP	G	A	Pts	PIM	PP	SH	GW
1989-90	London Knights	OHL	9	0	2	2	....	....	....	18	....	....	....	....	....	....	....	....	....	....	....	....	....	....	....	....	....	....
1990-91	London Knights	OHL	65	14	17	31	....	....	....	202	....	....	....	....	....	....	....	....	....	....	7	0	2	2	10	....	....	....
1991-92	London Knights	OHL	61	19	32	51	....	....	....	224	....	....	....	....	....	....	....	....	....	....	10	5	1	6	22	....	....	....
1992-93	Erie Panthers	ECHL	5	1	1	2	....	....	....	31	....	....	....	....	....	....	....	....	....	....	....	....	....	....	....	....	....	....
	Toledo Storm	ECHL	43	5	18	23	....	....	....	184	....	....	....	....	....	....	....	....	....	....	14	5	2	7	73	....	....	....
1993-94	Toledo Storm	ECHL	13	9	4	13	....	....	....	81	....	....	....	....	....	....	....	....	....	....	....	....	....	....	....	....	....	....
	Adirondack Red Wings	AHL	50	9	5	14	....	....	....	224	....	....	....	....	....	....	....	....	....	....	11	1	1	2	44	....	....	....
1994-95	Phoenix Roadrunners	IHL	42	5	6	11	....	....	....	171	....	....	....	....	....	....	....	....	....	....	....	....	....	....	....	....	....	....
1995-96	**Los Angeles Kings**	**NHL**	**33**	**3**	**2**	**5**	**3**	**2**	**5**	**104**	**1**	**0**	**0**	**23**	**13.0**	**10**	**2**	**15**	**0**	**–7**	....	....	....	....	....	....	....	....
	Phoenix Roadrunners	IHL	24	5	2	7	....	....	....	74	....	....	....	....	....	....	....	....	....	....	3	1	0	1	8	....	....	....
1996-97	**Los Angeles Kings**	**NHL**	**26**	**3**	**2**	**5**	**3**	**2**	**5**	**93**	**0**	**0**	**1**	**18**	**16.7**	**7**	**0**	**15**	**0**	**–8**	....	....	....	....	....	....	....	....
	Phoenix Roadrunners	IHL	28	2	11	13	....	....	....	58	....	....	....	....	....	....	....	....	....	....	....	....	....	....	....	....	....	....
1997-98	**San Jose Sharks**	**NHL**	**9**	**0**	**1**	**1**	**0**	**1**	**1**	**30**	**0**	**0**	**0**	**4**	**0.0**	**2**	**0**	**1**	**0**	**+1**	....	....	....	....	....	....	....	....
	Las Vegas Thunder	IHL	31	3	2	5	....	....	....	143	....	....	....	....	....	....	....	....	....	....	4	1	0	1	13	....	....	....
	NHL Totals		**68**	**6**	**5**	**11**	**6**	**5**	**11**	**227**	**1**	**0**	**1**	**45**	**13.3**	**19**	**2**	**31**	**0**		....	....	....	....	....	....	....	....

Signed as a free agent by **LA Kings**, July 7, 1994. Signed as a free agent by **San Jose**, August 15, 1997. Signed as a free agent by **Detroit**, July 21, 1998.

• POTVIN, DENIS

Denis Potvin D – L. 6', 205 lbs. b: Ottawa, Ont., 10/29/1953. NY Islanders' 1st choice, 1st overall, in 1973 Amateur Draft. **HHOF**

			REGULAR SEASON																		PLAYOFFS							
Season	Club	League	GP	G	A	Pts	AG	AA	APts	PIM	PP	SH	GW	S	%	TGF	PGF	TGA	PGA	+/-	GP	G	A	Pts	PIM	PP	SH	GW
1968-69	Ottawa 67's	OHA	46	12	25	37	....	....	....	83	....	....	....	....	....	....	....	....	....	....	....	....	....	....	....	....	....	....
1969-70	Ottawa 67's	OHA	42	13	18	31	....	....	....	97	....	....	....	....	....	....	....	....	....	....	....	....	....	....	....	....	....	....
1970-71	Ottawa 67's	OHA	57	20	58	78	....	....	....	200	....	....	....	....	....	....	....	....	....	....	....	....	....	....	....	....	....	....
1971-72	Ottawa 67's	OHA	48	15	45	60	....	....	....	188	....	....	....	....	....	....	....	....	....	....	....	....	....	....	....	....	....	....
1972-73	Ottawa 67's	OHA	61	35	88	123	....	....	....	232	....	....	....	....	....	....	....	....	....	....	....	....	....	....	....	....	....	....
1973-74	**New York Islanders**	**NHL**	**77**	**17**	**37**	**54**	**17**	**32**	**49**	**175**	**6**	**0**	**3**	**209**	**8.1**	**114**	**29**	**141**	**40**	**–16**	....	....	....	....	....	....	....	....
1974-75	**New York Islanders**	**NHL**	**79**	**21**	**55**	**76**	**19**	**43**	**62**	**105**	**5**	**2**	**4**	**211**	**10.0**	**153**	**48**	**111**	**34**	**+28**	**17**	**5**	**9**	**14**	**30**	**3**	**1**	**0**
1975-76	**New York Islanders**	**NHL**	**78**	**31**	**67**	**98**	**29**	**53**	**82**	**100**	**18**	**0**	**4**	**256**	**12.1**	**168**	**85**	**104**	**33**	**+12**	**13**	**5**	***14**	**19**	**32**	**2**	**0**	**1**
1976-77	Canada	C Cup	7	1	8	9	....	....	....	16	....	....	....	....	....	....	....	....	....	....	....	....	....	....	....	....	....	....
	New York Islanders	**NHL**	**80**	**25**	**55**	**80**	**24**	**45**	**69**	**103**	**7**	**1**	**4**	**241**	**10.4**	**173**	**56**	**92**	**17**	**+42**	**12**	**6**	**4**	**10**	**20**	**2**	**0**	**0**
1977-78	**New York Islanders**	**NHL**	**80**	**30**	**64**	**94**	**29**	**52**	**81**	**81**	**9**	**0**	**6**	**288**	**10.4**	**204**	**70**	**107**	**30**	**+57**	**7**	**2**	**2**	**4**	**6**	**0**	**0**	**0**
1978-79	**New York Islanders**	**NHL**	**73**	**31**	**70**	**101**	**28**	**54**	**82**	**58**	**12**	**3**	**2**	**237**	**13.1**	**203**	**75**	**91**	**34**	**+71**	**10**	**4**	**7**	**11**	**8**	**0**	**0**	**1**
	NHL All-Stars	Chal Cup	2	0	0	0	....	....	....	0	....	....	....	....	....	....	....	....	....	....	....	....	....	....	....	....	....	....
1979-80	**New York Islanders**	**NHL**	**31**	**8**	**33**	**41**	**7**	**25**	**32**	**44**	**4**	**0**	**0**	**98**	**8.2**	**72**	**26**	**48**	**15**	**+13**	**21**	**6**	**13**	**19**	**24**	**4**	**0**	**1**
1980-81	**New York Islanders**	**NHL**	**74**	**20**	**56**	**76**	**16**	**39**	**55**	**104**	**9**	**0**	**4**	**206**	**9.7**	**190**	**85**	**108**	**41**	**+38**	**18**	**8**	**17**	**25**	**16**	**6**	**1**	**2**
1981-82	Canada	C Cup	7	2	5	7	....	....	....	12	....	....	....	....	....	....	....	....	....	....	....	....	....	....	....	....	....	....
	New York Islanders	**NHL**	**60**	**24**	**37**	**61**	**19**	**24**	**43**	**83**	**11**	**1**	**4**	**169**	**14.2**	**148**	**56**	**77**	**23**	**+38**	**19**	**5**	**16**	**21**	**30**	**3**	**0**	**0**
1982-83	**New York Islanders**	**NHL**	**69**	**12**	**54**	**66**	**10**	**37**	**47**	**60**	**4**	**1**	**1**	**191**	**6.3**	**140**	**55**	**81**	**28**	**+32**	**20**	**8**	**12**	**20**	**22**	**4**	**0**	**1**
1983-84	**New York Islanders**	**NHL**	**78**	**22**	**63**	**85**	**18**	**43**	**61**	**87**	**11**	**1**	**3**	**246**	**8.9**	**178**	**50**	**105**	**32**	**+55**	**20**	**1**	**5**	**6**	**28**	**1**	**0**	**0**
1984-85	**New York Islanders**	**NHL**	**77**	**17**	**51**	**68**	**14**	**35**	**49**	**96**	**6**	**0**	**1**	**198**	**8.6**	**161**	**45**	**117**	**37**	**+36**	**10**	**3**	**2**	**5**	**10**	**1**	**0**	**1**
1985-86	**New York Islanders**	**NHL**	**74**	**21**	**38**	**59**	**17**	**25**	**42**	**76**	**8**	**1**	**4**	**168**	**12.5**	**133**	**39**	**93**	**33**	**+34**	**3**	**0**	**1**	**1**	**0**	**0**	**0**	**0**
	Canada	WEC-A	7	1	4	5	....	....	....	6	....	....	....	....	....	....	....	....	....	....	....	....	....	....	....	....	....	....
1986-87	**New York Islanders**	**NHL**	**58**	**12**	**30**	**42**	**10**	**22**	**32**	**70**	**8**	**0**	**1**	**147**	**8.2**	**93**	**44**	**78**	**23**	**–6**	**10**	**2**	**2**	**4**	**21**	**1**	**0**	**0**
1987-88	**New York Islanders**	**NHL**	**72**	**19**	**32**	**51**	**16**	**23**	**39**	**112**	**9**	**0**	**3**	**188**	**10.1**	**121**	**46**	**74**	**25**	**+26**	**5**	**1**	**4**	**5**	**6**	**1**	**0**	**0**
	NHL Totals		**1060**	**310**	**742**	**1052**	**273**	**552**	**825**	**1354**	**127**	**10**	**44**	**3053**	**10.2**	**2251**	**809**	**1427**	**445**		**185**	**56**	**108**	**164**	**253**	**28**	**2**	**7**

OHA First All-Star Team (1971, 1972, 1973) • Won Calder Memorial Trophy (1974) • NHL First All-Star Team (1975, 1976, 1978, 1979, 1981) • Won James Norris Trophy (1976, 1978, 1979) • NHL Second All-Star Team (1977, 1984)

Played in NHL All-Star Game (1974, 1975, 1976, 1977, 1978, 1981, 1983, 1984, 1988)

• POTVIN, JEAN

Jean Potvin D – R. 5'11", 188 lbs. b: Ottawa, Ont., 3/25/1949.

Season	Club	League	GP	G	A	Pts	AG	AA	APts	PIM	PP	SH	GW	S	%	TGF	PGF	TGA	PGA	+/-	GP	G	A	Pts	PIM	PP	SH	GW
1966-67	Hull Volants	QJHL	....	22	27	49	....	....	....	115	....	....	....	....	....	....	....	....	....	....	....	....	....	....	....	....	....	....
1967-68	Ottawa 67's	OHA	54	18	17	35	....	....	....	138	....	....	....	....	....	....	....	....	....	....	....	....	....	....	....	....	....	....
1968-69	Ottawa 67's	OHA	54	17	23	40	....	....	....	116	....	....	....	....	....	....	....	....	....	....	7	1	7	8	20	....	....	....
1969-70	Springfield Kings	AHL	61	3	5	8	....	....	....	42	....	....	....	....	....	....	....	....	....	....	14	0	2	2	24	....	....	....
1970-71	**Los Angeles Kings**	**NHL**	**4**	**1**	**3**	**4**	**1**	**3**	**4**	**2**	**0**	**0**	**0**	**5**	**20.0**	**8**	**1**	**3**	**1**	**+5**	....	....	....	....	....	....	....	....
	Springfield Kings	AHL	60	9	23	32	....	....	....	94	....	....	....	....	....	....	....	....	....	....	12	2	10	12	17	....	....	....
1971-72	**Los Angeles Kings**	**NHL**	**39**	**2**	**3**	**5**	**2**	**3**	**5**	**35**	**0**	**0**	**1**	**55**	**3.6**	**25**	**3**	**67**	**6**	**–39**	....	....	....	....	....	....	....	....
	Philadelphia Flyers	**NHL**	**29**	**3**	**12**	**15**	**3**	**11**	**14**	**6**	**2**	**0**	**1**	**23**	**13.0**	**22**	**16**	**13**	**1**	**–6**	....	....	....	....	....	....	....	....
1972-73	**Philadelphia Flyers**	**NHL**	**35**	**3**	**9**	**12**	**3**	**8**	**11**	**10**	**1**	**0**	**1**	**27**	**11.1**	**25**	**12**	**17**	**3**	**–1**	....	....	....	....	....	....	....	....
	New York Islanders	**NHL**	**10**	**0**	**3**	**3**	**0**	**2**	**2**	**12**	**0**	**0**	**0**	**18**	**0.0**	**15**	**2**	**22**	**6**	**–3**	....	....	....	....	....	....	....	....
1973-74	**New York Islanders**	**NHL**	**78**	**5**	**23**	**28**	**5**	**20**	**25**	**100**	**2**	**0**	**0**	**114**	**4.4**	**85**	**28**	**99**	**16**	**–26**	....	....	....	....	....	....	....	....
1974-75	**New York Islanders**	**NHL**	**73**	**9**	**24**	**33**	**8**	**19**	**27**	**59**	**6**	**1**	**4**	**115**	**7.8**	**85**	**39**	**56**	**7**	**–3**	**15**	**2**	**4**	**6**	**9**	**0**	**0**	**0**
1975-76	**New York Islanders**	**NHL**	**78**	**17**	**55**	**72**	**16**	**43**	**59**	**74**	**9**	**1**	**2**	**167**	**10.2**	**139**	**82**	**48**	**7**	**+16**	**13**	**0**	**1**	**1**	**2**	**0**	**0**	**0**
1976-77	**New York Islanders**	**NHL**	**79**	**10**	**36**	**46**	**10**	**29**	**39**	**26**	**1**	**1**	**0**	**124**	**8.1**	**86**	**37**	**38**	**3**	**+14**	**11**	**0**	**4**	**4**	**6**	**0**	**0**	**0**
1977-78	**New York Islanders**	**NHL**	**34**	**1**	**10**	**11**	**1**	**8**	**9**	**8**	**0**	**0**	**0**	**36**	**2.8**	**33**	**1**	**27**	**6**	**+11**	....	....	....	....	....	....	....	....
	Cleveland Barons	**NHL**	**40**	**3**	**14**	**17**	**3**	**11**	**14**	**30**	**0**	**0**	**1**	**85**	**3.5**	**58**	**6**	**76**	**20**	**–4**	....	....	....	....	....	....	....	....
1978-79	**Minnesota North Stars**	**NHL**	**64**	**5**	**16**	**21**	**5**	**12**	**17**	**65**	**2**	**2**	**1**	**89**	**5.6**	**67**	**11**	**73**	**7**	**–10**	....	....	....	....	....	....	....	....
	Oklahoma City Stars	CHL	9	3	7	10	....	....	....	10	....	....	....	....	....	....	....	....	....	....	....	....	....	....	....	....	....	....
1979-80	**New York Islanders**	**NHL**	**32**	**2**	**13**	**15**	**2**	**10**	**12**	**26**	**2**	**0**	**0**	**49**	**4.1**	**36**	**10**	**49**	**11**	**–12**	....	....	....	....	....	....	....	....
1980-81	**New York Islanders**	**NHL**	**18**	**2**	**3**	**5**	**2**	**2**	**4**	**25**	**2**	**0**	**1**	**16**	**12.5**	**14**	**3**	**17**	**2**	**–4**	....	....	....	....	....	....	....	....
	NHL Totals		**613**	**63**	**224**	**287**	**61**	**181**	**242**	**478**	**27**	**5**	**12**	**923**	**6.8**	**698**	**251**	**605**	**96**		**39**	**2**	**9**	**11**	**17**	**0**	**0**	**0**

Signed as a free agent by **LA Kings** (Springfield - AHL), November 15, 1969. Traded to **Philadelphia** by **LA Kings** with Ed Joyal, Bill Flett and Ross Lonsberry for Bill Lesuk, Jim Johnson and Serge Bernier, January 28, 1972. Traded to **NY Islanders** by **Philadelphia** with future considerations (Glen Irwin, May 18, 1973), for Terry Crisp, March 5, 1973. Traded to **Cleveland** by **NY Islanders** with Jean-Paul Parise and a 4th round choice in 1978 Entry Draft (later cancelled by Cleveland-Minnesota merger) for Wayne Merrick and Darcy Reiger, January 10, 1978. Placed on **Minnesota** Reserve List after **Cleveland-Minnesota** Dispersal Draft, June 15, 1978. Signed as a free agent by **NY Islanders**, June 10, 1979.

• POTVIN, MARC

Marc Potvin RW – R. 6'1", 200 lbs. b: Ottawa, Ont., 1/29/1967. Detroit's 9th choice, 169th overall, in 1986 Entry Draft.

Season	Club	League	GP	G	A	Pts	AG	AA	APts	PIM	PP	SH	GW	S	%	TGF	PGF	TGA	PGA	+/-	GP	G	A	Pts	PIM	PP	SH	GW
1985-86	Stratford Cullitons	OJHL	63	5	6	11	....	....	....	117	....	....	....	....	....	....	....	....	....	....	....	....	....	....	....	....	....	....
1986-87	Bowling Green University	CCHA	43	5	15	20	....	....	....	74	....	....	....	....	....	....	....	....	....	....	....	....	....	....	....	....	....	....
1987-88	Bowling Green University	CCHA	45	15	21	36	....	....	....	80	....	....	....	....	....	....	....	....	....	....	....	....	....	....	....	....	....	....
1988-89	Bowling Green University	CCHA	46	23	12	35	....	....	....	63	....	....	....	....	....	....	....	....	....	....	....	....	....	....	....	....	....	....
1989-90	Bowling Green University	CCHA	40	19	17	36	....	....	....	72	....	....	....	....	....	....	....	....	....	....	....	....	....	....	....	....	....	....
	Adirondack Red Wings	AHL	5	2	1	3	....	....	....	9	....	....	....	....	....	....	....	....	....	....	4	0	1	1	23	....	....	....
1990-91	**Detroit Red Wings**	**NHL**	**9**	**0**	**0**	**0**	**0**	**0**	**0**	**55**	**0**	**0**	**0**	**13**	**0.0**	**3**	**0**	**7**	**0**	**–4**	**6**	**0**	**0**	**0**	**32**	**0**	**0**	**0**
	Adirondack Red Wings	AHL	63	9	13	22	....	....	....	*365	....	....	....	....	....	....	....	....	....	....	....	....	....	....	....	....	....	....
1991-92	**Detroit Red Wings**	**NHL**	**5**	**1**	**0**	**1**	**1**	**0**	**1**	**52**	**0**	**0**	**0**	**4**	**25.0**	**1**	**0**	**3**	**0**	**–2**	**1**	**0**	**0**	**0**	**0**	**0**	**0**	**0**
	Adirondack Red Wings	AHL	51	13	16	29	....	....	....	314	....	....	....	....	....	....	....	....	....	....	19	5	4	9	57	....	....	....
1992-93	Adirondack Red Wings	AHL	37	8	12	20	....	....	....	109	....	....	....	....	....	....	....	....	....	....	....	....	....	....	....	....	....	....
	Los Angeles Kings	**NHL**	**20**	**0**	**1**	**1**	**0**	**1**	**1**	**61**	**0**	**0**	**0**	**7**	**0.0**	**1**	**0**	**11**	**0**	**–10**	**1**	**0**	**0**	**0**	**0**	**0**	**0**	**0**
1993-94	**Los Angeles Kings**	**NHL**	**3**	**0**	**0**	**0**	**0**	**0**	**0**	**26**	**0**	**0**	**0**	**1**	**0.0**	**0**	**0**	**3**	**0**	**–3**	....	....	....	....	....	....	....	....
	Hartford Whalers	**NHL**	**51**	**2**	**3**	**5**	**2**	**2**	**4**	**246**	**0**	**0**	**0**	**25**	**8.0**	**7**	**1**	**11**	**0**	**–5**	....	....	....	....	....	....	....	....
1994-95	**Boston Bruins**	**NHL**	**6**	**0**	**1**	**1**	**0**	**1**	**1**	**4**	**0**	**0**	**0**	**4**	**0.0**	**1**	**0**	**0**	**0**	**+1**	....	....	....	....	....	....	....	....
	Providence Bruins	AHL	21	4	14	18	....	....	....	84	....	....	....	....	....	....	....	....	....	....	12	2	4	6	25	....	....	....
1995-96	**Boston Bruins**	**NHL**	**27**	**0**	**0**	**0**	**0**	**0**	**0**	**12**	**0**	**0**	**0**	**14**	**0.0**	**1**	**0**	**3**	**0**	**–2**	**5**	**0**	**1**	**1**	**18**	**0**	**0**	**0**
	Providence Bruins	AHL	48	9	9	18	....	....	....	118	....	....	....	....	....	....	....	....	....	....	....	....	....	....	....	....	....	....
1996-97	Portland Pirates	AHL	71	17	15	32	....	....	....	222	....	....	....	....	....	....	....	....	....	....	5	0	0	0	12	....	....	....
1997-98	Chicago Wolves	IHL	81	4	8	12	....	....	....	170	....	....	....	....	....	....	....	....	....	....	10	0	0	0	22	....	....	....
	NHL Totals		**121**	**3**	**5**	**8**	**3**	**4**	**7**	**456**	**0**	**0**	**0**	**68**	**4.4**	**14**	**1**	**38**	**0**		**13**	**0**	**1**	**1**	**50**	**0**	**0**	**0**

Traded to **LA Kings** by **Detroit** with Jimmy Carson and Gary Shuchuk for Paul Coffey, Sylvain Couturier and Jim Hiller, January 29, 1993. Traded to **Hartford** by **LA Kings** for Doug Houda, November 3, 1993. Signed as a free agent by **Boston**, June 29, 1994.

• POUDRIER, DANIEL

Daniel Poudrier D – L. 6'2", 175 lbs. b: Thetford Mines, Que., 2/15/1964. Quebec's 6th choice, 131st overall, in 1982 Entry Draft.

Season	Club	League	GP	G	A	Pts	AG	AA	APts	PIM	PP	SH	GW	S	%	TGF	PGF	TGA	PGA	+/-	GP	G	A	Pts	PIM	PP	SH	GW
1980-81	Magog AAA	Midget	26	8	8	16	....	....	....	18	....	....	....	....	....	....	....	....	....	....	....	....	....	....	....	....	....	....
1981-82	Shawinigan Cataractes	QMJHL	64	6	18	24	....	....	....	20	....	....	....	....	....	....	....	....	....	....	14	1	1	2	2	....	....	....
1982-83	Shawinigan Cataractes	QMJHL	67	6	28	34	....	....	....	31	....	....	....	....	....	....	....	....	....	....	10	1	2	3	2	....	....	....
1983-84	Drummondville Voltigeurs	QMJHL	64	7	28	35	....	....	....	15	....	....	....	....	....	....	....	....	....	....	10	2	3	5	4	....	....	....
1984-85	Fredericton Express	AHL	1	0	0	0	....	....	....	0	....	....	....	....	....	....	....	....	....	....	....	....	....	....	....	....	....	....
	Muskegon Mohawks	IHL	82	9	30	39	....	....	....	12	....	....	....	....	....	....	....	....	....	....	17	2	6	8	2	....	....	....
1985-86	**Quebec Nordiques**	**NHL**	**13**	**1**	**5**	**6**	**1**	**3**	**4**	**10**	**0**	**0**	**1**	**6**	**16.7**	**11**	**1**	**11**	**3**	**+2**	....	....	....	....	....	....	....	....
	Fredericton Express	AHL	65	5	26	31	....	....	....	9	....	....	....	....	....	....	....	....	....	....	6	0	3	3	0	....	....	....
1986-87	**Quebec Nordiques**	**NHL**	**6**	**0**	**0**	**0**	**0**	**0**	**0**	**0**	**0**	**0**	**0**	**2**	**0.0**	**3**	**0**	**5**	**0**	**–2**	....	....	....	....	....	....	....	....
	Fredericton Express	AHL	69	8	18	26	....	....	....	11	....	....	....	....	....	....	....	....	....	....	....	....	....	....	....	....	....	....
1987-88	**Quebec Nordiques**	**NHL**	**6**	**0**	**0**	**0**	**0**	**0**	**0**	**0**	**0**	**0**	**0**	**0**	**0.0**	**4**	**3**	**3**	**1**	**–1**	....	....	....	....	....	....	....	....
	Fredericton Express	AHL	66	13	30	43	....	....	....	18	....	....	....	....	....	....	....	....	....	....	11	2	5	7	2	....	....	....
1988-89	Halifax Citadels	AHL	7	2	4	6	....	....	....	2	....	....	....	....	....	....	....	....	....	....	3	0	0	0	2	....	....	....
	HC Mont Blanc	France	18	7	5	12	....	....	....	8	....	....	....	....	....	....	....	....	....	....	....	....	....	....	....	....	....	....

			REGULAR SEASON																		PLAYOFFS							
Season	Club	League	GP	G	A	Pts	AG	AA	APts	PIM	PP	SH	GW	S	%	TGF	PGF	TGA	PGA	+/–	GP	G	A	Pts	PIM	PP	SH	GW
1989-90	Canada	Nat-Team	40	4	7	11	....	....	....	2	....	....	....	....	....	....	....	....	....	....	....	....	....	....	....	....	....	....
	WEV Wien	Austria	11	5	6	11	....	....	....	6	....	....	....	....	....	....	....	....	....	....	....	....	....	....	....	....	....	....
1990-91	EV Fussen	German 2	47	30	42	72	....	....	....	22	....	....	....	....	....	....	....	....	....	....	....	....	....	....	....	....	....	....
1991-92	St. Thomas Wildcats	ColHL	9	1	1	2	....	....	....	0	....	....	....	....	....	....	....	....	....	....	....	....	....	....	....	....	....	....
	NHL Totals		**25**	**1**	**5**	**6**	**1**	**3**	**4**	**10**	**0**	**0**	**1**	**8**	**12.5**	**18**	**4**	**19**	**4**		....	....	....	....	....	....	....	....

• POULIN, DAN

Dan Poulin D – R. 5'11", 185 lbs. b: Robertsville, Que., 9/19/1957. Philadelphia's 19th choice, 166th overall, in 1977 Amateur Draft.

Season	Club	League	GP	G	A	Pts	AG	AA	APts	PIM	PP	SH	GW	S	%	TGF	PGF	TGA	PGA	+/–	GP	G	A	Pts	PIM	PP	SH	GW
1974-75	Chicoutimi Sagueneens	QMJHL	68	15	46	61	....	....	....	43	....	....	....	....	....	....	....	....	....	....	....	....	....	....	....	....	....	....
1975-76	Chicoutimi Sagueneens	QMJHL	72	18	55	73	....	....	....	24	....	....	....	....	....	....	....	....	....	....	....	....	....	....	....	....	....	....
1976-77	Chicoutimi Sagueneens	QMJHL	72	21	74	95	....	....	....	50	....	....	....	....	....	....	....	....	....	....	....	....	....	....	....	....	....	....
1977-78	Kalamazoo Wings	IHL	43	7	20	27	....	....	....	44	....	....	....	....	....	....	....	....	....	....	....	....	....	....	....	....	....	....
	Muskegon Mohawks	IHL	2	0	1	1	....	....	....	0	....	....	....	....	....	....	....	....	....	....	....	....	....	....	....	....	....	....
1978-79	Erie Baldesw	EHL	68	35	53	88	....	....	....	79	....	....	....	....	....	....	....	....	....	....	....	....	....	....	....	....	....	....
1979-80	Erie Blades	EHL	65	33	*66	99	....	....	....	36	....	....	....	....	....	....	....	....	....	....	9	3	*12	15	12	....	....	....
1980-81	Oklahoma City Stars	CHL	58	16	32	48	....	....	....	32	....	....	....	....	....	....	....	....	....	....	3	0	0	0	0	....	....	....
1981-82	**Minnesota North Stars**	**NHL**	**3**	**1**	**1**	**2**	**1**	**1**	**2**	**2**	**0**	**0**	**0**	**8**	**12.5**	**4**	**1**	**3**	**1**	**+1**	....	....	....	....	....	....	....	....
	Nashville South Stars	CHL	76	29	56	85	....	....	....	104	....	....	....	....	....	....	....	....	....	....	3	2	2	4	2	....	....	....
1982-83	EHC Biel	Switz.	....	32	27	59	....	....	....	....	....	....	....	....	....	....	....	....	....	....	....	....	....	....	....	....	....	....
1983-84	EHC Biel	Swirz.	....	30	34	64	....	....	....	....	....	....	....	....	....	....	....	....	....	....	....	....	....	....	....	....	....	....
1984-85	EHC Biel	Switz.	38	27	34	61	....	....	....	....	....	....	....	....	....	....	....	....	....	....	....	1	1	2	....	....	....	....
1985-86	EHC Biel	Switz.	....	27	35	62	....	....	....	....	....	....	....	....	....	....	....	....	....	....	....	....	....	....	....	....	....	....
1986-87	EHC Biel	Switz.	....	14	19	33	....	....	....	....	....	....	....	....	....	....	....	....	....	....	....	....	....	....	....	....	....	....
1987-88	EHC Biel	Switz.	....	17	28	45	....	....	....	....	....	....	....	....	....	....	....	....	....	....	....	....	....	....	....	....	....	....
1988-89	EHC Biel	Switz.	....	19	20	39	....	....	....	....	....	....	....	....	....	....	....	....	....	....	2	1	0	1	....	....	....	....
	NHL Totals		**3**	**1**	**1**	**2**	**1**	**1**	**2**	**2**	**0**	**0**	**0**	**8**	**12.5**	**4**	**1**	**3**	**1**		....	....	....	....	....	....	....	....

QMJHL East First All-Star Team (1976) • CHL First All-Star Team (1982) • Won Bobby Orr Trophy (CHL's Top Defenseman) (1982)

Signed as a free agent by **Minnesota**, June 16, 1980.

• POULIN, DAVE

Dave Poulin C – L. 5'11", 190 lbs. b: Timmins, Ont., 12/17/1958.

Season	Club	League	GP	G	A	Pts	AG	AA	APts	PIM	PP	SH	GW	S	%	TGF	PGF	TGA	PGA	+/–	GP	G	A	Pts	PIM	PP	SH	GW
1978-79	University of Notre Dame	WCHA	37	28	31	59	....	....	....	32	....	....	....	....	....	....	....	....	....	....	....	....	....	....	....	....	....	....
1979-80	University of Notre Dame	WCHA	24	19	24	43	....	....	....	46	....	....	....	....	....	....	....	....	....	....	....	....	....	....	....	....	....	....
1980-81	University of Notre Dame	WCHA	35	13	22	35	....	....	....	53	....	....	....	....	....	....	....	....	....	....	....	....	....	....	....	....	....	....
1981-82	University of Notre Dame	CCHA	39	29	30	59	....	....	....	44	....	....	....	....	....	....	....	....	....	....	....	....	....	....	....	....	....	....
1982-83	Rogle	Sweden	32	35	27	62	....	....	....	64	....	....	....	....	....	....	....	....	....	....	....	....	....	....	....	....	....	....
	Philadelphia Flyers	**NHL**	**2**	**2**	**0**	**2**	**2**	**0**	**2**	**2**	**0**	**1**	**1**	**4**	**50.0**	**2**	**0**	**2**	**1**	**+1**	**3**	**1**	**3**	**4**	**9**	**0**	**0**	**0**
	Maine Mariners	AHL	16	7	9	16	....	....	....	2	....	....	....	....	....	....	....	....	....	....	....	....	....	....	....	....	....	....
1983-84	**Philadelphia Flyers**	**NHL**	**73**	**31**	**45**	**76**	**25**	**31**	**56**	**47**	**6**	**3**	**6**	**185**	**16.8**	**113**	**22**	**86**	**26**	**+31**	**3**	**0**	**0**	**0**	**2**	**0**	**0**	**0**
1984-85	**Philadelphia Flyers**	**NHL**	**73**	**30**	**44**	**74**	**25**	**30**	**55**	**59**	**1**	**4**	**5**	**174**	**17.2**	**104**	**16**	**78**	**33**	**+43**	**11**	**3**	**5**	**8**	**6**	**0**	**2**	**0**
1985-86	**Philadelphia Flyers**	**NHL**	**79**	**27**	**42**	**69**	**22**	**28**	**50**	**49**	**2**	**6**	**2**	**181**	**14.9**	**100**	**19**	**99**	**38**	**+20**	**5**	**2**	**0**	**2**	**2**	**1**	**0**	**0**
1986-87	**Philadelphia Flyers**	**NHL**	**75**	**25**	**45**	**70**	**22**	**33**	**55**	**53**	**1**	**3**	**5**	**155**	**16.1**	**96**	**10**	**75**	**36**	**+47**	**15**	**3**	**3**	**6**	**14**	**1**	**1**	**0**
	NHL All-Stars	RV'87	2	1	1	2	....	....	....	0	....	....	....	....	....	....	....	....	....	....	....	....	....	....	....	....	....	....
1987-88	**Philadelphia Flyers**	**NHL**	**68**	**19**	**32**	**51**	**16**	**23**	**39**	**32**	**1**	**5**	**3**	**125**	**15.2**	**62**	**5**	**79**	**39**	**+17**	**7**	**2**	**6**	**8**	**4**	**1**	**0**	**1**
1988-89	**Philadelphia Flyers**	**NHL**	**69**	**18**	**17**	**35**	**15**	**12**	**27**	**49**	**1**	**5**	**4**	**81**	**22.2**	**52**	**3**	**76**	**31**	**+4**	**19**	**6**	**5**	**11**	**16**	**0**	**2**	**2**
1989-90	**Philadelphia Flyers**	**NHL**	**28**	**9**	**8**	**17**	**8**	**6**	**14**	**12**	**0**	**0**	**1**	**46**	**19.6**	**20**	**0**	**30**	**15**	**+5**	....	....	....	....	....	....	....	....
	Boston Bruins	**NHL**	**32**	**6**	**19**	**25**	**5**	**14**	**19**	**12**	**0**	**1**	**0**	**42**	**14.3**	**37**	**4**	**33**	**11**	**+11**	**18**	**8**	**5**	**13**	**8**	**2**	**0**	**2**
1990-91	**Boston Bruins**	**NHL**	**31**	**8**	**12**	**20**	**7**	**9**	**16**	**25**	**0**	**2**	**0**	**60**	**13.3**	**29**	**2**	**32**	**10**	**+5**	**16**	**0**	**9**	**9**	**20**	**0**	**0**	**0**
1991-92	**Boston Bruins**	**NHL**	**18**	**4**	**4**	**8**	**4**	**3**	**7**	**18**	**0**	**1**	**1**	**31**	**12.9**	**11**	**1**	**19**	**7**	**–2**	**15**	**3**	**3**	**6**	**22**	**1**	**0**	**1**
1992-93	**Boston Bruins**	**NHL**	**84**	**16**	**33**	**49**	**13**	**23**	**36**	**62**	**0**	**5**	**0**	**112**	**14.3**	**69**	**2**	**75**	**37**	**+29**	**4**	**1**	**1**	**2**	**10**	**0**	**1**	**0**
1993-94	**Washington Capitals**	**NHL**	**63**	**6**	**19**	**25**	**6**	**15**	**21**	**52**	**0**	**1**	**0**	**64**	**9.4**	**35**	**0**	**67**	**31**	**–1**	**11**	**2**	**2**	**4**	**19**	**0**	**0**	**0**
1994-95	**Washington Capitals**	**NHL**	**29**	**4**	**5**	**9**	**7**	**7**	**14**	**10**	**0**	**2**	**0**	**30**	**13.3**	**15**	**1**	**24**	**12**	**+2**	**2**	**0**	**0**	**0**	**0**	**0**	**0**	**0**
	NHL Totals		**724**	**205**	**325**	**530**	**177**	**234**	**411**	**482**	**12**	**39**	**28**	**1290**	**15.9**	**745**	**85**	**775**	**327**		**129**	**31**	**42**	**73**	**132**	**6**	**6**	**6**

CCHA Second All-Star Team (1982) • Won Frank J. Selke Trophy (1987) • Won King Clancy Memorial Trophy (1993)

Played in NHL All-Star Game (1986, 1988)

Signed as a free agent by **Philadelphia**, March 8, 1983. Traded to **Boston** by **Philadelphia** for Ken Linseman, January 16, 1990. Signed as a free agent by **Washington**, August 3, 1993.

• POULIN, PATRICK

Patrick Poulin LW – L. 6'1", 210 lbs. b: Vanier, Que., 4/23/1973. Hartford's 3rd choice, 9th overall, in 1991 Entry Draft.

Season	Club	League	GP	G	A	Pts	AG	AA	APts	PIM	PP	SH	GW	S	%	TGF	PGF	TGA	PGA	+/–	GP	G	A	Pts	PIM	PP	SH	GW
1989-90	St-Hyacinthe Laser	QMJHL	60	25	26	51	....	....	....	55	....	....	....	....	....	....	....	....	....	....	12	1	9	10	5	....	....	....
1990-91	St-Hyacinthe Laser	QMJHL	56	32	38	70	....	....	....	82	....	....	....	....	....	....	....	....	....	....	4	0	2	2	23	....	....	....
1991-92	St-Hyacinthe Laser	QMJHL	56	52	86	*138	....	....	....	58	....	....	....	....	....	....	....	....	....	....	5	2	2	4	4	....	....	....
	Canada	WJC-A	7	2	2	4	....	....	....	2	....	....	....	....	....	....	....	....	....	....	....	....	....	....	....	....	....	....
	Hartford Whalers	**NHL**	**1**	**0**	**0**	**0**	**0**	**0**	**0**	**2**	**0**	**0**	**0**	**0**	**0.0**	**1**	**0**	**2**	**0**	**–1**	**7**	**2**	**1**	**3**	**0**	**1**	**0**	**0**
	Springfield Indians	AHL	....	....	....	....	....	....	....	....	....	....	....	....	....	....	....	....	....	....	1	0	0	0	0	....	....	....
1992-93	**Hartford Whalers**	**NHL**	**81**	**20**	**31**	**51**	**17**	**21**	**38**	**37**	**4**	**0**	**2**	**160**	**12.5**	**73**	**19**	**74**	**1**	**–19**	....	....	....	....	....	....	....	....
1993-94	**Hartford Whalers**	**NHL**	**9**	**2**	**1**	**3**	**2**	**1**	**3**	**11**	**1**	**0**	**0**	**13**	**15.4**	**2**	**1**	**9**	**0**	**–8**	....	....	....	....	....	....	....	....
	Chicago Blackhawks	**NHL**	**58**	**12**	**13**	**25**	**11**	**10**	**21**	**40**	**1**	**0**	**3**	**83**	**14.5**	**30**	**4**	**26**	**0**	**0**	**4**	**0**	**0**	**0**	**0**	**0**	**0**	**0**
1994-95	**Chicago Blackhawks**	**NHL**	**45**	**15**	**15**	**30**	**27**	**22**	**49**	**53**	**4**	**0**	**2**	**77**	**19.5**	**49**	**14**	**23**	**1**	**+13**	**16**	**4**	**1**	**5**	**8**	**1**	**0**	**0**
1995-96	**Chicago Blackhawks**	**NHL**	**38**	**7**	**8**	**15**	**7**	**7**	**14**	**16**	**0**	**0**	**0**	**40**	**17.5**	**23**	**1**	**15**	**0**	**+7**	....	....	....	....	....	....	....	....
	Indianapolis Ice	IHL	1	0	1	1	....	....	....	0	....	....	....	....	....	....	....	....	....	....	....	....	....	....	....	....	....	....
	Tampa Bay Lightning	**NHL**	**8**	**0**	**1**	**1**	**0**	**1**	**1**	**0**	**1**	**0**	**0**	**11**	**0.0**	**2**	**0**	**2**	**0**	**0**	**2**	**0**	**0**	**0**	**0**	**0**	**0**	**0**
1996-97	**Tampa Bay Lightning**	**NHL**	**73**	**12**	**14**	**26**	**13**	**12**	**25**	**56**	**2**	**3**	**1**	**124**	**9.7**	**36**	**7**	**67**	**22**	**–16**	....	....	....	....	....	....	....	....
1997-98	**Tampa Bay Lightning**	**NHL**	**44**	**2**	**7**	**9**	**2**	**7**	**9**	**19**	**0**	**0**	**0**	**49**	**4.1**	**14**	**0**	**37**	**20**	**–3**	....	....	....	....	....	....	....	....
	Montreal Canadiens	**NHL**	**34**	**4**	**6**	**10**	**5**	**6**	**11**	**8**	**0**	**1**	**1**	**39**	**10.3**	**19**	**2**	**26**	**8**	**–1**	**3**	**0**	**0**	**0**	**0**	**0**	**0**	**0**
	NHL Totals		**391**	**74**	**96**	**170**	**84**	**87**	**171**	**242**	**13**	**4**	**9**	**596**	**12.4**	**249**	**48**	**281**	**52**		**32**	**6**	**2**	**8**	**8**	**2**	**0**	**0**

QMJHL First All-Star Team (1992) • Canadian Major Junior Player of the Year (1992)

Traded to **Chicago** by **Hartford** with Eric Weinrich for Steve Larmer and Bryan Marchment, November 2, 1993. Traded to **Tampa Bay** by **Chicago** with Igor Ulanov and Chicago's 2nd round choice (later traded to New Jersey — New Jersey selected Pierre Dagenais) in 1996 Entry Draft for Enrico Ciccone and Tampa Bay's 2nd round choice (Jeff Paul) in 1996 Entry Draft, March 20, 1996. Traded to **Montreal** by **Tampa Bay** with Mick Vukota and Igor Ulanov for Stephane Richer, Darcy Tucker and David Wilkie, January 15, 1998.

• POUZAR, JAROSLAV

Jaroslav Pouzar LW – L. 5'11", 200 lbs. b: Cakovec, Czech., 1/23/1952. Edmonton's 4th choice, 83rd overall, in 1982 Entry Draft.

Season	Club	League	GP	G	A	Pts	AG	AA	APts	PIM	PP	SH	GW	S	%	TGF	PGF	TGA	PGA	+/–	GP	G	A	Pts	PIM	PP	SH	GW
1975-76	Motor Ceske Budejovice	Czech.	STATISTICS NOT AVAILABLE																									
	Czechoslovakia	Olympics	5	1	1	2	....	....	....	2	....	....	....	....	....	....	....	....	....	....	....	....	....	....	....	....	....	....
	Czechoslovakia	WEC-A	8	2	3	5	....	....	....	0	....	....	....	....	....	....	....	....	....	....	....	....	....	....	....	....	....	....
1976-77	Czechoslovakia	C Cup	5	2	0	2	....	....	....	4	....	....	....	....	....	....	....	....	....	....	....	....	....	....	....	....	....	....
	Motor Ceske Budejovice	Czech.	....	29	15	44	....	....	....	....	....	....	....	....	....	....	....	....	....	....	....	....	....	....	....	....	....	....
	Czechoslovakia	WEC-A	10	4	4	8	....	....	....	14	....	....	....	....	....	....	....	....	....	....	....	....	....	....	....	....	....	....
1977-78	Motor Ceske Budejovice	Czech.	STATISTICS NOT AVAILABLE																									
	Czechoslovakia	WEC-A	10	7	1	8	....	....	....	4	....	....	....	....	....	....	....	....	....	....	....	....	....	....	....	....	....	....
1978-79	Motor Ceske Budejovice	Czech.	23	10	7	17	....	....	....	....	....	....	....	....	....	....	....	....	....	....	....	....	....	....	....	....	....	....
	Czechoslovakia	WEC-A	8	4	3	7	....	....	....	6	....	....	....	....	....	....	....	....	....	....	....	....	....	....	....	....	....	....
1979-80	Motor Ceske Budejovice	Czech.	44	39	23	62	....	....	....	....	....	....	....	....	....	....	....	....	....	....	23	10	10	20	31	....	....	....
	Czechoslovakia	Olympics	6	8	5	13	....	....	....	8	....	....	....	....	....	....	....	....	....	....	....	....	....	....	....	....	....	....
1980-81	Motor Ceske Budejovice	Czech.	42	29	23	52	....	....	....	....	....	....	....	....	....	....	....	....	....	....	28	8	5	13	....	....	....	....
	Czechoslovakia	WEC-A	7	1	1	2	....	....	....	2	....	....	....	....	....	....	....	....	....	....	....	....	....	....	....	....	....	....
1981-82	Czechoslovakia	C Cup	6	1	1	2	....	....	....	4	....	....	....	....	....	....	....	....	....	....	....	....	....	....	....	....	....	....
	Motor Ceske Budejovice	Czech	34	19	17	36	....	....	....	32	....	....	....	....	....	....	....	....	....	....	....	....	....	....	....	....	....	....
	Czechoslovakia	WEC-A	10	3	1	4	....	....	....	6	....	....	....	....	....	....	....	....	....	....	....	....	....	....	....	....	....	....
1982-83	**Edmonton Oilers**	**NHL**	**74**	**15**	**18**	**33**	**12**	**12**	**24**	**57**	**2**	**0**	**2**	**86**	**17.4**	**53**	**7**	**29**	**0**	**+17**	**1**	**2**	**0**	**2**	**0**	**1**	**0**	**1**
1983-84	**Edmonton Oilers**	**NHL**	**67**	**13**	**19**	**32**	**10**	**13**	**23**	**44**	**2**	**0**	**0**	**87**	**14.9**	**83**	**15**	**51**	**0**	**+17**	**14**	**1**	**2**	**3**	**12**	**0**	**0**	**1**
1984-85	**Edmonton Oilers**	**NHL**	**33**	**4**	**8**	**12**	**3**	**5**	**8**	**28**	**0**	**0**	**1**	**36**	**11.1**	**20**	**3**	**14**	**0**	**+3**	**9**	**2**	**1**	**3**	**2**	**0**	**0**	**0**
1985-86	Iserlohn	Germany	44	20	31	51	....	....	....	39	....	....	....	....	....	....	....	....	....	....	....	....	....	....	....	....	....	....

Season	Club	League	GP	G	A	Pts	AG	AA	APts	PIM	PP	SH	GW	S	%	TGF	PGF	TGA	PGA	+/-	GP	G	A	Pts	PIM	PP	SH	GW
1986-87	Edmonton Oilers	NHL	12	2	3	5	2	2	4	6	0	0	1	11	18.2	10	0	7	0	+3	5	1	1	2	2	0	0	0
	Iserlohn	Germany	38	32	38	70				30																		
1987-88	SB Rosenheim	Germany	38	20	28	48				29																		
1988-89	SB Rosenheim	Germany	36	20	34	54				26											11	10	10	*20	22			
1989-90	SB Rosenheim	Germany	35	9	31	40				32											11	2	7	9	28			
1990-91	Augsburg	German 2	33	17	46	63				26																		
1991-92	SB Rosenheim	Germany	5	1	2	3				4																		
	NHL Totals		186	34	48	82	27	32	59	135	4	0	4	220	15.5	166	25	101	0		29	6	4	10	16	1	0	2

● POWIS, GEOFF   Geoff Powis   C – L. 6'1", 170 lbs.   b: Winnipeg, Man., 6/14/1945.

Season	Club	League	GP	G	A	Pts	AG	AA	APts	PIM	PP	SH	GW	S	%	TGF	PGF	TGA	PGA	+/-	GP	G	A	Pts	PIM	PP	SH	GW
1963-64	Moose Jaw Canucks	SJHL	48	23	21	44				45											5	0	1	1	2			
1964-65	Moose Jaw Canucks	SJHL	49	39	38	77				100																		
1965-66	Moose Jaw Canucks	SJHL	54	46	44	90				53											3	1	1	2	0			
1966-67	St. Louis Braves	CHL	57	8	15	23				23																		
1967-68	**Chicago Black Hawks**	**NHL**	2	0	0	0	0	0	0	0	0	0	0	0	0.0	0	0	0	0									
	Dallas Black Hawks	CHL	60	15	30	45				20											5	0	1	1	0			
1968-69	Port Huron Flags	IHL	71	48	36	84				28											3	4	2	6	2			
1969-70	Port Huron Flags	IHL	67	31	40	71				54											15	7	7	14	13			
1970-71	Port Huron–Toledo	IHL	52	21	22	43				30																		
1971-72	Toledo Hornets	IHL	27	5	15	20				6																		
1972-73	Seattle Totems	WHL	4	0	1	1				2																		
	Cranbrook Royals	WIHL	50	36	32	68																						
1973-74	Cranbrook Royals	WIHL	46	28	39	67																						
1974-75	Cranbrook Royals	WIHL	12	4	4	8				0																		
1975-76	Cranbrook Royals	WIHL	24	10	13	23				22																		
	NHL Totals		2	0	0	0	0	0	0	0	0	0	0	0	0.0	0	0	0	0									

IHL First All-Star Team (1969)

● POWIS, LYNN   Lynn Powis   C – L. 6', 175 lbs.   b: Maryfield, Sask., 7/7/1949.   Montreal's 7th choice, 68th overall, in 1969 Amateur Draft.

Season	Club	League	GP	G	A	Pts	AG	AA	APts	PIM	PP	SH	GW	S	%	TGF	PGF	TGA	PGA	+/-	GP	G	A	Pts	PIM	PP	SH	GW
1965-66	Melville Millionaires	SJHL	43	0	2	2				4																		
1966-67	Moose Jaw Canucks	WCJHL	52	13	18	31				17											14	5	4	9	4			
1967-68	University of Denver	WCHA	DID NOT PLAY – FRESHMAN																								
1968-69	University of Denver	WCHA	30	17	12	29				21																		
1969-70	University of Denver	WCHA	5	2	3	5				12																		
1970-71	Denver Spurs	WHL	59	14	13	27				13																		
1971-72	Nova Scotia Voyageurs	AHL	38	5	6	11				19											15	0	2	2	0			
1972-73	Omaha Knights	CHL	72	34	40	74				49											11	2	5	7	8			
1973-74	**Chicago Black Hawks**	**NHL**	57	8	13	21	8	11	19	6	1	0	2	71	11.3	30	4	17	1	+10	1	0	0	0	0	0	0	0
1974-75	**Kansas City Scouts**	**NHL**	73	11	20	31	10	16	26	19	3	0	0	149	7.4	39	18	79	4	-54								
1975-76	Providence Reds	AHL	52	30	31	61				54											10	5	4	9	12			
	Calgary Cowboys	WHA	21	4	10	14				2																		
1976-77	Calgary Cowboys	WHA	63	30	30	60				40																		
1977-78	Indianapolis Racers	WHA	14	4	6	10				2																		
	Winnipeg Jets	WHA	55	12	19	31				16											3	2	1	3	7			
1978-79	Duisburg SC	Germany	STATISTICS NOT AVAILABLE																								
1979-80	Duisberg SC	Germany	39	28	37	65				*162																		
1980-81	Duisberg SC	Germany	17	12	12	24				62																		
1981-82	EV Fussen	Germany	32	17	22	39				82																		
	NHL Totals		130	19	33	52	18	27	45	25	4	0	2	220	8.6	69	22	96	5		1	0	0	0	0	0	0	0
	Other Major League Totals		153	50	65	115				80											13	7	5	12	19			

Selected by **Dayton-Houston** (WHA) in 1972 WHA General Player Draft, February 12, 1972. Traded to **Atlanta** by **Montreal** for cash, June 9, 1972. Traded to **Chicago** by **Atlanta** for Mike Baumgartner, August 30, 1973. Claimed by **Kansas City** from **Chicago** in Expansion Draft, June 12, 1974. Traded to **St. Louis** by **Kansas City** with Kansas City's 2nd round choice (Brian Sutter) in 1976 Amateur Draft for Craig Patrick and Denis Dupere, June 18, 1975. Traded to **Calgary** (WHA) by **Providence** (AHL) for future considerations, February, 1976. Signed as a free agent by **Indianapolis** (WHA) after **Calgary** (WHA) franchise folded, May 31, 1977. Signed as a free agent by **Winnipeg** (WHA) following release by **Indianapolis** (WHA), December, 1977.

● PRAJSLER, PETR   Petr Prajsler   D – L. 6'2", 200 lbs.   b: Hradec Kralove, Czech., 9/21/1965.   Los Angeles' 5th choice, 93rd overall, in 1985 Entry Draft.

Season	Club	League	GP	G	A	Pts	AG	AA	APts	PIM	PP	SH	GW	S	%	TGF	PGF	TGA	PGA	+/-	GP	G	A	Pts	PIM	PP	SH	GW
1984-85	Tesla Pardubice	Czech.	29	4	1	5				24																		
1985-86	Tesla Pardubice	Czech.	27	5	5	10				24																		
1986-87	Tesla Pardubice	Czech.	41	3	4	7				49																		
1987-88	**Los Angeles Kings**	**NHL**	7	0	0	0	0	0	0	2	0	0	0	2	0.0	4	0	2	0	+2								
	New Haven Nighthawks	AHL	41	3	8	11				58																		
1988-89	**Los Angeles Kings**	**NHL**	2	0	3	3	0	2	2	0	0	0	0	1	0.0	6	2	0	0	+4	1	0	0	0	0	0	0	0
	New Haven Nighthawks	AHL	43	4	6	10				96											16	3	3	6	34			
1989-90	**Los Angeles Kings**	**NHL**	34	3	7	10	3	5	8	47	1	0	0	49	6.1	38	19	33	5	-9	3	0	0	0	0	0	0	0
	New Haven Nighthawks	AHL	6	1	7	8				2																		
1990-91	Phoenix Roadrunners	IHL	77	13	34	47				140											9	1	9	10	18			
1991-92	**Boston Bruins**	**NHL**	3	0	0	0	0	0	0	2	0	0	0	0	0.0	0	0	1	0	-1								
	Maine Mariners	AHL	61	12	33	45				88																		
1992-93			DID NOT PLAY																								
1993-94	Hradec Kralove	Czech.	17	0	4	4																						
	NHL Totals		46	3	10	13	3	7	10	51	1	0	0	55	5.5	40	21	36	5		4	0	0	0	0	0	0	0

Signed as a free agent by **Boston**, August 1, 1991.

● PRATT, KELLY   Kelly Pratt   RW – R. 5'9", 170 lbs.   b: High Prairie, Alta., 2/8/1953.

Season	Club	League	GP	G	A	Pts	AG	AA	APts	PIM	PP	SH	GW	S	%	TGF	PGF	TGA	PGA	+/-	GP	G	A	Pts	PIM	PP	SH	GW
1969-70	Red Deer Rustlers	Jr. B	20	3	4	7				56																		
1970-71	Kamloops Chiefs	BCJHL	STATISTICS NOT AVAILABLE																								
1971-72	Swift Current Broncos	WCJHL	63	36	29	65				114																		
1972-73	Swift Current Broncos	WCJHL	65	45	37	82				91																		
1973-74	Winnipeg Jets	WHA	46	4	6	10				50																		
	Jacksonville Barons	AHL	16	2	6	8				24																		
1974-75	**Pittsburgh Penguins**	**NHL**	22	0	6	6	0	5	5	15	0	0	0	28	0.0	10	2	10	3	+1								
	Hershey Bears	AHL	31	7	10	17				97											8	0	2	2	14			
1975-76	Hershey Bears	AHL	62	13	25	38				96											1	0	0	0	0			
1976-77	Hershey Bears	AHL	31	2	5	7				21																		
1977-78	Hampton Gulls	AHL	11	1	0	1				26																		
	San Diego Mariners	PCL	23	10	15	25				20																		
1978-79	Spokane Flyers	PCL	18	5	5	10				32																		
	Los Angeles Blades	PHL	9	6	2	8				9																		
	San Diego Hawks	PHL	16	3	4	7				4																		
	NHL Totals		22	0	6	6	0	5	5	15	0	0	0	28	0.0	10	2	10	3									
	Other Major League Totals		46	4	6	10				50																		

Selected by **Winnipeg** (WHA) in 1973 WHA Amateur Draft, June, 1973. Signed as a free agent by **Pittsburgh**, July 15, 1974. Traded to **Hershey** (AHL) by **Pittsburgh** for cash, August 28, 1975.

			REGULAR SEASON																		PLAYOFFS							
Season	Club	League	GP	G	A	Pts	AG	AA	APts	PIM	PP	SH	GW	S	%	TGF	PGF	TGA	PGA	+/–	GP	G	A	Pts	PIM	PP	SH	GW

• PRATT, NOLAN

Nolan Pratt D – L. 6′2″, 195 lbs. b: Fort McMurray, Alta., 8/14/1975. Hartford's 4th choice, 115th overall, in 1993 Entry Draft.

Season	Club	League	GP	G	A	Pts	AG	AA	APts	PIM	PP	SH	GW	S	%	TGF	PGF	TGA	PGA	+/–	GP	G	A	Pts	PIM	PP	SH	GW
1991-92	Portland Winter Hawks	WHL	22	2	9	11	....	....	....	13	....	....	....	....	....	....	....	....	....	....	6	1	3	4	12	....	....	....
1992-93	Portland Winter Hawks	WHL	70	4	19	23	....	....	....	97	....	....	....	....	....	....	....	....	....	....	16	2	7	9	31	....	....	....
1993-94	Portland Winter Hawks	WHL	72	4	32	36	....	....	....	105	....	....	....	....	....	....	....	....	....	....	10	1	2	3	14	....	....	....
1994-95	Portland Winter Hawks	WHL	72	6	37	43	....	....	....	196	....	....	....	....	....	....	....	....	....	....	9	1	6	7	10	....	....	....
1995-96	Springfield Falcons	AHL	62	2	6	8	....	....	....	72	....	....	....	....	....	....	....	....	....	....	2	0	0	0	0	....	....	....
	Richmond Renegades	ECHL	4	1	0	1	....	....	....	2	....	....	....	....	....	....	....	....	....	....	....	....	....	....	....	....	....	....
1996-97	**Hartford Whalers**	**NHL**	**9**	**0**	**2**	**2**	**0**	**2**	**2**	**6**	**0**	**0**	**0**	**4**	**0.0**	**4**	**0**	**6**	**2**	**0**	....	....	....	....	....	....	....	....
	Springfield Falcons	AHL	66	1	18	19	....	....	....	127	....	....	....	....	....	....	....	....	....	....	17	0	3	3	18	....	....	....
1997-98	**Carolina Hurricanes**	**NHL**	**23**	**0**	**2**	**2**	**0**	**2**	**2**	**44**	**0**	**0**	**0**	**11**	**0.0**	**10**	**0**	**14**	**2**	**–2**	....	....	....	....	....	....	....	....
	Beast of New Haven	AHL	54	3	15	18	....	....	....	135	....	....	....	....	....	....	....	....	....	....	....	....	....	....	....	....	....	....
	NHL Totals		**32**	**0**	**4**	**4**	**0**	**4**	**4**	**50**	**0**	**0**	**0**	**15**	**0.0**	**14**	**0**	**20**	**4**		....	....	....	....	....	....	....	....

• PRATT, TRACY

Tracy Pratt D – L. 6′2″, 195 lbs. b: New York City, NY, 3/8/1943.

Season	Club	League	GP	G	A	Pts	AG	AA	APts	PIM	PP	SH	GW	S	%	TGF	PGF	TGA	PGA	+/–	GP	G	A	Pts	PIM	PP	SH	GW
1960-61	Flin Flon Bombers	SJHL	59	3	13	16	....	....	....	83	....	....	....	....	....	....	....	....	....	....	....	....	....	....	....	....	....	....
1961-62	Flin Flon Bombers	SJHL	59	10	30	40	....	....	....	....	....	....	....	....	....	....	....	....	....	....	....	....	....	....	....	....	....	....
1962-63	Brandon Wheat Kings	MJHL	33	10	17	27	....	....	....	132	....	....	....	....	....	....	....	....	....	....	19	5	12	17	*73	....	....	....
1963-64	St. Paul Rangers	CHL	52	4	15	19	....	....	....	128	....	....	....	....	....	....	....	....	....	....	11	0	0	0	*49	....	....	....
1964-65	St. Paul Rangers	CHL	66	15	25	40	....	....	....	200	....	....	....	....	....	....	....	....	....	....	9	1	2	3	27	....	....	....
1965-66	St. Louis Braves	CHL	70	2	23	25	....	....	....	*206	....	....	....	....	....	....	....	....	....	....	5	1	2	3	6	....	....	....
1966-67	Portland Buckaroos	WHL	63	0	10	10	....	....	....	92	....	....	....	....	....	....	....	....	....	....	4	0	1	1	4	....	....	....
1967-68	**Oakland Seals**	**NHL**	**34**	**0**	**5**	**5**	**0**	**5**	**5**	**90**	**0**	**0**	**0**	**35**	**0.0**	**23**	**2**	**48**	**9**	**–18**	....	....	....	....	....	....	....	....
	Vancouver Canucks	WHL	29	1	8	9	....	....	....	73	....	....	....	....	....	....	....	....	....	....	....	....	....	....	....	....	....	....
1968-69	Vancouver Canucks	WHL	45	2	10	12	....	....	....	74	....	....	....	....	....	....	....	....	....	....	....	....	....	....	....	....	....	....
	Pittsburgh Penguins	**NHL**	**18**	**0**	**5**	**5**	**0**	**5**	**5**	**34**	**0**	**0**	**0**	**10**	**0.0**	**23**	**3**	**16**	**2**	**+6**	....	....	....	....	....	....	....	....
1969-70	**Pittsburgh Penguins**	**NHL**	**65**	**5**	**7**	**12**	**6**	**7**	**13**	**124**	**0**	**0**	**1**	**73**	**6.8**	**35**	**4**	**73**	**13**	**–29**	**10**	**0**	**1**	**1**	**51**	**0**	**0**	**0**
1970-71	**Buffalo Sabres**	**NHL**	**76**	**1**	**7**	**8**	**1**	**6**	**7**	**179**	**0**	**0**	**0**	**34**	**2.9**	**64**	**2**	**102**	**23**	**–17**	....	....	....	....	....	....	....	....
1971-72	**Buffalo Sabres**	**NHL**	**27**	**0**	**10**	**10**	**0**	**9**	**9**	**52**	**0**	**0**	**0**	**31**	**0.0**	**32**	**1**	**40**	**9**	**0**	....	....	....	....	....	....	....	....
	Cincinnati Swords	AHL	16	0	11	11	....	....	....	40	....	....	....	....	....	....	....	....	....	....	....	....	....	....	....	....	....	....
1972-73	**Buffalo Sabres**	**NHL**	**74**	**1**	**15**	**16**	**1**	**13**	**14**	**116**	**0**	**0**	**0**	**63**	**1.6**	**79**	**2**	**92**	**24**	**+9**	**6**	**0**	**0**	**0**	**6**	**0**	**0**	**0**
1973-74	**Buffalo Sabres**	**NHL**	**33**	**0**	**7**	**7**	**0**	**6**	**6**	**52**	**0**	**0**	**0**	**20**	**0.0**	**46**	**0**	**45**	**8**	**+9**	....	....	....	....	....	....	....	....
	Vancouver Canucks	**NHL**	**45**	**3**	**8**	**11**	**3**	**7**	**10**	**44**	**0**	**0**	**0**	**30**	**10.0**	**47**	**0**	**82**	**24**	**–11**	....	....	....	....	....	....	....	....
1974-75	**Vancouver Canucks**	**NHL**	**79**	**5**	**17**	**22**	**5**	**13**	**18**	**145**	**0**	**0**	**0**	**100**	**5.0**	**100**	**7**	**123**	**36**	**+6**	**3**	**0**	**0**	**0**	**5**	**0**	**0**	**0**
1975-76	**Vancouver Canucks**	**NHL**	**52**	**1**	**5**	**6**	**1**	**4**	**5**	**72**	**1**	**0**	**0**	**44**	**2.3**	**40**	**2**	**70**	**25**	**–7**	**2**	**0**	**0**	**0**	**0**	**0**	**0**	**0**
1976-77	**Colorado Rockies**	**NHL**	**66**	**1**	**10**	**11**	**1**	**8**	**9**	**110**	**0**	**0**	**0**	**53**	**1.9**	**57**	**4**	**113**	**33**	**–27**	....	....	....	....	....	....	....	....
	Toronto Maple Leafs	**NHL**	**11**	**0**	**1**	**1**	**0**	**1**	**1**	**8**	**0**	**0**	**0**	**4**	**0.0**	**2**	**0**	**10**	**1**	**–7**	**4**	**0**	**0**	**0**	**0**	**0**	**0**	**0**
	NHL Totals		**580**	**17**	**97**	**114**	**18**	**84**	**102**	**1026**	**1**	**0**	**1**	**497**	**3.4**	**548**	**27**	**814**	**207**		**25**	**0**	**1**	**1**	**62**	**0**	**0**	**0**

Played in NHL All-Star Game (1975)

Traded to **Chicago** by **NY Rangers** with Dave Richardson, Dick Meissner and Mel Pearson for John McKenzie and Ray Cullen, June 4, 1965. Claimed by **Oakland** from **Chicago** in Expansion Draft, June 6, 1967. Traded to **Pittsburgh** by **Oakland** with George Swarbrick and Bryan Watson for Earl Ingarfield Sr., Gene Ubriaco and Dick Mattiussi, January 30, 1969. Claimed by **Buffalo** from **Pittsburgh** in Expansion Draft, June 10, 1970. Traded to **Vancouver** by **Buffalo** with John Gould for Jerry Korab, December 27, 1973. Signed as a free agent by **Colorado**, September 12, 1976. Traded to **Toronto** by **Colorado** for Toronto's 3rd round choice (Randy Pierce) in 1977 Amateur Draft, March 8, 1977.

• PRENTICE, DEAN

Dean Prentice LW – L. 5′11″, 180 lbs. b: Shumacher, Ont., 10/5/1932.

Season	Club	League	GP	G	A	Pts	AG	AA	APts	PIM	PP	SH	GW	S	%	TGF	PGF	TGA	PGA	+/–	GP	G	A	Pts	PIM	PP	SH	GW
1950-51	Guelph Biltmores	OHA	51	20	16	36	....	....	....	26	....	....	....	....	....	....	....	....	....	....	4	1	1	2	15	....	....	....
1951-52	Guelph Biltmores	OHA	51	48	27	75	....	....	....	68	....	....	....	....	....	....	....	....	....	....	23	*21	10	31	28	....	....	....
1952-53	Guelph Biltmores	OHA	5	1	1	2	....	....	....	16	....	....	....	....	....	....	....	....	....	....	....	....	....	....	....	....	....	....
	New York Rangers	**NHL**	**55**	**6**	**3**	**9**	**9**	**4**	**13**	**20**	....	....	....	....	....	....	....	....	....	....	....	....	....	....	....	....	....	....
1953-54	**New York Rangers**	**NHL**	**52**	**4**	**13**	**17**	**6**	**18**	**24**	**18**	....	....	....	....	....	....	....	....	....	....	....	....	....	....	....	....	....	....
1954-55	**New York Rangers**	**NHL**	**70**	**16**	**15**	**31**	**23**	**19**	**42**	**20**	....	....	....	....	....	....	....	....	....	....	....	....	....	....	....	....	....	....
1955-56	**New York Rangers**	**NHL**	**70**	**24**	**18**	**42**	**35**	**22**	**57**	**44**	....	....	....	....	....	....	....	....	....	....	**5**	**1**	**0**	**1**	**2**	....	....	....
1956-57	**New York Rangers**	**NHL**	**68**	**19**	**23**	**42**	**26**	**27**	**53**	**38**	....	....	....	....	....	....	....	....	....	....	**5**	**0**	**2**	**2**	**4**	....	....	....
1957-58	**New York Rangers**	**NHL**	**38**	**13**	**9**	**22**	**17**	**10**	**27**	**14**	....	....	....	....	....	....	....	....	....	....	**6**	**1**	**3**	**4**	**4**	....	....	....
1958-59	**New York Rangers**	**NHL**	**70**	**17**	**33**	**50**	**22**	**35**	**57**	**11**	....	....	....	....	....	....	....	....	....	....	....	....	....	....	....	....	....	....
1959-60	**New York Rangers**	**NHL**	**70**	**32**	**34**	**66**	**40**	**35**	**75**	**43**	....	....	....	....	....	....	....	....	....	....	....	....	....	....	....	....	....	....
1960-61	**New York Rangers**	**NHL**	**56**	**20**	**25**	**45**	**24**	**25**	**49**	**17**	....	....	....	....	....	....	....	....	....	....	....	....	....	....	....	....	....	....
1961-62	**New York Rangers**	**NHL**	**68**	**22**	**38**	**60**	**27**	**39**	**66**	**20**	....	....	....	....	....	....	....	....	....	....	**3**	**0**	**2**	**2**	**0**	....	....	....
1962-63	**New York Rangers**	**NHL**	**49**	**13**	**25**	**38**	**16**	**26**	**42**	**18**	....	....	....	....	....	....	....	....	....	....	....	....	....	....	....	....	....	....
	Boston Bruins	**NHL**	**19**	**6**	**9**	**15**	**7**	**9**	**16**	**4**	....	....	....	....	....	....	....	....	....	....	....	....	....	....	....	....	....	....
1963-64	**Boston Bruins**	**NHL**	**70**	**23**	**16**	**39**	**31**	**18**	**49**	**37**	....	....	....	....	....	....	....	....	....	....	....	....	....	....	....	....	....	....
1964-65	**Boston Bruins**	**NHL**	**31**	**14**	**9**	**23**	**18**	**10**	**28**	**12**	....	....	....	....	....	....	....	....	....	....	....	....	....	....	....	....	....	....
1965-66	**Boston Bruins**	**NHL**	**50**	**7**	**22**	**29**	**8**	**22**	**30**	**10**	....	....	....	....	....	....	....	....	....	....	....	....	....	....	....	....	....	....
	Detroit Red Wings	**NHL**	**19**	**6**	**9**	**15**	**7**	**9**	**16**	**8**	....	....	....	....	....	....	....	....	....	....	**12**	**5**	**5**	**10**	**4**	....	....	....
1966-67	**Detroit Red Wings**	**NHL**	**68**	**23**	**22**	**45**	**28**	**23**	**51**	**18**	....	....	....	....	....	....	....	....	....	....	....	....	....	....	....	....	....	....
1967-68	**Detroit Red Wings**	**NHL**	**69**	**17**	**38**	**55**	**21**	**40**	**61**	**42**	**4**	**1**	**2**	**174**	**9.8**	**77**	**14**	**71**	**15**	**+7**	....	....	....	....	....	....	....	....
1968-69	**Detroit Red Wings**	**NHL**	**74**	**14**	**20**	**34**	**16**	**19**	**35**	**18**	**2**	**1**	**1**	**191**	**7.3**	**51**	**6**	**77**	**24**	**–8**	....	....	....	....	....	....	....	....
1969-70	**Pittsburgh Penguins**	**NHL**	**75**	**26**	**25**	**51**	**30**	**25**	**55**	**14**	**12**	**0**	**2**	**205**	**12.7**	**74**	**28**	**66**	**0**	**–20**	**10**	**2**	**5**	**7**	**8**	**1**	**0**	**0**
1970-71	**Pittsburgh Penguins**	**NHL**	**69**	**21**	**17**	**38**	**22**	**15**	**37**	**18**	**7**	**0**	**2**	**135**	**15.6**	**60**	**22**	**46**	**0**	**–8**	....	....	....	....	....	....	....	....
1971-72	**Minnesota North Stars**	**NHL**	**71**	**20**	**27**	**47**	**21**	**25**	**46**	**14**	**7**	**0**	**1**	**207**	**9.7**	**62**	**16**	**42**	**0**	**+4**	**7**	**3**	**0**	**3**	**0**	**0**	**0**	**1**
1972-73	**Minnesota North Stars**	**NHL**	**73**	**26**	**16**	**42**	**26**	**13**	**39**	**22**	**5**	**0**	**5**	**168**	**15.5**	**56**	**9**	**44**	**0**	**+3**	**6**	**1**	**0**	**1**	**16**	**1**	**0**	**0**
1973-74	**Minnesota North Stars**	**NHL**	**24**	**2**	**3**	**5**	**2**	**3**	**5**	**4**	**0**	**0**	**0**	**36**	**5.6**	**9**	**0**	**20**	**0**	**–11**	....	....	....	....	....	....	....	....
	NHL Totals		**1378**	**391**	**469**	**860**	**482**	**491**	**973**	**484**	**37**	**2**	**13**	**1116**	**35.0**	**389**	**95**	**366**	**39**		**54**	**13**	**17**	**30**	**38**	**2**	**0**	**1**

NHL Second All-Star Team (1960)

Played in NHL All-Star Game (1957, 1961, 1963, 1970)

Traded to **Boston** by **NY Rangers** for Don McKenney, February 6, 1963. Traded to **Detroit** by **Boston** for Ron Murphy, February 18, 1966. Claimed by **Pittsburgh** from **Detroit** in Intra-League Draft, June 11, 1969. Traded to **Minnesota** by **Pittsburgh** for cash, October 6, 1971.

• PRESLEY, WAYNE

Wayne Presley RW – R. 5′11″, 195 lbs. b: Dearborn, MI, 3/23/1965. Chicago's 2nd choice, 39th overall, in 1983 Entry Draft.

Season	Club	League	GP	G	A	Pts	AG	AA	APts	PIM	PP	SH	GW	S	%	TGF	PGF	TGA	PGA	+/–	GP	G	A	Pts	PIM	PP	SH	GW
1982-83	Kitchener Rangers	OHL	70	39	48	87	....	....	....	99	....	....	....	....	....	....	....	....	....	....	12	1	4	5	9	....	....	....
1983-84	Kitchener Rangers	OHL	70	63	76	139	....	....	....	156	....	....	....	....	....	....	....	....	....	....	16	12	16	28	38	....	....	....
1984-85	Kitchener Rangers	OHL	31	25	21	46	....	....	....	77	....	....	....	....	....	....	....	....	....	....	....	....	....	....	....	....	....	....
	Sault Ste. Marie Greyhounds	OHL	11	5	9	14	....	....	....	14	....	....	....	....	....	....	....	....	....	....	16	13	9	22	13	....	....	....
	Chicago Black Hawks	**NHL**	**3**	**0**	**1**	**1**	**0**	**1**	**1**	**0**	**0**	**0**	**0**	**0**	**0.0**	**1**	**0**	**0**	**0**	**+1**	....	....	....	....	....	....	....	....
1985-86	**Chicago Black Hawks**	**NHL**	**38**	**7**	**8**	**15**	**6**	**5**	**11**	**38**	**0**	**0**	**1**	**56**	**12.5**	**30**	**0**	**36**	**0**	**–6**	**3**	**0**	**0**	**0**	**0**	**0**	**0**	**0**
	Nova Scotia Oilers	AHL	29	6	9	15	....	....	....	22	....	....	....	....	....	....	....	....	....	....	....	....	....	....	....	....	....	....
1986-87	**Chicago Blackhawks**	**NHL**	**80**	**32**	**29**	**61**	**28**	**21**	**49**	**114**	**7**	**0**	**4**	**167**	**19.2**	**85**	**22**	**81**	**0**	**–18**	**4**	**1**	**0**	**1**	**9**	**0**	**0**	**0**
1987-88	United States	C Cup	5	1	0	1	....	....	....	12	....	....	....	....	....	....	....	....	....	....	....	....	....	....	....	....	....	....
	Chicago Blackhawks	**NHL**	**42**	**12**	**10**	**22**	**10**	**7**	**17**	**52**	**4**	**0**	**1**	**89**	**13.5**	**33**	**12**	**35**	**1**	**–13**	**5**	**0**	**0**	**0**	**4**	**0**	**0**	**0**
1988-89	**Chicago Blackhawks**	**NHL**	**72**	**21**	**19**	**40**	**18**	**13**	**31**	**100**	**4**	**3**	**4**	**132**	**15.9**	**52**	**14**	**56**	**15**	**–3**	**14**	**7**	**5**	**12**	**18**	**1**	**3**	**1**
1989-90	**Chicago Blackhawks**	**NHL**	**49**	**6**	**7**	**13**	**5**	**5**	**10**	**69**	**1**	**0**	**0**	**75**	**8.0**	**27**	**5**	**46**	**5**	**–19**	**19**	**9**	**6**	**15**	**29**	**1**	**1**	**1**
1990-91	**Chicago Blackhawks**	**NHL**	**71**	**15**	**19**	**34**	**14**	**14**	**28**	**122**	**1**	**0**	**3**	**141**	**10.6**	**55**	**13**	**35**	**4**	**+11**	**6**	**0**	**1**	**1**	**38**	**0**	**0**	**0**
1991-92	**San Jose Sharks**	**NHL**	**47**	**8**	**14**	**22**	**7**	**11**	**18**	**76**	**3**	**0**	**0**	**114**	**7.0**	**28**	**14**	**47**	**4**	**–29**	....	....	....	....	....	....	....	....
	Buffalo Sabres	**NHL**	**12**	**2**	**2**	**4**	**2**	**1**	**3**	**57**	**0**	**0**	**1**	**21**	**9.5**	**9**	**1**	**8**	**2**	**+2**	**7**	**3**	**3**	**6**	**14**	**0**	**0**	**0**
1992-93	**Buffalo Sabres**	**NHL**	**79**	**15**	**17**	**32**	**12**	**12**	**24**	**96**	**0**	**1**	**2**	**97**	**15.5**	**49**	**4**	**58**	**18**	**+5**	**8**	**1**	**0**	**1**	**6**	**0**	**1**	**1**
1993-94	**Buffalo Sabres**	**NHL**	**65**	**17**	**8**	**25**	**16**	**6**	**22**	**103**	**1**	**5**	**1**	**93**	**18.3**	**41**	**3**	**35**	**15**	**+18**	**7**	**2**	**1**	**3**	**14**	**1**	**0**	**1**
1994-95	**Buffalo Sabres**	**NHL**	**46**	**14**	**5**	**19**	**25**	**7**	**32**	**41**	**0**	**5**	**2**	**90**	**15.6**	**27**	**2**	**39**	**19**	**+5**	**5**	**3**	**1**	**4**	**8**	**0**	**1**	**1**
1995-96	**New York Rangers**	**NHL**	**61**	**4**	**6**	**10**	**4**	**5**	**9**	**71**	**0**	**1**	**2**	**85**	**4.7**	**19**	**0**	**34**	**22**	**+7**	....	....	....	....	....	....	....	....
	Toronto Maple Leafs	**NHL**	**19**	**2**	**2**	**4**	**2**	**2**	**4**	**14**	**1**	**0**	**0**	**28**	**7.1**	**7**	**2**	**19**	**10**	**–4**	**5**	**0**	**0**	**0**	**2**	**0**	**0**	**0**

Season	Club	League	REGULAR SEASON																		PLAYOFFS							
			GP	G	A	Pts	AG	AA	APts	PIM	PP	SH	GW	S	%	TGF	PGF	TGA	PGA	+/–	GP	G	A	Pts	PIM	PP	SH	GW
1996-97	St. John's Maple Leafs	AHL	2	0	0	0	....	....	....	0	....	....	....	....	....	....	....	....	....	....	....	....	....	....	....	....	....	....
	Detroit Vipers	IHL	42	7	16	23	....	....	....	80	....	....	....	....	....	....	....	....	....	....	18	0	4	4	50	....	....	....
1997-98	Detroit Vipers	IHL	16	1	5	6	....	....	....	47	....	....	....	....	....	....	....	....	....	....	23	4	6	10	60	....	....	....
	NHL Totals		684	155	147	302	149	110	259	953	22	15	21	1188	13.0	463	92	529	115		83	26	17	43	142	3	6	5

OHL First All-Star Team (1984)

Traded to **San Jose** by **Chicago** for San Jose's 3rd round choice (Bogdan Savenko) in 1993 Entry Draft, September 20, 1991. Traded to **Buffalo** by **San Jose** for Dave Snuggerud, March 9, 1992. Signed as a free agent by **NY Rangers**, August 31, 1995. Traded to **Toronto** by **NY Rangers** for Sergio Momesso, February 20, 1996.

• PRESTON, RICH

Rich "Cool Hand Luke" Preston RW – R. 6′, 185 lbs. b: Regina, Sask., 5/22/1952.

Season	Club	League	GP	G	A	Pts	AG	AA	APts	PIM	PP	SH	GW	S	%	TGF	PGF	TGA	PGA	+/–	GP	G	A	Pts	PIM	PP	SH	GW
1969-70	Regina Pats	SJHL	....	15	15	30	....	....	....	4	....	....	....	....	....	....	....	....	....	....	....	....	....	....	....	....	....	....
1970-71	University of Denver	WCHA	17	0	1	1	....	....	....	0	....	....	....	....	....	....	....	....	....	....	....	....	....	....	....	....	....	....
1971-72	University of Denver	WCHA	33	3	11	14	....	....	....	18	....	....	....	....	....	....	....	....	....	....	....	....	....	....	....	....	....	....
1972-73	University of Denver	WCHA	39	23	25	48	....	....	....	24	....	....	....	....	....	....	....	....	....	....	....	....	....	....	....	....	....	....
1973-74	University of Denver	WCHA	38	20	25	45	....	....	....	36	....	....	....	....	....	....	....	....	....	....	....	....	....	....	....	....	....	....
1974-75	Houston Aeros	WHA	78	20	21	41	....	....	....	10	....	....	....	....	....	....	....	....	....	....	13	1	6	7	6	....	....	....
1975-76	Houston Aeros	WHA	77	22	33	55	....	....	....	33	....	....	....	....	....	....	....	....	....	....	17	4	6	10	8	....	....	....
1976-77	Houston Aeros	WHA	80	38	41	79	....	....	....	54	....	....	....	....	....	....	....	....	....	....	11	3	5	8	10	....	....	....
1977-78	Houston Aeros	WHA	73	25	25	50	....	....	....	52	....	....	....	....	....	....	....	....	....	....	....	....	....	....	....	....	....	....
1978-79	Winnipeg Jets	WHA	80	28	32	60	....	....	....	88	....	....	....	....	....	....	....	....	....	....	10	8	5	13	15	....	....	....
1979-80	**Chicago Black Hawks**	**NHL**	80	31	30	61	28	23	51	70	12	2	5	205	15.1	106	38	75	23	+16	7	0	3	3	2	0	0	0
1980-81	**Chicago Black Hawks**	**NHL**	47	7	14	21	6	10	16	24	3	0	1	100	7.0	46	14	72	25	–15	3	0	1	1	0	0	0	0
1981-82	**Chicago Black Hawks**	**NHL**	75	15	28	43	12	19	31	30	1	1	1	122	12.3	84	15	94	25	0	15	2	4	6	21	0	0	0
1982-83	**Chicago Black Hawks**	**NHL**	79	25	28	53	21	19	40	64	4	0	2	161	15.5	97	23	80	20	+14	13	2	7	9	25	0	0	1
1983-84	**Chicago Black Hawks**	**NHL**	75	10	18	28	8	12	20	50	3	1	1	109	9.2	59	11	91	22	–21	5	0	1	1	4	0	0	0
1984-85	**New Jersey Devils**	**NHL**	75	12	15	27	10	10	20	26	1	0	1	106	11.3	48	6	85	19	–24	....	....	....	....	....	....	....	....
1985-86	**New Jersey Devils**	**NHL**	76	19	22	41	15	15	30	65	3	0	2	117	16.2	70	19	82	34	+3	....	....	....	....	....	....	....	....
1986-87	**Chicago Blackhawks**	**NHL**	73	8	9	17	7	6	13	19	0	0	1	55	14.5	30	2	59	23	–8	4	0	2	2	4	0	0	0
	NHL Totals		580	127	164	291	107	114	221	348	27	4	14	975	13.0	540	128	638	191		47	4	18	22	56	0	0	1
	Other Major League Totals		388	133	152	285	....	....	....	237	....	....	....	....	....	....	....	....	....		51	16	22	38	39	....	....	....

Won WHA Playoff MVP Trophy (1979)

Selected by **Houston** (WHA) in 1973 WHA Professional Player Draft, June, 1973. Traded to **Winnipeg** (WHA) by **Houston** (WHA) for cash, July 6, 1978. Claimed by **Chicago** from **Winnipeg** in Expansion Draft, June 13, 1979. Traded to **New Jersey** by **Chicago** with Don Dietrich for Bob McMillan and New Jersey's 5th round choice (Rick Herbert) in 1985 Entry Draft, June 19, 1984. Signed as a free agent by **Chicago**, July 14, 1986.

• PRESTON, YVES

Yves Preston LW – L. 5′11″, 180 lbs. b: Montreal, Que., 6/14/1956.

Season	Club	League	GP	G	A	Pts	AG	AA	APts	PIM	PP	SH	GW	S	%	TGF	PGF	TGA	PGA	+/–	GP	G	A	Pts	PIM	PP	SH	GW
1973-74	Chicoutimi Sagueneens	QMJHL	70	26	33	59	....	....	....	60	....	....	....	....	....	....	....	....	....	....	....	....	....	....	....	....	....	....
1974-75	Laval Nationales	QMJHL	64	18	33	51	....	....	....	44	....	....	....	....	....	....	....	....	....	....	....	....	....	....	....	....	....	....
1975-76	Laval Nationales	QMJHL	63	29	42	71	....	....	....	45	....	....	....	....	....	....	....	....	....	....	....	....	....	....	....	....	....	....
1976-77	Dayton Gems	IHL	10	0	0	0	....	....	....	2	....	....	....	....	....	....	....	....	....	....	....	....	....	....	....	....	....	....
1977-78	Milwaukee Admirals	IHL	80	37	37	74	....	....	....	51	....	....	....	....	....	....	....	....	....	....	1	0	0	0	0	....	....	....
1978-79	**Philadelphia Flyers**	**NHL**	9	3	1	4	3	1	4	0	0	0	1	7	42.9	6	2	6	0	–2	....	....	....	....	....	....	....	....
	Maine Mariners	AHL	73	35	32	67	....	....	....	38	....	....	....	....	....	....	....	....	....	....	10	6	4	10	19	....	....	....
1979-80	Maine Mariners	AHL	71	23	24	47	....	....	....	51	....	....	....	....	....	....	....	....	....	....	12	1	4	5	17	....	....	....
1980-81	**Philadelphia Flyers**	**NHL**	19	4	2	6	3	1	4	4	1	0	1	13	30.8	9	1	7	0	+1	....	....	....	....	....	....	....	....
	Wichita Wind	CHL	31	4	11	15	....	....	....	25	....	....	....	....	....	....	....	....	....	....	4	0	3	3	21	....	....	....
1981-82	Milwaukee Admirals	IHL	70	25	29	54	....	....	....	23	....	....	....	....	....	....	....	....	....	....	5	1	1	2	0	....	....	....
1982-83	Milwaukee Admirals	IHL	67	35	53	88	....	....	....	17	....	....	....	....	....	....	....	....	....	....	11	4	3	7	0	....	....	....
1983-84	Milwaukee Admirals	IHL	82	36	40	85	....	....	....	37	....	....	....	....	....	....	....	....	....	....	4	0	2	2	0	....	....	....
	NHL Totals		28	7	3	10	6	2	8	4	1	0	2	20	35.0	15	3	13	0		....	....	....	....	....	....	....	....

IHL Second All-Star Team (1978) • AHL First All-Star Team (1979)

Signed as a free agent by **Philadelphia**, October 9, 1978.

• PRIAKIN, SERGEI

Sergei Priakin RW – L. 6′3″, 210 lbs. b: Moscow, Soviet Union, 12/7/1963. Calgary's 12th choice, 252nd overall, in 1988 Entry Draft.

Season	Club	League	GP	G	A	Pts	AG	AA	APts	PIM	PP	SH	GW	S	%	TGF	PGF	TGA	PGA	+/–	GP	G	A	Pts	PIM	PP	SH	GW
1981-82	Soviet Wings	USSR	43	4	5	9	....	....	....	23	....	....	....	....	....	....	....	....	....	....	....	....	....	....	....	....	....	....
	Soviet Union	WJC-A	7	2	1	3	....	....	....	4	....	....	....	....	....	....	....	....	....	....	....	....	....	....	....	....	....	....
1982-83	Soviet Wings	USSR	35	11	9	20	....	....	....	18	....	....	....	....	....	....	....	....	....	....	....	....	....	....	....	....	....	....
	Soviet Union	WJC-A	7	2	4	6	....	....	....	13	....	....	....	....	....	....	....	....	....	....	....	....	....	....	....	....	....	....
1983-84	Soviet Wings	USSR	44	18	13	31	....	....	....	24	....	....	....	....	....	....	....	....	....	....	....	....	....	....	....	....	....	....
1984-85	Soviet Wings	USSR	32	14	9	23	....	....	....	10	....	....	....	....	....	....	....	....	....	....	....	....	....	....	....	....	....	....
1985-86	Soviet Wings	USSR	39	12	13	25	....	....	....	16	....	....	....	....	....	....	....	....	....	....	....	....	....	....	....	....	....	....
1986-87	Soviet Wings	USSR	40	12	20	32	....	....	....	18	....	....	....	....	....	....	....	....	....	....	....	....	....	....	....	....	....	....
	USSR	RV'87	2	0	0	0	....	....	....	12	....	....	....	....	....	....	....	....	....	....	....	....	....	....	....	....	....	....
	Soviet Union	WEC-A	8	0	2	2	....	....	....	8	....	....	....	....	....	....	....	....	....	....	....	....	....	....	....	....	....	....
1987-88	Soviet Union	C Cup	9	0	2	2	....	....	....	6	....	....	....	....	....	....	....	....	....	....	....	....	....	....	....	....	....	....
	Soviet Wings	USSR	44	10	15	25	....	....	....	16	....	....	....	....	....	....	....	....	....	....	....	....	....	....	....	....	....	....
1988-89	Soviet Wings	USSR	44	11	15	26	....	....	....	23	....	....	....	....	....	....	....	....	....	....	....	....	....	....	....	....	....	....
	Calgary Flames	**NHL**	2	0	0	0	0	0	0	2	0	0	0	2	0.0	1	0	0	0	+1	1	0	0	0	0	0	0	0
1989-90	Calgary Flames	FrTour	4	1	1	2	....	....	....	0	....	....	....	....	....	....	....	....	....	....	....	....	....	....	....	....	....	....
	Calgary Flames	**NHL**	20	2	2	4	2	1	3	0	0	0	1	17	11.8	8	0	15	0	–7	....	....	....	....	....	....	....	....
	Salt Lake Golden Eagles	IHL	3	1	0	1	....	....	....	0	....	....	....	....	....	....	....	....	....	....	....	....	....	....	....	....	....	....
	Soviet Union	WEC-A	3	0	1	1	....	....	....	2	....	....	....	....	....	....	....	....	....	....	....	....	....	....	....	....	....	....
1990-91	**Calgary Flames**	**NHL**	24	1	6	7	1	5	6	0	0	0	0	26	3.8	11	0	14	0	–3	....	....	....	....	....	....	....	....
	Salt Lake Golden Eagles	IHL	18	5	12	17	....	....	....	2	....	....	....	....	....	....	....	....	....	....	....	....	....	....	....	....	....	....
1991-92	Zurcher SC	Switz. B	42	21	25	46	....	....	....	24	....	....	....	....	....	....	....	....	....	....	....	....	....	....	....	....	....	....
1992-93	Soviet Wings	CIS	20	4	4	8	....	....	....	10	....	....	....	....	....	....	....	....	....	....	....	....	....	....	....	....	....	....
	Zurcher SC	Switz	23	12	5	17	....	....	....	12	....	....	....	....	....	....	....	....	....	....	4	2	1	3	4	....	....	....
1993-94	Zurcher SC	Switz	29	19	15	34	....	....	....	20	....	....	....	....	....	....	....	....	....	....	....	....	....	....	....	....	....	....
1994-95	Kiekko-Espoo	Finland	50	13	20	33	....	....	....	49	....	....	....	....	....	....	....	....	....	....	4	1	4	5	0	....	....	....
1995-96	Kiekko-Espoo	Finland	49	9	24	33	....	....	....	53	....	....	....	....	....	....	....	....	....	....	....	....	....	....	....	....	....	....
1996-97	Kiekko-Espoo	Finland	50	15	25	40	....	....	....	53	....	....	....	....	....	....	....	....	....	....	4	0	0	0	2	....	....	....
	NHL Totals		46	3	8	11	3	6	9	2	0	0	1	45	6.7	20	0	29	0		1	0	0	0	0	0	0	0

• PRICE, NOEL

Noel (Garry) Price D – L. 6′, 190 lbs. b: Brockville, Ont., 12/9/1935.

Season	Club	League	GP	G	A	Pts	AG	AA	APts	PIM	PP	SH	GW	S	%	TGF	PGF	TGA	PGA	+/–	GP	G	A	Pts	PIM	PP	SH	GW
1952-53	St. Michaels Majors	OHA	44	0	4	4	....	....	....	120	....	....	....	....	....	....	....	....	....	....	17	1	4	5	28	....	....	....
1953-54	St. Michaels Majors	OHA	58	6	5	11	....	....	....	157	....	....	....	....	....	....	....	....	....	....	8	1	2	3	31	....	....	....
1954-55	St. Michaels Majors	OHA	47	4	11	15	....	....	....	129	....	....	....	....	....	....	....	....	....	....	5	1	2	3	12	....	....	....
1955-56	St. Michael's Majors	OHA	46	10	22	32	....	....	....	84	....	....	....	....	....	....	....	....	....	....	8	1	0	1	8	....	....	....
1956-57	Rochester Americans	AHL	1	1	1	2	....	....	....	0	....	....	....	....	....	....	....	....	....	....	10	0	1	1	16	....	....	....
	Winnipeg Warriors	WHL	70	5	22	27	....	....	....	142	....	....	....	....	....	....	....	....	....	....	....	....	....	....	....	....	....	....
1957-58	**Toronto Maple Leafs**	**NHL**	1	0	0	0	0	0	0	5	....	....	....	....	....	....	....	....	....	....	....	....	....	....	....	....	....	....
	Rochester Americans	AHL	69	4	20	24	....	....	....	153	....	....	....	....	....	....	....	....	....	....	....	....	....	....	....	....	....	....
1958-59	**Toronto Maple Leafs**	**NHL**	28	0	0	0	0	0	0	4	....	....	....	....	....	....	....	....	....	....	5	0	0	0	2	....	....	....
1959-60	**New York Rangers**	**NHL**	6	0	0	0	0	0	0	2	....	....	....	....	....	....	....	....	....	....	....	....	....	....	....	....	....	....
	Springfield Indians	AHL	31	0	6	6	....	....	....	52	....	....	....	....	....	....	....	....	....	....	10	1	3	4	20	....	....	....
1960-61	**New York Rangers**	**NHL**	1	0	0	0	0	0	0	2	....	....	....	....	....	....	....	....	....	....	....	....	....	....	....	....	....	....
	Springfield Indians	AHL	71	6	21	27	....	....	....	97	....	....	....	....	....	....	....	....	....	....	8	1	4	5	30	....	....	....
1961-62	Springfield Indians	AHL	47	4	19	23	....	....	....	75	....	....	....	....	....	....	....	....	....	....	....	....	....	....	....	....	....	....
	Detroit Red Wings	**NHL**	20	0	1	1	0	1	1	6	....	....	....	....	....	....	....	....	....	....	....	....	....	....	....	....	....	....
1962-63	Baltimore Clippers	AHL	68	7	29	36	....	....	....	103	....	....	....	....	....	....	....	....	....	....	3	0	0	0	4	....	....	....
1963-64	Baltimore Clippers	AHL	72	6	35	41	....	....	....	109	....	....	....	....	....	....	....	....	....	....	....	....	....	....	....	....	....	....
1964-65	Baltimore Clippers	AHL	72	4	35	39	....	....	....	78	....	....	....	....	....	....	....	....	....	....	5	0	2	2	4	....	....	....

			REGULAR SEASON																		PLAYOFFS							
Season	Club	League	GP	G	A	Pts	AG	AA	APts	PIM	PP	SH	GW	S	%	TGF	PGF	TGA	PGA	+/–	GP	G	A	Pts	PIM	PP	SH	GW
1965-66	**Montreal Canadiens**	**NHL**	**15**	**0**	**6**	**6**	**0**	**6**	**6**	**8**	....	....	....	....	....	....	....	....	....	....	**3**	**0**	**1**	**1**	**0**	....	....	....
	Quebec Aces	AHL	55	8	20	28	....	....	....	48	....	....	....	....	....	....	....	....	....	....	....	....	....	....	....	....	....	....
1966-67	**Montreal Canadiens**	**NHL**	**24**	**0**	**3**	**3**	**0**	**3**	**3**	**8**	....	....	....	....	....	....	....	....	....	....	....	....	....	....	....	....	....	....
	Quebec Aces	AHL	47	3	23	26	....	....	....	60	....	....	....	....	....	....	....	....	....	....	5	1	4	5	2	....	....	....
1967-68	**Pittsburgh Penguins**	**NHL**	**70**	**6**	**27**	**33**	**7**	**28**	**35**	**48**	**1**	**0**	**2**	**187**	**3.2**	**97**	**17**	**105**	**18**	**–7**	....	....	....	....	....	....	....	....
1968-69	**Pittsburgh Penguins**	**NHL**	**73**	**2**	**18**	**20**	**2**	**17**	**19**	**61**	**1**	**0**	**0**	**152**	**1.3**	**65**	**13**	**99**	**17**	**–30**	....	....	....	....	....	....	....	....
1969-70	Springfield Kings	AHL	72	10	44	54	....	....	....	58	....	....	....	....	....	....	....	....	....	....	14	1	3	4	14	....	....	....
1970-71	**Los Angeles Kings**	**NHL**	**62**	**1**	**19**	**20**	**1**	**17**	**18**	**29**	**0**	**0**	**0**	**88**	**1.1**	**63**	**11**	**77**	**10**	**–15**	....	....	....	....	....	....	....	....
1971-72	Springfield Kings	AHL	9	1	3	4	....	....	....	6	....	....	....	....	....	....	....	....	....	....	....	....	....	....	....	....	....	....
	Nova Scotia Voyageurs	AHL	64	3	26	29	....	....	....	81	....	....	....	....	....	....	....	....	....	....	15	4	7	11	16	....	....	....
1972-73	**Atlanta Flames**	**NHL**	**54**	**1**	**13**	**14**	**1**	**11**	**12**	**38**	**0**	**0**	**0**	**70**	**1.4**	**51**	**11**	**61**	**14**	**–7**	....	....	....	....	....	....	....	....
1973-74	**Atlanta Flames**	**NHL**	**62**	**0**	**13**	**13**	**0**	**11**	**11**	**38**	**0**	**0**	**0**	**93**	**0.0**	**56**	**2**	**82**	**17**	**–11**	**4**	**0**	**0**	**0**	**6**	**0**	**0**	**0**
1974-75	**Atlanta Flames**	**NHL**	**80**	**4**	**14**	**18**	**4**	**11**	**15**	**82**	**1**	**1**	**0**	**101**	**4.0**	**66**	**6**	**81**	**21**	**0**	....	....	....	....	....	....	....	....
1975-76	**Atlanta Flames**	**NHL**	**3**	**0**	**0**	**0**	**0**	**0**	**0**	**2**	**0**	**0**	**0**	**1**	**0.0**	**0**	**0**	**0**	**0**	**0**	....	....	....	....	....	....	....	....
	Nova Scotia Voyageurs	AHL	73	2	37	39	....	....	....	55	....	....	....	....	....	....	....	....	....	....	8	0	7	7	12	....	....	....
	NHL Totals		**499**	**14**	**114**	**128**	**15**	**105**	**120**	**333**	**3**	**1**	**2**	**692**	**2.0**	**398**	**60**	**505**	**97**		**12**	**0**	**1**	**1**	**8**	**0**	**0**	**0**

WHL Prairie Division Second All-Star Team (1957) • AHL Second All-Star Team (1966) • AHL First All-Star Team (1970, 1972, 1976) • Won Eddie Shore Award (Outstanding Defenseman - AHL) (1970, 1972, 1976)

Played in NHL All-Star Game (1967)

Traded to **NY Rangers** by **Toronto** for Hank Ciesla, Bill Kennedy and future considerations, October 3, 1959. Loaned to **Detroit** by **NY Rangers** for Pete Goegan, February 16, 1962. Traded to **Montreal** by **NY Rangers** with Earl Ingarfield, Gord Labossiere and Dave McComb for Cesare Maniago and Garry Peters, June 8, 1965. Claimed by **Pittsburgh** from **Montreal** in Expansion Draft, June 6, 1967. Claimed by **LA Kings** (Springfield - AHL) from **Pittsburgh** in Reverse Draft, June 10, 1968. Traded to **Montreal** by **LA Kings** with Denis DeJordy, Dale Hoganson and Doug Robinson for Rogie Vachon, November 4, 1971. Traded to **Atlanta** by **Montreal** for cash and future considerations, August 14, 1972.

• PRICE, PAT

Pat Price D – L. 6′2″, 200 lbs. b: Nelson, B.C., 3/24/1955. NY Islanders' 1st choice, 11th overall, in 1975 Amateur Draft.

Season	Club	League	GP	G	A	Pts	AG	AA	APts	PIM	PP	SH	GW	S	%	TGF	PGF	TGA	PGA	+/–	GP	G	A	Pts	PIM	PP	SH	GW
1970-71	Saskatoon Blades	WCJHL	66	12	16	28	....	....	....	56	....	....	....	....	....	....	....	....	....	....	....	....	....	....	....	....	....	....
1971-72	Saskatoon Blades	WCJHL	66	10	48	58	....	....	....	85	....	....	....	....	....	....	....	....	....	....	....	....	....	....	....	....	....	....
1972-73	Saskatoon Blades	WCJHL	67	12	56	68	....	....	....	134	....	....	....	....	....	....	....	....	....	....	16	4	17	21	24	....	....	....
1973-74	Saskatoon Blades	WCJHL	68	27	68	95	....	....	....	147	....	....	....	....	....	....	....	....	....	....	6	3	4	7	13	....	....	....
1974-75	Canada	Summit	DID NOT PLAY																									
	Vancouver Blazers	WHA	68	5	29	34	....	....	....	15	....	....	....	....	....	....	....	....	....	....	....	....	....	....	....	....	....	....
1975-76	**New York Islanders**	**NHL**	**4**	**0**	**2**	**2**	**0**	**2**	**2**	**2**	**0**	**0**	**0**	**4**	**0.0**	**6**	**0**	**2**	**0**	**+4**	....	....	....	....	....	....	....	....
	Fort Worth Texans	CHL	72	6	44	50	....	....	....	119	....	....	....	....	....	....	....	....	....	....	....	....	....	....	....	....	....	....
1976-77	**New York Islanders**	**NHL**	**71**	**3**	**22**	**25**	**3**	**18**	**21**	**25**	**2**	**0**	**0**	**82**	**3.7**	**81**	**19**	**37**	**1**	**+26**	**10**	**0**	**1**	**1**	**2**	**0**	**0**	**0**
1977-78	**New York Islanders**	**NHL**	**52**	**2**	**10**	**12**	**2**	**8**	**10**	**27**	**0**	**0**	**1**	**50**	**4.0**	**60**	**5**	**30**	**0**	**+25**	**5**	**0**	**1**	**1**	**2**	**0**	**0**	**0**
	Rochester Americans	AHL	5	2	1	3	....	....	....	9	....	....	....	....	....	....	....	....	....	....	....	....	....	....	....	....	....	....
1978-79	**New York Islanders**	**NHL**	**55**	**3**	**11**	**14**	**3**	**8**	**11**	**50**	**0**	**0**	**0**	**48**	**6.3**	**60**	**4**	**38**	**0**	**+18**	**7**	**0**	**1**	**1**	**25**	**0**	**0**	**0**
1979-80	**Edmonton Oilers**	**NHL**	**75**	**11**	**21**	**32**	**10**	**16**	**26**	**134**	**2**	**0**	**0**	**95**	**11.6**	**98**	**16**	**113**	**35**	**+4**	**3**	**0**	**0**	**0**	**11**	**0**	**0**	**0**
1980-81	**Edmonton Oilers**	**NHL**	**59**	**8**	**24**	**32**	**7**	**17**	**24**	**193**	**0**	**0**	**0**	**90**	**8.9**	**82**	**22**	**91**	**24**	**–7**	....	....	....	....	....	....	....	....
	Pittsburgh Penguins	**NHL**	**13**	**0**	**10**	**10**	**0**	**7**	**7**	**33**	**0**	**0**	**0**	**25**	**0.0**	**18**	**2**	**17**	**3**	**+2**	**5**	**1**	**1**	**2**	**21**	**0**	**0**	**0**
1981-82	**Pittsburgh Penguins**	**NHL**	**77**	**7**	**31**	**38**	**6**	**20**	**26**	**322**	**2**	**0**	**0**	**107**	**6.5**	**98**	**13**	**107**	**24**	**+2**	**5**	**0**	**0**	**0**	**28**	**0**	**0**	**0**
1982-83	**Pittsburgh Penguins**	**NHL**	**38**	**1**	**11**	**12**	**1**	**8**	**9**	**104**	**0**	**0**	**0**	**57**	**1.8**	**36**	**8**	**63**	**16**	**–19**	....	....	....	....	....	....	....	....
	Quebec Nordiques	**NHL**	**14**	**1**	**2**	**3**	**1**	**1**	**2**	**28**	**0**	**0**	**0**	**8**	**12.5**	**18**	**0**	**28**	**7**	**–3**	**4**	**0**	**0**	**0**	**14**	**0**	**0**	**0**
1983-84	**Quebec Nordiques**	**NHL**	**72**	**3**	**25**	**28**	**2**	**17**	**19**	**188**	**0**	**0**	**2**	**59**	**5.1**	**107**	**16**	**93**	**22**	**+20**	**9**	**1**	**0**	**1**	**10**	**0**	**0**	**0**
1984-85	**Quebec Nordiques**	**NHL**	**68**	**1**	**26**	**27**	**1**	**18**	**19**	**118**	**0**	**0**	**0**	**55**	**1.8**	**80**	**3**	**84**	**24**	**+17**	**17**	**0**	**4**	**4**	**51**	**0**	**0**	**0**
1985-86	**Quebec Nordiques**	**NHL**	**54**	**3**	**13**	**16**	**2**	**9**	**11**	**82**	**0**	**0**	**0**	**49**	**6.1**	**54**	**3**	**73**	**22**	**0**	**3**	**0**	**1**	**1**	**4**	**0**	**0**	**0**
1986-87	**Quebec Nordiques**	**NHL**	**47**	**0**	**6**	**6**	**0**	**4**	**4**	**81**	**0**	**0**	**0**	**22**	**0.0**	**27**	**0**	**42**	**8**	**–7**	....	....	....	....	....	....	....	....
	Fredericton Express	AHL	7	0	0	0	....	....	....	14	....	....	....	....	....	....	....	....	....	....	....	....	....	....	....	....	....	....
	New York Rangers	**NHL**	**13**	**0**	**2**	**2**	**0**	**1**	**1**	**49**	**0**	**0**	**0**	**4**	**0.0**	**5**	**0**	**19**	**6**	**–8**	**6**	**0**	**1**	**1**	**27**	**0**	**0**	**0**
1987-88	**Minnesota North Stars**	**NHL**	**14**	**0**	**2**	**2**	**0**	**1**	**1**	**20**	**0**	**0**	**0**	**10**	**0.0**	**7**	**0**	**19**	**9**	**–3**	....	....	....	....	....	....	....	....
	Kalamazoo Wings	IHL	2	1	1	2	....	....	....	15	....	....	....	....	....	....	....	....	....	....	....	....	....	....	....	....	....	....
	NHL Totals		**726**	**43**	**218**	**261**	**38**	**155**	**193**	**1456**	**6**	**0**	**3**	**765**	**5.6**	**837**	**111**	**856**	**201**		**74**	**2**	**10**	**12**	**195**	**0**	**0**	**0**
	Other Major League Totals		68	5	29	34	....	....	....	15	....	....	....	....	....	....	....	....	....	....	....	....	....	....	....	....	....	....

WCJHL First All-Star Team (1974)

Selected by **Vancouver** (WHA) in 1974 WHA Amateur Draft, May, 1974. Claimed by **Edmonton** from **NY Islanders** in Expansion Draft, June 13, 1979. Traded to **Pittsburgh** by **Edmonton** for Pat Hughes, March 10, 1981. Claimed on waivers by **Quebec** from **Pittsburgh**, December 31, 1982. Traded to **NY Rangers** by **Quebec** for Lane Lambert, March 5, 1987. Traded to **Minnesota** by **NY Rangers** for Willi Plett, September 8, 1987.

• PRICE, TOM

Tom Price D – L. 6′1″, 190 lbs. b: Toronto, Ont., 7/12/1954. California's 5th choice, 57th overall, in 1974 Amateur Draft.

Season	Club	League	GP	G	A	Pts	AG	AA	APts	PIM	PP	SH	GW	S	%	TGF	PGF	TGA	PGA	+/–	GP	G	A	Pts	PIM	PP	SH	GW
1972-73	London Knights	OHA	62	4	10	14	....	....	....	104	....	....	....	....	....	....	....	....	....	....	....	....	....	....	....	....	....	....
1973-74	Ottawa 67's	OHA	61	7	33	40	....	....	....	80	....	....	....	....	....	....	....	....	....	....	....	....	....	....	....	....	....	....
1974-75	**California Golden Seals**	**NHL**	**3**	**0**	**0**	**0**	**0**	**0**	**0**	**4**	**0**	**0**	**0**	**2**	**0.0**	**1**	**0**	**3**	**1**	**–1**	....	....	....	....	....	....	....	....
	Salt Lake Golden Eagles	CHL	52	2	16	18	....	....	....	91	....	....	....	....	....	....	....	....	....	....	1	0	0	0	2	....	....	....
1975-76	**California Golden Seals**	**NHL**	**5**	**0**	**0**	**0**	**0**	**0**	**0**	**0**	**0**	**0**	**0**	**5**	**0.0**	**1**	**0**	**10**	**0**	**–9**	....	....	....	....	....	....	....	....
	Salt Lake City Golden Eagles	CHL	59	11	15	26	....	....	....	77	....	....	....	....	....	....	....	....	....	....	5	1	1	2	2	....	....	....
1976-77	**Cleveland Barons**	**NHL**	**2**	**0**	**0**	**0**	**0**	**0**	**0**	**0**	**0**	**0**	**0**	**2**	**0.0**	**0**	**0**	**4**	**0**	**–4**	....	....	....	....	....	....	....	....
	Salt Lake Golden Eagles	CHL	55	3	21	24	....	....	....	71	....	....	....	....	....	....	....	....	....	....	....	....	....	....	....	....	....	....
	Pittsburgh Penguins	**NHL**	**7**	**0**	**2**	**2**	**0**	**2**	**2**	**4**	**0**	**0**	**0**	**7**	**0.0**	**4**	**1**	**3**	**0**	**0**	....	....	....	....	....	....	....	....
1977-78	**Pittsburgh Penguins**	**NHL**	**10**	**0**	**0**	**0**	**0**	**0**	**0**	**0**	**0**	**0**	**0**	**3**	**0.0**	**2**	**0**	**6**	**0**	**–4**	....	....	....	....	....	....	....	....
	Grand Rapids Owls	IHL	9	1	8	9	....	....	....	30	....	....	....	....	....	....	....	....	....	....	....	....	....	....	....	....	....	....
	Binghamton Dusters	AHL	31	1	6	7	....	....	....	39	....	....	....	....	....	....	....	....	....	....	....	....	....	....	....	....	....	....
	Springfield Indians	AHL	21	0	9	9	....	....	....	23	....	....	....	....	....	....	....	....	....	....	4	1	2	2	6	....	....	....
1978-79	**Pittsburgh Penguins**	**NHL**	**2**	**0**	**0**	**0**	**0**	**0**	**0**	**4**	**0**	**0**	**0**	**0**	**0.0**	**0**	**0**	**2**	**0**	**–2**	....	....	....	....	....	....	....	....
	Binghamton Dusters	AHL	70	14	31	45	....	....	....	62	....	....	....	....	....	....	....	....	....	....	10	1	7	8	16	....	....	....
1979-80	Syracuse Firebirds	AHL	68	4	34	38	....	....	....	58	....	....	....	....	....	....	....	....	....	....	4	1	4	5	0	....	....	....
1980-81	Springfield Indians	AHL	51	2	24	26	....	....	....	56	....	....	....	....	....	....	....	....	....	....	....	....	....	....	....	....	....	....
1981-82	New Haven Nighthawks	AHL	57	3	20	23	....	....	....	52	....	....	....	....	....	....	....	....	....	....	4	0	0	0	2	....	....	....
1982-83	Saginaw Gears	IHL	26	1	8	9	....	....	....	18	....	....	....	....	....	....	....	....	....	....	....	....	....	....	....	....	....	....
1983-84	New Haven Nighthawks	AHL	77	2	23	25	....	....	....	54	....	....	....	....	....	....	....	....	....	....	....	....	....	....	....	....	....	....
1984-85			DID NOT PLAY																									
1985-86	New Haven Nighthawks	AHL	8	0	2	2	....	....	....	8	....	....	....	....	....	....	....	....	....	....	....	....	....	....	....	....	....	....
	NHL Totals		**29**	**0**	**2**	**2**	**0**	**2**	**2**	**12**	**0**	**0**	**0**	**19**	**0.0**	**8**	**1**	**28**	**1**		....	....	....	....	....	....	....	....

Transferred to **Cleveland** after **California** franchise relocated, August 26, 1976. Signed as a free agent by **Pittsburgh** following release by **Cleveland**, Februray 28, 1977.

• PRIESTLAY, KEN

Ken Priestlay C – L. 5′10″, 190 lbs. b: Richmond, B.C., 8/24/1967. Buffalo's 5th choice, 98th overall, in 1985 Entry Draft.

Season	Club	League	GP	G	A	Pts	AG	AA	APts	PIM	PP	SH	GW	S	%	TGF	PGF	TGA	PGA	+/–	GP	G	A	Pts	PIM	PP	SH	GW
1983-84	Victoria Cougars	WHL	55	10	18	28	....	....	....	31	....	....	....	....	....	....	....	....	....	....	....	....	....	....	....	....	....	....
1984-85	Victoria Cougars	WHL	50	25	37	62	....	....	....	48	....	....	....	....	....	....	....	....	....	....	....	....	....	....	....	....	....	....
1985-86	Victoria Cougars	WHL	72	73	72	145	....	....	....	45	....	....	....	....	....	....	....	....	....	....	....	....	....	....	....	....	....	....
	Rochester Americans	AHL	4	0	2	2	....	....	....	0	....	....	....	....	....	....	....	....	....	....	....	....	....	....	....	....	....	....
1986-87	Victoria Cougars	WHL	33	43	39	82	....	....	....	37	....	....	....	....	....	....	....	....	....	....	....	....	....	....	....	....	....	....
	Buffalo Sabres	**NHL**	**34**	**11**	**6**	**17**	**10**	**4**	**14**	**8**	**3**	**0**	**0**	**49**	**22.4**	**30**	**14**	**14**	**1**	**+3**	....	....	....	....	....	....	....	....
	Rochester Americans	AHL	....	....	....	....	....	....	....	....	....	....	....	....	....	....	....	....	....	....	8	3	2	5	4	....	....	....
1987-88	**Buffalo Sabres**	**NHL**	**33**	**5**	**12**	**17**	**4**	**9**	**13**	**35**	**1**	**1**	**0**	**63**	**7.9**	**38**	**15**	**37**	**10**	**–4**	**6**	**0**	**0**	**0**	**11**	**0**	**0**	**0**
	Rochester Americans	AHL	43	27	24	51	....	....	....	47	....	....	....	....	....	....	....	....	....	....	....	....	....	....	....	....	....	....
1988-89	**Buffalo Sabres**	**NHL**	**15**	**2**	**0**	**2**	**2**	**0**	**2**	**2**	**0**	**0**	**0**	**20**	**10.0**	**6**	**2**	**19**	**7**	**–8**	**3**	**0**	**0**	**0**	**2**	**0**	**0**	**0**
	Rochester Americans	AHL	64	56	37	93	....	....	....	60	....	....	....	....	....	....	....	....	....	....	....	....	....	....	....	....	....	....
1989-90	**Buffalo Sabres**	**NHL**	**35**	**7**	**7**	**14**	**6**	**5**	**11**	**14**	**1**	**0**	**1**	**66**	**10.6**	**23**	**5**	**23**	**4**	**–1**	**5**	**0**	**0**	**0**	**8**	**0**	**0**	**0**
	Rochester Americans	AHL	40	19	39	58	....	....	....	46	....	....	....	....	....	....	....	....	....	....	....	....	....	....	....	....	....	....
1990-91	Canada	Nat-Team	40	20	26	46	....	....	....	34	....	....	....	....	....	....	....	....	....	....	....	....	....	....	....	....	....	....
	Pittsburgh Penguins	**NHL**	**2**	**0**	**1**	**1**	**0**	**1**	**1**	**0**	**0**	**0**	**0**	**2**	**0.0**	**1**	**0**	**1**	**0**	**0**	....	....	....	....	....	....	....	....
1991-92	**Pittsburgh Penguins**	**NHL**	**49**	**2**	**8**	**10**	**2**	**6**	**8**	**4**	**0**	**0**	**0**	**20**	**10.0**	**14**	**4**	**10**	**5**	**+5**	....	....	....	....	....	....	....	....
	Muskegon Lumberjacks	IHL	13	4	11	15	....	....	....	6	....	....	....	....	....	....	....	....	....	....	13	5	11	16	10	....	....	....

			REGULAR SEASON																		PLAYOFFS							
Season	Club	League	GP	G	A	Pts	AG	AA	APts	PIM	PP	SH	GW	S	%	TGF	PGF	TGA	PGA	+/–	GP	G	A	Pts	PIM	PP	SH	GW
1992-93	Cleveland Lumberjacks	IHL	66	33	36	69				72											4	2	1	3	4			
1993-94	Kalamazoo Wings	IHL	25	9	5	14				34											5	2	1	3	2			
1994-95	Sheffield Steelers	Britain	28	55	32	87				18											8	9	8	17	32			
1995-96	Sheffield Steelers	Britain	36	58	40	98				28											8	8	5	13	4			
1996-97	Sheffield Steelers	Britain	34	25	12	37				24											8	4	5	9	2			
1997-98	Sheffield Steelers	Britain	27	11	24	35				24											9	3	3	6	2			
	NHL Totals		**168**	**27**	**34**	**61**	**24**	**25**	**49**	**63**	**5**	**1**	**1**	**220**	**12.3**	**112**	**40**	**104**	**27**		**14**	**0**	**0**	**0**	**21**	**0**	**0**	**0**

WHL West Second All-Star Team (1986, 1987)

Traded to **Pittsburgh** by **Buffalo** for Tony Tanti, March 5, 1991.

• PRIMEAU, KEITH

Keith Primeau C – L. 6'4", 210 lbs. b: Toronto, Ont., 11/24/1971. Detroit's 1st choice, 3rd overall, in 1990 Entry Draft.

1987-88	Hamilton Steelhawks	OHL	47	6	6	12				69											11	0	2	2	2			
1988-89	Niagara Falls Thunder	OHL	48	20	35	55				56											17	9	16	25	12			
1989-90	Niagara Falls Thunder	OHL	65	*57	70	*127				97											16	*16	17	*33	49			
1990-91	**Detroit Red Wings**	**NHL**	**58**	**3**	**12**	**15**	**3**	**9**	**12**	**106**	**0**	**0**	**1**	**33**	**9.1**	**24**	**3**	**33**	**0**	**–12**	**5**	**1**	**1**	**2**	**25**	**0**	**0**	**0**
	Adirondack Red Wings	AHL	6	3	5	8				8																		
1991-92	**Detroit Red Wings**	**NHL**	**35**	**6**	**10**	**16**	**5**	**7**	**12**	**83**	**0**	**0**	**0**	**27**	**22.2**	**24**	**1**	**16**	**2**	**+9**	**11**	**0**	**0**	**0**	**14**	**0**	**0**	**0**
	Adirondack Red Wings	AHL	42	21	24	45				89											9	1	7	8	27			
1992-93	**Detroit Red Wings**	**NHL**	**73**	**15**	**17**	**32**	**12**	**12**	**24**	**152**	**4**	**1**	**2**	**75**	**20.0**	**49**	**16**	**44**	**5**	**–6**	**7**	**0**	**2**	**2**	**26**	**0**	**0**	**0**
1993-94	**Detroit Red Wings**	**NHL**	**78**	**31**	**42**	**73**	**29**	**32**	**61**	**173**	**7**	**3**	**4**	**155**	**20.0**	**112**	**29**	**62**	**13**	**+34**	**7**	**0**	**2**	**2**	**6**	**0**	**0**	**0**
1994-95	**Detroit Red Wings**	**NHL**	**45**	**15**	**27**	**42**	**27**	**40**	**67**	**99**	**1**	**0**	**3**	**96**	**15.6**	**57**	**13**	**31**	**4**	**+17**	**17**	**4**	**5**	**9**	**45**	**2**	**0**	**0**
1995-96	**Detroit Red Wings**	**NHL**	**74**	**27**	**25**	**52**	**27**	**20**	**47**	**168**	**6**	**2**	**7**	**150**	**18.0**	**97**	**38**	**46**	**6**	**+19**	**17**	**1**	**4**	**5**	**28**	**0**	**0**	**0**
1996-97	Canada	W Cup	5	0	0	0				21																		
	Hartford Whalers	**NHL**	**75**	**26**	**25**	**51**	**28**	**22**	**50**	**161**	**6**	**3**	**2**	**169**	**15.4**	**78**	**21**	**71**	**11**	**–3**								
	Canada	WC-A	11	3	3	6				14																		
1997-98	**Carolina Hurricanes**	**NHL**	**81**	**26**	**37**	**63**	**31**	**36**	**67**	**110**	**7**	**3**	**2**	**180**	**14.4**	**103**	**30**	**73**	**19**	**+19**								
	Canada	Olympics	6	2	1	3				4																		
	Canada	WC-A	6	3	1	4				4																		
	NHL Totals		**519**	**149**	**195**	**344**	**162**	**178**	**340**	**1052**	**31**	**12**	**21**	**885**	**16.8**	**544**	**151**	**376**	**60**		**64**	**6**	**14**	**20**	**144**	**2**	**0**	**0**

OHL Second All-Star Team (1990)

Traded to **Hartford** by **Detroit** with Paul Coffey and Detroit's 1st round choice (Nikos Tselios) in 1997 Entry Draft for Brendan Shanahan and Brian Glynn, October 9, 1996. Transferred to **Carolina** after **Hartford** franchise relocated, June 25, 1997.

• PRIMEAU, KEVIN

Kevin Primeau RW – R. 6', 180 lbs. b: Edmonton, Alta., 1/3/1956.

1974-75	University of Alberta	CWUAA	33	12	15	27				23																		
1975-76	University of Alberta	CWUAA	34	10	10	20				29																		
1976-77	University of Alberta	CWUAA	34	20	14	34				49																		
1977-78	University of Alberta	CWUAA	25	13	16	29				36																		
	Edmonton Oilers	WHA	7	0	1	1				2											2	0	0	0	2			
1978-79	MC Davos	Switz.	STATISTICS NOT AVAILABLE																									
1979-80	Canada	Nat-Team	41	16	11	27				18											6	4	1	5	6			
	Canada	Olympics	6	4	1	5				6																		
1980-81	**Vancouver Canucks**	**NHL**	**2**	**0**	**0**	**0**	**0**	**0**	**0**	**4**	**0**	**0**	**0**	**0**	**0.0**	**0**	**0**	**0**	**0**	**0**								
	Dallas Black Hawks	CHL	45	14	9	23				22																		
	NHL Totals		**2**	**0**	**0**	**0**	**0**	**0**	**0**	**4**	**0**	**0**	**0**	**0**	**0.0**	**0**	**0**	**0**	**0**									
	Other Major League Totals		7	0	1	1				2											2	0	0	0	2			

Signed as a free agent by **Edmonton** (WHA), March 5, 1977. Signed as a free agent by **Vancouver**, 1980.

• PRIMEAU, WAYNE

Wayne Primeau C – L. 6'3", 193 lbs. b: Scarborough, Ont., 6/4/1976. Buffalo's 1st choice, 17th overall, in 1994 Entry Draft.

1992-93	Owen Sound Platers	OHL	66	10	27	37				108											8	1	4	5	0			
1993-94	Owen Sound Platers	OHL	65	25	50	75				75											9	1	6	7	8			
1994-95	Owen Sound Platers	OHL	66	34	62	96				84											10	4	0	10	15			
	Buffalo Sabres	**NHL**	**1**	**1**	**0**	**1**	**2**	**0**	**2**	**0**	**0**	**0**	**1**	**2**	**50.0**	**1**	**0**	**3**	**0**	**–2**								
1995-96	Owen Sound Platers	OHL	28	15	29	44				52																		
	Oshawa Generals	OHL	24	12	13	25				33											3	2	3	5	2			
	Buffalo Sabres	**NHL**	**2**	**0**	**0**	**0**	**0**	**0**	**0**	**0**	**0**	**0**	**0**	**0**	**0.0**	**0**	**0**	**0**	**0**	**0**								
	Rochester Americans	AHL	8	2	3	5				6											17	3	1	4	11			
1996-97	**Buffalo Sabres**	**NHL**	**45**	**2**	**4**	**6**	**2**	**4**	**6**	**64**	**1**	**0**	**0**	**25**	**8.0**	**7**	**1**	**8**	**0**	**–2**	**9**	**0**	**0**	**0**	**6**	**0**	**0**	**0**
	Rochester Americans	AHL	24	9	5	14				27											1	0	0	0	0			
1997-98	**Buffalo Sabres**	**NHL**	**69**	**6**	**6**	**12**	**7**	**6**	**13**	**87**	**2**	**0**	**1**	**51**	**11.8**	**24**	**4**	**18**	**7**	**+9**	**14**	**1**	**3**	**4**	**6**	**0**	**0**	**0**
	NHL Totals		**117**	**9**	**10**	**19**	**11**	**10**	**21**	**151**	**3**	**0**	**2**	**78**	**11.5**	**32**	**5**	**29**	**7**		**23**	**1**	**3**	**4**	**12**	**0**	**0**	**0**

• PROBERT, BOB

Bob Probert LW – L. 6'3", 225 lbs. b: Windsor, Ont., 6/5/1965. Detroit's 3rd choice, 46th overall, in 1983 Entry Draft.

1982-83	Brantford Alexanders	OHL	51	12	16	28				133											8	2	2	4	23			
1983-84	Brantford Alexanders	OHL	65	35	28	63				189											6	0	3	3	16			
1984-85	Hamilton Steelhawks	OHL	4	0	1	1				21																		
	Sault Ste. Marie Greyhounds	OHL	44	20	52	72				172											15	6	11	17	60			
1985-86	**Detroit Red Wings**	**NHL**	**44**	**8**	**13**	**21**	**6**	**9**	**15**	**186**	**3**	**0**	**0**	**46**	**17.4**	**30**	**9**	**35**	**0**	**–14**								
	Adirondack Red Wings	AHL	32	12	15	27				152											10	2	3	5	68			
1986-87	**Detroit Red Wings**	**NHL**	**63**	**13**	**11**	**24**	**11**	**8**	**19**	**221**	**2**	**0**	**0**	**56**	**23.2**	**27**	**5**	**28**	**0**	**–6**	**16**	**3**	**4**	**7**	**63**	**1**	**0**	**1**
	Adirondack Red Wings	AHL	7	1	4	5				15																		
1987-88	**Detroit Red Wings**	**NHL**	**74**	**29**	**33**	**62**	**25**	**23**	**48**	***398**	**15**	**0**	**5**	**126**	**23.0**	**111**	**42**	**63**	**0**	**+16**	**16**	**8**	**13**	**21**	**51**	**5**	**0**	**1**
1988-89	**Detroit Red Wings**	**NHL**	**25**	**4**	**2**	**6**	**3**	**1**	**4**	**106**	**1**	**0**	**0**	**23**	**17.4**	**13**	**6**	**18**	**0**	**–11**								
1989-90	**Detroit Red Wings**	**NHL**	**4**	**3**	**0**	**3**	**3**	**0**	**3**	**21**	**0**	**0**	**1**	**12**	**25.0**	**5**	**0**	**5**	**0**	**0**								
1990-91	**Detroit Red Wings**	**NHL**	**55**	**16**	**23**	**39**	**15**	**17**	**32**	**315**	**4**	**0**	**3**	**88**	**18.2**	**63**	**22**	**44**	**0**	**–3**	**6**	**1**	**2**	**3**	**50**	**0**	**0**	**0**
1991-92	**Detroit Red Wings**	**NHL**	**63**	**20**	**24**	**44**	**18**	**18**	**36**	**276**	**8**	**0**	**1**	**96**	**20.8**	**76**	**24**	**36**	**0**	**+16**	**11**	**1**	**6**	**7**	**28**	**0**	**0**	**0**
1992-93	**Detroit Red Wings**	**NHL**	**80**	**14**	**29**	**43**	**12**	**20**	**32**	**292**	**6**	**0**	**3**	**128**	**10.9**	**64**	**20**	**53**	**0**	**–9**	**7**	**0**	**3**	**3**	**10**	**0**	**0**	**0**
1993-94	**Detroit Red Wings**	**NHL**	**66**	**7**	**10**	**17**	**7**	**8**	**15**	**275**	**1**	**0**	**0**	**105**	**6.7**	**29**	**2**	**28**	**0**	**–1**	**7**	**1**	**1**	**2**	**8**	**0**	**0**	**0**
1994-95			DID NOT PLAY																									
1995-96	**Chicago Blackhawks**	**NHL**	**78**	**19**	**21**	**40**	**19**	**17**	**36**	**237**	**1**	**0**	**3**	**97**	**19.6**	**61**	**9**	**37**	**0**	**+15**	**10**	**0**	**2**	**2**	**23**	**0**	**0**	**0**
1996-97	**Chicago Blackhawks**	**NHL**	**82**	**9**	**14**	**23**	**10**	**12**	**22**	**326**	**1**	**0**	**3**	**111**	**8.1**	**47**	**12**	**38**	**0**	**–3**	**6**	**2**	**1**	**3**	**41**	**0**	**0**	**0**
1997-98	**Chicago Blackhawks**	**NHL**	**14**	**2**	**1**	**3**	**2**	**1**	**3**	**48**	**2**	**0**	**0**	**18**	**11.1**	**3**	**2**	**8**	**0**	**–7**								
	NHL Totals		**648**	**144**	**181**	**325**	**131**	**134**	**265**	**2701**	**44**	**0**	**19**	**906**	**15.9**	**529**	**153**	**383**	**0**		**79**	**16**	**32**	**48**	**274**	**6**	**0**	**2**

Played in NHL All-Star Game (1988)

Signed as a free agent by **Chicago**, July 23, 1994.

• PROCHAZKA, MARTIN

Martin Prochazka RW – R. 5'11", 180 lbs. b: Slany, Czech., 3/3/1972. Toronto's 6th choice, 135th overall, in 1991 Entry Draft.

1989-90	Poldi Kladno	Czech.	49	18	12	30																						
	Czechoslovakia	WJC-A	7	5	2	7				2																		
1990-91	Poldi Kladno	Czech.	50	19	10	29				21																		
	Czechoslovakia	WJC-A	7	4	1	5				0																		
1991-92	Dukla Jihlava	Czech.	44	18	11	29				2																		
	Czechoslovakia	WJC-A	7	0	2	2				0																		
1992-93	Poldi Kladno	Czech.	46	26	12	38																						
1993-94	Poldi Kladno	Czech.	43	24	16	40				0											2	2	0	2				
1994-95	Poldi Kladno	Czech.	41	25	33	58				18											11	8	4	12	4			
	Czech Republic	WC-A	8	2	1	3				2																		
1995-96	Poldi Kladno	Czech.	37	15	27	42															8	2	4	6				
	Czech Republic	WC-A	6	3	3	6				2																		

			REGULAR SEASON																		PLAYOFFS							
Season	Club	League	GP	G	A	Pts	AG	AA	APts	PIM	PP	SH	GW	S	%	TGF	PGF	TGA	PGA	+/–	GP	G	A	Pts	PIM	PP	SH	GW
1996-97	Czech Republic	W Cup	2	0	0	0	....	....	....	0	....	....	....	....	....	....	....	....	....	....	....	....	....	....	....	....	....	....
	AIK Solna	Sweden	49	16	23	39	....	....	....	38	....	....	....	....	....	....	....	....	....	....	7	2	3	5	8	....	....	....
	Czech Republic	WC-A	9	7	7	14	....	....	....	4	....	....	....	....	....	....	....	....	....	....	....	....	....	....	....	....	....	....
1997-98	**Toronto Maple Leafs**	**NHL**	**29**	**2**	**4**	**6**	**2**	**4**	**6**	**8**	**0**	**0**	**0**	**40**	**5.0**	**13**	**4**	**11**	**1**	**–1**	....	....	....	....	....	....	....	....
	Czech Republic	Olympics	6	1	1	2	....	....	....	0	....	....	....	....	....	....	....	....	....	....	....	....	....	....	....	....	....	....
	Czech Republic	WC-A	9	3	5	8	....	....	....	14	....	....	....	....	....	....	....	....	....	....	....	....	....	....	....	....	....	....
	NHL Totals		**29**	**2**	**4**	**6**	**2**	**4**	**6**	**8**	**0**	**0**	**0**	**40**	**5.0**	**13**	**4**	**11**	**1**		....	....	....	....	....	....	....	....

WC-A All-Star Team (1997)

• PROKHOROV, VITALI

Vitali Prokhorov LW – L. 5'9", 185 lbs. b: Moscow, USSR, 12/25/1966. St. Louis' 3rd choice, 64th overall, in 1992 Entry Draft.

Season	Club	League	GP	G	A	Pts	AG	AA	APts	PIM	PP	SH	GW	S	%	TGF	PGF	TGA	PGA	+/–	GP	G	A	Pts	PIM	PP	SH	GW
1983-84	Spartak Moscow	USSR	5	0	0	0	....	....	....	0	....	....	....	....	....	....	....	....	....	....	....	....	....	....	....	....	....	....
1984-85	Spartak Moscow	USSR	31	1	1	2	....	....	....	10	....	....	....	....	....	....	....	....	....	....	....	....	....	....	....	....	....	....
1985-86	Spartak Moscow	USSR	29	3	9	12	....	....	....	4	....	....	....	....	....	....	....	....	....	....	....	....	....	....	....	....	....	....
1986-87	Spartak Moscow	USSR	27	1	6	7	....	....	....	2	....	....	....	....	....	....	....	....	....	....	....	....	....	....	....	....	....	....
1987-88	Spartak Moscow	USSR	19	5	0	5	....	....	....	4	....	....	....	....	....	....	....	....	....	....	....	....	....	....	....	....	....	....
1988-89	Spartak Moscow	USSR	37	11	5	16	....	....	....	10	....	....	....	....	....	....	....	....	....	....	....	....	....	....	....	....	....	....
1989-90	Spartak Moscow	FrTour	1	0	0	0	....	....	....	0	....	....	....	....	....	....	....	....	....	....	....	....	....	....	....	....	....	....
	Spartak Moscow	USSR	43	13	8	21	....	....	....	35	....	....	....	....	....	....	....	....	....	....	....	....	....	....	....	....	....	....
1990-91	Spartak Moscow	FrTour	1	0	1	1	....	....	....	0	....	....	....	....	....	....	....	....	....	....	....	....	....	....	....	....	....	....
	Spartak Moscow	USSR	43	21	10	31	....	....	....	29	....	....	....	....	....	....	....	....	....	....	....	....	....	....	....	....	....	....
1991-92	Soviet Union	C Cup	5	1	2	3	....	....	....	4	....	....	....	....	....	....	....	....	....	....	....	....	....	....	....	....	....	....
	Spartak Moscow	CIS	38	13	19	32	....	....	....	68	....	....	....	....	....	....	....	....	....	....	....	....	....	....	....	....	....	....
	Russia	Olympics	8	2	4	6	....	....	....	6	....	....	....	....	....	....	....	....	....	....	....	....	....	....	....	....	....	....
	Russia	WC-A	6	0	3	3	....	....	....	4	....	....	....	....	....	....	....	....	....	....	....	....	....	....	....	....	....	....
1992-93	**St. Louis Blues**	**NHL**	**26**	**4**	**1**	**5**	**3**	**1**	**4**	**15**	**0**	**0**	**1**	**21**	**19.0**	**8**	**2**	**10**	**0**	**–4**	....	....	....	....	....	....	....	....
1993-94	**St. Louis Blues**	**NHL**	**55**	**15**	**10**	**25**	**14**	**8**	**22**	**20**	**3**	**0**	**1**	**85**	**17.6**	**30**	**4**	**32**	**0**	**–6**	**4**	**0**	**0**	**0**	**0**	**0**	**0**	**0**
	Peoria Rivermen	IHL	19	13	10	23	....	....	....	16	....	....	....	....	....	....	....	....	....	....	....	....	....	....	....	....	....	....
1994-95	Spartak Moscow	CIS	8	1	4	5	....	....	....	8	....	....	....	....	....	....	....	....	....	....	....	....	....	....	....	....	....	....
	St. Louis Blues	**NHL**	**2**	**0**	**0**	**0**	**0**	**0**	**0**	**0**	**0**	**0**	**0**	**0**	**0.0**	**1**	**0**	**0**	**0**	**+1**	....	....	....	....	....	....	....	....
	Peoria Rivermen	IHL	20	6	3	9	....	....	....	6	....	....	....	....	....	....	....	....	....	....	9	4	7	11	6	....	....	....
1995-96	Farjestads BK Karlstad	Sweden	37	7	11	18	....	....	....	61	....	....	....	....	....	....	....	....	....	....	8	2	0	2	31	....	....	....
	NHL Totals		**83**	**19**	**11**	**30**	**17**	**9**	**26**	**35**	**3**	**0**	**2**	**106**	**17.9**	**39**	**6**	**42**	**0**		**4**	**0**	**0**	**0**	**0**	**0**	**0**	**0**

• PROKOPEC, MIKE

Mike Prokopec RW – R. 6'2", 190 lbs. b: Toronto, Ont., 5/17/1974. Chicago's 7th choice, 161st overall, in 1992 Entry Draft.

Season	Club	League	GP	G	A	Pts	AG	AA	APts	PIM	PP	SH	GW	S	%	TGF	PGF	TGA	PGA	+/–	GP	G	A	Pts	PIM	PP	SH	GW
1991-92	Cornwall Royals	OHL	59	12	15	27	....	....	....	75	....	....	....	....	....	....	....	....	....	....	6	0	0	0	0	....	....	....
1992-93	Newmarket Royals	OHL	40	6	14	20	....	....	....	70	....	....	....	....	....	....	....	....	....	....	....	....	....	....	....	....	....	....
	Guelph Platers	OHL	28	10	14	24	....	....	....	27	....	....	....	....	....	....	....	....	....	....	5	1	0	1	14	....	....	....
1993-94	Guelph Platers	OHL	66	52	58	110	....	....	....	93	....	....	....	....	....	....	....	....	....	....	9	12	4	16	17	....	....	....
1994-95	Indianapolis Ice	IHL	70	21	12	33	....	....	....	80	....	....	....	....	....	....	....	....	....	....	....	....	....	....	....	....	....	....
1995-96	**Chicago Blackhawks**	**NHL**	**9**	**0**	**0**	**0**	**0**	**0**	**0**	**5**	**0**	**0**	**0**	**5**	**0.0**	**1**	**0**	**5**	**0**	**–4**	....	....	....	....	....	....	....	....
	Indianapolis Ice	IHL	67	18	22	40	....	....	....	131	....	....	....	....	....	....	....	....	....	....	5	2	0	2	4	....	....	....
1996-97	**Chicago Blackhawks**	**NHL**	**6**	**0**	**0**	**0**	**0**	**0**	**0**	**6**	**0**	**0**	**0**	**2**	**0.0**	**1**	**0**	**2**	**0**	**–1**	....	....	....	....	....	....	....	....
	Indianapolis Ice	IHL	57	13	18	31	....	....	....	143	....	....	....	....	....	....	....	....	....	....	....	....	....	....	....	....	....	....
	Detroit Vipers	IHL	3	2	0	2	....	....	....	4	....	....	....	....	....	....	....	....	....	....	8	2	1	3	14	....	....	....
1997-98	Worcester IceCats	AHL	62	21	25	46	....	....	....	112	....	....	....	....	....	....	....	....	....	....	11	1	2	3	10	....	....	....
	NHL Totals		**15**	**0**	**0**	**0**	**0**	**0**	**0**	**11**	**0**	**0**	**0**	**7**	**0.0**	**2**	**0**	**7**	**0**		....	....	....	....	....	....	....	....

Traded to **Ottawa** by **Chicago** for Denis Chasse, the rights to Kevin Bolibruck and future considerations, March 18, 1997.

• PRONGER, CHRIS

Chris Pronger D – L. 6'5", 220 lbs. b: Dryden, Ont., 10/10/1974. Hartford's 1st choice, 2nd overall, in 1993 Entry Draft.

Season	Club	League	GP	G	A	Pts	AG	AA	APts	PIM	PP	SH	GW	S	%	TGF	PGF	TGA	PGA	+/–	GP	G	A	Pts	PIM	PP	SH	GW
1991-92	Peterborough Petes	OHL	63	17	45	62	....	....	....	90	....	....	....	....	....	....	....	....	....	....	10	1	8	9	28	....	....	....
1992-93	Peterborough Petes	OHL	61	15	62	77	....	....	....	108	....	....	....	....	....	....	....	....	....	....	21	15	25	40	51	....	....	....
	Canada	WJC-A	7	1	3	4	....	....	....	6	....	....	....	....	....	....	....	....	....	....	....	....	....	....	....	....	....	....
1993-94	**Hartford Whalers**	**NHL**	**81**	**5**	**25**	**30**	**5**	**19**	**24**	**113**	**2**	**0**	**0**	**174**	**2.9**	**81**	**22**	**99**	**37**	**–3**	....	....	....	....	....	....	....	....
1994-95	**Hartford Whalers**	**NHL**	**43**	**5**	**9**	**14**	**9**	**13**	**22**	**54**	**3**	**0**	**1**	**94**	**5.3**	**40**	**11**	**55**	**14**	**–12**	....	....	....	....	....	....	....	....
1995-96	**St. Louis Blues**	**NHL**	**78**	**7**	**18**	**25**	**7**	**15**	**22**	**110**	**3**	**1**	**1**	**138**	**5.1**	**86**	**29**	**106**	**31**	**–18**	**13**	**1**	**5**	**6**	**16**	**0**	**0**	**0**
1996-97	**St. Louis Blues**	**NHL**	**79**	**11**	**24**	**35**	**12**	**21**	**33**	**143**	**4**	**0**	**0**	**147**	**7.5**	**103**	**26**	**90**	**28**	**+15**	**6**	**1**	**1**	**2**	**22**	**0**	**0**	**0**
	Canada	WC-A	9	0	2	2	....	....	....	12	....	....	....	....	....	....	....	....	....	....	....	....	....	....	....	....	....	....
1997-98	**St. Louis Blues**	**NHL**	**81**	**9**	**27**	**36**	**11**	**26**	**37**	**180**	**1**	**0**	**2**	**145**	**6.2**	**118**	**15**	**84**	**28**	**+47**	**10**	**1**	**9**	**10**	**26**	**0**	**0**	**0**
	Canada	Olympics	6	0	0	0	....	....	....	4	....	....	....	....	....	....	....	....	....	....	....	....	....	....	....	....	....	....
	NHL Totals		**362**	**37**	**103**	**140**	**44**	**94**	**138**	**600**	**13**	**1**	**4**	**698**	**5.3**	**428**	**103**	**434**	**138**		**29**	**3**	**15**	**18**	**64**	**0**	**0**	**0**

OHL First All-Star Team (1993) • Canadian Major Junior First All-Star Team (1993) • Canadian Major Junior Defenseman of the Year (1993) • NHL/Upper Deck All-Rookie Team (1994) • NHL Second All-Star Team (1998) • Won Bud Ice Plus/Minus Award (1998)

Traded to **St. Louis** by **Hartford** for Brendan Shanahan, July 27, 1995.

• PRONGER, SEAN

Sean Pronger C – L. 6'2", 205 lbs. b: Dryden, Ont., 11/30/1972. Vancouver's 3rd choice, 51st overall, in 1991 Entry Draft.

Season	Club	League	GP	G	A	Pts	AG	AA	APts	PIM	PP	SH	GW	S	%	TGF	PGF	TGA	PGA	+/–	GP	G	A	Pts	PIM	PP	SH	GW
1990-91	Bowling Green University	CCHA	40	3	7	10	....	....	....	30	....	....	....	....	....	....	....	....	....	....	....	....	....	....	....	....	....	....
1991-92	Bowling Green University	CCHA	34	9	7	16	....	....	....	28	....	....	....	....	....	....	....	....	....	....	....	....	....	....	....	....	....	....
1992-93	Bowling Green University	CCHA	39	23	23	46	....	....	....	35	....	....	....	....	....	....	....	....	....	....	....	....	....	....	....	....	....	....
1993-94	Bowling Green University	CCHA	38	17	17	34	....	....	....	38	....	....	....	....	....	....	....	....	....	....	....	....	....	....	....	....	....	....
1994-95	Knoxville Cherokees	ECHL	34	18	23	41	....	....	....	55	....	....	....	....	....	....	....	....	....	....	....	....	....	....	....	....	....	....
	Greensboro Monarchs	ECHL	2	0	2	2	....	....	....	0	....	....	....	....	....	....	....	....	....	....	....	....	....	....	....	....	....	....
	San Diego Gulls	IHL	8	0	0	0	....	....	....	2	....	....	....	....	....	....	....	....	....	....	....	....	....	....	....	....	....	....
1995-96	**Anaheim Mighty Ducks**	**NHL**	**7**	**0**	**1**	**1**	**0**	**1**	**1**	**6**	**0**	**0**	**0**	**3**	**0.0**	**2**	**0**	**2**	**0**	**0**	....	....	....	....	....	....	....	....
	Baltimore Bandits	AHL	72	16	17	33	....	....	....	61	....	....	....	....	....	....	....	....	....	....	12	3	7	10	16	....	....	....
1996-97	**Anaheim Mighty Ducks**	**NHL**	**39**	**7**	**7**	**14**	**7**	**6**	**13**	**20**	**1**	**0**	**1**	**43**	**16.3**	**23**	**2**	**18**	**3**	**+6**	**9**	**0**	**2**	**2**	**4**	**0**	**0**	**0**
	Baltimore Bandits	AHL	41	26	17	43	....	....	....	17	....	....	....	....	....	....	....	....	....	....	....	....	....	....	....	....	....	....
1997-98	**Anaheim Mighty Ducks**	**NHL**	**62**	**5**	**15**	**20**	**6**	**15**	**21**	**30**	**1**	**0**	**2**	**68**	**7.4**	**35**	**11**	**37**	**4**	**–9**	....	....	....	....	....	....	....	....
	Pittsburgh Penguins	**NHL**	**5**	**1**	**0**	**1**	**1**	**0**	**1**	**2**	**0**	**0**	**1**	**5**	**20.0**	**2**	**0**	**3**	**0**	**–1**	**5**	**0**	**0**	**0**	**4**	**0**	**0**	**0**
	NHL Totals		**113**	**13**	**23**	**36**	**14**	**22**	**36**	**58**	**2**	**0**	**4**	**119**	**10.9**	**62**	**13**	**60**	**7**		**14**	**0**	**2**	**2**	**8**	**0**	**0**	**0**

Signed as a free agent by **Anaheim**, February 14, 1995. Traded to **Pittsburgh** by **Anaheim** for the rights to Patrick Lalime, March 24, 1998.

• PRONOVOST, ANDRE

Andre Pronovost LW – L. 5'10", 188 lbs. b: Shawinigan Falls, Que., 7/9/1936.

Season	Club	League	GP	G	A	Pts	AG	AA	APts	PIM	PP	SH	GW	S	%	TGF	PGF	TGA	PGA	+/–	GP	G	A	Pts	PIM	PP	SH	GW
1953-54	Verdun Jr. Canadiens	QJHL	54	31	46	77	....	....	....	28	....	....	....	....	....	....	....	....	....	....	8	3	2	5	2	....	....	....
1954-55	Montreal Jr. Canadiens	QJHL	42	22	13	35	....	....	....	60	....	....	....	....	....	....	....	....	....	....	5	1	3	4	4	....	....	....
1955-56	Montreal Jr. Canadiens	QJHL	....	....	....	....	....	....	....	....	....	....	....	....	....	....	....	....	....	....	....	....	....	....	....	....	....	....
	Shawinigan Cataracts	QHL	3	0	1	1	....	....	....	4	....	....	....	....	....	....	....	....	....	....	....	....	....	....	....	....	....	....
1956-57	**Montreal Canadiens**	**NHL**	**64**	**10**	**11**	**21**	**14**	**13**	**27**	**58**	....	....	....	....	....	....	....	....	....	....	**8**	**1**	**0**	**1**	**4**	....	....	....
	Shawinigan Cataracts	QHL	7	2	2	4	....	....	....	11	....	....	....	....	....	....	....	....	....	....	....	....	....	....	....	....	....	....
1957-58	**Montreal Canadiens**	**NHL**	**66**	**16**	**12**	**28**	**21**	**13**	**34**	**55**	....	....	....	....	....	....	....	....	....	....	**10**	**2**	**0**	**2**	**16**	....	....	....
1958-59	**Montreal Canadiens**	**NHL**	**70**	**9**	**14**	**23**	**11**	**15**	**26**	**48**	....	....	....	....	....	....	....	....	....	....	**11**	**2**	**1**	**3**	**6**	....	....	....
1959-60	**Montreal Canadiens**	**NHL**	**69**	**12**	**19**	**31**	**15**	**19**	**34**	**61**	....	....	....	....	....	....	....	....	....	....	**8**	**1**	**2**	**3**	**0**	....	....	....
1960-61	**Montreal Canadiens**	**NHL**	**21**	**1**	**5**	**6**	**1**	**5**	**6**	**4**	....	....	....	....	....	....	....	....	....	....	....	....	....	....	....	....	....	....
	Boston Bruins	**NHL**	**47**	**11**	**11**	**22**	**13**	**11**	**24**	**30**	....	....	....	....	....	....	....	....	....	....	....	....	....	....	....	....	....	....
1961-62	**Boston Bruins**	**NHL**	**70**	**15**	**8**	**23**	**18**	**8**	**26**	**74**	....	....	....	....	....	....	....	....	....	....	....	....	....	....	....	....	....	....
1962-63	**Boston Bruins**	**NHL**	**21**	**0**	**2**	**2**	**0**	**2**	**2**	**6**	....	....	....	....	....	....	....	....	....	....	....	....	....	....	....	....	....	....
	Detroit Red Wings	**NHL**	**47**	**13**	**5**	**18**	**16**	**5**	**21**	**18**	....	....	....	....	....	....	....	....	....	....	**11**	**1**	**4**	**5**	**6**	....	....	....
1963-64	**Detroit Red Wings**	**NHL**	**70**	**7**	**16**	**23**	**9**	**18**	**27**	**54**	....	....	....	....	....	....	....	....	....	....	**14**	**4**	**3**	**7**	**26**	....	....	....
1964-65	**Detroit Red Wings**	**NHL**	**3**	**0**	**1**	**1**	**0**	**1**	**1**	**0**	....	....	....	....	....	....	....	....	....	....	....	....	....	....	....	....	....	....
	Pittsburgh Hornets	AHL	22	2	5	7	....	....	....	4	....	....	....	....	....	....	....	....	....	....	....	....	....	....	....	....	....	....
	Memphis Wings	CHL	55	23	38	61	....	....	....	75	....	....	....	....	....	....	....	....	....	....	....	....	....	....	....	....	....	....

Season	Club	League	GP	G	A	Pts	AG	AA	APts	PIM	PP	SH	GW	S	%	TGF	PGF	TGA	PGA	+/–	GP	G	A	Pts	PIM	PP	SH	GW
			REGULAR SEASON																		PLAYOFFS							
1965-66	Pittsburgh Hornets	AHL	72	25	21	46	....	....	....	64	....	....	....	....	....	....	....	....	....	....	3	0	1	1	0	....	....	....
1966-67	Memphis Wings	CHL	70	25	42	67	....	....	....	85	....	....	....	....	....	....	....	....	....	....	7	1	1	2	19	....	....	....
1967-68	**Minnesota North Stars**	**NHL**	**8**	**0**	**0**	**0**	**0**	**0**	**0**	**0**	**0**	**0**	**0**	**6**	**0.0**	**1**	**0**	**2**	**1**	**0**	**8**	**0**	**1**	**1**	**0**	**0**	**0**	**0**
	Memphis South Stars	CHL	60	20	18	38	....	....	....	43	....	....	....	....	....	....	....	....	....	....	3	2	1	3	0	....	....	....
1968-69	Phoenix Roadrunners	WHL	51	18	14	32	....	....	....	31	....	....	....	....	....	....	....	....	....	....	....	....	....	....	....	....	....	....
	Baltimore Clippers	AHL	25	1	4	5	....	....	....	2	....	....	....	....	....	....	....	....	....	....	4	0	0	0	0	....	....	....
1969-70	Muskegon Mohawks	IHL	71	50	57	107	....	....	....	55	....	....	....	....	....	....	....	....	....	....	6	0	3	3	8	....	....	....
1970-71	Muskegon Mohawks	IHL	60	18	24	42	....	....	....	24	....	....	....	....	....	....	....	....	....	....	6	2	0	2	2	....	....	....
1971-72	Jersey Devils	EHL	5	2	1	3	....	....	....	2	....	....	....	....	....	....	....	....	....	....	....	....	....	....	....	....	....	....
	NHL Totals		**556**	**94**	**104**	**198**	**118**	**110**	**228**	**408**	**0**	**0**	**0**	**6**	**1567**	**1**	**0**	**2**	**1**		**70**	**11**	**11**	**22**	**58**	**0**	**0**	**0**

IHL First All-Star Team (1970)

Played in NHL All-Star Game (1957, 1958, 1959, 1960)

Traded to **Boston** by **Montreal** for Jean-Guy Gendron, November 27, 1960. Traded to **Detroit** by **Boston** for Forbes Kennedy, December, 1962. Claimed by **Minnesota** from **Detroit** in Expansion Draft, June 6, 1967. Traded to **Montreal** by **Minnesota** for cash, September, 1969.

• PRONOVOST, JEAN

Jean Pronovost RW – R. 6', 185 lbs. b: Shawinigan Falls, Que., 12/18/1945.

Season	Club	League	GP	G	A	Pts	AG	AA	APts	PIM	PP	SH	GW	S	%	TGF	PGF	TGA	PGA	+/–	GP	G	A	Pts	PIM	PP	SH	GW
1963-64	Victoriaville Bruins	QJHL	STATISTICS NOT AVAILABLE																									
1964-65	Niagara Falls Flyers	OHA	54	30	40	70	....	....	....	40	....	....	....	....	....	....	....	....	....	....	11	4	8	12	8	....	....	....
1965-66	Niagara Falls Flyers	OHA	48	18	34	52	....	....	....	47	....	....	....	....	....	....	....	....	....	....	....	....	....	....	....	....	....	....
1966-67	Oklahoma City Blazers	CHL	68	21	24	45	....	....	....	81	....	....	....	....	....	....	....	....	....	....	11	5	2	7	12	....	....	....
1967-68	Oklahoma City Blazers	CHL	49	25	25	50	....	....	....	41	....	....	....	....	....	....	....	....	....	....	7	3	4	7	6	....	....	....
1968-69	**Pittsburgh Penguins**	**NHL**	**76**	**16**	**25**	**41**	**18**	**23**	**41**	**41**	**4**	**2**	**1**	**199**	**8.0**	**57**	**14**	**50**	**3**	**–4**	....	....	....	....	....	....	....	....
1969-70	**Pittsburgh Penguins**	**NHL**	**72**	**20**	**21**	**41**	**23**	**21**	**44**	**45**	**5**	**0**	**6**	**222**	**9.0**	**57**	**16**	**44**	**1**	**–2**	**10**	**3**	**4**	**7**	**2**	**1**	**1**	**0**
1970-71	**Pittsburgh Penguins**	**NHL**	**78**	**21**	**24**	**45**	**22**	**21**	**43**	**35**	**4**	**0**	**2**	**225**	**9.3**	**70**	**15**	**54**	**7**	**+8**	....	....	....	....	....	....	....	....
1971-72	**Pittsburgh Penguins**	**NHL**	**68**	**30**	**23**	**53**	**32**	**21**	**53**	**12**	**3**	**1**	**3**	**214**	**14.0**	**75**	**18**	**51**	**9**	**+15**	**4**	**1**	**1**	**2**	**0**	**0**	**1**	**0**
1972-73	**Pittsburgh Penguins**	**NHL**	**66**	**21**	**22**	**43**	**21**	**18**	**39**	**16**	**2**	**1**	**5**	**192**	**10.9**	**68**	**16**	**78**	**11**	**–15**	....	....	....	....	....	....	....	....
1973-74	**Pittsburgh Penguins**	**NHL**	**77**	**40**	**32**	**72**	**41**	**28**	**69**	**22**	**8**	**4**	**2**	**248**	**16.1**	**107**	**27**	**82**	**11**	**+9**	....	....	....	....	....	....	....	....
1974-75	**Pittsburgh Penguins**	**NHL**	**78**	**43**	**32**	**75**	**40**	**25**	**65**	**37**	**11**	**1**	**9**	**275**	**15.6**	**108**	**28**	**81**	**14**	**+13**	**9**	**3**	**3**	**6**	**6**	**0**	**0**	**0**
1975-76	**Pittsburgh Penguins**	**NHL**	**80**	**52**	**52**	**104**	**49**	**41**	**90**	**24**	**13**	**2**	**3**	**299**	**17.4**	**148**	**51**	**92**	**11**	**+16**	**3**	**0**	**0**	**0**	**2**	**0**	**0**	**0**
1976-77	**Pittsburgh Penguins**	**NHL**	**79**	**33**	**31**	**64**	**32**	**25**	**57**	**24**	**7**	**1**	**6**	**217**	**15.2**	**89**	**25**	**79**	**23**	**+8**	**3**	**2**	**1**	**3**	**2**	**1**	**0**	**0**
	Canada	WEC-A	7	2	2	4	....	....	....	0	....	....	....	....	....	....	....	....	....	....	....	....	....	....	....	....	....	....
1977-78	**Pittsburgh Penguins**	**NHL**	**79**	**40**	**25**	**65**	**39**	**20**	**59**	**50**	**12**	**2**	**5**	**219**	**18.3**	**102**	**36**	**106**	**24**	**–16**	....	....	....	....	....	....	....	....
	Canada	WEC-A	10	2	3	5	....	....	....	0	....	....	....	....	....	....	....	....	....	....	....	....	....	....	....	....	....	....
1978-79	**Atlanta Flames**	**NHL**	**75**	**28**	**39**	**67**	**25**	**30**	**55**	**30**	**4**	**2**	**8**	**151**	**18.5**	**86**	**22**	**48**	**5**	**+21**	**2**	**2**	**0**	**2**	**0**	**1**	**0**	**0**
1979-80	**Atlanta Flames**	**NHL**	**80**	**24**	**19**	**43**	**22**	**15**	**37**	**12**	**6**	**0**	**3**	**119**	**20.2**	**66**	**14**	**72**	**32**	**+12**	**4**	**0**	**0**	**0**	**2**	**0**	**0**	**0**
1980-81	**Washington Capitals**	**NHL**	**80**	**22**	**36**	**58**	**18**	**25**	**43**	**61**	**6**	**1**	**4**	**188**	**11.7**	**91**	**34**	**88**	**22**	**–9**	....	....	....	....	....	....	....	....
1981-82	**Washington Capitals**	**NHL**	**10**	**1**	**2**	**3**	**1**	**1**	**2**	**4**	**0**	**0**	**0**	**15**	**6.7**	**6**	**1**	**13**	**1**	**–7**	....	....	....	....	....	....	....	....
	Hershey Bears	AHL	64	35	31	66	....	....	....	18	....	....	....	....	....	....	....	....	....	....	5	1	1	2	0	....	....	....
	NHL Totals		**998**	**391**	**383**	**774**	**383**	**314**	**697**	**413**	**85**	**17**	**57**	**2783**	**14.0**	**1130**	**317**	**938**	**174**		**35**	**11**	**9**	**20**	**14**	**3**	**2**	**0**

Played in NHL All-Star Game (1975, 1976, 1977, 1978)

Traded to **Pittsburgh** by **Boston** for cash, May 21, 1968. Traded to **Atlanta** by **Pittsburgh** for Gregg Sheppard, September 6, 1978. Transferred to **Calgary** after **Atlanta** franchise relocated, June 23, 1980. Traded to **Washington** by **Calgary** for cash, July 1, 1980.

• PRONOVOST, MARCEL

Marcel Pronovost D – L. 6', 190 lbs. b: Shawinigan Falls, Que., 6/15/1930. **HHOF**

Season	Club	League	GP	G	A	Pts	AG	AA	APts	PIM	PP	SH	GW	S	%	TGF	PGF	TGA	PGA	+/–	GP	G	A	Pts	PIM	PP	SH	GW
1947-48	Windsor Spitfires	OHA	33	6	18	24	....	....	....	61	....	....	....	....	....	....	....	....	....	....	12	1	3	4	28	....	....	....
	Detroit Auto Club	IHL	19	5	3	8	....	....	....	53	....	....	....	....	....	....	....	....	....	....	....	....	....	....	....	....	....	....
1948-49	Windsor Spitfires	OHA	42	14	23	37	....	....	....	126	....	....	....	....	....	....	....	....	....	....	4	1	5	6	2	....	....	....
	Detroit Auto Club	IHL	9	4	4	8	....	....	....	24	....	....	....	....	....	....	....	....	....	....	6	3	1	4	15	....	....	....
1949-50	Omaha Knights	USHL	69	13	39	52	....	....	....	100	....	....	....	....	....	....	....	....	....	....	7	4	*9	*13	9	....	....	....
	Detroit Red Wings	**NHL**	....	....	....	....	....	....	....	....	....	....	....	....	....	....	....	....	....	....	**9**	**0**	**1**	**1**	**10**	....	....	....
1950-51	**Detroit Red Wings**	**NHL**	**37**	**1**	**6**	**7**	**1**	**8**	**9**	**20**	....	....	....	....	....	....	....	....	....	....	**6**	**0**	**0**	**0**	**0**	....	....	....
	Indianapolis Capitals	AHL	34	9	23	32	....	....	....	44	....	....	....	....	....	....	....	....	....	....	....	....	....	....	....	....	....	....
1951-52	**Detroit Red Wings**	**NHL**	**69**	**7**	**11**	**18**	**10**	**14**	**24**	**50**	....	....	....	....	....	....	....	....	....	....	**8**	**0**	**1**	**1**	**10**	....	....	....
1952-53	**Detroit Red Wings**	**NHL**	**68**	**8**	**19**	**27**	**12**	**27**	**39**	**72**	....	....	....	....	....	....	....	....	....	....	**8**	**0**	**0**	**0**	**6**	....	....	....
1953-54	**Detroit Red Wings**	**NHL**	**57**	**6**	**12**	**18**	**9**	**16**	**25**	**50**	....	....	....	....	....	....	....	....	....	....	**12**	**2**	**3**	**5**	**12**	....	....	....
1954-55	**Detroit Red Wings**	**NHL**	**70**	**9**	**25**	**34**	**13**	**32**	**45**	**90**	....	....	....	....	....	....	....	....	....	....	**11**	**1**	**2**	**3**	**6**	....	....	....
1955-56	**Detroit Red Wings**	**NHL**	**68**	**4**	**13**	**17**	**6**	**16**	**22**	**46**	....	....	....	....	....	....	....	....	....	....	**10**	**0**	**2**	**2**	**8**	....	....	....
1956-57	**Detroit Red Wings**	**NHL**	**70**	**7**	**9**	**16**	**9**	**10**	**19**	**38**	....	....	....	....	....	....	....	....	....	....	**5**	**0**	**0**	**0**	**6**	....	....	....
1957-58	**Detroit Red Wings**	**NHL**	**62**	**2**	**18**	**20**	**3**	**20**	**23**	**52**	....	....	....	....	....	....	....	....	....	....	**4**	**0**	**1**	**1**	**4**	....	....	....
1958-59	**Detroit Red Wings**	**NHL**	**69**	**11**	**21**	**32**	**14**	**22**	**36**	**44**	....	....	....	....	....	....	....	....	....	....	....	....	....	....	....	....	....	....
1959-60	**Detroit Red Wings**	**NHL**	**69**	**7**	**17**	**24**	**9**	**17**	**26**	**38**	....	....	....	....	....	....	....	....	....	....	**6**	**1**	**1**	**2**	**2**	....	....	....
1960-61	**Detroit Red Wings**	**NHL**	**70**	**6**	**11**	**17**	**7**	**11**	**18**	**44**	....	....	....	....	....	....	....	....	....	....	**9**	**2**	**3**	**5**	**0**	....	....	....
1961-62	**Detroit Red Wings**	**NHL**	**70**	**4**	**14**	**18**	**5**	**14**	**19**	**38**	....	....	....	....	....	....	....	....	....	....	....	....	....	....	....	....	....	....
1962-63	**Detroit Red Wings**	**NHL**	**69**	**4**	**9**	**13**	**5**	**9**	**14**	**48**	....	....	....	....	....	....	....	....	....	....	**11**	**1**	**4**	**5**	**8**	....	....	....
1963-64	**Detroit Red Wings**	**NHL**	**67**	**3**	**17**	**20**	**4**	**19**	**23**	**42**	....	....	....	....	....	....	....	....	....	....	**14**	**0**	**2**	**2**	**14**	....	....	....
1964-65	**Detroit Red Wings**	**NHL**	**68**	**1**	**15**	**16**	**1**	**16**	**17**	**45**	....	....	....	....	....	....	....	....	....	....	**7**	**0**	**3**	**3**	**4**	....	....	....
1965-66	**Toronto Maple Leafs**	**NHL**	**54**	**2**	**8**	**10**	**2**	**8**	**10**	**34**	....	....	....	....	....	....	....	....	....	....	**4**	**0**	**0**	**0**	**6**	....	....	....
1966-67	**Toronto Maple Leafs**	**NHL**	**58**	**2**	**12**	**14**	**2**	**12**	**14**	**28**	....	....	....	....	....	....	....	....	....	....	**12**	**1**	**0**	**1**	**8**	....	....	....
1967-68	**Toronto Maple Leafs**	**NHL**	**70**	**3**	**17**	**20**	**4**	**18**	**22**	**48**	**0**	**0**	**1**	**70**	**4.3**	**70**	**0**	**82**	**12**	**0**	....	....	....	....	....	....	....	....
1968-69	**Toronto Maple Leafs**	**NHL**	**34**	**1**	**2**	**3**	**1**	**2**	**3**	**20**	**0**	**0**	**0**	**18**	**5.6**	**18**	**1**	**26**	**7**	**–2**	....	....	....	....	....	....	....	....
1969-70	**Toronto Maple Leafs**	**NHL**	**7**	**0**	**1**	**1**	**0**	**1**	**1**	**4**	**0**	**0**	**0**	**2**	**0.0**	**10**	**0**	**6**	**1**	**+5**	....	....	....	....	....	....	....	....
	Tulsa Oilers	CHL	53	1	16	17	....	....	....	24	....	....	....	....	....	....	....	....	....	....	....	....	....	....	....	....	....	....
1970-71	Tulsa Oilers	CHL	17	0	0	0	....	....	....	4	....	....	....	....	....	....	....	....	....	....	2	0	0	0	0	....	....	....
	NHL Totals		**1206**	**88**	**257**	**345**	**117**	**292**	**409**	**851**	**0**	**0**	**1**	**90**	**97.8**	**98**	**1**	**114**	**20**		**134**	**8**	**23**	**31**	**104**	**0**	**0**	**0**

USHL First All-Star Team (1950) • Won Outstanding Rookie Cup (Top Rookie - USHL) (1950) • AHL Second All-Star Team (1951) • NHL Second All-Star Team (1958, 1959) • NHL First All-Star Team (1960, 1961)

Played in NHL All-Star Game (1950, 1954, 1955, 1957, 1958, 1959, 1960, 1961, 1963, 1965, 1968)

Traded to **Toronto** by **Detroit** with Aut Erickson, Larry Jeffrey, Ed Joyal and Lowell MacDonald for Billy Harris, Gary Jarrett and Andy Bathgate, May 20, 1965.

• PROPP, BRIAN

Brian Propp LW – L. 5'10", 195 lbs. b: Lanigan, Sask., 2/15/1959. Philadelphia's 1st choice, 14th overall, in 1979 Entry Draft.

Season	Club	League	GP	G	A	Pts	AG	AA	APts	PIM	PP	SH	GW	S	%	TGF	PGF	TGA	PGA	+/–	GP	G	A	Pts	PIM	PP	SH	GW
1975-76	Melville Millionaires	SJHL	57	76	92	168	....	....	....	36	....	....	....	....	....	....	....	....	....	....	....	....	....	....	....	....	....	....
1976-77	Brandon Wheat Kings	WCJHL	72	55	80	135	....	....	....	47	....	....	....	....	....	....	....	....	....	....	16	*14	12	26	5	....	....	....
1977-78	Brandon Wheat Kings	WCJHL	70	70	*112	*182	....	....	....	200	....	....	....	....	....	....	....	....	....	....	8	7	6	13	12	....	....	....
1978-79	Brandon Wheat Kings	WHL	71	*94	*100	*194	....	....	....	127	....	....	....	....	....	....	....	....	....	....	22	15	23	*38	40	....	....	....
	Canada	WJC-A	5	2	1	3	....	....	....	2	....	....	....	....	....	....	....	....	....	....	....	....	....	....	....	....	....	....
1979-80	**Philadelphia Flyers**	**NHL**	**80**	**34**	**41**	**75**	**31**	**32**	**63**	**54**	**4**	**0**	**3**	**209**	**16.3**	**118**	**23**	**51**	**1**	**+45**	**19**	**5**	**10**	**15**	**29**	**3**	**0**	**0**
1980-81	**Philadelphia Flyers**	**NHL**	**79**	**26**	**40**	**66**	**21**	**28**	**49**	**110**	**6**	**0**	**5**	**194**	**13.4**	**104**	**34**	**43**	**0**	**+27**	**12**	**6**	**6**	**12**	**32**	**0**	**0**	**0**
1981-82	**Philadelphia Flyers**	**NHL**	**80**	**44**	**47**	**91**	**35**	**31**	**66**	**117**	**13**	**0**	**6**	**290**	**15.2**	**130**	**49**	**65**	**3**	**+19**	**4**	**2**	**2**	**4**	**4**	**0**	**0**	**1**
	Canada	WEC-A	10	3	1	4	....	....	....	4	....	....	....	....	....	....	....	....	....	....	....	....	....	....	....	....	....	....
1982-83	**Philadelphia Flyers**	**NHL**	**80**	**40**	**42**	**82**	**33**	**29**	**62**	**72**	**13**	**1**	**12**	**250**	**16.0**	**108**	**28**	**59**	**14**	**+35**	**3**	**1**	**2**	**3**	**8**	**1**	**0**	**0**
	Canada	WEC-A	10	4	4	0	....	....	....	6	....	....	....	....	....	....	....	....	....	....	....	....	....	....	....	....	....	....
1983-84	**Philadelphia Flyers**	**NHL**	**79**	**39**	**53**	**92**	**31**	**36**	**67**	**37**	**11**	**1**	**4**	**301**	**13.0**	**141**	**29**	**89**	**26**	**+49**	**3**	**0**	**1**	**1**	**6**	**0**	**0**	**0**
1984-85	**Philadelphia Flyers**	**NHL**	**76**	**43**	**54**	**97**	**35**	**37**	**72**	**43**	**12**	**7**	**4**	**258**	**16.7**	**141**	**39**	**85**	**29**	**+46**	**19**	**8**	**10**	**18**	**6**	**4**	**1**	**2**
1985-86	**Philadelphia Flyers**	**NHL**	**72**	**40**	**57**	**97**	**32**	**38**	**70**	**47**	**11**	**2**	**5**	**317**	**12.6**	**153**	**64**	**80**	**23**	**+24**	**5**	**0**	**2**	**2**	**4**	**0**	**0**	**0**
1986-87	**Philadelphia Flyers**	**NHL**	**53**	**31**	**36**	**67**	**27**	**26**	**53**	**45**	**8**	**5**	**5**	**208**	**14.9**	**93**	**29**	**45**	**20**	**+39**	**26**	**12**	**16**	**28**	**10**	**5**	**1**	**3**
1987-88	Canada	C Cup	9	2	2	4	....	....	....	2	....	....	....	....	....	....	....	....	....	....	....	....	....	....	....	....	....	....
	Philadelphia Flyers	**NHL**	**74**	**27**	**49**	**76**	**23**	**35**	**58**	**76**	**7**	**2**	**6**	**257**	**10.5**	**119**	**49**	**86**	**24**	**+8**	**7**	**4**	**2**	**6**	**8**	**0**	**0**	**0**
1988-89	**Philadelphia Flyers**	**NHL**	**77**	**32**	**46**	**78**	**27**	**32**	**59**	**37**	**13**	**2**	**5**	**245**	**13.1**	**123**	**52**	**78**	**23**	**+16**	**18**	**14**	**0**	**23**	**14**	**5**	**1**	**1**
1989-90	**Philadelphia Flyers**	**NHL**	**40**	**13**	**15**	**28**	**11**	**11**	**22**	**31**	**5**	**0**	**0**	**108**	**12.0**	**40**	**14**	**30**	**7**	**+3**	....	....	....	....	....	....	....	....
	Boston Bruins	**NHL**	**14**	**3**	**9**	**12**	**3**	**6**	**9**	**10**	**0**	**1**	**0**	**45**	**6.7**	**19**	**6**	**16**	**5**	**+2**	**20**	**4**	**9**	**13**	**2**	**1**	**0**	**2**

Season	Club	League	GP	G	A	Pts	AG	AA	APts	PIM	PP	SH	GW	S	%	TGF	PGF	TGA	PGA	+/–	PO GP	PO G	PO A	PO Pts	PO PIM	PO PP	PO SH	PO GW
1990-91	Minnesota North Stars	FrTour	3	0	1	1	....	....	....	8	....	....	....	....	....	....	....	....	....	....	....	....	....	....	....	....	....	....
	Minnesota North Stars	**NHL**	**79**	**26**	**47**	**73**	**24**	**36**	**60**	**58**	**9**	**0**	**1**	**171**	**15.2**	**110**	**49**	**66**	**12**	**+7**	**23**	**8**	**15**	**23**	**28**	**8**	**0**	**3**
1991-92	**Minnesota North Stars**	**NHL**	**51**	**12**	**23**	**35**	**11**	**17**	**28**	**49**	**4**	**0**	**0**	**115**	**10.4**	**56**	**23**	**37**	**1**	**–3**	**1**	**0**	**0**	**0**	**0**	**0**	**0**	**0**
1992-93	**Minnesota North Stars**	**NHL**	**17**	**3**	**3**	**6**	**2**	**2**	**4**	**0**	**1**	**0**	**1**	**35**	**8.6**	**10**	**7**	**15**	**2**	**–10**	....	....	....	....	....	....	....	....
	Lugano	Switz.	24	21	6	27	....	....	....	32	....	....	....	....	....	....	....	....	....	....	9	5	1	6	28	....	....	....
	Canada	Nat-Team	3	3	1	4	....	....	....	2	....	....	....	....	....	....	....	....	....	....	....	....	....	....	....	....	....	....
1993-94	**Hartford Whalers**	**NHL**	**65**	**12**	**17**	**29**	**11**	**13**	**24**	**44**	**3**	**1**	**2**	**108**	**11.1**	**39**	**11**	**43**	**18**	**+3**	....	....	....	....	....	....	....	....
	NHL Totals		**1016**	**425**	**579**	**1004**	**357**	**409**	**766**	**830**	**120**	**22**	**59**	**3111**	**13.7**	**1504**	**506**	**896**	**208**		**160**	**64**	**84**	**148**	**151**	**27**	**3**	**12**

WCJHL All-Star Team (1978) • WHL All-Star Team (1979)

Played in NHL All-Star Game (1980, 1982, 1984, 1986, 1990)

Traded to **Boston** by **Philadelphia** for Boston's 2nd round choice (Terran Sandwith) in 1990 Entry Draft, March 2, 1990. Signed as a free agent by **Minnesota**, July 25, 1990. Signed as a free agent by **Hartford**, October 4, 1993.

• PROSPAL, VACLAV

Vaclav Prospal C – L. 6'2", 185 lbs. b: Ceske-Budejovice, Czech., 2/17/1975. Philadelphia's 2nd choice, 71st overall, in 1993 Entry Draft.

Season	Club	League	GP	G	A	Pts	AG	AA	APts	PIM	PP	SH	GW	S	%	TGF	PGF	TGA	PGA	+/–	PO GP	PO G	PO A	PO Pts	PO PIM	PO PP	PO SH	PO GW
1992-93	Motor Ceske Budejovice	Czech. Jr.	32	26	31	57	....	....	....	24	....	....	....	....	....	....	....	....	....	....	....	....	....	....	....	....	....	....
1993-94	Hershey Bears	AHL	55	14	21	35	....	....	....	38	....	....	....	....	....	....	....	....	....	....	2	0	0	0	2	....	....	....
	Czech Republic	WJC-A	7	1	1	2	....	....	....	16	....	....	....	....	....	....	....	....	....	....	....	....	....	....	....	....	....	....
1994-95	Hershey Bears	AHL	69	13	32	45	....	....	....	36	....	....	....	....	....	....	....	....	....	....	2	1	0	1	4	....	....	....
	Czech Republic	WJC-A	7	3	7	10	....	....	....	2	....	....	....	....	....	....	....	....	....	....	....	....	....	....	....	....	....	....
1995-96	Hershey Bears	AHL	68	15	36	51	....	....	....	59	....	....	....	....	....	....	....	....	....	....	5	2	4	6	2	....	....	....
1996-97	**Philadelphia Flyers**	**NHL**	**18**	**5**	**10**	**15**	**5**	**9**	**14**	**4**	**0**	**0**	**0**	**35**	**14.3**	**22**	**10**	**9**	**0**	**+3**	**5**	**1**	**3**	**4**	**4**	**0**	**0**	**0**
	Philadelphia Phantoms	AHL	63	32	63	95	....	....	....	70	....	....	....	....	....	....	....	....	....	....	....	....	....	....	....	....	....	....
1997-98	**Philadelphia Flyers**	**NHL**	**41**	**5**	**13**	**18**	**6**	**13**	**19**	**17**	**4**	**0**	**0**	**60**	**8.3**	**25**	**13**	**23**	**1**	**–10**	....	....	....	....	....	....	....	....
	Ottawa Senators	**NHL**	**15**	**1**	**6**	**7**	**1**	**6**	**7**	**4**	**0**	**0**	**0**	**28**	**3.6**	**9**	**4**	**6**	**0**	**–1**	**6**	**0**	**0**	**0**	**0**	**0**	**0**	**0**
	NHL Totals		**74**	**11**	**29**	**40**	**12**	**28**	**40**	**25**	**4**	**0**	**0**	**123**	**8.9**	**56**	**27**	**38**	**1**		**11**	**1**	**3**	**4**	**4**	**0**	**0**	**0**

AHL First All-Star Team (1997)

Traded to **Ottawa** by **Philadelphia** with Pat Falloon and Dallas' 2nd round choice (previously acquired, Ottawa selected Chris Bala) in 1998 Entry Draft for Alexandre Daigle, January 17, 1998.

• PROULX, CHRISTIAN

Christian Proulx D – L. 6', 185 lbs. b: Sherbrooke, Que., 12/10/1973. Montreal's 9th choice, 164th overall, in 1992 Entry Draft.

Season	Club	League	GP	G	A	Pts	AG	AA	APts	PIM	PP	SH	GW	S	%	TGF	PGF	TGA	PGA	+/–	PO GP	PO G	PO A	PO Pts	PO PIM	PO PP	PO SH	PO GW
1990-91	St-Jean Castors	QMJHL	67	1	8	9	....	....	....	73	....	....	....	....	....	....	....	....	....	....	....	....	....	....	....	....	....	....
1991-92	St-Jean Castors	QMJHL	68	1	17	18	....	....	....	180	....	....	....	....	....	....	....	....	....	....	....	....	....	....	....	....	....	....
1992-93	St-Jean Castors	QMJHL	70	3	34	37	....	....	....	147	....	....	....	....	....	....	....	....	....	....	4	0	0	0	12	....	....	....
	Fredericton Canadiens	AHL	2	1	0	1	....	....	....	2	....	....	....	....	....	....	....	....	....	....	4	0	0	0	0	....	....	....
1993-94	**Montreal Canadiens**	**NHL**	**7**	**1**	**2**	**3**	**1**	**2**	**3**	**20**	**0**	**0**	**0**	**11**	**9.1**	**6**	**1**	**5**	**0**	**0**	....	....	....	....	....	....	....	....
	Fredericton Canadiens	AHL	70	2	12	14	....	....	....	183	....	....	....	....	....	....	....	....	....	....	....	....	....	....	....	....	....	....
1994-95	Fredericton Canadiens	AHL	75	1	9	10	....	....	....	184	....	....	....	....	....	....	....	....	....	....	9	0	1	1	8	....	....	....
1995-96	San Francisco Spiders	IHL	80	1	15	16	....	....	....	154	....	....	....	....	....	....	....	....	....	....	4	0	0	0	6	....	....	....
1996-97	Milwaukee Admirals	IHL	74	3	4	7	....	....	....	145	....	....	....	....	....	....	....	....	....	....	1	0	0	0	2	....	....	....
1997-98	Hershey Bears	AHL	32	2	2	4	....	....	....	76	....	....	....	....	....	....	....	....	....	....	....	....	....	....	....	....	....	....
	Milwaukee Admirals	IHL	31	4	6	10	....	....	....	84	....	....	....	....	....	....	....	....	....	....	10	0	1	1	20	....	....	....
	NHL Totals		**7**	**1**	**2**	**3**	**1**	**2**	**3**	**20**	**0**	**0**	**0**	**11**	**9.1**	**6**	**1**	**5**	**0**		....	....	....	....	....	....	....	....

• PROVOST, CLAUDE

Claude Provost RW – R. 5'9", 168 lbs. b: Montreal, Que., 9/17/1933. d: 4/17/1984.

Season	Club	League	GP	G	A	Pts	AG	AA	APts	PIM	PP	SH	GW	S	%	TGF	PGF	TGA	PGA	+/–	PO GP	PO G	PO A	PO Pts	PO PIM	PO PP	PO SH	PO GW
1951-52	Montreal Nationale	QJHL	49	24	29	53	....	....	....	46	....	....	....	....	....	....	....	....	....	....	9	5	2	7	4	....	....	....
1952-53	Montreal Jr. Canadiens	QJHL	46	24	36	60	....	....	....	29	....	....	....	....	....	....	....	....	....	....	7	6	5	11	10	....	....	....
1953-54	Montreal Jr. Canadiens	QJHL	48	45	39	84	....	....	....	83	....	....	....	....	....	....	....	....	....	....	8	3	8	11	16	....	....	....
1954-55	Shawinigan Cataracts	QHL	61	25	23	48	....	....	....	44	....	....	....	....	....	....	....	....	....	....	13	6	3	9	6	....	....	....
1955-56	**Montreal Canadiens**	**NHL**	**60**	**13**	**16**	**29**	**19**	**20**	**39**	**30**	....	....	....	....	....	....	....	....	....	....	**10**	**3**	**3**	**6**	**12**	....	....	....
	Shawinigan Cataracts	QHL	9	7	8	15	....	....	....	12	....	....	....	....	....	....	....	....	....	....	....	....	....	....	....	....	....	....
1956-57	**Montreal Canadiens**	**NHL**	**67**	**16**	**14**	**30**	**22**	**16**	**38**	**24**	....	....	....	....	....	....	....	....	....	....	**10**	**0**	**1**	**1**	**8**	....	....	....
1957-58	**Montreal Canadiens**	**NHL**	**70**	**19**	**32**	**51**	**25**	**35**	**60**	**71**	....	....	....	....	....	....	....	....	....	....	**10**	**1**	**3**	**4**	**8**	....	....	....
1958-59	**Montreal Canadiens**	**NHL**	**69**	**16**	**22**	**38**	**20**	**23**	**43**	**37**	....	....	....	....	....	....	....	....	....	....	**11**	**6**	**2**	**8**	**2**	....	....	....
1959-60	**Montreal Canadiens**	**NHL**	**70**	**17**	**29**	**46**	**21**	**30**	**51**	**42**	....	....	....	....	....	....	....	....	....	....	**8**	**1**	**1**	**2**	**0**	....	....	....
1960-61	**Montreal Canadiens**	**NHL**	**49**	**11**	**4**	**15**	**13**	**4**	**17**	**32**	....	....	....	....	....	....	....	....	....	....	**6**	**1**	**3**	**4**	**4**	....	....	....
1961-62	**Montreal Canadiens**	**NHL**	**70**	**33**	**29**	**62**	**41**	**29**	**70**	**22**	....	....	....	....	....	....	....	....	....	....	**6**	**2**	**2**	**4**	**2**	....	....	....
1962-63	**Montreal Canadiens**	**NHL**	**67**	**20**	**30**	**50**	**25**	**31**	**56**	**26**	....	....	....	....	....	....	....	....	....	....	**5**	**0**	**1**	**1**	**2**	....	....	....
1963-64	**Montreal Canadiens**	**NHL**	**68**	**15**	**17**	**32**	**20**	**19**	**39**	**37**	....	....	....	....	....	....	....	....	....	....	**7**	**2**	**2**	**4**	**22**	....	....	....
1964-65	**Montreal Canadiens**	**NHL**	**70**	**27**	**37**	**64**	**35**	**40**	**75**	**28**	....	....	....	....	....	....	....	....	....	....	**13**	**2**	**6**	**8**	**12**	....	....	....
1965-66	**Montreal Canadiens**	**NHL**	**70**	**19**	**36**	**55**	**23**	**36**	**59**	**38**	....	....	....	....	....	....	....	....	....	....	**10**	**2**	**3**	**5**	**2**	....	....	....
1966-67	**Montreal Canadiens**	**NHL**	**64**	**11**	**13**	**24**	**13**	**13**	**26**	**16**	....	....	....	....	....	....	....	....	....	....	**7**	**1**	**1**	**2**	**0**	....	....	....
1967-68	**Montreal Canadiens**	**NHL**	**73**	**14**	**30**	**44**	**17**	**31**	**48**	**26**	**2**	**3**	**3**	**170**	**8.2**	**60**	**4**	**66**	**27**	**+17**	**13**	**2**	**8**	**10**	**10**	**1**	**0**	**1**
1968-69	**Montreal Canadiens**	**NHL**	**73**	**13**	**15**	**28**	**15**	**14**	**29**	**18**	**0**	**1**	**5**	**184**	**7.1**	**48**	**0**	**66**	**30**	**+12**	**10**	**2**	**2**	**4**	**2**	**0**	**0**	**0**
1969-70	**Montreal Canadiens**	**NHL**	**65**	**10**	**11**	**21**	**12**	**11**	**23**	**22**	**0**	**0**	**1**	**120**	**8.3**	**34**	**0**	**57**	**29**	**+6**	....	....	....	....	....	....	....	....
1970-71	Rosemont Nationale	QJHL	DID NOT PLAY – COACHING																									
	NHL Totals		**1005**	**254**	**335**	**589**	**321**	**352**	**673**	**469**	**2**	**4**	**9**	**474**	**53.6**	**142**	**4**	**189**	**86**		**126**	**25**	**38**	**63**	**86**	**1**	**0**	**1**

NHL First All-Star Team (1965) • Won Bill Masterton Trophy (1968)

Played in NHL All-Star Game (1956, 1957, 1958, 1959, 1960, 1961, 1962, 1963, 1964, 1965, 1967)

Traded to **LA Kings** by **Montreal** for cash, June 8, 1971.

• PRPIC, JOEL

Joel Prpic C – L. 6'6", 200 lbs. b: Sudbury, Ont., 9/25/1974. Boston's 9th choice, 233rd overall, in 1993 Entry Draft.

Season	Club	League	GP	G	A	Pts	AG	AA	APts	PIM	PP	SH	GW	S	%	TGF	PGF	TGA	PGA	+/–	PO GP	PO G	PO A	PO Pts	PO PIM	PO PP	PO SH	PO GW
1992-93	Waterloo Siskins	OJHL	45	17	43	60	....	....	....	160	....	....	....	....	....	....	....	....	....	....	....	....	....	....	....	....	....	....
1993-94	St. Lawrence University	ECAC	31	2	4	6	....	....	....	90	....	....	....	....	....	....	....	....	....	....	....	....	....	....	....	....	....	....
1994-95	St. Lawrence University	ECAC	32	7	10	17	....	....	....	62	....	....	....	....	....	....	....	....	....	....	....	....	....	....	....	....	....	....
1995-96	St. Lawrence University	ECAC	32	3	10	13	....	....	....	77	....	....	....	....	....	....	....	....	....	....	....	....	....	....	....	....	....	....
1996-97	St. Lawrence University	ECAC	34	10	8	18	....	....	....	57	....	....	....	....	....	....	....	....	....	....	....	....	....	....	....	....	....	....
1997-98	**Boston Bruins**	**NHL**	**1**	**0**	**0**	**0**	**0**	**0**	**0**	**2**	**0**	**0**	**0**	**0**	**0.0**	**0**	**0**	**0**	**0**	**0**	....	....	....	....	....	....	....	....
	Providence Bruins	AHL	73	17	18	35	....	....	....	53	....	....	....	....	....	....	....	....	....	....	....	....	....	....	....	....	....	....
	NHL Totals		**1**	**0**	**0**	**0**	**0**	**0**	**0**	**2**	**0**	**0**	**0**	**0**	**0.0**	**0**	**0**	**0**	**0**		....	....	....	....	....	....	....	....

• PRYOR, CHRIS

Chris Pryor D – R. 5'11", 210 lbs. b: St. Paul, MN, 1/23/1961.

Season	Club	League	GP	G	A	Pts	AG	AA	APts	PIM	PP	SH	GW	S	%	TGF	PGF	TGA	PGA	+/–	PO GP	PO G	PO A	PO Pts	PO PIM	PO PP	PO SH	PO GW
1979-80	University of New Hampshire	ECAC	27	9	13	22	....	....	....	27	....	....	....	....	....	....	....	....	....	....	....	....	....	....	....	....	....	....
1980-81	University of New Hampshire	ECAC	33	10	27	37	....	....	....	36	....	....	....	....	....	....	....	....	....	....	....	....	....	....	....	....	....	....
1981-82	University of New Hampshire	ECAC	35	3	16	19	....	....	....	36	....	....	....	....	....	....	....	....	....	....	....	....	....	....	....	....	....	....
1982-83	University of New Hampshire	ECAC	34	4	9	13	....	....	....	23	....	....	....	....	....	....	....	....	....	....	....	....	....	....	....	....	....	....
1983-84	Salt Lake Golden Eagles	CHL	72	7	21	28	....	....	....	215	....	....	....	....	....	....	....	....	....	....	5	1	2	3	11	....	....	....
1984-85	**Minnesota North Stars**	**NHL**	**4**	**0**	**0**	**0**	**0**	**0**	**0**	**16**	**0**	**0**	**0**	**2**	**0.0**	**0**	**0**	**4**	**2**	**–2**	....	....	....	....	....	....	....	....
	Springfield Indians	AHL	77	3	21	24	....	....	....	158	....	....	....	....	....	....	....	....	....	....	....	....	....	....	....	....	....	....
1985-86	**Minnesota North Stars**	**NHL**	**7**	**0**	**1**	**1**	**0**	**1**	**1**	**0**	**0**	**0**	**0**	**8**	**0.0**	**4**	**0**	**6**	**2**	**0**	....	....	....	....	....	....	....	....
	Springfield Indians	AHL	55	4	16	20	....	....	....	104	....	....	....	....	....	....	....	....	....	....	....	....	....	....	....	....	....	....
1986-87	**Minnesota North Stars**	**NHL**	**50**	**1**	**3**	**4**	**1**	**2**	**3**	**49**	**0**	**0**	**0**	**20**	**5.0**	**27**	**1**	**50**	**18**	**–6**	....	....	....	....	....	....	....	....
	Springfield Indians	AHL	5	0	2	2	....	....	....	17	....	....	....	....	....	....	....	....	....	....	....	....	....	....	....	....	....	....
1987-88	**Minnesota North Stars**	**NHL**	**3**	**0**	**0**	**0**	**0**	**0**	**0**	**6**	**0**	**0**	**0**	**3**	**0.0**	**0**	**0**	**1**	**0**	**–1**	....	....	....	....	....	....	....	....
	Kalamazoo Wings	IHL	56	4	16	20	....	....	....	171	....	....	....	....	....	....	....	....	....	....	....	....	....	....	....	....	....	....
	New York Islanders	**NHL**	**1**	**0**	**0**	**0**	**0**	**0**	**0**	**2**	**0**	**0**	**0**	**1**	**0.0**	**1**	**0**	**0**	**0**	**+1**	....	....	....	....	....	....	....	....
1988-89	**New York Islanders**	**NHL**	**7**	**0**	**0**	**0**	**0**	**0**	**0**	**25**	**0**	**0**	**0**	**2**	**0.0**	**2**	**0**	**11**	**3**	**–6**	....	....	....	....	....	....	....	....
	Springfield Indians	AHL	54	3	6	9	....	....	....	205	....	....	....	....	....	....	....	....	....	....	....	....	....	....	....	....	....	....
1989-90	**New York Islanders**	**NHL**	**10**	**0**	**0**	**0**	**0**	**0**	**0**	**24**	**0**	**0**	**0**	**2**	**0.0**	**0**	**0**	**8**	**1**	**–7**	....	....	....	....	....	....	....	....
	Springfield Indians	AHL	60	3	7	10	....	....	....	105	....	....	....	....	....	....	....	....	....	....	18	1	3	4	12	....	....	....

			REGULAR SEASON																		PLAYOFFS							
Season	Club	League	GP	G	A	Pts	AG	AA	APts	PIM	PP	SH	GW	S	%	TGF	PGF	TGA	PGA	+/–	GP	G	A	Pts	PIM	PP	SH	GW
1990-91	Capital District Islanders	AHL	41	1	8	9	....	....	....	94	....	....	....	....	....	....	....	....	....	....	....	....	....	....	....	....	....	....
1991-92	Capital District Islanders	AHL	22	0	3	3	....	....	....	12	....	....	....	....	....	....	....	....	....	....	7	2	2	4	18	....	....	....
1992-93	Capital District Islanders	AHL	3	0	0	0	....	....	....	6	....	....	....	....	....	....	....	....	....	....	....	....	....	....	....	....	....	....
	NHL Totals		**82**	**1**	**4**	**5**	**1**	**3**	**4**	**122**	**0**	**0**	**0**	**38**	**2.6**	**34**	**1**	**80**	**26**		....	....	....	....	....	....	....	....

Signed as a free agent by **Minnesota**, January 10, 1985. Traded to **NY Islanders** by **Minnesota** with future considerations for Gord Dineen, March 8, 1988.

• PULFORD, BOB

Bob "Pully" Pulford LW – L. 5'11", 188 lbs. b: Newton Robinson, Ont., 3/31/1936. **HHOF**

1953-54	Weston Dukes	Jr. B	STATISTICS NOT AVAILABLE																									
	Toronto Marlboros	OHA	17	5	9	14	....	....	....	12	....	....	....	....	....	....	....	....	....	....	15	4	7	11	12	....	....	....
1954-55	Toronto Marlboros	OHA	47	24	22	46	....	....	....	43	....	....	....	....	....	....	....	....	....	....	13	7	10	17	29	....	....	....
1955-56	Toronto Marlboros	OHA	48	30	25	55	....	....	....	87	....	....	....	....	....	....	....	....	....	....	11	*16	8	*24	2	....	....	....
1956-57	**Toronto Maple Leafs**	**NHL**	**65**	**11**	**11**	**22**	**15**	**13**	**28**	**32**	....	....	....	....	....	....	....	....	....	....	....	....	....	....	....	....	....	....
1957-58	**Toronto Maple Leafs**	**NHL**	**70**	**14**	**17**	**31**	**18**	**18**	**36**	**48**	....	....	....	....	....	....	....	....	....	....	....	....	....	....	....	....	....	....
1958-59	**Toronto Maple Leafs**	**NHL**	**70**	**23**	**14**	**37**	**29**	**15**	**44**	**53**	....	....	....	....	....	....	....	....	....	....	**12**	**4**	**4**	**8**	**8**	....	....	....
1959-60	**Toronto Maple Leafs**	**NHL**	**70**	**24**	**28**	**52**	**30**	**29**	**59**	**81**	....	....	....	....	....	....	....	....	....	....	**10**	**4**	**1**	**5**	**10**	....	....	....
1960-61	**Toronto Maple Leafs**	**NHL**	**40**	**11**	**18**	**29**	**13**	**18**	**31**	**41**	....	....	....	....	....	....	....	....	....	....	**5**	**0**	**0**	**0**	**8**	....	....	....
1961-62	**Toronto Maple Leafs**	**NHL**	**70**	**18**	**21**	**39**	**22**	**21**	**43**	**98**	....	....	....	....	....	....	....	....	....	....	**12**	**7**	**1**	**8**	**24**	....	....	....
1962-63	**Toronto Maple Leafs**	**NHL**	**70**	**19**	**25**	**44**	**23**	**26**	**49**	**49**	....	....	....	....	....	....	....	....	....	....	**10**	**2**	**5**	**7**	**14**	....	....	....
1963-64	**Toronto Maple Leafs**	**NHL**	**70**	**18**	**30**	**48**	**24**	**33**	**57**	**73**	....	....	....	....	....	....	....	....	....	....	**14**	**5**	**3**	**8**	**20**	....	....	....
1964-65	**Toronto Maple Leafs**	**NHL**	**65**	**19**	**20**	**39**	**24**	**22**	**46**	**46**	....	....	....	....	....	....	....	....	....	....	**6**	**1**	**1**	**2**	**16**	....	....	....
1965-66	**Toronto Maple Leafs**	**NHL**	**70**	**28**	**28**	**56**	**34**	**28**	**62**	**51**	....	....	....	....	....	....	....	....	....	....	**4**	**1**	**1**	**2**	**12**	....	....	....
1966-67	**Toronto Maple Leafs**	**NHL**	**67**	**17**	**28**	**45**	**21**	**29**	**50**	**28**	....	....	....	....	....	....	....	....	....	....	**12**	**1**	***10**	**11**	**12**	....	....	....
1967-68	**Toronto Maple Leafs**	**NHL**	**74**	**20**	**30**	**50**	**25**	**31**	**56**	**40**	**4**	**3**	**3**	**229**	**8.7**	**69**	**14**	**71**	**9**	**–7**	....	....	....	....	....	....	....	....
1968-69	**Toronto Maple Leafs**	**NHL**	**72**	**11**	**23**	**34**	**12**	**22**	**34**	**20**	**3**	**1**	**1**	**179**	**6.1**	**53**	**9**	**77**	**24**	**–9**	**4**	**0**	**0**	**0**	**2**	**0**	**0**	**0**
1969-70	**Toronto Maple Leafs**	**NHL**	**74**	**18**	**19**	**37**	**21**	**19**	**40**	**31**	**3**	**0**	**1**	**227**	**7.9**	**62**	**21**	**84**	**19**	**–24**	....	....	....	....	....	....	....	....
1970-71	**Los Angeles Kings**	**NHL**	**59**	**17**	**26**	**43**	**18**	**23**	**41**	**53**	**6**	**1**	**2**	**170**	**10.0**	**63**	**19**	**83**	**24**	**–15**	....	....	....	....	....	....	....	....
1971-72	**Los Angeles Kings**	**NHL**	**73**	**13**	**24**	**37**	**14**	**22**	**36**	**48**	**2**	**1**	**0**	**170**	**7.6**	**57**	**14**	**99**	**31**	**–25**	....	....	....	....	....	....	....	....
1972-73	**Los Angeles Kings**	**NHL**	DID NOT PLAY – COACHING																									
	NHL Totals		**1079**	**281**	**362**	**643**	**343**	**369**	**712**	**792**	**18**	**6**	**7**	**975**	**28.8**	**304**	**77**	**414**	**107**		**89**	**25**	**26**	**51**	**126**	**0**	**0**	**0**

Won Jack Adams Award (1975)

Played in NHL All-Star Game (1960, 1962, 1963, 1964, 1968)

Traded to **LA Kings** by **Toronto** for Garry Monahan and Brian Murphy, September 3, 1970.

• PULKKINEN, DAVE

Dave Pulkkinen LW/D – R. 6', 195 lbs. b: Kapuskasing, Ont., 5/18/1949. St. Louis' 8th choice, 77th overall, in 1969 Amateur Draft.

1968-69	Oshawa Generals	OHA	54	17	19	36	....	....	....	50	....	....	....	....	....	....	....	....	....	....	....	....	....	....	....	....	....	....
1969-70	Kansas City Blues	CHL	11	1	2	3	....	....	....	0	....	....	....	....	....	....	....	....	....	....	....	....	....	....	....	....	....	....
	Port Huron Flags	IHL	43	11	16	27	....	....	....	51	....	....	....	....	....	....	....	....	....	....	....	....	....	....	....	....	....	....
1970-71	Dayton Gems	IHL	1	0	0	0	....	....	....	0	....	....	....	....	....	....	....	....	....	....	....	....	....	....	....	....	....	....
	Port Huron–Toledo	IHL	25	3	12	15	....	....	....	8	....	....	....	....	....	....	....	....	....	....	....	....	....	....	....	....	....	....
1971-72	Kansas City Blues	CHL	70	12	46	58	....	....	....	49	....	....	....	....	....	....	....	....	....	....	....	....	....	....	....	....	....	....
1972-73	**New York Islanders**	**NHL**	**2**	**0**	**0**	**0**	**0**	**0**	**0**	**0**	**0**	**0**	**0**	**0**	**0.0**	**0**	**0**	**1**	**0**	**–1**	....	....	....	....	....	....	....	....
	New Haven Nighthawks	AHL	75	25	41	66	....	....	....	55	....	....	....	....	....	....	....	....	....	....	....	....	....	....	....	....	....	....
1973-74	Baltimore Clippers	AHL	60	11	24	35	....	....	....	39	....	....	....	....	....	....	....	....	....	....	2	0	1	1	0	....	....	....
1974-75	Syracuse Eagles	AHL	11	0	3	3	....	....	....	4	....	....	....	....	....	....	....	....	....	....	....	....	....	....	....	....	....	....
	NHL Totals		**2**	**0**	**0**	**0**	**0**	**0**	**0**	**0**	**0**	**0**	**0**	**0**	**0.0**	**0**	**0**	**1**	**0**		....	....	....	....	....	....	....	....

Traded to **NY Islanders** by **St. Louis** for cash, August, 1972.

• PURVES, JOHN

John Purves RW – R. 6'1", 201 lbs. b: Toronto, Ont., 2/12/1968. Washington's 6th choice, 103rd overall, in 1986 Entry Draft.

1984-85	Belleville Bulls	OHL	55	15	14	29	....	....	....	39	....	....	....	....	....	....	....	....	....	....	....	....	....	....	....	....	....	....
1985-86	Belleville Bulls	OHL	16	3	9	12	....	....	....	6	....	....	....	....	....	....	....	....	....	....	....	....	....	....	....	....	....	....
	Hamilton Steelhawks	OHL	36	13	28	41	....	....	....	36	....	....	....	....	....	....	....	....	....	....	....	....	....	....	....	....	....	....
1986-87	Hamilton Steelhawks	OHL	28	12	11	23	....	....	....	37	....	....	....	....	....	....	....	....	....	....	9	2	0	2	12	....	....	....
1987-88	Hamilton Steelhawks	OHL	64	39	44	83	....	....	....	65	....	....	....	....	....	....	....	....	....	....	14	7	18	25	4	....	....	....
1988-89	Niagara Falls Thunder	OHL	5	5	11	16	....	....	....	2	....	....	....	....	....	....	....	....	....	....	....	....	....	....	....	....	....	....
	North Bay Centennials	OHL	42	34	52	86	....	....	....	38	....	....	....	....	....	....	....	....	....	....	12	14	12	26	16	....	....	....
1989-90	Baltimore Skipjacks	AHL	75	29	35	64	....	....	....	12	....	....	....	....	....	....	....	....	....	....	9	5	7	12	4	....	....	....
1990-91	**Washington Capitals**	**NHL**	**7**	**1**	**0**	**1**	**1**	**0**	**1**	**0**	**0**	**0**	**1**	**8**	**12.5**	**3**	**0**	**6**	**0**	**–3**	....	....	....	....	....	....	....	....
	Baltimore Skipjacks	AHL	53	22	29	51	....	....	....	27	....	....	....	....	....	....	....	....	....	....	6	2	3	5	0	....	....	....
1991-92	Baltimore Skipjacks	AHL	78	43	46	89	....	....	....	47	....	....	....	....	....	....	....	....	....	....	....	....	....	....	....	....	....	....
1992-93	ESV Kaufbeuren	Germany	43	15	17	32	....	....	....	34	....	....	....	....	....	....	....	....	....	....	....	....	....	....	....	....	....	....
1993-94	Fort Wayne Komets	IHL	69	38	48	86	....	....	....	29	....	....	....	....	....	....	....	....	....	....	18	10	14	24	12	....	....	....
1994-95	Fort Wayne Komets	IHL	60	30	33	63	....	....	....	16	....	....	....	....	....	....	....	....	....	....	4	4	1	5	6	....	....	....
1995-96	San Francisco Spiders	IHL	75	56	49	105	....	....	....	32	....	....	....	....	....	....	....	....	....	....	4	0	3	3	0	....	....	....
1996-97	Kansas City Blades	IHL	66	25	47	72	....	....	....	17	....	....	....	....	....	....	....	....	....	....	3	0	0	0	0	....	....	....
1997-98	Kansas City Blades	IHL	21	6	10	16	....	....	....	9	....	....	....	....	....	....	....	....	....	....	....	....	....	....	....	....	....	....
	San Antonio Dragons	IHL	59	22	21	43	....	....	....	12	....	....	....	....	....	....	....	....	....	....	....	....	....	....	....	....	....	....
	NHL Totals		**7**	**1**	**0**	**1**	**1**	**0**	**1**	**0**	**0**	**0**	**1**	**8**	**12.5**	**3**	**0**	**6**	**0**		....	....	....	....	....	....	....	....

OHL Second All-Star Team (1989) • IHL Second All-Star Team (1996)

• PUSHOR, JAMIE

Jamie Pushor D – R. 6'3", 192 lbs. b: Lethbridge, Alta., 2/11/1973. Detroit's 2nd choice, 32nd overall, in 1991 Entry Draft.

1989-90	Lethbridge Hurricanes	WHL	10	0	2	2	....	....	....	2	....	....	....	....	....	....	....	....	....	....	....	....	....	....	....	....	....	....
1990-91	Lethbridge Hurricanes	WHL	71	1	13	14	....	....	....	193	....	....	....	....	....	....	....	....	....	....	....	....	....	....	....	....	....	....
1991-92	Lethbridge Hurricanes	WHL	49	2	15	17	....	....	....	232	....	....	....	....	....	....	....	....	....	....	5	0	0	0	33	....	....	....
1992-93	Lethbridge Hurricanes	WHL	72	6	22	28	....	....	....	200	....	....	....	....	....	....	....	....	....	....	4	0	1	1	9	....	....	....
1993-94	Adirondack Red Wings	AHL	73	1	17	18	....	....	....	124	....	....	....	....	....	....	....	....	....	....	12	0	0	0	22	....	....	....
1994-95	Adirondack Red Wings	AHL	58	2	11	13	....	....	....	129	....	....	....	....	....	....	....	....	....	....	4	0	1	1	0	....	....	....
1995-96	**Detroit Red Wings**	**NHL**	**5**	**0**	**1**	**1**	**0**	**1**	**1**	**17**	**0**	**0**	**0**	**6**	**0.0**	**4**	**0**	**4**	**2**	**+2**	....	....	....	....	....	....	....	....
	Adirondack Red Wings	AHL	65	2	16	18	....	....	....	126	....	....	....	....	....	....	....	....	....	....	3	0	0	0	5	....	....	....
1996-97	**Detroit Red Wings**	**NHL**	**75**	**4**	**7**	**11**	**4**	**6**	**10**	**129**	**0**	**0**	**0**	**63**	**6.3**	**46**	**1**	**56**	**12**	**+1**	**5**	**0**	**1**	**1**	**5**	**0**	**0**	**0**
1997-98	**Detroit Red Wings**	**NHL**	**54**	**2**	**5**	**7**	**2**	**5**	**7**	**71**	**0**	**0**	**0**	**43**	**4.7**	**33**	**1**	**44**	**14**	**+2**	....	....	....	....	....	....	....	....
	Anaheim Mighty Ducks	**NHL**	**10**	**0**	**2**	**2**	**0**	**2**	**2**	**10**	**0**	**0**	**0**	**8**	**0.0**	**8**	**0**	**12**	**5**	**+1**	....	....	....	....	....	....	....	....
	NHL Totals		**144**	**6**	**15**	**21**	**6**	**14**	**20**	**227**	**0**	**0**	**0**	**120**	**5.0**	**91**	**2**	**116**	**33**		**5**	**0**	**1**	**1**	**5**	**0**	**0**	**0**

Traded to **Anaheim** by **Detroit** with Detroit's 4th round choice (Viktor Wallin) in 1998 Entry Draft for Dmitri Mironov, March 24, 1998.

• PYATT, NELSON

Nelson Pyatt C – L. 6', 175 lbs. b: Port Arthur, Ont., 9/9/1953. Detroit's 2nd choice, 39th overall, in 1973 Amateur Draft.

1971-72	Oshawa Generals	OHA	54	17	29	46	....	....	....	27	....	....	....	....	....	....	....	....	....	....	....	....	....	....	....	....	....	....
1972-73	Oshawa Generals	OHA	26	13	19	32	....	....	....	7	....	....	....	....	....	....	....	....	....	....	....	....	....	....	....	....	....	....
1973-74	**Detroit Red Wings**	**NHL**	**5**	**0**	**0**	**0**	**0**	**0**	**0**	**0**	**0**	**0**	**0**	**1**	**0.0**	**0**	**0**	**2**	**0**	**–2**	....	....	....	....	....	....	....	....
	London Lions	Britain	61	35	28	63	....	....	....	4	....	....	....	....	....	....	....	....	....	....	....	....	....	....	....	....	....	....
1974-75	**Detroit Red Wings**	**NHL**	**9**	**0**	**0**	**0**	**0**	**0**	**0**	**2**	**0**	**0**	**0**	**6**	**0.0**	**1**	**0**	**3**	**0**	**–2**	....	....	....	....	....	....	....	....
	Virginia Wings	AHL	14	3	4	7	....	....	....	12	....	....	....	....	....	....	....	....	....	....	....	....	....	....	....	....	....	....
	Washington Capitals	**NHL**	**16**	**6**	**4**	**10**	**6**	**3**	**9**	**21**	**0**	**0**	**1**	**33**	**18.2**	**11**	**4**	**28**	**7**	**–14**	....	....	....	....	....	....	....	....
1975-76	**Washington Capitals**	**NHL**	**77**	**26**	**23**	**49**	**24**	**18**	**42**	**14**	**5**	**0**	**0**	**151**	**17.2**	**70**	**16**	**120**	**10**	**–56**	....	....	....	....	....	....	....	....
1976-77	**Colorado Rockies**	**NHL**	**77**	**23**	**22**	**45**	**22**	**18**	**40**	**20**	**2**	**0**	**4**	**158**	**14.6**	**60**	**7**	**72**	**2**	**–17**	....	....	....	....	....	....	....	....
1977-78	**Colorado Rockies**	**NHL**	**71**	**9**	**12**	**21**	**9**	**10**	**19**	**8**	**1**	**0**	**0**	**87**	**10.3**	**31**	**4**	**50**	**0**	**–23**	....	....	....	....	....	....	....	....

			REGULAR SEASON																		PLAYOFFS							
Season	Club	League	GP	G	A	Pts	AG	AA	APts	PIM	PP	SH	GW	S	%	TGF	PGF	TGA	PGA	+/–	GP	G	A	Pts	PIM	PP	SH	GW
1978-79	**Colorado Rockies**	**NHL**	**28**	**2**	**2**	**4**	**2**	**2**	**4**	**2**	**0**	**0**	**0**	**34**	**5.9**	**7**	**0**	**24**	**0**	**–17**	....	....	....	....	....	....	....	....
	Philadelphia Firebirds	AHL	7	3	1	4	....	....	....	0	....	....	....	....	....	....	....	....	....	....	....	....	....	....	....	....	....	....
1979-80	**Colorado Rockies**	**NHL**	**13**	**5**	**0**	**5**	**5**	**0**	**5**	**2**	**0**	**0**	**0**	**20**	**25.0**	**7**	**0**	**13**	**1**	**–5**	....	....	....	....	....	....	....	....
	Fort Worth Texans	CHL	45	20	17	37	....	....	....	11	....	....	....	....	....	....	....	....	....	....	15	5	1	6	2	....	....	....
	NHL Totals		**296**	**71**	**63**	**134**	**68**	**51**	**119**	**69**	**8**	**0**	**5**	**490**	**14.5**	**187**	**31**	**312**	**20**		....	....	....	....	....	....	....	....

Traded to **Washington** by **Detroit** for Washington's 3rd round choice (Allen Cameron) in 1975 Amateur Draft, February 28, 1975. Signed as a free agent by **Colorado**, September 1, 1976.

• QUENNEVILLE, JOEL

Joel "Herbie" Quenneville D – L. 6'1", 200 lbs. b: Windsor, Ont., 9/15/1958. Toronto's 1st choice, 21st overall, in 1978 Amateur Draft.

1975-76	Windsor Spitfires	OHA	66	15	33	48	....	....	....	61	....	....	....	....	....	....	....	....	....	....	....	....	....	....	....	....	....	....
1976-77	Windsor Spitfires	OHA	65	19	59	78	....	....	....	169	....	....	....	....	....	....	....	....	....	....	9	6	5	11	112	....	....	....
1977-78	Windsor Spitfires	OHA	66	27	76	103	....	....	....	114	....	....	....	....	....	....	....	....	....	....	6	2	3	5	17	....	....	....
1978-79	**Toronto Maple Leafs**	**NHL**	**61**	**2**	**9**	**11**	**2**	**7**	**9**	**60**	**0**	**0**	**1**	**56**	**3.6**	**41**	**2**	**42**	**10**	**+7**	**6**	**0**	**1**	**1**	**4**	**0**	**0**	**0**
	New Brunswick Hawks	AHL	16	1	10	11	....	....	....	10	....	....	....	....	....	....	....	....	....	....	....	....	....	....	....	....	....	....
1979-80	**Toronto Maple Leafs**	**NHL**	**32**	**1**	**4**	**5**	**1**	**3**	**4**	**24**	**1**	**0**	**0**	**56**	**1.8**	**25**	**2**	**33**	**8**	**–2**	....	....	....	....	....	....	....	....
	Colorado Rockies	**NHL**	**35**	**5**	**7**	**12**	**5**	**5**	**10**	**26**	**1**	**0**	**0**	**62**	**8.1**	**32**	**8**	**46**	**1**	**–21**	....	....	....	....	....	....	....	....
1980-81	**Colorado Rockies**	**NHL**	**71**	**10**	**24**	**34**	**8**	**17**	**25**	**86**	**3**	**0**	**1**	**107**	**9.3**	**91**	**28**	**106**	**19**	**–24**	....	....	....	....	....	....	....	....
1981-82	**Colorado Rockies**	**NHL**	**64**	**5**	**10**	**15**	**4**	**7**	**11**	**55**	**0**	**0**	**0**	**67**	**7.5**	**49**	**4**	**93**	**19**	**–29**	....	....	....	....	....	....	....	....
1982-83	**New Jersey Devils**	**NHL**	**74**	**5**	**12**	**17**	**4**	**8**	**12**	**46**	**0**	**1**	**0**	**85**	**5.9**	**66**	**3**	**106**	**30**	**–13**	....	....	....	....	....	....	....	....
1983-84	**Hartford Whalers**	**NHL**	**80**	**5**	**8**	**13**	**4**	**5**	**9**	**95**	**0**	**2**	**0**	**67**	**7.5**	**77**	**1**	**139**	**52**	**–11**	....	....	....	....	....	....	....	....
1984-85	**Hartford Whalers**	**NHL**	**79**	**6**	**16**	**22**	**5**	**11**	**16**	**96**	**0**	**0**	**2**	**75**	**8.0**	**80**	**2**	**135**	**42**	**–15**	....	....	....	....	....	....	....	....
1985-86	**Hartford Whalers**	**NHL**	**71**	**5**	**20**	**25**	**4**	**13**	**17**	**83**	**1**	**0**	**1**	**49**	**10.2**	**84**	**1**	**100**	**38**	**+21**	**10**	**0**	**2**	**2**	**12**	**0**	**0**	**0**
1986-87	**Hartford Whalers**	**NHL**	**37**	**3**	**7**	**10**	**3**	**5**	**8**	**24**	**0**	**1**	**1**	**19**	**15.8**	**31**	**0**	**44**	**20**	**+7**	**6**	**0**	**0**	**0**	**0**	**0**	**0**	**0**
1987-88	**Hartford Whalers**	**NHL**	**77**	**1**	**8**	**9**	**1**	**6**	**7**	**44**	**0**	**0**	**0**	**42**	**2.4**	**44**	**0**	**95**	**38**	**–13**	**6**	**0**	**2**	**2**	**2**	**0**	**0**	**0**
1988-89	**Hartford Whalers**	**NHL**	**69**	**4**	**7**	**11**	**3**	**5**	**8**	**32**	**0**	**0**	**0**	**45**	**8.9**	**53**	**1**	**77**	**28**	**+3**	**4**	**0**	**3**	**3**	**4**	**0**	**0**	**0**
1989-90	**Hartford Whalers**	**NHL**	**44**	**1**	**4**	**5**	**1**	**3**	**4**	**34**	**0**	**0**	**0**	**17**	**5.9**	**35**	**0**	**37**	**11**	**+9**	....	....	....	....	....	....	....	....
1990-91	**Washington Capitals**	**NHL**	**9**	**1**	**0**	**1**	**1**	**0**	**1**	**0**	**0**	**0**	**0**	**3**	**33.3**	**1**	**0**	**9**	**0**	**–8**	....	....	....	....	....	....	....	....
	Baltimore Skipjacks	AHL	59	6	13	19	....	....	....	58	....	....	....	....	....	....	....	....	....	....	6	1	1	2	6	....	....	....
1991-92	St. John's Maple Leafs	AHL	73	7	23	30	....	....	....	58	....	....	....	....	....	....	....	....	....	....	16	0	1	1	10	....	....	....
	NHL Totals		**803**	**54**	**136**	**190**	**46**	**95**	**141**	**705**	**6**	**4**	**6**	**750**	**7.2**	**709**	**52**	**1062**	**316**		**32**	**0**	**8**	**8**	**22**	**0**	**0**	**0**

OHA Second All-Star Team (1978) • AHL Second All-Star Team (1992)

Traded to **Colorado** by **Toronto** with Lanny McDonald for Pat Hickey and Wilf Paiement, December 29, 1979 Transferred to **New Jersey** after **Colorado** franchise relocated, June 30, 1982. Traded to **Calgary** by **New Jersey** with Steve Tambellini for Phil Russell and Mel Bridgeman, June 20, 1983. Traded to **Hartford** by **Calgary** with Richie Dunn for Mickey Volcan, July 5, 1983. Traded to **Washington** by **Hartford** for cash, October 3, 1990. Signed as a free agent by **Toronto**, July 30, 1991.

• QUINN, DAN

Dan Quinn C – L. 5'11", 182 lbs. b: Ottawa, Ont., 6/1/1965. Calgary's 1st choice, 13th overall, in 1983 Entry Draft.

1981-82	Belleville Bulls	OHL	67	19	32	51	....	....	....	41	....	....	....	....	....	....	....	....	....	....	....	....	....	....	....	....	....	....
1982-83	Belleville Bulls	OHL	70	59	88	147	....	....	....	27	....	....	....	....	....	....	....	....	....	....	4	2	6	8	2	....	....	....
1983-84	Belleville Bulls	OHL	24	23	36	59	....	....	....	12	....	....	....	....	....	....	....	....	....	....	....	....	....	....	....	....	....	....
	Calgary Flames	**NHL**	**54**	**19**	**33**	**52**	**15**	**22**	**37**	**20**	**11**	**0**	**1**	**103**	**18.4**	**68**	**32**	**48**	**9**	**–3**	**8**	**3**	**5**	**8**	**4**	**1**	**0**	**0**
1984-85	**Calgary Flames**	**NHL**	**74**	**20**	**38**	**58**	**16**	**26**	**42**	**22**	**7**	**0**	**3**	**143**	**14.0**	**85**	**33**	**54**	**11**	**+9**	**3**	**0**	**0**	**0**	**0**	**0**	**0**	**0**
1985-86	**Calgary Flames**	**NHL**	**78**	**30**	**42**	**72**	**24**	**28**	**52**	**44**	**17**	**3**	**3**	**191**	**15.7**	**96**	**44**	**102**	**38**	**–12**	**18**	**8**	**7**	**15**	**10**	**5**	**1**	**2**
1986-87	**Calgary Flames**	**NHL**	**16**	**3**	**6**	**9**	**3**	**4**	**7**	**14**	**1**	**0**	**0**	**27**	**11.1**	**12**	**7**	**11**	**0**	**–6**	....	....	....	....	....	....	....	....
	Pittsburgh Penguins	**NHL**	**64**	**28**	**43**	**71**	**24**	**31**	**55**	**40**	**10**	**3**	**4**	**157**	**17.8**	**92**	**30**	**76**	**28**	**+14**	....	....	....	....	....	....	....	....
	Canada	WEC-A	10	2	2	4	....	....	....	12	....	....	....	....	....	....	....	....	....	....	....	....	....	....	....	....	....	....
1987-88	**Pittsburgh Penguins**	**NHL**	**70**	**40**	**39**	**79**	**34**	**28**	**62**	**50**	**21**	**1**	**4**	**235**	**17.0**	**119**	**62**	**111**	**46**	**–8**	....	....	....	....	....	....	....	....
1988-89	**Pittsburgh Penguins**	**NHL**	**79**	**34**	**60**	**94**	**29**	**42**	**71**	**102**	**16**	**0**	**4**	**200**	**17.0**	**132**	**74**	**107**	**12**	**–37**	**11**	**6**	**3**	**9**	**10**	**4**	**0**	**1**
1989-90	**Pittsburgh Penguins**	**NHL**	**41**	**9**	**20**	**29**	**8**	**14**	**22**	**22**	**5**	**0**	**2**	**86**	**10.5**	**44**	**22**	**50**	**13**	**–15**	....	....	....	....	....	....	....	....
	Vancouver Canucks	**NHL**	**37**	**16**	**18**	**34**	**14**	**13**	**27**	**27**	**6**	**0**	**3**	**95**	**16.8**	**43**	**18**	**36**	**9**	**–2**	....	....	....	....	....	....	....	....
1990-91	**Vancouver Canucks**	**NHL**	**64**	**18**	**31**	**49**	**17**	**23**	**40**	**46**	**8**	**0**	**3**	**157**	**11.5**	**71**	**35**	**77**	**13**	**–28**	....	....	....	....	....	....	....	....
	St. Louis Blues	**NHL**	**14**	**4**	**7**	**11**	**4**	**5**	**9**	**20**	**4**	**0**	**2**	**26**	**15.4**	**13**	**8**	**10**	**0**	**–5**	**13**	**4**	**7**	**11**	**32**	**2**	**0**	**1**
1991-92	**Philadelphia Flyers**	**NHL**	**67**	**11**	**26**	**37**	**10**	**20**	**30**	**26**	**6**	**0**	**1**	**101**	**10.9**	**55**	**26**	**42**	**0**	**–13**	....	....	....	....	....	....	....	....
1992-93	**Minnesota North Stars**	**NHL**	**11**	**0**	**4**	**4**	**0**	**3**	**3**	**6**	**0**	**0**	**0**	**20**	**0.0**	**6**	**4**	**7**	**1**	**–4**	....	....	....	....	....	....	....	....
1993-94	SC Bern	Switz.	25	13	18	31	....	....	....	56	....	....	....	....	....	....	....	....	....	....	....	....	....	....	....	....	....	....
	Ottawa Senators	**NHL**	**13**	**7**	**0**	**7**	**7**	**0**	**7**	**6**	**2**	**0**	**3**	**31**	**22.6**	**14**	**4**	**17**	**7**	**0**	....	....	....	....	....	....	....	....
1994-95	EV Zug	Switz.	7	7	6	13	....	....	....	26	....	....	....	....	....	....	....	....	....	....	....	....	....	....	....	....	....	....
	Los Angeles Kings	**NHL**	**44**	**14**	**17**	**31**	**25**	**25**	**50**	**32**	**2**	**0**	**4**	**78**	**17.9**	**41**	**9**	**38**	**3**	**–3**	....	....	....	....	....	....	....	....
1995-96	**Ottawa Senators**	**NHL**	**28**	**6**	**18**	**24**	**6**	**15**	**21**	**24**	**4**	**0**	**0**	**62**	**9.7**	**33**	**12**	**32**	**3**	**–8**	....	....	....	....	....	....	....	....
	Detroit Vipers	IHL	4	0	5	5	....	....	....	2	....	....	....	....	....	....	....	....	....	....	....	....	....	....	....	....	....	....
	Philadelphia Flyers	**NHL**	**35**	**7**	**14**	**21**	**7**	**11**	**18**	**22**	**3**	**0**	**0**	**47**	**14.9**	**34**	**16**	**16**	**0**	**+2**	**12**	**1**	**4**	**5**	**6**	**1**	**0**	**0**
1996-97	**Pittsburgh Penguins**	**NHL**	**16**	**0**	**3**	**3**	**0**	**3**	**3**	**10**	**0**	**0**	**0**	**16**	**0.0**	**8**	**2**	**15**	**3**	**–6**	....	....	....	....	....	....	....	....
	NHL Totals		**805**	**266**	**419**	**685**	**243**	**313**	**556**	**533**	**123**	**7**	**37**	**1775**	**15.0**	**966**	**438**	**849**	**196**		**65**	**22**	**26**	**48**	**62**	**13**	**1**	**4**

Traded to **Pittsburgh** by **Calgary** for Mike Bullard, November 12, 1986. Traded to **Vancouver** by **Pittsburgh** with Dave Capuano and Andrew McBain for Rod Buskas, Barry Pederson and Tony Tanti, January 8, 1990. Traded to **St. Louis** by **Vancouver** with Garth Butcher for Geoff Courtnall, Robert Dirk, Sergio Momesso, Cliff Ronning and St. Louis' 5th round choice (Brian Loney) in 1992 Entry Draft, March 5, 1991. Traded to **Philadelphia** by **St. Louis** with Rod Brind'Amour for Ron Sutter and Murray Baron, September 22, 1991. Signed as a free agent by **Minnesota**, October 4, 1992. Signed as a free agent by **Ottawa**, March 15, 1994. Signed as a free agent by **LA Kings**, September 3, 1994. Signed as a free agent by **Ottawa**, August 1, 1995. Traded to **Philadelphia** by **Ottawa** for cash, January 23, 1996. Signed as a free agent by **Pittsburgh**, July 17, 1996.

• QUINN, PAT

Pat Quinn D – L. 6'3", 205 lbs. b: Hamilton, Ont., 1/29/1943.

1958-59	Hamilton Tiger Cubs	OHA	20	0	1	1	....	....	....	34	....	....	....	....	....	....	....	....	....	....	....	....	....	....	....	....	....	....
1959-60	Hamilton Tiger Cubs	OHA	27	0	1	1	....	....	....	58	....	....	....	....	....	....	....	....	....	....	....	....	....	....	....	....	....	....
1960-61	Hamilton Kilty B's	Jr. B	STATISTICS NOT AVAILABLE																									
1961-62	Hamilton Kilty B's	Jr. B	STATISTICS NOT AVAILABLE																									
1962-63	Edmonton Oil Kings	ASHL	STATISTICS NOT AVAILABLE																									
1963-64	Knoxville Knights	EHL	72	6	31	37	....	....	....	217	....	....	....	....	....	....	....	....	....	....	8	1	3	4	34	....	....	....
1964-65	Tulsa Oilers	CHL	70	3	32	35	....	....	....	202	....	....	....	....	....	....	....	....	....	....	3	0	0	0	9	....	....	....
1965-66	Memphis Wings	CHL	67	2	16	18	....	....	....	135	....	....	....	....	....	....	....	....	....	....	....	....	....	....	....	....	....	....
1966-67	Houston Apollos	CHL	15	0	3	3	....	....	....	66	....	....	....	....	....	....	....	....	....	....	....	....	....	....	....	....	....	....
	Seattle Totems	WHL	35	1	3	4	....	....	....	49	....	....	....	....	....	....	....	....	....	....	5	0	0	0	2	....	....	....
1967-68	Tulsa Oilers	CHL	51	3	15	18	....	....	....	178	....	....	....	....	....	....	....	....	....	....	11	1	4	5	19	....	....	....
1968-69	**Toronto Maple Leafs**	**NHL**	**40**	**2**	**7**	**9**	**2**	**7**	**9**	**95**	**0**	**0**	**1**	**42**	**4.8**	**39**	**1**	**33**	**5**	**+10**	**4**	**0**	**0**	**0**	**13**	**0**	**0**	**0**
	Tulsa Oilers	CHL	17	0	6	6	....	....	....	25	....	....	....	....	....	....	....	....	....	....	....	....	....	....	....	....	....	....
1969-70	**Toronto Maple Leafs**	**NHL**	**59**	**0**	**5**	**5**	**0**	**5**	**5**	**88**	**0**	**0**	**0**	**47**	**0.0**	**35**	**0**	**67**	**18**	**–14**	....	....	....	....	....	....	....	....
	Tulsa Oilers	CHL	2	0	1	1	....	....	....	6	....	....	....	....	....	....	....	....	....	....	....	....	....	....	....	....	....	....
1970-71	**Vancouver Canucks**	**NHL**	**76**	**2**	**11**	**13**	**2**	**10**	**12**	**149**	**0**	**0**	**0**	**76**	**2.6**	**69**	**0**	**103**	**36**	**+2**	....	....	....	....	....	....	....	....
1971-72	**Vancouver Canucks**	**NHL**	**57**	**2**	**3**	**5**	**2**	**3**	**5**	**63**	**0**	**0**	**0**	**37**	**5.4**	**32**	**1**	**71**	**12**	**–28**	....	....	....	....	....	....	....	....
1972-73	**Atlanta Flames**	**NHL**	**78**	**2**	**18**	**20**	**2**	**15**	**17**	**113**	**0**	**1**	**1**	**88**	**2.3**	**67**	**4**	**82**	**21**	**+2**	....	....	....	....	....	....	....	....
1973-74	**Atlanta Flames**	**NHL**	**77**	**5**	**27**	**32**	**5**	**23**	**28**	**94**	**0**	**0**	**1**	**93**	**5.4**	**86**	**1**	**92**	**22**	**+15**	**4**	**0**	**0**	**0**	**6**	**0**	**0**	**0**
1974-75	**Atlanta Flames**	**NHL**	**80**	**2**	**19**	**21**	**2**	**15**	**17**	**156**	**0**	**0**	**0**	**68**	**2.9**	**76**	**1**	**94**	**31**	**+12**	....	....	....	....	....	....	....	....
1975-76	**Atlanta Flames**	**NHL**	**80**	**2**	**11**	**13**	**2**	**9**	**11**	**134**	**0**	**1**	**0**	**58**	**3.4**	**70**	**1**	**77**	**13**	**+5**	**2**	**0**	**1**	**1**	**2**	**0**	**0**	**0**
1976-77	**Atlanta Flames**	**NHL**	**59**	**1**	**12**	**13**	**1**	**10**	**11**	**58**	**0**	**0**	**0**	**29**	**3.4**	**47**	**0**	**66**	**12**	**–7**	**1**	**0**	**0**	**0**	**0**	**0**	**0**	**0**
	NHL Totals		**606**	**18**	**113**	**131**	**18**	**97**	**115**	**950**	**0**	**2**	**3**	**538**	**3.3**	**521**	**9**	**685**	**170**		**11**	**0**	**1**	**1**	**21**	**0**	**0**	**0**

Won Jack Adams Award (1980)

Claimed by **Montreal** from **Detroit** in Intra-League Draft, June 15, 1966. Traded to **St. Louis** by **Montreal** with Ron Attwell for cash, June 14, 1967. Traded to **Toronto** by **St. Louis** for cash, March 25, 1968. Claimed by **Vancouver** from **Toronto** in Expansion Draft, June 10, 1970. Claimed by **Atlanta** from **Vancouver** in Expansion Draft, June 6, 1972.

• QUINNEY, KEN

Ken Quinney RW – R. 5'10", 186 lbs. b: New Westminster, B.C., 5/23/1965. Quebec's 9th choice, 203rd overall, in 1984 Entry Draft.

1981-82	Calgary Wranglers	WHL	63	11	17	28	....	....	....	55	....	....	....	....	....	....	....	....	....	....	2	0	0	0	15	....	....	....
1982-83	Calgary Wranglers	WHL	71	26	25	51	....	....	....	71	....	....	....	....	....	....	....	....	....	....	16	6	1	7	46	....	....	....
1983-84	Calgary Wranglers	WHL	71	64	54	118	....	....	....	38	....	....	....	....	....	....	....	....	....	....	4	5	2	7	0	....	....	....
1984-85	Calgary Wranglers	WHL	56	47	67	114	....	....	....	65	....	....	....	....	....	....	....	....	....	....	7	6	4	10	15	....	....	....
1985-86	Fredericton Express	AHL	61	11	26	37	....	....	....	34	....	....	....	....	....	....	....	....	....	....	6	2	2	4	9	....	....	....

			REGULAR SEASON																		PLAYOFFS							
Season	Club	League	GP	G	A	Pts	AG	AA	APts	PIM	PP	SH	GW	S	%	TGF	PGF	TGA	PGA	+/–	GP	G	A	Pts	PIM	PP	SH	GW
1986-87	Quebec Nordiques	NHL	25	2	7	9	2	5	7	16	1	0	0	22	9.1	13	2	11	2	+2	....	....	....	....	....	....	....	....
	Fredericton Express	AHL	48	14	27	41	....	....	....	20	....	....	....	....	....	....	....	....	....	....	....	....	....	....	....	....	....	....
1987-88	Quebec Nordiques	NHL	15	2	2	4	2	1	3	5	1	0	0	20	10.0	6	2	8	1	–3	....	....	....	....	....	....	....	....
	Fredericton Express	AHL	58	37	39	76	....	....	....	39	....	....	....	....	....	....	....	....	....	....	13	3	5	8	35	....	....	....
1988-89	Halifax Citadels	AHL	72	41	49	90	....	....	....	65	....	....	....	....	....	....	....	....	....	....	4	3	0	3	0	....	....	....
1989-90	Halifax Citadels	AHL	44	9	16	25	....	....	....	63	....	....	....	....	....	....	....	....	....	....	2	0	0	0	2	....	....	....
1990-91	Quebec Nordiques	NHL	19	3	4	7	3	3	6	2	1	0	0	19	15.8	17	4	16	1	–2	....	....	....	....	....	....	....	....
	Halifax Citadels	AHL	44	20	20	40	....	....	....	76	....	....	....	....	....	....	....	....	....	....	....	....	....	....	....	....	....	....
1991-92	Adirondack Red Wings	AHL	63	31	29	60	....	....	....	33	....	....	....	....	....	....	....	....	....	....	19	7	12	19	9	....	....	....
1992-93	Adirondack Red Wings	AHL	63	32	34	66	....	....	....	15	....	....	....	....	....	....	....	....	....	....	10	2	9	11	9	....	....	....
1993-94	Las Vegas Thunder	IHL	79	*55	53	108	....	....	....	52	....	....	....	....	....	....	....	....	....	....	5	3	3	6	2	....	....	....
1994-95	Las Vegas Thunder	IHL	78	40	42	82	....	....	....	40	....	....	....	....	....	....	....	....	....	....	10	3	2	5	9	....	....	....
1995-96	Las Vegas Thunder	IHL	66	33	36	69	....	....	....	59	....	....	....	....	....	....	....	....	....	....	9	2	5	7	15	....	....	....
1996-97	Las Vegas Thunder	IHL	71	27	36	63	....	....	....	39	....	....	....	....	....	....	....	....	....	....	2	0	0	0	0	....	....	....
1997-98	Las Vegas Thunder	IHL	82	34	57	91	....	....	....	19	....	....	....	....	....	....	....	....	....	....	4	1	2	3	2	....	....	....
	NHL Totals		59	7	13	20	7	9	16	23	3	0	0	61	11.5	36	8	35	4		....	....	....	....	....	....	....	....

WHL East First All-Star Team (1985) • IHL First All-Star Team (1994) • IHL Second All-Star Team (1998)

Signed as a free agent by **Detroit**, August 12, 1991.

• QUINT, DERON

Deron Quint D – L. 6'1", 182 lbs. b: Durham, NH, 3/12/1976. Winnipeg's 1st choice, 30th overall, in 1994 Entry Draft.

Season	Club	League	GP	G	A	Pts	AG	AA	APts	PIM	PP	SH	GW	S	%	TGF	PGF	TGA	PGA	+/–	GP	G	A	Pts	PIM	PP	SH	GW
1993-94	Seattle Thunderbirds	WHL	63	15	29	44	....	....	....	47	....	....	....	....	....	....	....	....	....	....	9	4	12	16	8	....	....	....
	United States	WJC-A	7	0	1	1	....	....	....	2	....	....	....	....	....	....	....	....	....	....	....	....	....	....	....	....	....	....
1994-95	Seattle Thunderbirds	WHL	65	29	60	89	....	....	....	82	....	....	....	....	....	....	....	....	....	....	3	1	2	3	6	....	....	....
	United States	WJC-A	7	3	3	6	....	....	....	6	....	....	....	....	....	....	....	....	....	....	....	....	....	....	....	....	....	....
1995-96	Winnipeg Jets	NHL	51	5	13	18	5	11	16	22	2	0	0	97	5.2	64	15	52	1	–2	....	....	....	....	....	....	....	....
	Springfield Falcons	AHL	11	2	3	5	....	....	....	4	....	....	....	....	....	....	....	....	....	....	10	2	3	5	6	....	....	....
	Seattle Thunderbirds	WHL	....	....	....	....	....	....	....	....	....	....	....	....	....	....	....	....	....	....	5	4	1	5	6	....	....	....
1996-97	Phoenix Coyotes	NHL	27	3	11	14	3	10	13	4	1	0	0	63	4.8	34	18	20	0	–4	7	0	2	2	0	0	0	0
	Springfield Falcons	AHL	43	6	18	24	....	....	....	20	....	....	....	....	....	....	....	....	....	....	12	2	7	9	4	....	....	....
1997-98	Phoenix Coyotes	NHL	32	4	7	11	5	7	12	16	1	0	1	61	6.6	27	10	24	1	–6	....	....	....	....	....	....	....	....
	Springfield Falcons	AHL	8	1	7	8	....	....	....	10	....	....	....	....	....	....	....	....	....	....	1	0	0	0	0	....	....	....
	NHL Totals		110	12	31	43	13	28	41	42	4	0	1	221	5.4	125	43	96	2		7	0	2	2	0	0	0	0

WHL West First All-Star Team (1995)

Transferred to **Phoenix** after **Winnipeg** franchise relocated, July 1, 1996.

• QUINTAL, STEPHANE

Stephane Quintal D – R. 6'3", 225 lbs. b: Boucherville, Que., 10/22/1968. Boston's 2nd choice, 14th overall, in 1987 Entry Draft.

Season	Club	League	GP	G	A	Pts	AG	AA	APts	PIM	PP	SH	GW	S	%	TGF	PGF	TGA	PGA	+/–	GP	G	A	Pts	PIM	PP	SH	GW
1985-86	Granby Bisons	QMJHL	67	2	17	19	....	....	....	144	....	....	....	....	....	....	....	....	....	....	....	....	....	....	....	....	....	....
1986-87	Granby Bisons	QMJHL	67	13	41	54	....	....	....	178	....	....	....	....	....	....	....	....	....	....	8	0	9	9	10	....	....	....
1987-88	Hull Olympiques	QMJHL	38	13	23	36	....	....	....	138	....	....	....	....	....	....	....	....	....	....	19	7	12	19	30	....	....	....
1988-89	Boston Bruins	NHL	26	0	1	1	0	1	1	29	0	0	0	23	0.0	13	1	19	2	–5	....	....	....	....	....	....	....	....
	Maine Mariners	AHL	16	4	10	14	....	....	....	28	....	....	....	....	....	....	....	....	....	....	....	....	....	....	....	....	....	....
1989-90	Boston Bruins	NHL	38	2	2	4	2	1	3	22	0	0	0	43	4.7	14	1	26	2	–11	....	....	....	....	....	....	....	....
	Maine Mariners	AHL	37	4	16	20	....	....	....	27	....	....	....	....	....	....	....	....	....	....	....	....	....	....	....	....	....	....
1990-91	Boston Bruins	NHL	45	2	6	8	2	5	7	89	1	0	0	54	3.7	34	2	34	4	+2	3	0	1	1	7	0	0	0
	Maine Mariners	AHL	23	1	5	6	....	....	....	30	....	....	....	....	....	....	....	....	....	....	....	....	....	....	....	....	....	....
1991-92	Boston Bruins	NHL	49	4	10	14	4	7	11	77	0	0	0	52	7.7	36	4	44	4	–8	....	....	....	....	....	....	....	....
	St. Louis Blues	NHL	26	0	6	6	0	4	4	32	0	0	0	19	0.0	23	2	32	8	–3	....	....	....	....	....	....	....	....
1992-93	St. Louis Blues	NHL	75	1	10	11	1	7	8	100	0	1	0	81	1.2	56	4	76	18	–6	4	1	2	3	6	1	0	0
1993-94	Winnipeg Jets	NHL	81	8	18	26	7	14	21	119	1	1	1	154	5.2	80	15	145	55	–25	9	0	0	0	8	0	0	0
1994-95	Winnipeg Jets	NHL	43	6	17	23	11	25	36	78	3	0	2	107	5.6	67	18	63	14	0	....	....	....	....	....	....	....	....
1995-96	Montreal Canadiens	NHL	68	2	14	16	2	11	13	117	0	1	1	104	1.9	72	15	83	22	–4	6	0	1	1	6	0	0	0
1996-97	Montreal Canadiens	NHL	71	7	15	22	7	13	20	100	1	0	0	139	5.0	80	7	100	37	+1	5	0	1	1	6	0	0	0
1997-98	Montreal Canadiens	NHL	71	6	10	16	7	10	17	97	0	0	0	88	6.8	61	2	68	22	+13	9	0	2	2	4	0	0	0
	NHL Totals		593	38	109	147	43	98	141	860	6	3	4	864	4.4	536	71	699	188		36	1	7	8	37	1	0	0

QMJHL First All-Star Team (1987)

Traded to **St. Louis** by **Boston** with Craig Janney for Adam Oates, February 7, 1992. Traded to **Winnipeg** by **St. Louis** with Nelson Emerson for Phil Housley, September 24, 1993. Traded to **Montreal** by **Winnipeg** for Montreal's 2nd round choice (Jason Doig) in 1995 Entry Draft, July 8, 1995.

• QUINTIN, JEAN-FRANCOIS

Jean-Francois Quintin LW – L. 6', 187 lbs. b: St. Jean, Que., 5/28/1969. Minnesota's 4th choice, 75th overall, in 1989 Entry Draft.

Season	Club	League	GP	G	A	Pts	AG	AA	APts	PIM	PP	SH	GW	S	%	TGF	PGF	TGA	PGA	+/–	GP	G	A	Pts	PIM	PP	SH	GW
1986-87	Shawinigan Cataractes	QMJHL	43	1	9	10	....	....	....	17	....	....	....	....	....	....	....	....	....	....	....	....	....	....	....	....	....	....
1987-88	Shawinigan Cataractes	QMJHL	70	28	70	98	....	....	....	143	....	....	....	....	....	....	....	....	....	....	11	5	8	13	26	....	....	....
1988-89	Shawinigan Cataractes	QMJHL	69	52	100	152	....	....	....	105	....	....	....	....	....	....	....	....	....	....	10	9	15	24	16	....	....	....
1989-90	Kalamazoo Wings	IHL	68	20	18	38	....	....	....	38	....	....	....	....	....	....	....	....	....	....	10	8	4	12	14	....	....	....
1990-91	Kalamazoo Wings	IHL	78	31	43	74	....	....	....	64	....	....	....	....	....	....	....	....	....	....	9	1	5	6	11	....	....	....
1991-92	San Jose Sharks	NHL	8	3	0	3	3	0	3	0	0	0	0	12	25.0	5	0	3	0	+2	....	....	....	....	....	....	....	....
	Kansas City Blades	IHL	21	4	6	10	....	....	....	29	....	....	....	....	....	....	....	....	....	....	13	2	10	12	29	....	....	....
1992-93	San Jose Sharks	NHL	14	2	5	7	2	3	5	4	0	0	0	12	16.7	9	4	9	0	–4	....	....	....	....	....	....	....	....
	Kansas City Blades	IHL	64	20	29	49	....	....	....	169	....	....	....	....	....	....	....	....	....	....	11	2	1	3	16	....	....	....
1993-94	Kansas City Blades	IHL	41	14	19	33	....	....	....	117	....	....	....	....	....	....	....	....	....	....	....	....	....	....	....	....	....	....
1994-95	Kansas City Blades	IHL	63	23	35	58	....	....	....	130	....	....	....	....	....	....	....	....	....	....	19	2	9	11	57	....	....	....
1995-96	Kansas City Blades	IHL	77	26	35	61	....	....	....	158	....	....	....	....	....	....	....	....	....	....	5	0	3	3	20	....	....	....
1996-97	Kansas City Blades	IHL	21	3	5	8	....	....	....	49	....	....	....	....	....	....	....	....	....	....	2	0	0	0	2	....	....	....
1997-98	Kansas City Blades	IHL	79	22	37	59	....	....	....	126	....	....	....	....	....	....	....	....	....	....	11	3	6	9	34	....	....	....
	NHL Totals		22	5	5	10	5	3	8	4	0	0	0	24	20.8	14	4	12	0		....	....	....	....	....	....	....	....

QMJHL Second All-Star Team (1989)

Claimed by **San Jose** from **Minnesota** in Dispersal Draft, May 30, 1991.

• RACINE, YVES

Yves Racine D – L. 6', 205 lbs. b: Matane, Que., 2/7/1969. Detroit's 1st choice, 11th overall, in 1987 Entry Draft.

Season	Club	League	GP	G	A	Pts	AG	AA	APts	PIM	PP	SH	GW	S	%	TGF	PGF	TGA	PGA	+/–	GP	G	A	Pts	PIM	PP	SH	GW
1986-87	Longueuil Chevaliers	QMJHL	70	7	43	50	....	....	....	50	....	....	....	....	....	....	....	....	....	....	20	3	11	14	14	....	....	....
1987-88	Victoriaville Tigres	QMJHL	69	10	84	94	....	....	....	150	....	....	....	....	....	....	....	....	....	....	5	0	0	0	13	....	....	....
	Adirondack Red Wings	AHL	....	....	....	....	....	....	....	....	....	....	....	....	....	....	....	....	....	....	9	4	2	6	2	....	....	....
1988-89	Victoriaville Tigres	QMJHL	63	23	85	108	....	....	....	95	....	....	....	....	....	....	....	....	....	....	16	3	*30	*33	41	....	....	....
	Canada	WJC-A	7	0	0	0	....	....	....	6	....	....	....	....	....	....	....	....	....	....	....	....	....	....	....	....	....	....
	Adirondack Red Wings	AHL	....	....	....	....	....	....	....	....	....	....	....	....	....	....	....	....	....	....	2	1	1	2	0	....	....	....
1989-90	Detroit Red Wings	NHL	28	4	9	13	3	6	9	23	1	0	0	49	8.2	30	9	24	0	–3	....	....	....	....	....	....	....	....
	Adirondack Red Wings	AHL	46	8	27	35	....	....	....	31	....	....	....	....	....	....	....	....	....	....	....	....	....	....	....	....	....	....
1990-91	Detroit Red Wings	NHL	62	7	40	47	6	30	36	33	2	0	1	131	5.3	82	27	57	3	+1	7	2	0	2	0	2	0	0
	Adirondack Red Wings	AHL	16	3	9	12	....	....	....	10	....	....	....	....	....	....	....	....	....	....	....	....	....	....	....	....	....	....
	Canada	WEC-A	4	0	0	0	....	....	....	0	....	....	....	....	....	....	....	....	....	....	....	....	....	....	....	....	....	....
1991-92	Detroit Red Wings	NHL	61	2	22	24	2	17	19	94	1	0	0	103	1.9	69	18	60	12	6	11	2	1	3	10	1	0	1
1992-93	Detroit Red Wings	NHL	80	9	31	40	7	21	28	80	5	0	0	163	5.5	114	38	79	13	+10	7	1	3	4	27	0	0	0
1993-94	Philadelphia Flyers	NHL	67	9	43	52	8	33	41	48	5	1	1	142	6.3	102	45	87	19	–11	....	....	....	....	....	....	....	....
	Canada	WC-A	8	1	2	3	....	....	....	8	....	....	....	....	....	....	....	....	....	....	....	....	....	....	....	....	....	....
1994-95	Montreal Canadiens	NHL	47	4	7	11	7	10	17	42	2	0	1	63	6.3	48	15	55	21	–1	....	....	....	....	....	....	....	....
1995-96	Montreal Canadiens	NHL	25	0	3	3	0	2	2	26	0	0	0	16	0.0	12	3	23	7	–7	....	....	....	....	....	....	....	....
	San Jose Sharks	NHL	32	1	16	17	1	13	14	28	0	0	0	35	2.9	45	10	50	12	–3	....	....	....	....	....	....	....	....

			REGULAR SEASON																		PLAYOFFS							
Season	Club	League	GP	G	A	Pts	AG	AA	APts	PIM	PP	SH	GW	S	%	TGF	PGF	TGA	PGA	+/–	GP	G	A	Pts	PIM	PP	SH	GW
1996-97	Kentucky Thoroughblades	AHL	4	0	1	1	....	....	....	2	....	....	....	....	....	....	....	....	....	....	....	....	....	....	....	....	....	....
	Quebec Rafales	IHL	6	0	4	4	....	....	....	4	....	....	....	....	....	....	....	....	....	....	....	....	....	....	....	....	....	....
	Calgary Flames	**NHL**	**46**	**1**	**15**	**16**	**1**	**13**	**14**	**24**	**1**	**0**	**0**	**82**	**1.2**	**55**	**20**	**32**	**1**	**+4**	....	....	....	....	....	....	....	....
1997-98	**Tampa Bay Lightning**	**NHL**	**60**	**0**	**8**	**8**	**0**	**8**	**8**	**41**	**0**	**0**	**0**	**76**	**0.0**	**31**	**8**	**59**	**13**	**–23**	....	....	....	....	....	....	....	....
	NHL Totals		**508**	**37**	**194**	**231**	**35**	**153**	**188**	**439**	**17**	**1**	**3**	**860**	**4.3**	**588**	**193**	**535**	**101**		**25**	**5**	**4**	**9**	**37**	**3**	**0**	**1**

QMJHL First-All Star Team (1988, 1989)

Traded to **Philadelphia** by **Detroit** with Detroit's 4th round choice (Sebastien Vallee) in 1994 Entry Draft for Terry Carkner, October 5, 1993. Traded to **Montreal** by **Philadelphia** for Kevin Haller, June 29, 1994. Claimed on waivers by **San Jose** from **Montreal**, January 23, 1996. Traded to **Calgary** by **San Jose** for cash, December 17, 1996. Signed as a free agent by **Tampa Bay**, July 16, 1997.

• RAGLAN, HERB

Herb Raglan RW – R. 6', 205 lbs. b: Peterborough, Ont., 8/5/1967. St. Louis' 1st choice, 37th overall, in 1985 Entry Draft.

Season	Club	League	GP	G	A	Pts	AG	AA	APts	PIM	PP	SH	GW	S	%	TGF	PGF	TGA	PGA	+/–	GP	G	A	Pts	PIM	PP	SH	GW
1983-84	Peterborough Bees	Midget	26	39	21	60	....	....	....	60	....	....	....	....	....	....	....	....	....	....	....	....	....	....	....	....	....	....
1984-85	Peterborough Petes	OHL	58	20	22	42	....	....	....	166	....	....	....	....	....	....	....	....	....	....	....	....	....	....	....	....	....	....
1985-86	Kingston Canadians	OHL	28	10	9	19	....	....	....	88	....	....	....	....	....	....	....	....	....	....	10	5	2	7	30	....	....	....
	St. Louis Blues	**NHL**	**7**	**0**	**0**	**0**	**0**	**0**	**0**	**5**	**0**	**0**	**0**	**4**	**0.0**	**0**	**0**	**3**	**0**	**–3**	**10**	**1**	**1**	**2**	**24**	**0**	**0**	**0**
1986-87	**St. Louis Blues**	**NHL**	**62**	**6**	**10**	**16**	**5**	**7**	**12**	**159**	**0**	**0**	**0**	**58**	**10.3**	**28**	**0**	**22**	**0**	**+6**	**4**	**0**	**0**	**0**	**2**	**0**	**0**	**0**
1987-88	**St. Louis Blues**	**NHL**	**73**	**10**	**15**	**25**	**9**	**11**	**20**	**190**	**0**	**0**	**2**	**95**	**10.5**	**37**	**0**	**47**	**0**	**–10**	**10**	**1**	**3**	**4**	**11**	**0**	**0**	**0**
1988-89	**St. Louis Blues**	**NHL**	**50**	**7**	**10**	**17**	**6**	**7**	**13**	**144**	**0**	**0**	**1**	**86**	**8.1**	**22**	**0**	**30**	**0**	**–8**	**8**	**1**	**2**	**3**	**13**	**0**	**0**	**0**
1989-90	**St. Louis Blues**	**NHL**	**11**	**0**	**1**	**1**	**0**	**1**	**1**	**21**	**0**	**0**	**0**	**13**	**0.0**	**2**	**0**	**7**	**0**	**–5**	....	....	....	....	....	....	....	....
1990-91	**St. Louis Blues**	**NHL**	**32**	**3**	**3**	**6**	**3**	**2**	**5**	**52**	**0**	**0**	**1**	**29**	**10.3**	**12**	**0**	**8**	**0**	**+4**	....	....	....	....	....	....	....	....
	Quebec Nordiques	**NHL**	**15**	**1**	**3**	**4**	**1**	**2**	**3**	**30**	**0**	**0**	**0**	**19**	**5.3**	**6**	**0**	**5**	**0**	**+1**	....	....	....	....	....	....	....	....
1991-92	**Quebec Nordiques**	**NHL**	**62**	**6**	**14**	**20**	**5**	**11**	**16**	**120**	**0**	**0**	**0**	**79**	**7.6**	**25**	**1**	**30**	**1**	**–5**	....	....	....	....	....	....	....	....
1992-93	Halifax Citadels	AHL	28	3	9	12	....	....	....	83	....	....	....	....	....	....	....	....	....	....	....	....	....	....	....	....	....	....
	Tampa Bay Lightning	**NHL**	**2**	**0**	**0**	**0**	**0**	**0**	**0**	**2**	**0**	**0**	**0**	**0**	**0.0**	**0**	**0**	**0**	**0**	**0**	....	....	....	....	....	....	....	....
	Atlanta Knights	IHL	24	4	10	14	....	....	....	139	....	....	....	....	....	....	....	....	....	....	9	3	3	6	32	....	....	....
1993-94	Kalamazoo Wings	IHL	29	6	11	17	....	....	....	112	....	....	....	....	....	....	....	....	....	....	5	0	0	0	32	....	....	....
	Ottawa Senators	**NHL**	**29**	**0**	**0**	**0**	**0**	**0**	**0**	**52**	**0**	**0**	**0**	**13**	**0.0**	**0**	**0**	**13**	**0**	**–13**	....	....	....	....	....	....	....	....
1994-95	Kalamazoo Wings	IHL	31	4	4	8	....	....	....	94	....	....	....	....	....	....	....	....	....	....	6	0	0	0	15	....	....	....
1995-96	Brantford Smoke	ColHL	69	46	38	84	....	....	....	267	....	....	....	....	....	....	....	....	....	....	12	9	6	15	58	....	....	....
1996-97	Central Texas Stampede	WPHL	33	14	18	32	....	....	....	131	....	....	....	....	....	....	....	....	....	....	10	7	3	10	30	....	....	....
	Brantford Smoke	ColHL	11	5	4	9	....	....	....	33	....	....	....	....	....	....	....	....	....	....	2	3	1	4	4	....	....	....
1997-98	Brantford Smoke	UHL	17	8	10	18	....	....	....	38	....	....	....	....	....	....	....	....	....	....	....	....	....	....	....	....	....	....
	NHL Totals		**343**	**33**	**56**	**89**	**29**	**41**	**70**	**775**	**0**	**0**	**4**	**396**	**8.3**	**132**	**1**	**165**	**1**		**32**	**3**	**6**	**9**	**50**	**0**	**0**	**0**

Traded to **Quebec** by **St. Louis** with Tony Twist and Andy Rymshaw for Darin Kimble, February 4, 1991. Traded to **Tampa Bay** by **Quebec** for Martin Simard, Steve Tuttle and Michel Mongeau, February 12, 1993. Signed as a free agent by **Ottawa**, January 1, 1994.

• RAGNARSSON, MARCUS

Marcus Ragnarsson D – L. 6'1", 215 lbs. b: Ostervala, Sweden, 8/13/1971. San Jose's 5th choice, 99th overall, in 1992 Entry Draft.

Season	Club	League	GP	G	A	Pts	AG	AA	APts	PIM	PP	SH	GW	S	%	TGF	PGF	TGA	PGA	+/–	GP	G	A	Pts	PIM	PP	SH	GW
1989-90	Djurgarden IF Stockholm	Sweden	13	0	2	2	....	....	....	0	....	....	....	....	....	....	....	....	....	....	1	0	0	0	0	....	....	....
1990-91	Djurgarden IF Stockholm	Sweden	35	4	1	5	....	....	....	12	....	....	....	....	....	....	....	....	....	....	7	0	0	0	6	....	....	....
1991-92	Djurgarden IF Stockholm	Sweden	40	8	5	13	....	....	....	14	....	....	....	....	....	....	....	....	....	....	10	0	1	1	4	....	....	....
1992-93	Djurgarden IF Stockholm	Sweden	35	3	3	6	....	....	....	53	....	....	....	....	....	....	....	....	....	....	6	0	3	3	8	....	....	....
1993-94	Djurgarden IF Stockholm	Sweden	19	0	4	4	....	....	....	24	....	....	....	....	....	....	....	....	....	....	....	....	....	....	....	....	....	....
1994-95	Djurgarden IF Stockholm	Sweden	38	7	9	16	....	....	....	20	....	....	....	....	....	....	....	....	....	....	3	0	0	0	4	....	....	....
	Sweden	WC-A	4	0	0	0	....	....	....	4	....	....	....	....	....	....	....	....	....	....	....	....	....	....	....	....	....	....
1995-96	**San Jose Sharks**	**NHL**	**71**	**8**	**31**	**39**	**8**	**25**	**33**	**42**	**4**	**0**	**0**	**94**	**8.5**	**100**	**37**	**90**	**3**	**–24**	....	....	....	....	....	....	....	....
1996-97	**San Jose Sharks**	**NHL**	**69**	**3**	**14**	**17**	**3**	**12**	**15**	**63**	**2**	**0**	**0**	**57**	**5.3**	**62**	**13**	**90**	**23**	**–18**	....	....	....	....	....	....	....	....
	Sweden	WC-A	11	2	1	3	....	....	....	10	....	....	....	....	....	....	....	....	....	....	....	....	....	....	....	....	....	....
1997-98	**San Jose Sharks**	**NHL**	**79**	**5**	**20**	**25**	**6**	**19**	**25**	**65**	**3**	**0**	**2**	**91**	**5.5**	**67**	**18**	**77**	**17**	**–11**	**6**	**0**	**0**	**0**	**4**	**0**	**0**	**0**
	Sweden	Olympics	3	0	1	1	....	....	....	0	....	....	....	....	....	....	....	....	....	....	....	....	....	....	....	....	....	....
	NHL Totals		**219**	**16**	**65**	**81**	**17**	**56**	**73**	**170**	**9**	**0**	**2**	**242**	**6.6**	**229**	**68**	**257**	**43**		**6**	**0**	**0**	**0**	**4**	**0**	**0**	**0**

• RAMAGE, ROB

Rob Ramage D – R. 6'2", 200 lbs. b: Byron, Ont., 1/11/1959. Colorado's 1st choice, 1st overall, in 1979 Entry Draft.

Season	Club	League	GP	G	A	Pts	AG	AA	APts	PIM	PP	SH	GW	S	%	TGF	PGF	TGA	PGA	+/–	GP	G	A	Pts	PIM	PP	SH	GW
1975-76	London Knights	OHA	65	12	31	43	....	....	....	113	....	....	....	....	....	....	....	....	....	....	5	0	1	1	11	....	....	....
1976-77	London Knights	OHA	65	15	58	73	....	....	....	177	....	....	....	....	....	....	....	....	....	....	20	3	11	14	55	....	....	....
	Canada	WJC-A	7	0	1	1	....	....	....	6	....	....	....	....	....	....	....	....	....	....	....	....	....	....	....	....	....	....
1977-78	London Knights	OHA	59	17	48	65	....	....	....	162	....	....	....	....	....	....	....	....	....	....	11	4	5	9	29	....	....	....
	Canada	WJC-A	6	1	3	4	....	....	....	6	....	....	....	....	....	....	....	....	....	....	....	....	....	....	....	....	....	....
1978-79	Birmingham Bulls	WHA	80	12	36	48	....	....	....	165	....	....	....	....	....	....	....	....	....	....	....	....	....	....	....	....	....	....
1979-80	**Colorado Rockies**	**NHL**	**75**	**8**	**20**	**28**	**7**	**15**	**22**	**135**	**4**	**0**	**3**	**218**	**3.7**	**87**	**21**	**126**	**20**	**–40**	....	....	....	....	....	....	....	....
1980-81	**Colorado Rockies**	**NHL**	**79**	**20**	**42**	**62**	**16**	**29**	**45**	**193**	**12**	**1**	**3**	**289**	**6.9**	**141**	**63**	**164**	**40**	**–46**	....	....	....	....	....	....	....	....
	Canada	WEC-A	8	0	1	1	....	....	....	0	....	....	....	....	....	....	....	....	....	....	....	....	....	....	....	....	....	....
1981-82	**Colorado Rockies**	**NHL**	**80**	**13**	**29**	**42**	**10**	**19**	**29**	**201**	**6**	**0**	**0**	**270**	**4.8**	**113**	**35**	**153**	**28**	**–47**	....	....	....	....	....	....	....	....
1982-83	**St. Louis Blues**	**NHL**	**78**	**16**	**35**	**51**	**13**	**24**	**37**	**193**	**7**	**0**	**3**	**279**	**5.7**	**143**	**47**	**138**	**33**	**–9**	**4**	**0**	**3**	**3**	**22**	**0**	**0**	**0**
1983-84	**St. Louis Blues**	**NHL**	**80**	**15**	**45**	**60**	**12**	**31**	**43**	**121**	**9**	**0**	**3**	**266**	**5.6**	**155**	**64**	**161**	**59**	**–11**	**11**	**1**	**8**	**9**	**32**	**1**	**0**	**1**
1984-85	**St. Louis Blues**	**NHL**	**80**	**7**	**31**	**38**	**6**	**21**	**27**	**178**	**1**	**0**	**0**	**285**	**2.5**	**136**	**41**	**142**	**40**	**–7**	**3**	**1**	**3**	**4**	**6**	**0**	**1**	**0**
1985-86	**St. Louis Blues**	**NHL**	**77**	**10**	**56**	**66**	**8**	**38**	**46**	**171**	**7**	**0**	**2**	**227**	**4.4**	**158**	**52**	**131**	**43**	**+18**	**19**	**1**	**10**	**11**	**66**	**0**	**0**	**0**
1986-87	**St. Louis Blues**	**NHL**	**59**	**11**	**28**	**39**	**10**	**20**	**30**	**108**	**6**	**0**	**3**	**160**	**6.9**	**95**	**41**	**86**	**20**	**–12**	**6**	**2**	**2**	**4**	**21**	**2**	**0**	**0**
1987-88	**St. Louis Blues**	**NHL**	**67**	**8**	**34**	**42**	**7**	**24**	**31**	**127**	**5**	**0**	**0**	**203**	**3.9**	**108**	**46**	**117**	**35**	**–20**	....	....	....	....	....	....	....	....
	Calgary Flames	**NHL**	**12**	**1**	**6**	**7**	**1**	**4**	**5**	**37**	**1**	**0**	**0**	**12**	**8.3**	**26**	**2**	**16**	**8**	**+16**	**9**	**1**	**3**	**4**	**21**	**1**	**0**	**0**
1988-89	**Calgary Flames**	**NHL**	**68**	**3**	**13**	**16**	**3**	**9**	**12**	**156**	**2**	**0**	**0**	**91**	**3.3**	**67**	**9**	**48**	**16**	**+26**	**20**	**1**	**11**	**12**	**26**	**1**	**0**	**0**
1989-90	**Toronto Maple Leafs**	**NHL**	**80**	**8**	**41**	**49**	**7**	**29**	**36**	**202**	**3**	**0**	**1**	**196**	**4.1**	**144**	**48**	**130**	**33**	**–1**	**5**	**1**	**2**	**3**	**20**	**0**	**0**	**0**
1990-91	**Toronto Maple Leafs**	**NHL**	**80**	**10**	**25**	**35**	**9**	**19**	**28**	**173**	**5**	**0**	**2**	**169**	**5.9**	**104**	**28**	**102**	**28**	**+2**	....	....	....	....	....	....	....	....
1991-92	**Minnesota North Stars**	**NHL**	**34**	**4**	**5**	**9**	**4**	**4**	**8**	**69**	**2**	**0**	**0**	**63**	**6.3**	**40**	**15**	**31**	**2**	**–4**	....	....	....	....	....	....	....	....
1992-93	**Tampa Bay Lightning**	**NHL**	**66**	**5**	**12**	**17**	**4**	**8**	**12**	**138**	**5**	**0**	**0**	**115**	**4.3**	**47**	**20**	**66**	**18**	**–21**	....	....	....	....	....	....	....	....
	Montreal Canadiens	**NHL**	**8**	**0**	**1**	**1**	**0**	**1**	**1**	**8**	**0**	**0**	**0**	**16**	**0.0**	**5**	**0**	**12**	**4**	**–3**	**7**	**0**	**0**	**0**	**4**	**0**	**0**	**0**
1993-94	**Montreal Canadiens**	**NHL**	**6**	**0**	**1**	**1**	**0**	**1**	**1**	**2**	**0**	**0**	**0**	**5**	**0.0**	**3**	**0**	**4**	**0**	**–1**	....	....	....	....	....	....	....	....
	Philadelphia Flyers	**NHL**	**15**	**0**	**1**	**1**	**0**	**1**	**1**	**14**	**0**	**0**	**0**	**18**	**0.0**	**3**	**0**	**21**	**7**	**–11**	....	....	....	....	....	....	....	....
	NHL Totals		**1044**	**139**	**425**	**564**	**117**	**297**	**414**	**2226**	**75**	**1**	**20**	**2882**	**4.8**	**1575**	**532**	**1648**	**434**		**84**	**8**	**42**	**50**	**218**	**5**	**1**	**1**
	Other Major League Totals		80	12	36	48	....	....	....	165	....	....	....	....	....	....	....	....	....		....	....	....	....	....	....	....	....

OHA First All-Star Team (1978) • WHA First All-Star Team (1979)

Played in NHL All-Star Game (1981, 1984, 1986, 1988)

Signed as an underage free agent by **Birmingham** (WHA), June, 1978. Traded to **St. Louis** by **New Jersey** for St. Louis' 1st round choice (John MacLean) in 1983 Entry Draft, June 9, 1982. Traded to **Calgary** by **St. Louis** with Rick Wamsley for Brett Hull and Steve Bozek, March 7, 1988. Traded to **Toronto** by **Calgary** for Toronto's 2nd round choice (Kent Manderville) in 1989 Entry Draft June 16, 1989. Claimed by **Minnesota** from **Toronto** in Expansion Draft, May 30, 1991. Claimed by **Tampa Bay** from **Minnesota** in Expansion Draft, June 18, 1992. Traded to **Montreal** by **Tampa Bay** for Eric Charron, Alain Cote and future considerations (Donald Dufresne, June 18, 1993), March 20, 1993. Traded to **Philadelphia** by **Montreal** for cash November 28, 1993.

• RAMSAY, CRAIG

Craig "Rammer" Ramsay LW – L. 5'10", 175 lbs. b: Weston, Ont., 3/17/1951. Buffalo's 2nd choice, 19th overall, in 1971 Amateur Draft.

Season	Club	League	GP	G	A	Pts	AG	AA	APts	PIM	PP	SH	GW	S	%	TGF	PGF	TGA	PGA	+/–	GP	G	A	Pts	PIM	PP	SH	GW
1967-68	Peterborough Petes	OHA	40	6	13	19	....	....	....	21	....	....	....	....	....	....	....	....	....	....	5	0	0	0	4	....	....	....
1968-69	Peterborough Petes	OHA	54	11	28	39	....	....	....	20	....	....	....	....	....	....	....	....	....	....	10	1	2	3	9	....	....	....
1969-70	Peterborough Petes	OHA	54	27	41	68	....	....	....	18	....	....	....	....	....	....	....	....	....	....	....	....	....	....	....	....	....	....
1970-71	Peterborough Petes	OHA	58	30	76	106	....	....	....	25	....	....	....	....	....	....	....	....	....	....	....	....	....	....	....	....	....	....
1971-72	Cincinnati Swords	AHL	19	5	7	12	....	....	....	4	....	....	....	....	....	....	....	....	....	....	....	....	....	....	....	....	....	....
	Buffalo Sabres	**NHL**	**57**	**6**	**10**	**16**	**6**	**9**	**15**	**0**	**0**	**0**	**2**	**43**	**14.0**	**32**	**3**	**28**	**4**	**+5**	....	....	....	....	....	....	....	....
1972-73	**Buffalo Sabres**	**NHL**	**76**	**11**	**17**	**28**	**11**	**14**	**25**	**15**	**0**	**1**	**1**	**89**	**12.4**	**46**	**0**	**46**	**13**	**+13**	**6**	**1**	**1**	**2**	**0**	**0**	**0**	**0**
1973-74	**Buffalo Sabres**	**NHL**	**78**	**20**	**26**	**46**	**20**	**22**	**42**	**0**	**1**	**2**	**3**	**154**	**13.0**	**69**	**4**	**85**	**37**	**+17**	....	....	....	....	....	....	....	....
1974-75	**Buffalo Sabres**	**NHL**	**80**	**26**	**38**	**64**	**24**	**30**	**54**	**26**	**1**	**7**	**7**	**200**	**13.0**	**90**	**5**	**77**	**43**	**+51**	**17**	**5**	**7**	**12**	**2**	**1**	**1**	**1**
1975-76	**Buffalo Sabres**	**NHL**	**80**	**22**	**49**	**71**	**20**	**39**	**59**	**34**	**1**	**1**	**0**	**134**	**16.4**	**100**	**9**	**76**	**29**	**+44**	**9**	**1**	**2**	**3**	**2**	**0**	**1**	**0**
1976-77	**Buffalo Sabres**	**NHL**	**80**	**20**	**41**	**61**	**19**	**33**	**52**	**20**	**2**	**3**	**2**	**145**	**13.8**	**92**	**15**	**68**	**28**	**+37**	**6**	**0**	**4**	**4**	**0**	**0**	**0**	**0**
1977-78	**Buffalo Sabres**	**NHL**	**80**	**28**	**43**	**71**	**27**	**35**	**62**	**18**	**2**	**5**	**3**	**159**	**17.6**	**105**	**17**	**73**	**23**	**+38**	**8**	**3**	**1**	**4**	**9**	**1**	**0**	**1**
1978-79	**Buffalo Sabres**	**NHL**	**80**	**26**	**31**	**57**	**24**	**24**	**48**	**10**	**4**	**3**	**3**	**113**	**23.0**	**90**	**19**	**88**	**38**	**+21**	**3**	**1**	**0**	**1**	**2**	**0**	**0**	**0**

			REGULAR SEASON																		PLAYOFFS							
Season	Club	League	GP	G	A	Pts	AG	AA	APts	PIM	PP	SH	GW	S	%	TGF	PGF	TGA	PGA	+/-	GP	G	A	Pts	PIM	PP	SH	GW
1979-80	**Buffalo Sabres**	**NHL**	**80**	**21**	**39**	**60**	**19**	**30**	**49**	**18**	**5**	**0**	**4**	**103**	**20.4**	**84**	**20**	**82**	**33**	**+15**	**10**	**0**	**6**	**6**	**4**	**0**	**0**	**0**
1980-81	**Buffalo Sabres**	**NHL**	**80**	**24**	**35**	**59**	**20**	**24**	**44**	**12**	**1**	**1**	**3**	**110**	**21.8**	**87**	**3**	**69**	**24**	**+39**	**8**	**2**	**4**	**6**	**4**	**0**	**0**	**1**
1981-82	**Buffalo Sabres**	**NHL**	**80**	**16**	**35**	**51**	**13**	**23**	**36**	**8**	**0**	**1**	**2**	**109**	**14.7**	**68**	**4**	**83**	**33**	**+14**	**4**	**1**	**1**	**2**	**0**	**0**	**0**	**1**
1982-83	**Buffalo Sabres**	**NHL**	**64**	**11**	**18**	**29**	**9**	**12**	**21**	**7**	**0**	**3**	**1**	**87**	**12.6**	**41**	**2**	**42**	**17**	**+14**	**10**	**2**	**3**	**5**	**4**	**0**	**0**	**0**
1983-84	**Buffalo Sabres**	**NHL**	**76**	**9**	**17**	**26**	**7**	**12**	**19**	**17**	**0**	**0**	**0**	**97**	**9.3**	**47**	**2**	**64**	**22**	**+3**	**3**	**0**	**1**	**1**	**0**	**0**	**0**	**0**
1984-85	**Buffalo Sabres**	**NHL**	**79**	**12**	**21**	**33**	**10**	**14**	**24**	**16**	**0**	**0**	**1**	**71**	**16.9**	**51**	**4**	**53**	**23**	**+17**	**5**	**1**	**1**	**2**	**0**	**0**	**0**	**0**
	NHL Totals		**1070**	**252**	**420**	**672**	**229**	**321**	**550**	**201**	**17**	**27**	**32**	**1614**	**15.6**	**1002**	**107**	**934**	**367**		**89**	**17**	**31**	**48**	**27**	**2**	**2**	**4**

Won Frank J. Selke Trophy (1985)

Played in NHL All-Star Game (1976)

• RAMSEY, MIKE

Mike Ramsey D – L. 6'3", 195 lbs. b: Minneapolis, MN, 12/3/1960. Buffalo's 1st choice, 11th overall, in 1979 Entry Draft.

Season	Club	League	GP	G	A	Pts	AG	AA	APts	PIM	PP	SH	GW	S	%	TGF	PGF	TGA	PGA	+/-	GP	G	A	Pts	PIM	PP	SH	GW
1978-79	University of Minnesota	WCHA	26	6	11	17	....	....	....	30	....	....	....	....	....	....	....	....	....	....	....	....	....	....	....	....	....	....
	United States	WJC-A	5	1	1	2	....	....	....	10	....	....	....	....	....	....	....	....	....	....	....	....	....	....	....	....	....	....
1979-80	United States	Nat-Team	56	11	22	33	....	....	....	55	....	....	....	....	....	....	....	....	....	....	....	....	....	....	....	....	....	....
	United States	Olympics	7	0	2	2	....	....	....	8	....	....	....	....	....	....	....	....	....	....	....	....	....	....	....	....	....	....
	Buffalo Sabres	**NHL**	**13**	**1**	**6**	**7**	**1**	**5**	**6**	**6**	**0**	**0**	**1**	**17**	**5.9**	**17**	**1**	**8**	**1**	**+9**	**13**	**1**	**2**	**3**	**12**	**1**	**0**	**1**
1980-81	**Buffalo Sabres**	**NHL**	**72**	**3**	**14**	**17**	**2**	**10**	**12**	**56**	**0**	**0**	**0**	**50**	**6.0**	**45**	**7**	**27**	**5**	**+16**	**8**	**0**	**3**	**3**	**20**	**0**	**0**	**0**
1981-82	**Buffalo Sabres**	**NHL**	**80**	**7**	**23**	**30**	**6**	**15**	**21**	**56**	**2**	**0**	**0**	**94**	**7.4**	**102**	**8**	**96**	**20**	**+18**	**4**	**1**	**1**	**2**	**14**	**0**	**0**	**0**
	United States	WEC-A	7	1	0	1	....	....	....	8	....	....	....	....	....	....	....	....	....	....	....	....	....	....	....	....	....	....
1982-83	**Buffalo Sabres**	**NHL**	**77**	**8**	**30**	**38**	**7**	**21**	**28**	**55**	**1**	**1**	**1**	**116**	**6.9**	**109**	**12**	**101**	**24**	**+20**	**10**	**4**	**4**	**8**	**15**	**0**	**0**	**1**
1983-84	**Buffalo Sabres**	**NHL**	**72**	**9**	**22**	**31**	**7**	**15**	**22**	**82**	**1**	**0**	**4**	**134**	**6.7**	**96**	**12**	**88**	**31**	**+27**	**3**	**0**	**1**	**1**	**6**	**0**	**0**	**0**
1984-85	United States	C Cup	6	1	1	2	....	....	....	6	....	....	....	....	....	....	....	....	....	....	....	....	....	....	....	....	....	....
	Buffalo Sabres	**NHL**	**79**	**8**	**22**	**30**	**7**	**15**	**22**	**102**	**3**	**0**	**2**	**160**	**5.0**	**115**	**27**	**85**	**28**	**+31**	**5**	**0**	**1**	**1**	**23**	**0**	**0**	**0**
1985-86	**Buffalo Sabres**	**NHL**	**76**	**7**	**21**	**28**	**6**	**14**	**20**	**117**	**1**	**0**	**1**	**154**	**4.5**	**104**	**14**	**124**	**35**	**+1**	....	....	....	....	....	....	....	....
1986-87	**Buffalo Sabres**	**NHL**	**80**	**8**	**31**	**39**	**7**	**22**	**29**	**109**	**2**	**1**	**0**	**154**	**5.2**	**110**	**22**	**151**	**64**	**+1**	....	....	....	....	....	....	....	....
	NHL All-Stars	RV'87	2	0	0	0	....	....	....	0	....	....	....	....	....	....	....	....	....	....	....	....	....	....	....	....	....	....
1987-88	United States	C Cup	5	0	1	1	....	....	....	2	....	....	....	....	....	....	....	....	....	....	....	....	....	....	....	....	....	....
	Buffalo Sabres	**NHL**	**63**	**5**	**16**	**21**	**4**	**11**	**15**	**77**	**1**	**0**	**0**	**94**	**5.3**	**76**	**16**	**103**	**49**	**+6**	**6**	**0**	**3**	**3**	**29**	**0**	**0**	**0**
1988-89	**Buffalo Sabres**	**NHL**	**56**	**2**	**14**	**16**	**2**	**10**	**12**	**84**	**0**	**0**	**1**	**63**	**3.2**	**62**	**6**	**75**	**24**	**+5**	**5**	**1**	**0**	**1**	**11**	**1**	**0**	**0**
1989-90	**Buffalo Sabres**	**NHL**	**73**	**4**	**21**	**25**	**3**	**15**	**18**	**47**	**1**	**0**	**2**	**91**	**4.4**	**86**	**9**	**85**	**29**	**+21**	**6**	**0**	**1**	**1**	**8**	**0**	**0**	**0**
1990-91	**Buffalo Sabres**	**NHL**	**71**	**6**	**14**	**20**	**5**	**11**	**16**	**46**	**0**	**0**	**1**	**87**	**6.9**	**80**	**1**	**100**	**35**	**+14**	**5**	**1**	**0**	**1**	**12**	**0**	**0**	**1**
1991-92	**Buffalo Sabres**	**NHL**	**66**	**3**	**14**	**17**	**3**	**11**	**14**	**67**	**0**	**0**	**1**	**55**	**5.5**	**52**	**3**	**84**	**43**	**+8**	**7**	**0**	**2**	**2**	**8**	**0**	**0**	**0**
1992-93	**Buffalo Sabres**	**NHL**	**33**	**2**	**8**	**10**	**2**	**5**	**7**	**20**	**0**	**0**	**0**	**27**	**7.4**	**29**	**0**	**33**	**8**	**+4**	....	....	....	....	....	....	....	....
	Pittsburgh Penguins	**NHL**	**12**	**1**	**2**	**3**	**1**	**1**	**2**	**8**	**0**	**0**	**0**	**8**	**12.5**	**20**	**0**	**9**	**2**	**+13**	**12**	**0**	**6**	**6**	**4**	**0**	**0**	**0**
1993-94	**Pittsburgh Penguins**	**NHL**	**65**	**2**	**2**	**4**	**2**	**2**	**4**	**22**	**0**	**0**	**0**	**31**	**6.5**	**31**	**0**	**51**	**16**	**–4**	**1**	**0**	**0**	**0**	**0**	**0**	**0**	**0**
1994-95	**Detroit Red Wings**	**NHL**	**33**	**1**	**2**	**3**	**2**	**3**	**5**	**23**	**0**	**0**	**0**	**29**	**3.4**	**24**	**1**	**19**	**7**	**+11**	**15**	**0**	**1**	**1**	**4**	**0**	**0**	**0**
1995-96	**Detroit Red Wings**	**NHL**	**47**	**2**	**4**	**6**	**2**	**3**	**5**	**35**	**0**	**0**	**0**	**35**	**5.7**	**35**	**0**	**28**	**10**	**+17**	**15**	**0**	**4**	**4**	**10**	**0**	**0**	**0**
1996-97	**Detroit Red Wings**	**NHL**	**2**	**0**	**0**	**0**	**0**	**0**	**0**	**0**	**0**	**0**	**0**	**3**	**0.0**	**1**	**0**	**2**	**1**	**0**	....	....	....	....	....	....	....	....
	NHL Totals		**1070**	**79**	**266**	**345**	**69**	**189**	**258**	**1012**	**12**	**2**	**14**	**1402**	**5.6**	**1194**	**139**	**1269**	**432**		**115**	**8**	**29**	**37**	**176**	**2**	**0**	**3**

Played in NHL All-Star Game (1982, 1983, 1985, 1986)

Traded to **Pittsburgh** by **Buffalo** for Bob Errey, March 22, 1993. Signed as a free agent by **Detroit**, August 3, 1994.

• RAMSEY, WAYNE

Wayne Ramsey D – L. 6', 185 lbs. b: Hamiota, Man., 1/31/1957. Buffalo's 5th choice, 104th overall, in 1977 Amateur Draft.

Season	Club	League	GP	G	A	Pts	AG	AA	APts	PIM	PP	SH	GW	S	%	TGF	PGF	TGA	PGA	+/-	GP	G	A	Pts	PIM	PP	SH	GW
1973-74	Brandon Wheat Kings	WCJHL	53	1	11	12	....	....	....	37	....	....	....	....	....	....	....	....	....	....	....	....	....	....	....	....	....	....
1974-75	Brandon Wheat Kings	WCJHL	21	1	0	1	....	....	....	17	....	....	....	....	....	....	....	....	....	....	5	1	2	3	7	....	....	....
1975-76	Brandon Wheat Kings	WCJHL	63	11	37	48	....	....	....	75	....	....	....	....	....	....	....	....	....	....	5	0	2	2	6	....	....	....
1976-77	Brandon Wheat Kings	WCJHL	72	16	60	76	....	....	....	136	....	....	....	....	....	....	....	....	....	....	16	4	*16	20	33	....	....	....
1977-78	**Buffalo Sabres**	**NHL**	**2**	**0**	**0**	**0**	**0**	**0**	**0**	**0**	**0**	**0**	**0**	**0**	**0.0**	**0**	**0**	**0**	**0**	**0**	....	....	....	....	....	....	....	....
	Hershey Bears	AHL	56	10	18	28	....	....	....	35	....	....	....	....	....	....	....	....	....	....	....	....	....	....	....	....	....	....
1978-79	Springfield Indians	AHL	15	4	5	9	....	....	....	8	....	....	....	....	....	....	....	....	....	....	....	....	....	....	....	....	....	....
	Milwaukee Admirals	IHL	3	1	2	3	....	....	....	2	....	....	....	....	....	....	....	....	....	....	....	....	....	....	....	....	....	....
	Toledo Goaldiggers	IHL	61	9	30	39	....	....	....	63	....	....	....	....	....	....	....	....	....	....	6	0	4	4	6	....	....	....
1979-80	Rochester Americans	AHL	68	6	29	35	....	....	....	58	....	....	....	....	....	....	....	....	....	....	....	....	....	....	....	....	....	....
1980-81	Port Huron Flags	IHL	61	9	29	38	....	....	....	53	....	....	....	....	....	....	....	....	....	....	4	1	1	2	4	....	....	....
	NHL Totals		**2**	**0**	**0**	**0**	**0**	**0**	**0**	**0**	**0**	**0**	**0**	**0**	**0.0**	**0**	**0**	**0**	**0**		....	....	....	....	....	....	....	....

Traded to **Toledo** (IHL) by **Milwaukee** (IHL) for Paul Tantardini, December, 1978.

• RANHEIM, PAUL

Paul Ranheim LW – R. 6'1", 210 lbs. b: St. Louis, MO, 1/25/1966. Calgary's 3rd choice, 38th overall, in 1984 Entry Draft.

Season	Club	League	GP	G	A	Pts	AG	AA	APts	PIM	PP	SH	GW	S	%	TGF	PGF	TGA	PGA	+/-	GP	G	A	Pts	PIM	PP	SH	GW
1983-84	Edina-Minnesota High	H.S.	26	16	24	40	....	....	....	6	....	....	....	....	....	....	....	....	....	....	....	....	....	....	....	....	....	....
1984-85	University of Wisconsin	WCHA	42	11	11	22	....	....	....	40	....	....	....	....	....	....	....	....	....	....	....	....	....	....	....	....	....	....
1985-86	University of Wisconsin	WCHA	33	17	17	34	....	....	....	34	....	....	....	....	....	....	....	....	....	....	....	....	....	....	....	....	....	....
	United States	WJC-A	7	6	3	9	....	....	....	8	....	....	....	....	....	....	....	....	....	....	....	....	....	....	....	....	....	....
1986-87	University of Wisconsin	WCHA	42	24	35	59	....	....	....	54	....	....	....	....	....	....	....	....	....	....	....	....	....	....	....	....	....	....
1987-88	University of Wisconsin	WCHA	44	36	26	62	....	....	....	63	....	....	....	....	....	....	....	....	....	....	....	....	....	....	....	....	....	....
1988-89	**Calgary Flames**	**NHL**	**5**	**0**	**0**	**0**	**0**	**0**	**0**	**0**	**0**	**0**	**0**	**4**	**0.0**	**2**	**0**	**5**	**0**	**–3**	....	....	....	....	....	....	....	....
	Salt Lake Golden Eagles	IHL	75	*68	29	97	....	....	....	16	....	....	....	....	....	....	....	....	....	....	14	5	5	10	8	....	....	....
1989-90	Calgary Flames	FrTour	4	2	0	2	....	....	....	0	....	....	....	....	....	....	....	....	....	....	....	....	....	....	....	....	....	....
	Calgary Flames	**NHL**	**80**	**26**	**28**	**54**	**22**	**20**	**42**	**23**	**1**	**3**	**4**	**197**	**13.2**	**72**	**5**	**51**	**11**	**+27**	**6**	**1**	**3**	**4**	**2**	**0**	**0**	**0**
	United States	WEC-A	9	4	0	4	....	....	....	6	....	....	....	....	....	....	....	....	....	....	....	....	....	....	....	....	....	....
1990-91	**Calgary Flames**	**NHL**	**39**	**14**	**16**	**30**	**13**	**12**	**25**	**4**	**2**	**0**	**2**	**108**	**13.0**	**56**	**14**	**32**	**10**	**+20**	**7**	**2**	**2**	**4**	**0**	**0**	**0**	**0**
1991-92	**Calgary Flames**	**NHL**	**80**	**23**	**20**	**43**	**21**	**15**	**36**	**32**	**1**	**3**	**3**	**159**	**14.5**	**65**	**6**	**59**	**16**	**+16**	....	....	....	....	....	....	....	....
	United States	WC-A	6	2	1	3	....	....	....	2	....	....	....	....	....	....	....	....	....	....	....	....	....	....	....	....	....	....
1992-93	**Calgary Flames**	**NHL**	**83**	**21**	**22**	**43**	**17**	**15**	**32**	**26**	**3**	**4**	**1**	**179**	**11.7**	**59**	**9**	**96**	**42**	**–4**	**6**	**0**	**1**	**1**	**0**	**0**	**0**	**0**
1993-94	**Calgary Flames**	**NHL**	**67**	**10**	**14**	**24**	**9**	**11**	**20**	**20**	**0**	**2**	**2**	**110**	**9.1**	**37**	**2**	**68**	**26**	**–7**	....	....	....	....	....	....	....	....
	Hartford Whalers	**NHL**	**15**	**0**	**3**	**3**	**0**	**2**	**2**	**2**	**0**	**0**	**0**	**21**	**0.0**	**5**	**0**	**20**	**4**	**–11**	....	....	....	....	....	....	....	....
1994-95	**Hartford Whalers**	**NHL**	**47**	**6**	**14**	**20**	**11**	**21**	**32**	**10**	**0**	**0**	**1**	**73**	**8.2**	**24**	**1**	**41**	**15**	**–3**	....	....	....	....	....	....	....	....
1995-96	**Hartford Whalers**	**NHL**	**73**	**10**	**20**	**30**	**10**	**16**	**26**	**14**	**0**	**1**	**1**	**126**	**7.9**	**39**	**2**	**56**	**17**	**–2**	....	....	....	....	....	....	....	....
1996-97	**Hartford Whalers**	**NHL**	**67**	**10**	**11**	**21**	**11**	**10**	**21**	**18**	**0**	**3**	**1**	**96**	**10.4**	**30**	**1**	**61**	**19**	**–13**	....	....	....	....	....	....	....	....
	United States	WC-A	8	2	0	2	....	....	....	2	....	....	....	....	....	....	....	....	....	....	....	....	....	....	....	....	....	....
1997-98	**Carolina Hurricanes**	**NHL**	**73**	**5**	**9**	**14**	**6**	**9**	**15**	**28**	**0**	**1**	**2**	**77**	**6.5**	**17**	**0**	**42**	**14**	**–11**	....	....	....	....	....	....	....	....
	NHL Totals		**629**	**125**	**157**	**282**	**120**	**131**	**251**	**177**	**7**	**17**	**17**	**1150**	**10.9**	**406**	**40**	**531**	**174**		**19**	**3**	**6**	**9**	**2**	**0**	**0**	**0**

WCHA Second All-Star Team (1987) • NCAA West First All-American Team (1988) • WCHA First All-Star Team (1988) • IHL Second All-Star Team (1989) • Won Garry F. Longman Memorial Trophy (Top Rookie - IHL) (1989)

Traded to **Hartford** by **Calgary** with Gary Suter and Ted Drury for James Patrick, Zarley Zalapski and Michael Nylander, March 10, 1994. Transferred to **Carolina** after **Hartford** franchise relocated, June 25, 1997.

• RASMUSSEN, ERIK

Erik Rasmussen C – L. 6'2", 205 lbs. b: Minneapolis, MN, 3/28/1977. Buffalo's 1st choice, 7th overall, in 1996 Entry Draft.

Season	Club	League	GP	G	A	Pts	AG	AA	APts	PIM	PP	SH	GW	S	%	TGF	PGF	TGA	PGA	+/-	GP	G	A	Pts	PIM	PP	SH	GW
1995-96	University of Minnesota	WCHA	40	16	32	48	....	....	....	55	....	....	....	....	....	....	....	....	....	....	....	....	....	....	....	....	....	....
	United States	WJC-A	6	0	1	1	....	....	....	16	....	....	....	....	....	....	....	....	....	....	....	....	....	....	....	....	....	....
1996-97	University of Minnesota	WCHA	34	15	12	27	....	....	....	*123	....	....	....	....	....	....	....	....	....	....	....	....	....	....	....	....	....	....
	United States	WJC-A	6	4	5	9	....	....	....	4	....	....	....	....	....	....	....	....	....	....	....	....	....	....	....	....	....	....
1997-98	**Buffalo Sabres**	**NHL**	**21**	**2**	**3**	**5**	**2**	**3**	**5**	**14**	**0**	**0**	**0**	**28**	**7.1**	**12**	**0**	**10**	**0**	**+2**	....	....	....	....	....	....	....	....
	Rochester Americans	AHL	53	9	14	23	....	....	....	83	....	....	....	....	....	....	....	....	....	....	1	0	0	0	5	....	....	....
	NHL Totals		**21**	**2**	**3**	**5**	**2**	**3**	**5**	**14**	**0**	**0**	**0**	**28**	**7.1**	**12**	**0**	**10**	**0**		....	....	....	....	....	....	....	....

• RATELLE, JEAN

Jean Ratelle C – L. 6'1", 180 lbs. b: Lac Ste. Jean, Que., 10/3/1940. **HHOF**

Season	Club	League	GP	G	A	Pts	AG	AA	APts	PIM	PP	SH	GW	S	%	TGF	PGF	TGA	PGA	+/-	GP	G	A	Pts	PIM	PP	SH	GW
1958-50	Guelph Biltmores	OHA	54	20	31	51	....	....	....	11	....	....	....	....	....	....	....	....	....	....	10	5	4	9	2	....	....	....
1959-60	Guelph Biltmores	OHA	48	39	47	86	....	....	....	15	....	....	....	....	....	....	....	....	....	....	5	3	5	8	4	....	....	....
	Trois-Rivieres Lions	EPHL	3	3	5	8	....	....	....	0	....	....	....	....	....	....	....	....	....	....	4	0	3	3	0	....	....	....

			REGULAR SEASON																		PLAYOFFS							
Season	**Club**	**League**	**GP**	**G**	**A**	**Pts**	**AG**	**AA**	**APts**	**PIM**	**PP**	**SH**	**GW**	**S**	**%**	**TGF**	**PGF**	**TGA**	**PGA**	**+/-**	**GP**	**G**	**A**	**Pts**	**PIM**	**PP**	**SH**	**GW**
1960-61	Guelph Royals	OHA	47	40	*61	101	....	....	....	10	....	....	....	....	....	....	....	....	....	....	14	6	11	17	6	....	....	....
	New York Rangers	**NHL**	**3**	**2**	**1**	**3**	**2**	**1**	**3**	**0**	....	....	....	....	....	....	....	....	....	....	....	....	....	....	....	....	....	....
1961-62	**New York Rangers**	**NHL**	**31**	**4**	**8**	**12**	**5**	**8**	**13**	**4**	....	....	....	....	....	....	....	....	....	....	....	....	....	....	....	....	....	....
	Kitchener-Waterloo Beavers	EPHL	32	10	29	39	....	....	....	8	....	....	....	....	....	....	....	....	....	....	7	2	6	8	2	....	....	....
1962-63	**New York Rangers**	**NHL**	**48**	**11**	**9**	**20**	**13**	**9**	**22**	**8**	....	....	....	....	....	....	....	....	....	....	....	....	....	....	....	....	....	....
	Baltimore Clippers	AHL	20	11	8	19	....	....	....	0	....	....	....	....	....	....	....	....	....	....	3	0	0	0	0	....	....	....
1963-64	**New York Rangers**	**NHL**	**15**	**0**	**7**	**7**	**0**	**8**	**8**	**6**	....	....	....	....	....	....	....	....	....	....	....	....	....	....	....	....	....	....
	Baltimore Clippers	AHL	57	20	26	46	....	....	....	2	....	....	....	....	....	....	....	....	....	....	....	....	....	....	....	....	....	....
1964-65	**New York Rangers**	**NHL**	**54**	**14**	**21**	**35**	**18**	**23**	**41**	**14**	....	....	....	....	....	....	....	....	....	....	....	....	....	....	....	....	....	....
	Baltimore Clippers	AHL	8	9	4	13	....	....	....	6	....	....	....	....	....	....	....	....	....	....	....	....	....	....	....	....	....	....
1965-66	**New York Rangers**	**NHL**	**67**	**21**	**30**	**51**	**25**	**30**	**55**	**10**	....	....	....	....	....	....	....	....	....	....	....	....	....	....	....	....	....	....
1966-67	**New York Rangers**	**NHL**	**41**	**6**	**5**	**11**	**7**	**5**	**12**	**4**	....	....	....	....	....	....	....	....	....	....	**4**	**0**	**0**	**0**	**2**	....	....	....
1967-68	**New York Rangers**	**NHL**	**74**	**32**	**46**	**78**	**40**	**48**	**88**	**18**	**10**	**0**	**5**	**180**	**17.8**	**98**	**25**	**50**	**0**	**+23**	**6**	**0**	**4**	**4**	**2**	**0**	**0**	**0**
1968-69	**New York Rangers**	**NHL**	**75**	**32**	**46**	**78**	**36**	**43**	**79**	**26**	**8**	**0**	**4**	**204**	**15.7**	**110**	**36**	**58**	**0**	**+16**	**4**	**1**	**0**	**1**	**0**	**1**	**0**	**0**
1969-70	**New York Rangers**	**NHL**	**75**	**32**	**42**	**74**	**37**	**42**	**79**	**28**	**10**	**0**	**6**	**198**	**16.2**	**93**	**29**	**57**	**1**	**+8**	**6**	**1**	**3**	**4**	**0**	**0**	**0**	**0**
1970-71	**New York Rangers**	**NHL**	**78**	**26**	**46**	**72**	**27**	**41**	**68**	**14**	**6**	**1**	**3**	**203**	**12.8**	**93**	**26**	**41**	**2**	**+28**	**13**	**2**	**9**	**11**	**8**	**0**	**0**	**0**
1971-72	**New York Rangers**	**NHL**	**63**	**46**	**63**	**109**	**49**	**58**	**107**	**4**	**5**	**1**	**6**	**183**	**25.1**	**140**	**39**	**41**	**1**	**+61**	**6**	**0**	**1**	**1**	**0**	**0**	**0**	**0**
1972-73	Canada	Summit	6	1	3	4	....	....	....	0	....	....	....	....	....	....	....	....	....	....	....	....	....	....	....	....	....	....
	New York Rangers	**NHL**	**78**	**41**	**53**	**94**	**41**	**44**	**85**	**12**	**11**	**0**	**4**	**241**	**17.0**	**123**	**35**	**67**	**3**	**+24**	**10**	**2**	**7**	**9**	**0**	**1**	**0**	**0**
1973-74	**New York Rangers**	**NHL**	**68**	**28**	**39**	**67**	**29**	**34**	**63**	**16**	**6**	**0**	**3**	**165**	**17.0**	**95**	**34**	**60**	**4**	**+5**	**13**	**2**	**4**	**6**	**0**	**0**	**0**	**1**
1974-75	**New York Rangers**	**NHL**	**79**	**36**	**55**	**91**	**33**	**43**	**76**	**26**	**15**	**0**	**6**	**205**	**17.6**	**129**	**63**	**65**	**0**	**+1**	**3**	**1**	**5**	**6**	**2**	**1**	**0**	**0**
1975-76	**New York Rangers**	**NHL**	**13**	**5**	**10**	**15**	**5**	**8**	**13**	**2**	**2**	**0**	**1**	**28**	**17.9**	**20**	**9**	**12**	**3**	**+2**	....	....	....	....	....	....	....	....
	Boston Bruins	**NHL**	**67**	**31**	**59**	**90**	**29**	**47**	**76**	**16**	**15**	**1**	**3**	**186**	**16.7**	**115**	**50**	**66**	**18**	**+17**	**12**	**8**	**8**	**16**	**4**	**5**	**0**	**1**
1976-77	**Boston Bruins**	**NHL**	**78**	**33**	**61**	**94**	**32**	**50**	**82**	**22**	**8**	**1**	**6**	**186**	**17.7**	**117**	**27**	**75**	**4**	**+19**	**14**	**5**	**12**	**17**	**4**	**1**	**0**	**1**
1977-78	**Boston Bruins**	**NHL**	**80**	**25**	**59**	**84**	**24**	**48**	**72**	**10**	**3**	**0**	**5**	**158**	**15.8**	**112**	**16**	**53**	**6**	**+49**	**15**	**3**	**7**	**10**	**0**	**0**	**0**	**0**
1978-79	**Boston Bruins**	**NHL**	**80**	**27**	**45**	**72**	**25**	**34**	**59**	**12**	**11**	**0**	**5**	**137**	**19.7**	**100**	**32**	**61**	**10**	**+17**	**11**	**7**	**6**	**13**	**2**	**2**	**0**	**2**
1979-80	**Boston Bruins**	**NHL**	**67**	**28**	**45**	**73**	**25**	**35**	**60**	**8**	**14**	**0**	**1**	**145**	**19.3**	**98**	**38**	**53**	**4**	**+11**	**3**	**0**	**0**	**0**	**0**	**0**	**0**	**0**
1980-81	**Boston Bruins**	**NHL**	**47**	**11**	**26**	**37**	**9**	**18**	**27**	**16**	**4**	**0**	**2**	**62**	**17.7**	**52**	**19**	**26**	**11**	**+18**	**3**	**0**	**0**	**0**	**0**	**0**	**0**	**0**
	NHL Totals		**1281**	**491**	**776**	**1267**	**511**	**677**	**1188**	**276**	**128**	**4**	**60**	**2481**	**19.8**	**1495**	**478**	**785**	**67**		**123**	**32**	**66**	**98**	**24**	**11**	**0**	**5**

Won Bill Masterton Trophy (1971) • NHL Second All-Star Team (1972) • Won Lady Byng Trophy (1972, 1976) • Won Lester B. Pearson Award (1972)
Played in NHL All-Star Game (1970, 1971, 1972, 1973, 1980)
Traded to **Boston** by **NY Rangers** with Brad Park for Phil Esposito and Carol Vadnais, November 7, 1975.

• RATHJE, MIKE

Mike Rathje D – L. 6'6", 220 lbs. b: Mannville, Alta., 5/11/1974. San Jose's 1st choice, 3rd overall, in 1992 Entry Draft.

1990-91	Medicine Hat Tigers	WHL	64	1	16	17	....	....	....	28	....	....	....	....	....	....	....	....	....	....	12	0	4	4	2	....	....	....
1991-92	Medicine Hat Tigers	WHL	67	11	23	34	....	....	....	109	....	....	....	....	....	....	....	....	....	....	4	0	1	1	2	....	....	....
1992-93	Medicine Hat Tigers	WHL	57	12	37	49	....	....	....	103	....	....	....	....	....	....	....	....	....	....	10	3	3	6	12	....	....	....
	Canada	WJC-A	7	2	2	4	....	....	....	12	....	....	....	....	....	....	....	....	....	....	....	....	....	....	....	....	....	....
	Kansas City Blades	IHL	....	....	....	....	....	....	....	....	....	....	....	....	....	....	....	....	....	....	5	0	0	0	12	....	....	....
1993-94	**San Jose Sharks**	**NHL**	**47**	**1**	**9**	**10**	**1**	**7**	**8**	**59**	**1**	**0**	**0**	**30**	**3.3**	**26**	**3**	**42**	**10**	**-9**	**1**	**0**	**0**	**0**	**0**	**0**	**0**	**0**
	Kansas City Blades	IHL	6	0	2	2	....	....	....	0	....	....	....	....	....	....	....	....	....	....	....	....	....	....	....	....	....	....
1994-95	**San Jose Sharks**	**NHL**	**42**	**2**	**7**	**9**	**4**	**10**	**14**	**29**	**0**	**0**	**0**	**38**	**5.3**	**42**	**5**	**53**	**15**	**-1**	**11**	**5**	**2**	**7**	**4**	**5**	**0**	**0**
	Kansas City Blades	IHL	6	0	1	1	....	....	....	7	....	....	....	....	....	....	....	....	....	....	....	....	....	....	....	....	....	....
1995-96	**San Jose Sharks**	**NHL**	**27**	**0**	**7**	**7**	**0**	**6**	**6**	**14**	**0**	**0**	**0**	**26**	**0.0**	**24**	**9**	**46**	**15**	**-16**	....	....	....	....	....	....	....	....
	Kansas City Blades	IHL	36	6	11	17	....	....	....	34	....	....	....	....	....	....	....	....	....	....	....	....	....	....	....	....	....	....
1996-97	**San Jose Sharks**	**NHL**	**31**	**0**	**8**	**8**	**0**	**7**	**7**	**21**	**0**	**0**	**0**	**22**	**0.0**	**26**	**3**	**31**	**7**	**-1**	....	....	....	....	....	....	....	....
1997-98	**San Jose Sharks**	**NHL**	**81**	**3**	**12**	**15**	**4**	**12**	**16**	**59**	**1**	**0**	**0**	**61**	**4.9**	**55**	**6**	**83**	**30**	**-4**	**6**	**1**	**0**	**1**	**6**	**1**	**0**	**0**
	NHL Totals		**228**	**6**	**43**	**49**	**9**	**42**	**51**	**182**	**2**	**0**	**0**	**177**	**3.4**	**173**	**26**	**255**	**77**		**18**	**6**	**2**	**8**	**10**	**6**	**0**	**0**

WHL East Second All-Star Team (1992, 1993)

• RATHWELL, JOHN

John "Jake" Rathwell RW – L. 6', 190 lbs. b: Temiscominque, Que., 8/12/1947.

1967-68	Espanola Bruins	Jr. B	STATISTICS NOT AVAILABLE																									
	Kitchener Rangers	OHA	9	0	0	0	....	....	....	7	....	....	....	....	....	....	....	....	....	....	....	....	....	....	....	....	....	....
	Peterborough Petes	OHA	14	2	2	4	....	....	....	4	....	....	....	....	....	....	....	....	....	....	....	....	....	....	....	....	....	....
1968-69	Clinton Comets	EHL	72	18	26	44	....	....	....	104	....	....	....	....	....	....	....	....	....	....	17	5	6	11	30	....	....	....
1969-70	Clinton Comets	EHL	74	*56	43	99	....	....	....	151	....	....	....	....	....	....	....	....	....	....	17	11	12	23	27	....	....	....
	Iowa Stars	CHL	....	....	....	....	....	....	....	....	....	....	....	....	....	....	....	....	....	....	3	0	0	0	4	....	....	....
1970-71	Salt Lake Golden Eagles	WHL	71	20	19	39	....	....	....	66	....	....	....	....	....	....	....	....	....	....	....	....	....	....	....	....	....	....
1971-72	Salt Lake Golden Eagles	WHL	30	5	6	11	....	....	....	20	....	....	....	....	....	....	....	....	....	....	....	....	....	....	....	....	....	....
	Portland Buckaroos	WHL	16	8	5	13	....	....	....	17	....	....	....	....	....	....	....	....	....	....	....	....	....	....	....	....	....	....
	Cincinnati Swords	AHL	14	6	6	12	....	....	....	4	....	....	....	....	....	....	....	....	....	....	10	2	2	4	17	....	....	....
1972-73	Cincinnati Swords	AHL	76	27	44	71	....	....	....	78	....	....	....	....	....	....	....	....	....	....	15	4	8	12	22	....	....	....
1973-74	San Diego Gulls	WHL	37	6	10	16	....	....	....	25	....	....	....	....	....	....	....	....	....	....	....	....	....	....	....	....	....	....
	Rochester Americans	AHL	26	5	5	10	....	....	....	24	....	....	....	....	....	....	....	....	....	....	5	2	2	4	10	....	....	....
1974-75	**Boston Bruins**	**NHL**	**1**	**0**	**0**	**0**	**0**	**0**	**0**	**0**	**0**	**0**	**0**	**0**	**0.0**	**0**	**0**	**0**	**0**	**0**	....	....	....	....	....	....	....	....
	Rochester Americans	AHL	68	10	12	22	....	....	....	45	....	....	....	....	....	....	....	....	....	....	10	2	0	2	4	....	....	....
	NHL Totals		**1**	**0**	**0**	**0**	**0**	**0**	**0**	**0**	**0**	**0**	**0**	**0**	**0.0**	**0**	**0**	**0**	**0**		....	....	....	....	....	....	....	....

Won WHL Rookie of the Year Award (1971)
Traded to **Minnesota** by **Montreal** for cash, June, 1968. Claimed by **Salt Lake** (CHL) from **Minnesota** in Reverse Draft, June, 1970. Traded to **Buffalo** (Portland-WHL) by **Salt Lake** (WHL) with Guyle Fielder for Lyle Bradley and Fred Hilts, January, 1972. Traded to **St. Louis** by **Buffalo** for Paul Curtis, June 14, 1973. Traded to **Boston** by **St. Louis** with St. Louis' 2nd round choice (Mark Howe) in 1974 Amateur Draft and cash for Don Awrey, October 5, 1973.

• RATUSHNY, DAN

Dan Ratushny D – R. 6'1", 205 lbs. b: Nepean, Ont., 10/29/1970. Winnipeg's 2nd choice, 25th overall, in 1989 Entry Draft.

1987-88	Nepean Raiders	OJHL	54	8	20	28	....	....	....	116	....	....	....	....	....	....	....	....	....	....	....	....	....	....	....	....	....	....
1988-89	Cornell University	ECAC	28	2	13	15	....	....	....	50	....	....	....	....	....	....	....	....	....	....	....	....	....	....	....	....	....	....
	Canada	Nat-Team	2	0	0	0	....	....	....	2	....	....	....	....	....	....	....	....	....	....	....	....	....	....	....	....	....	....
1989-90	Cornell University	ECAC	26	5	14	19	....	....	....	54	....	....	....	....	....	....	....	....	....	....	....	....	....	....	....	....	....	....
	Canada	WJC-A	7	2	2	4	....	....	....	4	....	....	....	....	....	....	....	....	....	....	....	....	....	....	....	....	....	....
1990-91	Cornell University	ECAC	26	7	24	31	....	....	....	52	....	....	....	....	....	....	....	....	....	....	....	....	....	....	....	....	....	....
	Canada	Nat-Team	12	0	1	1	....	....	....	6	....	....	....	....	....	....	....	....	....	....	....	....	....	....	....	....	....	....
1991-92	Canada	Nat-Team	58	5	13	18	....	....	....	50	....	....	....	....	....	....	....	....	....	....	....	....	....	....	....	....	....	....
	Canada	Olympics	8	0	0	0	....	....	....	4	....	....	....	....	....	....	....	....	....	....	....	....	....	....	....	....	....	....
	EHC Olten	Switz.	2	0	0	0	....	....	....	0	....	....	....	....	....	....	....	....	....	....	....	....	....	....	....	....	....	....
1992-93	Fort Wayne Komets	IHL	63	6	19	25	....	....	....	48	....	....	....	....	....	....	....	....	....	....	....	....	....	....	....	....	....	....
	Vancouver Canucks	**NHL**	**1**	**0**	**1**	**1**	**0**	**1**	**1**	**2**	**0**	**0**	**0**	**2**	**0.0**	**2**	**0**	**2**	**0**	**0**	....	....	....	....	....	....	....	....
1993-94	Hamilton Canucks	AHL	62	8	31	39	....	....	....	22	....	....	....	....	....	....	....	....	....	....	4	0	0	0	4	....	....	....
1994-95	Fort Wayne Komets	IHL	72	3	25	28	....	....	....	46	....	....	....	....	....	....	....	....	....	....	4	0	1	1	8	....	....	....
1995-96	Peoria Rivermen	IHL	45	7	15	22	....	....	....	45	....	....	....	....	....	....	....	....	....	....	12	3	4	7	10	....	....	....
	Carolina Monarchs	AHL	23	5	10	15	....	....	....	28	....	....	....	....	....	....	....	....	....	....	....	....	....	....	....	....	....	....
1996-97	Quebec Rafales	IHL	50	14	23	37	....	....	....	34	....	....	....	....	....	....	....	....	....	....	....	....	....	....	....	....	....	....
1997-98	Quebec Rafales	IHL	20	3	9	12	....	....	....	22	....	....	....	....	....	....	....	....	....	....	....	....	....	....	....	....	....	....
	Albany River Rats	AHL	39	8	5	13	....	....	....	10	....	....	....	....	....	....	....	....	....	....	9	0	3	3	8	....	....	....
	NHL Totals		**1**	**0**	**1**	**1**	**0**	**1**	**1**	**2**	**0**	**0**	**0**	**2**	**0.0**	**2**	**0**	**2**	**0**		....	....	....	....	....	....	....	....

ECAC First All-Star Team (1990, 1991)
Traded to **Vancouver** by **Winnipeg** for Vancouver's 9th round choice (Harijs Vitolinsh) in 1993 Entry Draft, March 22, 1993.

• RAUSSE, ERROL

Errol Rausse LW – L. 5'10", 180 lbs. b: Quesnel, B.C., 5/18/1959. Washington's 2nd choice, 24th overall, in 1979 Entry Draft.

1975-76	Langley Thunder	BCJHL	66	34	49	83	....	....	....	47	....	....	....	....	....	....	....	....	....	....	....	....	....	....	....	....	....	....
1976-77	Kamloops Blazers	WCHL	68	22	18	40	....	....	....	21	....	....	....	....	....	....	....	....	....	....	5	0	2	2	0	....	....	....
1977-78	Seattle Thunderbirds	WCJHL	72	62	92	154	....	....	....	60	....	....	....	....	....	....	....	....	....	....	....	....	....	....	....	....	....	....

			REGULAR SEASON																		PLAYOFFS							
Season	**Club**	**League**	**GP**	**G**	**A**	**Pts**	**AG**	**AA**	**APts**	**PIM**	**PP**	**SH**	**GW**	**S**	**%**	**TGF**	**PGF**	**TGA**	**PGA**	**+/–**	**GP**	**G**	**A**	**Pts**	**PIM**	**PP**	**SH**	**GW**
1978-79	Seattle Thunderbirds	WHL	71	65	47	112	....	....	....	17	....	....	....	....	....	....	....	....	....	....	....	....	....	....	....	....	....	....
	Canada	WJC-A	5	1	1	2	....	....	....	2	....	....	....	....	....	....	....	....	....	....	....	....	....	....	....	....	....	....
1979-80	**Washington Capitals**	**NHL**	**24**	**6**	**2**	**8**	**5**	**2**	**7**	**0**	**0**	**0**	**0**	**24**	**25.0**	**12**	**0**	**8**	**0**	**+4**	....	....	....	....	....	....	....	....
	Hershey Bears	AHL	53	14	17	31	....	....	....	2	....	....	....	....	....	....	....	....	....	....	11	7	7	14	2	....	....	....
1980-81	**Washington Capitals**	**NHL**	**5**	**1**	**1**	**2**	**1**	**1**	**2**	**0**	**0**	**0**	**0**	**3**	**33.3**	**3**	**0**	**2**	**0**	**+1**	....	....	....	....	....	....	....	....
	Hershey Bears	AHL	57	19	27	46	....	....	....	18	....	....	....	....	....	....	....	....	....	....	10	2	6	8	2	....	....	....
1981-82	**Washington Capitals**	**NHL**	**2**	**0**	**0**	**0**	**0**	**0**	**0**	**0**	**0**	**0**	**0**	**0**	**0.0**	**0**	**0**	**2**	**0**	**–2**	....	....	....	....	....	....	....	....
	Hershey Bears	AHL	59	18	25	43	....	....	....	6	....	....	....	....	....	....	....	....	....	....	5	0	4	4	2	....	....	....
1982-83	Hershey Bears	AHL	79	25	35	60	....	....	....	18	....	....	....	....	....	....	....	....	....	....	5	1	2	3	2	....	....	....
1983-84	Cortina	Italy	28	29	31	60	....	....	....	8	....	....	....	....	....	....	....	....	....	....	....	....	....	....	....	....	....	....
1984-85	HC Alleghe	Italy	26	39	45	84	....	....	....	10	....	....	....	....	....	....	....	....	....	....	8	11	14	*25	10	....	....	....
1985-86	HC Alleghe	Italy	35	43	60	103	....	....	....	56	....	....	....	....	....	....	....	....	....	....	4	5	6	11	0	....	....	....
1986-87	HC Alleghe	Italy	37	37	47	84	....	....	....	26	....	....	....	....	....	....	....	....	....	....	....	....	....	....	....	....	....	....
1987-88	HC Alleghe	Italy	36	43	50	93	....	....	....	22	....	....	....	....	....	....	....	....	....	....	....	....	....	....	....	....	....	....
1988-89	HC Alleghe	Italy	60	37	30	67	....	....	....	12	....	....	....	....	....	....	....	....	....	....	....	....	....	....	....	....	....	....
1989-90	HC Alleghe	Italy	45	36	64	100	....	....	....	28	....	....	....	....	....	....	....	....	....	....	....	....	....	....	....	....	....	....
1990-91	HC Alleghe	Italy	30	21	36	57	....	....	....	4	....	....	....	....	....	....	....	....	....	....	....	....	....	....	....	....	....	....
1991-92	HC Alleghe	Italy	27	15	31	46	....	....	....	6	....	....	....	....	....	....	....	....	....	....	....	....	....	....	....	....	....	....
1992-93	HC Alleghe	Italy	25	11	23	34	....	....	....	4	....	....	....	....	....	....	....	....	....	....	....	....	....	....	....	....	....	....
1993-94	HC Alleghe	Italy	10	5	5	10	....	....	....	6	....	....	....	....	....	....	....	....	....	....	....	....	....	....	....	....	....	....
	NHL Totals		**31**	**7**	**3**	**10**	**6**	**3**	**9**	**0**	**0**	**0**	**0**	**27**	**25.9**	**15**	**0**	**12**	**0**		....	....	....	....	....	....	....	....

• RAUTAKALLIO, PEKKA

Pekka Rautakallio D – L. 5′11″, 185 lbs. b: Pori, Finland, 7/25/1953.

Season	**Club**	**League**	**GP**	**G**	**A**	**Pts**	**AG**	**AA**	**APts**	**PIM**	**PP**	**SH**	**GW**	**S**	**%**	**TGF**	**PGF**	**TGA**	**PGA**	**+/–**	**GP**	**G**	**A**	**Pts**	**PIM**	**PP**	**SH**	**GW**
1968-69	Assat Pori	Finland	10	2	1	3	....	....	....	0	....	....	....	....	....	....	....	....	....	....	....	....	....	....	....	....	....	....
1969-70	Assat Pori	Finland	22	9	2	11	....	....	....	2	....	....	....	....	....	....	....	....	....	....	....	....	....	....	....	....	....	....
1970-71	Assat Pori	Finland	31	6	5	11	....	....	....	18	....	....	....	....	....	....	....	....	....	....	....	....	....	....	....	....	....	....
1971-72	Assat Pori	Finland	32	10	8	18	....	....	....	14	....	....	....	....	....	....	....	....	....	....	....	....	....	....	....	....	....	....
	Finland	WEC-A	4	0	0	0	....	....	....	0	....	....	....	....	....	....	....	....	....	....	....	....	....	....	....	....	....	....
1972-73	Assat Pori	Finland	34	23	12	35	....	....	....	21	....	....	....	....	....	....	....	....	....	....	....	....	....	....	....	....	....	....
	Finland	WEC-A	7	0	0	0	....	....	....	4	....	....	....	....	....	....	....	....	....	....	....	....	....	....	....	....	....	....
1973-74	Assat Pori	Finland	32	9	12	21	....	....	....	8	....	....	....	....	....	....	....	....	....	....	....	....	....	....	....	....	....	....
1974-75	Assat Pori	Finland	36	9	13	22	....	....	....	19	....	....	....	....	....	....	....	....	....	....	....	....	....	....	....	....	....	....
	Finland	WEC-A	10	0	3	3	....	....	....	0	....	....	....	....	....	....	....	....	....	....	....	....	....	....	....	....	....	....
1975-76	Phoenix Roadrunners	WHA	73	11	39	50	....	....	....	8	....	....	....	....	....	....	....	....	....	....	5	0	2	2	0	....	....	....
1976-77	Finland	C Cup	5	2	2	4	....	....	....	2	....	....	....	....	....	....	....	....	....	....	....	....	....	....	....	....	....	....
	Phoenix Roadrunners	WHA	78	4	31	35	....	....	....	8	....	....	....	....	....	....	....	....	....	....	....	....	....	....	....	....	....	....
	Finland	WEC-A	10	3	4	7	....	....	....	2	....	....	....	....	....	....	....	....	....	....	....	....	....	....	....	....	....	....
1977-78	Assat Pori	Finland	36	16	21	37	....	....	....	16	....	....	....	....	....	....	....	....	....	....	9	5	4	9	0	....	....	....
	Finland	WEC-A	10	4	3	7	....	....	....	2	....	....	....	....	....	....	....	....	....	....	....	....	....	....	....	....	....	....
1978-79	Assat Pori	Finland	36	25	28	53	....	....	....	26	....	....	....	....	....	....	....	....	....	....	8	5	9	14	2	....	....	....
	Finland	WEC-A	7	2	1	3	....	....	....	2	....	....	....	....	....	....	....	....	....	....	....	....	....	....	....	....	....	....
1979-80	**Atlanta Flames**	**NHL**	**79**	**5**	**25**	**30**	**5**	**19**	**24**	**18**	**1**	**0**	**1**	**104**	**4.8**	**100**	**18**	**60**	**0**	**+22**	**4**	**0**	**1**	**1**	**2**	**0**	**0**	**0**
1980-81	**Calgary Flames**	**NHL**	**76**	**11**	**45**	**56**	**9**	**31**	**40**	**64**	**3**	**0**	**1**	**129**	**8.5**	**118**	**34**	**88**	**3**	**–1**	**16**	**2**	**4**	**6**	**6**	**1**	**0**	**0**
1981-82	Finland	C Cup	5	0	1	1	....	....	....	2	....	....	....	....	....	....	....	....	....	....	....	....	....	....	....	....	....	....
	Calgary Flames	**NHL**	**80**	**17**	**51**	**68**	**13**	**34**	**47**	**40**	**5**	**0**	**3**	**176**	**9.7**	**151**	**44**	**129**	**14**	**–8**	**3**	**0**	**0**	**0**	**0**	**0**	**0**	**0**
1982-83	HIFK Helsinki	Finland	36	16	16	32	....	....	....	16	....	....	....	....	....	....	....	....	....	....	9	6	4	10	10	....	....	....
	Finland	WEC-A	10	1	7	8	....	....	....	0	....	....	....	....	....	....	....	....	....	....	....	....	....	....	....	....	....	....
1983-84	HIFK Helsinki	Finland	33	9	21	30	....	....	....	10	....	....	....	....	....	....	....	....	....	....	2	0	2	2	0	....	....	....
1984-85	HIFK Helsinki	Finland	29	12	18	30	....	....	....	18	....	....	....	....	....	....	....	....	....	....	....	....	....	....	....	....	....	....
1985-86	HIFK Helsinki	Finland	34	13	23	36	....	....	....	8	....	....	....	....	....	....	....	....	....	....	10	3	0	3	10	....	....	....
1986-87	HIFK Helsinki	Finland	42	15	25	40	....	....	....	10	....	....	....	....	....	....	....	....	....	....	5	5	1	6	5	....	....	....
	NHL Totals		**235**	**33**	**121**	**154**	**27**	**84**	**111**	**122**	**9**	**0**	**5**	**409**	**8.1**	**369**	**96**	**277**	**17**		**23**	**2**	**5**	**7**	**8**	**1**	**0**	**0**
	Other Major League Totals		151	15	70	85	....	....	....	16	....	....	....	....	....	....	....	....	....		5	0	2	2	0	....	....	....

EJC-A All-Star Team (1971) • Named Best Defenseman at EJC-A (1971) • Finnish First All-Star Team (1975, 1978, 1979, 1983, 1986)
Played in NHL All-Star Game (1982)
Signed as a free agent by **Phoenix** (WHA), June, 1975. Signed as a free agent by **Atlanta**, June 5, 1979. Transferred to **Calgary** after **Atlanta** franchise relocated, June 24, 1980.

• RAVLICH, MATT

Matt Ravlich D – L. 5′10″, 185 lbs. b: Sault Ste. Marie, Ont., 7/12/1938.

Season	**Club**	**League**	**GP**	**G**	**A**	**Pts**	**AG**	**AA**	**APts**	**PIM**	**PP**	**SH**	**GW**	**S**	**%**	**TGF**	**PGF**	**TGA**	**PGA**	**+/–**	**GP**	**G**	**A**	**Pts**	**PIM**	**PP**	**SH**	**GW**
1954-55	Woodstock Athletics	Jr. B	STATISTICS NOT AVAILABLE																									
	Galt Black Hawks	OHA	3	1	1	2	....	....	....	0	....	....	....	....	....	....	....	....	....	....	....	....	....	....	....	....	....	....
1955-56	St. Catharines Teepees	OHA	48	2	15	17	....	....	....	188	....	....	....	....	....	....	....	....	....	....	6	0	0	0	11	....	....	....
1956-57	St. Catharines Teepees	OHA	52	7	27	34	....	....	....	137	....	....	....	....	....	....	....	....	....	....	14	9	12	21	4	....	....	....
1957-58	St. Catharines Teepees	OHA	49	38	35	73	....	....	....	105	....	....	....	....	....	....	....	....	....	....	8	3	7	10	15	....	....	....
1958-59	Trois Rivieres Lions	QHL	61	14	31	45	....	....	....	58	....	....	....	....	....	....	....	....	....	....	8	2	3	5	7	....	....	....
1959-60	Sault Ste. Marie Greyhounds	EPHL	70	18	37	55	....	....	....	94	....	....	....	....	....	....	....	....	....	....	....	....	....	....	....	....	....	....
1960-61	Sault Ste. Marie Greyhounds	EPHL	55	5	25	30	....	....	....	104	....	....	....	....	....	....	....	....	....	....	12	0	2	2	0	....	....	....
1961-62	Providence Reds	AHL	69	10	29	39	....	....	....	112	....	....	....	....	....	....	....	....	....	....	3	0	2	2	0	....	....	....
1962-63	**Boston Bruins**	**NHL**	**2**	**1**	**0**	**1**	**1**	**0**	**1**	**0**	....	....	....	....	....	....	....	....	....	....	....	....	....	....	....	....	....	....
	Providence Reds	AHL	70	7	38	45	....	....	....	97	....	....	....	....	....	....	....	....	....	....	6	0	2	2	8	....	....	....
1963-64	Providence Reds	AHL	69	8	31	39	....	....	....	79	....	....	....	....	....	....	....	....	....	....	3	2	2	4	2	....	....	....
1964-65	Buffalo Bisons	AHL	8	1	5	6	....	....	....	12	....	....	....	....	....	....	....	....	....	....	....	....	....	....	....	....	....	....
	Chicago Black Hawks	**NHL**	**61**	**3**	**16**	**19**	**4**	**17**	**21**	**80**	....	....	....	....	....	....	....	....	....	....	**14**	**1**	**4**	**5**	**14**	....	....	....
1965-66	**Chicago Black Hawks**	**NHL**	**62**	**0**	**16**	**16**	**0**	**16**	**16**	**78**	....	....	....	....	....	....	....	....	....	....	**6**	**0**	**1**	**1**	**2**	....	....	....
1966-67	**Chicago Black Hawks**	**NHL**	**62**	**0**	**3**	**3**	**0**	**3**	**3**	**39**	....	....	....	....	....	....	....	....	....	....	....	....	....	....	....	....	....	....
1967-68	Dallas Black Hawks	CHL	15	1	8	9	....	....	....	55	....	....	....	....	....	....	....	....	....	....	5	0	1	1	2	....	....	....
	Chicago Black Hawks	**NHL**	....	....	....	....	....	....	....	....	....	....	....	....	....	....	....	....	....	....	**4**	**0**	**0**	**0**	**0**	....	....	....
1968-69	**Chicago Black Hawks**	**NHL**	**60**	**2**	**12**	**14**	**2**	**11**	**13**	**57**	**0**	**0**	**0**	**74**	**2.7**	**69**	**1**	**66**	**18**	**+20**	....	....	....	....	....	....	....	....
	Dallas Black Hawks	CHL	9	0	4	4	....	....	....	16	....	....	....	....	....	....	....	....	....	....	8	0	3	3	6	....	....	....
1969-70	**Detroit Red Wings**	**NHL**	**46**	**0**	**6**	**6**	**0**	**6**	**6**	**33**	**0**	**0**	**0**	**25**	**0.0**	**31**	**0**	**26**	**2**	**+7**	....	....	....	....	....	....	....	....
	Los Angeles Kings	**NHL**	**21**	**3**	**7**	**10**	**3**	**7**	**10**	**34**	**0**	**0**	**1**	**19**	**15.8**	**24**	**2**	**36**	**6**	**–8**	....	....	....	....	....	....	....	....
1970-71	**Los Angeles Kings**	**NHL**	**66**	**3**	**16**	**19**	**3**	**14**	**17**	**41**	**0**	**0**	**1**	**57**	**5.3**	**68**	**14**	**88**	**20**	**–14**	....	....	....	....	....	....	....	....
1971-72	Seattle Totems	WHL	8	0	2	2	....	....	....	2	....	....	....	....	....	....	....	....	....	....	....	....	....	....	....	....	....	....
	Boston Bruins	**NHL**	**25**	**0**	**1**	**1**	**0**	**1**	**1**	**2**	**0**	**0**	**0**	**13**	**0.0**	**13**	**0**	**9**	**0**	**+4**	....	....	....	....	....	....	....	....
	Boston Braves	AHL	20	1	6	7	....	....	....	14	....	....	....	....	....	....	....	....	....	....	8	1	3	4	14	....	....	....
1972-73	**Boston Bruins**	**NHL**	**5**	**0**	**1**	**1**	**0**	**1**	**1**	**0**	**0**	**0**	**0**	**1**	**0.0**	**1**	**0**	**7**	**1**	**–5**	....	....	....	....	....	....	....	....
	Boston Braves	AHL	67	5	15	20	....	....	....	71	....	....	....	....	....	....	....	....	....	....	9	2	4	6	21	....	....	....
1973-74	Boston Braves	AHL	50	4	20	24	....	....	....	21	....	....	....	....	....	....	....	....	....	....	....	....	....	....	....	....	....	....
	NHL Totals		**410**	**12**	**78**	**90**	**13**	**76**	**89**	**364**	**0**	**0**	**2**	**189**	**6.3**	**206**	**17**	**232**	**47**		**24**	**1**	**5**	**6**	**16**	**0**	**0**	**0**

Claimed by **Boston** from **Chicago** (Sault Ste. Marie-EPHL) in Inter-League Draft, June 12, 1961. Traded to **Chicago** by **Boston** with Jerry Toppazzini for Murray Balfour and Mike Draper, June 9, 1964. Claimed by **Detroit** from **Chicago** in Intra-League Draft, June 11, 1969. Claimed on waivers by **LA Kings** from **Detroit**, February 20, 1970. Claimed on waivers by **Boston** from **LA Kings**, November 3, 1971.

• RAY, ROB

Rob Ray RW – L. 6′, 203 lbs. b: Belleville, Ont., 6/8/1968. Buffalo's 5th choice, 97th overall, in 1986 Entry Draft.

Season	**Club**	**League**	**GP**	**G**	**A**	**Pts**	**AG**	**AA**	**APts**	**PIM**	**PP**	**SH**	**GW**	**S**	**%**	**TGF**	**PGF**	**TGA**	**PGA**	**+/–**	**GP**	**G**	**A**	**Pts**	**PIM**	**PP**	**SH**	**GW**
1985-86	Cornwall Royals	OHL	53	6	13	19	....	....	....	253	....	....	....	....	....	....	....	....	....	....	6	0	0	0	26	....	....	....
1986-87	Cornwall Royals	OHL	46	17	20	37	....	....	....	158	....	....	....	....	....	....	....	....	....	....	5	1	1	2	16	....	....	....
1987-88	Cornwall Royals	OHL	61	11	41	52	....	....	....	179	....	....	....	....	....	....	....	....	....	....	11	2	3	5	33	....	....	....
1988-89	Rochester Americans	AHL	74	11	18	29	....	....	....	*446	....	....	....	....	....	....	....	....	....	....	....	....	....	....	....	....	....	....
1989-90	**Buffalo Sabres**	**NHL**	**27**	**2**	**1**	**3**	**2**	**1**	**3**	**99**	**0**	**0**	**0**	**20**	**10.0**	**8**	**0**	**10**	**0**	**–2**	....	....	....	....	....	....	....	....
	Rochester Americans	AHL	43	2	13	15	....	....	....	335	....	....	....	....	....	....	....	....	....	....	17	1	3	4	115	....	....	....
1990-91	**Buffalo Sabres**	**NHL**	**66**	**8**	**8**	**16**	**7**	**6**	**13**	***350**	**0**	**0**	**1**	**54**	**14.8**	**24**	**1**	**34**	**0**	**–11**	**6**	**1**	**1**	**2**	**56**	**0**	**0**	**1**
	Rochester Americans	AHL	8	1	1	2	....	....	....	15	....	....	....	....	....	....	....	....	....	....	....	....	....	....	....	....	....	....
1991-92	**Buffalo Sabres**	**NHL**	**63**	**5**	**3**	**8**	**5**	**2**	**7**	**354**	**0**	**0**	**0**	**29**	**17.2**	**10**	**1**	**18**	**0**	**–9**	**7**	**0**	**0**	**0**	**2**	**0**	**0**	**0**

			REGULAR SEASON																		PLAYOFFS							
Season	Club	League	GP	G	A	Pts	AG	AA	APts	PIM	PP	SH	GW	S	%	TGF	PGF	TGA	PGA	+/-	GP	G	A	Pts	PIM	PP	SH	GW
1992-93	Buffalo Sabres	NHL	68	3	2	5	2	1	3	211	1	0	0	28	10.7	9	1	11	0	–3								
1993-94	Buffalo Sabres	NHL	82	3	4	7	3	3	6	274	0	0	0	34	8.8	15	0	13	0	+2	7	1	0	1	43	0	0	0
1994-95	Buffalo Sabres	NHL	47	0	3	3	0	4	4	173	0	0	0	7	0.0	6	0	10	0	–4	5	0	0	0	14	0	0	0
1995-96	Buffalo Sabres	NHL	71	3	6	9	3	5	8	287	0	0	0	21	14.3	12	0	20	0	–8								
1996-97	Buffalo Sabres	NHL	82	7	3	10	7	3	10	286	0	0	1	45	15.6	18	0	16	1	+3	12	0	1	1	28	0	0	0
1997-98	Buffalo Sabres	NHL	63	2	4	6	2	4	6	234	1	0	1	19	10.5	14	2	10	0	+2	10	0	0	0	24	0	0	0
	NHL Totals		569	33	34	67	31	29	60	2268	2	0	3	257	12.8	116	5	142	1		47	2	2	4	167	0	0	1

• REAUME, MARC

Marc Reaume D – L. 6'1", 185 lbs. b: La Salle, Ont., 2/7/1934.

Season	Club	League	GP	G	A	Pts	AG	AA	APts	PIM	PP	SH	GW	S	%	TGF	PGF	TGA	PGA	+/-	GP	G	A	Pts	PIM	PP	SH	GW
1950-51	St. Michael's Majors	OHA	5	0	0	0				2																		
1951-52	St. Michael's Majors	OHA	46	11	16	27				44											7	1	2	3	8			
1952-53	St. Michael's Majors	OHA	46	5	16	21				75											17	0	3	3	16			
1953-54	St. Michael's Majors	OHA	54	14	27	41				24											8	3	6	9	6			
1954-55	Toronto Maple Leafs	NHL	1	0	0	0	0	0	0	4											4	0	0	0	2			
	Pittsburgh Hornets	AHL	57	5	7	12				63											6	0	0	0	4			
1955-56	Toronto Maple Leafs	NHL	48	0	12	12	0	15	15	50											5	0	2	2	6			
	Pittsburgh Hornets	AHL	16	2	5	7				24																		
1956-57	Toronto Maple Leafs	NHL	63	6	14	20	8	16	24	81																		
1957-58	Toronto Maple Leafs	NHL	68	1	7	8	1	8	9	49																		
1958-59	Toronto Maple Leafs	NHL	51	1	5	6	1	5	6	67											10	0	0	0	0			
1959-60	Toronto Maple Leafs	NHL	36	0	1	1	0	1	1	6																		
	Detroit Red Wings	NHL	9	0	1	1	0	1	1	2											2	0	0	0	0			
1960-61	Detroit Red Wings	NHL	38	0	1	1	0	1	1	8																		
	Hershey Bears	AHL	33	2	7	9				30											8	0	1	1	4			
1961-62	Hershey Bears	AHL	70	3	18	21				42											7	1	2	3	6			
1962-63	Hershey Bears	AHL	69	5	23	28				42											13	2	4	6	34			
1963-64	Montreal Canadiens	NHL	3	0	0	0	0	0	0	2																		
	Hershey Bears	AHL	69	5	23	28				45											6	1	0	1	2			
1964-65	Tulsa Oilers	CHL	68	4	28	32				31											12	0	7	7	6			
1965-66	Rochester Americans	AHL	2	0	3	3				2																		
	Tulsa Oilers	CHL	68	8	25	33				43											11	1	0	1	0			
1966-67	Tulsa Oilers	CHL	62	7	18	25				59																		
	Rochester Americans	AHL	2	0	0	0				0																		
1967-68	Rochester Americans	AHL	70	8	22	30				40											11	2	4	6	10			
1968-69	Rochester Americans	AHL	11	0	6	6				2																		
	Vancouver Canucks	WHL	59	4	19	23				31											8	3	7	10	2			
1969-70	Vancouver Canucks	WHL	72	10	25	35				36											11	2	11	13	6			
1970-71	Vancouver Canucks	NHL	27	0	2	2	0	2	2	4	0	0	0	19	0.0	12	0	24	6	–6								
	Rochester Americans	AHL	6	0	3	3				6																		
	NHL Totals		344	8	43	51	10	49	59	273	0	0	0	19	42.1	12	0	24	6		21	0	2	2	8	0	0	0

AHL First All-Star Team (1963) • Won Eddie Shore Award (Outstanding Defenseman - AHL) (1963) • CHL Second All-Star Team (1966) • AHL Second All-Star Team (1968) • WHL First All-Star Team (1970) • Won Hal Laycoe Cup (WHL Top Defenseman) (1970)

Traded to **Detroit** by **Toronto** for Red Kelly, February 10, 1960. Traded to **Montreal** by **Detroit** (Hershey - AHL) for Ralph Keller and the loan of Chuck Hamilton, June 4, 1962. Claimed by **Toronto** (Tulsa-CHL) from **Montreal** in Inter-League Draft, June 9, 1964. NHL rights transferred to **Vancouver** after owners of **Vancouver** (WHL) franchise awarded NHL expansion team, May 22, 1970. • Suffered career-ending injuries in automobile accident, January 24, 1971.

• RECCHI, MARK

Mark Recchi RW – L. 5'10", 180 lbs. b: Kamloops, B.C., 2/1/1968. Pittsburgh's 4th choice, 67th overall, in 1988 Entry Draft.

Season	Club	League	GP	G	A	Pts	AG	AA	APts	PIM	PP	SH	GW	S	%	TGF	PGF	TGA	PGA	+/-	GP	G	A	Pts	PIM	PP	SH	GW
1985-86	New Westminster Bruins	WHL	72	21	40	61				55																		
1986-87	Kamloops Blazers	WHL	40	26	50	76				63											13	3	16	19	17			
1987-88	Kamloops Blazers	WHL	62	61	*93	154				75											17	10	*21	*31	18			
	Canada	WJC-A	7	0	5	5				4																		
1988-89	Pittsburgh Penguins	NHL	15	1	1	2	1	1	2	0	0	0	0	11	9.1	4	0	6	0	–2								
	Muskegon Lumberjacks	IHL	63	50	49	99				86											14	7	*14	*21	28			
1989-90	Pittsburgh Penguins	NHL	74	30	37	67	26	26	52	44	6	2	4	143	21.0	88	18	72	8	+6								
	Muskegon Lumberjacks	IHL	4	7	4	11				2																		
	Canada	WEC-A	5	0	2	2				2																		
1990-91	Pittsburgh Penguins	NHL	78	40	73	113	37	56	93	48	12	0	9	184	21.7	151	58	108	15	0	24	10	24	34	33	5	0	2
1991-92	Pittsburgh Penguins	NHL	58	33	37	70	30	28	58	78	16	1	4	156	21.2	100	49	83	16	–16								
	Philadelphia Flyers	NHL	22	10	17	27	9	13	22	18	4	0	1	54	18.5	36	19	31	9	–5								
1992-93	Philadelphia Flyers	NHL	84	53	70	123	44	48	92	95	15	4	6	274	19.3	163	57	116	11	+1								
	Canada	WC-A	8	2	5	7				2																		
1993-94	Philadelphia Flyers	NHL	84	40	67	107	37	52	89	46	11	0	5	217	18.4	155	56	107	6	–2								
1994-95	Philadelphia Flyers	NHL	10	2	3	5	4	4	8	12	1	0	2	17	11.8	6	3	9	0	–6								
	Montreal Canadiens	NHL	39	14	29	43	25	43	68	16	8	0	1	104	13.5	58	18	45	2	–3								
1995-96	Montreal Canadiens	NHL	82	28	50	78	28	41	69	69	11	2	6	191	14.7	115	43	59	7	+20	6	3	3	6	0	3	0	0
1996-97	Montreal Canadiens	NHL	82	34	46	80	36	41	77	58	7	2	3	202	16.8	112	34	103	24	–1	5	4	2	6	2	0	0	0
	Canada	WC-A	9	3	3	6				0																		
1997-98	Montreal Canadiens	NHL	82	32	42	74	38	41	79	51	9	1	6	216	14.8	107	48	59	11	+11	10	4	8	12	6	0	0	2
	Canada	Olympics	5	0	2	2				0																		
	NHL Totals		710	317	472	789	315	394	709	535	100	12	47	1769	17.9	1095	403	798	109		45	21	37	58	41	8	0	4

WHL West All-Star Team (1988) • IHL Second All-Star Team (1989) • NHL Second All-Star Team (1992)

Played in NHL All-Star Game (1991, 1993, 1994, 1997, 1998)

Traded to **Philadelphia** by **Pittsburgh** with Brian Benning and LA Kings' 1st round choice (previously acquired, Philadelphia selected Jason Bowen) in 1992 Entry Draft for Rick Tocchet, Kjell Samuelsson, Ken Wregget and Philadelphia's 3rd round choice (Dave Roche) in 1993 Entry Draft, February 19, 1992. Traded to **Montreal** by **Philadelphia** with Philadelphia's 3rd round choice (Martin Hohenberger) in 1995 Entry Draft for Eric Desjardins, Gilbert Dionne and John LeClair, February 9, 1995.

• REDDEN, WADE

Wade Redden D – L. 6'2", 193 lbs. b: Lloydminster, Sask., 6/12/1977. NY Islanders' 1st choice, 2nd overall, in 1995 Entry Draft.

Season	Club	League	GP	G	A	Pts	AG	AA	APts	PIM	PP	SH	GW	S	%	TGF	PGF	TGA	PGA	+/-	GP	G	A	Pts	PIM	PP	SH	GW
1993-94	Brandon Wheat Kings	WHL	63	4	35	39				98											14	2	4	6	10			
1994-95	Brandon Wheat Kings	WHL	64	14	46	60				83											18	5	10	15	8			
	Canada	WJC-A	7	3	2	5				0																		
1995-96	Brandon Wheat Kings	WHL	51	9	45	54				55											19	5	10	15	19			
	Canada	WJC-A	6	0	2	2				2																		
1996-97	Ottawa Senators	NHL	82	6	24	30	6	21	27	41	2	0	1	102	5.9	75	22	66	14	+1	7	1	3	4	2	0	0	0
1997-98	Ottawa Senators	NHL	80	8	14	22	9	14	23	27	3	0	2	103	7.8	67	13	54	17	+17	9	0	2	2	2	0	0	0
	NHL Totals		162	14	38	52	15	35	50	68	5	0	3	205	6.8	142	35	120	31		16	1	5	6	4	0	0	0

WHL East Second All-Star Team (1995) • WHL East First All-Star Team (1996) • Memorial Cup All-Star Team (1996)

Traded to **Ottawa** by **NY Islanders** with Damian Rhodes for Don Beaupre, Martin Straka and Bryan Berard, January 23, 1996.

• REDMOND, CRAIG

Craig Redmond D – L. 5'11", 190 lbs. b: Dawson Creek, B.C., 9/22/1965. Los Angeles' 1st choice, 6th overall, in 1984 Entry Draft.

Season	Club	League	GP	G	A	Pts	AG	AA	APts	PIM	PP	SH	GW	S	%	TGF	PGF	TGA	PGA	+/-	GP	G	A	Pts	PIM	PP	SH	GW
1980-81	Abbotsford Flyers	BCJHL	40	15	22	37																						
1981-82	Abbotsford Flyers	BCJHL	45	30	76	106				41																		
1982-83	University of Denver	WCHA	34	16	38	54				44																		
1983-84	Canada	Nat-Team	55	10	11	21				38																		
	Canada	Olympics	7	2	0	2				4																		
1984-85	Los Angeles Kings	NHL	79	6	33	39	5	22	27	57	1	0	0	113	5.3	102	23	101	14	–8	3	1	0	1	2	0	0	0
1985-86	Los Angeles Kings	NHL	73	6	18	24	5	12	17	57	3	0	0	116	5.2	71	19	99	13	–34								
	Canada	WEC-A	10	3	2	5				16																		
1986-87	Los Angeles Kings	NHL	16	1	7	8	1	5	6	8	0	0	0	18	5.6	19	5	19	4	–1								
	New Haven Nighthawks	AHL	5	2	2	4				6																		

			REGULAR SEASON																		PLAYOFFS							
Season	Club	League	GP	G	A	Pts	AG	AA	APts	PIM	PP	SH	GW	S	%	TGF	PGF	TGA	PGA	+/-	GP	G	A	Pts	PIM	PP	SH	GW
1987-88	**Los Angeles Kings**	**NHL**	**2**	**0**	**0**	**0**	**0**	**0**	**0**	**0**	**0**	**0**	**0**	**5**	**0.0**	**0**	**0**	**4**	**0**	**–4**	....	....	....	....	....	....	....	....
	New Haven Nighthawks	AHL	DID NOT PLAY – SUSPENDED																									
1988-89	Denver Rangers	IHL	10	0	13	13	....	....	....	6	....	....	....	....	....	....	....	....	....	....	....	....	....	....	....	....	....	....
	Edmonton Oilers	**NHL**	**21**	**3**	**10**	**13**	**3**	**7**	**10**	**12**	**3**	**0**	**0**	**29**	**10.3**	**26**	**16**	**24**	**4**	**–10**	....	....	....	....	....	....	....	....
	Cape Breton Oilers	AHL	44	13	22	35	....	....	....	28	....	....	....	....	....	....	....	....	....	....	....	....	....	....	....	....	....	....
1989-1995			DID NOT PLAY																									
1995-96	Cape Breton Oilers	AHL	43	2	18	20	....	....	....	80	....	....	....	....	....	....	....	....	....	....	....	....	....	....	....	....	....	....
	Atlanta Knights	IHL	25	0	5	5	....	....	....	10	....	....	....	....	....	....	....	....	....	....	3	0	1	1	0	....	....	....
	NHL Totals		**191**	**16**	**68**	**84**	**14**	**46**	**60**	**134**	**7**	**0**	**0**	**281**	**5.7**	**218**	**63**	**247**	**35**		**3**	**1**	**0**	**1**	**2**	**0**	**0**	**0**

• Suspended by **LA Kings** for refusing to report to **New Haven** (AHL), October, 1987. Traded to **Edmonton** by **LA Kings** for John Miner, August 10, 1988. Claimed by **NY Rangers** from **Edmonton** in Waiver Draft, October 3, 1988. Claimed on waivers by **Edmonton** from **NY Rangers**, November 1, 1988.

• REDMOND, DICK

Dick Redmond D – L. 5'11", 178 lbs. b: Kirkland Lake, Ont., 8/14/1949. Minnesota's 1st choice, 5th overall, in 1969 Amateur Draft.

Season	Club	League	GP	G	A	Pts	AG	AA	APts	PIM	PP	SH	GW	S	%	TGF	PGF	TGA	PGA	+/-	GP	G	A	Pts	PIM	PP	SH	GW
1966-67	Peterborough Petes	OHA	40	2	7	9	....	....	....	77	....	....	....	....	....	....	....	....	....	....	6	0	2	2	2	....	....	....
1967-68	Peterborough Petes	OHA	52	7	28	35	....	....	....	84	....	....	....	....	....	....	....	....	....	....	5	3	0	3	2	....	....	....
1968-69	Peterborough Petes	OHA	6	2	2	4	....	....	....	44	....	....	....	....	....	....	....	....	....	....	....	....	....	....	....	....	....	....
	St. Catherines Blackhawks	OHA	44	31	43	74	....	....	....	136	....	....	....	....	....	....	....	....	....	....	18	11	17	28	35	....	....	....
1969-70	**Minnesota North Stars**	**NHL**	**7**	**0**	**1**	**1**	**0**	**1**	**1**	**4**	**0**	**0**	**0**	**10**	**0.0**	**2**	**1**	**2**	**0**	**–1**	....	....	....	....	....	....	....	....
	Iowa Stars	CHL	56	7	23	30	....	....	....	65	....	....	....	....	....	....	....	....	....	....	11	2	8	10	26	....	....	....
1970-71	**Minnesota North Stars**	**NHL**	**9**	**0**	**2**	**2**	**0**	**2**	**2**	**16**	**0**	**0**	**0**	**11**	**0.0**	**2**	**0**	**6**	**2**	**–2**	....	....	....	....	....	....	....	....
	Cleveland Barons	AHL	49	6	13	19	....	....	....	69	....	....	....	....	....	....	....	....	....	....	....	....	....	....	....	....	....	....
	California Golden Seals	**NHL**	**11**	**2**	**4**	**6**	**2**	**4**	**6**	**12**	**1**	**0**	**0**	**35**	**5.7**	**25**	**5**	**29**	**3**	**–6**	....	....	....	....	....	....	....	....
1971-72	**California Golden Seals**	**NHL**	**74**	**10**	**35**	**45**	**11**	**32**	**43**	**76**	**1**	**0**	**0**	**254**	**3.9**	**111**	**36**	**102**	**17**	**–10**	....	....	....	....	....	....	....	....
1972-73	**California Golden Seals**	**NHL**	**24**	**3**	**13**	**16**	**3**	**11**	**14**	**22**	**1**	**0**	**0**	**63**	**4.8**	**29**	**9**	**44**	**9**	**–15**	....	....	....	....	....	....	....	....
	Chicago Black Hawks	**NHL**	**52**	**9**	**19**	**28**	**9**	**16**	**25**	**4**	**3**	**0**	**1**	**140**	**6.4**	**51**	**18**	**31**	**0**	**+2**	**13**	**4**	**2**	**6**	**2**	**0**	**0**	**2**
1973-74	**Chicago Black Hawks**	**NHL**	**76**	**17**	**42**	**59**	**17**	**36**	**53**	**69**	**5**	**0**	**4**	**246**	**6.9**	**117**	**40**	**58**	**7**	**+26**	**11**	**1**	**7**	**8**	**8**	**1**	**0**	**0**
1974-75	**Chicago Black Hawks**	**NHL**	**80**	**14**	**43**	**57**	**13**	**34**	**47**	**90**	**6**	**0**	**1**	**310**	**4.5**	**150**	**50**	**128**	**34**	**+6**	**8**	**2**	**3**	**5**	**0**	**1**	**0**	**0**
1975-76	**Chicago Black Hawks**	**NHL**	**53**	**9**	**27**	**36**	**8**	**21**	**29**	**25**	**5**	**0**	**1**	**165**	**5.5**	**70**	**20**	**60**	**9**	**+1**	**4**	**0**	**2**	**2**	**4**	**0**	**0**	**0**
1976-77	**Chicago Black Hawks**	**NHL**	**80**	**22**	**25**	**47**	**21**	**20**	**41**	**30**	**9**	**0**	**2**	**211**	**10.4**	**95**	**30**	**123**	**18**	**–40**	**2**	**0**	**1**	**1**	**0**	**0**	**0**	**0**
1977-78	**St. Louis Blues**	**NHL**	**28**	**4**	**11**	**15**	**4**	**9**	**13**	**16**	**2**	**0**	**0**	**93**	**4.3**	**25**	**13**	**31**	**5**	**–14**	....	....	....	....	....	....	....	....
	Atlanta Flames	**NHL**	**42**	**7**	**11**	**18**	**7**	**9**	**16**	**16**	**5**	**0**	**1**	**86**	**8.1**	**64**	**20**	**38**	**6**	**+12**	**2**	**1**	**0**	**1**	**0**	**0**	**0**	**0**
1978-79	**Boston Bruins**	**NHL**	**64**	**7**	**26**	**33**	**6**	**20**	**26**	**21**	**4**	**0**	**1**	**144**	**4.9**	**88**	**38**	**68**	**18**	**0**	**11**	**1**	**3**	**4**	**2**	**0**	**1**	**0**
1979-80	**Boston Bruins**	**NHL**	**76**	**14**	**33**	**47**	**13**	**25**	**38**	**39**	**6**	**0**	**5**	**166**	**8.4**	**135**	**41**	**75**	**18**	**+37**	**10**	**0**	**3**	**3**	**9**	**0**	**0**	**0**
1980-81	**Boston Bruins**	**NHL**	**78**	**15**	**20**	**35**	**12**	**14**	**26**	**60**	**6**	**2**	**0**	**152**	**9.9**	**97**	**24**	**91**	**22**	**+4**	**3**	**0**	**1**	**1**	**2**	**0**	**0**	**0**
1981-82	**Boston Bruins**	**NHL**	**17**	**0**	**0**	**0**	**0**	**0**	**0**	**4**	**0**	**0**	**0**	**14**	**0.0**	**5**	**0**	**14**	**2**	**–7**	**2**	**0**	**0**	**0**	**0**	**0**	**0**	**0**
	Erie Blades	AHL	31	8	12	20	....	....	....	14	....	....	....	....	....	....	....	....	....	....	....	....	....	....	....	....	....	....
	NHL Totals		**771**	**133**	**312**	**445**	**126**	**254**	**380**	**504**	**54**	**2**	**16**	**2100**	**6.3**	**1074**	**351**	**900**	**170**		**66**	**9**	**22**	**31**	**27**	**2**	**1**	**2**

OHA First All-Star Team (1969)

Traded to **California** by **Minnesota** with Tom Williams for Ted Hampson and Wayne Muloin, March 7, 1971. Traded to **Chicago** by **California** with Bobby Sheehan for Darryl Maggs, December 5, 1972. Traded to **St. Louis** by **Chicago** for Pierre Plante, August 9, 1977. Traded to **Atlanta** by **St. Louis** with Yves Belanger, Bob MacMillan and St. Louis' 2nd round choice (Mike Perovich) in 1979 Entry Draft for Phil Myre, Curt Bennett and Barry Gibbs, December 12, 1977. Traded to **Boston** by **Atlanta** for Gregg Sheppard, September 6, 1978.

• REDMOND, KEITH

Keith Redmond LW – L. 6'3", 208 lbs. b: Richmond Hill, Ont., 10/25/1972. Los Angeles' 2nd choice, 79th overall, in 1991 Entry Draft.

Season	Club	League	GP	G	A	Pts	AG	AA	APts	PIM	PP	SH	GW	S	%	TGF	PGF	TGA	PGA	+/-	GP	G	A	Pts	PIM	PP	SH	GW
1988-89	Nepean Raiders	COJHL	59	3	12	15	....	....	....	110	....	....	....	....	....	....	....	....	....	....	....	....	....	....	....	....	....	....
1989-90	Nepean Raiders	COJHL	40	14	10	24	....	....	....	169	....	....	....	....	....	....	....	....	....	....	....	....	....	....	....	....	....	....
1990-91	Bowling Green University	CCHA	35	1	3	4	....	....	....	72	....	....	....	....	....	....	....	....	....	....	....	....	....	....	....	....	....	....
1991-92	Bowling Green University	CCHA	8	0	0	0	....	....	....	14	....	....	....	....	....	....	....	....	....	....	....	....	....	....	....	....	....	....
	Belleville Bulls	OHL	16	1	7	8	....	....	....	52	....	....	....	....	....	....	....	....	....	....	....	....	....	....	....	....	....	....
	Detroit Jr. Red Wings	OHL	25	6	12	18	....	....	....	61	....	....	....	....	....	....	....	....	....	....	7	1	3	4	49	....	....	....
1992-93	Phoenix Roadrunners	IHL	53	6	10	16	....	....	....	285	....	....	....	....	....	....	....	....	....	....	....	....	....	....	....	....	....	....
	Muskegon Fury	ColHL	4	1	0	1	....	....	....	46	....	....	....	....	....	....	....	....	....	....	....	....	....	....	....	....	....	....
1993-94	**Los Angeles Kings**	**NHL**	**12**	**1**	**0**	**1**	**1**	**0**	**1**	**20**	**0**	**0**	**0**	**9**	**11.1**	**1**	**0**	**4**	**0**	**–3**	....	....	....	....	....	....	....	....
	Phoenix Roadrunners	IHL	43	8	10	18	....	....	....	196	....	....	....	....	....	....	....	....	....	....	....	....	....	....	....	....	....	....
1994-95	Phoenix Roadrunners	IHL	20	0	3	3	....	....	....	81	....	....	....	....	....	....	....	....	....	....	6	2	1	3	29	....	....	....
1995-96	Phoenix Roadrunners	IHL	34	5	3	8	....	....	....	164	....	....	....	....	....	....	....	....	....	....	1	0	0	0	0	....	....	....
	NHL Totals		**12**	**1**	**0**	**1**	**1**	**0**	**1**	**20**	**0**	**0**	**0**	**9**	**11.1**	**1**	**0**	**4**	**0**		....	....	....	....	....	....	....	....

• REDMOND, MICKEY

Mickey Redmond RW – R. 5'11", 185 lbs. b: Kirkland Lake, Ont., 12/27/1947.

Season	Club	League	GP	G	A	Pts	AG	AA	APts	PIM	PP	SH	GW	S	%	TGF	PGF	TGA	PGA	+/-	GP	G	A	Pts	PIM	PP	SH	GW
1963-64	Peterborough Petes	OHA	53	21	17	38	....	....	....	26	....	....	....	....	....	....	....	....	....	....	4	1	2	3	2	....	....	....
1964-65	Peterborough Petes	OHA	52	23	20	43	....	....	....	30	....	....	....	....	....	....	....	....	....	....	12	9	1	10	11	....	....	....
1965-66	Peterborough Petes	OHA	48	41	51	92	....	....	....	31	....	....	....	....	....	....	....	....	....	....	6	4	1	5	6	....	....	....
1966-67	Peterborough Petes	OHA	48	*51	44	95	....	....	....	44	....	....	....	....	....	....	....	....	....	....	6	2	5	7	14	....	....	....
	Houston Apollos	CHL	....	....	....	....	....	....	....	....	....	....	....	....	....	....	....	....	....	....	5	3	2	5	2	....	....	....
1967-68	**Montreal Canadiens**	**NHL**	**41**	**6**	**5**	**11**	**7**	**5**	**12**	**4**	**1**	**0**	**0**	**52**	**11.5**	**16**	**5**	**9**	**0**	**+2**	**2**	**0**	**0**	**0**	**0**	**0**	**0**	**0**
	Houston Apollos	CHL	15	9	8	17	....	....	....	9	....	....	....	....	....	....	....	....	....	....	....	....	....	....	....	....	....	....
1968-69	**Montreal Canadiens**	**NHL**	**65**	**9**	**15**	**24**	**10**	**14**	**24**	**12**	**1**	**0**	**0**	**118**	**7.6**	**39**	**4**	**19**	**0**	**+16**	**14**	**2**	**3**	**5**	**2**	**0**	**1**	**1**
1969-70	**Montreal Canadiens**	**NHL**	**75**	**27**	**27**	**54**	**31**	**27**	**58**	**61**	**3**	**0**	**2**	**279**	**9.7**	**83**	**18**	**42**	**0**	**+23**	....	....	....	....	....	....	....	....
1970-71	**Montreal Canadiens**	**NHL**	**40**	**14**	**15**	**29**	**15**	**13**	**28**	**35**	**2**	**0**	**1**	**116**	**12.1**	**47**	**13**	**22**	**0**	**+12**	....	....	....	....	....	....	....	....
	Detroit Red Wings	**NHL**	**21**	**6**	**8**	**14**	**6**	**7**	**13**	**7**	**2**	**0**	**1**	**68**	**8.8**	**22**	**8**	**16**	**0**	**–2**	....	....	....	....	....	....	....	....
1971-72	**Detroit Red Wings**	**NHL**	**78**	**42**	**29**	**71**	**45**	**26**	**71**	**34**	**10**	**0**	**5**	**271**	**15.5**	**104**	**37**	**80**	**0**	**–13**	....	....	....	....	....	....	....	....
1972-73	Canada	Summit	1	0	0	0	....	....	....	0	....	....	....	....	....	....	....	....	....	....	....	....	....	....	....	....	....	....
	Detroit Red Wings	**NHL**	**76**	**52**	**41**	**93**	**52**	**34**	**86**	**24**	**15**	**0**	**7**	**363**	**14.3**	**124**	**47**	**73**	**2**	**+6**	....	....	....	....	....	....	....	....
1973-74	**Detroit Red Wings**	**NHL**	**76**	**51**	**26**	**77**	**52**	**22**	**74**	**14**	**21**	**0**	**9**	**296**	**17.2**	**111**	**45**	**89**	**2**	**–21**	....	....	....	....	....	....	....	....
1974-75	**Detroit Red Wings**	**NHL**	**29**	**15**	**12**	**27**	**14**	**9**	**23**	**18**	**5**	**0**	**1**	**93**	**16.1**	**44**	**23**	**33**	**0**	**–12**	....	....	....	....	....	....	....	....
1975-76	**Detroit Red Wings**	**NHL**	**37**	**11**	**17**	**28**	**10**	**13**	**23**	**10**	**2**	**0**	**3**	**123**	**8.9**	**40**	**15**	**42**	**0**	**–17**	....	....	....	....	....	....	....	....
	NHL Totals		**538**	**233**	**195**	**428**	**242**	**170**	**412**	**219**	**62**	**0**	**29**	**1779**	**13.1**	**630**	**215**	**425**	**4**		**16**	**2**	**3**	**5**	**2**	**0**	**1**	**1**

NHL First All-Star Team (1973) • NHL Second All-Star Team (1974)

Played in NHL All-Star Game (1974)

Traded to **Detroit** by **Montreal** with Guy Charron and Bill Collins for Frank Mahovlich, January 13, 1971.

• REEDS, MARK

Mark Reeds RW – R. 5'10", 190 lbs. b: Burlington, Ont., 1/24/1960. St. Louis' 3rd choice, 86th overall, in 1979 Entry Draft.

Season	Club	League	GP	G	A	Pts	AG	AA	APts	PIM	PP	SH	GW	S	%	TGF	PGF	TGA	PGA	+/-	GP	G	A	Pts	PIM	PP	SH	GW
1976-77	Markham Waxers	Jr. B	24	17	23	40	....	....	....	62	....	....	....	....	....	....	....	....	....	....	....	....	....	....	....	....	....	....
	Toronto Marlboros	OHA	18	6	7	13	....	....	....	6	....	....	....	....	....	....	....	....	....	....	....	....	....	....	....	....	....	....
1977-78	Peterborough Petes	OHA	68	11	27	38	....	....	....	67	....	....	....	....	....	....	....	....	....	....	....	....	....	....	....	....	....	....
1978-79	Peterborough Petes	OHA	66	25	25	50	....	....	....	96	....	....	....	....	....	....	....	....	....	....	11	0	5	5	19	....	....	....
1979-80	Peterborough Petes	OHA	54	34	45	79	....	....	....	51	....	....	....	....	....	....	....	....	....	....	14	9	10	19	19	....	....	....
	Canada	WJC-A	5	1	0	1	....	....	....	2	....	....	....	....	....	....	....	....	....	....	....	....	....	....	....	....	....	....
1980-81	Salt Lake Golden Eagles	CHL	74	15	45	60	....	....	....	81	....	....	....	....	....	....	....	....	....	....	17	5	8	13	28	....	....	....
1981-82	**St. Louis Blues**	**NHL**	**9**	**1**	**3**	**4**	**1**	**2**	**3**	**0**	**0**	**0**	**0**	**8**	**12.5**	**6**	**0**	**3**	**0**	**+3**	**10**	**0**	**1**	**1**	**2**	**0**	**0**	**0**
	Salt Lake Golden Eagles	CHL	59	22	24	46	....	....	....	55	....	....	....	....	....	....	....	....	....	....	....	....	....	....	....	....	....	....
1982-83	**St. Louis Blues**	**NHL**	**20**	**5**	**14**	**19**	**4**	**10**	**14**	**8**	**0**	**0**	**1**	**34**	**14.7**	**26**	**3**	**17**	**2**	**+8**	**4**	**1**	**0**	**1**	**2**	**0**	**0**	**0**
	Salt Lake Golden Eagles	CHL	55	16	26	42	....	....	....	32	....	....	....	....	....	....	....	....	....	....	....	....	....	....	....	....	....	....
1983-84	**St. Louis Blues**	**NHL**	**65**	**11**	**14**	**25**	**9**	**9**	**18**	**23**	**3**	**1**	**0**	**72**	**15.3**	**33**	**5**	**48**	**17**	**–3**	**11**	**3**	**3**	**6**	**15**	**0**	**1**	**1**
1984-85	**St. Louis Blues**	**NHL**	**80**	**9**	**30**	**39**	**7**	**20**	**27**	**25**	**0**	**1**	**4**	**98**	**9.2**	**56**	**0**	**73**	**25**	**+8**	**3**	**0**	**0**	**0**	**0**	**0**	**0**	**0**
1985-86	**St. Louis Blues**	**NHL**	**78**	**10**	**28**	**38**	**8**	**19**	**27**	**28**	**0**	**0**	**2**	**108**	**9.3**	**56**	**2**	**77**	**34**	**+11**	**19**	**4**	**4**	**8**	**2**	**0**	**0**	**1**
1986-87	**St. Louis Blues**	**NHL**	**68**	**9**	**16**	**25**	**8**	**12**	**20**	**16**	**1**	**0**	**0**	**106**	**8.5**	**39**	**5**	**80**	**26**	**–20**	**6**	**0**	**1**	**1**	**2**	**0**	**0**	**0**
1987-88	**Hartford Whalers**	**NHL**	**38**	**0**	**7**	**7**	**0**	**5**	**5**	**31**	**0**	**0**	**0**	**36**	**0.0**	**13**	**0**	**35**	**9**	**–13**	....	....	....	....	....	....	....	....
1988-89	**Hartford Whalers**	**NHL**	**7**	**0**	**2**	**2**	**0**	**1**	**1**	**6**	**0**	**0**	**0**	**6**	**0.0**	**2**	**0**	**4**	**1**	**–1**	....	....	....	....	....	....	....	....
	Binghamton Whalers	AHL	69	26	34	60	....	....	....	18	....	....	....	....	....	....	....	....	....	....	....	....	....	....	....	....	....	....
1989-90	HC Fiemme	Italy	44	47	84	131	....	....	....	12	....	....	....	....	....	....	....	....	....	....	....	....	....	....	....	....	....	....

										REGULAR SEASON											PLAYOFFS							
Season	Club	League	GP	G	A	Pts	AG	AA	APts	PIM	PP	SH	GW	S	%	TGF	PGF	TGA	PGA	+/–	GP	G	A	Pts	PIM	PP	SH	GW
1990-91	HC Fiemme	Italy 2	36	8	47	55	....	....	....	18	....	....	....	....	....	....	....	....	....	....	....	....	....	....	....	....	....	....
1991-92			DID NOT PLAY																									
1992-93	Peoria Rivermen	IHL	16	4	2	6	....	....	....	8	....	....	....	....	....	....	....	....	....	....	1	0	0	0	0	....	....	....
	NHL Totals		**365**	**45**	**114**	**159**	**37**	**78**	**115**	**135**	**4**	**2**	**7**	**468**	**9.6**	**231**	**15**	**337**	**114**		**53**	**8**	**9**	**17**	**23**	**0**	**1**	**2**

Memorial Cup All-Star Team (1980)

Traded to **Hartford** by **St. Louis** for Hartford's 3rd round choice (Blair Atcheynum) in 1989 Entry Draft, October 5, 1987.

• REEKIE, JOE

Joe Reekie D – L. 6'3", 220 lbs. b: Victoria, B.C., 2/22/1965. Buffalo's 6th choice, 119th overall, in 1985 Entry Draft.

Season	Club	League	GP	G	A	Pts	AG	AA	APts	PIM	PP	SH	GW	S	%	TGF	PGF	TGA	PGA	+/–	GP	G	A	Pts	PIM	PP	SH	GW
1982-83	North Bay Centennials	OHL	59	2	9	11	....	....	....	49	....	....	....	....	....	....	....	....	....	....	8	0	1	1	11	....	....	....
1983-84	North Bay Centennials	OHL	9	1	0	1	....	....	....	18	....	....	....	....	....	....	....	....	....	....	....	....	....	....	....	....	....	....
	Cornwall Royals	OHL	53	6	27	33	....	....	....	166	....	....	....	....	....	....	....	....	....	....	3	0	0	0	4	....	....	....
1984-85	Cornwall Royals	OHL	65	19	63	82	....	....	....	134	....	....	....	....	....	....	....	....	....	....	9	4	13	17	18	....	....	....
1985-86	**Buffalo Sabres**	**NHL**	**3**	**0**	**0**	**0**	**0**	**0**	**0**	**14**	**0**	**0**	**0**	**1**	**0.0**	**2**	**0**	**4**	**0**	**–2**	....	....	....	....	....	....	....	....
	Rochester Americans	AHL	77	3	25	28	....	....	....	178	....	....	....	....	....	....	....	....	....	....	....	....	....	....	....	....	....	....
1986-87	**Buffalo Sabres**	**NHL**	**56**	**1**	**8**	**9**	**1**	**6**	**7**	**82**	**0**	**0**	**0**	**56**	**1.8**	**59**	**4**	**74**	**25**	**+6**	....	....	....	....	....	....	....	....
	Rochester Americans	AHL	22	0	6	6	....	....	....	52	....	....	....	....	....	....	....	....	....	....	....	....	....	....	....	....	....	....
1987-88	**Buffalo Sabres**	**NHL**	**30**	**1**	**4**	**5**	**1**	**3**	**4**	**68**	**0**	**0**	**0**	**23**	**4.3**	**28**	**0**	**39**	**8**	**–3**	**2**	**0**	**0**	**0**	**4**	**0**	**0**	**0**
1988-89	**Buffalo Sabres**	**NHL**	**15**	**1**	**3**	**4**	**1**	**2**	**3**	**26**	**1**	**0**	**0**	**14**	**7.1**	**19**	**1**	**18**	**6**	**+6**	....	....	....	....	....	....	....	....
	Rochester Americans	AHL	21	1	2	3	....	....	....	56	....	....	....	....	....	....	....	....	....	....	....	....	....	....	....	....	....	....
1989-90	**New York Islanders**	**NHL**	**31**	**1**	**8**	**9**	**1**	**6**	**7**	**43**	**0**	**0**	**1**	**22**	**4.5**	**35**	**1**	**38**	**17**	**+13**	....	....	....	....	....	....	....	....
	Springfield Indians	AHL	15	1	4	5	....	....	....	24	....	....	....	....	....	....	....	....	....	....	....	....	....	....	....	....	....	....
1990-91	**New York Islanders**	**NHL**	**66**	**3**	**16**	**19**	**3**	**12**	**15**	**96**	**0**	**0**	**2**	**70**	**4.3**	**65**	**3**	**76**	**31**	**+17**	....	....	....	....	....	....	....	....
	Capital District Islanders	AHL	2	1	0	1	....	....	....	0	....	....	....	....	....	....	....	....	....	....	....	....	....	....	....	....	....	....
1991-92	**New York Islanders**	**NHL**	**54**	**4**	**12**	**16**	**4**	**9**	**13**	**85**	**0**	**0**	**0**	**59**	**6.8**	**64**	**3**	**75**	**29**	**+15**	....	....	....	....	....	....	....	....
	Capital District Islanders	AHL	3	2	2	4	....	....	....	2	....	....	....	....	....	....	....	....	....	....	....	....	....	....	....	....	....	....
1992-93	**Tampa Bay Lightning**	**NHL**	**42**	**2**	**11**	**13**	**2**	**8**	**10**	**69**	**0**	**0**	**0**	**53**	**3.8**	**40**	**2**	**56**	**20**	**+2**	....	....	....	....	....	....	....	....
1993-94	**Tampa Bay Lightning**	**NHL**	**73**	**1**	**11**	**12**	**1**	**8**	**9**	**127**	**0**	**0**	**0**	**88**	**1.1**	**55**	**0**	**73**	**26**	**+8**	....	....	....	....	....	....	....	....
	Washington Capitals	**NHL**	**12**	**0**	**5**	**5**	**0**	**4**	**4**	**29**	**0**	**0**	**0**	**10**	**0.0**	**15**	**0**	**12**	**4**	**+7**	**11**	**2**	**1**	**3**	**29**	**0**	**1**	**1**
1994-95	**Washington Capitals**	**NHL**	**48**	**1**	**6**	**7**	**2**	**9**	**11**	**97**	**0**	**0**	**0**	**52**	**1.9**	**35**	**1**	**37**	**13**	**+10**	**7**	**0**	**0**	**0**	**2**	**0**	**0**	**0**
1995-96	**Washington Capitals**	**NHL**	**78**	**3**	**7**	**10**	**3**	**6**	**9**	**149**	**0**	**0**	**0**	**52**	**5.8**	**54**	**0**	**63**	**16**	**+7**	....	....	....	....	....	....	....	....
1996-97	**Washington Capitals**	**NHL**	**65**	**1**	**8**	**9**	**1**	**7**	**8**	**107**	**0**	**0**	**0**	**65**	**1.5**	**48**	**1**	**58**	**19**	**+8**	....	....	....	....	....	....	....	....
1997-98	**Washington Capitals**	**NHL**	**68**	**2**	**8**	**10**	**2**	**8**	**10**	**70**	**0**	**0**	**1**	**59**	**3.4**	**52**	**1**	**52**	**16**	**+15**	**21**	**1**	**2**	**3**	**20**	**0**	**0**	**0**
	NHL Totals		**641**	**21**	**107**	**128**	**22**	**88**	**110**	**1062**	**1**	**0**	**4**	**624**	**3.4**	**571**	**17**	**675**	**230**		**41**	**3**	**3**	**6**	**55**	**0**	**1**	**1**

• Re-entered NHL draft. Originally Hartford's 8th choice, 128th overall, in 1983 Entry Draft.

Traded to **NY Islanders** by **Buffalo** for NY Islanders' 6th round choice (Bill Pye) in 1989 Entry Draft, June 17, 1989. Claimed by **Tampa Bay** from **NY Islanders** in Expansion Draft, June 18, 1992. Traded to **Washington** by **Tampa Bay** for Enrico Ciccone, Washington's 3rd round choice (later traded to Anaheim — Anaheim selected Craig Reichert) in 1994 Entry Draft and the return of draft choices transferred in the Pat Elynuik trade, March 21, 1994.

• REGIER, DARCY

Darcy Regier D – L. 5'11", 190 lbs. b: Swift Current, Sask., 11/27/1956. California's 5th choice, 77th overall, in 1976 Amateur Draft.

Season	Club	League	GP	G	A	Pts	AG	AA	APts	PIM	PP	SH	GW	S	%	TGF	PGF	TGA	PGA	+/–	GP	G	A	Pts	PIM	PP	SH	GW
1973-74	Prince Albert Raiders	SJHL	48	1	10	11	....	....	....	63	....	....	....	....	....	....	....	....	....	....	....	....	....	....	....	....	....	....
1974-75	Lethbridge Broncos	WCJHL	67	11	25	36	....	....	....	78	....	....	....	....	....	....	....	....	....	....	....	....	....	....	....	....	....	....
1975-76	Lethbridge Broncos	WCJHL	53	5	22	27	....	....	....	125	....	....	....	....	....	....	....	....	....	....	7	1	1	2	9	....	....	....
1976-77	Salt Lake Golden Eagles	CHL	68	5	22	27	....	....	....	123	....	....	....	....	....	....	....	....	....	....	....	....	....	....	....	....	....	....
1977-78	**Cleveland Barons**	**NHL**	**15**	**0**	**1**	**1**	**0**	**1**	**1**	**28**	**0**	**0**	**0**	**8**	**0.0**	**6**	**0**	**14**	**3**	**–5**	....	....	....	....	....	....	....	....
	Binghamton Whalers	AHL	5	0	1	1	....	....	....	2	....	....	....	....	....	....	....	....	....	....	....	....	....	....	....	....	....	....
	Phoenix Roadrunners	CHL	16	0	5	5	....	....	....	43	....	....	....	....	....	....	....	....	....	....	....	....	....	....	....	....	....	....
	Fort Worth Texans	CHL	38	2	6	8	....	....	....	37	....	....	....	....	....	....	....	....	....	....	14	2	6	8	24	....	....	....
1978-79	Fort Worth Texans	CHL	59	1	15	16	....	....	....	98	....	....	....	....	....	....	....	....	....	....	5	0	1	1	2	....	....	....
1979-80	Indianapolis Checkers	CHL	79	0	18	18	....	....	....	52	....	....	....	....	....	....	....	....	....	....	7	0	1	1	20	....	....	....
1980-81	Indianapolis Checkers	CHL	76	2	18	20	....	....	....	77	....	....	....	....	....	....	....	....	....	....	5	0	1	1	27	....	....	....
1981-82	Indianapolis Checkers	CHL	80	4	17	21	....	....	....	98	....	....	....	....	....	....	....	....	....	....	13	1	4	5	20	....	....	....
1982-83	**New York Islanders**	**NHL**	**6**	**0**	**0**	**0**	**0**	**0**	**0**	**7**	**0**	**0**	**0**	**3**	**0.0**	**1**	**0**	**2**	**1**	**0**	....	....	....	....	....	....	....	....
	Indianapolis Checkers	CHL	74	3	28	31	....	....	....	102	....	....	....	....	....	....	....	....	....	....	11	0	4	4	21	....	....	....
1983-84	**New York Islanders**	**NHL**	**5**	**0**	**1**	**1**	**0**	**1**	**1**	**0**	**0**	**0**	**0**	**6**	**0.0**	**4**	**0**	**2**	**0**	**+2**	....	....	....	....	....	....	....	....
	Indianapolis Checkers	CHL	68	4	12	16	....	....	....	112	....	....	....	....	....	....	....	....	....	....	10	1	1	2	13	....	....	....
	NHL Totals		**26**	**0**	**2**	**2**	**0**	**2**	**2**	**35**	**0**	**0**	**0**	**17**	**0.0**	**11**	**0**	**18**	**4**		....	....	....	....	....	....	....	....

CHL First All-Star Team (1983)

Rights transferred to **Cleveland** after **California** franchise relocated, August 26, 1976. Traded to **NY Islanders** by **Cleveland** with Wayne Merrick for Jean-Paul Parise, Jean Potvin and the NY Islanders' 4th round choice in 1978 Amateur Draft (later cancelled by Cleveland-Minnesota merger), January 10, 1978.

• REICHEL, ROBERT

Robert Reichel C – L. 5'10", 185 lbs. b: Litvinov, Czech., 6/25/1971. Calgary's 5th choice, 70th overall, in 1989 Entry Draft.

Season	Club	League	GP	G	A	Pts	AG	AA	APts	PIM	PP	SH	GW	S	%	TGF	PGF	TGA	PGA	+/–	GP	G	A	Pts	PIM	PP	SH	GW
1987-88	CHZ Litvinov	Czech.	36	17	10	27	....	....	....	8	....	....	....	....	....	....	....	....	....	....	....	....	....	....	....	....	....	....
	Czechoslovakia	WJC-A	7	3	8	11	....	....	....	2	....	....	....	....	....	....	....	....	....	....	....	....	....	....	....	....	....	....
1988-89	CHZ Litvinov	Czech.	44	23	25	48	....	....	....	32	....	....	....	....	....	....	....	....	....	....	....	....	....	....	....	....	....	....
	Czechoslovakia	WJC-A	7	4	4	8	....	....	....	4	....	....	....	....	....	....	....	....	....	....	....	....	....	....	....	....	....	....
1989-90	CHZ Litvinov	Czech.	52	*49	34	*83	....	....	....	....	....	....	....	....	....	....	....	....	....	....	....	....	....	....	....	....	....	....
	Czechoslovakia	WJC-A	7	11	10	21	....	....	....	4	....	....	....	....	....	....	....	....	....	....	....	....	....	....	....	....	....	....
	Czechoslovakia	WEC-A	10	5	6	11	....	....	....	4	....	....	....	....	....	....	....	....	....	....	....	....	....	....	....	....	....	....
1990-91	**Calgary Flames**	**NHL**	**66**	**19**	**22**	**41**	**17**	**17**	**34**	**22**	**3**	**0**	**3**	**131**	**14.5**	**58**	**17**	**24**	**0**	**+17**	**6**	**1**	**1**	**2**	**0**	**1**	**0**	**0**
	Czechoslovakia	WEC-A	8	2	4	6	....	....	....	10	....	....	....	....	....	....	....	....	....	....	....	....	....	....	....	....	....	....
1991-92	Czechoslovakia	C Cup	5	1	2	3	....	....	....	6	....	....	....	....	....	....	....	....	....	....	....	....	....	....	....	....	....	....
	Calgary Flames	**NHL**	**77**	**20**	**34**	**54**	**18**	**26**	**44**	**32**	**8**	**0**	**3**	**181**	**11.0**	**77**	**36**	**41**	**1**	**+1**	....	....	....	....	....	....	....	....
	Czechoslovakia	WC-A	8	1	3	4	....	....	....	2	....	....	....	....	....	....	....	....	....	....	....	....	....	....	....	....	....	....
1992-93	**Calgary Flames**	**NHL**	**80**	**40**	**48**	**88**	**33**	**33**	**66**	**54**	**12**	**0**	**5**	**238**	**16.8**	**127**	**49**	**54**	**1**	**+25**	**6**	**2**	**4**	**6**	**2**	**2**	**0**	**0**
1993-94	**Calgary Flames**	**NHL**	**84**	**40**	**53**	**93**	**37**	**41**	**78**	**58**	**14**	**0**	**6**	**249**	**16.1**	**118**	**49**	**51**	**2**	**+20**	**7**	**0**	**5**	**5**	**0**	**0**	**0**	**0**
1994-95	Frankfurt Lions	Germany	21	19	24	43	....	....	....	41	....	....	....	....	....	....	....	....	....	....	....	....	....	....	....	....	....	....
	Calgary Flames	**NHL**	**48**	**18**	**17**	**35**	**32**	**25**	**57**	**28**	**5**	**0**	**2**	**160**	**11.3**	**50**	**20**	**32**	**0**	**–2**	**7**	**2**	**4**	**6**	**4**	**0**	**0**	**1**
1995-96	Frankfurt Lions	Germany	46	47	54	101	....	....	....	84	....	....	....	....	....	....	....	....	....	....	3	1	3	4	0	....	....	....
	Czech Republic	WC-A	8	4	4	8	....	....	....	0	....	....	....	....	....	....	....	....	....	....	....	....	....	....	....	....	....	....
1996-97	Czech Republic	W Cup	3	1	0	1	....	....	....	0	....	....	....	....	....	....	....	....	....	....	....	....	....	....	....	....	....	....
	Calgary Flames	**NHL**	**70**	**16**	**27**	**43**	**17**	**24**	**41**	**22**	**6**	**0**	**3**	**181**	**8.8**	**57**	**22**	**38**	**1**	**–2**	....	....	....	....	....	....	....	....
	New York Islanders	**NHL**	**12**	**5**	**14**	**19**	**5**	**12**	**17**	**4**	**0**	**1**	**0**	**33**	**15.2**	**22**	**5**	**10**	**0**	**+7**	....	....	....	....	....	....	....	....
	Czech Republic	WC-A	9	1	4	5	....	....	....	4	....	....	....	....	....	....	....	....	....	....	....	....	....	....	....	....	....	....
1997-98	**New York Islanders**	**NHL**	**82**	**25**	**40**	**65**	**29**	**39**	**68**	**32**	**8**	**0**	**2**	**201**	**12.4**	**97**	**48**	**61**	**1**	**–11**	....	....	....	....	....	....	....	....
	Czech Republic	Olympics	6	3	0	3	....	....	....	0	....	....	....	....	....	....	....	....	....	....	....	....	....	....	....	....	....	....
	Czech Republic	WC-A	8	0	4	4	....	....	....	0	....	....	....	....	....	....	....	....	....	....	....	....	....	....	....	....	....	....
	NHL Totals		**519**	**183**	**255**	**438**	**188**	**217**	**405**	**252**	**56**	**1**	**24**	**1374**	**13.3**	**606**	**246**	**311**	**6**		**26**	**5**	**14**	**19**	**6**	**3**	**0**	**1**

EJC-A All-Star Team (1988, 1989) • WJC-A All-Star Team (1990) • Named Best Forward at WJC-A (1990) • Czechoslovakian First All-Star Team (1990) • WEC-A All-Star Team (1990) • WC-A All-Star Team (1996)

Traded to **NY Islanders** by **Calgary** for Marty McInnis, Tyrone Garner and Calgary's 6th round choice (previously acquired, Calgary selected Ilja Demidov) in 1997 Entry Draft, March 18, 1997.

			REGULAR SEASON																		PLAYOFFS							
Season	Club	League	GP	G	A	Pts	AG	AA	APts	PIM	PP	SH	GW	S	%	TGF	PGF	TGA	PGA	+/–	GP	G	A	Pts	PIM	PP	SH	GW
● **REICHERT, CRAIG** Craig Reichert RW – R. 6'1", 200 lbs. b: Winnipeg, Man., 5/11/1974. Anaheim's 3rd choice, 67th overall, in 1994 Entry Draft.																												
1991-92	Spokane Chiefs	WHL	68	13	20	33	....	....	....	86	....	....	....	....	....	....	....	....	....	....	4	1	0	1	4	....	....	....
1992-93	Red Deer Rebels	WHL	66	32	33	65	....	....	....	62	....	....	....	....	....	....	....	....	....	....	4	3	1	4	2	....	....	....
1993-94	Red Deer Rebels	WHL	72	52	67	119	....	....	....	153	....	....	....	....	....	....	....	....	....	....	4	2	2	4	8	....	....	....
1994-95	San Diego Gulls	IHL	49	4	12	16	....	....	....	28	....	....	....	....	....	....	....	....	....	....	....	....	....	....	....	....	....	....
1995-96	Baltimore Bandits	AHL	68	10	17	27	....	....	....	50	....	....	....	....	....	....	....	....	....	....	1	0	0	0	0	....	....	....
1996-97	**Anaheim Mighty Ducks**	**NHL**	3	0	0	0	0	0	0	0	0	0	0	3	0.0	0	0	2	0	–2	....	....	....	....	....	....	....	....
	Baltimore Bandits	AHL	77	22	53	75	....	....	....	54	....	....	....	....	....	....	....	....	....	....	3	0	2	2	0	....	....	....
1997-98	Cincinnati Mighty Ducks	AHL	78	28	59	87	....	....	....	28	....	....	....	....	....	....	....	....	....	....	....	....	....	....	....	....	....	....
	NHL Totals		3	0	0	0	0	0	0	0	0	0	0	3	0.0	0	0	2	0		....	....	....	....	....	....	....	....
● **REID, DAVID** David Reid LW – L. 6'1", 217 lbs. b: Toronto, Ont., 5/15/1964. Boston's 4th choice, 60th overall, in 1982 Entry Draft.																												
1981-82	Peterborough Petes	OHL	68	10	32	42	....	....	....	41	....	....	....	....	....	....	....	....	....	....	9	2	3	5	11	....	....	....
1982-83	Peterborough Petes	OHL	70	23	34	57	....	....	....	33	....	....	....	....	....	....	....	....	....	....	4	3	1	4	0	....	....	....
1983-84	Peterborough Petes	OHL	60	33	64	97	....	....	....	12	....	....	....	....	....	....	....	....	....	....	....	....	....	....	....	....	....	....
	Boston Bruins	**NHL**	8	1	0	1	1	0	1	2	0	0	0	4	25.0	3	0	2	0	+1	....	....	....	....	....	....	....	....
1984-85	**Boston Bruins**	**NHL**	35	14	13	27	11	9	20	27	2	0	5	52	26.9	39	10	30	0	–1	5	1	0	1	0	0	0	0
	Hershey Bears	AHL	43	10	14	24	....	....	....	6	....	....	....	....	....	....	....	....	....	....	....	....	....	....	....	....	....	....
1985-86	**Boston Bruins**	**NHL**	37	10	10	20	8	7	15	10	4	0	1	53	18.9	34	15	17	0	+2	....	....	....	....	....	....	....	....
	Moncton Golden Flames	AHL	26	14	18	32	....	....	....	4	....	....	....	....	....	....	....	....	....	....	....	....	....	....	....	....	....	....
1986-87	**Boston Bruins**	**NHL**	12	3	3	6	3	2	5	0	0	0	0	19	15.8	6	0	7	0	–1	2	0	0	0	0	0	0	0
	Moncton Golden Flames	AHL	40	12	22	34	....	....	....	23	....	....	....	....	....	....	....	....	....	....	5	0	1	1	0	....	....	....
1987-88	**Boston Bruins**	**NHL**	3	0	0	0	0	0	0	0	0	0	0	2	0.0	0	0	0	0	0	....	....	....	....	....	....	....	....
	Maine Mariners	AHL	63	21	37	58	....	....	....	40	....	....	....	....	....	....	....	....	....	....	10	6	7	13	0	....	....	....
1988-89	**Toronto Maple Leafs**	**NHL**	77	9	21	30	8	15	23	22	1	1	0	87	10.3	49	5	61	29	+12	....	....	....	....	....	....	....	....
1989-90	**Toronto Maple Leafs**	**NHL**	70	9	19	28	8	14	22	9	0	4	1	97	9.3	41	0	80	31	–8	3	0	0	0	0	0	0	0
1990-91	**Toronto Maple Leafs**	**NHL**	69	15	13	28	14	10	24	18	1	8	0	110	13.6	41	4	77	30	–10	....	....	....	....	....	....	....	....
1991-92	**Boston Bruins**	**NHL**	43	7	7	14	6	5	11	27	2	1	0	70	10.0	32	5	33	11	+5	15	2	5	7	4	0	0	1
	Maine Mariners	AHL	12	1	5	6	....	....	....	4	....	....	....	....	....	....	....	....	....	....	....	....	....	....	....	....	....	....
1992-93	**Boston Bruins**	**NHL**	65	20	16	36	17	11	28	10	1	5	2	116	17.2	52	3	67	30	+12	....	....	....	....	....	....	....	....
1993-94	**Boston Bruins**	**NHL**	83	6	17	23	6	13	19	25	0	2	1	145	4.1	46	0	66	30	+10	13	2	1	3	2	0	1	0
1994-95	**Boston Bruins**	**NHL**	38	5	5	10	9	7	16	10	0	0	0	47	10.6	16	0	16	8	+8	5	0	0	0	0	0	0	0
	Providence Bruins	AHL	7	3	0	3	....	....	....	0	....	....	....	....	....	....	....	....	....	....	....	....	....	....	....	....	....	....
1995-96	**Boston Bruins**	**NHL**	63	23	21	44	23	17	40	4	1	6	3	160	14.4	58	3	67	26	+14	5	0	2	2	2	0	0	0
1996-97	**Dallas Stars**	**NHL**	82	19	20	39	20	18	38	10	1	1	4	135	14.1	50	2	55	19	+12	7	1	0	1	4	0	0	0
1997-98	**Dallas Stars**	**NHL**	65	6	12	18	7	12	19	14	3	0	1	90	6.7	29	12	45	13	–15	5	0	3	3	2	0	0	0
	NHL Totals		750	147	177	324	141	140	281	188	16	28	18	1187	12.4	496	59	623	227		60	6	11	17	14	0	1	1
Signed as a free agent by **Toronto**, June 23, 1988. Signed as a free agent by **Boston**, December 1, 1991. Signed as a free agent by **Dallas**, July 11, 1996.																												
● **REID, TOM** Tom Reid D – L. 6'1", 200 lbs. b: Fort Erie, Ont., 6/24/1946.																												
1963-64	Fort Frances Royals	MJHL	27	2	5	7	....	....	....	45	....	....	....	....	....	....	....	....	....	....	10	1	1	2	24	....	....	....
1964-65	St. Catharines Black Hawks	OHA	56	4	13	17	....	....	....	106	....	....	....	....	....	....	....	....	....	....	5	1	0	1	11	....	....	....
1965-66	St. Catharines Black Hawks	OHA	45	3	15	18	....	....	....	74	....	....	....	....	....	....	....	....	....	....	7	0	0	0	44	....	....	....
1966-67	St. Catharines Black Hawks	OHA	45	5	19	24	....	....	....	120	....	....	....	....	....	....	....	....	....	....	4	0	2	2	2	....	....	....
	St. Louis Braves	CHL	1	0	0	0	....	....	....	0	....	....	....	....	....	....	....	....	....	....	....	....	....	....	....	....	....	....
1967-68	**Chicago Black Hawks**	**NHL**	56	0	4	4	0	4	4	25	0	0	0	24	0.0	18	0	30	13	+1	9	0	0	0	2	0	0	0
	Dallas Black Hawks	CHL	3	0	1	1	....	....	....	0	....	....	....	....	....	....	....	....	....	....	....	....	....	....	....	....	....	....
1968-69	**Chicago Black Hawks**	**NHL**	30	0	3	3	0	3	3	12	0	0	0	6	0.0	12	0	18	2	–4	....	....	....	....	....	....	....	....
	Dallas Black Hawks	CHL	3	0	1	1	....	....	....	4	....	....	....	....	....	....	....	....	....	....	....	....	....	....	....	....	....	....
	Minnesota North Stars	**NHL**	18	0	4	4	0	4	4	38	0	0	0	16	0.0	16	2	32	5	–13	....	....	....	....	....	....	....	....
1969-70	**Minnesota North Stars**	**NHL**	66	1	7	8	1	7	8	51	0	0	1	89	1.1	63	2	86	15	–10	6	0	1	1	4	0	0	0
	Iowa Stars	CHL	9	0	5	5	....	....	....	8	....	....	....	....	....	....	....	....	....	....	....	....	....	....	....	....	....	....
1970-71	**Minnesota North Stars**	**NHL**	73	3	14	17	3	12	15	62	0	0	1	111	2.7	72	4	99	25	–6	12	0	6	6	20	0	0	0
1971-72	**Minnesota North Stars**	**NHL**	78	6	15	21	6	14	20	107	1	0	1	111	5.4	86	8	88	23	+13	7	1	4	5	17	0	0	0
1972-73	**Minnesota North Stars**	**NHL**	60	1	13	14	1	11	12	50	0	0	0	79	1.3	78	3	77	17	+15	6	0	2	2	4	0	0	0
1973-74	**Minnesota North Stars**	**NHL**	76	4	19	23	4	16	20	81	0	0	0	118	3.4	82	3	134	33	–22	....	....	....	....	....	....	....	....
1974-75	**Minnesota North Stars**	**NHL**	74	1	5	6	1	4	5	103	0	0	1	98	1.0	65	1	147	44	–39	....	....	....	....	....	....	....	....
1975-76	**Minnesota North Stars**	**NHL**	69	0	15	15	0	12	12	52	0	0	0	90	0.0	59	20	102	39	–24	....	....	....	....	....	....	....	....
1976-77	**Minnesota North Stars**	**NHL**	65	0	8	8	0	6	6	52	0	0	0	45	0.0	56	4	101	33	–16	2	0	0	0	2	0	0	0
1977-78	**Minnesota North Stars**	**NHL**	36	1	6	7	1	5	6	21	0	0	1	26	3.8	24	1	66	17	–26	....	....	....	....	....	....	....	....
	NHL Totals		701	17	113	130	17	98	115	654	1	0	5	813	2.1	631	48	980	266		42	1	13	14	49	0	0	0
Traded to **Minnesota** by **Chicago** with Bill Orban for Andre Boudrias and Mike McMahon, February, 1969.																												
● **REIERSON, DAVE** Dave Reierson D – R. 6', 185 lbs. b: Bashaw, Alta., 8/30/1964. Calgary's 1st choice, 29th overall, in 1982 Entry Draft.																												
1980-81	Prince Albert Raiders	SJHL	73	14	39	53	....	....	....	....	....	....	....	....	....	....	....	....	....	....	....	....	....	....	....	....	....	....
1981-82	Prince Albert Raiders	SJHL	60	20	51	71	....	....	....	163	....	....	....	....	....	....	....	....	....	....	27	3	25	28	42	....	....	....
1982-83	Michigan Tech Huskies	CCHA	38	2	14	16	....	....	....	52	....	....	....	....	....	....	....	....	....	....	....	....	....	....	....	....	....	....
1983-84	Michigan Tech Huskies	CCHA	38	4	15	19	....	....	....	63	....	....	....	....	....	....	....	....	....	....	....	....	....	....	....	....	....	....
1984-85	Michigan Tech Huskies	CCHA	36	5	27	32	....	....	....	76	....	....	....	....	....	....	....	....	....	....	....	....	....	....	....	....	....	....
1985-86	Michigan Tech Huiskies	WCHA	39	7	16	23	....	....	....	51	....	....	....	....	....	....	....	....	....	....	....	....	....	....	....	....	....	....
1986-87	Canada	Nat-Team	61	1	17	18	....	....	....	36	....	....	....	....	....	....	....	....	....	....	....	....	....	....	....	....	....	....
	Moncton Golden Flames	AHL	....	....	....	....	....	....	....	....	....	....	....	....	....	....	....	....	....	....	6	0	1	1	12	....	....	....
1987-88	Canada	Nat-Team	32	2	8	10	....	....	....	18	....	....	....	....	....	....	....	....	....	....	....	....	....	....	....	....	....	....
	Salt Lake Golden Eagles	IHL	48	10	19	29	....	....	....	42	....	....	....	....	....	....	....	....	....	....	16	2	14	16	30	....	....	....
1988-89	**Calgary Flames**	**NHL**	2	0	0	0	0	0	0	2	0	0	0	1	0.0	2	0	1	0	+1	....	....	....	....	....	....	....	....
	Salt Lake Golden Eagles	IHL	76	7	46	53	....	....	....	70	....	....	....	....	....	....	....	....	....	....	13	1	8	9	12	....	....	....
1989-90	Tappara Tampere	Finland	32	7	5	12	....	....	....	28	....	....	....	....	....	....	....	....	....	....	7	0	2	2	12	....	....	....
1990-91	Canada	Nat-Team	8	0	1	1	....	....	....	6	....	....	....	....	....	....	....	....	....	....	....	....	....	....	....	....	....	....
	Tappara Tampere	Finland	41	1	8	9	....	....	....	18	....	....	....	....	....	....	....	....	....	....	3	0	0	0	2	....	....	....
1991-92	Amiens SC	France	34	8	14	22	....	....	....	40	....	....	....	....	....	....	....	....	....	....	....	....	....	....	....	....	....	....
1992-93	Amiens SC	France	14	14	12	26	....	....	....	18	....	....	....	....	....	....	....	....	....	....	....	....	....	....	....	....	....	....
1993-94	Amiens SC	France	32	12	23	36	....	....	....	44	....	....	....	....	....	....	....	....	....	....	....	....	....	....	....	....	....	....
1994-95	Hannover Scorpions	Germany	43	8	14	22	....	....	....	38	....	....	....	....	....	....	....	....	....	....	5	1	0	1	2	....	....	....
1995-96	Augsburg Panthers	Germany	7	2	2	4	....	....	....	6	....	....	....	....	....	....	....	....	....	....	7	1	1	2	4	....	....	....
1996-97	Amiens SC	France	STATISTICS NOT AVAILABLE																									
1997-98	Amiens SC	EuroHL	6	1	2	3	....	....	....	8	....	....	....	....	....	....	....	....	....	....	....	....	....	....	....	....	....	....
	NHL Totals		2	0	0	0	0	0	0	2	0	0	0	1	0.0	2	0	1	0		....	....	....	....	....	....	....	....
● **REINHART, PAUL** Paul "Rhino" Reinhart D – L. 5'11", 205 lbs. b: Kitchener, Ont., 1/6/1960. Atlanta's 8th choice, 12th overall, in 1979 Entry Draft.																												
1975-76	Kitchener Rangers	OHA	53	6	33	39	....	....	....	42	....	....	....	....	....	....	....	....	....	....	8	1	2	3	4	....	....	....
1976-77	Kitchener Rangers	OHA	51	4	14	18	....	....	....	10	....	....	....	....	....	....	....	....	....	....	3	0	2	2	4	....	....	....
1977-78	Kitchener Rangers	OHA	47	17	20	45	....	....	....	15	....	....	....	....	....	....	....	....	....	....	9	4	6	10	29	....	....	....
1978-79	Kitchener Rangers	OHA	66	51	78	129	....	....	....	57	....	....	....	....	....	....	....	....	....	....	10	3	10	13	16	....	....	....
1979-80	**Atlanta Flames**	**NHL**	79	9	38	47	8	29	37	31	4	0	1	130	6.9	118	31	78	2	+11	....	....	....	....	....	....	....	....
1980-81	**Calgary Flames**	**NHL**	74	18	49	67	15	34	49	52	10	0	0	122	14.8	156	54	105	13	+10	16	1	14	15	16	1	0	0
1981-82	Canada	C Cup	2	0	0	0	....	....	....	2	....	....	....	....	....	....	....	....	....	....	....	....	....	....	....	....	....	....
	Calgary Flames	**NHL**	62	13	48	61	10	32	42	17	8	0	0	116	11.2	131	50	115	35	+1	3	0	1	1	2	0	0	0
	Canada	WEC-A	7	1	5	6	....	....	....	4	....	....	....	....	....	....	....	....	....	....	....	....	....	....	....	....	....	....
1982-83	**Calgary Flames**	**NHL**	78	17	58	75	14	40	54	28	5	0	1	152	11.2	154	59	125	31	+1	9	6	3	9	2	4	1	0
	Canada	WEC-A	6	2	4	6	....	....	....	2	....	....	....	....	....	....	....	....	....	....	....	....	....	....	....	....	....	....
1983-84	**Calgary Flames**	**NHL**	27	6	15	21	5	10	15	10	3	0	1	92	6.5	44	13	51	10	–10	11	6	11	17	2	0	1	0

			REGULAR SEASON																		PLAYOFFS							
Season	Club	League	GP	G	A	Pts	AG	AA	APts	PIM	PP	SH	GW	S	%	TGF	PGF	TGA	PGA	+/–	GP	G	A	Pts	PIM	PP	SH	GW
1984-85	**Calgary Flames**	**NHL**	**75**	**23**	**46**	**69**	**19**	**31**	**50**	**18**	**12**	**2**	**5**	**173**	**13.3**	**153**	**55**	**149**	**54**	**+3**	**4**	**1**	**1**	**2**	**0**	**0**	**0**	**0**
1985-86	**Calgary Flames**	**NHL**	**32**	**8**	**25**	**33**	**6**	**17**	**23**	**15**	**4**	**0**	**2**	**58**	**13.8**	**65**	**26**	**52**	**17**	**+4**	**21**	**5**	**13**	**18**	**4**	**4**	**0**	**0**
1986-87	**Calgary Flames**	**NHL**	**76**	**15**	**53**	**68**	**13**	**38**	**51**	**22**	**7**	**0**	**2**	**120**	**12.5**	**133**	**50**	**96**	**20**	**+7**	**4**	**0**	**1**	**1**	**6**	**0**	**0**	**0**
1987-88	**Calgary Flames**	**NHL**	**14**	**0**	**4**	**4**	**0**	**3**	**3**	**10**	**0**	**0**	**0**	**22**	**0.0**	**20**	**7**	**18**	**5**	**0**	**8**	**2**	**7**	**9**	**6**	**1**	**0**	**0**
1988-89	**Vancouver Canucks**	**NHL**	**64**	**7**	**50**	**57**	**6**	**35**	**41**	**44**	**3**	**0**	**1**	**133**	**5.3**	**121**	**60**	**80**	**15**	**–4**	**7**	**2**	**3**	**5**	**4**	**1**	**0**	**2**
1989-90	**Vancouver Canucks**	**NHL**	**67**	**17**	**40**	**57**	**15**	**29**	**44**	**30**	**9**	**1**	**1**	**139**	**12.2**	**118**	**48**	**89**	**21**	**+2**	....	....	....	....	....	....	....	....
	NHL Totals		**648**	**133**	**426**	**559**	**111**	**298**	**409**	**277**	**65**	**3**	**14**	**1257**	**10.6**	**1213**	**453**	**958**	**223**		**83**	**23**	**54**	**77**	**42**	**11**	**2**	**2**

Played in NHL All-Star Game (1985, 1989)

Transferred to **Calgary** after **Atlanta** franchise relocated, June 24, 1980. Traded to **Vancouver** by **Calgary** with Steve Bozek for Vancouver's 3rd round choice (Veli-Pekka Kautonen) in 1989 Entry Draft, September 6, 1988.

• RENAUD, MARK

Mark Renaud D – L. 6′, 185 lbs. b: Windsor, Ont., 2/21/1959. Hartford's 5th choice, 102nd overall, in 1979 Entry Draft.

Season	Club	League	GP	G	A	Pts	AG	AA	APts	PIM	PP	SH	GW	S	%	TGF	PGF	TGA	PGA	+/–	GP	G	A	Pts	PIM	PP	SH	GW
1975-76	Windsor Spitfires	OHA	66	3	15	18	....	....	....	42	....	....	....	....	....	....	....	....	....	....	....	....	....	....	....	....	....	....
1976-77	Niagara Falls Flyers	OHA	66	7	25	32	....	....	....	30	....	....	....	....	....	....	....	....	....	....	....	....	....	....	....	....	....	....
1977-78	Niagara Falls Flyers	OHA	68	6	24	30	....	....	....	57	....	....	....	....	....	....	....	....	....	....	....	....	....	....	....	....	....	....
1978-79	Niagara Falls Flyers	OHA	68	10	56	66	....	....	....	89	....	....	....	....	....	....	....	....	....	....	20	4	17	21	30	....	....	....
1979-80	**Hartford Whalers**	**NHL**	**13**	**0**	**2**	**2**	**0**	**2**	**2**	**4**	**0**	**0**	**0**	**9**	**0.0**	**9**	**0**	**10**	**0**	**–1**	....	....	....	....	....	....	....	....
	Springfield Indians	AHL	61	3	16	19	....	....	....	39	....	....	....	....	....	....	....	....	....	....	....	....	....	....	....	....	....	....
1980-81	**Hartford Whalers**	**NHL**	**4**	**1**	**0**	**1**	**1**	**0**	**1**	**0**	**0**	**0**	**0**	**1**	**100.0**	**2**	**0**	**3**	**1**	**0**	....	....	....	....	....	....	....	....
	Binghamton Whalers	AHL	73	6	44	50	....	....	....	56	....	....	....	....	....	....	....	....	....	....	6	0	2	2	2	....	....	....
1981-82	**Hartford Whalers**	**NHL**	**48**	**1**	**17**	**18**	**1**	**11**	**12**	**39**	**0**	**0**	**0**	**72**	**1.4**	**54**	**9**	**77**	**15**	**–17**	....	....	....	....	....	....	....	....
	Binghamton Whalers	AHL	33	3	19	22	....	....	....	70	....	....	....	....	....	....	....	....	....	....	....	....	....	....	....	....	....	....
1982-83	**Hartford Whalers**	**NHL**	**77**	**3**	**28**	**31**	**2**	**19**	**21**	**37**	**1**	**0**	**0**	**87**	**3.4**	**77**	**14**	**128**	**23**	**–42**	....	....	....	....	....	....	....	....
1983-84	**Buffalo Sabres**	**NHL**	**10**	**1**	**3**	**4**	**1**	**2**	**3**	**6**	**0**	**0**	**0**	**11**	**9.1**	**6**	**0**	**5**	**0**	**+1**	....	....	....	....	....	....	....	....
	Rochester Americans	AHL	64	9	33	42	....	....	....	52	....	....	....	....	....	....	....	....	....	....	15	2	8	10	39	....	....	....
1984-85	Rochester Americans	AHL	80	8	34	42	....	....	....	56	....	....	....	....	....	....	....	....	....	....	5	0	0	0	2	....	....	....
	NHL Totals		**152**	**6**	**50**	**56**	**5**	**34**	**39**	**86**	**1**	**0**	**0**	**180**	**3.3**	**148**	**23**	**223**	**39**		....	....	....	....	....	....	....	....

Claimed by **Buffalo** from **Hartford** in Waiver Draft, October 3, 1983.

• RENBERG, MIKAEL

Mikael Renberg RW – L. 6′2″, 218 lbs. b: Pitea, Sweden, 5/5/1972. Philadelphia's 3rd choice, 40th overall, in 1990 Entry Draft.

Season	Club	League	GP	G	A	Pts	AG	AA	APts	PIM	PP	SH	GW	S	%	TGF	PGF	TGA	PGA	+/–	GP	G	A	Pts	PIM	PP	SH	GW
1988-89	Pitea	Sweden 2	12	6	3	9	....	....	....	....	....	....	....	....	....	....	....	....	....	....	....	....	....	....	....	....	....	....
1989-90	Pitea	Sweden 2	29	15	19	34	....	....	....	....	....	....	....	....	....	....	....	....	....	....	....	....	....	....	....	....	....	....
1990-91	Lulea HF	Sweden	29	11	6	17	....	....	....	12	....	....	....	....	....	....	....	....	....	....	5	1	1	2	4	....	....	....
1991-92	Lulea HF	Sweden	38	8	15	23	....	....	....	20	....	....	....	....	....	....	....	....	....	....	2	0	0	0	0	....	....	....
	Sweden	WJC-A	7	6	4	10	....	....	....	8	....	....	....	....	....	....	....	....	....	....	....	....	....	....	....	....	....	....
1992-93	Lulea HF	Sweden	39	19	13	32	....	....	....	61	....	....	....	....	....	....	....	....	....	....	11	4	4	8	4	....	....	....
	Sweden	WC-A	8	5	3	8	....	....	....	6	....	....	....	....	....	....	....	....	....	....	....	....	....	....	....	....	....	....
1993-94	**Philadelphia Flyers**	**NHL**	**83**	**38**	**44**	**82**	**36**	**34**	**70**	**36**	**9**	**0**	**1**	**195**	**19.5**	**119**	**42**	**69**	**0**	**+8**	....	....	....	....	....	....	....	....
1994-95	Lulea HF	Sweden	10	9	4	13	....	....	....	16	....	....	....	....	....	....	....	....	....	....	....	....	....	....	....	....	....	....
	Philadelphia Flyers	**NHL**	**47**	**26**	**31**	**57**	**46**	**46**	**92**	**20**	**8**	**0**	**4**	**143**	**18.2**	**75**	**21**	**35**	**1**	**+20**	**15**	**6**	**7**	**13**	**6**	**2**	**0**	**0**
1995-96	**Philadelphia Flyers**	**NHL**	**51**	**23**	**20**	**43**	**23**	**16**	**39**	**45**	**9**	**0**	**4**	**198**	**11.6**	**68**	**28**	**33**	**1**	**+8**	**11**	**3**	**6**	**9**	**14**	**1**	**0**	**0**
1996-97	**Philadelphia Flyers**	**NHL**	**77**	**22**	**37**	**59**	**23**	**33**	**56**	**65**	**1**	**0**	**4**	**249**	**8.8**	**99**	**13**	**50**	**0**	**+36**	**18**	**5**	**6**	**11**	**4**	**2**	**0**	**0**
1997-98	**Tampa Bay Lightning**	**NHL**	**68**	**16**	**22**	**38**	**19**	**21**	**40**	**34**	**6**	**3**	**0**	**175**	**9.1**	**51**	**21**	**72**	**5**	**–37**	....	....	....	....	....	....	....	....
	Sweden	Olympics	4	1	2	3	....	....	....	4	....	....	....	....	....	....	....	....	....	....	....	....	....	....	....	....	....	....
	Sweden	WC-A	10	5	3	8	....	....	....	5	....	....	....	....	....	....	....	....	....	....	....	....	....	....	....	....	....	....
	NHL Totals		**326**	**125**	**154**	**279**	**147**	**150**	**297**	**200**	**33**	**3**	**13**	**960**	**13.0**	**412**	**125**	**259**	**7**		**44**	**14**	**19**	**33**	**24**	**5**	**0**	**0**

WC-A All-Star Team (1993) • NHL/Upper Deck All-Rookie Team (1994)

Traded to **Tampa Bay** by **Philadelphia** with Karl Dykhuis for Philadelphia's 1st round choices in 1998 (Simon Gagne), 1999, 2000 and 2001 Entry Drafts (previously acquired by Tampa Bay), August 20, 1997.

• REYNOLDS, BOBBY

Bobby Reynolds LW – L. 5′11″, 175 lbs. b: Flint, MI, 7/14/1967. Toronto's 10th choice, 190th overall, in 1985 Entry Draft.

Season	Club	League	GP	G	A	Pts	AG	AA	APts	PIM	PP	SH	GW	S	%	TGF	PGF	TGA	PGA	+/–	GP	G	A	Pts	PIM	PP	SH	GW
1983-84	St. Clair Shores	NAJHL	60	25	34	59	....	....	....	....	....	....	....	....	....	....	....	....	....	....	....	....	....	....	....	....	....	....
1984-85	St. Clair Shores	NAJHL	43	20	30	50	....	....	....	....	....	....	....	....	....	....	....	....	....	....	....	....	....	....	....	....	....	....
1985-86	Michigan State Spartans	CCHA	45	9	10	19	....	....	....	26	....	....	....	....	....	....	....	....	....	....	....	....	....	....	....	....	....	....
1986-87	Michigan State Spartans	CCHA	40	20	13	33	....	....	....	40	....	....	....	....	....	....	....	....	....	....	....	....	....	....	....	....	....	....
1987-88	Michigan State Spartans	CCHA	46	42	25	67	....	....	....	52	....	....	....	....	....	....	....	....	....	....	....	....	....	....	....	....	....	....
1988-89	Michigan State Spartans	CCHA	47	36	41	77	....	....	....	78	....	....	....	....	....	....	....	....	....	....	....	....	....	....	....	....	....	....
1989-90	**Toronto Maple Leafs**	**NHL**	**7**	**1**	**1**	**2**	**1**	**1**	**2**	**0**	**0**	**0**	**0**	**13**	**7.7**	**2**	**0**	**5**	**0**	**–3**	....	....	....	....	....	....	....	....
	Newmarket Saints	AHL	66	22	28	50	....	....	....	55	....	....	....	....	....	....	....	....	....	....	....	....	....	....	....	....	....	....
1990-91	Newmarket Saints	AHL	65	24	22	46	....	....	....	59	....	....	....	....	....	....	....	....	....	....	....	....	....	....	....	....	....	....
	Baltimore Skipjacks	AHL	14	4	9	13	....	....	....	8	....	....	....	....	....	....	....	....	....	....	6	2	2	4	10	....	....	....
1991-92	Baltimore Skipjacks	AHL	53	12	18	30	....	....	....	39	....	....	....	....	....	....	....	....	....	....	....	....	....	....	....	....	....	....
	Kalamazoo Wings	IHL	13	8	10	18	....	....	....	19	....	....	....	....	....	....	....	....	....	....	12	5	4	9	4	....	....	....
1992-93	Sauerland	German 2	45	54	69	123	....	....	....	97	....	....	....	....	....	....	....	....	....	....	....	....	....	....	....	....	....	....
1993-94	Sauerland	German 2	52	45	47	92	....	....	....	84	....	....	....	....	....	....	....	....	....	....	....	....	....	....	....	....	....	....
1994-95	Courmaosta	Italy	16	9	14	23	....	....	....	6	....	....	....	....	....	....	....	....	....	....	....	....	....	....	....	....	....	....
	Klagenfurt	Germany	7	2	5	7	....	....	....	6	....	....	....	....	....	....	....	....	....	....	7	4	5	9	29	....	....	....
1995-96	Ratingen Lions	Germany	46	41	32	73	....	....	....	36	....	....	....	....	....	....	....	....	....	....	3	1	1	2	0	....	....	....
1996-97	Ratingen Lions	Germany	48	21	16	37	....	....	....	28	....	....	....	....	....	....	....	....	....	....	6	1	1	2	52	....	....	....
	NHL Totals		**7**	**1**	**1**	**2**	**1**	**1**	**2**	**0**	**0**	**0**	**0**	**13**	**7.7**	**2**	**0**	**5**	**0**		....	....	....	....	....	....	....	....

CCHA Second All-Star Team (1988, 1989) • NCAA West First All-American Team (1989)

Traded to **Washington** by **Toronto** for Rob Mendel, March 5, 1991.

• RHEAUME, PASCAL

Pascal Rheaume C – L. 6′1″, 200 lbs. b: Quebec, Que., 6/21/1973.

Season	Club	League	GP	G	A	Pts	AG	AA	APts	PIM	PP	SH	GW	S	%	TGF	PGF	TGA	PGA	+/–	GP	G	A	Pts	PIM	PP	SH	GW
1991-92	Trois Rivières Draveurs	QMJHL	65	17	20	37	....	....	....	84	....	....	....	....	....	....	....	....	....	....	14	5	4	9	23	....	....	....
1992-93	Sherbrooke Faucons	QMJHL	65	28	34	62	....	....	....	88	....	....	....	....	....	....	....	....	....	....	14	6	5	11	31	....	....	....
1993-94	Albany River Rats	AHL	55	17	18	35	....	....	....	43	....	....	....	....	....	....	....	....	....	....	5	0	1	1	0	....	....	....
1994-95	Albany River Rats	AHL	78	19	25	44	....	....	....	46	....	....	....	....	....	....	....	....	....	....	14	3	6	9	19	....	....	....
1995-96	Albany River Rats	AHL	68	26	42	68	....	....	....	50	....	....	....	....	....	....	....	....	....	....	4	1	2	3	2	....	....	....
1996-97	**New Jersey Devils**	**NHL**	**2**	**1**	**0**	**1**	**1**	**0**	**1**	**0**	**0**	**0**	**0**	**5**	**20.0**	**1**	**0**	**0**	**0**	**+1**	....	....	....	....	....	....	....	....
	Albany River Rats	AHL	51	22	23	45	....	....	....	40	....	....	....	....	....	....	....	....	....	....	16	2	8	10	16	....	....	....
1997-98	**St. Louis Blues**	**NHL**	**48**	**6**	**9**	**15**	**7**	**9**	**16**	**35**	**1**	**0**	**0**	**45**	**13.3**	**33**	**8**	**21**	**0**	**+4**	**10**	**1**	**3**	**4**	**8**	**1**	**0**	**0**
	NHL Totals		**50**	**7**	**9**	**16**	**8**	**9**	**17**	**35**	**1**	**0**	**0**	**50**	**14.0**	**34**	**8**	**21**	**0**		**10**	**1**	**3**	**4**	**8**	**1**	**0**	**0**

Signed as a free agent by **New Jersey**, October 1, 1993. Claimed by **St. Louis** from **New Jersey** in NHL Waiver Draft, September 28, 1997.

• RIBBLE, PAT

Pat Ribble D – L. 6′4″, 210 lbs. b: Leamington, Ont., 4/26/1954. Atlanta's 3rd choice, 58th overall, in 1974 Amateur Draft.

Season	Club	League	GP	G	A	Pts	AG	AA	APts	PIM	PP	SH	GW	S	%	TGF	PGF	TGA	PGA	+/–	GP	G	A	Pts	PIM	PP	SH	GW
1972-73	Oshawa Generals	OHA	61	11	27	38	....	....	....	110	....	....	....	....	....	....	....	....	....	....	....	....	....	....	....	....	....	....
1973-74	Oshawa Generals	OHA	70	8	16	24	....	....	....	134	....	....	....	....	....	....	....	....	....	....	....	....	....	....	....	....	....	....
1974-75	Oshawa Generals	OHA	77	5	17	22	....	....	....	164	....	....	....	....	....	....	....	....	....	....	6	0	1	1	23	....	....	....
1975-76	**Atlanta Flames**	**NHL**	**3**	**0**	**0**	**0**	**0**	**0**	**0**	**0**	**0**	**0**	**0**	**0**	**0.0**	**2**	**0**	**2**	**0**	**0**	....	....	....	....	....	....	....	....
	Tulsa Oilers	CHL	73	3	22	25	....	....	....	98	....	....	....	....	....	....	....	....	....	....	9	0	3	3	10	....	....	....
1976-77	**Atlanta Flames**	**NHL**	**23**	**2**	**2**	**4**	**2**	**2**	**4**	**31**	**0**	**0**	**0**	**31**	**6.5**	**19**	**0**	**23**	**3**	**–1**	**2**	**0**	**0**	**0**	**6**	**0**	**0**	**0**
	Tulsa Oilers	CHL	51	9	20	29	....	....	....	140	....	....	....	....	....	....	....	....	....	....	....	....	....	....	....	....	....	....
1977-78	**Atlanta Flames**	**NHL**	**80**	**5**	**12**	**17**	**5**	**10**	**15**	**68**	**1**	**0**	**0**	**106**	**4.7**	**83**	**2**	**105**	**28**	**+4**	**2**	**0**	**1**	**1**	**2**	**0**	**0**	**0**
	Canada	WEC-A	10	0	0	0	....	....	....	15	....	....	....	....	....	....	....	....	....	....	....	....	....	....	....	....	....	....
1978-79	**Atlanta Flames**	**NHL**	**66**	**5**	**16**	**21**	**5**	**12**	**17**	**69**	**0**	**0**	**0**	**70**	**7.1**	**77**	**0**	**78**	**19**	**+18**	....	....	....	....	....	....	....	....
	Chicago Black Hawks	**NHL**	**12**	**1**	**3**	**4**	**1**	**2**	**3**	**8**	**0**	**0**	**1**	**12**	**8.3**	**11**	**0**	**4**	**0**	**+7**	**4**	**0**	**0**	**0**	**4**	**0**	**0**	**0**

Season	Club	League	REGULAR SEASON																		PLAYOFFS							
			GP	G	A	Pts	AG	AA	APts	PIM	PP	SH	GW	S	%	TGF	PGF	TGA	PGA	+/–	GP	G	A	Pts	PIM	PP	SH	GW
1979-80	**Chicago Black Hawks**	**NHL**	**23**	**1**	**2**	**3**	**1**	**2**	**3**	**14**	**0**	**0**	**0**	**15**	**6.7**	**11**	**1**	**19**	**1**	**–8**								
	Toronto Maple Leafs	**NHL**	**13**	**0**	**2**	**2**	**0**	**2**	**2**	**8**	**0**	**0**	**0**	**11**	**0.0**	**10**	**0**	**22**	**3**	**–9**								
	Washington Capitals	**NHL**	**19**	**1**	**5**	**6**	**1**	**4**	**5**	**30**	**0**	**0**	**0**	**15**	**6.7**	**17**	**0**	**20**	**5**	**+2**								
1980-81	**Washington Capitals**	**NHL**	**67**	**3**	**15**	**18**	**2**	**10**	**12**	**103**	**3**	**0**	**1**	**115**	**2.6**	**98**	**32**	**121**	**42**	**–13**								
1981-82	**Washington Capitals**	**NHL**	**12**	**1**	**2**	**3**	**1**	**1**	**2**	**14**	**0**	**0**	**0**	**15**	**6.7**	**11**	**0**	**17**	**2**	**–4**								
	Calgary Flames	**NHL**	**3**	**0**	**0**	**0**	**0**	**0**	**0**	**2**	**0**	**0**	**0**	**6**	**0.0**	**3**	**0**	**1**	**0**	**+2**								
	Oklahoma City Stars	CHL	43	1	9	10				44											2	0	0	0	6			
1982-83	**Calgary Flames**	**NHL**	**28**	**0**	**1**	**1**	**0**	**1**	**1**	**18**	**0**	**0**	**0**	**14**	**0.0**	**18**	**0**	**39**	**9**	**–12**								
	Colorado Flames	CHL	10	1	4	5				8																		
1983-84	Colorado Flames	CHL	53	4	27	31				60											6	0	2	2	4			
1984-85	Indianapolis Checkers	IHL	24	10	14	24				18											7	0	2	2	4			
	Salt Lake Golden Eagles	IHL	54	4	23	27				50																		
1985-86	Indianapolis Checkers	IHL	52	6	21	27				45											2	0	1	1	2			
1986-87	Salt Lake Golden Eagles	IHL	80	9	19	28				55											17	1	5	6	2			
	NHL Totals		**349**	**19**	**60**	**79**	**18**	**46**	**64**	**365**	**4**	**0**	**2**	**410**	**4.6**	**360**	**35**	**451**	**112**		**8**	**0**	**1**	**1**	**12**	**0**	**0**	**0**

CHL Second All-Star Team (1977, 1984)

Traded to **Chicago** by **Atlanta** with Tom Lysiak, Harold Phillipoff, Greg Fox and Miles Zaharko for Ivan Bolderiv, Phil Russell and Darcy Rota, March 13, 1979. Traded to **Toronto** by **Chicago** for Dave Hutchison, January 10, 1980. Traded to **Washington** by **Toronto** for Mike Kaszycki, February 16, 1980. Traded to **Calgary** by **Washington** with Washington's 2nd round choice (later traded to Montreal — Montreal selected Todd Francis) in 1983 Entry Draft for Randy Holt and Bobby Gould, November 25, 1981.

• RICCI, MIKE

Mike Ricci C – L. 6', 190 lbs. b: Scarborough, Ont., 10/27/1971. Philadelphia's 1st choice, 4th overall, in 1990 Entry Draft.

Season	Club	League	GP	G	A	Pts	AG	AA	APts	PIM	PP	SH	GW	S	%	TGF	PGF	TGA	PGA	+/–	GP	G	A	Pts	PIM	PP	SH	GW
1987-88	Peterborough Petes	OHL	41	24	37	61				20											8	5	5	10	4			
1988-89	Peterborough Petes	OHL	60	54	52	106				43											17	19	16	35	18			
	Canada	WJC-A	7	5	2	7				6																		
1989-90	Peterborough Petes	OHL	60	52	64	116				39											12	5	7	12	26			
	Canada	WJC-A	5	0	4	4				0																		
1990-91	**Philadelphia Flyers**	**NHL**	**68**	**21**	**20**	**41**	**19**	**15**	**34**	**64**	**9**	**0**	**4**	**121**	**17.4**	**69**	**28**	**58**	**9**	**–8**								
1991-92	**Philadelphia Flyers**	**NHL**	**78**	**20**	**36**	**56**	**18**	**27**	**45**	**93**	**11**	**2**	**0**	**149**	**13.4**	**83**	**29**	**90**	**26**	**–10**								
1992-93	**Quebec Nordiques**	**NHL**	**77**	**27**	**51**	**78**	**23**	**35**	**58**	**123**	**12**	**1**	**10**	**142**	**19.0**	**123**	**58**	**75**	**18**	**+8**	**6**	**0**	**6**	**6**	**8**	**0**	**0**	**0**
1993-94	**Quebec Nordiques**	**NHL**	**83**	**30**	**21**	**51**	**28**	**16**	**44**	**113**	**13**	**3**	**6**	**138**	**21.7**	**82**	**32**	**80**	**21**	**–9**								
	Canada	WC-A	8	2	1	3				8																		
1994-95	**Quebec Nordiques**	**NHL**	**48**	**15**	**21**	**36**	**27**	**31**	**58**	**40**	**9**	**0**	**1**	**73**	**20.5**	**56**	**25**	**35**	**9**	**+5**	**6**	**1**	**3**	**4**	**8**	**0**	**0**	**0**
1995-96	**Colorado Avalanche**	**NHL**	**62**	**6**	**21**	**27**	**6**	**17**	**23**	**52**	**3**	**0**	**1**	**73**	**8.2**	**60**	**29**	**41**	**11**	**+1**	**22**	**6**	**11**	**17**	**18**	**3**	**0**	**1**
1996-97	**Colorado Avalanche**	**NHL**	**63**	**13**	**19**	**32**	**14**	**17**	**31**	**59**	**5**	**0**	**3**	**74**	**17.6**	**55**	**22**	**36**	**0**	**–3**	**17**	**2**	**4**	**6**	**17**	**0**	**0**	**1**
1997-98	**Colorado Avalanche**	**NHL**	**6**	**0**	**4**	**4**	**0**	**4**	**4**	**2**	**0**	**0**	**0**	**5**	**0.0**	**4**	**0**	**4**	**0**	**0**								
	San Jose Sharks	**NHL**	**59**	**9**	**14**	**23**	**11**	**14**	**25**	**30**	**5**	**0**	**2**	**86**	**10.5**	**40**	**16**	**41**	**13**	**–4**	**6**	**1**	**3**	**4**	**6**	**0**	**0**	**0**
	NHL Totals		**544**	**141**	**207**	**348**	**146**	**176**	**322**	**576**	**67**	**6**	**27**	**861**	**16.4**	**572**	**239**	**460**	**107**		**57**	**10**	**27**	**37**	**57**	**3**	**0**	**2**

OHL Second All-Star Team (1989) • Canadian Major Junior Player of the Year (1990) • OHL First All-Star Team (1990)

Traded to **Quebec** by **Philadelphia** with Peter Forsberg, Steve Duchesne, Kerry Huffman, Ron Hextall, Chris Simon, Philadelphia's 1st round choice in the 1993 (Jocelyn Thibault) and 1994 (later traded to Toronto — later traded to Washington — Washington selected Nolan Baumgartner) Entry Drafts and cash for Eric Lindros, June 30, 1992. Transferred to **Colorado** after **Quebec** franchise relocated, June 21, 1995. Traded to **San Jose** by **Colorado** with Colorado's 2nd round choice (later traded to Buffalo - Buffalo selected Jaroslav Kristek) in 1998 Entry Draft for Shean Donovan and San Jose's 1st round choice (Alex Tanguay) in 1998 Entry Draft, November 21, 1997.

• RICE, STEVEN

Steven Rice RW – R. 6', 217 lbs. b: Kitchener, Ont., 5/26/1971. NY Rangers' 1st choice, 20th overall, in 1989 Entry Draft.

Season	Club	League	GP	G	A	Pts	AG	AA	APts	PIM	PP	SH	GW	S	%	TGF	PGF	TGA	PGA	+/–	GP	G	A	Pts	PIM	PP	SH	GW
1987-88	Kitchener Rangers	OHL	59	11	14	25				43											4	0	1	1	0			
1988-89	Kitchener Rangers	OHL	64	36	30	66				42											5	2	1	3	8			
1989-90	Kitchener Rangers	OHL	58	39	37	76				102											16	4	8	12	24			
	Canada	WJC-A	7	2	0	2				16																		
1990-91	Kitchener Rangers	OHL	29	30	30	60				43											6	5	6	11	2			
	Canada	WJC-A	7	4	1	5				8																		
	New York Rangers	**NHL**	**11**	**1**	**1**	**2**	**1**	**1**	**2**	**4**	**0**	**0**	**0**	**12**	**8.3**	**4**	**0**	**2**	**0**	**+2**	**2**	**2**	**1**	**3**	**6**	**1**	**0**	**0**
	Binghamton Rangers	AHL	8	4	1	5				12											5	2	0	2	2			
1991-92	**Edmonton Oilers**	**NHL**	**3**	**0**	**0**	**0**	**0**	**0**	**0**	**2**	**0**	**0**	**0**	**2**	**0.0**	**0**	**0**	**2**	**0**	**–2**								
	Cape Breton Oilers	AHL	45	32	20	52				38											5	4	4	8	10			
1992-93	**Edmonton Oilers**	**NHL**	**28**	**2**	**5**	**7**	**2**	**3**	**5**	**28**	**0**	**0**	**0**	**29**	**6.9**	**11**	**0**	**16**	**1**	**–4**								
	Cape Breton Oilers	AHL	51	34	28	62				63											14	4	6	10	22			
1993-94	**Edmonton Oilers**	**NHL**	**63**	**17**	**15**	**32**	**16**	**12**	**28**	**36**	**6**	**0**	**1**	**129**	**13.2**	**58**	**20**	**48**	**0**	**–10**								
1994-95	**Hartford Whalers**	**NHL**	**40**	**11**	**10**	**21**	**19**	**15**	**34**	**61**	**4**	**0**	**1**	**57**	**19.3**	**30**	**9**	**19**	**0**	**+2**								
1995-96	**Hartford Whalers**	**NHL**	**59**	**10**	**12**	**22**	**10**	**10**	**20**	**47**	**1**	**0**	**2**	**108**	**9.3**	**39**	**10**	**33**	**0**	**–4**								
1996-97	**Hartford Whalers**	**NHL**	**78**	**21**	**14**	**35**	**22**	**12**	**34**	**59**	**5**	**0**	**2**	**159**	**13.2**	**60**	**17**	**54**	**0**	**–11**								
1997-98	**Carolina Hurricanes**	**NHL**	**47**	**2**	**4**	**6**	**2**	**4**	**6**	**38**	**0**	**0**	**0**	**39**	**5.1**	**8**	**1**	**23**	**0**	**–16**								
	NHL Totals		**329**	**64**	**61**	**125**	**72**	**57**	**129**	**275**	**16**	**0**	**6**	**535**	**12.0**	**210**	**57**	**197**	**1**		**2**	**2**	**1**	**3**	**6**	**1**	**0**	**0**

Memorial Cup All-Star Team (1990) • OHL Second All-Star Team (1991) • AHL Second All-Star Team (1993)

Traded to **Edmonton** by **NY Rangers** with Bernie Nicholls and Louie DeBrusk for Mark Messier and future considerations, October 4, 1991. Signed as a free agent by **Hartford**, August 18, 1994. Transferred to **Carolina** after **Hartford** franchise relocated, June 25, 1997.

• RICHARD, HENRI

Henri "The Pocket Rocket" Richard C – R. 5'7", 160 lbs. b: Montreal, Que., 2/29/1936. **HHOF**

Season	Club	League	GP	G	A	Pts	AG	AA	APts	PIM	PP	SH	GW	S	%	TGF	PGF	TGA	PGA	+/–	GP	G	A	Pts	PIM	PP	SH	GW
1951-52	Montreal Nationale	QJHL	49	23	32	55				35											4	1	0	1	0			
1952-53	Montreal Nationale	QJHL	46	27	36	63				55											7	4	5	9	4			
	Montreal Royals	QSHL	1	0	0	0				0																		
1953-54	Montreal Jr. Canadiens	QJHL	54	*56	*53	*109				85											7	6	7	13	6			
1954-55	Montreal Jr. Canadiens	QJHL	44	*33	33	*66				65											4	3	1	4	2			
1955-56	**Montreal Canadiens**	**NHL**	**64**	**19**	**21**	**40**	**28**	**26**	**54**	**46**											**10**	**4**	**4**	**8**	**21**			
1956-57	**Montreal Canadiens**	**NHL**	**63**	**18**	**36**	**54**	**25**	**42**	**67**	**71**											**10**	**2**	**6**	**8**	**10**			
1957-58	**Montreal Canadiens**	**NHL**	**67**	**28**	***52**	**80**	**37**	**57**	**94**	**56**											**10**	**1**	**7**	**8**	**11**			
1958-59	**Montreal Canadiens**	**NHL**	**63**	**21**	**30**	**51**	**27**	**32**	**59**	**33**											**11**	**3**	**8**	**11**	**13**			
1959-60	**Montreal Canadiens**	**NHL**	**70**	**30**	**43**	**73**	**38**	**44**	**82**	**66**											**8**	**3**	**9**	***12**	**9**			
1960-61	**Montreal Canadiens**	**NHL**	**70**	**24**	**44**	**68**	**29**	**45**	**74**	**91**											**6**	**2**	**4**	**6**	**22**			
1961-62	**Montreal Canadiens**	**NHL**	**54**	**21**	**29**	**50**	**26**	**29**	**55**	**48**																		
1962-63	**Montreal Canadiens**	**NHL**	**67**	**23**	***50**	**73**	**28**	**53**	**81**	**57**											**5**	**1**	**1**	**2**	**2**			
1963-64	**Montreal Canadiens**	**NHL**	**66**	**14**	**39**	**53**	**18**	**43**	**61**	**73**											**7**	**1**	**1**	**2**	**9**			
1964-65	**Montreal Canadiens**	**NHL**	**53**	**23**	**29**	**52**	**29**	**31**	**60**	**43**											**13**	**7**	**4**	**11**	**24**			
1965-66	**Montreal Canadiens**	**NHL**	**62**	**22**	**39**	**61**	**27**	**39**	**66**	**47**											**8**	**1**	**4**	**5**	**2**			
1966-67	**Montreal Canadiens**	**NHL**	**65**	**21**	**34**	**55**	**26**	**35**	**61**	**28**											**10**	**4**	**6**	**10**	**2**			
1967-68	**Montreal Canadiens**	**NHL**	**54**	**9**	**19**	**28**	**11**	**20**	**31**	**16**	**2**	**0**	**3**	**123**	**7.3**	**36**	**9**	**23**	**0**	**+4**	**13**	**4**	**4**	**8**	**4**	**1**	**0**	**0**
1968-69	**Montreal Canadiens**	**NHL**	**64**	**15**	**37**	**52**	**17**	**35**	**52**	**45**	**2**	**0**	**0**	**210**	**7.1**	**78**	**7**	**48**	**2**	**+25**	**14**	**2**	**4**	**6**	**8**	**0**	**0**	**0**
1969-70	**Montreal Canadiens**	**NHL**	**62**	**16**	**36**	**52**	**18**	**36**	**54**	**61**	**2**	**0**	**4**	**204**	**7.8**	**72**	**8**	**40**	**0**	**+24**								
1970-71	**Montreal Canadiens**	**NHL**	**75**	**12**	**37**	**49**	**13**	**33**	**46**	**46**	**1**	**0**	**1**	**226**	**5.3**	**59**	**5**	**43**	**2**	**+13**	**20**	**5**	**7**	**12**	**20**	**0**	**0**	**1**
1971-72	**Montreal Canadiens**	**NHL**	**75**	**12**	**32**	**44**	**13**	**29**	**42**	**48**	**0**	**0**	**1**	**175**	**6.9**	**66**	**6**	**51**	**1**	**+10**	**6**	**0**	**3**	**3**	**4**	**0**	**0**	**0**
1972-73	**Montreal Canadiens**	**NHL**	**71**	**8**	**35**	**43**	**8**	**29**	**37**	**21**	**0**	**0**	**2**	**133**	**6.0**	**58**	**1**	**24**	**1**	**+34**	**17**	**6**	**4**	**10**	**14**	**0**	**0**	**2**
1973-74	**Montreal Canadiens**	**NHL**	**75**	**19**	**36**	**55**	**19**	**31**	**50**	**28**	**1**	**0**	**3**	**175**	**10.9**	**73**	**4**	**63**	**1**	**+7**	**6**	**2**	**2**	**4**	**2**	**0**	**0**	**0**
1974-75	**Montreal Canadiens**	**NHL**	**16**	**3**	**10**	**13**	**3**	**8**	**11**	**4**	**0**	**0**	**0**	**33**	**9.1**	**20**	**1**	**10**	**0**	**+9**	**6**	**1**	**2**	**3**	**4**	**0**	**0**	**0**
	NHL Totals		**1256**	**358**	**688**	**1046**	**440**	**697**	**1137**	**928**	**0**	**0**	**14**	**1279**	**28.0**	**462**	**41**	**302**	**7**		**180**	**49**	**80**	**129**	**181**	**1**	**0**	**3**

NHL First All-Star Team (1958) • NHL Second All-Star Team (1959, 1961, 1963) • Won Bill Masterton Trophy (1974)

Played in NHL All-Star Game (1956, 1957, 1958, 1959, 1960, 1961, 1963, 1965, 1967, 1974)

• RICHARD, JACQUES

Jacques Richard LW – L. 5'11", 180 lbs. b: Quebec City, Que., 10/7/1952. Atlanta's 1st choice, 2nd overall, in 1972 Amateur Draft.

Season	Club	League	GP	G	A	Pts	AG	AA	APts	PIM	PP	SH	GW	S	%	TGF	PGF	TGA	PGA	+/–	GP	G	A	Pts	PIM	PP	SH	GW
1967-68	Quebec Aces	QJHL	50	18	18	36																						
1968-69	Quebec Aces	QJHL	50	23	40	63				78																		
1969-70	Quebec Remparts	QJHL	53	62	64	126				170											15	11	14	25	30			

			REGULAR SEASON																		PLAYOFFS							
Season	Club	League	GP	G	A	Pts	AG	AA	APts	PIM	PP	SH	GW	S	%	TGF	PGF	TGA	PGA	+/–	GP	G	A	Pts	PIM	PP	SH	GW
1970-71	Quebec Remparts	QJHL	55	53	60	113	....	....	....	125	....	....	....	....	....	....	....	....	....	....	14	18	17	35	42	....	....	....
1971-72	Quebec Remparts	QMJHL	61	*71	89	*160	....	....	....	100	....	....	....	....	....	....	....	....	....	....	15	11	*26	*37	23	....	....	....
1972-73	**Atlanta Flames**	**NHL**	**74**	**13**	**18**	**31**	**13**	**15**	**28**	**32**	**4**	**0**	**2**	**165**	**7.9**	**48**	**15**	**57**	**0**	**–24**	....	....	....	....	....	....	....	....
1973-74	**Atlanta Flames**	**NHL**	**78**	**27**	**16**	**43**	**28**	**14**	**42**	**45**	**7**	**0**	**1**	**270**	**10.0**	**79**	**31**	**66**	**0**	**–18**	**4**	**0**	**0**	**0**	**2**	**0**	**0**	**0**
1974-75	**Atlanta Flames**	**NHL**	**63**	**17**	**12**	**29**	**16**	**9**	**25**	**31**	**3**	**0**	**1**	**172**	**9.9**	**44**	**12**	**49**	**1**	**–16**	....	....	....	....	....	....	....	....
1975-76	**Buffalo Sabres**	**NHL**	**73**	**12**	**23**	**35**	**11**	**18**	**29**	**31**	**3**	**0**	**5**	**104**	**11.5**	**62**	**11**	**47**	**0**	**+4**	**9**	**1**	**1**	**2**	**7**	**0**	**0**	**0**
1976-77	**Buffalo Sabres**	**NHL**	**21**	**2**	**0**	**2**	**2**	**0**	**2**	**16**	**0**	**0**	**0**	**20**	**10.0**	**6**	**0**	**9**	**0**	**–3**	....	....	....	....	....	....	....	....
	Hershey Bears	AHL	44	20	25	45	....	....	....	42	....	....	....	....	....	....	....	....	....	....	6	3	0	3	2	....	....	....
1977-78	Hershey Bears	AHL	54	25	23	48	....	....	....	29	....	....	....	....	....	....	....	....	....	....	....	....	....	....	....	....	....	....
1978-79	**Buffalo Sabres**	**NHL**	**61**	**10**	**15**	**25**	**9**	**11**	**20**	**26**	**0**	**0**	**1**	**85**	**11.8**	**37**	**3**	**26**	**0**	**+8**	**3**	**1**	**0**	**1**	**0**	**0**	**0**	**1**
1979-80	**Quebec Nordiques**	**NHL**	**14**	**3**	**12**	**15**	**3**	**9**	**12**	**4**	**0**	**0**	**0**	**45**	**6.7**	**18**	**8**	**19**	**2**	**–7**	....	....	....	....	....	....	....	....
	Rochester Americans	AHL	37	13	23	36	....	....	....	37	....	....	....	....	....	....	....	....	....	....	....	....	....	....	....	....	....	....
1980-81	**Quebec Nordiques**	**NHL**	**78**	**52**	**51**	**103**	**43**	**36**	**79**	**39**	**16**	**0**	**5**	**261**	**19.9**	**136**	**58**	**91**	**4**	**–9**	**5**	**2**	**4**	**6**	**14**	**1**	**0**	**0**
1981-82	**Quebec Nordiques**	**NHL**	**59**	**15**	**26**	**41**	**12**	**17**	**29**	**77**	**1**	**3**	**1**	**124**	**12.1**	**63**	**20**	**59**	**7**	**–9**	**10**	**1**	**0**	**1**	**9**	**0**	**0**	**0**
1982-83	**Quebec Nordiques**	**NHL**	**35**	**9**	**14**	**23**	**7**	**10**	**17**	**6**	**1**	**0**	**1**	**60**	**15.0**	**31**	**6**	**33**	**8**	**0**	**4**	**0**	**0**	**0**	**2**	**0**	**0**	**0**
	Fredericton Express	AHL	19	16	15	31	....	....	....	16	....	....	....	....	....	....	....	....	....	....	....	....	....	....	....	....	....	....
	NHL Totals		**556**	**160**	**187**	**347**	**144**	**139**	**283**	**307**	**35**	**3**	**17**	**1306**	**12.3**	**524**	**164**	**456**	**22**		**35**	**5**	**5**	**10**	**34**	**1**	**0**	**1**

QJHL First All-Star Team (1971) • QMJHL First All-Star Team (1972)

Traded to **Buffalo** by **Atlanta** for Larry Carriere and Buffalo's 1st round choice (later traded to Washington — Washington selected Greg Carroll) in 1976 Amateur Draft and cash, October 1, 1975. Signed as a free agent by **Quebec**, February 12, 1980.

• RICHARD, JEAN-MARC

Jean-Marc Richard D – L. 5′11″, 178 lbs. b: St.-Raymond, Que., 10/8/1966.

Season	Club	League	GP	G	A	Pts	AG	AA	APts	PIM	PP	SH	GW	S	%	TGF	PGF	TGA	PGA	+/–	GP	G	A	Pts	PIM	PP	SH	GW
1983-84	Chicoutimi Sagueneens	QMJHL	61	1	20	21	....	....	....	41	....	....	....	....	....	....	....	....	....	....	....	....	....	....	....	....	....	....
1984-85	Chicoutimi Sagueneens	QMJHL	68	10	61	71	....	....	....	57	....	....	....	....	....	....	....	....	....	....	....	....	....	....	....	....	....	....
1985-86	Chicoutimi Sagueneens	QMJHL	72	20	87	107	....	....	....	111	....	....	....	....	....	....	....	....	....	....	9	3	5	8	14	....	....	....
1986-87	Chicoutimi Sagueneens	QMJHL	67	21	81	102	....	....	....	105	....	....	....	....	....	....	....	....	....	....	16	6	25	31	28	....	....	....
1987-88	**Quebec Nordiques**	**NHL**	**4**	**2**	**1**	**3**	**2**	**1**	**3**	**2**	**1**	**0**	**0**	**5**	**40.0**	**3**	**2**	**4**	**0**	**–3**	....	....	....	....	....	....	....	....
	Fredericton Express	AHL	68	14	42	56	....	....	....	52	....	....	....	....	....	....	....	....	....	....	7	2	1	3	4	....	....	....
1988-89	Halifax Citadels	AHL	57	8	25	33	....	....	....	38	....	....	....	....	....	....	....	....	....	....	4	1	0	1	4	....	....	....
1989-90	**Quebec Nordiques**	**NHL**	**1**	**0**	**0**	**0**	**0**	**0**	**0**	**0**	**0**	**0**	**0**	**0**	**0.0**	**0**	**0**	**1**	**0**	**–1**	....	....	....	....	....	....	....	....
	Halifax Citadels	AHL	40	1	24	25	....	....	....	38	....	....	....	....	....	....	....	....	....	....	....	....	....	....	....	....	....	....
1990-91	Halifax Citadels	AHL	80	7	41	48	....	....	....	76	....	....	....	....	....	....	....	....	....	....	....	....	....	....	....	....	....	....
	Fort Wayne Komets	IHL	1	0	0	0	....	....	....	0	....	....	....	....	....	....	....	....	....	....	19	3	9	12	8	....	....	....
1991-92	Fort Wayne Komets	IHL	82	18	68	86	....	....	....	109	....	....	....	....	....	....	....	....	....	....	7	0	5	5	20	....	....	....
1992-93	San Diego Gulls	IHL	6	1	0	1	....	....	....	4	....	....	....	....	....	....	....	....	....	....	....	....	....	....	....	....	....	....
	Fort Wayne Komets	IHL	52	10	33	43	....	....	....	48	....	....	....	....	....	....	....	....	....	....	12	6	11	17	6	....	....	....
1993-94	Las Vegas Thunder	IHL	59	15	33	48	....	....	....	44	....	....	....	....	....	....	....	....	....	....	5	0	3	3	0	....	....	....
1994-95	Las Vegas Thunder	IHL	81	16	41	57	....	....	....	76	....	....	....	....	....	....	....	....	....	....	10	0	3	3	4	....	....	....
1995-96	Las Vegas Thunder	IHL	82	12	40	52	....	....	....	92	....	....	....	....	....	....	....	....	....	....	15	1	7	8	23	....	....	....
	NHL Totals		**5**	**2**	**1**	**3**	**2**	**1**	**3**	**2**	**1**	**0**	**0**	**5**	**40.0**	**3**	**2**	**5**	**0**		....	....	....	....	....	....	....	....

QMJHL First All-Star Team (1986, 1987) • IHL First All-Star Team (1992, 1994) • Won Governors' Trophy (Top Defenseman - IHL) (1992)

Signed as a free agent by **Quebec**, April 13, 1987. Signed as a free agent by **Fort Wayne** (IHL), September, 1991.

• RICHARD, MIKE

Mike Richard C – L. 5′10″, 190 lbs. b: Scarborough, Ont., 7/9/1966.

Season	Club	League	GP	G	A	Pts	AG	AA	APts	PIM	PP	SH	GW	S	%	TGF	PGF	TGA	PGA	+/–	GP	G	A	Pts	PIM	PP	SH	GW
1982-83	Don Mills Midgets	OHA	40	25	30	55	....	....	....	10	....	....	....	....	....	....	....	....	....	....	....	....	....	....	....	....	....	....
1983-84	Toronto Marlboros	OHL	66	19	17	36	....	....	....	12	....	....	....	....	....	....	....	....	....	....	9	2	1	3	0	....	....	....
1984-85	Toronto Marlboros	OHL	66	31	41	72	....	....	....	15	....	....	....	....	....	....	....	....	....	....	5	0	0	0	11	....	....	....
1985-86	Toronto Marlboros	OHL	63	32	48	80	....	....	....	28	....	....	....	....	....	....	....	....	....	....	4	1	1	2	2	....	....	....
1986-87	Toronto Marlboros	OHL	66	*57	50	107	....	....	....	38	....	....	....	....	....	....	....	....	....	....	....	....	....	....	....	....	....	....
	Baltimore Skipjacks	AHL	9	5	2	7	....	....	....	2	....	....	....	....	....	....	....	....	....	....	....	....	....	....	....	....	....	....
	Baltimore Skipjacks	AHL	9	5	2	7	....	....	....	2	....	....	....	....	....	....	....	....	....	....	....	....	....	....	....	....	....	....
1987-88	**Washington Capitals**	**NHL**	**4**	**0**	**0**	**0**	**0**	**0**	**0**	**0**	**0**	**0**	**0**	**5**	**0.0**	**1**	**1**	**1**	**0**	**–1**	....	....	....	....	....	....	....	....
	Binghamton Whalers	AHL	72	46	48	94	....	....	....	23	....	....	....	....	....	....	....	....	....	....	4	0	3	3	4	....	....	....
1988-89	Baltimore Skipjacks	AHL	80	44	63	107	....	....	....	51	....	....	....	....	....	....	....	....	....	....	....	....	....	....	....	....	....	....
1989-90	Washington Capitals	FrTour	1	0	0	0	....	....	....	0	....	....	....	....	....	....	....	....	....	....	....	....	....	....	....	....	....	....
	Washington Capitals	**NHL**	**3**	**0**	**2**	**2**	**0**	**1**	**1**	**0**	**0**	**0**	**0**	**5**	**0.0**	**6**	**2**	**5**	**1**	**0**	....	....	....	....	....	....	....	....
	Baltimore Skipjacks	AHL	53	41	42	83	....	....	....	14	....	....	....	....	....	....	....	....	....	....	11	4	*13	17	6	....	....	....
1990-91	Zurich SC	Switz.	36	28	23	51	....	....	....	....	....	....	....	....	....	....	....	....	....	....	....	1	3	4	....	....	....	....
1991-92	Milano Devils	Italy	18	20	26	46	....	....	....	4	....	....	....	....	....	....	....	....	....	....	12	7	11	18	4	....	....	....
1992-93	EHC Olten	Switz. B	36	46	46	....	....	....	....	....	....	....	....	....	....	....	....	....	....	....	....	....	....	....	....	....	....	....
1993-94	EHC Olten	Switz	35	29	19	48	....	....	....	50	....	....	....	....	....	....	....	....	....	....	....	....	....	....	....	....	....	....
1994-95	EHC Olten	Switz. B	STATISTICS NOT AVAILABLE																									
1995-96	Rapperswil-Jona	Switz	36	27	....	65	....	....	....	14	....	....	....	....	....	....	....	....	....	....	4	0	3	3	7	....	....	....
1996-97	Rapperswil-Jona	Switz	41	17	31	48	....	....	....	30	....	....	....	....	....	....	....	....	....	....	3	1	0	1	0	....	....	....
1997-98	Rapperswil-Jona	Switz.	22	12	19	31	....	....	....	25	....	....	....	....	....	....	....	....	....	....	7	5	4	9	4	....	....	....
	NHL Totals		**7**	**0**	**2**	**2**	**0**	**1**	**1**	**0**	**0**	**0**	**0**	**10**	**0.0**	**7**	**3**	**6**	**1**		....	....	....	....	....	....	....	....

Won Dudley "Red" Garrett Memorial Award (Top Rookie - AHL) (1987) • AHL Second All-Star Team (1990)

Signed as a free agent by **Washington**, October 9, 1987.

• RICHARDS, TODD

Todd Richards D – R. 6′, 194 lbs. b: Robindale, MN, 10/20/1966. Montreal's 3rd choice, 33rd overall, in 1985 Entry Draft.

Season	Club	League	GP	G	A	Pts	AG	AA	APts	PIM	PP	SH	GW	S	%	TGF	PGF	TGA	PGA	+/–	GP	G	A	Pts	PIM	PP	SH	GW
1984-85	Armstrong High Scool	H.S.	24	10	23	33	....	....	....	24	....	....	....	....	....	....	....	....	....	....	....	....	....	....	....	....	....	....
1985-86	University of Minnesota	WCHA	38	6	23	29	....	....	....	38	....	....	....	....	....	....	....	....	....	....	....	....	....	....	....	....	....	....
1986-87	University of Minnesota	WCHA	49	8	43	51	....	....	....	70	....	....	....	....	....	....	....	....	....	....	....	....	....	....	....	....	....	....
1987-88	University of Minnesota	WCHA	34	10	30	40	....	....	....	26	....	....	....	....	....	....	....	....	....	....	....	....	....	....	....	....	....	....
1988-89	University of Minnesota	WCHA	46	6	32	38	....	....	....	60	....	....	....	....	....	....	....	....	....	....	....	....	....	....	....	....	....	....
1989-90	Sherbrooke Canadiens	AHL	71	6	18	24	....	....	....	73	....	....	....	....	....	....	....	....	....	....	5	1	2	3	6	....	....	....
1990-91	Montreal Canadiens	FrTour	2	0	0	0	....	....	....	2	....	....	....	....	....	....	....	....	....	....	....	....	....	....	....	....	....	....
	Fredericton Canadiens	AHL	3	0	1	1	....	....	....	2	....	....	....	....	....	....	....	....	....	....	....	....	....	....	....	....	....	....
	Hartford Whalers	**NHL**	**2**	**0**	**4**	**4**	**0**	**3**	**3**	**2**	**0**	**0**	**0**	**4**	**0.0**	**5**	**5**	**6**	**2**	**–4**	**6**	**0**	**0**	**0**	**2**	**0**	**0**	**0**
	Springfield Indians	AHL	71	10	41	51	....	....	....	62	....	....	....	....	....	....	....	....	....	....	14	2	8	10	2	....	....	....
1991-92	**Hartford Whalers**	**NHL**	**6**	**0**	**0**	**0**	**0**	**0**	**0**	**2**	**0**	**0**	**0**	**3**	**0.0**	**6**	**2**	**6**	**0**	**–2**	**5**	**0**	**3**	**3**	**4**	**0**	**0**	**0**
	Springfield Indians	AHL	43	6	23	29	....	....	....	33	....	....	....	....	....	....	....	....	....	....	8	0	3	3	2	....	....	....
1992-93	Springfield Indians	AHL	78	13	42	55	....	....	....	53	....	....	....	....	....	....	....	....	....	....	9	1	5	6	2	....	....	....
1993-94	Las Vegas Thunder	IHL	80	11	35	46	....	....	....	122	....	....	....	....	....	....	....	....	....	....	5	1	4	5	18	....	....	....
1994-95	Las Vegas Thunder	IHL	80	12	49	61	....	....	....	130	....	....	....	....	....	....	....	....	....	....	9	1	2	3	6	....	....	....
1995-96	Orlando Solar Bears	IHL	81	19	54	73	....	....	....	59	....	....	....	....	....	....	....	....	....	....	23	4	9	13	8	....	....	....
1996-97	Orlando Solar Bears	IHL	82	9	36	45	....	....	....	134	....	....	....	....	....	....	....	....	....	....	10	0	1	1	4	....	....	....
1997-98	Orlando Solar Bears	IHL	75	6	37	43	....	....	....	68	....	....	....	....	....	....	....	....	....	....	17	3	8	11	13	....	....	....
	NHL Totals		**8**	**0**	**4**	**4**	**0**	**3**	**3**	**4**	**0**	**0**	**0**	**7**	**0.0**	**11**	**7**	**12**	**2**		**11**	**0**	**3**	**3**	**6**	**0**	**0**	**0**

WCHA Second All-Star Team (1987, 1988, 1989) • NCAA Championship All-Tournament Team (1989) • IHL Second All-Star Team (1994) • IHL First All-Star Team (1995, 1996) • Won Governors' Trophy (Top Defenseman - IHL) (1995)

Traded to **Hartford** by **Montreal** for future considerations, October 11, 1990.

• RICHARDS, TRAVIS

Travis Richards D – L. 6′1″, 185 lbs. b: Crystal, MN, 3/22/1970. Minnesota's 3rd choice, 169th overall, in 1988 Entry Draft.

Season	Club	League	GP	G	A	Pts	AG	AA	APts	PIM	PP	SH	GW	S	%	TGF	PGF	TGA	PGA	+/–	GP	G	A	Pts	PIM	PP	SH	GW
1986-87	Armstrong High School	H.S.	22	6	16	22	....	....	....	20	....	....	....	....	....	....	....	....	....	....	....	....	....	....	....	....	....	....
1987-88	Armstrong High School	H.S.	24	14	14	28	....	....	....		....	....	....	....	....	....	....	....	....	....	....	....	....	....	....	....	....	....
1988-89	University of Minnesota	WCHA	DID NOT PLAY – FRESHMAN																									
1989-90	University of Minnesota	WCHA	45	4	24	28	....	....	....	38	....	....	....	....	....	....	....	....	....	....	....	....	....	....	....	....	....	....
1990-91	University of Minnesota	WCHA	45	9	25	34	....	....	....	28	....	....	....	....	....	....	....	....	....	....	....	....	....	....	....	....	....	....
1991-92	University of Minnesota	WCHA	41	10	22	32	....	....	....	65	....	....	....	....	....	....	....	....	....	....	....	....	....	....	....	....	....	....

			REGULAR SEASON																		PLAYOFFS							
Season	Club	League	GP	G	A	Pts	AG	AA	APts	PIM	PP	SH	GW	S	%	TGF	PGF	TGA	PGA	+/–	GP	G	A	Pts	PIM	PP	SH	GW
1992-93	University of Minnesota	WCHA	42	12	26	38	....	....	....	52	....	....	....	....	....	....	....	....	....	....	....	....	....	....	....	....	....	....
	United States	WC-A	5	0	1	1	....	....	....	0	....	....	....	....	....	....	....	....	....	....	....	....	....	....	....	....	....	....
1993-94	United States	Nat-Team	51	1	11	12	....	....	....	38	....	....	....	....	....	....	....	....	....	....	....	....	....	....	....	....	....	....
	United States	Olympics	8	0	0	0	....	....	....	2	....	....	....	....	....	....	....	....	....	....	....	....	....	....	....	....	....	....
	Kalamazoo Wings	IHL	19	2	10	12	....	....	....	20	....	....	....	....	....	....	....	....	....	....	4	1	1	2	0	....	....	....
1994-95	**Dallas Stars**	**NHL**	**2**	**0**	**0**	**0**	**0**	**0**	**0**	**0**	**0**	**0**	**0**	**1**	**0.0**	**0**	**0**	**0**	**0**	**0**	....	....	....	....	....	....	....	....
	Kalamazoo Wings	IHL	63	4	16	20	....	....	....	53	....	....	....	....	....	....	....	....	....	....	15	1	5	6	12	....	....	....
1995-96	**Dallas Stars**	**NHL**	**1**	**0**	**0**	**0**	**0**	**0**	**0**	**2**	**0**	**0**	**0**	**0**	**0.0**	**0**	**0**	**1**	**0**	**–1**	....	....	....	....	....	....	....	....
	Michigan K-Wings	IHL	65	8	15	23	....	....	....	55	....	....	....	....	....	....	....	....	....	....	9	2	2	4	4	....	....	....
1996-97	Grand Rapids Griffins	IHL	77	10	13	23	....	....	....	83	....	....	....	....	....	....	....	....	....	....	5	1	3	4	2	....	....	....
1997-98	Grand Rapids Griffins	IHL	81	12	20	32	....	....	....	70	....	....	....	....	....	....	....	....	....	....	3	1	1	2	4	....	....	....
	NHL Totals		**3**	**0**	**0**	**0**	**0**	**0**	**0**	**2**	**0**	**0**	**0**	**1**	**0.0**	**0**	**0**	**1**	**0**		....	....	....	....	....	....	....	....

WCHA Second All-Star Team (1992, 1993) • IHL First All-Star Team (1995, 1996) • Won Governors' Trophy (Outstanding Defenseman - IHL) (1995)

Rights transferred to **Dallas** after **Minnesota** franchise relocated, June 9, 1993.

• RICHARDSON, DAVE

Dave Richardson LW – L. 5'9", 175 lbs. b: St. Boniface, Man., 12/11/1940.

Season	Club	League	GP	G	A	Pts	AG	AA	APts	PIM	PP	SH	GW	S	%	TGF	PGF	TGA	PGA	+/–	GP	G	A	Pts	PIM	PP	SH	GW
1957-58	Brandon Wheat Kings	MJHL	28	3	7	10	....	....	....	39	....	....	....	....	....	....	....	....	....	....	....	....	....	....	....	....	....	....
1958-59	Winnipeg Rangers	MJHL	31	10	13	23	....	....	....	60	....	....	....	....	....	....	....	....	....	....	4	0	1	1	9	....	....	....
1959-60	Winnipeg Rangers	MJHL	STATISTICS NOT AVAILABLE																									
1960-61	Winnipeg Rangers	MJHL	29	17	31	48	....	....	....	65	....	....	....	....	....	....	....	....	....	....	....	....	....	....	....	....	....	....
	Seattle Totems	WHL	2	0	0	0	....	....	....	4	....	....	....	....	....	....	....	....	....	....	....	....	....	....	....	....	....	....
1961-62	Los Angeles Blades	WHL	3	0	1	1	....	....	....	0	....	....	....	....	....	....	....	....	....	....	....	....	....	....	....	....	....	....
	Fort Wayne Komets	IHL	65	24	47	71	....	....	....	166	....	....	....	....	....	....	....	....	....	....	....	....	....	....	....	....	....	....
1962-63	Sudbury Wolves	EPHL	72	29	38	67	....	....	....	117	....	....	....	....	....	....	....	....	....	....	8	3	1	4	8	....	....	....
1963-64	**New York Rangers**	**NHL**	**34**	**3**	**1**	**4**	**4**	**1**	**5**	**21**	....	....	....	....	....	....	....	....	....	....	....	....	....	....	....	....	....	....
	Baltimore Clippers	AHL	37	9	15	24	....	....	....	88	....	....	....	....	....	....	....	....	....	....	....	....	....	....	....	....	....	....
1964-65	**New York Rangers**	**NHL**	**7**	**0**	**1**	**1**	**0**	**1**	**1**	**4**	....	....	....	....	....	....	....	....	....	....	....	....	....	....	....	....	....	....
	St. Paul Rangers	CHL	8	3	2	5	....	....	....	10	....	....	....	....	....	....	....	....	....	....	....	....	....	....	....	....	....	....
	Baltimore Clippers	AHL	47	17	23	40	....	....	....	89	....	....	....	....	....	....	....	....	....	....	3	0	0	0	2	....	....	....
1965-66	**Chicago Black Hawks**	**NHL**	**3**	**0**	**0**	**0**	**0**	**0**	**0**	**2**	....	....	....	....	....	....	....	....	....	....	....	....	....	....	....	....	....	....
	Buffalo Bisons	AHL	35	11	14	25	....	....	....	58	....	....	....	....	....	....	....	....	....	....	....	....	....	....	....	....	....	....
	St. Louis Braves	CHL	6	1	3	4	....	....	....	2	....	....	....	....	....	....	....	....	....	....	....	....	....	....	....	....	....	....
1966-67	Buffalo Bisons	AHL	71	13	35	48	....	....	....	54	....	....	....	....	....	....	....	....	....	....	....	....	....	....	....	....	....	....
1967-68	**Detroit Red Wings**	**NHL**	**1**	**0**	**0**	**0**	**0**	**0**	**0**	**0**	**0**	**0**	**0**	**0**	**0.0**	**0**	**0**	**0**	**0**	**0**	....	....	....	....	....	....	....	....
	Fort Worth–Memphis	CHL	46	21	28	49	....	....	....	71	....	....	....	....	....	....	....	....	....	....	13	3	6	9	17	....	....	....
1968-69	San Diego Gulls	WHL	51	9	12	21	....	....	....	55	....	....	....	....	....	....	....	....	....	....	....	....	....	....	....	....	....	....
1969-70	San Diego Gulls	WHL	24	4	6	10	....	....	....	35	....	....	....	....	....	....	....	....	....	....	....	....	....	....	....	....	....	....
1970-71			DID NOT PLAY																									
1971-72	St. Boniface Mohawks	CCHL	STATISTICS NOT AVAILABLE																									
1972-73	St. Boniface Mohawks	CCHL	....	33	55	*88	....	....	....	27	....	....	....	....	....	....	....	....	....	....	....	....	....	....	....	....	....	....
1973-74	Warroad Lakers	CCHL	24	14	14	28	....	....	....	....	....	....	....	....	....	....	....	....	....	....	....	....	....	....	....	....	....	....
	NHL Totals		**45**	**3**	**2**	**5**	**4**	**2**	**6**	**27**	**0**	**0**	**0**	**0**	**0.0**	**0**	**0**	**0**	**0**		....	....	....	....	....	....	....	....

Won Garry F. Longman Memorial Trophy (Top Rookie - IHL) (1962) • CCHA Second All-Star Team (1982)

Traded to **Chicago** by **NY Rangers** with Tracy Pratt, Mel Pearson and Dick Meissner for Ray Cullen and John McKenzie, June 4, 1965. Claimed by **Minnesota** from **Chicago** in Expansion Draft, June 6, 1967. Traded to **Detroit** by **Minnesota** with Jean-Guy Talbot for Duke Harris and Bob McCord, October 19, 1967.

• RICHARDSON, GLEN

Glen Richardson LW – L. 6'2", 200 lbs. b: Barrie, Ont., 9/20/1955. Vancouver's 4th choice, 64th overall, in 1975 Amateur Draft.

Season	Club	League	GP	G	A	Pts	AG	AA	APts	PIM	PP	SH	GW	S	%	TGF	PGF	TGA	PGA	+/–	GP	G	A	Pts	PIM	PP	SH	GW
1972-73	Kitchener Rangers	OHA	40	4	6	10	....	....	....	25	....	....	....	....	....	....	....	....	....	....	....	....	....	....	....	....	....	....
1973-74	Hamilton Fincups	OHA	65	11	17	28	....	....	....	64	....	....	....	....	....	....	....	....	....	....	....	....	....	....	....	....	....	....
1974-75	Hamilton Fincups	OHA	66	29	43	72	....	....	....	119	....	....	....	....	....	....	....	....	....	....	....	....	....	....	....	....	....	....
1975-76	**Vancouver Canucks**	**NHL**	**24**	**3**	**6**	**9**	**3**	**5**	**8**	**19**	**0**	**0**	**0**	**27**	**11.1**	**15**	**1**	**15**	**0**	**–1**	....	....	....	....	....	....	....	....
	Tulsa Oilers	CHL	45	10	10	20	....	....		27	....	....	....	....	....	....	....	....	....	....	9	4	1	5	4	....	....	....
1976-77	Tulsa Oilers	CHL	72	24	38	62	....	....	....	27	....	....	....	....	....	....	....	....		....	9	1	2	3	4	....	....	....
1977-78	Tulsa Oilers	CHL	69	11	18	29	....	....	....	24	....	....	....	....	....	....	....	....	....	....	7	2	1	3	12	....	....	....
	NHL Totals		**24**	**3**	**6**	**9**	**3**	**5**	**8**	**19**	**0**	**0**	**0**	**27**	**11.1**	**15**	**1**	**15**	**0**		....	....	....	....	....	....	....	....

• RICHARDSON, KEN

Ken Richardson C – L. 6', 190 lbs. b: North Bay, Ont., 4/12/1951.

Season	Club	League	GP	G	A	Pts	AG	AA	APts	PIM	PP	SH	GW	S	%	TGF	PGF	TGA	PGA	+/–	GP	G	A	Pts	PIM	PP	SH	GW
1968-69	Peterborough Petes	OHA	54	7	12	19	....	....	....	27	....	....	....	....	....	....	....	....	....	....	10	1	1	2	5	....	....	....
1969-70	Smith Falls Bears	Ott-Jr.	....	24	16	40	....	....	....	77	....	....	....	....	....	....	....	....	....	....	....	....	....	....	....	....	....	....
1970-71	Smith Falls Bears	Ott-Jr.	....	30	32	62	....	....	....	97	....	....	....	....	....	....	....	....	....	....	....	....	....	....	....	....	....	....
1971-72	Laurentian University	OUAA	....	16	10	26	....	....	....	21	....	....	....	....	....	....	....	....	....	....	....	....	....	....	....	....	....	....
1972-73	Laurentian University	OUAA	....	14	7	21	....	....	....	37	....	....	....	....	....	....	....	....	....	....	....	....	....	....	....	....	....	....
1973-74	Columbus Owls	IHL	58	11	22	33	....	....	....	29	....	....	....	....	....	....	....	....	....	....	4	5	2	7	10	....	....	....
1974-75	**St. Louis Blues**	**NHL**	**21**	**5**	**7**	**12**	**5**	**5**	**10**	**12**	**1**	**0**	**1**	**26**	**19.2**	**16**	**2**	**10**	**0**	**+4**	....	....	....	....	....	....	....	....
	Denver Spurs	CHL	30	10	11	21	....	....	....	20	....	....	....	....	....	....	....	....	....	....	2	2	1	3	0	....	....	....
1975-76	Providence Reds	AHL	3	0	1	1	....	....	....	4	....	....	....	....	....	....	....	....	....	....	....	....	....	....	....	....	....	....
	Oklahoma City Blazers	CHL	70	19	33	52	....	....	....	17	....	....	....	....	....	....	....	....	....	....	4	1	0	1	0	....	....	....
1976-77	Kansas City Blues	CHL	74	20	27	47	....	....	....	17	....	....	....	....	....	....	....	....	....	....	10	2	3	5	2	....	....	....
1977-78	**St. Louis Blues**	**NHL**	**12**	**2**	**5**	**7**	**2**	**4**	**6**	**2**	**0**	**0**	**0**	**14**	**14.3**	**9**	**0**	**6**	**1**	**+4**	....	....	....	....	....	....	....	....
	Salt Lake Golden Eagles	CHL	59	16	23	39	....	....	....	26	....	....	....	....	....	....	....	....	....	....	6	3	0	3	2	....	....	....
1978-79	**St. Louis Blues**	**NHL**	**16**	**1**	**1**	**2**	**1**	**1**	**2**	**2**	**0**	**0**	**0**	**6**	**16.7**	**5**	**0**	**26**	**16**	**–5**	....	....	....	....	....	....	....	....
	Salt Lake Golden Eagles	CHL	58	7	10	17	....	....	....	15	....	....	....	....	....	....	....	....	....	....	10	3	1	4	0	....	....	....
1979-80	Salt Lake Golden Eagles	CHL	61	4	16	20	....	....	....	24	....	....	....	....	....	....	....	....	....	....	11	0	1	1	2	....	....	....
	NHL Totals		**49**	**8**	**13**	**21**	**8**	**10**	**18**	**16**	**1**	**0**	**1**	**46**	**17.4**	**30**	**2**	**42**	**17**		....	....	....	....	....	....	....	....

Signed as a free agent by **St. Louis** (Columbus - IHL), September, 1973.

• RICHARDSON, LUKE

Luke Richardson D – L. 6'4", 210 lbs. b: Ottawa, Ont., 3/26/1969. Toronto's 1st choice, 7th overall, in 1987 Entry Draft.

Season	Club	League	GP	G	A	Pts	AG	AA	APts	PIM	PP	SH	GW	S	%	TGF	PGF	TGA	PGA	+/–	GP	G	A	Pts	PIM	PP	SH	GW
1985-86	Peterborough Petes	OHL	63	6	18	24	....	....	....	57	....	....	....	....	....	....	....	....	....	....	16	2	1	3	50	....	....	....
1986-87	Peterborough Petes	OHL	59	13	32	45	....	....	....	70	....	....	....	....	....	....	....	....	....	....	12	0	5	5	24	....	....	....
	Canada	WJC-A	6	0	0	0	....	....	....	0	....	....	....	....	....	....	....	....	....	....	....	....	....	....	....	....	....	....
1987-88	**Toronto Maple Leafs**	**NHL**	**78**	**4**	**6**	**10**	**3**	**4**	**7**	**90**	**0**	**0**	**0**	**49**	**8.2**	**48**	**1**	**93**	**21**	**–25**	**2**	**0**	**0**	**0**	**0**	**0**	**0**	**0**
1988-89	**Toronto Maple Leafs**	**NHL**	**55**	**2**	**7**	**9**	**2**	**5**	**7**	**106**	**0**	**0**	**0**	**59**	**3.4**	**42**	**1**	**76**	**20**	**–15**	....	....	....	....	....	....	....	....
1989-90	**Toronto Maple Leafs**	**NHL**	**67**	**4**	**14**	**18**	**3**	**10**	**13**	**122**	**0**	**0**	**0**	**80**	**5.0**	**76**	**6**	**83**	**12**	**–1**	**5**	**0**	**0**	**0**	**22**	**0**	**0**	**0**
1990-91	**Toronto Maple Leafs**	**NHL**	**78**	**1**	**9**	**10**	**1**	**7**	**8**	**238**	**0**	**0**	**0**	**68**	**1.5**	**46**	**1**	**102**	**29**	**–28**	....	....	....	....	....	....	....	....
1991-92	**Edmonton Oilers**	**NHL**	**75**	**2**	**19**	**21**	**2**	**14**	**16**	**118**	**0**	**0**	**0**	**85**	**2.4**	**64**	**7**	**101**	**35**	**–9**	**16**	**0**	**5**	**5**	**45**	**0**	**0**	**0**
1992-93	**Edmonton Oilers**	**NHL**	**82**	**3**	**10**	**13**	**2**	**7**	**9**	**142**	**0**	**2**	**0**	**78**	**3.8**	**55**	**2**	**107**	**36**	**–18**	....	....	....	....	....	....	....	....
1993-94	**Edmonton Oilers**	**NHL**	**69**	**2**	**6**	**8**	**2**	**5**	**7**	**131**	**0**	**0**	**0**	**92**	**2.2**	**47**	**0**	**83**	**23**	**–13**	....	....	....	....	....	....	....	....
	Canada	WC-A	8	0	1	1	....	....	....	6	....	....	....	....	....	....	....	....	....	....	....	....	....	....	....	....	....	....
1994-95	**Edmonton Oilers**	**NHL**	**46**	**3**	**10**	**13**	**5**	**15**	**20**	**40**	**1**	**1**	**1**	**51**	**5.9**	**40**	**4**	**72**	**30**	**–6**	....	....	....	....	....	....	....	....
1995-96	**Edmonton Oilers**	**NHL**	**82**	**2**	**9**	**11**	**2**	**7**	**9**	**108**	**0**	**0**	**0**	**61**	**3.3**	**55**	**4**	**113**	**35**	**–27**	....	....	....	....	....	....	....	....
	Canada	WC-A	8	0	0	0	....	....	....	12	....	....	....	....	....	....	....	....	....	....	....	....	....	....	....	....	....	....
1996-97	**Edmonton Oilers**	**NHL**	**82**	**1**	**11**	**12**	**1**	**10**	**11**	**91**	**0**	**0**	**0**	**67**	**1.5**	**68**	**3**	**80**	**24**	**+9**	**12**	**0**	**2**	**2**	**14**	**0**	**0**	**0**
1997-98	**Philadelphia Flyers**	**NHL**	**81**	**2**	**3**	**5**	**2**	**3**	**5**	**139**	**2**	**0**	**0**	**57**	**3.5**	**51**	**4**	**62**	**22**	**+7**	**5**	**0**	**0**	**0**	**0**	**0**	**0**	**0**
	NHL Totals		**795**	**26**	**104**	**130**	**25**	**87**	**112**	**1325**	**3**	**3**	**1**	**747**	**3.5**	**592**	**33**	**972**	**287**		**40**	**0**	**7**	**7**	**81**	**0**	**0**	**0**

Traded to **Edmonton** by **Toronto** with Vincent Damphousse, Peter Ing, Scott Thornton, future considerations and cash for Grant Fuhr, Glenn Anderson and Craig Berube, September 19, 1991. Signed as a free agent by **Philadelphia**, July 23, 1997.

			REGULAR SEASON																		PLAYOFFS							
Season	Club	League	GP	G	A	Pts	AG	AA	APts	PIM	PP	SH	GW	S	%	TGF	PGF	TGA	PGA	+/–	GP	G	A	Pts	PIM	PP	SH	GW

• RICHER, BOB

Bob Richer C – L. 5'10", 175 lbs. b: Cowansville, Que., 3/5/1951. Buffalo's 4th choice, 47th overall, in 1971 Amateur Draft.

Season	Club	League	GP	G	A	Pts	AG	AA	APts	PIM	PP	SH	GW	S	%	TGF	PGF	TGA	PGA	+/–	GP	G	A	Pts	PIM	PP	SH	GW
1969-70	Trois Rivieres Ducs	QJHL	50	22	29	51	....	....	....	87	....	....	....	....	....	....	....	....	....	....	....	....	....	....	....	....	....	....
1970-71	Trois Rivieres Ducs	QJHL	62	47	44	91	....	....	....	130	....	....	....	....	....	....	....	....	....	....	11	6	1	7	15	....	....	....
1971-72	Cincinnati Swords	AHL	1	0	0	0	....	....	....	2	....	....	....	....	....	....	....	....	....	....	....	....	....	....	....	....	....	....
	Charlotte Checkers	EHL	71	44	31	75	....	....	....	62	....	....	....	....	....	....	....	....	....	....	15	7	9	16	37	....	....	....
1972-73	**Buffalo Sabres**	**NHL**	**3**	**0**	**0**	**0**	**0**	**0**	**0**	**0**	**0**	**0**	**0**	**0**	**0.0**	**0**	**0**	**0**	**0**	**0**	....	....	....	....	....	....	....	....
	Cincinnati Swords	AHL	63	11	10	21	....	....	....	12	....	....	....	....	....	....	....	....	....	....	1	0	0	0	5	....	....	....
1973-74	Cincinnati Swords	AHL	71	9	11	20	....	....	....	25	....	....	....	....	....	....	....	....	....	....	5	0	0	0	0	....	....	....
	NHL Totals		**3**	**0**	**0**	**0**	**0**	**0**	**0**	**0**	**0**	**0**	**0**	**0**	**0.0**	**0**	**0**	**0**	**0**		....	....	....	....	....	....	....	....

• RICHER, STEPHANE

Stephane Richer RW – R. 6'2", 215 lbs. b: Ripon, Que., 6/7/1966. Montreal's 3rd choice, 29th overall, in 1984 Entry Draft.

Season	Club	League	GP	G	A	Pts	AG	AA	APts	PIM	PP	SH	GW	S	%	TGF	PGF	TGA	PGA	+/–	GP	G	A	Pts	PIM	PP	SH	GW
1983-84	Granby Bisons	QMJHL	67	39	37	76	....	....	....	58	....	....	....	....	....	....	....	....	....	....	3	1	1	2	4	....	....	....
1984-85	Granby Bisons	QMJHL	30	30	27	57	....	....	....	31	....	....	....	....	....	....	....	....	....	....	....	....	....	....	....	....	....	....
	Canada	WJC-A	7	4	3	7	....	....	....	2	....	....	....	....	....	....	....	....	....	....	....	....	....	....	....	....	....	....
	Chicoutimi Sagueneens	QMJHL	27	31	32	63	....	....	....	40	....	....	....	....	....	....	....	....	....	....	12	13	13	26	25	....	....	....
	Montreal Canadiens	**NHL**	**1**	**0**	**0**	**0**	**0**	**0**	**0**	**0**	**0**	**0**	**0**	**0**	**0.0**	**0**	**0**	**0**	**0**	**0**	....	....	....	....	....	....	....	....
	Sherbrooke Canadiens	AHL	....	....	....	....	....	....	....	....	....	....	....	....	....	....	....	....	....	....	9	6	3	9	10	....	....	....
1985-86	**Montreal Canadiens**	**NHL**	**65**	**21**	**16**	**37**	**17**	**11**	**28**	**50**	**5**	**0**	**2**	**112**	**18.8**	**57**	**24**	**32**	**0**	**+1**	**16**	**4**	**1**	**5**	**23**	**3**	**0**	**1**
1986-87	**Montreal Canadiens**	**NHL**	**57**	**20**	**19**	**39**	**17**	**14**	**31**	**80**	**4**	**0**	**3**	**109**	**18.3**	**54**	**14**	**30**	**1**	**+11**	**5**	**3**	**2**	**5**	**0**	**0**	**0**	**1**
	Sherbrooke Canadiens	AHL	12	10	4	14	....	....	....	11	....	....	....	....	....	....	....	....	....	....	....	....	....	....	....	....	....	....
1987-88	**Montreal Canadiens**	**NHL**	**72**	**50**	**28**	**78**	**43**	**20**	**63**	**72**	**16**	**0**	**11**	**263**	**19.0**	**103**	**42**	**50**	**1**	**+12**	**8**	**7**	**5**	**12**	**6**	**1**	**0**	**2**
1988-89	**Montreal Canadiens**	**NHL**	**68**	**25**	**35**	**60**	**21**	**25**	**46**	**61**	**11**	**0**	**6**	**214**	**11.7**	**77**	**33**	**40**	**0**	**+4**	**21**	**6**	**5**	**11**	**14**	**2**	**0**	**3**
1989-90	**Montreal Canadiens**	**NHL**	**75**	**51**	**40**	**91**	**44**	**29**	**73**	**46**	**9**	**0**	**8**	**269**	**19.0**	**111**	**31**	**45**	**0**	**+35**	**9**	**7**	**3**	**10**	**2**	**1**	**0**	**1**
1990-91	Montreal Canadiens	FrTour	4	2	1	3	....	....	....	8	....	....	....	....	....	....	....	....	....	....	....	....	....	....	....	....	....	....
	Montreal Canadiens	**NHL**	**75**	**31**	**30**	**61**	**29**	**23**	**52**	**53**	**9**	**0**	**4**	**221**	**14.0**	**76**	**22**	**54**	**0**	**0**	**13**	**9**	**5**	**14**	**6**	**1**	**0**	**1**
1991-92	**New Jersey Devils**	**NHL**	**74**	**29**	**35**	**64**	**26**	**26**	**52**	**25**	**5**	**1**	**6**	**240**	**12.1**	**91**	**28**	**67**	**3**	**–1**	**7**	**1**	**2**	**3**	**0**	**0**	**0**	**0**
1992-93	**New Jersey Devils**	**NHL**	**78**	**38**	**35**	**73**	**32**	**24**	**56**	**44**	**7**	**1**	**7**	**286**	**13.3**	**101**	**34**	**72**	**4**	**–1**	**5**	**2**	**2**	**4**	**2**	**1**	**0**	**0**
1993-94	**New Jersey Devils**	**NHL**	**80**	**36**	**36**	**72**	**34**	**28**	**62**	**16**	**7**	**3**	**9**	**217**	**16.6**	**97**	**21**	**52**	**7**	**+31**	**20**	**7**	**5**	**12**	**6**	**3**	**0**	**2**
1994-95	**New Jersey Devils**	**NHL**	**45**	**23**	**16**	**39**	**41**	**24**	**65**	**10**	**1**	**2**	**5**	**133**	**17.3**	**48**	**8**	**35**	**3**	**+8**	**19**	**6**	**15**	**21**	**2**	**3**	**1**	**2**
1995-96	**New Jersey Devils**	**NHL**	**73**	**20**	**12**	**32**	**20**	**10**	**30**	**30**	**3**	**4**	**3**	**192**	**10.4**	**42**	**7**	**57**	**14**	**–8**	....	....	....	....	....	....	....	....
1996-97	**Montreal Canadiens**	**NHL**	**63**	**22**	**24**	**46**	**23**	**21**	**44**	**32**	**2**	**0**	**2**	**126**	**17.5**	**63**	**15**	**52**	**4**	**0**	**5**	**0**	**0**	**0**	**0**	**0**	**0**	**0**
1997-98	**Montreal Canadiens**	**NHL**	**14**	**5**	**4**	**9**	**6**	**4**	**10**	**5**	**2**	**0**	**0**	**24**	**20.8**	**13**	**6**	**6**	**0**	**+1**	....	....	....	....	....	....	....	....
	Tampa Bay Lightning	**NHL**	**26**	**9**	**11**	**20**	**11**	**11**	**22**	**36**	**3**	**0**	**2**	**71**	**12.7**	**29**	**10**	**29**	**3**	**–7**	....	....	....	....	....	....	....	....
	NHL Totals		**866**	**380**	**341**	**721**	**364**	**270**	**634**	**560**	**84**	**11**	**68**	**2477**	**15.3**	**962**	**295**	**621**	**40**		**128**	**52**	**45**	**97**	**61**	**15**	**1**	**13**

QMJHL Rookie of the Year (1984) • QMJHL Second All-Star Team (1985)

Played in NHL All-Star Game (1990)

Traded to **New Jersey** by **Montreal** with Tom Chorske for Kirk Muller and Roland Melanson, September 20, 1991. Traded to **Montreal** by **New Jersey** for Lyle Odelein, August 22, 1996. Traded to **Tampa Bay** by **Montreal** with Darcy Tucker and David Wilkie for Patrick Poulin, Mick Vukota and Igor Ulanov, January 15, 1998.

• RICHER, STEPHANE J. G.

Stephane J. G. Richer D – R. 5'11", 190 lbs. b: Hull, Que., 4/28/1966.

Season	Club	League	GP	G	A	Pts	AG	AA	APts	PIM	PP	SH	GW	S	%	TGF	PGF	TGA	PGA	+/–	GP	G	A	Pts	PIM	PP	SH	GW
1983-84	Hull Olympiques	QMJHL	70	8	38	46	....	....	....	42	....	....	....	....	....	....	....	....	....	....	....	....	....	....	....	....	....	....
1984-85	Hull Olympiques	QMJHL	62	21	56	77	....	....	....	98	....	....	....	....	....	....	....	....	....	....	....	....	....	....	....	....	....	....
1985-86	Hull Olympiques	QMJHL	71	14	52	66	....	....	....	166	....	....	....	....	....	....	....	....	....	....	....	....	....	....	....	....	....	....
1986-87	Hull Olympiques	QMJHL	33	6	22	28	....	....	....	74	....	....	....	....	....	....	....	....	....	....	8	3	4	7	17	....	....	....
1987-88	Baltimore Skipjacks	AHL	22	0	3	3	....	....	....	6	....	....	....	....	....	....	....	....	....	....	....	....	....	....	....	....	....	....
	Sherbrooke Canadiens	AHL	41	4	7	11	....	....	....	46	....	....	....	....	....	....	....	....	....	....	5	1	0	1	10	....	....	....
1988-89	Sherbrooke Canadiens	AHL	70	7	26	33	....	....	....	158	....	....	....	....	....	....	....	....	....	....	6	1	2	3	18	....	....	....
1989-90	Sherbrooke Canadiens	AHL	60	10	12	22	....	....	....	85	....	....	....	....	....	....	....	....	....	....	12	4	9	13	16	....	....	....
1990-91	New Haven Nighthawks	AHL	3	0	1	1	....	....	....	0	....	....	....	....	....	....	....	....	....	....	....	....	....	....	....	....	....	....
	Phoenix Roadrunners	IHL	67	11	38	49	....	....	....	48	....	....	....	....	....	....	....	....	....	....	11	4	6	10	6	....	....	....
1991-92	Fredericton Canadiens	AHL	80	17	47	64	....	....	....	74	....	....	....	....	....	....	....	....	....	....	7	0	5	5	18	....	....	....
1992-93	**Tampa Bay Lightning**	**NHL**	**3**	**0**	**0**	**0**	**0**	**0**	**0**	**0**	**0**	**0**	**0**	**2**	**0.0**	**1**	**0**	**4**	**0**	**–3**	....	....	....	....	....	....	....	....
	Atlanta Knights	IHL	3	0	4	4	....	....	....	4	....	....	....	....	....	....	....	....	....	....	....	....	....	....	....	....	....	....
	Boston Bruins	**NHL**	**21**	**1**	**4**	**5**	**1**	**3**	**4**	**18**	**0**	**0**	**1**	**22**	**4.5**	**9**	**0**	**16**	**1**	**–6**	**3**	**0**	**0**	**0**	**0**	**0**	**0**	**0**
	Providence Bruins	AHL	53	8	20	28	....	....	....	60	....	....	....	....	....	....	....	....	....	....	....	....	....	....	....	....	....	....
1993-94	**Florida Panthers**	**NHL**	**2**	**0**	**1**	**1**	**0**	**1**	**1**	**0**	**0**	**0**	**0**	**3**	**0.0**	**2**	**2**	**2**	**1**	**–1**	....	....	....	....	....	....	....	....
	Cincinnati Cyclones	IHL	66	9	55	64	....	....	....	80	....	....	....	....	....	....	....	....	....	....	11	2	9	11	26	....	....	....
1994-95	Cincinnati Cyclones	IHL	80	16	53	69	....	....	....	67	....	....	....	....	....	....	....	....	....	....	10	2	7	9	18	....	....	....
	Florida Panthers	**NHL**	**1**	**0**	**0**	**0**	**0**	**0**	**0**	**2**	**0**	**0**	**0**	**0**	**0.0**	**0**	**0**	**0**	**0**	**0**	....	....	....	....	....	....	....	....
1995-96	Adler Mannheim	Germany	50	11	30	41	....	....	....	62	....	....	....	....	....	....	....	....	....	....	8	1	4	5	0	....	....	....
1996-97	Adler Mannheim	Germany	49	10	19	29	....	....	....	65	....	....	....	....	....	....	....	....	....	....	9	0	4	4	10	....	....	....
1997-98	Adler Mannheim	Germany	48	6	25	31	....	....	....	64	....	....	....	....	....	....	....	....	....	....	8	3	6	9	4	....	....	....
	NHL Totals		**27**	**1**	**5**	**6**	**1**	**4**	**5**	**20**	**0**	**0**	**1**	**27**	**3.7**	**12**	**2**	**22**	**2**		**3**	**0**	**0**	**0**	**0**	**0**	**0**	**0**

AHL Second All-Star Team (1992) • IHL Second All-Star Team (1994, 1995)

Signed as a free agent by **Montreal**, January 9, 1988. Signed as a free agent by **LA Kings**, July 11, 1990. Signed as a free agent by **Montreal**, September 17, 1991. Signed as a free agent by **Tampa Bay**, July 29, 1992. Traded to **Boston** by **Tampa Bay** for Bob Beers, October 28, 1992. Claimed by **Florida** from **Boston** in Expansion Draft, June 24, 1993.

• RICHMOND, STEVE

Steve Richmond D – L. 6'1", 205 lbs. b: Chicago, IL, 12/11/1959.

Season	Club	League	GP	G	A	Pts	AG	AA	APts	PIM	PP	SH	GW	S	%	TGF	PGF	TGA	PGA	+/–	GP	G	A	Pts	PIM	PP	SH	GW
1978-79	University of Michigan	CCHA	34	2	5	7	....	....	....	38	....	....	....	....	....	....	....	....	....	....	....	....	....	....	....	....	....	....
1979-80	University of Michigan	CCHA	38	10	19	29	....	....	....	26	....	....	....	....	....	....	....	....	....	....	....	....	....	....	....	....	....	....
1980-81	University of Michigan	CCHA	39	22	32	54	....	....	....	56	....	....	....	....	....	....	....	....	....	....	....	....	....	....	....	....	....	....
1981-82	University of Michigan	CCHA	38	6	30	36	....	....	....	68	....	....	....	....	....	....	....	....	....	....	....	....	....	....	....	....	....	....
1982-83	Tulsa Oilers	CHL	68	5	13	18	....	....	....	187	....	....	....	....	....	....	....	....	....	....	....	....	....	....	....	....	....	....
1983-84	**New York Rangers**	**NHL**	**26**	**2**	**5**	**7**	**2**	**3**	**5**	**110**	**0**	**0**	**0**	**16**	**12.5**	**24**	**0**	**21**	**3**	**+6**	**4**	**0**	**0**	**0**	**12**	**0**	**0**	**0**
	Tulsa Oilers	CHL	38	1	17	18	....	....	....	114	....	....	....	....	....	....	....	....	....	....	....	....	....	....	....	....	....	....
1984-85	**New York Rangers**	**NHL**	**34**	**0**	**5**	**5**	**0**	**3**	**3**	**90**	**0**	**0**	**0**	**14**	**0.0**	**21**	**1**	**42**	**6**	**–16**	....	....	....	....	....	....	....	....
	New Haven Nighthawks	AHL	37	3	10	13	....	....	....	122	....	....	....	....	....	....	....	....	....	....	....	....	....	....	....	....	....	....
1985-86	**New York Rangers**	**NHL**	**17**	**0**	**2**	**2**	**0**	**1**	**1**	**63**	**0**	**0**	**0**	**8**	**0.0**	**10**	**0**	**8**	**0**	**+2**	....	....	....	....	....	....	....	....
	New Haven Nighthawks	AHL	11	2	6	8	....	....	....	32	....	....	....	....	....	....	....	....	....	....	....	....	....	....	....	....	....	....
	Detroit Red Wings	**NHL**	**29**	**1**	**2**	**3**	**1**	**1**	**2**	**82**	**0**	**0**	**0**	**18**	**5.6**	**13**	**1**	**35**	**5**	**–18**	....	....	....	....	....	....	....	....
	Adirondack Red Wings	AHL	20	1	7	8	....	....	....	23	....	....	....	....	....	....	....	....	....	....	17	2	9	11	34	....	....	....
1986-87	**New Jersey Devils**	**NHL**	**44**	**1**	**7**	**8**	**1**	**5**	**6**	**143**	**0**	**0**	**0**	**31**	**3.2**	**34**	**0**	**55**	**9**	**–12**	....	....	....	....	....	....	....	....
1987-88	Utica Devils	AHL	79	6	27	33	....	....	....	141	....	....	....	....	....	....	....	....	....	....	....	....	....	....	....	....	....	....
	Flint Spirits	IHL	2	0	2	2	....	....	....	2	....	....	....	....	....	....	....	....	....	....	16	2	9	11	57	....	....	....
1988-89	**Los Angeles Kings**	**NHL**	**9**	**0**	**2**	**2**	**0**	**1**	**1**	**26**	**0**	**0**	**0**	**1**	**0.0**	**6**	**0**	**7**	**3**	**+2**	....	....	....	....	....	....	....	....
	New Haven Nighthawks	AHL	49	6	35	41	....	....	....	114	....	....	....	....	....	....	....	....	....	....	17	3	10	13	84	....	....	....
1989-90	Flint Spirits	IHL	10	1	3	4	....	....	....	19	....	....	....	....	....	....	....	....	....	....	4	0	1	1	16	....	....	....
1990-91	San Diego Gulls	IHL	12	3	7	10	....	....	....	19	....	....	....	....	....	....	....	....	....	....	....	....	....	....	....	....	....	....
	NHL Totals		**159**	**4**	**23**	**27**	**4**	**14**	**18**	**514**	**0**	**0**	**0**	**88**	**4.5**	**108**	**2**	**168**	**26**		**4**	**0**	**0**	**0**	**12**	**0**	**0**	**0**

Signed as a free agent by **NY Rangers**, June 22, 1982. Traded to **Detroit** by **NY Rangers** for Mike McEwen, December 26, 1985. Traded to **New Jersey** by **Detroit** for Sam St.Laurent, August 18, 1986. Signed as a free agent by **LA Kings**, July, 1988.

• RICHTER, BARRY

Barry Richter D – L. 6'2", 200 lbs. b: Madison, WI, 9/11/1970. Hartford's 2nd choice, 32nd overall, in 1988 Entry Draft.

Season	Club	League	GP	G	A	Pts	AG	AA	APts	PIM	PP	SH	GW	S	%	TGF	PGF	TGA	PGA	+/–	GP	G	A	Pts	PIM	PP	SH	GW
1987-88	Culver Military Academy	H.S.	35	24	29	53	....	....	....	18	....	....	....	....	....	....	....	....	....	....	....	....	....	....	....	....	....	....
1988-89	Culver Military Academy	H.S.	19	21	29	50	....	....	....	16	....	....	....	....	....	....	....	....	....	....	....	....	....	....	....	....	....	....
	United States	WJC-A	7	0	0	0	....	....	....	2	....	....	....	....	....	....	....	....	....	....	....	....	....	....	....	....	....	....
1989-90	University of Wisconsin	WCHA	42	13	23	36	....	....	....	36	....	....	....	....	....	....	....	....	....	....	....	....	....	....	....	....	....	....
	United States	WJC-A	7	3	1	4	....	....	....	0	....	....	....	....	....	....	....	....	....	....	....	....	....	....	....	....	....	....
1990-91	University of Wisconsin	WCHA	43	15	20	35	....	....	....	42	....	....	....	....	....	....	....	....	....	....	....	....	....	....	....	....	....	....

			REGULAR SEASON																		PLAYOFFS							
Season	Club	League	GP	G	A	Pts	AG	AA	APts	PIM	PP	SH	GW	S	%	TGF	PGF	TGA	PGA	+/–	GP	G	A	Pts	PIM	PP	SH	GW
1991-92	University of Wisconsin	WCHA	39	10	25	35	....	....	....	62	....	....	....	....	....	....	....	....	....	....	....	....	....	....	....	....	....	....
	United States	WC-A	4	1	0	1	....	....	....	4	....	....	....	....	....	....	....	....	....	....	....	....	....	....	....	....	....	....
1992-93	University of Wisconsin	WCHA	42	14	32	46	....	....	....	74	....	....	....	....	....	....	....	....	....	....	....	....	....	....	....	....	....	....
	United States	WC-A	6	0	0	0	....	....	....	8	....	....	....	....	....	....	....	....	....	....	....	....	....	....	....	....	....	....
1993-94	United States	Nat-Team	56	7	16	23	....	....	....	50	....	....	....	....	....	....	....	....	....	....	....	....	....	....	....	....	....	....
	United States	Olympics	8	0	3	3	....	....	....	4	....	....	....	....	....	....	....	....	....	....	....	....	....	....	....	....	....	....
	United States	WC-A	7	0	0	0	....	....	....	6	....	....	....	....	....	....	....	....	....	....	....	....	....	....	....	....	....	....
	Binghamton Rangers	AHL	21	0	9	9	....	....	....	12	....	....	....	....	....	....	....	....	....	....	....	....	....	....	....	....	....	....
1994-95	Binghamton Rangers	AHL	73	15	41	56	....	....	....	54	....	....	....	....	....	....	....	....	....	....	11	4	5	9	12	....	....	....
1995-96	**New York Rangers**	**NHL**	**4**	**0**	**1**	**1**	**0**	**1**	**1**	**0**	**0**	**0**	**0**	**3**	**0.0**	**2**	**0**	**1**	**1**	**+2**	....	....	....	....	....	....	....	....
	Binghamton Rangers	AHL	69	20	61	81	....	....	....	64	....	....	....	....	....	....	....	....	....	....	3	0	3	3	0	....	....	....
1996-97	**Boston Bruins**	**NHL**	**50**	**5**	**13**	**18**	**5**	**11**	**16**	**32**	**1**	**0**	**0**	**79**	**6.3**	**54**	**16**	**50**	**5**	**–7**	....	....	....	....	....	....	....	....
	Providence Bruins	AHL	19	2	6	8	....	....	....	4	....	....	....	....	....	....	....	....	....	....	10	4	4	8	4	....	....	....
1997-98	Providence Bruins	AHL	75	16	29	45	....	....	....	47	....	....	....	....	....	....	....	....	....	....	....	....	....	....	....	....	....	....
	NHL Totals		**54**	**5**	**14**	**19**	**5**	**12**	**17**	**32**	**1**	**0**	**0**	**82**	**6.1**	**56**	**16**	**51**	**6**		....	....	....	....	....	....	....	....

NCAA Championship All-Tournament Team (1992) • WCHA First All-Star Team (1993) • NCAA West First All-American Team (1993) • AHL First All-Star Team (1996) • Won Eddie Shore Plaque (Outstanding Defenseman - AHL) (1996)

Traded to **NY Rangers** by **Hartford** with Steve Larmer, Nick Kypreos and Hartford's 6th round choice (Yuri Litvinov) in 1994 Entry Draft for Darren Turcotte and James Patrick, November 2, 1993. Signed as a free agent by **Boston**, July 19, 1996.

• RICHTER, DAVE

Dave Richter D – R. 6'5", 225 lbs. b: St. Boniface, Man., 4/8/1960. Minnesota's 10th choice, 205th overall, in 1980 Entry Draft.

Season	Club	League	GP	G	A	Pts	AG	AA	APts	PIM	PP	SH	GW	S	%	TGF	PGF	TGA	PGA	+/–	GP	G	A	Pts	PIM	PP	SH	GW
1979-80	University of Michigan	WCHA	34	0	4	4	....	....	....	54	....	....	....	....	....	....	....	....	....	....	....	....	....	....	....	....	....	....
1980-81	University of Michigan	WCHA	36	2	13	15	....	....	....	56	....	....	....	....	....	....	....	....	....	....	....	....	....	....	....	....	....	....
1981-82	University of Michigan	WCHA	36	9	12	21	....	....	....	78	....	....	....	....	....	....	....	....	....	....	....	....	....	....	....	....	....	....
	Minnesota North Stars	**NHL**	**3**	**0**	**0**	**0**	**0**	**0**	**0**	**11**	**0**	**0**	**0**	**1**	**0.0**	**1**	**0**	**1**	**0**	**0**	....	....	....	....	....	....	....	....
	Nashville South Stars	CHL	2	0	1	1	....	....	....	0	....	....	....	....	....	....	....	....	....	....	....	....	....	....	....	....	....	....
1982-83	**Minnesota North Stars**	**NHL**	**6**	**0**	**0**	**0**	**0**	**0**	**0**	**4**	**0**	**0**	**0**	**3**	**0.0**	**5**	**0**	**5**	**0**	**0**	....	....	....	....	....	....	....	....
	Birmingham South Stars	CHL	69	6	17	23	....	....	....	211	....	....	....	....	....	....	....	....	....	....	13	3	1	4	36	....	....	....
1983-84	**Minnesota North Stars**	**NHL**	**42**	**2**	**3**	**5**	**2**	**2**	**4**	**132**	**0**	**0**	**0**	**22**	**9.1**	**19**	**0**	**33**	**6**	**–8**	**8**	**0**	**0**	**0**	**20**	**0**	**0**	**0**
	Salt Lake Golden Eagles	CHL	10	1	4	5	....	....	....	39	....	....	....	....	....	....	....	....	....	....	....	....	....	....	....	....	....	....
1984-85	**Minnesota North Stars**	**NHL**	**55**	**2**	**8**	**10**	**2**	**5**	**7**	**221**	**0**	**0**	**0**	**29**	**6.9**	**30**	**0**	**55**	**28**	**+3**	**9**	**1**	**0**	**1**	**39**	**0**	**0**	**0**
	Springfield Indians	AHL	3	0	0	0	....	....	....	2	....	....	....	....	....	....	....	....	....	....	....	....	....	....	....	....	....	....
1985-86	**Minnesota North Stars**	**NHL**	**14**	**0**	**3**	**3**	**0**	**2**	**2**	**29**	**0**	**0**	**0**	**5**	**0.0**	**5**	**0**	**13**	**2**	**–6**	....	....	....	....	....	....	....	....
	Philadelphia Flyers	**NHL**	**50**	**0**	**2**	**2**	**0**	**1**	**1**	**138**	**0**	**0**	**0**	**17**	**0.0**	**22**	**0**	**32**	**8**	**–2**	**5**	**0**	**0**	**0**	**21**	**0**	**0**	**0**
1986-87	**Vancouver Canucks**	**NHL**	**78**	**2**	**15**	**17**	**2**	**11**	**13**	**172**	**0**	**0**	**0**	**31**	**6.5**	**72**	**0**	**102**	**28**	**–2**	....	....	....	....	....	....	....	....
1987-88	**Vancouver Canucks**	**NHL**	**49**	**2**	**4**	**6**	**2**	**3**	**5**	**224**	**0**	**0**	**0**	**18**	**11.1**	**31**	**1**	**49**	**14**	**–5**	....	....	....	....	....	....	....	....
1988-89	**St. Louis Blues**	**NHL**	**66**	**1**	**5**	**6**	**1**	**4**	**5**	**99**	**0**	**0**	**0**	**23**	**4.3**	**33**	**0**	**77**	**23**	**–21**	....	....	....	....	....	....	....	....
1989-90	**St. Louis Blues**	**NHL**	**2**	**0**	**0**	**0**	**0**	**0**	**0**	**0**	**0**	**0**	**0**	**3**	**0.0**	**0**	**0**	**2**	**0**	**–2**	....	....	....	....	....	....	....	....
	Peoria Rivermen	IHL	9	1	4	5	....	....	....	30	....	....	....	....	....	....	....	....	....	....	....	....	....	....	....	....	....	....
	Phoenix Roadrunners	IHL	20	0	5	5	....	....	....	49	....	....	....	....	....	....	....	....	....	....	....	....	....	....	....	....	....	....
	Baltimore Skipjacks	AHL	13	0	1	1	....	....	....	13	....	....	....	....	....	....	....	....	....	....	....	....	....	....	....	....	....	....
	WEV Wien	Austria	10	0	0	0	....	....	....	2	....	....	....	....	....	....	....	....	....	....	....	....	....	....	....	....	....	....
1990-91	Albany Choppers	IHL	41	0	1	1	....	....	....	128	....	....	....	....	....	....	....	....	....	....	....	....	....	....	....	....	....	....
	Capital District Islanders	AHL	3	0	1	1	....	....	....	0	....	....	....	....	....	....	....	....	....	....	....	....	....	....	....	....	....	....
	NHL Totals		**305**	**9**	**40**	**49**	**9**	**28**	**37**	**1030**	**0**	**0**	**0**	**152**	**5.9**	**218**	**1**	**369**	**109**		**22**	**1**	**0**	**1**	**80**	**0**	**0**	**0**

CHL Second All-Star Team (1983)

Traded to **Philadelphia** by **Minnesota** with Bo Berglund for Ed Hospodar and Todd Bergen, November 29, 1985. Traded to **Vancouver** by **Philadelphia** with Rich Sutter and Vancouver's 3rd round choice (previously acquired, Vancouver selected Don Gibson) in 1986 Entry Draft for J.J. Daigneault and Vancouver's 2nd round choice (Kent Hawley) in 1986 Entry Draft, June 6, 19 Traded to **St. Louis** by **Vancouver** with Vancouver's 2nd round choice (Mikael Renberg) in 1990 Entry Draft for Robert Nordmark, September 6, 1988.

• RIDLEY, MIKE

Mike Ridley C – L. 6', 195 lbs. b: Winnipeg, Man., 7/8/1963.

Season	Club	League	GP	G	A	Pts	AG	AA	APts	PIM	PP	SH	GW	S	%	TGF	PGF	TGA	PGA	+/–	GP	G	A	Pts	PIM	PP	SH	GW
1983-84	University of Manitoba	GPAC	46	30	41	80	....	....	....	....	....	....	....	....	....	....	....	....	....	....	....	....	....	....	....	....	....	....
1984-85	University of Manitoba	GPAC	23	23	36	59	....	....	....	40	....	....	....	....	....	....	....	....	....	....	7	6	2	8	30	....	....	....
1985-86	**New York Rangers**	**NHL**	**80**	**22**	**43**	**65**	**18**	**29**	**47**	**69**	**7**	**0**	**6**	**150**	**14.7**	**97**	**31**	**96**	**30**	**0**	**16**	**6**	**8**	**14**	**26**	**2**	**0**	**1**
1986-87	**New York Rangers**	**NHL**	**38**	**16**	**20**	**36**	**14**	**14**	**28**	**20**	**4**	**0**	**1**	**81**	**19.8**	**60**	**17**	**40**	**5**	**–10**	....	....	....	....	....	....	....	....
	Washington Capitals	**NHL**	**40**	**16**	**10**	**04**	**13**	**14**	**27**	**20**	**6**	**0**	**3**	**68**	**22.1**	**51**	**13**	**42**	**3**	**–1**	**7**	**2**	**1**	**3**	**6**	**0**	**0**	**1**
1987-88	**Washington Capitals**	**NHL**	**70**	**28**	**31**	**59**	**24**	**22**	**46**	**22**	**12**	**0**	**3**	**134**	**20.9**	**94**	**38**	**58**	**3**	**+1**	**14**	**6**	**5**	**11**	**10**	**1**	**0**	**0**
1988-89	**Washington Capitals**	**NHL**	**80**	**41**	**48**	**89**	**35**	**34**	**69**	**49**	**16**	**0**	**9**	**187**	**21.9**	**117**	**45**	**57**	**2**	**+17**	**6**	**0**	**5**	**5**	**2**	**0**	**0**	**0**
1989-90	Washington Capitals	FrTour	4	2	0	2	....	....	....	10	....	....	....	....	....	....	....	....	....	....	....	....	....	....	....	....	....	....
	Washington Capitals	**NHL**	**74**	**30**	**43**	**73**	**26**	**31**	**57**	**27**	**8**	**3**	**3**	**124**	**24.2**	**94**	**26**	**94**	**26**	**0**	**14**	**3**	**4**	**7**	**8**	**0**	**1**	**0**
1990-91	**Washington Capitals**	**NHL**	**79**	**23**	**48**	**71**	**21**	**36**	**57**	**26**	**6**	**5**	**4**	**155**	**14.8**	**105**	**32**	**87**	**23**	**+9**	**11**	**3**	**4**	**7**	**8**	**1**	**0**	**1**
1991-92	**Washington Capitals**	**NHL**	**80**	**29**	**40**	**69**	**26**	**30**	**56**	**38**	**5**	**5**	**3**	**123**	**23.6**	**99**	**27**	**103**	**34**	**+3**	**7**	**0**	**11**	**11**	**0**	**0**	**0**	**0**
1992-93	**Washington Capitals**	**NHL**	**84**	**26**	**56**	**82**	**22**	**38**	**60**	**44**	**6**	**2**	**3**	**148**	**17.6**	**124**	**48**	**118**	**47**	**+5**	**6**	**1**	**5**	**6**	**0**	**1**	**0**	**0**
1993-94	**Washington Capitals**	**NHL**	**81**	**26**	**44**	**70**	**24**	**34**	**58**	**24**	**10**	**2**	**4**	**144**	**18.1**	**105**	**35**	**84**	**29**	**+15**	**11**	**4**	**6**	**10**	**6**	**0**	**0**	**0**
1994-95	**Toronto Maple Leafs**	**NHL**	**48**	**10**	**27**	**37**	**18**	**40**	**58**	**14**	**2**	**2**	**1**	**88**	**11.4**	**50**	**11**	**47**	**9**	**+1**	**7**	**3**	**1**	**4**	**2**	**1**	**0**	**1**
1995-96	**Vancouver Canucks**	**NHL**	**37**	**6**	**15**	**21**	**6**	**12**	**18**	**29**	**2**	**0**	**1**	**32**	**18.8**	**30**	**8**	**35**	**10**	**–3**	**5**	**0**	**0**	**0**	**2**	**0**	**0**	**0**
1996-97	**Vancouver Canucks**	**NHL**	**75**	**20**	**32**	**52**	**21**	**28**	**49**	**42**	**3**	**0**	**5**	**79**	**25.3**	**78**	**15**	**67**	**4**	**0**	....	....	....	....	....	....	....	....
1997-98	Manitoba Moose	IHL	4	2	2	4	....	....	....	0	....	....	....	....	....	....	....	....	....	....	....	....	....	....	....	....	....	....
	NHL Totals		**866**	**292**	**466**	**758**	**268**	**362**	**630**	**424**	**87**	**19**	**46**	**1513**	**19.3**	**1094**	**346**	**936**	**225**		**104**	**28**	**50**	**78**	**70**	**6**	**1**	**4**

Canadian University Player of the Year; CIAU All-Canadian, GPAC MVP and First All-Star Team (1984) • CIAU All-Canadian, GPAC First All-Star Team (1985) • NHL All-Rookie Team (1986)

Played in NHL All-Star Game (1989)

Signed as a free agent by **NY Rangers**, September 26, 1985. Traded to **Washington** by **NY Rangers** with Bob Crawford and Kelly Miller for Bob Carpenter and Washington's 2nd round choice (Jason Prosofsky) in 1989 Entry Draft, January 1, 1987. Traded to **Toronto** by **Washington** with St. Louis' 1st round choice (acquired earlier, Toronto selected Eric Fichaud) in 1994 Entry Draft for Rob Pearson and Philadelphia's 1st round choice (acquired earlier, Washington selected Nolan Baumgartner) in 1994 Entry Draft, June 28, 1994. Traded to **Vancouver** by **Toronto** for Sergio Momesso, July 8, 1995.

• RILEY, BILL

Bill Riley RW – R. 5'11", 195 lbs. b: Amherst, N.S., 9/20/1950.

Season	Club	League	GP	G	A	Pts	AG	AA	APts	PIM	PP	SH	GW	S	%	TGF	PGF	TGA	PGA	+/–	GP	G	A	Pts	PIM	PP	SH	GW
1973-74	Kitmat Seniors	B.C. Sr.	STATISTICS NOT AVAILABLE																									
1974-75	**Washington Capitals**	**NHL**	**1**	**0**	**0**	**0**	**0**	**0**	**0**	**0**	**0**	**0**	**0**	**0**	**0.0**	**0**	**0**	**1**	**0**	**–1**	....	....	....	....	....	....	....	....
	Dayton Gems	IHL	63	12	16	28	....	....	....	279	....	....	....	....	....	....	....	....	....	....	....	....	....	....	....	....	....	....
1975-76	Dayton Gems	IHL	69	35	31	66	....	....	....	301	....	....	....	....	....	....	....	....	....	....	....	....	....	....	....	....	....	....
1976-77	**Washington Capitals**	**NHL**	**43**	**13**	**14**	**27**	**12**	**11**	**23**	**124**	**5**	**0**	**2**	**45**	**28.9**	**43**	**13**	**26**	**0**	**+4**	....	....	....	....	....	....	....	....
	Dayton Gems	IHL	30	19	15	34	....	....	....	69	....	....	....	....	....	....	....	....	....	....	....	....	....	....	....	....	....	....
1977-78	**Washington Capitals**	**NHL**	**57**	**13**	**12**	**25**	**13**	**10**	**23**	**125**	**5**	**0**	**0**	**67**	**19.4**	**42**	**14**	**43**	**0**	**–15**	....	....	....	....	....	....	....	....
1978-79	**Washington Capitals**	**NHL**	**24**	**2**	**2**	**4**	**2**	**2**	**4**	**64**	**0**	**0**	**0**	**24**	**8.3**	**5**	**0**	**11**	**0**	**–6**	....	....	....	....	....	....	....	....
	Hershey Bears	AHL	51	15	15	30	....	....	....	118	....	....	....	....	....	....	....	....	....	....	4	1	0	1	8	....	....	....
1979-80	**Winnipeg Jets**	**NHL**	**14**	**3**	**2**	**5**	**3**	**2**	**5**	**7**	**2**	**0**	**1**	**11**	**27.3**	**8**	**4**	**4**	**0**	**0**	....	....	....	....	....	....	....	....
	Nova Scotia Voyageurs	AHL	63	31	33	64	....	....	....	157	....	....	....	....	....	....	....	....	....	....	4	0	0	0	2	....	....	....
1980-81	New Brunswick Hawks	AHL	46	12	25	37	....	....	....	107	....	....	....	....	....	....	....	....	....	....	12	3	3	6	49	....	....	....
1981-82	New Brunswick Hawks	AHL	80	32	30	62	....	....	....	104	....	....	....	....	....	....	....	....	....	....	15	8	8	16	6	....	....	....
1982-83	Moncton Alpines	AHL	73	33	30	63	....	....	....	134	....	....	....	....	....	....	....	....	....	....	....	....	....	....	....	....	....	....
1983-84	Nova Scotia Voyageurs	AHL	78	24	24	48	....	....	....	79	....	....	....	....	....	....	....	....	....	....	12	2	5	7	8	....	....	....
1984-85			DID NOT PLAY																									
1985-86	Moncton Junction Club	City Sr.	STATISTICS NOT AVAILABLE																									
1986-87	St. John's Capitals	Nfld.	STATISTICS NOT AVAILABLE																									

			REGULAR SEASON																		PLAYOFFS							
Season	Club	League	GP	G	A	Pts	AG	AA	APts	PIM	PP	SH	GW	S	%	TGF	PGF	TGA	PGA	+/–	GP	G	A	Pts	PIM	PP	SH	GW
1987-88	St. John's Capitals	Nfld.	37	39	63	102	....	....	....	43	....	....	....	....	....	....	....	....	....	....	....	....	....	....	....	....	....	....
1988-89	St. John's Capitals	Nfld.	29	25	36	61	....	....	....	....	....	....	....	....	....	....	....	....	....	....	....	....	....	....	....	....	....	....
1989-90	Amherst Ramblers	NSJHL	DID NOT PLAY – COACHING																									
	NHL Totals		**139**	**31**	**30**	**61**	**30**	**25**	**55**	**320**	**12**	**0**	**3**	**147**	**21.1**	**98**	**31**	**85**	**0**		....	....	....	....	....	....	....	....

Signed as a free agent by **Washington** to a five-game tryout contract, December 20, 1974. Signed as a free agent by **Washington**, January 19, 1977. Claimed by **Winnipeg** from **Washington** in Expansion Draft, June 3, 1979. Signed as a free agent by **Toronto**, February 25, 1981.

• RIOUX, GERRY

Gerry Rioux RW – R. 5'11", 195 lbs. b: Iroquois Falls, Ont., 2/17/1959.

Season	Club	League	GP	G	A	Pts	AG	AA	APts	PIM	PP	SH	GW	S	%	TGF	PGF	TGA	PGA	+/–	GP	G	A	Pts	PIM	PP	SH	GW
1976-77	Sault Ste. Marie Greyhounds	OHA	61	5	15	20	....	....	....	126	....	....	....	....	....	....	....	....	....	....	....	....	....	....	....	....	....	....
1977-78	Sault Ste. Marie Greyhounds	OHA	25	0	4	4	....	....	....	28	....	....	....	....	....	....	....	....	....	....	....	....	....	....	....	....	....	....
	Niagara Falls Flyers	OHA	29	2	5	7	....	....	....	34	....	....	....	....	....	....	....	....	....	....	....	....	....	....	....	....	....	....
1978-79	Windsor Spitfires	OHA	65	11	14	25	....	....	....	195	....	....	....	....	....	....	....	....	....	....	....	....	....	....	....	....	....	....
1979-80	**Winnipeg Jets**	**NHL**	**8**	**0**	**0**	**0**	**0**	**0**	**0**	**6**	**0**	**0**	**0**	**4**	**0.0**	**0**	**0**	**2**	**0**	**–2**	....	....	....	....	....	....	....	....
	Tulsa Oilers	CHL	57	9	11	20	....	....	....	172	....	....	....	....	....	....	....	....	....	....	....	....	....	....	....	....	....	....
1980-81	Tulsa Oilers	CHL	22	2	2	4	....	....	....	48	....	....	....	....	....	....	....	....	....	....	....	....	....	....	....	....	....	....
	Fort Wayne Komets	IHL	3	0	1	1	....	....	....	0	....	....	....	....	....	....	....	....	....	....	....	....	....	....	....	....	....	....
	NHL Totals		**8**	**0**	**0**	**0**	**0**	**0**	**0**	**6**	**0**	**0**	**0**	**4**	**0.0**	**0**	**0**	**2**	**0**		....	....	....	....	....	....	....	....

Signed as a free agent by **Winnipeg**, October, 1979.

• RIOUX, PIERRE

Pierre Rioux RW – R. 5'9", 165 lbs. b: Quebec City, Que., 2/1/1962.

Season	Club	League	GP	G	A	Pts	AG	AA	APts	PIM	PP	SH	GW	S	%	TGF	PGF	TGA	PGA	+/–	GP	G	A	Pts	PIM	PP	SH	GW
1979-80	Shawinigan Cataractes	QMJHL	70	27	47	74	....	....	....	24	....	....	....	....	....	....	....	....	....	....	7	2	2	4	4	....	....	....
1980-81	Shawinigan Cataractes	QMJHL	69	53	77	130	....	....	....	16	....	....	....	....	....	....	....	....	....	....	5	2	3	5	6	....	....	....
1981-82	Shawinigan Cataractes	QMJHL	57	*66	86	152	....	....	....	50	....	....	....	....	....	....	....	....	....	....	14	15	26	41	8	....	....	....
	Canada	WJC-A	7	3	3	6	....	....	....	4	....	....	....	....	....	....	....	....	....	....	....	....	....	....	....	....	....	....
1982-83	**Calgary Flames**	**NHL**	**14**	**1**	**2**	**3**	**1**	**1**	**2**	**4**	**0**	**0**	**0**	**9**	**11.1**	**4**	**0**	**8**	**1**	**–3**	....	....	....	....	....	....	....	....
	Colorado Flames	CHL	59	26	36	62	....	....	....	18	....	....	....	....	....	....	....	....	....	....	....	....	....	....	....	....	....	....
1983-84	Colorado Flames	CHL	65	37	46	83	....	....	....	22	....	....	....	....	....	....	....	....	....	....	6	2	7	9	4	....	....	....
1984-85	Moncton Golden Flames	AHL	69	25	66	91	....	....	....	14	....	....	....	....	....	....	....	....	....	....	....	....	....	....	....	....	....	....
1985-86	Moncton Golden Flames	AHL	5	0	0	0	....	....	....	0	....	....	....	....	....	....	....	....	....	....	....	....	....	....	....	....	....	....
	Binghamton Whalers	AHL	6	0	2	2	....	....	....	0	....	....	....	....	....	....	....	....	....	....	....	....	....	....	....	....	....	....
1986-87	Viry	France	....	42	*67	109	....	....	....	....	....	....	....	....	....	....	....	....	....	....	....	....	....	....	....	....	....	....
1987-88	Kalpa Kuopio	Finland	41	21	20	41	....	....	....	44	....	....	....	....	....	....	....	....	....	....	....	....	....	....	....	....	....	....
1988-89	Ratigen	German 2	45	36	64	100	....	....	....	36	....	....	....	....	....	....	....	....	....	....	....	....	....	....	....	....	....	....
1989-90	Bayreuth	German 2	54	81	78	159	....	....	....	16	....	....	....	....	....	....	....	....	....	....	....	....	....	....	....	....	....	....
1990-91	Bayreuth	German 2	50	57	71	128	....	....	....	78	....	....	....	....	....	....	....	....	....	....	....	....	....	....	....	....	....	....
1991-92	Bayreuth	German 2	43	29	58	87	....	....	....	24	....	....	....	....	....	....	....	....	....	....	....	....	....	....	....	....	....	....
1992-93	Bayrueth	German 2	45	41	52	93	....	....	....	14	....	....	....	....	....	....	....	....	....	....	....	....	....	....	....	....	....	....
1993-94	Dusseldorfer EG	Germany	42	12	24	36	....	....	....	8	....	....	....	....	....	....	....	....	....	....	....	....	....	....	....	....	....	....
1994-95	Dusseldorfer EG	Germany	43	17	37	54	....	....	....	8	....	....	....	....	....	....	....	....	....	....	10	1	10	11	6	....	....	....
1995-96	Augsburg Panthers	Germany	1	1	1	2	....	....	....	0	....	....	....	....	....	....	....	....	....	....	....	....	....	....	....	....	....	....
1996-97	Augsburg Panthers	Germany	27	14	16	30	....	....	....	2	....	....	....	....	....	....	....	....	....	....	4	3	1	4	0	....	....	....
1997-98	Augsburg Panthers	Germany	50	22	28	50	....	....	....	4	....	....	....	....	....	....	....	....	....	....	....	....	....	....	....	....	....	....
	NHL Totals		**14**	**1**	**2**	**3**	**1**	**1**	**2**	**4**	**0**	**0**	**0**	**9**	**11.1**	**4**	**0**	**8**	**1**		....	....	....	....	....	....	....	....

QMJHL First All-Star Team (1982) • AHL First All-Star Team (1985)

Signed as a free agent by **Calgary**, August 24, 1982.

• RISEBROUGH, DOUG

Doug Risebrough C – L. 5'11", 180 lbs. b: Guelph, Ont., 1/29/1954. Montreal's 2nd choice, 7th overall, in 1974 Amateur Draft.

Season	Club	League	GP	G	A	Pts	AG	AA	APts	PIM	PP	SH	GW	S	%	TGF	PGF	TGA	PGA	+/–	GP	G	A	Pts	PIM	PP	SH	GW
1971-72	Guelph GMCs	SOJHL	56	19	33	52	....	....	....	127	....	....	....	....	....	....	....	....	....	....	....	....	....	....	....	....	....	....
1972-73	Guelph Biltmores	SOJHL	60	*47	*60	*107	....	....	....	229	....	....	....	....	....	....	....	....	....	....	....	....	....	....	....	....	....	....
1973-74	Kitchener Rangers	OHA	46	25	27	52	....	....	....	114	....	....	....	....	....	....	....	....	....	....	....	....	....	....	....	....	....	....
1974-75	**Montreal Canadiens**	**NHL**	**64**	**15**	**32**	**47**	**14**	**25**	**39**	**198**	**2**	**0**	**2**	**111**	**13.5**	**69**	**7**	**35**	**0**	**+27**	**11**	**3**	**5**	**8**	**37**	**0**	**0**	**0**
	Nova Scotia Voyageurs	AHL	7	5	4	9	....	....	....	55	....	....	....	....	....	....	....	....	....	....	....	....	....	....	....	....	....	....
1975-76	**Montreal Canadiens**	**NHL**	**80**	**16**	**28**	**44**	**15**	**22**	**37**	**180**	**1**	**0**	**3**	**143**	**11.2**	**64**	**11**	**36**	**1**	**+18**	**13**	**0**	**3**	**3**	**30**	**0**	**0**	**0**
1976-77	**Montreal Canadiens**	**NHL**	**78**	**22**	**38**	**60**	**21**	**31**	**52**	**132**	**1**	**0**	**6**	**142**	**15.5**	**80**	**11**	**36**	**0**	**+33**	**12**	**2**	**3**	**5**	**16**	**0**	**0**	**0**
1977-78	**Montreal Canadiens**	**NHL**	**72**	**18**	**23**	**41**	**17**	**19**	**36**	**97**	**1**	**0**	**3**	**115**	**15.7**	**66**	**6**	**34**	**4**	**+30**	**15**	**2**	**2**	**4**	**17**	**0**	**1**	**1**
1978-79	**Montreal Canadiens**	**NHL**	**48**	**10**	**15**	**25**	**9**	**11**	**20**	**62**	**0**	**0**	**2**	**83**	**12.0**	**42**	**0**	**22**	**2**	**+22**	**15**	**1**	**6**	**7**	**32**	**0**	**0**	**1**
1979-80	**Montreal Canadiens**	**NHL**	**44**	**8**	**10**	**18**	**7**	**8**	**15**	**81**	**0**	**0**	**0**	**82**	**9.8**	**26**	**1**	**30**	**3**	**–2**	....	....	....	....	....	....	....	....
1980-81	**Montreal Canadiens**	**NHL**	**48**	**13**	**21**	**34**	**11**	**15**	**26**	**93**	**1**	**0**	**1**	**94**	**13.8**	**41**	**5**	**34**	**5**	**+7**	**3**	**1**	**0**	**1**	**0**	**1**	**0**	**0**
1981-82	**Montreal Canadiens**	**NHL**	**59**	**15**	**18**	**33**	**12**	**12**	**24**	**116**	**2**	**2**	**2**	**80**	**18.8**	**50**	**5**	**33**	**11**	**+23**	**5**	**2**	**1**	**3**	**11**	**0**	**0**	**0**
1982-83	**Calgary Flames**	**NHL**	**71**	**21**	**37**	**58**	**17**	**26**	**43**	**138**	**3**	**0**	**1**	**145**	**14.5**	**79**	**5**	**89**	**28**	**+13**	**9**	**1**	**3**	**4**	**18**	**0**	**0**	**0**
1983-84	**Calgary Flames**	**NHL**	**77**	**23**	**28**	**51**	**19**	**19**	**38**	**161**	**0**	**1**	**3**	**161**	**14.3**	**78**	**3**	**94**	**30**	**+11**	**11**	**2**	**1**	**3**	**25**	**0**	**0**	**0**
1984-85	**Calgary Flames**	**NHL**	**15**	**7**	**5**	**12**	**6**	**3**	**9**	**49**	**0**	**1**	**4**	**33**	**21.2**	**14**	**0**	**13**	**9**	**+10**	**4**	**0**	**3**	**3**	**12**	**0**	**0**	**0**
1985-86	**Calgary Flames**	**NHL**	**62**	**15**	**28**	**43**	**12**	**19**	**31**	**169**	**0**	**3**	**1**	**92**	**16.3**	**58**	**0**	**65**	**29**	**+22**	**22**	**7**	**9**	**16**	**38**	**0**	**1**	**1**
1986-87	**Calgary Flames**	**NHL**	**22**	**2**	**3**	**5**	**2**	**2**	**4**	**66**	**0**	**0**	**0**	**19**	**10.5**	**9**	**0**	**20**	**9**	**–2**	**4**	**0**	**1**	**1**	**2**	**0**	**0**	**0**
	NHL Totals		**740**	**185**	**286**	**471**	**162**	**212**	**374**	**1542**	**11**	**7**	**28**	**1300**	**14.2**	**676**	**54**	**541**	**131**		**124**	**21**	**37**	**58**	**238**	**1**	**2**	**3**

Traded to **Calgary** by **Montreal** with Montreal's 2nd round choice (later traded to Minnesota — Minnesota selected Frantisek Musil) in 1983 Entry Draft for Washington's 2nd round choice (previously acquired, Montreal selected Todd Francis) in 1983 Entry Draft and Calgary's 3rd round choice (Graeme Bonar) in 1984 Entry Draft, September 11, 1982.

• RISSLING, GARY

Gary Rissling LW – L. 5'9", 175 lbs. b: Saskatoon, Sask., 8/8/1956.

Season	Club	League	GP	G	A	Pts	AG	AA	APts	PIM	PP	SH	GW	S	%	TGF	PGF	TGA	PGA	+/–	GP	G	A	Pts	PIM	PP	SH	GW
1973-74	Edmonton Mets	AJHL	46	29	31	60	....	....	....	132	....	....	....	....	....	....	....	....	....	....	....	....	....	....	....	....	....	....
1974-75	Edmonton Oil Kings	WHL	69	19	35	54	....	....	....	228	....	....	....	....	....	....	....	....	....	....	....	....	....	....	....	....	....	....
1975-76	Edmonton Oil Kings	WCJHL	18	5	9	14	....	....	....	25	....	....	....	....	....	....	....	....	....	....	....	....	....	....	....	....	....	....
	Calgary Centennials	WCJHL	47	29	38	67	....	....	....	196	....	....	....	....	....	....	....	....	....	....	....	....	....	....	....	....	....	....
1976-77	Calgary Wranglers	WCJHL	68	40	40	80	....	....	....	317	....	....	....	....	....	....	....	....	....	....	9	9	7	16	12	....	....	....
1977-78	Port Huron Flags	IHL	79	29	34	63	....	....	....	341	....	....	....	....	....	....	....	....	....	....	17	7	10	17	131	....	....	....
1978-79	**Washington Capitals**	**NHL**	**26**	**3**	**3**	**6**	**3**	**2**	**5**	**127**	**1**	**0**	**1**	**16**	**18.8**	**11**	**1**	**15**	**0**	**–5**	....	....	....	....	....	....	....	....
	Hershey Bears	AHL	52	14	20	34	....	....	....	337	....	....	....	....	....	....	....	....	....	....	4	0	0	0	18	....	....	....
1979-80	**Washington Capitals**	**NHL**	**11**	**0**	**1**	**1**	**0**	**1**	**1**	**49**	**0**	**0**	**0**	**5**	**0.0**	**1**	**0**	**7**	**0**	**–6**	....	....	....	....	....	....	....	....
	Hershey Bears	AHL	46	16	24	40	....	....	....	279	....	....	....	....	....	....	....	....	....	....	14	3	5	8	*87	....	....	....
1980-81	Hershey Bears	AHL	4	1	1	2	....	....	....	74	....	....	....	....	....	....	....	....	....	....	....	....	....	....	....	....	....	....
	Birmingham Bulls	CHL	19	5	7	12	....	....	....	161	....	....	....	....	....	....	....	....	....	....	....	....	....	....	....	....	....	....
	Pittsburgh Penguins	**NHL**	**25**	**1**	**0**	**1**	**1**	**0**	**1**	**143**	**0**	**0**	**0**	**16**	**6.3**	**1**	**0**	**5**	**0**	**–4**	**5**	**0**	**1**	**1**	**4**	**0**	**0**	**0**
1981-82	**Pittsburgh Penguins**	**NHL**	**16**	**0**	**0**	**0**	**0**	**0**	**0**	**55**	**0**	**0**	**0**	**1**	**0.0**	**1**	**0**	**3**	**0**	**–2**	....	....	....	....	....	....	....	....
	Erie Blades	AHL	29	7	15	22	....	....	....	185	....	....	....	....	....	....	....	....	....	....	....	....	....	....	....	....	....	....
1982-83	**Pittsburgh Penguins**	**NHL**	**40**	**5**	**4**	**9**	**4**	**3**	**7**	**128**	**0**	**0**	**0**	**35**	**14.3**	**10**	**1**	**28**	**2**	**–17**	....	....	....	....	....	....	....	....
	Baltimore Skipjacks	AHL	38	14	17	31	....	....	....	136	....	....	....	....	....	....	....	....	....	....	....	....	....	....	....	....	....	....
1983-84	**Pittsburgh Penguins**	**NHL**	**47**	**4**	**13**	**17**	**3**	**9**	**12**	**297**	**1**	**0**	**1**	**40**	**10.0**	**24**	**5**	**32**	**4**	**–9**	....	....	....	....	....	....	....	....
	Baltimore Skipjacks	AHL	30	12	13	25	....	....	....	47	....	....	....	....	....	....	....	....	....	....	....	....	....	....	....	....	....	....
1984-85	**Pittsburgh Penguins**	**NHL**	**56**	**10**	**9**	**19**	**8**	**6**	**14**	**209**	**0**	**0**	**0**	**52**	**19.2**	**30**	**1**	**38**	**3**	**–6**	....	....	....	....	....	....	....	....
	Baltimore Skipjacks	AHL	22	9	17	26	....	....	....	60	....	....	....	....	....	....	....	....	....	....	....	....	....	....	....	....	....	....
1985-86	Baltimore Skipjacks	AHL	76	19	34	53	....	....	....	340	....	....	....	....	....	....	....	....	....	....	....	....	....	....	....	....	....	....
1986-87	Baltimore Skipjacks	AHL	66	15	23	38	....	....	....	285	....	....	....	....	....	....	....	....	....	....	....	....	....	....	....	....	....	....
	NHL Totals		**221**	**23**	**30**	**53**	**19**	**21**	**40**	**1008**	**2**	**0**	**2**	**165**	**13.9**	**78**	**8**	**128**	**9**		**5**	**0**	**1**	**1**	**4**	**0**	**0**	**0**

Signed as a free agent by **Washington**, December 4, 1978. Traded to **Pittsburgh** by **Washington** for Pittsburgh's 5th round choice (Peter Sidorkiewicz) in 1981 Entry Draft, January 2, 1981.

● **RITCHIE, BOB** Bob Ritchie LW – L. 5'10", 170 lbs. b: Laverlochere, Que., 2/20/1955. Philadelphia's 2nd choice, 54th overall, in 1975 Amateur Draft.

			REGULAR SEASON																		PLAYOFFS							
Season	Club	League	GP	G	A	Pts	AG	AA	APts	PIM	PP	SH	GW	S	%	TGF	PGF	TGA	PGA	+/–	GP	G	A	Pts	PIM	PP	SH	GW
1971-72	Sorel Black Hawks	QMJHL	62	18	24	42	....	....	....	31	....	....	....	....	....	....	....	....	....	....	4	1	1	2	15	....	....	....
1972-73	Sorel Black Hawks	QMJHL	50	13	30	43	....	....	....	20	....	....	....	....	....	....	....	....	....	....	....	....	....	....	....	....	....	....
1973-74	Sorel Black Hawks	QMJHL	70	37	58	95	....	....	....	23	....	....	....	....	....	....	....	....	....	....	....	....	....	....	....	....	....	....
1974-75	Sorel Black Hawks	QMJHL	72	55	56	111	....	....	....	48	....	....	....	....	....	....	....	....	....	....	....	....	....	....	....	....	....	....
1975-76	Richmond Robins	AHL	42	12	10	22	....	....	....	19	....	....	....	....	....	....	....	....	....	....	....	....	....	....	....	....	....	....
1976-77	**Philadelphia Flyers**	**NHL**	**1**	**0**	**0**	**0**	**0**	**0**	**0**	**0**	**0**	**0**	**0**	**1**	**0.0**	**0**	**0**	**0**	**0**	**0**	....	....	....	....	....	....	....	....
	Springfield Indians	AHL	54	19	25	44	....	....	....	20	....	....	....	....	....	....	....	....	....	....	....	....	....	....	....	....	....	....
	Detroit Red Wings	**NHL**	**17**	**6**	**2**	**8**	**6**	**2**	**8**	**10**	**1**	**0**	**0**	**33**	**18.2**	**12**	**3**	**25**	**3**	**–13**	....	....	....	....	....	....	....	....
1977-78	**Detroit Red Wings**	**NHL**	**11**	**2**	**2**	**4**	**2**	**2**	**4**	**0**	**1**	**0**	**0**	**18**	**11.1**	**5**	**2**	**4**	**0**	**–1**	....	....	....	....	....	....	....	....
	Kansas City Red Wings	CHL	52	15	21	36	....	....	....	16	....	....	....	....	....	....	....	....	....	....	....	....	....	....	....	....	....	....
	NHL Totals		**29**	**8**	**4**	**12**	**8**	**4**	**12**	**10**	**2**	**0**	**0**	**52**	**15.4**	**17**	**5**	**29**	**3**		....	....	....	....	....	....	....	....

Traded to **Detroit** by **Philadelphia** with Terry Murray, Steve Coates and Dave Kelly for Rick Lapointe and Mike Korney, February 17, 1977.

● **RIVARD, BOB** Bob Rivard C/LW – L. 5'8", 155 lbs. b: Sherbrooke, Que., 8/1/1939.

Season	Club	League	GP	G	A	Pts	AG	AA	APts	PIM	PP	SH	GW	S	%	TGF	PGF	TGA	PGA	+/–	GP	G	A	Pts	PIM	PP	SH	GW
1958-59	Peterborough Petes	OHA	10	3	2	5	....	....	....	4	....	....	....	....	....	....	....	....	....	....	19	0	2	2	0	....	....	....
1959-60	Peterborough Petes	OHA	48	22	31	53	....	....	....	18	....	....	....	....	....	....	....	....	....	....	12	8	11	19	10	....	....	....
	Montreal Royals	EPHL	....	....	....	....	....	....	....	....	....	....	....	....	....	....	....	....	....	....	4	0	0	0	2	....	....	....
1960-61	Toledo–Indianapolis	IHL	40	20	25	45	....	....	....	23	....	....	....	....	....	....	....	....	....	....	....	....	....	....	....	....	....	....
1961-62	Indianapolis Chiefs	IHL	68	40	51	91	....	....	....	33	....	....	....	....	....	....	....	....	....	....	....	....	....	....	....	....	....	....
1962-63	Fort Wayne Komets	IHL	70	20	36	56	....	....	....	25	....	....	....	....	....	....	....	....	....	....	11	8	2	10	6	....	....	....
1963-64	Fort Wayne Komets	IHL	70	34	62	96	....	....	....	38	....	....	....	....	....	....	....	....	....	....	12	3	11	14	4	....	....	....
1964-65	Fort Wayne Komets	IHL	70	46	70	116	....	....	....	44	....	....	....	....	....	....	....	....	....	....	9	7	8	15	2	....	....	....
1965-66	Fort Wayne Komets	IHL	70	42	*91	*133	....	....	....	32	....	....	....	....	....	....	....	....	....	....	6	4	5	9	2	....	....	....
1966-67	Quebec Aces	AHL	71	22	40	62	....	....	....	22	....	....	....	....	....	....	....	....	....	....	5	3	2	5	0	....	....	....
1967-68	**Pittsburgh Penguins**	**NHL**	**27**	**5**	**12**	**17**	**6**	**13**	**19**	**4**	**1**	**0**	**1**	**62**	**8.1**	**21**	**4**	**19**	**2**	**0**	....	....	....	....	....	....	....	....
	Baltimore Clippers	AHL	41	14	24	38	....	....	....	12	....	....	....	....	....	....	....	....	....	....	....	....	....	....	....	....	....	....
1968-69	Quebec–Baltimore	AHL	73	20	37	57	....	....	....	40	....	....	....	....	....	....	....	....	....	....	4	0	3	3	2	....	....	....
1969-70	Baltimore Clippers	AHL	68	21	35	56	....	....	....	16	....	....	....	....	....	....	....	....	....	....	5	2	3	5	0	....	....	....
1970-71	Baltimore Clippers	AHL	68	26	16	42	....	....	....	16	....	....	....	....	....	....	....	....	....	....	6	1	2	3	6	....	....	....
1971-72	Baltimore Clippers	AHL	75	23	35	58	....	....	....	18	....	....	....	....	....	....	....	....	....	....	18	*10	*15	*25	8	....	....	....
1972-73	Baltimore Clippers	AHL	76	25	50	75	....	....	....	28	....	....	....	....	....	....	....	....	....	....	....	....	....	....	....	....	....	....
1973-74	Baltimore Clippers	AHL	76	36	56	92	....	....	....	48	....	....	....	....	....	....	....	....	....	....	9	4	5	9	0	....	....	....
1974-75	Baltimore Clippers	AHL	46	14	23	37	....	....	....	26	....	....	....	....	....	....	....	....	....	....	....	....	....	....	....	....	....	....
	Fort Wayne Komets	IHL	24	7	14	21	....	....	....	16	....	....	....	....	....	....	....	....	....	....	....	....	....	....	....	....	....	....
1975-76	Lindsay Lancers	OHA Sr.	30	12	17	29	....	....	....	14	....	....	....	....	....	....	....	....	....	....	....	....	....	....	....	....	....	....
	NHL Totals		**27**	**5**	**12**	**17**	**6**	**13**	**19**	**4**	**1**	**0**	**1**	**62**	**8.1**	**21**	**4**	**19**	**2**		....	....	....	....	....	....	....	....

IHL First All-Star Team (1965) • IHL Second All-Star Team (1966) • Won Leo P. Lamoureux Memorial Trophy (Top Scorer - IHL) (1966) • Won Dudley "Red" Garrett Memorial Award (Top Rookie - AHL) (1967)

Claimed by **Pittsburgh** from **Montreal** in Expansion Draft, June 6, 1967.

● **RIVERS, JAMIE** Jamie Rivers D – L. 6', 190 lbs. b: Ottawa, Ont., 3/16/1975. St. Louis' 2nd choice, 63rd overall, in 1993 Entry Draft.

Season	Club	League	GP	G	A	Pts	AG	AA	APts	PIM	PP	SH	GW	S	%	TGF	PGF	TGA	PGA	+/–	GP	G	A	Pts	PIM	PP	SH	GW
1991-92	Sudbury Wolves	OHL	55	3	13	16	....	....	....	20	....	....	....	....	....	....	....	....	....	....	8	0	0	0	0	....	....	....
1992-93	Sudbury Wolves	OHL	62	12	43	55	....	....	....	20	....	....	....	....	....	....	....	....	....	....	14	7	19	26	4	....	....	....
1993-94	Sudbury Wolves	OHL	65	32	*89	121	....	....	....	58	....	....	....	....	....	....	....	....	....	....	10	1	9	10	14	....	....	....
1994-95	Sudbury Wolves	OHL	46	9	56	65	....	....	....	30	....	....	....	....	....	....	....	....	....	....	18	7	26	33	22	....	....	....
	Canada	WJC-A	7	3	3	6	....	....	....	2	....	....	....	....	....	....	....	....	....	....	....	....	....	....	....	....	....	....
1995-96	**St. Louis Blues**	**NHL**	**3**	**0**	**0**	**0**	**0**	**0**	**0**	**2**	**0**	**0**	**0**	**5**	**0.0**	**0**	**0**	**1**	**0**	**–1**	....	....	....	....	....	....	....	....
	Worcester IceCats	AHL	75	7	45	52	....	....	....	130	....	....	....	....	....	....	....	....	....	....	4	0	1	1	4	....	....	....
1996-97	**St. Louis Blues**	**NHL**	**15**	**2**	**5**	**7**	**2**	**4**	**6**	**6**	**1**	**0**	**0**	**9**	**22.2**	**11**	**5**	**11**	**1**	**–4**	....	....	....	....	....	....	....	....
	Worcester IceCats	AHL	63	8	35	43	....	....	....	83	....	....	....	....	....	....	....	....	....	....	5	1	2	3	14	....	....	....
1997-98	**St. Louis Blues**	**NHL**	**59**	**2**	**4**	**6**	**2**	**4**	**6**	**36**	**1**	**0**	**1**	**53**	**3.8**	**31**	**8**	**18**	**0**	**+5**	....	....	....	....	....	....	....	....
	NHL Totals		**77**	**4**	**9**	**13**	**4**	**8**	**12**	**44**	**2**	**0**	**1**	**67**	**6.0**	**42**	**13**	**30**	**1**		....	....	....	....	....	....	....	....

OHL First All-Star Team (1994) • Canadian Major Junior Second All-Star Team (1994) • OHL Second All-Star Team (1995) • AHL Second All-Star Team (1997)

● **RIVERS, SHAWN** Shawn Rivers D – L. 5'10", 185 lbs. b: Ottawa, Ont., 1/30/1971.

Season	Club	League	GP	G	A	Pts	AG	AA	APts	PIM	PP	SH	GW	S	%	TGF	PGF	TGA	PGA	+/–	GP	G	A	Pts	PIM	PP	SH	GW
1988-89	St. Lawrence University	ECAC	36	3	23	26	....	....	....	20	....	....	....	....	....	....	....	....	....	....	....	....	....	....	....	....	....	....
1989-90	St. Lawrence University	ECAC	26	3	14	17	....	....	....	29	....	....	....	....	....	....	....	....	....	....	....	....	....	....	....	....	....	....
1990-91	Sudbury Wolves	OHL	66	18	33	51	....	....	....	43	....	....	....	....	....	....	....	....	....	....	5	2	7	9	0	....	....	....
1991-92	Sudbury Wolves	OHL	64	26	54	80	....	....	....	34	....	....	....	....	....	....	....	....	....	....	11	0	4	4	10	....	....	....
1992-93	**Tampa Bay Lightning**	**NHL**	**4**	**0**	**2**	**2**	**0**	**1**	**1**	**2**	**0**	**0**	**0**	**3**	**0.0**	**2**	**0**	**4**	**0**	**–2**	....	....	....	....	....	....	....	....
	Atlanta Knights	IHL	78	9	34	43	....	....	....	101	....	....	....	....	....	....	....	....	....	....	9	1	3	4	8	....	....	....
1993-94	Atlanta Knights	IHL	76	6	30	36	....	....	....	88	....	....	....	....	....	....	....	....	....	....	12	1	4	5	21	....	....	....
1994-95	Chicago Wolves	IHL	68	8	29	37	....	....	....	69	....	....	....	....	....	....	....	....	....	....	3	0	1	1	0	....	....	....
1995-96	Chicago Wolves	IHL	21	3	4	7	....	....	....	22	....	....	....	....	....	....	....	....	....	....	....	....	....	....	....	....	....	....
	Atlanta Knights	IHL	45	2	16	18	....	....	....	22	....	....	....	....	....	....	....	....	....	....	....	....	....	....	....	....	....	....
	Syracuse Crunch	AHL	5	0	2	2	....	....	....	2	....	....	....	....	....	....	....	....	....	....	16	1	6	7	14	....	....	....
1996-97	Augsburg Panthers	Germany	48	8	20	28	....	....	....	22	....	....	....	....	....	....	....	....	....	....	4	1	2	3	0	....	....	....
1997-98	Lake Charles Ice Pirates	WPHL	5	3	3	6	....	....	....	2	....	....	....	....	....	....	....	....	....	....	....	....	....	....	....	....	....	....
	Springfield Falcons	AHL	3	0	0	0	....	....	....	0	....	....	....	....	....	....	....	....	....	....	....	....	....	....	....	....	....	....
	San Antonio Dragons	IHL	14	2	4	6	....	....	....	6	....	....	....	....	....	....	....	....	....	....	....	....	....	....	....	....	....	....
	NHL Totals		**4**	**0**	**2**	**2**	**0**	**1**	**1**	**2**	**0**	**0**	**0**	**3**	**0.0**	**2**	**0**	**4**	**0**		....	....	....	....	....	....	....	....

Signed as a free agent by **Tampa Bay**, June 29, 1992.

● **RIVERS, WAYNE** Wayne Rivers RW – R. 5'9", 177 lbs. b: Hamilton, Ont., 2/1/1942.

Season	Club	League	GP	G	A	Pts	AG	AA	APts	PIM	PP	SH	GW	S	%	TGF	PGF	TGA	PGA	+/–	GP	G	A	Pts	PIM	PP	SH	GW
1959-60	Hamilton Tiger Cubs	OHA	2	0	0	0	....	....	....	2	....	....	....	....	....	....	....	....	....	....	....	....	....	....	....	....	....	....
1960-61	Hamilton Red Wings	OHA	41	13	18	31	....	....	....	38	....	....	....	....	....	....	....	....	....	....	4	0	0	0	21	....	....	....
1961-62	Hamilton Red Wings	OHA	48	14	15	29	....	....	....	55	....	....	....	....	....	....	....	....	....	....	10	2	1	3	20	....	....	....
	Detroit Red Wings	**NHL**	**2**	**0**	**0**	**0**	**0**	**0**	**0**	**0**	....	....	....	....	....	....	....	....	....	....	....	....	....	....	....	....	....	....
	Hershey Bears	AHL	1	0	0	0	....	....	....	0	....	....	....	....	....	....	....	....	....	....	....	....	....	....	....	....	....	....
1962-63	Hershey Bears	AHL	52	15	31	46	....	....	....	42	....	....	....	....	....	....	....	....	....	....	12	0	0	0	13	....	....	....
1963-64	**Boston Bruins**	**NHL**	**12**	**2**	**7**	**9**	**3**	**8**	**11**	**6**	....	....	....	....	....	....	....	....	....	....	....	....	....	....	....	....	....	....
	Hershey Bears	AHL	36	20	6	26	....	....	....	24	....	....	....	....	....	....	....	....	....	....	....	....	....	....	....	....	....	....
1964-65	**Boston Bruins**	**NHL**	**58**	**6**	**17**	**23**	**8**	**18**	**26**	**72**	....	....	....	....	....	....	....	....	....	....	....	....	....	....	....	....	....	....
	Hershey Bears	AHL	14	6	8	14	....	....	....	0	....	....	....	....	....	....	....	....	....	....	....	....	....	....	....	....	....	....
1965-66	**Boston Bruins**	**NHL**	**2**	**1**	**1**	**2**	**1**	**1**	**2**	**2**	....	....	....	....	....	....	....	....	....	....	....	....	....	....	....	....	....	....
	Hershey Bears	AHL	65	37	30	67	....	....	....	81	....	....	....	....	....	....	....	....	....	....	3	1	0	1	2	....	....	....
1966-67	**Boston Bruins**	**NHL**	**8**	**2**	**1**	**3**	**2**	**1**	**3**	**6**	....	....	....	....	....	....	....	....	....	....	....	....	....	....	....	....	....	....
	Hershey Bears	AHL	54	30	37	67	....	....	....	59	....	....	....	....	....	....	....	....	....	....	5	0	2	2	4	....	....	....
1967-68	**St. Louis Blues**	**NHL**	**22**	**4**	**4**	**8**	**5**	**4**	**9**	**8**	**1**	**0**	**0**	**53**	**7.5**	**16**	**4**	**15**	**1**	**–2**	....	....	....	....	....	....	....	....
	Kansas City Blues	CHL	50	25	37	62	....	....	....	41	....	....	....	....	....	....	....	....	....	....	7	*6	1	7	9	....	....	....
1968-69	**New York Rangers**	**NHL**	**4**	**0**	**0**	**0**	**0**	**0**	**0**	**0**	**0**	**0**	**0**	**1**	**0.0**	**0**	**0**	**1**	**0**	**–1**	....	....	....	....	....	....	....	....
	Buffalo Bisons	AHL	67	30	37	67	....	....	....	35	....	....	....	....	....	....	....	....	....	....	6	3	5	8	0	....	....	....
1969-70	Buffalo Bisons	AHL	68	27	34	61	....	....	....	58	....	....	....	....	....	....	....	....	....	....	14	3	9	12	6	....	....	....
	Omaha Knights	CHL	....	....	....	....	....	....	....	....	....	....	....	....	....	....	....	....	....	....	6	3	4	7	7	....	....	....
1970-71	Baltimore Clippers	AHL	65	38	37	75	....	....	....	66	....	....	....	....	....	....	....	....	....	....	6	3	2	5	6	....	....	....
1971-72	Springfield Kings	AHL	68	*48	33	81	....	....	....	67	....	....	....	....	....	....	....	....	....	....	5	0	3	3	4	....	....	....
1972-73	New York Raiders	WHA	75	37	40	77	....	....	....	47	....	....	....	....	....	....	....	....	....	....	....	....	....	....	....	....	....	....
1973-74	New York-New Jersey	WHA	73	30	27	57	....	....	....	20	....	....	....	....	....	....	....	....	....	....	....	....	....	....	....	....	....	....
1974-75	San Diego Mariners	WHA	78	54	53	107	....	....	....	52	....	....	....	....	....	....	....	....	....	....	5	3	1	4	8	....	....	....

			REGULAR SEASON																		PLAYOFFS							
Season	Club	League	GP	G	A	Pts	AG	AA	APts	PIM	PP	SH	GW	S	%	TGF	PGF	TGA	PGA	+/–	GP	G	A	Pts	PIM	PP	SH	GW
1975-76	San Diego Mariners	WHA	71	19	25	44	....	....	....	24	....	....	....	....	....	....	....	....	....	....	11	4	4	8	4	....	....	....
1976-77	San Diego Mariners	WHA	60	18	31	49	....	....	....	40	....	....	....	....	....	....	....	....	....	....	7	1	1	2	2	....	....	....
1977-78	San Francisco Shamrocks	PHL	32	11	22	33	....	....	....	7	....	....	....	....	....	....	....	....	....	....	....	....	....	....	....	....	....	....
1978-79	San Francisco Shamrocks	PHL	15	4	5	9	....	....	....	25	....	....	....	....	....	....	....	....	....	....	....	....	....	....	....	....	....	....
	NHL Totals		108	15	30	45	19	32	51	94	1	0	0	54	27.8	16	4	16	1		....	....	....	....	....	....	....	....
	Other Major League Totals		357	158	176	334	....	....	....	183	....	....	....	....	....	....	....	....	....	....	23	8	6	14	14	....	....	....

AHL Second All-Star Team (1967, 1971) • CHL Second All-Star Team (1968) • AHL First All-Star Team (1972)

Claimed by **Boston** from **Detroit** in Intra-League Draft, June 4, 1963. Claimed by **St. Louis** from **Boston** in Expansion Draft, June 6, 1967. Traded to **NY Rangers** by **St. Louis** with Don Caley for Camille Henry, Bill Plager and Robbie Irons, June 13, 1968. Selected by **Ontario-Ottawa** (WHA) in 1972 WHA General Player Draft, February 12, 1972. Traded to **NY Raiders** (WHA) by **Ottawa** (WHA) for future considerations, July, 1972. Transferred to **San Diego** (WHA) after **New York-New Jersey** (WHA) franchise relocated, April 30, 1974.

• RIVET, CRAIG

Craig Rivet D – R. 6'1", 190 lbs. b: North Bay, Ont., 9/13/1974. Montreal's 4th choice, 68th overall, in 1992 Entry Draft.

Season	Club	League	GP	G	A	Pts	AG	AA	APts	PIM	PP	SH	GW	S	%	TGF	PGF	TGA	PGA	+/–	GP	G	A	Pts	PIM	PP	SH	GW
1991-92	Kingston Frontenacs	OHL	66	5	21	26	....	....	....	97	....	....	....	....	....	....	....	....	....	....	....	....	....	....	....	....	....	....
1992-93	Kingston Frontenacs	OHL	64	19	55	74	....	....	....	117	....	....	....	....	....	....	....	....	....	....	16	5	7	12	39	....	....	....
1993-94	Kingston Frontenacs	OHL	61	12	52	64	....	....	....	100	....	....	....	....	....	....	....	....	....	....	6	0	3	3	6	....	....	....
	Fredericton Canadiens	AHL	4	0	2	2	....	....	....	2	....	....	....	....	....	....	....	....	....	....	....	....	....	....	....	....	....	....
1994-95	Fredericton Canadiens	AHL	78	5	27	32	....	....	....	126	....	....	....	....	....	....	....	....	....	....	12	0	4	4	17	....	....	....
	Montreal Canadiens	NHL	5	0	1	1	0	1	1	5	0	0	0	2	0.0	2	0	0	0	+2	....	....	....	....	....	....	....	....
1995-96	Montreal Canadiens	NHL	19	1	4	5	1	3	4	54	0	0	0	9	11.1	11	0	7	0	+4	....	....	....	....	....	....	....	....
	Fredericton Canadiens	AHL	49	5	18	23	....	....	....	189	....	....	....	....	....	....	....	....	....	....	6	0	0	0	12	....	....	....
1996-97	Montreal Canadiens	NHL	35	0	4	4	0	4	4	54	0	0	0	24	0.0	27	0	23	3	+7	5	0	1	1	14	0	0	0
	Fredericton Canadiens	AHL	23	3	12	15	....	....	....	99	....	....	....	....	....	....	....	....	....	....	....	....	....	....	....	....	....	....
1997-98	Montreal Canadiens	NHL	61	0	2	2	0	2	2	93	0	0	0	26	0.0	21	0	32	8	–3	5	0	0	0	2	0	0	0
	NHL Totals		120	1	11	12	1	10	11	206	0	0	0	61	1.6	61	0	62	11		10	0	1	1	16	0	0	0

• RIZZUTO, GARTH

Garth Rizzuto C – L. 5'10", 175 lbs. b: Trail, B.C., 9/11/1947.

Season	Club	League	GP	G	A	Pts	AG	AA	APts	PIM	PP	SH	GW	S	%	TGF	PGF	TGA	PGA	+/–	GP	G	A	Pts	PIM	PP	SH	GW
1965-66	Moose Jaw Canucks	SJHL	22	5	11	16	....	....	....	16	....	....	....	....	....	....	....	....	....	....	5	0	2	2	14	....	....	....
1966-67	Moose Jaw Canucks	SJHL	55	24	31	55	....	....	....	133	....	....	....	....	....	....	....	....	....	....	14	7	16	23	59	....	....	....
1967-68	Dallas Black Hawks	CHL	47	5	14	19	....	....	....	17	....	....	....	....	....	....	....	....	....	....	5	2	1	3	4	....	....	....
1968-69	Dallas Black Hawks	CHL	72	30	29	59	....	....	....	71	....	....	....	....	....	....	....	....	....	....	11	2	4	6	10	....	....	....
1969-70	Dallas Black Hawks	CHL	72	20	42	62	....	....	....	55	....	....	....	....	....	....	....	....	....	....	....	....	....	....	....	....	....	....
1970-71	Vancouver Canucks	NHL	37	3	4	7	3	4	7	16	1	0	0	33	9.1	9	2	26	3	–16	....	....	....	....	....	....	....	....
	Rochester Americans	AHL	22	8	12	20	....	....	....	56	....	....	....	....	....	....	....	....	....	....	....	....	....	....	....	....	....	....
1971-72	Seattle Totems	WHL	23	4	15	19	....	....	....	36	....	....	....	....	....	....	....	....	....	....	....	....	....	....	....	....	....	....
	Rochester Americans	AHL	36	6	8	14	....	....	....	11	....	....	....	....	....	....	....	....	....	....	....	....	....	....	....	....	....	....
1972-73	Winnipeg Jets	WHA	61	10	10	20	....	....	....	32	....	....	....	....	....	....	....	....	....	....	14	0	1	1	14	....	....	....
1973-74	Winnipeg Jets	WHA	41	3	4	7	....	....	....	8	....	....	....	....	....	....	....	....	....	....	....	....	....	....	....	....	....	....
1974-75	Nelson Maple Leafs	WIHL	6	4	7	11	....	....	....	34	....	....	....	....	....	....	....	....	....	....	....	....	....	....	....	....	....	....
	NHL Totals		37	3	4	7	3	4	7	16	1	0	0	33	9.1	9	2	26	3		....	....	....	....	....	....	....	....
	Other Major League Totals		102	13	14	27	....	....	....	40	....	....	....	....	....	....	....	....	....	....	14	0	1	1	14	....	....	....

Claimed by **Vancouver** from **Chicago** in Expansion Draft, June 10, 1970. Signed as a free agent by **Winnipeg** (WHA), August, 1972.

• ROBERGE, MARIO

Mario Roberge LW – L. 5'11", 193 lbs. b: Quebec City, Que., 1/25/1964.

Season	Club	League	GP	G	A	Pts	AG	AA	APts	PIM	PP	SH	GW	S	%	TGF	PGF	TGA	PGA	+/–	GP	G	A	Pts	PIM	PP	SH	GW
1981-82	Quebec Remparts	QMJHL	8	0	3	3	....	....	....	2	....	....	....	....	....	....	....	....	....	....	....	....	....	....	....	....	....	....
1982-83	Quebec Remparts	QMJHL	69	3	27	30	....	....	....	153	....	....	....	....	....	....	....	....	....	....	....	....	....	....	....	....	....	....
1983-84	Quebec Remparts	QMJHL	60	12	28	40	....	....	....	253	....	....	....	....	....	....	....	....	....	....	5	0	1	1	22	....	....	....
1984-85	Riviere-Du-Loup 3 L's	RHL	STATISTICS NOT AVAILABLE																									
1985-86	Riviere-Du-Loup 3 L's	RHL	31	16	41	57	....	....	....	94	....	....	....	....	....	....	....	....	....	....	....	....	....	....	....	....	....	....
	St. John's Capitals	Nfld.	2	1	0	1	....	....	....	2	....	....	....	....	....	....	....	....	....	....	....	....	....	....	....	....	....	....
1986-87	Virginia Lancers	ACHL	52	25	43	68	....	....	....	178	....	....	....	....	....	....	....	....	....	....	12	5	9	14	62	....	....	....
1987-88	Port-Aux-Basques Mariners	Nfld.	37	24	64	88	....	....	....	152	....	....	....	....	....	....	....	....	....	....	....	....	....	....	....	....	....	....
1988-89	Sherbrooke Canadiens	AHL	58	4	9	13	....	....	....	249	....	....	....	....	....	....	....	....	....	....	6	0	2	2	8	....	....	....
1989-90	Sherbrooke Canadiens	AHL	73	13	27	40	....	....	....	247	....	....	....	....	....	....	....	....	....	....	12	5	2	7	53	....	....	....
1990-91	Montreal Canadiens	NHL	5	0	0	0	0	0	0	21	0	0	0	2	0.0	0	0	2	0	–2	12	0	0	0	24	0	0	0
	Fredericton Canadiens	AHL	68	12	27	39	....	....	....	*365	....	....	....	....	....	....	....	....	....	....	2	0	2	2	5	....	....	....
1991-92	Montreal Canadiens	NHL	20	2	1	3	2	1	3	62	0	0	0	7	28.6	4	0	1	0	+3	....	....	....	....	....	....	....	....
	Fredericton Canadiens	AHL	6	1	2	3	....	....	....	20	....	....	....	....	....	....	....	....	....	....	7	0	2	2	20	....	....	....
1992-93	Montreal Canadiens	NHL	50	4	4	8	3	3	6	142	0	0	3	23	17.4	14	1	11	0	+2	3	0	0	0	0	0	0	0
1993-94	Montreal Canadiens	NHL	28	1	2	3	1	2	3	55	0	0	0	5	20.0	4	0	6	0	–2	....	....	....	....	....	....	....	....
1994-95	Montreal Canadiens	NHL	9	0	0	0	0	0	0	34	0	0	0	0	0.0	0	0	2	0	–2	....	....	....	....	....	....	....	....
	Fredericton Canadiens	AHL	28	8	12	20	....	....	....	91	....	....	....	....	....	....	....	....	....	....	6	1	1	2	6	....	....	....
1995-96	Fredericton Canadiens	AHL	74	9	24	33	....	....	....	205	....	....	....	....	....	....	....	....	....	....	4	0	2	2	14	....	....	....
	NHL Totals		112	7	7	14	6	6	12	314	0	0	3	37	18.9	22	1	22	0		15	0	0	0	24	0	0	0

Signed as a free agent by **Montreal**, October 5, 1988.

• ROBERGE, SERGE

Serge Roberge RW – R. 6'1", 195 lbs. b: Quebec City, Que., 3/31/1965.

Season	Club	League	GP	G	A	Pts	AG	AA	APts	PIM	PP	SH	GW	S	%	TGF	PGF	TGA	PGA	+/–	GP	G	A	Pts	PIM	PP	SH	GW
1982-83	Quebec Remparts	QMJHL	9	0	0	0	....	....	....	30	....	....	....	....	....	....	....	....	....	....	....	....	....	....	....	....	....	....
	Hull Olympiques	QMJHL	22	0	4	4	....	....	....	115	....	....	....	....	....	....	....	....	....	....	....	....	....	....	....	....	....	....
1983-84	Drummondville Voltigeurs	QMJHL	58	1	7	8	....	....	....	287	....	....	....	....	....	....	....	....	....	....	10	0	2	2	*105	....	....	....
1984-85	Drummondville Voltigeurs	QMJHL	45	8	19	27	....	....	....	299	....	....	....	....	....	....	....	....	....	....	....	....	....	....	....	....	....	....
1985-86	Riviere-du-Loup 3 L's	RHL	31	6	8	14	....	....	....	180	....	....	....	....	....	....	....	....	....	....	....	....	....	....	....	....	....	....
1986-87	Virginia Lancers	ACHL	49	9	16	25	....	....	....	*353	....	....	....	....	....	....	....	....	....	....	12	4	2	6	*104	....	....	....
1987-88	Sherbrooke Canadiens	AHL	30	0	1	1	....	....	....	130	....	....	....	....	....	....	....	....	....	....	5	0	0	0	21	....	....	....
1988-89	Sherbrooke Canadiens	AHL	65	5	7	12	....	....	....	352	....	....	....	....	....	....	....	....	....	....	6	0	1	1	10	....	....	....
1989-90	Sherbrooke Canadiens	AHL	66	8	5	13	....	....	....	*343	....	....	....	....	....	....	....	....	....	....	12	2	0	2	44	....	....	....
1990-91	Quebec Nordiques	NHL	9	0	0	0	0	0	0	24	0	0	0	0	0.0	1	0	1	0	0	....	....	....	....	....	....	....	....
	Halifax Citadels	AHL	52	0	5	5	....	....	....	152	....	....	....	....	....	....	....	....	....	....	....	....	....	....	....	....	....	....
1991-92	Halifax Citadels	AHL	66	2	8	10	....	....	....	319	....	....	....	....	....	....	....	....	....	....	....	....	....	....	....	....	....	....
1992-93	Halifax Citadels	AHL	16	2	2	4	....	....	....	34	....	....	....	....	....	....	....	....	....	....	....	....	....	....	....	....	....	....
	Utica Devils	AHL	28	0	3	3	....	....	....	85	....	....	....	....	....	....	....	....	....	....	1	0	0	0	0	....	....	....
1993-94	Cape Breton Oilers	AHL	51	3	5	8	....	....	....	130	....	....	....	....	....	....	....	....	....	....	1	0	0	0	0	....	....	....
1994-95	Cornwall Aces	AHL	73	0	3	3	....	....	....	342	....	....	....	....	....	....	....	....	....	....	11	0	0	0	29	....	....	....
1995-96	Rochester Americans	AHL	32	0	1	1	....	....	....	42	....	....	....	....	....	....	....	....	....	....	....	....	....	....	....	....	....	....
	Fredericton Canadiens	AHL	14	1	1	2	....	....	....	45	....	....	....	....	....	....	....	....	....	....	7	0	0	0	10	....	....	....
1996-97	Quebec Rafales	IHL	61	2	4	6	....	....	....	273	....	....	....	....	....	....	....	....	....	....	....	....	....	....	....	....	....	....
1997-98	Quebec Rafales	IHL	35	2	0	2	....	....	....	115	....	....	....	....	....	....	....	....	....	....	....	....	....	....	....	....	....	....
	NHL Totals		9	0	0	0	0	0	0	24	0	0	0	0	0.0	1	0	1	0		....	....	....	....	....	....	....	....

Signed as a free agent by **Montreal**, January 25, 1988. Signed as a free agent by **Quebec**, December 28, 1990.

• ROBERT, RENE

Rene Robert RW – R. 5'10", 184 lbs. b: Trois Rivieres, Que., 12/31/1948.

Season	Club	League	GP	G	A	Pts	AG	AA	APts	PIM	PP	SH	GW	S	%	TGF	PGF	TGA	PGA	+/–	GP	G	A	Pts	PIM	PP	SH	GW
1967-68	Trois Rivieres Reds	QJHL	STATISTICS NOT AVAILABLE																									
	Tulsa Oilers	CHL	3	0	2	2	....	....	....	0	....	....	....	....	....	....	....	....	....	....	2	0	4	4	14	....	....	....
1968-69	Tulsa Oilers	CHL	59	21	30	51	....	....	....	57	....	....	....	....	....	....	....	....	....	....	7	4	3	7	2	....	....	....
1969-70	Vancouver Canucks	WHL	5	0	0	0	....	....	....	2	....	....	....	....	....	....	....	....	....	....	....	....	....	....	....	....	....	....
	Rochester Americans	AHL	49	23	40	63	....	....	....	57	....	....	....	....	....	....	....	....	....	....	....	....	....	....	....	....	....	....
1970-71	Toronto Maple Leafs	NHL	5	0	0	0	0	0	0	0	0	0	0	8	0.0	1	0	3	0	–2	....	....	....	....	....	....	....	....
	Tulsa Oilers	CHL	58	26	36	62	....	....	....	85	....	....	....	....	....	....	....	....	....	....	....	....	....	....	....	....	....	....
	Phoenix Roadrunners	WHL	7	4	3	7	....	....	....	6	....	....	....	....	....	....	....	....	....	....	10	5	3	8	7	....	....	....
1971-72	Pittsburgh Penguins	NHL	49	7	11	18	7	10	17	42	3	0	2	71	9.9	28	12	29	2	–11	....	....	....	....	....	....	....	....
	Buffalo Sabres	NHL	12	6	3	9	6	3	9	2	3	0	0	42	14.3	15	8	12	0	–5	....	....	....	....	....	....	....	....

			REGULAR SEASON																		PLAYOFFS							
Season	Club	League	GP	G	A	Pts	AG	AA	APts	PIM	PP	SH	GW	S	%	TGF	PGF	TGA	PGA	+/-	GP	G	A	Pts	PIM	PP	SH	GW
1972-73	**Buffalo Sabres**	**NHL**	**75**	**40**	**43**	**83**	**40**	**36**	**76**	**83**	**9**	**0**	**6**	**265**	**15.1**	**119**	**43**	**60**	**0**	**+16**	**6**	**5**	**3**	**8**	**2**	**1**	**0**	**1**
1973-74	**Buffalo Sabres**	**NHL**	**76**	**21**	**44**	**65**	**21**	**38**	**59**	**71**	**3**	**0**	**5**	**245**	**8.6**	**109**	**39**	**86**	**0**	**–16**	....	....	....	....	....	....	....	....
1974-75	**Buffalo Sabres**	**NHL**	**74**	**40**	**60**	**100**	**37**	**47**	**84**	**75**	**14**	**0**	**3**	**264**	**15.2**	**145**	**65**	**77**	**3**	**+6**	**16**	**5**	**8**	**13**	**16**	**0**	**0**	**3**
1975-76	**Buffalo Sabres**	**NHL**	**72**	**35**	**52**	**87**	**33**	**41**	**74**	**53**	**11**	**0**	**4**	**273**	**12.8**	**135**	**59**	**59**	**0**	**+17**	**9**	**3**	**2**	**5**	**6**	**0**	**0**	**0**
1976-77	**Buffalo Sabres**	**NHL**	**80**	**33**	**40**	**73**	**32**	**32**	**64**	**46**	**5**	**0**	**4**	**250**	**13.2**	**120**	**41**	**52**	**0**	**+27**	**6**	**5**	**2**	**7**	**20**	**1**	**0**	**0**
1977-78	**Buffalo Sabres**	**NHL**	**67**	**25**	**48**	**73**	**24**	**39**	**63**	**25**	**7**	**0**	**4**	**209**	**12.0**	**110**	**34**	**57**	**0**	**+19**	**7**	**2**	**0**	**2**	**23**	**0**	**0**	**0**
1978-79	**Buffalo Sabres**	**NHL**	**68**	**22**	**40**	**62**	**20**	**31**	**51**	**46**	**1**	**0**	**6**	**206**	**10.7**	**86**	**35**	**63**	**0**	**–12**	**3**	**2**	**2**	**4**	**4**	**0**	**0**	**0**
1979-80	**Colorado Rockies**	**NHL**	**69**	**28**	**35**	**63**	**25**	**27**	**52**	**79**	**10**	**0**	**0**	**248**	**11.3**	**95**	**42**	**88**	**15**	**–20**	....	....	....	....	....	....	....	....
1980-81	**Colorado Rockies**	**NHL**	**28**	**8**	**11**	**19**	**7**	**8**	**15**	**30**	**4**	**0**	**0**	**66**	**12.1**	**29**	**12**	**32**	**2**	**–13**	....	....	....	....	....	....	....	....
	Toronto Maple Leafs	**NHL**	**14**	**6**	**7**	**13**	**5**	**5**	**10**	**8**	**1**	**0**	**1**	**43**	**14.0**	**22**	**10**	**9**	**2**	**+5**	**3**	**0**	**2**	**2**	**2**	**0**	**0**	**0**
1981-82	**Toronto Maple Leafs**	**NHL**	**55**	**13**	**24**	**37**	**10**	**16**	**26**	**37**	**2**	**0**	**1**	**120**	**10.8**	**59**	**26**	**58**	**14**	**–11**	....	....	....	....	....	....	....	....
	NHL Totals		**744**	**284**	**418**	**702**	**267**	**333**	**600**	**597**	**73**	**0**	**36**	**2310**	**12.3**	**1073**	**426**	**685**	**38**		**50**	**22**	**19**	**41**	**73**	**2**	**0**	**4**

NHL Second All-Star Team (1975)

Played in NHL All-Star Game (1973, 1975)

Signed as a free agent by **Toronto** (Tulsa-CHL) to five-game tryout contract, March 20, 1968. Traded to **Vancouver** (WHL) by **Toronto** with Brad Selwood for Ron Ward, May, 1969. Traded to **Toronto** by **Vancouver** (WHL) for cash, May, 1970. Claimed by **Buffalo** from **Toronto** in Intra-League Draft, June 8, 1971. Claimed by **Pittsburgh** from **Buffalo** in Intra-League Draft, June 8, 1971. Traded to **Buffalo** by **Pittsburgh** for Eddie Shack, March 4, 1972. Traded to **Colorado** by **Buffalo** for John Van Boxmeer, October 5, 1979. Traded to **Toronto** by **Colorado** for Toronto's 3rd round choice (Ullrich Heimer) in the 1981 Entry Draft, January 30, 1981.

• ROBERTO, PHIL

Phil Roberto RW – R. 6'1", 190 lbs. b: Niagara Falls, Ont., 1/1/1949.

1965-66	Niagara Falls Flyers	OHA	2	2	0	2	....	....	....	0	....	....	....	....	....	....	....	....	....	....	6	1	1	2	6	....	....	....
1966-67	Niagara Falls Flyers	OHA	14	1	0	1	....	....	....	6	....	....	....	....	....	....	....	....	....	....	....	....	....	....	....	....	....	....
1967-68	Niagara Falls Flyers	OHA	53	19	20	39	....	....	....	92	....	....	....	....	....	....	....	....	....	....	19	13	14	27	*71	....	....	....
1968-69	Niagara Falls Flyers	OHA	52	29	65	94	....	....	....	152	....	....	....	....	....	....	....	....	....	....	14	7	15	22	38	....	....	....
1969-70	**Montreal Canadiens**	**NHL**	**8**	**0**	**1**	**1**	**0**	**1**	**1**	**8**	**0**	**0**	**0**	**5**	**0.0**	**3**	**1**	**1**	**0**	**+1**	....	....	....	....	....	....	....	....
	Montreal Voyageurs	AHL	54	20	19	39	....	....	....	160	....	....	....	....	....	....	....	....	....	....	8	3	1	4	19	....	....	....
1970-71	**Montreal Canadiens**	**NHL**	**39**	**14**	**7**	**21**	**15**	**6**	**21**	**76**	**2**	**0**	**3**	**88**	**15.9**	**29**	**2**	**23**	**6**	**+10**	**15**	**0**	**1**	**1**	**36**	**0**	**0**	**0**
	Montreal Voyageurs	AHL	32	19	22	41	....	....	....	127	....	....	....	....	....	....	....	....	....	....	....	....	....	....	....	....	....	....
1971-72	**Montreal Canadiens**	**NHL**	**27**	**3**	**2**	**5**	**3**	**2**	**5**	**22**	**0**	**0**	**0**	**35**	**8.6**	**10**	**0**	**9**	**2**	**+3**	....	....	....	....	....	....	....	....
	St. Louis Blues	**NHL**	**49**	**12**	**13**	**25**	**13**	**12**	**25**	**76**	**0**	**0**	**0**	**170**	**7.1**	**40**	**3**	**44**	**6**	**–1**	**11**	**7**	**6**	**13**	**29**	**3**	**0**	**1**
1972-73	**St. Louis Blues**	**NHL**	**77**	**20**	**22**	**42**	**20**	**18**	**38**	**99**	**2**	**0**	**5**	**275**	**7.3**	**69**	**8**	**90**	**17**	**–12**	**5**	**2**	**1**	**3**	**4**	**0**	**0**	**0**
1973-74	**St. Louis Blues**	**NHL**	**15**	**1**	**1**	**2**	**1**	**1**	**2**	**10**	**0**	**0**	**0**	**14**	**7.1**	**3**	**1**	**11**	**5**	**–4**	....	....	....	....	....	....	....	....
	Denver Spurs	WHL	8	5	4	9	....	....	....	40	....	....	....	....	....	....	....	....	....	....	....	....	....	....	....	....	....	....
1974-75	**St. Louis Blues**	**NHL**	**7**	**0**	**2**	**2**	**0**	**2**	**2**	**2**	**0**	**0**	**0**	**5**	**0.0**	**3**	**1**	**7**	**2**	**–3**	....	....	....	....	....	....	....	....
	Denver Spurs	CHL	8	3	2	5	....	....	....	12	....	....	....	....	....	....	....	....	....	....	....	....	....	....	....	....	....	....
	Detroit Red Wings	**NHL**	**46**	**13**	**27**	**40**	**12**	**21**	**33**	**30**	**5**	**0**	**2**	**113**	**11.5**	**55**	**19**	**50**	**4**	**–10**	....	....	....	....	....	....	....	....
1975-76	**Detroit Red Wings**	**NHL**	**37**	**1**	**7**	**8**	**1**	**5**	**6**	**68**	**0**	**0**	**0**	**55**	**1.8**	**19**	**2**	**25**	**6**	**–2**	....	....	....	....	....	....	....	....
	Kansas City Scouts	**NHL**	**37**	**7**	**15**	**22**	**7**	**12**	**19**	**42**	**3**	**0**	**0**	**89**	**7.9**	**35**	**12**	**52**	**18**	**–11**	....	....	....	....	....	....	....	....
1976-77	**Colorado Rockies**	**NHL**	**22**	**1**	**5**	**6**	**1**	**4**	**5**	**23**	**0**	**0**	**0**	**38**	**2.6**	**8**	**0**	**25**	**6**	**–11**	....	....	....	....	....	....	....	....
	Cleveland Barons	**NHL**	**21**	**3**	**4**	**7**	**3**	**3**	**6**	**8**	**0**	**0**	**0**	**32**	**9.4**	**13**	**0**	**20**	**0**	**–7**	....	....	....	....	....	....	....	....
1977-78	Birmingham Bulls	WHA	53	8	20	28	....	....	....	91	....	....	....	....	....	....	....	....	....	....	4	1	0	1	20	....	....	....
	NHL Totals		**385**	**75**	**106**	**181**	**76**	**87**	**163**	**464**	**12**	**0**	**10**	**919**	**8.2**	**287**	**49**	**357**	**72**		**31**	**9**	**8**	**17**	**69**	**3**	**0**	**1**
	Other Major League Totals		53	8	20	28	....	....	....	91	....	....	....	....	....	....	....	....	....		4	1	0	1	20	....	....	....

OHA Second All-Star Team (1969)

Traded to **St. Louis** by **Montreal** for Jimmy Roberts, December 13, 1971. Selected by **New England** (WHA) in 1972 WHA General Player Draft, February 12, 1972. Traded to **Detroit** by **St. Louis** with St. Louis' 3rd round pick (Blair Davidson) in 1975 Amateur Draft for Red Berenson, December 30, 1974. Traded to **Kansas City** by **Detroit** for Buster Harvey, January 14, 1976. Transferred to **Colorado** after **Kansas City** franchise relocated, July 15, 1976. Signed as a free agent by **Cleveland** after securing release from **Colorado**, December 24, 1976. Signed as a free agent by **Birmingham** (WHA), July, 1977.

• ROBERTS, DAVID

David Roberts LW – L. 6', 185 lbs. b: Alameda, CA, 5/28/1970. St. Louis' 5th choice, 114th overall, in 1989 Entry Draft.

1988-89	Avon Old Farms	H.S.	25	20	48	76	....	....	....	....	....	....	....	....	....	....	....	....	....	....	....	....	....	....	....	....	....	....
1989-90	University of Michigan	CCHA	42	21	32	53	....	....	....	46	....	....	....	....	....	....	....	....	....	....	....	....	....	....	....	....	....	....
1990-91	University of Michigan	CCHA	43	26	45	71	....	....	....	58	....	....	....	....	....	....	....	....	....	....	....	....	....	....	....	....	....	....
1991-92	University of Michigan	CCHA	44	16	42	58	....	....	....	68	....	....	....	....	....	....	....	....	....	....	....	....	....	....	....	....	....	....
1992-93	University of Michigan	CCHA	40	27	38	65	....	....	....	40	....	....	....	....	....	....	....	....	....	....	....	....	....	....	....	....	....	....
1993-94	United States	Nat-Team	49	17	28	45				68	....	....	....	....	....	....	....	....	....	....	....	....	....	....	....	....	....	....
	United States	Olympics	8	1	5	6	....	....	....	4	....	....	....	....	....	....	....	....	....	....	....	....	....	....	....	....	....	....
	St. Louis Blues	**NHL**	**1**	**0**	**0**	**0**	**0**	**0**	**0**	**2**	**0**	**0**	**0**	**1**	**0.0**	**0**	**0**	**0**	**0**	**0**	**3**	**0**	**0**	**0**	**12**	**0**	**0**	**0**
	Peoria Rivermen	IHL	10	4	6	10	....	....	....	4	....	....	....	....	....	....	....	....	....	....	....	....	....	....	....	....	....	....
1994-95	Peoria Rivermen	IHL	65	30	38	68	....	....	....	65	....	....	....	....	....	....	....	....	....	....	....	....	....	....	....	....	....	....
	St. Louis Blues	**NHL**	**19**	**6**	**5**	**11**	**11**	**7**	**18**	**10**	**3**	**0**	**2**	**41**	**14.6**	**15**	**5**	**8**	**0**	**+2**	**6**	**0**	**0**	**0**	**4**	**0**	**0**	**0**
1995-96	**St. Louis Blues**	**NHL**	**28**	**1**	**6**	**7**	**1**	**5**	**6**	**12**	**1**	**0**	**1**	**35**	**2.9**	**12**	**3**	**17**	**1**	**–7**	....	....	....	....	....	....	....	....
	Worcester IceCats	AHL	22	8	17	25	....	....	....	46	....	....	....	....	....	....	....	....	....	....	....	....	....	....	....	....	....	....
	Edmonton Oilers	**NHL**	**6**	**2**	**4**	**6**	**2**	**3**	**5**	**6**	**0**	**0**	**0**	**12**	**16.7**	**5**	**0**	**5**	**0**	**0**	....	....	....	....	....	....	....	....
1996-97	**Vancouver Canucks**	**NHL**	**58**	**10**	**17**	**27**	**11**	**15**	**26**	**51**	**1**	**1**	**1**	**74**	**13.5**	**38**	**5**	**29**	**7**	**+11**	....	....	....	....	....	....	....	....
1997-98	**Vancouver Canucks**	**NHL**	**13**	**1**	**1**	**2**	**1**	**1**	**2**	**4**	**0**	**0**	**0**	**14**	**7.1**	**3**	**0**	**6**	**2**	**–1**	....	....	....	....	....	....	....	....
	Syracuse Crunch	AHL	37	17	22	39	....	....	....	44	....	....	....	....	....	....	....	....	....	....	5	2	1	3	2	....	....	....
	NHL Totals		**125**	**20**	**33**	**53**	**26**	**31**	**57**	**85**	**5**	**1**	**4**	**177**	**11.3**	**73**	**13**	**65**	**10**		**9**	**0**	**0**	**0**	**16**	**0**	**0**	**0**

CCHA Second All-Star Team (1991, 1993) • NCAA West Second All-American Team (1991)

Traded to **Edmonton** by **St. Louis** for future considerations, March 12, 1996. Signed as a free agent by **Vancouver**, July 31, 1996.

• ROBERTS, DOUG

Doug Roberts RW – R. 6'2", 212 lbs. b: Detroit, MI, 10/28/1942.

1962-63	Michigan State Spartans	WCHA	....	7	6	13	....	....	....	....	....	....	....	....	....	....	....	....	....	....	....	....	....	....	....	....	....	....
1963-64	Michigan State Spartans	WCHA	22	21	14	35	....	....	....	16	....	....	....	....	....	....	....	....	....	....	....	....	....	....	....	....	....	....
1964-65	Michigan State Spartans	CCHA	29	28	33	61	....	....	....	42	....	....	....	....	....	....	....	....	....	....	....	....	....	....	....	....	....	....
1965-66	Memphis Wings	CHL	70	20	40	60		....	....	71	....	....	....	....	....	....	....	....	....	....	....	....	....	....	....	....	....	....
	Detroit Red Wings	**NHL**	**1**	**0**	**0**	**0**	**0**	**0**	**0**	**0**	....	....	....	....	....	....	....	....	....	....	....	....	....	....	....	....	....	....
1966-67	**Detroit Red Wings**	**NHL**	**13**	**3**	**1**	**4**	**4**	**1**	**5**	**0**	....	....	....	....	....	....	....	....	....	....	....	....	....	....	....	....	....	....
	Memphis Wings	CHL	57	11	18	29	....	....	....	116	....	....	....	....	....	....	....	....	....	....	....	....	....	....	....	....	....	....
1967-68	**Detroit Red Wings**	**NHL**	**37**	**8**	**9**	**17**	**10**	**9**	**19**	**12**	**1**	**0**	**1**	**60**	**13.3**	**28**	**7**	**21**	**0**	**0**	....	....	....	....	....	....	....	....
	Fort Worth Wings	CHL	28	8	17	25	....	....	....	73	....	....	....	....	....	....	....	....	....	....	13	5	8	13	16	....	....	....
1968-69	**Oakland Seals**	**NHL**	**76**	**1**	**19**	**20**	**1**	**18**	**19**	**79**	**0**	**0**	**0**	**114**	**0.9**	**103**	**17**	**122**	**23**	**–13**	**7**	**0**	**1**	**1**	**34**	**0**	**0**	**0**
1969-70	**Oakland Seals**	**NHL**	**76**	**6**	**25**	**31**	**7**	**25**	**32**	**107**	**0**	**0**	**1**	**137**	**4.4**	**94**	**21**	**126**	**16**	**–37**	**4**	**0**	**2**	**2**	**6**	**0**	**0**	**0**
1970-71	**California Golden Seals**	**NHL**	**78**	**4**	**13**	**17**	**4**	**11**	**15**	**94**	**1**	**0**	**0**	**128**	**3.1**	**65**	**7**	**134**	**20**	**–56**	....	....	....	....	....	....	....	....
1971-72	**Boston Bruins**	**NHL**	**3**	**1**	**0**	**1**	**1**	**0**	**1**	**0**	**0**	**0**	**0**	**3**	**33.3**	**1**	**0**	**0**	**0**	**+1**	....	....	....	....	....	....	....	....
	Boston Braves	AHL	74	35	40	75	....	....	....	107	....	....	....	....	....	....	....	....	....	....	9	1	4	5	21	....	....	....
1972-73	**Boston Bruins**	**NHL**	**45**	**4**	**7**	**11**	**4**	**6**	**10**	**7**	**0**	**0**	**2**	**67**	**6.0**	**26**	**2**	**11**	**0**	**+13**	**5**	**2**	**0**	**2**	**6**	**0**	**0**	**0**
	Boston Braves	AHL	7	2	3	5	....	....	....	0	....	....	....	....	....	....	....	....	....	....	....	....	....	....	....	....	....	....
1973-74	**Boston Bruins**	**NHL**	**7**	**0**	**1**	**1**	**0**	**1**	**1**	**2**	**0**	**0**	**0**	**11**	**0.0**	**3**	**0**	**1**	**0**	**+2**	....	....	....	....	....	....	....	....
	Detroit Red Wings	**NHL**	**57**	**12**	**25**	**37**	**12**	**22**	**34**	**33**	**2**	**0**	**1**	**84**	**14.3**	**52**	**4**	**57**	**0**	**–9**	....	....	....	....	....	....	....	....
1974-75	**Detroit Red Wings**	**NHL**	**26**	**4**	**4**	**8**	**4**	**3**	**7**	**8**	**4**	**0**	**0**	**26**	**15.4**	**20**	**10**	**18**	**1**	**–7**	....	....	....	....	....	....	....	....
	Virginia Wings	AHL	31	7	11	18	....	....	....	32	....	....	....	....	....	....	....	....	....	....	5	0	2	2	4	....	....	....
1975-76	New England Whalers	WHA	76	4	13	17	....	....	....	51	....	....	....	....	....	....	....	....	....	....	17	1	1	2	8	....	....	....

			REGULAR SEASON																		PLAYOFFS							
Season	Club	League	GP	G	A	Pts	AG	AA	APts	PIM	PP	SH	GW	S	%	TGF	PGF	TGA	PGA	+/–	GP	G	A	Pts	PIM	PP	SH	GW
1976-77	New England Whalers	WHA	64	3	18	21				33											2	0	0	0	0			
	Rhode Island Reds	AHL	8	2	4	6				4																		
1977-78	Jokerit Helsinki	Finland	31	4	2	6				38																		
	NHL Totals		419	43	104	147	47	96	143	342	8	0	5	630	6.8	392	68	490	60		16	2	3	5	46	0	0	0
	Other Major League Totals		140	7	31	38				84											19	1	1	2	8			

WCHA Second All-Star Team (1965) • NCAA West First All-American Team (1965) • Won Ken McKenzie Trophy (CHL's Rookie of the Year) (1966)

Played in NHL All-Star Game (1971)

Signed as a free agent by **Detroit**, June 12, 1965. Traded to **Oakland** by **Detroit** with Gary Jarrett, Howie Young and Chris Worthy for Bob Baun and Ron Harris, May 27, 1968. Traded to **Boston** by **California** for cash, September 4, 1971. Traded to **Detroit** by **Boston** for cash, November 23, 1973. Selected by **LA Sharks** (WHA) in 1972 WHA General Player Draft, February 12, 1972. Signed as a free agent by **New England** (WHA), September, 1975.

• ROBERTS, GARY

Gary Roberts LW – L. 6'1", 190 lbs. b: North York, Ont., 5/23/1966. Calgary's 2nd choice, 12th overall, in 1984 Entry Draft.

Season	Club	League	GP	G	A	Pts	AG	AA	APts	PIM	PP	SH	GW	S	%	TGF	PGF	TGA	PGA	+/–	GP	G	A	Pts	PIM	PP	SH	GW
1982-83	Ottawa 67's	OHL	53	12	8	20				83											5	1	0	1	19			
1983-84	Ottawa 67's	OHL	48	27	30	57				144											13	10	7	17	62			
1984-85	Ottawa 67's	OHL	59	44	62	106				186											5	2	8	10	10			
	Moncton Golden Flames	AHL	7	4	2	6				7																		
1985-86	Ottawa 67's	OHL	24	26	25	51				83																		
	Canada	WJC-A	7	6	3	9				6																		
	Guelph Platers	OHL	23	18	15	33				65											20	18	13	31	43			
1986-87	Calgary Flames	NHL	32	5	10	15	4	7	11	85	0	0	0	38	13.2	23	1	16	0	+6	2	0	0	0	4	0	0	0
	Moncton Golden Flames	AHL	38	20	18	38				72																		
1987-88	Calgary Flames	NHL	74	13	15	28	11	11	22	282	0	0	1	118	11.0	60	1	47	12	+24	9	2	3	5	29	0	0	0
1988-89	Calgary Flames	NHL	71	22	16	38	19	11	30	250	0	1	2	123	17.9	60	1	34	7	+32	22	5	7	12	57	0	0	0
1989-90	Calgary Flames	FrTour	4	1	0	1				6																		
	Calgary Flames	NHL	78	39	33	72	34	24	58	222	5	0	5	175	22.3	107	19	64	7	+31	6	2	5	7	41	0	0	0
1990-91	Calgary Flames	NHL	80	22	31	53	20	23	43	252	0	0	3	132	16.7	75	3	68	11	+15	7	1	3	4	18	0	0	0
1991-92	Calgary Flames	NHL	76	53	37	90	49	28	77	207	15	0	2	196	27.0	121	33	79	23	+32								
1992-93	Calgary Flames	NHL	58	38	41	79	32	28	60	172	8	3	4	166	22.9	104	26	55	9	+32	5	1	6	7	43	1	0	0
1993-94	Calgary Flames	NHL	73	41	43	84	38	33	71	145	12	3	5	202	20.3	128	49	63	21	+37	7	2	6	8	24	1	0	1
1994-95	Calgary Flames	NHL	8	2	2	4	4	3	7	43	2	0	0	20	10.0	8	5	3	1	+1								
1995-96	Calgary Flames	NHL	35	22	20	42	22	16	38	78	9	0	5	84	26.2	51	21	16	1	+15								
1996-97	DID NOT PLAY – INJURED																											
1997-98	Carolina Hurricanes	NHL	61	20	29	49	23	28	51	103	4	0	2	106	18.9	65	20	46	4	+3								
	NHL Totals		646	277	277	554	256	212	468	1839	55	7	29	1360	20.4	802	179	491	96		58	13	30	43	216	2	0	1

OHL Second All-Star Team (1985, 1986) • Won Bill Masterton Memorial Trophy (1996)

Played in NHL All-Star Game (1992, 1993)

• Placed on voluntary retired list to recover from neck and shoulder injuries, June 17, 1996. Traded to **Carolina** by **Calgary** with Trevor Kidd for Andrew Cassels and Jean-Sebastien Giguere, August 25, 1997.

• ROBERTS, GORDIE

Gordie Roberts D – L. 6'1", 195 lbs. b: Detroit, MI, 10/2/1957. Montreal's 7th choice, 54th overall, in 1977 Amateur Draft.

Season	Club	League	GP	G	A	Pts	AG	AA	APts	PIM	PP	SH	GW	S	%	TGF	PGF	TGA	PGA	+/–	GP	G	A	Pts	PIM	PP	SH	GW
1973-74	Detroit Jr. Red Wings	SOJHL	70	25	55	80				340																		
1974-75	Victoria Cougars	WHL	53	19	45	64				145											12	1	9	10	42			
1975-76	New England Whalers	WHA	77	3	19	22				102											17	2	9	11	36			
1976-77	New England Whalers	WHA	77	13	33	46				169											5	2	2	4	6			
1977-78	New England Whalers	WHA	78	15	46	61				118											14	0	5	5	29			
1978-79	New England Whalers	WHA	79	11	46	57				113											10	0	4	4	10			
1979-80	Hartford Whalers	NHL	80	8	28	36	7	21	28	89	1	0	1	107	7.5	135	16	133	20	+6	3	1	1	2	2	0	0	0
1980-81	Hartford Whalers	NHL	27	2	11	13	2	8	10	81	1	0	0	36	5.6	36	6	58	13	–15								
	Minnesota North Stars	NHL	50	6	31	37	5	22	27	94	3	0	0	83	7.2	73	21	66	16	+2	19	1	5	6	17	0	1	0
1981-82	Minnesota North Stars	NHL	79	4	30	34	3	20	23	119	0	0	0	104	3.8	127	33	119	24	–1	4	0	3	3	27	0	0	0
	United States	WEC-A	7	3	4	7				12																		
1982-83	Minnesota North Stars	NHL	80	3	41	44	2	28	30	103	2	0	1	127	2.4	135	35	108	26	+18	9	1	5	6	14	0	0	0
1983-84	Minnesota North Stars	NHL	77	8	45	53	6	31	37	132	1	1	0	131	6.1	147	35	136	38	+14	15	3	7	10	23	1	1	0
1984-85	United States	C Cup	6	1	0	1				6																		
	Minnesota North Stars	NHL	78	6	36	42	5	24	29	112	1	0	0	142	4.2	104	32	122	38	–12	9	1	6	7	6	0	0	0
1985-86	Minnesota North Stars	NHL	76	2	21	23	2	14	16	101	0	0	0	66	3.0	101	4	106	23	+14	5	0	4	4	8	0	0	0
1986-87	Minnesota North Stars	NHL	67	3	10	13	3	7	10	68	0	0	1	43	7.0	61	1	111	44	–7								
	United States	WEC-A	10	0	1	1				33																		
1987-88	Minnesota North Stars	NHL	48	1	10	11	1	7	8	103	0	0	0	33	3.0	37	3	80	29	–17								
	Philadelphia Flyers	NHL	11	1	2	3	1	1	2	15	0	0	0	9	11.1	19	2	13	3	+7								
	St. Louis Blues	NHL	11	1	3	4	1	2	3	25	0	0	0	10	10.0	14	1	19	6	0	10	1	2	3	33	0	0	0
1988-89	St. Louis Blues	NHL	77	2	24	26	2	17	19	90	0	0	0	52	3.8	91	12	111	39	+7	10	1	7	8	8	0	0	0
1989-90	St. Louis Blues	NHL	75	3	14	17	3	10	13	140	0	0	0	56	5.4	71	6	101	24	–12	10	0	2	2	26	0	0	0
1990-91	St. Louis Blues	NHL	3	0	1	1	0	1	1	8	0	0	0	2	0.0	2	0	3	0	–1								
	Peoria Rivermen	IHL	6	0	8	8				4																		
	Pittsburgh Penguins	NHL	61	3	12	15	3	9	12	70	0	0	0	22	13.6	67	0	69	20	+18	24	1	2	3	63	0	0	0
1991-92	Pittsburgh Penguins	NHL	73	2	22	24	2	17	19	87	1	0	1	29	6.9	78	4	72	17	+19	19	0	2	2	32	0	0	0
1992-93	Boston Bruins	NHL	65	5	12	17	4	8	12	105	0	0	1	40	12.5	74	6	67	22	+23	4	0	0	0	6	0	0	0
1993-94	Boston Bruins	NHL	59	1	6	7	1	5	6	40	0	0	0	19	5.3	30	0	47	4	–13	12	0	1	1	8	0	0	0
1994-95	Chicago Wolves	IHL	68	6	22	28				80											3	0	0	0	4			
1995-96	Minnesota Moose	IHL	37	1	12	13				44																		
	NHL Totals		1097	61	359	420	53	252	305	1582	10	1	5	1111	5.5	1402	217	1541	406		153	10	47	57	273	1	2	0
	Other Major League Totals		311	42	144	186				502											46	4	20	24	81			

Signed as an underage free agent by **New England** (WHA), August, 1975. Claimed by **Hartford** from **Montreal** in Expansion Draft, June 22, 1979. Traded to **Minnesota** by **Hartford** for Mike Fidler, December 16, 1980. Traded to **Philadelphia** by **Minnesota** for future considerations, February 8, 1988. Traded to **St. Louis** by **Philadelphia** for future considerations, March 8, 1988. Traded to **Pittsburgh** by **St. Louis** for Pittsburgh's 11th round choice (Wade Saltzman) in 1992 Entry Draft, October 2, 1990. Signed as a free agent by **Boston**, July 23, 1992.

• ROBERTS, JIM

Jim (James Drew) Roberts LW – L. 6'1", 198 lbs. b: Toronto, Ont., 6/8/1956. Minnesota's 2nd choice, 31st overall, in 1976 Amateur Draft.

Season	Club	League	GP	G	A	Pts	AG	AA	APts	PIM	PP	SH	GW	S	%	TGF	PGF	TGA	PGA	+/–	GP	G	A	Pts	PIM	PP	SH	GW
1973-74	Ottawa 67's	OHA	64	13	18	31				44																		
1974-75	Ottawa 67's	OHA	60	22	40	62				58																		
1975-76	Ottawa 67's	OHA	64	27	56	83				62																		
1976-77	Minnesota North Stars	NHL	53	11	8	19	11	6	17	14	1	0	0	73	15.1	33	3	39	0	–9	2	0	0	0	0	0	0	0
	New Haven Nighthawks	AHL	10	7	3	10				6																		
1977-78	Minnesota North Stars	NHL	42	4	14	18	4	11	15	19	0	0	0	75	5.3	36	11	43	4	–14								
	Fort Worth Texans	CHL	33	15	7	22				12																		
1978-79	Minnesota North Stars	NHL	11	2	1	3	2	1	3	0	0	0	0	8	25.0	5	1	9	0	–5								
	Oklahoma City Stars	CHL	66	21	22	43				34																		
1979-80	Cincinnati Stingers	CHL	26	8	10	18				11																		
	Maine Mariners	AHL	48	17	16	33				22											9	1	2	3	0			
	NHL Totals		106	17	23	40	17	18	35	33	1	0	0	156	10.9	74	15	91	4		2	0	0	0	0	0	0	0

Claimed by **Winnipeg** from **Minnesota** in Expansion Draft, June 13, 1979.

• ROBERTS, JIMMY

Jimmy Roberts D/RW – R. 5'10", 185 lbs. b: Toronto, Ont., 4/9/1940.

Season	Club	League	GP	G	A	Pts	AG	AA	APts	PIM	PP	SH	GW	S	%	TGF	PGF	TGA	PGA	+/–	GP	G	A	Pts	PIM	PP	SH	GW
1958-59	Peterborough Petes	OHA	54	2	8	10				34											19	0	0	0	2			
1959-60	Peterborough Petes	OHA	48	6	21	27				55											12	2	7	9	18			
	Montreal Royals	EPHL																			4	0	0	0	4			
1960-61	Montreal Royals	EPHL	51	7	18	25				55																		
1961-62	Hull-Ottawa Canadiens	EPHL	67	11	28	39				42											13	3	0	3	18			
1962-63	Hull-Ottawa Canadiens	EPHL	72	2	27	29				78											3	0	0	0	10			
	Cleveland Barons	AHL																			1	0	0	0	2			

Season	Club	League	GP	G	A	Pts	AG	AA	APts	PIM	PP	SH	GW	S	%	TGF	PGF	TGA	PGA	+/-	GP	G	A	Pts	PIM	PP	SH	GW
			REGULAR SEASON																		PLAYOFFS							
1963-64	Montreal Canadiens	NHL	15	0	1	1	0	1	1	2	....	....	....	....	....	....	....	....	....	....	7	0	1	1	14	....	....	....
	Cleveland Barons	AHL	9	1	3	4	....	....	....	4	....	....	....	....	....	....	....	....	....	....	....	....	....	....	....	....	....	....
	Quebec Aces	AHL	2	0	0	0	....	....	....	2	....	....	....	....	....	....	....	....	....	....	....	....	....	....	....	....	....	....
	Omaha Knights	CHL	46	18	19	37	....	....	....	47	....	....	....	....	....	....	....	....	....	....	....	....	....	....	....	....	....	....
1964-65	Montreal Canadiens	NHL	70	3	10	13	4	11	15	40	....	....	....	....	....	....	....	....	....	....	13	0	0	0	30	....	....	....
1965-66	Montreal Canadiens	NHL	70	5	5	10	6	5	11	20	....	....	....	....	....	....	....	....	....	....	10	1	1	2	10	....	....	....
1966-67	Montreal Canadiens	NHL	63	3	0	3	4	0	4	16	....	....	....	....	....	....	....	....	....	....	4	1	0	1	0	....	....	....
1967-68	St. Louis Blues	NHL	74	14	23	37	17	24	41	66	3	1	1	164	8.5	77	27	81	23	-8	18	4	1	5	20	0	0	1
1968-69	St. Louis Blues	NHL	72	14	19	33	16	18	34	81	2	1	1	129	10.9	63	13	64	27	+13	12	1	4	5	10	0	0	0
1969-70	St. Louis Blues	NHL	76	13	17	30	15	17	32	51	1	2	4	165	7.9	65	11	59	23	+18	16	2	3	5	29	0	0	0
1970-71	St. Louis Blues	NHL	72	13	18	31	14	16	30	77	2	1	0	123	10.6	78	16	85	30	+7	6	2	1	3	11	0	0	0
1971-72	St. Louis Blues	NHL	26	5	7	12	5	6	11	4	1	2	0	46	10.9	28	5	28	9	+4	....	....	....	....	....	....	....	....
	Montreal Canadiens	NHL	51	7	15	22	7	14	21	53	0	3	1	69	10.1	40	2	46	11	+3	6	1	0	1	0	0	0	1
1972-73	Montreal Canadiens	NHL	77	14	18	32	14	15	29	28	0	1	3	104	13.5	76	1	56	14	+33	17	0	2	2	22	0	0	0
1973-74	Montreal Canadiens	NHL	67	8	16	24	8	14	22	39	0	1	2	97	8.2	76	0	71	22	+27	6	0	0	0	4	0	0	0
1974-75	Montreal Canadiens	NHL	79	5	13	18	5	10	15	52	0	2	0	85	5.9	61	3	67	27	+18	11	2	2	4	2	0	0	0
1975-76	Montreal Canadiens	NHL	74	13	8	21	12	6	18	35	0	0	1	80	16.3	33	0	39	13	+7	13	3	1	4	2	0	1	0
1976-77	Montreal Canadiens	NHL	45	5	14	19	5	11	16	18	0	1	1	56	8.9	35	0	19	6	+22	14	3	0	3	6	0	1	1
1977-78	St. Louis Blues	NHL	75	4	10	14	4	8	12	39	0	0	1	70	5.7	49	5	87	23	-20	....	....	....	....	....	....	....	....
	NHL Totals		1006	126	194	320	136	176	312	621	9	15	15	1188	10.6	681	83	702	228		153	20	16	36	160	0	2	3

Played in NHL All-Star Game (1965, 1969, 1970)

Claimed by **St. Louis** from **Montreal** in Expansion Draft, June 6, 1967. Traded to **Montreal** by **St. Louis** for Phil Roberto, December 13, 1971. Traded to **St. Louis** by **Montreal** for St. Louis' 3rd round choice (Murray Meyers) in 1979 Amateur Draft, August 18, 1977.

• ROBERTSON, GEORDIE

Geordie "Robbie" Robertson RW – R. 6', 165 lbs. b: Victoria, B.C., 8/1/1959.

Season	Club	League	GP	G	A	Pts	AG	AA	APts	PIM	PP	SH	GW	S	%	TGF	PGF	TGA	PGA	+/-	GP	G	A	Pts	PIM	PP	SH	GW
1975-76	Nanaimo Clippers	BCJHL	STATISTICS NOT AVAILABLE																									
	Victoria Cougars	WCJHL	3	3	2	5	....	....	....	0	....	....	....	....	....	....	....	....	....	....	....	....	....	....	....	....	....	....
1976-77	Victoria Cougars	WCHL	72	39	44	83	....	....	....	107	....	....	....	....	....	....	....	....	....	....	....	....	....	....	....	....	....	....
1977-78	Victoria Cougars	WCJHL	61	64	72	136	....	....	....	85	....	....	....	....	....	....	....	....	....	....	13	15	11	26	42	....	....	....
1978-79	Victoria Cougars	WHL	54	31	42	73	....	....	....	94	....	....	....	....	....	....	....	....	....	....	14	15	10	25	22	....	....	....
1979-80	Rochester Americans	AHL	55	26	26	52	....	....	....	66	....	....	....	....	....	....	....	....	....	....	4	1	4	5	2	....	....	....
1980-81	Rochester Americans	AHL	20	3	3	6	....	....	....	19	....	....	....	....	....	....	....	....	....	....	....	....	....	....	....	....	....	....
1981-82	Rochester Americans	AHL	46	14	15	29	....	....	....	45	....	....	....	....	....	....	....	....	....	....	9	1	3	4	13	....	....	....
1982-83	Buffalo Sabres	NHL	5	1	2	3	1	1	2	7	0	0	0	10	10.0	5	4	2	0	-1	....	....	....	....	....	....	....	....
	Rochester Americans	AHL	72	46	73	119	....	....	....	83	....	....	....	....	....	....	....	....	....	....	16	8	6	14	23	....	....	....
1983-84	Rochester Americans	AHL	64	37	54	91	....	....	....	103	....	....	....	....	....	....	....	....	....	....	18	9	9	18	42	....	....	....
1984-85	Rochester Americans	AHL	70	27	48	75	....	....	....	91	....	....	....	....	....	....	....	....	....	....	5	0	1	1	4	....	....	....
1985-86	Adirondack Red Wings	AHL	79	36	56	92	....	....	....	99	....	....	....	....	....	....	....	....	....	....	15	4	6	10	25	....	....	....
1986-87	Adirondack Red Wings	AHL	63	28	41	69	....	....	....	94	....	....	....	....	....	....	....	....	....	....	....	....	....	....	....	....	....	....
1987-88	JyP HT Jyvaskyla	Finland	34	14	6	20	....	....	....	28	....	....	....	....	....	....	....	....	....	....	....	....	....	....	....	....	....	....
	Adirondack Red Wings	AHL	30	11	15	26	....	....	....	24	....	....	....	....	....	....	....	....	....	....	6	1	2	3	14	....	....	....
1988-89	Rochester Americans	AHL	32	11	12	23	....	....	....	12	....	....	....	....	....	....	....	....	....	....	....	....	....	....	....	....	....	....
	NHL Totals		5	1	2	3	1	1	2	7	0	0	0	10	10.0	5	4	2	0		....	....	....	....	....			

Signed as a free agent by **Buffalo**, September 5, 1979. Signed as a free agent by **Detroit**, July 9, 1985.

• ROBERTSON, TORRIE

Torrie Robertson LW – L. 5'11", 200 lbs. b: Victoria, B.C., 8/2/1961. Washington's 3rd choice, 55th overall, in 1980 Entry Draft.

Season	Club	League	GP	G	A	Pts	AG	AA	APts	PIM	PP	SH	GW	S	%	TGF	PGF	TGA	PGA	+/-	GP	G	A	Pts	PIM	PP	SH	GW
1978-79	Victoria Cougars	WHL	69	18	23	41	....	....	....	141	....	....	....	....	....	....	....	....	....	....	15	1	2	3	29	....	....	....
1979-80	Victoria Cougars	WHL	72	23	24	47	....	....	....	298	....	....	....	....	....	....	....	....	....	....	17	5	7	12	117	....	....	....
1980-81	Victoria Cougars	WHL	59	45	66	111	....	....	....	274	....	....	....	....	....	....	....	....	....	....	15	10	13	23	55	....	....	....
	Washington Capitals	NHL	3	0	0	0	0	0	0	0	0	0	0	3	0.0	0	0	2	0	-2	....	....	....	....	....	....	....	....
1981-82	Washington Capitals	NHL	54	8	13	21	6	9	15	204	2	0	0	46	17.4	20	6	23	0	-1	....	....	....	....	....	....	....	....
	Hershey Bears	AHL	21	5	3	8	....	....	....	60	....	....	....	....	....	....	....	....	....	....	....	....	....	....	....	....	....	....
1982-83	Washington Capitals	NHL	5	2	0	2	2	0	2	4	0	0	0	5	40.0	3	0	5	0	-2	....	....	....	....	....	....	....	....
	Hershey Bears	AHL	69	21	33	54	....	....	....	187	....	....	....	....	....	....	....	....	....	....	5	1	2	3	8	....	....	....
1983-84	Hartford Whalers	NHL	66	7	13	20	6	9	15	198	0	0	2	61	11.5	35	2	42	0	-9	....	....	....	....	....	....	....	....
1984-85	Hartford Whalers	NHL	74	11	30	41	9	20	29	337	1	0	3	72	15.3	58	14	57	0	-13	....	....	....	....	....	....	....	....
1985-86	Hartford Whalers	NHL	76	13	24	37	10	16	26	358	3	0	0	89	14.6	50	11	50	0	-11	10	1	0	1	67	0	0	0
1986-87	Hartford Whalers	NHL	20	1	0	1	1	0	1	98	0	0	1	19	5.3	6	0	12	0	-6	....	....	....	....	....	....	....	....
1987-88	Hartford Whalers	NHL	63	2	8	10	2	6	8	293	0	0	1	46	4.3	17	0	17	0	0	6	0	1	1	6	0	0	0
1988-89	Hartford Whalers	NHL	27	2	4	6	2	3	5	84	0	0	1	21	9.5	9	1	11	0	-3	....	....	....	....	....	....	....	....
	Detroit Red Wings	NHL	12	2	2	4	2	1	3	63	0	0	0	5	40.0	6	0	6	0	0	6	1	0	1	17	0	0	0
1989-90	Detroit Red Wings	NHL	42	1	5	6	1	4	5	112	0	0	0	20	5.0	11	0	14	0	-3	....	....	....	....	....	....	....	....
	Adirondack Red Wings	AHL	27	3	13	16	....	....	....	47	....	....	....	....	....	....	....	....	....	....	6	1	1	2	33	....	....	....
1990-91	Rochester Americans	AHL	1	0	1	1	....	....	....	0	....	....	....	....	....	....	....	....	....	....	....	....	....	....	....	....	....	....
	Albany Choppers	IHL	1	0	0	0	....	....	....	0	....	....	....	....	....	....	....	....	....	....	....	....	....	....	....	....	....	....
	NHL Totals		442	49	99	148	41	68	109	1751	7	0	8	387	12.7	223	34	239	0		22	2	1	3	90	0	0	0

Traded to **Hartford** by **Washington** for Greg Adams, October 3, 1983. Traded to **Detroit** by **Hartford** for Jim Pavese, March 7, 1989.

• ROBERTSSON, BERT

Bert Robertsson D – L. 6'3", 205 lbs. b: Sodertalje, Sweden, 6/30/1974. Vancouver's 8th choice, 254th overall, in 1993 Entry Draft.

Season	Club	League	GP	G	A	Pts	AG	AA	APts	PIM	PP	SH	GW	S	%	TGF	PGF	TGA	PGA	+/-	GP	G	A	Pts	PIM	PP	SH	GW
1992-93	Sodertalje SK	Sweden 2	23	2	1	3	....	....	....	24	....	....	....	....	....	....	....	....	....	....	....	....	....	....	....	....	....	....
1993-94	Sodertalje SK	Sweden 2	28	0	1	1	....	....	....	12	....	....	....	....	....	....	....	....	....	....	....	....	....	....	....	....	....	....
1994-95	Sodertalje SK	Sweden 2	23	1	2	3	....	....	....	24	....	....	....	....	....	....	....	....	....	....	....	....	....	....	....	....	....	....
1995-96	Syracuse Crunch	AHL	65	1	7	8	....	....	....	109	....	....	....	....	....	....	....	....	....	....	16	0	1	1	26	....	....	....
1996-97	Syracuse Crunch	AHL	80	4	9	13	....	....	....	132	....	....	....	....	....	....	....	....	....	....	3	1	0	1	4	....	....	....
1997-98	Vancouver Canucks	NHL	30	2	4	6	2	4	6	24	0	0	0	19	10.5	12	0	11	1	+2	....	....	....	....	....	....	....	....
	Syracuse Crunch	AHL	42	5	9	14	....	....	....	87	....	....	....	....	....	....	....	....	....	....	3	0	0	0	6	....	....	....
	NHL Totals		30	2	4	6	2	4	6	24	0	0	0	19	10.5	12	0	11	1		....	....	....	....	....	....	....	....

• ROBIDOUX, FLORENT

Florent Robidoux LW – L. 6'2", 190 lbs. b: Treheme, Man., 5/5/1960.

Season	Club	League	GP	G	A	Pts	AG	AA	APts	PIM	PP	SH	GW	S	%	TGF	PGF	TGA	PGA	+/-	GP	G	A	Pts	PIM	PP	SH	GW
1977-78	Estevan Bruins	SJHL	59	29	34	63	....	....	....	99	....	....	....	....	....	....	....	....	....	....	....	....	....	....	....	....	....	....
	New Westminster Bruins	WCJHL	8	1	1	2	....	....	....	12	....	....	....	....	....	....	....	....	....	....	16	1	4	5	35	....	....	....
1978-79	Portland Winter Hawks	WHL	70	36	41	77	....	....	....	73	....	....	....	....	....	....	....	....	....	....	25	11	16	27	20	....	....	....
1979-80	Portland Winter Hawks	WHL	70	43	57	100	....	....	....	157	....	....	....	....	....	....	....	....	....	....	8	5	2	7	10	....	....	....
1980-81	Chicago Black Hawks	NHL	39	6	2	8	5	1	6	75	1	0	0	31	19.4	11	2	15	0	-6	....	....	....	....	....	....	....	....
	New Brunswick Hawks	AHL	35	12	11	23	....	....	....	110	....	....	....	....	....	....	....	....	....	....	13	2	7	9	38	....	....	....
1981-82	Chicago Black Hawks	NHL	4	1	2	3	1	1	2	0	0	0	0	4	25.0	3	0	1	0	+2	....	....	....	....	....	....	....	....
	New Brunswick Hawks	AHL	69	31	35	66	....	....	....	200	....	....	....	....	....	....	....	....	....	....	15	*9	10	19	21	....	....	....
1982-83			DID NOT PLAY – INJURED																									
1983-84	Chicago Black Hawks	NHL	9	0	0	0	0	0	0	0	0	0	0	2	0.0	0	0	3	0	-3	....	....	....	....	....	....	....	....
	Springfield Indians	AHL	68	26	22	48	....	....	....	123	....	....	....	....	....	....	....	....	....	....	4	0	1	1	0	....	....	....
1984-85	Milwaukee Admirals	IHL	76	29	35	64	....	....	....	184	....	....	....	....	....	....	....	....	....	....	....	....	....	....	....	....	....	....
1985-86	Hershey Bears	AHL	47	6	3	9	....	....	....	81	....	....	....	....	....	....	....	....	....	....	3	0	0	0	15	....	....	....
1986-87	Milwaukee Admirals	IHL	15	2	7	9	....	....	....	16	....	....	....	....	....	....	....	....	....	....	6	3	3	6	13	....	....	....
	NHL Totals		52	7	4	11	6	2	8	75	1	0	0	37	18.9	14	2	19	0		....	....	....	....	....	....	....	....

WHL All-Star Team (1980)

Signed as a free agent by **Chicago**, October 20, 1979. Signed as a free agent by **Philadelphia**, October 8, 1985.

• ROBINSON, DOUG

Doug Robinson LW – L. 6'2", 197 lbs. b: St. Catharines, Ont., 8/27/1940.

Season	Club	League	REGULAR SEASON GP	G	A	Pts	AG	AA	APts	PIM	PP	SH	GW	S	%	TGF	PGF	TGA	PGA	+/–	PLAYOFFS GP	G	A	Pts	PIM	PP	SH	GW
1956-57	Guelph Biltmores	OHA	52	9	7	16	....	....	....	8	....	....	....	....	....	....	....	....	....	....	10	1	2	3	14	....	....	....
1957-58	Guelph Biltmores	OHA	6	2	1	3	....	....	....	2	....	....	....	....	....	....	....	....	....	....	....	....	....	....	....	....	....	....
	St. Catharines Teepees	OHA	....	....	....	....	....	....	....	....	....	....	....	....	....	....	....	....	....	....	6	0	1	1	0	....	....	....
1958-59	St. Catharines Teepees	OHA	52	12	11	23	....	....	....	10	....	....	....	....	....	....	....	....	....	....	7	0	3	3	0	....	....	....
1959-60	St. Catharines Teepees	OHA	48	15	20	35	....	....	....	4	....	....	....	....	....	....	....	....	....	....	17	3	4	7	6	....	....	....
1960-61	St. Catharines Teepees	OHA	48	36	30	66	....	....	....	22	....	....	....	....	....	....	....	....	....	....	6	3	1	4	20	....	....	....
	Sault Ste. Marie Thunderbirds	EPHL	....	....	....	....	....	....	....	....	....	....	....	....	....	....	....	....	....	....	1	0	0	0	2	....	....	....
1961-62	Sault Ste. Marie Thunderbirds	EPHL	70	33	26	59	....	....	....	32	....	....	....	....	....	....	....	....	....	....	....	....	....	....	....	....	....	....
	Buffalo Bisons	AHL	....	....	....	....	....	....	....	....	....	....	....	....	....	....	....	....	....	....	2	0	0	0	0	....	....	....
1962-63	Buffalo Bisons	AHL	72	36	37	73	....	....	....	8	....	....	....	....	....	....	....	....	....	....	13	*10	4	14	2	....	....	....
1963-64	Buffalo Bisons	AHL	46	22	27	49	....	....	....	22	....	....	....	....	....	....	....	....	....	....	....	....	....	....	....	....	....	....
	Chicago Black Hawks	**NHL**	....	....	....	....	....	....	....	....	....	....	....	....	....	....	....	....	....	....	**4**	**0**	**0**	**0**	**0**	....	....	....
1964-65	**Chicago Black Hawks**	**NHL**	**40**	**2**	**9**	**11**	**3**	**10**	**13**	**8**	....	....	....	....	....	....	....	....	....	....	....	....	....	....	....	....	....	....
	New York Rangers	**NHL**	**21**	**8**	**14**	**22**	**10**	**15**	**25**	**2**	....	....	....	....	....	....	....	....	....	....	....	....	....	....	....	....	....	....
1965-66	**New York Rangers**	**NHL**	**51**	**8**	**12**	**20**	**10**	**12**	**22**	**8**	....	....	....	....	....	....	....	....	....	....	....	....	....	....	....	....	....	....
	Baltimore Clippers	AHL	5	2	2	4	....	....	....	0	....	....	....	....	....	....	....	....	....	....	....	....	....	....	....	....	....	....
1966-67	**New York Rangers**	**NHL**	**1**	**0**	**0**	**0**	**0**	**0**	**0**	**0**	....	....	....	....	....	....	....	....	....	....	....	....	....	....	....	....	....	....
	Baltimore Clippers	AHL	63	39	33	72	....	....	....	89	....	....	....	....	....	....	....	....	....	....	9	4	6	10	2	....	....	....
1967-68	**Los Angeles Kings**	**NHL**	**34**	**9**	**9**	**18**	**11**	**9**	**20**	**6**	**1**	**0**	**0**	**63**	**14.3**	**29**	**3**	**22**	**0**	**+4**	**7**	**4**	**3**	**7**	**0**	**0**	**0**	**0**
	Springfield Kings	AHL	36	21	25	46	....	....	....	0	....	....	....	....	....	....	....	....	....	....	....	....	....	....	....	....	....	....
1968-69	**Los Angeles Kings**	**NHL**	**31**	**2**	**10**	**12**	**2**	**9**	**11**	**2**	**0**	**0**	**0**	**43**	**4.7**	**21**	**2**	**23**	**0**	**–4**	....	....	....	....	....	....	....	....
	Springfield Kings	AHL	42	14	20	34	....	....	....	6	....	....	....	....	....	....	....	....	....	....	....	....	....	....	....	....	....	....
1969-70	Springfield Kings	AHL	70	45	41	86	....	....	....	26	....	....	....	....	....	....	....	....	....	....	14	5	3	8	0	....	....	....
1970-71	**Los Angeles Kings**	**NHL**	**61**	**15**	**13**	**28**	**16**	**11**	**27**	**8**	**3**	**0**	**3**	**85**	**17.6**	**42**	**5**	**45**	**0**	**–8**	....	....	....	....	....	....	....	....
1971-72	Nova Scotia Voyageurs	AHL	27	10	17	27	....	....	....	4	....	....	....	....	....	....	....	....	....	....	....	....	....	....	....	....	....	....
	Seattle Totems	WHL	9	7	1	8	....	....	....	0	....	....	....	....	....	....	....	....	....	....	....	....	....	....	....	....	....	....
	NHL Totals		**239**	**44**	**67**	**111**	**52**	**66**	**118**	**34**	**4**	**0**	**3**	**191**	**23.0**	**92**	**10**	**90**	**0**		**11**	**4**	**3**	**7**	**0**	**0**	**0**	**0**

AHL Second All-Star Team (1963) • Won Dudley "Red" Garrett Memorial Award (Top Rookie - AHL) (1963) • AHL First All-Star Team (1970)

Traded to **NY Rangers** by **Chicago** with Wayne Hillman and John Brenneman for Camille Henry, Don Johns, Bill Taylor Jr. and Wally Chevrier, February 4, 1965. Claimed by **LA Kings** from **NY Rangers** in Expansion Draft, June 6, 1967. Traded to **Montreal** by **LA Kings** with Denis Dejordy, Dale Hoganson and Noel Price for Rogie Vachon, November 4, 1971.

• ROBINSON, LARRY

Larry "Big Bird" Robinson D – L. 6'4", 225 lbs. b: Winchester, Ont., 6/2/1951. Montreal's 4th choice, 20th overall, in 1971 Amateur Draft. **HHOF**

Season	Club	League	REGULAR SEASON GP	G	A	Pts	AG	AA	APts	PIM	PP	SH	GW	S	%	TGF	PGF	TGA	PGA	+/–	PLAYOFFS GP	G	A	Pts	PIM	PP	SH	GW
1969-70	Brockville Braves	OJHL	40	22	29	51	....	....	....	74	....	....	....	....	....	....	....	....	....	....	....	....	....	....	....	....	....	....
1970-71	Kitchener Rangers	OHA	61	12	39	51	....	....	....	65	....	....	....	....	....	....	....	....	....	....	....	....	....	....	....	....	....	....
1971-72	Nova Scotia Voyageurs	AHL	74	10	14	24	....	....	....	54	....	....	....	....	....	....	....	....	....	....	15	2	10	12	31	....	....	....
1972-73	Nova Scotia Voyageurs	AHL	38	6	33	39	....	....	....	33	....	....	....	....	....	....	....	....	....	....	....	....	....	....	....	....	....	....
	Montreal Canadiens	**NHL**	**36**	**2**	**4**	**6**	**2**	**3**	**5**	**20**	**0**	**0**	**1**	**36**	**5.6**	**23**	**1**	**19**	**0**	**+3**	**11**	**1**	**4**	**5**	**9**	**0**	**0**	**1**
1973-74	**Montreal Canadiens**	**NHL**	**78**	**6**	**20**	**26**	**6**	**17**	**23**	**66**	**0**	**0**	**1**	**98**	**6.1**	**111**	**6**	**92**	**19**	**+32**	**6**	**0**	**1**	**1**	**26**	**0**	**0**	**0**
1974-75	**Montreal Canadiens**	**NHL**	**80**	**14**	**47**	**61**	**13**	**37**	**50**	**76**	**1**	**0**	**2**	**102**	**13.7**	**142**	**17**	**83**	**19**	**+61**	**11**	**0**	**4**	**4**	**27**	**0**	**0**	**0**
1975-76	**Montreal Canadiens**	**NHL**	**80**	**10**	**30**	**40**	**9**	**24**	**33**	**59**	**2**	**0**	**0**	**130**	**7.7**	**113**	**16**	**63**	**16**	**+50**	**13**	**3**	**3**	**6**	**10**	**0**	**0**	**1**
1976-77	Canada	C Cup	7	0	0	0	....	....	....	0	....	....	....	....	....	....	....	....	....	....	....	....	....	....	....	....	....	....
	Montreal Canadiens	**NHL**	**77**	**19**	**66**	**85**	**18**	**54**	**72**	**45**	**3**	**0**	**3**	**199**	**9.5**	**218**	**34**	**74**	**10**	**+120**	**14**	**2**	**10**	**12**	**12**	**1**	**0**	**0**
1977-78	**Montreal Canadiens**	**NHL**	**80**	**13**	**52**	**65**	**13**	**43**	**56**	**39**	**3**	**2**	**5**	**154**	**8.4**	**196**	**45**	**107**	**27**	**+71**	**15**	**4**	***17**	***21**	**6**	**2**	**0**	**0**
1978-79	**Montreal Canadiens**	**NHL**	**67**	**16**	**45**	**61**	**15**	**34**	**49**	**33**	**4**	**0**	**1**	**147**	**10.9**	**156**	**41**	**82**	**17**	**+50**	**16**	**6**	**9**	**15**	**8**	**1**	**0**	**1**
	NHL All-Stars	Chal Cup	3	1	0	1	....	....	....	0	....	....	....	....	....	....	....	....	....	....	....	....	....	....	....	....	....	....
1979-80	**Montreal Canadiens**	**NHL**	**72**	**14**	**61**	**75**	**13**	**47**	**60**	**39**	**6**	**0**	**3**	**133**	**10.5**	**173**	**59**	**106**	**30**	**+38**	**10**	**0**	**4**	**4**	**2**	**0**	**0**	**0**
1980-81	**Montreal Canadiens**	**NHL**	**65**	**12**	**38**	**50**	**10**	**27**	**37**	**37**	**7**	**0**	**2**	**130**	**9.2**	**151**	**35**	**97**	**27**	**+46**	**3**	**0**	**1**	**1**	**2**	**0**	**0**	**0**
	Canada	WEC-A	6	1	1	2	....	....	....	2	....	....	....	....	....	....	....	....	....	....	....	....	....	....	....	....	....	....
1981-82	Canada	C Cup	7	0	1	1	....	....	....	2	....	....	....	....	....	....	....	....	....	....	....	....	....	....	....	....	....	....
	Montreal Canadiens	**NHL**	**71**	**12**	**47**	**59**	**9**	**31**	**40**	**41**	**5**	**1**	**0**	**141**	**8.5**	**165**	**33**	**104**	**29**	**+57**	**5**	**0**	**1**	**1**	**8**	**0**	**0**	**0**
1982-83	**Montreal Canadiens**	**NHL**	**71**	**14**	**49**	**63**	**11**	**34**	**45**	**33**	**6**	**0**	**1**	**147**	**9.5**	**151**	**41**	**116**	**39**	**+33**	**3**	**0**	**0**	**0**	**2**	**0**	**0**	**0**
1983-84	**Montreal Canadiens**	**NHL**	**74**	**9**	**34**	**43**	**7**	**23**	**30**	**39**	**4**	**0**	**1**	**141**	**6.4**	**127**	**40**	**117**	**34**	**+4**	**15**	**0**	**5**	**5**	**22**	**0**	**0**	**0**
1984-85	Canada	C Cup	8	1	2	3	....	....	....	2	....	....	....	....	....	....	....	....	....	....	....	....	....	....	....	....	....	....
	Montreal Canadiens	**NHL**	**76**	**14**	**33**	**47**	**11**	**22**	**33**	**44**	**6**	**0**	**3**	**120**	**11.7**	**136**	**32**	**97**	**26**	**+33**	**12**	**3**	**8**	**11**	**8**	**1**	**0**	**0**
1985-86	**Montreal Canadiens**	**NHL**	**78**	**19**	**63**	**82**	**15**	**42**	**57**	**39**	**10**	**0**	**1**	**167**	**11.4**	**191**	**65**	**127**	**30**	**+29**	**20**	**0**	**13**	**13**	**22**	**0**	**0**	**0**
1986-87	**Montreal Canadiens**	**NHL**	**70**	**13**	**37**	**50**	**11**	**27**	**38**	**44**	**6**	**0**	**3**	**122**	**10.7**	**129**	**41**	**74**	**10**	**+24**	**17**	**3**	**17**	**20**	**6**	**2**	**0**	**0**
1987-88	**Montreal Canadiens**	**NHL**	**53**	**6**	**34**	**40**	**5**	**24**	**29**	**30**	**2**	**0**	**1**	**96**	**6.3**	**105**	**31**	**59**	**11**	**+26**	**11**	**1**	**4**	**5**	**4**	**0**	**0**	**0**
1988-89	**Montreal Canadiens**	**NHL**	**74**	**4**	**26**	**30**	**3**	**18**	**21**	**22**	**0**	**0**	**0**	**79**	**5.1**	**99**	**23**	**60**	**7**	**+23**	**21**	**2**	**8**	**10**	**12**	**0**	**0**	**0**
1989-90	**Los Angeles Kings**	**NHL**	**64**	**7**	**32**	**39**	**6**	**23**	**29**	**34**	**1**	**0**	**1**	**80**	**8.8**	**112**	**28**	**101**	**24**	**+7**	**10**	**2**	**3**	**5**	**10**	**0**	**0**	**0**
1990-91	**Los Angeles Kings**	**NHL**	**62**	**1**	**22**	**23**	**1**	**17**	**18**	**16**	**0**	**0**	**0**	**70**	**1.4**	**84**	**13**	**72**	**23**	**+22**	**12**	**1**	**4**	**5**	**15**	**0**	**0**	**0**
1991-92	**Los Angeles Kings**	**NHL**	**56**	**3**	**10**	**13**	**3**	**7**	**10**	**37**	**0**	**0**	**0**	**46**	**6.5**	**53**	**7**	**66**	**21**	**+1**	**2**	**0**	**0**	**0**	**0**	**0**	**0**	**0**
	NHL Totals		**1384**	**208**	**750**	**958**	**181**	**554**	**735**	**793**	**66**	**3**	**29**	**2338**	**8.9**	**2635**	**608**	**1716**	**419**		**227**	**28**	**116**	**144**	**211**	**7**	**0**	**3**

NHL First All-Star Team (1977, 1979, 1980) • Won James Norris Trophy (1977, 1980) • NHL Plus/Minus Leader (1977) • NHL Second All-Star Team (1978, 1981, 1986) • Won Conn Smythe Trophy (1978) • WEC-A All-Star Team (1981) • Named Best Defenseman at WEC-A (1981)

Played in NHL All-Star Game (1974, 1976, 1977, 1978, 1980, 1982, 1986, 1988, 1989, 1992)

Signed as a free agent by **LA Kings**, July 26, 1989.

• ROBINSON, MOE

Moe Robinson D – L. 6'4", 175 lbs. b: Winchester, Ont., 5/29/1957. Montreal's 6th choice, 49th overall, in 1977 Amateur Draft.

Season	Club	League	REGULAR SEASON GP	G	A	Pts	AG	AA	APts	PIM	PP	SH	GW	S	%	TGF	PGF	TGA	PGA	+/–	PLAYOFFS GP	G	A	Pts	PIM	PP	SH	GW
1976-77	Kingston Canadians	OHA	48	5	15	20	....	....	....	35	....	....	....	....	....	....	....	....	....	....	....	....	....	....	....	....	....	....
1977-78	Nova Scotia Voyageurs	AHL	75	6	23	29	....	....	....	68	....	....	....	....	....	....	....	....	....	....	11	0	1	1	7	....	....	....
1978-79	Nova Scotia Voyageurs	AHL	78	4	23	27	....	....	....	92	....	....	....	....	....	....	....	....	....	....	9	1	1	2	6	....	....	....
1979-80	**Montreal Canadiens**	**NHL**	**1**	**0**	**0**	**0**	**0**	**0**	**0**	**0**	**0**	**0**	**0**	**0**	**0.0**	**0**	**0**	**0**	**0**	**0**	....	....	....	....	....	....	....	....
	Nova Scotia Voyageurs	AHL	64	5	35	40	....	....	....	82	....	....	....	....	....	....	....	....	....	....	6	0	2	2	4	....	....	....
1980-81	Oklahoma City Stars	CHL	56	4	22	26	....	....	....	55	....	....	....	....	....	....	....	....	....	....	3	0	2	2	0	....	....	....
	NHL Totals		**1**	**0**	**0**	**0**	**0**	**0**	**0**	**0**	**0**	**0**	**0**	**0**	**0.0**	**0**	**0**	**0**	**0**		....	....	....	....	....	....	....	....

• ROBINSON, ROB

Rob Robinson D – L. 6'1", 214 lbs. b: St. Catharines, Ont., 4/19/1967. St. Louis' 6th choice, 117th overall, in 1987 Entry Draft.

Season	Club	League	REGULAR SEASON GP	G	A	Pts	AG	AA	APts	PIM	PP	SH	GW	S	%	TGF	PGF	TGA	PGA	+/–	PLAYOFFS GP	G	A	Pts	PIM	PP	SH	GW
1985-86	University of Miami-Ohio	CCHA	38	1	9	10	....	....	....	24	....	....	....	....	....	....	....	....	....	....	....	....	....	....	....	....	....	....
1986-87	University of Miami-Ohio	CCHA	33	3	5	8	....	....	....	32	....	....	....	....	....	....	....	....	....	....	....	....	....	....	....	....	....	....
1987-88	University of Miami-Ohio	CCHA	35	1	3	4	....	....	....	56	....	....	....	....	....	....	....	....	....	....	....	....	....	....	....	....	....	....
1988-89	University of Miami-Ohio	CCHA	30	3	4	7	....	....	....	42	....	....	....	....	....	....	....	....	....	....	....	....	....	....	....	....	....	....
	Peoria Rivermen	IHL	11	2	0	2	....	....	....	6	....	....	....	....	....	....	....	....	....	....	....	....	....	....	....	....	....	....
1989-90	Peoria Rivermen	IHL	60	2	11	13	....	....	....	72	....	....	....	....	....	....	....	....	....	....	5	0	1	1	10	....	....	....
1990-91	Peoria Rivermen	IHL	79	2	21	23	....	....	....	42	....	....	....	....	....	....	....	....	....	....	19	0	6	6	8	....	....	....
1991-92	**St. Louis Blues**	**NHL**	**22**	**0**	**1**	**1**	**0**	**1**	**1**	**8**	**0**	**0**	**0**	**9**	**0.0**	**8**	**0**	**14**	**2**	**–4**	....	....	....	....	....	....	....	....
	Peoria Rivermen	IHL	35	1	10	11	....	....	....	29	....	....	....	....	....	....	....	....	....	....	10	0	2	2	12	....	....	....
1992-93	Peoria Rivermen	IHL	34	0	4	4	....	....	....	38	....	....	....	....	....	....	....	....	....	....	....	....	....	....	....	....	....	....
1993-94	Kalamazoo Wings	IHL	67	3	12	15	....	....	....	32	....	....	....	....	....	....	....	....	....	....	5	0	0	0	2	....	....	....
1994-95	Houston Aeros	IHL	70	3	12	15	....	....	....	54	....	....	....	....	....	....	....	....	....	....	4	0	1	1	4	....	....	....
1995-96	Syracuse Crunch	AHL	40	2	6	8	....	....	....	12	....	....	....	....	....	....	....	....	....	....	16	0	2	2	2	....	....	....
1995-96	Syracuse Crunch	IHL	40	2	6	8	....	....	....	12	....	....	....	....	....	....	....	....	....	....	16	0	2	2	2	....	....	....
1996-97	VEU Feldkirch	Austria	55	4	6	10	....	....	....	30	....	....	....	....	....	....	....	....	....	....	....	....	....	....	....	....	....	....
1996-97	VEU Feldkirch	Austria	55	4	6	10	....	....	....	30	....	....	....	....	....	....	....	....	....	....	....	....	....	....	....	....	....	....
1997-98	Frankfurt Lions	Germany	43	0	9	9	....	....	....	51	....	....	....	....	....	....	....	....	....	....	7	0	2	2	29	....	....	....
	NHL Totals		**22**	**0**	**1**	**1**	**0**	**1**	**1**	**8**	**0**	**0**	**0**	**9**	**0.0**	**8**	**0**	**14**	**2**		....	....	....	....	....	....	....	....

IHL Second All-Star Team (1991)

Traded to **Tampa Bay** by **St. Louis** for future considerations, June 19, 1992.

● ROBINSON, SCOTT

Scott Robinson RW – R. 6'2", 180 lbs. b: 100 Mile House, B.C., 3/29/1964.

			REGULAR SEASON																		PLAYOFFS							
Season	Club	League	GP	G	A	Pts	AG	AA	APts	PIM	PP	SH	GW	S	%	TGF	PGF	TGA	PGA	+/–	GP	G	A	Pts	PIM	PP	SH	GW
1982-83	Seattle Breakers	WHL	63	14	13	27	....	....	....	151	....	....	....	....	....	....	....	....	....	....	4	3	0	3	9	....	....	....
1983-84	Seattle Breakers	WHL	44	17	18	35	....	....	....	105	....	....	....	....	....	....	....	....	....	....	5	0	1	1	25	....	....	....
1984-85	Seattle Breakers	WHL	64	44	53	97	....	....	....	106	....	....	....	....	....	....	....	....	....	....	....	....	....	....	....	....	....	....
1985-86	University of Calgary	CWUAA	18	3	9	12	....	....	....	61	....	....	....	....	....	....	....	....	....	....	2	1	1	2	10	....	....	....
1986-87	University of Calgary	CWUAA	19	12	14	26	....	....	....	85	....	....	....	....	....	....	....	....	....	....	5	3	3	6	10	....	....	....
1987-88	University of Calgary	CWUAA	21	14	14	28	....	....	....	64	....	....	....	....	....	....	....	....	....	....	6	3	4	7	12	....	....	....
1988-89	Kalamazoo Wings	IHL	49	14	17	31	....	....	....	129	....	....	....	....	....	....	....	....	....	....	6	1	1	2	21	....	....	....
1989-90	**Minnesota North Stars**	**NHL**	**1**	**0**	**0**	**0**	**0**	**0**	**0**	**2**	**0**	**0**	**0**	**0**	**0.0**	**0**	**0**	**0**	**0**	**0**	....	....	....	....	....	....	....	....
	Kalamazoo Wings	IHL	48	13	12	25	....	....	....	97	....	....	....	....	....	....	....	....	....	....	10	4	7	11	21	....	....	....
1990-91	Kalamazoo Wings	IHL	27	7	9	16	....	....	....	36	....	....	....	....	....	....	....	....	....	....	11	2	1	3	32	....	....	....
1991-92	Kalamazoo Wings	IHL	78	29	27	56	....	....	....	58	....	....	....	....	....	....	....	....	....	....	11	2	6	8	*86	....	....	....
1992-93	Milwaukee Admirals	IHL	27	13	10	23	....	....	....	33	....	....	....	....	....	....	....	....	....	....	....	....	....	....	....	....	....	....
	NHL Totals		**1**	**0**	**0**	**0**	**0**	**0**	**0**	**2**	**0**	**0**	**0**	**0**	**0.0**	**0**	**0**	**0**	**0**		....	....	....	....	....	....	....	....

WHL West Second All-Star Team (1985)

Signed as a free agent by **Minnesota**, September 27, 1988.

● ROBITAILLE, LUC

Luc "Lucky" Robitaille LW – L. 6'1", 195 lbs. b: Montreal, Que., 2/17/1966. Los Angeles' 9th choice, 171st overall, in 1984 Entry Draft.

			REGULAR SEASON																		PLAYOFFS							
Season	Club	League	GP	G	A	Pts	AG	AA	APts	PIM	PP	SH	GW	S	%	TGF	PGF	TGA	PGA	+/–	GP	G	A	Pts	PIM	PP	SH	GW
1983-84	Hull Olympiques	QMJHL	70	32	53	85	....	....	....	48	....	....	....	....	....	....	....	....	....	....	....	....	....	....	....	....	....	....
1984-85	Hull Olympiques	QMJHL	64	55	94	149	....	....	....	115	....	....	....	....	....	....	....	....	....	....	5	4	2	6	27	....	....	....
1985-86	Hull Olympiques	QMJHL	63	68	123	191	....	....	....	91	....	....	....	....	....	....	....	....	....	....	15	17	27	44	28	....	....	....
	Canada	WJC-A	7	3	5	8	....	....	....	2	....	....	....	....	....	....	....	....	....	....	....	....	....	....	....	....	....	....
1986-87	**Los Angeles Kings**	**NHL**	**79**	**45**	**39**	**84**	**39**	**28**	**67**	**28**	**18**	**0**	**3**	**199**	**22.6**	**125**	**53**	**91**	**1**	**–18**	**5**	**1**	**4**	**5**	**2**	**0**	**0**	**0**
1987-88	**Los Angeles Kings**	**NHL**	**80**	**53**	**58**	**111**	**46**	**41**	**87**	**82**	**17**	**0**	**6**	**220**	**24.1**	**156**	**72**	**94**	**1**	**–9**	**5**	**2**	**5**	**7**	**18**	**2**	**0**	**1**
1988-89	**Los Angeles Kings**	**NHL**	**78**	**46**	**52**	**98**	**39**	**37**	**76**	**65**	**10**	**0**	**4**	**237**	**19.4**	**143**	**38**	**111**	**11**	**+5**	**11**	**2**	**6**	**8**	**10**	**0**	**0**	**1**
1989-90	**Los Angeles Kings**	**NHL**	**80**	**52**	**49**	**101**	**45**	**35**	**80**	**38**	**20**	**0**	**7**	**210**	**24.8**	**141**	**46**	**88**	**1**	**+8**	**10**	**5**	**5**	**10**	**10**	**1**	**0**	**1**
1990-91	**Los Angeles Kings**	**NHL**	**76**	**45**	**46**	**91**	**42**	**35**	**77**	**68**	**11**	**0**	**5**	**229**	**19.7**	**136**	**41**	**68**	**1**	**+28**	**12**	**12**	**4**	**16**	**22**	**5**	**0**	**2**
1991-92	Canada	C Cup	8	1	2	3	....	....	....	10	....	....	....	....	....	....	....	....	....	....	....	....	....	....	....	....	....	....
	Los Angeles Kings	**NHL**	**80**	**44**	**63**	**107**	**40**	**47**	**87**	**95**	**26**	**0**	**6**	**240**	**18.3**	**137**	**67**	**81**	**7**	**–4**	**6**	**3**	**4**	**7**	**12**	**1**	**0**	**1**
1992-93	**Los Angeles Kings**	**NHL**	**84**	**63**	**62**	**125**	**53**	**43**	**96**	**100**	**24**	**2**	**8**	**265**	**23.8**	**167**	**59**	**110**	**20**	**+18**	**24**	**9**	**13**	**22**	**28**	**4**	**0**	**2**
1993-94	**Los Angeles Kings**	**NHL**	**83**	**44**	**42**	**86**	**41**	**32**	**73**	**86**	**24**	**0**	**3**	**267**	**16.5**	**134**	**73**	**84**	**3**	**–20**	....	....	....	....	....	....	....	....
	Canada	WC-A	8	4	4	8	....	....	....	2	....	....	....	....	....	....	....	....	....	....	....	....	....	....	....	....	....	....
1994-95	**Pittsburgh Penguins**	**NHL**	**46**	**23**	**19**	**42**	**41**	**28**	**69**	**37**	**5**	**0**	**3**	**109**	**21.1**	**70**	**20**	**45**	**5**	**+10**	**12**	**7**	**4**	**11**	**26**	**0**	**0**	**2**
1995-96	**New York Rangers**	**NHL**	**77**	**23**	**46**	**69**	**23**	**38**	**61**	**80**	**11**	**0**	**4**	**223**	**10.3**	**103**	**42**	**48**	**0**	**+13**	**11**	**1**	**5**	**6**	**8**	**0**	**0**	**0**
1996-97	**New York Rangers**	**NHL**	**69**	**24**	**24**	**48**	**26**	**21**	**47**	**48**	**5**	**0**	**4**	**200**	**12.0**	**81**	**24**	**41**	**0**	**+16**	**15**	**4**	**7**	**11**	**4**	**0**	**0**	**0**
1997-98	**Los Angeles Kings**	**NHL**	**57**	**16**	**24**	**40**	**19**	**23**	**42**	**66**	**5**	**0**	**7**	**130**	**12.3**	**60**	**24**	**31**	**0**	**+5**	**4**	**1**	**2**	**3**	**6**	**0**	**0**	**0**
	NHL Totals		**889**	**478**	**524**	**1002**	**454**	**408**	**862**	**793**	**176**	**2**	**60**	**2529**	**18.9**	**1453**	**559**	**892**	**50**		**115**	**47**	**59**	**106**	**146**	**13**	**0**	**10**

QMJHL Second All-Star Team (1985) • QMJHL First All-Star Team (1986) • Canadian Major Junior Player of the Year (1986) • NHL All-Rookie Team (1987) • Won Calder Memorial Trophy (1987) • NHL Second All-Star Team (1987, 1992) • NHL First All-Star Team (1988, 1989, 1990, 1991, 1993)

Played in NHL All-Star Game (1988, 1989, 1990, 1991, 1992, 1993)

Traded to **Pittsburgh** by **LA Kings** for Rick Tocchet and Pittsburgh's 2nd round choice (Pavel Rosa) in 1995 Entry Draft, July 29, 1994. Traded to **NY Rangers** by **Pittsburgh** with Ulf Samuelsson for Petr Nedved and Sergei Zubov, August 31, 1995. Traded to **Los Angeles** by **NY Rangers** for Kevin Stevens, August 28, 1997.

● ROBITAILLE, MIKE

Mike Robitaille D – R. 5'11", 195 lbs. b: Midland, Ont., 2/12/1948.

			REGULAR SEASON																		PLAYOFFS							
Season	Club	League	GP	G	A	Pts	AG	AA	APts	PIM	PP	SH	GW	S	%	TGF	PGF	TGA	PGA	+/–	GP	G	A	Pts	PIM	PP	SH	GW
1963-64	Kitchener Rangers	OHA	1	0	0	0	....	....	....	0	....	....	....	....	....	....	....	....	....	....	....	....	....	....	....	....	....	....
1964-65	Kitchener Rangers	OHA	37	2	8	10	....	....	....	83	....	....	....	....	....	....	....	....	....	....	....	....	....	....	....	....	....	....
1965-66	Kitchener Greenshirts	OJHL	STATISTICS NOT AVAILABLE																									
	Kitchener Rangers	OHA	1	0	0	0	....	....	....	0	....	....	....	....	....	....	....	....	....	....	....	....	....	....	....	....	....	....
1966-67	Kitchener Rangers	OHA	40	7	30	37	....	....	....	70	....	....	....	....	....	....	....	....	....	....	13	2	6	8	15	....	....	....
1967-68	Kitchener Rangers	OHA	51	20	51	71	....	....	....	77	....	....	....	....	....	....	....	....	....	....	14	4	10	14	34	....	....	....
1968-69	Omaha Knights	CHL	43	5	35	40	....	....	....	52	....	....	....	....	....	....	....	....	....	....	7	1	3	4	9	....	....	....
1969-70	**New York Rangers**	**NHL**	**4**	**0**	**0**	**0**	**0**	**0**	**0**	**8**	**0**	**0**	**0**	**2**	**0.0**	**1**	**1**	**0**	**0**	**0**	....	....	....	....	....	....	....	....
	Omaha Knights	CHL	64	12	46	58	....	....	....	115	....	....	....	....	....	....	....	....	....	....	12	2	*14	16	15	....	....	....
	Buffalo Bisons	AHL	....	....	....	....	....	....	....	....	....	....	....	....	....	....	....	....	....	....	5	0	4	4	14	....	....	....
1970-71	**New York Rangers**	**NHL**	**11**	**1**	**1**	**2**	**1**	**1**	**2**	**7**	**1**	**0**	**0**	**12**	**8.3**	**3**	**1**	**3**	**0**	**–1**	....	....	....	....	....	....	....	....
	Omaha Knights	CHL	13	0	9	9	....	....	....	32	....	....	....	....	....	....	....	....	....	....	....	....	....	....	....	....	....	....
	Detroit Red Wings	**NHL**	**23**	**4**	**8**	**12**	**4**	**7**	**11**	**22**	**2**	**0**	**0**	**37**	**10.8**	**28**	**12**	**37**	**7**	**–14**		....	....	....	....	....	....	....
1971-72	**Buffalo Sabres**	**NHL**	**31**	**2**	**10**	**12**	**2**	**9**	**11**	**22**	**1**	**0**	**0**	**62**	**3.2**	**23**	**13**	**29**	**5**	**–14**	....	....	....	....	....	....	....	....
	Cincinnati Swords	AHL	8	0	1	1	....	....	....	12	....	....	....	....	....	....	....	....	....	....	....	....	....	....	....	....	....	....
1972-73	**Buffalo Sabres**	**NHL**	**65**	**4**	**17**	**21**	**4**	**14**	**18**	**40**	**0**	**0**	**0**	**182**	**2.2**	**74**	**8**	**60**	**3**	**+9**	**6**	**0**	**0**	**0**	**0**	**0**	**0**	**0**
1973-74	**Buffalo Sabres**	**NHL**	**71**	**2**	**18**	**20**	**2**	**16**	**18**	**60**	**2**	**0**	**0**	**185**	**1.1**	**83**	**9**	**91**	**19**	**+2**	....	....	....	....	....	....	....	....
1974-75	**Buffalo Sabres**	**NHL**	**3**	**0**	**1**	**1**	**0**	**1**	**1**	**0**	**0**	**0**	**0**	**4**	**0.0**	**5**	**0**	**7**	**4**	**+2**	....	....	....	....	....	....	....	....
	Vancouver Canucks	**NHL**	**63**	**2**	**22**	**24**	**2**	**17**	**19**	**31**	**0**	**0**	**0**	**157**	**1.3**	**85**	**14**	**83**	**29**	**+17**	**5**	**0**	**1**	**1**	**2**	**0**	**0**	**0**
1975-76	**Vancouver Canucks**	**NHL**	**71**	**8**	**19**	**27**	**7**	**15**	**22**	**69**	**2**	**0**	**0**	**164**	**4.9**	**90**	**16**	**95**	**29**	**+8**	**2**	**0**	**0**	**0**	**2**	**0**	**0**	**0**
1976-77	**Vancouver Canucks**	**NHL**	**40**	**0**	**9**	**9**	**0**	**7**	**7**	**21**	**0**	**0**	**0**	**54**	**0.0**	**39**	**7**	**57**	**12**	**–13**	....	....	....	....	....	....	....	....
	NHL Totals		**382**	**23**	**105**	**128**	**22**	**87**	**109**	**280**	**8**	**0**	**0**	**859**	**2.7**	**431**	**81**	**462**	**108**		**13**	**0**	**1**	**1**	**4**	**0**	**0**	**0**

OHA First All-Star Team (1968) • CHL First All-Star Team (1970) • Named CHL's Top Defenseman (1970)

Traded to **Detroit** by **NY Rangers** with Arnie Brown and Tom Miller for Bruce MacGregor and Larry Brown, February 2, 1971. Traded to **Buffalo** by **Detroit** with Don Luce for Joe Daley, May 25, 1971. Traded to **Vancouver** by **Buffalo** with Gerry Meehan for Jocelyn Guevremont and Bryan McSheffrey, October 14, 1974.

● ROBITAILLE, RANDY

Randy Robitaille C – L. 5'11", 195 lbs. b: Ottawa, Ont., 10/12/1975.

			REGULAR SEASON																		PLAYOFFS							
Season	Club	League	GP	G	A	Pts	AG	AA	APts	PIM	PP	SH	GW	S	%	TGF	PGF	TGA	PGA	+/–	GP	G	A	Pts	PIM	PP	SH	GW
1995-96	University of Miami-Ohio	CCHA	36	14	31	45	....	....	....	26	....	....	....	....	....	....	....	....	....	....	....	....	....	....	....	....	....	....
1996-97	University of Miami-Ohio	CCHA	39	27	34	61	....	....	....	44	....	....	....	....	....	....	....	....	....	....	....	....	....	....	....	....	....	....
	Boston Bruins	**NHL**	**1**	**0**	**0**	**0**	**0**	**0**	**0**	**0**	**0**	**0**	**0**	**0**	**0.0**	**0**	**0**	**0**	**0**	**0**	....	....	....	....	....	....	....	....
1997-98	**Boston Bruins**	**NHL**	**4**	**0**	**0**	**0**	**0**	**0**	**0**	**0**	**0**	**0**	**0**	**5**	**0.0**	**2**	**0**	**4**	**0**	**–2**	....	....	....	....	....	....	....	....
	Providence Bruins	AHL	48	15	29	44	....	....	....	16	....	....	....	....	....	....	....	....	....	....	....	....	....	....	....	....	....	....
	NHL Totals		**5**	**0**	**0**	**0**	**0**	**0**	**0**	**0**	**0**	**0**	**0**	**5**	**0.0**	**2**	**0**	**4**	**0**		....	....	....	....	....	....	....	....

CCHA First All-Star Team (1997) • NCAA West First All-American Team (1997)

Signed as a free agent by **Boston**, March 27, 1997.

● ROCHE, DAVE

Dave Roche C – L. 6'4", 227 lbs. b: Lindsay, Ont., 6/13/1975. Pittsburgh's 3rd choice, 62nd overall, in 1993 Entry Draft.

			REGULAR SEASON																		PLAYOFFS							
Season	Club	League	GP	G	A	Pts	AG	AA	APts	PIM	PP	SH	GW	S	%	TGF	PGF	TGA	PGA	+/–	GP	G	A	Pts	PIM	PP	SH	GW
1991-92	Peterborough Petes	OHL	62	10	17	27	....	....	....	134	....	....	....	....	....	....	....	....	....	....	10	0	0	0	34	....	....	....
1992-93	Peterborough Petes	OHL	56	40	60	100	....	....	....	105	....	....	....	....	....	....	....	....	....	....	21	14	15	29	42	....	....	....
1993-94	Peterborough Petes	OHL	34	15	22	37	....	....	....	127	....	....	....	....	....	....	....	....	....	....	....	....	....	....	....	....	....	....
	Windsor Spitfires	OHL	29	14	20	34	....	....	....	73	....	....	....	....	....	....	....	....	....	....	4	1	1	2	15	....	....	....
1994-95	Windsor Spitfires	OHL	66	55	59	114	....	....	....	180	....	....	....	....	....	....	....	....	....	....	10	9	6	15	16	....	....	....
1995-96	**Pittsburgh Penguins**	**NHL**	**71**	**7**	**7**	**14**	**7**	**6**	**13**	**130**	**0**	**0**	**1**	**65**	**10.8**	**24**	**1**	**28**	**0**	**–5**	**16**	**2**	**7**	**9**	**26**	**0**	**0**	**0**
1996-97	**Pittsburgh Penguins**	**NHL**	**61**	**5**	**5**	**10**	**5**	**4**	**9**	**155**	**2**	**0**	**0**	**53**	**9.4**	**15**	**4**	**24**	**0**	**–13**	....	....	....	....	....	....	....	....
	Cleveland Lumberjacks	IHL	18	5	5	10	....	....	....	25	....	....	....	....	....	....	....	....	....	....	13	6	3	9	*87	....	....	....
1997-98	Syracuse Crunch	AHL	73	12	20	32	....	....	....	307	....	....	....	....	....	....	....	....	....	....	5	2	0	2	10	....	....	....
	NHL Totals		**132**	**12**	**12**	**24**	**12**	**10**	**22**	**285**	**2**	**0**	**1**	**118**	**10.2**	**39**	**5**	**52**	**0**		**16**	**2**	**7**	**9**	**26**	**0**	**0**	**0**

OHL First All-Star Team (1995)

Traded to **Calgary** by **Pittsburgh** with Ken Wregget for German Titov and Todd Hlushko, June 17, 1998.

• ROCHEFORT, LEON

Leon Rochefort RW – R. 6', 185 lbs. b: Cap de la Madeleine, Que., 5/4/1939.

			REGULAR SEASON																		PLAYOFFS							
Season	Club	League	GP	G	A	Pts	AG	AA	APts	PIM	PP	SH	GW	S	%	TGF	PGF	TGA	PGA	+/–	GP	G	A	Pts	PIM	PP	SH	GW
1957-58	Guelph Biltmores	OHA	52	17	18	35	....	....	....	19	....	....	....	....	....	....	....	....	....	....	....	....	....	....	....	....	....	....
1958-59	Guelph Biltmores	OHA	54	16	19	35	....	....	....	16	....	....	....	....	....	....	....	....	....	....	10	8	4	12	4	....	....	....
1959-60	Trois-Rivieres Lions	EPHL	70	27	22	49	....	....	....	35	....	....	....	....	....	....	....	....	....	....	4	0	0	0	9	....	....	....
1960-61	New York Rangers	NHL	1	0	0	0	0	0	0	0	....	....	....	....	....	....	....	....	....	....	....	....	....	....	....	....	....	....
	Kitchener-Waterloo Beavers	EPHL	65	20	18	38	....	....	....	33	....	....	....	....	....	....	....	....	....	....	7	3	1	4	14	....	....	....
1961-62	Kitchener-Waterloo Beavers	EPHL	69	33	27	69	....	....	....	29	....	....	....	....	....	....	....	....	....	....	....	....	....	....	....	....	....	....
1962-63	New York Rangers	NHL	23	5	4	9	6	4	10	6	....	....	....	....	....	....	....	....	....	....	....	....	....	....	....	....	....	....
	Baltimore Clippers	AHL	50	14	20	34	....	....	....	12	....	....	....	....	....	....	....	....	....	....	....	....	....	....	....	....	....	....
1963-64	Montreal Canadiens	NHL	3	0	0	0	0	0	0	0	....	....	....	....	....	....	....	....	....	....	....	....	....	....	....	....	....	....
	Quebec Aces	AHL	71	27	25	52	....	....	....	14	....	....	....	....	....	....	....	....	....	....	9	4	3	7	2	....	....	....
1964-65	Montreal Canadiens	NHL	9	2	0	2	3	0	3	0	....	....	....	....	....	....	....	....	....	....	....	....	....	....	....	....	....	....
	Quebec Aces	AHL	41	18	21	38	....	....	....	12	....	....	....	....	....	....	....	....	....	....	5	0	3	3	6	....	....	....
1965-66	Montreal Canadiens	NHL	1	0	1	1	0	1	1	0	....	....	....	....	....	....	....	....	....	....	4	1	1	2	4	....	....	....
	Quebec Aces	AHL	71	35	37	72	....	....	....	12	....	....	....	....	....	....	....	....	....	....	6	5	3	8	0	....	....	....
1966-67	Montreal Canadiens	NHL	27	9	7	16	11	7	18	6	....	....	....	....	....	....	....	....	....	....	10	1	1	2	4	....	....	....
	Quebec Aces	AHL	8	3	2	5	....	....	....	2	....	....	....	....	....	....	....	....	....	....	....	....	....	....	....	....	....	....
1967-68	Philadelphia Flyers	NHL	74	21	21	42	26	22	48	16	4	2	1	237	8.9	57	12	54	8	–1	7	2	0	2	2	0	0	1
1968-69	Philadelphia Flyers	NHL	65	14	21	35	16	20	36	10	3	0	0	148	9.5	43	18	32	0	–7	3	0	0	0	0	0	0	0
1969-70	Los Angeles Kings	NHL	76	9	23	32	10	23	33	14	1	0	1	190	4.7	55	25	67	7	–30	....	....	....	....	....	....	....	....
1970-71	Montreal Canadiens	NHL	57	5	10	15	5	9	14	4	0	3	1	33	15.2	22	0	30	19	+11	10	0	0	0	6	0	0	0
	Montreal Voyageurs	AHL	10	1	6	7	....	....	....	0	....	....	....	....	....	....	....	....	....	....	....	....	....	....	....	....	....	....
1971-72	Detroit Red Wings	NHL	64	17	12	29	18	11	29	10	0	0	3	97	17.5	40	3	45	9	+1	....	....	....	....	....	....	....	....
1972-73	Detroit Red Wings	NHL	20	2	4	6	2	3	5	2	0	0	0	23	8.7	9	1	9	1	0	....	....	....	....	....	....	....	....
	Atlanta Flames	NHL	54	9	18	27	9	15	24	10	1	0	0	130	6.9	38	8	34	0	–4	....	....	....	....	....	....	....	....
1973-74	Atlanta Flames	NHL	56	10	12	22	10	10	20	13	1	0	1	107	9.3	41	5	52	4	–12	....	....	....	....	....	....	....	....
1974-75	Vancouver Canucks	NHL	76	18	11	29	17	9	26	2	2	0	3	124	14.5	45	7	47	4	–5	5	0	2	2	0	0	0	0
1975-76	Vancouver Canucks	NHL	11	0	3	3	0	2	2	0	0	0	0	13	0.0	4	0	10	2	–4	....	....	....	....	....	....	....	....
	Tulsa Oilers	CHL	60	25	40	65	....	....	....	2	....	....	....	....	....	....	....	....	....	....	9	2	5	7	6	....	....	....
	NHL Totals		617	121	147	268	133	136	269	93	12	5	10	1102	11.0	354	79	380	54		39	4	4	8	16	0	0	1

Played in NHL All-Star Game (1968)

Traded to **Montreal** by **NY Rangers** with Dave Balon, Len Ronson and Gump Worsley for Phil Goyette, Don Marshall and Jacques Plante, June 4, 1963. Claimed by **Philadelphia** from **Montreal** in Expansion Draft, June 6, 1967. Traded to **NY Rangers** by **Philadelphia** with Don Blackburn for Reggie Fleming, June 6, 1969. Traded to **LA Kings** by **NY Rangers** with Dennis Hextall for Real Lemieux, June 9, 1969. Traded to **Montreal** by **LA Kings** with Wayne Thomas and Greg Boddy for Larry Mickey, Lucien Grenier and Jack Norris, May 22, 1970. Traded to **Detroit** by **Montreal** for Kerry Ketter and cash, May 25, 1971. Traded to **Atlanta** by **Detroit** for Bill Hogaboam, November 28, 1972. Traded to **Vancouver** by **Atlanta** for cash, October 4, 1974.

• ROCHEFORT, NORMAND

Normand Rochefort D – L. 6'1", 214 lbs. b: Trois-Rivières, Que., 1/28/1961. Quebec's 1st choice, 24th overall, in 1980 Entry Draft.

Season	Club	League	GP	G	A	Pts	AG	AA	APts	PIM	PP	SH	GW	S	%	TGF	PGF	TGA	PGA	+/–	GP	G	A	Pts	PIM	PP	SH	GW
1977-78	Trois-Rivieres Draveurs	QMJHL	72	9	37	46	....	....	....	36	....	....	....	....	....	....	....	....	....	....	....	....	....	....	....	....	....	....
1978-79	Trois-Rivieres Draveurs	QMJHL	72	17	57	74	....	....	....	30	....	....	....	....	....	....	....	....	....	....	13	3	11	14	17	....	....	....
1979-80	Trois-Rivieres Draveurs	QMJHL	20	5	25	30	....	....	....	22	....	....	....	....	....	....	....	....	....	....	....	....	....	....	....	....	....	....
	Quebec Remparts	QMJHL	52	8	39	47	....	....	....	68	....	....	....	....	....	....	....	....	....	....	5	1	3	4	8	....	....	....
1980-81	Quebec Remparts	QMJHL	9	2	6	8	....	....	....	14	....	....	....	....	....	....	....	....	....	....	....	....	....	....	....	....	....	....
	Quebec Nordiques	NHL	56	3	7	10	2	5	7	51	0	0	0	77	3.9	63	6	85	17	–11	5	0	0	0	4	0	0	0
1981-82	Quebec Nordiques	NHL	72	4	14	18	3	9	12	115	0	0	1	105	3.8	102	6	102	25	+19	16	0	2	2	10	0	0	0
1982-83	Quebec Nordiques	NHL	62	6	17	23	5	12	17	40	1	0	1	104	5.8	99	16	94	22	+11	1	0	0	0	2	0	0	0
1983-84	Quebec Nordiques	NHL	75	2	22	24	2	15	17	47	0	0	1	84	2.4	104	5	93	35	+41	6	1	0	1	6	0	0	0
1984-85	Quebec Nordiques	NHL	73	3	21	24	2	14	16	74	1	0	1	113	2.7	95	6	107	30	+12	18	2	1	3	8	0	0	1
1985-86	Quebec Nordiques	NHL	26	5	4	9	4	3	7	30	2	0	0	51	9.8	35	5	28	7	+9	....	....	....	....	....	....	....	....
1986-87	Quebec Nordiques	NHL	70	6	9	15	5	6	11	46	0	0	0	92	6.5	74	4	85	17	+2	13	2	1	3	26	0	0	1
	NHL All-Stars	RV'87	1	0	0	0	....	....	....	0	....	....	....	....	....	....	....	....	....	....	....	....	....	....	....	....	....	....
1987-88	Canada	C Cup	9	1	2	3	....	....	....	8	....	....	....	....	....	....	....	....	....	....	....	....	....	....	....	....	....	....
	Quebec Nordiques	NHL	46	3	10	13	3	7	10	49	0	1	0	70	4.3	66	20	77	29	–2	....	....	....	....	....	....	....	....
1988-89	New York Rangers	NHL	11	1	5	6	1	4	5	18	0	0	1	14	7.1	12	1	13	2	0	....	....	....	....	....	....	....	....
1989-90	New York Rangers	NHL	31	3	1	4	3	1	4	24	0	0	1	30	10.0	26	0	37	13	+2	10	2	1	3	26	0	1	0
	Flint Spirits	IHL	7	3	2	5	....	....	....	4	....	....	....	....	....	....	....	....	....	....	....	....	....	....	....	....	....	....
1990-91	New York Rangers	NHL	44	3	7	10	3	5	8	35	0	0	0	34	8.8	33	0	38	15	+10	....	....	....	....	....	....	....	....
1991-92	New York Rangers	NHL	26	0	2	2	0	1	1	31	0	0	0	18	0.0	11	0	23	2	–10	....	....	....	....	....	....	....	....
1992-93	Eisbaren	Germany	17	4	2	6	....	....	....	21	....	....	....	....	....	....	....	....	....	....	....	....	....	....	....	....	....	....
1993-94	Tampa Bay Lightning	NHL	6	0	0	0	0	0	0	10	0	0	0	4	0.0	2	0	5	2	–1	....	....	....	....	....	....	....	....
	Atlanta Knights	IHL	65	5	7	12	....	....	....	43	....	....	....	....	....	....	....	....	....	....	13	0	2	2	6	....	....	....
1994-95	Denver Grizzlies	IHL	77	4	13	17	....	....	....	46	....	....	....	....	....	....	....	....	....	....	17	1	4	5	12	....	....	....
1995-96	San Francisco Spiders	IHL	77	3	12	15	....	....	....	45	....	....	....	....	....	....	....	....	....	....	4	0	0	0	2	....	....	....
1996-97	Kansas City Blades	IHL	77	7	14	21	....	....	....	28	....	....	....	....	....	....	....	....	....	....	3	1	0	1	2	....	....	....
1997-98	Kansas City Blades	IHL	52	1	3	4	....	....	....	48	....	....	....	....	....	....	....	....	....	....	11	1	2	3	8	....	....	....
	NHL Totals		598	39	119	158	33	82	115	570	4	1	6	796	4.9	722	69	787	216		69	7	5	12	82	0	1	2

Memorial Cup All-Star Team (1979) • QMJHL Second All-Star Team (1980)

Traded to **NY Rangers** by **Quebec** with Jason Lafreniere for Bruce Bell, Jari Gronstrand, Walt Poddubny and NY Rangers' 4th round choice (Eric Dubois) in 1989 Entry Draft, August 1, 1988. Signed as a free agent by **Tampa Bay**, September 27, 1993.

• ROENICK, JEREMY

Jeremy Roenick C – R. 6', 170 lbs. b: Boston, MA, 1/17/1970. Chicago's 1st choice, 8th overall, in 1988 Entry Draft.

Season	Club	League	GP	G	A	Pts	AG	AA	APts	PIM	PP	SH	GW	S	%	TGF	PGF	TGA	PGA	+/–	GP	G	A	Pts	PIM	PP	SH	GW
1987-88	Thayer Academy	H.S.	24	34	50	84	....	....	....	....	....	....	....	....	....	....	....	....	....	....	....	....	....	....	....	....	....	....
	United States	WJC-A	7	5	4	9	....	....	....	4	....	....	....	....	....	....	....	....	....	....	....	....	....	....	....	....	....	....
1988-89	Hull Olympiques	QMJHL	28	34	36	70	....	....	....	14	....	....	....	....	....	....	....	....	....	....	....	....	....	....	....	....	....	....
	United States	WJC-A	7	8	8	16	....	....	....	0	....	....	....	....	....	....	....	....	....	....	....	....	....	....	....	....	....	....
	Chicago Blackhawks	NHL	20	9	9	18	8	6	14	4	2	0	0	52	17.3	26	7	16	1	+4	10	1	3	4	7	1	0	1
1989-90	Chicago Blackhawks	NHL	78	26	40	66	22	29	51	54	6	0	4	173	15.0	86	28	64	8	+2	20	11	7	18	8	4	0	1
1990-91	Chicago Blackhawks	NHL	79	41	53	94	38	40	78	80	15	4	10	194	21.1	140	61	52	11	+38	6	3	5	8	4	1	0	1
	United States	WEC-A	9	5	6	11	....	....	....	8	....	....	....	....	....	....	....	....	....	....	....	....	....	....	....	....	....	....
1991-92	United States	C Cup	8	4	2	6	....	....	....	4	....	....	....	....	....	....	....	....	....	....	....	....	....	....	....	....	....	....
	Chicago Blackhawks	NHL	80	53	50	103	49	38	87	98	22	3	13	234	22.6	128	57	63	15	+23	18	12	10	22	12	4	0	3
1992-93	Chicago Blackhawks	NHL	84	50	57	107	42	39	81	86	22	3	3	255	19.6	132	67	64	14	+15	4	1	2	3	2	0	0	0
1993-94	Chicago Blackhawks	NHL	84	46	61	107	43	47	90	125	24	5	5	281	16.4	135	52	91	29	+21	6	1	6	7	2	0	0	1
1994-95	Koln	Germany	3	3	1	4	....	....	....	2	....	....	....	....	....	....	....	....	....	....	....	....	....	....	....	....	....	....
	Chicago Blackhawks	NHL	33	10	24	34	18	35	53	14	5	0	1	93	10.8	58	33	29	9	+5	8	1	2	3	16	0	0	0
1995-96	Chicago Blackhawks	NHL	66	32	35	67	32	29	61	109	12	4	2	171	18.7	92	36	64	17	+9	10	5	7	12	2	1	0	1
1996-97	Phoenix Coyotes	NHL	72	29	40	69	31	35	66	115	10	3	7	228	12.7	91	33	76	11	–7	6	2	4	6	4	0	0	0
1997-98	Phoenix Coyotes	NHL	79	24	32	56	28	31	59	103	6	1	3	182	13.2	88	38	66	21	+5	6	5	3	8	4	2	2	2
	United States	Olympics	4	0	1	1	....	....	....	6	....	....	....	....	....	....	....	....	....	....	....	....	....	....	....	....	....	....
	NHL Totals		675	320	401	721	311	329	640	788	124	23	48	1863	17.2	976	412	585	136		94	42	49	91	61	13	2	10

WJC-A All-Star Team (1989) • QMJHL Second All-Star Team (1989) • Canada Cup All-Star Team (1991)

Played in NHL All-Star Game (1991, 1992, 1993, 1994)

Traded to **Phoenix** by **Chicago** for Alexei Zhamnov, Craig Mills and Phoenix's 1st round choice (Ty Jones) in 1997 Entry Draft, August 16, 1996.

• ROGERS, JOHN

John Rogers RW – R. 5'11", 175 lbs. b: Paradise Hills, Sask., 4/10/1953. Minnesota's 2nd choice, 25th overall, in 1973 Amateur Draft.

			REGULAR SEASON																		PLAYOFFS							
Season	Club	League	GP	G	A	Pts	AG	AA	APts	PIM	PP	SH	GW	S	%	TGF	PGF	TGA	PGA	+/–	GP	G	A	Pts	PIM	PP	SH	GW
1969-70	Edmonton Oil Kings	Tier II	44	30	21	51	....	....	....	150	....	....	....	....	....	....	....	....	....	....	....	....	....	....	....	....	....	....
1970-71	Edmonton Oil Kings	WCJHL	47	27	16	43	....	....	....	218	....	....	....	....	....	....	....	....	....	....	....	....	....	....	....	....	....	....
1971-72	Edmonton Oil Kings	WCJHL	46	26	27	53	....	....	....	236	....	....	....	....	....	....	....	....	....	....	....	....	....	....	....	....	....	....
1972-73	Edmonton Oil Kings	WCJHL	68	63	41	104	....	....	....	219	....	....	....	....	....	....	....	....	....	....	....	....	....	....	....	....	....	....
1973-74	**Minnesota North Stars**	**NHL**	**10**	**2**	**4**	**6**	**2**	**3**	**5**	**0**	**0**	**0**	**0**	**13**	**15.4**	**7**	**0**	**7**	**1**	**+1**	....	....	....	....	....	....	....	....
	New Haven Nighthawks	AHL	54	16	18	34	....	....	....	73	....	....	....	....	....	....	....	....	....	....	10	1	1	2	0	....	....	....
1974-75	**Minnesota North Stars**	**NHL**	**4**	**0**	**0**	**0**	**0**	**0**	**0**	**0**	**0**	**0**	**0**	**2**	**0.0**	**0**	**0**	**1**	**0**	**–1**	....	....	....	....	....	....	....	....
	New Haven Nighthawks	AHL	54	16	18	34	....	....	....	41	....	....	....	....	....	....	....	....	....	....	2	0	0	0	0	....	....	....
1975-76	Edmonton Oilers	WHA	44	9	8	17	....	....	....	34	....	....	....	....	....	....	....	....	....	....	....	....	....	....	....	....	....	....
	Spokane Flyers	WIHL	6	6	2	8	....	....	....	0	....	....	....	....	....	....	....	....	....	....	....	....	....	....	....	....	....	....
	NHL Totals		**14**	**2**	**4**	**6**	**2**	**3**	**5**	**0**	**0**	**0**	**0**	**15**	**13.3**	**7**	**0**	**8**	**1**		....	....	....	....	....	....	....	....
	Other Major League Totals		44	9	8	17	....	....	....	34	....	....	....	....	....	....	....	....	....	....	....	....	....	....	....	....	....	....

Selected by **Edmonton** (WHA) in 1973 WHA Amateur Draft, June, 1973.

• ROGERS, MIKE

Mike Rogers C – L. 5'9", 170 lbs. b: Calgary, Alta., 10/24/1954. Vancouver's 4th choice, 77th overall, in 1974 Amateur Draft.

Season	Club	League	GP	G	A	Pts	AG	AA	APts	PIM	PP	SH	GW	S	%	TGF	PGF	TGA	PGA	+/–	GP	G	A	Pts	PIM	PP	SH	GW
1971-72	Calgary Centennials	WCJHL	66	27	30	57	....	....	....	19	....	....	....	....	....	....	....	....	....	....	....	....	....	....	....	....	....	....
1972-73	Calgary Centennials	WCJHL	67	54	58	122	....	....	....	44	....	....	....	....	....	....	....	....	....	....	6	8	5	13	2	....	....	....
1973-74	Calgary Centennials	WCJHL	66	67	73	140	....	....	....	32	....	....	....	....	....	....	....	....	....	....	14	13	16	29	6	....	....	....
1974-75	Edmonton Oilers	WHA	78	35	48	83	....	....	....	2	....	....	....	....	....	....	....	....	....	....	....	....	....	....	....	....	....	....
1975-76	Edmonton Oilers	WHA	44	12	15	27	....	....	....	10	....	....	....	....	....	....	....	....	....	....	....	....	....	....	....	....	....	....
	New England Whalers	WHA	36	18	14	32	....	....	....	10	....	....	....	....	....	....	....	....	....	....	17	5	8	13	2	....	....	....
1976-77	New England Whalers	WHA	78	25	57	82	....	....	....	10	....	....	....	....	....	....	....	....	....	....	5	1	1	2	2	....	....	....
1977-78	New England Whalers	WHA	80	28	43	71	....	....	....	46	....	....	....	....	....	....	....	....	....	....	14	5	6	11	8	....	....	....
1978-79	New England Whalers	WHA	80	27	45	72	....	....	....	31	....	....	....	....	....	....	....	....	....	....	10	2	6	8	2	....	....	....
1979-80	**Hartford Whalers**	**NHL**	**80**	**44**	**61**	**105**	**40**	**47**	**87**	**10**	**3**	**2**	**0**	**229**	**19.2**	**133**	**30**	**79**	**5**	**+29**	**3**	**0**	**3**	**3**	**0**	**0**	**0**	**0**
1980-81	**Hartford Whalers**	**NHL**	**80**	**40**	**65**	**105**	**33**	**46**	**79**	**32**	**10**	**4**	**1**	**242**	**16.5**	**133**	**45**	**150**	**40**	**–22**	....	....	....	....	....	....	....	....
	Canada	WEC-A	6	0	1	1	....	....	....	4	....	....	....	....	....	....	....	....	....	....	....	....	....	....	....	....	....	....
1981-82	**New York Rangers**	**NHL**	**80**	**38**	**65**	**103**	**30**	**43**	**73**	**43**	**6**	**1**	**2**	**213**	**17.8**	**138**	**48**	**113**	**25**	**+2**	**9**	**1**	**6**	**7**	**2**	**0**	**0**	**0**
1982-83	**New York Rangers**	**NHL**	**71**	**29**	**47**	**76**	**24**	**32**	**56**	**28**	**7**	**5**	**5**	**199**	**14.6**	**99**	**41**	**86**	**18**	**–10**	**1**	**0**	**0**	**0**	**0**	**0**	**0**	**0**
1983-84	**New York Rangers**	**NHL**	**78**	**23**	**38**	**61**	**19**	**26**	**45**	**45**	**6**	**3**	**2**	**186**	**12.4**	**89**	**39**	**93**	**19**	**–24**	**1**	**0**	**0**	**0**	**0**	**0**	**0**	**0**
1984-85	**New York Rangers**	**NHL**	**78**	**26**	**38**	**64**	**21**	**26**	**47**	**24**	**5**	**1**	**1**	**143**	**18.2**	**90**	**32**	**92**	**9**	**–25**	**3**	**0**	**4**	**4**	**4**	**0**	**0**	**0**
1985-86	**New York Rangers**	**NHL**	**9**	**1**	**3**	**4**	**1**	**2**	**3**	**2**	**1**	**0**	**1**	**20**	**5.0**	**7**	**2**	**3**	**0**	**+2**	....	....	....	....	....	....	....	....
	New Haven Nighthawks	AHL	20	9	15	24	....	....	....	28	....	....	....	....	....	....	....	....	....	....	....	....	....	....	....	....	....	....
	Edmonton Oilers	**NHL**	**8**	**1**	**0**	**1**	**1**	**0**	**1**	**0**	**0**	**0**	**0**	**6**	**16.7**	**2**	**0**	**4**	**0**	**–2**	....	....	....	....	....	....	....	....
	Nova Scotia Oilers	AHL	33	15	28	43	....	....	....	14	....	....	....	....	....	....	....	....	....	....	....	....	....	....	....	....	....	....
1986-87	Ambri-Piotta	Switz.	....	19	18	37	....	....	....	....	....	....	....	....	....	....	....	....	....	....	....	....	....	....	....	....	....	....
	NHL Totals		**484**	**202**	**317**	**519**	**169**	**222**	**391**	**184**	**38**	**16**	**12**	**1238**	**16.3**	**691**	**237**	**620**	**116**		**17**	**1**	**13**	**14**	**6**	**0**	**0**	**0**
	Other Major League Totals		396	145	222	367	....	....	....	109	....	....	....	....	....	....	....	....	....	....	46	13	21	34	14	....	....	....

Won Paul Daneau Trophy (WHA Most Gentlemanly Player) (1975)

Played in NHL All-Star Game (1981)

Selected by **Edmonton** (WHA) in 1974 WHA Amateur Draft, May, 1974. Traded to **New England** (WHA) by **Edmonton** (WHA) with future considerations for Wayne Carleton, January, 1976. Rights retained by **Hartford** prior to Expansion Draft, June 9, 1979. Traded to **NY Rangers** by **Hartford** with Hartford's 10th round choice (Simo Saarinen) in 1982 Entry Draft for Chris Kotsopoulos, Gerry McDonald and Doug Sulliman, October 2, 1981. Traded to **Edmonton** by **NY Rangers** for Larry Melnyk and Todd Strueby, December 20, 1985.

• ROHLICEK, JEFF

Jeff Rohlicek C – L. 6', 180 lbs. b: Park Ridge, IL, 1/27/1966. Vancouver's 2nd choice, 31st overall, in 1984 Entry Draft.

Season	Club	League	GP	G	A	Pts	AG	AA	APts	PIM	PP	SH	GW	S	%	TGF	PGF	TGA	PGA	+/–	GP	G	A	Pts	PIM	PP	SH	GW
1983-84	Portland Winter Hawks	WHL	71	44	53	97	....	....	....	22	....	....	....	....	....	....	....	....	....	....	14	13	8	21	10	....	....	....
1984-85	Portland Winter Hawks	WHL	10	5	13	18	....	....	....	2	....	....	....	....	....	....	....	....	....	....	....	....	....	....	....	....	....	....
	United States	WJC-A	7	0	2	2	....	....	....	2	....	....	....	....	....	....	....	....	....	....	....	....	....	....	....	....	....	....
	Kelowna Chiefs	WHL	49	34	39	73	....	....	....	24	....	....	....	....	....	....	....	....	....	....	6	3	6	9	2	....	....	....
1985-86	Spokane Chiefs	WHL	57	50	52	102	....	....	....	39	....	....	....	....	....	....	....	....	....	....	9	6	2	8	16	....	....	....
1986-87	Fredericton Express	AHL	70	19	37	56	....	....	....	22	....	....	....	....	....	....	....	....	....	....	....	....	....	....	....	....	....	....
1987-88	**Vancouver Canucks**	**NHL**	**7**	**0**	**0**	**0**	**0**	**0**	**0**	**4**	**0**	**0**	**0**	**2**	**0.0**	**0**	**0**	**4**	**0**	**–4**	....	....	....	....	....	....	....	....
	Fredericton Express	AHL	65	26	31	57	....	....	....	50	....	....	....	....	....	....	....	....	....	....	....	....	....	....	....	....	....	....
1988-89	**Vancouver Canucks**	**NHL**	**2**	**0**	**0**	**0**	**0**	**0**	**0**	**4**	**0**	**0**	**0**	**2**	**0.0**	**0**	**0**	**0**	**0**	**0**	....	....	....	....	....	....	....	....
	Milwaukee Admirals	IHL	78	47	63	110	....	....	....	106	....	....	....	....	....	....	....	....	....	....	11	6	6	12	8	....	....	....
1989-90	Springfield Indians	AHL	12	1	2	3	....	....	....	4	....	....	....	....	....	....	....	....	....	....	7	3	2	5	6	....	....	....
	Milwaukee Admirals	IHL	53	22	26	48	....	....	....	37	....	....	....	....	....	....	....	....	....	....	....	....	....	....	....	....	....	....
1990-91	New Haven Nighthawks	AHL	4	1	1	2	....	....	....	6	....	....	....	....	....	....	....	....	....	....	....	....	....	....	....	....	....	....
	Phoenix Roadrunners	IHL	74	29	31	60	....	....	....	67	....	....	....	....	....	....	....	....	....	....	10	7	6	13	12	....	....	....
1991-92	Phoenix Roadrunners	IHL	23	5	11	16	....	....	....	32	....	....	....	....	....	....	....	....	....	....	....	....	....	....	....	....	....	....
	Indianapolis Ice	IHL	59	25	32	57	....	....	....	28	....	....	....	....	....	....	....	....	....	....	....	....	....	....	....	....	....	....
1992-93	Milwaukee Admirals	IHL	11	1	1	2	....	....	....	8	....	....	....	....	....	....	....	....	....	....	....	....	....	....	....	....	....	....
	Toledo Storm	ECHL	8	5	8	13	....	....	....	14	....	....	....	....	....	....	....	....	....	....	....	....	....	....	....	....	....	....
	Adirondack Red Wings	AHL	29	6	16	22	....	....	....	20	....	....	....	....	....	....	....	....	....	....	11	4	5	9	10	....	....	....
1993-94	Toledo Storm	ECHL	57	28	54	82	....	....	....	36	....	....	....	....	....	....	....	....	....	....	....	....	....	....	....	....	....	....
	Nashville Knights	ECHL	4	1	1	2	....	....	....	24	....	....	....	....	....	....	....	....	....	....	2	1	0	1	2	....	....	....
1994-95	Chicago Wolves	IHL	10	4	4	8	....	....	....	13	....	....	....	....	....	....	....	....	....	....	....	....	....	....	....	....	....	....
	Fort Wayne Komets	IHL	22	9	14	23	....	....	....	8	....	....	....	....	....	....	....	....	....	....	4	1	2	3	4	....	....	....
1995-96	Fort Wayne Komets	IHL	38	8	12	20	....	....	....	34	....	....	....	....	....	....	....	....	....	....	....	....	....	....	....	....	....	....
1996-97	Mississippi Sea Wolves	ECHL	69	34	56	90	....	....	....	34	....	....	....	....	....	....	....	....	....	....	3	1	0	4	4	....	....	....
1997-98	Mississippi Sea Wolves	ECHL	29	7	15	22	....	....	....	30	....	....	....	....	....	....	....	....	....	....	....	....	....	....	....	....	....	....
	NHL Totals		**9**	**0**	**0**	**0**	**0**	**0**	**0**	**8**	**0**	**0**	**0**	**4**	**0.0**	**0**	**0**	**4**	**0**		....	....	....	....	....	....	....	....

WHL West Second All-Star Team (1985) • IHL First All-Star Team (1989)

Traded to **NY Islanders** by **Vancouver** for Jack Capuano, March 6, 1990.

• ROHLIN, LEIF

Leif Rohlin D – L. 6'1", 198 lbs. b: Vasteras, Sweden, 2/26/1968. Vancouver's 2nd choice, 33rd overall, in 1988 Entry Draft.

Season	Club	League	GP	G	A	Pts	AG	AA	APts	PIM	PP	SH	GW	S	%	TGF	PGF	TGA	PGA	+/–	GP	G	A	Pts	PIM	PP	SH	GW
1986-87	Vasteras IK	Sweden 2	27	2	5	7	....	....	....	12	....	....	....	....	....	....	....	....	....	....	12	0	2	2	8	....	....	....
1987-88	Vasteras IK	Sweden 2	30	2	15	17	....	....	....	46	....	....	....	....	....	....	....	....	....	....	7	0	4	4	8	....	....	....
	Sweden	WJC-A	7	1	1	2	....	....	....	10	....	....	....	....	....	....	....	....	....	....	....	....	....	....	....	....	....	....
1988-89	Vasteras IK	Sweden	22	3	7	10	....	....	....	18	....	....	....	....	....	....	....	....	....	....	....	....	....	....	....	....	....	....
1989-90	Vasteras IK	Sweden	32	3	6	9	....	....	....	40	....	....	....	....	....	....	....	....	....	....	2	0	0	0	2	....	....	....
1990-91	Vasteras IK	Sweden	40	4	10	14	....	....	....	46	....	....	....	....	....	....	....	....	....	....	4	0	1	1	8	....	....	....
1991-92	Vasteras IK	Sweden	39	4	6	10	....	....	....	52	....	....	....	....	....	....	....	....	....	....	....	....	....	....	....	....	....	....
1992-93	Vasteras IK	Sweden	37	5	7	12	....	....	....	24	....	....	....	....	....	....	....	....	....	....	2	0	0	0	0	....	....	....
1993-94	Vasteras IK	Sweden	40	6	14	20	....	....	....	26	....	....	....	....	....	....	....	....	....	....	4	0	1	1	6	....	....	....
	Sweden	Olympics	8	0	1	1	....	....	....	10	....	....	....	....	....	....	....	....	....	....	....	....	....	....	....	....	....	....
1994-95	Vasteras IK	Sweden	39	15	15	30	....	....	....	46	....	....	....	....	....	....	....	....	....	....	4	2	0	2	2	....	....	....
	Sweden	WC-A	8	0	3	3	....	....	....	0	....	....	....	....	....	....	....	....	....	....	....	....	....	....	....	....	....	....
1995-96	**Vancouver Canucks**	**NHL**	**56**	**6**	**16**	**22**	**6**	**13**	**19**	**32**	**1**	**0**	**0**	**72**	**8.3**	**68**	**24**	**56**	**12**	**0**	**5**	**0**	**0**	**0**	**0**	**0**	**0**	**0**
1996-97	Sweden	W Cup	1	0	0	0	....	....	....	2	....	....	....	....	....	....	....	....	....	....	....	....	....	....	....	....	....	....
	Vancouver Canucks	**NHL**	**40**	**2**	**8**	**10**	**2**	**7**	**9**	**8**	**0**	**0**	**0**	**37**	**5.4**	**32**	**2**	**31**	**5**	**+4**	....	....	....	....	....	....	....	....
1997-98	Ambri-Piotta	Switz.	40	7	29	36	....	....	....	28	....	....	....	....	....	....	....	....	....	....	14	3	4	7	32	....	....	....
	NHL Totals		**96**	**8**	**24**	**32**	**8**	**20**	**28**	**40**	**1**	**0**	**0**	**109**	**7.3**	**100**	**26**	**87**	**17**		**5**	**0**	**0**	**0**	**0**	**0**	**0**	**0**

• ROHLOFF, JON

Jon Rohloff D – R. 6', 221 lbs. b: Mankato, MN, 10/3/1969. Boston's 7th choice, 186th overall, in 1988 Entry Draft.

Season	Club	League	GP	G	A	Pts	AG	AA	APts	PIM	PP	SH	GW	S	%	TGF	PGF	TGA	PGA	+/–	GP	G	A	Pts	PIM	PP	SH	GW
1987-88	Grand Rapids High School	H.S.	23	10	13	23	....	....	....	....	....	....	....	....	....	....	....	....	....	....	....	....	....	....	....	....	....	....
1988-89	University of Minnesota-Duluth	WCHA	39	1	2	3	....	....	....	44	....	....	....	....	....	....	....	....	....	....	....	....	....	....	....	....	....	....
1989-90	University of Minnesota-Duluth	WCHA	5	0	1	1	....	....	....	6	....	....	....	....	....	....	....	....	....	....	....	....	....	....	....	....	....	....
1990-91	University of Minnesota-Duluth	WCHA	32	6	11	17	....	....	....	38	....	....	....	....	....	....	....	....	....	....	....	....	....	....	....	....	....	....

			REGULAR SEASON																		PLAYOFFS							
Season	Club	League	GP	G	A	Pts	AG	AA	APts	PIM	PP	SH	GW	S	%	TGF	PGF	TGA	PGA	+/–	GP	G	A	Pts	PIM	PP	SH	GW
1991-92	University of Minnesota-Duluth	WCHA	27	9	9	18	....	....	....	48	....	....	....	....	....	....	....	....	....	....	....	....	....	....	....	....	....	....
1992-93	University of Minnesota-Duluth	WCHA	36	15	20	35	....	....	....	87	....	....	....	....	....	....	....	....	....	....	....	....	....	....	....	....	....	....
1993-94	Providence Bruins	AHL	55	12	23	35	....	....	....	59	....	....	....	....	....	....	....	....	....	....	....	....	....	....	....	....	....	....
1994-95	Providence Bruins	AHL	4	2	1	3	....	....	....	6	....	....	....	....	....	....	....	....	....	....	....	....	....	....	....	....	....	....
	Boston Bruins	**NHL**	**34**	**3**	**8**	**11**	**5**	**12**	**17**	**39**	**0**	**0**	**1**	**51**	**5.9**	**22**	**2**	**22**	**3**	**+1**	**5**	**0**	**0**	**0**	**6**	**0**	**0**	**0**
1995-96	**Boston Bruins**	**NHL**	**79**	**1**	**12**	**13**	**1**	**10**	**11**	**59**	**1**	**0**	**0**	**106**	**0.9**	**58**	**14**	**58**	**6**	**–8**	**5**	**1**	**2**	**3**	**2**	**1**	**0**	**0**
1996-97	**Boston Bruins**	**NHL**	**37**	**3**	**5**	**8**	**3**	**4**	**7**	**31**	**1**	**0**	**0**	**69**	**4.3**	**29**	**8**	**42**	**7**	**–14**	....	....	....	....	....	....	....	....
	Providence Bruins	AHL	3	1	1	2	....	....	....	0	....	....	....	....	....	....	....	....	....	....	....	....	....	....	....	....	....	....
	United States	WC-A	8	0	2	2	....	....	....	10	....	....	....	....	....	....	....	....	....	....	....	....	....	....	....	....	....	....
1997-98	Providence Bruins	AHL	58	6	17	23	....	....	....	46	....	....	....	....	....	....	....	....	....	....	....	....	....	....	....	....	....	....
	NHL Totals		**150**	**7**	**25**	**32**	**9**	**26**	**35**	**129**	**2**	**0**	**1**	**226**	**3.1**	**109**	**24**	**122**	**16**		**10**	**1**	**2**	**3**	**8**	**1**	**0**	**0**

WCHA Second All-Star Team (1993)

• ROLFE, DALE

Dale Rolfe D – L. 6'4", 210 lbs. b: Timmins, Ont., 4/30/1940.

Season	Club	League	GP	G	A	Pts	AG	AA	APts	PIM	PP	SH	GW	S	%	TGF	PGF	TGA	PGA	+/–	GP	G	A	Pts	PIM	PP	SH	GW
1956-57	Barrie Flyers	OHA	52	18	16	34	....	....	....	37	....	....	....	....	....	....	....	....	....	....	3	0	0	0	2	....	....	....
1957-58	Barrie Flyers	OHA	50	5	22	27	....	....	....	83	....	....	....	....	....	....	....	....	....	....	4	0	0	0	8	....	....	....
1958-59	Barrie Flyers	OHA	44	9	25	34	....	....	....	132	....	....	....	....	....	....	....	....	....	....	6	1	4	5	24	....	....	....
1959-60	Barrie Flyers	OHA	48	8	39	47	....	....	....	127	....	....	....	....	....	....	....	....	....	....	6	1	6	7	25	....	....	....
	Boston Bruins	**NHL**	**3**	**0**	**0**	**0**	**0**	**0**	**0**	**0**	....	....	....	....	....	....	....	....	....	....	....	....	....	....	....	....	....	....
	Kingston Frontenacs	EPHL	2	0	1	1	....	....	....	2	....	....	....	....	....	....	....	....	....	....	....	....	....	....	....	....	....	....
1960-61	Portland Buckaroos	WHL	70	4	12	16	....	....	....	52	....	....	....	....	....	....	....	....	....	....	14	2	5	7	8	....	....	....
1961-62	Portland Buckaroos	WHL	70	7	15	22	....	....	....	65	....	....	....	....	....	....	....	....	....	....	7	1	2	3	8	....	....	....
1962-63	Hershey Bears	AHL	53	3	9	12	....	....	....	78	....	....	....	....	....	....	....	....	....	....	11	1	3	4	26	....	....	....
1963-64	Springfield Indians	AHL	71	2	16	18	....	....	....	103	....	....	....	....	....	....	....	....	....	....	....	....	....	....	....	....	....	....
1964-65	Springfield Indians	AHL	69	10	25	35	....	....	....	68	....	....	....	....	....	....	....	....	....	....	....	....	....	....	....	....	....	....
1965-66	Springfield Indians	AHL	71	5	27	32	....	....	....	94	....	....	....	....	....	....	....	....	....	....	6	0	1	1	16	....	....	....
1966-67	Springfield Indians	AHL	67	14	35	49	....	....	....	94	....	....	....	....	....	....	....	....	....	....	....	....	....	....	....	....	....	....
1967-68	**Los Angeles Kings**	**NHL**	**68**	**3**	**13**	**16**	**4**	**14**	**18**	**84**	**1**	**0**	**0**	**93**	**3.2**	**72**	**6**	**95**	**19**	**–10**	**7**	**0**	**1**	**1**	**14**	**0**	**0**	**0**
	Springfield Kings	AHL	6	1	5	6	....	....	....	2	....	....	....	....	....	....	....	....	....	....	....	....	....	....	....	....	....	....
1968-69	**Los Angeles Kings**	**NHL**	**75**	**3**	**19**	**22**	**3**	**18**	**21**	**85**	**0**	**0**	**0**	**151**	**2.0**	**76**	**7**	**116**	**23**	**–24**	**10**	**0**	**4**	**4**	**8**	**0**	**0**	**0**
1969-70	**Los Angeles Kings**	**NHL**	**55**	**1**	**9**	**10**	**1**	**9**	**10**	**77**	**0**	**0**	**0**	**115**	**0.9**	**43**	**5**	**94**	**31**	**–25**	....	....	....	....	....	....	....	....
	Detroit Red Wings	**NHL**	**20**	**2**	**9**	**11**	**2**	**9**	**11**	**12**	**0**	**0**	**1**	**62**	**3.2**	**27**	**4**	**21**	**7**	**+9**	**4**	**0**	**2**	**2**	**8**	**0**	**0**	**0**
1970-71	**Detroit Red Wings**	**NHL**	**44**	**3**	**9**	**12**	**3**	**8**	**11**	**48**	**0**	**0**	**0**	**90**	**3.3**	**44**	**5**	**65**	**13**	**–13**	....	....	....	....	....	....	....	....
	New York Rangers	**NHL**	**14**	**0**	**7**	**7**	**0**	**6**	**6**	**23**	**0**	**0**	**0**	**28**	**0.0**	**22**	**2**	**15**	**6**	**+11**	**13**	**0**	**1**	**1**	**14**	**0**	**0**	**0**
1971-72	**New York Rangers**	**NHL**	**68**	**2**	**14**	**16**	**2**	**13**	**15**	**67**	**0**	**0**	**0**	**166**	**1.2**	**93**	**3**	**64**	**15**	**+41**	**16**	**4**	**3**	**7**	**16**	**0**	**0**	**1**
1972-73	**New York Rangers**	**NHL**	**72**	**7**	**25**	**32**	**7**	**21**	**28**	**74**	**1**	**0**	**0**	**159**	**4.4**	**124**	**13**	**89**	**19**	**+41**	**8**	**0**	**5**	**5**	**6**	**0**	**0**	**0**
1973-74	**New York Rangers**	**NHL**	**48**	**3**	**12**	**15**	**3**	**10**	**13**	**56**	**0**	**1**	**0**	**98**	**3.1**	**74**	**3**	**68**	**13**	**+16**	**13**	**1**	**8**	**9**	**23**	**0**	**0**	**0**
1974-75	**New York Rangers**	**NHL**	**42**	**1**	**8**	**9**	**1**	**6**	**7**	**30**	**1**	**0**	**0**	**56**	**1.8**	**47**	**3**	**43**	**11**	**+12**	....	....	....	....	....	....	....	....
	NHL Totals		**509**	**25**	**125**	**150**	**26**	**114**	**140**	**556**	**3**	**1**	**1**	**1018**	**2.5**	**622**	**51**	**670**	**157**		**71**	**5**	**24**	**29**	**89**	**0**	**0**	**1**

AHL First All-Star Team (1967)

Traded to **Springfield** (AHL) by **Boston** with Bruce Gamble, Terry Gray and Randy Miller for Bob McCord, June, 1963. NHL rights transferred to **LA Kings** after NHL club purchased **Springfield** (AHL) franchise, May, 1967. Traded to **Detroit** by **LA Kings** with Gary Croteau and Larry Johnston for Brian Gibbons and Garry Monahan, February 20, 1970. Traded to **NY Rangers** by **Detroit** for Jim Krulicki, March 2, 1971.

• ROLSTON, BRIAN

Brian Rolston C – L. 6'2", 200 lbs. b: Flint, MI, 2/21/1973. New Jersey's 2nd choice, 11th overall, in 1991 Entry Draft.

Season	Club	League	GP	G	A	Pts	AG	AA	APts	PIM	PP	SH	GW	S	%	TGF	PGF	TGA	PGA	+/–	GP	G	A	Pts	PIM	PP	SH	GW
1990-91	Detroit Compuware	NAJHL	36	49	46	95	....	....	....	14	....	....	....	....	....	....	....	....	....	....	....	....	....	....	....	....	....	....
1991-92	Lake Superior State	CCHA	37	14	23	37	....	....	....	14	....	....	....	....	....	....	....	....	....	....	....	....	....	....	....	....	....	....
	United States	WJC-A	7	3	3	6	....	....	....	2	....	....	....	....	....	....	....	....	....	....	....	....	....	....	....	....	....	....
1992-93	Lake Superior State	CCHA	39	33	31	64	....	....	....	20	....	....	....	....	....	....	....	....	....	....	....	....	....	....	....	....	....	....
	United States	WJC-A	7	6	2	8	....	....	....	2	....	....	....	....	....	....	....	....	....	....	....	....	....	....	....	....	....	....
1993-94	United States	Nat-Team	41	20	28	48	....	....	....	36	....	....	....	....	....	....	....	....	....	....	....	....	....	....	....	....	....	....
	United States	Olympics	8	7	0	7	....	....	....	8	....	....	....	....	....	....	....	....	....	....	....	....	....	....	....	....	....	....
	Albany River Rats	AHL	17	5	5	10	....	....	....	8	....	....	....	....	....	....	....	....	....	....	5	1	2	3	0	....	....	....
1994-95	Albany River Rats	AHL	18	9	11	20	....	....	....	10	....	....	....	....	....	....	....	....	....	....	....	....	....	....	....	....	....	....
	New Jersey Devils	**NHL**	**40**	**7**	**11**	**18**	**12**	**16**	**28**	**17**	**2**	**0**	**3**	**92**	**7.6**	**28**	**5**	**18**	**0**	**+5**	**6**	**2**	**1**	**3**	**4**	**1**	**0**	**0**
1995-96	**New Jersey Devils**	**NHL**	**58**	**13**	**11**	**24**	**13**	**9**	**22**	**8**	**3**	**1**	**4**	**139**	**9.4**	**40**	**10**	**29**	**8**	**+9**	....	....	....	....	....	....	....	....
	United States	WC-A	8	3	4	7	....	....	....	4	....	....	....	....	....	....	....	....	....	....	....	....	....	....	....	....	....	....
1996-97	United States	W Cup	1	0	0	0	....	....	....	0	....	....	....	....	....	....	....	....	....	....	....	....	....	....	....	....	....	....
	New Jersey Devils	**NHL**	**81**	**18**	**27**	**45**	**19**	**24**	**43**	**20**	**2**	**2**	**3**	**237**	**7.6**	**64**	**14**	**50**	**6**	**+6**	**10**	**4**	**1**	**5**	**6**	**1**	**2**	**0**
1997-98	**New Jersey Devils**	**NHL**	**76**	**16**	**14**	**30**	**19**	**14**	**33**	**16**	**0**	**2**	**1**	**185**	**8.6**	**48**	**7**	**49**	**15**	**+7**	**6**	**1**	**0**	**1**	**2**	**0**	**1**	**0**
	NHL Totals		**255**	**54**	**63**	**117**	**63**	**63**	**126**	**61**	**7**	**5**	**11**	**653**	**8.3**	**180**	**36**	**146**	**29**		**22**	**7**	**2**	**9**	**12**	**2**	**3**	**0**

NCAA Championship All-Tournament Team (1992, 1993) • CCHA First All-Star Team (1993) • NCAA West Second All-American Team (1993)

• ROMANCHYCH, LARRY

Larry "Swoop" Romanchych RW – R. 6'1", 180 lbs. b: Vancouver, B.C., 9/7/1949. Chicago's 2nd choice, 24th overall, in 1969 Amateur Draft.

Season	Club	League	GP	G	A	Pts	AG	AA	APts	PIM	PP	SH	GW	S	%	TGF	PGF	TGA	PGA	+/–	GP	G	A	Pts	PIM	PP	SH	GW
1967-68	Brandon Wheat Kings	WCJHL	53	20	23	43	....	....	....	24	....	....	....	....	....	....	....	....	....	....	....	....	....	....	....	....	....	....
1968-69	Flin Flon Bombers	WCJHL	55	31	25	56	....	....	....	40	....	....	....	....	....	....	....	....	....	....	....	....	....	....	....	....	....	....
1969-70	Dallas Black Hawks	CHL	57	21	12	33	....	....	....	38	....	....	....	....	....	....	....	....	....	....	....	....	....	....	....	....	....	....
1970-71	**Chicago Black Hawks**	**NHL**	**10**	**0**	**2**	**2**	**0**	**2**	**2**	**2**	**0**	**0**	**0**	**10**	**0.0**	**2**	**1**	**1**	**0**	**0**	....	....	....	....	....	....	....	....
	Dallas Black Hawks	CHL	65	18	34	52	....	....	....	26	....	....	....	....	....	....	....	....	....	....	10	2	4	6	4	....	....	....
1971-72	Dallas Black Hawks	CHL	60	21	23	44	....	....	....	31	....	....	....	....	....	....	....	....	....	....	12	3	4	7	28	....	....	....
1972-73	**Atlanta Flames**	**NHL**	**70**	**18**	**30**	**48**	**18**	**25**	**43**	**39**	**4**	**0**	**2**	**157**	**11.5**	**72**	**15**	**68**	**0**	**–11**	....	....	....	....	....	....	....	....
1973-74	**Atlanta Flames**	**NHL**	**73**	**22**	**29**	**51**	**22**	**25**	**47**	**33**	**7**	**0**	**4**	**159**	**13.8**	**72**	**25**	**54**	**0**	**–7**	**4**	**2**	**2**	**4**	**4**	**0**	**0**	**0**
1974-75	**Atlanta Flames**	**NHL**	**53**	**8**	**12**	**20**	**7**	**9**	**16**	**16**	**2**	**0**	**0**	**64**	**12.5**	**43**	**20**	**33**	**1**	**–9**	....	....	....	....	....	....	....	....
1975-76	**Atlanta Flames**	**NHL**	**67**	**16**	**19**	**35**	**15**	**15**	**30**	**8**	**6**	**0**	**2**	**110**	**14.5**	**57**	**20**	**44**	**0**	**–7**	**2**	**0**	**0**	**0**	**0**	**0**	**0**	**0**
1976-77	**Atlanta Flames**	**NHL**	**25**	**4**	**5**	**9**	**4**	**4**	**8**	**4**	**0**	**0**	**0**	**42**	**9.5**	**12**	**2**	**13**	**0**	**–3**	**1**	**0**	**0**	**0**	**0**	**0**	**0**	**0**
	Tulsa Oilers	CHL	37	20	28	48	....	....	....	18	....	....	....	....	....	....	....	....	....	....	....	....	....	....	....	....	....	....
1977-78	Maine Mariners	AHL	79	17	34	51	....	....	....	23	....	....	....	....	....	....	....	....	....	....	12	*8	4	12	6	....	....	....
	NHL Totals		**298**	**68**	**97**	**165**	**66**	**80**	**146**	**102**	**19**	**0**	**8**	**542**	**12.5**	**258**	**83**	**213**	**1**		**7**	**2**	**2**	**4**	**4**	**0**	**0**	**0**

Claimed by **Atlanta** from **Chicago** in Expansion Draft, June 6, 1967.

• ROMANIUK, RUSSELL

Russell Romaniuk LW – L. 6', 195 lbs. b: Winnipeg, Man., 6/9/1970. Winnipeg's 2nd choice, 31st overall, in 1988 Entry Draft.

Season	Club	League	GP	G	A	Pts	AG	AA	APts	PIM	PP	SH	GW	S	%	TGF	PGF	TGA	PGA	+/–	GP	G	A	Pts	PIM	PP	SH	GW
1987-88	St. Boniface Saints	MJHL	STATISTICS NOT AVAILABLE																									
1988-89	University of North Dakota	WCHA	39	17	14	31	....	....	....	32	....	....	....	....	....	....	....	....	....	....	....	....	....	....	....	....	....	....
	Canada	Nat-Team	3	1	0	1	....	....	....	0	....	....	....	....	....	....	....	....	....	....	....	....	....	....	....	....	....	....
1989-90	University of North Dakota	WCHA	45	36	15	51	....	....	....	54	....	....	....	....	....	....	....	....	....	....	....	....	....	....	....	....	....	....
1990-91	University of North Dakota	WCHA	39	40	28	68	....	....	....	30	....	....	....	....	....	....	....	....	....	....	....	....	....	....	....	....	....	....
1991-92	**Winnipeg Jets**	**NHL**	**27**	**3**	**5**	**8**	**3**	**4**	**7**	**18**	**2**	**0**	**1**	**32**	**9.4**	**12**	**6**	**4**	**0**	**+2**	....	....	....	....	....	....	....	....
	Moncton Hawks	AHL	45	16	15	31	....	....	....	25	....	....	....	....	....	....	....	....	....	....	10	5	4	9	19	....	....	....
1992-93	**Winnipeg Jets**	**NHL**	**28**	**3**	**1**	**4**	**2**	**1**	**3**	**22**	**0**	**0**	**1**	**20**	**15.0**	**14**	**3**	**11**	**0**	**0**	**1**	**0**	**0**	**0**	**0**	**0**	**0**	**0**
	Moncton Hawks	AHL	28	18	8	26	....	....	....	40	....	....	....	....	....	....	....	....	....	....	5	0	4	4	2	....	....	....
	Fort Wayne Komets	IHL	4	2	0	2	....	....	....	7	....	....	....	....	....	....	....	....	....	....	....	....	....	....	....	....	....	....
1993-94	Canada	Nat-Team	34	8	9	17	....	....	....	17	....	....	....	....	....	....	....	....	....	....	....	....	....	....	....	....	....	....
	Winnipeg Jets	**NHL**	**24**	**4**	**8**	**12**	**4**	**6**	**10**	**6**	**3**	**0**	**0**	**36**	**11.1**	**16**	**5**	**24**	**2**	**–11**	....	....	....	....	....	....	....	....
	Moncton Hawks	AHL	18	16	8	24	....	....	....	24	....	....	....	....	....	....	....	....	....	....	17	2	6	8	30	....	....	....
1994-95	**Winnipeg Jets**	**NHL**	**6**	**0**	**0**	**0**	**0**	**0**	**0**	**0**	**0**	**0**	**0**	**3**	**0.0**	**0**	**0**	**4**	**1**	**–3**	....	....	....	....	....	....	....	....
	Springfield Falcons	AHL	17	5	7	12	....	....	....	29	....	....	....	....	....	....	....	....	....	....	....	....	....	....	....	....	....	....
1995-96	**Philadelphia Flyers**	**NHL**	**17**	**3**	**0**	**3**	**3**	**0**	**3**	**17**	**1**	**0**	**0**	**13**	**23.1**	**8**	**3**	**7**	**0**	**–2**	**1**	**0**	**0**	**0**	**0**	**0**	**0**	**0**
	Hershey Bears	AHL	27	19	10	29	....	....	....	43	....	....	....	....	....	....	....	....	....	....	....	....	....	....	....	....	....	....
1996-97	Manitoba Moose	IHL	46	14	13	27	....	....	....	43	....	....	....	....	....	....	....	....	....	....	....	....	....	....	....	....	....	....

			REGULAR SEASON																		PLAYOFFS							
Season	Club	League	GP	G	A	Pts	AG	AA	APts	PIM	PP	SH	GW	S	%	TGF	PGF	TGA	PGA	+/–	GP	G	A	Pts	PIM	PP	SH	GW
1997-98	Long Beach Ice Dogs	IHL	49	16	11	27	....	....	....	37	....	....	....	....	....	....	....	....	....	....	....	....	....	....	....	....	....	....
	Manitoba Moose	IHL	5	0	1	1	....	....	....	8	....	....	....	....	....	....	....	....	....	....	....	....	....	....	....	....	....	....
	Las Vegas Thunder	IHL	22	6	4	10	....	....	....	10	....	....	....	....	....	....	....	....	....	....	4	2	2	4	4	....	....	....
	NHL Totals		**102**	**13**	**14**	**27**	**12**	**11**	**23**	**63**	**6**	**0**	**2**	**104**	**12.5**	**50**	**17**	**50**	**3**		**2**	**0**	**0**	**0**	**0**	**0**	**0**	**0**

WCHA First All-Star Team (1991)

Traded to **Philadelphia** by **Winnipeg** for Jeff Finley, June 27, 1995.

• ROMBOUGH, DOUG

Doug Rombough C – L. 6'3", 215 lbs. b: Fergus, Ont., 7/8/1950. Buffalo's 8th choice, 97th overall, in 1970 Amateur Draft.

1968-69	St. Catharines Black Hawks	OHA	53	12	13	25	....	....	....	15	....	....	....	....	....	....	....	....	....	....	17	1	1	2	2	....	....	....
1969-70	St. Catharines Black Hawks	OHA	53	14	13	27	....	....	....	36	....	....	....	....	....	....	....	....	....	....	....	....	....	....	....	....	....	....
1970-71	Flint Generals	IHL	65	22	36	58	....	....	....	26	....	....	....	....	....	....	....	....	....	....	7	1	5	6	2	....	....	....
1971-72	Cincinnati Swords	AHL	76	22	26	48	....	....	....	42	....	....	....	....	....	....	....	....	....	....	10	4	4	8	22	....	....	....
1972-73	**Buffalo Sabres**	**NHL**	**5**	**2**	**0**	**2**	**2**	**0**	**2**	**0**	**0**	**0**	**0**	**3**	**66.7**	**2**	**0**	**0**	**0**	**+2**	....	....	....	....	....	....	....	....
	Cincinnati Swords	AHL	66	28	43	71	....	....	....	48	....	....	....	....	....	....	....	....	....	....	14	*10	8	18	26	....	....	....
1973-74	**Buffalo Sabres**	**NHL**	**46**	**6**	**9**	**15**	**6**	**8**	**14**	**27**	**0**	**0**	**1**	**38**	**15.8**	**22**	**2**	**18**	**0**	**+2**	....	....	....	....	....	....	....	....
	New York Islanders	**NHL**	**12**	**3**	**1**	**4**	**3**	**1**	**4**	**8**	**2**	**0**	**0**	**19**	**15.8**	**7**	**2**	**4**	**0**	**+1**	....	....	....	....	....	....	....	....
1974-75	**New York Islanders**	**NHL**	**28**	**5**	**6**	**11**	**5**	**5**	**10**	**6**	**0**	**0**	**0**	**35**	**14.3**	**18**	**4**	**8**	**0**	**+6**	....	....	....	....	....	....	....	....
	Minnesota North Stars	**NHL**	**40**	**6**	**9**	**15**	**6**	**7**	**13**	**33**	**0**	**0**	**1**	**63**	**9.5**	**22**	**5**	**17**	**1**	**+1**	....	....	....	....	....	....	....	....
1975-76	**Minnesota North Stars**	**NHL**	**19**	**2**	**2**	**4**	**2**	**2**	**4**	**6**	**0**	**0**	**1**	**9**	**22.2**	**3**	**0**	**11**	**4**	**–4**	....	....	....	....	....	....	....	....
	New Haven Nighthawks	AHL	42	5	20	25	....	....	....	28	....	....	....	....	....	....	....	....	....	....	3	0	0	0	0	....	....	....
1976-77	New Haven Nighthawks	AHL	4	0	0	0	....	....	....	0	....	....	....	....	....	....	....	....	....	....	....	....	....	....	....	....	....	....
	Dallas Black Hawks	CHL	70	21	25	46	....	....	....	24	....	....	....	....	....	....	....	....	....	....	5	1	0	1	0	....	....	....
1977-78	Fort Worth Texans	CHL	73	23	34	57	....	....	....	38	....	....	....	....	....	....	....	....	....	....	14	3	3	6	9	....	....	....
	NHL Totals		**150**	**24**	**27**	**51**	**24**	**23**	**47**	**80**	**2**	**0**	**3**	**167**	**14.4**	**74**	**13**	**58**	**5**		....	....	....	....	....	....	....	....

Traded to **NY Islanders** by **Buffalo** for Brian Spencer, March 10, 1974. Traded to **Minnesota** by **NY Islanders** with Ernie Hicke for Jean-Paul Parise, January 5, 1975.

• RONAN, ED

Ed Ronan RW – R. 6', 197 lbs. b: Quincy, MA, 3/21/1968. Montreal's 13th choice, 227th overall, in 1987 Entry Draft.

1986-87	Andover Academy	H.S.	22	10	22	32	....	....	....	10	....	....	....	....	....	....	....	....	....	....	....	....	....	....	....	....	....	....
1987-88	Boston University	H.E.	31	2	5	7	....	....	....	20	....	....	....	....	....	....	....	....	....	....	....	....	....	....	....	....	....	....
1988-89	Boston University	H.E.	36	4	11	15	....	....	....	34	....	....	....	....	....	....	....	....	....	....	....	....	....	....	....	....	....	....
1989-90	Boston University	H.E.	44	17	23	40	....	....	....	50	....	....	....	....	....	....	....	....	....	....	....	....	....	....	....	....	....	....
1990-91	Boston University	H.E.	41	16	19	35	....	....	....	38	....	....	....	....	....	....	....	....	....	....	....	....	....	....	....	....	....	....
1991-92	**Montreal Canadiens**	**NHL**	**3**	**0**	**0**	**0**	**0**	**0**	**0**	**0**	**0**	**0**	**0**	**1**	**0.0**	**0**	**0**	**0**	**0**	**0**	....	....	....	....	....	....	....	....
	Fredericton Canadiens	AHL	78	25	34	59	....	....	....	82	....	....	....	....	....	....	....	....	....	....	7	5	1	6	6	....	....	....
1992-93	**Montreal Canadiens**	**NHL**	**53**	**5**	**7**	**12**	**4**	**5**	**9**	**20**	**0**	**0**	**1**	**54**	**9.3**	**23**	**0**	**20**	**3**	**+6**	**14**	**2**	**3**	**5**	**10**	**0**	**0**	**0**
	Fredericton Canadiens	AHL	16	10	5	15	....	....	....	15	....	....	....	....	....	....	....	....	....	....	5	2	4	6	6	....	....	....
1993-94	**Montreal Canadiens**	**NHL**	**61**	**6**	**8**	**14**	**6**	**6**	**12**	**42**	**0**	**0**	**1**	**49**	**12.2**	**24**	**1**	**21**	**1**	**+3**	**7**	**1**	**0**	**1**	**0**	**0**	**0**	**0**
1994-95	**Montreal Canadiens**	**NHL**	**30**	**1**	**4**	**5**	**2**	**6**	**8**	**12**	**0**	**0**	**0**	**14**	**7.1**	**7**	**0**	**19**	**5**	**–7**	....	....	....	....	....	....	....	....
1995-96	**Winnipeg Jets**	**NHL**	**17**	**0**	**0**	**0**	**0**	**0**	**0**	**16**	**0**	**0**	**0**	**13**	**0.0**	**2**	**0**	**13**	**8**	**–3**	....	....	....	....	....	....	....	....
	Springfield Falcons	AHL	31	8	16	24	....	....	....	50	....	....	....	....	....	....	....	....	....	....	10	7	6	13	4	....	....	....
1996-97	**Buffalo Sabres**	**NHL**	**18**	**1**	**4**	**5**	**1**	**4**	**5**	**11**	**0**	**0**	**0**	**10**	**10.0**	**8**	**0**	**4**	**0**	**+4**	**6**	**1**	**0**	**1**	**6**	**0**	**0**	**0**
	Rochester Americans	AHL	47	13	21	34	....	....	....	62	....	....	....	....	....	....	....	....	....	....	....	....	....	....	....	....	....	....
1997-98	Providence Bruins	AHL	49	13	15	28	....	....	....	40	....	....	....	....	....	....	....	....	....	....	....	....	....	....	....	....	....	....
	NHL Totals		**182**	**13**	**23**	**36**	**13**	**21**	**34**	**101**	**0**	**0**	**2**	**141**	**9.2**	**64**	**1**	**77**	**17**		**27**	**4**	**3**	**7**	**16**	**0**	**0**	**0**

Signed as a free agent by **Winnipeg**, October 13, 1995. Signed as a free agent by **Buffalo**, September 5, 1996.

• RONNING, CLIFF

Cliff Ronning C – L. 5'8", 170 lbs. b: Burnaby, B.C., 10/1/1965. St. Louis' 6th choice, 134th overall, in 1984 Entry Draft.

1983-84	New Westminster Bruins	WHL	71	69	67	136	....	....	....	10	....	....	....	....	....	....	....	....	....	....	9	8	13	21	10	....	....	....
1984-85	New Westminster Bruins	WHL	70	*89	108	*197	....	....	....	20	....	....	....	....	....	....	....	....	....	....	11	10	14	24	4	....	....	....
1985-86	Canada	Nat-Team	71	55	63	118	....	....	....	....	....	....	....	....	....	....	....	....	....	....	....	....	....	....	....	....	....	....
	St. Louis Blues	**NHL**	....	....	....	....	....	....	....	....	**0**	**0**	**0**	**0**	**0.0**	**0**	**0**	**0**	**0**	**0**	**5**	**1**	**1**	**2**	**2**	**1**	**0**	**0**
1986-87	Canada	Nat-Team	26	17	16	33	....	....	....	12	....	....	....	....	....	....	....	....	....	....	....	....	....	....	....	....	....	....
	St. Louis Blues	**NHL**	**42**	**11**	**14**	**25**	**10**	**10**	**20**	**6**	**2**	**0**	**2**	**68**	**16.2**	**31**	**9**	**23**	**0**	**–1**	**4**	**0**	**1**	**1**	**0**	**0**	**0**	**0**
1987-88	**St. Louis Blues**	**NHL**	**26**	**5**	**8**	**13**	**4**	**6**	**10**	**12**	**1**	**0**	**1**	**38**	**13.2**	**16**	**6**	**4**	**0**	**+6**	....	....	....	....	....	....	....	....
1988-89	**St. Louis Blues**	**NHL**	**64**	**24**	**31**	**55**	**20**	**22**	**42**	**18**	**16**	**0**	**1**	**150**	**16.0**	**68**	**41**	**25**	**1**	**+3**	**7**	**1**	**3**	**4**	**0**	**1**	**0**	**0**
	Peoria Rivermen	IHL	12	11	20	31	....	....	....	8	....	....	....	....	....	....	....	....	....	....	....	....	....	....	....	....	....	....
1989-90	HC Asiago	Italy	36	67	49	116	....	....	....	25	....	....	....	....	....	....	....	....	....	....	6	7	12	19	4	....	....	....
1990-91	**St. Louis Blues**	**NHL**	**48**	**14**	**18**	**32**	**13**	**14**	**27**	**10**	**5**	**0**	**2**	**81**	**17.3**	**50**	**29**	**19**	**0**	**+2**	....	....	....	....	....	....	....	....
	Vancouver Canucks	**NHL**	**11**	**6**	**6**	**12**	**5**	**5**	**10**	**0**	**2**	**0**	**0**	**32**	**18.8**	**22**	**12**	**12**	**0**	**–2**	**6**	**6**	**3**	**9**	**12**	**2**	**0**	**2**
	Canada	WEC-A	10	1	4	5	....	....	....	8	....	....	....	....	....	....	....	....	....	....	....	....	....	....	....	....	....	....
1991-92	**Vancouver Canucks**	**NHL**	**80**	**24**	**47**	**71**	**22**	**35**	**57**	**42**	**6**	**0**	**2**	**216**	**11.1**	**97**	**33**	**48**	**2**	**+18**	**13**	**8**	**5**	**13**	**6**	**1**	**0**	**1**
1992-93	**Vancouver Canucks**	**NHL**	**79**	**29**	**56**	**85**	**24**	**38**	**62**	**30**	**10**	**0**	**2**	**209**	**13.9**	**102**	**33**	**50**	**0**	**+19**	**12**	**2**	**9**	**11**	**6**	**0**	**0**	**0**
1993-94	**Vancouver Canucks**	**NHL**	**76**	**25**	**43**	**68**	**23**	**33**	**56**	**42**	**10**	**0**	**4**	**197**	**12.7**	**106**	**49**	**51**	**1**	**+7**	**24**	**5**	**10**	**15**	**16**	**2**	**0**	**2**
1994-95	**Vancouver Canucks**	**NHL**	**41**	**6**	**19**	**25**	**11**	**28**	**39**	**27**	**3**	**0**	**2**	**93**	**6.5**	**40**	**20**	**24**	**0**	**–4**	**11**	**3**	**5**	**8**	**2**	**1**	**0**	**2**
1995-96	**Vancouver Canucks**	**NHL**	**79**	**22**	**45**	**67**	**22**	**37**	**59**	**42**	**5**	**0**	**1**	**187**	**11.8**	**92**	**18**	**59**	**1**	**+16**	**6**	**0**	**2**	**2**	**6**	**0**	**0**	**0**
1996-97	**Phoenix Coyotes**	**NHL**	**69**	**19**	**32**	**51**	**20**	**28**	**48**	**26**	**8**	**0**	**2**	**171**	**11.1**	**71**	**30**	**50**	**0**	**–9**	**7**	**0**	**7**	**7**	**12**	**0**	**0**	**0**
1997-98	**Phoenix Coyotes**	**NHL**	**80**	**11**	**44**	**55**	**13**	**43**	**56**	**36**	**3**	**0**	**0**	**197**	**5.6**	**72**	**30**	**40**	**3**	**+5**	**6**	**1**	**3**	**4**	**4**	**0**	**0**	**0**
	NHL Totals		**695**	**196**	**363**	**559**	**187**	**299**	**486**	**291**	**71**	**0**	**19**	**1639**	**12.0**	**767**	**310**	**405**	**8**		**101**	**27**	**49**	**76**	**66**	**8**	**0**	**7**

WHL First All-Star Team (1985)

Traded to **Vancouver** by **St. Louis** with Geoff Courtnall, Robert Dirk, Sergio Momesso and St. Louis' 5th round choice (Brian Loney) in 1992 Entry Draft for Dan Quinn and Garth Butcher, March 5, 1991. Signed as a free agent by **Phoenix**, July 1, 1996.

• RONSON, LEN

Len Ronson LW – L. 5'9", 175 lbs. b: Brantford, Ont., 7/8/1936.

1954-55	Galt Black Hawks	OHA	49	15	21	36	....	....	....	84	....	....	....	....	....	....	....	....	....	....	4	0	1	1	6	....	....	....
1955-56	St. Catharines Teepees	OHA	48	9	8	17	....	....	....	69	....	....	....	....	....	....	....	....	....	....	6	0	0	0	7	....	....	....
1956-57	Hamilton Tiger Cubs	OHA	1	0	0	0	....	....	....	0	....	....	....	....	....	....	....	....	....	....	....	....	....	....	....	....	....	....
	Chatham Maroons	OHA Sr.	18	2	2	4	....	....	....	26	....	....	....	....	....	....	....	....	....	....	....	....	....	....	....	....	....	....
	Indianapolis–Huntington	IHL	39	7	6	13	....	....	....	31	....	....	....	....	....	....	....	....	....	....	4	1	0	1	0	....	....	....
1957-58	Fort Wayne Komets	IHL	61	26	31	57	....	....	....	13	....	....	....	....	....	....	....	....	....	....	4	1	2	3	2	....	....	....
1958-59	Fort Wayne Komets	IHL	60	39	58	97	....	....	....	38	....	....	....	....	....	....	....	....	....	....	11	8	6	14	4	....	....	....
1959-60	Fort Wayne Komets	IHL	68	*62	47	109	....	....	....	53	....	....	....	....	....	....	....	....	....	....	13	7	10	*17	2	....	....	....
1960-61	**New York Rangers**	**NHL**	**13**	**2**	**1**	**3**	**2**	**1**	**3**	**10**	....	....	....	....	....	....	....	....	....	....	....	....	....	....	....	....	....	....
	Buffalo Bisons	AHL	2	0	0	0	....	....	....	2	....	....	....	....	....	....	....	....	....	....	....	....	....	....	....	....	....	....
	Kitchener-Waterloo Beavers	EPHL	32	17	10	27	....	....	....	4	....	....	....	....	....	....	....	....	....	....	7	2	0	2	14	....	....	....
1961-62	Kitchener-Waterloo Beavers	EPHL	61	34	44	78	....	....	....	25	....	....	....	....	....	....	....	....	....	....	7	3	4	7	22	....	....	....
1962-63	Baltimore Clippers	AHL	45	7	15	22	....	....	....	20	....	....	....	....	....	....	....	....	....	....	....	....	....	....	....	....	....	....
	Sudbury Wolves	EPHL	16	8	17	25	....	....	....	6	....	....	....	....	....	....	....	....	....	....	8	3	4	7	6	....	....	....
1963-64	Cleveland Barons	AHL	2	0	1	1	....	....	....	4	....	....	....	....	....	....	....	....	....	....	3	1	0	1	0	....	....	....
	Omaha Knights	CHL	63	29	47	76	....	....	....	45	....	....	....	....	....	....	....	....	....	....	10	*8	8	*16	0	....	....	....
1964-65	Providence Reds	AHL	71	25	21	46	....	....	....	24	....	....	....	....	....	....	....	....	....	....	....	....	....	....	....	....	....	....
1965-66	Portland Buckaroos	WHL	68	18	13	31	....	....	....	6	....	....	....	....	....	....	....	....	....	....	14	5	2	7	6	....	....	....
1966-67	San Diego Gulls	WHL	71	32	35	67	....	....	....	22	....	....	....	....	....	....	....	....	....	....	....	....	....	....	....	....	....	....
1967-68	San Diego Gulls	WHL	72	*45	35	80	....	....	....	53	....	....	....	....	....	....	....	....	....	....	7	2	5	7	4	....	....	....
1968-69	**Oakland Seals**	**NHL**	**5**	**0**	**0**	**0**	**0**	**0**	**0**	**0**	**0**	**0**	**0**	**6**	**0.0**	**2**	**1**	**4**	**0**	**–3**	....	....	....	....	....	....	....	....
	San Diego Gulls	WHL	47	24	17	41	....	....	....	34	....	....	....	....	....	....	....	....	....	....	7	1	5	6	0	....	....	....
1969-70	San Diego Gulls	WHL	72	*51	37	88	....	....	....	48	....	....	....	....	....	....	....	....	....	....	6	6	4	10	13	....	....	....
1970-71	San Diego Gulls	WHL	72	21	35	56	....	....	....	39	....	....	....	....	....	....	....	....	....	....	6	2	3	5	2	....	....	....

			REGULAR SEASON																		PLAYOFFS							
Season	Club	League	GP	G	A	Pts	AG	AA	APts	PIM	PP	SH	GW	S	%	TGF	PGF	TGA	PGA	+/–	GP	G	A	Pts	PIM	PP	SH	GW
1971-72	Fort Worth Wings	CHL	4	2	3	5	....	....	....	0	....	....	....	....	....	....	....	....	....	....	....	....	....	....	....	....	....	....
	San Diego Gulls	WHL	68	21	33	54	....	....	....	37	....	....	....	....	....	....	....	....	....	....	4	0	0	0	0	....	....	....
1972-73	San Diego Gulls	WHL	44	12	18	30	....	....	....	14	....	....	....	....	....	....	....	....	....	....	6	3	2	5	0	....	....	....
	NHL Totals		**18**	**2**	**1**	**3**	**2**	**1**	**3**	**10**	**0**	**0**	**0**	**6**	**33.3**	**2**	**1**	**4**	**0**		....	....	....	....	....	....	....	....

IHL Second All-Star Team (1959) • IHL First All-Star Team (1960) • WHL First All-Star Team (1968, 1970)

Traded to **Montreal** by **NY Rangers** with Dave Balon, Leon Rochefort and Gump Worsley for Phil Goyette, Don Marshall and Jacques Plante, June 4, 1963. Traded to **Portland** (WHL) by **Montreal** for cash, July, 1965. Traded to **San Diego** (WHL) by **Portland** (WHL), August, 1966. Claimed by **Montreal** from **San Diego** (WHL) in Reverse Draft, June, 1968. Traded to **Oakland** by **Montreal** for cash, August, 1968. Traded to **San Diego** (WHL) by **Oakland** for cash, November, 1968.

• ROONEY, STEVE

Steve Rooney LW – L. 6'2", 205 lbs. b: Canton, MA, 6/28/1962. Montreal's 8th choice, 88th overall, in 1981 Entry Draft.

Season	Club	League	GP	G	A	Pts	AG	AA	APts	PIM	PP	SH	GW	S	%	TGF	PGF	TGA	PGA	+/–	GP	G	A	Pts	PIM	PP	SH	GW
1980-81	Canton-Mass High School	H.S.	STATISTICS NOT AVAILABLE																									
1981-82	Providence College	ECAC	31	7	10	17	....	....	....	41	....	....	....	....	....	....	....	....	....	....	....	....	....	....	....	....	....	....
1982-83	Providence College	ECAC	42	10	20	30	....	....	....	31	....	....	....	....	....	....	....	....	....	....	....	....	....	....	....	....	....	....
1983-84	Providence College	ECAC	33	11	16	27	....	....	....	46	....	....	....	....	....	....	....	....	....	....	....	....	....	....	....	....	....	....
1984-85	Providence College	HE	31	7	10	17	....	....	....	41	....	....	....	....	....	....	....	....	....	....	....	....	....	....	....	....	....	....
	Montreal Canadiens	**NHL**	**3**	**1**	**0**	**1**	**1**	**0**	**1**	**7**	**1**	**0**	**0**	**3**	**33.3**	**2**	**1**	**2**	**0**	**–1**	**11**	**2**	**2**	**4**	**19**	**0**	**0**	**0**
1985-86	**Montreal Canadiens**	**NHL**	**38**	**2**	**3**	**5**	**2**	**2**	**4**	**114**	**1**	**0**	**0**	**24**	**8.3**	**14**	**3**	**15**	**0**	**–4**	**1**	**0**	**0**	**0**	**0**	**0**	**0**	**0**
1986-87	**Montreal Canadiens**	**NHL**	**2**	**0**	**0**	**0**	**0**	**0**	**0**	**22**	**0**	**0**	**0**	**2**	**0.0**	**0**	**0**	**0**	**0**	**0**	....	....	....	....	....	....	....	....
	Sherbrooke Canadiens	AHL	22	4	11	15	....	....	....	66	....	....	....	....	....	....	....	....	....	....	....	....	....	....	....	....	....	....
	Winnipeg Jets	**NHL**	**30**	**2**	**3**	**5**	**2**	**2**	**4**	**57**	**0**	**0**	**1**	**23**	**8.7**	**8**	**0**	**12**	**0**	**–4**	**8**	**0**	**0**	**0**	**34**	**0**	**0**	**0**
1987-88	**Winnipeg Jets**	**NHL**	**56**	**7**	**6**	**13**	**6**	**4**	**10**	**217**	**0**	**0**	**0**	**62**	**11.3**	**19**	**2**	**15**	**0**	**+2**	**5**	**1**	**0**	**1**	**33**	**0**	**0**	**0**
1988-89	**New Jersey Devils**	**NHL**	**25**	**3**	**1**	**4**	**3**	**1**	**4**	**79**	**0**	**0**	**1**	**23**	**13.0**	**5**	**1**	**13**	**0**	**–9**	....	....	....	....	....	....	....	....
1989-90	Utica Devils	AHL	59	9	16	25	....	....	....	134	....	....	....	....	....	....	....	....	....	....	5	0	1	1	19	....	....	....
1990-91	Phoenix Roadrunners	IHL	11	2	5	7	....	....	....	76	....	....	....	....	....	....	....	....	....	....	....	....	....	....	....	....	....	....
	New Haven	IHL	44	14	17	31	....	....	....	141	....	....	....	....	....	....	....	....	....	....	....	....	....	....	....	....	....	....
1991-92	Maine Mariners	AHL	13	2	3	5	....	....	....	17	....	....	....	....	....	....	....	....	....	....	....	....	....	....	....	....	....	....
	NHL Totals		**154**	**15**	**13**	**28**	**14**	**9**	**23**	**496**	**2**	**0**	**2**	**137**	**10.9**	**48**	**7**	**57**	**0**		**25**	**3**	**2**	**5**	**86**	**0**	**0**	**0**

Traded to **Winnipeg** by **Montreal** for Winnipeg's 3rd round choice (Francois Gravel) in 1987 Entry Draft, January 8, 1987. Traded to **New Jersey** by **Winnipeg** with Winnipeg's 3rd round choice (Brad Bombardir) in 1990 Entry Draft for Alain Chevrier and New Jersey's 7th round choice (Doug Evans) in 1989 Entry Draft, July 19, 1988.

• ROOT, BILL

Bill Root D – R. 6', 210 lbs. b: Toronto, Ont., 9/6/1959.

Season	Club	League	GP	G	A	Pts	AG	AA	APts	PIM	PP	SH	GW	S	%	TGF	PGF	TGA	PGA	+/–	GP	G	A	Pts	PIM	PP	SH	GW
1976-77	Niagara Falls Flyers	OHA	66	3	19	22	....	....	....	114	....	....	....	....	....	....	....	....	....	....	....	....	....	....	....	....	....	....
1977-78	Niagara Falls Flyers	OHA	67	6	11	17	....	....	....	61	....	....	....	....	....	....	....	....	....	....	....	....	....	....	....	....	....	....
1978-79	Niagara Falls Flyers	OHA	67	4	31	35	....	....	....	119	....	....	....	....	....	....	....	....	....	....	20	4	7	11	42	....	....	....
1979-80	Nova Scotia Voyageurs	AHL	55	4	15	19	....	....	....	57	....	....	....	....	....	....	....	....	....	....	6	1	1	2	2	....	....	....
1980-81	Nova Scotia Voyageurs	AHL	63	3	12	15	....	....	....	76	....	....	....	....	....	....	....	....	....	....	6	0	1	1	2	....	....	....
1981-82	Nova Scotia Voyageurs	AHL	77	6	25	31	....	....	....	105	....	....	....	....	....	....	....	....	....	....	9	1	0	1	4	....	....	....
1982-83	**Montreal Canadiens**	**NHL**	**46**	**2**	**3**	**5**	**2**	**2**	**4**	**24**	**0**	**0**	**0**	**44**	**4.5**	**42**	**2**	**44**	**9**	**+5**	....	....	....	....	....	....	....	....
	Nova Scotia Voyageurs	AHL	24	0	7	7	....	....	....	29	....	....	....	....	....	....	....	....	....	....	....	....	....	....	....	....	....	....
1983-84	**Montreal Canadiens**	**NHL**	**72**	**4**	**13**	**17**	**3**	**9**	**12**	**45**	**1**	**1**	**0**	**71**	**5.6**	**90**	**2**	**75**	**13**	**+26**	....	....	....	....	....	....	....	....
1984-85	**Toronto Maple Leafs**	**NHL**	**35**	**1**	**1**	**2**	**1**	**1**	**2**	**23**	**0**	**0**	**0**	**34**	**2.9**	**25**	**0**	**65**	**15**	**–25**	....	....	....	....	....	....	....	....
	St. Catharines Saints	AHL	28	5	9	14	....	....	....	10	....	....	....	....	....	....	....	....	....	....	....	....	....	....	....	....	....	....
1985-86	**Toronto Maple Leafs**	**NHL**	**27**	**0**	**1**	**1**	**0**	**1**	**1**	**29**	**0**	**0**	**0**	**34**	**0.0**	**28**	**5**	**48**	**17**	**–8**	**7**	**0**	**2**	**2**	**13**	**0**	**0**	**0**
	St. Catharines Saints	AHL	14	7	4	11	....	....	....	11	....	....	....	....	....	....	....	....	....	....	....	....	....	....	....	....	....	....
1986-87	**Toronto Maple Leafs**	**NHL**	**34**	**3**	**3**	**6**	**3**	**2**	**5**	**37**	**1**	**0**	**0**	**31**	**9.7**	**24**	**1**	**47**	**15**	**–9**	**13**	**1**	**0**	**1**	**12**	**0**	**0**	**0**
	Newmarket Saints	AHL	32	4	11	15	....	....	....	23	....	....	....	....	....	....	....	....	....	....	....	....	....	....	....	....	....	....
1987-88	**St. Louis Blues**	**NHL**	**9**	**0**	**0**	**0**	**0**	**0**	**0**	**6**	**0**	**0**	**0**	**6**	**0.0**	**4**	**0**	**13**	**2**	**–7**	....	....	....	....	....	....	....	....
	Philadelphia Flyers	**NHL**	**24**	**1**	**2**	**3**	**1**	**1**	**2**	**16**	**1**	**0**	**0**	**13**	**7.7**	**13**	**2**	**9**	**1**	**+3**	**2**	**0**	**0**	**0**	**0**	**0**	**0**	**0**
1988-89	Newmarket Saints	AHL	66	10	22	32	....	....	....	39	....	....	....	....	....	....	....	....	....	....	5	0	0	0	18	....	....	....
1989-90	Newmarket Saints	AHL	47	8	7	15	....	....	....	20	....	....	....	....	....	....	....	....	....	....	....	....	....	....	....	....	....	....
1990-91	Newmarket Saints	AHL	36	2	4	6	....	....	....	39	....	....	....	....	....	....	....	....	....	....	....	....	....	....	....	....	....	....
	NHL Totals		**247**	**11**	**23**	**34**	**10**	**16**	**26**	**180**	**3**	**1**	**0**	**233**	**4.7**	**226**	**12**	**301**	**72**		**22**	**1**	**2**	**3**	**25**	**0**	**0**	**0**

Signed as a free agent by **Montreal**, October 4, 1979. Traded to **Toronto** by **Montreal** with Montreal's 2nd round choice (Darryl Shannon) in 1986 Entry Draft for Dom Campedelli, August 21, 1984. Traded to **Hartford** by **Toronto** for Dave Semenko, September 8, 1987. Claimed by **St. Louis** from **Hartford** in Waiver Draft, October 5, 1987. Claimed on waivers by **Philadelphia** from **St. Louis**, November 26, 1987. Traded to **Toronto** by **Philadelphia** for Mike Stothers, June 21, 1988.

• ROTA, DARCY

Darcy Rota LW – L. 5'11", 180 lbs. b: Vancouver, B.C., 2/16/1953. Chicago's 1st choice, 13th overall, in 1973 Amateur Draft.

Season	Club	League	GP	G	A	Pts	AG	AA	APts	PIM	PP	SH	GW	S	%	TGF	PGF	TGA	PGA	+/–	GP	G	A	Pts	PIM	PP	SH	GW
1970-71	Edmonton Oil Kings	WCJHL	64	43	39	82	....	....	....	60	....	....	....	....	....	....	....	....	....	....	17	13	10	23	15	....	....	....
1971-72	Edmonton Oil Kings	WCJHL	67	51	54	105	....	....	....	68	....	....	....	....	....	....	....	....	....	....	16	8	9	17	11	....	....	....
1972-73	Edmonton Oil Kings	WCJHL	68	*73	56	129	....	....	....	104	....	....	....	....	....	....	....	....	....	....	4	5	4	9	14	....	....	....
1973-74	**Chicago Black Hawks**	**NHL**	**74**	**21**	**12**	**33**	**21**	**10**	**31**	**58**	**6**	**0**	**3**	**120**	**17.5**	**54**	**13**	**25**	**0**	**+16**	**11**	**3**	**0**	**3**	**11**	**0**	**0**	**0**
1974-75	**Chicago Black Hawks**	**NHL**	**78**	**22**	**22**	**44**	**20**	**17**	**37**	**93**	**5**	**0**	**2**	**158**	**13.9**	**66**	**9**	**56**	**0**	**+1**	**7**	**0**	**1**	**1**	**24**	**0**	**0**	**0**
1975-76	**Chicago Black Hawks**	**NHL**	**79**	**20**	**17**	**37**	**19**	**13**	**32**	**73**	**4**	**0**	**2**	**201**	**10.0**	**71**	**16**	**63**	**0**	**–8**	**4**	**1**	**0**	**1**	**2**	**1**	**0**	**0**
1976-77	**Chicago Black Hawks**	**NHL**	**76**	**24**	**22**	**46**	**23**	**18**	**41**	**82**	**4**	**0**	**3**	**148**	**16.2**	**72**	**13**	**66**	**0**	**–7**	**2**	**0**	**0**	**0**	**0**	**0**	**0**	**0**
1977-78	**Chicago Black Hawks**	**NHL**	**78**	**17**	**20**	**37**	**16**	**16**	**32**	**67**	**3**	**0**	**1**	**107**	**15.9**	**46**	**10**	**31**	**0**	**+5**	**4**	**0**	**0**	**0**	**2**	**0**	**0**	**0**
1978-79	**Chicago Black Hawks**	**NHL**	**63**	**13**	**17**	**30**	**12**	**13**	**25**	**77**	**1**	**0**	**1**	**116**	**11.2**	**40**	**3**	**47**	**0**	**–10**	....	....	....	....	....	....	....	....
	Atlanta Flames	**NHL**	**13**	**9**	**5**	**14**	**8**	**4**	**12**	**21**	**0**	**0**	**0**	**27**	**33.3**	**16**	**1**	**13**	**1**	**+3**	**2**	**0**	**1**	**1**	**26**	**0**	**0**	**0**
1979-80	**Atlanta Flames**	**NHL**	**44**	**10**	**8**	**18**	**9**	**6**	**15**	**49**	**0**	**0**	**1**	**70**	**14.3**	**30**	**3**	**24**	**0**	**+3**	....	....	....	....	....	....	....	....
	Vancouver Canucks	**NHL**	**26**	**5**	**6**	**11**	**5**	**5**	**10**	**29**	**0**	**0**	**2**	**53**	**9.4**	**15**	**3**	**24**	**3**	**–9**	**4**	**2**	**0**	**2**	**8**	**0**	**0**	**0**
1980-81	**Vancouver Canucks**	**NHL**	**80**	**25**	**31**	**56**	**21**	**22**	**43**	**124**	**7**	**0**	**5**	**178**	**14.0**	**87**	**18**	**61**	**2**	**+10**	**3**	**2**	**1**	**3**	**14**	**1**	**0**	**0**
1981-82	**Vancouver Canucks**	**NHL**	**51**	**20**	**20**	**40**	**16**	**13**	**29**	**139**	**2**	**0**	**0**	**80**	**25.0**	**50**	**11**	**33**	**0**	**+6**	**17**	**6**	**3**	**9**	**54**	**2**	**0**	**1**
1982-83	**Vancouver Canucks**	**NHL**	**73**	**42**	**39**	**81**	**35**	**27**	**62**	**88**	**9**	**0**	**5**	**173**	**24.3**	**104**	**30**	**61**	**0**	**+13**	**3**	**0**	**0**	**0**	**6**	**0**	**0**	**0**
1983-84	**Vancouver Canucks**	**NHL**	**59**	**28**	**20**	**48**	**23**	**14**	**37**	**73**	**6**	**0**	**0**	**127**	**22.0**	**71**	**22**	**62**	**1**	**–12**	**3**	**0**	**1**	**1**	**0**	**0**	**0**	**0**
	NHL Totals		**794**	**256**	**239**	**495**	**228**	**178**	**406**	**973**	**47**	**0**	**25**	**1558**	**16.4**	**722**	**152**	**566**	**7**		**60**	**14**	**7**	**21**	**147**	**4**	**0**	**1**

WCJHL Second All-Star Team (1972) • WCJHL First All-Star Team (1973)

Played in NHL All-Star Game (1984)

Traded to **Atlanta** by **Chicago** with Ivan Bolderiv and Phil Russell for Tom Lysiak, Pat Ribble, Harold Phillipoff, Greg Fox and Miles Zaharko, March 13, 1979. Traded to **Vancouver** by **Atlanta** with Ivan Bolderiv for Don Lever and Brad Smith, February 8, 1980.

• ROTA, RANDY

Randy Rota C/LW – L. 5'8", 170 lbs. b: Creston, B.C., 8/16/1950. California's 3rd choice, 33rd overall, in 1970 Amateur Draft.

Season	Club	League	GP	G	A	Pts	AG	AA	APts	PIM	PP	SH	GW	S	%	TGF	PGF	TGA	PGA	+/–	GP	G	A	Pts	PIM	PP	SH	GW
1967-68	Kamloops Rockets	BCJHL	....	*45	28	73	....	....	....	22	....	....	....	....	....	....	....	....	....	....	....	....	....	....	....	....	....	....
1968-69	Calgary Centennials	WCJHL	33	20	18	38	....	....	....	2	....	....	....	....	....	....	....	....	....	....	11	0	3	3	....	....	....	....
1969-70	Calgary Centennials	WCJHL	60	43	47	80	....	....	....	43	....	....	....	....	....	....	....	....	....	....	15	3	8	11	12	....	....	....
1970-71	Providence Reds	AHL	68	31	34	65	....	....	....	31	....	....	....	....	....	....	....	....	....	....	10	4	3	7	4	....	....	....
1971-72	Nova Scotia Voyageurs	AHL	72	32	23	55	....	....	....	24	....	....	....	....	....	....	....	....	....	....	15	6	4	10	2	....	....	....
1972-73	**Montreal Canadiens**	**NHL**	**2**	**1**	**1**	**2**	**1**	**1**	**2**	**0**	**0**	**0**	**1**	**4**	**25.0**	**3**	**0**	**1**	**0**	**+2**	....	....	....	....	....	....	....	....
	Nova Scotia Voyageurs	AHL	73	34	38	72	....	....	....	23	....	....	....	....	....	....	....	....	....	....	13	*10	7	17	10	....	....	....
1973-74	**Los Angeles Kings**	**NHL**	**58**	**10**	**6**	**16**	**10**	**5**	**15**	**16**	**0**	**0**	**0**	**93**	**10.8**	**29**	**5**	**34**	**2**	**–8**	**5**	**0**	**1**	**1**	**0**	**0**	**0**	**0**
1974-75	**Kansas City Scouts**	**NHL**	**80**	**15**	**18**	**33**	**14**	**14**	**28**	**30**	**3**	**0**	**0**	**182**	**8.2**	**52**	**14**	**81**	**4**	**–39**	....	....	....	....	....	....	....	....
1975-76	**Kansas City Scouts**	**NHL**	**71**	**12**	**14**	**26**	**11**	**11**	**22**	**14**	**2**	**0**	**1**	**146**	**8.2**	**39**	**8**	**70**	**1**	**–38**	....	....	....	....	....	....	....	....
1976-77	**Colorado Rockies**	**NHL**	**1**	**0**	**0**	**0**	**0**	**0**	**0**	**0**	**0**	**0**	**0**	**0**	**0.0**	**0**	**0**	**0**	**0**	**0**	....	....	....	....	....	....	....	....
	Oklahoma City Blazers	CHL	12	4	4	8	....	....	....	5	....	....	....	....	....	....	....	....	....	....	....	....	....	....	....	....	....	....
	Edmonton Oilers	WHA	40	9	6	15	....	....	....	8	....	....	....	....	....	....	....	....	....	....	5	3	2	5	0	....	....	....
1977-78	Edmonton Oilers	WHA	53	8	22	30	....	....	....	12	....	....	....	....	....	....	....	....	....	....	5	1	1	2	4	....	....	....
	NHL Totals		**212**	**38**	**39**	**77**	**36**	**31**	**67**	**60**	**5**	**0**	**2**	**425**	**8.9**	**123**	**27**	**186**	**7**		**5**	**0**	**1**	**1**	**0**	**0**	**0**	**0**
	Other Major League Totals		93	17	28	45	....	....	....	20	....	....	....	....	....	....	....	....	....		10	4	3	7	4	....	....	....

Traded to **Montreal** by **California** for Lyle Carter and John French, October, 1971. Traded to **LA Kings** by **Montreal** with Bob Murdoch for LA Kings' 1st round choice (Mario Tremblay) in 1974 Amateur Draft and cash, May 29, 1973. Claimed by **Kansas City** from **LA Kings** in Expansion Draft, June 12, 1974. Transferred to **Colorado** after **Kansas City** franchise relocated, July 15, 1976. Traded to **Edmonton** (WHA) by **Colorado** for cash, November, 1976.

• ROULSTON, TOM Tom Roulston C/RW – R. 6'1", 184 lbs. b: Winnipeg, Man., 11/20/1957. St. Louis' 3rd choice, 45th overall, in 1977 Amateur Draft.

			REGULAR SEASON																		PLAYOFFS							
Season	Club	League	GP	G	A	Pts	AG	AA	APts	PIM	PP	SH	GW	S	%	TGF	PGF	TGA	PGA	+/–	GP	G	A	Pts	PIM	PP	SH	GW
1975-76	Spruce Grove Mintos	AJHL	5	3	1	4	....	....	....	4	....	....	....	....	....	....	....	....	....	....	....	....	....	....	....	....	....	....
	Edmonton Oil Kings	WCJHL	1	0	0	0	....	....	....	0	....	....	....	....	....	....	....	....	....	....	....	....	....	....	....	....	....	....
	Winnipeg Clubs	WCJHL	60	18	17	35	....	....	....	56	....	....	....	....	....	....	....	....	....	....	....	....	....	....	....	....	....	....
1976-77	Winnipeg Monarchs	WCJHL	72	56	53	109	....	....	....	35	....	....	....	....	....	....	....	....	....	....	....	....	....	....	....	....	....	....
1977-78	Salt Lake Golden Eagles	CHL	21	2	1	3	....	....	....	2	....	....	....	....	....	....	....	....	....	....	....	....	....	....	....	....	....	....
	Port Huron Flags	IHL	49	27	36	63	....	....	....	24	....	....	....	....	....	....	....	....	....	....	16	*17	7	24	10	....	....	....
1978-79	Dallas Black Hawks	CHL	73	26	29	55	....	....	....	57	....	....	....	....	....	....	....	....	....	....	9	*6	6	12	11	....	....	....
1979-80	Houston Apollos	CHL	72	29	41	70	....	....	....	46	....	....	....	....	....	....	....	....	....	....	6	2	4	6	4	....	....	....
1980-81	**Edmonton Oilers**	**NHL**	**11**	**1**	**1**	**2**	**1**	**1**	**2**	**2**	**0**	**0**	**0**	**9**	**11.1**	**7**	**0**	**13**	**3**	**–3**	....	....	....	....	....	....	....	....
	Wichita Wind	CHL	69	*63	44	107	....	....	....	93	....	....	....	....	....	....	....	....	....	....	18	15	11	*26	44	....	....	....
1981-82	**Edmonton Oilers**	**NHL**	**35**	**11**	**3**	**14**	**9**	**2**	**11**	**22**	**0**	**1**	**0**	**54**	**20.4**	**20**	**3**	**25**	**2**	**–6**	**5**	**1**	**0**	**1**	**2**	**0**	**0**	**0**
	Wichita Wind	CHL	30	22	28	50	....	....	....	40	....	....	....	....	....	....	....	....	....	....	....	....	....	....	....	....	....	....
1982-83	**Edmonton Oilers**	**NHL**	**67**	**19**	**21**	**40**	**16**	**14**	**30**	**24**	**2**	**0**	**2**	**107**	**17.8**	**63**	**8**	**30**	**4**	**+29**	**16**	**1**	**2**	**3**	**0**	**0**	**0**	**0**
1983-84	**Edmonton Oilers**	**NHL**	**24**	**5**	**7**	**12**	**4**	**5**	**9**	**16**	**1**	**0**	**0**	**38**	**13.2**	**19**	**3**	**17**	**1**	**0**	....	....	....	....	....	....	....	....
	Pittsburgh Penguins	**NHL**	**53**	**11**	**17**	**28**	**9**	**12**	**21**	**8**	**3**	**0**	**0**	**110**	**10.0**	**45**	**17**	**61**	**2**	**–31**	....	....	....	....	....	....	....	....
1984-85	Baltimore Skipjacks	AHL	78	31	39	70	....	....	....	48	....	....	....	....	....	....	....	....	....	....	15	4	8	12	6	....	....	....
1985-86	**Pittsburgh Penguins**	**NHL**	**5**	**0**	**0**	**0**	**0**	**0**	**0**	**2**	**0**	**0**	**0**	**6**	**0.0**	**1**	**0**	**3**	**0**	**–2**	....	....	....	....	....	....	....	....
	Baltimore Skipjacks	AHL	73	38	49	87	....	....	....	38	....	....	....	....	....	....	....	....	....	....	....	....	....	....	....	....	....	....
1986-87	Salzburger	Austria	19	18	19	37	....	....	....	28	....	....	....	....	....	....	....	....	....	....	....	....	....	....	....	....	....	....
	Landshut	Germany	20	23	12	35	....	....	....	25	....	....	....	....	....	....	....	....	....	....	....	....	....	....	....	....	....	....
1987-88	SB Rosenheim	Germany	21	10	13	23	....	....	....	34	....	....	....	....	....	....	....	....	....	....	....	....	....	....	....	....	....	....
1988-89	HC Fiemme	Italy	36	40	47	87	....	....	....	26	....	....	....	....	....	....	....	....	....	....	....	....	....	....	....	....	....	....
	HC Davos	Switz.	1	0	1	1	....	....	....	0	....	....	....	....	....	....	....	....	....	....	12	10	7	17	....	....	....	....
	NHL Totals		**195**	**47**	**49**	**96**	**39**	**34**	**73**	**74**	**6**	**1**	**2**	**324**	**14.5**	**155**	**31**	**149**	**12**		**21**	**2**	**2**	**4**	**2**	**0**	**0**	**0**

CHL First All-Star Team (1981)

Traded to **Edmonton** by **St. Louis** with Risto Siltanen for Joe Micheletti, August 7, 1979. Traded to **Pittsburgh** by **Edmonton** for Kevin McClelland and Pittsburgh's 6th round choice (Emanuel Viveiros) in 1984 Entry Draft, December 5, 1983.

• ROUPE, MAGNUS Magnus Roupe LW – L. 6', 189 lbs. b: Stockholm, Sweden, 3/23/1963. Philadelphia's 9th choice, 182nd overall, in 1982 Entry Draft.

			REGULAR SEASON																		PLAYOFFS							
Season	Club	League	GP	G	A	Pts	AG	AA	APts	PIM	PP	SH	GW	S	%	TGF	PGF	TGA	PGA	+/–	GP	G	A	Pts	PIM	PP	SH	GW
1981-82	Farjestad BK Karlstad	Sweden	24	5	3	8	....	....	....	8	....	....	....	....	....	....	....	....	....	....	2	0	0	0	0	....	....	....
	Sweden	WJC-A	7	7	3	10	....	....	....	4	....	....	....	....	....	....	....	....	....	....	....	....	....	....	....	....	....	....
1982-83	Farjestad BK Karlstad	Sweden	29	7	4	11	....	....	....	16	....	....	....	....	....	....	....	....	....	....	6	1	1	2	8	....	....	....
	Sweden	WJC-A	6	1	2	3	....	....	....	....	....	....	....	....	....	....	....	....	....	....	....	....	....	....	....	....	....	....
1983-84	Farjestad BK Karlstad	Sweden	36	2	3	5	....	....	....	38	....	....	....	....	....	....	....	....	....	....	....	....	....	....	....	....	....	....
1984-85	Farjestad BK Karlstad	Sweden	31	9	6	15	....	....	....	16	....	....	....	....	....	....	....	....	....	....	3	1	0	1	0	....	....	....
1985-86	Farjestad BK Karlstad	Sweden	35	11	10	21	....	....	....	38	....	....	....	....	....	....	....	....	....	....	8	3	2	5	18	....	....	....
1986-87	Farjestad BK Karlstad	Sweden	31	11	6	17	....	....	....	58	....	....	....	....	....	....	....	....	....	....	7	0	2	2	10	....	....	....
1987-88	Sweden	C Cup	5	1	1	2	....	....	....	4	....	....	....	....	....	....	....	....	....	....	....	....	....	....	....	....	....	....
	Philadelphia Flyers	**NHL**	**33**	**2**	**4**	**6**	**2**	**3**	**5**	**32**	**1**	**0**	**0**	**37**	**5.4**	**11**	**2**	**15**	**0**	**–6**	....	....	....	....	....	....	....	....
	Hershey Bears	AHL	23	6	16	22	....	....	....	10	....	....	....	....	....	....	....	....	....	....	11	3	4	7	31	....	....	....
1988-89	**Philadelphia Flyers**	**NHL**	**7**	**1**	**1**	**2**	**1**	**1**	**2**	**10**	**0**	**0**	**0**	**15**	**6.7**	**2**	**0**	**1**	**0**	**+1**	....	....	....	....	....	....	....	....
	Hershey Bears	AHL	12	2	6	8	....	....	....	17	....	....	....	....	....	....	....	....	....	....	....	....	....	....	....	....	....	....
	Farjestad BK Karlstad	Sweden	18	9	41	13	....	....	....	58	....	....	....	....	....	....	....	....	....	....	2	0	1	1	6	....	....	....
1989-90	Farjestad BK Karlstad	Sweden	39	19	17	36	....	....	....	66	....	....	....	....	....	....	....	....	....	....	9	1	2	3	14	....	....	....
	Sweden	WEC-A	10	0	3	3	....	....	....	8	....	....	....	....	....	....	....	....	....	....	....	....	....	....	....	....	....	....
1990-91	Farjestad BK Karlstad	Sweden	39	9	10	19	....	....	....	54	....	....	....	....	....	....	....	....	....	....	8	2	5	7	12	....	....	....
1991-92	Farjestad BK Karlstad	Sweden	39	3	9	12	....	....	....	22	....	....	....	....	....	....	....	....	....	....	6	0	0	0	4	....	....	....
	NHL Totals		**40**	**3**	**5**	**8**	**3**	**4**	**7**	**42**	**1**	**0**	**0**	**52**	**5.8**	**13**	**2**	**16**	**0**		....	....	....	....	....	....	....	....

• ROUSE, BOB Bob Rouse D – R. 6'1", 210 lbs. b: Surrey, B.C., 6/18/1964. Minnesota's 3rd choice, 80th overall, in 1982 Entry Draft.

			REGULAR SEASON																		PLAYOFFS							
Season	Club	League	GP	G	A	Pts	AG	AA	APts	PIM	PP	SH	GW	S	%	TGF	PGF	TGA	PGA	+/–	GP	G	A	Pts	PIM	PP	SH	GW
1980-81	Billings Bighorns	WHL	70	0	13	13	....	....	....	116	....	....	....	....	....	....	....	....	....	....	5	0	0	0	2	....	....	....
1981-82	Billings Bighorns	WHL	71	7	22	29	....	....	....	209	....	....	....	....	....	....	....	....	....	....	5	0	2	2	10	....	....	....
1982-83	Nanaimo Islanders	WHL	29	7	20	27	....	....	....	86	....	....	....	....	....	....	....	....	....	....	....	....	....	....	....	....	....	....
	Lethbridge Broncos	WHL	42	8	30	38	....	....	....	82	....	....	....	....	....	....	....	....	....	....	20	2	13	15	55	....	....	....
1983-84	Lethbridge Broncos	WHL	71	18	42	60	....	....	....	101	....	....	....	....	....	....	....	....	....	....	5	0	1	1	28	....	....	....
	Minnesota North Stars	**NHL**	**1**	**0**	**0**	**0**	**0**	**0**	**0**	**0**	**0**	**0**	**0**	**0**	**0.0**	**0**	**0**	**0**	**0**	**0**	....	....	....	....	....	....	....	....
1984-85	**Minnesota North Stars**	**NHL**	**63**	**2**	**9**	**11**	**2**	**6**	**8**	**113**	**0**	**0**	**0**	**80**	**2.5**	**48**	**1**	**83**	**22**	**–14**	....	....	....	....	....	....	....	....
	Springfield Indians	AHL	8	0	3	3	....	....	....	6	....	....	....	....	....	....	....	....	....	....	....	....	....	....	....	....	....	....
1985-86	**Minnesota North Stars**	**NHL**	**75**	**1**	**14**	**15**	**1**	**9**	**10**	**151**	**0**	**0**	**1**	**91**	**1.1**	**97**	**2**	**112**	**32**	**+15**	**3**	**0**	**0**	**0**	**0**	**0**	**0**	**0**
1986-87	**Minnesota North Stars**	**NHL**	**72**	**2**	**10**	**12**	**2**	**7**	**9**	**179**	**0**	**0**	**0**	**71**	**2.8**	**63**	**1**	**103**	**47**	**+6**	....	....	....	....	....	....	....	....
	Canada	WEC-A	4	0	0	0	....	....	....	4	....	....	....	....	....	....	....	....	....	....	....	....	....	....	....	....	....	....
1987-88	**Minnesota North Stars**	**NHL**	**74**	**0**	**12**	**12**	**0**	**9**	**9**	**168**	**0**	**0**	**0**	**62**	**0.0**	**48**	**1**	**125**	**48**	**–30**	....	....	....	....	....	....	....	....
1988-89	**Minnesota North Stars**	**NHL**	**66**	**4**	**13**	**17**	**3**	**9**	**12**	**124**	**0**	**0**	**1**	**66**	**6.1**	**59**	**0**	**92**	**28**	**–5**	....	....	....	....	....	....	....	....
	Washington Capitals	**NHL**	**13**	**0**	**2**	**2**	**0**	**1**	**1**	**36**	**0**	**0**	**0**	**19**	**0.0**	**16**	**3**	**16**	**5**	**+2**	**6**	**2**	**0**	**2**	**4**	**0**	**0**	**0**
1989-90	Washington Capitals	FrTour	4	0	0	0	....	....	....	4	....	....	....	....	....	....	....	....	....	....	....	....	....	....	....	....	....	....
	Washington Capitals	**NHL**	**70**	**4**	**16**	**20**	**3**	**11**	**14**	**123**	**0**	**0**	**2**	**72**	**5.6**	**73**	**7**	**93**	**25**	**–2**	**15**	**2**	**3**	**5**	**47**	**1**	**0**	**0**
1990-91	**Washington Capitals**	**NHL**	**47**	**5**	**15**	**20**	**5**	**11**	**16**	**65**	**1**	**0**	**0**	**50**	**10.0**	**44**	**4**	**57**	**10**	**–7**	....	....	....	....	....	....	....	....
	Toronto Maple Leafs	**NHL**	**13**	**2**	**4**	**6**	**2**	**3**	**5**	**10**	**1**	**0**	**0**	**15**	**13.3**	**14**	**3**	**28**	**6**	**–11**	....	....	....	....	....	....	....	....
1991-92	**Toronto Maple Leafs**	**NHL**	**79**	**3**	**19**	**22**	**3**	**14**	**17**	**97**	**1**	**0**	**0**	**115**	**2.6**	**68**	**9**	**112**	**33**	**–20**	....	....	....	....	....	....	....	....
1992-93	**Toronto Maple Leafs**	**NHL**	**82**	**3**	**11**	**14**	**2**	**8**	**10**	**130**	**0**	**1**	**1**	**78**	**3.8**	**64**	**2**	**84**	**29**	**+7**	**21**	**3**	**8**	**11**	**29**	**1**	**0**	**1**
1993-94	**Toronto Maple Leafs**	**NHL**	**63**	**5**	**11**	**16**	**5**	**8**	**13**	**101**	**1**	**1**	**0**	**77**	**6.5**	**57**	**8**	**66**	**25**	**+8**	**18**	**0**	**3**	**3**	**29**	**0**	**0**	**0**
1994-95	**Detroit Red Wings**	**NHL**	**48**	**1**	**7**	**8**	**2**	**10**	**12**	**36**	**0**	**0**	**1**	**51**	**2.0**	**45**	**4**	**41**	**14**	**+14**	**18**	**0**	**3**	**3**	**8**	**0**	**0**	**0**
1995-96	**Detroit Red Wings**	**NHL**	**58**	**0**	**6**	**6**	**0**	**5**	**5**	**48**	**0**	**0**	**0**	**49**	**0.0**	**39**	**0**	**43**	**9**	**+5**	**7**	**0**	**1**	**1**	**4**	**0**	**0**	**0**
1996-97	**Detroit Red Wings**	**NHL**	**70**	**4**	**9**	**13**	**4**	**8**	**12**	**58**	**0**	**2**	**0**	**70**	**5.7**	**44**	**0**	**49**	**13**	**+8**	**20**	**0**	**0**	**0**	**55**	**0**	**0**	**0**
1997-98	**Detroit Red Wings**	**NHL**	**71**	**1**	**11**	**12**	**1**	**11**	**12**	**57**	**0**	**0**	**0**	**54**	**1.9**	**38**	**1**	**61**	**15**	**–8**	**22**	**0**	**3**	**3**	**16**	**0**	**0**	**0**
	NHL Totals		**965**	**37**	**169**	**206**	**35**	**130**	**165**	**1496**	**4**	**4**	**6**	**1020**	**3.6**	**817**	**46**	**1165**	**361**		**130**	**7**	**21**	**28**	**192**	**2**	**0**	**1**

WHL East First All-Star Team (1984)

Traded to **Washington** by **Minnesota** with Dino Ciccarelli for Mike Gartner and Larry Murphy, March 7, 1989. Traded to **Toronto** by **Washington** with Peter Zezel for Al Iafrate, January 16, 1991. Signed as a free agent by **Detroit**, August 5, 1994. Signed as a free agent by **San Jose**, June 14, 1998.

• ROUSSEAU, BOBBY Bobby Rousseau RW – R. 5'10", 178 lbs. b: Montreal, Que., 7/26/1940.

			REGULAR SEASON																		PLAYOFFS							
Season	Club	League	GP	G	A	Pts	AG	AA	APts	PIM	PP	SH	GW	S	%	TGF	PGF	TGA	PGA	+/–	GP	G	A	Pts	PIM	PP	SH	GW
1955-56	St-Jean Braves	QJHL	44	*53	32	85	....	....	....	25	....	....	....	....	....	....	....	....	....	....	....	....	....	....	....	....	....	....
1956-57	Hull-Ottawa Jr. Canadiens	Ott-Jr.	28	7	15	22	....	....	....	18	....	....	....	....	....	....	....	....	....	....	....	....	....	....	....	....	....	....
	Hull Ottawa Jr. Canadiens	EOHL	15	4	2	6	....	....	....	2	....	....	....	....	....	....	....	....	....	....	....	....	....	....	....	....	....	....
1957-58	Hull-Ottawa Jr. Canadiens	Ott-Jr.	27	24	27	51	....	....	....	64	....	....	....	....	....	....	....	....	....	....	....	....	....	....	....	....	....	....
	Hull-Ottawa Jr. Canadiens	EOHL	36	26	26	52	....	....	....	14	....	....	....	....	....	....	....	....	....	....	....	....	....	....	....	....	....	....
1958-59	Hull-Ottawa Jr. Canadiens	Ott-Jr.	STATISTICS NOT AVAILABLE																									
	Hull-Ottawa Jr. Canadiens	EOHL	18	7	18	25	....	....	....	26	....	....	....	....	....	....	....	....	....	....	3	1	1	2	2	....	....	....
	Rochester Americans	AHL	2	0	0	0	....	....	....	0	....	....	....	....	....	....	....	....	....	....	....	....	....	....	....	....	....	....
1959-60	Hull-Ottawa Jr. Canadiens	Ott-Jr.	STATISTICS NOT AVAILABLE																									
	Canada	Olympics	7	5	4	9	....	....	....	2	....	....	....	....	....	....	....	....	....	....	....	....	....	....	....	....	....	....
	Hull-Ottawa Canadiens	EPHL	4	4	2	6	....	....	....	4	....	....	....	....	....	....	....	....	....	....	....	....	....	....	....	....	....	....
1960-61	**Montreal Canadiens**	**NHL**	**15**	**1**	**2**	**3**	**1**	**2**	**3**	**4**	....	....	....	....	....	....	....	....	....	....	....	....	....	....	....	....	....	....
	Hull-Ottawa Canadiens	EPHL	38	34	26	60	....	....	....	18	....	....	....	....	....	....	....	....	....	....	14	*12	7	*19	10	....	....	....
1961-62	**Montreal Canadiens**	**NHL**	**70**	**21**	**24**	**45**	**26**	**24**	**50**	**26**	....	....	....	....	....	....	....	....	....	....	**6**	**0**	**2**	**2**	**0**	....	....	....
1962-63	**Montreal Canadiens**	**NHL**	**62**	**19**	**18**	**37**	**23**	**19**	**42**	**15**	....	....	....	....	....	....	....	....	....	....	**5**	**0**	**1**	**1**	**2**	....	....	....
1963-64	**Montreal Canadiens**	**NHL**	**70**	**25**	**31**	**56**	**33**	**34**	**67**	**32**	....	....	....	....	....	....	....	....	....	....	**7**	**1**	**1**	**2**	**2**	....	....	....
1964-65	**Montreal Canadiens**	**NHL**	**66**	**12**	**35**	**47**	**15**	**30**	**53**	**26**	....	....	....	....	....	....	....	....	....	....	**13**	**5**	**8**	**13**	**24**	....	....	....
1965-66	**Montreal Canadiens**	**NHL**	**70**	**30**	***48**	**78**	**37**	**49**	**86**	**20**	....	....	....	....	....	....	....	....	....	....	**10**	**4**	**4**	**8**	**6**	....	....	....
1966-67	**Montreal Canadiens**	**NHL**	**68**	**19**	**44**	**63**	**23**	**46**	**69**	**58**	....	....	....	....	....	....	....	....	....	....	**10**	**1**	**7**	**8**	**4**	....	....	....
1967-68	**Montreal Canadiens**	**NHL**	**74**	**19**	**46**	**65**	**23**	**48**	**71**	**47**	**7**	**1**	**5**	**183**	**10.4**	**97**	**40**	**47**	**2**	**+12**	**13**	**2**	**4**	**6**	**8**	**0**	**0**	**1**

			REGULAR SEASON																		PLAYOFFS							
Season	Club	League	GP	G	A	Pts	AG	AA	APts	PIM	PP	SH	GW	S	%	TGF	PGF	TGA	PGA	+/–	GP	G	A	Pts	PIM	PP	SH	GW
1968-69	**Montreal Canadiens**	**NHL**	**76**	**30**	**40**	**70**	**34**	**38**	**72**	**59**	**3**	**0**	**8**	**278**	**10.8**	**112**	**28**	**69**	**12**	**+27**	**14**	**3**	**2**	**5**	**8**	**0**	**2**	**1**
1969-70	**Montreal Canadiens**	**NHL**	**72**	**24**	**34**	**58**	**28**	**34**	**62**	**30**	**5**	**2**	**4**	**228**	**10.5**	**91**	**30**	**80**	**22**	**+3**	....	....	....	....	....	....	....	....
1970-71	**Minnesota North Stars**	**NHL**	**63**	**4**	**20**	**24**	**4**	**18**	**22**	**12**	**0**	**0**	**0**	**122**	**3.3**	**30**	**3**	**25**	**1**	**+3**	**12**	**2**	**6**	**8**	**0**	**1**	**0**	**1**
1971-72	**New York Rangers**	**NHL**	**78**	**21**	**36**	**57**	**22**	**33**	**55**	**12**	**4**	**1**	**6**	**180**	**11.7**	**96**	**46**	**49**	**7**	**+8**	**16**	**6**	**11**	**17**	**7**	**0**	**0**	**1**
1972-73	**New York Rangers**	**NHL**	**78**	**8**	**37**	**45**	**8**	**31**	**39**	**14**	**2**	**0**	**3**	**150**	**5.3**	**72**	**37**	**37**	**3**	**+1**	**10**	**2**	**3**	**5**	**4**	**0**	**0**	**0**
1973-74	**New York Rangers**	**NHL**	**72**	**10**	**41**	**51**	**10**	**36**	**46**	**4**	**6**	**0**	**0**	**87**	**11.5**	**75**	**49**	**24**	**0**	**+2**	**12**	**1**	**8**	**9**	**4**	**1**	**0**	**0**
1974-75	**New York Rangers**	**NHL**	**8**	**2**	**2**	**4**	**2**	**2**	**4**	**0**	**2**	**0**	**1**	**9**	**22.2**	**6**	**5**	**3**	**0**	**–2**	....	....	....	....	....	....	....	....
	NHL Totals		**942**	**245**	**458**	**703**	**289**	**452**	**741**	**359**	**29**	**4**	**27**	**1237**	**19.8**	**579**	**238**	**334**	**47**		**128**	**27**	**57**	**84**	**69**	**2**	**2**	**4**

Won Calder Memorial Trophy (1962) • NHL Second All-Star Team (1966)

Played in NHL All-Star Game (1965, 1967, 1969)

Traded to **Minnesota** by **Montreal** for Claude Larose, June 10, 1970. Traded to **NY Rangers** by **Minnesota** to complete transaction that sent Bob Nevin to Minnesota (May 25, 1971), June 8, 1971.

• ROUTHIER, JEAN-MARC

Jean-Marc Routhier RW – R. 6'2", 190 lbs. b: Quebec City, Que., 2/2/1968. Quebec's 2nd choice, 39th overall, in 1986 Entry Draft.

Season	Club	League	GP	G	A	Pts	AG	AA	APts	PIM	PP	SH	GW	S	%	TGF	PGF	TGA	PGA	+/–	GP	G	A	Pts	PIM	PP	SH	GW
1984-85	St. Foy Midgets	Midget	41	13	22	35	....	....	....	68	....	....	....	....	....	....	....	....	....	....	....	....	....	....	....	....	....	....
1985-86	Hull Olympiques	QMJHL	71	18	16	34	....	....	....	111	....	....	....	....	....	....	....	....	....	....	15	3	6	9	27	....	....	....
1986-87	Hull Olympiques	QMJHL	59	17	18	35	....	....	....	98	....	....	....	....	....	....	....	....	....	....	....	....	....	....	....	....	....	....
1987-88	Victoriaville Tigers	QMJHL	57	16	28	44	....	....	....	267	....	....	....	....	....	....	....	....	....	....	2	0	0	0	5	....	....	....
1988-89	Halifax Citadels	AHL	52	13	13	26	....	....	....	189	....	....	....	....	....	....	....	....	....	....	4	1	1	2	16	....	....	....
1989-90	**Quebec Nordiques**	**NHL**	**8**	**0**	**0**	**0**	**0**	**0**	**0**	**9**	**0**	**0**	**0**	**8**	**0.0**	**0**	**0**	**3**	**0**	**–3**	....	....	....	....	....	....	....	....
	Halifax Citadels	AHL	17	4	8	12	....	....	....	29	....	....	....	....	....	....	....	....	....	....	....	....	....	....	....	....	....	....
	NHL Totals		**8**	**0**	**0**	**0**	**0**	**0**	**0**	**9**	**0**	**0**	**0**	**8**	**0.0**	**0**	**0**	**3**	**0**		....	....	....	....	....	....	....	....

• ROWE, MIKE

Mike Rowe D – L. 6'1", 208 lbs. b: Kingston, Ont., 3/8/1965. Pittsburgh's 3rd choice, 59th overall, in 1983 Entry Draft.

Season	Club	League	GP	G	A	Pts	AG	AA	APts	PIM	PP	SH	GW	S	%	TGF	PGF	TGA	PGA	+/–	GP	G	A	Pts	PIM	PP	SH	GW
1981-82	Toronto Marlboros	OHA	58	4	4	8	....	....	....	214	....	....	....	....	....	....	....	....	....	....	10	0	0	0	63	....	....	....
1982-83	Toronto Marlboros	OHL	64	4	29	33	....	....	....	262	....	....	....	....	....	....	....	....	....	....	4	0	1	1	19	....	....	....
1983-84	Toronto Marlboros	OHL	59	9	36	45	....	....	....	208	....	....	....	....	....	....	....	....	....	....	9	0	5	5	45	....	....	....
1984-85	Toronto Marlboros	OHL	66	17	34	51	....	....	....	202	....	....	....	....	....	....	....	....	....	....	....	....	....	....	....	....	....	....
	Pittsburgh Penguins	**NHL**	**6**	**0**	**0**	**0**	**0**	**0**	**0**	**7**	**0**	**0**	**0**	**6**	**0.0**	**2**	**0**	**12**	**3**	**–7**	....	....	....	....	....	....	....	....
	Baltimore Clippers	AHL	....	....	....	....	....	....	....	....	....	....	....	....	....	....	....	....	....	....	3	0	0	0	0	....	....	....
1985-86	**Pittsburgh Penguins**	**NHL**	**3**	**0**	**0**	**0**	**0**	**0**	**0**	**4**	**0**	**0**	**0**	**5**	**0.0**	**0**	**0**	**1**	**0**	**–1**	....	....	....	....	....	....	....	....
	Baltimore Skipjacks	AHL	67	0	5	5	....	....	....	107	....	....	....	....	....	....	....	....	....	....	....	....	....	....	....	....	....	....
1986-87	**Pittsburgh Penguins**	**NHL**	**2**	**0**	**0**	**0**	**0**	**0**	**0**	**0**	**0**	**0**	**0**	**1**	**0.0**	**0**	**0**	**2**	**0**	**–2**	....	....	....	....	....	....	....	....
	Baltimore Skipjacks	AHL	79	1	18	19	....	....	....	64	....	....	....	....	....	....	....	....	....	....	....	....	....	....	....	....	....	....
1987-88	Muskegon Lumberjacks	IHL	80	8	21	29	....	....	....	137	....	....	....	....	....	....	....	....	....	....	6	0	0	0	13	....	....	....
1988-89	Whitley Warriors	Britain	35	34	86	120	....	....	....	122	....	....	....	....	....	....	....	....	....	....	5	6	5	11	24	....	....	....
1989-90	Fife Flyers	Britain	29	22	30	52	....	....	....	107	....	....	....	....	....	....	....	....	....	....	5	1	4	5	24	....	....	....
1990-91	Basingstoke Beavers	Britain	36	39	63	109	....	....	....	*239	....	....	....	....	....	....	....	....	....	....	....	....	....	....	....	....	....	....
	Murrayfield Racers	Britain	....	....	....	....	....	....	....	....	....	....	....	....	....	....	....	....	....	....	7	6	7	13	18	....	....	....
1991-92	Whitley Warriors	Britain	36	32	48	80	....	....	....	146	....	....	....	....	....	....	....	....	....	....	7	2	7	9	12	....	....	....
1992-93	Whitley Warriors	Britain	34	17	61	78	....	....	....	100	....	....	....	....	....	....	....	....	....	....	6	1	7	8	10	....	....	....
1993-94	Whitley Warriors	Britain	43	16	53	69	....	....	....	110	....	....	....	....	....	....	....	....	....	....	5	0	1	1	23	....	....	....
1994-95	Whitley Warriors	Britain	37	9	30	39	....	....	....	100	....	....	....	....	....	....	....	....	....	....	6	2	6	8	43	....	....	....
	NHL Totals		**11**	**0**	**0**	**0**	**0**	**0**	**0**	**11**	**0**	**0**	**0**	**12**	**0.0**	**2**	**0**	**15**	**3**		....	....	....	....	....	....	....	....

• ROWE, TOM

Tom Rowe RW – R. 6', 190 lbs. b: Lynn, MA, 5/23/1956. Washington's 3rd choice, 37th overall, in 1976 Amateur Draft.

Season	Club	League	GP	G	A	Pts	AG	AA	APts	PIM	PP	SH	GW	S	%	TGF	PGF	TGA	PGA	+/–	GP	G	A	Pts	PIM	PP	SH	GW
1973-74	London Knights	OHA	70	30	39	69	....	....	....	99	....	....	....	....	....	....	....	....	....	....	....	....	....	....	....	....	....	....
1974-75	London Knights	OHA	63	19	15	34	....	....	....	137	....	....	....	....	....	....	....	....	....	....	....	....	....	....	....	....	....	....
1975-76	London Knights	OHA	60	39	55	94	....	....	....	98	....	....	....	....	....	....	....	....	....	....	5	1	3	4	14	....	....	....
1976-77	**Washington Capitals**	**NHL**	**12**	**1**	**2**	**3**	**1**	**2**	**3**	**2**	**0**	**0**	**0**	**22**	**4.5**	**9**	**2**	**13**	**0**	**–6**	....	....	....	....	....	....	....	....
	Springfield Indians	AHL	67	19	23	42	....	....	....	117	....	....	....	....	....	....	....	....	....	....	....	....	....	....	....	....	....	....
	United States	WEC-A	2	0	0	0	....	....	....	2	....	....	....	....	....	....	....	....	....	....	....	....	....	....	....	....	....	....
1977-78	**Washington Capitals**	**NHL**	**63**	**13**	**8**	**21**	**13**	**7**	**20**	**82**	**1**	**0**	**0**	**116**	**11.2**	**31**	**1**	**48**	**0**	**–18**	....	....	....	....	....	....	....	....
1978-79	**Washington Capitals**	**NHL**	**69**	**31**	**30**	**61**	**28**	**23**	**51**	**137**	**4**	**0**	**4**	**205**	**15.1**	**93**	**20**	**79**	**0**	**–6**	....	....	....	....	....	....	....	....
1979-80	**Washington Capitals**	**NHL**	**41**	**10**	**17**	**27**	**9**	**13**	**22**	**76**	**4**	**0**	**2**	**107**	**9.3**	**47**	**17**	**40**	**1**	**–9**	....	....	....	....	....	....	....	....
	Hartford Whalers	**NHL**	**20**	**6**	**4**	**10**	**5**	**3**	**8**	**30**	**1**	**0**	**1**	**41**	**14.6**	**17**	**1**	**19**	**0**	**–3**	**3**	**2**	**0**	**2**	**0**	**0**	**0**	**0**
1980-81	**Hartford Whalers**	**NHL**	**74**	**13**	**28**	**41**	**11**	**20**	**31**	**190**	**1**	**0**	**1**	**143**	**9.1**	**65**	**9**	**66**	**0**	**–10**	....	....	....	....	....	....	....	....
1981-82	**Hartford Whalers**	**NHL**	**21**	**4**	**0**	**4**	**3**	**0**	**3**	**36**	**1**	**1**	**0**	**47**	**8.5**	**5**	**1**	**18**	**3**	**–11**	....	....	....	....	....	....	....	....
	Binghamton Whalers	AHL	8	5	3	8	....	....	....	36	....	....	....	....	....	....	....	....	....	....	....	....	....	....	....	....	....	....
	Washington Capitals	**NHL**	**6**	**1**	**1**	**2**	**1**	**1**	**2**	**18**	**0**	**0**	**0**	**9**	**11.1**	**4**	**0**	**4**	**0**	**0**	....	....	....	....	....	....	....	....
	Hershey Bears	AHL	34	17	17	34	....	....	....	89	....	....	....	....	....	....	....	....	....	....	5	3	4	7	33	....	....	....
1982-83	**Detroit Red Wings**	**NHL**	**51**	**6**	**10**	**16**	**5**	**7**	**12**	**44**	**0**	**0**	**1**	**65**	**9.2**	**28**	**2**	**43**	**0**	**–17**	....	....	....	....	....	....	....	....
	Adirondack Red Wings	AHL	20	16	7	23	....	....	....	26	....	....	....	....	....	....	....	....	....	....	....	....	....	....	....	....	....	....
1983-84	Moncton Alpines	AHL	50	28	16	44	....	....	....	86	....	....	....	....	....	....	....	....	....	....	....	....	....	....	....	....	....	....
	NHL Totals		**357**	**85**	**100**	**185**	**76**	**76**	**152**	**615**	**12**	**1**	**9**	**755**	**11.3**	**299**	**53**	**330**	**4**		**3**	**2**	**0**	**2**	**0**	**0**	**0**	**0**

Traded to **Hartford** by **Washington** for Greg Adams, October 3, 1983. Signed as a free agent by **Washington**, January 31, 1982. Signed as a free agent by **Detroit**, August 9, 1982. Signed as a free agent by **Edmonton**, September 29, 1983.

• ROY, ANDRE

Andre Roy LW – L. 6'3", 202 lbs. b: Port Chester, NY, 2/8/1975. Boston's 5th choice, 151st overall, in 1994 Entry Draft.

Season	Club	League	GP	G	A	Pts	AG	AA	APts	PIM	PP	SH	GW	S	%	TGF	PGF	TGA	PGA	+/–	GP	G	A	Pts	PIM	PP	SH	GW
1993-94	Beauport Harfangs	QMJHL	33	6	7	13	....	....	....	125	....	....	....	....	....	....	....	....	....	....	....	....	....	....	....	....	....	....
	Chicoutimi Sagueneens	QMJHL	32	4	14	18	....	....	....	152	....	....	....	....	....	....	....	....	....	....	25	3	6	9	94	....	....	....
1994-95	Chicoutimi Sagueneens	QMJHL	20	15	8	23	....	....	....	90	....	....	....	....	....	....	....	....	....	....	....	....	....	....	....	....	....	....
	Drummondville Voltigeurs	QMJHL	34	18	13	31	....	....	....	233	....	....	....	....	....	....	....	....	....	....	4	2	0	2	34	....	....	....
1995-96	**Boston Bruins**	**NHL**	**3**	**0**	**0**	**0**	**0**	**0**	**0**	**0**	**0**	**0**	**0**	**0**	**0.0**	**0**	**0**	**0**	**0**	**0**	....	....	....	....	....	....	....	....
	Providence Bruins	AHL	58	7	8	15	....	....	....	167	....	....	....	....	....	....	....	....	....	....	1	0	0	0	10	....	....	....
1996-97	**Boston Bruins**	**NHL**	**10**	**0**	**2**	**2**	**0**	**2**	**2**	**12**	**0**	**0**	**0**	**12**	**0.0**	**2**	**0**	**7**	**0**	**–5**	....	....	....	....	....	....	....	....
	Providence Bruins	AHL	50	17	11	28	....	....	....	234	....	....	....	....	....	....	....	....	....	....	....	....	....	....	....	....	....	....
1997-98	Providence Bruins	AHL	36	3	11	14	....	....	....	154	....	....	....	....	....	....	....	....	....	....	....	....	....	....	....	....	....	....
	Charlotte Checkers	ECHL	27	10	8	18	....	....	....	132	....	....	....	....	....	....	....	....	....	....	7	2	3	5	34	....	....	....
	NHL Totals		**13**	**0**	**2**	**2**	**0**	**2**	**2**	**12**	**0**	**0**	**0**	**12**	**0.0**	**2**	**0**	**7**	**0**		....	....	....	....	....	....	....	....

• ROY, JEAN-YVES

Jean-Yves Roy RW – L. 5'10", 180 lbs. b: Rosemere, Que., 2/17/1969.

Season	Club	League	GP	G	A	Pts	AG	AA	APts	PIM	PP	SH	GW	S	%	TGF	PGF	TGA	PGA	+/–	GP	G	A	Pts	PIM	PP	SH	GW
1989-90	University of Maine	H.E.	46	*39	26	65	....	....	....	52	....	....	....	....	....	....	....	....	....	....	....	....	....	....	....	....	....	....
1990-91	University of Maine	H.E.	43	37	45	82	....	....	....	62	....	....	....	....	....	....	....	....	....	....	....	....	....	....	....	....	....	....
1991-92	University of Maine	H.E.	35	32	24	56	....	....	....	62	....	....	....	....	....	....	....	....	....	....	....	....	....	....	....	....	....	....
	Canada	Nat-Team	13	10	4	14	....	....	....	6	....	....	....	....	....	....	....	....	....	....	....	....	....	....	....	....	....	....
1992-93	Canada	Nat-Team	23	9	6	15	....	....	....	35	....	....	....	....	....	....	....	....	....	....	....	....	....	....	....	....	....	....
	Binghamton Rangers	AHL	49	13	15	28	....	....	....	21	....	....	....	....	....	....	....	....	....	....	14	5	2	7	4	....	....	....
1993-94	Binghamton Rangers	AHL	65	41	24	65	....	....	....	33	....	....	....	....	....	....	....	....	....	....	....	....	....	....	....	....	....	....
	Canada	Nat-Team	6	3	2	5	....	....	....	2	....	....	....	....	....	....	....	....	....	....	....	....	....	....	....	....	....	....
	Canada	Olympics	8	1	0	1	....	....	....	0	....	....	....	....	....	....	....	....	....	....	....	....	....	....	....	....	....	....
1994-95	Binghamton Rangers	AHL	67	41	36	77	....	....	....	28	....	....	....	....	....	....	....	....	....	....	11	4	6	10	12	....	....	....
	New York Rangers	**NHL**	**3**	**1**	**0**	**1**	**2**	**0**	**2**	**2**	**0**	**0**	**0**	**8**	**12.5**	**1**	**0**	**2**	**0**	**–1**	....	....	....	....	....	....	....	....
1995-96	**Ottawa Senators**	**NHL**	**4**	**1**	**1**	**2**	**1**	**1**	**2**	**2**	**0**	**0**	**0**	**6**	**16.7**	**4**	**0**	**1**	**0**	**+3**	....	....	....	....	....	....	....	....
	P.E.I. Senators	AHL	67	40	55	95	....	....	....	64	....	....	....	....	....	....	....	....	....	....	5	4	8	12	6	....	....	....

			REGULAR SEASON																		PLAYOFFS							
Season	Club	League	GP	G	A	Pts	AG	AA	APts	PIM	PP	SH	GW	S	%	TGF	PGF	TGA	PGA	+/–	GP	G	A	Pts	PIM	PP	SH	GW
1996-97	**Boston Bruins**	**NHL**	**52**	**10**	**15**	**25**	**11**	**13**	**24**	**22**	**2**	**0**	**1**	**100**	**10.0**	**43**	**7**	**48**	**4**	**–8**	....	....	....	....	....	....	....	....
	Providence Bruins	AHL	27	9	16	25	....	....	....	30	....	....	....	....	....	....	....	....	....	....	10	2	7	9	2	....	....	....
1997-98	**Boston Bruins**	**NHL**	**2**	**0**	**0**	**0**	**0**	**0**	**0**	**0**	**0**	**0**	**0**	**1**	**0.0**	**0**	**0**	**0**	**0**	**0**	....	....	....	....	....	....	....	....
	Providence Bruins	AHL	65	28	34	62	....	....	....	60	....	....	....	....	....	....	....	....	....	....	....	....	....	....	....	....	....	....
	NHL Totals		**61**	**12**	**16**	**28**	**14**	**14**	**28**	**26**	**2**	**0**	**1**	**115**	**10.4**	**48**	**7**	**51**	**4**		....	....	....	....	....	....	....	....

NCAA East Second All-American Team (1990) • Hockey East First All-Star Team (1991) • NCAA East First All-American Team (1991, 1992) • NCAA Championship All-Tournament Team (1991) • Hockey East Second All-Star Team (1992)

Signed as a free agent by **NY Rangers**, July 20, 1992. Traded to **Ottawa** by **NY Rangers** for Steve Larouche, October 5, 1995. Signed as a free agent by **Boston**, July 15, 1996.

• ROY, STEPHANE

Stephane Roy C – L. 6', 190 lbs. b: Ste. Foy, Que., 6/29/1967. Minnesota's 4th choice, 51st overall, in 1985 Entry Draft.

Season	Club	League	GP	G	A	Pts	AG	AA	APts	PIM	PP	SH	GW	S	%	TGF	PGF	TGA	PGA	+/–	GP	G	A	Pts	PIM	PP	SH	GW
1983-84	Chicoutimi Sagueneens	QMJHL	67	12	26	38	....	....	....	25	....	....	....	....	....	....	....	....	....	....	....	....	....	....	....	....	....	....
1984-85	Chicoutimi–Granby	QMJHL	68	28	53	81	....	....	....	34	....	....	....	....	....	....	....	....	....	....	....	....	....	....	....	....	....	....
1985-86	Granby Bisons	QMJHL	61	33	52	85	....	....	....	68	....	....	....	....	....	....	....	....	....	....	....	....	....	....	....	....	....	....
	Canada	Nat-Team	10	0	1	1	....	....	....	4	....	....	....	....	....	....	....	....	....	....	....	....	....	....	....	....	....	....
1986-87	Granby Bisons	QMJHL	45	23	44	67	....	....	....	54	....	....	....	....	....	....	....	....	....	....	7	2	3	5	50	....	....	....
	Canada	Nat-Team	9	1	2	3	....	....	....	4	....	....	....	....	....	....	....	....	....	....	....	....	....	....	....	....	....	....
	Canada	WJC-A	6	0	1	1	....	....	....	6	....	....	....	....	....	....	....	....	....	....	....	....	....	....	....	....	....	....
1987-88	**Minnesota North Stars**	**NHL**	**12**	**1**	**0**	**1**	**1**	**0**	**1**	**0**	**0**	**0**	**0**	**14**	**7.1**	**2**	**0**	**9**	**1**	**–6**	....	....	....	....	....	....	....	....
	Kalamazoo Wings	IHL	58	21	12	33	....	....	....	52	....	....	....	....	....	....	....	....	....	....	5	1	2	3	11	....	....	....
1988-89	Halifax Citadels	AHL	42	8	16	24	....	....	....	28	....	....	....	....	....	....	....	....	....	....	1	0	0	0	0	....	....	....
	Kalamazoo Wings	IHL	20	5	4	9	....	....	....	27	....	....	....	....	....	....	....	....	....	....	....	....	....	....	....	....	....	....
1989-90			DID NOT PLAY																									
1990-91	Canada	Nat-Team	52	22	22	44	....	....	....	6	....	....	....	....	....	....	....	....	....	....	....	....	....	....	....	....	....	....
1991-92	EHC Olten	Switz. 2	STATISTICS NOT AVAILABLE																									
1992-93	EHC Olten	Switz. 2	STATISTICS NOT AVAILABLE																									
1993-94	EHC Olten	Switz.	3	1	2	3	....	....	....	2	....	....	....	....	....	....	....	....	....	....	....	....	....	....	....	....	....	....
1994-95	EHC Olten	Switz. 2	STATISTICS NOT AVAILABLE																									
1995-96	Memphis River Kings	CHL	60	18	44	62	....	....	....	33	....	....	....	....	....	....	....	....	....	....	6	1	2	3	8	....	....	....
1996-97	Memphis River Kings	CHL	38	16	28	44	....	....	....	25	....	....	....	....	....	....	....	....	....	....	....	....	....	....	....	....	....	....
	NHL Totals		**12**	**1**	**0**	**1**	**1**	**0**	**1**	**0**	**0**	**0**	**0**	**14**	**7.1**	**2**	**0**	**9**	**1**		....	....	....	....	....	....	....	....

Traded to **Quebec** by **Minnesota** for future considerations, December 15, 1988.

• RUCCHIN, STEVE

Steve Rucchin C – L. 6'3", 215 lbs. b: London, Ont., 7/4/1971. Anaheim's 1st choice, 2nd overall, in 1994 Supplemental Draft.

Season	Club	League	GP	G	A	Pts	AG	AA	APts	PIM	PP	SH	GW	S	%	TGF	PGF	TGA	PGA	+/–	GP	G	A	Pts	PIM	PP	SH	GW
1990-91	University of Western Ontario	OUAA	34	13	16	29	....	....	....	14	....	....	....	....	....	....	....	....	....	....	....	....	....	....	....	....	....	....
1991-92	University of Western Ontario	OUAA	37	28	34	62	....	....	....	36	....	....	....	....	....	....	....	....	....	....	....	....	....	....	....	....	....	....
1992-93	University of Western Ontario	OUAA	34	22	26	48	....	....	....	16	....	....	....	....	....	....	....	....	....	....	....	....	....	....	....	....	....	....
1993-94	University of Western Ontario	OUAA	35	30	23	53	....	....	....	30	....	....	....	....	....	....	....	....	....	....	....	....	....	....	....	....	....	....
1994-95	San Diego Gulls	IHL	41	11	15	26	....	....	....	14	....	....	....	....	....	....	....	....	....	....	....	....	....	....	....	....	....	....
	Anaheim Mighty Ducks	**NHL**	**43**	**6**	**11**	**17**	**11**	**16**	**27**	**23**	**0**	**0**	**1**	**59**	**10.2**	**24**	**0**	**27**	**10**	**+7**	....	....	....	....	....	....	....	....
1995-96	**Anaheim Mighty Ducks**	**NHL**	**64**	**19**	**25**	**44**	**19**	**20**	**39**	**12**	**8**	**1**	**4**	**113**	**16.8**	**65**	**30**	**53**	**21**	**+3**	....	....	....	....	....	....	....	....
1996-97	**Anaheim Mighty Ducks**	**NHL**	**79**	**19**	**48**	**67**	**20**	**43**	**63**	**24**	**6**	**1**	**2**	**153**	**12.4**	**105**	**32**	**63**	**16**	**+26**	**8**	**1**	**2**	**3**	**10**	**0**	**0**	**0**
1997-98	**Anaheim Mighty Ducks**	**NHL**	**72**	**17**	**36**	**53**	**20**	**35**	**55**	**13**	**8**	**1**	**3**	**131**	**13.0**	**82**	**24**	**72**	**22**	**+8**	....	....	....	....	....	....	....	....
	Canada	WC-A	6	1	2	3	....	....	....	2	....	....	....	....	....	....	....	....	....	....	....	....	....	....	....	....	....	....
	NHL Totals		**258**	**61**	**120**	**181**	**70**	**114**	**184**	**72**	**22**	**3**	**10**	**456**	**13.4**	**276**	**86**	**215**	**69**		**8**	**1**	**2**	**3**	**10**	**0**	**0**	**0**

• RUCINSKI, MIKE

Mike Rucinski C – L. 5'11", 190 lbs. b: Wheeling, IL, 12/12/1963.

Season	Club	League	GP	G	A	Pts	AG	AA	APts	PIM	PP	SH	GW	S	%	TGF	PGF	TGA	PGA	+/–	GP	G	A	Pts	PIM	PP	SH	GW
1983-84	University of Illinois-Chicago	CCHA	33	17	26	43	....	....	....	12	....	....	....	....	....	....	....	....	....	....	....	....	....	....	....	....	....	....
1984-85	University of Illinois-Chicago	CCHA	40	29	32	61	....	....	....	28	....	....	....	....	....	....	....	....	....	....	....	....	....	....	....	....	....	....
1985-86	University of Illinois-Chicago	CCHA	37	16	31	47	....	....	....	18	....	....	....	....	....	....	....	....	....	....	....	....	....	....	....	....	....	....
1986-87	Moncton Golden Flames	AHL	42	5	9	14	....	....	....	14	....	....	....	....	....	....	....	....	....	....	....	....	....	....	....	....	....	....
	Salt Lake Golden Eagles	IHL	20	16	25	41	....	....	....	19	....	....	....	....	....	....	....	....	....	....	17	9	*18	*27	28	....	....	....
1987-88	Saginaw Hawks	IHL	44	19	31	50	....	....	....	32	....	....	....	....	....	....	....	....	....	....	10	1	9	10	10	....	....	....
	Chicago Blackhawks	**NHL**	....	....	....	....	....	....	....	....	....	....	....	....	....	....	....	....	....	....	**2**	**0**	**0**	**0**	**0**	....	....	....
1988-89	**Chicago Blackhawks**	**NHL**	**1**	**0**	**0**	**0**	**0**	**0**	**0**	**0**	**0**	**0**	**0**	**0**	**0.0**	**0**	**0**	**0**	**0**	**0**	....	....	....	....	....	....	....	....
	Saginaw Hawks	IHL	81	35	72	107	....	....	....	40	....	....	....	....	....	....	....	....	....	....	6	2	4	6	14	....	....	....
1989-90	Indianapolis Ice	IHL	80	28	41	69	....	....	....	27	....	....	....	....	....	....	....	....	....	....	13	3	8	11	8	....	....	....
	NHL Totals		**1**	**0**	**0**	**0**	**0**	**0**	**0**	**0**	**0**	**0**	**0**	**0**	**0.0**	**0**	**0**	**0**	**0**		**2**	**0**	**0**	**0**	**0**	**0**	**0**	**0**

Signed as a free agent by **Calgary**, August 10, 1986. Signed as a free agent by **Chicago**, July 8, 1987.

• RUCINSKI, MIKE

Mike Rucinski D – L. 5'11", 179 lbs. b: Trenton, MI, 3/30/1975. Hartford's 8th choice, 217th overall, in 1995 Entry Draft.

Season	Club	League	GP	G	A	Pts	AG	AA	APts	PIM	PP	SH	GW	S	%	TGF	PGF	TGA	PGA	+/–	GP	G	A	Pts	PIM	PP	SH	GW
1992-93	Detroit Jr. Red Wings	OHL	66	6	13	19	....	....	....	59	....	....	....	....	....	....	....	....	....	....	15	0	4	4	12	....	....	....
1993-94	Detroit Jr. Red Wings	OHL	66	2	26	28	....	....	....	58	....	....	....	....	....	....	....	....	....	....	17	0	7	7	15	....	....	....
1994-95	Detroit Jr. Red Wings	OHL	64	9	18	27	....	....	....	61	....	....	....	....	....	....	....	....	....	....	21	3	3	6	8	....	....	....
1995-96	Detroit Jr. Whalers	OHL	51	10	26	36	....	....	....	65	....	....	....	....	....	....	....	....	....	....	11	2	4	6	14	....	....	....
1996-97	Richmond Renegades	ECHL	61	20	23	43	....	....	....	85	....	....	....	....	....	....	....	....	....	....	8	2	6	8	18	....	....	....
	Springfield Falcons	AHL	6	0	1	1	....	....	....	0	....	....	....	....	....	....	....	....	....	....	....	....	....	....	....	....	....	....
1997-98	**Carolina Hurricanes**	**NHL**	**9**	**0**	**1**	**1**	**0**	**1**	**1**	**2**	**0**	**0**	**0**	**3**	**0.0**	**3**	**0**	**3**	**0**	**0**	....	....	....	....	....	....	....	....
	Beast of New Haven	AHL	65	5	17	22	....	....	....	50	....	....	....	....	....	....	....	....	....	....	1	0	0	0	0	....	....	....
	Cleveland Lumberjacks	IHL	2	0	0	0	....	....	....	4	....	....	....	....	....	....	....	....	....	....	....	....	....	....	....	....	....	....
	NHL Totals		**9**	**0**	**1**	**1**	**0**	**1**	**1**	**2**	**0**	**0**	**0**	**3**	**0.0**	**3**	**0**	**3**	**0**		....	....	....	....	....	....	....	....

• RUCINSKY, MARTIN

Martin Rucinsky LW – L. 6', 198 lbs. b: Most, Czech., 3/11/1971. Edmonton's 2nd choice, 20th overall, in 1991 Entry Draft.

Season	Club	League	GP	G	A	Pts	AG	AA	APts	PIM	PP	SH	GW	S	%	TGF	PGF	TGA	PGA	+/–	GP	G	A	Pts	PIM	PP	SH	GW
1988-89	CHZ Litvinov	Czech.	3	1	0	1	....	....	....	2	....	....	....	....	....	....	....	....	....	....	....	....	....	....	....	....	....	....
1989-90	CHZ Litvinov	Czech.	47	17	9	26	....	....	....	....	....	....	....	....	....	....	....	....	....	....	....	....	....	....	....	....	....	....
1990-91	CHZ Litvinov	Czech.	56	24	20	44	....	....	....	69	....	....	....	....	....	....	....	....	....	....	....	....	....	....	....	....	....	....
	Czechoslovakia	WJC-A	7	9	5	14	....	....	....	2	....	....	....	....	....	....	....	....	....	....	....	....	....	....	....	....	....	....
1991-92	Czechoslovakia	C Cup	4	0	2	2	....	....	....	4	....	....	....	....	....	....	....	....	....	....	....	....	....	....	....	....	....	....
	Edmonton Oilers	**NHL**	**2**	**0**	**0**	**0**	**0**	**0**	**0**	**0**	**0**	**0**	**0**	**1**	**0.0**	**0**	**0**	**3**	**0**	**3**	....	....	....	....	....	....	....	....
	Cape Breton Oilers	AHL	35	11	12	23	....	....	....	34	....	....	....	....	....	....	....	....	....	....	....	....	....	....	....	....	....	....
	Quebec Nordiques	**NHL**	**4**	**1**	**1**	**2**	**1**	**1**	**2**	**2**	**0**	**0**	**0**	**4**	**25.0**	**3**	**0**	**2**	**0**	**+1**	....	....	....	....	....	....	....	....
	Halifax Citadels	AHL	7	1	1	2	....	....	....	6	....	....	....	....	....	....	....	....	....	....	....	....	....	....	....	....	....	....
1992-93	**Quebec Nordiques**	**NHL**	**77**	**18**	**30**	**48**	**15**	**21**	**36**	**51**	**4**	**0**	**1**	**133**	**13.5**	**74**	**21**	**41**	**4**	**+16**	**6**	**1**	**1**	**2**	**4**	**1**	**0**	**0**
1993-94	**Quebec Nordiques**	**NHL**	**60**	**9**	**23**	**32**	**8**	**18**	**26**	**58**	**4**	**0**	**1**	**96**	**9.4**	**49**	**17**	**30**	**2**	**+4**	....	....	....	....	....	....	....	....
	Czech Republic	WC-A	6	2	2	4	....	....	....	8	....	....	....	....	....	....	....	....	....	....	....	....	....	....	....	....	....	....
1994-95	CHZ Litvinov	Czech.	13	12	10	22	....	....	....	54	....	....	....	....	....	....	....	....	....	....	....	....	....	....	....	....	....	....
	Quebec Nordiques	**NHL**	**20**	**3**	**6**	**9**	**5**	**9**	**14**	**14**	**0**	**0**	**0**	**32**	**9.4**	**12**	**0**	**9**	**2**	**+5**	....	....	....	....	....	....	....	....
1995-96	Zbrojovka Vsetin	Czech.	1	1	1	2	....	....	....	0	....	....	....	....	....	....	....	....	....	....	....	....	....	....	....	....	....	....
	Colorado Avalanche	**NHL**	**22**	**4**	**11**	**15**	**4**	**9**	**13**	**14**	**0**	**0**	**1**	**39**	**10.3**	**21**	**3**	**10**	**2**	**+10**	....	....	....	....	....	....	....	....
	Montreal Canadiens	**NHL**	**56**	**25**	**35**	**60**	**25**	**29**	**54**	**54**	**9**	**2**	**3**	**142**	**17.6**	**81**	**28**	**64**	**19**	**+8**	....	....	....	....	....	....	....	....
1996-97	Czech Republic	W Cup	3	0	0	0	....	....	....	2	....	....	....	....	....	....	....	....	....	....	....	....	....	....	....	....	....	....
	Montreal Canadiens	**NHL**	**70**	**28**	**27**	**55**	**30**	**24**	**54**	**62**	**6**	**3**	**3**	**172**	**16.3**	**74**	**22**	**69**	**10**	**+1**	**5**	**0**	**0**	**0**	**4**	**0**	**0**	**0**
1997-98	**Montreal Canadiens**	**NHL**	**78**	**21**	**32**	**53**	**25**	**31**	**56**	**84**	**5**	**3**	**3**	**192**	**10.9**	**76**	**22**	**50**	**9**	**+13**	**10**	**3**	**0**	**3**	**4**	**1**	**0**	**0**
	Czech Republic	Olympics	6	3	1	4	....	....	....	4	....	....	....	....	....	....	....	....	....	....	....	....	....	....	....	....	....	....
	NHL Totals		**389**	**109**	**165**	**274**	**113**	**142**	**255**	**339**	**28**	**8**	**12**	**811**	**13.4**	**390**	**113**	**278**	**56**		**21**	**4**	**1**	**5**	**12**	**2**	**0**	**0**

WJC-A All-Star Team (1991)

Traded to **Quebec** by **Edmonton** for Ron Tugnutt and Brad Zavisha, March 10, 1992. Transferred to **Colorado** after **Quebec** franchise relocated, June 21, 1995. Traded to **Montreal** by **Colorado** with Andrei Kovalenko and Jocelyn Thibault for Patrick Roy and Mike Keane, December 6, 1995.

			REGULAR SEASON																		PLAYOFFS							
Season	Club	League	GP	G	A	Pts	AG	AA	APts	PIM	PP	SH	GW	S	%	TGF	PGF	TGA	PGA	+/–	GP	G	A	Pts	PIM	PP	SH	GW

● **RUFF, JASON** Jason Ruff LW – L. 6'2", 192 lbs. b: Kelowna, B.C., 1/27/1970. St Louis' 2nd choice, 96th overall, in 1990 Entry Draft.

Season	Club	League	GP	G	A	Pts	AG	AA	APts	PIM	PP	SH	GW	S	%	TGF	PGF	TGA	PGA	+/–	GP	G	A	Pts	PIM	PP	SH	GW
1987-88	Lethbridge Hurricanes	WHL	69	25	22	47	....	....	....	109	....	....	....	....	....	....	....	....	....	....	....	....	....	....	....	....	....	....
1988-89	Lethbridge Hurricanes	WHL	69	42	38	80	....	....	....	127	....	....	....	....	....	....	....	....	....	....	....	....	....	....	....	....	....	....
1989-90	Lethbridge Hurricanes	WHL	72	55	64	119	....	....	....	114	....	....	....	....	....	....	....	....	....	....	19	9	10	19	18	....	....	....
1990-91	Lethbridge Hurricanes	WHL	66	61	75	136	....	....	....	154	....	....	....	....	....	....	....	....	....	....	16	12	17	29	18	....	....	....
	Peoria Rivermen	IHL	....	....	....	....	....	....	....	....	....	....	....	....	....	....	....	....	....	....	5	0	0	0	2	....	....	....
1991-92	Peoria Rivermen	IHL	67	27	45	72	....	....	....	148	....	....	....	....	....	....	....	....	....	....	10	7	7	14	19	....	....	....
1992-93	**St. Louis Blues**	**NHL**	**7**	**2**	**1**	**3**	**2**	**1**	**3**	**8**	**1**	**0**	**1**	**7**	**28.6**	**6**	**3**	**4**	**0**	**–1**	....	....	....	....	....	....	....	....
	Peoria Rivermen	IHL	40	22	21	43	....	....	....	81	....	....	....	....	....	....	....	....	....	....	....	....	....	....	....	....	....	....
	Tampa Bay Lightning	**NHL**	**1**	**0**	**0**	**0**	**0**	**0**	**0**	**0**	**0**	**0**	**0**	**1**	**0.0**	**0**	**0**	**0**	**0**	**0**	....	....	....	....	....	....	....	....
	Atlanta Knights	IHL	26	11	14	25	....	....	....	90	....	....	....	....	....	....	....	....	....	....	7	2	1	3	26	....	....	....
1993-94	**Tampa Bay Lightning**	**NHL**	**6**	**1**	**2**	**3**	**1**	**2**	**3**	**2**	**0**	**0**	**0**	**14**	**7.1**	**4**	**0**	**2**	**0**	**+2**	....	....	....	....	....	....	....	....
	Atlanta Knights	IHL	71	24	25	49	....	....	....	122	....	....	....	....	....	....	....	....	....	....	14	6	*17	23	41	....	....	....
1994-95	Atlanta Knights	IHL	64	42	34	76	....	....	....	161	....	....	....	....	....	....	....	....	....	....	3	3	1	4	10	....	....	....
1995-96	Atlanta Knights	IHL	59	39	33	72	....	....	....	135	....	....	....	....	....	....	....	....	....	....	2	0	0	0	16	....	....	....
1996-97	Quebec Rafales	IHL	80	35	50	85	....	....	....	93	....	....	....	....	....	....	....	....	....	....	9	8	5	13	10	....	....	....
1997-98	Quebec Rafales	IHL	54	21	24	45	....	....	....	77	....	....	....	....	....	....	....	....	....	....	....	....	....	....	....	....	....	....
	Cleveland Lumberjacks	IHL	6	2	3	5	....	....	....	9	....	....	....	....	....	....	....	....	....	....	10	6	6	12	4	....	....	....
	NHL Totals		**14**	**3**	**3**	**6**	**3**	**3**	**6**	**10**	**1**	**0**	**1**	**22**	**13.6**	**10**	**3**	**6**	**0**		....	....	....	....	....	....	....	....

WHL East First All-Star Team (1991)

Traded to **Tampa Bay** by **St. Louis** with future considerations for Doug Crossman, Basil McRae and Tampa Bay's 4th round choice (Andrei Petrakov) in 1996 Entry Draft, January 28, 1993.

● **RUFF, LINDY** Lindy Ruff D/LW – L. 6'2", 201 lbs. b: Warburg, Alta., 2/17/1960. Buffalo's 2nd choice, 32nd overall, in 1979 Entry Draft.

Season	Club	League	GP	G	A	Pts	AG	AA	APts	PIM	PP	SH	GW	S	%	TGF	PGF	TGA	PGA	+/–	GP	G	A	Pts	PIM	PP	SH	GW
1976-77	Taber Golden Suns	AJHL	60	13	33	46	....	....	....	112	....	....	....	....	....	....	....	....	....	....	....	....	....	....	....	....	....	....
	Lethbridge Broncos	WCJHL	2	0	2	2	....	....	....	0	....	....	....	....	....	....	....	....	....	....	....	....	....	....	....	....	....	....
1977-78	Lethbridge Broncos	WCJHL	66	9	24	33	....	....	....	219	....	....	....	....	....	....	....	....	....	....	8	2	8	10	4	....	....	....
1978-79	Lethbridge Broncos	WHL	24	9	18	27	....	....	....	108	....	....	....	....	....	....	....	....	....	....	6	0	1	1	0	....	....	....
1979-80	**Buffalo Sabres**	**NHL**	**63**	**5**	**14**	**19**	**5**	**11**	**16**	**38**	**1**	**0**	**0**	**77**	**6.5**	**56**	**18**	**40**	**0**	**–2**	**8**	**1**	**1**	**2**	**19**	**0**	**0**	**0**
1980-81	**Buffalo Sabres**	**NHL**	**65**	**8**	**18**	**26**	**7**	**13**	**20**	**121**	**1**	**0**	**2**	**97**	**8.2**	**70**	**14**	**54**	**1**	**+3**	**6**	**3**	**1**	**4**	**23**	**1**	**0**	**1**
1981-82	**Buffalo Sabres**	**NHL**	**79**	**16**	**32**	**48**	**13**	**21**	**34**	**194**	**3**	**0**	**6**	**183**	**8.7**	**101**	**25**	**87**	**12**	**+1**	**4**	**0**	**0**	**0**	**28**	**0**	**0**	**0**
1982-83	**Buffalo Sabres**	**NHL**	**60**	**12**	**17**	**29**	**10**	**12**	**22**	**130**	**2**	**0**	**1**	**110**	**10.9**	**60**	**9**	**43**	**7**	**+15**	**10**	**4**	**2**	**6**	**47**	**0**	**0**	**0**
1983-84	**Buffalo Sabres**	**NHL**	**58**	**14**	**31**	**45**	**11**	**21**	**32**	**101**	**3**	**0**	**4**	**126**	**11.1**	**72**	**14**	**50**	**7**	**+15**	**3**	**1**	**0**	**1**	**9**	**0**	**0**	**0**
1984-85	**Buffalo Sabres**	**NHL**	**39**	**13**	**11**	**24**	**11**	**7**	**18**	**45**	**2**	**0**	**2**	**71**	**18.3**	**36**	**6**	**33**	**2**	**–1**	**5**	**2**	**4**	**6**	**15**	**1**	**0**	**0**
1985-86	**Buffalo Sabres**	**NHL**	**54**	**20**	**12**	**32**	**16**	**8**	**24**	**158**	**5**	**1**	**4**	**131**	**15.3**	**58**	**13**	**44**	**7**	**+8**	....	....	....	....	....	....	....	....
1986-87	**Buffalo Sabres**	**NHL**	**50**	**6**	**14**	**20**	**5**	**10**	**15**	**74**	**0**	**1**	**1**	**95**	**6.3**	**43**	**7**	**67**	**19**	**–12**	....	....	....	....	....	....	....	....
1987-88	**Buffalo Sabres**	**NHL**	**77**	**2**	**23**	**25**	**2**	**16**	**18**	**179**	**0**	**0**	**0**	**106**	**1.9**	**47**	**5**	**86**	**35**	**–9**	**6**	**0**	**2**	**2**	**23**	**0**	**0**	**0**
1988-89	**Buffalo Sabres**	**NHL**	**63**	**6**	**11**	**17**	**5**	**8**	**13**	**86**	**0**	**0**	**0**	**69**	**8.7**	**41**	**3**	**78**	**23**	**–17**	....	....	....	....	....	....	....	....
	New York Rangers	**NHL**	**13**	**0**	**5**	**5**	**0**	**4**	**4**	**31**	**0**	**0**	**0**	**19**	**0.0**	**13**	**4**	**19**	**4**	**–6**	**2**	**0**	**0**	**0**	**17**	**0**	**0**	**0**
1989-90	**New York Rangers**	**NHL**	**56**	**3**	**6**	**9**	**3**	**4**	**7**	**80**	**0**	**0**	**2**	**59**	**5.1**	**24**	**3**	**38**	**7**	**–10**	**8**	**0**	**3**	**3**	**12**	**0**	**0**	**0**
1990-91	**New York Rangers**	**NHL**	**14**	**0**	**1**	**1**	**0**	**1**	**1**	**27**	**0**	**0**	**0**	**10**	**0.0**	**2**	**0**	**4**	**0**	**–2**	....	....	....	....	....	....	....	....
1991-92	Rochester Americans	AHL	62	10	24	34	....	....	....	110	....	....	....	....	....	....	....	....	....	....	13	0	4	4	18	....	....	....
1992-93	San Diego Gulls	IHL	81	10	32	42	....	....	....	100	....	....	....	....	....	....	....	....	....	....	14	1	6	7	26	....	....	....
	NHL Totals		**691**	**105**	**195**	**300**	**88**	**136**	**224**	**1264**	**17**	**2**	**22**	**1153**	**9.1**	**623**	**121**	**643**	**124**		**52**	**11**	**13**	**24**	**193**	**2**	**0**	**1**

Traded to **NY Rangers** by **Buffalo** for NY Rangers' 5th round choice (Richard Smehlik) in 1990 Entry Draft, March 7, 1989.

● **RUHNKE, KENT** Kent Ruhnke RW – R. 6'1", 190 lbs. b: Toronto, Ont., 9/18/1952.

Season	Club	League	GP	G	A	Pts	AG	AA	APts	PIM	PP	SH	GW	S	%	TGF	PGF	TGA	PGA	+/–	GP	G	A	Pts	PIM	PP	SH	GW
1971-72	University of Toronto	OUAA	....	9	6	15	....	....	....	10	....	....	....	....	....	....	....	....	....	....	....	....	....	....	....	....	....	....
1972-73	University of Toronto	OUAA	....	22	13	35	....	....	....	6	....	....	....	....	....	....	....	....	....	....	....	....	....	....	....	....	....	....
1973-74	University of Toronto	OUAA	....	27	13	40	....	....	....	8	....	....	....	....	....	....	....	....	....	....	....	....	....	....	....	....	....	....
	Barrie Flyers	OHA Sr.	1	1	0	1	....	....	....	0	....	....	....	....	....	....	....	....	....	....	....	....	....	....	....	....	....	....
1974-75	University of Toronto	OUAA	....	10	5	15	....	....	....	10	....	....	....	....	....	....	....	....	....	....	....	....	....	....	....	....	....	....
1975-76	University of Toronto	OUAA	....	29	15	44	....	....	....	6	....	....	....	....	....	....	....	....	....	....	....	....	....	....	....	....	....	....
	Boston Bruins	**NHL**	**2**	**0**	**1**	**1**	**0**	**1**	**1**	**0**	**0**	**0**	**0**	**2**	**0.0**	**1**	**0**	**0**	**0**	**+1**	....	....	....	....	....	....	....	....
1976-77	Winnipeg Jets	WHA	51	11	11	22	....	....	....	2	....	....	....	....	....	....	....	....	....	....	....	....	....	....	....	....	....	....
1977-78	Winnipeg Jets	WHA	21	8	9	17	....	....	....	2	....	....	....	....	....	....	....	....	....	....	5	2	0	2	0	....	....	....
	Binghamto Dusters	AHL	47	14	20	34	....	....	....	2	....	....	....	....	....	....	....	....	....	....	....	....	....	....	....	....	....	....
1978-79	Riessersee	Germany	49	42	37	79	....	....	....	4	....	....	....	....	....	....	....	....	....	....	....	....	....	....	....	....	....	....
	NHL Totals		**2**	**0**	**1**	**1**	**0**	**1**	**1**	**0**	**0**	**0**	**0**	**2**	**0.0**	**1**	**0**	**0**	**0**		....	....	....	....	....	....	....	....
	Other Major League Totals		72	19	20	39	....	....	....	4	....	....	....	....	....	....	....	....	....	....	5	2	0	2	0	....	....	....

Signed to a pro try-out contract by **Boston**, March, 1976. Signed as a free agent by **Winnipeg** (WHA), July, 1976.

● **RUMBLE, DARREN** Darren Rumble D – L. 6'1", 200 lbs. b: Barrie, Ont., 1/23/1969. Philadelphia's 1st choice, 20th overall, in 1987 Entry Draft.

Season	Club	League	GP	G	A	Pts	AG	AA	APts	PIM	PP	SH	GW	S	%	TGF	PGF	TGA	PGA	+/–	GP	G	A	Pts	PIM	PP	SH	GW
1986-87	Kitchener Rangers	OHL	64	11	32	43	....	....	....	44	....	....	....	....	....	....	....	....	....	....	4	0	1	1	9	....	....	....
1987-88	Kitchener Rangers	OHL	55	15	50	65	....	....	....	64	....	....	....	....	....	....	....	....	....	....	....	....	....	....	....	....	....	....
1988-89	Kitchener Rangers	OHL	46	11	28	39	....	....	....	25	....	....	....	....	....	....	....	....	....	....	5	1	0	1	2	....	....	....
1989-90	Hershey Bears	AHL	57	2	13	15	....	....	....	31	....	....	....	....	....	....	....	....	....	....	....	....	....	....	....	....	....	....
1990-91	**Philadelphia Flyers**	**NHL**	**3**	**1**	**0**	**1**	**1**	**0**	**1**	**0**	**0**	**0**	**0**	**2**	**50.0**	**2**	**0**	**1**	**0**	**+1**	....	....	....	....	....	....	....	....
	Hershey Bears	AHL	73	6	35	41	....	....	....	48	....	....	....	....	....	....	....	....	....	....	3	0	5	5	2	....	....	....
1991-92	Hershey Bears	AHL	79	12	54	66	....	....	....	118	....	....	....	....	....	....	....	....	....	....	6	0	3	3	2	....	....	....
1992-93	**Ottawa Senators**	**NHL**	**69**	**3**	**13**	**16**	**2**	**9**	**11**	**61**	**0**	**0**	**0**	**92**	**3.3**	**38**	**4**	**75**	**17**	**–24**	....	....	....	....	....	....	....	....
	New Haven Nighthawks	AHL	2	1	0	1	....	....	....	0	....	....	....	....	....	....	....	....	....	....	....	....	....	....	....	....	....	....
1993-94	**Ottawa Senators**	**NHL**	**70**	**6**	**9**	**15**	**6**	**7**	**13**	**116**	**0**	**0**	**0**	**95**	**6.3**	**40**	**3**	**125**	**38**	**–50**	....	....	....	....	....	....	....	....
	P.E.I. Senators	AHL	3	2	0	2	....	....	....	0	....	....	....	....	....	....	....	....	....	....	....	....	....	....	....	....	....	....
1994-95	P.E.I. Senators	AHL	70	7	46	53	....	....	....	77	....	....	....	....	....	....	....	....	....	....	11	0	6	6	4	....	....	....
1995-96	**Philadelphia Flyers**	**NHL**	**5**	**0**	**0**	**0**	**0**	**0**	**0**	**4**	**0**	**0**	**0**	**7**	**0.0**	**3**	**0**	**3**	**0**	**0**	....	....	....	....	....	....	....	....
	Hershey Bears	AHL	58	13	37	50	....	....	....	83	....	....	....	....	....	....	....	....	....	....	5	0	0	0	6	....	....	....
1996-97	**Philadelphia Flyers**	**NHL**	**10**	**0**	**0**	**0**	**0**	**0**	**0**	**0**	**0**	**0**	**0**	**9**	**0.0**	**6**	**1**	**7**	**0**	**–2**	....	....	....	....	....	....	....	....
	Philadelphia Phantoms	AHL	72	18	44	62	....	....	....	83	....	....	....	....	....	....	....	....	....	....	7	0	3	3	19	....	....	....
1997-98	Adler Mannheim	EuroHL	4	0	1	1	....	....	....	4	....	....	....	....	....	....	....	....	....	....	....	....	....	....	....	....	....	....
	Adler Mannheim	Germany	21	2	7	9	....	....	....	18	....	....	....	....	....	....	....	....	....	....	....	....	....	....	....	....	....	....
	San Antonio Dragons	IHL	46	7	22	29	....	....	....	47	....	....	....	....	....	....	....	....	....	....	....	....	....	....	....	....	....	....
	NHL Totals		**157**	**10**	**22**	**32**	**9**	**16**	**25**	**181**	**0**	**0**	**0**	**205**	**4.9**	**89**	**8**	**211**	**55**		....	....	....	....	....	....	....	....

AHL Second All-Star Team (1995) • AHL First All-Star Team (1997) • Won Eddie Shore Plaque (Outstanding Defenseman - AHL) (1997)

Claimed by **Ottawa** from **Philadelphia** in Expansion Draft, June 18, 1992. Signed as a free agent by **Philadelphia**, July 31, 1995.

● **RUNDQVIST, THOMAS** Thomas Rundqvist C – L. 6'3", 195 lbs. b: Vimmerby, Sweden, 5/4/1960. Montreal's 12th choice, 206th overall, in 1983 Entry Draft.

Season	Club	League	GP	G	A	Pts	AG	AA	APts	PIM	PP	SH	GW	S	%	TGF	PGF	TGA	PGA	+/–	GP	G	A	Pts	PIM	PP	SH	GW
1978-79	Farjestad BK Karlstad	Sweden	15	2	5	7	....	....	....	8	....	....	....	....	....	....	....	....	....	....	....	0	1	1	2	....	....	....
1979-80	Farjestad BK Karlstad	Sweden	36	9	6	15	....	....	....	28	....	....	....	....	....	....	....	....	....	....	....	....	....	....	....	....	....	....
	Sweden	WJC-A	5	1	2	3	....	....	....	6	....	....	....	....	....	....	....	....	....	....	....	....	....	....	....	....	....	....
1980-81	Farjestad BK Karlstad	Sweden	36	15	19	34	....	....	....	22	....	....	....	....	....	....	....	....	....	....	7	1	2	3	0	....	....	....
1981-82	Farjestad BK Karlstad	Sweden	36	14	13	27	....	....	....	30	....	....	....	....	....	....	....	....	....	....	2	0	1	1	2	....	....	....
	Sweden	WEC-A	9	1	2	3	....	....	....	2	....	....	....	....	....	....	....	....	....	....	....	....	....	....	....	....	....	....
1982-83	Farjestad BK Karlstad	Sweden	36	22	21	43	....	....	....	28	....	....	....	....	....	....	....	....	....	....	8	3	*8	11	6	....	....	....
	Sweden	WEC-A	10	1	3	4	....	....	....	2	....	....	....	....	....	....	....	....	....	....	....	....	....	....	....	....	....	....
1983-84	Farjestad BK Karlstad	Sweden	36	13	22	35	....	....	....	38	....	....	....	....	....	....	....	....	....	....	....	....	....	....	....	....	....	....
1984-85	**Montreal Canadiens**	**NHL**	**2**	**0**	**1**	**1**	**0**	**1**	**1**	**0**	**0**	**0**	**0**	**1**	**0.0**	**1**	**0**	**0**	**0**	**+1**	....	....	....	....	....	....	....	....
	Sherbrooke Canadiens	AHL	73	19	39	58	....	....	....	16	....	....	....	....	....	....	....	....	....	....	17	*5	14	19	4	....	....	....
1985-86	Farjestad BK Karlstad	Sweden	32	9	17	26	....	....	....	27	....	....	....	....	....	....	....	....	....	....	8	2	4	6	2	....	....	....
	Sweden	WEC-A	10	2	3	5	....	....	....	8	....	....	....	....	....	....	....	....	....	....	....	....	....	....	....	....	....	....

			REGULAR SEASON																		PLAYOFFS							
Season	**Club**	**League**	**GP**	**G**	**A**	**Pts**	**AG**	**AA**	**APts**	**PIM**	**PP**	**SH**	**GW**	**S**	**%**	**TGF**	**PGF**	**TGA**	**PGA**	**+/–**	**GP**	**G**	**A**	**Pts**	**PIM**	**PP**	**SH**	**GW**
1986-87	Farjestad BK Karlstad	Sweden	35	13	22	35	....	....	....	38	....	....	....	....	....	....	....	....	....	....	7	2	5	7	2	....	....	....
	Sweden	WEC-A	10	1	2	3	....	....	....	4	....	....	....	....	....	....	....	....	....	....	....	....	....	....	....	....	....	....
1987-88	Sweden	C Cup	6	0	2	2	....	....	....	10	....	....	....	....	....	....	....	....	....	....	....	....	....	....	....	....	....	....
	Farjestad BK Karlstad	Sweden	40	15	22	37	....	....	....	40	....	....	....	....	....	....	....	....	....	....	9	3	7	10	6	....	....	....
	Sweden	Olympics	8	0	3	3	....	....	....	0	....	....	....	....	....	....	....	....	....	....	....	....	....	....	....	....	....	....
1988-89	Farjestad BK Karlstad	Sweden	37	15	26	41	....	....	....	44	....	....	....	....	....	....	....	....	....	....	2	2	1	3	2	....	....	....
	Sweden	WEC-A	9	1	2	3	....	....	....	6	....	....	....	....	....	....	....	....	....	....	....	....	....	....	....	....	....	....
1989-90	Farjestad BK Karlstad	Sweden	40	16	29	45	....	....	....	30	....	....	....	....	....	....	....	....	....	....	10	8	4	12	0	....	....	....
	Sweden	WEC-A	10	3	8	11	....	....	....	6	....	....	....	....	....	....	....	....	....	....	....	....	....	....	....	....	....	....
1990-91	Farjestad BK Karlstad	Sweden	39	12	21	33	....	....	....	22	....	....	....	....	....	....	....	....	....	....	8	5	*7	*12	6	....	....	....
	Sweden	WEC-A	10	6	4	10	....	....	....	4	....	....	....	....	....	....	....	....	....	....	....	....	....	....	....	....	....	....
1991-92	Sweden	C Cup	6	2	2	4	....	....	....	2	....	....	....	....	....	....	....	....	....	....	....	....	....	....	....	....	....	....
	Farjestad BK Karlstad	Sweden	39	10	28	38	....	....	....	54	....	....	....	....	....	....	....	....	....	....	6	3	2	5	8	....	....	....
	Sweden	Olympics	8	3	4	7	....	....	....	8	....	....	....	....	....	....	....	....	....	....	....	....	....	....	....	....	....	....
1992-93	Farjestad BK Karlstad	Sweden	37	8	17	25	....	....	....	40	....	....	....	....	....	....	....	....	....	....	3	0	0	0	2	....	....	....
	Sweden	WC-A	8	1	4	5	....	....	....	0	....	....	....	....	....	....	....	....	....	....	....	....	....	....	....	....	....	....
1993-94	VEU Feldkirch	Austria	53	20	37	57	....	....	....	18	....	....	....	....	....	....	....	....	....	....	....	....	....	....	....	....	....	....
1994-95	VEU Feldkirch	Austria	28	9	15	24	....	....	....	32	....	....	....	....	....	....	....	....	....	....	8	2	3	5	6	....	....	....
1995-96	VEU Feldkirch	Austria	39	15	39	54	....	....	....	35	....	....	....	....	....	....	....	....	....	....	....	....	....	....	....	....	....	....
1996-97	VEU Feldkirch	Austria	52	11	34	45	....	....	....	61	....	....	....	....	....	....	....	....	....	....	....	....	....	....	....	....	....	....
	VEU Feldkirch	EuroHL	10	6	7	13	....	....	....	4	....	....	....	....	....	....	....	....	....	....	....	....	....	....	....	....	....	....
	NHL Totals		**2**	**0**	**1**	**1**	**0**	**1**	**1**	**0**	**0**	**0**	**0**	**1**	**0.0**	**1**	**0**	**0**	**0**		....	....	....	....	....	....	....	....

Swedish World All-Star Team (1988, 1989, 1990, 1991) • Swedish Player of the Year (1991) • WEC-A All-Star Team (1991)

• RUOTSALAINEN, REIJO

Reijo "Rex" Ruotsalainen D – R. 5'8", 170 lbs. b: Oulu, Finland, 4/1/1960. NY Rangers' 5th choice, 119th overall, in 1980 Entry Draft.

Season	Club	League	GP	G	A	Pts	AG	AA	APts	PIM	PP	SH	GW	S	%	TGF	PGF	TGA	PGA	+/–	GP	G	A	Pts	PIM	PP	SH	GW
1976-77	Finland	WJC-A	7	2	4	6	....	....	....	6	....	....	....	....	....	....	....	....	....	....	....	....	....	....	....	....	....	....
1977-78	Karpat Oulu	Finland	30	9	14	23	....	....	....	4	....	....	....	....	....	....	....	....	....	....	....	....	....	....	....	....	....	....
	Finland	WJC-A	6	3	3	6	....	....	....	2	....	....	....	....	....	....	....	....	....	....	....	....	....	....	....	....	....	....
	Finland	WEC-A	9	2	0	2	....	....	....	2	....	....	....	....	....	....	....	....	....	....	....	....	....	....	....	....	....	....
1978-79	Karpat Oulu	Finland	36	14	8	22	....	....	....	47	....	....	....	....	....	....	....	....	....	....	....	....	....	....	....	....	....	....
	Finland	WJC-A	6	0	3	3	....	....	....	0	....	....	....	....	....	....	....	....	....	....	....	....	....	....	....	....	....	....
	Finland	WEC-A	6	2	0	2	....	....	....	2	....	....	....	....	....	....	....	....	....	....	....	....	....	....	....	....	....	....
1979-80	Karpat Oulu	Finland	30	15	13	28	....	....	....	31	....	....	....	....	....	....	....	....	....	....	6	5	2	7	0	....	....	....
	Finland	WJC-A	5	4	3	7	....	....	....	2	....	....	....	....	....	....	....	....	....	....	....	....	....	....	....	....	....	....
1980-81	Karpat Oulu	Finland	36	28	23	51	....	....	....	28	....	....	....	....	....	....	....	....	....	....	12	*7	4	11	6	....	....	....
	Finland	WEC-A	8	3	4	7	....	....	....	4	....	....	....	....	....	....	....	....	....	....	....	....	....	....	....	....	....	....
1981-82	Finland	C Cup	5	0	1	1	....	....	....	2	....	....	....	....	....	....	....	....	....	....	....	....	....	....	....	....	....	....
	New York Rangers	**NHL**	**78**	**18**	**38**	**56**	**14**	**25**	**39**	**27**	**7**	**0**	**3**	**247**	**7.3**	**128**	**43**	**72**	**5**	**+18**	**10**	**4**	**5**	**9**	**2**	**2**	**0**	**1**
1982-83	**New York Rangers**	**NHL**	**77**	**16**	**53**	**69**	**13**	**37**	**50**	**22**	**5**	**0**	**4**	**230**	**7.0**	**141**	**44**	**77**	**7**	**+27**	**9**	**4**	**2**	**6**	**6**	**1**	**0**	**1**
1983-84	**New York Rangers**	**NHL**	**74**	**20**	**39**	**59**	**16**	**26**	**42**	**26**	**5**	**0**	**4**	**287**	**7.0**	**130**	**40**	**79**	**6**	**+17**	**5**	**1**	**1**	**2**	**2**	**1**	**0**	**1**
1984-85	**New York Rangers**	**NHL**	**80**	**28**	**45**	**73**	**23**	**30**	**53**	**32**	**10**	**0**	**2**	**255**	**11.0**	**123**	**53**	**99**	**2**	**–27**	**3**	**2**	**0**	**2**	**6**	**1**	**0**	**0**
	Finland	WEC-A	10	0	4	4	....	....	....	6	....	....	....	....	....	....	....	....	....	....	....	....	....	....	....	....	....	....
1985-86	**New York Rangers**	**NHL**	**80**	**17**	**42**	**59**	**14**	**28**	**42**	**47**	**6**	**0**	**2**	**228**	**7.5**	**130**	**49**	**62**	**3**	**+22**	**16**	**0**	**8**	**8**	**6**	**0**	**0**	**0**
1986-87	SC Bern	Switz.	36	26	28	54	....	....	....	....	....	....	....	....	....	....	....	....	....	....	....	....	....	....	....	....	....	....
	Edmonton Oilers	**NHL**	**16**	**5**	**8**	**13**	**4**	**6**	**10**	**6**	**3**	**0**	**1**	**52**	**9.6**	**33**	**10**	**17**	**2**	**+8**	**21**	**2**	**5**	**7**	**10**	**1**	**0**	**1**
1987-88	Finland	C Cup	4	0	0	0	....	....	....	2	....	....	....	....	....	....	....	....	....	....	....	....	....	....	....	....	....	....
	HV71	Sweden	40	10	22	32	....	....	....	26	....	....	....	....	....	....	....	....	....	....	2	0	1	1	2	....	....	....
	Finland	Olympics	8	4	2	6	....	....	....	0	....	....	....	....	....	....	....	....	....	....	....	....	....	....	....	....	....	....
1988-89	SC Bern	Switz.	36	17	30	47	....	....	....	....	....	....	....	....	....	....	....	....	....	....	9	4	8	12	....	....	....	....
	Finland	WEC-A	10	2	4	6	....	....	....	6	....	....	....	....	....	....	....	....	....	....	....	....	....	....	....	....	....	....
1989-90	**New Jersey Devils**	**NHL**	**31**	**2**	**5**	**7**	**2**	**4**	**6**	**14**	**1**	**0**	**0**	**52**	**3.8**	**27**	**10**	**24**	**0**	**–4**	....	....	....	....	....	....	....	....
	Edmonton Oilers	**NHL**	**10**	**1**	**7**	**8**	**1**	**5**	**6**	**6**	**0**	**0**	**0**	**28**	**3.6**	**16**	**8**	**11**	**2**	**–1**	**22**	**2**	**11**	**13**	**12**	**1**	**0**	**0**
1990-91	SC Bern	Switz.	36	13	25	38	....	....	....	....	....	....	....	....	....	....	....	....	....	....	10	5	9	14	....	....	....	....
1991-92	SC Bern	Switz.	46	11	22	33	....	....	....	28	....	....	....	....	....	....	....	....	....	....	....	....	....	....	....	....	....	....
1992-93	SC Bern	Switz.	31	7	16	23	....	....	....	30	....	....	....	....	....	....	....	....	....	....	5	1	2	3	8	....	....	....
1993-94	Tappara Tampere	Finland	6	2	4	6	....	....	....	2	....	....	....	....	....	....	....	....	....	....	....	....	....	....	....	....	....	....
1994-95	SC Bern	Switz.	19	3	7	10	....	....	....	20	....	....	....	....	....	....	....	....	....	....	6	1	5	6	4	....	....	....
1995-96	Zürcher SC	Switz.	18	4	11	15	....	....	....	4	....	....	....	....	....	....	....	....	....	....	....	....	....	....	....	....	....	....
	Kalpa Kuozio	Finland	16	3	5	8	....	....	....	4	....	....	....	....	....	....	....	....	....	....	....	....	....	....	....	....	....	....
	NHL Totals		**446**	**107**	**237**	**344**	**87**	**161**	**248**	**180**	**37**	**0**	**16**	**1379**	**7.8**	**728**	**257**	**441**	**30**		**86**	**15**	**32**	**47**	**44**	**7**	**0**	**4**

WJC-A All-Star Team (1980) • Named Best Defenseman at WJC-A (1980) • Finnish First All-Star Team (1980, 1981)

Played in NHL All-Star Game (1986)

Traded to **Edmonton** by **NY Rangers** with Clark Donatelli, Ville Kentala, Jim Wiemer and future considerations (Stu Kulak, March 10, 1987) for Mike Golden, Don Jackson and Miloslav Horava, October 2, 1986. Claimed by **New Jersey** from **Edmonton** in Waiver Draft, October 5, 1987. Traded to **Edmonton** by **New Jersey** for Jeff Sharples, March 6, 1990.

• RUPP, DUANE

Duane Rupp D – L. 6'1", 195 lbs. b: MacNutt, Sask., 3/29/1938.

Season	Club	League	GP	G	A	Pts	AG	AA	APts	PIM	PP	SH	GW	S	%	TGF	PGF	TGA	PGA	+/–	GP	G	A	Pts	PIM	PP	SH	GW
1955-56	Melville Millionaires	SJHL	1	0	1	1	....	....	....	0	....	....	....	....	....	....	....	....	....	....	....	....	....	....	....	....	....	....
1956-57	Flin Flon Bombers	SJHL	55	4	20	24	....	....	....	20	....	....	....	....	....	....	....	....	....	....	10	2	1	3	2	....	....	....
1957-58	Flin Flon Bombers	SJHL	55	9	25	34	....	....	....	27	....	....	....	....	....	....	....	....	....	....	12	0	0	0	4	....	....	....
1958-59	Indianapolis–Fort Wayne	IHL	58	5	11	16	....	....	....	22	....	....	....	....	....	....	....	....	....	....	11	0	1	1	11	....	....	....
1959-60	Fort Wayne Komets	IHL	67	10	44	54	....	....	....	22	....	....	....	....	....	....	....	....	....	....	13	1	6	7	0	....	....	....
1960-61	Kitchener-Waterloo Beavers	EPHL	69	10	14	24	....	....	....	26	....	....	....	....	....	....	....	....	....	....	7	1	1	2	6	....	....	....
1961-62	Springfield Indians	AHL	27	7	9	16	....	....	....	10	....	....	....	....	....	....	....	....	....	....	....	....	....	....	....	....	....	....
	Vancouver Canucks	WHL	35	3	13	16	....	....	....	14	....	....	....	....	....	....	....	....	....	....	....	....	....	....	....	....	....	....
1962-63	**New York Rangers**	**NHL**	**2**	**0**	**0**	**0**	**0**	**0**	**0**	**0**	....	....	....	....	....	....	....	....	....	....	....	....	....	....	....	....	....	....
	Baltimore Clippers	AHL	71	4	17	21	....	....	....	42	....	....	....	....	....	....	....	....	....		3	0	2	2	11	....	....	....
1963-64	Baltimore Clippers	AHL	61	2	9	11	....	....	....	65	....	....	....	....	....	....	....	....	....	....	....	....	....	....	....	....	....	....
	Rochester Americans	AHL	15	1	4	5	....	....	....	16	....	....	....	....	....	....	....	....	....		2	0	1	1	0	....	....	....
1964-65	**Toronto Maple Leafs**	**NHL**	**2**	**0**	**0**	**0**	**0**	**0**	**0**	**0**	....	....	....	....	....	....	....	....	....	....	....	....	....	....	....	....	....	....
	Rochester Americans	AHL	71	4	30	34	....	....	....	50	....	....	....	....	....	....	....	....	....	....	10	1	7	8	18	....	....	....
1965-66	**Toronto Maple Leafs**	**NHL**	**2**	**0**	**1**	**1**	**0**	**1**	**1**	**0**	....	....	....	....	....	....	....	....	....	....	....	....	....	....	....	....	....	....
	Rochester Americans	AHL	70	7	34	41	....	....	....	86	....	....	....	....	....	....	....	....	....	....	12	0	8	8	30	....	....	....
1966-67	**Toronto Maple Leafs**	**NHL**	**3**	**0**	**0**	**0**	**0**	**0**	**0**	**0**	....	....	....	....	....	....	....	....	....	....	....	....	....	....	....	....	....	....
	Rochester Americans	AHL	59	7	35	42	....	....	....	84	....	....	....	....	....	....	....	....	....	....	13	0	5	5	13	....	....	....
1967-68	**Toronto Maple Leafs**	**NHL**	**71**	**1**	**8**	**9**	**1**	**8**	**9**	**42**	**0**	**0**	**0**	**79**	**1.3**	**69**	**1**	**63**	**11**	**+16**	....	....	....	....	....	....	....	....
1968-69	**Minnesota North Stars**	**NHL**	**29**	**2**	**1**	**3**	**2**	**1**	**3**	**8**	**1**	**0**	**0**	**36**	**5.6**	**25**	**4**	**36**	**6**	**–9**	....	....	....	....	....	....	....	....
	Cleveland Barons	AHL	13	3	6	9	....	....	....	38	....	....	....	....	....	....	....	....	....	....	....	....	....	....	....	....	....	....
	Pittsburgh Penguins	**NHL**	**30**	**3**	**10**	**13**	**3**	**9**	**12**	**24**	**0**	**0**	**0**	**69**	**4.3**	**35**	**14**	**41**	**7**	**–13**	....	....	....	....	....	....	....	....
1969-70	**Pittsburgh Penguins**	**NHL**	**64**	**2**	**14**	**16**	**2**	**14**	**16**	**18**	**1**	**0**	**0**	**105**	**1.9**	**63**	**22**	**78**	**26**	**–11**	**6**	**2**	**2**	**4**	**2**	**0**	**0**	**0**
1970-71	**Pittsburgh Penguins**	**NHL**	**59**	**5**	**28**	**33**	**5**	**25**	**30**	**34**	**1**	**0**	**1**	**152**	**3.3**	**83**	**36**	**68**	**11**	**–10**	....	....	....	....	....	....	....	....
1971-72	**Pittsburgh Penguins**	**NHL**	**34**	**4**	**18**	**22**	**4**	**16**	**20**	**32**	**0**	**0**	**0**	**91**	**4.4**	**54**	**6**	**62**	**14**	**0**	**4**	**0**	**0**	**0**	**6**	**0**	**0**	**0**
	Hershey Bears	AHL	38	2	21	23	....	....	....	36	....	....	....	....	....	....	....	....	....	....	....	....	....	....	....	....	....	....
1972-73	**Pittsburgh Penguins**	**NHL**	**78**	**7**	**13**	**20**	**7**	**11**	**18**	**62**	**2**	**1**	**2**	**132**	**5.3**	**102**	**22**	**106**	**23**	**–3**	....	....	....	....	....	....	....	....
1973-74	Hershey Bears	AHL	67	7	27	34	....	....	....	32	....	....	....	....	....	....	....	....	....	....	14	1	5	6	8	....	....	....
1974-75	Vancouver Blazers	WHA	72	3	26	29	....	....	....	45	....	....	....	....	....	....	....	....	....	....	....	....	....	....	....	....	....	....

Season	Club	League	GP	G	A	Pts	AG	AA	APts	PIM	PP	SH	GW	S	%	TGF	PGF	TGA	PGA	+/–	GP	G	A	Pts	PIM	PP	SH	GW
			REGULAR SEASON																		PLAYOFFS							
1975-76	Calgary Cowboys	WHA	42	0	16	16	....	....	....	33	....	....	....	....	....	....	....	....	....	....	7	0	2	2	8	....	....	....
	Rochester Americans	AHL	4	1	6	7	....	....	....	2	....	....	....	....	....	....	....	....	....	....	....	....	....	....	....	....	....	....
1976-77	Rochester Americans	AHL	41	3	8	11	....	....	....	12	....	....	....	....	....	....	....	....	....	....	2	0	0	0	0	....	....	....
	NHL Totals		**374**	**24**	**93**	**117**	**24**	**85**	**109**	**220**	**5**	**1**	**3**	**664**	**3.6**	**431**	**105**	**454**	**98**		**10**	**2**	**2**	**4**	**8**	**0**	**0**	**0**
	Other Major League Totals		114	3	42	45	....	....	....	78	....	....	....	....	....	....	....	....	....	....	7	0	2	2	8	....	....	....

AHL Second All-Star Team (1966, 1967, 1974)

Played in NHL All-Star Game (1968)

Traded to **Toronto** by **NY Rangers** with Ed Ehrenverth for Lou Angotti and Ed Lawson, June 25, 1964. Claimed by **Minnesota** from **Toronto** in Intra-League Draft, June 12, 1968. Traded to **Pittsburgh** by **Minnesota** for Leo Boivin, January 24, 1969. Signed as a free agent by **Vancouver** (WHA), June, 1974. Transferred to **Calgary** (WHA) after **Vancouver** (WHA) franchise relocated, May, 1975.

• RUSKOWSKI, TERRY

Terry "Roscoe" Ruskowski   C – L. 5′10″, 178 lbs.   b: Prince Albert, Sask., 12/31/1954.   Chicago's 4th choice, 70th overall, in 1974 Amateur Draft.

Season	Club	League	GP	G	A	Pts	AG	AA	APts	PIM	PP	SH	GW	S	%	TGF	PGF	TGA	PGA	+/–	GP	G	A	Pts	PIM	PP	SH	GW
1971-72	Swift Current Broncos	WCJHL	67	13	38	51	....	....	....	177	....	....	....	....	....	....	....	....	....	....	....	....	....	....	....	....	....	....
1972-73	Swift Current Broncos	WCJHL	53	25	64	89	....	....	....	136	....	....	....	....	....	....	....	....	....	....	....	....	....	....	....	....	....	....
1973-74	Swift Current Broncos	WCJHL	68	40	93	133	....	....	....	243	....	....	....	....	....	....	....	....	....	....	13	5	*23	28	23	....	....	....
1974-75	Houston Aeros	WHA	71	10	36	46	....	....	....	134	....	....	....	....	....	....	....	....	....	....	13	4	2	6	15	....	....	....
1975-76	Houston Aeros	WHA	65	14	35	49	....	....	....	100	....	....	....	....	....	....	....	....	....	....	16	6	10	16	*64	....	....	....
1976-77	Houston Aeros	WHA	80	24	60	84	....	....	....	146	....	....	....	....	....	....	....	....	....	....	11	6	11	17	*67	....	....	....
1977-78	Houston Aeros	WHA	78	15	57	72	....	....	....	170	....	....	....	....	....	....	....	....	....	....	4	1	1	2	5	....	....	....
1978-79	Winnipeg Jets	WHA	75	20	66	86	....	....	....	211	....	....	....	....	....	....	....	....	....	....	8	1	*12	13	23	....	....	....
1979-80	**Chicago Black Hawks**	**NHL**	**74**	**15**	**55**	**70**	**14**	**42**	**56**	**252**	**6**	**1**	**3**	**90**	**16.7**	**94**	**33**	**82**	**28**	**+7**	**4**	**0**	**0**	**0**	**22**	**0**	**0**	**0**
1980-81	**Chicago Black Hawks**	**NHL**	**72**	**8**	**51**	**59**	**7**	**36**	**43**	**225**	**2**	**0**	**2**	**88**	**9.1**	**80**	**22**	**103**	**26**	**–19**	**3**	**0**	**2**	**2**	**11**	**0**	**0**	**0**
1981-82	**Chicago Black Hawks**	**NHL**	**60**	**7**	**30**	**37**	**6**	**20**	**26**	**120**	**2**	**0**	**0**	**69**	**10.1**	**62**	**19**	**67**	**11**	**–13**	**11**	**1**	**2**	**3**	**53**	**0**	**0**	**0**
1982-83	**Chicago Black Hawks**	**NHL**	**5**	**0**	**2**	**2**	**0**	**1**	**1**	**12**	**0**	**0**	**0**	**4**	**0.0**	**2**	**0**	**2**	**0**	**0**	....	....	....	....	....	....	....	....
	Los Angeles Kings	**NHL**	**71**	**14**	**30**	**44**	**11**	**21**	**32**	**127**	**4**	**1**	**2**	**71**	**19.7**	**64**	**11**	**94**	**25**	**–16**	....	....	....	....	....	....	....	....
1983-84	**Los Angeles Kings**	**NHL**	**77**	**7**	**25**	**32**	**6**	**17**	**23**	**89**	**0**	**2**	**1**	**51**	**13.7**	**43**	**4**	**83**	**20**	**–24**	....	....	....	....	....	....	....	....
1984-85	**Los Angeles Kings**	**NHL**	**78**	**16**	**33**	**49**	**13**	**22**	**35**	**144**	**2**	**0**	**2**	**74**	**21.6**	**79**	**11**	**82**	**16**	**+2**	**3**	**0**	**2**	**2**	**0**	**0**	**0**	**0**
1985-86	**Pittsburgh Penguins**	**NHL**	**73**	**26**	**37**	**63**	**21**	**25**	**46**	**162**	**11**	**0**	**7**	**91**	**28.6**	**115**	**56**	**50**	**1**	**+10**	....	....	....	....	....	....	....	....
1986-87	**Pittsburgh Penguins**	**NHL**	**70**	**14**	**37**	**51**	**12**	**27**	**39**	**145**	**5**	**0**	**2**	**71**	**19.7**	**89**	**38**	**43**	**0**	**+8**	....	....	....	....	....	....	....	....
1987-88	**Minnesota North Stars**	**NHL**	**47**	**5**	**12**	**17**	**4**	**9**	**13**	**76**	**2**	**0**	**0**	**33**	**15.2**	**25**	**6**	**43**	**9**	**–15**	....	....	....	....	....	....	....	....
1988-89	**Minnesota North Stars**	**NHL**	**3**	**1**	**1**	**2**	**1**	**1**	**2**	**2**	**0**	**0**	**0**	**2**	**50.0**	**2**	**0**	**1**	**0**	**+1**	....	....	....	....	....	....	....	....
	NHL Totals		**630**	**113**	**313**	**426**	**95**	**221**	**316**	**1354**	**34**	**4**	**19**	**644**	**17.5**	**655**	**200**	**650**	**136**		**21**	**1**	**6**	**7**	**86**	**0**	**0**	**0**
	Other Major League Totals		369	83	254	337	....	....	....	761	....	....	....	....	....	....	....	....	....	....	52	18	36	54	174	....	....	....

Selected by **Houston** (WHA) in 1974 WHA Amateur Draft, May, 1974. Traded to **Winnipeg** (WHA) by **Houston** (WHA) for cash, July, 1978. Reclaimed by **Chicago** from **Winnipeg** prior to Expansion Draft, June 9, 1979. Traded to **LA Kings** by **Chicago** for Larry Goodenough and LA Kings' 3rd round choice (Trent Yawney) in 1984 Entry Draft, October 24, 1982. Signed as a free agent by **Pittsburgh**, October 3, 1985. Signed as a free agent by **Minnesota**, July, 1987.

• RUSSELL, CAM

Cam Russell   D – L. 6′4″, 200 lbs.   b: Halifax, N.S., 1/12/1969.   Chicago's 3rd choice, 50th overall, in 1987 Entry Draft.

Season	Club	League	GP	G	A	Pts	AG	AA	APts	PIM	PP	SH	GW	S	%	TGF	PGF	TGA	PGA	+/–	GP	G	A	Pts	PIM	PP	SH	GW
1985-86	Hull Olympiques	QMJHL	56	3	4	7	....	....	....	24	....	....	....	....	....	....	....	....	....	....	15	0	2	2	4	....	....	....
1986-87	Hull Olympiques	QMJHL	66	3	16	19	....	....	....	119	....	....	....	....	....	....	....	....	....	....	8	0	1	1	16	....	....	....
1987-88	Hull Olympiques	QMJHL	53	9	18	27	....	....	....	141	....	....	....	....	....	....	....	....	....	....	19	2	5	7	39	....	....	....
1988-89	Hull Olympiques	QMJHL	66	8	32	40	....	....	....	109	....	....	....	....	....	....	....	....	....	....	9	2	6	8	6	....	....	....
1989-90	**Chicago Blackhawks**	**NHL**	**19**	**0**	**1**	**1**	**0**	**1**	**1**	**27**	**0**	**0**	**0**	**10**	**0.0**	**9**	**1**	**13**	**2**	**–3**	**1**	**0**	**0**	**0**	**0**	**0**	**0**	**0**
	Indianapolis Ice	IHL	46	3	15	18	....	....	....	114	....	....	....	....	....	....	....	....	....	....	9	0	1	1	24	....	....	....
1990-91	**Chicago Blackhawks**	**NHL**	**3**	**0**	**0**	**0**	**0**	**0**	**0**	**5**	**0**	**0**	**0**	**0**	**0.0**	**2**	**0**	**1**	**0**	**+1**	**1**	**0**	**0**	**0**	**0**	**0**	**0**	**0**
	Indianapolis Ice	IHL	53	5	9	14	....	....	....	125	....	....	....	....	....	....	....	....	....	....	6	0	2	2	30	....	....	....
1991-92	**Chicago Blackhawks**	**NHL**	**19**	**0**	**0**	**0**	**0**	**0**	**0**	**34**	**0**	**0**	**0**	**9**	**0.0**	**2**	**0**	**12**	**2**	**–8**	**12**	**0**	**2**	**2**	**2**	**0**	**0**	**0**
	Indianapolis Ice	IHL	41	4	9	13	....	....	....	78	....	....	....	....	....	....	....	....	....	....	....	....	....	....	....	....	....	....
1992-93	**Chicago Blackhawks**	**NHL**	**67**	**2**	**4**	**6**	**2**	**3**	**5**	**151**	**0**	**0**	**0**	**49**	**4.1**	**32**	**2**	**32**	**7**	**+5**	**4**	**0**	**0**	**0**	**0**	**0**	**0**	**0**
1993-94	**Chicago Blackhawks**	**NHL**	**67**	**1**	**7**	**8**	**1**	**5**	**6**	**200**	**0**	**0**	**0**	**41**	**2.4**	**37**	**0**	**31**	**4**	**+10**	....	....	....	....	....	....	....	....
1994-95	**Chicago Blackhawks**	**NHL**	**33**	**1**	**3**	**4**	**2**	**4**	**6**	**88**	**0**	**0**	**0**	**18**	**5.6**	**17**	**1**	**12**	**0**	**+4**	**16**	**0**	**3**	**3**	**8**	**0**	**0**	**0**
1995-96	**Chicago Blackhawks**	**NHL**	**61**	**2**	**2**	**4**	**2**	**2**	**4**	**129**	**0**	**0**	**0**	**22**	**9.1**	**26**	**0**	**19**	**1**	**+8**	**6**	**0**	**0**	**0**	**2**	**0**	**0**	**0**
1996-97	**Chicago Blackhawks**	**NHL**	**44**	**1**	**1**	**2**	**1**	**1**	**2**	**65**	**0**	**0**	**0**	**19**	**5.3**	**10**	**0**	**19**	**1**	**–8**	**4**	**0**	**0**	**0**	**4**	**0**	**0**	**0**
1997-98	**Chicago Blackhawks**	**NHL**	**41**	**1**	**1**	**2**	**1**	**1**	**2**	**79**	**0**	**0**	**1**	**18**	**5.6**	**16**	**0**	**14**	**1**	**+3**	....	....	....	....	....	....	....	....
	NHL Totals		**354**	**8**	**19**	**27**	**9**	**17**	**26**	**778**	**0**	**0**	**1**	**186**	**4.3**	**151**	**4**	**153**	**18**		**44**	**0**	**5**	**5**	**16**	**0**	**0**	**0**

• RUSSELL, PHIL

Phil Russell   D – R. 6′2″, 205 lbs.   b: Edmonton, Alta., 7/21/1952.   Chicago's 1st choice, 13th overall, in 1972 Amateur Draft.

Season	Club	League	GP	G	A	Pts	AG	AA	APts	PIM	PP	SH	GW	S	%	TGF	PGF	TGA	PGA	+/–	GP	G	A	Pts	PIM	PP	SH	GW
1970-71	Edmonton Oil Kings	WCJHL	34	4	16	20	....	....	....	113	....	....	....	....	....	....	....	....	....	....	17	1	7	8	47	....	....	....
1971-72	Edmonton Oil Kings	WCJHL	64	14	45	59	....	....	....	*331	....	....	....	....	....	....	....	....	....	....	16	1	9	10	15	....	....	....
1972-73	**Chicago Black Hawks**	**NHL**	**76**	**6**	**19**	**25**	**6**	**16**	**22**	**156**	**1**	**0**	**0**	**119**	**5.0**	**99**	**7**	**72**	**11**	**+31**	**16**	**0**	**3**	**3**	**49**	**0**	**0**	**0**
1973-74	**Chicago Black Hawks**	**NHL**	**75**	**10**	**25**	**35**	**10**	**22**	**32**	**184**	**0**	**1**	**0**	**123**	**8.1**	**112**	**8**	**61**	**4**	**+47**	**9**	**0**	**1**	**1**	**41**	**0**	**0**	**0**
1974-75	**Chicago Black Hawks**	**NHL**	**80**	**5**	**24**	**29**	**5**	**19**	**24**	**260**	**1**	**0**	**1**	**187**	**2.7**	**108**	**24**	**100**	**23**	**+7**	**8**	**1**	**3**	**4**	**23**	**0**	**0**	**0**
1975-76	**Chicago Black Hawks**	**NHL**	**74**	**9**	**29**	**38**	**8**	**23**	**31**	**194**	**7**	**0**	**0**	**180**	**5.0**	**102**	**26**	**119**	**23**	**–20**	**4**	**0**	**1**	**1**	**17**	**0**	**0**	**0**
1976-77	**Chicago Black Hawks**	**NHL**	**76**	**9**	**36**	**45**	**9**	**29**	**38**	**233**	**1**	**0**	**2**	**178**	**5.1**	**124**	**31**	**120**	**28**	**+1**	**2**	**0**	**1**	**1**	**2**	**0**	**0**	**0**
	Canada	WEC-A	10	0	3	3	....	....	....	16	....	....	....	....	....	....	....	....	....	....	....	....	....	....	....	....	....	....
1977-78	**Chicago Black Hawks**	**NHL**	**57**	**6**	**20**	**26**	**6**	**16**	**22**	**139**	**0**	**1**	**1**	**132**	**4.5**	**79**	**12**	**62**	**14**	**+19**	....	....	....	....	....	....	....	....
1978-79	**Chicago Black Hawks**	**NHL**	**66**	**8**	**23**	**31**	**7**	**18**	**25**	**122**	**1**	**1**	**1**	**147**	**5.4**	**78**	**16**	**97**	**28**	**–7**	....	....	....	....	....	....	....	....
	Atlanta Flames	**NHL**	**13**	**1**	**6**	**7**	**1**	**5**	**6**	**28**	**1**	**0**	**0**	**19**	**5.3**	**24**	**5**	**24**	**6**	**+1**	**2**	**0**	**0**	**0**	**9**	**0**	**0**	**0**
1979-80	**Atlanta Flames**	**NHL**	**80**	**5**	**31**	**36**	**5**	**24**	**29**	**115**	**1**	**0**	**1**	**104**	**4.8**	**104**	**6**	**103**	**19**	**+14**	**4**	**0**	**1**	**1**	**6**	**0**	**0**	**0**
1980-81	**Calgary Flames**	**NHL**	**80**	**6**	**23**	**29**	**5**	**16**	**21**	**104**	**1**	**1**	**1**	**109**	**5.5**	**127**	**9**	**155**	**54**	**+17**	**16**	**2**	**7**	**9**	**29**	**0**	**0**	**0**
1981-82	**Calgary Flames**	**NHL**	**71**	**4**	**25**	**29**	**3**	**17**	**20**	**110**	**0**	**0**	**0**	**114**	**3.5**	**101**	**2**	**142**	**49**	**+6**	**3**	**0**	**1**	**1**	**2**	**0**	**0**	**0**
1982-83	**Calgary Flames**	**NHL**	**78**	**13**	**18**	**31**	**11**	**12**	**23**	**112**	**0**	**1**	**2**	**116**	**11.2**	**96**	**0**	**120**	**26**	**+2**	**9**	**1**	**4**	**5**	**24**	**0**	**0**	**0**
1983-84	**New Jersey Devils**	**NHL**	**76**	**9**	**22**	**31**	**7**	**15**	**22**	**96**	**0**	**0**	**0**	**123**	**7.3**	**81**	**9**	**128**	**29**	**–27**	....	....	....	....	....	....	....	....
1984-85	**New Jersey Devils**	**NHL**	**66**	**4**	**16**	**20**	**3**	**11**	**14**	**110**	**0**	**1**	**0**	**73**	**5.5**	**66**	**2**	**112**	**34**	**–14**	....	....	....	....	....	....	....	....
1985-86	**New Jersey Devils**	**NHL**	**30**	**2**	**3**	**5**	**2**	**2**	**4**	**51**	**0**	**0**	**0**	**22**	**9.1**	**20**	**1**	**46**	**10**	**–17**	....	....	....	....	....	....	....	....
1985-86	**Buffalo Sabres**	**NHL**	**12**	**2**	**3**	**5**	**2**	**2**	**4**	**12**	**0**	**0**	**0**	**15**	**13.3**	**7**	**0**	**18**	**3**	**–8**	....	....	....	....	....	....	....	....
	Canada	WEC-A	8	0	1	1	....	....	....	10	....	....	....	....	....	....	....	....	....	....	....	....	....	....	....	....	....	....
1986-87	**Buffalo Sabres**	**NHL**	**6**	**0**	**2**	**2**	**0**	**1**	**1**	**12**	**0**	**0**	**0**	**2**	**0.0**	**6**	**0**	**8**	**2**	**0**	....	....	....	....	....	....	....	....
1987-88	Kalamazoo Wings	IHL	27	2	9	11	....	....	....	35	....	....	....	....	....	....	....	....	....	....	....	....	....	....	....	....	....	....
	NHL Totals		**1016**	**99**	**325**	**424**	**90**	**248**	**338**	**2038**	**14**	**6**	**9**	**1763**	**5.6**	**1334**	**158**	**1487**	**363**		**73**	**4**	**22**	**26**	**202**	**0**	**0**	**0**

WCJHL All-Star Team (1972)

Played in NHL All-Star Game (1976, 1977, 1985)

Traded to **Atlanta** by **Chicago** with Ivan Bolderiv and Darcy Rota for Tom Lysiak, Pat Ribble, Harold Phillipoff, Greg Fox and Miles Zaharko, March 13, 1979. Transferred to **Calgary** after **Atlanta** franchise relocated, June 24, 1980. Traded to **New Jersey** by **Calgary** with Mel Bridgeman for Steve Tambellini and Joel Quenneville, June 20, 1983. Traded to **Buffalo** by **New Jersey** for Buffalo's 12th round choice (Doug Kirton) in 1986 Entry Draft, March 11, 1986.

• RUUTTU, CHRISTIAN

Christian Ruuttu   C – L. 5′11″, 194 lbs.   b: Lappeenranta, Finland, 2/20/1964.   Buffalo's 9th choice, 139th overall, in 1983 Entry Draft.

Season	Club	League	GP	G	A	Pts	AG	AA	APts	PIM	PP	SH	GW	S	%	TGF	PGF	TGA	PGA	+/–	GP	G	A	Pts	PIM	PP	SH	GW
1982-83	Assat Pori	Finland	36	15	18	33	....	....	....	34	....	....	....	....	....	....	....	....	....	....	....	....	....	....	....	....	....	....
	Finland	WJC-A	7	2	2	4	....	....	....	14	....	....	....	....	....	....	....	....	....	....	....	....	....	....	....	....	....	....
1983-84	Assat Pori	Finland	37	18	42	60	....	....	....	72	....	....	....	....	....	....	....	....	....	....	9	2	5	7	12	....	....	....
	Finland	WJC-A	7	0	1	1	....	....	....	8	....	....	....	....	....	....	....	....	....	....	....	....	....	....	....	....	....	....
1984-85	Assat Pori	Finland	32	14	32	46	....	....	....	34	....	....	....	....	....	....	....	....	....	....	8	1	6	7	8	....	....	....
	Finland	WEC-A	6	1	1	2	....	....	....	16	....	....	....	....	....	....	....	....	....	....	....	....	....	....	....	....	....	....
1985-86	HIFK Helsinki	Finland	36	16	38	54	....	....	....	47	....	....	....	....	....	....	....	....	....	....	10	3	6	9	8	....	....	....
	Finland	WEC-A	10	2	5	7	....	....	....	12	....	....	....	....	....	....	....	....	....	....	....	....	....	....	....	....	....	....
1986-87	**Buffalo Sabres**	**NHL**	**76**	**22**	**43**	**65**	**19**	**31**	**50**	**62**	**3**	**1**	**1**	**167**	**13.2**	**96**	**31**	**67**	**11**	**+9**	....	....	....	....	....	....	....	....
	Finland	WEC-A	10	0	0	0	....	....	....	18	....	....	....	....	....	....	....	....	....	....	....	....	....	....	....	....	....	....
1987-88	Finland	C Cup	5	2	1	3	....	....	....	10	....	....	....	....	....	....	....	....	....	....	....	....	....	....	....	....	....	....
	Buffalo Sabres	**NHL**	**73**	**26**	**45**	**71**	**22**	**32**	**54**	**85**	**8**	**1**	**4**	**185**	**14.1**	**95**	**39**	**86**	**27**	**–3**	**6**	**2**	**5**	**7**	**4**	**1**	**0**	**0**
1988-89	**Buffalo Sabres**	**NHL**	**67**	**14**	**46**	**60**	**12**	**32**	**44**	**98**	**5**	**0**	**1**	**149**	**9.4**	**84**	**30**	**64**	**23**	**+13**	**2**	**0**	**0**	**0**	**2**	**0**	**0**	**0**

			REGULAR SEASON															PLAYOFFS							
Season	Club	League	GP	G	A	Pts	AG	AA	APts	PIM	PP	SH	GW	S	%	TGF	PGF	TGA	PGA	+/-	GP	G	A	Pts	PIM	PP	SH	GW

Season	Club	League	GP	G	A	Pts	AG	AA	APts	PIM	PP	SH	GW	S	%	TGF	PGF	TGA	PGA	+/-	GP	G	A	Pts	PIM	PP	SH	GW
1989-90	Buffalo Sabres	NHL	75	19	41	60	16	29	45	66	4	1	2	160	11.9	81	17	83	28	+9	6	0	0	0	4	0	0	0
	Finland	WEC-A	9	5	3	8				4																		
1990-91	Buffalo Sabres	NHL	77	16	34	50	15	26	41	96	2	3	1	155	10.3	78	26	90	32	-6	6	1	3	4	29	0	1	0
	Finland	WEC-A	10	7	3	10				10																		
1991-92	Finland	C Cup	6	1	5	6				4																		
	Buffalo Sabres	NHL	70	4	21	25	4	16	20	76	0	2	1	108	3.7	42	12	74	37	-7	3	0	0	0	6	0	0	0
	Finland	WC-A	5	0	1	1				6																		
1992-93	Chicago Blackhawks	NHL	84	17	37	54	14	25	39	134	3	1	6	187	9.1	76	20	62	20	+14	4	0	0	0	2	0	0	0
1993-94	Chicago Blackhawks	NHL	54	9	20	29	8	15	23	68	1	1	1	96	9.4	36	8	46	14	-4	6	0	0	0	2	0	0	0
	Finland	WC-A	4	2	2	4				4																		
1994-95	HIFK Helsinki	Finland	20	4	8	12				24																		
	Chicago Blackhawks	NHL	20	2	5	7	4	7	11	6	0	0	1	25	8.0	10	0	10	3	+3								
	Vancouver Canucks	NHL	25	5	6	11	9	9	18	23	0	0	1	44	11.4	17	1	9	4	+11	9	1	1	2	0	0	1	0
1995-96	Vastra Frolunda	Sweden	32	13	25	38				98											12	4	7	11	24			
	Finland	WC-A	6	0	2	2				2																		
1996-97	Finland	W Cup	4	1	0	1				2																		
1997-98	HIFK Helsinki	Finland	44	11	28	39				32											9	3	3	6	8			
	NHL Totals		621	134	298	432	123	222	345	714	26	10	19	1276	10.5	615	184	591	199		42	4	9	13	49	1	2	0

Finnish First All-Star Team (1986)

Played in NHL All-Star Game (1988)

Traded to **Winnipeg** by **Buffalo** with future considerations for Stephane Beauregard, June 15, 1992. Traded to **Chicago** by **Winnipeg** for Stephane Beauregard, August 10, 1992. Traded to **Vancouver** by **Chicago** for Murray Craven, March 10, 1995.

● RUZICKA, VLADIMIR

Vladimir Ruzicka   C – L. 6'3", 215 lbs.   b: Most, Czech., 6/6/1963.   Toronto's 5th choice, 73rd overall, in 1982 Entry Draft.

Season	Club	League	GP	G	A	Pts	AG	AA	APts	PIM	PP	SH	GW	S	%	TGF	PGF	TGA	PGA	+/-	GP	G	A	Pts	PIM	PP	SH	GW
1979-80	CHZ Litvinov	Czech.	9	1	1	2				0																		
1980-81	CHZ Litvinov	Czech.	41	12	13	25				10																		
	Czechoslovakia	WJC-A	5	5	0	5				2																		
1981-82	CHZ Litvinov	Czech.	44	27	22	49				50																		
	Czechoslovakia	WJC A	7	8	1	9				6																		
1982-83	CHZ Litvinov	Czech.	43	22	24	46				40																		
	Czechoslovakia	WJC-A	7	12	8	20				6																		
	Czechoslovakia	WEC-A	10	3	1	4				4																		
1983-84	CHZ Litvinov	Czech.	44	31	23	54				50																		
	Czechoslovakia	Olympics	7	4	6	10				0																		
1984-85	Czechoslovakia	C Cup	5	0	0	0				2																		
	CHZ Litvinov	Czech.	41	38	22	60				29																		
	Czechoslovakia	WEC-A	10	8	3	11				0																		
1985-86	CHZ Litvinov	Czech.	43	41	32	73																						
	Czechoslovakia	WEC-A	10	4	11	15				0																		
1986-87	CHZ Litvinov	Czech.	39	29	21	50				46																		
	Czechoslovakia	WEC-A	10	3	3	6				10																		
1987-88	Czechoslovakia	C Cup	6	2	0	2				0																		
	Dukla Trencin	Czech.	44	*38	27	65				70																		
	Czechoslovakia	Olympics	8	4	3	7				12																		
1988-89	Dukla Trencin	Czech.	45	*46	38	*84				42																		
	Czechoslovakia	WEC-A	10	7	7	14				2																		
1989-90	CHZ Litvinov	Czech.	32	21	23	44																						
	Edmonton Oilers	NHL	25	11	6	17	9	4	13	10	4	0	1	52	21.2	24	13	32	0	-21								
1990-91	Boston Bruins	NHL	29	8	8	16	7	6	13	19	4	0	0	51	15.7	22	7	14	0	+1	17	2	11	13	0	1	0	2
1991-92	Boston Bruins	NHL	77	39	36	75	36	27	63	48	18	0	6	228	17.1	106	54	63	1	-10	13	2	3	5	2	2	0	0
1992-93	Boston Bruins	NHL	60	19	22	41	16	15	31	38	7	0	2	146	13.0	60	23	43	0	-6								
1993-94	Ottawa Senators	NHL	42	6	13	18	6	10	15	14	4	0	0	64	7.8	32	16	37	0	-21								
1994-95	Slavia Praha	Czech.	41	27	24	51																3	2	0	2				
1995-96	Slavia Praha	Czech.	37	21	*44	*65															5	2	1	3				
1996-97	Slavia Praha	Czech.	44	22	32	64				40																		
1997-98	Slavia Praha	Czech.	49	20	40	60				60											5	0	6	6	6			
	Czech Republic	Olympics	6	3	0	3				0																		
	NHL Totals		233	82	85	167	73	62	135	129	37	0	9	541	15.2	244	113	189	1		30	4	14	18	2	3	0	2

EJC-A All-Star Team (1981) • WJC-A All-Star Team (1982, 1983) • WEC-A All-Star Team (1985) • Czechoslovakian Player of the Year (1986, 1988) • Czechoslovakian First All-Star Team (1988, 1989)

Traded to **Edmonton** by **Toronto** for Edmonton's 4th round choice (Greg Walters) in 1990 Entry Draft, December 21, 1989. Traded to **Boston** by **Edmonton** for Greg Hawgood, October 22, 1990. Signed as a free agent by **Ottawa**, August 12, 1993.

● RYAN, TERRY

Terry Ryan   LW – L. 6'2", 198 lbs.   b: St. John's, Nfld., 1/14/1977.   Montreal's 1st choice, 8th overall, in 1995 Entry Draft.

Season	Club	League	GP	G	A	Pts	AG	AA	APts	PIM	PP	SH	GW	S	%	TGF	PGF	TGA	PGA	+/-	GP	G	A	Pts	PIM	PP	SH	GW
1993-94	Tri-City Americans	WHL	61	16	17	33				176											4	0	1	1	25			
1994-95	Tri-City Americans	WHL	70	50	60	110				207											17	12	15	27	36			
1995-96	Tri-City Americans	WHL	59	32	37	69				133											5	0	0	0	4			
	Fredericton Canadiens	AHL																			3	0	0	0	2			
1996-97	Red Deer Rebels	WHL	16	13	22	35				10											16	18	6	24	32			
	Montreal Canadiens	NHL	3	0	0	0	0	0	0	0	0	0	0	0	0.0	0	0	0	0									
1997-98	**Montreal Canadiens**	NHL	4	0	0	0	0	0	0	31	0	0	0	0	0.0	0	0	0	0									
	Fredericton Canadiens	AHL	71	21	18	39				256											3	1	1	2	0			
	NHL Totals		7	0	0	0	0	0	0	31	0	0	0	0	0.0	0	0	0	0									

WHL West Second All-Star Team (1995)

● RYCHEL, WARREN

Warren Rychel   LW – L. 6', 205 lbs.   b: Tecumseh, Ont., 5/12/1967.

Season	Club	League	GP	G	A	Pts	AG	AA	APts	PIM	PP	SH	GW	S	%	TGF	PGF	TGA	PGA	+/-	GP	G	A	Pts	PIM	PP	SH	GW
1984-85	Sudbury Wolves	OHL	35	5	8	13				74																		
	Guelph Platers	OHL	29	1	3	4				48																		
1985-86	Guelph Platers	OHL	38	14	5	19				119																		
	Ottawa 67's	OHL	29	11	18	29				54																		
1986-87	Ottawa 67's	OHL	28	11	7	18				57																		
	Kitchener Rangers	OHL	21	5	5	10				39											4	0	0	0	9			
1987-88	Peoria Rivermen	IHL	7	2	1	3				7											1	0	0	0	0			
	Saginaw Hawks	IHL	51	2	7	9				113																		
1988-89	**Chicago Blackhawks**	NHL	2	0	0	0	0	0	0	17	0	0	0	3	0.0	0	0	1	0	-1								
	Saginaw Hawks	IHL	50	15	14	29				226											6	0	0	0	51			
1989-90	Indianapolis Ice	IHL	77	23	16	39				374											14	1	3	4	64			
1990-91	Indianapolis Ice	IHL	68	33	30	63				338											5	2	1	3	30			
	Chicago Blackhawks	NHL																			3	1	3	4	2	1	0	1
1991-92	Moncton Hawks	AHL	36	14	15	29				211																		
	Kalamazoo Wings	IHL	45	15	20	35				165											8	0	3	3	51			
1992-93	**Los Angeles Kings**	NHL	70	6	7	13	5	5	10	314	0	0	1	67	9.0	20	2	42	9	-15	23	6	7	13	39	0	0	2
1993-94	**Los Angeles Kings**	NHL	80	10	9	19	9	7	16	322	0	0	3	105	9.5	32	1	52	2	-19								
1994-95	**Los Angeles Kings**	NHL	7	0	0	0	0	0	0	7	0	0	0	0	0.0	0	0	0	0	-5								
	Toronto Maple Leafs	NHL	26	1	6	7	2	9	11	101	0	0	0	34	2.9	11	0	10	0	+1	3	0	0	0	0	0	0	0
1995-96	**Colorado Avalanche**	NHL	52	6	2	8	6	2	8	147	0	0	1	45	13.3	13	0	7	0	+6	12	1	0	1	23	0	0	0

			REGULAR SEASON																		PLAYOFFS							
Season	Club	League	GP	G	A	Pts	AG	AA	APts	PIM	PP	SH	GW	S	%	TGF	PGF	TGA	PGA	+/–	GP	G	A	Pts	PIM	PP	SH	GW
1996-97	**Anaheim Mighty Ducks**	**NHL**	70	10	7	17	11	6	17	218	1	1	1	59	16.9	29	1	22	0	+6	11	0	2	2	19	0	0	0
1997-98	**Anaheim Mighty Ducks**	**NHL**	63	5	6	11	6	6	12	198	1	0	0	62	8.1	23	5	29	1	–10	....	....	....	....	....	....	....	....
	Colorado Avalanche	**NHL**	8	0	0	0	0	0	0	23	0	0	0	4	0.0	0	0	1	0	–1	6	0	0	0	24	0	0	0
	NHL Totals		378	38	37	75	39	35	74	1359	2	1	6	386	9.8	129	9	170	12		58	8	12	20	107	1	0	3

Signed as a free agent by **Chicago**, September 19, 1986. Traded to **Winnipeg** by **Chicago** with Troy Murray for Bryan Marchment and Chris Norton, July 22, 1991. Traded to **Minnesota** by **Winnipeg** for Tony Joseph, December 30, 1991. Signed as a free agent by **LA Kings**, October 1, 1992. Traded to **Washington** by **LA Kings** for Randy Burridge, February 10, 1995. Traded to **Toronto** by **Washington** for Toronto's 4th round choice (Sebastien Charpentier) in 1995 Entry Draft, February 10, 1995. Traded to **Colorado** by **Toronto** for cash, October 2, 1995. Signed as a free agent by **Anaheim**, August 21, 1996. Traded to **Colorado** by **Anaheim** with future considerations for Josef Marha, March 24, 1998.

• RYMSHA, ANDY

Andy Rymsha D – L. 6'3", 210 lbs. b: St. Catharines, Ont., 12/10/1968. St. Louis' 5th choice, 82nd overall, in 1987 Entry Draft.

Season	Club	League	GP	G	A	Pts	AG	AA	APts	PIM	PP	SH	GW	S	%	TGF	PGF	TGA	PGA	+/–	GP	G	A	Pts	PIM	PP	SH	GW
1985-86	St. Catharines Falcons	OJHL	39	6	13	19	....	....	....	170	....	....	....	....	....	....	....	....	....	....	....	....	....	....	....	....	....	....
1986-87	Western Michigan Broncos	CCHA	41	7	12	19	....	....	....	60	....	....	....	....	....	....	....	....	....	....	....	....	....	....	....	....	....	....
1987-88	Western Michigan Broncos	CCHA	42	5	6	11	....	....	....	114	....	....	....	....	....	....	....	....	....	....	....	....	....	....	....	....	....	....
1988-89	Western Michigan Broncos	CCHA	35	3	4	7	....	....	....	139	....	....	....	....	....	....	....	....	....	....	....	....	....	....	....	....	....	....
1989-90	Western Michigan Broncos	CCHA	37	1	10	11	....	....	....	108	....	....	....	....	....	....	....	....	....	....	....	....	....	....	....	....	....	....
1990-91	Halifax Citadels	AHL	12	1	2	3	....	....	....	22	....	....	....	....	....	....	....	....	....	....	....	....	....	....	....	....	....	....
	Peoria Rivermen	IHL	45	2	9	11	....	....	....	64	....	....	....	....	....	....	....	....	....	....	....	....	....	....	....	....	....	....
1991-92	**Quebec Nordiques**	**NHL**	6	0	0	0	0	0	0	23	0	0	0	4	0.0	1	0	4	0	–3	....	....	....	....	....	....	....	....
	Halifax Citadels	AHL	44	4	7	11	....	....	....	54	....	....	....	....	....	....	....	....	....	....	....	....	....	....	....	....	....	....
	New Haven Nighthawks	AHL	16	0	5	5	....	....	....	20	....	....	....	....	....	....	....	....	....	....	....	....	....	....	....	....	....	....
1992-93	Canada	Nat-Team	6	8	2	10	....	....	....	16	....	....	....	....	....	....	....	....	....	....	....	....	....	....	....	....	....	....
	Halifax Citadels	AHL	43	4	6	10	....	....	....	62	....	....	....	....	....	....	....	....	....	....	....	....	....	....	....	....	....	....
1993-94	Detroit Falcons	ColHL	48	24	38	62	....	....	....	48	....	....	....	....	....	....	....	....	....	....	....	....	....	....	....	....	....	....
	Bracknell Bees	Britain	14	16	13	29	....	....	....	40	....	....	....	....	....	....	....	....	....	....	....	....	....	....	....	....	....	....
1994-95	HC Asiago	Italy	8	4	7	11	....	....	....	18	....	....	....	....	....	....	....	....	....	....	....	....	....	....	....	....	....	....
	WEV Wein	Austria	29	21	21	42	....	....	....	*124	....	....	....	....	....	....	....	....	....	....	3	3	0	3	6	....	....	....
1995-96	San Francisco Spiders	IHL	76	33	27	60	....	....	....	84	....	....	....	....	....	....	....	....	....	....	4	0	2	2	8	....	....	....
1996-97	Kaufbeurer Adler	Germany	26	8	12	20	....	....	....	68	....	....	....	....	....	....	....	....	....	....	....	....	....	....	....	....	....	....
1997-98	Star Bulls Rosenheim	Germany	48	16	17	33	....	....	....	116	....	....	....	....	....	....	....	....	....	....	....	....	....	....	....	....	....	....
	NHL Totals		6	0	0	0	0	0	0	23	0	0	0	4	0.0	1	0	4	0		....	....	....	....	....	....	....	....

Traded to **Quebec** by **St. Louis** with Tony Twist and Herb Raglan for Darin Kimble February 4, 1991.

• SAARINEN, SIMO

Simo Saarinen D – L. 5'8", 185 lbs. b: Helsinki, Finland, 2/14/1963. NY Rangers' 10th choice, 193rd overall, in 1982 Entry Draft.

Season	Club	League	GP	G	A	Pts	AG	AA	APts	PIM	PP	SH	GW	S	%	TGF	PGF	TGA	PGA	+/–	GP	G	A	Pts	PIM	PP	SH	GW
1980-81	HIFK Helsinki	Finland	20	1	0	1	....	....	....	4	....	....	....	....	....	....	....	....	....	....	2	0	0	0	0	....	....	....
1981-82	HIFK Helsinki	Finland	36	5	10	15	....	....	....	20	....	....	....	....	....	....	....	....	....	....	8	1	3	4	6	....	....	....
	Finland	WJC-A	7	3	3	6	....	....	....	6	....	....	....	....	....	....	....	....	....	....	....	....	....	....	....	....	....	....
1982-83	HIFK Helsinki	Finland	36	9	6	15	....	....	....	24	....	....	....	....	....	....	....	....	....	....	9	0	1	1	14	....	....	....
	Finland	WJC-A	7	3	3	6	....	....	....	4	....	....	....	....	....	....	....	....	....	....	....	....	....	....	....	....	....	....
1983-84	HIFK Helsinki	Finland	36	7	7	14	....	....	....	32	....	....	....	....	....	....	....	....	....	....	2	0	0	0	0	....	....	....
	Finland	Olympics	6	1	0	1	....	....	....	14	....	....	....	....	....	....	....	....	....	....	....	....	....	....	....	....	....	....
1984-85	**New York Rangers**	**NHL**	8	0	0	0	0	0	0	0	0	0	0	8	0.0	5	1	8	0	–4	....	....	....	....	....	....	....	....
1985-86	New Haven Nighthawks	AHL	13	3	4	7	....	....	....	11	....	....	....	....	....	....	....	....	....	....	....	....	....	....	....	....	....	....
1986-87	HIFK Helsinki	Finland	36	1	6	7	....	....	....	12	....	....	....	....	....	....	....	....	....	....	5	1	1	2	2	....	....	....
1987-88	HIFK Helsinki	Finland	39	8	11	19	....	....	....	29	....	....	....	....	....	....	....	....	....	....	6	2	2	4	2	....	....	....
	Finland	Olympics	7	0	2	2	....	....	....	4	....	....	....	....	....	....	....	....	....	....	....	....	....	....	....	....	....	....
1988-89	HIFK Helsinki	Finland	34	1	7	8	....	....	....	14	....	....	....	....	....	....	....	....	....	....	2	0	1	1	0	....	....	....
	Finland	WEC-A	5	0	0	0	....	....	....	2	....	....	....	....	....	....	....	....	....	....	....	....	....	....	....	....	....	....
1989-90	HIFK Helsinki	Finland	41	9	11	20	....	....	....	38	....	....	....	....	....	....	....	....	....	....	2	0	1	1	2	....	....	....
	Finland	WEC-A	7	0	3	3	....	....	....	8	....	....	....	....	....	....	....	....	....	....	....	....	....	....	....	....	....	....
1990-91	HIFK Helsinki	Finland	27	3	7	10	....	....	....	12	....	....	....	....	....	....	....	....	....	....	....	....	....	....	....	....	....	....
1991-92	HIFK Helsinki	Finland	43	5	18	23	....	....	....	14	....	....	....	....	....	....	....	....	....	....	....	....	....	....	....	....	....	....
	Finland	Olympics	5	0	1	1	....	....	....	6	....	....	....	....	....	....	....	....	....	....	....	....	....	....	....	....	....	....
1992-93	HIFK Helsinki	Finland	46	7	5	12	....	....	....	22	....	....	....	....	....	....	....	....	....	....	....	....	....	....	....	....	....	....
1993-94	HIFK Helsinki	Finland	40	4	5	9	....	....	....	38	....	....	....	....	....	....	....	....	....	....	....	....	....	....	....	....	....	....
1994-95	HIFK Helsinki	Finland	42	7	7	14	....	....	....	40	....	....	....	....	....	....	....	....	....	....	3	0	0	0	2	....	....	....
1995-96	HIFK Helsinki	Finland	30	4	3	7	....	....	....	32	....	....	....	....	....	....	....	....	....	....	1	1	0	1	0	....	....	....
	NHL Totals		8	0	0	0	0	0	0	0	0	0	0	8	0.0	5	1	8	0		....	....	....	....	....	....	....	....

WJC-A All-Star Team (1983) • Finnish First All-Star Team (1988)

• SABOL, SHAUN

Shaun Sabol D – L. 6'3", 230 lbs. b: Minneapolis, MN, 7/13/1966. Philadelphia's 9th choice, 209th overall, in 1986 Entry Draft.

Season	Club	League	GP	G	A	Pts	AG	AA	APts	PIM	PP	SH	GW	S	%	TGF	PGF	TGA	PGA	+/–	GP	G	A	Pts	PIM	PP	SH	GW
1983-84	St. Paul Volcans	USHL	47	6	10	16	....	....	....	32	....	....	....	....	....	....	....	....	....	....	....	....	....	....	....	....	....	....
1984-85	St. Paul Volcans	USHL	47	4	13	17	....	....	....	137	....	....	....	....	....	....	....	....	....	....	....	....	....	....	....	....	....	....
1985-86	St. Paul Volcans	USHL	46	10	19	29	....	....	....	129	....	....	....	....	....	....	....	....	....	....	....	....	....	....	....	....	....	....
1986-87	University of Wisconsin	WCHA	40	7	16	23	....	....	....	98	....	....	....	....	....	....	....	....	....	....	....	....	....	....	....	....	....	....
1987-88	University of Wisconsin	WCHA	8	4	3	7	....	....	....	10	....	....	....	....	....	....	....	....	....	....	....	....	....	....	....	....	....	....
	Hershey Bears	AHL	51	1	9	10	....	....	....	66	....	....	....	....	....	....	....	....	....	....	2	0	0	0	5	....	....	....
1988-89	Hershey Bears	AHL	58	7	11	18	....	....	....	134	....	....	....	....	....	....	....	....	....	....	12	0	2	2	35	....	....	....
1989-90	**Philadelphia Flyers**	**NHL**	2	0	0	0	0	0	0	0	0	0	0	2	0.0	1	0	1	0	0	....	....	....	....	....	....	....	....
	Hershey Bears	AHL	46	6	16	22	....	....	....	49	....	....	....	....	....	....	....	....	....	....	....	....	....	....	....	....	....	....
1990-91	Hershey Bears	AHL	59	6	13	19	....	....	....	136	....	....	....	....	....	....	....	....	....	....	7	0	1	1	34	....	....	....
1991-92	Binghamton Rangers	AHL	72	5	19	24	....	....	....	123	....	....	....	....	....	....	....	....	....	....	11	1	2	3	10	....	....	....
	NHL Totals		2	0	0	0	0	0	0	0	0	0	0	2	0.0	1	0	1	0		....	....	....	....	....	....	....	....

Traded to **NY Rangers** by **Philadelphia** for future considerations, August 5, 1991.

• SABOURIN, GARY

Gary Sabourin RW – R. 5'11", 180 lbs. b: Parry Sound, Ont., 12/4/1943.

Season	Club	League	GP	G	A	Pts	AG	AA	APts	PIM	PP	SH	GW	S	%	TGF	PGF	TGA	PGA	+/–	GP	G	A	Pts	PIM	PP	SH	GW
1962-63	Guelph Royals	OHA	42	14	26	40	....	....	....	119	....	....	....	....	....	....	....	....	....	....	....	....	....	....	....	....	....	....
1963-64	Kitchener Rangers	OHA	53	16	34	50	....	....	....	111	....	....	....	....	....	....	....	....	....	....	....	....	....	....	....	....	....	....
	St. Paul Rangers	CHL	6	2	1	3	....	....	....	9	....	....	....	....	....	....	....	....	....	....	2	0	0	0	0	....	....	....
1964-65	St. Paul Rangers	CHL	59	16	22	38	....	....	....	92	....	....	....	....	....	....	....	....	....	....	11	0	7	7	16	....	....	....
1965-66	Minnesota Rangers	CHL	66	11	30	41	....	....	....	118	....	....	....	....	....	....	....	....	....	....	7	3	1	4	16	....	....	....
1966-67	Omaha Knights	CHL	70	23	25	48	....	....	....	121	....	....	....	....	....	....	....	....	....	....	12	2	2	4	12	....	....	....
1967-68	**St. Louis Blues**	**NHL**	50	13	10	23	16	10	26	50	0	2	2	121	10.7	36	2	25	2	+11	18	4	2	6	30	1	0	1
	Kansas City Blues	CHL	18	8	10	18	....	....	....	16	....	....	....	....	....	....	....	....	....	....	....	....	....	....	....	....	....	....
1968-69	**St. Louis Blues**	**NHL**	75	25	23	48	28	22	50	58	3	0	3	228	11.0	61	12	27	1	+23	12	6	5	11	12	1	2	0
1969-70	**St. Louis Blues**	**NHL**	72	28	14	42	32	14	46	61	11	0	5	246	11.4	78	37	50	0	–9	16	5	0	5	10	0	1	1
1970-71	**St. Louis Blues**	**NHL**	59	14	17	31	15	15	30	56	2	0	2	160	8.8	48	8	36	0	+4	....	....	....	....	....	....	....	....
1971-72	**St. Louis Blues**	**NHL**	77	28	17	45	30	15	45	52	4	0	7	236	11.9	63	13	48	1	+3	11	3	3	6	6	0	0	0
1972-73	**St. Louis Blues**	**NHL**	76	21	27	48	21	23	44	30	1	0	2	240	8.8	68	9	64	0	–5	5	1	1	2	0	0	0	1
1973-74	**St. Louis Blues**	**NHL**	54	7	23	30	7	20	27	27	1	0	0	126	5.6	46	8	47	0	–9	....	....	....	....	....	....	....	....
1974-75	**Toronto Maple Leafs**	**NHL**	55	5	18	23	5	14	19	26	1	0	0	114	4.4	33	7	43	4	–13	....	....	....	....	....	....	....	....
1975-76	**California Golden Seals**	**NHL**	76	21	28	49	20	22	42	33	4	0	3	172	12.2	71	19	59	0	–7	....	....	....	....	....	....	....	....
1976-77	**Cleveland Barons**	**NHL**	33	7	11	18	7	9	16	4	2	0	1	76	9.2	27	6	27	0	–6	....	....	....	....	....	....	....	....
	NHL Totals		627	169	188	357	181	164	345	397	29	2	25	1719	9.8	531	121	426	8		62	19	11	30	58	2	3	3

Played in NHL All-Star Game (1970, 1971)

Traded to **St. Louis** by **NY Rangers** with Bob Plager, Gord Kannegiesser and Tim Eccelstone for Rod Seiling, June 6, 1967. Traded to **Toronto** by **St. Louis** for Ed Johnston, May 27, 1974. Traded to **California** by **Toronto** for Stan Weir, June 20, 1975. Transferred to **Cleveland** after **California** franchise relocated, August 26, 1976.

● SABOURIN, KEN

Ken Sabourin D – L. 6'3", 205 lbs. b: Scarborough, Ont., 4/28/1966. Calgary's 2nd choice, 33rd overall, in 1984 Entry Draft.

			REGULAR SEASON																		PLAYOFFS							
Season	Club	League	GP	G	A	Pts	AG	AA	APts	PIM	PP	SH	GW	S	%	TGF	PGF	TGA	PGA	+/–	GP	G	A	Pts	PIM	PP	SH	GW
1982-83	Sault Ste. Marie Greyhounds	OHL	58	0	8	8	....	....	....	90	....	....	....	....	....	....	....	....	....	....	10	0	0	0	14	....	....	....
1983-84	Sault Ste. Marie Greyhounds	OHL	63	7	14	21	....	....	....	157	....	....	....	....	....	....	....	....	....	....	9	0	1	1	25	....	....	....
1984-85	Sault Ste. Marie Greyhounds	OHL	63	5	19	24	....	....	....	139	....	....	....	....	....	....	....	....	....	....	16	1	4	5	10	....	....	....
1985-86	Sault Ste. Marie Greyhounds	OHL	25	1	5	6	....	....	....	77	....	....	....	....	....	....	....	....	....	....	....	....	....	....	....	....	....	....
	Cornwall Royals	OHL	37	3	12	15	....	....	....	94	....	....	....	....	....	....	....	....	....	....	6	1	2	3	6	....	....	....
	Moncton Golden Flames	AHL	3	0	0	0	....	....	....	0	....	....	....	....	....	....	....	....	....	....	6	0	1	1	2	....	....	....
1986-87	Moncton Golden Flames	AHL	75	1	10	11	....	....	....	166	....	....	....	....	....	....	....	....	....	....	6	0	1	1	27	....	....	....
1987-88	Salt Lake Golden Eagles	IHL	71	2	8	10	....	....	....	186	....	....	....	....	....	....	....	....	....	....	16	1	6	7	57	....	....	....
1988-89	**Calgary Flames**	**NHL**	**6**	**0**	**1**	**1**	**0**	**1**	**1**	**26**	**0**	**0**	**0**	**2**	**0.0**	**6**	**0**	**3**	**0**	**+3**	**1**	**0**	**0**	**0**	**0**	**0**	**0**	**0**
	Salt Lake Golden Eagles	IHL	74	2	18	20	....	....	....	197	....	....	....	....	....	....	....	....	....	....	11	0	1	1	26	....	....	....
1989-90	Calgary Flames	FrTour	3	0	0	0	....	....	....	6	....	....	....	....	....	....	....	....	....	....	....	....	....	....	....	....	....	....
	Calgary Flames	**NHL**	**5**	**0**	**0**	**0**	**0**	**0**	**0**	**10**	**0**	**0**	**0**	**3**	**0.0**	**5**	**0**	**4**	**0**	**+1**	....	....	....	....	....	....	....	....
	Salt Lake Golden Eagles	IHL	76	5	19	24	....	....	....	336	....	....	....	....	....	....	....	....	....	....	11	0	2	2	40	....	....	....
1990-91	**Calgary Flames**	**NHL**	**16**	**1**	**3**	**4**	**1**	**2**	**3**	**36**	**0**	**0**	**0**	**9**	**11.1**	**15**	**0**	**8**	**2**	**+9**	....	....	....	....	....	....	....	....
	Salt Lake Golden Eagles	IHL	28	2	15	17	....	....	....	77	....	....	....	....	....	....	....	....	....	....	....	....	....	....	....	....	....	....
	Washington Capitals	**NHL**	**28**	**1**	**4**	**5**	**1**	**3**	**4**	**81**	**0**	**0**	**0**	**14**	**7.1**	**22**	**0**	**17**	**1**	**+6**	**11**	**0**	**0**	**0**	**34**	**0**	**0**	**0**
1991-92	**Washington Capitals**	**NHL**	**19**	**0**	**0**	**0**	**0**	**0**	**0**	**48**	**0**	**0**	**0**	**12**	**0.0**	**7**	**0**	**13**	**1**	**–5**	....	....	....	....	....	....	....	....
	Baltimore Skipjacks	AHL	30	3	8	11	....	....	....	106	....	....	....	....	....	....	....	....	....	....	....	....	....	....	....	....	....	....
1992-93	Baltimore Skipjacks	AHL	30	5	14	19	....	....	....	68	....	....	....	....	....	....	....	....	....	....	....	....	....	....	....	....	....	....
	Salt Lake Golden Eagles	IHL	52	2	11	13	....	....	....	140	....	....	....	....	....	....	....	....	....	....	....	....	....	....	....	....	....	....
1993-94	Milwaukee Admirals	IHL	81	6	13	19	....	....	....	279	....	....	....	....	....	....	....	....	....	....	4	0	0	0	10	....	....	....
1994-95	Milwaukee Admirals	IHL	75	3	16	19	....	....	....	297	....	....	....	....	....	....	....	....	....	....	15	1	1	2	69	....	....	....
1995-96	Milwaukee Admirals	IHL	82	2	8	10	....	....	....	252	....	....	....	....	....	....	....	....	....	....	5	0	1	1	24	....	....	....
1996-97	Milwaukee Admirals	IHL	81	2	9	11	....	....	....	233	....	....	....	....	....	....	....	....	....	....	3	0	0	0	2	....	....	....
1997-98	Milwaukee Admirals	IHL	71	1	5	6	....	....	....	172	....	....	....	....	....	....	....	....	....	....	10	0	1	1	55	....	....	....
	NHL Totals		**74**	**2**	**8**	**10**	**2**	**6**	**8**	**201**	**0**	**0**	**0**	**40**	**5.0**	**55**	**0**	**45**	**4**		**12**	**0**	**0**	**0**	**34**	**0**	**0**	**0**

Traded to **Washington** by **Calgary** for Paul Fenton, January 24, 1991. Traded to **Calgary** by **Washington** for future considerations, December 16, 1992. Traded to **Quebec** by **Washington** with Paul MacDermid for Mike Hough, January 20, 1993.

● SACCO, DAVID

David Sacco RW – R. 6', 180 lbs. b: Malden, MA, 7/31/1970. Toronto's 4th choice, 195th overall, in 1988 Entry Draft.

			REGULAR SEASON																		PLAYOFFS							
Season	Club	League	GP	G	A	Pts	AG	AA	APts	PIM	PP	SH	GW	S	%	TGF	PGF	TGA	PGA	+/–	GP	G	A	Pts	PIM	PP	SH	GW
1987-88	Medford-Mass High School	H.S.	STATISTICS NOT AVAILABLE																									
1988-89	Boston University	H.E.	35	14	29	43	....	....	....	40	....	....	....	....	....	....	....	....	....	....	....	....	....	....	....	....	....	....
1989-90	Boston University	H.E.	3	0	4	4	....	....	....	2	....	....	....	....	....	....	....	....	....	....	....	....	....	....	....	....	....	....
1990-91	Boston University	H.E.	40	21	40	61	....	....	....	24	....	....	....	....	....	....	....	....	....	....	....	....	....	....	....	....	....	....
1991-92	Boston University	H.E.	34	13	32	45	....	....	....	30	....	....	....	....	....	....	....	....	....	....	....	....	....	....	....	....	....	....
1992-93	Boston University	H.E.	40	25	37	62	....	....	....	86	....	....	....	....	....	....	....	....	....	....	....	....	....	....	....	....	....	....
	United States	WC-A	6	0	0	0	....	....	....	0	....	....	....	....	....	....	....	....	....	....	....	....	....	....	....	....	....	....
1993-94	United States	Nat-Team	32	8	20	28	....	....	....	88	....	....	....	....	....	....	....	....	....	....	....	....	....	....	....	....	....	....
	United States	Olympics	8	3	5	8	....	....	....	12	....	....	....	....	....	....	....	....	....	....	....	....	....	....	....	....	....	....
	Toronto Maple Leafs	**NHL**	**4**	**1**	**1**	**2**	**1**	**1**	**2**	**4**	**1**	**0**	**0**	**4**	**25.0**	**2**	**2**	**2**	**0**	**–2**	....	....	....	....	....	....	....	....
	St. John's Maple Leafs	AHL	5	3	1	4	....	....	....	2	....	....	....	....	....	....	....	....	....	....	....	....	....	....	....	....	....	....
1994-95	San Diego Gulls	IHL	45	11	25	36	....	....	....	57	....	....	....	....	....	....	....	....	....	....	4	3	1	4	0	....	....	....
	Anaheim Mighty Ducks	**NHL**	**8**	**0**	**2**	**2**	**0**	**3**	**3**	**0**	**0**	**0**	**0**	**5**	**0.0**	**4**	**1**	**6**	**0**	**–3**	....	....	....	....	....	....	....	....
1995-96	**Anaheim Mighty Ducks**	**NHL**	**23**	**4**	**10**	**14**	**4**	**8**	**12**	**18**	**2**	**0**	**0**	**26**	**15.4**	**22**	**7**	**14**	**0**	**+1**	....	....	....	....	....	....	....	....
	Baltimore Bandits	AHL	25	14	16	30	....	....	....	18	....	....	....	....	....	....	....	....	....	....	2	0	1	1	4	....	....	....
1996-97	Baltimore Bandits	AHL	51	18	38	56	....	....	....	30	....	....	....	....	....	....	....	....	....	....	1	0	2	2	0	....	....	....
	SC Bern	Switz.	16	5	12	17	....	....	....	47	....	....	....	....	....	....	....	....	....	....	....	....	....	....	....	....	....	....
	SC Bern	EuroHL	3	0	0	0	....	....	....	0	....	....	....	....	....	....	....	....	....	....	....	....	....	....	....	....	....	....
	NHL Totals		**35**	**5**	**13**	**18**	**5**	**12**	**17**	**22**	**3**	**0**	**0**	**35**	**14.3**	**28**	**10**	**22**	**0**		....	....	....	....	....	....	....	....

NCAA East First All-American Team (1992, 1993) • Hockey East First All-Star Team (1992, 1993)

Traded to **Anaheim** by **Toronto** for Terry Yake, September 28, 1994. Signed as a free agent by **NY Islanders**, September 6, 1996.

● SACCO, JOE

Joe Sacco LW – L. 6'1", 195 lbs. b: Medford, MA, 2/4/1969. Toronto's 4th choice, 71st overall, in 1987 Entry Draft.

			REGULAR SEASON																		PLAYOFFS							
Season	Club	League	GP	G	A	Pts	AG	AA	APts	PIM	PP	SH	GW	S	%	TGF	PGF	TGA	PGA	+/–	GP	G	A	Pts	PIM	PP	SH	GW
1986-87	Medford-Mass High School	H.S.	21	22	32	54	....	....	....	....	....	....	....	....	....	....	....	....	....	....	....	....	....	....	....	....	....	....
1987-88	Boston University	H.E.	34	16	20	36	....	....	....	40	....	....	....	....	....	....	....	....	....	....	....	....	....	....	....	....	....	....
1988-89	Boston University	H.E.	33	21	19	40	....	....	....	66	....	....	....	....	....	....	....	....	....	....	....	....	....	....	....	....	....	....
	United States	WJC-A	7	3	1	4	....	....	....	2	....	....	....	....	....	....	....	....	....	....	....	....	....	....	....	....	....	....
1989-90	Boston University	H.E.	44	28	24	52	....	....	....	70	....	....	....	....	....	....	....	....	....	....	....	....	....	....	....	....	....	....
	United States	WEC-A	10	1	1	2	....	....	....	2	....	....	....	....	....	....	....	....	....	....	....	....	....	....	....	....	....	....
1990-91	**Toronto Maple Leafs**	**NHL**	**20**	**0**	**5**	**5**	**0**	**4**	**4**	**2**	**0**	**0**	**0**	**20**	**0.0**	**7**	**3**	**11**	**2**	**–5**	....	....	....	....	....	....	....	....
	Newmarket Saints	AHL	49	18	17	35	....	....	....	24	....	....	....	....	....	....	....	....	....	....	....	....	....	....	....	....	....	....
	United States	WEC-A	10	1	0	1	....	....	....	6	....	....	....	....	....	....	....	....	....	....	....	....	....	....	....	....	....	....
1991-92	United States	Nat-Team	50	11	26	37	....	....	....	61	....	....	....	....	....	....	....	....	....	....	....	....	....	....	....	....	....	....
	United States	Olympics	8	0	2	2	....	....	....	0	....	....	....	....	....	....	....	....	....	....	....	....	....	....	....	....	....	....
	United States	WC-A	6	1	0	1	....	....	....	4	....	....	....	....	....	....	....	....	....	....	....	....	....	....	....	....	....	....
	Toronto Maple Leafs	**NHL**	**17**	**7**	**4**	**11**	**6**	**3**	**9**	**4**	**0**	**0**	**1**	**40**	**17.5**	**16**	**0**	**8**	**0**	**+8**	....	....	....	....	....	....	....	....
	St. John's Maple Leafs	AHL	....	....	....	....	....	....	....	....	....	....	....	....	....	....	....	....	....	....	1	1	1	2	0	....	....	....
1992-93	**Toronto Maple Leafs**	**NHL**	**23**	**4**	**4**	**8**	**3**	**3**	**6**	**8**	**0**	**0**	**0**	**38**	**10.5**	**13**	**2**	**16**	**1**	**–4**	....	....	....	....	....	....	....	....
	St. John's Maple Leafs	AHL	37	14	16	30	....	....	....	45	....	....	....	....	....	....	....	....	....	....	7	6	4	10	2	....	....	....
1993-94	**Anaheim Mighty Ducks**	**NHL**	**84**	**19**	**18**	**37**	**18**	**14**	**32**	**61**	**3**	**1**	**2**	**206**	**9.2**	**52**	**10**	**70**	**17**	**–11**	....	....	....	....	....	....	....	....
	United States	WC-A	8	0	1	1	....	....	....	14	....	....	....	....	....	....	....	....	....	....	....	....	....	....	....	....	....	....
1994-95	**Anaheim Mighty Ducks**	**NHL**	**41**	**10**	**8**	**18**	**18**	**12**	**30**	**23**	**2**	**0**	**0**	**77**	**13.0**	**22**	**4**	**33**	**7**	**–8**	....	....	....	....	....	....	....	....
1995-96	**Anaheim Mighty Ducks**	**NHL**	**76**	**13**	**14**	**27**	**13**	**11**	**24**	**40**	....	....	....	....	....	....	....	....	....	....	....	....	....	....	....	....	....	....
	United States	WC-A	8	2	4	6	....	....	....	2	....	....	....	....	....	....	....	....	....	....	....	....	....	....	....	....	....	....
1996-97	**Anaheim Mighty Ducks**	**NHL**	**77**	**12**	**17**	**29**	**13**	**15**	**28**	**35**	**1**	**1**	**2**	**131**	**9.2**	**38**	**2**	**50**	**15**	**+1**	**11**	**2**	**0**	**2**	**2**	**0**	**0**	**0**
1997-98	**Anaheim Mighty Ducks**	**NHL**	**55**	**8**	**11**	**19**	**9**	**11**	**20**	**24**	**0**	**2**	**2**	**90**	**8.9**	**27**	**1**	**40**	**13**	**–1**	....	....	....	....	....	....	....	....
	New York Islanders	**NHL**	**25**	**3**	**3**	**6**	**4**	**3**	**7**	**10**	**0**	**0**	**0**	**32**	**9.4**	**9**	**0**	**11**	**3**	**+1**	....	....	....	....	....	....	....	....
	NHL Totals		**418**	**76**	**84**	**160**	**84**	**76**	**160**	**207**	**6**	**4**	**7**	**634**	**12.0**	**184**	**22**	**239**	**58**		**11**	**2**	**0**	**2**	**2**	**0**	**0**	**0**

Claimed by **Anaheim** from **Toronto** in Expansion Draft, June 24, 1993. Traded to **NY Islanders** by **Anaheim** with J.J. Daigneault and Mark Janssens for Travis Green, Doug Houda and Tony Tuzzolino, February 6, 1998.

● SACHARUK, LAWRENCE

Lawrence Sacharuk D – R. 6', 200 lbs. b: Saskatoon, Sask., 9/16/1952. NY Rangers' 3rd choice, 21st overall, in 1972 Amateur Draft.

			REGULAR SEASON																		PLAYOFFS							
Season	Club	League	GP	G	A	Pts	AG	AA	APts	PIM	PP	SH	GW	S	%	TGF	PGF	TGA	PGA	+/–	GP	G	A	Pts	PIM	PP	SH	GW
1967-68	Saskatoon Blades	WCJHL	34	6	2	8	....	....	....	4	....	....	....	....	....	....	....	....	....	....	....	....	....	....	....	....	....	....
1968-69	Saskatoon Blades	WCJHL	56	5	11	16	....	....	....	39	....	....	....	....	....	....	....	....	....	....	....	....	....	....	....	....	....	....
1969-70	Niagara Falls Flyers	OHA	51	19	18	37	....	....	....	47	....	....	....	....	....	....	....	....	....	....	....	....	....	....	....	....	....	....
1970-71	Saskatoon Blades	WCJHL	59	27	58	85	....	....	....	42	....	....	....	....	....	....	....	....	....	....	....	....	....	....	....	....	....	....
1971-72	Saskatoon Blades	WCJHL	65	50	36	86	....	....	....	57	....	....	....	....	....	....	....	....	....	....	....	....	....	....	....	....	....	....
1972-73	**New York Rangers**	**NHL**	**8**	**1**	**0**	**1**	**1**	**0**	**1**	**0**	**0**	**0**	**0**	**9**	**11.1**	**4**	**0**	**5**	**0**	**–1**	....	....	....	....	....	....	....	....
	Providence Reds	AHL	64	14	35	49	....	....	....	42	....	....	....	....	....	....	....	....	....	....	4	0	1	1	0	....	....	....
1973-74	**New York Rangers**	**NHL**	**23**	**2**	**4**	**6**	**2**	**3**	**5**	**4**	**1**	**0**	**2**	**50**	**4.0**	**20**	**5**	**16**	**1**	**0**	....	....	....	....	....	....	....	....
	Providence Reds	AHL	42	27	35	62	....	....	....	26	....	....	....	....	....	....	....	....	....	....	15	1	*14	15	4	....	....	....
1974-75	**St. Louis Blues**	**NHL**	**76**	**20**	**22**	**42**	**19**	**17**	**36**	**24**	**11**	**0**	**1**	**207**	**9.7**	**87**	**32**	**69**	**5**	**–9**	**2**	**1**	**1**	**2**	**2**	**0**	**0**	**0**
1975-76	**New York Rangers**	**NHL**	**42**	**6**	**7**	**13**	**6**	**5**	**11**	**14**	**4**	**0**	**2**	**70**	**8.6**	**32**	**21**	**26**	**1**	**–14**	....	....	....	....	....	....	....	....
1976-77	**New York Rangers**	**NHL**	**2**	**0**	**0**	**0**	**0**	**0**	**0**	**0**	**0**	**0**	**0**	**2**	**0.0**	**1**	**1**	**1**	**0**	**–1**	....	....	....	....	....	....	....	....
	New Haven Nighthawks	AHL	55	23	31	54	....	....	....	18	....	....	....	....	....	....	....	....	....	....	....	....	....	....	....	....	....	....
1977-78	New Haven Nighthawks	AHL	72	19	37	58	....	....	....	12	....	....	....	....	....	....	....	....	....	....	11	0	5	5	0	....	....	....
1978-79	Indianapolis Racers	WHA	15	2	9	11	....	....	....	25	....	....	....	....	....	....	....	....	....	....	....	....	....	....	....	....	....	....

			REGULAR SEASON																		PLAYOFFS							
Season	Club	League	GP	G	A	Pts	AG	AA	APts	PIM	PP	SH	GW	S	%	TGF	PGF	TGA	PGA	+/–	GP	G	A	Pts	PIM	PP	SH	GW
1979-80	Birmingham Bulls	CHL	80	11	29	40	....	....	....	28	....	....	....	....	....	....	....	....	....	....	4	0	0	0	0	....	....	....
1980-81	EC Sparkasse Innsbruck	Austria	34	35	23	58	....	....	....	34	....	....	....	....	....	....	....	....	....	....	....	....	....	....	....	....	....	....
1981-82	WAT Stadlau	Austria	....	12	10	22	....	....	....	....	....	....	....	....	....	....	....	....	....	....	....	....	....	....	....	....	....	....
	NHL Totals		**151**	**29**	**33**	**62**	**28**	**25**	**53**	**42**	**16**	**0**	**5**	**338**	**8.6**	**144**	**59**	**117**	**7**		**2**	**1**	**1**	**2**	**2**	**0**	**0**	**0**
	Other Major League Totals		15	2	9	11	....	....	....	25	....	....	....	....	....	....	....	....	....		....	....	....	....	....	....	....	....

WCJHL Second All-Star Team (1972)

Selected by **NY Raiders** (WHA) in 1972 WHA General Player Draft, February 12, 1972. Traded to **NY Rangers** by **St. Louis** for Bob MacMillan, September 20, 1975. Traded to **St. Louis** by **NY Rangers** with NY Rangers' 1st round choice (Lucien DeBlois) in 1977 Amateur Draft for Greg Polis, August 29, 1974. Signed as a free agent by **Indianapolis** (WHA), July, 1978.

• SAGANIUK, ROCKY

Rocky (Ray) Saganiuk RW/C – R. 5'8", 185 lbs. b: Myrnam, Alta., 10/15/1957. Toronto's 4th choice, 29th overall, in 1977 Amateur Draft.

Season	Club	League	GP	G	A	Pts	AG	AA	APts	PIM	PP	SH	GW	S	%	TGF	PGF	TGA	PGA	+/–	GP	G	A	Pts	PIM	PP	SH	GW
1974-75	Taber Gold Suns	AJHL	50	21	32	53	....	....	....	124	....	....	....	....	....	....	....	....	....	....	....	....	....	....	....	....	....	....
1975-76	Taber Gold Suns	AJHL	49	42	32	74	....	....	....	169	....	....	....	....	....	....	....	....	....	....	....	....	....	....	....	....	....	....
	Kamloops Chiefs	WCJHL	4	0	0	0	....	....	....	0	....	....	....	....	....	....	....	....	....	....	....	....	....	....	....	....	....	....
	Lethbridge Broncos	WCJHL	6	2	1	3	....	....	....	0	....	....	....	....	....	....	....	....	....	....	5	2	1	3	6	....	....	....
1976-77	Lethbridge Broncos	WCHL	72	60	48	108	....	....	....	203	....	....	....	....	....	....	....	....	....	....	15	6	5	11	21	....	....	....
1977-78	Dallas Black Hawks	CHL	42	16	13	29	....	....	....	71	....	....	....	....	....	....	....	....	....	....	....	....	....	....	....	....	....	....
1978-79	**Toronto Maple Leafs**	**NHL**	**16**	**3**	**5**	**8**	**3**	**4**	**7**	**9**	**1**	**0**	**1**	**30**	**10.0**	**15**	**4**	**10**	**0**	**+1**	**3**	**1**	**0**	**1**	**5**	**0**	**0**	**0**
	New Brunswick Hawks	AHL	62	*47	29	76	....	....	....	91	....	....	....	....	....	....	....	....	....	....	....	....	....	....	....	....	....	....
1979-80	**Toronto Maple Leafs**	**NHL**	**75**	**24**	**23**	**47**	**22**	**18**	**40**	**52**	**3**	**0**	**4**	**164**	**14.6**	**67**	**9**	**63**	**0**	**–5**	**3**	**0**	**0**	**0**	**10**	**0**	**0**	**0**
1980-81	**Toronto Maple Leafs**	**NHL**	**71**	**12**	**18**	**30**	**10**	**13**	**23**	**52**	**2**	**0**	**3**	**113**	**10.6**	**51**	**9**	**58**	**0**	**–16**	....	....	....	....	....	....	....	....
1981-82	**Toronto Maple Leafs**	**NHL**	**65**	**17**	**16**	**33**	**13**	**11**	**24**	**49**	**0**	**0**	**1**	**100**	**17.0**	**47**	**0**	**63**	**0**	**–16**	....	....	....	....	....	....	....	....
1982-83	**Toronto Maple Leafs**	**NHL**	**3**	**0**	**0**	**0**	**0**	**0**	**0**	**2**	**0**	**0**	**0**	**0**	**0.0**	**0**	**0**	**3**	**0**	**–3**	....	....	....	....	....	....	....	....
	St. Catharines Saints	AHL	61	26	23	49	....	....	....	83	....	....	....	....	....	....	....	....	....	....	....	....	....	....	....	....	....	....
1983-84	**Pittsburgh Penguins**	**NHL**	**29**	**1**	**3**	**4**	**1**	**2**	**3**	**37**	**0**	**0**	**0**	**30**	**3.3**	**7**	**0**	**23**	**4**	**–12**	....	....	....	....	....	....	....	....
	Baltimore Skipjacks	AHL	5	1	1	2	....	....	....	0	....	....	....	....	....	....	....	....	....	....	....	....	....	....	....	....	....	....
1984-85	St. Catharines Saints	AHL	4	1	1	2	....	....	....	11	....	....	....	....	....	....	....	....	....	....	....	....	....	....	....	....	....	....
1985-86			DID NOT PLAY																									
1986-87	Brantford Motts Clamatos	OHA Sr.	STATISTICS NOT AVAILABLE																									
1987-88	Ayr Bruins	Britain	14	19	20	39	....	....	....	50	....	....	....	....	....	....	....	....	....	....	....	....	....	....	....	....	....	....
1988-89	Ayr Bruins	Britain	22	27	28	55	....	....	....	82	....	....	....	....	....	....	....	....	....	....	....	....	....	....	....	....	....	....
1989-90	Ayr Bruins	Britain	DID NOT PLAY – COACHING																									
1990-91	Peterborough Pirates	Britain	DID NOT PLAY – COACHING																									
1991-92	Peterborough Pirates	Britain	4	6	4	10	....	....	....	2	....	....	....	....	....	....	....	....	....	....	....	....	....	....	....	....	....	....
1992-93	Peterborough Pirates	Britain	DID NOT PLAY – COACHING																									
1993-94	Murrayfield Racers	Britain	3	4	3	7	....	....	....	4	....	....	....	....	....	....	....	....	....	....	....	....	....	....	....	....	....	....
1994-95	Durham Wasps	Britain	2	1	2	3	....	....	....	6	....	....	....	....	....	....	....	....	....	....	....	....	....	....	....	....	....	....
	Blackburn Hawks	Britain	DID NOT PLAY – COACHING																									
	NHL Totals		**259**	**57**	**65**	**122**	**49**	**48**	**97**	**201**	**6**	**0**	**9**	**437**	**13.0**	**187**	**22**	**220**	**4**		**6**	**1**	**0**	**1**	**15**	**0**	**0**	**0**

AHL First All-Star Team (1979) • Won Les Cunningham Award (MVP - AHL) (1979)

Traded to **Pittsburgh** by **Toronto** with Vincent Tremblay for Pat Graham and Nick Ricci, August 15, 1983.

• ST. AMOUR, MARTIN

Martin St. Amour LW – L. 6'3", 194 lbs. b: Montreal, Que., 1/30/1970. Montreal's 2nd choice, 34th overall, in 1988 Entry Draft.

Season	Club	League	GP	G	A	Pts	AG	AA	APts	PIM	PP	SH	GW	S	%	TGF	PGF	TGA	PGA	+/–	GP	G	A	Pts	PIM	PP	SH	GW
1986-87	Laval Canadiens	Midget	52	55	95	150	....	....	....	58	....	....	....	....	....	....	....	....	....	....	....	....	....	....	....	....	....	....
1987-88	Verdun Jr. Canadiens	QMJHL	61	20	50	70	....	....	....	111	....	....	....	....	....	....	....	....	....	....	....	....	....	....	....	....	....	....
1988-89	Verdun Jr. Canadiens	QMJHL	28	19	17	36	....	....	....	87	....	....	....	....	....	....	....	....	....	....	....	....	....	....	....	....	....	....
	Trois-Rivieres Draveurs	QMJHL	26	8	21	29	....	....	....	69	....	....	....	....	....	....	....	....	....	....	4	1	2	3	0	....	....	....
1989-90	Trois-Rivieres Draveurs	QMJHL	60	57	79	136	....	....	....	162	....	....	....	....	....	....	....	....	....	....	7	7	9	16	19	....	....	....
	Sherbrooke Canadiens	AHL	....	....	....	....	....	....	....	....	....	....	....	....	....	....	....	....	....	....	1	0	0	0	0	....	....	....
1990-91	Fredericton Canadiens	AHL	45	13	16	29	....	....	....	51	....	....	....	....	....	....	....	....	....	....	1	0	0	0	0	....	....	....
1991-92	Cincinnati Cyclones	ECHL	60	44	44	88	....	....	....	183	....	....	....	....	....	....	....	....	....	....	9	4	9	13	18	....	....	....
1992-93	**Ottawa Senators**	**NHL**	**1**	**0**	**0**	**0**	**0**	**0**	**0**	**2**	**0**	**0**	**0**	**2**	**0.0**	**0**	**0**	**0**	**0**	**0**	....	....	....	....	....	....	....	....
	New Haven Nighthawks	AHL	71	21	39	60	....	....	....	78	....	....	....	....	....	....	....	....	....	....	....	....	....	....	....	....	....	....
1993-94	P.E.I. Senators	AHL	37	13	12	25	....	....	....	65	....	....	....	....	....	....	....	....	....	....	....	....	....	....	....	....	....	....
	Providence Bruins	AHL	12	0	3	3	....	....	....	22	....	....	....	....	....	....	....	....	....	....	....	....	....	....	....	....	....	....
1994-95	Whitley Warriors	Britain	2	1	1	2	....	....	....	16	....	....	....	....	....	....	....	....	....	....	....	....	....	....	....	....	....	....
1995-96	San Francisco Spiders	IHL	4	0	2	2	....	....	....	6	....	....	....	....	....	....	....	....	....	....	....	....	....	....	....	....	....	....
	Los Angeles Ice Dogs	IHL	1	0	0	0	....	....	....	0	....	....	....	....	....	....	....	....	....	....	....	....	....	....	....	....	....	....
	San Diego Gulls	WCHL	53	*61	48	*109	....	....	....	....	....	....	....	....	....	....	....	....	....	....	9	6	7	13	10	....	....	....
1996-97	San Diego Gulls	WCHL	59	*60	67	*127	....	....	....	170	....	....	....	....	....	....	....	....	....	....	8	*8	4	12	23	....	....	....
1997-98	San Diego Gulls	WCHL	61	35	44	79	....	....	....	203	....	....	....	....	....	....	....	....	....	....	12	11	7	18	28	....	....	....
	NHL Totals		**1**	**0**	**0**	**0**	**0**	**0**	**0**	**2**	**0**	**0**	**0**	**2**	**0.0**	**0**	**0**	**0**	**0**		....	....	....	....	....	....	....	....

WCHL First All-Star Team (1996, 1997) • Named WCHL's MVP (1997)

Signed as a free agent by **Ottawa**, July 16, 1992.

• ST. LAURENT, ANDRE

Andre St. Laurent C – R. 5'10", 180 lbs. b: Rouyn-Noranda, Que., 2/16/1953. NY Islanders' 3rd choice, 49th overall, in 1973 Amateur Draft.

Season	Club	League	GP	G	A	Pts	AG	AA	APts	PIM	PP	SH	GW	S	%	TGF	PGF	TGA	PGA	+/–	GP	G	A	Pts	PIM	PP	SH	GW
1970-71	Montreal Jr. Canadiens	OHA	60	13	27	40	....	....	....	127	....	....	....	....	....	....	....	....	....	....	....	....	....	....	....	....	....	....
1971-72	Montreal Jr. Canadiens	QMJHL	63	18	34	52	....	....	....	161	....	....	....	....	....	....	....	....	....	....	....	....	....	....	....	....	....	....
1972-73	Montreal Jr. Canadiens	QMJHL	64	52	48	100	....	....	....	245	....	....	....	....	....	....	....	....	....	....	4	1	2	3	0	....	....	....
1973-74	**New York Islanders**	**NHL**	**42**	**5**	**9**	**14**	**5**	**8**	**13**	**18**	**0**	**0**	**0**	**75**	**6.7**	**17**	**1**	**15**	**0**	**+1**	....	....	....	....	....	....	....	....
	Fort Worth Wings	CHL	32	14	19	33	....	....	....	53	....	....	....	....	....	....	....	....	....	....	5	2	2	4	12	....	....	....
1974-75	**New York Islanders**	**NHL**	**78**	**14**	**27**	**41**	**13**	**21**	**34**	**60**	**1**	**0**	**0**	**186**	**7.5**	**62**	**7**	**33**	**0**	**+22**	**15**	**2**	**2**	**4**	**6**	**1**	**0**	**0**
1975-76	**New York Islanders**	**NHL**	**67**	**9**	**17**	**26**	**8**	**13**	**21**	**56**	**0**	**0**	**2**	**101**	**8.9**	**38**	**2**	**23**	**1**	**+14**	**13**	**1**	**5**	**6**	**15**	**0**	**0**	**0**
	Fort Worth Texans	CHL	3	1	2	3	....	....	....	2	....	....	....	....	....	....	....	....	....	....	....	....	....	....	....	....	....	....
1976-77	**New York Islanders**	**NHL**	**72**	**10**	**13**	**23**	**10**	**11**	**21**	**55**	**2**	**0**	**3**	**96**	**10.4**	**41**	**4**	**29**	**0**	**+8**	**12**	**1**	**2**	**3**	**6**	**0**	**0**	**1**
1977-78	**New York Islanders**	**NHL**	**2**	**0**	**0**	**0**	**0**	**0**	**0**	**2**	**0**	**0**	**0**	**5**	**0.0**	**0**	**0**	**0**	**0**	**0**	....	....	....	....	....	....	....	....
	Detroit Red Wings	**NHL**	**77**	**31**	**39**	**70**	**30**	**32**	**62**	**108**	**10**	**0**	**4**	**193**	**16.1**	**90**	**30**	**66**	**13**	**+7**	**7**	**1**	**1**	**2**	**4**	**0**	**0**	**0**
1978-79	**Detroit Red Wings**	**NHL**	**76**	**18**	**31**	**49**	**16**	**24**	**40**	**124**	**4**	**1**	**1**	**158**	**11.4**	**66**	**22**	**91**	**16**	**–31**	....	....	....	....	....	....	....	....
1979-80	**Los Angeles Kings**	**NHL**	**77**	**6**	**24**	**30**	**5**	**18**	**23**	**88**	**1**	**0**	**0**	**121**	**5.0**	**42**	**9**	**62**	**16**	**–13**	**4**	**1**	**0**	**1**	**0**	**0**	**1**	**1**
1980-81	**Los Angeles Kings**	**NHL**	**22**	**10**	**6**	**16**	**8**	**4**	**12**	**63**	**0**	**0**	**2**	**33**	**30.3**	**20**	**0**	**12**	**0**	**+8**	**3**	**0**	**1**	**1**	**9**	**0**	**0**	**0**
	Fort Worth Texans	CHL	12	1	14	15	....	....	....	36	....	....	....	....	....	....	....	....	....	....	....	....	....	....	....	....	....	....
	Houston Apollos	CHL	3	1	0	1	....	....	....	4	....	....	....	....	....	....	....	....	....	....	....	....	....	....	....	....	....	....
1981-82	**Los Angeles Kings**	**NHL**	**16**	**2**	**4**	**6**	**2**	**3**	**5**	**28**	**0**	**1**	**0**	**27**	**7.4**	**10**	**1**	**19**	**12**	**+2**	....	....	....	....	....	....	....	....
	New Haven Nighthawks	AHL	28	7	9	16	....	....	....	58	....	....	....	....	....	....	....	....	....	....	....	....	....	....	....	....	....	....
	Pittsburgh Penguins	**NHL**	**18**	**8**	**5**	**13**	**6**	**3**	**9**	**4**	**1**	**0**	**1**	**33**	**24.2**	**20**	**2**	**21**	**8**	**+5**	**5**	**2**	**1**	**3**	**8**	**0**	**0**	**0**
1982-83	**Pittsburgh Penguins**	**NHL**	**70**	**13**	**9**	**22**	**11**	**6**	**17**	**105**	....	....	....	....	....	....	....	....	....	....	....	....	....	....	....	....	....	....
1983-84	**Pittsburgh Penguins**	**NHL**	**8**	**2**	**0**	**2**	**2**	**0**	**2**	**21**	....	....	....	....	....	....	....	....	....	....	....	....	....	....	....	....	....	....
	Detroit Red Wings	**NHL**	**19**	**1**	**3**	**4**	**1**	**2**	**3**	**17**	....	....	....	....	....	....	....	....	....	....	....	....	....	....	....	....	....	....
	Adirondack Red Wings	AHL	50	26	43	69	....	....	....	129	....	....	....	....	....	....	....	....	....	....	7	4	4	8	23	....	....	....
1984-85	Adirondack Red Wings	AHL	35	10	23	33	....	....	....	68	....	....	....	....	....	....	....	....	....	....	....	....	....	....	....	....	....	....
	NHL Totals		**644**	**129**	**187**	**316**	**117**	**145**	**262**	**749**	**19**	**2**	**13**	**1028**	**12.5**	**406**	**78**	**371**	**66**		**59**	**8**	**12**	**20**	**48**	**1**	**1**	**2**

Traded to **Detroit** by **NY Islanders** for Michel Bergeron, October 20, 1977. Traded to **LA Kings** by **Detroit** with Detroit's 1st round choice (Larry Murphy) in 1980 Entry Draft and 1st round choice (Doug Smith) in 1981 Entry Draft for Dale McCourt, August 22, 1979. Claimed on waivers by **Pittsburgh** from **LA Kings**, February 23, 1982. Traded to **Detroit** by **Pittsburgh** for future considerations, October 24, 1983.

• ST. MARSEILLE, FRANK

Frank St. Marseille RW – R. 5'11", 180 lbs. b: Levack, Ont., 12/14/1939.

Season	Club	League	GP	G	A	Pts	AG	AA	APts	PIM	PP	SH	GW	S	%	TGF	PGF	TGA	PGA	+/–	GP	G	A	Pts	PIM	PP	SH	GW
1961-62	New Haven Blades	EHL	3	0	0	0	....	....	....	9	....	....	....	....	....	....	....	....	....	....	....	....	....	....	....	....	....	....
1962-63	Sudbury Wolves	EPHL	3	0	2	2	....	....	....	0	....	....	....	....	....	....	....	....	....	....	....	....	....	....	....	....	....	....
	Chatham Maroons	OHA Sr.	45	17	22	39	....	....	....	49	....	....	....	....	....	....	....	....	....	....	10	4	1	5	4	....	....	....
1963-64	Chatham Maroons	IHL	70	31	33	64	....	....	....	21	....	....	....	....	....	....	....	....	....	....	....	....	....	....	....	....	....	....
1964-65	Port Huron Flags	IHL	70	38	59	97	....	....	....	57	....	....	....	....	....	....	....	....	....	....	7	2	5	7	24	....	....	....

Season	Club	League	GP	G	A	Pts	AG	AA	APts	PIM	PP	SH	GW	S	%	TGF	PGF	TGA	PGA	+/–	GP	G	A	Pts	PIM	PP	SH	GW
			REGULAR SEASON																		PLAYOFFS							
1965-66	Port Huron Flags	IHL	68	45	45	90	....	....	....	28	....	....	....	....	....	....	....	....	....	....	9	6	6	12	12	....	....	....
1966-67	Port Huron Flags	IHL	72	41	77	118	....	....	....	46	....	....	....	....	....	....	....	....	....	....	....	....	....	....	....	....	....	....
1967-68	**St. Louis Blues**	**NHL**	**57**	**16**	**16**	**32**	**20**	**17**	**37**	**12**	**1**	**0**	**1**	**147**	**10.9**	**40**	**6**	**23**	**0**	**+11**	**18**	**5**	**8**	**13**	**0**	**4**	**0**	**0**
	Kansas City Blues	CHL	11	7	8	15	....	....	....	0	....	....	....	....	....	....	....	....	....	....	....	....	....	....	....	....	....	....
1968-69	**St. Louis Blues**	**NHL**	**72**	**12**	**26**	**38**	**13**	**24**	**37**	**22**	**3**	**0**	**3**	**169**	**7.1**	**55**	**16**	**19**	**0**	**+20**	**12**	**3**	**3**	**6**	**2**	**0**	**0**	**0**
1969-70	**St. Louis Blues**	**NHL**	**74**	**16**	**43**	**59**	**18**	**43**	**61**	**18**	**3**	**0**	**1**	**166**	**9.6**	**90**	**47**	**46**	**0**	**–3**	**15**	**6**	**7**	**13**	**4**	**3**	**1**	**0**
1970-71	**St. Louis Blues**	**NHL**	**77**	**19**	**32**	**51**	**20**	**28**	**48**	**26**	**3**	**0**	**5**	**217**	**8.8**	**72**	**26**	**42**	**0**	**+4**	**6**	**2**	**1**	**3**	**4**	**2**	**0**	**1**
1971-72	**St. Louis Blues**	**NHL**	**78**	**16**	**36**	**52**	**17**	**33**	**50**	**32**	**1**	**0**	**1**	**228**	**7.0**	**67**	**15**	**48**	**1**	**+5**	**11**	**3**	**5**	**8**	**6**	**1**	**0**	**0**
1972-73	**St. Louis Blues**	**NHL**	**45**	**7**	**18**	**25**	**7**	**15**	**22**	**8**	**3**	**0**	**0**	**119**	**5.9**	**38**	**11**	**33**	**0**	**–6**	....	....	....	....	....	....	....	....
	Los Angeles Kings	**NHL**	**29**	**7**	**4**	**11**	**7**	**3**	**10**	**2**	**2**	**0**	**2**	**65**	**10.8**	**20**	**4**	**17**	**0**	**–1**	....	....	....	....	....	....	....	....
1973-74	**Los Angeles Kings**	**NHL**	**78**	**14**	**36**	**50**	**14**	**31**	**45**	**40**	**2**	**0**	**1**	**190**	**7.4**	**71**	**14**	**62**	**6**	**+1**	**5**	**0**	**0**	**0**	**0**	**0**	**0**	**0**
1974-75	**Los Angeles Kings**	**NHL**	**80**	**17**	**36**	**53**	**16**	**28**	**44**	**46**	**0**	**0**	**1**	**168**	**10.1**	**72**	**10**	**54**	**4**	**+12**	**3**	**0**	**1**	**1**	**0**	**0**	**0**	**0**
1975-76	**Los Angeles Kings**	**NHL**	**68**	**10**	**16**	**26**	**9**	**13**	**22**	**20**	**2**	**0**	**1**	**66**	**15.2**	**33**	**10**	**37**	**0**	**–14**	**9**	**0**	**0**	**0**	**0**	**0**	**0**	**0**
1976-77	**Los Angeles Kings**	**NHL**	**49**	**6**	**22**	**28**	**6**	**18**	**24**	**16**	**1**	**0**	**0**	**74**	**8.1**	**46**	**7**	**39**	**1**	**+1**	**9**	**1**	**0**	**1**	**2**	**0**	**0**	**0**
	Fort Worth Texans	CHL	16	6	12	18	....	....	....	4	....	....	....	....	....	....	....	....	....	....	....	....	....	....	....	....	....	....
1977-78	Nova Scotia Voyageurs	AHL	74	14	14	28	....	....	....	38	....	....	....	....	....	....	....	....	....	....	11	3	2	5	0	....	....	....
	NHL Totals		**707**	**140**	**285**	**425**	**147**	**253**	**400**	**242**	**21**	**0**	**16**	**1609**	**8.7**	**604**	**166**	**420**	**12**		**88**	**20**	**25**	**45**	**18**	**10**	**1**	**1**

IHL Second All-Star Team (1967)

Played in NHL All-Star Game (1970)

Signed as a free agent by **St. Louis**, November 23, 1967. Traded to **LA Kings** by **St. Louis** for Paul Curtis, January 27, 1973.

• ST. SAUVEUR, CLAUDE

Claude St. Sauveur C – L. 6'1", 185 lbs. b: Sherbrooke, Que., 1/2/1952. California's 4th choice, 54th overall, in 1972 Amateur Draft.

Season	Club	League	GP	G	A	Pts	AG	AA	APts	PIM	PP	SH	GW	S	%	TGF	PGF	TGA	PGA	+/–	GP	G	A	Pts	PIM	PP	SH	GW
1969-70	Sherbrooke Castors	QJHL	26	23	18	41	....	....	....	6	....	....	....	....	....	....	....	....	....	....	....	....	....	....	....	....	....	....
1970-71	Sherbrooke Castors	QMJHL	62	52	67	119	....	....	....	80	....	....	....	....	....	....	....	....	....	....	10	11	9	20	10	....	....	....
1971-72	Sherbrooke Castors	QMJHL	60	53	58	111	....	....	....	97	....	....	....	....	....	....	....	....	....	....	4	1	2	3	4	....	....	....
1972-73	Roanoke Valley Rebels	EHL	62	55	52	107	....	....	....	99	....	....	....	....	....	....	....	....	....	....	16	11	13	24	0	....	....	....
	Philadelphia Blazers	WHA	2	1	0	1	....	....	....	0	....	....	....	....	....	....	....	....	....	....	....	....	....	....	....	....	....	....
1973-74	Vancouver Blazers	WHA	70	38	30	68	....	....	....	55	....	....	....	....	....	....	....	....	....	....	....	....	....	....	....	....	....	....
1974-75	Vancouver Blazers	WHA	76	24	23	47	....	....	....	32	....	....	....	....	....	....	....	....	....	....	....	....	....	....	....	....	....	....
1975-76	**Atlanta Flames**	**NHL**	**79**	**24**	**24**	**48**	**22**	**19**	**41**	**23**	**11**	**0**	**2**	**171**	**14.0**	**67**	**32**	**41**	**0**	**–6**	**2**	**0**	**0**	**0**	**0**	**0**	**0**	**0**
1976-77	Calgary Cowboys	WHA	17	0	3	3	....	....	....	2	....	....	....	....	....	....	....	....	....	....	....	....	....	....	....	....	....	....
	Tidewater Sharks	SHL	6	5	7	12	....	....	....	0	....	....	....	....	....	....	....	....	....	....	....	....	....	....	....	....	....	....
	Edmonton Oilers	WHA	15	5	7	12	....	....	....	2	....	....	....	....	....	....	....	....	....	....	5	1	0	1	0	....	....	....
1977-78	Indianapolis Racers	WHA	72	36	42	78	....	....	....	24	....	....	....	....	....	....	....	....	....	....	....	....	....	....	....	....	....	....
1978-79	Indianapolis Racers	WHA	17	4	2	6	....	....	....	12	....	....	....	....	....	....	....	....	....	....	....	....	....	....	....	....	....	....
	Cincinnati Stingers	WHA	16	4	5	9	....	....	....	4	....	....	....	....	....	....	....	....	....	....	....	....	....	....	....	....	....	....
1979-80	Milwaukee Admirals	IHL	43	38	57	95	....	....	....	91	....	....	....	....	....	....	....	....	....	....	1	0	0	0	0	....	....	....
1980-81	Milwaukee Admirals	IHL	54	34	2	62	....	....	....	88	....	....	....	....	....	....	....	....	....	....	5	2	3	5	6	....	....	....
	NHL Totals		**79**	**24**	**24**	**48**	**22**	**19**	**41**	**23**	**11**	**0**	**2**	**171**	**14.0**	**67**	**32**	**41**	**0**		**2**	**0**	**0**	**0**	**0**	**0**	**0**	**0**
	Other Major League Totals		285	112	112	224	....	....	....	131	....	....	....	....	....	....	....	....	....		5	1	0	1	0	....	....	....

QMJHL First All-Star Team (1972) • EHL Rookie of the Year (1973) • IHL Second All-Star Team (1980)

Selected by **Miami-Philadelphia** (WHA) in 1972 WHA General Player Draft, February 12, 1972. Transferred to **Vancouver** (WHA) after **Philadelphia** (WHA) franchise relocated, May, 1973. Traded to **Atlanta** by **California** for cash, September 23, 1975. WHA rights transferred to **Calgary** (WHA) after **Vancouver** (WHA) franchise relocated, May 7, 1975. Traded to **Edmonton** (WHA) by **Calgary** (WHA) with Wayne Connelly for cash, January, 1977. Traded to **Indianapolis** (WHA) by **Edmonton** (WHA) with Blair MacDonald, Barry Wilkins, Rusty Patenaude and Kevin Devine for Dave Inkpen and Mike Zuke, September, 1977. Signed as a free agent by **Cincinnati** (WHA) after **Indianapolis** (WHA) franchise folded, December 15, 1978.

• SAKIC, JOE

Joe Sakic C – L. 5'11", 185 lbs. b: Burnaby, B.C., 7/7/1969. Quebec's 2nd choice, 15th overall, in 1987 Entry Draft.

Season	Club	League	GP	G	A	Pts	AG	AA	APts	PIM	PP	SH	GW	S	%	TGF	PGF	TGA	PGA	+/–	GP	G	A	Pts	PIM	PP	SH	GW
1986-87	Swift Current Broncos	WHL	72	60	73	133	....	....	....	31	....	....	....	....	....	....	....	....	....	....	4	0	1	1	0	....	....	....
	Canada	Nat-Team	1	0	0	0	....	....	....	0	....	....	....	....	....	....	....	....	....	....	....	....	....	....	....	....	....	....
1987-88	Swift Current Broncos	WHL	64	*78	82	*160	....	....	....	64	....	....	....	....	....	....	....	....	....	....	10	11	13	24	12	....	....	....
	Canada	WJC-A	7	3	1	4	....	....	....	2	....	....	....	....	....	....	....	....	....	....	....	....	....	....	....	....	....	....
1988-89	**Quebec Nordiques**	**NHL**	**70**	**23**	**39**	**62**	**20**	**27**	**47**	**24**	**10**	**0**	**2**	**148**	**15.5**	**96**	**59**	**86**	**12**	**–36**	....	....	....	....	....	....	....	....
1989-90	**Quebec Nordiques**	**NHL**	**80**	**39**	**63**	**102**	**34**	**45**	**79**	**27**	**8**	**1**	**2**	**234**	**16.7**	**139**	**58**	**132**	**11**	**–40**	....	....	....	....	....	....	....	....
1990-91	**Quebec Nordiques**	**NHL**	**80**	**48**	**61**	**109**	**44**	**46**	**90**	**24**	**12**	**3**	**7**	**245**	**19.0**	**132**	**48**	**164**	**54**	**–26**	....	....	....	....	....	....	....	....
	Canada	WEC-A	10	6	5	11	....	....	....	0	....	....	....	....	....	....	....	....	....	....	....	....	....	....	....	....	....	....
1991-92	**Quebec Nordiques**	**NHL**	**69**	**29**	**65**	**94**	**26**	**49**	**75**	**20**	**6**	**3**	**1**	**217**	**13.4**	**124**	**46**	**97**	**24**	**+5**	....	....	....	....	....	....	....	....
1992-93	**Quebec Nordiques**	**NHL**	**78**	**48**	**57**	**105**	**40**	**39**	**79**	**40**	**20**	**2**	**4**	**264**	**18.2**	**160**	**76**	**104**	**27**	**–3**	**6**	**3**	**3**	**6**	**2**	**1**	**0**	**0**
1993-94	**Quebec Nordiques**	**NHL**	**84**	**28**	**64**	**92**	**26**	**50**	**76**	**18**	**10**	**1**	**9**	**279**	**10.0**	**121**	**49**	**105**	**25**	**–8**	....	....	....	....	....	....	....	....
	Canada	WC-A	8	4	3	7	....	....	....	0	....	....	....	....	....	....	....	....	....	....	....	....	....	....	....	....	....	....
1994-95	**Quebec Nordiques**	**NHL**	**47**	**19**	**43**	**62**	**34**	**63**	**97**	**30**	**3**	**2**	**5**	**157**	**12.1**	**82**	**36**	**49**	**10**	**+7**	**6**	**4**	**1**	**5**	**0**	**1**	**1**	**1**
1995-96	**Colorado Avalanche**	**NHL**	**82**	**51**	**69**	**120**	**50**	**57**	**107**	**44**	**17**	**6**	**7**	**339**	**15.0**	**159**	**74**	**85**	**14**	**+14**	**22**	***18**	**16**	***34**	**14**	**6**	**0**	**6**
1996-97	Canada	W Cup	8	2	2	4	....	....	....	6	....	....	....	....	....	....	....	....	....	....	....	....	....	....	....	....	....	....
	Colorado Avalanche	**NHL**	**65**	**22**	**52**	**74**	**23**	**46**	**69**	**34**	**10**	**2**	**5**	**261**	**8.4**	**107**	**58**	**67**	**8**	**–10**	**17**	**8**	***17**	**25**	**14**	**3**	**0**	**0**
1997-98	**Colorado Avalanche**	**NHL**	**64**	**27**	**36**	**63**	**32**	**35**	**67**	**50**	**12**	**1**	**2**	**254**	**10.6**	**90**	**45**	**53**	**8**	**0**	**6**	**2**	**3**	**5**	**6**	**0**	**1**	**2**
	Canada	Olympics	4	1	2	3	....	....	....	4	....	....	....	....	....	....	....	....	....	....	....	....	....	....	....	....	....	....
	NHL Totals		**719**	**334**	**549**	**883**	**329**	**457**	**786**	**311**	**108**	**21**	**44**	**2398**	**13.9**	**1200**	**549**	**941**	**193**		**57**	**35**	**40**	**75**	**36**	**11**	**2**	**9**

WHL East Second All-Star Team (1987) • Canadian Major Junior Player of the Year (1988) • WHL East First All-Star Team (1988) • Won Conn Smythe Trophy (1996)

Played in NHL All-Star Game (1990, 1991, 1992, 1993, 1994, 1996, 1998)

Transferred to **Colorado** after **Quebec** franchise relocated, June 21, 1995.

• SALEI, RUSLAN

Ruslan Salei D – L. 6'2", 205 lbs. b: Minsk, USSR, 11/2/1974. Anaheim's 1st choice, 9th overall, in 1996 Entry Draft.

Season	Club	League	GP	G	A	Pts	AG	AA	APts	PIM	PP	SH	GW	S	%	TGF	PGF	TGA	PGA	+/–	GP	G	A	Pts	PIM	PP	SH	GW
1992-93	Dynamo Minsk	CIS	9	1	0	1	....	....	....	10	....	....	....	....	....	....	....	....	....	....	....	....	....	....	....	....	....	....
1993-94	Tivali Minsk	CIS	39	2	3	5	....	....	....	50	....	....	....	....	....	....	....	....	....	....	....	....	....	....	....	....	....	....
	Belarus	WC-C1	6	1	1	2	....	....	....	10	....	....	....	....	....	....	....	....	....	....	....	....	....	....	....	....	....	....
1994-95	Tivali Minsk	CIS	51	4	2	6	....	....	....	44	....	....	....	....	....	....	....	....	....	....	....	....	....	....	....	....	....	....
	Belarus	WC-C1	4	0	1	1	....	....	....	4	....	....	....	....	....	....	....	....	....	....	....	....	....	....	....	....	....	....
1995-96	Las Vegas Thunder	IHL	76	7	23	30	....	....	....	123	....	....	....	....	....	....	....	....	....	....	15	3	7	10	18	....	....	....
1996-97	**Anaheim Mighty Ducks**	**NHL**	**30**	**0**	**1**	**1**	**0**	**1**	**1**	**37**	**0**	**0**	**0**	**14**	**0.0**	**12**	**1**	**20**	**1**	**–8**	....	....	....	....	....	....	....	....
	Baltimore Bandits	AHL	12	1	4	5	....	....	....	12	....	....	....	....	....	....	....	....	....	....	....	....	....	....	....	....	....	....
	Las Vegas Thunder	IHL	8	0	2	2	....	....	....	24	....	....	....	....	....	....	....	....	....	....	3	2	1	3	6	....	....	....
1997-98	**Anaheim Mighty Ducks**	**NHL**	**66**	**5**	**10**	**15**	**6**	**10**	**16**	**70**	**1**	**0**	**0**	**104**	**4.8**	**53**	**12**	**49**	**15**	**+7**	....	....	....	....	....	....	....	....
	Cincinnati Mighty Ducks	AHL	6	3	6	9	....	....	....	14	....	....	....	....	....	....	....	....	....	....	....	....	....	....	....	....	....	....
	Belarus	Olympics	7	1	0	1	....	....	....	4	....	....	....	....	....	....	....	....	....	....	....	....	....	....	....	....	....	....
	Belarus	WC-A	2	1	0	1	....	....	....	2	....	....	....	....	....	....	....	....	....	....	....	....	....	....	....	....	....	....
	NHL Totals		**96**	**5**	**11**	**16**	**6**	**11**	**17**	**107**	**1**	**0**	**0**	**118**	**4.2**	**65**	**13**	**69**	**16**		....	....	....	....	....	....	....	....

• SALESKI, DON

Don "Big Bird" Saleski RW – R. 6'3", 205 lbs. b: Moose Jaw, Sask., 11/10/1949. Philadelphia's 6th choice, 64th overall, in 1969 Amateur Draft.

Season	Club	League	GP	G	A	Pts	AG	AA	APts	PIM	PP	SH	GW	S	%	TGF	PGF	TGA	PGA	+/–	GP	G	A	Pts	PIM	PP	SH	GW
1966-67	Regina Pats	SJHL	38	3	2	5	....	....	....	6	....	....	....	....	....	....	....	....	....	....	3	0	0	0	0	....	....	....
1967-68	Regina Pats	SJHL	58	6	9	15	....	....	....	34	....	....	....	....	....	....	....	....	....	....	....	....	....	....	....	....	....	....
1968-69	Regina Pats	SJHL	STATISTICS NOT AVAILABLE																									
1969-70	Winnipeg–Saskatoon	WCJHL	5	1	1	2	....	....	....	10	....	....	....	....	....	....	....	....	....	....	....	....	....	....	....	....	....	....
1970-71	Quebec Aces	AHL	72	9	7	16	....	....	....	51	....	....	....	....	....	....	....	....	....	....	1	0	0	0	0	....	....	....
1971-72	**Philadelphia Flyers**	**NHL**	**1**	**0**	**0**	**0**	**0**	**0**	**0**	**0**	**0**	**0**	**0**	**2**	**0.0**	**0**	**0**	**1**	**0**	**–1**	....	....	....	....	....	....	....	....
	Richmond Robins	AHL	73	22	35	57	....	....	....	111	....	....	....	....	....	....	....	....	....	....	....	....	....	....	....	....	....	....
1972-73	**Philadelphia Flyers**	**NHL**	**78**	**12**	**9**	**21**	**12**	**8**	**20**	**205**	**1**	**1**	**2**	**158**	**7.6**	**36**	**3**	**57**	**4**	**–20**	**11**	**1**	**2**	**3**	**4**	**0**	**0**	**0**
1973-74	**Philadelphia Flyers**	**NHL**	**77**	**15**	**25**	**40**	**15**	**22**	**37**	**131**	**2**	**2**	**3**	**157**	**9.6**	**60**	**8**	**32**	**1**	**+21**	**17**	**2**	**7**	**9**	**24**	**0**	**0**	**0**
1974-75	**Philadelphia Flyers**	**NHL**	**63**	**10**	**18**	**28**	**9**	**14**	**23**	**107**	**0**	**0**	**2**	**113**	**8.8**	**39**	**1**	**34**	**3**	**+7**	**17**	**2**	**3**	**5**	**25**	**0**	**0**	**1**
1975-76	**Philadelphia Flyers**	**NHL**	**78**	**21**	**26**	**47**	**20**	**20**	**40**	**68**	**1**	**1**	**4**	**224**	**9.4**	**74**	**7**	**47**	**13**	**+33**	**16**	**6**	**5**	**11**	**47**	**0**	**1**	**1**
1976-77	**Philadelphia Flyers**	**NHL**	**74**	**22**	**16**	**38**	**21**	**13**	**34**	**33**	**2**	**2**	**6**	**156**	**14.1**	**68**	**8**	**51**	**15**	**+24**	**10**	**0**	**0**	**0**	**12**	**0**	**0**	**0**
1977-78	**Philadelphia Flyers**	**NHL**	**70**	**27**	**18**	**45**	**26**	**15**	**41**	**44**	**5**	**4**	**1**	**163**	**16.6**	**69**	**10**	**40**	**15**	**+34**	**11**	**2**	**0**	**2**	**19**	**0**	**0**	**1**

Season	Club	League	GP	G	A	Pts	AG	AA	APts	PIM	PP	SH	GW	S	%	TGF	PGF	TGA	PGA	+/-	GP	G	A	Pts	PIM	PP	SH	GW
			REGULAR SEASON																		PLAYOFFS							
1978-79	Philadelphia Flyers	NHL	35	11	5	16	10	4	14	14	1	1	2	75	14.7	25	4	24	6	+3	....	....	....	....	....	....	....	....
	Colorado Rockies	NHL	16	2	0	2	2	0	2	4	0	0	0	50	4.0	5	1	20	6	–10	....	....	....	....	....	....	....	....
1979-80	Colorado Rockies	NHL	51	8	8	16	7	6	13	23	0	0	0	68	11.8	31	4	54	10	–17	....	....	....	....	....	....	....	....
	Fort Worth Texans	CHL	19	9	6	15	....	....	....	18	....	....	....	....	....	....	....	....	....	....	14	5	6	11	20	....	....	....
	NHL Totals		543	128	125	253	122	102	224	629	12	11	20	1166	11.0	407	46	360	73		82	13	17	30	131	0	1	3

Traded to **Colorado** by **Philadelphia** for future considerations, March 3, 1979.

• SALMING, BORJE

Borje "King" Salming D – L. 6'1", 193 lbs. b: Kiruna, Sweden, 4/17/1951. **HHOF**

Season	Club	League	GP	G	A	Pts	AG	AA	APts	PIM	PP	SH	GW	S	%	TGF	PGF	TGA	PGA	+/-	GP	G	A	Pts	PIM	PP	SH	GW
1970-71	Brynas IF Gavle	Sweden	14	0	5	5	....	....	....	6	....	....	....	....	....	....	....	....	....	....	13	2	1	3	16	....	....	....
1971-72	Brynas IF Gavle	Sweden	14	1	1	2	....	....	....	20	....	....	....	....	....	....	....	....	....	....	14	0	4	4	30	....	....	....
	Sweden	WEC-A	4	0	0	0	....	....	....	6	....	....	....	....	....	....	....	....	....	....	....	....	....	....	....	....	....	....
1972-73	Brynas IF Gavle	Sweden	14	2	3	5	....	....	....	10	....	....	....	....	....	....	....	....	....	....	12	3	1	4	24	....	....	....
	Sweden	WEC-A	10	4	6	10	....	....	....	8	....	....	....	....	....	....	....	....	....	....	....	....	....	....	....	....	....	....
1973-74	Toronto Maple Leafs	NHL	76	5	34	39	5	29	34	48	3	0	0	130	3.8	115	22	78	23	+38	4	0	1	1	4	0	0	0
1974-75	Toronto Maple Leafs	NHL	60	12	25	37	11	20	31	34	4	1	1	136	8.8	96	22	109	39	+4	7	0	4	4	6	0	0	0
1975-76	Toronto Maple Leafs	NHL	78	16	41	57	15	32	47	70	8	0	1	194	8.2	177	53	134	43	+33	10	3	4	7	9	1	0	0
1976-77	Sweden	C Cup	5	4	3	7	....	....	....	2	....	....	....	....	....	....	....	....	....	....	....	....	....	....	....	....	....	....
	Toronto Maple Leafs	NHL	76	12	66	78	11	54	65	46	1	0	0	186	6.5	182	48	120	31	+45	9	3	6	9	6	2	0	0
1977-78	Toronto Maple Leafs	NHL	80	16	60	76	15	49	64	70	6	0	5	258	6.2	157	50	111	34	+30	6	2	2	4	6	0	0	1
1978-79	Toronto Maple Leafs	NHL	78	17	56	73	15	43	58	76	4	0	2	230	7.4	149	46	103	36	+36	6	0	1	1	8	0	0	0
	NHL All-Stars	Chal Cup	3	0	0	0	....	....	....	2	....	....	....	....	....	....	....	....	....	....	....	....	....	....	....	....	....	....
1979-80	Toronto Maple Leafs	NHL	74	19	52	71	17	40	57	94	4	0	1	222	8.6	174	56	155	41	+4	3	1	1	2	2	1	0	0
1980-81	Toronto Maple Leafs	NHL	72	5	61	66	4	43	47	154	1	1	1	210	2.4	146	58	131	43	0	3	0	2	2	4	0	0	0
1981-82	Sweden	C Cup	5	0	2	2	....	....	....	10	....	....	....	....	....	....	....	....	....	....	....	....	....	....	....	....	....	....
	Toronto Maple Leafs	NHL	69	12	44	56	9	29	38	170	1	0	0	175	6.9	143	37	155	53	+4	....	....	....	....	....	....	....	....
1982-83	Toronto Maple Leafs	NHL	69	7	38	45	6	26	32	104	2	1	0	110	6.4	129	40	131	39	–3	4	1	4	5	10	1	0	0
1983-84	Toronto Maple Leafs	NHL	68	5	38	43	4	26	30	92	2	1	0	160	3.1	121	33	182	60	–34	....	....	....	....	....	....	....	....
1984-85	Toronto Maple Leafs	NHL	73	6	33	39	5	22	27	76	3	0	0	181	3.3	115	39	147	45	–26	....	....	....	....	....	....	....	....
1985-86	Toronto Maple Leafs	NHL	41	7	15	22	6	10	16	48	3	1	1	71	9.9	67	24	66	16	–7	10	1	6	7	14	0	0	0
1986-87	Toronto Maple Leafs	NHL	56	4	16	20	3	12	15	42	0	1	1	71	5.6	89	8	92	28	+17	13	0	3	3	14	0	0	0
1987-88	Toronto Maple Leafs	NHL	66	2	24	26	2	17	19	82	1	0	0	92	2.2	105	18	114	34	+7	6	1	3	4	8	0	0	0
1988-89	Toronto Maple Leafs	NHL	63	3	17	20	3	12	15	86	1	0	0	58	5.2	75	13	92	37	+7	....	....	....	....	....	....	....	....
	Sweden	WEC-A	8	1	1	2	....	....	....	8	....	....	....	....	....	....	....	....	....	....	....	....	....	....	....	....	....	....
1989-90	Detroit Red Wings	NHL	49	2	17	19	2	12	14	52	2	0	0	52	3.8	71	13	57	19	+20	....	....	....	....	....	....	....	....
1990-91	AIK Solna	Sweden	36	4	9	13	....	....	....	46	....	....	....	....	....	....	....	....	....	....	....	....	....	....	....	....	....	....
1991-92	Sweden	C Cup	6	0	0	0	....	....	....	10	....	....	....	....	....	....	....	....	....	....	....	....	....	....	....	....	....	....
	AIK Solna	Sweden	38	6	14	20	....	....	....	*98	....	....	....	....	....	....	....	....	....	....	3	0	2	2	6	....	....	....
	Sweden	Olympics	8	4	3	7	....	....	....	4	....	....	....	....	....	....	....	....	....	....	....	....	....	....	....	....	....	....
1992-93	AIK Solna	Sweden	6	1	0	1	....	....	....	10	....	....	....	....	....	....	....	....	....	....	....	....	....	....	....	....	....	....
	NHL Totals		1148	150	637	787	133	476	609	1344	46	6	13	2536	5.9	2111	580	1977	621		81	12	37	49	91	5	0	1

Named Best Defenseman at EJC-A (1969) • WEC-A All-Star Team (1973) • NHL Second All-Star Team (1975, 1976, 1978, 1979, 1980) • Canada Cup All-Star Team (1976) • NHL First All-Star Team (1977) • Swedish World All-Star Team (1989)

Played in NHL All-Star Game (1976, 1977, 1978)

Signed as a free agent by **Toronto**, May 12, 1973. Signed as a free agent by **Detroit**, June 12, 1989.

• SALOVAARA, JOHN BARRY

John Barry Salovaara D – R. 5'10", 180 lbs. b: Cooksville, Ont., 1/7/1948.

Season	Club	League	GP	G	A	Pts	AG	AA	APts	PIM	PP	SH	GW	S	%	TGF	PGF	TGA	PGA	+/-	GP	G	A	Pts	PIM	PP	SH	GW
1965-66	St. Catharines Black Hawks	OHA	47	3	13	16	....	....	....	67	....	....	....	....	....	....	....	....	....	....	7	0	2	2	8	....	....	....
1966-67	St. Catharines Black Hawks	OHA	48	7	18	25	....	....	....	99	....	....	....	....	....	....	....	....	....	....	6	1	1	2	4	....	....	....
1967-68	St. Catharines Black Hawks	OHA	38	6	20	26	....	....	....	96	....	....	....	....	....	....	....	....	....	....	....	....	....	....	....	....	....	....
1968-69	Greensboro Generals	EHL	57	6	15	21	....	....	....	106	....	....	....	....	....	....	....	....	....	....	8	0	1	1	19	....	....	....
	Dallas Black Hawks	CHL	4	0	1	1	....	....	....	8	....	....	....	....	....	....	....	....	....	....	....	....	....	....	....	....	....	....
1969-70	Greensboro Generals	EHL	74	11	35	46	....	....	....	141	....	....	....	....	....	....	....	....	....	....	16	1	13	14	45	....	....	....
1970-71	Greensboro Generals	EHL	72	15	53	68	....	....	....	95	....	....	....	....	....	....	....	....	....	....	9	0	7	7	29	....	....	....
1971-72	Fort Worth Wings	CHL	34	3	14	17	....	....	....	42	....	....	....	....	....	....	....	....	....	....	....	....	....	....	....	....	....	....
	Tidewater Wings	AHL	36	0	13	13	....	....	....	36	....	....	....	....	....	....	....	....	....	....	....	....	....	....	....	....	....	....
1972-73	Tidewater Wings	AHL	76	4	26	30	....	....	....	92	....	....	....	....	....	....	....	....	....	....	13	3	1	4	16	....	....	....
1973-74	Baltimore Clippers	AHL	70	8	25	33	....	....	....	95	....	....	....	....	....	....	....	....	....	....	9	1	5	6	22	....	....	....
1974-75	Detroit Red Wings	NHL	27	0	2	2	0	2	2	18	0	0	0	18	0.0	15	0	31	5	–11	....	....	....	....	....	....	....	....
	Virginia Wings	AHL	43	2	17	19	....	....	....	50	....	....	....	....	....	....	....	....	....	....	5	1	0	1	7	....	....	....
1975-76	Detroit Red Wings	NHL	63	2	11	13	2	9	11	52	1	0	1	57	3.5	36	1	48	6	–7	....	....	....	....	....	....	....	....
	New Haven Nighthawks	AHL	6	1	3	4	....	....	....	14	....	....	....	....	....	....	....	....	....	....	....	....	....	....	....	....	....	....
	NHL Totals		90	2	13	15	2	11	13	70	1	0	1	75	2.7	51	1	79	11		....	....	....	....	....	....	....	....

Traded to **Detroit** (Tidewater - AHL) by **Chicago** (Greensboro-EHL) for cash, June 15, 1971.

• SALVIAN, DAVE

Dave Salvian RW – L. 5'10", 170 lbs. b: Toronto, Ont., 9/9/1955. NY Islanders' 2nd choice, 29th overall, in 1975 Amateur Draft.

Season	Club	League	GP	G	A	Pts	AG	AA	APts	PIM	PP	SH	GW	S	%	TGF	PGF	TGA	PGA	+/-	GP	G	A	Pts	PIM	PP	SH	GW
1972-73	St. Catharines Black Hawks	OHA	51	12	12	24	....	....	....	66	....	....	....	....	....	....	....	....	....	....	....	....	....	....	....	....	....	....
1973-74	St. Catharines Black Hawks	OHA	66	36	61	97	....	....	....	113	....	....	....	....	....	....	....	....	....	....	....	....	....	....	....	....	....	....
1974-75	St. Catharines Black Hawks	OHA	57	44	48	92	....	....	....	81	....	....	....	....	....	....	....	....	....	....	....	....	....	....	....	....	....	....
1975-76	Fort Worth Texans	CHL	74	38	21	59	....	....	....	72	....	....	....	....	....	....	....	....	....	....	....	....	....	....	....	....	....	....
1976-77	Fort Worth Texans	CHL	75	36	24	60	....	....	....	57	....	....	....	....	....	....	....	....	....	....	6	1	2	3	2	....	....	....
	New York Islanders	NHL	....	....	....	....	....	....	....	....	....	....	....	....	....	....	....	....	....	....	1	0	1	1	2	....	....	....
1977-78	Fort Worth Texans	CHL	68	12	22	34	....	....	....	58	....	....	....	....	....	....	....	....	....	....	14	3	3	6	10	....	....	....
1978-79	Fort Worth Texans	CHL	56	11	13	24	....	....	....	45	....	....	....	....	....	....	....	....	....	....	....	....	....	....	....	....	....	....
	Fort Wayne Komets	IHL	14	1	2	3	....	....	....	2	....	....	....	....	....	....	....	....	....	....	13	3	3	6	6	....	....	....
1979-80	Dallas Black Hawks	CHL	76	24	19	43	....	....	....	22	....	....	....	....	....	....	....	....	....	....	....	....	....	....	....	....	....	....
	NHL Totals		0	0	0	0	0	0	0	0	0	0	0	0	0.0	0	0	0	0		1	0	1	1	2	0	0	0

OHA Second All-Star Team (1975)

• SAMPSON, GARY

Gary Sampson LW – L. 6', 190 lbs. b: Atikokan, Ont., 8/24/1959.

Season	Club	League	GP	G	A	Pts	AG	AA	APts	PIM	PP	SH	GW	S	%	TGF	PGF	TGA	PGA	+/-	GP	G	A	Pts	PIM	PP	SH	GW
1978-79	Boston College	ECAC	30	10	18	28	....	....	....	4	....	....	....	....	....	....	....	....	....	....	....	....	....	....	....	....	....	....
1979-80	Boston College	ECAC	24	6	18	24	....	....	....	8	....	....	....	....	....	....	....	....	....	....	....	....	....	....	....	....	....	....
1980-81	Boston College	ECAC	31	8	16	24	....	....	....	8	....	....	....	....	....	....	....	....	....	....	....	....	....	....	....	....	....	....
1981-82	Boston College	ECAC	21	7	11	18	....	....	....	22	....	....	....	....	....	....	....	....	....	....	....	....	....	....	....	....	....	....
1982-83	United States	Nat-Team	40	11	20	31	....	....	....	8	....	....	....	....	....	....	....	....	....	....	....	....	....	....	....	....	....	....
1983-84	United States	Nat-Team	57	21	18	39	....	....	....	10	....	....	....	....	....	....	....	....	....	....	....	....	....	....	....	....	....	....
	United States	Olympics	6	1	2	3	....	....	....	2	....	....	....	....	....	....	....	....	....	....	....	....	....	....	....	....	....	....
	Washington Capitals	NHL	15	1	1	2	1	1	2	6	0	0	0	17	5.9	5	0	4	0	+1	8	1	0	1	0	0	0	0
1984-85	Washington Capitals	NHL	46	10	15	25	8	10	18	13	0	1	0	53	18.9	38	0	23	5	+20	4	0	0	0	0	0	0	0
	Binghamton Whalers	AHL	5	2	2	4	....	....	....	2	....	....	....	....	....	....	....	....	....	....	....	....	....	....	....	....	....	....
1985-86	Washington Capitals	NHL	19	1	4	5	1	3	4	2	0	0	1	17	5.9	5	1	9	2	–3	....	....	....	....	....	....	....	....
	Binghamton Whalers	AHL	49	9	21	30	....	....	....	16	....	....	....	....	....	....	....	....	....	....	6	2	2	4	4	....	....	....
1986-87	Washington Capitals	NHL	25	1	2	3	1	1	2	4	0	0	0	14	7.1	6	0	19	4	–9	....	....	....	....	....	....	....	....
	Binghamton Whalers	AHL	37	12	16	28	....	....	....	10	....	....	....	....	....	....	....	....	....	....	11	4	2	6	0	....	....	....
1987-88	Baltimore Skipjacks	AHL	16	2	4	6	....	....	....	4	....	....	....	....	....	....	....	....	....	....	....	....	....	....	....	....	....	....
	NHL Totals		105	13	22	35	11	15	26	25	0	1	1	101	12.9	54	1	55	11		12	1	0	1	0	0	0	0

Signed as a free agent by **Washington**, February 21, 1984.

• SAMSONOV, SERGEI Sergei Samsonov LW – R. 5'8", 184 lbs. b: Moscow, USSR, 10/27/1978. Boston's 2nd choice, 8th overall, in 1997 Entry Draft.

Season	Club	League	GP	G	A	Pts	AG	AA	APts	PIM	PP	SH	GW	S	%	TGF	PGF	TGA	PGA	+/–	GP	G	A	Pts	PIM	PP	SH	GW
1994-95	CSKA Moscow	CIS Jr.	50	110	72	182	....	....	....	....	....	....	....	....	....	....	....	....	....	....	....	....	....	....	....	....	....	....
	CSKA Moscow	CIS	13	2	2	4	....	....	....	14	....	....	....	....	....	....	....	....	....	....	2	0	0	0	0	....	....	....
1995-96	CSKA Moscow	CIS	51	21	17	38	....	....	....	12	....	....	....	....	....	....	....	....	....	....	3	1	1	2	4	....	....	....
	Russia	WJC-A	7	4	2	6	....	....	....	0	....	....	....	....	....	....	....	....	....	....	....	....	....	....	....	....	....	....
1996-97	Detroit Vipers	IHL	73	29	35	64	....	....	....	18	....	....	....	....	....	....	....	....	....	....	19	8	4	12	12	....	....	....
	Russia	WJC-A	6	6	1	7	....	....	....	0	....	....	....	....	....	....	....	....	....	....	....	....	....	....	....	....	....	....
1997-98	**Boston Bruins**	**NHL**	**81**	**22**	**25**	**47**	**26**	**24**	**50**	**8**	**7**	**0**	**3**	**159**	**13.8**	**64**	**22**	**33**	**0**	**+9**	**6**	**2**	**5**	**7**	**0**	**0**	**0**	**1**
	NHL Totals		**81**	**22**	**25**	**47**	**26**	**24**	**50**	**8**	**7**	**0**	**3**	**159**	**13.8**	**64**	**22**	**33**	**0**		**6**	**2**	**5**	**7**	**0**	**0**	**0**	**1**

EJC-A All-Star Team (1995, 1996) • Named Best Forward at EJC-A (1995) • WJC-A All-Star Team (1997) • Won Garry F. Longman Memorial Trophy (Top Rookie - IHL) (1997) • NHL All-Rookie Team (1998 • Won Calder Memorial Trophy (1998)

• SAMUELSSON, KJELL Kjell Samuelsson D – R. 6'6", 235 lbs. b: Tyngsryd, Sweden, 10/18/1958. NY Rangers' 4th choice, 119th overall, in 1984 Entry Draft.

Season	Club	League	GP	G	A	Pts	AG	AA	APts	PIM	PP	SH	GW	S	%	TGF	PGF	TGA	PGA	+/–	GP	G	A	Pts	PIM	PP	SH	GW
1977-78	Tyngsryd	Sweden 2	20	3	0	3	....	....	....	41	....	....	....	....	....	....	....	....	....	....	....	....	....	....	....	....	....	....
1978-79	Tyngsryd	Sweden 2	24	3	4	7	....	....	....	67	....	....	....	....	....	....	....	....	....	....	....	....	....	....	....	....	....	....
1979-80	Tyngsryd	Sweden 2	26	5	4	9	....	....	....	45	....	....	....	....	....	....	....	....	....	....	....	....	....	....	....	....	....	....
1980-81	Tyngsryd	Sweden 2	35	6	7	13	....	....	....	61	....	....	....	....	....	....	....	....	....	....	2	0	1	1	14	....	....	....
1981-82	Tyngsryd	Sweden 2	33	11	14	25	....	....	....	68	....	....	....	....	....	....	....	....	....	....	3	0	2	2	2	....	....	....
1982-83	Tyngsryd	Sweden 2	32	11	6	17	....	....	....	57	....	....	....	....	....	....	....	....	....	....	....	....	....	....	....	....	....	....
1983-84	Leksands IF	Sweden	36	6	6	12	....	....	....	59	....	....	....	....	....	....	....	....	....	....	....	....	....	....	....	....	....	....
1984-85	Leksands IF	Sweden	35	9	5	14	....	....	....	34	....	....	....	....	....	....	....	....	....	....	....	....	....	....	....	....	....	....
1985-86	**New York Rangers**	**NHL**	**9**	**0**	**0**	**0**	**0**	**0**	**0**	**10**	**0**	**0**	**0**	**7**	**0.0**	**4**	**0**	**8**	**3**	**–1**	**9**	**0**	**1**	**1**	**8**	**0**	**0**	**0**
	New Haven Nighthawks	AHL	56	6	21	27	....	....	....	87	....	....	....	....	....	....	....	....	....	....	3	0	0	0	10	....	....	....
1986-87	**New York Rangers**	**NHL**	**30**	**2**	**6**	**8**	**2**	**4**	**6**	**50**	**0**	**0**	**0**	**20**	**10.0**	**39**	**7**	**39**	**5**	**–2**	....	....	....	....	....	....	....	....
	Philadelphia Flyers	**NHL**	**46**	**1**	**6**	**7**	**1**	**4**	**5**	**86**	**0**	**0**	**0**	**28**	**3.6**	**35**	**2**	**52**	**10**	**–9**	**26**	**0**	**4**	**4**	**25**	**0**	**0**	**0**
1987-88	**Philadelphia Flyers**	**NHL**	**74**	**6**	**24**	**30**	**5**	**17**	**22**	**184**	**3**	**0**	**0**	**118**	**5.1**	**117**	**29**	**92**	**32**	**+28**	**7**	**2**	**5**	**7**	**23**	**0**	**0**	**1**
1988-89	**Philadelphia Flyers**	**NHL**	**69**	**3**	**14**	**17**	**3**	**10**	**13**	**140**	**0**	**1**	**0**	**60**	**5.0**	**80**	**3**	**108**	**44**	**+13**	**19**	**1**	**3**	**4**	**24**	**0**	**0**	**0**
1989-90	**Philadelphia Flyers**	**NHL**	**66**	**5**	**17**	**22**	**4**	**12**	**16**	**91**	**0**	**0**	**1**	**88**	**5.7**	**88**	**4**	**110**	**46**	**+20**	....	....	....	....	....	....	....	....
1990-91	**Philadelphia Flyers**	**NHL**	**70**	**9**	**19**	**28**	**8**	**14**	**22**	**82**	**1**	**0**	**3**	**101**	**8.9**	**74**	**7**	**112**	**49**	**+4**	....	....	....	....	....	....	....	....
	Sweden	WEC-A	10	2	2	4	....	....	....	12	....	....	....	....	....	....	....	....	....	....	....	....	....	....	....	....	....	....
1991-92	Sweden	C Cup	6	1	0	1	....	....	....	16	....	....	....	....	....	....	....	....	....	....	....	....	....	....	....	....	....	....
	Philadelphia Flyers	**NHL**	**54**	**4**	**9**	**13**	**4**	**7**	**11**	**76**	**0**	**0**	**0**	**63**	**6.3**	**44**	**2**	**69**	**28**	**+1**	....	....	....	....	....	....	....	....
	Pittsburgh Penguins	**NHL**	**20**	**1**	**2**	**3**	**1**	**1**	**2**	**34**	**0**	**0**	**1**	**28**	**3.6**	**21**	**0**	**31**	**10**	**0**	**15**	**0**	**3**	**3**	**12**	**0**	**0**	**0**
1992-93	**Pittsburgh Penguins**	**NHL**	**63**	**3**	**6**	**9**	**2**	**4**	**6**	**106**	**0**	**0**	**1**	**63**	**4.8**	**61**	**3**	**64**	**31**	**+25**	**12**	**0**	**3**	**3**	**2**	**0**	**0**	**0**
1993-94	**Pittsburgh Penguins**	**NHL**	**59**	**5**	**8**	**13**	**5**	**6**	**11**	**118**	**1**	**0**	**0**	**57**	**8.8**	**61**	**5**	**59**	**21**	**+18**	**6**	**0**	**0**	**0**	**26**	**0**	**0**	**0**
1994-95	**Pittsburgh Penguins**	**NHL**	**41**	**1**	**6**	**7**	**2**	**9**	**11**	**54**	**0**	**0**	**0**	**37**	**2.7**	**39**	**2**	**52**	**23**	**+8**	**11**	**0**	**1**	**1**	**32**	**0**	**0**	**0**
1995-96	**Philadelphia Flyers**	**NHL**	**75**	**3**	**11**	**14**	**3**	**9**	**12**	**81**	**0**	**0**	**1**	**62**	**4.8**	**70**	**1**	**67**	**18**	**+20**	**12**	**1**	**0**	**1**	**24**	**0**	**0**	**0**
1996-97	**Philadelphia Flyers**	**NHL**	**34**	**4**	**3**	**7**	**4**	**3**	**7**	**47**	**0**	**0**	**0**	**36**	**11.1**	**31**	**0**	**19**	**5**	**+17**	**5**	**0**	**0**	**0**	**2**	**0**	**0**	**0**
1997-98	**Philadelphia Flyers**	**NHL**	**49**	**0**	**3**	**3**	**0**	**3**	**3**	**28**	**0**	**0**	**0**	**23**	**0.0**	**27**	**0**	**33**	**15**	**+9**	**1**	**0**	**0**	**0**	**0**	**0**	**0**	**0**
	NHL Totals		**767**	**47**	**134**	**181**	**44**	**103**	**147**	**1187**	**5**	**1**	**7**	**791**	**5.9**	**791**	**65**	**915**	**340**		**123**	**4**	**20**	**24**	**178**	**0**	**0**	**1**

Played in NHL All-Star Game (1988)

Traded to **Philadelphia** by **NY Rangers** with NY Rangers' 2nd round choice (Patrik Juhlin) in 1989 Entry Draft for Bob Froese, December 18, 1986. Traded to **Pittsburgh** by **Philadelphia** with Rick Tocchet, Ken Wregget and Philadelphia's 3rd round choice (Dave Roche) in 1993 Entry Draft for Mark Recchi, Brian Benning and LA Kings' 1st round choice (previously acquired, Philadelphia selected Jason Bowen) in 1992 Entry Draft, February 19, 1992. Signed as a free agent by **Philadelphia**, August 31, 1995.

• SAMUELSSON, ULF Ulf Samuelsson D – L. 6'1", 205 lbs. b: Fagersta, Sweden, 3/26/1964. Hartford's 4th choice, 67th overall, in 1982 Entry Draft.

Season	Club	League	GP	G	A	Pts	AG	AA	APts	PIM	PP	SH	GW	S	%	TGF	PGF	TGA	PGA	+/–	GP	G	A	Pts	PIM	PP	SH	GW
1981-82	Leksands IF	Sweden	31	3	1	4	....	....	....	40	....	....	....	....	....	....	....	....	....	....	....	....	....	....	....	....	....	....
	Sweden	WJC-A	7	1	2	3	....	....	....	10	....	....	....	....	....	....	....	....	....	....	....	....	....	....	....	....	....	....
1982-83	Leksands IF	Sweden	33	9	6	15	....	....	....	72	....	....	....	....	....	....	....	....	....	....	....	....	....	....	....	....	....	....
	Sweden	WJC-A	1	0	1	1	....	....	....	....	....	....	....	....	....	....	....	....	....	....	....	....	....	....	....	....	....	....
1983-84	Leksands IF	Sweden	36	5	11	16	....	....	....	53	....	....	....	....	....	....	....	....	....	....	....	....	....	....	....	....	....	....
	Sweden	WJC-A	7	1	4	5	....	....	....	18	....	....	....	....	....	....	....	....	....	....	....	....	....	....	....	....	....	....
1984-85	**Hartford Whalers**	**NHL**	**41**	**2**	**6**	**8**	**2**	**4**	**6**	**83**	**0**	**0**	**0**	**32**	**6.3**	**41**	**3**	**53**	**9**	**–6**	....	....	....	....	....	....	....	....
	Binghamton Whalers	AHL	36	5	11	16	....	....	....	92	....	....	....	....	....	....	....	....	....	....	....	....	....	....	....	....	....	....
	Sweden	WEC-A	9	1	2	3	....	....	....	22	....	....	....	....	....	....	....	....	....	....	....	....	....	....	....	....	....	....
1985-86	**Hartford Whalers**	**NHL**	**80**	**5**	**19**	**24**	**4**	**13**	**17**	**174**	**0**	**1**	**1**	**72**	**6.9**	**103**	**13**	**109**	**26**	**+7**	**10**	**1**	**2**	**3**	**38**	**0**	**0**	**1**
1986-87	**Hartford Whalers**	**NHL**	**78**	**2**	**31**	**33**	**2**	**22**	**24**	**162**	**0**	**0**	**0**	**104**	**1.9**	**120**	**18**	**111**	**37**	**+28**	**5**	**0**	**1**	**1**	**41**	**-2**	**0**	**0**
	NHL All-Stars	RV'87	2	0	0	0	....	....	....	0	....	....	....	....	....	....	....	....	....	....	....	....	....	....	....	....	....	....
1987-88	**Hartford Whalers**	**NHL**	**76**	**8**	**33**	**41**	**7**	**23**	**30**	**159**	**3**	**0**	**0**	**156**	**5.1**	**96**	**32**	**113**	**39**	**–10**	**5**	**0**	**0**	**0**	**8**	**0**	**0**	**0**
1988-89	**Hartford Whalers**	**NHL**	**71**	**9**	**26**	**35**	**8**	**18**	**26**	**181**	**3**	**0**	**2**	**122**	**7.4**	**111**	**34**	**87**	**33**	**+23**	**4**	**0**	**2**	**2**	**4**	**0**	**0**	**0**
1989-90	**Hartford Whalers**	**NHL**	**55**	**2**	**11**	**13**	**2**	**8**	**10**	**177**	**0**	**0**	**0**	**57**	**3.5**	**57**	**4**	**57**	**19**	**+15**	**7**	**1**	**0**	**1**	**2**	**0**	**0**	**0**
	Sweden	WEC-A	7	2	0	2	....	....	....	18	....	....	....	....	....	....	....	....	....	....	....	....	....	....	....	....	....	....
1990-91	**Hartford Whalers**	**NHL**	**62**	**3**	**18**	**21**	**3**	**14**	**17**	**174**	**0**	**0**	**0**	**110**	**2.7**	**62**	**4**	**57**	**12**	**+13**	....	....	....	....	....	....	....	....
	Pittsburgh Penguins	**NHL**	**14**	**1**	**4**	**5**	**1**	**3**	**4**	**37**	**0**	**0**	**0**	**15**	**6.7**	**15**	**0**	**15**	**4**	**+4**	**20**	**3**	**2**	**5**	**34**	**1**	**0**	**1**
1991-92	Sweden	C Cup	3	0	0	0	....	....	....	4	....	....	....	....	....	....	....	....	....	....	....	....	....	....	....	....	....	....
	Pittsburgh Penguins	**NHL**	**62**	**1**	**14**	**15**	**1**	**11**	**12**	**206**	**1**	**0**	**1**	**75**	**1.3**	**69**	**9**	**83**	**25**	**+2**	**21**	**0**	**2**	**2**	**39**	**0**	**0**	**0**
1992-93	**Pittsburgh Penguins**	**NHL**	**77**	**3**	**26**	**29**	**2**	**18**	**20**	**249**	**0**	**0**	**1**	**96**	**3.1**	**116**	**14**	**100**	**34**	**+36**	**12**	**1**	**5**	**6**	**24**	**0**	**0**	**0**
1993-94	**Pittsburgh Penguins**	**NHL**	**80**	**5**	**24**	**29**	**5**	**19**	**24**	**199**	**1**	**0**	**0**	**106**	**4.7**	**111**	**17**	**102**	**31**	**+23**	**6**	**0**	**1**	**1**	**18**	**0**	**0**	**0**
1994-95	Leksands IF	Sweden	2	0	0	0	....	....	....	8	....	....	....	....	....	....	....	....	....	....	....	....	....	....	....	....	....	....
	Pittsburgh Penguins	**NHL**	**44**	**1**	**15**	**16**	**2**	**22**	**24**	**113**	**0**	**0**	**0**	**47**	**2.1**	**57**	**8**	**63**	**25**	**+11**	**7**	**0**	**2**	**2**	**8**	**0**	**0**	**0**
1995-96	**New York Rangers**	**NHL**	**74**	**1**	**18**	**19**	**1**	**15**	**16**	**122**	**0**	**0**	**0**	**66**	**1.5**	**63**	**8**	**68**	**22**	**+9**	**11**	**1**	**5**	**6**	**16**	**0**	**0**	**0**
1996-97	**New York Rangers**	**NHL**	**73**	**6**	**11**	**17**	**6**	**10**	**16**	**138**	**1**	**0**	**1**	**77**	**7.8**	**63**	**4**	**67**	**21**	**+3**	**15**	**0**	**2**	**2**	**30**	**0**	**0**	**0**
1997-98	**New York Rangers**	**NHL**	**73**	**3**	**9**	**12**	**4**	**9**	**13**	**122**	**0**	**0**	**2**	**59**	**5.1**	**38**	**1**	**54**	**18**	**+1**	....	....	....	....	....	....	....	....
	Sweden	Olympics	3	0	1	1	....	....	....	4	....	....	....	....	....	....	....	....	....	....	....	....	....	....	....	....	....	....
	NHL Totals		**960**	**52**	**265**	**317**	**50**	**209**	**259**	**2296**	**9**	**1**	**8**	**1194**	**4.4**	**1112**	**169**	**1139**	**355**		**123**	**7**	**24**	**31**	**262**	**-1**	**0**	**2**

EJC-A All-Star Team (1982)

Traded to **Pittsburgh** by **Hartford** with Ron Francis and Grant Jennings for John Cullen, Jeff Parker and Zarley Zalapski, March 4, 1991. Traded to **NY Rangers** by **Pittsburgh** with Luc Robitaille for Petr Nedved and Sergei Zubov, August 31, 1995.

• SANDELIN, SCOTT Scott Sandelin D – R. 6', 200 lbs. b: Hibbing, MN, 8/8/1964. Montreal's 5th choice, 40th overall, in 1982 Entry Draft.

Season	Club	League	GP	G	A	Pts	AG	AA	APts	PIM	PP	SH	GW	S	%	TGF	PGF	TGA	PGA	+/–	GP	G	A	Pts	PIM	PP	SH	GW
1981-82	Hibbing High School	H.S.	20	5	15	20	....	....	....	30	....	....	....	....	....	....	....	....	....	....	....	....	....	....	....	....	....	....
1982-83	University of North Dakota	WCHA	21	0	4	4	....	....	....	10	....	....	....	....	....	....	....	....	....	....	....	....	....	....	....	....	....	....
1983-84	University of North Dakota	WCHA	41	4	23	27	....	....	....	24	....	....	....	....	....	....	....	....	....	....	....	....	....	....	....	....	....	....
	United States	WJC-A	7	0	1	1	....	....	....	10	....	....	....	....	....	....	....	....	....	....	....	....	....	....	....	....	....	....
1984-85	University of North Dakota	WCHA	38	4	17	21	....	....	....	30	....	....	....	....	....	....	....	....	....	....	....	....	....	....	....	....	....	....
1985-86	University of North Dakota	WCHA	40	7	31	38	....	....	....	38	....	....	....	....	....	....	....	....	....	....	....	....	....	....	....	....	....	....
	Sherbrooke Canadiens	AHL	6	0	2	2	....	....	....	2	....	....	....	....	....	....	....	....	....	....	....	....	....	....	....	....	....	....
	United States	WEC-A	10	2	0	2	....	....	....	2	....	....	....	....	....	....	....	....	....	....	....	....	....	....	....	....	....	....
1986-87	**Montreal Canadiens**	**NHL**	**1**	**0**	**0**	**0**	**0**	**0**	**0**	**0**	**0**	**0**	**0**	**0**	**0.0**	**1**	**0**	**0**	**0**	**+1**	....	....	....	....	....	....	....	....
	Sherbrooke Canadiens	AHL	74	7	22	29	....	....	....	35	....	....	....	....	....	....	....	....	....	....	16	2	4	6	2	....	....	....
1987-88	**Montreal Canadiens**	**NHL**	**8**	**0**	**1**	**1**	**0**	**1**	**1**	**2**	**0**	**0**	**0**	**5**	**0.0**	**8**	**1**	**7**	**0**	**0**	....	....	....	....	....	....	....	....
	Sherbrooke Canadiens	AHL	58	8	14	22	....	....	....	35	....	....	....	....	....	....	....	....	....	....	4	0	2	2	0	....	....	....
1988-89	Sherbrooke Canadiens	AHL	12	0	0	9	....	....	....	8	....	....	....	....	....	....	....	....	....	....	....	....	....	....	....	....	....	....
	Hershey Bears	AHL	39	6	9	15	....	....	....	38	....	....	....	....	....	....	....	....	....	....	8	2	1	3	4	....	....	....
1989-90	Hershey Bears	AHL	70	4	27	31	....	....	....	38	....	....	....	....	....	....	....	....	....	....	....	....	....	....	....	....	....	....

			REGULAR SEASON																		PLAYOFFS							
Season	Club	League	GP	G	A	Pts	AG	AA	APts	PIM	PP	SH	GW	S	%	TGF	PGF	TGA	PGA	+/–	GP	G	A	Pts	PIM	PP	SH	GW
1990-91	**Philadelphia Flyers**	**NHL**	**15**	**0**	**3**	**3**	**0**	**2**	**2**	**0**	**0**	**0**	**0**	**4**	**0.0**	**11**	**2**	**12**	**0**	**–3**	....	....	....	....	....	....	....	....
	Hershey Bears	AHL	39	3	10	13	....	....	....	21	....	....	....	....	....	....	....	....	....	....	7	1	2	3	0	....	....	....
1991-92	**Minnesota North Stars**	**NHL**	**1**	**0**	**0**	**0**	**0**	**0**	**0**	**0**	**0**	**0**	**0**	**1**	**0.0**	**0**	**0**	**1**	**0**	**–1**	....	....	....	....	....	....	....	....
	Kalamazoo Wings	IHL	49	3	18	21	....	....	....	32	....	....	....	....	....	....	....	....	....	....	11	1	1	2	2	....	....	....
	NHL Totals		**25**	**0**	**4**	**4**	**0**	**3**	**3**	**2**	**0**	**0**	**0**	**10**	**0.0**	**20**	**3**	**20**	**0**		....	....	....	....	....	....	....	....

WCHA First All-Star Team (1986)

Traded to **Philadelphia** by **Montreal** for J.J. Daigneault, November 7, 1988. Signed as a free agent by **Minnesota**, August 21, 1991.

• SANDERSON, DEREK

Derek "Turk" Sanderson C – L. 6', 185 lbs. b: Niagara Falls, Ont., 6/16/1946.

Season	Club	League	GP	G	A	Pts	AG	AA	APts	PIM	PP	SH	GW	S	%	TGF	PGF	TGA	PGA	+/–	GP	G	A	Pts	PIM	PP	SH	GW
1962-63	Niagara Falls Flyers	OHA	2	0	0	0	....	....	....	10	....	....	....	....	....	....	....	....	....	....	1	0	0	0	0	....	....	....
1963-64	Niagara Falls Flyers	OHA	42	12	15	27	....	....	....	42	....	....	....	....	....	....	....	....	....	....	4	0	1	1	0	....	....	....
1964-65	Niagara Falls Flyers	OHA	55	19	46	65	....	....	....	128	....	....	....	....	....	....	....	....	....	....	11	9	8	17	26	....	....	....
1965-66	Niagara Falls Flyers	OHA	48	33	43	76	....	....	....	*238	....	....	....	....	....	....	....	....	....	....	6	6	0	6	*72	....	....	....
	Boston Bruins	**NHL**	**2**	**0**	**0**	**0**	**0**	**0**	**0**	**0**	....	....	....	....	....	....	....	....	....	....	....	....	....	....	....	....	....	....
	Oklahoma City Blazers	CHL	2	1	0	1	....	....	....	0	....	....	....	....	....	....	....	....	....	....	4	0	4	4	5	....	....	....
1966-67	Niagara Falls Flyers	OHA	47	41	*60	*101	....	....	....	193	....	....	....	....	....	....	....	....	....	....	13	8	*17	25	*70	....	....	....
	Boston Bruins	**NHL**	**2**	**0**	**0**	**0**	**0**	**0**	**0**	**0**	....	....	....	....	....	....	....	....	....	....	....	....	....	....	....	....	....	....
	Oklahoma City Blazers	CHL	....	....	....	....	....	....	....	....	....	....	....	....	....	....	....	....	....	....	2	0	0	0	0	....	....	....
1967-68	**Boston Bruins**	**NHL**	**71**	**24**	**25**	**49**	**30**	**26**	**56**	**98**	**4**	**1**	**6**	**187**	**12.8**	**60**	**6**	**50**	**7**	**+11**	**4**	**0**	**2**	**2**	**9**	**0**	**0**	**0**
1968-69	**Boston Bruins**	**NHL**	**61**	**26**	**22**	**48**	**29**	**21**	**50**	**146**	**1**	**3**	**3**	**194**	**13.4**	**62**	**6**	**41**	**20**	**+35**	**9**	***8**	**2**	**10**	**36**	**0**	**2**	**3**
1969-70	**Boston Bruins**	**NHL**	**50**	**18**	**23**	**41**	**21**	**23**	**44**	**118**	**5**	**5**	**2**	**179**	**10.1**	**56**	**15**	**54**	**21**	**+8**	**14**	**5**	**4**	**9**	***72**	**1**	**0**	**2**
1970-71	**Boston Bruins**	**NHL**	**71**	**29**	**34**	**63**	**30**	**30**	**60**	**130**	**1**	**6**	**0**	**217**	**13.4**	**82**	**3**	**69**	**29**	**+39**	**7**	**2**	**1**	**3**	**13**	**0**	**0**	**0**
1971-72	**Boston Bruins**	**NHL**	**78**	**25**	**33**	**58**	**27**	**30**	**57**	**108**	**0**	**7**	**2**	**198**	**12.6**	**73**	**1**	**86**	**39**	**+25**	**11**	**1**	**1**	**2**	**44**	**0**	**1**	**0**
1972-73	Philadelphia Blazers	WHA	8	3	3	6	....	....	....	69	....	....	....	....	....	....	....	....	....	....	....	....	....	....	....	....	....	....
	Boston Bruins	**NHL**	**25**	**5**	**10**	**15**	**5**	**8**	**13**	**38**	**0**	**2**	**0**	**41**	**12.2**	**18**	**0**	**20**	**13**	**+11**	**5**	**1**	**2**	**3**	**13**	**0**	**0**	**0**
1973-74	**Boston Bruins**	**NHL**	**29**	**8**	**12**	**20**	**8**	**10**	**18**	**48**	**0**	**0**	**1**	**64**	**12.5**	**31**	**2**	**23**	**11**	**+17**	....	....	....	....	....	....	....	....
	Boston Braves	AHL	3	4	3	7	....	....	....	2	....	....	....	....	....	....	....	....	....	....	....	....	....	....	....	....	....	....
1974-75	**New York Rangers**	**NHL**	**75**	**25**	**25**	**50**	**23**	**20**	**43**	**106**	**3**	**2**	**3**	**188**	**13.3**	**80**	**10**	**83**	**23**	**+10**	**3**	**0**	**0**	**0**	**0**	**0**	**0**	**0**
1975-76	**New York Rangers**	**NHL**	**8**	**0**	**0**	**0**	**0**	**0**	**0**	**4**	**0**	**0**	**0**	**29**	**0.0**	**0**	**0**	**13**	**5**	**–8**	....	....	....	....	....	....	....	....
	St. Louis Blues	**NHL**	**65**	**24**	**43**	**67**	**22**	**34**	**56**	**59**	**6**	**6**	**1**	**171**	**14.0**	**86**	**23**	**90**	**40**	**+13**	**3**	**1**	**0**	**1**	**0**	**1**	**0**	**0**
1976-77	**St. Louis Blues**	**NHL**	**32**	**8**	**13**	**21**	**8**	**11**	**19**	**26**	**3**	**0**	**2**	**53**	**15.1**	**27**	**9**	**27**	**1**	**–8**	....	....	....	....	....	....	....	....
	Vancouver Canucks	**NHL**	**16**	**7**	**9**	**16**	**7**	**7**	**14**	**30**	**2**	**2**	**1**	**21**	**33.3**	**25**	**8**	**17**	**5**	**+5**	....	....	....	....	....	....	....	....
	Kansas City Blues	CHL	8	4	3	7	....	....	....	6	....	....	....	....	....	....	....	....	....	....	....	....	....	....	....	....	....	....
1977-78	**Pittsburgh Penguins**	**NHL**	**13**	**3**	**1**	**4**	**3**	**1**	**4**	**0**	**1**	**0**	**0**	**11**	**27.3**	**5**	**1**	**15**	**5**	**–6**	....	....	....	....	....	....	....	....
	Tulsa Oilers	CHL	4	0	0	0	....	....	....	0	....	....	....	....	....	....	....	....	....	....	....	....	....	....	....	....	....	....
	Kansas City Red Wings	CHL	4	1	3	4	....	....	....	0	....	....	....	....	....	....	....	....	....	....	....	....	....	....	....	....	....	....
	NHL Totals		**598**	**202**	**250**	**452**	**213**	**221**	**434**	**911**	**26**	**34**	**21**	**1553**	**13.0**	**605**	**84**	**588**	**219**		**56**	**18**	**12**	**30**	**187**	**2**	**3**	**5**
	Other Major League Totals		8	3	3	6	....	....	....	69	....	....	....	....	....	....	....	....	....		....	....	....	....	....	....	....	....

Won Calder Memorial Trophy (1968)

Selected by **Miami-Philadelphia** (WHA) in 1972 WHA General Player Draft, February 12, 1972. Signed as a free agent by **Boston** after securing release from **Philadelphia** (WHA), February, 1973. Traded to **NY Rangers** by **Boston** for Walt McKechnie, June 12, 1974. Traded to **St. Louis** by **NY Rangers** for NY Rangers' 1st round choice (previously acquired, NY Rangers selected Lucien DeBlois) in 1977 Amateur Draft, October 30, 1975. Signed as a free agent by **Pittsburgh**, March 14, 1978.

• SANDERSON, GEOFF

Geoff Sanderson LW – L. 6', 185 lbs. b: Hay River, N.W.T., 2/1/1972. Hartford's 2nd choice, 36th overall, in 1990 Entry Draft.

Season	Club	League	GP	G	A	Pts	AG	AA	APts	PIM	PP	SH	GW	S	%	TGF	PGF	TGA	PGA	+/–	GP	G	A	Pts	PIM	PP	SH	GW
1988-89	Swift Current Broncos	WHL	58	17	11	28	....	....	....	16	....	....	....	....	....	....	....	....	....	....	12	3	5	8	6	....	....	....
1989-90	Swift Current Broncos	WHL	70	32	62	94	....	....	....	56	....	....	....	....	....	....	....	....	....	....	4	1	4	5	8	....	....	....
1990-91	Swift Current Broncos	WHL	70	62	50	112	....	....	....	57	....	....	....	....	....	....	....	....	....	....	3	1	2	3	4	....	....	....
	Hartford Whalers	**NHL**	**2**	**1**	**0**	**1**	**1**	**0**	**1**	**0**	**0**	**0**	**0**	**2**	**50.0**	**1**	**0**	**3**	**0**	**–2**	**3**	**0**	**0**	**0**	**0**	**0**	**0**	**0**
	Springfield Indians	AHL	....	....	....	....	....	....	....	....	....	....	....	....	....	....	....	....	....	....	1	0	0	0	2	....	....	....
1991-92	**Hartford Whalers**	**NHL**	**64**	**13**	**18**	**31**	**12**	**14**	**26**	**18**	**2**	**0**	**1**	**98**	**13.3**	**49**	**5**	**59**	**20**	**+5**	**7**	**1**	**0**	**1**	**2**	**0**	**0**	**0**
1992-93	**Hartford Whalers**	**NHL**	**82**	**46**	**43**	**89**	**38**	**29**	**67**	**28**	**21**	**2**	**4**	**271**	**17.0**	**113**	**53**	**92**	**11**	**–21**	....	....	....	....	....	....	....	....
	Canada	WC-A	8	3	3	6	....	....	....	2	....	....	....	....	....	....	....	....	....	....	....	....	....	....	....	....	....	....
1993-94	**Hartford Whalers**	**NHL**	**82**	**41**	**26**	**67**	**38**	**20**	**58**	**42**	**15**	**1**	**6**	**266**	**15.4**	**98**	**40**	**74**	**3**	**–13**	....	....	....	....	....	....	....	....
	Canada	WC-A	8	4	2	6	....	....	....	8	....	....	....	....	....	....	....	....	....	....	....	....	....	....	....	....	....	....
1994-95	HPK Hameenlinna	Finland	12	6	4	10	....	....	....	24	....	....	....	....	....	....	....	....	....	....	....	....	....	....	....	....	....	....
	Hartford Whalers	**NHL**	**46**	**18**	**14**	**32**	**32**	**21**	**53**	**24**	**4**	**0**	**4**	**170**	**10.6**	**42**	**16**	**37**	**1**	**–10**	....	....	....	....	....	....	....	....
1995-96	**Hartford Whalers**	**NHL**	**81**	**34**	**31**	**65**	**34**	**25**	**59**	**40**	**6**	**0**	**7**	**314**	**10.8**	**88**	**30**	**66**	**8**	**0**	....	....	....	....	....	....	....	....
1996-97	**Hartford Whalers**	**NHL**	**82**	**36**	**31**	**67**	**38**	**27**	**65**	**29**	**12**	**1**	**4**	**297**	**12.1**	**90**	**35**	**65**	**1**	**–9**	....	....	....	....	....	....	....	....
	Canada	WC-A	11	3	2	5	....	....	....	2	....	....	....	....	....	....	....	....	....	....	....	....	....	....	....	....	....	....
1997-98	**Carolina Hurricanes**	**NHL**	**40**	**7**	**10**	**17**	**8**	**10**	**18**	**14**	**2**	**0**	**0**	**96**	**7.3**	**29**	**11**	**23**	**1**	**–4**	....	....	....	....	....	....	....	....
	Vancouver Canucks	**NHL**	**9**	**0**	**3**	**3**	**0**	**3**	**3**	**4**	**0**	**0**	**0**	**29**	**0.0**	**5**	**1**	**5**	**0**	**–1**	....	....	....	....	....	....	....	....
	Buffalo Sabres	**NHL**	**26**	**4**	**5**	**9**	**5**	**5**	**10**	**20**	**0**	**0**	**2**	**72**	**5.6**	**17**	**7**	**5**	**1**	**+6**	**14**	**3**	**1**	**4**	**4**	**1**	**0**	**1**
	NHL Totals		**514**	**200**	**181**	**381**	**206**	**154**	**360**	**219**	**62**	**4**	**28**	**1615**	**12.4**	**532**	**198**	**429**	**46**		**24**	**4**	**1**	**5**	**6**	**1**	**0**	**1**

Played in NHL All-Star Game (1994, 1997)

Transferred to **Carolina** after **Hartford** franchise relocated, June 25, 1997. Traded to **Vancouver** by **Carolina** with Sean Burke and Enrico Ciccone for Kirk McLean and Martin Gelinas, January 3, 1998. Traded to **Buffalo** by **Vancouver** for Brad May and future considerations, February 4, 1998.

• SANDLAK, JIM

Jim Sandlak RW – R. 6'4", 219 lbs. b: Kitchener, Ont., 12/12/1966. Hartford's 1st choice, 5th overall, in 1985 Entry Draft.

Season	Club	League	GP	G	A	Pts	AG	AA	APts	PIM	PP	SH	GW	S	%	TGF	PGF	TGA	PGA	+/–	GP	G	A	Pts	PIM	PP	SH	GW
1982-83	Kitchener Rangers	OHL	38	26	25	51	....	....	....	100	....	....	....	....	....	....	....	....	....	....	....	....	....	....	....	....	....	....
1983-84	London Knights	OHL	68	23	18	41	....	....	....	143	....	....	....	....	....	....	....	....	....	....	8	1	11	12	13	....	....	....
1984-85	London Knights	OHL	58	40	24	64	....	....	....	128	....	....	....	....	....	....	....	....	....	....	8	3	2	5	14	....	....	....
	Canada	WJC-A	5	1	0	1	....	....	....	6	....	....	....	....	....	....	....	....	....	....	....	....	....	....	....	....	....	....
1985-86	London Knights	OHL	16	8	14	22	....	....	....	38	....	....	....	....	....	....	....	....	....	....	5	2	3	5	24	....	....	....
	Vancouver Canucks	**NHL**	**23**	**1**	**3**	**4**	**1**	**2**	**3**	**10**	**0**	**0**	**0**	**34**	**2.9**	**9**	**3**	**10**	**0**	**–4**	**3**	**0**	**1**	**1**	**0**	**0**	**0**	**0**
	Canada	WJC-A	7	5	7	12	....	....	....	16	....	....	....	....	....	....	....	....	....	....	....	....	....	....	....	....	....	....
1986-87	**Vancouver Canucks**	**NHL**	**78**	**15**	**21**	**36**	**13**	**15**	**28**	**66**	**2**	**0**	**3**	**114**	**13.2**	**57**	**19**	**42**	**0**	**–4**	....	....	....	....	....	....	....	....
1987-88	**Vancouver Canucks**	**NHL**	**49**	**16**	**15**	**31**	**14**	**11**	**25**	**81**	**6**	**0**	**2**	**96**	**16.7**	**52**	**21**	**41**	**1**	**–9**	....	....	....	....	....	....	....	....
	Fredericton Express	AHL	24	10	15	25	....	....	....	47	....	....	....	....	....	....	....	....	....	....	....	....	....	....	....	....	....	....
1988-89	**Vancouver Canucks**	**NHL**	**72**	**20**	**20**	**40**	**17**	**14**	**31**	**99**	**9**	**0**	**4**	**164**	**12.2**	**64**	**20**	**36**	**0**	**+8**	**6**	**1**	**1**	**2**	**2**	**0**	**0**	**0**
1989-90	**Vancouver Canucks**	**NHL**	**70**	**15**	**8**	**23**	**13**	**6**	**19**	**104**	**1**	**0**	**2**	**135**	**11.1**	**41**	**7**	**49**	**0**	**–15**	....	....	....	....	....	....	....	....
1990-91	**Vancouver Canucks**	**NHL**	**59**	**7**	**6**	**13**	**6**	**5**	**11**	**125**	**4**	**0**	**0**	**88**	**8.0**	**22**	**7**	**35**	**0**	**–20**	....	....	....	....	....	....	....	....
1991-92	**Vancouver Canucks**	**NHL**	**66**	**16**	**24**	**40**	**15**	**18**	**33**	**176**	**3**	**0**	**2**	**122**	**13.1**	**58**	**10**	**27**	**1**	**+22**	**13**	**4**	**6**	**10**	**22**	**2**	**0**	**0**
1992-93	**Vancouver Canucks**	**NHL**	**59**	**10**	**18**	**28**	**8**	**12**	**20**	**122**	**1**	**0**	**1**	**104**	**9.6**	**44**	**14**	**35**	**7**	**+2**	**6**	**2**	**2**	**4**	**4**	**0**	**0**	**0**
1993-94	**Hartford Whalers**	**NHL**	**27**	**6**	**2**	**8**	**6**	**2**	**8**	**32**	**2**	**0**	**1**	**32**	**18.8**	**16**	**2**	**9**	**1**	**+6**	....	....	....	....	....	....	....	....
1994-95	**Hartford Whalers**	**NHL**	**13**	**0**	**0**	**0**	**0**	**0**	**0**	**0**	**0**	**0**	**0**	**13**	**0.0**	**2**	**0**	**12**	**0**	**–10**	....	....	....	....	....	....	....	....
1995-96	**Vancouver Canucks**	**NHL**	**33**	**4**	**2**	**6**	**4**	**2**	**6**	**6**	**0**	**1**	**1**	**44**	**9.1**	**13**	**1**	**18**	**3**	**–3**	**5**	**0**	**0**	**0**	**2**	**0**	**0**	**0**
	Syracuse Crunch	AHL	12	6	1	7	....	....	....	16	....	....	....	....	....	....	....	....	....	....	....	....	....	....	....	....	....	....
	NHL Totals		**549**	**110**	**119**	**229**	**97**	**87**	**184**	**821**	**28**	**1**	**16**	**946**	**11.6**	**378**	**104**	**314**	**13**		**33**	**7**	**10**	**17**	**30**	**2**	**0**	**0**

Named Best Forward at WJC-A (1986) • NHL All-Rookie Team (1987)

Traded to **Hartford** by **Vancouver** to complete transaction that sent Murray Craven to Vancouver (March 22, 1993), May 17, 1993.

• SANDSTROM, TOMAS

Tomas Sandstrom RW – L. 6'2", 205 lbs. b: Jakobstad, Finland, 9/4/1964. NY Rangers' 2nd choice, 36th overall, in 1982 Entry Draft.

Season	Club	League	GP	G	A	Pts	AG	AA	APts	PIM	PP	SH	GW	S	%	TGF	PGF	TGA	PGA	+/–	GP	G	A	Pts	PIM	PP	SH	GW
1981-82	Fagersta	Sweden 2	32	28	11	39	....	....	....	74	....	....	....	....	....	....	....	....	....	....	....	....	....	....	....	....	....	....
1982-83	Brynas IF Gavle	Sweden	36	23	14	37	....	....	....	50	....	....	....	....	....	....	....	....	....	....	....	....	....	....	....	....	....	....
	Sweden	WJC-A	7	9	3	12	....	....	....	....	....	....	....	....	....	....	....	....	....	....	....	....	....	....	....	....	....	....
1983-84	Brynas IF Gavle	Sweden	34	19	10	29	....	....	....	81	....	....	....	....	....	....	....	....	....	....	....	....	....	....	....	....	....	....
	Sweden	WJC-A	7	4	3	7	....	....	....	12	....	....	....	....	....	....	....	....	....	....	....	....	....	....	....	....	....	....
	Sweden	Olympics	7	2	1	3	....	....	....	6	....	....	....	....	....	....	....	....	....	....	....	....	....	....	....	....	....	....

			REGULAR SEASON																		PLAYOFFS							
Season	Club	League	GP	G	A	Pts	AG	AA	APts	PIM	PP	SH	GW	S	%	TGF	PGF	TGA	PGA	+/–	GP	G	A	Pts	PIM	PP	SH	GW
1984-85	Sweden	C Cup	8	1	1	2	....	....	....	2	....	....	....	....	....	....	....	....	....	....	....	....	....	....	....	....	....	....
	New York Rangers	**NHL**	**74**	**29**	**29**	**58**	**24**	**20**	**44**	**51**	**5**	**0**	**3**	**190**	**15.3**	**84**	**25**	**58**	**2**	**+3**	**3**	**0**	**2**	**2**	**0**	**0**	**0**	**0**
	Sweden	WEC-A	10	3	6	9	....	....	....	18	....	....	....	....	....	....	....	....	....	....	....	....	....	....	....	....	....	....
1985-86	**New York Rangers**	**NHL**	**73**	**25**	**29**	**54**	**20**	**19**	**39**	**109**	**8**	**2**	**1**	**238**	**10.5**	**80**	**39**	**53**	**8**	**–4**	**16**	**4**	**6**	**10**	**20**	**0**	**0**	**1**
1986-87	**New York Rangers**	**NHL**	**64**	**40**	**34**	**74**	**35**	**25**	**60**	**60**	**13**	**0**	**5**	**240**	**16.7**	**100**	**36**	**56**	**0**	**+8**	**6**	**1**	**2**	**3**	**20**	**0**	**0**	**0**
	NHL All-Stars	RV'87	1	0	0	0	....	....	....	0	....	....	....	....	....	....	....	....	....	....	....	....	....	....	....	....	....	....
	Sweden	WEC A	8	4	6	10	....	....	....	6	....	....	....	....	....	....	....	....	....	....	....	....	....	....	....	....	....	....
1987-88	**New York Rangers**	**NHL**	**69**	**28**	**40**	**68**	**24**	**28**	**52**	**95**	**11**	**0**	**3**	**204**	**13.7**	**109**	**52**	**67**	**4**	**–6**	....	....	....	....	....	....	....	....
1988-89	**New York Rangers**	**NHL**	**79**	**32**	**56**	**88**	**27**	**39**	**66**	**148**	**11**	**2**	**4**	**240**	**13.3**	**132**	**52**	**90**	**15**	**+5**	**4**	**3**	**2**	**5**	**12**	**2**	**0**	**0**
	Sweden	WEC-A	10	4	3	7	....	....	....	14	....	....	....	....	....	....	....	....	....	....	....	....	....	....	....	....	....	....
1989-90	**New York Rangers**	**NHL**	**48**	**19**	**19**	**38**	**16**	**14**	**30**	**100**	**6**	**0**	**3**	**166**	**11.4**	**53**	**24**	**40**	**1**	**–10**	....	....	....	....	....	....	....	....
	Los Angeles Kings	**NHL**	**28**	**13**	**20**	**33**	**11**	**14**	**25**	**28**	**1**	**1**	**0**	**83**	**15.7**	**45**	**16**	**35**	**5**	**–1**	**10**	**5**	**4**	**9**	**19**	**0**	**0**	**0**
1990-91	**Los Angeles Kings**	**NHL**	**68**	**45**	**44**	**89**	**42**	**33**	**75**	**106**	**16**	**0**	**6**	**221**	**20.4**	**128**	**41**	**60**	**0**	**+27**	**10**	**4**	**4**	**8**	**14**	**3**	**0**	**0**
1991-92	Sweden	C Cup	6	1	2	3	....	....	....	8	....	....	....	....	....	....	....	....	....	....	....	....	....	....	....	....	....	....
	Los Angeles Kings	**NHL**	**49**	**17**	**22**	**39**	**16**	**17**	**33**	**70**	**5**	**0**	**4**	**147**	**11.6**	**58**	**18**	**43**	**1**	**–2**	**6**	**0**	**3**	**3**	**8**	**0**	**0**	**0**
1992-93	**Los Angeles Kings**	**NHL**	**39**	**25**	**27**	**52**	**21**	**18**	**39**	**57**	**8**	**0**	**3**	**134**	**18.7**	**71**	**25**	**34**	**0**	**+12**	**24**	**8**	**17**	**25**	**12**	**2**	**0**	**2**
1993-94	**Los Angeles Kings**	**NHL**	**51**	**17**	**24**	**41**	**16**	**19**	**35**	**59**	**4**	**0**	**2**	**121**	**14.0**	**68**	**32**	**51**	**3**	**–12**	....	....	....	....	....	....	....	....
	Pittsburgh Penguins	**NHL**	**27**	**6**	**11**	**17**	**6**	**8**	**14**	**24**	**0**	**0**	**1**	**72**	**8.3**	**25**	**2**	**22**	**4**	**+5**	**6**	**0**	**0**	**0**	**4**	**0**	**0**	**0**
1994-95	Malmo IF	Sweden	12	10	5	15	....	....	....	14	....	....	....	....	....	....	....	....	....	....	....	....	....	....	....	....	....	....
	Pittsburgh Penguins	**NHL**	**47**	**21**	**23**	**44**	**37**	**34**	**71**	**42**	**4**	**1**	**3**	**116**	**18.1**	**56**	**17**	**51**	**13**	**+1**	**12**	**3**	**3**	**6**	**16**	**2**	**0**	**0**
1995-96	**Pittsburgh Penguins**	**NHL**	**58**	**35**	**35**	**70**	**35**	**29**	**64**	**69**	**17**	**1**	**2**	**187**	**18.7**	**120**	**59**	**64**	**7**	**+4**	**18**	**4**	**2**	**6**	**30**	**0**	**0**	**1**
1996-97	**Pittsburgh Penguins**	**NHL**	**40**	**9**	**15**	**24**	**10**	**13**	**23**	**33**	**1**	**1**	**0**	**73**	**12.3**	**38**	**10**	**30**	**6**	**+4**	....	....	....	....	....	....	....	....
	Detroit Red Wings	**NHL**	**34**	**9**	**9**	**18**	**10**	**8**	**18**	**36**	**0**	**1**	**2**	**66**	**13.6**	**32**	**10**	**26**	**6**	**+2**	**20**	**0**	**4**	**4**	**24**	**0**	**0**	**0**
1997-98	**Anaheim Mighty Ducks**	**NHL**	**77**	**9**	**8**	**17**	**11**	**8**	**19**	**64**	**2**	**1**	**0**	**136**	**6.6**	**40**	**13**	**54**	**2**	**–25**	....	....	....	....	....	....	....	....
	Sweden	Olympics	4	0	1	1	....	....	....	0	....	....	....	....	....	....	....	....	....	....	....	....	....	....	....	....	....	....
	NHL Totals		**925**	**379**	**445**	**824**	**361**	**346**	**707**	**1151**	**112**	**10**	**42**	**2634**	**14.4**	**1239**	**471**	**834**	**77**		**135**	**32**	**49**	**81**	**179**	**9**	**0**	**4**

EJC-A All-Star Team (1982) • Named Best Forward at EJC-A (1982) • WJC-A All-Star Team (1983) • Named Best Forward at WJC-A (1983) • NHL All-Rookie Team (1985)
Played in NHL All-Star Game (1988, 1991)

Traded to **LA Kings** by **NY Rangers** with Tony Granato for Bernie Nicholls, January 20, 1990. Traded to **Pittsburgh** by **LA Kings** with Shawn McEachern for Marty McSorley and Jim Paek, February 16, 1994. Traded to **Detroit** by **Pittsburgh** for Greg Johnson, January 27, 1997. Signed as a free agent by **Anaheim**, October 20, 1997.

• SANDWITH, TERRAN

Terran Sandwith D – L. 6'4", 210 lbs. b: Edmonton, Alta., 4/17/1972. Philadelphia's 4th choice, 42nd overall, in 1990 NHL Entry Draft.

Season	Club	League	GP	G	A	Pts	AG	AA	APts	PIM	PP	SH	GW	S	%	TGF	PGF	TGA	PGA	+/–	GP	G	A	Pts	PIM	PP	SH	GW
1988-89	Tri-City Americans	WHL	31	0	0	0	....	....	....	29	....	....	....	....	....	....	....	....	....	....	6	0	0	0	4	....	....	....
1989-90	Tri-City Americans	WHL	70	4	14	18	....	....	....	92	....	....	....	....	....	....	....	....	....	....	7	0	2	2	14	....	....	....
1990-91	Tri-City Americans	WHL	46	5	17	22	....	....	....	132	....	....	....	....	....	....	....	....	....	....	7	1	0	1	14	....	....	....
1991-92	Brandon Wheat Kings	WHL	41	6	14	20	....	....	....	145	....	....	....	....	....	....	....	....	....	....	....	....	....	....	....	....	....	....
	Saskatoon Blades	WHL	18	2	5	7	....	....	....	53	....	....	....	....	....	....	....	....	....	....	18	2	1	3	28	....	....	....
1992-93	Hershey Bears	AHL	61	1	12	13	....	....	....	140	....	....	....	....	....	....	....	....	....	....	....	....	....	....	....	....	....	....
1993-94	Hershey Bears	AHL	62	3	5	8	....	....	....	169	....	....	....	....	....	....	....	....	....	....	2	0	1	1	4	....	....	....
1994-95	Hershey Bears	AHL	11	1	1	2	....	....	....	32	....	....	....	....	....	....	....	....	....	....	....	....	....	....	....	....	....	....
	Kansas City Blades	IHL	25	0	3	3	....	....	....	73	....	....	....	....	....	....	....	....	....	....	....	....	....	....	....	....	....	....
1995-96	Canada	Nat-Team	47	3	12	15	....	....	....	63	....	....	....	....	....	....	....	....	....	....	....	....	....	....	....	....	....	....
	Cape Breton Oilers	AHL	5	0	2	2	....	....	....	4	....	....	....	....	....	....	....	....	....	....	....	....	....	....	....	....	....	....
1996-97	Hamilton Bulldogs	AHL	78	3	6	9	....	....	....	213	....	....	....	....	....	....	....	....	....	....	22	0	2	2	27	....	....	....
1997-98	**Edmonton Oilers**	**NHL**	**8**	**0**	**0**	**0**	**0**	**0**	**0**	**6**	**0**	**0**	**0**	**4**	**0.0**	**3**	**0**	**8**	**1**	**–4**	....	....	....	....	....	....	....	....
	Hamilton Bulldogs	AHL	54	4	8	12	....	....	....	131	....	....	....	....	....	....	....	....	....	....	9	0	0	0	10	....	....	....
	NHL Totals		**8**	**0**	**0**	**0**	**0**	**0**	**0**	**6**	**0**	**0**	**0**	**4**	**0.0**	**3**	**0**	**8**	**1**		....	....	....	....	....	....	....	....

Signed as a free agent by **Edmonton**, April 10, 1996. Signed as a free agent by **Anaheim**, July 14, 1998.

• SANIPASS, EVERETT

Everett Sanipass LW – L. 6'2", 204 lbs. b: Big Cove, N.B., 2/13/1968. Chicago's 1st choice, 14th overall, in 1986 Entry Draft.

Season	Club	League	GP	G	A	Pts	AG	AA	APts	PIM	PP	SH	GW	S	%	TGF	PGF	TGA	PGA	+/–	GP	G	A	Pts	PIM	PP	SH	GW
1983-84	Moncton Flyers	Midget	37	43	26	69	....	....	....	....	....	....	....	....	....	....	....	....	....	....	....	....	....	....	....	....	....	....
1984-85	Verdun Jr. Canadiens	QMJHL	38	0	11	19	....	....	....	84	....	....	....	....	....	....	....	....	....	....	12	2	5	7	68	....	....	....
1985-86	Verdun Jr. Canadiens	QMJHL	67	23	66	89	....	....	....	320	....	....	....	....	....	....	....	....	....	....	5	0	2	2	16	....	....	....
1986-87	Verdun Jr. Canadiens	QMJHL	23	17	34	51	....	....	....	165	....	....	....	....	....	....	....	....	....	....	....	....	....	....	....	....	....	....
	Canada	WJC-A	6	3	2	5	....	....	....	8	....	....	....	....	....	....	....	....	....	....	....	....	....	....	....	....	....	....
	Granby Bisons	QMJHL	12	17	14	31	....	....	....	55	....	....	....	....	....	....	....	....	....	....	8	6	4	10	48	....	....	....
	Chicago Blackhawks	**NHL**	**7**	**1**	**3**	**4**	**1**	**2**	**3**	**2**	**0**	**0**	**0**	**9**	**11.1**	**6**	**0**	**3**	**0**	**+3**	....	....	....	....	....	....	....	....
1987-88	**Chicago Blackhawks**	**NHL**	**57**	**8**	**12**	**20**	**7**	**9**	**16**	**126**	**0**	**0**	**0**	**55**	**14.5**	**27**	**4**	**32**	**0**	**–9**	**2**	**2**	**0**	**2**	**2**	**0**	**0**	**0**
1988-89	**Chicago Blackhawks**	**NHL**	**50**	**6**	**9**	**15**	**5**	**6**	**11**	**164**	**0**	**0**	**2**	**51**	**11.8**	**26**	**6**	**28**	**1**	**–7**	**3**	**0**	**0**	**0**	**2**	**0**	**0**	**0**
	Saginaw Hawks	IHL	23	9	12	21	....	....	....	76	....	....	....	....	....	....	....	....	....	....	....	....	....	....	....	....	....	....
1989-90	**Chicago Blackhawks**	**NHL**	**12**	**2**	**2**	**4**	**2**	**1**	**3**	**17**	**0**	**0**	**0**	**16**	**12.5**	**7**	**0**	**8**	**1**	**0**	....	....	....	....	....	....	....	....
	Indianapolis Ice	IHL	33	15	13	28	....	....	....	121	....	....	....	....	....	....	....	....	....	....	....	....	....	....	....	....	....	....
	Quebec Nordiques	**NHL**	**9**	**3**	**3**	**6**	**3**	**2**	**5**	**8**	**2**	**0**	**0**	**16**	**18.8**	**9**	**5**	**8**	**0**	**–4**	....	....	....	....	....	....	....	....
1990-91	**Quebec Nordiques**	**NHL**	**29**	**5**	**5**	**10**	**5**	**4**	**9**	**41**	**1**	**0**	**0**	**38**	**13.2**	**13**	**2**	**26**	**0**	**–15**	....	....	....	....	....	....	....	....
	Halifax Citadels	AHL	14	11	7	18	....	....	....	41	....	....	....	....	....	....	....	....	....	....	....	....	....	....	....	....	....	....
1991-92	Halifax Citadels	AHL	7	3	5	8	....	....	....	31	....	....	....	....	....	....	....	....	....	....	....	....	....	....	....	....	....	....
1992-93	Halifax Citadels	AHL	9	1	3	4	....	....	....	36	....	....	....	....	....	....	....	....	....	....	....	....	....	....	....	....	....	....
1993-94	Richibucto Schooners	NBSHL	....	....	....	....	....	....	....	....	....	....	....	....	....	....	....	....	....	....	7	10	9	19	25	....	....	....
1994-95	East Hant's Penguins	NBSHL	21	9	31	30	....	....	....	....	....	....	....	....	....	....	....	....	....	....	....	....	....	....	....	....	....	....
	NHL Totals		**164**	**25**	**34**	**59**	**23**	**24**	**47**	**358**	**3**	**0**	**2**	**185**	**13.5**	**88**	**17**	**105**	**2**		**5**	**2**	**0**	**2**	**4**	**0**	**0**	**0**

QMJHL First All-Star Team (1987)

Traded to **Quebec** by **Chicago** with Mario Doyon and Dan Vincelette for Greg Millen, Michel Goulet and Quebec's 6th round choice (Kevin St.Jacques) in 1991 Entry Draft, March 5, 1990.

• SARAULT, YVES

Yves Sarault LW – L. 6'1", 170 lbs. b: Valleyfield, Que., 12/23/1972. Montreal's 4th choice, 61st overall, in 1991 Entry Draft.

Season	Club	League	GP	G	A	Pts	AG	AA	APts	PIM	PP	SH	GW	S	%	TGF	PGF	TGA	PGA	+/–	GP	G	A	Pts	PIM	PP	SH	GW
1989-90	Victoriaville Tigres	QMJHL	70	12	28	40	....	....	....	140	....	....	....	....	....	....	....	....	....	....	16	0	3	3	26	....	....	....
1990-91	St-Jean Lynx	QMJHL	56	22	24	46	....	....	....	113	....	....	....	....	....	....	....	....	....	....	....	....	....	....	....	....	....	....
1991-92	St-Jean Lynx	QMJHL	50	28	38	66	....	....	....	96	....	....	....	....	....	....	....	....	....	....	....	....	....	....	....	....	....	....
	Trois-Rivières Draveurs	QMJHL	18	15	14	29	....	....	....	12	....	....	....	....	....	....	....	....	....	....	....	....	....	....	....	....	....	....
1992-93	Fredericton Canadiens	AHL	59	14	17	31	....	....	....	41	....	....	....	....	....	....	....	....	....	....	15	10	10	20	18	....	....	....
	Wheeling Thunderbirds	ECHL	2	1	3	4	....	....	....	0	....	....	....	....	....	....	....	....	....	....	3	0	1	1	2	....	....	....
1993-94	Fredericton Canadiens	AHL	60	13	14	27	....	....	....	72	....	....	....	....	....	....	....	....	....	....	....	....	....	....	....	....	....	....
1994-95	Fredericton Canadiens	AHL	69	24	21	45	....	....	....	96	....	....	....	....	....	....	....	....	....	....	13	2	1	3	33	....	....	....
	Montreal Canadiens	**NHL**	**8**	**0**	**1**	**1**	**0**	**1**	**1**	**0**	**0**	**0**	**0**	**9**	**0.0**	**1**	**0**	**2**	**0**	**–1**	....	....	....	....	....	....	....	....
1995-96	**Montreal Canadiens**	**NHL**	**14**	**0**	**0**	**0**	**0**	**0**	**0**	**4**	**0**	**0**	**0**	**14**	**0.0**	**0**	**0**	**7**	**0**	**–7**	....	....	....	....	....	....	....	....
	Calgary Flames	**NHL**	**11**	**2**	**1**	**3**	**2**	**1**	**3**	**4**	**0**	**0**	**1**	**12**	**16.7**	**6**	**1**	**7**	**0**	**–2**	....	....	....	....	....	....	....	....
	Saint John Flames	AHL	26	10	12	22	....	....	....	34	....	....	....	....	....	....	....	....	....	....	16	6	2	8	33	....	....	....
1996-97	**Colorado Avalanche**	**NHL**	**28**	**2**	**1**	**3**	**2**	**1**	**3**	**6**	**0**	**0**	**0**	**41**	**4.9**	**6**	**1**	**5**	**0**	**0**	**5**	**0**	**0**	**0**	**2**	**0**	**0**	**0**
	Hershey Bears	AHL	6	2	3	5	....	....	....	8	....	....	....	....	....	....	....	....	....	....	....	....	....	....	....	....	....	....
1997-98	**Colorado Avalanche**	**NHL**	**2**	**1**	**0**	**1**	**1**	**0**	**1**	**0**	**0**	**0**	**0**	**1**	**100.0**	**1**	**0**	**0**	**0**	**+1**	....	....	....	....	....	....	....	....
	Hershey Bears	AHL	63	23	36	59	....	....	....	43	....	....	....	....	....	....	....	....	....	....	7	1	2	3	14	....	....	....
	NHL Totals		**63**	**5**	**3**	**8**	**5**	**3**	**8**	**14**	**0**	**0**	**1**	**77**	**6.5**	**14**	**2**	**21**	**0**		**5**	**0**	**0**	**0**	**2**	**0**	**0**	**0**

QMJHL Second All-Star Team (1992)

Traded to **Calgary** by **Montreal** with Craig Ferguson for Calgary's 8th round choice (Petr Kubos) in 1997 Entry Draft, November 26, 1995. Signed as a free agent by **Colorado**, September 13, 1996.

• SARGENT, GARY

Gary Sargent D – L. 5'10", 210 lbs. b: Red Lake, MN, 2/8/1954. Los Angeles' 1st choice, 48th overall, in 1974 Amateur Draft.

Season	Club	League	GP	G	A	Pts	AG	AA	APts	PIM	PP	SH	GW	S	%	TGF	PGF	TGA	PGA	+/–	GP	G	A	Pts	PIM	PP	SH	GW
1972-73	Bemidji State University	NCAA II	30	23	24	47	....	....	....	....	....	....	....	....	....	....	....	....	....	....	....	....	....	....	....	....	....	....
1972-73	United States	Nat-Team	7	1	4	5	....	....	....	0	....	....	....	....	....	....	....	....	....	....	....	....	....	....	....	....	....	....
1973-74	Fargo Moorheads	MWJHL	47	37	46	83	....	....	....	78	....	....	....	....	....	....	....	....	....	....	....	....	....	....	....	....	....	....
	United States	WJC-A	3	0	2	2	....	....	....	0	....	....	....	....	....	....	....	....	....	....	....	....	....	....	....	....	....	....

			REGULAR SEASON																		PLAYOFFS							
Season	Club	League	GP	G	A	Pts	AG	AA	APts	PIM	PP	SH	GW	S	%	TGF	PGF	TGA	PGA	+/–	GP	G	A	Pts	PIM	PP	SH	GW
1974-75	Springfield Indians	AHL	27	7	17	24	....	....	....	46	....	....	....	....	....	....	....	....	....	....	....	....	....	....	....	....	....	....
1975-76	Los Angeles Kings	NHL	63	8	16	24	7	13	20	36	3	0	1	87	9.2	59	10	59	7	–3	....	....	....	....	....	....	....	....
1976-77	United States	C Cup	5	0	0	0	....	....	....	2	....	....	....	....	....	....	....	....	....	....	....	....	....	....	....	....	....	....
	Los Angeles Kings	NHL	80	14	40	54	13	32	45	65	8	0	2	200	7.0	151	54	118	28	+7	9	3	4	7	6	2	0	0
1977-78	Los Angeles Kings	NHL	72	7	34	41	7	28	35	52	3	0	1	182	3.8	133	41	95	21	+18	2	0	0	0	0	0	0	0
1978-79	Minnesota North Stars	NHL	79	12	32	44	11	24	35	39	8	0	1	182	6.6	145	43	135	23	–10	....	....	....	....	....	....	....	....
1979-80	Minnesota North Stars	NHL	52	13	21	34	12	16	28	22	3	0	1	129	10.1	91	32	54	7	+12	4	2	1	3	2	1	0	1
1980-81	Minnesota North Stars	NHL	23	4	7	11	3	5	8	36	2	0	0	42	9.5	31	11	24	3	–1	....	....	....	....	....	....	....	....
1981-82	Minnesota North Stars	NHL	15	0	5	5	0	3	3	18	0	0	0	24	0.0	25	8	13	1	+5	....	....	....	....	....	....	....	....
1982-83	Minnesota North Stars	NHL	18	3	6	9	2	4	6	5	1	0	0	30	10.0	27	8	19	5	+5	5	0	2	2	0	0	0	0
	NHL Totals		402	61	161	222	55	125	180	273	28	0	6	876	7.0	662	207	517	95		20	5	7	12	8	3	0	1

Signed as a free agent by **Minnesota** from **LA Kings**, June 30, 1978. LA Kings received Rick Hampton, Steve Jensen and Dave Gardner as compensation.

• SARNER, CRAIG

Craig Sarner RW – L. 5′11″, 185 lbs. b: St. Paul, MN, 6/20/1949.

Season	Club	League	GP	G	A	Pts	AG	AA	APts	PIM	PP	SH	GW	S	%	TGF	PGF	TGA	PGA	+/–	GP	G	A	Pts	PIM	PP	SH	GW
1968-69	University of Minnesota	WCHA	28	5	0	5	....	....	....	4	....	....	....	....	....	....	....	....	....	....	....	....	....	....	....	....	....	....
1969-70	University of Minnesota	WCHA	33	13	10	23	....	....	....	2	....	....	....	....	....	....	....	....	....	....	....	....	....	....	....	....	....	....
1970-71	University of Minnesota	WCHA	29	12	19	31	....	....	....	17	....	....	....	....	....	....	....	....	....	....	....	....	....	....	....	....	....	....
1971-72	United States	Nat-Team	STATISTICS NOT AVAILABLE																									
	United States	Olympics	6	4	6	10	....	....	....	0	....	....	....	....	....	....	....	....	....	....	....	....	....	....	....	....	....	....
	United States	WEC-B	6	4	4	8	....	....	....	....	....	....	....	....	....	....	....	....	....	....	....	....	....	....	....	....	....	....
	Oklahoma City Blazers	CHL	5	1	0	1	....	....	....	0	....	....	....	....	....	....	....	....	....	....	....	....	....	....	....	....	....	....
1972-73	Boston Braves	AHL	74	27	27	54	....	....	....	16	....	....	....	....	....	....	....	....	....	....	5	2	3	5	2	....	....	....
1973-74	Boston Braves	AHL	66	15	26	41	....	....	....	18	....	....	....	....	....	....	....	....	....	....	....	....	....	....	....	....	....	....
1974-75	Boston Bruins	NHL	7	0	0	0	0	0	0	0	0	0	0	5	0.0	3	0	7	1	–3	....	....	....	....	....	....	....	....
	Rochester Americans	AHL	47	14	13	27	....	....	....	26	....	....	....	....	....	....	....	....	....	....	12	4	3	7	4	....	....	....
1975-76	Minnesota Fighting Saints	WHA	1	0	0	0	....	....	....	0	....	....	....	....	....	....	....	....	....	....	....	....	....	....	....	....	....	....
	United States	Nat-Team	STATISTICS NOT AVAILABLE																									
	United States	WEC-A	10	2	1	3	....	....	....	13	....	....	....	....	....	....	....	....	....	....	....	....	....	....	....	....	....	....
1976-77	EC Kolner	Germany	41	35	26	61	....	....	....	100	....	....	....	....	....	....	....	....	....	....	....	....	....	....	....	....	....	....
1977-78	EC Kolner	Germany	STATISTICS NOT AVAILABLE																									
1978-79	Berlin Sports Club	Germany	....	52	64	116	....	....	....	....	....	....	....	....	....	....	....	....	....	....	8	1	1	2	4	....	....	....
	United States	WEC-A	8	1	1	2	....	....	....	4	....	....	....	....	....	....	....	....	....	....	....	....	....	....	....	....	....	....
1979-80	HC Davos	Switz.	....	19	10	29	....	....	....	....	....	....	....	....	....	....	....	....	....	....	....	....	....	....	....	....	....	....
1980-81	HC Davos	Switz.	....	16	14	30	....	....	....	....	....	....	....	....	....	....	....	....	....	....	....	....	....	....	....	....	....	....
	NHL Totals		7	0	0	0	0	0	0	0	0	0	0	5	0.0	3	0	7	1		....	....	....	....	....	....	....	....
	Other Major League Totals		1	0	0	0	....	....	....	0	....	....	....	....	....	....	....	....	....	....	....	....	....	....	....	....	....	....

Selected by **Minnesota** (WHA) in 1972 WHA General Player Draft, February 12, 1972. Signed as a free agent by **Boston**, March, 1972.

• SARRAZIN, DICK

Dick Sarrazin RW – R. 6′, 185 lbs. b: St. Gabriel-de-Brandon, Que., 1/22/1946.

Season	Club	League	GP	G	A	Pts	AG	AA	APts	PIM	PP	SH	GW	S	%	TGF	PGF	TGA	PGA	+/–	GP	G	A	Pts	PIM	PP	SH	GW
1963-64	St. Jerome Alouettes	QJHL	44	15	28	43	....	....	....	6	....	....	....	....	....	....	....	....	....	....	....	....	....	....	....	....	....	....
1964-65	St. Jerome Alouettes	QJHL	50	25	25	50	....	....	....	14	....	....	....	....	....	....	....	....	....	....	....	....	....	....	....	....	....	....
1965-66	St. Jerome Alouettes	QJHL	50	33	32	65	....	....	....	54	....	....	....	....	....	....	....	....	....	....	....	....	....	....	....	....	....	....
1966-67	Johnstown–New Jersey	EHL	69	26	28	54	....	....	....	20	....	....	....	....	....	....	....	....	....	....	16	3	4	7	2	....	....	....
1967-68	Quebec Aces	AHL	69	17	19	36	....	....	....	27	....	....	....	....	....	....	....	....	....	....	15	3	4	7	2	....	....	....
1968-69	Philadelphia Flyers	NHL	54	16	30	46	18	28	46	14	6	1	3	128	12.5	59	23	49	6	–7	4	0	0	0	0	0	0	0
	Quebec Aces	AHL	19	7	6	13	....	....	....	4	....	....	....	....	....	....	....	....	....	....	....	....	....	....	....	....	....	....
1969-70	Philadelphia Flyers	NHL	18	1	1	2	1	1	2	4	1	0	0	32	3.1	10	3	10	1	–2	....	....	....	....	....	....	....	....
	Quebec Aces	AHL	50	10	20	30	....	....	....	18	....	....	....	....	....	....	....	....	....	....	6	0	1	1	2	....	....	....
1970-71	Quebec Aces	AHL	70	21	53	74	....	....	....	39	....	....	....	....	....	....	....	....	....	....	10	5	6	11	23	....	....	....
1971-72	Philadelphia Flyers	NHL	28	3	4	7	3	4	7	4	1	0	1	38	7.9	14	6	10	2	0	....	....	....	....	....	....	....	....
	Richmond Robins	AHL	42	11	11	22	....	....	....	4	....	....	....	....	....	....	....	....	....	....	....	....	....	....	....	....	....	....
1972-73	New England Whalers	WHA	35	4	7	11	....	....	....	0	....	....	....	....	....	....	....	....	....	....	....	....	....	....	....	....	....	....
	Chicago Cougars	WHA	33	3	8	11	....	....	....	2	....	....	....	....	....	....	....	....	....	....	....	....	....	....	....	....	....	....
1973-74	Jacksonville Barons	AHL	76	20	34	54	....	....	....	18	....	....	....	....	....	....	....	....	....	....	....	....	....	....	....	....	....	....
1974-75	Syracuse Eagles	AHL	75	33	37	70	....	....	....	6	....	....	....	....	....	....	....	....	....	....	1	0	2	2	0	....	....	....
1975-76	Baltimore Clippers	AHL	55	14	13	27	....	....	....	14	....	....	....	....	....	....	....	....	....	....	....	....	....	....	....	....	....	....
	NHL Totals		100	20	35	55	22	33	55	22	8	1	4	198	10.1	83	32	69	9		4	0	0	0	0	0	0	0
	Other Major League Totals		68	7	15	22	....	....	....	2	....	....	....	....	....	....	....	....	....	....	....	....	....	....	....	....	....	....

Traded to **Philadelphia** (Quebec - AHL) by **Detroit** for cash, October, 1967. Selected by **New England** (WHA) in 1972 WHA General Player Draft, February 12, 1972. Traded to **Chicago** (WHA) by **New England** (WHA) for cash and future considerations, January, 1973. Selected by **Phoenix** (WHA) from **Chicago** (WHA) in 1974 WHA Expansion Draft, May, 1974.

• SASSER, GRANT

Grant Sasser C – R. 5′10″, 175 lbs. b: Portland, OR, 2/13/1964. Pittsburgh's 4th choice, 94th overall, in 1982 Entry Draft.

Season	Club	League	GP	G	A	Pts	AG	AA	APts	PIM	PP	SH	GW	S	%	TGF	PGF	TGA	PGA	+/–	GP	G	A	Pts	PIM	PP	SH	GW
1980-81	Fort Saskatchewan Traders	SJHL	54	33	49	82	....	....	....	49	....	....	....	....	....	....	....	....	....	....	....	....	....	....	....	....	....	....
1981-82	Portland Winter Hawks	WHL	49	19	23	42	....	....	....	32	....	....	....	....	....	....	....	....	....	....	15	5	6	11	13	....	....	....
1982-83	Portland Winter Hawks	WHL	70	54	65	119	....	....	....	39	....	....	....	....	....	....	....	....	....	....	14	12	15	27	4	....	....	....
1983-84	Portland Winter Hawks	WHL	66	44	69	113	....	....	....	24	....	....	....	....	....	....	....	....	....	....	14	5	8	13	2	....	....	....
	Pittsburgh Penguins	NHL	3	0	0	0	0	0	0	0	0	0	0	2	0.0	1	0	3	0	–2	....	....	....	....	....	....	....	....
1984-85	Baltimore Skipjacks	AHL	60	5	7	12	....	....	....	12	....	....	....	....	....	....	....	....	....	....	....	....	....	....	....	....	....	....
	Muskegon Mohawks	IHL	10	1	4	5	....	....	....	18	....	....	....	....	....	....	....	....	....	....	....	....	....	....	....	....	....	....
	NHL Totals		3	0	0	0	0	0	0	0	0	0	0	2	0.0	1	0	3	0		....	....	....	....	....	....	....	....

• SATAN, MIROSLAV

Miroslav Satan C – L. 6′1″, 195 lbs. b: Topolcany, Czech., 10/22/1974. Edmonton's 6th choice, 111th overall, in 1993 Entry Draft.

Season	Club	League	GP	G	A	Pts	AG	AA	APts	PIM	PP	SH	GW	S	%	TGF	PGF	TGA	PGA	+/–	GP	G	A	Pts	PIM	PP	SH	GW
1991-92	Topocalny	Czech. 2	9	2	1	3	....	....	....	6	....	....	....	....	....	....	....	....	....	....	....	....	....	....	....	....	....	....
1992-93	Dukla Trencin	Czech.	38	11	6	17	....	....	....	....	....	....	....	....	....	....	....	....	....	....	....	....	....	....	....	....	....	....
1993-94	Dukla Trencin	Slovakia	30	32	16	48	....	....	....	16	....	....	....	....	....	....	....	....	....	....	....	....	....	....	....	....	....	....
	Slovakia	WJC-C	4	6	7	13	....	....	....	4	....	....	....	....	....	....	....	....	....	....	....	....	....	....	....	....	....	....
	Slovakia	Olympics	8	9	0	9	....	....	....	0	....	....	....	....	....	....	....	....	....	....	....	....	....	....	....	....	....	....
	Slovakia	WC-C1	6	7	1	8	....	....	....	18	....	....	....	....	....	....	....	....	....	....	....	....	....	....	....	....	....	....
1994-95	Cape Breton Oilers	AHL	25	24	16	40	....	....	....	15	....	....	....	....	....	....	....	....	....	....	....	....	....	....	....	....	....	....
	Detroit Vipers	IHL	8	1	3	4	....	....	....	4	....	....	....	....	....	....	....	....	....	....	....	....	....	....	....	....	....	....
	San Diego Gulls	IHL	6	0	2	2	....	....	....	6	....	....	....	....	....	....	....	....	....	....	....	....	....	....	....	....	....	....
	Slovakia	WC-B	7	7	6	13	....	....	....	4	....	....	....	....	....	....	....	....	....	....	....	....	....	....	....	....	....	....
1995-96	Edmonton Oilers	NHL	62	18	17	35	18	14	32	22	6	0	4	113	15.9	57	19	39	1	0	....	....	....	....	....	....	....	....
	Slovakia	WC-A	5	0	3	3	....	....	....	6	....	....	....	....	....	....	....	....	....	....	....	....	....	....	....	....	....	....
1996-97	Slovakia	W Cup	3	0	0	0	....	....	....	2	....	....	....	....	....	....	....	....	....	....	....	....	....	....	....	....	....	....
	Edmonton Oilers	NHL	64	17	11	28	18	10	28	22	5	0	2	90	18.9	41	13	32	0	–4	....	....	....	....	....	....	....	....
	Buffalo Sabres	NHL	12	8	2	10	8	2	10	4	2	0	1	29	27.6	12	3	8	0	+1	7	0	0	0	0	0	0	0
1997-98	Buffalo Sabres	NHL	79	22	24	46	26	23	49	34	9	0	4	139	15.8	64	25	38	1	+2	14	5	4	9	4	4	0	1
	NHL Totals		217	65	54	119	70	49	119	82	22	0	11	371	17.5	174	60	117	2		21	5	4	9	4	4	0	1

Named Best Forward at WC-C1 (1994) • WC-B All-Star Team (1995)

Traded to **Buffalo** by **Edmonton** for Barrie Moore and Craig Millar, March 18, 1997.

• SATHER, GLEN

Glen "Slats" Sather LW – L. 5′11″, 180 lbs. b: High River, Alta., 9/2/1943.

Season	Club	League	GP	G	A	Pts	AG	AA	APts	PIM	PP	SH	GW	S	%	TGF	PGF	TGA	PGA	+/–	GP	G	A	Pts	PIM	PP	SH	GW
1963-64	Edmonton Oil Kings	WCJHL	14	13	14	27	....	....	....	22	....	....	....	....	....	....	....	....	....	....	....	....	....	....	....	....	....	....
1964-65	Memphis Wings	CHL	69	19	29	48	....	....	....	98	....	....	....	....	....	....	....	....	....	....	....	....	....	....	....	....	....	....
1965-66	Oklahoma City Blazers	CHL	64	13	12	25	....	....	....	76	....	....	....	....	....	....	....	....	....	....	9	4	4	8	14	....	....	....
1966-67	Oklahoma City Blazers	CHL	57	14	19	33	....	....	....	147	....	....	....	....	....	....	....	....	....	....	11	2	6	8	24	....	....	....
	Boston Bruins	NHL	5	0	0	0	0	0	0	0	....	....	....	....	....	....	....	....	....	....	....	....	....	....	....	....	....	....
1967-68	Boston Bruins	NHL	65	8	12	20	10	13	23	34	0	2	1	55	14.5	33	4	39	19	+9	3	0	0	0	0	0	0	0
1968-69	Boston Bruins	NHL	76	4	11	15	4	10	14	67	0	1	1	51	7.8	25	1	46	26	+4	10	0	0	0	18	0	0	0

			REGULAR SEASON																		PLAYOFFS							
Season	Club	League	GP	G	A	Pts	AG	AA	APts	PIM	PP	SH	GW	S	%	TGF	PGF	TGA	PGA	+/–	GP	G	A	Pts	PIM	PP	SH	GW
1969-70	**Pittsburgh Penguins**	**NHL**	**76**	**12**	**14**	**26**	**14**	**14**	**28**	**114**	**2**	**0**	**0**	**127**	**9.4**	**36**	**8**	**67**	**26**	**–13**	**10**	**0**	**2**	**2**	**17**	**0**	**0**	**0**
1970-71	**Pittsburgh Penguins**	**NHL**	**46**	**8**	**3**	**11**	**8**	**3**	**11**	**96**	**1**	**1**	**0**	**64**	**12.5**	**13**	**2**	**27**	**16**	**0**	....	....	....	....	....	....	....	....
	New York Rangers	**NHL**	**31**	**2**	**0**	**2**	**2**	**0**	**2**	**52**	**0**	**0**	**1**	**18**	**11.1**	**3**	**0**	**14**	**11**	**0**	**13**	**0**	**1**	**1**	**18**	**0**	**0**	**0**
1971-72	**New York Rangers**	**NHL**	**76**	**5**	**9**	**14**	**5**	**8**	**13**	**77**	**0**	**0**	**0**	**52**	**9.6**	**18**	**1**	**40**	**21**	**–2**	**16**	**0**	**1**	**1**	**22**	**0**	**0**	**0**
1972-73	**New York Rangers**	**NHL**	**77**	**11**	**15**	**26**	**11**	**13**	**24**	**64**	**1**	**1**	**2**	**69**	**15.9**	**47**	**1**	**37**	**7**	**+16**	**9**	**0**	**0**	**0**	**7**	**0**	**0**	**0**
1973-74	**New York Rangers**	**NHL**	**2**	**0**	**0**	**0**	**0**	**0**	**0**	**0**	**0**	**0**	**0**	**0**	**0.0**	**0**	**0**	**0**	**0**	**0**	....	....	....	....	....	....	....	....
	St. Louis Blues	**NHL**	**69**	**15**	**29**	**44**	**15**	**25**	**40**	**82**	**4**	**0**	**5**	**106**	**14.2**	**62**	**17**	**69**	**15**	**–9**	....	....	....	....	....	....	....	....
1974-75	**Montreal Canadiens**	**NHL**	**63**	**6**	**10**	**16**	**6**	**8**	**14**	**44**	**0**	**1**	**0**	**23**	**26.1**	**29**	**1**	**23**	**9**	**+14**	**11**	**1**	**1**	**2**	**4**	**0**	**0**	**0**
1975-76	**Minnesota North Stars**	**NHL**	**72**	**9**	**10**	**19**	**8**	**8**	**16**	**94**	**1**	**0**	**1**	**73**	**12.3**	**32**	**3**	**63**	**26**	**–8**	....	....	....	....	....	....	....	....
1976-77	Edmonton Oilers	WHA	81	19	34	53	....	....	....	77	....	....	....	....	....	....	....	....	....	....	5	1	1	2	2	....	....	....
	NHL Totals		**658**	**80**	**113**	**193**	**83**	**102**	**185**	**724**	**9**	**6**	**11**	**638**	**12.5**	**298**	**38**	**425**	**176**		**72**	**1**	**5**	**6**	**86**	**0**	**0**	**0**
	Other Major League Totals		81	19	34	53	....	....	....	77	....	....	....	....	....	....	....	....	....		5	1	1	2	2	....	....	....

Won Jack Adams Award (1986)

Claimed by **Boston** from **Memphis** (CHL) in Inter-League Draft, June 8, 1965. Selected by **Pittsburgh** from **Boston** in Intra-League Draft, June 11, 1969. Traded to **NY Rangers** by **Pittsburgh** for Syl Apps Jr., January 26, 1971. Selected by **Edmonton** (WHA) in 1972 WHA General Player Draft, February 12, 1972. Traded to **St. Louis** by **NY Rangers** with Rene Villemeure for Jack Egers, October 28, 1973. Traded to **Montreal** by **St. Louis** to complete transaction that sent Rik Wilson to St. Louis (May 27, 1974), June 14, 1974. Traded to **Minnesota** by **Montreal** for Minnesota's 3rd round choice (Alain Cote) in 1977 Amateur Draft and cash, July 9, 1975.

• SAUNDERS, BERNIE

Bernie Saunders LW – R. 6', 190 lbs. b: Montreal, Que., 6/21/1956.

Season	Club	League	GP	G	A	Pts	AG	AA	APts	PIM	PP	SH	GW	S	%	TGF	PGF	TGA	PGA	+/–	GP	G	A	Pts	PIM	PP	SH	GW
1976-77	Western Michigan University	CCHA	37	24	16	40	....	....	....	24	....	....	....	....	....	....	....	....	....	....	....	....	....	....	....	....	....	....
1977-78	Western Michigan University	CCHA	33	22	29	51	....	....	....	30	....	....	....	....	....	....	....	....	....	....	....	....	....	....	....	....	....	....
1978-79	Western Michigan University	CCHA	36	23	21	44	....	....	....	11	....	....	....	....	....	....	....	....	....	....	....	....	....	....	....	....	....	....
	Kalamazoo Wings	IHL	3	1	3	4	....	....	....	0	....	....	....	....	....	....	....	....	....	....	....	....	....	....	....	....	....	....
1979-80	**Quebec Nordiques**	**NHL**	**4**	**0**	**0**	**0**	**0**	**0**	**0**	**0**	**0**	**0**	**0**	**4**	**0.0**	**1**	**0**	**2**	**0**	**–1**	....	....	....	....	....	....	....	....
	Cincinnati Stingers	CHL	29	13	11	24	....	....	....	16	....	....	....	....	....	....	....	....	....	....	....	....	....	....	....	....	....	....
	Syracuse Firebirds	AHL	38	23	17	40	....	....	....	29	....	....	....	....	....	....	....	....	....	....	4	1	0	1	2	....	....	....
1980-81	**Quebec Nordiques**	**NHL**	**6**	**0**	**1**	**1**	**0**	**1**	**1**	**8**	**0**	**0**	**0**	**5**	**0.0**	**1**	**0**	**2**	**0**	**–1**	....	....	....	....	....	....	....	....
	Nova Scotia Voyageurs	AHL	69	17	21	38	....	....	....	88	....	....	....	....	....	....	....	....	....	....	6	1	1	2	4	....	....	....
1981-82	Kalamazoo Wings	IHL	70	38	37	75	....	....	....	57	....	....	....	....	....	....	....	....	....	....	5	3	2	5	6	....	....	....
1982-83			DID NOT PLAY																									
1983-84	Kalamazoo Wings	IHL	1	0	0	0	....	....	....	0	....	....	....	....	....	....	....	....	....	....	....	....	....	....	....	....	....	....
	NHL Totals		**10**	**0**	**1**	**1**	**0**	**1**	**1**	**8**	**0**	**0**	**0**	**9**	**0.0**	**2**	**0**	**4**	**0**		....	....	....	....	....	....	....	....

CCHA Second All-Star Team (1978)

Signed as a free agent by **Quebec**, May 29, 1979.

• SAUNDERS, DAVID

David Saunders LW – L. 6'1", 195 lbs. b: Ottawa, Ont., 5/20/1966. Vancouver's 3rd choice, 52nd overall, in 1984 Entry Draft.

Season	Club	League	GP	G	A	Pts	AG	AA	APts	PIM	PP	SH	GW	S	%	TGF	PGF	TGA	PGA	+/–	GP	G	A	Pts	PIM	PP	SH	GW
1983-84	St. Lawrence University	ECAC	32	10	21	31	....	....	....	24	....	....	....	....	....	....	....	....	....	....	....	....	....	....	....	....	....	....
1984-85	St. Lawrence University	ECAC	27	7	9	16	....	....	....	16	....	....	....	....	....	....	....	....	....	....	....	....	....	....	....	....	....	....
1985-86	St. Lawrence University	ECAC	29	15	19	34	....	....	....	26	....	....	....	....	....	....	....	....	....	....	....	....	....	....	....	....	....	....
1986-87	St. Lawrence University	ECAC	34	18	34	52	....	....	....	44	....	....	....	....	....	....	....	....	....	....	....	....	....	....	....	....	....	....
1987-88	**Vancouver Canucks**	**NHL**	**56**	**7**	**13**	**20**	**6**	**9**	**15**	**10**	**1**	**0**	**3**	**100**	**7.0**	**30**	**7**	**50**	**12**	**–15**	....	....	....	....	....	....	....	....
	Fredericton Express	AHL	14	9	7	16	....	....	....	6	....	....	....	....	....	....	....	....	....	....	8	1	0	1	12	....	....	....
	Flint Spirits	IHL	8	5	5	10		....	....	2	....	....	....	....	....	....	....	....	....	....	....	....	....	....	....	....	....	....
1988-89	Milwaukee Admirals	IHL	21	6	12	18			....	21	....	....	....	....	....	....	....	....	....	....	....	....	....	....	....	....	....	....
	Canada	Nat-Team	6	1	3	4	....	....	....	2	....	....	....	....	....	....	....	....	....	....	....	....	....	....	....	....	....	....
	NHL Totals		**56**	**7**	**13**	**20**	**6**	**9**	**15**	**10**	**1**	**0**	**3**	**100**	**7.0**	**30**	**7**	**50**	**12**		....	....	....	....	....	....	....	....

• SAUVE, JEAN-FRANCOIS

Jean-François "Frankie" Sauve C L. 5'6", 175 lbs. b: Ste. Genevieve, Que., 1/23/1960.

Season	Club	League	GP	G	A	Pts	AG	AA	APts	PIM	PP	SH	GW	S	%	TGF	PGF	TGA	PGA	+/–	GP	G	A	Pts	PIM	PP	SH	GW
1977-78	Trois-Rivieres Draveurs	QMJHL	6	2	3	5	....	....		0	....	....	....	....	....	....	....	....	....	....	....	....	....	....	....	....	....	....
1978-79	Trois-Rivieres Draveurs	QMJHL	72	65	111	*176	....	....	....	31	....	....	....	....	....	....	....	....	....	....	13	*19	*19	*38	4	....	....	....
1979-80	Trois-Rivieres Draveurs	QMJHL	72	63	*124	*187	....	....	....	31	....	....	....	....	....	....	....	....	....	....	7	5	9	14	0	....	....	....
	Rochester Americans	AHL	3	1	1	2	....	....	....	0	....	....	....	....	....	....	....	....	....	....	4	1	2	3	2	....	....	....
1980-81	**Buffalo Sabres**	**NHL**	**20**	**5**	**9**	**14**	**4**	**6**	**10**	**12**	**3**	**0**	**0**	**26**	**19.2**	**20**	**8**	**14**	**0**	**–2**	**5**	**2**	**0**	**2**	**0**	**1**	**0**	**0**
	Rochester Americans	AHL	56	29	54	83	....	....	....	21	....	....	....	....	....	....	....	....	....	....	....	....	....	....	....	....	....	....
1981-82	**Buffalo Sabres**	**NHL**	**69**	**19**	**36**	**55**	**15**	**24**	**39**	**46**	**5**	**0**	**1**	**119**	**16.0**	**85**	**31**	**47**	**0**	**+7**	**2**	**0**	**2**	**2**	**0**	**0**	**0**	**0**
	Rochester Americans	AHL	7	5	8	13	....	....	....	4	....	....	....	....	....	....	....	....	....	....	....	....	....	....	....	....	....	....
1982-83	**Buffalo Sabres**	**NHL**	**9**	**0**	**4**	**4**	**0**	**3**	**3**	**9**	**0**	**0**	**0**	**15**	**0.0**	**5**	**1**	**4**	**0**	**0**	....	....	....	....	....	....	....	....
	Rochester Americans	AHL	73	30	69	99	....	....	....	10	....	....	....	....	....	....	....	....	....	....	16	7	*21	*28	2	....	....	....
1983-84	**Quebec Nordiques**	**NHL**	**39**	**10**	**17**	**27**	**8**	**12**	**20**	**2**	**5**	**0**	**0**	**43**	**23.3**	**39**	**26**	**9**	**0**	**+4**	**9**	**2**	**5**	**7**	**2**	**2**	**0**	**1**
	Fredericton Express	AHL	26	19	31	50	....	....	....	23	....	....	....	....	....	....	....	....	....	....	....	....	....	....	....	....	....	....
1984-85	**Quebec Nordiques**	**NHL**	**64**	**13**	**29**	**42**	**11**	**20**	**31**	**21**	**8**	**0**	**1**	**85**	**15.3**	**71**	**43**	**18**	**1**	**+11**	**18**	**5**	**5**	**10**	**8**	**2**	**0**	**0**
1985-86	**Quebec Nordiques**	**NHL**	**75**	**16**	**40**	**56**	**13**	**27**	**40**	**20**	**13**	**0**	**1**	**100**	**16.0**	**74**	**64**	**23**	**0**	**–13**	**2**	**0**	**0**	**0**	**0**	**0**	**0**	**0**
1986-87	**Quebec Nordiques**	**NHL**	**14**	**2**	**3**	**5**	**2**	**2**	**4**	**4**	**2**	**0**	**0**	**14**	**14.3**	**10**	**10**	**4**	**0**	**–4**	....	....	....	....	....	....	....	....
	HC Fribourg	Switz.	....	33	*53	*86	....	....	....	....	....	....	....	....	....	....	....	....	....	....	....	....	....	....	....	....	....	....
1987-88	HC Fribourg	Switz.	36	35	*47	82	....	....	....	....	....	....	....	....	....	....	....	....	....	....	....	....	....	....	....	....	....	....
1988-89	HC Fribourg	Switz.	....	24	35	59	....	....	....	....	....	....	....	....	....	....	....	....	....	....	2	0	2	2	....	....	....	....
	Adirondack Red Wings	AHL	16	7	19	26	....	....	....	18	....	....	....	....	....	....	....	....	....	....	17	6	12	18	6	....	....	....
1989-90	ASG Tours	France 2	STATISTICS NOT AVAILABLE																									
1990-91	ASG Tours	France	23	21	29	50	....	....	....	....	....	....	....	....	....	....	....	....	....	....	....	....	....	....	....	....	....	....
	NHL Totals		**290**	**65**	**138**	**203**	**53**	**94**	**147**	**114**	**36**	**0**	**3**	**402**	**16.2**	**304**	**183**	**119**	**1**		**36**	**9**	**12**	**21**	**10**	**5**	**0**	**1**

QMJHL Second All-Star Team (1979) • QMJHL First All-Star Team (1980) • AHL Second All-Star Team (1981)

Signed as a free agent by **Buffalo**, November 1, 1979. Traded to **Quebec** by **Buffalo** with Tony McKegney, Andre Savard and Buffalo's 3rd round choice (Iiro Jarvi) in 1983 Entry Draft for Real Cloutier and Quebec's 1st round choice (Adam Creighton) in 1983 Entry Draft, June 8, 1983.

• SAVAGE, BRIAN

Brian Savage LW – L. 6'1", 190 lbs. b: Sudbury, Ont., 2/24/1971. Montreal's 11th choice, 171st overall, in 1991 Entry Draft.

Season	Club	League	GP	G	A	Pts	AG	AA	APts	PIM	PP	SH	GW	S	%	TGF	PGF	TGA	PGA	+/–	GP	G	A	Pts	PIM	PP	SH	GW
1990-91	University of Miami-Ohio	CCHA	28	5	6	11	....	....	....	26	....	....	....	....	....	....	....	....	....	....	....	....	....	....	....	....	....	....
1991-92	University of Miami-Ohio	CCHA	40	24	16	40	....	....	....	43	....	....	....	....	....	....	....	....	....	....	....	....	....	....	....	....	....	....
1992-93	University of Miami-Ohio	CCHA	38	*37	21	58	....	....	....	44	....	....	....	....	....	....	....	....	....	....	....	....	....	....	....	....	....	....
	Canada	Nat-Team	9	3	0	3	....	....	....	12	....	....	....	....	....	....	....	....	....	....	....	....	....	....	....	....	....	....
	Canada	WC-A	8	1	0	1	....	....	....	2	....	....	....	....	....	....	....	....	....	....	....	....	....	....	....	....	....	....
1993-94	Canada	Nat-Team	51	20	26	46	....	....	....	38	....	....	....	....	....	....	....	....	....	....	....	....	....	....	....	....	....	....
	Canada	Olympics	8	2	2	4	....	....	....	6	....	....	....	....	....	....	....	....	....	....	....	....	....	....	....	....	....	....
	Montreal Canadiens	**NHL**	**3**	**1**	**0**	**1**	**1**	**0**	**1**	**0**	**0**	**0**	**0**	**3**	**33.3**	**1**	**0**	**1**	**0**	**0**	**3**	**0**	**2**	**2**	**0**	**0**	**0**	**0**
	Fredericton Canadiens	AHL	17	12	15	27	....	....	....	4	....	....	....	....	....	....	....	....	....	....	....	....	....	....	....	....	....	....
1994-95	**Montreal Canadiens**	**NHL**	**37**	**12**	**7**	**19**	**21**	**10**	**31**	**27**	**0**	**0**	**0**	**64**	**18.8**	**30**	**2**	**27**	**4**	**+5**	....	....	....	....	....	....	....	....
1995-96	**Montreal Canadiens**	**NHL**	**75**	**25**	**8**	**33**	**25**	**7**	**32**	**28**	**4**	**0**	**4**	**150**	**16.7**	**55**	**16**	**47**	**0**	**–8**	**6**	**0**	**2**	**2**	**2**	**0**	**0**	**0**
1996-97	**Montreal Canadiens**	**NHL**	**81**	**23**	**37**	**60**	**24**	**33**	**57**	**39**	**5**	**0**	**2**	**219**	**10.5**	**80**	**20**	**74**	**0**	**–14**	**5**	**1**	**1**	**2**	**0**	**0**	**0**	**0**
1997-98	**Montreal Canadiens**	**NHL**	**64**	**26**	**17**	**43**	**31**	**17**	**48**	**36**	**8**	**0**	**7**	**152**	**17.1**	**60**	**16**	**33**	**0**	**+11**	**9**	**0**	**2**	**2**	**6**	**0**	**0**	**0**
	NHL Totals		**260**	**87**	**69**	**156**	**102**	**67**	**169**	**130**	**17**	**0**	**13**	**588**	**14.8**	**226**	**54**	**182**	**4**		**23**	**1**	**7**	**8**	**8**	**0**	**0**	**0**

CCHA First All-Star Team (1993) • NCAA West Second All-American Team (1993)

• SAVAGE, JOEL

Joel Savage RW – R. 5'11", 205 lbs. b: Surrey, B.C., 12/25/1969. Buffalo's 1st choice, 13th overall, in 1988 Entry Draft.

Season	Club	League	GP	G	A	Pts	AG	AA	APts	PIM	PP	SH	GW	S	%	TGF	PGF	TGA	PGA	+/–	GP	G	A	Pts	PIM	PP	SH	GW
1985-86	Kelowna Packers	BCJHL	43	10	12	22	....	....	....	76	....	....	....	....	....	....	....	....	....	....	11	2	1	3	6	....	....	....
1986-87	Victoria Cougars	WHL	68	14	13	27	....	....	....	48	....	....	....	....	....	....	....	....	....	....	5	2	0	2	0	....	....	....
1987-88	Victoria Cougars	WHL	69	37	32	69	....	....	....	73	....	....	....	....	....	....	....	....	....	....	....	....	....	....	....	....	....	....
1988-89	Victoria Cougars	WHL	60	17	30	47	....	....	....	95	....	....	....	....	....	....	....	....	....	....	6	1	1	2	8	....	....	....
1989-90	Rochester Americans	AHL	43	6	7	13	....	....	....	39	....	....	....	....	....	....	....	....	....	....	5	0	1	1	4	....	....	....
1990-91	**Buffalo Sabres**	**NHL**	**3**	**0**	**1**	**1**	**0**	**1**	**1**	**0**	**0**	**0**	**0**	**2**	**0.0**	**2**	**1**	**3**	**0**	**–2**	....	....	....	....	....	....	....	....
	Rochester Americans	AHL	61	25	19	44	....	....	....	45	....	....	....	....	....	....	....	....	....	....	15	3	3	6	8	....	....	....

			REGULAR SEASON																		PLAYOFFS							
Season	Club	League	GP	G	A	Pts	AG	AA	APts	PIM	PP	SH	GW	S	%	TGF	PGF	TGA	PGA	+/–	GP	G	A	Pts	PIM	PP	SH	GW
1991-92	Rochester Americans	AHL	59	8	14	22	....	....	....	39	....	....	....	....	....	....	....	....	....	....	9	2	0	2	8	....	....	....
1992-93	Rochester Americans	AHL	6	1	1	2	....	....	....	6	....	....	....	....	....	....	....	....	....	....	3	0	0	0	12	....	....	....
	Fort Wayne Komets	IHL	46	21	16	37	....	....	....	60	....	....	....	....	....	....	....	....	....	....	10	3	5	8	22	....	....	....
1993-94	Fort Wayne Komets	IHL	31	2	11	13	....	....	....	29	....	....	....	....	....	....	....	....	....	....	....	....	....	....	....	....	....	....
	San Diego Gulls	IHL	20	0	2	2	....	....	....	4	....	....	....	....	....	....	....	....	....	....	....	....	....	....	....	....	....	....
	Kalamazoo Wings	IHL	4	2	1	3	....	....	....	0	....	....	....	....	....	....	....	....	....	....	2	0	0	0	4	....	....	....
1994-95	Canada	Nat-Team	37	10	17	27	....	....	....	47	....	....	....	....	....	....	....	....	....	....	....	....	....	....	....	....	....	....
1995-96	Star Bulls Rosenheim	Germany	50	16	38	54	....	....	....	62	....	....	....	....	....	....	....	....	....	....	4	0	3	3	18	....	....	....
1996-97	Star Bulls Rosenheim	Germany	46	8	19	27	....	....	....	108	....	....	....	....	....	....	....	....	....	....	3	0	2	2	2	....	....	....
1997-98	HC Lugano	Switz.	11	1	3	4	....	....	....	8	....	....	....	....	....	....	....	....	....	....	....	....	....	....	....	....	....	....
	Frankfurt Lions	Germany	27	7	14	21	....	....	....	40	....	....	....	....	....	....	....	....	....	....	....	....	....	....	....	....	....	....
	NHL Totals		**3**	**0**	**1**	**1**	**0**	**1**	**1**	**0**	**0**	**0**	**0**	**2**	**0.0**	**2**	**1**	**3**	**0**		....	....	....	....	....	....	....	....

WHL West Second All-Star Team (1988)

Signed as a free agent by **Anaheim**, September 19, 1993.

• SAVAGE, REGGIE

Reggie Savage C – L. 5'10", 192 lbs. b: Montreal, Que., 5/1/1970. Washington's 1st choice, 15th overall, in 1988 Entry Draft.

1986-87	Richelieu Midgets	Midget	42	82	57	139	....	....	....	44	....	....	....	....	....	....	....	....	....	....	....	....	....	....	....	....	....	....
1987-88	Victoriaville Tigres	QMJHL	68	68	54	122	....	....	....	77	....	....	....	....	....	....	....	....	....	....	5	2	3	5	8	....	....	....
1988-89	Victoriaville Tigres	QMJHL	54	58	55	113	....	....	....	178	....	....	....	....	....	....	....	....	....	....	16	15	13	28	52	....	....	....
	Canada	WJC-A	7	4	5	9	....	....	....	4	....	....	....	....	....	....	....	....	....	....	....	....	....	....	....	....	....	....
1989-90	Victoriaville Tigres	QMJHL	63	51	43	94	....	....	....	79	....	....	....	....	....	....	....	....	....	....	16	13	10	23	40	....	....	....
1990-91	**Washington Capitals**	**NHL**	**1**	**0**	**0**	**0**	**0**	**0**	**0**	**0**	**0**	**0**	**0**	**2**	**0.0**	**0**	**0**	**1**	**0**	**–1**	....	....	....	....	....	....	....	....
	Baltimore Skipjacks	AHL	62	32	29	61	....	....	....	10	....	....	....	....	....	....	....	....	....	....	6	1	1	2	6	....	....	....
1991-92	Baltimore Skipjacks	AHL	77	42	28	70	....	....	....	51	....	....	....	....	....	....	....	....	....	....	....	....	....	....	....	....	....	....
1992-93	**Washington Capitals**	**NHL**	**16**	**2**	**3**	**5**	**2**	**2**	**4**	**12**	**2**	**0**	**0**	**20**	**10.0**	**9**	**4**	**9**	**0**	**–4**	....	....	....	....	....	....	....	....
	Baltimore Skipjacks	AHL	40	37	18	55	....	....	....	28	....	....	....	....	....	....	....	....	....	....	....	....	....	....	....	....	....	....
1993-94	**Quebec Nordiques**	**NHL**	**17**	**3**	**4**	**7**	**3**	**3**	**6**	**16**	**1**	**0**	**0**	**25**	**12.0**	**9**	**3**	**3**	**0**	**+3**	....	....	....	....	....	....	....	....
	Cornwall Aces	AHL	33	21	13	34	....	....	....	56	....	....	....	....	....	....	....	....	....	....	....	....	....	....	....	....	....	....
1994-95	Cornwall Aces	AHL	34	13	7	20	....	....	....	56	....	....	....	....	....	....	....	....	....	....	14	5	6	11	40	....	....	....
1995-96	Atlanta Knights	IHL	66	22	14	36	....	....	....	118	....	....	....	....	....	....	....	....	....	....	....	....	....	....	....	....	....	....
	Syracuse Crunch	AHL	10	9	5	14	....	....	....	28	....	....	....	....	....	....	....	....	....	....	16	9	6	15	54	....	....	....
1996-97	Springfield Falcons	AHL	68	32	25	57	....	....	....	103	....	....	....	....	....	....	....	....	....	....	17	6	7	13	24	....	....	....
1997-98	Kansas City Blades	IHL	51	6	10	16	....	....	....	60	....	....	....	....	....	....	....	....	....	....	....	....	....	....	....	....	....	....
	San Antonio Dragons	IHL	22	6	12	18	....	....	....	24	....	....	....	....	....	....	....	....	....	....	....	....	....	....	....	....	....	....
	Orlando Solar Bears	IHL	10	5	5	10	....	....	....	18	....	....	....	....	....	....	....	....	....	....	17	2	9	11	60	....	....	....
	NHL Totals		**34**	**5**	**7**	**12**	**5**	**5**	**10**	**28**	**3**	**0**	**0**	**47**	**10.6**	**18**	**7**	**13**	**0**		....	....	....	....	....	....	....	....

Traded to **Quebec** by **Washington** with Paul MacDermid for Mike Hough, June 20, 1993. Signed as a free agent by **Phoenix**, August 28, 1996.

• SAVARD, ANDRE

Andre Savard C – L. 6'1", 185 lbs. b: Temiscamingue, Que., 2/9/1953. Boston's 1st choice, 6th overall, in 1973 Amateur Draft.

1969-70	Quebec Remparts	QJHL	56	23	60	83	....	....	....	126	....	....	....	....	....	....	....	....	....	....	15	9	13	22	30	....	....	....
1970-71	Quebec Remparts	QJHL	61	50	89	139	....	....	....	150	....	....	....	....	....	....	....	....	....	....	14	9	17	26	56	....	....	....
1971-72	Quebec Remparts	QMJHL	33	32	46	78	....	....	....	107	....	....	....	....	....	....	....	....	....	....	....	....	....	....	....	....	....	....
1972-73	Quebec Remparts	QMJHL	56	67	84	*151	....	....	....	147	....	....	....	....	....	....	....	....	....	....	15	8	*24	*42	33	....	....	....
1973-74	**Boston Bruins**	**NHL**	**72**	**16**	**14**	**30**	**16**	**12**	**28**	**39**	**0**	**0**	**1**	**88**	**18.2**	**41**	**1**	**24**	**0**	**+16**	**16**	**3**	**2**	**5**	**24**	**0**	**0**	**0**
1974-75	**Boston Bruins**	**NHL**	**77**	**19**	**25**	**44**	**18**	**20**	**38**	**45**	**0**	**0**	**2**	**150**	**12.7**	**62**	**2**	**47**	**3**	**+16**	**3**	**1**	**1**	**2**	**2**	**0**	**0**	**1**
1975-76	**Boston Bruins**	**NHL**	**79**	**17**	**23**	**40**	**16**	**18**	**34**	**60**	**0**	**0**	**3**	**182**	**9.3**	**58**	**2**	**56**	**4**	**+4**	**12**	**1**	**4**	**5**	**9**	**0**	**0**	**0**
1976-77	**Buffalo Sabres**	**NHL**	**80**	**25**	**35**	**60**	**24**	**28**	**52**	**30**	**4**	**0**	**4**	**160**	**15.6**	**89**	**17**	**69**	**6**	**+9**	**6**	**0**	**1**	**1**	**2**	**0**	**0**	**0**
1977-78	**Buffalo Sabres**	**NHL**	**80**	**19**	**20**	**39**	**18**	**16**	**34**	**40**	**2**	**0**	**0**	**127**	**15.0**	**56**	**5**	**51**	**1**	**+1**	**6**	**0**	**0**	**0**	**4**	**0**	**0**	**0**
1978-79	**Buffalo Sabres**	**NHL**	**65**	**18**	**22**	**40**	**16**	**17**	**33**	**20**	**2**	**2**	**1**	**97**	**18.6**	**59**	**6**	**59**	**8**	**–2**	**3**	**0**	**2**	**2**	**2**	**0**	**0**	**0**
1979-80	**Buffalo Sabres**	**NHL**	**33**	**3**	**10**	**13**	**3**	**8**	**11**	**16**	**0**	**0**	**2**	**36**	**8.3**	**16**	**0**	**14**	**2**	**+4**	**8**	**1**	**1**	**2**	**2**	**0**	**0**	**0**
	Rochester Americans	AHL	25	11	17	28	....	....	....	4	....	....	....	....	....	....	....	....	....	....	....	....	....	....	....	....	....	....
1980-81	**Buffalo Sabres**	**NHL**	**79**	**31**	**43**	**74**	**26**	**30**	**56**	**63**	**2**	**2**	**4**	**149**	**20.8**	**110**	**24**	**65**	**11**	**+32**	**8**	**4**	**2**	**6**	**17**	**1**	**0**	**0**
1981-82	**Buffalo Sabres**	**NHL**	**62**	**18**	**20**	**38**	**14**	**13**	**27**	**24**	**2**	**1**	**3**	**118**	**15.3**	**50**	**4**	**60**	**19**	**+5**	**4**	**0**	**1**	**1**	**5**	**0**	**0**	**0**
1982-83	**Buffalo Sabres**	**NHL**	**68**	**16**	**25**	**41**	**13**	**17**	**30**	**28**	**3**	**2**	**2**	**122**	**13.1**	**53**	**7**	**45**	**10**	**+11**	**10**	**0**	**4**	**4**	**8**	**0**	**0**	**0**
1983-84	**Quebec Nordiques**	**NHL**	**60**	**20**	**24**	**44**	**16**	**16**	**32**	**38**	**0**	**2**	**2**	**100**	**20.0**	**58**	**2**	**65**	**26**	**+17**	**9**	**3**	**0**	**3**	**2**	**0**	**2**	**1**
1984-85	**Quebec Nordiques**	**NHL**	**35**	**9**	**10**	**19**	**7**	**7**	**14**	**8**	**1**	**1**	**1**	**55**	**16.4**	**25**	**2**	**44**	**18**	**–3**	....	....	....	....	....	....	....	....
	NHL Totals		**790**	**211**	**271**	**482**	**187**	**202**	**389**	**411**	**16**	**10**	**25**	**1384**	**15.2**	**677**	**72**	**599**	**108**		**85**	**13**	**18**	**31**	**77**	**1**	**2**	**2**

QJHL Second All-Star Team (1971) • QMJHL First All-Star Team (1973)

Signed as a free agent by **Buffalo**, June 11, 1976. Traded to **Quebec** by **Buffalo** with Tony McKegney, Jean-Francois Sauve and Buffalo's 3rd round choice (Iiro Jarvi) in 1983 Entry Draft for Real Cloutier and Quebec's 1st round choice (Adam Creighton) in 1983 Entry Draft, June 8, 1983.

• SAVARD, DENIS

Denis Savard C – R. 5'10", 175 lbs. b: Pointe Gatineau, Que., 2/4/1961. Chicago's 1st choice, 3rd overall, in 1980 Entry Draft.

1977-78	Montreal Jr. Canadiens	QMJHL	72	37	79	116	....	....	....	22	....	....	....	....	....	....	....	....	....	....	....	....	....	....	....	....	....	....
1978-79	Montreal Jr. Canadiens	QMJHL	70	46	*112	158	....	....	....	88	....	....	....	....	....	....	....	....	....	....	11	5	6	11	46	....	....	....
1979-80	Montreal Jr. Canadiens	QMJHL	72	63	118	181	....	....	....	93	....	....	....	....	....	....	....	....	....	....	10	7	16	23	8	....	....	....
1980-81	**Chicago Black Hawks**	**NHL**	**76**	**28**	**47**	**75**	**23**	**33**	**56**	**47**	**4**	**0**	**3**	**159**	**17.6**	**102**	**20**	**64**	**9**	**+27**	**3**	**0**	**0**	**0**	**0**	**0**	**0**	**0**
1981-82	**Chicago Black Hawks**	**NHL**	**80**	**32**	**87**	**119**	**25**	**58**	**83**	**82**	**8**	**0**	**4**	**231**	**13.9**	**149**	**57**	**95**	**3**	**0**	**15**	**11**	**7**	**18**	**52**	**5**	**0**	**2**
1982-83	**Chicago Black Hawks**	**NHL**	**78**	**35**	**86**	**121**	**29**	**60**	**89**	**99**	**13**	**0**	**4**	**213**	**16.4**	**153**	**61**	**67**	**1**	**+26**	**13**	**8**	**9**	**17**	**22**	**3**	**0**	**1**
1983-84	**Chicago Black Hawks**	**NHL**	**75**	**37**	**57**	**94**	**30**	**39**	**69**	**71**	**12**	**0**	**5**	**210**	**17.6**	**121**	**53**	**83**	**2**	**–13**	**5**	**1**	**3**	**4**	**9**	**0**	**0**	**0**
1984-85	**Chicago Black Hawks**	**NHL**	**79**	**38**	**67**	**105**	**31**	**45**	**76**	**56**	**7**	**0**	**1**	**266**	**14.3**	**133**	**47**	**70**	**0**	**+16**	**15**	**9**	**20**	**29**	**20**	**3**	**0**	**0**
1985-86	**Chicago Black Hawks**	**NHL**	**80**	**47**	**69**	**116**	**38**	**46**	**84**	**111**	**14**	**1**	**8**	**279**	**16.8**	**149**	**47**	**103**	**8**	**+7**	**3**	**4**	**1**	**5**	**6**	**2**	**0**	**0**
1986-87	**Chicago Blackhawks**	**NHL**	**70**	**40**	**50**	**90**	**35**	**36**	**71**	**108**	**7**	**0**	**7**	**237**	**16.9**	**116**	**38**	**68**	**5**	**+15**	**4**	**1**	**0**	**1**	**12**	**0**	**0**	**0**
1987-88	**Chicago Blackhawks**	**NHL**	**80**	**44**	**87**	**131**	**38**	**62**	**100**	**95**	**14**	**7**	**6**	**270**	**16.3**	**158**	**77**	**112**	**35**	**+4**	**5**	**4**	**3**	**7**	**17**	**0**	**1**	**1**
1988-89	**Chicago Blackhawks**	**NHL**	**58**	**23**	**59**	**82**	**20**	**42**	**62**	**110**	**7**	**5**	**1**	**182**	**12.6**	**106**	**52**	**87**	**28**	**–5**	**16**	**8**	**11**	**19**	**10**	**2**	**1**	**1**
1989-90	**Chicago Blackhawks**	**NHL**	**60**	**27**	**53**	**80**	**23**	**38**	**61**	**56**	**10**	**2**	**4**	**181**	**14.9**	**97**	**39**	**64**	**14**	**+8**	**20**	**7**	**15**	**22**	**41**	**4**	**0**	**1**
1990-91	Montreal Canadiens	FrTour	4	3	3	6	....	....	....	4	....	....	....	....	....	....	....	....	....	....	....	....	....	....	....	....	....	....
	Montreal Canadiens	**NHL**	**70**	**28**	**31**	**59**	**26**	**23**	**49**	**52**	**7**	**2**	**0**	**187**	**15.0**	**76**	**29**	**51**	**3**	**–1**	**13**	**2**	**11**	**13**	**35**	**1**	**0**	**0**
1991-92	**Montreal Canadiens**	**NHL**	**77**	**28**	**42**	**70**	**26**	**32**	**58**	**73**	**12**	**1**	**5**	**174**	**16.1**	**92**	**40**	**51**	**5**	**+6**	**11**	**3**	**9**	**12**	**8**	**1**	**0**	**0**
1992-93	**Montreal Canadiens**	**NHL**	**63**	**16**	**34**	**50**	**13**	**23**	**36**	**90**	**4**	**1**	**2**	**99**	**16.2**	**63**	**19**	**55**	**12**	**+1**	**14**	**0**	**5**	**5**	**4**	**0**	**0**	**0**
1993-94	**Tampa Bay Lightning**	**NHL**	**74**	**18**	**28**	**46**	**17**	**22**	**39**	**106**	**2**	**1**	**2**	**181**	**9.9**	**69**	**21**	**71**	**22**	**–1**	....	....	....	....	....	....	....	....
1994-95	**Tampa Bay Lightning**	**NHL**	**31**	**6**	**11**	**17**	**11**	**16**	**27**	**10**	**1**	**0**	**1**	**56**	**10.7**	**18**	**6**	**22**	**4**	**–6**	....	....	....	....	....	....	....	....
	Chicago Blackhawks	**NHL**	**12**	**4**	**4**	**8**	**7**	**6**	**13**	**8**	**1**	**0**	**0**	**26**	**15.4**	**13**	**5**	**7**	**2**	**+3**	**16**	**7**	**11**	**18**	**10**	**3**	**0**	**0**
1995-96	**Chicago Blackhawks**	**NHL**	**69**	**13**	**35**	**48**	**13**	**29**	**42**	**102**	**2**	**0**	**1**	**110**	**11.8**	**65**	**15**	**30**	**0**	**+20**	**10**	**1**	**2**	**3**	**8**	**0**	**0**	**0**
1996-97	**Chicago Blackhawks**	**NHL**	**64**	**9**	**18**	**27**	**10**	**16**	**26**	**60**	**2**	**0**	**2**	**82**	**11.0**	**40**	**15**	**37**	**2**	**–10**	**6**	**0**	**2**	**2**	**2**	**0**	**0**	**0**
	NHL Totals		**1196**	**473**	**865**	**1338**	**415**	**626**	**1041**	**1336**	**127**	**20**	**56**	**3143**	**15.0**	**1720**	**641**	**1137**	**155**		**169**	**66**	**109**	**175**	**256**	**24**	**2**	**6**

QMJHL First All-Star Team (1980) • NHL Second All-Star Team (1983)

Played in NHL All-Star Game (1982, 1983, 1984, 1986, 1988, 1991, 1996)

Traded to **Montreal** by **Chicago** for Chris Chelios and Montreal's 2nd round choice (Michael Pomichter) in 1991 Entry Draft, June 29, 1990. Signed as a free agent by **Tampa Bay**, July 29, 1993. Traded to **Chicago** by **Tampa Bay** for Chicago's 6th round choice (Xavier Delisle) in 1996 Entry Draft, April 6, 1995.

• SAVARD, JEAN

Jean Savard C – R. 5'11", 172 lbs. b: Verdun, Que., 4/26/1957. Chicago's 1st choice, 19th overall, in 1977 Amateur Draft.

1974-75	Montreal Jr. Canadiens	QMJHL	72	35	24	59	....	....	....	44	....	....	....	....	....	....	....	....	....	....	....	....	....	....	....	....	....	....
1975-76	Quebec Remparts	QMJHL	68	25	42	67	....	....	....	58	....	....	....	....	....	....	....	....	....	....	....	....	....	....	....	....	....	....
1976-77	Quebec Remparts	QMJHL	72	*84	96	*180	....	....	....	110	....	....	....	....	....	....	....	....	....	....	....	....	....	....	....	....	....	....
1977-78	**Chicago Black Hawks**	**NHL**	**31**	**7**	**11**	**18**	**7**	**9**	**16**	**20**	**2**	**0**	**2**	**37**	**18.9**	**24**	**3**	**15**	**0**	**+6**	....	....	....	....	....	....	....	....
	Dallas Black Hawks	CHL	41	17	18	35	....	....	....	28	....	....	....	....	....	....	....	....	....	....	13	4	4	8	32	....	....	....
1978-79	**Chicago Black Hawks**	**NHL**	**11**	**0**	**1**	**1**	**0**	**1**	**1**	**9**	**0**	**0**	**0**	**7**	**0.0**	**1**	**0**	**3**	**0**	**–2**	....	....	....	....	....	....	....	....
	New Brunswick Hawks	AHL	60	26	29	55	....	....	....	85	....	....	....	....	....	....	....	....	....	....	5	2	2	4	0	....	....	....
1979-80	**Hartford Whalers**	**NHL**	**1**	**0**	**0**	**0**	**0**	**0**	**0**	**0**	**0**	**0**	**0**	**1**	**0.0**	**0**	**0**	**0**	**0**	**0**	....	....	....	....	....	....	....	....
	Springfield Indians	AHL	78	28	43	71	....	....	....	60	....	....	....	....	....	....	....	....	....	....	....	....	....	....	....	....	....	....

			REGULAR SEASON																		PLAYOFFS							
Season	Club	League	GP	G	A	Pts	AG	AA	APts	PIM	PP	SH	GW	S	%	TGF	PGF	TGA	PGA	+/–	GP	G	A	Pts	PIM	PP	SH	GW
1980-81	Binghamton Whalers	AHL	52	13	27	40				70																		
1981-82	Zurich SC	Switz.	28	28	22	50				20																		
1982-83	Salt Lake Golden Eagles	CHL	3	0	2	2				4																		
1983-84	Zurich SC	Switz.	STATISTICS NOT AVAILABLE																									
1984-85	Salzburger	Austria	11	9	10	19				48																		
	NHL Totals		**43**	**7**	**12**	**19**	**7**	**10**	**17**	**29**	**2**	**0**	**2**	**45**	**15.6**	**25**	**3**	**18**	**0**									

QMJHL First All-Star Team (1977)

Claimed by **Hartford** from **Chicago** in Expansion Draft, June 13, 1979.

• SAVARD, MARC

Marc Savard C – L. 5'10", 174 lbs. b: Ottawa, Ont., 7/17/1977. NY Rangers' 3rd choice, 91st overall, in 1995 Entry Draft.

Season	Club	League	GP	G	A	Pts	AG	AA	APts	PIM	PP	SH	GW	S	%	TGF	PGF	TGA	PGA	+/–	GP	G	A	Pts	PIM	PP	SH	GW
1993-94	Oshawa Generals	OHL	61	18	39	57				20											5	4	3	7	8			
1994-95	Oshawa Generals	OHL	66	43	96	*139				78											7	5	6	11	8			
1995-96	Oshawa Generals	OHL	48	28	59	87				77											5	4	5	9	6			
1996-97	Oshawa Generals	OHL	64	43	*87	*130				94											18	13	*24	*37	20			
1997-98	**New York Rangers**	**NHL**	**28**	**1**	**5**	**6**	**1**	**5**	**6**	**4**	**0**	**0**	**0**	**32**	**3.1**	**9**	**5**	**9**	**1**	**–4**								
	Hartford Wolf Pack	AHL	58	21	53	74				66											15	8	19	27	24			
	NHL Totals		**28**	**1**	**5**	**6**	**1**	**5**	**6**	**4**	**0**	**0**	**0**	**32**	**3.1**	**9**	**5**	**9**	**1**									

OHL Second All-Star Team (1995)

• SAVARD, SERGE

Serge "The Senator" Savard D – L. 6'3", 210 lbs. b: Montreal, Que., 1/22/1946. **HHOF**

Season	Club	League	GP	G	A	Pts	AG	AA	APts	PIM	PP	SH	GW	S	%	TGF	PGF	TGA	PGA	+/–	GP	G	A	Pts	PIM	PP	SH	GW
1963-64	Montreal Jr. Canadiens	OHA	56	3	31	34				72											17	1	7	8	30			
1964-65	Montreal Jr. Canadiens	OHA	56	14	33	47				81											7	2	3	5	8			
	Omaha Knights	CHL	2	0	0	0				0											4	0	1	1	4			
1965-66	Montreal Jr. Canadiens	OHA	20	8	10	18				33											10	1	4	5	20			
1966-67	**Montreal Canadiens**	**NHL**	**2**	**0**	**0**	**0**	**0**	**0**	**0**	**0**																		
	Houston Apollos	CHL	68	7	25	32				155											5	1	3	4	17			
	Quebec Aces	AHL																			1	0	0	0	2			
1967-68	**Montreal Canadiens**	**NHL**	**67**	**2**	**13**	**15**	**2**	**14**	**16**	**34**	**1**	**0**	**0**	**59**	**3.4**	**51**	**5**	**40**	**7**	**+13**	**6**	**2**	**0**	**2**	**0**	**0**	**2**	**1**
1968-69	**Montreal Canadiens**	**NHL**	**74**	**8**	**23**	**31**	**9**	**22**	**31**	**73**	**0**	**0**	**2**	**98**	**8.2**	**93**	**4**	**62**	**6**	**+33**	**14**	**4**	**6**	**10**	**24**	**1**	**1**	**0**
1969-70	**Montreal Canadiens**	**NHL**	**64**	**12**	**19**	**31**	**14**	**19**	**33**	**38**	**5**	**3**	**2**	**151**	**7.9**	**96**	**26**	**92**	**26**	**+4**								
1970-71	**Montreal Canadiens**	**NHL**	**37**	**5**	**10**	**15**	**5**	**9**	**14**	**30**	**0**	**1**	**0**	**55**	**9.1**	**48**	**6**	**40**	**9**	**+11**								
1971-72	**Montreal Canadiens**	**NHL**	**23**	**1**	**8**	**9**	**1**	**7**	**8**	**16**	**0**	**0**	**0**	**45**	**2.2**	**43**	**6**	**21**	**5**	**+21**	**6**	**0**	**0**	**0**	**10**	**0**	**0**	**0**
1972-73	Canada	Summit	5	0	2	2				0																		
	Montreal Canadiens	**NHL**	**74**	**7**	**32**	**39**	**7**	**27**	**34**	**58**	**2**	**1**	**0**	**106**	**6.6**	**147**	**14**	**85**	**22**	**+70**	**17**	**3**	**8**	**11**	**22**	**0**	**0**	**0**
1973-74	**Montreal Canadiens**	**NHL**	**67**	**4**	**14**	**18**	**4**	**12**	**16**	**49**	**1**	**0**	**1**	**98**	**4.1**	**105**	**17**	**98**	**30**	**+20**	**6**	**1**	**1**	**2**	**4**	**0**	**0**	**0**
1974-75	**Montreal Canadiens**	**NHL**	**80**	**20**	**40**	**60**	**19**	**32**	**51**	**64**	**7**	**1**	**2**	**165**	**12.1**	**171**	**37**	**97**	**34**	**+71**	**11**	**1**	**7**	**8**	**2**	**0**	**0**	**0**
1975-76	**Montreal Canadiens**	**NHL**	**71**	**8**	**39**	**47**	**7**	**31**	**38**	**38**	**1**	**1**	**1**	**112**	**7.1**	**125**	**19**	**75**	**21**	**+52**	**13**	**3**	**6**	**9**	**6**	**1**	**1**	**2**
1976-77	Canada	C Cup	7	0	3	3				0																		
	Montreal Canadiens	**NHL**	**78**	**9**	**33**	**42**	**9**	**27**	**36**	**35**	**0**	**0**	**1**	**110**	**8.2**	**168**	**18**	**93**	**22**	**+79**	**14**	**2**	**7**	**9**	**2**	**1**	**0**	**1**
1977-78	**Montreal Canadiens**	**NHL**	**77**	**8**	**34**	**42**	**8**	**28**	**36**	**24**	**4**	**0**	**1**	**103**	**7.8**	**155**	**33**	**88**	**28**	**+62**	**15**	**1**	**7**	**8**	**8**	**0**	**0**	**0**
1978-79	**Montreal Canadiens**	**NHL**	**80**	**7**	**26**	**33**	**6**	**20**	**26**	**30**	**1**	**2**	**0**	**82**	**8.5**	**135**	**12**	**104**	**27**	**+46**	**16**	**2**	**7**	**9**	**6**	**1**	**0**	**1**
	NHL All-Stars	Chal Cup	3	0	0	0				0																		
1979-80	**Montreal Canadiens**	**NHL**	**46**	**5**	**8**	**13**	**5**	**6**	**11**	**18**	**0**	**0**	**1**	**45**	**11.1**	**58**	**8**	**68**	**16**	**–2**	**2**	**0**	**0**	**0**	**0**	**0**	**0**	**0**
1980-81	**Montreal Canadiens**	**NHL**	**77**	**4**	**13**	**17**	**3**	**9**	**12**	**30**	**0**	**0**	**1**	**63**	**6.3**	**93**	**1**	**108**	**28**	**+12**	**3**	**0**	**0**	**0**	**0**	**0**	**0**	**0**
1981-82	**Winnipeg Jets**	**NHL**	**47**	**2**	**5**	**7**	**2**	**3**	**5**	**26**	**0**	**0**	**1**	**41**	**4.9**	**67**	**0**	**94**	**19**	**–8**	**4**	**0**	**0**	**0**	**2**	**0**	**0**	**0**
1982-83	**Winnipeg Jets**	**NHL**	**76**	**4**	**16**	**20**	**3**	**11**	**14**	**29**	**0**	**0**	**0**	**51**	**7.8**	**88**	**1**	**155**	**44**	**–24**	**3**	**0**	**0**	**0**	**2**	**0**	**0**	**0**
	NHL Totals		**1040**	**106**	**333**	**439**	**104**	**277**	**381**	**592**	**22**	**9**	**13**	**1384**	**7.7**	**1643**	**207**	**1320**	**344**		**130**	**19**	**49**	**68**	**88**	**4**	**4**	**5**

CHL Second All-Star Team (1967) • Won Ken McKenzie Trophy (CHL's Rookie of the Year) (1967) • Won Conn Smythe Trophy (1969) • NHL Second All-Star Team (1979) • Won Bill Masterton Trophy (1979)

Played in NHL All-Star Game (1970, 1973, 1977, 1978)

Claimed by **Winnipeg** from **Montreal** in Waiver Draft, October 5, 1981.

• SAWYER, KEVIN

Kevin Sawyer LW – L. 6'2", 205 lbs. b: Christina Lake, B.C., 2/21/1974.

Season	Club	League	GP	G	A	Pts	AG	AA	APts	PIM	PP	SH	GW	S	%	TGF	PGF	TGA	PGA	+/–	GP	G	A	Pts	PIM	PP	SH	GW
1992-93	Spokane Chiefs	WHL	62	4	3	7				274											8	1	1	2	13			
1993-94	Spokane Chiefs	WHL	60	10	15	25				350											3	0	1	1	6			
1994-95	Spokane Chiefs	WHL	54	7	9	16				365											11	2	0	2	58			
	Peoria Rivermen	IHL																			2	0	0	0	12			
1995-96	**St. Louis Blues**	**NHL**	**6**	**0**	**0**	**0**	**0**	**0**	**0**	**23**	**0**	**0**	**0**	**1**	**0.0**	**0**	**0**	**2**	**0**	**–2**								
	Worcester IceCats	AHL	41	3	4	7				268																		
	Boston Bruins	**NHL**	**2**	**0**	**0**	**0**	**0**	**0**	**0**	**5**	**0**	**0**	**0**	**0**	**0.0**	**1**	**0**	**0**	**0**	**+1**								
	Providence Bruins	AHL	4	0	0	0				29											4	0	1	1	9			
1996-97	**Boston Bruins**	**NHL**	**2**	**0**	**0**	**0**	**0**	**0**	**0**	**0**	**0**	**0**	**0**	**0**	**0.0**	**0**	**0**	**0**	**0**	**0**								
	Providence Bruins	AHL	60	8	9	17				367											6	0	0	0	32			
1997-98	Michigan K-Wings	IHL	60	2	5	7				398											3	0	0	0	23			
	NHL Totals		**10**	**0**	**0**	**0**	**0**	**0**	**0**	**28**	**0**	**0**	**0**	**1**	**0.0**	**1**	**0**	**2**	**0**									

Signed as a free agent by **St. Louis**, February 28, 1995. Traded to **Boston** by **St. Louis** with Steve Staios for Steve Leach, March 8, 1996. Signed as a free agent by **Dallas**, August 19, 1997.

• SCAMURRA, PETER

Peter Scamurra D – L. 6'3", 185 lbs. b: Buffalo, NY, 2/23/1955. Washington's 2nd choice, 19th overall, in 1975 Amateur Draft.

Season	Club	League	GP	G	A	Pts	AG	AA	APts	PIM	PP	SH	GW	S	%	TGF	PGF	TGA	PGA	+/–	GP	G	A	Pts	PIM	PP	SH	GW
1972-73	Niagara Falls Flyers	OJHL	55	12	30	42				48																		
1973-74	University of Wisconsin	WCHA	13	2	1	3				12																		
	Peterborough Petes	OHA	35	3	11	14				12																		
	Canada	WJC-A	5	1	0	1				8																		
1974-75	Peterborough Petes	OHA	62	12	40	52				45																		
1975-76	**Washington Capitals**	**NHL**	**58**	**2**	**13**	**15**	**2**	**10**	**12**	**33**	**1**	**0**	**0**	**49**	**4.1**	**44**	**3**	**92**	**13**	**–38**								
	Richmond Robins	AHL	18	2	1	3				12																		
1976-77	**Washington Capitals**	**NHL**	**21**	**0**	**2**	**2**	**0**	**2**	**2**	**8**	**0**	**0**	**0**	**19**	**0.0**	**13**	**1**	**20**	**2**	**–6**								
	Springfield Indians	AHL	11	2	5	7				6																		
1977-78	Binghamton Dusters	AHL	13	2	2	4				20																		
1978-79	**Washington Capitals**	**NHL**	**30**	**3**	**5**	**8**	**3**	**4**	**7**	**12**	**0**	**1**	**0**	**26**	**11.5**	**33**	**1**	**61**	**16**	**–13**								
1979-80	**Washington Capitals**	**NHL**	**23**	**3**	**5**	**8**	**3**	**4**	**7**	**6**	**1**	**0**	**0**	**16**	**18.8**	**18**	**2**	**22**	**5**	**–1**								
1980-81	Saipa Lappeenranta	Finland	16	1	3	4				10																		
	Binghamton Whalers	AHL	6	1	2	3				4																		
	NHL Totals		**132**	**8**	**25**	**33**	**8**	**20**	**28**	**59**	**2**	**1**	**0**	**110**	**7.3**	**108**	**7**	**195**	**36**									

OHA Second All-Star Team (1975)

• SCATCHARD, DAVE

Dave Scatchard C – R. 6'2", 200 lbs. b: Hinton, Alta., 2/20/1976. Vancouver's 3rd choice, 42nd overall, in 1994 Entry Draft.

Season	Club	League	GP	G	A	Pts	AG	AA	APts	PIM	PP	SH	GW	S	%	TGF	PGF	TGA	PGA	+/–	GP	G	A	Pts	PIM	PP	SH	GW
1993-94	Portland Winter Hawks	WHL	47	9	11	20				46											10	2	1	3	4			
1994-95	Portland Winter Hawks	WHL	71	20	30	50				148											8	0	3	3	21			
1995-96	Portland Winter Hawks	WHL	59	19	28	47				146											7	1	8	9	14			
	Syracuse Crunch	AHL	1	0	0	0				0											15	2	5	7	29			
1996-97	Syracuse Crunch	AHL	26	8	7	15				65																		
1997-98	**Vancouver Canucks**	**NHL**	**76**	**13**	**11**	**24**	**15**	**11**	**26**	**165**	**0**	**0**	**1**	**85**	**15.3**	**30**	**2**	**35**	**3**	**–4**								
	NHL Totals		**76**	**13**	**11**	**24**	**15**	**11**	**26**	**165**	**0**	**0**	**1**	**85**	**15.3**	**30**	**2**	**35**	**3**									

REGULAR SEASON / PLAYOFFS

• SCEVIOUR, DARIN

Darin Sceviour RW – R. 5'10", 185 lbs. b: Lacombe, Alta., 11/30/1965. Chicago's 5th choice, 101st overall, in 1984 Entry Draft.

Season	Club	League	GP	G	A	Pts	AG	AA	APts	PIM	PP	SH	GW	S	%	TGF	PGF	TGA	PGA	+/-	GP	G	A	Pts	PIM	PP	SH	GW
1981-82	Red Deer Rustlers	Midget	64	55	67	122	....	....	....	87	....	....	....	....	....	....	....	....	....	....	....	....	....	....	....	....	....	....
1982-83	Lethbridge Broncos	WHL	64	9	17	26	....	....	....	45	....	....	....	....	....	....	....	....	....	....	17	8	0	8	9	....	....	....
1983-84	Lethbridge Broncos	WHL	71	37	28	65	....	....	....	28	....	....	....	....	....	....	....	....	....	....	5	2	2	4	0	....	....	....
1984-85	Lethbridge Broncos	WHL	67	39	36	75	....	....	....	37	....	....	....	....	....	....	....	....	....	....	4	2	2	4	0	....	....	....
1985-86	Nova Scotia Oilers	AHL	31	4	3	7	....	....	....	6	....	....	....	....	....	....	....	....	....	....	....	....	....	....	....	....	....	....
	Saginaw Generals	IHL	24	9	11	20	....	....	....	7	....	....	....	....	....	....	....	....	....	....	11	8	5	13	5	....	....	....
1986-87	**Chicago Blackhawks**	**NHL**	**1**	**0**	**0**	**0**	**0**	**0**	**0**	**0**	**0**	**0**	**0**	**1**	**0.0**	**0**	**0**	**0**	**0**	**0**	....	....	....	....	....	....	....	....
	Canada	Nat-Team	5	2	0	2	....	....	....	17	....	....	....	....	....	....	....	....	....	....	....	....	....	....	....	....	....	....
	Saginaw Generals	IHL	37	13	18	31	....	....	....	4	....	....	....	....	....	....	....	....	....	....	10	10	2	12	0	....	....	....
	NHL Totals		**1**	**0**	**0**	**0**	**0**	**0**	**0**	**0**	**0**	**0**	**0**	**1**	**0.0**	**0**	**0**	**0**	**0**		....	....	....	....	....	....	....	....

• SCHAMEHORN, KEVIN

Kevin Schamehorn RW – R. 5'9", 185 lbs. b: Calgary, Alta., 7/28/1956. Detroit's 4th choice, 58th overall, in 1976 Amateur Draft.

Season	Club	League	GP	G	A	Pts	AG	AA	APts	PIM	PP	SH	GW	S	%	TGF	PGF	TGA	PGA	+/-	GP	G	A	Pts	PIM	PP	SH	GW
1973-74	Bellingham Blazers	BCHL	58	17	8	25	....	....	....	293	....	....	....	....	....	....	....	....	....	....	....	....	....	....	....	....	....	....
	New Westminster Bruins	WCJHL	2	1	1	2	....	....	....	7	....	....	....	....	....	....	....	....	....	....	4	0	0	0	0	....	....	....
1974-75	New Westminster Bruins	WCJHL	37	14	6	20	....	....	....	175	....	....	....	....	....	....	....	....	....	....	18	7	11	18	13	....	....	....
1975-76	New Westminster Bruinas	WCJHL	62	32	42	74	....	....	....	276	....	....	....	....	....	....	....	....	....	....	17	8	9	17	68	....	....	....
1976-77	**Detroit Red Wings**	**NHL**	**3**	**0**	**0**	**0**	**0**	**0**	**0**	**9**	**0**	**0**	**0**	**1**	**0.0**	**0**	**0**	**1**	**0**	**–1**	....	....	....	....	....	....	....	....
	Kalamazoo Wings	IHL	77	27	32	59	....	....	....	314	....	....	....	....	....	....	....	....	....	....	10	3	9	12	76	....	....	....
1977-78	Kansas City Red Wings	CHL	36	5	3	8	....	....	....	113	....	....	....	....	....	....	....	....	....	....	....	....	....	....	....	....	....	....
	Kalamazoo Wings	IHL	39	18	14	32	....	....	....	144	....	....	....	....	....	....	....	....	....	....	7	1	3	4	65	....	....	....
1978-79	Kalamazoo Wings	IHL	80	45	57	102	....	....	....	245	....	....	....	....	....	....	....	....	....	....	15	*15	9	24	60	....	....	....
1979-80	**Detroit Red Wings**	**NHL**	**2**	**0**	**0**	**0**	**0**	**0**	**0**	**4**	**0**	**0**	**0**	**0**	**0.0**	**1**	**0**	**3**	**0**	**–2**	....	....	....	....	....	....	....	....
	Adirondack Red Wings	AHL	60	10	13	23	....	....	....	145	....	....	....	....	....	....	....	....	....	....	5	0	0	0	13	....	....	....
1980-81	**Los Angeles Kings**	**NHL**	**5**	**0**	**0**	**0**	**0**	**0**	**0**	**4**	**0**	**0**	**0**	**2**	**0.0**	**0**	**0**	**1**	**0**	**–1**	....	....	....	....	....	....	....	....
	Rochester Americans	AHL	27	6	10	16	....	....	....	44	....	....	....	....	....	....	....	....	....	....	....	....	....	....	....	....	....	....
	Houston Apollos	CHL	26	7	9	16	....	....	....	43	....	....	....	....	....	....	....	....	....	....	....	....	....	....	....	....	....	....
1981-82	Kalamazoo Wings	IHL	75	38	27	65	....	....	....	113	....	....	....	....	....	....	....	....	....	....	5	1	2	3	25	....	....	....
1982-83	Kalamazoo Wings	IHL	58	38	29	67	....	....	....	78	....	....	....	....	....	....	....	....	....	....	9	6	3	9	24	....	....	....
1983-84	Kalamazoo Wings	IHL	76	37	31	68	....	....	....	154	....	....	....	....	....	....	....	....	....	....	3	0	2	2	9	....	....	....
1984-85	Kalamazoo Wings	IHL	80	35	43	78	....	....	....	154	....	....	....	....	....	....	....	....	....	....	11	4	3	7	31	....	....	....
1985-86	Milwaukee Admirals	IHL	82	47	34	81	....	....	....	101	....	....	....	....	....	....	....	....	....	....	5	1	3	4	4	....	....	....
1986-87	Milwaukee Admirals	IHL	82	35	35	70	....	....	....	102	....	....	....	....	....	....	....	....	....	....	6	3	3	6	6	....	....	....
1987-88	Milwaukee Admirals	IHL	57	17	19	36	....	....	....	122	....	....	....	....	....	....	....	....	....	....	....	....	....	....	....	....	....	....
	Flint Spirits	IHL	19	3	11	14	....	....	....	32	....	....	....	....	....	....	....	....	....	....	....	....	....	....	....	....	....	....
1988-89			DID NOT PLAY																									
1989-90	Kalamazoo Wings	IHL	9	1	2	3	....	....	....	0	....	....	....	....	....	....	....	....	....	....	....	....	....	....	....	....	....	....
	NHL Totals		**10**	**0**	**0**	**0**	**0**	**0**	**0**	**17**	**0**	**0**	**0**	**3**	**0.0**	**1**	**0**	**5**	**0**		....	....	....	....	....	....	....	....

Signed as a free agent by **LA Kings**, October 18, 1980.

• SCHELLA, JOHN

John Schella D – R. 6', 180 lbs. b: Port Arthur, Ont., 5/9/1947.

Season	Club	League	GP	G	A	Pts	AG	AA	APts	PIM	PP	SH	GW	S	%	TGF	PGF	TGA	PGA	+/-	GP	G	A	Pts	PIM	PP	SH	GW
1964-65	Fort William Canadians	TBJHL	....	6	16	22	....	....	....	131	....	....	....	....	....	....	....	....	....	....	....	....	....	....	....	....	....	....
1965-66	Fort William Canadians	TBJHL	....	8	29	37	....	....	....	....	....	....	....	....	....	....	....	....	....	....	....	....	....	....	....	....	....	....
1966-67	Peterborough Petes	OHA	47	11	11	22	....	....	....	182	....	....	....	....	....	....	....	....	....	....	6	2	3	5	12	....	....	....
1967-68	Houston Apollos	CHL	39	5	2	7	....	....	....	110	....	....	....	....	....	....	....	....	....	....	....	....	....	....	....	....	....	....
1968-69	Denver Spurs	WHL	69	4	22	26	....	....	....	152	....	....	....	....	....	....	....	....	....	....	....	....	....	....	....	....	....	....
1969-70	Denver Spurs	WHL	67	7	30	37	....	....	....	198	....	....	....	....	....	....	....	....	....	....	....	....	....	....	....	....	....	....
1970-71	**Vancouver Canucks**	**NHL**	**38**	**0**	**5**	**5**	**0**	**4**	**4**	**58**	**0**	**0**	**0**	**29**	**0.0**	**17**	**0**	**40**	**18**	**–5**	....	....	....	....	....	....	....	....
	Rochester Americans	AHL	33	3	14	17	....	....	....	118	....	....	....	....	....	....	....	....	....	....	....	....	....	....	....	....	....	....
1971-72	**Vancouver Canucks**	**NHL**	**77**	**2**	**13**	**15**	**2**	**12**	**14**	**166**	**0**	**0**	**0**	**107**	**1.9**	**59**	**2**	**127**	**41**	**–29**	....	....	....	....	....	....	....	....
1972-73	Houston Aeros	WHA	77	2	24	26	....	....	....	*239	....	....	....	....	....	....	....	....	....	....	10	0	2	2	12	....	....	....
1973-74	Houston Aeros	WHA	73	12	19	31	....	....	....	170	....	....	....	....	....	....	....	....	....	....	14	2	6	8	42	....	....	....
1974-75	Houston Aeros	WHA	78	10	42	52	....	....	....	176	....	....	....	....	....	....	....	....	....	....	13	0	8	8	12	....	....	....
1975-76	Houston Aeros	WHA	74	6	32	38	....	....	....	106	....	....	....	....	....	....	....	....	....	....	17	1	6	7	38	....	....	....
1976-77	Houston Aeros	WHA	20	0	6	6	....	....	....	28	....	....	....	....	....	....	....	....	....	....	6	1	2	3	6	....	....	....
1977-78	Houston Aeros	WHA	63	9	20	29	....	....	....	125	....	....	....	....	....	....	....	....	....	....	6	0	1	1	33	....	....	....
1978-79	San Diego Mariners	PCL	58	6	21	27	....	....	....	145	....	....	....	....	....	....	....	....	....	....	....	....	....	....	....	....	....	....
	Binghamton Dusters	AHL	2	1	1	2	....	....	....	0	....	....	....	....	....	....	....	....	....	....	10	0	0	0	12	....	....	....
	NHL Totals		**115**	**2**	**18**	**20**	**2**	**16**	**18**	**224**	**0**	**0**	**0**	**136**	**1.5**	**76**	**2**	**167**	**59**		....	....	....	....	....	....	....	....
	Other Major League Totals		385	39	143	182	....	....	....	844	....	....	....	....	....	....	....	....	....		66	4	25	29	143	....	....	....

Claimed by **Vancouver** from **Montreal** in Expansion Draft, June 10, 1970. Selected by **Dayton-Houston** (WHA) in 1972 WHA General Player Draft, February 12, 1972. Claimed by **NY Islanders** from **Vancouver** in Expansion Draft, June 6, 1972.

• SCHINKEL, KEN

Ken Schinkel RW – R. 5'10", 172 lbs. b: Jansen, Sask., 11/27/1932.

Season	Club	League	GP	G	A	Pts	AG	AA	APts	PIM	PP	SH	GW	S	%	TGF	PGF	TGA	PGA	+/-	GP	G	A	Pts	PIM	PP	SH	GW
1952-53	St. Catharines Teepees	OHA	56	21	22	43	....	....	....	34	....	....	....	....	....	....	....	....	....	....	3	0	1	1	0	....	....	....
1953-54	Springfield Indians	QHL	39	3	14	17	....	....	....	6	....	....	....	....	....	....	....	....	....	....	....	....	....	....	....	....	....	....
	Syracuse Warriors	AHL	28	7	14	21	....	....	....	4	....	....	....	....	....	....	....	....	....	....	....	....	....	....	....	....	....	....
1954-55	Pembroke Lumber Kings	NOHA	57	9	23	32	....	....	....	18	....	....	....	....	....	....	....	....	....	....	5	1	1	2	2	....	....	....
1955-56	Springfield Indians	AHL	57	18	16	34	....	....	....	42	....	....	....	....	....	....	....	....	....	....	....	....	....	....	....	....	....	....
1956-57	Springfield Indians	AHL	64	22	36	58	....	....	....	2	....	....	....	....	....	....	....	....	....	....	....	....	....	....	....	....	....	....
1957-58	Springfield Indians	AHL	70	11	27	38	....	....	....	40	....	....	....	....	....	....	....	....	....	....	13	3	3	6	2	....	....	....
1958-59	Springfield Indians	AHL	70	*43	42	85	....	....	....	19	....	....	....	....	....	....	....	....	....	....	....	....	....	....	....	....	....	....
1959-60	**New York Rangers**	**NHL**	**69**	**13**	**16**	**29**	**16**	**16**	**32**	**27**	....	....	....	....	....	....	....	....	....	....	....	....	....	....	....	....	....	....
1960-61	**New York Rangers**	**NHL**	**38**	**2**	**6**	**8**	**2**	**6**	**8**	**18**	....	....	....	....	....	....	....	....	....	....	....	....	....	....	....	....	....	....
	Springfield Indians	AHL	28	13	8	21	....	....	....	25	....	....	....	....	....	....	....	....	....	....	7	3	3	6	9	....	....	....
1961-62	**New York Rangers**	**NHL**	**65**	**7**	**21**	**28**	**8**	**21**	**29**	**17**	....	....	....	....	....	....	....	....	....	....	**2**	**1**	**0**	**1**	**0**	....	....	....
1962-63	**New York Rangers**	**NHL**	**69**	**6**	**9**	**15**	**7**	**9**	**16**	**15**	....	....	....	....	....	....	....	....	....	....	....	....	....	....	....	....	....	....
1963-64	**New York Rangers**	**NHL**	**4**	**0**	**0**	**0**	**0**	**0**	**0**	**0**	....	....	....	....	....	....	....	....	....	....	....	....	....	....	....	....	....	....
	Baltimore Clippers	AHL	64	23	33	56	....	....	....	35	....	....	....	....	....	....	....	....	....	....	....	....	....	....	....	....	....	....
1964-65	Baltimore Clippers	AHL	72	30	41	71	....	....	....	16	....	....	....	....	....	....	....	....	....	....	5	1	2	3	0	....	....	....
1965-66	Baltimore Clippers	AHL	72	30	45	75	....	....	....	31	....	....	....	....	....	....	....	....	....	....	....	....	....	....	....	....	....	....
1966-67	**New York Rangers**	**NHL**	**20**	**6**	**3**	**9**	**7**	**3**	**10**	**0**	....	....	....	....	....	....	....	....	....	....	**4**	**0**	**1**	**1**	**0**	....	....	....
	Baltimore Clippers	AHL	51	25	31	56	....	....	....	29	....	....	....	....	....	....	....	....	....	....	....	....	....	....	....	....	....	....
1967-68	**Pittsburgh Penguins**	**NHL**	**57**	**14**	**25**	**39**	**17**	**26**	**43**	**19**	**2**	**0**	**3**	**185**	**7.6**	**54**	**12**	**63**	**11**	**–10**	....	....	....	....	....	....	....	....
1968-69	**Pittsburgh Penguins**	**NHL**	**76**	**18**	**34**	**52**	**20**	**32**	**52**	**18**	**8**	**1**	**2**	**226**	**8.0**	**71**	**25**	**90**	**5**	**–39**	....	....	....	....	....	....	....	....
1969-70	**Pittsburgh Penguins**	**NHL**	**72**	**20**	**25**	**45**	**23**	**25**	**48**	**19**	**4**	**0**	**5**	**225**	**8.9**	**62**	**18**	**73**	**3**	**–26**	**10**	**4**	**1**	**5**	**4**	**1**	**0**	**0**
1970-71	**Pittsburgh Penguins**	**NHL**	**50**	**15**	**19**	**34**	**16**	**17**	**33**	**6**	**3**	**0**	**1**	**120**	**12.5**	**48**	**23**	**44**	**0**	**–19**	....	....	....	....	....	....	....	....
1971-72	**Pittsburgh Penguins**	**NHL**	**74**	**15**	**30**	**45**	**16**	**27**	**43**	**8**	**1**	**0**	**1**	**154**	**9.7**	**65**	**15**	**63**	**3**	**–10**	**3**	**2**	**0**	**2**	**0**	**0**	**0**	**0**
1972-73	**Pittsburgh Penguins**	**NHL**	**42**	**11**	**10**	**21**	**11**	**8**	**19**	**16**	**1**	**0**	**2**	**79**	**13.9**	**29**	**6**	**36**	**3**	**–10**	....	....	....	....	....	....	....	....
	NHL Totals		**636**	**127**	**198**	**325**	**143**	**190**	**333**	**163**	**19**	**1**	**14**	**989**	**12.8**	**329**	**99**	**369**	**25**		**19**	**7**	**2**	**9**	**4**	**1**	**0**	**0**

AHL Second All-Star Team (1959)

Played in NHL All-Star Game (1968, 1969)

Claimed by **Pittsburgh** from **NY Rangers** in Expansion Draft, June 6, 1967.

• SCHLEGEL, BRAD

Brad Schlegel D – R. 5'10", 188 lbs. b: Kitchener, Ont., 7/22/1968. Washington's 8th choice, 144th overall, in 1988 Entry Draft.

Season	Club	League	GP	G	A	Pts	AG	AA	APts	PIM	PP	SH	GW	S	%	TGF	PGF	TGA	PGA	+/-	GP	G	A	Pts	PIM	PP	SH	GW
1984-85	Kitchener Dutchmen	Midget	40	30	50	80	....	....	....	70	....	....	....	....	....	....	....	....	....	....	....	....	....	....	....	....	....	....
1985-86	London Knights	OHL	62	2	13	15	....	....	....	35	....	....	....	....	....	....	....	....	....	....	5	0	0	0	4	....	....	....
1986-87	London Knights	OHL	65	4	23	27	....	....	....	24	....	....	....	....	....	....	....	....	....	....	....	....	....	....	....	....	....	....
1987-88	London Knights	OHL	66	13	63	76	....	....	....	49	....	....	....	....	....	....	....	....	....	....	12	8	17	25	6	....	....	....
1988-89	Canada	Nat-Team	60	2	22	24	....	....	....	30	....	....	....	....	....	....	....	....	....	....	....	....	....	....	....	....	....	....

Season	Club	League	REGULAR SEASON																			PLAYOFFS							
			GP	G	A	Pts	AG	AA	APts	PIM	PP	SH	GW	S	%	TGF	PGF	TGA	PGA	+/–	GP	G	A	Pts	PIM	PP	SH	GW
1989-90	Canada	Nat-Team	72	7	25	32	....	....	....	44	....	....	....	....	....	....	....	....	....	....	....	....	....	....	....	....	....	....
1990-91	Canada	Nat-Team	59	8	20	28	....	....	....	64	....	....	....	....	....	....	....	....	....	....	....	....	....	....	....	....	....	....
	Canada	WEC-A	10	0	1	1	....	....	....	6	....	....	....	....	....	....	....	....	....	....	....	....	....	....	....	....	....	....
1991-92	Canada	Nat-Team	61	3	18	21	....	....	....	84	....	....	....	....	....	....	....	....	....	....	....	....	....	....	....	....	....	....
	Canada	Olympics	8	1	2	3	....	....	....	4	....	....	....	....	....	....	....	....	....	....	....	....	....	....	....	....	....	....
	Washington Capitals	**NHL**	**15**	**0**	**1**	**1**	**0**	**1**	**1**	**0**	**0**	**0**	**0**	**7**	**0.0**	**6**	**1**	**10**	**1**	**–4**	**7**	**0**	**1**	**1**	**2**	**0**	**0**	**0**
	Baltimore Skipjacks	AHL	2	0	1	1	....	....	....	0	....	....	....	....	....	....	....	....	....	....	....	....	....	....	....	....	....	....
	Canada	WC-A	3	0	0	0	....	....	....	2	....	....	....	....	....	....	....	....	....	....	....	....	....	....	....	....	....	....
1992-93	**Washington Capitals**	**NHL**	**7**	**0**	**1**	**1**	**0**	**1**	**1**	**6**	**0**	**0**	**0**	**8**	**0.0**	**3**	**0**	**3**	**1**	**+1**	....	....	....	....	....	....	....	....
	Baltimore Skipjacks	AHL	61	3	20	23	....	....	....	40	....	....	....	....	....	....	....	....	....	....	7	0	5	5	6	....	....	....
1993-94	**Calgary Flames**	**NHL**	**26**	**1**	**6**	**7**	**1**	**5**	**6**	**4**	**0**	**0**	**0**	**24**	**4.2**	**14**	**3**	**21**	**6**	**–4**	....	....	....	....	....	....	....	....
	Saint John Flames	AHL	21	2	8	10	....	....	....	6	....	....	....	....	....	....	....	....	....	....	7	0	1	1	6	....	....	....
	Canada	Nat-Team	4	0	0	0	....	....	....	2	....	....	....	....	....	....	....	....	....	....	....	....	....	....	....	....	....	....
	Canada	Olympics	8	0	0	0	....	....	....	6	....	....	....	....	....	....	....	....	....	....	....	....	....	....	....	....	....	....
1994-95	VSV Villach	Austria	28	7	26	33	....	....	....	40	....	....	....	....	....	....	....	....	....	....	12	1	11	12	44	....	....	....
	Canada	Nat-Team	4	0	1	1	....	....	....	2	....	....	....	....	....	....	....	....	....	....	....	....	....	....	....	....	....	....
	Canada	WC-A	8	0	3	3	....	....	....	12	....	....	....	....	....	....	....	....	....	....	....	....	....	....	....	....	....	....
1995-96	VSV Villach	Austria	24	5	18	23	....	....	....	18	....	....	....	....	....	....	....	....	....	....	....	....	....	....	....	....	....	....
	Hannover Scorpions	Germany	26	1	16	17	....	....	....	34	....	....	....	....	....	....	....	....	....	....	2	0	0	0	0	....	....	....
1996-97	VSV Villach	Austria	49	3	29	32	....	....	....	103	....	....	....	....	....	....	....	....	....	....	....	....	....	....	....	....	....	....
	NHL Totals		**48**	**1**	**8**	**9**	**1**	**7**	**8**	**10**	**0**	**0**	**0**	**39**	**2.6**	**23**	**4**	**34**	**8**		**7**	**0**	**1**	**1**	**2**	**0**	**0**	**0**

OHL Second All-Star Team (1988)

Traded to **Calgary** by **Washington** for Calgary's 7th round choice (Andrew Brunette) in 1993 Entry Draft, June 26, 1993.

• SCHLIEBENER, ANDY

Andy Schliebener D – L. 6', 200 lbs. b: Ottawa, Ont., 8/16/1962. Vancouver's 2nd choice, 49th overall, in 1980 Entry Draft.

Season	Club	League	GP	G	A	Pts	AG	AA	APts	PIM	PP	SH	GW	S	%	TGF	PGF	TGA	PGA	+/–	GP	G	A	Pts	PIM	PP	SH	GW
1979-80	Peterborough Petes	OHA	68	8	20	28	....	....	....	47	....	....	....	....	....	....	....	....	....	....	....	....	....	....	....	....	....	....
1980-81	Peterborough Petes	OHA	68	9	48	57	....	....	....	144	....	....	....	....	....	....	....	....	....	....	5	1	3	4	4	....	....	....
1981-82	Peterborough Petes	OHL	14	1	9	10	....	....	....	25	....	....	....	....	....	....	....	....	....	....	....	....	....	....	....	....	....	....
	Niagara Falls Flyers	OHL	27	6	26	32	....	....	....	33	....	....	....	....	....	....	....	....	....	....	5	3	5	8	14	....	....	....
	Dallas Black Hawks	CHL	8	2	2	4	....	....	....	4	....	....	....	....	....	....	....	....	....	....	9	0	4	4	10	....	....	....
	Vancouver Canucks	**NHL**	**22**	**0**	**1**	**1**	**0**	**1**	**1**	**10**	**0**	**0**	**0**	**19**	**0.0**	**13**	**0**	**27**	**3**	**–11**	**3**	**0**	**0**	**0**	**0**	**0**	**0**	**0**
1982-83	Fredericton Express	AHL	76	4	15	19	....	....	....	20	....	....	....	....	....	....	....	....	....	....	10	0	3	3	7	....	....	....
1983-84	**Vancouver Canucks**	**NHL**	**51**	**2**	**10**	**12**	**2**	**7**	**9**	**48**	**0**	**0**	**0**	**62**	**3.2**	**42**	**8**	**49**	**6**	**–9**	**3**	**0**	**0**	**0**	**0**	**0**	**0**	**0**
	Fredericton Express	AHL	27	1	6	7	....	....	....	27	....	....	....	....	....	....	....	....	....	....	....	....	....	....	....	....	....	....
1984-85	**Vancouver Canucks**	**NHL**	**11**	**0**	**0**	**0**	**0**	**0**	**0**	**16**	**0**	**0**	**0**	**6**	**0.0**	**3**	**0**	**17**	**3**	**–11**	....	....	....	....	....	....	....	....
	Fredericton Express	AHL	47	1	11	12	....	....	....	58	....	....	....	....	....	....	....	....	....	....	....	....	....	....	....	....	....	....
1985-86	Fredericton Express	AHL	73	3	9	12	....	....	....	60	....	....	....	....	....	....	....	....	....	....	6	0	1	1	10	....	....	....
	NHL Totals		**84**	**2**	**11**	**13**	**2**	**8**	**10**	**74**	**0**	**0**	**0**	**87**	**2.3**	**58**	**8**	**93**	**12**		**6**	**0**	**0**	**0**	**0**	**0**	**0**	**0**

• SCHMAUTZ, BOBBY

Bobby Schmautz RW – R. 5'9", 172 lbs. b: Saskatoon, Sask., 3/28/1945.

Season	Club	League	GP	G	A	Pts	AG	AA	APts	PIM	PP	SH	GW	S	%	TGF	PGF	TGA	PGA	+/–	GP	G	A	Pts	PIM	PP	SH	GW
1961-62	Medicine Hat Monarchs	SSHL	26	12	9	21	....	....	....	39	....	....	....	....	....	....	....	....	....	....	6	3	2	5	17	....	....	....
1962-63	Saskatoon Jr. Quakers	SJHL	54	28	31	59	....	....	....	42	....	....	....	....	....	....	....	....	....	....	....	....	....	....	....	....	....	....
	Saskatoon Quakers	SSHL	....	....	....	....	....	....	....	....	....	....	....	....	....	....	....	....	....	....	7	1	1	2	0	....	....	....
1963-64	Saskatoon Jr. Quakers	SJHL	60	55	43	98	....	....	....	114	....	....	....	....	....	....	....	....	....	....	12	12	12	24	20	....	....	....
1964-65	Saskatoon Blades	SJHL	44	45	34	79	....	....	....	103	....	....	....	....	....	....	....	....	....	....	5	4	2	6	10	....	....	....
	Los Angeles Blades	WHL	5	0	1	1	....	....	....	0	....	....	....	....	....	....	....	....	....	....	....	....	....	....	....	....	....	....
1965-66	Los Angeles Blades	WHL	70	7	16	23	....	....	....	27	....	....	....	....	....	....	....	....	....	....	....	....	....	....	....	....	....	....
1966-67	Los Angeles Blades	WHL	37	3	7	10	....	....	....	19	....	....	....	....	....	....	....	....	....	....	....	....	....	....	....	....	....	....
1967-68	**Chicago Black Hawks**	**NHL**	**13**	**3**	**2**	**5**	**4**	**2**	**6**	**6**	**0**	**0**	**1**	**27**	**11.1**	**9**	**0**	**11**	**3**	**+1**	**11**	**2**	**3**	**5**	**2**	**0**	**0**	**1**
	Dallas Black Hawks	CHL	54	23	23	46	....	....	....	83	....	....	....	....	....	....	....	....	....	....	....	....	....	....	....	....	....	....
1968-69	**Chicago Black Hawks**	**NHL**	**63**	**9**	**7**	**16**	**10**	**7**	**17**	**37**	**3**	**0**	**1**	**81**	**11.1**	**32**	**9**	**29**	**1**	**–5**	....	....	....	....	....	....	....	....
1969-70	Salt Lake–Seattle	WHL	66	32	27	59	....	....	....	89	....	....	....	....	....	....	....	....	....	....	3	0	2	2	5	....	....	....
1970-71	Seattle Totems	WHL	42	16	21	37	....	....	....	59	....	....	....	....	....	....	....	....	....	....	....	....	....	....	....	....	....	....
	Vancouver Canucks	**NHL**	**26**	**5**	**5**	**10**	**5**	**4**	**9**	**14**	**0**	**0**	**0**	**64**	**7.8**	**18**	**1**	**17**	**2**	**+2**	....	....	....	....	....	....	....	....
1971-72	**Vancouver Canucks**	**NHL**	**60**	**12**	**13**	**25**	**13**	**12**	**25**	**82**	**1**	**0**	**0**	**137**	**8.8**	**40**	**5**	**50**	**5**	**–10**	....	....	....	....	....	....	....	....
	Rochester Americans	AHL	7	7	8	15	....	....	....	8	....	....	....	....	....	....	....	....	....	....	....	....	....	....	....	....	....	....
1972-73	**Vancouver Canucks**	**NHL**	**77**	**38**	**33**	**71**	**38**	**28**	**66**	**137**	**5**	**0**	**5**	**263**	**14.4**	**100**	**25**	**104**	**12**	**–17**	....	....	....	....	....	....	....	....
1973-74	**Vancouver Canucks**	**NHL**	**49**	**26**	**19**	**45**	**27**	**16**	**43**	**58**	**8**	**2**	**3**	**164**	**15.9**	**63**	**21**	**58**	**16**	**0**	....	....	....	....	....	....	....	....
	Boston Bruins	**NHL**	**27**	**7**	**13**	**20**	**7**	**11**	**18**	**31**	**1**	**0**	**1**	**62**	**11.3**	**34**	**5**	**23**	**0**	**+6**	**16**	**3**	**6**	**9**	**44**	**0**	**0**	**0**
1974-75	**Boston Bruins**	**NHL**	**56**	**21**	**30**	**51**	**19**	**24**	**43**	**63**	**1**	**0**	**2**	**156**	**13.5**	**80**	**12**	**56**	**11**	**+23**	**3**	**1**	**5**	**6**	**6**	**0**	**0**	**0**
1975-76	**Boston Bruins**	**NHL**	**75**	**28**	**34**	**62**	**26**	**27**	**53**	**116**	**7**	**0**	**7**	**243**	**11.5**	**105**	**44**	**62**	**14**	**+13**	**11**	**2**	**8**	**10**	**13**	**0**	**0**	**1**
1976-77	**Boston Bruins**	**NHL**	**57**	**23**	**29**	**52**	**22**	**24**	**46**	**62**	**4**	**0**	**2**	**177**	**13.0**	**89**	**19**	**46**	**1**	**+25**	**14**	***11**	**1**	**12**	**10**	**4**	**0**	**1**
1977-78	**Boston Bruins**	**NHL**	**54**	**27**	**27**	**54**	**26**	**22**	**48**	**87**	**4**	**3**	**6**	**174**	**15.5**	**73**	**23**	**33**	**7**	**+24**	**15**	**7**	**8**	**15**	**11**	**2**	**0**	**1**
1978-79	**Boston Bruins**	**NHL**	**65**	**20**	**22**	**42**	**18**	**17**	**35**	**77**	**6**	**1**	**4**	**199**	**10.1**	**69**	**24**	**73**	**27**	**–1**	**11**	**2**	**2**	**4**	**6**	**1**	**0**	**0**
1979-80	**Boston Bruins**	**NHL**	**20**	**8**	**6**	**14**	**7**	**5**	**12**	**8**	**4**	**0**	**0**	**40**	**20.0**	**24**	**10**	**17**	**2**	**–1**	....	....	....	....	....	....	....	....
	Edmonton Oilers	**NHL**	**29**	**8**	**8**	**16**	**7**	**6**	**13**	**20**	**2**	**0**	**0**	**46**	**17.4**	**21**	**4**	**21**	**0**	**–4**	....	....	....	....	....	....	....	....
	Colorado Rockies	**NHL**	**20**	**9**	**4**	**13**	**8**	**3**	**11**	**53**	**2**	**1**	**1**	**66**	**13.6**	**22**	**6**	**29**	**3**	**–10**	....	....	....	....	....	....	....	....
1980-81	**Vancouver Canucks**	**NHL**	**73**	**27**	**34**	**61**	**22**	**24**	**46**	**137**	**9**	**0**	**3**	**205**	**13.2**	**95**	**36**	**65**	**1**	**–5**	**3**	**0**	**0**	**0**	**0**	**0**	**0**	**0**
	NHL Totals		**764**	**271**	**286**	**557**	**259**	**232**	**491**	**988**	**57**	**7**	**36**	**2104**	**12.9**	**874**	**244**	**694**	**105**		**84**	**28**	**33**	**61**	**92**	**7**	**0**	**4**

Played in NHL All-Star Game (1973, 1974)

Claimed by **St. Louis** from **Chicago** in Intra-League Draft, June 11, 1969. Traded to **Montreal** by **St. Louis** with Norm Beaudin for Ernie Wakely, June 27, 1969. Traded to **Salt Lake** (WHL) by **Montreal** for cash, August, 1969. Traded to **Seattle** (WHL) by **Salt Lake** (WHL) for Guyle Fielder, November, 1969. Traded to **Vancouver** by **Seattle** (WHL) for the loan of Jim Wiste and Ed Hatoum for remainder of 1970-71 season, February 9, 1971. Traded to **Boston** by **Vancouver** for Fred O'Donnell and Chris Oddleifson, February 7, 1974. Traded to **Edmonton** by **Boston** for Dan Newman, December 10, 1979. Traded to **Colorado** by **Edmonton** for Don Ashby, February 25, 1980. Signed as a free agent by **Vancouver**, October 2, 1980.

• SCHMAUTZ, CLIFF

Cliff Schmautz RW – R. 5'10", 165 lbs. b: Saskatoon, Sask., 3/17/1939.

Season	Club	League	GP	G	A	Pts	AG	AA	APts	PIM	PP	SH	GW	S	%	TGF	PGF	TGA	PGA	+/–	GP	G	A	Pts	PIM	PP	SH	GW
1956-57	Saskatoon Jr. Quakers	SJHL	47	9	10	19	....	....	....	65	....	....	....	....	....	....	....	....	....	....	....	....	....	....	....	....	....	....
1957-58	Saskatoon Jr. Quakers	SJHL	33	10	16	26	....	....	....	58	....	....	....	....	....	....	....	....	....	....	....	....	....	....	....	....	....	....
1958-59	Weyburn–Moose Jaw	SJHL	42	33	32	65	....	....	....	90	....	....	....	....	....	....	....	....	....	....	....	....	....	....	....	....	....	....
	Nelson Maple Leafs	WIHL	2	0	1	1	....	....	....	6	....	....	....	....	....	....	....	....	....	....	....	....	....	....	....	....	....	....
1959-60	Omaha Knights	IHL	63	32	20	52	....	....	....	[illegible]	....	....	....	....	....	....	....	....	....	....	....	....	....	....	....	....	....	....
	Calgary Stampeders	WHL	5	1	1	2	....	....	....	11	....	....	....	....	....	....	....	....	....	....	....	....	....	....	....	....	....	....
1960-61	Sault Ste. Marie Thunderbirds	EPHL	70	32	20	52	....	....	....	91	....	....	....	....	....	....	....	....	....	....	12	7	6	13	4	....	....	....
1961-62	Sault Ste. Marie Thunderbirds	EPHL	24	6	9	15	....	....	....	24	....	....	....	....	....	....	....	....	....	....	....	....	....	....	....	....	....	....
	Buffalo Bisons	AHL	43	14	13	27	....	....	....	29	....	....	....	....	....	....	....	....	....	....	4	0	0	0	12	....	....	....
1962-63	Buffalo Bisons	AHL	64	24	15	39	....	....	....	24	....	....	....	....	....	....	....	....	....	....	13	8	4	12	4	....	....	....
1963-64	Buffalo Bisons	AHL	26	3	7	10	....	....	....	6	....	....	....	....	....	....	....	....	....	....	....	....	....	....	....	....	....	....
	Portland Buckaroos	WHL	34	7	7	14	....	....	....	22	....	....	....	....	....	....	....	....	....	....	5	2	3	5	2	....	....	....
1964-65	Portland Buckaroos	WHL	66	17	42	59	....	....	....	84	....	....	....	....	....	....	....	....	....	....	10	3	2	5	0	....	....	....
1965-66	Portland Buckaroos	WHL	72	*46	58	*104	....	....	....	47	....	....	....	....	....	....	....	....	....	....	14	9	7	16	17	....	....	....
1966-67	Portland Buckaroos	WHL	66	28	29	57	....	....	....	53	....	....	....	....	....	....	....	....	....	....	4	2	1	3	2	....	....	....
1967-68	Portland Buckaroos	WHL	69	26	33	59	....	....	....	[illegible]	....	....	....	....	....	....	....	....	....	....	12	*7	4	11	4	....	....	....
1968-69	Portland Buckaroos	WHL	53	27	29	56	....	....	....	28	....	....	....	....	....	....	....	....	....	....	11	*10	4	*14	4	....	....	....
1969-70	Portland Buckaroos	WHL	70	40	33	73	....	....	....	23	....	....	....	....	....	....	....	....	....	....	11	6	6	12	6	....	....	....
1970-71	**Buffalo Sabres**	**NHL**	**26**	**5**	**7**	**12**	**5**	**6**	**11**	**10**	**2**	**0**	**0**	**44**	**11.4**	**19**	**11**	**19**	**0**	**–11**	....	....	....	....	....	....	....	....
	Philadelphia Flyers	**NHL**	**30**	**8**	**12**	**20**	**8**	**11**	**19**	**23**	**0**	**0**	**2**	**65**	**12.3**	**30**	**11**	**16**	**0**	**+3**	....	....	....	....	....	....	....	....
1971-72	Portland Buckaroos	WHL	68	40	37	77	....	....	....	44	....	....	....	....	....	....	....	....	....	....	11	6	2	8	2	....	....	....

			REGULAR SEASON																		PLAYOFFS							
Season	Club	League	GP	G	A	Pts	AG	AA	APts	PIM	PP	SH	GW	S	%	TGF	PGF	TGA	PGA	+/–	GP	G	A	Pts	PIM	PP	SH	GW
1972-73	Portland Buckaroos	WHL	54	30	21	51	....	....	....	47	....	....	....	....	....	....	....	....	....	....	....	....	....	....	....	....	....	....
1973-74			DID NOT PLAY																									
1974-75	Portland Buckaroos	WHL	....	11	8	19	....	....	....	8	....	....	....	....	....	....	....	....	....	....	....	....	....	....	....	....	....	....
	NHL Totals		**56**	**13**	**19**	**32**	**13**	**17**	**30**	**33**	**2**	**0**	**2**	**109**	**11.9**	**49**	**22**	**35**	**0**		....	....	....	....	....	....	....	....

WHL First All-Star Team (1966) • WHL Second All-Star Team (1972)

Traded to **Portland** (WHL) by **Buffalo** (AHL) for Pat Hannigan, December, 1963. Claimed by **Buffalo** from **Portland** (WHL) in Inter-League Draft, June 9, 1970. Claimed on waivers by **Philadelphia** from **Buffalo**, December 28, 1970. Traded to **Portland** (WHL) by **Philadelphia** for cash, September, 1971.

• SCHMIDT, NORM

Norm Schmidt D – R. 5'11", 190 lbs. b: Sault Ste. Marie, Ont., 1/24/1963. Pittsburgh's 3rd choice, 70th overall, in 1981 Entry Draft.

Season	Club	League	GP	G	A	Pts	AG	AA	APts	PIM	PP	SH	GW	S	%	TGF	PGF	TGA	PGA	+/–	GP	G	A	Pts	PIM	PP	SH	GW
1979-80	Sault Ste. Marie Thunderbirds	OJHL	18	8	16	24	....	....	....	....	....	....	....	....	....	....	....	....	....	....	....	....	....	....	....	....	....	....
1980-81	Oshawa Generals	OHA	65	12	25	37	....	....	....	73	....	....	....	....	....	....	....	....	....	....	11	2	5	7	25	....	....	....
1981-82	Oshawa Generals	OHL	67	13	48	61	....	....	....	172	....	....	....	....	....	....	....	....	....	....	....	....	....	....	....	....	....	....
1982-83	Oshawa Generals	OHL	61	21	49	70	....	....	....	114	....	....	....	....	....	....	....	....	....	....	17	4	16	20	47	....	....	....
1983-84	**Pittsburgh Penguins**	**NHL**	**34**	**6**	**12**	**18**	**5**	**8**	**13**	**12**	**0**	**0**	**0**	**56**	**10.7**	**38**	**5**	**39**	**5**	**–1**	....	....	....	....	....	....	....	....
	Baltimore Skipjacks	AHL	43	4	12	16	....	....	....	31	....	....	....	....	....	....	....	....	....	....	....	....	....	....	....	....	....	....
1984-85	Baltimore Skipjacks	AHL	33	0	22	22	....	....	....	31	....	....	....	....	....	....	....	....	....	....	....	....	....	....	....	....	....	....
1985-86	**Pittsburgh Penguins**	**NHL**	**66**	**15**	**14**	**29**	**12**	**9**	**21**	**57**	**3**	**0**	**0**	**141**	**10.6**	**87**	**20**	**78**	**18**	**+7**	....	....	....	....	....	....	....	....
1986-87	**Pittsburgh Penguins**	**NHL**	**20**	**1**	**5**	**6**	**1**	**4**	**5**	**4**	**1**	**0**	**0**	**32**	**3.1**	**16**	**5**	**22**	**3**	**–8**	....	....	....	....	....	....	....	....
	Baltimore Skipjacks	AHL	36	4	7	11	....	....	....	25	....	....	....	....	....	....	....	....	....	....	....	....	....	....	....	....	....	....
1987-88	**Pittsburgh Penguins**	**NHL**	**5**	**1**	**2**	**3**	**1**	**1**	**2**	**0**	**0**	**0**	**0**	**13**	**7.7**	**8**	**5**	**2**	**0**	**+1**	....	....	....	....	....	....	....	....
	NHL Totals		**125**	**23**	**33**	**56**	**19**	**22**	**41**	**73**	**4**	**0**	**0**	**242**	**9.5**	**149**	**35**	**141**	**26**		....	....	....	....	....	....	....	....

OHL Second All-Star Team (1983)

• SCHNEIDER, ANDY

Andy Schneider LW – L. 5'9", 170 lbs. b: Edmonton, Alta., 3/29/1972.

Season	Club	League	GP	G	A	Pts	AG	AA	APts	PIM	PP	SH	GW	S	%	TGF	PGF	TGA	PGA	+/–	GP	G	A	Pts	PIM	PP	SH	GW
1990-91	Swift Current Broncos	WHL	69	12	74	86	....	....	....	103	....	....	....	....	....	....	....	....	....	....	3	0	0	0	2	....	....	....
1991-92	Swift Current Broncos	WHL	63	44	60	104	....	....	....	120	....	....	....	....	....	....	....	....	....	....	8	4	9	13	8	....	....	....
	Canada	WJC-A	7	0	0	0	....	....	....	6	....	....	....	....	....	....	....	....	....	....	....	....	....	....	....	....	....	....
1992-93	Swift Current Broncos	WHL	38	19	66	85	....	....	....	78	....	....	....	....	....	....	....	....	....	....	17	13	*26	*39	40	....	....	....
	New Haven Nighthawks	AHL	19	2	2	4	....	....	....	13	....	....	....	....	....	....	....	....	....	....	....	....	....	....	....	....	....	....
1993-94	**Ottawa Senators**	**NHL**	**10**	**0**	**0**	**0**	**0**	**0**	**0**	**15**	**0**	**0**	**0**	**4**	**0.0**	**0**	**0**	**6**	**0**	**–6**	....	....	....	....	....	....	....	....
	P.E.I. Senators	AHL	61	15	46	61	....	....	....	119	....	....	....	....	....	....	....	....	....	....	....	....	....	....	....	....	....	....
1994-95	Leksands IF	Sweden	39	6	8	14	....	....	....	71	....	....	....	....	....	....	....	....	....	....	4	1	1	2	31	....	....	....
	Canada	Nat-Team	3	1	0	1	....	....	....	0	....	....	....	....	....	....	....	....	....	....	....	....	....	....	....	....	....	....
	P.E.I. Senators	AHL	10	1	5	6	....	....	....	25	....	....	....	....	....	....	....	....	....	....	11	5	5	10	11	....	....	....
1995-96	Minnesota Moose	IHL	81	12	28	40	....	....	....	85	....	....	....	....	....	....	....	....	....	....	....	....	....	....	....	....	....	....
1996-97	Manitoba Moose	IHL	79	14	37	51	....	....	....	142	....	....	....	....	....	....	....	....	....	....	....	....	....	....	....	....	....	....
1997-98	ECR Revier Lowen	Germany	26	3	12	15	....	....	....	46	....	....	....	....	....	....	....	....	....	....	....	....	....	....	....	....	....	....
	Schwenningen Wild Wings	Germany	22	7	13	20	....	....	....	91	....	....	....	....	....	....	....	....	....	....	....	....	....	....	....	....	....	....
	NHL Totals		**10**	**0**	**0**	**0**	**0**	**0**	**0**	**15**	**0**	**0**	**0**	**4**	**0.0**	**0**	**0**	**6**	**0**		....	....	....	....	....	....	....	....

WHL East Second All-Star Team (1993)

Signed as a free agent by **Ottawa**, October 9, 1992.

• SCHNEIDER, MATHIEU

Mathieu Schneider D – L. 5'11", 192 lbs. b: New York, NY, 6/12/1969. Montreal's 4th choice, 44th overall, in 1987 Entry Draft.

Season	Club	League	GP	G	A	Pts	AG	AA	APts	PIM	PP	SH	GW	S	%	TGF	PGF	TGA	PGA	+/–	GP	G	A	Pts	PIM	PP	SH	GW
1986-87	Cornwall Royals	OHL	63	7	29	36	....	....	....	75	....	....	....	....	....	....	....	....	....	....	5	0	0	0	22	....	....	....
1987-88	Cornwall Royals	OHL	48	21	40	61	....	....	....	83	....	....	....	....	....	....	....	....	....	....	11	2	6	8	14	....	....	....
	United States	WJC-A	7	0	2	2	....	....	....	16	....	....	....	....	....	....	....	....	....	....	....	....	....	....	....	....	....	....
	Montreal Canadiens	**NHL**	**4**	**0**	**0**	**0**	**0**	**0**	**0**	**2**	**0**	**0**	**0**	**2**	**0.0**	**1**	**0**	**2**	**0**	**–1**	....	....	....	....	....	....	....	....
	Sherbrooke Canadiens	AHL	....	....	....	....	....	....	....	....	....	....	....	....	....	....	....	....	....	....	3	0	3	3	12	....	....	....
1988-89	Cornwall Royals	OHL	59	16	57	73	....	....	....	96	....	....	....	....	....	....	....	....	....	....	18	7	20	27	30	....	....	....
1989-90	**Montreal Canadiens**	**NHL**	**44**	**7**	**14**	**21**	**6**	**10**	**16**	**25**	**5**	**0**	**1**	**84**	**8.3**	**57**	**16**	**53**	**14**	**+2**	**9**	**1**	**3**	**4**	**31**	**1**	**0**	**0**
	Sherbrooke Canadiens	AHL	28	6	13	19	....	....	....	20	....	....	....	....	....	....	....	....	....	....	....	....	....	....	....	....	....	....
1990-91	Montreal Canadiens	FrTour	3	0	1	1	....	....	....	12	....	....	....	....	....	....	....	....	....	....	....	....	....	....	....	....	....	....
	Montreal Canadiens	**NHL**	**69**	**10**	**20**	**30**	**9**	**15**	**24**	**63**	**5**	**0**	**3**	**164**	**6.1**	**98**	**33**	**75**	**17**	**+7**	**13**	**2**	**7**	**9**	**18**	**1**	**0**	**0**
1991-92	**Montreal Canadiens**	**NHL**	**78**	**8**	**24**	**32**	**7**	**18**	**25**	**72**	**2**	**0**	**1**	**194**	**4.1**	**107**	**41**	**75**	**19**	**+10**	**10**	**1**	**4**	**5**	**6**	**1**	**0**	**0**
1992-93	**Montreal Canadiens**	**NHL**	**60**	**13**	**31**	**44**	**11**	**21**	**32**	**91**	**3**	**0**	**2**	**169**	**7.7**	**100**	**33**	**82**	**23**	**+8**	**11**	**1**	**2**	**3**	**16**	**0**	**0**	**0**
1993-94	**Montreal Canadiens**	**NHL**	**75**	**20**	**32**	**52**	**19**	**25**	**44**	**62**	**11**	**0**	**4**	**193**	**10.4**	**119**	**48**	**86**	**30**	**+15**	**1**	**0**	**0**	**0**	**0**	**0**	**0**	**0**
1994-95	**Montreal Canadiens**	**NHL**	**30**	**5**	**15**	**20**	**9**	**22**	**31**	**49**	**2**	**0**	**0**	**82**	**6.1**	**39**	**13**	**38**	**9**	**–3**	....	....	....	....	....	....	....	....
	New York Islanders	**NHL**	**13**	**3**	**6**	**9**	**5**	**9**	**14**	**30**	**1**	**0**	**2**	**36**	**8.3**	**20**	**7**	**26**	**8**	**–5**	....	....	....	....	....	....	....	....
1995-96	**New York Islanders**	**NHL**	**65**	**11**	**36**	**47**	**11**	**29**	**40**	**93**	**7**	**0**	**1**	**155**	**7.1**	**103**	**49**	**103**	**31**	**–18**	....	....	....	....	....	....	....	....
	Toronto Maple Leafs	**NHL**	**13**	**2**	**5**	**7**	**2**	**4**	**6**	**10**	**0**	**0**	**0**	**36**	**5.6**	**18**	**12**	**10**	**2**	**–2**	**6**	**0**	**4**	**4**	**8**	**0**	**0**	**0**
1996-97	United States	W Cup	7	2	0	2	....	....	....	8	....	....	....	....	....	....	....	....	....	....	....	....	....	....	....	....	....	....
	Toronto Maple Leafs	**NHL**	**26**	**5**	**7**	**12**	**5**	**6**	**11**	**20**	**1**	**0**	**1**	**63**	**7.9**	**37**	**10**	**27**	**3**	**+3**	....	....	....	....	....	....	....	....
1997-98	**Toronto Maple Leafs**	**NHL**	**76**	**11**	**26**	**37**	**13**	**25**	**38**	**44**	**4**	**1**	**1**	**181**	**6.1**	**89**	**32**	**89**	**20**	**–12**	....	....	....	....	....	....	....	....
	United States	Olympics	4	0	0	0	....	....	....	6	....	....	....	....	....	....	....	....	....	....	....	....	....	....	....	....	....	....
	NHL Totals		**553**	**95**	**216**	**311**	**97**	**184**	**281**	**561**	**41**	**1**	**16**	**1359**	**7.0**	**788**	**294**	**666**	**176**		**50**	**5**	**20**	**25**	**79**	**3**	**0**	**0**

OHL First All-Star Team (1988, 1989)

Played in NHL All-Star Game (1996)

Traded to **NY Islanders** by **Montreal** with Kirk Muller and Craig Darby for Pierre Turgeon and Vladimir Malakhov, April 5, 1995. Traded to **Toronto** by **NY Islanders** with Wendel Clark and D.J. Smith for Darby Hendrickson, Sean Haggerty, Kenny Jonsson and Toronto's 1st round choice (Roberto Luongo) in 1997 Entry Draft, March 13, 1996.

• SCHOCK, DANNY

Danny Schock LW – L. 5'11", 180 lbs. b: Terrace Bay, Ont., 12/30/1948. Boston's 1st choice, 12th overall, in 1968 Amateur Draft.

Season	Club	League	GP	G	A	Pts	AG	AA	APts	PIM	PP	SH	GW	S	%	TGF	PGF	TGA	PGA	+/–	GP	G	A	Pts	PIM	PP	SH	GW
1966-67	Estevan Bruins	WCJHL	55	29	29	58	....	....	....	66	....	....	....	....	....	....	....	....	....	....	12	5	1	6	30	....	....	....
1967-68	Estevan Bruins	WCJHL	52	33	30	63	....	....	....	159	....	....	....	....	....	....	....	....	....	....	14	6	15	21	10	....	....	....
1968-69	Oklahoma City Blazers	CHL	66	20	32	52	....	....	....	52	....	....	....	....	....	....	....	....	....	....	12	3	6	9	21	....	....	....
1969-70	Oklahoma City Blazers	CHL	3	1	0	1	....	....	....	8	....	....	....	....	....	....	....	....	....	....	....	....	....	....	....	....	....	....
	Salt Lake Golden Eagles	WHL	55	20	18	38	....	....	....	12	....	....	....	....	....	....	....	....	....	....	....	....	....	....	....	....	....	....
	Boston Bruins	**NHL**	....	....	....	....	....	....	....	....	....	....	....	....	....	....	....	....	....	....	**1**	**0**	**0**	**0**	**0**	....	....	....
1970-71	**Boston Bruins**	**NHL**	**6**	**0**	**0**	**0**	**0**	**0**	**0**	**0**	**0**	**0**	**0**	**1**	**0.0**	**0**	**0**	**1**	**0**	**–1**	....	....	....	....	....	....	....	....
	Philadelphia Flyers	**NHL**	**14**	**1**	**2**	**3**	**1**	**2**	**3**	**0**	**0**	**0**	**0**	**7**	**14.3**	**6**	**0**	**5**	**0**	**+1**	....	....	....	....	....	....	....	....
	Quebec Aces	AHL	7	2	1	3	....	....	....	0	....	....	....	....	....	....	....	....	....	....	....	....	....	....	....	....	....	....
1971-72	Richmond Robins	AHL	74	24	17	41	....	....	....	36	....	....	....	....	....	....	....	....	....	....	....	....	....	....	....	....	....	....
1972-73	Richmond Robins	AHL	74	48	36	84	....	....	....	37	....	....	....	....	....	....	....	....	....	....	4	1	3	4	0	....	....	....
1973-74	Richmond Robins	AHL	54	23	28	51	....	....	....	8	....	....	....	....	....	....	....	....	....	....	5	0	2	2	0	....	....	....
1974-75	Syracuse Eagles	AHL	4	3	0	3	....	....	....	0	....	....	....	....	....	....	....	....	....	....	....	....	....	....	....	....	....	....
	Greensboro Generals	SHL	24	5	18	23	....	....	....	2	....	....	....	....	....	....	....	....	....	....	....	....	....	....	....	....	....	....
	Syracuse Blazers	NAHL	3	0	1	1	....	....	....	2	....	....	....	....	....	....	....	....	....	....	....	....	....	....	....	....	....	....
1975-76			DID NOT PLAY																									
1976-77	Richmond Wildcats	SHL	1	0	0	0	....	....	....	0	....	....	....	....	....	....	....	....	....	....	....	....	....	....	....	....	....	....
	NHL Totals		**20**	**1**	**2**	**3**	**1**	**2**	**3**	**0**	**0**	**0**	**0**	**8**	**12.5**	**6**	**0**	**6**	**0**		**1**	**0**	**0**	**0**	**0**	**0**	**0**	**0**

Traded to **Philadelphia** by **Boston** with Rick MacLeish for Mike Walton, February 1, 1971.

• SCHOCK, RON

Ron Schock C – L. 5'11", 180 lbs. b: Chapleau, Ont., 12/19/1943.

Season	Club	League	GP	G	A	Pts	AG	AA	APts	PIM	PP	SH	GW	S	%	TGF	PGF	TGA	PGA	+/–	GP	G	A	Pts	PIM	PP	SH	GW
1961-62	Niagara Falls Flyers	OHA	50	18	27	45	....	....	....	17	....	....	....	....	....	....	....	....	....	....	26	10	22	32	29	....	....	....
1962-63	Niagara Falls Flyers	OHA	46	23	48	71	....	....	....	66	....	....	....	....	....	....	....	....	....	....	9	5	11	16	19	....	....	....
	Kingston Frontenacs	EPHL	1	0	1	1	....	....	....	0	....	....	....	....	....	....	....	....	....	....	....	....	....	....	....	....	....	....
1963-64	Niagara Falls Flyers	OHA	44	38	36	74	....	....	....	30	....	....	....	....	....	....	....	....	....	....	4	2	1	3	2	....	....	....
	Boston Bruins	**NHL**	**5**	**1**	**2**	**3**	**1**	**2**	**3**	**0**	....	....	....	....	....	....	....	....	....	....	....	....	....	....	....	....	....	....
	Minneapolis Bruins	CHL	....	....	....	....	....	....	....	....	....	....	....	....	....	....	....	....	....	....	2	0	3	3	0	....	....	....
1964-65	**Boston Bruins**	**NHL**	**33**	**4**	**7**	**11**	**5**	**8**	**13**	**14**	....	....	....	....	....	....	....	....	....	....	....	....	....	....	....	....	....	....

			REGULAR SEASON																		PLAYOFFS							
Season	Club	League	GP	G	A	Pts	AG	AA	APts	PIM	PP	SH	GW	S	%	TGF	PGF	TGA	PGA	+/–	GP	G	A	Pts	PIM	PP	SH	GW
1965-66	**Boston Bruins**	**NHL**	**24**	**2**	**2**	**4**	**2**	**2**	**4**	**6**	....	....	....	....	....	....	....	....	....	....	....	....	....	....	....	....	....	....
	San Francisco Seals	WHL	43	11	21	32	....	....	....	28	....	....	....	....	....	....	....	....	....	....	7	1	5	6	6	....	....	....
1966-67	**Boston Bruins**	**NHL**	**66**	**10**	**20**	**30**	**12**	**21**	**33**	**8**	....	....	....	....	....	....	....	....	....	....	....	....	....	....	....	....	....	....
	St. Louis Blues	**NHL**	**55**	**9**	**9**	**18**	**11**	**9**	**20**	**17**	**4**	**0**	**1**	**116**	**7.8**	**28**	**9**	**37**	**1**	**–17**	**12**	**1**	**2**	**3**	**0**	**0**	**0**	**1**
	Kansas City Blues	CHL	10	2	8	10	....	....	....	2	....	....	....	....	....	....	....	....	....	....	....	....	....	....	....	....	....	....
1968-69	**St. Louis Blues**	**NHL**	**67**	**12**	**27**	**39**	**13**	**25**	**38**	**14**	**4**	**0**	**3**	**157**	**7.6**	**51**	**11**	**39**	**2**	**+3**	**12**	**1**	**2**	**3**	**6**	**0**	**0**	**0**
1969-70	**Pittsburgh Penguins**	**NHL**	**76**	**8**	**21**	**29**	**9**	**21**	**30**	**40**	**4**	**1**	**1**	**160**	**5.0**	**49**	**17**	**54**	**15**	**–7**	**10**	**1**	**6**	**7**	**7**	**0**	**0**	**0**
1970-71	**Pittsburgh Penguins**	**NHL**	**71**	**14**	**26**	**40**	**15**	**23**	**38**	**20**	**2**	**2**	**1**	**148**	**9.5**	**50**	**8**	**62**	**22**	**+2**	....	....	....	....	....	....	....	....
1971-72	**Pittsburgh Penguins**	**NHL**	**77**	**17**	**29**	**46**	**18**	**26**	**44**	**22**	**3**	**2**	**1**	**151**	**11.3**	**60**	**11**	**96**	**37**	**–10**	**4**	**1**	**0**	**1**	**6**	**0**	**0**	**0**
1972-73	**Pittsburgh Penguins**	**NHL**	**78**	**13**	**36**	**49**	**13**	**30**	**43**	**23**	**2**	**3**	**1**	**143**	**9.1**	**63**	**7**	**94**	**26**	**–12**	....	....	....	....	....	....	....	....
1973-74	**Pittsburgh Penguins**	**NHL**	**77**	**14**	**29**	**43**	**14**	**25**	**39**	**22**	**0**	**2**	**3**	**138**	**10.1**	**55**	**5**	**100**	**23**	**–27**	....	....	....	....	....	....	....	....
1974-75	**Pittsburgh Penguins**	**NHL**	**80**	**23**	**63**	**86**	**21**	**50**	**71**	**36**	**3**	**2**	**3**	**172**	**13.4**	**113**	**18**	**100**	**27**	**+22**	**9**	**0**	**4**	**4**	**10**	**0**	**0**	**0**
1975-76	**Pittsburgh Penguins**	**NHL**	**80**	**18**	**44**	**62**	**17**	**35**	**52**	**28**	**2**	**1**	**3**	**161**	**11.2**	**82**	**7**	**94**	**21**	**+2**	**3**	**0**	**1**	**1**	**0**	**0**	**0**	**0**
1976-77	**Pittsburgh Penguins**	**NHL**	**80**	**17**	**32**	**49**	**16**	**26**	**42**	**10**	**3**	**1**	**4**	**154**	**11.0**	**69**	**8**	**85**	**18**	**–6**	**3**	**0**	**1**	**1**	**0**	**0**	**0**	**0**
1977-78	**Buffalo Sabres**	**NHL**	**40**	**4**	**4**	**8**	**4**	**3**	**7**	**0**	**0**	**0**	**2**	**19**	**21.1**	**10**	**0**	**16**	**1**	**–5**	**2**	**0**	**0**	**0**	**0**	**0**	**0**	**0**
1978-79	Hershey Bears	AHL	79	21	45	66	....	....	....	21	....	....	....	....	....	....	....	....	....	....	4	0	2	2	0	....	....	....
1979-80	Rochester Americans	AHL	40	10	18	28	....	....	....	12	....	....	....	....	....	....	....	....	....	....	....	....	....	....	....	....	....	....
	NHL Totals		**909**	**166**	**351**	**517**	**171**	**306**	**477**	**260**	**27**	**14**	**23**	**1519**	**10.9**	**630**	**101**	**777**	**193**		**55**	**4**	**16**	**20**	**29**	**0**	**0**	**1**

Claimed by **St. Louis** from **Boston** in Expansion Draft, June 6, 1967. Traded to **Pittsburgh** by **St. Louis** with Craig Cameron for Lou Angotti and Pittsburgh's 1st choice (Gene Carr) in 1971 Amateur Draft, June 6, 1969. Traded to **Buffalo** by **Pittsburgh** for Brian Spencer, September 20, 1977.

• SCHOENFELD, JIM

Jim Schoenfeld D – L. 6'2", 200 lbs. b: Galt, Ont., 9/4/1952. Buffalo's 1st choice, 5th overall, in 1972 Amateur Draft.

1969-70	London Knights	OHA	16	1	4	5	....	....	....	81	....	....	....	....	....	....	....	....	....	....	....	....	....	....	....	....	....	....
	Hamilton Red Wings	OHA	32	2	12	14	....	....	....	54	....	....	....	....	....	....	....	....	....	....	....	....	....	....	....	....	....	....
1970-71	Hamilton Red Wings	OHA	25	3	19	22	....	....	....	120	....	....	....	....	....	....	....	....	....	....	....	....	....	....	....	....	....	....
	Niagara Falls Flyers	OHA	30	3	9	12	....	....	....	85	....	....	....	....	....	....	....	....	....	....	....	....	....	....	....	....	....	....
1971-72	Niagara Falls Flyers	OHA	40	6	46	52	....	....	....	215	....	....	....	....	....	....	....	....	....	....	....	....	....	....	....	....	....	....
1972-73	**Buffalo Sabres**	**NHL**	**66**	**4**	**15**	**19**	**4**	**13**	**17**	**178**	**1**	**0**	**0**	**91**	**4.4**	**84**	**6**	**78**	**12**	**+12**	**6**	**2**	**1**	**3**	**4**	**0**	**0**	**0**
1973-74	**Buffalo Sabres**	**NHL**	**28**	**1**	**8**	**9**	**1**	**7**	**8**	**56**	**0**	**0**	**0**	**49**	**2.0**	**27**	**1**	**43**	**8**	**–9**	....	....	....	....	....	....	....	....
	Cincinnati Swords	AHL	2	0	2	2	....	....	....	4	....	....	....	....	....	....	....	....	....	....	....	....	....	....	....	....	....	....
1974-75	**Buffalo Sabres**	**NHL**	**68**	**1**	**19**	**20**	**1**	**15**	**16**	**184**	**0**	**0**	**0**	**148**	**0.7**	**109**	**3**	**101**	**30**	**+35**	**17**	**1**	**4**	**5**	**38**	**1**	**0**	**0**
1975-76	**Buffalo Sabres**	**NHL**	**56**	**2**	**22**	**24**	**2**	**17**	**19**	**114**	**0**	**0**	**0**	**112**	**1.8**	**103**	**3**	**82**	**22**	**+40**	**8**	**0**	**3**	**3**	**33**	**0**	**0**	**0**
1976-77	**Buffalo Sabres**	**NHL**	**65**	**7**	**25**	**32**	**7**	**20**	**27**	**97**	**2**	**0**	**2**	**181**	**3.9**	**115**	**17**	**88**	**18**	**+28**	**6**	**0**	**0**	**0**	**12**	**0**	**0**	**0**
1977-78	**Buffalo Sabres**	**NHL**	**60**	**2**	**20**	**22**	**2**	**16**	**18**	**89**	**0**	**0**	**0**	**114**	**1.8**	**101**	**10**	**81**	**14**	**+24**	**8**	**0**	**1**	**1**	**28**	**0**	**0**	**0**
1978-79	**Buffalo Sabres**	**NHL**	**46**	**8**	**17**	**25**	**7**	**13**	**20**	**67**	**6**	**0**	**0**	**99**	**8.1**	**81**	**15**	**77**	**19**	**+8**	**3**	**0**	**1**	**1**	**0**	**0**	**0**	**0**
1979-80	**Buffalo Sabres**	**NHL**	**77**	**9**	**27**	**36**	**8**	**21**	**29**	**72**	**4**	**0**	**1**	**114**	**7.9**	**130**	**11**	**88**	**29**	**+60**	**14**	**0**	**3**	**3**	**18**	**0**	**0**	**0**
1980-81	**Buffalo Sabres**	**NHL**	**71**	**8**	**25**	**33**	**7**	**17**	**24**	**110**	**3**	**0**	**0**	**101**	**7.9**	**115**	**7**	**111**	**31**	**+28**	**8**	**0**	**0**	**0**	**14**	**0**	**0**	**0**
1981-82	**Buffalo Sabres**	**NHL**	**13**	**3**	**2**	**5**	**2**	**1**	**3**	**30**	**0**	**0**	**1**	**21**	**14.3**	**14**	**0**	**11**	**2**	**+5**	....	....	....	....	....	....	....	....
	Detroit Red Wings	**NHL**	**39**	**5**	**9**	**14**	**4**	**6**	**10**	**69**	**0**	**0**	**0**	**87**	**5.7**	**49**	**1**	**58**	**12**	**+2**	....	....	....	....	....	....	....	....
1982-83	**Detroit Red Wings**	**NHL**	**57**	**1**	**10**	**11**	**1**	**7**	**8**	**18**	**0**	**0**	**1**	**68**	**1.5**	**46**	**2**	**80**	**22**	**–14**	....	....	....	....	....	....	....	....
1983-84	**Boston Bruins**	**NHL**	**39**	**0**	**2**	**2**	**0**	**1**	**1**	**20**	**0**	**0**	**0**	**35**	**0.0**	**41**	**0**	**33**	**10**	**+18**	....	....	....	....	....	....	....	....
1984-85	Rochester Americans	AHL	DID NOT PLAY – COACHING																									
	Buffalo Sabres	**NHL**	**34**	**0**	**3**	**3**	**0**	**2**	**2**	**28**	**0**	**0**	**0**	**37**	**0.0**	**27**	**0**	**42**	**15**	**0**	**5**	**0**	**0**	**0**	**4**	**0**	**0**	**0**
	NHL Totals		**719**	**51**	**204**	**255**	**46**	**156**	**202**	**1132**	**16**	**0**	**5**	**1267**	**4.1**	**1042**	**78**	**973**	**244**		**75**	**3**	**13**	**16**	**151**	**1**	**0**	**0**

OHA Second All-Star Team (1972) • NHL Second All-Star Team (1980)

Played in NHL All-Star Game (1977, 1980)

Traded to **Detroit** by **Buffalo** with Danny Gare and Derek Smith for Mike Foligno, Dale McCourt and Brent Peterson, December 2, 1981. Signed as a free agent by **Boston**, August 19, 1983. Signed as a free agent by **Buffalo**, December 6, 1984.

• SCHOFIELD, DWIGHT

Dwight Schofield D – L. 6'3", 195 lbs. b: Waltham, MA, 3/25/1956. Detroit's 5th choice, 76th overall, in 1976 Amateur Draft.

1974-75	London Knights	OHA	70	6	16	22	....	....	....	124	....	....	....	....	....	....	....	....	....	....	....	....	....	....	....	....	....	....
1975-76	London Knights	OHA	59	14	29	43	....	....	....	121	....	....	....	....	....	....	....	....	....	....	....	....	....	....	....	....	....	....
1976-77	**Detroit Red Wings**	**NHL**	**3**	**1**	**0**	**1**	**1**	**0**	**1**	**2**	**0**	**0**	**0**	**3**	**33.3**	**3**	**0**	**3**	**0**	**0**	....	....	....	....	....	....	....	....
	Kalamazoo Wings	IHL	73	20	41	61	....	....	....	180	....	....	....	....	....	....	....	....	....	....	10	4	7	11	61	....	....	....
1977-78	Kansas City Red Wings	CHL	22	3	7	10	....	....	....	58	....	....	....	....	....	....	....	....	....	....	....	....	....	....	....	....	....	....
	Kalamazoo Wings	IHL	3	3	6	9	....	....	....	21	....	....	....	....	....	....	....	....	....	....	....	....	....	....	....	....	....	....
1978-79	Kansas City Red Wings	CHL	13	1	4	5	....	....	....	20	....	....	....	....	....	....	....	....	....	....	....	....	....	....	....	....	....	....
	Kalamazoo Wings	IHL	47	8	29	37	....	....	....	199	....	....	....	....	....	....	....	....	....	....	....	....	....	....	....	....	....	....
	Fort Wayne Komets	IHL	14	2	3	5	....	....	....	54	....	....	....	....	....	....	....	....	....	....	13	0	9	9	28	....	....	....
1979-80	Dayton Gems	IHL	71	15	47	62	....	....	....	257	....	....	....	....	....	....	....	....	....	....	....	....	....	....	....	....	....	....
	Tulsa Oilers	CHL	1	0	0	0	....	....	....	0	....	....	....	....	....	....	....	....	....	....	....	....	....	....	....	....	....	....
1980-81	Milwaukee Admirals	IHL	82	18	41	59	....	....	....	327	....	....	....	....	....	....	....	....	....	....	7	2	5	7	28	....	....	....
1981-82	Nova Scotia Voyageurs	AHL	75	7	24	31	....	....	....	*335	....	....	....	....	....	....	....	....	....	....	9	1	3	4	41	....	....	....
1982-83	**Montreal Canadiens**	**NHL**	**2**	**0**	**0**	**0**	**0**	**0**	**0**	**7**	**0**	**0**	**0**	**0**	**0.0**	**1**	**0**	**0**	**0**	**+1**	....	....	....	....	....	....	....	....
	Nova Scotia Voyageurs	AHL	73	10	21	31	....	....	....	248	....	....	....	....	....	....	....	....	....	....	7	0	3	3	21	....	....	....
1983-84	**St. Louis Blues**	**NHL**	**70**	**4**	**10**	**14**	**3**	**7**	**10**	**219**	**0**	**0**	**1**	**48**	**8.3**	**51**	**6**	**55**	**7**	**–3**	**4**	**0**	**0**	**0**	**26**	**0**	**0**	**0**
	Toledo Goaldiggers	IHL	3	2	2	4	....	....	....	4	....	....	....	....	....	....	....	....	....	....	....	....	....	....	....	....	....	....
1984-85	**St. Louis Blues**	**NHL**	**43**	**1**	**4**	**5**	**1**	**3**	**4**	**184**	**0**	**0**	**0**	**14**	**7.1**	**9**	**0**	**13**	**0**	**–4**	**2**	**0**	**0**	**0**	**15**	**0**	**0**	**0**
1985-86	**Washington Capitals**	**NHL**	**50**	**1**	**2**	**3**	**1**	**1**	**2**	**127**	**0**	**0**	**0**	**13**	**7.7**	**17**	**0**	**12**	**0**	**+5**	**3**	**0**	**0**	**0**	**14**	**0**	**0**	**0**
1986-87	**Pittsburgh Penguins**	**NHL**	**25**	**1**	**6**	**7**	**1**	**4**	**5**	**59**	**0**	**0**	**0**	**9**	**11.1**	**24**	**1**	**21**	**2**	**+4**	....	....	....	....	....	....	....	....
	Baltimore Skipjacks	AHL	20	1	5	6	....	....	....	58	....	....	....	....	....	....	....	....	....	....	....	....	....	....	....	....	....	....
1987-88	**Winnipeg Jets**	**NHL**	**18**	**0**	**0**	**0**	**0**	**0**	**0**	**33**	**0**	**0**	**0**	**3**	**0.0**	**3**	**0**	**6**	**0**	**3**	....	....	....	....	....	....	....	....
	Kalamazoo Wings	IHL	34	2	7	9	....	....	....	150	....	....	....	....	....	....	....	....	....	....	....	....	....	....	....	....	....	....
	NHL Totals		**211**	**8**	**22**	**30**	**7**	**15**	**22**	**631**	**0**	**0**	**1**	**90**	**8.9**	**108**	**7**	**110**	**9**		**9**	**0**	**0**	**0**	**55**	**0**	**0**	**0**

Signed as a free agent by **Montreal**, September 20, 1982. Claimed by **St. Louis** from **Montreal** in Waiver Draft, October 3, 1983. Claimed by **Washington** from **St. Louis** in Waiver Draft, October 7, 1985. Traded to **Pittsburgh** by **Washington** for cash, October 8, 1986. Signed as a free agent by **Winnipeg**, July, 1987.

• SCHREIBER, WALLY

Wally Schreiber RW – R. 5'11", 180 lbs. b: Edmonton, Alta., 4/15/1962. Washington's 5th choice, 152nd overall, in 1982 Entry Draft.

1980-81	Fort Saskatchewan Traders	SJHL	55	39	41	80	....	....	....	105	....	....	....	....	....	....	....	....	....	....	....	....	....	....	....	....	....	....
1981-82	Regina Pats	WHL	68	56	68	124	....	....	....	68	....	....	....	....	....	....	....	....	....	....	20	12	12	24	34	....	....	....
1982-83	Fort Wayne Komets	IHL	67	24	34	58	....	....	....	23	....	....	....	....	....	....	....	....	....	....	....	....	....	....	....	....	....	....
1983-84	Fort Wayne Komets	IHL	82	47	66	*113	....	....	....	44	....	....	....	....	....	....	....	....	....	....	6	3	3	6	6	....	....	....
1984-85	Fort Wayne Komets	IHL	81	51	58	109	....	....	....	45	....	....	....	....	....	....	....	....	....	....	13	3	7	10	10	....	....	....
1985-86	Fort Wayne Komets	IHL	72	37	52	89	....	....	....	38	....	....	....	....	....	....	....	....	....	....	15	10	8	18	6	....	....	....
1986-87	Canada	Nat-Team	70	40	37	77	....	....	....	27	....	....	....	....	....	....	....	....	....	....	....	....	....	....	....	....	....	....
1987-88	Canada	Nat-Team	61	24	15	39	....	....	....	34	....	....	....	....	....	....	....	....	....	....	....	....	....	....	....	....	....	....
	Canada	Olympics	8	1	2	3	....	....	....	2	....	....	....	....	....	....	....	....	....	....	....	....	....	....	....	....	....	....
	Minnesota North Stars	**NHL**	**16**	**6**	**5**	**11**	**5**	**4**	**9**	**2**	**1**	**2**	**1**	**29**	**20.7**	**18**	**5**	**21**	**4**	**–4**	....	....	....	....	....	....	....	....
1988-89	**Minnesota North Stars**	**NHL**	**25**	**2**	**5**	**7**	**2**	**4**	**6**	**10**	**1**	**0**	**1**	**41**	**4.9**	**11**	**5**	**22**	**11**	**–5**	....	....	....	....	....	....	....	....
	Fort Wayne Komets	IHL	32	15	16	31	....	....	....	51	....	....	....	....	....	....	....	....	....	....	....	....	....	....	....	....	....	....
	Kalamazoo Wings	IHL	5	5	7	12	....	....	....	2	....	....	....	....	....	....	....	....	....	....	....	....	....	....	....	....	....	....
1989-90	Schwenninger ERC	Germany	36	25	29	54	....	....	....	28	....	....	....	....	....	....	....	....	....	....	10	7	13	20	4	....	....	....
1990-91	Schwenninger ERC	Germany	41	27	47	74	....	....	....	34	....	....	....	....	....	....	....	....	....	....	....	....	....	....	....	....	....	....
1991-92	Schwenninger ERC	Germany	44	32	43	75	....	....	....	31	....	....	....	....	....	....	....	....	....	....	....	....	....	....	....	....	....	....
	Canada	Olympics	8	2	2	4	....	....	....	2	....	....	....	....	....	....	....	....	....	....	....	....	....	....	....	....	....	....
1992-93	Schwenninger ERC	Germany	44	23	31	54	....	....	....	28	....	....	....	....	....	....	....	....	....	....	....	....	....	....	....	....	....	....
1993-94	EC Hedos Munich	Germany	44	25	30	55	....	....	....	27	....	....	....	....	....	....	....	....	....	....	....	....	....	....	....	....	....	....
	Canada	Olympics	8	1	0	1	....	....	....	2	....	....	....	....	....	....	....	....	....	....	....	....	....	....	....	....	....	....
1994-95	EV Landshut	Germany	42	27	27	54	....	....	....	26	....	....	....	....	....	....	....	....	....	....	18	11	*15	*20	20	....	....	....

			REGULAR SEASON																		PLAYOFFS							
Season	Club	League	GP	G	A	Pts	AG	AA	APts	PIM	PP	SH	GW	S	%	TGF	PGF	TGA	PGA	+/–	GP	G	A	Pts	PIM	PP	SH	GW
1995-96	EV Landshut	Germany	50	25	30	55	....	....	....	46	....	....	....	....	....	....	....	....	....	....	11	5	9	14	22	....	....	....
1996-97	EV Landshut	Germany	47	22	29	51	....	....	....	12	....	....	....	....	....	....	....	....	....	....	7	1	9	10	2	....	....	....
1997-98	EV Landshut	Germany	48	17	19	36	....	....	....	43	....	....	....	....	....	....	....	....	....	....	6	1	6	7	2	....	....	....
	NHL Totals		**41**	**8**	**10**	**18**	**7**	**8**	**15**	**12**	**2**	**2**	**2**	**70**	**11.4**	**29**	**10**	**43**	**15**		....	....	....	....	....	....	....	....

IHL First All-Star Team (1984, 1985) • Won Leo P. Lamoureux Memorial Trophy (Top Scorer - IHL) (1984) • IHL Second All-Star Team (1986)

Signed as a free agent by **Minnesota**, May 26, 1987.

• SCHULTE, PAXTON

Paxton Schulte LW – L. 6'2", 217 lbs. b: Onaway, Alta., 7/16/1972. Quebec's 7th choice, 124th overall, in 1992 Entry Draft.

Season	Club	League	GP	G	A	Pts	AG	AA	APts	PIM	PP	SH	GW	S	%	TGF	PGF	TGA	PGA	+/–	GP	G	A	Pts	PIM	PP	SH	GW
1990-91	University of North Dakota	WCHA	38	2	4	6	....	....	....	32	....	....	....	....	....	....	....	....	....	....	....	....	....	....	....	....	....	....
1991-92	Spokane Chiefs	WHL	70	42	42	84	....	....	....	222	....	....	....	....	....	....	....	....	....	....	10	2	8	10	48	....	....	....
1992-93	Spokane Chiefs	WHL	45	38	35	73	....	....	....	142	....	....	....	....	....	....	....	....	....	....	10	5	6	11	12	....	....	....
1993-94	**Quebec Nordiques**	**NHL**	**1**	**0**	**0**	**0**	**0**	**0**	**0**	**2**	**0**	**0**	**0**	**0**	**0.0**	**0**	**0**	**0**	**0**	**0**	....	....	....	....	....	....	....	....
	Cornwall Aces	AHL	56	15	15	30	....	....	....	102	....	....	....	....	....	....	....	....	....	....	....	....	....	....	....	....	....	....
1994-95	Cornwall Aces	AHL	74	14	22	36	....	....	....	217	....	....	....	....	....	....	....	....	....	....	14	3	3	6	29	....	....	....
1995-96	Cornwall Aces	AHL	69	25	31	56	....	....	....	171	....	....	....	....	....	....	....	....	....	....	....	....	....	....	....	....	....	....
	Saint John Flames	AHL	14	4	5	9	....	....	....	25	....	....	....	....	....	....	....	....	....	....	14	4	7	11	40	....	....	....
1996-97	**Calgary Flames**	**NHL**	**1**	**0**	**0**	**0**	**0**	**0**	**0**	**2**	**0**	**0**	**0**	**1**	**0.0**	**1**	**0**	**0**	**0**	**+1**	....	....	....	....	....	....	....	....
	Saint John Flames	AHL	71	14	23	37	....	....	....	274	....	....	....	....	....	....	....	....	....	....	4	2	0	2	35	....	....	....
1997-98	Saint John Flames	AHL	59	8	17	25	....	....	....	133	....	....	....	....	....	....	....	....	....	....	....	....	....	....	....	....	....	....
	Las Vegas Thunder	IHL	10	0	1	1	....	....	....	32	....	....	....	....	....	....	....	....	....	....	4	0	0	0	4	....	....	....
	NHL Totals		**2**	**0**	**0**	**0**	**0**	**0**	**0**	**4**	**0**	**0**	**0**	**1**	**0.0**	**1**	**0**	**0**	**0**		....	....	....	....	....	....	....	....

Transferred to **Colorado** after **Quebec** franchise relocated, July 1, 1995. Traded to **Calgary** by **Colorado** for Vesa Viitakoski, March 19, 1996.

• SCHULTZ, DAVE

Dave "The Hammer" Schultz LW – L. 6'1", 190 lbs. b: Waldheim, Sask., 10/14/1949. Philadelphia's 5th choice, 52nd overall, in 1969 Amateur Draft.

Season	Club	League	GP	G	A	Pts	AG	AA	APts	PIM	PP	SH	GW	S	%	TGF	PGF	TGA	PGA	+/–	GP	G	A	Pts	PIM	PP	SH	GW
1967-68	Swift Current Broncos	WCJHL	59	35	34	69	....	....	....	138	....	....	....	....	....	....	....	....	....	....	....	....	....	....	....	....	....	....
1968-69	Swift Current Broncos	WCJHL	33	16	16	32	....	....	....	65	....	....	....	....	....	....	....	....	....	....	....	....	....	....	....	....	....	....
	Sorel Black Hawks	QJHL	STATISTICS NOT AVAILABLE																									
1969-70	Salem Rebels	EHL	67	32	37	69	....	....	....	*356	....	....	....	....	....	....	....	....	....	....	5	2	3	5	23	....	....	....
	Quebec Aces	AHL	8	0	0	0	....	....	....	13	....	....	....	....	....	....	....	....	....	....	....	....	....	....	....	....	....	....
1970-71	Quebec Aces	AHL	71	14	23	37	....	....	....	*382	....	....	....	....	....	....	....	....	....	....	1	0	0	0	15	....	....	....
1971-72	**Philadelphia Flyers**	**NHL**	**1**	**0**	**0**	**0**	**0**	**0**	**0**	**0**	**0**	**0**	**0**	**0**	**0.0**	**1**	**0**	**1**	**0**	**0**	....	....	....	....	....	....	....	....
	Richmond Robins	AHL	76	18	28	46	....	....	....	*392	....	....	....	....	....	....	....	....	....	....	....	....	....	....	....	....	....	....
1972-73	**Philadelphia Flyers**	**NHL**	**76**	**9**	**12**	**21**	**9**	**10**	**19**	***259**	**0**	**0**	**2**	**63**	**14.3**	**29**	**0**	**25**	**0**	**+4**	**11**	**1**	**0**	**1**	***51**	**0**	**0**	**0**
1973-74	**Philadelphia Flyers**	**NHL**	**73**	**20**	**16**	**36**	**20**	**14**	**34**	***348**	**2**	**0**	**3**	**95**	**21.1**	**48**	**2**	**20**	**0**	**+26**	**17**	**2**	**4**	**6**	***139**	**0**	**0**	**1**
1974-75	**Philadelphia Flyers**	**NHL**	**76**	**9**	**17**	**26**	**8**	**13**	**21**	***472**	**0**	**0**	**0**	**93**	**9.7**	**46**	**2**	**28**	**0**	**+16**	**17**	**2**	**3**	**5**	***83**	**0**	**0**	**0**
1975-76	**Philadelphia Flyers**	**NHL**	**71**	**13**	**19**	**32**	**12**	**15**	**27**	**307**	**0**	**0**	**3**	**91**	**14.3**	**48**	**0**	**24**	**0**	**+24**	**16**	**2**	**2**	**4**	***90**	**0**	**0**	**0**
1976-77	**Los Angeles Kings**	**NHL**	**76**	**10**	**20**	**30**	**10**	**16**	**26**	**232**	**2**	**0**	**2**	**122**	**8.2**	**51**	**6**	**53**	**0**	**–8**	**9**	**1**	**1**	**2**	**45**	**1**	**0**	**0**
1977-78	**Los Angeles Kings**	**NHL**	**8**	**2**	**0**	**2**	**2**	**0**	**2**	***27**	**0**	**0**	**0**	**10**	**20.0**	**4**	**0**	**3**	**0**	**+1**	....	....	....	....	....	....	....	....
	Pittsburgh Penguins	**NHL**	**66**	**9**	**25**	**34**	**9**	**20**	**29**	***378**	**0**	**0**	**1**	**102**	**8.8**	**56**	**3**	**62**	**0**	**–9**	....	....	....	....	....	....	....	....
1978-79	**Pittsburgh Penguins**	**NHL**	**47**	**4**	**9**	**13**	**4**	**7**	**11**	**157**	**0**	**0**	**0**	**50**	**8.0**	**24**	**0**	**27**	**1**	**–2**	....	....	....	....	....	....	....	....
	Buffalo Sabres	**NHL**	**28**	**2**	**3**	**5**	**2**	**2**	**4**	**86**	**0**	**0**	**0**	**16**	**12.5**	**7**	**1**	**18**	**0**	**–12**	**3**	**0**	**2**	**2**	**4**	**0**	**0**	**0**
1979-80	**Buffalo Sabres**	**NHL**	**13**	**1**	**0**	**1**	**1**	**0**	**1**	**28**	**0**	**0**	**0**	**1**	**100.0**	**2**	**0**	**2**	**0**	**0**	....	....	....	....	....	....	....	....
	Rochester Americans	AHL	56	10	14	24	....	....	....	248	....	....	....	....	....	....	....	....	....	....	4	1	0	1	12	....	....	....
	NHL Totals		**535**	**79**	**121**	**200**	**77**	**97**	**174**	**2294**	**4**	**0**	**11**	**643**	**12.3**	**316**	**14**	**263**	**1**		**73**	**8**	**12**	**20**	**412**	**1**	**0**	**1**

Traded to **LA Kings** by **Philadelphia** for LA Kings' 4th round pick (Yves Guillemette) in 1977 Amateur Draft and 2nd choice (later traded to Colorado — Colorado selected Merlin Malinowski) in 1978 Amateur Draft, September 29, 1976. Traded to **Pittsburgh** by **LA Kings** with Gene Carr and LA Kings' 4th round choice (Shane Pearsall) in 1976 Amateur Draft for Hartland Monahan and Syl Apps Jr., November 2, 1977. Traded to **Buffalo** by **Pittsburgh** for Gary McAdam, February 6, 1979.

• SCHULTZ, RAY

Ray Schultz D – L. 6'2", 199 lbs. b: Red Deer, Alta., 11/14/1976. Ottawa's 8th choice, 184th overall, in 1995 Entry Draft.

Season	Club	League	GP	G	A	Pts	AG	AA	APts	PIM	PP	SH	GW	S	%	TGF	PGF	TGA	PGA	+/–	GP	G	A	Pts	PIM	PP	SH	GW
1993-94	Tri-City Americans	WHL	3	0	0	0	....	....	....	11	....	....	....	....	....	....	....	....	....	....	....	....	....	....	....	....	....	....
1994-95	Tri-City Americans	WHL	63	1	8	9	....	....	....	209	....	....	....	....	....	....	....	....	....	....	11	0	0	0	16	....	....	....
1995-96	Calgary Hitmen	WHL	66	3	17	20	....	....	....	282	....	....	....	....	....	....	....	....	....	....	....	....	....	....	....	....	....	....
1996-97	Calgary Hitmen	WHL	32	3	17	20	....	....	....	141	....	....	....	....	....	....	....	....	....	....	....	....	....	....	....	....	....	....
	Kelowna Rockets	WHL	23	3	11	14	....	....	....	63	....	....	....	....	....	....	....	....	....	....	6	0	2	2	12	....	....	....
1997-98	**New York Islanders**	**NHL**	**13**	**0**	**1**	**1**	**0**	**1**	**1**	**45**	**0**	**0**	**0**	**4**	**0.0**	**5**	**0**	**2**	**0**	**+3**	....	....	....	....	....	....	....	....
	Kentucky Thoroughblades	AHL	51	2	4	6	....	....	....	179	....	....	....	....	....	....	....	....	....	....	1	0	0	0	25	....	....	....
	NHL Totals		**13**	**0**	**1**	**1**	**0**	**1**	**1**	**45**	**0**	**0**	**0**	**4**	**0.0**	**5**	**0**	**2**	**0**		....	....	....	....	....	....	....	....

Signed as a free agent by **NY Islanders**, June 9, 1997.

• SCHURMAN, MAYNARD

Maynard "M.F." Schurman LW – L. 6'3", 205 lbs. b: Summerdale, P.E.I., 7/16/1957.

Season	Club	League	GP	G	A	Pts	AG	AA	APts	PIM	PP	SH	GW	S	%	TGF	PGF	TGA	PGA	+/–	GP	G	A	Pts	PIM	PP	SH	GW
1975-76	Mount Allison University	AUAA	20	3	1	4	....	....	....	4	....	....	....	....	....	....	....	....	....	....	....	....	....	....	....	....	....	....
1976-77	Mount Allison University	AUAA	20	14	13	27	....	....	....	23	....	....	....	....	....	....	....	....	....	....	....	....	....	....	....	....	....	....
1977-78	Spokane Flyers	WIHL	....	20	42	62	....	....	....	113	....	....	....	....	....	....	....	....	....	....	....	....	....	....	....	....	....	....
1978-79	Maine Mariners	AHL	10	0	0	0	....	....	....	15	....	....	....	....	....	....	....	....	....	....	....	....	....	....	....	....	....	....
	Milwaukee Admirals	IHL	61	23	30	53	....	....	....	83	....	....	....	....	....	....	....	....	....	....	8	3	2	5	0	....	....	....
1979-80	**Hartford Whalers**	**NHL**	**7**	**0**	**0**	**0**	**0**	**0**	**0**	**0**	**0**	**0**	**0**	**5**	**0.0**	**0**	**0**	**1**	**0**	**–1**	....	....	....	....	....	....	....	....
	Springfield Indians	AHL	64	5	15	20	....	....	....	24	....	....	....	....	....	....	....	....	....	....	....	....	....	....	....	....	....	....
1980-81	Hampton Aces	EHL	66	13	43	56	....	....	....	49	....	....	....	....	....	....	....	....	....	....	....	....	....	....	....	....	....	....
1981-82	Charlottetown Islanders	PEI Sr.	STATISTICS NOT AVAILABLE																		....	....	....	....	....	....	....	....
1982-83	Wichita Wind	CHL	38	14	19	33	....	....	....	24	....	....	....	....	....	....	....	....	....	....	....	....	....	....	....	....	....	....
1983-84	Maine Mariners	AHL	43	5	15	20	....	....	....	50	....	....	....	....	....	....	....	....	....	....	....	....	....	....	....	....	....	....
	NHL Totals		**7**	**0**	**0**	**0**	**0**	**0**	**0**	**0**	**0**	**0**	**0**	**5**	**0.0**	**0**	**0**	**1**	**0**		....	....	....	....	....	....	....	....

Signed as a free agent by **Philadelphia**, September, 1978. Claimed by **Hartford** from **Philadelphia** in Expansion Draft, June 13, 1979.

• SCHUTT, ROD

Rod Schutt LW – L. 5'10", 185 lbs. b: Bancroft, Ont., 10/13/1956. Montreal's 2nd choice, 13th overall, in 1976 Amateur Draft.

Season	Club	League	GP	G	A	Pts	AG	AA	APts	PIM	PP	SH	GW	S	%	TGF	PGF	TGA	PGA	+/–	GP	G	A	Pts	PIM	PP	SH	GW
1972-73	Pembroke Lumber Kings	CJHL	55	31	55	86	....	....	....	61	....	....	....	....	....	....	....	....	....	....	....	....	....	....	....	....	....	....
1973-74	Sudbury Wolves	OHA	67	15	41	56	....	....	....	47	....	....	....	....	....	....	....	....	....	....	....	....	....	....	....	....	....	....
1974-75	Sudbury Wolves	OHA	69	43	61	104	....	....	....	66	....	....	....	....	....	....	....	....	....	....	15	13	9	22	2	....	....	....
1975-76	Sudbury Wolves	OHA	63	72	63	135	....	....	....	42	....	....	....	....	....	....	....	....	....	....	17	18	16	34	13	....	....	....
1976-77	Nova Scotia Voyageurs	AHL	80	33	51	84	....	....	....	56	....	....	....	....	....	....	....	....	....	....	12	8	8	16	4	....	....	....
1977-78	**Montreal Canadiens**	**NHL**	**2**	**0**	**0**	**0**	**0**	**0**	**0**	**0**	**0**	**0**	**0**	**0**	**0.0**	**0**	**0**	**0**	**0**	**0**	....	....	....	....	....	....	....	....
	Nova Scotia Voyageurs	AHL	77	36	44	80	....	....	....	57	....	....	....	....	....	....	....	....	....	....	11	4	7	11	2	....	....	....
1978-79	**Pittsburgh Penguins**	**NHL**	**74**	**24**	**21**	**45**	**22**	**16**	**38**	**33**	**3**	**0**	**2**	**181**	**13.3**	**74**	**21**	**63**	**1**	**–9**	**7**	**2**	**0**	**2**	**4**	**0**	**0**	**0**
1979-80	**Pittsburgh Penguins**	**NHL**	**73**	**18**	**21**	**39**	**16**	**16**	**32**	**43**	**3**	**0**	**2**	**170**	**10.6**	**60**	**14**	**54**	**0**	**–8**	**5**	**2**	**1**	**3**	**6**	**0**	**0**	**0**
1980-81	**Pittsburgh Penguins**	**NHL**	**80**	**25**	**35**	**60**	**21**	**24**	**45**	**55**	**11**	**0**	**5**	**206**	**12.1**	**88**	**27**	**75**	**1**	**–13**	**5**	**3**	**3**	**6**	**16**	**1**	**0**	**1**
1981-82	**Pittsburgh Penguins**	**NHL**	**35**	**9**	**12**	**21**	**7**	**8**	**15**	**42**	**0**	**0**	**3**	**73**	**12.3**	**29**	**2**	**24**	**0**	**+3**	**5**	**1**	**2**	**3**	**0**	**0**	**0**	**0**
	Erie Blades	AHL	35	12	15	27	....	....	....	40	....	....	....	....	....	....	....	....	....	....	....	....	....	....	....	....	....	....
1982-83	**Pittsburgh Penguins**	**NHL**	**5**	**0**	**0**	**0**	**0**	**0**	**0**	**0**	**0**	**0**	**0**	**6**	**0.0**	**1**	**0**	**3**	**0**	**–2**	....	....	....	....	....	....	....	....
	Baltimore Skipjacks	AHL	64	34	53	87	....	....	....	24	....	....	....	....	....	....	....	....	....	....	....	....	....	....	....	....	....	....
1983-84	**Pittsburgh Penguins**	**NHL**	**11**	**1**	**3**	**4**	**1**	**2**	**3**	**4**	**0**	**0**	**0**	**13**	**7.7**	**6**	**1**	**5**	**0**	**0**	....	....	....	....	....	....	....	....
	Baltimore Skipjacks	AHL	36	15	19	34	....	....	....	48	....	....	....	....	....	....	....	....	....	....	10	3	1	4	22	....	....	....
1984-85	Muskegon Mohawks	IHL	79	44	46	90	....	....	....	58	....	....	....	....	....	....	....	....	....	....	17	10	13	23	10	....	....	....
1985-86	**Toronto Maple Leafs**	**NHL**	**6**	**0**	**0**	**0**	**0**	**0**	**0**	**0**	**0**	**0**	**0**	**2**	**0.0**	**0**	**0**	**2**	**0**	**–2**	....	....	....	....	....	....	....	....
	St. Catharines Saints	AHL	70	21	28	49	....	....	....	44	....	....	....	....	....	....	....	....	....	....	13	7	4	11	18	....	....	....
	NHL Totals		**286**	**77**	**92**	**169**	**67**	**66**	**133**	**177**	**17**	**0**	**12**	**651**	**11.8**	**258**	**65**	**226**	**2**		**22**	**8**	**6**	**14**	**26**	**1**	**0**	**1**

OHA First All-Star Team (1975, 1976) • Won Dudley "Red" Garrett Memorial Award (Top Rookie - AHL) (1977)

Traded to **Pittsburgh** by **Montreal** for Pittsburgh's 1st round choice (Mark Hunter) in 1981 Entry Draft, October 18, 1978. Signed as a free agent by **Toronto**, October 3, 1985.

• SCISSONS, SCOTT Scott Scissons C – L. 6'1", 201 lbs. b: Saskatoon, Sask., 10/29/1971. NY Islanders' 1st choice, 6th overall, in 1990 Entry Draft.

Season	Club	League	GP	G	A	Pts	AG	AA	APts	PIM	PP	SH	GW	S	%	TGF	PGF	TGA	PGA	+/–	Playoffs GP	G	A	Pts	PIM	PP	SH	GW
			REGULAR SEASON																		PLAYOFFS							
1988-89	Saskatoon Blades	WHL	71	30	56	86	....	....	....	65	....	....	....	....	....	....	....	....	....	....	7	0	4	4	16	....	....	....
1989-90	Saskatoon Blades	WHL	61	40	47	87	....	....	....	81	....	....	....	....	....	....	....	....	....	....	10	3	8	11	6	....	....	....
1990-91	Saskatoon Blades	WHL	57	24	53	77	....	....	....	61	....	....	....	....	....	....	....	....	....	....	....	....	....	....	....	....	....	....
	New York Islanders	**NHL**	**1**	**0**	**0**	**0**	**0**	**0**	**0**	**0**	**0**	**0**	**0**	**1**	**0.0**	**0**	**0**	**0**	**0**	**0**	....	....	....	....	....	....	....	....
1991-92	Canada	Nat-Team	26	4	8	12	....	....	....	31	....	....	....	....	....	....	....	....	....	....	....	....	....	....	....	....	....	....
1992-93	Capital District Islanders	AHL	43	14	30	44	....	....	....	33	....	....	....	....	....	....	....	....	....	....	4	0	0	0	0	....	....	....
	New York Islanders	**NHL**	....	....	....	....	....	....	....	....	....	....	....	....	....	....	....	....	....	....	**1**	**0**	**0**	**0**	**0**	....	....	....
1993-94	**New York Islanders**	**NHL**	**1**	**0**	**0**	**0**	**0**	**0**	**0**	**0**	**0**	**0**	**0**	**0**	**0.0**	**0**	**0**	**0**	**0**	**0**	....	....	....	....	....	....	....	....
	Salt Lake Golden Eagles	IHL	72	10	26	36	....	....	....	123	....	....	....	....	....	....	....	....	....	....	....	....	....	....	....	....	....	....
1994-95	Denver Grizzlies	IHL	7	2	3	5	....	....	....	6	....	....	....	....	....	....	....	....	....	....	....	....	....	....	....	....	....	....
	Minnesota Moose	IHL	23	7	9	16	....	....	....	6	....	....	....	....	....	....	....	....	....	....	....	....	....	....	....	....	....	....
	NHL Totals		**2**	**0**	**0**	**0**	**0**	**0**	**0**	**0**	**0**	**0**	**0**	**1**	**0.0**	**0**	**0**	**0**	**0**		**1**	**0**	**0**	**0**	**0**	**0**	**0**	**0**

• SCREMIN, CLAUDIO Claudio Scremin D – R. 6'2", 205 lbs. b: Burnaby, B.C., 5/28/1968. Washington's 12th choice, 204th overall, in 1988 Entry Draft.

Season	Club	League	GP	G	A	Pts	AG	AA	APts	PIM	PP	SH	GW	S	%	TGF	PGF	TGA	PGA	+/–	Playoffs GP	G	A	Pts	PIM	PP	SH	GW
1984-85	B.C. Wrigley Midgets	Midget	71	24	100	124	....	....	....	....	....	....	....	....	....	....	....	....	....	....	....	....	....	....	....	....	....	....
1985-86	Richmond Sockeyes	BCJHL	62	8	35	43	....	....	....	....	....	....	....	....	....	....	....	....	....	....	....	....	....	....	....	....	....	....
1985-86	Richmond Sockeyes	BCJHL	62	8	35	43	....	....	....	....	....	....	....	....	....	....	....	....	....	....	....	....	....	....	....	....	....	....
1986-87	University of Maine	H.E.	15	0	1	1	....	....	....	2	....	....	....	....	....	....	....	....	....	....	....	....	....	....	....	....	....	....
1987-88	University of Maine	H.E.	44	6	18	24	....	....	....	22	....	....	....	....	....	....	....	....	....	....	....	....	....	....	....	....	....	....
1988-89	University of Maine	H.E.	45	5	24	29	....	....	....	42	....	....	....	....	....	....	....	....	....	....	....	....	....	....	....	....	....	....
1989-90	University of Maine	H.E.	45	4	26	30	....	....	....	14	....	....	....	....	....	....	....	....	....	....	....	....	....	....	....	....	....	....
1990-91	Kansas City Blades	IHL	77	7	14	21	....	....	....	60	....	....	....	....	....	....	....	....	....	....	....	....	....	....	....	....	....	....
1991-92	**San Jose Sharks**	**NHL**	**13**	**0**	**0**	**0**	**0**	**0**	**0**	**25**	**0**	**0**	**0**	**18**	**0.0**	**9**	**0**	**17**	**4**	**–4**	....	....	....	....	....	....	....	....
	Kansas City Blades	IHL	70	5	23	28	....	....	....	44	....	....	....	....	....	....	....	....	....	....	15	1	6	7	14	....	....	....
1992-93	**San Jose Sharks**	**NHL**	**4**	**0**	**1**	**1**	**0**	**1**	**1**	**4**	**0**	**0**	**0**	**4**	**0.0**	**6**	**0**	**9**	**2**	**–1**	....	....	....	....	....	....	....	....
	Kansas City Blades	IHL	75	10	22	32	....	....	....	93	....	....	....	....	....	....	....	....	....	....	12	0	5	5	18	....	....	....
1993-94	Varese HC	Italy	7	2	4	6	....	....	....	11	....	....	....	....	....	....	....	....	....	....	....	....	....	....	....	....	....	....
	Varese HC	Alpenliga	28	10	12	22	....	....	....	20	....	....	....	....	....	....	....	....	....	....	....	....	....	....	....	....	....	....
	Kansas City Blades	IHL	38	7	17	24	....	....	....	39	....	....	....	....	....	....	....	....	....	....	....	....	....	....	....	....	....	....
1994-95	Kansas City Blades	IHL	61	8	30	38	....	....	....	29	....	....	....	....	....	....	....	....	....	....	20	8	12	20	14	....	....	....
1995-96	Kansas City Blades	IHL	79	6	47	53	....	....	....	83	....	....	....	....	....	....	....	....	....	....	5	0	1	1	6	....	....	....
1996-97	Kansas City Blades	IHL	69	7	25	32	....	....	....	71	....	....	....	....	....	....	....	....	....	....	3	1	1	2	2	....	....	....
1997-98	Kansas City Blades	IHL	81	12	46	58	....	....	....	66	....	....	....	....	....	....	....	....	....	....	11	2	12	14	4	....	....	....
	NHL Totals		**17**	**0**	**1**	**1**	**0**	**1**	**1**	**29**	**0**	**0**	**0**	**22**	**0.0**	**15**	**0**	**26**	**6**		....	....	....	....	....	....	....	....

Traded to **Minnesota** by **Washington** for Don Beaupre, November 1, 1988. Signed as a free agent by **San Jose**, September 3, 1991.

• SCRUTON, HOWARD Howard Scruton D – L. 6'3", 190 lbs. b: Toronto, Ont., 10/6/1962.

Season	Club	League	GP	G	A	Pts	AG	AA	APts	PIM	PP	SH	GW	S	%	TGF	PGF	TGA	PGA	+/–	Playoffs GP	G	A	Pts	PIM	PP	SH	GW
1979-80	Niagara Falls Flyers	OHA	51	1	3	4	....	....	....	76	....	....	....	....	....	....	....	....	....	....	10	1	2	3	14	....	....	....
1980-81	Niagara Falls Flyers	OHA	28	5	9	14	....	....	....	56	....	....	....	....	....	....	....	....	....	....	....	....	....	....	....	....	....	....
	Kingston Canadians	OHA	25	0	10	10	....	....	....	23	....	....	....	....	....	....	....	....	....	....	14	0	4	4	25	....	....	....
1981-82	Kingston Canadians	OHL	56	6	29	35	....	....	....	80	....	....	....	....	....	....	....	....	....	....	....	....	....	....	....	....	....	....
	New Haven Nighthawks	AHL	1	1	0	1	....	....	....	0	....	....	....	....	....	....	....	....	....	....	2	0	0	0	0	....	....	....
1982-83	**Los Angeles Kings**	**NHL**	**4**	**0**	**4**	**4**	**0**	**3**	**3**	**9**	**0**	**0**	**0**	**4**	**0.0**	**5**	**0**	**10**	**1**	**–4**	....	....	....	....	....	....	....	....
	New Haven Nighthawks	AHL	74	6	7	13	....	....	....	40	....	....	....	....	....	....	....	....	....	....	12	0	1	1	12	....	....	....
1983-84	New Haven Nighthawks	AHL	33	1	4	5	....	....	....	21	....	....	....	....	....	....	....	....	....	....	....	....	....	....	....	....	....	....
1984-85	New Haven Nighthawks	AHL	74	1	6	7	....	....	....	31	....	....	....	....	....	....	....	....	....	....	....	....	....	....	....	....	....	....
	NHL Totals		**4**	**0**	**4**	**4**	**0**	**3**	**3**	**9**	**0**	**0**	**0**	**4**	**0.0**	**5**	**0**	**10**	**1**		....	....	....	....	....	....	....	....

Signed as a free agent by **LA Kings**, August 5, 1981.

• SEABROOKE, GLEN Glen Seabrooke C – L. 6', 190 lbs. b: Peterborough, Ont., 9/11/1967. Philadelphia's 1st choice, 21st overall, in 1985 Entry Draft.

Season	Club	League	GP	G	A	Pts	AG	AA	APts	PIM	PP	SH	GW	S	%	TGF	PGF	TGA	PGA	+/–	Playoffs GP	G	A	Pts	PIM	PP	SH	GW
1983-84	Peterborough Midgets	Midget	29	36	31	67	....	....	....	31	....	....	....	....	....	....	....	....	....	....	....	....	....	....	....	....	....	....
1984-85	Peterborough Petes	OHL	45	21	13	34	....	....	....	49	....	....	....	....	....	....	....	....	....	....	16	3	5	8	4	....	....	....
1985-86	Peterborough Petes	OHL	19	8	12	20	....	....	....	33	....	....	....	....	....	....	....	....	....	....	14	9	7	16	14	....	....	....
1986-87	Peterborough Petes	OHL	48	30	39	69	....	....	....	29	....	....	....	....	....	....	....	....	....	....	4	3	3	6	6	....	....	....
	Philadelphia Flyers	**NHL**	**10**	**1**	**4**	**5**	**1**	**3**	**4**	**2**	**0**	**0**	**0**	**10**	**10.0**	**8**	**3**	**3**	**0**	**+2**	....	....	....	....	....	....	....	....
1987-88	**Philadelphia Flyers**	**NHL**	**6**	**0**	**1**	**1**	**0**	**1**	**1**	**2**	**0**	**0**	**0**	**3**	**0.0**	**2**	**1**	**2**	**0**	**–1**	....	....	....	....	....	....	....	....
	Hershey Bears	AHL	73	32	46	78	....	....	....	39	....	....	....	....	....	....	....	....	....	....	7	4	5	9	2	....	....	....
1988-89	**Philadelphia Flyers**	**NHL**	**3**	**0**	**1**	**1**	**0**	**1**	**1**	**0**	**0**	**0**	**0**	**0**	**0.0**	**1**	**0**	**2**	**0**	**–1**	....	....	....	....	....	....	....	....
	Hershey Bears	AHL	51	23	15	38	....	....	....	19	....	....	....	....	....	....	....	....	....	....	....	....	....	....	....	....	....	....
	NHL Totals		**19**	**1**	**6**	**7**	**1**	**5**	**6**	**4**	**0**	**0**	**0**	**13**	**7.7**	**11**	**4**	**7**	**0**		....	....	....	....	....	....	....	....

• SECORD, AL Al Secord LW – L. 6'1", 205 lbs. b: Sudbury, Ont., 3/3/1958. Boston's 1st choice, 16th overall, in 1978 Amateur Draft.

Season	Club	League	GP	G	A	Pts	AG	AA	APts	PIM	PP	SH	GW	S	%	TGF	PGF	TGA	PGA	+/–	Playoffs GP	G	A	Pts	PIM	PP	SH	GW
1974-75	Wexford Raiders	MTHL	41	5	13	18	....	....	....	104	....	....	....	....	....	....	....	....	....	....	....	....	....	....	....	....	....	....
1975-76	Hamilton Fincups	OHA	63	9	13	22	....	....	....	117	....	....	....	....	....	....	....	....	....	....	....	....	....	....	....	....	....	....
1976-77	St. Catharines Fincups	OHA	57	32	34	66	....	....	....	343	....	....	....	....	....	....	....	....	....	....	14	4	3	7	46	....	....	....
	Canada	WJC-A	7	2	2	4	....	....	....	8	....	....	....	....	....	....	....	....	....	....	....	....	....	....	....	....	....	....
1977-78	Hamilton Fincups	OHA	59	28	22	50	....	....	....	185	....	....	....	....	....	....	....	....	....	....	20	8	11	19	71	....	....	....
1978-79	**Boston Bruins**	**NHL**	**71**	**16**	**7**	**23**	**15**	**5**	**20**	**125**	**0**	**0**	**0**	**80**	**20.0**	**33**	**0**	**26**	**0**	**+7**	**4**	**0**	**0**	**0**	**4**	**0**	**0**	**0**
	Rochester Americans	AHL	4	4	2	6	....	....	....	40	....	....	....	....	....	....	....	....	....	....	....	....	....	....	....	....	....	....
1979-80	**Boston Bruins**	**NHL**	**77**	**23**	**16**	**39**	**21**	**12**	**33**	**170**	**1**	**0**	**2**	**155**	**14.8**	**68**	**2**	**47**	**1**	**+20**	**10**	**0**	**3**	**3**	**65**	**0**	**0**	**0**
1980-81	**Boston Bruins**	**NHL**	**18**	**0**	**3**	**3**	**0**	**2**	**2**	**42**	**0**	**0**	**0**	**11**	**0.0**	**5**	**1**	**2**	**0**	**+2**	....	....	....	....	....	....	....	....
	Springfield Indians	AHL	8	3	5	8	....	....	....	21	....	....	....	....	....	....	....	....	....	....	....	....	....	....	....	....	....	....
	Chicago Black Hawks	**NHL**	**41**	**13**	**9**	**22**	**11**	**6**	**17**	**145**	**3**	**0**	**2**	**111**	**11.7**	**38**	**11**	**32**	**1**	**–4**	**3**	**4**	**0**	**4**	**14**	**0**	**0**	**0**
1981-82	**Chicago Black Hawks**	**NHL**	**80**	**44**	**31**	**75**	**35**	**20**	**55**	**303**	**14**	**0**	**6**	**215**	**20.5**	**135**	**53**	**99**	**0**	**–17**	**15**	**2**	**5**	**7**	**61**	**2**	**0**	**1**
1982-83	**Chicago Black Hawks**	**NHL**	**80**	**54**	**32**	**86**	**45**	**22**	**67**	**180**	**20**	**0**	**6**	**239**	**22.6**	**155**	**56**	**66**	**1**	**+34**	**12**	**4**	**7**	**11**	**66**	**1**	**0**	**0**
1983-84	**Chicago Black Hawks**	**NHL**	**14**	**4**	**4**	**8**	**3**	**3**	**6**	**77**	**1**	**0**	**3**	**35**	**11.4**	**23**	**9**	**7**	**0**	**+7**	**5**	**3**	**4**	**7**	**28**	**0**	**0**	**1**
1984-85	**Chicago Black Hawks**	**NHL**	**51**	**15**	**11**	**26**	**12**	**7**	**19**	**193**	**6**	**0**	**2**	**110**	**13.6**	**60**	**20**	**40**	**0**	**0**	**15**	**7**	**9**	**16**	**42**	**1**	**0**	**1**
1985-86	**Chicago Black Hawks**	**NHL**	**80**	**40**	**36**	**76**	**32**	**24**	**56**	**201**	**12**	**0**	**3**	**210**	**19.0**	**139**	**48**	**84**	**1**	**+8**	**2**	**0**	**2**	**2**	**26**	**0**	**0**	**0**
1986-87	**Chicago Blackhawks**	**NHL**	**77**	**29**	**29**	**58**	**25**	**21**	**46**	**196**	**5**	**0**	**3**	**179**	**16.2**	**86**	**20**	**86**	**0**	**–20**	**4**	**0**	**0**	**0**	**21**	**0**	**0**	**0**
	Canada	WEC-A	10	0	2	2	....	....	....	16	....	....	....	....	....	....	....	....	....	....	....	....	....	....	....	....	....	....
1987-88	**Toronto Maple Leafs**	**NHL**	**74**	**15**	**27**	**42**	**13**	**19**	**32**	**221**	**2**	**0**	**0**	**149**	**10.1**	**80**	**21**	**80**	**0**	**–21**	**6**	**1**	**0**	**1**	**16**	**0**	**0**	**0**
1988-89	**Toronto Maple Leafs**	**NHL**	**40**	**5**	**10**	**15**	**4**	**7**	**11**	**71**	**1**	**0**	**1**	**52**	**9.6**	**20**	**5**	**28**	**0**	**–13**	....	....	....	....	....	....	....	....
	Philadelphia Flyers	**NHL**	**20**	**1**	**0**	**1**	**1**	**0**	**1**	**38**	**0**	**0**	**0**	**15**	**6.7**	**3**	**0**	**10**	**0**	**–7**	**14**	**0**	**4**	**4**	**31**	**0**	**0**	**0**
1989-90	**Chicago Blackhawks**	**NHL**	**43**	**14**	**7**	**21**	**12**	**5**	**17**	**131**	**1**	**0**	**0**	**68**	**20.6**	**36**	**1**	**30**	**0**	**+5**	**12**	**0**	**0**	**0**	**8**	**0**	**0**	**0**
1990-1994			DID NOT PLAY – RETIRED																									
1994-95	Chicago Wolves	IHL	59	13	20	33	....	....	....	195	....	....	....	....	....	....	....	....	....	....	3	1	1	2	19	....	....	....
1995-96	Chicago Wolves	IHL	47	8	8	16	....	....	....	108	....	....	....	....	....	....	....	....	....	....	9	1	0	4	4	....	....	....
	NHL Totals		**766**	**273**	**222**	**495**	**229**	**153**	**382**	**2093**	**66**	**0**	**28**	**1629**	**16.8**	**881**	**247**	**637**	**4**		**102**	**21**	**34**	**55**	**382**	**4**	**0**	**3**

Played in NHL All-Star Game (1982, 1983)

Traded to **Chicago** by **Boston** for Mike O'Connell, December 18, 1980. Traded to **Toronto** by **Chicago** with Ed Olczyk for Rick Vaive, Steve Thomas and Bob McGill, September 3, 1987. Traded to **Philadelphia** by **Toronto** for Philadelphia's 5th round choice (Keith Carney) in 1989 Entry Draft, February 7, 1989. Signed as a free agent by **Chicago**, August 7, 1989 . Signed as a free agent by **Chicago Wolves** (IHL), September 10, 1994.

• SEDLBAUER, RON Ron Sedlbauer LW – L. 6'3", 195 lbs. b: Burlington, Ont., 10/22/1954. Vancouver's 1st choice, 23rd overall, in 1974 Amateur Draft.

Season	Club	League	GP	G	A	Pts	AG	AA	APts	PIM	PP	SH	GW	S	%	TGF	PGF	TGA	PGA	+/–	Playoffs GP	G	A	Pts	PIM	PP	SH	GW
1971-72	Hamilton Red Wings	OHA	61	18	8	26	....	....	....	43	....	....	....	....	....	....	....	....	....	....	....	....	....	....	....	....	....	
1972-73	Hamilton Red Wings	OHA	58	13	20	33	....	....	....	92	....	....	....	....	....	....	....	....	....	....	....	....	....	....	....	....	....	....
1973-74	Kitchener Rangers	OHA	61	20	25	54	....	....	....	83	....	....	....	....	....	....	....	....	....	....	....	....	....	....	....	....	....	....
1974-75	**Vancouver Canucks**	**NHL**	**26**	**3**	**4**	**7**	**3**	**3**	**6**	**17**	**0**	**0**	**1**	**43**	**7.0**	**12**	**1**	**15**	**0**	**–4**	**5**	**0**	**0**	**0**	**10**	**0**	**0**	**0**
	Seattle Totems	CHL	53	23	13	36	....	....	....	100	....	....	....	....	....	....	....	....	....	....	....	....	....	....	....	....	....	....

			REGULAR SEASON																		PLAYOFFS							
Season	Club	League	GP	G	A	Pts	AG	AA	APts	PIM	PP	SH	GW	S	%	TGF	PGF	TGA	PGA	+/–	GP	G	A	Pts	PIM	PP	SH	GW
1975-76	Vancouver Canucks	NHL	56	19	13	32	18	10	28	66	5	0	3	135	14.1	60	20	48	4	–4	2	0	0	0	0	0	0	0
	Tulsa Oilers	CHL	4	1	1	2	....	....	....	9	....	....	....	....	....	....	....	....	....	....	....	....	....	....	....	....	....	....
1976-77	Vancouver Canucks	NHL	70	18	20	38	17	16	33	29	0	1	3	129	14.0	54	3	49	10	+12	....	....	....	....	....	....	....	....
	Tulsa Oilers	CHL	8	4	6	10	....	....	....	28	....	....	....	....	....	....	....	....	....	....	....	....	....	....	....	....	....	....
1977-78	Vancouver Canucks	NHL	62	18	12	30	17	10	27	25	1	0	1	119	15.1	43	6	52	9	–6	....	....	....	....	....	....	....	....
	Tulsa Oilers	CHL	5	6	1	7	....	....	....	2	....	....	....	....	....	....	....	....	....	....	....	....	....	....	....	....	....	....
1978-79	Vancouver Canucks	NHL	79	40	16	56	36	12	48	26	15	0	5	225	17.8	87	35	86	0	–34	3	0	1	1	9	0	0	0
1979-80	Vancouver Canucks	NHL	32	10	4	14	9	3	12	7	0	0	0	74	13.5	28	5	28	0	–5	....	....	....	....	....	....	....	....
	Chicago Black Hawks	NHL	45	13	10	23	12	8	20	14	1	0	0	132	9.8	48	7	40	0	+1	7	1	1	2	6	1	0	1
1980-81	Chicago Black Hawks	NHL	39	12	3	15	10	2	12	12	3	0	0	69	17.4	25	7	25	0	–7	....	....	....	....	....	....	....	....
	Toronto Maple Leafs	NHL	21	10	4	14	8	3	11	14	5	0	2	45	22.2	24	12	15	0	–3	2	0	1	1	2	0	0	0
1981-82	Cincinnati Tigers	CHL	73	27	20	47	....	....	....	49	....	....	....	....	....	....	....	....	....	....	4	3	0	3	0	....	....	....
	NHL Totals		430	143	86	229	130	67	197	210	30	1	15	971	14.7	381	96	358	23		19	1	3	4	27	1	0	1

Traded to **Chicago** by **Vancouver** for Dave Logan and Harold Phillipoff, December 21, 1979. Traded to **Toronto** by **Chicago** for cash, February 18, 1981.

• SEFTEL, STEVE

Steve Seftel LW – L. 6'3", 200 lbs. b: Kitchener, Ont., 5/14/1968. Washington's 2nd choice, 40th overall, in 1986 Entry Draft.

Season	Club	League	GP	G	A	Pts	AG	AA	APts	PIM	PP	SH	GW	S	%	TGF	PGF	TGA	PGA	+/–	GP	G	A	Pts	PIM	PP	SH	GW
1984-85	Kitchener Greenshirts	Midget	69	58	52	110	....	....	....	176	....	....	....	....	....	....	....	....	....	....	....	....	....	....	....	....	....	....
1985-86	Kingston Canadians	OHL	42	11	16	27	....	....	....	53	....	....	....	....	....	....	....	....	....	....	....	....	....	....	....	....	....	....
1986-87	Kingston Canadians	OHL	54	21	43	64	....	....	....	55	....	....	....	....	....	....	....	....	....	....	12	1	4	5	9	....	....	....
1987-88	Kingston Canadians	OHL	66	32	43	75	....	....	....	51	....	....	....	....	....	....	....	....	....	....	....	....	....	....	....	....	....	....
	Binghamton Whalers	AHL	3	0	0	0	....	....	....	2	....	....	....	....	....	....	....	....	....	....	....	....	....	....	....	....	....	....
1988-89	Baltimore Skipjacks	AHL	58	12	15	27	....	....	....	70	....	....	....	....	....	....	....	....	....	....	....	....	....	....	....	....	....	....
1989-90	Baltimore Skipjacks	AHL	74	10	19	29	....	....	....	52	....	....	....	....	....	....	....	....	....	....	12	4	3	7	10	....	....	....
1990-91	Washington Capitals	NHL	4	0	0	0	0	0	0	2	0	0	0	2	0.0	0	0	2	0	–2	....	....	....	....	....	....	....	....
	Baltimore Skipjacks	AHL	66	22	22	44	....	....	....	46	....	....	....	....	....	....	....	....	....	....	6	0	0	0	14	....	....	....
1991-92	Baltimore Skipjacks	AHL	18	2	6	8	....	....	....	27	....	....	....	....	....	....	....	....	....	....	....	....	....	....	....	....	....	....
	NHL Totals		4	0	0	0	0	0	0	2	0	0	0	2	0.0	0	0	2	0		....	....	....	....	....	....	....	....

• SEGUIN, DAN

Dan Seguin LW – L. 5'8", 165 lbs. b: Sudbury, Ont., 6/7/1948.

Season	Club	League	GP	G	A	Pts	AG	AA	APts	PIM	PP	SH	GW	S	%	TGF	PGF	TGA	PGA	+/–	GP	G	A	Pts	PIM	PP	SH	GW
1966-67	Kitchener Rangers	OHA	48	13	32	45	....	....	....	78	....	....	....	....	....	....	....	....	....	....	13	1	3	4	21	....	....	....
1967-68	Kitchener Rangers	OHA	43	20	49	69	....	....	....	65	....	....	....	....	....	....	....	....	....	....	19	10	15	25	62	....	....	....
1968-69	Memphis South Stars	CHL	72	25	32	57	....	....	....	60	....	....	....	....	....	....	....	....	....	....	....	....	....	....	....	....	....	....
1969-70	Iowa Stars	CHL	72	20	49	69	....	....	....	43	....	....	....	....	....	....	....	....	....	....	10	3	7	10	12	....	....	....
1970-71	Minnesota North Stars	NHL	11	1	1	2	1	1	2	4	0	0	0	4	25.0	3	0	4	2	+1	....	....	....	....	....	....	....	....
	Vancouver Canucks	NHL	25	0	5	5	0	4	4	46	0	0	0	17	0.0	5	1	15	1	–10	....	....	....	....	....	....	....	....
	Rochester Americans	AHL	14	3	3	6	....	....	....	4	....	....	....	....	....	....	....	....	....	....	....	....	....	....	....	....	....	....
1971-72	Rochester Americans	AHL	66	15	24	39	....	....	....	82	....	....	....	....	....	....	....	....	....	....	....	....	....	....	....	....	....	....
1972-73	Seattle Totems	WHL	72	32	47	79	....	....	....	66	....	....	....	....	....	....	....	....	....	....	....	....	....	....	....	....	....	....
1973-74	Vancouver Canucks	NHL	1	1	0	1	1	0	1	0	0	0	0	3	33.3	2	0	1	0	+1	....	....	....	....	....	....	....	....
	Seattle Totems	WHL	67	26	35	61	....	....	....	54	....	....	....	....	....	....	....	....	....	....	....	....	....	....	....	....	....	....
1974-75	Seattle Totems	CHL	73	*37	47	84	....	....	....	26	....	....	....	....	....	....	....	....	....	....	....	....	....	....	....	....	....	....
1975-76	Tulsa Oilers	CHL	62	22	28	50	....	....	....	56	....	....	....	....	....	....	....	....	....	....	9	1	1	2	2	....	....	....
1976-77	Rhode Island Reds	AHL	80	27	37	64	....	....	....	31	....	....	....	....	....	....	....	....	....	....	....	....	....	....	....	....	....	....
	NHL Totals		37	2	6	8	2	5	7	50	0	0	0	24	8.3	10	1	20	3		....	....	....	....	....	....	....	....

CHL Second All-Star Team (1970, 1975) • WHL First All-Star Team (1973)

Traded to **Minnesota** by **NY Rangers** with Wayne Hillman and Joey Johnston for Dave Balon, June 12, 1968. Claimed on waivers by **Vancouver** from **Minnesota**, November 23, 1970. Traded to **Rhode Island** (AHL) by **Vancouver** for cash, October, 1976.

• SEGUIN, STEVE

Steve Seguin LW/RW – L. 6'2", 200 lbs. b: Cornwall, Ont., 4/10/1964. Los Angeles' 2nd choice, 48th overall, in 1982 Entry Draft.

Season	Club	League	GP	G	A	Pts	AG	AA	APts	PIM	PP	SH	GW	S	%	TGF	PGF	TGA	PGA	+/–	GP	G	A	Pts	PIM	PP	SH	GW
1979-80	Cornwall Majors	Midget	55	61	48	109	....	....	....	....	....	....	....	....	....	....	....	....	....	....	....	....	....	....	....	....	....	....
1980-81	Kingston Canadians	OHA	49	8	8	16	....	....	....	18	....	....	....	....	....	....	....	....	....	....	....	....	....	....	....	....	....	....
1981-82	Kingston Canadians	OHL	62	23	31	54	....	....	....	75	....	....	....	....	....	....	....	....	....	....	4	0	2	2	4	....	....	....
1982-83	Kingston Canadians	OHL	19	8	17	25	....	....	....	42	....	....	....	....	....	....	....	....	....	....	....	....	....	....	....	....	....	....
	Peterborough Petes	OHL	44	16	30	46	....	....	....	22	....	....	....	....	....	....	....	....	....	....	4	0	1	1	2	....	....	....
1983-84	Peterborough Petes	OHL	67	55	51	106	....	....	....	84	....	....	....	....	....	....	....	....	....	....	8	8	8	16	11	....	....	....
1984-85	Los Angeles Kings	NHL	5	0	0	0	0	0	0	9	0	0	0	5	0.0	0	0	5	0	–5	....	....	....	....	....	....	....	....
	New Haven Nighthawks	AHL	58	18	7	25	....	....	....	39	....	....	....	....	....	....	....	....	....	....	....	....	....	....	....	....	....	....
1985-86	New Haven Nighthawks	AHL	2	0	0	0	....	....	....	0	....	....	....	....	....	....	....	....	....	....	....	....	....	....	....	....	....	....
	Hershey Bears	AHL	75	25	29	54	....	....	....	91	....	....	....	....	....	....	....	....	....	....	15	2	0	2	22	....	....	....
1986-87	Smith's Falls Rideaus	OHA Sr.	STATISTICS NOT AVAILABLE																									
1987-88	Hershey Bears	AHL	1	0	0	0	....	....	....	0	....	....	....	....	....	....	....	....	....	....	....	....	....	....	....	....	....	....
	Baltimore Skipjacks	AHL	45	17	18	35	....	....	....	63	....	....	....	....	....	....	....	....	....	....	....	....	....	....	....	....	....	....
	NHL Totals		5	0	0	0	0	0	0	9	0	0	0	5	0.0	0	0	5	0		....	....	....	....	....	....	....	....

• SEILING, RIC

Ric Seiling RW/C – R. 6'1", 180 lbs. b: Elmira, Ont., 12/15/1957. Buffalo's 1st choice, 14th overall, in 1977 Amateur Draft.

Season	Club	League	GP	G	A	Pts	AG	AA	APts	PIM	PP	SH	GW	S	%	TGF	PGF	TGA	PGA	+/–	GP	G	A	Pts	PIM	PP	SH	GW
1974-75	Hamilton Red Wings	OHA	68	33	30	63	....	....	....	74	....	....	....	....	....	....	....	....	....	....	....	....	....	....	....	....	....	....
1975-76	Hamilton Fincups	OHA	59	35	51	86	....	....	....	49	....	....	....	....	....	....	....	....	....	....	14	14	13	27	19	....	....	....
1976-77	St. Catharines Fincups	OHA	62	49	61	110	....	....	....	103	....	....	....	....	....	....	....	....	....	....	14	6	6	12	36	....	....	....
	Canada	WJC-A	7	3	1	4	....	....	....	10	....	....	....	....	....	....	....	....	....	....	....	....	....	....	....	....	....	....
1977-78	Buffalo Sabres	NHL	80	19	19	38	18	15	33	33	2	0	4	114	16.7	64	5	46	0	+13	8	0	2	2	7	0	0	0
1978-79	Buffalo Sabres	NHL	78	20	22	42	18	17	35	56	2	0	4	136	14.7	68	9	51	7	+15	3	0	1	1	2	0	0	0
1979-80	Buffalo Sabres	NHL	80	25	35	60	23	27	50	54	5	1	2	155	16.1	102	14	66	8	+30	14	5	4	9	6	0	0	0
1980-81	Buffalo Sabres	NHL	74	30	27	57	25	19	44	80	2	1	4	140	21.4	80	11	65	16	+20	8	2	2	4	2	0	0	0
1981-82	Buffalo Sabres	NHL	57	22	25	47	17	17	34	58	7	1	3	112	19.6	69	21	54	13	+7	4	1	1	2	2	1	0	0
1982-83	Buffalo Sabres	NHL	75	19	22	41	16	15	31	41	6	0	2	127	15.0	80	18	74	14	+2	10	2	3	5	6	0	0	0
1983-84	Buffalo Sabres	NHL	78	13	22	35	10	15	25	42	0	3	0	135	9.6	65	3	67	15	+10	3	0	0	0	2	0	0	0
1984-85	Buffalo Sabres	NHL	73	16	15	31	13	10	23	86	2	3	3	118	13.6	59	5	49	25	+30	5	4	1	5	4	0	0	0
1985-86	Buffalo Sabres	NHL	69	12	13	25	10	9	19	74	0	0	1	85	14.1	38	2	59	18	–5	....	....	....	....	....	....	....	....
1986-87	Detroit Red Wings	NHL	74	3	8	11	3	6	9	49	0	0	0	35	8.6	17	0	55	34	–4	7	0	0	0	5	0	0	0
1987-88	Adirondack Red Wings	AHL	70	16	13	29	....	....	....	34	....	....	....	....	....	....	....	....	....	....	9	2	2	4	47	....	....	....
	NHL Totals		738	179	208	387	153	150	303	573	26	9	23	1157	15.5	642	88	586	150		62	14	14	28	36	1	0	0

Memorial Cup All-Star Team (1976)

Traded to **Detroit** by **Buffalo** for future considerations, October 7, 1986.

• SEILING, ROD

Rod "Sod" Seiling D – L. 6', 195 lbs. b: Kitchener, Ont., 11/14/1944.

Season	Club	League	GP	G	A	Pts	AG	AA	APts	PIM	PP	SH	GW	S	%	TGF	PGF	TGA	PGA	+/–	GP	G	A	Pts	PIM	PP	SH	GW
1960-61	St. Michael's Majors	OHA	3	0	0	0	....	....	....	2	....	....	....	....	....	....	....	....	....	....	4	0	0	0	0	....	....	....
1961-62	St. Michael's Majors	OHA	31	24	26	50	....	....	....	14	....	....	....	....	....	....	....	....	....	....	4	2	1	3	0	....	....	....
1962-63	Neil McNeil Maroons	Tor-Jr.	38	29	48	77	....	....	....	32	....	....	....	....	....	....	....	....	....	....	16	5	13	18	16	....	....	....
	Toronto Maple Leafs	NHL	1	0	1	1	0	1	1	0	....	....	....	....	....	....	....	....	....	....	....	....	....	....	....	....	....	....
	Sudbury Wolves	EPHL	3	2	2	4	....	....	....	0	....	....	....	....	....	....	....	....	....	....	....	....	....	....	....	....	....	....
	Rochester Americans	AHL	1	1	0	1	....	....	....	0	....	....	....	....	....	....	....	....	....	....	....	....	....	....	....	....	....	....
1963-64	Toronto Marlboros	OHA	41	13	54	67	....	....	....	74	....	....	....	....	....	....	....	....	....	....	9	5	14	19	14	....	....	....
	Canada	Olympics	7	4	2	6	....	....	....	6	....	....	....	....	....	....	....	....	....	....	....	....	....	....	....	....	....	....
	Rochester Americans	AHL	2	0	0	0	....	....	....	0	....	....	....	....	....	....	....	....	....	....	....	....	....	....	....	....	....	....
	New York Rangers	NHL	2	0	1	1	0	1	1	0	....	....	....	....	....	....	....	....	....	....	....	....	....	....	....	....	....	....
1964-65	New York Rangers	NHL	68	4	22	26	5	24	29	44	....	....	....	....	....	....	....	....	....	....	....	....	....	....	....	....	....	....
1965-66	New York Rangers	NHL	52	5	10	15	6	10	16	24	....	....	....	....	....	....	....	....	....	....	....	....	....	....	....	....	....	....
	Minnesota Rangers	CHL	13	3	5	8	....	....	....	4	....	....	....	....	....	....	....	....	....	....	....	....	....	....	....	....	....	....
1966-67	New York Rangers	NHL	12	1	1	2	1	1	2	6	....	....	....	....	....	....	....	....	....	....	....	....	....	....	....	....	....	....
	Baltimore Clippers	AHL	46	10	20	30	....	....	....	38	....	....	....	....	....	....	....	....	....	....	9	2	2	4	14	....	....	....

| | | | REGULAR SEASON | | | | | | | | | | | | | | | | | | PLAYOFFS | | | | | | | |
Season	Club	League	GP	G	A	Pts	AG	AA	APts	PIM	PP	SH	GW	S	%	TGF	PGF	TGA	PGA	+/-	GP	G	A	Pts	PIM	PP	SH	GW
1967-68	New York Rangers	NHL	71	5	11	16	6	11	17	44	0	0	1	119	4.2	69	5	48	7	+23	6	1	1	2	4	0	0	0
1968-69	New York Rangers	NHL	73	4	17	21	4	16	20	73	0	0	1	154	2.6	85	16	82	19	+6	4	1	0	1	2	0	0	0
1969-70	New York Rangers	NHL	76	5	21	26	6	21	27	68	0	0	0	176	2.8	113	10	80	18	+41	2	0	0	0	0	0	0	0
1970-71	New York Rangers	NHL	68	5	22	27	5	19	24	34	0	0	3	137	3.6	85	13	58	16	+30	13	1	1	2	12	0	0	0
1971-72	New York Rangers	NHL	78	5	36	41	5	33	38	62	0	1	2	168	3.0	127	7	92	25	+53	16	1	4	5	10	1	0	0
1972-73	Canada	Summit	3	0	0	0				0																		
	New York Rangers	NHL	72	9	33	42	9	28	37	36	1	1	2	155	5.8	125	12	90	20	+43								
1973-74	New York Rangers	NHL	68	7	23	30	7	20	27	32	0	0	2	104	6.7	98	6	96	20	+16	13	0	2	2	19	0	0	0
1974-75	New York Rangers	NHL	4	0	1	1	0	1	1	0	0	0	0	4	0.0	1	0	7	2	-4								
	Washington Capitals	NHL	1	0	0	0	0	0	0	0	0	0	0	0	0.0	0	0	0	0									
	Toronto Maple Leafs	NHL	60	5	12	17	5	9	14	40	1	1	1	94	5.3	76	7	89	28	+8	7	0	0	0	0	0	0	0
1975-76	Toronto Maple Leafs	NHL	77	3	16	19	3	13	16	46	0	0	0	108	2.8	78	3	96	32	+11	10	0	1	1	6	0	0	0
1976-77	St. Louis Blues	NHL	79	3	26	29	3	21	24	36	2	0	1	142	2.1	100	14	118	33	+1	4	0	0	0	2	0	0	0
1977-78	St. Louis Blues	NHL	78	1	11	12	1	9	10	40	0	0	0	98	1.0	54	3	129	30	-48								
1978-79	St. Louis Blues	NHL	3	0	1	1	0	1	1	4	0	0	0	3	0.0	2	0	5	2	-1								
	Atlanta Flames	NHL	36	0	4	4	0	3	3	12	0	0	0	28	0.0	29	0	29	8	+8	2	0	0	0	0	0	0	0
NHL Totals			979	62	269	331	66	242	308	601	4	3	11	1492	4.2	1042	96	1019	260		77	4	8	12	55	1	0	0

Played in NHL All-Star Game (1972)

Traded to **NY Rangers** by **Toronto** with Dick Duff, Arnie Brown and Bill Collins for Andy Bathgate and Don McKenney, February 4, 1964. Claimed by **St. Louis** from **NY Rangers** in Expansion Draft, June 6, 1967. Traded to **NY Rangers** by **St. Louis** for Gary Sabourin, Bob Plager, Gord Kannegiesser and Tim Eccelstone, June 6, 1967. Claimed on waivers by **Washington** from **NY Rangers**, October 29, 1974. Traded to **Toronto** by **Washington** for Tim Eccelstone and Willie Brossart, November 2, 1974. Signed as a free agent by **St. Louis**, September 9, 1976. Traded to **Atlanta** by **St. Louis** for cash, November 4, 1978.

● SEJBA, JIRI

Jiri Sejba   LW – L. 5'10", 185 lbs. b: Pardubice, Czech., 7/22/1962. Buffalo's 9th choice, 182nd overall, in 1985 Entry Draft.

Season	Club	League	GP	G	A	Pts	AG	AA	APts	PIM	PP	SH	GW	S	%	TGF	PGF	TGA	PGA	+/-	GP	G	A	Pts	PIM	PP	SH	GW
1984-85	Czechoslovakia	WEC-A	9	4	3	7				2																		
1985-86	Czechoslovakia	WEC-A	9	2	4	6				6																		
1986-87	HC Pardubice	Czech.	34	23	11	34																						
	Czechoslovakia	WEC-A	10	1	3	4				12																		
1987-88	Czechoslovakia	C Cup	5	1	2	3				2																		
	HC Pardubice	Czech.	23	10	15	25																						
	Czechoslovakia	Olympics	8	3	1	4				16																		
1988-89	HC Pardubice	Czech.	44	38	21	59				68																		
	Czechoslovakia	WEC-A	10	0	1	1																						
1989-90	HC Pardubice	Czech.	26	11	14	25																						
1990-91	**Buffalo Sabres**	**NHL**	11	0	2	2	0	2	2	8	0	0	0	10	0.0	4	0	9	0	-5								
	Rochester Americans	AHL	31	15	13	28				54											14	6	7	13	29			
1991-92	Rochester Americans	AHL	59	27	31	58				36											2	0	0	0	0			
1992-93	STATISTICS NOT AVAILABLE																											
1993-94	HC Pardubice	Czech.	42	12	18	30				0																		
1994-95	HC Pardubice	Czech.	36	16	16	32																						
1995-96	Slovan Bratislava	Slovakia	36	11	17	28				44																		
1996-97	Slovan Bratislava	Slovakia	43	8	23	31															2	3	1	4				
NHL Totals			11	0	2	2	0	2	2	8	0	0	0	10	0.0	4	0	9	0									

● SELANNE, TEEMU

Teemu Selanne   RW – R. 6', 200 lbs. b: Helsinki, Finland, 7/3/1970. Winnipeg's 1st choice, 10th overall, in 1988 Entry Draft.

Season	Club	League	GP	G	A	Pts	AG	AA	APts	PIM	PP	SH	GW	S	%	TGF	PGF	TGA	PGA	+/-	GP	G	A	Pts	PIM	PP	SH	GW
1987-88	Jokerit Helsinki	Fin-Jr.	33	43	23	66				18											5	4	3	7	2			
1988-89	Jokerit Helsinki	Finland 2	5	1	1	2				0																		
	Jokerit Helsinki	Finland 2	34	35	33	68				12											5	7	3	10	4			
1989-90	Jokerit Helsinki	Finland	11	4	8	12				10																		
1990-91	Jokerit Helsinki	Finland	42	33	25	58				12																		
	Finland	WEC-A	10	6	5	11				2																		
1991-92	Finland	C Cup	6	1	1	2				2																		
	Jokerit Helsinki	Finland	44	*39	23	62				20											10	10	7	17	18			
	Finland	Olympics	8	7	4	11				6																		
1992-93	**Winnipeg Jets**	**NHL**	84	*76	56	132	64	38	102	45	24	0	7	387	19.6	165	67	93	3	+8	6	4	2	6	2	2	0	2
1993-94	Winnipeg Jets	NHL	51	25	29	54	23	22	45	22	11	0	2	191	13.1	81	38	66	0	-23								
1994-95	Jokerit Helsinki	Finland	20	7	12	19				6																		
	Winnipeg Jets	**NHL**	45	22	26	48	39	38	77	2	8	2	1	167	13.2	75	32	44	2	+1								
1995-96	Winnipeg Jets	NHL	51	24	48	72	24	39	63	18	6	1	4	163	14.7	98	47	52	4	+3								
	Anaheim Mighty Ducks	NHL	28	16	20	36	16	16	32	4	3	0	1	104	15.4	48	23	24	1	+2								
	Finland	WC-A	6	5	3	8				0																		
1996-97	Finland	W Cup	4	3	2	5				0																		
	Anaheim Mighty Ducks	NHL	78	51	58	109	54	51	105	34	11	1	8	273	18.7	137	46	70	7	+28	11	7	3	10	4	3	0	1
1997-98	Anaheim Mighty Ducks	NHL	73	52	34	86	61	33	94	30	10	1	10	268	19.4	112	34	72	6	+12								
	Finland	Olympics	4	4	6	10				8																		
NHL Totals			410	266	271	537	281	237	518	155	73	5	33	1553	17.1	716	287	421	23		17	11	5	16	6	5	0	3

EJC-A All-Star Team (1988) • Won Calder Memorial Trophy (1993) • NHL First All-Star Team (1993, 1997) • NHL/Upper Deck All-Rookie Team (1993) • NHL Second All-Star Team (1998)
Played in NHL All-Star Game (1993, 1994, 1996, 1997, 1998)

Traded to **Anaheim** by **Winnipeg** with Marc Chouinard and Winnipeg's 4th round choice (later traded to Toronto — later traded to Montreal — Montreal selected Kim Staal) in 1996 Entry Draft for Chad Kilger, Oleg Tverdovsky and Anaheim's 3rd round choice (Per-Anton Lundstrom) in 1996 Entry Draft, February 7, 1996.

● SELBY, BRIT

Brit Selby   LW – L. 5'10", 175 lbs. b: Kingston, Ont., 3/27/1945.

Season	Club	League	GP	G	A	Pts	AG	AA	APts	PIM	PP	SH	GW	S	%	TGF	PGF	TGA	PGA	+/-	GP	G	A	Pts	PIM	PP	SH	GW
1960-61	Toronto Marlboros	OHA	2	0	0	0				0																		
1961-62	Lakeshore Maroons	Jr. B	STATISTICS NOT AVAILABLE																									
	Toronto Marlboros	OHA	3	1	1	2				0																		
1962-63	Toronto Marlboros	OHA	33	24	15	39				22											11	6	11	17	28			
1963-64	Toronto Marlboros	OHA	48	24	28	52				34											9	2	3	5	4			
1964-65	Toronto Marlboros	OHA	52	45	43	88				58											19	*11	10	21	18			
	Toronto Maple Leafs	**NHL**	3	2	0	2	3	0	3	2																		
1965-66	Toronto Maple Leafs	NHL	61	14	13	27	17	13	30	26											4	0	0	0	0			
1966-67	Toronto Maple Leafs	NHL	6	1	1	2	1	1	2	0																		
	Vancouver Canucks	WHL	15	5	1	6				12																		
1967-68	Philadelphia Flyers	NHL	56	15	15	30	19	16	35	24	4	0	1	88	17.0	45	9	39	0	-3	7	1	1	2	4	0	0	0
1968-69	Philadelphia Flyers	NHL	63	10	13	23	11	12	23	23	1	0	3	116	8.6	37	4	57	13	-11	4	0	0	0	0	0	0	0
	Toronto Maple Leafs	NHL	14	2	2	4	2	2	4	19	0	0	0	18	11.1	8	2	7	1	0								
1969-70	Toronto Maple Leafs	NHL	74	10	13	23	12	13	25	40	1	0	1	88	11.4	46	7	65	21	-5								
1970-71	Toronto Maple Leafs	NHL	11	0	1	1	0	1	1	6	0	0	0	7	0.0	1	0	7	3	-3								
	St. Louis Blues	NHL	56	1	4	5	1	4	5	23	0	0	0	33	3.0	14	1	25	2	-10	1	0	0	0	0	0	0	0
1971-72	St. Louis Blues	NHL	6	0	0	0	0	0	0	0	0	0	0	7	0.0	3	0	5	2	-2								
	Kansas City Blues	CHL	63	11	24	35				82																		

			REGULAR SEASON																		PLAYOFFS							
Season	Club	League	GP	G	A	Pts	AG	AA	APts	PIM	PP	SH	GW	S	%	TGF	PGF	TGA	PGA	+/–	GP	G	A	Pts	PIM	PP	SH	GW
1972-73	Quebec Nordiques	WHA	7	0	1	1	....	....	....	4	....	....	....	....	....	....	....	....	....	....	....	....	....	....	....	....	....	....
	New England Whalers	WHA	65	13	29	42	....	....	....	48	....	....	....	....	....	....	....	....	....	....	13	3	4	7	13	....	....	....
1973-74	Toronto Toros	WHA	64	9	17	26	....	....	....	21	....	....	....	....	....	....	....	....	....	....	10	1	3	4	2	....	....	....
1974-75	Toronto Toros	WHA	17	1	4	5	....	....	....	0	....	....	....	....	....	....	....	....	....	....	....	....	....	....	....	....	....	....
	NHL Totals		**350**	**55**	**62**	**117**	**66**	**62**	**128**	**163**	**6**	**0**	**7**	**357**	**15.4**	**154**	**23**	**205**	**40**		**16**	**1**	**1**	**2**	**8**	**0**	**0**	**0**
	Other Major League Totals		153	23	51	74	....	....	....	73	....	....	....	....	....	....	....	....	....		23	4	7	11	15	....	....	....

Won Calder Memorial Trophy (1966)

Claimed by **Philadelphia** from **Toronto** in Expansion Draft, June 6, 1967. Traded to **Toronto** by **Philadelphia** with Forbes Kennedy for Gerry Meehan, Bill Sutherland and Mike Byers, March 2, 1969. Traded to **St. Louis** by **Toronto** for Bob Baun, November 13, 1970. Selected by **Dayton-Houston** (WHA) in 1972 WHA General Player Draft, February 12, 1972. WHA rights traded to **Quebec** (WHA) by **Houston** (WHA) for future considerations, June, 1972. Traded to **Philadelphia** (WHA) by **Quebec** (WHA) with Jean Gravel for Frank Golembrosky and Michel Rouleau, October, 1972. Traded to **New England** (WHA) by **Philadelphia** (WHA) for Bob Brown, October, 1972. Traded to **Toronto Toros** (WHA) by **New England** (WHA) for Bob Charlebois, September, 1973.

• SELF, STEVE

Steve Self C – L. 5'9", 170 lbs. b: Peterborough, Ont., 5/9/1950.

Season	Club	League	GP	G	A	Pts	AG	AA	APts	PIM	PP	SH	GW	S	%	TGF	PGF	TGA	PGA	+/–	GP	G	A	Pts	PIM	PP	SH	GW
1971-72	Colby College	NCAA	....	29	28	57	....	....	....	....	....	....	....	....	....	....	....	....	....	....	....	....	....	....	....	....	....	....
1972-73	New England–Greensboro	EHL	77	50	40	90	....	....	....	92	....	....	....	....	....	....	....	....	....	....	7	2	2	4	0	....	....	....
1973-74	Greensboro Generals	SHL	11	5	4	9	....	....	....	19	....	....	....	....	....	....	....	....	....	....	....	....	....	....	....	....	....	....
	Flint–Dayton	IHL	51	23	22	45	....	....	....	48	....	....	....	....	....	....	....	....	....	....	4	4	4	8	0	....	....	....
1974-75	Dayton Gems	IHL	74	56	47	103	....	....	....	77	....	....	....	....	....	....	....	....	....	....	14	7	7	14	6	....	....	....
1975-76	Dayton Gems	IHL	78	36	37	73	....	....	....	91	....	....	....	....	....	....	....	....	....	....	15	10	8	18	8	....	....	....
1976-77	**Washington Capitals**	**NHL**	**3**	**0**	**0**	**0**	**0**	**0**	**0**	**0**	**0**	**0**	**0**	**3**	**0.0**	**1**	**0**	**4**	**0**	**–3**	....	....	....	....	....	....	....	....
	Dayton Gems	IHL	78	44	41	85	....	....	....	33	....	....	....	....	....	....	....	....	....	....	4	0	1	1	0	....	....	....
	NHL Totals		**3**	**0**	**0**	**0**	**0**	**0**	**0**	**0**	**0**	**0**	**0**	**3**	**0.0**	**1**	**0**	**4**	**0**		....	....	....	....	....	....	....	....

NCAA (College Div.) East All-American Team (1972)

Signed as a free agent by **Washington** to a three-game tryout contract, October 10, 1976.

• SELIVANOV, ALEXANDER

Alexander Selivanov RW – L. 6', 206 lbs. b: Moscow, USSR, 3/23/1971. Philadelphia's 4th choice, 140th overall, in 1994 Entry Draft.

Season	Club	League	GP	G	A	Pts	AG	AA	APts	PIM	PP	SH	GW	S	%	TGF	PGF	TGA	PGA	+/–	GP	G	A	Pts	PIM	PP	SH	GW
1988-89	Spartak Moscow	USSR	1	0	0	0	....	....	....	0	....	....	....	....	....	....	....	....	....	....	....	....	....	....	....	....	....	....
1989-90	Spartak Moscow	USSR	4	0	0	0	....	....	....	0	....	....	....	....	....	....	....	....	....	....	....	....	....	....	....	....	....	....
1990-91	Spartak Moscow	USSR	21	3	1	4	....	....	....	6	....	....	....	....	....	....	....	....	....	....	....	....	....	....	....	....	....	....
1991-92	Spartak Moscow	CIS	31	6	7	13	....	....	....	16	....	....	....	....	....	....	....	....	....	....	....	....	....	....	....	....	....	....
1992-93	Spartak Moscow	CIS	42	12	19	31	....	....	....	66	....	....	....	....	....	....	....	....	....	....	3	2	0	2	2	....	....	....
1993-94	Spartak Moscow	CIS	45	30	11	41	....	....	....	50	....	....	....	....	....	....	....	....	....	....	6	5	1	6	2	....	....	....
1994-95	Atlanta Knights	IHL	4	0	3	3	....	....	....	2	....	....	....	....	....	....	....	....	....	....	....	....	....	....	....	....	....	....
	Chicago Wolves	IHL	14	4	1	5	....	....	....	8	....	....	....	....	....	....	....	....	....	....	....	....	....	....	....	....	....	....
	Tampa Bay Lightning	**NHL**	**43**	**10**	**6**	**16**	**18**	**9**	**27**	**14**	**4**	**0**	**3**	**94**	**10.6**	**32**	**10**	**24**	**0**	**–2**	....	....	....	....	....	....	....	....
1995-96	**Tampa Bay Lightning**	**NHL**	**79**	**31**	**21**	**52**	**31**	**17**	**48**	**93**	**13**	**0**	**5**	**215**	**14.4**	**79**	**29**	**47**	**0**	**+3**	**6**	**2**	**2**	**4**	**6**	**0**	**0**	**1**
1996-97	**Tampa Bay Lightning**	**NHL**	**69**	**15**	**18**	**33**	**16**	**16**	**32**	**61**	**3**	**0**	**4**	**187**	**8.0**	**53**	**17**	**40**	**1**	**–3**	....	....	....	....	....	....	....	....
1997-98	**Tampa Bay Lightning**	**NHL**	**70**	**16**	**19**	**35**	**19**	**19**	**38**	**85**	**4**	**0**	**3**	**206**	**7.8**	**50**	**19**	**70**	**1**	**–38**	....	....	....	....	....	....	....	....
	NHL Totals		**261**	**72**	**64**	**136**	**84**	**61**	**145**	**253**	**24**	**0**	**15**	**702**	**10.3**	**214**	**75**	**181**	**2**		**6**	**2**	**2**	**4**	**6**	**0**	**0**	**1**

Traded to **Tampa Bay** by **Philadelphia** for Philadelphia's 4th round choice (previously acquired, Philadelphia selected Radovan Somik) in 1995 Entry Draft, September 6, 1994.

• SELWOOD, BRAD

Brad Selwood D – L. 6'1", 200 lbs. b: Leamington, Ont., 3/18/1948. Toronto's 1st choice, 10th overall, in 1968 Amateur Draft.

Season	Club	League	GP	G	A	Pts	AG	AA	APts	PIM	PP	SH	GW	S	%	TGF	PGF	TGA	PGA	+/–	GP	G	A	Pts	PIM	PP	SH	GW
1967-68	Niagara Falls Flyers	OHA	54	10	23	33	....	....	....	75	....	....	....	....	....	....	....	....	....	....	19	6	11	17	35	....	....	....
1968-69	Tulsa Oilers	CHL	70	7	32	39	....	....	....	118	....	....	....	....	....	....	....	....	....	....	....	....	....	....	....	....	....	....
1969-70	Vancouver Canucks	WHL	72	9	24	33	....	....	....	93	....	....	....	....	....	....	....	....	....	....	11	1	9	10	26	....	....	....
1970-71	**Toronto Maple Leafs**	**NHL**	**28**	**2**	**10**	**12**	**2**	**9**	**11**	**13**	**2**	**0**	**0**	**31**	**6.5**	**25**	**6**	**30**	**4**	**–7**	....	....	....	....	....	....	....	....
	Tulsa Oilers	CHL	13	1	1	2	....	....	....	4	....	....	....	....	....	....	....	....	....	....	....	....	....	....	....	....	....	....
1971-72	**Toronto Maple Leafs**	**NHL**	**72**	**4**	**17**	**21**	**4**	**15**	**19**	**58**	**2**	**0**	**1**	**108**	**3.7**	**58**	**9**	**58**	**16**	**+7**	**5**	**0**	**0**	**0**	**4**	**0**	**0**	**0**
1972-73	New England Whalers	WHA	75	13	21	34	....	....	....	114	....	....	....	....	....	....	....	....	....	....	15	3	5	8	22	....	....	....
1973-74	New England Whalers	WHA	76	9	28	37	....	....	....	91	....	....	....	....	....	....	....	....	....	....	7	0	2	2	11	....	....	....
1974-75	Canada	Summit	4	0	0	0	....	....	....	4	....	....	....	....	....	....	....	....	....	....	....	....	....	....	....	....	....	....
	New England Whalers	WHA	77	4	35	39	....	....	....	117	....	....	....	....	....	....	....	....	....	....	5	1	0	1	11	....	....	....
1975-76	New England Whalers	WHA	40	2	10	12	....	....	....	28	....	....	....	....	....	....	....	....	....	....	17	2	2	4	27	....	....	....
1976-77	New England Whalers	WHA	41	4	12	16	....	....	....	71	....	....	....	....	....	....	....	....	....	....	5	0	0	0	2	....	....	....
1977-78	New England Whalers	WHA	80	6	25	31	....	....	....	88	....	....	....	....	....	....	....	....	....	....	14	0	3	3	8	....	....	....
1978-79	New England Whalers	WHA	42	4	12	16	....	....	....	47	....	....	....	....	....	....	....	....	....	....	....	....	....	....	....	....	....	....
1979-80	**Los Angeles Kings**	**NHL**	**63**	**1**	**13**	**14**	**1**	**10**	**11**	**82**	**1**	**0**	**0**	**78**	**1.3**	**63**	**17**	**88**	**28**	**–14**	**1**	**0**	**0**	**0**	**0**	**0**	**0**	**0**
1980-81	Houston Apollos	CHL	30	0	9	9	....	....	....	37	....	....	....	....	....	....	....	....	....	....	....	....	....	....	....	....	....	....
	Fort Worth Texans	CHL	33	2	14	16	....	....	....	53	....	....	....	....	....	....	....	....	....	....	5	0	0	0	4	....	....	....
1981-82	New Haven Nighthawks	AHL	23	2	4	6	....	....	....	30	....	....	....	....	....	....	....	....	....	....	....	....	....	....	....	....	....	....
	NHL Totals		**163**	**7**	**40**	**47**	**7**	**34**	**41**	**153**	**5**	**0**	**1**	**217**	**3.2**	**146**	**32**	**176**	**48**		**6**	**0**	**0**	**0**	**4**	**0**	**0**	**0**
	Other Major League Totals		431	42	143	185	....	....	....	556	....	....	....	....	....	....	....	....	....		63	6	12	18	81	....	....	....

Won WHL Rookie of the Year Award (1970)

Traded to **Vancouver** (WHL) by **Toronto** with Rene Robert for Ron Ward, May, 1969. Traded to **Toronto** by **Vancouver** (WHL) for cash, May, 1970. Selected by **New England** (WHA) in 1972 WHA General Player Draft, February 12, 1972. Claimed by **Montreal** from **Toronto** in Intra-League Draft, June 5, 1972. Reclaimed by **Montreal** from **Hartford** prior to Expansion Draft, June 9, 1979. Traded to **LA Kings** by **Montreal** with Montreal's 4th round choice (David Gans) in 1982 Entry Draft for LA Kings' 4th round choice (John Devoe) in 1982 Entry Draft, September 14, 1979.

• SEMAK, ALEXANDER

Alexander Semak C – R. 5'10", 185 lbs. b: Ufa, USSR, 2/11/1966. New Jersey's 12th choice, 207th overall, in 1988 Entry Draft.

Season	Club	League	GP	G	A	Pts	AG	AA	APts	PIM	PP	SH	GW	S	%	TGF	PGF	TGA	PGA	+/–	GP	G	A	Pts	PIM	PP	SH	GW
1982-83	Ufa Salavat	USSR	13	2	1	3	....	....	....	4	....	....	....	....	....	....	....	....	....	....	....	....	....	....	....	....	....	....
1983-84	Ufa Salavat	USSR 2	STATISTICS NOT AVAILABLE																		....	....	....	....	....	....	....	....
	Soviet Union	WJC-A	7	0	4	4	....	....	....	2	....	....	....	....	....	....	....	....	....	....	....	....	....	....	....	....	....	....
1984-85	Ufa Salavat	USSR 2	47	19	17	36	....	....	....	64	....	....	....	....	....	....	....	....	....	....	....	....	....	....	....	....	....	....
	Soviet Union	WJC-A	7	7	4	11	....	....	....	12	....	....	....	....	....	....	....	....	....	....	....	....	....	....	....	....	....	....
1985-86	Ufa Salavat	USSR	22	9	7	16	....	....	....	22	....	....	....	....	....	....	....	....	....	....	....	....	....	....	....	....	....	....
	Soviet Union	WJC-A	7	3	6	9	....	....	....	4	....	....	....	....	....	....	....	....	....	....	....	....	....	....	....	....	....	....
1986-87	Moscow Dynamo	USSR	40	20	8	28	....	....	....	32	....	....	....	....	....	....	....	....	....	....	....	....	....	....	....	....	....	....
	USSR	RV'87	2	0	0	0	....	....	....	0	....	....	....	....	....	....	....	....	....	....	....	....	....	....	....	....	....	....
	Soviet Union	WEC-A	10	1	0	1	....	....	....	4	....	....	....	....	....	....	....	....	....	....	....	....	....	....	....	....	....	....
1987-88	Soviet Union	C Cup	7	3	0	3	....	....	....	10	....	....	....	....	....	....	....	....	....	....	....	....	....	....	....	....	....	....
	Moscow Dynamo	USSR	47	21	14	35	....	....	....	40	....	....	....	....	....	....	....	....	....	....	....	....	....	....	....	....	....	....
1988-89	Moscow Dynamo	USSR	44	18	10	28	....	....	....	22	....	....	....	....	....	....	....	....	....	....	....	....	....	....	....	....	....	....
1989-90	Moscow Dynamo	FrTour	1	2	0	2	....	....	....	0	....	....	....	....	....	....	....	....	....	....	....	....	....	....	....	....	....	....
	Moscow Dynamo	USSR	43	23	11	34	....	....	....	33	....	....	....	....	....	....	....	....	....	....	....	....	....	....	....	....	....	....
	Moscow Dynamo	SuperS	5	1	2	3	....	....	....	2	....	....	....	....	....	....	....	....	....	....	....	....	....	....	....	....	....	....
	Soviet Union	WEC-A	10	2	2	4	....	....	....	6	....	....	....	....	....	....	....	....	....	....	....	....	....	....	....	....	....	....
1990-91	Moscow Dynamo	FrTour	1	1	0	1	....	....	....	2	....	....	....	....	....	....	....	....	....	....	....	....	....	....	....	....	....	....
	Moscow Dynamo	USSR	46	17	21	38	....	....	....	48	....	....	....	....	....	....	....	....	....	....	....	....	....	....	....	....	....	....
	Moscow Dynamo	SuperS	7	3	4	7	....	....	....	2	....	....	....	....	....	....	....	....	....	....	....	....	....	....	....	....	....	....
	Soviet Union	WEC-A	10	5	5	10	....	....	....	8	....	....	....	....	....	....	....	....	....	....	....	....	....	....	....	....	....	....
1991-92	Soviet Union	C Cup	5	2	1	3	....	....	....	7	....	....	....	....	....	....	....	....	....	....	....	....	....	....	....	....	....	....
	Moscow Dynamo	CIS	26	10	13	23	....	....	....	26	....	....	....	....	....	....	....	....	....	....	....	....	....	....	....	....	....	....
	New Jersey Devils	**NHL**	**25**	**5**	**6**	**11**	**5**	**4**	**9**	**0**	**0**	**0**	**1**	**45**	**11.1**	**18**	**2**	**11**	**0**	**+5**	**1**	**0**	**0**	**0**	**0**	**0**	**0**	**0**
	Utica Devils	AHL	7	3	2	5	....	....	....	0	....	....	....	....	....	....	....	....	....	....	....	....	....	....	....	....	....	....
1992-93	**New Jersey Devils**	**NHL**	**82**	**37**	**42**	**79**	**31**	**29**	**60**	**70**	**4**	**1**	**6**	**217**	**17.1**	**102**	**17**	**75**	**14**	**+24**	**5**	**1**	**1**	**2**	**0**	**0**	**0**	**0**
1993-94	**New Jersey Devils**	**NHL**	**54**	**12**	**17**	**29**	**11**	**13**	**24**	**22**	**2**	**2**	**2**	**88**	**13.6**	**38**	**12**	**23**	**3**	**+6**	**2**	**0**	**0**	**0**	**0**	**0**	**0**	**0**
1994-95	Ufa Salavat	CIS	9	9	6	15	....	....	....	4	....	....	....	....	....	....	....	....	....	....	....	....	....	....	....	....	....	....
	New Jersey Devils	**NHL**	**19**	**2**	**6**	**8**	**4**	**9**	**13**	**13**	**0**	**0**	**0**	**32**	**6.3**	**13**	**3**	**15**	**1**	**–4**	....	....	....	....	....	....	....	....
	Tampa Bay Lightning	**NHL**	**22**	**5**	**5**	**10**	**9**	**7**	**16**	**12**	**0**	**0**	**1**	**39**	**12.8**	**12**	**2**	**13**	**0**	**–3**	....	....	....	....	....	....	....	....
1995-96	**New York Islanders**	**NHL**	**69**	**20**	**14**	**34**	**20**	**11**	**31**	**68**	**6**	**0**	**2**	**128**	**15.6**	**49**	**15**	**38**	**0**	**–4**	....	....	....	....	....	....	....	....

Season	Club	League	REGULAR SEASON GP	G	A	Pts	AG	AA	APts	PIM	PP	SH	GW	S	%	TGF	PGF	TGA	PGA	+/–	PLAYOFFS GP	G	A	Pts	PIM	PP	SH	GW
1996-97	Russia	W Cup	1	0	0	0	....	....	....	0	....	....	....	....	....	....	....	....	....	....	....	....	....	....	....	....	....	....
	Vancouver Canucks	**NHL**	**18**	**2**	**1**	**3**	**2**	**1**	**3**	**2**	**1**	**0**	**0**	**12**	**16.7**	**5**	**1**	**6**	**0**	**–2**	....	....	....	....	....	....	....	....
	Syracuse Crunch	AHL	23	10	14	24	....	....	....	12	....	....	....	....	....	....	....	....	....	....	....	....	....	....	....	....	....	....
	Las Vegas Thunder	IHL	13	11	13	24	....	....	....	10	....	....	....	....	....	....	....	....	....	....	3	0	4	4	4	....	....	....
1997-98	Chicago Wolves	IHL	67	26	35	61	....	....	....	90	....	....	....	....	....	....	....	....	....	....	22	10	17	27	35	....	....	....
	NHL Totals		**289**	**83**	**91**	**174**	**82**	**74**	**156**	**187**	**13**	**3**	**12**	**561**	**14.8**	**237**	**52**	**181**	**18**		**8**	**1**	**1**	**2**	**0**	**0**	**0**	**0**

Named Best Forward at EJC-A (1984) • USSR First All-Star Team (1991) • Won "Bud" Poile Trophy (Playoff MVP - IHL) (1998)

Traded to **Tampa Bay** by **New Jersey** with Ben Hankinson for Shawn Chambers and Danton Cole, March 14, 1995. Traded to **NY Islanders** by **Tampa Bay** for NY Islanders' 5th round choice (Karel Betik) in 1997 Entry Draft, September 14, 1995. Claimed by **Vancouver** from **NY Islanders** in NHL Waiver Draft, September 30, 1996.

• SEMCHUK, BRANDY

Brandy Semchuk RW – R. 6'1", 185 lbs. b: Calgary, Alta., 9/22/1971. Los Angeles' 2nd choice, 28th overall, in 1990 Entry Draft.

Season	Club	League	GP	G	A	Pts	AG	AA	APts	PIM	PP	SH	GW	S	%	TGF	PGF	TGA	PGA	+/–	GP	G	A	Pts	PIM	PP	SH	GW
1988-89	Canada	Nat-Team	42	11	11	22	....	....	....	14	....	....	....	....	....	....	....	....	....	....	....	....	....	....	....	....	....	....
1989-90	Canada	Nat-Team	60	9	15	24	....	....	....	14	....	....	....	....	....	....	....	....	....	....	....	....	....	....	....	....	....	....
1990-91	Lethbridge Hurricanes	WHL	14	9	8	17	....	....	....	10	....	....	....	....	....	....	....	....	....	....	15	8	5	13	18	....	....	....
	New Haven Nighthawks	AHL	21	1	4	5	....	....	....	6	....	....	....	....	....	....	....	....	....	....	....	....	....	....	....	....	....	....
1991-92	Phoenix Roadrunners	IHL	15	1	5	6	....	....	....	6	....	....	....	....	....	....	....	....	....	....	....	....	....	....	....	....	....	....
	Raleigh IceCaps	ECHL	5	1	2	3	....	....	....	16	....	....	....	....	....	....	....	....	....	....	2	1	0	1	4	....	....	....
1992-93	**Los Angeles Kings**	**NHL**	**1**	**0**	**0**	**0**	**0**	**0**	**0**	**2**	**0**	**0**	**0**	**0**	**0.0**	**0**	**0**	**0**	**0**	**0**	....	....	....	....	....	....	....	....
	Phoenix Roadrunners	IHL	56	13	12	25	....	....	....	58	....	....	....	....	....	....	....	....	....	....	....	....	....	....	....	....	....	....
1993-94	Erie Panthers	ECHL	44	17	15	32	....	....	....	37	....	....	....	....	....	....	....	....	....	....	....	....	....	....	....	....	....	....
	Phoenix Roadrunners	IHL	2	0	0	0	....	....	....	6	....	....	....	....	....	....	....	....	....	....	....	....	....	....	....	....	....	....
1994-95	Nashville Knights	ECHL	9	3	2	5	....	....	....	2	....	....	....	....	....	....	....	....	....	....	....	....	....	....	....	....	....	....
	San Antonio Iguanas	CHL	30	18	16	34	....	....	....	34	....	....	....	....	....	....	....	....	....	....	13	1	5	6	33	....	....	....
1995-96	San Antonio Iguanas	CHL	12	5	2	7	....	....	....	43	....	....	....	....	....	....	....	....	....	....	....	....	....	....	....	....	....	....
1996-97	San Antonio Iguanas	CHL	10	4	6	10	....	....	....	2	....	....	....	....	....	....	....	....	....	....	....	....	....	....	....	....	....	....
	Columbus Cottonmouths	CHL	13	5	5	10	....	....	....	8	....	....	....	....	....	....	....	....	....	....	3	0	1	1	12	....	....	....
1997-98	Shreveport Mudbugs	WPHL	34	20	11	31	....	....	....	33	....	....	....	....	....	....	....	....	....	....	....	....	....	....	....	....	....	....
	Fresno Fighting Falcons	WCHL	25	20	18	38	....	....	....	21	....	....	....	....	....	....	....	....	....	....	5	2	3	5	0	....	....	....
	NHL Totals		**1**	**0**	**0**	**0**	**0**	**0**	**0**	**2**	**0**	**0**	**0**	**0**	**0.0**	**0**	**0**	**0**	**0**		....	....	....	....	....	....	....	....

• SEMENKO, DAVE

Dave "Sam" Semenko LW – L. 6'3", 200 lbs. b: Winnipeg, Man., 7/12/1957. Minnesota's 2nd choice, 25th overall, in 1977 Amateur Draft.

Season	Club	League	GP	G	A	Pts	AG	AA	APts	PIM	PP	SH	GW	S	%	TGF	PGF	TGA	PGA	+/–	GP	G	A	Pts	PIM	PP	SH	GW
1974-75	Brandon Travellers	Jr. A	42	11	17	28	....	....	....	55	....	....	....	....	....	....	....	....	....	....	....	....	....	....	....	....	....	....
	Brandon Wheat Kings	WCJHL	12	2	1	3	....	....	....	12	....	....	....	....	....	....	....	....	....	....	....	....	....	....	....	....	....	....
1975-76	Brandon Wheat Kings	WCJHL	72	8	5	13	....	....	....	194	....	....	....	....	....	....	....	....	....	....	....	....	....	....	....	....	....	....
1976-77	Brandon Wheat Kings	WCJHL	61	27	33	60	....	....	....	265	....	....	....	....	....	....	....	....	....	....	16	3	4	7	61	....	....	....
1977-78	Brandon Wheat Kings	WCJHL	7	10	5	15	....	....	....	40	....	....	....	....	....	....	....	....	....	....	....	....	....	....	....	....	....	....
	Edmonton Oilers	WHA	65	6	6	12	....	....	....	140	....	....	....	....	....	....	....	....	....	....	5	0	0	0	8	....	....	....
1978-79	Edmonton Oilers	WHA	77	10	14	24	....	....	....	158	....	....	....	....	....	....	....	....	....	....	11	4	2	6	29	....	....	....
1979-80	**Edmonton Oilers**	**NHL**	**67**	**6**	**7**	**13**	**5**	**5**	**10**	**135**	**1**	**0**	**1**	**43**	**14.0**	**26**	**5**	**34**	**0**	**–13**	**3**	**0**	**0**	**0**	**2**	**0**	**0**	**0**
1980-81	**Edmonton Oilers**	**NHL**	**58**	**11**	**8**	**19**	**9**	**6**	**15**	**80**	**4**	**0**	**2**	**42**	**26.2**	**29**	**11**	**22**	**0**	**–4**	**8**	**0**	**0**	**0**	**5**	**0**	**0**	**0**
	Wichita Wind	CHL	14	1	2	3	....	....	....	40	....	....	....	....	....	....	....	....	....	....	....	....	....	....	....	....	....	....
1981-82	**Edmonton Oilers**	**NHL**	**59**	**12**	**12**	**24**	**9**	**8**	**17**	**194**	**4**	**0**	**1**	**54**	**22.2**	**45**	**12**	**26**	**0**	**+7**	**4**	**0**	**0**	**0**	**2**	**0**	**0**	**0**
1982-83	**Edmonton Oilers**	**NHL**	**75**	**12**	**15**	**27**	**10**	**10**	**20**	**141**	**0**	**0**	**1**	**69**	**17.4**	**62**	**7**	**36**	**0**	**+10**	**15**	**1**	**1**	**2**	**69**	**0**	**0**	**0**
1983-84	**Edmonton Oilers**	**NHL**	**52**	**0**	**11**	**17**	**5**	**7**	**12**	**118**	**0**	**0**	**2**	**39**	**15.4**	**34**	**2**	**23**	**0**	**+9**	**19**	**5**	**5**	**10**	**44**	**0**	**0**	**1**
1984-85	**Edmonton Oilers**	**NHL**	**69**	**6**	**12**	**18**	**5**	**8**	**13**	**172**	**0**	**0**	**1**	**50**	**12.0**	**34**	**2**	**27**	**0**	**+5**	**14**	**0**	**0**	**0**	**39**	**0**	**0**	**0**
1985-86	**Edmonton Oilers**	**NHL**	**69**	**6**	**12**	**18**	**5**	**8**	**13**	**141**	**0**	**0**	**0**	**51**	**11.8**	**40**	**3**	**38**	**0**	**–1**	**6**	**0**	**0**	**0**	**32**	**0**	**0**	**0**
1986-87	**Edmonton Oilers**	**NHL**	**5**	**0**	**0**	**0**	**0**	**0**	**0**	**0**	**0**	**0**	**0**	**1**	**0.0**	**2**	**0**	**2**	**0**	**0**	....	....	....	....	....	....	....	....
	Hartford Whalers	**NHL**	**51**	**4**	**8**	**12**	**3**	**6**	**9**	**87**	**0**	**0**	**0**	**31**	**12.9**	**21**	**3**	**25**	**0**	**–7**	**4**	**0**	**0**	**0**	**15**	**0**	**0**	**0**
1987-88	**Toronto Maple Leafs**	**NHL**	**70**	**2**	**3**	**5**	**2**	**2**	**4**	**107**	**0**	**0**	**0**	**12**	**16.7**	**8**	**3**	**13**	**0**	**–8**	....	....	....	....	....	....	....	....
	NHL Totals		**575**	**65**	**88**	**153**	**53**	**60**	**113**	**1175**	**9**	**0**	**8**	**392**	**16.6**	**301**	**48**	**246**	**0**		**73**	**6**	**6**	**12**	**208**	**0**	**0**	**1**
	Other Major League Totals		142	16	20	36	....	....	....	298	....	....	....	....	....	....	....	....	....		16	4	2	6	37	....	....	....

Selected by **Houston** (WHA) in 1977 WHA Amateur Draft, May, 1977. WHA rights traded to **Edmonton** (WHA) by **Houston** (WHA) for future considerations, November, 1978. Reclaimed by **Minnesota** from **Edmonton** prior to Expansion Draft, June 9, 1979. Traded to **Edmonton** by **Minnesota** for Edmonton's 2nd round (Neal Broten) and 3rd round (Kevin Maxwell) choices in 1979 Entry Draft, August 9, 1979. Traded to **Hartford** by **Edmonton** for Hartford's 3rd round choice (Trevor Sim) in 1988 Entry Draft, December 12, 1986. Traded to **Toronto** by **Hartford** for Bill Root, September 8, 1987.

• SEMENOV, ANATOLI

Anatoli Semenov C/LW – L. 6'2", 190 lbs. b: Moscow, USSR, 3/5/1962. Edmonton's 5th choice, 120th overall, in 1989 Entry Draft.

Season	Club	League	GP	G	A	Pts	AG	AA	APts	PIM	PP	SH	GW	S	%	TGF	PGF	TGA	PGA	+/–	GP	G	A	Pts	PIM	PP	SH	GW
1979-80	Moscow Dynamo	USSR	8	3	0	3	....	....	....	2	....	....	....	....	....	....	....	....	....	....	....	....	....	....	....	....	....	....
1980-81	Moscow Dynamo	USSR	47	18	14	32	....	....	....	18	....	....	....	....	....	....	....	....	....	....	....	....	....	....	....	....	....	....
	Soviet Union	WJC-A	5	3	2	5	....	....	....	6	....	....	....	....	....	....	....	....	....	....	....	....	....	....	....	....	....	....
1981-82	Moscow Dynamo	USSR	44	12	14	26	....	....	....	28	....	....	....	....	....	....	....	....	....	....	....	....	....	....	....	....	....	....
	Soviet Union	WJC-A	7	5	8	13	....	....	....	22	....	....	....	....	....	....	....	....	....	....	....	....	....	....	....	....	....	....
1982-83	Moscow Dynamo	USSR	44	22	18	40	....	....	....	26	....	....	....	....	....	....	....	....	....	....	....	....	....	....	....	....	....	....
	USSR	SuperS	3	1	0	1	....	....	....	2	....	....	....	....	....	....	....	....	....	....	....	....	....	....	....	....	....	....
1983-84	Moscow Dynamo	USSR	19	10	5	15	....	....	....	14	....	....	....	....	....	....	....	....	....	....	....	....	....	....	....	....	....	....
1984-85	Soviet Union	C Cup	6	3	1	4	....	....	....	2	....	....	....	....	....	....	....	....	....	....	....	....	....	....	....	....	....	....
	Moscow Dynamo	USSR	30	17	12	29	....	....	....	32	....	....	....	....	....	....	....	....	....	....	....	....	....	....	....	....	....	....
1985-86	Moscow Dynamo	USSR	32	18	17	35	....	....	....	19	....	....	....	....	....	....	....	....	....	....	....	....	....	....	....	....	....	....
	Moscow Dynamo	SuperS	DID NOT PLAY																									
1986-87	Moscow Dynamo	USSR	40	15	29	44	....	....	....	32	....	....	....	....	....	....	....	....	....	....	....	....	....	....	....	....	....	....
	USSR	RV'87	1	1	0	1	....	....	....	0	....	....	....	....	....	....	....	....	....	....	....	....	....	....	....	....	....	....
	Soviet Union	WEC A	10	2	1	3	....	....	....	16	....	....	....	....	....	....	....	....	....	....	....	....	....	....	....	....	....	....
1987-88	Soviet Union	C Cup	9	2	5	7	....	....	....	2	....	....	....	....	....	....	....	....	....	....	....	....	....	....	....	....	....	....
	Moscow Dynamo	USSR	32	17	8	25	....	....	....	22	....	....	....	....	....	....	....	....	....	....	....	....	....	....	....	....	....	....
	Soviet Union	Olympics	8	2	4	6	....	....	....	6	....	....	....	....	....	....	....	....	....	....	....	....	....	....	....	....	....	....
1988-89	Moscow Dynamo	USSR	31	9	12	21	....	....	....	24	....	....	....	....	....	....	....	....	....	....	....	....	....	....	....	....	....	....
	Dynamo Riga	SuperS	7	1	3	4	....	....	....	0	....	....	....	....	....	....	....	....	....	....	....	....	....	....	....	....	....	....
1989-90	Moscow Dynamo	FrTour	1	1	1	2	....	....	....	0	....	....	....	....	....	....	....	....	....	....	....	....	....	....	....	....	....	....
	Moscow Dynamo	USSR	48	13	20	33	....	....	....	16	....	....	....	....	....	....	....	....	....	....	....	....	....	....	....	....	....	....
	Moscow Dynamo	SuperS	5	1	1	2	....	....	....	2	....	....	....	....	....	....	....	....	....	....	....	....	....	....	....	....	....	....
	Edmonton Oilers	**NHL**	....	....	....	....	....	....	....	....	....	....	....	....	....	....	....	....	....	....	**2**	**0**	**0**	**0**	**0**	....	....	....
1990-91	**Edmonton Oilers**	**NHL**	**57**	**15**	**16**	**31**	**14**	**12**	**26**	**26**	**3**	**1**	**1**	**101**	**14.9**	**56**	**9**	**37**	**7**	**+17**	**12**	**5**	**5**	**10**	**6**	**0**	**0**	**0**
1991-92	**Edmonton Oilers**	**NHL**	**59**	**20**	**22**	**42**	**18**	**17**	**35**	**16**	**3**	**0**	**3**	**105**	**19.0**	**60**	**12**	**53**	**17**	**+12**	**8**	**1**	**1**	**2**	**6**	**0**	**0**	**0**
1992-93	**Tampa Bay Lightning**	**NHL**	**13**	**2**	**3**	**5**	**2**	**2**	**4**	**4**	**0**	**0**	**0**	**14**	**14.3**	**9**	**3**	**11**	**0**	**–5**	....	....	....	....	....	....	....	....
	Vancouver Canucks	**NHL**	**62**	**10**	**34**	**44**	**8**	**23**	**31**	**28**	**3**	**2**	**1**	**88**	**11.4**	**76**	**19**	**56**	**20**	**+21**	**12**	**1**	**3**	**4**	**0**	**0**	**0**	**0**
1993-94	**Anaheim Mighty Ducks**	**NHL**	**49**	**11**	**19**	**30**	**10**	**15**	**25**	**12**	**4**	**0**	**2**	**103**	**10.7**	**46**	**18**	**42**	**10**	**–4**	....	....	....	....	....	....	....	....
1994-95	**Anaheim Mighty Ducks**	**NHL**	**15**	**3**	**4**	**7**	**5**	**6**	**11**	**4**	**2**	**0**	**0**	**33**	**9.1**	**9**	**2**	**21**	**4**	**–10**	....	....	....	....	....	....	....	....
	Philadelphia Flyers	**NHL**	**26**	**1**	**2**	**3**	**2**	**3**	**5**	**6**	**0**	**0**	**0**	**36**	**2.8**	**9**	**4**	**7**	**0**	**–2**	**15**	**2**	**4**	**6**	**0**	**0**	**0**	**0**
1995-96	**Philadelphia Flyers**	**NHL**	**44**	**3**	**13**	**16**	**3**	**11**	**14**	**14**	**0**	**0**	**2**	**55**	**5.5**	**19**	**1**	**15**	**0**	**+3**	....	....	....	....	....	....	....	....
	Anaheim Mighty Ducks	**NHL**	**12**	**1**	**9**	**10**	**1**	**7**	**8**	**10**	**0**	**0**	**0**	**24**	**4.2**	**17**	**10**	**11**	**0**	**–4**	....	....	....	....	....	....	....	....
1996-97	**Buffalo Sabres**	**NHL**	**25**	**2**	**4**	**6**	**2**	**4**	**6**	**2**	**1**	**0**	**1**	**21**	**9.5**	**9**	**2**	**17**	**7**	**–3**	....	....	....	....	....	....	....	....
1997-98	Yekaterinburg	CIS	8	0	0	0	....	....	....	0	....	....	....	....	....	....	....	....	....	....	....	....	....	....	....	....	....	....
	NHL Totals		**362**	**68**	**126**	**194**	**65**	**100**	**165**	**122**	**16**	**3**	**10**	**580**	**11.7**	**310**	**80**	**270**	**65**		**49**	**9**	**13**	**22**	**12**	**0**	**0**	**0**

USSR First All-Star Team (1985)

Claimed by **Tampa Bay** from **Edmonton** in Expansion Draft, June 18, 1992. Traded to **Vancouver** by **Tampa Bay** for Dave Capuano and Vancouver's 4th round choice (later traded to New Jersey — later traded to Calgary — Calgary selected Ryan Duthie) in 1994 Entry Draft, November 3, 1992. Claimed by **Anaheim** from **Vancouver** in Expansion Draft, June 24, 1993. Traded to **Philadelphia** by **Anaheim** for Milos Holan, March 8, 1995. Traded to **Anaheim** by **Philadelphia** with Mike Crowley for Brian Wesenberg, March 19, 1996. Signed as a free agent by **Buffalo**, September 17, 1996.

REGULAR SEASON / PLAYOFFS

● **SEPPA, JYRKI** Jyrki Seppa D – L. 6'1", 190 lbs. b: Tampere, Finland, 11/14/1961. Winnipeg's 3rd choice, 43rd overall, in 1981 Entry Draft.

Season	Club	League	GP	G	A	Pts	AG	AA	APts	PIM	PP	SH	GW	S	%	TGF	PGF	TGA	PGA	+/–	GP	G	A	Pts	PIM	PP	SH	GW
1980-81	Ilves Tampere	Finland	34	3	4	7	....	....	....	14	....	....	....	....	....	....	....	....	....	....	2	0	0	0	5	....	....	....
	Finland	WJC-A	5	2	0	2	....	....	....	4	....	....	....	....	....	....	....	....	....	....	....	....	....	....	....	....	....	....
1981-82	Jokerit Helsinki	Finland	31	6	1	7	....	....	....	12	....	....	....	....	....	....	....	....	....	....	....	....	....	....	....	....	....	....
1982-83	Sherbrooke Jets	AHL	72	2	13	15	....	....	....	66	....	....	....	....	....	....	....	....	....	....	....	....	....	....	....	....	....	....
1983-84	**Winnipeg Jets**	**NHL**	**13**	**0**	**2**	**2**	**0**	**1**	**1**	**6**	**0**	**0**	**0**	**7**	**0.0**	**5**	**2**	**12**	**0**	**–9**	....	....	....	....	....	....	....	....
	Sherbrooke Jets	AHL	60	5	35	40	....	....	....	43	....	....	....	....	....	....	....	....	....	....	....	....	....	....	....	....	....	....
1984-85	HPK Hameenlinna	Finland2	23	4	3	7	....	....	....	24	....	....	....	....	....	....	....	....	....	....	....	....	....	....	....	....	....	....
1985-86	Jokerit Helsinki	Finland	32	2	7	9	....	....	....	36	....	....	....	....	....	....	....	....	....	....	....	....	....	....	....	....	....	....
	NHL Totals		**13**	**0**	**2**	**2**	**0**	**1**	**1**	**6**	**0**	**0**	**0**	**7**	**0.0**	**5**	**2**	**12**	**0**		....	....	....	....	....	....	....	....

● **SERAFINI, RON** Ron Serafini D – R. 5'11", 180 lbs. b: Highland Park, MI, 10/31/1953. California's 2nd choice, 50th overall, in 1973 Amateur Draft.

Season	Club	League	GP	G	A	Pts	AG	AA	APts	PIM	PP	SH	GW	S	%	TGF	PGF	TGA	PGA	+/–	GP	G	A	Pts	PIM	PP	SH	GW
1971-72	St. Catharines Black Hawks	OHA	61	6	17	23	....	....	....	164	....	....	....	....	....	....	....	....	....	....	....	....	....	....	....	....	....	....
1972-73	St. Catharines Black Hawks	OHA	63	17	25	42	....	....	....	221	....	....	....	....	....	....	....	....	....	....	....	....	....	....	....	....	....	....
1973-74	**California Golden Seals**	**NHL**	**2**	**0**	**0**	**0**	**0**	**0**	**0**	**2**	**0**	**0**	**0**	**0**	**0.0**	**2**	**0**	**5**	**1**	**–2**	....	....	....	....	....	....	....	....
	Salt Lake Golden Eagles	WHL	74	8	31	39	....	....	....	202	....	....	....	....	....	....	....	....	....	....	5	0	0	0	2	....	....	....
1974-75	Denver Spurs	CHL	75	7	21	28	....	....	....	83	....	....	....	....	....	....	....	....	....	....	2	0	1	1	9	....	....	....
1975-76	Cincinnati Stingers	WHA	16	0	2	2	....	....	....	15	....	....	....	....	....	....	....	....	....	....	....	....	....	....	....	....	....	....
	Tucson Mavericks	CHL	20	1	3	4	....	....	....	39	....	....	....	....	....	....	....	....	....	....	....	....	....	....	....	....	....	....
	Hampton Gulls	SHL	27	4	20	24	....	....	....	20	....	....	....	....	....	....	....	....	....	....	9	1	7	8	10	....	....	....
1976-77	Salt Lake Golden Eagles	CHL	31	3	5	8	....	....	....	29	....	....	....	....	....	....	....	....	....	....	....	....	....	....	....	....	....	....
	Oklahoma City Blazers	CHL	10	1	0	1	....	....	....	17	....	....	....	....	....	....	....	....	....	....	....	....	....	....	....	....	....	....
	Winston-Salem Polar Bears	SHL	8	1	2	3	....	....	....	4	....	....	....	....	....	....	....	....	....	....	....	....	....	....	....	....	....	....
	Hampton Gulls	SHL	9	0	6	6	....	....	....	10	....	....	....	....	....	....	....	....	....	....	....	....	....	....	....	....	....	....
	NHL Totals		**2**	**0**	**0**	**0**	**0**	**0**	**0**	**2**	**0**	**0**	**0**	**0**	**0.0**	**2**	**0**	**5**	**1**		....	....	....	....	....	....	....	....
	Other Major League Totals		16	0	2	2	....	....	....	15	....	....	....	....	....	....	....	....	....		....	....	....	....	....	....	....	....

Selected by **Cleveland** (WHA) in 1973 WHA Amateur Draft, June, 1973. Traded to **St. Louis** by **California** for Glenn Patrick, July 18, 1974. WHA rights claimed by **Phoenix** (WHA) from **Cleveland** (WHA) in WHA Expansion Draft, June, 1975. Traded to **Cincinnati** (WHA) by **Phoenix** (WHA) for Gary Veneruzzo, November, 1975.

● **SEROWIK, JEFF** Jeff Serowik D – R. 6'1", 210 lbs. b: Manchester, NH, 1/10/1967. Toronto's 5th choice, 85th overall, in 1985 Entry Draft.

Season	Club	League	GP	G	A	Pts	AG	AA	APts	PIM	PP	SH	GW	S	%	TGF	PGF	TGA	PGA	+/–	GP	G	A	Pts	PIM	PP	SH	GW
1984-85	Lawrence Academy	H.S.	21	12	12	24	....	....	....	....	....	....	....	....	....	....	....	....	....	....	....	....	....	....	....	....	....	....
1985-86	Lawrence Academy	H.S.	24	8	25	33	....	....	....	....	....	....	....	....	....	....	....	....	....	....	....	....	....	....	....	....	....	....
1986-87	Providence College	H.E.	33	3	8	11	....	....	....	22	....	....	....	....	....	....	....	....	....	....	....	....	....	....	....	....	....	....
1987-88	Providence College	H.E.	33	3	9	12	....	....	....	44	....	....	....	....	....	....	....	....	....	....	....	....	....	....	....	....	....	....
1988-89	Providence College	H.E.	35	3	14	17	....	....	....	48	....	....	....	....	....	....	....	....	....	....	....	....	....	....	....	....	....	....
1989-90	Providence College	H.E.	35	6	19	25	....	....	....	34	....	....	....	....	....	....	....	....	....	....	....	....	....	....	....	....	....	....
1990-91	**Toronto Maple Leafs**	**NHL**	**1**	**0**	**0**	**0**	**0**	**0**	**0**	**0**	**0**	**0**	**0**	**1**	**0.0**	**0**	**0**	**0**	**0**	**0**	....	....	....	....	....	....	....	....
	Newmarket Saints	AHL	60	8	15	23	....	....	....	45	....	....	....	....	....	....	....	....	....	....	....	....	....	....	....	....	....	....
1991-92	St. John's Maple Leafs	AHL	78	11	34	45	....	....	....	60	....	....	....	....	....	....	....	....	....	....	16	4	9	13	22	....	....	....
1992-93	St. John's Maple Leafs	AHL	77	19	35	54	....	....	....	92	....	....	....	....	....	....	....	....	....	....	9	1	5	6	8	....	....	....
1993-94	Cincinnati Cyclones	IHL	79	6	21	27	....	....	....	98	....	....	....	....	....	....	....	....	....	....	7	0	1	1	8	....	....	....
1994-95	**Boston Bruins**	**NHL**	**1**	**0**	**0**	**0**	**0**	**0**	**0**	**0**	**0**	**0**	**0**	**0**	**0.0**	**1**	**0**	**0**	**0**	**+1**	....	....	....	....	....	....	....	....
	Providence Bruins	AHL	78	28	34	62	....	....	....	102	....	....	....	....	....	....	....	....	....	....	13	4	6	10	10	....	....	....
1995-96	Indianapolis Ice	IHL	69	20	23	43	....	....	....	86	....	....	....	....	....	....	....	....	....	....	....	....	....	....	....	....	....	....
	Las Vegas Thunder	IHL	13	7	6	13	....	....	....	18	....	....	....	....	....	....	....	....	....	....	15	6	5	11	16	....	....	....
1996-97	Las Vegas Thunder	IHL	42	5	19	24	....	....	....	34	....	....	....	....	....	....	....	....	....	....	3	0	0	0	4	....	....	....
1997-98	Kansas City Blades	IHL	77	14	35	49	....	....	....	50	....	....	....	....	....	....	....	....	....	....	11	2	5	7	12	....	....	....
	NHL Totals		**2**	**0**	**0**	**0**	**0**	**0**	**0**	**0**	**0**	**0**	**0**	**1**	**0.0**	**1**	**0**	**0**	**0**		....	....	....	....	....	....	....	....

Hockey East Second All-Star Team (1990) • Won Eddie Shore Award (Outstanding Defenseman - AHL) (1995)

Signed as a free agent by **Florida**, July 20, 1993. Signed as a free agent by **Boston**, June 29, 1994. Signed as a free agent by **Chicago**, August 10, 1995.

● **SERVINIS, GEORGE** George Servinis LW – L. 5'11", 180 lbs. b: Toronto, Ont., 4/29/1962.

Season	Club	League	GP	G	A	Pts	AG	AA	APts	PIM	PP	SH	GW	S	%	TGF	PGF	TGA	PGA	+/–	GP	G	A	Pts	PIM	PP	SH	GW
1980-81	Wexford Raiders	MTHL	40	35	45	80	....	....	....	....	....	....	....	....	....	....	....	....	....	....	....	....	....	....	....	....	....	....
1981-82	Aurora Tigers	OJHL	55	62	55	117	....	....	....	....	....	....	....	....	....	....	....	....	....	....	....	....	....	....	....	....	....	....
1982-83	RPI Engineers	ECAC	28	35	29	64	....	....	....	22	....	....	....	....	....	....	....	....	....	....	....	....	....	....	....	....	....	....
1983-84	RPI Engineers	ECAC	12	5	13	18	....	....	....	14	....	....	....	....	....	....	....	....	....	....	....	....	....	....	....	....	....	....
	Canada	Nat-Team	43	13	11	24	....	....	....	33	....	....	....	....	....	....	....	....	....	....	....	....	....	....	....	....	....	....
1984-85	RPI Engineers	ECAC	35	34	25	59	....	....	....	44	....	....	....	....	....	....	....	....	....	....	....	....	....	....	....	....	....	....
1985-86	Springfield Indians	AHL	30	2	14	16	....	....	....	19	....	....	....	....	....	....	....	....	....	....	....	....	....	....	....	....	....	....
1986-87	Indianapolis Checkers	IHL	70	41	54	95	....	....	....	54	....	....	....	....	....	....	....	....	....	....	....	....	....	....	....	....	....	....
1987-88	**Minnesota North Stars**	**NHL**	**5**	**0**	**0**	**0**	**0**	**0**	**0**	**0**	**0**	**0**	**0**	**8**	**0.0**	**0**	**0**	**2**	**0**	**–2**	....	....	....	....	....	....	....	....
	Kalamazoo Wings	IHL	49	34	21	55	....	....	....	54	....	....	....	....	....	....	....	....	....	....	6	3	1	4	2	....	....	....
1988-89	HC Villach	Austria	37	32	35	67	....	....	....	....	....	....	....	....	....	....	....	....	....	....	....	....	....	....	....	....	....	....
	NHL Totals		**5**	**0**	**0**	**0**	**0**	**0**	**0**	**0**	**0**	**0**	**0**	**8**	**0.0**	**0**	**0**	**2**	**0**		....	....	....	....	....	....	....	....

NCAA Championship All-Tournament Team (1985)

Signed as a free agent by **Minnesota**, August 13, 1985.

● **SEVCIK, JAROSLAV** Jaroslav Sevcik LW – R. 5'9", 170 lbs. b: Brno, Czech., 5/15/1965. Quebec's 9th choice, 177th overall, in 1987 Entry Draft.

Season	Club	League	GP	G	A	Pts	AG	AA	APts	PIM	PP	SH	GW	S	%	TGF	PGF	TGA	PGA	+/–	GP	G	A	Pts	PIM	PP	SH	GW
1984-85	Dukla Trencin	Czech.	31	3	4	7	....	....	....	6	....	....	....	....	....	....	....	....	....	....	....	....	....	....	....	....	....	....
	Czechoslovakia	WJC-A	7	1	0	1	....	....	....	2	....	....	....	....	....	....	....	....	....	....	....	....	....	....	....	....	....	....
1985-86	Dukla Trencin	Czech.	22	0	1	1	....	....	....	6	....	....	....	....	....	....	....	....	....	....	....	....	....	....	....	....	....	....
1986-87	Zetor Brno	Czech.	42	14	9	23	....	....	....	14	....	....	....	....	....	....	....	....	....	....	....	....	....	....	....	....	....	....
1987-88	Fredericton Express	AHL	32	9	7	16	....	....	....	6	....	....	....	....	....	....	....	....	....	....	....	....	....	....	....	....	....	....
1988-89	Halifax Citadels	AHL	78	17	41	58	....	....	....	17	....	....	....	....	....	....	....	....	....	....	4	1	1	2	2	....	....	....
1989-90	**Quebec Nordiques**	**NHL**	**13**	**0**	**2**	**2**	**0**	**1**	**1**	**2**	**0**	**0**	**0**	**9**	**0.0**	**5**	**1**	**9**	**0**	**–5**	....	....	....	....	....	....	....	....
	Halifax Citadels	AHL	50	17	17	34	....	....	....	36	....	....	....	....	....	....	....	....	....	....	3	0	1	1	0	....	....	....
1990-91	Halifax Citadels	AHL	66	16	26	42	....	....	....	22	....	....	....	....	....	....	....	....	....	....	....	....	....	....	....	....	....	....
1991-92	SC Rapperswill	Switz.2	10	5	3	8	....	....	....	14	....	....	....	....	....	....	....	....	....	....	....	....	....	....	....	....	....	....
1992-93	Panda's Rotterdam	Holland	22	13	18	31	....	....	....	26	....	....	....	....	....	....	....	....	....	....	5	2	4	6	0	....	....	....
1993-94	SPG Nijmegan	Holland	27	14	23	37	....	....	....	26	....	....	....	....	....	....	....	....	....	....	2	0	2	2	0	....	....	....
1994-95	Villach HC	Austria	28	16	*43	54	....	....	....	18	....	....	....	....	....	....	....	....	....	....	12	5	9	14	12	....	....	....
1995-96	Ratingen Lions	Germany	17	3	10	13	....	....	....	8	....	....	....	....	....	....	....	....	....	....	....	....	....	....	....	....	....	....
	KAC Klagenfurt	Austria	26	11	24	35	....	....	....	12	....	....	....	....	....	....	....	....	....	....	....	....	....	....	....	....	....	....
1996-97	Kapfenberger	Austria	41	13	16	29	....	....	....	45	....	....	....	....	....	....	....	....	....	....	....	....	....	....	....	....	....	....
	NHL Totals		**13**	**0**	**2**	**2**	**0**	**1**	**1**	**2**	**0**	**0**	**0**	**9**	**0.0**	**5**	**1**	**9**	**0**		....	....	....	....	....	....	....	....

● **SEVERYN, BRENT** Brent Severyn LW – L. 6'2", 211 lbs. b: Vegreville, Alta., 2/22/1966. Winnipeg's 5th choice, 99th overall, in 1984 Entry Draft.

Season	Club	League	GP	G	A	Pts	AG	AA	APts	PIM	PP	SH	GW	S	%	TGF	PGF	TGA	PGA	+/–	GP	G	A	Pts	PIM	PP	SH	GW
1983-84	Seattle Thunderbirds	WHL	72	14	22	36	....	....	....	49	....	....	....	....	....	....	....	....	....	....	....	....	....	....	....	....	....	....
1984-85	Seattle Thunderbirds	WHL	38	8	32	40	....	....	....	54	....	....	....	....	....	....	....	....	....	....	....	....	....	....	....	....	....	....
	Brandon Wheat Kings	WHL	26	7	16	23	....	....	....	57	....	....	....	....	....	....	....	....	....	....	....	....	....	....	....	....	....	....
1985-86	Seattle Thunderbirds	WHL	33	11	20	31	....	....	....	164	....	....	....	....	....	....	....	....	....	....	....	....	....	....	....	....	....	....
	Saskatoon Blades	WHL	9	1	4	5	....	....	....	38	....	....	....	....	....	....	....	....	....	....	....	....	....	....	....	....	....	....
1986-87	University of Alberta	CWUAA	43	7	19	26	....	....	....	171	....	....	....	....	....	....	....	....	....	....	....	....	....	....	....	....	....	....
1987-88	University of Alberta	CWUAA	46	21	29	50	....	....	....	178	....	....	....	....	....	....	....	....	....	....	....	....	....	....	....	....	....	....
1988-89	Halifax Citadels	AHL	47	2	12	14	....	....	....	141	....	....	....	....	....	....	....	....	....	....	....	....	....	....	....	....	....	....
1989-90	**Quebec Nordiques**	**NHL**	**35**	**0**	**2**	**2**	**0**	**1**	**1**	**42**	**0**	**0**	**0**	**28**	**0.0**	**16**	**0**	**38**	**3**	**–19**	....	....	....	....	....	....	....	....
	Halifax Citadels	AHL	43	6	9	15	....	....	....	105	....	....	....	....	....	....	....	....	....	....	6	1	2	3	49	....	....	....
1990-91	Halifax Citadels	AHL	50	7	26	33	....	....	....	202	....	....	....	....	....	....	....	....	....	....	....	....	....	....	....	....	....	....
1991-92	Utica Devils	AHL	80	11	33	44	....	....	....	211	....	....	....	....	....	....	....	....	....	....	4	0	1	1	4	....	....	....

Season	Club	League	GP	G	A	Pts	AG	AA	APts	PIM	PP	SH	GW	S	%	TGF	PGF	TGA	PGA	+/-	GP	G	A	Pts	PIM	PP	SH	GW
1992-93	Utica Devils	AHL	77	20	32	52				240												5	0	0	0	35			
1993-94	Florida Panthers	NHL	67	4	7	11	4	5	9	156	1	0	1	93	4.3	37	6	45	13	−1								
1994-95	Florida Panthers	NHL	9	1	1	2	2	1	3	37	1	0	0	10	10.0	4	2	6	1	−3								
	New York Islanders	NHL	19	1	3	4	2	4	6	34	0	0	0	22	4.5	12	0	13	2	+1								
1995-96	New York Islanders	NHL	65	1	8	9	1	7	8	180	0	0	0	40	2.5	36	0	48	15	+3								
1996-97	Colorado Avalanche	NHL	66	1	4	5	1	4	5	193	0	0	0	55	1.8	10	0	16	0	−6	8	0	0	0	12	0	0	0
1997-98	Anaheim Mighty Ducks	NHL	37	1	3	4	1	3	4	133	0	0	0	27	3.7	9	0	12	0	−3								
	NHL Totals		298	9	28	37	11	25	36	775	2	0	1	275	3.3	124	8	178	34		8	0	0	0	12	0	0	0

AHL First All-Star Team (1993)

Signed as a free agent by **Quebec**, July 15, 1988. Traded to **New Jersey** by **Quebec** for Dave Marcinyshyn, June 3, 1991. Traded to **Winnipeg** by **New Jersey** for Winnipeg's 6th round choice (Ryan Smart) in 1994 Entry Draft, September 30, 1993. Traded to **Florida** by **Winnipeg** for Milan Tichy, October 3, 1993. Traded to **NY Islanders** by **Florida** for NY Islanders' 4th round choice (Dave Duerden) in 1995 Entry Draft, March 3, 1995. Traded to **Colorado** by **NY Islanders** for Colorado's 3rd round choice (later traded to Calgary — later traded to Hartford — Carolina selected Francis Lessard) in 1997 Entry Draft, September 4, 1996. Claimed by **Anaheim** from **Colorado** in NHL Waiver Draft, September 28, 1998.

● SEVIGNY, PIERRE
Pierre Sevigny LW – L. 6', 195 lbs. b: Trois-Rivières, Que., 9/8/1971. Montreal's 4th choice, 51st overall, in 1989 Entry Draft.

Season	Club	League	GP	G	A	Pts	AG	AA	APts	PIM	PP	SH	GW	S	%	TGF	PGF	TGA	PGA	+/-	GP	G	A	Pts	PIM	PP	SH	GW
1988-89	Verdun Jr. Canadiens	QMJHL	67	27	43	70				88																		
1989-90	St-Hyacinthe Laser	QMJHL	67	47	72	119				205											12	8	8	16	42			
1990-91	St-Hyacinthe Laser	QMJHL	60	36	46	82				203																		
	Canada	WJC-A	7	4	2	6				8																		
1991-92	Fredericton Canadiens	AHL	74	22	37	59				145											7	1	1	2	26			
1992-93	Fredericton Canadiens	AHL	80	36	40	76				113											5	1	1	2	2			
1993-94	Montreal Canadiens	NHL	43	4	5	9	4	4	8	42	1	0	1	19	21.1	17	1	10	0	+6	3	0	1	1	0	0	0	0
1994-95	Montreal Canadiens	NHL	19	0	0	0	0	0	0	15	0	0	0	6	0.0	1	0	6	0	−5								
1995-96	Fredericton Canadiens	AHL	76	39	42	81				188											10	5	9	14	20			
1996-97	Montreal Canadiens	NHL	13	0	0	0	0	0	0	5	0	0	0	1	0.0	1	0	1	0									
	Fredericton Canadiens	AHL	32	9	17	26				58																		
1997-98	New York Rangers	NHL	3	0	0	0	0	0	0	2	0	0	0	1	0.0	1	0	1	0									
	Hartford	AHL	40	18	13	31				94											12	3	6	8	14			
	NHL Totals		78	4	5	9	4	4	8	64	1	0	1	27	14.8	20	1	18	0		3	0	1	1	0	0	0	0

QMJHL First All-Star Team (1981)

QMJHL Second All-Star Team (1990, 1991)

Signed as a free agent by **NY Rangers**, August 26, 1997.

● SHACK, EDDIE
Eddie "The Entertainer" Shack LW – L. 6'1", 200 lbs. b: Sudbury, Ont., 2/11/1937.

Season	Club	League	GP	G	A	Pts	AG	AA	APts	PIM	PP	SH	GW	S	%	TGF	PGF	TGA	PGA	+/-	GP	G	A	Pts	PIM	PP	SH	GW
1952-53	Guelph Biltmores	OHA	21	2	6	8				45																		
1953-54	Guelph Biltmores	OHA	54	13	9	22				46											1	1	0	1	4			
1954-55	Guelph Biltmores	OHA	19	6	7	13				35											2	0	0	0	4			
1955-56	Guelph Biltmores	OHA	48	23	49	72				93											3	1	0	1	10			
1956-57	Guelph Biltmores	OHA	52	47	*57	104				129											10	4	10	14	53			
1957-58	Providence Reds	AHL	35	16	18	34				98																		
1958-59	New York Rangers	NHL	67	7	14	21	9	15	24	109																		
1959-60	New York Rangers	NHL	62	8	10	18	10	10	20	110																		
	Springfield Indians	AHL	9	3	4	7				10																		
1960-61	New York Rangers	NHL	12	1	2	3	1	2	3	17																		
	Toronto Maple Leafs	NHL	55	14	14	28	17	14	31	90											4	0	0	0	2			
1961-62	Toronto Maple Leafs	NHL	44	7	14	21	8	14	22	62											9	0	0	0	18			
1962-63	Toronto Maple Leafs	NHL	63	16	9	25	20	9	29	97											10	2	1	3	11			
1963-64	Toronto Maple Leafs	NHL	64	11	10	21	14	11	25	128											13	0	1	1	25			
1964-65	Toronto Maple Leafs	NHL	67	5	9	14	6	10	16	68											5	1	0	1	8			
1965-66	Toronto Maple Leafs	NHL	63	26	17	43	32	17	49	88											4	2	1	3	33			
	Rochester Americans	AHL	8	3	4	7				12																		
1966-67	Toronto Maple Leafs	NHL	63	11	14	25	13	14	27	58											8	0	0	0	8			
1967-68	Boston Bruins	NHL	70	23	19	42	28	20	48	107	4	0	6	195	11.8	60	8	52	1	+1	4	0	1	1	6	0	0	0
1968-69	Boston Bruins	NHL	50	11	11	22	12	10	22	74	1	0	3	125	8.8	34	4	29	1	+2	9	0	2	2	23	0	0	0
1969-70	Los Angeles Kings	NHL	73	22	12	34	25	12	37	113	4	0	2	203	10.8	54	10	83	1	−38								
1970-71	Los Angeles Kings	NHL	11	2	2	4	2	2	4	8	0	0	1	13	15.4	6	3	7	1	−3								
	Buffalo Sabres	NHL	56	25	17	42	26	15	41	93	10	0	4	192	13.0	69	34	65	1	−29								
1971-72	Buffalo Sabres	NHL	50	11	14	25	12	13	25	34	4	0	0	92	12.0	42	19	34	0	−11								
	Pittsburgh Penguins	NHL	18	5	9	14	5	8	13	12	4	0	2	47	10.6	24	11	8	0	+5	4	0	1	1	15	0	0	0
1972-73	Pittsburgh Penguins	NHL	74	25	20	45	25	17	42	84	8	0	3	192	13.0	76	30	57	1	−10								
1973-74	Toronto Maple Leafs	NHL	59	7	8	15	7	7	14	74	4	0	1	78	9.0	36	8	27	0	+1	4	1	0	1	2	0	0	0
1974-75	Toronto Maple Leafs	NHL	26	2	1	3	2	1	3	11	1	0	0	18	11.1	3	2	10	1	−8								
	Oklahoma City Blazers	CHL	8	3	4	7				10																		
1975-76			DID NOT PLAY																									
1976-77	Whitby Warriors	OHA Sr.	9	5	4	9				8																		
	NHL Totals		1047	239	226	465	274	221	495	1437	40	0	22	1155	20.7	404	129	372	7		74	6	7	13	151	0	0	0

Played in NHL All-Star Game (1962, 1963, 1964)

Traded to **Detroit** by **NY Rangers** with Bill Gadsby for Red Kelly and Billy McNeil, February 4, 1960. Kelly refused to report and transaction was cancelled. Traded to **Toronto** by **NY Rangers** for Pat Hannigan and John Wilson, November, 1960. Traded to **Boston** by **Toronto** for Murray Oliver and cash, May 15, 1967. Traded to **LA Kings** by **Boston** with Ross Lonsberry for Ken Turlik and LA Kings' 1st round choices in 1971 (Ron Jones) and 1973 (Andre Savard) Amateur Drafts, May 14, 1969. Traded to **Buffalo** by **LA Kings** with Dick Duff for Mike McMahon Jr., November 25, 1970. Traded to **Pittsburgh** by **Buffalo** for Rene Robert, March 4, 1972. Traded to **Toronto** by **Pittsburgh** for cash, July 3, 1973.

● SHAFRANOV, KONSTANTIN
Konstantin Shafranov RW – l 5'11", 176 lbs. b: Kamenogorsk, USSR, 9/11/1968. St. Louis' 10th choice, 229th overall, in 1996 Entry Draft.

Season	Club	League	GP	G	A	Pts	AG	AA	APts	PIM	PP	SH	GW	S	%	TGF	PGF	TGA	PGA	+/-	GP	G	A	Pts	PIM	PP	SH	GW
1989-90	Torpedo Ust-Kamenogorsk	USSR	28	6	8	14				16																		
1990-91	Torpedo Ust-Kamenogorsk	USSR	40	16	6	22				32																		
1991-92	Torpedo Ust-Kamenogorsk	CIS	36	10	6	16				40																		
1992-93	Torpedo Ust-Kamenogorsk	CIS	42	19	19	38				26											1	0	1	1	0			
	Kazakhstan	WC-C	7	10	9	19				4																		
1993-94	Detroit Falcons	ColHL	4	3	2	5				0																		
	Torpedo Ust-Kamenogorsk	CIS	27	18	21	39				6																		
	Kazakhstan	WC-C1	6	7	5	12				44																		
1994-95	Magnitogorsk	CIS	47	21	30	51				24											7	5	4	9	12			
1995-96	Magnitogorsk	CIS	6	3	3	6				0																		
	Fort Wayne Komets	IHL	74	46	28	74				26											5	1	2	3	4			
1996-97	St. Louis Blues	NHL	5	2	1	3	2	1	3	0	0	0	0	8	25.0	3	0	2	0	+1								
	Worcester IceCats	AHL	62	23	25	48				16											5	0	2	2	0			
1997-98	Fort Wayne Komets	IHL	67	28	52	80				50											4	2	4	6	2			
	Kazakhstan	Olympics	7	4	3	7				6																		
	Kazakhstan	WC-A	3	0	0	0				0																		
	NHL Totals		5	2	1	3	2	1	3	0	0	0	0	8	25.0	3	0	2	0									

Won Garry F. Longman Memorial Trophy (Top Rookie - IHL) (1996) • IHL Second All-Star Team (1998)

			REGULAR SEASON																		PLAYOFFS							
Season	Club	League	GP	G	A	Pts	AG	AA	APts	PIM	PP	SH	GW	S	%	TGF	PGF	TGA	PGA	+/-	GP	G	A	Pts	PIM	PP	SH	GW

• SHAKES, PAUL

Paul Shakes D – R. 5'10", 175 lbs. b: Collingwood, Ont., 9/4/1952. California's 3rd choice, 38th overall, in 1972 Amateur Draft.

Season	Club	League	GP	G	A	Pts	AG	AA	APts	PIM	PP	SH	GW	S	%	TGF	PGF	TGA	PGA	+/-	GP	G	A	Pts	PIM	PP	SH	GW
1969-70	St. Catharines Black Hawks	OHA	42	7	24	31	....	....	....	50	....	....	....	....	....	....	....	....	....	....	....	....	....	....	....	....	....	....
1970-71	St. Catharines Black Hawks	OHA	60	14	57	71	....	....	....	49	....	....	....	....	....	....	....	....	....	....	....	....	....	....	....	....	....	....
1971-72	St. Catharines Black Hawks	OHA	61	20	48	68	....	....	....	61	....	....	....	....	....	....	....	....	....	....	....	....	....	....	....	....	....	....
1972-73	Salt Lake Golden Eagles	WHL	71	11	31	42	....	....	....	59	....	....	....	....	....	....	....	....	....	....	9	1	3	4	8	....	....	....
1973-74	**California Golden Seals**	**NHL**	**21**	**0**	**4**	**4**	**0**	**3**	**3**	**12**	**0**	**0**	**0**	**29**	**0.0**	**14**	**0**	**30**	**3**	**–13**	....	....	....	....	....	....	....	....
	Salt Lake Golden Eagles	WHL	54	3	35	38	....	....	....	40	....	....	....	....	....	....	....	....	....	....	5	0	1	1	7	....	....	....
1974-75	Springfield Indians	AHL	74	11	32	43	....	....	....	60	....	....	....	....	....	....	....	....	....	....	17	4	9	13	17	....	....	....
1975-76	Salt Lake City Golden Eagles	CHL	26	3	16	19	....	....	....	16	....	....	....	....	....	....	....	....	....	....	....	....	....	....	....	....	....	....
	NHL Totals		**21**	**0**	**4**	**4**	**0**	**3**	**3**	**12**	**0**	**0**	**0**	**29**	**0.0**	**14**	**0**	**30**	**3**		....	....	....	....	....	....	....	....

OHA First All-Star Team (1972)

• SHALDYBIN, YEVGENY

Yevgeny Shaldybin D – L. 6'2", 198 lbs. b: Novosibirsk, USSR, 7/29/1975. Boston's 6th choice, 151st overall, in 1995 Entry Draft.

Season	Club	League	GP	G	A	Pts	AG	AA	APts	PIM	PP	SH	GW	S	%	TGF	PGF	TGA	PGA	+/-	GP	G	A	Pts	PIM	PP	SH	GW
1993-94	Torpedo Yaroslavl	CIS	14	0	0	0	....	....	....	0	....	....	....	....	....	....	....	....	....	....	....	....	....	....	....	....	....	....
1994-95	Torpedo Yaroslavl	CIS	42	2	5	7	....	....	....	10	....	....	....	....	....	....	....	....	....	....	4	0	1	1	0	....	....	....
1995-96	Torpedo Yaroslavl	CIS	41	0	2	2	....	....	....	10	....	....	....	....	....	....	....	....	....	....	3	0	1	1	2	....	....	....
1996-97	**Boston Bruins**	**NHL**	**3**	**1**	**0**	**1**	**1**	**0**	**1**	**0**	**0**	**0**	**0**	**5**	**20.0**	**1**	**0**	**3**	**0**	**–2**	....	....	....	....	....	....	....	....
	Providence Bruins	AHL	69	4	13	17	....	....	....	28	....	....	....	....	....	....	....	....	....	....	3	0	0	0	0	....	....	....
1997-98	Providence Bruins	AHL	63	5	7	12	....	....	....	54	....	....	....	....	....	....	....	....	....	....	....	....	....	....	....	....	....	....
	NHL Totals		**3**	**1**	**0**	**1**	**1**	**0**	**1**	**0**	**0**	**0**	**0**	**5**	**20.0**	**1**	**0**	**3**	**0**		....	....	....	....	....	....	....	....

• SHANAHAN, BRENDAN

Brendan Shanahan LW – R. 6'3", 218 lbs. b: Mimico, Ont., 1/23/1969. New Jersey's 1st choice, 2nd overall, in 1987 Entry Draft.

Season	Club	League	GP	G	A	Pts	AG	AA	APts	PIM	PP	SH	GW	S	%	TGF	PGF	TGA	PGA	+/-	GP	G	A	Pts	PIM	PP	SH	GW
1985-86	London Knights	OHL	59	28	34	62	....	....	....	70	....	....	....	....	....	....	....	....	....	....	5	5	5	10	5	....	....	....
1986-87	London Knights	OHL	56	39	53	92	....	....	....	92	....	....	....	....	....	....	....	....	....	....	....	....	....	....	....	....	....	....
	Canada	WJC-A	6	4	3	7	....	....	....	4	....	....	....	....	....	....	....	....	....	....	....	....	....	....	....	....	....	....
1987-88	**New Jersey Devils**	**NHL**	**65**	**7**	**19**	**26**	**6**	**14**	**20**	**131**	**2**	**0**	**2**	**72**	**9.7**	**34**	**11**	**43**	**0**	**–20**	**12**	**2**	**1**	**3**	**44**	**1**	**0**	**0**
1988-89	**New Jersey Devils**	**NHL**	**68**	**22**	**28**	**50**	**19**	**20**	**39**	**115**	**9**	**0**	**0**	**152**	**14.5**	**73**	**27**	**44**	**0**	**+2**	....	....	....	....	....	....	....	....
1989-90	**New Jersey Devils**	**NHL**	**73**	**30**	**42**	**72**	**26**	**30**	**56**	**137**	**8**	**0**	**5**	**196**	**15.3**	**115**	**35**	**66**	**1**	**+15**	**6**	**3**	**3**	**6**	**20**	**1**	**0**	**1**
1990-91	**New Jersey Devils**	**NHL**	**75**	**29**	**37**	**66**	**27**	**28**	**55**	**141**	**7**	**0**	**2**	**195**	**14.9**	**91**	**31**	**58**	**2**	**+4**	**7**	**3**	**5**	**8**	**12**	**2**	**0**	**0**
1991-92	Canada	C Cup	8	2	0	2	....	....	....	6	....	....	....	....	....	....	....	....	....	....	....	....	....	....	....	....	....	....
	St. Louis Blues	**NHL**	**80**	**33**	**36**	**69**	**30**	**27**	**57**	**171**	**13**	**0**	**2**	**215**	**15.3**	**105**	**44**	**65**	**1**	**–3**	**6**	**2**	**3**	**5**	**14**	**1**	**0**	**0**
1992-93	**St. Louis Blues**	**NHL**	**71**	**51**	**43**	**94**	**43**	**29**	**72**	**174**	**18**	**0**	**8**	**232**	**22.0**	**131**	**61**	**61**	**1**	**+10**	**11**	**4**	**3**	**7**	**18**	**2**	**0**	**0**
1993-94	**St. Louis Blues**	**NHL**	**81**	**52**	**50**	**102**	**49**	**39**	**88**	**211**	**15**	**7**	**8**	**397**	**13.1**	**145**	**69**	**106**	**21**	**–9**	**4**	**2**	**5**	**7**	**4**	**0**	**0**	**0**
	Canada	WC-A	6	4	3	7	....	....	....	6	....	....	....	....	....	....	....	....	....	....	....	....	....	....	....	....	....	....
1994-95	Dusseldorfer EG	Germany	3	5	3	8	....	....	....	4	....	....	....	....	....	....	....	....	....	....	....	....	....	....	....	....	....	....
	St. Louis Blues	**NHL**	**45**	**20**	**21**	**41**	**36**	**31**	**67**	**136**	**6**	**2**	**6**	**153**	**13.1**	**56**	**15**	**46**	**12**	**+7**	**5**	**4**	**5**	**9**	**14**	**1**	**0**	**1**
1995-96	**Hartford Whalers**	**NHL**	**74**	**44**	**34**	**78**	**44**	**28**	**72**	**125**	**17**	**2**	**6**	**280**	**15.7**	**109**	**51**	**78**	**22**	**+2**	....	....	....	....	....	....	....	....
1996-97	Canada	W Cup	7	3	3	6	....	....	....	8	....	....	....	....	....	....	....	....	....	....	....	....	....	....	....	....	....	....
	Hartford Whalers	**NHL**	**2**	**1**	**0**	**1**	**1**	**0**	**1**	**0**	**0**	**1**	**0**	**13**	**7.7**	**2**	**0**	**1**	**0**	**+1**	....	....	....	....	....	....	....	....
	Detroit Red Wings	**NHL**	**79**	**46**	**41**	**87**	**49**	**36**	**85**	**131**	**20**	**2**	**7**	**323**	**14.2**	**126**	**49**	**52**	**6**	**+31**	**20**	**9**	**8**	**17**	**43**	**2**	**0**	**2**
1997-98	**Detroit Red Wings**	**NHL**	**75**	**28**	**29**	**57**	**33**	**28**	**61**	**154**	**15**	**1**	**9**	**266**	**10.5**	**80**	**36**	**45**	**7**	**+6**	**20**	**5**	**4**	**9**	**22**	**3**	**0**	**2**
	Canada	Olympics	6	2	0	2	....	....	....	0	....	....	....	....	....	....	....	....	....	....	....	....	....	....	....	....	....	....
	NHL Totals		**788**	**363**	**380**	**743**	**363**	**310**	**673**	**1626**	**130**	**15**	**55**	**2494**	**14.6**	**1067**	**429**	**665**	**73**		**91**	**34**	**37**	**71**	**191**	**13**	**0**	**6**

NHL First All-Star Team (1994)

Played in NHL All-Star Game (1994, 1996, 1997, 1998)

Signed as a free agent by **St. Louis**, July 25, 1991. Traded to **Hartford** by **St. Louis** for Chris Pronger, July 27, 1995. Traded to **Detroit** by **Hartford** with Brian Glynn for Paul Coffey, Keith Primeau and Detroit's 1st round choice (Nikos Tselios) in 1997 Entry Draft, October 9, 1996.

• SHANAHAN, SEAN

Sean Shanahan C/RW – R. 6'3", 205 lbs. b: Toronto, Ont., 2/8/1951.

Season	Club	League	GP	G	A	Pts	AG	AA	APts	PIM	PP	SH	GW	S	%	TGF	PGF	TGA	PGA	+/-	GP	G	A	Pts	PIM	PP	SH	GW
1968-69	Kitchener Rangers	OHA	50	3	8	11	....	....	....	37	....	....	....	....	....	....	....	....	....	....	....	....	....	....	....	....	....	....
1969-70	Toronto Marlboros	OHA	19	2	4	6	....	....	....	5	....	....	....	....	....	....	....	....	....	....	....	....	....	....	....	....	....	....
1970-71	Toronto Marlboros	OHA	6	0	0	0	....	....	....	0	....	....	....	....	....	....	....	....	....	....	....	....	....	....	....	....	....	....
	Oshawa Generals	OHA	24	1	4	5	....	....	....	14	....	....	....	....	....	....	....	....	....	....	....	....	....	....	....	....	....	....
1971-72	Providence College	ECAC	23	13	15	28	....	....	....		....	....	....	....	....	....	....	....	....	....	....	....	....	....	....	....	....	....
1972-73	Providence College	ECAC	25	13	23	36	....	....	....	8	....	....	....	....	....	....	....	....	....	....	....	....	....	....	....	....	....	....
1973-74	Nova Scotia Voyageurs	AHL	63	13	14	27	....	....	....	65	....	....	....	....	....	....	....	....	....	....	6	1	0	1	6	....	....	....
1974-75	Nova Scotia Voyageurs	AHL	67	12	10	22	....	....	....	159	....	....	....	....	....	....	....	....	....	....	6	0	0	0	58	....	....	....
1975-76	**Montreal Canadiens**	**NHL**	**4**	**0**	**0**	**0**	**0**	**0**	**0**	**0**	**0**	**0**	**0**	**0**	**0.0**	**0**	**0**	**1**	**0**	**–1**	....	....	....	....	....	....	....	....
	Nova Scotia Voyageurs	AHL	64	18	26	44	....	....	....	91	....	....	....	....	....	....	....	....	....	....	9	4	6	10	11	....	....	....
1976-77	**Colorado Rockies**	**NHL**	**30**	**1**	**3**	**4**	**1**	**2**	**3**	**40**	**0**	**0**	**0**	**33**	**3.0**	**10**	**0**	**21**	**0**	**–11**	....	....	....	....	....	....	....	....
	Rhode Island Reds	AHL	10	0	1	1	....	....	....	11	....	....	....	....	....	....	....	....	....	....	....	....	....	....	....	....	....	....
	Dallas Black Hawks	CHL	7	0	0	0	....	....	....	25	....	....	....	....	....	....	....	....	....	....	5	1	0	1	19	....	....	....
1977-78	**Boston Bruins**	**NHL**	**6**	**0**	**0**	**0**	**0**	**0**	**0**	**7**	**0**	**0**	**0**	**2**	**0.0**	**1**	**0**	**2**	**0**	**–1**	....	....	....	....	....	....	....	....
	Rochester Americans	AHL	66	20	23	43	....	....	....	156	....	....	....	....	....	....	....	....	....	....	6	2	3	5	10	....	....	....
1978-79	Cincinnati Stingers	WHA	4	0	0	0	....	....	....	7	....	....	....	....	....	....	....	....	....	....	....	....	....	....	....	....	....	....
	NHL Totals		**40**	**1**	**3**	**4**	**1**	**2**	**3**	**47**	**0**	**0**	**0**	**35**	**2.9**	**11**	**0**	**24**	**0**		....	....	....	....	....	....	....	....
	Other Major League Totals		4	0	0	0	....	....	....	7	....	....	....	....	....	....	....	....	....	....	....	....	....	....	....	....	....	....

Signed as a free agent by **Montreal**, September, 1973. Traded to **Colorado** by **Montreal** with Ron Andruff for cash, September 13, 1976. Signed as a free agent by **Boston**, October 13, 1977. Signed as a free agent by **Detroit**, June 6, 1978. Signed as a free agent by **Cincinnati** (WHA) to 10-game tryout contract, October 24, 1978.

• SHAND, DAVE

Dave Shand D – R. 6'2", 200 lbs. b: Cold Lake, Alta., 8/11/1956. Atlanta's 1st choice, 8th overall, in 1976 Amateur Draft.

Season	Club	League	GP	G	A	Pts	AG	AA	APts	PIM	PP	SH	GW	S	%	TGF	PGF	TGA	PGA	+/-	GP	G	A	Pts	PIM	PP	SH	GW
1973-74	University of Michigan	WCHA	34	2	8	10	....	....	....	50	....	....	....	....	....	....	....	....	....	....	....	....	....	....	....	....	....	....
1974-75	University of Michigan	WCHA	10	0	4	4	....	....	....	20	....	....	....	....	....	....	....	....	....	....	....	....	....	....	....	....	....	....
	Peterborough Petes	OHA	33	4	11	15	....	....	....	30	....	....	....	....	....	....	....	....	....	....	11	1	4	5	17	....	....	....
1975-76	Peterborough Petes	OHA	62	9	37	46	....	....	....	169	....	....	....	....	....	....	....	....	....	....	....	....	....	....	....	....	....	....
1976-77	**Atlanta Flames**	**NHL**	**55**	**5**	**11**	**16**	**5**	**9**	**14**	**62**	**0**	**0**	**1**	**79**	**6.3**	**51**	**1**	**42**	**13**	**+21**	**3**	**0**	**0**	**0**	**33**	**0**	**0**	**0**
	Nova Scotia Voyageurs	AHL	9	0	5	5	....	....	....	21	....	....	....	....	....	....	....	....	....	....	....	....	....	....	....	....	....	....
1977-78	**Atlanta Flames**	**NHL**	**80**	**2**	**23**	**25**	**2**	**19**	**21**	**94**	**0**	**0**	**0**	**83**	**2.4**	**85**	**4**	**81**	**23**	**+23**	**2**	**0**	**0**	**0**	**4**	**0**	**0**	**0**
	Canada	WEC-A	10	0	3	3	....	....	....	6	....	....	....	....	....	....	....	....	....	....	....	....	....	....	....	....	....	....
1978-79	**Atlanta Flames**	**NHL**	**79**	**4**	**22**	**26**	**4**	**17**	**21**	**64**	**0**	**1**	**0**	**81**	**4.9**	**107**	**1**	**104**	**21**	**+23**	**2**	**0**	**0**	**0**	**20**	**0**	**0**	**0**
	Canada	WEC-A	7	0	0	0	....	....	....	8	....	....	....	....	....	....	....	....	....	....	....	....	....	....	....	....	....	....
1979-80	**Atlanta Flames**	**NHL**	**74**	**3**	**7**	**10**	**3**	**5**	**8**	**104**	**0**	**0**	**1**	**47**	**6.4**	**54**	**0**	**65**	**12**	**+1**	**4**	**0**	**1**	**1**	**0**	**0**	**0**	**0**
1980-81	**Toronto Maple Leafs**	**NHL**	**47**	**0**	**4**	**4**	**0**	**3**	**3**	**60**	**0**	**0**	**0**	**31**	**0.0**	**36**	**4**	**63**	**17**	**–14**	**3**	**0**	**0**	**0**	**0**	**0**	**0**	**0**
	New Brunswick Hawks	AHL	2	0	0	0	....	....	....	2	....	....	....	....	....	....	....	....	....	....	....	....	....	....	....	....	....	....
1981-82	Cincinnati Tigers	CHL	76	8	37	45	....	....	....	206	....	....	....	....	....	....	....	....	....	....	4	0	4	4	9	....	....	....
1982-83	**Toronto Maple Leafs**	**NHL**	**1**	**0**	**1**	**1**	**0**	**1**	**1**	**2**	**0**	**0**	**0**	**0**	**0.0**	**2**	**0**	**0**	**0**	**+2**	**4**	**1**	**0**	**1**	**13**	**0**	**0**	**0**
	St. Catharines Saints	AHL	69	9	32	41	....	....	....	154	....	....	....	....	....	....	....	....	....	....	....	....	....	....	....	....	....	....
1983-84	**Washington Capitals**	**NHL**	**72**	**4**	**15**	**19**	**3**	**10**	**13**	**124**	**0**	**0**	**0**	**53**	**7.5**	**66**	**3**	**45**	**5**	**+23**	**8**	**0**	**1**	**1**	**13**	**0**	**0**	**0**
	Hershey Bears	AHL	2	0	1	1	....	....	....	2	....	....	....	....	....	....	....	....	....	....	....	....	....	....	....	....	....	....
1984-85	**Washington Capitals**	**NHL**	**13**	**1**	**1**	**2**	**1**	**1**	**2**	**34**	**0**	**0**	**0**	**13**	**7.7**	**6**	**0**	**5**	**0**	**+1**	....	....	....	....	....	....	....	....
	Binghamton Whalers	AHL	8	0	1	1	....	....	....	10	....	....	....	....	....	....	....	....	....	....	....	....	....	....	....	....	....	....
1985-86	KAC Klagenfurter	Austria	44	11	21	32	....	....	....	110	....	....	....	....	....	....	....	....	....	....	....	....	....	....	....	....	....	....

			REGULAR SEASON																		PLAYOFFS							
Season	Club	League	GP	G	A	Pts	AG	AA	APts	PIM	PP	SH	GW	S	%	TGF	PGF	TGA	PGA	+/–	GP	G	A	Pts	PIM	PP	SH	GW
1986-87	KAC Klagenfurter	Austria	26	4	21	25	....	....	....	95	....	....	....	....	....	....	....	....	....	....	....	....	....	....	....	....	....	....
1987-88	KAC Klagenfurter	Austria	STATISTICS NOT AVAILABLE																									
1988-89	KAC Klagenfurter	Austria	39	5	25	30	....	....	....	98	....	....	....	....	....	....	....	....	....	....	....	....	....	....	....	....	....	....
	NHL Totals		**421**	**19**	**84**	**103**	**18**	**65**	**83**	**544**	**0**	**1**	**2**	**387**	**4.9**	**407**	**13**	**405**	**91**		**26**	**1**	**2**	**3**	**83**	**0**	**0**	**0**

OHA Second All-Star Team (1976) • CHL Second All-Star Team (1982)

Transferred to **Calgary** after **Atlanta** franchise relocated, June 24, 1980. Traded to **Toronto** by **Calgary** with Calgary's 3rd round choice (later traded to Washington — Washington selected Torrie Robertson) in 1980 Entry Draft for Toronto's 2nd round choice (Kevin LaVallee) in 1980 Entry Draft, June 10, 1980. Traded to **Washington** by **Toronto** for Lee Norwood, October 6, 1983.

• SHANK, DANIEL

Daniel Shank RW – R. 5'10", 190 lbs. b: Montreal, Que., 5/12/1967.

Season	Club	League	GP	G	A	Pts	AG	AA	APts	PIM	PP	SH	GW	S	%	TGF	PGF	TGA	PGA	+/–	GP	G	A	Pts	PIM	PP	SH	GW
1984-85	Longueuil Chevaliers	QMJHL	55	26	29	55	....	....	....	139	....	....	....	....	....	....	....	....	....	....	....	....	....	....	....	....	....	....
1985-86	Shawinigan Cataracts	QMJHL	51	34	38	72	....	....	....	184	....	....	....	....	....	....	....	....	....	....	....	....	....	....	....	....	....	....
1986-87	Hull Olympiques	QMJHL	46	26	43	69	....	....	....	325	....	....	....	....	....	....	....	....	....	....	....	....	....	....	....	....	....	....
1987-88	Hull Olympiques	QMJHL	42	23	34	57	....	....	....	274	....	....	....	....	....	....	....	....	....	....	5	3	2	5	16	....	....	....
1988-89	Adirondack Red Wings	AHL	42	5	20	25	....	....	....	113	....	....	....	....	....	....	....	....	....	....	17	11	8	19	102	....	....	....
1989-90	**Detroit Red Wings**	**NHL**	**57**	**11**	**13**	**24**	**9**	**9**	**18**	**143**	**0**	**0**	**1**	**61**	**18.0**	**32**	**0**	**31**	**0**	**+1**	....	....	....	....	....	....	....	....
	Adirondack Red Wings	AHL	14	8	8	16	....	....	....	36	....	....	....	....	....	....	....	....	....	....	....	....	....	....	....	....	....	....
1990-91	**Detroit Red Wings**	**NHL**	**7**	**0**	**1**	**1**	**0**	**1**	**1**	**14**	**0**	**0**	**0**	**4**	**0.0**	**5**	**0**	**5**	**0**	**0**	....	....	....	....	....	....	....	....
	Adirondack Red Wings	AHL	60	26	49	75	....	....	....	278	....	....	....	....	....	....	....	....	....	....	....	....	....	....	....	....	....	....
1991-92	Adirondack Red Wings	AHL	27	13	21	34	....	....	....	112	....	....	....	....	....	....	....	....	....	....	....	....	....	....	....	....	....	....
	Hartford Whalers	**NHL**	**13**	**2**	**0**	**2**	**2**	**0**	**2**	**18**	**0**	**0**	**0**	**10**	**20.0**	**4**	**2**	**6**	**0**	**–4**	**5**	**0**	**0**	**0**	**22**	**0**	**0**	**0**
	Springfield Indians	AHL	31	9	19	28	....	....	....	83	....	....	....	....	....	....	....	....	....	....	8	8	0	8	48	....	....	....
1992-93	San Diego Gulls	IHL	77	39	53	92	....	....	....	*495	....	....	....	....	....	....	....	....	....	....	14	5	10	15	*131	....	....	....
1993-94	San Diego Gulls	IHL	63	27	36	63	....	....	....	273	....	....	....	....	....	....	....	....	....	....	....	....	....	....	....	....	....	....
	Phoenix Roadrunners	IHL	7	4	6	10	....	....	....	26	....	....	....	....	....	....	....	....	....	....	....	....	....	....	....	....	....	....
1994-95	Minnesota Moose	IHL	19	4	11	15	....	....	....	30	....	....	....	....	....	....	....	....	....	....	....	....	....	....	....	....	....	....
	Detroit Vipers	IHL	54	44	27	71	....	....	....	142	....	....	....	....	....	....	....	....	....	....	5	2	2	4	6	....	....	....
1995-96	Las Vegas Thunder	IHL	49	36	29	65	....	....	....	191	....	....	....	....	....	....	....	....	....	....	....	....	....	....	....	....	....	....
	Detroit Vipers	IHL	29	14	19	33	....	....	....	96	....	....	....	....	....	....	....	....	....	....	12	4	5	9	38	....	....	....
1996-97	San Antonio Dragons	IHL	81	33	58	91	....	....	....	293	....	....	....	....	....	....	....	....	....	....	9	3	3	6	32	....	....	....
1997-98	San Antonio Dragons	IHL	80	39	43	82	....	....	....	141	....	....	....	....	....	....	....	....	....	....	....	....	....	....	....	....	....	....
	NHL Totals		**77**	**13**	**14**	**27**	**11**	**10**	**21**	**175**	**0**	**0**	**1**	**75**	**17.3**	**41**	**2**	**42**	**0**		**5**	**0**	**0**	**0**	**22**	**0**	**0**	**0**

IHL First All-Star Team (1993)

Signed as a free agent by **Detroit**, May 26, 1989. Traded to **Hartford** by **Detroit** for Chris Tancill, December 18, 1991.

• SHANNON, DARRIN

Darrin Shannon LW – L. 6'2", 210 lbs. b: Barrie, Ont., 12/8/1969. Pittsburgh's 2nd choice, 4th overall, in 1988 Entry Draft.

Season	Club	League	GP	G	A	Pts	AG	AA	APts	PIM	PP	SH	GW	S	%	TGF	PGF	TGA	PGA	+/–	GP	G	A	Pts	PIM	PP	SH	GW
1986-87	Windsor Spitfires	OHL	60	16	67	83	....	....	....	116	....	....	....	....	....	....	....	....	....	....	14	4	6	10	8	....	....	....
1987-88	Windsor Spitfires	OHL	43	33	41	74	....	....	....	49	....	....	....	....	....	....	....	....	....	....	12	6	12	18	9	....	....	....
1988-89	Windsor Spitfires	OHL	54	33	48	81	....	....	....	47	....	....	....	....	....	....	....	....	....	....	4	1	6	7	2	....	....	....
	Canada	WJC-A	7	1	3	4	....	....	....	10	....	....	....	....	....	....	....	....	....	....	....	....	....	....	....	....	....	....
	Buffalo Sabres	**NHL**	**3**	**0**	**0**	**0**	**0**	**0**	**0**	**0**	**0**	**0**	**0**	**0**	**0.0**	**0**	**0**	**2**	**0**	**–2**	**2**	**0**	**0**	**0**	**0**	**0**	**0**	**0**
1989-90	**Buffalo Sabres**	**NHL**	**17**	**2**	**7**	**9**	**2**	**5**	**7**	**4**	**0**	**0**	**0**	**20**	**10.0**	**12**	**0**	**7**	**1**	**+6**	**6**	**0**	**1**	**1**	**4**	**0**	**0**	**0**
	Rochester Americans	AHL	50	20	23	43	....	....	....	25	....	....	....	....	....	....	....	....	....	....	9	4	1	5	2	....	....	....
1990-91	**Buffalo Sabres**	**NHL**	**34**	**8**	**6**	**14**	**7**	**5**	**12**	**12**	**1**	**0**	**0**	**56**	**14.3**	**20**	**1**	**37**	**7**	**–11**	**6**	**1**	**2**	**3**	**4**	**0**	**0**	**0**
	Rochester Americans	AHL	49	26	34	60	....	....	....	56	....	....	....	....	....	....	....	....	....	....	10	3	5	8	22	....	....	....
1991-92	**Buffalo Sabres**	**NHL**	**1**	**0**	**1**	**1**	**0**	**1**	**1**	**0**	**0**	**0**	**0**	**2**	**0.0**	**1**	**0**	**0**	**0**	**+1**	....	....	....	....	....	....	....	....
	Winnipeg Jets	**NHL**	**68**	**13**	**26**	**39**	**12**	**20**	**32**	**41**	**3**	**0**	**3**	**91**	**14.3**	**63**	**20**	**55**	**17**	**+5**	**7**	**0**	**1**	**1**	**10**	**0**	**0**	**0**
1992-93	**Winnipeg Jets**	**NHL**	**84**	**20**	**40**	**60**	**17**	**27**	**44**	**91**	**12**	**0**	**2**	**116**	**17.2**	**107**	**40**	**97**	**26**	**–4**	**6**	**2**	**4**	**6**	**6**	**1**	**0**	**0**
1993-94	**Winnipeg Jets**	**NHL**	**77**	**21**	**37**	**58**	**20**	**29**	**49**	**87**	**9**	**0**	**2**	**124**	**16.9**	**73**	**26**	**85**	**20**	**–18**	....	....	....	....	....	....	....	....
1994-95	**Winnipeg Jets**	**NHL**	**19**	**5**	**3**	**8**	**9**	**4**	**13**	**14**	**3**	**0**	**1**	**26**	**19.2**	**18**	**13**	**16**	**5**	**–6**	....	....	....	....	....	....	....	....
1995-96	**Winnipeg Jets**	**NHL**	**63**	**5**	**18**	**23**	**5**	**15**	**20**	**28**	**0**	**0**	**1**	**74**	**6.8**	**40**	**7**	**48**	**10**	**–5**	**6**	**1**	**0**	**1**	**6**	**0**	**0**	**0**
1996-97	**Phoenix Coyotes**	**NHL**	**82**	**11**	**13**	**24**	**12**	**11**	**23**	**41**	**1**	**0**	**2**	**104**	**10.6**	**48**	**5**	**59**	**20**	**+4**	**7**	**3**	**1**	**4**	**4**	**0**	**0**	**1**
1997-98	**Phoenix Coyotes**	**NHL**	**58**	**2**	**12**	**14**	**2**	**12**	**14**	**26**	**0**	**0**	**0**	**57**	**3.5**	**24**	**0**	**38**	**18**	**+4**	**5**	**0**	**1**	**1**	**4**	**0**	**0**	**0**
	NHL Totals		**506**	**87**	**163**	**250**	**88**	**129**	**215**	**344**	**29**	**0**	**11**	**670**	**13.0**	**406**	**112**	**444**	**124**		**45**	**7**	**10**	**17**	**38**	**1**	**0**	**1**

Canadian Major Junior Scholastic Player of the Year (1988)

Traded to **Buffalo** by **Pittsburgh** with Doug Bodger for Tom Barrasso and Buffalo's 3rd round choice (Joe Dziedzic) in 1990 Entry Draft, November 12, 1988. Traded to **Winnipeg** by **Buffalo** with Mike Hartman and Dean Kennedy for Dave McLlwain, Gord Donnelly, Winnipeg's 5th round choice (Yuri Khmylev) in 1992 Entry Draft and future considerations, October 11, 1991. Transferred to **Phoenix** after **Winnipeg** franchise relocated, July 1, 1996.

• SHANNON, DARRYL

Darryl Shannon D – L. 6'2", 208 lbs. b: Barrie, Ont., 6/21/1968. Toronto's 2nd choice, 36th overall, in 1986 Entry Draft.

Season	Club	League	GP	G	A	Pts	AG	AA	APts	PIM	PP	SH	GW	S	%	TGF	PGF	TGA	PGA	+/–	GP	G	A	Pts	PIM	PP	SH	GW
1985-86	Windsor Spitfires	OHL	57	6	21	27	....	....	....	52	....	....	....	....	....	....	....	....	....	....	16	5	6	11	22	....	....	....
1986-87	Windsor Spitfires	OHL	64	23	27	50	....	....	....	83	....	....	....	....	....	....	....	....	....	....	14	4	8	12	18	....	....	....
1987-88	Windsor Spitfires	OHL	60	16	67	83	....	....	....	116	....	....	....	....	....	....	....	....	....	....	12	3	8	11	17	....	....	....
1988-89	**Toronto Maple Leafs**	**NHL**	**14**	**1**	**3**	**4**	**1**	**2**	**3**	**6**	**0**	**0**	**0**	**16**	**6.3**	**19**	**2**	**13**	**1**	**+5**	....	....	....	....	....	....	....	....
	Newmarket Saints	AHL	61	5	24	29	....	....	....	37	....	....	....	....	....	....	....	....	....	....	5	0	3	3	10	....	....	....
1989-90	**Toronto Maple Leafs**	**NHL**	**10**	**0**	**1**	**1**	**0**	**1**	**1**	**12**	**0**	**0**	**0**	**16**	**0.0**	**5**	**0**	**15**	**0**	**–10**	....	....	....	....	....	....	....	....
	Newmarket Saints	AHL	47	4	15	19	....	....	....	58	....	....	....	....	....	....	....	....	....	....	....	....	....	....	....	....	....	....
1990-91	**Toronto Maple Leafs**	**NHL**	**10**	**0**	**1**	**1**	**0**	**1**	**1**	**0**	**0**	**0**	**0**	**3**	**0.0**	**5**	**0**	**4**	**0**	**+1**	....	....	....	....	....	....	....	....
	Newmarket Saints	AHL	47	2	14	16	....	....	....	51	....	....	....	....	....	....	....	....	....	....	....	....	....	....	....	....	....	....
1991-92	**Toronto Maple Leafs**	**NHL**	**48**	**2**	**8**	**10**	**2**	**6**	**8**	**23**	**1**	**0**	**0**	**50**	**4.0**	**22**	**7**	**34**	**2**	**–17**	....	....	....	....	....	....	....	....
1992-93	**Toronto Maple Leafs**	**NHL**	**16**	**0**	**0**	**0**	**0**	**0**	**0**	**11**	**0**	**0**	**0**	**10**	**0.0**	**3**	**0**	**9**	**1**	**–5**	....	....	....	....	....	....	....	....
	St. John's Maple Leafs	AHL	7	1	1	2	....	....	....	4	....	....	....	....	....	....	....	....	....	....	....	....	....	....	....	....	....	....
1993-94	**Winnipeg Jets**	**NHL**	**20**	**0**	**4**	**4**	**0**	**3**	**3**	**18**	**0**	**0**	**0**	**14**	**0.0**	**11**	**1**	**20**	**4**	**–6**	....	....	....	....	....	....	....	....
	Moncton Hawks	AHL	37	1	10	11	....	....	....	62	....	....	....	....	....	....	....	....	....	....	20	1	7	8	32	....	....	....
1994-95	**Winnipeg Jets**	**NHL**	**40**	**5**	**9**	**14**	**9**	**13**	**22**	**48**	**0**	**1**	**0**	**42**	**11.9**	**26**	**0**	**30**	**5**	**+1**	....	....	....	....	....	....	....	....
1995-96	**Winnipeg Jets**	**NHL**	**48**	**2**	**7**	**9**	**2**	**6**	**8**	**72**	**0**	**0**	**0**	**34**	**5.9**	**34**	**1**	**50**	**22**	**+5**	....	....	....	....	....	....	....	....
	Buffalo Sabres	**NHL**	**26**	**2**	**6**	**8**	**2**	**5**	**7**	**20**	**0**	**0**	**0**	**25**	**8.0**	**31**	**2**	**35**	**16**	**+10**	....	....	....	....	....	....	....	....
1996-97	**Buffalo Sabres**	**NHL**	**82**	**4**	**19**	**23**	**4**	**17**	**21**	**112**	**1**	**0**	**1**	**94**	**4.3**	**78**	**4**	**74**	**23**	**+23**	**12**	**2**	**3**	**5**	**8**	**0**	**0**	**0**
1997-98	**Buffalo Sabres**	**NHL**	**76**	**3**	**19**	**22**	**4**	**19**	**23**	**56**	**1**	**0**	**1**	**85**	**3.5**	**71**	**14**	**57**	**26**	**+26**	**15**	**2**	**4**	**6**	**8**	**0**	**1**	**0**
	NHL Totals		**390**	**19**	**77**	**96**	**24**	**73**	**97**	**378**	**3**	**1**	**2**	**389**	**4.9**	**305**	**31**	**341**	**100**		**27**	**4**	**7**	**11**	**16**	**0**	**1**	**0**

OHL Second All-Star Team (1987) • OHL First All-Star Team (1988)

Signed as a free agent by **Winnipeg**, June 30, 1993. Traded to **Buffalo** by **Winnipeg** with Michal Grosek for Craig Muni, February 15, 1996.

• SHANTZ, JEFF

Jeff Shantz C – R. 6', 185 lbs. b: Duchess, Alta., 10/10/1973. Chicago's 2nd choice, 36th overall, in 1992 Entry Draft.

Season	Club	League	GP	G	A	Pts	AG	AA	APts	PIM	PP	SH	GW	S	%	TGF	PGF	TGA	PGA	+/–	GP	G	A	Pts	PIM	PP	SH	GW
1990-91	Regina Pats	WHL	69	16	21	37	....	....	....	22	....	....	....	....	....	....	....	....	....	....	8	2	2	4	2	....	....	....
1991-92	Regina Pats	WHL	72	39	50	89	....	....	....	75	....	....	....	....	....	....	....	....	....	....	....	....	....	....	....	....	....	....
1992-93	Regina Pats	WHL	64	29	54	83	....	....	....	75	....	....	....	....	....	....	....	....	....	....	13	2	12	14	14	....	....	....
1993-94	**Chicago Blackhawks**	**NHL**	**52**	**3**	**13**	**16**	**3**	**10**	**13**	**30**	**0**	**0**	**0**	**56**	**5.4**	**19**	**1**	**34**	**2**	**–14**	**6**	**0**	**0**	**0**	**6**	**0**	**0**	**0**
	Indianapolis Ice	IHL	19	5	9	14	....	....	....	20	....	....	....	....	....	....	....	....	....	....	....	....	....	....	....	....	....	....
1994-95	Indianapolis Ice	IHL	32	9	15	24	....	....	....	20	....	....	....	....	....	....	....	....	....	....	....	....	....	....	....	....	....	....
	Chicago Blackhawks	**NHL**	**45**	**6**	**12**	**18**	**11**	**18**	**29**	**33**	**0**	**2**	**0**	**58**	**10.3**	**24**	**4**	**12**	**3**	**+11**	**16**	**3**	**1**	**4**	**2**	**0**	**0**	**0**
1995-96	**Chicago Blackhawks**	**NHL**	**78**	**6**	**14**	**20**	**6**	**11**	**17**	**24**	**1**	**2**	**0**	**72**	**8.3**	**29**	**1**	**39**	**23**	**+12**	**10**	**2**	**3**	**5**	**6**	**0**	**0**	**0**
1996-97	**Chicago Blackhawks**	**NHL**	**69**	**9**	**21**	**30**	**10**	**19**	**29**	**28**	**0**	**1**	**1**	**86**	**10.5**	**41**	**3**	**42**	**15**	**+11**	**6**	**0**	**4**	**4**	**6**	**0**	**0**	**0**
1997-98	**Chicago Blackhawks**	**NHL**	**61**	**11**	**20**	**31**	**13**	**19**	**32**	**36**	**1**	**2**	**2**	**69**	**15.9**	**38**	**8**	**43**	**13**	**0**	....	....	....	....	....	....	....	....
	NHL Totals		**305**	**35**	**80**	**115**	**43**	**77**	**120**	**151**	**2**	**7**	**3**	**341**	**10.3**	**151**	**17**	**170**	**56**		**38**	**5**	**8**	**13**	**20**	**0**	**0**	**0**

WHL East First All-Star Team (1993)

• SHARIFJANOV, VADIM

Vadim Sharifjanov RW – L. 5'11", 210 lbs. b: Ufa, USSR, 12/23/1975. New Jersey's 1st choice, 25th overall, in 1994 Entry Draft.

			REGULAR SEASON																		PLAYOFFS							
Season	Club	League	GP	G	A	Pts	AG	AA	APts	PIM	PP	SH	GW	S	%	TGF	PGF	TGA	PGA	+/–	GP	G	A	Pts	PIM	PP	SH	GW
1992-93	Ufa Salavat	CIS	37	6	4	10	....	....	....	16	....	....	....	....	....	....	....	....	....	....	2	1	0	1	0	....	....	....
1993-94	Ufa Salavat	CIS	46	10	6	16	....	....	....	36	....	....	....	....	....	....	....	....	....	....	5	3	0	3	4	....	....	....
1994-95	CSKA Moscow	CIS	34	7	3	10	....	....	....	26	....	....	....	....	....	....	....	....	....	....	2	0	0	0	0	....	....	....
	Albany River Rats	AHL	1	1	1	2	....	....	....	0	....	....	....	....	....	....	....	....	....	....	9	3	3	6	10	....	....	....
1995-96	Albany River Rats	AHL	69	14	28	42	....	....	....	28	....	....	....	....	....	....	....	....	....	....	....	....	....	....	....	....	....	....
1996-97	**New Jersey Devils**	**NHL**	**2**	**0**	**0**	**0**	**0**	**0**	**0**	**0**	**0**	**0**	**0**	**4**	**0.0**	**0**	**0**	**0**	**0**	**0**	....	....	....	....	....	....	....	....
	Albany River Rats	AHL	70	14	27	41	....	....	....	89	....	....	....	....	....	....	....	....	....	....	10	3	3	6	6	....	....	....
1997-98	Albany River Rats	AHL	72	23	27	50	....	....	....	69	....	....	....	....	....	....	....	....	....	....	12	4	9	13	6	....	....	....
	NHL Totals		**2**	**0**	**0**	**0**	**0**	**0**	**0**	**0**	**0**	**0**	**0**	**4**	**0.0**	**0**	**0**	**0**	**0**		....	....	....	....	....	....	....	....

• SHARPLES, JEFF

Jeff Sharples D – L. 6'1", 195 lbs. b: Terrace, B.C., 7/28/1967. Detroit's 2nd choice, 29th overall, in 1985 Entry Draft.

Season	Club	League	GP	G	A	Pts	AG	AA	APts	PIM	PP	SH	GW	S	%	TGF	PGF	TGA	PGA	+/–	GP	G	A	Pts	PIM	PP	SH	GW
1983-84	Kelowna Wings	WHL	72	9	24	33	....	....	....	51	....	....	....	....	....	....	....	....	....	....	....	....	....	....	....	....	....	....
1984-85	Kelowna Wings	WHL	72	12	41	53	....	....	....	90	....	....	....	....	....	....	....	....	....	....	6	0	1	1	6	....	....	....
1985-86	Spokane Chiefs	WHL	3	0	0	0	....	....	....	4	....	....	....	....	....	....	....	....	....	....	....	....	....	....	....	....	....	....
	Portland Winter Hawks	WHL	19	2	6	8	....	....	....	44	....	....	....	....	....	....	....	....	....	....	15	2	6	8	6	....	....	....
1986-87	Portland Winter Hawks	WHL	44	25	35	60	....	....	....	92	....	....	....	....	....	....	....	....	....	....	20	7	15	22	23	....	....	....
	Detroit Red Wings	**NHL**	**3**	**0**	**1**	**1**	**0**	**1**	**1**	**2**	**0**	**0**	**0**	**1**	**0.0**	**2**	**0**	**2**	**0**	**0**	**2**	**0**	**0**	**0**	**2**	**0**	**0**	**0**
1987-88	**Detroit Red Wings**	**NHL**	**56**	**10**	**25**	**35**	**9**	**18**	**27**	**42**	**2**	**0**	**0**	**94**	**10.6**	**78**	**27**	**41**	**3**	**+13**	**4**	**0**	**3**	**3**	**4**	**0**	**0**	**0**
	Adirondack Red Wings	AHL	4	2	1	3	....	....	....	4	....	....	....	....	....	....	....	....	....	....	....	....	....	....	....	....	....	....
1988-89	**Detroit Red Wings**	**NHL**	**46**	**4**	**9**	**13**	**3**	**6**	**9**	**26**	**3**	**0**	**0**	**48**	**8.3**	**46**	**14**	**29**	**2**	**+5**	**1**	**0**	**0**	**0**	**0**	**0**	**0**	**0**
	Adirondack Red Wings	AHL	10	0	4	4	....	....	....	8	....	....	....	....	....	....	....	....	....	....	....	....	....	....	....	....	....	....
1989-90	Adirondack Red Wings	AHL	9	2	5	7	....	....	....	6	....	....	....	....	....	....	....	....	....	....	....	....	....	....	....	....	....	....
	Cape Breton Oilers	AHL	38	4	13	17	....	....	....	28	....	....	....	....	....	....	....	....	....	....	....	....	....	....	....	....	....	....
	Utica Devils	AHL	13	2	5	7	....	....	....	19	....	....	....	....	....	....	....	....	....	....	5	1	2	3	15	....	....	....
1990-91	Utica Devils	AHL	64	16	29	45	....	....	....	42	....	....	....	....	....	....	....	....	....	....	....	....	....	....	....	....	....	....
1991-92	Capital District Islanders	AHL	31	3	12	15	....	....	....	18	....	....	....	....	....	....	....	....	....	....	7	6	5	11	4	....	....	....
1992-93	Kansas City Blades	IHL	39	5	21	26	....	....	....	43	....	....	....	....	....	....	....	....	....	....	8	0	0	0	6	....	....	....
1993-94	Las Vegas Thunder	IHL	68	18	32	50	....	....	....	68	....	....	....	....	....	....	....	....	....	....	5	2	1	3	6	....	....	....
1994-95	Las Vegas Thunder	IHL	72	20	33	53	....	....	....	63	....	....	....	....	....	....	....	....	....	....	10	4	4	8	18	....	....	....
1995-96	Las Vegas Thunder	IHL	41	6	14	20	....	....	....	56	....	....	....	....	....	....	....	....	....	....	....	....	....	....	....	....	....	....
	Utah Grizzlies	IHL	31	2	15	17	....	....	....	18	....	....	....	....	....	....	....	....	....	....	21	3	10	13	16	....	....	....
1996-97	Utah Grizzlies	IHL	49	9	26	35	....	....	....	54	....	....	....	....	....	....	....	....	....	....	7	0	2	2	10	....	....	....
1997-98	Utah Grizzlies	IHL	76	10	28	38	....	....	....	82	....	....	....	....	....	....	....	....	....	....	4	1	1	2	6	....	....	....
	NHL Totals		**105**	**14**	**35**	**49**	**12**	**25**	**37**	**70**	**5**	**0**	**0**	**143**	**9.8**	**126**	**41**	**72**	**5**		**7**	**0**	**3**	**3**	**6**	**0**	**0**	**0**

WHL West Second All-Star Team (1985)

Traded to **Edmonton** by **Detroit** with Petr Klima, Joe Murphy and Adam Graves for Jimmy Carson, Kevin McClelland and Edmonton's 5th round choice (later traded to Montreal — Montreal selected Brad Layzell) in 1991 Entry Draft, November 2, 1989. Traded to **New Jersey** by **Edmonton** for Reijo Ruotsalainen, March 6, 1990.

• SHARPLEY, GLEN

Glen Sharpley C – R. 6', 190 lbs. b: York, Ont., 9/6/1956. Minnesota's 1st choice, 3rd overall, in 1976 Amateur Draft.

Season	Club	League	GP	G	A	Pts	AG	AA	APts	PIM	PP	SH	GW	S	%	TGF	PGF	TGA	PGA	+/–	GP	G	A	Pts	PIM	PP	SH	GW
1973-74	Hull Festivals	QMJHL	52	14	30	44	....	....	....	64	....	....	....	....	....	....	....	....	....	....	....	....	....	....	....	....	....	....
1974-75	Hull Festivals	QMJHL	68	24	45	69	....	....	....	99	....	....	....	....	....	....	....	....	....	....	....	....	....	....	....	....	....	....
1975-76	Hull Festivals	QMJHL	69	60	74	134	....	....	....	99	....	....	....	....	....	....	....	....	....	....	....	....	....	....	....	....	....	....
1976-77	**Minnesota North Stars**	**NHL**	**80**	**25**	**32**	**57**	**24**	**26**	**50**	**48**	**2**	**1**	**6**	**206**	**12.1**	**67**	**13**	**93**	**18**	**–21**	**2**	**0**	**0**	**0**	**4**	**0**	**0**	**0**
1977-78	**Minnesota North Stars**	**NHL**	**79**	**22**	**33**	**55**	**21**	**27**	**48**	**42**	**6**	**0**	**3**	**215**	**10.2**	**76**	**24**	**107**	**22**	**–33**	....	....	....	....	....	....	....	....
	Canada	WEC-A	10	1	3	4	....	....	....	16	....	....	....	....	....	....	....	....	....	....	....	....	....	....	....	....	....	....
1978-79	**Minnesota North Stars**	**NHL**	**80**	**19**	**34**	**53**	**17**	**26**	**43**	**30**	**5**	**0**	**1**	**162**	**11.7**	**81**	**18**	**88**	**7**	**–18**	....	....	....	....	....	....	....	....
1979-80	**Minnesota North Stars**	**NHL**	**51**	**20**	**27**	**47**	**18**	**21**	**39**	**38**	**6**	**0**	**0**	**109**	**18.3**	**62**	**16**	**49**	**2**	**–1**	**9**	**1**	**6**	**7**	**4**	**0**	**0**	**0**
1980-81	**Minnesota North Stars**	**NHL**	**28**	**12**	**12**	**24**	**10**	**8**	**18**	**18**	**6**	**0**	**0**	**52**	**23.1**	**32**	**11**	**25**	**0**	**–4**	....	....	....	....	....	....	....	....
	Chicago Black Hawks	**NHL**	**35**	**10**	**16**	**26**	**8**	**11**	**19**	**12**	**4**	**0**	**0**	**64**	**15.6**	**44**	**12**	**39**	**13**	**+6**	**1**	**0**	**2**	**2**	**0**	**0**	**0**	**0**
1981-82	**Chicago Black Hawks**	**NHL**	**36**	**9**	**7**	**16**	**7**	**5**	**12**	**11**	**0**	**0**	**2**	**38**	**23.7**	**24**	**1**	**31**	**10**	**+2**	**15**	**6**	**3**	**9**	**16**	**0**	**0**	**0**
1982-1985			DID NOT PLAY																									
1985-86	Baltimore Skipjacks	AHL	7	0	3	3	....	....	....	4	....	....	....	....	....	....	....	....	....	....	....	....	....	....	....	....	....	....
	Peoria Rivermen	IHL	50	26	37	63	....	....	....	32	....	....	....	....	....	....	....	....	....	....	....	....	....	....	....	....	....	....
1986-87	Salt Lake Golden Eagles	IHL	32	10	15	25	....	....	....	14	....	....	....	....	....	....	....	....	....	....	....	....	....	....	....	....	....	....
	Dundee Rockets	Britain	15	31	40	71	....	....	....	49	....	....	....	....	....	....	....	....	....	....	5	6	13	19	10	....	....	....
	NHL Totals		**389**	**117**	**161**	**278**	**105**	**124**	**229**	**199**	**29**	**1**	**12**	**846**	**13.8**	**386**	**95**	**432**	**72**		**27**	**7**	**11**	**18**	**24**	**0**	**0**	**0**

QMJHL West First All-Star Team (1976)

Traded to **Chicago** by **Minnesota** for Ken Solheim and Chicago's 2nd round choice (Tom Hirsch) in 1981 Entry Draft, December 29, 1980.

• SHAUNESSY, SCOTT

Scott Shaunessy D/LW – L. 6'4", 220 lbs. b: Newport, RI, 1/22/1964. Quebec's 8th choice, 200th overall, in 1983 Entry Draft.

Season	Club	League	GP	G	A	Pts	AG	AA	APts	PIM	PP	SH	GW	S	%	TGF	PGF	TGA	PGA	+/–	GP	G	A	Pts	PIM	PP	SH	GW
1982-83	St. John's Prep	H.S.	23	7	32	39	....	....	....	....	....	....	....	....	....	....	....	....	....	....	....	....	....	....	....	....	....	....
1983-84	Boston University	ECAC	40	6	22	28	....	....	....	48	....	....	....	....	....	....	....	....	....	....	....	....	....	....	....	....	....	....
1984-85	Boston University	H.E.	42	7	15	22	....	....	....	87	....	....	....	....	....	....	....	....	....	....	....	....	....	....	....	....	....	....
1985-86	Boston University	H.E.	38	6	13	19	....	....	....	31	....	....	....	....	....	....	....	....	....	....	....	....	....	....	....	....	....	....
1986-87	Boston University	H.E.	32	2	13	15	....	....	....	71	....	....	....	....	....	....	....	....	....	....	....	....	....	....	....	....	....	....
	Quebec Nordiques	**NHL**	**3**	**0**	**0**	**0**	**0**	**0**	**0**	**7**	**0**	**0**	**0**	**0**	**0.0**	**0**	**0**	**1**	**0**	**–1**	....	....	....	....	....	....	....	....
1987-88	Fredericton Express	AHL	60	0	9	9	....	....	....	257	....	....	....	....	....	....	....	....	....	....	1	0	0	0	2	....	....	....
1988-89	**Quebec Nordiques**	**NHL**	**4**	**0**	**0**	**0**	**0**	**0**	**0**	**16**	**0**	**0**	**0**	**0**	**0.0**	**1**	**0**	**2**	**1**	**0**	....	....	....	....	....	....	....	....
	Halifax Citadels	AHL	41	3	10	13	....	....	....	106	....	....	....	....	....	....	....	....	....	....	....	....	....	....	....	....	....	....
1989-90	Halifax Citadels	AHL	27	3	5	8	....	....	....	105	....	....	....	....	....	....	....	....	....	....	....	....	....	....	....	....	....	....
	Fort Wayne Komets	IHL	45	3	9	12	....	....	....	267	....	....	....	....	....	....	....	....	....	....	5	0	1	1	31	....	....	....
1990-91	Albany Choppers	IHL	34	3	9	12	....	....	....	126	....	....	....	....	....	....	....	....	....	....	....	....	....	....	....	....	....	....
	Muskegon Lumberjacks	IHL	23	1	4	5	....	....	....	104	....	....	....	....	....	....	....	....	....	....	5	0	0	0	21	....	....	....
1991-92	Fort Wayne Komets	IHL	53	3	8	11	....	....	....	243	....	....	....	....	....	....	....	....	....	....	7	0	1	1	27	....	....	....
1992-93	Cincinnati Cyclones	IHL	71	2	7	9	....	....	....	222	....	....	....	....	....	....	....	....	....	....	....	....	....	....	....	....	....	....
	NHL Totals		**7**	**0**	**0**	**0**	**0**	**0**	**0**	**23**	**0**	**0**	**0**	**0**	**0.0**	**1**	**0**	**3**	**1**		....	....	....	....	....	....	....	....

Hockey East Second All-Star Team (1985) • Hockey East First All-Star Team (1986)

• SHAW, BRAD

Brad Shaw D – R. 6', 190 lbs. b: Cambridge, Ont., 4/28/1964. Detroit's 5th choice, 86th overall, in 1982 Entry Draft.

Season	Club	League	GP	G	A	Pts	AG	AA	APts	PIM	PP	SH	GW	S	%	TGF	PGF	TGA	PGA	+/–	GP	G	A	Pts	PIM	PP	SH	GW
1980-81	Kitchener Greenshirts	Midget	62	14	58	72	....	....	....	14	....	....	....	....	....	....	....	....	....	....	....	....	....	....	....	....	....	....
1981-82	Ottawa 67's	OHL	68	13	59	72	....	....	....	24	....	....	....	....	....	....	....	....	....	....	15	1	13	14	4	....	....	....
1982-83	Ottawa 67's	OHL	63	12	66	78	....	....	....	24	....	....	....	....	....	....	....	....	....	....	9	2	9	11	4	....	....	....
	Canada	WJC-A	7	1	1	2	....	....	....	2	....	....	....	....	....	....	....	....	....	....	....	....	....	....	....	....	....	....
1983-84	Ottawa 67's	OHL	68	11	71	82	....	....	....	75	....	....	....	....	....	....	....	....	....	....	13	2	*27	29	9	....	....	....
	Canada	WJC-A	7	0	2	2	....	....	....	0	....	....	....	....	....	....	....	....	....	....	....	....	....	....	....	....	....	....
1984-85	Binghamton Whalers	AHL	24	1	10	11	....	....	....	4	....	....	....	....	....	....	....	....	....	....	8	1	8	9	6	....	....	....
	Salt Lake Golden Eagles	IHL	44	3	29	32	....	....	....	25	....	....	....	....	....	....	....	....	....	....	....	....	....	....	....	....	....	....
1985-86	**Hartford Whalers**	**NHL**	**8**	**0**	**2**	**2**	**0**	**1**	**1**	**4**	**0**	**0**	**0**	**17**	**0.0**	**8**	**3**	**6**	**0**	**–1**	....	....	....	....	....	....	....	....
	Binghamton Whalers	AHL	64	10	44	54	....	....	....	33	....	....	....	....	....	....	....	....	....	....	5	0	2	2	6	....	....	....
1986-87	**Hartford Whalers**	**NHL**	**2**	**0**	**0**	**0**	**0**	**0**	**0**	**0**	**0**	**0**	**0**	**2**	**0.0**	**1**	**0**	**1**	**0**	**0**	....	....	....	....	....	....	....	....
	Binghamton Whalers	AHL	77	9	30	39	....	....	....	43	....	....	....	....	....	....	....	....	....	....	12	1	8	9	2	....	....	....
1987-88	**Hartford Whalers**	**NHL**	**1**	**0**	**0**	**0**	**0**	**0**	**0**	**0**	**0**	**0**	**0**	**1**	**0.0**	**1**	**1**	**1**	**0**	**–1**	....	....	....	....	....	....	....	....
	Binghamton Whalers	AHL	73	12	50	62	....	....	....	50	....	....	....	....	....	....	....	....	....	....	4	0	5	5	4	....	....	....
1988-89	Varese HC	Italy	35	10	30	40	....	....	....	44	....	....	....	....	....	....	....	....	....	....	11	4	8	12	13	....	....	....
	Canada	Nat-Team	4	1	0	1	....	....	....	2	....	....	....	....	....	....	....	....	....	....	....	....	....	....	....	....	....	....
	Hartford Whalers	**NHL**	**3**	**1**	**0**	**1**	**1**	**0**	**1**	**0**	**1**	**0**	**0**	**2**	**50.0**	**3**	**1**	**1**	**0**	**+1**	**3**	**1**	**0**	**1**	**0**	**0**	**0**	**0**
1989-90	**Hartford Whalers**	**NHL**	**64**	**3**	**32**	**35**	**3**	**23**	**26**	**30**	**3**	**0**	**0**	**65**	**4.6**	**82**	**28**	**72**	**20**	**+2**	**7**	**2**	**5**	**7**	**0**	**1**	**0**	**0**
1990-91	**Hartford Whalers**	**NHL**	**72**	**4**	**28**	**32**	**4**	**21**	**25**	**29**	**2**	**0**	**1**	**129**	**3.1**	**88**	**40**	**81**	**23**	**–10**	**6**	**1**	**2**	**3**	**2**	**0**	**0**	**0**
1991-92	**Hartford Whalers**	**NHL**	**62**	**3**	**22**	**25**	**3**	**17**	**20**	**44**	**0**	**0**	**0**	**100**	**3.0**	**77**	**31**	**63**	**18**	**+1**	**3**	**0**	**1**	**1**	**4**	**0**	**0**	**0**

Season	Club	League	REGULAR SEASON																		PLAYOFFS							
			GP	G	A	Pts	AG	AA	APts	PIM	PP	SH	GW	S	%	TGF	PGF	TGA	PGA	+/–	GP	G	A	Pts	PIM	PP	SH	GW
1992-93	**Ottawa Senators**	**NHL**	**81**	**7**	**34**	**41**	**6**	**23**	**29**	**34**	**4**	**0**	**0**	**166**	**4.2**	**106**	**49**	**160**	**56**	**–47**	....	....	....	....	....	....	....	....
1993-94	**Ottawa Senators**	**NHL**	**66**	**4**	**19**	**23**	**4**	**15**	**19**	**59**	**1**	**0**	**0**	**113**	**3.5**	**63**	**20**	**116**	**32**	**–41**	....	....	....	....	....	....	....	....
1994-95	**Ottawa Senators**	**NHL**	**2**	**0**	**0**	**0**	**0**	**0**	**0**	**0**	**0**	**0**	**0**	**3**	**0.0**	**3**	**0**	**1**	**1**	**+3**	....	....	....	....	....	....	....	....
	Atlanta Knights	IHL	26	1	18	19	....	....	....	17	....	....	....	....	....	....	....	....	....	....	5	3	4	7	9	....	....	....
1995-96	Detroit Vipers	IHL	79	7	54	61	....	....	....	46	....	....	....	....	....	....	....	....	....	....	8	2	3	5	8	....	....	....
1996-97	Detroit Vipers	IHL	59	6	32	38	....	....	....	30	....	....	....	....	....	....	....	....	....	....	21	2	9	11	10	....	....	....
1997-98	Detroit Vipers	IHL	64	2	33	35	....	....	....	47	....	....	....	....	....	....	....	....	....	....	23	1	11	12	30	....	....	....
	NHL Totals		**361**	**22**	**137**	**159**	**21**	**100**	**121**	**200**	**11**	**0**	**1**	**598**	**3.7**	**432**	**173**	**502**	**150**		**19**	**4**	**8**	**12**	**6**	**1**	**0**	**0**

OHL First All-Star Team (1984) • Won Eddie Shore Award (Outstanding Defenseman - AHL) (1987) • NHL All-Rookie Team (1990) • IHL First All-Star Team (1997)

Traded to **Hartford** by **Detroit** for Hartford's 8th round choice (Urban Nordin) in 1984 Entry Draft, May 29, 1984. Traded to **New Jersey** by **Hartford** for cash, June 13, 1992. Claimed by **Ottawa** from **New Jersey** in Expansion Draft, June 18, 1992.

• SHAW, DAVID

David Shaw D – R. 6'2", 205 lbs. b: St. Thomas, Ont., 5/25/1964. Quebec's 1st choice, 13th overall, in 1982 Entry Draft.

Season	Club	League	GP	G	A	Pts	AG	AA	APts	PIM	PP	SH	GW	S	%	TGF	PGF	TGA	PGA	+/–	GP	G	A	Pts	PIM	PP	SH	GW
1981-82	Kitchener Rangers	OHL	68	6	25	31	....	....	....	94	....	....	....	....	....	....	....	....	....	....	15	2	2	4	51	....	....	....
1982-83	Kitchener Rangers	OHL	57	18	56	74	....	....	....	78	....	....	....	....	....	....	....	....	....	....	12	2	10	12	18	....	....	....
	Quebec Nordiques	**NHL**	**2**	**0**	**0**	**0**	**0**	**0**	**0**	**0**	**0**	**0**	**0**	**0**	**0.0**	**0**	**0**	**1**	**0**	**–1**	....	....	....	....	....	....	....	....
1983-84	Kitchener Rangers	OHL	58	14	34	48	....	....	....	73	....	....	....	....	....	....	....	....	....	....	16	4	9	13	12	....	....	....
	Quebec Nordiques	**NHL**	**3**	**0**	**0**	**0**	**0**	**0**	**0**	**0**	**0**	**0**	**0**	**3**	**0.0**	**2**	**0**	**0**	**0**	**+2**	....	....	....	....	....	....	....	....
1984-85	**Quebec Nordiques**	**NHL**	**14**	**0**	**0**	**0**	**0**	**0**	**0**	**11**	**0**	**0**	**0**	**10**	**0.0**	**4**	**0**	**9**	**0**	**–5**	....	....	....	....	....	....	....	....
	Fredericton Express	AHL	48	7	6	13	....	....	....	73	....	....	....	....	....	....	....	....	....	....	2	0	0	0	7	....	....	....
1985-86	**Quebec Nordiques**	**NHL**	**73**	**7**	**19**	**26**	**6**	**13**	**19**	**78**	**2**	**0**	**2**	**126**	**5.6**	**105**	**18**	**94**	**21**	**+14**	....	....	....	....	....	....	....	....
1986-87	**Quebec Nordiques**	**NHL**	**75**	**0**	**19**	**19**	**0**	**14**	**14**	**69**	**0**	**0**	**0**	**136**	**0.0**	**55**	**15**	**99**	**24**	**–35**	....	....	....	....	....	....	....	....
1987-88	**New York Rangers**	**NHL**	**68**	**7**	**25**	**32**	**6**	**18**	**24**	**100**	**5**	**0**	**1**	**141**	**5.0**	**95**	**47**	**93**	**37**	**–8**	....	....	....	....	....	....	....	....
1988-89	**New York Rangers**	**NHL**	**63**	**6**	**11**	**17**	**5**	**8**	**13**	**88**	**3**	**1**	**1**	**85**	**7.1**	**84**	**10**	**85**	**25**	**+14**	**4**	**0**	**2**	**2**	**30**	**0**	**0**	**0**
1989-90	**New York Rangers**	**NHL**	**22**	**2**	**10**	**12**	**2**	**7**	**9**	**22**	**1**	**1**	**0**	**24**	**8.3**	**24**	**6**	**31**	**10**	**–3**	....	....	....	....	....	....	....	....
1990-91	**New York Rangers**	**NHL**	**77**	**2**	**10**	**12**	**2**	**8**	**10**	**89**	**0**	**0**	**1**	**61**	**3.3**	**77**	**0**	**105**	**36**	**+8**	**6**	**0**	**0**	**0**	**11**	**0**	**0**	**0**
1991-92	**New York Rangers**	**NHL**	**10**	**0**	**1**	**1**	**0**	**1**	**1**	**15**	**0**	**0**	**0**	**6**	**0.0**	**7**	**0**	**10**	**4**	**+1**	....	....	....	....	....	....	....	....
	Edmonton Oilers	**NHL**	**12**	**1**	**1**	**2**	**1**	**1**	**2**	**8**	**0**	**0**	**0**	**15**	**6.7**	**3**	**0**	**16**	**5**	**–8**	....	....	....	....	....	....	....	....
	Minnesota North Stars	**NHL**	**37**	**0**	**7**	**7**	**0**	**5**	**5**	**49**	**0**	**0**	**0**	**49**	**0.0**	**38**	**12**	**33**	**2**	**–5**	**7**	**2**	**2**	**4**	**10**	**1**	**0**	**0**
1992-93	**Boston Bruins**	**NHL**	**77**	**10**	**14**	**24**	**8**	**10**	**18**	**108**	**1**	**1**	**1**	**122**	**8.2**	**79**	**12**	**75**	**18**	**+10**	**4**	**0**	**1**	**1**	**6**	**0**	**0**	**0**
1993-94	**Boston Bruins**	**NHL**	**55**	**1**	**9**	**10**	**1**	**7**	**8**	**85**	**0**	**0**	**0**	**107**	**0.9**	**43**	**1**	**67**	**14**	**–11**	**13**	**1**	**2**	**3**	**16**	**0**	**0**	**1**
1994-95	**Boston Bruins**	**NHL**	**44**	**3**	**4**	**7**	**5**	**6**	**11**	**36**	**1**	**0**	**0**	**58**	**5.2**	**29**	**4**	**41**	**7**	**–9**	**5**	**0**	**1**	**1**	**4**	**0**	**0**	**0**
1995-96	**Tampa Bay Lightning**	**NHL**	**66**	**1**	**11**	**12**	**1**	**9**	**10**	**64**	**0**	**0**	**0**	**90**	**1.1**	**62**	**7**	**66**	**16**	**+5**	**6**	**0**	**1**	**1**	**4**	**0**	**0**	**0**
1996-97	**Tampa Bay Lightning**	**NHL**	**57**	**1**	**10**	**11**	**1**	**9**	**10**	**72**	**0**	**0**	**0**	**59**	**1.7**	**45**	**11**	**39**	**6**	**+1**	....	....	....	....	....	....	....	....
1997-98	**Tampa Bay Lightning**	**NHL**	**14**	**0**	**2**	**2**	**0**	**2**	**2**	**12**	**0**	**0**	**0**	**12**	**0.0**	**5**	**0**	**12**	**5**	**–2**	....	....	....	....	....	....	....	....
	Las Vegas Thunder	IHL	26	6	13	19	....	....	....	28	....	....	....	....	....	....	....	....	....	....	....	....	....	....	....	....	....	....
	NHL Totals		**769**	**41**	**153**	**194**	**38**	**118**	**156**	**906**	**13**	**3**	**6**	**1104**	**3.7**	**757**	**143**	**876**	**230**		**45**	**3**	**9**	**12**	**81**	**1**	**0**	**1**

OHL First All-Star Team (1984) • Memorial Cup All-Star Team (1984)

Traded to **NY Rangers** by **Quebec** with John Ogrodnick for Jeff Jackson and Terry Carkner, September 30, 1987. Traded to **Edmonton** by **NY Rangers** for Jeff Beukeboom, November 12, 1991. Traded to **Minnesota** by **Edmonton** for Brian Glynn, January 21, 1992. Traded to **Boston** by **Minnesota** for future considerations, September 2, 1992. Traded to **Tampa Bay** by **Boston** for Detroit's 3rd round choice (previously acquired, Boston selected Jason Doyle) in 1996 Entry Draft, August 17, 1995. Traded to **San Jose** by **Tampa Bay** with Bryan Marchment and Tampa Bay's 1st round choice (later traded to Nashville - Nashville selected David Legwand) in 1998 Entry Draft for Andrei Nazarov and Florida's 1st round choice (previously acquired, Tampa Bay selected David Legwand) in 1998 Entry Draft, March 24, 1998.

• SHEDDEN, DOUG

Doug Shedden C – R. 6', 185 lbs. b: Wallaceburg, Ont., 4/29/1961. Pittsburgh's 4th choice, 93rd overall, in 1980 Entry Draft.

Season	Club	League	GP	G	A	Pts	AG	AA	APts	PIM	PP	SH	GW	S	%	TGF	PGF	TGA	PGA	+/–	GP	G	A	Pts	PIM	PP	SH	GW
1977-78	Hamilton Fincups	OHA	32	1	9	10	....	....	....	32	....	....	....	....	....	....	....	....	....	....	....	....	....	....	....	....	....	....
	Kitchener Rangers	OHA	18	5	7	12	....	....	....	14	....	....	....	....	....	....	....	....	....	....	....	....	....	....	....	....	....	....
1978-79	Kitchener Rangers	OHA	66	16	42	58	....	....	....	20	....	....	....	....	....	....	....	....	....	....	....	....	....	....	....	....	....	....
1979-80	Kitchener Rangers	OHA	16	10	16	26	....	....	....	26	....	....	....	....	....	....	....	....	....	....	....	....	....	....	....	....	....	....
	Sault Ste. Marie Greyhounds	OHA	45	30	44	74	....	....	....	59	....	....	....	....	....	....	....	....	....	....	....	....	....	....	....	....	....	....
1980-81	Sault Ste. Marie Greyhounds	OHA	66	51	72	123	....	....	....	114	....	....	....	....	....	....	....	....	....	....	19	16	22	38	10	....	....	....
1981-82	**Pittsburgh Penguins**	**NHL**	**38**	**10**	**15**	**25**	**8**	**10**	**18**	**12**	**4**	**0**	**2**	**76**	**13.2**	**41**	**17**	**26**	**0**	**–2**	....	....	....	....	....	....	....	....
	Erie Blades	AHL	17	4	6	10	....	....	....	14	....	....	....	....	....	....	....	....	....	....	....	....	....	....	....	....	....	....
1982-83	**Pittsburgh Penguins**	**NHL**	**80**	**24**	**43**	**67**	**20**	**30**	**50**	**54**	**4**	**1**	**2**	**175**	**13.7**	**101**	**33**	**97**	**9**	**–20**	....	....	....	....	....	....	....	....
1983-84	**Pittsburgh Penguins**	**NHL**	**67**	**22**	**35**	**57**	**18**	**24**	**42**	**20**	**6**	**1**	**1**	**159**	**13.8**	**83**	**31**	**100**	**10**	**–38**	....	....	....	....	....	....	....	....
1984-85	**Pittsburgh Penguins**	**NHL**	**80**	**35**	**32**	**67**	**29**	**22**	**51**	**30**	**12**	**0**	**3**	**203**	**17.2**	**95**	**43**	**103**	**0**	**–51**	....	....	....	....	....	....	....	....
1985-86	**Pittsburgh Penguins**	**NHL**	**67**	**32**	**34**	**66**	**26**	**23**	**49**	**32**	**19**	**0**	**5**	**179**	**17.9**	**114**	**55**	**66**	**0**	**–7**	....	....	....	....	....	....	....	....
	Detroit Red Wings	**NHL**	**11**	**2**	**3**	**5**	**2**	**2**	**4**	**2**	**2**	**0**	**0**	**33**	**6.1**	**15**	**6**	**10**	**0**	**–1**	....	....	....	....	....	....	....	....
1986-87	**Detroit Red Wings**	**NHL**	**33**	**6**	**12**	**18**	**5**	**9**	**14**	**6**	**1**	**0**	**1**	**51**	**11.8**	**35**	**7**	**25**	**0**	**+3**	....	....	....	....	....	....	....	....
	Adirondack Red Wings	AHL	5	2	2	4	....	....	....	4	....	....	....	....	....	....	....	....	....	....	....	....	....	....	....	....	....	....
	Quebec Nordiques	**NHL**	**16**	**0**	**2**	**2**	**0**	**1**	**1**	**8**	**0**	**0**	**0**	**29**	**0.0**	**4**	**0**	**9**	**0**	**–5**	....	....	....	....	....	....	....	....
	Fredericton Express	AHL	15	12	6	18	....	....	....	0	....	....	....	....	....	....	....	....	....	....	....	....	....	....	....	....	....	....
1987-88	Baltimore Skipjacks	AHL	80	37	51	88	....	....	....	32	....	....	....	....	....	....	....	....	....	....	....	....	....	....	....	....	....	....
1988-89	**Toronto Maple Leafs**	**NHL**	**1**	**0**	**0**	**0**	**0**	**0**	**0**	**2**	**0**	**0**	**0**	**2**	**0.0**	**0**	**0**	**1**	**0**	**–1**	....	....	....	....	....	....	....	....
	Newmarket Saints	AHL	29	14	26	40	....	....	....	6	....	....	....	....	....	....	....	....	....	....	....	....	....	....	....	....	....	....
1989-90	Newmarket Saints	AHL	47	26	33	59	....	....	....	12	....	....	....	....	....	....	....	....	....	....	....	....	....	....	....	....	....	....
1990-91	**Toronto Maple Leafs**	**NHL**	**23**	**8**	**10**	**18**	**7**	**8**	**15**	**10**	**4**	**0**	**0**	**35**	**22.9**	**28**	**10**	**16**	**0**	**+2**	....	....	....	....	....	....	....	....
	Newmarket Saints	AHL	47	15	34	49	....	....	....	16	....	....	....	....	....	....	....	....	....	....	....	....	....	....	....	....	....	....
1991-92	Bolzano HC	Italy	29	28	22	50	....	....	....	22	....	....	....	....	....	....	....	....	....	....	....	....	....	....	....	....	....	....
	HC Davos	Switz.	15	15	28	43	....	....	....	....	....	....	....	....	....	....	....	....	....	....	....	....	....	....	....	....	....	....
1992-93	Muskegon	IHL	18	16	21	37	....	....	....	18	....	....	....	....	....	....	....	....	....	....	....	....	....	....	....	....	....	....
	NHL Totals		**416**	**139**	**186**	**325**	**115**	**129**	**244**	**176**	**52**	**2**	**14**	**942**	**14.8**	**516**	**202**	**453**	**19**		....	....	....	....	....	....	....	....

Traded to **Detroit** by **Pittsburgh** for Ron Duguay, March 11, 1986. Traded to **Quebec** by **Detroit** with Basil McRae and John Ogrodnick for Brent Ashton, Gilbert Delorme and Mark Kumpel, January 17, 1987. Signed as a free agent by **Toronto**, August 4, 1988.

• SHEEHAN, BOBBY

Bobby Sheehan C – L. 5'7", 155 lbs. b: Weymouth, MA, 1/11/1949. Montreal's 3rd choice, 32nd overall, in 1969 Amateur Draft.

Season	Club	League	GP	G	A	Pts	AG	AA	APts	PIM	PP	SH	GW	S	%	TGF	PGF	TGA	PGA	+/–	GP	G	A	Pts	PIM	PP	SH	GW
1966-67	Halifax Canadiens	NSJHL	50	*64	51	115	....	....	....	21	....	....	....	....	....	....	....	....	....	....	17	*24	*28	*52	19	....	....	....
1967-68	Halifax Canadiens	NSJHL	44	51	47	98	....	....	....	25	....	....	....	....	....	....	....	....	....	....	4	6	5	11	0	....	....	....
1968-69	St. Catharines Black Hawks	OHA	44	44	41	85	....	....	....	6	....	....	....	....	....	....	....	....	....	....	18	10	13	23	2	....	....	....
1969-70	**Montreal Canadiens**	**NHL**	**16**	**2**	**1**	**3**	**2**	**1**	**3**	**2**	**0**	**0**	**0**	**20**	**10.0**	**5**	**0**	**5**	**0**	**0**	....	....	....	....	....	....	....	....
	Montreal Voyageurs	AHL	46	16	27	43	....	....	....	8	....	....	....	....	....	....	....	....	....	....	8	2	2	4	4	....	....	....
1970-71	**Montreal Canadiens**	**NHL**	**29**	**6**	**5**	**11**	**6**	**4**	**10**	**2**	**1**	**0**	**1**	**33**	**18.2**	**13**	**3**	**6**	**0**	**+4**	**6**	**0**	**0**	**0**	**0**	**0**	**0**	**0**
	Montreal Voyageurs	AHL	35	24	21	45	....	....	....	14	....	....	....	....	....	....	....	....	....	....	....	....	....	....	....	....	....	....
1971-72	**California Golden Seals**	**NHL**	**78**	**20**	**26**	**46**	**21**	**24**	**45**	**12**	**2**	**1**	**3**	**170**	**11.8**	**59**	**10**	**70**	**4**	**–17**	....	....	....	....	....	....	....	....
1972-73	New York Raiders	WHA	75	35	53	88	....	....	....	34	....	....	....	....	....	....	....	....	....	....	....	....	....	....	....	....	....	....
1973-74	New York-New Jersey	WHA	50	12	8	20	....	....	....	16	....	....	....	....	....	....	....	....	....	....	....	....	....	....	....	....	....	....
	Edmonton Oilers	WHA	10	1	3	4	....	....	....	12	....	....	....	....	....	....	....	....	....	....	....	....	....	....	....	....	....	....
1974-75	Edmonton Oilers	WHA	77	19	39	58	....	....	....	16	....	....	....	....	....	....	....	....	....	....	....	....	....	....	....	....	....	....
1975-76	**Chicago Black Hawks**	**NHL**	**78**	**11**	**20**	**31**	**10**	**16**	**26**	**18**	**2**	**0**	**0**	**129**	**8.5**	**39**	**7**	**36**	**0**	**–4**	**4**	**0**	**0**	**0**	**0**	**0**	**0**	**0**
1976-77	**Detroit Red Wings**	**NHL**	**34**	**5**	**4**	**9**	**5**	**3**	**8**	**2**	**0**	**0**	**0**	**45**	**11.1**	**12**	**0**	**24**	**2**	**–10**	....	....	....	....	....	....	....	....
	Rhode Island Reds	AHL	36	28	26	54	....	....	....	18	....	....	....	....	....	....	....	....	....	....	....	....	....	....	....	....	....	....
1977-78	Indianapolis Racers	WHA	29	8	7	15	....	....	....	6	....	....	....	....	....	....	....	....	....	....	....	....	....	....	....	....	....	....
	New Haven Nighthawks	AHL	43	13	26	39	....	....	....	14	....	....	....	....	....	....	....	....	....	....	15	7	5	12	4	....	....	....
1978-79	New Haven Nighthawks	AHL	70	33	48	81	....	....	....	26	....	....	....	....	....	....	....	....	....	....	....	....	....	....	....	....	....	....
	New York Rangers	**NHL**	....	....	....	....	....	....	....	....	**0**	**0**	**0**	**0**	**0.0**	**0**	**0**	**0**	**0**	**0**	**15**	**4**	**3**	**7**	**8**	**1**	**0**	**0**
1979-80	New Haven Nighthawks	AHL	13	8	7	15	....	....	....	2	....	....	....	....	....	....	....	....	....	....	....	....	....	....	....	....	....	....
	Colorado Rockies	**NHL**	**30**	**3**	**4**	**7**	**3**	**3**	**6**	**2**	**1**	**0**	**0**	**39**	**7.7**	**14**	**1**	**24**	**4**	**–7**	....	....	....	....	....	....	....	....
	Fort Worth Texans	CHL	31	18	20	38	....	....	....	14	....	....	....	....	....	....	....	....	....	....	....	....	....	....	....	....	....	....
1980-81	**Colorado Rockies**	**NHL**	**41**	**1**	**3**	**4**	**1**	**2**	**3**	**10**	**0**	**0**	**0**	**28**	**3.6**	**9**	**0**	**18**	**4**	**–5**	....	....	....	....	....	....	....	....
	United States	WEC A	0	1	1	2	....	....	....	0	....	....	....	....	....	....	....	....	....	....	....	....	....	....	....	....	....	....

Season	Club	League	GP	G	A	Pts	AG	AA	APts	PIM	PP	SH	GW	S	%	TGF	PGF	TGA	PGA	+/–	Playoffs GP	G	A	Pts	PIM	PP	SH	GW
			REGULAR SEASON																		PLAYOFFS							
1981-82	Los Angeles Kings	NHL	4	0	0	0	0	0	0	2	0	0	0	7	0.0	0	0	3	1	–2	....	....	....	....	....	....	....	....
	New Haven Nighthawks	AHL	74	21	17	38	....	....	....	32	....	....	....	....	....	....	....	....	....	....	4	0	2	2	0	....	....	....
1982-83	Binghamton Whalers	AHL	48	7	18	25	....	....	....	6	....	....	....	....	....	....	....	....	....	....	5	1	1	2	0	....	....	....
	NHL Totals		310	48	63	111	48	53	101	50	6	1	4	471	10.2	151	21	186	15		25	4	3	7	8	1	0	0
	Other Major League Totals		241	75	110	185	....	....	....	84	....	....	....	....	....	....	....	....	....		....	....	....	....	....	....	....	....

AHL Second All-Star Team (1979)

Traded to **California** by **Montreal** for cash, May 25, 1971. Selected by **New England** (WHA) in 1972 WHA General Player Draft, February 12, 1972. Rights traded to **Chicago** by **California** with Dick Redmond for Darryl Maggs, December 5, 1972. WHA rights traded to **NY Raiders** (WHA) by **New England** (WHA) for NY Raiders' 1st (Glenn Goldup) and 4th (Tom Colley) round choices in 1973 WHA Amateur Draft, August, 1972. Traded to **Edmonton** (WHA) by **New York-New Jersey** (WHA) for future considerations (Bob Falkenberg, May, 1974), March, 1974. Signed as a free agent by **Detroit**, October 8, 1976. Signed as a free agent by **Indianapolis** (WHA), July, 1977. Signed as a free agent by **NY Rangers**, October 1, 1978. Traded to **Colorado** by **New Haven** (AHL) for Dennis Owchar and Larry Skinner, May 12, 1979. Signed as a free agent by **LA Kings**, July 8, 1981.

• SHEEHY, NEIL

Neil Sheehy D – R. 6′2″, 214 lbs. b: International Falls, MN, 2/9/1960.

Season	Club	League	GP	G	A	Pts	AG	AA	APts	PIM	PP	SH	GW	S	%	TGF	PGF	TGA	PGA	+/–	Playoffs GP	G	A	Pts	PIM	PP	SH	GW
1979-80	Harvard University	ECAC	13	0	0	0	....	....	....	10	....	....	....	....	....	....	....	....	....	....	....	....	....	....	....	....	....	....
1980-81	Harvard University	ECAC	26	4	8	12	....	....	....	22	....	....	....	....	....	....	....	....	....	....	....	....	....	....	....	....	....	....
1981-82	Harvard University	ECAC	30	7	11	18	....	....	....	46	....	....	....	....	....	....	....	....	....	....	....	....	....	....	....	....	....	....
1982-83	Harvard University	ECAC	34	5	13	18	....	....	....	48	....	....	....	....	....	....	....	....	....	....	....	....	....	....	....	....	....	....
1983-84	Calgary Flames	NHL	1	1	0	1	1	0	1	2	0	0	0	1	100.0	1	0	1	0	0	4	0	0	0	4	0	0	0
	Colorado Flames	CHL	74	5	18	23	....	....	....	151	....	....	....	....	....	....	....	....	....	....	....	....	....	....	....	....	....	....
1984-85	Calgary Flames	NHL	31	3	4	7	2	3	5	109	0	0	0	42	7.1	28	0	25	2	+5	....	....	....	....	....	....	....	....
	Moncton Golden Flames	AHL	34	6	9	15	....	....	....	101	....	....	....	....	....	....	....	....	....	....	....	....	....	....	....	....	....	....
	United States	WEC-A	8	0	0	0	....	....	....	14	....	....	....	....	....	....	....	....	....	....	....	....	....	....	....	....	....	....
1985-86	Calgary Flames	NHL	65	2	16	18	2	11	13	271	1	0	0	59	3.4	59	8	74	22	–1	22	0	2	2	79	0	0	0
	Moncton Golden Flames	AHL	4	1	1	2	....	....	....	21	....	....	....	....	....	....	....	....	....	....	....	....	....	....	....	....	....	....
1986-87	Calgary Flames	NHL	54	4	6	10	3	4	7	151	0	0	0	45	8.9	49	0	49	11	+11	6	0	0	0	21	0	0	0
1987-88	Calgary Flames	NHL	36	2	6	8	2	4	6	73	0	0	0	27	7.4	43	0	44	17	+16	....	....	....	....	....	....	....	....
	Hartford Whalers	NHL	26	1	4	5	1	3	4	116	0	0	0	13	7.7	19	2	25	5	–3	1	0	0	0	7	0	0	0
1988-89	Washington Capitals	NHL	72	3	4	7	3	3	6	179	0	0	0	22	13.6	41	0	62	20	–1	6	0	0	0	19	0	0	0
1989-90	Washington Capitals	FrTour	3	0	0	0	....	....	....	0	....	....	....	....	....	....	....	....	....	....	....	....	....	....	....	....	....	....
	Washington Capitals	NHL	59	1	5	6	1	4	5	291	0	0	0	32	3.1	35	0	36	9	+8	13	0	1	1	92	0	0	0
1990-91	Washington Capitals	NHL	....	....	....	....	....	....	....	....	....	....	....	....	....	....	....	....	....	....	2	0	0	0	19	....	....	....
1991-92	Calgary Flames	NHL	35	1	2	3	1	1	2	119	0	0	0	19	5.3	20	0	33	6	–7	....	....	....	....	....	....	....	....
	Salt Lake Golden Eagles	IHL	6	0	0	0	....	....	....	34	....	....	....	....	....	....	....	....	....	....	....	....	....	....	....	....	....	....
	United States	WC-A	6	0	0	0	....	....	....	2	....	....	....	....	....	....	....	....	....	....	....	....	....	....	....	....	....	....
	NHL Totals		379	18	47	65	16	33	49	1311	1	0	0	260	6.9	295	10	349	92		54	0	3	3	241	0	0	0

Signed as a free agent by **Calgary**, August 16, 1983. Traded to **Hartford** by **Calgary** with Carey Wilson and rights to Lane MacDonald for Dana Murzyn and Shane Churla, January 3, 1988. Traded to **Washington** by **Hartford** with Mike Millar for Grant Jennings and Ed Kastelic, July 6, 1988. Signed as a free agent by **Calgary**, September 3, 1991.

• SHEEHY, TIM

Tim Sheehy RW – R. 6′1″, 185 lbs. b: Fort Frances, Ont., 9/3/1948. **USHOF**

Season	Club	League	GP	G	A	Pts	AG	AA	APts	PIM	PP	SH	GW	S	%	TGF	PGF	TGA	PGA	+/–	Playoffs GP	G	A	Pts	PIM	PP	SH	GW
1967-68	Boston College	ECAC	30	27	30	57	....	....	....	....	....	....	....	....	....	....	....	....	....	....	....	....	....	....	....	....	....	....
1968-69	Boston College	ECAC	26	19	41	60	....	....	....	36	....	....	....	....	....	....	....	....	....	....	....	....	....	....	....	....	....	....
	United States	WEC-A	10	1	4	5	....	....	....	8	....	....	....	....	....	....	....	....	....	....	....	....	....	....	....	....	....	....
1969-70	Boston College	ECAC	24	28	40	68	....	....	....	20	....	....	....	....	....	....	....	....	....	....	....	....	....	....	....	....	....	....
1970-71	United States	Nat-Team	STATISTICS NOT AVAILABLE																									
	United States	WEC-A	10	1	2	3	....	....	....	6	....	....	....	....	....	....	....	....	....	....	....	....	....	....	....	....	....	....
	United States	Olympics	6	4	1	5	....	....	....	0	....	....	....	....	....	....	....	....	....	....	....	....	....	....	....	....	....	....
1972-73	New England Whalers	WHA	78	33	38	71	....	....	....	30	....	....	....	....	....	....	....	....	....	....	15	9	14	23	13	....	....	....
1973-74	New England Whalers	WHA	77	29	29	58	....	....	....	22	....	....	....	....	....	....	....	....	....	....	7	4	2	6	4	....	....	....
1974-75	New England Whalers	WHA	52	20	13	33	....	....	....	18	....	....	....	....	....	....	....	....	....	....	....	....	....	....	....	....	....	....
	Edmonton Oilers	WHA	29	8	20	28	....	....	....	4	....	....	....	....	....	....	....	....	....	....	....	....	....	....	....	....	....	....
1975-76	Edmonton Oilers	WHA	81	34	31	65	....	....	....	17	....	....	....	....	....	....	....	....	....	....	4	2	2	4	0	....	....	....
1976-77	Edmonton Oilers	WHA	28	15	8	23	....	....	....	4	....	....	....	....	....	....	....	....	....	....	....	....	....	....	....	....	....	....
	Birmingham Bulls	WHA	50	26	21	47	....	....	....	44	....	....	....	....	....	....	....	....	....	....	....	....	....	....	....	....	....	....
1977-78	Detroit Red Wings	NHL	15	0	0	0	0	0	0	0	0	0	0	17	0.0	4	2	15	0	–13	....	....	....	....	....	....	....	....
	Kansas City Red Wings	CHL	16	2	6	8	....	....	....	4	....	....	....	....	....	....	....	....	....	....	....	....	....	....	....	....	....	....
	New England Whalers	WHA	25	8	11	19	....	....	....	12	....	....	....	....	....	....	....	....	....	....	13	1	3	4	9	....	....	....
1978-79	Springfield Indians	AHL	49	9	19	28	....	....	....	17	....	....	....	....	....	....	....	....	....	....	....	....	....	....	....	....	....	....
	Utica Mohawks	NEHL	21	14	12	26	....	....	....	21	....	....	....	....	....	....	....	....	....	....	....	....	....	....	....	....	....	....
1979-80	Hartford Whalers	NHL	12	2	1	3	2	1	3	0	0	0	0	15	13.3	7	0	1	0	+6	....	....	....	....	....	....	....	....
	Cincinnati Stingers	CHL	10	4	5	9	....	....	....	4	....	....	....	....	....	....	....	....	....	....	....	....	....	....	....	....	....	....
	Springfield Indians	AHL	52	25	21	46	....	....	....	10	....	....	....	....	....	....	....	....	....	....	....	....	....	....	....	....	....	....
	NHL Totals		27	2	1	3	2	1	3	0	0	0	0	32	6.3	11	2	16	0		....	....	....	....	....	....	....	....
	Other Major League Totals		420	173	171	344	....	....	....	151	....	....	....	....	....	....	....	....	....	....	39	16	21	37	26	....	....	....

ECAC Second All-Star Team (1969) • NCAA East First All-American Team (1969, 1970) • ECAC First All-Star Team (1970)

Selected by **New England** (WHA) in 1972 WHA General Player Draft, February 12, 1972. Traded to **Edmonton** (WHA) by **New England** (WHA) for Ron Climie, February, 1975. Traded to **Birmingham** (WHA) by **Edmonton** (WHA) for Gavin Kirk and Tom Simpson, December, 1976. Traded to **Detroit** by **Birmingham** (WHA) with Vaclav Nedomansky for Steve Durbano, Dave Hanson and future considerations, November, 1977. Traded to **New England** (WHA) by **Detroit** for cash, February 12, 1978.

• SHELTON, DOUG

Doug Shelton RW – R. 5′10″, 175 lbs. b: Woodstock, Ont., 6/27/1945.

Season	Club	League	GP	G	A	Pts	AG	AA	APts	PIM	PP	SH	GW	S	%	TGF	PGF	TGA	PGA	+/–	Playoffs GP	G	A	Pts	PIM	PP	SH	GW
1962-63	Ingersoll Rockets	Jr. B	STATISTICS NOT AVAILABLE																									
1963-64	St. Catharines Black Hawks	OHA	56	3	9	12	....	....	....	16	....	....	....	....	....	....	....	....	....	....	13	0	0	0	0	....	....	....
1964-65	St. Catharines Black Hawks	OHA	56	8	8	16	....	....	....	16	....	....	....	....	....	....	....	....	....	....	5	0	0	0	4	....	....	....
1965-66	St. Catharines Black Hawks	OHA	48	36	24	60	....	....	....	16	....	....	....	....	....	....	....	....	....	....	7	1	2	3	10	....	....	....
	St. Louis Braves	CHL	....	....	....	....	....	....	....	....	....	....	....	....	....	....	....	....	....	....	2	0	0	0	0	....	....	....
1966-67	St. Louis Braves	CHL	68	11	23	34	....	....	....	4	....	....	....	....	....	....	....	....	....	....	....	....	....	....	....	....	....	....
1967-68	Chicago Black Hawks	NHL	5	0	1	1	0	1	1	2	0	0	0	1	0.0	1	0	4	0	–3	....	....	....	....	....	....	....	....
	Dallas Black Hawks	CHL	65	19	39	58	....	....	....	22	....	....	....	....	....	....	....	....	....	....	5	0	2	2	0	....	....	....
1968-69	Dallas Black Hawks	CHL	69	17	27	44	....	....	....	30	....	....	....	....	....	....	....	....	....	....	11	3	4	7	10	....	....	....
1969-70	Denver Spurs	WHL	20	2	3	5	....	....	....	0	....	....	....	....	....	....	....	....	....	....	....	....	....	....	....	....	....	....
	Springfield Kings	AHL	28	1	4	5	....	....	....	4	....	....	....	....	....	....	....	....	....	....	14	4	8	12	6	....	....	....
	NHL Totals		5	0	1	1	0	1	1	2	0	0	0	1	0.0	1	0	4	0		....	....	....	....	....	....	....	....

Traded to **Minnesota** by **Chicago** to complete transaction that sent Andre Boudrias to Chicago (February 14, 1969), June, 1969. Claimed by **Denver** (WHL) from **Minnesota** in Reverse Draft, June, 1969.

• SHEPPARD, GREGG

Gregg Sheppard C – L. 5′8″, 170 lbs. b: North Battleford, Sask., 4/23/1949.

Season	Club	League	GP	G	A	Pts	AG	AA	APts	PIM	PP	SH	GW	S	%	TGF	PGF	TGA	PGA	+/–	Playoffs GP	G	A	Pts	PIM	PP	SH	GW
1965-66	Estevan Bruins	SJHL	1	1	1	2	....	....	....	0	....	....	....	....	....	....	....	....	....	....	1	0	0	0	0	....	....	....
1966-67	Estevan Bruins	WCJHL	52	44	24	68	....	....	....	14	....	....	....	....	....	....	....	....	....	....	12	11	9	20	4	....	....	....
1967-68	Estevan Bruins	WCJHL	58	35	46	81	....	....	....	68	....	....	....	....	....	....	....	....	....	....	14	13	7	20	6	....	....	....
1968-69	Estevan Bruins	WCJHL	54	42	42	84	....	....	....	33	....	....	....	....	....	....	....	....	....	....	10	1	7	8	0	....	....	....
	Oklahoma City Blazers	CHL	4	0	0	0	....	....	....	0	....	....	....	....	....	....	....	....	....	....	....	....	....	....	....	....	....	....
1969-70	Oklahoma City Blazers	CHL	65	26	29	55	....	....	....	19	....	....	....	....	....	....	....	....	....	....	....	....	....	....	....	....	....	....
	Salt Lake Golden Eagles	WHL	5	0	0	0	....	....	....	2	....	....	....	....	....	....	....	....	....	....	....	....	....	....	....	....	....	....
1970-71	Oklahoma City Blazers	CHL	68	25	50	75	....	....	....	45	....	....	....	....	....	....	....	....	....	....	5	2	3	5	5	....	....	....
1971-72	Oklahoma City Blazers	CHL	72	*41	52	93	....	....	....	43	....	....	....	....	....	....	....	....	....	....	6	4	7	11	4	....	....	....
1972-73	Boston Bruins	NHL	64	24	26	50	24	22	46	18	0	2	3	151	15.9	62	0	30	5	+37	5	2	1	3	0	0	1	1
	Boston Braves	AHL	8	5	5	10	....	....	....	2	....	....	....	....	....	....	....	....	....	....	....	....	....	....	....	....	....	....
1973-74	Boston Bruins	NHL	75	16	31	47	16	27	43	21	0	3	3	168	9.5	70	1	71	25	+23	16	11	8	19	4	0	2	2
1974-75	Boston Bruins	NHL	76	30	48	78	28	38	66	19	5	7	4	249	12.0	125	25	80	23	+43	3	3	1	4	5	0	0	0
1975-76	Boston Bruins	NHL	70	31	43	74	29	34	63	28	5	2	4	222	14.0	117	44	75	26	+24	12	5	6	11	6	1	0	1
1976-77	Boston Bruins	NHL	77	31	36	67	30	29	59	20	8	1	5	247	12.6	96	34	82	23	+3	14	5	7	12	8	1	1	2
1977-78	Boston Bruins	NHL	54	23	36	59	22	29	51	24	5	1	7	160	14.4	79	25	56	21	+19	15	2	10	12	6	0	0	0

			REGULAR SEASON																		PLAYOFFS							
Season	Club	League	GP	G	A	Pts	AG	AA	APts	PIM	PP	SH	GW	S	%	TGF	PGF	TGA	PGA	+/–	GP	G	A	Pts	PIM	PP	SH	GW
1978-79	Pittsburgh Penguins	NHL	60	15	22	37	14	17	31	9	3	1	2	134	11.2	64	18	65	27	+8	7	1	2	3	0	1	0	0
1979-80	Pittsburgh Penguins	NHL	76	13	24	37	12	18	30	20	3	0	2	136	9.6	67	17	97	25	–22	5	1	1	2	0	0	0	0
1980-81	Pittsburgh Penguins	NHL	47	11	17	28	9	12	21	49	3	0	1	85	12.9	42	12	77	34	–13	5	2	4	6	2	1	0	0
1981-82	Pittsburgh Penguins	NHL	58	11	10	21	9	7	16	35	0	0	1	81	13.6	38	2	75	48	+9	....	....	....	....	....	....	....	....
	NHL Totals		657	205	293	498	193	233	426	243	32	17	32	1633	12.6	760	178	708	257		82	32	40	72	31	4	4	6

CHL Second All-Star Team (1971) • CHL First All-Star Team (1972) • Won Tommy Ivan Trophy (CHL's MVP) (1972)

Played in NHL All-Star Game (1976)

Traded to **Atlanta** by **Boston** for Dick Redmond, Spetember 6, 1978. Traded to **Pittsburgh** by **Atlanta** for Jean Pronovost, September 6, 1978.

• SHEPPARD, RAY

Ray Sheppard RW – R. 6'1", 195 lbs. b: Pembroke, Ont., 5/27/1966. Buffalo's 3rd choice, 60th overall, in 1984 Entry Draft.

Season	Club	League	GP	G	A	Pts	AG	AA	APts	PIM	PP	SH	GW	S	%	TGF	PGF	TGA	PGA	+/–	GP	G	A	Pts	PIM	PP	SH	GW
1983-84	Cornwall Royals	OHL	68	44	36	80	....	....	....	69	....	....	....	....	....	....	....	....	....	....	....	....	....	....	....	....	....	....
1984-85	Cornwall Royals	OHL	49	25	33	58	....	....	....	51	....	....	....	....	....	....	....	....	....	....	9	2	12	14	4	....	....	....
1985-86	Cornwall Royals	OHL	63	*81	61	*142	....	....	....	25	....	....	....	....	....	....	....	....	....	....	6	7	4	11	0	....	....	....
1986-87	Rochester Americans	AHL	55	18	13	31	....	....	....	11	....	....	....	....	....	....	....	....	....	....	15	12	3	15	2	....	....	....
1987-88	Buffalo Sabres	NHL	74	38	27	65	33	19	52	14	15	0	5	173	22.0	84	32	58	0	–6	6	1	1	2	2	1	0	0
1988-89	Buffalo Sabres	NHL	67	22	21	43	19	15	34	15	7	0	4	147	15.0	79	30	57	1	–7	1	0	1	1	0	0	0	0
1989-90	Buffalo Sabres	NHL	18	4	2	6	3	1	4	0	1	0	1	31	12.9	11	3	5	0	+3	....	....	....	....	....	....	....	....
	Rochester Americans	AHL	5	3	5	8	....	....	....	2	....	....	....	....	....	....	....	....	....	....	17	8	7	15	9	....	....	....
1990-91	New York Rangers	NHL	59	24	23	47	22	17	39	21	7	0	5	129	18.6	63	23	32	0	+8	....	....	....	....	....	....	....	....
1991-92	Detroit Red Wings	NHL	74	36	26	62	33	20	53	27	11	1	4	178	20.2	90	27	56	0	+7	11	6	2	8	4	3	0	0
1992-93	Detroit Red Wings	NHL	70	32	34	66	27	23	50	29	10	0	1	183	17.5	92	36	50	1	+7	7	2	3	5	0	2	0	0
1993-94	Detroit Red Wings	NHL	82	52	41	93	49	32	81	26	19	0	5	260	20.0	124	46	68	3	+13	7	2	1	3	4	0	0	0
1994-95	Detroit Red Wings	NHL	43	30	10	40	53	15	68	17	11	0	5	125	24.0	60	24	27	2	+11	17	4	3	7	5	2	0	0
1995-96	Detroit Red Wings	NHL	5	2	2	4	2	2	4	2	0	0	1	9	22.2	5	2	3	0	0	....	....	....	....	....	....	....	....
	San Jose Sharks	NHL	51	27	19	46	27	15	42	10	12	0	4	170	15.9	63	24	62	4	–19	....	....	....	....	....	....	....	....
	Florida Panthers	NHL	14	8	2	10	8	2	10	4	2	0	2	52	15.4	11	3	8	0	0	21	8	8	16	4	3	0	0
1996-97	Florida Panthers	NHL	68	29	31	60	31	27	58	4	13	0	7	226	12.8	78	31	43	0	+4	5	2	0	2	0	1	0	0
1997-98	Florida Panthers	NHL	61	14	17	31	16	17	33	21	5	0	1	136	10.3	52	25	40	0	–13	....	....	....	....	....	....	....	....
	Carolina Hurricanes	NHL	10	4	2	6	5	2	7	2	2	0	1	33	12.1	12	5	5	0	+2	....	....	....	....	....	....	....	....
	NHL Totals		696	322	257	579	328	207	535	192	115	1	46	1852	17.4	824	311	514	11		75	25	19	44	19	12	0	0

OHL First All-Star Team (1986) • NHL All-Rookie Team (1988)

Traded to **NY Rangers** by **Buffalo** for cash and future considerations, July 9, 1990. Signed as a free agent by **Detroit**, August 5, 1991. Traded to **San Jose** by **Detroit** for Igor Larionov and future considerations, October 24, 1995. Traded to **Florida** by **San Jose** with San Jose's 4th round choice (Joey Tetarenko) in 1996 Entry Draft for Florida's 2nd (later traded to Chicago — Chicago selected Geoff Peters) and 4th (Matt Bradley) round choices in 1996 Entry Draft, March 16, 1996. Traded to **Carolina** by **Florida** for Kirk McLean, March 24, 1998.

• SHERVEN, GORD

Gord Sherven C – R. 6', 185 lbs. b: Gravelbourg, Sask., 8/21/1963. Edmonton's 9th choice, 197th overall, in 1981 Entry Draft.

Season	Club	League	GP	G	A	Pts	AG	AA	APts	PIM	PP	SH	GW	S	%	TGF	PGF	TGA	PGA	+/–	GP	G	A	Pts	PIM	PP	SH	GW
1980-81	Weyburn Red Wings	SJHL	44	35	34	69	....	....	....	....	....	....	....	....	....	....	....	....	....	....	....	....	....	....	....	....	....	....
1981-82	University of North Dakota	WCHA	46	18	25	43	....	....	....	16	....	....	....	....	....	....	....	....	....	....	....	....	....	....	....	....	....	....
1982-83	University of North Dakota	WCHA	36	12	21	33	....	....	....	16	....	....	....	....	....	....	....	....	....	....	....	....	....	....	....	....	....	....
	Canada	WJC-A	7	1	3	4	....	....	....	0	....	....	....	....	....	....	....	....	....	....	....	....	....	....	....	....	....	....
	Canada	WEC-A	9	2	1	3	....	....	....	2	....	....	....	....	....	....	....	....	....	....	....	....	....	....	....	....	....	....
1983-84	Canada	Nat-Team	46	9	13	22	....	....	....	13	....	....	....	....	....	....	....	....	....	....	....	....	....	....	....	....	....	....
	Edmonton Oilers	NHL	2	1	0	1	1	0	1	0	0	0	0	5	20.0	1	0	0	0	+1	....	....	....	....	....	....	....	....
1984-85	Edmonton Oilers	NHL	37	9	7	16	7	5	12	10	1	0	1	49	18.4	22	2	22	0	–2	....	....	....	....	....	....	....	....
	Minnesota North Stars	NHL	32	2	12	14	2	8	10	8	0	0	1	49	4.1	21	0	33	15	+3	3	0	0	0	0	0	0	0
	Nova Scotia Voyageurs	AHL	5	4	5	9	....	....	....	5	....	....	....	....	....	....	....	....	....	....	....	....	....	....	....	....	....	....
1985-86	Minnesota North Stars	NHL	13	0	2	2	0	1	1	11	0	0	0	8	0.0	4	0	8	5	+1	....	....	....	....	....	....	....	....
	Springfield Indians	AHL	11	3	7	10	....	....	....	8	....	....	....	....	....	....	....	....	....	....	....	....	....	....	....	....	....	....
	Edmonton Oilers	NHL	5	1	1	2	1	1	2	4	0	0	0	6	16.7	2	0	2	0	0	....	....	....	....	....	....	....	....
	Nova Scotia Oilers	AHL	38	14	17	31	....	....	....	4	....	....	....	....	....	....	....	....	....	....	....	....	....	....	....	....	....	....
1986-87	Canada	Nat-Team	56	14	22	36	....	....	....	30	....	....	....	....	....	....	....	....	....	....	....	....	....	....	....	....	....	....
	Hartford Whalers	NHL	7	0	0	0	0	0	0	0	0	0	0	7	0.0	0	0	6	0	–6	....	....	....	....	....	....	....	....
1987-88	Canada	Nat-Team	53	12	16	28	....	....	....	26	....	....	....	....	....	....	....	....	....	....	....	....	....	....	....	....	....	....
	Canada	Olympics	8	4	4	8	....	....	....	4	....	....	....	....	....	....	....	....	....	....	....	....	....	....	....	....	....	....
	Hartford Whalers	NHL	1	0	0	0	0	0	0	0	0	0	0	2	0.0	0	0	0	0	0	....	....	....	....	....	....	....	....
1988-89	SB Rosenheim	Germany	18	10	15	25	....	....	....	6	....	....	....	....	....	....	....	....	....	....	7	3	4	7	6	....	....	....
1989-90	SB Rosenheim	Germany	36	*36	21	57	....	....	....	20	....	....	....	....	....	....	....	....	....	....	10	8	4	12	14	....	....	....
1990-91	SB Rosenheim	Germany	43	33	44	77	....	....	....	42	....	....	....	....	....	....	....	....	....	....	11	*16	8	*24	6	....	....	....
1991-92	SB Rosenheim	Germany	37	19	40	59	....	....	....	26	....	....	....	....	....	....	....	....	....	....	....	....	....	....	....	....	....	....
1992-93	Zurcher	Switz.	DID NOT PLAY																									
1993-94	EC Hedos Munich	Germany	43	21	27	48	....	....	....	29	....	....	....	....	....	....	....	....	....	....	....	....	....	....	....	....	....	....
1994-95	EC Hedos Munich	Germany	27	16	21	37	....	....	....	12	....	....	....	....	....	....	....	....	....	....	....	....	....	....	....	....	....	....
	Star Bulls Rosenheim	Germany	15	4	16	20	....	....	....	10	....	....	....	....	....	....	....	....	....	....	7	3	5	8	2	....	....	....
1995-96	Dusseldorfer EG	Germany	50	20	42	62	....	....	....	36	....	....	....	....	....	....	....	....	....	....	13	6	9	15	4	....	....	....
1996-97	Dusseldorfer EG	Germany	40	13	17	30	....	....	....	12	....	....	....	....	....	....	....	....	....	....	4	1	2	3	6	....	....	....
1997-98	Dusseldorfer EG	Germany	44	9	15	24	....	....	....	14	....	....	....	....	....	....	....	....	....	....	3	0	1	1	2	....	....	....
	NHL Totals		97	13	22	35	11	15	26	33	1	0	2	126	10.3	50	2	71	20		3	0	0	0	0	0	0	0

Traded to **Minnesota** by **Edmonton** with Terry Martin for Mark Napier, January 24, 1985. Traded to **Edmonton** by **Minnesota** with Don Biggs for Marc Habscheid, Dan Barber and Emanuel Viveiros, December 20, 1985. Claimed by **Hartford** from **Edmonton** in Waiver Draft, October 6, 1986.

• SHEVALIER, JEFF

Jeff Shevalier LW – L. 5'11", 180 lbs. b: Mississauga, Ont., 3/14/1974. Los Angeles' 4th choice, 111th overall, in 1992 Entry Draft.

Season	Club	League	GP	G	A	Pts	AG	AA	APts	PIM	PP	SH	GW	S	%	TGF	PGF	TGA	PGA	+/–	GP	G	A	Pts	PIM	PP	SH	GW
1991-92	North Bay Centennials	OHL	64	28	29	57	....	....	....	26	....	....	....	....	....	....	....	....	....	....	21	5	11	16	25	....	....	....
1992-93	North Bay Centennials	OHL	62	59	54	113	....	....	....	46	....	....	....	....	....	....	....	....	....	....	2	1	2	3	4	....	....	....
1993-94	North Bay Centennials	OHL	64	52	49	101	....	....	....	52	....	....	....	....	....	....	....	....	....	....	17	8	14	22	18	....	....	....
1994-95	Phoenix Roadrunners	IHL	68	31	39	70	....	....	....	44	....	....	....	....	....	....	....	....	....	....	9	5	4	9	0	....	....	....
	Los Angeles Kings	NHL	1	1	0	1	2	0	2	0	0	0	0	1	100.0	1	0	0	0	+1	....	....	....	....	....	....	....	....
1995-96	Phoenix Roadrunners	IHL	79	29	38	67	....	....	....	72	....	....	....	....	....	....	....	....	....	....	4	2	2	4	2	....	....	....
1996-97	Los Angeles Kings	NHL	26	4	9	13	4	8	12	6	1	0	0	42	9.5	18	4	20	0	–6	....	....	....	....	....	....	....	....
	Phoenix Roadrunners	IHL	46	16	21	37	....	....	....	26	....	....	....	....	....	....	....	....	....	....	....	....	....	....	....	....	....	....
1997-98	Springfield Falcons	AHL	66	23	30	53	....	....	....	38	....	....	....	....	....	....	....	....	....	....	4	1	1	2	0	....	....	....
	NHL Totals		27	5	9	14	6	8	14	6	1	0	0	43	11.6	19	4	20	0		....	....	....	....	....	....	....	....

OHL First All-Star Team (1994)

• SHINSKE, RICK

Rick Shinske C – L. 5'11", 165 lbs. b: Weyburn, Sask., 5/31/1955. California's 6th choice, 111th overall, in 1975 Amateur Draft.

Season	Club	League	GP	G	A	Pts	AG	AA	APts	PIM	PP	SH	GW	S	%	TGF	PGF	TGA	PGA	+/–	GP	G	A	Pts	PIM	PP	SH	GW
1971-72	Kamloops Blazers	BCJHL	48	3	9	12	....	....	....	74	....	....	....	....	....	....	....	....	....	....	....	....	....	....	....	....	....	....
1972-73	Kamloops Blazers	BCJHL	61	28	*90	*118	....	....	....	97	....	....	....	....	....	....	....	....	....	....	....	....	....	....	....	....	....	....
	Calgary Centennials	WHL	1	0	0	0	....	....	....	0	....	....	....	....	....	....	....	....	....	....	....	....	....	....	....	....	....	....
1973-74	Calgary Centennials	WHL	67	12	43	55	....	....	....	18	....	....	....	....	....	....	....	....	....	....	13	1	8	9	4	....	....	....
1974-75	Calgary Centennials	WHL	17	3	13	16	....	....	....	18	....	....	....	....	....	....	....	....	....	....	....	....	....	....	....	....	....	....
	New Westminster Bruins	WHL	48	20	44	64	....	....	....	54	....	....	....	....	....	....	....	....	....	....	18	7	11	18	18	....	....	....
1975-76	New Westminster Bruins	WHL	70	52	91	143	....	....	....	86	....	....	....	....	....	....	....	....	....	....	17	7	23	30	26	....	....	....
	Salt Lake City Golden Eagles	CHL	4	0	2	2	....	....	....	0	....	....	....	....	....	....	....	....	....	....	....	....	....	....	....	....	....	....
1976-77	Cleveland Barons	NHL	5	0	0	0	0	0	0	2	0	0	0	3	0.0	1	1	5	1	–4	....	....	....	....	....	....	....	....
	Salt Lake Golden Eagles	CHL	70	22	48	70	....	....	....	18	....	....	....	....	....	....	....	....	....	....	....	....	....	....	....	....	....	....
1977-78	Cleveland Barons	NHL	47	5	12	17	5	10	15	6	1	0	1	40	12.5	21	3	30	0	–12	....	....	....	....	....	....	....	....
	Phoenix Roadrunners	CHL	14	3	8	11	....	....	....	0	....	....	....	....	....	....	....	....	....	....	....	....	....	....	....	....	....	....
	Binghamton Dusters	AHL	17	8	9	17	....	....	....	2	....	....	....	....	....	....	....	....	....	....	....	....	....	....	....	....	....	....
1978-79	St. Louis Blues	NHL	11	0	4	4	0	3	3	2	0	0	0	7	0.0	6	1	8	0	–3	....	....	....	....	....	....	....	....
	Salt Lake Golden Eagles	CHL	66	22	*66	*88	....	....	....	31	....	....	....	....	....	....	....	....	....	....	10	3	7	10	6	....	....	....
1979-80	Adirondack Red Wings	AHL	78	22	58	80	....	....	....	20	....	....	....	....	....	....	....	....	....	....	5	0	3	3	0	....	....	....

			REGULAR SEASON																		PLAYOFFS							
Season	**Club**	**League**	**GP**	**G**	**A**	**Pts**	**AG**	**AA**	**APts**	**PIM**	**PP**	**SH**	**GW**	**S**	**%**	**TGF**	**PGF**	**TGA**	**PGA**	**+/–**	**GP**	**G**	**A**	**Pts**	**PIM**	**PP**	**SH**	**GW**
1980-81	Adirondack Red Wings	AHL	46	20	35	55	....	....	....	46	....	....	....	....	....	....	....	....	....	....	....	....	....	....	....	....	....	....
1981-82	Adirondack Red Wings	AHL	35	10	23	33	....	....	....	0	....	....	....	....	....	....	....	....	....	....	5	2	4	6	0	....	....	....
1982-83	New Haven Nighthawks	AHL	45	10	27	37	....	....	....	12	....	....	....	....	....	....	....	....	....	....	12	3	6	9	2	....	....	....
	NHL Totals		**63**	**5**	**16**	**21**	**5**	**13**	**18**	**10**	**1**	**0**	**1**	**50**	**10.0**	**28**	**5**	**43**	**1**		....	....	....	....	....	....	....	....

Won George Parsons Trophy (Memorial Cup Tournament Most Sportsmanlike Player) (1976) • CHL First All-Star Team (1979)

Rights transferred to **Cleveland** after **California** franchise relocated, August 26, 1976. Claimed by **Minnesota** in **Cleveland-Minnesota** Dispersal Draft, June 15, 1978. Claimed on waivers by **St. Louis** from **Minnesota**, August 12, 1978. Signed as a free agent by **Detroit**, September, 1979.

• SHIRES, JIM

Jim Shires LW – L. 6′, 180 lbs. b: Edmonton, Alta., 11/15/1945.

1963-64	Edmonton Oil Kings	SJHL	2	0	0	0	....	....	....	4	....	....	....	....	....	....	....	....	....	....	....	....	....	....	....	....	....	....
1964-65	University of Denver	WCHA	DID NOT PLAY – FRESHMAN																									
1965-66	University of Denver	WCHA	26	8	10	18	....	....	....	18	....	....	....	....	....	....	....	....	....	....	....	....	....	....	....	....	....	....
1966-67	University of Denver	WCHA	30	8	19	27	....	....	....	39	....	....	....	....	....	....	....	....	....	....	....	....	....	....	....	....	....	....
1967-68	University of Denver	WCHA	34	15	23	38	....	....	....	43	....	....	....	....	....	....	....	....	....	....	....	....	....	....	....	....	....	....
1968-69	Omaha Knights	CHL	9	0	2	2	....	....	....	4	....	....	....	....	....	....	....	....	....	....	....	....	....	....	....	....	....	....
	Denver Spurs	WHL	20	2	2	4	....	....	....	6	....	....	....	....	....	....	....	....	....	....	....	....	....	....	....	....	....	....
	Amarillo Wranglers	CHL	34	10	18	28	....	....	....	43	....	....	....	....	....	....	....	....	....	....	....	....	....	....	....	....	....	....
1969-70	Fort Worth Wings	CHL	69	16	18	34	....	....	....	61	....	....	....	....	....	....	....	....	....	....	7	1	1	2	21	....	....	....
1970-71	**Detroit Red Wings**	**NHL**	**20**	**2**	**1**	**3**	**2**	**1**	**3**	**22**	**1**	**0**	**0**	**22**	**9.1**	**4**	**1**	**6**	**0**	**–3**	....	....	....	....	....	....	....	....
	Fort Worth Wings	CHL	48	13	25	38	....	....	....	97	....	....	....	....	....	....	....	....	....	....	4	0	0	0	2	....	....	....
1971-72	**St. Louis Blues**	**NHL**	**18**	**0**	**3**	**3**	**0**	**3**	**3**	**8**	**0**	**0**	**0**	**14**	**0.0**	**3**	**1**	**16**	**1**	**–13**	....	....	....	....	....	....	....	....
	Denver Spurs	WHL	42	18	27	45	....	....	....	82	....	....	....	....	....	....	....	....	....	....	9	2	3	5	15	....	....	....
1972-73	Denver Spurs	WHL	32	10	7	17	....	....	....	45	....	....	....	....	....	....	....	....	....	....	....	....	....	....	....	....	....	....
	Pittsburgh Penguins	**NHL**	**18**	**1**	**2**	**3**	**1**	**2**	**3**	**2**	**0**	**0**	**0**	**22**	**4.5**	**6**	**0**	**14**	**0**	**–8**	....	....	....	....	....	....	....	....
1973-74	San Diego Gulls	WHL	68	26	34	60	....	....	....	44	....	....	....	....	....	....	....	....	....	....	4	2	2	4	0	....	....	....
1974-75	Fort Wayne Komets	IHL	21	3	9	12	....	....	....	12	....	....	....	....	....	....	....	....	....	....	....	....	....	....	....	....	....	....
	NHL Totals		**56**	**3**	**6**	**9**	**3**	**6**	**9**	**32**	**1**	**0**	**0**	**58**	**5.2**	**13**	**2**	**36**	**1**		....	....	....	....	....	....	....	....

• Rights retained by Detroit as territorial exemption (Edmonton-WCJHL), June, 1968. Traded to **St. Louis** by **Detroit** for Rick Sentes, May 12, 1971. Traded to **Pittsburgh** by **St. Louis** for Joe Noris, January 8, 1973.

• SHMYR, PAUL

Paul Shmyr D – L. 5′11″, 170 lbs. b: Cudworth, Sask., 1/18/1946.

1966-67	Vancouver Canucks	WHL	1	0	0	0	....	....	....	0	....	....	....	....	....	....	....	....	....	....	....	....	....	....	....	....	....	....
	Fort Wayne Komets	IHL	70	3	18	21	....	....	....	89	....	....	....	....	....	....	....	....	....	....	11	3	3	6	19	....	....	....
1967-68	Dallas Black Hawks	CHL	70	5	15	20	....	....	....	73	....	....	....	....	....	....	....	....	....	....	5	0	0	0	0	....	....	....
1968-69	**Chicago Black Hawks**	**NHL**	**3**	**1**	**0**	**1**	**1**	**0**	**1**	**8**	**0**	**0**	**0**	**5**	**20.0**	**4**	**0**	**4**	**0**	**0**	....	....	....	....	....	....	....	....
	Dallas Black Hawks	CHL	69	7	39	46	....	....	....	118	....	....	....	....	....	....	....	....	....	....	11	4	12	16	17	....	....	....
	Portland Buckaroos	WHL	....	....	....	....	....	....	....	....	....	....	....	....	....	....	....	....	....	....	1	0	1	1	0	....	....	....
1969-70	**Chicago Black Hawks**	**NHL**	**24**	**0**	**4**	**4**	**0**	**4**	**4**	**26**	**0**	**0**	**0**	**13**	**0.0**	**18**	**1**	**8**	**2**	**+11**	**8**	**1**	**2**	**3**	**0**	**0**	**0**	**0**
	Dallas Black Hawks	CHL	48	3	21	24	....	....	....	88	....	....	....	....	....	....	....	....	....	....	....	....	....	....	....	....	....	....
1970-71	**Chicago Black Hawks**	**NHL**	**57**	**1**	**12**	**13**	**1**	**11**	**12**	**41**	**0**	**0**	**1**	**35**	**2.9**	**28**	**0**	**34**	**9**	**+3**	**9**	**0**	**0**	**0**	**17**	**0**	**0**	**0**
1971-72	**California Golden Seals**	**NHL**	**69**	**6**	**21**	**27**	**6**	**19**	**25**	**156**	**0**	**0**	**0**	**82**	**7.3**	**81**	**3**	**127**	**22**	**–27**	....	....	....	....	....	....	....	....
1972-73	Cleveland Crusaders	WHA	73	5	43	48	....	....	....	169	....	....	....	....	....	....	....	....	....	....	8	1	3	4	19	....	....	....
1973-74	Cleveland Crusaders	WHA	78	13	31	44	....	....	....	165	....	....	....	....	....	....	....	....	....	....	5	0	4	4	31	....	....	....
1974-75	Canada	Summit	7	0	2	2	....	....	....	6	....	....	....	....	....	....	....	....	....	....	....	....	....	....	....	....	....	....
	Cleveland Crusaders	WHA	49	7	14	21	....	....	....	103	....	....	....	....	....	....	....	....	....	....	5	2	1	3	15	....	....	....
1975-76	Cleveland Crusaders	WHA	70	6	44	50	....	....	....	101	....	....	....	....	....	....	....	....	....	....	....	....	....	....	....	....	....	....
1976-77	San Diego Mariners	WHA	81	13	37	50	....	....	....	103	....	....	....	....	....	....	....	....	....	....	7	0	2	2	8	....	....	....
1977-78	Edmonton Oilers	WHA	80	9	40	49	....	....	....	100	....	....	....	....	....	....	....	....	....	....	5	1	3	4	11	....	....	....
1978-79	Edmonton Oilers	WHA	80	8	39	47	....	....	....	119	....	....	....	....	....	....	....	....	....	....	13	1	5	6	23	....	....	....
1979-80	**Minnesota North Stars**	**NHL**	**63**	**3**	**15**	**18**	**3**	**11**	**14**	**84**	**0**	**0**	**1**	**82**	**3.7**	**72**	**1**	**56**	**10**	**+25**	**14**	**2**	**1**	**3**	**23**	**1**	**0**	**1**
1980-81	**Minnesota North Stars**	**NHL**	**61**	**1**	**9**	**10**	**1**	**6**	**7**	**79**	**0**	**0**	**0**	**62**	**1.6**	**49**	**2**	**63**	**20**	**+4**	**3**	**0**	**0**	**0**	**4**	**0**	**0**	**0**
1981-82	**Hartford Whalers**	**NHL**	**66**	**1**	**11**	**12**	**1**	**7**	**8**	**134**	**0**	**0**	**0**	**44**	**2.3**	**62**	**6**	**90**	**23**	**–11**	....	....	....	....	....	....	....	....
	NHL Totals		**343**	**13**	**72**	**85**	**13**	**58**	**71**	**528**	**0**	**0**	**2**	**323**	**4.0**	**314**	**13**	**382**	**86**		**34**	**3**	**3**	**6**	**44**	**1**	**0**	**1**
	Other Major League Totals		511	61	248	309	....	....	....	860	....	....	....	....	....	....	....	....	....		43	5	18	23	107	....	....	....

WHA First All-Star Team (1973, 1974, 1976) • Won Dennis A. Murphy Trophy (WHA Top Defenseman) (1976) • WHA Second All-Star Team (1979)

Traded to **Chicago** by **NY Rangers** for Camille Henry, August 17, 1967. Traded to **California** by **Chicago** with Gilles Marotte for Gerry Desjardins, October 18, 1971. Selected by **Miami-Philadelphia** (WHA) in 1972 WHA General Player Draft, February 12, 1972. WHA rights traded to **Cleveland** (WHA) by **Philadelphia** (WHA) for future considerations, Spetember, 1972. Traded to **San Diego** (WHA) by **Minnesota** (WHA) with Gerry Pinder for Ray Adduono, Bob Wall and cash, September, 1976. Signed as a free agent by **Edmonton** (WHA) after **San Diego** (WHA) franchise folded, August, 1977. Claimed by **Minnesota** in **Cleveland-Minnesota** Dispersal Draft, June 15, 1978. Reclaimed by **Minnesota** from **Edmonton** prior to Expansion Draft, June 9, 1979. Signed as a free agent by **Hartford**, October, 1981.

• SHOEBOTTOM, BRUCE

Bruce Shoebottom D – L. 6′2″, 200 lbs. b: Windsor, Ont., 8/20/1965. Los Angeles' 1st choice, 47th overall, in 1983 Entry Draft.

1981-82	Peterborough Petes	OHA	51	0	4	4	....	....	....	67	....	....	....	....	....	....	....	....	....	....	....	....	....	....	....	....	....	....
1982-83	Peterborough Petes	OHL	34	2	10	12	....	....	....	106	....	....	....	....	....	....	....	....	....	....	....	....	....	....	....	....	....	....
1983-84	Peterborough Petes	OHL	16	0	5	5	....	....	....	73	....	....	....	....	....	....	....	....	....	....	....	....	....	....	....	....	....	....
1984-85	Peterborough Petes	OHL	60	2	15	17	....	....	....	143	....	....	....	....	....	....	....	....	....	....	17	0	4	4	26	....	....	....
1985-86	New Haven Nighthawks	AHL	6	2	0	2	....	....	....	12	....	....	....	....	....	....	....	....	....	....	....	....	....	....	....	....	....	....
	Binghamton Whalers	AHL	62	7	5	12	....	....	....	249	....	....	....	....	....	....	....	....	....	....	....	....	....	....	....	....	....	....
1986-87	Fort Wayne Komets	IHL	75	2	10	12	....	....	....	309	....	....	....	....	....	....	....	....	....	....	10	0	0	0	31	....	....	....
1987-88	**Boston Bruins**	**NHL**	**3**	**0**	**1**	**1**	**0**	**1**	**1**	**0**	**0**	**0**	**0**	**2**	**0.0**	**1**	**0**	**4**	**0**	**–3**	**4**	**1**	**0**	**1**	**42**	**0**	**0**	**1**
	Maine Mariners	AHL	70	2	12	14	....	....	....	338	....	....	....	....	....	....	....	....	....	....	....	....	....	....	....	....	....	....
1988-89	**Boston Bruins**	**NHL**	**29**	**1**	**3**	**4**	**1**	**2**	**3**	**44**	**0**	**0**	**0**	**19**	**5.3**	**13**	**0**	**8**	**0**	**+5**	**10**	**0**	**2**	**2**	**35**	**0**	**0**	**0**
	Maine Mariners	AHL	44	0	8	8	....	....	....	265	....	....	....	....	....	....	....	....	....	....	....	....	....	....	....	....	....	....
1989-90	**Boston Bruins**	**NHL**	**2**	**0**	**0**	**0**	**0**	**0**	**0**	**4**	**0**	**0**	**0**	**3**	**0.0**	**0**	**0**	**0**	**0**	**0**	....	....	....	....	....	....	....	....
	Maine Mariners	AHL	66	3	11	14	....	....	....	228	....	....	....	....	....	....	....	....	....	....	....	....	....	....	....	....	....	....
1990-91	**Boston Bruins**	**NHL**	**1**	**0**	**0**	**0**	**0**	**0**	**0**	**5**	**0**	**0**	**0**	**0**	**0.0**	**0**	**0**	**1**	**0**	**–1**	....	....	....	....	....	....	....	....
	Maine Mariners	AHL	71	2	8	10	....	....	....	238	....	....	....	....	....	....	....	....	....	....	1	0	0	0	14	....	....	....
1991-92	Peoria Rivermen	IHL	79	4	12	16	....	....	....	234	....	....	....	....	....	....	....	....	....	....	10	0	0	0	33	....	....	....
1992-93	Rochester Americans	AHL	65	7	5	12	....	....	....	253	....	....	....	....	....	....	....	....	....	....	14	0	0	0	19	....	....	....
1993-94	Oklahoma City Blazers	CHL	43	4	11	15	....	....	....	236	....	....	....	....	....	....	....	....	....	....	1	0	0	0	14	....	....	....
1994-95			DID NOT PLAY																									
1995-96	San Diego Gulls	WCHL	DID NOT PLAY – COACHING																									
1996-97	San Diego Gulls	WCHL	38	6	6	12	....	....	....	288	....	....	....	....	....	....	....	....	....	....	2	0	0	0	24	....	....	....
1997-98	Austin Ice-Bats	WPHL	9	0	4	4	....	....	....	37	....	....	....	....	....	....	....	....	....	....	4	0	0	0	14	....	....	....
	NHL Totals		**35**	**1**	**4**	**5**	**1**	**3**	**4**	**53**	**0**	**0**	**0**	**24**	**4.2**	**14**	**0**	**13**	**0**		**14**	**1**	**2**	**3**	**77**	**0**	**0**	**1**

Traded to **Washington** by **LA Kings** for Bryan Erickson, October 31, 1985. Signed as a free agent by **Boston**, July 20, 1987.

• SHORT, STEVE

Steve Short LW – L. 6′2″, 210 lbs. b: Roseville, MN, 4/6/1954. Philadelphia's 7th choice, 142nd overall, in 1974 Amateur Draft.

1973-74	Minnesota Jr. Stars	MWJHL	54	28	47	75	....	....	....	103	....	....	....	....	....	....	....	....	....	....	....	....	....	....	....	....	....	....
	United States	WJC-A	5	1	2	3	....	....	....	14	....	....	....	....	....	....	....	....	....	....	....	....	....	....	....	....	....	....
1974-75	Philadelphia Firebirds	NAHL	12	6	1	7	....	....	....	25	....	....	....	....	....	....	....	....	....	....	....	....	....	....	....	....	....	....
	Richmond Robins	AHL	43	5	11	16	....	....	....	106	....	....	....	....	....	....	....	....	....	....	5	0	0	0	12	....	....	....
1975-76	Richmond Robins	AHL	74	5	14	19	....	....	....	*302	....	....	....	....	....	....	....	....	....	....	8	1	0	1	15	....	....	....
1976-77	Springfield Indians	AHL	24	0	3	3	....	....	....	72	....	....	....	....	....	....	....	....	....	....	....	....	....	....	....	....	....	....
	Fort Worth Texans	CHL	48	5	9	14	....	....	....	135	....	....	....	....	....	....	....	....	....	....	6	2	1	3	*33	....	....	....
1977-78	**Los Angeles Kings**	**NHL**	**5**	**0**	**0**	**0**	**0**	**0**	**0**	**2**	**0**	**0**	**0**	**1**	**0.0**	**1**	**0**	**6**	**0**	**–5**	....	....	....	....	....	....	....	....
	Springfield Indians	AHL	67	2	20	22	....	....	....	236	....	....	....	....	....	....	....	....	....	....	4	0	0	0	0	....	....	....
1978-79	**Detroit Red Wings**	**NHL**	**1**	**0**	**0**	**0**	**0**	**0**	**0**	**0**	**0**	**0**	**0**	**1**	**0.0**	**0**	**0**	**0**	**0**	**0**	....	....	....	....	....	....	....	....
	Kansas City Red Wings	CHL	51	3	11	14	....	....	....	*216	....	....	....	....	....	....	....	....	....	....	4	0	2	2	26	....	....	....

			REGULAR SEASON																		PLAYOFFS							
Season	Club	League	GP	G	A	Pts	AG	AA	APts	PIM	PP	SH	GW	S	%	TGF	PGF	TGA	PGA	+/–	GP	G	A	Pts	PIM	PP	SH	GW
1979-80	Adirondack Red Wings	AHL	66	1	8	9	....	....	....	167	....	....	....	....	....	....	....	....	....	....	3	0	0	0	6	....	....	....
1980-81	Adirondack Red Wings	AHL	63	2	7	9	....	....	....	75	....	....	....	....	....	....	....	....	....	....	16	0	1	1	20	....	....	....
1981-82	Kalamazoo Wings	IHL	1	0	0	0	....	....	....	2	....	....	....	....	....	....	....	....	....	....	....	....	....	....	....	....	....	....
	NHL Totals		**6**	**0**	**0**	**0**	**0**	**0**	**0**	**2**	**0**	**0**	**0**	**2**	**0.0**	**1**	**0**	**6**	**0**		....	....	....	....	....	....	....	....

Traded to **LA Kings** by **Philadelphia** for Paul Evans, June 17, 1977. Traded to **Detroit** by **LA Kings** for Steve Carlson, December 6, 1978.

• SHUCHUK, GARY

Gary Shuchuk RW – R. 5′11″, 190 lbs. b: Edmonton, Alta., 2/17/1967. Detroit's 1st choice, 22nd overall, in 1988 Supplemental Draft.

Season	Club	League	GP	G	A	Pts	AG	AA	APts	PIM	PP	SH	GW	S	%	TGF	PGF	TGA	PGA	+/–	GP	G	A	Pts	PIM	PP	SH	GW
1986-87	University of Wisconsin	WCHA	42	19	11	30	....	....	....	72	....	....	....	....	....	....	....	....	....	....	....	....	....	....	....	....	....	....
1987-88	University of Wisconsin	WCHA	44	7	22	29	....	....	....	70	....	....	....	....	....	....	....	....	....	....	....	....	....	....	....	....	....	....
1988-89	University of Wisconsin	WCHA	46	18	19	37	....	....	....	102	....	....	....	....	....	....	....	....	....	....	....	....	....	....	....	....	....	....
1989-90	University of Wisconsin	WCHA	45	*41	39	*80	....	....	....	70	....	....	....	....	....	....	....	....	....	....	....	....	....	....	....	....	....	....
1990-91	**Detroit Red Wings**	**NHL**	**6**	**1**	**2**	**3**	**1**	**2**	**3**	**6**	**0**	**0**	**0**	**8**	**12.5**	**4**	**0**	**4**	**1**	**+1**	**3**	**0**	**0**	**0**	**0**	**0**	**0**	**0**
	Adirondack Red Wings	AHL	59	23	24	47	....	....	....	32	....	....	....	....	....	....	....	....	....	....	....	....	....	....	....	....	....	....
1991-92	Adirondack Red Wings	AHL	79	32	48	80	....	....	....	48	....	....	....	....	....	....	....	....	....	....	19	4	9	13	18	....	....	....
1992-93	Adirondack Red Wings	AHL	47	24	53	77	....	....	....	66	....	....	....	....	....	....	....	....	....	....	....	....	....	....	....	....	....	....
	Los Angeles Kings	**NHL**	**25**	**2**	**4**	**6**	**2**	**3**	**5**	**16**	**0**	**0**	**0**	**24**	**8.3**	**11**	**1**	**11**	**1**	**0**	**17**	**2**	**2**	**4**	**12**	**0**	**0**	**1**
1993-94	**Los Angeles Kings**	**NHL**	**56**	**3**	**4**	**7**	**3**	**3**	**6**	**30**	**0**	**0**	**1**	**55**	**5.5**	**12**	**0**	**33**	**13**	**–8**	....	....	....	....	....	....	....	....
1994-95	**Los Angeles Kings**	**NHL**	**22**	**3**	**6**	**9**	**5**	**9**	**14**	**6**	**0**	**0**	**0**	**16**	**18.8**	**11**	**0**	**16**	**3**	**–2**	....	....	....	....	....	....	....	....
	Phoenix Roadrunners	IHL	13	8	7	15	....	....	....	12	....	....	....	....	....	....	....	....	....	....	....	....	....	....	....	....	....	....
1995-96	**Los Angeles Kings**	**NHL**	**33**	**4**	**10**	**14**	**4**	**8**	**12**	**12**	**0**	**0**	**0**	**22**	**18.2**	**23**	**1**	**20**	**1**	**+3**	....	....	....	....	....	....	....	....
	Phoenix Roadrunners	IHL	33	8	21	29	....	....	....	76	....	....	....	....	....	....	....	....	....	....	4	1	0	1	4	....	....	....
1996-97	Houston Aeros	IHL	55	18	23	41	....	....	....	48	....	....	....	....	....	....	....	....	....	....	13	5	2	7	18	....	....	....
1997-98	Herisau	Switz.	40	15	33	48	....	....	....	60	....	....	....	....	....	....	....	....	....	....	....	....	....	....	....	....	....	....
	NHL Totals		**142**	**13**	**26**	**39**	**15**	**25**	**40**	**70**	**0**	**0**	**1**	**125**	**10.4**	**61**	**2**	**84**	**19**		**20**	**2**	**2**	**4**	**12**	**0**	**0**	**1**

WCHA First All-Star Team (1990) • NCAA West First All-American Team (1990)

Traded to **LA Kings** by **Detroit** with Jimmy Carson and Marc Potvin for Paul Coffey, Sylvain Couturier and Jim Hiller, January 29, 1993.

• SHUDRA, RON

Ron Shudra D – L. 6′2″, 192 lbs. b: Winnipeg, Man., 11/28/1967. Edmonton's 3rd choice, 63rd overall, in 1986 Entry Draft.

Season	Club	League	GP	G	A	Pts	AG	AA	APts	PIM	PP	SH	GW	S	%	TGF	PGF	TGA	PGA	+/–	GP	G	A	Pts	PIM	PP	SH	GW
1984-85	Red Deer Rustlers	AJHL	57	14	57	71	....	....	....	70	....	....	....	....	....	....	....	....	....	....	....	....	....	....	....	....	....	....
1985-86	Kamloops Blazers	WHL	72	10	40	50	....	....	....	81	....	....	....	....	....	....	....	....	....	....	16	1	11	12	11	....	....	....
1986-87	Kamloops Blazers	WHL	71	49	70	119	....	....	....	68	....	....	....	....	....	....	....	....	....	....	11	7	3	10	10	....	....	....
1987-88	**Edmonton Oilers**	**NHL**	**10**	**0**	**5**	**5**	**0**	**4**	**4**	**6**	**0**	**0**	**0**	**8**	**0.0**	**8**	**0**	**3**	**0**	**+5**	....	....	....	....	....	....	....	....
	Nova Scotia Oilers	AHL	49	7	15	22	....	....	....	21	....	....	....	....	....	....	....	....	....	....	....	....	....	....	....	....	....	....
1988-89	Cape Breton Oilers	AHL	5	0	0	0	....	....	....	0	....	....	....	....	....	....	....	....	....	....	....	....	....	....	....	....	....	....
	Denver Rangers	IHL	64	11	14	25	....	....	....	44	....	....	....	....	....	....	....	....	....	....	2	0	0	0	0	....	....	....
1989-90	Fort Wayne Komets	IHL	67	11	16	27	....	....	....	48	....	....	....	....	....	....	....	....	....	....	2	0	0	0	0	....	....	....
1990-91	Solihull Barons	Britain	36	24	53	77	....	....	....	70	....	....	....	....	....	....	....	....	....	....	6	7	9	16	10	....	....	....
1991-92	Sheffield Steelers	Britain	32	78	70	148	....	....	....	42	....	....	....	....	....	....	....	....	....	....	6	15	14	29	4	....	....	....
1992-93	Sheffield Steelers	Britain	26	32	46	78	....	....	....	36	....	....	....	....	....	....	....	....	....	....	....	....	....	....	....	....	....	....
1993-94	Sheffield Steelers	Britain	34	31	48	79	....	....	....	69	....	....	....	....	....	....	....	....	....	....	8	8	16	24	6	....	....	....
1994-95	Sheffield Steelers	Britain	43	25	38	63	....	....	....	83	....	....	....	....	....	....	....	....	....	....	8	5	8	13	2	....	....	....
1995-96	Sheffield Steelers	Britain	36	23	31	54	....	....	....	56	....	....	....	....	....	....	....	....	....	....	8	2	4	6	2	....	....	....
1996-97	Sheffield Steelers	Britain	41	13	16	29	....	....	....	12	....	....	....	....	....	....	....	....	....	....	8	3	1	4	4	....	....	....
1997-98	Sheffield Steelers	Britain	38	8	16	24	....	....	....	18	....	....	....	....	....	....	....	....	....	....	9	1	2	3	0	....	....	....
	NHL Totals		**10**	**0**	**5**	**5**	**0**	**4**	**4**	**6**	**0**	**0**	**0**	**8**	**0.0**	**8**	**0**	**3**	**0**		....	....	....	....	....	....	....	....

WHL West Second All-Star Team (1986, 1987) • Memorial Cup All-Star Team (1986)

Traded to **NY Rangers** by **Edmonton** for Jeff Crossman, October 27, 1988.

• SHUTT, STEVE

Steve Shutt LW – L. 5′11″, 185 lbs. b: Toronto, Ont., 7/1/1952. Montreal's 1st choice, 4th overall, in 1972 Amateur Draft. **HHOF**

Season	Club	League	GP	G	A	Pts	AG	AA	APts	PIM	PP	SH	GW	S	%	TGF	PGF	TGA	PGA	+/–	GP	G	A	Pts	PIM	PP	SH	GW
1968-69	North York Rangers	MTHL	17	10	17	27	....	....	....	....	....	....	....	....	....	....	....	....	....	....	....	....	....	....	....	....	....	....
	Toronto Marlboros	OHA	....	....	....	....	....	....	....	....	....	....	....	....	....	....	....	....	....	....	5	1	3	4	2	....	....	....
1969-70	Toronto Marlboros	OHA	49	11	14	25	....	....	....	93	....	....	....	....	....	....	....	....	....	....	....	....	....	....	....	....	....	....
1970-71	Toronto Marlboros	OHA	62	70	53	123	....	....	....	85	....	....	....	....	....	....	....	....	....	....	....	....	....	....	....	....	....	....
1971-72	Toronto Marlboros	OHA	58	*63	49	112	....	....	....	60	....	....	....	....	....	....	....	....	....	....	....	....	....	....	....	....	....	....
1972-73	**Montreal Canadiens**	**NHL**	**50**	**8**	**8**	**16**	**8**	**7**	**15**	**24**	**1**	**0**	**2**	**55**	**14.5**	**24**	**2**	**17**	**0**	**+5**	**1**	**0**	**0**	**0**	**0**	**0**	**0**	**0**
	Nova Scotia Voyageurs	AHL	6	4	1	5	....	....	....	2	....	....	....	....	....	....	....	....	....	....	....	....	....	....	....	....	....	....
1973-74	**Montreal Canadiens**	**NHL**	**70**	**15**	**20**	**35**	**15**	**17**	**32**	**17**	**3**	**0**	**1**	**131**	**11.5**	**52**	**11**	**22**	**0**	**+19**	**6**	**5**	**3**	**8**	**9**	**1**	**0**	**0**
1974-75	**Montreal Canadiens**	**NHL**	**77**	**30**	**35**	**65**	**28**	**28**	**56**	**40**	**3**	**0**	**5**	**165**	**18.2**	**106**	**17**	**49**	**0**	**+40**	**9**	**1**	**6**	**7**	**4**	**0**	**0**	**0**
1975-76	**Montreal Canadiens**	**NHL**	**80**	**45**	**34**	**79**	**42**	**27**	**69**	**47**	**7**	**0**	**7**	**223**	**20.2**	**128**	**22**	**36**	**3**	**+73**	**13**	**7**	**8**	**15**	**2**	**3**	**0**	**0**
1976-77	Canada	C Cup	6	1	2	3	....	....	....	8	....	....	....	....	....	....	....	....	....	....	....	....	....	....	....	....	....	....
	Montreal Canadiens	**NHL**	**80**	***60**	**45**	**105**	**58**	**37**	**95**	**28**	**8**	**0**	**9**	**294**	**20.4**	**159**	**32**	**39**	**0**	**+88**	**14**	**8**	**10**	**18**	**2**	**2**	**0**	**3**
1977-78	**Montreal Canadiens**	**NHL**	**80**	**49**	**37**	**86**	**48**	**30**	**78**	**24**	**16**	**0**	**7**	**243**	**20.2**	**145**	**42**	**47**	**0**	**+56**	**15**	**9**	**8**	**17**	**20**	**3**	**0**	**0**
1978-79	**Montreal Canadiens**	**NHL**	**72**	**37**	**40**	**77**	**34**	**31**	**65**	**31**	**10**	**0**	**6**	**192**	**19.3**	**109**	**27**	**45**	**0**	**+37**	**11**	**4**	**7**	**11**	**6**	**1**	**0**	**0**
	NHL All-Stars	Chal Cup	2	0	1	1	....	....	....	0	....	....	....	....	....	....	....	....	....	....	....	....	....	....	....	....	....	....
1979-80	**Montreal Canadiens**	**NHL**	**77**	**47**	**42**	**89**	**43**	**32**	**75**	**34**	**17**	**0**	**4**	**224**	**21.0**	**149**	**42**	**62**	**0**	**+45**	**10**	**6**	**3**	**9**	**6**	**2**	**0**	**2**
1980-81	**Montreal Canadiens**	**NHL**	**77**	**35**	**38**	**73**	**29**	**27**	**56**	**51**	**7**	**0**	**3**	**232**	**15.1**	**115**	**35**	**50**	**0**	**+30**	**3**	**2**	**1**	**3**	**4**	**0**	**0**	**0**
1981-82	**Montreal Canadiens**	**NHL**	**57**	**31**	**24**	**55**	**25**	**16**	**41**	**40**	**5**	**0**	**3**	**154**	**20.1**	**77**	**16**	**37**	**0**	**+24**	....	....	....	....	....	....	....	....
1982-83	**Montreal Canadiens**	**NHL**	**78**	**35**	**22**	**57**	**29**	**15**	**44**	**26**	**8**	**0**	**0**	**202**	**17.3**	**85**	**28**	**49**	**0**	**+8**	**3**	**1**	**0**	**1**	**0**	**0**	**0**	**0**
1983-84	**Montreal Canadiens**	**NHL**	**63**	**14**	**23**	**37**	**11**	**16**	**27**	**29**	**4**	**0**	**2**	**146**	**9.6**	**50**	**16**	**52**	**0**	**–18**	**11**	**7**	**2**	**9**	**8**	**2**	**0**	**0**
1984-85	**Montreal Canadiens**	**NHL**	**10**	**2**	**0**	**2**	**2**	**0**	**2**	**9**	**1**	**0**	**0**	**17**	**11.8**	**7**	**3**	**2**	**0**	**+2**	....	....	....	....	....	....	....	....
	Los Angeles Kings	**NHL**	**59**	**16**	**25**	**41**	**13**	**17**	**30**	**10**	**5**	**0**	**1**	**127**	**12.6**	**58**	**18**	**56**	**0**	**–16**	**3**	**0**	**0**	**0**	**4**	**0**	**0**	**0**
	NHL Totals		**930**	**424**	**393**	**817**	**385**	**300**	**685**	**410**	**95**	**0**	**50**	**2405**	**17.6**	**1264**	**311**	**563**	**3**		**99**	**50**	**48**	**98**	**65**	**14**	**0**	**5**

OHA Second All-Star Team (1971) • OHA First All-Star Team (1972) • NHL First All-Star Team (1977) • NHL Second All-Star Team (1978, 1980)

Played in NHL All-Star Game (1976, 1978, 1981)

Traded to **LA Kings** by **Montreal** for future considerations, November 19, 1984. Claimed on waivers by **Montreal** from **LA Kings**, June 18, 1985.

• SILK, DAVE

Dave Silk RW – R. 5′11″, 190 lbs. b: Scituate, MA, 1/1/1958. NY Rangers' 4th choice, 59th overall, in 1978 Amateur Draft.

Season	Club	League	GP	G	A	Pts	AG	AA	APts	PIM	PP	SH	GW	S	%	TGF	PGF	TGA	PGA	+/–	GP	G	A	Pts	PIM	PP	SH	GW
1976-77	Boston University	ECAC	34	35	30	65	....	....	....	50	....	....	....	....	....	....	....	....	....	....	....	....	....	....	....	....	....	....
1977-78	Boston University	ECAC	28	27	31	58	....	....	....	57	....	....	....	....	....	....	....	....	....	....	....	....	....	....	....	....	....	....
1978-79	Boston University	ECAC	23	8	12	20	....	....	....	20	....	....	....	....	....	....	....	....	....	....	....	....	....	....	....	....	....	....
1979-80	United States	Nat-Team	56	12	36	48	....	....	....	32	....	....	....	....	....	....	....	....	....	....	....	....	....	....	....	....	....	....
	United States	Olympics	7	2	3	5	....	....	....	0	....	....	....	....	....	....	....	....	....	....	....	....	....	....	....	....	....	....
	New York Rangers	**NHL**	**2**	**0**	**0**	**0**	**0**	**0**	**0**	**0**	**0**	**0**	**0**	**4**	**0.0**	**1**	**0**	**0**	**0**	**+1**	....	....	....	....	....	....	....	....
	New Haven Nighthawks	AHL	11	1	9	10	....	....	....	0	....	....	....	....	....	....	....	....	....	....	9	1	2	3	12	....	....	....
1980-81	**New York Rangers**	**NHL**	**59**	**14**	**12**	**26**	**12**	**8**	**20**	**58**	**2**	**0**	**1**	**124**	**11.3**	**38**	**9**	**58**	**5**	**–24**	....	....	....	....	....	....	....	....
	New Haven Nighthawks	AHL	12	0	4	4	....	....	....	34	....	....	....	....	....	....	....	....	....	....	3	0	0	0	0	....	....	....
1981-82	**New York Rangers**	**NHL**	**64**	**15**	**20**	**35**	**12**	**13**	**25**	**39**	**1**	**0**	**0**	**111**	**13.5**	**57**	**12**	**29**	**1**	**+17**	**9**	**2**	**4**	**6**	**4**	**0**	**0**	**1**
1982-83	**New York Rangers**	**NHL**	**16**	**1**	**1**	**2**	**1**	**1**	**2**	**15**	**0**	**0**	**0**	**10**	**10.0**	**3**	**1**	**5**	**0**	**–3**	....	....	....	....	....	....	....	....
	Tulsa Oilers	CHL	40	20	29	57	....	....	....	67	....	....	....	....	....	....	....	....	....	....	....	....	....	....	....	....	....	....
	Binghamton Whalers	AHL	9	1	2	3	....	....	....	29	....	....	....	....	....	....	....	....	....	....	....	....	....	....	....	....	....	....
1983-84	**Boston Bruins**	**NHL**	**35**	**13**	**17**	**30**	**10**	**12**	**22**	**64**	**5**	**0**	**1**	**62**	**21.0**	**42**	**15**	**16**	**0**	**+11**	**3**	**0**	**0**	**0**	**7**	**0**	**0**	**0**
	Hershey Bears	AHL	15	11	10	21	....	....	....	22	....	....	....	....	....	....	....	....	....	....	....	....	....	....	....	....	....	....
1984-85	**Boston Bruins**	**NHL**	**29**	**7**	**5**	**12**	**6**	**3**	**9**	**22**	**0**	**0**	**0**	**40**	**17.5**	**20**	**7**	**11**	**1**	**+3**	....	....	....	....	....	....	....	....
	Detroit Red Wings	**NHL**	**12**	**2**	**0**	**2**	**2**	**0**	**2**	**10**	**0**	**0**	**0**	**7**	**28.6**	**2**	**1**	**8**	**1**	**–6**	....	....	....	....	....	....	....	....
1985-86	**Winnipeg Jets**	**NHL**	**32**	**2**	**4**	**6**	**2**	**3**	**5**	**63**	**0**	**0**	**1**	**30**	**6.7**	**10**	**0**	**19**	**13**	**–6**	**1**	**0**	**0**	**0**	**2**	**0**	**0**	**0**
	Sherbrooke Canadiens	AHL	18	5	14	19	....	....	....	18	....	....	....	....	....	....	....	....	....	....	....	....	....	....	....	....	....	....
1986-87	Mannheimer ERC	Germany	36	15	31	46	....	....	....	68	....	....	....	....	....	....	....	....	....	....	....	....	....	....	....	....	....	....

			REGULAR SEASON																		PLAYOFFS							
Season	Club	League	GP	G	A	Pts	AG	AA	APts	PIM	PP	SH	GW	S	%	TGF	PGF	TGA	PGA	+/–	GP	G	A	Pts	PIM	PP	SH	GW
1987-88	Mannheimer ERC	Germany	36	25	30	55	....	....	....	71	....	....	....	....	....	....	....	....	....	....	9	4	7	11	21	....	....	....
1988-89	SC Preussen Berlin	Germany	35	25	34	59	....	....	....	49	....	....	....	....	....	....	....	....	....	....	5	4	5	9	4	....	....	....
1989-90	SC Preussen Berlin	Germany	40	28	23	51	....	....	....	59	....	....	....	....	....	....	....	....	....	....	10	5	4	9	4	....	....	....
	NHL Totals		**249**	**54**	**59**	**113**	**45**	**40**	**85**	**271**	**8**	**0**	**3**	**388**	**13.9**	**173**	**45**	**146**	**21**		**13**	**2**	**4**	**6**	**13**	**0**	**0**	**1**

NCAA Championship All-Tournament Team (1977, 1978) • ECAC Second All-Star Team (1978)

Traded to **Boston** by **NY Rangers** for Dave Barr, October 5, 1983. Claimed on waivers by **Detroit** from **Boston**, December 21, 1984. Signed as a free agent by **Winnipeg**, September 30, 1985.

• SILLINGER, MIKE

Mike Sillinger C – R. 5'10", 190 lbs. b: Regina, Sask., 6/29/1971. Detroit's 1st choice, 11th overall, in 1989 Entry Draft.

Season	Club	League	GP	G	A	Pts	AG	AA	APts	PIM	PP	SH	GW	S	%	TGF	PGF	TGA	PGA	+/–	GP	G	A	Pts	PIM	PP	SH	GW
1987-88	Regina Pats	WHL	67	18	25	43	....	....	....	17	....	....	....	....	....	....	....	....	....	....	4	2	2	4	0	....	....	....
1988-89	Regina Pats	WHL	72	53	78	131	....	....	....	52	....	....	....	....	....	....	....	....	....	....	....	....	....	....	....	....	....	....
1989-90	Regina Pats	WHL	70	57	72	129	....	....	....	41	....	....	....	....	....	....	....	....	....	....	11	12	10	22	2	....	....	....
	Adirondack Red Wings	AHL	....	....	....	....	....	....	....	....	....	....	....	....	....	....	....	....	....	....	1	0	0	0	0	....	....	....
1990-91	Regina Pats	WHL	57	50	66	116	....	....	....	42	....	....	....	....	....	....	....	....	....	....	8	6	9	15	4	....	....	....
	Canada	WJC-A	7	4	2	6	....	....	....	2	....	....	....	....	....	....	....	....	....	....	....	....	....	....	....	....	....	....
	Detroit Red Wings	**NHL**	**3**	**0**	**1**	**1**	**0**	**1**	**1**	**0**	**0**	**0**	**0**	**6**	**0.0**	**1**	**0**	**3**	**0**	**–2**	**3**	**0**	**1**	**1**	**0**	**0**	**0**	**0**
1991-92	Adirondack Red Wings	AHL	64	25	41	66	....	....	....	26	....	....	....	....	....	....	....	....	....	....	15	9	*19	*28	12	....	....	....
	Detroit Red Wings	**NHL**	....	....	....	....	....	....	....	....	....	....	....	....	....	....	....	....	....	....	**8**	**2**	**2**	**4**	**2**	....	....	....
1992-93	**Detroit Red Wings**	**NHL**	**51**	**4**	**17**	**21**	**3**	**12**	**15**	**16**	**0**	**0**	**0**	**47**	**8.5**	**29**	**0**	**50**	**21**	**0**	....	....	....	....	....	....	....	....
	Adirondack Red Wings	AHL	15	10	20	30	....	....	....	31	....	....	....	....	....	....	....	....	....	....	11	5	13	18	10	....	....	....
1993-94	**Detroit Red Wings**	**NHL**	**62**	**8**	**21**	**29**	**7**	**16**	**23**	**10**	**0**	**1**	**1**	**91**	**8.8**	**41**	**7**	**45**	**13**	**+2**	....	....	....	....	....	....	....	....
1994-95	Wien	Austria	13	13	14	27	....	....	....	10	....	....	....	....	....	....	....	....	....	....	....	....	....	....	....	....	....	....
	Detroit Red Wings	**NHL**	**13**	**2**	**6**	**8**	**4**	**9**	**13**	**2**	**0**	**0**	**0**	**11**	**18.2**	**9**	**2**	**4**	**0**	**+3**	....	....	....	....	....	....	....	....
	Anaheim Mighty Ducks	**NHL**	**15**	**2**	**5**	**7**	**4**	**7**	**11**	**6**	**2**	**0**	**0**	**28**	**7.1**	**16**	**8**	**8**	**1**	**+1**	....	....	....	....	....	....	....	....
1995-96	**Anaheim Mighty Ducks**	**NHL**	**62**	**13**	**21**	**34**	**13**	**17**	**30**	**32**	**7**	**0**	**2**	**143**	**9.1**	**52**	**29**	**48**	**5**	**–20**	....	....	....	....	....	....	....	....
	Vancouver Canucks	**NHL**	**12**	**1**	**3**	**4**	**1**	**2**	**3**	**6**	**0**	**1**	**0**	**16**	**6.3**	**5**	**0**	**5**	**2**	**+2**	**6**	**0**	**0**	**0**	**2**	**0**	**0**	**0**
1996-97	**Vancouver Canucks**	**NHL**	**78**	**17**	**20**	**37**	**18**	**18**	**36**	**25**	**3**	**3**	**2**	**112**	**15.2**	**53**	**5**	**80**	**29**	**–3**	....	....	....	....	....	....	....	....
1997-98	**Vancouver Canucks**	**NHL**	**48**	**10**	**9**	**19**	**12**	**9**	**21**	**34**	**1**	**2**	**1**	**56**	**17.9**	**25**	**3**	**41**	**5**	**–14**	....	....	....	....	....	....	....	....
	Philadelphia Flyers	**NHL**	**27**	**11**	**11**	**22**	**13**	**11**	**24**	**16**	**1**	**2**	**0**	**40**	**27.5**	**28**	**9**	**21**	**5**	**+3**	**3**	**1**	**0**	**1**	**0**	**0**	**0**	**0**
	NHL Totals		**371**	**68**	**114**	**182**	**75**	**102**	**177**	**147**	**14**	**9**	**6**	**550**	**12.4**	**259**	**63**	**305**	**81**		**20**	**3**	**3**	**6**	**4**	**0**	**0**	**0**

WHL East Second All-Star Team (1990) • WHL East First All-Star Team (1991)

Traded to **Anaheim** by **Detroit** with Jason York for Stu Grimson, Mark Ferner and Anaheim's 6th round choice (Magnus Nilsson) in 1996 Entry Draft, April 4, 1995. Traded to **Vancouver** by **Anaheim** for Roman Oksiuta, March 15, 1996. Traded to **Philadelphia** by **Vancouver** for Philadelphia's 5th round choice (traded back to Philadelphia — Philadelphia selected Garrett Prosofsky) in 1998 Entry Draft, February 5, 1998.

• SILTALA, MIKE

Mike Siltala RW – R. 5'9", 170 lbs. b: Toronto, Ont., 8/5/1963. Washington's 4th choice, 89th overall, in 1981 Entry Draft.

Season	Club	League	GP	G	A	Pts	AG	AA	APts	PIM	PP	SH	GW	S	%	TGF	PGF	TGA	PGA	+/–	GP	G	A	Pts	PIM	PP	SH	GW
1979-80	Sault Ste. Marie Greyhounds	Midget	57	78	83	161	....	....	....	....	....	....	....	....	....	....	....	....	....	....	....	....	....	....	....	....	....	....
1980-81	Kingston Canadians	OHA	63	18	22	40	....	....	....	23	....	....	....	....	....	....	....	....	....	....	14	5	6	11	20	....	....	....
1981-82	Kingston Canadians	OHL	59	38	49	87	....	....	....	70	....	....	....	....	....	....	....	....	....	....	4	2	3	5	9	....	....	....
	Washington Capitals	**NHL**	**3**	**1**	**0**	**1**	**1**	**0**	**1**	**2**	**0**	**0**	**0**	**2**	**50.0**	**2**	**0**	**3**	**0**	**–1**	....	....	....	....	....	....	....	....
1982-83	Kingston Canadians	OHL	50	53	61	114	....	....	....	45	....	....	....	....	....	....	....	....	....	....	....	....	....	....	....	....	....	....
	Hershey Bears	AHL	9	0	3	3	....	....	....	2	....	....	....	....	....	....	....	....	....	....	....	....	....	....	....	....	....	....
1983-84	Hershey Bears	AHL	50	15	17	32	....	....	....	29	....	....	....	....	....	....	....	....	....	....	....	....	....	....	....	....	....	....
1984-85	Binghamton Whalers	AHL	75	42	36	78	....	....	....	53	....	....	....	....	....	....	....	....	....	....	5	5	5	10	0	....	....	....
1985-86	Binghamton Whalers	AHL	50	25	22	47	....	....	....	36	....	....	....	....	....	....	....	....	....	....	2	3	0	3	0	....	....	....
1986-87	**New York Rangers**	**NHL**	**1**	**0**	**0**	**0**	**0**	**0**	**0**	**0**	**0**	**0**	**0**	**0**	**0.0**	**1**	**0**	**0**	**0**	**+1**	....	....	....	....	....	....	....	....
	New Haven Nighthawks	AHL	17	13	6	19	....	....	....	20	....	....	....	....	....	....	....	....	....	....	....	....	....	....	....	....	....	....
1987-88	**New York Rangers**	**NHL**	**3**	**0**	**0**	**0**	**0**	**0**	**0**	**0**	**0**	**0**	**0**	**3**	**0.0**	**1**	**0**	**1**	**0**	**0**	....	....	....	....	....	....	....	....
	New Haven Nighthawks	AHL	32	17	20	37	....	....	....	8	....	....	....	....	....	....	....	....	....	....	....	....	....	....	....	....	....	....
	Colorado Rangers	IHL	38	22	28	50	....	....	....	28	....	....	....	....	....	....	....	....	....	....	....	....	....	....	....	....	....	....
1988-89	Schwenninger ERC	Germany	26	15	20	35	....	....	....	22	....	....	....	....	....	....	....	....	....	....	3	1	0	1	2	....	....	....
	NHL Totals		**7**	**1**	**0**	**1**	**1**	**0**	**1**	**2**	**0**	**0**	**0**	**5**	**20.0**	**4**	**0**	**4**	**0**		....	....	....	....	....	....	....	....

OHL First All-Star Team (1983) • AHL Second All-Star Team (1985)

Signed as a free agent by **NY Rangers**, August 15, 1986. Traded to **LA Kings** by **NY Rangers** with Gord Walker for Joe Paterson, January 21, 1988.

• SILTANEN, RISTO

Risto "The Incredible Hulk" Siltanen D – R. 5'9", 158 lbs. b: Tampere, Finland, 10/31/1958. St. Louis' 13th choice, 173rd overall, in 1978 Amateur Draft.

Season	Club	League	GP	G	A	Pts	AG	AA	APts	PIM	PP	SH	GW	S	%	TGF	PGF	TGA	PGA	+/–	GP	G	A	Pts	PIM	PP	SH	GW
1976-77	Ilves Tampere	Finland	36	10	7	17	....	....	....	28	....	....	....	....	....	....	....	....	....	....	....	....	....	....	....	....	....	....
	Finland	WJC-A	7	4	2	6	....	....	....	8	....	....	....	....	....	....	....	....	....	....	....	....	....	....	....	....	....	....
	Finland	WEC-A	10	1	1	2	....	....	....	6	....	....	....	....	....	....	....	....	....	....	....	....	....	....	....	....	....	....
1977-78	Ilves Tampere	Finland	36	7	8	15	....	....	....	42	....	....	....	....	....	....	....	....	....	....	7	1	1	2	10	....	....	....
	Finland	WJC-A	4	0	3	3	....	....	....	4	....	....	....	....	....	....	....	....	....	....	....	....	....	....	....	....	....	....
	Finland	WEC-A	10	0	2	2	....	....	....	6	....	....	....	....	....	....	....	....	....	....	....	....	....	....	....	....	....	....
1978-79	Finland	Nat-Team	11	2	0	2	....	....	....	6	....	....	....	....	....	....	....	....	....	....	....	....	....	....	....	....	....	....
	Edmonton Oilers	WHA	20	3	4	7	....	....	....	4	....	....	....	....	....	....	....	....	....	....	11	0	9	9	4	....	....	....
1979-80	**Edmonton Oilers**	**NHL**	**64**	**6**	**29**	**35**	**5**	**22**	**27**	**26**	**1**	**0**	**0**	**116**	**5.2**	**95**	**34**	**70**	**0**	**–9**	**2**	**0**	**0**	**0**	**2**	**0**	**0**	**0**
1980-81	**Edmonton Oilers**	**NHL**	**79**	**17**	**36**	**53**	**14**	**25**	**39**	**54**	**7**	**1**	**3**	**209**	**8.1**	**143**	**60**	**107**	**29**	**+5**	**9**	**2**	**0**	**2**	**8**	**2**	**0**	**1**
1981-82	Finland	C Cup	5	1	1	2	....	....	....	6	....	....	....	....	....	....	....	....	....	....	....	....	....	....	....	....	....	....
	Edmonton Oilers	**NHL**	**63**	**15**	**48**	**63**	**12**	**32**	**44**	**26**	**6**	**0**	**1**	**143**	**10.5**	**126**	**52**	**71**	**10**	**+13**	**5**	**3**	**2**	**5**	**10**	**1**	**0**	**0**
1982-83	**Hartford Whalers**	**NHL**	**74**	**5**	**25**	**30**	**4**	**17**	**21**	**28**	**3**	**0**	**0**	**155**	**3.2**	**99**	**26**	**141**	**29**	**–39**	....	....	....	....	....	....	....	....
	Finland	WEC-A	6	0	1	1	....	....	....	8	....	....	....	....	....	....	....	....	....	....	....	....	....	....	....	....	....	....
1983-84	**Hartford Whalers**	**NHL**	**75**	**15**	**38**	**53**	**12**	**26**	**38**	**34**	**12**	**0**	**0**	**163**	**9.2**	**127**	**57**	**98**	**7**	**–21**	....	....	....	....	....	....	....	....
1984-85	**Hartford Whalers**	**NHL**	**76**	**12**	**33**	**45**	**10**	**22**	**32**	**30**	**8**	**0**	**2**	**174**	**6.9**	**126**	**61**	**93**	**4**	**–24**	....	....	....	....	....	....	....	....
1985-86	**Hartford Whalers**	**NHL**	**52**	**8**	**22**	**30**	**6**	**15**	**21**	**30**	**6**	**0**	**1**	**126**	**6.3**	**92**	**47**	**44**	**1**	**+2**	....	....	....	....	....	....	....	....
	Quebec Nordiques	**NHL**	**13**	**2**	**5**	**7**	**2**	**3**	**5**	**6**	**2**	**0**	**0**	**53**	**3.8**	**24**	**10**	**18**	**3**	**–1**	**3**	**0**	**1**	**1**	**2**	**0**	**0**	**0**
1986-87	**Quebec Nordiques**	**NHL**	**66**	**10**	**29**	**39**	**9**	**21**	**30**	**32**	**8**	**0**	**1**	**130**	**7.7**	**91**	**57**	**36**	**0**	**–2**	**13**	**1**	**9**	**10**	**8**	**1**	**0**	**0**
	Fredericton Express	AHL	6	2	4	6	....	....	....	6	....	....	....	....	....	....	....	....	....	....	....	....	....	....	....	....	....	....
1987-88	SC Bern	Switz.	38	13	13	26	....	....	....	....	....	....	....	....	....	....	....	....	....	....	....	....	....	....	....	....	....	....
1988-89	Ilves Tampere	Finland	43	19	20	39	....	....	....	32	....	....	....	....	....	....	....	....	....	....	5	2	1	3	6	....	....	....
1989-90	Ilves Tampere	Finland	44	16	17	33	....	....	....	40	....	....	....	....	....	....	....	....	....	....	9	2	6	8	4	....	....	....
1990-91	Ilves Tampere	Finland	37	11	13	24	....	....	....	32	....	....	....	....	....	....	....	....	....	....	....	....	....	....	....	....	....	....
1991-92	Ilves Tampere	Finland	44	4	9	13	....	....	....	22	....	....	....	....	....	....	....	....	....	....	....	....	....	....	....	....	....	....
1992-93	TuTo	Finland2	43	17	21	38	....	....	....	110	....	....	....	....	....	....	....	....	....	....	6	0	0	0	8	....	....	....
1993-94	TuTo	Finland2	46	12	23	35	....	....	....	44	....	....	....	....	....	....	....	....	....	....	5	1	1	2	2	....	....	....
1994-95	TPS Turku	Finland	44	10	14	24	....	....	....	52	....	....	....	....	....	....	....	....	....	....	....	....	....	....	....	....	....	....
1995-96	TPS Turku	Finland	45	6	6	12	....	....	....	44	....	....	....	....	....	....	....	....	....	....	....	....	....	....	....	....	....	....
	NHL Totals		**562**	**90**	**265**	**355**	**74**	**183**	**257**	**266**	**53**	**1**	**8**	**1269**	**7.1**	**923**	**404**	**678**	**83**		**32**	**6**	**12**	**18**	**30**	**4**	**0**	**1**
	Other Major League Totals		20	3	4	7	....	....	....	4	....	....	....	....	....	....	....	....	....	....	11	0	9	9	4	....	....	....

WJC-A All-Star Team (1977, 1978) • Finnish First All-Star Team (1977, 1989, 1990) • Finnish Rookie of the Year (1977)

Signed as a free agent by **Edmonton** (WHA), June, 1978. Reclaimed by **St. Louis** from **Edmonton** prior to Expansion Draft, June 9, 1979. Traded to **Edmonton** by **St. Louis** with Tom Roulston for Joe Micheletti, August 7, 1979. Traded to **Hartford** by **Edmonton** with rights to Brent Loney for Ken Linseman and Don Nachbaur, August 19, 1982. Traded to **Quebec** by **Hartford** for John Anderson, March 8, 1986.

• SIM, TREVOR

Trevor Sim RW – L. 6'2", 192 lbs. b: Calgary, Alta., 6/9/1970. Edmonton's 3rd choice, 53rd overall, in 1988 Entry Draft.

Season	Club	League	GP	G	A	Pts	AG	AA	APts	PIM	PP	SH	GW	S	%	TGF	PGF	TGA	PGA	+/–	GP	G	A	Pts	PIM	PP	SH	GW
1986-87	Seattle Thunderbirds	WHL	4	2	0	2	....	....	....	0	....	....	....	....	....	....	....	....	....	....	....	....	....	....	....	....	....	....
1987-88	Seattle Thunderbirds	WHL	67	17	18	35	....	....	....	87	....	....	....	....	....	....	....	....	....	....	....	....	....	....	....	....	....	....
1988-89	Regina Pats	WHL	21	4	8	12	....	....	....	48	....	....	....	....	....	....	....	....	....	....	....	....	....	....	....	....	....	....
	Swift Current Broncos	WHL	42	16	19	35	....	....	....	69	....	....	....	....	....	....	....	....	....	....	11	10	6	16	20	....	....	....
1989-90	Swift Current Broncos	WHL	6	3	2	5	....	....	....	21	....	....	....	....	....	....	....	....	....	....	....	....	....	....	....	....	....	....
	Kamloops Blazers	WHL	43	27	35	62	....	....	....	53	....	....	....	....	....	....	....	....	....	....	17	3	13	16	28	....	....	....
	Edmonton Oilers	**NHL**	**3**	**0**	**1**	**1**	**0**	**1**	**1**	**2**	**0**	**0**	**0**	**0**	**0.0**	**1**	**0**	**1**	**0**	**0**	....	....	....	....	....	....	....	....
1990-91	Cape Breton Oilers	AHL	62	20	9	29	....	....	....	39	....	....	....	....	....	....	....	....	....	....	2	0	0	0	0	....	....	....

			REGULAR SEASON																		PLAYOFFS							
Season	Club	League	GP	G	A	Pts	AG	AA	APts	PIM	PP	SH	GW	S	%	TGF	PGF	TGA	PGA	+/–	GP	G	A	Pts	PIM	PP	SH	GW
1991-92	Cape Breton Oilers	AHL	2	0	1	1				0																		
	Winston-Salem Thunderbirds	ECHL	53	25	29	54				110											5	7	2	9	4			
1992-93	Canada	Nat-Team	53	24	19	43				49																		
1993-94	Milwaukee Admirals	IHL	32	7	13	20				10											4	1	0	1	0			
1994-95	Syracuse Crunch	AHL	3	2	0	2				0																		
	Milwaukee Admirals	IHL	37	9	10	19				26											7	1	2	3	4			
1995-96	HC Asiago	Italy	7	1	4	5				12																		
	Milwaukee Admirals	IHL	7	0	0	0				0																		
	Raleigh IceCaps	ECHL	28	11	17	28				26											4	0	0	0	0			
1996-97	Orlando Solar Bears	IHL	58	9	21	30				32											2	0	1	1	0			
1997-98	New Orleans Brass	ECHL	13	4	11	15				23											4	0	3	3	2			
	Orlando Solar Bears	IHL	36	8	3	11				17																		
	NHL Totals		**3**	**0**	**1**	**1**	**0**	**1**	**1**	**2**	**0**	**0**	**0**	**0**	**0.0**	**1**	**0**	**1**	**0**									

• SIMARD, MARTIN

Martin Simard RW – R. 6'1", 215 lbs. b: Montreal, Que., 6/25/1966.

Season	Club	League	GP	G	A	Pts	AG	AA	APts	PIM	PP	SH	GW	S	%	TGF	PGF	TGA	PGA	+/–	GP	G	A	Pts	PIM	PP	SH	GW
1983-84	Quebec Remparts	QMJHL	59	6	10	16				26											4	0	0	0	0			
1984-85	Granby Bisons	QMJHL	58	22	31	53				78											8	3	7	10	21			
1985-86	Granby Bisons	QMJHL	54	32	28	60				129																		
	Hull Olympiques	QMJHL	14	8	8	16				55											14	8	19	27	19			
1986-87	Granby Bisons	QMJHL	41	30	47	77				105											8	3	7	10	21			
1987-88	Salt Lake Golden Eagles	IHL	82	8	23	31				281											19	6	3	9	100			
1988-89	Salt Lake Golden Eagles	IHL	71	13	15	28				221											14	4	0	4	45			
1989-90	Salt Lake Golden Eagles	IHL	59	22	23	45				151											11	5	8	13	12			
1990-91	**Calgary Flames**	**NHL**	**16**	**0**	**2**	**2**	**0**	**2**	**2**	**53**	**0**	**0**	**0**	**7**	**0.0**	**5**	**0**	**5**	**0**	**0**								
	Salt Lake Golden Eagles	IHL	54	24	25	49				113											4	3	0	3	20			
1991-92	**Calgary Flames**	**NHL**	**21**	**1**	**3**	**4**	**1**	**2**	**3**	**119**	**1**	**0**	**0**	**11**	**9.1**	**7**	**1**	**10**	**0**	**–4**								
	Salt Lake Golden Eagles	IHL	11	3	7	10				51																		
	Halifax Citadels	AHL	10	5	3	8				26																		
1992-93	**Tampa Bay Lightning**	**NHL**	**7**	**0**	**0**	**0**	**0**	**0**	**0**	**11**	**0**	**0**	**0**	**1**	**0.0**	**1**	**0**	**2**	**0**	**–1**								
	Atlanta Knights	IHL	19	5	5	10				77																		
	Halifax Citadels	AHL	13	3	4	7				17																		
1993-94	Cornwall Aces	AHL	57	10	10	20				152											7	3	1	4	7			
1994-95	Milwaukee Admirals	IHL	57	7	5	12				100											5	0	0	0	2			
1995-96	Providence Bruins	AHL	69	13	25	38				137											4	1	1	2	6			
1996-97	Providence Bruins	AHL	69	13	25	38				137											9	1	0	1	10			
1997-98	Springfield Falcons	AHL	35	9	5	14				89																		
	NHL Totals		**44**	**1**	**5**	**6**	**1**	**4**	**5**	**183**	**1**	**0**	**0**	**19**	**5.3**	**13**	**1**	**17**	**0**									

Signed as a free agent by **Calgary**, May 19, 1987. Traded to **Quebec** by **Calgary** for Greg Smyth, March 10, 1992. Traded to **Tampa Bay** by **Quebec** to complete transaction that sent Tim Hunter to Quebec (June 19, 1992), September 14, 1992. Traded to **Quebec** by **Tampa Bay** with Steve Tuttle and Michel Mongeau for Herb Ragglan, February 12, 1993. Signed as a free agent by **Phoenix**, August 6, 1997.

• SIMMER, CHARLIE

Charlie "Chaz" Simmer LW – L. 6'3", 210 lbs. b: Terrace Bay, Ont., 3/20/1954. California's 4th choice, 39th overall, in 1974 Amateur Draft.

Season	Club	League	GP	G	A	Pts	AG	AA	APts	PIM	PP	SH	GW	S	%	TGF	PGF	TGA	PGA	+/–	GP	G	A	Pts	PIM	PP	SH	GW
1971-72	Kenora Muskies	MJHL	45	14	31	45				77																		
1972-73	Kenora Muskies	MJHL	48	43	*68	*111				57																		
1973-74	Sault Ste. Marie Greyhounds	OHA	70	45	54	99				137																		
1974-75	**California Golden Seals**	**NHL**	**35**	**8**	**13**	**21**	**7**	**10**	**17**	**26**	**2**	**0**	**0**	**46**	**17.4**	**28**	**8**	**24**	**2**	**–2**								
	Salt Lake Golden Eagles	CHL	47	12	29	41				86																		
1975-76	**California Golden Seals**	**NHL**	**21**	**1**	**1**	**2**	**1**	**1**	**2**	**22**	**1**	**0**	**0**	**12**	**8.3**	**4**	**2**	**15**	**4**	**–9**								
	Salt Lake City Golden Eagles	CHL	42	23	16	39				96																		
1976-77	**Cleveland Barons**	**NHL**	**24**	**2**	**0**	**2**	**2**	**0**	**2**	**16**	**1**	**0**	**0**	**42**	**4.8**	**8**	**4**	**21**	**6**	**–11**								
	Salt Lake Golden Eagles	CHL	51	32	30	62				37																		
1977-78	**Los Angeles Kings**	**NHL**	**3**	**0**	**0**	**0**	**0**	**0**	**0**	**2**	**0**	**0**	**0**	**4**	**0.0**	**0**	**0**	**0**	**0**	**0**								
	Springfield Indians	AHL	75	42	41	83				100											4	0	1	1	5			
1978-79	**Los Angeles Kings**	**NHL**	**38**	**21**	**27**	**48**	**19**	**21**	**40**	**16**	**8**	**0**	**0**	**112**	**18.8**	**76**	**31**	**37**	**1**	**+9**	**2**	**1**	**0**	**1**	**2**	**1**	**0**	**0**
	Springfield Indians	AHL	39	13	23	36				33																		
1979-80	**Los Angeles Kings**	**NHL**	**64**	***56**	**45**	**101**	**51**	**35**	**86**	**65**	**21**	**0**	**8**	**213**	**26.3**	**146**	**56**	**44**	**1**	**+47**	**3**	**2**	**0**	**2**	**0**	**1**	**0**	**0**
1980-81	**Los Angeles Kings**	**NHL**	**65**	**56**	**49**	**105**	**46**	**34**	**80**	**62**	**23**	**0**	**9**	**171**	**32.7**	**152**	**62**	**59**	**0**	**+31**								
1981-82	**Los Angeles Kings**	**NHL**	**50**	**15**	**24**	**39**	**12**	**16**	**28**	**42**	**3**	**0**	**2**	**88**	**17.0**	**69**	**29**	**52**	**5**	**–7**	**10**	**4**	**7**	**11**	**22**	**1**	**0**	**1**
1982-83	**Los Angeles Kings**	**NHL**	**80**	**29**	**51**	**80**	**24**	**35**	**59**	**51**	**11**	**1**	**1**	**183**	**15.8**	**128**	**53**	**89**	**14**	**0**								
	Canada	WEC-A	10	2	3	5				8																		
1983-84	**Los Angeles Kings**	**NHL**	**79**	**44**	**48**	**92**	**36**	**33**	**69**	**78**	**13**	**1**	**4**	**188**	**23.4**	**125**	**41**	**79**	**2**	**+7**								
1984-85	**Los Angeles Kings**	**NHL**	**5**	**1**	**0**	**1**	**1**	**0**	**1**	**4**	**0**	**0**	**0**	**8**	**12.5**	**1**	**0**	**5**	**0**	**–4**								
	Boston Bruins	**NHL**	**63**	**33**	**30**	**63**	**27**	**20**	**47**	**35**	**12**	**0**	**5**	**128**	**25.8**	**90**	**33**	**44**	**1**	**+14**	**5**	**2**	**2**	**4**	**2**	**0**	**0**	**0**
1985-86	**Boston Bruins**	**NHL**	**55**	**36**	**24**	**60**	**29**	**16**	**45**	**42**	**14**	**0**	**5**	**141**	**25.5**	**92**	**45**	**35**	**0**	**+12**	**3**	**0**	**0**	**0**	**4**	**0**	**0**	**0**
1986-87	**Boston Bruins**	**NHL**	**80**	**29**	**40**	**69**	**25**	**29**	**54**	**59**	**11**	**0**	**4**	**137**	**21.2**	**117**	**38**	**59**	**0**	**+20**	**1**	**0**	**0**	**0**	**2**	**0**	**0**	**0**
1987-88	**Pittsburgh Penguins**	**NHL**	**50**	**11**	**17**	**28**	**9**	**12**	**21**	**24**	**5**	**0**	**3**	**58**	**19.0**	**54**	**26**	**22**	**0**	**+6**								
1988-89	Frankfurt	Germany	36	19	32	51				68											4	1	2	3	13			
1989-90			DID NOT PLAY																									
1990-91	San Diego Gulls	IHL	43	16	7	23				63																		
1991-92	San Diego Gulls	IHL	1	0	0	0				0																		
	NHL Totals		**712**	**342**	**369**	**711**	**289**	**262**	**551**	**544**	**125**	**2**	**41**	**1531**	**22.3**	**1090**	**428**	**585**	**36**		**24**	**9**	**9**	**18**	**32**	**3**	**0**	**1**

CHL Second All-Star Team (1977) • AHL Second All-Star Team (1978) • NHL First All-Star Team (1980, 1981) • Won Bill Masterton Trophy (1986)

Played in NHL All-Star Game (1981, 1984)

Transferred to **Cleveland** after **California** franchise relocated, August 26, 1976. Signed as a free agent by **LA Kings**, August 8, 1977. Traded to **Boston** by **LA Kings** for Boston's 1st round choice (Dan Gratton) in 1985 Entry Draft, October 24, 1985. Claimed by **Pittsburgh** from **Boston** in Waiver Draft, October 5, 1987.

• SIMMONS, AL

Al Simmons D – R. 6', 170 lbs. b: Winnipeg, Man., 9/25/1951. California's 6th choice, 85th overall, in 1971 Amateur Draft.

Season	Club	League	GP	G	A	Pts	AG	AA	APts	PIM	PP	SH	GW	S	%	TGF	PGF	TGA	PGA	+/–	GP	G	A	Pts	PIM	PP	SH	GW
1970-71	Winnipeg Jets	WCJHL	65	14	39	53				89																		
1971-72	**California Golden Seals**	**NHL**	**1**	**0**	**0**	**0**	**0**	**0**	**0**	**0**	**0**	**0**	**0**	**4**	**0.0**	**3**	**0**	**4**	**0**	**–1**								
	Columbus Seals	IHL	60	2	12	14				26																		
1972-73	Salt Lake Golden Eagles	WHL	72	19	22	41				50											9	1	4	5	6			
1973-74	**Boston Bruins**	**NHL**	**3**	**0**	**0**	**0**	**0**	**0**	**0**	**0**	**0**	**0**	**0**	**1**	**0.0**	**0**	**0**	**1**	**0**	**–1**	**1**	**0**	**0**	**0**	**0**	**0**	**0**	**0**
	Boston Braves	AHL	75	5	32	37				41																		
1974-75	Rochester Americans	AHL	68	7	36	43				60											12	2	5	7	13			
1975-76	**Boston Bruins**	**NHL**	**7**	**0**	**1**	**1**	**0**	**1**	**1**	**21**	**0**	**0**	**0**	**6**	**0.0**	**6**	**0**	**9**	**3**	**0**								
	Rochester Americans	AHL	5	0	5	5				13																		
	Providence Reds	AHL	56	2	23	27				48											3	0	2	2	0			
	NHL Totals		**11**	**0**	**1**	**1**	**0**	**1**	**1**	**21**	**0**	**0**	**0**	**11**	**0.0**	**9**	**0**	**14**	**3**		**1**	**0**	**0**	**0**	**0**	**0**	**0**	**0**

AHL Second All-Star Team (1976)

Claimed by **San Diego** (WHL) from **California** in Reverse Draft, June 13, 1973. Traded to **Boston** by **San Diego** for cash, February 7, 1974. Traded to **NY Rangers** by **Boston** for cash, November 14, 1975.

• SIMON, CHRIS

Chris Simon LW – L. 6'3", 219 lbs. b: Wawa, Ont., 1/30/1972. Philadelphia's 2nd choice, 25th overall, in 1990 Entry Draft.

Season	Club	League	GP	G	A	Pts	AG	AA	APts	PIM	PP	SH	GW	S	%	TGF	PGF	TGA	PGA	+/–	GP	G	A	Pts	PIM	PP	SH	GW
1988-89	Ottawa 67's	OHL	36	4	2	6				31																		
1989-90	Ottawa 67's	OHL	57	36	38	74				146											3	2	1	3	4			
1990-91	Ottawa 67's	OHL	20	16	6	22				69											17	5	9	14	59			
1991-92	Ottawa 67's	OHL	2	1	1	2				24																		
	Sault Ste. Marie Greyhounds	OHL	31	19	25	44				143											11	5	8	13	49			
1992-93	**Quebec Nordiques**	**NHL**	**16**	**1**	**1**	**2**	**1**	**1**	**2**	**67**	**0**	**0**	**1**	**15**	**6.7**	**6**	**0**	**8**	**0**	**–2**	**5**	**0**	**0**	**0**	**26**	**0**	**0**	**0**
	Halifax Citadels	AHL	36	12	6	18				131																		
1993-94	**Quebec Nordiques**	**NHL**	**37**	**4**	**4**	**8**	**4**	**3**	**7**	**132**	**0**	**0**	**1**	**39**	**10.3**	**16**	**2**	**16**	**0**	**–2**								

			REGULAR SEASON																		PLAYOFFS							
Season	Club	League	GP	G	A	Pts	AG	AA	APts	PIM	PP	SH	GW	S	%	TGF	PGF	TGA	PGA	+/–	GP	G	A	Pts	PIM	PP	SH	GW
1994-95	**Quebec Nordiques**	**NHL**	29	3	9	12	5	13	18	106	0	0	0	33	9.1	20	1	6	1	+14	6	1	1	2	19	0	0	1
1995-96	**Colorado Avalanche**	**NHL**	64	16	18	34	16	15	31	250	4	0	1	105	15.2	51	11	30	0	+10	12	1	2	3	11	0	0	0
1996-97	**Washington Capitals**	**NHL**	42	9	13	22	10	11	21	165	3	0	1	89	10.1	37	7	32	1	–1	....	....	....	....	....	....	....	....
1997-98	**Washington Capitals**	**NHL**	28	7	10	17	8	10	18	38	4	0	1	71	9.9	34	15	20	0	–1	18	1	0	1	26	0	0	0
	NHL Totals		216	40	55	95	44	53	97	758	11	0	5	352	11.4	164	36	112	2		41	3	3	6	82	0	0	1

Traded to **Quebec** by **Philadelphia** with Peter Forsberg, Steve Duchesne, Kerry Huffman, Mike Ricci, Ron Hextall, Philadelphia's 1st round choice in the 1993 (Jocelyn Thibault) and 1994 (later traded to Toronto — later traded to Washington — Washington selected Nolan Baumgartner) Entry Drafts and cash for Eric Lindros, June 30, 1992. Transferred to **Coloradeo** after **Quebec** franchise relocated, July 1, 1995. Traded to **Washington** by **Colorado** with Curtis Leschyshyn for Keith Jones and Washington's 1st (Scott Parker) and 4th (later traded back to Washington — Washington selected Krys Barch) round choices in 1998 Entry Draft, November 2, 1996.

• SIMON, JASON

Jason Simon LW – L. 6'1", 210 lbs. b: Sarnia, Ont., 3/21/1969. New Jersey's 9th choice, 215th overall, in 1989 Entry Draft.

Season	Club	League	GP	G	A	Pts	AG	AA	APts	PIM	PP	SH	GW	S	%	TGF	PGF	TGA	PGA	+/–	GP	G	A	Pts	PIM	PP	SH	GW
1986-87	London Knights	OHL	33	1	2	3	....	....	....	33	....	....	....	....	....	....	....	....	....	....	....	....	....	....	....	....	....	....
	Sudbury Wolves	OHL	26	2	3	5	....	....	....	50	....	....	....	....	....	....	....	....	....	....	....	....	....	....	....	....	....	....
1987-88	Sudbury Wolves	OHL	26	5	7	12	....	....	....	35	....	....	....	....	....	....	....	....	....	....	....	....	....	....	....	....	....	....
	Hamilton Steelhawks	OHL	29	5	13	18	....	....	....	124	....	....	....	....	....	....	....	....	....	....	11	0	2	2	15	....	....	....
1988-89	Windsor Spitfires	OHL	62	23	39	62	....	....	....	193	....	....	....	....	....	....	....	....	....	....	4	1	4	5	13	....	....	....
1989-90	Utica Devils	AHL	16	3	4	7	....	....	....	28	....	....	....	....	....	....	....	....	....	....	2	0	0	0	12	....	....	....
	Nashville Knights	ECHL	13	4	3	7	....	....	....	81	....	....	....	....	....	....	....	....	....	....	5	1	3	4	17	....	....	....
1990-91	Utica Devils	AHL	50	2	12	14	....	....	....	189	....	....	....	....	....	....	....	....	....	....	....	....	....	....	....	....	....	....
	Johnstown Chiefs	ECHL	22	11	9	20	....	....	....	55	....	....	....	....	....	....	....	....	....	....	....	....	....	....	....	....	....	....
1991-92	Utica Devils	AHL	1	0	0	0	....	....	....	12	....	....	....	....	....	....	....	....	....	....	....	....	....	....	....	....	....	....
	San Diego Gulls	IHL	13	1	4	5	....	....	....	45	....	....	....	....	....	....	....	....	....	....	3	0	1	1	9	....	....	....
1992-93	Detroit Falcons	ColHL	11	7	13	20	....	....	....	38	....	....	....	....	....	....	....	....	....	....	....	....	....	....	....	....	....	....
	Flint Generals	ColHL	44	17	32	49	....	....	....	202	....	....	....	....	....	....	....	....	....	....	....	....	....	....	....	....	....	....
1993-94	Salt Lake Golden Eagles	IHL	50	7	7	14	....	....	....	*323	....	....	....	....	....	....	....	....	....	....	....	....	....	....	....	....	....	....
	New York Islanders	**NHL**	4	0	0	0	0	0	0	34	0	0	0	0	0.0	0	0	0	0	0	....	....	....	....	....	....	....	....
	Detroit Falcons	ColHL	13	9	16	25	....	....	....	87	....	....	....	....	....	....	....	....	....	....	....	....	....	....	....	....	....	....
1994-95	Denver Grizzlies	IHL	61	3	6	9	....	....	....	300	....	....	....	....	....	....	....	....	....	....	1	0	0	0	12	....	....	....
1995-96	Springfield Falcons	AHL	18	2	2	4	....	....	....	90	....	....	....	....	....	....	....	....	....	....	7	1	0	1	26	....	....	....
1996-97	**Phoenix Coyotes**	**NHL**	1	0	0	0	0	0	0	0	0	0	0	0	0.0	0	0	1	0	–1	....	....	....	....	....	....	....	....
	Las Vegas Thunder	IHL	64	4	3	7	....	....	....	402	....	....	....	....	....	....	....	....	....	....	3	0	0	0	0	....	....	....
1997-98	Hershey Bears	AHL	26	0	1	1	....	....	....	170	....	....	....	....	....	....	....	....	....	....	....	....	....	....	....	....	....	....
	Quebec Rafales	IHL	30	6	3	9	....	....	....	127	....	....	....	....	....	....	....	....	....	....	....	....	....	....	....	....	....	....
	NHL Totals		5	0	0	0	0	0	0	34	0	0	0	0	0.0	0	0	1	0		....	....	....	....	....	....	....	....

Signed as a free agent by **NY Islanders**, January 6, 1994. Signed as a free agent by **Winnipeg**, August 9, 1995. Transferred to **Colorado** after **Winnipeg** franchise relocated, July 1, 1996. Signed as a free agent by **Colorado**, August 22, 1997.

• SIMON, TODD

Todd Simon C – R. 5'10", 188 lbs. b: Toronto, Ont., 4/21/1972. Buffalo's 10th choice, 203rd overall, in 1992 Entry Draft.

Season	Club	League	GP	G	A	Pts	AG	AA	APts	PIM	PP	SH	GW	S	%	TGF	PGF	TGA	PGA	+/–	GP	G	A	Pts	PIM	PP	SH	GW
1989-90	Niagara Falls Thunder	OHL	9	0	1	1	....	....	....	2	....	....	....	....	....	....	....	....	....	....	11	3	1	4	2	....	....	....
1990-91	Niagara Falls Thunder	OHL	65	51	74	125	....	....	....	35	....	....	....	....	....	....	....	....	....	....	14	7	8	15	12	....	....	....
1991-92	Niagara Falls Thunder	OHL	66	53	93	*146	....	....	....	72	....	....	....	....	....	....	....	....	....	....	17	17	24	*41	36	....	....	....
1992-93	Rochester Americans	AHL	67	27	66	93	....	....	....	54	....	....	....	....	....	....	....	....	....	....	12	3	14	17	15	....	....	....
1993-94	**Buffalo Sabres**	**NHL**	15	0	1	1	0	1	1	0	0	0	0	14	0.0	3	2	4	0	–3	5	1	0	1	0	1	0	1
	Rochester Americans	AHL	55	33	52	85	....	....	....	79	....	....	....	....	....	....	....	....	....	....	....	....	....	....	....	....	....	....
1994-95	Rochester Americans	AHL	69	25	65	90	....	....	....	78	....	....	....	....	....	....	....	....	....	....	5	0	2	2	21	....	....	....
1995-96	Las Vegas Thunder	IHL	52	26	48	74	....	....	....	48	....	....	....	....	....	....	....	....	....	....	....	....	....	....	....	....	....	....
	Detroit Vipers	IHL	29	19	16	35	....	....	....	20	....	....	....	....	....	....	....	....	....	....	12	2	12	14	6	....	....	....
1996-97	Detroit Vipers	IHL	80	21	51	72	....	....	....	46	....	....	....	....	....	....	....	....	....	....	18	4	6	10	12	....	....	....
1997-98	Cincinnati Cyclones	IHL	81	33	72	105	....	....	....	115	....	....	....	....	....	....	....	....	....	....	9	2	4	6	12	....	....	....
	NHL Totals		15	0	1	1	0	1	1	0	0	0	0	14	0.0	3	2	4	0		5	1	0	1	0	1	0	1

OHL First All-Star Team (1992) • Canadian Major Junior First All-Star Team (1992) • IHL First All-Star Team (1996)

• SIMONETTI, FRANK

Frank Simonetti D – R. 6'1", 190 lbs. b: Melrose, MA, 9/11/1962.

Season	Club	League	GP	G	A	Pts	AG	AA	APts	PIM	PP	SH	GW	S	%	TGF	PGF	TGA	PGA	+/–	GP	G	A	Pts	PIM	PP	SH	GW
1983-84	Norwich University	ECAC II	18	9	19	28	....	....	....	32	....	....	....	....	....	....	....	....	....	....	....	....	....	....	....	....	....	....
1984-85	**Boston Bruins**	**NHL**	43	1	5	6	1	3	4	26	0	0	0	36	2.8	32	2	35	4	–1	5	0	1	1	2	0	0	0
	Hershey Bears	AHL	31	0	6	6	....	....	....	14	....	....	....	....	....	....	....	....	....	....	....	....	....	....	....	....	....	....
1985-86	**Boston Bruins**	**NHL**	17	1	0	1	1	0	1	14	0	0	0	8	12.5	7	0	10	2	–1	3	0	0	0	0	0	0	0
	Moncton Golden Flames	AHL	5	0	0	0	....	....	....	2	....	....	....	....	....	....	....	....	....	....	....	....	....	....	....	....	....	....
1986-87	**Boston Bruins**	**NHL**	25	1	0	1	1	0	1	17	0	0	0	11	9.1	10	0	18	2	–6	4	0	0	0	6	0	0	0
	Moncton Golden Flames	AHL	7	0	1	1	....	....	....	6	....	....	....	....	....	....	....	....	....	....	....	....	....	....	....	....	....	....
1987-88	**Boston Bruins**	**NHL**	30	2	3	5	2	2	4	19	0	0	1	20	10.0	13	0	13	1	+1	....	....	....	....	....	....	....	....
	Maine Mariners	AHL	7	0	1	1	....	....	....	4	....	....	....	....	....	....	....	....	....	....	2	0	0	0	2	....	....	....
	NHL Totals		115	5	8	13	5	5	10	76	0	0	1	75	6.7	62	2	76	9		12	0	1	1	8	0	0	0

NCAA (College Div.) East All-American Team (1984)

Signed as a free agent by **Boston**, October 4, 1984.

• SIMPSON, BOBBY

Bobby Simpson LW – L. 6', 190 lbs. b: Caughnawaga, Que., 11/17/1956. Atlanta's 3rd choice, 28th overall, in 1976 Amateur Draft.

Season	Club	League	GP	G	A	Pts	AG	AA	APts	PIM	PP	SH	GW	S	%	TGF	PGF	TGA	PGA	+/–	GP	G	A	Pts	PIM	PP	SH	GW
1973-74	Sherbrooke Beavers	QMJHL	64	6	21	27	....	....	....	138	....	....	....	....	....	....	....	....	....	....	....	....	....	....	....	....	....	....
1974-75	Sherbrooke Beavers	QMJHL	69	38	47	85	....	....	....	146	....	....	....	....	....	....	....	....	....	....	13	10	12	22	26	....	....	....
1975-76	Sherbrooke Beavers	QMJHL	68	56	77	133	....	....	....	126	....	....	....	....	....	....	....	....	....	....	17	11	14	25	19	....	....	....
1976-77	**Atlanta Flames**	**NHL**	72	13	10	23	12	8	20	45	0	0	2	118	11.0	42	3	37	0	+2	2	0	1	1	0	0	0	0
1977-78	**Atlanta Flames**	**NHL**	55	10	8	18	10	7	17	49	0	0	1	91	11.0	31	1	30	0	0	2	0	0	0	2	0	0	0
	Tulsa Oilers	CHL	14	8	8	16	....	....	....	34	....	....	....	....	....	....	....	....	....	....	....	....	....	....	....	....	....	....
1978-79	Tulsa Oilers	CHL	49	14	19	33	....	....	....	38	....	....	....	....	....	....	....	....	....	....	....	....	....	....	....	....	....	....
1979-80	**St. Louis Blues**	**NHL**	18	2	2	4	2	2	4	0	0	0	0	20	10.0	7	1	8	0	–2	....	....	....	....	....	....	....	....
	Salt Lake Golden Eagles	CHL	41	19	12	31	....	....	....	58	....	....	....	....	....	....	....	....	....	....	12	4	5	9	9	....	....	....
1980-81	Salt Lake Golden Eagles	CHL	8	2	1	3	....	....	....	4	....	....	....	....	....	....	....	....	....	....	....	....	....	....	....	....	....	....
	Muskegon Mohawks	IHL	42	17	26	43	....	....	....	42	....	....	....	....	....	....	....	....	....	....	3	2	1	3	0	....	....	....
1981-82	**Pittsburgh Penguins**	**NHL**	26	9	9	18	7	6	13	4	0	0	1	37	24.3	25	0	28	0	–3	2	0	0	0	0	0	0	0
	Erie Blades	AHL	48	25	23	48	....	....	....	45	....	....	....	....	....	....	....	....	....	....	....	....	....	....	....	....	....	....
1982-83	**Pittsburgh Penguins**	**NHL**	4	1	0	1	1	0	1	0	0	0	0	3	33.3	1	0	2	0	–1	....	....	....	....	....	....	....	....
	Baltimore Skipjacks	AHL	61	24	27	51	....	....	....	24	....	....	....	....	....	....	....	....	....	....	....	....	....	....	....	....	....	....
1983-84	Baltimore Skipjacks	AHL	71	16	16	32	....	....	....	36	....	....	....	....	....	....	....	....	....	....	10	7	5	12	8	....	....	....
1984-85	Indianapolis Checkers	IHL	55	16	24	40	....	....	....	65	....	....	....	....	....	....	....	....	....	....	....	....	....	....	....	....	....	....
	Salt Lake Golden Eagles	IHL	28	7	11	18	....	....	....	25	....	....	....	....	....	....	....	....	....	....	7	1	0	1	19	....	....	....
1985-86	Salt Lake Golden Eagles	IHL	74	6	38	44	....	....	....	37	....	....	....	....	....	....	....	....	....	....	5	2	3	5	8	....	....	....
1986-87	Salt Lake Golden Eagles	IHL	9	2	3	5	....	....	....	12	....	....	....	....	....	....	....	....	....	....	....	....	....	....	....	....	....	....
	Peoria Rivermen	IHL	58	14	29	43	....	....	....	32	....	....	....	....	....	....	....	....	....	....	....	....	....	....	....	....	....	....
	NHL Totals		175	35	29	64	32	23	55	98	0	0	4	269	13.0	106	5	105	0		6	0	1	1	2	0	0	0

Traded to **St. Louis** by **Atlanta** for Curt Bennett, May 24, 1979. Claimed by **St. Louis** as a fill-in during Expansion Draft, June 13, 1979. Signed as a free agent by **Pittsburgh**, October 1, 1981.

• SIMPSON, CRAIG

Craig Simpson LW – R. 6'2", 195 lbs. b: London, Ont., 2/15/1967. Pittsburgh's 1st choice, 2nd overall, in 1985 Entry Draft.

Season	Club	League	GP	G	A	Pts	AG	AA	APts	PIM	PP	SH	GW	S	%	TGF	PGF	TGA	PGA	+/–	GP	G	A	Pts	PIM	PP	SH	GW
1982-83	London Diamonds	Jr. B	....	48	63	*111	....	....	....	....	....	....	....	....	....	....	....	....	....	....	....	....	....	....	....	....	....	....
1983-84	Michigan State Spartans	CCHA	46	14	43	57	....	....	....	38	....	....	....	....	....	....	....	....	....	....	....	....	....	....	....	....	....	....
1984-85	Michigan State Spartans	CCHA	42	31	53	84	....	....	....	33	....	....	....	....	....	....	....	....	....	....	....	....	....	....	....	....	....	....
1985-86	**Pittsburgh Penguins**	**NHL**	76	11	17	28	9	11	20	49	2	1	0	74	14.9	46	13	32	0	+1	....	....	....	....	....	....	....	....
1986-87	**Pittsburgh Penguins**	**NHL**	72	26	25	51	23	18	41	57	7	0	3	133	19.5	87	21	55	0	+11	....	....	....	....	....	....	....	....
1987-88	**Pittsburgh Penguins**	**NHL**	21	13	13	26	11	9	20	34	4	0	3	59	22.0	34	10	23	4	+5	....	....	....	....	....	....	....	....
	Edmonton Oilers	**NHL**	59	43	21	64	37	15	52	43	18	0	5	118	36.4	104	41	49	1	+15	19	13	6	19	26	3	0	3
1988-89	**Edmonton Oilers**	**NHL**	66	35	41	76	30	29	59	80	17	0	4	121	28.9	102	44	62	1	–3	7	2	0	2	10	1	0	1

			REGULAR SEASON																		PLAYOFFS							
Season	Club	League	GP	G	A	Pts	AG	AA	APts	PIM	PP	SH	GW	S	%	TGF	PGF	TGA	PGA	+/–	GP	G	A	Pts	PIM	PP	SH	GW
1989-90	Edmonton Oilers	NHL	80	29	32	61	25	23	48	180	7	0	2	129	22.5	94	33	65	2	–2	22	*16	15	*31	8	6	0	3
1990-91	Edmonton Oilers	NHL	75	30	27	57	28	20	48	66	15	0	5	143	21.0	83	37	54	0	–8	18	5	11	16	12	1	0	0
1991-92	Edmonton Oilers	NHL	79	24	37	61	22	28	50	80	6	0	2	128	18.8	101	34	60	1	+8	1	0	0	0	0	0	0	0
1992-93	Edmonton Oilers	NHL	60	24	22	46	20	15	35	36	12	0	3	91	26.4	70	36	49	1	–14								
1993-94	Buffalo Sabres	NHL	22	8	8	16	7	6	13	8	2	0	2	28	28.6	25	10	18	0	–3								
1994-95	Buffalo Sabres	NHL	24	4	7	11	7	10	17	26	1	0	0	20	20.0	13	6	12	0	–5								
	NHL Totals		634	247	250	497	219	184	403	659	91	1	29	1044	23.7	759	285	479	10		67	36	32	68	56	11	0	7

CCHA First All-Star Team (1985) • NCAA West First All-American Team (1985)

Traded to **Edmonton** by **Pittsburgh** with Dave Hannan, Moe Mantha and Chris Joseph for Paul Coffey, Dave Hunter and Wayne Van Dorp, November 24, 1987. Traded to **Buffalo** by **Edmonton** for Jozef Cierny and Buffalo's 4th round choice (Jussi Tarvainen) in 1994 Entry Draft, September 1, 1993.

• SIMPSON, REID

Reid Simpson LW – L. 6'2", 220 lbs. b: Flin Flon, Man., 5/21/1969. Philadelphia's 3rd choice, 72nd overall, in 1989 Entry Draft.

1985-86	New Westminster Bruins	WHL	2	0	0	0				0																		
1986-87	Prince Albert Raiders	WHL	47	3	8	11				105																		
1987-88	Prince Albert Raiders	WHL	72	13	14	27				164											10	1	0	1	43			
1988-89	Prince Albert Raiders	WHL	59	26	29	55				264											4	2	1	3	30			
1989-90	Prince Albert Raiders	WHL	29	15	17	32				121											14	4	7	11	34			
	Hershey Bears	AHL	28	2	2	4				175																		
1990-91	Hershey Bears	AHL	54	9	15	24				183											1	0	0	0	0			
1991-92	Philadelphia Flyers	NHL	1	0	0	0	0	0	0	0	0	0	0	0	0.0	0	0	0	0	0								
	Hershey Bears	AHL	60	11	7	18				145																		
1992-93	Minnesota North Stars	NHL	1	0	0	0	0	0	0	5	0	0	0	0	0.0	0	0	0	0	0								
	Kalamazoo Wings	IHL	45	5	5	10				193																		
1993-94	Kalamazoo Wings	IHL	5	0	0	0				16																		
	Albany River Rats	AHL	37	9	5	14				135											5	1	1	2	18			
1994-95	Albany River Rats	AHL	70	18	25	43				268											14	1	8	9	13			
	New Jersey Devils	NHL	9	0	0	0	0	0	0	27	0	0	0	5	0.0	1	0	2	0	–1								
1995-96	New Jersey Devils	NHL	23	1	5	6	1	4	5	79	0	0	0	8	12.5	7	0	5	0	+2								
	Albany River Rats	AHL	6	1	3	4				17																		
1996-97	New Jersey Devils	NHL	27	0	4	4	0	4	4	60	0	0	0	17	0.0	6	1	5	0	0	5	0	0	0	29	0	0	0
	Albany River Rats	AHL	3	0	0	0				10																		
1997-98	New Jersey Devils	NHL	6	0	0	0	0	0	0	16	0	0	0	5	0.0	2	0	4	0	–2								
	Chicago Blackhawks	NHL	38	3	2	5	4	2	6	102	1	0	0	19	15.8	7	2	6	0	–1								
	NHL Totals		105	4	11	15	5	10	15	289	1	0	0	54	7.4	23	3	22	0		5	0	0	0	29	0	0	0

Signed as a free agent by **Minnesota**, December 14, 1992. Transferred to **Dallas** after **Minnesota** franchise relocated, June 9, 1993. Traded to **New Jersey** by **Dallas** with Roy Mitchell for future considerations, March 21, 1994. Traded to **Chicago** by **New Jersey** for Chicago's 4th round choice (Mikko Jokela) in 1998 Entry Draft and future considerations, January 8, 1998.

• SIMPSON, TODD

Todd Simpson D – L. 6'3", 215 lbs. b: North Vancouver, B.C., 5/28/1973.

1991-92	Brown University	ECAC	14	1	3	4				18																		
1992-93	Tri-City Americans	WHL	69	5	18	23				196											4	0	0	0	13			
1993-94	Tri-City Americans	WHL	12	2	3	5				32																		
	Saskatoon Blades	WHL	51	7	19	26				175											16	0	1	1	29			
1994-95	Saint John Flames	AHL	80	3	10	13				321											5	0	0	0	4			
1995-96	Calgary Flames	NHL	6	0	0	0	0	0	0	32	0	0	0	3	0.0	1	0	1	0	0								
	Saint John Flames	AHL	66	4	13	17				277											16	2	3	5	32			
1996-97	Calgary Flames	NHL	82	1	13	14	1	11	12	208	0	0	0	85	1.2	51	0	91	26	–14								
1997-98	Calgary Flames	NHL	53	1	5	6	1	5	6	109	0	0	1	51	2.0	38	1	64	17	–10								
	NHL Totals		141	2	18	20	2	16	18	349	0	0	1	139	1.4	90	1	156	43									

Signed as free agent by **Calgary**, July 6, 1994.

• SIMS, AL

Al Sims D – L. 6', 182 lbs. b: Toronto, Ont., 4/18/1953. Boston's 4th choice, 47th overall, in 1973 Amateur Draft.

1971-72	Cornwall Royals	QMJHL	58	6	24	30				65											16	2	9	11	15			
1972-73	Cornwall Royals	QMJHL	62	13	62	75				54											12	2	5	7	8			
1973-74	Boston Bruins	NHL	76	3	9	12	3	8	11	22	0	0	1	111	2.7	116	1	69	18	+64	16	0	0	0	12	0	0	0
1974-75	Boston Bruins	NHL	75	4	8	12	4	6	10	73	0	0	0	102	3.9	97	3	85	20	+29								
1975-76	Boston Bruins	NHL	48	4	3	7	4	2	6	43	0	0	0	61	6.6	41	5	47	17	+6	1	0	0	0	0	0	0	0
	Rochester Americans	AHL	21	4	5	9				12											7	1	4	5	11			
1976-77	Boston Bruins	NHL	1	0	0	0	0	0	0	0	0	0	0	1	0.0	1	0	0	0	+1	2	0	0	0	0	0	0	0
	Rochester Americans	AHL	80	10	32	42				42											12	2	9	11	12			
1977-78	Boston Bruins	NHL	43	2	8	10	2	7	9	6	0	0	1	55	3.6	28	0	20	3	+11	8	0	0	0	0	0	0	0
	Rochester Americans	AHL	31	6	13	19				12																		
1978-79	Boston Bruins	NHL	67	9	20	29	8	15	23	28	0	0	2	128	7.0	91	16	92	39	+22	11	0	2	2	0	0	0	0
	Rochester Americans	AHL	3	0	1	1				4																		
1979-80	Hartford Whalers	NHL	76	10	31	41	9	24	33	30	2	0	1	141	7.1	125	19	131	34	+9	3	0	0	0	2	0	0	0
1980-81	Hartford Whalers	NHL	80	16	36	52	13	25	38	68	5	0	1	182	8.8	133	40	153	40	–20								
1981-82	Los Angeles Kings	NHL	8	1	1	2	1	1	2	16	0	0	0	14	7.1	11	0	18	4	–3								
	New Haven Nighthawks	AHL	51	4	27	31				53																		
1982-83	Los Angeles Kings	NHL	1	0	0	0	0	0	0	0	0	0	0	1	0.0	0	0	0	0	0								
	New Haven Nighthawks	AHL	76	18	50	68				46											12	3	3	6	10			
1983-84	Servette	Switz.	STATISTICS NOT AVAILABLE																									
1984-85	EV Landshut	Germany	20	8	16	24				36																		
	New Haven Nighthawks	AHL	13	3	6	9				2																		
1985-86	SC Preussen Berlin	Germany	17	7	11	18				29																		
1986-87	Fife Flyers	Britain	36	52	86	138				95											5	6	11	17	0			
1987-88	Fife Flyers	Britain	30	33	42	75				51											6	5	11	16	2			
	NHL Totals		475	49	116	165	44	88	132	286	7	0	6	796	6.2	643	84	615	175		41	0	2	2	14	0	0	0

QMJHL First All-Star Team (1973) • AHL Second All-Star Team (1977, 1983)

Claimed by **Hartford** from **Boston** in Expansion Draft, June 13, 1979. Claimed by **LA Kings** from **Hartford** in Waiver Draft, October 5, 1981.

• SINISALO, ILKKA

Ilkka Sinisalo HW – L. 6', 185 lbs. b: Hauho, Finland, 7/10/1958.

1977-78	HIFK Helsinki	Finland	36	9	3	12				18																		
	Finland	WJC-A	6	1	7	8				4																		
1978-79	HIFK Helsinki	Finland	30	6	4	10				16											6	4	1	5	2			
1979-80	HIFK Helsinki	Finland	35	16	9	25				16											7	1	3	4	4			
1980-81	HIFK Helsinki	Finland	36	27	17	44				14											6	5	3	8	4			
	Finland	WEC-A	6	0	1	1				4																		
1981-82	Finland	C Cup	5	1	0	1				6																		
	Philadelphia Flyers	NHL	66	15	22	37	12	15	27	22	1	0	0	87	17.2	51	10	23	0	+18	4	0	2	2	0	0	0	0
	Finland	WEC-A	5	1	1	2				6																		
1982-83	Philadelphia Flyers	NHL	61	21	29	50	17	20	37	16	3	0	0	126	16.7	65	10	39	2	+18	3	1	1	2	0	0	0	0
	Finland	WEC-A	8	0	2	2				4																		
1983-84	Philadelphia Flyers	NHL	73	29	17	46	23	12	35	29	2	3	4	165	17.6	70	7	53	12	+22	2	2	0	2	0	1	0	0
1984-85	Philadelphia Flyers	NHL	70	36	37	73	29	25	54	16	7	1	8	166	21.7	105	33	54	14	+32	19	6	1	7	0	2	0	3
1985-86	Philadelphia Flyers	NHL	74	39	37	76	31	25	56	31	19	1	7	187	20.9	104	46	55	14	+17	5	2	2	4	2	0	0	0
1986-87	Philadelphia Flyers	NHL	42	10	21	31	9	15	24	8	3	1	1	80	12.5	52	17	26	5	+14	18	5	1	6	4	0	0	1
1987-88	Philadelphia Flyers	NHL	68	25	17	42	21	12	33	30	6	2	4	148	16.9	71	24	61	16	+2	7	4	2	6	0	1	0	0
1988-89	Philadelphia Flyers	NHL	13	1	6	7	1	4	5	2	0	0	0	15	6.7	13	1	10	4	+6	8	1	1	2	0	0	1	1
1989-90	Philadelphia Flyers	NHL	50	23	23	46	20	16	36	26	4	3	4	102	22.5	66	12	58	10	+6								
1990-91	Minnesota North Stars	FrTour	3	1	1	2				2																		
	Minnesota North Stars	NHL	46	5	12	17	5	9	14	24	1	1	1	68	7.4	27	4	39	6	–10								
	Los Angeles Kings	NHL	7	0	0	0	0	0	0	2	0	0	0	4	0.0	6	0	2	0	+4	2	0	1	1	0	0	0	0

			REGULAR SEASON																		PLAYOFFS							
Season	Club	League	GP	G	A	Pts	AG	AA	APts	PIM	PP	SH	GW	S	%	TGF	PGF	TGA	PGA	+/–	GP	G	A	Pts	PIM	PP	SH	GW
1991-92	**Los Angeles Kings**	**NHL**	**3**	**0**	**1**	**1**	**0**	**1**	**1**	**2**	**0**	**0**	**0**	**3**	**0.0**	**3**	**0**	**3**	**0**	**0**	....	....	....	....	....	....	....	....
	Phoenix Roadrunners	IHL	42	19	21	40	....	....	....	32	....	....	....	....	....	....	....	....	....	....	....	....	....	....	....	....	....	....
1992-93	HPK Hameelinna	Finland	46	13	16	29	....	....	....	55	....	....	....	....	....	....	....	....	....	....	12	2	3	5	8	....	....	....
1993-94	Ilves Tampere	Finland	12	1	6	7	....	....	....	10	....	....	....	....	....	....	....	....	....	....	....	....	....	....	....	....	....	....
1994-95	Ilves Tampere	Finland	30	2	7	9	....	....	....	45	....	....	....	....	....	....	....	....	....	....	....	....	....	....	....	....	....	....
	Keikko Espoo	Finland	16	7	7	14	....	....	....	6	....	....	....	....	....	....	....	....	....	....	4	0	3	3	4	....	....	....
1995-96	Keikko Espoo	Finland	44	7	12	19	....	....	....	36	....	....	....	....	....	....	....	....	....	....	....	....	....	....	....	....	....	....
	NHL Totals		**582**	**204**	**222**	**426**	**168**	**154**	**322**	**208**	**46**	**12**	**29**	**1151**	**17.7**	**633**	**164**	**423**	**83**		**68**	**21**	**11**	**32**	**6**	**4**	**1**	**5**

Signed as a free agent by **Philadelphia**, February 14, 1981. Signed as a free agent by **Minnesota**, July 3, 1990. Traded to **LA Kings** by **Minnesota** for LA Kings' 8th round choice (Michael Burkett) in 1991 Entry Draft, March 5, 1991.

• SIREN, VILLE

Ville Siren D – L. 6'2", 191 lbs. b: Tampere, Finland, 2/11/1964. Hartford's 3rd choice, 23rd overall, in 1983 Entry Draft.

Season	Club	League	GP	G	A	Pts	AG	AA	APts	PIM	PP	SH	GW	S	%	TGF	PGF	TGA	PGA	+/–	GP	G	A	Pts	PIM	PP	SH	GW
1982-83	Ilves Tampere	Finland	29	3	2	5	....	....	....	42	....	....	....	....	....	....	....	....	....	....	8	1	3	4	8	....	....	....
	Finland	WJC-A	7	1	1	2	....	....	....	6	....	....	....	....	....	....	....	....	....	....	....	....	....	....	....	....	....	....
1983-84	Ilves Tampere	Finland	36	1	10	11	....	....	....	40	....	....	....	....	....	....	....	....	....	....	2	0	0	0	2	....	....	....
	Finland	WJC-A	6	0	2	2	....	....	....	4	....	....	....	....	....	....	....	....	....	....	....	....	....	....	....	....	....	....
	Finland	Olympics	6	0	1	1	....	....	....	2	....	....	....	....	....	....	....	....	....	....	....	....	....	....	....	....	....	....
1984-85	Ilves Tampere	Finland	36	11	13	24	....	....	....	24	....	....	....	....	....	....	....	....	....	....	9	0	2	2	10	....	....	....
	Finland	WEC-A	5	0	0	0	....	....	....	8	....	....	....	....	....	....	....	....	....	....	....	....	....	....	....	....	....	....
1985-86	**Pittsburgh Penguins**	**NHL**	**60**	**4**	**8**	**12**	**3**	**5**	**8**	**32**	**1**	**0**	**0**	**58**	**6.9**	**55**	**11**	**59**	**7**	**–8**	....	....	....	....	....	....	....	....
1986-87	**Pittsburgh Penguins**	**NHL**	**69**	**5**	**17**	**22**	**4**	**12**	**16**	**50**	**1**	**0**	**0**	**84**	**6.0**	**102**	**22**	**87**	**15**	**+8**	....	....	....	....	....	....	....	....
1987-88	Finland	C Cup	5	0	0	0	....	....	....	6	....	....	....	....	....	....	....	....	....	....	....	....	....	....	....	....	....	....
	Pittsburgh Penguins	**NHL**	**58**	**1**	**20**	**21**	**1**	**14**	**15**	**62**	**0**	**0**	**0**	**53**	**1.9**	**87**	**20**	**78**	**25**	**+14**	....	....	....	....	....	....	....	....
1988-89	**Pittsburgh Penguins**	**NHL**	**12**	**1**	**0**	**1**	**1**	**0**	**1**	**14**	**0**	**0**	**0**	**11**	**9.1**	**9**	**0**	**9**	**0**	**0**	....	....	....	....	....	....	....	....
	Minnesota North Stars	**NHL**	**38**	**2**	**10**	**12**	**2**	**7**	**9**	**58**	**0**	**0**	**0**	**39**	**5.1**	**47**	**17**	**32**	**2**	**0**	**4**	**0**	**0**	**0**	**4**	**0**	**0**	**0**
1989-90	**Minnesota North Stars**	**NHL**	**53**	**1**	**13**	**14**	**1**	**9**	**10**	**60**	**0**	**0**	**0**	**53**	**1.9**	**62**	**14**	**51**	**4**	**+1**	**3**	**0**	**0**	**0**	**2**	**0**	**0**	**0**
1990-91	HPK Hameenlina	Finland	44	4	9	13	....	....	....	90	....	....	....	....	....	....	....	....	....	....	8	1	1	2	37	....	....	....
	Finland	WEC-A	10	2	2	4	....	....	....	16	....	....	....	....	....	....	....	....	....	....	....	....	....	....	....	....	....	....
1991-92	Finland	C Cup	6	0	1	1	....	....	....	15	....	....	....	....	....	....	....	....	....	....	....	....	....	....	....	....	....	....
	Ilves Tampere	Finland	43	8	14	22	....	....	....	88	....	....	....	....	....	....	....	....	....	....	....	....	....	....	....	....	....	....
	Finland	Olympics	8	0	2	2	....	....	....	16	....	....	....	....	....	....	....	....	....	....	....	....	....	....	....	....	....	....
1992-93	Lulea HF	Sweden	37	4	11	15	....	....	....	84	....	....	....	....	....	....	....	....	....	....	11	0	0	0	*22	....	....	....
	Finland	WC-A	6	0	0	0	....	....	....	6	....	....	....	....	....	....	....	....	....	....	....	....	....	....	....	....	....	....
1993-94	Lulea HF	Sweden	40	4	11	15	....	....	....	65	....	....	....	....	....	....	....	....	....	....	....	....	....	....	....	....	....	....
1994-95	Vasteras IK	Sweden	37	1	4	5	....	....	....	44	....	....	....	....	....	....	....	....	....	....	4	0	1	1	4	....	....	....
1995-96	SC Bern	Switz.	6	1	0	1	....	....	....	6	....	....	....	....	....	....	....	....	....	....	11	3	7	10	18	....	....	....
1996-97	SC Bern	Switz.	42	10	11	21	....	....	....	72	....	....	....	....	....	....	....	....	....	....	12	1	5	6	*47	....	....	....
1997-98	SC Bern	EuroHL	6	1	3	4	....	....	....	10	....	....	....	....	....	....	....	....	....	....	....	....	....	....	....	....	....	....
	SC Bern	Switz.	36	3	9	12	....	....	....	96	....	....	....	....	....	....	....	....	....	....	7	1	4	5	26	....	....	....
	NHL Totals		**290**	**14**	**68**	**82**	**12**	**47**	**59**	**276**	**2**	**0**	**0**	**298**	**4.7**	**362**	**84**	**316**	**53**		**7**	**0**	**0**	**0**	**6**	**0**	**0**	**0**

Traded to **Pittsburgh** by **Hartford** for Pat Boutette, November 16, 1984. Traded to **Minnesota** by **Pittsburgh** with Steve Gotaas for Gord Dineen and Scott Bjudstad, December 17, 1988.

• SIROIS, BOB

Bob Sirois RW – L. 6', 178 lbs. b: Montreal, Que., 2/6/1954. Philadelphia's 2nd choice, 53rd overall, in 1974 Amateur Draft.

Season	Club	League	GP	G	A	Pts	AG	AA	APts	PIM	PP	SH	GW	S	%	TGF	PGF	TGA	PGA	+/–	GP	G	A	Pts	PIM	PP	SH	GW
1970-71	Rosemount Nationale	QJHL	59	24	30	54	....	....	....	37	....	....	....	....	....	....	....	....	....	....	....	....	....	....	....	....	....	....
1971-72	Laval Nationale	QMJHL	59	20	44	64	....	....	....	58	....	....	....	....	....	....	....	....	....	....	....	....	....	....	....	....	....	....
1972-73	Laval Nationale	QMJHL	6	5	3	8	....	....	....	6	....	....	....	....	....	....	....	....	....	....	....	....	....	....	....	....	....	....
	Montreal Jr. Canadiens	QMJHL	57	46	51	97	....	....	....	55	....	....	....	....	....	....	....	....	....	....	....	....	....	....	....	....	....	....
1973-74	Montreal Jr. Canadiens	QMJHL	67	72	81	153	....	....	....	77	....	....	....	....	....	....	....	....	....	....	....	....	....	....	....	....	....	....
1974-75	**Philadelphia Flyers**	**NHL**	**3**	**1**	**0**	**1**	**1**	**0**	**1**	**4**	**0**	**0**	**0**	**3**	**33.3**	**1**	**0**	**0**	**0**	**+1**	....	....	....	....	....	....	....	....
	Richmond Robins	AHL	53	26	23	49	....	....	....	38	....	....	....	....	....	....	....	....	....	....	....	....	....	....	....	....	....	....
1975-76	**Philadelphia Flyers**	**NHL**	**1**	**0**	**0**	**0**	**0**	**0**	**0**	**0**	**0**	**0**	**0**	**0**	**0.0**	**0**	**0**	**0**	**0**	**0**	....	....	....	....	....	....	....	....
	Richmond Robins	AHL	26	14	18	32	....	....	....	10	....	....	....	....	....	....	....	....	....	....	....	....	....	....	....	....	....	....
	Washington Capitals	**NHL**	**43**	**10**	**19**	**29**	**9**	**15**	**24**	**6**	**4**	**0**	**0**	**109**	**9.2**	**34**	**12**	**55**	**0**	**–33**	....	....	....	....	....	....	....	....
1976-77	**Washington Capitals**	**NHL**	**45**	**13**	**22**	**35**	**12**	**18**	**30**	**2**	**1**	**0**	**1**	**100**	**13.0**	**43**	**5**	**38**	**1**	**+1**	....	....	....	....	....	....	....	....
1977-78	**Washington Capitals**	**NHL**	**72**	**24**	**37**	**61**	**23**	**30**	**53**	**6**	**5**	**0**	**1**	**189**	**12.7**	**92**	**25**	**83**	**5**	**–11**	....	....	....	....	....	....	....	....
1978-79	**Washington Capitals**	**NHL**	**73**	**29**	**25**	**54**	**26**	**19**	**45**	**6**	**9**	**0**	**3**	**207**	**14.0**	**86**	**29**	**72**	**9**	**–6**	....	....	....	....	....	....	....	....
1979-80	**Washington Capitals**	**NHL**	**49**	**15**	**17**	**32**	**14**	**13**	**27**	**18**	**4**	**1**	**2**	**110**	**13.6**	**46**	**15**	**46**	**10**	**–5**	....	....	....	....	....	....	....	....
	Hershey Bears	AHL	2	1	1	2	....	....	....	0	....	....	....	....	....	....	....	....	....	....	....	....	....	....	....	....	....	....
1980-81	Lausanne HC	Switz.	STATISTICS NOT AVAILABLE																									
1981-82	Hershey Bears	AHL	13	2	6	8	....	....	....	0	....	....	....	....	....	....	....	....	....	....	....	....	....	....	....	....	....	....
	NHL Totals		**286**	**92**	**120**	**212**	**85**	**95**	**180**	**42**	**23**	**1**	**7**	**718**	**12.8**	**302**	**86**	**294**	**25**		....	....	....	....	....	....	....	....

Played in NHL All-Star Game (1978)

Traded to **Washington** by **Philadelphia** for future considerations (John Paddock, September 1, 1976), December 15, 1975.

• SITTLER, DARRYL

Darryl Sittler C – L. 6', 190 lbs. b: Kitchener, Ont., 9/18/1950. Toronto's 1st choice, 8th overall, in 1970 Amateur Draft. **HHOF**

Season	Club	League	GP	G	A	Pts	AG	AA	APts	PIM	PP	SH	GW	S	%	TGF	PGF	TGA	PGA	+/–	GP	G	A	Pts	PIM	PP	SH	GW
1967-68	London Nationals	OHA	54	22	41	63	....	....	....	84	....	....	....	....	....	....	....	....	....	....	5	5	2	7	6	....	....	....
1968-69	London Nationals	OHA	53	34	65	99	....	....	....	90	....	....	....	....	....	....	....	....	....	....	6	2	5	7	11	....	....	....
1969-70	London Nationals	OHA	54	42	48	90	....	....	....	126	....	....	....	....	....	....	....	....	....	....	....	....	....	....	....	....	....	....
1970-71	**Toronto Maple Leafs**	**NHL**	**49**	**10**	**8**	**18**	**10**	**7**	**17**	**37**	**3**	**0**	**3**	**131**	**7.6**	**31**	**7**	**23**	**2**	**+3**	**6**	**2**	**1**	**3**	**31**	**1**	**0**	**0**
1971-72	**Toronto Maple Leafs**	**NHL**	**74**	**15**	**17**	**32**	**16**	**15**	**31**	**44**	**1**	**0**	**4**	**174**	**8.6**	**46**	**5**	**48**	**3**	**–4**	**3**	**0**	**0**	**0**	**2**	**0**	**0**	**0**
1972-73	**Toronto Maple Leafs**	**NHL**	**78**	**29**	**48**	**77**	**29**	**40**	**69**	**69**	**8**	**0**	**1**	**331**	**8.8**	**102**	**26**	**102**	**15**	**–11**	....	....	....	....	....	....	....	....
1973-74	**Toronto Maple Leafs**	**NHL**	**78**	**38**	**46**	**84**	**39**	**40**	**79**	**55**	**11**	**0**	**6**	**270**	**14.1**	**112**	**28**	**72**	**0**	**+12**	**4**	**2**	**1**	**3**	**6**	**1**	**0**	**0**
1974-75	**Toronto Maple Leafs**	**NHL**	**72**	**36**	**44**	**80**	**33**	**35**	**68**	**47**	**12**	**1**	**2**	**273**	**13.2**	**107**	**39**	**93**	**15**	**–10**	**7**	**2**	**1**	**3**	**15**	**1**	**0**	**0**
1975-76	**Toronto Maple Leafs**	**NHL**	**79**	**41**	**59**	**100**	**38**	**47**	**85**	**90**	**11**	**1**	**2**	**346**	**11.8**	**129**	**35**	**111**	**29**	**+12**	**10**	**5**	**7**	**12**	**19**	**2**	**0**	**1**
1976-77	Canada	C Cup	7	4	2	6	....	....	....	4	....	....	....	....	....	....	....	....	....	....	....	....	....	....	....	....	....	....
	Toronto Maple Leafs	**NHL**	**73**	**38**	**52**	**90**	**36**	**42**	**78**	**89**	**12**	**1**	**5**	**307**	**12.4**	**124**	**42**	**92**	**18**	**+8**	**9**	**5**	**16**	**21**	**4**	**3**	**0**	**0**
1977-78	**Toronto Maple Leafs**	**NHL**	**80**	**45**	**72**	**117**	**44**	**59**	**103**	**100**	**14**	**0**	**8**	**311**	**14.5**	**141**	**41**	**69**	**3**	**+34**	**13**	**3**	**8**	**11**	**12**	**2**	**0**	**0**
1978-79	**Toronto Maple Leafs**	**NHL**	**70**	**36**	**51**	**87**	**33**	**39**	**72**	**69**	**12**	**0**	**4**	**290**	**12.4**	**122**	**41**	**80**	**8**	**+9**	**6**	**5**	**4**	**9**	**17**	**2**	**0**	**0**
	NHL All-Stars	Chal Cup	3	0	1	1	....	....	....	0	....	....	....	....	....	....	....	....	....	....	....	....	....	....	....	....	....	....
1979-80	**Toronto Maple Leafs**	**NHL**	**73**	**40**	**57**	**97**	**36**	**44**	**80**	**62**	**17**	**1**	**5**	**315**	**12.7**	**130**	**43**	**97**	**13**	**+3**	**3**	**1**	**2**	**3**	**10**	**1**	**0**	**0**
1980-81	**Toronto Maple Leafs**	**NHL**	**80**	**43**	**53**	**96**	**36**	**37**	**73**	**77**	**14**	**2**	**2**	**267**	**16.1**	**142**	**52**	**120**	**22**	**–8**	**3**	**0**	**0**	**0**	**4**	**0**	**0**	**0**
1981-82	**Toronto Maple Leafs**	**NHL**	**38**	**18**	**20**	**38**	**14**	**13**	**27**	**24**	**5**	**2**	**0**	**127**	**14.2**	**52**	**19**	**59**	**12**	**–14**	....	....	....	....	....	....	....	....
	Philadelphia Flyers	**NHL**	**35**	**14**	**18**	**32**	**11**	**12**	**23**	**50**	**5**	**1**	**2**	**114**	**12.3**	**44**	**9**	**59**	**23**	**–1**	**4**	**3**	**1**	**4**	**6**	**1**	**0**	**0**
	Canada	WEC-A	10	4	3	7	....	....	....	2	....	....	....	....	....	....	....	....	....	....	....	....	....	....	....	....	....	....
1982-83	**Philadelphia Flyers**	**NHL**	**80**	**43**	**40**	**83**	**35**	**28**	**63**	**60**	**10**	**0**	**8**	**231**	**18.6**	**111**	**30**	**66**	**2**	**+17**	**3**	**1**	**0**	**1**	**4**	**0**	**0**	**0**
	Canada	WEC-A	10	3	1	4	....	....	....	12	....	....	....	....	....	....	....	....	....	....	....	....	....	....	....	....	....	....
1983-84	**Philadelphia Flyers**	**NHL**	**76**	**27**	**36**	**63**	**22**	**24**	**46**	**38**	**11**	**1**	**3**	**212**	**12.7**	**90**	**26**	**64**	**13**	**+13**	**3**	**0**	**2**	**2**	**7**	**0**	**0**	**0**
1984-85	**Detroit Red Wings**	**NHL**	**61**	**11**	**16**	**27**	**9**	**11**	**20**	**37**	**4**	**0**	**2**	**113**	**9.7**	**49**	**11**	**57**	**9**	**–10**	**2**	**0**	**2**	**2**	**0**	**0**	**0**	**0**
	NHL Totals		**1096**	**484**	**637**	**1121**	**441**	**493**	**934**	**948**	**150**	**10**	**57**	**3812**	**12.7**	**1532**	**454**	**1212**	**187**		**76**	**29**	**45**	**74**	**137**	**14**	**0**	**1**

OHA Second All-Star Team (1969) • Canada Cup All-Star Team (1976) • NHL Second All-Star Team (1978)

Played in NHL All-Star Game (1975, 1978, 1980, 1983)

Traded to **Philadelphia** by **Toronto** for Rich Costello, Hartford's 2nd round choice (previously acquired, Toronto selected Peter Ihnacek) in 1982 Entry Draft and future considerations (Ken Strong), January 20, 1982. Traded to **Detroit** by **Philadelphia** for Murray Craven and Joe Paterson, October 10, 1984.

• SJOBERG, LARS-ERIK

Lars-Erik Sjoberg D – L. 5'8", 179 lbs. b: Falun, Sweden, 4/5/1944. Deceased.

Season	Club	League	GP	G	A	Pts	AG	AA	APts	PIM	PP	SH	GW	S	%	TGF	PGF	TGA	PGA	+/–	GP	G	A	Pts	PIM	PP	SH	GW
1967-68	Sweden	Olympics	7	0	0	0	....	....	....	4	....	....	....	....	....	....	....	....	....	....	....	....	....	....	....	....	....	....
1968-69	Sweden	WEC-A	9	3	2	5	....	....	....	2	....	....	....	....	....	....	....	....	....	....	....	....	....	....	....	....	....	....
1969-70	Vastra Frolunda	Sweden	14	2	1	3	....	....	....	10	....	....	....	....	....	....	....	....	....	....	....	....	....	....	....	....	....	....
	Sweden	WEC-A	10	1	1	2	....	....	....	0	....	....	....	....	....	....	....	....	....	....	....	....	....	....	....	....	....	....
1970-71	Vastra Frolunda	Sweden	13	8	4	12	....	....	....	6	....	....	....	....	....	....	....	....	....	....	....	....	....	....	....	....	....	....

Season	Club	League	GP	G	A	Pts	AG	AA	APts	PIM	PP	SH	GW	S	%	TGF	PGF	TGA	PGA	+/-	GP	G	A	Pts	PIM	PP	SH	GW
1971-72	Vastra Frolunda	Sweden	27	4	11	15				4																		
	Sweden	Olympics	6	1	1	2				2																		
	Sweden	WEC-A	10	1	1	2				0																		
1972-73	Vastra Frolunda	Sweden	14	1	6	7				0																		
	Sweden	WEC-A	10	1	2	3				2																		
1973-74	Vastra Frolunda	Sweden	41	4	35	39				21																		
	Sweden	WEC-A	9	1	0	1				2																		
1974-75	Winnipeg Jets	WHA	75	7	53	60				30																		
1975-76	Winnipeg Jets	WHA	81	5	36	41				12												13	0	5	5	12			
1976-77	Sweden	C Cup	5	0	3	3				6																		
	Winnipeg Jets	WHA	52	2	38	40				31												20	0	6	6	22			
1977-78	Winnipeg Jets	WHA	78	11	39	50				72												9	0	9	9	4			
1978-79	Winnipeg Jets	WHA	9	0	3	3				6												10	1	2	3	4			
1979-80	**Winnipeg Jets**	**NHL**	79	7	27	34	6	21	27	48	3	1	0	145	4.8	87	21	137	36	-35								
	NHL Totals		79	7	27	34	6	21	27	48	3	1	0	145	4.8	87	21	137	36									
	Other Major League Totals		295	25	169	194				147											52	1	22	23	42			

Swedish Player of the Year (1969) • WEC-A All-Star Team (1974) • Named Best Defenseman at WEC-A (1974) • WHA First All-Star Team (1978) • Won Dennis A. Murphy Trophy (WHA Top Defenseman) (1978)

Signed as a free agent by **Winnipeg** (WHA), May 23, 1974. Rights retained by **Winnipeg** prior to Expansion Draft, June 9, 1979.

● SJODIN, TOMMY
Tommy Sjodin D – R. 5'11", 190 lbs. b: Timra, Sweden, 8/13/1965. Minnesota's 10th choice, 237th overall, in 1985 Entry Draft.

Season	Club	League	GP	G	A	Pts	AG	AA	APts	PIM	PP	SH	GW	S	%	TGF	PGF	TGA	PGA	+/-	GP	G	A	Pts	PIM	PP	SH	GW
1983-84	Timra	Sweden 2	16	4	4	8				6											6	0			4			
1984-85	Timra	Sweden 2	23	8	11	19				14																		
1985-86	Timra	Sweden 2	32	13	12	25				40																		
1986-87	Brynas IF Gavle	Sweden	29	0	4	4				24																		
1987-88	Brynas IF Gavle	Sweden	40	6	9	15				28																		
1988-89	Brynas IF Gavle	Sweden	40	8	11	19				52											5	1	0	1	6			
1989-90	Brynas IF Gavle	Sweden	40	14	14	28				46											5	0	0	0	2			
1990-91	Brynas IF Gavle	Sweden	38	12	17	29				77											2	0	1	1	2			
1991-92	Brynas IF Gavle	Sweden	40	6	16	22				46											5	0	3	3	4			
	Sweden	Olympics	8	4	1	5				2																		
	Sweden	WC-A	8	3	0	1				6																		
1992-93	**Minnesota North Stars**	**NHL**	77	7	29	36	6	20	26	30	5	0	1	175	4.0	90	70	45	0	-25								
1993-94	**Dallas Stars**	**NHL**	7	0	2	2	0	2	2	4	0	0	0	8	0.0	6	4	3	0	-1								
	Kalamazoo Wings	IHL	38	12	32	44				22																		
	Quebec Nordiques	**NHL**	22	1	9	10	1	7	8	18	1	0	0	46	2.2	26	10	11	0	+5								
	Sweden	WC-A	8	0	0	0				6																		
1994-95	HC Lugano	Switz.	36	17	27	44				36											5	3	2	5	2			
	Sweden	WC-A	8	2	3	5				6																		
1995-96	HC Lugano	Switz.	30	3	21	24				26											4	2	2	4	2			
	Sweden	WC-A	6	1	1	2				0																		
1996-97	HC Bolzano	Italy	6	2	2	4				0																		
	HC Lugano	Switz.	45	23	28	51				55											8	2	4	6	2			
1997-98	HC Lugano	Switz.	20	12	10	31				36											7	4	1	5	0			
	NHL Totals		106	8	40	48	7	29	36	52	6	0	1	229	3.5	122	84	59	0									

Swedish World All-Star Team (1992, 1995) • Swedish Player of the Year (1992) • WC-A All-Star Team (1995)

Transferred to **Dallas** after **Minnesota** franchise relocated, June 9, 1993. Traded to **Quebec** by **Dallas** with Dallas' 3rd round choice (Chris Drury) in 1994 Entry Draft for rights to Emanuel Fernandez, February 13, 1994.

● SKAARE, BJORNE
Bjorne Skaare C L. 6', 180 lbs. b: Oslo, Norway, 10/29/1958. Deceased. Detroit's 6th choice, 62nd overall, in 1978 Amateur Draft.

Season	Club	League	GP	G	A	Pts	AG	AA	APts	PIM	PP	SH	GW	S	%	TGF	PGF	TGA	PGA	+/-	GP	G	A	Pts	PIM	PP	SH	GW
1976-77	Farjestad BK Karlstad	Swe-Jr.	40	21	20	41				8																		
	Farjestad BK Karlstad	Sweden	9	1	0	1				2																		
1977-78	Ottawa 67's	OHA	38	12	30	42				72																		
1978-79	**Detroit Red Wings**	**NHL**	1	0	0	0	0	0	0	0	0	0	0	1	0.0	0	0	0	0	0								
	Kansas City Red Wings	CHL	37	8	26	34				18																		
1979-80	Furuset IF	Norway 2			STATISTICS	NOT	AVAILABLE																					
1980-81	Furuset IF	Norway	33	*38	*34	*72				49																		
1981-82	Kac-Sparkasse	Austria		27	31	58																						
1982-83	Kac-Sparkasse	Austria 2			STATISTICS	NOT	AVAILABLE																					
1983-84	Tulsa Oilers	CHL	2	1	1	2				5											9	2	7	9	2			
1984-85	Furuset Oslo	Norway	35	32	35	67				35																		
	NHL Totals		1	0	0	0	0	0	0	0	0	0	0	1	0.0	0	0	0	0	0								

● SKALDE, JARROD
Jarrod Skalde C L. 6', 175 lbs. b: Niagara Falls, Ont., 2/26/1971. New Jersey's 3rd choice, 26th overall, in 1989 Entry Draft.

Season	Club	League	GP	G	A	Pts	AG	AA	APts	PIM	PP	SH	GW	S	%	TGF	PGF	TGA	PGA	+/-	GP	G	A	Pts	PIM	PP	SH	GW
1987-88	Oshawa Generals	OHL	60	12	16	28				24											7	2	1	3	2			
1988-89	Oshawa Generals	OHL	65	38	38	76				36											6	1	5	6	2			
1989-90	Oshawa Generals	OHL	62	40	52	92				66											17	10	7	17	6			
1990-91	Oshawa 67's	OHL	15	8	14	22				14																		
	Belleville Bulls	OHL	40	30	52	82				21											6	9	6	15	10			
	New Jersey Devils	**NHL**	1	0	1	1	0	1	1	0	0	0	0	1	0.0	1	0	1	0	0								
	Utica Devils	AHL	3	3	2	5				0																		
1991-92	**New Jersey Devils**	**NHL**	15	2	4	6	2	3	5	4	0	0	2	25	8.0	8	0	9	0	-1								
	Utica Devils	AHL	62	20	20	40				56											4	3	1	4	8			
1992-93	**New Jersey Devils**	**NHL**	11	0	2	2	0	1	1	4	0	0	0	4	0.0			15	8	-3								
	Utica Devils	AHL	59	21	39	60				76											5	0	2	2	19			
	Cincinnati Cyclones	IHL	4	1	2	3				4																		
1993-94	**Anaheim Mighty Ducks**	**NHL**	20	5	4	9	5	3	8	10	2	0	2	25	20.0	17	6	14	0	-3								
	San Diego Gulls	IHL	57	25	38	63				79											9	3	12	15	10			
1994-95	Las Vegas Thunder	IHL	74	34	41	75				103											9	2	4	6	8			
1995-96	Baltimore Bandits	AHL	11	2	6	8				55																		
	Calgary Flames	**NHL**	1	0	0	0	0	0	0	0	0	0	0	0	0.0	0	0	0	0	0								
	Saint John Flames	AHL	68	27	40	67				98											16	4	9	13	6			
1996-97	Saint John Flames	AHL	65	32	36	68				94											3	0	0	0	14			
1997-98	**San Jose Sharks**	**NHL**	22	4	6	10	5	6	11	14	0	0	0	30	13.3	15	2	15	0	-2								
	Kentucky Thoroughblades	AHL	6	2	6	8				10																		
	Chicago Blackhawks	**NHL**	4	0	1	1	0	1	1	2	0	0	0	4	0.0				0									
	Indianapolis Ice	IHL	2	0	2	2				0																		
	Dallas Stars	**NHL**	1	0	0	0	0	0	0	0	0	0	0	0	0.0	0	0	0	0	0								
	Chicago Blackhawks	**NHL**	3	0	0	0	0	0	0	0	0	0	0	0	0.0				0									
	Kentucky Thoroughblades	AHL	17	3	9	12				38											3	3	0	3	6			
	NHL Totals		78	11	18	29	12	15	27	36	2	0	4	97	11.3	45	8	54	8									

OHL Second All-Star Team (1991)

Claimed by **Anaheim** from **New Jersey** in Expansion Draft, June 24, 1993. Signed as a free agent by **Anaheim**, May 31, 1995. Traded to **Calgary** by **Anaheim** for Bobby Marshall, October 30, 1995. Signed as a free agent by **San Jose**, August 14, 1997. Claimed on waivers by **Chicago** from **San Jose**, January 8, 1998. Claimed on waivers by **San Jose** from **Chicago**, January 23, 1998. Claimed on waivers by **Dallas** from **San Jose**, January 27, 1998. Claimed on waivers by **Chicago** from **Dallas**, February 10, 1998. Claimed on waivers by **San Jose** from **Chicago**, March 6, 1998.

● SKARDA, RANDY
Randy Skarda D – R. 6'1", 205 lbs. b: St. Paul, MN, 5/5/1968. St. Louis' 8th choice, 157th overall, in 1986 Entry Draft.

Season	Club	League	GP	G	A	Pts	PIM
1984-85	St. Thomas Academy	H.S.	23	14	42	56	
1985-86	St. Thomas Academy	H.S.	23	15	27	42	
1986-87	University of Minnesota	WCHA	43	3	10	13	77

			REGULAR SEASON																		PLAYOFFS							
Season	**Club**	**League**	**GP**	**G**	**A**	**Pts**	**AG**	**AA**	**APts**	**PIM**	**PP**	**SH**	**GW**	**S**	**%**	**TGF**	**PGF**	**TGA**	**PGA**	**+/–**	**GP**	**G**	**A**	**Pts**	**PIM**	**PP**	**SH**	**GW**
1987-88	University of Minnesota	WCHA	42	19	26	45	....	....	....	102	....	....	....	....	....	....	....	....	....	....	....	....	....	....	....	....	....	....
	United States	WJC-A	6	1	2	3	....	....	....	26	....	....	....	....	....	....	....	....	....	....	....	....	....	....	....	....	....	....
1988-89	University of Minnesota	WCHA	43	6	24	30	....	....	....	91	....	....	....	....	....	....	....	....	....	....	....	....	....	....	....	....	....	....
1989-90	**St. Louis Blues**	**NHL**	**25**	**0**	**5**	**5**	**0**	**4**	**4**	**11**	**0**	**0**	**0**	**8**	**0.0**	**20**	**1**	**17**	**0**	**+2**	....	....	....	....	....	....	....	....
	Peoria Rivermen	IHL	38	7	17	24	....	....	....	40	....	....	....	....	....	....	....	....	....	....	4	0	0	0	0	....	....	....
1990-91	Peoria Rivermen	IHL	78	8	34	42	....	....	....	126	....	....	....	....	....	....	....	....	....	....	19	3	5	8	22	....	....	....
1991-92	**St. Louis Blues**	**NHL**	**1**	**0**	**0**	**0**	**0**	**0**	**0**	**0**	**0**	**0**	**0**	**0**	**0.0**	**0**	**0**	**0**	**0**	**0**	....	....	....	....	....	....	....	....
	Peoria Rivermen	IHL	57	8	24	32	....	....	....	64	....	....	....	....	....	....	....	....	....	....	7	0	0	0	14	....	....	....
1992-93	Milwaukee Admirals	IHL	54	3	9	12	....	....	....	104	....	....	....	....	....	....	....	....	....	....	....	....	....	....	....	....	....	....
1993-94	P.E.I. Senators	AHL	20	1	3	4	....	....	....	14	....	....	....	....	....	....	....	....	....	....	....	....	....	....	....	....	....	....
	Hershey Bears	AHL	4	0	2	2	....	....	....	0	....	....	....	....	....	....	....	....	....	....	....	....	....	....	....	....	....	....
	Johnstown Chiefs	ECHL	9	1	6	7	....	....	....	6	....	....	....	....	....	....	....	....	....	....	....	....	....	....	....	....	....	....
	NHL Totals		**26**	**0**	**5**	**5**	**0**	**4**	**4**	**11**	**0**	**0**	**0**	**8**	**0.0**	**20**	**1**	**17**	**0**		....	....	....	....	....	....	....	....

WCHA First All-Star Team (1988)

NCAA West Second All-American Team (1988) • WCHA First All-Star Team (1988)

• SKINNER, LARRY

Larry Skinner C – L. 5′11″, 180 lbs. b: Vancouver, B.C., 4/21/1956. Kansas City's 4th choice, 92nd overall, in 1976 Amateur Draft.

Season	**Club**	**League**	**GP**	**G**	**A**	**Pts**	**AG**	**AA**	**APts**	**PIM**	**PP**	**SH**	**GW**	**S**	**%**	**TGF**	**PGF**	**TGA**	**PGA**	**+/–**	**GP**	**G**	**A**	**Pts**	**PIM**	**PP**	**SH**	**GW**
1972-73	Nepean Raiders	OJHL	....	13	35	58	....	....	....	15	....	....	....	....	....	....	....	....	....	....	....	....	....	....	....	....	....	....
1973-74	Winnipeg Monarchs	MJHL	STATISTICS NOT AVAILABLE																									
1974-75	Winnipeg Jets	WCJHL	70	33	62	95	....	....	....	17	....	....	....	....	....	....	....	....	....	....	....	....	....	....	....	....	....	....
1975-76	Ottawa 67's	OHA	58	37	78	115	....	....	....	8	....	....	....	....	....	....	....	....	....	....	12	8	8	16	8	....	....	....
1976-77	**Colorado Rockies**	**NHL**	**19**	**4**	**5**	**9**	**4**	**4**	**8**	**6**	**3**	**0**	**0**	**40**	**10.0**	**11**	**7**	**21**	**4**	**–13**	....	....	....	....	....	....	....	....
	Rhode Island Reds	AHL	46	22	34	56	....	....	....	11	....	....	....	....	....	....	....	....	....	....	....	....	....	....	....	....	....	....
1977-78	**Colorado Rockies**	**NHL**	**14**	**3**	**5**	**8**	**3**	**4**	**7**	**0**	**1**	**0**	**0**	**28**	**10.7**	**12**	**2**	**8**	**0**	**+2**	**2**	**0**	**0**	**0**	**0**	**0**	**0**	**0**
	Phoenix Roadrunners	CHL	20	4	6	10	....	....	....	9	....	....	....	....	....	....	....	....	....	....	....	....	....	....	....	....	....	....
	Hampton Gulls	AHL	15	7	9	16	....	....	....	6	....	....	....	....	....	....	....	....	....	....	....	....	....	....	....	....	....	....
	Springfield Indians	AHL	14	1	5	6	....	....	....	2	....	....	....	....	....	....	....	....	....	....	....	....	....	....	....	....	....	....
1978-79	**Colorado Rockies**	**NHL**	**12**	**3**	**2**	**5**	**3**	**2**	**5**	**2**	**1**	**0**	**0**	**13**	**23.1**	**9**	**4**	**10**	**0**	**–5**	....	....	....	....	....	....	....	....
	Philadelphia Firebirds	AHL	67	34	33	67	....	....	....	34	....	....	....	....	....	....	....	....	....	....	....	....	....	....	....	....	....	....
1979-80	**Colorado Rockies**	**NHL**	**2**	**0**	**0**	**0**	**0**	**0**	**0**	**0**	**0**	**0**	**0**	**2**	**0.0**	**0**	**0**	**2**	**0**	**–2**	....	....	....	....	....	....	....	....
	Fort Worth Texans	CHL	10	5	7	12	....	....	....	8	....	....	....	....	....	....	....	....	....	....	....	....	....	....	....	....	....	....
	New Haven Nighthawks	AHL	63	18	53	71	....	....	....	38	....	....	....	....	....	....	....	....	....	....	10	5	10	15	0	....	....	....
1980-81	Springfield Indians	AHL	48	21	40	61	....	....	....	36	....	....	....	....	....	....	....	....	....	....	7	3	8	11	4	....	....	....
1981-82	Hershey Bears	AHL	18	5	14	19	....	....	....	2	....	....	....	....	....	....	....	....	....	....	5	2	7	9	0	....	....	....
	Innsbruck	Austria	....	21	28	49	....	....	....	....	....	....	....	....	....	....	....	....	....	....	....	....	....	....	....	....	....	....
1982-83	Hershey Bears	AHL	14	8	9	17	....	....	....	2	....	....	....	....	....	....	....	....	....	....	4	1	0	1	0	....	....	....
1983-84	Paris Volants	France	STATISTICS NOT AVAILABLE																									
1984-85	Paris Volants	France	25	*44	16	60	....	....	....	....	....	....	....	....	....	....	....	....	....	....	....	....	....	....	....	....	....	....
1985-86	Paris Volants	France	STATISTICS NOT AVAILABLE																									
1986-87	Paris Volants	France	25	50	35	85	....	....	....	....	....	....	....	....	....	....	....	....	....	....	....	....	....	....	....	....	....	....
1987-88	Paris Volants	France	25	30	23	53	....	....	....	38	....	....	....	....	....	....	....	....	....	....	....	....	....	....	....	....	....	....
	NHL Totals		**47**	**10**	**12**	**22**	**10**	**10**	**20**	**8**	**5**	**0**	**0**	**83**	**12.0**	**32**	**13**	**41**	**4**		**2**	**0**	**0**	**0**	**0**	**0**	**0**	**0**

Transferred to **Colorado** after **Kansas City** franchise relocated, July 15, 1977. Selected by **Colorado** as a fill-in during Expansion Draft, June 13, 1979. Traded to **New Haven** (AHL) by **Colorado** with Dennis Owchar for Bobby Sheehan, August, 1979.

• SKRIKO, PETRI

Petri Skriko LW – L. 5′10″, 175 lbs. b: Lappeenranta, Finland, 3/12/1962. Vancouver's 7th choice, 157th overall, in 1981 Entry Draft.

Season	**Club**	**League**	**GP**	**G**	**A**	**Pts**	**AG**	**AA**	**APts**	**PIM**	**PP**	**SH**	**GW**	**S**	**%**	**TGF**	**PGF**	**TGA**	**PGA**	**+/–**	**GP**	**G**	**A**	**Pts**	**PIM**	**PP**	**SH**	**GW**
1979-80	SaiPa Lappeenranta	Finland 2	36	25	20	45	....	....	....	8	....	....	....	....	....	....	....	....	....	....	....	....	....	....	....	....	....	....
1980-81	SaiPa Lappeenranta	Finland	36	20	13	33	....	....	....	14	....	....	....	....	....	....	....	....	....	....	....	....	....	....	....	....	....	....
	Finland	WJC-A	5	3	3	6	....	....	....	10	....	....	....	....	....	....	....	....	....	....	....	....	....	....	....	....	....	....
1981-82	SaiPa Lappeenranta	Finland	33	19	27	46	....	....	....	24	....	....	....	....	....	....	....	....	....	....	....	....	....	....	....	....	....	....
	Finland	WJC-A	7	8	7	15	....	....	....	4	....	....	....	....	....	....	....	....	....	....	....	....	....	....	....	....	....	....
1982-83	SaiPa Lappeenranta	Finland	36	23	12	35	....	....	....	12	....	....	....	....	....	....	....	....	....	....	....	....	....	....	....	....	....	....
	Finland	WEC-A	10	4	2	6	....	....	....	6	....	....	....	....	....	....	....	....	....	....	....	....	....	....	....	....	....	....
1983-84	SaiPa Lappeenranta	Finland	32	25	26	51	....	....	....	13	....	....	....	....	....	....	....	....	....	....	....	....	....	....	....	....	....	....
	Finland	Olympics	6	6	4	10	....	....	....	8	....	....	....	....	....	....	....	....	....	....	....	....	....	....	....	....	....	....
1984-85	**Vancouver Canucks**	**NHL**	**72**	**21**	**14**	**35**	**17**	**9**	**26**	**10**	**3**	**0**	**2**	**154**	**13.6**	**51**	**9**	**70**	**2**	**–26**	....	....	....	....	....	....	....	....
	Finland	WEC-A	10	2	2	4	....	....	....	0	....	....	....	....	....	....	....	....	....	....	....	....	....	....	....	....	....	....
1985-86	**Vancouver Canucks**	**NHL**	**80**	**38**	**40**	**78**	**30**	**27**	**57**	**34**	**12**	**1**	**2**	**192**	**19.8**	**117**	**44**	**121**	**31**	**–17**	**3**	**0**	**0**	**0**	**0**	**0**	**0**	**0**
1986-87	**Vancouver Canucks**	**NHL**	**76**	**33**	**41**	**74**	**29**	**30**	**59**	**44**	**10**	**6**	**4**	**224**	**14.7**	**108**	**35**	**100**	**23**	**–4**	....	....	....	....	....	....	....	....
	Finland	WEC-A	10	1	1	2	....	....	....	2	....	....	....	....	....	....	....	....	....	....	....	....	....	....	....	....	....	....
1987-88	Finland	C Cup	5	0	1	1	....	....	....	2	....	....	....	....	....	....	....	....	....	....	....	....	....	....	....	....	....	....
	Vancouver Canucks	**NHL**	**73**	**30**	**34**	**64**	**26**	**24**	**50**	**32**	**10**	**2**	**2**	**172**	**17.4**	**92**	**32**	**89**	**17**	**–12**	....	....	....	....	....	....	....	....
1988-89	**Vancouver Canucks**	**NHL**	**74**	**30**	**36**	**66**	**25**	**25**	**50**	**57**	**9**	**0**	**5**	**204**	**14.7**	**93**	**38**	**72**	**14**	**–3**	**7**	**1**	**5**	**6**	**0**	**0**	**0**	**0**
1989-90	**Vancouver Canucks**	**NHL**	**77**	**15**	**33**	**48**	**13**	**24**	**37**	**36**	**3**	**1**	**2**	**172**	**8.7**	**77**	**26**	**99**	**27**	**–21**	....	....	....	....	....	....	....	....
1990-91	**Vancouver Canucks**	**NHL**	**20**	**4**	**4**	**8**	**4**	**3**	**7**	**8**	**0**	**1**	**2**	**47**	**8.5**	**12**	**4**	**22**	**5**	**–9**	....	....	....	....	....	....	....	....
	Boston Bruins	**NHL**	**28**	**5**	**14**	**19**	**5**	**11**	**16**	**9**	**1**	**0**	**3**	**73**	**6.8**	**36**	**11**	**23**	**2**	**+4**	**18**	**4**	**4**	**8**	**4**	**3**	**0**	**0**
1991-92	Finland	C Cup	6	3	2	5	....	....	....	2	....	....	....	....	....	....	....	....	....	....	....	....	....	....	....	....	....	....
	Boston Bruins	**NHL**	**9**	**1**	**0**	**1**	**1**	**0**	**1**	**6**	**1**	**0**	**0**	**20**	**5.0**	**4**	**3**	**4**	**0**	**–3**	....	....	....	....	....	....	....	....
	Winnipeg Jets	**NHL**	**15**	**2**	**3**	**5**	**2**	**2**	**4**	**4**	**0**	**0**	**0**	**27**	**7.4**	**12**	**3**	**10**	**0**	**–1**	....	....	....	....	....	....	....	....
	Finland	Olympics	8	1	4	5	....	....	....	4	....	....	....	....	....	....	....	....	....	....	....	....	....	....	....	....	....	....
1992-93	**San Jose Sharks**	**NHL**	**17**	**4**	**3**	**7**	**3**	**2**	**5**	**6**	**2**	**1**	**0**	**35**	**11.4**	**9**	**4**	**17**	**4**	**–8**	....	....	....	....	....	....	....	....
	Kiekko-Espoo	Finland	18	5	4	9	....	....	....	8	....	....	....	....	....	....	....	....	....	....	....	....	....	....	....	....	....	....
	NHL Totals		**541**	**183**	**222**	**405**	**155**	**157**	**312**	**246**	**51**	**12**	**22**	**1320**	**13.9**	**611**	**209**	**627**	**125**		**28**	**5**	**9**	**14**	**4**	**3**	**0**	**0**

Finnish Rookie of the Year (1981) • WJC-A All-Star Team (1982) • Named Best Forward at WJC-A (1982) • Finnish First All-Star Team (1984)

Traded to **Boston** by **Vancouver** for Boston's 2nd round choice (Mike Peca) in 1992 Entry Draft, January 16, 1991. Traded to **Winnipeg** by **Boston** for Brent Ashton, October 29, 1991. Signed as a free agent by **San Jose**, August 27, 1992.

• SKRUDLAND, BRIAN

Brian Skrudland C – L. 6′, 195 lbs. b: Peace River, Alta., 7/31/1963.

Season	**Club**	**League**	**GP**	**G**	**A**	**Pts**	**AG**	**AA**	**APts**	**PIM**	**PP**	**SH**	**GW**	**S**	**%**	**TGF**	**PGF**	**TGA**	**PGA**	**+/–**	**GP**	**G**	**A**	**Pts**	**PIM**	**PP**	**SH**	**GW**
1980-81	Saskatoon Blades	WHL	66	15	27	42	....	....	....	97	....	....	....	....	....	....	....	....	....	....	....	....	....	....	....	....	....	....
1981-82	Saskatoon Blades	WHL	71	27	29	56	....	....	....	135	....	....	....	....	....	....	....	....	....	....	5	0	1	1	2	....	....	....
1982-83	Saskatoon Blades	WHL	71	35	59	94	....	....	....	42	....	....	....	....	....	....	....	....	....	....	6	1	3	4	19	....	....	....
1983-84	Nova Scotia Voyageurs	AHL	56	13	12	25	....	....	....	55	....	....	....	....	....	....	....	....	....	....	12	2	8	10	14	....	....	....
1984-85	Sherbrooke Canadiens	AHL	70	22	28	50	....	....	....	109	....	....	....	....	....	....	....	....	....	....	17	9	8	17	23	....	....	....
1985-86	**Montreal Canadiens**	**NHL**	**65**	**9**	**13**	**22**	**7**	**9**	**16**	**57**	**0**	**2**	**0**	**62**	**14.5**	**30**	**0**	**33**	**6**	**+3**	**20**	**2**	**4**	**6**	**76**	**0**	**0**	**1**
1986-87	**Montreal Canadiens**	**NHL**	**79**	**11**	**17**	**28**	**10**	**12**	**22**	**107**	**0**	**1**	**0**	**72**	**15.3**	**54**	**1**	**57**	**22**	**+18**	**14**	**1**	**5**	**6**	**29**	**0**	**0**	**0**
1987-88	**Montreal Canadiens**	**NHL**	**79**	**12**	**24**	**36**	**10**	**17**	**27**	**112**	**0**	**1**	**3**	**96**	**12.5**	**55**	**0**	**60**	**19**	**+14**	**11**	**1**	**5**	**6**	**24**	**0**	**0**	**0**
1988-89	**Montreal Canadiens**	**NHL**	**71**	**12**	**29**	**41**	**10**	**20**	**30**	**84**	**1**	**1**	**5**	**98**	**12.2**	**60**	**3**	**53**	**18**	**+22**	**21**	**3**	**7**	**10**	**40**	**0**	**0**	**0**
1989-90	**Montreal Canadiens**	**NHL**	**59**	**11**	**31**	**42**	**9**	**22**	**31**	**56**	**4**	**0**	**1**	**70**	**15.7**	**65**	**15**	**40**	**11**	**+21**	**11**	**3**	**5**	**8**	**30**	**0**	**0**	**1**
1990-91	Montreal Canadiens	FrTour	4	0	0	0	....	....	....	12	....	....	....	....	....	....	....	....	....	....	....	....	....	....	....	....	....	....
	Montreal Canadiens	**NHL**	**57**	**15**	**19**	**34**	**14**	**14**	**28**	**85**	**1**	**1**	**2**	**71**	**21.1**	**48**	**5**	**44**	**13**	**+12**	**13**	**3**	**10**	**13**	**42**	**1**	**0**	**0**
1991-92	**Montreal Canadiens**	**NHL**	**42**	**3**	**3**	**6**	**3**	**2**	**5**	**36**	**0**	**0**	**1**	**51**	**5.9**	**14**	**0**	**29**	**11**	**–4**	**11**	**1**	**1**	**2**	**20**	**0**	**0**	**0**
1992-93	**Montreal Canadiens**	**NHL**	**23**	**5**	**3**	**8**	**4**	**2**	**6**	**55**	**0**	**2**	**1**	**29**	**17.2**	**9**	**0**	**13**	**5**	**+1**	....	....	....	....	....	....	....	....
	Calgary Flames	**NHL**	**16**	**2**	**4**	**6**	**2**	**3**	**5**	**10**	**0**	**0**	**0**	**22**	**9.1**	**9**	**0**	**11**	**5**	**+3**	**6**	**0**	**3**	**3**	**12**	**0**	**0**	**0**
1993-94	**Florida Panthers**	**NHL**	**79**	**15**	**25**	**40**	**14**	**19**	**33**	**136**	**0**	**2**	**1**	**110**	**13.6**	**49**	**1**	**67**	**32**	**+13**	....	....	....	....	....	....	....	....
1994-95	**Florida Panthers**	**NHL**	**47**	**5**	**9**	**14**	**9**	**13**	**22**	**88**	**1**	**0**	**0**	**44**	**11.4**	**24**	**1**	**36**	**13**	**0**	....	....	....	....	....	....	....	....
1995-96	**Florida Panthers**	**NHL**	**79**	**7**	**20**	**27**	**7**	**16**	**23**	**129**	**0**	**1**	**1**	**90**	**7.8**	**47**	**1**	**65**	**25**	**+6**	**21**	**1**	**3**	**4**	**18**	**0**	**0**	**0**

			REGULAR SEASON																		PLAYOFFS							
Season	Club	League	GP	G	A	Pts	AG	AA	APts	PIM	PP	SH	GW	S	%	TGF	PGF	TGA	PGA	+/–	GP	G	A	Pts	PIM	PP	SH	GW
1996-97	Florida Panthers	NHL	51	5	13	18	5	11	16	48	0	0	2	57	8.8	22	0	33	15	+4	....	....	....	....	....	....	....	....
1997-98	New York Rangers	NHL	59	5	6	11	6	6	12	39	0	0	1	42	11.9	13	0	31	14	–4	....	....	....	....	....	....	....	....
	Dallas Stars	NHL	13	2	0	2	2	0	2	10	0	0	0	13	15.4	2	0	7	3	–2	17	0	1	1	16	0	0	0
	NHL Totals		819	119	216	335	112	166	278	1052	7	11	18	927	12.8	501	27	579	212		145	15	44	59	307	1	0	2

Won Jack A. Butterfield Trophy (Playoff MVP - AHL) (1985)

Signed as a free agent by **Montreal**, September 13, 1983. Traded to **Calgary** by **Montreal** for Gary Leeman, January 28, 1993. Claimed by **Florida** from **Calgary** in Expansion Draft, June 24, 1993. Signed as a free agent by **NY Rangers**, August 21, 1997. Traded to **Dallas** by **NY Rangers** with Mike Keane and NY Rangers' 6th round choice (Pavel Patera) in 1998 Entry Draft for Todd Harvey, Bob Errey and Dallas' 4th round choice (Boyd Kane) in 1998 Entry Draft, March 24, 1998.

• SLANEY, JOHN

John Slaney D – L. 6', 185 lbs. b: St. John's, Nfld., 2/7/1972. Washington's 1st choice, 9th overall, in 1990 Entry Draft.

Season	Club	League	GP	G	A	Pts	AG	AA	APts	PIM	PP	SH	GW	S	%	TGF	PGF	TGA	PGA	+/–	GP	G	A	Pts	PIM	PP	SH	GW
1988-89	Cornwall Royals	OHL	66	16	43	59	....	....	....	23	....	....	....	....	....	....	....	....	....	....	18	8	16	24	10	....	....	....
1989-90	Cornwall Royals	OHL	64	38	59	97	....	....	....	68	....	....	....	....	....	....	....	....	....	....	6	0	8	8	11	....	....	....
1990-91	Cornwall Royals	OHL	34	21	25	46	....	....	....	28	....	....	....	....	....	....	....	....	....	....	....	....	....	....	....	....	....	....
	Canada	WJC-A	7	1	2	3	....	....	....	6	....	....	....	....	....	....	....	....	....	....	....	....	....	....	....	....	....	....
1991-92	Cornwall Royals	OHL	34	19	41	60	....	....	....	43	....	....	....	....	....	....	....	....	....	....	6	3	8	11	0	....	....	....
	Canada	WJC-A	7	1	3	4	....	....	....	6	....	....	....	....	....	....	....	....	....	....	....	....	....	....	....	....	....	....
	Baltimore Skipjacks	AHL	6	2	4	6	....	....	....	0	....	....	....	....	....	....	....	....	....	....	....	....	....	....	....	....	....	....
1992-93	Baltimore Skipjacks	AHL	79	20	46	66	....	....	....	60	....	....	....	....	....	....	....	....	....	....	7	0	7	7	8	....	....	....
1993-94	Washington Capitals	NHL	47	7	9	16	7	7	14	27	3	0	1	70	10.0	43	8	36	4	+3	11	1	1	2	2	1	0	0
	Portland Pirates	AHL	29	14	13	27	....	....	....	17	....	....	....	....	....	....	....	....	....	....	....	....	....	....	....	....	....	....
1994-95	Washington Capitals	NHL	16	0	3	3	0	4	4	6	0	0	0	21	0.0	8	4	7	0	–3	....	....	....	....	....	....	....	....
	Portland Pirates	AHL	8	3	10	13	....	....	....	4	....	....	....	....	....	....	....	....	....	....	7	1	3	4	4	....	....	....
1995-96	Colorado Avalanche	NHL	7	0	3	3	0	2	2	4	0	0	0	12	0.0	9	2	6	1	+2	....	....	....	....	....	....	....	....
	Cornwall Aces	AHL	5	0	4	4	....	....	....	2	....	....	....	....	....	....	....	....	....	....	....	....	....	....	....	....	....	....
	Los Angeles Kings	NHL	31	6	11	17	6	9	15	10	3	1	0	63	9.5	45	16	26	2	+5	....	....	....	....	....	....	....	....
1996-97	Los Angeles Kings	NHL	32	3	11	14	3	10	13	4	1	0	1	60	5.0	35	10	38	3	–10	....	....	....	....	....	....	....	....
	Phoenix Roadrunners	IHL	35	9	25	34	....	....	....	8	....	....	....	....	....	....	....	....	....	....	....	....	....	....	....	....	....	....
1997-98	Phoenix Coyotes	NHL	55	3	14	17	4	14	18	24	1	0	1	74	4.1	46	15	42	8	–3	....	....	....	....	....	....	....	....
	Las Vegas Thunder	IHL	5	2	2	4	....	....	....	10	....	....	....	....	....	....	....	....	....	....	....	....	....	....	....	....	....	....
	NHL Totals		188	19	51	70	20	46	66	75	8	1	3	300	6.3	186	55	155	18		11	1	1	2	2	1	0	0

OHL First All-Star Team (1990) • Canadian Major Junior Defenseman of the Year (1990) • OHL Second All-Star Team (1991)

Traded to **Colorado** by **Washington** for Philadelphia's 3rd round choice (previously acquired, Washington selected Shawn McNeil) in 1996 Entry Draft, July 12, 1995. Traded to **LA Kings** by **Colorado** for Winnipeg's 6th round choice (previously acquired, Colorado selected Brian Willsie) in 1996 Entry Draft, December 28, 1995. Signed as a free agent by **Phoenix**, August 19, 1997. Claimed by **Nashville** from **Phoenix** in Expansion Draft, June 26, 1998.

• SLEGR, JIRI

Jiri Slegr D – L. 6'1", 205 lbs. b: Jihlava, Czech., 5/30/1971. Vancouver's 3rd choice, 23rd overall, in 1990 Entry Draft.

Season	Club	League	GP	G	A	Pts	AG	AA	APts	PIM	PP	SH	GW	S	%	TGF	PGF	TGA	PGA	+/–	GP	G	A	Pts	PIM	PP	SH	GW
1987-88	CHZ Litvinov	Czech.	4	1	1	2	....	....	....	0	....	....	....	....	....	....	....	....	....	....	....	....	....	....	....	....	....	....
1988-89	CHZ Litvinov	Czech.	8	0	0	0	....	....	....	4	....	....	....	....	....	....	....	....	....	....	....	....	....	....	....	....	....	....
1989-90	CHZ Litvinov	Czech.	51	4	15	19	....	....	....	....	....	....	....	....	....	....	....	....	....	....	....	....	....	....	....	....	....	....
	Czechoslovakia	WJC-A	7	3	4	7	....	....	....	18	....	....	....	....	....	....	....	....	....	....	....	....	....	....	....	....	....	....
1990-91	CHZ Litvinov	Czech.	47	11	36	47	....	....	....	26	....	....	....	....	....	....	....	....	....	....	....	....	....	....	....	....	....	....
	Czechoslovakia	WJC-A	7	0	0	0	....	....	....	14	....	....	....	....	....	....	....	....	....	....	....	....	....	....	....	....	....	....
	Czechoslovakia	WEC-A	9	2	1	3	....	....	....	32	....	....	....	....	....	....	....	....	....	....	....	....	....	....	....	....	....	....
1991-92	Czechoslovakia	C Cup	5	0	1	1	....	....	....	25	....	....	....	....	....	....	....	....	....	....	....	....	....	....	....	....	....	....
	Chemopetrol Litvinov	Czech.	42	9	23	32	....	....	....	38	....	....	....	....	....	....	....	....	....	....	....	....	....	....	....	....	....	....
	Czechoslovakia	Olympics	8	1	1	2	....	....	....	14	....	....	....	....	....	....	....	....	....	....	....	....	....	....	....	....	....	....
1992-93	Vancouver Canucks	NHL	41	4	22	26	3	16	18	109	2	0	0	89	4.5	61	16	43	14	+16	5	0	3	3	4	0	0	0
	Hamilton Canucks	AHL	21	4	14	18	....	....	....	42	....	....	....	....	....	....	....	....	....	....	....	....	....	....	....	....	....	....
1993-94	Vancouver Canucks	NHL	78	5	33	38	5	25	30	86	1	0	0	160	3.1	86	31	61	6	0	....	....	....	....	....	....	....	....
1994-95	Chemopetrol Litvinov	Czech.	11	3	10	13	....	....	....	80	....	....	....	....	....	....	....	....	....	....	....	....	....	....	....	....	....	....
	Vancouver Canucks	NHL	19	1	5	6	2	7	9	32	0	0	1	42	2.4	21	4	17	0	0	....	....	....	....	....	....	....	....
	Edmonton Oilers	NHL	12	1	5	6	2	7	9	14	1	0	0	27	3.7	12	4	17	4	–5	....	....	....	....	....	....	....	....
1995-96	Edmonton Oilers	NHL	57	4	13	17	4	11	15	74	0	1	1	91	4.4	50	8	56	13	–1	....	....	....	....	....	....	....	....
	Cape Breton Oilers	AHL	4	1	2	3	....	....	....	4	....	....	....	....	....	....	....	....	....	....	....	....	....	....	....	....	....	....
1996-97	Czech Republic	W Cup	3	0	0	0	....	....	....	6	....	....	....	....	....	....	....	....	....	....	....	....	....	....	....	....	....	....
	Chemopetrol Litvinov	Czech.	1	0	0	0	....	....	....	0	....	....	....	....	....	....	....	....	....	....	....	....	....	....	....	....	....	....
	Sodertalje SK	Sweden	30	4	14	18	....	....	....	62	....	....	....	....	....	....	....	....	....	....	....	....	....	....	....	....	....	....
	Czech Republic	WC-A	8	1	1	2	....	....	....	35	....	....	....	....	....	....	....	....	....	....	....	....	....	....	....	....	....	....
1997-98	Pittsburgh Penguins	NHL	73	5	12	17	6	12	18	109	1	1	0	131	3.8	62	9	53	10	+10	6	0	4	4	2	0	0	0
	Czech Republic	Olympics	6	1	0	1	....	....	....	8	....	....	....	....	....	....	....	....	....	....	....	....	....	....	....	....	....	....
	Czech Republic	WC-A	6	0	1	1	....	....	....	20	....	....	....	....	....	....	....	....	....	....	....	....	....	....	....	....	....	....
	NHL Totals		280	20	90	110	22	77	99	424	5	2	2	540	3.7	292	72	247	47		11	0	7	7	6	0	0	0

WJC-A All-Star Team (1990) • Named Best Defenseman at WJC-A (1991) • Czechoslovakian First All-Star Team (1991)

Traded to **Edmonton** by **Vancouver** for Roman Oksiuta, April 7, 1995. Traded to **Pittsburgh** by **Edmonton** for Pittsburgh's 3rd round choice (later traded to New Jersey — New Jersey selected Brian Gionta) in 1998 Entry Draft, August 12, 1997.

• SLEIGHER, LOUIS

Louis Sleigher RW – R. 5'11", 200 lbs. b: Nouvelle, Que., 10/23/1958. Montreal's 24th choice, 233rd overall, in 1978 Amateur Draft.

Season	Club	League	GP	G	A	Pts	AG	AA	APts	PIM	PP	SH	GW	S	%	TGF	PGF	TGA	PGA	+/–	GP	G	A	Pts	PIM	PP	SH	GW
1976-77	Chicoutimi Sagueneens	QMJHL	70	53	48	101	....	....	....	49	....	....	....	....	....	....	....	....	....	....	8	5	3	8	9	....	....	....
1977-78	Chicoutimi Sagueneens	QMJHL	71	65	54	119	....	....	....	125	....	....	....	....	....	....	....	....	....	....	....	....	....	....	....	....	....	....
1978-79	Birmingham Bulls	WHA	62	26	12	38	....	....	....	46	....	....	....	....	....	....	....	....	....	....	....	....	....	....	....	....	....	....
1979-80	Quebec Nordiques	NHL	2	0	1	1	0	1	1	0	0	0	0	0	0.0	1	0	0	0	+1	....	....	....	....	....	....	....	....
	Syracuse Firebirds	AHL	58	28	15	43	....	....	....	37	....	....	....	....	....	....	....	....	....	....	1	0	1	1	15	....	....	....
1980-81	Erie Blades	EHL	50	39	29	68	....	....	....	129	....	....	....	....	....	....	....	....	....	....	8	6	4	10	12	....	....	....
1981-82	Quebec Nordiques	NHL	8	0	0	0	0	0	0	0	0	0	0	3	0.0	1	0	4	1	–2	....	....	....	....	....	....	....	....
	Fredericton Express	AHL	59	32	34	66	....	....	....	37	....	....	....	....	....	....	....	....	....	....	....	....	....	....	....	....	....	....
1982-83	Quebec Nordiques	NHL	51	14	10	24	11	7	18	49	0	0	1	55	25.5	31	0	31	8	+8	4	0	0	0	4	0	0	0
	Fredericton Express	AHL	12	8	2	10	....	....	....	9	....	....	....	....	....	....	....	....	....	....	....	....	....	....	....	....	....	....
1983-84	Quebec Nordiques	NHL	44	15	19	34	12	13	25	32	3	1	1	74	20.3	56	8	25	0	+23	7	1	1	2	42	0	0	0
1984-85	Quebec Nordiques	NHL	6	1	2	3	1	1	2	0	0	0	1	12	8.3	3	0	4	0	–1	....	....	....	....	....	....	....	....
	Boston Bruins	NHL	70	12	19	31	10	13	23	45	0	0	2	102	11.8	41	1	44	2	–2	5	0	0	0	4	0	0	0
1985-86	Boston Bruins	NHL	13	4	2	6	3	1	4	20	0	0	1	18	22.2	7	2	9	0	–4	1	0	0	0	14	0	0	0
	NHL Totals		194	46	53	99	37	36	73	146	3	1	6	264	17.4	140	11	117	11		17	1	1	2	64	0	0	0
	Other Major League Totals		62	26	12	38	....	....	....	46	....	....	....	....	....	....	....	....	....	....	....	....	....	....	....	....	....	....

Signed as an underage free agent by **Birmingham** (WHA), September, 1978. Signed as a free agent by **Quebec**, September 11, 1980. Traded to **Boston** by **Quebec** for Luc Dufour and Boston's 4th round choice (Peter Massey) in 1985 Entry Draft, October 25, 1984.

• SLY, DARRYL

Darryl Sly D – R. 5'11", 185 lbs. b: Collingwood, Ont., 4/3/1939.

Season	Club	League	GP	G	A	Pts	AG	AA	APts	PIM	PP	SH	GW	S	%	TGF	PGF	TGA	PGA	+/–	GP	G	A	Pts	PIM	PP	SH	GW
1956-57	St. Michael's Majors	OHA	46	7	7	14	....	....	....	35	....	....	....	....	....	....	....	....	....	....	1	0	0	0	4	....	....	....
1957-58	St. Michael's Majors	OHA	62	10	20	30	....	....	....	61	....	....	....	....	....	....	....	....	....	....	9	2	4	6	12	....	....	....
1958-59	St. Michael's Majors	OHA	48	8	16	24	....	....	....	58	....	....	....	....	....	....	....	....	....	....	15	0	3	3	42	....	....	....
	Kitchener-Waterloo Dutchmen	OHA Sr.	1	0	0	0	....	....	....	0	....	....	....	....	....	....	....	....	....	....	....	....	....	....	....	....	....	....
1959-60	Kitchener-Waterloo Dutchmen	OHA Sr.	47	4	8	12	....	....	....	63	....	....	....	....	....	....	....	....	....	....	8	1	1	2	14	....	....	....
	Canada	Olympics	7	1	1	2	....	....	....	9	....	....	....	....	....	....	....	....	....	....	....	....	....	....	....	....	....	....
1960-61	Galt Terriers	OHA Sr.	....	5	9	14	....	....	....	12	....	....	....	....	....	....	....	....	....	....	15	7	8	15	24	....	....	....
	Trail Smoke Eaters	WIHL	13	7	12	19	....	....	....	....	....	....	....	....	....	....	....	....	....	....	....	....	....	....	....	....	....	....
	Canada	Nat-Team	18	12	6	18	....	....	....	*46	....	....	....	....	....	....	....	....	....	....	....	....	....	....	....	....	....	....
	Canada	WEC-A	7	4	2	6	....	....	....	6	....	....	....	....	....	....	....	....	....	....	....	....	....	....	....	....	....	....
	Rochester Americans	AHL	2	0	0	0	....	....	....	0	....	....	....	....	....	....	....	....	....	....	....	....	....	....	....	....	....	....
1961-62	Rochester Americans	AHL	70	8	16	24	....	....	....	50	....	....	....	....	....	....	....	....	....	....	2	0	0	0	0	....	....	....
1962-63	Rochester Americans	AHL	70	4	14	18	....	....	....	52	....	....	....	....	....	....	....	....	....	....	2	0	0	0	7	....	....	....

			REGULAR SEASON																		PLAYOFFS							
Season	Club	League	GP	G	A	Pts	AG	AA	APts	PIM	PP	SH	GW	S	%	TGF	PGF	TGA	PGA	+/–	GP	G	A	Pts	PIM	PP	SH	GW
1963-64	Rochester Americans	AHL	72	16	16	32	....	....	....	41	....	....	....	....	....	....	....	....	....	....	2	0	0	0	0	....	....	....
1964-65	Rochester Americans	AHL	72	3	18	21	....	....	....	56	....	....	....	....	....	....	....	....	....	....	10	1	2	3	8	....	....	....
1965-66	**Toronto Maple Leafs**	**NHL**	**2**	**0**	**0**	**0**	**0**	**0**	**0**	**0**	....	....	....	....	....	....	....	....	....	....	....	....	....	....	....	....	....	....
	Rochester Americans	AHL	67	5	15	20	....	....	....	49	....	....	....	....	....	....	....	....	....	....	12	2	2	4	12	....	....	....
1966-67	Rochester Americans	AHL	72	8	25	33	....	....	....	56	....	....	....	....	....	....	....	....	....	....	13	1	0	1	14	....	....	....
1967-68	**Toronto Maple Leafs**	**NHL**	**17**	**0**	**0**	**0**	**0**	**0**	**0**	**4**	**0**	**0**	**0**	**2**	**0.0**	**0**	**0**	**5**	**4**	**–1**	....	....	....	....	....	....	....	....
	Rochester Americans	AHL	52	3	22	25	....	....	....	36	....	....	....	....	....	....	....	....	....	....	11	1	6	7	12	....	....	....
1968-69	Vancouver Canucks	WHL	74	6	16	22	....	....	....	45	....	....	....	....	....	....	....	....	....	....	8	0	1	1	8	....	....	....
1969-70	**Minnesota North Stars**	**NHL**	**29**	**1**	**0**	**1**	**1**	**0**	**1**	**6**	**0**	**0**	**0**	**20**	**5.0**	**15**	**2**	**25**	**7**	**–5**	....	....	....	....	....	....	....	....
	Iowa Stars	CHL	10	0	8	8	....	....	....	2	....	....	....	....	....	....	....	....	....	....	11	1	8	9	8	....	....	....
1970-71	**Vancouver Canucks**	**NHL**	**31**	**0**	**2**	**2**	**0**	**2**	**2**	**10**	**0**	**0**	**0**	**13**	**0.0**	**12**	**2**	**22**	**11**	**–1**	....	....	....	....	....	....	....	....
	Rochester Americans	AHL	37	3	4	7	....	....	....	28	....	....	....	....	....	....	....	....	....	....	....	....	....	....	....	....	....	....
1971-72	Barrie Flyers	OHA Sr.	33	7	17	24	....	....	....	32	....	....	....	....	....	....	....	....	....	....	....	....	....	....	....	....	....	....
1972-73	Barrie Flyers	OHA Sr.	41	3	19	22	....	....	....	42	....	....	....	....	....	....	....	....	....	....	....	....	....	....	....	....	....	....
	Rochester Americans	AHL	1	1	2	3	....	....	....	0	....	....	....	....	....	....	....	....	....	....	....	....	....	....	....	....	....	....
1973-74	Barrie Flyers	OHA Sr.	31	3	12	15	....	....	....	15	....	....	....	....	....	....	....	....	....	....	....	....	....	....	....	....	....	....
	Rochester Americans	AHL	1	0	0	0	....	....	....	2	....	....	....	....	....	....	....	....	....	....	....	....	....	....	....	....	....	....
1974-75	Barrie Flyers	OHA Sr.	40	4	10	14	....	....	....	28	....	....	....	....	....	....	....	....	....	....	....	....	....	....	....	....	....	....
1975-76	Barrie Flyers	OHA Sr.	44	4	16	20	....	....	....	24	....	....	....	....	....	....	....	....	....	....	....	....	....	....	....	....	....	....
1976-77	Barrie Flyers	OHA Sr.	34	1	10	11	....	....	....	26	....	....	....	....	....	....	....	....	....	....	....	....	....	....	....	....	....	....
1977-78	Barrie Flyers	OHA Sr.	38	0	5	5	....	....	....	16	....	....	....	....	....	....	....	....	....	....	....	....	....	....	....	....	....	....
	NHL Totals		**79**	**1**	**2**	**3**	**1**	**2**	**3**	**20**	**0**	**0**	**0**	**35**	**2.9**	**27**	**4**	**52**	**22**		....	....	....	....	....	....	....	....

WEC-A All-Star Team (1961) • WHL Second All-Star Team (1969)

Traded to **Vancouver** (WHL) by **Toronto** for cash, October, 1968. Claimed by **Minnesota** from **Vancouver** (WHL) in Intra-League Draft, June 10, 1969. Claimed by **Vancouver** from **Minnesota** in Expansion Draft, June 10, 1970.

• SMAIL, DOUG

Doug Smail LW – L. 5'9", 175 lbs. b: Moose Jaw, Sask., 9/2/1957.

1977-78	University of North Dakota	WCHA	38	22	28	50	....	....	....	52	....	....	....	....	....	....	....	....	....	....	....	....	....	....	....	....	....	....
1978-79	University of North Dakota	WCHA	35	24	34	58	....	....	....	46	....	....	....	....	....	....	....	....	....	....	....	....	....	....	....	....	....	....
1979-80	University of North Dakota	WCHA	40	43	44	87	....	....	....	70	....	....	....	....	....	....	....	....	....	....	....	....	....	....	....	....	....	....
1980-81	**Winnipeg Jets**	**NHL**	**30**	**10**	**8**	**18**	**8**	**6**	**14**	**45**	**1**	**3**	**1**	**58**	**17.2**	**24**	**1**	**39**	**9**	**–7**	....	....	....	....	....	....	....	....
1981-82	**Winnipeg Jets**	**NHL**	**72**	**17**	**18**	**35**	**13**	**12**	**25**	**55**	**2**	**1**	**1**	**97**	**17.5**	**50**	**3**	**88**	**19**	**–22**	**4**	**0**	**0**	**0**	**0**	**0**	**0**	**0**
1982-83	**Winnipeg Jets**	**NHL**	**80**	**15**	**29**	**44**	**12**	**20**	**32**	**32**	**0**	**3**	**3**	**113**	**13.3**	**61**	**0**	**94**	**33**	**0**	**3**	**0**	**0**	**0**	**6**	**0**	**0**	**0**
1983-84	**Winnipeg Jets**	**NHL**	**66**	**20**	**17**	**37**	**16**	**12**	**28**	**62**	**1**	**4**	**2**	**122**	**16.4**	**49**	**2**	**69**	**17**	**–5**	**3**	**0**	**1**	**1**	**7**	**0**	**0**	**0**
1984-85	**Winnipeg Jets**	**NHL**	**80**	**31**	**35**	**66**	**25**	**24**	**49**	**45**	**0**	**3**	**5**	**154**	**20.1**	**94**	**8**	**101**	**27**	**+12**	**8**	**2**	**1**	**3**	**4**	**0**	**1**	**0**
1985-86	**Winnipeg Jets**	**NHL**	**73**	**16**	**26**	**42**	**13**	**17**	**30**	**32**	**1**	**3**	**4**	**150**	**10.7**	**61**	**5**	**97**	**31**	**–10**	**3**	**1**	**0**	**1**	**0**	**0**	**0**	**0**
1986-87	**Winnipeg Jets**	**NHL**	**78**	**25**	**18**	**43**	**22**	**13**	**35**	**36**	**0**	**2**	**4**	**132**	**18.9**	**66**	**2**	**66**	**20**	**+18**	**10**	**4**	**0**	**4**	**10**	**0**	**1**	**0**
1987-88	**Winnipeg Jets**	**NHL**	**71**	**15**	**16**	**31**	**13**	**11**	**24**	**34**	**0**	**3**	**5**	**110**	**13.6**	**43**	**0**	**70**	**32**	**+5**	**5**	**1**	**0**	**1**	**22**	**0**	**0**	**0**
1988-89	**Winnipeg Jets**	**NHL**	**47**	**14**	**15**	**29**	**12**	**11**	**23**	**52**	**0**	**2**	**0**	**68**	**20.6**	**42**	**0**	**44**	**14**	**+12**	....	....	....	....	....	....	....	....
1989-90	**Winnipeg Jets**	**NHL**	**79**	**25**	**24**	**49**	**22**	**17**	**39**	**63**	**1**	**1**	**6**	**165**	**15.2**	**78**	**7**	**72**	**16**	**+15**	**5**	**1**	**0**	**1**	**0**	**0**	**0**	**0**
1990-91	**Winnipeg Jets**	**NHL**	**15**	**1**	**2**	**3**	**1**	**2**	**3**	**10**	**0**	**0**	**0**	**18**	**5.6**	**4**	**1**	**13**	**4**	**–6**	....	....	....	....	....	....	....	....
	Minnesota North Stars	**NHL**	**57**	**7**	**13**	**20**	**6**	**10**	**16**	**38**	**0**	**2**	**0**	**89**	**7.9**	**25**	**0**	**39**	**12**	**–2**	**1**	**0**	**0**	**0**	**0**	**0**	**0**	**0**
1991-92	**Quebec Nordiques**	**NHL**	**46**	**10**	**18**	**28**	**9**	**14**	**23**	**47**	**0**	**1**	**1**	**72**	**13.9**	**35**	**3**	**63**	**20**	**–11**	....	....	....	....	....	....	....	....
1992-93	**Ottawa Senators**	**NHL**	**51**	**4**	**10**	**14**	**3**	**7**	**10**	**51**	**0**	**0**	**0**	**73**	**5.5**	**19**	**0**	**78**	**25**	**–34**	....	....	....	....	....	....	....	....
	San Diego Gulls	IHL	9	2	1	3	....	....	....	20	....	....	....	....	....	....	....	....	....	....	9	3	2	5	20	....	....	....
1993-94	Fife Flyers	Britain	41	62	80	142	....	....	....	66	....	....	....	....	....	....	....	....	....	....	7	9	9	18	8	....	....	....
1994-95	Cardiff Devils	Britain	3	2	5	7	....	....	....	2	....	....	....	....	....	....	....	....	....	....	....	....	....	....	....	....	....	....
	Fife Flyers	Britain	15	20	9	29	....	....	....	26	....	....	....	....	....	....	....	....	....	....	6	5	9	14	12	....	....	....
1995-96	Cardiff Devils	Britain	16	12	14	26	....	....	....	14	....	....	....	....	....	....	....	....	....	....	6	3	5	8	10	....	....	....
	NHL Totals		**845**	**210**	**249**	**459**	**175**	**176**	**351**	**602**	**6**	**28**	**32**	**1421**	**14.8**	**651**	**32**	**933**	**279**		**42**	**9**	**2**	**11**	**49**	**0**	**2**	**0**

NCAA Championship All-Tournament Team (1980) • NCAA Championship Tournament MVP (1980)

Played in NHL All-Star Game (1990)

Signed as a free agent by **Winnipeg**, May 22, 1980. Traded to **Minnesota** by **Winnipeg** for Don Barber, November 7, 1990. Signed as a free agent by **Quebec**, August 30, 1991. Signed as a free agent by **Ottawa**, August 30, 1992.

• SMEDSMO, DALE

Dale Smedsmo LW – L. 6'1", 195 lbs. b: Roseau, MN, 4/23/1951. Toronto's 7th choice, 93rd overall, in 1971 Amateur Draft.

1970-71	Bemidji State University	NCAA	24	16	5	21	....	....	....	52	....	....	....	....	....	....	....	....	....	....	....	....	....	....	....	....	....	....
1971-72	Bemidji State University	NCAA	STATISTICS NOT AVAILABLE																									
	Tulsa Oilers	CHL	6	0	2	2	....	....	....	0	....	....	....	....	....	....	....	....	....	....	....	....	....	....	....	....	....	....
1972-73	**Toronto Maple Leafs**	**NHL**	**4**	**0**	**0**	**0**	**0**	**0**	**0**	**0**	**0**	**0**	**0**	**2**	**0.0**	**0**	**0**	**0**	**0**	**0**	....	....	....	....	....	....	....	....
	Tulsa Oilers	CHL	64	12	18	30	....	....	....	185	....	....	....	....	....	....	....	....	....	....	....	....	....	....	....	....	....	....
1973-74	Tulsa Oilers	CHL	63	11	15	26	....	....	....	214	....	....	....	....	....	....	....	....	....	....	....	....	....	....	....	....	....	....
1974-75	Saginaw Gears	IHL	12	4	1	5	....	....	....	39	....	....	....	....	....	....	....	....	....	....	....	....	....	....	....	....	....	....
	Hampton Gulls	SHL	33	12	5	17	....	....	....	134	....	....	....	....	....	....	....	....	....	....	....	....	....	....	....	....	....	....
	Oklahoma City Blazers	CHL	20	3	3	6	....	....	....	51	....	....	....	....	....	....	....	....	....	....	5	0	0	0	14	....	....	....
1975-76	Cincinnati Stingers	WHA	66	8	14	22	....	....	....	187	....	....	....	....	....	....	....	....	....	....	....	....	....	....	....	....	....	....
1976-77	Hampton Gulls	SHL	14	1	7	8	....	....	....	47	....	....	....	....	....	....	....	....	....	....	....	....	....	....	....	....	....	....
	New England Whalers	WHA	15	2	0	2	....	....	....	54	....	....	....	....	....	....	....	....	....	....	....	....	....	....	....	....	....	....
	Rhode Island Reds	AHL	2	0	0	0	....	....	....	5	....	....	....	....	....	....	....	....	....	....	....	....	....	....	....	....	....	....
	Binghamton Dusters	NAHL	2	1	1	2	....	....	....	2	....	....	....	....	....	....	....	....	....	....	....	....	....	....	....	....	....	....
	Cincinnati Stingers	WHA	23	0	5	5	....	....	....	43	....	....	....	....	....	....	....	....	....	....	2	0	1	1	0	....	....	....
1977-78	Indianapolis Racers	WHA	6	0	3	3	....	....	....	7	....	....	....	....	....	....	....	....	....	....	....	....	....	....	....	....	....	....
	Long Beach Sharks-Rockets	PHL	40	16	32	48	....	....	....	*162	....	....	....	....	....	....	....	....	....	....	....	....	....	....	....	....	....	....
1978-79	Tucson Rustlers	PHL	55	15	24	39	....	....	....	*144	....	....	....	....	....	....	....	....	....	....	....	....	....	....	....	....	....	....
	Los Angeles Blades	PHL	2	0	0	0	....	....	....	*16	....	....	....	....	....	....	....	....	....	....	....	....	....	....	....	....	....	....
	NHL Totals		**4**	**0**	**0**	**0**	**0**	**0**	**0**	**0**	**0**	**0**	**0**	**2**	**0.0**	**0**	**0**	**0**	**0**		....	....	....	....	....	....	....	....
	Other Major League Totals		110	10	22	32	....	....	....	291	....	....	....	....	....	....	....	....	....		2	0	1	1	0	....	....	....

Selected by **Minnesota** (WHA) in 1972 WHA General Player Draft, February 12, 1972. WHA rights claimed on waivers by **Cincinnati** (WHA) from **Minnesota** (WHA), September, 1975. Traded to **New England** (WHA) by **Cincinnati** (WHA) for cash, November, 1976. Traded to **Cincinnati** (WHA) by **New England** (WHA) for future considerations, February, 1977. Signed as a free agent by **Indianapolis** (WHA), March, 1978.

• SMEHLIK, RICHARD

Richard Smehlik D – L. 6'3", 222 lbs. b: Ostrava, Czech., 1/23/1970. Buffalo's 3rd choice, 97th overall, in 1990 Entry Draft.

1988-89	TJ Vitkovice	Czech.	38	2	5	7	....	....	....	12	....	....	....	....	....	....	....	....	....	....	....	....	....	....	....	....	....	....
1989-90	TJ Vitkovice	Czech.	51	5	4	9	....	....	....	....	....	....	....	....	....	....	....	....	....	....	....	....	....	....	....	....	....	....
	Czechoslovakia	WJC-A	7	0	1	1	....	....	....	4	....	....	....	....	....	....	....	....	....	....	....	....	....	....	....	....	....	....
1990-91	Dukla Jihlava	Czech.	58	4	3	7	....	....	....	22	....	....	....	....	....	....	....	....	....	....	....	....	....	....	....	....	....	....
	Czechoslovakia	WEC-A	8	1	2	3	....	....	....	8	....	....	....	....	....	....	....	....	....	....	....	....	....	....	....	....	....	....
1991-92	Czechoslovakia	C Cup	5	0	1	1	....	....	....	2	....	....	....	....	....	....	....	....	....	....	....	....	....	....	....	....	....	....
	TJ Vitkovice	Czech.	47	9	10	19	....	....	....	42	....	....	....	....	....	....	....	....	....	....	....	....	....	....	....	....	....	....
	Czechoslovakia	Olympics	8	0	1	1	....	....	....	2	....	....	....	....	....	....	....	....	....	....	....	....	....	....	....	....	....	....
	Czechoslovakia	WC-A	8	0	0	0	....	....	....	4	....	....	....	....	....	....	....	....	....	....	....	....	....	....	....	....	....	....
1992-93	**Buffalo Sabres**	**NHL**	**80**	**4**	**27**	**31**	**3**	**18**	**21**	**59**	**0**	**0**	**0**	**82**	**4.9**	**86**	**4**	**115**	**42**	**+9**	**8**	**0**	**4**	**4**	**2**	**0**	**0**	**0**
1993-94	**Buffalo Sabres**	**NHL**	**84**	**14**	**27**	**41**	**13**	**21**	**34**	**69**	**3**	**3**	**1**	**106**	**13.2**	**107**	**27**	**86**	**28**	**+22**	**7**	**0**	**2**	**2**	**10**	**0**	**0**	**0**
1994-95	TJ Vitkovice	Czech.	13	5	2	7	....	....	....	12	....	....	....	....	....	....	....	....	....	....	....	....	....	....	....	....	....	....
	Buffalo Sabres	**NHL**	**39**	**4**	**7**	**11**	**7**	**10**	**17**	**46**	**0**	**1**	**1**	**49**	**8.2**	**46**	**7**	**49**	**15**	**+5**	**5**	**0**	**0**	**0**	**2**	**0**	**0**	**0**
1995-96			DID NOT PLAY – INJURED																									

			REGULAR SEASON																		PLAYOFFS							
Season	Club	League	GP	G	A	Pts	AG	AA	APts	PIM	PP	SH	GW	S	%	TGF	PGF	TGA	PGA	+/–	GP	G	A	Pts	PIM	PP	SH	GW
1996-97	**Buffalo Sabres**	**NHL**	62	11	19	30	12	17	29	43	2	0	1	100	11.0	76	14	59	16	+19	12	0	2	2	4	0	0	0
1997-98	**Buffalo Sabres**	**NHL**	72	3	17	20	4	17	21	62	0	1	0	90	3.3	68	12	75	30	+11	15	0	2	2	6	0	0	0
	Czech Republic	Olympics	6	0	1	1	....	....	....	4	....	....	....	....	....	....	....	....	....	....	....	....	....	....	....	....	....	....
	NHL Totals		337	36	97	133	39	83	122	279	5	5	3	427	8.4	383	64	384	131		47	0	10	10	24	0	0	0

• Missed entire 1995-96 season after undergoing off-season knee surgery, August 11, 1995.

• SMITH, BARRY

Barry Smith C – L. 5′11″, 178 lbs. b: Surrey, B.C., 4/25/1955. Boston's 2nd choice, 32nd overall, in 1975 Amateur Draft.

1971-72	Vancouver Nats	WCJHL	41	9	15	24	....	....	....	39	....	....	....	....	....	....	....	....	....	....	....	....	....	....	....	....	....	....
1972-73	Vancouver Nats	WCJHL	30	5	6	11	....	....	....	13	....	....	....	....	....	....	....	....	....	....	....	....	....	....	....	....	....	....
	New Westminster Bruins	WCJHL	32	5	6	11	....	....	....	46	....	....	....	....	....	....	....	....	....	....	5	0	0	0	0	....	....	....
1973-74	New Westminster Briuns	WCJHL	65	8	10	18	....	....	....	61	....	....	....	....	....	....	....	....	....	....	11	2	1	3	12	....	....	....
1974-75	New Westminster Bruins	WCJHL	65	19	24	43	....	....	....	50	....	....	....	....	....	....	....	....	....	....	18	7	6	13	14	....	....	....
	Canada	WJC-A	....	1	2	3	....	....	....	....	....	....	....	....	....	....	....	....	....	....	....	....	....	....	....	....	....	....
1975-76	**Boston Bruins**	**NHL**	19	1	0	1	1	0	1	2	0	0	0	8	12.5	2	0	10	3	–5	....	....	....	....	....	....	....	....
	Rochester Americans	AHL	50	14	22	36	....	....	....	14	....	....	....	....	....	....	....	....	....	....	7	4	4	8	5	....	....	....
1976-77	Rochester Americans	AHL	79	9	13	22	....	....	....	16	....	....	....	....	....	....	....	....	....	....	12	3	2	5	4	....	....	....
1977-78	Rochester Americans	AHL	81	16	16	32	....	....	....	22	....	....	....	....	....	....	....	....	....	....	6	2	1	3	0	....	....	....
1978-79	Rochester Americans	AHL	80	23	43	66	....	....	....	46	....	....	....	....	....	....	....	....	....	....	....	....	....	....	....	....	....	....
1979-80	**Colorado Rockies**	**NHL**	33	2	3	5	2	2	4	4	0	1	0	21	9.5	8	0	33	14	–11	....	....	....	....	....	....	....	....
	Rochester Americans	AHL	35	3	7	10	....	....	....	14	....	....	....	....	....	....	....	....	....	....	....	....	....	....	....	....	....	....
	Birmingham Bulls	CHL	13	2	0	2	....	....	....	43	....	....	....	....	....	....	....	....	....	....	4	1	1	2	0	....	....	....
1980-81	**Colorado Rockies**	**NHL**	62	4	4	8	3	3	6	4	0	0	0	38	10.5	20	0	56	34	–2	....	....	....	....	....	....	....	....
	Fort Worth Texans	CHL	14	2	5	7	....	....	....	14	....	....	....	....	....	....	....	....	....	....	....	....	....	....	....	....	....	....
	NHL Totals		114	7	7	14	6	5	11	10	0	1	0	67	10.4	30	0	99	51		....	....	....	....	....	....	....	....

Memorial Cup All-Star Team (1975) • Won Stafford Smythe Memorial Trophy (Memorial Cup Tournament MVP) (1975)

Signed as a free agent by **Colorado**, September 14, 1979.

• SMITH, BOBBY

Bobby Smith C – L. 6′4″, 210 lbs. b: North Sydney, N.S., 2/12/1958. Minnesota's 10th choice, 1st overall, in 1978 Amateur Draft.

1975-76	Ottawa 67's	OHA	62	24	34	58	....	....	....	21	....	....	....	....	....	....	....	....	....	....	....	....	....	....	....	....	....	....
1976-77	Ottawa 67's	OHA	64	*65	70	135	....	....	....	52	....	....	....	....	....	....	....	....	....	....	19	16	16	32	29	....	....	....
1977-78	Ottawa 67's	OHA	61	69	*123	*192	....	....	....	44	....	....	....	....	....	....	....	....	....	....	16	15	15	30	10	....	....	....
	Canada	WJC-A	3	1	4	5	....	....	....	0	....	....	....	....	....	....	....	....	....	....	....	....	....	....	....	....	....	....
1978-79	**Minnesota North Stars**	**NHL**	80	30	44	74	27	34	61	39	9	0	4	244	12.3	92	30	71	1	–8	....	....	....	....	....	....	....	....
	Canada	WEC-A	8	5	3	8	....	....	....	0	....	....	....	....	....	....	....	....	....	....	....	....	....	....	....	....	....	....
1979-80	**Minnesota North Stars**	**NHL**	61	27	56	83	24	43	67	24	9	0	3	223	12.1	107	35	56	0	+16	15	1	13	14	9	1	0	0
1980-81	**Minnesota North Stars**	**NHL**	78	29	64	93	24	45	69	73	13	0	7	242	12.0	125	56	68	0	+1	19	8	17	25	13	2	0	0
1981-82	**Minnesota North Stars**	**NHL**	80	43	71	114	34	47	81	82	20	0	4	261	16.5	149	57	82	0	+10	4	2	4	6	5	0	0	0
	Canada	WEC-A	10	1	5	6	....	....	....	0	....	....	....	....	....	....	....	....	....	....	....	....	....	....	....	....	....	....
1982-83	**Minnesota North Stars**	**NHL**	77	24	53	77	20	37	57	81	12	0	3	190	12.6	107	50	78	1	–20	9	6	4	10	17	3	0	2
1983-84	**Minnesota North Stars**	**NHL**	10	3	6	9	2	4	6	9	1	0	0	21	14.3	12	5	9	1	–1	....	....	....	....	....	....	....	....
	Montreal Canadiens	**NHL**	70	26	37	63	21	25	46	62	6	1	3	179	14.5	88	30	69	4	–7	15	2	7	9	8	1	0	1
1984-85	**Montreal Canadiens**	**NHL**	65	16	40	56	13	27	40	59	8	0	1	146	11.0	72	37	45	1	–9	12	5	6	11	30	3	0	1
1985-86	**Montreal Canadiens**	**NHL**	79	31	55	86	25	37	62	55	5	0	7	202	15.3	121	40	77	6	+10	20	7	8	15	22	3	0	3
1986-87	**Montreal Canadiens**	**NHL**	80	28	47	75	24	34	58	72	11	0	7	197	14.2	117	48	63	0	+6	17	9	9	18	19	2	0	0
1987-88	**Montreal Canadiens**	**NHL**	78	27	66	93	23	47	70	78	8	0	4	198	13.6	119	47	62	3	+13	11	3	4	7	8	1	0	0
1988-89	**Montreal Canadiens**	**NHL**	80	32	51	83	27	36	63	69	6	0	3	195	16.4	115	46	44	0	+25	21	11	8	19	46	5	0	1
1989-90	**Montreal Canadiens**	**NHL**	53	12	14	26	10	10	20	35	4	0	2	102	11.8	40	10	34	0	–4	11	1	4	5	6	0	0	0
1990-91	Minnesota North Stars	Fr-Tour	3	0	1	1				0																		
	Minnesota North Stars	**NHL**	73	15	31	46	14	23	37	60	7	0	2	121	12.4	65	25	55	6	–9	23	8	8	16	56	2	0	5
1991-92	**Minnesota North Stars**	**NHL**	68	9	37	46	8	28	36	109	3	0	1	129	7.0	60	26	58	0	–24	7	1	4	5	6	1	0	0
1992-93	**Minnesota North Stars**	**NHL**	45	5	7	12	4	5	9	10	0	0	0	50	9.4	19	7	21	0	–9	....	....	....	....	....	....	....	....
	NHL Totals		1077	357	679	1036	300	482	782	917	125	1	51	2703	13.2	1408	549	892	23		184	64	96	160	245	24	0	13

OHA Second All-Star Team (1976, 1977) • Memorial Cup All-Star Team (1977) • Won George Parsons Trophy (Memorial Cup Tournament Most Sportsmanlike Player) (1977) • OHA First All-Star Team (1978) • Canadian Major Junior Player of the Year (1978) • Won Calder Memorial Trophy (1979)

Played in NHL All-Star Game (1981, 1982, 1989, 1991)

Traded to **Montreal** by **Minnesota** for Keith Acton, Mark Napier and Toronto's 3rd round choice (acquired earlier, Minnesota selected Ken Hodge Jr.) in 1984 Entry Draft, October 28, 1983. Traded to **Minnesota** by **Montreal** for Minnesota's 4th round choice (Louis Bernard) in 1992 Entry Draft, August 7, 1990.

• SMITH, BRAD

Brad "Motor City Smitty" Smith RW – R. 6′1″, 195 lbs. b: Windsor, Ont., 4/13/1958. Vancouver's 5th choice, 57th overall, in 1978 Amateur Draft.

1975-76	Windsor Spitfires	OHA	4	4	2	6	....	....	....	4	....	....	....	....	....	....	....	....	....	....	....	....	....	....	....	....	....	....
1976-77	Windsor Spitfires	OHA	66	37	53	90	....	....	....	154	....	....	....	....	....	....	....	....	....	....	9	4	10	14	20	....	....	....
1977-78	Windsor Spitfires	OHA	20	8	26	34	....	....	....	39	....	....	....	....	....	....	....	....	....	....	....	....	....	....	....	....	....	....
	Sudbury Wolves	OHA	46	21	21	42	....	....	....	183	....	....	....	....	....	....	....	....	....	....	....	....	....	....	....	....	....	....
	Kalamazoo Wings	IHL	....	....	....	....	....	....	....	....	....	....	....	....	....	....	....	....	....	....	3	0	1	1	15	....	....	....
1978-79	**Vancouver Canucks**	**NHL**	2	0	0	0	0	0	0	2	0	0	0	0	0.0	0	0	3	0	–3	....	....	....	....	....	....	....	....
	Dallas Black Hawks	CHL	60	17	18	35	....	....	....	143	....	....	....	....	....	....	....	....	....	....	9	1	3	4	22	....	....	....
1979-80	**Vancouver Canucks**	**NHL**	19	1	3	4	1	2	3	50	0	0	0	14	7.1	9	0	13	0	–4	....	....	....	....	....	....	....	....
	Atlanta Flames	**NHL**	4	0	0	0	0	0	0	4	0	0	0	0	0.0	2	0	1	0	+1	....	....	....	....	....	....	....	....
	Dallas Black Hawks	CHL	51	26	16	42	....	....	....	138	....	....	....	....	....	....	....	....	....	....	....	....	....	....	....	....	....	....
1980-81	**Calgary Flames**	**NHL**	45	7	4	11	6	3	9	65	1	0	1	51	13.7	16	2	22	0	–8	....	....	....	....	....	....	....	....
	Birmingham Bulls	CHL	10	5	6	11	....	....	....	13	....	....	....	....	....	....	....	....	....	....	....	....	....	....	....	....	....	....
	Detroit Red Wings	**NHL**	20	5	2	7	4	1	5	93	0	0	0	31	16.1	10	2	21	1	–12	....	....	....	....	....	....	....	....
1981-82	**Detroit Red Wings**	**NHL**	33	2	0	2	2	0	2	80	0	0	1	25	8.0	4	0	11	0	–7	....	....	....	....	....	....	....	....
	Adirondack Red Wings	AHL	34	10	5	15	....	....	....	126	....	....	....	....	....	....	....	....	....	....	5	0	0	0	8	....	....	....
1982-83	**Detroit Red Wings**	**NHL**	1	0	0	0	0	0	0	0	0	0	0	0	0.0	0	0	1	0	–1	....	....	....	....	....	....	....	....
	Adirondack Red Wings	AHL	74	20	30	50	....	....	....	132	....	....	....	....	....	....	....	....	....	....	6	1	1	2	10	....	....	....
1983-84	**Detroit Red Wings**	**NHL**	8	2	1	3	2	1	3	36	0	0	0	10	20.0	3	0	5	0	–2	....	....	....	....	....	....	....	....
	Adirondack Red Wings	AHL	46	15	29	44	....	....	....	128	....	....	....	....	....	....	....	....	....	....	7	1	1	2	26	....	....	....
1984-85	**Detroit Red Wings**	**NHL**	1	1	0	1	1	0	1	5	0	0	0	4	25.0	1	0	1	0	0	3	0	1	1	5	0	0	0
	Adirondack Red Wings	AHL	75	33	39	72	....	....	....	89	....	....	....	....	....	....	....	....	....	....	....	....	....	....	....	....	....	....
1985-86	**Toronto Maple Leafs**	**NHL**	42	5	17	22	4	11	15	84	0	0	0	46	10.9	41	3	46	0	–8	6	2	1	3	20	1	0	0
	St. Catharines Saints	AHL	31	13	29	42	....	....	....	79	....	....	....	....	....	....	....	....	....	....	....	....	....	....	....	....	....	....
1986-87	**Toronto Maple Leafs**	**NHL**	47	5	7	12	4	5	9	172	0	0	2	45	11.1	25	1	9	0	+15	11	1	1	2	24	0	0	1
	NHL Totals		222	28	34	62	24	23	47	591	1	0	4	226	12.4	111	8	133	1		20	3	3	6	49	1	0	1

Traded to **Atlanta** by **Vancouver** with Don Lever for Ivan Bolderiv and Darcy Rota, February 8, 1980. Transferred to **Calgary** after **Atlanta** franchise relocated, June 24, 1980. Traded to **Detroit** by **Calgary** for future considerations (Rick Vasko, May 28, 1981), February 24, 1981. Signed as a free agent by **Toronto**, July 2, 1985.

• SMITH, BRIAN D.

Brian D. Smith LW – R. 5′11″, 170 lbs. b: Ottawa, Ont., 9/6/1940. d: 8/2/1995.

1960-61	Montreal Royals	EPHL	1	0	0	0	....	....	....	0	....	....	....	....	....	....	....	....	....	....	....	....	....	....	....	....	....	....
	Hull-Ottawa Canadiens	EPHL	2	0	1	1	....	....	....	0	....	....	....	....	....	....	....	....	....	....	5	1	0	1	0	....	....	....
1961-62	Hull-Ottawa Canadiens	EPHL	50	16	15	31	....	....	....	35	....	....	....	....	....	....	....	....	....	....	8	4	3	7	2	....	....	....
1962-63	Hull-Ottawa Canadiens	EPHL	72	24	34	58	....	....	....	40	....	....	....	....	....	....	....	....	....	....	3	0	0	0	0	....	....	....
1963-64			DID NOT PLAY																									
1964-65	Springfield Indians	AHL	70	22	12	34	....	....	....	32	....	....	....	....	....	....	....	....	....	....	....	....	....	....	....	....	....	....
1965-66	Springfield Indians	AHL	69	20	18	38	....	....	....	15	....	....	....	....	....	....	....	....	....	....	6	0	2	2	4	....	....	....
1966-67	Springfield Indians	AHL	68	30	31	61	....	....	....	15	....	....	....	....	....	....	....	....	....	....	....	....	....	....	....	....	....	....
1967-68	**Los Angeles Kings**	**NHL**	58	10	9	19	12	9	21	33	1	0	3	92	10.9	33	5	32	2	–2	7	0	0	0	0	0	0	0
1968-69	**Minnesota North Stars**	**NHL**	9	0	1	1	0	1	1	0	0	0	0	14	0.0	1	1	7	0	–7	....	....	....	....	....	....	....	....
	Memphis South Stars	CHL	21	5	7	12	....	....	....	11	....	....	....	....	....	....	....	....	....	....	....	....	....	....	....	....	....	....
	Phoenix Roadrunners	WHL	21	1	3	4	....	....	....	0	....	....	....	....	....	....	....	....	....	....	....	....	....	....	....	....	....	....

Season	Club	League	Regular Season GP	G	A	Pts	AG	AA	APts	PIM	PP	SH	GW	S	%	TGF	PGF	TGA	PGA	+/-	Playoffs GP	G	A	Pts	PIM	PP	SH	GW
1969-70	Denver Spurs	WHL	60	17	25	42	....	....	....	15	....	....	....	....	....	....	....	....	....	....	....	....	....	....	....	....	....	....
1970-71			DID NOT PLAY – RETIRED																									
1971-72			DID NOT PLAY – RETIRED																									
1972-73	Houston Aeros	WHA	48	7	6	13	....	....	....	19	....	....	....	....	....	....	....	....	....	....	10	0	2	2	0	....	....	....
	NHL Totals		**67**	**10**	**10**	**20**	**12**	**10**	**22**	**33**	**1**	**0**	**3**	**106**	**9.4**	**34**	**6**	**39**	**2**		**7**	**0**	**0**	**0**	**0**	**0**	**0**	**0**
	Other Major League Totals		48	7	6	13	....	....	....	19	....	....	....	....	....	....	....	....	....		10	0	2	2	0	....	....	....

Traded to **Springfield** (AHL) by **Montreal** with the loan of Gary Bergman, Wayne Boddy, Fred Hilts, Lorne O'Donnell and John Rodger for Terry Gray, Bruce Cline, Wayne Larkin, John Chasczewski and Ted Harris, June, 1963. NHL rights transferred to **LA Kings** after NHL club purchased **Springfield** (AHL) franchise, May, 1967. Traded to **Montreal** by **LA Kings** with Yves Locas for Larry Cahan, July 1, 1968. Traded to **Minnesota** by **Montreal** for cash, November 15, 1968. Traded to **Phoenix** (WHL) by **Minnesota** with Milan Marcetta for Tom Polanic, February 11, 1969. Signed as a free agent by **Houston** (WHA), September, 1972.

• SMITH, D.J.

D.J. (Denis) Smith D – L. 6'1", 200 lbs. b: Windsor, Ont., 5/13/1977. NY Islanders' 3rd choice, 41st overall, in 1995 Entry Draft.

Season	Club	League	GP	G	A	Pts	AG	AA	APts	PIM	PP	SH	GW	S	%	TGF	PGF	TGA	PGA	+/-	GP	G	A	Pts	PIM	PP	SH	GW
1994-95	Windsor Spitfires	OHL	61	4	13	17	....	....	....	201	....	....	....	....	....	....	....	....	....	....	10	1	3	4	41	....	....	....
1995-96	Windsor Spitfires	OHL	64	14	45	59	....	....	....	260	....	....	....	....	....	....	....	....	....	....	7	1	7	8	23	....	....	....
	St. John's Maple Leafs	AHL	1	0	0	0	....	....	....	0	....	....	....	....	....	....	....	....	....	....	....	....	....	....	....	....	....	....
1996-97	Windsor Spitfires	OHL	63	15	52	67	....	....	....	190	....	....	....	....	....	....	....	....	....	....	5	1	7	8	11	....	....	....
	Toronto Maple Leafs	**NHL**	**8**	**0**	**1**	**1**	**0**	**1**	**1**	**7**	**0**	**0**	**0**	**4**	**0.0**	**2**	**0**	**8**	**1**	**–5**	....	....	....	....	....	....	....	....
	St. John's Maple Leafs	AHL	....	....	....	....	....	....	....	....	....	....	....	....	....	....	....	....	....	....	1	0	0	0	0	....	....	....
1997-98	St. John's Maple Leafs	AHL	65	4	11	15	....	....	....	237	....	....	....	....	....	....	....	....	....	....	4	0	0	0	4	....	....	....
	NHL Totals		**8**	**0**	**1**	**1**	**0**	**1**	**1**	**7**	**0**	**0**	**0**	**4**	**0.0**	**2**	**0**	**8**	**1**		....	....	....	....	....	....	....	....

OHL Second All-Star Team (1997)

Traded to **Toronto** by **NY Islanders** with Wendel Clark and Mathieu Schneider for Darby Hendrickson, Sean Haggerty, Kenny Jonsson and Toronto's 1st round choice (Roberto Luongo) in 1997 Entry Draft, March 13, 1996.

• SMITH, DALLAS

Dallas Smith D – L. 5'11", 180 lbs. b: Hamiota, Man., 10/10/1941.

Season	Club	League	GP	G	A	Pts	AG	AA	APts	PIM	PP	SH	GW	S	%	TGF	PGF	TGA	PGA	+/-	GP	G	A	Pts	PIM	PP	SH	GW
1958-59	Estevan Bruins	SJHL	47	5	15	20	....	....	....	41	....	....	....	....	....	....	....	....	....	....	14	4	2	6	16	....	....	....
1959-60	Estevan Bruins	SJHL	59	12	33	45	....	....	....	98	....	....	....	....	....	....	....	....	....	....	....	....	....	....	....	....	....	....
	Boston Bruins	**NHL**	**5**	**1**	**1**	**2**	**1**	**1**	**2**	**0**	....	....	....	....	....	....	....	....	....	....	....	....	....	....	....	....	....	....
1960-61	**Boston Bruins**	**NHL**	**70**	**1**	**9**	**10**	**1**	**9**	**10**	**79**	....	....	....	....	....	....	....	....	....	....	....	....	....	....	....	....	....	....
1961-62	**Boston Bruins**	**NHL**	**7**	**0**	**0**	**0**	**0**	**0**	**0**	**10**	....	....	....	....	....	....	....	....	....	....	....	....	....	....	....	....	....	....
	Hull-Ottawa Canadiens	EPHL	3	0	0	0	....	....	....	0	....	....	....	....	....	....	....	....	....	....	....	....	....	....	....	....	....	....
	Pittsburgh Hornets	AHL	55	1	12	13	....	....	....	93	....	....	....	....	....	....	....	....	....	....	....	....	....	....	....	....	....	....
1962-63	Portland Buckaroos	WHL	68	4	18	22	....	....	....	64	....	....	....	....	....	....	....	....	....	....	7	1	2	3	14	....	....	....
1963-64	Portland Buckaroos	WHL	64	4	14	18	....	....	....	57	....	....	....	....	....	....	....	....	....	....	5	1	0	1	6	....	....	....
1964-65	San Francisco Seals	WHL	70	14	16	30	....	....	....	79	....	....	....	....	....	....	....	....	....	....	....	....	....	....	....	....	....	....
1965-66	**Boston Bruins**	**NHL**	**2**	**0**	**0**	**0**	**0**	**0**	**0**	**2**	....	....	....	....	....	....	....	....	....	....	....	....	....	....	....	....	....	....
	Oklahoma City Blazers	CHL	69	5	23	28	....	....	....	52	....	....	....	....	....	....	....	....	....	....	9	0	5	5	10	....	....	....
1966-67	**Boston Bruins**	**NHL**	**33**	**0**	**1**	**1**	**0**	**1**	**1**	**24**	....	....	....	....	....	....	....	....	....	....	....	....	....	....	....	....	....	....
	Oklahoma City Blazers	CHL	29	3	9	12	....	....	....	44	....	....	....	....	....	....	....	....	....	....	11	2	0	2	20	....	....	....
1967-68	**Boston Bruins**	**NHL**	**74**	**4**	**23**	**27**	**5**	**24**	**29**	**65**	**0**	**0**	**1**	**159**	**2.5**	**114**	**5**	**98**	**22**	**+33**	**4**	**0**	**2**	**2**	**0**	**0**	**0**	**0**
1968-69	**Boston Bruins**	**NHL**	**75**	**4**	**24**	**28**	**4**	**23**	**27**	**74**	**0**	**1**	**0**	**131**	**3.1**	**121**	**2**	**108**	**33**	**+44**	**10**	**0**	**3**	**3**	**16**	**0**	**0**	**0**
1969-70	**Boston Bruins**	**NHL**	**75**	**7**	**17**	**24**	**8**	**17**	**25**	**119**	**1**	**1**	**1**	**160**	**4.4**	**79**	**1**	**109**	**40**	**+9**	**14**	**0**	**3**	**3**	**19**	**0**	**0**	**0**
1970-71	**Boston Bruins**	**NHL**	**73**	**7**	**38**	**45**	**7**	**34**	**41**	**68**	**0**	**2**	**1**	**159**	**4.4**	**154**	**4**	**84**	**28**	**+94**	**7**	**0**	**3**	**3**	**26**	**0**	**0**	**0**
1971-72	**Boston Bruins**	**NHL**	**78**	**8**	**22**	**30**	**8**	**20**	**28**	**132**	**0**	**1**	**1**	**111**	**7.2**	**119**	**2**	**107**	**24**	**+34**	**15**	**0**	**4**	**4**	**22**	**0**	**0**	**0**
1972-73	**Boston Bruins**	**NHL**	**78**	**4**	**27**	**31**	**4**	**23**	**27**	**72**	**0**	**0**	**0**	**130**	**3.1**	**118**	**3**	**101**	**24**	**+38**	**5**	**0**	**2**	**2**	**2**	**0**	**0**	**0**
1973-74	**Boston Bruins**	**NHL**	**77**	**6**	**21**	**27**	**6**	**18**	**24**	**64**	**0**	**0**	**0**	**112**	**5.4**	**98**	**0**	**91**	**19**	**+26**	**16**	**1**	**7**	**8**	**20**	**0**	**0**	**0**
1974-75	**Boston Bruins**	**NHL**	**79**	**3**	**20**	**23**	**3**	**16**	**19**	**84**	**0**	**0**	**1**	**146**	**2.1**	**104**	**1**	**99**	**26**	**+30**	**3**	**0**	**2**	**2**	**4**	**0**	**0**	**0**
1975-76	**Boston Bruins**	**NHL**	**77**	**7**	**25**	**32**	**7**	**20**	**27**	**103**	**0**	**0**	**0**	**125**	**5.6**	**128**	**5**	**110**	**29**	**+42**	**11**	**2**	**2**	**4**	**19**	**0**	**0**	**1**
1976-77	**Boston Bruins**	**NHL**	**58**	**2**	**20**	**22**	**2**	**16**	**18**	**40**	**0**	**0**	**0**	**66**	**3.0**	**81**	**2**	**75**	**12**	**+16**	....	....	....	....	....	....	....	....
	Canada	WEC-A	10	0	2	2	....	....	....	4	....	....	....	....	....	....	....	....	....	....	....	....	....	....	....	....	....	....
1977-78	**New York Rangers**	**NHL**	**29**	**1**	**4**	**5**	**1**	**3**	**4**	**23**	**0**	**0**	**0**	**35**	**2.9**	**21**	**1**	**37**	**6**	**–11**	**1**	**0**	**1**	**1**	**0**	**0**	**0**	**0**
	NHL Totals		**890**	**55**	**252**	**307**	**57**	**225**	**282**	**959**	**1**	**5**	**5**	**1334**	**4.1**	**1137**	**26**	**1019**	**263**		**86**	**3**	**29**	**32**	**128**	**0**	**0**	**1**

CHL Second All-Star Team (1966) • NHL Plus/Minus Leader (1968)

Played in NHL All-Star Game (1971, 1972, 1973, 1974)

Signed as a free agent by **NY Rangers**, December 19, 1977.

• SMITH, DENNIS

Dennis Smith D – L. 5'11", 190 lbs. b: Detroit, MI, 7/27/1964.

Season	Club	League	GP	G	A	Pts	AG	AA	APts	PIM	PP	SH	GW	S	%	TGF	PGF	TGA	PGA	+/-	GP	G	A	Pts	PIM	PP	SH	GW
1981-82	Kingston Canadians	OHL	48	2	24	26	....	....	....	84	....	....	....	....	....	....	....	....	....	....	4	0	2	2	0	....	....	....
1982-83	Kingston Canadians	OHL	58	6	30	36	....	....	....	100	....	....	....	....	....	....	....	....	....	....	....	....	....	....	....	....	....	....
1983-84	Kingston Canadians	OHL	62	10	41	51	....	....	....	165	....	....	....	....	....	....	....	....	....	....	....	....	....	....	....	....	....	....
	Erie Golden Blades	ACHL	2	1	1	2	....	....	....	2	....	....	....	....	....	....	....	....	....	....	9	2	4	6	8	....	....	....
1984-85	Osby	Sweden	30	15	15	30	....	....	....	74	....	....	....	....	....	....	....	....	....	....	....	....	....	....	....	....	....	....
	Erie Golden Blades	ACHL	19	5	20	25	....	....	....	67	....	....	....	....	....	....	....	....	....	....	12	1	4	5	52	....	....	....
1985-86	Peoria Rivermen	IHL	70	5	15	20	....	....	....	102	....	....	....	....	....	....	....	....	....	....	10	0	2	2	18	....	....	....
1986-87	Adirondack Red Wings	AHL	64	4	24	28	....	....	....	120	....	....	....	....	....	....	....	....	....	....	6	0	0	0	8	....	....	....
1987-88	Adirondack Red Wings	AHL	75	6	24	30	....	....	....	213	....	....	....	....	....	....	....	....	....	....	11	2	2	4	47	....	....	....
1988-89	Adirondack Red Wings	AHL	75	5	35	40	....	....	....	176	....	....	....	....	....	....	....	....	....	....	17	1	6	7	47	....	....	....
1989-90	**Washington Capitals**	**NHL**	**4**	**0**	**0**	**0**	**0**	**0**	**0**	**0**	**0**	**0**	**0**	**0**	**0.0**	**2**	**0**	**2**	**0**	**0**	....	....	....	....	....	....	....	....
	Baltimore Skipjacks	AHL	74	8	25	33	....	....	....	103	....	....	....	....	....	....	....	....	....	....	12	0	3	3	65	....	....	....
1990-91	**Los Angeles Kings**	**NHL**	**4**	**0**	**0**	**0**	**0**	**0**	**0**	**4**	**0**	**0**	**0**	**1**	**0.0**	**5**	**1**	**2**	**1**	**+3**	....	....	....	....	....	....	....	....
	New Haven Nighthawks	AHL	61	7	25	32	....	....	....	148	....	....	....	....	....	....	....	....	....	....	....	....	....	....	....	....	....	....
1991-92	Maine Mariners	AHL	59	2	32	34	....	....	....	63	....	....	....	....	....	....	....	....	....	....	....	....	....	....	....	....	....	....
	Baltimore Skipjacks	AHL	17	1	4	5	....	....	....	23	....	....	....	....	....	....	....	....	....	....	....	....	....	....	....	....	....	....
1992-93	VEU Feldkirch	Austria	25	7	19	26	....	....	....	....	....	....	....	....	....	....	....	....	....	....	....	....	....	....	....	....	....	....
1993-94			STATISTICS NOT AVAILABLE																									
1994-95	Kalamazoo Wings	IHL	39	4	1	5	....	....	....	53	....	....	....	....	....	....	....	....	....	....	13	0	2	2	33	....	....	....
1995-96	Michigan K-Wings	IHL	49	0	10	10	....	....	....	62	....	....	....	....	....	....	....	....	....	....	10	0	0	0	6	....	....	....
	NHL Totals		**8**	**0**	**0**	**0**	**0**	**0**	**0**	**4**	**0**	**0**	**0**	**1**	**0.0**	**7**	**1**	**4**	**1**		....	....	....	....	....	....	....	....

AHL Second All-Star Team (1990)

Signed as a free agent by **Detroit**, December 2, 1986. Signed as a free agent by **Washington**, July 25, 1989. Signed as a free agent by **LA Kings**, September 28, 1990. Signed as a free agent by **Boston**, August 2, 1991. Traded to **Washington** by **Boston** with John Byce for Brent Hughes and future considerations, February 24, 1992.

• SMITH, DEREK

Derek Smith C/LW – L. 5'11", 180 lbs. b: Quebec City, Que., 7/31/1954. Buffalo's 10th choice, 168th overall, in 1974 Amateur Draft.

Season	Club	League	GP	G	A	Pts	AG	AA	APts	PIM	PP	SH	GW	S	%	TGF	PGF	TGA	PGA	+/-	GP	G	A	Pts	PIM	PP	SH	GW
1971-72	Ottawa 67's	OHA	53	6	11	17	....	....	....	10	....	....	....	....	....	....	....	....	....	....	....	....	....	....	....	....	....	....
1972-73	Ottawa 67's	OHA	63	52	46	98	....	....	....	32	....	....	....	....	....	....	....	....	....	....	....	....	....	....	....	....	....	....
1973-74	Ottawa 67's	OHA	69	47	45	92	....	....	....	40	....	....	....	....	....	....	....	....	....	....	....	....	....	....	....	....	....	....
1974-75	Charlotte Checkers	SHL	4	4	3	7	....	....	....	0	....	....	....	....	....	....	....	....	....	....	....	....	....	....	....	....	....	....
	Hershey Bears	AHL	64	11	16	27	....	....	....	10	....	....	....	....	....	....	....	....	....	....	11	7	3	10	0	....	....	....
1975-76	Hershey Bears	AHL	67	28	32	60	....	....	....	14	....	....	....	....	....	....	....	....	....	....	10	4	5	9	4	....	....	....
	Buffalo Sabres	**NHL**	....	....	....	....	....	....	....	....	....	....	....	....	....	....	....	....	....	....	**1**	**0**	**0**	**0**	**0**	....	....	....
1976-77	**Buffalo Sabres**	**NHL**	**5**	**0**	**0**	**0**	**0**	**0**	**0**	**0**	**0**	**0**	**0**	**0**	**0.0**	**0**	**0**	**1**	**0**	**–1**	....	....	....	....	....	....	....	....
	Hershey Bears	AHL	65	31	31	62	....	....	....	20	....	....	....	....	....	....	....	....	....	....	6	3	1	4	2	....	....	....
1977-78	**Buffalo Sabres**	**NHL**	**36**	**3**	**3**	**6**	**3**	**2**	**5**	**0**	**0**	**0**	**0**	**25**	**12.0**	**9**	**1**	**12**	**0**	**–4**	**8**	**3**	**3**	**6**	**7**	**0**	**0**	**0**
	Hershey Bears	AHL	5	2	2	4	....	....	....	2	....	....	....	....	....	....	....	....	....	....	....	....	....	....	....	....	....	....
1978-79	**Buffalo Sabres**	**NHL**	**43**	**14**	**12**	**26**	**13**	**9**	**22**	**8**	**3**	**0**	**0**	**85**	**16.5**	**35**	**9**	**32**	**1**	**–5**	....	....	....	....	....	....	....	....
1979-80	**Buffalo Sabres**	**NHL**	**79**	**24**	**39**	**63**	**22**	**30**	**52**	**16**	**8**	**0**	**3**	**137**	**17.5**	**102**	**33**	**36**	**0**	**+33**	**13**	**5**	**7**	**12**	**4**	**3**	**0**	**1**
1980-81	**Buffalo Sabres**	**NHL**	**69**	**21**	**43**	**64**	**17**	**30**	**47**	**12**	**11**	**0**	**2**	**166**	**12.7**	**99**	**41**	**44**	**0**	**+14**	**8**	**1**	**4**	**5**	**2**	**1**	**0**	**0**
1981-82	**Buffalo Sabres**	**NHL**	**12**	**3**	**1**	**4**	**2**	**1**	**3**	**2**	**0**	**0**	**0**	**15**	**20.0**	**9**	**2**	**8**	**1**	**0**	....	....	....	....	....	....	....	....
1981-82	**Detroit Red Wings**	**NHL**	**49**	**6**	**14**	**20**	**5**	**9**	**14**	**10**	**0**	**0**	**0**	**82**	**7.3**	**34**	**5**	**36**	**3**	**–4**	....	....	....	....	....	....	....	....

			REGULAR SEASON																		PLAYOFFS							
Season	Club	League	GP	G	A	Pts	AG	AA	APts	PIM	PP	SH	GW	S	%	TGF	PGF	TGA	PGA	+/–	GP	G	A	Pts	PIM	PP	SH	GW
1982-83	**Detroit Red Wings**	**NHL**	**42**	**7**	**4**	**11**	**6**	**3**	**9**	**12**	**1**	**0**	**0**	**50**	**14.0**	**24**	**2**	**31**	**2**	**–7**	....	....	....	....	....	....	....	....
	Adirondack Red Wings	AHL	11	6	4	10	....	....	....	2	....	....	....	....	....	....	....	....	....	....	6	1	2	3	0	....	....	....
1983-84	Adirondack Red Wings	AHL	61	16	29	45	....	....	....	10	....	....	....	....	....	....	....	....	....	....	10	1	0	0	0	....	....	....
	NHL Totals		**335**	**78**	**116**	**194**	**68**	**84**	**152**	**60**	**23**	**0**	**5**	**560**	**13.9**	**312**	**93**	**200**	**7**		**30**	**9**	**14**	**23**	**13**	**4**	**0**	**1**

Traded to **Detroit** by **Buffalo** with Danny Gare and Jim Schoenfeld for Mike Foligno, Dale McCourt and Brent Peterson, December 2, 1981.

• SMITH, DERRICK

Derrick Smith LW – L. 6'2", 215 lbs. b: Scarborough, Ont., 1/22/1965. Philadelphia's 2nd choice, 44th overall, in 1983 Entry Draft.

Season	Club	League	GP	G	A	Pts	AG	AA	APts	PIM	PP	SH	GW	S	%	TGF	PGF	TGA	PGA	+/–	GP	G	A	Pts	PIM	PP	SH	GW
1981-82	Wexford Raiders	MTHL	45	35	47	82	....	....	....	40	....	....	....	....	....	....	....	....	....	....	....	....	....	....	....	....	....	....
1982-83	Peterborough Petes	OHL	70	16	19	35	....	....	....	47	....	....	....	....	....	....	....	....	....	....	....	....	....	....	....	....	....	....
1983-84	Peterborough Petes	OHL	70	30	36	66	....	....	....	31	....	....	....	....	....	....	....	....	....	....	8	4	4	8	7	....	....	....
1984-85	**Philadelphia Flyers**	**NHL**	**77**	**17**	**22**	**39**	**14**	**15**	**29**	**31**	**0**	**1**	**4**	**140**	**12.1**	**60**	**2**	**38**	**8**	**+28**	**19**	**2**	**5**	**7**	**16**	**0**	**0**	**0**
1985-86	**Philadelphia Flyers**	**NHL**	**69**	**6**	**6**	**12**	**5**	**4**	**9**	**57**	**0**	**0**	**2**	**108**	**5.6**	**38**	**0**	**25**	**1**	**+14**	**4**	**0**	**0**	**0**	**10**	**0**	**0**	**0**
1986-87	**Philadelphia Flyers**	**NHL**	**71**	**11**	**21**	**32**	**10**	**15**	**25**	**34**	**0**	**0**	**0**	**150**	**7.3**	**51**	**0**	**60**	**5**	**–4**	**26**	**6**	**4**	**10**	**26**	**0**	**0**	**1**
1987-88	**Philadelphia Flyers**	**NHL**	**76**	**16**	**8**	**24**	**14**	**6**	**20**	**104**	**0**	**0**	**1**	**155**	**10.3**	**40**	**0**	**71**	**11**	**–20**	**7**	**0**	**0**	**0**	**6**	**0**	**0**	**0**
1988-89	**Philadelphia Flyers**	**NHL**	**74**	**16**	**14**	**30**	**14**	**10**	**24**	**43**	**0**	**1**	**3**	**115**	**13.9**	**45**	**0**	**66**	**17**	**–4**	**19**	**5**	**2**	**7**	**12**	**0**	**2**	**1**
1989-90	**Philadelphia Flyers**	**NHL**	**55**	**3**	**6**	**9**	**3**	**4**	**7**	**32**	**0**	**0**	**0**	**72**	**4.2**	**22**	**0**	**47**	**10**	**–15**	....	....	....	....	....	....	....	....
1990-91	**Philadelphia Flyers**	**NHL**	**72**	**11**	**10**	**21**	**10**	**8**	**18**	**37**	**0**	**1**	**2**	**100**	**11.0**	**32**	**1**	**44**	**13**	**0**	....	....	....	....	....	....	....	....
1991-92	**Minnesota North Stars**	**NHL**	**33**	**2**	**4**	**6**	**2**	**3**	**5**	**33**	**0**	**0**	**0**	**29**	**6.9**	**9**	**0**	**26**	**9**	**–8**	**7**	**1**	**0**	**1**	**9**	**0**	**0**	**1**
	Kalamazoo Wings	IHL	6	1	5	6	....	....	....	4	....	....	....	....	....	....	....	....	....	....	....	....	....	....	....	....	....	....
1992-93	**Minnesota North Stars**	**NHL**	**9**	**0**	**1**	**1**	**0**	**1**	**1**	**2**	**0**	**0**	**0**	**3**	**0.0**	**1**	**0**	**3**	**0**	**–2**	....	....	....	....	....	....	....	....
	Kalamazoo Wings	IHL	52	22	13	35	....	....	....	43	....	....	....	....	....	....	....	....	....	....	....	....	....	....	....	....	....	....
1993-94	**Dallas Stars**	**NHL**	**1**	**0**	**0**	**0**	**0**	**0**	**0**	**0**	**0**	**0**	**0**	**1**	**0.0**	**0**	**0**	**1**	**0**	**–1**	....	....	....	....	....	....	....	....
	Kalamazoo Wings	IHL	77	44	37	81	....	....	....	90	....	....	....	....	....	....	....	....	....	....	5	0	0	0	18	....	....	....
1994-95	Kalamazoo Wings	IHL	68	30	21	51	....	....	....	103	....	....	....	....	....	....	....	....	....	....	16	3	8	11	8	....	....	....
1995-96	Michigan K-Wings	IHL	69	15	26	41	....	....	....	79	....	....	....	....	....	....	....	....	....	....	10	4	3	7	16	....	....	....
1996-97	Michigan K-Wings	IHL	68	8	21	29	....	....	....	55	....	....	....	....	....	....	....	....	....	....	4	1	0	1	16	....	....	....
1997-98	Michigan K-Wings	IHL	64	15	26	41	....	....	....	39	....	....	....	....	....	....	....	....	....	....	4	1	1	2	2	....	....	....
	NHL Totals		**537**	**82**	**92**	**174**	**72**	**66**	**138**	**373**	**0**	**3**	**12**	**873**	**9.4**	**298**	**3**	**381**	**74**		**82**	**14**	**11**	**25**	**79**	**0**	**2**	**3**

IHL Second All-Star Team (1994)

Claimed on waivers by **Minnesota** from **Philadelphia**, October 26, 1991. Transferred to **Dallas** after **Minnesota** franchise relocated, June 9, 1993.

• SMITH, DOUG

Doug Smith C – R. 5'11", 186 lbs. b: Ottawa, Ont., 5/17/1963. Los Angeles' 10th choice, 2nd overall, in 1981 Entry Draft.

Season	Club	League	GP	G	A	Pts	AG	AA	APts	PIM	PP	SH	GW	S	%	TGF	PGF	TGA	PGA	+/–	GP	G	A	Pts	PIM	PP	SH	GW
1979-80	Ottawa 67's	OHA	64	23	34	57	....	....	....	45	....	....	....	....	....	....	....	....	....	....	11	2	0	2	33	....	....	....
1980-81	Ottawa 67's	OHA	54	45	56	101	....	....	....	61	....	....	....	....	....	....	....	....	....	....	7	5	6	11	13	....	....	....
1981-82	Ottawa 67's	OHA	1	1	2	3	....	....	....	17	....	....	....	....	....	....	....	....	....	....	....	....	....	....	....	....	....	....
	Los Angeles Kings	**NHL**	**80**	**16**	**14**	**30**	**13**	**9**	**22**	**64**	**1**	**0**	**1**	**141**	**11.3**	**53**	**3**	**78**	**15**	**–13**	**10**	**3**	**2**	**5**	**11**	**1**	**0**	**0**
1982-83	**Los Angeles Kings**	**NHL**	**42**	**11**	**11**	**22**	**9**	**8**	**17**	**12**	**1**	**0**	**1**	**87**	**12.6**	**27**	**5**	**38**	**2**	**–14**	....	....	....	....	....	....	....	....
1983-84	**Los Angeles Kings**	**NHL**	**72**	**16**	**20**	**36**	**13**	**14**	**27**	**28**	**6**	**0**	**0**	**146**	**11.0**	**50**	**12**	**76**	**5**	**–33**	....	....	....	....	....	....	....	....
1984-85	**Los Angeles Kings**	**NHL**	**62**	**21**	**20**	**41**	**17**	**14**	**31**	**58**	**3**	**1**	**1**	**146**	**14.4**	**54**	**12**	**69**	**12**	**–15**	**3**	**1**	**0**	**1**	**4**	**0**	**0**	**0**
1985-86	**Los Angeles Kings**	**NHL**	**48**	**8**	**9**	**17**	**6**	**6**	**12**	**56**	**1**	**1**	**0**	**115**	**7.0**	**32**	**5**	**90**	**34**	**–29**	....	....	....	....	....	....	....	....
	Buffalo Sabres	**NHL**	**30**	**10**	**11**	**21**	**8**	**7**	**15**	**73**	**3**	**1**	**3**	**72**	**13.9**	**33**	**9**	**26**	**4**	**+2**	....	....	....	....	....	....	....	....
1986-87	**Buffalo Sabres**	**NHL**	**62**	**16**	**24**	**40**	**14**	**17**	**31**	**106**	**7**	**0**	**2**	**158**	**10.1**	**61**	**28**	**73**	**20**	**–20**	....	....	....	....	....	....	....	....
	Rochester Americans	AHL	15	5	6	11	....	....	....	35	....	....	....	....	....	....	....	....	....	....	....	....	....	....	....	....	....	....
1987-88	**Buffalo Sabres**	**NHL**	**70**	**9**	**19**	**28**	**8**	**14**	**22**	**117**	**1**	**0**	**0**	**136**	**6.6**	**47**	**9**	**78**	**30**	**–10**	**1**	**0**	**0**	**0**	**0**	**0**	**0**	**0**
1988-89	**Edmonton Oilers**	**NHL**	**19**	**1**	**1**	**2**	**1**	**1**	**2**	**9**	**0**	**0**	**0**	**15**	**6.7**	**6**	**0**	**8**	**1**	**–1**	....	....	....	....	....	....	....	....
	Cape Breton Oilers	AHL	24	11	11	22	....	....	....	69	....	....	....	....	....	....	....	....	....	....	....	....	....	....	....	....	....	....
	Vancouver Canucks	**NHL**	**10**	**3**	**4**	**7**	**3**	**3**	**6**	**4**	**1**	**0**	**1**	**12**	**25.0**	**8**	**2**	**5**	**2**	**+3**	**4**	**0**	**0**	**0**	**6**	**0**	**0**	**0**
1989-90	**Vancouver Canucks**	**NHL**	**30**	**3**	**4**	**7**	**3**	**3**	**6**	**72**	**0**	**1**	**0**	**40**	**7.5**	**18**	**3**	**22**	**8**	**+1**	....	....	....	....	....	....	....	....
	Pittsburgh Penguins	**NHL**	**10**	**1**	**1**	**2**	**1**	**1**	**2**	**25**	**0**	**0**	**0**	**11**	**9.1**	**2**	**0**	**5**	**1**	**–2**	....	....	....	....	....	....	....	....
1990-91	EC Graz	Austria	42	33	36	69	....	....	....	....	....	....	....	....	....	....	....	....	....	....	....	....	....	....	....	....	....	....
1991-92	EC Graz	Austria	00	15	10	20	....	....	....	....	....	....	....	....	....	....	....	....	....	....	....	....	....	....	....	....	....	....
1991-92	EC Graz	Austria	30	15	13	28	....	....	....	....	....	....	....	....	....	....	....	....	....	....	....	....	....	....	....	....	....	....
	NHL Totals		**535**	**115**	**138**	**253**	**96**	**97**	**193**	**624**	**24**	**4**	**9**	**1079**	**10.7**	**391**	**88**	**568**	**134**		**18**	**4**	**2**	**6**	**21**	**1**	**0**	**0**

Traded to **Buffalo** by **LA Kings** with Brian Engblom for Sean McKenna, Larry Playfair and Ken Baumgartner, January 30, 1986. Claimed by **Edmonton** from **Buffalo** in NHL Waiver Draft, October 3, 1988. Traded to **Vancouver** by **Edmonton** with Greg C. Adams for John LeBlanc and Vancouver's 5th round choice (Peter White) in 1989 Entry Draft, March 7, 1989. Traded to **Pittsburgh** by **Vancouver** for cash, February 26, 1990.

• SMITH, FLOYD

Floyd Smith RW – R. 5'10", 180 lbs. b: Perth, Ont., 5/16/1935.

Season	Club	League	GP	G	A	Pts	AG	AA	APts	PIM	PP	SH	GW	S	%	TGF	PGF	TGA	PGA	+/–	GP	G	A	Pts	PIM	PP	SH	GW
1952-53	Galt Black Hawks	OHA	6	0	1	1	....	....	....	0	....	....	....	....	....	....	....	....	....	....	....	....	....	....	....	....	....	....
	Inkerman Rockets	NYOHL	STATISTICS NOT AVAILABLE																									
1953-54	Inkerman Rockets	NYOHL	STATISTICS NOT AVAILABLE																									
1954-55	Galt Black Hawks	OHA	46	29	40	69	....	....	....	60	....	....	....	....	....	....	....	....	....	....	4	1	4	5	0	....	....	....
	Boston Bruins	**NHL**	**3**	**0**	**1**	**1**	**0**	**1**	**1**	**0**	....	....	....	....	....	....	....	....	....	....	....	....	....	....	....	....	....	....
1955-56	Hershey Bears	AHL	49	10	19	29	....	....	....	31	....	....	....	....	....	....	....	....	....	....	....	....	....	....	....	....	....	....
1956-57	**Boston Bruins**	**NHL**	**23**	**0**	**0**	**0**	**0**	**0**	**0**	**6**	....	....	....	....	....	....	....	....	....	....	....	....	....	....	....	....	....	....
	Hershey Bears	AHL	41	12	25	37	....	....	....	32	....	....	....	....	....	....	....	....	....	....	6	0	1	1	8	....	....	....
1957-58	Springfield Indians	AHL	70	25	50	75	....	....	....	60	....	....	....	....	....	....	....	....	....	....	13	2	11	13	4	....	....	....
1958-59	Springfield Indians	AHL	68	25	32	57	....	....	....	34	....	....	....	....	....	....	....	....	....	....	....	....	....	....	....	....	....	....
1959-60	Springfield Indians	AHL	71	31	51	82	....	....	....	26	....	....	....	....	....	....	....	....	....	....	10	1	5	6	10	....	....	....
1960-61	**New York Rangers**	**NHL**	**29**	**5**	**9**	**14**	**6**	**9**	**15**	**0**	....	....	....	....	....	....	....	....	....	....	....	....	....	....	....	....	....	....
	Springfield Indians	AHL	40	10	27	46	....	....	....	26	....	....	....	....	....	....	....	....	....	....	....	....	....	....	....	....	....	....
1961-62	Springfield Indians	AHL	69	*41	36	77	....	....	....	19	....	....	....	....	....	....	....	....	....	....	11	0	4	4	2	....	....	....
1962-63	**Detroit Red Wings**	**NHL**	**61**	**9**	**17**	**26**	**11**	**18**	**29**	**10**	....	....	....	....	....	....	....	....	....	....	**11**	**2**	**3**	**5**	**4**	....	....	....
	Pittsburgh Hornets	AHL	16	8	7	15	....	....	....	6	....	....	....	....	....	....	....	....	....	....	....	....	....	....	....	....	....	....
1963-64	**Detroit Red Wings**	**NHL**	**52**	**18**	**13**	**31**	**24**	**14**	**38**	**22**	....	....	....	....	....	....	....	....	....	....	**14**	**4**	**3**	**7**	**4**	....	....	....
	Pittsburgh Hornets	AHL	21	14	17	31	....	....	....	14	....	....	....	....	....	....	....	....	....	....	....	....	....	....	....	....	....	....
1964-65	**Detroit Red Wings**	**NHL**	**67**	**16**	**29**	**45**	**20**	**31**	**51**	**44**	....	....	....	....	....	....	....	....	....	....	**7**	**1**	**3**	**4**	**4**	....	....	....
1965-66	**Detroit Red Wings**	**NHL**	**66**	**21**	**28**	**49**	**25**	**28**	**53**	**20**	....	....	....	....	....	....	....	....	....	....	**12**	**5**	**2**	**7**	**4**	....	....	....
1966-67	**Detroit Red Wings**	**NHL**	**54**	**11**	**14**	**25**	**13**	**14**	**27**	**8**	....	....	....	....	....	....	....	....	....	....	....	....	....	....	....	....	....	....
	Pittsburgh Hornets	AHL	13	5	9	14	....	....	....	10	....	....	....	....	....	....	....	....	....	....	....	....	....	....	....	....	....	....
1967-68	**Detroit Red Wings**	**NHL**	**57**	**18**	**21**	**39**	**22**	**22**	**44**	**14**	**5**	**1**	**2**	**132**	**13.6**	**59**	**15**	**42**	**2**	**+4**	....	....	....	....	....	....	....	....
	Toronto Maple Leafs	**NHL**	**6**	**6**	**1**	**7**	**7**	**1**	**8**	**0**	**1**	**0**	**1**	**19**	**31.6**	**13**	**2**	**4**	**0**	**+7**	....	....	....	....	....	....	....	....
1968-69	**Toronto Maple Leafs**	**NHL**	**64**	**15**	**19**	**34**	**17**	**18**	**35**	**22**	**2**	**0**	**2**	**120**	**12.5**	**61**	**14**	**38**	**5**	**+14**	**4**	**0**	**0**	**0**	**0**	**0**	**0**	**0**
1969-70	**Toronto Maple Leafs**	**NHL**	**61**	**4**	**14**	**18**	**5**	**14**	**19**	**13**	**0**	**0**	**0**	**73**	**5.5**	**30**	**4**	**31**	**2**	**–3**	....	....	....	....	....	....	....	....
1970-71	**Buffalo Sabres**	**NHL**	**77**	**6**	**11**	**17**	**6**	**10**	**16**	**46**	**0**	**2**	**0**	**80**	**7.5**	**32**	**5**	**65**	**26**	**–12**	....	....	....	....	....	....	....	....
1971-72	**Buffalo Sabres**	**NHL**	**6**	**0**	**1**	**1**	**0**	**1**	**1**	**2**	**0**	**0**	**0**	**1**	**0.0**	**0**	**0**	**5**	**1**	**–4**	....	....	....	....	....	....	....	....
	NHL Totals		**616**	**129**	**178**	**307**	**156**	**181**	**337**	**207**	**8**	**3**	**5**	**425**	**30.4**	**195**	**40**	**185**	**36**		**48**	**12**	**11**	**23**	**16**	**0**	**0**	**0**

AHL Second All-Star Team (1960, 1962)

Traded to **NY Rangers** by **Boston** for Don Simmons, September, 1956. Claimed by **Detroit** from **NY Rangers** in Intra-League Draft, June, 1962. Traded to **Toronto** by **Detroit** with Norm Ullman and Paul Henderson for Frank Mahovlich, Pete Stemkowski, Garry Unger and NHL rights to Carl Brewer, March 3, 1968. Traded to **Buffalo** by **Toronto** for cash, August 31, 1970.

• SMITH, GEOFF

Geoff Smith D – L. 6'3", 194 lbs. b: Edmonton, Alta., 3/7/1969. Edmonton's 2nd choice, 63rd overall, in 1987 Entry Draft.

Season	Club	League	GP	G	A	Pts	AG	AA	APts	PIM	PP	SH	GW	S	%	TGF	PGF	TGA	PGA	+/–	GP	G	A	Pts	PIM	PP	SH	GW
1986-87	St. Albert Saints	AJHL	57	7	28	35	....	....	....	101	....	....	....	....	....	....	....	....	....	....	....	....	....	....	....	....	....	....
1987-88	University of North Dakota	WCHA	42	4	12	16	....	....	....	34	....	....	....	....	....	....	....	....	....	....	....	....	....	....	....	....	....	....
1988-89	University of North Dakota	WCHA	9	0	1	1	....	....	....	8	....	....	....	....	....	....	....	....	....	....	....	....	....	....	....	....	....	....
	Canada	WJC-A	7	0	1	1	....	....	....	4	....	....	....	....	....	....	....	....	....	....	....	....	....	....	....	....	....	....
	Kamloops Blazers	WHL	32	4	31	35	....	....	....	29	....	....	....	....	....	....	....	....	....	....	6	1	3	4	12	....	....	....
1989-90	**Edmonton Oilers**	**NHL**	**74**	**4**	**11**	**15**	**3**	**8**	**11**	**52**	**1**	**0**	**0**	**66**	**6.1**	**77**	**13**	**72**	**21**	**+13**	**3**	**0**	**0**	**0**	**0**	**0**	**0**	**0**
1990-91	**Edmonton Oilers**	**NHL**	**59**	**1**	**12**	**13**	**1**	**9**	**10**	**55**	**0**	**0**	**0**	**66**	**1.5**	**57**	**6**	**55**	**17**	**+13**	**4**	**0**	**0**	**0**	**0**	**0**	**0**	**0**
1991-92	**Edmonton Oilers**	**NHL**	**74**	**2**	**16**	**18**	**2**	**12**	**14**	**43**	**0**	**0**	**0**	**61**	**3.3**	**74**	**12**	**101**	**34**	**–5**	**5**	**0**	**1**	**1**	**6**	**0**	**0**	**0**

Season	Club	League	GP	G	A	Pts	AG	AA	APts	PIM	PP	SH	GW	S	%	TGF	PGF	TGA	PGA	+/–	GP	G	A	Pts	PIM	PP	SH	GW
1992-93	Edmonton Oilers	NHL	78	4	14	18	3	10	13	30	0	1	0	67	6.0	50	4	100	43	–11	....	....	....	....	....	....	....	....
	Canada	WC-A	8	0	0	0	....	....	....	4	....	....	....	....	....	....	....	....	....	....	....	....	....	....	....	....	....	....
1993-94	Edmonton Oilers	NHL	21	0	3	3	0	2	2	12	0	0	0	23	0.0	17	3	34	10	–10	....	....	....	....	....	....	....	....
	Florida Panthers	NHL	56	1	5	6	1	4	5	38	0	0	0	44	2.3	40	1	62	20	–3	....	....	....	....	....	....	....	....
1994-95	Florida Panthers	NHL	47	2	4	6	4	6	10	22	0	0	0	40	5.0	24	1	49	21	–5	....	....	....	....	....	....	....	....
1995-96	Florida Panthers	NHL	31	3	7	10	3	6	9	20	2	0	0	34	8.8	24	3	40	15	–4	1	0	0	0	2	0	0	0
1996-97	Florida Panthers	NHL	3	0	0	0	0	0	0	2	0	0	0	2	0.0	2	1	0	0	+1	....	....	....	....	....	....	....	....
	Carolina Monarchs	AHL	27	3	4	7	....	....	....	20	....	....	....	....	....	....	....	....	....	....	....	....	....	....	....	....	....	....
1997-98	New York Rangers	NHL	15	1	1	2	1	1	2	6	1	0	0	11	9.1	7	1	15	5	–4	....	....	....	....	....	....	....	....
	Hartford Wolf Pack	AHL	59	1	12	13	....	....	....	34	....	....	....	....	....	....	....	....	....	....	....	....	....	....	....	....	....	....
	NHL Totals		**458**	**18**	**73**	**91**	**18**	**58**	**76**	**280**	**4**	**1**	**0**	**414**	**4.3**	**372**	**45**	**528**	**186**		**13**	**0**	**1**	**1**	**8**	**0**	**0**	**0**

WHL West Second All-Star Team (1989) • NHL All-Rookie Team (1990)

Traded to **Florida** by **Edmonton** with Edmonton's 4th round choice (David Nemirovsky) in 1994 Entry Draft for Florida's 3rd round choice (Corey Neilson) in 1994 Entry Draft and St. Louis' 6th round choice (previously acquired and later traded to Winnipeg — Winnipeg selected Chris Kibermanis) in 1994 Entry Draft, December 6, 1993.

• SMITH, GORD

Gord Smith D – L. 5'10", 175 lbs. b: Perth, Ont., 11/17/1949.

Season	Club	League	GP	G	A	Pts	AG	AA	APts	PIM	PP	SH	GW	S	%	TGF	PGF	TGA	PGA	+/–	GP	G	A	Pts	PIM	PP	SH	GW
1968-69	Cornwall Royals	QJHL	STATISTICS NOT AVAILABLE																									
1969-70	New Haven Blades	EHL	72	4	20	24	....	....	....	92	....	....	....	....	....	....	....	....	....	....	11	0	3	3	36	....	....	....
	Omaha Knights	CHL	....	....	....	....	....	....	....	....	....	....	....	....	....	....	....	....	....	....	5	0	0	0	8	....	....	....
1970-71	New Haven Blades	EHL	73	7	24	31	....	....	....	253	....	....	....	....	....	....	....	....	....	....	14	1	5	6	66	....	....	....
1971-72	New Haven Blades	EHL	74	3	33	36	....	....	....	188	....	....	....	....	....	....	....	....	....	....	7	1	5	6	18	....	....	....
1972-73	Springfield Kings	AHL	72	3	29	32	....	....	....	134	....	....	....	....	....	....	....	....	....	....	....	....	....	....	....	....	....	....
1973-74	Springfield Kings	AHL	75	13	54	67	....	....	....	118	....	....	....	....	....	....	....	....	....	....	....	....	....	....	....	....	....	....
1974-75	Washington Capitals	NHL	63	3	8	11	3	6	9	56	2	0	0	54	5.6	49	7	125	27	–56	....	....	....	....	....	....	....	....
	Richmond Robins	AHL	15	1	4	5	....	....	....	23	....	....	....	....	....	....	....	....	....	....	....	....	....	....	....	....	....	....
1975-76	Washington Capitals	NHL	25	1	2	3	1	2	3	28	1	0	0	10	10.0	17	2	44	7	–22	....	....	....	....	....	....	....	....
	Richmond Robins	AHL	50	2	13	15	....	....	....	80	....	....	....	....	....	....	....	....	....	....	8	0	4	4	28	....	....	....
1976-77	Washington Capitals	NHL	79	1	12	13	1	10	11	92	1	0	0	72	1.4	63	5	112	27	–27	....	....	....	....	....	....	....	....
1977-78	Washington Capitals	NHL	80	4	7	11	4	6	10	78	0	0	1	57	7.0	55	2	98	25	–20	....	....	....	....	....	....	....	....
1978-79	Washington Capitals	NHL	39	0	1	1	0	1	1	22	0	0	0	11	0.0	22	1	42	14	–7	....	....	....	....	....	....	....	....
	Hershey Bears	AHL	33	1	16	17	....	....	....	54	....	....	....	....	....	....	....	....	....	....	4	0	2	2	6	....	....	....
1979-80	Winnipeg Jets	NHL	13	0	0	0	0	0	0	8	0	0	0	3	0.0	3	0	11	3	–5	....	....	....	....	....	....	....	....
	Tulsa Oilers	CHL	64	5	16	21	....	....	....	55	....	....	....	....	....	....	....	....	....	....	3	0	0	0	2	....	....	....
1980-81	New Haven Nighthawks	AHL	58	1	11	12	....	....	....	94	....	....	....	....	....	....	....	....	....	....	4	0	0	0	2	....	....	....
1981-82	Springfield Indians	AHL	80	4	12	16	....	....	....	80	....	....	....	....	....	....	....	....	....	....	....	....	....	....	....	....	....	....
1982-83	Maine Mariners	AHL	35	0	8	8	....	....	....	49	....	....	....	....	....	....	....	....	....	....	17	0	3	3	21	....	....	....
	NHL Totals		**299**	**9**	**30**	**39**	**9**	**25**	**34**	**284**	**4**	**0**	**1**	**207**	**4.3**	**209**	**17**	**432**	**103**		....	....	....	....	....	....	....	....

EHL North First All-Star Team (1971, 1972) • AHL First All-Star Team (1974) • Won Eddie Shore Award (Outstanding Defenseman - AHL) (1974) • AHL Second All-Star Team (1976) • CHL Second All-Star Team (1980)

Signed as a free agent by **LA Kings**, May 22, 1970. Claimed by **Washington** from **LA Kings** in Expansion Draft, June 12, 1974. Claimed by **Winnipeg** from **Washington** in Expansion Draft, June 13, 1979. Traded to **NY Rangers** by **Winnipeg** for cash, August 6, 1980.

• SMITH, GREG

Greg Smith D – L. 6', 195 lbs. b: Ponoka, Alta., 7/8/1955. California's 4th choice, 57th overall, in 1975 Amateur Draft.

Season	Club	League	GP	G	A	Pts	AG	AA	APts	PIM	PP	SH	GW	S	%	TGF	PGF	TGA	PGA	+/–	GP	G	A	Pts	PIM	PP	SH	GW
1973-74	Colorado College	WCHA	31	7	13	20	....	....	....	80	....	....	....	....	....	....	....	....	....	....	....	....	....	....	....	....	....	....
1974-75	Colorado College	WCHA	36	10	24	34	....	....	....	75	....	....	....	....	....	....	....	....	....	....	....	....	....	....	....	....	....	....
1975-76	Colorado College	WCHA	34	18	19	37	....	....	....	123	....	....	....	....	....	....	....	....	....	....	....	....	....	....	....	....	....	....
	California Golden Seals	NHL	1	0	1	1	0	1	1	2	0	0	0	1	0.0	1	1	1	0	–1	....	....	....	....	....	....	....	....
	Salt Lake City Golden Eagles	CHL	5	0	2	2	....	....	....	2	....	....	....	....	....	....	....	....	....	....	5	1	2	3	4	....	....	....
1976-77	Cleveland Barons	NHL	74	9	17	26	9	14	23	65	4	0	2	128	7.0	64	21	86	12	–31	....	....	....	....	....	....	....	....
	Canada	WEC-A	10	1	1	2	....	....	....	4	....	....	....	....	....	....	....	....	....	....	....	....	....	....	....	....	....	....
1977-78	Cleveland Barons	NHL	80	7	30	37	7	24	31	92	2	0	0	148	4.7	119	24	158	37	–26	....	....	....	....	....	....	....	....
1978-79	Minnesota North Stars	NHL	80	5	27	32	5	21	26	147	1	0	1	193	2.6	99	14	127	21	–21	....	....	....	....	....	....	....	....
	Canada	WEC-A	5	0	0	0	....	....	....	12	....	....	....	....	....	....	....	....	....	....	....	....	....	....	....	....	....	....
1979-80	Minnesota North Stars	NHL	55	5	13	18	5	10	15	103	1	1	1	91	5.5	63	10	62	8	–1	12	0	1	1	9	0	0	0
1980-81	Minnesota North Stars	NHL	74	5	21	26	4	15	19	126	1	0	1	99	5.1	83	8	96	28	+7	19	1	5	6	39	0	1	0
1981-82	Detroit Red Wings	NHL	69	10	22	32	8	15	23	79	2	0	1	154	6.5	99	10	143	32	–22	....	....	....	....	....	....	....	....
1982-83	Detroit Red Wings	NHL	73	4	26	30	3	18	21	79	0	0	0	92	4.3	100	4	123	34	+7	....	....	....	....	....	....	....	....
1983-84	Detroit Red Wings	NHL	75	3	20	23	2	14	16	108	0	0	1	63	4.8	83	2	100	25	+6	4	1	0	1	8	0	0	0
1984-85	Detroit Red Wings	NHL	73	2	18	20	2	12	14	117	0	0	0	54	3.7	61	4	115	32	–26	3	0	0	0	7	0	0	0
1985-86	Detroit Red Wings	NHL	62	5	19	24	4	13	17	84	0	0	0	53	9.4	55	8	100	39	–14	....	....	....	....	....	....	....	....
	Washington Capitals	NHL	14	0	3	3	0	2	2	10	0	0	0	6	0.0	13	1	13	4	+3	9	2	1	3	9	0	1	0
1986-87	Washington Capitals	NHL	45	0	9	9	0	6	6	31	0	0	0	30	0.0	32	3	43	8	–6	7	0	0	0	11	0	0	0
1987-88	Washington Capitals	NHL	54	1	6	7	1	4	5	67	0	0	0	31	3.2	36	1	42	12	+5	9	0	0	0	23	0	0	0
	NHL Totals		**829**	**56**	**232**	**288**	**50**	**169**	**219**	**1110**	**11**	**1**	**7**	**1143**	**4.9**	**908**	**111**	**1209**	**292**		**63**	**4**	**7**	**11**	**106**	**0**	**2**	**0**

Signed as a free agent by **California**, March, 1975. Transferred to **Cleveland** after **California** franchise relocated, August 26, 1976. Protected by **Minnesota** prior to **Cleveland-Minnesota** Dispersal Draft, June 15, 1978. Traded to **Detroit** by **Minnesota** with rights to Don Murdoch and Minnesota's 1st round choice (Murray Craven) in 1982 Entry Draft for Detroit's 1st round choice (Brian Bellows) in 1982 Entry Draft, August 21, 1981. Traded to **Washington** by **Detroit** with John Barrett for Darren Veitch, March 10, 1986.

• SMITH, JASON

Jason Smith D – R. 6'3", 205 lbs. b: Calgary, Alta., 11/2/1973. New Jersey's 6th choice, 18th overall, in 1992 Entry Draft.

Season	Club	League	GP	G	A	Pts	AG	AA	APts	PIM	PP	SH	GW	S	%	TGF	PGF	TGA	PGA	+/–	GP	G	A	Pts	PIM	PP	SH	GW
1990-91	Regina Pats	WHL	2	0	0	0	....	....	....	7	....	....	....	....	....	....	....	....	....	....	4	0	0	0	2	....	....	....
1991-92	Regina Pats	WHL	62	9	29	38	....	....	....	168	....	....	....	....	....	....	....	....	....	....	....	....	....	....	....	....	....	....
1992-93	Regina Pats	WHL	64	14	52	66	....	....	....	175	....	....	....	....	....	....	....	....	....	....	13	4	8	12	39	....	....	....
	Canada	WJC-A	7	1	3	4	....	....	....	10	....	....	....	....	....	....	....	....	....	....	....	....	....	....	....	....	....	....
	Utica Devils	AHL	....	....	....	....	....	....	....	....	....	....	....	....	....	....	....	....	....	....	1	0	0	0	2	....	....	....
1993-94	New Jersey Devils	NHL	41	0	5	5	0	4	4	43	0	0	0	47	0.0	24	1	20	4	+7	6	0	0	0	7	0	0	0
	Albany River Rats	AHL	20	6	3	9	....	....	....	31	....	....	....	....	....	....	....	....	....	....	....	....	....	....	....	....	....	....
1994-95	New Jersey Devils	NHL	2	0	0	0	0	0	0	0	0	0	0	5	0.0	1	0	4	0	–3	....	....	....	....	....	....	....	....
	Albany River Rats	AHL	7	0	2	2	....	....	....	15	....	....	....	....	....	....	....	....	....	....	11	2	2	4	19	....	....	....
1995-96	New Jersey Devils	NHL	64	2	1	3	2	1	3	86	0	0	0	52	3.8	41	0	36	0	+5	....	....	....	....	....	....	....	....
1996-97	New Jersey Devils	NHL	57	1	2	3	1	2	3	38	0	0	0	48	2.1	28	1	35	0	–8	....	....	....	....	....	....	....	....
	Toronto Maple Leafs	NHL	21	0	5	5	0	4	4	16	0	0	0	26	0.0	15	0	24	5	–4	....	....	....	....	....	....	....	....
1997-98	Toronto Maple Leafs	NHL	81	3	13	16	4	13	17	100	0	0	0	97	3.1	57	0	90	28	–5	....	....	....	....	....	....	....	....
	NHL Totals		**266**	**6**	**26**	**32**	**7**	**24**	**31**	**283**	**0**	**0**	**0**	**275**	**2.2**	**166**	**2**	**209**	**37**		**6**	**0**	**0**	**0**	**7**	**0**	**0**	**0**

WHL East First All-Star Team (1993) • Canadian Major Junior First All-Star Team (1993)

Traded to **Toronto** by **New Jersey** with Steve Sullivan and the rights to Alyn McCauley for Doug Gilmour, Dave Ellett and New Jersey's 4th round choice (previously acquired — later traded to Edmonton — Edmonton selected Kristian Antila) in 1998 Entry Draft, February 25, 1997.

• SMITH, RANDY

Randy Smith C – L. 6'4", 200 lbs. b: Saskatoon, Sask., 7/7/1965. St. Louis' 7th choice, 88th overall, in 1973 Amateur Draft.

Season	Club	League	GP	G	A	Pts	AG	AA	APts	PIM	PP	SH	GW	S	%	TGF	PGF	TGA	PGA	+/–	GP	G	A	Pts	PIM	PP	SH	GW
1983-84	Saskatoon Blades	WHL	69	19	21	40	....	....	....	53	....	....	....	....	....	....	....	....	....	....	....	....	....	....	....	....	....	....
1984-85	Saskatoon Blades	WHL	25	6	16	22	....	....	....	9	....	....	....	....	....	....	....	....	....	....	....	....	....	....	....	....	....	....
	Calgary Wranglers	WHL	46	28	35	63	....	....	....	17	....	....	....	....	....	....	....	....	....	....	8	4	3	7	0	....	....	....
1985-86	Saskatoon Blades	WHL	70	60	86	146	....	....	....	44	....	....	....	....	....	....	....	....	....	....	9	4	9	13	4	....	....	....
	Minnesota North Stars	NHL	1	0	0	0	0	0	0	0	0	0	0	0	0.0	0	0	0	0	0	....	....	....	....	....	....	....	....
1986-87	Minnesota North Stars	NHL	2	0	0	0	0	0	0	0	0	0	0	0	0.0	1	1	2	0	–2	....	....	....	....	....	....	....	....
	Springfield Indians	AHL	75	20	44	64	....	....	....	24	....	....	....	....	....	....	....	....	....	....	....	....	....	....	....	....	....	....
1987-88	Kalamazoo Wings	IHL	77	13	43	56	....	....	....	54	....	....	....	....	....	....	....	....	....	....	6	0	8	8	2	....	....	....
1988-89	Maine Mariners	AHL	33	9	16	25	....	....	....	34	....	....	....	....	....	....	....	....	....	....	....	....	....	....	....	....	....	....
	Kalamazoo Wings	IHL	23	4	9	13	....	....	....	2	....	....	....	....	....	....	....	....	....	....	....	....	....	....	....	....	....	....
1989-90	Kalamazoo Wings	IHL	8	1	2	3	....	....	....	12	....	....	....	....	....	....	....	....	....	....	....	....	....	....	....	....	....	....
	Salt Lake Golden Eagles	IHL	30	5	6	11	....	....	....	10	....	....	....	....	....	....	....	....	....	....	3	0	0	0	0	....	....	....

Season	Club	League	GP	G	A	Pts	AG	AA	APts	PIM	PP	SH	GW	S	%	TGF	PGF	TGA	PGA	+/–	GP	G	A	Pts	PIM	PP	SH	GW
			REGULAR SEASON																		PLAYOFFS							
1990-91	Canada	Nat-Team	58	17	39	56	....	....	....	42	....	....	....	....	....	....	....	....	....	....	....	....	....	....	....	....	....	....
	Canada	WEC-A	10	0	0	0	....	....	....	8	....	....	....	....	....	....	....	....	....	....	....	....	....	....	....	....	....	....
1991-92	Canada	Nat-Team	59	20	25	45	....	....	....	24	....	....	....	....	....	....	....	....	....	....	....	....	....	....	....	....	....	....
	Canada	Olympics	8	1	7	8	....	....	....	4	....	....	....	....	....	....	....	....	....	....	....	....	....	....	....	....	....	....
	Canada	WC-A	6	1	0	1	....	....	....	4	....	....	....	....	....	....	....	....	....	....	....	....	....	....	....	....	....	....
1992-93	Klagenfurt	Germany	39	26	18	44	....	....	....	....	....	....	....	....	....	....	....	....	....	....	....	....	....	....	....	....	....	....
1993-94	Las Vegas Thunder	IHL	53	7	7	14	....	....	....	78	....	....	....	....	....	....	....	....	....	....	....	....	....	....	....	....	....	....
1994-95	Edinburgh Racers	Britain	44	53	84	167	....	....	....	....	....	....	....	....	....	....	....	....	....	....	....	....	....	....	....	....	....	....
1995-96	Cardiff Devils	Britain	55	87	76	163	....	....	....	50	....	....	....	....	....	....	....	....	....	....	....	....	....	....	....	....	....	....
	NHL Totals		**3**	**0**	**0**	**0**	**0**	**0**	**0**	**0**	**0**	**0**	**0**	**0**	**0.0**	**1**	**1**	**2**	**0**		....	....	....	....	....	....	....	....

Signed as a free agent by **Minnesota**, May 12, 1986.

• SMITH, RICK

Rick Smith D – L. 5′11″, 190 lbs. b: Hamilton, Ont., 6/29/1948. Boston's 2nd choice, 7th overall, in 1966 Amateur Draft.

Season	Club	League	GP	G	A	Pts	AG	AA	APts	PIM	PP	SH	GW	S	%	TGF	PGF	TGA	PGA	+/–	GP	G	A	Pts	PIM	PP	SH	GW
1965-66	Hamilton Red Wings	OHA	47	2	16	18	....	....	....	60	....	....	....	....	....	....	....	....	....	....	5	1	1	2	6	....	....	....
1966-67	Hamilton Red Wings	OHA	48	2	17	19	....	....	....	74	....	....	....	....	....	....	....	....	....	....	17	4	14	18	35	....	....	....
1967-68	Hamilton Red Wings	OHA	49	5	36	41	....	....	....	123	....	....	....	....	....	....	....	....	....	....	11	2	9	11	33	....	....	....
1968-69	**Boston Bruins**	**NHL**	**48**	**0**	**5**	**5**	**0**	**5**	**5**	**29**	**0**	**0**	**0**	**28**	**0.0**	**34**	**0**	**22**	**2**	**+14**	**9**	**0**	**0**	**0**	**6**	**0**	**0**	**0**
	Oklahoma City Blazers	CHL	19	5	10	15	....	....	....	37	....	....	....	....	....	....	....	....	....	....	....	....	....	....	....	....	....	....
1969-70	**Boston Bruins**	**NHL**	**69**	**2**	**8**	**10**	**2**	**8**	**10**	**65**	**0**	**0**	**1**	**94**	**2.1**	**62**	**2**	**66**	**18**	**+12**	**14**	**1**	**3**	**4**	**17**	**0**	**0**	**0**
1970-71	**Boston Bruins**	**NHL**	**67**	**4**	**19**	**23**	**4**	**17**	**21**	**44**	**0**	**0**	**1**	**79**	**5.1**	**63**	**0**	**48**	**15**	**+30**	**6**	**0**	**0**	**0**	**0**	**0**	**0**	**0**
1971-72	**Boston Bruins**	**NHL**	**61**	**2**	**12**	**14**	**2**	**11**	**13**	**46**	**0**	**0**	**0**	**81**	**2.5**	**90**	**2**	**56**	**21**	**+53**	....	....	....	....	....	....	....	....
	California Golden Seals	**NHL**	**17**	**1**	**4**	**5**	**1**	**4**	**5**	**26**	**0**	**0**	**0**	**23**	**4.3**	**16**	**0**	**38**	**5**	**–17**	....	....	....	....	....	....	....	....
1972-73	**California Golden Seals**	**NHL**	**64**	**9**	**24**	**33**	**9**	**20**	**29**	**77**	**3**	**0**	**0**	**126**	**7.1**	**95**	**25**	**141**	**28**	**–43**	....	....	....	....	....	....	....	....
1973-74	Minnesota Fighting Saints	WHA	71	10	28	38	....	....	....	98	....	....	....	....	....	....	....	....	....	....	11	0	1	1	22	....	....	....
1974-75	Canada	Summit	7	0	0	0	....	....	....	12	....	....	....	....	....	....	....	....	....	....	....	....	....	....	....	....	....	....
	Minnesota Fighting Saints	WHA	78	9	29	38	....	....	....	112	....	....	....	....	....	....	....	....	....	....	12	2	7	9	6	....	....	....
1975-76	Minnesota Fighting Saints	WHA	51	1	32	33	....	....	....	50	....	....	....	....	....	....	....	....	....	....	....	....	....	....	....	....	....	....
	St. Louis Blues	**NHL**	**24**	**1**	**7**	**8**	**1**	**5**	**6**	**18**	**0**	**0**	**0**	**32**	**3.1**	**20**	**5**	**35**	**14**	**+2**	**3**	**0**	**1**	**1**	**4**	**0**	**0**	**0**
1976-77	**St. Louis Blues**	**NHL**	**18**	**0**	**1**	**1**	**0**	**1**	**1**	**6**	**0**	**0**	**0**	**11**	**0.0**	**11**	**0**	**21**	**7**	**–3**	....	....	....	....	....	....	....	....
	Kansas City Blues	CHL	7	1	6	7	....	....	....	11	....	....	....	....	....	....	....	....	....	....	....	....	....	....	....	....	....	....
	Boston Bruins	**NHL**	**46**	**6**	**16**	**22**	**6**	**13**	**19**	**30**	**0**	**0**	**0**	**72**	**8.3**	**70**	**1**	**55**	**9**	**+23**	**14**	**0**	**9**	**9**	**14**	**0**	**0**	**0**
1977-78	**Boston Bruins**	**NHL**	**79**	**7**	**29**	**36**	**7**	**24**	**31**	**69**	**0**	**0**	**0**	**116**	**6.0**	**140**	**8**	**87**	**25**	**+70**	**15**	**1**	**5**	**6**	**18**	**0**	**0**	**0**
1978-79	**Boston Bruins**	**NHL**	**65**	**7**	**18**	**25**	**6**	**14**	**20**	**46**	**0**	**0**	**1**	**78**	**9.0**	**83**	**0**	**78**	**15**	**+20**	**11**	**0**	**4**	**4**	**12**	**0**	**0**	**0**
1979-80	**Boston Bruins**	**NHL**	**78**	**8**	**18**	**26**	**7**	**14**	**21**	**62**	**0**	**0**	**2**	**85**	**9.4**	**78**	**0**	**76**	**20**	**+22**	**6**	**1**	**1**	**2**	**2**	**0**	**0**	**0**
1980-81	**Detroit Red Wings**	**NHL**	**11**	**0**	**2**	**2**	**0**	**1**	**1**	**6**	**0**	**0**	**0**	**7**	**0.0**	**5**	**0**	**11**	**1**	**–5**	....	....	....	....	....	....	....	....
	Washington Capitals	**NHL**	**40**	**5**	**4**	**9**	**4**	**3**	**7**	**36**	**2**	**0**	**2**	**35**	**14.3**	**44**	**7**	**43**	**13**	**+7**	....	....	....	....	....	....	....	....
	NHL Totals		**687**	**52**	**167**	**219**	**49**	**140**	**189**	**560**	**5**	**0**	**7**	**867**	**6.0**	**819**	**50**	**777**	**193**		**78**	**3**	**23**	**26**	**73**	**0**	**0**	**0**
	Other Major League Totals		200	20	89	109	....	....	....	260	....	....	....	....	....	....	....	....	....	....	23	2	8	10	28	....	....	....

OHA Second All-Star Team (1968)

Traded to **California** by **Boston** with Reggie Leach and Bob Stewart for Carol Vadnais and Don O'Donoghue, February 23, 1972. Selected by **Miami-Philadelphia** (WHA) in 1972 WHA General Player Draft, February 12, 1972. WHA rights traded to **Minnesota** (WHA) by **Philadelphia** (WHA) for Bill Young, cash and future considerations, May, 1972. Traded to **St. Louis** by **California** for cash, October 22, 1975. Traded to **Boston** by **St. Louis** for Joe Zanussi, December 20, 1976. Claimed by **Detroit** from **Boston** in Waiver Draft, October 10, 1980. Claimed on waivers by **Washington** from **Detroit**, November 7, 1980.

• SMITH, RON

Ron Smith D – R. 6′, 185 lbs. b: Port Hope, Ont., 11/19/1952. NY Islanders' 6th choice, 49th overall, in 1972 Amateur Draft.

Season	Club	League	GP	G	A	Pts	AG	AA	APts	PIM	PP	SH	GW	S	%	TGF	PGF	TGA	PGA	+/–	GP	G	A	Pts	PIM	PP	SH	GW
1970-71	Sorel Eperviers	QJHL	42	4	12	16	....	....	....	152	....	....	....	....	....	....	....	....	....	....	2	0	2	2	2	....	....	....
1971-72	Cornwall Royals	QMJHL	56	8	27	35	....	....	....	55	....	....	....	....	....	....	....	....	....	....	16	4	3	7	24	....	....	....
1972-73	**New York Islanders**	**NHL**	**11**	**1**	**1**	**2**	**1**	**1**	**2**	**14**	**0**	**0**	**0**	**10**	**10.0**	**4**	**0**	**12**	**0**	**–8**	....	....	....	....	....	....	....	....
	New Haven Nighthawks	AHL	53	6	11	17	....	....	....	83	....	....	....	....	....	....	....	....	....	....	....	....	....	....	....	....	....	....
1973-74	Fort Worth Wings	CHL	72	1	16	17	....	....	....	103	....	....	....	....	....	....	....	....	....	....	5	1	1	2	2	....	....	....
1974-75	Fort Worth Texans	CHL	75	6	19	25	....	....	....	97	....	....	....	....	....	....	....	....	....	....	....	....	....	....	....	....	....	....
	NHL Totals		**11**	**1**	**1**	**2**	**1**	**1**	**2**	**14**	**0**	**0**	**0**	**10**	**10.0**	**4**	**0**	**12**	**0**									

• SMITH, STEVE

Steve Smith D – L. 6′4″, 215 lbs. b: Glasgow, Scotland, 4/30/1963. Edmonton's 5th choice, 111th overall, in 1981 Entry Draft.

Season	Club	League	GP	G	A	Pts	AG	AA	APts	PIM	PP	SH	GW	S	%	TGF	PGF	TGA	PGA	+/–	GP	G	A	Pts	PIM	PP	SH	GW
1980-81	London Knights	OHA	62	4	12	16	....	....	....	141	....	....	....	....	....	....	....	....	....	....	....	....	....	....	....	....	....	....
1981-82	London Knights	OHL	58	10	36	46	....	....	....	207	....	....	....	....	....	....	....	....	....	....	4	1	2	3	13	....	....	....
1982-83	London Knights	OHL	50	6	35	41	....	....	....	133	....	....	....	....	....	....	....	....	....	....	3	1	0	1	10	....	....	....
	Moncton Alpines	AHL	2	0	0	0	....	....	....	0	....	....	....	....	....	....	....	....	....	....	....	....	....	....	....	....	....	....
1983-84	Moncton Alpines	AHL	64	1	8	9	....	....	....	176	....	....	....	....	....	....	....	....	....	....	....	....	....	....	....	....	....	....
1984-85	**Edmonton Oilers**	**NHL**	**2**	**0**	**0**	**0**	**0**	**0**	**0**	**2**	**0**	**0**	**0**	**3**	**0.0**	**1**	**0**	**3**	**0**	**–2**	....	....	....	....	....	....	....	....
	Nova Scotia Voyageurs	AHL	68	2	28	30	....	....	....	161	....	....	....	....	....	....	....	....	....	....	5	0	3	3	40	....	....	....
1985-86	**Edmonton Oilers**	**NHL**	**55**	**4**	**20**	**24**	**3**	**13**	**16**	**166**	**1**	**0**	**1**	**74**	**5.4**	**71**	**8**	**40**	**7**	**+30**	**6**	**0**	**1**	**1**	**14**	**0**	**0**	**0**
	Nova Scotia Oilers	AHL	4	0	2	2	....	....	....	11	....	....	....	....	....	....	....	....	....	....	....	....	....	....	....	....	....	....
1986-87	**Edmonton Oilers**	**NHL**	**62**	**7**	**15**	**22**	**6**	**11**	**17**	**165**	**2**	**0**	**1**	**71**	**9.9**	**71**	**8**	**66**	**14**	**+11**	**15**	**1**	**3**	**4**	**45**	**0**	**0**	**0**
1987-88	**Edmonton Oilers**	**NHL**	**79**	**12**	**43**	**55**	**10**	**31**	**41**	**286**	**5**	**0**	**1**	**116**	**10.3**	**140**	**37**	**97**	**34**	**+40**	**19**	**1**	**11**	**12**	**55**	**1**	**0**	**0**
1988-89	**Edmonton Oilers**	**NHL**	**35**	**3**	**19**	**22**	**3**	**13**	**16**	**97**	**0**	**0**	**0**	**47**	**6.4**	**52**	**17**	**44**	**14**	**+5**	**7**	**2**	**2**	**4**	**20**	**0**	**0**	**1**
1989-90	**Edmonton Oilers**	**NHL**	**75**	**7**	**34**	**41**	**6**	**24**	**30**	**171**	**3**	**0**	**1**	**125**	**5.6**	**125**	**52**	**86**	**19**	**+6**	**22**	**5**	**10**	**15**	**37**	**0**	**1**	**1**
1990-91	**Edmonton Oilers**	**NHL**	**77**	**13**	**41**	**54**	**12**	**31**	**43**	**193**	**4**	**0**	**2**	**114**	**11.4**	**121**	**38**	**101**	**32**	**+14**	**18**	**1**	**2**	**3**	**45**	**1**	**0**	**0**
1991-92	Canada	C Cup	8	0	1	1	....	....	....	30	....	....	....	....	....	....	....	....	....	....	....	....	....	....	....	....	....	....
	Chicago Blackhawks	**NHL**	**76**	**9**	**21**	**30**	**8**	**16**	**24**	**304**	**3**	**0**	**1**	**153**	**5.9**	**122**	**40**	**89**	**30**	**+23**	**18**	**1**	**11**	**12**	**16**	**1**	**0**	**0**
1992-93	**Chicago Blackhawks**	**NHL**	**78**	**10**	**47**	**57**	**8**	**32**	**40**	**214**	**7**	**1**	**2**	**212**	**4.7**	**142**	**66**	**100**	**44**	**+12**	**4**	**0**	**0**	**0**	**10**	**0**	**0**	**0**
1993-94	**Chicago Blackhawks**	**NHL**	**57**	**5**	**22**	**27**	**5**	**17**	**22**	**174**	**1**	**0**	**1**	**89**	**5.6**	**71**	**21**	**76**	**21**	**–5**	....	....	....	....	....	....	....	....
1994-95	**Chicago Blackhawks**	**NHL**	**48**	**1**	**12**	**13**	**2**	**18**	**20**	**128**	**0**	**0**	**0**	**43**	**2.3**	**47**	**9**	**50**	**18**	**+6**	**16**	**0**	**1**	**1**	**26**	**0**	**0**	**0**
1995-96	**Chicago Blackhawks**	**NHL**	**37**	**0**	**9**	**9**	**0**	**7**	**7**	**71**	**0**	**0**	**0**	**17**	**0.0**	**39**	**4**	**40**	**17**	**+12**	**6**	**0**	**0**	**0**	**16**	**0**	**0**	**0**
1996-97	**Chicago Blackhawks**	**NHL**	**21**	**0**	**0**	**0**	**0**	**0**	**0**	**29**	**0**	**0**	**0**	**7**	**0.0**	**15**	**0**	**17**	**6**	**+4**	**3**	**0**	**0**	**0**	**4**	**0**	**0**	**0**
	NHL Totals		**702**	**71**	**283**	**354**	**63**	**213**	**276**	**2000**	**26**	**1**	**10**	**1071**	**6.6**	**1017**	**300**	**817**	**256**		**134**	**11**	**41**	**52**	**288**	**3**	**1**	**2**

Played in NHL All-Star Game (1991)

Traded to **Chicago** by **Edmonton** for Dave Manson and Chicago's 3rd round choice (Kirk Maltby) in 1992 Entry Draft, October 2, 1991.

• SMITH, STEVE

Steve Smith D – L. 5′9″, 215 lbs. b: Trenton, Ont., 4/4/1963. Philadelphia's 2nd choice, 16th overall, in 1981 Entry Draft.

Season	Club	League	GP	G	A	Pts	AG	AA	APts	PIM	PP	SH	GW	S	%	TGF	PGF	TGA	PGA	+/–	GP	G	A	Pts	PIM	PP	SH	GW
1979-80	Belleville Bulls	Tier II	41	8	25	33	....	....	....	105	....	....	....	....	....	....	....	....	....	....	....	....	....	....	....	....	....	....
1980-81	Sault Ste. Marie Greyhounds	OHA	61	3	37	40	....	....	....	143	....	....	....	....	....	....	....	....	....	....	19	0	6	6	60	....	....	....
1981-82	Sault Ste. Marie Greyhounds	OHL	50	7	20	27	....	....	....	179	....	....	....	....	....	....	....	....	....	....	12	0	2	2	23	....	....	....
	Philadelphia Flyers	**NHL**	**8**	**0**	**1**	**1**	**0**	**1**	**1**	**0**	**0**	**0**	**0**	**9**	**0.0**	**2**	**0**	**7**	**3**	**–2**	....	....	....	....	....	....	....	....
1982-83	Sault Ste. Marie Greyhounds	OHL	55	11	33	44	....	....	....	139	....	....	....	....	....	....	....	....	....	....	16	0	8	8	28	....	....	....
1983-84	Springfield Indians	AHL	70	4	25	29	....	....	....	77	....	....	....	....	....	....	....	....	....	....	4	0	0	0	0	....	....	....
1984-85	**Philadelphia Flyers**	**NHL**	**2**	**0**	**0**	**0**	**0**	**0**	**0**	**7**	**0**	**0**	**0**	**0**	**0.0**	**3**	**1**	**0**	**0**	**+2**	....	....	....	....	....	....	....	....
	Hershey Bears	AHL	65	10	20	30	....	....	....	83	....	....	....	....	....	....	....	....	....	....	....	....	....	....	....	....	....	....
1985-86	**Phialdelphia**	**NHL**	**2**	**0**	**0**	**0**	**0**	**0**	**0**	**2**	....	....	....	....	....	....	....	....	....	....	....	....	....	....	....	....	....	....
	Hershey Bears	AHL	49	1	11	12	....	....	....	96	....	....	....	....	....	....	....	....	....	....	16	2	4	6	43	....	....	....
1986-87	**Philadelphia Flyers**	**NHL**	**2**	**0**	**0**	**0**	**0**	**0**	**0**	**6**	**0**	**0**	**0**	**1**	**0.0**	**0**	**0**	**2**	**0**	**–2**	....	....	....	....	....	....	....	....
	Hershey Bears	AHL	66	11	26	37	....	....	....	191	....	....	....	....	....	....	....	....	....	....	5	0	2	2	8	....	....	....
1987-88	**Philadelphia Flyers**	**NHL**	**1**	**0**	**0**	**0**	**0**	**0**	**0**	**0**	....	....	....	....	....	....	....	....	....	....	....	....	....	....	....	....	....	....
	Hershey Bears	AHL	66	10	19	29	....	....	....	132	....	....	....	....	....	....	....	....	....	....	12	2	10	12	35	....	....	....
1988-89	**Buffalo Sabres**	**NHL**	**3**	**0**	**0**	**0**	**0**	**0**	**0**	**0**	**0**	**0**	**0**	**2**	**0.0**	**2**	**0**	**2**	**0**	**0**	....	....	....	....	....	....	....	....
	Rochester Americans	AHL	48	2	12	14	....	....	....	79	....	....	....	....	....	....	....	....	....	....	....	....	....	....	....	....	....	....
1989-90	Rochester Americans	AHL	42	3	15	18	....	....	....	107	....	....	....	....	....	....	....	....	....	....	17	0	5	5	27	....	....	....
1990-91	Rochester Americans	AHL	37	2	4	6	....	....	....	74	....	....	....	....	....	....	....	....	....	....	5	0	0	0	4	....	....	....

Season	Club	League	GP	G	A	Pts	AG	AA	APts	PIM	PP	SH	GW	S	%	TGF	PGF	TGA	PGA	+/–	GP	G	A	Pts	PIM	PP	SH	GW
			REGULAR SEASON																		PLAYOFFS							
1991-92	Rochester Americans	AHL	3	1	0	1				0																		
	Zell-A-See	Austria	28	11	6	17																						
1992-93	SG Brunico	Italy	19	6	22	28				4																		
	NHL Totals		**18**	**0**	**1**	**1**	**0**	**1**	**1**	**15**	**0**	**0**	**0**	**12**	**0.0**	**7**	**1**	**11**	**3**									

OHL Second All-Star Team (1981,1982, 1983)

Claimed by **Buffalo** from **Philadelphia** in Waiver Draft, October 3, 1988.

• SMITH, STU G.

Stu G. Smith D – R. 6′1″, 205 lbs. b: Toronto, Ont., 3/17/1960. Hartford's 2nd choice, 39th overall, in 1979 Entry Draft.

Season	Club	League	GP	G	A	Pts	AG	AA	APts	PIM	PP	SH	GW	S	%	TGF	PGF	TGA	PGA	+/–	GP	G	A	Pts	PIM	PP	SH	GW
1977-78	Peterborough Petes	OHA	67	1	18	19				112																		
1978-79	Peterborough Petes	OHA	64	5	35	40				172											19	2	7	9	56			
1979-80	Peterborough Petes	OHA	62	12	40	52				119											14	1	13	14	16			
	Hartford Whalers	**NHL**	**4**	**0**	**0**	**0**	**0**	**0**	**0**	**0**	**0**	**0**	**0**	**3**	**0.0**	**4**	**0**	**5**	**0**	**–1**								
1980-81	**Hartford Whalers**	**NHL**	**38**	**1**	**7**	**8**	**1**	**5**	**6**	**55**	**0**	**0**	**0**	**34**	**2.9**	**35**	**2**	**61**	**14**	**–14**								
	Binghamton Whalers	AHL	42	3	9	12				63																		
1981-82	**Hartford Whalers**	**NHL**	**17**	**0**	**3**	**3**	**0**	**2**	**2**	**15**	**0**	**0**	**0**	**14**	**0.0**	**8**	**0**	**21**	**6**	**–7**								
	Binghamton Whalers	AHL	61	4	21	25				121											15	2	7	9	22			
1982-83	**Hartford Whalers**	**NHL**	**18**	**1**	**0**	**1**	**1**	**0**	**1**	**25**	**0**	**0**	**0**	**21**	**4.8**	**12**	**1**	**34**	**7**	**–16**								
	Binghamton Whalers	AHL	50	3	8	11				97											5	0	1	1	12			
1983-84	Binghamton Whalers	AHL	54	3	22	25				95																		
1984-85	New Haven Nighthawks	AHL	79	4	17	21				87																		
	NHL Totals		**77**	**2**	**10**	**12**	**2**	**7**	**9**	**95**	**0**	**0**	**0**	**72**	**2.8**	**59**	**3**	**121**	**27**									

Signed as a free agent by **LA Kings**, November 8, 1984.

• SMITH, VERN

Vern Smith D – L. 6′1″, 190 lbs. b: Winnipeg, Man., 5/30/1964. NY Islanders' 2nd choice, 42nd overall, in 1982 Entry Draft.

Season	Club	League	GP	G	A	Pts	AG	AA	APts	PIM	PP	SH	GW	S	%	TGF	PGF	TGA	PGA	+/–	GP	G	A	Pts	PIM	PP	SH	GW
1981-82	Lethbridge Broncos	WHL	72	5	38	43				73											12	0	2	2	8			
1982-83	Lethbridge Broncos	WHL	30	2	10	12				54																		
	Nanaimo Islanders	WHL	42	6	21	27				62																		
1983-84	New Westminster Bruins	WHL	69	13	44	57				94											9	6	6	12	12			
1984-85	**New York Islanders**	**NHL**	**1**	**0**	**0**	**0**	**0**	**0**	**0**	**0**	**0**	**0**	**0**	**0**	**0.0**	**1**	**0**	**1**	**0**	**0**								
	Springfield Indians	AHL	76	6	20	26				115											4	0	2	2	9			
1985-86	Springfield Indians	AHL	55	3	11	14				83																		
1986-87	Springfield Indians	AHL	41	1	10	11				58																		
1987-88	Springfield Indians	AHL	64	5	22	27				78																		
1988-89	Springfield Indians	AHL	80	3	26	29				121																		
1989-90	Phoenix Roadrunners	IHL	48	4	19	23				37																		
1990-91	New Haven Nighthawks	AHL	9	0	1	1				2																		
	Albany Choppers	IHL	46	5	15	20				48																		
1991-92	Phoenix Roadrunners	IHL	16	1	2	3				25																		
	New Haven Nighthawks	AHL	4	0	0	0				5																		
	Capital District Islanders	AHL	17	1	5	6				6																		
	Erie Panthers	ECHL	8	3	5	8				6																		
	NHL Totals		**1**	**0**	**0**	**0**	**0**	**0**	**0**	**0**	**0**	**0**	**0**	**0**	**0.0**	**1**	**0**	**1**	**0**									

• SMOLINSKI, BRYAN

Bryan Smolinski C – R. 6′1″, 200 lbs. b: Toledo, OH, 12/27/1971. Boston's 3rd choice, 21st overall, in 1990 Entry Draft.

Season	Club	League	GP	G	A	Pts	AG	AA	APts	PIM	PP	SH	GW	S	%	TGF	PGF	TGA	PGA	+/–	GP	G	A	Pts	PIM	PP	SH	GW
1989-90	Michigan State Spartans	CCHA	35	9	13	22				34																		
	United States	WJC-A	7	2	3	5				8																		
1990-91	Michigan State Spartans	CCHA	35	9	12	21				24																		
1991-92	Michigan State Spartans	CCHA	41	28	33	61				55																		
1992-93	Michigan State Spartans	CCHA	40	31	37	*68				93																		
	Boston Bruins	**NHL**	**9**	**1**	**3**	**4**	**1**	**2**	**3**	**0**	**0**	**0**	**0**	**10**	**10.0**	**5**	**1**	**1**	**0**	**+3**	**4**	**1**	**0**	**1**	**2**	**0**	**0**	**0**
1993-94	**Boston Bruins**	**NHL**	**83**	**31**	**20**	**51**	**29**	**15**	**44**	**82**	**4**	**3**	**5**	**179**	**17.3**	**69**	**14**	**60**	**9**	**+4**	**13**	**5**	**4**	**9**	**4**	**2**	**0**	**0**
1994-95	**Boston Bruins**	**NHL**	**44**	**18**	**13**	**31**	**32**	**19**	**51**	**31**	**6**	**0**	**5**	**121**	**14.9**	**40**	**13**	**35**	**5**	**–3**	**5**	**0**	**1**	**1**	**4**	**0**	**0**	**0**
1995-96	**Pittsburgh Penguins**	**NHL**	**81**	**24**	**40**	**64**	**24**	**33**	**57**	**69**	**8**	**2**	**1**	**229**	**10.5**	**94**	**24**	**85**	**21**	**+6**	**18**	**5**	**4**	**9**	**10**	**0**	**0**	**1**
1996-97	United States	W Cup	6	0	5	5				0																		
	Detroit Vipers	IHL	6	5	7	12				10																		
	New York Islanders	**NHL**	**64**	**28**	**28**	**56**	**30**	**25**	**55**	**25**	**9**	**0**	**1**	**183**	**15.3**	**78**	**21**	**49**	**1**	**+9**								
1997-98	**New York Islanders**	**NHL**	**81**	**13**	**30**	**43**	**15**	**29**	**44**	**34**	**3**	**0**	**4**	**203**	**6.4**	**68**	**21**	**66**	**3**	**–16**								
	United States	WC-A	6	3	1	4				10																		
	NHL Totals		**362**	**115**	**134**	**249**	**131**	**123**	**254**	**241**	**30**	**5**	**16**	**925**	**12.4**	**354**	**94**	**296**	**39**		**40**	**11**	**9**	**20**	**20**	**2**	**0**	**1**

CCHA First All-Star Team (1993) • NCAA West First All-American Team (1993)

Traded to **Pittsburgh** by **Boston** with Glen Murray and Boston's 3rd round choice (Boyd Kane) in 1996 Entry Draft for Kevin Stevens and Shawn McEachern, August 2, 1995. Traded to **NY Islanders** by **Pittsburgh** for Darius Kasparaitis and Andreas Johansson, November 17, 1996.

• SMRKE, JOHN

John Smrke LW – L. 5′11″, 205 lbs. b: Chicoutimi, Que., 2/25/1956. St. Louis' 3rd choice, 25th overall, in 1976 Amateur Draft.

Season	Club	League	GP	G	A	Pts	AG	AA	APts	PIM	PP	SH	GW	S	%	TGF	PGF	TGA	PGA	+/–	GP	G	A	Pts	PIM	PP	SH	GW
1973-74	Toronto Marlboros	OHA	70	23	28	51				18																		
1974-75	Toronto Marlboros	OHA	61	43	54	97				39																		
1975-76	Toronto Marlboros	OHA	64	39	46	85				32																		
1976-77	Kansas City Blues	CHL	70	25	26	51				8											5	2	0	2	2			
1977-78	**St. Louis Blues**	**NHL**	**18**	**2**	**4**	**6**	**2**	**3**	**5**	**11**	**0**	**0**	**0**	**20**	**10.0**	**11**	**3**	**15**	**0**	**–7**								
	Salt Lake Golden Eagles	CHL	60	25	45	70				21											6	4	2	6	2			
1978-79	**St. Louis Blues**	**NHL**	**55**	**6**	**8**	**14**	**5**	**6**	**11**	**20**	**0**	**1**	**0**	**72**	**8.3**	**21**	**0**	**63**	**18**	**–24**								
	Salt Lake Golden Eagles	CHL	11	5	7	12				0																		
1979-80	**Quebec Nordiques**	**NHL**	**30**	**3**	**5**	**8**	**3**	**4**	**7**	**2**	**0**	**0**	**0**	**32**	**9.4**	**17**	**0**	**18**	**4**	**+3**								
	Syracuse Firebirds	AHL	19	5	5	10				2											4	1	0	1	2			
1980-81	Binghamton Whalers	AHL	9	1	2	3				0																		
	Houston Apollos	CHL	33	7	4	11				16																		
1981-82	Cincinnati Tigers	CHL	45	6	7	13				4											4	0	0	0	25			
1982-83			DID NOT PLAY																									
1983-84			DID NOT PLAY																									
1984-85	Auronzo	Italy	25	29	22	51				12											2	5	2	7	0			
1985-86	Campbellton Tigers	NNBSL	40	37	57	94				31											6	2	9	11				
	NHL Totals		**103**	**11**	**17**	**28**	**10**	**13**	**23**	**33**	**0**	**1**	**0**	**124**	**8.9**	**49**	**3**	**96**	**22**									

Won George Parsons Trophy (Memorial Cup Tournament Most Sportsmanlike Player) (1975)

Claimed by **Quebec** from **St. Louis** in Expansion Draft, June 13, 1979.

• SMYL, STAN

Stan "Steamer" Smyl RW – R. 5′8″, 185 lbs. b: Glendon, Alta., 1/28/1958. Vancouver's 3rd choice, 40th overall, in 1978 Amateur Draft.

Season	Club	League	GP	G	A	Pts	AG	AA	APts	PIM	PP	SH	GW	S	%	TGF	PGF	TGA	PGA	+/–	GP	G	A	Pts	PIM	PP	SH	GW
1974-75	Bellingham Blazers	BCJHL	STATISTICS NOT AVAILABLE																									
	New Westminster Bruins	WCJHL																			3	0	0	0	15			
1975-76	New Westminster Bruins	WCJHL	72	32	42	74				169											19	8	6	14	58			
1976-77	New Westminster Bruins	WCJHL	72	36	31	66				200											13	6	7	13	51			
1977-78	New Westminster Bruins	WCJHL	53	29	47	76				211											20	14	21	35	43			
	Canada	WJC-A	6	1	1	2				6																		
1978-79	**Vancouver Canucks**	**NHL**	**62**	**14**	**24**	**38**	**13**	**18**	**31**	**89**	**4**	**0**	**0**	**122**	**11.5**	**62**	**24**	**44**	**0**	**–6**	**2**	**1**	**1**	**2**	**0**	**0**	**0**	**0**
	Dallas Black Hawks	CHL	3	1	1	2				9																		
1979-80	**Vancouver Canucks**	**NHL**	**77**	**31**	**47**	**78**	**28**	**36**	**64**	**204**	**11**	**0**	**3**	**182**	**17.0**	**107**	**29**	**53**	**3**	**+28**	**4**	**0**	**2**	**2**	**14**	**0**	**0**	**0**
1980-81	**Vancouver Canucks**	**NHL**	**80**	**25**	**38**	**63**	**21**	**27**	**48**	**171**	**6**	**1**	**2**	**209**	**12.0**	**92**	**32**	**72**	**4**	**–8**	**3**	**1**	**2**	**3**	**0**	**0**	**0**	**0**
1981-82	**Vancouver Canucks**	**NHL**	**80**	**34**	**44**	**78**	**27**	**29**	**56**	**144**	**10**	**2**	**5**	**222**	**15.3**	**126**	**40**	**96**	**28**	**+18**	**17**	**9**	**9**	**18**	**25**	**1**	**0**	**1**
1982-83	**Vancouver Canucks**	**NHL**	**74**	**38**	**50**	**88**	**31**	**35**	**66**	**114**	**15**	**1**	**2**	**215**	**17.7**	**124**	**52**	**85**	**7**	**–6**	**4**	**3**	**2**	**5**	**12**	**1**	**0**	**1**
1983-84	**Vancouver Canucks**	**NHL**	**80**	**24**	**43**	**67**	**19**	**29**	**48**	**136**	**8**	**0**	**4**	**205**	**11.7**	**106**	**40**	**106**	**19**	**–21**	**4**	**2**	**1**	**3**	**4**	**0**	**0**	**0**

Season	Club	League	GP	G	A	Pts	AG	AA	APts	PIM	PP	SH	GW	S	%	TGF	PGF	TGA	PGA	+/–	GP	G	A	Pts	PIM	PP	SH	GW
			REGULAR SEASON																		PLAYOFFS							
1984-85	Vancouver Canucks	NHL	80	27	37	64	22	25	47	100	6	2	1	182	14.8	95	25	111	23	–18	....	....	....	....	....	....	....	....
	Canada	WEC-A	10	1	1	2	....	....	....	6	....	....	....	....	....	....	....	....	....	....	....	....	....	....	....	....	....	....
1985-86	Vancouver Canucks	NHL	73	27	35	62	22	23	45	144	3	4	1	165	16.4	90	23	117	30	–20	....	....	....	....	....	....	....	....
1986-87	Vancouver Canucks	NHL	66	20	23	43	17	17	34	84	5	2	2	113	17.7	78	30	85	17	–20	....	....	....	....	....	....	....	....
1987-88	Vancouver Canucks	NHL	57	12	25	37	10	18	28	110	5	1	0	96	12.5	58	18	53	8	–5	....	....	....	....	....	....	....	....
1988-89	Vancouver Canucks	NHL	75	7	18	25	6	13	19	102	1	0	0	89	7.9	47	8	45	6	0	7	0	0	0	9	0	0	0
1989-90	Vancouver Canucks	NHL	47	1	15	16	1	11	12	71	0	0	0	58	1.7	29	5	45	7	–14	....	....	....	....	....	....	....	....
1990-91	Vancouver Canucks	NHL	45	2	12	14	2	9	11	87	0	0	0	45	4.4	21	1	26	1	–5	....	....	....	....	....	....	....	....
	NHL Totals		896	262	411	673	219	290	509	1556	74	13	20	1903	13.8	1035	327	938	153		41	16	17	33	64	2	0	2

Memorial Cup All-Star Team (1978) • Won Stafford Smythe Memorial Trophy (Memorial Cup Tournament MVP) (1978)

• SMYTH, BRAD

Brad Smyth RW – R. 6′, 200 lbs. b: Ottawa, Ont., 3/13/1973.

Season	Club	League	GP	G	A	Pts	AG	AA	APts	PIM	PP	SH	GW	S	%	TGF	PGF	TGA	PGA	+/–	GP	G	A	Pts	PIM	PP	SH	GW
1990-91	London Knights	OHL	29	2	6	8	....	....	....	22	....	....	....	....	....	....	....	....	....	....	....	....	....	....	....	....	....	....
1991-92	London Knights	OHL	58	17	18	35	....	....	....	93	....	....	....	....	....	....	....	....	....	....	10	2	0	2	8	....	....	....
1992-93	London Knights	OHL	66	54	55	109	....	....	....	118	....	....	....	....	....	....	....	....	....	....	12	7	8	15	25	....	....	....
1993-94	Cincinnati Cyclones	IHL	30	7	3	10	....	....	....	54	....	....	....	....	....	....	....	....	....	....	....	....	....	....	....	....	....	....
	Birmingham Bulls	ECHL	29	26	30	56	....	....	....	38	....	....	....	....	....	....	....	....	....	....	10	8	8	16	19	....	....	....
1994-95	Springfield Falcons	AHL	3	0	0	0	....	....	....	7	....	....	....	....	....	....	....	....	....	....	....	....	....	....	....	....	....	....
	Birmingham Bulls	ECHL	36	33	35	68	....	....	....	52	....	....	....	....	....	....	....	....	....	....	3	5	2	7	0	....	....	....
	Cincinnati Cyclones	IHL	26	2	11	13	....	....	....	34	....	....	....	....	....	....	....	....	....	....	1	0	0	0	2	....	....	....
1995-96	Florida Panthers	NHL	7	1	1	2	1	1	2	4	1	0	0	12	8.3	3	3	3	0	–3	....	....	....	....	....	....	....	....
	Carolina Monarchs	AHL	68	*68	58	*126	....	....	....	80	....	....	....	....	....	....	....	....	....	....	....	....	....	....	....	....	....	....
1996-97	Florida Panthers	NHL	8	1	0	1	1	0	1	2	0	0	0	10	10.0	1	0	4	0	–3	....	....	....	....	....	....	....	....
	Los Angeles Kings	NHL	44	8	8	16	8	7	15	74	0	0	1	74	10.8	24	5	26	0	–7	....	....	....	....	....	....	....	....
	Phoenix Roadrunners	IHL	3	5	2	7	....	....	....	0	....	....	....	....	....	....	....	....	....	....	....	....	....	....	....	....	....	....
1997-98	Los Angeles Kings	NHL	9	1	3	4	1	3	4	4	0	0	0	12	8.3	5	3	3	0	–1	....	....	....	....	....	....	....	....
	New York Rangers	NHL	1	0	0	0	0	0	0	0	0	0	0	1	0.0	0	0	0	0	0	....	....	....	....	....	....	....	....
	Hartford Wolf Pack	AHL	57	29	33	62	....	....	....	79	....	....	....	....	....	....	....	....	....	....	15	12	8	20	11	....	....	....
	NHL Totals		69	11	12	23	11	11	22	84	1	0	1	109	10.1	33	11	36	0		....	....	....	....	....	....	....	....

AHL First All-Star Team (1996) • Won John B. Sollenberger Trophy (Top Scorer - AHL) (1996) • Won Les Cunningham Plaque (MVP - AHL) (1996)

Signed as a free agent by **Florida**, October 4, 1993. Traded to **LA Kings** by **Florida** for LA Kings' 3rd round choice (Vratislav Czech) in 1997 Entry Draft, November 28, 1996. Traded to **NY Rangers** by **LA Kings** for future considerations, November 14, 1997.

• SMYTH, GREG

Greg Smyth D – R. 6′3″, 212 lbs. b: Oakville, Ont., 4/23/1966. Philadelphia's 1st choice, 22nd overall, in 1984 Entry Draft.

Season	Club	League	GP	G	A	Pts	AG	AA	APts	PIM	PP	SH	GW	S	%	TGF	PGF	TGA	PGA	+/–	GP	G	A	Pts	PIM	PP	SH	GW
1983-84	London Knights	OHL	64	4	21	25	....	....	....	252	....	....	....	....	....	....	....	....	....	....	6	1	0	1	24	....	....	....
1984-85	London Knights	OHL	47	7	16	23	....	....	....	188	....	....	....	....	....	....	....	....	....	....	8	2	2	4	27	....	....	....
1985-86	London Knights	OHL	46	12	42	54	....	....	....	199	....	....	....	....	....	....	....	....	....	....	4	1	2	3	28	....	....	....
	Hershey Bears	AHL	2	0	1	1	....	....	....	5	....	....	....	....	....	....	....	....	....	....	8	0	0	0	60	....	....	....
1986-87	Philadelphia Flyers	NHL	1	0	0	0	0	0	0	0	....	....	....	....	....	....	....	....	....	....	1	0	0	0	2	....	....	....
	Hershey Bears	AHL	35	0	2	2	....	....	....	158	....	....	....	....	....	....	....	....	....	....	2	0	0	0	19	....	....	....
1987-88	Philadelphia Flyers	NHL	48	1	6	7	1	4	5	192	0	0	0	29	3.4	34	0	48	12	–2	5	0	0	0	38	0	0	0
	Hershey Bears	AHL	21	0	10	10	....	....	....	102	....	....	....	....	....	....	....	....	....	....	....	....	....	....	....	....	....	....
1988-89	Quebec Nordiques	NHL	10	0	1	1	0	1	1	70	0	0	0	3	0.0	2	0	11	0	–9	....	....	....	....	....	....	....	....
	Halifax Citadels	AHL	43	3	9	12	....	....	....	310	....	....	....	....	....	....	....	....	....	....	4	0	1	1	35	....	....	....
1989-90	Quebec Nordiques	NHL	13	0	0	0	0	0	0	57	0	0	0	4	0.0	3	0	12	1	–8	....	....	....	....	....	....	....	....
	Halifax Citadels	AHL	49	5	14	19	....	....	....	235	....	....	....	....	....	....	....	....	....	....	6	1	0	1	52	....	....	....
1990-91	Quebec Nordiques	NHL	1	0	0	0	0	0	0	0	0	0	0	0	0.0	0	0	0	0	0	....	....	....	....	....	....	....	....
	Halifax Citadels	AHL	56	6	23	29	....	....	....	340	....	....	....	....	....	....	....	....	....	....	....	....	....	....	....	....	....	....
1991-92	Quebec Nordiques	NHL	29	0	2	2	0	1	1	138	0	0	0	24	0.0	12	1	23	2	–10	....	....	....	....	....	....	....	....
	Halifax Citadels	AHL	9	1	3	4	....	....	....	35	....	....	....	....	....	....	....	....	....	....	....	....	....	....	....	....	....	....
	Calgary Flames	NHL	7	1	1	2	1	1	2	15	0	0	0	10	10.0	10	0	6	3	+7	....	....	....	....	....	....	....	....
1992-93	Calgary Flames	NHL	35	1	2	3	1	1	2	95	1	0	0	14	7.1	15	1	13	1	+2	....	....	....	....	....	....	....	....
	Salt Lake Golden Eagles	IHL	5	0	1	1	....	....	....	31	....	....	....	....	....	....	....	....	....	....	....	....	....	....	....	....	....	....
1993-94	Florida Panthers	NHL	12	1	0	1	1	0	1	37	0	0	0	4	25.0	2	0	2	0	0	....	....	....	....	....	....	....	....
	Toronto Maple Leafs	NHL	11	0	1	1	0	1	1	38	0	0	0	3	0.0	3	0	5	0	–2	....	....	....	....	....	....	....	....
	Chicago Blackhawks	NHL	38	0	0	0	0	0	0	108	0	0	0	29	0.0	19	2	22	3	–2	6	0	0	0	0	0	0	0
1994-95	Chicago Blackhawks	NHL	22	0	3	3	0	4	4	33	0	0	0	10	0.0	7	0	5	0	+2	....	....	....	....	....	....	....	....
	Indianapolis Ice	IHL	2	0	0	0	....	....	....	0	....	....	....	....	....	....	....	....	....	....	....	....	....	....	....	....	....	....
1995-96	Chicago Wolves	IHL	15	1	3	4	....	....	....	53	....	....	....	....	....	....	....	....	....	....	....	....	....	....	....	....	....	....
	Los Angeles Ice Dogs	IHL	41	2	7	9	....	....	....	231	....	....	....	....	....	....	....	....	....	....	....	....	....	....	....	....	....	....
1996-97	Toronto Maple Leafs	NHL	2	0	0	0	0	0	0	0	0	0	0	1	0.0	0	0	1	1	0	....	....	....	....	....	....	....	....
	St. John's Maple Leafs	AHL	43	2	4	6	....	....	....	273	....	....	....	....	....	....	....	....	....	....	5	0	1	1	14	....	....	....
1997-98	St. John's Maple Leafs	AHL	63	5	6	11	....	....	....	353	....	....	....	....	....	....	....	....	....	....	4	0	1	1	6	....	....	....
	NHL Totals		229	4	16	20	4	13	17	783	1	0	0	131	3.1	107	4	148	23		12	0	0	0	40	0	0	0

OHL Second All-Star Team (1986)

Traded to **Quebec** by **Philadelphia** with Philadelphia's 3rd round choice (John Tanner) in the 1989 Entry Draft for Terry Carkner, July 25, 1988. Traded to **Calgary** by **Quebec** for Martin Simard, March 10, 1992. Signed as a free agent by **Florida**, August 10, 1993. Traded to **Toronto** by **Florida** for cash, December 7, 1993. Claimed on waivers by **Chicago** from **Toronto**, January 8, 1994. Signed as a free agent by **Toronto**, August 22, 1996.

• SMYTH, KEVIN

Kevin Smyth LW – L. 6′2″, 217 lbs. b: Banff, Alta., 11/22/1973. Hartford's 4th choice, 79th overall, in 1992 Entry Draft.

Season	Club	League	GP	G	A	Pts	AG	AA	APts	PIM	PP	SH	GW	S	%	TGF	PGF	TGA	PGA	+/–	GP	G	A	Pts	PIM	PP	SH	GW
1990-91	Moose Jaw Warriors	WHL	66	30	45	75	....	....	....	96	....	....	....	....	....	....	....	....	....	....	6	1	1	2	0	....	....	....
1991-92	Moose Jaw Warriors	WHL	71	30	55	85	....	....	....	114	....	....	....	....	....	....	....	....	....	....	4	1	3	4	6	....	....	....
1992-93	Moose Jaw Warriors	WHL	64	44	38	82	....	....	....	111	....	....	....	....	....	....	....	....	....	....	....	....	....	....	....	....	....	....
1993-94	Hartford Whalers	NHL	21	3	2	5	3	2	5	10	0	0	0	8	37.5	7	1	7	0	–1	....	....	....	....	....	....	....	....
	Springfield Indians	AHL	42	22	27	49	....	....	....	72	....	....	....	....	....	....	....	....	....	....	6	4	5	9	0	....	....	....
1994-95	Springfield Falcons	AHL	57	17	22	39	....	....	....	72	....	....	....	....	....	....	....	....	....	....	....	....	....	....	....	....	....	....
	Hartford Whalers	NHL	16	1	5	6	2	7	9	13	0	0	0	20	5.0	9	1	11	0	–3	....	....	....	....	....	....	....	....
1995-96	Hartford Whalers	NHL	21	2	1	3	2	1	3	8	1	0	0	27	7.4	5	1	9	0	–5	....	....	....	....	....	....	....	....
	Springfield Falcons	AHL	47	15	33	48	....	....	....	87	....	....	....	....	....	....	....	....	....	....	10	5	5	10	8	....	....	....
1996-97	Orlando Solar Bears	IHL	38	14	17	31	....	....	....	49	....	....	....	....	....	....	....	....	....	....	10	1	2	3	6	....	....	....
1997-98	Orlando Solar Bears	IHL	43	10	5	15	....	....	....	59	....	....	....	....	....	....	....	....	....	....	1	0	0	0	2	....	....	....
	NHL Totals		58	6	8	14	7	10	17	31	1	0	0	55	10.9	21	3	27	0		....	....	....	....	....	....	....	....

• SMYTH, RYAN

Ryan Smyth LW – L. 6′1″, 195 lbs. b: Banff, Alta., 2/21/1976. Edmonton's 4th choice, 6th overall, in 1994 Entry Draft.

Season	Club	League	GP	G	A	Pts	AG	AA	APts	PIM	PP	SH	GW	S	%	TGF	PGF	TGA	PGA	+/–	GP	G	A	Pts	PIM	PP	SH	GW
1991-92	Moose Jaw Warriors	WHL	2	0	0	0	....	....	....	0	....	....	....	....	....	....	....	....	....	....	....	....	....	....	....	....	....	....
1992-93	Moose Jaw Warriors	WHL	64	19	14	33	....	....	....	59	....	....	....	....	....	....	....	....	....	....	....	....	....	....	....	....	....	....
1993-94	Moose Jaw Warriors	WHL	72	50	55	105	....	....	....	88	....	....	....	....	....	....	....	....	....	....	....	....	....	....	....	....	....	....
1994-95	Moose Jaw Warriors	WHL	50	41	45	86	....	....	....	66	....	....	....	....	....	....	....	....	....	....	10	6	9	15	22	....	....	....
	Canada	WJC-A	7	2	5	7	....	....	....	4	....	....	....	....	....	....	....	....	....	....	....	....	....	....	....	....	....	....
	Edmonton Oilers	NHL	3	0	0	0	0	0	0	0	0	0	0	2	0.0	0	0	1	0	–1	....	....	....	....	....	....	....	....
1995-96	Edmonton Oilers	NHL	48	2	9	11	2	7	9	28	1	0	0	65	3.1	18	1	27	0	–10	....	....	....	....	....	....	....	....
	Cape Breton Oilers	AHL	9	6	5	11	....	....	....	4	....	....	....	....	....	....	....	....	....	....	....	....	....	....	....	....	....	....
1996-97	Edmonton Oilers	NHL	82	39	22	61	42	19	61	76	20	0	4	265	14.7	92	40	62	3	–7	12	5	5	10	12	1	0	2
1997-98	Edmonton Oilers	NHL	65	20	13	33	23	13	36	44	10	0	2	205	9.8	51	29	46	0	–24	12	1	3	4	16	1	0	0
	NHL Totals		198	61	44	105	67	39	106	148	31	0	6	537	11.4	161	70	136	3		24	6	8	14	28	2	0	2

WHL East Second All-Star Team (1995)

			REGULAR SEASON																		PLAYOFFS							
Season	**Club**	**League**	**GP**	**G**	**A**	**Pts**	**AG**	**AA**	**APts**	**PIM**	**PP**	**SH**	**GW**	**S**	**%**	**TGF**	**PGF**	**TGA**	**PGA**	**+/–**	**GP**	**G**	**A**	**Pts**	**PIM**	**PP**	**SH**	**GW**

• SNELL, CHRIS

Chris Snell D – L. 5'11", 200 lbs. b: Regina, Sask., 5/12/1971. Buffalo's 8th choice, 145th overall, in 1991 Entry Draft.

Season	Club	League	GP	G	A	Pts	AG	AA	APts	PIM	PP	SH	GW	S	%	TGF	PGF	TGA	PGA	+/–	GP	G	A	Pts	PIM	PP	SH	GW
1989-90	Ottawa 67's	OHL	63	18	62	80	....	....	....	36	....	....	....	....	....	....	....	....	....	....	3	2	4	6	4	....	....	....
1990-91	Ottawa 67's	OHL	54	23	59	82	....	....	....	58	....	....	....	....	....	....	....	....	....	....	17	3	14	17	8	....	....	....
	Canada	WJC-A	7	0	4	4	....	....	....	0	....	....	....	....	....	....	....	....	....	....	....	....	....	....	....	....	....	....
1991-92	Rochester Americans	AHL	65	5	27	32	....	....	....	66	....	....	....	....	....	....	....	....	....	....	10	2	1	3	6	....	....	....
1992-93	Rochester Americans	AHL	76	14	57	71	....	....	....	83	....	....	....	....	....	....	....	....	....	....	17	5	8	13	39	....	....	....
1993-94	**Toronto Maple Leafs**	**NHL**	**2**	**0**	**0**	**0**	**0**	**0**	**0**	**2**	**0**	**0**	**0**	**4**	**0.0**	**0**	**0**	**1**	**0**	**–1**	....	....	....	....	....	....	....	....
	St. John's Maple Leafs	AHL	75	22	74	96	....	....	....	92	....	....	....	....	....	....	....	....	....	....	11	1	15	16	10	....	....	....
1994-95	Phoenix Roadrunners	IHL	57	15	49	64	....	....	....	122	....	....	....	....	....	....	....	....	....	....	....	....	....	....	....	....	....	....
	Los Angeles Kings	**NHL**	**32**	**2**	**7**	**9**	**4**	**10**	**14**	**22**	**0**	**2**	**0**	**45**	**4.4**	**20**	**8**	**25**	**6**	**–7**	....	....	....	....	....	....	....	....
1995-96	Phoenix Roadrunners	IHL	40	9	22	31	....	....	....	113	....	....	....	....	....	....	....	....	....	....	....	....	....	....	....	....	....	....
	Binghamton Rangers	AHL	32	7	25	32	....	....	....	48	....	....	....	....	....	....	....	....	....	....	4	2	2	4	6	....	....	....
1996-97	Indianapolis Ice	IHL	73	22	45	67	....	....	....	130	....	....	....	....	....	....	....	....	....	....	2	0	0	0	2	....	....	....
1997-98	Monroe Moccasins	WPHL	69	4	11	15	....	....	....	66	....	....	....	....	....	....	....	....	....	....	....	....	....	....	....	....	....	....
	NHL Totals		**34**	**2**	**7**	**9**	**4**	**10**	**14**	**24**	**0**	**2**	**0**	**49**	**4.1**	**20**	**8**	**26**	**6**		....	....	....	....	....	....	....	....

OHL First All-Star Team (1990, 1991) • AHL First All-Star Team (1994) • Won Eddie Shore Plaque (Top Defenseman - AHL) (1994) • IHL First All-Star Team (1995) • IHL Second All-Star Team (1997)

Signed as a free agent by **Toronto**, August 3, 1993. Traded to **LA Kings** by **Toronto** with Eric Lacroix and Toronto's 4th round choice (Eric Belanger) in 1996 Entry Draft for Dixon Ward, Guy Leveque and Kelly Fairchild, October 3, 1994. Traded to **NY Rangers** by **LA Kings** for Steve Larouche, January 14, 1996. Signed as a free agent by **Chicago**, August 16, 1996.

• SNELL, RON

Ron Snell RW – R. 5'10", 158 lbs. b: Regina, Sask., 8/11/1948. Pittsburgh's 2nd choice, 14th overall, in 1968 Amateur Draft.

Season	Club	League	GP	G	A	Pts	AG	AA	APts	PIM	PP	SH	GW	S	%	TGF	PGF	TGA	PGA	+/–	GP	G	A	Pts	PIM	PP	SH	GW
1966-67	Regina Pats	WCJHL	56	24	29	53	....	....	....	43	....	....	....	....	....	....	....	....	....	....	16	11	6	17	4	....	....	....
1967-68	Regina Pats	WCJHL	60	56	55	111	....	....	....	86	....	....	....	....	....	....	....	....	....	....	....	....	....	....	....	....	....	....
1968-69	**Pittsburgh Penguins**	**NHL**	**4**	**3**	**1**	**4**	**3**	**1**	**4**	**6**	**2**	**0**	**1**	**9**	**33.3**	**6**	**2**	**0**	**0**	**+4**	....	....	....	....	....	....	....	....
	Amarillo Wranglers	CHL	69	26	19	45	....	....	....	43	....	....	....	....	....	....	....	....	....	....	....	....	....	....	....	....	....	....
1969-70	**Pittsburgh Penguins**	**NHL**	**3**	**0**	**1**	**1**	**0**	**1**	**1**	**0**	**0**	**0**	**0**	**3**	**0.0**	**1**	**0**	**3**	**0**	**–2**	....	....	....	....	....	....	....	....
	Baltimore Clippers	AHL	68	24	29	53	....	....	....	40	....	....	....	....	....	....	....	....	....	....	5	0	0	0	2	....	....	....
1970-71	Amarillo Wranglers	CHL	72	25	22	47	....	....	....	69	....	....	....	....	....	....	....	....	....	....	....	....	....	....	....	....	....	....
1971-72	Hershey Bears	AHL	76	22	31	53	....	....	....	29	....	....	....	....	....	....	....	....	....	....	4	0	1	1	12	....	....	....
1972-73	Hershey Bears	AHL	75	33	38	71	....	....	....	90	....	....	....	....	....	....	....	....	....	....	7	1	5	6	4	....	....	....
1973-74	Winnipeg Jets	WHA	70	24	25	49	....	....	....	32	....	....	....	....	....	....	....	....	....	....	4	0	0	0	0	....	....	....
1974-75	Winnipeg Jets	WHA	20	0	0	0	....	....	....	8	....	....	....	....	....	....	....	....	....	....	....	....	....	....	....	....	....	....
	Cape Cod Codders	NAHL	25	17	12	29	....	....	....	49	....	....	....	....	....	....	....	....	....	....	....	....	....	....	....	....	....	....
1975-76	Cape Cod Codders	NAHL	33	26	26	52	....	....	....	24	....	....	....	....	....	....	....	....	....	....	....	....	....	....	....	....	....	....
	Buffalo Norsemen	NAHL	3	1	2	3	....	....	....	2	....	....	....	....	....	....	....	....	....	....	....	....	....	....	....	....	....	....
	Rochester Americans	AHL	37	10	12	22	....	....	....	13	....	....	....	....	....	....	....	....	....	....	2	0	0	0	6	....	....	....
	NHL Totals		**7**	**3**	**2**	**5**	**3**	**2**	**5**	**6**	**2**	**0**	**1**	**12**	**25.0**	**7**	**2**	**3**	**0**		....	....	....	....	....	....	....	....
	Other Major League Totals		90	24	25	49	....	....	....	40	....	....	....	....	....	....	....	....	....		4	0	0	0	0	....	....	....

Selected by **Winnipeg** (WHA) in 1972 WHA General Player Draft, February 12, 1972. Traded to **Hershey** (AHL) by **Pittsburgh** for cash, June, 1973.

• SNELL, TED

Ted Snell RW – R. 5'9", 190 lbs. b: Ottawa, Ont., 5/28/1946.

Season	Club	League	GP	G	A	Pts	AG	AA	APts	PIM	PP	SH	GW	S	%	TGF	PGF	TGA	PGA	+/–	GP	G	A	Pts	PIM	PP	SH	GW
1962-63	Niagara Falls Flyers	OHA	50	20	20	40	....	....	....	17	....	....	....	....	....	....	....	....	....	....	25	7	9	16	6	....	....	....
1963-64	Niagara Falls Flyers	OHA	56	13	27	40	....	....	....	43	....	....	....	....	....	....	....	....	....	....	4	0	1	1	12	....	....	....
1954-65	Niagara Falls Flyers	OHA	56	26	23	49	....	....	....	26	....	....	....	....	....	....	....	....	....	....	11	3	7	10	10	....	....	....
1965-66	Hershey Bears	AHL	4	1	0	1	....	....	....	2	....	....	....	....	....	....	....	....	....	....	....	....	....	....	....	....	....	....
	Niagara Falls Flyers	OHA	47	18	25	43	....	....	....	73	....	....	....	....	....	....	....	....	....	....	6	2	1	3	4	....	....	....
	Oklahoma City Blazers	CHL	....	....	....	....	....	....	....	....	....	....	....	....	....	....	....	....	....	....	1	0	0	0	0	....	....	....
1966-67	Hershey Bears	AHL	34	4	8	12	....	....	....	4	....	....	....	....	....	....	....	....	....	....	1	0	0	0	0	....	....	....
1967-68	Hershey Bears	AHL	67	11	29	40	....	....	....	23	....	....	....	....	....	....	....	....	....	....	5	0	0	0	0	....	....	....
1968-69	Phoenix Roadrunners	WHL	54	6	9	15	....	....	....	25	....	....	....	....	....	....	....	....	....	....	....	....	....	....	....	....	....	....
	Hershey Bears	AHL	20	4	5	9	....	....	....	4	....	....	....	....	....	....	....	....	....	....	11	4	5	9	2	....	....	....
1969-70	Hershey Bears	AHL	58	12	23	35	....	....	....	24	....	....	....	....	....	....	....	....	....	....	7	3	4	7	0	....	....	....
1970-71	Hershey Bears	AHL	72	12	28	40	....	....	....	13	....	....	....	....	....	....	....	....	....	....	4	1	0	1	0	....	....	....
1971-72	Hershey Bears	AHL	68	12	18	30	....	....	....	4	....	....	....	....	....	....	....	....	....	....	4	0	0	0	2	....	....	....
1972-73	Hershey Bears	AHL	72	29	35	64	....	....	....	23	....	....	....	....	....	....	....	....	....	....	6	0	3	3	0	....	....	....
1973-74	**Pittsburgh Penguins**	**NHL**	**55**	**4**	**12**	**16**	**4**	**10**	**14**	**8**	**0**	**0**	**0**	**64**	**6.3**	**19**	**1**	**62**	**22**	**–22**	....	....	....	....	....	....	....	....
1974-75	**Kansas City Scouts**	**NHL**	**29**	**3**	**2**	**5**	**3**	**2**	**5**	**8**	**0**	**1**	**0**	**25**	**12.0**	**9**	**0**	**37**	**20**	**–8**	....	....	....	....	....	....	....	....
	Detroit Red Wings	**NHL**	**20**	**0**	**4**	**4**	**0**	**3**	**3**	**6**	**0**	**0**	**0**	**12**	**0.0**	**12**	**5**	**17**	**0**	**–10**	....	....	....	....	....	....	....	....
	Virginia Wings	AHL	24	5	3	8	....	....	....	17	....	....	....	....	....	....	....	....	....	....	5	1	0	1	0	....	....	....
1975-76	Hershey Bears	AHL	74	4	15	19	....	....	....	24	....	....	....	....	....	....	....	....	....	....	10	0	0	0	0	....	....	....
	NHL Totals		**104**	**7**	**18**	**25**	**7**	**15**	**22**	**22**	**0**	**1**	**0**	**101**	**6.9**	**40**	**6**	**116**	**42**		....	....	....	....	....	....	....	....

Claimed by **Hershey** (AHL) from **Boston** in Reverse Draft, June, 1968. Traded to **Phoenix** (WHL) by **Hershey** (AHL) for cash, June, 1968. Traded to **Hershey** (AHL) by **Phoenix** (WHL) for cash, October, 1969. Signed as a free agent by **Pittsburgh**, October, 1973. Claimed by **Kansas City** from **Pittsburgh** in Expansion Draft, June 12, 1974. Traded to **Detroit** by **Kansas City** with Bart Crashley and Larry Giroux for Guy Charron and Claude Houde, December 14, 1974.

• SNEPSTS, HAROLD

Harold Snepsts D – L. 6'3", 210 lbs. b: Edmonton, Alta., 10/24/1954. Vancouver's 3rd choice, 59th overall, in 1974 Amateur Draft.

Season	Club	League	GP	G	A	Pts	AG	AA	APts	PIM	PP	SH	GW	S	%	TGF	PGF	TGA	PGA	+/–	GP	G	A	Pts	PIM	PP	SH	GW
1972-73	Edmonton Oil Kings	WHL	68	2	24	26	....	....	....	155	....	....	....	....	....	....	....	....	....	....	11	0	1	1	54	....	....	....
1973-74	Edmonton Oil Kings	WHL	68	8	41	49	....	....	....	239	....	....	....	....	....	....	....	....	....	....	....	....	....	....	....	....	....	....
1974-75	**Vancouver Canucks**	**NHL**	**27**	**1**	**2**	**3**	**1**	**2**	**3**	**30**	**0**	**1**	**0**	**18**	**5.6**	**14**	**2**	**16**	**4**	**0**	....	....	....	....	....	....	....	....
	Seattle Totems	CHL	19	1	6	7	....	....	....	58	....	....	....	....	....	....	....	....	....	....	....	....	....	....	....	....	....	....
1975-76	**Vancouver Canucks**	**NHL**	**78**	**3**	**15**	**18**	**3**	**12**	**15**	**125**	**0**	**0**	**1**	**74**	**4.1**	**80**	**4**	**93**	**27**	**+10**	**2**	**0**	**0**	**0**	**4**	**0**	**0**	**0**
1976-77	**Vancouver Canucks**	**NHL**	**79**	**4**	**18**	**22**	**4**	**15**	**19**	**149**	**0**	**0**	**1**	**101**	**4.0**	**85**	**2**	**112**	**24**	**–5**	....	....	....	....	....	....	....	....
1977-78	**Vancouver Canucks**	**NHL**	**75**	**4**	**16**	**20**	**4**	**13**	**17**	**118**	**0**	**0**	**0**	**95**	**4.2**	**71**	**0**	**115**	**28**	**–16**	....	....	....	....	....	....	....	....
1978-79	**Vancouver Canucks**	**NHL**	**76**	**7**	**24**	**31**	**6**	**18**	**24**	**130**	**4**	**0**	**0**	**115**	**6.1**	**84**	**20**	**123**	**32**	**–27**	**3**	**0**	**0**	**0**	**0**	**0**	**0**	**0**
1979-80	**Vancouver Canucks**	**NHL**	**79**	**3**	**20**	**23**	**3**	**15**	**18**	**202**	**0**	**0**	**0**	**103**	**2.9**	**90**	**6**	**111**	**34**	**+7**	**4**	**0**	**2**	**2**	**8**	**0**	**0**	**0**
1980-81	**Vancouver Canucks**	**NHL**	**76**	**3**	**16**	**19**	**2**	**11**	**13**	**212**	**0**	**0**	**1**	**77**	**3.9**	**79**	**2**	**126**	**52**	**+3**	**3**	**0**	**0**	**0**	**8**	**0**	**0**	**0**
1981-82	**Vancouver Canucks**	**NHL**	**68**	**3**	**14**	**17**	**2**	**9**	**11**	**153**	**0**	**0**	**0**	**69**	**4.3**	**89**	**0**	**101**	**34**	**+22**	**17**	**0**	**4**	**4**	**50**	**0**	**0**	**0**
1982-83	**Vancouver Canucks**	**NHL**	**46**	**2**	**8**	**10**	**2**	**6**	**8**	**80**	**0**	**1**	**1**	**40**	**5.0**	**31**	**0**	**71**	**23**	**–17**	**4**	**1**	**1**	**2**	**8**	**0**	**0**	**0**
1983-84	**Vancouver Canucks**	**NHL**	**79**	**4**	**16**	**20**	**3**	**11**	**14**	**152**	**0**	**0**	**0**	**77**	**5.2**	**59**	**0**	**119**	**41**	**–19**	**4**	**0**	**1**	**1**	**15**	**0**	**0**	**0**
1984-85	**Minnesota North Stars**	**NHL**	**71**	**0**	**7**	**7**	**0**	**5**	**5**	**232**	**0**	**0**	**0**	**50**	**0.0**	**44**	**1**	**90**	**28**	**–19**	**9**	**0**	**0**	**0**	**24**	**0**	**0**	**0**
1985-86	**Detroit Red Wings**	**NHL**	**35**	**0**	**6**	**6**	**0**	**4**	**4**	**75**	**0**	**0**	**0**	**12**	**0.0**	**20**	**0**	**43**	**16**	**–7**	....	....	....	....	....	....	....	....
1986-87	**Detroit Red Wings**	**NHL**	**54**	**1**	**13**	**14**	**1**	**9**	**10**	**129**	**0**	**0**	**0**	**38**	**2.6**	**46**	**0**	**56**	**17**	**+7**	**11**	**0**	**2**	**2**	**18**	**0**	**0**	**0**
1987-88	**Detroit Red Wings**	**NHL**	**31**	**1**	**4**	**5**	**1**	**3**	**4**	**67**	**0**	**0**	**0**	**20**	**5.0**	**27**	**0**	**29**	**5**	**+3**	**10**	**0**	**0**	**0**	**40**	**0**	**0**	**0**
	Adirondack Red Wings	AHL	3	0	2	2	....	....	....	14	....	....	....	....	....	....	....	....	....	....	....	....	....	....	....	....	....	....
1988-89	**Vancouver Canucks**	**NHL**	**59**	**0**	**8**	**8**	**0**	**6**	**6**	**69**	**0**	**0**	**0**	**27**	**0.0**	**21**	**0**	**54**	**30**	**–3**	**7**	**0**	**1**	**1**	**6**	**0**	**0**	**0**
1989-90	**Vancouver Canucks**	**NHL**	**39**	**1**	**3**	**4**	**1**	**2**	**3**	**26**	**1**	**0**	**1**	**13**	**7.7**	**16**	**1**	**39**	**27**	**+3**	....	....	....	....	....	....	....	....
	St. Louis Blues	**NHL**	**7**	**0**	**1**	**1**	**0**	**1**	**1**	**10**	**0**	**0**	**0**	**2**	**0.0**	**3**	**0**	**10**	**3**	**–4**	**11**	**0**	**3**	**3**	**38**	**0**	**0**	**0**
1990-91	**St. Louis Blues**	**NHL**	**54**	**1**	**4**	**5**	**1**	**3**	**4**	**50**	**0**	**0**	**1**	**33**	**3.0**	**37**	**0**	**48**	**14**	**+3**	**8**	**0**	**0**	**0**	**12**	**0**	**0**	**0**
	NHL Totals		**1033**	**38**	**195**	**233**	**34**	**145**	**179**	**2009**	**5**	**2**	**6**	**964**	**3.9**	**896**	**38**	**1356**	**439**		**93**	**1**	**14**	**15**	**231**	**0**	**0**	**0**

Played in NHL All-Star Game (1977, 1982)

Traded to **Minnesota** by **Vancouver** for Al MacAdam, June 21, 1984. Signed as a free agent by **Detroit**, July 31, 1985. Signed as a free agent by **Vancouver**, October 6, 1988. Traded to **St. Louis** by **Vancouver** with Rich Sutter and St. Louis' 2nd round choice (Craig Johnson) in 1990 Entry Draft for Adrien Plavsic, Montreal's 1st round choice (previously acquired, Vancouver selected Shawn Antoski) in 1990 Entry Draft and St. Louis' 2nd round choice (later traded to Montreal — Montreal selected Craig Darby) in 1991 Entry Draft, March 6, 1990.

• SNOW, SANDY

Sandy (William) Snow RW – R. 6', 175 lbs. b: Glace Bay, N.S., 11/11/1946.

Season	Club	League	GP	G	A	Pts	AG	AA	APts	PIM	PP	SH	GW	S	%	TGF	PGF	TGA	PGA	+/–	GP	G	A	Pts	PIM	PP	SH	GW
1963-64	Hamilton Red Wings	OHA	41	11	15	26	....	....	....	17	....	....	....	....	....	....	....	....	....	....	....	....	....	....	....	....	....	....
1964-65	Weyburn Red Wings	SJHL	52	43	28	71	....	....	....	35	....	....	....	....	....	....	....	....	....	....	15	*14	10	24	26	....	....	....
1965-66	Hamilton Red Wings	OHA	46	22	25	47	....	....	....	64	....	....	....	....	....	....	....	....	....	....	5	2	0	2	0	....	....	....
	Memphis Wings	CHL	4	0	1	1	....	....	....	0	....	....	....	....	....	....	....	....	....	....	....	....	....	....	....	....	....	....
1966-67	Hamilton Red Wings	OHA	48	13	20	33	....	....	....	52	....	....	....	....	....	....	....	....	....	....	8	1	1	2	8	....	....	....

			REGULAR SEASON																			PLAYOFFS							
Season	Club	League	GP	G	A	Pts	AG	AA	APts	PIM	PP	SH	GW	S	%	TGF	PGF	TGA	PGA	+/–	GP	G	A	Pts	PIM	PP	SH	GW
1967-68	Fort Worth Wings	CHL	56	13	13	26	....	....	....	17	....	....	....	....	....	....	....	....	....	....	11	1	2	3	4	....	....	....
1968-69	**Detroit Red Wings**	**NHL**	**3**	**0**	**0**	**0**	**0**	**0**	**0**	**2**	**0**	**0**	**0**	**1**	**0.0**	**0**	**0**	**0**	**0**	**0**	....	....	....	....	....	....	....	....
	Fort Worth Wings	CHL	60	13	21	34	....	....	....	19	....	....	....	....	....	....	....	....	....	....	....	....	....	....	....	....	....	....
1969-70	Phoenix Roadrunners	WHL	72	17	14	31	....	....	....	10	....	....	....	....	....	....	....	....	....	....	....	....	....	....	....	....	....	....
1970-71	Phoenix Roadrunners	WHL	11	1	0	1	....	....	....	5	....	....	....	....	....	....	....	....	....	....	....	....	....	....	....	....	....	....
	Kansas City Blues	CHL	12	2	4	6	....	....	....	2	....	....	....	....	....	....	....	....	....	....	....	....	....	....	....	....	....	....
	Flint Generals	IHL	26	7	23	30	....	....	....	4	....	....	....	....	....	....	....	....	....	....	7	3	4	7	0	....	....	....
1971-72	Flint Generals	IHL	55	30	27	57	....	....	....	8	....	....	....	....	....	....	....	....	....	....	4	0	2	2	0	....	....	....
1972-73	Flint Generals	IHL	63	28	35	63	....	....	....	12	....	....	....	....	....	....	....	....	....	....	2	1	0	1	0	....	....	....
1973-74	Brantford Forresters	OHA Sr.	9	3	2	5	....	....	....	0	....	....	....	....	....	....	....	....	....	....	....	....	....	....	....	....	....	....
	NHL Totals		**3**	**0**	**0**	**0**	**0**	**0**	**0**	**2**	**0**	**0**	**0**	**1**	**0.0**	**0**	**0**	**0**	**0**		....	....	....	....	....	....	....	....

Traded to **NY Rangers** by **Detroit** with Terry Sawchuk for Larry Jeffrey, June 17, 1969. Traded to **Phoenix** (WHL) by **NY Rangers** with Don Caley for Pete McDuffe, July, 1969. Traded to **Kansas City** (CHL) by **Phoenix** (WHL) for cash, December, 1970.

● SNUGGERUD, DAVE

Dave Snuggerud RW – L. 6', 190 lbs. b: Minnetonka, MN, 6/20/1966. Buffalo's 1st choice, 1st overall, in 1987 Supplemental Draft.

Season	Club	League	GP	G	A	Pts	AG	AA	APts	PIM	PP	SH	GW	S	%	TGF	PGF	TGA	PGA	+/–	GP	G	A	Pts	PIM	PP	SH	GW
1984-85	Minnesota Jr. Stars	USHL	48	38	35	73	....	....	....	26	....	....	....	....	....	....	....	....	....	....	....	....	....	....	....	....	....	....
1985-86	University of Minnesota	WCHA	42	14	18	32	....	....	....	47	....	....	....	....	....	....	....	....	....	....	....	....	....	....	....	....	....	....
1986-87	University of Minnesota	WCHA	39	30	29	59	....	....	....	38	....	....	....	....	....	....	....	....	....	....	....	....	....	....	....	....	....	....
1987-88	United States	Nat-Team	51	14	21	35	....	....	....	26	....	....	....	....	....	....	....	....	....	....	....	....	....	....	....	....	....	....
	United States	Olympics	6	3	2	5	....	....	....	4	....	....	....	....	....	....	....	....	....	....	....	....	....	....	....	....	....	....
1988-89	University of Minnesota	WCHA	45	29	20	49	....	....	....	39	....	....	....	....	....	....	....	....	....	....	....	....	....	....	....	....	....	....
	United States	WEC-A	10	4	1	5	....	....	....	2	....	....	....	....	....	....	....	....	....	....	....	....	....	....	....	....	....	....
1989-90	**Buffalo Sabres**	**NHL**	**80**	**14**	**16**	**30**	**12**	**11**	**23**	**41**	**1**	**2**	**2**	**120**	**11.7**	**53**	**4**	**69**	**28**	**+8**	**6**	**0**	**0**	**0**	**2**	**0**	**0**	**0**
1990-91	**Buffalo Sabres**	**NHL**	**80**	**9**	**15**	**24**	**8**	**11**	**19**	**32**	**0**	**4**	**2**	**128**	**7.0**	**46**	**2**	**91**	**34**	**–13**	**6**	**1**	**3**	**4**	**4**	**0**	**1**	**0**
1991-92	**Buffalo Sabres**	**NHL**	**55**	**3**	**15**	**18**	**3**	**11**	**14**	**36**	**0**	**0**	**0**	**75**	**4.0**	**28**	**3**	**53**	**25**	**–3**	....	....	....	....	....	....	....	....
	San Jose Sharks	**NHL**	**11**	**0**	**1**	**1**	**0**	**1**	**1**	**4**	**0**	**0**	**0**	**19**	**0.0**	**3**	**0**	**20**	**5**	**–12**	....	....	....	....	....	....	....	....
1992-93	**San Jose Sharks**	**NHL**	**25**	**4**	**5**	**9**	**3**	**3**	**6**	**14**	**0**	**1**	**1**	**51**	**7.8**	**13**	**0**	**32**	**16**	**–3**	....	....	....	....	....	....	....	....
	Philadelphia Flyers	**NHL**	**14**	**0**	**2**	**2**	**0**	**1**	**1**	**0**	**0**	**0**	**0**	**10**	**0.0**	**2**	**0**	**3**	**1**	**0**	....	....	....	....	....	....	....	....
1993-94			DID NOT PLAY																									
1994-95	Minnesota Moose	IHL	72	25	23	48	....	....	....	57	....	....	....	....	....	....	....	....	....	....	3	0	1	1	2	....	....	....
	NHL Totals		**265**	**30**	**54**	**84**	**26**	**38**	**64**	**127**	**1**	**7**	**5**	**403**	**7.4**	**145**	**9**	**268**	**109**		**12**	**1**	**3**	**4**	**6**	**0**	**1**	**0**

WCHA Second All-Star Team (1989)

Traded to **San Jose** by **Buffalo** for Wayne Presley, March 9, 1992. Traded to **Philadelphia** by **San Jose** for Mark Pederson and future considerations, December 19, 1992.

● SOBCHUK, DENNIS

Dennis Sobchuk C – L. 6'2", 176 lbs. b: Lang, Sask., 1/12/1954. Philadelphia's 10th choice, 89th overall, in 1974 Amateur Draft.

Season	Club	League	GP	G	A	Pts	AG	AA	APts	PIM	PP	SH	GW	S	%	TGF	PGF	TGA	PGA	+/–	GP	G	A	Pts	PIM	PP	SH	GW
1970-71	Estevan Bruins	WCJHL	8	1	1	2	....	....	....	14	....	....	....	....	....	....	....	....	....	....	....	....	....	....	....	....	....	....
1971-72	Regina Pats	WCJHL	68	56	67	123	....	....	....	115	....	....	....	....	....	....	....	....	....	....	15	9	*18	*27	50	....	....	....
1972-73	Regina Pats	WCJHL	66	67	80	147	....	....	....	128	....	....	....	....	....	....	....	....	....	....	4	3	3	6	28	....	....	....
1973-74	Regina Pats	WCJHL	66	68	78	146	....	....	....	78	....	....	....	....	....	....	....	....	....	....	16	10	21	*31	20	....	....	....
1974-75	Phoenix Roadrunners	WHA	78	32	45	77	....	....	....	36	....	....	....	....	....	....	....	....	....	....	5	4	1	5	2	....	....	....
1975-76	Cincinnati Stingers	WHA	79	32	40	72	....	....	....	74	....	....	....	....	....	....	....	....	....	....	....	....	....	....	....	....	....	....
1976-77	Cincinnati Stingers	WHA	81	44	52	96	....	....	....	38	....	....	....	....	....	....	....	....	....	....	3	0	1	1	2	....	....	....
1977-78	Cincinnati Stingers	WHA	23	5	9	14	....	....	....	22	....	....	....	....	....	....	....	....	....	....	....	....	....	....	....	....	....	....
	Edmonton Oilers	WHA	13	6	3	9	....	....	....	4	....	....	....	....	....	....	....	....	....	....	5	1	0	1	4	....	....	....
1978-79	Edmonton Oilers	WHA	74	26	37	63	....	....	....	31	....	....	....	....	....	....	....	....	....	....	12	6	6	12	4	....	....	....
1979-80	**Detroit Red Wings**	**NHL**	**33**	**4**	**6**	**10**	**4**	**5**	**9**	**0**	**0**	**0**	**0**	**47**	**8.5**	**13**	**3**	**21**	**0**	**–11**	....	....	....	....	....	....	....	....
	Adirondack Red Wings	AHL	15	6	4	10	....	....	....	6	....	....	....	....	....	....	....	....	....	....	4	0	1	1	0	....	....	....
1980-81	Birmingham Bulls	CHL	5	1	3	4	....	....	....	0	....	....	....	....	....	....	....	....	....	....	....	....	....	....	....	....	....	....
1981-82	ECS Innsbruck	Austria	STATISTICS NOT AVAILABLE																									
1982-83	Moncton Alpines	AHL	20	5	12	17	....	....	....	0	....	....	....	....	....	....	....	....	....	....	....	....	....	....	....	....	....	....
	Quebec Nordiques	**NHL**	**2**	**1**	**0**	**1**	**1**	**0**	**1**	**2**	**0**	**0**	**0**	**2**	**50.0**	**1**	**0**	**0**	**0**	**+1**	....	....	....	....	....	....	....	....
	Fredericton Express	AHL	29	12	17	29	....	....	....	2	....	....	....	....	....	....	....	....	....	....	12	8	4	12	10	....	....	....
	NHL Totals		**35**	**5**	**6**	**11**	**5**	**5**	**10**	**2**	**0**	**0**	**0**	**49**	**10.2**	**14**	**3**	**21**	**0**		....	....	....	....	....	....	....	....
	Other Major League Totals		340	145	180	331	....	....	....	205	....	....	....	....	....	....	....	....	....	....	25	11	8	19	12	....	....	....

WCJHL Second All-Star Team (1972)

Signed as a free agent by **Cincinnati** (WHA), April, 1973. Loaned to **Phoenix** (WHA) by **Cincinnati** (WHA) for 1974-75 season, June, 1974. Traded to **Edmonton** (WHA) by **Cincinnati** (WHA) for the rights to Dave Debol and future considerations, December, 1977. Reclaimed by **Philadelphia** from **Edmonton** prior to Expansion Draft, June 9, 1979. Traded to **Detroit** by **Philadelphia** for Detroit's 5th round choice (Dave Michayluk) in 1981 Entry Draft, September 4, 1979. Signed as a free agent by **Quebec**, March 7, 1982.

● SOBCHUK, GENE

Gene Sobchuk LW/C – L. 5'9", 160 lbs. b: Lang, Sask., 2/19/1951. Deceased. NY Rangers' 10th choice, 109th overall, in 1971 Amateur Draft.

Season	Club	League	GP	G	A	Pts	AG	AA	APts	PIM	PP	SH	GW	S	%	TGF	PGF	TGA	PGA	+/–	GP	G	A	Pts	PIM	PP	SH	GW
1969-70	Weyburn Red Wings	SJHL	....	22	*36	58	....	....	....	28	....	....	....	....	....	....	....	....	....	....	....	....	....	....	....	....	....	....
1970-71	Regina Pats	WCJHL	66	17	37	54	....	....	....	74	....	....	....	....	....	....	....	....	....	....	....	....	....	....	....	....	....	....
1971-72	Des Moines Oak Leafs	IHL	56	16	18	34	....	....	....	16	....	....	....	....	....	....	....	....	....	....	....	....	....	....	....	....	....	....
1972-73	Rochester Americans	AHL	58	22	16	38	....	....	....	29	....	....	....	....	....	....	....	....	....	....	6	1	4	5	4	....	....	....
1973-74	**Vancouver Canucks**	**NHL**	**1**	**0**	**0**	**0**	**0**	**0**	**0**	**0**	**0**	**0**	**0**	**0**	**0.0**	**0**	**0**	**0**	**0**	**0**	....	....	....	....	....	....	....	....
	Virginia Wings	AHL	18	12	5	17	....	....	....	14	....	....	....	....	....	....	....	....	....	....	....	....	....	....	....	....	....	....
	Seattle Totems	WHL	55	15	19	34	....	....	....	30	....	....	....	....	....	....	....	....	....	....	....	....	....	....	....	....	....	....
1974-75	Phoenix Roadrunners	WHA	3	1	0	1	....	....	....	0	....	....	....	....	....	....	....	....	....	....	....	....	....	....	....	....	....	....
	Tulsa Oilers	CHL	73	35	28	63	....	....	....	65	....	....	....	....	....	....	....	....	....	....	2	1	0	1	2	....	....	....
1975-76	Cincinnati Stingers	WHA	78	24	18	42	....	....	....	37	....	....	....	....	....	....	....	....	....	....	....	....	....	....	....	....	....	....
1976-77	Oklahoma City Blazers	CHL	29	4	11	15	....	....	....	6	....	....	....	....	....	....	....	....	....	....	....	....	....	....	....	....	....	....
	Springfield Indians	AHL	3	1	0	1	....	....	....	0	....	....	....	....	....	....	....	....	....	....	....	....	....	....	....	....	....	....
1977-78	Hampton Gulls	AHL	37	3	5	8	....	....	....	2	....	....	....	....	....	....	....	....	....	....	....	....	....	....	....	....	....	....
	NHL Totals		**1**	**0**	**0**	**0**	**0**	**0**	**0**	**0**	**0**	**0**	**0**	**0**	**0.0**	**0**	**0**	**0**	**0**		....	....	....	....	....	....	....	....
	Other Major League Totals		81	25	18	43	....	....	....	37	....	....	....	....	....	....	....	....	....	....	....	....	....	....	....	....	....	....

Selected by **LA Sharks** (WHA) in 1972 WHA General Player Draft, February 12, 1972. Claimed by **Vancouver** (Seattle-WHL) from **NY Rangers** in Reverse Draft, June, 1973. Claimed by **Cincinnati** (WHA) from **LA Sharks** (WHA) prior to WHA Expansion Draft, June, 1974. Loaned to **Phoenix** (WHA) by **Cincinnati** (WHA) for 1974-75 season, June, 1974.

● SOLHEIM, KEN

Ken Solheim LW – L. 6'3", 210 lbs. b: Hythe, Alta., 3/27/1961. Chicago's 4th choice, 30th overall, in 1980 Entry Draft.

Season	Club	League	GP	G	A	Pts	AG	AA	APts	PIM	PP	SH	GW	S	%	TGF	PGF	TGA	PGA	+/–	GP	G	A	Pts	PIM	PP	SH	GW
1977-78	St. Albert Saints	AJHL	60	26	16	42	....	....	....	31	....	....	....	....	....	....	....	....	....	....	....	....	....	....	....	....	....	....
1978-79	St. Albert Saints	AJHL	60	47	42	89	....	....	....	63	....	....	....	....	....	....	....	....	....	....	....	....	....	....	....	....	....	....
1979-80	Medicine Hat Tigers	WHL	72	54	33	87	....	....	....	50	....	....	....	....	....	....	....	....	....	....	13	1	6	7	6	....	....	....
1980-81	Medicine Hat Tigers	WHL	64	*68	43	111	....	....	....	87	....	....	....	....	....	....	....	....	....	....	5	5	4	9	2	....	....	....
	Chicago Black Hawks	**NHL**	**5**	**2**	**0**	**2**	**2**	**0**	**2**	**0**	**0**	**0**	**0**	**8**	**25.0**	**2**	**0**	**5**	**0**	**–3**	....	....	....	....	....	....	....	....
	Minnesota North Stars	**NHL**	**5**	**2**	**1**	**3**	**2**	**1**	**3**	**0**	**0**	**0**	**0**	**9**	**22.2**	**4**	**0**	**1**	**0**	**+3**	**2**	**1**	**0**	**1**	**0**	**0**	**0**	**0**
1981-82	**Minnesota North Stars**	**NHL**	**29**	**4**	**5**	**9**	**3**	**3**	**6**	**4**	**2**	**0**	**2**	**46**	**8.7**	**17**	**3**	**22**	**0**	**–8**	**1**	**0**	**1**	**1**	**2**	**0**	**0**	**0**
	Nashville South Stars	CHL	44	23	18	41	....	....	....	40	....	....	....	....	....	....	....	....	....	....	....	....	....	....	....	....	....	....
1982-83	**Minnesota North Stars**	**NHL**	**25**	**2**	**4**	**6**	**2**	**3**	**5**	**4**	**0**	**0**	**1**	**34**	**5.9**	**11**	**0**	**10**	**0**	**+1**	....	....	....	....	....	....	....	....
	Detroit Red Wings	**NHL**	**10**	**0**	**0**	**0**	**0**	**0**	**0**	**2**	**0**	**0**	**0**	**5**	**0.0**	**0**	**0**	**2**	**0**	**–2**	....	....	....	....	....	....	....	....
	Birmingham South Stars	CHL	22	14	3	17	....	....	....	4	....	....	....	....	....	....	....	....	....	....	....	....	....	....	....	....	....	....
1983-84	Adirondack Red Wings	AHL	61	24	20	44	....	....	....	13	....	....	....	....	....	....	....	....	....	....	7	1	1	2	0	....	....	....
1984-85	**Minnesota North Stars**	**NHL**	**55**	**8**	**10**	**18**	**7**	**7**	**14**	**19**	**4**	**0**	**1**	**87**	**9.2**	**33**	**17**	**32**	**1**	**–15**	....	....	....	....	....	....	....	....
	Springfield Indians	AHL	17	6	8	14	....	....	....	0	....	....	....	....	....	....	....	....	....	....	4	2	0	2	2	....	....	....
1985-86	**Edmonton Oilers**	**NHL**	**6**	**1**	**0**	**1**	**1**	**0**	**1**	**5**	**0**	**0**	**0**	**8**	**12.5**	**4**	**0**	**6**	**0**	**–2**	....	....	....	....	....	....	....	....
	Nova Scotia Oilers	AHL	71	19	27	46	....	....	....	45	....	....	....	....	....	....	....	....	....	....	....	....	....	....	....	....	....	....
	NHL Totals		**135**	**19**	**20**	**39**	**17**	**14**	**31**	**34**	**6**	**0**	**4**	**197**	**9.6**	**71**	**20**	**78**	**1**		**3**	**1**	**1**	**2**	**2**	**0**	**0**	**0**

WHL All-Star Team (1981)

Traded to **Minnesota** by **Chicago** with Chicago's 2nd round choice (Tom Hirsch) in 1981 Entry Draft for Glen Sharpley, December 29, 1980. Traded to **Detroit** by **Minnesota** for future considerations, March 8, 1983. Traded to **Minnesota** by **Detroit** for future considerations, September 20, 1984. Signed as a free agent by **Edmonton**, August 15, 1985.

Season	Club	League	GP	G	A	Pts	AG	AA	APts	PIM	PP	SH	GW	S	%	TGF	PGF	TGA	PGA	+/-	GP	G	A	Pts	PIM	PP	SH	GW
			REGULAR SEASON																		PLAYOFFS							

• SOMMER, ROY

Roy Sommer LW/C – L. 6', 185 lbs. b: Oakland, CA, 4/5/1957. Toronto's 7th choice, 101st overall, in 1977 Amateur Draft.

Season	Club	League	GP	G	A	Pts	AG	AA	APts	PIM	PP	SH	GW	S	%	TGF	PGF	TGA	PGA	+/-	GP	G	A	Pts	PIM	PP	SH	GW
1974-75	Spruce Grove Mets	AJHL	85	20	21	41	....	....	....	200	....	....	....	....	....	....	....	....	....	....	....	....	....	....	....	....	....	....
	Edmonton Oil Kings	WHL	1	0	0	0	....	....	....	5	....	....	....	....	....	....	....	....	....	....	....	....	....	....	....	....	....	....
1975-76	Calgary Centennials	WHL	70	13	24	37	....	....	....	155	....	....	....	....	....	....	....	....	....	....	....	....	....	....	....	....	....	....
1976-77	Calgary Centennials	WCJHL	50	16	22	38	....	....	....	111	....	....	....	....	....	....	....	....	....	....	9	5	9	14	8	....	....	....
1977-78	Saginaw Gears	IHL	12	2	3	5	....	....	....	2	....	....	....	....	....	....	....	....	....	....	....	....	....	....	....	....	....	....
	Grand Rapids Owls	IHL	45	20	18	38	....	....	....	67	....	....	....	....	....	....	....	....	....	....	....	....	....	....	....	....	....	....
1978-79	Spokane Flyers	PHL	45	19	30	49	....	....	....	196	....	....	....	....	....	....	....	....	....	....	....	....	....	....	....	....	....	....
1979-80	Grand Rapids Owls	IHL	9	1	4	5	....	....	....	32	....	....	....	....	....	....	....	....	....	....	....	....	....	....	....	....	....	....
	Houston Apollos	CHL	69	24	31	55	....	....	....	246	....	....	....	....	....	....	....	....	....	....	6	2	2	4	8	....	....	....
1980-81	**Edmonton Oilers**	**NHL**	**3**	**1**	**0**	**1**	**1**	**0**	**1**	**7**	**0**	**0**	**0**	**1**	**100.0**	**1**	**0**	**1**	**0**	**0**	....	....	....	....	....	....	....	....
	Wichita Wind	CHL	57	13	22	35	....	....	....	212	....	....	....	....	....	....	....	....	....	....	14	3	2	5	61	....	....	....
1981-82	Wichita Wind	CHL	76	17	28	45	....	....	....	193	....	....	....	....	....	....	....	....	....	....	....	....	....	....	....	....	....	....
1982-83	Wichita Wind	CHL	73	22	39	61	....	....	....	130	....	....	....	....	....	....	....	....	....	....	....	....	....	....	....	....	....	....
1983-84	Maine Mariners	AHL	67	7	10	17	....	....	....	202	....	....	....	....	....	....	....	....	....	....	14	6	1	7	24	....	....	....
1984-85	Maine Mariners	AHL	80	12	13	25	....	....	....	175	....	....	....	....	....	....	....	....	....	....	11	4	2	6	27	....	....	....
1985-86	Indianapolis Checkers	IHL	37	9	10	19	....	....	....	118	....	....	....	....	....	....	....	....	....	....	....	....	....	....	....	....	....	....
	Muskegon Lumberjacks	IHL	27	5	8	13	....	....	....	109	....	....	....	....	....	....	....	....	....	....	12	2	4	6	*92	....	....	....
1986-87	Muskegon Lumberjacks	IHL	65	14	13	27	....	....	....	219	....	....	....	....	....	....	....	....	....	....	15	3	3	6	44	....	....	....
	NHL Totals		**3**	**1**	**0**	**1**	**1**	**0**	**1**	**7**	**0**	**0**	**0**	**1**	**100.0**	**1**	**0**	**1**	**0**		....	....	....	....	....	....	....	....

Signed as a free agent by **Edmonton**, January 1, 1980. Signed as a free agent by **New Jersey**, September 25, 1982.

• SONGIN, TOM

Tom Songin RW – R. 6'3", 195 lbs. b: Norwood, MA, 12/20/1953.

Season	Club	League	GP	G	A	Pts	AG	AA	APts	PIM	PP	SH	GW	S	%	TGF	PGF	TGA	PGA	+/-	GP	G	A	Pts	PIM	PP	SH	GW
1973-74	Boston College	ECAC	5	0	1	1	....	....	....	4	....	....	....	....	....	....	....	....	....	....	....	....	....	....	....	....	....	....
1974-75	Boston College	ECAC	28	13	27	40	....	....	....	44	....	....	....	....	....	....	....	....	....	....	....	....	....	....	....	....	....	....
1975-76	Boston College	ECAC	22	9	7	16	....	....	....	24	....	....	....	....	....	....	....	....	....	....	....	....	....	....	....	....	....	....
1976-77	Boston College	ECAC	27	7	7	14	....	....	....	24	....	....	....	....	....	....	....	....	....	....	....	....	....	....	....	....	....	....
1977-78	Long Beach Sharks-Rockets	PHL	42	25	25	50	....	....	....	66	....	....	....	....	....	....	....	....	....	....	....	....	....	....	....	....	....	....
1978-79	**Boston Bruins**	**NHL**	**17**	**3**	**1**	**4**	**3**	**1**	**4**	**0**	**1**	**0**	**0**	**16**	**18.8**	**5**	**2**	**6**	**0**	**–3**	....	....	....	....	....	....	....	....
	Rochester Americans	AHL	59	21	38	59	....	....	....	92	....	....	....	....	....	....	....	....	....	....	....	....	....	....	....	....	....	....
1979-80	**Boston Bruins**	**NHL**	**17**	**1**	**3**	**4**	**1**	**2**	**3**	**16**	**0**	**0**	**0**	**14**	**7.1**	**5**	**0**	**5**	**0**	**0**	....	....	....	....	....	....	....	....
	Binghamton Dusters	AHL	63	24	39	63	....	....	....	36	....	....	....	....	....	....	....	....	....	....	....	....	....	....	....	....	....	....
1980-81	**Boston Bruins**	**NHL**	**9**	**1**	**1**	**2**	**1**	**1**	**2**	**6**	**0**	**0**	**1**	**10**	**10.0**	**5**	**1**	**4**	**0**	**0**	....	....	....	....	....	....	....	....
	Springfield Indians	AHL	57	26	32	58	....	....	....	68	....	....	....	....	....	....	....	....	....	....	2	0	1	1	24	....	....	....
1981-82	Erie Blades	AHL	53	10	26	36	....	....	....	10	....	....	....	....	....	....	....	....	....	....	....	....	....	....	....	....	....	....
1982-83	Birmingham South Stars	CHL	5	0	1	1	....	....	....	2	....	....	....	....	....	....	....	....	....	....	....	....	....	....	....	....	....	....
	NHL Totals		**43**	**5**	**5**	**10**	**5**	**4**	**9**	**22**	**1**	**0**	**1**	**40**	**12.5**	**15**	**3**	**15**	**0**		....	....	....	....	....	....	....	....

Signed as a free agent by **Boston**, October 10, 1978.

• SOURAY, SHELDON

Sheldon Souray D – L. 6'2", 210 lbs. b: Elk Point, Alta., 7/13/1976. New Jersey's 3rd choice, 71st overall, in 1994 Entry Draft.

Season	Club	League	GP	G	A	Pts	AG	AA	APts	PIM	PP	SH	GW	S	%	TGF	PGF	TGA	PGA	+/-	GP	G	A	Pts	PIM	PP	SH	GW
1992-93	Tri-City Americans	WHL	2	0	0	0	....	....	....	0	....	....	....	....	....	....	....	....	....	....	....	....	....	....	....	....	....	....
1993-94	Tri-City Americans	WHL	42	3	6	9	....	....	....	122	....	....	....	....	....	....	....	....	....	....	....	....	....	....	....	....	....	....
1994-95	Tri-City Americans	WHL	40	2	24	26	....	....	....	140	....	....	....	....	....	....	....	....	....	....	....	....	....	....	....	....	....	....
	Prince George Cougars	WHL	11	2	3	5	....	....	....	23	....	....	....	....	....	....	....	....	....	....	....	....	....	....	....	....	....	....
	Albany River Rats	AHL	7	0	2	2	....	....	....	8	....	....	....	....	....	....	....	....	....	....	....	....	....	....	....	....	....	....
1995-96	Prince George Cougars	WHL	32	9	18	27	....	....	....	91	....	....	....	....	....	....	....	....	....	....	....	....	....	....	....	....	....	....
	Kelowna Rockets	WHL	27	7	20	27	....	....	....	94	....	....	....	....	....	....	....	....	....	....	6	0	5	5	2	....	....	....
	Albany River Rats	AHL	6	0	2	2	....	....	....	12	....	....	....	....	....	....	....	....	....	....	4	0	1	1	4	....	....	....
1996-97	Albany River Rats	AHL	70	2	11	13	....	....	....	160	....	....	....	....	....	....	....	....	....	....	16	2	3	5	47	....	....	....
1997-98	**New Jersey Devils**	**NHL**	**60**	**3**	**7**	**10**	**4**	**7**	**11**	**85**	**0**	**0**	**1**	**74**	**4.1**	**39**	**4**	**20**	**3**	**+18**	**3**	**0**	**1**	**1**	**2**	**0**	**0**	**0**
	Albany River Rats	AHL	6	0	0	0	....	....	....	8	....	....	....	....	....	....	....	....	....	....	....	....	....	....	....	....	....	....
	NHL Totals		**60**	**3**	**7**	**10**	**4**	**7**	**11**	**85**	**0**	**0**	**1**	**74**	**4.1**	**39**	**4**	**20**	**3**		**3**	**0**	**1**	**1**	**2**	**0**	**0**	**0**

WHL West Second All-Star Team (1996)

• SPECK, FRED

Fred Speck C – L. 5'9", 160 lbs. b: Thorold, Ont., 7/22/1947.

Season	Club	League	GP	G	A	Pts	AG	AA	APts	PIM	PP	SH	GW	S	%	TGF	PGF	TGA	PGA	+/-	GP	G	A	Pts	PIM	PP	SH	GW
1962-63	Hamilton Red Wings	OHA	1	0	0	0	....	....	....	0	....	....	....	....	....	....	....	....	....	....	....	....	....	....	....	....	....	....
1963-64	Hamilton Red Wings	OHA	17	2	6	8	....	....	....	20	....	....	....	....	....	....	....	....	....	....	....	....	....	....	....	....	....	....
1964-65	Hamilton Red Wings	OHA	41	16	18	34	....	....	....	108	....	....	....	....	....	....	....	....	....	....	....	....	....	....	....	....	....	....
1965-66	Hamilton Red Wings	OHA	48	20	37	57	....	....	....	123	....	....	....	....	....	....	....	....	....	....	5	1	2	3	8	....	....	....
1966-67	Hamilton Red Wings	OHA	39	23	32	55	....	....	....	67	....	....	....	....	....	....	....	....	....	....	13	4	6	10	14	....	....	....
1967-68	Hamilton Red Wings	OHA	52	31	54	85	....	....	....	115	....	....	....	....	....	....	....	....	....	....	11	6	8	14	15	....	....	....
	Fort Worth Wings	CHL	1	1	1	2	....	....	....	2	....	....	....	....	....	....	....	....	....	....	3	1	3	4	4	....	....	....
1968-69	**Detroit Red Wings**	**NHL**	**5**	**0**	**0**	**0**	**0**	**0**	**0**	**2**	**0**	**0**	**0**	**6**	**0.0**	**0**	**0**	**0**	**0**	**0**	....	....	....	....	....	....	....	....
	Fort Worth Wings	CHL	63	21	24	45	....	....	....	26	....	....	....	....	....	....	....	....	....	....	....	....	....	....	....	....	....	....
1969-70	**Detroit Red Wings**	**NHL**	**5**	**0**	**0**	**0**	**0**	**0**	**0**	**0**	**0**	**0**	**0**	**8**	**0.0**	**0**	**0**	**2**	**0**	**–2**	....	....	....	....	....	....	....	....
	Fort Worth Wings	CHL	67	30	46	76	....	....	....	47	....	....	....	....	....	....	....	....	....	....	7	0	3	3	7	....	....	....
	San Diego Gulls	WHL	....	....	....	....	....	....	....	....	....	....	....	....	....	....	....	....	....	....	2	0	0	0	0	....	....	....
1970-71	Baltimore Clippers	AHL	72	31	*61	*92	....	....	....	40	....	....	....	....	....	....	....	....	....	....	6	4	5	9	4	....	....	....
1971-72	**Vancouver Canucks**	**NHL**	**18**	**1**	**2**	**3**	**1**	**2**	**3**	**0**	**0**	**0**	**0**	**23**	**4.3**	**3**	**0**	**18**	**0**	**–15**	....	....	....	....	....	....	....	....
	Seattle Totems	WHL	6	3	3	6	....	....	....	0	....	....	....	....	....	....	....	....	....	....	....	....	....	....	....	....	....	....
	Cleveland Barons	AHL	27	6	8	14	....	....	....	21	....	....	....	....	....	....	....	....	....	....	6	0	1	1	6	....	....	....
1972-73	Minnesota Fighting Saints	WHA	47	13	16	29	....	....	....	52	....	....	....	....	....	....	....	....	....	....	....	....	....	....	....	....	....	....
	Los Angeles Sharks	WHA	28	3	13	16	....	....	....	22	....	....	....	....	....	....	....	....	....	....	6	3	2	5	2	....	....	....
1973-74	Los Angeles Sharks	WHA	18	2	5	7	....	....	....	4	....	....	....	....	....	....	....	....	....	....	....	....	....	....	....	....	....	....
	Greensboro Generals	SHL	8	1	3	4	....	....	....	19	....	....	....	....	....	....	....	....	....	....	....	....	....	....	....	....	....	....
1974-75	Michigan-Baltimore	WHA	30	4	8	12	....	....	....	18	....	....	....	....	....	....	....	....	....	....	....	....	....	....	....	....	....	....
	Syracuse Blazers	NAHL	17	11	23	34	....	....	....	16	....	....	....	....	....	....	....	....	....	....	....	....	....	....	....	....	....	....
1975-76	Baltimore Clippers	AHL	76	23	52	75	....	....	....	93	....	....	....	....	....	....	....	....	....	....	....	....	....	....	....	....	....	....
1976-77	Brantford Alexanders	OHA Sr.	27	16	21	37	....	....	....	29	....	....	....	....	....	....	....	....	....	....	....	....	....	....	....	....	....	....
	NHL Totals		**28**	**1**	**2**	**3**	**1**	**2**	**3**	**2**	**0**	**0**	**0**	**37**	**2.7**	**3**	**0**	**20**	**0**		....	....	....	....	....	....	....	....
	Other Major League Totals		123	22	42	64	....	....	....	96	....	....	....	....	....	....	....	....	....	....	6	3	2	5	2	....	....	....

AHL First All-Star Team (1971) • Won Dudley "Red" Garrett Memorial Award (Top Rookie - AHL) (1971) • Won John B. Sollenberger Trophy (Top Scorer - AHL) (1971) • Won Les Cunningham Award (MVP - AHL) (1971)

Claimed by **Vancouver** from **Detroit** in Intra-League Draft, June 8, 1971. Selected by **Minnesota** (WHA) in 1972 WHA General Player Draft, February 12, 1972. Traded to **Minnesota** by **Vancouver** for cash, August, 1972. Traded to **LA Sharks** (WHA) by **Minnesota** (WHA) for Bill Young, February, 1973. Transferred to **Michigan** (WHA) after **LA Sharks** (WHA) franchise relocated, April 11, 1974.

• SPEER, BILL

Bill Speer D – L. 5'11", 205 lbs. b: Lindsay, Ont., 3/20/1942. Deceased.

Season	Club	League	GP	G	A	Pts	AG	AA	APts	PIM	PP	SH	GW	S	%	TGF	PGF	TGA	PGA	+/-	GP	G	A	Pts	PIM	PP	SH	GW
1959-60	St. Catharines Teepees	OHA	43	1	6	7	....	....	....	53	....	....	....	....	....	....	....	....	....	....	16	0	1	1	10	....	....	....
1960-61	St. Catharines Teepees	OHA	42	5	22	27	....	....	....	70	....	....	....	....	....	....	....	....	....	....	6	0	2	2	8	....	....	....
1961-62	St. Catharines Teepees	OHA	38	6	24	30	....	....	....	96	....	....	....	....	....	....	....	....	....	....	6	0	0	0	8	....	....	....
	Sault Ste. Marie Thunderbirds	EPHL	4	0	0	0	....	....	....	2	....	....	....	....	....	....	....	....	....	....	....	....	....	....	....	....	....	....
1962-63	Knoxville Knights	EHL	68	10	44	54	....	....	....	46	....	....	....	....	....	....	....	....	....	....	5	1	0	1	4	....	....	....
1963-64	Springfield Indians	AHL	28	2	4	6	....	....	....	10	....	....	....	....	....	....	....	....	....	....	....	....	....	....	....	....	....	....
1964-65	Cleveland Barons	AHL	71	4	16	20	....	....	....	54	....	....	....	....	....	....	....	....	....	....	....	....	....	....	....	....	....	....
1965-66	Cleveland Barons	AHL	70	3	16	19	....	....	....	36	....	....	....	....	....	....	....	....	....	....	12	2	2	4	6	....	....	....
1966-67	Buffalo Bisons	AHL	64	6	25	31	....	....	....	52	....	....	....	....	....	....	....	....	....	....	....	....	....	....	....	....	....	....
1967-68	**Pittsburgh Penguins**	**NHL**	**68**	**3**	**13**	**16**	**4**	**14**	**18**	**44**	**1**	**0**	**0**	**101**	**3.0**	**56**	**11**	**70**	**11**	**–14**	....	....	....	....	....	....	....	....
	Baltimore Clippers	AHL	5	0	5	5	....	....	....	8	....	....	....	....	....	....	....	....	....	....	....	....	....	....	....	....	....	....

Season	Club	League	GP	G	A	Pts	AG	AA	APts	PIM	PP	SH	GW	S	%	TGF	PGF	TGA	PGA	+/–	GP	G	A	Pts	PIM	PP	SH	GW
			REGULAR SEASON																		PLAYOFFS							
1968-69	**Pittsburgh Penguins**	**NHL**	**34**	**1**	**4**	**5**	**1**	**4**	**5**	**27**	**1**	**0**	**1**	**43**	**2.3**	**23**	**4**	**44**	**9**	**–16**	....	....	....	....	....	....	....	....
	Baltimore Clippers	AHL	13	1	4	5	....	....	....	21	....	....	....	....	....	....	....	....	....	....	....	....	....	....	....	....	....	....
	Amarillo Wranglers	CHL	7	1	1	2	....	....	....	14	....	....	....	....	....	....	....	....	....	....	....	....	....	....	....	....	....	....
1969-70	**Boston Bruins**	**NHL**	**27**	**1**	**3**	**4**	**1**	**3**	**4**	**4**	**0**	**0**	**0**	**5**	**20.0**	**16**	**1**	**15**	**6**	**+6**	**8**	**1**	**0**	**1**	**4**	**0**	**0**	**0**
	Salt Lake Golden Eagles	WHL	19	1	3	4	....	....	....	47	....	....	....	....	....	....	....	....	....	....	....	....	....	....	....	....	....	....
1970-71	**Boston Bruins**	**NHL**	**1**	**0**	**0**	**0**	**0**	**0**	**0**	**4**	**0**	**0**	**0**	**0**	**0.0**	**0**	**0**	**0**	**0**	**0**	....	....	....	....	....	....	....	....
	Hershey Bears	AHL	27	2	6	8	....	....	....	42	....	....	....	....	....	....	....	....	....	....	....	....	....	....	....	....	....	....
	Providence Reds	AHL	25	3	19	22	....	....	....	35	....	....	....	....	....	....	....	....	....	....	10	1	6	7	6	....	....	....
1971-72	Boston Braves	AHL	7	0	0	0	....	....	....	2	....	....	....	....	....	....	....	....	....	....	....	....	....	....	....	....	....	....
	Providence Reds	AHL	52	5	27	32	....	....	....	36	....	....	....	....	....	....	....	....	....	....	5	2	2	4	8	....	....	....
1972-73	New York Raiders	WHA	69	3	23	26	....	....	....	40	....	....	....	....	....	....	....	....	....	....	....	....	....	....	....	....	....	....
1973-74	New York-New Jersey	WHA	66	1	3	4	....	....	....	30	....	....	....	....	....	....	....	....	....	....	....	....	....	....	....	....	....	....
1974-75	Orillia Terriers	OHA Sr.	13	0	11	11	....	....	....	18	....	....	....	....	....	....	....	....	....	....	....	....	....	....	....	....	....	....
	NHL Totals		**130**	**5**	**20**	**25**	**6**	**21**	**27**	**79**	**2**	**0**	**1**	**149**	**3.4**	**95**	**16**	**129**	**26**		**8**	**1**	**0**	**1**	**4**	**0**	**0**	**0**
	Other Major League Totals		135	4	26	30	....	....	....	70	....	....	....	....	....	....	....	....	....		....	....	....	....	....	....	....	....

Traded to **Cleveland** (AHL) by **Springfield** (AHL) for Pete Shearer, September, 1964. Traded to **Pittsburgh** (AHL) by **Cleveland** (AHL) for cash, August, 1966. Loaned to **Buffalo** (AHL) by **Pittsburgh** (AHL) for 1966-67 season, September, 1966. Traded to **Pittsburgh** by **Cleveland** (AHL) for cash, September, 1967. Claimed by **Boston** from **Pittsburgh** in Intra-League Draft, June 11, 1969. Traded to **Providence** (AHL) by **Boston** for cash, February, 1971. Selected by **NY Raiders** (WHA) in 1972 WHA General Player Draft, February 12, 1972. Claimed by **NY Islanders** from **Providence** (AHL) in Inter-League Draft, June, 1972.

• SPEERS, TED

Ted Speers RW – R. 5′11″, 200 lbs. b: Ann Arbor, MI, 1/28/1961.

Season	Club	League	GP	G	A	Pts	AG	AA	APts	PIM	PP	SH	GW	S	%	TGF	PGF	TGA	PGA	+/–	GP	G	A	Pts	PIM	PP	SH	GW
1979-80	University of Michigan	WCHA	30	13	16	29	....	....	....	16	....	....	....	....	....	....	....	....	....	....	....	....	....	....	....	....	....	....
1980-81	University of Michigan	WCHA	39	22	23	45	....	....	....	20	....	....	....	....	....	....	....	....	....	....	....	....	....	....	....	....	....	....
1981-82	University of Michigan	WCHA	38	23	16	39	....	....	....	46	....	....	....	....	....	....	....	....	....	....	....	....	....	....	....	....	....	....
1982-83	University of Michigan	CCHA	36	18	41	59	....	....	....	40	....	....	....	....	....	....	....	....	....	....	....	....	....	....	....	....	....	....
1983-84	Adirondack Red Wings	AHL	79	15	25	40	....	....	....	27	....	....	....	....	....	....	....	....	....	....	7	2	1	3	9	....	....	....
1984-85	Adirondack Red Wings	AHL	80	22	31	53	....	....	....	40	....	....	....	....	....	....	....	....	....	....	....	....	....	....	....	....	....	....
1985-86	**Detroit Red Wings**	**NHL**	**4**	**1**	**1**	**2**	**1**	**1**	**2**	**0**	**0**	**0**	**0**	**6**	**16.7**	**4**	**0**	**4**	**2**	**+2**	....	....	....	....	....	....	....	....
	Adirondack Red Wings	AHL	74	32	35	67	....	....	....	20	....	....	....	....	....	....	....	....	....	....	15	7	5	12	9	....	....	....
1986-87	Adirondack Red Wings	AHL	80	24	37	61	....	....	....	39	....	....	....	....	....	....	....	....	....	....	11	2	0	2	4	....	....	....
	NHL Totals		**4**	**1**	**1**	**2**	**1**	**1**	**2**	**0**	**0**	**0**	**0**	**6**	**16.7**	**4**	**0**	**4**	**2**		....	....	....	....	....	....	....	....

CCHA First All-Star Team (1983)

Signed as a free agent by **Detroit**, September, 1983.

• SPENCER, BRIAN

Brian Spencer LW – L. 5′11″, 185 lbs. b: Fort St. James, B.C., 9/3/1949. d: 6/3/1988. Toronto's 5th choice, 55th overall, in 1969 Amateur Draft.

Season	Club	League	GP	G	A	Pts	AG	AA	APts	PIM	PP	SH	GW	S	%	TGF	PGF	TGA	PGA	+/–	GP	G	A	Pts	PIM	PP	SH	GW
1967-68	Calgary Centennials	WCJHL	56	14	12	26	....	....	....	29	....	....	....	....	....	....	....	....	....	....	....	....	....	....	....	....	....	....
1968-69	Estevan–Swift Current	WCJHL	53	19	29	48	....	....	....	120	....	....	....	....	....	....	....	....	....	....	4	3	1	4	14	....	....	....
1969-70	**Toronto Maple Leafs**	**NHL**	**9**	**0**	**0**	**0**	**0**	**0**	**0**	**12**	**0**	**0**	**0**	**8**	**0.0**	**1**	**0**	**5**	**0**	**–4**	....	....	....	....	....	....	....	....
	Tulsa Oilers	CHL	66	13	19	32	....	....	....	186	....	....	....	....	....	....	....	....	....	....	....	....	....	....	....	....	....	....
1970-71	**Toronto Maple Leafs**	**NHL**	**50**	**9**	**15**	**24**	**9**	**13**	**22**	**115**	**3**	**0**	**1**	**61**	**14.8**	**38**	**10**	**26**	**0**	**+2**	**6**	**0**	**1**	**1**	**17**	**0**	**0**	**0**
	Tulsa Oilers	CHL	23	6	8	14	....	....	....	103	....	....	....	....	....	....	....	....	....	....	....	....	....	....	....	....	....	....
1971-72	**Toronto Maple Leafs**	**NHL**	**36**	**1**	**5**	**6**	**1**	**5**	**6**	**65**	**0**	**0**	**0**	**31**	**3.2**	**16**	**1**	**13**	**0**	**+2**	....	....	....	....	....	....	....	....
	Tulsa Oilers	CHL	20	7	7	14	....	....	....	115	....	....	....	....	....	....	....	....	....	....	....	....	....	....	....	....	....	....
1972-73	**New York Islanders**	**NHL**	**78**	**14**	**24**	**38**	**14**	**20**	**34**	**90**	**0**	**0**	**2**	**163**	**8.6**	**52**	**6**	**94**	**1**	**–47**	....	....	....	....	....	....	....	....
1973-74	**New York Islanders**	**NHL**	**54**	**5**	**16**	**21**	**5**	**14**	**19**	**65**	**0**	**0**	**0**	**114**	**4.4**	**29**	**5**	**42**	**2**	**–16**	....	....	....	....	....	....	....	....
	Buffalo Sabres	**NHL**	**13**	**3**	**2**	**5**	**3**	**2**	**5**	**4**	**1**	**0**	**0**	**21**	**14.3**	**6**	**1**	**8**	**0**	**–3**	....	....	....	....	....	....	....	....
1974-75	**Buffalo Sabres**	**NHL**	**73**	**12**	**29**	**41**	**11**	**23**	**34**	**77**	**1**	**0**	**1**	**126**	**9.5**	**65**	**6**	**42**	**0**	**+17**	**16**	**0**	**4**	**4**	**8**	**0**	**0**	**0**
1975-76	**Buffalo Sabres**	**NHL**	**77**	**13**	**26**	**39**	**12**	**20**	**32**	**70**	**0**	**0**	**1**	**84**	**15.5**	**57**	**1**	**42**	**0**	**+14**	**9**	**1**	**0**	**1**	**4**	**0**	**0**	**0**
1976-77	**Buffalo Sabres**	**NHL**	**77**	**14**	**15**	**29**	**13**	**12**	**25**	**55**	**1**	**0**	**2**	**78**	**17.9**	**44**	**4**	**40**	**0**	**0**	**6**	**0**	**0**	**0**	**0**	**0**	**0**	**0**
1977-78	**Pittsburgh Penguins**	**NHL**	**79**	**9**	**11**	**20**	**9**	**9**	**18**	**81**	**0**	**0**	**1**	**101**	**8.9**	**37**	**2**	**54**	**1**	**–18**	....	....	....	....	....	....	....	....
1978-79	**Pittsburgh Penguins**	**NHL**	**7**	**0**	**0**	**0**	**0**	**0**	**0**	**0**	**0**	**0**	**0**	**2**	**0.0**	**0**	**0**	**0**	**0**	**0**	....	....	....	....	....	....	....	....
	Binghamton Dusters	AHL	39	5	9	14	....	....	....	58	....	....	....	....	....	....	....	....	....	....	....	....	....	....	....	....	....	....
1979-80	Springfield Indians	AHL	9	1	1	2	....	....	....	0	....	....	....	....	....	....	....	....	....	....	....	....	....	....	....	....	....	....
	Hershey Bears	AHL	30	0	4	4	....	....	....	23	....	....	....	....	....	....	....	....	....	....	....	....	....	....	....	....	....	....
	NHL Totals		**553**	**80**	**143**	**223**	**77**	**118**	**195**	**634**	**6**	**0**	**8**	**789**	**10.1**	**345**	**36**	**366**	**4**		**37**	**1**	**5**	**6**	**29**	**0**	**0**	**0**

Claimed by **NY Islanders** from **Toronto** in Expansion Draft, June 6, 1972. Traded to **Buffalo** by **NY Islanders** for Doug Rombough, March 10, 1974. Traded to **Pittsburgh** by **Buffalo** for Ron Schock, September, 1977.

• SPENCER, IRV

Irv Spencer D – L. 5′10″, 180 lbs. b: Sudbury, Ont., 12/4/1937.

Season	Club	League	GP	G	A	Pts	AG	AA	APts	PIM	PP	SH	GW	S	%	TGF	PGF	TGA	PGA	+/–	GP	G	A	Pts	PIM	PP	SH	GW
1954-55	Kitchener Canucks	OHA	49	10	9	19	....	....	....	65	....	....	....	....	....	....	....	....	....	....	....	....	....	....	....	....	....	....
1955-56	Kitchener Canucks	OHA	48	4	9	13	....	....	....	36	....	....	....	....	....	....	....	....	....	....	8	1	0	1	16	....	....	....
1956-57	Peterborough Petes	OHA	45	6	26	32	....	....	....	68	....	....	....	....	....	....	....	....	....	....	....	....	....	....	....	....	....	....
	Hull-Ottawa Canadiens	QHL	8	1	2	3	....	....	....	2	....	....	....	....	....	....	....	....	....	....	....	....	....	....	....	....	....	....
1957-58	Peterborough Petes	OHA	52	8	31	39	....	....	....	76	....	....	....	....	....	....	....	....	....	....	5	3	1	4	8	....	....	....
	Montreal Royals	QHL	3	0	1	1	....	....	....	2	....	....	....	....	....	....	....	....	....	....	....	....	....	....	....	....	....	....
1958-59	Montreal Royals	QHL	45	6	12	18	....	....	....	55	....	....	....	....	....	....	....	....	....	....	8	1	2	3	8	....	....	....
1959-60	**New York Rangers**	**NHL**	**32**	**1**	**2**	**3**	**1**	**2**	**3**	**20**	....	....	....	....	....	....	....	....	....	....	....	....	....	....	....	....	....	....
	Trois-Rivieres Lions	EPHL	18	3	4	7	....	....	....	8	....	....	....	....	....	....	....	....	....	....	....	....	....	....	....	....	....	....
	Springfield Indians	AHL	14	0	5	5	....	....	....	12	....	....	....	....	....	....	....	....	....	....	....	....	....	....	....	....	....	....
1960-61	**New York Rangers**	**NHL**	**56**	**1**	**8**	**9**	**1**	**8**	**9**	**30**	....	....	....	....	....	....	....	....	....	....	....	....	....	....	....	....	....	....
1961-62	**New York Rangers**	**NHL**	**43**	**2**	**10**	**12**	**2**	**10**	**12**	**31**	....	....	....	....	....	....	....	....	....	....	**1**	**0**	**0**	**0**	**2**	....	....	....
1962-63	**Boston Bruins**	**NHL**	**69**	**5**	**17**	**22**	**6**	**18**	**24**	**34**	....	....	....	....	....	....	....	....	....	....	....	....	....	....	....	....	....	....
1963-64	**Detroit Red Wings**	**NHL**	**25**	**3**	**0**	**3**	**4**	**0**	**4**	**8**	....	....	....	....	....	....	....	....	....	....	**11**	**0**	**0**	**0**	**0**	....	....	....
	Cincinnati Wings	CHL	23	3	8	11	....	....	....	34	....	....	....	....	....	....	....	....	....	....	....	....	....	....	....	....	....	....
	Pittsburgh Hornets	AHL	18	5	8	13	....	....	....	2	....	....	....	....	....	....	....	....	....	....	....	....	....	....	....	....	....	....
1964-65	Pittsburgh Hornets	AHL	72	18	22	40	....	....	....	45	....	....	....	....	....	....	....	....	....	....	4	0	0	0	0	....	....	....
	Detroit Red Wings	**NHL**	....	....	....	....	....	....	....	....	....	....	....	....	....	....	....	....	....	....	**1**	**0**	**0**	**0**	**4**	....	....	....
1965-66	Memphis Wings	CHL	54	12	21	33	....	....	....	14	....	....	....	....	....	....	....	....	....	....	....	....	....	....	....	....	....	....
	Pittsburgh Hornets	AHL	19	4	11	15	....	....	....	26	....	....	....	....	....	....	....	....	....	....	....	....	....	....	....	....	....	....
	Detroit Red Wings	**NHL**	....				....	....	....	....	....	....	....	....	....	....	....	....	....	....	**3**	**0**	**0**	**0**	**2**	....	....	....
1966-67	Pittsburgh Hornets	AHL	2	0	1	1	....	....	....	0	....	....	....	....	....	....	....	....	....	....	....	....	....	....	....	....	....	....
	Memphis Wings	CHL	30	2	6	8	....	....	....	8	....	....	....	....	....	....	....	....	....	....	7	0	5	5	4	....	....	....
1967-68	**Detroit Red Wings**	**NHL**	**5**	**0**	**1**	**1**	**0**	**1**	**1**	**4**	**0**	**0**	**0**	**7**	**0.0**	**5**	**1**	**7**	**2**	**–1**	....	....	....	....	....	....	....	....
	Fort Worth Wings	CHL	55	7	31	38	....	....	....	42	....	....	....	....	....	....	....	....	....	....	13	3	3	6	12	....	....	....
1968-69	Fort Worth Wings	CHL	49	7	18	25	....	....	....	24	....	....	....	....	....	....	....	....	....	....	....	....	....	....	....	....	....	....
1969-70	San Diego Gulls	WHL	62	13	25	38	....	....	....	26	....	....	....	....	....	....	....	....	....	....	6	0	3	3	8	....	....	....
1970-71	San Diego Gulls	WHL	45	2	15	17	....	....	....	24	....	....	....	....	....	....	....	....	....	....	6	2	0	2	19	....	....	....
1971-72	Fort Worth Wings	CHL	1	0	0	0	....	....	....	0	....	....	....	....	....	....	....	....	....	....	....	....	....	....	....	....	....	....
1972-73	Philadelphia Blazers	WHA	54	2	27	29	....	....	....	43	....	....	....	....	....	....	....	....	....	....	....	....	....	....	....	....	....	....
	Rhode Island Reds	EHL	11	3	3	6	....	....	....	4	....	....	....	....	....	....	....	....	....	....	....	....	....	....	....	....	....	....
1973-74	Vancouver Blazers	WHA	19	0	1	1	....	....	....	6	....	....	....	....	....	....	....	....	....	....	....	....	....	....	....	....	....	....
	NHL Totals		**230**	**12**	**38**	**50**	**14**	**39**	**53**	**127**	**0**	**0**	**0**	**7**	**171.4**	**5**	**1**	**7**	**2**		**16**	**0**	**0**	**0**	**8**	**0**	**0**	**0**
	Other Major League Totals		73	2	28	30	....	....	....	49	....	....	....	....	....	....	....	....	....		....	....	....	....	....	....	....	....

CHL First All-Star Team (1968)

Claimed by **NY Rangers** from **Montreal** in Intra-League Draft, June 10, 1959. Claimed by **Boston** from **NY Rangers** in Intra-League Draft, June 4, 1962. Claimed by **Detroit** from **Boston** in Intra-League Draft, June 4, 1963. Traded to **San Diego** (WHL) by **Detroit** for cash, August, 1970. Traded to **Detroit** by **San Diego** (WHL) for cash, May, 1971. Claimed by **Vancouver** from **Tidewater** (AHL) in Inter-League Draft, June, 1971. Traded to **Detroit** by **Vancouver** with Bob Dillabough for Gary Bredin and John Cunniff, June 8, 1971. Signed as a free agent by **Philadelphia** (WHA), June, 1972. Transferred to **Vancouver** (WHA) after **Philadelphia** (WHA) franchise relocated, May, 1973.

• SPRING, COREY

Corey Spring RW – R. 6'4", 214 lbs. b: Cranbrook, B.C., 5/31/1971.

Season	Club	League	GP	G	A	Pts	AG	AA	APts	PIM	PP	SH	GW	S	%	TGF	PGF	TGA	PGA	+/–	GP	G	A	Pts	PIM	PP	SH	GW
			REGULAR SEASON																		PLAYOFFS							
1991-92	University of Alaska-Anchorage	NCAA	35	3	8	11	....	....	....	30	....	....	....	....	....	....	....	....	....	....	....	....	....	....	....	....	....	....
1992-93	University of Alaska-Anchorage	CCHA	28	5	5	10	....	....	....	20	....	....	....	....	....	....	....	....	....	....	....	....	....	....	....	....	....	....
1993-94	University of Alaska-Anchorage	CCHA	38	19	18	37	....	....	....	34	....	....	....	....	....	....	....	....	....	....	....	....	....	....	....	....	....	....
1994-95	University of Alaska-Anchorage	CCHA	33	18	14	32	....	....	....	56	....	....	....	....	....	....	....	....	....	....	....	....	....	....	....	....	....	....
1995-96	Atlanta Knights	IHL	73	14	14	28	....	....	....	104	....	....	....	....	....	....	....	....	....	....	2	0	0	0	0	....	....	....
1996-97	Adirondack Red Wings	AHL	69	20	26	46	....	....	....	118	....	....	....	....	....	....	....	....	....	....	4	0	0	0	14	....	....	....
1997-98	**Tampa Bay Lightning**	**NHL**	**8**	**1**	**0**	**1**	**1**	**0**	**1**	**10**	**0**	**0**	**0**	**12**	**8.3**	**1**	**0**	**2**	**0**	**–1**	....	....	....	....	....	....	....	....
	Adirondack Red Wings	AHL	57	19	25	44	....	....	....	120	....	....	....	....	....	....	....	....	....	....	3	0	0	0	6	....	....	....
	NHL Totals		**8**	**1**	**0**	**1**	**1**	**0**	**1**	**10**	**0**	**0**	**0**	**12**	**8.3**	**1**	**0**	**2**	**0**		....	....	....	....	....	....	....	....

Signed as a free agent by **Tampa Bay**, July 24, 1995.

• SPRING, DON

Don Spring D – L. 5'11", 195 lbs. b: Maracaibo, Venezuela, 6/15/1959.

Season	Club	League	GP	G	A	Pts	AG	AA	APts	PIM	PP	SH	GW	S	%	TGF	PGF	TGA	PGA	+/–	GP	G	A	Pts	PIM	PP	SH	GW
1976-77	University of Alberta	CWUAA	34	1	6	7	....	....	....	24	....	....	....	....	....	....	....	....	....	....	....	....	....	....	....	....	....	....
1977-78	University of Alberta	CWUAA	30	6	14	20	....	....	....	12	....	....	....	....	....	....	....	....	....	....	....	....	....	....	....	....	....	....
1978-79	University of Alberta	CWUAA	42	7	29	36	....	....	....	27	....	....	....	....	....	....	....	....	....	....	....	....	....	....	....	....	....	....
1979-80	Canada	Nat-Team	51	1	23	24	....	....	....	20	....	....	....	....	....	....	....	....	....	....	....	....	....	....	....	....	....	....
	Canada	Olympics	6	0	1	1	....	....	....	0	....	....	....	....	....	....	....	....	....	....	....	....	....	....	....	....	....	....
1980-81	**Winnipeg Jets**	**NHL**	**80**	**1**	**18**	**19**	**1**	**13**	**14**	**18**	**0**	**0**	**0**	**51**	**2.0**	**67**	**1**	**139**	**33**	**–40**	....	....	....	....	....	....	....	....
1981-82	**Winnipeg Jets**	**NHL**	**78**	**0**	**16**	**16**	**0**	**11**	**11**	**21**	**0**	**0**	**0**	**67**	**0.0**	**71**	**1**	**105**	**22**	**–13**	**4**	**0**	**0**	**0**	**4**	**0**	**0**	**0**
1982-83	**Winnipeg Jets**	**NHL**	**80**	**0**	**16**	**16**	**0**	**11**	**11**	**37**	**0**	**0**	**0**	**50**	**0.0**	**80**	**0**	**103**	**23**	**0**	**2**	**0**	**0**	**0**	**6**	**0**	**0**	**0**
1983-84	**Winnipeg Jets**	**NHL**	**21**	**0**	**4**	**4**	**0**	**3**	**3**	**4**	**0**	**0**	**0**	**10**	**0.0**	**16**	**0**	**28**	**7**	**–5**	....	....	....	....	....	....	....	....
	Sherbrooke Jets	AHL	50	0	17	17	....	....	....	21	....	....	....	....	....	....	....	....	....	....	....	....	....	....	....	....	....	....
1984-85	EV Essen	Germany	36	8	19	27	....	....	....	32	....	....	....	....	....	....	....	....	....	....	18	3	13	16	12	....	....	....
	NHL Totals		**259**	**1**	**54**	**55**	**1**	**38**	**39**	**80**	**0**	**0**	**0**	**178**	**0.6**	**234**	**2**	**375**	**85**		**6**	**0**	**0**	**0**	**10**	**0**	**0**	**0**

Signed as a free agent by **Winnipeg**, May 22, 1980.

• SPRING, FRANK

Frank Spring RW – R. 6'3", 216 lbs. b: Cranbrook, B.C., 10/19/1949. Boston's 2nd choice, 4th overall, in 1969 Amateur Draft.

Season	Club	League	GP	G	A	Pts	AG	AA	APts	PIM	PP	SH	GW	S	%	TGF	PGF	TGA	PGA	+/–	GP	G	A	Pts	PIM	PP	SH	GW
1967-68	Edmonton Oil Kings	WCJHL	57	24	27	51	....	....	....	85	....	....	....	....	....	....	....	....	....	....	13	3	4	7	12	....	....	....
1968-69	Edmonton Oil Kings	WCJHL	41	9	16	25	....	....	....	60	....	....	....	....	....	....	....	....	....	....	17	10	2	12	16	....	....	....
1969-70	**Boston Bruins**	**NHL**	**1**	**0**	**0**	**0**	**0**	**0**	**0**	**0**	**0**	**0**	**0**	**0**	**0.0**	**0**	**0**	**0**	**0**	**0**	....	....	....	....	....	....	....	....
	Oklahoma City Blazers	CHL	62	17	22	39	....	....	....	55	....	....	....	....	....	....	....	....	....	....	....	....	....	....	....	....	....	....
1970-71	Hershey Bears	AHL	43	12	12	24	....	....	....	32	....	....	....	....	....	....	....	....	....	....	....	....	....	....	....	....	....	....
1971-72	Richmond Robins	AHL	75	12	19	31	....	....	....	61	....	....	....	....	....	....	....	....	....	....	....	....	....	....	....	....	....	....
1972-73	Richmond Robins	AHL	70	12	19	31	....	....	....	96	....	....	....	....	....	....	....	....	....	....	4	1	1	2	6	....	....	....
1973-74	**St. Louis Blues**	**NHL**	**2**	**0**	**0**	**0**	**0**	**0**	**0**	**0**	**0**	**0**	**0**	**2**	**0.0**	**0**	**0**	**0**	**0**	**0**	....	....	....	....	....	....	....	....
	Denver Spurs	WHL	47	17	11	28	....	....	....	41	....	....	....	....	....	....	....	....	....	....	....	....	....	....	....	....	....	....
	Richmond Robins	AHL	18	0	5	5	....	....	....	25	....	....	....	....	....	....	....	....	....	....	....	....	....	....	....	....	....	....
1974-75	**St. Louis Blues**	**NHL**	**3**	**0**	**0**	**0**	**0**	**0**	**0**	**0**	**0**	**0**	**0**	**3**	**0.0**	**1**	**0**	**2**	**0**	**–1**	....	....	....	....	....	....	....	....
	Denver Spurs	CHL	31	19	9	28	....	....	....	27	....	....	....	....	....	....	....	....	....	....	....	....	....	....	....	....	....	....
	California Golden Seals	**NHL**	**28**	**3**	**8**	**11**	**3**	**6**	**9**	**6**	**1**	**0**	**0**	**43**	**7.0**	**16**	**3**	**12**	**0**	**+1**	....	....	....	....	....	....	....	....
1975-76	**California Golden Seals**	**NHL**	**1**	**0**	**2**	**2**	**0**	**2**	**2**	**0**	**0**	**0**	**0**	**1**	**0.0**	**2**	**1**	**0**	**0**	**+1**	....	....	....	....	....	....	....	....
	Salt Lake City Golden Eagles	CHL	75	*44	29	73	....	....	....	50	....	....	....	....	....	....	....	....	....	....	5	0	0	0	8	....	....	....
1976-77	**Cleveland Barons**	**NHL**	**26**	**11**	**10**	**21**	**11**	**8**	**19**	**6**	**5**	**0**	**0**	**49**	**22.4**	**26**	**12**	**22**	**0**	**–8**	....	....	....	....	....	....	....	....
	Salt Lake Golden Eagles	CHL	19	8	10	18	....	....	....	12	....	....	....	....	....	....	....	....	....	....	....	....	....	....	....	....	....	....
1977-78	New Haven Nighthawks	AHL	45	14	11	25	....	....	....	35	....	....	....	....	....	....	....	....	....	....	13	2	4	6	0	....	....	....
	Indianapolis Racers	WHA	13	2	4	6	....	....	....	2	....	....	....	....	....	....	....	....	....	....	....	....	....	....	....	....	....	....
	NHL Totals		**61**	**14**	**20**	**34**	**14**	**16**	**30**	**12**	**6**	**0**	**0**	**98**	**14.3**	**45**	**16**	**36**	**0**		....	....	....	....	....	....	....	....
	Other Major League Totals		13	2	4	6	....	....	....	2	....	....	....	....	....	....	....	....	....	....	....	....	....	....	....	....	....	....

CHL Second All-Star Team (1976)

Claimed by **Philadelphia** from **Boston** in Intra-League Draft, June 8, 1971. Selected by **Chicago** (WHA) in 1972 WHA General Player Draft, February 12, 1972. Traded to **St. Louis** by **Philadelphia** for Ray Schultz, December, 1973. Traded to **California** by **St. Louis** for Bruce Affleck, January 9, 1975. Transferred to **Cleveland** after **California** franchise relocated, August 26, 1976. Signed as a free agent by **Indianapolis** (WHA), September, 1977.

• SPRUCE, ANDY

Andy Spruce LW – L. 5'11", 178 lbs. b: London, Ont., 4/17/1954. Vancouver's 5th choice, 95th overall, in 1974 Amateur Draft.

Season	Club	League	GP	G	A	Pts	AG	AA	APts	PIM	PP	SH	GW	S	%	TGF	PGF	TGA	PGA	+/–	GP	G	A	Pts	PIM	PP	SH	GW
1971-72	London Knights	OHA	33	1	9	10	....	....	....	17	....	....	....	....	....	....	....	....	....	....	....	....	....	....	....	....	....	....
1972-73	London Knights	OHA	63	34	69	103	....	....	....	69	....	....	....	....	....	....	....	....	....	....	....	....	....	....	....	....	....	....
1973-74	London Knights	OHA	39	12	0	51	....	....	....	18	....	....	....	....	....	....	....	....	....	....	....	....	....	....	....	....	....	....
1974-75	Seattle Totems	CHL	65	17	31	48	....	....	....	104	....	....	....	....	....	....	....	....	....	....	....	....	....	....	....	....	....	....
1975-76	Tulsa Oilers	CHL	75	29	46	75	....	....	....	100	....	....	....	....	....	....	....	....	....	....	9	1	7	8	8	....	....	....
1976-77	**Vancouver Canucks**	**NHL**	**51**	**9**	**6**	**15**	**9**	**5**	**14**	**37**	**2**	**0**	**0**	**54**	**16.7**	**21**	**4**	**39**	**2**	**–20**	....	....	....	....	....	....	....	....
	Tulsa Oilers	CHL	20	6	14	20	....	....	....	35	....	....	....	....	....	....	....	....	....	....	9	3	6	*9	21	....	....	....
1977-78	**Colorado Rockies**	**NHL**	**74**	**19**	**21**	**40**	**18**	**17**	**35**	**43**	**3**	**0**	**1**	**119**	**16.0**	**68**	**10**	**77**	**12**	**–7**	**2**	**0**	**2**	**2**	**0**	**0**	**0**	**0**
1978-79	**Colorado Rockies**	**NHL**	**47**	**3**	**15**	**18**	**3**	**11**	**14**	**31**	**0**	**0**	**0**	**57**	**5.3**	**35**	**12**	**42**	**1**	**–18**	....	....	....	....	....	....	....	....
1979-80	Fort Worth Texans	CHL	77	31	41	72	....	....	....	97	....	....	....	....	....	....	....	....	....	....	15	8	6	14	10	....	....	....
1980-81	Springfield Indians	AHL	79	15	38	53	....	....	....	108	....	....	....	....	....	....	....	....	....	....	7	2	3	5	17	....	....	....
1981-82	Erie Blades	AHL	76	8	17	23	....	....	....	95	....	....	....	....	....	....	....	....	....	....	....	....	....	....	....	....	....	....
	NHL Totals		**172**	**31**	**42**	**73**	**30**	**33**	**63**	**111**	**5**	**0**	**1**	**230**	**13.5**	**124**	**26**	**158**	**15**		**2**	**0**	**2**	**2**	**0**	**0**	**0**	**0**

Signed as a free agent by **Colorado**, October 5, 1977.

• SRSEN, TOMAS

Tomas Srsen RW – L. 5'11", 180 lbs. b: Olomouc, Czech., 8/25/1966. Edmonton's 6th choice, 147th overall, in 1987 Entry Draft.

Season	Club	League	GP	G	A	Pts	AG	AA	APts	PIM	PP	SH	GW	S	%	TGF	PGF	TGA	PGA	+/–	GP	G	A	Pts	PIM	PP	SH	GW
1984-85	Olomovc	Czech.2	31	14	8	22	....	....	....	20	....	....	....	....	....	....	....	....	....	....	....	....	....	....	....	....	....	....
1985-86	Zetor Brno	Czech.	40	6	5	11	....	....	....	44	....	....	....	....	....	....	....	....	....	....	....	....	....	....	....	....	....	....
	Czechoslovakia	WJC-A	7	0	2	2	....	....	....	6	....	....	....	....	....	....	....	....	....	....	....	....	....	....	....	....	....	....
1986-87	Zetor Brno	Czech.	40	15	8	23	....	....	....	44	....	....	....	....	....	....	....	....	....	....	....	....	....	....	....	....	....	....
1987-88	Zetor Brno	Czech.	45	24	8	32	....	....	....	114	....	....	....	....	....	....	....	....	....	....	....	....	....	....	....	....	....	....
1988-89	Dukla Jihlava	Czech.	42	19	11	30	....	....	....	48	....	....	....	....	....	....	....	....	....	....	....	....	....	....	....	....	....	....
1989-90	Dukla Jihlava	Czech.	25	5	10	15	....	....	....	....	....	....	....	....	....	....	....	....	....	....	....	....	....	....	....	....	....	....
	Zetor Brno	Czech.	5	3	5	8	....	....	....	....	....	....	....	....	....	....	....	....	....	....	....	....	....	....	....	....	....	....
1990-91	**Edmonton Oilers**	**NHL**	**2**	**0**	**0**	**0**	**0**	**0**	**0**	**0**	**0**	**0**	**0**	**2**	**0.0**	**0**	**0**	**0**	**0**	**0**	....	....	....	....	....	....	....	....
	Cape Breton Oilers	AHL	72	32	26	58	....	....	....	100	....	....	....	....	....	....	....	....	....	....	4	3	1	4	6	....	....	....
1991-92	Cape Breton Oilers	AHL	68	19	27	46	....	....	....	79	....	....	....	....	....	....	....	....	....	....	5	2	2	4	4	....	....	....
1992-93	Leksands IF	Sweden	39	20	6	26	....	....	....	48	....	....	....	....	....	....	....	....	....	....	2	1	1	2	2	....	....	....
1993-94	Rogle BK	Sweden	40	*28	13	41	....	....	....	72	....	....	....	....	....	....	....	....	....	....	....	....	....	....	....	....	....	....
	Czech Republic	Olympics	8	2	3	5	....	....	....	8	....	....	....	....	....	....	....	....	....	....	....	....	....	....	....	....	....	....
	Czech Republic	WC-A	6	1	1	2	....	....	....	2	....	....	....	....	....	....	....	....	....	....	....	....	....	....	....	....	....	....
1994-95	Rogle BK	Sweden	16	3	1	4	....	....	....	30	....	....	....	....	....	....	....	....	....	....	....	....	....	....	....	....	....	....
	Dadak Vsetin	Czech.	24	9	18	27	....	....	....	....	....	....	....	....	....	....	....	....	....	....	11	6	3	9	....	....	....	....
	Czech Republic	WC-A	8	1	1	2	....	....	....	6	....	....	....	....	....	....	....	....	....	....	....	....	....	....	....	....	....	....
1995-96	Dadak Vsetin	Czech.	31	8	18	26	....	....	....	....	....	....	....	....	....	....	....	....	....	....	12	4	5	9	....	....	....	....
1996-97	Petra Vsetin	Czech.	52	16	36	52	....	....	....	92	....	....	....	....	....	....	....	....	....	....	10	7	*10	*17	38	....	....	....
1997-98	Petra Vsetin	EuroHL	10	3	6	9	....	....	....	12	....	....	....	....	....	....	....	....	....	....	....	....	....	....	....	....	....	....
	Petra Vsetin	Czech.	50	13	31	44	....	....	....	107	....	....	....	....	....	....	....	....	....	....	10	5	3	8	20	....	....	....
	NHL Totals		**2**	**0**	**0**	**0**	**0**	**0**	**0**	**0**	**0**	**0**	**0**	**2**	**0.0**	**0**	**0**	**0**	**0**		....	....	....	....	....	....	....	....

			REGULAR SEASON																		PLAYOFFS							
Season	Club	League	GP	G	A	Pts	AG	AA	APts	PIM	PP	SH	GW	S	%	TGF	PGF	TGA	PGA	+/-	GP	G	A	Pts	PIM	PP	SH	GW

• STACKHOUSE, RON Ron "Stack" Stackhouse D – R. 6'3", 210 lbs. b: Haliburton, Ont., 8/26/1949. Oakland's 2nd choice, 18th overall, in 1969 Amateur Draft.

Season	Club	League	GP	G	A	Pts	AG	AA	APts	PIM	PP	SH	GW	S	%	TGF	PGF	TGA	PGA	+/-	GP	G	A	Pts	PIM	PP	SH	GW
1967-68	Peterborough Petes	OHA	49	13	9	22	....	....	....	88	....	....	....	....	....	....	....	....	....	....	5	0	3	3	20	....	....	....
1968-69	Peterborough Petes	OHA	54	15	31	46	....	....	....	52	....	....	....	....	....	....	....	....	....	....	10	6	4	10	14	....	....	....
1969-70	Providence Reds	AHL	65	1	5	6	....	....	....	37	....	....	....	....	....	....	....	....	....	....	....	....	....	....	....	....	....	....
	Seattle Totems	WHL	....	....	....	....	....	....	....	....	....	....	....	....	....	....	....	....	....	....	5	0	0	0	0	....	....	....
1970-71	**California Golden Seals**	**NHL**	**78**	**8**	**24**	**32**	**8**	**21**	**29**	**73**	**3**	**0**	**2**	**135**	**5.9**	**109**	**28**	**140**	**31**	**–28**	....	....	....	....	....	....	....	....
1971-72	**California Golden Seals**	**NHL**	**5**	**1**	**3**	**4**	**1**	**3**	**4**	**6**	**0**	**0**	**0**	**13**	**7.7**	**9**	**1**	**12**	**4**	**0**	....	....	....	....	....	....	....	....
	Detroit Red Wings	**NHL**	**74**	**5**	**25**	**30**	**5**	**23**	**28**	**83**	**1**	**0**	**0**	**117**	**4.3**	**103**	**18**	**113**	**20**	**–8**	....	....	....	....	....	....	....	....
1972-73	**Detroit Red Wings**	**NHL**	**78**	**5**	**29**	**34**	**5**	**24**	**29**	**82**	**0**	**0**	**0**	**129**	**3.9**	**109**	**8**	**102**	**23**	**+22**	....	....	....	....	....	....	....	....
1973-74	**Detroit Red Wings**	**NHL**	**33**	**2**	**14**	**16**	**2**	**12**	**14**	**33**	**0**	**0**	**0**	**46**	**4.3**	**57**	**10**	**49**	**3**	**+1**	....	....	....	....	....	....	....	....
	Pittsburgh Penguins	**NHL**	**36**	**4**	**15**	**19**	**4**	**13**	**17**	**33**	**0**	**0**	**1**	**67**	**6.0**	**50**	**7**	**41**	**10**	**+12**	....	....	....	....	....	....	....	....
1974-75	**Pittsburgh Penguins**	**NHL**	**72**	**15**	**45**	**60**	**14**	**35**	**49**	**52**	**6**	**1**	**0**	**152**	**9.9**	**135**	**46**	**102**	**26**	**+13**	**9**	**2**	**6**	**8**	**10**	**1**	**0**	**0**
1975-76	**Pittsburgh Penguins**	**NHL**	**80**	**11**	**60**	**71**	**10**	**47**	**57**	**76**	**1**	**0**	**2**	**228**	**4.8**	**162**	**50**	**120**	**27**	**+19**	**3**	**0**	**0**	**0**	**0**	**0**	**0**	**0**
1976-77	**Pittsburgh Penguins**	**NHL**	**80**	**7**	**34**	**41**	**7**	**28**	**35**	**72**	**3**	**1**	**0**	**219**	**3.2**	**136**	**34**	**118**	**27**	**+11**	**3**	**2**	**1**	**3**	**0**	**0**	**0**	**0**
1977-78	**Pittsburgh Penguins**	**NHL**	**50**	**5**	**15**	**20**	**5**	**12**	**17**	**36**	**3**	**0**	**1**	**115**	**4.3**	**68**	**15**	**87**	**18**	**–16**	....	....	....	....	....	....	....	....
1978-79	**Pittsburgh Penguins**	**NHL**	**75**	**10**	**33**	**43**	**9**	**25**	**34**	**54**	**3**	**1**	**1**	**173**	**5.8**	**123**	**25**	**99**	**22**	**+21**	**7**	**0**	**0**	**0**	**4**	**0**	**0**	**0**
1979-80	**Pittsburgh Penguins**	**NHL**	**78**	**6**	**27**	**33**	**5**	**21**	**26**	**36**	**2**	**0**	**1**	**166**	**3.6**	**116**	**17**	**123**	**40**	**+16**	**5**	**1**	**0**	**1**	**18**	**1**	**0**	**0**
1980-81	**Pittsburgh Penguins**	**NHL**	**74**	**6**	**29**	**35**	**5**	**20**	**25**	**86**	**2**	**0**	**1**	**127**	**4.7**	**111**	**29**	**136**	**43**	**–11**	**4**	**0**	**1**	**1**	**6**	**0**	**0**	**0**
1981-82	**Pittsburgh Penguins**	**NHL**	**76**	**2**	**19**	**21**	**2**	**13**	**15**	**102**	**0**	**0**	**0**	**95**	**2.1**	**91**	**14**	**134**	**46**	**–11**	**1**	**0**	**0**	**0**	**0**	**0**	**0**	**0**
	NHL Totals		**889**	**87**	**372**	**459**	**82**	**297**	**379**	**824**	**24**	**3**	**9**	**1782**	**4.9**	**1379**	**302**	**1376**	**340**		**32**	**5**	**8**	**13**	**38**	**2**	**0**	**0**

OHA Second All-Star Team (1969)

Played in NHL All-Star Game (1980)

Traded to **Detroit** by **California** for Tom Webster, October 22, 1971. Traded to **Pittsburgh** by **Detroit** for Jack Lynch and Jim Rutherford, January 18, 1974.

• STAIOS, STEVE Steve Staios D – R. 6', 185 lbs. b: Hamilton, Ont., 7/28/1973. St. Louis' 1st choice, 27th overall, in 1991 Entry Draft.

Season	Club	League	GP	G	A	Pts	AG	AA	APts	PIM	PP	SH	GW	S	%	TGF	PGF	TGA	PGA	+/-	GP	G	A	Pts	PIM	PP	SH	GW
1990-91	Niagara Falls Thunder	OHL	66	17	29	46	....	....	....	115	....	....	....	....	....	....	....	....	....	....	12	2	3	5	10	....	....	....
1991-92	Niagara Falls Thunder	OHL	65	11	42	53	....	....	....	122	....	....	....	....	....	....	....	....	....	....	17	7	8	15	27	....	....	....
1992-93	Niagara Falls Thunder	OHL	12	4	14	18	....	....	....	30	....	....	....	....	....	....	....	....	....	....	....	....	....	....	....	....	....	....
	Sudbury Wolves	OHL	53	13	44	57	....	....	....	67	....	....	....	....	....	....	....	....	....	....	11	5	6	11	22	....	....	....
1993-94	Peoria Rivermen	IHL	38	3	9	12	....	....	....	42	....	....	....	....	....	....	....	....	....	....	....	....	....	....	....	....	....	....
1994-95	Peoria Rivermen	IHL	60	3	13	16	....	....	....	64	....	....	....	....	....	....	....	....	....	....	6	0	0	0	10	....	....	....
1995-96	Peoria Rivermen	IHL	6	0	1	1	....	....	....	14	....	....	....	....	....	....	....	....	....	....	....	....	....	....	....	....	....	....
	Worcester IceCats	AHL	57	1	11	12	....	....	....	114	....	....	....	....	....	....	....	....	....	....	....	....	....	....	....	....	....	....
	Boston Bruins	**NHL**	**12**	**0**	**0**	**0**	**0**	**0**	**0**	**4**	**0**	**0**	**0**	**4**	**0.0**	**0**	**0**	**5**	**0**	**–5**	**3**	**0**	**0**	**0**	**0**	**0**	**0**	**0**
	Providence Bruins	AHL	7	1	4	5	....	....	....	8	....	....	....	....	....	....	....	....	....	....	....	....	....	....	....	....	....	....
1996-97	**Boston Bruins**	**NHL**	**54**	**3**	**8**	**11**	**3**	**7**	**10**	**71**	**0**	**0**	**0**	**56**	**5.4**	**28**	**1**	**58**	**5**	**–26**	....	....	....	....	....	....	....	....
	Vancouver Canucks	**NHL**	**9**	**0**	**6**	**6**	**0**	**5**	**5**	**20**	**0**	**0**	**0**	**10**	**0.0**	**7**	**0**	**6**	**1**	**+2**	....	....	....	....	....	....	....	....
1997-98	**Vancouver Canucks**	**NHL**	**77**	**3**	**4**	**7**	**4**	**4**	**8**	**134**	**0**	**0**	**1**	**45**	**6.7**	**29**	**0**	**35**	**3**	**–3**	....	....	....	....	....	....	....	....
	NHL Totals		**152**	**6**	**18**	**24**	**7**	**16**	**23**	**229**	**0**	**0**	**1**	**115**	**5.2**	**64**	**1**	**104**	**9**		**3**	**0**	**0**	**0**	**0**	**0**	**0**	**0**

Traded to **Boston** by **St. Louis** with Kevin Sawyer for Steve Leach, March 8, 1996. Claimed on waivers by **Vancouver** from **Boston**, March 18, 1997.

• STAJDUHAR, NICK Nick Stajduhar D – L. 6'3", 200 lbs. b: Kitchener, Ont., 12/6/1974. Edmonton's 2nd choice, 16th overall, in 1990 Entry Draft.

Season	Club	League	GP	G	A	Pts	AG	AA	APts	PIM	PP	SH	GW	S	%	TGF	PGF	TGA	PGA	+/-	GP	G	A	Pts	PIM	PP	SH	GW
1990-91	London Knights	OHL	66	3	12	15	....	....	....	51	....	....	....	....	....	....	....	....	....	....	7	0	0	0	2	....	....	....
1991-92	London Knights	OHL	66	6	15	21	....	....	....	62	....	....	....	....	....	....	....	....	....	....	10	1	4	5	10	....	....	....
1992-93	London Knights	OHL	49	15	45	60	....	....	....	58	....	....	....	....	....	....	....	....	....	....	12	4	11	15	10	....	....	....
1993-94	London Knights	OHL	52	34	52	86	....	....	....	58	....	....	....	....	....	....	....	....	....	....	5	0	2	2	8	....	....	....
	Canada	WJC A	7	1	4	5	....	....	....	8	....	....	....	....	....	....	....	....	....	....	....	....	....	....	....	....	....	....
1994-95	Cape Breton Oilers	AHL	54	12	26	38	....	....	....	55	....	....	....	....	....	....	....	....	....	....	....	....	....	....	....	....	....	....
1995-96	Canada	Nat Team	46	7	21	28	....	....	....	60	....	....	....	....	....	....	....	....	....	....	....	....	....	....	....	....	....	....
	Edmonton Oilers	**NHL**	**2**	**0**	**0**	**0**	**0**	**0**	**0**	**4**	**0**	**0**	**0**	**1**	**0.0**	**2**	**0**	**0**	**0**	**+2**	....	....	....	....	....	....	....	....
	Cape Breton Oilers	AHL	8	2	0	2	....	....	....	11	....	....	....	....	....	....	....	....	....	....	....	....	....	....	....	....	....	....
1996-97	Hamilton Bulldogs	AHL	11	1	2	3	....	....	....	2	....	....	....	....	....	....	....	....	....	....	....	....	....	....	....	....	....	....
	Quebec Rafales	IHL	7	1	3	4	....	....	....	2	....	....	....	....	....	....	....	....	....	....	....	....	....	....	....	....	....	....
	Pensacola Ice Pilots	ECHL	30	0	15	24	....	....	....	32	....	....	....	....	....	....	....	....	....	....	12	1	6	7	34	....	....	....
1997-98	Fort Wayne Komets	IHL	15	2	0	2	....	....	....	27	....	....	....	....	....	....	....	....	....	....	....	....	....	....	....	....	....	....
	Pensacola Ice Pilots	ECHL	19	4	8	12	....	....	....	36	....	....	....	....	....	....	....	....	....	....	19	5	21	26	10	....	....	....
	NHL Totals		**2**	**0**	**0**	**0**	**0**	**0**	**0**	**4**	**0**	**0**	**0**	**1**	**0.0**	**2**	**0**	**0**	**0**		....	....	....	....	....	....	....	....

OHL First All-Star Team (1994)

• STAMLER, LORNE Lorne Stamler LW – L. 6', 190 lbs. b: Winnipeg, Man., 8/9/1951. Los Angeles' 7th choice, 103rd overall, in 1971 Amateur Draft.

Season	Club	League	GP	G	A	Pts	AG	AA	APts	PIM	PP	SH	GW	S	%	TGF	PGF	TGA	PGA	+/-	GP	G	A	Pts	PIM	PP	SH	GW
1968-69	Toronto Marlboros	OHA	25	2	3	5	....	....	....	14	....	....	....	....	....	....	....	....	....	....	1	0	0	0	0	....	....	....
1969-70	Toronto Marlboros	OHA	51	6	12	18	....	....	....	32	....	....	....	....	....	....	....	....	....	....	....	....	....	....	....	....	....	....
1970-71	Michigan Tech Huskies	WCHA	32	8	5	13	....	....	....	8	....	....	....	....	....	....	....	....	....	....	....	....	....	....	....	....	....	....
1971-72	Michigan Tech Huskies	WCHA	32	20	12	32	....	....	....	20	....	....	....	....	....	....	....	....	....	....	....	....	....	....	....	....	....	....
1972-73	Michigan Tech Huskies	WCHA	37	11	17	28	....	....	....	22	....	....	....	....	....	....	....	....	....	....	....	....	....	....	....	....	....	....
1973-74	Michigan Tech Huskies	WCHA	39	26	30	56	....	....	....	36	....	....	....	....	....	....	....	....	....	....	....	....	....	....	....	....	....	....
1974-75	Springfield Indians	AHL	43	16	9	25	....	....	....	5	....	....	....	....	....	....	....	....	....	....	17	5	8	13	8	....	....	....
1975-76	Fort Worth Texans	CHL	76	33	33	66	....	....	....	12	....	....	....	....	....	....	....	....	....	....	....	....	....	....	....	....	....	....
1976-77	**Los Angeles Kings**	**NHL**	**7**	**2**	**1**	**3**	**2**	**1**	**3**	**2**	**0**	**0**	**0**	**8**	**25.0**	**3**	**0**	**3**	**0**	**0**	....	....	....	....	....	....	....	....
	Fort Worth Texans	CHL	48	19	21	40	....	....	....	12	....	....	....	....	....	....	....	....	....	....	5	*4	2	6	0	....	....	....
1977-78	**Los Angeles Kings**	**NHL**	**2**	**0**	**0**	**0**	**0**	**0**	**0**	**0**	**0**	**0**	**0**	**1**	**0.0**	**0**	**0**	**0**	**0**	**0**	....	....	....	....	....	....	....	....
	Springfield Indians	AHL	70	18	34	52	....	....	....	4	....	....	....	....	....	....	....	....	....	....	....	....	....	....	....	....	....	....
1978-79	**Toronto Maple Leafs**	**NHL**	**45**	**4**	**3**	**7**	**4**	**2**	**6**	**2**	**0**	**0**	**1**	**31**	**12.9**	**9**	**1**	**27**	**13**	**–6**	....	....	....	....	....	....	....	....
	New Brunswick Hawks	AHL	14	9	1	10	....	....	....	4	....	....	....	....	....	....	....	....	....	....	5	2	1	3	9	....	....	....
1979-80	**Winnipeg Jets**	**NHL**	**62**	**8**	**7**	**15**	**7**	**5**	**12**	**12**	**0**	**0**	**0**	**89**	**9.0**	**23**	**0**	**59**	**7**	**–29**	....	....	....	....	....	....	....	....
	Tulsa Oilers	CHL	6	8	3	11	....	....	....	0	....	....	....	....	....	....	....	....	....	....	....	....	....	....	....	....	....	....
1980-81	Indianapolis Checkers	CHL	42	7	6	13	....	....	....	25	....	....	....	....	....	....	....	....	....	....	....	....	....	....	....	....	....	....
1981-82	Indianapolis Checkers	CHL	53	5	7	12	....	....	....	8	....	....	....	....	....	....	....	....	....	....	13	4	2	6	0	....	....	....
1982-83	Indianapolis Checkers	CHL	38	4	4	8	....	....	....	0	....	....	....	....	....	....	....	....	....	....	13	2	0	2	0	....	....	....
1983-84	Indianapolis Checkers	CHL	15	3	2	5	....	....	....	0	....	....	....	....	....	....	....	....	....	....	....	....	....	....	....	....	....	....
	NHL Totals		**116**	**14**	**11**	**25**	**13**	**8**	**21**	**16**	**0**	**0**	**1**	**129**	**10.9**	**35**	**1**	**89**	**20**		....	....	....	....	....	....	....	....

WCHA Second All-Star Team (1974)

Traded to **Toronto** by **LA Kings** with Dave Hutchison for Brian Glennie, Scott Garland, Kurt Walker and Toronto's 2nd round choice (Mark Hardy) in 1979 Entry Draft, June 14, 1978. Claimed by **Winnipeg** from **Toronto** in Expansion Draft, June 13, 1979. Signed as a free agent by **NY Islanders**, October 8, 1980.

• STANDING, GEORGE George Standing RW – R. 5'10", 190 lbs. b: Toronto, Ont., 8/3/1941.

Season	Club	League	GP	G	A	Pts	AG	AA	APts	PIM	PP	SH	GW	S	%	TGF	PGF	TGA	PGA	+/-	GP	G	A	Pts	PIM	PP	SH	GW
1957-58	Toronto Marlboros	OHA	2	1	0	1	....	....	....	0	....	....	....	....	....	....	....	....	....	....	....	....	....	....	....	....	....	....
1958-59	Toronto Marlboros	OHA	26	1	2	3	....	....	....	18	....	....	....	....	....	....	....	....	....	....	....	....	....	....	....	....	....	....
1959-60	Toronto Marlboros	OHA	45	1	1	2	....	....	....	4	....	....	....	....	....	....	....	....	....	....	4	0	0	0	0	....	....	....
1960-61	Toronto Marlboros	OHA	48	18	24	42	....	....	....	69	....	....	....	....	....	....	....	....	....	....	....	....	....	....	....	....	....	....
1961-62	North Bay Trappers	EPHL	1	0	0	0	....	....	....	2	....	....	....	....	....	....	....	....	....	....	....	....	....	....	....	....	....	....
	Guelph Royals	OHA	10	5	5	10	....	....	....	18	....	....	....	....	....	....	....	....	....	....	....	....	....	....	....	....	....	....
	St. Catharines Teepees	OHA	39	17	19	36	....	....	....	25	....	....	....	....	....	....	....	....	....	....	6	0	2	2	20	....	....	....
1962-63			DID NOT PLAY																									
1963-64	Nashville Dixie Flyers	EHL	72	20	33	53	....	....	....	39	....	....	....	....	....	....	....	....	....	....	3	0	0	0	0	....	....	....
1964-65	Nashville Dixie Flyers	EHL	67	54	34	88	....	....	....	79	....	....	....	....	....	....	....	....	....	....	13	4	10	14	4	....	....	....
1965-66	Nashville Dixie Flyers	EHL	72	30	36	66	....	....	....	36	....	....	....	....	....	....	....	....	....	....	11	1	5	0	4	....	....	....
1966-67	Nashville Dixie Flyers	EHL	72	47	40	87	....	....	....	46	....	....	....	....	....	....	....	....	....	....	14	*14	8	*22	4	....	....	....
1967-68	**Minnesota North Stars**	**NHL**	**2**	**0**	**0**	**0**	**0**	**0**	**0**	**0**	**0**	**0**	**0**	**1**	**0.0**	**1**	**1**	**1**	**0**	**–1**	....	....	....	....	....	....	....	....
	Memphis South Stars	CHL	63	20	15	35	....	....	....	34	....	....	....	....	....	....	....	....	....	....	3	0	3	3	0	....	....	....

Season	Club	League	GP	G	A	Pts	AG	AA	APts	PIM	PP	SH	GW	S	%	TGF	PGF	TGA	PGA	+/–	GP	G	A	Pts	PIM	PP	SH	GW
			REGULAR SEASON																		PLAYOFFS							
1968-69	Memphis South Stars	CHL	13	3	3	6	....	....	....	14	....	....	....	....	....	....	....	....	....	....	....	....	....	....	....	....	....	....
	Jacksonville Rockets	EHL	36	15	20	35	....	....	....	6	....	....	....	....	....	....	....	....	....	....	4	1	2	3	0	....	....	....
1969-70	Nashville Dixie Flyers	EHL	74	30	45	75	....	....	....	35	....	....	....	....	....	....	....	....	....	....	....	....	....	....	....	....	....	....
1970-71	Nashville Dixie Flyers	EHL	36	10	15	25	....	....	....	7	....	....	....	....	....	....	....	....	....	....	4	1	2	3	0	....	....	....
1971-72	St. Petersburg Suns	EHL	15	3	7	10	....	....	....	6	....	....	....	....	....	....	....	....	....	....	....	....	....	....	....	....	....	....
	NHL Totals		**2**	**0**	**0**	**0**	**0**	**0**	**0**	**0**	**0**	**0**	**0**	**1**	**0.0**	**1**	**1**	**1**	**0**		....	....	....	....	....	....	....	....

EHL South First All-Star Team (1965) • EHL South Second All-Star Team (1967)

Signed as a free agent by **Minnesota**, September, 1967.

• STANFIELD, FRED

Fred Stanfield LW – L. 5′10″, 185 lbs. b: Toronto, Ont., 5/4/1944.

Season	Club	League	GP	G	A	Pts	AG	AA	APts	PIM	PP	SH	GW	S	%	TGF	PGF	TGA	PGA	+/–	GP	G	A	Pts	PIM	PP	SH	GW
1961-62	St. Catharines Teepees	OHA	49	11	15	26	....	....	....	19	....	....	....	....	....	....	....	....	....	....	6	0	0	0	2	....	....	....
1962-63	St. Catharines Teepees	OHA	48	28	39	67	....	....	....	25	....	....	....	....	....	....	....	....	....	....	....	....	....	....	....	....	....	....
1963-64	St. Catharines Teepees	OHA	56	34	75	109	....	....	....	29	....	....	....	....	....	....	....	....	....	....	13	15	12	27	4	....	....	....
1964-65	**Chicago Black Hawks**	**NHL**	**58**	**7**	**10**	**17**	**9**	**11**	**20**	**14**	....	....	....	....	....	....	....	....	....	....	**14**	**2**	**1**	**3**	**2**	....	....	....
1965-66	**Chicago Black Hawks**	**NHL**	**39**	**2**	**2**	**4**	**2**	**2**	**4**	**2**	....	....	....	....	....	....	....	....	....	....	**5**	**0**	**0**	**0**	**2**	....	....	....
	St. Louis Braves	CHL	24	7	11	18	....	....	....	2	....	....	....	....	....	....	....	....	....	....	....	....	....	....	....	....	....	....
1966-67	**Chicago Black Hawks**	**NHL**	**10**	**1**	**0**	**1**	**1**	**0**	**1**	**0**	....	....	....	....	....	....	....	....	....	....	**1**	**0**	**0**	**0**	**0**	....	....	....
	St. Louis Braves	CHL	37	20	21	41	....	....	....	10	....	....	....	....	....	....	....	....	....	....	....	....	....	....	....	....	....	....
1967-68	**Boston Bruins**	**NHL**	**73**	**20**	**44**	**64**	**25**	**46**	**71**	**10**	**3**	**0**	**1**	**215**	**9.3**	**95**	**30**	**57**	**1**	**+9**	**4**	**0**	**1**	**1**	**0**	**0**	**0**	**0**
1968-69	**Boston Bruins**	**NHL**	**71**	**25**	**29**	**54**	**28**	**27**	**55**	**22**	**6**	**0**	**1**	**199**	**12.6**	**80**	**26**	**63**	**5**	**–4**	**10**	**2**	**2**	**4**	**0**	**1**	**0**	**0**
1969-70	**Boston Bruins**	**NHL**	**73**	**23**	**35**	**58**	**27**	**35**	**62**	**14**	**13**	**0**	**3**	**254**	**9.1**	**107**	**63**	**50**	**13**	**+7**	**14**	**4**	**12**	**16**	**6**	**2**	**0**	**0**
1970-71	**Boston Bruins**	**NHL**	**75**	**24**	**52**	**76**	**25**	**46**	**71**	**12**	**8**	**0**	**3**	**267**	**9.0**	**153**	**74**	**48**	**1**	**+32**	**7**	**3**	**4**	**7**	**0**	**1**	**0**	**0**
1971-72	**Boston Bruins**	**NHL**	**78**	**23**	**56**	**79**	**25**	**51**	**76**	**12**	**5**	**1**	**4**	**168**	**13.7**	**112**	**48**	**45**	**1**	**+20**	**15**	**7**	**9**	**16**	**0**	**1**	**0**	**0**
1972-73	**Boston Bruins**	**NHL**	**78**	**20**	**58**	**78**	**20**	**49**	**69**	**10**	**7**	**0**	**2**	**214**	**9.3**	**142**	**63**	**68**	**1**	**+12**	**5**	**1**	**1**	**2**	**0**	**0**	**0**	**0**
1973-74	**Minnesota North Stars**	**NHL**	**71**	**16**	**28**	**44**	**16**	**24**	**40**	**10**	**3**	**0**	**2**	**218**	**7.3**	**73**	**24**	**69**	**6**	**–14**	....	....	....	....	....	....	....	....
1974-75	**Minnesota North Stars**	**NHL**	**40**	**8**	**18**	**26**	**7**	**14**	**21**	**12**	**2**	**0**	**1**	**107**	**7.5**	**40**	**22**	**35**	**3**	**–14**	....	....	....	....	....	....	....	....
	Buffalo Sabres	**NHL**	**32**	**12**	**21**	**33**	**11**	**17**	**28**	**4**	**6**	**0**	**2**	**77**	**15.6**	**54**	**27**	**20**	**2**	**+9**	**17**	**2**	**4**	**6**	**0**	**0**	**0**	**0**
1975-76	**Buffalo Sabres**	**NHL**	**80**	**18**	**30**	**48**	**17**	**24**	**41**	**4**	**2**	**1**	**3**	**112**	**16.1**	**78**	**28**	**60**	**15**	**+5**	**9**	**0**	**1**	**1**	**0**	**0**	**0**	**0**
1976-77	**Buffalo Sabres**	**NHL**	**79**	**9**	**14**	**23**	**9**	**11**	**20**	**6**	**2**	**0**	**2**	**69**	**13.0**	**37**	**19**	**20**	**0**	**–2**	**5**	**0**	**0**	**0**	**0**	**0**	**0**	**0**
1977-78	**Buffalo Sabres**	**NHL**	**57**	**3**	**8**	**11**	**3**	**7**	**10**	**2**	**0**	**0**	**0**	**38**	**7.9**	**21**	**12**	**21**	**4**	**–8**	....	....	....	....	....	....	....	....
1978-79	Hershey Bears	AHL	50	19	41	60	....	....	....	4	....	....	....	....	....	....	....	....	....	....	....	....	....	....	....	....	....	....
	NHL Totals		**914**	**211**	**405**	**616**	**225**	**364**	**589**	**134**	**57**	**2**	**24**	**1938**	**10.9**	**992**	**436**	**556**	**52**		**106**	**21**	**35**	**56**	**10**	**5**	**0**	**0**

Traded to **Boston** by **Chicago** with Phil Esposito and Ken Hodge for Gilles Marotte, Pit Martin and Jack Norris, May 15, 1967. Traded to **Minnesota** by **Boston** for Gilles Gilbert, May 22, 1973. Traded to **Buffalo** by **Minnesota** for Norm Gratton and Buffalo's 3rd round choice (Ron Zanussi) in 1976 Amateur Draft, January 27, 1975.

• STANFIELD, JIM

Jim Stanfield C/RW – L. 5′10″, 160 lbs. b: Toronto, Ont., 1/1/1947.

Season	Club	League	GP	G	A	Pts	AG	AA	APts	PIM	PP	SH	GW	S	%	TGF	PGF	TGA	PGA	+/–	GP	G	A	Pts	PIM	PP	SH	GW
1964-65	St. Catharines Teepees	OHA	3	0	1	1	....	....	....	0	....	....	....	....	....	....	....	....	....	....	....	....	....	....	....	....	....	....
1965-66	St. Catharines Teepees	OHA	45	7	10	17	....	....	....	42	....	....	....	....	....	....	....	....	....	....	2	0	0	0	4	....	....	....
1966-67	London Nationals	OHA	45	32	19	51	....	....	....	53	....	....	....	....	....	....	....	....	....	....	6	6	2	8	0	....	....	....
1967-68	Dallas Black Hawks	CHL	24	5	5	10	....	....	....	6	....	....	....	....	....	....	....	....	....	....	....	....	....	....	....	....	....	....
1968-69	Dallas Black Hawks	CHL	66	24	15	39	....	....	....	16	....	....	....	....	....	....	....	....	....	....	11	5	3	8	2	....	....	....
1969-70	**Los Angeles Kings**	**NHL**	**1**	**0**	**0**	**0**	**0**	**0**	**0**	**0**	**0**	**0**	**0**	**0**	**0.0**	**0**	**0**	**0**	**0**	**0**	....	....	....	....	....	....	....	....
	Dallas Black Hawks	CHL	55	18	11	29	....	....	....	8	....	....	....	....	....	....	....	....	....	....	....	....	....	....	....	....	....	....
	Springfield Kings	AHL	18	11	5	16	....	....	....	2	....	....	....	....	....	....	....	....	....	....	14	*8	9	*17	2	....	....	....
1970-71	**Los Angeles Kings**	**NHL**	**2**	**0**	**0**	**0**	**0**	**0**	**0**	**0**	**0**	**0**	**0**	**8**	**0.0**	**2**	**1**	**0**	**0**	**+1**	....	....	....	....	....	....	....	....
	Springfield Kings	AHL	45	7	19	26	....	....	....	22	....	....	....	....	....	....	....	....	....	....	11	1	0	1	6	....	....	....
1971-72	**Los Angeles Kings**	**NHL**	**4**	**0**	**1**	**1**	**0**	**1**	**1**	**0**	**0**	**0**	**0**	**7**	**0.0**	**0**	**0**	**1**	**0**	**–1**	....	....	....	....	....	....	....	....
	Springfield Kings	AHL	64	30	26	56	....	....	....	11	....	....	....	....	....	....	....	....	....	....	3	0	0	0	0	....	....	....
1972-73	San Diego Gulls	WHL	21	9	14	23	....	....	....	4	....	....	....	....	....	....	....	....	....	....	....	....	....	....	....	....	....	....
	Portland Buckaroos	WHL	47	15	8	23	....	....	....	7	....	....	....	....	....	....	....	....	....	....	....	....	....	....	....	....	....	....
1973-74	San Diego Gulls	WHL	32	4	14	18	....	....	....	2	....	....	....	....	....	....	....	....	....	....	....	....	....	....	....	....	....	....
	Denver Spurs	WHL	35	15	21	36	....	....	....	4	....	....	....	....	....	....	....	....	....	....	....	....	....	....	....	....	....	....
1974-75	Spokane Jets	WIHL	47	45	57	*102	....	....	....	6	....	....	....	....	....	....	....	....	....	....	....	....	....	....	....	....	....	....
1975-76	Spokane Jets	WIHL	33	33	21	54	....	....	....	2	....	....	....	....	....	....	....	....	....	....	....	....	....	....	....	....	....	....
	Buffalo Norsemen	NAHL	27	10	19	29	....	....	....	0	....	....	....	....	....	....	....	....	....	....	4	1	1	2	0	....	....	....
1976-77	Spokane Jets	WIHL	....	10	16	26	....	....	....	4	....	....	....	....	....	....	....	....	....	....	....	....	....	....	....	....	....	....
	NHL Totals		**7**	**0**	**1**	**1**	**0**	**1**	**1**	**0**	**0**	**0**	**0**	**15**	**0.0**	**2**	**1**	**1**	**0**		....	....	....	....	....	....	....	....

Traded to **LA Kings** by **Chicago** with Gilles Marotte and Denis Dejordy for Bryan Campbell, Bill White and Gerry Desjardins, February 20, 1970. Traded to **Portland** (WHL) by **LA Kings** with Mike Keeler and Glen Toner for John VanHorlick, December, 1972. Traded to **Philadelphia** by **Portland** (WHL) for cash, May, 1973. Traded to **San Diego** (WHL) by **Philadelphia** with Tom Trevalyn and Bob Hurlburt for Bruce Cowick, May, 1973. Traded to **St. Louis** (Denver-WHL) by **San Diego** (WHL) for Bernie MacNeil, January, 1974.

• STANKIEWICZ, MYRON

Myron Stankiewicz LW – L. 5′11″, 185 lbs. b: Kitchener, Ont., 12/4/1935.

Season	Club	League	GP	G	A	Pts	AG	AA	APts	PIM	PP	SH	GW	S	%	TGF	PGF	TGA	PGA	+/–	GP	G	A	Pts	PIM	PP	SH	GW
1952-53	Kitchener Greenshirts	OHA	18	0	3	3	....	....	....	2	....	....	....	....	....	....	....	....	....	....	....	....	....	....	....	....	....	....
1953-54	Barrie Flyers	OHA	19	0	6	6	....	....	....	0	....	....	....	....	....	....	....	....	....	....	....	....	....	....	....	....	....	....
1954-55	Kitchener–Galt	OHA	40	8	10	18	....	....	....	52	....	....	....	....	....	....	....	....	....	....	4	0	0	0	9	....	....	....
1955-56	Toledo–Indianapolis	IHL	54	16	10	26	....	....	....	76	....	....	....	....	....	....	....	....	....	....	....	....	....	....	....	....	....	....
1956-57	Toledo–Indianapolis	IHL	58	16	16	32	....	....	....	52	....	....	....	....	....	....	....	....	....	....	6	0	0	0	4	....	....	....
1957-58	Indianapolis Chiefs	IHL	63	25	36	61	....	....	....	58	....	....	....	....	....	....	....	....	....	....	11	2	4	6	12	....	....	....
1958-59	Edmonton Flyers	WHL	35	4	11	15	....	....	....	19	....	....	....	....	....	....	....	....	....	....	....	....	....	....	....	....	....	....
	Quebec Aces	QHL	20	4	2	6	....	....	....	6	....	....	....	....	....	....	....	....	....	....	....	....	....	....	....	....	....	....
1959-60	Quebec Aces	AHL	62	10	11	21	....	....	....	66	....	....	....	....	....	....	....	....	....	....	....	....	....	....	....	....	....	....
1960-61	Sudbury Wolves	EPHL	37	9	10	19	....	....	....	27	....	....	....	....	....	....	....	....	....	....	....	....	....	....	....	....	....	....
	Hershey Bears	AHL	33	2	11	13	....	....	....	39	....	....	....	....	....	....	....	....	....	....	....	....	....	....	....	....	....	....
1961-62	Hershey Bears	AHL	70	20	33	53	....	....	....	66	....	....	....	....	....	....	....	....	....	....	7	2	2	4	4	....	....	....
1962-63	Hershey Bears	AHL	68	21	43	64	....	....	....	30	....	....	....	....	....	....	....	....	....	....	15	3	4	7	21	....	....	....
1963-64	Hershey Bears	AHL	72	25	41	66	....	....	....	65	....	....	....	....	....	....	....	....	....	....	6	1	1	2	21	....	....	....
1964-65	Hershey Bears	AHL	72	28	36	64	....	....	....	59	....	....	....	....	....	....	....	....	....	....	15	2	6	8	16	....	....	....
1965-66	Hershey Bears	AHL	72	28	30	58	....	....	....	53	....	....	....	....	....	....	....	....	....	....	3	1	0	1	2	....	....	....
1966-67	Hershey Bears	AHL	70	8	23	31	....	....	....	42	....	....	....	....	....	....	....	....	....	....	4	1	0	1	5	....	....	....
1967-68	Hershey Bears	AHL	65	23	27	50	....	....	....	49	....	....	....	....	....	....	....	....	....	....	1	0	0	0	0	....	....	....
1968-69	**St. Louis Blues**	**NHL**	**16**	**0**	**2**	**2**	**0**	**2**	**2**	**11**	**0**	**0**	**0**	**17**	**0.0**	**6**	**0**	**8**	**0**	**–2**	....	....	....	....	....	....	....	....
	Omaha Knights	CHL	5	1	2	3	....	....	....	8	....	....	....	....	....	....	....	....	....	....	....	....	....	....	....	....	....	....
	Philadelphia Flyers	**NHL**	**19**	**0**	**5**	**5**	**0**	**5**	**5**	**25**	**0**	**0**	**0**	**43**	**0.0**	**7**	**0**	**18**	**0**	**–11**	**1**	**0**	**0**	**0**	**0**	**0**	**0**	**0**
	Quebec Aces	AHL	15	6	6	12	....	....	....	5	....	....	....	....	....	....	....	....	....	....	15	5	8	13	10	....	....	....
	NHL Totals		**35**	**0**	**7**	**7**	**0**	**7**	**7**	**36**	**0**	**0**	**0**	**60**	**0.0**	**13**	**0**	**26**	**0**		**1**	**0**	**0**	**0**	**0**	**0**	**0**	**0**

Traded to **Quebec** (QHL) by **Detroit** (Edmonton-WHL) for Roger Dejordy, January, 1959. Traded to **Hershey** (AHL) by **Quebec** (AHL) with Al Millar for Claude Dufour, June, 1960. Claimed by **St. Louis** from **Hershey** (AHL) in Inter-League Draft, June 11, 1968. Claimed on waivers by **Philadelphia** from **St. Louis**, January 16, 1969.

• STANLEY, ALLAN

Allan "Snowshoes" Stanley D – L. 6′1″, 170 lbs. b: Timmins, Ont., 3/1/1926. **HHOF**

Season	Club	League	GP	G	A	Pts	AG	AA	APts	PIM	PP	SH	GW	S	%	TGF	PGF	TGA	PGA	+/–	GP	G	A	Pts	PIM	PP	SH	GW
1943-44	Boston Olympics	EHL	40	10	32	42	....	....	....	10	....	....	....	....	....	....	....	....	....	....	....	....	....	....	....	....	....	....
1944-45	Porcupine Combines	NOHA	....	5	4	9	....	....	....	7	....	....	....	....	....	....	....	....	....	....	....	....	....	....	....	....	....	....
1945-46	Boston Olympics	EHL	30	8	15	23	....	....	....	35	....	....	....	....	....	....	....	....	....	....	....	....	....	....	....	....	....	....
1946-47	Providence Reds	AHL	54	8	13	21	....	....	....	32	....	....	....	....	....	....	....	....	....	....	....	....	....	....	....	....	....	....
1947-48	Boston Olympics	QSHL	1	0	0	0	....	....	....	0	....	....	....	....	....	....	....	....	....	....	....	....	....	....	....	....	....	....
	Providence Reds	AHL	68	9	32	41	....	....	....	81	....	....	....	....	....	....	....	....	....	....	5	0	0	0	4	....	....	....
1948-49	**New York Rangers**	**NHL**	**40**	**2**	**8**	**10**	**3**	**13**	**16**	**22**	....	....	....	....	....	....	....	....	....	....	....	....	....	....	....	....	....	....
	Providence Reds	AHL	23	7	16	23	....	....	....	24	....	....	....	....	....	....	....	....	....	....	....	....	....	....	....	....	....	....
1949-50	**New York Rangers**	**NHL**	**55**	**4**	**4**	**8**	**5**	**5**	**10**	**58**	....	....	....	....	....	....	....	....	....	....	**12**	**2**	**5**	**7**	**10**	....	....	....
1950-51	**New York Rangers**	**NHL**	**70**	**7**	**14**	**21**	**9**	**18**	**27**	**75**	....	....	....	....	....	....	....	....	....	....	....	....	....	....	....	....	....	....
1951-52	**New York Rangers**	**NHL**	**50**	**5**	**14**	**19**	**7**	**18**	**25**	**52**	....	....	....	....	....	....	....	....	....	....	....	....	....	....	....	....	....	....
1952-53	**New York Rangers**	**NHL**	**70**	**5**	**12**	**17**	**8**	**17**	**25**	**52**	....	....	....	....	....	....	....	....	....	....	....	....	....	....	....	....	....	....

Season	Club	League	GP	G	A	Pts	AG	AA	APts	PIM	PP	SH	GW	S	%	TGF	PGF	TGA	PGA	+/–	GP	G	A	Pts	PIM	PP	SH	GW
			REGULAR SEASON																		PLAYOFFS							
1953-54	**New York Rangers**	**NHL**	**10**	**0**	**2**	**2**	**0**	**3**	**3**	**11**	....	....	....	....	....	....	....	....	....	....	....	....	....	....	....	....	....	....
	Vancouver Canucks	WHL	47	6	30	36	....	....	....	43	....	....	....	....	....	....	....	....	....	....	13	2	5	7	10	....	....	....
1954-55	**New York Rangers**	**NHL**	**12**	**0**	**1**	**1**	**0**	**1**	**1**	**2**	....	....	....	....	....	....	....	....	....	....	....	....	....	....	....	....	....	....
	Chicago Black Hawks	**NHL**	**52**	**10**	**15**	**25**	**14**	**19**	**33**	**22**	....	....	....	....	....	....	....	....	....	....	....	....	....	....	....	....	....	....
1955-56	**Chicago Black Hawks**	**NHL**	**59**	**4**	**14**	**18**	**6**	**17**	**23**	**70**	....	....	....	....	....	....	....	....	....	....	....	....	....	....	....	....	....	....
1956-57	**Boston Bruins**	**NHL**	**60**	**6**	**25**	**31**	**8**	**29**	**37**	**45**	....	....	....	....	....	....	....	....	....	....	....	....	....	....	....	....	....	....
1957-58	**Boston Bruins**	**NHL**	**69**	**6**	**25**	**31**	**8**	**27**	**35**	**37**	....	....	....	....	....	....	....	....	....	....	**12**	**1**	**3**	**4**	**6**	....	....	....
1958-59	**Toronto Maple Leafs**	**NHL**	**70**	**1**	**22**	**23**	**1**	**23**	**24**	**47**	....	....	....	....	....	....	....	....	....	....	**12**	**0**	**3**	**3**	**2**	....	....	....
1959-60	**Toronto Maple Leafs**	**NHL**	**64**	**10**	**23**	**33**	**12**	**24**	**36**	**22**	....	....	....	....	....	....	....	....	....	....	**10**	**2**	**3**	**5**	**2**	....	....	....
1960-61	**Toronto Maple Leafs**	**NHL**	**68**	**9**	**25**	**34**	**11**	**25**	**36**	**42**	....	....	....	....	....	....	....	....	....	....	**5**	**0**	**3**	**3**	**0**	....	....	....
1961-62	**Toronto Maple Leafs**	**NHL**	**60**	**9**	**26**	**35**	**11**	**26**	**37**	**24**	....	....	....	....	....	....	....	....	....	....	**12**	**0**	**3**	**3**	**6**	....	....	....
1962-63	**Toronto Maple Leafs**	**NHL**	**61**	**4**	**15**	**19**	**5**	**16**	**21**	**22**	....	....	....	....	....	....	....	....	....	....	**10**	**1**	**6**	**7**	**8**	....	....	....
1963-64	**Toronto Maple Leafs**	**NHL**	**70**	**6**	**21**	**27**	**8**	**23**	**31**	**60**	....	....	....	....	....	....	....	....	....	....	**14**	**1**	**6**	**7**	**20**	....	....	....
1964-65	**Toronto Maple Leafs**	**NHL**	**64**	**2**	**15**	**17**	**3**	**16**	**19**	**30**	....	....	....	....	....	....	....	....	....	....	**6**	**0**	**1**	**1**	**12**	....	....	....
1965-66	**Toronto Maple Leafs**	**NHL**	**59**	**4**	**14**	**18**	**5**	**14**	**19**	**35**	....	....	....	....	....	....	....	....	....	....	**1**	**0**	**0**	**0**	**0**	....	....	....
1966-67	**Toronto Maple Leafs**	**NHL**	**53**	**1**	**12**	**13**	**1**	**12**	**13**	**20**	....	....	....	....	....	....	....	....	....	....	**12**	**0**	**2**	**2**	**10**	....	....	....
1967-68	**Toronto Maple Leafs**	**NHL**	**64**	**1**	**13**	**14**	**1**	**14**	**15**	**16**	**0**	**0**	**0**	**61**	**1.6**	**62**	**0**	**63**	**7**	**+6**	....	....	....	....	....	....	....	....
1968-69	**Philadelphia Flyers**	**NHL**	**64**	**4**	**13**	**17**	**4**	**12**	**16**	**28**	**2**	**0**	**0**	**75**	**5.3**	**62**	**29**	**49**	**12**	**–4**	**3**	**0**	**1**	**1**	**4**	**0**	**0**	**0**
	NHL Totals		**1244**	**100**	**333**	**433**	**130**	**372**	**502**	**792**	**2**	**0**	**0**	**136**	**73.5**	**124**	**29**	**112**	**19**		**109**	**7**	**36**	**43**	**80**	**0**	**0**	**0**

EHL First All-Star Team (1944) • WHL First All-Star Team (1954) • NHL Second All-Star Team (1960, 1961, 1966)

Played in NHL All-Star Game (1955, 1957, 1960, 1962, 1963, 1967, 1968)

Traded to **NY Rangers** by **Providence** (AHL) for Ed Kullman, Elwyn Morris, cash and future considerations (Ken Davies, June, 1949), December, 1948. Traded to **Chicago** by **NY Rangers** with Nick Mickoski and Dick Lamoureux for Bill Gadsby and Pete Conacher, November 23, 1954. Traded to **Boston** by **Chicago** for cash, October 8, 1956. Traded to **Toronto** by **Boston** for Jim Morrison, October, 1958. Claimed by **Philadelphia** (Quebec - AHL) from **Toronto** in Reverse Draft, June 13, 1968.

• STANLEY, DARYL

Daryl Stanley D/LW – L. 6′2″, 200 lbs. b: Winnipeg, Man., 12/2/1962.

Season	Club	League	GP	G	A	Pts	AG	AA	APts	PIM	PP	SH	GW	S	%	TGF	PGF	TGA	PGA	+/–	GP	G	A	Pts	PIM	PP	SH	GW
1979-80	New Westminster Bruins	WHL	64	2	12	14	....	....	....	110	....	....	....	....	....	....	....	....	....	....	....	....	....	....	....	....	....	....
1980-81	New Westminster Bruins	WHL	66	7	27	34	....	....	....	127	....	....	....	....	....	....	....	....	....	....	....	....	....	....	....	....	....	....
1981-82	Saskatoon Blades	WHL	65	7	25	32	....	....	....	175	....	....	....	....	....	....	....	....	....	....	5	1	1	2	14	....	....	....
	Maine Mariners	AHL	....	....	....	....	....	....	....	....	....	....	....	....	....	....	....	....	....	....	2	0	2	2	2	....	....	....
1982-83	Maine Mariners	AHL	44	2	5	7	....	....	....	95	....	....	....	....	....	....	....	....	....	....	2	0	0	0	0	....	....	....
	Toledo Goaldiggers	IHL	5	0	2	2	....	....	....	2	....	....	....	....	....	....	....	....	....	....	....	....	....	....	....	....	....	....
1983-84	**Philadelphia Flyers**	**NHL**	**23**	**1**	**4**	**5**	**1**	**3**	**4**	**71**	**0**	**0**	**1**	**14**	**7.1**	**23**	**0**	**22**	**3**	**+4**	**3**	**0**	**0**	**0**	**19**	**0**	**0**	**0**
	Springfield Indians	AHL	51	4	10	14	....	....	....	122	....	....	....	....	....	....	....	....	....	....	....	....	....	....	....	....	....	....
1984-85	Hershey Bears	AHL	24	0	7	7	....	....	....	33	....	....	....	....	....	....	....	....	....	....	....	....	....	....	....	....	....	....
1985-86	**Philadelphia Flyers**	**NHL**	**33**	**0**	**2**	**2**	**0**	**1**	**1**	**69**	**0**	**0**	**0**	**7**	**0.0**	**6**	**0**	**12**	**1**	**–5**	**1**	**0**	**0**	**0**	**2**	**0**	**0**	**0**
	Hershey Bears	AHL	27	0	4	4	....	....	....	88	....	....	....	....	....	....	....	....	....	....	....	....	....	....	....	....	....	....
1986-87	**Philadelphia Flyers**	**NHL**	**33**	**1**	**2**	**3**	**1**	**1**	**2**	**76**	**0**	**0**	**1**	**22**	**4.5**	**15**	**0**	**11**	**2**	**+6**	**13**	**0**	**0**	**0**	**9**	**0**	**0**	**0**
1987-88	**Vancouver Canucks**	**NHL**	**57**	**2**	**7**	**9**	**2**	**5**	**7**	**151**	**0**	**0**	**0**	**27**	**7.4**	**36**	**1**	**65**	**18**	**–12**	....	....	....	....	....	....	....	....
1988-89	**Vancouver Canucks**	**NHL**	**20**	**3**	**1**	**4**	**3**	**1**	**4**	**14**	**0**	**0**	**1**	**12**	**25.0**	**6**	**0**	**3**	**0**	**+3**	....	....	....	....	....	....	....	....
1989-90	**Vancouver Canucks**	**NHL**	**23**	**1**	**1**	**2**	**1**	**1**	**2**	**27**	**0**	**0**	**1**	**7**	**14.3**	**7**	**0**	**9**	**0**	**–2**	....	....	....	....	....	....	....	....
	NHL Totals		**189**	**8**	**17**	**25**	**8**	**12**	**20**	**408**	**0**	**0**	**4**	**89**	**9.0**	**93**	**1**	**122**	**24**		**17**	**0**	**0**	**0**	**30**	**0**	**0**	**0**

Signed as a free agent by **Philadelphia**, October 9, 1981. Traded to **Vancouver** by **Philadelphia** with Darren Jensen for Wendell Young and Vancouver's 3rd round choice (Kimbi Daniels) in 1980 Entry Draft, August 31, 1987.

• STANTON, PAUL

Paul Stanton D – R. 6′1″, 195 lbs. b: Boston, MA, 6/22/1967. Pittsburgh's 8th choice, 149th overall, in 1985 Entry Draft.

Season	Club	League	GP	G	A	Pts	AG	AA	APts	PIM	PP	SH	GW	S	%	TGF	PGF	TGA	PGA	+/–	GP	G	A	Pts	PIM	PP	SH	GW
1984-85	Catholic Memorial High	H.S.	20	16	21	37	....	....	....	17	....	....	....	....	....	....	....	....	....	....	....	....	....	....	....	....	....	....
1985-86	University of Wisconsin	WCHA	36	4	6	10	....	....	....	16	....	....	....	....	....	....	....	....	....	....	....	....	....	....	....	....	....	....
1986-87	University of Wisconsin	WCHA	41	5	17	22	....	....	....	70	....	....	....	....	....	....	....	....	....	....	....	....	....	....	....	....	....	....
1987-88	University of Wisconsin	WCHA	45	9	38	47	....	....	....	98	....	....	....	....	....	....	....	....	....	....	....	....	....	....	....	....	....	....
1988-89	University of Wisconsin	WCHA	45	7	29	36	....	....	....	126	....	....	....	....	....	....	....	....	....	....	....	....	....	....	....	....	....	....
1989-90	Muskegon Lumberjacks	IHL	77	5	27	32	....	....	....	61	....	....	....	....	....	....	....	....	....	....	15	2	4	6	21	....	....	....
1990-91	**Pittsburgh Penguins**	**NHL**	**75**	**5**	**18**	**23**	**5**	**14**	**19**	**40**	**1**	**0**	**1**	**72**	**6.9**	**78**	**7**	**91**	**31**	**+11**	**22**	**1**	**2**	**3**	**24**	**0**	**0**	**0**
1991-92	**Pittsburgh Penguins**	**NHL**	**54**	**2**	**8**	**10**	**2**	**6**	**8**	**62**	**0**	**0**	**0**	**70**	**2.9**	**45**	**8**	**56**	**11**	**–8**	**21**	**1**	**7**	**8**	**42**	**0**	**0**	**0**
1992-93	**Pittsburgh Penguins**	**NHL**	**77**	**4**	**12**	**16**	**3**	**8**	**11**	**97**	**2**	**0**	**1**	**106**	**3.8**	**81**	**15**	**72**	**13**	**+7**	**1**	**0**	**1**	**1**	**0**	**0**	**0**	**0**
1993-94	**Boston Bruins**	**NHL**	**71**	**3**	**7**	**10**	**3**	**5**	**8**	**54**	**1**	**0**	**1**	**136**	**2.2**	**56**	**11**	**60**	**8**	**–7**	....	....	....	....	....	....	....	....
1994-95	Providence Bruins	AHL	8	4	4	8	....	....	....	4	....	....	....	....	....	....	....	....	....	....	....	....	....	....	....	....	....	....
	New York Islanders	**NHL**	**18**	**0**	**4**	**4**	**0**	**6**	**6**	**9**	**0**	**0**	**0**	**28**	**0.0**	**11**	**5**	**13**	**1**	**–6**	....	....	....	....	....	....	....	....
	Denver Grizzlies	IHL	11	2	6	8	....	....	....	15	....	....	....	....	....	....	....	....	....	....	....	....	....	....	....	....	....	....
	United States	WC-A	6	2	1	3	....	....	....	4	....	....	....	....	....	....	....	....	....	....	....	....	....	....	....	....	....	....
1995-96	Adler Mannheim	Germany	47	12	24	36	....	....	....	88	....	....	....	....	....	....	....	....	....	....	9	2	5	7	8	....	....	....
	United States	WC-A	7	0	0	0	....	....	....	4	....	....	....	....	....	....	....	....	....	....	....	....	....	....	....	....	....	....
1996-97	Adler Mannheim	Germany	50	5	26	31	....	....	....	64	....	....	....	....	....	....	....	....	....	....	9	2	4	6	26	....	....	....
1997-98	Adler Mannheim	EuroHL	5	3	0	3	....	....	....	31	....	....	....	....	....	....	....	....	....	....	....	....	....	....	....	....	....	....
	Adler Mannheim	Germany	47	10	25	35	....	....	....	72	....	....	....	....	....	....	....	....	....	....	10	4	6	10	22	....	....	....
	United States	WC-A	5	0	0	0	....	....	....	0	....	....	....	....	....	....	....	....	....	....	....	....	....	....	....	....	....	....
	NHL Totals		**295**	**14**	**49**	**63**	**13**	**39**	**52**	**262**	**4**	**0**	**3**	**412**	**3.4**	**271**	**46**	**292**	**64**		**44**	**2**	**10**	**12**	**66**	**0**	**0**	**0**

WCHA Second All-Star Team (1988) • NCAA West First All-American Team (1988) • WCHA First All-Star Team (1989)

Traded to **Boston** by **Pittsburgh** for Boston's 3rd round choice (Greg Crozier) in 1994 Entry Draft, October 8, 1993. Traded to **NY Islanders** by **Boston** for NY Islanders' 8th round choice (later traded to Ottawa — Ottawa selected Ray Schultz) in 1995 Entry Draft, February 10, 1995.

• STAPLETON, BRIAN

Brian Stapleton RW – R. 6′2″, 190 lbs. b: Fort Erie, Ont., 12/25/1951.

Season	Club	League	GP	G	A	Pts	AG	AA	APts	PIM	PP	SH	GW	S	%	TGF	PGF	TGA	PGA	+/–	GP	G	A	Pts	PIM	PP	SH	GW
1971-72	Brown University	ECAC	25	4	9	13	....	....	....	23	....	....	....	....	....	....	....	....	....	....	....	....	....	....	....	....	....	....
1972-73	Brown University	ECAC	25	12	12	24	....	....	....	54	....	....	....	....	....	....	....	....	....	....	....	....	....	....	....	....	....	....
1973-74	Brown University	ECAC	23	8	18	26	....	....	....	40	....	....	....	....	....	....	....	....	....	....	....	....	....	....	....	....	....	....
1974-75	Fort Wayne–Dayton	IHL	69	14	19	33	....	....	....	66	....	....	....	....	....	....	....	....	....	....	14	2	2	4	4	....	....	....
1975-76	**Washington Capitals**	**NHL**	**1**	**0**	**0**	**0**	**0**	**0**	**0**	**0**	**0**	**0**	**0**	**0**	**0.0**	**0**	**0**	**2**	**0**	**–2**	....	....	....	....	....	....	....	....
	Dayton Gems	IHL	74	24	34	60	....	....	....	69	....	....	....	....	....	....	....	....	....	....	15	7	8	15	4	....	....	....
1976-77	Dayton Gems	IHL	68	20	46	66	....	....	....	21	....	....	....	....	....	....	....	....	....	....	4	2	0	2	0	....	....	....
	NHL Totals		**1**	**0**	**0**	**0**	**0**	**0**	**0**	**0**	**0**	**0**	**0**	**0**	**0.0**	**0**	**0**	**2**	**0**		....	....	....	....	....	....	....	....

Signed as a free agent by **Washington** to three-game tryout contract, October, 1975.

• STAPLETON, MIKE

Mike Stapleton C – R. 5′10″, 183 lbs. b: Sarnia, Ont., 5/5/1966. Chicago's 7th choice, 132nd overall, in 1984 Entry Draft.

Season	Club	League	GP	G	A	Pts	AG	AA	APts	PIM	PP	SH	GW	S	%	TGF	PGF	TGA	PGA	+/–	GP	G	A	Pts	PIM	PP	SH	GW
1983-84	Cornwall Royals	OHL	70	24	45	69	....	....	....	94	....	....	....	....	....	....	....	....	....	....	3	1	2	3	4	....	....	....
1984-85	Cornwall Royals	OHL	56	41	44	85	....	....	....	68	....	....	....	....	....	....	....	....	....	....	9	2	4	6	23	....	....	....
1985-86	Cornwall Royals	OHL	56	39	64	103	....	....	....	74	....	....	....	....	....	....	....	....	....	....	6	2	3	5	2	....	....	....
	Canada	WJC-A	7	3	3	6	....	....	....	6	....	....	....	....	....	....	....	....	....	....	....	....	....	....	....	....	....	....
1986-87	Canada	Nat-Team	21	2	4	6	....	....	....	4	....	....	....	....	....	....	....	....	....	....	....	....	....	....	....	....	....	....
	Chicago Blackhawks	**NHL**	**39**	**3**	**6**	**9**	**3**	**4**	**7**	**6**	**0**	**0**	**0**	**54**	**5.6**	**17**	**0**	**32**	**6**	**–9**	**4**	**0**	**0**	**0**	**2**	**0**	**0**	**0**
1987-88	**Chicago Blackhawks**	**NHL**	**53**	**2**	**9**	**11**	**2**	**6**	**8**	**59**	**0**	**0**	**1**	**50**	**4.0**	**19**	**8**	**39**	**18**	**–10**	....	....	....	....	....	....	....	....
	Saginaw Hawks	IHL	31	11	19	30	....	....	....	52	....	....	....	....	....	....	....	....	....	....	10	5	6	11	10	....	....	....
1988-89	**Chicago Blackhawks**	**NHL**	**7**	**0**	**1**	**1**	**0**	**1**	**1**	**7**	**0**	**0**	**0**	**6**	**0.0**	**2**	**0**	**3**	**0**	**–1**	....	....	....	....	....	....	....	....
	Saginaw Hawks	IHL	69	21	47	68	....	....	....	162	....	....	....	....	....	....	....	....	....	....	6	1	3	4	4	....	....	....
1989-90	Indianapolis Ice	IHL	16	5	10	15	....	....	....	6	....	....	....	....	....	....	....	....	....	....	13	9	10	19	38	....	....	....
1990-91	**Chicago Blackhawks**	**NHL**	**7**	**0**	**1**	**1**	**0**	**1**	**1**	**2**	**0**	**0**	**0**	**6**	**0.0**	**1**	**0**	**1**	**0**	**0**	....	....	....	....	....	....	....	....
	Indianapolis Ice	IHL	75	29	52	81	....	....	....	76	....	....	....	....	....	....	....	....	....	....	7	1	4	5	0	....	....	....
1991-92	**Chicago Blackhawks**	**NHL**	**19**	**4**	**4**	**8**	**4**	**3**	**7**	**8**	**1**	**0**	**0**	**32**	**12.5**	**9**	**2**	**9**	**2**	**0**	....	....	....	....	....	....	....	....
	Indianapolis Ice	IHL	50	18	40	58	....	....	....	65	....	....	....	....	....	....	....	....	....	....	....	....	....	....	....	....	....	....
1992-93	**Pittsburgh Penguins**	**NHL**	**78**	**4**	**9**	**13**	**3**	**6**	**9**	**10**	**0**	**1**	**1**	**78**	**5.1**	**20**	**6**	**35**	**13**	**–8**	**4**	**0**	**0**	**0**	**0**	**0**	**0**	**0**

			REGULAR SEASON																		PLAYOFFS							
Season	Club	League	GP	G	A	Pts	AG	AA	APts	PIM	PP	SH	GW	S	%	TGF	PGF	TGA	PGA	+/–	GP	G	A	Pts	PIM	PP	SH	GW
1993-94	**Pittsburgh Penguins**	**NHL**	**58**	**7**	**4**	**11**	**7**	**3**	**10**	**18**	**3**	**0**	**0**	**59**	**11.9**	**17**	**8**	**29**	**16**	**–4**	....	....	....	....	....	....	....	....
	Edmonton Oilers	**NHL**	**23**	**5**	**9**	**14**	**5**	**7**	**12**	**28**	**1**	**0**	**0**	**43**	**11.6**	**20**	**5**	**17**	**1**	**–1**	....	....	....	....	....	....	....	....
1994-95	**Edmonton Oilers**	**NHL**	**46**	**6**	**11**	**17**	**11**	**16**	**27**	**21**	**3**	**0**	**2**	**59**	**10.2**	**27**	**9**	**36**	**6**	**–12**	....	....	....	....	....	....	....	....
1995-96	**Winnipeg Jets**	**NHL**	**58**	**10**	**14**	**24**	**10**	**11**	**21**	**37**	**3**	**1**	**0**	**91**	**11.0**	**43**	**10**	**54**	**17**	**–4**	**6**	**0**	**0**	**0**	**21**	**0**	**0**	**0**
1996-97	**Phoenix Coyotes**	**NHL**	**55**	**4**	**11**	**15**	**4**	**10**	**14**	**36**	**2**	**0**	**1**	**74**	**5.4**	**23**	**9**	**29**	**11**	**–4**	**7**	**0**	**0**	**0**	**14**	**0**	**0**	**0**
1997-98	**Phoenix Coyotes**	**NHL**	**64**	**5**	**5**	**10**	**6**	**5**	**11**	**36**	**1**	**1**	**1**	**69**	**7.2**	**20**	**5**	**30**	**11**	**–4**	**6**	**0**	**0**	**0**	**2**	**0**	**0**	**0**
	NHL Totals		**507**	**50**	**84**	**134**	**55**	**73**	**128**	**268**	**14**	**3**	**6**	**621**	**8.1**	**218**	**62**	**314**	**101**		**27**	**0**	**0**	**0**	**39**	**0**	**0**	**0**

Signed as a free agent by **Pittsburgh**, September 30, 1992. Claimed on waivers by **Edmonton** from **Pittsburgh**, February 19, 1994. Signed as a free agent by **Winnipeg**, August 18, 1995. Transferred to **Phoenix** after **Winnipeg** franchise relocated, July 1, 1996.

• STAPLETON, PAT

Pat Stapleton D – L. 5'8", 180 lbs. b: Sarnia, Ont., 7/4/1940.

Season	Club	League	GP	G	A	Pts	AG	AA	APts	PIM	PP	SH	GW	S	%	TGF	PGF	TGA	PGA	+/–	GP	G	A	Pts	PIM	PP	SH	GW
1957-58	Sarnia Legionnaires	Jr. B	STATISTICS NOT AVAILABLE																									
1958-59	St. Catharines Teepees	OHA	49	10	26	36	....	....	....	18	....	....	....	....	....	....	....	....	....	....	7	0	0	0	6	....	....	....
1959-60	St. Catharines Teepees	OHA	47	12	35	47	....	....	....	83	....	....	....	....	....	....	....	....	....	....	17	5	12	17	32	....	....	....
	Buffalo Bisons	AHL	1	0	0	0	....	....	....	2	....	....	....	....	....	....	....	....	....	....	....	....	....	....	....	....	....	....
1960-61	Sault Ste. Marie Thunderbirds	EPHL	59	5	43	48	....	....	....	22	....	....	....	....	....	....	....	....	....	....	12	1	8	9	2	....	....	....
1961-62	**Boston Bruins**	**NHL**	**69**	**2**	**5**	**7**	**2**	**5**	**7**	**42**	....	....	....	....	....	....	....	....	....	....	....	....	....	....	....	....	....	....
1962-63	**Boston Bruins**	**NHL**	**21**	**0**	**3**	**3**	**0**	**3**	**3**	**8**	....	....	....	....	....	....	....	....	....	....	....	....	....	....	....	....	....	....
	Kingston Frontenacs	EPHL	49	10	26	36	....	....	....	92	....	....	....	....	....	....	....	....	....	....	5	4	2	6	12	....	....	....
1963-64	Portland Buckaroos	WHL	70	5	44	49	....	....	....	80	....	....	....	....	....	....	....	....	....	....	5	1	6	7	0	....	....	....
1964-65	Portland Buckaroos	WHL	70	29	57	86	....	....	....	61	....	....	....	....	....	....	....	....	....	....	10	3	4	7	16	....	....	....
1965-66	**Chicago Black Hawks**	**NHL**	**55**	**4**	**30**	**34**	**5**	**30**	**35**	**52**	....	....	....	....	....	....	....	....	....	....	**6**	**2**	**3**	**5**	**4**	....	....	....
	St. Louis Braves	CHL	14	2	4	6	....	....	....	6	....	....	....	....	....	....	....	....	....	....	....	....	....	....	....	....	....	....
1966-67	**Chicago Black Hawks**	**NHL**	**70**	**3**	**31**	**34**	**4**	**32**	**36**	**54**	....	....	....	....	....	....	....	....	....	....	**6**	**1**	**1**	**2**	**12**	....	....	....
1967-68	**Chicago Black Hawks**	**NHL**	**67**	**4**	**34**	**38**	**5**	**36**	**41**	**34**	**0**	**0**	**0**	**38**	**10.5**	**98**	**12**	**90**	**8**	**+4**	**11**	**0**	**4**	**4**	**4**	**0**	**0**	**0**
1968-69	**Chicago Black Hawks**	**NHL**	**75**	**6**	**50**	**56**	**7**	**47**	**54**	**44**	**0**	**0**	**0**	**112**	**5.4**	**160**	**41**	**124**	**28**	**+23**	....	....	....	....	....	....	....	....
1969-70	**Chicago Black Hawks**	**NHL**	**49**	**4**	**38**	**42**	**5**	**38**	**43**	**28**	**1**	**0**	**1**	**106**	**3.8**	**97**	**24**	**63**	**8**	**+18**	....	....	....	....	....	....	....	....
1970-71	**Chicago Black Hawks**	**NHL**	**76**	**7**	**44**	**51**	**7**	**39**	**46**	**30**	**4**	**0**	**0**	**130**	**5.4**	**161**	**44**	**84**	**16**	**+49**	**18**	**3**	**14**	**17**	**4**	**1**	**1**	**0**
1971-72	**Chicago Black Hawks**	**NHL**	**78**	**3**	**38**	**41**	**3**	**35**	**38**	**47**	**2**	**0**	**2**	**133**	**2.3**	**150**	**41**	**89**	**21**	**+41**	**8**	**2**	**2**	**4**	**4**	**2**	**0**	**0**
1972-73	Canada	Summit	7	0	0	0	....	....	....	6	....	....	....	....	....	....	....	....	....	....	....	....	....	....	....	....	....	....
	Chicago Black Hawks	**NHL**	**75**	**10**	**21**	**31**	**10**	**18**	**28**	**14**	**2**	**0**	**2**	**128**	**7.8**	**112**	**26**	**89**	**22**	**+19**	**16**	**2**	***15**	**17**	**10**	**1**	**0**	**0**
1973-74	Chicago Cougars	WHA	78	6	52	58	....	....	....	44	....	....	....	....	....	....	....	....	....	....	12	0	13	13	36	....	....	....
1974-75	Canada	Summit	8	0	3	3	....	....	....	12	....	....	....	....	....	....	....	....	....	....	....	....	....	....	....	....	....	....
	Chicago Cougars	WHA	68	4	30	34	....	....	....	38	....	....	....	....	....	....	....	....	....	....	....	....	....	....	....	....	....	....
1975-76	Indianapolis Racers	WHA	80	4	40	44	....	....	....	48	....	....	....	....	....	....	....	....	....	....	7	0	2	2	2	....	....	....
1976-77	Indianapolis Racers	WHA	81	8	45	53	....	....	....	29	....	....	....	....	....	....	....	....	....	....	9	2	6	8	0	....	....	....
1977-78	Cincinnati Stingers	WHA	65	4	45	49	....	....	....	28	....	....	....	....	....	....	....	....	....	....	....	....	....	....	....	....	....	....
	NHL Totals		**635**	**43**	**294**	**337**	**48**	**283**	**331**	**353**	**9**	**0**	**5**	**647**	**6.6**	**778**	**188**	**539**	**103**		**65**	**10**	**39**	**49**	**38**	**4**	**1**	**0**
	Other Major League Totals		372	26	212	238	....	....	....	187	....	....	....	....	....	....	....	....	....	....	28	2	21	23	38	....	....	....

WHL Second All-Star Team (1964) • WHL First All-Star Team (1965) • Won Hal Laycoe Cup (WHL Top Defenseman) (1965) • NHL Second All-Star Team (1966, 1971, 1972) • WHA First All-Star Team (1974) • Won Dennis A. Murphy Trophy (WHA Top Defenseman) (1974) • WHA Second All-Star Team (1976)

Played in NHL All-Star Game (1967, 1969, 1971, 1972)

Claimed by **Boston** from **Chicago** in Intra-League Draft, June 13, 1961. Traded to **Toronto** by **Boston** with Orland Kurtenbach and Andy Hebenton for Ron Stewart, June 8, 1965. Claimed by **Chicago** from **Toronto** in Intra-League Draft, June 9, 1965. Selected by **LA Sharks** (WHA) in 1972 WHA General Player Draft, February 12, 1972. WHA rights traded to **Chicago** (WHA) by **LA Sharks** (WHA) for cash, September, 1973. Selected by **Indianapolis** (WHA) from **Chicago** (WHA) in WHA Dispersal Draft, June, 1975. WHA rights transferred to **Cincinnati** (WHA) in Special Dispersal Auction after **Indianapolis** (WHA) refused to honour his contract, November, 1977.

• STARIKOV, SERGEI

Sergei Starikov D – L. 5'10", 225 lbs. b: Chelyabinski, Soviet Union, 12/4/1958. New Jersey's 7th choice, 152nd overall, in 1989 Entry Draft.

Season	Club	League	GP	G	A	Pts	AG	AA	APts	PIM	PP	SH	GW	S	%	TGF	PGF	TGA	PGA	+/–	GP	G	A	Pts	PIM	PP	SH	GW
1976-77	Traktor Chelyabinsk	USSR	35	2	4	6	....	....	....	28	....	....	....	....	....	....	....	....	....	....	....	....	....	....	....	....	....	....
	Soviet Union	WJC-A	7	1	2	3	....	....	....	8	....	....	....	....	....	....	....	....	....	....	....	....	....	....	....	....	....	....
1977-78	Traktor Chelyabinsk	USSR	36	3	5	8	....	....	....	26	....	....	....	....	....	....	....	....	....	....	....	....	....	....	....	....	....	....
	Soviet Union	WJC-A	7	1	5	6	....	....	....	2	....	....	....	....	....	....	....	....	....	....	....	....	....	....	....	....	....	....
1978-79	Traktor Chelyabinsk	USSR	44	6	8	14	....	....	....	34	....	....	....	....	....	....	....	....	....	....	....	....	....	....	....	....	....	....
	USSR	Chal Cup	3	0	1	1	....	....	....	0	....	....	....	....	....	....	....	....	....	....	....	....	....	....	....	....	....	....
	Soviet Wings	SuperS	4	1	3	4	....	....	....	4	....	....	....	....	....	....	....	....	....	....	....	....	....	....	....	....	....	....
	Soviet Union	WEC-A	1	0	1	1	....	....	....	2	....	....	....	....	....	....	....	....	....	....	....	....	....	....	....	....	....	....
1979-80	CSKA Moscow	USSR	39	10	8	18	....	....	....	14	....	....	....	....	....	....	....	....	....	....	....	....	....	....	....	....	....	....
	CSKA Moscow	SuperS	5	0	2	2	....	....	....	0	....	....	....	....	....	....	....	....	....	....	....	....	....	....	....	....	....	....
	Soviet Union	Olympics	7	1	6	7	....	....	....	0	....	....	....	....	....	....	....	....	....	....	....	....	....	....	....	....	....	....
1980-81	CSKA Moscow	USSR	49	4	8	12	....	....	....	26	....	....	....	....	....	....	....	....	....	....	....	....	....	....	....	....	....	....
1981-82	CSKA Moscow	USSR	40	1	4	5	....	....	....	14	....	....	....	....	....	....	....	....	....	....	....	....	....	....	....	....	....	....
1982-83	CSKA Moscow	USSR	44	6	14	20	....	....	....	14	....	....	....	....	....	....	....	....	....	....	....	....	....	....	....	....	....	....
	USSR	SuperS	5	1	0	1	....	....	....	2	....	....	....	....	....	....	....	....	....	....	....	....	....	....	....	....	....	....
	Soviet Union	WEC-A	10	1	4	5	....	....	....	0	....	....	....	....	....	....	....	....	....	....	....	....	....	....	....	....	....	....
1983-84	CSKA Moscow	USSR	44	11	7	18	....	....	....	20	....	....	....	....	....	....	....	....	....	....	....	....	....	....	....	....	....	....
	Soviet Union	Olympics	7	1	1	2	....	....	....	2	....	....	....	....	....	....	....	....	....	....	....	....	....	....	....	....	....	....
1984-85	Soviet Union	C Cup	6	0	3	3	....	....	....	2	....	....	....	....	....	....	....	....	....	....	....	....	....	....	....	....	....	....
	CSKA Moscow	USSR	40	3	10	13	....	....	....	12	....	....	....	....	....	....	....	....	....	....	....	....	....	....	....	....	....	....
	Soviet Union	WEC-A	10	0	4	4	....	....	....	2	....	....	....	....	....	....	....	....	....	....	....	....	....	....	....	....	....	....
1985-86	CSKA Moscow	USSR	37	3	2	5	....	....	....	6	....	....	....	....	....	....	....	....	....	....	....	....	....	....	....	....	....	....
	CSKA Moscow	SuperS	6	0	0	0	....	....	....	0	....	....	....	....	....	....	....	....	....	....	....	....	....	....	....	....	....	....
	Soviet Union	WEC-A	10	0	2	2	....	....	....	0	....	....	....	....	....	....	....	....	....	....	....	....	....	....	....	....	....	....
1986-87	CSKA Moscow	USSR	34	4	2	6	....	....	....	8	....	....	....	....	....	....	....	....	....	....	....	....	....	....	....	....	....	....
	USSR	RV'87	2	0	1	1	....	....	....	0	....	....	....	....	....	....	....	....	....	....	....	....	....	....	....	....	....	....
	Soviet Union	WEC-A	10	4	2	6	....	....	....	8	....	....	....	....	....	....	....	....	....	....	....	....	....	....	....	....	....	....
1987-88	CSKA Moscow	USSR	38	2	11	13	....	....	....	12	....	....	....	....	....	....	....	....	....	....	....	....	....	....	....	....	....	....
	Soviet Union	Olympics	5	0	2	2	....	....	....	4	....	....	....	....	....	....	....	....	....	....	....	....	....	....	....	....	....	....
1988-89	CSKA Moscow	USSR	30	3	3	6	....	....	....	4	....	....	....	....	....	....	....	....	....	....	....	....	....	....	....	....	....	....
	CSKA Moscow	SuperS	5	0	2	2	....	....	....	2	....	....	....	....	....	....	....	....	....	....	....	....	....	....	....	....	....	....
1989-90	**New Jersey Devils**	**NHL**	**16**	**0**	**1**	**1**	**0**	**1**	**1**	**8**	**0**	**0**	**0**	**6**	**0.0**	**11**	**0**	**26**	**7**	**–8**	....	....	....	....	....	....	....	....
	Utica Devils	AHL	43	8	11	19	....	....	....	14	....	....	....	....	....	....	....	....	....	....	4	0	3	3	0	....	....	....
1990-91	Utica Devils	AHL	51	2	7	9	....	....	....	26	....	....	....	....	....	....	....	....	....	....	....	....	....	....	....	....	....	....
1991-92	San Diego Gulls	IHL	70	7	31	38	....	....	....	42	....	....	....	....	....	....	....	....	....	....	4	0	0	0	0	....	....	....
1992-93	San Diego Gulls	IHL	42	0	9	9	....	....	....	12	....	....	....	....	....	....	....	....	....	....	....	....	....	....	....	....	....	....
	NHL Totals		**16**	**0**	**1**	**1**	**0**	**1**	**1**	**8**	**0**	**0**	**0**	**6**	**0.0**	**11**	**0**	**26**	**7**		....	....	....	....	....	....	....	....

• STASTNY, ANTON

Anton Stastny LW – L. 6', 188 lbs. b: Bratislava, Czech., 8/5/1959. Quebec's 4th choice, 83rd overall, in 1979 Entry Draft.

Season	Club	League	GP	G	A	Pts	AG	AA	APts	PIM	PP	SH	GW	S	%	TGF	PGF	TGA	PGA	+/–	GP	G	A	Pts	PIM	PP	SH	GW
1977-78	Slovan Bratislava	Czech.	44	19	17	36	....	....	....	22	....	....	....	....	....	....	....	....	....	....	....	....	....	....	....	....	....	....
	Czechoslovakia	WJC-A	6	4	2	6	....	....	....	4	....	....	....	....	....	....	....	....	....	....	....	....	....	....	....	....	....	....
1978-79	Slovan Bratislava	Czech.	44	32	19	51	....	....	....	38	....	....	....	....	....	....	....	....	....	....	....	....	....	....	....	....	....	....
	Czechoslovakia	WJC-A	6	3	4	7	....	....	....	6	....	....	....	....	....	....	....	....	....	....	....	....	....	....	....	....	....	....
	Czechoslovakia	WEC-A	8	5	1	6	....	....	....	2	....	....	....	....	....	....	....	....	....	....	....	....	....	....	....	....	....	....
1979-80	Slovan Bratislava	Czech.	40	30	30	60	....	....	....	33	....	....	....	....	....	....	....	....	....	....	....	....	....	....	....	....	....	....
	Czechoslovakia	Olympics	6	4	4	8	....	....	....	2	....	....	....	....	....	....	....	....	....	....	....	....	....	....	....	....	....	....
1980-81	**Quebec Nordiques**	**NHL**	**80**	**39**	**46**	**85**	**32**	**32**	**64**	**12**	**12**	**0**	**4**	**177**	**22.0**	**123**	**39**	**80**	**0**	**+4**	**5**	**4**	**3**	**7**	**2**	**2**	**0**	**0**
1981-82	**Quebec Nordiques**	**NHL**	**68**	**26**	**46**	**72**	**21**	**30**	**51**	**16**	**10**	**0**	**4**	**135**	**19.3**	**107**	**43**	**94**	**1**	**–29**	**16**	**5**	**10**	**15**	**10**	**3**	**0**	**0**
1982-83	**Quebec Nordiques**	**NHL**	**79**	**32**	**60**	**92**	**26**	**42**	**68**	**25**	**10**	**0**	**7**	**169**	**18.9**	**136**	**40**	**71**	**0**	**+25**	**4**	**2**	**2**	**4**	**0**	**0**	**0**	**0**
1983-84	**Quebec Nordiques**	**NHL**	**69**	**25**	**37**	**62**	**20**	**25**	**45**	**14**	**7**	**0**	**0**	**145**	**17.2**	**106**	**37**	**57**	**0**	**+12**	**9**	**2**	**5**	**7**	**7**	**0**	**0**	**0**
1984-85	**Quebec Nordiques**	**NHL**	**79**	**38**	**42**	**80**	**31**	**28**	**59**	**30**	**9**	**0**	**3**	**176**	**21.6**	**119**	**29**	**73**	**1**	**+18**	**16**	**3**	**3**	**6**	**6**	**1**	**0**	**1**
1985-86	**Quebec Nordiques**	**NHL**	**74**	**31**	**43**	**74**	**25**	**29**	**54**	**19**	**8**	**0**	**4**	**163**	**19.0**	**107**	**31**	**68**	**0**	**+8**	**3**	**1**	**1**	**2**	**0**	**0**	**0**	**0**
1986-87	**Quebec Nordiques**	**NHL**	**77**	**27**	**35**	**62**	**23**	**25**	**48**	**8**	**6**	**0**	**5**	**172**	**15.7**	**81**	**23**	**55**	**0**	**+3**	**13**	**3**	**8**	**11**	**6**	**0**	**0**	**0**
1987-88	**Quebec Nordiques**	**NHL**	**69**	**27**	**45**	**72**	**23**	**32**	**55**	**14**	**15**	**0**	**4**	**177**	**15.3**	**108**	**62**	**55**	**0**	**–9**	....	....	....	....	....	....	....	....

			REGULAR SEASON																		PLAYOFFS							
Season	Club	League	GP	G	A	Pts	AG	AA	APts	PIM	PP	SH	GW	S	%	TGF	PGF	TGA	PGA	+/–	GP	G	A	Pts	PIM	PP	SH	GW
1988-89	Quebec Nordiques	NHL	55	7	30	37	6	21	27	12	3	0	0	84	8.3	58	26	52	1	–19	....	....	....	....	....	....	....	....
	Halifax Citadels	AHL	16	9	5	14	....	....	....	4	....	....	....	....	....	....	....	....	....	....	....	....	....	....	....	....	....	....
1989-90	HC Fribourg	Switz.	36	25	22	47	....	....	....	....	....	....	....	....	....	....	....	....	....	....	3	3	4	7	....	....	....	....
1990-91	EHC Olten	Switz.	36	26	14	40	....	....	....	....	....	....	....	....	....	....	....	....	....	....	10	10	16	26	....	....	....	....
1991-92	EHC Olten	Switz.	33	20	19	39	....	....	....	66	....	....	....	....	....	....	....	....	....	....	....	....	....	....	....	....	....	....
1992-93			DID NOT PLAY																									
1993-94	Slovan Bratislava	Czech.	11	6	8	14	....	....	....	2	....	....	....	....	....	....	....	....	....	....	....	....	....	....	....	....	....	....
	NHL Totals		650	252	384	636	207	264	471	150	80	0	31	1398	18.0	945	330	605	3		66	20	32	52	31	6	0	1

WJC-A All-Star Team (1978)

• Re-entered NHL draft. Originally Philadelphia's 19th choice, 198th overall, in 1978 Amateur Draft.

• STASTNY, MARIAN

Marian Stastny RW – L. 5'10", 195 lbs. b: Bratislava, Czech., 1/8/1953.

Season	Club	League	GP	G	A	Pts	AG	AA	APts	PIM	PP	SH	GW	S	%	TGF	PGF	TGA	PGA	+/–	GP	G	A	Pts	PIM	PP	SH	GW
1974-75	Slovak Bratislava	Czech.	....	36	27	63	....	....	....	....	....	....	....	....	....	....	....	....	....	....	....	....	....	....	....	....	....	....
	Czechoslovakia	WEC-A	5	3	1	4	....	....	....	0	....	....	....	....	....	....	....	....	....	....	....	....	....	....	....	....	....	....
1975-76	Slovan Bratislava	Czech.	STATISTICS NOT AVAILABLE																									
	Czechoslovakia	WEC-A	8	2	4	6	....	....	....	2	....	....	....	....	....	....	....	....	....	....	....	....	....	....	....	....	....	....
1976-77	Czechoslovakia	C Cup	7	1	4	5	....	....	....	2	....	....	....	....	....	....	....	....	....	....	....	....	....	....	....	....	....	....
	Slovan Bratislava	Czech.	44	28	24	52	....	....	....	....	....	....	....	....	....	....	....	....	....	....	....	....	....	....	....	....	....	....
	Czechoslovakia	WEC-A	10	7	4	11	....	....	....	2	....	....	....	....	....	....	....	....	....	....	....	....	....	....	....	....	....	....
1977-78	Slovan Bratislava	Czech.	44	33	23	56	....	....	....	58	....	....	....	....	....	....	....	....	....	....	....	....	....	....	....	....	....	....
	Czechoslovakia	WEC-A	9	4	5	9	....	....	....	4	....	....	....	....	....	....	....	....	....	....	....	....	....	....	....	....	....	....
1978-79	Slovan Bratislava	Czech.	....	39	*35	*74	....	....	....	....	....	....	....	....	....	....	....	....	....	....	14	12	8	20	....	....	....	....
	Czechoslovakia	WEC-A	8	0	5	5	....	....	....	2	....	....	....	....	....	....	....	....	....	....	....	....	....	....	....	....	....	....
1979-80	Ducla Trenchin	Czech.	13	7	8	15	....	....	....	....	....	....	....	....	....	....	....	....	....	....	....	....	....	....	....	....	....	....
	Slovan Bratislava	Czech.	21	20	15	35	....	....	....	....	....	....	....	....	....	....	....	....	....	....	19	10	11	21	6	....	....	....
	Czechoslovakia	Olympics	6	5	6	11	....	....	....	4	....	....	....	....	....	....	....	....	....	....	....	....	....	....	....	....	....	....
1980-81			DID NOT PLAY																									
1981-82	**Quebec Nordiques**	**NHL**	74	35	54	89	28	36	64	27	13	0	3	176	19.9	124	39	89	4	0	16	3	14	17	5	1	0	0
1982-83	**Quebec Nordiques**	**NHL**	60	36	43	79	30	30	60	32	13	0	3	169	21.3	107	34	53	0	+20	2	0	0	0	0	0	0	0
1983-84	**Quebec Nordiques**	**NHL**	68	20	32	52	16	22	38	26	4	0	5	113	17.7	80	20	59	0	+1	9	2	3	5	2	0	0	1
1984-85	**Quebec Nordiques**	**NHL**	50	7	14	21	6	9	15	4	0	0	1	45	15.6	32	3	28	0	+1	2	0	0	0	0	0	0	0
1985-86	**Toronto Maple Leafs**	**NHL**	70	23	30	53	18	20	38	21	7	0	0	132	17.4	87	24	71	2	–6	3	0	0	0	0	0	0	0
1986-87	HC Sierre	Switz.	....	20	30	50	....	....	....	....	....	....	....	....	....	....	....	....	....	....	....	....	....	....	....	....	....	....
	NHL Totals		322	121	173	294	98	117	215	110	37	0	12	635	19.1	430	120	300	6		32	5	17	22	7	1	0	1

Played in NHL All-Star Game (1983)

Signed as a free agent by **Quebec**, August 26, 1980. Signed as a free agent by **Toronto**, August 12, 1985.

• STASTNY, PETER

Peter Stastny C – L. 6'1", 200 lbs. b: Bratislava, Czech., 9/18/1956.

Season	Club	League	GP	G	A	Pts	AG	AA	APts	PIM	PP	SH	GW	S	%	TGF	PGF	TGA	PGA	+/–	GP	G	A	Pts	PIM	PP	SH	GW
1974-75	Czechoslovakia	WJC-A	....	4	0	4	....	....	....	....	....	....	....	....	....	....	....	....	....	....	....	....	....	....	....	....	....	....
1975-76	Slovan Bratislava	Czech.	32	19	9	28	....	....	....	....	....	....	....	....	....	....	....	....	....	....	....	....	....	....	....	....	....	....
	Czechoslovakia	WJC-A	4	1	1	2	....	....	....	0	....	....	....	....	....	....	....	....	....	....	....	....	....	....	....	....	....	....
	Czechoslovakia	WEC-A	9	8	4	12	....	....	....	0	....	....	....	....	....	....	....	....	....	....	....	....	....	....	....	....	....	....
1976-77	Czechoslovakia	C Cup	7	0	4	4	....	....	....	2	....	....	....	....	....	....	....	....	....	....	....	....	....	....	....	....	....	....
	Slovan Bratislava	Czech.	44	25	27	52	....	....	....	....	....	....	....	....	....	....	....	....	....	....	....	....	....	....	....	....	....	....
	Czechoslovakia	WEC-A	10	3	5	8	....	....	....	0	....	....	....	....	....	....	....	....	....	....	....	....	....	....	....	....	....	....
1977-78	Slovan Bratislava	Czech.	42	29	24	53	....	....	....	28	....	....	....	....	....	....	....	....	....	....	....	....	....	....	....	....	....	....
	Czechoslovakia	WEC-A	10	5	6	11	....	....	....	7	....	....	....	....	....	....	....	....	....	....	....	....	....	....	....	....	....	....
1978-79	Slovan Bratislava	Czech.	39	32	23	55	....	....	....	21	....	....	....	....	....	....	....	....	....	....	....	....	....	....	....	....	....	....
	Czechoslovakia	WEC-A	8	2	3	5	....	....	....	6	....	....	....	....	....	....	....	....	....	....	....	....	....	....	....	....	....	....
1979-80	Slovan Bratislava	Czech.	41	26	26	52	....	....	....	58	....	....	....	....	....	....	....	....	....	....	....	....	....	....	....	....	....	....
	Czechoslovakia	Olympics	6	7	7	14	....	....	....	6	....	....	....	....	....	....	....	....	....	....	....	....	....	....	....	....	....	....
1980-81	**Quebec Nordiques**	**NHL**	77	39	70	109	32	49	81	37	11	2	4	232	16.8	147	49	99	12	+11	5	2	8	10	7	1	0	0
1981-82	**Quebec Nordiques**	**NHL**	80	46	93	139	37	62	99	91	16	3	3	227	20.3	173	65	125	7	–10	12	7	11	18	10	4	0	1
1982-83	**Quebec Nordiques**	**NHL**	75	47	77	124	39	53	92	78	5	0	4	201	23.4	153	40	93	8	+28	4	3	2	5	10	1	0	0
1983-84	**Quebec Nordiques**	**NHL**	80	46	73	119	37	50	87	73	11	0	4	189	24.3	156	43	97	6	+22	9	2	7	9	31	2	0	0
1984-85	Canada	C Cup	8	1	2	3	....	....	....	0	....	....	....	....	....	....	....	....	....	....	....	....	....	....	....	....	....	....
	Quebec Nordiques	**NHL**	75	32	68	100	26	46	72	95	7	1	9	207	15.5	140	40	81	4	+23	18	4	19	23	24	1	0	2
1985-86	**Quebec Nordiques**	**NHL**	76	41	81	122	33	54	87	60	15	0	8	207	19.8	167	77	92	4	+2	3	0	1	1	2	0	0	0
1986-87	**Quebec Nordiques**	**NHL**	64	24	53	77	21	38	59	43	12	0	4	157	15.3	112	51	83	1	–21	13	6	9	15	12	2	1	1
1987-88	**Quebec Nordiques**	**NHL**	76	46	65	111	39	46	85	69	20	0	2	199	23.1	146	78	77	11	+2	....	....	....	....	....	....	....	....
1988-89	**Quebec Nordiques**	**NHL**	72	35	50	85	30	35	65	117	13	0	5	195	17.9	114	54	94	11	–23	....	....	....	....	....	....	....	....
1989-90	**Quebec Nordiques**	**NHL**	62	24	38	62	21	27	48	24	10	0	0	131	18.3	83	39	97	8	–45	....	....	....	....	....	....	....	....
	New Jersey Devils	**NHL**	12	5	6	11	4	4	8	16	2	0	1	25	20.0	15	8	9	1	–1	6	3	2	5	2	1	0	1
1990-91	**New Jersey Devils**	**NHL**	77	18	42	60	17	32	49	53	4	0	3	117	15.4	92	39	53	0	0	7	3	4	7	2	1	0	2
1991-92	**New Jersey Devils**	**NHL**	66	24	38	62	22	29	51	42	10	1	3	142	16.9	102	35	63	2	+6	7	3	7	10	19	0	0	0
1992-93	**New Jersey Devils**	**NHL**	62	17	23	40	14	16	30	22	7	0	3	106	16.0	70	34	45	4	–5	5	0	2	2	2	0	0	0
1993-94	Slovan Bratislava	Slovakia	4	0	4	4	....	....	....	0	....	....	....	....	....	....	....	....	....	....	....	....	....	....	....	....	....	....
	Slovakia	Olympics	8	5	4	9	....	....	....	9	....	....	....	....	....	....	....	....	....	....	....	....	....	....	....	....	....	....
	St. Louis Blues	**NHL**	17	5	11	16	5	8	13	4	2	0	1	30	16.7	20	12	10	0	–2	4	0	0	0	2	0	0	0
1994-95	**St. Louis Blues**	**NHL**	6	1	1	2	2	1	3	0	0	0	0	9	11.1	3	0	2	0	+1	....	....	....	....	....	....	....	....
	Slovakia	WC-B	6	8	8	16	....	....	....	0	....	....	....	....	....	....	....	....	....	....	....	....	....	....	....	....	....	....
	NHL Totals		977	450	789	1239	379	550	929	824	145	7	54	2374	19.0	1693	664	1120	79		93	33	72	106	123	13	1	7

Czechoslovakian Player of the Year (1980) • Won Calder Memorial Trophy (1981) • WC-B All-Star Team (1995) • Named Best Forward at WC-B (1995)

Played in NHL All-Star Game (1981, 1982, 1983, 1984, 1986, 1988)

Signed as a free agent by **Quebec**, August 26, 1980. Traded to **New Jersey** by **Quebec** for Craig Wolanin and future considerations (Randy Velischek, August 13, 1990), March 6, 1990. Signed as a free agent by **St. Louis**, March 9, 1994.

• STASZAK, RAY

Ray Staszak RW – R. 6', 200 lbs. b: Philadelphia, PA, 12/1/1962.

Season	Club	League	GP	G	A	Pts	AG	AA	APts	PIM	PP	SH	GW	S	%	TGF	PGF	TGA	PGA	+/–	GP	G	A	Pts	PIM	PP	SH	GW
1982-83	Austin Mavericks	USHL	30	18	13	31	....	....	....	....	....	....	....	....	....	....	....	....	....	....	....	....	....	....	....	....	....	....
1983-84	University of Illinois-Chicago	CCHA	31	15	17	32	....	....	....	42	....	....	....	....	....	....	....	....	....	....	....	....	....	....	....	....	....	....
1984-85	University of Illinois-Chicago	CCHA	38	37	35	72	....	....	....	98	....	....	....	....	....	....	....	....	....	....	....	....	....	....	....	....	....	....
1985-86	**Detroit Red Wings**	**NHL**	4	0	1	1	0	1	1	7	0	0	0	5	0.0	2	0	8	3	–3	....	....	....	....	....	....	....	....
	Adirondack Red Wings	AHL	26	13	8	21	....	....	....	41	....	....	....	....	....	....	....	....	....	....	16	2	3	5	70	....	....	....
	NHL Totals		4	0	1	1	0	1	1	7	0	0	0	5	0.0	2	0	8	3		....	....	....	....	....	....	....	....

CCHA First All-Star Team (1985)

Signed as a free agent by **Detroit**, July 31, 1985.

• STEEN, ANDERS

Anders Steen C – L. 6'1", 204 lbs. b: Nykoping, Sweden, 4/28/1955.

Season	Club	League	GP	G	A	Pts	AG	AA	APts	PIM	PP	SH	GW	S	%	TGF	PGF	TGA	PGA	+/–	GP	G	A	Pts	PIM	PP	SH	GW
1974-75	Farjestad–Karlstad	Sweden	13	1	1	2	....	....	....	0	....	....	....	....	....	....	....	....	....	....	....	....	....	....	....	....	....	....
	Sweden	WJC-A	5	1	1	2	....	....	....	....	....	....	....	....	....	....	....	....	....	....	....	....	....	....	....	....	....	....
1975-76	Farjestad–Karlstad	Sweden	32	21	7	28	....	....	....	8	....	....	....	....	....	....	....	....	....	....	....	1	0	1	2	....	....	....
1976-77	Farjestad–Karlstad	Sweden	32	17	20	37	....	....	....	17	....	....	....	....	....	....	....	....	....	....	5	2	0	2	2	....	....	....
1977-78	Farjestad–Karlstad	Sweden	35	22	12	34	....	....	....	35	....	....	....	....	....	....	....	....	....	....	....	....	....	....	....	....	....	....
1978-79	Farjestad–Karlstad	Sweden	35	18	16	34	....	....	....	42	....	....	....	....	....	....	....	....	....	....	....	1	0	1	0	....	....	....
1979-80	Farjestad–Farlstad	Sweden	36	*29	16	*45	....	....	....	46	....	....	....	....	....	....	....	....	....	....	....	....	....	....	....	....	....	....
1980-81	**Winnipeg Jets**	**NHL**	42	5	11	16	4	8	12	22	3	0	1	57	8.8	18	7	35	2	–22	....	....	....	....	....	....	....	....
	Tulsa Oilers	CHL	21	11	14	25	....	....	....	28	....	....	....	....	....	....	....	....	....	....	7	0	4	4	10	....	....	....

			REGULAR SEASON																		PLAYOFFS							
Season	Club	League	GP	G	A	Pts	AG	AA	APts	PIM	PP	SH	GW	S	%	TGF	PGF	TGA	PGA	+/-	GP	G	A	Pts	PIM	PP	SH	GW
1981-82	Farjestad–Karlstad	Sweden	30	14	5	19	....	....	....	34	....	....	....	....	....	....	....	....	....	....	2	1	1	2	4	....	....	....
1982-83	Farjestad–Karlstad	Sweden	23	9	9	18	....	....	....	20	....	....	....	....	....	....	....	....	....	....	4	0	1	1	2	....	....	....
1983-84	Farjestad–Farlstad	Sweden	11	1	0	1	....	....	....	0	....	....	....	....	....	....	....	....	....	....	....	....	....	....	....	....	....	....
	NHL Totals		42	5	11	16	4	8	12	22	3	0	1	57	8.8	18	7	35	2		....	....	....	....	....	....	....	....

Signed as a free agent by **Winnipeg**, March 26, 1980.

• STEEN, THOMAS

Thomas Steen C – L. 5′11″, 190 lbs. b: Grums, Sweden, 6/8/1960. Winnipeg's 5th choice, 103rd overall, in 1979 Entry Draft.

Season	Club	League	GP	G	A	Pts	AG	AA	APts	PIM	PP	SH	GW	S	%	TGF	PGF	TGA	PGA	+/-	GP	G	A	Pts	PIM	PP	SH	GW
1976-77	Leksands IF	Sweden	2	1	1	2	....	....	....	2	....	....	....	....	....	....	....	....	....	....	....	....	....	....	....	....	....	....
1977-78	Leksands IF	Sweden	35	5	6	11	....	....	....	30	....	....	....	....	....	....	....	....	....	....	....	....	....	....	....	....	....	....
	Sweden	WJC-A	7	3	3	6	....	....	....	4	....	....	....	....	....	....	....	....	....	....	....	....	....	....	....	....	....	....
1978-79	Leksands IF	Sweden	23	13	4	17	....	....	....	35	....	....	....	....	....	....	....	....	....	....	2	0	0	0	0	....	....	....
	Sweden	WJC-A	6	5	1	6	....	....	....	6	....	....	....	....	....	....	....	....	....	....	....	....	....	....	....	....	....	....
1979-80	Leksands IF	Sweden	18	7	7	14	....	....	....	14	....	....	....	....	....	....	....	....	....	....	2	0	0	0	6	....	....	....
	Sweden	WJC-A	5	2	4	6	....	....	....	12	....	....	....	....	....	....	....	....	....	....	....	....	....	....	....	....	....	....
1980-81	Farjestad–Karlstad	Sweden	32	16	23	39	....	....	....	30	....	....	....	....	....	....	....	....	....	....	7	4	2	6	8	....	....	....
	Sweden	WEC-A	8	1	3	4	....	....	....	6	....	....	....	....	....	....	....	....	....	....	....	....	....	....	....	....	....	....
1981-82	Sweden	C Cup	3	0	0	0	....	....	....	2	....	....	....	....	....	....	....	....	....	....	....	....	....	....	....	....	....	....
	Winnipeg Jets	**NHL**	73	15	29	44	12	19	31	42	4	0	1	133	11.3	78	16	46	0	+16	4	0	4	4	2	0	0	0
1982-83	**Winnipeg Jets**	**NHL**	75	26	33	59	21	23	44	60	5	0	3	156	16.7	82	12	81	5	–6	3	0	2	2	0	0	0	0
1983-84	**Winnipeg Jets**	**NHL**	78	20	45	65	16	31	47	69	5	3	2	181	11.0	85	25	93	28	–5	3	0	1	1	9	0	0	0
1984-85	Sweden	C Cup	8	7	1	8	....	....	....	4	....	....	....	....	....	....	....	....	....	....	....	....	....	....	....	....	....	....
	Winnipeg Jets	**NHL**	79	30	54	84	25	37	62	80	7	2	4	238	12.6	118	37	108	26	–1	8	2	3	5	17	2	0	0
1985-86	**Winnipeg Jets**	**NHL**	78	17	47	64	14	31	45	76	2	3	1	195	8.7	94	31	129	37	–29	3	1	1	2	4	0	1	0
	Sweden	WEC-A	8	8	3	11	....	....	....	16	....	....	....	....	....	....	....	....	....	....	....	....	....	....	....	....	....	....
1986-87	**Winnipeg Jets**	**NHL**	75	17	33	50	15	24	39	59	3	3	1	143	11.9	88	23	76	18	+7	10	3	4	7	8	0	1	1
1987-88	**Winnipeg Jets**	**NHL**	76	16	38	54	14	27	41	53	3	1	1	167	9.6	91	35	100	33	–11	5	1	5	6	2	1	0	0
1988-89	**Winnipeg Jets**	**NHL**	80	27	61	88	23	43	66	80	9	1	2	173	15.6	125	39	113	41	+14	....	....	....	....	....	....	....	....
	Sweden	WEC-A	10	2	4	6	....	....	....	10	....	....	....	....	....	....	....	....	....	....	....	....	....	....	....	....	....	....
1989-90	**Winnipeg Jets**	**NHL**	53	18	48	66	16	34	50	35	5	0	3	129	14.0	84	32	60	10	+2	7	2	5	7	16	1	0	0
1990-91	**Winnipeg Jets**	**NHL**	58	19	48	67	17	36	53	49	7	0	3	125	15.2	91	42	54	2	–3	....	....	....	....	....	....	....	....
1991-92	Sweden	C Cup	6	0	3	3	....	....	....	11	....	....	....	....	....	....	....	....	....	....	....	....	....	....	....	....	....	....
	Winnipeg Jets	**NHL**	38	13	25	38	12	19	31	29	10	0	0	75	17.3	60	28	29	2	+5	7	2	4	6	2	2	0	0
1992-93	**Winnipeg Jets**	**NHL**	80	22	50	72	18	34	52	75	6	0	6	150	14.7	102	45	68	3	–8	6	1	3	4	2	1	0	0
1993-94	**Winnipeg Jets**	**NHL**	76	19	32	51	18	25	43	32	6	0	1	137	13.9	80	33	100	15	–38	....	....	....	....	....	....	....	....
1994-95	**Winnipeg Jets**	**NHL**	31	5	10	15	9	15	24	14	2	0	0	32	15.6	20	7	26	0	–13	....	....	....	....	....	....	....	....
1995-96	Frankfurt Lions	Germany	4	1	0	1	....	....	....	2	....	....	....	....	....	....	....	....	....	....	3	0	1	1	6	....	....	....
1996-97	Eisbaren Berlin	Germany	49	15	18	33	....	....	....	48	....	....	....	....	....	....	....	....	....	....	8	0	2	2	27	....	....	....
1997-98	Eisbaren Berlin	Germany	43	4	7	11	....	....	....	20	....	....	....	....	....	....	....	....	....	....	10	3	4	7	10	....	....	....
	NHL Totals		950	264	553	817	230	398	628	753	74	13	28	2034	13.0	1198	405	1083	220		56	12	32	44	62	7	2	1

WJC-A All-Star Team (1979) • Swedish World All-Star Team (1981, 1985, 1986)

• STEFANIW, MORRIS

Morris Stefaniw C – L. 5′11″, 170 lbs. b: North Battleford, Sask., 1/10/1948.

Season	Club	League	GP	G	A	Pts	AG	AA	APts	PIM	PP	SH	GW	S	%	TGF	PGF	TGA	PGA	+/-	GP	G	A	Pts	PIM	PP	SH	GW
1964-65	Estevan Bruins	SJHL	54	52	44	96	....	....	....	64	....	....	....	....	....	....	....	....	....	....	6	4	2	6	10	....	....	....
1965-66	Estevan Bruins	SJHL	60	52	66	118	....	....	....	51	....	....	....	....	....	....	....	....	....	....	12	7	12	19	18	....	....	....
1966-67	Estevan Bruins	WCJHL	55	36	58	94	....	....	....	28	....	....	....	....	....	....	....	....	....	....	13	2	10	12	4	....	....	....
1967-68	Oklahoma City Blazers	CHL	37	11	15	26	....	....	....	11	....	....	....	....	....	....	....	....	....	....	....	....	....	....	....	....	....	....
	Phoenix Roadrunners	WHL	17	8	0	8	....	....	....	2	....	....	....	....	....	....	....	....	....	....	4	0	0	0	2	....	....	....
1968-69	Phoenix Roadrunners	WHL	68	12	15	27	....	....	....	50	....	....	....	....	....	....	....	....	....	....	....	....	....	....	....	....	....	....
1969-70	Phoenix Roadrunners	WHL	72	7	22	29	....	....	....	33	....	....	....	....	....	....	....	....	....	....	....	....	....	....	....	....	....	....
1970-71	Omaha Knights	CHL	70	19	41	60	....	....	....	98	....	....	....	....	....	....	....	....	....	....	11	*7	9	16	6	....	....	....
1971-72	Providence Reds	AHL	70	11	20	31	....	....	....	16	....	....	....	....	....	....	....	....	....	....	5	3	3	6	12	....	....	....
1972-73	**Atlanta Flames**	**NHL**	13	1	1	2	1	1	2	2	0	1	0	16	6.3	3	1	12	7	–3	....	....	....	....	....	....	....	....
	Nova Scotia Voyageurs	AHL	64	30	*71	101	....	....	....	80	....	....	....	....	....	....	....	....	....	....	13	8	*17	*25	12	....	....	....
1973-74	Nova Scotia Voyageurs	AHL	27	3	12	15	....	....	....	42	....	....	....	....	....	....	....	....	....	....	....	....	....	....	....	....	....	....
	Albuquerque 6-Guns	CHL	41	7	22	29	....	....	....	24	....	....	....	....	....	....	....	....	....	....	....	....	....	....	....	....	....	....
1974-75	Baltimore Clippers	AHL	46	11	18	29	....	....	....	50	....	....	....	....	....	....	....	....	....	....	....	....	....	....	....	....	....	....
	Johnstown Jets	NAHL	17	1	5	6	....	....	....	6	....	....	....	....	....	....	....	....	....	....	....	....	....	....	....	....	....	....
1975-76	Baltimore Clippers	AHL	76	7	39	46	....	....	....	48	....	....	....	....	....	....	....	....	....	....	....	....	....	....	....	....	....	....
	NHL Totals		13	1	1	2	1	1	2	2	0	1	0	16	6.3	3	1	12	7		....	....	....	....	....	....	....	....

AHL Second All-Star Team (1973)

Traded to **Phoenix** (WHL) by **Boston** for cash, February, 1969. Traded to **NY Rangers** by **Phoenix** (WHL) for cash, October, 1970. Claimed by **Atlanta** from **NY Rangers** in Expansion Draft, June 6, 1972. Traded to **Kansas City** by **Atlanta** for cash, September, 1974.

• STEFANSKI, BUD

Bud (Edward) Stefanski C – L. 5′10″, 170 lbs. b: South Porcupine, Ont., 4/28/1955. NY Rangers' 9th choice, 154th overall, in 1975 Amateur Draft.

Season	Club	League	GP	G	A	Pts	AG	AA	APts	PIM	PP	SH	GW	S	%	TGF	PGF	TGA	PGA	+/-	GP	G	A	Pts	PIM	PP	SH	GW
1973-74	Oshawa Generals	OHA	67	25	32	57	....	....	....	22	....	....	....	....	....	....	....	....	....	....	....	....	....	....	....	....	....	....
1974-75	Oshawa Generals	OHA	61	18	48	66	....	....	....	35	....	....	....	....	....	....	....	....	....	....	....	....	....	....	....	....	....	....
1975-76	Port Huron Flags	IHL	71	26	30	56	....	....	....	59	....	....	....	....	....	....	....	....	....	....	15	4	4	8	16	....	....	....
1976-77	Port Huron Flags	IHL	77	49	54	103	....	....	....	61	....	....	....	....	....	....	....	....	....	....	....	....	....	....	....	....	....	....
	New Haven Nighthawks	AHL	....	....	....	....	....	....	....	....	....	....	....	....	....	....	....	....	....	....	2	1	0	1	0	....	....	....
1977-78	**New York Rangers**	**NHL**	1	0	0	0	0	0	0	0	0	0	0	1	0.0	0	0	1	0	–1	....	....	....	....	....	....	....	....
	New Haven Nighthawks	AHL	79	27	37	64	....	....	....	61	....	....	....	....	....	....	....	....	....	....	15	5	4	9	6	....	....	....
1978-79	New Haven Nighthawks	AHL	51	18	40	58	....	....	....	71	....	....	....	....	....	....	....	....	....	....	10	3	7	10	21	....	....	....
1979-80	Tulsa Oilers	CHL	71	19	44	63	....	....	....	61	....	....	....	....	....	....	....	....	....	....	3	0	0	0	9	....	....	....
1980-81	Heraklith Villacher	Austria	34	32	40	72	....	....	....	71	....	....	....	....	....	....	....	....	....	....	....	....	....	....	....	....	....	....
	New Haven Nighthawks	AHL	20	9	18	27	....	....	....	46	....	....	....	....	....	....	....	....	....	....	4	0	1	1	8	....	....	....
1981-82	Heraklith Villacher	Austria	....	23	46	69	....	....	....	....	....	....	....	....	....	....	....	....	....	....	....	9	17	26	....	....	....	....
	New Haven Nighthawks	AHL	16	6	5	11	....	....	....	24	....	....	....	....	....	....	....	....	....	....	4	2	1	3	11	....	....	....
1982-83	Springfield Indians	AHL	80	30	40	70	....	....	....	65	....	....	....	....	....	....	....	....	....	....	....	....	....	....	....	....	....	....
1983-84	Maine Mariners	AHL	57	26	24	50	....	....	....	47	....	....	....	....	....	....	....	....	....	....	17	*12	9	21	16	....	....	....
1984-85	Maine Mariners	AHL	75	19	34	53	....	....	....	67	....	....	....	....	....	....	....	....	....	....	11	1	7	8	12	....	....	....
1985-86	Maine Mariners	AHL	68	32	39	71	....	....	....	70	....	....	....	....	....	....	....	....	....	....	2	0	0	0	6	....	....	....
1986-87	Maine Mariners	AHL	29	9	12	21	....	....	....	34	....	....	....	....	....	....	....	....	....	....	....	....	....	....	....	....	....	....
	NHL Totals		1	0	0	0	0	0	0	0	0	0	0	1	0.0	0	0	1	0		....	....	....	....	....	....	....	....

Won Jack A. Butterfield Trophy (Playoff MVP - AHL) (1984)

Traded to **Winnipeg** by **NY Rangers** for cash and future considerations, October 12, 1979.

• STEMKOWSKI, PETE

Pete "Stemmer" Stemkowski C – L. 6′1″, 196 lbs. b: Winnipeg, Man., 8/25/1943.

Season	Club	League	GP	G	A	Pts	AG	AA	APts	PIM	PP	SH	GW	S	%	TGF	PGF	TGA	PGA	+/-	GP	G	A	Pts	PIM	PP	SH	GW
1960-61	Winnipeg Monarchs	MJHL	31	22	16	38	....	....	....	29	....	....	....	....	....	....	....	....	....	....	....	....	....	....	....	....	....	....
1961-62	Winnipeg Monarchs	MJHL	40	31	34	65	....	....	....	100	....	....	....	....	....	....	....	....	....	....	8	3	7	10	22	....	....	....
1962-63	Winnipeg Monarchs	MJHL	5	6	3	9	....	....	....	8	....	....	....	....	....	....	....	....	....	....	....	....	....	....	....	....	....	....
	Toronto Marlboros	OHA	23	16	27	43	....	....	....	44	....	....	....	....	....	....	....	....	....	....	11	7	17	24	26	....	....	....
1963-64	Toronto Marlboros	OHA	51	42	61	103	....	....	....	89	....	....	....	....	....	....	....	....	....	....	9	5	9	14	8	....	....	....
1963-64	**Toronto Maple Leafs**	**NHL**	1	0	0	0	0	0	0	2	....	....	....	....	....	....	....	....	....	....	....	....	....	....	....	....	....	....
	Rochester Americans	AHL	3	1	1	2	....	....	....	0	....	....	....	....	....	....	....	....	....	....	....	....	....	....	....	....	....	....
1964-65	**Toronto Maple Leafs**	**NHL**	36	5	15	20	6	16	22	33	....	....	....	....	....	....	....	....	....	....	6	0	3	3	7	....	....	....
	Rochester Americans	AHL	35	17	22	39	....	....	....	52	....	....	....	....	....	....	....	....	....	....	....	....	....	....	....	....	....	....
1965-66	**Toronto Maple Leafs**	**NHL**	56	4	12	16	5	12	17	55	....	....	....	....	....	....	....	....	....	....	4	0	0	0	26	....	....	....
	Rochester Americans	AHL	7	5	5	10	....	....	....	8	....	....	....	....	....	....	....	....	....	....	....	....	....	....	....	....	....	....
1966-67	**Toronto Maple Leafs**	**NHL**	68	13	22	35	16	23	39	75	....	....	....	....	....	....	....	....	....	....	12	5	7	12	20	....	....	....
1967-68	**Toronto Maple Leafs**	**NHL**	60	7	15	22	9	16	25	82	0	0	1	141	5.0	28	3	30	0	–5	....	....	....	....	....	....	....	....
	Detroit Red Wings	**NHL**	13	3	6	9	4	6	10	4	0	0	0	38	7.9	13	0	20	3	–4	....	....	....	....	....	....	....	....

			REGULAR SEASON																		PLAYOFFS							
Season	Club	League	GP	G	A	Pts	AG	AA	APts	PIM	PP	SH	GW	S	%	TGF	PGF	TGA	PGA	+/–	GP	G	A	Pts	PIM	PP	SH	GW
1968-69	**Detroit Red Wings**	**NHL**	**71**	**21**	**31**	**52**	**24**	**29**	**53**	**81**	**3**	**2**	**4**	**209**	**10.0**	**65**	**9**	**75**	**20**	**+1**	....	....	....	....	....	....	....	....
1969-70	**Detroit Red Wings**	**NHL**	**76**	**25**	**24**	**49**	**29**	**24**	**53**	**114**	**4**	**1**	**6**	**268**	**9.3**	**75**	**16**	**68**	**22**	**+13**	**4**	**1**	**1**	**2**	**6**	**0**	**0**	**1**
1970-71	**Detroit Red Wings**	**NHL**	**10**	**2**	**2**	**4**	**2**	**2**	**4**	**8**	**1**	**0**	**0**	**31**	**6.5**	**8**	**3**	**10**	**4**	**–1**	....	....	....	....	....	....	....	....
	New York Rangers	**NHL**	**68**	**16**	**29**	**45**	**17**	**26**	**43**	**61**	**4**	**0**	**2**	**244**	**6.6**	**63**	**10**	**46**	**9**	**+16**	**13**	**3**	**2**	**5**	**6**	**0**	**0**	**2**
1971-72	**New York Rangers**	**NHL**	**59**	**11**	**17**	**28**	**12**	**15**	**27**	**53**	**1**	**0**	**1**	**159**	**6.9**	**40**	**5**	**35**	**2**	**+2**	**16**	**4**	**8**	**12**	**18**	**0**	**0**	**1**
1972-73	**New York Rangers**	**NHL**	**78**	**22**	**37**	**59**	**22**	**31**	**53**	**71**	**2**	**0**	**1**	**200**	**11.0**	**78**	**10**	**47**	**7**	**+28**	**10**	**4**	**2**	**6**	**6**	**1**	**0**	**1**
1973-74	**New York Rangers**	**NHL**	**78**	**25**	**45**	**70**	**26**	**39**	**65**	**74**	**2**	**0**	**2**	**232**	**10.8**	**89**	**8**	**97**	**19**	**+3**	**13**	**6**	**6**	**12**	**35**	**1**	**0**	**0**
1974-75	**New York Rangers**	**NHL**	**77**	**24**	**35**	**59**	**22**	**28**	**50**	**63**	**3**	**0**	**0**	**159**	**15.1**	**78**	**10**	**86**	**15**	**–3**	**3**	**1**	**0**	**1**	**10**	**0**	**0**	**0**
1975-76	**New York Rangers**	**NHL**	**75**	**13**	**28**	**41**	**12**	**22**	**34**	**49**	**1**	**0**	**2**	**126**	**10.3**	**50**	**4**	**73**	**20**	**–7**	....	....	....	....	....	....	....	....
1976-77	**New York Rangers**	**NHL**	**61**	**2**	**13**	**15**	**2**	**11**	**13**	**8**	**0**	**1**	**0**	**56**	**3.6**	**22**	**1**	**60**	**25**	**–14**	....	....	....	....	....	....	....	....
1977-78	**Los Angeles Kings**	**NHL**	**80**	**13**	**18**	**31**	**13**	**15**	**28**	**33**	**0**	**0**	**2**	**134**	**9.7**	**35**	**1**	**47**	**14**	**+1**	2	1	0	1	2	0	0	0
1978-79	Springfield Indians	AHL	24	3	12	15	....	....	....	8	....	....	....	....	....	....	....	....	....	....	....	....	....	....	....	....	....	....
	NHL Totals		**967**	**206**	**349**	**555**	**221**	**315**	**536**	**866**	**21**	**4**	**21**	**1997**	**10.3**	**644**	**80**	**694**	**160**		**83**	**25**	**29**	**54**	**136**	**2**	**0**	**5**

Played in NHL All-Star Game (1968)

Traded to **Detroit** by **Toronto** with Frank Mahovlich, Garry Unger and rights to Carl Brewer for Norm Ullman, Paul Henderson and Floyd Smith, March 3, 1968. Traded to **NY Rangers** by **Detroit** for Larry Brown, October 31, 1970. Signed as a free agent by **LA Kings**, August 31, 1977.

• STENLUND, VERN

Vern Stenlund C – L. 6'1", 178 lbs. b: Thunder Bay, Ont., 4/11/1956. California's 2nd choice, 23rd overall, in 1976 Amateur Draft.

Season	Club	League	GP	G	A	Pts	AG	AA	APts	PIM	PP	SH	GW	S	%	TGF	PGF	TGA	PGA	+/–	GP	G	A	Pts	PIM	PP	SH	GW
1972-73	Chatham Maroons	SOJHL	40	28	36	64	....	....	....	11	....	....	....	....	....	....	....	....	....	....	....	....	....	....	....	....	....	....
1973-74	London Knights	OHA	66	17	27	44	....	....	....	16	....	....	....	....	....	....	....	....	....	....	....	....	....	....	....	....	....	....
1974-75	London Knights	OHA	70	23	37	60	....	....	....	20	....	....	....	....	....	....	....	....	....	....	....	....	....	....	....	....	....	....
1975-76	London Knights	OHA	64	44	75	119	....	....	....	24	....	....	....	....	....	....	....	....	....	....	....	....	....	....	....	....	....	....
1976-77	**Cleveland Barons**	**NHL**	**4**	**0**	**0**	**0**	**0**	**0**	**0**	**0**	**0**	**0**	**0**	**1**	**0.0**	**0**	**0**	**3**	**0**	**–3**	....	....	....	....	....	....	....	....
	Salt Lake Golden Eagles	CHL	67	13	17	30	....	....	....	10	....	....	....	....	....	....	....	....	....	....	....	....	....	....	....	....	....	....
1977-78	Phoenix Roadrunners	CHL	19	0	7	7	....	....	....	0	....	....	....	....	....	....	....	....	....	....	....	....	....	....	....	....	....	....
1978-79			DID NOT PLAY																									
1979-80			DID NOT PLAY																									
1980-81	SK Djerv	Norway	36	36	28	64	....	....	....	45	....	....	....	....	....	....	....	....	....	....	....	....	....	....	....	....	....	....
	NHL Totals		**4**	**0**	**0**	**0**	**0**	**0**	**0**	**0**	**0**	**0**	**0**	**1**	**0.0**	**0**	**0**	**3**	**0**		....	....	....	....	....	....	....	....

Transferred to **Cleveland** after **California** franchise relocated, August 26, 1976.

• STEPHENSON, BOB

Bob Stephenson RW – R. 6'1", 187 lbs. b: Saskatoon, Sask., 2/1/1954.

Season	Club	League	GP	G	A	Pts	AG	AA	APts	PIM	PP	SH	GW	S	%	TGF	PGF	TGA	PGA	+/–	GP	G	A	Pts	PIM	PP	SH	GW
1974-75	St. Francis Xavier X-Men	AUAA	18	*21	24	45	....	....	....	67	....	....	....	....	....	....	....	....	....	....	....	....	....	....	....	....	....	....
1975-76	St. Francis Xavier X-Men	AUAA	16	*22	16	38	....	....	....	38	....	....	....	....	....	....	....	....	....	....	....	....	....	....	....	....	....	....
1976-77	St. Francis Xavier X-Men	AUAA	19	20	23	43	....	....	....	39	....	....	....	....	....	....	....	....	....	....	....	....	....	....	....	....	....	....
1977-78	Birmingham Bulls	WHA	39	7	6	13	....	....	....	33	....	....	....	....	....	....	....	....	....	....	....	....	....	....	....	....	....	....
	Hampton Gulls	AHL	1	0	0	0	....	....	....	0	....	....	....	....	....	....	....	....	....	....	....	....	....	....	....	....	....	....
	Flint Generals	IHL	6	2	5	7	....	....	....	7	....	....	....	....	....	....	....	....	....	....	....	....	....	....	....	....	....	....
	Tulsa Oilers	CHL	9	1	1	2	....	....	....	7	....	....	....	....	....	....	....	....	....	....	....	....	....	....	....	....	....	....
1978-79	Birmingham Bulls	WHA	80	12	36	48	....	....	....	165	....	....	....	....	....	....	....	....	....	....	....	....	....	....	....	....	....	....
1979-80	**Hartford Whalers**	**NHL**	**4**	**0**	**1**	**1**	**0**	**1**	**1**	**0**	**0**	**0**	**0**	**3**	**0.0**	**4**	**0**	**2**	**0**	**+2**	....	....	....	....	....	....	....	....
	Springfield Indians	AHL	28	10	18	28	....	....	....	40	....	....	....	....	....	....	....	....	....	....	....	....	....	....	....	....	....	....
	Toronto Maple Leafs	**NHL**	**14**	**2**	**2**	**4**	**2**	**2**	**4**	**4**	**0**	**0**	**0**	**10**	**20.0**	**5**	**0**	**13**	**1**	**–7**	....	....	....	....	....	....	....	....
	New Brunswick Hawks	AHL	10	6	2	8	....	....	....	4	....	....	....	....	....	....	....	....	....	....	12	2	1	3	0	....	....	....
1980-81	Springfield Indians	AHL	27	5	2	7	....	....	....	43	....	....	....	....	....	....	....	....	....	....	....	....	....	....	....	....	....	....
	NHL Totals		**18**	**2**	**3**	**5**	**2**	**3**	**5**	**4**	**0**	**0**	**0**	**13**	**15.4**	**9**	**0**	**15**	**1**		....	....	....	....	....	....	....	....
	Other Major League Totals		119	19	42	61	....	....	....	198	....	....	....	....	....	....	....	....	....		....	....	....	....	....	....	....	....

Signed as a free agent by **Birmingham** (WHA), September, 1977. Claimed by **Hartford** from **Birmingham** (WHA) in WHA Dispersal Draft, June, 1979. Traded to **Toronto** by **Hartford** for Pat Boutette, December 24, 1979.

• STERN, RON

Ron Stern RW – R. 6', 195 lbs. b: Ste. Agathe, Que., 1/11/1967. Vancouver's 3rd choice, 70th overall, in 1986 Entry Draft.

Season	Club	League	GP	G	A	Pts	AG	AA	APts	PIM	PP	SH	GW	S	%	TGF	PGF	TGA	PGA	+/–	GP	G	A	Pts	PIM	PP	SH	GW
1984-85	Longueuil Chevaliers	QMJHL	67	6	14	20	....	....	....	170	....	....	....	....	....	....	....	....	....	....	....	....	....	....	....	....	....	....
1985-86	Longueuil Chevaliers	QMJHL	70	39	33	72	....	....	....	317	....	....	....	....	....	....	....	....	....	....	....	....	....	....	....	....	....	....
1986-87	Longueuil Chevaliers	QMJHL	56	32	39	71	....	....	....	266	....	....	....	....	....	....	....	....	....	....	19	11	9	20	55	....	....	....
1987-88	**Vancouver Canucks**	**NHL**	**15**	**0**	**0**	**0**	**0**	**0**	**0**	**52**	**0**	**0**	**0**	**7**	**0.0**	**0**	**0**	**7**	**0**	**–7**	....	....	....	....	....	....	....	....
	Fredericton Express	AHL	2	1	0	1	....	....	....	4	....	....	....	....	....	....	....	....	....	....	....	....	....	....	....	....	....	....
	Flint Spirits	IHL	55	14	19	33	....	....	....	294	....	....	....	....	....	....	....	....	....	....	16	8	8	16	94	....	....	....
1988-89	**Vancouver Canucks**	**NHL**	**17**	**1**	**0**	**1**	**1**	**0**	**1**	**49**	**0**	**0**	**0**	**13**	**7.7**	**2**	**0**	**8**	**0**	**–6**	**3**	**0**	**1**	**1**	**17**	**0**	**0**	**0**
	Milwaukee Admirals	IHL	45	19	23	42	....	....	....	280	....	....	....	....	....	....	....	....	....	....	5	1	0	1	11	....	....	....
1989-90	**Vancouver Canucks**	**NHL**	**34**	**2**	**3**	**5**	**2**	**2**	**4**	**208**	**0**	**0**	**0**	**27**	**7.4**	**9**	**0**	**26**	**0**	**–17**	....	....	....	....	....	....	....	....
	Milwaukee Admirals	IHL	26	8	9	17	....	....	....	165	....	....	....	....	....	....	....	....	....	....	....	....	....	....	....	....	....	....
1990-91	**Vancouver Canucks**	**NHL**	**31**	**2**	**3**	**5**	**2**	**2**	**4**	**171**	**0**	**0**	**0**	**30**	**6.7**	**8**	**1**	**21**	**0**	**–14**	....	....	....	....	....	....	....	....
	Milwaukee Admirals	IHL	7	2	2	4	....	....	....	81	....	....	....	....	....	....	....	....	....	....	....	....	....	....	....	....	....	....
	Calgary Flames	**NHL**	**13**	**1**	**3**	**4**	**1**	**2**	**3**	**69**	**0**	**0**	**0**	**15**	**6.7**	**5**	**0**	**5**	**0**	**0**	**7**	**1**	**3**	**4**	**14**	**0**	**0**	**0**
1991-92	**Calgary Flames**	**NHL**	**72**	**13**	**9**	**22**	**12**	**7**	**19**	**338**	**0**	**1**	**1**	**96**	**13.5**	**35**	**0**	**47**	**12**	**0**	....	....	....	....	....	....	....	....
1992-93	**Calgary Flames**	**NHL**	**70**	**10**	**15**	**25**	**8**	**10**	**18**	**207**	**0**	**0**	**1**	**82**	**12.2**	**34**	**0**	**34**	**4**	**+4**	**6**	**0**	**0**	**0**	**43**	**0**	**0**	**0**
1993-94	**Calgary Flames**	**NHL**	**71**	**9**	**20**	**29**	**8**	**15**	**23**	**243**	**0**	**1**	**3**	**105**	**8.6**	**43**	**0**	**39**	**2**	**+6**	**7**	**2**	**0**	**2**	**12**	**0**	**0**	**0**
1994-95	**Calgary Flames**	**NHL**	**39**	**9**	**4**	**13**	**16**	**6**	**22**	**163**	**1**	**0**	**0**	**69**	**13.0**	**24**	**1**	**27**	**8**	**+4**	**7**	**3**	**1**	**4**	**8**	**1**	**1**	**0**
1995-96	**Calgary Flames**	**NHL**	**52**	**10**	**5**	**15**	**10**	**4**	**14**	**111**	**0**	**0**	**1**	**64**	**15.6**	**29**	**4**	**35**	**12**	**+2**	**4**	**0**	**2**	**2**	**8**	**0**	**0**	**0**
1996-97	**Calgary Flames**	**NHL**	**79**	**7**	**10**	**17**	**7**	**9**	**16**	**157**	**0**	**1**	**1**	**98**	**7.1**	**25**	**0**	**44**	**15**	**–4**	....	....	....	....	....	....	....	....
1997-98	**Calgary Flames**	**NHL**	DID NOT PLAY – INJURED																									
	NHL Totals		**493**	**64**	**72**	**136**	**67**	**57**	**124**	**1768**	**1**	**3**	**7**	**606**	**10.6**	**214**	**6**	**293**	**53**		**34**	**6**	**7**	**13**	**102**	**1**	**1**	**0**

Traded to **Calgary** by **Vancouver** with Kevan Guy for Dana Murzyn, March 5, 1991. • Missed entire 1997-98 season after undergoing knee surgery, October, 1997.

• STEVENS, JOHN

John Stevens D – L. 6'1", 195 lbs. b: Campbellton, N.B., 5/4/1966. Philadelphia's 5th choice, 47th overall, in 1984 Entry Draft.

Season	Club	League	GP	G	A	Pts	AG	AA	APts	PIM	PP	SH	GW	S	%	TGF	PGF	TGA	PGA	+/–	GP	G	A	Pts	PIM	PP	SH	GW
1983-84	Oshawa Generals	OHL	70	1	10	11	....	....	....	71	....	....	....	....	....	....	....	....	....	....	7	0	1	1	6	....	....	....
1984-85	Oshawa Generals	OHL	44	2	10	12	....	....	....	61	....	....	....	....	....	....	....	....	....	....	5	0	2	2	4	....	....	....
	Hershey Bears	AHL	3	0	0	0	....	....	....	0	....	....	....	....	....	....	....	....	....	....	....	....	....	....	....	....	....	....
1985-86	Oshawa Generals	OHL	65	1	7	8	....	....	....	146	....	....	....	....	....	....	....	....	....	....	6	0	2	2	14	....	....	....
	Kalamazoo Wings	IHL	6	0	1	1	....	....	....	8	....	....	....	....	....	....	....	....	....	....	6	0	3	3	9	....	....	....
1986-87	**Philadelphia Flyers**	**NHL**	**6**	**0**	**2**	**2**	**0**	**1**	**1**	**14**	**0**	**0**	**0**	**2**	**0.0**	**6**	**1**	**5**	**0**	**0**	....	....	....	....	....	....	....	....
	Hershey Bears	AHL	63	1	15	16	....	....	....	131	....	....	....	....	....	....	....	....	....	....	3	0	0	0	7	....	....	....
1987-88	**Philadelphia Flyers**	**NHL**	**3**	**0**	**0**	**0**	**0**	**0**	**0**	**0**	**0**	**0**	**0**	**0**	**0.0**	**1**	**0**	**2**	**0**	**–1**	....	....	....	....	....	....	....	....
	Hershey Bears	AHL	59	1	15	16	....	....	....	108	....	....	....	....	....	....	....	....	....	....	....	....	....	....	....	....	....	....
1988-89	Hershey Bears	AHL	78	3	13	16	....	....	....	129	....	....	....	....	....	....	....	....	....	....	12	1	1	2	29	....	....	....
1989-90	Hershey Bears	AHL	79	3	10	13	....	....	....	193	....	....	....	....	....	....	....	....	....	....	....	....	....	....	....	....	....	....
1990-91	**Hartford Whalers**	**NHL**	**14**	**0**	**1**	**1**	**0**	**1**	**1**	**11**	**0**	**0**	**0**	**7**	**0.0**	**6**	**0**	**10**	**4**	**0**	....	....	....	....	....	....	....	....
	Springfield Indians	AHL	65	0	12	12	....	....	....	139	....	....	....	....	....	....	....	....	....	....	18	0	6	6	35	....	....	....
1991-92	**Hartford Whalers**	**NHL**	**21**	**0**	**4**	**4**	**0**	**3**	**3**	**19**	**0**	**0**	**0**	**13**	**0.0**	**19**	**3**	**24**	**4**	**–4**	....	....	....	....	....	....	....	....
	Springfield Indians	AHL	45	1	12	13	....	....	....	73	....	....	....	....	....	....	....	....	....	....	11	1	3	4	27	....	....	....
1992-93	Springfield Indians	AHL	74	1	19	20	....	....	....	111	....	....	....	....	....	....	....	....	....	....	15	0	1	1	18	....	....	....
1993-94	**Hartford Whalers**	**NHL**	**9**	**0**	**3**	**3**	**0**	**2**	**2**	**4**	**0**	**0**	**0**	**3**	**0.0**	**9**	**0**	**5**	**0**	**+4**	....	....	....	....	....	....	....	....
	Springfield Indians	AHL	71	3	9	12	....	....	....	85	....	....	....	....	....	....	....	....	....	....	3	0	0	0	0	....	....	....
1994-95	Springfield Falcons	AHL	79	5	15	20	....	....	....	122	....	....	....	....	....	....	....	....	....	....	....	....	....	....	....	....	....	....
1995-96	Springfield Falcons	AHL	69	0	19	19	....	....	....	95	....	....	....	....	....	....	....	....	....	....	10	0	1	1	31	....	....	....
1996-97	Philadelphia Phantoms	AHL	74	2	18	20	....	....	....	116	....	....	....	....	....	....	....	....	....	....	10	0	2	2	8	....	....	....
1997-98	Philadelphia Phantoms	AHL	50	1	9	10	....	....	....	76	....	....	....	....	....	....	....	....	....	....	20	0	6	6	44	....	....	....
	NHL Totals		**53**	**0**	**10**	**10**	**0**	**7**	**7**	**48**	**0**	**0**	**0**	**25**	**0.0**	**41**	**4**	**46**	**8**		....	....	....	....	....	....	....	....

Signed as a free agent by **Hartford**, July 30, 1990. Signed as a free agent by **Philadelphia**, August 6, 1996.

• STEVENS, KEVIN Kevin Stevens LW – L. 6'3", 217 lbs. b: Brockton, MA, 4/15/1965. Los Angeles' 6th choice, 112th overall, in 1983 Entry Draft.

			REGULAR SEASON																		PLAYOFFS							
Season	Club	League	GP	G	A	Pts	AG	AA	APts	PIM	PP	SH	GW	S	%	TGF	PGF	TGA	PGA	+/–	GP	G	A	Pts	PIM	PP	SH	GW
1982-83	Silver Lake-Minnesota High	H.S.	18	24	27	51	....	....	....	....	....	....	....	....	....	....	....	....	....	....	....	....	....	....	....	....	....	....
1983-84	Boston College	ECAC	37	6	14	20	....	....	....	36	....	....	....	....	....	....	....	....	....	....	....	....	....	....	....	....	....	....
1984-85	Boston College	H.E.	40	13	23	36	....	....	....	36	....	....	....	....	....	....	....	....	....	....	....	....	....	....	....	....	....	....
1985-86	Boston College	H.E.	42	17	27	44	....	....	....	56	....	....	....	....	....	....	....	....	....	....	....	....	....	....	....	....	....	....
1986-87	Boston College	H.E.	39	35	35	70	....	....	....	54	....	....	....	....	....	....	....	....	....	....	....	....	....	....	....	....	....	....
	United States	WEC-A	8	1	1	2	....	....	....	10	....	....	....	....	....	....	....	....	....	....	....	....	....	....	....	....	....	....
1987-88	United States	Nat-Team	44	22	23	45	....	....	....	52	....	....	....	....	....	....	....	....	....	....	....	....	....	....	....	....	....	....
	United States	Olympics	5	1	3	4	....	....	....	2	....	....	....	....	....	....	....	....	....	....	....	....	....	....	....	....	....	....
	Pittsburgh Penguins	**NHL**	**16**	**5**	**2**	**7**	**4**	**1**	**5**	**8**	**2**	**0**	**0**	**22**	**22.7**	**18**	**8**	**16**	**0**	**–6**	....	....	....	....	....	....	....	....
1988-89	**Pittsburgh Penguins**	**NHL**	**24**	**12**	**3**	**15**	**10**	**2**	**12**	**19**	**4**	**0**	**3**	**52**	**23.1**	**22**	**7**	**23**	**0**	**–8**	**11**	**3**	**7**	**10**	**16**	**0**	**0**	**0**
	Muskegon Lumberjacks	IHL	45	24	41	65	....	....	....	113	....	....	....	....	....	....	....	....	....	....	....	....	....	....	....	....	....	....
1989-90	**Pittsburgh Penguins**	**NHL**	**76**	**29**	**41**	**70**	**25**	**29**	**54**	**171**	**12**	**0**	**1**	**179**	**16.2**	**109**	**38**	**92**	**8**	**–13**	....	....	....	....	....	....	....	....
	United States	WEC-A	10	5	2	7	....	....	....	18	....	....	....	....	....	....	....	....	....	....	....	....	....	....	....	....	....	....
1990-91	**Pittsburgh Penguins**	**NHL**	**80**	**40**	**46**	**86**	**37**	**35**	**72**	**133**	**18**	**0**	**6**	**253**	**15.8**	**143**	**60**	**86**	**2**	**–1**	**24**	***17**	**16**	**33**	**53**	**7**	**0**	**4**
1991-92	**Pittsburgh Penguins**	**NHL**	**80**	**54**	**69**	**123**	**50**	**52**	**102**	**254**	**19**	**0**	**4**	**325**	**16.6**	**175**	**69**	**99**	**1**	**+8**	**21**	**13**	**15**	**28**	**28**	**4**	**0**	**3**
1992-93	**Pittsburgh Penguins**	**NHL**	**72**	**55**	**56**	**111**	**46**	**38**	**84**	**177**	**26**	**0**	**5**	**326**	**16.9**	**166**	**70**	**80**	**1**	**+17**	**12**	**5**	**11**	**16**	**22**	**4**	**0**	**0**
1993-94	**Pittsburgh Penguins**	**NHL**	**83**	**41**	**47**	**88**	**38**	**36**	**74**	**155**	**21**	**0**	**4**	**284**	**14.4**	**138**	**69**	**94**	**1**	**–24**	**6**	**1**	**1**	**2**	**10**	**0**	**0**	**0**
1994-95	**Pittsburgh Penguins**	**NHL**	**27**	**15**	**12**	**27**	**27**	**18**	**45**	**51**	**6**	**0**	**4**	**80**	**18.8**	**33**	**13**	**20**	**0**	**0**	**12**	**4**	**7**	**11**	**21**	**3**	**0**	**1**
1995-96	**Boston Bruins**	**NHL**	**41**	**10**	**13**	**23**	**10**	**11**	**21**	**49**	**3**	**0**	**1**	**101**	**9.9**	**53**	**19**	**33**	**0**	**+1**	....	....	....	....	....	....	....	....
	Los Angeles Kings	**NHL**	**20**	**3**	**10**	**13**	**3**	**8**	**11**	**22**	**3**	**0**	**0**	**69**	**4.3**	**17**	**9**	**19**	**0**	**–11**	....	....	....	....	....	....	....	....
	United States	WC-A	8	4	3	7	....	....	....	12	....	....	....	....	....	....	....	....	....	....	....	....	....	....	....	....	....	....
1996-97	**Los Angeles Kings**	**NHL**	**69**	**14**	**20**	**34**	**15**	**18**	**33**	**96**	**4**	**0**	**1**	**175**	**8.0**	**68**	**21**	**74**	**0**	**–27**	....	....	....	....	....	....	....	....
1997-98	**New York Rangers**	**NHL**	**80**	**14**	**27**	**41**	**16**	**26**	**42**	**130**	**5**	**0**	**3**	**144**	**9.7**	**60**	**17**	**50**	**0**	**–7**	....	....	....	....	....	....	....	....
	NHL Totals		**668**	**292**	**346**	**638**	**281**	**274**	**555**	**1265**	**123**	**0**	**32**	**2010**	**14.5**	**1002**	**400**	**686**	**13**		**86**	**43**	**57**	**100**	**150**	**18**	**0**	**8**

Hockey East First All-Star Team (1987) • NCAA East Second All-American Team (1987) • NHL Second All-Star Team (1991, 1993) • NHL First All-Star Team (1992)

Played in NHL All-Star Game (1991, 1992, 1993)

Rights traded to **Pittsburgh** by **LA Kings** for Anders Hakansson, September 9, 1983. Traded to **Boston** by **Pittsburgh** with Shawn McEachern for Glen Murray, Bryan Smolinski and Boston's 3rd round choice (Boyd Kane) in 1996 Entry Draft, August 2, 1995. Traded to **LA Kings** by **Boston** for Rick Tocchet, January 25, 1996. Traded to **NY Rangers** by **Los Angeles** for Luc Robitaille, August 28, 1997.

• STEVENS, MIKE Mike Stevens LW – L. 6', 202 lbs. b: Kitchener, Ont., 12/30/1965. Vancouver's 1st choice, 58th overall, in 1984 Entry Draft.

1982-83	Kitchener Jr. Rangers	OJHL	29	5	18	23	....	....	....	86	....	....	....	....	....	....	....	....	....	....	....	....	....	....	....	....	....	....
	Kitchener Rangers	OHL	13	0	4	4	....	....	....	16	....	....	....	....	....	....	....	....	....	....	12	0	1	1	9	....	....	....
1983-84	Kitchener Rangers	OHL	66	19	21	40	....	....	....	109	....	....	....	....	....	....	....	....	....	....	16	10	7	17	40	....	....	....
1984-85	Kitchener Rangers	OHL	37	17	18	35	....	....	....	121	....	....	....	....	....	....	....	....	....	....	4	1	1	2	8	....	....	....
	Vancouver Canucks	**NHL**	**6**	**0**	**3**	**3**	**0**	**2**	**2**	**6**	**0**	**0**	**0**	**10**	**0.0**	**3**	**0**	**5**	**0**	**–2**	....	....	....	....	....	....	....	....
1985-86	Fredericton Express	AHL	79	12	19	31	....	....	....	208	....	....	....	....	....	....	....	....	....	....	6	1	1	2	35	....	....	....
1986-87	Fredericton Express	AHL	71	7	18	25	....	....	....	258	....	....	....	....	....	....	....	....	....	....	....	....	....	....	....	....	....	....
1987-88	**Boston Bruins**	**NHL**	**7**	**0**	**1**	**1**	**0**	**1**	**1**	**9**	**0**	**0**	**0**	**5**	**0.0**	**1**	**0**	**1**	**0**	**0**	....	....	....	....	....	....	....	....
	Maine Mariners	AHL	63	30	25	55	....	....	....	265	....	....	....	....	....	....	....	....	....	....	7	1	2	3	37	....	....	....
1988-89	**New York Islanders**	**NHL**	**9**	**1**	**0**	**1**	**1**	**0**	**1**	**14**	**0**	**0**	**0**	**9**	**11.1**	**2**	**0**	**3**	**0**	**–1**	....	....	....	....	....	....	....	....
	Springfield Indians	AHL	42	17	13	30	....	....	....	120	....	....	....	....	....	....	....	....	....	....	....	....	....	....	....	....	....	....
1989-90	Springfield Indians	AHl	28	12	10	22	....	....	....	75	....	....	....	....	....	....	....	....	....	....	....	....	....	....	....	....	....	....
	Toronto Maple Leafs	**NHL**	**1**	**0**	**0**	**0**	**0**	**0**	**0**	**0**	**0**	**0**	**0**	**2**	**0.0**	**0**	**0**	**0**	**0**	**0**	....	....	....	....	....	....	....	....
	Newmarket Saints	AHL	46	16	28	44	....	....	....	86	....	....	....	....	....	....	....	....	....	....	....	....	....	....	....	....	....	....
1990-91	Newmarket Saints	AHL	68	24	23	47	....	....	....	229	....	....	....	....	....	....	....	....	....	....	....	....	....	....	....	....	....	....
1991-92	St. John's Maple Leafs	AHL	30	13	11	24	....	....	....	65	....	....	....	....	....	....	....	....	....	....	....	....	....	....	....	....	....	....
	Binghamton Rangers	AHL	44	15	15	30	....	....	....	87	....	....	....	....	....	....	....	....	....	....	11	7	6	13	45	....	....	....
1992-93	Binghamton Rangers	AHL	68	31	61	92	....	....	....	230	....	....	....	....	....	....	....	....	....	....	14	5	5	10	63	....	....	....
1993-94	Saint John Flames	AHL	79	20	37	57	....	....	....	293	....	....	....	....	....	....	....	....	....	....	6	1	3	4	34	....	....	....
1994-95	Cincinnati Cyclones	IHL	80	34	43	77	....	....	....	274	....	....	....	....	....	....	....	....	....	....	10	6	3	9	16	....	....	....
1995-96	Cleveland Lumberjacks	IHL	81	31	43	74	....	....	....	252	....	....	....	....	....	....	....	....	....	....	3	1	0	1	8	....	....	....
1996-97	Cleveland Lumberjacks	IHL	6	1	4	5	....	....	....	32	....	....	....	....	....	....	....	....	....	....	....	....	....	....	....	....	....	....
	Cincinnati Cyclones	IHL	46	16	18	34	....	....	....	140	....	....	....	....	....	....	....	....	....	....	3	0	2	2	8	....	....	....
1997-98	Schwenningen Wild Wings	Germany	50	18	32	50	....	....	....	197	....	....	....	....	....	....	....	....	....	....	....	....	....	....	....	....	....	....
	NHL Totals		**23**	**1**	**4**	**5**	**1**	**3**	**4**	**29**	**0**	**0**	**0**	**26**	**3.8**	**6**	**0**	**9**	**0**		....	....	....	....	....	....	....	....

Traded to **Boston** by **Vancouver** for cash, October 6, 1987. Signed as a free agent by **NY Islanders**, August 20, 1988. Traded to **Toronto** by **NY Islanders** with Gilles Thibaudeau for Jack Capuano, Paul Gagne and Derek Laxdal, December 20, 1989. Traded to **NY Rangers** by **Toronto** for Guy Larose, December 26, 1991. Signed as a free agent by **Calgary**, August 10, 1993.

• STEVENS, SCOTT Scott Stevens D – L. 6'2", 215 lbs. b: Kitchener, Ont., 4/1/1964. Washington's 1st choice, 5th overall, in 1982 Entry Draft.

1980-81	Kitchener Jr. Rangers	OJHL	39	7	33	40	....	....	....	82	....	....	....	....	....	....	....	....	....	....	....	....	....	....	....	....	....	....
	Kitchener Rangers	OHA	1	0	0	0	....	....	....	0	....	....	....	....	....	....	....	....	....	....	....	....	....	....	....	....	....	....
1981-82	Kitchener Rangers	OHL	68	6	36	42	....	....	....	158	....	....	....	....	....	....	....	....	....	....	15	1	10	11	71	....	....	....
1982-83	**Washington Capitals**	**NHL**	**77**	**9**	**16**	**25**	**7**	**11**	**18**	**195**	**0**	**0**	**0**	**121**	**7.4**	**91**	**3**	**81**	**7**	**+14**	**4**	**1**	**0**	**1**	**26**	**0**	**0**	**0**
	Canada	WEC-A	10	0	2	2	....	....	....	8	....	....	....	....	....	....	....	....	....	....	....	....	....	....	....	....	....	....
1983-84	**Washington Capitals**	**NHL**	**78**	**13**	**32**	**45**	**10**	**22**	**32**	**201**	**7**	**0**	**2**	**155**	**8.4**	**128**	**29**	**87**	**14**	**+26**	**8**	**1**	**8**	**9**	**21**	**1**	**0**	**0**
1984-85	**Washington Capitals**	**NHL**	**80**	**21**	**44**	**65**	**17**	**30**	**47**	**221**	**16**	**0**	**5**	**170**	**12.4**	**147**	**50**	**109**	**31**	**+19**	**5**	**0**	**1**	**1**	**20**	**0**	**0**	**0**
	Canada	WEC-A	8	1	2	3	....	....	....	6	....	....	....	....	....	....	....	....	....	....	....	....	....	....	....	....	....	....
1985-86	**Washington Capitals**	**NHL**	**73**	**15**	**38**	**53**	**12**	**25**	**37**	**165**	**3**	**0**	**2**	**121**	**12.4**	**133**	**35**	**122**	**24**	**0**	**9**	**3**	**8**	**11**	**12**	**2**	**0**	**2**
1986-87	**Washington Capitals**	**NHL**	**77**	**10**	**51**	**61**	**9**	**37**	**46**	**283**	**2**	**0**	**0**	**165**	**6.1**	**150**	**45**	**115**	**23**	**+13**	**7**	**0**	**5**	**5**	**19**	**0**	**0**	**0**
	Canada	WEC-A	2	0	1	1	....	....	....	2	....	....	....	....	....	....	....	....	....	....	....	....	....	....	....	....	....	....
1987-88	**Washington Capitals**	**NHL**	**80**	**12**	**60**	**72**	**10**	**43**	**53**	**184**	**5**	**1**	**2**	**231**	**5.2**	**158**	**62**	**124**	**42**	**+14**	**13**	**1**	**11**	**12**	**46**	**0**	**0**	**0**
1988-89	**Washington Capitals**	**NHL**	**80**	**7**	**61**	**68**	**6**	**43**	**49**	**225**	**6**	**0**	**3**	**195**	**3.6**	**163**	**66**	**134**	**38**	**+1**	**6**	**1**	**4**	**5**	**11**	**0**	**0**	**0**
	Canada	WEC-A	7	2	1	3	....	....	....	2	....	....	....	....	....	....	....	....	....	....	....	....	....	....	....	....	....	....
1989-90	Washington Capitals	FrTour	4	1	4	5	....	....	....	15	....	....	....	....	....	....	....	....	....	....	....	....	....	....	....	....	....	....
	Washington Capitals	**NHL**	**56**	**11**	**29**	**40**	**9**	**21**	**30**	**154**	**7**	**0**	**0**	**143**	**7.7**	**99**	**34**	**87**	**23**	**+1**	**15**	**2**	**7**	**9**	**25**	**1**	**0**	**0**
1990-91	**St. Louis Blues**	**NHL**	**78**	**5**	**44**	**49**	**5**	**33**	**38**	**150**	**1**	**0**	**1**	**160**	**3.1**	**142**	**37**	**117**	**35**	**+23**	**13**	**0**	**3**	**3**	**36**	**0**	**0**	**0**
1991-92	Canada	C Cup	8	1	0	1	....	....	....	4	....	....	....	....	....	....	....	....	....	....	....	....	....	....	....	....	....	....
	New Jersey Devils	**NHL**	**68**	**17**	**42**	**59**	**16**	**32**	**48**	**124**	**7**	**1**	**2**	**156**	**10.9**	**120**	**28**	**87**	**19**	**+24**	**7**	**2**	**1**	**3**	**29**	**2**	**0**	**1**
1992-93	**New Jersey Devils**	**NHL**	**81**	**12**	**45**	**57**	**10**	**31**	**41**	**120**	**8**	**0**	**1**	**146**	**8.2**	**128**	**39**	**125**	**50**	**+14**	**5**	**2**	**2**	**4**	**10**	**1**	**0**	**0**
1993-94	**New Jersey Devils**	**NHL**	**83**	**18**	**60**	**78**	**17**	**46**	**63**	**112**	**5**	**1**	**4**	**215**	**8.4**	**153**	**38**	**93**	**31**	**+53**	**20**	**2**	**9**	**11**	**42**	**2**	**0**	**1**
1994-95	**New Jersey Devils**	**NHL**	**48**	**2**	**20**	**22**	**4**	**29**	**33**	**56**	**1**	**0**	**1**	**111**	**1.8**	**54**	**10**	**56**	**16**	**+4**	**20**	**1**	**7**	**8**	**24**	**0**	**0**	**1**
1995-96	**New Jersey Devils**	**NHL**	**82**	**5**	**23**	**28**	**5**	**19**	**24**	**100**	**2**	**1**	**1**	**174**	**2.9**	**80**	**17**	**86**	**30**	**+7**	....	....	....	....	....	....	....	....
1996-97	Canada	W Cup	8	0	2	2	....	....	....	4	....	....	....	....	....	....	....	....	....	....	....	....	....	....	....	....	....	....
	New Jersey Devils	**NHL**	**79**	**5**	**19**	**24**	**5**	**17**	**22**	**70**	**0**	**0**	**1**	**166**	**3.0**	**92**	**12**	**69**	**15**	**+26**	**10**	**0**	**4**	**4**	**2**	**0**	**0**	**0**
1997-98	**New Jersey Devils**	**NHL**	**80**	**4**	**22**	**26**	**5**	**21**	**26**	**80**	**1**	**0**	**1**	**94**	**4.3**	**62**	**2**	**71**	**30**	**+19**	**6**	**1**	**0**	**1**	**8**	**0**	**0**	**0**
	Canada	Olympics	6	0	0	0	....	....	....	2	....	....	....	....	....	....	....	....	....	....	....	....	....	....	....	....	....	....
	NHL Totals		**1200**	**166**	**606**	**772**	**147**	**460**	**607**	**2440**	**71**	**4**	**26**	**2523**	**6.6**	**1900**	**507**	**1563**	**428**		**148**	**17**	**70**	**87**	**331**	**9**	**0**	**5**

NHL Plus/Minus Leader (1994)

NHL All-Rookie Team (1983) • NHL First All-Star Team (1988, 1994) • NHL Second All-Star Team (1992, 1997) • Won Alka-Seltzer Plus Award (1994)

Played in NHL All-Star Game (1985, 1989, 1991, 1992, 1993, 1994, 1996, 1997, 1998)

Signed as a free agent by **St. Louis**, July 16, 1990. Transferred to **New Jersey** from **St. Louis** as compensation for St. Louis' signing of free agent Brendan Shanahan, September 3, 1991.

• STEVENSON, JEREMY Jeremy Stevenson LW – L. 6'2", 220 lbs. b: San Bernadino, CA, 7/28/1974. Anaheim's 10th choice, 262nd overall, in 1994 Entry Draft.

1990-91	Cornwall Royals	OHL	58	13	20	33	....	....	....	124	....	....	....	....	....	....	....	....	....	....	....	....	....	....	....	....	....	....
1991-92	Cornwall Royals	OHL	63	15	23	38	....	....	....	176	....	....	....	....	....	....	....	....	....	....	6	3	1	4	4	....	....	....
1992-93	Newmarket Royals	OHL	54	28	28	56	....	....	....	144	....	....	....	....	....	....	....	....	....	....	5	5	1	6	28	....	....	....
1993-94	Newmarket Royals	OHL	9	2	4	6	....	....	....	27	....	....	....	....	....	....	....	....	....	....	....	....	....	....	....	....	....	....
	Sault Ste. Marie Greyhounds	OHL	48	18	19	37	....	....	....	183	....	....	....	....	....	....	....	....	....	....	14	1	1	2	23	....	....	....

			REGULAR SEASON																		PLAYOFFS							
Season	Club	League	GP	G	A	Pts	AG	AA	APts	PIM	PP	SH	GW	S	%	TGF	PGF	TGA	PGA	+/–	GP	G	A	Pts	PIM	PP	SH	GW
1994-95	Greensboro Monarchs	ECHL	43	14	13	27	....	....	....	231	....	....	....	....	....	....	....	....	....	....	17	6	11	17	64	....	....	....
1995-96	**Anaheim Mighty Ducks**	**NHL**	3	0	1	1	0	1	1	12	0	0	0	1	0.0	1	0	0	0	+1	....	....	....	....	....	....	....	....
	Baltimore Bandits	AHL	60	11	10	21	....	....	....	295	....	....	....	....	....	....	....	....	....	....	12	4	2	6	23	....	....	....
1996-97	**Anaheim Mighty Ducks**	**NHL**	5	0	0	0	0	0	0	14	0	0	0	1	0.0	0	0	1	0	–1	....	....	....	....	....	....	....	....
	Baltimore Bandits	AHL	25	8	8	16	....	....	....	125	....	....	....	....	....	....	....	....	....	....	3	0	0	0	8	....	....	....
1997-98	**Anaheim Mighty Ducks**	**NHL**	45	3	5	8	4	5	9	101	0	0	1	43	7.0	11	0	15	0	–4	....	....	....	....	....	....	....	....
	Cincinnati Mighty Ducks	AHL	10	5	0	5	....	....	....	34	....	....	....	....	....	....	....	....	....	....	....	....	....	....	....	....	....	....
	NHL Totals		53	3	6	9	4	6	10	127	0	0	1	45	6.7	12	0	16	0		....	....	....	....	....	....	....	....

• Re-entered NHL draft. Originally Winnipeg's 3rd choice, 60th overall, in 1992 Entry Draft.

• STEVENSON, SHAYNE

Shayne Stevenson RW – R. 6'1", 190 lbs. b: Newmarket, Ont., 10/26/1970. Boston's 3rd choice, 17th overall, in 1989 Entry Draft.

Season	Club	League	GP	G	A	Pts	AG	AA	APts	PIM	PP	SH	GW	S	%	TGF	PGF	TGA	PGA	+/–	GP	G	A	Pts	PIM	PP	SH	GW
1985-86	Barrie Colts	OJHL	38	14	23	37	....	....	....	75	....	....	....	....	....	....	....	....	....	....	....	....	....	....	....	....	....	....
1986-87	London Knights	OHL	61	7	15	22	....	....	....	56	....	....	....	....	....	....	....	....	....	....	....	....	....	....	....	....	....	....
1987-88	London Knights	OHL	36	14	25	39	....	....	....	56	....	....	....	....	....	....	....	....	....	....	....	....	....	....	....	....	....	....
	Kitchener Rangers	OHL	30	10	25	35	....	....	....	48	....	....	....	....	....	....	....	....	....	....	4	1	1	2	4	....	....	....
1988-89	Kitchener Rangers	OHL	56	25	51	76	....	....	....	86	....	....	....	....	....	....	....	....	....	....	5	2	3	5	4	....	....	....
1989-90	Kitchener Rangers	OHL	56	28	61	89	....	....	....	225	....	....	....	....	....	....	....	....	....	....	17	16	21	*37	31	....	....	....
1990-91	**Boston Bruins**	**NHL**	14	0	0	0	0	0	0	26	0	0	0	8	0.0	3	0	7	0	–4	....	....	....	....	....	....	....	....
	Maine Mariners	AHL	58	22	28	50	....	....	....	112	....	....	....	....	....	....	....	....	....	....	....	....	....	....	....	....	....	....
1991-92	**Boston Bruins**	**NHL**	5	0	1	1	0	1	1	2	0	0	0	3	0.0	2	0	1	0	+1	....	....	....	....	....	....	....	....
	Maine Mariners	AHL	54	10	23	33	....	....	....	150	....	....	....	....	....	....	....	....	....	....	....	....	....	....	....	....	....	....
1992-93	**Tampa Bay Lightning**	**NHL**	8	0	1	1	0	1	1	7	0	0	0	4	0.0	1	0	6	0	–5	....	....	....	....	....	....	....	....
	Atlanta Knights	IHL	53	17	17	34	....	....	....	160	....	....	....	....	....	....	....	....	....	....	6	0	2	2	21	....	....	....
1993-94	Brunico	Alpenliga	16	8	15	23	....	....	....	66	....	....	....	....	....	....	....	....	....	....	....	....	....	....	....	....	....	....
	Fort Wayne Komets	IHL	22	3	5	8	....	....	....	116	....	....	....	....	....	....	....	....	....	....	....	....	....	....	....	....	....	....
	Muskegon Fury	ColHL	1	2	0	2	....	....	....	0	....	....	....	....	....	....	....	....	....	....	....	....	....	....	....	....	....	....
	St. Thomas Wildcats	ColHL	6	3	3	6	....	....	....	15	....	....	....	....	....	....	....	....	....	....	2	0	2	2	9	....	....	....
1994-95	Utica Blizzard	ColHL	43	17	40	57	....	....	....	37	....	....	....	....	....	....	....	....	....	....	6	0	3	3	11	....	....	....
1995-96	Utica Blizzard	ColHL	27	11	21	32	....	....	....	72	....	....	....	....	....	....	....	....	....	....	....	....	....	....	....	....	....	....
1996-97	Utica Blizzard	ColHL	10	2	6	8	....	....	....	18	....	....	....	....	....	....	....	....	....	....	....	....	....	....	....	....	....	....
	Saginaw Wheels	ColHL	17	2	23	25	....	....	....	30	....	....	....	....	....	....	....	....	....	....	....	....	....	....	....	....	....	....
	Brantford Smoke	ColHL	10	3	9	12	....	....	....	25	....	....	....	....	....	....	....	....	....	....	6	3	5	8	24	....	....	....
1997-98	Port Huron Border Cats	UHL	18	8	9	17	....	....	....	27	....	....	....	....	....	....	....	....	....	....	3	2	0	2	4	....	....	....
	NHL Totals		27	0	2	2	0	2	2	35	0	0	0	15	0.0	6	0	14	0		....	....	....	....	....	....	....	....

Claimed by **Tampa Bay** from **Boston** in Expansion Draft, June 18, 1992.

• STEVENSON, TURNER

Turner Stevenson RW – R. 6'3", 215 lbs. b: Prince George, B.C., 5/18/1972. Montreal's 1st choice, 12th overall, in 1990 Entry Draft.

Season	Club	League	GP	G	A	Pts	AG	AA	APts	PIM	PP	SH	GW	S	%	TGF	PGF	TGA	PGA	+/–	GP	G	A	Pts	PIM	PP	SH	GW
1988-89	Seattle Thunderbirds	WHL	69	15	12	27	....	....	....	84	....	....	....	....	....	....	....	....	....	....	....	....	....	....	....	....	....	....
1989-90	Seattle Thunderbirds	WHL	62	29	32	61	....	....	....	276	....	....	....	....	....	....	....	....	....	....	13	3	2	5	35	....	....	....
1990-91	Seattle Thunderbirds	WHL	57	36	27	63	....	....	....	222	....	....	....	....	....	....	....	....	....	....	6	1	5	6	15	....	....	....
	Fredericton Canadiens	AHL	....	....	....	....	....	....	....	....	....	....	....	....	....	....	....	....	....	....	4	0	0	0	5	....	....	....
1991-92	Seattle Thunderbirds	WHL	58	20	32	52	....	....	....	264	....	....	....	....	....	....	....	....	....	....	15	9	3	12	55	....	....	....
	Canada	WJC-A	7	0	2	2	....	....	....	14	....	....	....	....	....	....	....	....	....	....	....	....	....	....	....	....	....	....
1992-93	**Montreal Canadiens**	**NHL**	1	0	0	0	0	0	0	0	0	0	0	1	0.0	0	0	1	0	–1	....	....	....	....	....	....	....	....
	Fredericton Canadiens	AHL	79	25	34	59	....	....	....	102	....	....	....	....	....	....	....	....	....	....	5	2	3	5	11	....	....	....
1993-94	**Montreal Canadiens**	**NHL**	2	0	0	0	0	0	0	2	0	0	0	0	0.0	0	0	2	0	–2	3	0	2	2	0	0	0	0
	Fredericton Canadiens	AHL	66	19	28	47	....	....	....	155	....	....	....	....	....	....	....	....	....	....	....	....	....	....	....	....	....	....
1994-95	Fredericton Canadiens	AHL	37	12	12	24	....	....	....	109	....	....	....	....	....	....	....	....	....	....	....	....	....	....	....	....	....	....
	Montreal Canadiens	**NHL**	41	6	1	7	11	1	12	86	0	0	1	35	17.1	10	0	11	1	0	....	....	....	....	....	....	....	....
1995-96	**Montreal Canadiens**	**NHL**	80	9	16	25	9	13	22	167	0	0	2	101	8.9	39	2	39	0	–2	6	0	1	1	2	0	0	0
1996-97	**Montreal Canadiens**	**NHL**	65	8	13	21	8	11	19	97	1	0	0	76	10.5	29	2	41	0	–14	5	1	1	2	2	0	0	0
1997-98	**Montreal Canadiens**	**NHL**	63	4	6	10	5	6	11	110	1	0	0	43	9.3	13	1	20	0	–8	10	3	4	7	12	0	0	0
	NHL Totals		252	27	36	63	33	31	64	462	2	0	3	256	10.5	91	5	114	1		24	4	8	12	16	0	0	0

WHL West First All-Star Team (1992) • Memorial Cup All-Star Team (1992)

• STEWART, ALLAN

Allan Stewart LW – L. 6', 195 lbs. b: Fort St. John, B.C., 1/31/1964. New Jersey's 9th choice, 213th overall, in 1983 Entry Draft.

Season	Club	League	GP	G	A	Pts	AG	AA	APts	PIM	PP	SH	GW	S	%	TGF	PGF	TGA	PGA	+/–	GP	G	A	Pts	PIM	PP	SH	GW
1981-82	Prince Albert Raiders	SJHL	46	9	25	34	....	....	....	53	....	....	....	....	....	....	....	....	....	....	....	....	....	....	....	....	....	....
1982-83	Prince Albert Raiders	WHL	70	25	34	59	....	....	....	272	....	....	....	....	....	....	....	....	....	....	....	....	....	....	....	....	....	....
1983-84	Prince Albert Raiders	WHL	67	44	39	83	....	....	....	216	....	....	....	....	....	....	....	....	....	....	5	1	2	3	29	....	....	....
	Maine Mariners	AHL	....	....	....	....	....	....	....	....	....	....	....	....	....	....	....	....	....	....	3	0	0	0	0	....	....	....
1984-85	Maine Mariners	AHL	75	8	11	19	....	....	....	241	....	....	....	....	....	....	....	....	....	....	11	1	2	3	58	....	....	....
1985-86	**New Jersey Devils**	**NHL**	4	0	0	0	0	0	0	21	0	0	0	0	0.0	0	0	1	0	–1	....	....	....	....	....	....	....	....
	Maine Mariners	AHL	58	7	12	19	....	....	....	181	....	....	....	....	....	....	....	....	....	....	....	....	....	....	....	....	....	....
1986-87	**New Jersey Devils**	**NHL**	7	1	0	1	1	0	1	26	0	0	0	8	12.5	3	0	9	2	–4	....	....	....	....	....	....	....	....
	Maine Mariners	AHL	74	14	24	38	....	....	....	143	....	....	....	....	....	....	....	....	....	....	....	....	....	....	....	....	....	....
1987-88	**New Jersey Devils**	**NHL**	1	0	0	0	0	0	0	0	0	0	0	0	0.0	2	0	0	0	+2	....	....	....	....	....	....	....	....
	Utica Devils	AHL	49	8	17	25	....	....	....	129	....	....	....	....	....	....	....	....	....	....	....	....	....	....	....	....	....	....
1988-89	**New Jersey Devils**	**NHL**	6	0	2	2	0	1	1	15	0	0	0	4	0.0	2	0	4	0	–2	....	....	....	....	....	....	....	....
	Utica Devils	AHL	72	9	23	32	....	....	....	110	....	....	....	....	....	....	....	....	....	....	5	1	0	1	4	....	....	....
1989-90	Utica Devils	AHL	1	0	0	0	....	....	....	0	....	....	....	....	....	....	....	....	....	....	1	0	0	0	11	....	....	....
1990-91	**New Jersey Devils**	**NHL**	41	5	2	7	5	2	7	159	0	0	0	33	15.2	16	0	32	10	–6	....	....	....	....	....	....	....	....
	Utica Devils	AHL	9	2	0	2	....	....	....	9	....	....	....	....	....	....	....	....	....	....	....	....	....	....	....	....	....	....
1991-92	**New Jersey Devils**	**NHL**	1	0	0	0	0	0	0	5	0	0	0	0	0.0	0	0	0	0	0	....	....	....	....	....	....	....	....
	Boston Bruins	**NHL**	4	0	0	0	0	0	0	17	0	0	0	1	0.0	0	0	1	0	–1	....	....	....	....	....	....	....	....
1992-93	Moncton Hawks	AHL	45	3	8	11	....	....	....	118	....	....	....	....	....	....	....	....	....	....	2	1	0	1	20	....	....	....
	NHL Totals		64	6	4	10	6	3	9	243	0	0	0	46	13.0	23	0	47	12		....	....	....	....	....	....	....	....

Traded to **Boston** by **New Jersey** for future considerations, October 16, 1991. Signed as a free agent by **Winnipeg**, October 5, 1992.

• STEWART, BILL

Bill Stewart D – R. 6'2", 190 lbs. b: Toronto, Ont., 10/6/1957. Buffalo's 3rd choice, 68th overall, in 1977 Amateur Draft

Season	Club	League	GP	G	A	Pts	AG	AA	APts	PIM	PP	SH	GW	S	%	TGF	PGF	TGA	PGA	+/–	GP	G	A	Pts	PIM	PP	SH	GW
1973-74	Dixie Beehives	OJHL	41	9	24	33	....	....	....	38	....	....	....	....	....	....	....	....	....	....	....	....	....	....	....	....	....	....
1974-75	Kitchener Rangers	OHA	55	6	15	21	....	....	....	70	....	....	....	....	....	....	....	....	....	....	....	....	....	....	....	....	....	....
1975-76	Kitchener Rangers	OHA	4	1	3	4	....	....	....	4	....	....	....	....	....	....	....	....	....	....	....	....	....	....	....	....	....	....
	St. Catharines Flyers	OHA	48	9	31	40	....	....	....	57	....	....	....	....	....	....	....	....	....	....	4	0	3	3	8	....	....	....
1976-77	Niagara Falls Flyers	OHA	59	18	37	55	....	....	....	202	....	....	....	....	....	....	....	....	....	....	....	....	....	....	....	....	....	....
1977-78	**Buffalo Sabres**	**NHL**	13	2	0	2	2	0	2	15	0	0	1	12	16.7	6	0	5	0	+1	8	0	2	2	0	0	0	0
	Hershey Bears	AHL	54	6	18	24	....	....	....	92	....	....	....	....	....	....	....	....	....	....	....	....	....	....	....	....	....	....
1978-79	**Buffalo Sabres**	**NHL**	68	1	17	18	1	13	14	101	0	0	0	87	1.1	76	4	80	13	+5	1	0	1	1	0	0	0	0
1979-80	Rochester Americans	AHL	63	12	28	40	....	....	....	189	....	....	....	....	....	....	....	....	....	....	4	1	2	3	42	....	....	....
1980-81	Rochester Americans	AHL	6	1	6	7	....	....	....	12	....	....	....	....	....	....	....	....	....	....	....	....	....	....	....	....	....	....
	St. Louis Blues	**NHL**	60	2	21	23	2	15	17	114	0	0	0	62	3.2	84	3	70	14	+19	4	1	0	1	11	0	0	0
	Salt Lake Golden Eagles	CHL	2	0	0	0	....	....	....	2	....	....	....	....	....	....	....	....	....	....	....	....	....	....	....	....	....	....
1981-82	**St. Louis Blues**	**NHL**	22	0	5	5	0	3	3	26	0	0	0	21	0.0	21	1	29	4	–5	....	....	....	....	....	....	....	....
	Salt Lake Golden Eagles	CHL	40	2	12	14	....	....	....	93	....	....	....	....	....	....	....	....	....	....	10	0	6	6	12	....	....	....
1982-83	**St. Louis Blues**	**NHL**	7	0	0	0	0	0	0	8	0	0	0	5	0.0	3	0	7	3	–1	....	....	....	....	....	....	....	....
	Salt Lake Golden Eagles	CHL	62	10	42	52	....	....	....	143	....	....	....	....	....	....	....	....	....	....	5	1	4	5	8	....	....	....
1983-84	**Toronto Maple Leafs**	**NHL**	56	2	17	19	2	12	14	116	0	0	0	42	4.8	61	2	86	26	–1	....	....	....	....	....	....	....	....
1984-85	**Toronto Maple Leafs**	**NHL**	27	0	2	2	0	1	1	32	0	0	0	9	0.0	21	0	28	4	–3	....	....	....	....	....	....	....	....
	St. Catharines Saints	AHL	12	2	5	7	....	....	....	11	....	....	....	....	....	....	....	....	....	....	....	....	....	....	....	....	....	....
1985-86	**Minnesota North Stars**	**NHL**	8	0	2	2	0	1	1	13	0	0	0	3	0.0	7	0	6	1	+2	....	....	....	....	....	....	....	....
	Springfield Indians	AHL	59	7	19	26	....	....	....	135	....	....	....	....	....	....	....	....	....	....	....	....	....	....	....	....	....	....
1986-87	SG Brunico	Italy	40	20	21	41	....	....	....	91	....	....	....	....	....	....	....	....	....	....	....	....	....	....	....	....	....	....

			REGULAR SEASON																		PLAYOFFS							
Season	Club	League	GP	G	A	Pts	AG	AA	APts	PIM	PP	SH	GW	S	%	TGF	PGF	TGA	PGA	+/–	GP	G	A	Pts	PIM	PP	SH	GW
1987-88	SG Brunico	Italy	34	8	35	43	....	....	....	62	....	....	....	....	....	....	....	....	....	....	....	....	....	....	....	....	....	....
1988-89	Milano	Italy	18	4	11	15	....	....	....	24	....	....	....	....	....	....	....	....	....	....	....	....	....	....	....	....	....	....
1989-90	Milano Saima	Italy2	STATISTICS NOT AVAILABLE																									
1990-91	Milano Saima	Italy	34	11	33	44	....	....	....	52	....	....	....	....	....	....	....	....	....	....	....	....	....	....	....	....	....	....
1991-92	Milano Devils	Italy	29	3	22	25	....	....	....	28	....	....	....	....	....	....	....	....	....	....	....	....	....	....	....	....	....	....
1992-93	Milano Lions	Italy	23	3	8	11	....	....	....	54	....	....	....	....	....	....	....	....	....	....	....	....	....	....	....	....	....	....
1993-94	Val Gardena	Italy	19	3	7	10	....	....	....	17	....	....	....	....	....	....	....	....	....	....	....	....	....	....	....	....	....	....
1994-95	Courmaosta	Italy	36	2	15	17	....	....	....	70	....	....	....	....	....	....	....	....	....	....	....	....	....	....	....	....	....	....
	NHL Totals		261	7	64	71	7	45	52	424	0	0	1	241	2.9	279	10	317	65		13	1	3	4	11	0	0	0

Claimed by Buffalo as a fill-in during Expansion Draft, June 13, 1979. Traded to **St. Louis** by **Buffalo** for Bob Hess, October 30, 1980. Signed as a free agent by **Toronto**, September 10, 1983. Signed as a free agent by **Minnesota**, September 15, 1985.

• STEWART, BLAIR

Blair Stewart C – R. 5'11", 185 lbs. b: Winnipeg, Man., 3/15/1953. Detroit's 5th choice, 75th overall, in 1973 Amateur Draft.

Season	Club	League	GP	G	A	Pts	AG	AA	APts	PIM	PP	SH	GW	S	%	TGF	PGF	TGA	PGA	+/–	GP	G	A	Pts	PIM	PP	SH	GW
1971-72	Winnipeg Jets	WCJHL	44	8	10	18	....	....	....	112	....	....	....	....	....	....	....	....	....	....	....	....	....	....	....	....	....	....
1972-73	Winnipeg Jets	WCJHL	68	24	36	60	....	....	....	151	....	....	....	....	....	....	....	....	....	....	....	....	....	....	....	....	....	....
1973-74	**Detroit Red Wings**	**NHL**	17	0	4	4	0	3	3	16	0	0	0	22	0.0	8	0	14	0	–6	....	....	....	....	....	....	....	....
	Virginia Wings	AHL	54	9	13	22	....	....	....	99	....	....	....	....	....	....	....	....	....	....	....	....	....	....	....	....	....	....
1974-75	Virginia Wings	AHL	26	7	10	17	....	....	....	93	....	....	....	....	....	....	....	....	....	....	....	....	....	....	....	....	....	....
	Detroit Red Wings	**NHL**	19	0	5	5	0	4	4	38	0	0	0	31	0.0	9	1	13	0	–5	....	....	....	....	....	....	....	....
	Washington Capitals	**NHL**	2	1	0	1	1	0	1	2	0	0	0	4	25.0	1	0	3	0	–2	....	....	....	....	....	....	....	....
1975-76	**Washington Capitals**	**NHL**	74	13	14	27	12	11	23	113	0	0	0	88	14.8	44	6	100	9	–53	....	....	....	....	....	....	....	....
1976-77	**Washington Capitals**	**NHL**	34	5	2	7	5	2	7	85	0	0	0	41	12.2	14	0	21	1	–6	....	....	....	....	....	....	....	....
	Springfield Indians	AHL	4	1	3	4	....	....	....	11	....	....	....	....	....	....	....	....	....	....	....	....	....	....	....	....	....	....
1977-78	**Washington Capitals**	**NHL**	8	0	1	1	0	1	1	9	0	0	0	4	0.0	2	0	5	0	–3	....	....	....	....	....	....	....	....
	Hershey Bears	AHL	20	9	9	18	....	....	....	46	....	....	....	....	....	....	....	....	....	....	....	....	....	....	....	....	....	....
1978-79	**Washington Capitals**	**NHL**	45	7	12	19	6	9	15	48	0	0	0	56	12.5	34	1	33	1	+1	....	....	....	....	....	....	....	....
	Hershey Bears	AHL	23	16	8	24	....	....	....	49	....	....	....	....	....	....	....	....	....	....	....	....	....	....	....	....	....	....
1979-80	**Quebec Nordiques**	**NHL**	30	8	6	14	7	5	12	15	0	1	2	53	15.1	22	4	24	8	+2	....	....	....	....	....	....	....	....
	Syracuse Firebirds	AHL	20	9	10	19	....	....	....	35	....	....	....	....	....	....	....	....	....	....	4	1	1	2	27	....	....	....
1980-81	Houston Apollos	CHL	9	1	0	1	....	....	....	24	....	....	....	....	....	....	....	....	....	....	....	....	....	....	....	....	....	....
	Fort Worth Texans	CHL	38	12	9	21	....	....	....	48	....	....	....	....	....	....	....	....	....	....	5	1	2	3	18	....	....	....
	NHL Totals		229	34	44	78	31	35	66	326	0	1	2	299	11.4	134	12	213	19		....	....	....	....	....	....	....	....

Traded to **Washington** by **Detroit** for Mike Bloom, March 9, 1975. Claimed by **Quebec** from **Washington** in Expansion Draft, June 13, 1979.

• STEWART, CAM

Cam Stewart LW – L. 5'11", 196 lbs. b: Kitchener, Ont., 9/18/1971. Boston's 4th choice, 63rd overall, in 1990 Entry Draft.

Season	Club	League	GP	G	A	Pts	AG	AA	APts	PIM	PP	SH	GW	S	%	TGF	PGF	TGA	PGA	+/–	GP	G	A	Pts	PIM	PP	SH	GW
1989-90	Elmira Sugar Kings	OJHL	46	44	95	139	....	....	....	172	....	....	....	....	....	....	....	....	....	....	....	....	....	....	....	....	....	....
1990-91	University of of Michigan	CCHA	44	8	24	32	....	....	....	122	....	....	....	....	....	....	....	....	....	....	....	....	....	....	....	....	....	....
1991-92	University of Michigan	CCHA	44	13	15	28	....	....	....	106	....	....	....	....	....	....	....	....	....	....	....	....	....	....	....	....	....	....
1992-93	University of Michigan	CCHA	39	20	39	59	....	....	....	69	....	....	....	....	....	....	....	....	....	....	....	....	....	....	....	....	....	....
1993-94	**Boston Bruins**	**NHL**	57	3	6	9	3	5	8	66	0	0	1	55	5.5	19	0	29	4	–6	8	0	3	3	7	0	0	0
	Providence Bruins	AHL	14	3	2	5	....	....	....	5	....	....	....	....	....	....	....	....	....	....	....	....	....	....	....	....	....	....
1994-95	**Boston Bruins**	**NHL**	5	0	0	0	0	0	0	2	0	0	0	2	0.0	1	0	2	1	0	....	....	....	....	....	....	....	....
	Providence Bruins	AHL	31	13	11	24	....	....	....	38	....	....	....	....	....	....	....	....	....	....	9	2	5	7	0	....	....	....
1995-96	**Boston Bruins**	**NHL**	6	0	0	0	0	0	0	0	0	0	0	2	0.0	0	0	2	0	–2	5	1	0	1	2	0	0	0
	Providence Bruins	AHL	54	17	25	42	....	....	....	39	....	....	....	....	....	....	....	....	....	....	....	....	....	....	....	....	....	....
1996-97	**Boston Bruins**	**NHL**	15	0	1	1	0	1	1	4	0	0	0	21	0.0	3	0	5	0	–2	....	....	....	....	....	....	....	....
	Providence Bruins	AHL	18	4	3	7	....	....	....	37	....	....	....	....	....	....	....	....	....	....	....	....	....	....	....	....	....	....
	Cincinnati Cyclones	IHL	7	3	2	5	....	....	....	8	....	....	....	....	....	....	....	....	....	....	1	0	0	0	0	....	....	....
1997-98	Houston Aeros	IHL	63	18	27	45	....	....	....	51	....	....	....	....	....	....	....	....	....	....	4	0	1	1	18	....	....	....
	NHL Totals		83	3	7	10	3	6	9	72	0	0	1	80	3.8	23	0	38	5		13	1	3	4	9	0	0	0

• STEWART, JOHN A.

John A. Stewart LW – L. 6', 180 lbs. b: Eriksdale, Man., 5/16/1950. Pittsburgh's 2nd choice, 21st overall, in 1970 Amateur Draft.

Season	Club	League	GP	G	A	Pts	AG	AA	APts	PIM	PP	SH	GW	S	%	TGF	PGF	TGA	PGA	+/–	GP	G	A	Pts	PIM	PP	SH	GW
1967-68	Winnipeg Jets	WCJHL	24	7	8	15	....	....	....	33	....	....	....	....	....	....	....	....	....	....	....	....	....	....	....	....	....	....
1968-69	Winnipeg Jets	WCJHL	4	3	1	4	....	....	....	5	....	....	....	....	....	....	....	....	....	....	....	....	....	....	....	....	....	....
	Sorel Eperviers	QJHL	STATISTICS NOT AVAILABLE																									
1969-70	Flin Flon Bombers	WCJHL	25	10	13	23	....	....	....	71	....	....	....	....	....	....	....	....	....	....	....	....	....	....	....	....	....	....
1970-71	**Pittsburgh Penguins**	**NHL**	15	2	1	3	2	1	3	9	1	0	0	25	8.0	8	4	13	0	–9	....	....	....	....	....	....	....	....
	Amarillo Wranglers	CHL	57	19	15	34	....	....	....	92	....	....	....	....	....	....	....	....	....	....	....	....	....	....	....	....	....	....
1971-72	**Pittsburgh Penguins**	**NHL**	25	2	8	10	2	7	9	23	0	0	0	33	6.1	16	3	19	0	–6	....	....	....	....	....	....	....	....
	Hershey Bears	AHL	46	10	17	27	....	....	....	32	....	....	....	....	....	....	....	....	....	....	4	1	2	3	4	....	....	....
1972-73	**Atlanta Flames**	**NHL**	68	17	17	34	17	14	31	30	2	0	3	168	10.1	53	16	47	1	–9	....	....	....	....	....	....	....	....
	Nova Scotia Voyageurs	AHL	5	3	3	6	....	....	....	7	....	....	....	....	....	....	....	....	....	....	....	....	....	....	....	....	....	....
1973-74	**Atlanta Flames**	**NHL**	74	18	15	33	18	13	31	41	3	0	3	143	12.6	53	7	43	0	+3	4	0	0	0	10	0	0	0
1974-75	**California Golden Seals**	**NHL**	76	19	19	38	18	15	33	55	2	0	2	191	9.9	62	15	95	6	–42	....	....	....	....	....	....	....	....
1975-76	Cleveland Crusaders	WHA	79	12	21	33	....	....	....	42	....	....	....	....	....	....	....	....	....	....	3	0	0	0	2	....	....	....
1976-77	Minnesota Fighting Saints	WHA	15	3	3	6	....	....	....	2	....	....	....	....	....	....	....	....	....	....	....	....	....	....	....	....	....	....
	Birmingham Bulls	WHA	1	0	0	0	....	....	....	0	....	....	....	....	....	....	....	....	....	....	....	....	....	....	....	....	....	....
1977-78	Philadelphia Firebirds	AHL	70	23	15	38	....	....	....	90	....	....	....	....	....	....	....	....	....	....	4	1	3	4	2	....	....	....
	NHL Totals		258	58	60	118	57	50	107	158	8	0	8	560	10.4	192	45	217	7		4	0	0	0	10	0	0	0
	Other Major League Totals		95	15	24	39	....	....	....	44	....	....	....	....	....	....	....	....	....	....	3	0	0	0	2	....	....	....

Selected by **Alberta** (WHA) in 1972 WHA General Player Draft, February 12, 1972. Claimed by **Atlanta** from **Pittsburgh** in Expansion Draft, June 6, 1972. Traded to **California** by **Atlanta** for Hilliard Graves, July 18, 1974. WHA rights traded to **Cleveland** (WHA) by **Edmonton** (WHA) for future considerations, June, 1975. Transferred to **Minnesota** (WHA) after **Cleveland** (WHA) franchise relocated, July, 1976. Signed as a free agent by **Birmingham** (WHA) after **Minnesota** (WHA) franchise folded, January, 1977.

• STEWART, JOHN C.

John C. "J.C." Stewart C – L. 6', 180 lbs. b: Toronto, Ont., 1/2/1954. Montreal's 11th choice, 105th overall, in 1974 Amateur Draft.

Season	Club	League	GP	G	A	Pts	AG	AA	APts	PIM	PP	SH	GW	S	%	TGF	PGF	TGA	PGA	+/–	GP	G	A	Pts	PIM	PP	SH	GW
1971-72	Markham Waxers	MTHL	STATISTICS NOT AVAILABLE																									
1972-73	Bowling Green University	CCHA	35	20	31	51	....	....	....	26	....	....	....	....	....	....	....	....	....	....	....	....	....	....	....	....	....	....
1973-74	Bowling Green University	CCHA	39	27	43	70	....	....	....	50	....	....	....	....	....	....	....	....	....	....	....	....	....	....	....	....	....	....
1974-75	Cleveland Crusaders	WHA	59	4	7	11	....	....	....	8	....	....	....	....	....	....	....	....	....	....	1	0	0	0	0	....	....	....
	Cape Cod Codders	NAHL	13	5	11	16	....	....	....	14	....	....	....	....	....	....	....	....	....	....	....	....	....	....	....	....	....	....
1975-76	Cleveland Crusaders	WHA	42	2	9	11	....	....	....	15	....	....	....	....	....	....	....	....	....	....	....	....	....	....	....	....	....	....
	Syracuse Blazers	NAHL	23	11	17	28	....	....	....	29	....	....	....	....	....	....	....	....	....	....	....	....	....	....	....	....	....	....
1976-77	Birmingham Bulls	WHA	52	17	24	41	....	....	....	33	....	....	....	....	....	....	....	....	....	....	....	....	....	....	....	....	....	....
	Syracuse Blazers	NAHL	18	18	36	54	....	....	....	4	....	....	....	....	....	....	....	....	....	....	....	....	....	....	....	....	....	....
1977-78	Birmingham Bulls	WHA	48	13	26	39	....	....	....	52	....	....	....	....	....	....	....	....	....	....	5	1	1	2	6	....	....	....
	Philadelphia Firebirds	AHL	24	11	13	24	....	....	....	44	....	....	....	....	....	....	....	....	....	....	....	....	....	....	....	....	....	....
1978-79	Birmingham Bulls	WHA	71	24	26	50	....	....	....	108	....	....	....	....	....	....	....	....	....	....	....	....	....	....	....	....	....	....
1979-80	**Quebec Nordiques**	**NHL**	2	0	0	0	0	0	0	0	0	0	0	4	0.0	0	0	2	0	–2	....	....	....	....	....	....	....	....
	Syracuse Firebirds	AHL	71	28	40	68	....	....	....	59	....	....	....	....	....	....	....	....	....	....	2	0	0	0	0	....	....	....
1980-81	Birmingham Bulls	CHL	57	22	32	55	....	....	....	57	....	....	....	....	....	....	....	....	....	....	....	....	....	....	....	....	....	....
	Binghamton Whalers	AHL	18	10	10	20	....	....	....	29	....	....	....	....	....	....	....	....	....	....	6	4	2	6	2	....	....	....
1981-82	Berliner SC	Germany	35	12	17	29	....	....	....	46	....	....	....	....	....	....	....	....	....	....	....	....	....	....	....	....	....	....
	NHL Totals		2	0	0	0	0	0	0	0	0	0	0	4	0.0	0	0	2	0		....	....	....	....	....	....	....	....

CCHA Second All-Star Team (1974)

Selected by **Cleveland** (WHA) in 1973 WHA Amateur Draft, May, 1974. Transferred to **Minnesota** (WHA) after **Cleveland** (WHA) franchise relocated, July, 1976. Signed as a free agent by **Birmingham** (WHA) after **Minnesota** (WHA) franchise folded, January, 1977. Claimed by **Quebec** from **Birmingham** (WHA) in WHA Dispersal Draft, June 9, 1979. Signed as a free agent by **Calgary**, August, 1980. Traded to **Hartford** by **Calgary** for future considerations, February, 1981.

			REGULAR SEASON																	PLAYOFFS							
Season	Club	League	GP	G	A	Pts	AG	AA	APts	PIM	PP	SH	GW	S	%	TGF	PGF	TGA	PGA	+/–	GP	G	A	Pts	PIM	PP	SH	GW

● **STEWART, PAUL** Paul Stewart LW/D – L. 6'1", 205 lbs. b: Boston, MA, 3/21/1954.

1975-76	Binghamton Dusters	NAHL	46	3	4	7	....	....	....	273	....	....	....	....	....	....	....	....	....	....	....	....	....	....	....	....	....	....
1976-77	Edmonton Oilers	WHA	2	0	0	0	....	....	....	2	....	....	....	....	....	....	....	....	....	....	....	....	....	....	....	....	....	....
	New Haven Nighthawks	AHL	1	0	0	0	....	....	....	6	....	....	....	....	....	....	....	....	....	....	....	....	....	....	....	....	....	....
	Binghamton Dusters	NAHL	60	4	13	17	....	....	....	232	....	....	....	....	....	....	....	....	....	....	10	1	1	32	35	....	....	....
1977-78	Cincinnati Stingers	WHA	40	1	5	6	....	....	....	241	....	....	....	....	....	....	....	....	....	....	....	....	....	....	....	....	....	....
	Binghamton Dusters	AHL	21	5	2	7	....	....	....	69	....	....	....	....	....	....	....	....	....	....	....	....	....	....	....	....	....	....
1978-79	Cincinnati Stingers	WHA	23	2	1	3	....	....	....	45	....	....	....	....	....	....	....	....	....	....	3	0	0	0	0	....	....	....
	Philadelphia Firebirds	AHL	16	2	0	2	....	....	....	92	....	....	....	....	....	....	....	....	....	....	....	....	....	....	....	....	....	....
	Binghamton Dusters	AHL	7	1	2	3	....	....	....	40	....	....	....	....	....	....	....	....	....	....	....	....	....	....	....	....	....	....
1979-80	**Quebec Nordiques**	**NHL**	**21**	**2**	**0**	**2**	**2**	**0**	**2**	**74**	**0**	**0**	**0**	**9**	**22.2**	**7**	**0**	**8**	**0**	**–1**	....	....	....	....	....	....	....	....
	Cincinnati Stingers	CHL	20	1	2	3	....	....	....	79	....	....	....	....	....	....	....	....	....	....	....	....	....	....	....	....	....	....
	Birmingham Bulls	CHL	10	0	0	0	....	....	....	56	....	....	....	....	....	....	....	....	....	....	....	....	....	....	....	....	....	....
1980-81	Binghamton Whalers	AHL	15	2	1	3	....	....	....	59	....	....	....	....	....	....	....	....	....	....	....	....	....	....	....	....	....	....
1981-82	Cape Cod Buccaneers	ACHL	5	0	2	2	....	....	....	20	....	....	....	....	....	....	....	....	....	....	....	....	....	....	....	....	....	....
1982-83	Mohawk Valley Stars	ACHL	....	....	....	....	....	....	....	....	....	....	....	....	....	....	....	....	....	....	2	0	0	0	2	....	....	....
	NHL Totals		**21**	**2**	**0**	**2**	**2**	**0**	**2**	**74**	**0**	**0**	**0**	**9**	**22.2**	**7**	**0**	**8**	**0**		....	....	....	....	....	....	....	....
	Other Major League Totals		65	3	6	9	....	....	....	288	....	....	....	....	....	....	....	....	....	....	3	0	0	0	0	....	....	....

Signed as a free agent by **Edmonton** (WHA), October, 1976. Signed as a free agent by **Cincinnati** (WHA), December, 1977. Claimed by **Quebec** from **Cincinnati** (WHA) in WHA Dispersal Draft, June 9, 1979.

● **STEWART, RALPH** Ralph Stewart C – L. 6'1", 190 lbs. b: Fort William, Ont., 12/2/1948. **USHOF**

1965-66	Montreal Jr. Canadiens	OHA	46	7	9	16	....	....	....	28	....	....	....	....	....	....	....	....	....	....	10	0	0	0	2	....	....	....
1966-67	Montreal Jr. Canadiens	OHA	48	6	23	29	....	....	....	49	....	....	....	....	....	....	....	....	....	....	6	4	1	5	0	....	....	....
1967-68	Montreal Jr. Canadiens	OHA	43	17	31	48	....	....	....	28	....	....	....	....	....	....	....	....	....	....	11	5	4	9	8	....	....	....
1968-69	Vancouver Canucks	WHL	6	0	1	1	....	....	....	0	....	....	....	....	....	....	....	....	....	....	....	....	....	....	....	....	....	....
	Houston Apollos	CHL	44	10	17	27	....	....	....	10	....	....	....	....	....	....	....	....	....	....	3	0	0	0	0	....	....	....
1969-70	Kansas City Blues	CHL	72	21	21	42	....	....	....	37	....	....	....	....	....	....	....	....	....	....	....	....	....	....	....	....	....	....
1970-71	**Vancouver Canucks**	**NHL**	**3**	**0**	**1**	**1**	**0**	**1**	**1**	**0**	**0**	**0**	**0**	**2**	**0.0**	**2**	**1**	**2**	**0**	**–1**	....	....	....	....	....	....	....	....
	Rochester Americans	AHL	66	27	16	43	....	....	....	14	....	....	....	....	....	....	....	....	....	....	....	....	....	....	....	....	....	....
1971-72	Seattle Totems	WHL	16	2	6	8	....	....	....	4	....	....	....	....	....	....	....	....	....	....	....	....	....	....	....	....	....	....
	Tidewater Wings	AHL	20	3	8	11	....	....	....	8	....	....	....	....	....	....	....	....	....	....	....	....	....	....	....	....	....	....
	Fort Worth Wings	CHL	38	21	36	57	....	....	....	23	....	....	....	....	....	....	....	....	....	....	7	6	6	12	6	....	....	....
1972-73	Fort Worth Wings	CHL	39	29	36	65	....	....	....	23	....	....	....	....	....	....	....	....	....	....	....	....	....	....	....	....	....	....
	New York Islanders	**NHL**	**31**	**4**	**10**	**14**	**4**	**8**	**12**	**4**	**0**	**0**	**0**	**68**	**5.9**	**21**	**2**	**30**	**0**	**–11**	....	....	....	....	....	....	....	....
1973-74	**New York Islanders**	**NHL**	**67**	**23**	**20**	**43**	**23**	**17**	**40**	**6**	**2**	**5**	**2**	**178**	**12.9**	**54**	**11**	**69**	**19**	**–7**	....	....	....	....	....	....	....	....
1974-75	**New York Islanders**	**NHL**	**70**	**16**	**24**	**40**	**15**	**19**	**34**	**12**	**6**	**1**	**2**	**145**	**11.0**	**55**	**18**	**58**	**12**	**–9**	**13**	**3**	**3**	**6**	**2**	**1**	**0**	**0**
1975-76	**New York Islanders**	**NHL**	**31**	**6**	**7**	**13**	**6**	**5**	**11**	**2**	**0**	**1**	**1**	**28**	**21.4**	**19**	**1**	**16**	**1**	**+3**	**6**	**1**	**1**	**2**	**0**	**1**	**0**	**0**
	Fort Worth Texans	CHL	3	2	5	7	....	....	....	2	....	....	....	....	....	....	....	....	....	....	....	....	....	....	....	....	....	....
1976-77	**Vancouver Canucks**	**NHL**	**34**	**6**	**8**	**14**	**6**	**6**	**12**	**4**	**0**	**0**	**1**	**54**	**11.1**	**23**	**1**	**26**	**7**	**+3**	....	....	....	....	....	....	....	....
	Tulsa Oilers	CHL	43	24	26	50	....	....	....	14	....	....	....	....	....	....	....	....	....	....	....	....	....	....	....	....	....	....
1977-78	**Vancouver Canucks**	**NHL**	**16**	**2**	**3**	**5**	**2**	**2**	**4**	**0**	**1**	**0**	**0**	**28**	**7.1**	**5**	**1**	**15**	**1**	**–10**	....	....	....	....	....	....	....	....
	Tulsa Oilers	CHL	50	16	29	45	....	....	....	12	....	....	....	....	....	....	....	....	....	....	7	6	3	0	0	....	....	....
1978-79	Fort Worth Texans	CHL	76	15	33	48	....	....	....	8	....	....	....	....	....	....	....	....	....	....	5	0	0	0	4	....	....	....
	NHL Totals		**252**	**57**	**73**	**130**	**56**	**58**	**114**	**28**	**9**	**7**	**6**	**503**	**11.3**	**179**	**35**	**216**	**40**		**19**	**4**	**4**	**8**	**2**	**2**	**0**	**0**

Claimed by **Vancouver** from **Montreal** in Expansion Draft, June 10, 1970. Traded to **Detroit** by **Vancouver** for Jim Niekamp, March 6, 1972. Traded to **NY Islanders** by **Detroit** with Bob Cook for Ken Murray and Brian Lavender, January 17, 1973. Traded to **Vancouver** by **NY Islanders** with Dave Fortier for cash, October 6, 1976.

● **STEWART, ROBERT** Robert Stewart D – L. 6'1", 206 lbs. b: Charlottetown, P.E.I., 11/10/1950. Boston's 4th choice, 13th overall, in 1970 Amateur Draft.

1967-68	Oshawa Generals	OHA	50	2	11	13	....	....	....	172	....	....	....	....	....	....	....	....	....	....	....	....	....	....	....	....	....	....
1968-69	Oshawa Generals	OHA	52	7	32	39	....	....	....	226	....	....	....	....	....	....	....	....	....	....	....	....	....	....	....	....	....	....
1969-70	Oshawa Generals	OHA	44	11	24	35	....	....	....	159	....	....	....	....	....	....	....	....	....	....	....	....	....	....	....	....	....	....
1970-71	Oklahoma City Blazers	CHL	61	6	16	22	....	....	....	270	....	....	....	....	....	....	....	....	....	....	5	0	1	1	23	....	....	....
1971-72	**Boston Bruins**	**NHL**	**8**	**0**	**0**	**0**	**0**	**0**	**0**	**15**	**0**	**0**	**0**	**0**	**0.0**	**5**	**0**	**2**	**0**	**+3**	....	....	....	....	....	....	....	....
	Oklahoma City Blazers	CHL	10	1	3	4	....	....	....	34	....	....	....	....	....	....	....	....	....	....	....	....	....	....	....	....	....	....
	Boston Braves	AHL	39	1	7	8	....	....	....	102	....	....	....	....	....	....	....	....	....	....	....	....	....	....	....	....	....	....
	California Golden Seals	**NHL**	**16**	**1**	**2**	**3**	**1**	**2**	**3**	**44**	**0**	**0**	**0**	**18**	**5.6**	**13**	**0**	**27**	**3**	**–11**	....	....	....	....	....	....	....	....
1972-73	**California Golden Seals**	**NHL**	**63**	**4**	**17**	**21**	**4**	**14**	**18**	**101**	**0**	**0**	**0**	**93**	**4.2**	**68**	**1**	**139**	**26**	**–46**	....	....	....	....	....	....	....	....
1973-74	**California Golden Seals**	**NHL**	**47**	**2**	**5**	**7**	**2**	**4**	**6**	**69**	**1**	**0**	**0**	**42**	**4.8**	**38**	**4**	**91**	**15**	**–42**	....	....	....	....	....	....	....	....
1974-75	**California Golden Seals**	**NHL**	**67**	**5**	**12**	**17**	**5**	**9**	**14**	**93**	**0**	**0**	**1**	**87**	**5.7**	**71**	**2**	**122**	**35**	**–18**	....	....	....	....	....	....	....	....
1975-76	**California Golden Seals**	**NHL**	**76**	**4**	**17**	**21**	**4**	**13**	**17**	**112**	**2**	**0**	**0**	**67**	**6.0**	**71**	**13**	**122**	**30**	**–34**	....	....	....	....	....	....	....	....
1976-77	**Cleveland Barons**	**NHL**	**73**	**1**	**12**	**13**	**1**	**10**	**11**	**108**	**0**	**0**	**0**	**69**	**1.4**	**67**	**2**	**119**	**23**	**–31**	....	....	....	....	....	....	....	....
1977-78	**Cleveland Barons**	**NHL**	**72**	**2**	**15**	**17**	**2**	**12**	**14**	**84**	**0**	**0**	**0**	**57**	**3.5**	**80**	**3**	**131**	**29**	**–25**	....	....	....	....	....	....	....	....
1978-79	**St. Louis Blues**	**NHL**	**78**	**5**	**13**	**18**	**5**	**10**	**15**	**47**	**1**	**0**	**0**	**57**	**8.8**	**76**	**2**	**149**	**47**	**–28**	....	....	....	....	....	....	....	....
1979-80	**St. Louis Blues**	**NHL**	**10**	**0**	**1**	**1**	**0**	**1**	**1**	**4**	**0**	**0**	**0**	**7**	**0.0**	**7**	**0**	**9**	**1**	**–1**	....	....	....	....	....	....	....	....
	Pittsburgh Penguins	**NHL**	**65**	**3**	**7**	**10**	**3**	**5**	**8**	**52**	**0**	**0**	**0**	**53**	**5.7**	**57**	**3**	**99**	**18**	**–27**	**5**	**1**	**1**	**2**	**2**	**0**	**0**	**0**
	NHL Totals		**575**	**27**	**101**	**128**	**27**	**80**	**107**	**809**	**4**	**0**	**1**	**552**	**4.9**	**553**	**30**	**1010**	**227**		**5**	**1**	**1**	**2**	**2**	**0**	**0**	**0**

OHA First All-Star Team (1970)

Traded to **California** by **Boston** with Reggie Leach and Rick Smith for Carol Vadnais and Don O'Donoghue, February 23, 1972. Transferred to **Cleveland** after **California** franchise relocated, August 26, 1976. Claimed as a fill-in by **Minnesota** during **Cleveland-Minnesota** Dispersal Draft, June 15, 1978. Traded to **St. Louis** by **Minnesota** for St. Louis' 2nd round choice (Jali Wahlsten) in 1981 Entry Draft and future considerations, June 15, 1978. Traded to **Pittsburgh** by **St. Louis** for Blair Chapman, November 13, 1979.

● **STEWART, RON** Ron "Stew" Stewart C – R. 5'11", 171 lbs. b: Calgary, Alta., 7/11/1932.

1949-50	Toronto Marlboros	OHA	30	2	5	7	....	....	....	41	....	....	....	....	....	....	....	....	....	....	5	0	1	1	8	....	....	....
1950-51	Toronto Marlboros	OHA	53	22	23	45	....	....	....	49	....	....	....	....	....	....	....	....	....	....	13	6	8	14	31	....	....	....
1951-52	Toronto Marlboros	OHA	21	9	10	19	....	....	....	57	....	....	....	....	....	....	....	....	....	....	....	....	....	....	....	....	....	....
	Barrie Flyers	OHA	29	13	18	31	....	....	....	43	....	....	....	....	....	....	....	....	....	....	....	....	....	....	....	....	....	....
	Guelph Biltmores	OHA	....	....	....	....	....	....	....	....	....	....	....	....	....	....	....	....	....	....	23	17	14	31	14	....	....	....
1952-53	**Toronto Maple Leafs**	**NHL**	**70**	**13**	**22**	**35**	**20**	**31**	**51**	**29**	....	....	....	....	....	....	....	....	....	....	....	....	....	....	....	....	....	....
1953-54	**Toronto Maple Leafs**	**NHL**	**70**	**14**	**11**	**25**	**21**	**15**	**36**	**72**	....	....	....	....	....	....	....	....	....	....	**5**	**0**	**1**	**1**	**10**	....	....	....
1954-55	**Toronto Maple Leafs**	**NHL**	**53**	**14**	**5**	**19**	**20**	**6**	**26**	**20**	....	....	....	....	....	....	....	....	....	....	**4**	**0**	**0**	**0**	**2**	....	....	....
1955-56	**Toronto Maple Leafs**	**NHL**	**69**	**13**	**14**	**27**	**19**	**17**	**36**	**35**	....	....	....	....	....	....	....	....	....	....	**5**	**1**	**1**	**2**	**2**	....	....	....
1956-57	**Toronto Maple Leafs**	**NHL**	**65**	**15**	**20**	**35**	**20**	**23**	**43**	**28**	....	....	....	....	....	....	....	....	....	....	....	....	....	....	....	....	....	....
1957-58	**Toronto Maple Leafs**	**NHL**	**70**	**15**	**24**	**39**	**20**	**26**	**46**	**51**	....	....	....	....	....	....	....	....	....	....	....	....	....	....	....	....	....	....
1958-59	**Toronto Maple Leafs**	**NHL**	**70**	**21**	**13**	**34**	**27**	**14**	**41**	**23**	....	....	....	....	....	....	....	....	....	....	**12**	**3**	**3**	**6**	**6**	....	....	....
1959-60	**Toronto Maple Leafs**	**NHL**	**67**	**14**	**20**	**34**	**17**	**20**	**37**	**28**	....	....	....	....	....	....	....	....	....	....	**10**	**0**	**2**	**2**	**2**	....	....	....
1960-61	**Toronto Maple Leafs**	**NHL**	**51**	**13**	**12**	**25**	**16**	**12**	**28**	**8**	....	....	....	....	....	....	....	....	....	....	**5**	**1**	**0**	**1**	**2**	....	....	....
1961-62	**Toronto Maple Leafs**	**NHL**	**60**	**8**	**9**	**17**	**10**	**9**	**19**	**14**	....	....	....	....	....	....	....	....	....	....	**11**	**1**	**6**	**7**	**4**	....	....	....
1962-63	**Toronto Maple Leafs**	**NHL**	**63**	**16**	**16**	**32**	**20**	**17**	**37**	**26**	....	....	....	....	....	....	....	....	....	....	**10**	**4**	**0**	**4**	**2**	....	....	....
1963-64	**Toronto Maple Leafs**	**NHL**	**65**	**14**	**5**	**19**	**18**	**5**	**23**	**46**	....	....	....	....	....	....	....	....	....	....	**14**	**0**	**4**	**4**	**24**	....	....	....
1964-65	**Toronto Maple Leafs**	**NHL**	**65**	**16**	**11**	**27**	**20**	**12**	**32**	**33**	....	....	....	....	....	....	....	....	....	....	**6**	**0**	**1**	**1**	**2**	....	....	....
1965-66	**Boston Bruins**	**NHL**	**70**	**20**	**16**	**36**	**24**	**16**	**40**	**17**	....	....	....	....	....	....	....	....	....	....	....	....	....	....	....	....	....	....
1966-67	**Boston Bruins**	**NHL**	**56**	**14**	**10**	**24**	**17**	**10**	**27**	**31**	....	....	....	....	....	....	....	....	....	....	....	....	....	....	....	....	....	....
1967-68	**St. Louis Blues**	**NHL**	**19**	**7**	**5**	**12**	**9**	**5**	**14**	**11**	**1**	**1**	**2**	**69**	**10.1**	**17**	**7**	**22**	**5**	**–7**	....	....	....	....	....	....	....	....
	New York Rangers	**NHL**	**55**	**7**	**7**	**14**	**9**	**7**	**16**	**19**	**0**	**0**	**1**	**101**	**6.9**	**32**	**5**	**44**	**13**	**–4**	**6**	**1**	**1**	**2**	**2**	**0**	**0**	**0**
1968-69	**New York Rangers**	**NHL**	**75**	**18**	**11**	**29**	**20**	**10**	**30**	**20**	**1**	**2**	**5**	**184**	**9.8**	**41**	**3**	**68**	**19**	**–11**	**4**	**0**	**1**	**1**	**0**	**0**	**0**	**0**
1969-70	**New York Rangers**	**NHL**	**76**	**14**	**10**	**24**	**16**	**10**	**26**	**14**	**1**	**4**	**5**	**109**	**12.8**	**35**	**4**	**45**	**21**	**+7**	**6**	**0**	**0**	**0**	**2**	**0**	**0**	**0**
1970-71	**New York Rangers**	**NHL**	**76**	**5**	**6**	**11**	**5**	**5**	**10**	**19**	**0**	**2**	**1**	**52**	**9.6**	**19**	**2**	**30**	**22**	**+9**	**13**	**1**	**0**	**1**	**0**	**0**	**1**	**0**

Season	Club	League	REGULAR SEASON GP	G	A	Pts	AG	AA	APts	PIM	PP	SH	GW	S	%	TGF	PGF	TGA	PGA	+/–	PLAYOFFS GP	G	A	Pts	PIM	PP	SH	GW
1971-72	Providence Reds	AHL	18	6	5	11	....	....	....	2	....	....	....	....	....	....	....	....	....	....	....	....	....	....	....	....	....	....
	Vancouver Canucks	**NHL**	**42**	**3**	**1**	**4**	**3**	**1**	**4**	**10**	**0**	**0**	**0**	**19**	**15.8**	**8**	**0**	**34**	**23**	**–3**	....	....	....	....	....	....	....	....
	New York Rangers	**NHL**	**13**	**0**	**2**	**2**	**0**	**2**	**2**	**2**	**0**	**0**	**0**	**10**	**0.0**	**3**	**1**	**10**	**2**	**–6**	**8**	**2**	**1**	**3**	**0**	**0**	**0**	**0**
1972-73	**New York Rangers**	**NHL**	**11**	**0**	**1**	**1**	**0**	**1**	**1**	**0**	**0**	**0**	**0**	**8**	**0.0**	**2**	**0**	**3**	**1**	**0**	....	....	....	....	....	....	....	....
	New York Islanders	**NHL**	**22**	**2**	**2**	**4**	**2**	**2**	**4**	**4**	**2**	**0**	**0**	**11**	**18.2**	**10**	**4**	**34**	**11**	**–17**	....	....	....	....	....	....	....	....
	NHL Totals		**1353**	**276**	**253**	**529**	**353**	**276**	**629**	**560**	**5**	**9**	**14**	**563**	**49.0**	**167**	**26**	**290**	**117**		**119**	**14**	**21**	**35**	**60**	**0**	**1**	**0**

Played in NHL All-Star Game (1955, 1962, 1963, 1964)

Traded to **Boston** by **Toronto** for Orland Kurtenbach, Andy Hebenton and Pat Stapleton, June 8, 1965. Claimed by **St. Louis** from **Boston** in Expansion Draft, June 6, 1967. Traded to **NY Rangers** by **St. Louis** with Ron Attwell for Red Berenson and Barclay Plager, November 29, 1967. Traded to **Vancouver** by **NY Rangers** with Dave Balon and Wayne Connelly for Gary Doak and Jim Wiste, November 16, 1971. Traded to **NY Rangers** by **Vancouver** for cash, March 5, 1972. Traded to **NY Islanders** by **NY Rangers** for cash, November 14, 1972.

• STEWART, RYAN

Ryan Stewart C – R. 6′1″, 175 lbs. b: Houston, B.C., 6/1/1967. Winnipeg's 14th choice, 18th overall, in 1985 Entry Draft.

Season	Club	League	GP	G	A	Pts	AG	AA	APts	PIM	PP	SH	GW	S	%	TGF	PGF	TGA	PGA	+/–	GP	G	A	Pts	PIM	PP	SH	GW
1983-84	Kamloops Jr. Oilers	WHL	69	31	38	69	....	....	....	88	....	....	....	....	....	....	....	....	....	....	16	7	7	14	19	....	....	....
1984-85	Kamloops Blazers	WHL	54	33	37	70	....	....	....	92	....	....	....	....	....	....	....	....	....	....	11	6	6	12	34	....	....	....
1985-86	Kamloops Blazers	WHL	10	7	11	18	....	....	....	27	....	....	....	....	....	....	....	....	....	....	....	....	....	....	....	....	....	....
	Prince Albert Raiders	WHL	52	45	33	78	....	....	....	55	....	....	....	....	....	....	....	....	....	....	15	7	8	15	21	....	....	....
	Winnipeg Jets	**NHL**	**3**	**1**	**0**	**1**	**1**	**0**	**1**	**0**	**0**	**0**	**0**	**5**	**20.0**	**1**	**0**	**1**	**0**	**0**	....	....	....	....	....	....	....	....
1986-87	Brandon Wheat Kings	WHL	15	7	9	16	....	....	....	15	....	....	....	....	....	....	....	....	....	....	....	....	....	....	....	....	....	....
	Portland Winter Hawks	WHL	7	5	2	7	....	....	....	12	....	....	....	....	....	....	....	....	....	....	17	7	11	18	34	....	....	....
1987-88	Moncton Hawks	AHL	48	5	18	23	....	....	....	83	....	....	....	....	....	....	....	....	....	....	....	....	....	....	....	....	....	....
1988-89	Maine Mariners	AHL	7	1	0	1	....	....	....	7	....	....	....	....	....	....	....	....	....	....	....	....	....	....	....	....	....	....
	Moncton Hawks	AHL	1	0	0	0	....	....	....	0	....	....	....	....	....	....	....	....	....	....	....	....	....	....	....	....	....	....
1989-90			STATISTICS NOT AVAILABLE																									
1990-91	Albany Choppers	IHL	1	0	0	0	....	....	....	10	....	....	....	....	....	....	....	....	....	....	....	....	....	....	....	....	....	....
1991-92	Swindon Wildcats	Britain	34	79	65	144	....	....	....	....	....	....	....	....	....	....	....	....	....	....	6	20	13	33	10	....	....	....
1992-93	Swindon Wildcats	Britain	31	71	57	128	....	....	....	66	....	....	....	....	....	....	....	....	....	....	6	8	5	13	6	....	....	....
	NHL Totals		**3**	**1**	**0**	**1**	**1**	**0**	**1**	**0**	**0**	**0**	**0**	**5**	**20.0**	**1**	**0**	**1**	**0**		....	....	....	....	....	....	....	....

• STIENBURG, TREVOR

Trevor Stienburg RW – R. 6′1″, 200 lbs. b: Kingston, Ont., 5/13/1966. Quebec's 1st choice, 15th overall, in 1984 Entry Draft.

Season	Club	League	GP	G	A	Pts	AG	AA	APts	PIM	PP	SH	GW	S	%	TGF	PGF	TGA	PGA	+/–	GP	G	A	Pts	PIM	PP	SH	GW
1982-83	Brockville Braves	Jr. B	47	39	30	69	....	....	....	182	....	....	....	....	....	....	....	....	....	....	....	....	....	....	....	....	....	....
1983-84	Guelph Platers	OHL	65	33	18	51	....	....	....	104	....	....	....	....	....	....	....	....	....	....	....	....	....	....	....	....	....	....
1984-85	Guelph Platers	OHL	18	7	12	19	....	....	....	38	....	....	....	....	....	....	....	....	....	....	....	....	....	....	....	....	....	....
	London Knights	OHL	22	9	11	20	....	....	....	45	....	....	....	....	....	....	....	....	....	....	8	1	3	4	22	....	....	....
1985-86	**Quebec Nordiques**	**NHL**	**2**	**1**	**0**	**1**	**1**	**0**	**1**	**0**	**0**	**0**	**0**	**6**	**16.7**	**2**	**0**	**2**	**0**	**0**	**1**	**0**	**0**	**0**	**0**	**0**	**0**	**0**
	London Knights	OHL	31	12	18	30	....	....	....	88	....	....	....	....	....	....	....	....	....	....	5	0	0	0	20	....	....	....
1986-87	**Quebec Nordiques**	**NHL**	**6**	**1**	**0**	**1**	**1**	**0**	**1**	**12**	**0**	**0**	**1**	**6**	**16.7**	**1**	**0**	**1**	**0**	**0**	....	....	....	....	....	....	....	....
	Fredericton Express	AHL	48	14	12	26	....	....	....	123	....	....	....	....	....	....	....	....	....	....	....	....	....	....	....	....	....	....
1987-88	**Quebec Nordiques**	**NHL**	**8**	**0**	**1**	**1**	**0**	**1**	**1**	**24**	**0**	**0**	**0**	**3**	**0.0**	**1**	**0**	**2**	**0**	**–1**	....	....	....	....	....	....	....	....
	Fredericton Express	AHL	55	12	24	36	....	....	....	279	....	....	....	....	....	....	....	....	....	....	13	3	3	6	115	....	....	....
1988-89	**Quebec Nordiques**	**NHL**	**55**	**6**	**3**	**9**	**5**	**2**	**7**	**125**	**1**	**0**	**0**	**65**	**9.2**	**17**	**3**	**31**	**0**	**–17**	....	....	....	....	....	....	....	....
1989-90	Halifax Citadels	AHL	11	3	3	6	....	....	....	36	....	....	....	....	....	....	....	....	....	....	....	....	....	....	....	....	....	....
1990-91	Halifax Citadels	AHL	41	16	7	23	....	....	....	190	....	....	....	....	....	....	....	....	....	....	....	....	....	....	....	....	....	....
1991-92	New Haven Nighthawks	AHL	66	17	22	39	....	....	....	201	....	....	....	....	....	....	....	....	....	....	1	0	0	0	2	....	....	....
1992-93	Springfield Indians	AHL	65	14	20	34	....	....	....	244	....	....	....	....	....	....	....	....	....	....	10	0	0	0	31	....	....	....
1993-94	Springfield Indians	AHL	47	4	10	14	....	....	....	134	....	....	....	....	....	....	....	....	....	....	....	....	....	....	....	....	....	....
	NHL Totals		**71**	**8**	**4**	**12**	**7**	**3**	**10**	**161**	**1**	**0**	**1**	**80**	**10.0**	**21**	**3**	**36**	**0**		**1**	**0**	**0**	**0**	**0**	**0**	**0**	**0**

Signed as a free agent by **Hartford**, July 21, 1992.

• STILES, TONY

Tony Stiles D – L. 5′11″, 200 lbs. b: Carstairs, Alta., 8/12/1959.

Season	Club	League	GP	G	A	Pts	AG	AA	APts	PIM	PP	SH	GW	S	%	TGF	PGF	TGA	PGA	+/–	GP	G	A	Pts	PIM	PP	SH	GW
1980-81	Michigan Tech Huskies	CCHA	44	10	20	30	....	....	....	58	....	....	....	....	....	....	....	....	....	....	....	....	....	....	....	....	....	....
1981-82	Michigan Tech Huskies	CCHA	38	7	14	21	....	....	....	26	....	....	....	....	....	....	....	....	....	....	....	....	....	....	....	....	....	....
1982-83	Colorado Flames	CHL	58	2	7	9	....	....	....	53	....	....	....	....	....	....	....	....	....	....	1	0	0	0	0	....	....	....
1983-84	**Calgary Flames**	**NHL**	**30**	**2**	**7**	**9**	**2**	**5**	**7**	**20**	**0**	**0**	**0**	**19**	**10.5**	**34**	**0**	**24**	**4**	**+14**	....	....	....	....	....	....	....	....
	Colorado Flames	CHL	39	3	18	21	....	....	....	24	....	....	....	....	....	....	....	....	....	....	1	0	0	0	0	....	....	....
1984-85	Moncton Golden Flames	AHL	79	5	9	14	....	....	....	46	....	....	....	....	....	....	....	....	....	....	....	....	....	....	....	....	....	....
1985-86	Moncton Golden Flames	AHL	20	0	2	2	....	....	....	18	....	....	....	....	....	....	....	....	....	....	....	....	....	....	....	....	....	....
	Fredericton Express	AHL	9	0	1	1	....	....	....	9	....	....	....	....	....	....	....	....	....	....	....	....	....	....	....	....	....	....
1986-87	Canada	Nat-Team	70	4	18	22	....	....	....	58	....	....	....	....	....	....	....	....	....	....	....	....	....	....	....	....	....	....
1987-88	Canada	Nat-Team	58	0	8	8	....	....	....	44	....	....	....	....	....	....	....	....	....	....	....	....	....	....	....	....	....	....
	Canada	Olympics	5	0	0	0	....	....	....	0	....	....	....	....	....	....	....	....	....	....	....	....	....	....	....	....	....	....
	NHL Totals		**30**	**2**	**7**	**9**	**2**	**5**	**7**	**20**	**0**	**0**	**0**	**19**	**10.5**	**34**	**0**	**24**	**4**		....	....	....	....	....	....	....	....

Signed as a free agent by **Calgary**, September 17, 1982. Traded to **Quebec** by **Calgary** for Tom Thornbury, January 16, 1986.

• STILLMAN, CORY

Cory Stillman C – L. 6′, 180 lbs. b: Peterborough, Ont., 12/20/1973. Calgary's 1st choice, 6th overall, in 1992 Entry Draft.

Season	Club	League	GP	G	A	Pts	AG	AA	APts	PIM	PP	SH	GW	S	%	TGF	PGF	TGA	PGA	+/–	GP	G	A	Pts	PIM	PP	SH	GW
1990-91	Windsor Spitfires	OHL	64	31	70	101	....	....	....	31	....	....	....	....	....	....	....	....	....	....	11	3	6	9	8	....	....	....
1991-92	Windsor Spitfires	OHL	53	29	61	90	....	....	....	59	....	....	....	....	....	....	....	....	....	....	7	2	4	6	8	....	....	....
1992-93	Peterborough Petes	OHL	61	25	55	80	....	....	....	55	....	....	....	....	....	....	....	....	....	....	18	3	8	11	18	....	....	....
	Canada	Nat-Team	1	0	0	0	....	....	....	0	....	....	....	....	....	....	....	....	....	....	....	....	....	....	....	....	....	....
1993-94	Saint John Flames	AHL	79	35	48	83	....	....	....	52	....	....	....	....	....	....	....	....	....	....	7	2	4	6	16	....	....	....
1994-95	Saint John Flames	AHL	63	28	53	81	....	....	....	70	....	....	....	....	....	....	....	....	....	....	5	0	2	2	2	....	....	....
	Calgary Flames	**NHL**	**10**	**0**	**2**	**2**	**0**	**3**	**3**	**2**	**0**	**0**	**0**	**7**	**0.0**	**3**	**1**	**1**	**0**	**+1**	....	....	....	....	....	....	....	....
1995-96	**Calgary Flames**	**NHL**	**74**	**16**	**19**	**35**	**16**	**15**	**31**	**41**	**4**	**1**	**3**	**132**	**12.1**	**56**	**29**	**38**	**6**	**–5**	**2**	**1**	**1**	**2**	**0**	**0**	**0**	**0**
1996-97	**Calgary Flames**	**NHL**	**58**	**6**	**20**	**26**	**6**	**18**	**24**	**14**	**2**	**0**	**0**	**112**	**5.4**	**41**	**19**	**28**	**0**	**–6**	....	....	....	....	....	....	....	....
1997-98	**Calgary Flames**	**NHL**	**72**	**27**	**22**	**49**	**32**	**21**	**53**	**40**	**9**	**4**	**1**	**178**	**15.2**	**65**	**23**	**67**	**16**	**–9**	....	....	....	....	....	....	....	....
	NHL Totals		**214**	**49**	**63**	**112**	**54**	**57**	**111**	**97**	**15**	**5**	**4**	**429**	**11.4**	**165**	**72**	**134**	**22**		**2**	**1**	**1**	**2**	**0**	**0**	**0**	**0**

• STOCK, P.J.

P.J. Stock LW – L. 5′10″, 190 lbs. b: Victoriaville, Que., 5/26/1975.

Season	Club	League	GP	G	A	Pts	AG	AA	APts	PIM	PP	SH	GW	S	%	TGF	PGF	TGA	PGA	+/–	GP	G	A	Pts	PIM	PP	SH	GW
1994-95	Victoriaville Tigres	QMJHL	70	9	46	55	....	....	....	386	....	....	....	....	....	....	....	....	....	....	4	0	0	0	60	....	....	....
1995-96	Victoriaville Tigres	QMJHL	67	19	43	62	....	....	....	432	....	....	....	....	....	....	....	....	....	....	12	5	4	9	79	....	....	....
1996-97	St. Francis Xavier X-Men	AUAA	27	11	20	31	....	....	....	110	....	....	....	....	....	....	....	....	....	....	3	0	4	4	14	....	....	....
1997-98	Hartford Wolf Pack	AHL	41	8	8	16	....	....	....	202	....	....	....	....	....	....	....	....	....	....	11	1	3	4	79	....	....	....
	New York Rangers	**NHL**	**38**	**2**	**3**	**5**	**2**	**3**	**5**	**114**	....	....	....	....	....	....	....	....	....	....	....	....	....	....	....	....	....	....
	NHL Totals		**38**	**2**	**3**	**5**	**2**	**3**	**5**	**114**	**0**	**0**	**0**	**0**	**0.0**	**0**	**0**	**0**	**0**		....	....	....	....	....	....	....	....

Signed as a free agent by **NY Rangers**, November 18, 1997.

• STOJANOV, ALEK

Alek Stojanov RW – L. 6′4″, 225 lbs. b: Windsor, Ont., 4/25/1973. Vancouver's 1st choice, 7th overall, in 1991 Entry Draft.

Season	Club	League	GP	G	A	Pts	AG	AA	APts	PIM	PP	SH	GW	S	%	TGF	PGF	TGA	PGA	+/–	GP	G	A	Pts	PIM	PP	SH	GW
1989-90	Dukes of Hamilton	OHL	37	4	4	8	....	....	....	91	....	....	....	....	....	....	....	....	....	....	....	....	....	....	....	....	....	....
1990-91	Dukes of Hamilton	OHL	62	25	20	45	....	....	....	181	....	....	....	....	....	....	....	....	....	....	4	1	1	2	14	....	....	....
1991-92	Guelph Platers	OHL	33	12	15	27	....	....	....	91	....	....	....	....	....	....	....	....	....	....	....	....	....	....	....	....	....	....
1992-93	Guelph Platers	OHL	36	27	28	55	....	....	....	62	....	....	....	....	....	....	....	....	....	....	....	....	....	....	....	....	....	....
	Newmarket Royals	OHL	14	9	7	16	....	....	....	26	....	....	....	....	....	....	....	....	....	....	7	1	3	4	26	....	....	....
	Hamilton Canucks	AHL	4	4	0	4	....	....	....	0	....	....	....	....	....	....	....	....	....	....	....	....	....	....	....	....	....	....
1993-94	Hamilton Canucks	AHL	4	0	1	1	....	....	....	5	....	....	....	....	....	....	....	....	....	....	....	....	....	....	....	....	....	....
1994-95	Syracuse Crunch	AHL	73	18	12	30	....	....	....	270	....	....	....	....	....	....	....	....	....	....	....	....	....	....	....	....	....	....
	Vancouver Canucks	**NHL**	**4**	**0**	**0**	**0**	**0**	**0**	**0**	**13**	**0**	**0**	**0**	**1**	**0.0**	**0**	**0**	**2**	**0**	**–2**	**5**	**0**	**0**	**0**	**2**	**0**	**0**	**0**

Season	Club	League	GP	G	A	Pts	AG	AA	APts	PIM	PP	SH	GW	S	%	TGF	PGF	TGA	PGA	+/–	GP	G	A	Pts	PIM	PP	SH	GW
			REGULAR SEASON																		PLAYOFFS							
1995-96	**Vancouver Canucks**	**NHL**	**58**	**0**	**1**	**1**	**0**	**1**	**1**	**123**	**0**	**0**	**0**	**16**	**0.0**	**7**	**0**	**19**	**0**	**–12**								
	Pittsburgh Penguins	**NHL**	**10**	**1**	**0**	**1**	**1**	**0**	**1**	**7**	**0**	**0**	**0**	**4**	**25.0**	**1**	**0**	**2**	**0**	**–1**	**9**	**0**	**0**	**0**	**19**	**0**	**0**	**0**
1996-97	**Pittsburgh Penguins**	**NHL**	**35**	**1**	**4**	**5**	**1**	**4**	**5**	**79**	**0**	**0**	**0**	**11**	**9.1**	**8**	**0**	**5**	**0**	**+3**								
1997-98	Syracuse Crunch	AHL	41	5	4	9				215											3	1	0	1	4			
	NHL Totals		**107**	**2**	**5**	**7**	**2**	**5**	**7**	**222**	**0**	**0**	**0**	**32**	**6.3**	**16**	**0**	**28**	**0**		**14**	**0**	**0**	**0**	**21**	**0**	**0**	**0**

Traded to **Pittsburgh** by **Vancouver** for Markus Naslund, March 20, 1996.

• STOLTZ, ROLAND

Roland Stoltz RW – R. 6'1", 191 lbs. b: Oeverkalix, Sweden, 8/15/1954.

Season	Club	League	GP	G	A	Pts	AG	AA	APts	PIM	PP	SH	GW	S	%	TGF	PGF	TGA	PGA	+/–	GP	G	A	Pts	PIM	PP	SH	GW
1975-76	Skelleftea AIK	Sweden	32	15	10	25				8											3	0	1	1	2			
1976-77	Skelleftea AIK	Sweden	32	12	5	17				16																		
1977-78	Skelleftea AIK	Sweden	34	13	13	26				14											5	0	1	1	2			
1978-79	Skelleftea AIK	Sweden	36	16	12	28				26																		
1979-80	Skelleftea AIK	Sweden	36	15	9	24				44																		
1980-81	Skelleftea AIK	Sweden	35	18	19	37				34											3	0	0	0	0			
1981-82	**Washington Capitals**	**NHL**	**14**	**2**	**2**	**4**	**2**	**1**	**3**	**14**	**0**	**0**	**0**	**6**	**33.3**	**7**	**2**	**12**	**4**	**–3**								
	Skelleftea AIK	Sweden	20	7	7	14				24																		
1982-83	Skelleftea AIK	Sweden	31	4	8	12				26																		
1983-84	Skelleftea AIK	Sweden	35	8	22	30				36																		
1984-85	Skelleftea AIK	Sweden	36	17	17	34				36																		
1985-86			DID NOT PLAY																									
1986-87	Skelleftea AIK	Sweden	34	7	11	18				38																		
	NHL Totals		**14**	**2**	**2**	**4**	**2**	**1**	**3**	**14**	**0**	**0**	**0**	**6**	**33.3**	**7**	**2**	**12**	**4**									

Signed as a free agent by **Washington**, June 5, 1981.

• STONE, STEVE

Steve Stone RW – R. 5'8", 170 lbs. b: Toronto, Ont., 9/26/1952. Vancouver's 9th choice, 131st overall, in 1972 Amateur Draft.

Season	Club	League	GP	G	A	Pts	AG	AA	APts	PIM	PP	SH	GW	S	%	TGF	PGF	TGA	PGA	+/–	GP	G	A	Pts	PIM	PP	SH	GW
1970-71	Niagara Falls Flyers	OHA	57	18	35	53				36																		
1971-72	Niagara Falls Flyers	OHA	62	30	62	92				25																		
1972-73	Des Moines Capitols	IHL	74	35	49	84				10											3	2	0	2	0			
1973-74	**Vancouver Canucks**	**NHL**	**2**	**0**	**0**	**0**	**0**	**0**	**0**	**0**	**0**	**0**	**0**	**1**	**0.0**	**0**	**0**	**2**	**0**	**–2**								
	Seattle Totems	WHL	77	23	32	55				28																		
1974-75	Des Moines Oak Leafs	IHL	72	12	14	26				67																		
1975-76	Port Huron Flags	IHL	78	19	42	61				47											15	4	3	7	9			
1976-77	Port Huron Flags	IHL	2	0	1	1				0																		
	NHL Totals		**2**	**0**	**0**	**0**	**0**	**0**	**0**	**0**	**0**	**0**	**0**	**1**	**0.0**	**0**	**0**	**2**	**0**									

• STORM, JIM

Jim Storm LW – L. 6'2", 200 lbs. b: Milford, MI, 2/5/1971. Hartford's 5th choice, 75th overall, in 1991 Entry Draft.

Season	Club	League	GP	G	A	Pts	AG	AA	APts	PIM	PP	SH	GW	S	%	TGF	PGF	TGA	PGA	+/–	GP	G	A	Pts	PIM	PP	SH	GW
1990-91	Michigan Tech Huskies	WCHA	36	16	18	34				46																		
1991-92	Michigan Tech Huskies	WCHA	39	25	33	58				12																		
1992-93	Michigan Tech Huskies	WCHA	33	22	32	54				30																		
1993-94	**Hartford Whalers**	**NHL**	**68**	**6**	**10**	**16**	**6**	**8**	**14**	**27**	**1**	**0**	**0**	**84**	**7.1**	**34**	**1**	**35**	**6**	**+4**								
	United States	Nat-Team	28	8	12	20				14																		
1994-95	**Hartford Whalers**	**NHL**	**6**	**0**	**3**	**3**	**0**	**4**	**4**	**0**	**0**	**0**	**0**	**3**	**0.0**	**3**	**0**	**1**	**0**	**+2**								
	Springfield Falcons	AHL	33	11	11	22				20																		
1995-96	**Dallas Stars**	**NHL**	**10**	**1**	**2**	**3**	**1**	**2**	**3**	**17**	**0**	**0**	**1**	**11**	**9.1**	**3**	**1**	**3**	**0**	**–1**								
	Michigan K-Wings	IHL	60	18	33	51				27											10	4	8	12	2			
1996-97	Michigan K-Wings	IHL	75	25	24	49				27											4	0	1	1	4			
1997-98	Utah Grizzlies	IHL	5	0	0	0				2																		
	NHL Totals		**84**	**7**	**15**	**22**	**7**	**14**	**21**	**44**	**1**	**0**	**1**	**98**	**7.1**	**40**	**2**	**39**	**6**									

Signed as a free agent by **Dallas**, September 13, 1995. Signed as a free agent by **NY Islanders**, July 21, 1997.

• STOTHERS, MIKE

Mike Stothers D – L. 6'4", 212 lbs. b: Toronto, Ont., 2/22/1962. Philadelphia's 1st choice, 21st overall, in 1980 Entry Draft.

Season	Club	League	GP	G	A	Pts	AG	AA	APts	PIM	PP	SH	GW	S	%	TGF	PGF	TGA	PGA	+/–	GP	G	A	Pts	PIM	PP	SH	GW
1979-80	Kingston Canadians	OHA	66	4	23	27				137																		
1980-81	Kingston Canadians	OHA	66	4	22	26				237											14	0	3	3	27			
1981-82	Kingston Canadians	OHL	61	1	20	21				203											4	0	1	1	8			
	Maine Mariners	AHL	5	0	0	0				4											1	0	0	0	0			
1982-83	Maine Mariners	AHL	80	2	16	18				139											12	0	0	0	21			
1983-84	Maine Mariners	AHL	61	2	10	12				109											17	0	1	1	34			
1984-85	**Philadelphia Flyers**	**NHL**	**1**	**0**	**0**	**0**	**0**	**0**	**0**	**0**	**0**	**0**	**0**	**0**	**0.0**	**0**	**0**	**1**	**0**	**–1**								
	Hershey Bears	AHL	60	8	18	26				142																		
1985-86	**Philadelphia Flyers**	**NHL**	**6**	**0**	**1**	**1**	**0**	**1**	**1**	**6**	**0**	**0**	**0**	**1**	**0.0**	**3**	**1**	**1**	**0**	**+1**	**3**	**0**	**0**	**0**	**4**	**0**	**0**	**0**
	Hershey Bears	AHL	66	4	9	13				221											13	0	3	3	88			
1986-87	**Philadelphia Flyers**	**NHL**	**2**	**0**	**0**	**0**	**0**	**0**	**0**	**4**	**0**	**0**	**0**	**2**	**0.0**	**1**	**0**	**1**	**0**	**0**	**2**	**0**	**0**	**0**	**7**	**0**	**0**	**0**
	Hershey Bears	AHL	75	5	11	16				283											5	0	0	0	10			
1987-88	**Philadelphia Flyers**	**NHL**	**3**	**0**	**0**	**0**	**0**	**0**	**0**	**13**	**0**	**0**	**0**	**0**	**0.0**	**0**	**0**	**2**	**1**	**–1**								
	Hershey Bears	AHL	13	3	2	5				55																		
	Toronto Maple Leafs	**NHL**	**18**	**0**	**1**	**1**	**0**	**1**	**1**	**42**	**0**	**0**	**0**	**0**	**0.0**	**3**	**0**	**10**	**1**	**–6**								
	Newmarket Saints	AHL	38	1	9	10				69																		
1988-89	Hershey Bears	AHL	76	4	11	15				262											9	0	2	2	29			
1989-90	Hershey Bears	AHL	56	1	6	7				170																		
1990-91	Hershey Bears	AHL	72	5	6	11				234											7	0	1	1	9			
1991-92	Hershey Bears	AHL	70	3	8	11				152											6	0	1	1	6			
	NHL Totals		**30**	**0**	**2**	**2**	**0**	**2**	**2**	**65**	**0**	**0**	**0**	**3**	**0.0**	**7**	**1**	**15**	**2**		**5**	**0**	**0**	**0**	**11**	**0**	**0**	**0**

Traded to **Toronto** by **Philadelphia** for future considerations, December 4, 1987. Traded to **Philadelphia** by **Toronto** for Bill Root, June 21, 1988.

• STOUGHTON, BLAINE

Blaine "Stash" Stoughton RW – R. 5'11", 185 lbs. b: Gilbert Plains, Man., 3/13/1953. Pittsburgh's 1st choice, 7th overall, in 1973 Amateur Draft.

Season	Club	League	GP	G	A	Pts	AG	AA	APts	PIM	PP	SH	GW	S	%	TGF	PGF	TGA	PGA	+/–	GP	G	A	Pts	PIM	PP	SH	GW
1969-70	Flin Flon Bombers	WCJHL	59	19	20	39				181											17	4	2	6	69			
1970-71	Flin Flon Bombers	WCJHL	35	26	24	50				96											17	13	13	26	61			
1971-72	Flin Flon Bombers	WCJHL	68	*60	66	126				121											7	4	6	10	27			
1972-73	Flin Flon Bombers	WCJHL	66	58	60	118				86											9	9	5	14	18			
1973-74	**Pittsburgh Penguins**	**NHL**	**34**	**5**	**6**	**11**	**5**	**5**	**10**	**8**	**0**	**0**	**0**	**52**	**9.6**	**18**	**0**	**31**	**1**	**–12**								
	Hershey Bears	AHL	47	23	17	40				35																		
1974-75	**Toronto Maple Leafs**	**NHL**	**78**	**23**	**14**	**37**	**21**	**11**	**32**	**24**	**4**	**0**	**1**	**161**	**14.3**	**63**	**12**	**69**	**11**	**–7**	**7**	**4**	**2**	**6**	**2**	**1**	**0**	**1**
1975-76	**Toronto Maple Leafs**	**NHL**	**43**	**6**	**11**	**17**	**6**	**9**	**15**	**8**	**1**	**0**	**0**	**60**	**10.0**	**29**	**5**	**28**	**2**	**–2**								
	Oklahoma City Blazers	CHL	30	14	22	36				24											4	0	0	0	2			
1976-77	Cincinnati Stingers	WHA	81	52	52	104				39											4	0	3	3	2			
1977-78	Cincinnati Stingers	WHA	30	6	13	19				36																		
	Indianapolis Racers	WHA	47	13	13	26				28																		
1978-79	Indianapolis Racers	WHA	25	9	9	18				16																		
	New England Whalers	WHA	36	9	3	12				2											7	4	3	7	4			
1979-80	**Hartford Whalers**	**NHL**	**80**	***56**	**44**	**100**	**51**	**34**	**85**	**16**	**16**	**2**	**0**	**234**	**23.9**	**134**	**31**	**104**	**10**	**+9**	**1**	**0**	**0**	**0**	**0**	**0**	**0**	**0**
1980-81	**Hartford Whalers**	**NHL**	**71**	**43**	**30**	**73**	**36**	**21**	**57**	**56**	**10**	**2**	**6**	**212**	**20.3**	**114**	**33**	**115**	**17**	**–17**								
1981-82	**Hartford Whalers**	**NHL**	**80**	**52**	**39**	**91**	**41**	**26**	**67**	**57**	**13**	**1**	**4**	**266**	**19.5**	**129**	**51**	**102**	**7**	**–17**								
1982-83	**Hartford Whalers**	**NHL**	**72**	**45**	**31**	**76**	**37**	**21**	**58**	**27**	**10**	**0**	**8**	**207**	**21.7**	**108**	**31**	**103**	**3**	**–23**								
1983-84	**Hartford Whalers**	**NHL**	**54**	**23**	**14**	**37**	**19**	**9**	**28**	**4**	**7**	**0**	**2**	**103**	**22.3**	**57**	**24**	**46**	**0**	**–13**								
	New York Rangers	**NHL**	**14**	**5**	**2**	**7**	**4**	**1**	**5**	**4**	**1**	**0**	**1**	**27**	**18.5**	**9**	**4**	**17**	**0**	**–12**								

			REGULAR SEASON																		PLAYOFFS							
Season	**Club**	**League**	**GP**	**G**	**A**	**Pts**	**AG**	**AA**	**APts**	**PIM**	**PP**	**SH**	**GW**	**S**	**%**	**TGF**	**PGF**	**TGA**	**PGA**	**+/–**	**GP**	**G**	**A**	**Pts**	**PIM**	**PP**	**SH**	**GW**
1984-85	New Haven Nighthawks	AHL	60	20	25	45	....	....	....	35	....	....	....	....	....	....	....	....	....	....	....	....	....	....	....	....	....	....
1986-87			DID NOT PLAY																									
1987-88	HC Asiago	Italy	15	10	16	26	....	....	....	2	....	....	....	....	....	....	....	....	....	....	....	....	....	....	....	....	....	....
	NHL Totals		**526**	**258**	**191**	**449**	**220**	**137**	**357**	**204**	**62**	**5**	**31**	**1322**	**19.5**	**661**	**191**	**615**	**51**		**8**	**4**	**2**	**6**	**2**	**1**	**0**	**1**
	Other Major League Totals		219	89	90	179	....	....	....	121	....	....	....	....	....	....	....	....	....	....	11	4	6	10	6	....	....	....

WCJHL All-Star Team (1972)

Played in NHL All-Star Game (1982)

Selected by **Quebec** (WHA) in 1973 WHA Amateur Draft, June, 1973. Traded to **Toronto** by **Pittsburgh** with future considerations for Rick Kehoe, September 13, 1974. WHA rights claimed by **Cincinnati** (WHA) from **Quebec** (WHA) prior to WHA Expansion Draft, June, 1975. Traded to **Indianapolis** (WHA) by **Cincinnati** (WHA) with Gilles Marotte for Bryon Baltimore and Hugh Harris, December, 1977. Traded to **New England** (WHA) by **Indianapolis** (WHA) with Dave Inkpen for cash, December, 1978. Claimed by **Hartford** from **Toronto** in Expansion Draft, June 13, 1979. Traded to **NY Rangers** by **Hartford** for Scot Kleinendorst, February 27, 1984.

• STOYANOVICH, STEVE

Steve Stoyanovich C – R. 6'2", 205 lbs. b: London, Ont., 5/2/1957. NY Islanders' 5th choice, 69th overall, in 1977 Amateur Draft.

Season	Club	League	GP	G	A	Pts	AG	AA	APts	PIM	PP	SH	GW	S	%	TGF	PGF	TGA	PGA	+/–	GP	G	A	Pts	PIM	PP	SH	GW
1976-77	RPI Engineers	ECAC	DID NOT PLAY – FRESHMAN																									
1977-78	RPI Engineers	ECAC	28	22	30	52	....	....	....	24	....	....	....	....	....	....	....	....	....	....	....	....	....	....	....	....	....	....
1978-79	RPI Engineers	ECAC	28	17	30	47	....	....	....	32	....	....	....	....	....	....	....	....	....	....	....	....	....	....	....	....	....	....
1979-80	RPI Engineers	ECAC	17	9	15	24	....	....	....	16	....	....	....	....	....	....	....	....	....	....	....	....	....	....	....	....	....	....
1980-81			DID NOT PLAY																									
1981-82	Indianapolis Checkers	CHL	80	42	30	72	....	....	....	55	....	....	....	....	....	....	....	....	....	....	13	7	8	15	20	....	....	....
1982-83	Indianapolis Checkers	CHL	79	41	43	84	....	....	....	65	....	....	....	....	....	....	....	....	....	....	13	6	3	9	4	....	....	....
1983-84	**Hartford Whalers**	**NHL**	**23**	**3**	**5**	**8**	**2**	**3**	**5**	**11**	**0**	**0**	**1**	**60**	**5.0**	**13**	**2**	**12**	**0**	**–1**	....	....	....	....	....	....	....	....
	Binghamton Whalers	AHL	21	11	8	19	....	....	....	0	....	....	....	....	....	....	....	....	....	....	....	....	....	....	....	....	....	....
1984-85	Groden	Italy	26	31	35	66	....	....	....	28	....	....	....	....	....	....	....	....	....	....	8	14	6	20	16	....	....	....
1985-86	Groden	Italy	36	53	35	88	....	....	....	52	....	....	....	....	....	....	....	....	....	....	4	8	5	13	8	....	....	....
1986-87	L'Avalese	Italy 2	STATISTICS NOT AVAILABLE																									
1987-88	L'Avalese	Italy	35	37	47	84	....	....	....	79	....	....	....	....	....	....	....	....	....	....	....	....	....	....	....	....	....	....
1988-89	Alleghe	Italy	12	10	14	24	....	....	....	16	....	....	....	....	....	....	....	....	....	....	....	....	....	....	....	....	....	....
	NHL Totals		**23**	**3**	**5**	**8**	**2**	**3**	**5**	**11**	**0**	**0**	**1**	**60**	**5.0**	**13**	**2**	**12**	**0**		....	....	....	....	....	....	....	....

CHL First All-Star Team (1983)

Traded to **Hartford** by **NY Islanders** for Hartford's 5th round choice (Tommy Hedlund) in 1985 Entry Draft, August 19, 1983.

• STRAKA, MARTIN

Martin Straka C – L. 5'10", 178 lbs. b: Plzen, Czech., 9/3/1972. Pittsburgh's 1st choice, 19th overall, in 1992 Entry Draft.

Season	Club	League	GP	G	A	Pts	AG	AA	APts	PIM	PP	SH	GW	S	%	TGF	PGF	TGA	PGA	+/–	GP	G	A	Pts	PIM	PP	SH	GW
1989-90	Skoda Plzen	Czech.	1	0	3	3	....	....	....	....	....	....	....	....	....	....	....	....	....	....	....	....	....	....	....	....	....	....
1990-91	Skoda Plzen	Czech.	47	7	24	31	....	....	....	6	....	....	....	....	....	....	....	....	....	....	....	....	....	....	....	....	....	....
	Czechoslovakia	WJC-A	6	1	5	6	....	....	....	0	....	....	....	....	....	....	....	....	....	....	....	....	....	....	....	....	....	....
1991-92	Skoda Plzen	Czech.	50	27	28	55	....	....	....	20	....	....	....	....	....	....	....	....	....	....	....	....	....	....	....	....	....	....
	Czechoslovakia	WJC-A	7	2	6	8	....	....	....	4	....	....	....	....	....	....	....	....	....	....	....	....	....	....	....	....	....	....
1992-93	**Pittsburgh Penguins**	**NHL**	**42**	**3**	**13**	**16**	**2**	**9**	**11**	**29**	**0**	**0**	**1**	**28**	**10.7**	**21**	**4**	**15**	**0**	**+2**	**11**	**2**	**1**	**3**	**2**	**0**	**0**	**0**
	Cleveland Lumberjacks	IHL	4	4	3	7	....	....	....	0	....	....	....	....	....	....	....	....	....	....	....	....	....	....	....	....	....	....
1993-94	**Pittsburgh Penguins**	**NHL**	**84**	**30**	**34**	**64**	**28**	**26**	**54**	**24**	**2**	**0**	**6**	**130**	**23.1**	**98**	**7**	**70**	**3**	**+24**	**6**	**1**	**0**	**1**	**2**	**0**	**0**	**0**
	Czech Republic	WC-A	3	1	0	1	....	....	....	4	....	....	....	....	....	....	....	....	....	....	....	....	....	....	....	....	....	....
1994-95	Interconex Plzen	Czech.	19	10	11	21	....	....	....	18	....	....	....	....	....	....	....	....	....	....	....	....	....	....	....	....	....	....
	Pittsburgh Penguins	**NHL**	**31**	**4**	**12**	**16**	**7**	**18**	**25**	**16**	**0**	**0**	**0**	**36**	**11.1**	**26**	**5**	**22**	**1**	**0**	....	....	....	....	....	....	....	....
	Ottawa Senators	**NHL**	**6**	**1**	**1**	**2**	**2**	**1**	**3**	**0**	**0**	**0**	**0**	**13**	**7.7**	**4**	**2**	**3**	**0**	**–1**	....	....	....	....	....	....	....	....
1995-96	**Ottawa Senators**	**NHL**	**43**	**9**	**16**	**25**	**9**	**13**	**22**	**29**	**5**	**0**	**1**	**63**	**14.3**	**36**	**14**	**38**	**2**	**–14**	....	....	....	....	....	....	....	....
	New York Islanders	**NHL**	**22**	**2**	**10**	**12**	**2**	**8**	**10**	**6**	**0**	**0**	**0**	**18**	**11.1**	**21**	**6**	**21**	**0**	**–6**	....	....	....	....	....	....	....	....
	Florida Panthers	**NHL**	**12**	**2**	**4**	**6**	**2**	**3**	**5**	**6**	**1**	**0**	**0**	**17**	**11.8**	**9**	**2**	**6**	**0**	**+1**	**13**	**2**	**2**	**4**	**2**	**0**	**0**	**0**
1996-97	Czech Republic	W Cup	1	0	0	0	....	....	....	0	....	....	....	....	....	....	....	....	....	....	....	....	....	....	....	....	....	....
	Florida Panthers	**NHL**	**55**	**7**	**22**	**29**	**7**	**19**	**26**	**12**	**2**	**0**	**1**	**94**	**7.4**	**50**	**15**	**26**	**0**	**+9**	**4**	**0**	**0**	**0**	**0**	**0**	**0**	**0**
1997-98	**Pittsburgh Penguins**	**NHL**	**75**	**19**	**23**	**42**	**22**	**22**	**44**	**28**	**4**	**3**	**4**	**117**	**16.2**	**57**	**13**	**59**	**14**	**–1**	**6**	**2**	**0**	**2**	**2**	**0**	**1**	**0**
	Czech Republic	Olympics	6	1	2	3	....	....	....	0	....	....	....	....	....	....	....	....	....	....	....	....	....	....	....	....	....	....
	NHL Totals		**370**	**77**	**135**	**212**	**81**	**119**	**200**	**150**	**14**	**3**	**13**	**516**	**14.9**	**322**	**68**	**260**	**20**		**40**	**7**	**3**	**10**	**8**	**0**	**1**	**0**

Czechoslovakian First All-Star Team (1992)

Traded to **Ottawa** by **Pittsburgh** for Troy Murray and Norm Maciver, April 7, 1995. Traded to **NY Islanders** by **Ottawa** with Don Beaupre and Bryan Berard for Damian Rhodes and Wade Redden, January 23, 1996. Claimed on waivers by **Florida** from **NY Islanders**, March 15, 1996. Signed as a free agent by **Pittsburgh**, August 6, 1997.

• STRATTON, ART

Art Stratton C/LW – L. 5'11", 170 lbs. b: Winnipeg, Man., 10/8/1935.

Season	Club	League	GP	G	A	Pts	AG	AA	APts	PIM	PP	SH	GW	S	%	TGF	PGF	TGA	PGA	+/–	GP	G	A	Pts	PIM	PP	SH	GW
1953-54	Winnipeg Barons	MJHL	36	17	28	45	....	....	....	39	....	....	....	....	....	....	....	....	....	....	6	0	5	5	0	....	....	....
1954-55	Winnipeg Barons	MJHL	32	*50	26	*76	....	....	....	39	....	....	....	....	....	....	....	....	....	....	5	3	3	6	0	....	....	....
	Warroad Lakers	USHL	STATISTICS NOT AVAILABLE																									
1955-56	St. Catharines Teepees	OHA	48	37	42	79	....	....	....	49	....	....	....	....	....	....	....	....	....	....	6	1	3	4	17	....	....	....
	Cleveland Barons	AHL	1	0	0	0	....	....	....	0	....	....	....	....	....	....	....	....	....	....	1	0	1	1	2	....	....	....
1956-57	North Bay Trappers	NOHA	60	29	34	63	....	....	....	23	....	....	....	....	....	....	....	....	....	....	13	5	8	13	12	....	....	....
1957-58	Winnipeg Warriors	WHL	70	23	53	76	....	....	....	12	....	....	....	....	....	....	....	....	....	....	7	4	1	5	4	....	....	....
1958-59	Cleveland Barons	AHL	62	29	47	76	....	....	....	40	....	....	....	....	....	....	....	....	....	....	7	1	3	4	2	....	....	....
1959-60	**New York Rangers**	**NHL**	**18**	**2**	**5**	**7**	**2**	**5**	**7**	**2**	....	....	....	....	....	....	....	....	....	....	....	....	....	....	....	....	....	....
	Springfield Indians	AHL	46	12	44	56	....	....	....	29	....	....	....	....	....	....	....	....	....	....	....	....	....	....	....	....	....	....
1960-61	Springfield Indians	AHL	48	16	41	57	....	....	....	16	....	....	....	....	....	....	....	....	....	....	....	....	....	....	....	....	....	....
	Kitchener-Waterloo Beavers	EPHL	16	7	5	12	....	....	....	4	....	....	....	....	....	....	....	....	....	....	7	0	2	2	0	....	....	....
1961-62	Buffalo Bisons	AHL	63	15	24	39	....	....	....	52	....	....	....	....	....	....	....	....	....	....	6	1	3	4	2	....	....	....
1962-63	Buffalo Bisons	AHL	70	20	*70	90	....	....	....	18	....	....	....	....	....	....	....	....	....	....	13	4	*15	19	2	....	....	....
1963-64	**Detroit Red Wings**	**NHL**	**5**	**0**	**3**	**3**	**0**	**3**	**3**	**2**	....	....	....	....	....	....	....	....	....	....	....	....	....	....	....	....	....	....
	Pittsburgh Hornets	AHL	66	17	*65	82	....	....	....	29	....	....	....	....	....	....	....	....	....	....	5	0	2	2	4	....	....	....
1964-65	Buffalo Bisons	AHL	71	25	*84	*109	....	....	....	32	....	....	....	....	....	....	....	....	....	....	9	1	5	6	4	....	....	....
1965-66	**Chicago Black Hawks**	**NHL**	**2**	**0**	**0**	**0**	**0**	**0**	**0**	**0**	....	....	....	....	....	....	....	....	....	....	....	....	....	....	....	....	....	....
	St. Louis Braves	CHL	66	28	*66	*94	....	....	....	14	....	....	....	....	....	....	....	....	....	....	5	0	1	1	2	....	....	....
1966-67	St. Louis Braves	CHL	67	34	56	*90	....	....	....	46	....	....	....	....	....	....	....	....	....	....	....	....	....	....	....	....	....	....
1967-68	**Pittsburgh Penguins**	**NHL**	**58**	**16**	**21**	**37**	**20**	**22**	**42**	**16**	**5**	**0**	**2**	**105**	**15.2**	**44**	**10**	**42**	**2**	**–6**	....	....	....	....	....	....	....	....
	Philadelphia Flyers	**NHL**	**12**	**0**	**4**	**4**	**0**	**4**	**4**	**4**	**0**	**0**	**0**	**18**	**0.0**	**5**	**3**	**6**	**0**	**–4**	**5**	**0**	**0**	**0**	**0**	**0**	**0**	**0**
1968-69	Seattle Totems	WHL	66	15	44	59	....	....	....	58	....	....	....	....	....	....	....	....	....	....	4	0	0	0	4	....	....	....
1969-70	Seattle Totems	WHL	59	24	55	79	....	....	....	22	....	....	....	....	....	....	....	....	....	....	....	....	....	....	....	....	....	....
1970-71	Seattle Totems	WHL	71	17	31	48	....	....	....	40	....	....	....	....	....	....	....	....	....	....	....	....	....	....	....	....	....	....
1971-72	Seattle Totems	WHL	11	1	6	7	....	....	....	6	....	....	....	....	....	....	....	....	....	....	....	....	....	....	....	....	....	....
	Tidewater Wings	AHL	61	15	41	56	....	....	....	54	....	....	....	....	....	....	....	....	....	....	....	....	....	....	....	....	....	....
1972-73	Tidewater Wings	AHL	76	30	50	80	....	....	....	32	....	....	....	....	....	....	....	....	....	....	12	4	4	8	0	....	....	....
1973-74	Rochester Americans	AHL	76	24	*71	95	....	....	....	118	....	....	....	....	....	....	....	....	....	....	6	2	6	8	4	....	....	....
1974-75	Richmond Robins	AHL	29	8	18	26	....	....	....	10	....	....	....	....	....	....	....	....	....	....	7	1	2	3	10	....	....	....
1975-76	Hampton Gulls	SHL	70	14	64	78	....	....	....	112	....	....	....	....	....	....	....	....	....	....	9	2	3	5	2	....	....	....
	NHL Totals		**95**	**18**	**33**	**51**	**22**	**34**	**56**	**24**	**5**	**0**	**2**	**123**	**14.6**	**49**	**13**	**48**	**2**		**5**	**0**	**0**	**0**	**0**	**0**	**0**	**0**

Won WHL Prairie Division Rookie of the Year Award (1958) • AHL First All-Star Team (1963, 1964, 1965) • Won Les Cunningham Award (MVP - AHL) (1965, 1974) • Won John B. Sollenberger Trophy (Top Scorer - AHL) (1965) • CHL First All-Star Team (1966, 1967) • Won Tommy Ivan Trophy (CHL's MVP) (1966, 1967) • AHL Second All-Star Team (1974) • SHL Second All-Star Team (1976) • Named SHL's MVP (1976)

Claimed by **Detroit** from **NY Rangers** (Buffalo - AHL) in Inter-League Draft, June 4, 1963. Traded to **Chicago** by **Detroit** with Ian Cushenan and John Miszuk for Ron Murphy and Aut Erickson, June 9, 1964. Claimed by **Pittsburgh** from **Chicago** in Expansion Draft, June 6, 1967. Traded to **Philadelphia** by **Pittsburgh** for Wayne Hicks and cash, February 27, 1968 Traded to **Seattle** (WHL) by **Philadelphia** with the loan of Ray Larose and Bob Courcy for Earl Heiskala, June, 1968. Traded to **Detroit** by **Seattle** (WHL) for Bob Sneddon, November, 1971. Claimed by **Rochester** (AHL) from **Detroit** in Reverse Draft, June, 1973.

			REGULAR SEASON																		PLAYOFFS							
Season	Club	League	GP	G	A	Pts	AG	AA	APts	PIM	PP	SH	GW	S	%	TGF	PGF	TGA	PGA	+/−	GP	G	A	Pts	PIM	PP	SH	GW
● STRONG, KEN	Ken Strong	LW – L. 5'11", 185 lbs.				b: Toronto, Ont., 5/9/1963.				Philadelphia's 4th choice, 58th overall, in 1981 Entry Draft.																		
1979-80	Streetsville Derbys	Jr. B	35	47	51	98				116																		
1980-81	Peterborough Petes	OHA	64	17	36	53				52												5	2	1	3	18			
1981-82	Peterborough Petes	OHL	42	21	22	43				69												9	8	11	19	23			
1982-83	Peterborough Petes	OHL	57	41	48	89				80												4	2	2	4	4			
	Toronto Maple Leafs	**NHL**	2	0	0	0	0	0	0	0	0	0	0	2	0	0	0	0	0	0								
1983-84	**Toronto Maple Leafs**	**NHL**	2	0	2	2	0	1	1	2	0	0	0	3	0.0	2	0	4	2	0								
	St. Catharines Saints	AHL	78	27	45	72				78											7	3	3	6	4			
1984-85	**Toronto Maple Leafs**	**NHL**	11	2	0	2	2	0	2	4	0	0	0	19	10.5	3	0	8	2	−3								
	St. Catharines Saints	AHL	45	15	19	34				41																		
1985-86	St. Catharines Saints	AHL	33	16	25	41				14											3	0	1	1	0			
1986-87	Adirondack Red Wings	AHL	31	7	13	20				18											11	6	7	13	12			
	EHC Chur	Switz.		9	5	14																						
1987-88	Villach HC	Austria	22	29	25	54																						
1988-89	Villach HC	Austria	46	42	*57	*99																						
1989-90	Villach HC	Austria	37	32	45	77				52																		
1990-91	Villach HC	Austria	43	*40	42	82																						
1991-92	Villach HC	Austria	44	*48	41	89																						
1992-93	Villach HC	Austria	46	34	34	68																						
1993-94	Villach HC	Austria	48	33	42	75																						
	Austria	Olympics	7	3	1	4				12																		
	Austria	WC-A	6	2	0	2				8																		
1994-95	Val Gardena	Italy	28	15	24	39				26																		
	Austria	WC-A	7	0	1	1				4																		
1995-96	Villach HC	Austria	33	23	23	46				65																		
1996-97	Kafenberger	Austria	43	25	27	42				70																		
	NHL Totals		**15**	**2**	**2**	**4**	**2**	**1**	**3**	**6**	**0**	**0**	**0**	**24**	**8.3**	**5**	**0**	**12**	**4**									

Traded to **Toronto** by **Philadelphia** to complete transaction that sent Darryl Sittler to Philadelphia, January 20, 1982.

Season	Club	League	GP	G	A	Pts	AG	AA	APts	PIM	PP	SH	GW	S	%	TGF	PGF	TGA	PGA	+/−	GP	G	A	Pts	PIM	PP	SH	GW
● STRUCH, DAVID	David Struch	C – L. 5'10", 180 lbs.				b: Flin Flon, Man., 2/11/1971.				Calgary's 11th choice, 195th overall, in 1991 Entry Draft.																		
1988-89	Saskatoon Blades	WHL	66	20	31	51				18											8	2	3	5	6			
1989-90	Saskatoon Blades	WHL	68	40	37	77				67											10	8	5	13	6			
1990-91	Saskatoon Blades	WHL	72	45	57	102				69																		
1991-92	Saskatoon Blades	WHL	47	29	26	55				34											22	8	15	23	26			
	Salt Lake Golden Eagles	IHL	12	4	1	5				8																		
1992-93	Salt Lake Golden Eagles	IHL	78	20	22	42				73																		
1993-94	**Calgary Flames**	**NHL**	4	0	0	0	0	0	0	4	0	0	0	3	0.0	2	0	4	0	−2								
	Saint John Flames	AHL	58	18	25	43				87											7	0	1	1	4			
1994-95	Saint John Flames	AHL	7	0	1	1				4																		
1995-96	Saint John Flames	AHL	45	10	15	25				57											3	0	1	1	4			
1996-97	EC Graz	Austria	26	6	16	22				18																		
	Waco Wizards	WPHL	11	4	7	11				0																		
	NHL Totals		**4**	**0**	**0**	**0**	**0**	**0**	**0**	**4**	**0**	**0**	**0**	**3**	**0.0**	**2**	**0**	**4**	**0**									

Season	Club	League	GP	G	A	Pts	AG	AA	APts	PIM	PP	SH	GW	S	%	TGF	PGF	TGA	PGA	+/−	GP	G	A	Pts	PIM	PP	SH	GW
● STRUDWICK, JASON	Jason Strudwick	D – L. 6'3", 207 lbs.				b: Edmonton, Alta., 7/17/1975.				NY Islanders' 3rd choice, 63rd overall, in 1994 Entry Draft.																		
1993-94	Kamloops Blazers	WHL	61	6	8	14				118											19	0	4	4	24			
1994-95	Kamloops Blazers	WHL	72	3	11	14				183											21	1	1	2	39			
1995-96	**New York Islanders**	**NHL**	1	0	0	0	0	0	0	7	0	0	0	0	0	0	0	0	0	0								
	Worcester IceCats	AHL	60	2	7	9				119											4	0	1	1	0			
1996-97	Kentucky Thoroughblades	AHL	80	1	9	10				198											4	0	0	0	0			
1997-98	**New York Islanders**	**NHL**	17	0	1	1	0	1	1	36	0	0	0	3	0.0	4	0	3	0	+1								
	Kentucky Thoroughblades	AHL	39	3	1	4				87																		
	Vancouver Canucks	**NHL**	11	0	1	1	0	1	1	29	0	0	0	5	0.0	4	0	11	4	−3								
	Syracuse Crunch	AHL																			3	0	0	0	6			
	NHL Totals		**29**	**0**	**2**	**2**	**0**	**2**	**2**	**72**	**0**	**0**	**0**	**8**	**0.0**	**8**	**0**	**14**	**4**									

Traded to **Vancouver** by **NY Islanders** for Gino Odjick, March 23, 1998.

Season	Club	League	GP	G	A	Pts	AG	AA	APts	PIM	PP	SH	GW	S	%	TGF	PGF	TGA	PGA	+/−	GP	G	A	Pts	PIM	PP	SH	GW
● STRUEBY, TODD	Todd Strueby	LW – L. 6'1", 185 lbs.				b: Lannigan, Sask., 6/15/1963.				Edmonton's 2nd choice, 29th overall, in 1981 Entry Draft.																		
1979-80	Notre Dame Hounds	AJHL	58	44	61	105				112																		
1980-81	Regina Pats	WHL	71	18	27	45				99											11	3	6	9	19			
1981-82	Saskatoon Blades	WHL	61	60	58	118				160											5	2	2	4	6			
	Canada	WJC-A	7	0	5	5				4																		
	Edmonton Oilers	**NHL**	3	0	0	0	0	0	0	0	0	0	0	1	0.0	0	0	0	0	0								
1982-83	Saskatoon Blades	WHL	65	40	70	110				119											6	3	3	6	19			
	Edmonton Oilers	**NHL**	1	0	0	0	0	0	0	0	0	0	0	1	0.0	0	0	2	0	−2								
1983-84	**Edmonton Oilers**	**NHL**	1	0	1	1	0	1	1	2	0	0	0	1	0.0	2	0	0	0	+2								
	Moncton Alpines	AHL	72	17	25	42				38																		
1984-85	Nova Scotia Voyageurs	AHL	38	2	3	5				29																		
	Muskegon Mohawks	IHL	27	19	12	31				55											17	4	10	14	27			
1985-86	Muskegon Lumberjacks	IHL	58	25	40	65				191											14	7	5	12	51			
1986-87	Muskegon Lumberjacks	IHL	82	28	41	69				208											13	4	6	10	53			
1987-88	Fort Wayne Komets	IHL	68	29	27	56				211											4	0	0	0	14			
1988-89	Canada	Nat-Team	61	18	20	38				112																		
1989-90	EHC Freiburg	Germany	25	13	12	25				76																		
	Canada	Nat-Team	16	12	3	15				35																		
1990-91	EHC Freiburg	Germany	7	0	3	3				10																		
	Canada	Nat-Team	31	12	13	25				49																		
1991-92	Salt Lake Golden Eagles	IHL	61	15	16	31				72											3	1	0	1	6			
	NHL Totals		**5**	**0**	**1**	**1**	**0**	**1**	**1**	**2**	**0**	**0**	**0**	**3**	**0.0**	**2**	**0**	**2**	**0**									

WHL First All-Star Team (1982) • WHL Second All-Star Team (1983)

Traded to **NY Rangers** by **Edmonton** with Larry Melnyk for Mike Rogers, December, 1985.

Season	Club	League	GP	G	A	Pts	AG	AA	APts	PIM	PP	SH	GW	S	%	TGF	PGF	TGA	PGA	+/−	GP	G	A	Pts	PIM	PP	SH	GW
● STUMPEL, JOZEF	Jozef "Stumpy" Stumpel	C – R. 6'3", 210 lbs.				b: Nitra, Czech., 7/20/1972.				Boston's 2nd choice, 40th overall, in 1991 Entry Draft.																		
1989-90	AC Nitra	Czech. 2	38	12	11	23																						
1990-91	AC Nitra	Czech.	49	23	22	45				14																		
	Czechoslovakia	WJC-A	7	4	4	8				2																		
1991-92	Kolner Haie	Germany	37	20	19	39				35																		
	Boston Bruins	**NHL**	4	1	0	1	1	0	1	0	0	0	0	3	33.3	2	0	1	0	+1								
1992-93	**Boston Bruins**	**NHL**	13	1	3	4	1	2	3	4	0	0	0	8	12.5	4	0	7	0	−3								
	Providence Bruins	AHL	56	31	61	92				26											6	4	4	8	0			
1993-94	**Boston Bruins**	**NHL**	59	8	15	23	7	12	19	14	0	0	1	62	12.9	30	8	19	1	+4	13	1	7	8	4	0	0	0
	Providence Bruins	AHL	17	5	12	17																							
1994-95	Kolner Haie	Germany	25	16	23	39				18																		
	Boston Bruins	**NHL**	44	5	13	18	9	19	28	8	1	0	2	46	10.9	34	10	22	2	+4	5	0	0	0	0	0	0	0
1995-96	**Boston Bruins**	**NHL**	76	18	36	54	18	29	47	14	5	0	2	158	11.4	75	30	53	0	−8	5	1	2	3	0	0	0	0

			REGULAR SEASON																		PLAYOFFS							
Season	**Club**	**League**	**GP**	**G**	**A**	**Pts**	**AG**	**AA**	**APts**	**PIM**	**PP**	**SH**	**GW**	**S**	**%**	**TGF**	**PGF**	**TGA**	**PGA**	**+/–**	**GP**	**G**	**A**	**Pts**	**PIM**	**PP**	**SH**	**GW**
1996-97	Slovakia	W Cup	3	0	0	0	....	....	....	0	....	....	....	....	....	....	....	....	....	....	....	....	....	....	....	....	....	....
	Boston Bruins	**NHL**	**78**	**21**	**55**	**76**	**22**	**49**	**71**	**14**	**6**	**0**	**1**	**168**	**12.5**	**95**	**29**	**89**	**1**	**–22**	....	....	....	....	....	....	....	....
	Slovakia	WC-A	8	2	1	3	....	....	....	4	....	....	....	....	....	....	....	....	....	....	....	....	....	....	....	....	....	....
1997-98	**Los Angeles Kings**	**NHL**	**77**	**21**	**58**	**79**	**25**	**57**	**82**	**53**	**4**	**0**	**2**	**162**	**13.0**	**99**	**31**	**64**	**13**	**+17**	**4**	**1**	**2**	**3**	**2**	**0**	**0**	**0**
	Slovakia	WC-A	4	1	2	3	....	....	....	6	....	....	....	....	....	....	....	....	....	....	....	....	....	....	....	....	....	....
	NHL Totals		**351**	**75**	**180**	**255**	**83**	**168**	**251**	**107**	**16**	**0**	**8**	**607**	**12.4**	**339**	**108**	**255**	**17**		**27**	**3**	**11**	**14**	**6**	**0**	**0**	**0**

Traded to **LA Kings** by **Boston** with Sandy Moger and Boston's 4th round choice (later traded to New Jersey — New Jersey selected Pierre Dagenais) in 1998 Entry Draft for Dimitri Kristich and Byron Dafoe, August 29, 1997.

• STUMPF, ROBERT

Robert Stumpf RW/D – R. 6'1", 195 lbs. b: Milo, Alta., 4/25/1953. Philadelphia's 3rd choice, 40th overall, in 1973 Amateur Draft.

Season	Club	League	GP	G	A	Pts	AG	AA	APts	PIM	PP	SH	GW	S	%	TGF	PGF	TGA	PGA	+/–	GP	G	A	Pts	PIM	PP	SH	GW
1968-69	Red Deer Rustlers	AJHL	....	1	8	9	....	....	....	11	....	....	....	....	....	....	....	....	....	....	....	....	....	....	....	....	....	....
1969-70	Red Deer Rustlers	AJHL	37	13	16	29	....	....	....	138	....	....	....	....	....	....	....	....	....	....	....	....	....	....	....	....	....	....
1970-71	Estevan Bruins	WCJHL	64	3	28	31	....	....	....	174	....	....	....	....	....	....	....	....	....	....	4	1	1	2	0	....	....	....
1971-72	New Westminster Bruins	WCJHL	66	7	43	50	....	....	....	226	....	....	....	....	....	....	....	....	....	....	5	0	3	3	4	....	....	....
1972-73	New Westminster Bruins	WCJHL	46	19	43	62	....	....	....	93	....	....	....	....	....	....	....	....	....	....	3	4	2	6	28	....	....	....
1973-74	Richmond Robins	AHL	6	0	4	4	....	....	....	6	....	....	....	....	....	....	....	....	....	....	....	....	....	....	....	....	....	....
	Denver Spurs	WHL	67	18	20	38	....	....	....	85	....	....	....	....	....	....	....	....	....	....	....	....	....	....	....	....	....	....
1974-75	**St. Louis Blues**	**NHL**	**7**	**1**	**1**	**2**	**1**	**1**	**2**	**16**	**0**	**0**	**0**	**8**	**12.5**	**8**	**0**	**11**	**5**	**+2**	....	....	....	....	....	....	....	....
	Denver Spurs	CHL	34	3	14	17	....	....	....	72	....	....	....	....	....	....	....	....	....	....	....	....	....	....	....	....	....	....
	Pittsburgh Penguins	**NHL**	**3**	**0**	**0**	**0**	**0**	**0**	**0**	**4**	**0**	**0**	**0**	**1**	**0.0**	**1**	**0**	**5**	**0**	**–4**	....	....	....	....	....	....	....	....
	Hershey Bears	AHL	17	2	4	6	....	....	....	18	....	....	....	....	....	....	....	....	....	....	....	....	....	....	....	....	....	....
1975-76	Hershey Bears	AHL	69	2	22	24	....	....	....	128	....	....	....	....	....	....	....	....	....	....	10	1	2	3	4	....	....	....
	NHL Totals		**10**	**1**	**1**	**2**	**1**	**1**	**2**	**20**	**0**	**0**	**0**	**9**	**11.1**	**9**	**0**	**16**	**5**		....	....	....	....	....	....	....	....

Traded to **St. Louis** by **Philadelphia** for George Pesut, November, 1973. Traded to **Pittsburgh** by **St. Louis** for Bernie Lukowich, January 20, 1975.

• STURGEON, PETER

Peter Sturgeon LW – L. 6'2", 198 lbs. b: Whitehorse, Yukon, 2/12/1954. Boston's 3rd choice, 36th overall, in 1974 Amateur Draft.

Season	Club	League	GP	G	A	Pts	AG	AA	APts	PIM	PP	SH	GW	S	%	TGF	PGF	TGA	PGA	+/–	GP	G	A	Pts	PIM	PP	SH	GW
1971-72	Kitchener Rangers	OHA	26	1	5	6	....	....	....	8	....	....	....	....	....	....	....	....	....	....	....	....	....	....	....	....	....	....
1972-73	Chatham Maroons	OJHL	48	41	33	74	....	....	....	44	....	....	....	....	....	....	....	....	....	....	....	....	....	....	....	....	....	....
	Kitchener Rangers	OHA	5	1	1	2	....	....	....	0	....	....	....	....	....	....	....	....	....	....	....	....	....	....	....	....	....	....
1973-74	Kitchener Rangers	OHA	70	39	48	87	....	....	....	42	....	....	....	....	....	....	....	....	....	....	....	....	....	....	....	....	....	....
1974-75	Rochester Americans	AHL	32	6	11	17	....	....	....	19	....	....	....	....	....	....	....	....	....	....	....	....	....	....	....	....	....	....
1975-76	Baltimore Clippers	AHL	4	0	1	1	....	....	....	7	....	....	....	....	....	....	....	....	....	....	....	....	....	....	....	....	....	....
	Rochester Americans	AHL	1	0	0	0	....	....	....	0	....	....	....	....	....	....	....	....	....	....	....	....	....	....	....	....	....	....
	Binghamton Dusters	NAHL	67	18	15	33	....	....	....	62	....	....	....	....	....	....	....	....	....	....	....	....	....	....	....	....	....	....
1976-77	Columbus Owls	IHL	48	16	13	29	....	....	....	55	....	....	....	....	....	....	....	....	....	....	7	1	1	2	24	....	....	....
1977-78	Rochester Americans	AHL	12	0	1	1	....	....	....	21	....	....	....	....	....	....	....	....	....	....	....	....	....	....	....	....	....	....
	Dayton-Grand Rapids	IHL	6	2	1	3	....	....	....	24	....	....	....	....	....	....	....	....	....	....	....	....	....	....	....	....	....	....
	Phoenix Roadrunners	PHL	42	12	14	26	....	....	....	13	....	....	....	....	....	....	....	....	....	....	....	....	....	....	....	....	....	....
1978-79	Grand Rapids Owls	IHL	6	2	1	3	....	....	....	34	....	....	....	....	....	....	....	....	....	....	....	....	....	....	....	....	....	....
1979-80	**Colorado Rockies**	**NHL**	**2**	**0**	**0**	**0**	**0**	**0**	**0**	**0**	**0**	**0**	**0**	**1**	**0.0**	**0**	**0**	**0**	**0**	**0**	....	....	....	....	....	....	....	....
	Fort Worth Texans	CHL	22	8	12	20	....	....	....	10	....	....	....	....	....	....	....	....	....	....	15	2	6	8	6	....	....	....
1980-81	**Colorado Rockies**	**NHL**	**4**	**0**	**1**	**1**	**0**	**1**	**1**	**2**	**0**	**0**	**0**	**4**	**0.0**	**1**	**0**	**1**	**0**	**0**	....	....	....	....	....	....	....	....
	Fort Worth Texans	CHL	52	5	14	19	....	....	....	21	....	....	....	....	....	....	....	....	....	....	....	....	....	....	....	....	....	....
1981-82	Georgetown Terriers	OHA Sr.	....	36	55	91	....	....	....	....	....	....	....	....	....	....	....	....	....	....	....	....	....	....	....	....	....	....
	NHL Totals		**6**	**0**	**1**	**1**	**0**	**1**	**1**	**2**	**0**	**0**	**0**	**5**	**0.0**	**1**	**0**	**1**	**0**		....	....	....	....	....	....	....	....

Signed as a free agent by **Colorado**, July 10, 1979.

• STURM, MARCO

Marco Sturm C – L. 5'11", 178 lbs. b: Dingolfing, Germany, 9/8/1978. San Jose's 2nd choice, 21st overall, in 1996 Entry Draft.

Season	Club	League	GP	G	A	Pts	AG	AA	APts	PIM	PP	SH	GW	S	%	TGF	PGF	TGA	PGA	+/–	GP	G	A	Pts	PIM	PP	SH	GW
1994-95	Germany	WJC-A	7	0	0	0	....	....	....	6	....	....	....	....	....	....	....	....	....	....	....	....	....	....	....	....	....	....
1995-96	EV Landshut	Germany	47	12	20	32	....	....	....	50	....	....	....	....	....	....	....	....	....	....	11	1	3	4	18	....	....	....
	Germany	WJC-A	6	4	6	10	....	....	....	51	....	....	....	....	....	....	....	....	....	....	....	....	....	....	....	....	....	....
1996-97	EV Landshut	Germany	46	16	27	43	....	....	....	40	....	....	....	....	....	....	....	....	....	....	7	1	4	5	6	....	....	....
	Germany	WC-A	8	1	1	2	....	....	....	4	....	....	....	....	....	....	....	....	....	....	....	....	....	....	....	....	....	....
1997-98	**San Jose Sharks**	**NHL**	**74**	**10**	**20**	**30**	**12**	**19**	**31**	**40**	**2**	**0**	**3**	**118**	**8.5**	**52**	**16**	**44**	**6**	**–2**	**2**	**0**	**0**	**0**	**0**	**0**	**0**	**0**
	Germany	Olympics	2	0	0	0	....	....	....	0	....	....	....	....	....	....	....	....	....	....	....	....	....	....	....	....	....	....
	NHL Totals		**74**	**10**	**20**	**30**	**12**	**19**	**31**	**40**	**2**	**0**	**3**	**118**	**8.5**	**52**	**16**	**44**	**6**		**2**	**0**	**0**	**0**	**0**	**0**	**0**	**0**

• SUIKKANEN, KAI

Kai Suikkanen D – L. 6'2", 205 lbs. b: Opiskelija, Finland, 9/29/1960.

Season	Club	League	GP	G	A	Pts	AG	AA	APts	PIM	PP	SH	GW	S	%	TGF	PGF	TGA	PGA	+/–	GP	G	A	Pts	PIM	PP	SH	GW
1977-78	Karpat Oulu	Finland	35	21	6	27	....	....	....	19	....	....	....	....	....	....	....	....	....	....	....	....	....	....	....	....	....	....
	Finland	WJC-A	6	5	3	8	....	....	....	9	....	....	....	....	....	....	....	....	....	....	....	....	....	....	....	....	....	....
1978-79	Karpat Oulu	Finland	36	16	6	22	....	....	....	65	....	....	....	....	....	....	....	....	....	....	....	....	....	....	....	....	....	....
	Finland	WJC-A	6	1	2	3	....	....	....	0	....	....	....	....	....	....	....	....	....	....	....	....	....	....	....	....	....	....
1979-80	Karpat Oulu	Finland	36	21	17	38	....	....	....	18	....	....	....	....	....	....	....	....	....	....	6	0	3	3	6	....	....	....
1980-81	Karpat Oulu	Finland	33	20	11	31	....	....	....	60	....	....	....	....	....	....	....	....	....	....	11	5	2	7	32	....	....	....
1981-82	**Buffalo Sabres**	**NHL**	**1**	**0**	**0**	**0**	**0**	**0**	**0**	**0**	**0**	**0**	**0**	**0**	**0.0**	**0**	**0**	**1**	**0**	**–1**	....	....	....	....	....	....	....	....
	Rochester Americans	AHL	71	34	33	67	....	....	....	32	....	....	....	....	....	....	....	....	....	....	9	4	2	6	4	....	....	....
1982-83	**Buffalo Sabres**	**NHL**	**1**	**0**	**0**	**0**	**0**	**0**	**0**	**0**	**0**	**0**	**0**	**1**	**0.0**	**1**	**0**	**0**	**0**	**+1**	....	....	....	....	....	....	....	....
	Rochester Americans	AHL	66	33	44	77	....	....	....	65	....	....	....	....	....	....	....	....	....	....	16	7	7	14	21	....	....	....
1983-84	Rochester Americans	AHL	15	7	10	17	....	....	....	2	....	....	....	....	....	....	....	....	....	....	....	....	....	....	....	....	....	....
	Karpat Oulu	Finland	23	9	4	13	....	....	....	20	....	....	....	....	....	....	....	....	....	....	10	6	4	10	8	....	....	....
1984-85	Karpat Oulu	Finland	22	8	6	14	....	....	....	47	....	....	....	....	....	....	....	....	....	....	7	2	3	5	4	....	....	....
1985-86	Karpat Oulu	Finland	33	26	10	36	....	....	....	34	....	....	....	....	....	....	....	....	....	....	4	0	0	0	24	....	....	....
	Finland	WEC-A	10	0	3	3	....	....	....	4	....	....	....	....	....	....	....	....	....	....	....	....	....	....	....	....	....	....
1986-87	Karpat Oulu	Finland	44	24	25	49	....	....	....	30	....	....	....	....	....	....	....	....	....	....	9	*7	1	8	6	....	....	....
1987-88	Karpat Oulu	Finland	26	17	14	31	....	....	....	25	....	....	....	....	....	....	....	....	....	....	....	....	....	....	....	....	....	....
	Finland	Olympics	8	1	0	1	....	....	....	4	....	....	....	....	....	....	....	....	....	....	....	....	....	....	....	....	....	....
1988-89	Karpat Oulu	Finland	33	13	10	23	....	....	....	16	....	....	....	....	....	....	....	....	....	....	....	....	....	....	....	....	....	....
1989-90	Karpat Oulu	Finland2	DID NOT PLAY																									
1990-91	TPS Turku	Finland	41	4	3	7	....	....	....	6	....	....	....	....	....	....	....	....	....	....	9	1	1	2	2	....	....	....
	NHL Totals		**2**	**0**	**0**	**0**	**0**	**0**	**0**	**0**	**0**	**0**	**0**	**1**	**0.0**	**1**	**0**	**1**	**0**		....	....	....	....	....	....	....	....

Signed as a free agent by **Buffalo**, August 31, 1981.

• SULLIMAN, DOUG

Doug Sulliman RW – L. 6'2", 210 lbs. b: Glace Bay, N.S., 8/29/1959. NY Rangers' 1st choice, 13th overall, in 1979 Entry Draft.

Season	Club	League	GP	G	A	Pts	AG	AA	APts	PIM	PP	SH	GW	S	%	TGF	PGF	TGA	PGA	+/–	GP	G	A	Pts	PIM	PP	SH	GW
1976-77	Kitchener Rangers	OHA	65	30	41	71	....	....	....	123	....	....	....	....	....	....	....	....	....	....	....	....	....	....	....	....	....	....
1977-78	Kitchener Rangers	OHA	68	50	39	89	....	....	....	87	....	....	....	....	....	....	....	....	....	....	9	5	7	12	24	....	....	....
1978-79	Kitchener Rangers	OHA	68	38	77	115	....	....	....	88	....	....	....	....	....	....	....	....	....	....	10	5	7	12	7	....	....	....
1979-80	**New York Rangers**	**NHL**	**31**	**4**	**7**	**11**	**4**	**5**	**9**	**2**	**1**	**0**	**0**	**26**	**15.4**	**23**	**5**	**18**	**0**	**0**	....	....	....	....	....	....	....	....
	New Haven Nighthawks	AHL	31	9	7	16	....	....	....	9	....	....	....	....	....	....	....	....	....	....	....	....	....	....	....	....	....	....
1980-81	**New York Rangers**	**NHL**	**32**	**4**	**1**	**5**	**3**	**1**	**4**	**32**	**0**	**0**	**0**	**56**	**7.1**	**11**	**0**	**24**	**4**	**–9**	**3**	**1**	**0**	**1**	**0**	**0**	**0**	**0**
	New Haven Nighthawks	AHL	45	10	16	26	....	....	....	18	....	....	....	....	....	....	....	....	....	....	1	0	0	0	0	....	....	....
1981-82	**Hartford Whalers**	**NHL**	**77**	**29**	**40**	**69**	**23**	**26**	**49**	**39**	**5**	**0**	**4**	**195**	**14.9**	**106**	**34**	**113**	**28**	**–13**	....	....	....	....	....	....	....	....
1982-83	**Hartford Whalers**	**NHL**	**77**	**22**	**19**	**41**	**18**	**13**	**31**	**14**	**8**	**0**	**0**	**162**	**13.6**	**73**	**23**	**126**	**19**	**–57**	....	....	....	....	....	....	....	....
1983-84	**Hartford Whalers**	**NHL**	**67**	**6**	**13**	**19**	**5**	**9**	**14**	**20**	**0**	**0**	**0**	**130**	**4.6**	**32**	**1**	**58**	**16**	**–11**	....	....	....	....	....	....	....	....
1984-85	**New Jersey Devils**	**NHL**	**57**	**22**	**16**	**38**	**18**	**11**	**29**	**4**	**6**	**0**	**1**	**112**	**19.6**	**59**	**21**	**50**	**1**	**–11**	....	....	....	....	....	....	....	....
1985-86	**New Jersey Devils**	**NHL**	**73**	**21**	**22**	**43**	**17**	**15**	**32**	**20**	**6**	**1**	**5**	**139**	**15.1**	**65**	**16**	**80**	**21**	**–10**	....	....	....	....	....	....	....	....
1986-87	**New Jersey Devils**	**NHL**	**78**	**27**	**26**	**53**	**23**	**19**	**42**	**14**	**4**	**1**	**4**	**148**	**18.2**	**76**	**18**	**109**	**34**	**–17**	....	....	....	....	....	....	....	....

										REGULAR SEASON											PLAYOFFS							
Season	Club	League	GP	G	A	Pts	AG	AA	APts	PIM	PP	SH	GW	S	%	TGF	PGF	TGA	PGA	+/-	GP	G	A	Pts	PIM	PP	SH	GW
1987-88	**New Jersey Devils**	**NHL**	**59**	**16**	**14**	**30**	**14**	**10**	**24**	**22**	**8**	**1**	**0**	**89**	**18.0**	**44**	**18**	**40**	**6**	**–8**	**9**	**0**	**3**	**3**	**2**	**0**	**0**	**0**
1988-89	**Philadelphia Flyers**	**NHL**	**52**	**6**	**6**	**12**	**5**	**4**	**9**	**8**	**0**	**1**	**1**	**52**	**11.5**	**20**	**0**	**38**	**10**	**–8**	**4**	**0**	**0**	**0**	**0**	**0**	**0**	**0**
1989-90	**Philadelphia Flyers**	**NHL**	**28**	**3**	**4**	**7**	**3**	**3**	**6**	**0**	**0**	**0**	**0**	**28**	**10.7**	**13**	**0**	**9**	**0**	**+4**	....	....	....	....	....	....	....	....
	NHL Totals		**631**	**160**	**168**	**328**	**133**	**116**	**249**	**175**	**38**	**4**	**15**	**1137**	**14.1**	**522**	**136**	**665**	**139**		**16**	**1**	**3**	**4**	**2**	**0**	**0**	**0**

Traded to **Hartford** by **NY Rangers** with Chris Kotsopoulos and Gerry McDonald for Mike Rogers and NY Rangers' 10th round choice (Simo Saarinen) in 1982 Entry Draft, October 2, 1981. Signed as a free agent by **New Jersey**, July 11, 1984. Claimed by **Philadelphia** from **New Jersey** in Waiver Draft, October 3, 1988.

• SULLIVAN, BOB

Bob Sullivan LW – R. 6', 210 lbs. b: Noranda, Que., 11/29/1957. NY Rangers' 8th choice, 116th overall, in 1977 Amateur Draft.

Season	Club	League	GP	G	A	Pts	AG	AA	APts	PIM	PP	SH	GW	S	%	TGF	PGF	TGA	PGA	+/-	GP	G	A	Pts	PIM	PP	SH	GW
1974-75	St. Jerome Alouettes	QMJHL	56	29	47	76	....	....	....	31	....	....	....	....	....	....	....	....	....	....	....	....	....	....	....	....	....	....
1975-76	Chicoutimi Sagueneens	QMJHL	68	20	22	42	....	....	....	34	....	....	....	....	....	....	....	....	....	....	5	4	2	6	0	....	....	....
1976-77	Chicoutimi Sagueneens	QMJHL	71	45	65	110	....	....	....	80	....	....	....	....	....	....	....	....	....	....	8	3	7	10	13	....	....	....
1977-78	Dalhousie University	AUAA	5	5	1	6	....	....	....	....	....	....	....	....	....	....	....	....	....	....	....	....	....	....	....	....	....	....
	New Haven Nighthawks	AHL	2	0	0	0	....	....	....	0	....	....	....	....	....	....	....	....	....	....	....	....	....	....	....	....	....	....
	Toledo Goaldiggers	IHL	65	27	27	54	....	....	....	60	....	....	....	....	....	....	....	....	....	....	17	3	9	12	16	....	....	....
1978-79	Toledo Goaldiggers	IHL	1	0	1	1	....	....	....	0	....	....	....	....	....	....	....	....	....	....	....	....	....	....	....	....	....	....
	Los Angeles Blades	PHL	21	7	14	21	....	....	....	42	....	....	....	....	....	....	....	....	....	....	....	....	....	....	....	....	....	....
1979-80	Toledo Goaldiggers	IHL	56	30	26	56	....	....	....	68	....	....	....	....	....	....	....	....	....	....	4	0	4	4	6	....	....	....
1980-81	Toledo Goaldiggers	IHL	79	32	52	84	....	....	....	69	....	....	....	....	....	....	....	....	....	....	....	....	....	....	....	....	....	....
1981-82	Binghamton Whalers	AHL	74	47	43	90	....	....	....	44	....	....	....	....	....	....	....	....	....	....	....	....	....	....	....	....	....	....
1982-83	**Hartford Whalers**	**NHL**	**62**	**18**	**19**	**37**	**15**	**13**	**28**	**18**	**5**	**0**	**0**	**93**	**19.4**	**47**	**8**	**56**	**0**	**–17**	....	....	....	....	....	....	....	....
	Binghamton Whalers	AHL	18	18	14	32	....	....	....	2	....	....	....	....	....	....	....	....	....	....	....	....	....	....	....	....	....	....
1983-84	Binghamton Whalers	AHL	76	33	47	80	....	....	....	48	....	....	....	....	....	....	....	....	....	....	....	....	....	....	....	....	....	....
1984-85	HC Bolzano	Italy	26	*47	40	87	....	....	....	28	....	....	....	....	....	....	....	....	....	....	9	*17	6	23	6	....	....	....
1985-86	HC Bozano	Italy	36	54	53	107	....	....	....	76	....	....	....	....	....	....	....	....	....	....	7	8	11	19	6	....	....	....
1986-87	SC Preussen Berlin	Switz.2	STATISTICS NOT AVAILABLE																									
1987-88	HC Asiago	Italy	21	25	21	46	....	....	....	29	....	....	....	....	....	....	....	....	....	....	....	....	....	....	....	....	....	....
	NHL Totals		**62**	**18**	**19**	**37**	**15**	**13**	**28**	**18**	**5**	**0**	**0**	**93**	**19.4**	**47**	**8**	**56**	**0**		....	....	....	....	....	....	....	....

AHL First All-Star Team (1982) • Won Dudley "Red" Garrett Memorial Award (Top Rookie - AHL) (1982)

Signed as a free agent by **Hartford**, August 24, 1982.

• SULLIVAN, BRIAN

Brian Sullivan RW – R. 6'4", 195 lbs. b: South Windsor, CT, 4/23/1969. New Jersey's 3rd choice, 65th overall, in 1987 Entry Draft.

Season	Club	League	GP	G	A	Pts	AG	AA	APts	PIM	PP	SH	GW	S	%	TGF	PGF	TGA	PGA	+/-	GP	G	A	Pts	PIM	PP	SH	GW
1985-86	South Windsor High	H.S.	....	39	50	89	....	....	....	....	....	....	....	....	....	....	....	....	....	....	....	....	....	....	....	....	....	....
1987-88	Northeastern University	H.E.	37	20	12	32	....	....	....	18	....	....	....	....	....	....	....	....	....	....	....	....	....	....	....	....	....	....
1988-89	Northeastern University	H.E.	34	13	14	27	....	....	....	65	....	....	....	....	....	....	....	....	....	....	....	....	....	....	....	....	....	....
1989-90	Northeastern University	H.E.	34	24	21	45	....	....	....	72	....	....	....	....	....	....	....	....	....	....	....	....	....	....	....	....	....	....
1990-91	Northeastern University	H.E.	32	17	23	40	....	....	....	75	....	....	....	....	....	....	....	....	....	....	....	....	....	....	....	....	....	....
1991-92	Utica Devils	AHL	70	23	24	47	....	....	....	58	....	....	....	....	....	....	....	....	....	....	4	0	4	4	6	....	....	....
1992-93	**New Jersey Devils**	**NHL**	**2**	**0**	**1**	**1**	**0**	**1**	**1**	**0**	**0**	**0**	**0**	**2**	**0.0**	**1**	**0**	**2**	**0**	**–1**	....	....	....	....	....	....	....	....
	Utica Devils	AHL	75	30	27	57	....	....	....	88	....	....	....	....	....	....	....	....	....	....	5	0	0	0	12	....	....	....
1993-94	Albany River Rats	AHL	77	31	30	61	....	....	....	140	....	....	....	....	....	....	....	....	....	....	5	1	1	2	18	....	....	....
1994-95	San Diego Gulls	IHL	74	24	23	47	....	....	....	97	....	....	....	....	....	....	....	....	....	....	5	0	1	1	7	....	....	....
1995-96			DID NOT PLAY																									
1996-97	San Antonio Dragons	IHL	77	22	24	46	....	....	....	115	....	....	....	....	....	....	....	....	....	....	9	1	2	3	11	....	....	....
1997-98	Grand Rapids Griffins	IHL	54	12	7	19	....	....	....	49	....	....	....	....	....	....	....	....	....	....	....	....	....	....	....	....	....	....
	Springfield Falcons	AHL	11	2	4	6	....	....	....	29	....	....	....	....	....	....	....	....	....	....	1	0	0	0	0	....	....	....
	NHL Totals		**2**	**0**	**1**	**1**	**0**	**1**	**1**	**0**	**0**	**0**	**0**	**2**	**0.0**	**1**	**0**	**2**	**0**		....	....	....	....	....	....	....	....

Signed as a free agent by **Anaheim**, August 31, 1994.

• SULLIVAN, MIKE

Mike Sullivan C – L. 6'2", 190 lbs. b: Marshfield, MA, 2/27/1968. NY Rangers' 4th choice, 69th overall, in 1987 Entry Draft.

Season	Club	League	GP	G	A	Pts	AG	AA	APts	PIM	PP	SH	GW	S	%	TGF	PGF	TGA	PGA	+/-	GP	G	A	Pts	PIM	PP	SH	GW
1986-87	Boston University	H.E.	37	13	18	31	....	....	....	18	....	....	....	....	....	....	....	....	....	....	....	....	....	....	....	....	....	....
1987-88	Boston University	H.E.	30	18	22	40	....	....	....	30	....	....	....	....	....	....	....	....	....	....	....	....	....	....	....	....	....	....
	United States	WJC-A	6	0	2	2	....	....	....	14	....	....	....	....	....	....	....	....	....	....	....	....	....	....	....	....	....	....
1988-89	Boston University	H.E.	36	19	17	36	....	....	....	30	....	....	....	....	....	....	....	....	....	....	....	....	....	....	....	....	....	....
1989-90	Boston University	H.E.	38	11	20	31	....	....	....	26	....	....	....	....	....	....	....	....	....	....	....	....	....	....	....	....	....	....
1990-91	San Diego Gulls	IHL	74	12	23	35	....	....	....	27	....	....	....	....	....	....	....	....	....	....	....	....	....	....	....	....	....	....
1991-92	**San Jose Sharks**	**NHL**	**64**	**8**	**11**	**19**	**7**	**8**	**15**	**15**	**1**	**0**	**1**	**72**	**11.1**	**38**	**10**	**54**	**8**	**–18**	....	....	....	....	....	....	....	....
	Kansas City Blades	IHL	10	2	8	10	....	....	....	8	....	....	....	....	....	....	....	....	....	....	....	....	....	....	....	....	....	....
1992-93	**San Jose Sharks**	**NHL**	**81**	**6**	**8**	**14**	**5**	**5**	**10**	**30**	**0**	**2**	**0**	**95**	**6.3**	**33**	**2**	**113**	**40**	**–42**	....	....	....	....	....	....	....	....
1993-94	**San Jose Sharks**	**NHL**	**26**	**2**	**2**	**4**	**2**	**2**	**4**	**4**	**0**	**2**	**1**	**21**	**9.5**	**8**	**0**	**21**	**10**	**–3**	....	....	....	....	....	....	....	....
	Kansas City Blades	IHL	6	3	3	6	....	....	....	0	....	....	....	....	....	....	....	....	....	....	....	....	....	....	....	....	....	....
	Calgary Flames	**NHL**	**19**	**2**	**3**	**5**	**2**	**2**	**4**	**6**	**0**	**2**	**0**	**27**	**7.4**	**6**	**0**	**5**	**1**	**+2**	**7**	**1**	**1**	**2**	**8**	**0**	**1**	**0**
	Saint John Flames	AHL	5	2	0	2	....	....	....	4	....	....	....	....	....	....	....	....	....	....	....	....	....	....	....	....	....	....
1994-95	**Calgary Flames**	**NHL**	**38**	**4**	**7**	**11**	**7**	**10**	**17**	**14**	**0**	**0**	**2**	**31**	**12.9**	**19**	**0**	**28**	**7**	**–2**	**7**	**3**	**5**	**8**	**2**	**0**	**1**	**1**
1995-96	**Calgary Flames**	**NHL**	**81**	**9**	**12**	**21**	**9**	**10**	**19**	**24**	**0**	**1**	**1**	**106**	**8.5**	**30**	**0**	**69**	**33**	**–6**	**4**	**0**	**0**	**0**	**0**	**0**	**0**	**0**
1996-97	**Calgary Flames**	**NHL**	**67**	**5**	**6**	**11**	**5**	**5**	**10**	**10**	**0**	**3**	**2**	**64**	**7.8**	**17**	**0**	**45**	**17**	**–11**	....	....	....	....	....	....	....	....
	United States	WC-A	8	1	2	3	....	....	....	2	....	....	....	....	....	....	....	....	....	....	....	....	....	....	....	....	....	....
1997-98	**Boston Bruins**	**NHL**	**77**	**5**	**13**	**18**	**6**	**13**	**19**	**34**	**0**	**0**	**2**	**83**	**6.0**	**32**	**1**	**45**	**13**	**–1**	**6**	**0**	**1**	**1**	**2**	**0**	**0**	**0**
	NHL Totals		**453**	**41**	**62**	**103**	**43**	**55**	**98**	**137**	**1**	**10**	**9**	**499**	**8.2**	**183**	**13**	**380**	**129**		**24**	**4**	**7**	**11**	**12**	**0**	**2**	**1**

Rights traded to **Minnesota** by **NY Rangers** with Paul Jerrard, the rights to Bret Barnett, and LA Kings' 3rd round choice (previously acquired, Minnesota selected Murray Garbutt) in 1989 Entry Draft for Brian Lawton, Igor Liba and the rights to Eric Bennett, October 11, 1988. Signed as a free agent by **San Jose**, August 9, 1991. Claimed on waivers by **Calgary** from **San Jose**, January 6, 1994. Traded to **Boston** by **Calgary** for Boston's 7th round choice (Radek Duda) in 1998 Entry Draft, June 21, 1997. Claimed by **Nashville** from **Boston** in Expansion Draft, June 26, 1998.

• SULLIVAN, PETER

Peter "Silky" Sullivan C – R. 5'9", 165 lbs. b: Toronto, Ont., 7/25/1951. Montreal's 12th choice, 95th overall, in 1971 Amateur Draft.

Season	Club	League	GP	G	A	Pts	AG	AA	APts	PIM	PP	SH	GW	S	%	TGF	PGF	TGA	PGA	+/-	GP	G	A	Pts	PIM	PP	SH	GW
1968-69	Peterborough Petes	OHA	4	1	0	1	....	....	....	0	....	....	....	....	....	....	....	....	....	....	....	....	....	....	....	....	....	....
1969-70	Oshawa Generals	OHA	52	40	30	70	....	....	....	16	....	....	....	....	....	....	....	....	....	....	....	....	....	....	....	....	....	....
1970-71	Oshawa Generals	OHA	61	29	23	52	....	....	....	26	....	....	....	....	....	....	....	....	....	....	....	....	....	....	....	....	....	....
1971-72	Mount Royal College	AJHL	26	14	19	33	....	....	....	4	....	....	....	....	....	....	....	....	....	....	....	....	....	....	....	....	....	....
	St. Petersburg Suns	FHL	5	2	1	3	....	....	....	0	....	....	....	....	....	....	....	....	....	....	....	....	....	....	....	....	....	....
	Muskegon Mohawks	IHL	1	0	0	0	....	....	....	0	....	....	....	....	....	....	....	....	....	....	....	....	....	....	....	....	....	....
1972-73	Nova Scotia Voyageurs	AHL	39	10	14	24	....	....	....	8	....	....	....	....	....	....	....	....	....	....	13	1	0	1	2	....	....	....
1973-74	Nova Scotia Voyageurs	AHL	74	30	40	70	....	....	....	22	....	....	....	....	....	....	....	....	....	....	6	5	4	9	2	....	....	....
1974-75	Nova Scotia Voyageurs	AHL	75	*44	60	104	....	....	....	48	....	....	....	....	....	....	....	....	....	....	6	2	6	8	5	....	....	....
1975-76	Winnipeg Jets	WHA	78	32	39	71	....	....	....	22	....	....	....	....	....	....	....	....	....	....	13	6	7	13	0	....	....	....
1976-77	Winnipeg Jets	WHA	78	31	52	83	....	....	....	10	....	....	....	....	....	....	....	....	....	....	20	7	12	19	2	....	....	....
1977-78	Winnipeg Jets	WHA	77	16	39	55	....	....	....	43	....	....	....	....	....	....	....	....	....	....	9	3	4	7	4	....	....	....
1978-79	Winnipeg Jets	WHA	80	46	40	86	....	....	....	24	....	....	....	....	....	....	....	....	....	....	10	5	9	14	2	....	....	....
1979-80	**Winnipeg Jets**	**NHL**	**79**	**24**	**35**	**59**	**22**	**27**	**49**	**20**	**5**	**0**	**3**	**166**	**14.5**	**84**	**34**	**98**	**3**	**–45**	....	....	....	....	....	....	....	....
1980-81	**Winnipeg Jets**	**NHL**	**47**	**4**	**19**	**23**	**3**	**13**	**16**	**20**	**2**	**0**	**0**	**42**	**9.5**	**33**	**16**	**37**	**3**	**–17**	....	....	....	....	....	....	....	....
1981-82	Wichita Wind	CHL	15	12	11	23	....	....	....	0	....	....	....	....	....	....	....	....	....	....	7	5	2	7	0	....	....	....
	HC Langnau	Switz.	....	37	24	61	....	....	....	....	....	....	....	....	....	....	....	....	....	....	....	....	....	....	....	....	....	....
1982-83	HC Langnau	Switz.	....	31	33	64	....	....	....	....	....	....	....	....	....	....	....	....	....	....	....	....	....	....	....	....	....	....
1983-84	SC Bern	Switz.2	....	46	39	85	....	....	....	....	....	....	....	....	....	....	....	....	....	....	....	....	....	....	....	....	....	....

			REGULAR SEASON																		PLAYOFFS							
Season	Club	League	GP	G	A	Pts	AG	AA	APts	PIM	PP	SH	GW	S	%	TGF	PGF	TGA	PGA	+/–	GP	G	A	Pts	PIM	PP	SH	GW
1984-85	HC Langnau	Switz.	....	53	29	82																						
	Moncton Golden Flames	AHL	5	2	3	5				0																		
1985-86	Langnau	Switz.	36	34	27	61																						
	NHL Totals		**126**	**28**	**54**	**82**	**25**	**40**	**65**	**40**	**7**	**0**	**3**	**208**	**13.5**	**117**	**50**	**135**	**6**									
	Other Major League Totals		313	125	170	295				107											52	21	32	53	8			

AHL Second All-Star Team (1975)

Signed as a free agent by **Winnipeg** (WHA), August, 1975. Rights retained by **Winnipeg** prior to Expansion Draft, June 9, 1979.

• SULLIVAN, STEVE

Steve Sullivan C – R. 5'9", 155 lbs. b: Timmins, Ont., 7/6/1974. New Jersey's 10th choice, 233rd overall, in 1994 Entry Draft.

Season	Club	League	GP	G	A	Pts	AG	AA	APts	PIM	PP	SH	GW	S	%	TGF	PGF	TGA	PGA	+/–	GP	G	A	Pts	PIM	PP	SH	GW
1992-93	Sault Ste. Marie Greyhounds	OHL	62	36	27	63				44											16	3	8	11	18			
1993-94	Sault Ste. Marie Greyhounds	OHL	63	51	62	113				82											14	9	16	25	22			
1994-95	Albany River Rats	AHL	75	31	50	81				124											14	4	7	11	10			
1995-96	**New Jersey Devils**	**NHL**	**16**	**5**	**4**	**9**	**5**	**3**	**8**	**8**	**2**	**0**	**1**	**23**	**21.7**	**18**	**8**	**7**	**0**	**+3**								
	Albany River Rats	AHL	53	33	42	75				127											4	3	0	3	6			
1996-97	**New Jersey Devils**	**NHL**	**33**	**8**	**14**	**22**	**8**	**12**	**20**	**14**	**2**	**0**	**2**	**63**	**12.7**	**30**	**9**	**12**	**0**	**+9**								
	Albany River Rats	AHL	15	8	7	15				16																		
	Toronto Maple Leafs	**NHL**	**21**	**5**	**11**	**16**	**5**	**10**	**15**	**23**	**1**	**0**	**1**	**45**	**11.1**	**22**	**6**	**11**	**0**	**+5**								
1997-98	**Toronto Maple Leafs**	**NHL**	**63**	**10**	**18**	**28**	**12**	**18**	**30**	**40**	**1**	**0**	**1**	**112**	**8.9**	**44**	**9**	**44**	**1**	**–8**								
	NHL Totals		**133**	**28**	**47**	**75**	**30**	**43**	**73**	**85**	**6**	**0**	**5**	**243**	**11.5**	**114**	**32**	**74**	**1**									

AHL First All-Star Team (1996)

Traded to **Toronto** by **New Jersey** with Jason Smith and the rights to Alyn McCauley for Doug Gilmour, Dave Ellett and a conditional draft choice, February 25, 1997.

• SUMMANEN, RAIMO

Raimo Summanen LW – L. 5'11", 185 lbs. b: Jyvaskyla, Finland, 3/2/1962. Edmonton's 6th choice, 125th overall, in 1982 Entry Draft.

Season	Club	League	GP	G	A	Pts	AG	AA	APts	PIM	PP	SH	GW	S	%	TGF	PGF	TGA	PGA	+/–	GP	G	A	Pts	PIM	PP	SH	GW
1981-82	Kiekkoreipas	Finland	36	15	6	21				17											2	2	0	2	0			
	Finland	WJC-A	7	7	9	16				0																		
1982-83	Ilves Tampere	Finland	36	*45	15	60				36											8	7	3	10	2			
	Finland	WEC-A	9	0	3	3				0																		
1983-84	Ilves Tampere	Finland	37	28	19	47				26																		
	Finland	Olympics	6	4	6	10				4																		
	Edmonton Oilers	**NHL**	**2**	**1**	**4**	**5**	**1**	**3**	**4**	**2**	**0**	**0**	**0**	**3**	**33.3**	**7**	**1**	**2**	**0**	**+4**	**5**	**1**	**4**	**5**	**0**	**0**	**0**	**0**
1984-85	**Edmonton Oilers**	**NHL**	**9**	**0**	**4**	**4**	**0**	**3**	**3**	**0**	**0**	**0**	**0**	**5**	**0.0**	**7**	**1**	**7**	**0**	**–1**								
	Nova Scotia Voyageurs	AHL	66	20	33	53				2											5	1	2	3	0			
1985-86	**Edmonton Oilers**	**NHL**	**73**	**19**	**18**	**37**	**15**	**12**	**27**	**16**	**1**	**0**	**4**	**83**	**22.9**	**58**	**4**	**47**	**0**	**+7**	**5**	**1**	**1**	**2**	**0**	**0**	**0**	**0**
1986-87	**Edmonton Oilers**	**NHL**	**48**	**10**	**7**	**17**	**9**	**5**	**14**	**15**	**0**	**0**	**0**	**55**	**18.2**	**26**	**1**	**26**	**0**	**–1**								
	Vancouver Canucks	**NHL**	**10**	**4**	**4**	**8**	**3**	**3**	**6**	**0**	**1**	**0**	**0**	**18**	**22.2**	**11**	**4**	**8**	**0**	**–1**								
	Finland	WEC-A	10	2	0	2				2																		
1987-88	Finland	C Cup	5	1	1	2				0																		
	Vancouver Canucks	**NHL**	**9**	**2**	**3**	**5**	**2**	**2**	**4**	**2**	**0**	**0**	**0**	**11**	**18.2**	**7**	**1**	**10**	**0**	**–4**								
	Fredericton Express	AHL	20	7	15	22				38																		
	Flint Spirits	IHL	7	1	1	2				0																		
1988-89	Ilves Tampere	Finland	44	35	46	*81				22											5	4	3	7	6			
1989-90	Ilves Tampere	Finland	40	39	31	70				42											9	3	4	7	8			
	Finland	WEC-A	10	5	3	8				10																		
1990-91	Ilves Tampere	Finland	39	25	30	55				67											8	*6	2	8	20			
	Finland	WEC-A	10	1	1	2				6																		
1991-92	Finland	C Cup	6	0	1	1				0																		
	Ilves Tampere	Finland	26	13	9	22				94																		
	Finland	Olympics	8	2	0	2				6																		
1992-93	TPS Turku	Finland	47	17	20	37				50																		
1993-94	Jokerit Helsinki	Finland	25	9	3	12				44																		
	SC Bern	Switz.	10	6	13	19				24																		
1994-95	TPS Turku	Finland	47	23	26	49				53											12	7	4	11	29			
	Finland	WC-A	8	1	1	2				0																		
	NHL Totals		**151**	**36**	**40**	**76**	**30**	**28**	**58**	**35**	**2**	**0**	**4**	**175**	**20.6**	**116**	**12**	**100**	**0**		**10**	**2**	**5**	**7**	**0**	**0**	**0**	**0**

Finnish First All-Star Team (1983, 1984, 1989, 1990)

Traded to **Vancouver** by **Edmonton** for Moe Lemay, March 10, 1987.

• SUNDBLAD, NIKLAS

Niklas Sundblad RW – R. 6'1", 200 lbs. b: Stockholm, Sweden, 1/3/1973. Calgary's 1st choice, 19th overall, in 1991 Entry Draft.

Season	Club	League	GP	G	A	Pts	AG	AA	APts	PIM	PP	SH	GW	S	%	TGF	PGF	TGA	PGA	+/–	GP	G	A	Pts	PIM	PP	SH	GW
1990-91	AIK Stockholm	Sweden	39	1	3	4				14																		
1991-92	AIK Stockholm	Sweden	33	9	2	11				20											3	3	1	4	0			
	Sweden	WJC-A	7	2	3	5				10																		
1992-93	AIK Stockholm	Sweden	22	5	4	9				56																		
	Sweden	WJC-A	7	0	3	3				10																		
1993-94	Saint John Flames	AHL	76	13	19	32				75											4	1	1	2	2			
1994-95	Saint John Flames	AHL	72	9	5	14				151											2	0	0	0	6			
1995-96	**Calgary Flames**	**NHL**	**2**	**0**	**0**	**0**	**0**	**0**	**0**	**0**	**0**	**0**	**0**	**3**	**0.0**	**0**	**0**	**0**	**0**	**0**								
	Saint John Flames	AHL	74	16	20	36				66											16	0	4	4	14			
1996-97	TPS Turku	Finland	50	15	21	36				93											11	2	2	4	24			
	Sweden	WC-A	11	2	1	3				22																		
1997-98	TPS Turku	Finland	47	17	16	33				68											4	0	0	0	6			
	NHL Totals		**2**	**0**	**0**	**0**	**0**	**0**	**0**	**0**	**0**	**0**	**0**	**3**	**0.0**	**0**	**0**	**0**	**0**									

• SUNDIN, MATS

Mats Sundin C/RW – R. 6'4", 215 lbs. b: Bromma, Sweden, 2/13/1971. Quebec's 1st choice, 1st overall, in 1989 Entry Draft.

Season	Club	League	GP	G	A	Pts	AG	AA	APts	PIM	PP	SH	GW	S	%	TGF	PGF	TGA	PGA	+/–	GP	G	A	Pts	PIM	PP	SH	GW
1988-89	Nacka	Sweden 2	25	10	8	18				18																		
1989-90	Djurgarden IF Stockholm	Sweden	34	10	8	18				16											8	7	0	7	4			
	Sweden	WJC-A	7	5	2	7				6																		
	Sweden	WEC-A	4	0	0	0				0																		
1990-91	**Quebec Nordiques**	**NHL**	**80**	**23**	**36**	**59**	**21**	**27**	**48**	**58**	**4**	**0**	**0**	**155**	**14.8**	**90**	**27**	**90**	**3**	**–24**								
	Sweden	WEC-A	10	7	5	12				12																		
1991-92	Sweden	C Cup	6	2	4	6				16																		
	Quebec Nordiques	**NHL**	**80**	**33**	**43**	**76**	**30**	**32**	**62**	**103**	**8**	**2**	**2**	**231**	**14.3**	**106**	**36**	**104**	**15**	**–19**								
	Sweden	WC-A	8	2	6	8				8																		
1992-93	**Quebec Nordiques**	**NHL**	**80**	**47**	**67**	**114**	**39**	**46**	**85**	**96**	**13**	**4**	**9**	**215**	**21.9**	**154**	**70**	**89**	**26**	**+21**	**6**	**3**	**1**	**4**	**6**	**1**	**0**	**0**
1993-94	**Quebec Nordiques**	**NHL**	**84**	**32**	**53**	**85**	**30**	**41**	**71**	**60**	**6**	**2**	**4**	**226**	**14.2**	**114**	**39**	**100**	**26**	**+1**								
	Sweden	WC-A	8	5	9	14				4																		
1994-95	Djurgarden IF Stockholm	Sweden	12	7	2	9				14																		
	Toronto Maple Leafs	**NHL**	**47**	**23**	**24**	**47**	**41**	**35**	**76**	**14**	**9**	**0**	**4**	**173**	**13.3**	**58**	**24**	**44**	**5**	**–5**	**7**	**5**	**4**	**9**	**4**	**2**	**0**	**1**
1995-96	**Toronto Maple Leafs**	**NHL**	**76**	**33**	**50**	**83**	**33**	**41**	**74**	**46**	**7**	**6**	**7**	**301**	**11.0**	**111**	**47**	**73**	**17**	**+8**	**6**	**3**	**1**	**4**	**4**	**2**	**0**	**1**
1996-97	Sweden	W Cup	4	4	3	7				4																		
	Toronto Maple Leafs	**NHL**	**82**	**41**	**53**	**94**	**44**	**47**	**91**	**59**	**7**	**4**	**8**	**281**	**14.6**	**125**	**35**	**103**	**19**	**+6**								
1997-98	**Toronto Maple Leafs**	**NHL**	**82**	**33**	**41**	**74**	**39**	**40**	**79**	**49**	**9**	**1**	**5**	**219**	**15.1**	**96**	**31**	**88**	**20**	**–3**								
	Sweden	Olympics	4	3	0	3				4																		
	Sweden	WC-A	10	5	6	11				6																		
	NHL Totals		**611**	**265**	**367**	**632**	**277**	**309**	**586**	**485**	**63**	**19**	**39**	**1801**	**14.7**	**854**	**309**	**691**	**131**		**19**	**11**	**6**	**17**	**14**	**5**	**0**	**2**

Swedish World All-Star Team (1991, 1992, 1994, 1997) • Canada Cup All-Star Team (1991) • WC-A All-Star Team (1992) • Named Best Forward at WC-A (1992) • World Cup All-Star Team (1996)

Played in NHL All-Star Game (1996, 1997, 1998)

Traded to **Toronto** by **Quebec** with Garth Butcher, Todd Warriner and Philadelphia's 1st round choice (previously acquired by Quebec — later traded to Washington — Washington selected Nolan Baumgartner) in 1994 Entry Draft for Wendel Clark, Sylvain Lefebvre, Landon Wilson and Toronto's 1st round choice (Jeffrey Kealty) in 1994 Entry Draft, June 28, 1994.

Season	Club	League	GP	G	A	Pts	AG	AA	APts	PIM	PP	SH	GW	S	%	TGF	PGF	TGA	PGA	+/–	GP	G	A	Pts	PIM	PP	SH	GW
			REGULAR SEASON																		PLAYOFFS							

• SUNDIN, RONNIE

Ronnie Sundin D – L. 6'1", 220 lbs. b: Ludvika, Sweden, 10/3/1970. NY Rangers' 8th choice, 237th overall, in 1996 Entry Draft.

Season	Club	League	GP	G	A	Pts	AG	AA	APts	PIM	PP	SH	GW	S	%	TGF	PGF	TGA	PGA	+/–	GP	G	A	Pts	PIM	PP	SH	GW
1991-92	Mora	Sweden 2	35	2	5	7	....	....	....	18	....	....	....	....	....	....	....	....	....	....	2	0	0	0	0	....	....	....
1992-93	Vastra Frolunda	Sweden	17	2	3	5	....	....	....	12	....	....	....	....	....	....	....	....	....	....	....	....	....	....	....	....	....	....
1993-94	Vastra Frolunda	Sweden	38	0	9	9	....	....	....	42	....	....	....	....	....	....	....	....	....	....	4	0	0	0	0	....	....	....
1994-95	Vastra Frolunda	Sweden	11	3	4	7	....	....	....	6	....	....	....	....	....	....	....	....	....	....	....	....	....	....	....	....	....	....
1995-96	Vastra Frolunda	Sweden	40	3	6	9	....	....	....	18	....	....	....	....	....	....	....	....	....	....	13	1	4	5	10	....	....	....
	Sweden	WC-A	1	0	0	0	....	....	....	0	....	....	....	....	....	....	....	....	....	....	....	....	....	....	....	....	....	....
1996-97	Vastra Frolunda	Sweden	47	3	14	17	....	....	....	24	....	....	....	....	....	....	....	....	....	....	3	1	0	1	2	....	....	....
	Sweden	WC-A	8	0	0	0	....	....	....	0	....	....	....	....	....	....	....	....	....	....	....	....	....	....	....	....	....	....
1997-98	**New York Rangers**	**NHL**	**1**	**0**	**0**	**0**	**0**	**0**	**0**	**0**	**0**	**0**	**0**	**0**	**0.0**	**0**	**0**	**0**	**0**	**0**	....	....	....	....	....	....	....	....
	Hartford Wolf Pack	AHL	67	3	19	22	....	....	....	59	....	....	....	....	....	....	....	....	....	....	14	2	5	7	15	....	....	....
	NHL Totals		**1**	**0**	**0**	**0**	**0**	**0**	**0**	**0**	**0**	**0**	**0**	**0**	**0.0**	**0**	**0**	**0**	**0**		....	....	....	....	....	....	....	....

• SUNDSTROM, NIKLAS

Niklas Sundstrom LW – L. 6', 185 lbs. b: Ornskoldsvik, Sweden, 6/6/1975. NY Rangers' 1st choice, 8th overall, in 1993 Entry Draft.

Season	Club	League	GP	G	A	Pts	AG	AA	APts	PIM	PP	SH	GW	S	%	TGF	PGF	TGA	PGA	+/–	GP	G	A	Pts	PIM	PP	SH	GW
1991-92	MoDo Ornskoldsvik	Sweden	9	1	3	4	....	....	....	0	....	....	....	....	....	....	....	....	....	....	....	....	....	....	....	....	....	....
1992-93	MoDo Ornskoldsvik	Sweden	40	7	11	18	....	....	....	18	....	....	....	....	....	....	....	....	....	....	3	0	0	0	0	....	....	....
	Sweden	WJC-A	7	10	4	14	....	....	....	0	....	....	....	....	....	....	....	....	....	....	....	....	....	....	....	....	....	....
1993-94	MoDo Ornskoldsvik	Sweden	37	7	12	19	....	....	....	28	....	....	....	....	....	....	....	....	....	....	11	4	3	7	2	....	....	....
	Sweden	WJC-A	7	4	7	11	....	....	....	10	....	....	....	....	....	....	....	....	....	....	....	....	....	....	....	....	....	....
1994-95	MoDo Ornskoldsvik	Sweden	33	8	13	21	....	....	....	30	....	....	....	....	....	....	....	....	....	....	....	....	....	....	....	....	....	....
	Sweden	WJC-A	7	4	4	8	....	....	....	8	....	....	....	....	....	....	....	....	....	....	....	....	....	....	....	....	....	....
1995-96	**New York Rangers**	**NHL**	**82**	**9**	**12**	**21**	**9**	**10**	**19**	**14**	**1**	**1**	**2**	**90**	**10.0**	**34**	**1**	**59**	**28**	**+2**	**11**	**4**	**3**	**7**	**4**	**1**	**0**	**0**
1996-97	Sweden	W Cup	4	2	2	4	....	....	....	0	....	....	....	....	....	....	....	....	....	....	....	....	....	....	....	....	....	....
	New York Rangers	**NHL**	**82**	**24**	**28**	**52**	**26**	**25**	**51**	**20**	**5**	**1**	**4**	**132**	**18.2**	**87**	**14**	**78**	**28**	**+23**	**9**	**0**	**5**	**5**	**2**	**0**	**0**	**0**
1997-98	**New York Rangers**	**NHL**	**70**	**19**	**28**	**47**	**22**	**27**	**49**	**24**	**4**	**0**	**1**	**115**	**16.5**	**70**	**18**	**69**	**17**	**0**	....	....	....	....	....	....	....	....
	Sweden	Olympics	4	1	1	2	....	....	....	2	....	....	....	....	....	....	....	....	....	....	....	....	....	....	....	....	....	....
	Sweden	WC-A	10	1	5	6	....	....	....	8	....	....	....	....	....	....	....	....	....	....	....	....	....	....	....	....	....	....
	NHL Totals		**234**	**52**	**68**	**120**	**57**	**62**	**119**	**58**	**10**	**2**	**7**	**337**	**15.4**	**191**	**33**	**206**	**73**		**20**	**4**	**8**	**12**	**6**	**1**	**0**	**0**

EJC-A All-Star Team (1993) • WJC-A All-Star Team (1994) • Named Best Forward at WJC-A (1994)

• SUNDSTROM, PATRIK

Patrik Sundstrom C – L. 6'1", 200 lbs. b: Skelleftea, Sweden, 12/14/1961. Vancouver's 8th choice, 175th overall, in 1980 Entry Draft.

Season	Club	League	GP	G	A	Pts	AG	AA	APts	PIM	PP	SH	GW	S	%	TGF	PGF	TGA	PGA	+/–	GP	G	A	Pts	PIM	PP	SH	GW
1978-79	IF Bjorkloven Umea	Sweden	1	0	0	0	....	....	....	0	....	....	....	....	....	....	....	....	....	....	....	....	....	....	....	....	....	....
1979-80	IF Bjorkloven Umea	Sweden	26	5	7	12	....	....	....	20	....	....	....	....	....	....	....	....	....	....	3	1	0	1	4	....	....	....
	Sweden	WJC-A	5	0	1	1	....	....	....	4	....	....	....	....	....	....	....	....	....	....	....	....	....	....	....	....	....	....
1980-81	IF Bjorkloven Umea	Sweden	36	10	18	28	....	....	....	30	....	....	....	....	....	....	....	....	....	....	....	....	....	....	....	....	....	....
	Sweden	WJC-A	5	7	0	7	....	....	....	8	....	....	....	....	....	....	....	....	....	....	....	....	....	....	....	....	....	....
	Sweden	WEC-A	7	4	0	4	....	....	....	2	....	....	....	....	....	....	....	....	....	....	....	....	....	....	....	....	....	....
1981-82	Sweden	C Cup	5	0	2	2	....	....	....	4	....	....	....	....	....	....	....	....	....	....	....	....	....	....	....	....	....	....
	IF Bjorkloven Umea	Sweden	36	22	13	35	....	....	....	38	....	....	....	....	....	....	....	....	....	....	7	3	4	7	6	....	....	....
	Sweden	WEC A	10	5	2	7	....	....	....	8	....	....	....	....	....	....	....	....	....	....	....	....	....	....	....	....	....	....
1982-83	**Vancouver Canucks**	**NHL**	**74**	**23**	**23**	**46**	**19**	**16**	**35**	**30**	**6**	**0**	**5**	**156**	**14.7**	**72**	**26**	**77**	**11**	**–20**	**4**	**0**	**0**	**0**	**2**	**0**	**0**	**0**
1983-84	**Vancouver Canucks**	**NHL**	**78**	**30**	**53**	**91**	**31**	**36**	**67**	**37**	**7**	**0**	**7**	**216**	**17.6**	**129**	**48**	**102**	**10**	**–11**	**4**	**0**	**1**	**1**	**7**	**0**	**0**	**0**
1984-85	Sweden	C Cup	8	1	6	7	....	....	....	6	....	....	....	....	....	....	....	....	....	....	....	....	....	....	....	....	....	....
	Vancouver Canucks	**NHL**	**71**	**25**	**43**	**68**	**20**	**29**	**49**	**46**	**5**	**0**	**2**	**186**	**13.4**	**98**	**28**	**102**	**15**	**–17**	....	....	....	....	....	....	....	....
1985-86	**Vancouver Canucks**	**NHL**	**79**	**18**	**48**	**66**	**14**	**32**	**46**	**28**	**6**	**1**	**0**	**155**	**11.6**	**100**	**39**	**81**	**12**	**–8**	**3**	**1**	**0**	**1**	**0**	**1**	**0**	**0**
1986-87	**Vancouver Canucks**	**NHL**	**72**	**29**	**42**	**71**	**25**	**30**	**55**	**40**	**12**	**1**	**0**	**141**	**20.6**	**102**	**30**	**84**	**21**	**+9**	....	....	....	....	....	....	....	....
1987-88	**New Jersey Devils**	**NHL**	**78**	**15**	**36**	**51**	**13**	**26**	**39**	**42**	**9**	**1**	**0**	**126**	**11.9**	**77**	**34**	**100**	**41**	**–16**	**18**	**7**	**13**	**20**	**14**	**3**	**0**	**1**
1988-89	**New Jersey Devils**	**NHL**	**65**	**28**	**41**	**69**	**24**	**29**	**53**	**36**	**12**	**1**	**4**	**156**	**17.9**	**110**	**43**	**82**	**37**	**+22**	....	....	....	....	....	....	....	....
1989-90	**New Jersey Devils**	**NHL**	**74**	**27**	**49**	**76**	**23**	**35**	**58**	**34**	**8**	**1**	**0**	**142**	**19.0**	**116**	**33**	**94**	**26**	**+15**	**6**	**1**	**3**	**4**	**2**	**0**	**0**	**0**
1990-91	**New Jersey Devils**	**NHL**	**71**	**15**	**31**	**46**	**14**	**23**	**37**	**48**	**4**	**1**	**1**	**96**	**15.6**	**78**	**24**	**68**	**21**	**+7**	**2**	**0**	**0**	**0**	**0**	**0**	**0**	**0**
1991-92	**New Jersey Devils**	**NHL**	**17**	**1**	**3**	**4**	**1**	**2**	**3**	**8**	**1**	**0**	**0**	**16**	**6.3**	**8**	**2**	**12**	**1**	**–5**	....	....	....	....	....	....	....	....
	Utica Devils	AHL	1	0	0	0	....	....	....	0	....	....	....	....	....	....	....	....	....	....	....	....	....	....	....	....	....	....
	NHL Totals		**679**	**219**	**369**	**588**	**184**	**258**	**442**	**349**	**70**	**6**	**19**	**1390**	**15.8**	**890**	**307**	**802**	**195**		**37**	**9**	**17**	**26**	**25**	**4**	**0**	**1**

WJC-A All-Star Team (1981) • Named Best Forward at WJC-A (1981) • Swedish World All-Star Team (1982) • Swedish Player of the Year (1982)

Traded to **New Jersey** by **Vancouver** with Vancouver's 4th round choice (Matt Ruchty) in 1988 Entry Draft for Kirk McLean and Greg Adams, September 15, 1987.

• SUNDSTROM, PETER

Peter Sundstrom LW – L. 6', 180 lbs. b: Skelleftea, Sweden, 12/14/1961. NY Rangers' 8th choice, 50th overall, in 1981 Entry Draft.

Season	Club	League	GP	G	A	Pts	AG	AA	APts	PIM	PP	SH	GW	S	%	TGF	PGF	TGA	PGA	+/–	GP	G	A	Pts	PIM	PP	SH	GW
1978-79	IF Bjorkloven Umea	Sweden	1	0	0	0	....	....	....	0	....	....	....	....	....	....	....	....	....	....	....	....	....	....	....	....	....	....
1979-80	IF Bjorkloven Umea	Sweden	8	0	0	0	....	....	....	4	....	....	....	....	....	....	....	....	....	....	....	....	....	....	....	....	....	....
1980-81	IF Bjorkloven Umea	Sweden	29	7	2	9	....	....	....	8	....	....	....	....	....	....	....	....	....	....	....	....	....	....	....	....	....	....
	Sweden	WJC-A	5	2	3	5	....	....	....	4	....	....	....	....	....	....	....	....	....	....	....	....	....	....	....	....	....	....
1981-82	IF Bjorkloven Umea	Sweden	35	10	14	24	....	....	....	18	....	....	....	....	....	....	....	....	....	....	7	2	1	3	0	....	....	....
	Sweden	WEC-A	8	3	1	4	....	....	....	2	....	....	....	....	....	....	....	....	....	....	....	....	....	....	....	....	....	....
1982-83	IF Bjorkloven Umea	Sweden	33	14	11	25	....	....	....	26	....	....	....	....	....	....	....	....	....	....	3	2	0	2	4	....	....	....
	Sweden	WEC-A	10	3	3	6	....	....	....	4	....	....	....	....	....	....	....	....	....	....	....	....	....	....	....	....	....	....
1983-84	**New York Rangers**	**NHL**	**77**	**22**	**22**	**44**	**18**	**15**	**33**	**24**	**0**	**2**	**4**	**153**	**14.4**	**68**	**3**	**72**	**10**	**+3**	**5**	**1**	**3**	**4**	**0**	**1**	**0**	**0**
1984-85	Sweden	C Cup	8	2	2	4	....	....	....	8	....	....	....	....	....	....	....	....	....	....	....	....	....	....	....	....	....	....
	New York Rangers	**NHL**	**76**	**18**	**25**	**43**	**15**	**17**	**32**	**34**	**0**	**2**	**2**	**157**	**11.5**	**60**	**0**	**110**	**24**	**–26**	**3**	**0**	**0**	**0**	**0**	**0**	**0**	**0**
1985-86	**New York Rangers**	**NHL**	**53**	**8**	**15**	**23**	**6**	**10**	**16**	**12**	**0**	**0**	**1**	**63**	**12.7**	**30**	**0**	**25**	**2**	**+7**	**1**	**0**	**0**	**0**	**2**	**0**	**0**	**0**
	New Haven Nighthawks	AHL	8	3	6	9	....	....	....	4	....	....	....	....	....	....	....	....	....	....	....	....	....	....	....	....	....	....
1986-87	IF Bjorkloven Umea	Sweden	36	22	16	38	....	....	....	44	....	....	....	....	....	....	....	....	....	....	6	2	*5	7	8	....	....	....
	Sweden	WEC-A	10	1	1	2	....	....	....	8	....	....	....	....	....	....	....	....	....	....	....	....	....	....	....	....	....	....
1987-88	**Washington Capitals**	**NHL**	**76**	**8**	**17**	**25**	**7**	**12**	**19**	**34**	**0**	**1**	**1**	**89**	**9.0**	**35**	**0**	**54**	**17**	**–2**	**14**	**2**	**0**	**2**	**6**	**0**	**1**	**1**
1988-89	**Washington Capitals**	**NHL**	**35**	**4**	**2**	**6**	**3**	**1**	**4**	**12**	**0**	**0**	**0**	**39**	**10.3**	**11**	**0**	**23**	**7**	**–5**	....	....	....	....	....	....	....	....
1989-90	**New Jersey Devils**	**NHL**	**21**	**1**	**2**	**3**	**1**	**1**	**2**	**4**	**0**	**0**	**0**	**16**	**6.3**	**9**	**0**	**12**	**4**	**+1**	....	....	....	....	....	....	....	....
	Utica Devils	AHL	31	11	18	29	....	....	....	6	....	....	....	....	....	....	....	....	....	....	5	4	1	5	0	....	....	....
1990-91	Malmo IF	Sweden	40	12	19	31	....	....	....	50	....	....	....	....	....	....	....	....	....	....	2	1	0	1	4	....	....	....
1991-92	Malmo IF	Sweden	40	10	17	27	....	....	....	36	....	....	....	....	....	....	....	....	....	....	10	*5	6	*11	2	....	....	....
1992-93	Malmo IF	Sweden	40	11	15	26	....	....	....	36	....	....	....	....	....	....	....	....	....	....	6	1	0	1	18	....	....	....
1993-94	Malmo IF	Sweden	40	4	14	18	....	....	....	28	....	....	....	....	....	....	....	....	....	....	11	5	2	7	8	....	....	....
1994-95	Malmo IF	Sweden	40	9	13	22	....	....	....	30	....	....	....	....	....	....	....	....	....	....	9	1	4	5	2	....	....	....
	NHL Totals		**338**	**61**	**83**	**144**	**50**	**56**	**106**	**120**	**0**	**5**	**8**	**517**	**11.8**	**213**	**3**	**296**	**64**		**23**	**3**	**3**	**6**	**8**	**1**	**1**	**1**

Traded to **Washington** by **NY Rangers** for Washington's 5th round choice (Martin Bergeron) in 1988 Entry Draft, August 27, 1987. Traded to **New Jersey** by **Washington** for New Jersey's 10th round choice (Rob Leask) in 1991 Entry Draft, June 19, 1989.

• SUTER, GARY

Gary Suter D – L. 6', 205 lbs. b: Madison, WI, 6/24/1964. Calgary's 4th choice, 180th overall, in 1984 Entry Draft.

Season	Club	League	GP	G	A	Pts	AG	AA	APts	PIM	PP	SH	GW	S	%	TGF	PGF	TGA	PGA	+/–	GP	G	A	Pts	PIM	PP	SH	GW
1983-84	University of Wisconsin	WCHA	35	4	18	22	....	....	....	32	....	....	....	....	....	....	....	....	....	....	....	....	....	....	....	....	....	....
	United States	WJC-A	7	1	1	2	....	....	....	12	....	....	....	....	....	....	....	....	....	....	....	....	....	....	....	....	....	....
1984-85	University of Wisconsin	WCHA	39	12	39	51	....	....	....	110	....	....	....	....	....	....	....	....	....	....	....	....	....	....	....	....	....	....
	United States	WEC-A	10	1	2	3	....	....	....	22	....	....	....	....	....	....	....	....	....	....	....	....	....	....	....	....	....	....
1985-86	**Calgary Flames**	**NHL**	**80**	**18**	**50**	**68**	**14**	**33**	**47**	**141**	**9**	**0**	**4**	**195**	**9.2**	**156**	**69**	**106**	**30**	**+11**	**10**	**2**	**8**	**10**	**8**	**0**	**0**	**1**
1986-87	**Calgary Flames**	**NHL**	**68**	**9**	**40**	**49**	**8**	**29**	**37**	**70**	**4**	**0**	**0**	**152**	**5.9**	**106**	**51**	**85**	**20**	**–10**	**6**	**0**	**3**	**3**	**10**	**0**	**0**	**0**
1987-88	United States	C Cup	5	0	3	3	....	....	....	9	....	....	....	....	....	....	....	....	....	....	....	....	....	....	....	....	....	....
	Calgary Flames	**NHL**	**75**	**21**	**70**	**91**	**18**	**50**	**68**	**124**	**6**	**1**	**3**	**204**	**10.3**	**186**	**79**	**100**	**32**	**+39**	**9**	**1**	**9**	**10**	**6**	**0**	**1**	**0**
1988-89	**Calgary Flames**	**NHL**	**63**	**13**	**49**	**62**	**11**	**35**	**46**	**78**	**8**	**0**	**1**	**216**	**6.0**	**141**	**71**	**60**	**16**	**+26**	**5**	**0**	**3**	**3**	**10**	**0**	**0**	**0**
1989-90	Calgary Flames	FrTour	4	0	1	1	....	....	....	2	....	....	....	....	....	....	....	....	....	....	....	....	....	....	....	....	....	....
	Calgary Flames	**NHL**	**76**	**16**	**60**	**76**	**14**	**43**	**57**	**97**	**5**	**0**	**1**	**211**	**7.6**	**160**	**82**	**83**	**9**	**+4**	**6**	**0**	**1**	**1**	**14**	**0**	**0**	**0**
1990-91	**Calgary Flames**	**NHL**	**79**	**12**	**58**	**70**	**11**	**44**	**55**	**102**	**6**	**0**	**1**	**258**	**4.7**	**164**	**78**	**78**	**18**	**+26**	**7**	**1**	**6**	**7**	**12**	**1**	**0**	**0**
1991-92	United States	C Cup	8	1	3	4	....	....	....	4	....	....	....	....	....	....	....	....	....	....	....	....	....	....	....	....	....	....
	Calgary Flames	**NHL**	**70**	**12**	**43**	**55**	**11**	**32**	**43**	**128**	**4**	**0**	**0**	**189**	**6.3**	**139**	**64**	**103**	**29**	**+1**	....	....	....	....	....	....	....	....
	United States	WC-A	6	0	1	1	....	....	....	6	....	....	....	....	....	....	....	....	....	....	....	....	....	....	....	....	....	....

			REGULAR SEASON																		PLAYOFFS							
Season	Club	League	GP	G	A	Pts	AG	AA	APts	PIM	PP	SH	GW	S	%	TGF	PGF	TGA	PGA	+/–	GP	G	A	Pts	PIM	PP	SH	GW
1992-93	**Calgary Flames**	**NHL**	**81**	**23**	**58**	**81**	**19**	**40**	**59**	**112**	**10**	**1**	**2**	**263**	**8.7**	**161**	**70**	**125**	**33**	**–1**	**6**	**2**	**3**	**5**	**8**	**0**	**1**	**0**
1993-94	**Calgary Flames**	**NHL**	**25**	**4**	**9**	**13**	**4**	**7**	**11**	**20**	**2**	**1**	**0**	**51**	**7.8**	**26**	**11**	**24**	**6**	**–3**	....	....	....	....	....	....	....	....
	Chicago Blackhawks	**NHL**	**16**	**2**	**3**	**5**	**2**	**2**	**4**	**18**	**2**	**0**	**0**	**35**	**5.7**	**25**	**15**	**34**	**15**	**–9**	**6**	**3**	**2**	**5**	**6**	**2**	**0**	**0**
1994-95	**Chicago Blackhawks**	**NHL**	**48**	**10**	**27**	**37**	**18**	**40**	**58**	**42**	**5**	**0**	**0**	**144**	**6.9**	**89**	**43**	**43**	**11**	**+14**	**12**	**2**	**5**	**7**	**10**	**1**	**0**	**0**
1995-96	**Chicago Blackhawks**	**NHL**	**82**	**20**	**47**	**67**	**20**	**38**	**58**	**80**	**12**	**2**	**4**	**242**	**8.3**	**137**	**58**	**103**	**27**	**+3**	**10**	**3**	**3**	**6**	**8**	**2**	**0**	**1**
1996-97	United States	W Cup	6	0	2	2	....	....	....	6	....	....	....	....	....	....	....	....	....	....	....	....	....	....	....	....	....	....
	Chicago Blackhawks	**NHL**	**82**	**7**	**21**	**28**	**7**	**19**	**26**	**70**	**3**	**0**	**0**	**225**	**3.1**	**98**	**35**	**83**	**16**	**–4**	**6**	**1**	**4**	**5**	**8**	**0**	**0**	**0**
1997-98	**Chicago Blackhawks**	**NHL**	**73**	**14**	**28**	**42**	**16**	**27**	**43**	**74**	**5**	**2**	**0**	**199**	**7.0**	**78**	**32**	**62**	**17**	**+1**	....	....	....	....	....	....	....	....
	United States	Olympics	4	0	0	0	....	....	....	2	....	....	....	....	....	....	....	....	....	....	....	....	....	....	....	....	....	....
	NHL Totals		**918**	**181**	**563**	**744**	**173**	**439**	**612**	**1156**	**81**	**7**	**16**	**2584**	**7.0**	**1666**	**758**	**1089**	**279**		**83**	**15**	**47**	**62**	**100**	**6**	**2**	**2**

Won Calder Memorial Trophy (1986) • NHL All-Rookie Team (1986) • NHL Second All-Star Team (1988)

Played in NHL All-Star Game (1986, 1988, 1989, 1991)

Traded to **Hartford** by **Calgary** with Paul Ranheim and Ted Drury for James Patrick, Zarley Zalapski and Michael Nylander, March 10, 1994. Traded to **Chicago** by **Hartford** with Randy Cunneyworth and Hartford's 3rd round choice (later traded to Vancouver — Vancouver selected Larry Courville) in 1995 Entry Draft for Frantisek Kucera and Jocelyn Lemieux, March 11, 1994. Signed as a free agent by **San Jose**, July 1, 1998.

• SUTHERLAND, BILL

Bill Sutherland C – L. 5'10", 160 lbs. b: Regina, Sask., 11/10/1934.

Season	Club	League	GP	G	A	Pts	AG	AA	APts	PIM	PP	SH	GW	S	%	TGF	PGF	TGA	PGA	+/–	GP	G	A	Pts	PIM	PP	SH	GW
1952-53	St. Boniface Canadians	MJHL	1	0	1	1	....	....	....	0	....	....	....	....	....	....	....	....	....	....	....	....	....	....	....	....	....	....
1953-54	St. Boniface Canadians	MJHL	25	25	18	43	....	....	....	42	....	....	....	....	....	....	....	....	....	....	18	*12	*18	*30	24	....	....	....
1954-55	St. Boniface Canadians	MJHL	25	25	35	60	....	....	....	33	....	....	....	....	....	....	....	....	....	....	....	....	....	....	....	....	....	....
1955-56	Cincinnati Mohawks	IHL	53	25	31	56	....	....	....	24	....	....	....	....	....	....	....	....	....	....	....	....	....	....	....	....	....	....
1956-57	Cincinnati Mohawks	IHL	58	27	26	53	....	....	....	30	....	....	....	....	....	....	....	....	....	....	7	1	1	2	4	....	....	....
1957-58	Cincinnati Mohawks	IHL	60	*55	39	94	....	....	....	43	....	....	....	....	....	....	....	....	....	....	....	....	....	....	....	....	....	....
	Shawinigan Cataracts	QHL	2	0	1	1	....	....	....	0	....	....	....	....	....	....	....	....	....	....	....	....	....	....	....	....	....	....
1958-59	Rochester Americans	AHL	1	0	0	0	....	....	....	0	....	....	....	....	....	....	....	....	....	....	....	....	....	....	....	....	....	....
	Montreal Royals	QHL	47	27	16	43	....	....	....	32	....	....	....	....	....	....	....	....	....	....	7	*7	3	*10	13	....	....	....
1959-60	Montreal Royals	EPHL	65	35	40	75	....	....	....	40	....	....	....	....	....	....	....	....	....	....	14	3	7	10	13	....	....	....
1960-61	Cleveland Barons	AHL	58	19	14	33	....	....	....	30	....	....	....	....	....	....	....	....	....	....	4	0	0	0	12	....	....	....
1961-62	Cleveland Barons	AHL	70	20	28	48	....	....	....	49	....	....	....	....	....	....	....	....	....	....	6	0	2	2	4	....	....	....
1962-63	Quebec Aces	AHL	45	21	17	38	....	....	....	22	....	....	....	....	....	....	....	....	....	....	....	....	....	....	....	....	....	....
	Montreal Canadiens	**NHL**	....	....	....	....	....	....	....	....	....	....	....	....	....	....	....	....	....	....	**2**	**0**	**0**	**0**	**0**	....	....	....
1963-64	Quebec Aces	AHL	49	22	33	55	....	....	....	32	....	....	....	....	....	....	....	....	....	....	9	2	7	9	22	....	....	....
1964-65	Quebec Aces	AHL	58	25	35	60	....	....	....	50	....	....	....	....	....	....	....	....	....	....	5	3	2	5	6	....	....	....
1965-66	Quebec Aces	AHL	48	24	25	49	....	....	....	24	....	....	....	....	....	....	....	....	....	....	6	3	3	6	2	....	....	....
1966-67	Quebec Aces	AHL	67	40	38	78	....	....	....	27	....	....	....	....	....	....	....	....	....	....	5	3	4	7	4	....	....	....
1967-68	**Philadelphia Flyers**	**NHL**	**60**	**20**	**9**	**29**	**25**	**9**	**34**	**6**	**5**	**2**	**1**	**98**	**20.4**	**40**	**12**	**41**	**14**	**+1**	**7**	**1**	**3**	**4**	**0**	**1**	**0**	**0**
1968-69	**Toronto Maple Leafs**	**NHL**	**44**	**7**	**5**	**12**	**8**	**5**	**13**	**14**	**0**	**0**	**0**	**53**	**13.2**	**19**	**1**	**23**	**2**	**–3**	....	....	....	....	....	....	....	....
	Philadelphia Flyers	**NHL**	**12**	**7**	**3**	**10**	**8**	**3**	**11**	**4**	**1**	**1**	**0**	**23**	**30.4**	**13**	**3**	**10**	**5**	**+5**	**4**	**1**	**1**	**2**	**0**	**1**	**0**	**0**
1969-70	**Philadelphia Flyers**	**NHL**	**51**	**15**	**17**	**32**	**17**	**17**	**34**	**30**	**3**	**0**	**1**	**103**	**14.6**	**44**	**8**	**48**	**10**	**–2**	....	....	....	....	....	....	....	....
1970-71	**Philadelphia Flyers**	**NHL**	**1**	**0**	**0**	**0**	**0**	**0**	**0**	**0**	**0**	**0**	**0**	**0**	**0.0**	**0**	**0**	**0**	**0**	**0**	....	....	....	....	....	....	....	....
	St. Louis Blues	**NHL**	**68**	**19**	**20**	**39**	**20**	**18**	**38**	**41**	**11**	**0**	**3**	**106**	**17.9**	**68**	**24**	**31**	**0**	**+13**	**1**	**0**	**0**	**0**	**0**	**0**	**0**	**0**
1971-72	**St. Louis Blues**	**NHL**	**9**	**2**	**3**	**5**	**2**	**3**	**5**	**2**	**0**	**1**	**0**	**7**	**28.6**	**9**	**3**	**8**	**6**	**+4**	....	....	....	....	....	....	....	....
	Detroit Red Wings	**NHL**	**5**	**0**	**1**	**1**	**0**	**1**	**1**	**2**	**0**	**0**	**0**	**3**	**0.0**	**1**	**0**	**2**	**0**	**–1**	....	....	....	....	....	....	....	....
	Tidewater Wings	AHL	40	6	10	16	....	....	....	26	....	....	....	....	....	....	....	....	....	....	....	....	....	....	....	....	....	....
1972-73	Winnipeg Jets	WHA	48	6	16	22	....	....	....	34	....	....	....	....	....	....	....	....	....	....	14	5	9	14	9	....	....	....
1973-74	Winnipeg Jets	WHA	12	4	5	9	....	....	....	6	....	....	....	....	....	....	....	....	....	....	4	0	0	0	4	....	....	....
	NHL Totals		**250**	**70**	**58**	**128**	**80**	**56**	**136**	**99**	**20**	**4**	**5**	**393**	**17.8**	**194**	**51**	**163**	**37**		**14**	**2**	**4**	**6**	**0**	**2**	**0**	**0**
	Other Major League Totals		60	10	21	31	....	....	....	40	....	....	....	....	....	....	....	....	....		18	5	9	14	13	....	....	....

IHL Second All-Star Team (1958)

Traded to **Quebec** (AHL) by **Montreal** for cash, July, 1962. NHL rights transferred to **Philadelphia** after NHL club purchased **Quebec** (AHL) franchise, May 8, 1967. Claimed by **Minnesota** from **Philadelphia** in Intra-League Draft, June 12, 1968. Claimed by **Toronto** from **Minnesota** in Intra-League Draft, June 12, 1968. Traded to **Philadelphia** by **Toronto** with Mike Byers and Gerry Meehan for Brit Selby and Forbes Kennedy, March 2, 1969. Traded to **St. Louis** by **Philadelphia** for cash, October 19, 1970. Traded to **Detroit** by **St. Louis** for cash, November 9, 1971. Selected by **Winnipeg** (WHA) in 1972 WHA General Player Draft, February 12, 1972.

• SUTTER, BRENT

Brent "Pup" Sutter C – R. 6', 188 lbs. b: Viking, Alta., 6/10/1962. NY Islanders' 1st choice, 17th overall, in 1980 Entry Draft.

Season	Club	League	GP	G	A	Pts	AG	AA	APts	PIM	PP	SH	GW	S	%	TGF	PGF	TGA	PGA	+/–	GP	G	A	Pts	PIM	PP	SH	GW
1977-78	Red Deer Rustlers	AJHL	60	12	18	30	....	....	....	33	....	....	....	....	....	....	....	....	....	....	....	....	....	....	....	....	....	....
1978-79	Red Deer Rustlers	AJHL	60	42	42	84	....	....	....	79	....	....	....	....	....	....	....	....	....	....	....	....	....	....	....	....	....	....
1979-80	Red Deer Rustlers	AJHL	59	70	101	171	....	....	....	....	....	....	....	....	....	....	....	....	....	....	....	....	....	....	....	....	....	....
	Lethbridge Broncos	WHL	5	1	0	1	....	....	....	2	....	....	....	....	....	....	....	....	....	....	....	....	....	....	....	....	....	....
1980-81	Lethbridge Broncos	WHL	68	54	54	108	....	....	....	116	....	....	....	....	....	....	....	....	....	....	9	6	4	10	51	....	....	....
	New York Islanders	**NHL**	**3**	**2**	**2**	**4**	**2**	**1**	**3**	**0**	**0**	**0**	**1**	**2**	**100.0**	**4**	**1**	**1**	**0**	**+2**	....	....	....	....	....	....	....	....
1981-82	Lethbridge Broncos	WHL	34	46	33	79	....	....	....	162	....	....	....	....	....	....	....	....	....	....	....	....	....	....	....	....	....	....
	New York Islanders	**NHL**	**43**	**21**	**22**	**43**	**17**	**15**	**32**	**114**	**3**	**0**	**1**	**93**	**22.6**	**59**	**15**	**16**	**0**	**+28**	**19**	**2**	**6**	**8**	**36**	**0**	**0**	**0**
1982-83	**New York Islanders**	**NHL**	**80**	**21**	**19**	**40**	**17**	**13**	**30**	**128**	**1**	**0**	**3**	**149**	**14.1**	**58**	**6**	**39**	**1**	**+14**	**20**	**10**	**11**	**21**	**26**	**3**	**0**	**0**
1983-84	**New York Islanders**	**NHL**	**69**	**34**	**15**	**49**	**27**	**10**	**37**	**69**	**7**	**0**	**6**	**154**	**22.1**	**73**	**16**	**61**	**8**	**+4**	**20**	**4**	**10**	**14**	**18**	**0**	**1**	**3**
1984-85	Canada	C Cup	8	2	2	4	....	....	....	10	....	....	....	....	....	....	....	....	....	....	....	....	....	....	....	....	....	....
	New York Islanders	**NHL**	**72**	**42**	**60**	**102**	**34**	**41**	**75**	**51**	**12**	**0**	**4**	**194**	**21.6**	**145**	**40**	**85**	**22**	**+42**	**10**	**3**	**3**	**6**	**14**	**1**	**0**	**2**
1985-86	**New York Islanders**	**NHL**	**61**	**24**	**31**	**55**	**19**	**21**	**40**	**74**	**10**	**0**	**2**	**135**	**17.8**	**75**	**24**	**60**	**20**	**+11**	**3**	**0**	**1**	**1**	**2**	**0**	**0**	**0**
	Canada	WEC-A	8	4	7	11	....	....	....	8	....	....	....	....	....	....	....	....	....	....	....	....	....	....	....	....	....	....
1986-87	**New York Islanders**	**NHL**	**69**	**27**	**36**	**63**	**23**	**26**	**49**	**73**	**6**	**3**	**8**	**177**	**15.3**	**93**	**32**	**63**	**25**	**+23**	**5**	**1**	**0**	**1**	**4**	**1**	**0**	**0**
1987-88	Canada	C Cup	9	1	3	4	....	....	....	6	....	....	....	....	....	....	....	....	....	....	....	....	....	....	....	....	....	....
	New York Islanders	**NHL**	**70**	**29**	**31**	**60**	**25**	**22**	**47**	**55**	**11**	**2**	**2**	**162**	**17.9**	**87**	**33**	**74**	**33**	**+13**	**6**	**2**	**1**	**3**	**18**	**0**	**1**	**1**
1988-89	**New York Islanders**	**NHL**	**77**	**29**	**34**	**63**	**25**	**24**	**49**	**77**	**17**	**2**	**2**	**187**	**15.5**	**95**	**46**	**94**	**33**	**–12**	....	....	....	....	....	....	....	....
1989-90	**New York Islanders**	**NHL**	**67**	**33**	**35**	**68**	**28**	**25**	**53**	**65**	**17**	**3**	**3**	**198**	**16.7**	**97**	**42**	**76**	**30**	**+9**	**5**	**2**	**3**	**5**	**2**	**2**	**0**	**1**
1990-91	**New York Islanders**	**NHL**	**75**	**21**	**32**	**53**	**19**	**24**	**43**	**49**	**6**	**2**	**4**	**186**	**11.3**	**85**	**32**	**91**	**30**	**–8**	....	....	....	....	....	....	....	....
1991-92	Canada	C Cup	8	3	1	4	....	....	....	6	....	....	....	....	....	....	....	....	....	....	....	....	....	....	....	....	....	....
	Chicago Blackhawks	**NHL**	**61**	**18**	**32**	**50**	**16**	**24**	**40**	**30**	**7**	**1**	**2**	**185**	**9.7**	**72**	**33**	**56**	**12**	**–5**	**18**	**3**	**5**	**8**	**22**	**1**	**0**	**1**
	New York Islanders	**NHL**	**8**	**4**	**6**	**10**	**4**	**4**	**8**	**6**	**1**	**0**	**1**	**21**	**19.0**	**14**	**6**	**13**	**0**	**–5**	....	....	....	....	....	....	....	....
1992-93	**Chicago Blackhawks**	**NHL**	**65**	**20**	**34**	**54**	**17**	**23**	**40**	**67**	**8**	**2**	**3**	**151**	**13.2**	**84**	**44**	**53**	**23**	**+10**	**4**	**1**	**1**	**2**	**4**	**0**	**0**	**0**
1993-94	**Chicago Blackhawks**	**NHL**	**73**	**9**	**29**	**38**	**8**	**22**	**30**	**43**	**3**	**2**	**0**	**127**	**7.1**	**60**	**13**	**60**	**30**	**+17**	**6**	**0**	**0**	**0**	**2**	**0**	**0**	**0**
1994-95	**Chicago Blackhawks**	**NHL**	**47**	**7**	**8**	**15**	**12**	**12**	**24**	**51**	**1**	**0**	**1**	**65**	**10.8**	**27**	**3**	**32**	**14**	**+6**	**16**	**1**	**2**	**3**	**4**	**0**	**0**	**0**
1995-96	**Chicago Blackhawks**	**NHL**	**80**	**13**	**27**	**40**	**13**	**22**	**35**	**56**	**0**	**0**	**3**	**102**	**12.7**	**52**	**1**	**66**	**29**	**+14**	**10**	**1**	**1**	**2**	**6**	**0**	**0**	**0**
1996-97	**Chicago Blackhawks**	**NHL**	**39**	**7**	**7**	**14**	**7**	**6**	**13**	**18**	**0**	**0**	**1**	**62**	**11.3**	**27**	**0**	**23**	**6**	**+10**	**2**	**0**	**0**	**0**	**6**	**0**	**0**	**0**
1997-98	**Chicago Blackhawks**	**NHL**	**52**	**2**	**6**	**8**	**2**	**6**	**8**	**28**	**0**	**1**	**0**	**43**	**4.7**	**12**	**1**	**27**	**10**	**–6**	....	....	....	....	....	....	....	....
	NHL Totals		**1111**	**363**	**466**	**829**	**315**	**341**	**656**	**1054**	**110**	**18**	**47**	**2393**	**15.2**	**1219**	**388**	**990**	**326**		**144**	**30**	**44**	**74**	**164**	**8**	**2**	**8**

Played in NHL All-Star Game (1985)

Traded to **Chicago** by **NY Islanders** with Brad Lauer for Adam Creighton and Steve Thomas, October 25, 1991.

• SUTTER, BRIAN

Brian Sutter LW – L. 5'11", 173 lbs. b: Viking, Alta., 10/7/1956. St. Louis' 2nd choice, 20th overall, in 1976 Amateur Draft.

Season	Club	League	GP	G	A	Pts	AG	AA	APts	PIM	PP	SH	GW	S	%	TGF	PGF	TGA	PGA	+/–	GP	G	A	Pts	PIM	PP	SH	GW
1972-73	Red Deer Rustlers	AJHL	51	27	40	67	....	....	....	54	....	....	....	....	....	....	....	....	....	....	....	....	....	....	....	....	....	....
1973-74	Red Deer Rustlers	AJHL	59	42	54	96	....	....	....	139	....	....	....	....	....	....	....	....	....	....	....	....	....	....	....	....	....	....
1974-75	Lethbridge Broncos	WHL	53	34	47	81	....	....	....	134	....	....	....	....	....	....	....	....	....	....	6	0	1	1	39	....	....	....
	Canada	WJC-A	5	1	4	5	....	....	....	2	....	....	....	....	....	....	....	....	....	....	....	....	....	....	....	....	....	....
1975-76	Lethbridge Broncos	WHL	72	36	56	92	....	....	....	233	....	....	....	....	....	....	....	....	....	....	7	3	4	7	45	....	....	....
1976-77	**St. Louis Blues**	**NHL**	**35**	**4**	**10**	**14**	**4**	**8**	**12**	**82**	**0**	**0**	**0**	**49**	**8.2**	**26**	**7**	**27**	**0**	**–8**	**4**	**1**	**0**	**1**	**14**	**0**	**0**	**0**
	Kansas City Blues	CHL	38	15	23	38	....	....	....	47	....	....	....	....	....	....	....	....	....	....	....	....	....	....	....	....	....	....
1977-78	**St. Louis Blues**	**NHL**	**78**	**9**	**13**	**22**	**9**	**11**	**20**	**123**	**4**	**0**	**1**	**98**	**9.2**	**42**	**10**	**71**	**1**	**–38**	....	....	....	....	....	....	....	....
1978-79	**St. Louis Blues**	**NHL**	**77**	**41**	**39**	**80**	**37**	**30**	**67**	**165**	**12**	**0**	**3**	**177**	**23.2**	**118**	**39**	**81**	**0**	**–2**	....	....	....	....	....	....	....	....
1979-80	**St. Louis Blues**	**NHL**	**71**	**23**	**35**	**58**	**21**	**27**	**48**	**156**	**6**	**0**	**1**	**173**	**13.3**	**101**	**30**	**68**	**0**	**+3**	**3**	**0**	**0**	**0**	**4**	**0**	**0**	**0**
1980-81	**St. Louis Blues**	**NHL**	**78**	**35**	**34**	**69**	**29**	**24**	**53**	**232**	**17**	**0**	**4**	**203**	**17.2**	**114**	**41**	**63**	**2**	**+12**	**11**	**6**	**3**	**9**	**77**	**3**	**0**	**0**
1981-82	**St. Louis Blues**	**NHL**	**74**	**39**	**36**	**75**	**31**	**24**	**55**	**239**	**14**	**0**	**3**	**195**	**20.0**	**108**	**38**	**74**	**2**	**–2**	**10**	**8**	**6**	**14**	**49**	**0**	**0**	**1**

Season	Club	League	GP	G	A	Pts	AG	AA	APts	PIM	PP	SH	GW	S	%	TGF	PGF	TGA	PGA	+/–	Playoffs GP	G	A	Pts	PIM	PP	SH	GW
			REGULAR SEASON																		PLAYOFFS							
1982-83	St. Louis Blues	NHL	79	46	30	76	38	21	59	254	11	0	4	204	22.5	115	38	79	2	0	4	2	1	3	10	2	0	0
1983-84	St. Louis Blues	NHL	76	32	51	83	26	35	61	162	14	2	3	192	16.7	126	51	103	22	–6	11	1	5	6	22	1	0	0
1984-85	St. Louis Blues	NHL	77	37	37	74	30	25	55	121	14	0	7	181	20.4	108	36	81	20	+11	3	2	1	3	2	2	0	0
1985-86	St. Louis Blues	NHL	44	19	23	42	15	15	30	87	8	0	1	92	20.7	61	23	59	9	–12	9	1	2	3	22	0	0	0
1986-87	St. Louis Blues	NHL	14	3	3	6	3	2	5	18	3	0	0	22	13.6	13	7	11	0	–5	....	....	....	....	....	....	....	....
1987-88	St. Louis Blues	NHL	76	15	22	37	13	16	29	147	4	1	2	99	15.2	55	14	89	32	–16	10	0	3	3	49	0	0	0
	NHL Totals		779	303	333	636	256	238	494	1786	107	3	29	1685	18.0	087	334	006	90		65	21	21	42	249	8	0	1

Won Jack Adams Award (1991)

Played in NHL All-Star Game (1982, 1983, 1985)

• SUTTER, DARRYL

Darryl Sutter LW – L. 5'11", 176 lbs. b: Viking, Alta., 8/19/1958. Chicago's 2nd choice, 179th overall, in 1978 Amateur Draft.

Season	Club	League	GP	G	A	Pts	AG	AA	APts	PIM	PP	SH	GW	S	%	TGF	PGF	TGA	PGA	+/–	Playoffs GP	G	A	Pts	PIM	PP	SH	GW
1974-75	Red Deer Rustlers	AJHL	60	16	20	36	....	....	....	43	....	....	....	....	....	....	....	....	....	....	....	....	....	....	....	....	....	....
1975-76	Red Deer Rustlers	AJHL	60	43	93	136	....	....	....	82	....	....	....	....	....	....	....	....	....	....	....	....	....	....	....	....	....	....
1976-77	Red Deer Rustlers	AJHL	56	55	*78	*133	....	....	....	131	....	....	....	....	....	....	....	....	....	....	....	....	....	....	....	....	....	....
	Lethbridge Broncos	WCJHL	1	1	0	1	....	....	....	0	....	....	....	....	....	....	....	....	....	....	15	3	7	10	13	....	....	....
1977-78	Lethbridge Broncos	WCJHL	68	22	48	81	....	....	....	119	....	....	....	....	....	....	....	....	....	....	8	4	9	13	2	....	....	....
1978-79	Lethbridge Broncos	WHL	68	33	48	81	....	....	....	119	....	....	....	....	....	....	....	....	....	....	8	4	9	13	2	....	....	....
	New Brunswick Hawks	AHL	19	7	6	13	....	....	....	6	....	....	....	....	....	....	....	....	....	....	5	1	2	3	0	....	....	....
	Iwakura Tomakomai	Japan	20	28	13	41	....	....	....	....	....	....	....	....	....	....	....	....	....	....	....	....	....	....	....	....	....	....
1979-80	Chicago Black Hawks	NHL	8	2	0	2	2	0	2	2	0	0	0	3	66.7	2	0	1	0	+1	7	3	1	4	2	2	0	1
	New Brunswick Hawks	AHL	69	35	31	66	....	....	....	69	....	....	....	....	....	....	....	....	....	....	12	6	6	12	8	....	....	....
1980-81	Chicago Black Hawks	NHL	76	40	22	62	33	15	48	86	14	0	4	179	22.3	98	28	86	15	–1	3	3	1	4	2	1	0	0
1981-82	Chicago Black Hawks	NHL	40	23	12	35	18	8	26	31	4	3	0	102	22.5	53	13	46	6	0	3	0	1	1	2	0	0	0
1982-83	Chicago Black Hawks	NHL	80	31	30	61	25	21	46	53	10	0	5	169	18.3	96	26	55	3	+18	13	4	6	10	8	0	0	0
1983-84	Chicago Black Hawks	NHL	59	20	20	40	16	14	30	44	8	0	4	135	14.8	63	23	60	2	–18	5	1	1	2	0	0	0	0
1984-85	Chicago Black Hawks	NHL	49	20	18	38	16	12	28	12	2	0	2	90	22.2	56	12	36	0	+8	15	12	7	19	12	2	0	4
1985-86	Chicago Black Hawks	NHL	50	17	10	27	14	7	21	44	3	0	2	89	19.1	41	7	49	0	–15	3	1	2	3	0	1	0	0
1986-87	Chicago Blackhawks	NHL	44	8	6	14	7	4	11	16	1	0	0	62	12.9	21	1	23	0	–3	2	0	0	0	0	0	0	0
	NHL Totals		406	161	118	279	131	81	212	288	42	3	17	829	19.4	430	110	356	26		51	24	19	43	26	6	0	5

AHL Second All-Star Team (1980) • Won Dudley "Red" Garrett Memorial Award (Top Rookie - AHL) (1980)

• SUTTER, DUANE

Duane "Dog" Sutter RW – R. 6'1", 185 lbs. b: Viking, Alta., 3/16/1960. NY Islanders' 2nd choice, 17th overall, in 1979 Entry Draft.

Season	Club	League	GP	G	A	Pts	AG	AA	APts	PIM	PP	SH	GW	S	%	TGF	PGF	TGA	PGA	+/–	Playoffs GP	G	A	Pts	PIM	PP	SH	GW
1976-77	Red Deer Rustlers	AJHL	60	9	26	35	....	....	....	76	....	....	....	....	....	....	....	....	....	....	....	....	....	....	....	....	....	....
	Lethbridge Broncos	WCJHL	1	0	1	1	....	....	....	2	....	....	....	....	....	....	....	....	....	....	8	0	1	1	15	....	....	....
1977-78	Red Deer Rustlers	AJHL	59	47	53	100	....	....	....	218	....	....	....	....	....	....	....	....	....	....	....	....	....	....	....	....	....	....
	Lethbridge Broncos	WCJHL	5	1	5	6	....	....	....	19	....	....	....	....	....	....	....	....	....	....	8	1	4	5	10	....	....	....
1978-79	Lethbridge Broncos	WHL	71	50	75	125	....	....	....	212	....	....	....	....	....	....	....	....	....	....	19	11	12	23	43	....	....	....
1979-80	Lethbridge Broncos	WHL	21	18	16	34	....	....	....	74	....	....	....	....	....	....	....	....	....	....	....	....	....	....	....	....	....	....
	New York Islanders	NHL	56	15	9	24	14	7	21	55	0	0	1	75	20.0	32	2	25	0	+5	21	3	7	10	74	0	0	0
1980-81	New York Islanders	NHL	23	7	11	18	6	8	14	26	1	0	1	48	14.6	19	4	23	0	–8	12	3	1	4	10	0	0	0
1981-82	New York Islanders	NHL	77	18	35	53	14	23	37	100	4	0	0	140	12.9	81	14	45	1	+23	19	5	5	10	57	0	0	2
1982-83	New York Islanders	NHL	75	13	19	32	11	13	24	118	1	0	2	122	10.7	47	5	35	1	+8	20	9	12	21	43	2	0	1
1983-84	New York Islanders	NHL	78	17	23	40	14	16	30	94	2	0	1	137	12.4	62	8	52	0	+2	21	1	3	4	48	0	0	0
1984-85	New York Islanders	NHL	78	17	24	41	14	16	30	174	1	0	1	125	13.6	58	8	62	0	–12	10	0	2	2	47	0	0	0
1985-86	New York Islanders	NHL	80	20	33	53	16	22	38	157	4	0	1	151	13.2	87	18	57	3	+15	3	0	0	0	16	0	0	0
1986-87	New York Islanders	NHL	80	14	17	31	12	12	24	169	1	0	1	152	9.2	57	9	56	9	+1	14	1	0	1	26	0	0	0
1987-88	Chicago Blackhawks	NHL	37	7	9	16	6	6	12	70	3	0	0	74	9.5	36	9	39	14	+2	5	0	0	0	21	0	0	0
1988-89	Chicago Blackhawks	NHL	75	7	9	16	6	6	12	214	0	0	1	83	8.4	23	0	35	1	–11	16	3	1	4	15	0	0	2
1989-90	Chicago Blackhawks	NHL	72	4	14	18	3	10	13	156	0	0	1	70	5.7	26	1	27	0	–2	20	1	1	2	48	0	0	0
	NHL Totals		731	139	203	342	116	139	255	1333	17	0	10	1177	11.8	528	78	456	30		101	20	32	58	405	2	0	5

Traded to **Chicago** by **NY Islanders** for Chicago's 2nd round choice (Wayne Doucet) in 1988 Entry Draft, September 9, 1987.

• SUTTER, RICH

Rich Sutter RW – R. 5'11", 188 lbs. b: Viking, Alta., 12/2/1963. Pittsburgh's 2nd choice, 10th overall, in 1982 Entry Draft.

Season	Club	League	GP	G	A	Pts	AG	AA	APts	PIM	PP	SH	GW	S	%	TGF	PGF	TGA	PGA	+/–	Playoffs GP	G	A	Pts	PIM	PP	SH	GW
1979-80	Red Deer Rustlers	AJHL	60	13	19	32	....	....	....	157	....	....	....	....	....	....	....	....	....	....	....	....	....	....	....	....	....	....
1980-81	Lethbridge Broncos	WHL	72	23	18	41	....	....	....	255	....	....	....	....	....	....	....	....	....	....	9	3	1	4	35	....	....	....
1981-82	Lethbridge Broncos	WHL	57	38	31	69	....	....	....	263	....	....	....	....	....	....	....	....	....	....	12	3	3	6	55	....	....	....
1982-83	Lethbridge Broncos	WHL	64	37	30	67	....	....	....	200	....	....	....	....	....	....	....	....	....	....	17	14	9	23	43	....	....	....
	Pittsburgh Penguins	NHL	4	0	0	0	0	0	0	0	0	0	0	3	0.0	1	0	3	0	–2	....	....	....	....	....	....	....	....
1983-84	Pittsburgh Penguins	NHL	5	0	0	0	0	0	0	0	0	0	0	2	0.0	0	0	2	0	–2	....	....	....	....	....	....	....	....
	Baltimore Skipjacks	AHL	2	0	1	1	....	....	....	0	....	....	....	....	....	....	....	....	....	....	....	....	....	....	....	....	....	....
	Philadelphia Flyers	NHL	70	16	12	28	13	8	21	93	2	0	1	133	12.0	46	3	33	0	+10	3	0	0	0	15	0	0	0
1984-85	Philadelphia Flyers	NHL	56	6	10	16	5	7	12	89	0	0	0	62	9.7	25	0	28	3	0	11	3	0	3	10	0	0	0
	Hershey Bears	AHL	13	3	7	10	....	....	....	14	....	....	....	....	....	....	....	....	....	....	....	....	....	....	....	....	....	....
1985-86	Philadelphia Flyers	NHL	78	14	25	39	11	17	28	199	0	0	2	124	11.3	58	1	35	6	+28	5	2	0	2	19	0	0	0
1986-87	Vancouver Canucks	NHL	74	20	22	42	17	16	33	113	3	0	2	166	12.0	62	13	74	8	–17	....	....	....	....	....	....	....	....
1987-88	Vancouver Canucks	NHL	80	15	15	30	13	11	24	165	2	1	2	132	11.4	50	6	69	21	–4	....	....	....	....	....	....	....	....
1988-89	Vancouver Canucks	NHL	75	17	15	32	14	11	25	122	1	3	4	125	13.6	49	5	69	28	+3	7	2	1	3	12	0	0	0
1989-90	Vancouver Canucks	NHL	62	9	9	18	8	6	14	133	0	1	1	100	9.0	32	0	55	22	–1	....	....	....	....	....	....	....	....
	St. Louis Blues	NHL	12	2	0	2	2	0	2	22	0	0	0	22	9.1	5	0	9	2	–2	12	2	1	3	39	0	1	1
1990-91	St. Louis Blues	NHL	77	16	11	27	15	8	23	122	0	2	2	130	12.3	43	0	58	21	+6	13	4	2	6	16	0	0	1
1991-92	St. Louis Blues	NHL	77	9	16	25	8	12	20	107	0	1	3	113	8.0	40	0	48	15	+7	6	0	0	0	8	0	0	0
1992-93	St. Louis Blues	NHL	84	13	14	27	11	10	21	100	0	2	1	148	8.8	42	1	77	32	–4	11	0	1	1	10	0	0	0
1993-94	Chicago Blackhawks	NHL	83	12	14	26	11	11	22	108	0	0	2	122	9.8	36	2	47	5	–8	6	0	0	0	2	0	0	0
1994-95	Chicago Blackhawks	NHL	15	0	0	0	0	0	0	28	0	0	0	17	0.0	4	0	4	1	+1	....	....	....	....	....	....	....	....
	Tampa Bay Lightning	NHL	4	0	0	0	0	0	0	0	0	0	0	3	0.0	0	0	0	0	0	....	....	....	....	....	....	....	....
	Atlanta Knights	IHL	4	0	5	5	....	....	....	0	....	....	....	....	....	....	....	....	....	....	....	....	....	....	....	....	....	....
	Toronto Maple Leafs	NHL	18	0	3	3	0	4	4	10	0	0	0	19	0.0	3	0	11	1	–7	4	0	0	0	2	0	0	0
	NHL Totals		874	149	166	315	128	121	249	1411	8	10	20	1421	10.5	496	31	622	165		78	13	5	18	133	0	1	2

Traded to **Philadelphia** by **Pittsburgh** with Pittsburgh's 2nd (Greg Smyth) and 3rd (David McLay) round choices in 1984 Entry Draft for Andy Brickley, Mark Taylor, Ron Flockhart and Philadelphia's 1st (Roger Belanger) and 3rd (later traded to Vancouver — Vancouver selected Mike Steves) in 1984 Entry Draft, October 23, 1983. Traded to **Vancouver** by **Philadelphia** with Dave Richter and Vancouver's 3rd round choice (previously acquired, Vancouver selected Don Gibson) in 1986 Entry Draft for J.J. Daigneault and Vancouver's 2nd round choice (Kent Hawley) in 1986 Entry Draft, June 6, 1986. Traded to **St. Louis** by **Vancouver** with Harold Snepts and St. Louis' 2nd round choice (previously acquired, St. Louis selected Craig Johnson) in 1990 Entry Draft for Adrien Plavsic, Montreal's 1st round choice (previously acquired, Vancouver selected Shawn Antoski) in 1990 Entry Draft and St. Louis' 2nd round choice (later traded to Montreal — Montreal selected Craig Darby) in 1991 Entry Draft, March 6, 1990. Claimed by **Chicago** from **St. Louis** in Waiver Draft, October 3, 1993. Traded to **Tampa Bay** by **Chicago** with Paul Ysebaert for Jim Cummins, Tom Tilley and Jeff Buchanan, February 22, 1995. Traded to **Toronto** by **Tampa Bay** for cash, March 13, 1995.

• SUTTER, RON

Ron Sutter C – R. 6', 180 lbs. b: Viking, Alta., 12/2/1963. Philadelphia's 2nd choice, 4th overall, in 1982 Entry Draft.

Season	Club	League	GP	G	A	Pts	AG	AA	APts	PIM	PP	SH	GW	S	%	TGF	PGF	TGA	PGA	+/–	Playoffs GP	G	A	Pts	PIM	PP	SH	GW
1979-80	Red Deer Rustlers	AJHL	60	12	33	45	....	....	....	44	....	....	....	....	....	....	....	....	....	....	....	....	....	....	....	....	....	....
1980-81	Lethbridge Broncos	WHL	72	13	32	45	....	....	....	152	....	....	....	....	....	....	....	....	....	....	9	2	5	7	29	....	....	....
1981-82	Lethbridge Broncos	WHL	59	38	54	92	....	....	....	207	....	....	....	....	....	....	....	....	....	....	12	6	5	11	28	....	....	....
	Lethbridge Broncos	WHL	58	35	48	83	....	....	....	08	....	....	....	....	....	....	....	....	....	....	20	*22	*19	*41	45	....	....	....
	Philadelphia Flyers	NHL	10	1	1	2	1	1	2	9	0	0	1	4	25.0	4	0	4	0	0	....	....	....	....	....	....	....	....
1983-84	Philadelphia Flyers	NHL	79	19	32	51	15	22	37	101	5	3	3	145	13.1	76	20	71	19	+4	3	0	0	0	22	0	0	0
1984-85	Philadelphia Flyers	NHL	73	16	29	45	13	20	33	94	2	0	5	140	11.4	66	5	66	18	+13	19	4	8	12	28	0	0	1
1985-86	Philadelphia Flyers	NHL	75	18	42	60	14	28	42	159	0	0	4	145	12.4	75	3	62	16	+26	5	0	2	2	10	0	0	0
1986-87	Philadelphia Flyers	NHL	39	10	17	27	9	12	21	69	0	0	0	68	14.7	33	0	35	12	+10	16	1	7	8	12	0	0	0
1987-88	Philadelphia Flyers	NHL	69	8	25	33	7	18	25	146	1	0	0	107	7.5	43	1	78	27	–9	7	0	1	1	26	0	0	0
1988-89	Philadelphia Flyers	NHL	55	26	22	48	22	15	37	80	4	1	2	106	24.5	62	6	51	20	+25	19	1	9	10	51	0	0	0
1989-90	Philadelphia Flyers	NHL	75	22	26	48	19	19	38	104	0	2	6	157	14.0	68	1	94	29	+2	....	....	....	....	....	....	....	....
	Canada	WEC A	10	1	1	2	....	....	....	4	....	....	....	....	....	....	....	....	....	....	....	....	....	....	....	....	....	....
1990-91	Philadelphia Flyers	NHL	80	17	28	45	16	21	37	92	2	0	1	149	11.4	65	7	93	37	+2	....	....	....	....	....	....	....	....

			REGULAR SEASON																		PLAYOFFS							
Season	Club	League	GP	G	A	Pts	AG	AA	APts	PIM	PP	SH	GW	S	%	TGF	PGF	TGA	PGA	+/-	GP	G	A	Pts	PIM	PP	SH	GW
1991-92	**St. Louis Blues**	**NHL**	**68**	**19**	**27**	**46**	**17**	**20**	**37**	**91**	**5**	**4**	**1**	**106**	**17.9**	**71**	**18**	**60**	**16**	**+9**	**6**	**1**	**3**	**4**	**8**	**1**	**0**	**0**
1992-93	**St. Louis Blues**	**NHL**	**59**	**12**	**15**	**27**	**10**	**10**	**20**	**99**	**4**	**0**	**3**	**90**	**13.3**	**43**	**15**	**43**	**4**	**–11**	....	....	....	....	....	....	....	....
1993-94	**St. Louis Blues**	**NHL**	**36**	**6**	**12**	**18**	**6**	**9**	**15**	**46**	**1**	**0**	**2**	**42**	**14.3**	**28**	**5**	**27**	**3**	**–1**	....	....	....	....	....	....	....	....
	Quebec Nordiques	**NHL**	**37**	**9**	**13**	**22**	**8**	**10**	**18**	**44**	**4**	**0**	**0**	**66**	**13.6**	**37**	**10**	**36**	**12**	**+3**	....	....	....	....	....	....	....	....
1994-95	**New York Islanders**	**NHL**	**27**	**1**	**4**	**5**	**2**	**6**	**8**	**21**	**0**	**0**	**1**	**29**	**3.4**	**7**	**0**	**25**	**10**	**–8**	....	....	....	....	....	....	....	....
1995-96	Phoenix Roadrunners	IHL	25	6	13	19	....	....	....	28	....	....	....	....	....	....	....	....	....	....	....	....	....	....	....	....	....	....
	Boston Bruins	**NHL**	**18**	**5**	**7**	**12**	**5**	**6**	**11**	**24**	**0**	**1**	**0**	**34**	**14.7**	**20**	**0**	**15**	**5**	**+10**	**5**	**0**	**0**	**0**	**8**	**0**	**0**	**0**
1996-97	**San Jose Sharks**	**NHL**	**78**	**5**	**7**	**12**	**5**	**6**	**11**	**65**	**1**	**2**	**1**	**78**	**6.4**	**22**	**1**	**46**	**17**	**–8**	....	....	....	....	....	....	....	....
1997-98	**San Jose Sharks**	**NHL**	**57**	**2**	**7**	**9**	**2**	**7**	**9**	**22**	**0**	**0**	**1**	**57**	**3.5**	**14**	**0**	**25**	**9**	**–2**	**6**	**1**	**0**	**1**	**14**	**0**	**0**	**0**
	NHL Totals		**935**	**196**	**314**	**510**	**171**	**230**	**401**	**1266**	**29**	**13**	**31**	**1523**	**12.9**	**734**	**92**	**831**	**254**		**86**	**8**	**30**	**38**	**179**	**1**	**0**	**1**

Traded to **St. Louis** by **Philadelphia** with Murray Baron for Dan Quinn and Rod Brind'Amour, September 22, 1991. Traded to **Quebec** by **St. Louis** with Garth Butcher and Bob Bassen for Steve Duchesne and Denis Chasse, January 23, 1994. Traded to **NY Islanders** by **Quebec** with Quebec's 1st round choice (Brett Lindros) in 1994 Entry Draft for Uwe Krupp and NY Islanders' 1st round choice (Wade Belak) in 1994 Entry Draft, June 28, 1994. Signed as a free agent by **Boston**, March 9, 1996. Signed as a free agent by **San Jose**, October 12, 1996.

• SUTTON, KEN

Ken Sutton D – L. 6', 200 lbs. b: Edmonton, Alta., 11/5/1969. Buffalo's 4th choice, 98th overall, in 1989 Entry Draft.

Season	Club	League	GP	G	A	Pts	AG	AA	APts	PIM	PP	SH	GW	S	%	TGF	PGF	TGA	PGA	+/-	GP	G	A	Pts	PIM	PP	SH	GW
1987-88	Calgary Canucks	AJHL	53	13	43	56	....	....	....	228	....	....	....	....	....	....	....	....	....	....	....	....	....	....	....	....	....	....
1988-89	Saskatoon Blades	WHL	71	22	31	53	....	....	....	104	....	....	....	....	....	....	....	....	....	....	8	2	5	7	12	....	....	....
1989-90	Rochester Americans	AHL	57	5	14	19	....	....	....	83	....	....	....	....	....	....	....	....	....	....	11	1	6	7	15	....	....	....
1990-91	**Buffalo Sabres**	**NHL**	**15**	**3**	**6**	**9**	**3**	**5**	**8**	**13**	**2**	**0**	**0**	**26**	**11.5**	**25**	**9**	**15**	**1**	**+2**	**6**	**0**	**1**	**1**	**2**	**0**	**0**	**0**
	Rochester Americans	AHL	62	7	24	31	....	....	....	65	....	....	....	....	....	....	....	....	....	....	3	1	1	2	14	....	....	....
1991-92	**Buffalo Sabres**	**NHL**	**64**	**2**	**18**	**20**	**2**	**14**	**16**	**71**	**0**	**0**	**0**	**81**	**2.5**	**69**	**14**	**76**	**26**	**+5**	**7**	**0**	**2**	**2**	**4**	**0**	**0**	**0**
1992-93	**Buffalo Sabres**	**NHL**	**63**	**8**	**14**	**22**	**7**	**10**	**17**	**30**	**1**	**0**	**2**	**77**	**10.4**	**71**	**1**	**81**	**8**	**–3**	**8**	**3**	**1**	**4**	**8**	**0**	**0**	**0**
1993-94	**Buffalo Sabres**	**NHL**	**78**	**4**	**20**	**24**	**4**	**15**	**19**	**71**	**1**	**0**	**0**	**95**	**4.2**	**72**	**25**	**61**	**8**	**–6**	**4**	**0**	**0**	**0**	**2**	**0**	**0**	**0**
1994-95	**Buffalo Sabres**	**NHL**	**12**	**1**	**2**	**3**	**2**	**3**	**5**	**30**	**0**	**0**	**1**	**12**	**8.3**	**10**	**4**	**8**	**0**	**–2**	....	....	....	....	....	....	....	....
	Edmonton Oilers	**NHL**	**12**	**3**	**1**	**4**	**5**	**1**	**6**	**12**	**0**	**0**	**0**	**28**	**10.7**	**9**	**2**	**13**	**5**	**–1**	....	....	....	....	....	....	....	....
1995-96	**Edmonton Oilers**	**NHL**	**32**	**0**	**8**	**8**	**0**	**7**	**7**	**39**	**0**	**0**	**0**	**38**	**0.0**	**28**	**8**	**46**	**14**	**–12**	....	....	....	....	....	....	....	....
	St. Louis Blues	**NHL**	**6**	**0**	**0**	**0**	**0**	**0**	**0**	**4**	**0**	**0**	**0**	**3**	**0.0**	**1**	**0**	**2**	**0**	**–1**	**1**	**0**	**0**	**0**	**0**	**0**	**0**	**0**
	Worcester IceCats	AHL	32	4	16	20	....	....	....	60	....	....	....	....	....	....	....	....	....	....	4	0	2	2	21	....	....	....
1996-97	Manitoba Moose	IHL	20	3	10	13	....	....	....	48	....	....	....	....	....	....	....	....	....	....	....	....	....	....	....	....	....	....
	Albany River Rats	AHL	61	6	13	19	....	....	....	79	....	....	....	....	....	....	....	....	....	....	16	4	8	12	55	....	....	....
1997-98	**New Jersey Devils**	**NHL**	**13**	**0**	**0**	**0**	**0**	**0**	**0**	**6**	**0**	**0**	**0**	**5**	**0.0**	**5**	**0**	**4**	**0**	**+1**	....	....	....	....	....	....	....	....
	Albany River Rats	AHL	10	0	7	7	....	....	....	15	....	....	....	....	....	....	....	....	....	....	....	....	....	....	....	....	....	....
	San Jose Sharks	**NHL**	**8**	**0**	**0**	**0**	**0**	**0**	**0**	**15**	**0**	**0**	**0**	**7**	**0.0**	**2**	**0**	**6**	**0**	**–4**	....	....	....	....	....	....	....	....
	NHL Totals		**303**	**21**	**69**	**90**	**23**	**55**	**78**	**291**	**4**	**0**	**3**	**372**	**5.6**	**292**	**63**	**312**	**62**		**26**	**3**	**4**	**7**	**16**	**0**	**0**	**0**

Memorial Cup All-Star Team (1989)

Traded to **Edmonton** by **Buffalo** for Scott Pearson, April 7, 1995. Traded to **St. Louis** by **Edmonton** with Igor Kravchuk for Jeff Norton and Donald Dufresne, January 4, 1996. Traded to **New Jersey** by **St. Louis** with St. Louis' 2nd round choice in 1999 Entry Draft for Mike Peluso and Ricard Persson, November 26, 1996. Traded to **San Jose** by **New Jersey** with John MacLean for Doug Bodger and Dody Wood, December 7, 1997.

• SUZOR, MARK

Mark Suzor D – L. 6'1", 212 lbs. b: Windsor, Ont., 11/5/1956. Philadelphia's 1st choice, 17th overall, in 1976 Amateur Draft.

Season	Club	League	GP	G	A	Pts	AG	AA	APts	PIM	PP	SH	GW	S	%	TGF	PGF	TGA	PGA	+/-	GP	G	A	Pts	PIM	PP	SH	GW
1973-74	Kingston Canadians	OHA	68	6	9	15	....	....	....	13	....	....	....	....	....	....	....	....	....	....	....	....	....	....	....	....	....	....
1974-75	Kingston Canadians	OHA	70	14	44	58	....	....	....	104	....	....	....	....	....	....	....	....	....	....	....	....	....	....	....	....	....	....
1975-76	Kingston Canadians	OHA	48	16	30	46	....	....	....	108	....	....	....	....	....	....	....	....	....	....	....	....	....	....	....	....	....	....
1976-77	**Philadelphia Flyers**	**NHL**	**4**	**0**	**1**	**1**	**0**	**1**	**1**	**4**	**0**	**0**	**0**	**4**	**0.0**	**2**	**0**	**1**	**1**	**+2**	....	....	....	....	....	....	....	....
	Springfield Indians	AHL	74	24	25	49	....	....	....	108	....	....	....	....	....	....	....	....	....	....	....	....	....	....	....	....	....	....
1977-78	**Colorado Rockies**	**NHL**	**60**	**4**	**15**	**19**	**4**	**12**	**16**	**56**	**2**	**0**	**0**	**89**	**4.5**	**47**	**12**	**76**	**6**	**–35**	....	....	....	....	....	....	....	....
1978-79	Rochester Americans	AHL	24	4	6	10	....	....	....	16	....	....	....	....	....	....	....	....	....	....	....	....	....	....	....	....	....	....
	Saginaw Gears	IHL	29	12	12	24	....	....	....	43	....	....	....	....	....	....	....	....	....	....	....	....	....	....	....	....	....	....
	Grand Rapids Owls	IHL	2	0	2	2	....	....	....	0	....	....	....	....	....	....	....	....	....	....	....	....	....	....	....	....	....	....
	Muskegon Mohawks	IHL	16	1	5	6	....	....	....	6	....	....	....	....	....	....	....	....	....	....	....	....	....	....	....	....	....	....
1979-80	Binghamton Dusters	AHL	7	0	1	1	....	....	....	2	....	....	....	....	....	....	....	....	....	....	....	....	....	....	....	....	....	....
	Grand Rapids Owls	IHL	58	20	33	53	....	....	....	109	....	....	....	....	....	....	....	....	....	....	....	....	....	....	....	....	....	....
1980-81	Toledo Goaldiggers	IHL	8	1	2	3	....	....	....	0	....	....	....	....	....	....	....	....	....	....	....	....	....	....	....	....	....	....
	NHL Totals		**64**	**4**	**16**	**20**	**4**	**13**	**17**	**60**	**2**	**0**	**0**	**93**	**4.3**	**49**	**12**	**77**	**7**									

Traded to **Colorado** by **Philadelphia** for Barry Dean, August 5, 1977. Traded to **Boston** by **Colorado** for Clayton Pachal, October 11, 1978.

• SVEHLA, ROBERT

Robert Svehla D – R. 6'1", 190 lbs. b: Martin, Czech., 1/2/1969. Calgary's 4th choice, 78th overall, in 1992 Entry Draft.

Season	Club	League	GP	G	A	Pts	AG	AA	APts	PIM	PP	SH	GW	S	%	TGF	PGF	TGA	PGA	+/-	GP	G	A	Pts	PIM	PP	SH	GW
1989-90	Dukla Trencin	Czech.	29	4	3	7	....	....	....	....	....	....	....	....	....	....	....	....	....	....	....	....	....	....	....	....	....	....
1990-91	Dukla Trencin	Czech.	52	16	9	25	....	....	....	62	....	....	....	....	....	....	....	....	....	....	....	....	....	....	....	....	....	....
1991-92	Dukla Trencin	Czech.	51	23	28	51	....	....	....	74	....	....	....	....	....	....	....	....	....	....	....	....	....	....	....	....	....	....
	Czechoslovakia	Olympics	8	2	1	3	....	....	....	8	....	....	....	....	....	....	....	....	....	....	....	....	....	....	....	....	....	....
	Czechoslovakia	WC-A	8	4	4	8	....	....	....	14	....	....	....	....	....	....	....	....	....	....	....	....	....	....	....	....	....	....
1992-93	Malmo IF	Sweden	40	19	10	29	....	....	....	86	....	....	....	....	....	....	....	....	....	....	6	0	1	1	14	....	....	....
1993-94	Malmo IF	Sweden	37	14	25	39	....	....	....	127	....	....	....	....	....	....	....	....	....	....	10	5	1	6	23	....	....	....
	Slovakia	Olympics	8	2	4	6	....	....	....	26	....	....	....	....	....	....	....	....	....	....	....	....	....	....	....	....	....	....
1994-95	Malmo IF	Sweden	32	11	13	24	....	....	....	83	....	....	....	....	....	....	....	....	....	....	9	2	3	5	6	....	....	....
	Florida Panthers	**NHL**	**5**	**1**	**1**	**2**	**2**	**1**	**3**	**0**	**1**	**0**	**0**	**6**	**16.7**	**7**	**2**	**2**	**0**	**+3**	....	....	....	....	....	....	....	....
	Slovakia	WC-B	4	0	6	6	....	....	....	10	....	....	....	....	....	....	....	....	....	....	....	....	....	....	....	....	....	....
1995-96	**Florida Panthers**	**NHL**	**81**	**8**	**49**	**57**	**8**	**40**	**48**	**94**	**7**	**0**	**0**	**146**	**5.5**	**124**	**53**	**89**	**15**	**–3**	**22**	**0**	**6**	**6**	**32**	**0**	**0**	**0**
1996-97	Slovakia	W Cup	3	0	3	3	....	....	....	4	....	....	....	....	....	....	....	....	....	....	....	....	....	....	....	....	....	....
	Florida Panthers	**NHL**	**82**	**13**	**32**	**45**	**14**	**28**	**42**	**86**	**5**	**0**	**3**	**159**	**8.2**	**100**	**33**	**82**	**17**	**+2**	**5**	**1**	**4**	**5**	**4**	**1**	**0**	**0**
1997-98	**Florida Panthers**	**NHL**	**79**	**9**	**34**	**43**	**11**	**33**	**44**	**113**	**3**	**0**	**0**	**144**	**6.3**	**109**	**41**	**107**	**36**	**–3**	....	....	....	....	....	....	....	....
	Slovakia	Olympics	2	0	1	1	....	....	....	0	....	....	....	....	....	....	....	....	....	....	....	....	....	....	....	....	....	....
	Slovakia	WC-A	6	1	1	2	....	....	....	14	....	....	....	....	....	....	....	....	....	....	....	....	....	....	....	....	....	....
	NHL Totals		**247**	**31**	**116**	**147**	**35**	**102**	**137**	**293**	**16**	**0**	**3**	**455**	**6.8**	**340**	**129**	**280**	**68**		**27**	**1**	**10**	**11**	**36**	**1**	**0**	**0**

Czechoslovakian First All-Star Team (1992) • Named Best Defenseman at WC-A (1992) • WC-B All-Star Team (1995)

Played in NHL All-Star Game (1997)

Traded to **Florida** by **Calgary** with Magnus Svensson for Florida's 3rd round choice (Dmitri Vlasenkov) in 1996 Entry Draft and 4th round choice (Ryan Ready) in 1997 Entry Draft, September 29, 1994.

• SVEJKOVSKY, JAROSLAV

Jaroslav Svejkovsky RW – R. 5'11", 185 lbs. b: Plzen, Czech., 10/1/1976. Washington's 2nd choice, 17th overall, in 1996 Entry Draft.

Season	Club	League	GP	G	A	Pts	AG	AA	APts	PIM	PP	SH	GW	S	%	TGF	PGF	TGA	PGA	+/-	GP	G	A	Pts	PIM	PP	SH	GW
1993-94	Skoda Plzen	Czech.	8	0	0	0	....	....	....	8	....	....	....	....	....	....	....	....	....	....	....	....	....	....	....	....	....	....
1994-95	Tabor	Czech. 2	11	6	7	13	....	....	....	....	....	....	....	....	....	....	....	....	....	....	....	....	....	....	....	....	....	....
1995-96	Tri-City Americans	WHL	70	58	43	101	....	....	....	118	....	....	....	....	....	....	....	....	....	....	11	10	9	19	8	....	....	....
1996-97	**Washington Capitals**	**NHL**	**19**	**7**	**3**	**10**	**7**	**3**	**10**	**4**	**2**	**0**	**1**	**30**	**23.3**	**10**	**3**	**8**	**0**	**–1**	....	....	....	....	....	....	....	....
	Portland Pirates	AHL	54	38	28	66	....	....	....	56	....	....	....	....	....	....	....	....	....	....	5	2	0	2	6	....	....	....
1997-98	**Washington Capitals**	**NHL**	**17**	**4**	**1**	**5**	**5**	**1**	**6**	**10**	**2**	**0**	**1**	**29**	**13.8**	**8**	**4**	**9**	**0**	**–5**	**1**	**0**	**0**	**0**	**2**	**0**	**0**	**0**
	Portland Pirates	AHL	16	12	7	19	....	....	....	16	....	....	....	....	....	....	....	....	....	....	7	1	2	3	2	....	....	....
	NHL Totals		**36**	**11**	**4**	**15**	**12**	**4**	**16**	**14**	**4**	**0**	**2**	**59**	**18.6**	**18**	**7**	**17**	**0**		**1**	**0**	**0**	**0**	**2**	**0**	**0**	**0**

WHL West Second All-Star Team (1996) • Won Dudley "Red" Garrett Memorial Trophy (Top Rookie - AHL) (1997)

• SVENSSON, LEIF

Leif Svensson D – L. 6'3", 190 lbs. b: Harnosand, Sweden, 7/8/1951.

Season	Club	League	GP	G	A	Pts	AG	AA	APts	PIM	PP	SH	GW	S	%	TGF	PGF	TGA	PGA	+/-	GP	G	A	Pts	PIM	PP	SH	GW
1971-72	Nacka	Sweden	7	1	5	6	....	....	....	6	....	....	....	....	....	....	....	....	....	....	....	....	....	....	....	....	....	....
1972-73	Sodertalje SK	Sweden	4	0	0	0	....	....	....	0	....	....	....	....	....	....	....	....	....	....	14	5	1	6	14	....	....	....
1973-74	Sodertalje SK	Sweden	STATISTICS NOT AVAILABLE																									
1974-75	Djurgarden IF Stockholm	Sweden	28	2	6	8	....	....	....	30	....	....	....	....	....	....	....	....	....	....	....	....	....	....	....	....	....	....
1975-76	Djurgarden IF Stockholm	Sweden	36	5	15	20	....	....	....	48	....	....	....	....	....	....	....	....	....	....	....	....	....	....	....	....	....	....
1976-77	Djurgarden IF Stockholm	Sweden	31	7	15	22	....	....	....	....	....	....	....	....	....	....	....	....	....	....	....	....	....	....	....	....	....	....
1977-78	Djurgarden IF Stockholm	Sweden	29	2	7	9	....	....	....	34	....	....	....	....	....	....	....	....	....	....	....	....	....	....	....	....	....	....

			REGULAR SEASON																		PLAYOFFS							
Season	Club	League	GP	G	A	Pts	AG	AA	APts	PIM	PP	SH	GW	S	%	TGF	PGF	TGA	PGA	+/-	GP	G	A	Pts	PIM	PP	SH	GW
1978-79	**Washington Capitals**	**NHL**	**74**	**2**	**29**	**31**	**2**	**22**	**24**	**28**	**0**	**0**	**0**	**72**	**2.8**	**102**	**19**	**118**	**32**	**-3**	....	....	....	....	....	....	....	....
	Sweden	WEC-A	8	0	0	0	....	....	....	6	....	....	....	....	....	....	....	....	....	....	....	....	....	....	....	....	....	....
1979-80	**Washington Capitals**	**NHL**	**47**	**4**	**11**	**15**	**4**	**8**	**12**	**21**	**0**	**0**	**0**	**41**	**9.8**	**34**	**3**	**62**	**21**	**-10**	....	....	....	....	....	....	....	....
1980-81	Djurgarden IF Stockholm	Sweden	18	1	2	3	....	....	....	20	....	....	....	....	....	....	....	....	....	....	....	....	....	....	....	....	....	....
1981-82	Djurgarden IF Stockholm	Sweden	18	2	3	5	....	....	....	28	....	....	....	....	....	....	....	....	....	....	....	....	....	....	....	....	....	....
	NHL Totals		**121**	**6**	**40**	**46**	**6**	**30**	**36**	**49**	**0**	**0**	**0**	**113**	**5.3**	**136**	**22**	**180**	**53**		....	....	....	....	....	....	....	....

Signed as a free agent by **Washington**, June 10, 1978.

• SVENSSON, MAGNUS

Magnus Svensson D – L. 5'11", 180 lbs. b: Tranas, Sweden, 3/1/1963. Calgary's 13th choice, 250th overall, in 1987 Entry Draft.

Season	Club	League	GP	G	A	Pts	AG	AA	APts	PIM	PP	SH	GW	S	%	TGF	PGF	TGA	PGA	+/-	GP	G	A	Pts	PIM	PP	SH	GW
1983-84	Leksands IF	Sweden	35	3	8	11	....	....	....	20	....	....	....	....	....	....	....	....	....	....	....	....	....	....	....	....	....	....
1984-85	Leksands IF	Sweden	35	8	7	15	....	....	....	22	....	....	....	....	....	....	....	....	....	....	....	....	....	....	....	....	....	....
1985-86	Leksands IF	Sweden	36	6	9	15	....	....	....	62	....	....	....	....	....	....	....	....	....	....	....	....	....	....	....	....	....	....
1986-87	Leksands IF	Sweden	33	8	16	24	....	....	....	42	....	....	....	....	....	....	....	....	....	....	....	....	....	....	....	....	....	....
	Sweden	WEC-A	2	0	0	0	....	....	....	4	....	....	....	....	....	....	....	....	....	....	....	....	....	....	....	....	....	....
1987-88	Leksands IF	Sweden	40	12	11	23	....	....	....	20	....	....	....	....	....	....	....	....	....	....	3	0	0	0	8	....	....	....
1988-89	Leksands IF	Sweden	39	15	22	37	....	....	....	40	....	....	....	....	....	....	....	....	....	....	9	3	5	8	8	....	....	....
1989-90	Leksans IF	Sweden	26	11	12	23	....	....	....	60	....	....	....	....	....	....	....	....	....	....	1	0	0	0	0	....	....	....
	Sweden	WEC-A	10	2	1	3	....	....	....	8	....	....	....	....	....	....	....	....	....	....	....	....	....	....	....	....	....	....
1990-91	HC Lugano	Switz.	33	16	20	36	....	....	....	....	....	....	....	....	....	....	....	....	....	....	11	3	2	5	....	....	....	....
1991-92	Leksands IF	Sweden	22	4	10	14	....	....	....	32	....	....	....	....	....	....	....	....	....	....	....	....	....	....	....	....	....	....
1992-93	Leksands IF	Sweden	37	10	17	27	....	....	....	36	....	....	....	....	....	....	....	....	....	....	2	0	2	2	0	....	....	....
1993-94	Leksands IF	Sweden	39	13	16	29	....	....	....	22	....	....	....	....	....	....	....	....	....	....	4	3	1	4	0	....	....	....
	Sweden	Olympics	7	4	1	5	....	....	....	6	....	....	....	....	....	....	....	....	....	....	....	....	....	....	....	....	....	....
	Sweden	WC-A	8	8	1	9	....	....	....	8	....	....	....	....	....	....	....	....	....	....	....	....	....	....	....	....	....	....
1994-95	HC Davos	Switz.	35	8	25	33	....	....	....	46	....	....	....	....	....	....	....	....	....	....	5	2	2	4	8	....	....	....
	Florida Panthers	**NHL**	**19**	**2**	**5**	**7**	**4**	**7**	**11**	**10**	**1**	**0**	**0**	**41**	**4.9**	**23**	**5**	**16**	**3**	**+5**	....	....	....	....	....	....	....	....
1995-96	**Florida Panthers**	**NHL**	**27**	**2**	**9**	**11**	**2**	**7**	**9**	**21**	**2**	**0**	**1**	**58**	**3.4**	**26**	**15**	**12**	**0**	**-1**	....	....	....	....	....	....	....	....
1996-97	Leksands IF	Sweden	45	8	17	25	....	....	....	62	....	....	....	....	....	....	....	....	....	....	9	1	2	3	35	....	....	....
	Sweden	WC-A	10	0	6	6	....	....	....	16	....	....	....	....	....	....	....	....	....	....	....	....	....	....	....	....	....	....
1997-98	HV-71 Jonkoping	Sweden	16	0	2	2	....	....	....	2	....	....	....	....	....	....	....	....	....	....	....	....	....	....	....	....	....	....
	Leksands IF	EuroHL	6	2	2	4	....	....	....	18	....	....	....	....	....	....	....	....	....	....	....	....	....	....	....	....	....	....
	Leksands IF	Sweden	42	2	23	25	....	....	....	52	....	....	....	....	....	....	....	....	....	....	4	0	1	1	6	....	....	....
	NHL Totals		**46**	**4**	**14**	**18**	**6**	**14**	**20**	**31**	**3**	**0**	**1**	**99**	**4.0**	**49**	**20**	**28**	**3**		....	....	....	....	....	....	....	....

Swedish World All-Star Team (1994) • WC-A All-Star Team (1994) • Named Best Defenseman at WC-A (1994)

Traded to **Florida** by **Calgary** with Robert Svehla for Florida's 3rd round choice (Dmitri Vlasenkov) in 1996 Entry Draft and future considerations, September 29, 1994.

• SVOBODA, PETR

Petr Svoboda D – L. 6'1", 195 lbs. b: Most, Czech., 2/14/1966. Montreal's 1st choice, 5th overall, in 1984 Entry Draft.

Season	Club	League	GP	G	A	Pts	AG	AA	APts	PIM	PP	SH	GW	S	%	TGF	PGF	TGA	PGA	+/-	GP	G	A	Pts	PIM	PP	SH	GW
1982-83	CHZ Litvinov	Czech.	4	0	0	0	....	....	....	2	....	....	....	....	....	....	....	....	....	....	....	....	....	....	....	....	....	....
1983-84	CHZ Litvinov	Czech.	18	3	1	4	....	....	....	20	....	....	....	....	....	....	....	....	....	....	....	....	....	....	....	....	....	....
	Czechoslovakia	WJC-A	7	0	4	4	....	....	....	16	....	....	....	....	....	....	....	....	....	....	....	....	....	....	....	....	....	....
1984-85	**Montreal Canadiens**	**NHL**	**73**	**4**	**27**	**31**	**3**	**18**	**21**	**65**	**0**	**0**	**1**	**80**	**5.0**	**79**	**21**	**43**	**1**	**+16**	**7**	**1**	**1**	**2**	**12**	**0**	**0**	**0**
1985-86	**Montreal Canadiens**	**NHL**	**73**	**1**	**18**	**19**	**1**	**12**	**13**	**93**	**0**	**0**	**0**	**63**	**1.6**	**89**	**9**	**58**	**2**	**+24**	**8**	**0**	**0**	**0**	**21**	**0**	**0**	**0**
1986-87	**Montreal Canadiens**	**NHL**	**70**	**5**	**17**	**22**	**4**	**12**	**16**	**63**	**1**	**0**	**1**	**80**	**6.3**	**76**	**12**	**50**	**0**	**+14**	**14**	**0**	**5**	**5**	**10**	**0**	**0**	**0**
1987-88	**Montreal Canadiens**	**NHL**	**69**	**7**	**22**	**29**	**6**	**16**	**22**	**149**	**2**	**0**	**1**	**138**	**5.1**	**113**	**16**	**57**	**6**	**+46**	**10**	**0**	**5**	**5**	**12**	**0**	**0**	**0**
1988-89	**Montreal Canadiens**	**NHL**	**71**	**8**	**37**	**45**	**7**	**26**	**33**	**147**	**4**	**0**	**1**	**131**	**6.1**	**114**	**38**	**63**	**15**	**+28**	**21**	**1**	**11**	**12**	**16**	**0**	**0**	**0**
1989-90	**Montreal Canadiens**	**NHL**	**60**	**5**	**31**	**36**	**4**	**22**	**26**	**98**	**2**	**0**	**2**	**90**	**5.6**	**94**	**30**	**48**	**4**	**+20**	**10**	**0**	**5**	**5**	**7**	**0**	**0**	**0**
1990-91	Montreal Canadiens	FrTour	3	0	0	0	....	....	....	27	....	....	....	....	....	....	....	....	....	....	....	....	....	....	....	....	....	....
	Montreal Canadiens	**NHL**	**60**	**4**	**22**	**26**	**4**	**17**	**21**	**52**	**3**	**0**	**1**	**67**	**6.0**	**72**	**20**	**66**	**19**	**+5**	**2**	**0**	**1**	**1**	**2**	**0**	**0**	**0**
1991-92	**Montreal Canadiens**	**NHL**	**58**	**5**	**16**	**21**	**5**	**12**	**17**	**94**	**1**	**0**	**3**	**88**	**5.7**	**65**	**21**	**44**	**9**	**+9**	....	....	....	....	....	....	....	....
	Buffalo Sabres	**NHL**	**13**	**1**	**6**	**7**	**1**	**4**	**5**	**52**	**0**	**0**	**0**	**23**	**4.3**	**15**	**12**	**21**	**10**	**-8**	**7**	**1**	**4**	**5**	**6**	**0**	**1**	**0**
1992-93	**Buffalo Sabres**	**NHL**	**40**	**2**	**24**	**26**	**2**	**16**	**18**	**59**	**1**	**0**	**1**	**61**	**3.3**	**63**	**24**	**46**	**10**	**+3**	....	....	....	....	....	....	....	....
1993-94	**Buffalo Sabres**	**NHL**	**60**	**2**	**14**	**16**	**2**	**11**	**13**	**89**	**1**	**0**	**0**	**80**	**2.5**	**65**	**25**	**36**	**7**	**+11**	**3**	**0**	**0**	**0**	**4**	**0**	**0**	**0**
1994-95	CHZ Litvinov	Czech.	8	2	0	2	....	....	....	50	....	....	....	....	....	....	....	....	....	....	....	....	....	....	....	....	....	....
	Buffalo Sabres	**NHL**	**26**	**0**	**5**	**5**	**0**	**7**	**7**	**60**	**0**	**0**	**0**	**22**	**0.0**	**16**	**6**	**22**	**7**	**-5**	....	....	....	....	....	....	....	....
	Philadelphia Flyers	**NHL**	**11**	**0**	**3**	**3**	**0**	**4**	**4**	**10**	**0**	**0**	**0**	**17**	**0.0**	**9**	**2**	**11**	**4**	**0**	**14**	**0**	**4**	**4**	**8**	**0**	**0**	**0**
1995-96	**Philadelphia Flyers**	**NHL**	**73**	**1**	**28**	**29**	**1**	**23**	**24**	**105**	**0**	**0**	**0**	**91**	**1.1**	**87**	**27**	**45**	**13**	**+28**	**12**	**0**	**6**	**6**	**22**	**0**	**0**	**0**
1996-97	**Philadelphia Flyers**	**NHL**	**67**	**2**	**12**	**14**	**2**	**11**	**13**	**94**	**1**	**0**	**0**	**36**	**5.6**	**54**	**3**	**53**	**12**	**+10**	**16**	**1**	**2**	**3**	**16**	**0**	**0**	**0**
1997-98	**Philadelphia Flyers**	**NHL**	**56**	**3**	**15**	**18**	**4**	**15**	**19**	**83**	**2**	**0**	**0**	**44**	**6.8**	**53**	**16**	**29**	**11**	**+19**	**3**	**0**	**1**	**1**	**4**	**0**	**0**	**0**
	Czech Republic	Olympics	6	1	1	2	....	....	....	39	....	....	....	....	....	....	....	....	....	....	....	....	....	....	....	....	....	....
	NHL Totals		**880**	**50**	**297**	**347**	**46**	**226**	**272**	**1313**	**18**	**0**	**11**	**1111**	**4.5**	**1064**	**282**	**692**	**130**		**127**	**4**	**45**	**49**	**140**	**0**	**1**	**0**

EJC-A All-Star Team (1983) • Named Best Defenseman at EJC-A (1983)

Traded to **Buffalo** by **Montreal** for Kevin Haller, March 10, 1992. Traded to **Philadelphia** by **Buffalo** for Garry Galley, April 7, 1995.

• SWAIN, GARRY

Garry Swain C – L. 5'8", 164 lbs. b: Welland, Ont., 9/11/1947. Pittsburgh's 1st choice, 4th overall, in 1968 Amateur Draft.

Season	Club	League	GP	G	A	Pts	AG	AA	APts	PIM	PP	SH	GW	S	%	TGF	PGF	TGA	PGA	+/-	GP	G	A	Pts	PIM	PP	SH	GW
1966-67	Niagara Falls Flyers	OHA	48	10	19	29	....	....	....	51	....	....	....	....	....	....	....	....	....	....	13	3	6	9	2	....	....	....
1967-68	Niagara Falls Flyers	OHA	54	41	62	103	....	....	....	79	....	....	....	....	....	....	....	....	....	....	19	9	16	25	35	....	....	....
1968-69	**Pittsburgh Penguins**	**NHL**	**9**	**1**	**1**	**2**	**1**	**1**	**2**	**0**	**0**	**0**	**0**	**17**	**5.9**	**2**	**0**	**4**	**1**	**-1**	....	....	....	....	....	....	....	....
	Amarillo Wranglers	CHL	69	20	27	47	....	....	....	51	....	....	....	....	....	....	....	....	....	....	....	....	....	....	....	....	....	....
1969-70	Baltimore Clippers	AHL	72	4	9	13	....	....	....	26	....	....	....	....	....	....	....	....	....	....	5	0	0	0	2	....	....	....
1970-71	Amarillo Wranglers	CHL	71	17	31	48	....	....	....	87	....	....	....	....	....	....	....	....	....	....	....	....	....	....	....	....	....	....
1971-72	Fort Wayne Komets	IHL	60	26	26	52	....	....	....	60	....	....	....	....	....	....	....	....	....	....	8	0	4	4	16	....	....	....
1972-73	Baltimore Clippers	AHL	76	14	24	38	....	....	....	69	....	....	....	....	....	....	....	....	....	....	....	....	....	....	....	....	....	....
1973-74	Baltimore Clippers	AHL	12	2	7	9	....	....	....	10	....	....	....	....	....	....	....	....	....	....	9	5	4	9	18	....	....	....
	Charlotte Checkers	SHL	68	34	*64	*98	....	....	....	84	....	....	....	....	....	....	....	....	....	....	....	....	....	....	....	....	....	....
1974-75	New England Whalers	WHA	66	7	15	22	....	....	....	18	....	....	....	....	....	....	....	....	....	....	6	0	3	3	41	....	....	....
1975-76	New England Whalers	WHA	79	10	16	26	....	....	....	46	....	....	....	....	....	....	....	....	....	....	17	3	2	5	15	....	....	....
1976-77	New England Whalers	WHA	26	5	2	7	....	....	....	6	....	....	....	....	....	....	....	....	....	....	2	0	0	0	0	....	....	....
	Rhode Island Reds	AHL	17	1	6	7	....	....	....	19	....	....	....	....	....	....	....	....	....	....	....	....	....	....	....	....	....	....
	NHL Totals		**9**	**1**	**1**	**2**	**1**	**1**	**2**	**0**	**0**	**0**	**0**	**17**	**5.9**	**2**	**0**	**4**	**1**		....	....	....	....	....	....	....	....
	Other Major League Totals		171	22	33	55	....	....	....	70	....	....	....	....	....	....	....	....	....	....	25	3	5	8	56	....	....	....

SHL Second All-Star Team (1974)

Selected by **Calgary-Cleveland** (WHA) in 1972 WHA General Player Draft, February 12, 1972. WHA rights traded to **New England** (WHA) by **Cleveland** (WHA) for future considerations, September, 1974.

• SWARBRICK, GEORGE

George Swarbrick RW – R. 5'10", 175 lbs. b: Moose Jaw, Sask., 2/16/1942.

Season	Club	League	GP	G	A	Pts	AG	AA	APts	PIM	PP	SH	GW	S	%	TGF	PGF	TGA	PGA	+/-	GP	G	A	Pts	PIM	PP	SH	GW
1958-59	Moose Jaw Canucks	SJHL	2	0	0	0	....	....	....	0	....	....	....	....	....	....	....	....	....	....	....	....	....	....	....	....	....	....
1959-60	Moose Jaw Canucks	SJHL	59	17	13	30	....	....	....	48	....	....	....	....	....	....	....	....	....	....	....	....	....	....	....	....	....	....
1960-61	Moose Jaw Canucks	SJHL	50	17	17	34	....	....	....	94	....	....	....	....	....	....	....	....	....	....	6	1	3	4	6	....	....	....
	Victoria Cougars	WHL	3	0	0	0	....	....	....	0	....	....	....	....	....	....	....	....	....	....	....	....	....	....	....	....	....	....
1961-62	Moose Jaw Canucks	SJHL	55	40	36	76	....	....	....	76	....	....	....	....	....	....	....	....	....	....	....	....	....	....	....	....	....	....
1962-63	Moose Jaw Pla-Mors	SSHL	38	29	28	57	....	....	....	62	....	....	....	....	....	....	....	....	....	....	5	5	2	7	11	....	....	....
1963-64	Canada	Olympics	7	3	3	6	....	....	....	2	....	....	....	....	....	....	....	....	....	....	....	....	....	....	....	....	....	....
	Moose Jaw Pla-Mors	SSHL	....	....	....	....	....	....	....	....	....	....	....	....	....	....	....	....	....	....	5	7	8	15	23	....	....	....
1964-65	San Francisco Seals	WHL	70	22	22	44	....	....	....	66	....	....	....	....	....	....	....	....	....	....	....	....	....	....	....	....	....	....
1965-66	San Francisco Seals	WHL	71	20	21	41	....	....	....	89	....	....	....	....	....	....	....	....	....	....	7	2	3	5	8	....	....	....
1966-67	California Seals	WHL	71	31	22	53	....	....	....	75	....	....	....	....	....	....	....	....	....	....	6	1	3	4	16	....	....	....
1967-68	**Oakland Seals**	**NHL**	**49**	**13**	**5**	**18**	**16**	**5**	**21**	**62**	**3**	**1**	**2**	**86**	**15.1**	**28**	**7**	**38**	**0**	**-17**	....	....	....	....	....	....	....	....
1968-69	**Oakland Seals**	**NHL**	**50**	**3**	**13**	**16**	**3**	**12**	**15**	**75**	**1**	**0**	**1**	**121**	**2.5**	**27**	**6**	**38**	**4**	**-13**	....	....	....	....	....	....	....	....
	Pittsburgh Penguins	**NHL**	**19**	**1**	**6**	**7**	**1**	**6**	**7**	**28**	**0**	**0**	**0**	**27**	**3.7**	**9**	**2**	**12**	**1**	**-4**	....	....	....	....	....	....	....	....

Season	Club	League	GP	G	A	Pts	AG	AA	APts	PIM	PP	SH	GW	S	%	TGF	PGF	TGA	PGA	+/–	GP	G	A	Pts	PIM	PP	SH	GW
			REGULAR SEASON																		PLAYOFFS							
1969-70	**Pittsburgh Penguins**	**NHL**	**12**	**0**	**1**	**1**	**0**	**1**	**1**	**8**	**0**	**0**	**0**	**38**	**0.0**	**5**	**0**	**5**	**0**	**0**	....	....	....	....	....	....	....	....
	Baltimore Clippers	AHL	56	19	22	41	....	....	....	81	....	....	....	....	....	....	....	....	....	....	4	0	3	3	8	....	....	....
1970-71	**Philadelphia Flyers**	**NHL**	**2**	**0**	**0**	**0**	**0**	**0**	**0**	**0**	**0**	**0**	**0**	**4**	**0.0**	**2**	**2**	**2**	**0**	**–2**	....	....	....	....	....	....	....	....
	Baltimore Clippers	AHL	34	4	7	11	....	....	....	54	....	....	....	....	....	....	....	....	....	....	....	....	....	....	....	....	....	....
	Hershey Bears	AHL	24	10	8	18	....	....	....	56	....	....	....	....	....	....	....	....	....	....	4	0	2	2	6	....	....	....
1971-72	San Diego Gulls	WHL	54	25	19	44	....	....	....	105	....	....	....	....	....	....	....	....	....	....	4	0	0	0	7	....	....	....
1972-73	San Diego Gulls	WHL	64	13	23	36	....	....	....	115	....	....	....	....	....	....	....	....	....	....	6	1	2	3	22	....	....	....
1973-74	Omaha Knights	CHL	65	23	30	53	....	....	....	89	....	....	....	....	....	....	....	....	....	....	5	2	2	4	20	....	....	....
1974-75	Long Island Cougars	NAHL	68	31	47	78	....	....	....	171	....	....	....	....	....	....	....	....	....	....	10	6	5	11	....	....	....	....
1975-76	Erie Blades	NAHL	27	10	9	19	....	....	....	46	....	....	....	....	....	....	....	....	....	....	5	3	2	5	13	....	....	....
1976-77	Philadelphia Firebirds	NAHL	74	32	27	59	....	....	....	91	....	....	....	....	....	....	....	....	....	....	4	1	2	3	6	....	....	....
	NHL Totals		**132**	**17**	**25**	**42**	**20**	**24**	**44**	**173**	**4**	**1**	**3**	**276**	**6.2**	**71**	**17**	**95**	**5**		....	....	....	....	....	....	....	....

Won WHL Rookie of the Year Award (1965)

NHL rights transferred to **California** after owners of **San Francisco** (WHL) franchise awarded NHL expansion team, April 5, 1966. Traded to **Pittsburgh** by **Oakland** with Bryan Watson and Tracy Pratt for Earl Ingarfield Sr., Gene Ubriaco and Dick Mattiussi, January 30, 1969. Traded to **Philadelphia** by **Pittsburgh** for Terry Ball, June 11, 1970. Signed as a free agent by **Atlanta** (Omaha-CHL), October 30, 1973. Traded to **Syracuse** (AHL) by **Atlanta** for cash, August, 1974.

• SWEENEY, BOB

Bob Sweeney C/RW – R. 6'3", 200 lbs. b: Concord, MA, 1/25/1964. Boston's 6th choice, 123rd overall, in 1982 Entry Draft.

Season	Club	League	GP	G	A	Pts	AG	AA	APts	PIM	PP	SH	GW	S	%	TGF	PGF	TGA	PGA	+/–	GP	G	A	Pts	PIM	PP	SH	GW
1981-82	Acton-Mass High School	H.S.	STATISTICS NOT AVAILABLE																									
1982-83	Boston College	ECAC	30	17	11	28	....	....	....	10	....	....	....	....	....	....	....	....	....	....	....	....	....	....	....	....	....	....
1983-84	Boston College	ECAC	23	14	7	21	....	....	....	10	....	....	....	....	....	....	....	....	....	....	....	....	....	....	....	....	....	....
1984-85	Boston College	H.E.	44	32	32	64	....	....	....	43	....	....	....	....	....	....	....	....	....	....	....	....	....	....	....	....	....	....
1985-86	Boston College	H.E.	41	15	24	39	....	....	....	52	....	....	....	....	....	....	....	....	....	....	....	....	....	....	....	....	....	....
1986-87	**Boston Bruins**	**NHL**	**14**	**2**	**4**	**6**	**2**	**3**	**5**	**21**	**0**	**0**	**0**	**13**	**15.4**	**8**	**2**	**11**	**0**	**–5**	**3**	**0**	**0**	**0**	**0**	**0**	**0**	**0**
	Moncton Golden Flames	AHL	58	29	26	55	....	....	....	81	....	....	....	....	....	....	....	....	....	....	4	0	2	2	13	....	....	....
1987-88	**Boston Bruins**	**NHL**	**80**	**22**	**23**	**45**	**19**	**16**	**35**	**73**	**6**	**0**	**7**	**118**	**18.6**	**72**	**19**	**42**	**0**	**+11**	**23**	**6**	**8**	**14**	**66**	**1**	**1**	**1**
1988-89	**Boston Bruins**	**NHL**	**75**	**14**	**14**	**28**	**12**	**10**	**22**	**99**	**2**	**1**	**3**	**117**	**12.0**	**50**	**15**	**65**	**11**	**–19**	**10**	**2**	**4**	**6**	**19**	**0**	**0**	**0**
1989-90	**Boston Bruins**	**NHL**	**70**	**22**	**24**	**46**	**19**	**17**	**36**	**93**	**5**	**2**	**6**	**147**	**15.0**	**70**	**19**	**64**	**15**	**+2**	**20**	**0**	**2**	**2**	**30**	**0**	**0**	**0**
1990-91	**Boston Bruins**	**NHL**	**80**	**15**	**33**	**48**	**14**	**25**	**39**	**115**	**0**	**1**	**2**	**116**	**12.9**	**71**	**6**	**71**	**18**	**+12**	**17**	**4**	**2**	**6**	**45**	**0**	**0**	**1**
1991-92	**Boston Bruins**	**NHL**	**63**	**6**	**14**	**20**	**5**	**11**	**16**	**103**	**0**	**1**	**1**	**70**	**8.6**	**35**	**6**	**60**	**22**	**–9**	**14**	**1**	**0**	**1**	**25**	**0**	**1**	**0**
	Maine Mariners	AHL	1	1	0	1	....	....	....	0	....	....	....	....	....	....	....	....	....	....	....	....	....	....	....	....	....	....
1992-93	**Buffalo Sabres**	**NHL**	**80**	**21**	**26**	**47**	**17**	**18**	**35**	**118**	**4**	**3**	**3**	**120**	**17.5**	**80**	**20**	**90**	**32**	**+2**	**8**	**2**	**2**	**4**	**8**	**0**	**0**	**1**
1993-94	**Buffalo Sabres**	**NHL**	**60**	**11**	**14**	**25**	**10**	**11**	**21**	**94**	**3**	**3**	**1**	**76**	**14.5**	**35**	**5**	**41**	**14**	**+3**	**1**	**0**	**0**	**0**	**0**	**0**	**0**	**0**
1994-95	**Buffalo Sabres**	**NHL**	**45**	**5**	**4**	**9**	**9**	**6**	**15**	**18**	**1**	**2**	**0**	**47**	**10.6**	**21**	**7**	**26**	**6**	**–6**	**5**	**0**	**0**	**0**	**4**	**0**	**0**	**0**
1995-96	**New York Islanders**	**NHL**	**66**	**6**	**6**	**12**	**6**	**5**	**11**	**59**	**0**	**1**	**1**	**54**	**11.1**	**18**	**0**	**68**	**27**	**–23**	....	....	....	....	....	....	....	....
	Calgary Flames	**NHL**	**6**	**1**	**1**	**2**	**1**	**1**	**2**	**6**	**0**	**0**	**0**	**8**	**12.5**	**6**	**1**	**2**	**0**	**+3**	**2**	**0**	**0**	**0**	**0**	**0**	**0**	**0**
1996-97	Quebec Rafales	IHL	69	10	21	31	....	....	....	120	....	....	....	....	....	....	....	....	....	....	9	2	0	2	8	....	....	....
1997-98	ECR Revier Lowen	Germany	27	9	4	13	....	....	....	77	....	....	....	....	....	....	....	....	....	....	....	....	....	....	....	....	....	....
	Frankfurt Lions	Germany	20	7	8	15	....	....	....	32	....	....	....	....	....	....	....	....	....	....	7	1	3	4	6	....	....	....
	NHL Totals		**639**	**125**	**163**	**288**	**114**	**123**	**237**	**799**	**21**	**14**	**24**	**886**	**14.1**	**466**	**100**	**540**	**145**		**103**	**15**	**18**	**33**	**197**	**1**	**2**	**3**

Hockey East Second All-Star Team (1985)

Claimed on waivers by **Buffalo** from **Boston**, October 9, 1992. Claimed by **NY Islanders** from **Buffalo** in NHL Waiver Draft, October 2, 1995. Traded to **Calgary** by **NY Islanders** for Pat Conacher and Calgary's 6th round choice (traded back to Calgary — Calgary selected Ilja Demidov) in 1997 Entry Draft, March 20, 1996.

• SWEENEY, DON

Don Sweeney D – L. 5'10", 184 lbs. b: St. Stephen, N.B., 8/17/1966. Boston's 8th choice, 166th overall, in 1984 Entry Draft.

Season	Club	League	GP	G	A	Pts	AG	AA	APts	PIM	PP	SH	GW	S	%	TGF	PGF	TGA	PGA	+/–	GP	G	A	Pts	PIM	PP	SH	GW
1983-84	St. Paul High School	H.S.	22	33	26	59	....	....	....	....	....	....	....	....	....	....	....	....	....	....	....	....	....	....	....	....	....	....
1984-85	Harvard University	ECAC	29	3	7	10	....	....	....	30	....	....	....	....	....	....	....	....	....	....	....	....	....	....	....	....	....	....
1985-86	Harvard University	ECAC	31	4	5	9	....	....	....	12	....	....	....	....	....	....	....	....	....	....	....	....	....	....	....	....	....	....
1986-87	Harvard University	ECAC	34	7	4	11	....	....	....	22	....	....	....	....	....	....	....	....	....	....	....	....	....	....	....	....	....	....
1987-88	Harvard University	ECAC	30	6	23	29	....	....	....	37	....	....	....	....	....	....	....	....	....	....	....	....	....	....	....	....	....	....
	Maine Mariners	AHL	....	....	....	....	....	....	....	....	....	....	....	....	....	....	....	....	....	....	6	1	3	4	0	....	....	....
1988-89	**Boston Bruins**	**NHL**	**36**	**3**	**5**	**8**	**3**	**4**	**7**	**20**	**0**	**0**	**0**	**35**	**8.6**	**23**	**1**	**38**	**10**	**–6**	....	....	....	....	....	....	....	....
	Maine Mariners	AHL	42	8	17	25	....	....	....	24	....	....	....	....	....	....	....	....	....	....	....	....	....	....	....	....	....	....
1989-90	**Boston Bruins**	**NHL**	**58**	**3**	**5**	**8**	**3**	**4**	**7**	**58**	**0**	**0**	**0**	**49**	**6.1**	**41**	**0**	**41**	**11**	**+11**	**21**	**1**	**5**	**6**	**18**	**1**	**0**	**0**
	Maine Mariners	AHL	11	0	8	8	....	....	....	8	....	....	....	....	....	....	....	....	....	....	....	....	....	....	....	....	....	....
1990-91	**Boston Bruins**	**NHL**	**77**	**8**	**13**	**21**	**7**	**10**	**17**	**67**	**0**	**1**	**3**	**102**	**7.8**	**67**	**1**	**89**	**25**	**+2**	**19**	**3**	**0**	**3**	**25**	**0**	**0**	**0**
1991-92	**Boston Bruins**	**NHL**	**75**	**3**	**11**	**14**	**3**	**8**	**11**	**74**	**0**	**0**	**1**	**92**	**3.3**	**50**	**0**	**97**	**38**	**–9**	**15**	**0**	**0**	**0**	**10**	**0**	**0**	**0**
1992-93	**Boston Bruins**	**NHL**	**84**	**7**	**27**	**34**	**6**	**18**	**24**	**68**	**0**	**1**	**0**	**107**	**6.5**	**94**	**0**	**88**	**28**	**+34**	**4**	**0**	**0**	**0**	**4**	**0**	**0**	**0**
1993-94	**Boston Bruins**	**NHL**	**75**	**6**	**15**	**21**	**6**	**12**	**18**	**50**	**1**	**2**	**2**	**136**	**4.4**	**85**	**3**	**83**	**30**	**+29**	**12**	**2**	**1**	**3**	**4**	**0**	**0**	**1**
1994-95	**Boston Bruins**	**NHL**	**47**	**3**	**19**	**22**	**5**	**28**	**33**	**24**	**1**	**0**	**2**	**102**	**2.9**	**65**	**20**	**51**	**12**	**+6**	**5**	**0**	**0**	**0**	**4**	**0**	**0**	**0**
1995-96	**Boston Bruins**	**NHL**	**77**	**4**	**24**	**28**	**4**	**20**	**24**	**42**	**2**	**0**	**3**	**142**	**2.8**	**98**	**20**	**111**	**29**	**–4**	**5**	**0**	**2**	**2**	**6**	**0**	**0**	**0**
1996-97	**Boston Bruins**	**NHL**	**82**	**3**	**23**	**26**	**3**	**20**	**23**	**39**	**0**	**0**	**0**	**113**	**2.7**	**92**	**12**	**115**	**30**	**–5**	....	....	....	....	....	....	....	....
	Canada	WC-A	11	1	3	4	....	....	....	6	....	....	....	....	....	....	....	....	....	....	....	....	....	....	....	....	....	....
1997-98	**Boston Bruins**	**NHL**	**59**	**1**	**15**	**16**	**1**	**15**	**16**	**24**	**0**	**0**	**0**	**55**	**1.8**	**53**	**2**	**46**	**7**	**+12**	....	....	....	....	....	....	....	....
	NHL Totals		**670**	**41**	**157**	**198**	**41**	**139**	**180**	**466**	**4**	**4**	**11**	**933**	**4.4**	**668**	**59**	**759**	**220**		**81**	**6**	**8**	**14**	**71**	**1**	**0**	**1**

NCAA East All-American Team (1988) • ECAC First All-Star Team (1988)

• SWEENEY, TIM

Tim Sweeney LW – L. 5'11", 185 lbs. b: Boston, MA, 4/12/1967. Calgary's 7th choice, 122nd overall, in 1985 Entry Draft.

Season	Club	League	GP	G	A	Pts	AG	AA	APts	PIM	PP	SH	GW	S	%	TGF	PGF	TGA	PGA	+/–	GP	G	A	Pts	PIM	PP	SH	GW
1984-85	Weymouth North High School	H.S.	22	32	56	88	....	....	....	....	....	....	....	....	....	....	....	....	....	....	....	....	....	....	....	....	....	....
1985-86	Boston College	H.E.	32	8	4	12	....	....	....	8	....	....	....	....	....	....	....	....	....	....	....	....	....	....	....	....	....	....
1986-87	Boston College	H.E.	38	31	18	49	....	....	....	28	....	....	....	....	....	....	....	....	....	....	....	....	....	....	....	....	....	....
1987-88	Boston College	H.E.	18	9	11	20	....	....	....	18	....	....	....	....	....	....	....	....	....	....	....	....	....	....	....	....	....	....
1988-89	Boston College	H.E.	39	29	44	73	....	....	....	26	....	....	....	....	....	....	....	....	....	....	....	....	....	....	....	....	....	....
1989-90	Salt Lake Golden Eagles	IHL	81	46	51	97	....	....	....	32	....	....	....	....	....	....	....	....	....	....	11	5	4	9	4	....	....	....
1990-91	**Calgary Flames**	**NHL**	**42**	**7**	**9**	**16**	**6**	**7**	**13**	**8**	**0**	**0**	**4**	**40**	**17.5**	**24**	**1**	**33**	**11**	**+1**	....	....	....	....	....	....	....	....
	Salt Lake Golden Eagles	IHL	31	19	16	35	....	....	....	8	....	....	....	....	....	....	....	....	....	....	4	3	3	6	0	....	....	....
1991-92	United States	Nat-Team	21	9	11	20	....	....	....	10	....	....	....	....	....	....	....	....	....	....	....	....	....	....	....	....	....	....
	United States	Olympics	8	3	4	7	....	....	....	6	....	....	....	....	....	....	....	....	....	....	....	....	....	....	....	....	....	....
	Calgary Flames	**NHL**	**11**	**1**	**2**	**3**	**1**	**1**	**2**	**4**	**0**	**0**	**1**	**16**	**6.3**	**4**	**0**	**9**	**5**	**0**	....	....	....	....	....	....	....	....
1992-93	**Boston Bruins**	**NHL**	**14**	**1**	**7**	**8**	**1**	**5**	**6**	**6**	**0**	**0**	**0**	**15**	**6.7**	**10**	**0**	**9**	**0**	**+1**	**3**	**0**	**0**	**0**	**0**	**0**	**0**	**0**
	Providence Bruins	AHL	60	41	55	96	....	....	....	32	....	....	....	....	....	....	....	....	....	....	3	2	2	4	0	....	....	....
1993-94	**Anaheim Mighty Ducks**	**NHL**	**78**	**16**	**27**	**43**	**15**	**21**	**36**	**49**	**6**	**1**	**2**	**114**	**14.0**	**62**	**18**	**50**	**9**	**+3**	....	....	....	....	....	....	....	....
	United States	WC-A	8	3	2	5	....	....	....	0	....	....	....	....	....	....	....	....	....	....	....	....	....	....	....	....	....	....
1994-95	**Anaheim Mighty Ducks**	**NHL**	**13**	**1**	**1**	**2**	**2**	**1**	**3**	**2**	**0**	**0**	**0**	**11**	**9.1**	**6**	**0**	**16**	**7**	**–3**	....	....	....	....	....	....	....	....
	Providence Bruins	AHL	2	2	2	4	....	....	....	0	....	....	....	....	....	....	....	....	....	....	13	8	*17	*25	6	....	....	....
1995-96	**Boston Bruins**	**NHL**	**41**	**8**	**8**	**16**	**8**	**7**	**15**	**14**	**1**	**0**	**2**	**47**	**17.0**	**20**	**4**	**22**	**10**	**+4**	**1**	**0**	**0**	**0**	**2**	**0**	**0**	**0**
	Providence Bruins	AHL	34	17	22	39	....	....	....	12	....	....	....	....	....	....	....	....	....	....	....	....	....	....	....	....	....	....
1996-97	**Boston Bruins**	**NHL**	**36**	**10**	**11**	**21**	**11**	**10**	**21**	**14**	**2**	**0**	**2**	**65**	**15.4**	**34**	**6**	**34**	**6**	**0**	....	....	....	....	....	....	....	....
	Providence Bruins	AHL	23	11	22	33	....	....	....	6	....	....	....	....	....	....	....	....	....	....	....	....	....	....	....	....	....	....
1997-98	**New York Rangers**	**NHL**	**56**	**11**	**18**	**29**	**13**	**18**	**31**	**26**	**2**	**0**	**1**	**75**	**14.7**	**42**	**11**	**25**	**1**	**+7**	....	....	....	....	....	....	....	....
	Hartford	AHL	7	2	6	8	....	....	....	8	....	....	....	....	....	....	....	....	....	....	....	....	....	....	....	....	....	....
	NHL Totals		**291**	**55**	**83**	**138**	**57**	**70**	**127**	**123**	**11**	**1**	**12**	**383**	**14.4**	**202**	**40**	**198**	**49**		**4**	**0**	**0**	**0**	**2**	**0**	**0**	**0**

Hockey East First All-Star Team (1989) • NCAA East Second All-American Team (1989) • IHL Second All-Star Team (1990) • AHL Second All-Star Team (1993)

Signed as a free agent by **Boston**, September 16, 1992. Claimed by **Anaheim** from **Boston** in Expansion Draft, June 24, 1993. Signed as a free agent by **Boston**, August 9, 1995. Signed as a free agent by **NY Rangers**, September 15, 1997.

• SYDOR, DARRYL

Darryl Sydor D – L. 6', 195 lbs. b: Edmonton, Alta., 5/13/1972. Los Angeles' 1st choice, 7th overall, in 1990 Entry Draft.

Season	Club	League	GP	G	A	Pts	AG	AA	APts	PIM	PP	SH	GW	S	%	TGF	PGF	TGA	PGA	+/–	GP	G	A	Pts	PIM	PP	SH	GW
1987-88	Edmonton Mets	AJHL	38	10	11	21	....	....	....	54	....	....	....	....	....	....	....	....	....	....	....	....	....	....	....	....	....	....
1988-89	Kamloops Blazers	WHL	65	12	14	26	....	....	....	86	....	....	....	....	....	....	....	....	....	....	15	1	4	5	19	....	....	....
1989-90	Kamloops Blazers	WHL	67	29	66	95	....	....	....	129	....	....	....	....	....	....	....	....	....	....	17	2	9	11	28	....	....	....

Season	Club	League	GP	G	A	Pts	AG	AA	APts	PIM	PP	SH	GW	S	%	TGF	PGF	TGA	PGA	+/-	GP	G	A	Pts	PIM	PP	SH	GW
			REGULAR SEASON																		PLAYOFFS							
1990-91	Kamloops Blazers	WHL	66	27	78	105	....	....	....	88	....	....	....	....	....	....	....	....	....	....	12	3	*22	25	10	....	....	....
1991-92	Kamloops Blazers	WHL	29	9	39	48	....	....	....	43	....	....	....	....	....	....	....	....	....	....	17	3	15	18	18	....	....	....
	Canada	WJC-A	7	3	1	4	....	....	....	4	....	....	....	....	....	....	....	....	....	....	....	....	....	....	....	....	....	....
	Los Angeles Kings	**NHL**	**18**	**1**	**5**	**6**	**1**	**4**	**5**	**22**	**0**	**0**	**0**	**18**	**5.6**	**17**	**5**	**15**	**0**	**-3**	....	....	....	....	....	....	....	....
1992-93	**Los Angeles Kings**	**NHL**	**80**	**6**	**23**	**29**	**5**	**16**	**21**	**63**	**0**	**0**	**1**	**112**	**5.4**	**81**	**15**	**100**	**32**	**-2**	**24**	**3**	**8**	**11**	**16**	**2**	**0**	**0**
1993-94	**Los Angeles Kings**	**NHL**	**84**	**8**	**27**	**35**	**7**	**21**	**28**	**94**	**1**	**0**	**0**	**146**	**5.5**	**81**	**19**	**93**	**22**	**-9**	....	....	....	....	....	....	....	....
	Canada	WC-A	8	0	1	1	....	....	....	4	....	....	....	....	....	....	....	....	....	....	....	....	....	....	....	....	....	....
1994-95	**Los Angeles Kings**	**NHL**	**48**	**4**	**19**	**23**	**7**	**28**	**35**	**36**	**3**	**0**	**0**	**96**	**4.2**	**61**	**8**	**76**	**21**	**-2**	....	....	....	....	....	....	....	....
1995-96	**Los Angeles Kings**	**NHL**	**58**	**1**	**11**	**12**	**1**	**9**	**10**	**34**	**1**	**0**	**0**	**84**	**1.2**	**59**	**12**	**82**	**24**	**-11**	....	....	....	....	....	....	....	....
	Dallas Stars	**NHL**	**26**	**2**	**6**	**8**	**2**	**5**	**7**	**41**	**1**	**0**	**0**	**33**	**6.1**	**17**	**5**	**13**	**0**	**-1**	....	....	....	....	....	....	....	....
	Canada	WC-A	8	0	1	1	....	....	....	0	....	....	....	....	....	....	....	....	....	....	....	....	....	....	....	....	....	....
1996-97	**Dallas Stars**	**NHL**	**82**	**8**	**40**	**48**	**8**	**35**	**43**	**51**	**2**	**0**	**2**	**142**	**5.6**	**108**	**33**	**39**	**1**	**+37**	**7**	**0**	**2**	**2**	**0**	**0**	**0**	**0**
1997-98	**Dallas Stars**	**NHL**	**79**	**11**	**35**	**46**	**13**	**34**	**47**	**51**	**4**	**1**	**1**	**166**	**6.6**	**109**	**54**	**45**	**7**	**+17**	**17**	**0**	**5**	**5**	**14**	**0**	**0**	**0**
	NHL Totals		**475**	**41**	**166**	**207**	**44**	**152**	**196**	**392**	**12**	**1**	**4**	**797**	**5.1**	**533**	**151**	**463**	**107**		**48**	**3**	**15**	**18**	**30**	**2**	**0**	**0**

Played in NHL All-Star Game (1998)

WHL West First All-Star Team (1990, 1991, 1992)

Traded to **Dallas** by **LA Kings** with LA Kings' 5th round choice (Ryan Christie) in 1996 Entry Draft for Shane Churla and Doug Zmolek, February 17, 1996.

• SYKES, BOB

Bob Sykes LW – L. 6', 200 lbs. b: Sudbury, Ont., 9/26/1951. Toronto's 5th choice, 65th overall, in 1971 Amateur Draft.

Season	Club	League	GP	G	A	Pts	AG	AA	APts	PIM	PP	SH	GW	S	%	TGF	PGF	TGA	PGA	+/-	GP	G	A	Pts	PIM	PP	SH	GW
1969-70	Sudbury Wolves	NOHA	45	18	23	41	....	....	....	79	....	....	....	....	....	....	....	....	....	....	....	....	....	....	....	....	....	....
1970-71	Sudbury Wolves	NOHA	48	48	59	107	....	....	....	26	....	....	....	....	....	....	....	....	....	....	....	....	....	....	....	....	....	....
1971-72	St. Louis University	CCHA	32	16	23	39	....	....	....	22	....	....	....	....	....	....	....	....	....	....	....	....	....	....	....	....	....	....
1972-73	St. Louis University	CCHA	15	17	22	39	....	....	....	16	....	....	....	....	....	....	....	....	....	....	....	....	....	....	....	....	....	....
1973-74	Oklahoma City Blazers	CHL	50	13	11	24	....	....	....	19	....	....	....	....	....	....	....	....	....	....	8	2	1	3	2	....	....	....
1974-75	**Toronto Maple Leafs**	**NHL**	**2**	**0**	**0**	**0**	**0**	**0**	**0**	**0**	**0**	**0**	**0**	**1**	**0.0**	**0**	**0**	**2**	**0**	**-2**	....	....	....	....	....	....	....	....
	Oklahoma City Blazers	CHL	73	30	21	51	....	....	....	24	....	....	....	....	....	....	....	....	....	....	5	1	2	3	0	....	....	....
1975-76	Oklahoma City Blazers	CHL	52	17	6	23	....	....	....	44	....	....	....	....	....	....	....	....	....	....	....	....	....	....	....	....	....	....
	Saginaw Gears	IHL	1	0	3	3	....	....	....	0	....	....	....	....	....	....	....	....	....	....	....	....	....	....	....	....	....	....
1976-77	Orillia Terriers	OHA Sr.	10	2	1	3	....	....	....	11	....	....	....	....	....	....	....	....	....	....	....	....	....	....	....	....	....	....
	NHL Totals		**2**	**0**	**0**	**0**	**0**	**0**	**0**	**0**	**0**	**0**	**0**	**1**	**0.0**	**0**	**0**	**2**	**0**		....	....	....	....	....	....	....	....

• SYKES, PHIL

Phil "Psycho" Sykes LW – L. 6', 175 lbs. b: Dawson Creek, B.C., 3/18/1959.

Season	Club	League	GP	G	A	Pts	AG	AA	APts	PIM	PP	SH	GW	S	%	TGF	PGF	TGA	PGA	+/-	GP	G	A	Pts	PIM	PP	SH	GW
1978-79	University of North Dakota	WCHA	41	9	5	14	....	....	....	16	....	....	....	....	....	....	....	....	....	....	....	....	....	....	....	....	....	....
1979-80	University of North Dakota	WCHA	37	22	27	49	....	....	....	34	....	....	....	....	....	....	....	....	....	....	....	....	....	....	....	....	....	....
1980-81	University of North Dakota	WCHA	38	28	34	62	....	....	....	22	....	....	....	....	....	....	....	....	....	....	....	....	....	....	....	....	....	....
1981-82	University of North Dakota	WCHA	37	22	27	49	....	....	....	34	....	....	....	....	....	....	....	....	....	....	....	....	....	....	....	....	....	....
1982-83	**Los Angeles Kings**	**NHL**	**7**	**2**	**0**	**2**	**2**	**0**	**2**	**2**	**0**	**0**	**0**	**5**	**40.0**	**3**	**0**	**2**	**0**	**+1**	....	....	....	....	....	....	....	....
	New Haven Nighthawks	AHL	71	19	26	45	....	....	....	111	....	....	....	....	....	....	....	....	....	....	12	2	2	4	21	....	....	....
1983-84	**Los Angeles Kings**	**NHL**	**3**	**0**	**0**	**0**	**0**	**0**	**0**	**2**	**0**	**0**	**0**	**2**	**0.0**	**0**	**0**	**1**	**0**	**-1**	....	....	....	....	....	....	....	....
	New Haven Nighthawks	AHL	77	29	37	66	....	....	....	101	....	....	....	....	....	....	....	....	....	....	....	....	....	....	....	....	....	....
1984-85	**Los Angeles Kings**	**NHL**	**79**	**17**	**15**	**32**	**14**	**10**	**24**	**38**	**1**	**2**	**2**	**96**	**17.7**	**49**	**3**	**78**	**14**	**-18**	**3**	**0**	**1**	**1**	**4**	**0**	**0**	**0**
1985-86	**Los Angeles Kings**	**NHL**	**76**	**20**	**24**	**44**	**16**	**16**	**32**	**97**	**1**	**2**	**4**	**132**	**15.2**	**61**	**10**	**125**	**48**	**-26**	....	....	....	....	....	....	....	....
	Canada	WEC-A	9	0	0	0	....	....	....	4	....	....	....	....	....	....	....	....	....	....	....	....	....	....	....	....	....	....
1986-87	**Los Angeles Kings**	**NHL**	**58**	**6**	**15**	**21**	**5**	**11**	**16**	**133**	**0**	**1**	**0**	**62**	**9.7**	**31**	**1**	**51**	**31**	**+10**	**5**	**0**	**1**	**1**	**8**	**0**	**0**	**0**
1987-88	**Los Angeles Kings**	**NHL**	**40**	**9**	**12**	**21**	**8**	**9**	**17**	**82**	**3**	**1**	**0**	**61**	**14.8**	**36**	**6**	**31**	**6**	**+5**	**4**	**0**	**0**	**0**	**0**	**0**	**0**	**0**
1988-89	**Los Angeles Kings**	**NHL**	**23**	**0**	**1**	**1**	**0**	**1**	**1**	**8**	**0**	**0**	**0**	**5**	**0.0**	**4**	**0**	**7**	**0**	**-3**	**3**	**0**	**0**	**0**	**8**	**0**	**0**	**0**
	New Haven Nighthawks	AHL	34	9	17	26	....	....	....	23	....	....	....	....	....	....	....	....	....	....	....	....	....	....	....	....	....	....
1989-90	New Haven Nighthawks	AHL	25	3	12	15	....	....	....	32	....	....	....	....	....	....	....	....	....	....	....	....	....	....	....	....	....	....
	Winnipeg Jets	**NHL**	**48**	**9**	**6**	**15**	**8**	**4**	**12**	**26**	**0**	**1**	**0**	**50**	**18.0**	**22**	**0**	**38**	**8**	**-8**	**4**	**0**	**0**	**0**	**0**	**0**	**0**	**0**
	Moncton Hawks	AHL	5	0	1	1	....	....	....	20	....	....	....	....	....	....	....	....	....	....	....	....	....	....	....	....	....	....
1990-91	**Winnipeg Jets**	**NHL**	**70**	**12**	**10**	**22**	**11**	**8**	**19**	**59**	**0**	**2**	**0**	**65**	**18.5**	**40**	**0**	**63**	**14**	**-9**	....	....	....	....	....	....	....	....
1991-92	**Winnipeg Jets**	**NHL**	**52**	**4**	**2**	**6**	**4**	**1**	**5**	**72**	**0**	**0**	**2**	**34**	**11.8**	**11**	**0**	**41**	**18**	**-12**	**7**	**0**	**1**	**1**	**9**	**0**	**0**	**0**
	NHL Totals		**456**	**79**	**85**	**164**	**68**	**60**	**128**	**519**	**5**	**9**	**8**	**512**	**15.4**	**257**	**20**	**437**	**139**		**26**	**0**	**3**	**3**	**29**	**0**	**0**	**0**

NCAA Championship All-Tournament Team (1980, 1982) • WCHA First All-Star Team (1982) • NCAA Championship Tournament MVP (1982)

Signed as a free agent by **LA Kings**, April 5, 1982. Traded to **Winnipeg** by **LA Kings** for Brad Jones, December 1, 1989.

• SYKORA, MICHAL

Michal Sykora D – L. 6'5", 225 lbs. b: Pardubice, Czech., 7/5/1973. San Jose's 6th choice, 123rd overall, in 1992 Entry Draft.

Season	Club	League	GP	G	A	Pts	AG	AA	APts	PIM	PP	SH	GW	S	%	TGF	PGF	TGA	PGA	+/-	GP	G	A	Pts	PIM	PP	SH	GW
1990-91	Pardubice	Czech.	2	0	0	0	....	....	....	....	....	....	....	....	....	....	....	....	....	....	....	....	....	....	....	....	....	....
1991-92	Tacoma Rockets	WHL	61	13	23	36	....	....	....	66	....	....	....	....	....	....	....	....	....	....	4	0	2	2	2	....	....	....
1992-93	Tacoma Rockets	WHL	70	23	50	73	....	....	....	73	....	....	....	....	....	....	....	....	....	....	7	4	8	12	2	....	....	....
1993-94	**San Jose Sharks**	**NHL**	**22**	**1**	**4**	**5**	**1**	**3**	**4**	**14**	**0**	**0**	**0**	**22**	**4.5**	**13**	**1**	**23**	**7**	**-4**	....	....	....	....	....	....	....	....
	Kansas City Blades	IHL	47	5	11	16	....	....	....	30	....	....	....	....	....	....	....	....	....	....	....	....	....	....	....	....	....	....
1994-95	Kansas City Blades	IHL	36	1	10	11	....	....	....	30	....	....	....	....	....	....	....	....	....	....	....	....	....	....	....	....	....	....
	San Jose Sharks	**NHL**	**16**	**0**	**4**	**4**	**0**	**6**	**6**	**10**	**0**	**0**	**0**	**6**	**0.0**	**11**	**0**	**12**	**7**	**+6**	....	....	....	....	....	....	....	....
1995-96	**San Jose Sharks**	**NHL**	**79**	**4**	**16**	**20**	**4**	**13**	**17**	**54**	**1**	**0**	**0**	**80**	**5.0**	**69**	**1**	**123**	**41**	**-14**	....	....	....	....	....	....	....	....
	Czech Republic	WC-A	8	0	1	1	....	....	....	6	....	....	....	....	....	....	....	....	....	....	....	....	....	....	....	....	....	....
1996-97	Czech Republic	W Cup	2	0	0	0	....	....	....	2	....	....	....	....	....	....	....	....	....	....	....	....	....	....	....	....	....	....
	San Jose Sharks	**NHL**	**35**	**2**	**5**	**7**	**2**	**4**	**6**	**59**	**1**	**0**	**0**	**39**	**5.1**	**26**	**3**	**29**	**6**	**0**	....	....	....	....	....	....	....	....
	Chicago Blackhawks	**NHL**	**28**	**1**	**9**	**10**	**1**	**8**	**9**	**10**	**0**	**0**	**0**	**38**	**2.6**	**18**	**3**	**11**	**0**	**+4**	**1**	**0**	**0**	**0**	**0**	**0**	**0**	**0**
1997-98	**Chicago Blackhawks**	**NHL**	**28**	**1**	**3**	**4**	**1**	**3**	**4**	**12**	**0**	**0**	**0**	**35**	**2.9**	**12**	**5**	**17**	**0**	**-10**	....	....	....	....	....	....	....	....
	Indianapolis Ice	IHL	6	0	0	0	....	....	....	4	....	....	....	....	....	....	....	....	....	....	....	....	....	....	....	....	....	....
	HC Pardubice	Czech.	1	1	0	1	....	....	....	2	....	....	....	....	....	....	....	....	....	....	....	....	....	....	....	....	....	....
	NHL Totals		**208**	**9**	**41**	**50**	**9**	**37**	**46**	**159**	**2**	**0**	**0**	**220**	**4.1**	**149**	**13**	**215**	**61**		**1**	**0**	**0**	**0**	**0**	**0**	**0**	**0**

WHL West First All-Star Team (1993) • WC-A All-Star Team (1996)

Traded to **Chicago** by **San Jose** with Chris Terreri and Ulf Dahlen for Ed Belfour, January 25, 1997.

• SYKORA, PETR

Petr Sykora C – L. 6', 190 lbs. b: Plzen, Czech., 11/19/1976. New Jersey's 1st choice, 18th overall, in 1995 Entry Draft.

Season	Club	League	GP	G	A	Pts	AG	AA	APts	PIM	PP	SH	GW	S	%	TGF	PGF	TGA	PGA	+/-	GP	G	A	Pts	PIM	PP	SH	GW
1992-93	Skoda Plzen	Czech.	19	12	5	17	....	....	....	....	....	....	....	....	....	....	....	....	....	....	....	....	....	....	....	....	....	....
1993-94	Skoda Plzen	Czech.	37	10	16	26	....	....	....	....	....	....	....	....	....	....	....	....	....	....	4	0	1	1	....	....	....	....
	Czech Republic	WJC-A	7	6	2	8	....	....	....	6	....	....	....	....	....	....	....	....	....	....	....	....	....	....	....	....	....	....
	Cleveland Lumberjacks	IHL	13	4	5	9	....	....	....	8	....	....	....	....	....	....	....	....	....	....	....	....	....	....	....	....	....	....
1994-95	Detroit Vipers	IHL	29	12	17	29	....	....	....	16	....	....	....	....	....	....	....	....	....	....	....	....	....	....	....	....	....	....
	Czech Republic	WJC-A	3	0	0	0	....	....	....	0	....	....	....	....	....	....	....	....	....	....	....	....	....	....	....	....	....	....
1995-96	**New Jersey Devils**	**NHL**	**63**	**18**	**24**	**42**	**18**	**20**	**38**	**32**	**8**	**0**	**3**	**128**	**14.1**	**62**	**25**	**30**	**0**	**+7**	....	....	....	....	....	....	....	....
	Albany River Rats	AHL	5	4	1	5	....	....	....	0	....	....	....	....	....	....	....	....	....	....	....	....	....	....	....	....	....	....
1996-97	Czech Republic	W Cup	2	0	1	1	....	....	....	0	....	....	....	....	....	....	....	....	....	....	....	....	....	....	....	....	....	....
	New Jersey Devils	**NHL**	**19**	**1**	**2**	**3**	**1**	**2**	**3**	**4**	**0**	**0**	**0**	**26**	**3.8**	**8**	**3**	**13**	**0**	**-8**	**2**	**0**	**0**	**0**	**2**	**0**	**0**	**0**
	Albany River Rats	AHL	43	20	25	45	....	....	....	48	....	....	....	....	....	....	....	....	....	....	4	1	4	5	2	....	....	....
1997-98	**New Jersey Devils**	**NHL**	**58**	**16**	**20**	**36**	**19**	**19**	**38**	**22**	**3**	**1**	**4**	**130**	**12.3**	**50**	**22**	**33**	**5**	**0**	**2**	**0**	**0**	**0**	**0**	**0**	**0**	**0**
	Czech Republic	WC-A	6	0	2	2	....	....	....	2	....	....	....	....	....	....	....	....	....	....	....	....	....	....	....	....	....	....
	NHL Totals		**140**	**35**	**46**	**81**	**38**	**41**	**79**	**58**	**11**	**1**	**7**	**284**	**12.3**	**120**	**50**	**76**	**5**		**4**	**0**	**0**	**0**	**2**	**0**	**0**	**0**

NHL All-Rookie Team (1998)

• SZURA, JOE

Joe Szura C – L. 6'3", 185 lbs. b: Fort William, Ont., 12/18/1938.

Season	Club	League	GP	G	A	Pts	AG	AA	APts	PIM	PP	SH	GW	S	%	TGF	PGF	TGA	PGA	+/-	GP	G	A	Pts	PIM	PP	SH	GW
1956-57	Fort William Canadians	TBJHL	....	27	*36	*63	....	....	....	14	....	....	....	....	....	....	....	....	....	....	8	3	4	7	0	....	....	....
1957-58	Fort William Canadians	TBJHL	....	10	21	31	....	....	....	2	....	....	....	....	....	....	....	....	....	....	4	1	5	6	0	....	....	....
1958-59	Fort William Canadians	TBJHL	....	13	27	*40	....	....	....	20	....	....	....	....	....	....	....	....	....	....	....	....	....	....	....	....	....	....
1959-60	Montreal Royals	EPHL	14	2	3	5	....	....	....	4	....	....	....	....	....	....	....	....	....	....	6	0	1	1	0	....	....	....
	Hull-Ottawa Canadiens	EPHL	26	5	8	13	....	....	....	4	....	....	....	....	....	....	....	....	....	....	....	....	....	....	....	....	....	....

			REGULAR SEASON																		PLAYOFFS							
Season	**Club**	**League**	**GP**	**G**	**A**	**Pts**	**AG**	**AA**	**APts**	**PIM**	**PP**	**SH**	**GW**	**S**	**%**	**TGF**	**PGF**	**TGA**	**PGA**	**+/–**	**GP**	**G**	**A**	**Pts**	**PIM**	**PP**	**SH**	**GW**
1960-61	Montreal–Hull-Ottawa	EPHL	65	10	24	34	....	....	....	20	....	....	....	....	....	....	....	....	....	....	....	....	....	....	....	....	....	....
1961-62	North Bay Trappers	EPHL	68	27	35	62	....	....	....	24	....	....	....	....	....	....	....	....	....	....	....	....	....	....	....	....	....	....
1962-63	Cleveland Barons	AHL	72	15	29	44	....	....	....	20	....	....	....	....	....	....	....	....	....	....	7	1	1	2	2	....	....	....
1963-64	Cleveland Barons	AHL	72	23	44	67	....	....	....	33	....	....	....	....	....	....	....	....	....	....	9	*13	6	*19	2	....	....	....
1964-65	Cleveland Barons	AHL	67	29	30	59	....	....	....	26	....	....	....	....	....	....	....	....	....	....	....	....	....	....	....	....	....	....
1965-66	Cleveland Barons	AHL	72	46	30	76	....	....	....	22	....	....	....	....	....	....	....	....	....	....	12	1	4	5	8	....	....	....
1966-67	Cleveland Barons	AHL	68	27	42	69	....	....	....	32	....	....	....	....	....	....	....	....	....	....	3	0	0	0	4	....	....	....
1967-68	**Oakland Seals**	**NHL**	**20**	**1**	**3**	**4**	**1**	**3**	**4**	**10**	**0**	**0**	**0**	**18**	**5.6**	**9**	**1**	**12**	**0**	**–4**	....	....	....	....	....	....	....	....
	Buffalo Bisons	AHL	43	13	22	35	....	....	....	16	....	....	....	....	....	....	....	....	....	....	5	3	1	4	2	....	....	....
1968-69	**Oakland Seals**	**NHL**	**70**	**9**	**12**	**21**	**10**	**11**	**21**	**20**	**0**	**0**	**1**	**102**	**8.8**	**40**	**4**	**42**	**1**	**–5**	**7**	**2**	**3**	**5**	**2**	**1**	**0**	**0**
1969-70	Providence Reds	AHL	72	21	46	67	....	....	....	23	....	....	....	....	....	....	....	....	....	....	....	....	....	....	....	....	....	....
1970-71	Providence Reds	AHL	70	21	53	74	....	....	....	39	....	....	....	....	....	....	....	....	....	....	10	5	6	11	23	....	....	....
1971-72	Baltimore Clippers	AHL	73	38	38	76	....	....	....	20	....	....	....	....	....	....	....	....	....	....	18	1	10	11	12	....	....	....
1972-73	Los Angeles Sharks	WHA	72	13	32	45	....	....	....	25	....	....	....	....	....	....	....	....	....	....	2	0	0	0	0	....	....	....
1973-74	Houston Aeros	WHA	42	8	7	15	....	....	....	4	....	....	....	....	....	....	....	....	....	....	10	0	0	0	0	....	....	....
1974-75	Cape Cod Codders	NAHL	10	3	2	5	....	....	....	0	....	....	....	....	....	....	....	....	....	....	....	....	....	....	....	....	....	....
	NHL Totals		**90**	**10**	**15**	**25**	**11**	**14**	**25**	**30**	**0**	**0**	**1**	**120**	**8.3**	**49**	**5**	**54**	**1**		**7**	**2**	**3**	**5**	**2**	**1**	**0**	**0**
	Other Major League Totals		114	21	39	60	....	....	....	29	....	....	....	....	....	....	....	....	....		12	0	0	0	0	....	....	....

AHL First All-Star Team (1966)

Claimed by **Oakland** from **Montreal** in Expansion Draft, June 6, 1967. Selected by **LA Sharks** (WHA) in 1972 WHA General Player Draft, February 12, 1972. Traded to **Houston** (WHA) by **LA Sharks** (WHA) for Brian McDonald, August, 1974.

• TAFT, JOHN

John Taft D – L. 6'2", 185 lbs. b: Minneapolis, MN, 3/8/1954. Detroit's 5th choice, 81st overall, in 1974 Amateur Draft.

Season	Club	League	GP	G	A	Pts	AG	AA	APts	PIM	PP	SH	GW	S	%	TGF	PGF	TGA	PGA	+/–	GP	G	A	Pts	PIM	PP	SH	GW
1972-73	University of Wisconsin	WCHA	40	9	18	27	....	....	....	28	....	....	....	....	....	....	....	....	....	....	....	....	....	....	....	....	....	....
1973-74	University of Wisconsin	WCHA	36	1	17	18	....	....	....	20	....	....	....	....	....	....	....	....	....	....	....	....	....	....	....	....	....	....
1974-75	University of Wisconsin	WCHA	11	11	17	28	....	....	....	22	....	....	....	....	....	....	....	....	....	....	....	....	....	....	....	....	....	....
	United States	Nat-Team	18	1	4	5	....	....	....	....	....	....	....	....	....	....	....	....	....	....	....	....	....	....	....	....	....	....
	United States	WEC-A	10	1	2	3	....	....	....	4	....	....	....	....	....	....	....	....	....	....	....	....	....	....	....	....	....	....
1975-76	United States	Nat-Team	51	9	34	43	....	....	....	66	....	....	....	....	....	....	....	....	....	....	....	....	....	....	....	....	....	....
	United States	Olympics	6	1	2	3	....	....	....	8	....	....	....	....	....	....	....	....	....	....	....	....	....	....	....	....	....	....
1976-77	University of Wisconsin	WCHA	42	15	43	58	....	....	....	41	....	....	....	....	....	....	....	....	....	....	....	....	....	....	....	....	....	....
1977-78	Kansas City Red Wings	CHL	71	5	22	27	....	....	....	25	....	....	....	....	....	....	....	....	....	....	....	....	....	....	....	....	....	....
1978-79	**Detroit Red Wings**	**NHL**	**15**	**0**	**2**	**2**	**0**	**2**	**2**	**4**	**0**	**0**	**0**	**13**	**0.0**	**14**	**0**	**13**	**1**	**+2**	....	....	....	....	....	....	....	....
	Kansas City Red Wings	CHL	61	8	24	32	....	....	....	48	....	....	....	....	....	....	....	....	....	....	4	0	2	2	0	....	....	....
1979-80	Adirondack Red Wings	AHL	47	1	7	8	....	....	....	25	....	....	....	....	....	....	....	....	....	....	....	....	....	....	....	....	....	....
1980-81	Salt Lake Golden Eagles	CHL	68	8	19	27	....	....	....	68	....	....	....	....	....	....	....	....	....	....	17	1	2	3	33	....	....	....
1981-82	Salt Lake Golden Eagles	CHL	70	6	16	22	....	....	....	46	....	....	....	....	....	....	....	....	....	....	1	0	0	0	0	....	....	....
1982-83	Salt Lake Golden Eagles	CHL	77	5	25	30	....	....	....	65	....	....	....	....	....	....	....	....	....	....	6	0	0	0	8	....	....	....
	NHL Totals		**15**	**0**	**2**	**2**	**0**	**2**	**2**	**4**	**0**	**0**	**0**	**13**	**0.0**	**14**	**0**	**13**	**1**		....	....	....	....	....	....	....	....

NCAA Championship All-Tournament Team (1973, 1977) • WEC-B All-Star Team (1974) • WCHA Second All-Star Team (1977)

Signed as a free agent by **St. Louis**, July 14, 1980.

• TAGLIANETTI, PETER

Peter Taglianetti D – L. 6'2", 195 lbs. b: Framingham, MA, 8/15/1963. Winnipeg's 4th choice, 43rd overall, in 1983 Entry Draft.

Season	Club	League	GP	G	A	Pts	AG	AA	APts	PIM	PP	SH	GW	S	%	TGF	PGF	TGA	PGA	+/–	GP	G	A	Pts	PIM	PP	SH	GW
1981-82	Providence College	ECAC	2	0	0	0	....	....	....	2	....	....	....	....	....	....	....	....	....	....	....	....	....	....	....	....	....	....
1982-83	Providence College	ECAC	43	4	17	21	....	....	....	68	....	....	....	....	....	....	....	....	....	....	....	....	....	....	....	....	....	....
1983-84	Providence College	ECAC	30	4	25	29	....	....	....	68	....	....	....	....	....	....	....	....	....	....	....	....	....	....	....	....	....	....
1984-85	Providence College	H.E.	35	6	18	24	....	....	....	32	....	....	....	....	....	....	....	....	....	....	....	....	....	....	....	....	....	....
	Winnipeg Jets	**NHL**	**1**	**0**	**0**	**0**	**0**	**0**	**0**	**0**	**0**	**0**	**0**	**2**	**0.0**	**2**	**1**	**1**	**1**	**+1**	**1**	**0**	**0**	**0**	**0**	**0**	**0**	**0**
1985-86	**Winnipeg Jets**	**NHL**	**18**	**0**	**0**	**0**	**0**	**0**	**0**	**48**	**0**	**0**	**0**	**8**	**0.0**	**9**	**0**	**14**	**4**	**–1**	**3**	**0**	**0**	**0**	**2**	**0**	**0**	**0**
	Sherbrooke Canadiens	AHL	24	1	18	9	....	....	....	75	....	....	....	....	....	....	....	....	....	....	....	....	....	....	....	....	....	....
1986-87	**Winnipeg Jets**	**NHL**	**3**	**0**	**0**	**0**	**0**	**0**	**0**	**12**	**0**	**0**	**0**	**2**	**0.0**	**2**	**0**	**6**	**0**	**–4**	....	....	....	....	....	....	....	....
	Sherbrooke Canadiens	AHL	54	5	14	19	....	....	....	104	....	....	....	....	....	....	....	....	....	....	10	2	5	7	25	....	....	....
1987-88	**Winnipeg Jets**	**NHL**	**70**	**6**	**17**	**23**	**5**	**12**	**17**	**182**	**2**	**0**	**1**	**92**	**6.5**	**66**	**26**	**72**	**19**	**–13**	**5**	**1**	**1**	**2**	**12**	**0**	**0**	**0**
1988-89	**Winnipeg Jets**	**NHL**	**66**	**1**	**14**	**15**	**1**	**10**	**11**	**226**	**1**	**0**	**0**	**72**	**1.4**	**62**	**3**	**115**	**33**	**–23**	....	....	....	....	....	....	....	....
1989-90	**Winnipeg Jets**	**NHL**	**49**	**3**	**6**	**9**	**3**	**4**	**7**	**136**	**0**	**0**	**1**	**57**	**5.3**	**51**	**1**	**42**	**12**	**+20**	**5**	**0**	**0**	**0**	**6**	**0**	**0**	**0**
	Moncton Hawks	AHL	3	0	2	2	....	....	....	2	....	....	....	....	....	....	....	....	....	....	....	....	....	....	....	....	....	....
1990-91	**Minnesota North Stars**	**NHL**	**16**	**0**	**1**	**1**	**0**	**1**	**1**	**14**	**0**	**0**	**0**	**15**	**0.0**	**16**	**2**	**20**	**6**	**0**	....	....	....	....	....	....	....	....
	Pittsburgh Penguins	**NHL**	**39**	**3**	**8**	**11**	**3**	**6**	**9**	**93**	**0**	**0**	**0**	**25**	**12.0**	**51**	**0**	**50**	**15**	**+16**	**19**	**0**	**3**	**3**	**49**	**0**	**0**	**0**
1991-92	**Pittsburgh Penguins**	**NHL**	**44**	**1**	**3**	**4**	**1**	**2**	**3**	**57**	**0**	**0**	**0**	**23**	**4.3**	**37**	**0**	**49**	**19**	**+7**	....	....	....	....	....	....	....	....
1992-93	**Tampa Bay Lightning**	**NHL**	**61**	**1**	**8**	**9**	**1**	**5**	**6**	**150**	**0**	**0**	**0**	**60**	**1.7**	**48**	**0**	**76**	**36**	**+8**	....	....	....	....	....	....	....	....
	Pittsburgh Penguins	**NHL**	**11**	**1**	**4**	**5**	**1**	**3**	**4**	**34**	**0**	**0**	**0**	**18**	**5.6**	**15**	**0**	**12**	**1**	**+4**	**11**	**1**	**2**	**3**	**16**	**0**	**0**	**0**
1993-94	**Pittsburgh Penguins**	**NHL**	**60**	**2**	**12**	**14**	**2**	**9**	**11**	**142**	**0**	**0**	**0**	**57**	**3.5**	**45**	**0**	**54**	**14**	**+5**	**5**	**0**	**2**	**2**	**16**	**0**	**0**	**0**
1994-95	**Pittsburgh Penguins**	**NHL**	**13**	**0**	**1**	**1**	**0**	**1**	**1**	**12**	**0**	**0**	**0**	**5**	**0.0**	**14**	**0**	**15**	**2**	**+1**	**4**	**0**	**0**	**0**	**2**	**0**	**0**	**0**
	Cleveland Lumberjacks	IHL	3	0	1	1	....	....	....	7	....	....	....	....	....	....	....	....	....	....	4	0	0	0	19	....	....	....
1995-96	Providence Bruins	AHL	34	0	6	6	....	....	....	44	....	....	....	....	....	....	....	....	....	....	....	....	....	....	....	....	....	....
	NHL Totals		**451**	**18**	**74**	**92**	**17**	**53**	**70**	**1106**	**3**	**0**	**2**	**436**	**4.1**	**418**	**33**	**526**	**162**		**53**	**2**	**8**	**10**	**103**	**0**	**0**	**0**

ECAC Second All-Star Team (1984) • Hockey East First All-Star Team (1985)

Traded to **Minnesota** by **Winnipeg** for future considerations, September 30, 1990. Traded to **Pittsburgh** by **Minnesota** with Larry Murphy for Chris Dahlquist and Jim Johnson, December 11, 1990. Claimed by **Tampa Bay** from **Pittsburgh** in Expansion Draft, June 18, 1992. Traded to **Pittsburgh** by **Tampa Bay** for Pittsburgh's 3rd round choice (later traded to Florida — Florida selected Steve Washburn) in 1993 Entry Draft, March 22, 1993. Signed as a free agent by **Boston**, August 9, 1995.

• TALAFOUS, DEAN

Dean Talafous RW – R. 6'4", 180 lbs. b: Duluth, MN, 8/25/1953. Atlanta's 4th choice, 53rd overall, in 1973 Amateur Draft.

Season	Club	League	GP	G	A	Pts	AG	AA	APts	PIM	PP	SH	GW	S	%	TGF	PGF	TGA	PGA	+/–	GP	G	A	Pts	PIM	PP	SH	GW
1971-72	University of Wisconsin	WCHA	37	10	24	34	....	....	....	42	....	....	....	....	....	....	....	....	....	....	....	....	....	....	....	....	....	....
1972-73	University of Wisconsin	WCHA	38	18	31	49	....	....	....	34	....	....	....	....	....	....	....	....	....	....	....	....	....	....	....	....	....	....
	United States	Nat-Team	7	2	8	10	....	....	....	....	....	....	....	....	....	....	....	....	....	....	....	....	....	....	....	....	....	....
1973-74	University of Wisconsin	WCHA	34	17	29	46	....	....	....	29	....	....	....	....	....	....	....	....	....	....	....	....	....	....	....	....	....	....
1974-75	**Atlanta Flames**	**NHL**	**18**	**1**	**4**	**5**	**1**	**3**	**4**	**13**	**0**	**0**	**0**	**22**	**4.5**	**13**	**3**	**17**	**0**	**–7**	....	....	....	....	....	....	....	....
	Omaha Knights	CHL	11	3	5	8	....	....	....	10	....	....	....	....	....	....	....	....	....	....	....	....	....	....	....	....	....	....
	Minnesota North Stars	**NHL**	**43**	**8**	**17**	**25**	**7**	**13**	**20**	**6**	**0**	**0**	**2**	**68**	**11.8**	**36**	**8**	**46**	**1**	**–17**	....	....	....	....	....	....	....	....
1975-76	**Minnesota North Stars**	**NHL**	**79**	**18**	**30**	**48**	**17**	**24**	**41**	**18**	**4**	**1**	**2**	**137**	**13.1**	**78**	**23**	**67**	**0**	**–12**	....	....	....	....	....	....	....	....
1976-77	United States	C Cup	5	2	2	4	....	....	....	8	....	....	....	....	....	....	....	....	....	....	....	....	....	....	....	....	....	....
	Minnesota North Stars	**NHL**	**80**	**22**	**27**	**49**	**21**	**22**	**43**	**10**	**9**	**0**	**2**	**185**	**11.9**	**87**	**44**	**72**	**0**	**–29**	**2**	**0**	**0**	**0**	**0**	**0**	**0**	**0**
1977-78	**Minnesota North Stars**	**NHL**	**75**	**13**	**16**	**29**	**13**	**13**	**26**	**25**	**2**	**0**	**2**	**80**	**16.3**	**51**	**13**	**55**	**1**	**–16**	....	....	....	....	....	....	....	....
1978-79	**New York Rangers**	**NHL**	**68**	**13**	**16**	**29**	**12**	**12**	**24**	**29**	**2**	**2**	**3**	**88**	**14.8**	**45**	**6**	**53**	**19**	**+5**	....	....	....	....	....	....	....	....
1979-80	**New York Rangers**	**NHL**	**55**	**10**	**20**	**30**	**9**	**15**	**24**	**26**	**4**	**0**	**0**	**69**	**14.5**	**49**	**15**	**44**	**11**	**+1**	**5**	**1**	**2**	**3**	**9**	**1**	**0**	**0**
1980-81	**New York Rangers**	**NHL**	**50**	**13**	**17**	**30**	**11**	**12**	**23**	**28**	**1**	**2**	**0**	**73**	**17.8**	**45**	**4**	**49**	**10**	**+2**	**14**	**3**	**5**	**8**	**2**	**0**	**0**	**0**
1981-82	United States	C Cup	6	3	2	5	....	....	....	0	....	....	....	....	....	....	....	....	....	....	....	....	....	....	....	....	....	....
	New York Rangers	**NHL**	**29**	**6**	**7**	**13**	**5**	**5**	**10**	**8**	**1**	**0**	**2**	**33**	**18.2**	**21**	**3**	**25**	**4**	**–3**	....	....	....	....	....	....	....	....
	NHL Totals		**497**	**104**	**154**	**258**	**96**	**119**	**215**	**163**	**23**	**5**	**13**	**755**	**13.8**	**425**	**119**	**428**	**46**		**21**	**4**	**7**	**11**	**11**	**1**	**0**	**0**

NCAA Championship All-Tournament Team (1973) • NCAA Championship Tournament MVP (1973)

Traded to **Minnesota** by **Atlanta** with Dwight Bialowas for Barry Gibbs, January 3, 1975. Signed as a free agent by **NY Rangers**, July 17, 1978.

			REGULAR SEASON																		PLAYOFFS							
Season	Club	League	GP	G	A	Pts	AG	AA	APts	PIM	PP	SH	GW	S	%	TGF	PGF	TGA	PGA	+/-	GP	G	A	Pts	PIM	PP	SH	GW

• TALAKOSKI, RON

Ron Talakoski RW – R. 6'3", 220 lbs. b: Thunder Bay, Ont., 6/1/1962.

Season	Club	League	GP	G	A	Pts	AG	AA	APts	PIM	PP	SH	GW	S	%	TGF	PGF	TGA	PGA	+/-	GP	G	A	Pts	PIM	PP	SH	GW
1982-83	University of Manitoba	GPAC	31	12	11	23	....	....	....	51	....	....	....	....	....	....	....	....	....	....	....	....	....	....	....	....	....	....
1983-84	University of Manitoba	GPAC	DID NOT PLAY																									
1984-85	University of Manitoba	GPAC	11	4	4	8	....	....	....	77	....	....	....	....	....	....	....	....	....	....	....	....	....	....	....	....	....	....
1985-86	University of Manitoba	GPAC	DID NOT PLAY																									
1986-87	**New York Rangers**	**NHL**	3	0	0	0	0	0	0	21	0	0	0	1	0.0	2	0	1	0	+1	....	....	....	....	....	....	....	....
	New Haven Nighthawks	AHL	26	2	2	4	....	....	....	58	....	....	....	....	....	....	....	....	....	....	1	0	0	0	0	....	....	....
	Flint Spirits	IHL	3	2	1	3	....	....	....	12	....	....	....	....	....	....	....	....	....	....	....	....	....	....	....	....	....	....
1987-88	**New York Rangers**	**NHL**	6	0	1	1	0	1	1	12	0	0	0	6	0.0	3	0	3	0	0	....	....	....	....	....	....	....	....
	Colorado Rangers	IHL	62	24	19	43	....	....	....	104	....	....	....	....	....	....	....	....	....	....	10	1	4	5	17	....	....	....
	NHL Totals		9	0	1	1	0	1	1	33	0	0	0	7	0.0	5	0	4	0		....	....	....	....	....	....	....	....

Signed as a free agent by **NY Rangers**, October 3, 1986.

• TALBOT, JEAN-GUY

Jean-Guy Talbot D – L. 5'11", 170 lbs. b: Cap de La Madeliene, Que., 7/11/1932.

Season	Club	League	GP	G	A	Pts	AG	AA	APts	PIM	PP	SH	GW	S	%	TGF	PGF	TGA	PGA	+/-	GP	G	A	Pts	PIM	PP	SH	GW
1949-50	Trois-Rivieres Reds	QJHL	36	3	4	7	....	....	....	79	....	....	....	....	....	....	....	....	....	....	9	0	3	3	12	....	....	....
1950-51	Trois-Rivieres Flambeaux	QJHL	44	7	22	29	....	....	....	*136	....	....	....	....	....	....	....	....	....	....	8	0	1	1	18	....	....	....
	Shawinigan Cataracts	QSHL	1	0	0	0	....	....	....	0	....	....	....	....	....	....	....	....	....	....	....	....	....	....	....	....	....	....
1951-52	Trois-Rivieres Flambeaux	QJHL	43	12	36	48	....	....	....	132	....	....	....	....	....	....	....	....	....	....	4	1	0	1	12	....	....	....
1952-53	Quebec Aces	QSHL	24	2	4	6	....	....	....	33	....	....	....	....	....	....	....	....	....	....	....	....	....	....	....	....	....	....
1953-54	Quebec Aces	QHL	67	9	11	20	....	....	....	58	....	....	....	....	....	....	....	....	....	....	23	2	2	4	14	....	....	....
1954-55	**Montreal Canadiens**	**NHL**	3	0	1	1	0	1	1	0	....	....	....	....	....	....	....	....	....	....	....	....	....	....	....	....	....	....
	Shawinigan Cataracts	QHL	59	6	28	34	....	....	....	82	....	....	....	....	....	....	....	....	....	....	13	2	5	7	14	....	....	....
1955-56	**Montreal Canadiens**	**NHL**	66	1	13	14	1	16	17	80	....	....	....	....	....	....	....	....	....	....	9	0	2	2	4	....	....	....
1956-57	**Montreal Canadiens**	**NHL**	59	0	13	13	0	15	15	70	....	....	....	....	....	....	....	....	....	....	10	0	2	2	10	....	....	....
1957-58	**Montreal Canadiens**	**NHL**	55	4	15	19	5	16	21	65	....	....	....	....	....	....	....	....	....	....	10	0	3	3	12	....	....	....
1958-59	**Montreal Canadiens**	**NHL**	69	4	17	21	5	18	23	77	....	....	....	....	....	....	....	....	....	....	11	0	1	1	10	....	....	....
1959-60	**Montreal Canadiens**	**NHL**	69	1	14	15	1	14	15	60	....	....	....	....	....	....	....	....	....	....	8	1	1	2	8	....	....	....
1960-61	**Montreal Canadiens**	**NHL**	70	5	26	31	6	26	32	143	....	....	....	....	....	....	....	....	....	....	6	1	1	2	10	....	....	....
1961-62	**Montreal Canadiens**	**NHL**	70	5	42	47	6	43	49	90	....	....	....	....	....	....	....	....	....	....	6	1	1	2	10	....	....	....
1962-63	**Montreal Canadiens**	**NHL**	70	3	22	25	4	23	27	51	....	....	....	....	....	....	....	....	....	....	5	0	0	0	8	....	....	....
1963-64	**Montreal Canadiens**	**NHL**	66	1	13	14	1	14	15	83	....	....	....	....	....	....	....	....	....	....	7	0	2	2	10	....	....	....
1964-65	**Montreal Canadiens**	**NHL**	67	8	14	22	10	15	25	64	....	....	....	....	....	....	....	....	....	....	13	0	1	1	22	....	....	....
1965-66	**Montreal Canadiens**	**NHL**	59	1	14	15	1	14	15	50	....	....	....	....	....	....	....	....	....	....	10	0	2	2	8	....	....	....
1966-67	**Montreal Canadiens**	**NHL**	68	3	5	8	4	5	9	51	....	....	....	....	....	....	....	....	....	....	10	0	0	0	0	....	....	....
1967-68	**Minnesota North Stars**	**NHL**	4	0	0	0	0	0	0	4	0	0	0	7	0.0	2	0	9	1	–6	....	....	....	....	....	....	....	....
	Detroit Red Wings	**NHL**	32	0	3	3	0	3	3	10	0	0	0	11	0.0	13	0	26	13	0	....	....	....	....	....	....	....	....
	St. Louis Blues	**NHL**	23	0	4	4	0	4	4	2	0	0	0	29	0.0	19	1	21	6	+3	17	0	2	2	8	0	0	0
1968-69	**St. Louis Blues**	**NHL**	69	5	4	9	6	4	10	24	0	0	1	67	7.5	41	2	49	19	+9	12	0	2	2	6	0	0	0
1969-70	**St. Louis Blues**	**NHL**	75	2	15	17	2	15	17	40	0	1	0	60	3.3	62	7	46	9	+18	16	1	6	7	16	0	0	0
1970-71	**St. Louis Blues**	**NHL**	5	0	0	0	0	0	0	6	0	0	0	3	0.0	1	0	4	0	–3	....	....	....	....	....	....	....	....
	Buffalo Sabres	**NHL**	57	0	7	7	0	6	6	36	0	0	0	41	0.0	41	2	73	14	–20	....	....	....	....	....	....	....	....
	NHL Totals		1056	43	242	285	52	252	304	1006	0	1	1	218	19.7	179	12	228	62		150	4	26	30	142	0	0	0

QHL First All-Star Team (1955) • NHL First All-Star Team (1962)

Played in NHL All-Star Game (1956, 1957, 1958, 1960, 1962, 1965, 1967)

Claimed by **Minnesota** from **Montreal** in Expansion Draft, June 6, 1967. Traded to **Detroit** by **Minnesota** for Bob McCord, October 19, 1967. Claimed on waivers by **St. Louis** from **Detroit**, January 13, 1968. Traded to **Buffalo** by **St. Louis** with Larry Keenan for Bob Baun, November 4, 1970.

• TALLON, DALE

Dale Tallon D – L. 6'1", 195 lbs. b: Noranda, Que., 10/19/1950. Vancouver's 1st choice, 2nd overall, in 1970 Amateur Draft.

Season	Club	League	GP	G	A	Pts	AG	AA	APts	PIM	PP	SH	GW	S	%	TGF	PGF	TGA	PGA	+/-	GP	G	A	Pts	PIM	PP	SH	GW
1967-68	Oshawa Generals	OHA	50	12	31	43	....	....	....	88	....	....	....	....	....	....	....	....	....	....	....	....	....	....	....	....	....	....
1968-69	Toronto Marlboros	OHA	48	17	32	49	....	....	....	80	....	....	....	....	....	....	....	....	....	....	6	6	2	8	8	....	....	....
1969-70	Toronto Marlboros	OHA	54	39	40	79	....	....	....	128	....	....	....	....	....	....	....	....	....	....	....	....	....	....	....	....	....	....
1970-71	**Vancouver Canucks**	**NHL**	78	14	42	56	15	37	52	58	5	0	1	232	6.0	134	48	124	13	–25	....	....	....	....	....	....	....	....
1971-72	**Vancouver Canucks**	**NHL**	69	17	27	44	18	25	43	78	11	0	1	240	7.1	84	27	92	11	–24	....	....	....	....	....	....	....	....
1972-73	Canada	Summit	DID NOT PLAY																									
	Vancouver Canucks	**NHL**	75	13	24	37	13	20	33	83	5	0	1	170	7.6	102	29	128	25	–30	....	....	....	....	....	....	....	....
1973-74	**Chicago Black Hawks**	**NHL**	65	15	19	34	15	16	31	36	3	0	3	98	15.3	43	8	24	1	+12	11	1	3	4	29	1	0	0
1974-75	**Chicago Black Hawks**	**NHL**	35	5	10	15	5	8	13	28	0	0	0	34	14.7	25	6	18	3	+4	8	1	3	4	4	0	0	0
	Dallas Black Hawks	CHL	7	1	4	5	....	....	....	14	....	....	....	....	....	....	....	....	....	....	....	....	....	....	....	....	....	....
1975-76	**Chicago Black Hawks**	**NHL**	80	15	47	62	14	37	51	101	7	1	5	161	9.3	141	49	130	27	–11	4	0	1	1	8	0	0	0
1976-77	**Chicago Black Hawks**	**NHL**	70	5	16	21	5	13	18	65	1	0	0	107	4.7	74	15	101	21	–21	2	0	1	1	0	0	0	0
1977-78	**Chicago Black Hawks**	**NHL**	75	4	20	24	4	16	20	66	2	1	2	93	4.3	61	4	70	16	+3	4	0	2	2	0	0	0	0
1978-79	**Pittsburgh Penguins**	**NHL**	63	5	24	29	5	18	23	35	2	0	3	91	5.5	83	18	101	21	–15	....	....	....	....	....	....	....	....
1979-80	**Pittsburgh Penguins**	**NHL**	32	5	9	14	5	7	12	18	4	0	1	46	10.9	25	12	24	7	–4	4	0	0	0	4	0	0	0
	Syracuse Firebirds	AHL	6	0	1	1	....	....	....	4	....	....	....	....	....	....	....	....	....	....	....	....	....	....	....	....	....	....
	NHL Totals		642	98	238	336	99	197	296	568	40	2	17	1272	7.7	772	216	812	145		33	2	10	12	45	1	0	0

Played in NHL All-Star Game (1971, 1972)

Traded to **Chicago** by **Vancouver** for Jerry Korab and Gary Smith, May 14, 1973. Traded to **Pittsburgh** by **Chicago** for Pittsburgh's 2nd round choice (Ken Solheim) in 1980 Entry Draft, October 9, 1978. Claimed by **Pittsburgh** as a fill-in during Expansion Draft, June 13, 1979.

• TAMBELLINI, STEVE

Steve Tambellini C – L. 6', 190 lbs. b: Trail, B.C., 5/14/1958. NY Islanders' 1st choice, 15th overall, in 1978 Amateur Draft.

Season	Club	League	GP	G	A	Pts	AG	AA	APts	PIM	PP	SH	GW	S	%	TGF	PGF	TGA	PGA	+/-	GP	G	A	Pts	PIM	PP	SH	GW
1975-76	Lethbridge Broncos	WCJHL	72	38	59	97	....	....	....	42	....	....	....	....	....	....	....	....	....	....	7	3	6	9	2	....	....	....
1976-77	Lethbridge Broncos	WCJHL	55	42	42	84	....	....	....	23	....	....	....	....	....	....	....	....	....	....	15	10	11	21	0	....	....	....
1977-78	Lethbridge Broncos	WCJHL	66	75	80	155	....	....	....	32	....	....	....	....	....	....	....	....	....	....	8	10	5	15	5	....	....	....
	Canada	WJC-A	6	2	2	4	....	....	....	0	....	....	....	....	....	....	....	....	....	....	....	....	....	....	....	....	....	....
1978-79	**New York Islanders**	**NHL**	1	0	0	0	0	0	0	0	0	0	0	3	0.0	0	0	1	0	–1	....	....	....	....	....	....	....	....
	Fort Worth Texans	CHL	73	25	27	52	....	....	....	32	....	....	....	....	....	....	....	....	....	....	5	0	1	1	0	....	....	....
1979-80	**New York Islanders**	**NHL**	45	5	8	13	5	6	11	4	0	0	0	63	7.9	21	1	21	0	–1	....	....	....	....	....	....	....	....
1980-81	**New York Islanders**	**NHL**	61	19	17	36	16	12	28	17	2	0	4	112	17.0	49	11	51	1	–12	....	....	....	....	....	....	....	....
	Colorado Rockies	**NHL**	13	6	12	18	5	8	13	2	2	0	1	33	18.2	22	7	16	0	–1	....	....	....	....	....	....	....	....
	Canada	WEC-A	8	0	3	3	....	....	....	4	....	....	....	....	....	....	....	....	....	....	....	....	....	....	....	....	....	....
1981-82	**Colorado Rockies**	**NHL**	79	29	30	59	23	20	43	14	9	0	0	185	15.7	83	24	93	1	–33	....	....	....	....	....	....	....	....
1982-83	**New Jersey Devils**	**NHL**	73	25	18	43	21	12	33	14	6	1	4	153	16.3	67	19	82	7	–27	....	....	....	....	....	....	....	....
1983-84	**Calgary Flames**	**NHL**	73	15	10	25	12	7	19	16	1	0	2	99	15.2	40	1	47	0	–8	2	0	1	1	0	0	0	0
1984-85	**Calgary Flames**	**NHL**	47	19	10	29	16	7	23	4	1	2	2	103	18.4	39	1	40	10	+8	....	....	....	....	....	....	....	....
	Moncton Golden Flames	AHL	7	2	5	7	....	....	....	0	....	....	....	....	....	....	....	....	....	....	....	....	....	....	....	....	....	....
1985-86	**Vancouver Canucks**	**NHL**	48	15	15	30	12	10	22	12	6	0	2	89	16.9	36	14	40	0	–18	....	....	....	....	....	....	....	....
1986-87	**Vancouver Canucks**	**NHL**	72	16	20	36	14	14	28	14	9	0	0	162	9.9	67	49	41	1	–22	....	....	....	....	....	....	....	....
1987-88	**Vancouver Canucks**	**NHL**	41	11	10	21	9	7	16	8	3	1	1	91	12.1	32	15	39	5	–17	....	....	....	....	....	....	....	....
	Canada	Olympics	8	1	3	4	....	....	....	2	....	....	....	....	....	....	....	....	....	....	....	....	....	....	....	....	....	....
	NHL Totals		553	160	150	310	133	103	236	105	39	4	16	1093	14.6	456	142	471	25		2	0	1	1	0	0	0	0

Traded to **Colorado** by **NY Islanders** with Glenn Resch for Mike McEwen and Jari Kaarela, March 10, 1981. Transferred to **New Jersey** after **Colorado** franchise relocated, June 30, 1982. Traded to **Calgary** by **New Jersey** with Joel Quenneville for Mel Bridgeman and Phil Russell, June 20, 1983. Signed as a free agent by **Vancouver**, August 28, 1985.

• TAMER, CHRIS

Chris Tamer D – L. 6'2", 212 lbs. b: Dearborn, MI, 11/17/1970. Pittsburgh's 3rd choice, 68th overall, in 1990 Entry Draft.

Season	Club	League	GP	G	A	Pts	AG	AA	APts	PIM	PP	SH	GW	S	%	TGF	PGF	TGA	PGA	+/-	GP	G	A	Pts	PIM	PP	SH	GW
1989-90	University of Michigan	CCHA	42	2	7	9	....	....	....	147	....	....	....	....	....	....	....	....	....	....	....	....	....	....	....	....	....	....
1990-91	University of Michigan	CCHA	45	8	19	27	....	....	....	130	....	....	....	....	....	....	....	....	....	....	....	....	....	....	....	....	....	....
1991-92	University of Michigan	CCHA	43	4	15	19	....	....	....	125	....	....	....	....	....	....	....	....	....	....	....	....	....	....	....	....	....	....
1992-93	University of Michigan	CCHA	39	5	18	23	....	....	....	113	....	....	....	....	....	....	....	....	....	....	....	....	....	....	....	....	....	....
1993-94	**Pittsburgh Penguins**	**NHL**	12	0	0	0	0	0	0	9	0	0	0	10	0.0	7	0	5	1	+3	5	0	0	0	2	0	0	0
	Cleveland Lumberjacks	IHL	53	1	2	3	....	....	....	160	....	....	....	....	....	....	....	....	....	....	....	....	....	....	....	....	....	....

			REGULAR SEASON																		PLAYOFFS							
Season	Club	League	GP	G	A	Pts	AG	AA	APts	PIM	PP	SH	GW	S	%	TGF	PGF	TGA	PGA	+/–	GP	G	A	Pts	PIM	PP	SH	GW
1994-95	Cleveland Lumberjacks	IHL	48	4	10	14	....	....	....	204	....	....	....	....	....	....	....	....	....	....	....	....	....	....	....	....	....	....
	Pittsburgh Penguins	**NHL**	**36**	**2**	**0**	**2**	**4**	**0**	**4**	**82**	**0**	**0**	**0**	**26**	**7.7**	**18**	**0**	**22**	**4**	**0**	**4**	**0**	**0**	**0**	**18**	**0**	**0**	**0**
1995-96	**Pittsburgh Penguins**	**NHL**	**70**	**4**	**10**	**14**	**4**	**8**	**12**	**153**	**0**	**0**	**1**	**75**	**5.3**	**82**	**2**	**89**	**29**	**+20**	**18**	**0**	**7**	**7**	**24**	**0**	**0**	**0**
1996-97	**Pittsburgh Penguins**	**NHL**	**45**	**2**	**4**	**6**	**2**	**4**	**6**	**131**	**0**	**1**	**0**	**56**	**3.6**	**26**	**0**	**61**	**10**	**–25**	**4**	**0**	**0**	**0**	**4**	**0**	**0**	**0**
1997-98	**Pittsburgh Penguins**	**NHL**	**79**	**0**	**7**	**7**	**0**	**7**	**7**	**181**	**0**	**0**	**0**	**55**	**0.0**	**36**	**1**	**45**	**14**	**+4**	**6**	**0**	**1**	**1**	**4**	**0**	**0**	**0**
	NHL Totals		**242**	**8**	**21**	**29**	**10**	**19**	**29**	**556**	**0**	**1**	**1**	**222**	**3.6**	**169**	**3**	**222**	**58**		**37**	**0**	**8**	**8**	**52**	**0**	**0**	**0**

• TANCILL, CHRIS

Chris Tancill C – L. 5'10", 185 lbs. b: Livonia, MI, 2/7/1968. Hartford's 1st choice, 15th overall, in 1989 Supplemental Draft.

Season	Club	League	GP	G	A	Pts	AG	AA	APts	PIM	PP	SH	GW	S	%	TGF	PGF	TGA	PGA	+/–	GP	G	A	Pts	PIM	PP	SH	GW
1986-87	University of Wisconsin	WCHA	40	9	23	32	....	....	....	26	....	....	....	....	....	....	....	....	....	....	....	....	....	....	....	....	....	....
1987-88	University of Wisconsin	WCHA	44	13	14	27	....	....	....	48	....	....	....	....	....	....	....	....	....	....	....	....	....	....	....	....	....	....
1988-89	University of Wisconsin	WCHA	44	20	23	43	....	....	....	50	....	....	....	....	....	....	....	....	....	....	....	....	....	....	....	....	....	....
1989-90	University of Wisconsin	WCHA	45	39	32	71	....	....	....	44	....	....	....	....	....	....	....	....	....	....	....	....	....	....	....	....	....	....
1990-91	**Hartford Whalers**	**NHL**	**9**	**1**	**1**	**2**	**1**	**1**	**2**	**4**	**0**	**1**	**0**	**6**	**16.7**	**5**	**0**	**3**	**0**	**+2**	....	....	....	....	....	....	....	....
	Springfield Indians	AHL	72	37	35	72	....	....	....	46	....	....	....	....	....	....	....	....	....	....	17	8	4	12	32	....	....	....
1991-92	**Hartford Whalers**	**NHL**	**10**	**0**	**0**	**0**	**0**	**0**	**0**	**2**	**0**	**0**	**0**	**13**	**0.0**	**3**	**0**	**9**	**0**	**–6**	....	....	....	....	....	....	....	....
	Springfield Indians	AHL	17	12	7	19	....	....	....	20	....	....	....	....	....	....	....	....	....	....	....	....	....	....	....	....	....	....
	Detroit Red Wings	**NHL**	**1**	**0**	**0**	**0**	**0**	**0**	**0**	**0**	**0**	**0**	**0**	**0**	**0.0**	**0**	**0**	**0**	**0**	**0**	....	....	....	....	....	....	....	....
	Adirondack Red Wings	AHL	50	36	34	70	....	....	....	42	....	....	....	....	....	....	....	....	....	....	19	7	9	16	31	....	....	....
1992-93	**Detroit Red Wings**	**NHL**	**4**	**1**	**0**	**1**	**1**	**0**	**1**	**2**	**0**	**0**	**0**	**3**	**33.3**	**1**	**0**	**4**	**1**	**–2**	....	....	....	....	....	....	....	....
	Adirondack Red Wings	AHL	68	*59	43	102	....	....	....	62	....	....	....	....	....	....	....	....	....	....	10	7	7	14	10	....	....	....
1993-94	**Dallas Stars**	**NHL**	**12**	**1**	**3**	**4**	**1**	**2**	**3**	**8**	**0**	**0**	**0**	**18**	**5.6**	**9**	**5**	**11**	**0**	**–7**	....	....	....	....	....	....	....	....
	Kalamazoo Wings	IHL	60	41	54	95	....	....	....	55	....	....	....	....	....	....	....	....	....	....	5	0	2	2	8	....	....	....
1994-95	Kansas City Blades	IHL	64	31	28	59	....	....	....	40	....	....	....	....	....	....	....	....	....	....	....	....	....	....	....	....	....	....
	San Jose Sharks	**NHL**	**26**	**3**	**11**	**14**	**5**	**16**	**21**	**10**	**0**	**1**	**0**	**39**	**7.7**	**15**	**0**	**19**	**5**	**+1**	**11**	**1**	**1**	**2**	**8**	**0**	**0**	**0**
1995-96	**San Jose Sharks**	**NHL**	**45**	**7**	**16**	**23**	**7**	**13**	**20**	**20**	**0**	**1**	**0**	**93**	**7.5**	**30**	**2**	**55**	**15**	**–12**	....	....	....	....	....	....	....	....
	Kansas City Blades	IHL	27	12	16	28	....	....	....	18	....	....	....	....	....	....	....	....	....	....	....	....	....	....	....	....	....	....
	United States	WC-A	7	5	2	7	....	....	....	10	....	....	....	....	....	....	....	....	....	....	....	....	....	....	....	....	....	....
1996-97	**San Jose Sharks**	**NHL**	**25**	**4**	**0**	**4**	**4**	**0**	**4**	**8**	**1**	**0**	**0**	**20**	**20.0**	**5**	**1**	**10**	**1**	**–5**	....	....	....	....	....	....	....	....
	Kentucky Thoroughblades	AHL	42	19	26	45	....	....	....	31	....	....	....	....	....	....	....	....	....	....	4	2	0	2	2	....	....	....
	United States	WC-A	8	2	3	5	....	....	....	2	....	....	....	....	....	....	....	....	....	....	....	....	....	....	....	....	....	....
1997-98	**Dallas Stars**	**NHL**	**2**	**0**	**1**	**1**	**0**	**1**	**1**	**0**	**0**	**0**	**0**	**1**	**0.0**	**1**	**0**	**2**	**0**	**–1**	....	....	....	....	....	....	....	....
	Michigan K-Wings	IHL	70	30	39	69	....	....	....	86	....	....	....	....	....	....	....	....	....	....	4	3	0	3	14	....	....	....
	NHL Totals		**134**	**17**	**32**	**49**	**19**	**33**	**52**	**54**	**1**	**3**	**0**	**193**	**8.8**	**69**	**8**	**113**	**22**		**11**	**1**	**1**	**2**	**8**	**0**	**0**	**0**

NCAA Championship All-Tournament Team (1990) • NCAA Championship Tournament MVP (1990) • AHL First All-Star Team (1992, 1993)

Traded to **Detroit** by **Hartford** for Daniel Shank, December 18, 1991. Signed as a free agent by **Dallas**, August 28, 1993. Signed as a free agent by **San Jose**, August 24, 1994. Signed as a free agent by **Dallas**, August 6, 1997.

• TANGUAY, CHRIS

Chris Tanguay RW – R. 5'10", 190 lbs. b: Beauport, Que., 8/4/1962. Quebec's 7th choice, 171st overall, in 1980 Entry Draft.

Season	Club	League	GP	G	A	Pts	AG	AA	APts	PIM	PP	SH	GW	S	%	TGF	PGF	TGA	PGA	+/–	GP	G	A	Pts	PIM	PP	SH	GW
1979-80	Trois-Rivieres Draveurs	QJHL	65	24	20	44	....	....	....	39	....	....	....	....	....	....	....	....	....	....	7	3	2	5	6	....	....	....
1980-81	Trois-Rivieres Draveurs	QJHL	72	45	39	84	....	....	....	34	....	....	....	....	....	....	....	....	....	....	19	12	8	20	27	....	....	....
1981-82	Trois-Rivieres Draveurs	QJHL	59	52	55	107	....	....	....	27	....	....	....	....	....	....	....	....	....	....	24	16	13	29	11	....	....	....
	Quebec Nordiques	**NHL**	**2**	**0**	**0**	**0**	**0**	**0**	**0**	**0**	**0**	**0**	**0**	**0**	**0.0**	**0**	**0**	**0**	**0**	**0**	....	....	....	....	....	....	....	....
1982-83	Fredericton Express	AHL	48	6	7	13	....	....	....	4	....	....	....	....	....	....	....	....	....	....	....	....	....	....	....	....	....	....
	Milwaukee Admirals	IHL	14	8	11	19	....	....	....	6	....	....	....	....	....	....	....	....	....	....	....	....	....	....	....	....	....	....
1983-84	Fredericton Express	AHL	3	2	0	2	....	....	....	0	....	....	....	....	....	....	....	....	....	....	....	....	....	....	....	....	....	....
	Milwaukee Admirals	IHL	74	44	50	94	....	....	....	23	....	....	....	....	....	....	....	....	....	....	4	0	2	2	0	....	....	....
1984-85	Muskegon Mohawks	IHL	19	1	8	9	....	....	....	9	....	....	....	....	....	....	....	....	....	....	....	....	....	....	....	....	....	....
	Rimouski Mariners	RHL	6	10	8	18	....	....	....	....	....	....	....	....	....	....	....	....	....	....	....	....	....	....	....	....	....	....
1985-86	Rimouski Mariners	RHL	8	12	10	22	....	....	....	4	....	....	....	....	....	....	....	....	....	....	....	....	....	....	....	....	....	....
	Auronzo	Italy	24	35	49	84	....	....	....	10	....	....	....	....	....	....	....	....	....	....	4	2	1	3	2	....	....	....
1986-87	Milwaukee Admirals	IHL	3	0	0	0	....	....	....	0	....	....	....	....	....	....	....	....	....	....	....	....	....	....	....	....	....	....
	Riviere du Loup 3 L's	RHL	29	37	29	66	....	....	....	4	....	....	....	....	....	....	....	....	....	....	12	*12	12	*24	....	....	....	....
	NHL Totals		**2**	**0**	**0**	**0**	**0**	**0**	**0**	**0**	**0**	**0**	**0**	**0**	**0.0**	**0**	**0**	**0**	**0**		....	....	....	....	....	....	....	....

IHL Second All-Star Team (1984)

• TANNAHILL, DON

Don Tannahill LW – L. 5'11", 178 lbs. b: Penetang, Ont., 2/21/1949. Boston's 1st choice, 3rd overall, in 1969 Amateur Draft.

Season	Club	League	GP	G	A	Pts	AG	AA	APts	PIM	PP	SH	GW	S	%	TGF	PGF	TGA	PGA	+/–	GP	G	A	Pts	PIM	PP	SH	GW
1966-67	Niagara Falls Flyers	OHA	45	8	13	21	....	....	....	15	....	....	....	....	....	....	....	....	....	....	13	0	4	4	0	....	....	....
1967-68	Niagara Falls Flyers	OHA	54	29	49	78	....	....	....	30	....	....	....	....	....	....	....	....	....	....	18	7	11	18	18	....	....	....
1968-69	Niagara Falls Flyers	OHA	54	48	41	89	....	....	....	131	....	....	....	....	....	....	....	....	....	....	14	17	6	23	10	....	....	....
1969-70	Oklahoma City Blazers	CHL	27	10	12	22	....	....	....	14	....	....	....	....	....	....	....	....	....	....	....	....	....	....	....	....	....	....
1970-71	Oklahoma City Blazers	CHL	69	27	36	63	....	....	....	22	....	....	....	....	....	....	....	....	....	....	5	2	2	4	0	....	....	....
1971-72	Boston Braves	AHL	76	30	44	74	....	....	....	23	....	....	....	....	....	....	....	....	....	....	9	5	1	6	2	....	....	....
1972-73	**Vancouver Canucks**	**NHL**	**78**	**22**	**21**	**43**	**22**	**18**	**40**	**21**	**2**	**1**	**3**	**186**	**11.8**	**68**	**10**	**95**	**8**	**–29**	....	....	....	....	....	....	....	....
1973-74	**Vancouver Canucks**	**NHL**	**33**	**8**	**12**	**20**	**8**	**10**	**18**	**4**	**0**	**0**	**1**	**43**	**18.6**	**29**	**5**	**23**	**0**	**+1**	....	....	....	....	....	....	....	....
1974-75	Minnesota Fighting Saints	WHA	72	23	30	53	....	....	....	20	....	....	....	....	....	....	....	....	....	....	10	2	4	6	0	....	....	....
1975-76	Calgary Cowboys	WHA	78	25	24	49	....	....	....	10	....	....	....	....	....	....	....	....	....	....	10	2	5	7	8	....	....	....
1976-77	Calgary Cowboys	WHA	72	10	22	32	....	....	....	4	....	....	....	....	....	....	....	....	....	....	....	....	....	....	....	....	....	....
1977-78	Salt Lake Golden Eagles	CHL	7	3	3	6	....	....	....	0	....	....	....	....	....	....	....	....	....	....	....	....	....	....	....	....	....	....
	Barrie Flyers	OHA Sr.	23	10	16	26	....	....	....	0	....	....	....	....	....	....	....	....	....	....	....	....	....	....	....	....	....	....
	NHL Totals		**111**	**30**	**33**	**63**	**30**	**28**	**58**	**25**	**2**	**1**	**4**	**229**	**13.1**	**97**	**15**	**118**	**8**		....	....	....	....	....	....	....	....
	Other Major League Totals		222	58	76	134	....	....	....	34	....	....	....	....	....	....	....	....	....	....	20	4	9	13	8	....	....	....

OHA Second All-Star Team (1969) • AHL Second All-Star Team (1972)

Selected by **Chicago** (WHA) in 1972 WHA General Player Draft, February 12, 1972. Claimed by **Vancouver** from **Boston** in Intra-League Draft, June 5, 1972. WHA rights traded to **Minnesota** (WHA) by **Chicago** (WHA) for future considerations, June, 1974. Traded to **Calgary** (WHA) by **Minnesota** (WHA) with George Morrison and cash for John McKenzie, Wally Olds, and Joe Micheletti, September, 1975. Traded to **Edmonton** (WHA) by **Calgary** (WHA) for cash, August, 1977.

• TANTI, TONY

Tony Tanti RW – L. 5'9", 180 lbs. b: Toronto, Ont., 9/7/1963. Chicago's 1st choice, 12th overall, in 1981 Entry Draft.

Season	Club	League	GP	G	A	Pts	AG	AA	APts	PIM	PP	SH	GW	S	%	TGF	PGF	TGA	PGA	+/–	GP	G	A	Pts	PIM	PP	SH	GW
1979-80	St. Michael's Buzzers	Jr. B	37	31	27	58	....	....	....	67	....	....	....	....	....	....	....	....	....	....	....	....	....	....	....	....	....	....
1980-81	Oshawa Generals	OHA	67	81	69	150	....	....	....	197	....	....	....	....	....	....	....	....	....	....	11	7	8	15	41	....	....	....
1981-82	Oshawa Generals	OHL	57	62	64	126	....	....	....	138	....	....	....	....	....	....	....	....	....	....	12	14	12	26	15	....	....	....
	Chicago Black Hawks	**NHL**	**2**	**0**	**0**	**0**	**0**	**0**	**0**	**0**	**0**	**0**	**0**	**0**	**0.0**	**1**	**0**	**1**	**0**	**0**	....	....	....	....	....	....	....	....
1982-83	Oshawa Generals	OHL	30	34	28	62	....	....	....	35	....	....	....	....	....	....	....	....	....	....	....	....	....	....	....	....	....	....
	Chicago Black Hawks	**NHL**	**1**	**1**	**0**	**1**	**1**	**0**	**1**	**0**	**0**	**0**	**0**	**5**	**20.0**	**1**	**0**	**1**	**0**	**0**	....	....	....	....	....	....	....	....
	Vancouver Canucks	**NHL**	**39**	**8**	**8**	**16**	**7**	**6**	**13**	**16**	**4**	**0**	**0**	**81**	**9.9**	**30**	**10**	**29**	**0**	**–9**	**4**	**0**	**1**	**1**	**0**	**0**	**0**	**0**
1983-84	**Vancouver Canucks**	**NHL**	**79**	**45**	**41**	**86**	**36**	**28**	**64**	**50**	**19**	**1**	**6**	**247**	**18.2**	**123**	**48**	**95**	**8**	**–12**	**4**	**1**	**2**	**3**	**0**	**0**	**0**	**0**
1984-85	**Vancouver Canucks**	**NHL**	**68**	**39**	**20**	**59**	**32**	**14**	**46**	**45**	**14**	**0**	**4**	**212**	**18.4**	**90**	**29**	**95**	**13**	**–21**	....	....	....	....	....	....	....	....
	Canada	WEC-A	10	5	2	7	....	....	....	12	....	....	....	....	....	....	....	....	....	....	....	....	....	....	....	....	....	....
1985-86	**Vancouver Canucks**	**NHL**	**77**	**39**	**33**	**72**	**31**	**22**	**53**	**85**	**17**	**0**	**5**	**213**	**18.3**	**114**	**53**	**73**	**4**	**–8**	**3**	**0**	**1**	**1**	**11**	**0**	**0**	**0**
	Canada	WEC-A	8	5	3	8	....	....	....	22	....	....	....	....	....	....	....	....	....	....	....	....	....	....	....	....	....	....
1986-87	**Vancouver Canucks**	**NHL**	**77**	**41**	**38**	**79**	**36**	**28**	**64**	**84**	**15**	**0**	**7**	**242**	**16.9**	**113**	**40**	**75**	**7**	**+5**	....	....	....	....	....	....	....	....
	Canada	WEC-A	10	6	2	8	....	....	....	6	....	....	....	....	....	....	....	....	....	....	....	....	....	....	....	....	....	....
1987-88	**Vancouver Canucks**	**NHL**	**73**	**40**	**37**	**77**	**34**	**26**	**60**	**90**	**20**	**0**	**4**	**202**	**19.8**	**114**	**45**	**83**	**13**	**–1**	....	....	....	....	....	....	....	....
1988-89	**Vancouver Canucks**	**NHL**	**77**	**24**	**25**	**49**	**20**	**18**	**38**	**69**	**8**	**0**	**3**	**211**	**11.4**	**75**	**32**	**60**	**7**	**–10**	**7**	**0**	**5**	**5**	**4**	**0**	**0**	**0**
1989-90	**Vancouver Canucks**	**NHL**	**41**	**14**	**18**	**32**	**12**	**13**	**25**	**50**	**5**	**0**	**0**	**103**	**13.6**	**48**	**17**	**35**	**5**	**+1**	....	....	....	....	....	....	....	....
	Pittsburgh Penguins	**NHL**	**37**	**14**	**18**	**32**	**12**	**13**	**25**	**22**	**7**	**0**	**0**	**89**	**15.7**	**51**	**22**	**41**	**1**	**–11**	....	....	....	....	....	....	....	....
1990-91	**Pittsburgh Penguins**	**NHL**	**46**	**6**	**12**	**18**	**5**	**9**	**14**	**44**	**3**	**0**	**0**	**74**	**8.1**	**37**	**14**	**22**	**0**	**+1**	....	....	....	....	....	....	....	....
	Buffalo Sabres	**NHL**	**10**	**1**	**7**	**8**	**1**	**5**	**6**	**6**	**0**	**0**	**0**	**19**	**5.3**	**11**	**4**	**5**	**0**	**+2**	**5**	**2**	**0**	**2**	**8**	**1**	**0**	**0**
1991-92	**Buffalo Sabres**	**NHL**	**70**	**15**	**16**	**31**	**14**	**12**	**26**	**100**	**6**	**1**	**0**	**133**	**11.3**	**52**	**18**	**55**	**17**	**–4**	**7**	**0**	**3**	**3**	**4**	**0**	**0**	**0**
1992-93	Preussen Berlin	Germany	34	14	17	31	....	....	....	73	....	....	....	....	....	....	....	....	....	....	....	....	....	....	....	....	....	....
1993-94	Preussen Berlin	Germany	41	13	19	32	....	....	....	44	....	....	....	....	....	....	....	....	....	....	....	....	....	....	....	....	....	....
1994-95	Preussen Berlin	Germany	42	25	33	58	....	....	....	114	....	....	....	....	....	....	....	....	....	....	9	2	2	4	8	....	....	....

Season	Club	League	GP	G	A	Pts	AG	AA	APts	PIM	PP	SH	GW	S	%	TGF	PGF	TGA	PGA	+/-	GP	G	A	Pts	PIM	PP	SH	GW
							REGULAR SEASON														PLAYOFFS							
1995-96	Preussen Berlin	Germany	43	32	28	60	....	....	....	56	....	....	....	....	....	....	....	....	....	....	11	9	5	14	16	....	....	....
1996-97	Berlin Capitals	Germany	43	14	25	39	....	....	....	42	....	....	....	....	....	....	....	....	....	....	4	0	2	2	6	....	....	....
1997-98	Berlin Capitals	Germany	41	6	24	30	....	....	....	84	....	....	....	....	....	....	....	....	....	....	....	....	....	....	....	....	....	....
	NHL Totals		**697**	**287**	**273**	**560**	**241**	**194**	**435**	**661**	**118**	**2**	**29**	**1831**	**15.7**	**860**	**332**	**670**	**75**		**30**	**3**	**12**	**15**	**27**	**1**	**0**	**0**

OHA First All-Star Team (1981) • OHL Second All-Star Team (1982)

Played in NHL All-Star Game (1986)

Traded to **Vancouver** by **Chicago** for Curt Fraser, January 6, 1983. Traded to **Pittsburgh** by **Vancouver** with Rod Buskas and Barry Pederson for Dave Capuano, Andrew McBain and Dan Quinn, January 8, 1990. Traded to **Buffalo** by **Pittsburgh** for Ken Priestlay, March 5, 1991.

• TARDIF, MARC

Marc Tardif LW – L. 6', 195 lbs. b: Granby, Que., 6/12/1949. Montreal's 2nd choice, 2nd overall, in 1969 Amateur Draft.

Season	Club	League	GP	G	A	Pts	AG	AA	APts	PIM	PP	SH	GW	S	%	TGF	PGF	TGA	PGA	+/-	GP	G	A	Pts	PIM	PP	SH	GW
1966-67	Thetford Mines Canadiens	QJHL	....	36	44	80	....	....	....	....	....	....	....	....	....	....	....	....	....	....	....	....	....	....	....	....	....	....
1967-68	Montreal Jr. Canadiens	OHA	54	32	34	66	....	....	....	62	....	....	....	....	....	....	....	....	....	....	11	3	9	12	18	....	....	....
1968-69	Montreal Jr. Canadiens	OHA	51	31	41	72	....	....	....	121	....	....	....	....	....	....	....	....	....	....	14	19	12	31	60	....	....	....
1969-70	**Montreal Canadiens**	**NHL**	**18**	**3**	**2**	**5**	**3**	**2**	**5**	**27**	**1**	**0**	**0**	**25**	**12.0**	**10**	**4**	**6**	**0**	**0**	....	....	....	....	....	....	....	....
	Montreal Voyageurs	AHL	45	27	31	58	....	....	....	70	....	....	....	....	....	....	....	....	....	....	8	3	6	9	29	....	....	....
1970-71	**Montreal Canadiens**	**NHL**	**76**	**19**	**30**	**49**	**20**	**26**	**46**	**133**	**4**	**0**	**2**	**144**	**13.2**	**77**	**21**	**34**	**3**	**+25**	**20**	**3**	**1**	**4**	**40**	**0**	**0**	**0**
1971-72	**Montreal Canadiens**	**NHL**	**75**	**31**	**22**	**53**	**33**	**20**	**53**	**81**	**9**	**0**	**4**	**203**	**15.3**	**83**	**27**	**43**	**2**	**+15**	**6**	**2**	**3**	**5**	**9**	**0**	**0**	**1**
1972-73	**Montreal Canadiens**	**NHL**	**76**	**25**	**25**	**50**	**25**	**21**	**46**	**48**	**3**	**0**	**4**	**152**	**16.4**	**71**	**21**	**32**	**0**	**+18**	**14**	**6**	**6**	**12**	**6**	**2**	**0**	**2**
1973-74	Los Angeles Sharks	WHA	75	40	30	70	....	....	....	47	....	....	....	....	....	....	....	....	....	....	....	....	....	....	....	....	....	....
1974-75	Canada	Summit	5	0	2	2	....	....	....	10	....	....	....	....	....	....	....	....	....	....	....	....	....	....	....	....	....	....
	Michigan Stags	WHA	23	12	5	17	....	....	....	9	....	....	....	....	....	....	....	....	....	....	....	....	....	....	....	....	....	....
	Quebec Nordiques	WHA	53	38	34	72	....	....	....	70	....	....	....	....	....	....	....	....	....	....	15	*10	11	21	10	....	....	....
1975-76	Quebec Nordiques	WHA	81	*71	*77	*148	....	....	....	79	....	....	....	....	....	....	....	....	....	....	2	1	0	1	2	....	....	....
1976-77	Quebec Nordiques	WHA	62	49	60	109	....	....	....	65	....	....	....	....	....	....	....	....	....	....	12	4	10	14	8	....	....	....
1977-78	Quebec Nordiques	WHA	78	*65	*89	*154	....	....	....	50	....	....	....	....	....	....	....	....	....	....	11	6	9	15	11	....	....	....
1978-79	Quebec Nordiques	WHA	74	41	55	96	....	....	....	98	....	....	....	....	....	....	....	....	....	....	4	6	2	8	4	....	....	....
1979-80	**Quebec Nordiques**	**NHL**	**58**	**33**	**35**	**68**	**30**	**27**	**57**	**30**	**9**	**0**	**4**	**229**	**14.4**	**87**	**26**	**75**	**1**	**-13**	....	....	....	....	....	....	....	....
1980-81	**Quebec Nordiques**	**NHL**	**63**	**23**	**31**	**54**	**19**	**22**	**41**	**35**	**11**	**0**	**3**	**144**	**16.0**	**74**	**32**	**46**	**0**	**-4**	**5**	**1**	**3**	**4**	**2**	**0**	**0**	**0**
1981-82	**Quebec Nordiques**	**NHL**	**75**	**39**	**31**	**70**	**31**	**20**	**51**	**55**	**14**	**0**	**3**	**166**	**23.5**	**107**	**51**	**71**	**0**	**-15**	**13**	**1**	**2**	**3**	**16**	**0**	**0**	**0**
1982-83	**Quebec Nordiques**	**NHL**	**76**	**21**	**31**	**52**	**17**	**21**	**38**	**34**	**4**	**0**	**3**	**116**	**18.1**	**78**	**28**	**50**	**0**	**0**	**4**	**0**	**0**	**0**	**2**	**0**	**0**	**0**
	NHL Totals		**517**	**194**	**207**	**401**	**178**	**159**	**337**	**443**	**55**	**0**	**23**	**1179**	**16.5**	**587**	**210**	**357**	**6**		**62**	**13**	**15**	**28**	**75**	**2**	**0**	**3**
	Other Major League Totals		446	316	350	666	....	....	....	418	....	....	....	....	....	....	....	....	....	....	44	27	32	59	35	....	....	....

OHA First All-Star Team (1969) • WHA Second All-Star Team (1975) • WHA First All-Star Team (1976, 1977, 1978) • Won W. D. (Bill) Hunter Trophy (WHA Scoring Leader) (1976, 1978) • Won Gary Davidson Trophy (WHA MVP) (1976, 1978)

Played in NHL All-Star Game (1982)

Selected by **LA Sharks** (WHA) in 1972 WHA General Player Draft, February 12, 1972. Transferred to **Michigan** (WHA) after **LA Sharks** (WHA) franchise relocated, April 11, 1974. Traded to **Quebec** (WHA) by **Michigan** (WHA) with Steve Sutherland for Alain Caron, Pierre Guite and Michel Rouleau, December, 1974. Claimed by **Quebec** from **Montreal** in Expansion Draft, June 13, 1979.

• TARDIF, PATRICE

Patrice Tardif C – L. 6'2", 202 lbs. b: Thetford Mines, Que., 10/30/1970. St. Louis' 3rd choice, 54th overall, in 1990 Entry Draft.

Season	Club	League	GP	G	A	Pts	AG	AA	APts	PIM	PP	SH	GW	S	%	TGF	PGF	TGA	PGA	+/-	GP	G	A	Pts	PIM	PP	SH	GW
1989-90	Champlain Junior College	QCAA	27	58	36	94	....	....	....	36	....	....	....	....	....	....	....	....	....	....	....	....	....	....	....	....	....	....
1990-91	University of Maine	H.E.	36	13	12	25	....	....	....	10	....	....	....	....	....	....	....	....	....	....	....	....	....	....	....	....	....	....
1991-92	University of Maine	H.E.	31	18	20	38	....	....	....	14	....	....	....	....	....	....	....	....	....	....	....	....	....	....	....	....	....	....
1992-93	University of Maine	H.E.	45	23	25	48	....	....	....	22	....	....	....	....	....	....	....	....	....	....	....	....	....	....	....	....	....	....
1993-94	University of Maine	H.E.	34	18	15	33	....	....	....	42	....	....	....	....	....	....	....	....	....	....	....	....	....	....	....	....	....	....
	Peoria Rivermen	IHL	11	4	4	8	....	....	....	21	....	....	....	....	....	....	....	....	....	....	4	2	0	2	4	....	....	....
1994-95	Peoria Rivermen	IHL	53	27	18	45	....	....	....	83	....	....	....	....	....	....	....	....	....	....	....	....	....	....	....	....	....	....
	St. Louis Blues	**NHL**	**27**	**3**	**10**	**13**	**5**	**15**	**20**	**29**	**1**	**0**	**0**	**46**	**6.5**	**20**	**6**	**11**	**1**	**+4**	....	....	....	....	....	....	....	....
1995-96	**St. Louis Blues**	**NHL**	**23**	**3**	**0**	**3**	**3**	**0**	**3**	**12**	**0**	**0**	**1**	**21**	**14.3**	**4**	**1**	**5**	**0**	**-2**	....	....	....	....	....	....	....	....
	Worcester IceCats	AHL	30	13	13	26	....	....	....	69	....	....	....	....	....	....	....	....	....	....	....	....	....	....	....	....	....	....
	Los Angeles Kings	**NHL**	**15**	**1**	**1**	**2**	**1**	**1**	**2**	**37**	**1**	**0**	**0**	**29**	**3.4**	**4**	**3**	**10**	**0**	**-9**	....	....	....	....	....	....	....	....
1996-97	Phoenix Roadrunners	IHL	9	0	3	3	....	....	....	13	....	....	....	....	....	....	....	....	....	....	....	....	....	....	....	....	....	....
	Detroit Vipers	IHL	66	24	23	47	....	....	....	70	....	....	....	....	....	....	....	....	....	....	11	0	1	1	8	....	....	....
1997-98	Rochester Americans	AHL	41	13	13	26	....	....	....	68	....	....	....	....	....	....	....	....	....	....	....	....	....	....	....	....	....	....
	Detroit Vipers	IHL	28	10	9	19	....	....	....	24	....	....	....	....	....	....	....	....	....	....	15	3	7	10	14	....	....	....
	NHL Totals		**65**	**7**	**11**	**18**	**9**	**16**	**25**	**78**	**2**	**0**	**1**	**96**	**7.3**	**28**	**10**	**26**	**1**		....	....	....	....	....	....	....	....

Traded to **LA Kings** by **St. Louis** with Craig Johnson, Roman Vopat, St. Louis' 5th round choice (Peter Hogan) in 1996 Entry Draft and 1st round choice (Matt Zultek) in 1997 Entry Draft for Wayne Gretzky, February 27, 1996. Signed as a free agent by **Buffalo**, September 9, 1997.

• TATARINOV, MIKHAIL

Mikhail Tatarinov D – L. 5'10", 195 lbs. b: Angarsk, USSR, 7/16/1966. Washington's 10th choice, 225th overall, in 1984 Entry Draft.

Season	Club	League	GP	G	A	Pts	AG	AA	APts	PIM	PP	SH	GW	S	%	TGF	PGF	TGA	PGA	+/-	GP	G	A	Pts	PIM	PP	SH	GW
1983-84	Sokol Kiev	USSR	38	7	3	10	....	....	....	46	....	....	....	....	....	....	....	....	....	....	....	....	....	....	....	....	....	....
	Soviet Union	WJC-A	7	1	2	3	....	....	....	0	....	....	....	....	....	....	....	....	....	....	....	....	....	....	....	....	....	....
1984-85	Sokol Kiev	USSR	34	3	6	9	....	....	....	54	....	....	....	....	....	....	....	....	....	....	....	....	....	....	....	....	....	....
	Soviet Union	WJC-A	5	1	2	3	....	....	....	6	....	....	....	....	....	....	....	....	....	....	....	....	....	....	....	....	....	....
1985-86	Sokol Kiev	USSR	37	7	5	12	....	....	....	41	....	....	....	....	....	....	....	....	....	....	....	....	....	....	....	....	....	....
	Soviet Union	WJC-A	7	2	5	7	....	....	....	16	....	....	....	....	....	....	....	....	....	....	....	....	....	....	....	....	....	....
1986-87	Moscow Dynamo	USSR	40	10	8	18	....	....	....	43	....	....	....	....	....	....	....	....	....	....	....	....	....	....	....	....	....	....
	USSR	RV'87	2	0	1	1	....	....	....	0	....	....	....	....	....	....	....	....	....	....	....	....	....	....	....	....	....	....
1987-88	Moscow Dynamo	USSR	30	2	2	4	....	....	....	8	....	....	....	....	....	....	....	....	....	....	....	....	....	....	....	....	....	....
1988-89	Moscow Dynamo	USSR	4	1	0	1	....	....	....	2	....	....	....	....	....	....	....	....	....	....	....	....	....	....	....	....	....	....
1989-90	Moscow Dynamo	FrTour	1	1	2	3	....	....	....	0	....	....	....	....	....	....	....	....	....	....	....	....	....	....	....	....	....	....
	Moscow Dynamo	USSR	44	11	10	21	....	....	....	34	....	....	....	....	....	....	....	....	....	....	....	....	....	....	....	....	....	....
	Moscow Dynamo	SuperS	5	0	1	1	....	....	....	0	....	....	....	....	....	....	....	....	....	....	....	....	....	....	....	....	....	....
	Soviet Union	WEC-A	10	3	8	11	....	....	....	20	....	....	....	....	....	....	....	....	....	....	....	....	....	....	....	....	....	....
1990-91	Moscow Dynamo	FrTour	1	0	0	0	....	....	....	2	....	....	....	....	....	....	....	....	....	....	....	....	....	....	....	....	....	....
	Moscow Dynamo	USSR	11	5	4	9	....	....	....	6	....	....	....	....	....	....	....	....	....	....	....	....	....	....	....	....	....	....
	Washington Capitals	**NHL**	**65**	**8**	**15**	**23**	**7**	**11**	**18**	**82**	**3**	**1**	**1**	**145**	**5.5**	**75**	**24**	**58**	**3**	**-4**	....	....	....	....	....	....	....	....
1991-92	Soviet Union	C Cup	5	0	1	1	....	....	....	17	....	....	....	....	....	....	....	....	....	....	....	....	....	....	....	....	....	....
	Quebec Nordiques	**NHL**	**66**	**11**	**27**	**38**	**10**	**20**	**30**	**72**	**5**	**0**	**1**	**191**	**5.8**	**104**	**32**	**88**	**24**	**+8**	....	....	....	....	....	....	....	....
1992-93	**Quebec Nordiques**	**NHL**	**28**	**2**	**6**	**8**	**2**	**4**	**6**	**28**	**1**	**0**	**0**	**46**	**4.3**	**34**	**13**	**22**	**7**	**+6**	....	....	....	....	....	....	....	....
1993-94	**Boston Bruins**	**NHL**	**2**	**0**	**0**	**0**	**0**	**0**	**0**	**2**	**0**	**0**	**0**	**4**	**0.0**	**2**	**2**	**0**	**0**	**0**	....	....	....	....	....	....	....	....
	Providence Bruins	AHL	3	0	3	3	....	....	....	0	....	....	....	....	....	....	....	....	....	....	....	....	....	....	....	....	....	....
	NHL Totals		**161**	**21**	**48**	**69**	**19**	**35**	**54**	**184**	**9**	**1**	**2**	**386**	**5.4**	**215**	**71**	**168**	**34**		....	....	....	....	....	....	....	....

Named Best Defenseman at EJC-A (1984) • WJC-A All-Star Team (1985, 1986) • Named Best Defenseman at WJC-A (1986) • USSR First All-Star Team (1990) • WEC-A All-Star Team (1990) • Named Best Defenseman at WEC-A (1990)

Traded to **Quebec** by **Washington** for Toronto's 2nd round choice (previously acquired, Washington selected Eric Lavigne) in 1991 Entry Draft, June 22, 1991. Signed as a free agent by **Boston**, July 30, 1993.

• TAYLOR, CHRIS

Chris Taylor C – L. 6', 189 lbs. b: Stratford, Ont., 3/6/1972. NY Islanders' 2nd choice, 27th overall, in 1990 Entry Draft.

Season	Club	League	GP	G	A	Pts	AG	AA	APts	PIM	PP	SH	GW	S	%	TGF	PGF	TGA	PGA	+/-	GP	G	A	Pts	PIM	PP	SH	GW
1988-89	London Knights	OHL	62	7	16	23	....	....	....	52	....	....	....	....	....	....	....	....	....	....	15	0	2	2	15	....	....	....
1989-90	London Knights	OHL	66	45	60	105	....	....	....	60	....	....	....	....	....	....	....	....	....	....	6	3	2	5	6	....	....	....
1990-91	London Knights	OHL	65	50	78	128	....	....	....	50	....	....	....	....	....	....	....	....	....	....	7	4	8	12	6	....	....	....
1991-92	London Knights	OHL	66	48	74	122	....	....	....	57	....	....	....	....	....	....	....	....	....	....	10	8	16	24	9	....	....	....
1992-93	Capital District Islanders	AHL	77	19	43	62	....	....	....	32	....	....	....	....	....	....	....	....	....	....	4	0	1	1	2	....	....	....
1993-94	Salt Lake Golden Eagles	IHL	79	21	20	41	....	....	....	38	....	....	....	....	....	....	....	....	....	....	....	....	....	....	....	....	....	....
1994-95	Denver Grizzlies	IHL	78	38	48	86	....	....	....	47	....	....	....	....	....	....	....	....	....	....	14	7	6	13	10	....	....	....
	New York Islanders	**NHL**	**10**	**0**	**3**	**3**	**0**	**4**	**4**	**2**	**0**	**0**	**0**	**13**	**0.0**	**8**	**4**	**5**	**2**	**+1**	....	....	....	....	....	....	....	....
1995-96	**New York Islanders**	**NHL**	**11**	**0**	**1**	**1**	**0**	**1**	**1**	**2**	**0**	**0**	**0**	**4**	**0.0**	**3**	**0**	**2**	**0**	**+1**	....	....	....	....	....	....	....	....
	Utah Grizzlies	IHL	50	18	23	41	....	....	....	60	....	....	....	....	....	....	....	....	....	....	22	5	11	16	26	....	....	....

			REGULAR SEASON																		PLAYOFFS							
Season	Club	League	GP	G	A	Pts	AG	AA	APts	PIM	PP	SH	GW	S	%	TGF	PGF	TGA	PGA	+/–	GP	G	A	Pts	PIM	PP	SH	GW
1996-97	**New York Islanders**	**NHL**	**1**	**0**	**0**	**0**	**0**	**0**	**0**	**0**	**0**	**0**	**0**	**1**	**0.0**	**0**	**0**	**0**	**0**	**0**	....	....	....	....	....	....	....	....
	Utah Grizzlies	IHL	71	27	40	67	....	....	....	24	....	....	....	....	....	....	....	....	....	....	7	1	2	3	0	....	....	....
1997-98	Utah Grizzlies	IHL	79	28	56	84	....	....	....	66	....	....	....	....	....	....	....	....	....	....	4	0	2	2	6	....	....	....
	NHL Totals		**22**	**0**	**4**	**4**	**0**	**5**	**5**	**4**	**0**	**0**	**0**	**18**	**0.0**	**11**	**4**	**7**	**2**		....	....	....	....	....	....	....	....

Signed as a free agent by **LA Kings**, July 25, 1997.

• TAYLOR, DAVE

Dave "Stitch" Taylor RW – R. 6', 190 lbs. b: Levack, Ont., 12/4/1955. Los Angeles' 14th choice, 210th overall, in 1975 Amateur Draft.

Season	Club	League	GP	G	A	Pts	AG	AA	APts	PIM	PP	SH	GW	S	%	TGF	PGF	TGA	PGA	+/–	GP	G	A	Pts	PIM	PP	SH	GW
1974-75	Clarkson College	ECAC	32	20	34	54	....	....	....	....	....	....	....	....	....	....	....	....	....	....	....	....	....	....	....	....	....	....
1975-76	Clarkson College	ECAC	31	26	33	59	....	....	....	....	....	....	....	....	....	....	....	....	....	....	....	....	....	....	....	....	....	....
1976-77	Clarkson College	ECAC	34	*41	*67	*108	....	....	....	....	....	....	....	....	....	....	....	....	....	....	....	....	....	....	....	....	....	....
	Fort Worth Texans	CHL	7	2	4	6	....	....	....	6	....	....	....	....	....	....	....	....	....	....	....	....	....	....	....	....	....	....
1977-78	**Los Angeles Kings**	**NHL**	**64**	**22**	**21**	**43**	**21**	**17**	**38**	**47**	**4**	**0**	**3**	**122**	**18.0**	**58**	**11**	**34**	**1**	**+14**	**2**	**0**	**0**	**0**	**5**	**0**	**0**	**0**
1978-79	**Los Angeles Kings**	**NHL**	**78**	**43**	**48**	**91**	**39**	**37**	**76**	**124**	**13**	**0**	**4**	**238**	**18.1**	**133**	**45**	**66**	**5**	**+27**	**2**	**0**	**0**	**0**	**2**	**0**	**0**	**0**
1979-80	**Los Angeles Kings**	**NHL**	**61**	**37**	**53**	**90**	**34**	**41**	**75**	**72**	**12**	**0**	**7**	**170**	**21.8**	**132**	**48**	**48**	**3**	**+39**	**4**	**2**	**1**	**3**	**4**	**0**	**0**	**0**
1980-81	**Los Angeles Kings**	**NHL**	**72**	**47**	**65**	**112**	**39**	**46**	**85**	**130**	**13**	**0**	**3**	**206**	**22.8**	**165**	**62**	**56**	**0**	**+47**	**4**	**2**	**2**	**4**	**10**	**1**	**0**	**0**
1981-82	**Los Angeles Kings**	**NHL**	**78**	**39**	**67**	**106**	**31**	**44**	**75**	**130**	**13**	**0**	**3**	**232**	**16.8**	**149**	**56**	**101**	**4**	**–4**	**10**	**4**	**6**	**10**	**20**	**3**	**0**	**0**
1982-83	**Los Angeles Kings**	**NHL**	**46**	**21**	**37**	**58**	**17**	**26**	**43**	**76**	**6**	**0**	**1**	**117**	**17.9**	**86**	**36**	**46**	**0**	**+4**	....	....	....	....	....	....	....	....
	Canada	WEC-A	10	1	4	5	....	....	....	4	....	....	....	....	....	....	....	....	....	....	....	....	....	....	....	....	....	....
1983-84	**Los Angeles Kings**	**NHL**	**63**	**20**	**49**	**69**	**16**	**33**	**49**	**91**	**6**	**0**	**2**	**150**	**13.3**	**99**	**32**	**75**	**5**	**–3**	....	....	....	....	....	....	....	....
1984-85	**Los Angeles Kings**	**NHL**	**79**	**41**	**51**	**92**	**34**	**35**	**69**	**132**	**11**	**2**	**6**	**175**	**23.4**	**140**	**55**	**81**	**9**	**+13**	**3**	**2**	**2**	**4**	**8**	**0**	**0**	**0**
	Canada	WEC-A	10	3	2	5	....	....	....	4	....	....	....	....	....	....	....	....	....	....	....	....	....	....	....	....	....	....
1985-86	**Los Angeles Kings**	**NHL**	**76**	**33**	**38**	**71**	**26**	**25**	**51**	**110**	**11**	**0**	**1**	**203**	**16.3**	**111**	**38**	**99**	**10**	**–16**	....	....	....	....	....	....	....	....
	Canada	WEC-A	10	3	4	7	....	....	....	12	....	....	....	....	....	....	....	....	....	....	....	....	....	....	....	....	....	....
1986-87	**Los Angeles Kings**	**NHL**	**67**	**18**	**44**	**62**	**16**	**32**	**48**	**84**	**9**	**1**	**3**	**115**	**15.7**	**91**	**38**	**70**	**17**	**0**	**5**	**2**	**3**	**5**	**6**	**1**	**0**	**0**
1987-88	**Los Angeles Kings**	**NHL**	**68**	**26**	**41**	**67**	**22**	**29**	**51**	**129**	**9**	**0**	**2**	**149**	**17.4**	**114**	**51**	**69**	**2**	**–4**	**5**	**3**	**3**	**6**	**6**	**2**	**0**	**0**
1988-89	**Los Angeles Kings**	**NHL**	**70**	**26**	**37**	**63**	**22**	**26**	**48**	**80**	**7**	**0**	**4**	**141**	**18.4**	**101**	**30**	**61**	**0**	**+10**	**11**	**1**	**5**	**6**	**19**	**1**	**0**	**0**
1989-90	**Los Angeles Kings**	**NHL**	**58**	**15**	**26**	**41**	**13**	**19**	**32**	**96**	**2**	**0**	**1**	**100**	**15.0**	**65**	**9**	**39**	**0**	**+17**	**6**	**4**	**4**	**8**	**2**	**2**	**0**	**0**
1990-91	**Los Angeles Kings**	**NHL**	**73**	**23**	**30**	**53**	**21**	**23**	**44**	**148**	**6**	**0**	**2**	**122**	**18.9**	**81**	**14**	**40**	**0**	**+27**	**12**	**2**	**1**	**3**	**12**	**0**	**0**	**1**
1991-92	**Los Angeles Kings**	**NHL**	**77**	**10**	**19**	**29**	**9**	**14**	**23**	**63**	**0**	**0**	**2**	**81**	**12.3**	**45**	**2**	**33**	**0**	**+10**	**6**	**1**	**1**	**2**	**20**	**0**	**0**	**0**
1992-93	**Los Angeles Kings**	**NHL**	**48**	**6**	**9**	**15**	**5**	**6**	**11**	**49**	**1**	**0**	**1**	**53**	**11.3**	**22**	**3**	**37**	**19**	**+1**	**22**	**3**	**5**	**8**	**31**	**0**	**2**	**0**
1993-94	**Los Angeles Kings**	**NHL**	**33**	**4**	**3**	**7**	**4**	**2**	**6**	**28**	**0**	**1**	**2**	**39**	**10.3**	**15**	**0**	**27**	**11**	**–1**	....	....	....	....	....	....	....	....
	NHL Totals		**1111**	**431**	**638**	**1069**	**369**	**455**	**824**	**1589**	**123**	**4**	**47**	**2413**	**17.9**	**1607**	**530**	**982**	**86**		**92**	**26**	**33**	**59**	**145**	**10**	**2**	**1**

Played in NHL All-Star Game (1981, 1982, 1986, 1994)

NHL Second All-Star Team (1981) • Won Bill Masterton Memorial Trophy (1991) • Won King Clancy Memorial Trophy (1991)

Played in NHL All-Star Game (1981, 1982, 1986, 1994)

• TAYLOR, MARK

Mark Taylor C – L. 6', 190 lbs. b: Vancouver, B.C., 1/26/1958. Philadelphia's 9th choice, 100th overall, in 1978 Amateur Draft.

Season	Club	League	GP	G	A	Pts	AG	AA	APts	PIM	PP	SH	GW	S	%	TGF	PGF	TGA	PGA	+/–	GP	G	A	Pts	PIM	PP	SH	GW
1975-76	Langley Thunder	BCJHL	63	49	79	128	....	....	....	48	....	....	....	....	....	....	....	....	....	....	....	....	....	....	....	....	....	....
1976-77	University of North Dakota	WCHA	31	16	19	35	....	....	....	20	....	....	....	....	....	....	....	....	....	....	....	....	....	....	....	....	....	....
1977-78	University of North Dakota	WCHA	37	18	22	40	....	....	....	28	....	....	....	....	....	....	....	....	....	....	....	....	....	....	....	....	....	....
1978-79	University of North Dakota	WCHA	42	24	59	83	....	....	....	28	....	....	....	....	....	....	....	....	....	....	....	....	....	....	....	....	....	....
1979-80	University of North Dakota	WCHA	40	33	59	92	....	....	....	30	....	....	....	....	....	....	....	....	....	....	....	....	....	....	....	....	....	....
1980-81	Maine Mariners	AHL	79	19	50	69	....	....	....	56	....	....	....	....	....	....	....	....	....	....	20	5	16	*21	20	....	....	....
1981-82	**Philadelphia Flyers**	**NHL**	**2**	**0**	**0**	**0**	**0**	**0**	**0**	**0**	**0**	**0**	**0**	**1**	**0.0**	**0**	**0**	**1**	**0**	**–1**	....	....	....	....	....	....	....	....
	Maine Mariners	AHL	75	32	48	80	....	....	....	42	....	....	....	....	....	....	....	....	....	....	4	2	3	5	4	....	....	....
1982-83	**Philadelphia Flyers**	**NHL**	**61**	**8**	**25**	**33**	**7**	**17**	**24**	**24**	**0**	**1**	**3**	**73**	**11.0**	**51**	**7**	**39**	**20**	**+25**	**3**	**0**	**0**	**0**	**0**	**0**	**0**	**0**
1983-84	**Philadelphia Flyers**	**NHL**	**1**	**0**	**0**	**0**	**0**	**0**	**0**	**0**	**0**	**0**	**0**	**0**	**0.0**	**0**	**0**	**0**	**0**	**0**	....	....	....	....	....	....	....	....
	Pittsburgh Penguins	**NHL**	**59**	**24**	**31**	**55**	**19**	**21**	**40**	**24**	**9**	**1**	**1**	**107**	**22.4**	**84**	**30**	**95**	**21**	**–20**	....	....	....	....	....	....	....	....
1984-85	**Pittsburgh Penguins**	**NHL**	**47**	**7**	**10**	**17**	**6**	**7**	**13**	**19**	**0**	**1**	**1**	**46**	**15.2**	**24**	**1**	**39**	**9**	**–7**	....	....	....	....	....	....	....	....
	Washington Capitals	**NHL**	**9**	**1**	**1**	**2**	**1**	**1**	**2**	**2**	**0**	**0**	**0**	**10**	**10.0**	**4**	**1**	**4**	**0**	**–1**	....	....	....	....	....	....	....	....
1985-86	**Washington Capitals**	**NHL**	**30**	**2**	**1**	**3**	**2**	**1**	**3**	**4**	**0**	**0**	**0**	**23**	**8.7**	**7**	**0**	**13**	**2**	**–4**	**3**	**0**	**0**	**0**	**0**	**0**	**0**	**0**
	Binghamton Whalers	AHL	43	19	38	57	....	....	....	27	....	....	....	....	....	....	....	....	....	....	....	....	....	....	....	....	....	....
1986-87	Binghamton Whalers	AHL	67	16	37	53	....	....	....	40	....	....	....	....	....	....	....	....	....	....	13	2	6	8	9	....	....	....
1987-88	Uzwil	Switz. B	....	23	39	62	....	....	....	....	....	....	....	....	....	....	....	....	....	....	....	....	....	....	....	....	....	....
	NHL Totals		**209**	**42**	**68**	**110**	**35**	**47**	**82**	**73**	**9**	**3**	**5**	**260**	**16.2**	**170**	**39**	**191**	**52**		**6**	**0**	**0**	**0**	**0**	**0**	**0**	**0**

NCAA Championship All-Tournament Team (1979) • WCHA First All-Star Team (1980) • NCAA West First All-American Team (1980)

Traded to **Pittsburgh** by **Philadelphia** with Ron Flockhart, Andy Brickley and Philadelphia's 1st (Roger Belanger) and 3rd (later traded to Vancouver — Vancouver selected Mike Stevens) round choices in 1984 Entry Draft for Ron Sutter and Pittsburgh's 2nd (Greg Smyth) and 3rd (David McClay) round choices in 1984 Entry Draft, October 23, 1983. Traded to **Washington** by **Pittsburgh** for Jim McGeough, March 12, 1985.

• TAYLOR, TED

Ted Taylor LW – L. 6', 175 lbs. b: Oak Lake, Man., 2/25/1942.

Season	Club	League	GP	G	A	Pts	AG	AA	APts	PIM	PP	SH	GW	S	%	TGF	PGF	TGA	PGA	+/–	GP	G	A	Pts	PIM	PP	SH	GW
1959-60	Brandon Wheat Kings	MJHL	32	14	12	26	....	....	....	54	....	....	....	....	....	....	....	....	....	....	22	4	16	20	10	....	....	....
1960-61	Brandon Wheat Kings	MJHL	32	28	30	58	....	....	....	53	....	....	....	....	....	....	....	....	....	....	9	5	5	10	18	....	....	....
	Vancouver Canucks	WHL	1	0	0	0	....	....	....	0	....	....	....	....	....	....	....	....	....	....	....	....	....	....	....	....	....	....
1961-62	Brandon Wheat Kings	MJHL	40	28	32	60	....	....	....	72	....	....	....	....	....	....	....	....	....	....	20	14	9	23	*40	....	....	....
1962-63	Sudbury Wolves	EPHL	56	22	23	45	....	....	....	76	....	....	....	....	....	....	....	....	....	....	....	....	....	....	....	....	....	....
	Baltimore Clippers	AHL	14	5	7	12	....	....	....	17	....	....	....	....	....	....	....	....	....	....	3	0	0	0	4	....	....	....
1963-64	Baltimore Clippers	AHL	6	0	2	2	....	....	....	6	....	....	....	....	....	....	....	....	....	....	....	....	....	....	....	....	....	....
	St. Paul Rangers	CHL	59	18	30	48	....	....	....	97	....	....	....	....	....	....	....	....	....	....	11	2	2	4	4	....	....	....
1964-65	**New York Rangers**	**NHL**	**4**	**0**	**0**	**0**	**0**	**0**	**0**	**4**	....	....	....	....	....	....	....	....	....	....	....	....	....	....	....	....	....	....
	Baltimore Clippers	AHL	68	25	28	53	....	....	....	74	....	....	....	....	....	....	....	....	....	....	3	0	0	0	4	....	....	....
1965-66	**New York Rangers**	**NHL**	**4**	**0**	**1**	**1**	**0**	**1**	**1**	**2**	....	....	....	....	....	....	....	....	....	....	....	....	....	....	....	....	....	....
	Baltimore Clippers	AHL	62	21	30	51	....	....	....	98	....	....	....	....	....	....	....	....	....	....	....	....	....	....	....	....	....	....
1966-67	**Detroit Red Wings**	**NHL**	**2**	**0**	**0**	**0**	**0**	**0**	**0**	**0**	....	....	....	....	....	....	....	....	....	....	....	....	....	....	....	....	....	....
	Pittsburgh Hornets	AHL	69	20	38	58	....	....	....	91	....	....	....	....	....	....	....	....	....	....	9	3	2	5	8	....	....	....
1967-68	**Minnesota North Stars**	**NHL**	**31**	**3**	**5**	**8**	**4**	**5**	**9**	**34**	**1**	**0**	**0**	**67**	**4.5**	**14**	**2**	**21**	**2**	**–7**	....	....	....	....	....	....	....	....
	Rochester Americans	AHL	37	14	16	30	....	....	....	54	....	....	....	....	....	....	....	....	....	....	11	5	5	10	29	....	....	....
1968-69	Vancouver Canucks	WHL	64	15	29	44	....	....	....	121	....	....	....	....	....	....	....	....	....	....	8	1	4	5	4	....	....	....
1969-70	Vancouver Canucks	WHL	66	36	35	71	....	....	....	97	....	....	....	....	....	....	....	....	....	....	11	9	8	17	46	....	....	....
1970-71	**Vancouver Canucks**	**NHL**	**56**	**11**	**16**	**27**	**11**	**14**	**25**	**53**	**1**	**1**	**1**	**82**	**13.4**	**39**	**3**	**61**	**16**	**–9**	....	....	....	....	....	....	....	....
1971-72	**Vancouver Canucks**	**NHL**	**69**	**9**	**13**	**22**	**10**	**12**	**22**	**88**	**0**	**0**	**0**	**82**	**11.0**	**32**	**0**	**55**	**3**	**–20**	....	....	....	....	....	....	....	....
1972-73	Houston Aeros	WHA	72	34	42	76	....	....	....	101	....	....	....	....	....	....	....	....	....	....	10	3	1	4	10	....	....	....
1973-74	Houston Aeros	WHA	75	21	23	44	....	....	....	143	....	....	....	....	....	....	....	....	....	....	14	4	8	12	60	....	....	....
1974-75	Houston Aeros	WHA	73	26	27	53	....	....	....	130	....	....	....	....	....	....	....	....	....	....	11	2	5	7	22	....	....	....
1975-76	Houston Aeros	WHA	68	15	26	41	....	....	....	88	....	....	....	....	....	....	....	....	....	....	11	2	2	4	17	....	....	....
1976-77	Houston Aeros	WHA	78	16	35	51	....	....	....	90	....	....	....	....	....	....	....	....	....	....	11	4	4	8	28	....	....	....
1977-78	Houston Aeros	WHA	54	11	11	22	....	....	....	46	....	....	....	....	....	....	....	....	....	....	6	3	1	4	10	....	....	....
	NHL Totals		**166**	**23**	**35**	**58**	**25**	**32**	**57**	**181**	**2**	**1**	**1**	**231**	**10.0**	**85**	**5**	**137**	**21**		....	....	....	....	....	....	....	....
	Other Major League Totals		420	123	164	287				598											63	18	21	39	147			

Traded to **Montreal** by **NY Rangers** with Gary Peters for Red Berenson, June 13, 1966. Claimed by **Detroit** from **Montreal** in Intra-League Draft, June 15, 1966. Claimed by **Minnesota** from **Detroit** in Expansion Draft, June 6, 1967. Traded to **Toronto** by **Minnesota** with Duke Harris, Murray Hall, Len Lunde, Don Johns and the loan of Carl Wetzel for Milan Marcetta and Jean-Paul Parise, December 26, 1967. NHL rights transferred to **Vancouver** after owners of **Vancouver** (WHL) franchise awarded NHL expansion team, May 22, 1970. Selected by **Dayton-Houston** (WHA) in 1972 WHA General Player Draft, February 12, 1972. Claimed by **NY Islanders** from **Vancouver** in Expansion Draft, June 6, 1972.

• TAYLOR, TIM

Tim Taylor C – L. 6'1", 185 lbs. b: Stratford, Ont., 2/6/1969. Washington's 2nd choice, 36th overall, in 1988 Entry Draft.

Season	Club	League	GP	G	A	Pts	AG	AA	APts	PIM	PP	SH	GW	S	%	TGF	PGF	TGA	PGA	+/–	GP	G	A	Pts	PIM	PP	SH	GW
1986-87	London Knights	OHL	34	7	9	16	....	....	....	11	....	....	....	....	....	....	....	....	....	....	....	....	....	....	....	....	....	....
1987-88	London Knights	OHL	64	46	50	96	....	....	....	66	....	....	....	....	....	....	....	....	....	....	12	9	9	18	26	....	....	....
1988-89	London Knights	OHL	61	34	80	114	....	....	....	93	....	....	....	....	....	....	....	....	....	....	21	*21	25	*46	58	....	....	....
1989-90	Baltimore Skipjacks	AHL	79	31	36	67	....	....	....	124	....	....	....	....	....	....	....	....	....	....	9	2	2	4	13	....	....	....
1990-91	Baltimore Skipjacks	AHL	79	25	42	67	....	....	....	75	....	....	....	....	....	....	....	....	....	....	5	0	1	1	4	....	....	....

			REGULAR SEASON																		PLAYOFFS							
Season	Club	League	GP	G	A	Pts	AG	AA	APts	PIM	PP	SH	GW	S	%	TGF	PGF	TGA	PGA	+/–	GP	G	A	Pts	PIM	PP	SH	GW
1991-92	Baltimore Skipjacks	AHL	65	9	18	27				131																		
1992-93	Baltimore Skipjacks	AHL	41	15	16	31				49																		
	Hamilton Canucks	AHL	36	15	22	37				37																		
1993-94	**Detroit Red Wings**	**NHL**	**1**	**1**	**0**	**1**	**1**	**0**	**1**	**0**	**0**	**0**	**0**	**4**	**25.0**	**1**	**0**	**2**	**0**	**–1**								
	Adirondack Red Wings	AHL	79	36	*81	*117				86											12	2	10	12	12			
1994-95	**Detroit Red Wings**	**NHL**	**22**	**0**	**4**	**4**	**0**	**6**	**6**	**16**	**0**	**0**	**0**	**21**	**0.0**	**10**	**3**	**4**	**0**	**+3**	**6**	**0**	**1**	**1**	**12**	**0**	**0**	**0**
1995-96	**Detroit Red Wings**	**NHL**	**72**	**11**	**14**	**25**	**11**	**11**	**22**	**39**	**1**	**1**	**4**	**81**	**13.6**	**32**	**3**	**20**	**2**	**+11**	**18**	**0**	**4**	**4**	**4**	**0**	**0**	**0**
1996-97	**Detroit Red Wings**	**NHL**	**44**	**3**	**4**	**7**	**3**	**4**	**7**	**52**	**0**	**1**	**0**	**44**	**6.8**	**17**	**3**	**26**	**6**	**–6**	**2**	**0**	**0**	**0**	**0**	**0**	**0**	**0**
1997-98	**Boston Bruins**	**NHL**	**79**	**20**	**11**	**31**	**23**	**11**	**34**	**57**	**1**	**3**	**0**	**127**	**15.7**	**44**	**7**	**73**	**20**	**–16**	**6**	**0**	**0**	**0**	**10**	**0**	**0**	**0**
	NHL Totals		**218**	**35**	**33**	**68**	**38**	**32**	**70**	**164**	**2**	**5**	**4**	**277**	**12.6**	**104**	**16**	**125**	**28**		**32**	**0**	**5**	**5**	**26**	**0**	**0**	**0**

AHL First All-Star Team (1994) • Won John B. Sollenberger Trophy (Top Scorer - AHL) (1994)

Traded to **Vancouver** by **Washington** for Eric Murano, January 29, 1993. Signed as a free agent by **Detroit**, July 28, 1993. Claimed by **Boston** from **Detroit** in NHL Waiver Draft, September 28, 1998.

• TEAL, JEFF

Jeff Teal RW – L. 6'3", 205 lbs. b: Edina, MN, 5/30/1960. Montreal's 6th choice, 82nd overall, in 1980 Entry Draft.

1979-80	University of Minnesota	WCHA	37	10	15	25				30																		
1980-81	University of Minnesota	WCHA	45	15	9	24				38																		
1981-82	University of Minnesota	WCHA	37	13	9	22				36																		
	Nova Scotia Voyageurs	AHL	7	0	1	1				0											6	1	1	2	2			
1982-83	Nova Scotia Voyageurs	AHL	76	8	20	28				14											7	0	1	1	2			
1983-84	Nova Scotia Voyageurs	AHL	15	8	4	12				2																		
1984-85	**Montreal Canadiens**	**NHL**	**6**	**0**	**1**	**1**	**0**	**1**	**1**	**0**	**0**	**0**	**0**	**4**	**0.0**	**1**	**0**	**1**	**0**	**0**								
	Sherbrooke Canadiens	AHL	69	18	24	42				16											17	4	8	12	8			
	NHL Totals		**6**	**0**	**1**	**1**	**0**	**1**	**1**	**0**	**0**	**0**	**0**	**4**	**0.0**	**1**	**0**	**1**	**0**									

• TEAL, VICTOR

Victor "Skeeter" Teal RW – R. 6'1", 160 lbs. b: St. Catharines, Ont., 8/10/1949. St. Louis' 3rd choice, 42nd overall, in 1969 Amateur Draft.

1965-66	St. Catharines Black Hawks	OHA																			4	0	0	0	0			
1966-67	St. Catharines Black Hawks	OHA	47	15	15	30				4											6	1	0	1	2			
1967-68	St. Catharines Black Hawks	OHA	54	34	29	63				29											5	1	5	6	0			
1968-69	St. Catharines Black Hawks	OHA	51	30	53	83				55											18	8	18	26	11			
1969-70	Kansas City Blues	CHL	58	8	13	21				28																		
1970-71			DID NOT PLAY																									
1971-72	Galt Terriers	OHA Sr.	36	36	27	63				11																		
1972-73	New Haven Nighthawks	AHL	69	18	34	52				6																		
1973-74	**New York Islanders**	**NHL**	**1**	**0**	**0**	**0**	**0**	**0**	**0**	**0**	**0**	**0**	**0**	**4**	**0.0**	**0**	**0**	**0**	**1**	**+1**								
	Fort Worth Wings	CHL	72	33	43	76				8											5	0	1	1	0			
1974-75	Fort Worth Texans	CHL	69	27	29	56				20																		
1975-76	Erie Blades	NAHL	63	36	27	63				4											2	0	2	2	0			
1976-77	Cambridge Hornets	OHA Sr.	12	14	7	21				0																		
	NHL Totals		**1**	**0**	**0**	**0**	**0**	**0**	**0**	**0**	**0**	**0**	**0**	**4**	**0.0**	**0**	**0**	**0**	**1**									

CHL Second All-Star Team (1974)

• TEBBUTT, GREG

Greg Tebbutt D – L. 6'3", 215 lbs. b: North Vancouver, B.C., 5/11/1957. Minnesota's 7th choice, 130th overall, in 1977 Amateur Draft.

1975-76	Victoria Cougars	WHL	51	3	4	7				217											15	2	0	2	43			
1976-77	Victoria Cougars	WCJHL	29	7	12	19				98																		
	Regina Pats	WCJHL	40	8	17	25				138																		
1977-78	Flin Flon Bombers	WCJHL	55	28	46	74				270											15	11	17	28	45			
1978-79	Binghamton Whalers	AHL	33	8	9	17				50																		
	Birmingham Bulls	WHA	38	2	5	7				83																		
1979-80	**Quebec Nordiques**	**NHL**	**2**	**0**	**1**	**1**	**0**	**1**	**1**	**4**	**0**	**0**	**0**	**0**	**0.0**	**1**	**0**	**2**	**0**	**–1**								
	Syracuse Firebirds	AHL	14	2	3	5				35																		
	Erie Blades	EHL	48	20	53	73				138											9	*11	*12	*23	32			
1980-81	Erie Blades	EHL	35	16	37	53				93											8	0	*12	12	28			
1981-82	Fort Wayne Komets	IHL	49	13	34	47				148											9	3	1	4	16			
1982-83	Baltimore Skipjacks	AHL	80	28	56	84				140																		
1983-84	**Pittsburgh Penguins**	**NHL**	**24**	**0**	**2**	**2**	**0**	**1**	**1**	**31**	**0**	**0**	**0**	**38**	**0.0**	**18**	**2**	**47**	**5**	**–26**								
	Baltimore Skipjacks	AHL	44	12	42	54				125											10	0	6	6	20			
1984-85	Baltimore Skipjacks	AHL	2	0	0	0				4																		
	Muskegon Mohawks	IHL	73	23	55	78				220											17	3	9	12	87			
1985-86	Milwaukee Admirals	IHL	77	20	49	69				226											5	0	3	3	8			
1986-87	Saginaw Generals	IHL	81	27	59	86				215											8	6	5	11	34			
1987-88	Baltimore Skipjacks	AHL	24	1	14	15				72																		
	NHL Totals		**26**	**0**	**3**	**3**	**0**	**2**	**2**	**35**	**0**	**0**	**0**	**38**	**0.0**	**19**	**2**	**49**	**5**									
	Other Major League Totals		38	2	5	7				83																		

AHL First All-Star Team (1983) • Won Eddie Shore Award (Outstanding Defenseman - AHL) (1983) • IHL Second All-Star Team (1985) • IHL First All-Star Team (1987)

Selected by **Birmingham** (WHA) in 1977 WHA Amateur Draft, June, 1977. Reclaimed by **Minnesota** from **Birmingham** (WHA) prior to Expansion Draft, June 9, 1979. Claimed by **Quebec** from **Minnesota** on waivers, August 13, 1979. Signed as a free agent by **Pittsburgh**, July 22, 1983.

• TEPPER, STEPHEN

Stephen Tepper RW – R. 6'4", 215 lbs. b: Santa Ana, CA, 3/10/1969. Chicago's 7th choice, 134th overall, in 1987 Entry Draft.

1986-87	Westboro-Mass High School	H.S.	25	34	18	52																						
1987-88	Westboro-Mass High School	H.S.	24	39	24	63																						
1988-89	University of Maine	H.E.	26	3	9	12				32																		
1989-90	University of Maine	H.E.	41	10	6	16				68																		
1990-91	University of Maine	H.E.	38	6	11	17				58																		
1991-92	University of Maine	H.E.	16	0	3	3				20																		
1992-93	**Chicago Blackhawks**	**NHL**	**1**	**0**	**0**	**0**	**0**	**0**	**0**	**0**	**0**	**0**	**0**	**0**	**0.0**	**0**	**0**	**0**	**0**	**0**								
	Indianapolis Ice	IHL	12	0	1	1				40																		
	Kansas City Blades	IHL	32	4	10	14				51											4	0	1	1	6			
1993-94	Fort Worth Fire	CHL	25	23	11	34				54																		
	Roanoke Express	ECHL	9	2	2	4				33																		
	Kansas City Blades	IHL	23	1	3	4				52																		
1994-95	Fort Worth Fire	CHL	35	26	22	48				63																		
	Cape Breton Oilers	AHL	26	1	4	5				16																		
1995-96	Cape Breton Oilers	AHL	52	8	14	22				74																		
	NHL Totals		**1**	**0**	**0**	**0**	**0**	**0**	**0**	**0**	**0**	**0**	**0**	**0**	**0.0**	**0**	**0**	**0**	**0**									

• TERBENCHE, PAUL

Paul Terbenche D – L. 5'10", 170 lbs. b: Port Hope, Ont., 9/16/1945.

1964-65	St. Catharines Black Hawks	OHA	56	3	23	26				63											5	0	0	0	4			
1965-66	St. Catharines Black Hawks	OHA	48	5	31	36				26											7	1	4	5	2			
	St. Louis Braves	CHL	2	0	0	0				0											5	0	2	2	0			
1966-67	St. Louis Braves	CHL	63	4	14	18				39																		
1967-68	**Chicago Black Hawks**	**NHL**	**68**	**3**	**7**	**10**	**4**	**7**	**11**	**8**	**0**	**0**	**1**	**65**	**4.6**	**22**	**2**	**35**	**4**	**–11**	**6**	**0**	**0**	**0**	**0**	**0**	**0**	**0**
1968-69	Dallas Black Hawks	CHL	26	0	4	4				2											11	0	3	3	2			
1969-70	Portland Buckaroos	WHL	66	5	15	20				8											3	0	0	0	0			
1970-71	**Buffalo Sabres**	**NHL**	**3**	**0**	**0**	**0**	**0**	**0**	**0**	**2**	**0**	**0**	**0**	**1**	**0.0**	**0**	**0**	**3**	**0**	**–3**								
	Salt Lake Golden Eagles	WHL	51	4	20	24				16																		
1971-72	**Buffalo Sabres**	**NHL**	**9**	**0**	**0**	**0**	**0**	**0**	**0**	**2**	**0**	**0**	**0**	**7**	**0.0**	**0**	**0**	**16**	**3**	**–13**								
	Salt Lake Golden Eagles	WHL	64	1	31	32				10																		
1972-73	**Buffalo Sabres**	**NHL**	**42**	**0**	**7**	**7**	**0**	**6**	**6**	**8**	**0**	**0**	**0**	**20**	**0.0**	**32**	**0**	**32**	**7**	**+7**	**6**	**0**	**0**	**0**	**0**	**0**	**0**	**0**
1973-74	**Buffalo Sabres**	**NHL**	**67**	**2**	**12**	**14**	**2**	**10**	**12**	**8**	**0**	**0**	**0**	**42**	**4.8**	**49**	**6**	**47**	**7**	**+3**								

			REGULAR SEASON																		PLAYOFFS							
Season	Club	League	GP	G	A	Pts	AG	AA	APts	PIM	PP	SH	GW	S	%	TGF	PGF	TGA	PGA	+/–	GP	G	A	Pts	PIM	PP	SH	GW
1974-75	Vancouver Blazers	WHA	60	3	14	17	....	....	....	10	....	....	....	....	....	....	....	....	....	....	....	....	....	....	....	....	....	....
1975-76	Calgary Cowboys	WHA	58	2	4	6	....	....	....	22	....	....	....	....	....	....	....	....	....	....	10	0	6	6	6	....	....	....
1976-77	Calgary Cowboys	WHA	80	9	24	33	....	....	....	30	....	....	....	....	....	....	....	....	....	....	....	....	....	....	....	....	....	....
1977-78	Birmingham Bulls	WHA	11	1	0	1	....	....	....	0	....	....	....	....	....	....	....	....	....	....	....	....	....	....	....	....	....	....
	Hampton Gulls	AHL	26	0	9	9	....	....	....	11	....	....	....	....	....	....	....	....	....	....	....	....	....	....	....	....	....	....
	Springfield Indians	AHL	8	0	5	5	....	....	....	4	....	....	....	....	....	....	....	....	....	....	....	....	....	....	....	....	....	....
	Houston Aeros	WHA	....	....	....	....	....	....	....	....	....	....	....	....	....	....	....	....	....	....	6	1	1	2	0	....	....	....
1978-79	Winnipeg Jets	WHA	68	3	22	25	....	....	....	12	....	....	....	....	....	....	....	....	....	....	10	1	1	2	4	....	....	....
1979-80	Birmingham Bulls	CHL	63	3	14	17	....	....	....	20	....	....	....	....	....	....	....	....	....	....	4	0	2	2	2	....	....	....
1980-81	Birmingham Bulls	CHL	41	2	2	4	....	....	....	26	....	....	....	....	....	....	....	....	....	....	....	....	....	....	....	....	....	....
	NHL Totals		**189**	**5**	**26**	**31**	**6**	**23**	**29**	**28**	**0**	**0**	**1**	**135**	**3.7**	**103**	**8**	**133**	**21**		**12**	**0**	**0**	**0**	**0**	**0**	**0**	**0**
	Other Major League Totals		277	18	64	82	....	....	....	74	....	....	....	....	....	....	....	....	....	....	26	2	8	10	10	....	....	....

Claimed by **Buffalo** from **Chicago** in Expansion Draft, June, 1970. Selected by **Dayton-Houston** in 1972 WHA General Player Draft, February 12, 1972. Claimed by **Kansas City** from **Buffalo** in Expansion Draft, June, 1974. Signed as a free agent by **Vancouver** (WHA), July, 1974. Transferred to **Calgary** (WHA) after **Vancouver** (WHA) franchise relocated, June, 1975. Signed as a free agent by **Birmingham** (WHA) after **Calgary** (WHA) franchise folded, May, 1977. Traded to **Houston** (WHA) by **Birmingham** (WHA) for future considerations, February, 1978. Traded to **Winnipeg** (WHA) by **Houston** (WHA) for cash, July, 1978. Retained by **Winnipeg** prior to Expansion Draft, June 9, 1979. Traded to **Atlanta** by **Winnipeg** for future considerations, August, 1979.

• TERRION, GREG

Greg "Tubby" Terrion LW – L. 5'11", 190 lbs. b: Marmora, Ont., 5/2/1960. Los Angeles' 3rd choice, 33rd overall, in 1980 Entry Draft.

Season	Club	League	GP	G	A	Pts	AG	AA	APts	PIM	PP	SH	GW	S	%	TGF	PGF	TGA	PGA	+/–	GP	G	A	Pts	PIM	PP	SH	GW
1977-78	Hamilton Fincups	OHA	64	11	30	41	....	....	....	43	....	....	....	....	....	....	....	....	....	....	....	....	....	....	....	....	....	....
1978-79	Brantford Alexanders	OHA	59	27	28	55	....	....	....	48	....	....	....	....	....	....	....	....	....	....	....	....	....	....	....	....	....	....
1979-80	Brantford Alexanders	OHA	67	44	78	122	....	....	....	13	....	....	....	....	....	....	....	....	....	....	11	4	7	11	14	....	....	....
1980-81	**Los Angeles Kings**	**NHL**	**73**	**12**	**25**	**37**	**10**	**17**	**27**	**99**	**2**	**0**	**2**	**92**	**13.0**	**48**	**9**	**46**	**6**	**–1**	**3**	**1**	**0**	**1**	**4**	**1**	**0**	**0**
1981-82	**Los Angeles Kings**	**NHL**	**61**	**15**	**22**	**37**	**12**	**15**	**27**	**23**	**1**	**0**	**3**	**106**	**14.2**	**61**	**15**	**67**	**9**	**–12**	....	....	....	....	....	....	....	....
1982-83	**Toronto Maple Leafs**	**NHL**	**74**	**16**	**16**	**32**	**13**	**11**	**24**	**59**	**0**	**3**	**1**	**73**	**21.9**	**50**	**2**	**82**	**31**	**–3**	**4**	**1**	**2**	**3**	**2**	**0**	**0**	**0**
	New Haven Nighthawks	AHL	4	0	1	1	....	....	....	7	....	....	....	....	....	....	....	....	....	....	....	....	....	....	....	....	....	....
1983-84	**Toronto Maple Leafs**	**NHL**	**79**	**15**	**24**	**39**	**12**	**16**	**28**	**36**	**0**	**2**	**2**	**92**	**16.3**	**63**	**3**	**109**	**43**	**–6**	....	....	....	....	....	....	....	....
1984-85	**Toronto Maple Leafs**	**NHL**	**72**	**14**	**17**	**31**	**11**	**11**	**22**	**20**	**1**	**4**	**0**	**91**	**15.4**	**46**	**4**	**101**	**44**	**–15**	....	....	....	....	....	....	....	....
1985-86	**Toronto Maple Leafs**	**NHL**	**76**	**10**	**22**	**32**	**8**	**15**	**23**	**31**	**0**	**2**	**1**	**105**	**9.5**	**46**	**0**	**77**	**26**	**–5**	**10**	**0**	**3**	**3**	**17**	**0**	**0**	**0**
1986-87	**Toronto Maple Leafs**	**NHL**	**67**	**7**	**8**	**15**	**6**	**6**	**12**	**6**	**0**	**2**	**0**	**55**	**12.7**	**27**	**0**	**59**	**27**	**–5**	**13**	**0**	**2**	**2**	**14**	**0**	**0**	**0**
1987-88	**Toronto Maple Leafs**	**NHL**	**59**	**4**	**16**	**20**	**3**	**11**	**14**	**65**	**1**	**0**	**1**	**57**	**7.0**	**30**	**1**	**57**	**22**	**–6**	**5**	**0**	**2**	**2**	**4**	**0**	**0**	**0**
	Newmarket Saints	AHL	4	1	3	4	....	....	....	6	....	....	....	....	....	....	....	....	....	....	....	....	....	....	....	....	....	....
1988-89	Newmarket Saints	AHL	60	15	34	49	....	....	....	64	....	....	....	....	....	....	....	....	....	....	4	0	1	1	2	....	....	....
	NHL Totals		**561**	**93**	**150**	**243**	**75**	**102**	**177**	**339**	**5**	**13**	**10**	**671**	**13.9**	**371**	**34**	**598**	**208**		**35**	**2**	**9**	**11**	**41**	**1**	**0**	**0**

Traded to **Toronto** by **LA Kings** for Toronto's 4th round choice (later traded to Detroit — Detroit selected David Korol) in 1983 Entry Draft, October 19, 1982.

• TERRY, BILL

Bill Terry C – R. 5'8", 175 lbs. b: Toronto, Ont., 7/13/1961.

Season	Club	League	GP	G	A	Pts	AG	AA	APts	PIM	PP	SH	GW	S	%	TGF	PGF	TGA	PGA	+/–	GP	G	A	Pts	PIM	PP	SH	GW
1978-79	Sault Ste. Marie Greyhounds	OHA	68	28	21	49	....	....	....	85	....	....	....	....	....	....	....	....	....	....	....	....	....	....	....	....	....	....
1979-80	Sault Ste. Marie Greyhounds	OHA	68	21	34	55	....	....	....	64	....	....	....	....	....	....	....	....	....	....	....	....	....	....	....	....	....	....
1980-81	Michigan Tech Huskies	WCHA	40	23	19	42	....	....	....	12	....	....	....	....	....	....	....	....	....	....	....	....	....	....	....	....	....	....
1981-82	Michigan Tech Huskies	CCHA	35	26	24	50	....	....	....	37	....	....	....	....	....	....	....	....	....	....	....	....	....	....	....	....	....	....
1982-83	Michigan Tech Huskies	CCHA	37	19	29	48	....	....	....	37	....	....	....	....	....	....	....	....	....	....	....	....	....	....	....	....	....	....
1983-84	Michigan Tech Huskies	CCHA	40	23	17	40	....	....	....	40	....	....	....	....	....	....	....	....	....	....	....	....	....	....	....	....	....	....
	Toledo Goaldiggers	IHL	3	2	2	4	....	....	....	4	....	....	....	....	....	....	....	....	....	....	....	....	....	....	....	....	....	....
1984-85				DID NOT PLAY																								
1985-86	Kalamazoo Wings	IHL	78	43	66	109	....	....	....	28	....	....	....	....	....	....	....	....	....	....	6	6	4	10	8	....	....	....
1986-87	Kalamazoo Wings	IHL	27	11	22	33	....	....	....	8	....	....	....	....	....	....	....	....	....	....	....	....	....	....	....	....	....	....
1987-88	**Minnesota North Stars**	**NHL**	**5**	**0**	**0**	**0**	**0**	**0**	**0**	**0**	**0**	**0**	**0**	**3**	**0.0**	**0**	**0**	**4**	**0**	**–4**	....	....	....	....	....	....	....	....
	Kalamazoo Wings	IHL	77	31	54	85	....	....	....	75	....	....	....	....	....	....	....	....	....	....	7	5	5	10	6	....	....	....
1988-89	HC Ajoie	Switz.	....	9	5	14	....	....	....	....	....	....	....	....	....	....	....	....	....	....	....	10	*15	25	....	....	....	....
	NHL Totals		**5**	**0**	**0**	**0**	**0**	**0**	**0**	**0**	**0**	**0**	**0**	**3**	**0.0**	**0**	**0**	**4**	**0**		....	....	....	....	....	....	....	....

IHL Second All-Star Team (1986)

Signed as a free agent by **Detroit**, September, 1986. Signed as a free agent by **Minnesota**, September, 1987.

• THEBERGE, GREG

Greg Theberge D – R. 5'10", 185 lbs. b: Peterborough, Ont., 9/3/1959. Washington's 5th choice, 109th overall, in 1979 Entry Draft.

Season	Club	League	GP	G	A	Pts	AG	AA	APts	PIM	PP	SH	GW	S	%	TGF	PGF	TGA	PGA	+/–	GP	G	A	Pts	PIM	PP	SH	GW
1976-77	Peterborough Petes	OHA	65	10	22	32	....	....	....	47	....	....	....	....	....	....	....	....	....	....	....	....	....	....	....	....	....	....
1977-78	Peterborough Petes	OHA	66	13	54	67	....	....	....	88	....	....	....	....	....	....	....	....	....	....	19	3	12	15	18	....	....	....
1978-79	Peterborough Petes	OHA	63	20	60	80	....	....	....	90	....	....	....	....	....	....	....	....	....	....	19	8	9	17	40	....	....	....
1979-80	**Washington Capitals**	**NHL**	**12**	**0**	**1**	**1**	**0**	**1**	**1**	**0**	**0**	**0**	**0**	**21**	**0.0**	**9**	**5**	**7**	**0**	**–3**	....	....	....	....	....	....	....	....
	Hershey Bears	AHL	58	7	22	29	....	....	....	31	....	....	....	....	....	....	....	....	....	....	16	5	6	11	18	....	....	....
1980-81	**Washington Capitals**	**NHL**	**1**	**1**	**0**	**1**	**1**	**0**	**1**	**0**	**0**	**0**	**0**	**1**	**100.0**	**1**	**0**	**3**	**0**	**–2**	....	....	....	....	....	....	....	....
	Hershey Bears	AHL	78	12	53	65	....	....	....	117	....	....	....	....	....	....	....	....	....	....	10	0	4	4	12	....	....	....
1981-82	**Washington Capitals**	**NHL**	**57**	**5**	**32**	**37**	**4**	**21**	**25**	**49**	**2**	**0**	**0**	**150**	**3.3**	**90**	**29**	**71**	**2**	**–8**	....	....	....	....	....	....	....	....
1982-83	**Washington Capitals**	**NHL**	**70**	**8**	**28**	**36**	**7**	**19**	**26**	**20**	**7**	**0**	**1**	**136**	**5.9**	**90**	**53**	**40**	**0**	**–3**	**4**	**0**	**1**	**1**	**0**	**0**	**0**	**0**
	Hershey Bears	AHL	6	1	5	6	....	....	....	2	....	....	....	....	....	....	....	....	....	....	....	....	....	....	....	....	....	....
1983-84	**Washington Capitals**	**NHL**	**13**	**1**	**2**	**3**	**1**	**1**	**2**	**4**	**1**	**0**	**0**	**19**	**5.3**	**7**	**5**	**6**	**0**	**–4**	....	....	....	....	....	....	....	....
	Hershey Bears	AHL	41	3	27	30	....	....	....	25	....	....	....	....	....	....	....	....	....	....	....	....	....	....	....	....	....	....
	NHL Totals		**153**	**15**	**63**	**78**	**13**	**42**	**55**	**73**	**10**	**0**	**1**	**327**	**4.6**	**197**	**92**	**127**	**2**		**4**	**0**	**1**	**1**	**0**	**0**	**0**	**0**

OHA First All-Star Team (1979) • AHL Second All-Star Team (1981)

• THELIN, MATS

Mats Thelin D – L. 5'10", 185 lbs. b: Stockholm, Sweden, 3/30/1961. Boston's 6th choice, 140th overall, in 1981 Entry Draft.

Season	Club	League	GP	G	A	Pts	AG	AA	APts	PIM	PP	SH	GW	S	%	TGF	PGF	TGA	PGA	+/–	GP	G	A	Pts	PIM	PP	SH	GW
1980-81	AIK Solna	Sweden	9	0	0	0	....	....	....	4	....	....	....	....	....	....	....	....	....	....	5	0	0	0	6	....	....	....
1981-82	AIK Solna	Sweden	36	2	2	4	....	....	....	28	....	....	....	....	....	....	....	....	....	....	7	0	1	1	16	....	....	....
	Sweden	WEC-A	10	0	0	0	....	....	....	8	....	....	....	....	....	....	....	....	....	....	....	....	....	....	....	....	....	....
1982-83	AIK Solna	Sweden	28	6	4	10	....	....	....	50	....	....	....	....	....	....	....	....	....	....	3	1	1	2	4	....	....	....
	Sweden	WEC-A	5	0	3	3	....	....	....	4	....	....	....	....	....	....	....	....	....	....	....	....	....	....	....	....	....	....
1983-84	AIK Solna	Sweden	16	4	1	5	....	....	....	20	....	....	....	....	....	....	....	....	....	....	....	....	....	....	....	....	....	....
	Sweden	Olympics	7	0	1	1	....	....	....	4	....	....	....	....	....	....	....	....	....	....	....	....	....	....	....	....	....	....
1984-85	Sweden	C Cup	8	1	3	4	....	....	....	14	....	....	....	....	....	....	....	....	....	....	....	....	....	....	....	....	....	....
	Boston Bruins	**NHL**	**73**	**5**	**13**	**18**	**4**	**9**	**13**	**9**	**0**	**0**	**2**	**91**	**5.5**	**82**	**7**	**81**	**15**	**+9**	**5**	**0**	**0**	**0**	**6**	**0**	**0**	**0**
1985-86	**Boston Bruins**	**NHL**	**31**	**2**	**3**	**5**	**2**	**2**	**4**	**29**	**1**	**0**	**0**	**29**	**6.9**	**28**	**1**	**41**	**17**	**+3**	....	....	....	....	....	....	....	....
	Moncton Golden Flames	AHL	2	0	1	1	....	....	....	0	....	....	....	....	....	....	....	....	....	....	....	....	....	....	....	....	....	....
1986-87	**Boston Bruins**	**NHL**	**59**	**1**	**3**	**4**	**1**	**2**	**3**	**69**	**0**	**0**	**0**	**39**	**2.6**	**33**	**0**	**43**	**2**	**–8**	....	....	....	....	....	....	....	....
1987-88	AIK Solna	Sweden	39	2	8	10	....	....	....	56	....	....	....	....	....	....	....	....	....	....	1	0	0	0	0	....	....	....
1988-89	AIK Solna	Sweden	38	6	16	22	....	....	....	62	....	....	....	....	....	....	....	....	....	....	2	0	2	2	0	....	....	....
1989-90	AIK Solna	Sweden	15	3	4	7	....	....	....	20	....	....	....	....	....	....	....	....	....	....	2	0	0	0	2	....	....	....
1990-91	AIK Solna	Sweden	37	1	3	4	....	....	....	54	....	....	....	....	....	....	....	....	....	....	....	....	....	....	....	....	....	....
1991-92	AIK Solna	Sweden	36	0	5	5	....	....	....	79	....	....	....	....	....	....	....	....	....	....	3	0	0	0	2	....	....	....
1992-93	AIK Solna	Sweden	22	0	3	3	....	....	....	22	....	....	....	....	....	....	....	....	....	....	....	....	....	....	....	....	....	....
	NHL Totals		**163**	**8**	**19**	**27**	**7**	**13**	**20**	**107**	**1**	**0**	**2**	**159**	**5.0**	**143**	**8**	**165**	**34**		**5**	**0**	**0**	**0**	**6**	**0**	**0**	**0**

• THELVEN, MICHAEL

Michael Thelven D – R. 5'11", 185 lbs. b: Stockholm, Sweden, 1/7/1961. Boston's 8th choice, 186th overall, in 1980 Entry Draft.

Season	Club	League	GP	G	A	Pts	AG	AA	APts	PIM	PP	SH	GW	S	%	TGF	PGF	TGA	PGA	+/–	GP	G	A	Pts	PIM	PP	SH	GW
1978-79	Djurgarden IF Stockholm	Sweden	10	0	1	1	....	....	....	8	....	....	....	....	....	....	....	....	....	....	....	....	....	....	....	....	....	....
1979-80				STATISTICS NOT AVAILABLE																								
1980-81	Djurgarden IF Stockholm	Sweden	28	2	4	6	....	....	....	38	....	....	....	....	....	....	....	....	....	....	....	....	....	....	....	....	....	....
1981-82	Djurgarden IF Stockholm	Sweden	34	5	3	8	....	....	....	53	....	....	....	....	....	....	....	....	....	....	6	2	1	3	2	....	....	....
1982-83	Djurgarden IF Stockholm	Sweden	30	3	14	17	....	....	....	50	....	....	....	....	....	....	....	....	....	....	7	1	2	3	12	....	....	....
1983-84	Djurgarden IF Stockholm	Sweden	27	6	7	13	....	....	....	51	....	....	....	....	....	....	....	....	....	....	5	1	1	2	6	....	....	....
	Sweden	Olympics	4	1	3	4	....	....	....	4	....	....	....	....	....	....	....	....	....	....	....	....	....	....	....	....	....	....

			REGULAR SEASON																		PLAYOFFS							
Season	Club	League	GP	G	A	Pts	AG	AA	APts	PIM	PP	SH	GW	S	%	TGF	PGF	TGA	PGA	+/–	GP	G	A	Pts	PIM	PP	SH	GW
1984-85	Sweden	C Cup	8	0	3	3	....	....	....	14	....	....	....	....	....	....	....	....	....	....	....	....	....	....	....	....	....	....
	Djurgarden IF Stockholm	Sweden	33	8	13	21	....	....	....	54	....	....	....	....	....	....	....	....	....	....	8	0	2	2	2	....	....	....
	Sweden	WEC-A	10	0	2	2	....	....	....	10	....	....	....	....	....	....	....	....	....	....	....	....	....	....	....	....	....	....
1985-86	**Boston Bruins**	**NHL**	**60**	**6**	**20**	**26**	**5**	**13**	**18**	**48**	**1**	**0**	**0**	**108**	**5.6**	**77**	**21**	**73**	**24**	**+7**	**3**	**0**	**0**	**0**	**0**	**0**	**0**	**0**
1986-87	**Boston Bruins**	**NHL**	**34**	**5**	**15**	**20**	**4**	**11**	**15**	**18**	**3**	**0**	**0**	**60**	**8.3**	**47**	**12**	**38**	**1**	**–2**	....	....	....	....	....	....	....	....
1987-88	Sweden	C Cup	6	0	3	3	....	....	....	10	....	....	....	....	....	....	....	....	....	....	....	....	....	....	....	....	....	....
	Boston Bruins	**NHL**	**67**	**6**	**25**	**31**	**5**	**18**	**23**	**57**	**1**	**0**	**1**	**106**	**5.7**	**74**	**17**	**61**	**16**	**+12**	**21**	**3**	**3**	**6**	**26**	**1**	**0**	**0**
1988-89	**Boston Bruins**	**NHL**	**40**	**3**	**18**	**21**	**3**	**13**	**16**	**71**	**1**	**1**	**0**	**68**	**4.4**	**57**	**19**	**42**	**14**	**+10**	**10**	**1**	**7**	**8**	**8**	**0**	**0**	**1**
1989-90	**Boston Bruins**	**NHL**	**6**	**0**	**2**	**2**	**0**	**1**	**1**	**23**	**0**	**0**	**0**	**8**	**0.0**	**5**	**0**	**2**	**0**	**+3**	....	....	....	....	....	....	....	....
	NHL Totals		**207**	**20**	**80**	**100**	**17**	**56**	**73**	**217**	**6**	**1**	**1**	**350**	**5.7**	**260**	**69**	**216**	**55**		**34**	**4**	**10**	**14**	**34**	**1**	**0**	**1**

Swedish World All-Star Team (1984, 1985)

• THERIEN, CHRIS

Chris Therien D – L. 6'5", 230 lbs. b: Ottawa, Ont., 12/14/1971. Philadelphia's 7th choice, 47th overall, in 1990 Entry Draft.

Season	Club	League	GP	G	A	Pts	AG	AA	APts	PIM	PP	SH	GW	S	%	TGF	PGF	TGA	PGA	+/–	GP	G	A	Pts	PIM	PP	SH	GW
1989-90	Northwood Prep School	H.S.	31	35	37	72	....	....	....	54	....	....	....	....	....	....	....	....	....	....	....	....	....	....	....	....	....	....
1990-91	Providence College	H.E.	36	4	18	22	....	....	....	36	....	....	....	....	....	....	....	....	....	....	....	....	....	....	....	....	....	....
1991-92	Providence College	H.E.	36	16	25	41	....	....	....	38	....	....	....	....	....	....	....	....	....	....	....	....	....	....	....	....	....	....
1992-93	Providence College	H.E.	33	8	11	19	....	....	....	52	....	....	....	....	....	....	....	....	....	....	....	....	....	....	....	....	....	....
	Canada	Nat-Team	8	1	4	5	....	....	....	8	....	....	....	....	....	....	....	....	....	....	....	....	....	....	....	....	....	....
1993-94	Canada	Nat-Team	59	7	15	22	....	....	....	46	....	....	....	....	....	....	....	....	....	....	....	....	....	....	....	....	....	....
	Canada	Olympics	4	0	0	0	....	....	....	4	....	....	....	....	....	....	....	....	....	....	....	....	....	....	....	....	....	....
	Hershey Bears	AHL	6	0	0	0	....	....	....	2	....	....	....	....	....	....	....	....	....	....	....	....	....	....	....	....	....	....
1994-95	Hershey Bears	AHL	34	3	13	16	....	....	....	27	....	....	....	....	....	....	....	....	....	....	....	....	....	....	....	....	....	....
	Philadelphia Flyers	**NHL**	**48**	**3**	**10**	**13**	**5**	**15**	**20**	**38**	**1**	**0**	**0**	**53**	**5.7**	**44**	**5**	**37**	**6**	**+8**	**15**	**0**	**0**	**0**	**10**	**0**	**0**	**0**
1995-96	**Philadelphia Flyers**	**NHL**	**82**	**6**	**17**	**23**	**6**	**14**	**20**	**89**	**3**	**0**	**1**	**123**	**4.9**	**75**	**10**	**61**	**12**	**+16**	**12**	**0**	**0**	**0**	**18**	**0**	**0**	**0**
1996-97	**Philadelphia Flyers**	**NHL**	**71**	**2**	**22**	**24**	**2**	**19**	**21**	**64**	**0**	**0**	**0**	**107**	**1.9**	**71**	**8**	**52**	**16**	**+27**	**19**	**1**	**6**	**7**	**6**	**0**	**0**	**1**
1997-98	**Philadelphia Flyers**	**NHL**	**78**	**3**	**16**	**19**	**4**	**16**	**20**	**80**	**1**	**0**	**1**	**102**	**2.9**	**68**	**12**	**71**	**20**	**+5**	**5**	**0**	**1**	**1**	**4**	**0**	**0**	**0**
	NHL Totals		**279**	**14**	**65**	**79**	**17**	**64**	**81**	**271**	**5**	**0**	**2**	**385**	**3.6**	**258**	**35**	**221**	**54**		**51**	**1**	**7**	**8**	**38**	**0**	**0**	**1**

Hockey East Second All-Star Team (1993) • NHL/Upper Deck All-Rookie Team (1995)

• THERRIEN, GASTON

Gaston Therrien D – R. 5'10", 185 lbs. b: Montreal, Que., 5/27/1960. Quebec's 5th choice, 129th overall, in 1980 Entry Draft.

Season	Club	League	GP	G	A	Pts	AG	AA	APts	PIM	PP	SH	GW	S	%	TGF	PGF	TGA	PGA	+/–	GP	G	A	Pts	PIM	PP	SH	GW
1977-78	Quebec Remparts	QMJHL	72	17	60	77	....	....	....	73	....	....	....	....	....	....	....	....	....	....	....	....	....	....	....	....	....	....
1978-79	Quebec Remparts	QMJHL	65	10	52	62	....	....	....	126	....	....	....	....	....	....	....	....	....	....	6	1	5	6	24	....	....	....
1979-80	Quebec Remparts	QMJHL	71	39	86	125	....	....	....	152	....	....	....	....	....	....	....	....	....	....	3	1	2	3	6	....	....	....
1980-81	**Quebec Nordiques**	**NHL**	**3**	**0**	**1**	**1**	**0**	**1**	**1**	**2**	**0**	**0**	**0**	**10**	**0.0**	**4**	**1**	**4**	**0**	**–1**	....	....	....	....	....	....	....	....
	Rochester Americans	AHL	18	2	10	12	....	....	....	6	....	....	....	....	....	....	....	....	....	....	....	....	....	....	....	....	....	....
1981-82	**Quebec Nordiques**	**NHL**	**14**	**0**	**7**	**7**	**0**	**5**	**5**	**6**	**0**	**0**	**0**	**15**	**0.0**	**17**	**4**	**11**	**0**	**+2**	**9**	**0**	**1**	**1**	**4**	**0**	**0**	**0**
	Fredericton Express	AHL	61	11	42	53	....	....	....	79	....	....	....	....	....	....	....	....	....	....	....	....	....	....	....	....	....	....
1982-83	**Quebec Nordiques**	**NHL**	**5**	**0**	**0**	**0**	**0**	**0**	**0**	**4**	**0**	**0**	**0**	**5**	**0.0**	**1**	**1**	**4**	**0**	**–4**	....	....	....	....	....	....	....	....
	Fredericton Express	AHL	41	3	10	13	....	....	....	60	....	....	....	....	....	....	....	....	....	....	....	....	....	....	....	....	....	....
	Erie Blades	ACHL	3	1	4	5	....	....	....	0	....	....	....	....	....	....	....	....	....	....	....	....	....	....	....	....	....	....
1983-1986			DID NOT PLAY																									
1986-87	Villard de Lans	France	29	36	48	84	....	....	....	....	....	....	....	....	....	....	....	....	....	....	....	....	....	....	....	....	....	....
1987-88	Villard de Lans	France	28	18	31	49	....	....	....	45	....	....	....	....	....	....	....	....	....	....	....	....	....	....	....	....	....	....
1988-89	Villard de Lans	France	39	26	33	59	....	....	....	56	....	....	....	....	....	....	....	....	....	....	....	....	....	....	....	....	....	....
	NHL Totals		**22**	**0**	**8**	**8**	**0**	**6**	**6**	**12**	**0**	**0**	**0**	**30**	**0.0**	**22**	**6**	**19**	**0**		**9**	**0**	**1**	**1**	**4**	**0**	**0**	**0**

QMJHL First All-Star Team (1980)

• THIBAUDEAU, GILLES

Gilles Thibaudeau C – L. 5'10", 165 lbs. b: Montreal, Que., 3/4/1963.

Season	Club	League	GP	G	A	Pts	AG	AA	APts	PIM	PP	SH	GW	S	%	TGF	PGF	TGA	PGA	+/–	GP	G	A	Pts	PIM	PP	SH	GW
1983-84	St. Antoine Saints	Jr. B	38	63	77	140	....	....	....	146	....	....	....	....	....	....	....	....	....	....	....	....	....	....	....	....	....	....
1984-85	Sherbrooke Canadiens	AHL	7	2	4	6	....	....	....	2	....	....	....	....	....	....	....	....	....	....	....	....	....	....	....	....	....	....
	Flint Generals	IHL	71	52	45	97	....	....	....	81	....	....	....	....	....	....	....	....	....	....	7	3	1	4	18	....	....	....
1985-86	Sherbrooke Canadiens	AHL	61	15	23	38	....	....	....	20	....	....	....	....	....	....	....	....	....	....	....	....	....	....	....	....	....	....
1986-87	**Montreal Canadiens**	**NHL**	**9**	**1**	**3**	**4**	**1**	**2**	**3**	**0**	**0**	**0**	**0**	**10**	**10.0**	**6**	**0**	**1**	**0**	**+5**	....	....	....	....	....	....	....	....
	Sherbrooke Canadiens	AHL	62	27	40	67	....	....	....	26	....	....	....	....	....	....	....	....	....	....	....	....	....	....	....	....	....	....
1987-88	**Montreal Canadiens**	**NHL**	**17**	**5**	**6**	**11**	**4**	**4**	**8**	**0**	**2**	**0**	**1**	**25**	**20.0**	**16**	**5**	**5**	**0**	**+6**	**8**	**3**	**3**	**6**	**2**	**1**	**0**	**0**
	Sherbrooke Canadiens	AHL	59	39	57	96	....	....	....	45	....	....	....	....	....	....	....	....	....	....	....	....	....	....	....	....	....	....
1988-89	**Montreal Canadiens**	**NHL**	**32**	**6**	**6**	**12**	**5**	**4**	**9**	**6**	**1**	**0**	**0**	**42**	**14.3**	**25**	**6**	**14**	**0**	**+5**	....	....	....	....	....	....	....	....
1989-90	**New York Islanders**	**NHL**	**20**	**4**	**4**	**8**	**3**	**3**	**6**	**17**	**0**	**0**	**0**	**23**	**17.4**	**11**	**1**	**8**	**0**	**+2**	....	....	....	....	....	....	....	....
	Springfield Indians	AHL	6	5	8	13	....	....	....	0	....	....	....	....	....	....	....	....	....	....	....	....	....	....	....	....	....	....
	Toronto Maple Leafs	**NHL**	**21**	**7**	**11**	**18**	**6**	**8**	**14**	**13**	**3**	**0**	**2**	**44**	**15.9**	**31**	**13**	**12**	**0**	**+6**	....	....	....	....	....	....	....	....
	Newmarket Saints	AHL	10	7	13	20	....	....	....	4	....	....	....	....	....	....	....	....	....	....	....	....	....	....	....	....	....	....
1990-91	**Toronto Maple Leafs**	**NHL**	**20**	**2**	**7**	**9**	**2**	**5**	**7**	**4**	**0**	**0**	**0**	**36**	**5.6**	**19**	**3**	**26**	**3**	**–7**	....	....	....	....	....	....	....	....
	Newmarket Saints	AHL	60	34	37	71	....	....	....	28	....	....	....	....	....	....	....	....	....	....	....	....	....	....	....	....	....	....
1991-92	HC Lugano	Switz.	33	29	17	46	....	....	....	12	....	....	....	....	....	....	....	....	....	....	4	6	3	9	2	....	....	....
1992-93	HC Davos	Switz. B	36	*50	25	75	....	....	....	....	....	....	....	....	....	....	....	....	....	....	....	....	....	....	....	....	....	....
1993-94	HC Davos	Switz. B	36	32	15	47	....	....	....	8	....	....	....	....	....	....	....	....	....	....	4	2	0	2	6	....	....	....
1994-95	HC Davos	Switz.	36	17	20	37	....	....	....	24	....	....	....	....	....	....	....	....	....	....	5	5	4	9	0	....	....	....
1995-96	SC Rapperswil-Jona	Switz.	36	26	27	53	....	....	....	12	....	....	....	....	....	....	....	....	....	....	4	4	1	5	4	....	....	....
1996-97	SC Rapperswil-Jona	Switz.	45	25	16	41	....	....	....	26	....	....	....	....	....	....	....	....	....	....	3	0	1	1	25	....	....	....
1997-98	SC Rapperswil-Jona	Switz.	40	18	29	47	....	....	....	32	....	....	....	....	....	....	....	....	....	....	7	6	3	9	2	....	....	....
	NHL Totals		**119**	**25**	**37**	**62**	**21**	**26**	**47**	**40**	**6**	**0**	**3**	**180**	**13.9**	**108**	**28**	**66**	**3**		**8**	**3**	**3**	**6**	**2**	**1**	**0**	**0**

IHL Second All-Star Team (1985) • Won Garry F. Longman Memorial Trophy (Top Rookie - IHL) (1985)

Signed as a free agent by **Montreal**, October 9, 1984. Signed as a free agent by **NY Islanders**, September, 1989. Traded to **Toronto** by **NY Islanders** with Mike Stevens for Jack Capuano, Paul Gagne and Derek Laxdal, December 20, 1989.

• THIFFAULT, LEO

Leo Thiffault LW – L. 5'10", 175 lbs. b: Drummondville, Que., 12/16/1944.

Season	Club	League	GP	G	A	Pts	AG	AA	APts	PIM	PP	SH	GW	S	%	TGF	PGF	TGA	PGA	+/–	GP	G	A	Pts	PIM	PP	SH	GW
1962-63	Montreal Jr. Canadiens	OHA	50	9	9	18	....	....	....	64	....	....	....	....	....	....	....	....	....	....	10	1	1	2	2	....	....	....
1963-64	Montreal Jr. Canadiens	OHA	55	23	38	61	....	....	....	44	....	....	....	....	....	....	....	....	....	....	17	7	12	19	22	....	....	....
1964-65	Peterborough Petes	OHA	56	33	52	85	....	....	....	52	....	....	....	....	....	....	....	....	....	....	12	4	10	14	8	....	....	....
	Quebec Aces	AHL	2	0	0	0	....	....	....	0	....	....	....	....	....	....	....	....	....	....	....	....	....	....	....	....	....	....
1965-66	Houston Apollos	CPHL	69	19	26	45	....	....	....	55	....	....	....	....	....	....	....	....	....	....	....	....	....	....	....	....	....	....
1966-67	Houston Apollos	CHL	47	7	15	22	....	....	....	37	....	....	....	....	....	....	....	....	....	....	2	0	0	0	0	....	....	....
	Cleveland Barons	AHL	5	1	1	2	....	....	....	4	....	....	....	....	....	....	....	....	....	....	....	....	....	....	....	....	....	....
1967-68	Memphis South Stars	CHL	66	22	32	54	....	....	....	52	....	....	....	....	....	....	....	....	....	....	3	0	1	1	6	....	....	....
	Minnesota North Stars	**NHL**	....	....	....	....	....	....	....	....	....	....	....	....	....	....	....	....	....	....	**5**	**0**	**0**	**0**	**0**	....	....	....
1968-69	Phoenix Roadrunners	WHL	70	16	24	40	....	....	....	25	....	....	....	....	....	....	....	....	....	....	....	....	....	....	....	....	....	....
1969-1972			DID NOT PLAY – RETIRED																									
1972-73	Phoenix Roadrunners	WHL	70	12	35	47	....	....	....	57	....	....	....	....	....	....	....	....	....	....	5	1	0	1	5	....	....	....
1973-74	Tulsa Oilers	CHL	1	0	1	1	....	....	....	0	....	....	....	....	....	....	....	....	....	....	....	....	....	....	....	....	....	....
	Phoenix Roadrunners	WHL	35	5	6	11	....	....	....	26	....	....	....	....	....	....	....	....	....	....	2	0	0	0	0	....	....	....
	NHL Totals		**0**	**0**	**0**	**0**	**0**	**0**	**0**	**0**	**0**	**0**	**0**	**0**	**0.0**	**0**	**0**	**0**	**0**		**5**	**0**	**0**	**0**	**0**	**0**	**0**	**0**

Rights traded to **Minnesota** by **Montreal** with Bill Plager and the rights to Barrie Meissner for Bryan Watson, June 6, 1967. Traded to **Phoenix** (WHL) by **Minnesota** with Bob Charlebois for Walt McKechnie, June, 1968.

• THOMAS, REG

Reg Thomas LW – L. 5'10", 185 lbs. b: Lambeth, Ont., 4/21/1953. Chicago's 2nd choice, 29th overall, in 1973 Amateur Draft.

Season	Club	League	GP	G	A	Pts	AG	AA	APts	PIM	PP	SH	GW	S	%	TGF	PGF	TGA	PGA	+/–	GP	G	A	Pts	PIM	PP	SH	GW
1970-71	London Knights	OHA	58	35	35	70	....	....	....	29	....	....	....	....	....	....	....	....	....	....	....	....	....	....	....	....	....	....
1971-72	London Knights	OHA	61	49	55	104	....	....	....	38	....	....	....	....	....	....	....	....	....	....	....	....	....	....	....	....	....	....
1972-73	London Knights	OHA	61	52	83	135	....	....	....	41	....	....	....	....	....	....	....	....	....	....	....	....	....	....	....	....	....	....
1973-74	Los Angeles Sharks	WHA	72	14	21	35	....	....	....	22	....	....	....	....	....	....	....	....	....	....	....	....	....	....	....	....	....	....
1974-75	Michigan-Baltimore	WHA	50	8	13	21	....	....	....	42	....	....	....	....	....	....	....	....	....	....	....	....	....	....	....	....	....	....

			REGULAR SEASON																		PLAYOFFS							
Season	Club	League	GP	G	A	Pts	AG	AA	APts	PIM	PP	SH	GW	S	%	TGF	PGF	TGA	PGA	+/–	GP	G	A	Pts	PIM	PP	SH	GW
1975-76	Indianapolis Racers	WHA	80	23	17	40	....	....	....	23	....	....	....	....	....	....	....	....	....	....	7	1	0	1	4	....	....	....
1976-77	Indianapolis Racers	WHA	79	25	30	55	....	....	....	34	....	....	....	....	....	....	....	....	....	....	9	7	9	16	4	....	....	....
1977-78	Indianapolis Racers	WHA	49	15	16	31	....	....	....	44	....	....	....	....	....	....	....	....	....	....	....	....	....	....	....	....	....	....
	Cincinnati Stingers	WHA	18	4	2	6	....	....	....	12	....	....	....	....	....	....	....	....	....	....	....	....	....	....	....	....	....	....
1978-79	Cincinnati Stingers	WHA	80	32	39	71	....	....	....	22	....	....	....	....	....	....	....	....	....	....	3	1	1	2	0	....	....	....
1979-80	**Quebec Nordiques**	**NHL**	**39**	**9**	**7**	**16**	**8**	**5**	**13**	**6**	**2**	**0**	**0**	**89**	**10.1**	**24**	**4**	**28**	**3**	**–5**	....	....	....	....	....	....	....	....
	New Brunswick Hawks	AHL	31	20	20	40	....	....	....	18	....	....	....	....	....	....	....	....	....	....	....	....	....	....	....	....	....	....
1980-81	Nova Scotia Voyageurs	AHL	74	36	43	79	....	....	....	90	....	....	....	....	....	....	....	....	....	....	4	1	6	7	2	....	....	....
1981-82	Cincinnati Tigers	CHL	80	47	63	110	....	....	....	55	....	....	....	....	....	....	....	....	....	....	4	2	2	4	2	....	....	....
1982-83	St. Catharines Saints	AHL	80	35	57	92	....	....	....	22	....	....	....	....	....	....	....	....	....	....	....	....	....	....	....	....	....	....
1983-84	Schops WAT Stadlau	Austria	28	29	33	62	....	....	....	....	....	....	....	....	....	....	....	....	....	....	....	....	....	....	....	....	....	....
1984-85	Schops WAT Stadlau	Austria	34	24	30	54	....	....	....	20	....	....	....	....	....	....	....	....	....	....	....	....	....	....	....	....	....	....
	NHL Totals		**39**	**9**	**7**	**16**	**8**	**5**	**13**	**6**	**2**	**0**	**0**	**89**	**10.1**	**24**	**4**	**28**	**3**		....	....	....	....	....	....	....	....
	Other Major League Totals		428	121	138	259	....	....	....	199	....	....	....	....	....	....	....	....	....	....	19	9	10	19	8	....	....	....

OHA First All-Star Team (1973) • CHL First All-Star Team (1982) • AHL First All-Star Team (1983)

Selected by **LA Sharks** (WHA) in 1973 WHA Professional Player Draft, June, 1973. Transferred to **Michigan** (WHA) after **LA Sharks** (WHA) franchise relocated, May, 1974. Claimed by **Indianapolis** (WHA) from **Michigan-Baltimore** (WHA) in WHA Dispersal Draft, June, 1975. Traded to **Cincinnati** (WHA) by **Indianapolis** (WHA) with Darryl Maggs for Claude Larose and Rich Leduc, February, 1978. Claimed by **Edmonton** from **Chicago** in Expansion Draft, June 13, 1979. Traded to **Toronto** by **Edmonton** for Toronto's 6th round choice (Steve Smith) in 1981 Entry Draft, August 22, 1979. Traded to **Quebec** by **Toronto** for Dave Farrish and Terry Martin, December 13, 1979. Signed as a free agent by **Toronto**, July 21, 1981.

• THOMAS, SCOTT

Scott Thomas RW – R. 6'2", 195 lbs. b: Buffalo, NY, 1/18/1970. Buffalo's 2nd choice, 56th overall, in 1989 Entry Draft.

Season	Club	League	GP	G	A	Pts	AG	AA	APts	PIM	PP	SH	GW	S	%	TGF	PGF	TGA	PGA	+/–	GP	G	A	Pts	PIM	PP	SH	GW
1987-88	Nichols High School	H.S.	16	23	39	62	....	....	....	62	....	....	....	....	....	....	....	....	....	....	....	....	....	....	....	....	....	....
1988-89	Nichols High School	H.S.	17	38	52	90	....	....	....	....	....	....	....	....	....	....	....	....	....	....	....	....	....	....	....	....	....	....
1989-90	Clarkson College	ECAC	34	19	13	32	....	....	....	95	....	....	....	....	....	....	....	....	....	....	....	....	....	....	....	....	....	....
1990-91	Clarkson College	ECAC	40	28	14	42	....	....	....	89	....	....	....	....	....	....	....	....	....	....	....	....	....	....	....	....	....	....
1991-92	Clarkson College	ECAC	29	22	20	42	....	....	....	57	....	....	....	....	....	....	....	....	....	....	....	....	....	....	....	....	....	....
	Rochester Americans	AHL	....	....	....	....	....	....	....	....	....	....	....	....	....	....	....	....	....	....	9	0	1	1	17	....	....	....
1992-93	**Buffalo Sabres**	**NHL**	**7**	**1**	**1**	**2**	**1**	**1**	**2**	**15**	**0**	**0**	**0**	**4**	**25.0**	**3**	**0**	**1**	**0**	**+2**	....	....	....	....	....	....	....	....
	Rochester Americans	AHL	65	32	27	59	....	....	....	38	....	....	....	....	....	....	....	....	....	....	17	8	5	13	6	....	....	....
1993-94	**Buffalo Sabres**	**NHL**	**32**	**2**	**2**	**4**	**2**	**2**	**4**	**8**	**1**	**0**	**0**	**26**	**7.7**	**9**	**2**	**13**	**0**	**–6**	....	....	....	....	....	....	....	....
	Rochester Americans	AHL	11	4	5	9	....	....	....	0	....	....	....	....	....	....	....	....	....	....	....	....	....	....	....	....	....	....
1994-95	Rochester Americans	AHL	55	21	25	46	....	....	....	115	....	....	....	....	....	....	....	....	....	....	5	4	0	4	4	....	....	....
1995-96	Cincinnati Cyclones	IHL	78	32	28	60	....	....	....	54	....	....	....	....	....	....	....	....	....	....	17	*13	2	15	4	....	....	....
1996-97	Cincinnati Cyclones	IHL	71	32	29	61	....	....	....	46	....	....	....	....	....	....	....	....	....	....	3	0	0	0	0	....	....	....
1997-98	Detroit Vipers	IHL	44	11	16	27	....	....	....	18	....	....	....	....	....	....	....	....	....	....	....	....	....	....	....	....	....	....
	Manitoba Moose	IHL	26	12	4	16	....	....	....	8	....	....	....	....	....	....	....	....	....	....	3	0	1	1	2	....	....	....
	NHL Totals		**39**	**3**	**3**	**6**	**3**	**3**	**6**	**23**	**1**	**0**	**0**	**30**	**10.0**	**12**	**2**	**14**	**0**		....	....	....	....	....	....	....	....

• THOMAS, STEVE

Steve Thomas LW – L. 5'11", 190 lbs. b: Stockport, England, 7/15/1963.

Season	Club	League	GP	G	A	Pts	AG	AA	APts	PIM	PP	SH	GW	S	%	TGF	PGF	TGA	PGA	+/–	GP	G	A	Pts	PIM	PP	SH	GW
1981-82	Markham Waxers	MTHL	48	68	57	125	....	....	....	113	....	....	....	....	....	....	....	....	....	....	....	....	....	....	....	....	....	....
1982-83	Toronto Marlboros	OHL	61	18	20	38	....	....	....	42	....	....	....	....	....	....	....	....	....	....	....	....	....	....	....	....	....	....
1983-84	Toronto Marlboros	OHL	70	51	54	105	....	....	....	77	....	....	....	....	....	....	....	....	....	....	....	....	....	....	....	....	....	....
1984-85	St. Catharines Saints	AHL	64	42	48	90	....	....	....	56	....	....	....	....	....	....	....	....	....	....	....	....	....	....	....	....	....	....
1984-85	**Toronto Maple Leafs**	**NHL**	**18**	**1**	**1**	**2**	**1**	**1**	**2**	**2**	**0**	**0**	**0**	**26**	**3.8**	**6**	**3**	**16**	**0**	**–13**	....	....	....	....	....	....	....	....
1985-86	**Toronto Maple Leafs**	**NHL**	**65**	**20**	**37**	**57**	**16**	**25**	**41**	**36**	**5**	**0**	**5**	**197**	**10.2**	**77**	**17**	**75**	**0**	**–15**	**10**	**6**	**8**	**14**	**9**	**3**	**0**	**0**
	St. Catharines Saints	AHL	19	18	14	32	....	....	....	35	....	....	....	....	....	....	....	....	....	....	....	....	....	....	....	....	....	....
1986-87	**Toronto Maple Leafs**	**NHL**	**78**	**35**	**27**	**62**	**30**	**20**	**50**	**114**	**3**	**0**	**7**	**245**	**14.3**	**91**	**16**	**78**	**0**	**–3**	**13**	**2**	**3**	**5**	**13**	**0**	**0**	**0**
1987-88	**Chicago Blackhawks**	**NHL**	**30**	**13**	**13**	**26**	**11**	**9**	**20**	**40**	**5**	**0**	**3**	**69**	**18.8**	**41**	**17**	**23**	**0**	**+1**	**3**	**1**	**2**	**3**	**6**	**0**	**0**	**0**
1988-89	**Chicago Blackhawks**	**NHL**	**45**	**21**	**19**	**40**	**18**	**13**	**31**	**69**	**8**	**0**	**0**	**124**	**16.9**	**51**	**19**	**44**	**10**	**–2**	**12**	**3**	**5**	**8**	**10**	**1**	**0**	**2**
1989-90	**Chicago Blackhawks**	**NHL**	**76**	**40**	**30**	**70**	**35**	**21**	**56**	**91**	**13**	**0**	**7**	**235**	**17.0**	**97**	**29**	**71**	**0**	**–3**	**20**	**7**	**6**	**13**	**33**	**1**	**0**	**3**
1990-91	**Chicago Blackhawks**	**NHL**	**69**	**19**	**35**	**54**	**17**	**27**	**44**	**129**	**2**	**0**	**3**	**192**	**9.9**	**66**	**13**	**45**	**0**	**+8**	**6**	**1**	**2**	**3**	**15**	**0**	**0**	**0**
	Canada	WEC-A	10	5	3	8	....	....	....	12	....	....	....	....	....	....	....	....	....	....	....	....	....	....	....	....	....	....
1991-92	**Chicago Blackhawks**	**NHL**	**11**	**2**	**6**	**8**	**2**	**4**	**6**	**26**	**0**	**0**	**1**	**35**	**5.7**	**11**	**3**	**15**	**4**	**–3**	....	....	....	....	....	....	....	....
	New York Islanders	**NHL**	**71**	**28**	**42**	**70**	**26**	**32**	**58**	**71**	**3**	**0**	**2**	**210**	**13.3**	**93**	**33**	**52**	**3**	**+11**	....	....	....	....	....	....	....	....
	Canada	WC-A	5	2	2	4	....	....	....	4	....	....	....	....	....	....	....	....	....	....	....	....	....	....	....	....	....	....
1992-93	**New York Islanders**	**NHL**	**79**	**37**	**50**	**87**	**31**	**34**	**65**	**111**	**12**	**0**	**7**	**264**	**14.0**	**131**	**58**	**70**	**0**	**+3**	**18**	**9**	**8**	**17**	**37**	**0**	**0**	**0**
1993-94	**New York Islanders**	**NHL**	**78**	**42**	**33**	**75**	**39**	**25**	**64**	**139**	**17**	**0**	**5**	**249**	**16.9**	**103**	**45**	**68**	**1**	**–9**	**4**	**1**	**0**	**1**	**8**	**1**	**0**	**0**
	Canada	WC-A	6	1	5	6	....	....	....	0	....	....	....	....	....	....	....	....	....	....	....	....	....	....	....	....	....	....
1994-95	**New York Islanders**	**NHL**	**47**	**11**	**15**	**26**	**19**	**22**	**41**	**60**	**3**	**0**	**2**	**133**	**8.3**	**33**	**13**	**34**	**0**	**–14**	....	....	....	....	....	....	....	....
1995-96	**New Jersey Devils**	**NHL**	**81**	**26**	**35**	**61**	**26**	**29**	**55**	**98**	**6**	**0**	**6**	**192**	**13.5**	**81**	**28**	**55**	**0**	**–2**	....	....	....	....	....	....	....	....
	Canada	WC-A	8	2	3	5	....	....	....	29	....	....	....	....	....	....	....	....	....	....	....	....	....	....	....	....	....	....
1996-97	**New Jersey Devils**	**NHL**	**57**	**15**	**19**	**34**	**16**	**17**	**33**	**46**	**1**	**0**	**2**	**124**	**12.1**	**48**	**10**	**29**	**0**	**+9**	**10**	**1**	**1**	**2**	**18**	**0**	**0**	**0**
1997-98	**New Jersey Devils**	**NHL**	**55**	**14**	**10**	**24**	**16**	**10**	**26**	**32**	**3**	**0**	**4**	**111**	**12.6**	**38**	**9**	**25**	**0**	**+4**	**6**	**0**	**3**	**3**	**2**	**0**	**0**	**0**
	NHL Totals		**860**	**324**	**372**	**696**	**303**	**289**	**592**	**1064**	**81**	**0**	**54**	**2406**	**13.5**	**967**	**313**	**700**	**18**		**102**	**31**	**38**	**69**	**151**	**6**	**0**	**5**

Won Dudley "Red" Garrett Memorial Trophy (Top Rookie - AHL) (1985) • AHL First All-Star Team (1985)

Signed as a free agent by **Toronto,** May 12, 1984. Traded to **Chicago** by **Toronto** with Rick Vaive and Bob McGill for Al Secord and Ed Olczyk, September 3, 1987. Traded to **NY Islanders** by **Chicago** with Adam Creighton for Brent Sutter and Brad Lauer, October 25, 1991. Traded to **New Jersey** by **NY Islanders** for Claude Lemieux, October 3, 1995. Signed as a free agent by **Toronto**, July 12, 1998.

• THOMLINSON, DAVE

Dave Thomlinson LW – L. 6'1", 215 lbs. b: Edmonton, Alta., 10/22/1966. Toronto's 3rd choice, 43rd overall, in 1985 Entry Draft.

Season	Club	League	GP	G	A	Pts	AG	AA	APts	PIM	PP	SH	GW	S	%	TGF	PGF	TGA	PGA	+/–	GP	G	A	Pts	PIM	PP	SH	GW
1984-85	Brandon Wheat Kings	WHL	26	13	14	27	....	....	....	70	....	....	....	....	....	....	....	....	....	....	....	....	....	....	....	....	....	....
1985-86	Brandon Wheat Kings	WHL	53	25	20	45	....	....	....	116	....	....	....	....	....	....	....	....	....	....	....	....	....	....	....	....	....	....
1986-87	Brandon Wheat Kings	WHL	2	0	1	1	....	....	....	9	....	....	....	....	....	....	....	....	....	....	....	....	....	....	....	....	....	....
	Moose Jaw Warriors	WHL	70	44	36	80	....	....	....	117	....	....	....	....	....	....	....	....	....	....	9	7	3	10	19	....	....	....
1987-88	Peoria Rivermen	IHL	74	27	30	57	....	....	....	56	....	....	....	....	....	....	....	....	....	....	7	4	3	7	11	....	....	....
1988-89	Peoria Rivermen	IHL	64	27	29	56	....	....	....	154	....	....	....	....	....	....	....	....	....	....	3	0	1	1	8	....	....	....
1989-90	**St. Louis Blues**	**NHL**	**19**	**1**	**2**	**3**	**1**	**1**	**2**	**12**	**0**	**0**	**0**	**17**	**5.9**	**4**	**0**	**8**	**0**	**–4**	....	....	....	....	....	....	....	....
	Peoria Rivermen	IHL	59	27	40	67	....	....	....	87	....	....	....	....	....	....	....	....	....	....	5	1	1	2	15	....	....	....
1990-91	**St. Louis Blues**	**NHL**	**3**	**0**	**0**	**0**	**0**	**0**	**0**	**0**	**0**	**0**	**0**	**0**	**0.0**	**0**	**0**	**3**	**0**	**–3**	**9**	**3**	**1**	**4**	**4**	**1**	**0**	**1**
	Peoria Rivermen	IHL	80	53	54	107	....	....	....	107	....	....	....	....	....	....	....	....	....	....	11	6	7	13	28	....	....	....
1991-92	**Boston Bruins**	**NHL**	**12**	**0**	**1**	**1**	**0**	**1**	**1**	**17**	**0**	**0**	**0**	**12**	**0.0**	**2**	**0**	**5**	**1**	**–2**	....	....	....	....	....	....	....	....
	Maine Mariners	AHL	25	9	11	20	....	....	....	36	....	....	....	....	....	....	....	....	....	....	....	....	....	....	....	....	....	....
1992-93	Binghamton Rangers	AHL	54	25	35	60	....	....	....	61	....	....	....	....	....	....	....	....	....	....	12	2	5	7	8	....	....	....
1993-94	**Los Angeles Kings**	**NHL**	**7**	**0**	**0**	**0**	**0**	**0**	**0**	**21**	**0**	**0**	**0**	**6**	**0.0**	**0**	**0**	**6**	**0**	**–6**	....	....	....	....	....	....	....	....
	Phoenix Roadrunners	IHL	39	10	15	25	....	....	....	70	....	....	....	....	....	....	....	....	....	....	....	....	....	....	....	....	....	....
1994-95	**Los Angeles Kings**	**NHL**	**1**	**0**	**0**	**0**	**0**	**0**	**0**	**0**	**0**	**0**	**0**	**0**	**0.0**	**0**	**0**	**1**	**0**	**–1**	....	....	....	....	....	....	....	....
	Phoenix Roadrunners	IHL	77	30	40	70	....	....	....	87	....	....	....	....	....	....	....	....	....	....	9	5	3	8	8	....	....	....
1995-96	Phoenix Roadrunners	IHL	48	10	13	23	....	....	....	65	....	....	....	....	....	....	....	....	....	....	4	1	0	1	2	....	....	....
1996-97	Phoenix Roadrunners	IHL	67	16	24	40	....	....	....	40	....	....	....	....	....	....	....	....	....	....	....	....	....	....	....	....	....	....
1997-98	Manitoba Moose	IHL	28	1	4	5	....	....	....	22	....	....	....	....	....	....	....	....	....	....	....	....	....	....	....	....	....	....
	NHL Totals		**42**	**1**	**3**	**4**	**1**	**2**	**3**	**50**	**0**	**0**	**0**	**35**	**2.9**	**6**	**0**	**23**	**1**		**9**	**3**	**1**	**4**	**4**	**1**	**0**	**1**

Signed as a free agent by **St. Louis**, June 4, 1987. Signed as a free agent by **Boston**, July 30, 1991. Signed as a free agent by **NY Rangers**, September 4, 1992. Signed as a free agent by **LA Kings**, July 22, 1993.

• THOMPSON, BRENT

Brent Thompson D – L. 6'2", 200 lbs. b: Calgary, Alta., 1/9/1971. Los Angeles' 1st choice, 39th overall, in 1989 Entry Draft.

Season	Club	League	GP	G	A	Pts	AG	AA	APts	PIM	PP	SH	GW	S	%	TGF	PGF	TGA	PGA	+/–	GP	G	A	Pts	PIM	PP	SH	GW
1988-89	Medicine Hat Tigers	WHL	72	3	10	13	....	....	....	160	....	....	....	....	....	....	....	....	....	....	3	0	0	0	2	....	....	....
1989-90	Medicine Hat Tigers	WHL	68	10	35	45	....	....	....	167	....	....	....	....	....	....	....	....	....	....	3	0	1	1	14	....	....	....
1990-91	Medicine Hat Tigers	WHL	51	5	40	45	....	....	....	87	....	....	....	....	....	....	....	....	....	....	12	1	7	8	16	....	....	....
	Phoenix Roadrunners	IHL	....	....	....	....	....	....	....	....	....	....	....	....	....	....	....	....	....	....	4	0	1	1	6	....	....	....
1991-92	**Los Angeles Kings**	**NHL**	**27**	**0**	**5**	**5**	**0**	**4**	**4**	**89**	**0**	**0**	**0**	**18**	**0.0**	**17**	**0**	**25**	**1**	**–7**	**4**	**0**	**0**	**0**	**4**	**0**	**0**	**0**
	Phoenix Roadrunners	IHL	42	4	13	17	....	....	....	139	....	....	....	....	....	....	....	....	....	....	....	....	....	....	....	....	....	....

			REGULAR SEASON																		PLAYOFFS							
Season	**Club**	**League**	**GP**	**G**	**A**	**Pts**	**AG**	**AA**	**APts**	**PIM**	**PP**	**SH**	**GW**	**S**	**%**	**TGF**	**PGF**	**TGA**	**PGA**	**+/–**	**GP**	**G**	**A**	**Pts**	**PIM**	**PP**	**SH**	**GW**
1992-93	**Los Angeles Kings**	**NHL**	**30**	**0**	**4**	**4**	**0**	**3**	**3**	**76**	**0**	**0**	**0**	**18**	**0.0**	**17**	**0**	**26**	**5**	**–4**	....	....	....	....	....	....	....	....
	Phoenix Roadrunners	IHL	22	0	5	5	....	....	....	112	....	....	....	....	....	....	....	....	....	....	....	....	....	....	....	....	....	....
1993-94	**Los Angeles Kings**	**NHL**	**24**	**1**	**0**	**1**	**1**	**0**	**1**	**81**	**0**	**0**	**0**	**9**	**11.1**	**13**	**1**	**15**	**2**	**–1**	....	....	....	....	....	....	....	....
	Phoenix Roadrunners	IHL	26	1	11	12	....	....	....	118	....	....	....	....	....	....	....	....	....	....	....	....	....	....	....	....	....	....
1994-95	**Winnipeg Jets**	**NHL**	**29**	**0**	**0**	**0**	**0**	**0**	**0**	**78**	**0**	**0**	**0**	**16**	**0.0**	**7**	**1**	**25**	**2**	**–17**	....	....	....	....	....	....	....	....
1995-96	**Winnipeg Jets**	**NHL**	**10**	**0**	**1**	**1**	**0**	**1**	**1**	**21**	**0**	**0**	**0**	**7**	**0.0**	**6**	**0**	**10**	**2**	**–2**	....	....	....	....	....	....	....	....
	Springfield Falcons	AHL	58	2	10	12	....	....	....	203	....	....	....	....	....	....	....	....	....	....	10	1	4	5	*55	....	....	....
1996-97	**Phoenix Coyotes**	**NHL**	**1**	**0**	**0**	**0**	**0**	**0**	**0**	**7**	**0**	**0**	**0**	**0**	**0.0**	**0**	**0**	**1**	**0**	**–1**	....	....	....	....	....	....	....	....
	Springfield Falcons	AHL	64	2	15	17	....	....	....	215	....	....	....	....	....	....	....	....	....	....	17	0	2	2	31	....	....	....
	Phoenix Roadrunners	IHL	12	0	1	1	....	....	....	67	....	....	....	....	....	....	....	....	....	....	....	....	....	....	....	....	....	....
1997-98	Hartford Wolf Pack	AHL	77	4	15	19	....	....	....	308	....	....	....	....	....	....	....	....	....	....	15	0	4	4	25	....	....	....
	NHL Totals		**121**	**1**	**10**	**11**	**1**	**8**	**9**	**352**	**0**	**0**	**0**	**68**	**1.5**	**60**	**2**	**102**	**12**		**4**	**0**	**0**	**0**	**4**	**0**	**0**	**0**

WHL East Second All-Star Team (1991)

Traded to **Winnipeg** by **LA Kings** with future considerations for the rights to Ruslan Batyrshin and Winnipeg's 2nd round choice (Marian Cisar) in 1996 Entry Draft, August 8, 1994. Transferred to **Phoenix** after **Winnipeg** franchise relocated, July 1, 1996. Signed as a free agent by **NY Rangers**, August 26, 1997.

• THOMPSON, ERROL

Errol "Spud" Thompson LW – L. 5'9", 185 lbs. b: Summerside, P.E.I., 5/28/1950. Toronto's 2nd choice, 22nd overall, in 1970 Amateur Draft.

Season	Club	League	GP	G	A	Pts	AG	AA	APts	PIM	PP	SH	GW	S	%	TGF	PGF	TGA	PGA	+/–	GP	G	A	Pts	PIM	PP	SH	GW
1966-67	Halifax Jr. Canadians	NSJHL	47	28	32	60	....	....	....	29	....	....	....	....	....	....	....	....	....	....	17	15	9	24	9	....	....	....
1967-68	Halifax Jr. Canadians	NSJHL	45	41	40	81	....	....	....	55	....	....	....	....	....	....	....	....	....	....	11	6	7	13	12	....	....	....
1968-69	Halifax Jr. Canadians	NSJHL	30	11	18	29	....	....	....	25	....	....	....	....	....	....	....	....	....	....	....	....	....	....	....	....	....	....
1969-70	Charlottetown Royals	PEI Sr.	....	13	23	36	....	....	....	....	....	....	....	....	....	....	....	....	....	....	3	1	3	4	0	....	....	....
1970-71	**Toronto Maple Leafs**	**NHL**	**1**	**0**	**0**	**0**	**0**	**0**	**0**	**0**	**0**	**0**	**0**	**0**	**0.0**	**0**	**0**	**1**	**0**	**–1**	....	....	....	....	....	....	....	....
	Tulsa Oilers	CHL	65	15	14	29	....	....	....	37	....	....	....	....	....	....	....	....	....	....	....	....	....	....	....	....	....	....
1971-72	Tulsa Oilers	CHL	46	21	21	42	....	....	....	30	....	....	....	....	....	....	....	....	....	....	13	4	6	10	8	....	....	....
1972-73	**Toronto Maple Leafs**	**NHL**	**68**	**13**	**19**	**32**	**13**	**16**	**29**	**8**	**2**	**0**	**1**	**137**	**9.5**	**55**	**11**	**43**	**3**	**+4**	....	....	....	....	....	....	....	....
1973-74	**Toronto Maple Leafs**	**NHL**	**56**	**7**	**8**	**15**	**7**	**7**	**14**	**6**	**0**	**0**	**2**	**74**	**9.5**	**25**	**1**	**31**	**9**	**+2**	**2**	**0**	**1**	**1**	**0**	**0**	**0**	**0**
1974-75	**Toronto Maple Leafs**	**NHL**	**65**	**25**	**17**	**42**	**23**	**13**	**36**	**12**	**3**	**1**	**4**	**202**	**12.4**	**65**	**10**	**66**	**10**	**–1**	**6**	**0**	**0**	**0**	**9**	**0**	**0**	**0**
1975-76	**Toronto Maple Leafs**	**NHL**	**75**	**43**	**37**	**80**	**40**	**29**	**69**	**26**	**13**	**1**	**7**	**210**	**20.5**	**120**	**36**	**75**	**19**	**+28**	**10**	**3**	**3**	**6**	**0**	**2**	**1**	**0**
1976-77	**Toronto Maple Leafs**	**NHL**	**41**	**21**	**16**	**37**	**20**	**13**	**33**	**8**	**8**	**1**	**2**	**109**	**19.3**	**62**	**22**	**63**	**13**	**–10**	**9**	**2**	**0**	**2**	**0**	**0**	**0**	**1**
1977-78	**Toronto Maple Leafs**	**NHL**	**59**	**17**	**22**	**39**	**16**	**18**	**34**	**10**	**4**	**1**	**2**	**132**	**12.9**	**67**	**12**	**43**	**5**	**+17**	....	....	....	....	....	....	....	....
	Detroit Red Wings	**NHL**	**14**	**5**	**1**	**6**	**5**	**1**	**6**	**2**	**1**	**0**	**0**	**27**	**18.5**	**12**	**6**	**10**	**0**	**–4**	**7**	**2**	**1**	**3**	**2**	**1**	**0**	**1**
1978-79	**Detroit Red Wings**	**NHL**	**70**	**23**	**31**	**54**	**21**	**24**	**45**	**26**	**8**	**0**	**3**	**163**	**14.1**	**84**	**42**	**70**	**0**	**–28**	....	....	....	....	....	....	....	....
1979-80	**Detroit Red Wings**	**NHL**	**77**	**34**	**14**	**48**	**31**	**11**	**42**	**22**	**8**	**2**	**3**	**164**	**20.7**	**77**	**19**	**94**	**26**	**–10**	....	....	....	....	....	....	....	....
1980-81	**Detroit Red Wings**	**NHL**	**39**	**14**	**12**	**26**	**12**	**8**	**20**	**52**	**5**	**0**	**2**	**83**	**16.9**	**44**	**15**	**41**	**8**	**–4**	....	....	....	....	....	....	....	....
	Pittsburgh Penguins	**NHL**	**34**	**6**	**8**	**14**	**5**	**6**	**11**	**12**	**0**	**0**	**1**	**54**	**11.1**	**24**	**2**	**33**	**2**	**–9**	....	....	....	....	....	....	....	....
	NHL Totals		**599**	**208**	**185**	**393**	**193**	**146**	**339**	**184**	**52**	**6**	**27**	**1355**	**15.4**	**635**	**176**	**570**	**95**		**34**	**7**	**5**	**12**	**11**	**3**	**1**	**2**

Traded to **Detroit** by **Toronto** with Toronto's 1st (Brent Peterson) and 2nd (Al Jensen) round choices in 1978 Amateur Draft and Toronto's 1st round choice (Mike Blaisdell) in 1980 Entry Draft for Dan Maloney and Detroit's 2nd round choice (Craig Muni) in 1980 Entry Draft, March 13, 1978. Traded to **Pittsburgh** by **Detroit** for Gary McAdam, January 8, 1981.

• THOMPSON, ROCKY

Rocky Thompson D – R. 6'2", 192 lbs. b: Calgary, Alta., 8/8/1977. Calgary's 1st choice, 72nd overall, in 1995 Entry Draft.

Season	Club	League	GP	G	A	Pts	AG	AA	APts	PIM	PP	SH	GW	S	%	TGF	PGF	TGA	PGA	+/–	GP	G	A	Pts	PIM	PP	SH	GW
1993-94	Medicine Hat Tigers	WHL	68	1	4	5	....	....	....	166	....	....	....	....	....	....	....	....	....	....	3	0	0	0	2	....	....	....
1994-95	Medicine Hat Tigers	WHL	63	1	6	7	....	....	....	220	....	....	....	....	....	....	....	....	....	....	5	0	0	0	17	....	....	....
1995-96	Medicine Hat Tigers	WHL	71	9	20	29	....	....	....	260	....	....	....	....	....	....	....	....	....	....	5	2	3	5	26	....	....	....
	Saint John Flames	AHL	4	0	0	0	....	....	....	33	....	....	....	....	....	....	....	....	....	....	....	....	....	....	....	....	....	....
1996-97	Medicine Hat Tigers	WHL	47	6	9	15	....	....	....	170	....	....	....	....	....	....	....	....	....	....	....	....	....	....	....	....	....	....
	Swift Current Broncos	WHL	22	3	5	8	....	....	....	90	....	....	....	....	....	....	....	....	....	....	10	1	2	3	22	....	....	....
1997-98	**Calgary Flames**	**NHL**	**12**	**0**	**0**	**0**	**0**	**0**	**0**	**61**	**0**	**0**	**0**	**3**	**0.0**	**1**	**0**	**1**	**0**	**0**	....	....	....	....	....	....	....	....
	Saint John Flames	AHL	51	3	0	3	....	....	....	187	....	....	....	....	....	....	....	....	....	....	18	1	1	2	47	....	....	....
	NHL Totals		**12**	**0**	**0**	**0**	**0**	**0**	**0**	**61**	**0**	**0**	**0**	**3**	**0.0**	**1**	**0**	**1**	**0**		....	....	....	....	....	....	....	....

• THOMSON, FLOYD

Floyd Thomson LW – L. 6', 190 lbs. b: Sudbury, Ont., 6/14/1949.

Season	Club	League	GP	G	A	Pts	AG	AA	APts	PIM	PP	SH	GW	S	%	TGF	PGF	TGA	PGA	+/–	GP	G	A	Pts	PIM	PP	SH	GW
1968-69	Falconbridge-Garson	NOHA	STATISTICS NOT AVAILABLE																									
1969-70	Fort Wayne Komets	IHL	69	10	19	29	....	....	....	81	....	....	....	....	....	....	....	....	....	....	3	0	1	1	0	....	....	....
1970-71	Kansas City Blues	CHL	72	15	18	33	....	....	....	73	....	....	....	....	....	....	....	....	....	....	....	....	....	....	....	....	....	....
1971-72	**St. Louis Blues**	**NHL**	**49**	**4**	**6**	**10**	**4**	**5**	**9**	**48**	**0**	**0**	**2**	**69**	**5.8**	**22**	**1**	**30**	**0**	**–9**	....	....	....	....	....	....	....	....
	Kansas City Blues	CHL	6	1	5	6	....	....	....	0	....	....	....	....	....	....	....	....	....	....	....	....	....	....	....	....	....	....
	Denver Spurs	WHL	17	6	6	12	....	....	....	8	....	....	....	....	....	....	....	....	....	....	9	2	2	4	14	....	....	....
1972-73	**St. Louis Blues**	**NHL**	**75**	**14**	**20**	**34**	**14**	**17**	**31**	**71**	**1**	**0**	**1**	**98**	**14.3**	**49**	**3**	**50**	**2**	**–2**	**5**	**0**	**1**	**1**	**2**	**0**	**0**	**0**
1973-74	**St. Louis Blues**	**NHL**	**77**	**11**	**22**	**33**	**11**	**19**	**30**	**58**	**0**	**0**	**1**	**125**	**8.8**	**46**	**2**	**63**	**0**	**–19**	....	....	....	....	....	....	....	....
1974-75	**St. Louis Blues**	**NHL**	**77**	**9**	**27**	**36**	**8**	**21**	**29**	**106**	**0**	**0**	**0**	**111**	**8.1**	**61**	**2**	**53**	**7**	**+13**	**2**	**0**	**1**	**1**	**0**	**0**	**0**	**0**
1975-76	**St. Louis Blues**	**NHL**	**58**	**8**	**10**	**18**	**7**	**8**	**15**	**25**	**0**	**0**	**1**	**71**	**11.3**	**28**	**2**	**33**	**3**	**–4**	....	....	....	....	....	....	....	....
1976-77	**St. Louis Blues**	**NHL**	**58**	**7**	**8**	**15**	**7**	**6**	**13**	**11**	**0**	**1**	**2**	**46**	**15.2**	**27**	**0**	**41**	**15**	**+1**	**3**	**0**	**0**	**0**	**4**	**0**	**0**	**0**
	Kansas City Blues	CHL	13	3	11	14	....	....	....	16	....	....	....	....	....	....	....	....	....	....	....	....	....	....	....	....	....	....
1977-78	**St. Louis Blues**	**NHL**	**6**	**1**	**1**	**2**	**1**	**1**	**2**	**4**	**0**	**0**	**0**	**4**	**25.0**	**2**	**0**	**5**	**0**	**–3**	....	....	....	....	....	....	....	....
	Salt Lake Golden Eagles	CHL	69	26	26	52	....	....	....	45	....	....	....	....	....	....	....	....	....	....	6	2	1	3	2	....	....	....
1978-79	Salt Lake Golden Eagles	CHL	76	41	40	81	....	....	....	96	....	....	....	....	....	....	....	....	....	....	10	5	4	9	11	....	....	....
1979-80	**St. Louis Blues**	**NHL**	**11**	**2**	**3**	**5**	**2**	**2**	**4**	**18**	**0**	**0**	**0**	**13**	**15.4**	**6**	**0**	**8**	**1**	**–1**	....	....	....	....	....	....	....	....
	Salt Lake Golden Eagles	CHL	73	23	41	63	....	....	....	49	....	....	....	....	....	....	....	....	....	....	13	6	8	14	11	....	....	....
1980-81	Salt Lake Golden Eagles	CHL	76	24	33	57	....	....	....	104	....	....	....	....	....	....	....	....	....	....	17	3	4	7	0	....	....	....
1981-82	Salt Lake Golden Eagles	CHL	74	17	28	45	....	....	....	83	....	....	....	....	....	....	....	....	....	....	9	1	0	1	4	....	....	....
	NHL Totals		**411**	**56**	**97**	**153**	**54**	**79**	**133**	**341**	**1**	**1**	**7**	**537**	**10.4**	**241**	**10**	**283**	**28**		**10**	**0**	**2**	**2**	**6**	**0**	**0**	**0**

CHL Second All-Star Team (1978) • CHL First All-Star Team (1979)

Signed as a free agent by **St. Louis**, October 1, 1970.

• THOMSON, JIM

Jim Thomson RW – R. 6'1", 220 lbs. b: Edmonton, Alta., 12/30/1965. Washington's 3rd choice, 185th overall, in 1984 Entry Draft.

Season	Club	League	GP	G	A	Pts	AG	AA	APts	PIM	PP	SH	GW	S	%	TGF	PGF	TGA	PGA	+/–	GP	G	A	Pts	PIM	PP	SH	GW
1982-83	Markham Waxers	MTHL	35	6	7	13	....	....	....	81	....	....	....	....	....	....	....	....	....	....	....	....	....	....	....	....	....	....
1983-84	Toronto Marlboros	OHL	60	10	18	28	....	....	....	68	....	....	....	....	....	....	....	....	....	....	9	1	0	1	26	....	....	....
1984-85	Toronto Marlboros	OHL	63	23	28	51	....	....	....	122	....	....	....	....	....	....	....	....	....	....	5	3	1	4	25	....	....	....
	Binghamton Whalers	AHL	4	0	0	0	....	....	....	2	....	....	....	....	....	....	....	....	....	....	....	....	....	....	....	....	....	....
1985-86	Binghamton Whalers	AHL	59	15	9	24	....	....	....	195	....	....	....	....	....	....	....	....	....	....	....	....	....	....	....	....	....	....
1986-87	**Washington Capitals**	**NHL**	**10**	**0**	**0**	**0**	**0**	**0**	**0**	**35**	**0**	**0**	**0**	**5**	**0.0**	**0**	**0**	**2**	**0**	**–2**	....	....	....	....	....	....	....	....
	Binghamton Whalers	AHL	57	13	10	23	....	....	....	360	....	....	....	....	....	....	....	....	....	....	10	0	1	1	40	....	....	....
1987-88	Binghamton Whalers	AHL	25	8	9	17	....	....	....	64	....	....	....	....	....	....	....	....	....	....	4	1	2	3	7	....	....	....
1988-89	**Washington Capitals**	**NHL**	**14**	**2**	**0**	**2**	**2**	**0**	**2**	**53**	**0**	**0**	**0**	**9**	**22.2**	**3**	**0**	**6**	**0**	**–3**	....	....	....	....	....	....	....	....
	Baltimore Skipjacks	AHL	41	25	16	41	....	....	....	129	....	....	....	....	....	....	....	....	....	....	....	....	....	....	....	....	....	....
	Hartford Whalers	**NHL**	**5**	**0**	**0**	**0**	**0**	**0**	**0**	**14**	**0**	**0**	**0**	**3**	**0.0**	**0**	**0**	**3**	**0**	**–3**	....	....	....	....	....	....	....	....
1989-90	Binghamton Whalers	AHL	8	1	2	3	....	....	....	30	....	....	....	....	....	....	....	....	....	....	....	....	....	....	....	....	....	....
	New Jersey Devils	**NHL**	**3**	**0**	**0**	**0**	**0**	**0**	**0**	**31**	**0**	**0**	**0**	**3**	**0.0**	**0**	**0**	**3**	**0**	**–3**	....	....	....	....	....	....	....	....
	Utica Devils	AHL	60	20	23	43	....	....	....	124	....	....	....	....	....	....	....	....	....	....	4	1	0	1	19	....	....	....
1990-91	**Los Angeles Kings**	**NHL**	**8**	**1**	**0**	**1**	**1**	**0**	**1**	**19**	**0**	**0**	**1**	**6**	**16.7**	**1**	**0**	**1**	**0**	**0**	....	....	....	....	....	....	....	....
	New Haven Nighthawks	AHL	27	5	8	13	....	....	....	121	....	....	....	....	....	....	....	....	....	....	....	....	....	....	....	....	....	....
1991-92	**Los Angeles Kings**	**NHL**	**45**	**1**	**2**	**3**	**1**	**1**	**2**	**162**	**0**	**0**	**0**	**24**	**4.2**	**5**	**0**	**6**	**0**	**–1**	....	....	....	....	....	....	....	....
	Phoenix Roadrunners	IHL	2	1	0	1	....	....	....	0	....	....	....	....	....	....	....	....	....	....	....	....	....	....	....	....	....	....

			REGULAR SEASON																		PLAYOFFS							
Season	Club	League	GP	G	A	Pts	AG	AA	APts	PIM	PP	SH	GW	S	%	TGF	PGF	TGA	PGA	+/–	GP	G	A	Pts	PIM	PP	SH	GW
1992-93	Ottawa Senators	NHL	15	0	1	1	0	1	1	41	0	0	0	21	0.0	1	0	12	0	–11	...							
	Los Angeles Kings	NHL	9	0	0	0	0	0	0	56	0	0	0	2	0.0	1	0	2	0	–1	1	0	0	0	0	0	0	0
	Phoenix Roadrunners	IHL	14	4	5	9				44																		
1993-94	Anaheim Mighty Ducks	NHL	6	0	0	0	0	0	0	5	0	0	0	0	0.0	0	0	0	0	0								
	NHL Totals		115	4	3	7	4	2	6	416	0	0	1	74	5.4	11	0	35	0		1	0	0	0	0	0	0	0

Traded to **Hartford** by **Washington** for Scot Kleinendorst, March 6, 1989. Traded to **New Jersey** by **Hartford** for Chris Cihocki, October 31, 1989. Signed as a free agent by **LA Kings**, July 2, 1990. Claimed by **Minnesota** from **LA Kings** in Expansion Draft, May 30, 1991. Traded to **LA Kings** by **Minnesota** with Randy Gilhen, Charlie Huddy and NY Rangers' 4th round choice (previously acquired, LA Kings selected Alexei Zhitnik) in 1991 Entry Draft for Todd Elik, June 22, 1991. Claimed by **Ottawa** from **LA Kings** in Expansion Draft, June 18, 1992. Traded to **LA Kings** by **Ottawa** with Marc Fortier for Bob Kudelski and Shawn McCosh, December 19, 1992. Claimed by **Anaheim** from **LA Kings** in Expansion Draft, June 24, 1993.

● THORNBURY, TOM
Tom Thornbury   D – R. 5'11", 175 lbs.   b: Lindsay, Ont., 3/17/1963.   Pittsburgh's 2nd choice, 49th overall, in 1981 Entry Draft.

Season	Club	League	GP	G	A	Pts	AG	AA	APts	PIM	PP	SH	GW	S	%	TGF	PGF	TGA	PGA	+/–	GP	G	A	Pts	PIM	PP	SH	GW
1979-80	Aurora Tigers	OJHL	44	19	30	49				84																			
1980-81	Niagara Falls Flyers	OHA	60	15	2	17				136												12	1	5	6	31			
1981-82	Niagara Falls Flyers	OHL	43	11	22	33				65												1	0	0	0	2			
1982-83	North Bay Centennials	OHL	17	6	9	15				30																			
	Cornwall Royals	OHL	50	21	35	56				66												8	2	4	6	8			
1983-84	**Pittsburgh Penguins**	**NHL**	14	1	8	9	1	5	6	16	0	0	0	44	2.3	16	9	26	0	–19								
	Baltimore Skipjacks	AHL	65	17	46	63				64												10	2	15	17	8			
1984-85	Baltimore Skipjacks	AHL	22	4	12	16				21																			
	Fredericton Express	AHL	53	11	16	27				26												6	0	2	2	5			
1985-86	Fredericton Express	AHL	24	0	15	15				30																			
	Muskegon Lumberjacks	IHL	9	0	8	8				8																			
	Moncton Golden Flames	AHL	40	6	12	18				38												7	0	2	2	10			
1986-87	Canada	Nat-Team	19	0	10	10				22																			
	Kolner Haie	Germany	26	10	16	26				40												9	2	8	10				
1987-88	Kolner Haie	Germany	46	10	23	33				72																			
1988-89	Kolner Haie	Germany	34	15	26	41				36												9	1	9	10	2			
1989-90	Kolner Haie	Germany	44	14	18	32				50																			
1990-91	Kolner Haie	Germany	39	12	32	44				83																			
1991-92	Kolner Haie	Germany	31	14	15	29				62																			
1992-93	Frankfurt Lions	German3	51	51	64	115				144																			
1993-94	Frankfurt Lions	German 2	39	10	8	18				82																			
	NHL Totals		14	1	8	9	1	5	6	16	0	0	0	44	2.3	16	9	26	0									

AHL Second All-Star Team (1984)

Traded to **Quebec** by **Pittsburgh** for Brian Ford, December 6, 1984. Traded to **Calgary** by **Quebec** for Tony Stiles, January 16, 1986.

● THORNTON, JOE
Joe Thornton   C – L. 6'4", 198 lbs.   b: London, Ont., 7/2/1979.   Boston's 1st choice, 1st overall, in 1997 Entry Draft.

Season	Club	League	GP	G	A	Pts	AG	AA	APts	PIM	PP	SH	GW	S	%	TGF	PGF	TGA	PGA	+/–	GP	G	A	Pts	PIM	PP	SH	GW
1995-96	Sault Ste. Marie Greyhounds	OHL	66	30	46	76				53												4	1	1	2	11			
1996-97	Sault Ste. Marie Greyhounds	OHL	59	41	81	122				123												11	11	8	19	24			
	Canada	WJC-A	7	2	2	4				0																			
1997-98	**Boston Bruins**	**NHL**	55	3	4	7	4	4	8	19	0	0	1	33	9.1	9	2	13	0	–6	6	0	0	0	9	0	0	0
	NHL Totals		55	3	4	7	4	4	8	19	0	0	1	33	9.1	9	2	13	0		6	0	0	0	9	0	0	0

Canadian Major Junior Rookie of the Year (1996) ● OHL Second All-Star Team (1997)

● THORNTON, SCOTT
Scott Thornton   C – L. 6'3", 210 lbs.   b: London, Ont., 1/9/1971.   Toronto's 1st choice, 3rd overall, in 1989 Entry Draft.

Season	Club	League	GP	G	A	Pts	AG	AA	APts	PIM	PP	SH	GW	S	%	TGF	PGF	TGA	PGA	+/–	GP	G	A	Pts	PIM	PP	SH	GW
1987-88	Belleville Bulls	OHL	62	11	19	30				54												6	0	1	1	2			
1988-89	Belleville Bulls	OHL	59	28	34	62				103												5	1	1	2	6			
1989-90	Belleville Bulls	OHL	47	21	28	49				91												11	2	10	12	15			
1990-91	Belleville Bulls	OHL	3	2	1	3				2												6	0	7	7	14			
	Canada	WJC-A	7	3	1	4				0																			
	Toronto Maple Leafs	**NHL**	33	1	3	4	1	2	3	30	0	0	0	31	3.2	9	0	26	2	–15								
	Newmarket Saints	AHL	5	1	0	1				4																			
1991-92	**Edmonton Oilers**	**NHL**	15	0	1	1	0	1	1	43	0	0	0	11	0.0	2	0	8	0	–6	1	0	0	0	0	0	0	0
	Cape Breton Oilers	AHL	49	9	14	23				40												5	1	0	1	8			
1992-93	**Edmonton Oilers**	**NHL**	9	0	1	1	0	1	1	0	0	0	0	7	0.0	1	0	5	0	–4								
	Cape Breton Oilers	AHL	58	23	27	50				102												16	1	2	3	35			
1993-94	**Edmonton Oilers**	**NHL**	61	4	7	11	4	5	9	104	0	0	0	65	6.2	21	2	41	7	–15								
	Cape Breton Oilers	AHL	2	1	1	2				31																			
1994-95	**Edmonton Oilers**	**NHL**	47	10	12	22	18	18	36	89	0	1	1	69	14.5	32	4	47	15	–4								
1995-96	**Edmonton Oilers**	**NHL**	77	9	9	18	9	7	16	149	0	2	3	95	9.5	27	2	76	26	–25								
1996-97	**Montreal Canadiens**	**NHL**	73	10	10	20	11	9	20	128	1	1	1	110	9.1	27	3	54	11	–19	5	1	0	1	2	0	0	0
1997-98	**Montreal Canadiens**	**NHL**	67	6	9	15	7	9	16	158	1	0	1	51	11.8	24	3	25	4	0	9	0	2	2	10	0	0	0
	NHL Totals		382	40	52	92	50	52	102	701	2	4	6	439	9.1	143	14	282	65		15	1	2	3	12	0	0	0

Traded to **Edmonton** by **Toronto** with Vincent Damphousse, Peter Ing, Luke Richardson, future considerations and cash for Grant Fuhr, Glenn Anderson and Craig Berube, September 19, 1991. Traded to **Montreal** by **Edmonton** for Andrei Kovalenko, September 6, 1996.

● THURLBY, TOM
Tom Thurlby   D – L. 5'10", 175 lbs.   b: Kingston, Ont., 11/9/1938.

Season	Club	League	GP	G	A	Pts	AG	AA	APts	PIM	PP	SH	GW	S	%	TGF	PGF	TGA	PGA	+/–	GP	G	A	Pts	PIM	PP	SH	GW
1955-56	Kitchener Canucks	OHA	35	2	4	6				4												8	2	4	6	4			
1956-57	Peterborough Petes	OHA	52	8	7	15				30																			
1957-58	Peterborough Petes	OHA	52	7	10	17				28												5	2	0	2	8			
1958-59	Peterborough Petes	OHA	54	9	19	28				34												19	0	3	3	18			
1959-60	Montreal Royals	EPHL	68	4	12	16				57												11	0	1	1	14			
1960-61	Kingston Frontenacs	EPHL	44	3	11	14				37																			
	Winnipeg–Portland	WHL	23	4	3	7				17												14	2	3	5	17			
1961-62	San Francisco Seals	WHL	70	4	17	21				36												2	0	0	0	0			
1962-63	San Francisco Seals	WHL	70	12	24	36				41												17	3	5	8	4			
1963-64	San Francisco Seals	WHL	61	7	10	17				14												11	4	6	10	12			
1964-65	San Francisco Seals	WHL	70	11	22	33				32																			
1965-66	San Francisco Seals	WHL	71	13	17	30				26												7	1	1	2	4			
1966-67	California Seals	WHL	72	10	16	26				26												6	0	0	0	2			
1967-68	**Oakland Seals**	**NHL**	20	1	1	2	1	1	2	4	0	0	0	27	3.7	5	3	8	0	–6								
	Vancouver Canucks	WHL	47	4	11	15				20																			
1968-69	Houston Apollos	CHL	53	3	7	10				8												3	0	0	0	0			
1969-70	Muskegon Mohawks	IHL	60	5	19	24				28												6	0	3	3	2			
1970-71	DID NOT PLAY																											
1971-72	Kingston Aces	OHA Sr.	36	5	20	25				24																			
1972-73	Kingston Aces	OHA Sr.	31	2	9	11				20																			
	NHL Totals		20	1	1	2	1	1	2	4	0	0	0	27	3.7	5	3	8	0									

Claimed by **Boston** from **Montreal** in Intra-League Draft, June 7, 1960. NHL rights transferred to **California** after owners of **San Francisco** (WHL) franchise awarded NHL expansion team, April 5, 1966.

THYER, MARIO — Mario Thyer C – L. 5'11", 170 lbs. b: Montreal, Que., 9/29/1966.

Season	Club	League	GP	G	A	Pts	AG	AA	APts	PIM	PP	SH	GW	S	%	TGF	PGF	TGA	PGA	+/-	GP	G	A	Pts	PIM	PP	SH	GW
1987-88	University of Maine	H.E.	44	24	42	66				4																		
1988-89	University of Maine	H.E.	9	9	7	16				0																		
1989-90	**Minnesota North Stars**	**NHL**	5	0	0	0	0	0	0	0	0	0	0	4	0.0	0	0	3	0	-3	1	0	0	0	2	0	0	0
	Kalamazoo Wings	IHL	68	19	42	61				12											10	2	6	8	4			
1990-91	Kalamazoo Wings	IHL	75	15	51	66				15											10	4	5	9	2			
1991-92	Kalamazoo Wings	IHL	46	17	28	45				0																		
	Binghamton Rangers	AHI	9	2	7	9				0											3	0	0	0	0			
1992-93	Cincinnati Cyclones	IHL	77	13	36	49				26																		
1993-94	Portland Pirates	AHL	3	0	0	0				0																		
	NHL Totals		5	0	0	0	0	0	0	0	0	0	0	4	0.0	0	0	3	0		1	0	0	0	2	0	0	0

Signed as a free agent by **Minnesota**, July 12, 1989. Traded to **NY Rangers** by **Minnesota** with Minnesota's 3rd round choice (Maxim Galanov) in 1993 Entry Draft for Mark Janssens, March 10, 1992. Traded to **Minnesota** by **NY Rangers** for future considerations, July 16, 1992.

TICHY, MILAN — Milan Tichy D – L. 6'3", 198 lbs. b: Plzen, Czech., 9/22/1969. Chicago's 6th choice, 153rd overall, in 1989 Entry Draft.

Season	Club	League	GP	G	A	Pts	AG	AA	APts	PIM	PP	SH	GW	S	%	TGF	PGF	TGA	PGA	+/-	GP	G	A	Pts	PIM	PP	SH	GW
1987-88	Skoda Plzen	Czech.	30	1	3	4				20																		
	Czechoslovakia	WJC-A	7	1	2	3				2																		
1988-89	Skoda Plzen	Czech.	36	1	12	13				44																		
1989-90	Dukla Trencin	Czech.	51	14	8	22																						
1990-91	Dukla Trencin	Czech.	41	9	12	21				72																		
1991-92	Indianapolis Ice	IHL	49	6	23	29				28																		
1992-93	**Chicago Blackhawks**	**NHL**	13	0	1	1	0	1	1	30	0	0	0	12	0.0	10	2	5	4	+7								
	Indianapolis Ice	IHL	49	7	32	39				62											4	0	5	5	14			
1993-94	Moncton Hawks	AHL	48	1	20	21				103											20	3	3	6	12			
1994-95	**New York Islanders**	**NHL**	2	0	0	0	0	0	0	2	0	0	0	1	0.0	0	0	1	0	-1								
	Denver Grizzlies	IHL	71	18	36	54				90											17	4	9	13	12			
1995-96	**New York Islanders**	**NHL**	8	0	4	4	0	3	3	8	0	0	0	6	0.0	0	8	0	7	2	+3							
	Utah Grizzlies	IHL	21	1	12	13				26																		
	ZPS Zlin	Czech.	8	0	3	3															4	0	0	0				
	NHL Totals		23	0	5	5	0	4	4	40	0	0	0	19	0.0	0	18	2	13	6									

WJC-A All-Star Team (1989)

Claimed by **Florida** from **Chicago** in Expansion Draft, June 24, 1993. Traded to **Winnipeg** by **Florida** for Brent Severyn, October 3, 1993. Signed as a free agent by **NY Islanders**, August 2, 1994.

TIDEY, ALEX — Alex Tidey RW – R. 6', 182 lbs. b: Vancouver, B.C., 1/5/1955. Buffalo's 10th choice, 143rd overall, in 1975 Amateur Draft.

Season	Club	League	GP	G	A	Pts	AG	AA	APts	PIM	PP	SH	GW	S	%	TGF	PGF	TGA	PGA	+/-	GP	G	A	Pts	PIM	PP	SH	GW
1972-73	Vancouver Nats	WCJHL	1	0	1	1				0																		
1973-74	Kamloops Chiefs	WCJHL	64	10	12	22				52																		
1974-75	Lethbridge Broncos	WCJHL	68	42	54	96				78																		
1975-76	San Diego Mariners	WHA	74	16	11	27				46											11	3	6	9	10			
1976-77	**Buffalo Sabres**	**NHL**	3	0	0	0	0	0	0	0	0	0	0	3	0.0	0	0	1	0	-1	2	0	0	0	0	0	0	0
	Hershey Bears	AHL	74	25	38	63				55											6	1	5	6	4			
1977-78	**Buffalo Sabres**	**NHL**	1	0	0	0	0	0	0	0	0	0	0	2	0.0	0	0	1	0	-1								
	Hershey Bears	AHL	49	14	19	33				36																		
1978-79	Hershey Bears	AHL	79	31	30	61				60											4	1	0	1	0			
1979-80	**Edmonton Oilers**	**NHL**	5	0	0	0	0	0	0	8	0	0	0	4	0.0	0	0	3	0	-3								
	Rochester Americans	AHL	9	2	3	5				6																		
	Cincinnati Stingers	CHL	10	3	2	5				10																		
	Houston Apollos	CHL	40	20	29	49				29											6	5	4	9	6			
1980-81	Houston Apollos	CHL	17	9	8	17				12																		
	Springfield Indians	AHL	30	9	7	16				34											5	1	1	2	0			
	NHL Totals		9	0	0	0	0	0	0	8	0	0	0	9	0.0	0	0	5	0		2	0	0	0	0	0	0	0
	Other Major League Totals		74	16	11	27				46											11	3	6	9	10			

Selected by **San Diego** (WHA) in 1975 WHA Amateur Draft, May, 1975. Traded to **Edmonton** by **Buffalo** for John Gould, November 13, 1979. Signed as a free agent by **LA Kings**, August, 1980.

TIKKANEN, ESA — Esa Tikkanen LW – L. 6'1", 190 lbs. b: Helsinki, Finland, 1/25/1965. Edmonton's 4th choice, 82nd overall, in 1983 Entry Draft.

Season	Club	League	GP	G	A	Pts	AG	AA	APts	PIM	PP	SH	GW	S	%	TGF	PGF	TGA	PGA	+/-	GP	G	A	Pts	PIM	PP	SH	GW
1981-82	Regina Capitals	SJHL	59	38	37	75				216																		
	Regina Pats	WHL	2	0	0	0				0																		
1982-83	HIFK Helsinki	Fin.-Jr.	30	34	31	65				104											4	4	3	7	10			
	Finland	WJC-A	7	2	3	5				4																		
	HIFK Helsinki	Finland																			1	0	0	0	0			
1983-84	HIFK Helsinki	Fin.-Jr.	6	5	9	14				13											4	4	3	7	8			
	Finland	WJC-A	7	8	3	11				12																		
	HIFK Helsinki	Finland	36	19	11	30				30											2	0	0	0	0			
1984-85	HIFK Helsinki	Finland	36	21	33	54				42																		
	Finland	WJC-A	7	7	12	19				10																		
	Finland	WEC-A	10	4	5	9				12																		
	Edmonton Oilers	**NHL**																			3	0	0	0	2			
1985-86	**Edmonton Oilers**	**NHL**	35	7	6	13	6	4	10	28	0	0	2	44	15.9	22	3	14	0	+5	8	3	2	5	7	0	0	0
	Nova Scotia Oilers	AHL	15	4	8	12				17																		
1986-87	**Edmonton Oilers**	**NHL**	76	34	44	78	29	32	61	120	7	0	6	126	27.0	125	27	54	0	+44	21	7	2	9	22	1	0	1
	NHL All-Stars	RV'87	2	0	1	1				2																		
1987-88	Finland	C Cup	5	0	1	1																						
	Edmonton Oilers	**NHL**	80	23	51	74	20	36	56	153	6	1	2	142	16.2	113	39	60	7	+21	19	10	17	27	72	5	0	1
1988-89	**Edmonton Oilers**	**NHL**	67	31	47	78	26	33	59	92	8	8	4	151	20.5	109	37	79	17	+10	7	1	3	4	12	0	0	0
	Finland	WEC-A	8	4	4	8				14																		
1989-90	**Edmonton Oilers**	**NHL**	79	30	33	63	26	24	50	161	6	4	6	199	15.1	103	41	74	29	+17	22	13	11	24	26	2	2	0
1990-91	**Edmonton Oilers**	**NHL**	79	27	42	69	25	32	57	85	3	2	6	235	11.5	113	35	98	42	+22	18	12	8	20	24	3	0	3
1991-92	Finland	C Cup	6	2	2	4				6																		
	Edmonton Oilers	**NHL**	40	12	16	28	11	12	23	44	6	2	1	117	10.3	48	24	47	15	-8	16	5	3	8	8	1	0	1
1992-93	**Edmonton Oilers**	**NHL**	66	14	19	33	12	13	25	76	2	4	3	162	8.6	64	24	75	24	-11								
	New York Rangers	**NHL**	15	2	5	7	2	3	5	18	0	0	0	40	5.0	14	3	29	5	-13								
	Finland	WC-A	6	0	0	0				2																		
1993-94	**New York Rangers**	**NHL**	83	22	32	54	21	25	46	114	5	3	4	257	8.6	93	35	69	16	+5	23	4	4	8	34	0	0	1
1994-95	HIFK Helsinki	Finland	19	2	11	13				16																		
	St. Louis Blues	**NHL**	43	12	23	35	21	34	55	22	5	1	2	107	11.2	57	21	46	23	+13	7	2	2	4	20	1	0	1
1995-96	**St. Louis Blues**	**NHL**	11	1	4	5	1	3	4	18	0	1	0	19	5.3	11	5	8	3	+1								
	New Jersey Devils	**NHL**	9	0	2	2	0	2	2	4	0	0	0	15	0.0	3	1	11	3	-6								
	Vancouver Canucks	**NHL**	38	13	24	37	13	20	33	14	8	0	2	61	21.3	55	27	23	1	+6	6	3	2	5	2	2	0	0
	Finland	WC-A	1	0	0	0				0																		
1996-97	**Vancouver Canucks**	**NHL**	62	12	15	27	13	13	26	66	4	1	2	103	11.7	54	21	47	5	-9								
	New York Rangers	**NHL**	14	1	2	3	1	2	3	6	0	1	0	30	3.3	8	2	9	3	0	15	9	3	12	26	3	1	3

			REGULAR SEASON																		PLAYOFFS							
Season	Club	League	GP	G	A	Pts	AG	AA	APts	PIM	PP	SH	GW	S	%	TGF	PGF	TGA	PGA	+/–	GP	G	A	Pts	PIM	PP	SH	GW
1997-98	**Florida Panthers**	**NHL**	**28**	**1**	**8**	**9**	**1**	**8**	**9**	**16**	**0**	**0**	**0**	**34**	**2.9**	**14**	**5**	**24**	**8**	**–7**	....	....	....	....	....	....	....	....
	Finland	Olympics	6	1	1	2	....	....	....	0	....	....	....	....	....	....	....	....	....	....	....	....	....	....	....	....	....	....
	Washington Capitals	**NHL**	**20**	**2**	**10**	**12**	**2**	**10**	**12**	**2**	**1**	**0**	**2**	**33**	**6.1**	**17**	**8**	**14**	**1**	**–4**	**21**	**3**	**3**	**6**	**20**	**1**	**0**	**0**
	NHL Totals		**845**	**244**	**383**	**627**	**230**	**306**	**536**	**1039**	**59**	**29**	**41**	**1875**	**13.0**	**1023**	**358**	**781**	**202**		**186**	**72**	**60**	**132**	**275**	**19**	**3**	**11**

WJC-A All-Star Team (1985)

Traded to **NY Rangers** by **Edmonton** for Doug Weight, March 17, 1993. Traded to **St. Louis** by **NY Rangers** with Doug Lidster for Petr Nedved, July 24, 1994. Traded to **New Jersey** by **St. Louis** for New Jersey's 3rd round choice (later traded to Colorado — Colorado selected Ville Nielnen) in 1997 Entry Draft, November 1, 1995. Traded to **Vancouver** by **New Jersey** for Vancouver's 2nd round choice (Wesley Mason) in 1996 Entry Draft, November 23, 1995. Traded to **NY Rangers** by **Vancouver** with Russ Courtnall for Sergei Nemchinov and Brian Noonan, March 8, 1997. Signed as a free agent by **Florida**, September 17, 1998. Traded to **Washington** by **Florida** for Dwayne Hay and future considerations, March 9, 1998.

• TILEY, BRAD

Brad Tiley D – L. 6'1", 185 lbs. b: Markdale, Ont., 7/5/1971. Boston's 4th choice, 84th overall, in 1991 Entry Draft.

Season	Club	League	GP	G	A	Pts	AG	AA	APts	PIM	PP	SH	GW	S	%	TGF	PGF	TGA	PGA	+/–	GP	G	A	Pts	PIM	PP	SH	GW
1988-89	Sault Ste. Marie Greyhounds	OHL	50	4	11	15	....	....	....	31	....	....	....	....	....	....	....	....	....	....	....	....	....	....	....	....	....	....
1989-90	Sault Ste. Marie Greyhounds	OHL	66	9	32	41	....	....	....	47	....	....	....	....	....	....	....	....	....	....	....	....	....	....	....	....	....	....
1990-91	Sault Ste. Marie Greyhounds	OHL	66	11	55	66	....	....	....	29	....	....	....	....	....	....	....	....	....	....	14	4	15	19	12	....	....	....
1991-92	Maine Mariners	AHL	62	7	22	29	....	....	....	36	....	....	....	....	....	....	....	....	....	....	....	....	....	....	....	....	....	....
1992-93	Phoenix Roadrunners	IHL	46	11	27	38	....	....	....	35	....	....	....	....	....	....	....	....	....	....	....	....	....	....	....	....	....	....
	Binghamton Rangers	AHL	26	6	10	16	....	....	....	19	....	....	....	....	....	....	....	....	....	....	8	0	1	1	2	....	....	....
1993-94	Binghamton Rangers	AHL	29	6	10	16	....	....	....	6	....	....	....	....	....	....	....	....	....	....	....	....	....	....	....	....	....	....
	Phoenix Roadrunners	IHL	35	8	15	23	....	....	....	21	....	....	....	....	....	....	....	....	....	....	....	....	....	....	....	....	....	....
1994-95	Detroit Vipers	IHL	56	7	19	26	....	....	....	32	....	....	....	....	....	....	....	....	....	....	....	....	....	....	....	....	....	....
	Fort Wayne Komets	IHL	14	1	6	7	....	....	....	2	....	....	....	....	....	....	....	....	....	....	3	1	2	3	0	....	....	....
1995-96	Orlando Solar Bears	IHL	69	11	23	34	....	....	....	82	....	....	....	....	....	....	....	....	....	....	23	2	4	6	16	....	....	....
1996-97	Phoenix Roadrunners	IHL	66	8	28	36	....	....	....	34	....	....	....	....	....	....	....	....	....	....	....	....	....	....	....	....	....	....
	Long Beach Ice Dogs	IHL	3	1	0	1	....	....	....	2	....	....	....	....	....	....	....	....	....	....	....	....	....	....	....	....	....	....
1997-98	**Phoenix Coyotes**	**NHL**	**1**	**0**	**0**	**0**	**0**	**0**	**0**	**0**	....	....	....	....	....	....	....	....	....	....	....	....	....	....	....	....	....	....
	Springfield Falcons	AHL	60	10	31	41	....	....	....	36	....	....	....	....	....	....	....	....	....	....	4	0	4	4	2	....	....	....
	NHL Totals		**1**	**0**	**0**	**0**	**0**	**0**	**0**	**0**	**0**	**0**	**0**	**0**	**0.0**	**0**	**0**	**0**	**0**		....	....	....	....	....	....	....	....

Memorial Cup All-Star Team (1991)

Signed as a free agent by **NY Rangers**, September 4, 1992. Traded to **LA Kings** by **NY Rangers** for LA Kings' 11th round choice (Jamie Butt) in 1994 Entry Draft, January 28, 1994. Signed as a free agent by **Phoenix**, September 4, 1997.

• TILLEY, TOM

Tom Tilley D – R. 6', 190 lbs. b: Trenton, Ont., 3/28/1965. St. Louis' 10th choice, 196th overall, in 1984 Entry Draft.

Season	Club	League	GP	G	A	Pts	AG	AA	APts	PIM	PP	SH	GW	S	%	TGF	PGF	TGA	PGA	+/–	GP	G	A	Pts	PIM	PP	SH	GW
1983-84	Orillia Travelways	OJHL	38	16	35	51	....	....	....	113	....	....	....	....	....	....	....	....	....	....	....	....	....	....	....	....	....	....
1984-85	Michigan State Spartans	CCHA	37	1	5	6	....	....	....	58	....	....	....	....	....	....	....	....	....	....	....	....	....	....	....	....	....	....
1985-86	Michigan State Spartans	CCHA	42	9	25	34	....	....	....	48	....	....	....	....	....	....	....	....	....	....	....	....	....	....	....	....	....	....
1986-87	Michigan State Spartans	CCHA	42	7	14	21	....	....	....	48	....	....	....	....	....	....	....	....	....	....	....	....	....	....	....	....	....	....
1987-88	Michigan State Spartans	CCHA	46	8	18	26	....	....	....	44	....	....	....	....	....	....	....	....	....	....	....	....	....	....	....	....	....	....
1988-89	**St. Louis Blues**	**NHL**	**70**	**1**	**22**	**23**	**1**	**15**	**16**	**47**	**0**	**0**	**0**	**77**	**1.3**	**63**	**10**	**77**	**25**	**+1**	**10**	**1**	**2**	**3**	**17**	**0**	**0**	**0**
1989-90	**St. Louis Blues**	**NHL**	**34**	**0**	**5**	**5**	**0**	**4**	**4**	**6**	**0**	**0**	**0**	**19**	**0.0**	**27**	**0**	**19**	**2**	**+10**	....	....	....	....	....	....	....	....
	Peoria Rivermen	IHL	22	1	8	9	....	....	....	13	....	....	....	....	....	....	....	....	....	....	....	....	....	....	....	....	....	....
1990-91	**St. Louis Blues**	**NHL**	**22**	**2**	**4**	**6**	**2**	**3**	**5**	**4**	**0**	**0**	**0**	**28**	**7.1**	**22**	**0**	**18**	**1**	**+5**	....	....	....	....	....	....	....	....
	Peoria Rivermen	IHL	48	7	38	45	....	....	....	53	....	....	....	....	....	....	....	....	....	....	13	2	9	11	25	....	....	....
1991-92	Milano Devils	Italy	18	7	13	20	....	....	....	12	....	....	....	....	....	....	....	....	....	....	12	5	12	17	10	....	....	....
	Canada	Nat-Team	4	0	1	1	....	....	....	0	....	....	....	....	....	....	....	....	....	....	....	....	....	....	....	....	....	....
1992-93	Milano Devils	Italy	14	8	3	11	....	....	....	2	....	....	....	....	....	....	....	....	....	....	8	1	5	6	4	....	....	....
	Milano Devils	Alpenliga	32	5	17	22	....	....	....	21	....	....	....	....	....	....	....	....	....	....	....	....	....	....	....	....	....	....
1993-94	**St. Louis Blues**	**NHL**	**48**	**1**	**7**	**8**	**1**	**5**	**6**	**32**	**0**	**0**	**0**	**41**	**2.4**	**28**	**7**	**25**	**7**	**+3**	**4**	**0**	**1**	**1**	**2**	**0**	**0**	**0**
1994-95	Atlanta Knights	IHL	10	2	6	8	....	....	....	14	....	....	....	....	....	....	....	....	....	....	....	....	....	....	....	....	....	....
	Indianapolis Ice	IHL	25	2	13	15	....	....	....	19	....	....	....	....	....	....	....	....	....	....	....	....	....	....	....	....	....	....
	Canada	WC-A	8	0	0	0	....	....	....	14	....	....	....	....	....	....	....	....	....	....	....	....	....	....	....	....	....	....
1995-96	Milwaukee Admirals	IHL	80	11	68	79	....	....	....	58	....	....	....	....	....	....	....	....	....	....	4	2	2	4	4	....	....	....
1996-97	Milwaukee Admirals	IHL	25	1	10	11	....	....	....	8	....	....	....	....	....	....	....	....	....	....	3	0	1	1	0	....	....	....
1997-98	Chicago Wolves	IHL	73	9	49	58	....	....	....	49	....	....	....	....	....	....	....	....	....	....	22	2	17	19	14	....	....	....
	NHL Totals		**174**	**4**	**38**	**42**	**4**	**27**	**31**	**89**	**0**	**0**	**0**	**165**	**2.4**	**140**	**17**	**139**	**35**		**14**	**1**	**3**	**4**	**19**	**0**	**0**	**0**

CCHA First All-Star Team (1988) • IHL Second All-Star Team (1991, 1996)

Traded to **Tampa Bay** by **St. Louis** for Adam Creighton, October 6, 1994. Traded to **Chicago** by **Tampa Bay** with Jim Cummins and Jeff Buchanan for Paul Ysebaert and Rich Sutter, February 22, 1995.

• TIMANDER, MATTIAS

Mattias Timander D – L. 6'3", 210 lbs. b: Solleftea, Sweden, 4/16/1974. Boston's 7th choice, 208th overall, in 1992 Entry Draft.

Season	Club	League	GP	G	A	Pts	AG	AA	APts	PIM	PP	SH	GW	S	%	TGF	PGF	TGA	PGA	+/–	GP	G	A	Pts	PIM	PP	SH	GW
1992-93	MoDo AIK	Sweden	1	0	0	0	....	....	....	0	....	....	....	....	....	....	....	....	....	....	....	....	....	....	....	....	....	....
1993-94	MoDo AIK	Sweden	23	2	2	4	....	....	....	6	....	....	....	....	....	....	....	....	....	....	11	2	0	2	10	....	....	....
	Sweden	WJC-A	7	0	1	1	....	....	....	0	....	....	....	....	....	....	....	....	....	....	....	....	....	....	....	....	....	....
1994-95	MoDo AIK	Sweden	39	8	9	17	....	....	....	24	....	....	....	....	....	....	....	....	....	....	....	....	....	....	....	....	....	....
1995-96	MoDo AIK	Sweden	37	4	10	14	....	....	....	34	....	....	....	....	....	....	....	....	....	....	7	1	1	2	8	....	....	....
1996-97	**Boston Bruins**	**NHL**	**41**	**1**	**8**	**9**	**1**	**7**	**8**	**14**	**0**	**0**	**0**	**62**	**1.6**	**38**	**8**	**43**	**4**	**–9**	....	....	....	....	....	....	....	....
	Providence Bruins	AHL	32	3	11	14	....	....	....	20	....	....	....	....	....	....	....	....	....	....	10	1	1	2	12	....	....	....
1997-98	**Boston Bruins**	**NHL**	**23**	**1**	**1**	**2**	**1**	**1**	**2**	**6**	**0**	**0**	**0**	**17**	**5.9**	**8**	**2**	**17**	**2**	**–9**	....	....	....	....	....	....	....	....
	Providence Bruins	AHL	31	3	7	10	....	....	....	25	....	....	....	....	....	....	....	....	....	....	....	....	....	....	....	....	....	....
	NHL Totals		**64**	**2**	**9**	**11**	**2**	**8**	**10**	**20**	**0**	**0**	**0**	**79**	**2.5**	**46**	**10**	**60**	**6**		....	....	....	....	....	....	....	....

• TINORDI, MARK

Mark Tinordi D – L. 6'4", 213 lbs. b: Red Deer, Alta., 5/9/1966.

Season	Club	League	GP	G	A	Pts	AG	AA	APts	PIM	PP	SH	GW	S	%	TGF	PGF	TGA	PGA	+/–	GP	G	A	Pts	PIM	PP	SH	GW
1982-83	Lethbridge Broncos	WHL	64	0	4	4	....	....	....	50	....	....	....	....	....	....	....	....	....	....	20	1	1	2	6	....	....	....
1983-84	Lethbridge Broncos	WHL	72	5	14	19	....	....	....	53	....	....	....	....	....	....	....	....	....	....	5	0	1	1	7	....	....	....
1984-85	Lethbridge Broncos	WHL	58	10	15	25	....	....	....	134	....	....	....	....	....	....	....	....	....	....	4	0	2	2	12	....	....	....
1985-86	Lethbridge Broncos	WHL	58	8	30	38	....	....	....	139	....	....	....	....	....	....	....	....	....	....	8	1	3	4	15	....	....	....
1986-87	Calgary Wranglers	WHL	61	29	37	66	....	....	....	148	....	....	....	....	....	....	....	....	....	....	....	....	....	....	....	....	....	....
	New Haven Nighthawks	AHL	2	0	0	0	....	....	....	2	....	....	....	....	....	....	....	....	....	....	2	0	0	0	0	....	....	....
1987-88	**New York Rangers**	**NHL**	**24**	**1**	**2**	**3**	**1**	**1**	**2**	**50**	**0**	**0**	**0**	**13**	**7.7**	**11**	**1**	**16**	**1**	**–5**	....	....	....	....	....	....	....	....
	Colorado Rangers	IHL	41	8	19	27	....	....	....	150	....	....	....	....	....	....	....	....	....	....	11	1	5	6	31	....	....	....
1988-89	**Minnesota North Stars**	**NHL**	**47**	**2**	**3**	**5**	**2**	**2**	**4**	**107**	**0**	**0**	**0**	**39**	**5.1**	**25**	**0**	**53**	**19**	**–9**	**5**	**0**	**0**	**0**	**0**	**0**	**0**	**0**
	Kalamazoo Wings	IHL	10	0	0	0	....	....	....	35	....	....	....	....	....	....	....	....	....	....	....	....	....	....	....	....	....	....
1989-90	**Minnesota North Stars**	**NHL**	**66**	**3**	**7**	**10**	**3**	**5**	**8**	**240**	**1**	**0**	**0**	**50**	**6.0**	**49**	**2**	**76**	**29**	**0**	**7**	**0**	**1**	**1**	**16**	**0**	**0**	**0**
1990-91	Minnesota North Stars	FrTour	4	0	0	0	....	....	....	24	....	....	....	....	....	....	....	....	....	....	....	....	....	....	....	....	....	....
	Minnesota North Stars	**NHL**	**69**	**5**	**27**	**32**	**5**	**20**	**25**	**189**	**1**	**0**	**2**	**92**	**5.4**	**92**	**29**	**94**	**32**	**+1**	**23**	**5**	**6**	**11**	**78**	**4**	**0**	**0**
1991-92	Canada	C Cup	3	0	0	0	....	....	....	2	....	....	....	....	....	....	....	....	....	....	....	....	....	....	....	....	....	....
	Minnesota North Stars	**NHL**	**63**	**4**	**24**	**28**	**4**	**18**	**22**	**179**	**4**	**0**	**0**	**93**	**4.3**	**84**	**32**	**92**	**27**	**–13**	**7**	**1**	**2**	**3**	**11**	**0**	**0**	**0**
1992-93	**Minnesota North Stars**	**NHL**	**69**	**15**	**27**	**42**	**12**	**18**	**30**	**157**	**7**	**0**	**2**	**122**	**12.3**	**110**	**31**	**118**	**38**	**–1**	....	....	....	....	....	....	....	....
1993-94	**Dallas Stars**	**NHL**	**61**	**6**	**18**	**24**	**6**	**14**	**20**	**143**	**1**	**0**	**0**	**112**	**5.4**	**80**	**20**	**79**	**25**	**+6**	....	....	....	....	....	....	....	....
1994-95	**Washington Capitals**	**NHL**	**42**	**3**	**9**	**12**	**5**	**13**	**18**	**71**	**2**	**0**	**1**	**71**	**4.2**	**31**	**7**	**42**	**13**	**–5**	**1**	**0**	**0**	**0**	**2**	**0**	**0**	**0**
1995-96	**Washington Capitals**	**NHL**	**71**	**3**	**10**	**13**	**3**	**8**	**11**	**113**	**2**	**0**	**0**	**82**	**3.7**	**64**	**13**	**61**	**36**	**+26**	**6**	**0**	**0**	**0**	**16**	**0**	**0**	**0**
1996-97	**Washington Capitals**	**NHL**	**56**	**2**	**6**	**8**	**2**	**5**	**7**	**118**	**0**	**0**	**0**	**53**	**3.8**	**42**	**1**	**58**	**20**	**+3**	....	....	....	....	....	....	....	....
1997-98	**Washington Capitals**	**NHL**	**47**	**8**	**9**	**17**	**9**	**9**	**18**	**39**	**0**	**1**	**0**	**57**	**14.0**	**48**	**2**	**44**	**7**	**+9**	**21**	**1**	**2**	**3**	**42**	**0**	**0**	**0**
	NHL Totals		**615**	**52**	**142**	**194**	**52**	**113**	**165**	**1406**	**18**	**1**	**5**	**784**	**6.6**	**636**	**138**	**733**	**247**		**70**	**7**	**11**	**18**	**165**	**4**	**0**	**0**

Played in NHL All-Star Game (1992)

Signed as a free agent by **NY Rangers**, January 4, 1987. Traded to **Minnesota** by **NY Rangers** with Paul Jerrard, the rights to Bret Barnett and Mike Sullivan, and LA Kings' 3rd round choice (previously acquired, Minnesota selected Murray Garbutt) in 1989 Entry Draft for Brian Lawton, Igor Liba and the rights to Eric Bennett, October 11, 1988. Transferred to **Dallas** after **Minnesota** franchise relocated, June 9, 1993. Traded to **Washington** by **Dallas** with Rich Mrozik for Kevin Hatcher, January 18, 1995.

• TIPPETT, DAVE

Dave Tippett LW – L. 5'10", 180 lbs. b: Moosomin, Sask., 8/25/1961.

Season	Club	League	GP	G	A	Pts	AG	AA	APts	PIM	PP	SH	GW	S	%	TGF	PGF	TGA	PGA	+/-	GP	G	A	Pts	PIM	PP	SH	GW
			REGULAR SEASON																		PLAYOFFS							
1979-80	Prince Albert Raiders	SJHL	85	72	95	167																						
1980-81	Prince Albert Raiders	SJHL	84	62	93	155																						
1981-82	University of North Dakota	WCHA	43	13	28	41				20																		
1982-83	University of North Dakota	WCHA	36	15	31	46				24																		
1983-84	Canada	Nat-Team	66	14	19	33				24																		
	Canada	Olympics	7	1	1	2				2																		
	Hartford Whalers	**NHL**	**17**	**4**	**2**	**6**	**3**	**1**	**4**	**2**	**0**	**1**	**0**	**25**	**16.0**	**8**	**0**	**17**	**8**	**–1**								
1984-85	**Hartford Whalers**	**NHL**	**80**	**7**	**12**	**19**	**6**	**8**	**14**	**12**	**0**	**0**	**0**	**98**	**7.1**	**30**	**3**	**88**	**37**	**–24**								
1985-86	**Hartford Whalers**	**NHL**	**80**	**14**	**20**	**34**	**11**	**13**	**24**	**18**	**0**	**2**	**1**	**118**	**11.9**	**51**	**3**	**87**	**48**	**+9**	**10**	**2**	**2**	**4**	**4**	**0**	**1**	**0**
1986-87	**Hartford Whalers**	**NHL**	**80**	**9**	**22**	**31**	**8**	**16**	**24**	**42**	**0**	**3**	**2**	**120**	**7.5**	**41**	**1**	**77**	**37**	**0**	**6**	**0**	**2**	**2**	**4**	**0**	**0**	**0**
1987-88	**Hartford Whalers**	**NHL**	**80**	**16**	**21**	**37**	**14**	**15**	**29**	**32**	**1**	**2**	**2**	**126**	**12.7**	**51**	**4**	**88**	**37**	**–4**	**6**	**0**	**0**	**0**	**2**	**0**	**0**	**0**
1988-89	**Hartford Whalers**	**NHL**	**80**	**17**	**24**	**41**	**14**	**17**	**31**	**45**	**1**	**2**	**1**	**165**	**10.3**	**75**	**9**	**120**	**48**	**–6**	**4**	**0**	**1**	**1**	**0**	**0**	**0**	**0**
1989-90	**Hartford Whalers**	**NHL**	**66**	**8**	**19**	**27**	**7**	**14**	**21**	**32**	**0**	**1**	**3**	**91**	**8.8**	**36**	**0**	**64**	**28**	**0**	**7**	**1**	**3**	**4**	**2**	**0**	**0**	**0**
1990-91	**Washington Capitals**	**NHL**	**61**	**6**	**9**	**15**	**5**	**7**	**12**	**24**	**0**	**0**	**2**	**68**	**8.8**	**31**	**0**	**56**	**12**	**–13**	**10**	**2**	**3**	**5**	**8**	**0**	**0**	**0**
1991-92	**Washington Capitals**	**NHL**	**30**	**2**	**10**	**12**	**2**	**7**	**9**	**16**	**0**	**0**	**0**	**26**	**7.7**	**14**	**1**	**18**	**7**	**+2**	**7**	**0**	**1**	**1**	**0**	**0**	**0**	**0**
	Canada	Nat-Team	1	0	0	0				4																		
	Canada	Olympics	7	1	2	3				10																		
1992-93	**Pittsburgh Penguins**	**NHL**	**74**	**6**	**19**	**25**	**5**	**13**	**18**	**56**	**0**	**1**	**1**	**64**	**9.4**	**30**	**0**	**46**	**21**	**+5**	**12**	**1**	**4**	**5**	**14**	**0**	**0**	**0**
1993-94	**Philadelphia Flyers**	**NHL**	**73**	**4**	**11**	**15**	**4**	**8**	**12**	**38**	**0**	**2**	**1**	**45**	**8.9**	**18**	**0**	**68**	**30**	**–20**								
1994-95	Houston Aeros	IHL	75	18	48	66				56											4	1	2	3	4			
	NHL Totals		**721**	**93**	**169**	**262**	**79**	**119**	**198**	**317**	**2**	**14**	**13**	**946**	**9.8**	**385**	**21**	**729**	**313**		**62**	**6**	**16**	**22**	**34**	**0**	**1**	**0**

WCHA Second All-Star Team (1983)

Signed as a free agent by **Hartford**, February 29, 1984. Traded to **Washington** by **Hartford** for Washington's 6th round choice (Jarrett Reid) in 1992 Entry Draft, September 30, 1990. Signed as a free agent by **Pittsburgh**, August 25, 1992. Signed as a free agent by **Philadelphia**, August 30, 1993.

• TITANIC, MORRIS

Morris Titanic LW – L. 6'1", 180 lbs. b: Toronto, Ont., 1/7/1953. Buffalo's 1st choice, 12th overall, in 1973 Amateur Draft.

Season	Club	League	GP	G	A	Pts	AG	AA	APts	PIM	PP	SH	GW	S	%	TGF	PGF	TGA	PGA	+/-	GP	G	A	Pts	PIM	PP	SH	GW
1970-71	Niagara Falls Flyers	OHA	59	27	17	44				61																		
1971-72	Niagara Falls Flyers	OHA	64	29	28	57				105																		
1972-73	Sudbury Wolves	OHA	63	61	60	121				80																		
1973-74	Cincinnati Swords	AHL	62	31	28	59				47											5	4	2	6	0			
1974-75	**Buffalo Sabres**	**NHL**	**17**	**0**	**0**	**0**	**0**	**0**	**0**	**0**	**0**	**0**	**0**	**6**	**0.0**	**4**	**2**	**7**	**1**	**–4**								
	Hershey Bears	AHL	34	9	17	26				64											6	3	3	6	16			
1975-76	**Buffalo Sabres**	**NHL**	**2**	**0**	**0**	**0**	**0**	**0**	**0**	**0**	**0**	**0**	**0**	**2**	**0.0**	**1**	**0**	**0**	**0**	**+1**								
	Hershey Bears	AHL	35	6	13	19				10											10	2	1	3	8			
1976-77			DID NOT PLAY																									
1977-78	Hershey Bears	AHL	69	10	20	30				54																		
1978-79	Milwaukee Admirals	IHL	75	26	44	70				31											8	3	1	4	0			
1979-80	Rochester Americans	AHL	25	3	3	6				6																		
	NHL Totals		**19**	**0**	**0**	**0**	**0**	**0**	**0**	**0**	**0**	**0**	**0**	**8**	**0.0**	**5**	**2**	**7**	**1**									

OHA First All-Star Team (1973)

• TITOV, GERMAN

German Titov C – L. 6'1", 190 lbs. b: Moscow, USSR, 10/10/1965. Calgary's 10th choice, 252nd overall, in 1993 Entry Draft.

Season	Club	League	GP	G	A	Pts	AG	AA	APts	PIM	PP	SH	GW	S	%	TGF	PGF	TGA	PGA	+/-	GP	G	A	Pts	PIM	PP	SH	GW
1986-87	Khimik Voskresensk	USSR	23	1	0	1				10																		
1987-88	Khimik Voskresensk	USSR	39	6	5	11				10																		
1988-89	Khimik Voskresensk	USSR	44	10	3	13				24																		
1989-90	Khimik Voskresensk	FrTour	1	0	0	0				0																		
	Khimik Voskresensk	USSR	44	6	14	20				10																		
	Khimik Voskresensk	SuperS	6	0	0	0				0																		
1990-91	Khimik Voskresensk	FrTour	1	0	0	0				0																		
	Khimik Voskresensk	USSR	45	13	11	24				28																		
	Khimik Voskresensk	SuperS	7	2	5	7				0																		
1991-92	Khimik Voskresensk	CIS	42	18	13	31				36																		
1992-93	TPS Turku	Finland	47	25	19	44				49											12	6	12	17	10			
	Russia	WC-A	0	4	2	6				0																		
1993-94	**Calgary Flames**	**NHL**	**76**	**27**	**18**	**45**	**25**	**14**	**39**	**28**	**8**	**3**	**2**	**153**	**17.6**	**77**	**21**	**67**	**31**	**+20**	**7**	**2**	**1**	**3**	**4**	**1**	**0**	**0**
1994-95	TPS Turku	Finland	14	6	6	12				20																		
	Calgary Flames	**NHL**	**40**	**12**	**12**	**24**	**21**	**18**	**39**	**16**	**3**	**2**	**3**	**88**	**13.6**	**35**	**6**	**33**	**10**	**+6**	**7**	**5**	**3**	**8**	**10**	**0**	**1**	**0**
1995-96	**Calgary Flames**	**NHL**	**82**	**28**	**39**	**67**	**28**	**32**	**60**	**24**	**13**	**2**	**2**	**214**	**13.1**	**116**	**42**	**78**	**13**	**+9**	**4**	**0**	**2**	**2**	**0**	**0**	**0**	**0**
1996-97	**Calgary Flames**	**NHL**	**79**	**22**	**30**	**52**	**23**	**27**	**50**	**36**	**12**	**0**	**4**	**192**	**11.5**	**75**	**32**	**64**	**9**	**–12**								
1997-98	**Calgary Flames**	**NHL**	**68**	**18**	**22**	**40**	**21**	**21**	**42**	**38**	**6**	**1**	**2**	**133**	**13.5**	**70**	**15**	**66**	**10**	**–1**								
	Russia	Olympics	6	1	0	1				6																		
	NHL Totals		**345**	**107**	**121**	**228**	**118**	**112**	**230**	**142**	**42**	**8**	**13**	**780**	**13.7**	**373**	**116**	**308**	**73**		**18**	**7**	**6**	**13**	**14**	**1**	**1**	**0**

Traded to **Pittsburgh** by **Calgary** with Todd Hlushko for Ken Wregget and Dave Roche, June 17, 1998.

• TKACHUK, KEITH

Keith Tkachuk LW – L. 6'2", 210 lbs. b: Melrose, MA, 3/28/1972. Winnipeg's 1st choice, 19th overall, in 1990 Entry Draft.

Season	Club	League	GP	G	A	Pts	AG	AA	APts	PIM	PP	SH	GW	S	%	TGF	PGF	TGA	PGA	+/-	GP	G	A	Pts	PIM	PP	SH	GW
1989-90	Malden Catholic High School	H.S.	6	12	14	26																						
1990-91	Boston University	H.E.	36	17	23	40				70																		
1991-92	United States	Nat-Team	45	10	10	20				141																		
	United States	WJC-A	7	3	4	7				6																		
	United States	Olympics	8	1	1	2				12																		
	Winnipeg Jets	**NHL**	**17**	**3**	**5**	**8**	**3**	**4**	**7**	**28**	**2**	**0**	**0**	**22**	**13.6**	**12**	**5**	**7**	**0**	**0**	**7**	**3**	**0**	**3**	**30**	**0**	**0**	**0**
1992-93	**Winnipeg Jets**	**NHL**	**83**	**28**	**23**	**51**	**23**	**16**	**39**	**201**	**12**	**0**	**2**	**199**	**14.1**	**92**	**39**	**67**	**1**	**–13**	**6**	**4**	**0**	**4**	**14**	**1**	**0**	**0**
1993-94	**Winnipeg Jets**	**NHL**	**84**	**41**	**40**	**81**	**38**	**31**	**69**	**255**	**22**	**3**	**3**	**218**	**18.8**	**125**	**56**	**97**	**16**	**–12**								
1994-95	**Winnipeg Jets**	**NHL**	**48**	**22**	**29**	**51**	**39**	**43**	**82**	**152**	**7**	**2**	**2**	**129**	**17.1**	**72**	**29**	**59**	**12**	**–4**								
1995-96	**Winnipeg Jets**	**NHL**	**76**	**50**	**48**	**98**	**49**	**39**	**88**	**156**	**20**	**2**	**6**	**249**	**20.1**	**140**	**61**	**94**	**26**	**+11**	**6**	**1**	**2**	**3**	**22**	**0**	**0**	**0**
1996-97	United States	W-Cup	7	5	1	6				44																		
	Phoenix Coyotes	**NHL**	**81**	***52**	**34**	**86**	**56**	**30**	**86**	**228**	**9**	**2**	**7**	**296**	**17.6**	**121**	**36**	**96**	**10**	**–1**	**7**	**6**	**0**	**6**	**7**	**2**	**0**	**0**
1997-98	**Phoenix Coyotes**	**NHL**	**69**	**40**	**26**	**66**	**47**	**25**	**72**	**147**	**11**	**0**	**8**	**232**	**17.2**	**98**	**34**	**61**	**8**	**+9**	**6**	**3**	**3**	**6**	**10**	**0**	**0**	**0**
	United States	Olympics	4	0	2	2				6																		
	NHL Totals		**458**	**236**	**205**	**441**	**255**	**188**	**443**	**1167**	**83**	**9**	**28**	**1345**	**17.5**	**658**	**260**	**481**	**73**		**32**	**17**	**5**	**22**	**83**	**3**	**0**	**0**

NHL Second All-Star Team (1995, 1998)

Played in NHL All-Star Game (1997, 1998)

Transferred to **Phoenix** after **Winnipeg** franchise relocated, July 1, 1996.

• TKACZUK, WALT

Walt Tkaczuk C – L. 6', 185 lbs. b: Emsdetten, Germany, 9/29/1947.

Season	Club	League	GP	G	A	Pts	AG	AA	APts	PIM	PP	SH	GW	S	%	TGF	PGF	TGA	PGA	+/-	GP	G	A	Pts	PIM	PP	SH	GW
1963-64	Kitchener Rangers	OHA	21	5	5	10				4																		
1964-65	Kitchener Rangers	OHA	7	1	2	3				6																		
1965-66	Kitchener Rangers	OHA	47	12	31	43				39											19	7	*23	30	13			
1966-67	Kitchener Rangers	OHA	48	23	47	70				85											13	6	8	14	23			
	Omaha Knights	CHL																			3	2	0	2	2			
1967-68	Kitchener Rangers	OHA	52	37	56	93				81											19	*17	*20	*37	58			
	New York Rangers	**NHL**	**2**	**0**	**0**	**0**	**0**	**0**	**0**	**0**	**0**	**0**	**0**	**0**	**0.0**	**0**	**0**	**1**	**0**	**–1**								
1968-69	**New York Rangers**	**NHL**	**71**	**12**	**24**	**36**	**13**	**23**	**36**	**28**	**0**	**0**	**1**	**130**	**9.2**	**43**	**8**	**46**	**0**	**–11**	**4**	**0**	**1**	**1**	**6**	**0**	**0**	**0**
	Buffalo Bisons	AHL	5	2	7	9				9																		
1969-70	**New York Rangers**	**NHL**	**76**	**27**	**50**	**77**	**31**	**50**	**81**	**38**	**5**	**0**	**2**	**203**	**13.3**	**96**	**18**	**53**	**1**	**+26**	**6**	**2**	**1**	**3**	**17**	**1**	**0**	**0**
1970-71	**New York Rangers**	**NHL**	**77**	**26**	**49**	**75**	**27**	**43**	**70**	**48**	**5**	**1**	**4**	**212**	**12.3**	**97**	**23**	**58**	**2**	**+18**	**13**	**1**	**5**	**6**	**14**	**0**	**0**	**1**
1971-72	**New York Rangers**	**NHL**	**76**	**24**	**42**	**66**	**26**	**38**	**64**	**65**	**3**	**2**	**2**	**231**	**10.4**	**89**	**15**	**57**	**17**	**+34**	**16**	**4**	**6**	**10**	**35**	**0**	**0**	**2**
1972-73	**New York Rangers**	**NHL**	**76**	**27**	**39**	**66**	**27**	**33**	**60**	**59**	**6**	**1**	**7**	**264**	**10.2**	**106**	**25**	**67**	**21**	**+35**	**10**	**7**	**2**	**9**	**8**	**1**	**0**	**1**
1973-74	**New York Rangers**	**NHL**	**71**	**21**	**42**	**63**	**21**	**36**	**57**	**58**	**3**	**3**	**0**	**218**	**9.6**	**84**	**21**	**65**	**17**	**+15**	**13**	**0**	**5**	**5**	**22**	**0**	**0**	**0**

			REGULAR SEASON																		PLAYOFFS							
Season	Club	League	GP	G	A	Pts	AG	AA	APts	PIM	PP	SH	GW	S	%	TGF	PGF	TGA	PGA	+/–	GP	G	A	Pts	PIM	PP	SH	GW
1974-75	**New York Rangers**	**NHL**	**62**	**11**	**25**	**36**	**10**	**20**	**30**	**34**	**2**	**0**	**1**	**134**	**8.2**	**65**	**24**	**56**	**16**	**+1**	**3**	**1**	**2**	**3**	**5**	**0**	**0**	**0**
1975-76	**New York Rangers**	**NHL**	**78**	**8**	**28**	**36**	**7**	**22**	**29**	**56**	**1**	**0**	**1**	**142**	**5.6**	**44**	**4**	**81**	**31**	**–10**	....	....	....	....	....	....	....	....
1976-77	**New York Rangers**	**NHL**	**80**	**12**	**38**	**50**	**11**	**31**	**42**	**38**	**1**	**1**	**0**	**139**	**8.6**	**69**	**5**	**68**	**15**	**+11**	....	....	....	....	....	....	....	....
1977-78	**New York Rangers**	**NHL**	**80**	**26**	**40**	**66**	**25**	**33**	**58**	**30**	**6**	**1**	**3**	**144**	**18.1**	**86**	**13**	**91**	**33**	**+15**	**3**	**0**	**2**	**2**	**0**	**0**	**0**	**0**
1978-79	**New York Rangers**	**NHL**	**77**	**15**	**27**	**42**	**14**	**21**	**35**	**38**	**4**	**0**	**0**	**134**	**11.2**	**73**	**8**	**80**	**35**	**+20**	**18**	**4**	**7**	**11**	**10**	**0**	**1**	**0**
1979-80	**New York Rangers**	**NHL**	**76**	**12**	**25**	**37**	**11**	**19**	**30**	**36**	**4**	**2**	**2**	**128**	**9.4**	**67**	**13**	**55**	**20**	**+19**	**7**	**0**	**1**	**1**	**2**	**0**	**0**	**0**
1980-81	**New York Rangers**	**NHL**	**43**	**6**	**22**	**28**	**5**	**15**	**20**	**28**	**1**	**0**	**0**	**67**	**9.0**	**40**	**2**	**38**	**13**	**+13**	....	....	....	....	....	....	....	....
	NHL Totals		**945**	**227**	**451**	**678**	**228**	**384**	**612**	**556**	**41**	**11**	**23**	**2146**	**10.6**	**959**	**179**	**816**	**221**		**93**	**19**	**32**	**51**	**119**	**2**	**1**	**4**

OHA First All-Star Team (1968)
Played in NHL All-Star Game (1970)

• TOAL, MIKE

Mike Toal C – R. 6′, 175 lbs. b: Red Deer, Alta., 3/23/1959. Edmonton's 5th choice, 105th overall, in 1979 Entry Draft.

Season	Club	League	GP	G	A	Pts	AG	AA	APts	PIM	PP	SH	GW	S	%	TGF	PGF	TGA	PGA	+/–	GP	G	A	Pts	PIM	PP	SH	GW
1976-77	Victoria Cougars	WCJHL	29	6	12	18	....	....	....	25	....	....	....	....	....	....	....	....	....	....	....	....	....	....	....	....	....	....
	Calgary Centennials	WCJHL	34	10	11	21	....	....	....	11	....	....	....	....	....	....	....	....	....	....	....	....	....	....	....	....	....	....
1977-78	Billings Bighorns	WCJHL	69	30	34	64	....	....	....	48	....	....	....	....	....	....	....	....	....	....	19	5	13	18	4			
1978-79	Portland Winter Hawks	WHL	71	38	83	121	....	....	....	32	....	....	....	....	....	....	....	....	....	....	....	....	....	....	....	....	....	....
1979-80	**Edmonton Oilers**	**NHL**	**3**	**0**	**0**	**0**	**0**	**0**	**0**	**0**	**0**	**0**	**0**	**1**	**0.0**	**0**	**0**	**0**	**0**	**0**	....	....	....	....	....	....	....	....
	Houston Apollos	CHL	76	31	45	76	....	....	....	47	....	....	....	....	....	....	....	....	....	....	6	1	0	1	2			
1980-81	Rochester Americans	AHL	14	0	0	0	....	....	....	84	....	....	....	....	....	....	....	....	....	....	....	....	....	....	....	....	....	....
	Wichita Wind	CHL	70	16	18	34	....	....	....	63	....	....	....	....	....	....	....	....	....	....	....	....	....	....	....	....	....	....
1981-82	Wichita Wind	CHL	55	15	15	30	....	....	....	14	....	....	....	....	....	....	....	....	....	....	1	0	0	0	0	....	....	....
	NHL Totals		**3**	**0**	**0**	**0**	**0**	**0**	**0**	**0**	**0**	**0**	**0**	**1**	**0.0**	**0**	**0**	**0**	**0**		....	....	....	....	....	....	....	....

• TOCCHET, RICK

Rick Tocchet RW – R. 6′, 205 lbs. b: Scarborough, Ont., 4/9/1964. Philadelphia's 5th choice, 125th overall, in 1983 Entry Draft.

Season	Club	League	GP	G	A	Pts	AG	AA	APts	PIM	PP	SH	GW	S	%	TGF	PGF	TGA	PGA	+/–	GP	G	A	Pts	PIM	PP	SH	GW
1981-82	Sault Ste. Marie Greyhounds	OHL	59	7	15	22	....	....	....	184	....	....	....	....	....	....	....	....	....	....	11	1	1	2	28	....	....	....
1982-83	Sault Ste. Marie Greyhounds	OHL	66	32	34	66	....	....	....	146	....	....	....	....	....	....	....	....	....	....	16	4	13	17	67	....	....	....
1983-84	Sault Ste. Marie Greyhounds	OHL	64	44	64	108	....	....	....	209	....	....	....	....	....	....	....	....	....	....	16	*22	14	*36	41	....	....	....
1984-85	**Philadelphia Flyers**	**NHL**	**75**	**14**	**25**	**39**	**11**	**17**	**28**	**181**	**0**	**0**	**0**	**112**	**12.5**	**50**	**4**	**42**	**2**	**+6**	**19**	**3**	**4**	**7**	**72**	**0**	**0**	**2**
1985-86	**Philadelphia Flyers**	**NHL**	**69**	**14**	**21**	**35**	**11**	**14**	**25**	**284**	**3**	**0**	**1**	**107**	**13.1**	**56**	**7**	**41**	**4**	**+12**	**5**	**1**	**2**	**3**	**26**	**0**	**0**	**0**
1986-87	**Philadelphia Flyers**	**NHL**	**69**	**21**	**26**	**47**	**18**	**19**	**37**	**288**	**1**	**1**	**5**	**147**	**14.3**	**68**	**6**	**58**	**12**	**+16**	**26**	**11**	**10**	**21**	**72**	**0**	**1**	**2**
1987-88	Canada	C Cup	7	3	2	5	....	....	....	8	....	....	....	....	....	....	....	....	....	....	....	....	....	....	....	....	....	....
	Philadelphia Flyers	**NHL**	**65**	**31**	**33**	**64**	**27**	**23**	**50**	**301**	**1**	**0**	**3**	**0**	**0.0**	**87**	**32**	**62**	**10**	**+3**	**5**	**1**	**4**	**5**	**55**	**2**	**1**	**0**
1988-89	**Philadelphia Flyers**	**NHL**	**66**	**45**	**36**	**81**	**38**	**25**	**63**	**183**	**16**	**1**	**5**	**220**	**20.5**	**113**	**49**	**68**	**3**	**–1**	**16**	**6**	**6**	**12**	**69**	**2**	**0**	**1**
1989-90	**Philadelphia Flyers**	**NHL**	**75**	**37**	**59**	**96**	**32**	**42**	**74**	**196**	**15**	**1**	**0**	**269**	**13.8**	**119**	**43**	**89**	**17**	**+4**	....	....	....	....	....	....	....	....
	Canada	WEC-A	10	4	2	6	....	....	....	14	....	....	....	....	....	....	....	....	....	....	....	....	....	....	....	....	....	....
1990-91	**Philadelphia Flyers**	**NHL**	**70**	**40**	**31**	**71**	**37**	**23**	**60**	**150**	**8**	**0**	**5**	**217**	**18.4**	**117**	**46**	**77**	**8**	**+2**	....	....	....	....	....	....	....	....
1991-92	Canada	C Cup	8	1	1	2	....	....	....	10	....	....	....	....	....	....	....	....	....	....	....	....	....	....	....	....	....	....
	Pittsburgh Penguins	**NHL**	**19**	**14**	**16**	**30**	**13**	**12**	**25**	**49**	**4**	**1**	**1**	**59**	**23.7**	**42**	**12**	**22**	**4**	**+12**	**14**	**6**	**13**	**19**	**24**	**3**	**0**	**1**
	Philadelphia Flyers	**NHL**	**42**	**13**	**16**	**29**	**12**	**12**	**24**	**102**	**4**	**0**	**1**	**107**	**12.1**	**44**	**17**	**24**	**0**	**+3**	....	....	....	....	....	....	....	....
1992-93	**Pittsburgh Penguins**	**NHL**	**80**	**48**	**61**	**109**	**40**	**42**	**82**	**252**	**20**	**4**	**5**	**240**	**20.0**	**165**	**62**	**83**	**8**	**+28**	**12**	**7**	**6**	**13**	**24**	**1**	**0**	**0**
1993-94	**Pittsburgh Penguins**	**NHL**	**51**	**14**	**26**	**40**	**13**	**20**	**33**	**134**	**5**	**1**	**2**	**150**	**9.3**	**67**	**28**	**58**	**4**	**–15**	**6**	**2**	**3**	**5**	**20**	**1**	**0**	**1**
1994-95	**Los Angeles Kings**	**NHL**	**36**	**18**	**17**	**35**	**32**	**25**	**57**	**70**	**7**	**1**	**3**	**95**	**18.9**	**54**	**22**	**41**	**1**	**–8**	....	....	....	....	....	....	....	....
1995-96	**Los Angeles Kings**	**NHL**	**44**	**13**	**23**	**36**	**13**	**19**	**32**	**117**	**4**	**0**	**0**	**100**	**13.0**	**49**	**14**	**32**	**0**	**+3**	....	....	....	....	....	....	....	....
	Boston Bruins	**NHL**	**27**	**16**	**8**	**24**	**16**	**7**	**23**	**64**	**6**	**0**	**3**	**85**	**18.8**	**39**	**16**	**16**	**0**	**+7**	**5**	**4**	**0**	**4**	**21**	**3**	**0**	**1**
1996-97	**Boston Bruins**	**NHL**	**40**	**16**	**14**	**30**	**17**	**12**	**29**	**67**	**3**	**0**	**1**	**120**	**13.3**	**45**	**11**	**37**	**0**	**–3**	....	....	....	....	....	....	....	....
	Washington Capitals	**NHL**	**13**	**5**	**5**	**10**	**5**	**4**	**9**	**31**	**1**	**0**	**1**	**37**	**13.5**	**15**	**2**	**13**	**0**	**0**	....	....	....	....	....	....	....	....
1997-98	**Phoenix Coyotes**	**NHL**	**68**	**26**	**19**	**45**	**31**	**19**	**50**	**157**	**8**	**0**	**6**	**161**	**16.1**	**71**	**29**	**43**	**2**	**+1**	**6**	**6**	**2**	**8**	**25**	**3**	**0**	**0**
	NHL Totals		**909**	**385**	**436**	**821**	**366**	**335**	**701**	**2626**	**106**	**10**	**42**	**2226**	**17.3**	**1201**	**400**	**806**	**75**		**114**	**47**	**50**	**97**	**408**	**15**	**2**	**8**

Played in NHL All-Star Game (1989, 1990, 1991, 1993)

Traded to **Pittsburgh** by **Philadelphia** with Kjell Samuelsson, Ken Wregget and Philadelphia's 3rd round choice (Dave Roche) in 1993 Entry Draft for Mark Recchi, Brian Benning and LA Kings' 1st round choice (previously acquired, Philadelphia selected Jason Bowen) in 1992 Entry Draft, February 19, 1992 Traded to **LA Kings** by **Pittsburgh** with Pittsburgh's 2nd round choice (Pavel Rosa) in 1995 Entry Draft for Luc Robitaille, July 29, 1994. Traded to **Boston** by **LA Kings** for Kevin Stevens, January 25, 1996. Traded to **Washington** by **Boston** with Bill Ranford and Adam Oates for Jim Carey, Anson Carter, Jason Allison and Washington's 3rd round choice (Lee Goren) in 1997 Entry Draft, March 1, 1997. Signed as a free agent by **Phoenix**, July 23, 1997.

• TODD, KEVIN

Kevin "Rat" Todd C – L. 5′10″, 180 lbs. b: Winnipeg, Man., 5/4/1968. New Jersey's 7th choice, 129th overall, in 1986 Entry Draft.

Season	Club	League	GP	G	A	Pts	AG	AA	APts	PIM	PP	SH	GW	S	%	TGF	PGF	TGA	PGA	+/–	GP	G	A	Pts	PIM	PP	SH	GW
1985-86	Prince Albert Raiders	WHL	55	14	25	39	....	....	....	19	....	....	....	....	....	....	....	....	....	....	20	7	6	13	29	....	....	....
1986-87	Prince Albert Raiders	WHL	71	39	46	85	....	....	....	92	....	....	....	....	....	....	....	....	....	....	8	2	5	7	17	....	....	....
1987-88	Prince Albert Raiders	WHL	72	49	72	121	....	....	....	83	....	....	....	....	....	....	....	....	....	....	10	8	11	19	27	....	....	....
1988-89	**New Jersey Devils**	**NHL**	**1**	**0**	**0**	**0**	**0**	**0**	**0**	**0**	**0**	**0**	**0**	**0**	**0.0**	**0**	**0**	**1**	**0**	**–1**	....	....	....	....	....	....	....	....
	Utica Devils	AHL	78	26	45	71	....	....	....	62	....	....	....	....	....	....	....	....	....	....	4	2	0	2	6	....	....	....
1989-90	Utica Devils	AHL	71	18	36	54	....	....	....	72	....	....	....	....	....	....	....	....	....	....	5	2	4	6	2	....	....	....
1990-91	**New Jersey Devils**	**NHL**	**1**	**0**	**0**	**0**	**0**	**0**	**0**	**0**	**0**	**0**	**0**	**0**	**0.0**	**0**	**0**	**1**	**0**	**–1**	**1**	**0**	**0**	**0**	**6**	**0**	**0**	**0**
	Utica Devils	AHL	75	37	*81	*118	....	....	....	75	....	....	....	....	....	....	....	....	....	....	....	....	....	....	....	....	....	....
1991-92	**New Jersey Devils**	**NHL**	**80**	**21**	**42**	**63**	**19**	**32**	**51**	**69**	**2**	**0**	**2**	**131**	**16.0**	**88**	**21**	**60**	**1**	**+8**	**7**	**3**	**2**	**5**	**8**	**1**	**0**	**0**
1992-93	**New Jersey Devils**	**NHL**	**30**	**5**	**5**	**10**	**4**	**3**	**7**	**16**	**0**	**0**	**2**	**48**	**10.4**	**21**	**4**	**24**	**3**	**–4**	....	....	....	....	....	....	....	....
	Utica Devils	AHL	2	2	1	3	....	....	....	0	....	....	....	....	....	....	....	....	....	....	....	....	....	....	....	....	....	....
	Edmonton Oilers	**NHL**	**25**	**4**	**9**	**13**	**3**	**6**	**9**	**10**	**0**	**0**	**1**	**39**	**10.3**	**18**	**2**	**21**	**0**	**–5**	....	....	....	....	....	....	....	....
1993-94	**Chicago Blackhawks**	**NHL**	**35**	**5**	**6**	**11**	**5**	**5**	**10**	**16**	**1**	**0**	**1**	**49**	**10.2**	**18**	**4**	**16**	**0**	**–2**	....	....	....	....	....	....	....	....
	Los Angeles Kings	**NHL**	**12**	**3**	**8**	**11**	**3**	**6**	**9**	**8**	**3**	**0**	**0**	**16**	**18.8**	**14**	**5**	**13**	**3**	**–1**	....	....	....	....	....	....	....	....
1994-95	**Los Angeles Kings**	**NHL**	**33**	**3**	**8**	**11**	**5**	**12**	**17**	**12**	**0**	**0**	**1**	**34**	**8.8**	**15**	**0**	**30**	**10**	**–5**	....	....	....	....	....	....	....	....
1995-96	**Los Angeles Kings**	**NHL**	**74**	**16**	**27**	**43**	**16**	**22**	**38**	**38**	**0**	**2**	**4**	**132**	**12.1**	**51**	**4**	**72**	**31**	**+6**	....	....	....	....	....	....	....	....
1996-97	**Anaheim Mighty Ducks**	**NHL**	**65**	**9**	**21**	**30**	**10**	**19**	**29**	**44**	**0**	**0**	**1**	**95**	**9.5**	**47**	**12**	**51**	**9**	**–7**	**4**	**0**	**0**	**0**	**2**	**0**	**0**	**0**
1997-98	**Anaheim Mighty Ducks**	**NHL**	**27**	**4**	**7**	**11**	**5**	**7**	**12**	**12**	**3**	**0**	**1**	**30**	**13.3**	**18**	**9**	**14**	**0**	**–5**	....	....	....	....	....	....	....	....
	Long Beach Ice Dogs	IHL	30	18	28	46	....	....	....	54	....	....	....	....	....	....	....	....	....	....	13	1	10	11	38	....	....	....
	NHL Totals		**383**	**70**	**133**	**203**	**70**	**112**	**182**	**225**	**9**	**2**	**13**	**574**	**12.2**	**290**	**61**	**303**	**57**		**12**	**3**	**2**	**5**	**16**	**1**	**0**	**0**

AHL First All-Star Team (1991) • Won Les Cunningham Plaque (MVP - AHL) (1991) • Won John B. Sollenberger Trophy (Leading Scorer - AHL) (1991) • NHL/Upper Deck All-Rookie Team (1992)

Traded to **Edmonton** by **New Jersey** with Zdeno Ciger for Bernie Nicholls, January 13, 1993. Traded to **Chicago** by **Edmonton** for Adam Bennett, October 7, 1993. Traded to **LA Kings** by **Chicago** for LA Kings' 4th round choice (Steve McLaren) in 1994 Entry Draft, March 21, 1994. Signed as a free agent by **Pittsburgh**, July 10, 1996. Claimed on waivers by **Anaheim** from **Pittsburgh**, October 4, 1996.

• TOMALTY, GLENN

Glenn Tomalty LW – L. 6′1″, 205 lbs. b: Lachute, Que., 7/23/1954.

Season	Club	League	GP	G	A	Pts	AG	AA	APts	PIM	PP	SH	GW	S	%	TGF	PGF	TGA	PGA	+/–	GP	G	A	Pts	PIM	PP	SH	GW
1977-78	Concordia University	OUAA	STATISTICS NOT AVAILABLE																									
	Grand Rapids Owls	IHL	3	0	0	0	....	....	....	5	....	....	....	....	....	....	....	....	....	....	....	....	....	....	....	....	....	....
1978-79	Cape Cod Freedoms	NEHL	41	24	23	47	....	....	....	51	....	....	....	....	....	....	....	....	....	....	....	....	....	....	....	....	....	....
	Utica Mohawks	NEHL	27	9	11	20	....	....	....	16	....	....	....	....	....	....	....	....	....	....	....	....	....	....	....	....	....	....
1979-80	**Winnipeg Jets**	**NHL**	**1**	**0**	**0**	**0**	**0**	**0**	**0**	**0**	**0**	**0**	**0**	**1**	**0.0**	**0**	**0**	**0**	**0**	**0**	....	....	....	....	....	....	....	....
	Dayton Gems	IHL	61	29	32	61	....	....	....	86	....	....	....	....	....	....	....	....	....	....	....	....	....	....	....	....	....	....
	Tulsa Oilers	CHL	22	5	2	7	....	....	....	59	....	....	....	....	....	....	....	....	....	....	3	1	1	2	17	....	....	....
1980-81	Tulsa Oilers	CHL	12	4	2	6	....	....	....	34	....	....	....	....	....	....	....	....	....	....	....	....	....	....	....	....	....	....
	Fort Wayne Komets	IHL	67	22	26	48	....	....	....	225	....	....	....	....	....	....	....	....	....	....	12	4	4	8	21	....	....	....
1981-82	Brussel HC	Holland	21	34	52	86	....	....	....	42	....	....	....	....	....	....	....	....	....	....	....	....	....	....	....	....	....	....
	NHL Totals		**1**	**0**	**0**	**0**	**0**	**0**	**0**	**0**	**0**	**0**	**0**	**1**	**0.0**	**0**	**0**	**0**	**0**		....	....	....	....	....	....	....	....

Signed as a free agent by **Winnipeg**, October 1, 1979.

• TOMLAK, MIKE

Mike Tomlak C/LW – L. 6′3″, 205 lbs. b: Thunder Bay, Ont., 10/17/1964. Toronto's 10th choice, 217th overall, in 1983 Entry Draft.

Season	Club	League	GP	G	A	Pts	AG	AA	APts	PIM	PP	SH	GW	S	%	TGF	PGF	TGA	PGA	+/–	GP	G	A	Pts	PIM	PP	SH	GW
1982-83	Cornwall Royals	OHL	70	18	49	67	....	....	....	26	....	....	....	....	....	....	....	....	....	....	....	....	....	....	....	....	....	....
1983-84	Cornwall Royals	OHL	64	24	64	88	....	....	....	21	....	....	....	....	....	....	....	....	....	....	....	....	....	....	....	....	....	....
1984-85	Cornwall Royals	OHL	66	30	70	100	....	....	....	9	....	....	....	....	....	....	....	....	....	....	....	....	....	....	....	....	....	....

			REGULAR SEASON																		PLAYOFFS							
Season	**Club**	**League**	**GP**	**G**	**A**	**Pts**	**AG**	**AA**	**APts**	**PIM**	**PP**	**SH**	**GW**	**S**	**%**	**TGF**	**PGF**	**TGA**	**PGA**	**+/–**	**GP**	**G**	**A**	**Pts**	**PIM**	**PP**	**SH**	**GW**
1985-86	University of Western Ontario	OUAA	38	28	20	48	....	....	....	45	....	....	....	....	....	....	....	....	....	....	....	....	....	....	....	....	....	....
	Canada	Nat-Team	3	1	1	2	....	....	....	0	....	....	....	....	....	....	....	....	....	....	....	....	....	....	....	....	....	....
1986-87	University of Western Ontario	OUAA	38	16	30	46	....	....	....	10	....	....	....	....	....	....	....	....	....	....	....	....	....	....	....	....	....	....
1987-88	University of Western Ontario	OUAA	39	24	52	76	....	....	....	....	....	....	....	....	....	....	....	....	....	....	....	....	....	....	....	....	....	....
1988-89	University of Western Ontario	OUAA	35	16	34	50	....	....	....	....	....	....	....	....	....	....	....	....	....	....	....	....	....	....	....	....	....	....
1989-90	**Hartford Whalers**	**NHL**	**70**	**7**	**14**	**21**	**6**	**10**	**16**	**48**	**1**	**1**	**2**	**64**	**10.9**	**25**	**2**	**32**	**14**	**+5**	**7**	**0**	**1**	**1**	**2**	**0**	**0**	**0**
1990-91	**Hartford Whalers**	**NHL**	**64**	**8**	**8**	**16**	**7**	**6**	**13**	**55**	**0**	**1**	**0**	**69**	**11.6**	**24**	**0**	**46**	**13**	**–9**	**3**	**0**	**0**	**0**	**2**	**0**	**0**	**0**
	Springfield Indians	AHL	15	4	9	13	....	....	....	15	....	....	....	....	....	....	....	....	....	....	....	....	....	....	....	....	....	....
1991-92	**Hartford Whalers**	**NHL**	**6**	**0**	**0**	**0**	**0**	**0**	**0**	**0**	**0**	**0**	**0**	**10**	**0.0**	**0**	**0**	**5**	**3**	**–2**	....	....	....	....	....	....	....	....
	Springfield Indians	AHL	39	16	21	37	....	....	....	24	....	....	....	....	....	....	....	....	....	....	....	....	....	....	....	....	....	....
1992-93	Springfield Indians	AHL	38	16	21	37	....	....	....	56	....	....	....	....	....	....	....	....	....	....	5	1	1	2	2	....	....	....
1993-94	**Hartford Whalers**	**NHL**	**1**	**0**	**0**	**0**	**0**	**0**	**0**	**0**	**0**	**0**	**0**	**2**	**0.0**	**0**	**0**	**0**	**0**	**0**	....	....	....	....	....	....	....	....
	Springfield Indians	AHL	79	44	56	100	....	....	....	53	....	....	....	....	....	....	....	....	....	....	4	2	5	7	4	....	....	....
1994-95	Milwaukee Admirals	IHL	63	27	41	68	....	....	....	54	....	....	....	....	....	....	....	....	....	....	15	4	5	9	8	....	....	....
1995-96	Milwaukee Admirals	IHL	82	11	32	43	....	....	....	68	....	....	....	....	....	....	....	....	....	....	5	0	2	2	6	....	....	....
1996-97	Milwaukee Admirals	IHL	47	8	23	31	....	....	....	44	....	....	....	....	....	....	....	....	....	....	....	....	....	....	....	....	....	....
1997-98	Milwaukee Admirals	IHL	82	19	32	51	....	....	....	62	....	....	....	....	....	....	....	....	....	....	10	1	3	4	10	....	....	....
	NHL Totals		**141**	**15**	**22**	**37**	**13**	**16**	**29**	**103**	**1**	**2**	**2**	**145**	**10.3**	**49**	**2**	**83**	**30**		**10**	**0**	**1**	**1**	**4**	**0**	**0**	**0**

Signed as a free agent by **Hartford**, November 14, 1988.

• TOMLINSON, DAVE

Dave Tomlinson C – L. 5′11″, 180 lbs. b: North Vancouver, B.C., 5/8/1969. Toronto's 1st choice, 3rd overall, in 1989 Supplemental Draft.

Season	Club	League	GP	G	A	Pts	AG	AA	APts	PIM	PP	SH	GW	S	%	TGF	PGF	TGA	PGA	+/–	GP	G	A	Pts	PIM	PP	SH	GW
1987-88	Boston University	H.E.	34	16	20	36	....	....	....	28	....	....	....	....	....	....	....	....	....	....	....	....	....	....	....	....	....	....
1988-89	Boston University	H.E.	34	16	30	46	....	....	....	40	....	....	....	....	....	....	....	....	....	....	....	....	....	....	....	....	....	....
1989-90	Boston University	H.E.	43	15	22	37	....	....	....	53	....	....	....	....	....	....	....	....	....	....	....	....	....	....	....	....	....	....
1990-91	Boston University	H.E.	41	30	30	60	....	....	....	55	....	....	....	....	....	....	....	....	....	....	....	....	....	....	....	....	....	....
1991-92	**Toronto Maple Leafs**	**NHL**	**3**	**0**	**0**	**0**	**0**	**0**	**0**	**2**	**0**	**0**	**0**	**6**	**0.0**	**1**	**0**	**2**	**0**	**–1**	....	....	....	....	....	....	....	....
	St. John's Maple Leafs	AHL	75	23	34	57	....	....	....	75	....	....	....	....	....	....	....	....	....	....	12	4	5	9	6	....	....	....
1992-93	**Toronto Maple Leafs**	**NHL**	**3**	**0**	**0**	**0**	**0**	**0**	**0**	**2**	**0**	**0**	**0**	**1**	**0.0**	**0**	**0**	**0**	**0**	**0**	....	....	....	....	....	....	....	....
	St. John's Maple Leafs	AHL	70	36	48	84	....	....	....	115	....	....	....	....	....	....	....	....	....	....	9	1	4	5	8	....	....	....
1993-94	**Winnipeg Jets**	**NHL**	**31**	**1**	**3**	**4**	**1**	**2**	**3**	**24**	**0**	**0**	**0**	**29**	**3.4**	**6**	**0**	**18**	**0**	**–12**	....	....	....	....	....	....	....	....
	Moncton Hawks	AHL	39	23	23	46	....	....	....	38	....	....	....	....	....	....	....	....	....	....	20	6	6	12	24	....	....	....
1994-95	Cincinnati Cyclones	IHL	78	38	72	110	....	....	....	79	....	....	....	....	....	....	....	....	....	....	10	7	3	10	8	....	....	....
	Florida Panthers	**NHL**	**5**	**0**	**0**	**0**	**0**	**0**	**0**	**0**	**0**	**0**	**0**	**0**	**0.0**	**0**	**0**	**2**	**0**	**–2**	....	....	....	....	....	....	....	....
1995-96	Cincinnati Cyclones	IHL	81	39	57	96	....	....	....	127	....	....	....	....	....	....	....	....	....	....	17	4	12	16	18	....	....	....
1996-97	Adler Mannheim	Germany	49	19	32	51	....	....	....	66	....	....	....	....	....	....	....	....	....	....	9	3	4	7	6	....	....	....
1997-98	Adler Mannheim	EuroHL	4	2	1	3	....	....	....	6	....	....	....	....	....	....	....	....	....	....	....	....	....	....	....	....	....	....
	Adler Mannheim	Germany	44	20	30	50	....	....	....	58	....	....	....	....	....	....	....	....	....	....	10	4	11	15	10	....	....	....
	NHL Totals		**42**	**1**	**3**	**4**	**1**	**2**	**3**	**28**	**0**	**0**	**0**	**36**	**2.8**	**7**	**0**	**22**	**0**		....	....	....	....	....	....	....	....

IHL Second All-Star Team (1996)

Traded to **Florida** by **Toronto** for cash, July 30, 1993. Traded to **Winnipeg** by **Florida** for Jason Cirone, August 3, 1993. Signed as a free agent by **Florida**, June 23, 1994.

• TOMLINSON, KIRK

Kirk Tomlinson C – L. 5′10″, 175 lbs. b: Toronto, Ont., 5/2/1968. Minnesota's 7th choice, 75th overall, in 1986 Entry Draft.

Season	Club	League	GP	G	A	Pts	AG	AA	APts	PIM	PP	SH	GW	S	%	TGF	PGF	TGA	PGA	+/–	GP	G	A	Pts	PIM	PP	SH	GW
1984-85	New Westminster Bruins	WHL	66	9	14	23	....	....	....	48	....	....	....	....	....	....	....	....	....	....	11	1	3	4	20	....	....	....
1985-86	Hamilton Steelhawks	OHL	58	28	23	51	....	....	....	230	....	....	....	....	....	....	....	....	....	....	....	....	....	....	....	....	....	....
1986-87	Hamilton Steelhawks	OHL	65	33	37	70	....	....	....	169	....	....	....	....	....	....	....	....	....	....	9	4	6	10	28	....	....	....
1987-88	Hamilton Steelhawks	OHL	23	10	18	28	....	....	....	72	....	....	....	....	....	....	....	....	....	....	....	....	....	....	....	....	....	....
	Oshawa Generals	OHL	26	10	13	23	....	....	....	128	....	....	....	....	....	....	....	....	....	....	6	4	4	8	16	....	....	....
	Minnesota North Stars	**NHL**	**1**	**0**	**0**	**0**	**0**	**0**	**0**	**0**	**0**	**0**	**0**	**0**	**0.0**	**0**	**0**	**0**	**0**	**0**	....	....	....	....	....	....	....	....
1988-89	Kalamazoo Wings	IHL	3	0	0	0	....	....	....	12	....	....	....	....	....	....	....	....	....	....	....	....	....	....	....	....	....	....
	Kitchener Rangers	OHA	43	29	30	59	....	....	....	131	....	....	....	....	....	....	....	....	....	....	5	2	4	6	2	....	....	....
1989-90			DID NOT PLAY																									
1990-91	Nashville Knights	ECHL	57	35	47	83	....	....	....	385	....	....	....	....	....	....	....	....	....	....	....	....	....	....	....	....	....	....
	Adirondack Red Wings	AHL	8	0	2	2	....	....	....	62	....	....	....	....	....	....	....	....	....	....	2	0	0	0	5	....	....	....
1991-92	Adirondack Red Wings	AHL	54	3	12	15	....	....	....	*356	....	....	....	....	....	....	....	....	....	....	8	1	0	1	17	....	....	....
1992-93	Adirondack Red Wings	AHL	50	8	12	20	....	....	....	224	....	....	....	....	....	....	....	....	....	....	9	0	1	1	32	....	....	....
1993-94	Las Vegas Thunder	IHL	15	2	6	8	....	....	....	95	....	....	....	....	....	....	....	....	....	....	....	....	....	....	....	....	....	....
1994-95	Fort Wayne Komets	IHL	13	0	1	1	....	....	....	82	....	....	....	....	....	....	....	....	....	....	....	....	....	....	....	....	....	....
	Peoria Rivermen	IHL	41	11	9	20	....	....	....	171	....	....	....	....	....	....	....	....	....	....	9	0	1	1	17	....	....	....
1995-96	Peoria Rivermen	IHL	24	3	6	0	....	....	....	59	....	....	....	....	....	....	....	....	....	....	....	....	....	....	....	....	....	....
	NHL Totals		**1**	**0**	**0**	**0**	**0**	**0**	**0**	**0**	**0**	**0**	**0**	**0**	**0.0**	**0**	**0**	**0**	**0**		....	....	....	....	....	....	....	....

• TOMS, JEFF

Jeff Toms LW – L. 6′5″, 200 lbs. b: Swift Current, Sask., 6/4/1974. New Jersey's 10th choice, 210th overall, in 1992 Entry Draft.

Season	Club	League	GP	G	A	Pts	AG	AA	APts	PIM	PP	SH	GW	S	%	TGF	PGF	TGA	PGA	+/–	GP	G	A	Pts	PIM	PP	SH	GW
1991-92	Sault Ste. Marie Greyhounds	OHL	36	9	5	14	....	....	....	0	....	....	....	....	....	....	....	....	....	....	16	0	1	1	2	....	....	....
1992-93	Sault Ste. Marie Greyhounds	OHL	59	16	23	39	....	....	....	20	....	....	....	....	....	....	....	....	....	....	16	4	4	8	7	....	....	....
1993-94	Sault Ste. Marie Greyhounds	OHL	64	52	45	97	....	....	....	19	....	....	....	....	....	....	....	....	....	....	14	11	4	15	2	....	....	....
1994-95	Atlanta Knights	IHL	40	7	8	15	....	....	....	10	....	....	....	....	....	....	....	....	....	....	4	0	0	0	4	....	....	....
1995-96	**Tampa Bay Lightning**	**NHL**	**1**	**0**	**0**	**0**	**0**	**0**	**0**	**0**	**0**	**0**	**0**	**1**	**0.0**	**0**	**0**	**0**	**0**	**0**	....	....	....	....	....	....	....	....
	Atlanta Knights	IHL	68	16	18	34	....	....	....	10	....	....	....	....	....	....	....	....	....	....	1	0	0	0	0	....	....	....
1996-97	**Tampa Bay Lightning**	**NHL**	**34**	**2**	**8**	**10**	**2**	**7**	**9**	**10**	**0**	**0**	**1**	**53**	**3.8**	**12**	**1**	**9**	**0**	**+2**	....	....	....	....	....	....	....	....
	Adirondack Red Wings	AHL	37	11	16	27	....	....	....	8	....	....	....	....	....	....	....	....	....	....	4	1	2	3	0	....	....	....
1997-98	**Tampa Bay Lightning**	**NHL**	**13**	**1**	**2**	**3**	**1**	**2**	**3**	**7**	**0**	**0**	**0**	**14**	**7.1**	**4**	**0**	**11**	**1**	**–6**	....	....	....	....	....	....	....	....
	Washington Capitals	**NHL**	**33**	**3**	**4**	**7**	**4**	**4**	**8**	**8**	**0**	**0**	**1**	**55**	**5.5**	**7**	**0**	**19**	**1**	**–11**	**1**	**0**	**0**	**0**	**0**	**0**	**0**	**0**
	NHL Totals		**81**	**6**	**14**	**20**	**7**	**13**	**20**	**25**	**0**	**0**	**2**	**123**	**4.9**	**23**	**1**	**39**	**2**		**1**	**0**	**0**	**0**	**0**	**0**	**0**	**0**

Traded to **Tampa Bay** by **New Jersey** for Vancouver's 4th round choice (previously acquired by Tampa Bay — later traded to Calgary — Calgary selected Ryan Duthie) in 1994 Entry Draft, May 31, 1994. Claimed by on waivers by **Washington** from **Tampa Bay**, November 19, 1997.

• TONELLI, JOHN

John Tonelli LW – L. 6′1″, 200 lbs. b: Milton, Ont., 3/23/1957. NY Islanders' 2nd choice, 33rd overall, in 1977 Amateur Draft.

Season	Club	League	GP	G	A	Pts	AG	AA	APts	PIM	PP	SH	GW	S	%	TGF	PGF	TGA	PGA	+/–	GP	G	A	Pts	PIM	PP	SH	GW
1973-74	Toronto Marlboros	OHA	69	18	37	55	....	....	....	62	....	....	....	....	....	....	....	....	....	....	....	....	....	....	....	....	....	....
1974-75	Toronto Marlboros	OHA	70	49	86	135	....	....	....	85	....	....	....	....	....	....	....	....	....	....	....	....	....	....	....	....	....	....
1975-76	Houston Aeros	WHA	79	17	14	31	....	....	....	66	....	....	....	....	....	....	....	....	....	....	17	7	7	14	18	....	....	....
1976-77	Houston Aeros	WHA	80	24	31	55	....	....	....	109	....	....	....	....	....	....	....	....	....	....	11	3	4	7	12	....	....	....
1977-78	Houston Aeros	WHA	65	23	41	64	....	....	....	103	....	....	....	....	....	....	....	....	....	....	6	1	3	4	8	....	....	....
1978-79	**New York Islanders**	**NHL**	**73**	**17**	**39**	**56**	**15**	**30**	**45**	**44**	**1**	**0**	**4**	**113**	**15.0**	**88**	**12**	**47**	**0**	**+29**	**10**	**1**	**6**	**7**	**0**	**0**	**0**	**0**
1979-80	**New York Islanders**	**NHL**	**77**	**14**	**30**	**44**	**13**	**23**	**36**	**49**	**3**	**0**	**2**	**103**	**13.6**	**68**	**10**	**52**	**2**	**+8**	**21**	**7**	**9**	**16**	**18**	**0**	**0**	**0**
1980-81	**New York Islanders**	**NHL**	**70**	**20**	**32**	**52**	**16**	**22**	**38**	**57**	**2**	**0**	**3**	**114**	**17.5**	**72**	**15**	**49**	**0**	**+8**	**16**	**5**	**8**	**13**	**16**	**0**	**0**	**2**
1981-82	**New York Islanders**	**NHL**	**80**	**35**	**58**	**93**	**28**	**38**	**66**	**57**	**5**	**0**	**5**	**165**	**21.2**	**139**	**29**	**67**	**5**	**+48**	**19**	**6**	**10**	**16**	**18**	**1**	**0**	**1**
1982-83	**New York Islanders**	**NHL**	**76**	**31**	**40**	**71**	**25**	**28**	**53**	**55**	**8**	**1**	**4**	**166**	**18.7**	**110**	**27**	**58**	**5**	**+30**	**20**	**7**	**11**	**18**	**20**	**0**	**0**	**2**
1983-84	**New York Islanders**	**NHL**	**73**	**27**	**40**	**67**	**22**	**27**	**49**	**66**	**5**	**1**	**7**	**105**	**25.7**	**90**	**13**	**69**	**13**	**+21**	**17**	**1**	**3**	**4**	**31**	**0**	**0**	**0**
1984-85	Canada	C Cup	8	3	6	9	....	....	....	2	....	....	....	....	....	....	....	....	....	....	....	....	....	....	....	....	....	....
	New York Islanders	**NHL**	**80**	**42**	**58**	**100**	**34**	**39**	**73**	**95**	**8**	**1**	**3**	**197**	**21.3**	**158**	**42**	**77**	**11**	**+50**	**10**	**1**	**8**	**9**	**10**	**0**	**0**	**0**
1985-86	**New York Islanders**	**NHL**	**65**	**20**	**41**	**61**	**16**	**27**	**43**	**50**	**3**	**0**	**1**	**139**	**14.4**	**94**	**22**	**66**	**16**	**+22**	....	....	....	....	....	....	....	....
	Calgary Flames	**NHL**	**9**	**3**	**4**	**7**	**2**	**3**	**5**	**10**	**1**	**0**	**1**	**18**	**16.7**	**12**	**1**	**12**	**0**	**–1**	**22**	**7**	**9**	**16**	**40**	**1**	**0**	**1**
1986-87	**Calgary Flames**	**NHL**	**78**	**20**	**31**	**51**	**17**	**22**	**39**	**72**	**10**	**0**	**3**	**150**	**13.3**	**93**	**32**	**63**	**0**	**–2**	**3**	**0**	**0**	**0**	**4**	**0**	**0**	**0**
1987-88	**Calgary Flames**	**NHL**	**74**	**17**	**41**	**58**	**15**	**29**	**44**	**84**	**6**	**0**	**1**	**128**	**13.3**	**101**	**38**	**53**	**0**	**+10**	**6**	**2**	**5**	**7**	**8**	**2**	**0**	**1**
1988-89	**Los Angeles Kings**	**NHL**	**77**	**31**	**33**	**64**	**26**	**23**	**49**	**110**	**1**	**1**	**3**	**156**	**19.9**	**94**	**13**	**83**	**11**	**+9**	**6**	**0**	**0**	**0**	**8**	**0**	**0**	**0**
1989-90	**Los Angeles Kings**	**NHL**	**73**	**31**	**37**	**68**	**27**	**26**	**53**	**62**	**15**	**0**	**4**	**163**	**19.0**	**88**	**36**	**60**	**0**	**–8**	**10**	**1**	**2**	**3**	**6**	**0**	**0**	**0**

			REGULAR SEASON																		PLAYOFFS							
Season	Club	League	GP	G	A	Pts	AG	AA	APts	PIM	PP	SH	GW	S	%	TGF	PGF	TGA	PGA	+/–	GP	G	A	Pts	PIM	PP	SH	GW
1990-91	**Los Angeles Kings**	**NHL**	**71**	**14**	**16**	**30**	**13**	**12**	**25**	**49**	**2**	**0**	**5**	**84**	**16.7**	**51**	**16**	**33**	**1**	**+3**	**12**	**2**	**4**	**6**	**12**	**1**	**0**	**0**
1991-92	**Chicago Blackhawks**	**NHL**	**33**	**1**	**7**	**8**	**1**	**5**	**6**	**37**	**0**	**0**	**1**	**29**	**3.4**	**20**	**8**	**11**	**1**	**+2**	....	....	....	....	....	....	....	....
	Quebec Nordiques	**NHL**	**19**	**2**	**4**	**6**	**2**	**3**	**5**	**14**	**2**	**0**	**0**	**16**	**12.5**	**11**	**7**	**11**	**0**	**–7**	....	....	....	....	....	....	....	....
	NHL Totals		**1028**	**325**	**511**	**836**	**272**	**357**	**629**	**911**	**72**	**4**	**47**	**1846**	**17.6**	**1289**	**321**	**811**	**65**		**172**	**40**	**75**	**115**	**200**	**5**	**0**	**7**
	Other Major League Totals		224	64	86	150	....	....	....	278	....	....	....	....	....	....	....	....	....	....	34	11	14	25	38	....	....	....

OHA First All-Star Team (1975) • NHL Second All-Star Team (1982, 1985) • Canada Cup All-Star Team (1984) • Named Canada Cup MVP (1984)

Played in NHL All-Star Game (1982, 1985)

Signed as an underage free agent by **Houston** (WHA), March, 1975. NHL rights reclaimed by **NY Islanders** after **Houston** (WHA) franchise folded, July 6, 1978. Traded to **Calgary** by **NY Islanders** for Richard Kromm and Steve Konroyd, March 11, 1986. Signed as a free agent by **LA Kings**, June 29, 1988. Signed as a free agent by **Chicago**, June 30, 1991. Traded to **Quebec** by **Chicago** for future considerations, February 18, 1992.

• TOOKEY, TIM

Tim Tookey C – L. 5′11″, 185 lbs. b: Edmonton, Alta., 8/29/1960. Washington's 4th choice, 88th overall, in 1979 Entry Draft.

Season	Club	League	GP	G	A	Pts	AG	AA	APts	PIM	PP	SH	GW	S	%	TGF	PGF	TGA	PGA	+/–	GP	G	A	Pts	PIM	PP	SH	GW
1977-78	Portland Winter Hawks	WCJHL	72	16	15	31	....	....	....	55	....	....	....	....	....	....	....	....	....	....	8	2	2	4	5	....	....	....
1978-79	Portland Winter Hawks	WHL	56	33	47	80	....	....	....	55	....	....	....	....	....	....	....	....	....	....	25	6	14	20	6	....	....	....
1979-80	Portland Winter Hawks	WHL	70	58	83	141	....	....	....	55	....	....	....	....	....	....	....	....	....	....	8	2	5	7	4	....	....	....
1980-81	**Washington Capitals**	**NHL**	**29**	**10**	**13**	**23**	**8**	**9**	**17**	**18**	**6**	**0**	**1**	**33**	**30.3**	**27**	**17**	**23**	**7**	**–6**	....	....	....	....	....	....	....	....
	Hershey Bears	AHL	47	20	38	58	....	....	....	129	....	....	....	....	....	....	....	....	....	....	....	....	....	....	....	....	....	....
1981-82	**Washington Capitals**	**NHL**	**28**	**8**	**8**	**16**	**6**	**5**	**11**	**35**	**5**	**0**	**0**	**52**	**15.4**	**21**	**9**	**21**	**0**	**–9**	....	....	....	....	....	....	....	....
	Hershey Bears	AHL	14	4	9	13	....	....	....	10	....	....	....	....	....	....	....	....	....	....	....	....	....	....	....	....	....	....
	Fredericton Express	AHL	16	6	10	16	....	....	....	16	....	....	....	....	....	....	....	....	....	....	....	....	....	....	....	....	....	....
1982-83	**Quebec Nordiques**	**NHL**	**12**	**1**	**6**	**7**	**1**	**4**	**5**	**4**	**0**	**0**	**0**	**8**	**12.5**	**9**	**1**	**6**	**0**	**+2**	....	....	....	....	....	....	....	....
	Fredericton Express	AHL	53	24	43	67	....	....	....	24	....	....	....	....	....	....	....	....	....	....	9	5	4	9	0	....	....	....
1983-84	**Pittsburgh Penguins**	**NHL**	**8**	**0**	**2**	**2**	**0**	**1**	**1**	**2**	**0**	**0**	**0**	**7**	**0.0**	**2**	**0**	**4**	**0**	**–2**	....	....	....	....	....	....	....	....
	Baltimore Skipjacks	AHL	58	16	28	44	....	....	....	25	....	....	....	....	....	....	....	....	....	....	8	1	1	2	2	....	....	....
1984-85	Baltimore Skipjacks	AHL	74	25	43	68	....	....	....	74	....	....	....	....	....	....	....	....	....	....	15	8	10	18	13	....	....	....
1985-86	Hershey Bears	AHL	69	35	*62	97	....	....	....	66	....	....	....	....	....	....	....	....	....	....	18	*11	8	19	10	....	....	....
1986-87	**Philadelphia Flyers**	**NHL**	**2**	**0**	**0**	**0**	**0**	**0**	**0**	**0**	**0**	**0**	**0**	**1**	**0.0**	**1**	**1**	**0**	**0**	**0**	**10**	**1**	**3**	**4**	**2**	**0**	**0**	**0**
	Hershey Bears	AHL	80	51	*73	*124	....	....	....	45	....	....	....	....	....	....	....	....	....	....	5	5	4	9	0	....	....	....
1987-88	**Los Angeles Kings**	**NHL**	**20**	**1**	**6**	**7**	**1**	**4**	**5**	**8**	**0**	**0**	**0**	**28**	**3.6**	**8**	**1**	**9**	**0**	**–2**	....	....	....	....	....	....	....	....
	New Haven Nighthawks	AHL	11	6	7	13	....	....	....	2	....	....	....	....	....	....	....	....	....	....	....	....	....	....	....	....	....	....
1988-89	**Los Angeles Kings**	**NHL**	**7**	**2**	**1**	**3**	**2**	**1**	**3**	**4**	**0**	**0**	**0**	**8**	**25.0**	**5**	**1**	**7**	**0**	**–3**	....	....	....	....	....	....	....	....
	New Haven Nighthawks	AHL	33	11	18	29	....	....	....	30	....	....	....	....	....	....	....	....	....	....	....	....	....	....	....	....	....	....
	Muskegon Lumberjacks	IHL	18	7	14	21	....	....	....	7	....	....	....	....	....	....	....	....	....	....	8	2	9	11	4	....	....	....
1989-90	Hershey Bears	AHL	42	18	22	40	....	....	....	28	....	....	....	....	....	....	....	....	....	....	....	....	....	....	....	....	....	....
1990-91	Hershey Bears	AHL	51	17	42	59	....	....	....	43	....	....	....	....	....	....	....	....	....	....	5	0	5	5	0	....	....	....
1991-92	Hershey Bears	AHL	80	36	69	105	....	....	....	63	....	....	....	....	....	....	....	....	....	....	6	4	2	6	4	....	....	....
1992-93	Hershey Bears	AHL	80	38	70	108	....	....	....	63	....	....	....	....	....	....	....	....	....	....	....	....	....	....	....	....	....	....
1993-94	Hershey Bears	AHL	66	32	57	89	....	....	....	43	....	....	....	....	....	....	....	....	....	....	11	4	9	13	8	....	....	....
1994-95	Providence Bruins	AHL	50	14	30	44	....	....	....	28	....	....	....	....	....	....	....	....	....	....	1	0	1	1	2	....	....	....
	NHL Totals		**106**	**22**	**36**	**58**	**18**	**24**	**42**	**71**	**11**	**0**	**1**	**137**	**16.1**	**73**	**30**	**70**	**7**		**10**	**1**	**3**	**4**	**2**	**0**	**0**	**0**

AHL Second All-Star Team (1986, 1992) • Won Jack A. Butterfield Trophy (Playoff MVP - AHL) (1986) • AHL First All-Star Team (1987) • Won John B. Sollenberger Trophy (Top Scorer - AHL) (1987) • Won Les Cunningham Award (MVP - AHL) (1987) • Won Fred T. Hunt Memorial Trophy (Sportsmanship - AHL) (1993)

Traded to **Quebec** by **Washington** with Washington's 7th round choice (Daniel Poudrier) in 1982 Entry Draft for Lee Norwood and Quebec's 6th round choice (Mats Kilstrom) in 1982 Entry Draft, February 1, 1982. Signed as a free agent by **Pittsburgh**, September 12, 1983. Signed as a free agent by **Philadelphia**, July 11, 1985. Claimed by **LA Kings** from **Philadelphia** in Waiver Draft, October 5, 1987. Traded to **Pittsburgh** by **LA Kings** for Pat Mayer, March 7, 1989. Signed as a free agent by **Philadelphia**, June 30, 1989.

• TOOMEY, SEAN

Sean Toomey LW – L. 6′1″, 200 lbs. b: St. Paul, MN, 6/27/1965. Minnesota's 8th choice, 141st overall, in 1983 Entry Draft.

Season	Club	League	GP	G	A	Pts	AG	AA	APts	PIM	PP	SH	GW	S	%	TGF	PGF	TGA	PGA	+/–	GP	G	A	Pts	PIM	PP	SH	GW
1982-83	St. Paul Cretin High	H.S.	23	48	32	80	....	....	....		....	....	....	....	....	....	....	....	....	....	....	....	....	....	....	....	....	....
1983-84	University of Minnesota-Duluth	WCHA	29	3	5	8	....	....	....	8	....	....	....	....	....	....	....	....	....	....	....	....	....	....	....	....	....	....
1984-85	University of Minnesota-Duluth	WCHA	43	6	7	13	....	....	....	14	....	....	....	....	....	....	....	....	....	....	....	....	....	....	....	....	....	....
1985-86	University of Minnesota-Duluth	WCHA	33	23	11	34	....	....	....	10	....	....	....	....	....	....	....	....	....	....	....	....	....	....	....	....	....	....
1986-87	University of Minnesota-Duluth	WCHA	39	26	17	43	....	....	....	34	....	....	....	....	....	....	....	....	....	....	....	....	....	....	....	....	....	....
	Minnesota North Stars	**NHL**	**1**	**0**	**0**	**0**	**0**	**0**	**0**	**0**	**0**	**0**	**0**	**2**	**0.0**	**0**	**0**	**1**	**0**	**–1**	....	....	....	....	....	....	....	....
	Indianapolis Checkers	IHL	13	3	3	6	....	....	....	0	....	....	....	....	....	....	....	....	....	....	5	2	2	4	2	....	....	....
1987-88	Baltimore Skipjacks	AHL	49	15	18	33	....	....	....	12	....	....	....	....	....	....	....	....	....	....	....	....	....	....	....	....	....	....
	Kalamazoo Wings	IHL	23	12	5	17	....	....	....	2	....	....	....	....	....	....	....	....	....	....	4	1	3	4	0	....	....	....
1988-89	Assat Pori	Finland	34	14	13	27	....	....	....	18	....	....	....	....	....	....	....	....	....	....	5	3	0	3	0	....	....	....
	NHL Totals		**1**	**0**	**0**	**0**	**0**	**0**	**0**	**0**	**0**	**0**	**0**	**2**	**0.0**	**0**	**0**	**1**	**0**		....	....	....	....	....	....	....	....

• TOPOROWSKI, SHAYNE

Shayne Toporowski RW – R. 6′2″, 210 lbs. b: Paddockwood, Sask., 8/6/1975. Los Angeles' 1st choice, 42nd overall, in 1993 Entry Draft.

Season	Club	League	GP	G	A	Pts	AG	AA	APts	PIM	PP	SH	GW	S	%	TGF	PGF	TGA	PGA	+/–	GP	G	A	Pts	PIM	PP	SH	GW
1991-92	Prince Albert Raiders	WHL	6	2	0	2	....	....	....	2	....	....	....	....	....	....	....	....	....	....	7	2	1	3	6	....	....	....
1992-93	Prince Albert Raiders	WHL	72	25	32	57	....	....	....	235	....	....	....	....	....	....	....	....	....	....	....	....	....	....	....	....	....	....
1993-94	Prince Albert Raiders	WHL	68	37	45	82	....	....	....	183	....	....	....	....	....	....	....	....	....	....	....	....	....	....	....	....	....	....
1994-95	Prince Albert Raiders	WHL	72	36	38	74	....	....	....	151	....	....	....	....	....	....	....	....	....	....	15	10	8	18	25	....	....	....
1995-96	St. John's Maple Leafs	AHL	72	11	26	37	....	....	....	216	....	....	....	....	....	....	....	....	....	....	4	1	1	2	4	....	....	....
1996-97	**Toronto Maple Leafs**	**NHL**	**3**	**0**	**0**	**0**	**0**	**0**	**0**	**7**	**0**	**0**	**0**	**3**	**0.0**	**0**	**0**	**0**	**0**	**0**	....	....	....	....	....	....	....	....
	St. John's Maple Leafs	AHL	72	20	17	37	....	....	....	210	....	....	....	....	....	....	....	....	....	....	11	3	2	5	16	....	....	....
1997-98	Worcester IceCats	AHL	73	9	21	30	....	....	....	128	....	....	....	....	....	....	....	....	....	....	11	5	3	8	44	....	....	....
	NHL Totals		**3**	**0**	**0**	**0**	**0**	**0**	**0**	**7**	**0**	**0**	**0**	**3**	**0.0**	**0**	**0**	**0**	**0**		....	....	....	....	....	....	....	....

Traded to **Toronto** by **LA Kings** with Dixon Ward, Guy Leveque and Kelly Fairchild for Eric Lacroix, Chris Snell and Toronto's 4th round choice (Eric Belanger) in 1996 Entry Draft, October 3, 1994. Signed as a free agent by **St. Louis**, September 9, 1997.

• TORGAYEV, PAVEL

Pavel Torgayev LW – L. 6′1″, 187 lbs. b: Gorky, USSR, 1/25/1966. Calgary's 13th choice, 279th overall, in 1994 Entry Draft.

Season	Club	League	GP	G	A	Pts	AG	AA	APts	PIM	PP	SH	GW	S	%	TGF	PGF	TGA	PGA	+/–	GP	G	A	Pts	PIM	PP	SH	GW
1982-83	Torpedo Gorky	USSR	4	0	0	0	....	....	....	0	....	....	....	....	....	....	....	....	....	....	....	....	....	....	....	....	....	....
1983-84	Torpedo Gorky	USSR	27	2	3	5	....	....	....	8	....	....	....	....	....	....	....	....	....	....	....	....	....	....	....	....	....	....
1984-85	Torpedo Gorky	USSR	47	11	5	16	....	....	....	52	....	....	....	....	....	....	....	....	....	....	....	....	....	....	....	....	....	....
	Soviet Union	WJC-A	7	2	2	4	....	....	....	8	....	....	....	....	....	....	....	....	....	....	....	....	....	....	....	....	....	....
1985-86	Torpedo Gorky	USSR	38	1	4	5	....	....	....	18	....	....	....	....	....	....	....	....	....	....	....	....	....	....	....	....	....	....
	Soviet Union	WJC-A	7	2	2	4	....	....	....	6	....	....	....	....	....	....	....	....	....	....	....	....	....	....	....	....	....	....
1986-87	Torpedo Gorky	USSR	40	6	9	15	....	....	....	30	....	....	....	....	....	....	....	....	....	....	....	....	....	....	....	....	....	....
1987-88	Torpedo Gorky	USSR	25	7	4	11	....	....	....	14	....	....	....	....	....	....	....	....	....	....	....	....	....	....	....	....	....	....
1988-89	Torpedo Gorky	USSR	26	6	3	9	....	....	....	17	....	....	....	....	....	....	....	....	....	....	....	....	....	....	....	....	....	....
1989-90	Torpedo Gorky	USSR	48	18	5	23	....	....	....	64	....	....	....	....	....	....	....	....	....	....	....	....	....	....	....	....	....	....
1990-91	Torpedo Nizhny	USSR	37	10	5	15	....	....	....	22	....	....	....	....	....	....	....	....	....	....	....	....	....	....	....	....	....	....
1991-92	Torpedo Nizhny	CIS	45	13	5	18	....	....	....	46	....	....	....	....	....	....	....	....	....	....	....	....	....	....	....	....	....	....
1992-93	Torpedo Nizhny	CIS	5	1	0	1	....	....	....	4	....	....	....	....	....	....	....	....	....	....	....	....	....	....	....	....	....	....
	Kiekko-67	Finland 2	30	16	20	36	....	....	....	48	....	....	....	....	....	....	....	....	....	....	....	....	....	....	....	....	....	....
1993-94	TPS Turku	Finland	47	19	11	30	....	....	....	60	....	....	....	....	....	....	....	....	....	....	3	0	1	1	14	....	....	....
	Russia	Olympics	8	2	1	3	....	....	....	10	....	....	....	....	....	....	....	....	....	....	....	....	....	....	....	....	....	....
1994-95	JyP HT Jyvaskyla	Finland	50	13	18	31	....	....	....	44	....	....	....	....	....	....	....	....	....	....	4	0	1	1	25	....	....	....
	Russia	WC-A	6	0	2	2	....	....	....	4	....	....	....	....	....	....	....	....	....	....	....	....	....	....	....	....	....	....
1995-96	**Calgary Flames**	**NHL**	**41**	**6**	**10**	**16**	**6**	**8**	**14**	**14**	**0**	**0**	**0**	**50**	**12.0**	**21**	**2**	**18**	**1**	**+2**	**1**	**0**	**0**	**0**	**0**	**0**	**0**	**0**
	Saint John Flames	AHL	16	11	6	17	....	....	....	18	....	....	....	....	....	....	....	....	....	....	....	....	....	....	....	....	....	....
1996-97	HC Lugano	Switz.	34	18	21	39	....	....	....	87	....	....	....	....	....	....	....	....	....	....	8	3	3	6	10	....	....	....
1997-98	HC Davos	Switz.	38	20	27	47	....	....	....	85	....	....	....	....	....	....	....	....	....	....	17	6	9	15	14	....	....	....
	NHL Totals		**41**	**6**	**10**	**16**	**6**	**8**	**14**	**14**	**0**	**0**	**0**	**50**	**12.0**	**21**	**2**	**18**	**1**		**1**	**0**	**0**	**0**	**0**	**0**	**0**	**0**

TORKKI, JARI

Jari Torkki   LW – L. 5'11", 185 lbs.   b: Rauma, Finland, 8/11/1965.   Chicago's 6th choice, 119th overall, in 1983 Entry Draft.

Season	Club	League	GP	G	A	Pts	AG	AA	APts	PIM	PP	SH	GW	S	%	TGF	PGF	TGA	PGA	+/-	GP	G	A	Pts	PIM	PP	SH	GW
1981-82	Lukko Rauma	Finland	1	0	0	0	....	....	....	0																		
1982-83	Lukko Rauma	Finland	34	13	17	30				34																		
1983-84	Lukko Rauma	Finland 2	....																									
	Finland	WJC-A	7	4	2	6				10																		
1984-85	Lukko Rauma	Finland	36	25	21	46				40																		
	Finland	WJC-A	7	5	4	9				8																		
1985-86	Lukko Rauma	Finland	32	22	18	40				40																		
1986-87	Lukko Rauma	Finland	44	27	8	35				42																		
	Finland	WEC-A	10	5	2	7				12																		
1987-88	Lukko Rauma	Finland	43	23	24	47				54												8	4	3	7	12		
	Finland	Olympics	4	1	0	1				2																		
1988-89	**Chicago Blackhawks**	**NHL**	4	1	0	1	1	0	1	0	1	0	0	2	50.0	2	1	3	0	–2							
	Saginaw Hawks	IHL	72	30	42	72				22												6	2	1	3	4		
1989-90	Indianapolis Ice	IHL	66	25	29	54				50												11	5	2	7	8		
1990-91	Lukko Rauma	Finland	44	23	26	49				52																		
1991-92	Lukko Rauma	Finland	44	16	19	35				34																		
1992-93	Lukko Rauma	Finland	48	17	14	31				38																		
1993-94	Lukko Rauma	Finland	46	14	18	32				22																		
1994-95	Lukko Rauma	Finland	33	14	30	44				48												9	2	0	2	4		
1995-96	Lukko Rauma	Finland	48	16	20	36				50												8	0	1	1	10		
1996-97	Star Bulls Rosenheim	Germany	47	17	18	35				80												3	0	1	1	6		
1997-98	Star Bulls Rosenheim	Germany	41	10	14	24				20																		
	NHL Totals		**4**	**1**	**0**	**1**	**1**	**0**	**1**	**0**	**1**	**0**	**0**	**2**	**50.0**	**2**	**1**	**3**	**0**									

TORMANEN, ANTTI

Antti Tormanen   RW – L. 6'1", 198 lbs.   b: Espoo, Finland, 9/19/1970.   Ottawa's 10th choice, 274th overall, in 1994 Entry Draft.

Season	Club	League	GP	G	A	Pts	AG	AA	APts	PIM	PP	SH	GW	S	%	TGF	PGF	TGA	PGA	+/-	GP	G	A	Pts	PIM	PP	SH	GW
1990-91	Jokerit Helsinki	Finland	44	12	9	21				70																		
1991-92	Jokerit Helsinki	Finland	40	18	11	29				18																		
1992-93	Jokerit Helsinki	Finland	21	2	0	2				8																		
1993-94	Jokerit Helsinki	Finland	46	20	18	38				46																		
1994-95	Jokerit Helsinki	Finland	50	19	13	32				32												11	7	3	11	20		
	Finland	WC-A	5	0	0	0				2																		
1995-96	**Ottawa Senators**	**NHL**	50	7	8	15	7	7	14	28	0	0	0	68	10.3	21	1	35	0	–15							
	P.E.I. Senators	AHL	22	6	11	17				17												5	2	3	5	2		
1996-97	Finland	W Cup	DID NOT PLAY																								
	Jokerit Helsinki	Finland	50	18	14	32				54												9	3	5	8	10		
	Finland	WC-A	5	0	1	1				2																		
1997-98	Jokerit Helsinki	Finland	48	20	14	34				37												8	3	2	5	12		
	Finland	Olympics	5	0	0	0				0																		
	Finland	WC-A	10	3	2	5				6																		
	NHL Totals		**50**	**7**	**8**	**15**	**7**	**7**	**14**	**28**	**0**	**0**	**0**	**68**	**10.3**	**21**	**1**	**35**	**0**									

TOWNSHEND, GRAEME

Graeme Townshend   RW – R. 6'2", 225 lbs.   b: Kingston, Jamaica, 10/2/1965.

Season	Club	League	GP	G	A	Pts	AG	AA	APts	PIM	PP	SH	GW	S	%	TGF	PGF	TGA	PGA	+/-	GP	G	A	Pts	PIM	PP	SH	GW
1985-86	RPI Engineers	ECAC	29	1	7	8				52																		
1986-87	RPI Engineers	ECAC	29	6	1	7				50																		
1987-88	RPI Engineers	ECAC	32	6	14	20				64																		
1988-89	RPI Engineers	ECAC	31	6	16	22				50																		
	Maine Mariners	AHL	5	2	1	3				11																		
1989-90	**Boston Bruins**	**NHL**	4	0	0	0	0	0	0	7	0	0	0	3	0.0	0	0	1	0	–1							
	Maine Mariners	AHL	64	15	13	28				162																		
1990-91	**Boston Bruins**	**NHL**	18	2	5	7	2	4	6	12	0	0	0	10	20.0	10	0	9	0	+1							
	Maine Mariners	AHL	49	18	10	28				119												2	2	0	2	4		
1991-92	**New York Islanders**	**NHL**	7	1	2	3	1	1	2	0	0	0	0	6	16.7	8	0	2	0	+6							
	Capital District Islanders	AHL	81	14	23	37				94												4	0	2	2	4		
1992-93	**New York Islanders**	**NHL**	2	0	0	0	0	0	0	0	0	0	0	0	0.0	0	0	0	0								
	Capital District Islanders	AHL	67	29	21	50				45												2	0	0	0	0		
1993-94	**Ottawa Senators**	**NHL**	14	0	0	0	0	0	0	9	0	0	0	5	0.0	0	0	7	0	–7							
	P.E.I. Senators	AHL	56	16	13	29				107																		
1994-95	Houston Aeros	IHL	71	19	21	40				204												4	0	2	2	22		
1995-96	Minnesota Moose	IHL	3	0	0	0				0																		
	Houston Aeros	IHL	63	21	11	32				97																		
1996-97	Houston Aeros	IHL	74	21	15	36				68												3	0	0	0	2		
1997-98	Utah Grizzlies	IHL	1	0	0	0				0																		
	Houston Aeros	IHL	1	0	0	0				0																		
	Lake Charles Ice Pirates	WPHL	68	43	44	87				67												4	0	4	4	14		
	NHL Totals		**45**	**3**	**7**	**10**	**3**	**5**	**8**	**28**	**0**	**0**	**0**	**24**	**12.5**	**18**	**0**	**19**	**0**									

Signed as a free agent by **Boston**, May 12, 1989. Signed as a free agent by **NY Islanders**, September 3, 1991. Signed as a free agent by **Ottawa**, August 24, 1993.

TRADER, LARRY

Larry Trader   D – L. 6'1", 180 lbs.   b: Barry's Bay, Ont., 7/7/1963.   Detroit's 3rd choice, 86th overall, in 1981 Entry Draft.

Season	Club	League	GP	G	A	Pts	AG	AA	APts	PIM	PP	SH	GW	S	%	TGF	PGF	TGA	PGA	+/-	GP	G	A	Pts	PIM	PP	SH	GW
1979-80	Gloucester Rangers	OJHL	50	13	20	33				70																		
1980-81	London Knights	OHA	68	5	23	28				132																		
1981-82	London Knights	OHL	60	19	37	56				161												4	0	1	1	6		
1982-83	London Knights	OHL	39	16	28	44				67												3	0	1	1	6		
	Canada	WJC-A	7	2	3	5				8																		
	Detroit Red Wings	**NHL**	15	0	2	2	0	1	1	6	0	0	0	7		1		16	1	–9							
	Adirondack Red Wings	AHL	6	2	2	4				4												6	2	1	3	10		
1983-84	Adirondack Red Wings	AHL	80	13	28	41				89												6	1	1	2	4		
1984-85	**Detroit Red Wings**	**NHL**	40	3	7	10	2	5	7	39	1	0	0	47	6.4	44	7	29	3	+11	3	0	0	0	0	0	0	0
	Adirondack Red Wings	AHL	6	0	4	4				0																		
1985-86	Adirondack Red Wings	AHL	64	10	46	56				77												17	6	*16	*22	14		
1986-87	Canada	Nat Team	40	4	10	20				56																		
	St. Louis Blues	**NHL**	5	0	0	0	0	0	0	8	0	0	0	3	0.0	3	1	7	0	–5							
1987-88	**St. Louis Blues**	**NHL**	1	0	0	0	0	0	0	2	0	0	0	1	0.0	0	1	0	0	–1							
	Montreal Canadiens	**NHL**	30	2	4	6	2	3	5	19	1	0	0	18	11.1	22	2	20	2	+2							
	Sherbrooke Canadiens	AHL	11	2	2	4				25																		
1988-89	Binghamton Whalers	AHL	65	11	40	51				72																		
1989-90	Klagenfurter AC	Austria	35	12	22	34				79																		
1990-91	Brunico HC	Italy	36	8	23	31				44																		
1991-92	Brunico HC	Italy	21	3	16	19				51																		
1992-93	Brunico HC	Italy	17	11	14	25				24																		
1992-93	Zell-am-Zee	Austria	4	1	1	2																						
1993-94	Varese HC	Italy	7	2	3	5				40																		
	NHL Totals		**91**	**5**	**13**	**18**	**4**	**9**	**13**	**74**	**2**	**0**	**0**	**77**	**6.5**	**76**	**11**	**73**	**6**		**3**	**0**	**0**	**0**	**0**	**0**	**0**	**0**

AHL Second All-Star Team (1986)

Traded to **St. Louis** by **Detroit** for Lee Norwood, August 7, 1986. Traded to **Montreal** by **St. Louis** with St. Louis' 3rd round choice (Pierre Sevigny) in 1989 Entry Draft for Gaston Gingras and Montreal's 3rd round choice (later traded to Winnipeg — Winnipeg selected Kris Draper) in 1989 Entry Draft, October 13, 1987. Signed as a free agent by **Hartford**, August 3, 1988.

REGULAR SEASON / PLAYOFFS

• TRAPP, DOUG

Doug Trapp LW – L. 6', 180 lbs. b: Balcarres, Sask., 11/28/1965. Buffalo's 2nd choice, 39th overall, in 1984 Entry Draft.

Season	Club	League	GP	G	A	Pts	AG	AA	APts	PIM	PP	SH	GW	S	%	TGF	PGF	TGA	PGA	+/–	GP	G	A	Pts	PIM	PP	SH	GW
1981-82	Regina Pats	SJHL	43	25	28	53	....	....	....	102	....	....	....	....	....	....	....	....	....	....	....	....	....	....	....	....	....	....
1982-83	Regina Pats	WHL	71	23	28	51	....	....	....	123	....	....	....	....	....	....	....	....	....	....	5	0	2	2	18	....	....	....
1983-84	Regina Pats	WHL	59	43	50	93	....	....	....	44	....	....	....	....	....	....	....	....	....	....	23	12	12	24	38	....	....	....
1984-85	Regina Pats	WHL	72	48	60	108	....	....	....	81	....	....	....	....	....	....	....	....	....	....	8	7	7	14	2	....	....	....
1985-86	Rochester Americans	AHL	75	21	42	63	....	....	....	86	....	....	....	....	....	....	....	....	....	....	....	....	....	....	....	....	....	....
1986-87	**Buffalo Sabres**	**NHL**	**2**	**0**	**0**	**0**	**0**	**0**	**0**	**0**	**0**	**0**	**0**	**1**	**0.0**	**0**	**0**	**0**	**0**	**0**	....	....	....	....	....	....	....	....
	Rochester Americans	AHL	68	27	35	62	....	....	....	80	....	....	....	....	....	....	....	....	....	....	16	0	9	9	5	....	....	....
	NHL Totals		**2**	**0**	**0**	**0**	**0**	**0**	**0**	**0**	**0**	**0**	**0**	**1**	**0.0**	**0**	**0**	**0**	**0**		....	....	....	....	....	....	....	....

• TRAVERSE, PATRICK

Patrick Traverse D – L. 6'3", 190 lbs. b: Montreal, Que., 3/14/1974. Ottawa's 3rd choice, 50th overall, in 1992 Entry Draft.

Season	Club	League	GP	G	A	Pts	AG	AA	APts	PIM	PP	SH	GW	S	%	TGF	PGF	TGA	PGA	+/–	GP	G	A	Pts	PIM	PP	SH	GW
1991-92	Shawinigan Cataractes	QMJHL	59	3	11	14	....	....	....	12	....	....	....	....	....	....	....	....	....	....	10	0	0	0	4	....	....	....
1992-93	St-Jean Lynx	QMJHL	68	6	30	36	....	....	....	24	....	....	....	....	....	....	....	....	....	....	4	0	1	1	2	....	....	....
	New Haven Nighthawks	AHL	2	0	0	0	....	....	....	2	....	....	....	....	....	....	....	....	....	....	....	....	....	....	....	....	....	....
1993-94	St-Jean Lynx	QMJHL	66	15	37	52	....	....	....	30	....	....	....	....	....	....	....	....	....	....	5	0	4	4	4	....	....	....
	P.E.I. Senators	AHL	3	0	1	1	....	....	....	2	....	....	....	....	....	....	....	....	....	....	....	....	....	....	....	....	....	....
1994-95	P.E.I. Senators	AHL	70	5	13	18	....	....	....	19	....	....	....	....	....	....	....	....	....	....	7	0	2	2	0	....	....	....
1995-96	**Ottawa Senators**	**NHL**	**5**	**0**	**0**	**0**	**0**	**0**	**0**	**2**	**0**	**0**	**0**	**2**	**0.0**	**1**	**0**	**2**	**0**	**–1**	....	....	....	....	....	....	....	....
	P.E.I. Senators	AHL	55	4	21	25	....	....	....	32	....	....	....	....	....	....	....	....	....	....	5	1	2	3	2	....	....	....
1996-97	Worcester IceCats	AHL	24	0	4	4	....	....	....	23	....	....	....	....	....	....	....	....	....	....	....	....	....	....	....	....	....	....
	Grand Rapids Griffins	IHL	10	2	1	3	....	....	....	10	....	....	....	....	....	....	....	....	....	....	2	0	1	1	2	....	....	....
1997-98	Hershey Bears	AHL	71	14	15	29	....	....	....	67	....	....	....	....	....	....	....	....	....	....	7	1	3	4	4	....	....	....
	NHL Totals		**5**	**0**	**0**	**0**	**0**	**0**	**0**	**2**	**0**	**0**	**0**	**2**	**0.0**	**1**	**0**	**2**	**0**		....	....	....	....	....	....	....	....

• TREBIL, DANIEL

Daniel Trebil D – R. 6'3", 210 lbs. b: Edina, MN, 4/10/1974. New Jersey's 7th choice, 138th overall, in 1992 Entry Draft.

Season	Club	League	GP	G	A	Pts	AG	AA	APts	PIM	PP	SH	GW	S	%	TGF	PGF	TGA	PGA	+/–	GP	G	A	Pts	PIM	PP	SH	GW
1991-92	Jefferson-Minnesota High	H.S.	28	7	26	33	....	....	....	6	....	....	....	....	....	....	....	....	....	....	....	....	....	....	....	....	....	....
1992-93	University of Minnesota	WCHA	36	2	11	13	....	....	....	16	....	....	....	....	....	....	....	....	....	....	....	....	....	....	....	....	....	....
1993-94	University of Minnesota	WCHA	42	1	21	22	....	....	....	24	....	....	....	....	....	....	....	....	....	....	....	....	....	....	....	....	....	....
1994-95	University of Minnesota	WCHA	44	10	33	43	....	....	....	10	....	....	....	....	....	....	....	....	....	....	....	....	....	....	....	....	....	....
1995-96	University of Minnesota	WCHA	42	11	35	46	....	....	....	36	....	....	....	....	....	....	....	....	....	....	....	....	....	....	....	....	....	....
1996-97	**Anaheim Mighty Ducks**	**NHL**	**29**	**3**	**3**	**6**	**3**	**3**	**6**	**23**	**0**	**0**	**0**	**30**	**10.0**	**27**	**5**	**23**	**6**	**+5**	**9**	**0**	**1**	**1**	**6**	**0**	**0**	**0**
	Baltimore Bandits	AHL	49	4	20	24	....	....	....	38	....	....	....	....	....	....	....	....	....	....	....	....	....	....	....	....	....	....
1997-98	**Anaheim Mighty Ducks**	**NHL**	**21**	**0**	**1**	**1**	**0**	**1**	**1**	**2**	**0**	**0**	**0**	**11**	**0.0**	**7**	**1**	**15**	**1**	**–8**	....	....	....	....	....	....	....	....
	Cincinnati Mighty Ducks	AHL	32	5	15	20	....	....	....	21	....	....	....	....	....	....	....	....	....	....	....	....	....	....	....	....	....	....
	United States	WC-A	4	0	0	0	....	....	....	0	....	....	....	....	....	....	....	....	....	....	....	....	....	....	....	....	....	....
	NHL Totals		**50**	**3**	**4**	**7**	**3**	**4**	**7**	**25**	**0**	**0**	**0**	**41**	**7.3**	**34**	**6**	**38**	**7**		**9**	**0**	**1**	**1**	**6**	**0**	**0**	**0**

WCHA Second All-Star Team (1996) • NCAA West Second All-American Team (1996)

Signed as a free agent by **Anaheim**, May 30, 1996.

• TREDWAY, BROCK

Brock Tredway RW – R. 6', 180 lbs. b: Highland Creek, Ont., 6/23/1959.

Season	Club	League	GP	G	A	Pts	AG	AA	APts	PIM	PP	SH	GW	S	%	TGF	PGF	TGA	PGA	+/–	GP	G	A	Pts	PIM	PP	SH	GW
1977-78	Cornell University	ECAC	22	28	12	40	....	....	....	2	....	....	....	....	....	....	....	....	....	....	....	....	....	....	....	....	....	....
1978-79	Cornell University	ECAC	29	31	29	60	....	....	....	8	....	....	....	....	....	....	....	....	....	....	....	....	....	....	....	....	....	....
1979-80	Cornell University	ECAC	31	25	35	60	....	....	....	10	....	....	....	....	....	....	....	....	....	....	....	....	....	....	....	....	....	....
1980-81	Cornell University	ECAC	31	29	17	46	....	....	....	0	....	....	....	....	....	....	....	....	....	....	....	....	....	....	....	....	....	....
1981-82	New Haven Nighthawks	AHL	80	35	24	59	....	....	....	7	....	....	....	....	....	....	....	....	....	....	4	3	3	6	0	....	....	....
	Los Angeles Kings	**NHL**	....	....	....	....	....	....	....	....	....	....	....	....	....	....	....	....	....	....	**1**	**0**	**0**	**0**	**0**	....	....	....
1982-83	New Haven Nighthawks	AHL	74	15	26	41	....	....	....	9	....	....	....	....	....	....	....	....	....	....	12	1	7	8	2	....	....	....
1983-84	New Haven Nighthawks	AHL	70	21	42	63	....	....	....	4	....	....	....	....	....	....	....	....	....	....	....	....	....	....	....	....	....	....
1984-85	Klagenfurter AC	Austria	39	19	21	40	....	....	....	20	....	....	....	....	....	....	....	....	....	....	....	....	....	....	....	....	....	....
1985-86	New Haven Nighthawks	AHL	39	2	6	8	....	....	....	0	....	....	....	....	....	....	....	....	....	....	....	....	....	....	....	....	....	....
	NHL Totals		**0**	**0**	**0**	**0**	**0**	**0**	**0**	**0**	**0**	**0**	**0**	**0**	**0.0**	**0**	**0**	**0**	**0**		**1**	**0**	**0**	**0**	**0**	**0**	**0**	**0**

ECAC Second All-Star Team (1979)

Signed as a free agent by **LA Kings**, May 11, 1981.

• TREMBLAY, BRENT

Brent Tremblay D – L. 6'2", 192 lbs. b: North Bay, Ont., 11/1/1957. Washington's 8th choice, 127th overall, in 1977 Amateur Draft.

Season	Club	League	GP	G	A	Pts	AG	AA	APts	PIM	PP	SH	GW	S	%	TGF	PGF	TGA	PGA	+/–	GP	G	A	Pts	PIM	PP	SH	GW
1975-76	Hull Festivals	QMJHL	72	2	18	20	....	....	....	129	....	....	....	....	....	....	....	....	....	....	....	....	....	....	....	....	....	....
1976-77	Trois-Rivieres Draveurs	QMJHL	60	9	17	26	....	....	....	131	....	....	....	....	....	....	....	....	....	....	....	....	....	....	....	....	....	....
1977-78	Port Huron Flags	IHL	61	7	25	32	....	....	....	231	....	....	....	....	....	....	....	....	....	....	17	5	8	15	74	....	....	....
	Hershey Bears	AHL	11	0	1	1	....	....	....	15	....	....	....	....	....	....	....	....	....	....	....	....	....	....	....	....	....	....
1978-79	**Washington Capitals**	**NHL**	**1**	**0**	**0**	**0**	**0**	**0**	**0**	**0**	**0**	**0**	**0**	**1**	**0.0**	**0**	**0**	**0**	**0**	**0**	....	....	....	....	....	....	....	....
	Hershey Bears	AHL	75	2	16	18	....	....	....	109	....	....	....	....	....	....	....	....	....	....	4	0	0	0	9	....	....	....
1979-80	**Washington Capitals**	**NHL**	**9**	**1**	**0**	**1**	**1**	**0**	**1**	**6**	**0**	**0**	**0**	**6**	**16.7**	**4**	**0**	**4**	**1**	**+1**	....	....	....	....	....	....	....	....
	Hershey Bears	AHL	26	2	11	13	....	....	....	54	....	....	....	....	....	....	....	....	....	....	....	....	....	....	....	....	....	....
	NHL Totals		**10**	**1**	**0**	**1**	**1**	**0**	**1**	**6**	**0**	**0**	**0**	**7**	**14.3**	**4**	**0**	**4**	**1**		....	....	....	....	....	....	....	....

QMJHL West Division Second All-Star Team (1976)

• TREMBLAY, GILLES

Gilles Tremblay LW – L. 5'10", 170 lbs. b: Montmorency, Que., 12/17/1938.

Season	Club	League	GP	G	A	Pts	AG	AA	APts	PIM	PP	SH	GW	S	%	TGF	PGF	TGA	PGA	+/–	GP	G	A	Pts	PIM	PP	SH	GW
1956-57	Hull-Ottawa Jr. Canadiens	Ott-Jr.	18	3	4	7	....	....	....	2	....	....	....	....	....	....	....	....	....	....	....	....	....	....	....	....	....	....
	Hull-Ottawa Jr. Canadiens	EOHL	8	0	2	2	....	....	....	2	....	....	....	....	....	....	....	....	....	....	....	....	....	....	....	....	....	....
	Hull-Ottawa Jr. Canadiens	QHL	14	2	1	3	....	....	....	0	....	....	....	....	....	....	....	....	....	....	....	....	....	....	....	....	....	....
1957-58	Hull-Ottawa Jr. Canadiens	Ott-Jr.	27	15	12	27	....	....	....	6	....	....	....	....	....	....	....	....	....	....	....	....	....	....	....	....	....	....
	Hull-Ottawa Jr. Canadiens	EOHL	36	13	19	32	....	....	....	10	....	....	....	....	....	....	....	....	....	....	....	....	....	....	....	....	....	....
1958-59	Hull-Ottawa Canadiens	EOHL	3	1	0	1	....	....	....	4	....	....	....	....	....	....	....	....	....	....	3	1	0	1	0	....	....	....
	Rochester Americans	AHL	3	1	1	2	....	....	....	2	....	....	....	....	....	....	....	....	....	....	....	....	....	....	....	....	....	....
1959-60	Hull-Ottawa Canadiens	EPHL	67	32	51	83	....	....	....	45	....	....	....	....	....	....	....	....	....	....	7	4	3	7	8	....	....	....
1960-61	**Montreal Canadiens**	**NHL**	**45**	**7**	**11**	**18**	**8**	**11**	**19**	**4**	....	....	....	....	....	....	....	....	....	....	**6**	**1**	**3**	**4**	**0**	....	....	....
	Hull-Ottawa Canadiens	EPHL	14	9	11	20	....	....	....	12	....	....	....	....	....	....	....	....	....	....	....	....	....	....	....	....	....	....
1961-62	**Montreal Canadiens**	**NHL**	**70**	**32**	**22**	**54**	**39**	**22**	**61**	**28**	....	....	....	....	....	....	....	....	....	....	**6**	**1**	**0**	**1**	**2**	....	....	....
1962-63	**Montreal Canadiens**	**NHL**	**60**	**25**	**24**	**49**	**31**	**25**	**56**	**42**	....	....	....	....	....	....	....	....	....	....	**5**	**2**	**0**	**2**	**0**	....	....	....
1963-64	**Montreal Canadiens**	**NHL**	**61**	**22**	**15**	**37**	**29**	**17**	**46**	**21**	....	....	....	....	....	....	....	....	....	....	**2**	**0**	**0**	**0**	**0**	....	....	....
1964-65	**Montreal Canadiens**	**NHL**	**26**	**9**	**7**	**16**	**11**	**8**	**19**	**16**	....	....	....	....	....	....	....	....	....	....	....	....	....	....	....	....	....	....
1965-66	**Montreal Canadiens**	**NHL**	**70**	**27**	**21**	**48**	**33**	**21**	**54**	**24**	....	....	....	....	....	....	....	....	....	....	**10**	**4**	**5**	**9**	**0**	....	....	....
1966-67	**Montreal Canadiens**	**NHL**	**62**	**13**	**19**	**32**	**16**	**20**	**36**	**16**	....	....	....	....	....	....	....	....	....	....	**10**	**0**	**1**	**1**	**0**	....	....	....
1967-68	**Montreal Canadiens**	**NHL**	**71**	**23**	**28**	**51**	**28**	**29**	**57**	**8**	**7**	**1**	**2**	**215**	**10.7**	**80**	**14**	**65**	**27**	**+28**	**9**	**1**	**5**	**6**	**2**	**0**	**0**	**0**
1968-69	**Montreal Canadiens**	**NHL**	**44**	**10**	**15**	**25**	**11**	**14**	**25**	**2**	**0**	**0**	**0**	**95**	**10.5**	**48**	**4**	**51**	**22**	**+15**	....	....	....	....	....	....	....	....
	NHL Totals		**509**	**168**	**162**	**330**	**206**	**167**	**373**	**161**	**7**	**1**	**2**	**310**	**54.2**	**128**	**18**	**116**	**49**		**48**	**9**	**14**	**23**	**4**	**0**	**0**	**0**

Played in NHL All-Star Game (1965, 1967)

• TREMBLAY, J.C.

J.C. (Jean-Claude) Tremblay D – L. 5'11", 170 lbs. b: Bagotville, Que., 1/22/1939. Deceased.

Season	Club	League	GP	G	A	Pts	AG	AA	APts	PIM	PP	SH	GW	S	%	TGF	PGF	TGA	PGA	+/–	GP	G	A	Pts	PIM	PP	SH	GW
1957-58	Hull-Ottawa Jr. Canadiens	Ott-Jr.	24	7	12	19	....	....	....	8	....	....	....	....	....	....	....	....	....	....	....	....	....	....	....	....	....	....
	Hull-Ottawa Jr. Canadiens	EOHL	34	5	17	22	....	....	....	16	....	....	....	....	....	....	....	....	....	....	....	....	....	....	....	....	....	....
1958-59	Hull-Ottawa Canadiens	EOHL	26	4	13	17	....	....	....	22	....	....	....	....	....	....	....	....	....	....	1	0	1	1	9	....	....	....
	Rochester Americans	AHL	3	0	0	0	....	....	....	0	....	....	....	....	....	....	....	....	....	....	....	....	....	....	....	....	....	....
1959-60	**Montreal Canadiens**	**NHL**	**11**	**0**	**1**	**1**	**0**	**1**	**1**	**0**	....	....	....	....	....	....	....	....	....	....	....	....	....	....	....	....	....	....
	Hull-Ottawa Canadiens	EPHL	55	25	31	56	....	....	....	55	....	....	....	....	....	....	....	....	....	....	7	1	4	5	2	....	....	....
1960-61	**Montreal Canadiens**	**NHL**	**29**	**1**	**3**	**4**	**1**	**3**	**4**	**18**	....	....	....	....	....	....	....	....	....	....	**5**	**0**	**0**	**0**	**2**	....	....	....
	Hull-Ottawa Canadiens	EPHL	37	7	33	40	....	....	....	28	....	....	....	....	....	....	....	....	....	....	....	....	....	....	....	....	....	....
1961-62	**Montreal Canadiens**	**NHL**	**70**	**3**	**17**	**20**	**4**	**17**	**21**	**18**	....	....	....	....	....	....	....	....	....	....	**6**	**0**	**2**	**2**	**2**	....	....	....

Season	Club	League	GP	G	A	Pts	AG	AA	APts	PIM	PP	SH	GW	S	%	TGF	PGF	TGA	PGA	+/-	GP	G	A	Pts	PIM	PP	SH	GW
1962-63	Montreal Canadiens	NHL	69	1	17	18	1	18	19	10											5	0	0	0	0			
1963-64	Montreal Canadiens	NHL	70	5	16	21	7	18	25	24											7	2	1	3	9			
1964-65	Montreal Canadiens	NHL	68	3	17	20	4	18	22	22											13	1	*9	10	18			
1965-66	Montreal Canadiens	NHL	59	6	29	35	7	29	36	8											10	2	9	11	2			
1966-67	Montreal Canadiens	NHL	60	8	26	34	10	27	37	14											10	4	6	2				
1967-68	Montreal Canadiens	NHL	73	4	26	30	5	27	32	18		1	0	1	105	3.8	116	29	88	29	+28	13	3	6	9	2	0	1	1
1968-69	Montreal Canadiens	NHL	75	7	32	39	8	30	38	18	2	0	1	139	5.0	146	29	118	30	+29	13	1	4	5	6	0	1	0
1969-70	Montreal Canadiens	NHL	58	2	19	21	2	19	21	7	1	0	0	77	2.6	72	21	55	9	+5								
1970-71	Montreal Canadiens	NHL	76	11	52	63	11	46	57	23	5	0	2	122	9.0	153	63	102	28	+16	20	3	14	17	15	1	0	3
1971-72	Montreal Canadiens	NHL	76	6	51	57	6	47	53	24	3	0	2	130	4.6	167	51	91	27	+52	6	0	2	2	0	0	0	0
1972-73	Quebec Nordiques	WHA	75	14	*75	89				32																		
1973-74	Quebec Nordiques	WHA	68	9	44	53				100																		
1974-75	Quebec Nordiques	WHA	68	16	56	72				18											11	0	10	10	2			
1975-76	Quebec Nordiques	WHA	80	12	*77	89				18											5	0	3	3	0			
1976-77	Quebec Nordiques	WHA	53	4	31	35				16											17	2	9	11	2			
1977-78	Quebec Nordiques	WHA	54	5	37	42				26											1	0	1	1	0			
1978-79	Quebec Nordiques	WHA	56	6	38	44				8																		
	NHL Totals		794	57	306	363	66	300	366	204	12	0	8	573	9.9	654	193	454	123		108	14	51	65	58	1	2	4
	Other Major League Totals		454	66	358	424				216											34	2	23	25	4			

NHL Second All-Star Team (1968) • NHL First All-Star Team (1971) • WHA First All-Star Team (1973, 1975, 1976) • Won Dennis A. Murphy Trophy (WHA Top Defenseman) (1973, 1975) • WHA Second All-Star Team (1974)

Played in NHL All-Star Game (1959, 1965, 1967, 1968, 1969, 1971, 1972)

Selected by **LA Sharks** (WHA) in 1972 WHA General Player Draft, February 12, 1972. Traded to **Quebec** (WHA) by **LA Sharks** (WHA) for future considerations, August, 1972.

● TREMBLAY, MARIO

Mario Tremblay   RW – R. 6', 185 lbs.   b: Montreal, Que., 2/9/1956.   Montreal's 4th choice, 12th overall, in 1974 Amateur Draft.

Season	Club	League	GP	G	A	Pts	AG	AA	APts	PIM	PP	SH	GW	S	%	TGF	PGF	TGA	PGA	+/-	GP	G	A	Pts	PIM	PP	SH	GW
1972-73	Montreal Jr. Canadiens	QMJHL	56	43	37	80				155											4	0	1	1	4			
1973-74	Montreal Jr. Canadiens	QMJHL	47	49	51	100				154											7	1	3	4	17			
1974-75	Montreal Canadiens	NHL	63	21	18	39	19	14	33	108	0	0	1	127	16.5	60	4	33	0	+23	11	0	1	1	7	0	0	0
	Nova Scotia Voyageurs	AHL	15	10	8	18				4																		
1975-76	Montreal Canadiens	NHL	71	11	16	27	10	13	23	88	1	0	2	94	11.7	38	4	29	0	+5	10	0	1	1	27	0	0	0
1976-77	Montreal Canadiens	NHL	74	18	28	46	17	23	40	61	4	0	3	139	12.9	69	7	37	0	+25	14	3	0	3	9	0	0	0
1977-78	Montreal Canadiens	NHL	56	10	14	24	10	11	21	44	0	1	0	89	11.2	34	1	29	2	+6	5	2	1	3	16	0	0	1
1978-79	Montreal Canadiens	NHL	76	30	29	59	27	22	49	74	3	0	4	163	18.4	78	6	55	6	+23	13	3	4	7	13	0	0	0
1979-80	Montreal Canadiens	NHL	77	16	26	42	14	20	34	105	0	0	2	192	8.3	60	5	51	2	+6	10	0	11	11	14	0	0	0
1980-81	Montreal Canadiens	NHL	77	25	38	63	21	27	48	123	4	1	0	254	9.8	91	20	57	2	+16	3	0	0	0	9	0	0	0
1981-82	Montreal Canadiens	NHL	80	33	40	73	26	26	52	66	7	0	4	205	16.1	105	28	53	0	+24	5	4	1	5	24	0	0	1
1982-83	Montreal Canadiens	NHL	80	30	37	67	25	26	51	87	7	0	4	175	17.1	101	20	52	0	+29	3	0	1	1	7	0	0	0
1983-84	Montreal Canadiens	NHL	67	14	25	39	11	17	28	112	3	0	3	133	10.5	68	16	51	1	+2	15	3	6	9	31	0	0	1
1984-85	Montreal Canadiens	NHL	75	31	35	66	25	24	49	120	14	0	6	193	16.1	96	30	45	0	+21	12	2	6	8	30	1	0	0
1985-86	Montreal Canadiens	NHL	56	19	20	39	15	13	28	55	3	0	3	119	16.0	62	13	45	0	+4								
	NHL Totals		852	258	326	584	220	236	456	1043	46	2	36	1883	13.7	862	154	537	13		101	20	29	49	187	1	0	4

● TREMBLAY, YANNICK

Yannick Tremblay   D – R. 6'2", 185 lbs.   b: Pointe-aux-Trembles, Que., 11/15/1975.   Toronto's 4th choice, 145th overall, in 1995 Entry Draft.

Season	Club	League	GP	G	A	Pts	AG	AA	APts	PIM	PP	SH	GW	S	%	TGF	PGF	TGA	PGA	+/-	GP	G	A	Pts	PIM	PP	SH	GW
1993-94	St. Thomas University	AUAA	25	2	3	5				10																		
1994-95	Beauport Harfangs	QMJHL	70	10	32	42				22											17	6	8	14	6			
1995-96	Beauport Harfangs	QMJHL	61	12	33	45				42											20	3	16	19	18			
	St. John's Maple Leafs	AHL	3	0	1	1				0																		
1996-97	Toronto Maple Leafs	NHL	5	0	0	0	0	0	0	0	0	0	0	2	0.0	0	0	4	0	-4								
	St. John's Maple Leafs	AHL	67	7	25	32				34											11	2	9	11	0			
1997-98	Toronto Maple Leafs	NHL	38	2	4	6	2	4	6	6	1	0	0	45	4.4	18	5	19	0	-6								
	St. John's Maple Leafs	AHL	17	3	7	10				4											4	0	1	1	5			
	NHL Totals		43	2	4	6	2	4	6	6	1	0	0	47	4.3	18	5	23	0									

● TREPANIER, PASCAL

Pascal Trepanier   D – R. 6', 205 lbs.   b: Gaspe, Que., 4/9/1973.

Season	Club	League	GP	G	A	Pts	AG	AA	APts	PIM	PP	SH	GW	S	%	TGF	PGF	TGA	PGA	+/-	GP	G	A	Pts	PIM	PP	SH	GW
1991-92	Trois-Rivieres Draveurs	QMJHL	53	4	18	22				125											15	3	5	8	21			
1992-93	Sherbrooke Faucons	QMJHL	59	15	33	48				130											15	5	7	12	36			
1993-94	Sherbrooke Faucons	QMJHL	48	16	41	57				67											12	1	8	9	14			
1994-95	Dayton Bombers	ECHL	36	10	28	44				113											9	2	4	6	20			
	Kalamazoo Wings	IHL	14	1	2	3				4																		
	Cornwall Aces	AHL	4	0	0	0				9											14	2	7	9	32			
1995-96	Cornwall Aces	AHL	70	13	20	33				142											8	1	2	3	24			
1996-97	Hershey Bears	AHL	73	14	39	53				151											23	6	13	19	59			
1997-98	Colorado Avalanche	NHL	15	0	1	1	0	1	1	18	0	0	0	9	0.0	2	0	4	0	-2								
	Hershey Bears	AHL	43	13	18	31				105											7	4	2	6	8			
	NHL Totals		15	0	1	1	0	1	1	18	0	0	0	9	0.0	2	0	4	0									

AHL Second All-Star Team (1997)

Signed as a free agent by **Colorado**, August 30, 1995.

● TRIMPER, TIM

Tim Trimper   LW – L. 5'9", 184 lbs.   b: Windsor, Ont., 9/28/1959.   Chicago's 2nd choice, 28th overall, in 1979 Entry Draft.

Season	Club	League	GP	G	A	Pts	AG	AA	APts	PIM	PP	SH	GW	S	%	TGF	PGF	TGA	PGA	+/-	GP	G	A	Pts	PIM	PP	SH	GW
1976-77	Peterborough Petes	OHA	62	14	11	25				95																		
1977-78	Peterborough Petes	OHA	50	26	34	60				73											21	8	8	16	25			
1978-79	Peterborough Petes	OHA	66	62	46	108				97											17	7	24	31	25			
1979-80	Chicago Black Hawks	NHL	30	6	10	16	5	8	13	10	2	0	1	65	9.2	29	16	20	0	-7	1	0	0	0	2	0	0	0
	New Brunswick Hawks	AHL	43	26	31	57				18																		
1980-81	Winnipeg Jets	NHL	56	15	14	29	12	10	22	28	1	0	1	95	15.8	39	2	69	1	-31								
	New Brunswick Hawks	AHL	19	7	8	15				21																		
	Hershey Bears	AHL	47	20	38	58				129																		
1981-82	Winnipeg Jets	NHL	74	8	8	16	6	5	11	100	0	1	0	68	11.8	26	0	57	24	-7	1	0	0	0	0	0	0	0
1982-83	Winnipeg Jets	NHL	5	0	0	0	0	0	0	0	0	0	0	2	0.0	0	0	5	3	-2								
	Sherbrooke Jets	AHL	68	20	30	50				53																		
1983-84	Winnipeg Jets	NHL	5	0	0	0	0	0	0	0	0	0	0	1	0.0	1	0	0	0	+1								
	Sherbrooke Jets	AHL	31	10	24	34				26																		
	Salt Lake Golden Eagles	IHL	35	18	27	45				26											5	4	3	7	0			
1984-85	Minnesota North Stars	NHL	20	1	4	5	1	3	4	15	0	0	0	28	3.6	7	0	16	0	-9								
	Springfield Indians	AHL	60	27	34	61				84											4	1	3	4	9			
	NHL Totals		190	30	36	66	24	26	50	153	3	1	2	259	11.6	102	18	167	28		2	0	0	0	2	0	0	0

OHA Second All-Star Team (1979) • Memorial Cup All-Star Team (1979)

Traded to **Winnipeg** by **Chicago** with Doug Lecuyer for Peter Marsh, December 1, 1980. Traded to **Minnesota** by **Winnipeg** for Jordy Douglas, January 12, 1984.

• TRNKA, PAVEL

Pavel Trnka D – L. 6'3", 200 lbs. b: Plzen, Czech., 7/27/1976. Anaheim's 5th choice, 106th overall, in 1994 Entry Draft.

			REGULAR SEASON																		PLAYOFFS							
Season	Club	League	GP	G	A	Pts	AG	AA	APts	PIM	PP	SH	GW	S	%	TGF	PGF	TGA	PGA	+/–	GP	G	A	Pts	PIM	PP	SH	GW
1993-94	Skoda Plzen	Czech.	12	0	1	1	....	....	....	....	....	....	....	....	....	....	....	....	....	....	....	....	....	....	....	....	....	....
1994-95	Poldi Kladno	Czech.	28	0	5	5	....	....	....	24	....	....	....	....	....	....	....	....	....	....	....	....	....	....	....	....	....	....
1994-95	Czech Republic	WJC-A	7	0	0	0	....	....	....	8	....	....	....	....	....	....	....	....	....	....	....	....	....	....	....	....	....	....
	Interconex Plzen	Czech.	6	0	0	0	....	....	....	0	....	....	....	....	....	....	....	....	....	....	....	....	....	....	....	....	....	....
1995-96	Baltimore Bandits	AHL	69	2	6	8	....	....	....	44	....	....	....	....	....	....	....	....	....	....	6	0	0	0	2	....	....	....
1996-97	Baltimore Bandits	AHL	69	6	14	20	....	....	....	86	....	....	....	....	....	....	....	....	....	....	3	0	0	0	2	....	....	....
1997-98	**Anaheim Mighty Ducks**	**NHL**	**48**	**3**	**4**	**7**	**4**	**4**	**8**	**40**	**1**	**0**	**0**	**46**	**6.5**	**30**	**6**	**36**	**8**	**–4**	....	....	....	....	....	....	....	....
	Cincinnati Mighty Ducks	AHL	23	3	5	8	....	....	....	28	....	....	....	....	....	....	....	....	....	....	....	....	....	....	....	....	....	....
	NHL Totals		**48**	**3**	**4**	**7**	**4**	**4**	**8**	**40**	**1**	**0**	**0**	**46**	**6.5**	**30**	**6**	**36**	**8**		....	....	....	....	....	....	....	....

• TROTTIER, BRYAN

Bryan "Trots" Trottier C – L. 5'11", 195 lbs. b: Val Marie, Sask., 7/17/1956. NY Islanders' 2nd choice, 22nd overall, in 1974 Amateur Draft.

Season	Club	League	GP	G	A	Pts	AG	AA	APts	PIM	PP	SH	GW	S	%	TGF	PGF	TGA	PGA	+/–	GP	G	A	Pts	PIM	PP	SH	GW
1972-73	Swift Current Broncos	WCJHL	67	16	29	45	....	....	....	10	....	....	....	....	....	....	....	....	....	....	....	....	....	....	....	....	....	....
1973-74	Swift Current Broncos	WCJHL	68	41	71	112	....	....	....	76	....	....	....	....	....	....	....	....	....	....	13	7	8	15	8	....	....	....
1974-75	Lethbridge Broncos	WCJHL	67	46	*98	144	....	....	....	103	....	....	....	....	....	....	....	....	....	....	6	2	5	7	14	....	....	....
	Canada	WJC-A	....	5	2	7	....	....	....	....	....	....	....	....	....	....	....	....	....	....	....	....	....	....	....	....	....	....
1975-76	**New York Islanders**	**NHL**	**80**	**32**	**63**	**95**	**30**	**50**	**80**	**21**	**11**	**1**	**5**	**178**	**18.0**	**129**	**63**	**40**	**2**	**+28**	**13**	**1**	**7**	**8**	**8**	**0**	**0**	**0**
1976-77	**New York Islanders**	**NHL**	**76**	**30**	**42**	**72**	**29**	**34**	**63**	**34**	**11**	**1**	**6**	**175**	**17.1**	**103**	**33**	**46**	**4**	**+28**	**12**	**2**	**8**	**10**	**2**	**0**	**0**	**0**
1977-78	**New York Islanders**	**NHL**	**77**	**46**	***77**	**123**	**45**	**63**	**108**	**46**	**13**	**2**	**6**	**193**	**23.8**	**156**	**55**	**55**	**6**	**+52**	**7**	**0**	**3**	**3**	**4**	**0**	**0**	**0**
1978-79	**New York Islanders**	**NHL**	**76**	**47**	***87**	***134**	**43**	**67**	**110**	**50**	**15**	**0**	**8**	**187**	**25.1**	**189**	**66**	**51**	**4**	**+76**	**10**	**2**	**4**	**6**	**13**	**0**	**0**	**1**
	NHL All-Stars	Chal Cup	3	1	1	2	....	....	....	2	....	....	....	....	....	....	....	....	....	....	....	....	....	....	....	....	....	....
1979-80	**New York Islanders**	**NHL**	**78**	**42**	**62**	**104**	**38**	**48**	**86**	**68**	**15**	**0**	**6**	**186**	**22.6**	**139**	**46**	**74**	**12**	**+31**	**21**	***12**	**17**	***29**	**16**	**4**	**2**	**2**
1980-81	**New York Islanders**	**NHL**	**73**	**31**	**72**	**103**	**26**	**51**	**77**	**74**	**9**	**2**	**5**	**156**	**19.9**	**151**	**53**	**73**	**24**	**+49**	***18**	**11**	***18**	**29**	**34**	**4**	**2**	**1**
1981-82	Canada	C Cup	7	3	8	11	....	....	....	6	....	....	....	....	....	....	....	....	....	....	....	....	....	....	....	....	....	....
	New York Islanders	**NHL**	**80**	**50**	**79**	**129**	**40**	**52**	**92**	**88**	**18**	**2**	**10**	**217**	**23.0**	**177**	**51**	**82**	**26**	**+70**	**19**	**6**	***23**	***29**	**40**	**2**	**0**	**2**
1982-83	**New York Islanders**	**NHL**	**80**	**34**	**55**	**89**	**28**	**38**	**66**	**68**	**13**	**0**	**5**	**179**	**19.0**	**139**	**46**	**75**	**19**	**+37**	**17**	**8**	**12**	**20**	**18**	**3**	**0**	**1**
1983-84	**New York Islanders**	**NHL**	**68**	**40**	**71**	**111**	**32**	**48**	**80**	**59**	**7**	**3**	**4**	**194**	**20.6**	**156**	**35**	**58**	**7**	**+70**	**21**	**8**	**6**	**14**	**49**	**1**	**0**	**0**
1984-85	United States	C Cup	6	2	3	5	....	....	....	8	....	....	....	....	....	....	....	....	....	....	....	....	....	....	....	....	....	....
	New York Islanders	**NHL**	**68**	**28**	**31**	**59**	**23**	**21**	**44**	**47**	**4**	**5**	**3**	**159**	**17.6**	**95**	**21**	**88**	**19**	**+5**	**10**	**4**	**2**	**6**	**8**	**1**	**0**	**1**
1985-86	**New York Islanders**	**NHL**	**78**	**37**	**59**	**96**	**30**	**40**	**70**	**72**	**5**	**1**	**3**	**185**	**20.0**	**138**	**44**	**93**	**28**	**+29**	**3**	**1**	**1**	**2**	**2**	**0**	**0**	**0**
1986-87	**New York Islanders**	**NHL**	**80**	**23**	**64**	**87**	**20**	**46**	**66**	**50**	**13**	**0**	**1**	**194**	**11.9**	**126**	**54**	**95**	**26**	**+3**	**14**	**8**	**5**	**13**	**12**	**3**	**0**	**2**
1987-88	**New York Islanders**	**NHL**	**77**	**30**	**52**	**82**	**26**	**37**	**63**	**48**	**15**	**0**	**3**	**176**	**17.0**	**110**	**48**	**81**	**29**	**+10**	**6**	**0**	**0**	**0**	**10**	**0**	**0**	**0**
1988-89	**New York Islanders**	**NHL**	**73**	**17**	**28**	**45**	**14**	**20**	**34**	**44**	**5**	**0**	**3**	**163**	**10.4**	**79**	**25**	**102**	**41**	**–7**	....	....	....	....	....	....	....	....
1989-90	**New York Islanders**	**NHL**	**59**	**13**	**11**	**24**	**11**	**8**	**19**	**29**	**4**	**0**	**0**	**84**	**15.5**	**40**	**8**	**64**	**21**	**–11**	**4**	**1**	**0**	**1**	**4**	**0**	**0**	**0**
1990-91	**Pittsburgh Penguins**	**NHL**	**52**	**9**	**19**	**28**	**8**	**14**	**22**	**24**	**0**	**1**	**0**	**68**	**13.2**	**37**	**1**	**48**	**17**	**+5**	**23**	**3**	**4**	**7**	**49**	**0**	**0**	**2**
1991-92	**Pittsburgh Penguins**	**NHL**	**63**	**11**	**18**	**29**	**10**	**14**	**24**	**54**	**3**	**1**	**0**	**102**	**10.8**	**49**	**10**	**76**	**26**	**–11**	**21**	**4**	**3**	**7**	**8**	**0**	**0**	**0**
1992-93			DID NOT PLAY																									
1993-94	**Pittsburgh Penguins**	**NHL**	**41**	**4**	**11**	**15**	**4**	**8**	**12**	**36**	**0**	**0**	**0**	**45**	**8.9**	**19**	**1**	**45**	**15**	**–12**	**2**	**0**	**0**	**0**	**0**	**0**	**0**	**0**
	NHL Totals		**1279**	**524**	**901**	**1425**	**457**	**659**	**1116**	**912**	**161**	**19**	**68**	**2841**	**18.4**	**2032**	**660**	**1246**	**326**		**221**	**71**	**113**	**184**	**277**	**18**	**4**	**12**

Won King Clancy Memorial Trophy (1989) • WCJHL First All-Star Team (1975) • Won Calder Memorial Trophy (1976) • NHL First All-Star Team (1978, 1979) • NHL Plus/Minus Leader (1979) • Won Art Ross Trophy (1979) • Won Hart Trophy (1979) • Won Conn Smythe Trophy (1980) • NHL Second All-Star Team (1982, 1984) • Won Bud Man of the Year Award (1988)

Played in NHL All-Star Game (1976, 1978, 1980, 1982, 1983, 1985, 1986, 1992)

Signed as a free agent by **Pittsburgh**, July 20, 1990. Signed as a free agent by **Pittsburgh**, June 22, 1993.

• TROTTIER, GUY

Guy "The Mouse" Trottier RW – R. 5'8", 165 lbs. b: Hull, Que., 4/1/1941.

Season	Club	League	GP	G	A	Pts	AG	AA	APts	PIM	PP	SH	GW	S	%	TGF	PGF	TGA	PGA	+/–	GP	G	A	Pts	PIM	PP	SH	GW
1962-63	Prescot-Kemptville	Ott-Sr.	STATISTICS NOT AVAILABLE																									
1963-64	Port Huron Flags	IHL	42	19	15	34	....	....	....	52	....	....	....	....	....	....	....	....	....	....	7	1	0	1	2	....	....	....
	Philadelphia Ramblers	EHL	27	14	16	30	....	....	....	38	....	....	....	....	....	....	....	....	....	....	....	....	....	....	....	....	....	....
1964-65	Dayton Gems	IHL	68	46	42	88	....	....	....	56	....	....	....	....	....	....	....	....	....	....	....	....	....	....	....	....	....	....
1965-66	Dayton Gems	IHL	66	68	64	132	....	....	....	16	....	....	....	....	....	....	....	....	....	....	11	10	9	19	21	....	....	....
1966-67	Dayton Gems	IHL	68	*71	64	135	....	....	....	23	....	....	....	....	....	....	....	....	....	....	4	0	5	5	0	....	....	....
1967-68	Buffalo Bisons	AHL	41	16	19	35	....	....	....	6	....	....	....	....	....	....	....	....	....	....	4	2	4	6	2	....	....	....
1968-69	**New York Rangers**	**NHL**	**2**	**0**	**0**	**0**	**0**	**0**	**0**	**0**	**0**	**0**	**0**	**6**	**0.0**	**0**	**0**	**0**	**0**	**0**	....	....	....	....	....	....	....	....
	Buffalo Bisons	AHL	72	*45	37	82	....	....	....	21	....	....	....	....	....	....	....	....	....	....	6	4	3	7	0	....	....	....
1969-70	Buffalo Bisons	AHL	71	*55	33	88	....	....	....	8	....	....	....	....	....	....	....	....	....	....	9	6	2	8	9	....	....	....
1970-71	**Toronto Maple Leafs**	**NHL**	**61**	**19**	**5**	**24**	**20**	**4**	**24**	**21**	**7**	**0**	**3**	**106**	**17.9**	**36**	**15**	**33**	**0**	**–12**	**5**	**0**	**0**	**0**	**0**	**0**	**0**	**0**
1971-72	**Toronto Maple Leafs**	**NHL**	**52**	**9**	**12**	**21**	**10**	**11**	**21**	**16**	**2**	**0**	**1**	**81**	**11.1**	**27**	**10**	**29**	**0**	**–12**	**4**	**1**	**0**	**1**	**16**	**0**	**0**	**0**
1972-73	Ottawa Nationals	WHA	72	26	32	58	....	....	....	25	....	....	....	....	....	....	....	....	....	....	5	1	2	3	0	....	....	....
1973-74	Toronto Toros	WHA	71	27	35	62	....	....	....	58	....	....	....	....	....	....	....	....	....	....	12	5	5	10	4	....	....	....
1974-75	Toronto Toros	WHA	6	2	2	4	....	....	....	2	....	....	....	....	....	....	....	....	....	....	....	....	....	....	....	....	....	....
	Michigan Stags	WHA	17	5	4	9	....	....	....	2	....	....	....	....	....	....	....	....	....	....	....	....	....	....	....	....	....	....
	Dayton Gems	IHL	20	12	5	17	....	....	....	6	....	....	....	....	....	....	....	....	....	....	13	4	1	5	5	....	....	....
1975-76	Buffalo Norsemen	NAHL	56	36	22	58	....	....	....	59	....	....	....	....	....	....	....	....	....	....	1	0	0	0	20	....	....	....
	NHL Totals		**115**	**28**	**17**	**45**	**30**	**15**	**45**	**37**	**9**	**0**	**4**	**193**	**14.5**	**63**	**25**	**62**	**0**		**9**	**1**	**0**	**1**	**16**	**0**	**0**	**0**
	Other Major League Totals		166	60	73	133	....	....	....	87	....	....	....	....	....	....	....	....	....	....	17	6	7	13	4	....	....	....

IHL Second All-Star Team (1965, 1966) • IHL First All-Star Team (1967) • AHL First All-Star Team (1969, 1970)

Traded to **NY Rangers** by **Buffalo** (AHL) for cash, December, 1968. Claimed by **Toronto** from **NY Rangers** in Intra-League Draft, June 9, 1970. Selected by **Dayton-Houston** (WHA) in 1972 WHA General Player Draft, February 12, 1972. WHA rights traded to **Ottawa** (WHA) by **Houston** (WHA) for cash, June, 1972. Transferred to **Toronto** (WHA) after **Ottawa** (WHA) franchise relocated, May, 1973. Traded to **Michigan** (WHA) by **Toronto** (WHA) for Toronto's 4th round choice (Rick Bourbonnais) in 1975 WHA Amateur Draft, November, 1974.

• TROTTIER, ROCKY

Rocky Trottier RW – L. 5'11", 185 lbs. b: Climax, Sask., 4/11/1964. New Jersey's 1st choice, 8th overall, in 1982 Entry Draft.

Season	Club	League	GP	G	A	Pts	AG	AA	APts	PIM	PP	SH	GW	S	%	TGF	PGF	TGA	PGA	+/–	GP	G	A	Pts	PIM	PP	SH	GW
1980-81	Saskatoon Blades	WHL	34	9	15	24	....	....	....	26	....	....	....	....	....	....	....	....	....	....	....	....	....	....	....	....	....	....
	Billings Bighorns	WHL	28	2	11	13	....	....	....	41	....	....	....	....	....	....	....	....	....	....	5	0	0	0	0	....	....	....
1981-82	Billings Bighorns	WHL	28	13	21	34	....	....	....	36	....	....	....	....	....	....	....	....	....	....	....	....	....	....	....	....	....	....
1982-83	Nanaimo Islanders	WHL	34	13	22	35	....	....	....	12	....	....	....	....	....	....	....	....	....	....	....	....	....	....	....	....	....	....
	Medicine Hat Tigers	WHL	20	5	9	14	....	....	....	11	....	....	....	....	....	....	....	....	....	....	5	0	2	2	2	....	....	....
	Wichita Wind	CHL	2	0	1	1	....	....	....	0	....	....	....	....	....	....	....	....	....	....	....	....	....	....	....	....	....	....
1983-84	Medicine Hat Tigers	WHL	65	34	50	84	....	....	....	41	....	....	....	....	....	....	....	....	....	....	14	5	10	15	13	....	....	....
	New Jersey Devils	**NHL**	**5**	**1**	**1**	**2**	**1**	**1**	**2**	**0**	**0**	**0**	**0**	**2**	**50.0**	**2**	**0**	**3**	**0**	**–1**	....	....	....	....	....	....	....	....
1984-85	**New Jersey Devils**	**NHL**	**33**	**5**	**3**	**8**	**4**	**2**	**6**	**2**	**0**	**0**	**0**	**30**	**16.7**	**12**	**0**	**15**	**0**	**–3**	....	....	....	....	....	....	....	....
	Maine Mariners	AHL	34	17	16	33	....	....	....	4	....	....	....	....	....	....	....	....	....	....	10	2	0	2	15	....	....	....
1985-86	Maine Mariners	AHL	66	12	19	31	....	....	....	42	....	....	....	....	....	....	....	....	....	....	....	....	....	....	....	....	....	....
1986-87	Maine Mariners	AHL	77	9	14	23	....	....	....	41	....	....	....	....	....	....	....	....	....	....	....	....	....	....	....	....	....	....
1987-88	Rogle	Sweden2	21	8	5	13	....	....	....	10	....	....	....	....	....	....	....	....	....	....	2	0	0	0	0	....	....	....
1988-89			DID NOT PLAY																									
1989-90	Hershey Bears	AHL	49	15	13	28	....	....	....	18	....	....	....	....	....	....	....	....	....	....	....	....	....	....	....	....	....	....
	NHL Totals		**38**	**6**	**4**	**10**	**5**	**3**	**8**	**2**	**0**	**0**	**0**	**32**	**18.8**	**14**	**0**	**18**	**0**		....	....	....	....	....	....	....	....

• TSULYGIN, NIKOLAI

Nikolai Tsulygin D – R. 6'3", 210 lbs. b: Ufa, USSR, 5/29/1975. Anaheim's 2nd choice, 30th overall, in 1993 Entry Draft.

Season	Club	League	GP	G	A	Pts	AG	AA	APts	PIM	PP	SH	GW	S	%	TGF	PGF	TGA	PGA	+/–	GP	G	A	Pts	PIM	PP	SH	GW
1992-93	Ufa Salavat	CIS	42	5	4	9	....	....	....	21	....	....	....	....	....	....	....	....	....	....	2	0	0	0	0	....	....	....
	Russia	WJC-A	5	0	0	0	....	....	....	2	....	....	....	....	....	....	....	....	....	....	....	....	....	....	....	....	....	....
1993-94	Ufa Salavat	CIS	43	0	14	14	....	....	....	24	....	....	....	....	....	....	....	....	....	....	5	0	1	1	0	....	....	....
	Russia	WJC-A	7	1	2	3	....	....	....	12	....	....	....	....	....	....	....	....	....	....	....	....	....	....	....	....	....	....
1994-95	CSKA Moscow	CIS	16	0	0	0	....	....	....	12	....	....	....	....	....	....	....	....	....	....	....	....	....	....	....	....	....	....
	Ufa Salavat	CIS	13	2	2	4	....	....	....	10	....	....	....	....	....	....	....	....	....	....	7	0	0	0	4	....	....	....
1995-96	Baltimore Bandits	AHL	78	3	18	21	....	....	....	109	....	....	....	....	....	....	....	....	....	....	12	0	5	5	18	....	....	....

			REGULAR SEASON																		PLAYOFFS							
Season	Club	League	GP	G	A	Pts	AG	AA	APts	PIM	PP	SH	GW	S	%	TGF	PGF	TGA	PGA	+/-	GP	G	A	Pts	PIM	PP	SH	GW
1996-97	**Anaheim Mighty Ducks**	**NHL**	**22**	**0**	**1**	**1**	**0**	**1**	**1**	**8**	**0**	**0**	**0**	**10**	**0.0**	**5**	**0**	**10**	**0**	**–5**								
	Baltimore Bandits	AHL	17	4	13	17				8											3	0	0	0	0			
	Fort Wayne Komets	IHL	5	2	1	3				8																		
1997-98	Cincinnati Mighty Ducks	AHL	77	5	31	36				63																		
	NHL Totals		**22**	**0**	**1**	**1**	**0**	**1**	**1**	**8**	**0**	**0**	**0**	**10**	**0.0**	**5**	**0**	**10**	**0**									

• TSYGUROV, DENIS

Denis Tsygurov D – L. 6'3", 198 lbs. b: Chelyabinsk, USSR, 2/26/1971. Buffalo's 1st choice, 38th overall, in 1993 Entry Draft.

Season	Club	League	GP	G	A	Pts	AG	AA	APts	PIM	PP	SH	GW	S	%	TGF	PGF	TGA	PGA	+/-	GP	G	A	Pts	PIM	PP	SH	GW
1988-89	Traktor Chelyabinsk	USSR	8	0	0	0				2																		
1989-90	Traktor Chelyabinsk	USSR	27	0	1	1				18																		
1990-91	Traktor Chelyabinsk	USSR	26	0	1	1				16																		
1991-92	Lada Togliatti	CIS	29	3	2	5				6																		
1992-93	Lada Togliatti	CIS	37	7	13	20				29											10	1	1	2	6			
1993-94	**Buffalo Sabres**	**NHL**	**8**	**0**	**0**	**0**	**0**	**0**	**0**	**8**	**0**	**0**	**0**	**3**	**0.0**	**4**	**0**	**5**	**0**	**–1**								
	Rochester Americans	AHL	24	1	10	11				10											1	0	1	1	0			
1994-95	Lada Togliatti	CIS	10	3	7	10				6																		
	Buffalo Sabres	**NHL**	**4**	**0**	**0**	**0**	**0**	**0**	**0**	**4**	**0**	**0**	**0**	**4**	**0.0**	**1**	**0**	**2**	**0**	**–1**								
	Los Angeles Kings	**NHL**	**21**	**0**	**0**	**0**	**0**	**0**	**0**	**11**	**0**	**0**	**0**	**16**	**0.0**	**8**	**0**	**13**	**3**	**–2**								
1995-96	**Los Angeles Kings**	**NHL**	**18**	**1**	**5**	**6**	**1**	**4**	**5**	**22**	**1**	**0**	**0**	**21**	**4.8**	**22**	**5**	**20**	**3**	**0**								
	Phoenix Roadrunners	IHL	17	1	3	4				10																		
	Lada Togliatti	CIS	3	0	0	0				4																		
1996-97	Lada Togliatti	Russia	8	2	1	3				0																		
	Opava	Czech.	17	1	4	5				50																		
1997-98	Long Beach Ice Dogs	IHL	15	1	4	5				8																		
	NHL Totals		**51**	**1**	**5**	**6**	**1**	**4**	**5**	**45**	**1**	**0**	**0**	**44**	**2.3**	**35**	**5**	**40**	**6**									

Traded to **LA Kings** by **Buffalo** with Philippe Boucher and Grant Fuhr for Alexei Zhitnik, Robb Stauber, Charlie Huddy and LA Kings' 5th round choice (Marian Menhart) in 1995 Entry Draft, February 14, 1995.

• TSYPLAKOV, VLADIMIR

Vladimir Tsyplakov LW – L. 6', 185 lbs. b: Moscow, USSR, 4/18/1969. Los Angeles' 4th choice, 59th overall, in 1995 Entry Draft.

Season	Club	League	GP	G	A	Pts	AG	AA	APts	PIM	PP	SH	GW	S	%	TGF	PGF	TGA	PGA	+/-	GP	G	A	Pts	PIM	PP	SH	GW
1988-89	Minsk Dynamo	USSR	19	6	1	7				4																		
	Soviet Union	WJC-A	7	1	0	1				8																		
1989-90	Minsk Dynamo	USSR	47	11	6	17				20																		
1990-91	Minsk Dynamo	USSR	28	6	5	11				14																		
1991-92	Minsk Dynamo	CIS	29	10	9	19				16																		
1992-93	Detroit Falcons	ColHL	44	33	43	76				20											6	5	4	9	6			
	Indianapolis Ice	IHL	11	6	7	13				4											5	1	1	2	2			
1993-94	Fort Wayne Komets	IHL	63	31	32	63				51											14	6	8	14	16			
1994-95	Fort Wayne Komets	IHL	79	38	40	78				39											4	2	4	6	2			
1995-96	**Los Angeles Kings**	**NHL**	**23**	**5**	**5**	**10**	**5**	**4**	**9**	**4**	**0**	**0**	**0**	**40**	**12.5**	**16**	**4**	**11**	**0**	**+1**								
	Las Vegas Thunder	IHL	9	5	6	11				4																		
1996-97	**Los Angeles Kings**	**NHL**	**67**	**16**	**23**	**39**	**17**	**20**	**37**	**12**	**1**	**0**	**2**	**118**	**13.6**	**57**	**11**	**38**	**0**	**+8**								
1997-98	**Los Angeles Kings**	**NHL**	**73**	**18**	**34**	**52**	**21**	**33**	**54**	**18**	**2**	**0**	**1**	**113**	**15.9**	**75**	**14**	**50**	**4**	**+15**	**4**	**0**	**1**	**1**	**8**	**0**	**0**	**0**
	Belarus	Olympics	5	1	1	2				2																		
	NHL Totals		**163**	**39**	**62**	**101**	**43**	**57**	**100**	**34**	**3**	**0**	**3**	**271**	**14.4**	**148**	**29**	**99**	**4**		**4**	**0**	**1**	**1**	**8**	**0**	**0**	**0**

• TUCKER, DARCY

Darcy Tucker C – L. 5'10", 179 lbs. b: Castor, Alta., 3/15/1975. Montreal's 8th choice, 151st overall, in 1993 Entry Draft.

Season	Club	League	GP	G	A	Pts	AG	AA	APts	PIM	PP	SH	GW	S	%	TGF	PGF	TGA	PGA	+/-	GP	G	A	Pts	PIM	PP	SH	GW
1991-92	Kamloops Blazers	WHL	26	3	10	13				32											9	0	1	1	16			
1992-93	Kamloops Blazers	WHL	67	31	58	89				155											13	7	6	13	34			
1993-94	Kamloops Blazers	WHL	66	52	88	140				143											19	9	*18	*27	43			
1994-95	Kamloops Blazers	WHL	64	64	73	137				94											21	*16	15	*31	19			
	Canada	WJC-A	7	0	4	4				0																		
1995-96	**Montreal Canadiens**	**NHL**	**3**	**0**	**0**	**0**	**0**	**0**	**0**	**0**	**0**	**0**	**0**	**1**	**0.0**	**0**	**0**	**1**	**0**	**–1**								
	Fredericton Canadiens	AHL	74	29	64	93				174											7	7	3	10	14			
1996-97	**Montreal Canadiens**	**NHL**	**73**	**7**	**13**	**20**	**7**	**11**	**18**	**110**	**1**	**0**	**3**	**62**	**11.3**	**31**	**4**	**32**	**0**	**–5**	**4**	**0**	**0**	**0**	**0**	**0**	**0**	**0**
1997-98	**Montreal Canadiens**	**NHL**	**39**	**1**	**5**	**6**	**1**	**5**	**6**	**57**	**0**	**0**	**0**	**19**	**5.3**	**9**	**1**	**21**	**7**	**–6**								
	Tampa Bay Lightning	**NHL**	**35**	**6**	**8**	**14**	**7**	**8**	**15**	**89**	**1**	**1**	**0**	**44**	**13.6**	**21**	**1**	**33**	**5**	**–8**								
	NHL Totals		**150**	**14**	**26**	**40**	**15**	**24**	**39**	**256**	**2**	**1**	**3**	**126**	**11.1**	**61**	**6**	**87**	**12**		**4**	**0**	**0**	**0**	**0**	**0**	**0**	**0**

WHL West First All-Star Team (1994, 1995) • Canadian Major Junior First All-Star Team (1994) • Memorial Cup All-Star Team (1994, 1995) • Won Stafford Smythe Memorial Trophy (Memorial Cup Tournament MVP) (1994) • Won Dudley "Red" Garrett Memorial Trophy (Top Rookie - AHL) (1996)

Traded to **Tampa Bay** by **Montreal** with Stephane Richer and David Wilkie for Patrick Poulin, Mick Vukota and Igor Ulanov, January 15, 1998.

• TUCKER, JOHN

John Tucker C – R. 6', 200 lbs. b: Windsor, Ont., 9/29/1964. Buffalo's 4th choice, 31st overall, in 1983 Entry Draft.

Season	Club	League	GP	G	A	Pts	AG	AA	APts	PIM	PP	SH	GW	S	%	TGF	PGF	TGA	PGA	+/-	GP	G	A	Pts	PIM	PP	SH	GW
1981-82	Kitchener Rangers	OHL	67	16	32	48				32											15	2	3	5	2			
1982-83	Kitchener Rangers	OHL	70	60	80	140				33											11	5	9	14	10			
1983-84	Kitchener Rangers	OHL	39	40	60	100				25											12	12	18	30	8			
	Buffalo Sabres	**NHL**	**21**	**12**	**4**	**16**	**10**	**3**	**13**	**4**	**5**	**0**	**2**	**40**	**30.0**	**22**	**8**	**12**	**0**	**+2**	**3**	**1**	**0**	**1**	**0**	**0**	**0**	**0**
1984-85	**Buffalo Sabres**	**NHL**	**64**	**22**	**27**	**49**	**18**	**18**	**36**	**21**	**11**	**0**	**3**	**112**	**19.6**	**76**	**39**	**31**	**0**	**+6**	**5**	**1**	**5**	**6**	**0**	**0**	**0**	**0**
1985-86	**Buffalo Sabres**	**NHL**	**75**	**31**	**34**	**65**	**25**	**23**	**48**	**39**	**8**	**0**	**3**	**146**	**21.2**	**92**	**37**	**56**	**1**	**0**								
1986-87	**Buffalo Sabres**	**NHL**	**54**	**17**	**34**	**51**	**15**	**25**	**40**	**21**	**4**	**0**	**0**	**104**	**16.3**	**67**	**21**	**51**	**2**	**–3**								
1987-88	**Buffalo Sabres**	**NHL**	**45**	**19**	**19**	**38**	**16**	**14**	**30**	**20**	**6**	**0**	**0**	**93**	**20.4**	**59**	**23**	**32**	**0**	**+4**	**6**	**7**	**3**	**10**	**18**	**4**	**0**	**2**
1988-89	**Buffalo Sabres**	**NHL**	**60**	**13**	**31**	**44**	**11**	**22**	**33**	**31**	**3**	**0**	**1**	**94**	**13.8**	**65**	**22**	**50**	**2**	**–5**	**3**	**0**	**3**	**3**	**0**	**0**	**0**	**0**
1989-90	**Buffalo Sabres**	**NHL**	**8**	**1**	**2**	**3**	**1**	**1**	**2**	**2**	**1**	**0**	**0**	**8**	**12.5**	**4**	**1**	**7**	**1**	**–3**								
	Washington Capitals	**NHL**	**38**	**9**	**19**	**28**	**8**	**14**	**22**	**10**	**1**	**0**	**1**	**61**	**14.8**	**51**	**17**	**23**	**0**	**+11**	**12**	**1**	**7**	**8**	**4**	**0**	**0**	**0**
1990-91	**Buffalo Sabres**	**NHL**	**18**	**1**	**3**	**4**	**1**	**2**	**3**	**4**	**0**	**0**	**0**	**16**	**6.3**	**8**	**3**	**5**	**0**	**0**								
	New York Islanders	**NHL**	**20**	**3**	**4**	**7**	**3**	**3**	**6**	**4**	**1**	**0**	**0**	**19**	**15.8**	**11**	**1**	**11**	**0**	**–1**								
1991-92	Asiago	Italy	18	16	21	37				6											11	7	13	20	15			
1992-93	**Tampa Bay Lightning**	**NHL**	**78**	**17**	**39**	**56**	**14**	**27**	**41**	**69**	**5**	**1**	**1**	**179**	**9.5**	**94**	**35**	**94**	**23**	**–12**								
1993-94	**Tampa Bay Lightning**	**NHL**	**66**	**17**	**23**	**40**	**16**	**18**	**34**	**28**	**2**	**0**	**6**	**126**	**13.5**	**59**	**9**	**58**	**17**	**+9**								
1994-95	**Tampa Bay Lightning**	**NHL**	**46**	**12**	**13**	**25**	**21**	**19**	**40**	**14**	**2**	**0**	**1**	**81**	**14.8**	**38**	**11**	**52**	**15**	**–10**								
1995-96	**Tampa Bay Lightning**	**NHL**	**63**	**3**	**7**	**10**	**3**	**6**	**9**	**18**	**0**	**1**	**0**	**53**	**5.7**	**22**	**1**	**59**	**30**	**–8**	**2**	**0**	**0**	**0**	**2**	**0**	**0**	**0**
1996-97	Milano 24	Alpenliga	30	12	29	41				88																		
1997-98	Kokudo Toyko	Japan	39	27	47	74				53																		
	NHL Totals		**656**	**177**	**259**	**436**	**162**	**195**	**357**	**285**	**49**	**2**	**18**	**1132**	**15.6**	**668**	**228**	**541**	**91**		**31**	**10**	**18**	**28**	**24**	**4**	**0**	**2**

OHL First All-Star Team (1984)

Traded to **Washington** by **Buffalo** for future considerations, January 5, 1990. Traded to **Buffalo** by **Washington** for cash, July 3, 1990. Traded to **NY Islanders** by **Buffalo** for future considerations, January 21, 1991. Signed as a free agent by **Tampa Bay**, August 5, 1992.

• TUDOR, ROB

Rob Tudor RW/C – R. 5'11", 188 lbs. b: Cupar, Sask., 6/30/1956. Vancouver's 5th choice, 98th overall, in 1976 Amateur Draft.

Season	Club	League	GP	G	A	Pts	AG	AA	APts	PIM	PP	SH	GW	S	%	TGF	PGF	TGA	PGA	+/-	GP	G	A	Pts	PIM	PP	SH	GW
1972-73	Regina Pats	WHL	5	0	1	1				0																		
1973-74	Regina Pats	WHL	68	17	17	34				60																		
1974-75	Regina Pats	WHL	68	48	48	96				125											11	5	6	11	20			
1975-76	Regina Pats	WHL	72	46	60	106				228											6	6	3	9	15			
1976-77	Fort Wayne Komets	IHL	78	34	60	94				108											9	11	8	19	26			
1977-78	Tulsa Oilers	CHL	65	23	33	56				58											7	1	2	3	37			
1978-79	**Vancouver Canucks**	**NHL**	**24**	**4**	**4**	**8**	**4**	**3**	**7**	**19**	**0**	**0**	**0**	**51**	**7.8**	**12**	**1**	**12**	**1**	**0**	**2**	**0**	**0**	**0**	**0**	**0**	**0**	**0**
	Dallas Black Hawks	CHL	51	27	37	64				80																		
1979-80	**Vancouver Canucks**	**NHL**	**2**	**0**	**0**	**0**	**0**	**0**	**0**	**0**	**0**	**0**	**0**	**0**	**0.0**	**0**	**0**	**0**	**0**	**0**	**1**	**0**	**0**	**0**	**0**	**0**	**0**	**0**
	Dallas Black Hawks	CHL	74	39	41	80				177																		
1980-81	Dallas Black Hawks	CHL	79	31	32	63				155											6	0	1	1	25			
1981-82	Dallas Black Hawks	CHL	80	32	47	79				132											15	7	13	20	56			

			REGULAR SEASON																		PLAYOFFS							
Season	Club	League	GP	G	A	Pts	AG	AA	APts	PIM	PP	SH	GW	S	%	TGF	PGF	TGA	PGA	+/–	GP	G	A	Pts	PIM	PP	SH	GW
1982-83	**St. Louis Blues**	**NHL**	**2**	**0**	**0**	**0**	**0**	**0**	**0**	**0**	**0**	**0**	**0**	**0**	**0.0**	**0**	**0**	**0**	**0**	**0**	....	....	....	....	....	....	....	....
	Salt Lake Golden Eagles	CHL	76	37	30	67	....	....	....	168	....	....	....	....	....	....	....	....	....	....	6	1	4	5	2	....	....	....
1983-84	Salt Lake Golden Eagles	CHL	32	10	12	22	....	....	....	35	....	....	....	....	....	....	....	....	....	....	5	1	2	3	21	....	....	....
	Kolner EC	Germany	28	9	8	17	....	....	....	82	....	....	....	....	....	....	....	....	....	....	....	....	....	....	....	....	....	....
1984-85	Nova Scotia Voyageurs	AHL	22	6	6	12	....	....	....	40	....	....	....	....	....	....	....	....	....	....	....	....	....	....	....	....	....	....
	New Haven Nighthawks	AHL	52	9	11	20	....	....	....	45	....	....	....	....	....	....	....	....	....	....	....	....	....	....	....	....	....	....
1985-86	Fort Wayne Komets	IHL	13	6	8	14	....	....	....	7	....	....	....	....	....	....	....	....	....	....	15	4	2	6	35	....	....	....
	NHL Totals		**28**	**4**	**4**	**8**	**4**	**3**	**7**	**19**	**0**	**0**	**0**	**51**	**7.8**	**12**	**1**	**12**	**1**		**3**	**0**	**0**	**0**	**0**	**0**	**0**	**0**

CHL Second All-Star Team (1980)

Signed as a free agent by **St. Louis**, July 22, 1982.

• TUER, ALLAN

Allan Tuer D – L. 6′, 190 lbs. b: North Battleford, Sask., 7/19/1963. Los Angeles' 8th choice, 186th overall, in 1981 Entry Draft.

1980-81	Regina Pats	WHL	31	0	7	7	....	....	....	58	....	....	....	....	....	....	....	....	....	....	8	0	1	1	37	....	....	....
1981-82	Regina Pats	WHL	63	2	18	20	....	....	....	*486	....	....	....	....	....	....	....	....	....	....	13	0	3	3	117	....	....	....
1982-83	Regina Pats	WHL	71	3	27	30	....	....	....	229	....	....	....	....	....	....	....	....	....	....	5	0	0	0	37	....	....	....
1983-84	New Haven Nighthawks	AHL	78	0	20	20	....	....	....	195	....	....	....	....	....	....	....	....	....	....	....	....	....	....	....	....	....	....
1984-85	New Haven Nighthawks	AHL	56	0	7	7	....	....	....	241	....	....	....	....	....	....	....	....	....	....	....	....	....	....	....	....	....	....
1985-86	**Los Angeles Kings**	**NHL**	**45**	**0**	**1**	**1**	**0**	**1**	**1**	**150**	**0**	**0**	**0**	**14**	**0.0**	**5**	**1**	**23**	**3**	**–16**	....	....	....	....	....	....	....	....
	New Haven Nighthawks	AHL	8	1	0	1	....	....	....	53	....	....	....	....	....	....	....	....	....	....	....	....	....	....	....	....	....	....
1986-87	New Haven Nighthawks	AHL	69	1	14	15	....	....	....	273	....	....	....	....	....	....	....	....	....	....	5	0	1	1	48	....	....	....
1987-88	**Minnesota North Stars**	**NHL**	**6**	**1**	**0**	**1**	**1**	**0**	**1**	**29**	**0**	**0**	**0**	**1**	**100.0**	**1**	**0**	**5**	**1**	**–3**	....	....	....	....	....	....	....	....
	Kalamazoo Wings	IHL	68	2	15	17	....	....	....	303	....	....	....	....	....	....	....	....	....	....	7	0	0	0	34	....	....	....
1988-89	**Hartford Whalers**	**NHL**	**4**	**0**	**0**	**0**	**0**	**0**	**0**	**23**	**0**	**0**	**0**	**0**	**0.0**	**0**	**0**	**2**	**0**	**–2**	....	....	....	....	....	....	....	....
	Binghamton Whalers	AHL	43	1	7	8	....	....	....	234	....	....	....	....	....	....	....	....	....	....	....	....	....	....	....	....	....	....
1989-90	**Hartford Whalers**	**NHL**	**2**	**0**	**0**	**0**	**0**	**0**	**0**	**6**	**0**	**0**	**0**	**0**	**0.0**	**1**	**0**	**2**	**0**	**–1**	....	....	....	....	....	....	....	....
	Binghamton Whalers	AHL	58	3	7	10	....	....	....	56	....	....	....	....	....	....	....	....	....	....	....	....	....	....	....	....	....	....
1990-91	San Diego Gulls	IHL	60	0	5	5	....	....	....	305	....	....	....	....	....	....	....	....	....	....	....	....	....	....	....	....	....	....
1991-92	New Haven Nighthawks	AHL	68	2	10	12	....	....	....	199	....	....	....	....	....	....	....	....	....	....	4	0	1	1	12	....	....	....
1992-93	Cincinnati Cyclones	IHL	52	1	9	10	....	....	....	248	....	....	....	....	....	....	....	....	....	....	....	....	....	....	....	....	....	....
	Cleveland Lumberjacks	IHL	13	1	4	5	....	....	....	29	....	....	....	....	....	....	....	....	....	....	2	0	0	0	4	....	....	....
	NHL Totals		**57**	**1**	**1**	**2**	**1**	**1**	**2**	**208**	**0**	**0**	**0**	**15**	**6.7**	**7**	**1**	**32**	**4**		....	....	....	....	....	....	....	....

Signed as a free agent by **Edmonton**, August 18, 1986. Claimed by **Minnesota** from **Edmonton** in Waiver Draft, October 5, 1987. Signed as a free agent by **Hartford**, July 12, 1988.

• TUOMAINEN, MARKO

Marko Tuomainen RW – R. 6′3″, 203 lbs. b: Kuopio, Finland, 4/25/1972. Edmonton's 10th choice, 205th overall, in 1992 Entry Draft.

1989-90	KalPa Kuopio	Finland	5	0	0	0	....	....	....	0	....	....	....	....	....	....	....	....	....	....	....	....	....	....	....	....	....	....
1990-91	KalPa Kuopio	Finland	30	2	1	3	....	....	....	2	....	....	....	....	....	....	....	....	....	....	8	0	0	0	6	....	....	....
1991-92	Clarkson University	ECAC	28	11	12	23	....	....	....	32	....	....	....	....	....	....	....	....	....	....	....	....	....	....	....	....	....	....
	Finland	WJC-A	7	1	4	5	....	....	....	14	....	....	....	....	....	....	....	....	....	....	....	....	....	....	....	....	....	....
1992-93	Clarkson University	ECAC	35	25	30	55	....	....	....	26	....	....	....	....	....	....	....	....	....	....	....	....	....	....	....	....	....	....
1993-94	Clarkson University	ECAC	34	23	29	52	....	....	....	60	....	....	....	....	....	....	....	....	....	....	....	....	....	....	....	....	....	....
1994-95	Clarkson University	ECAC	37	23	38	61	....	....	....	34	....	....	....	....	....	....	....	....	....	....	....	....	....	....	....	....	....	....
	Edmonton Oilers	**NHL**	**4**	**0**	**0**	**0**	**0**	**0**	**0**	**0**	**0**	**0**	**0**	**5**	**0.0**	**2**	**0**	**2**	**0**	**0**	....	....	....	....	....	....	....	....
1995-96	Cape Breton Oilers	AHL	58	25	35	60	....	....	....	71	....	....	....	....	....	....	....	....	....	....	....	....	....	....	....	....	....	....
1996-97	Hamilton Bulldogs	AHL	79	31	21	52	....	....	....	130	....	....	....	....	....	....	....	....	....	....	22	7	5	12	4	....	....	....
	Finland	WC-A	8	0	1	1	....	....	....	8	....	....	....	....	....	....	....	....	....	....	....	....	....	....	....	....	....	....
1997-98	HIFK Helsinki	Finland	46	13	9	22	....	....	....	20	....	....	....	....	....	....	....	....	....	....	9	0	3	3	0	....	....	....
	NHL Totals		**4**	**0**	**0**	**0**	**0**	**0**	**0**	**0**	**0**	**0**	**0**	**5**	**0.0**	**2**	**0**	**2**	**0**		....	....	....	....	....	....	....	....

ECAC First All-Star Team (1993, 1995) • NCAA East Second All-American Team (1995)

• TURCOTTE, ALFIE

Alfie Turcotte C – L. 5′11″, 185 lbs. b: Gary, IN, 6/5/1965. Montreal's 1st choice, 17th overall, in 1983 Entry Draft.

1981-82	Detroit Compuware	NAJHL	93	131	152	283	....	....	....	40	....	....	....	....	....	....	....	....	....	....	....	....	....	....	....	....	....	....
1982-83	Nanaimo Islanders	WHL	36	23	27	50	....	....	....	22	....	....	....	....	....	....	....	....	....	....	....	....	....	....	....	....	....	....
	Portland Winter Hawks	WHL	39	26	51	77	....	....	....	26	....	....	....	....	....	....	....	....	....	....	14	14	18	32	9	....	....	....
1983-84	Portland Winter Hawks	WHL	32	22	41	63	....	....	....	39	....	....	....	....	....	....	....	....	....	....	....	....	....	....	....	....	....	....
	United States	WJC-A	7	2	9	11	....	....	....	2	....	....	....	....	....	....	....	....	....	....	....	....	....	....	....	....	....	....
	Montreal Canadiens	**NHL**	**30**	**7**	**7**	**14**	**6**	**5**	**11**	**10**	**5**	**0**	**0**	**33**	**21.2**	**18**	**8**	**19**	**0**	**–9**	....	....	....	....	....	....	....	....
1984-85	**Montreal Canadiens**	**NHL**	**53**	**8**	**16**	**24**	**7**	**11**	**18**	**35**	**3**	**0**	**1**	**59**	**13.6**	**42**	**20**	**23**	**0**	**–1**	**5**	**0**	**0**	**0**	**0**	**0**	**0**	**0**
1985-86	**Montreal Canadiens**	**NHL**	**2**	**0**	**0**	**0**	**0**	**0**	**0**	**2**	**0**	**0**	**0**	**0**	**0.0**	**0**	**0**	**0**	**0**	**0**	....	....	....	....	....	....	....	....
	Sherbrooke Canadiens	AHL	75	29	36	65	....	....	....	60	....	....	....	....	....	....	....	....	....	....	....	....	....	....	....	....	....	....
	United States	WEC-A	9	0	2	2	....	....	....	8	....	....	....	....	....	....	....	....	....	....	....	....	....	....	....	....	....	....
1986-87	Nova Scotia Oilers	AHL	70	27	41	68	....	....	....	37	....	....	....	....	....	....	....	....	....	....	5	2	4	6	2	....	....	....
1987-88	**Winnipeg Jets**	**NHL**	**3**	**0**	**0**	**0**	**0**	**0**	**0**	**0**	**0**	**0**	**0**	**3**	**0.0**	**1**	**0**	**5**	**0**	**–4**	....	....	....	....	....	....	....	....
	Baltimore Skipjacks	AHL	33	21	33	54	....	....	....	42	....	....	....	....	....	....	....	....	....	....	....	....	....	....	....	....	....	....
	Moncton Hawks	AHL	25	12	25	37	....	....	....	18	....	....	....	....	....	....	....	....	....	....	....	....	....	....	....	....	....	....
	Sherbrooke Canadiens	AHL	8	3	8	11	....	....	....	4	....	....	....	....	....	....	....	....	....	....	....	....	....	....	....	....	....	....
1988-89	**Winnipeg Jets**	**NHL**	**14**	**1**	**3**	**4**	**1**	**2**	**3**	**2**	**0**	**0**	**0**	**10**	**10.0**	**7**	**1**	**12**	**0**	**–6**	....	....	....	....	....	....	....	....
	Moncton Hawks	AHL	54	27	39	66	....	....	....	74	....	....	....	....	....	....	....	....	....	....	10	3	9	12	17	....	....	....
1989-90	**Washington Capitals**	**NHL**	**4**	**0**	**2**	**2**	**0**	**1**	**1**	**0**	**0**	**0**	**0**	**4**	**0.0**	**3**	**1**	**2**	**0**	**0**	....	....	....	....	....	....	....	....
	Baltimore Skipjacks	AHL	65	26	40	66	....	....	....	42	....	....	....	....	....	....	....	....	....	....	12	7	9	16	14	....	....	....
1990-91	**Washington Capitals**	**NHL**	**6**	**1**	**1**	**2**	**1**	**1**	**2**	**0**	**0**	**0**	**1**	**8**	**12.5**	**3**	**0**	**4**	**0**	**–1**	....	....	....	....	....	....	....	....
	Baltimore Skipjacks	AHL	65	33	52	85	....	....	....	20	....	....	....	....	....	....	....	....	....	....	6	3	3	6	4	....	....	....
1991-92	VSV Villach	Austria	45	43	*61	*104	....	....	....	....	....	....	....	....	....	....	....	....	....	....	....	....	....	....	....	....	....	....
	HC Lugano	Switz.	2	1	3	4	....	....	....	....	....	....	....	....	....	....	....	....	....	....	....	....	....	....	....	....	....	....
1992-93	VSV Villach	Austria	56	26	*75	101	....	....	....	....	....	....	....	....	....	....	....	....	....	....	....	....	....	....	....	....	....	....
1993-94	VSV Villach	Austria	51	26	*63	*89	....	....	....	....	....	....	....	....	....	....	....	....	....	....	....	....	....	....	....	....	....	....
1994-95	Schwenningen Wild Wings	Germany	33	7	40	47	....	....	....	30	....	....	....	....	....	....	....	....	....	....	11	7	5	12	12	....	....	....
1995-96			DID NOT PLAY																									
1996-97	Schwenningen Wild Wings	Germany	1	0	0	0	....	....	....	0	....	....	....	....	....	....	....	....	....	....	....	....	....	....	....	....	....	....
1997-98	Frankfurt Lions	Germany	26	2	6	8	....	....	....	12	....	....	....	....	....	....	....	....	....	....	7	0	0	0	0	....	....	....
	NHL Totals		**112**	**17**	**29**	**46**	**15**	**20**	**35**	**49**	**8**	**0**	**2**	**117**	**14.5**	**74**	**30**	**65**	**0**		**5**	**0**	**0**	**0**	**0**	**0**	**0**	**0**

Won Stafford Smythe Memorial Trophy (Memorial Cup Tournament MVP) (1983) • AHL Second All-Star Team (1988)

Traded to **Edmonton** by **Montreal** for future considerations, June 25, 1986. Traded to **Montreal** by **Edmonton** for cash, May 14, 1987. Traded to **Winnipeg** by **Montreal** for future considerations, January 14, 1988. Signed as a free agent by **Boston**, June 27, 1989. Traded to **Washington** by **Boston** for Mike Millar, October 2, 1989.

• TURCOTTE, DARREN

Darren Turcotte C – L. 6′, 178 lbs. b: Boston, MA, 3/2/1968. NY Rangers' 6th choice, 114th overall, in 1986 Entry Draft.

1984-85	North Bay Centennials	OHL	62	33	32	65	....	....	....	28	....	....	....	....	....	....	....	....	....	....	8	0	2	2	0	....	....	....
1985-86	North Bay Centennials	OHL	62	35	37	72	....	....	....	35	....	....	....	....	....	....	....	....	....	....	10	3	4	7	8	....	....	....
1986-87	North Bay Centennials	OHL	55	30	48	78	....	....	....	20	....	....	....	....	....	....	....	....	....	....	18	12	8	20	6	....	....	....
	United States	WJC-A	7	6	4	10	....	....	....	8	....	....	....	....	....	....	....	....	....	....	....	....	....	....	....	....	....	....
1987-88	North Bay Centennials	OHL	32	30	33	63	....	....	....	16	....	....	....	....	....	....	....	....	....	....	4	3	0	3	4	....	....	....
	United States	WJC-A	7	2	2	4	....	....	....	6	....	....	....	....	....	....	....	....	....	....	....	....	....	....	....	....	....	....
	Colorado Rangers	IHL	8	4	3	7	....	....	....	9	....	....	....	....	....	....	....	....	....	....	6	2	6	8	8	....	....	....
1988-89	**New York Rangers**	**NHL**	**20**	**7**	**3**	**10**	**6**	**2**	**8**	**4**	**2**	**0**	**2**	**49**	**14.3**	**15**	**5**	**10**	**0**	**0**	**1**	**0**	**0**	**0**	**0**	**0**	**0**	**0**
	Denver Rangers	IHL	40	21	28	49	....	....	....	32	....	....	....	....	....	....	....	....	....	....	....	....	....	....	....	....	....	....
1989-90	**New York Rangers**	**NHL**	**76**	**32**	**34**	**66**	**28**	**24**	**52**	**32**	**10**	**1**	**4**	**205**	**15.6**	**89**	**44**	**69**	**27**	**+3**	**10**	**1**	**6**	**7**	**4**	**0**	**0**	**1**
1990-91	**New York Rangers**	**NHL**	**74**	**26**	**41**	**67**	**24**	**31**	**55**	**37**	**15**	**2**	**3**	**212**	**12.3**	**94**	**47**	**94**	**42**	**–5**	**6**	**1**	**2**	**3**	**0**	**1**	**0**	**0**
1991-92	**New York Rangers**	**NHL**	**71**	**30**	**23**	**53**	**27**	**17**	**44**	**57**	**13**	**1**	**4**	**216**	**13.9**	**85**	**42**	**51**	**19**	**+11**	**8**	**4**	**0**	**4**	**6**	**2**	**1**	**0**
1992-93	**New York Rangers**	**NHL**	**71**	**25**	**28**	**53**	**21**	**19**	**40**	**40**	**7**	**3**	**3**	**213**	**11.7**	**81**	**35**	**73**	**24**	**–3**	....	....	....	....	....	....	....	....
	United States	WC-A	6	2	1	3	....	....	....	0	....	....	....	....	....	....	....	....	....	....	....	....	....	....	....	....	....	....
1993-94	**New York Rangers**	**NHL**	**13**	**2**	**4**	**6**	**2**	**3**	**5**	**13**	**0**	**0**	**0**	**17**	**11.8**	**8**	**5**	**5**	**0**	**–2**	....	....	....	....	....	....	....	....
	Hartford Whalers	**NHL**	**19**	**2**	**11**	**13**	**2**	**8**	**10**	**4**	**0**	**0**	**0**	**43**	**4.7**	**21**	**8**	**29**	**5**	**–11**	....	....	....	....	....	....	....	....

			REGULAR SEASON																		PLAYOFFS							
Season	Club	League	GP	G	A	Pts	AG	AA	APts	PIM	PP	SH	GW	S	%	TGF	PGF	TGA	PGA	+/–	GP	G	A	Pts	PIM	PP	SH	GW
1994-95	**Hartford Whalers**	**NHL**	**47**	**17**	**18**	**35**	**30**	**26**	**56**	**22**	**3**	**1**	**3**	**121**	**14.0**	**47**	**14**	**45**	**13**	**+1**	....	....	....	....	....	....	....	....
1995-96	**Winnipeg Jets**	**NHL**	**59**	**16**	**16**	**32**	**16**	**13**	**29**	**26**	**2**	**0**	**2**	**134**	**11.9**	**46**	**11**	**58**	**20**	**–3**	....	....	....	....	....	....	....	....
	San Jose Sharks	**NHL**	**9**	**6**	**5**	**11**	**6**	**4**	**10**	**4**	**0**	**1**	**2**	**33**	**18.2**	**14**	**2**	**7**	**3**	**+8**	....	....	....	....	....	....	....	....
1996-97	**San Jose Sharks**	**NHL**	**65**	**16**	**21**	**37**	**17**	**19**	**36**	**16**	**3**	**1**	**4**	**126**	**12.7**	**56**	**21**	**53**	**10**	**–8**	....	....	....	....	....	....	....	....
1997-98	**St. Louis Blues**	**NHL**	**62**	**12**	**6**	**18**	**14**	**6**	**20**	**26**	**3**	**0**	**1**	**75**	**16.0**	**29**	**6**	**33**	**16**	**+6**	**10**	**0**	**0**	**0**	**2**	**0**	**0**	**0**
	NHL Totals		**586**	**191**	**210**	**401**	**193**	**172**	**365**	**281**	**58**	**10**	**28**	**1444**	**13.2**	**585**	**240**	**527**	**179**		**35**	**6**	**8**	**14**	**12**	**3**	**1**	**1**

Played in NHL All-Star Game (1991)

Traded to **Hartford** by **NY Rangers** with James Patrick for Steve Larmer, Nick Kypreos, Barry Richter and Hartford's 6th round choice (Yuri Litvinov) in 1994 Entry Draft, November 2, 1993. Traded to **Winnipeg** by **Hartford** for Nelson Emerson, October 6, 1995. Traded to **San Jose** by **Winnipeg** with Dallas' 2nd round choice (previously acquired and later traded to Chicago — Chicago selected Remi Royer) in 1996 Entry Draft for Craig Janney, March 18, 1996. Traded to **St. Louis** by **San Jose** for Stephane Matteau, July 24, 1997. Traded to **Nashville** by **St. Louis** for future considerations, June 26, 1998.

• TURGEON, PIERRE

Pierre Turgeon C – L. 6'1", 195 lbs. b: Rouyn, Que., 8/28/1969. Buffalo's 1st choice, 1st overall, in 1987 Entry Draft.

Season	Club	League	GP	G	A	Pts	AG	AA	APts	PIM	PP	SH	GW	S	%	TGF	PGF	TGA	PGA	+/–	GP	G	A	Pts	PIM	PP	SH	GW
1985-86	Granby Bisons	QMJHL	69	47	67	114	....	....	....	31	....	....	....	....	....	....	....	....	....	....	....	....	....	....	....	....	....	....
	Canada	Nat-Team	11	2	4	6	....	....	....	2	....	....	....	....	....	....	....	....	....	....	....	....	....	....	....	....	....	....
1986-87	Granby Bisons	QMJHL	58	69	85	154	....	....	....	8	....	....	....	....	....	....	....	....	....	....	7	9	6	15	15	....	....	....
	Canada	WJC-A	6	3	0	3	....	....	....	2	....	....	....	....	....	....	....	....	....	....	....	....	....	....	....	....	....	....
1987-88	**Buffalo Sabres**	**NHL**	**76**	**14**	**28**	**42**	**12**	**20**	**32**	**34**	**8**	**0**	**3**	**101**	**13.9**	**68**	**28**	**48**	**0**	**–8**	**6**	**4**	**3**	**7**	**4**	**3**	**0**	**0**
1988-89	**Buffalo Sabres**	**NHL**	**80**	**34**	**54**	**88**	**29**	**38**	**67**	**26**	**19**	**0**	**5**	**182**	**18.7**	**117**	**53**	**87**	**21**	**–2**	**5**	**3**	**5**	**8**	**2**	**1**	**0**	**0**
1989-90	**Buffalo Sabres**	**NHL**	**80**	**40**	**66**	**106**	**35**	**47**	**82**	**29**	**17**	**1**	**10**	**193**	**20.7**	**140**	**61**	**86**	**17**	**+10**	**6**	**2**	**4**	**6**	**2**	**0**	**0**	**1**
1990-91	**Buffalo Sabres**	**NHL**	**78**	**32**	**47**	**79**	**29**	**36**	**65**	**26**	**13**	**2**	**3**	**174**	**18.4**	**114**	**36**	**80**	**16**	**+14**	**6**	**3**	**1**	**4**	**6**	**1**	**0**	**0**
1991-92	**Buffalo Sabres**	**NHL**	**8**	**2**	**6**	**8**	**2**	**4**	**6**	**4**	**0**	**0**	**0**	**14**	**14.3**	**8**	**4**	**9**	**4**	**–1**	....	....	....	....	....	....	....	....
	New York Islanders	**NHL**	**69**	**38**	**49**	**87**	**35**	**37**	**72**	**16**	**13**	**0**	**6**	**193**	**19.7**	**111**	**41**	**75**	**13**	**+8**	....	....	....	....	....	....	....	....
1992-93	**New York Islanders**	**NHL**	**83**	**58**	**74**	**132**	**49**	**51**	**100**	**26**	**24**	**0**	**10**	**301**	**19.3**	**166**	**76**	**93**	**2**	**–1**	**11**	**6**	**7**	**13**	**0**	**0**	**0**	**0**
1993-94	**New York Islanders**	**NHL**	**69**	**38**	**56**	**94**	**36**	**43**	**79**	**18**	**10**	**4**	**6**	**254**	**15.0**	**120**	**46**	**76**	**16**	**+14**	**4**	**0**	**1**	**1**	**0**	**0**	**0**	**0**
1994-95	**New York Islanders**	**NHL**	**34**	**13**	**14**	**27**	**23**	**21**	**44**	**10**	**2**	**0**	**2**	**93**	**14.0**	**29**	**12**	**41**	**12**	**–12**	....	....	....	....	....	....	....	....
	Montreal Canadiens	**NHL**	**15**	**11**	**9**	**20**	**19**	**13**	**32**	**4**	**5**	**2**	**2**	**67**	**16.4**	**25**	**6**	**7**	**0**	**+12**	....	....	....	....	....	....	....	....
1995-96	**Montreal Canadiens**	**NHL**	**80**	**38**	**58**	**96**	**38**	**47**	**85**	**44**	**17**	**1**	**6**	**297**	**12.8**	**128**	**57**	**63**	**11**	**+19**	**6**	**2**	**4**	**6**	**2**	**0**	**0**	**0**
1996-97	**Montreal Canadiens**	**NHL**	**9**	**1**	**10**	**11**	**1**	**9**	**10**	**2**	**0**	**0**	**0**	**22**	**4.5**	**19**	**9**	**6**	**0**	**+4**	....	....	....	....	....	....	....	....
	St. Louis Blues	**NHL**	**69**	**25**	**49**	**74**	**27**	**43**	**70**	**12**	**5**	**0**	**7**	**194**	**12.9**	**97**	**30**	**72**	**9**	**+4**	**5**	**1**	**1**	**2**	**2**	**1**	**0**	**0**
1997-98	**St. Louis Blues**	**NHL**	**60**	**22**	**46**	**68**	**26**	**45**	**71**	**24**	**6**	**0**	**4**	**140**	**15.7**	**90**	**32**	**48**	**3**	**+13**	**10**	**4**	**4**	**8**	**2**	**2**	**0**	**0**
	NHL Totals		**810**	**366**	**566**	**932**	**361**	**454**	**815**	**275**	**139**	**10**	**64**	**2225**	**16.4**	**1232**	**491**	**791**	**124**		**59**	**25**	**30**	**55**	**20**	**8**	**0**	**1**

Won Lady Byng Memorial Trophy (1993)

Played in NHL All-Star Game (1990, 1993, 1994, 1996)

Traded to **NY Islanders** by **Buffalo** with Uwe Krupp, Benoit Hogue and Dave McLlwain for Pat Lafontaine, Randy Hillier, Randy Wood and NY Islanders' 4th round choice (Dean Melanson) in 1992 Entry Draft, October 25, 1991. Traded to **Montreal** by **NY Islanders** with Vladimir Malakhov for Kirk Muller, Mathieu Schneider and Craig Darby, April 5, 1995. Traded to **St. Louis** by **Montreal** with Rory Fitzpatrick and Craig Conroy for Murray Baron, Shayne Corson and St. Louis' 5th round choice (Gennady Razin) in 1997 Entry Draft, October 29, 1996.

• TURGEON, SYLVAIN

Sylvain Turgeon LW – L. 6', 200 lbs. b: Noranda, Que., 1/17/1965. Hartford's 1st choice, 2nd overall, in 1983 Entry Draft.

Season	Club	League	GP	G	A	Pts	AG	AA	APts	PIM	PP	SH	GW	S	%	TGF	PGF	TGA	PGA	+/–	GP	G	A	Pts	PIM	PP	SH	GW
1981-82	Hull Olympiques	QMJHL	57	33	40	73	....	....	....	78	....	....	....	....	....	....	....	....	....	....	14	11	11	22	16	....	....	....
1982-83	Hull Olympiques	QMJHL	67	54	109	163	....	....	....	103	....	....	....	....	....	....	....	....	....	....	7	8	7	15	10	....	....	....
	Canada	WJC-A	7	4	2	6	....	....	....	8	....	....	....	....	....	....	....	....	....	....	....	....	....	....	....	....	....	....
1983-84	**Hartford Whalers**	**NHL**	**76**	**40**	**32**	**72**	**32**	**22**	**54**	**55**	**18**	**0**	**3**	**237**	**16.9**	**106**	**46**	**71**	**0**	**–11**	....	....	....	....	....	....	....	....
1984-85	**Hartford Whalers**	**NHL**	**64**	**31**	**31**	**62**	**25**	**21**	**46**	**67**	**11**	**0**	**3**	**185**	**16.8**	**95**	**42**	**63**	**0**	**–10**	....	....	....	....	....	....	....	....
1985-86	**Hartford Whalers**	**NHL**	**76**	**45**	**34**	**79**	**36**	**23**	**59**	**88**	**13**	**0**	**5**	**249**	**18.1**	**115**	**41**	**73**	**0**	**+1**	**9**	**2**	**3**	**5**	**4**	**0**	**0**	**0**
1986-87	**Hartford Whalers**	**NHL**	**41**	**23**	**13**	**36**	**20**	**9**	**29**	**45**	**6**	**0**	**4**	**137**	**16.8**	**47**	**15**	**35**	**0**	**–3**	**6**	**1**	**2**	**3**	**4**	**0**	**0**	**0**
1987-88	**Hartford Whalers**	**NHL**	**71**	**23**	**26**	**49**	**20**	**18**	**38**	**71**	**13**	**0**	**3**	**247**	**9.3**	**85**	**44**	**46**	**0**	**–5**	**6**	**0**	**0**	**0**	**4**	**0**	**0**	**0**
1988-89	**Hartford Whalers**	**NHL**	**42**	**16**	**14**	**30**	**14**	**10**	**24**	**40**	**7**	**0**	**1**	**122**	**13.1**	**44**	**18**	**37**	**0**	**–11**	**4**	**0**	**2**	**2**	**4**	**0**	**0**	**0**
1989-90	**New Jersey Devils**	**NHL**	**72**	**30**	**17**	**47**	**26**	**12**	**38**	**81**	**7**	**0**	**3**	**218**	**13.8**	**77**	**20**	**65**	**0**	**–8**	**1**	**0**	**0**	**0**	**0**	**0**	**0**	**0**
1990-91	**Montreal Canadiens**	**NHL**	**19**	**5**	**7**	**12**	**5**	**5**	**10**	**20**	**1**	**0**	**1**	**41**	**12.2**	**17**	**7**	**12**	**0**	**–2**	**5**	**0**	**0**	**0**	**2**	**0**	**0**	**0**
1991-92	**Montreal Canadiens**	**NHL**	**56**	**9**	**11**	**20**	**8**	**8**	**16**	**39**	**6**	**0**	**1**	**99**	**9.1**	**42**	**26**	**21**	**1**	**–4**	**5**	**1**	**0**	**1**	**4**	**0**	**0**	**0**
1992-93	**Ottawa Senators**	**NHL**	**72**	**25**	**18**	**43**	**21**	**12**	**33**	**104**	**8**	**0**	**2**	**249**	**10.0**	**65**	**30**	**84**	**0**	**–29**	....	....	....	....	....	....	....	....
1993-94	**Ottawa Senators**	**NHL**	**47**	**11**	**15**	**26**	**10**	**12**	**22**	**52**	**7**	**0**	**2**	**116**	**9.5**	**40**	**19**	**47**	**1**	**–25**	....	....	....	....	....	....	....	....
1994-95	**Ottawa Senators**	**NHL**	**33**	**11**	**8**	**19**	**19**	**12**	**31**	**29**	**2**	**0**	**1**	**83**	**13.3**	**22**	**5**	**18**	**0**	**–1**	....	....	....	....	....	....	....	....
1995-96	Houston Aeros	IHL	65	28	31	59	....	....	....	66	....	....	....	....	....	....	....	....	....	....	....	....	....	....	....	....	....	....
1996-97	Wedemark Scorpions	Germany	10	4	6	10	....	....	....	12	....	....	....	....	....	....	....	....	....	....	8	5	2	7	41	....	....	....
1997-98	ECR Revier Lowen	Germany	27	11	15	26	....	....	....	24	....	....	....	....	....	....	....	....	....	....	....	....	....	....	....	....	....	....
	NHL Totals		**669**	**269**	**226**	**495**	**236**	**164**	**400**	**691**	**99**	**0**	**29**	**1983**	**13.6**	**755**	**313**	**552**	**2**		**36**	**4**	**7**	**11**	**22**	**0**	**0**	**0**

QMJHL First All-Star Team (1983) • NHL All-Rookie Team (1984)

Played in NHL All-Star Game (1986)

Traded to **New Jersey** by **Hartford** for Pat Verbeek, June 17, 1989. Traded to **Montreal** by **New Jersey** for Claude Lemieux, September 4, 1990. Claimed by **Ottawa** from **Montreal** in Expansion Draft, June 18, 1992.

• TURNBULL, IAN

Ian "Bull" Turnbull D – L. 6', 200 lbs. b: Montreal, Que., 12/22/1953. Toronto's 3rd choice, 15th overall, in 1973 Amateur Draft.

Season	Club	League	GP	G	A	Pts	AG	AA	APts	PIM	PP	SH	GW	S	%	TGF	PGF	TGA	PGA	+/–	GP	G	A	Pts	PIM	PP	SH	GW
1968-69	West Island Flyers	Jr. B	....	6	17	23	....	....	....	....	....	....	....	....	....	....	....	....	....	....	....	....	....	....	....	....	....	....
1969-70	Montreal Jr. Canadiens	OHA	53	4	21	25	....	....	....	88	....	....	....	....	....	....	....	....	....	....	....	....	....	....	....	....	....	....
1970-71	Montreal Jr. Canadiens	OHA	59	17	45	62	....	....	....	85	....	....	....	....	....	....	....	....	....	....	....	....	....	....	....	....	....	....
1971-72	Montreal Jr. Canadiens	OHA	63	34	48	82	....	....	....	85	....	....	....	....	....	....	....	....	....	....	....	....	....	....	....	....	....	....
1972-73	Ottawa 67's	OHA	60	31	50	81	....	....	....	98	....	....	....	....	....	....	....	....	....	....	....	....	....	....	....	....	....	....
1973-74	**Toronto Maple Leafs**	**NHL**	**78**	**8**	**27**	**35**	**8**	**23**	**31**	**74**	**2**	**0**	**2**	**231**	**3.5**	**101**	**23**	**88**	**22**	**+12**	**4**	**0**	**0**	**0**	**8**	**0**	**0**	**0**
1974-75	**Toronto Maple Leafs**	**NHL**	**22**	**6**	**7**	**13**	**6**	**5**	**11**	**44**	**1**	**0**	**0**	**69**	**8.7**	**31**	**7**	**38**	**8**	**–6**	**7**	**0**	**2**	**2**	**4**	**0**	**0**	**0**
	Oklahoma City Blazers	CHL	8	2	1	3	....	....	....	15	....	....	....	....	....	....	....	....	....	....	....	....	....	....	....	....	....	....
1975-76	**Toronto Maple Leafs**	**NHL**	**76**	**20**	**36**	**56**	**19**	**28**	**47**	**90**	**7**	**1**	**3**	**262**	**7.6**	**153**	**48**	**118**	**37**	**+24**	**10**	**2**	**9**	**11**	**29**	**1**	**0**	**0**
1976-77	**Toronto Maple Leafs**	**NHL**	**80**	**22**	**57**	**79**	**21**	**46**	**67**	**84**	**4**	**2**	**0**	**316**	**7.0**	**195**	**50**	**128**	**30**	**+47**	**9**	**4**	**4**	**8**	**10**	**4**	**0**	**0**
1977-78	**Toronto Maple Leafs**	**NHL**	**77**	**14**	**47**	**61**	**13**	**38**	**51**	**77**	**3**	**1**	**3**	**241**	**5.8**	**151**	**41**	**125**	**21**	**+6**	**13**	**6**	**10**	**16**	**10**	**1**	**0**	**0**
1978-79	**Toronto Maple Leafs**	**NHL**	**80**	**12**	**51**	**63**	**11**	**39**	**50**	**80**	**4**	**0**	**0**	**239**	**5.0**	**141**	**41**	**145**	**38**	**–7**	**6**	**0**	**4**	**4**	**27**	**0**	**0**	**0**
1979-80	**Toronto Maple Leafs**	**NHL**	**75**	**11**	**28**	**39**	**10**	**21**	**31**	**90**	**3**	**0**	**0**	**202**	**5.4**	**111**	**22**	**133**	**21**	**–23**	**3**	**0**	**3**	**3**	**2**	**0**	**0**	**0**
1980-81	**Toronto Maple Leafs**	**NHL**	**80**	**19**	**47**	**66**	**16**	**33**	**49**	**104**	**8**	**0**	**1**	**262**	**7.3**	**159**	**66**	**169**	**48**	**–17**	**3**	**1**	**0**	**1**	**4**	**0**	**0**	**0**
1981-82	**Toronto Maple Leafs**	**NHL**	**12**	**0**	**2**	**2**	**0**	**1**	**1**	**8**	**0**	**0**	**0**	**26**	**0.0**	**16**	**3**	**24**	**7**	**–4**	....	....	....	....	....	....	....	....
	Los Angeles Kings	**NHL**	**42**	**11**	**15**	**26**	**9**	**10**	**19**	**81**	**1**	**0**	**1**	**120**	**9.2**	**60**	**15**	**57**	**12**	**0**	....	....	....	....	....	....	....	....
	New Haven Nighthawks	AHL	13	1	7	8	....	....	....	4	....	....	....	....	....	....	....	....	....	....	3	0	0	0	0	....	....	....
1982-83	**Pittsburgh Penguins**	**NHL**	**6**	**0**	**0**	**0**	**0**	**0**	**0**	**4**	**0**	**0**	**0**	**6**	**0.0**	**2**	**1**	**4**	**0**	**–3**	....	....	....	....	....	....	....	....
	Baltimore Skipjacks	AHL	13	3	8	11	....	....	....	10	....	....	....	....	....	....	....	....	....	....	....	....	....	....	....	....	....	....
	NHL Totals		**628**	**123**	**317**	**440**	**113**	**244**	**357**	**736**	**33**	**4**	**10**	**1974**	**6.2**	**1120**	**306**	**1029**	**244**		**55**	**13**	**32**	**45**	**94**	**6**	**0**	**0**

OHA Second All-Star Team (1972, 1973)

Played in NHL All-Star Game (1977)

Traded to **LA Kings** by **Toronto** for Billy Harris and John Gibson, November 11, 1981. Signed as a free agent by **Pittsburgh**, October 4, 1982.

• TURNBULL, PERRY

Perry Turnbull C – L. 6'2", 200 lbs. b: Bentley, Alta., 3/9/1959. St. Louis' 1st choice, 2nd overall, in 1979 Entry Draft.

Season	Club	League	GP	G	A	Pts	AG	AA	APts	PIM	PP	SH	GW	S	%	TGF	PGF	TGA	PGA	+/–	GP	G	A	Pts	PIM	PP	SH	GW
1974-75	The Pas Red Devils	AJHL	69	6	4	10	....	....	....	134	....	....	....	....	....	....	....	....	....	....	....	....	....	....	....	....	....	....
1975-76	The Pas Red Devils	AJHL	45	27	23	50	....	....	....	140	....	....	....	....	....	....	....	....	....	....	....	....	....	....	....	....	....	....
	Calgary Centennials	WHL	19	6	7	13	....	....	....	14	....	....	....	....	....	....	....	....	....	....	....	....	....	....	....	....	....	....
1976-77	Calgary Centennials	WCJHL	10	8	5	13	....	....	....	33	....	....	....	....	....	....	....	....	....	....	....	....	....	....	....	....	....	....
	Portland Winter Hawks	WCJHL	58	23	30	53	....	....	....	249	....	....	....	....	....	....	....	....	....	....	10	2	1	3	36	....	....	....
1977-78	Portland Winter Hawks	WCJHL	57	36	27	63	....	....	....	318	....	....	....	....	....	....	....	....	....	....	8	2	3	5	44	....	....	....
1978-79	Portland Winter Hawks	WHL	70	75	43	118	....	....	....	191	....	....	....	....	....	....	....	....	....	....	20	10	8	18	33	....	....	....
1979-80	**St. Louis Blues**	**NHL**	**80**	**16**	**19**	**35**	**14**	**16**	**30**	**124**	**0**	**0**	**1**	**139**	**11.5**	**58**	**11**	**58**	**0**	**–11**	**3**	**1**	**1**	**2**	**2**	**1**	**0**	**0**
1980-81	**St. Louis Blues**	**NHL**	**75**	**34**	**22**	**56**	**28**	**15**	**43**	**209**	**5**	**0**	**5**	**209**	**16.3**	**85**	**15**	**55**	**0**	**+15**	....	....	....	....	....	....	....	....
1981-82	**St. Louis Blues**	**NHL**	**79**	**33**	**26**	**59**	**26**	**17**	**43**	**161**	**2**	**0**	**2**	**215**	**15.3**	**83**	**13**	**87**	**2**	**–15**	**5**	**3**	**2**	**5**	**11**	**1**	**0**	**0**

			REGULAR SEASON																		PLAYOFFS							
Season	Club	League	GP	G	A	Pts	AG	AA	APts	PIM	PP	SH	GW	S	%	TGF	PGF	TGA	PGA	+/–	GP	G	A	Pts	PIM	PP	SH	GW
1982-83	**St. Louis Blues**	**NHL**	**79**	**32**	**15**	**47**	**26**	**10**	**36**	**172**	**6**	**0**	**1**	**205**	**15.6**	**63**	**10**	**74**	**1**	**–20**	**4**	**1**	**0**	**1**	**14**	**0**	**0**	**0**
1983-84	**St. Louis Blues**	**NHL**	**32**	**14**	**8**	**22**	**11**	**5**	**16**	**81**	**1**	**0**	**0**	**84**	**16.7**	**32**	**9**	**26**	**1**	**–2**	....	....	....	....	....	....	....	....
	Montreal Canadiens	**NHL**	**40**	**6**	**7**	**13**	**5**	**5**	**10**	**59**	**2**	**0**	**1**	**67**	**9.0**	**19**	**4**	**28**	**1**	**–12**	**9**	**1**	**2**	**3**	**10**	**0**	**0**	**0**
1984-85	**Winnipeg Jets**	**NHL**	**66**	**22**	**21**	**43**	**18**	**14**	**32**	**130**	**2**	**0**	**1**	**138**	**15.9**	**76**	**11**	**58**	**2**	**+9**	**8**	**0**	**1**	**1**	**26**	**0**	**0**	**0**
1985-86	**Winnipeg Jets**	**NHL**	**80**	**20**	**31**	**51**	**16**	**21**	**37**	**183**	**6**	**0**	**2**	**168**	**11.9**	**74**	**13**	**80**	**1**	**–18**	**3**	**0**	**1**	**1**	**11**	**0**	**0**	**0**
1986-87	**Winnipeg Jets**	**NHL**	**26**	**1**	**5**	**6**	**1**	**4**	**5**	**44**	**0**	**0**	**0**	**29**	**3.4**	**12**	**3**	**11**	**0**	**–2**	**1**	**0**	**0**	**0**	**10**	**0**	**0**	**0**
1987-88	**St. Louis Blues**	**NHL**	**51**	**10**	**9**	**19**	**9**	**6**	**15**	**82**	**0**	**0**	**2**	**62**	**16.1**	**30**	**0**	**22**	**0**	**+8**	**1**	**0**	**0**	**0**	**2**	**0**	**0**	**0**
	Peoria Rivermen	IHL	3	5	0	5	....	....	....	4	....	....	....	....	....	....	....	....	....	....	....	....	....	....	....	....	....	....
1988-89	HC Asiago	Italy	32	31	27	58	....	....	....	*131	....	....	....	....	....	....	....	....	....	....	....	....	....	....	....	....	....	....
1989-90	HC Bolzano	Italy	35	25	30	55	....	....	....	73	....	....	....	....	....	....	....	....	....	....	....	....	....	....	....	....	....	....
1990-91	HC Bolzano	Italy	18	14	8	22	....	....	....	29	....	....	....	....	....	....	....	....	....	....	10	8	3	11	41	....	....	....
	NHL Totals		**608**	**188**	**163**	**351**	**154**	**112**	**266**	**1245**	**27**	**0**	**15**	**1316**	**14.3**	**532**	**89**	**499**	**8**		**34**	**6**	**7**	**13**	**86**	**2**	**0**	**0**

Traded to **Montreal** by **St. Louis** for Doug Wickenheiser, Gilbert Delorme and Greg Paslawski, December 21, 1983. Traded to **Winnipeg** by **Montreal** for Lucien DeBlois, June 14, 1984. Traded to **St. Louis** by **Winnipeg** for St. Louis' 5th round choice (Ken Gernander) in 1987 Entry Draft, June 5, 1987.

• TURNBULL, RANDY

Randy Turnbull D – R. 6′, 185 lbs. b: Bentley, Alta., 2/7/1962. Calgary's 1st choice, 97th overall, in 1980 Entry Draft.

Season	Club	League	GP	G	A	Pts	AG	AA	APts	PIM	PP	SH	GW	S	%	TGF	PGF	TGA	PGA	+/–	GP	G	A	Pts	PIM	PP	SH	GW
1977-78	Fort Saskatchewan Traders	AJHL	47	1	3	4	....	....	....	172	....	....	....	....	....	....	....	....	....	....	....	....	....	....	....	....	....	....
1978-79	Fort Saskatchewan Traders	AJHL	51	4	30	34	....	....	....	367	....	....	....	....	....	....	....	....	....	....	4	0	0	0	2	....	....	....
	Portland Winter Hawks	WHL	1	0	0	0	....	....	....	7	....	....	....	....	....	....	....	....	....	....	4	0	0	0	2	....	....	....
1979-80	Portland Winter Hawks	WHL	72	4	25	29	....	....	....	355	....	....	....	....	....	....	....	....	....	....	8	0	1	1	50	....	....	....
1980-81	Portland Winter Hawks	WHL	56	1	31	32	....	....	....	295	....	....	....	....	....	....	....	....	....	....	8	0	1	1	86	....	....	....
1981-82	Portland Winter Hawks	WHL	69	5	19	24	....	....	....	430	....	....	....	....	....	....	....	....	....	....	15	1	9	10	100	....	....	....
	Calgary Flames	**NHL**	**1**	**0**	**0**	**0**	**0**	**0**	**0**	**2**	**0**	**0**	**0**	**0**	**0.0**	**0**	**0**	**1**	**0**	**–1**	....	....	....	....	....	....	....	....
1982-83	Colorado Flames	CHL	65	2	1	3	....	....	....	292	....	....	....	....	....	....	....	....	....	....	6	0	1	1	7	....	....	....
1983-84	New Haven Nighthawks	AHL	8	0	0	0	....	....	....	46	....	....	....	....	....	....	....	....	....	....	....	....	....	....	....	....	....	....
	Peoria Prancers	IHL	73	3	18	21	....	....	....	213	....	....	....	....	....	....	....	....	....	....	....	....	....	....	....	....	....	....
1984-85	Salt Lake Golden Eagles	IHL	81	10	14	24	....	....	....	282	....	....	....	....	....	....	....	....	....	....	7	0	0	0	41	....	....	....
1985-86	Salt Lake Golden Eagles	IHL	77	6	14	20	....	....	....	236	....	....	....	....	....	....	....	....	....	....	5	0	1	1	15	....	....	....
1986-87	Salt Lake Golden Eagles	IHL	60	2	6	8	....	....	....	212	....	....	....	....	....	....	....	....	....	....	10	0	0	0	56	....	....	....
1987-88	Flint Spirits	IHL	1	0	0	0	....	....	....	2	....	....	....	....	....	....	....	....	....	....	....	....	....	....	....	....	....	....
	NHL Totals		**1**	**0**	**0**	**0**	**0**	**0**	**0**	**2**	**0**	**0**	**0**	**0**	**0.0**	**0**	**0**	**1**	**0**		....	....	....	....	....	....	....	....

• TURNER, BRAD

Brad Turner D – R. 6′2″, 205 lbs. b: Winnipeg, Man., 5/25/1968. Minnesota's 6th choice, 58th overall, in 1986 Entry Draft.

Season	Club	League	GP	G	A	Pts	AG	AA	APts	PIM	PP	SH	GW	S	%	TGF	PGF	TGA	PGA	+/–	GP	G	A	Pts	PIM	PP	SH	GW
1984-85	Darien-Minnesota High	H.S.	24	32	34	66	....	....	....	....	....	....	....	....	....	....	....	....	....	....	....	....	....	....	....	....	....	....
1985-86	Calgary Canucks	AJHL	52	14	21	35	....	....	....	109	....	....	....	....	....	....	....	....	....	....	....	....	....	....	....	....	....	....
1986-87	University of Michigan	CCHA	40	3	10	13	....	....	....	40	....	....	....	....	....	....	....	....	....	....	....	....	....	....	....	....	....	....
1987-88	University of Michigan	CCHA	39	3	11	14	....	....	....	52	....	....	....	....	....	....	....	....	....	....	....	....	....	....	....	....	....	....
1988-89	University of Michigan	CCHA	33	3	8	11	....	....	....	38	....	....	....	....	....	....	....	....	....	....	....	....	....	....	....	....	....	....
1989-90	University of Michigan	CCHA	32	8	9	17	....	....	....	34	....	....	....	....	....	....	....	....	....	....	....	....	....	....	....	....	....	....
1990-91	Capital District Islanders	AHL	31	1	2	3	....	....	....	8	....	....	....	....	....	....	....	....	....	....	....	....	....	....	....	....	....	....
	Richmond Renegades	ECHL	40	16	25	41	....	....	....	31	....	....	....	....	....	....	....	....	....	....	....	....	....	....	....	....	....	....
1991-92	**New York Islanders**	**NHL**	**3**	**0**	**0**	**0**	**0**	**0**	**0**	**0**	**0**	**0**	**0**	**1**	**0.0**	**1**	**0**	**0**	**0**	**+1**	....	....	....	....	....	....	....	....
	Capital District Islanders	AHL	35	3	6	9	....	....	....	17	....	....	....	....	....	....	....	....	....	....	....	....	....	....	....	....	....	....
	New Haven Nighthawks	AHL	32	6	11	17	....	....	....	58	....	....	....	....	....	....	....	....	....	....	....	....	....	....	....	....	....	....
1992-93	Capital District Islanders	AHL	65	8	11	19	....	....	....	71	....	....	....	....	....	....	....	....	....	....	3	0	0	0	2	....	....	....
1993-94	Canada	Nat-Team	30	6	9	15	....	....	....	21	....	....	....	....	....	....	....	....	....	....	....	....	....	....	....	....	....	....
	Cornwall Aces	AHL	29	3	13	16	....	....	....	19	....	....	....	....	....	....	....	....	....	....	4	1	1	2	4	....	....	....
1994-95	TuTo Turku	Finland	43	3	9	12	....	....	....	114	....	....	....	....	....	....	....	....	....	....	....	....	....	....	....	....	....	....
1995-96	WEV Wien	Austria	31	7	14	21	....	....	....	100	....	....	....	....	....	....	....	....	....	....	....	....	....	....	....	....	....	....
1996-97	Manchester Storm	Britain	21	3	8	11	....	....	....	12	....	....	....	....	....	....	....	....	....	....	6	2	0	2	4	....	....	....
1997-98	Manchester Storm	Britain	11	1	1	2	....	....	....	4	....	....	....	....	....	....	....	....	....	....	....	....	....	....	....	....	....	....
	Manchester Storm	EuroHL	5	1	3	4	....	....	....	4	....	....	....	....	....	....	....	....	....	....	....	....	....	....	....	....	....	....
	NHL Totals		**3**	**0**	**0**	**0**	**0**	**0**	**0**	**0**	**0**	**0**	**0**	**1**	**0.0**	**1**	**0**	**0**	**0**		....	....	....	....	....	....	....	....

Signed as a free agent by **NY Islanders**, June 4, 1991.

• TURNER, DEAN

Dean Turner D – L. 6′2″, 215 lbs. b: Dearborn, MI, 6/22/1958. NY Rangers' 3rd choice, 44th overall, in 1978 Amateur Draft.

Season	Club	League	GP	G	A	Pts	AG	AA	APts	PIM	PP	SH	GW	S	%	TGF	PGF	TGA	PGA	+/–	GP	G	A	Pts	PIM	PP	SH	GW
1976-77	University of Michigan	WCHA	45	13	18	31	....	....	....	106	....	....	....	....	....	....	....	....	....	....	....	....	....	....	....	....	....	....
1977-78	University of Michigan	WCHA	36	5	14	19	....	....	....	88	....	....	....	....	....	....	....	....	....	....	....	....	....	....	....	....	....	....
1978-79	**New York Rangers**	**NHL**	**1**	**0**	**0**	**0**	**0**	**0**	**0**	**0**	**0**	**0**	**0**	**0**	**0.0**	**0**	**0**	**1**	**0**	**–1**	....	....	....	....	....	....	....	....
	New Haven Nighthawks	AHL	76	9	25	34	....	....	....	275	....	....	....	....	....	....	....	....	....	....	6	0	0	0	9	....	....	....
1979-80	**Colorado Rockies**	**NHL**	**27**	**1**	**0**	**1**	**1**	**0**	**1**	**51**	**0**	**0**	**0**	**24**	**4.2**	**17**	**1**	**22**	**6**	**0**	....	....	....	....	....	....	....	....
	New Haven Nighthawks	AHL	6	1	3	4	....	....	....	10	....	....	....	....	....	....	....	....	....	....	....	....	....	....	....	....	....	....
	Fort Worth Texans	CHL	39	5	23	28	....	....	....	81	....	....	....	....	....	....	....	....	....	....	15	0	5	5	39	....	....	....
1980-81	**Colorado Rockies**	**NHL**	**4**	**0**	**0**	**0**	**0**	**0**	**0**	**4**	**0**	**0**	**0**	**0**	**0.0**	**2**	**0**	**6**	**0**	**–4**	....	....	....	....	....	....	....	....
	Fort Worth Texans	CHL	44	5	9	14	....	....	....	103	....	....	....	....	....	....	....	....	....	....	....	....	....	....	....	....	....	....
	Springfield Indians	AHL	11	2	7	9	....	....	....	31	....	....	....	....	....	....	....	....	....	....	6	4	5	9	7	....	....	....
1981-82	Rochester Americans	AHL	75	8	46	54	....	....	....	155	....	....	....	....	....	....	....	....	....	....	9	0	4	4	6	....	....	....
1982-83	**Los Angeles Kings**	**NHL**	**3**	**0**	**0**	**0**	**0**	**0**	**0**	**4**	**0**	**0**	**0**	**1**	**0.0**	**1**	**0**	**1**	**0**	**0**	....	....	....	....	....	....	....	....
	New Haven Nighthawks	AHL	66	14	20	34	....	....	....	129	....	....	....	....	....	....	....	....	....	....	12	2	3	5	34	....	....	....
	NHL Totals		**35**	**1**	**0**	**1**	**1**	**0**	**1**	**59**	**0**	**0**	**0**	**25**	**4.0**	**20**	**1**	**30**	**6**		....	....	....	....	....	....	....	....

Traded to **Colorado** by **NY Rangers** with Pat Hickey, Mike McEwen, Lucien DeBlois and future considerations (Bobby Crawford, January 15, 1980) for Barry Beck, November 2, 1979. Signed as a free agent by **Buffalo**, September 24, 1981. Traded to **LA Kings** by **Buffalo** for cash, September 9, 1982.

• TUTT, BRIAN

Brian Tutt D – L. 6′1″, 195 lbs. b: Swalwell, Alta., 6/9/1962. Philadelphia's 6th choice, 126th overall, in 1980 Entry Draft.

Season	Club	League	GP	G	A	Pts	AG	AA	APts	PIM	PP	SH	GW	S	%	TGF	PGF	TGA	PGA	+/–	GP	G	A	Pts	PIM	PP	SH	GW
1979-80	Calgary Canucks	AJHL	59	6	14	20	....	....	....	55	....	....	....	....	....	....	....	....	....	....	....	....	....	....	....	....	....	....
	Calgary Wranglers	WHL	2	0	0	0	....	....	....	2	....	....	....	....	....	....	....	....	....	....	4	0	1	1	6	....	....	....
1980-81	Calgary Wranglers	WHL	72	10	41	51	....	....	....	111	....	....	....	....	....	....	....	....	....	....	22	3	11	14	30	....	....	....
1981-82	Calgary Wranglers	WHL	40	2	16	18	....	....	....	85	....	....	....	....	....	....	....	....	....	....	9	2	2	4	22	....	....	....
1982-83	Maine Mariners	AHL	31	0	0	0	....	....	....	28	....	....	....	....	....	....	....	....	....	....	....	....	....	....	....	....	....	....
	Toledo Goaldiggers	IHL	23	5	10	15	....	....	....	26	....	....	....	....	....	....	....	....	....	....	11	1	7	8	16	....	....	....
1983-84	Springfield Indians	AHL	1	0	0	0	....	....	....	2	....	....	....	....	....	....	....	....	....	....	....	....	....	....	....	....	....	....
	Toledo Goaldiggers	IHL	82	7	44	51	....	....	....	79	....	....	....	....	....	....	....	....	....	....	13	0	6	6	16	....	....	....
1984-85	Hershey Bears	AHL	3	0	0	0	....	....	....	8	....	....	....	....	....	....	....	....	....	....	....	....	....	....	....	....	....	....
	Kalamazoo Wings	IHL	80	8	45	53	....	....	....	62	....	....	....	....	....	....	....	....	....	....	11	2	4	6	19	....	....	....
1985-86	Kalamazoo Wings	IHL	82	11	39	50	....	....	....	129	....	....	....	....	....	....	....	....	....	....	6	1	6	7	11	....	....	....
1986-87	Maine Mariners	AHL	41	6	15	21	....	....	....	19	....	....	....	....	....	....	....	....	....	....	....	....	....	....	....	....	....	....
	Kalamazoo Wings	IHL	19	2	7	9	....	....	....	10	....	....	....	....	....	....	....	....	....	....	....	....	....	....	....	....	....	....
1987-88	New Haven Nighthawks	AHL	32	1	12	13	....	....	....	33	....	....	....	....	....	....	....	....	....	....	....	....	....	....	....	....	....	....
1988-89	Baltimore Skipjacks	AHL	6	1	5	6	....	....	....	6	....	....	....	....	....	....	....	....	....	....	....	....	....	....	....	....	....	....
	Canada	Nat-Team	63	0	19	19	....	....	....	87	....	....	....	....	....	....	....	....	....	....	....	....	....	....	....	....	....	....
1989-90	**Washington Capitals**	**NHL**	**7**	**1**	**0**	**1**	**1**	**0**	**1**	**2**	**0**	**0**	**0**	**5**	**20.0**	**3**	**0**	**7**	**0**	**–4**	....	....	....	....	....	....	....	....
	Baltimore Skipjacks	AHL	67	2	13	15	....	....	....	80	....	....	....	....	....	....	....	....	....	....	9	1	0	1	4	....	....	....
1990-91	Canada	Nat-Team	10	4	3	7	....	....	....	14	....	....	....	....	....	....	....	....	....	....	....	....	....	....	....	....	....	....
	Furuset Oslo	Norway	35	13	24	37	....	....	....	100	....	....	....	....	....	....	....	....	....	....	6	3	2	5	....	....	....	....
1991-92	Furuset Oslo	Norway	28	7	9	16	....	....	....	96	....	....	....	....	....	....	....	....	....	....	....	....	....	....	....	....	....	....
	Canada	Nat-Team	6	0	1	1	....	....	....	6	....	....	....	....	....	....	....	....	....	....	....	....	....	....	....	....	....	....
	Canada	Olympics	8	0	0	0	....	....	....	4	....	....	....	....	....	....	....	....	....	....	....	....	....	....	....	....	....	....
	Canada	WC-A	5	0	0	0	....	....	....	8	....	....	....	....	....	....	....	....	....	....	....	....	....	....	....	....	....	....
1992-93	Ilves Tampere	Finland	46	5	18	23	....	....	....	*148	....	....	....	....	....	....	....	....	....	....	3	1	1	2	0	....	....	....
1993-94	Farjestads BK Karstad	Sweden	21	1	3	4	....	....	....	32	....	....	....	....	....	....	....	....	....	....	....	....	....	....	....	....	....	....
1994-95	Ilves Tampere	Finland	25	1	3	4	....	....	....	42	....	....	....	....	....	....	....	....	....	....	....	....	....	....	....	....	....	....
	Canada	WC-A	7	0	0	0	....	....	....	6	....	....	....	....	....	....	....	....	....	....	....	....	....	....	....	....	....	....

			REGULAR SEASON																		PLAYOFFS							
Season	Club	League	GP	G	A	Pts	AG	AA	APts	PIM	PP	SH	GW	S	%	TGF	PGF	TGA	PGA	+/–	GP	G	A	Pts	PIM	PP	SH	GW
1995-96	Schwenningen Wild Wings	Germany	31	4	14	18	....	....	....	71	....	....	....	....	....	....	....	....	....	....	....	....	....	....	....	....	....	....
1996-97	Schwenningen Wild Wings	Germany	31	4	14	18	....	....	....	71	....	....	....	....	....	....	....	....	....	....	5	2	3	5	12	....	....	....
1997-98	Hannover Scorpions	Germany	49	3	14	17	....	....	....	86	....	....	....	....	....	....	....	....	....	....	4	0	1	1	8	....	....	....
	NHL Totals		**7**	**1**	**0**	**1**	**1**	**0**	**1**	**2**	**0**	**0**	**0**	**5**	**20.0**	**3**	**0**	**7**	**0**		....	....	....	....	....	....	....	....

IHL Second All-Star Team (1984, 1985)

Signed as a free agent by **Washington**, July 25, 1989.

• TUTTLE, STEVE

Steve Tuttle RW – R. 6'1", 197 lbs. b: Vancouver, B.C., 1/5/1966. St. Louis' 5th choice, 113th overall, in 1984 Entry Draft.

Season	Club	League	GP	G	A	Pts	AG	AA	APts	PIM	PP	SH	GW	S	%	TGF	PGF	TGA	PGA	+/–	GP	G	A	Pts	PIM	PP	SH	GW
1983-84	Richmond Sockeyes	BCJHL	46	46	34	80	....	....	....	22	....	....	....	....	....	....	....	....	....	....	....	....	....	....	....	....	....	....
1984-85	University of Wisconsin	WCHA	28	3	4	7	....	....	....	0	....	....	....	....	....	....	....	....	....	....	....	....	....	....	....	....	....	....
1985-86	University of Wisconsin	WCHA	32	2	10	12	....	....	....	2	....	....	....	....	....	....	....	....	....	....	....	....	....	....	....	....	....	....
1986-87	University of Wisconsin	WCHA	42	31	21	52	....	....	....	14	....	....	....	....	....	....	....	....	....	....	....	....	....	....	....	....	....	....
1987-88	University of Wisconsin	WCHA	45	27	39	66	....	....	....	18	....	....	....	....	....	....	....	....	....	....	....	....	....	....	....	....	....	....
1988-89	**St. Louis Blues**	**NHL**	**53**	**13**	**12**	**25**	**11**	**8**	**19**	**6**	**0**	**1**	**3**	**82**	**15.9**	**37**	**0**	**60**	**26**	**+3**	**6**	**1**	**2**	**3**	**0**	**0**	**0**	**0**
1989-90	**St. Louis Blues**	**NHL**	**71**	**12**	**10**	**22**	**10**	**7**	**17**	**4**	**1**	**1**	**1**	**92**	**13.0**	**29**	**2**	**42**	**9**	**–6**	**5**	**0**	**1**	**1**	**2**	**0**	**0**	**0**
1990-91	**St. Louis Blues**	**NHL**	**20**	**3**	**6**	**9**	**3**	**5**	**8**	**2**	**0**	**0**	**0**	**16**	**18.8**	**14**	**1**	**12**	**1**	**+2**	**6**	**0**	**3**	**3**	**0**	**0**	**0**	**0**
	Peoria Rivermen	IHL	42	24	32	56	....	....	....	8	....	....	....	....	....	....	....	....	....	....	....	....	....	....	....	....	....	....
1991-92	Peoria Rivermen	IHL	71	43	46	89	....	....	....	22	....	....	....	....	....	....	....	....	....	....	10	4	8	12	4	....	....	....
1992-93	Milwaukee Admirals	IHL	51	27	34	61	....	....	....	12	....	....	....	....	....	....	....	....	....	....	4	0	2	2	2	....	....	....
	Halifax Citadels	AHL	22	11	17	28	....	....	....	2	....	....	....	....	....	....	....	....	....	....	....	....	....	....	....	....	....	....
1993-94	Milwaukee Admirals	IHL	78	27	44	71	....	....	....	34	....	....	....	....	....	....	....	....	....	....	4	0	2	2	4	....	....	....
1994-95	Peoria Rivermen	IHL	38	14	13	27	....	....	....	14	....	....	....	....	....	....	....	....	....	....	....	....	....	....	....	....	....	....
	Milwaukee Admirals	IHL	21	3	1	4	....	....	....	8	....	....	....	....	....	....	....	....	....	....	....	....	....	....	....	....	....	....
1995-96	Milwaukee Admirals	IHL	81	32	35	67	....	....	....	36	....	....	....	....	....	....	....	....	....	....	5	1	2	3	0	....	....	....
1996-97	Milwaukee Admirals	IHL	71	25	19	44	....	....	....	20	....	....	....	....	....	....	....	....	....	....	3	1	1	2	2	....	....	....
1997-98	Milwaukee Admirals	IHL	37	7	6	13	....	....	....	26	....	....	....	....	....	....	....	....	....	....	10	3	4	7	2	....	....	....
	NHL Totals		**144**	**28**	**28**	**56**	**24**	**20**	**44**	**12**	**1**	**2**	**4**	**190**	**14.7**	**80**	**3**	**114**	**36**		**17**	**1**	**6**	**7**	**2**	**0**	**0**	**0**

ECAC Second All-Star Team (1985) • WCHA Second All-Star Team (1988) • NCAA West Second All-American Team (1988) • IHL First All-Star Team (1992)

Traded to **Tampa Bay** by **St. Louis** with Pat Jablonski, Darin Kimble, and Rob Robinson for future considerations, June 19, 1992. Traded to **Quebec** by **Tampa Bay** with Martin Simard and Michel Mongeau for Herb Raglan, February 12, 1993.

• TUZZOLINO, TONY

Tony Tuzzolino RW – R. 6'2", 180 lbs. b: Buffalo, NY, 10/9/1975. Quebec's 7th choice, 113th overall, in 1994 Entry Draft.

Season	Club	League	GP	G	A	Pts	AG	AA	APts	PIM	PP	SH	GW	S	%	TGF	PGF	TGA	PGA	+/–	GP	G	A	Pts	PIM	PP	SH	GW
1993-94	Michigan State Spartans	CCHA	35	4	3	7	....	....	....	46	....	....	....	....	....	....	....	....	....	....	....	....	....	....	....	....	....	....
1994-95	Michigan State Spartans	CCHA	39	9	18	27	....	....	....	81	....	....	....	....	....	....	....	....	....	....	....	....	....	....	....	....	....	....
1995-96	Michigan State Spartans	CCHA	41	12	17	29	....	....	....	120	....	....	....	....	....	....	....	....	....	....	....	....	....	....	....	....	....	....
1996-97	Michigan State Spartans	CCHA	39	14	18	32	....	....	....	120	....	....	....	....	....	....	....	....	....	....	....	....	....	....	....	....	....	....
1997-98	**Anaheim Mighty Ducks**	**NHL**	**1**	**0**	**0**	**0**	**0**	**0**	**0**	**2**	**0**	**0**	**0**	**0**	**0.0**	**0**	**0**	**2**	**0**	**–2**	....	....	....	....	....	....	....	....
	Kentucky Thoroughblades	AHL	35	9	14	23	....	....	....	83	....	....	....	....	....	....	....	....	....	....	....	....	....	....	....	....	....	....
	Cincinnati Mighty Ducks	AHL	13	3	3	6	....	....	....	6	....	....	....	....	....	....	....	....	....	....	....	....	....	....	....	....	....	....
	NHL Totals		**1**	**0**	**0**	**0**	**0**	**0**	**0**	**2**	**0**	**0**	**0**	**0**	**0.0**	**0**	**0**	**2**	**0**		....	....	....	....	....	....	....	....

Signed as a free agent by **NY Islanders**, April 26, 1997. Traded to **Anaheim** by **NY Islanders** with Travis Green and Doug Houda for Joe Sacco, J.J. Daigneault and Mark Janssens, February 6, 1998.

• TVERDOVSKY, OLEG

Oleg Tverdovsky D – L. 6', 185 lbs. b: Donetsk, USSR, 5/18/1976. Anaheim's 1st choice, 2nd overall, in 1994 Entry Draft.

Season	Club	League	GP	G	A	Pts	AG	AA	APts	PIM	PP	SH	GW	S	%	TGF	PGF	TGA	PGA	+/–	GP	G	A	Pts	PIM	PP	SH	GW
1992-93	Soviet Wings	CIS	21	0	1	1	....	....	....	6	....	....	....	....	....	....	....	....	....	....	6	0	0	0	0	....	....	....
1993-94	Soviet Wings	CIS	46	4	10	14	....	....	....	22	....	....	....	....	....	....	....	....	....	....	3	1	0	1	2	....	....	....
	Russia	WJC-A	7	1	5	6	....	....	....	6	....	....	....	....	....	....	....	....	....	....	....	....	....	....	....	....	....	....
1994-95	Brandon Wheat Kings	WHL	7	1	4	5	....	....	....	4	....	....	....	....	....	....	....	....	....	....	....	....	....	....	....	....	....	....
	Anaheim Mighty Ducks	**NHL**	**36**	**3**	**9**	**12**	**5**	**13**	**18**	**14**	**1**	**1**	**0**	**26**	**11.5**	**32**	**7**	**35**	**4**	**–6**	....	....	....	....	....	....	....	....
1995-96	**Anaheim Mighty Ducks**	**NHL**	**51**	**7**	**15**	**22**	**7**	**12**	**19**	**35**	**2**	**0**	**0**	**84**	**8.3**	**50**	**10**	**43**	**3**	**0**	....	....	....	....	....	....	....	....
	Winnipeg Jets	**NHL**	**31**	**0**	**8**	**8**	**0**	**7**	**7**	**6**	**0**	**0**	**0**	**35**	**0.0**	**25**	**8**	**26**	**2**	**–7**	**6**	**0**	**1**	**1**	**0**	**0**	**0**	**0**
	Russia	WC-A	3	0	1	1	....	....	....	0	....	....	....	....	....	....	....	....	....	....	....	....	....	....	....	....	....	....
1996-97	Russia	W Cup	4	1	0	1	....	....	....	0	....	....	....	....	....	....	....	....	....	....	....	....	....	....	....	....	....	....
	Phoenix Coyotes	**NHL**	**82**	**10**	**45**	**55**	**11**	**40**	**51**	**30**	**3**	**1**	**2**	**144**	**6.9**	**121**	**46**	**96**	**16**	**–5**	**7**	**0**	**1**	**1**	**0**	**0**	**0**	**0**
1997-98	Hamilton Bulldogs	AHL	9	8	6	14	....	....	....	2	....	....	....	....	....	....	....	....	....	....	....	....	....	....	....	....	....	....
	Phoenix Coyotes	**NHL**	**46**	**7**	**12**	**19**	**8**	**12**	**20**	**12**	**4**	**0**	**1**	**83**	**8.4**	**50**	**21**	**31**	**3**	**+1**	**6**	**0**	**7**	**7**	**0**	**0**	**0**	**0**
	NHL Totals		**246**	**27**	**89**	**116**	**31**	**84**	**115**	**97**	**10**	**2**	**3**	**372**	**7.3**	**278**	**92**	**231**	**20**		**19**	**0**	**9**	**9**	**0**	**0**	**0**	**0**

EJC-A All-Star Team (1994)

Played in NHL All-Star Game (1997)

Traded to **Winnipeg** by **Anaheim** with Chad Kilger and Anaheim's 3rd round choice (Per-Anton Lundstrom) in 1996 Entry Draft for Teemu Selanne, Marc Chouinard and Winnipeg's 4th round choice (later traded to Toronto — later traded to Montreal — Montreal selected Kim Staal) in 1996 Entry Draft, February 7, 1996. Transferred to **Phoenix** after **Winnipeg** franchise relocated, July 1, 1996.

• TWIST, TONY

Tony Twist LW – L. 6'1", 220 lbs. b: Sherwood Park, Alta., 5/9/1968. St. Louis' 9th choice, 177th overall, in 1988 Entry Draft.

Season	Club	League	GP	G	A	Pts	AG	AA	APts	PIM	PP	SH	GW	S	%	TGF	PGF	TGA	PGA	+/–	GP	G	A	Pts	PIM	PP	SH	GW
1986-87	Saskatoon Blades	WHL	64	0	8	8	....	....	....	181	....	....	....	....	....	....	....	....	....	....	....	....	....	....	....	....	....	....
1987-88	Saskatoon Blades	WHL	55	1	8	9	....	....	....	226	....	....	....	....	....	....	....	....	....	....	10	1	1	2	6	....	....	....
1988-89	Peoria Rivermen	IHL	67	3	8	11	....	....	....	312	....	....	....	....	....	....	....	....	....	....	....	....	....	....	....	....	....	....
1989-90	**St. Louis Blues**	**NHL**	**28**	**0**	**0**	**0**	**0**	**0**	**0**	**124**	**0**	**0**	**0**	**2**	**0.0**	**3**	**0**	**5**	**0**	**–2**	....	....	....	....	....	....	....	....
	Peoria Rivermen	IHL	36	1	5	6	....	....	....	200	....	....	....	....	....	....	....	....	....	....	5	0	1	1	8	....	....	....
1990-91	Peoria Rivermen	IHL	38	2	10	12	....	....	....	244	....	....	....	....	....	....	....	....	....	....	....	....	....	....	....	....	....	....
	Quebec Nordiques	**NHL**	**24**	**0**	**0**	**0**	**0**	**0**	**0**	**104**	**0**	**0**	**0**	**2**	**0.0**	**1**	**0**	**5**	**0**	**–4**	....	....	....	....	....	....	....	....
1991-92	**Quebec Nordiques**	**NHL**	**44**	**0**	**1**	**1**	**0**	**1**	**1**	**164**	**0**	**0**	**0**	**9**	**0.0**	**4**	**0**	**7**	**0**	**–3**	....	....	....	....	....	....	....	....
1992-93	**Quebec Nordiques**	**NHL**	**34**	....	**2**	**2**	**0**	**1**	**1**	**64**	**0**	**0**	**0**	**14**	**0.0**	**4**	**0**	**4**	**0**	**0**	....	....	....	....	....	....	....	....
1993-94	**Quebec Nordiques**	**NHL**	**49**	**0**	**4**	**4**	**0**	**3**	**3**	**101**	**0**	**0**	**0**	**15**	**0.0**	**8**	**0**	**9**	**0**	**–1**	....	....	....	....	....	....	....	....
1994-95	**St. Louis Blues**	**NHL**	**28**	**3**	**0**	**3**	**5**	**0**	**5**	**89**	**0**	**0**	**1**	**8**	**37.5**	**5**	**0**	**5**	**0**	**0**	**1**	**0**	**0**	**0**	**6**	**0**	**0**	**0**
1995-96	**St. Louis Blues**	**NHL**	**51**	**3**	**2**	**5**	**3**	**2**	**5**	**100**	**0**	**0**	**1**	**12**	**25.0**	**8**	**0**	**9**	**0**	**–1**	**10**	**1**	**1**	**2**	**16**	**0**	**0**	**0**
1996-97	**St. Louis Blues**	**NHL**	**64**	**1**	**2**	**3**	**1**	**2**	**3**	**121**	**0**	**0**	**0**	**21**	**4.8**	**7**	**0**	**15**	**0**	**–8**	**6**	**0**	**0**	**0**	**0**	**0**	**0**	**0**
1997-98	**St. Louis Blues**	**NHL**	**60**	**1**	**1**	**2**	**1**	**1**	**2**	**105**	**0**	**0**	**0**	**17**	**5.9**	**7**	**1**	**11**	**1**	**–4**	....	....	....	....	....	....	....	....
	NHL Totals		**382**	**8**	**12**	**20**	**10**	**10**	**20**	**972**	**0**	**0**	**2**	**100**	**8.0**	**47**	**1**	**70**	**1**		**17**	**1**	**1**	**2**	**22**	**0**	**0**	**0**

Traded to **Quebec** by **St. Louis** with Herb Raglan and Andy Rymsha for Darin Kimble, February 4, 1991. Signed as a free agent by **St. Louis**, August 16, 1994.

• UBRIACO, GENE

Gene Ubriaco LW/C – L. 5'8", 157 lbs. b: Sault Ste. Marie, Ont., 12/26/1937.

Season	Club	League	GP	G	A	Pts	AG	AA	APts	PIM	PP	SH	GW	S	%	TGF	PGF	TGA	PGA	+/–	GP	G	A	Pts	PIM	PP	SH	GW
1954-55	St. Michael's Majors	OHA	28	2	5	7	....	....	....	14	....	....	....	....	....	....	....	....	....	....	4	1	1	2	0	....	....	....
1955-56	St. Michael's Majors	OHA	48	26	16	42	....	....	....	44	....	....	....	....	....	....	....	....	....	....	8	3	4	7	6	....	....	....
1956-57	St. Michael's Majors	OHA	52	22	32	54	....	....	....	49	....	....	....	....	....	....	....	....	....	....	4	1	3	4	0	....	....	....
1957-58	St. Michael's Majors	OHA	39	19	18	37	....	....	....	43	....	....	....	....	....	....	....	....	....	....	9	10	6	16	4	....	....	....
1958-59	New Westminster Royals	WHL	63	19	19	38	....	....	....	33	....	....	....	....	....	....	....	....	....	....	....	....	....	....	....	....	....	....
1959-60	Sudbury Wolves	EPHL	70	30	32	62	....	....	....	40	....	....	....	....	....	....	....	....	....	....	14	2	4	6	12	....	....	....
1960-61	Sudbury Wolves	EPHL	24	4	12	16	....	....	....	27	....	....	....	....	....	....	....	....	....	....	....	....	....	....	....	....	....	....
	Rochester Americans	AHL	60	16	24	40	....	....	....	15	....	....	....	....	....	....	....	....	....	....	....	....	....	....	....	....	....	....
1961-62	Pittsburgh Hornets	AHL	44	13	12	25	....	....	....	14	....	....	....	....	....	....	....	....	....	....	....	....	....	....	....	....	....	....
1962-63	Rochester Americans	AHL	72	22	48	70	....	....	....	21	....	....	....	....	....	....	....	....	....	....	2	1	0	1	0	....	....	....
1963-64	Hershey Bears	AHL	72	13	45	58	....	....	....	36	....	....	....	....	....	....	....	....	....	....	6	5	3	8	2	....	....	....
1964-65	Hershey Bears	AHL	63	15	32	47	....	....	....	12	....	....	....	....	....	....	....	....	....	....	15	3	6	9	0	....	....	....
1965-66	Hershey Bears	AHL	72	42	44	86	....	....	....	18	....	....	....	....	....	....	....	....	....	....	3	1	1	2	0	....	....	....
1966-67	Hershey Bears	AHL	69	38	43	81	....	....	....	50	....	....	....	....	....	....	....	....	....	....	5	0	0	3	2	....	....	....
1967-68	**Pittsburgh Penguins**	**NHL**	**65**	**18**	**15**	**33**	**22**	**10**	**38**	**16**	**3**	**0**	**3**	**119**	**15.1**	**39**	**12**	**40**	**0**	**–13**	....	....	....	....	....	....	....	....
	Baltimore Clippers	AHL	6	1	4	5	....	....	....	6	....	....	....	....	....	....	....	....	....	....	....	....	....	....	....	....	....	....

			REGULAR SEASON																		PLAYOFFS							
Season	Club	League	GP	G	A	Pts	AG	AA	APts	PIM	PP	SH	GW	S	%	TGF	PGF	TGA	PGA	+/–	GP	G	A	Pts	PIM	PP	SH	GW
1968-69	**Pittsburgh Penguins**	**NHL**	**49**	**15**	**11**	**26**	**17**	**10**	**27**	**14**	**4**	**0**	**2**	**100**	**15.0**	**38**	**11**	**27**	**0**	**0**	....	....	....	....	....	....	....	....
	Oakland Seals	**NHL**	**26**	**4**	**7**	**11**	**4**	**7**	**11**	**14**	**1**	**0**	**0**	**39**	**10.3**	**18**	**6**	**18**	**1**	**–5**	**7**	**2**	**0**	**2**	**2**	**0**	**0**	**0**
1969-70	**Oakland Seals**	**NHL**	**16**	**1**	**1**	**2**	**1**	**1**	**2**	**4**	**0**	**0**	**0**	**13**	**7.7**	**2**	**0**	**3**	**0**	**–1**	....	....	....	....	....	....	....	....
	Providence Reds	AHL	8	2	6	8	....	....	....	8	....	....	....	....	....	....	....	....	....	....	....	....	....	....	....	....	....	....
	Chicago Black Hawks	**NHL**	**21**	**1**	**1**	**2**	**1**	**1**	**2**	**2**	**0**	**0**	**0**	**7**	**14.3**	**2**	**1**	**2**	**0**	**–1**	**4**	**0**	**0**	**0**	**2**	**0**	**0**	**0**
	NHL Totals		**177**	**39**	**35**	**74**	**45**	**35**	**80**	**50**	**8**	**0**	**5**	**278**	**14.0**	**99**	**30**	**90**	**1**		**11**	**2**	**0**	**2**	**4**	**0**	**0**	**0**

AHL Second All-Star Team (1966)

Traded to **Hershey** (AHL) by **Toronto** with Bruce Draper for Les Duff, September, 1963. Traded to **Pittsburgh** by **Hershey** (AHL) for Jeannot Gilbert, October, 1967. Traded to **Oakland** by **Pittsburgh** with Earl Ingarfield Sr. and Dick Mattiussi for Bryan Watson, George Swarbrick and Tracy Pratt, January 30, 1969. Traded to **Chicago** by **Oakland** for Howie Menard, December, 1969.

• ULANOV, IGOR

Igor Ulanov D – L. 6'1", 205 lbs. b: Krasnokamsk, USSR, 10/1/1969. Winnipeg's 8th choice, 203rd overall, in 1991 Entry Draft.

Season	Club	League	GP	G	A	Pts	AG	AA	APts	PIM	PP	SH	GW	S	%	TGF	PGF	TGA	PGA	+/–	GP	G	A	Pts	PIM	PP	SH	GW
1990-91	Khimik Voskresensk	FrTour	1	0	0	0	....	....	....	2	....	....	....	....	....	....	....	....	....	....	....	....	....	....	....	....	....	....
	Khimik Voskresensk	USSR	41	2	2	4	....	....	....	52	....	....	....	....	....	....	....	....	....	....	....	....	....	....	....	....	....	....
	Khimik Voskresensk	SuperS	6	0	1	1	....	....	....	6	....	....	....	....	....	....	....	....	....	....	....	....	....	....	....	....	....	....
1991-92	Khimik Voskresensk	CIS	27	1	4	5	....	....	....	24	....	....	....	....	....	....	....	....	....	....	....	....	....	....	....	....	....	....
	Winnipeg Jets	**NHL**	**27**	**2**	**9**	**11**	**2**	**7**	**9**	**67**	**0**	**0**	**0**	**23**	**8.7**	**23**	**0**	**21**	**3**	**+5**	**7**	**0**	**0**	**0**	**39**	**0**	**0**	**0**
	Moncton Hawks	AHL	3	0	1	1	....	....	....	16	....	....	....	....	....	....	....	....	....	....	....	....	....	....	....	....	....	....
1992-93	**Winnipeg Jets**	**NHL**	**56**	**2**	**14**	**16**	**2**	**10**	**12**	**124**	**0**	**0**	**0**	**26**	**7.7**	**62**	**1**	**65**	**10**	**+6**	**4**	**0**	**0**	**0**	**4**	**0**	**0**	**0**
	Moncton Hawks	AHL	9	1	3	4	....	....	....	26	....	....	....	....	....	....	....	....	....	....	....	....	....	....	....	....	....	....
	Fort Wayne Komets	IHL	3	0	1	1	....	....	....	29	....	....	....	....	....	....	....	....	....	....	....	....	....	....	....	....	....	....
1993-94	**Winnipeg Jets**	**NHL**	**74**	**0**	**17**	**17**	**0**	**13**	**13**	**165**	**0**	**0**	**0**	**46**	**0.0**	**55**	**3**	**83**	**20**	**–11**	....	....	....	....	....	....	....	....
	Russia	WC-A	6	1	0	1	....	....	....	20	....	....	....	....	....	....	....	....	....	....	....	....	....	....	....	....	....	....
1994-95	**Winnipeg Jets**	**NHL**	**19**	**1**	**3**	**4**	**2**	**4**	**6**	**27**	**0**	**0**	**0**	**13**	**7.7**	**10**	**0**	**17**	**5**	**–2**	....	....	....	....	....	....	....	....
	Washington Capitals	**NHL**	**3**	**0**	**1**	**1**	**0**	**1**	**1**	**2**	**0**	**0**	**0**	**0**	**0.0**	**4**	**0**	**1**	**0**	**+3**	**2**	**0**	**0**	**0**	**4**	**0**	**0**	**0**
1995-96	**Chicago Blackhawks**	**NHL**	**53**	**1**	**8**	**9**	**1**	**7**	**8**	**92**	**0**	**0**	**0**	**24**	**4.2**	**31**	**0**	**22**	**3**	**+12**	....	....	....	....	....	....	....	....
	Indianapolis Ice	IHL	1	0	0	0	....	....	....	0	....	....	....	....	....	....	....	....	....	....	....	....	....	....	....	....	....	....
	Tampa Bay Lightning	**NHL**	**11**	**2**	**1**	**3**	**2**	**1**	**3**	**24**	**0**	**0**	**1**	**13**	**15.4**	**9**	**0**	**11**	**1**	**–1**	**5**	**0**	**0**	**0**	**15**	**0**	**0**	**0**
1996-97	Russia	W Cup	1	0	0	0	....	....	....	4	....	....	....	....	....	....	....	....	....	....	....	....	....	....	....	....	....	....
	Tampa Bay Lightning	**NHL**	**59**	**1**	**7**	**8**	**1**	**6**	**7**	**108**	**0**	**0**	**0**	**56**	**1.8**	**37**	**2**	**46**	**13**	**+2**	....	....	....	....	....	....	....	....
1997-98	**Tampa Bay Lightning**	**NHL**	**45**	**2**	**7**	**9**	**2**	**7**	**9**	**85**	**1**	**0**	**0**	**32**	**6.3**	**26**	**2**	**43**	**14**	**–5**	....	....	....	....	....	....	....	....
	Montreal Canadiens	**NHL**	**4**	**0**	**1**	**1**	**0**	**1**	**1**	**12**	**0**	**0**	**0**	**4**	**0.0**	**1**	**0**	**5**	**2**	**–2**	**10**	**1**	**4**	**5**	**12**	**0**	**0**	**0**
	NHL Totals		**351**	**11**	**68**	**79**	**12**	**57**	**69**	**706**	**1**	**0**	**1**	**237**	**4.6**	**258**	**8**	**314**	**71**		**28**	**1**	**4**	**5**	**74**	**0**	**0**	**0**

Traded to **Washington** by **Winnipeg** with Mike Eagles for Washington's 3rd (later traded to Dallas — Dallas selected Sergei Gusev) and 5th (Brian Elder) round choices in 1995 Entry Draft, April 7, 1995. Traded to **Chicago** by **Washington** for Chicago's 3rd round choice (Dave Weninger) in 1996 Entry Draft, October 17, 1995. Traded to **Tampa Bay** by **Chicago** with Patrick Poulin and Chicago's 2nd round choice (later traded to New Jersey — New Jersey selected Pierre Dagenais) in 1996 Entry Draft for Enrico Ciccone and Tampa Bay's 2nd round choice (Jeff Paul) in 1996 Entry Draft, March 20, 1996. Traded to **Montreal** by **Tampa Bay** with Patrick Poulin and Mick Vukota for Stephane Richer, Darcy Tucker and David Wilkie, January 15, 1998.

• ULLMAN, NORM

Norm Ullman C – L. 5'10", 175 lbs. b: Provost, Alta., 12/26/1935. **HHOF**

Season	Club	League	GP	G	A	Pts	AG	AA	APts	PIM	PP	SH	GW	S	%	TGF	PGF	TGA	PGA	+/–	GP	G	A	Pts	PIM	PP	SH	GW
1951-52	Edmonton Oil Kings	WCJHL	1	1	0	1	....	....	....	0	....	....	....	....	....	....	....	....	....	....	1	0	0	0	0	....	....	....
1952-53	Edmonton Oil Kings	WCJHL	36	29	*47	*76	....	....	....	4	....	....	....	....	....	....	....	....	....	....	13	4	6	10	0	....	....	....
1953-54	Edmonton Oil Kings	WCJHL	36	56	45	101	....	....	....	17	....	....	....	....	....	....	....	....	....	....	10	11	*26	*37	0	....	....	....
	Edmonton Flyers	WHL	1	1	0	1	....	....	....	0	....	....	....	....	....	....	....	....	....	....	....	....	....	....	....	....	....	....
1954-55	Edmonton Flyers	WHL	60	25	34	59	....	....	....	23	....	....	....	....	....	....	....	....	....	....	9	3	1	4	6	....	....	....
1955-56	**Detroit Red Wings**	**NHL**	**66**	**9**	**9**	**18**	**13**	**11**	**24**	**26**	....	....	....	....	....	....	....	....	....	....	**10**	**1**	**3**	**4**	**13**	....	....	....
1956-57	**Detroit Red Wings**	**NHL**	**64**	**16**	**36**	**52**	**22**	**42**	**64**	**47**	....	....	....	....	....	....	....	....	....	....	**5**	**1**	**1**	**2**	**6**	....	....	....
1957-58	**Detroit Red Wings**	**NHL**	**69**	**23**	**28**	**51**	**30**	**31**	**61**	**38**	....	....	....	....	....	....	....	....	....	....	**4**	**0**	**2**	**2**	**4**	....	....	....
1958-59	**Detroit Red Wings**	**NHL**	**69**	**22**	**36**	**58**	**28**	**39**	**67**	**42**	....	....	....	....	....	....	....	....	....	....	....	....	....	....	....	....	....	....
1959-60	**Detroit Red Wings**	**NHL**	**70**	**24**	**34**	**58**	**30**	**35**	**65**	**46**	....	....	....	....	....	....	....	....	....	....	**6**	**2**	**2**	**4**	**0**	....	....	....
1960-61	**Detroit Red Wings**	**NHL**	**70**	**28**	**42**	**70**	**34**	**43**	**77**	**34**	....	....	....	....	....	....	....	....	....	....	**11**	**0**	**4**	**4**	**4**	....	....	....
1961-62	**Detroit Red Wings**	**NHL**	**70**	**26**	**38**	**64**	**32**	**39**	**71**	**54**	....	....	....	....	....	....	....	....	....	....	....	....	....	....	....	....	....	....
1962-63	**Detroit Red Wings**	**NHL**	**70**	**26**	**30**	**56**	**32**	**31**	**63**	**53**	....	....	....	....	....	....	....	....	....	....	**11**	**4**	***12**	***16**	**14**	....	....	....
1963-64	**Detroit Red Wings**	**NHL**	**61**	**21**	**30**	**51**	**28**	**33**	**61**	**55**	....	....	....	....	....	....	....	....	....	....	**14**	**7**	**10**	**17**	**6**	....	....	....
1964-65	**Detroit Red Wings**	**NHL**	**70**	***42**	**41**	**83**	**55**	**45**	**100**	**70**	....	....	....	....	....	....	....	....	....	....	**7**	**6**	**4**	**10**	**2**	....	....	....
1965-66	**Detroit Red Wings**	**NHL**	**70**	**31**	**41**	**72**	**38**	**41**	**79**	**35**	....	....	....	....	....	....	....	....	....	....	**12**	***6**	**9**	***15**	**12**	....	....	....
1966-67	**Detroit Red Wings**	**NHL**	**68**	**26**	**44**	**70**	**32**	**46**	**78**	**26**	....	....	....	....	....	....	....	....	....	....	....	....	....	....	....	....	....	....
1967-68	**Detroit Red Wings**	**NHL**	**58**	**30**	**25**	**55**	**37**	**26**	**63**	**26**	**7**	**0**	**4**	**189**	**15.9**	**68**	**16**	**77**	**12**	**–13**	....	....	....	....	....	....	....	....
	Toronto Maple Leafs	**NHL**	**13**	**5**	**12**	**17**	**6**	**13**	**19**	**2**	**1**	**0**	**0**	**39**	**12.8**	**21**	**2**	**7**	**0**	**+12**	....	....	....	....	....	....	....	....
1968-69	**Toronto Maple Leafs**	**NHL**	**75**	**35**	**42**	**77**	**40**	**40**	**80**	**41**	**13**	**0**	**2**	**247**	**14.2**	**99**	**26**	**55**	**1**	**+19**	**4**	**1**	**0**	**1**	**0**	**0**	**0**	**0**
1969-70	**Toronto Maple Leafs**	**NHL**	**74**	**18**	**42**	**60**	**21**	**42**	**63**	**37**	**4**	**1**	**0**	**207**	**8.7**	**90**	**20**	**55**	**5**	**+20**	....	....	....	....	....	....	....	....
1970-71	**Toronto Maple Leafs**	**NHL**	**73**	**34**	**51**	**85**	**36**	**45**	**81**	**24**	**11**	**1**	**4**	**226**	**15.0**	**104**	**29**	**66**	**5**	**+14**	**6**	**0**	**2**	**2**	**2**	**0**	**0**	**0**
1971-72	**Toronto Maple Leafs**	**NHL**	**77**	**23**	**50**	**73**	**25**	**46**	**71**	**26**	**9**	**0**	**1**	**204**	**11.3**	**97**	**31**	**64**	**6**	**+8**	**5**	**1**	**3**	**4**	**2**	**0**	**0**	**0**
1972-73	**Toronto Maple Leafs**	**NHL**	**65**	**20**	**35**	**55**	**20**	**29**	**49**	**10**	**3**	**0**	**1**	**174**	**11.5**	**77**	**14**	**85**	**4**	**–18**	....	....	....	....	....	....	....	....
1973-74	**Toronto Maple Leafs**	**NHL**	**78**	**22**	**47**	**69**	**22**	**41**	**63**	**12**	**4**	**0**	**2**	**178**	**12.4**	**86**	**17**	**59**	**0**	**+10**	**4**	**1**	**1**	**2**	**0**	**0**	**0**	**0**
1974-75	**Toronto Maple Leafs**	**NHL**	**80**	**9**	**26**	**35**	**8**	**20**	**28**	**8**	**1**	**0**	**0**	**117**	**7.7**	**54**	**13**	**62**	**9**	**–12**	**7**	**0**	**0**	**0**	**2**	**0**	**0**	**0**
1975-76	Edmonton Oilers	WHA	77	31	56	87	....	....	....	12	....	....	....	....	....	....	....	....	....	....	4	1	3	4	2	....	....	....
1976-77	Edmonton Oilers	WHA	67	16	27	43	....	....	....	28	....	....	....	....	....	....	....	....	....	....	5	0	3	3	0	....	....	....
	NHL Totals		**1410**	**490**	**739**	**1229**	**589**	**738**	**1327**	**712**	**53**	**2**	**14**	**1581**	**31.0**	**696**	**168**	**530**	**42**		**106**	**30**	**53**	**83**	**67**	**0**	**0**	**0**
	Other Major League Totals		144	47	83	130	....	....	....	40	....	....	....	....	....	....	....	....	....		9	1	6	7	2	....	....	....

NHL First All-Star Team (1965) • NHL Second All-Star Team (1967)

Played in NHL All-Star Game (1955, 1960, 1961, 1962, 1963, 1964, 1965, 1967, 1968, 1969, 1974)

Traded to **Toronto** by **Detroit** with Floyd Smith and Paul Henderson for Frank Mahovlich, Pete Stemkowski, Garry Unger and the rights to Carl Brewer, March 3, 1968. Selected by **Edmonton** (WHA) in 1972 General Player Draft, February 12, 1972.

• UNGER, GARRY

Garry "Iron Man" Unger C – L. 5'11", 170 lbs. b: Calgary, Alta., 12/7/1947.

Season	Club	League	GP	G	A	Pts	AG	AA	APts	PIM	PP	SH	GW	S	%	TGF	PGF	TGA	PGA	+/–	GP	G	A	Pts	PIM	PP	SH	GW
1966-67	London Nationals	OHA	48	38	35	73	....	....	....	60	....	....	....	....	....	....	....	....	....	....	6	2	5	7	27	....	....	....
	Rochester Americans	AHL	1	0	0	0	....	....	....	0	....	....	....	....	....	....	....	....	....	....	1	0	0	0	0	....	....	....
	Tulsa Oilers	CHL	2	2	0	2	....	....	....	2	....	....	....	....	....	....	....	....	....	....	....	....	....	....	....	....	....	....
1967-68	London Nationals	OHA	2	4	1	5	....	....	....	2	....	....	....	....	....	....	....	....	....	....	....	....	....	....	....	....	....	....
	Toronto Maple Leafs	**NHL**	**15**	**1**	**1**	**2**	**1**	**1**	**2**	**4**	**0**	**0**	**0**	**15**	**6.7**	**3**	**1**	**7**	**0**	**–5**	....	....	....	....	....	....	....	....
	Tulsa Oilers	CHL	9	3	5	8	....	....	....	6	....	....	....	....	....	....	....	....	....	....	....	....	....	....	....	....	....	....
	Rochester Americans	AHL	5	1	3	4	....	....	....	6	....	....	....	....	....	....	....	....	....	....	....	....	....	....	....	....	....	....
	Detroit Red Wings	**NHL**	**13**	**5**	**10**	**15**	**6**	**10**	**16**	**2**	**0**	**0**	**0**	**42**	**11.9**	**20**	**3**	**13**	**0**	**+4**	....	....	....	....	....	....	....	....
1968-69	**Detroit Red Wings**	**NHL**	**76**	**24**	**20**	**44**	**27**	**19**	**46**	**33**	**5**	**1**	**4**	**186**	**12.9**	**71**	**20**	**48**	**3**	**+6**	....	....	....	....	....	....	....	....
1969-70	**Detroit Red Wings**	**NHL**	**76**	**42**	**24**	**66**	**49**	**24**	**73**	**67**	**12**	**0**	**4**	**234**	**17.9**	**89**	**19**	**46**	**0**	**+24**	**4**	**0**	**1**	**1**	**6**	**0**	**0**	**0**
1970-71	**Detroit Red Wings**	**NHL**	**51**	**13**	**14**	**27**	**14**	**12**	**26**	**63**	**0**	**0**	**1**	**157**	**8.3**	**35**	**6**	**64**	**3**	**–32**	....	....	....	....	....	....	....	....
	St. Louis Blues	**NHL**	**28**	**15**	**14**	**29**	**16**	**12**	**28**	**41**	**7**	**0**	**3**	**122**	**12.3**	**36**	**18**	**22**	**0**	**–4**	**6**	**3**	**2**	**5**	**20**	**0**	**1**	**0**
1971-72	**St. Louis Blues**	**NHL**	**78**	**36**	**34**	**70**	**39**	**31**	**70**	**104**	**14**	**1**	**4**	**321**	**11.2**	**96**	**28**	**83**	**7**	**–8**	**11**	**4**	**5**	**9**	**35**	**2**	**0**	**1**
1972-73	**St. Louis Blues**	**NHL**	**78**	**41**	**39**	**80**	**41**	**33**	**74**	**119**	**13**	**1**	**5**	**342**	**12.0**	**103**	**34**	**69**	**7**	**+7**	**5**	**1**	**2**	**3**	**2**	**0**	**0**	**0**
1973-74	**St. Louis Blues**	**NHL**	**78**	**33**	**35**	**68**	**34**	**30**	**64**	**96**	**9**	**1**	**4**	**327**	**10.1**	**93**	**36**	**83**	**9**	**–17**	....	....	....	....	....	....	....	....
1974-75	**St. Louis Blues**	**NHL**	**80**	**36**	**44**	**80**	**33**	**35**	**68**	**123**	**10**	**0**	**8**	**349**	**10.3**	**100**	**34**	**83**	**16**	**–1**	**2**	**1**	**3**	**4**	**6**	**0**	**0**	**0**
1975-76	**St. Louis Blues**	**NHL**	**80**	**39**	**44**	**83**	**36**	**35**	**71**	**95**	**13**	**0**	**3**	**357**	**10.9**	**110**	**43**	**79**	**13**	**+1**	**3**	**2**	**1**	**3**	**7**	**0**	**0**	**0**
1976-77	**St. Louis Blues**	**NHL**	**80**	**30**	**27**	**57**	**29**	**22**	**51**	**56**	**7**	**0**	**5**	**235**	**12.8**	**85**	**33**	**66**	**2**	**–12**	**4**	**0**	**1**	**1**	**2**	**0**	**0**	**0**
1977-78	**St. Louis Blues**	**NHL**	**80**	**32**	**20**	**52**	**31**	**16**	**47**	**66**	**10**	**0**	**5**	**238**	**13.4**	**69**	**25**	**82**	**3**	**–35**	....	....	....	....	....	....	....	....
	Canada	WEC-A	10	0	0	0	....	....	....	30	....	....	....	....	....	....	....	....	....	....	....	....	....	....	....	....	....	....
1978-79	**St. Louis Blues**	**NHL**	**80**	**30**	**26**	**56**	**27**	**20**	**47**	**44**	**3**	**0**	**3**	**182**	**16.5**	**84**	**19**	**113**	**4**	**–44**	....	....	....	....	....	....	....	....
	Canada	WEC-A	7	2	1	3	....	....	....	12	....	....	....	....	....	....	....	....	....	....	....	....	....	....	....	....	....	....
1979-80	**Atlanta Flames**	**NHL**	**79**	**17**	**16**	**33**	**15**	**12**	**27**	**39**	**1**	**0**	**3**	**170**	**10.0**	**55**	**9**	**51**	**7**	**+2**	**4**	**0**	**3**	**3**	**2**	**0**	**0**	**0**
1980-81	**Los Angeles Kings**	**NHL**	**58**	**10**	**10**	**20**	**8**	**7**	**15**	**40**	**1**	**0**	**0**	**67**	**14.9**	**29**	**3**	**43**	**0**	**–17**	....	....	....	....	....	....	....	....
	Edmonton Oilers	**NHL**	**13**	**0**	**0**	**0**	**0**	**0**	**0**	**6**	**0**	**0**	**0**	**13**	**0.0**	**1**	**1**	**9**	**0**	**–9**	**8**	**0**	**0**	**0**	**2**	**0**	**0**	**0**
1981-82	**Edmonton Oilers**	**NHL**	**46**	**7**	**13**	**20**	**6**	**9**	**15**	**69**	**0**	**0**	**2**	**62**	**11.3**	**32**	**4**	**30**	**10**	**+8**	**4**	**1**	**0**	**1**	**23**	**0**	**0**	**0**

			REGULAR SEASON																		PLAYOFFS							
Season	Club	League	GP	G	A	Pts	AG	AA	APts	PIM	PP	SH	GW	S	%	TGF	PGF	TGA	PGA	+/–	GP	G	A	Pts	PIM	PP	SH	GW
1982-83	**Edmonton Oilers**	**NHL**	**16**	**2**	**0**	**2**	**2**	**0**	**2**	**8**	**0**	**0**	**0**	**14**	**14.3**	**4**	**1**	**4**	**2**	**+1**	**1**	**0**	**0**	**0**	**0**	**0**	**0**	**0**
	Moncton Alpines	AHL	8	2	3	5	....	....	....	0	....	....	....	....	....	....	....	....	....	....	....	....	....	....	....	....	....	....
1983-84			DID NOT PLAY																									
1984-85			DID NOT PLAY																									
1985-86	Dundee Rockets	Britain	35	86	48	134	....	....	....	64	....	....	....	....	....	....	....	....	....	....	6	7	6	13	44	....	....	....
1986-87	Peterborough Pirates	Britain	30	95	*143	*238	....	....	....	58	....	....	....	....	....	....	....	....	....	....	8	17	15	32	38	....	....	....
	NHL Totals		**1105**	**413**	**391**	**804**	**414**	**328**	**742**	**1075**	**105**	**4**	**54**	**3433**	**12.0**	**1115**	**337**	**995**	**86**		**52**	**12**	**18**	**30**	**105**	**2**	**1**	**1**

Played in NHL All-Star Game (1972, 1973, 1974, 1975, 1976, 1977, 1978)

Traded to **Detroit** by **Toronto** with Frank Mahovlich, Pete Stemkowski and rights to Carl Brewer for Norm Ullman, Paul Henderson and Floyd Smith, March 3, 1968. Traded to **St. Louis** by **Detroit** with Wayne Connelly for Red Berenson and Tim Eccelstone, February 6, 1971. Traded to **Atlanta** by **St. Louis** for Ed Kea, Don Laurence and Atlanta's 2nd round choice (Hakan Nordin) in 1981 Entry Draft, October 10, 1979. Transferred to **Calgary** after **Atlanta** franchise relocated, June 24, 1980. Traded to **LA Kings** by **Calgary** for Bert Wilson and Randy Holt, June 6, 1980. Traded to **Edmonton** by **LA Kings** for Edmonton's 7th round choice (Craig Hurley) in 1981 Entry Draft, March 10, 1981.

• USTORF, STEFAN

Stefan Ustorf C – L. 6', 185 lbs. b: Kaufbeuren, Germany, 1/3/1974. Washington's 3rd choice, 53rd overall, in 1992 Entry Draft.

Season	Club	League	GP	G	A	Pts	AG	AA	APts	PIM	PP	SH	GW	S	%	TGF	PGF	TGA	PGA	+/–	GP	G	A	Pts	PIM	PP	SH	GW
1990-91	Kaufbeuren Jr. Eagles	Germany	37	33	34	67	....	....	....	78	....	....	....	....	....	....	....	....	....	....	....	....	....	....	....	....	....	....
	Germany	WJC-B	7	5	5	10	....	....	....	2	....	....	....	....	....	....	....	....	....	....	....	....	....	....	....	....	....	....
1991-92	Kaufbeuren Eagles	Germany	41	2	22	24	....	....	....	46	....	....	....	....	....	....	....	....	....	....	5	2	7	9	6	....	....	....
	Germany	WJC-A	5	0	2	2	....	....	....	4	....	....	....	....	....	....	....	....	....	....	....	....	....	....	....	....	....	....
	Germany	WO-A	6	1	1	2	....	....	....	0	....	....	....	....	....	....	....	....	....	....	....	....	....	....	....	....	....	....
1992-93	Kaufbeuren Eagles	Germany	37	14	18	32	....	....	....	32	....	....	....	....	....	....	....	....	....	....	3	1	0	1	10	....	....	....
	Germany	WC-A	4	1	1	2	....	....	....	26	....	....	....	....	....	....	....	....	....	....	....	....	....	....	....	....	....	....
1993-94	Kaufbeuren Eagles	Germany	38	10	20	30	....	....	....	21	....	....	....	....	....	....	....	....	....	....	3	0	0	0	4	....	....	....
	Germany	WJC-A	7	3	3	4	....	....	....	2	....	....	....	....	....	....	....	....	....	....	....	....	....	....	....	....	....	....
	Germany	Olympics	8	1	2	3	....	....	....	2	....	....	....	....	....	....	....	....	....	....	....	....	....	....	....	....	....	....
1994-95	Portland Pirates	AHL	63	21	38	59	....	....	....	51	....	....	....	....	....	....	....	....	....	....	7	1	6	7	7	....	....	....
1995-96	**Washington Capitals**	**NHL**	**48**	**7**	**10**	**17**	**7**	**8**	**15**	**14**	**0**	**0**	**1**	**39**	**17.9**	**26**	**1**	**18**	**1**	**+8**	**5**	**0**	**0**	**0**	**0**	**0**	**0**	**0**
	Portland Pirates	AHL	8	1	4	5	....	....	....	6	....	....	....	....	....	....	....	....	....	....	....	....	....	....	....	....	....	....
1996-97	Germany	W Cup	4	0	2	2	....	....	....	2	....	....	....	....	....	....	....	....	....	....	....	....	....	....	....	....	....	....
	Washington Capitals	**NHL**	**6**	**0**	**0**	**0**	**0**	**0**	**0**	**2**	**0**	**0**	**0**	**7**	**0.0**	**0**	**0**	**3**	**0**	**–3**	....	....	....	....	....	....	....	....
	Portland Pirates	AHL	36	7	17	24	....	....	....	27	....	....	....	....	....	....	....	....	....	....	....	....	....	....	....	....	....	....
1997-98	Berlin Capitals	Germany	45	17	23	40	....	....	....	54	....	....	....	....	....	....	....	....	....	....	....	....	....	....	....	....	....	....
	Germany	Olympics	4	0	0	0	....	....	....	0	....	....	....	....	....	....	....	....	....	....	....	....	....	....	....	....	....	....
	NHL Totals		**54**	**7**	**10**	**17**	**7**	**8**	**15**	**16**	**0**	**0**	**1**	**46**	**15.2**	**26**	**1**	**21**	**1**		**5**	**0**	**0**	**0**	**0**	**0**	**0**	**0**

• VACHON, NICK

Nick Vachon C – L. 5'10", 185 lbs. b: Montreal, Que., 7/20/1972. Toronto's 11th choice, 241st overall, in 1990 Entry Draft.

Season	Club	League	GP	G	A	Pts	AG	AA	APts	PIM	PP	SH	GW	S	%	TGF	PGF	TGA	PGA	+/–	GP	G	A	Pts	PIM	PP	SH	GW
1989-90	Govenor Dummer High School	H.S.	20	20	22	42	....	....	....	....	....	....	....	....	....	....	....	....	....	....	....	....	....	....	....	....	....	....
1990-91	Boston University	H.E.	8	0	1	1	....	....	....	4	....	....	....	....	....	....	....	....	....	....	....	....	....	....	....	....	....	....
1991-92	Boston University	H.E.	16	6	7	13	....	....	....	10	....	....	....	....	....	....	....	....	....	....	....	....	....	....	....	....	....	....
	Portland Winter Hawks	WHL	25	9	19	28	....	....	....	46	....	....	....	....	....	....	....	....	....	....	6	0	3	3	14	....	....	....
1992-93	Portland Winter Hawks	WHL	66	33	58	91	....	....	....	100	....	....	....	....	....	....	....	....	....	....	16	11	7	18	34	....	....	....
1993-94	Atlanta Knights	IHL	3	1	1	2	....	....	....	0	....	....	....	....	....	....	....	....	....	....	....	....	....	....	....	....	....	....
	Knoxville Cherokees	ECHL	61	29	57	86	....	....	....	139	....	....	....	....	....	....	....	....	....	....	3	0	0	0	2	....	....	....
1994-95	Phoenix Roadrunners	IHL	64	13	26	39	....	....	....	137	....	....	....	....	....	....	....	....	....	....	9	1	2	3	24	....	....	....
1995-96	Phoenix Roadrunners	IHL	73	13	17	30	....	....	....	168	....	....	....	....	....	....	....	....	....	....	1	0	0	0	2	....	....	....
1996-97	Phoenix Roadrunners	IHL	16	3	3	6	....	....	....	18	....	....	....	....	....	....	....	....	....	....	....	....	....	....	....	....	....	....
	New York Islanders	**NHL**	**1**	**0**	**0**	**0**	**0**	**0**	**0**	**0**	**0**	**0**	**0**	**0**	**0.0**	**0**	**0**	**1**	**0**	**–1**	....	....	....	....	....	....	....	....
	Utah Grizzlies	IHL	33	3	5	8	....	....	....	110	....	....	....	....	....	....	....	....	....	....	....	....	....	....	....	....	....	....
	Long Beach Ice Dogs	IHL	13	1	2	3	....	....	....	42	....	....	....	....	....	....	....	....	....	....	18	1	2	3	43	....	....	....
1997-98	Springfield Falcons	AHL	7	0	0	0	....	....	....	16	....	....	....	....	....	....	....	....	....	....	....	....	....	....	....	....	....	....
	Long Beach Ice Dogs	IHL	56	3	6	9	....	....	....	113	....	....	....	....	....	....	....	....	....	....	....	....	....	....	....	....	....	....
	NHL Totals		**1**	**0**	**0**	**0**	**0**	**0**	**0**	**0**	**0**	**0**	**0**	**0**	**0.0**	**0**	**0**	**1**	**0**		....	....	....	....	....	....	....	....

Signed as a free agent by **LA Kings**, September 12, 1995. Traded to **NY Islanders** by **LA Kings** for Chris Marinucci, November 19, 1996.

• VADNAIS, CAROL

Carol Vadnais LW – L. 6'1", 185 lbs. b: Montreal, Que., 9/25/1945.

Season	Club	League	GP	G	A	Pts	AG	AA	APts	PIM	PP	SH	GW	S	%	TGF	PGF	TGA	PGA	+/–	GP	G	A	Pts	PIM	PP	SH	GW
1963-64	Notre Dame Monarchs	QJHL	44	39	49	88	....	....	....	90	....	....	....	....	....	....	....	....	....	....	....	....	....	....	....	....	....	....
1964-65	Montreal Jr. Canadiens	OHA	56	9	16	25	....	....	....	74	....	....	....	....	....	....	....	....	....	....	7	1	0	1	13	....	....	....
1965-66	Montreal Jr. Canadiens	OHA	48	9	14	23	....	....	....	184	....	....	....	....	....	....	....	....	....	....	10	1	4	5	24	....	....	....
1966-67	**Montreal Canadiens**	**NHL**	**11**	**0**	**3**	**3**	**0**	**3**	**3**	**35**	....	....	....	....	....	....	....	....	....	....	**1**	**0**	**0**	**0**	**2**	....	....	....
	Houston Apollos	CHL	21	5	5	10	....	....	....	45	....	....	....	....	....	....	....	....	....	....	....	....	....	....	....	....	....	....
1967-68	**Montreal Canadiens**	**NHL**	**31**	**1**	**1**	**2**	**1**	**1**	**2**	**31**	**0**	**0**	**0**	**25**	**4.0**	**14**	**2**	**18**	**4**	**–2**	**1**	**0**	**0**	**0**	**0**	**0**	**0**	**0**
	Houston Apollos	CHL	36	5	21	26	....	....	....	178	....	....	....	....	....	....	....	....	....	....	....	....	....	....	....	....	....	....
1968-69	**Oakland Seals**	**NHL**	**76**	**15**	**27**	**42**	**17**	**25**	**42**	**151**	**4**	**0**	**4**	**274**	**5.5**	**118**	**28**	**133**	**25**	**–18**	**7**	**1**	**4**	**5**	**10**	**1**	**0**	**0**
1969-70	**Oakland Seals**	**NHL**	**76**	**24**	**20**	**44**	**28**	**20**	**48**	**212**	**7**	**0**	**0**	**245**	**9.8**	**81**	**29**	**103**	**27**	**–24**	**4**	**2**	**1**	**3**	**15**	**2**	**0**	**0**
1970-71	**California Golden Seals**	**NHL**	**42**	**10**	**16**	**26**	**10**	**14**	**24**	**91**	**3**	**1**	**3**	**146**	**6.8**	**61**	**16**	**63**	**15**	**–3**	....	....	....	....	....	....	....	....
1971-72	**California Golden Seals**	**NHL**	**52**	**14**	**20**	**34**	**15**	**18**	**33**	**106**	**7**	**0**	**2**	**139**	**10.1**	**86**	**27**	**104**	**25**	**–20**	....	....	....	....	....	....	....	....
	Boston Bruins	**NHL**	**16**	**4**	**6**	**10**	**4**	**5**	**9**	**37**	**0**	**0**	**0**	**37**	**10.8**	**36**	**3**	**41**	**10**	**+2**	**15**	**0**	**2**	**2**	**43**	**0**	**0**	**0**
1972-73	**Boston Bruins**	**NHL**	**78**	**7**	**24**	**31**	**7**	**20**	**27**	**127**	**1**	**0**	**3**	**150**	**4.7**	**117**	**8**	**98**	**10**	**+21**	**5**	**0**	**0**	**0**	**8**	**0**	**0**	**0**
1973-74	**Boston Bruins**	**NHL**	**78**	**16**	**43**	**59**	**16**	**37**	**53**	**123**	**6**	**0**	**1**	**187**	**8.6**	**175**	**57**	**100**	**17**	**+35**	**16**	**1**	**12**	**13**	**42**	**1**	**0**	**0**
1974-75	**Boston Bruins**	**NHL**	**79**	**18**	**56**	**74**	**17**	**44**	**61**	**129**	**6**	**0**	**2**	**256**	**7.0**	**181**	**68**	**127**	**24**	**+10**	**3**	**1**	**5**	**6**	**0**	**0**	**0**	**0**
1975-76	**Boston Bruins**	**NHL**	**12**	**2**	**5**	**7**	**2**	**4**	**6**	**17**	**1**	**0**	**0**	**33**	**6.1**	**23**	**8**	**23**	**9**	**+1**	....	....	....	....	....	....	....	....
	New York Rangers	**NHL**	**64**	**20**	**30**	**50**	**19**	**24**	**43**	**104**	**7**	**0**	**1**	**197**	**10.2**	**145**	**49**	**143**	**30**	**–17**	....	....	....	....	....	....	....	....
1976-77	Canada	C Cup	DID NOT PLAY																									
	New York Rangers	**NHL**	**74**	**11**	**37**	**48**	**11**	**30**	**41**	**131**	**3**	**1**	**0**	**169**	**6.5**	**138**	**46**	**149**	**37**	**–20**	....	....	....	....	....	....	....	....
	Canada	WEC-A	10	3	1	4	....	....	....	33	....	....	....	....	....	....	....	....	....	....	....	....	....	....	....	....	....	....
1977-78	**New York Rangers**	**NHL**	**80**	**6**	**40**	**46**	**6**	**33**	**39**	**115**	**3**	**1**	**1**	**164**	**3.7**	**140**	**59**	**141**	**35**	**–25**	**3**	**0**	**2**	**2**	**16**	**0**	**0**	**0**
1978-79	**New York Rangers**	**NHL**	**77**	**8**	**37**	**45**	**7**	**28**	**35**	**86**	**4**	**1**	**1**	**149**	**5.4**	**116**	**37**	**111**	**46**	**+14**	**18**	**2**	**9**	**11**	**13**	**0**	**0**	**0**
1979-80	**New York Rangers**	**NHL**	**66**	**3**	**20**	**23**	**3**	**15**	**18**	**118**	**1**	**0**	**1**	**82**	**3.7**	**86**	**15**	**97**	**25**	**–1**	**9**	**1**	**2**	**3**	**6**	**0**	**0**	**0**
1980-81	**New York Rangers**	**NHL**	**74**	**3**	**20**	**23**	**2**	**14**	**16**	**91**	**1**	**0**	**0**	**118**	**2.5**	**86**	**9**	**102**	**44**	**+19**	**14**	**1**	**3**	**4**	**26**	**0**	**0**	**0**
1981-82	**New York Rangers**	**NHL**	**50**	**5**	**6**	**11**	**4**	**4**	**8**	**45**	**1**	**0**	**0**	**43**	**11.6**	**47**	**2**	**70**	**23**	**–2**	**10**	**1**	**0**	**1**	**4**	**0**	**0**	**0**
1982-83	**New Jersey Devils**	**NHL**	**51**	**2**	**7**	**9**	**2**	**5**	**7**	**64**	**1**	**0**	**0**	**33**	**6.1**	**37**	**5**	**81**	**17**	**–32**	....	....	....	....	....	....	....	....
	NHL Totals		**1087**	**169**	**418**	**587**	**171**	**344**	**515**	**1813**	**56**	**4**	**19**	**2447**	**6.9**	**1687**	**468**	**1704**	**423**		**106**	**10**	**40**	**50**	**185**	**4**	**0**	**0**

Played in NHL All-Star Game (1969, 1970, 1972, 1975, 1976, 1978)

Claimed by **Oakland** from **Montreal** in Intra-League Draft, June 12, 1968 Traded to **Boston** by **California** with Don O'Donoghue for Reggie Leach, Rick Smith and Bob Stewart, February 23, 1972. Traded to **NY Rangers** by **Boston** with Phil Esposito for Brad Park, Jean Ratalle and Joe Zanussi, November 7, 1975. Claimed by **New Jersey** from **Boston** in Waiver Draft, June, 1982.

• VAIC, LUBOMIR

Lubomir Vaic C – L. 5'9", 178 lbs. b: Spisska Nova Ves, Czech., 3/6/1977. Vancouver's 8th choice, 227th overall, in 1996 Entry Draft.

Season	Club	League	GP	G	A	Pts	AG	AA	APts	PIM	PP	SH	GW	S	%	TGF	PGF	TGA	PGA	+/–	GP	G	A	Pts	PIM	PP	SH	GW
1993-94	SKP PS Poprad	Slovakia	28	10	6	16	....	....	....	10	....	....	....	....	....	....	....	....	....	....	....	....	....	....	....	....	....	....
	Slovakia	WJC-C	4	3	2	5	....	....	....	2	....	....	....	....	....	....	....	....	....	....	....	....	....	....	....	....	....	....
1994-95	Spisska Nova Ves	Slovakia	19	5	4	9	....	....	....	2	....	....	....	....	....	....	....	....	....	....	....	....	....	....	....	....	....	....
1995-96	HC Kosice	Slovakia	36	7	19	26	....	....	....	10	....	....	....	....	....	....	....	....	....	....	13	0	7	7	....	....	....	....
	Slovakia	WJC-A	6	2	4	6	....	....	....	25	....	....	....	....	....	....	....	....	....	....	....	....	....	....	....	....	....	....
1996-97	HC Kosice	Slovakia	36	13	12	25	....	....	....	....	....	....	....	....	....	....	....	....	....	....	7	2	0	2	....	....	....	....
	Slovakia	WJC-A	6	1	7	8	....	....	....	10	....	....	....	....	....	....	....	....	....	....	....	....	....	....	....	....	....	....
1997-98	**Vancouver Canucks**	**NHL**	**5**	**1**	**1**	**2**	**1**	**1**	**2**	**2**	**0**	**0**	**0**	**8**	**12.5**	**3**	**0**	**5**	**0**	**–2**	....	....	....	....	....	....	....	....
	Syracuse Crunch	AHL	50	12	15	27	....	....	....	22	....	....	....	....	....	....	....	....	....	....	3	0	0	0	4	....	....	....
	NHL Totals		**5**	**1**	**1**	**2**	**1**	**1**	**2**	**2**	**0**	**0**	**0**	**8**	**12.5**	**3**	**0**	**5**	**0**		....	....	....	....	....	....	....	....

● VAIL, ERIC Eric "Big Train" Vail LW – L. 6'1", 220 lbs. b: Timmins, Ont., 9/16/1953. Atlanta's 3rd choice, 21st overall, in 1973 Amateur Draft.

			REGULAR SEASON																		PLAYOFFS							
Season	Club	League	GP	G	A	Pts	AG	AA	APts	PIM	PP	SH	GW	S	%	TGF	PGF	TGA	PGA	+/–	GP	G	A	Pts	PIM	PP	SH	GW
1970-71	Niagara Falls Flyers	OHA	59	18	30	48	....	....	....	76	....	....	....	....	....	....	....	....	....	....	....	....	....	....	....	....	....	....
1971-72	Niagara Falls Flyers	OHA	60	25	48	73	....	....	....	122	....	....	....	....	....	....	....	....	....	....	....	....	....	....	....	....	....	....
1972-73	Sault Ste. Marie Greyhounds	OHA	38	29	31	60	....	....	....	50	....	....	....	....	....	....	....	....	....	....	....	....	....	....	....	....	....	....
	Sudbury Wolves	OHA	25	19	26	45	....	....	....	30	....	....	....	....	....	....	....	....	....	....	....	....	....	....	....	....	....	....
1973-74	**Atlanta Flames**	**NHL**	**23**	**2**	**9**	**11**	**2**	**8**	**10**	**30**	**2**	**0**	**1**	**44**	**4.5**	**18**	**4**	**12**	**0**	**+2**	**1**	**0**	**0**	**0**	**2**	**0**	**0**	**0**
	Omaha Knights	CHL	37	10	18	28	....	....	....	54	....	....	....	....	....	....	....	....	....	....	....	....	....	....	....	....	....	....
1974-75	**Atlanta Flames**	**NHL**	**72**	**39**	**21**	**60**	**36**	**17**	**53**	**46**	**6**	**0**	**4**	**177**	**22.0**	**79**	**24**	**56**	**2**	**+1**	....	....	....	....	....	....	....	....
1975-76	**Atlanta Flames**	**NHL**	**60**	**16**	**31**	**47**	**15**	**24**	**39**	**34**	**2**	**0**	**1**	**127**	**12.6**	**75**	**21**	**49**	**2**	**+7**	**2**	**0**	**0**	**0**	**0**	**0**	**0**	**0**
1976-77	**Atlanta Flames**	**NHL**	**78**	**32**	**39**	**71**	**31**	**32**	**63**	**22**	**12**	**1**	**3**	**208**	**15.4**	**107**	**26**	**76**	**4**	**+9**	**3**	**1**	**3**	**4**	**0**	**0**	**0**	**1**
	Canada	WEC-A	9	4	1	5	....	....	....	18	....	....	....	....	....	....	....	....	....	....	....	....	....	....	....	....	....	....
1977-78	**Atlanta Flames**	**NHL**	**79**	**22**	**36**	**58**	**21**	**29**	**50**	**16**	**8**	**0**	**6**	**178**	**12.4**	**98**	**29**	**68**	**2**	**+3**	**2**	**1**	**1**	**2**	**0**	**0**	**0**	**0**
1978-79	**Atlanta Flames**	**NHL**	**80**	**35**	**48**	**83**	**32**	**37**	**69**	**53**	**5**	**1**	**5**	**203**	**17.2**	**139**	**37**	**83**	**6**	**+25**	**2**	**0**	**1**	**1**	**2**	**0**	**0**	**0**
1979-80	**Atlanta Flames**	**NHL**	**77**	**28**	**25**	**53**	**25**	**19**	**44**	**22**	**6**	**0**	**3**	**193**	**14.5**	**98**	**23**	**75**	**5**	**+5**	**4**	**3**	**1**	**4**	**2**	**1**	**0**	**1**
1980-81	**Calgary Flames**	**NHL**	**64**	**28**	**36**	**64**	**23**	**25**	**48**	**23**	**12**	**0**	**6**	**164**	**17.1**	**92**	**32**	**57**	**5**	**+8**	**6**	**0**	**0**	**0**	**0**	**0**	**0**	**0**
1981-82	**Calgary Flames**	**NHL**	**6**	**4**	**1**	**5**	**3**	**1**	**4**	**0**	**1**	**0**	**0**	**8**	**50.0**	**7**	**4**	**4**	**0**	**–1**	....	....	....	....	....	....	....	....
	Oklahoma City Stars	CHL	3	0	3	3	....	....	....	0	....	....	....	....	....	....	....	....	....	....	....	....	....	....	....	....	....	....
	Detroit Red Wings	**NHL**	**52**	**10**	**14**	**24**	**8**	**9**	**17**	**35**	**3**	**0**	**0**	**86**	**11.6**	**43**	**15**	**54**	**5**	**–21**	....	....	....	....	....	....	....	....
	Adirondack Red Wings	AHL	10	3	4	7	....	....	....	0	....	....	....	....	....	....	....	....	....	....	....	....	....	....	....	....	....	....
1982-83	Adirondack Red Wings	AHL	74	20	29	49	....	....	....	33	....	....	....	....	....	....	....	....	....	....	5	1	1	2	0	....	....	....
	NHL Totals		**591**	**216**	**260**	**476**	**196**	**201**	**397**	**281**	**57**	**2**	**29**	**1388**	**15.6**	**756**	**215**	**534**	**31**		**20**	**5**	**6**	**11**	**6**	**1**	**0**	**2**

Won Calder Memorial Trophy (1975)

Played in NHL All-Star Game (1977)

Transferred to **Calgary** after **Atlanta** franchise relocated, June 24, 1980. Traded to **Detroit** by **Calgary** for Gary McAdam and Detroit's 4th round choice (John Bekkers) in 1983 Entry Draft, November 10, 1981.

● VAIVE, RICK Rick "Squiddly" Vaive RW – R. 6'1", 198 lbs. b: Ottawa, Ont., 5/14/1959. Vancouver's 1st choice, 5th overall, in 1979 Entry Draft.

Season	Club	League	GP	G	A	Pts	AG	AA	APts	PIM	PP	SH	GW	S	%	TGF	PGF	TGA	PGA	+/–	GP	G	A	Pts	PIM	PP	SH	GW
1976-77	Sherbrooke Beavers	QMJHL	67	51	59	110	....	....	....	91	....	....	....	....	....	....	....	....	....	....	18	10	13	23	78	....	....	....
1977-78	Sherbrooke Beavers	QMJHL	68	76	79	155	....	....	....	199	....	....	....	....	....	....	....	....	....	....	9	8	4	12	38	....	....	....
	Canada	WJC-A	6	3	0	3	....	....	....	4	....	....	....	....	....	....	....	....	....	....	....	....	....	....	....	....	....	....
1978-79	Birmingham Bulls	WHA	75	26	33	59	....	....	....	*248	....	....	....	....	....	....	....	....	....	....	....	....	....	....	....	....	....	....
1979-80	**Vancouver Canucks**	**NHL**	**47**	**13**	**8**	**21**	**12**	**6**	**18**	**111**	**1**	**0**	**4**	**89**	**14.6**	**29**	**2**	**39**	**0**	**–12**	....	....	....	....	....	....	....	....
	Toronto Maple Leafs	**NHL**	**22**	**9**	**7**	**16**	**8**	**5**	**13**	**77**	**2**	**0**	**1**	**55**	**16.4**	**24**	**5**	**24**	**1**	**–4**	**3**	**1**	**0**	**1**	**11**	**0**	**0**	**0**
1980-81	**Toronto Maple Leafs**	**NHL**	**75**	**33**	**29**	**62**	**27**	**20**	**47**	**229**	**8**	**2**	**1**	**195**	**16.9**	**93**	**23**	**99**	**13**	**–16**	**3**	**1**	**0**	**1**	**4**	**0**	**0**	**0**
1981-82	**Toronto Maple Leafs**	**NHL**	**77**	**54**	**35**	**89**	**43**	**23**	**66**	**157**	**12**	**5**	**6**	**267**	**20.2**	**119**	**29**	**106**	**28**	**+12**	....	....	....	....	....	....	....	....
	Canada	WEC-A	9	3	1	4	....	....	....	12	....	....	....	....	....	....	....	....	....	....	....	....	....	....	....	....	....	....
1982-83	**Toronto Maple Leafs**	**NHL**	**78**	**51**	**28**	**79**	**42**	**19**	**61**	**105**	**18**	**3**	**8**	**296**	**17.2**	**121**	**47**	**109**	**22**	**–13**	**4**	**2**	**5**	**7**	**6**	**0**	**0**	**0**
1983-84	**Toronto Maple Leafs**	**NHL**	**76**	**52**	**41**	**93**	**42**	**28**	**70**	**114**	**17**	**0**	**6**	**261**	**19.9**	**135**	**55**	**96**	**4**	**–12**	....	....	....	....	....	....	....	....
1984-85	**Toronto Maple Leafs**	**NHL**	**72**	**35**	**33**	**68**	**29**	**22**	**51**	**112**	**13**	**0**	**2**	**258**	**13.6**	**109**	**42**	**95**	**2**	**–26**	....	....	....	....	....	....	....	....
	Canada	WEC-A	10	6	2	8	....	....	....	16	....	....	....	....	....	....	....	....	....	....	....	....	....	....	....	....	....	....
1985-86	**Toronto Maple Leafs**	**NHL**	**61**	**33**	**31**	**64**	**26**	**21**	**47**	**85**	**12**	**0**	**1**	**225**	**14.7**	**86**	**28**	**88**	**11**	**–19**	**9**	**6**	**2**	**8**	**9**	**3**	**0**	**0**
1986-87	**Toronto Maple Leafs**	**NHL**	**73**	**32**	**34**	**66**	**28**	**25**	**53**	**61**	**8**	**1**	**6**	**214**	**15.0**	**109**	**31**	**70**	**4**	**+12**	**13**	**4**	**2**	**6**	**23**	**1**	**0**	**0**
1987-88	**Chicago Blackhawks**	**NHL**	**76**	**43**	**26**	**69**	**37**	**18**	**55**	**108**	**19**	**0**	**6**	**229**	**18.8**	**119**	**62**	**77**	**0**	**–20**	**5**	**6**	**2**	**8**	**38**	**5**	**0**	**0**
1988-89	**Chicago Blackhawks**	**NHL**	**30**	**12**	**13**	**25**	**10**	**9**	**19**	**60**	**9**	**0**	**1**	**57**	**21.1**	**45**	**29**	**22**	**1**	**–5**	....	....	....	....	....	....	....	....
	Buffalo Sabres	**NHL**	**28**	**19**	**13**	**32**	**16**	**9**	**25**	**64**	**7**	**0**	**3**	**81**	**23.5**	**46**	**21**	**19**	**1**	**+7**	**5**	**2**	**1**	**3**	**8**	**2**	**0**	**0**
1989-90	**Buffalo Sabres**	**NHL**	**70**	**29**	**19**	**48**	**25**	**14**	**39**	**74**	**8**	**0**	**4**	**195**	**14.9**	**102**	**50**	**43**	**0**	**+9**	**6**	**4**	**2**	**6**	**6**	**4**	**0**	**1**
1990-91	**Buffalo Sabres**	**NHL**	**71**	**25**	**27**	**52**	**23**	**20**	**43**	**74**	**9**	**0**	**3**	**155**	**16.1**	**75**	**29**	**35**	**0**	**+11**	**6**	**1**	**2**	**3**	**6**	**1**	**0**	**0**
1991-92	**Buffalo Sabres**	**NHL**	**20**	**1**	**3**	**4**	**1**	**2**	**3**	**14**	**0**	**0**	**0**	**25**	**4.0**	**10**	**3**	**9**	**0**	**–2**	....	....	....	....	....	....	....	....
	Rochester Americans	AHL	12	4	9	13	....	....	....	4	....	....	....	....	....	....	....	....	....	....	16	4	4	8	10	....	....	....
1992-93	Hamilton Canucks	AHL	38	16	15	31	....	....	....	34	....	....	....	....	....	....	....	....	....	....	....	....	....	....	....	....	....	....
	NHL Totals		**876**	**441**	**347**	**788**	**369**	**241**	**610**	**1445**	**143**	**11**	**52**	**2602**	**16.9**	**1222**	**456**	**931**	**87**		**54**	**27**	**16**	**43**	**111**	**16**	**0**	**1**
	Other Major League Totals		75	26	33	59	....	....	....	248	....	....	....	....	....	....	....	....	....		....	....	....	....	....	....	....	....

Played in NHL All-Star Game (1982, 1983, 1984)

Signed as an underage free agent by **Birmingham** (WHA), May, 1978. Traded to **Toronto** by **Vancouver** with Bill Derlago for Tiger Williams and Jerry Butler, February 18, 1980. Traded to **Chicago** by **Toronto** with Steve Thomas and Bob McGill for Al Secord and Ed Olczyk, September 3, 1987. Traded to **Buffalo** by **Chicago** for Adam Creighton, December 26, 1988. Signed as a free agent by **Vancouver**, September 2, 1992.

● VALENTINE, CHRIS Chris Valentine C – R. 6', 190 lbs. b: Belleville, Ont., 12/6/1961. Washington's 10th choice, 194th overall, in 1981 Entry Draft.

Season	Club	League	GP	G	A	Pts	AG	AA	APts	PIM	PP	SH	GW	S	%	TGF	PGF	TGA	PGA	+/–	GP	G	A	Pts	PIM	PP	SH	GW
1978-79	St. Louis University	WCHA	34	27	44	71	....	....	....	52	....	....	....	....	....	....	....	....	....	....	....	....	....	....	....	....	....	....
1979-80	Sorel Black Hawks	QMJHL	72	48	80	128	....	....	....	76	....	....	....	....	....	....	....	....	....	....	....	....	....	....	....	....	....	....
1980-81	Sorel Black Hawks	QMJHL	72	65	77	142	....	....	....	176	....	....	....	....	....	....	....	....	....	....	7	5	5	10	8	....	....	....
1981-82	**Washington Capitals**	**NHL**	**60**	**30**	**37**	**67**	**24**	**24**	**48**	**92**	**18**	**0**	**5**	**154**	**19.5**	**97**	**52**	**62**	**2**	**–15**	....	....	....	....	....	....	....	....
	Hershey Bears	AHL	19	12	9	21	....	....	....	69	....	....	....	....	....	....	....	....	....	....	....	....	....	....	....	....	....	....
1982-83	**Washington Capitals**	**NHL**	**23**	**7**	**10**	**17**	**6**	**7**	**13**	**14**	**1**	**0**	**1**	**24**	**29.2**	**23**	**9**	**16**	**0**	**–2**	**2**	**0**	**0**	**0**	**4**	**0**	**0**	**0**
	Hershey Bears	AHL	51	31	38	69	....	....	....	66	....	....	....	....	....	....	....	....	....	....	....	....	....	....	....	....	....	....
1983-84	**Washington Capitals**	**NHL**	**22**	**6**	**5**	**11**	**5**	**3**	**8**	**21**	**2**	**0**	**1**	**33**	**18.2**	**14**	**5**	**17**	**0**	**–8**	....	....	....	....	....	....	....	....
	Hershey Bears	AHL	47	15	44	59	....	....	....	41	....	....	....	....	....	....	....	....	....	....	....	....	....	....	....	....	....	....
1984-85	Dusseldorfer EG	Germany	36	*37	42	*79	....	....	....	74	....	....	....	....	....	....	....	....	....	....	4	1	3	4	24	....	....	....
1985-86	Dusseldorfer EG	Germany	45	36	*67	*103	....	....	....	98	....	....	....	....	....	....	....	....	....	....	....	....	....	....	....	....	....	....
1986-87	Dusseldorfer EG	Germany	42	28	50	78	....	....	....	71	....	....	....	....	....	....	....	....	....	....	8	4	11	15	....	....	....	....
1987-88	Dusseldorfer EG	Germany	43	34	50	84	....	....	....	63	....	....	....	....	....	....	....	....	....	....	....	....	....	....	....	....	....	....
1988-89	Dusseldorfer EG	Germany	36	27	47	74	....	....	....	34	....	....	....	....	....	....	....	....	....	....	11	4	10	14	27	....	....	....
1989-90	Dusseldorfer EG	Germany	36	27	*39	66	....	....	....	35	....	....	....	....	....	....	....	....	....	....	11	5	10	15	22	....	....	....
1990-91	Dusseldorfer EG	Germany	42	22	52	74	....	....	....	76	....	....	....	....	....	....	....	....	....	....	12	8	13	21	8	....	....	....
1991-92	Dusseldorfer EG	Germany	44	32	49	81	....	....	....	56	....	....	....	....	....	....	....	....	....	....	10	10	8	18	16	....	....	....
1992-93	Dusseldorfer EG	Germany	44	26	*44	*70	....	....	....	56	....	....	....	....	....	....	....	....	....	....	....	....	....	....	....	....	....	....
1993-94	Dusseldorfer EG	Germany	43	19	*40	59	....	....	....	52	....	....	....	....	....	....	....	....	....	....	....	....	....	....	....	....	....	....
1994-95	Dusseldorfer EG	Germany	42	16	34	50	....	....	....	102	....	....	....	....	....	....	....	....	....	....	10	10	7	17	16	....	....	....
1995-96	Dusseldorfer EG	Germany	26	9	8	17	....	....	....	22	....	....	....	....	....	....	....	....	....	....	12	5	10	15	30	....	....	....
	NHL Totals		**105**	**43**	**52**	**95**	**35**	**34**	**69**	**127**	**21**	**0**	**7**	**211**	**20.4**	**134**	**66**	**95**	**2**		**2**	**0**	**0**	**0**	**4**	**0**	**0**	**0**

CCHA Second All-Star Team (1979)

● VALIQUETTE, JACK Jack Valiquette C – L. 6'2", 195 lbs. b: St. Thomas, Ont., 3/18/1954. Toronto's 1st choice, 13th overall, in 1974 Amateur Draft.

Season	Club	League	GP	G	A	Pts	AG	AA	APts	PIM	PP	SH	GW	S	%	TGF	PGF	TGA	PGA	+/–	GP	G	A	Pts	PIM	PP	SH	GW
1971-72	Laurentian University	OUAA	....	0	3	3	....	....	....	6	....	....	....	....	....	....	....	....	....	....	....	....	....	....	....	....	....	....
1972-73	St. Mary's Lincolns	Jr. B	42	47	41	88	....	....	....	25	....	....	....	....	....	....	....	....	....	....	....	....	....	....	....	....	....	....
1973-74	Sault Ste. Marie Greyhounds	OHA	69	*63	72	*135	....	....	....	38	....	....	....	....	....	....	....	....	....	....	....	....	....	....	....	....	....	....
1974-75	**Toronto Maple Leafs**	**NHL**	**1**	**0**	**0**	**0**	**0**	**0**	**0**	**0**	**0**	**0**	**0**	**1**	**0.0**	**0**	**0**	**4**	**0**	**–4**	....	....	....	....	....	....	....	....
	Oklahoma City Blazers	CHL	76	22	51	73	....	....	....	52	....	....	....	....	....	....	....	....	....	....	5	0	1	1	0	....	....	....
1975-76	**Toronto Maple Leafs**	**NHL**	**45**	**10**	**23**	**33**	**9**	**18**	**27**	**30**	**1**	**1**	**1**	**111**	**9.0**	**44**	**10**	**46**	**4**	**–8**	**10**	**2**	**3**	**5**	**2**	**0**	**0**	**0**
	Oklahoma City Blazers	CHL	32	15	8	23	....	....	....	25	....	....	....	....	....	....	....	....	....	....	....	....	....	....	....	....	....	....
1976-77	**Toronto Maple Leafs**	**NHL**	**66**	**15**	**30**	**45**	**14**	**24**	**38**	**7**	**0**	**3**	**1**	**121**	**12.4**	**59**	**2**	**73**	**21**	**+5**	....	....	....	....	....	....	....	....
1977-78	**Toronto Maple Leafs**	**NHL**	**60**	**8**	**13**	**21**	**8**	**11**	**19**	**15**	**3**	**0**	**2**	**49**	**16.3**	**35**	**9**	**26**	**2**	**+2**	**13**	**1**	**3**	**4**	**2**	**1**	**0**	**0**
	Tulsa Oilers	CHL	7	7	5	12	....	....	....	2	....	....	....	....	....	....	....	....	....	....	....	....	....	....	....	....	....	....
1978-79	**Colorado Rockies**	**NHL**	**76**	**23**	**34**	**57**	**21**	**26**	**47**	**12**	**8**	**2**	**3**	**159**	**14.5**	**84**	**30**	**114**	**18**	**–42**	....	....	....	....	....	....	....	....
1979-80	**Colorado Rockies**	**NHL**	**77**	**25**	**25**	**50**	**23**	**19**	**42**	**8**	**6**	**0**	**2**	**157**	**15.9**	**88**	**28**	**75**	**8**	**–7**	....	....	....	....	....	....	....	....
1980-81	**Colorado Rockies**	**NHL**	**25**	**3**	**9**	**12**	**2**	**6**	**8**	**7**	**0**	**0**	**0**	**28**	**10.7**	**19**	**6**	**28**	**3**	**–12**	....	....	....	....	....	....	....	....
	Fort Worth Texans	CHL	37	18	18	36	....	....	....	4	....	....	....	....	....	....	....	....	....	....	....	....	....	....	....	....	....	....
	NHL Totals		**350**	**84**	**134**	**218**	**77**	**104**	**181**	**79**	**18**	**6**	**9**	**626**	**13.4**	**329**	**85**	**366**	**56**		**23**	**3**	**6**	**9**	**4**	**1**	**0**	**0**

Traded to **Colorado** by **Toronto** for Colorado's 2nd round choice (Gary Yaremchuk) in 1981 Entry Draft, October 19, 1978.

• VALK, GARRY Garry Valk LW – L. 6'1", 205 lbs. b: Edmonton, Alta., 11/27/1967. Vancouver's 5th choice, 108th overall, in 1987 Entry Draft.

			REGULAR SEASON																		PLAYOFFS							
Season	Club	League	GP	G	A	Pts	AG	AA	APts	PIM	PP	SH	GW	S	%	TGF	PGF	TGA	PGA	+/–	GP	G	A	Pts	PIM	PP	SH	GW
1986-87	Sherwood Park Crusaders	AJHL	59	42	44	86	....	....	....	204	....	....	....	....	....	....	....	....	....	....	....	....	....	....	....	....	....	....
1987-88	University of North Dakota	WCHA	38	23	12	35	....	....	....	64	....	....	....	....	....	....	....	....	....	....	....	....	....	....	....	....	....	....
1988-89	University of North Dakota	WCHA	40	14	17	31	....	....	....	71	....	....	....	....	....	....	....	....	....	....	....	....	....	....	....	....	....	....
1989-90	University of North Dakota	WCHA	43	22	17	39	....	....	....	92	....	....	....	....	....	....	....	....	....	....	....	....	....	....	....	....	....	....
1990-91	**Vancouver Canucks**	**NHL**	**59**	**10**	**11**	**21**	**9**	**8**	**17**	**67**	**1**	**0**	**1**	**90**	**11.1**	**37**	**12**	**51**	**3**	**–23**	**5**	**0**	**0**	**0**	**20**	**0**	**0**	**0**
	Milwaukee Admirals	IHL	10	12	4	16	....	....	....	13	....	....	....	....	....	....	....	....	....	....	3	0	0	0	2	....	....	....
1991-92	**Vancouver Canucks**	**NHL**	**65**	**8**	**17**	**25**	**7**	**13**	**20**	**56**	**2**	**1**	**2**	**93**	**8.6**	**41**	**7**	**49**	**18**	**+3**	**4**	**0**	**0**	**0**	**5**	**0**	**0**	**0**
1992-93	**Vancouver Canucks**	**NHL**	**48**	**6**	**7**	**13**	**5**	**5**	**10**	**77**	**0**	**0**	**2**	**46**	**13.0**	**20**	**0**	**28**	**14**	**+6**	**7**	**0**	**1**	**1**	**12**	**0**	**0**	**0**
	Hamilton Canucks	AHL	7	3	6	9	....	....	....	6	....	....	....	....	....	....	....	....	....	....	....	....	....	....	....	....	....	....
1993-94	**Anaheim Mighty Ducks**	**NHL**	**78**	**18**	**27**	**45**	**17**	**21**	**38**	**100**	**4**	**1**	**5**	**165**	**10.9**	**68**	**15**	**72**	**27**	**+8**	....	....	....	....	....	....	....	....
1994-95	**Anaheim Mighty Ducks**	**NHL**	**36**	**3**	**6**	**9**	**5**	**9**	**14**	**34**	**0**	**0**	**0**	**53**	**5.7**	**17**	**2**	**26**	**7**	**–4**	....	....	....	....	....	....	....	....
1995-96	**Anaheim Mighty Ducks**	**NHL**	**79**	**12**	**12**	**24**	**12**	**10**	**22**	**125**	**1**	**1**	**2**	**108**	**11.1**	**39**	**5**	**55**	**29**	**+8**	....	....	....	....	....	....	....	....
1996-97	**Anaheim Mighty Ducks**	**NHL**	**53**	**7**	**7**	**14**	**7**	**6**	**13**	**53**	**0**	**0**	**1**	**68**	**10.3**	**22**	**0**	**30**	**6**	**–2**	....	....	....	....	....	....	....	....
	Pittsburgh Penguins	**NHL**	**17**	**3**	**4**	**7**	**3**	**4**	**7**	**25**	**0**	**0**	**0**	**32**	**9.4**	**8**	**2**	**14**	**2**	**–6**	....	....	....	....	....	....	....	....
1997-98	**Pittsburgh Penguins**	**NHL**	**39**	**2**	**1**	**3**	**2**	**1**	**3**	**33**	**0**	**0**	**0**	**32**	**6.3**	**4**	**0**	**9**	**2**	**–3**	....	....	....	....	....	....	....	....
	NHL Totals		**474**	**69**	**92**	**161**	**67**	**77**	**144**	**570**	**8**	**3**	**13**	**687**	**10.0**	**256**	**43**	**334**	**108**		**16**	**0**	**1**	**1**	**37**	**0**	**0**	**0**

OHA First All-Star Team (1974)

Claimed by **Anaheim** from **Vancouver** in NHL Waiver Draft, October 3, 1993. Traded to **Pittsburgh** by **Anaheim** for Jean-Jacques Daigneault, February 21, 1997.

• VALLIS, LINDSAY Lindsay Vallis D – R. 6'3", 207 lbs. b: Winnipeg, Man., 1/12/1971. Montreal's 1st choice, 13th overall, in 1989 Entry Draft.

Season	Club	League	GP	G	A	Pts	AG	AA	APts	PIM	PP	SH	GW	S	%	TGF	PGF	TGA	PGA	+/–	GP	G	A	Pts	PIM	PP	SH	GW
1987-88	Seattle Thunderbirds	WHL	68	31	45	76	....	....	....	65	....	....	....	....	....	....	....	....	....	....	....	....	....	....	....	....	....	....
1988-89	Seattle Thunderbirds	WHL	63	21	32	53	....	....	....	48	....	....	....	....	....	....	....	....	....	....	....	....	....	....	....	....	....	....
1989-90	Seattle Thunderbirds	WHL	65	34	43	77	....	....	....	68	....	....	....	....	....	....	....	....	....	....	13	6	5	11	14	....	....	....
1990-91	Seattle Thunderbirds	WHL	72	41	38	79	....	....	....	119	....	....	....	....	....	....	....	....	....	....	6	1	3	4	17	....	....	....
	Fredericton Canadiens	AHL	....	....	....	....	....	....	....	....	....	....	....	....	....	....	....	....	....	....	7	0	0	0	6	....	....	....
1991-92	Fredericton Canadiens	AHL	71	10	19	29	....	....	....	84	....	....	....	....	....	....	....	....	....	....	4	0	1	1	7	....	....	....
1992-93	Fredericton Canadiens	AHL	65	18	16	34	....	....	....	38	....	....	....	....	....	....	....	....	....	....	5	0	2	2	10	....	....	....
1993-94	**Montreal Canadiens**	**NHL**	**1**	**0**	**0**	**0**	**0**	**0**	**0**	**0**	**0**	**0**	**0**	**0**	**0.0**	**0**	**0**	**0**	**0**	**0**	....	....	....	....	....	....	....	....
	Fredericton Canadiens	AHL	75	9	30	39	....	....	....	103	....	....	....	....	....	....	....	....	....	....	....	....	....	....	....	....	....	....
1994-95	Worcester IceCats	AHL	14	0	7	7	....	....	....	28	....	....	....	....	....	....	....	....	....	....	....	....	....	....	....	....	....	....
1995-96	Worcester IceCats	AHL	65	9	19	28	....	....	....	81	....	....	....	....	....	....	....	....	....	....	4	0	2	2	4	....	....	....
1996-97	Bakersfield Fog	WCHL	58	26	65	91	....	....	....	82	....	....	....	....	....	....	....	....	....	....	4	0	3	3	0	....	....	....
1997-98	Bakersfield Fog	WCHL	41	21	24	45	....	....	....	34	....	....	....	....	....	....	....	....	....	....	4	1	2	3	26	....	....	....
	NHL Totals		**1**	**0**	**0**	**0**	**0**	**0**	**0**	**0**	**0**	**0**	**0**	**0**	**0.0**	**0**	**0**	**0**	**0**		....	....	....	....	....	....	....	....

WCHL Second All-Star Team (1997)

• VAN ALLEN, SHAUN Shaun Van Allen C – L. 6'1", 200 lbs. b: Calgary, Alta., 8/29/1967. Edmonton's 4th choice, 105th overall, in 1987 Entry Draft.

Season	Club	League	GP	G	A	Pts	AG	AA	APts	PIM	PP	SH	GW	S	%	TGF	PGF	TGA	PGA	+/–	GP	G	A	Pts	PIM	PP	SH	GW
1984-85	Swift Current Broncos	WHL	61	12	20	32	....	....	....	136	....	....	....	....	....	....	....	....	....	....	....	....	....	....	....	....	....	....
1985-86	Saskatoon Blades	WHL	55	12	11	23	....	....	....	43	....	....	....	....	....	....	....	....	....	....	13	4	8	12	28	....	....	....
1986-87	Saskatoon Blades	WHL	72	38	59	97	....	....	....	116	....	....	....	....	....	....	....	....	....	....	11	4	6	10	24	....	....	....
1987-88	Milwaukee Admirals	IHL	40	14	28	42	....	....	....	34	....	....	....	....	....	....	....	....	....	....	....	....	....	....	....	....	....	....
	Nova Scotia Oilers	AHL	19	4	10	14	....	....	....	17	....	....	....	....	....	....	....	....	....	....	4	1	1	2	4	....	....	....
1988-89	Cape Breton Oilers	AHL	76	32	42	74	....	....	....	81	....	....	....	....	....	....	....	....	....	....	....	....	....	....	....	....	....	....
1989-90	Cape Breton Oilers	AHL	61	25	44	69	....	....	....	83	....	....	....	....	....	....	....	....	....	....	4	0	2	2	8	....	....	....
1990-91	**Edmonton Oilers**	**NHL**	**2**	**0**	**0**	**0**	**0**	**0**	**0**	**0**	**0**	**0**	**0**	**0**	**0.0**	**0**	**0**	**0**	**0**	**0**	....	....	....	....	....	....	....	....
	Cape Breton Oilers	AHL	76	25	75	100	....	....	....	182	....	....	....	....	....	....	....	....	....	....	4	0	1	1	8	....	....	....
1991-92	Cape Breton Oilers	AHL	77	29	*84	*113	....	....	....	80	....	....	....	....	....	....	....	....	....	....	5	3	7	10	14	....	....	....
1992-93	**Edmonton Oilers**	**NHL**	**21**	**1**	**4**	**5**	**1**	**3**	**4**	**6**	**0**	**0**	**0**	**19**	**5.3**	**8**	**4**	**6**	**0**	**–2**	....	....	....	....	....	....	....	....
	Cape Breton Oilers	AHL	43	14	62	76	....	....	....	68	....	....	....	....	....	....	....	....	....	....	15	8	9	17	18	....	....	....
1993-94	**Anaheim Mighty Ducks**	**NHL**	**80**	**8**	**25**	**33**	**7**	**19**	**26**	**64**	**2**	**2**	**1**	**104**	**7.7**	**58**	**15**	**52**	**9**	**0**	....	....	....	....	....	....	....	....
1994-95	**Anaheim Mighty Ducks**	**NHL**	**45**	**8**	**21**	**29**	**14**	**31**	**45**	**32**	**1**	**1**	**1**	**68**	**11.8**	**37**	**10**	**45**	**14**	**–4**	....	....	....	....	....	....	....	....
1995-96	**Anaheim Mighty Ducks**	**NHL**	**49**	**8**	**17**	**25**	**8**	**14**	**22**	**41**	**0**	**0**	**2**	**78**	**10.3**	**44**	**8**	**34**	**11**	**+13**	....	....	....	....	....	....	....	....
1996-97	**Ottawa Senators**	**NHL**	**80**	**11**	**14**	**25**	**12**	**12**	**24**	**35**	**1**	**1**	**2**	**123**	**8.9**	**36**	**3**	**48**	**7**	**–8**	**7**	**0**	**1**	**1**	**4**	**0**	**0**	**0**
1997-98	**Ottawa Senators**	**NHL**	**80**	**4**	**15**	**19**	**5**	**15**	**20**	**48**	**0**	**0**	**0**	**104**	**3.8**	**31**	**2**	**47**	**22**	**+4**	**11**	**0**	**1**	**1**	**10**	**0**	**0**	**0**
	NHL Totals		**357**	**40**	**96**	**136**	**47**	**94**	**141**	**226**	**4**	**4**	**6**	**496**	**8.1**	**214**	**42**	**232**	**63**		**18**	**0**	**2**	**2**	**14**	**0**	**0**	**0**

AHL Second All-Star Team (1991) • Won John B. Sollenberger Trophy (Top Scorer - AHL) (1992) • AHL First All-Star Team (1992)

Signed as a free agent by **Anaheim**, July 22, 1993. Traded to **Ottawa** by **Anaheim** with Jason York for Ted Drury and the rights to Marc Moro, October 1, 1996.

• VAN BOXMEER, JOHN John "Boxy" Van Boxmeer D – R. 6', 190 lbs. b: Petrolia, Ont., 11/20/1952. Montreal's 4th choice, 14th overall, in 1972 Amateur Draft.

Season	Club	League	GP	G	A	Pts	AG	AA	APts	PIM	PP	SH	GW	S	%	TGF	PGF	TGA	PGA	+/–	GP	G	A	Pts	PIM	PP	SH	GW
1971-72	Guelph CMC's	OJHL	56	30	42	72	....	....	....	160	....	....	....	....	....	....	....	....	....	....	....	....	....	....	....	....	....	....
1972-73	Nova Scotia Voyageurs	AHL	76	5	29	34	....	....	....	139	....	....	....	....	....	....	....	....	....	....	13	1	6	7	26	....	....	....
1973-74	**Montreal Canadiens**	**NHL**	**20**	**1**	**4**	**5**	**1**	**3**	**4**	**18**	**1**	**0**	**0**	**12**	**8.3**	**9**	**1**	**12**	**1**	**–3**	**1**	**0**	**0**	**0**	**0**	**0**	**0**	**0**
	Nova Scotia Voyageurs	AHL	47	8	20	28	....	....	....	78	....	....	....	....	....	....	....	....	....	....	....	....	....	....	....	....	....	....
1974-75	**Montreal Canadiens**	**NHL**	**9**	**0**	**2**	**2**	**0**	**2**	**2**	**0**	**0**	**0**	**0**	**10**	**0.0**	**3**	**0**	**4**	**0**	**–1**	....	....	....	....	....	....	....	....
	Nova Scotia Voyageurs	AHL	43	4	15	19	....	....	....	68	....	....	....	....	....	....	....	....	....	....	6	1	3	4	9	....	....	....
1975-76	**Montreal Canadiens**	**NHL**	**46**	**6**	**11**	**17**	**6**	**9**	**15**	**31**	**0**	**0**	**1**	**88**	**6.8**	**41**	**5**	**19**	**0**	**+17**	....	....	....	....	....	....	....	....
1976-77	**Montreal Canadiens**	**NHL**	**4**	**0**	**1**	**1**	**0**	**1**	**1**	**0**	**0**	**0**	**0**	**5**	**0.0**	**3**	**1**	**1**	**0**	**+1**	....	....	....	....	....	....	....	....
	Colorado Rockies	**NHL**	**41**	**2**	**11**	**13**	**2**	**9**	**11**	**32**	**0**	**0**	**0**	**88**	**2.3**	**39**	**15**	**50**	**6**	**–20**	....	....	....	....	....	....	....	....
1977-78	**Colorado Rockies**	**NHL**	**80**	**12**	**42**	**54**	**12**	**34**	**46**	**87**	**5**	**0**	**0**	**202**	**4.0**	**129**	**41**	**124**	**24**	**–12**	**2**	**0**	**1**	**1**	**2**	**0**	**0**	**0**
1978-79	**Colorado Rockies**	**NHL**	**76**	**9**	**34**	**43**	**8**	**26**	**34**	**46**	**4**	**0**	**0**	**189**	**4.8**	**106**	**36**	**119**	**23**	**–26**	....	....	....	....	....	....	....	....
1979-80	**Buffalo Sabres**	**NHL**	**80**	**11**	**40**	**51**	**10**	**31**	**41**	**55**	**4**	**0**	**1**	**198**	**5.6**	**138**	**40**	**63**	**5**	**+40**	**14**	**3**	**5**	**8**	**12**	**2**	**0**	**2**
1980-81	**Buffalo Sabres**	**NHL**	**80**	**18**	**51**	**69**	**15**	**36**	**51**	**69**	**6**	**1**	**2**	**258**	**7.0**	**139**	**52**	**96**	**7**	**–2**	**8**	**1**	**8**	**9**	**7**	**0**	**0**	**0**
1981-82	**Buffalo Sabres**	**NHL**	**69**	**14**	**54**	**68**	**11**	**36**	**47**	**62**	**3**	**0**	**1**	**120**	**11.7**	**82**	**32**	**34**	**4**	**+20**	**4**	**0**	**1**	**1**	**6**	**0**	**0**	**0**
	Canada	WEC-A	8	2	0	2	....	....	....	8	....	....	....	....	....	....	....	....	....	....	....	....	....	....	....	....	....	....
1982-83	**Buffalo Sabres**	**NHL**	**65**	**6**	**21**	**27**	**5**	**14**	**19**	**53**	**1**	**0**	**1**	**144**	**4.2**	**89**	**20**	**69**	**7**	**+7**	**9**	**1**	**0**	**1**	**10**	**1**	**0**	**0**
1983-84	**Quebec Nordiques**	**NHL**	**18**	**5**	**3**	**8**	**4**	**2**	**6**	**12**	**4**	**0**	**0**	**33**	**15.2**	**34**	**15**	**25**	**5**	**–1**	....	....	....	....	....	....	....	....
	Fredericton Express	AHL	45	10	34	44	....	....	....	40	....	....	....	....	....	....	....	....	....	....	7	2	5	7	8	....	....	....
1984-85	Rochester Americans	AHL	2	0	0	0	....	....	....	2	....	....	....	....	....	....	....	....	....	....	....	....	....	....	....	....	....	....
1985-86	Rochester Americans	AHL	DID NOT PLAY – COACHING																									
	NHL Totals		**588**	**84**	**274**	**358**	**74**	**203**	**277**	**465**	**28**	**1**	**6**	**1407**	**6.0**	**812**	**258**	**616**	**82**		**38**	**5**	**15**	**20**	**37**	**3**	**0**	**2**

Traded to **Colorado** by **Montreal** for Colorado's 3rd round choice (Craig Levie) in 1979 Entry Draft and cash, November 24, 1976. Traded to **Buffalo** by **Colorado** for Rene Robert, October 5, 1979. Claimed by **Quebec** from **Buffalo** in Waiver Draft, October 3, 1983.

• VANDENBUSSCHE, RYAN Ryan Vandenbussche RW – R. 5'11", 187 lbs. b: Simcoe, Ont., 2/28/1973. Toronto's 9th choice, 173rd overall, in 1992 Entry Draft.

Season	Club	League	GP	G	A	Pts	AG	AA	APts	PIM	PP	SH	GW	S	%	TGF	PGF	TGA	PGA	+/–	GP	G	A	Pts	PIM	PP	SH	GW
1990-91	Cornwall Royals	OHL	49	3	8	11	....	....	....	139	....	....	....	....	....	....	....	....	....	....	....	....	....	....	....	....	....	....
1991-92	Cornwall Royals	OHL	61	13	15	28	....	....	....	232	....	....	....	....	....	....	....	....	....	....	6	0	2	2	9	....	....	....
1992-93	Newmarket Royals	OHL	30	15	12	27	....	....	....	161	....	....	....	....	....	....	....	....	....	....	....	....	....	....	....	....	....	....
	Guelph Platers	OHL	29	3	14	17	....	....	....	99	....	....	....	....	....	....	....	....	....	....	5	1	3	4	13	....	....	....
	St. John's Maple Leafs	AHL	1	0	0	0	....	....	....	0	....	....	....	....	....	....	....	....	....	....	....	....	....	....	....	....	....	....
1993-94	St. John's Maple Leafs	AHL	44	4	10	14	....	....	....	124	....	....	....	....	....	....	....	....	....	....	....	....	....	....	....	....	....	....
	Springfield Indians	AHL	9	1	2	3	....	....	....	29	....	....	....	....	....	....	....	....	....	....	5	0	0	0	16	....	....	....
1994-95	St. John's Maple Leafs	AHL	53	2	13	15	....	....	....	239	....	....	....	....	....	....	....	....	....	....	3	0	0	0	17	....	....	....
1995-96	Binghamton Rangers	AHL	68	3	17	20	....	....	....	240	....	....	....	....	....	....	....	....	....	....	4	0	0	0	9	....	....	....
1996-97	**New York Rangers**	**NHL**	**11**	**1**	**0**	**1**	**1**	**0**	**1**	**30**	**0**	**0**	**0**	**4**	**25.0**	**1**	**0**	**3**	**0**	**–2**	....	....	....	....	....	....	....	....
	Binghamton Rangers	AHL	38	8	11	19	....	....	....	133	....	....	....	....	....	....	....	....	....	....	....	....	....	....	....	....	....	....

			REGULAR SEASON																		PLAYOFFS							
Season	**Club**	**League**	**GP**	**G**	**A**	**Pts**	**AG**	**AA**	**APts**	**PIM**	**PP**	**SH**	**GW**	**S**	**%**	**TGF**	**PGF**	**TGA**	**PGA**	**+/–**	**GP**	**G**	**A**	**Pts**	**PIM**	**PP**	**SH**	**GW**
1997-98	**New York Rangers**	**NHL**	**16**	**1**	**0**	**1**	**1**	**0**	**1**	**38**	**0**	**0**	**0**	**2**	**50.0**	**1**	**0**	**3**	**0**	**–2**	....	....	....	....	....	....	....	....
	Hartford Wolf Pack	AHL	15	2	0	2	....	....	....	45	....	....	....	....	....	....	....	....	....	....	....	....	....	....	....	....	....	....
	Chicago Blackhawks	**NHL**	**4**	**0**	**1**	**1**	**0**	**1**	**1**	**5**	**0**	**0**	**0**	**0**	**0.0**	**1**	**0**	**1**	**0**	**0**	....	....	....	....	....	....	....	....
	Indianapolis Ice	IHL	3	1	1	2	....	....	....	4	....	....	....	....	....	....	....	....	....	....	....	....	....	....	....	....	....	....
	NHL Totals		**31**	**2**	**1**	**3**	**2**	**1**	**3**	**73**	**0**	**0**	**0**	**6**	**33.3**	**3**	**0**	**7**	**0**		....	....	....	....	....	....	....	....

Signed as a free agent by **NY Rangers**, August 22, 1995. Traded to **Chicago** by **NY Rangers** for Ryan Risidore, March 24, 1998.

• VAN DORP, WAYNE

Wayne Van Dorp LW – L. 6'4", 225 lbs. b: Vancouver, B.C., 5/19/1961.

Season	Club	League	GP	G	A	Pts	AG	AA	APts	PIM	PP	SH	GW	S	%	TGF	PGF	TGA	PGA	+/–	GP	G	A	Pts	PIM	PP	SH	GW
1978-79	Billington Bulls	BCJHL	61	18	30	48	....	....	....	66	....	....	....	....	....	....	....	....	....	....	....	....	....	....	....	....	....	....
1979-80	Seattle Breakers	WHL	68	8	13	21	....	....	....	195	....	....	....	....	....	....	....	....	....	....	12	3	1	4	33	....	....	....
1980-81	Seattle Breakers	WHL	63	22	30	52	....	....	....	242	....	....	....	....	....	....	....	....	....	....	5	1	0	1	10	....	....	....
1981-82	Feenstra Flyers Heerenveen	Neth.	22	11	7	18	....	....	....	44	....	....	....	....	....	....	....	....	....	....	12	1	4	5	34	....	....	....
1982-83	Feenstra Flyers Heerenveen	Neth.	23	7	12	19	....	....	....	40	....	....	....	....	....	....	....	....	....	....	15	4	5	9	20	....	....	....
1983-84	Erie Blades	ACHL	45	19	18	37	....	....	....	202	....	....	....	....	....	....	....	....	....	....	8	1	2	3	46	....	....	....
1984-85	GIJS Groningen	Neth.	29	38	46	84	....	....	....	112	....	....	....	....	....	....	....	....	....	....	6	6	2	8	23	....	....	....
	Erie Blades	ACHL	7	9	8	17	....	....	....	21	....	....	....	....	....	....	....	....	....	....	10	0	2	2	62	....	....	....
1985-86	GIJS Groningen	Neth.	29	19	24	43	....	....	....	81	....	....	....	....	....	....	....	....	....	....	8	9	*12	21	6	....	....	....
	Holland	WEC-B	7	0	0	0	....	....	....	0	....	....	....	....	....	....	....	....	....	....	....	....	....	....	....	....	....	....
1986-87	Rochester Americans	AHL	47	7	3	10	....	....	....	192	....	....	....	....	....	....	....	....	....	....	....	....	....	....	....	....	....	....
	Edmonton Oilers	**NHL**	**3**	**0**	**0**	**0**	**0**	**0**	**0**	**25**	**0**	**0**	**0**	**3**	**0.0**	**0**	**0**	**1**	**0**	**–1**	**3**	**0**	**0**	**0**	**2**	**0**	**0**	**0**
	Nova Scotia Oilers	AHL	11	2	3	5	....	....	....	37	....	....	....	....	....	....	....	....	....	....	5	0	0	0	56	....	....	....
1987-88	**Pittsburgh Penguins**	**NHL**	**25**	**1**	**3**	**4**	**1**	**2**	**3**	**75**	**0**	**0**	**0**	**15**	**6.7**	**7**	**0**	**5**	**0**	**+2**	....	....	....	....	....	....	....	....
	Nova Scotia Oilers	AHL	12	2	2	4	....	....	....	87	....	....	....	....	....	....	....	....	....	....	....	....	....	....	....	....	....	....
1988-89	Rochester Americans	AHL	28	3	6	9	....	....	....	202	....	....	....	....	....	....	....	....	....	....	....	....	....	....	....	....	....	....
	Saginaw Hawks	IHL	11	4	3	7	....	....	....	60	....	....	....	....	....	....	....	....	....	....	....	....	....	....	....	....	....	....
	Chicago Blackhawks	**NHL**	**8**	**0**	**0**	**0**	**0**	**0**	**0**	**23**	**0**	**0**	**0**	**4**	**0.0**	**3**	**0**	**2**	**0**	**+1**	**16**	**0**	**1**	**1**	**17**	**0**	**0**	**0**
1989-90	**Chicago Blackhawks**	**NHL**	**61**	**7**	**4**	**11**	**6**	**3**	**9**	**303**	**0**	**0**	**1**	**38**	**18.4**	**23**	**0**	**26**	**0**	**–3**	**8**	**0**	**0**	**0**	**23**	**0**	**0**	**0**
1990-91	**Quebec Nordiques**	**NHL**	**4**	**1**	**0**	**1**	**1**	**0**	**1**	**30**	**0**	**0**	**0**	**2**	**50.0**	**1**	**0**	**0**	**0**	**+1**	....	....	....	....	....	....	....	....
1991-92	**Quebec Nordiques**	**NHL**	**24**	**3**	**5**	**8**	**3**	**4**	**7**	**109**	**0**	**0**	**0**	**19**	**15.8**	**9**	**1**	**3**	**0**	**+5**	....	....	....	....	....	....	....	....
	Halifax Citadels	AHL	15	5	5	10	....	....	....	54	....	....	....	....	....	....	....	....	....	....	....	....	....	....	....	....	....	....
1992-93	HC Fiemme	Italy	9	1	1	2	....	....	....	24	....	....	....	....	....	....	....	....	....	....	....	....	....	....	....	....	....	....
	Milwaukee Admirals	IHL	19	1	4	5	....	....	....	57	....	....	....	....	....	....	....	....	....	....	....	....	....	....	....	....	....	....
	NHL Totals		**125**	**12**	**12**	**24**	**11**	**9**	**20**	**565**	**0**	**0**	**1**	**81**	**14.8**	**43**	**1**	**37**	**0**		**27**	**0**	**1**	**1**	**42**	**0**	**0**	**0**

Signed as a free agent by **Buffalo**, October, 1986. Traded to **Edmonton** by **Buffalo** with Normand Lacombe and Buffalo's 4th round choice (Peter Ericksson) in 1987 Entry Draft for Lee Fogolin, Mark Napier and Edmonton's 4th round choice (John Bradley) in 1987 Entry Draft, March 6, 1987. Traded to **Pittsburgh** by **Edmonton** with Paul Coffey and Dave Hunter for Craig Simpson, Dave Hannan, Moe Mantha and Chris Joseph, November 24, 1987. Traded to **Buffalo** by **Pittsburgh** for future considerations, September 30, 1988. Traded to **Chicago** by **Buffalo** for Chicago's 7th round choice (Viktor Gordijuk) in 1990 Entry Draft, February 16, 1989. Claimed by **Quebec** from **Chicago** in Waiver Draft, October 1, 1990.

• VAN IMPE, DARREN

Darren Van Impe D – L. 6'1", 195 lbs. b: Saskatoon, Sask., 5/18/1973. NY Islanders' 7th choice, 170th overall, in 1993 Entry Draft.

Season	Club	League	GP	G	A	Pts	AG	AA	APts	PIM	PP	SH	GW	S	%	TGF	PGF	TGA	PGA	+/–	GP	G	A	Pts	PIM	PP	SH	GW
1990-91	Prince Albert Raiders	WHL	70	15	45	60	....	....	....	57	....	....	....	....	....	....	....	....	....	....	3	1	1	2	2	....	....	....
1991-92	Prince Albert Raiders	WHL	69	9	37	46	....	....	....	129	....	....	....	....	....	....	....	....	....	....	8	1	5	6	10	....	....	....
1992-93	Red Deer Rebels	WHL	54	23	47	70	....	....	....	118	....	....	....	....	....	....	....	....	....	....	4	2	5	7	16	....	....	....
1993-94	Red Deer Rebels	WHL	58	20	64	84	....	....	....	125	....	....	....	....	....	....	....	....	....	....	4	2	4	6	6	....	....	....
1994-95	San Diego Gulls	IHL	76	6	17	23	....	....	....	74	....	....	....	....	....	....	....	....	....	....	5	0	0	0	0	....	....	....
	Anaheim Mighty Ducks	**NHL**	**1**	**0**	**1**	**1**	**0**	**1**	**1**	**4**	**0**	**0**	**0**	**0**	**0.0**	**1**	**0**	**1**	**0**	**0**	....	....	....	....	....	....	....	....
1995-96	**Anaheim Mighty Ducks**	**NHL**	**16**	**1**	**2**	**3**	**1**	**2**	**3**	**14**	**0**	**0**	**1**	**13**	**7.7**	**12**	**1**	**6**	**3**	**+8**	....	....	....	....	....	....	....	....
	Baltimore Bandits	AHL	63	11	47	58	....	....	....	79	....	....	....	....	....	....	....	....	....	....	....	....	....	....	....	....	....	....
1996-97	**Anaheim Mighty Ducks**	**NHL**	**74**	**4**	**19**	**23**	**4**	**17**	**21**	**90**	**2**	**0**	**0**	**107**	**3.7**	**67**	**15**	**51**	**2**	**+3**	**9**	**0**	**2**	**2**	**16**	**0**	**0**	**0**
1997-98	**Anaheim Mighty Ducks**	**NHL**	**19**	**1**	**3**	**4**	**1**	**3**	**4**	**4**	**0**	**0**	**0**	**21**	**4.8**	**8**	**2**	**16**	**0**	**–10**	....	....	....	....	....	....	....	....
	Boston Bruins	**NHL**	**50**	**2**	**8**	**10**	**2**	**8**	**10**	**36**	**2**	**0**	**0**	**50**	**4.0**	**37**	**9**	**25**	**1**	**+4**	**6**	**2**	**1**	**3**	**0**	**1**	**0**	**1**
	NHL Totals		**160**	**8**	**33**	**41**	**8**	**31**	**39**	**148**	**4**	**0**	**1**	**191**	**4.2**	**125**	**27**	**99**	**6**		**15**	**2**	**3**	**5**	**16**	**1**	**0**	**1**

WHL East First All-Star Team (1993, 1994)

Traded to **Anaheim** by **NY Islanders** for Anaheim's 8th round choice (Mike Broda) in 1995 Entry Draft, August 31, 1994. Claimed on waivers by **Boston** from **Anaheim**, November 26, 1997.

• VAN IMPE, ED

Ed Van Impe D – L. 5'10", 205 lbs. b: Saskatoon, Sask., 5/27/1940.

Season	Club	League	GP	G	A	Pts	AG	AA	APts	PIM	PP	SH	GW	S	%	TGF	PGF	TGA	PGA	+/–	GP	G	A	Pts	PIM	PP	SH	GW
1956-57	Saskatoon Quakers	SJHL	1	0	0	0	....	....	....	0	....	....	....	....	....	....	....	....	....	....	....	....	....	....	....	....	....	....
1957-58	Saskatoon Quakers	SJHL	49	2	2	4	....	....	....	58	....	....	....	....	....	....	....	....	....	....	....	....	....	....	....	....	....	....
1958-59	Saskatoon Quakers	SJHL	48	0	23	23	....	....	....	*150	....	....	....	....	....	....	....	....	....	....	5	0	2	2	24	....	....	....
1959-60	Saskatoon Quakers	SJHL	58	11	42	53	....	....	....	136	....	....	....	....	....	....	....	....	....	....	7	1	2	3	4	....	....	....
1960-61	Calgary Stampeders	WHL	66	4	15	19	....	....	....	123	....	....	....	....	....	....	....	....	....	....	5	0	2	2	16	....	....	....
1961-62	Buffalo Bisons	AHL	70	0	19	19	....	....	....	172	....	....	....	....	....	....	....	....	....	....	11	0	1	1	*25	....	....	....
1962-63	Buffalo Bisons	AHL	65	3	12	15	....	....	....	*196	....	....	....	....	....	....	....	....	....	....	13	1	4	5	34	....	....	....
1963-64	Buffalo Bisons	AHL	70	4	22	26	....	....	....	*193	....	....	....	....	....	....	....	....	....	....	....	....	....	....	....	....	....	....
1964-65	Buffalo Bisons	AHL	72	5	6	11	....	....	....	197	....	....	....	....	....	....	....	....	....	....	9	0	0	0	26	....	....	....
1965-66	Buffalo Bisons	AHL	70	9	28	37	....	....	....	153	....	....	....	....	....	....	....	....	....	....	....	....	....	....	....	....	....	....
1966-67	**Chicago Black Hawks**	**NHL**	**61**	**8**	**11**	**19**	**10**	**11**	**21**	**111**	....	....	....	....	....	....	....	....	....	....	**6**	**0**	**0**	**0**	**8**	....	....	....
1967-68	**Philadelphia Flyers**	**NHL**	**67**	**4**	**13**	**17**	**5**	**14**	**19**	**141**	**4**	**0**	**1**	**129**	**3.1**	**66**	**16**	**70**	**15**	**–5**	**7**	**0**	**4**	**4**	**11**	**0**	**0**	**0**
1968-69	**Philadelphia Flyers**	**NHL**	**68**	**7**	**12**	**19**	**8**	**11**	**19**	**112**	**1**	**0**	**0**	**118**	**5.9**	**66**	**13**	**81**	**15**	**–13**	**1**	**0**	**0**	**0**	**17**	**0**	**0**	**0**
1969-70	**Philadelphia Flyers**	**NHL**	**65**	**0**	**10**	**10**	**0**	**10**	**10**	**117**	**0**	**0**	**0**	**81**	**0.0**	**52**	**1**	**74**	**22**	**–1**	....	....	....	....	....	....	....	....
1970-71	**Philadelphia Flyers**	**NHL**	**77**	**0**	**11**	**11**	**0**	**10**	**10**	**80**	**0**	**0**	**0**	**70**	**0.0**	**46**	**2**	**77**	**20**	**–13**	**4**	**0**	**1**	**1**	**8**	**0**	**0**	**0**
1971-72	**Philadelphia Flyers**	**NHL**	**73**	**4**	**9**	**13**	**4**	**8**	**12**	**78**	**0**	**0**	**0**	**110**	**3.6**	**62**	**1**	**95**	**26**	**–8**	....	....	....	....	....	....	....	....
1972-73	**Philadelphia Flyers**	**NHL**	**72**	**1**	**11**	**12**	**1**	**9**	**10**	**76**	**0**	**0**	**0**	**66**	**1.5**	**81**	**2**	**97**	**40**	**+22**	**11**	**0**	**0**	**0**	**16**	**0**	**0**	**0**
1973-74	**Philadelphia Flyers**	**NHL**	**77**	**2**	**16**	**18**	**2**	**14**	**16**	**119**	**0**	**0**	**1**	**76**	**2.6**	**74**	**1**	**64**	**22**	**+31**	**17**	**1**	**2**	**3**	**41**	**0**	**0**	**0**
1974-75	**Philadelphia Flyers**	**NHL**	**78**	**1**	**17**	**18**	**1**	**13**	**14**	**109**	**0**	**0**	**0**	**57**	**1.8**	**71**	**3**	**68**	**39**	**+39**	**17**	**0**	**4**	**4**	**28**	**0**	**0**	**0**
1975-76	**Philadelphia Flyers**	**NHL**	**40**	**0**	**8**	**8**	**0**	**6**	**6**	**60**	**0**	**0**	**0**	**15**	**0.0**	**39**	**0**	**43**	**20**	**+16**	....	....	....	....	....	....	....	....
	Pittsburgh Penguins	**NHL**	**12**	**0**	**5**	**5**	**0**	**4**	**4**	**16**	**0**	**0**	**0**	**7**	**0.0**	**17**	**0**	**16**	**3**	**+4**	**3**	**0**	**1**	**1**	**2**	**0**	**0**	**0**
1976-77	**Pittsburgh Penguins**	**NHL**	**10**	**0**	**3**	**3**	**0**	**2**	**2**	**6**	**0**	**0**	**0**	**3**	**0.0**	**5**	**0**	**8**	**1**	**–2**	....	....	....	....	....	....	....	....
	NHL Totals		**700**	**27**	**126**	**153**	**31**	**112**	**143**	**1025**	**5**	**0**	**2**	**732**	**3.7**	**579**	**39**	**693**	**223**		**66**	**1**	**12**	**13**	**131**	**0**	**0**	**0**

Played in NHL All-Star Game (1969, 1974, 1975)

Claimed by **Philadelphia** from **Chicago** in Expansion Draft, June 6, 1967. Traded to **Pittsburgh** by **Philadelphia** with Bobby Taylor for Gary Inness and future considerations, March 9, 1976.

• VARADA, VACLAV

Vaclav Varada RW – L. 6', 200 lbs. b: Vsetin, Czech., 4/26/1976. San Jose's 4th choice, 89th overall, in 1994 Entry Draft.

Season	Club	League	GP	G	A	Pts	AG	AA	APts	PIM	PP	SH	GW	S	%	TGF	PGF	TGA	PGA	+/–	GP	G	A	Pts	PIM	PP	SH	GW
1992-93	TJ Vitkovice	Czech.	1	0	0	0	....	....	....	....	....	....	....	....	....	....	....	....	....	....	....	....	....	....	....	....	....	....
1993-94	TJ Vitkovice	Czech.	24	6	7	13	....	....	....	....	....	....	....	....	....	....	....	....	....	....	5	1	1	2	....	....	....	....
1994-95	Tacoma Rockets	WHL	68	50	38	88	....	....	....	108	....	....	....	....	....	....	....	....	....	....	4	4	3	7	11	....	....	....
	Czech Republic	WJC-A	7	6	4	10	....	....	....	25	....	....	....	....	....	....	....	....	....	....	....	....	....	....	....	....	....	....
1995-96	Kelowna Rockets	WHL	59	39	46	85	....	....	....	100	....	....	....	....	....	....	....	....	....	....	6	3	3	6	16	....	....	....
	Czech Republic	WJC-A	6	5	1	6	....	....	....	8	....	....	....	....	....	....	....	....	....	....	....	....	....	....	....	....	....	....
	Buffalo Sabres	**NHL**	**1**	**0**	**0**	**0**	**0**	**0**	**0**	**0**	**0**	**0**	**0**	**2**	**0.0**	**0**	**0**	**0**	**0**	**0**	....	....	....	....	....	....	....	....
	Rochester Americans	AHL	5	3	0	3	....	....	....	4	....	....	....	....	....	....	....	....	....	....	....	....	....	....	....	....	....	....
1996-97	**Buffalo Sabres**	**NHL**	**5**	**0**	**0**	**0**	**0**	**0**	**0**	**2**	**0**	**0**	**0**	**2**	**0.0**	**0**	**0**	**0**	**0**	**0**	....	....	....	....	....	....	....	....
	Rochester Americans	AHL	53	23	25	48	....	....	....	81	....	....	....	....	....	....	....	....	....	....	10	1	6	7	27	....	....	....
1997-98	**Buffalo Sabres**	**NHL**	**27**	**5**	**6**	**11**	**6**	**6**	**12**	**15**	**0**	**0**	**1**	**27**	**18.5**	**13**	**0**	**13**	**0**	**0**	**15**	**3**	**4**	**7**	**18**	**0**	**0**	**0**
	Rochester Americans	AHL	45	30	26	56	....	....	....	74	....	....	....	....	....	....	....	....	....	....	....	....	....	....	....	....	....	....
	NHL Totals		**33**	**5**	**6**	**11**	**6**	**6**	**12**	**17**	**0**	**0**	**1**	**31**	**16.1**	**13**	**0**	**13**	**0**		**15**	**3**	**4**	**7**	**18**	**0**	**0**	**0**

Traded to **Buffalo** by **San Jose** with Martin Spahnel, an optional 1st round choice in 1996 Entry Draft and Philadelphia's 4th round choice (previously acquired, Buffalo selected Mike Martone) in 1996 Entry Draft for Doug Bodger, November 16, 1995.

● VARIS, PETRI

Petri Varis LW – L. 6'1", 200 lbs. b: Varkaus, Finland, 5/13/1969. San Jose's 7th choice, 132nd overall, in 1993 Entry Draft.

			REGULAR SEASON																		PLAYOFFS							
Season	Club	League	GP	G	A	Pts	AG	AA	APts	PIM	PP	SH	GW	S	%	TGF	PGF	TGA	PGA	+/–	GP	G	A	Pts	PIM	PP	SH	GW
1990-91	KooKoo Espoo	Finland 2	44	20	31	51	....	....	....	42	....	....	....	....	....	....	....	....	....	....	....	....	....	....	....	....	....	....
1991-92	Assat Pori	Finland	36	13	23	36	....	....	....	24	....	....	....	....	....	....	....	....	....	....	....	....	....	....	....	....	....	....
1992-93	Assat Pori	Finland	46	14	35	49	....	....	....	42	....	....	....	....	....	....	....	....	....	....	8	2	2	4	12	....	....	....
1993-94	Jokerit Helsinki	Finland	31	14	15	29	....	....	....	16	....	....	....	....	....	....	....	....	....	....	11	3	4	7	6	....	....	....
	Finland	Olympics	5	1	1	2	....	....	....	2	....	....	....	....	....	....	....	....	....	....	....	....	....	....	....	....	....	....
1994-95	Jokerit Helsinki	Finland	47	21	20	41	....	....	....	53	....	....	....	....	....	....	....	....	....	....	11	7	2	9	10	....	....	....
1995-96	Jokerit Helsinki	Finland	50	28	28	56	....	....	....	22	....	....	....	....	....	....	....	....	....	....	11	12	7	19	6	....	....	....
1996-97	Jokerit Helsinki	Finland	50	*36	23	*59	....	....	....	38	....	....	....	....	....	....	....	....	....	....	9	7	4	11	14	....	....	....
	Finland	WC-A	8	2	3	5	....	....	....	2	....	....	....	....	....	....	....	....	....	....	....	....	....	....	....	....	....	....
1997-98	**Chicago Blackhawks**	**NHL**	**1**	**0**	**0**	**0**	**0**	**0**	**0**	**0**	**0**	**0**	**0**	**0**	**0.0**	**0**	**0**	**0**	**0**	**0**	....	....	....	....	....	....	....	....
	Indianapolis Ice	IHL	77	18	54	72	....	....	....	32	....	....	....	....	....	....	....	....	....	....	5	3	4	7	4	....	....	....
	NHL Totals		**1**	**0**	**0**	**0**	**0**	**0**	**0**	**0**	**0**	**0**	**0**	**0**	**0.0**	**0**	**0**	**0**	**0**		....	....	....	....	....	....	....	....

Finnish Rookie of the Year (1992)

Rights traded to **Chicago** by **San Jose** with San Jose's 6th round choice in 1998 Entry Draft for Murray Craven, July 25, 1997.

● VARLAMOV, SERGEI

Sergei Varlamov LW – L. 5'11", 190 lbs. b: Kiev, USSR, 7/21/1978.

			REGULAR SEASON																		PLAYOFFS							
Season	Club	League	GP	G	A	Pts	AG	AA	APts	PIM	PP	SH	GW	S	%	TGF	PGF	TGA	PGA	+/–	GP	G	A	Pts	PIM	PP	SH	GW
1995-96	Swift Current Broncos	WHL	55	23	21	44	....	....	....	65	....	....	....	....	....	....	....	....	....	....	....	....	....	....	....	....	....	....
1996-97	Swift Current Broncos	WHL	72	46	39	85	....	....	....	94	....	....	....	....	....	....	....	....	....	....	10	3	8	11	10	....	....	....
	Saint John Flames	AHL	1	0	0	0	....	....	....	0	....	....	....	....	....	....	....	....	....	....	....	....	....	....	....	....	....	....
1997-98	Swift Current Broncos	WHL	72	*66	53	*119	....	....	....	132	....	....	....	....	....	....	....	....	....	....	12	10	5	15	28	....	....	....
	Calgary Flames	**NHL**	**1**	**0**	**0**	**0**	**0**	**0**	**0**	**0**	....	....	....	....	....	....	....	....	....	....	....	....	....	....	....	....	....	....
	Saint John Flames	AHL	....	....	....	....	....	....	....	....	....	....	....	....	....	....	....	....	....	....	3	0	0	0	0	....	....	....
	NHL Totals		**1**	**0**	**0**	**0**	**0**	**0**	**0**	**0**	**0**	**0**	**0**	**0**	**0.0**	**0**	**0**	**0**	**0**		....	....	....	....	....	....	....	....

Signed as a free agent by **Calgary**, September 18, 1996.

● VARVIO, JARKKO

Jarkko Varvio RW – R. 5'9", 175 lbs. b: Tampere, Finland, 4/28/1972. Minnesota's 1st choice, 34th overall, in 1992 Entry Draft.

			REGULAR SEASON																		PLAYOFFS							
Season	Club	League	GP	G	A	Pts	AG	AA	APts	PIM	PP	SH	GW	S	%	TGF	PGF	TGA	PGA	+/–	GP	G	A	Pts	PIM	PP	SH	GW
1989-90	Ilves Tampere	Finland	1	0	0	0	....	....	....	0	....	....	....	....	....	....	....	....	....	....	....	....	....	....	....	....	....	....
1990-91	Ilves Tampere	Finland	37	10	7	17	....	....	....	6	....	....	....	....	....	....	....	....	....	....	....	....	....	....	....	....	....	....
	Finland	WJC-A	7	5	4	9	....	....	....	4	....	....	....	....	....	....	....	....	....	....	....	....	....	....	....	....	....	....
1991-92	HPK Hameenlinna	Finland	41	25	9	34	....	....	....	6	....	....	....	....	....	....	....	....	....	....	....	....	....	....	....	....	....	....
	Finland	WJC-A	7	8	1	9	....	....	....	8	....	....	....	....	....	....	....	....	....	....	....	....	....	....	....	....	....	....
	Finland	WC-A	8	9	1	10	....	....	....	4	....	....	....	....	....	....	....	....	....	....	....	....	....	....	....	....	....	....
1992-93	HPK Hameenlinna	Finland	40	29	19	48	....	....	....	16	....	....	....	....	....	....	....	....	....	....	12	3	2	5	8	....	....	....
	Finland	WC-A	6	2	0	2	....	....	....	6	....	....	....	....	....	....	....	....	....	....	....	....	....	....	....	....	....	....
1993-94	**Dallas Stars**	**NHL**	**8**	**2**	**3**	**5**	**2**	**2**	**4**	**4**	**0**	**0**	**1**	**17**	**11.8**	**6**	**2**	**3**	**0**	**+1**	....	....	....	....	....	....	....	....
	Kalamazoo Wings	IHL	58	29	16	45	....	....	....	18	....	....	....	....	....	....	....	....	....	....	1	0	0	0	0	....	....	....
1994-95	HPK Hameenlinna	Finland	19	7	8	15	....	....	....	4	....	....	....	....	....	....	....	....	....	....	....	....	....	....	....	....	....	....
	Dallas Stars	**NHL**	**5**	**1**	**1**	**2**	**2**	**1**	**3**	**0**	**1**	**0**	**0**	**9**	**11.1**	**3**	**1**	**1**	**0**	**+1**	....	....	....	....	....	....	....	....
	Kalamazoo Wings	IHL	7	0	0	0	....	....	....	2	....	....	....	....	....	....	....	....	....	....	....	....	....	....	....	....	....	....
1995-96	Lukko Rauma	Finland	47	14	13	27	....	....	....	32	....	....	....	....	....	....	....	....	....	....	8	5	0	5	4	....	....	....
1996-97	Lukko Rauma	Finland	40	9	11	20	....	....	....	40	....	....	....	....	....	....	....	....	....	....	....	....	....	....	....	....	....	....
	Finland	WC-A	8	0	0	0	....	....	....	4	....	....	....	....	....	....	....	....	....	....	....	....	....	....	....	....	....	....
1997-98	Tappara Tampere	Finland	47	19	13	32	....	....	....	22	....	....	....	....	....	....	....	....	....	....	4	0	2	2	4	....	....	....
	NHL Totals		**13**	**3**	**4**	**7**	**4**	**3**	**7**	**4**	**1**	**0**	**1**	**26**	**11.5**	**9**	**3**	**4**	**0**		....	....	....	....	....	....	....	....

WC-A All-Star Team (1992) • Finnish First All-Star Team (1993)

Rights transferred to **Dallas** after **Minnesota** franchise relocated, June 9, 1993.

● VASILEVSKI, ALEXANDER

Alexander Vasilevski RW – L. 5'11", 190 lbs. b: Kiev, USSR, 1/8/1975. St. Louis' 9th choice, 271st overall, in 1993 Entry Draft.

			REGULAR SEASON																		PLAYOFFS							
Season	Club	League	GP	G	A	Pts	AG	AA	APts	PIM	PP	SH	GW	S	%	TGF	PGF	TGA	PGA	+/–	GP	G	A	Pts	PIM	PP	SH	GW
1992-93	Victoria Cougars	WHL	71	27	25	52	....	....	....	52	....	....	....	....	....	....	....	....	....	....	....	....	....	....	....	....	....	....
1993-94	Victoria Cougars	WHL	69	34	51	85	....	....	....	78	....	....	....	....	....	....	....	....	....	....	....	....	....	....	....	....	....	....
1994-95	Prince George Cougars	WHL	48	32	34	66	....	....	....	52	....	....	....	....	....	....	....	....	....	....	....	....	....	....	....	....	....	....
	Brandon Wheat Kings	WHL	23	6	11	17	....	....	....	39	....	....	....	....	....	....	....	....	....	....	18	3	6	9	34	....	....	....
1995-96	**St. Louis Blues**	**NHL**	**1**	**0**	**0**	**0**	**0**	**0**	**0**	**0**	**0**	**0**	**0**	**0**	**0.0**	**0**	**0**	**1**	**0**	**–1**	....	....	....	....	....	....	....	....
	Worcester IceCats	AHL	69	18	21	39	....	....	....	112	....	....	....	....	....	....	....	....	....	....	4	2	1	3	10	....	....	....
1996-97	**St. Louis Blues**	**NHL**	**3**	**0**	**0**	**0**	**0**	**0**	**0**	**2**	**0**	**0**	**0**	**3**	**0.0**	**0**	**0**	**1**	**0**	**–1**	....	....	....	....	....	....	....	....
	Worcester IceCats	AHL	61	9	23	32	....	....	....	100	....	....	....	....	....	....	....	....	....	....	....	....	....	....	....	....	....	....
	Grand Rapids Griffins	IHL	10	1	5	6	....	....	....	43	....	....	....	....	....	....	....	....	....	....	5	0	1	1	19	....	....	....
1997-98	Hamilton Bulldogs	AHL	41	3	14	17	....	....	....	60	....	....	....	....	....	....	....	....	....	....	....	....	....	....	....	....	....	....
	Detroit Vipers	IHL	9	1	1	2	....	....	....	7	....	....	....	....	....	....	....	....	....	....	....	....	....	....	....	....	....	....
	NHL Totals		**4**	**0**	**0**	**0**	**0**	**0**	**0**	**2**	**0**	**0**	**0**	**3**	**0.0**	**0**	**0**	**2**	**0**		....	....	....	....	....	....	....	....

● VASILIEV, ANDREI

Andrei Vasiliev LW – R. 5'9", 180 lbs. b: Voskresensk, USSR, 3/30/1972. NY Islanders' 11th choice, 248th overall, in 1992 Entry Draft.

			REGULAR SEASON																		PLAYOFFS							
Season	Club	League	GP	G	A	Pts	AG	AA	APts	PIM	PP	SH	GW	S	%	TGF	PGF	TGA	PGA	+/–	GP	G	A	Pts	PIM	PP	SH	GW
1991-92	CSKA Moscow	CIS	28	7	2	9	....	....	....	2	....	....	....	....	....	....	....	....	....	....	....	....	....	....	....	....	....	....
1992-93	Khimik Voskresensk	CIS	34	4	8	12	....	....	....	20	....	....	....	....	....	....	....	....	....	....	....	....	....	....	....	....	....	....
1993-94	CSKA Moscow	CIS	46	17	6	23	....	....	....	8	....	....	....	....	....	....	....	....	....	....	3	1	0	1	0	....	....	....
1994-95	Denver Grizzlies	IHL	74	28	37	65	....	....	....	48	....	....	....	....	....	....	....	....	....	....	13	9	4	13	22	....	....	....
	New York Islanders	**NHL**	**2**	**0**	**0**	**0**	**0**	**0**	**0**	**2**	**0**	**0**	**0**	**2**	**0.0**	**0**	**0**	**0**	**0**	**0**	....	....	....	....	....	....	....	....
1995-96	**New York Islanders**	**NHL**	**10**	**2**	**5**	**7**	**2**	**4**	**6**	**2**	**0**	**0**	**1**	**12**	**16.7**	**12**	**4**	**4**	**0**	**+4**	....	....	....	....	....	....	....	....
	Utah Grizzlies	IHL	43	26	20	46	....	....	....	34	....	....	....	....	....	....	....	....	....	....	22	12	4	16	18	....	....	....
1996-97	**New York Islanders**	**NHL**	**3**	**0**	**0**	**0**	**0**	**0**	**0**	**2**	**0**	**0**	**0**	**1**	**0.0**	**0**	**0**	**3**	**0**	**–3**	....	....	....	....	....	....	....	....
	Utah Grizzlies	IHL	56	16	18	34	....	....	....	42	....	....	....	....	....	....	....	....	....	....	7	4	1	5	0	....	....	....
	NHL Totals		**15**	**2**	**5**	**7**	**2**	**4**	**6**	**6**	**0**	**0**	**1**	**15**	**13.3**	**12**	**4**	**7**	**0**		....	....	....	....	....	....	....	....

● VASKE, DENNIS

Dennis Vaske D – L. 6'2", 210 lbs. b: Rockford, IL, 10/11/1967. NY Islanders' 2nd choice, 38th overall, in 1986 Entry Draft.

			REGULAR SEASON																		PLAYOFFS							
Season	Club	League	GP	G	A	Pts	AG	AA	APts	PIM	PP	SH	GW	S	%	TGF	PGF	TGA	PGA	+/–	GP	G	A	Pts	PIM	PP	SH	GW
1985-86	Armstrong-Minnesota High	H.S.	20	9	13	22	....	....	....	....	....	....	....	....	....	....	....	....	....	....	....	....	....	....	....	....	....	....
1986-87	University of Minnesota-Duluth	WCHA	33	0	2	2	....	....	....	40	....	....	....	....	....	....	....	....	....	....	....	....	....	....	....	....	....	....
1987-88	University of Minnesota-Duluth	WCHA	39	1	6	7	....	....	....	90	....	....	....	....	....	....	....	....	....	....	....	....	....	....	....	....	....	....
1988-89	University of Minnesota-Duluth	WCHA	37	9	19	28	....	....	....	86	....	....	....	....	....	....	....	....	....	....	....	....	....	....	....	....	....	....
1989-90	University of Minnesota-Duluth	WCHA	37	5	24	29	....	....	....	72	....	....	....	....	....	....	....	....	....	....	....	....	....	....	....	....	....	....
1990-91	**New York Islanders**	**NHL**	**5**	**0**	**0**	**0**	**0**	**0**	**0**	**2**	**0**	**0**	**0**	**3**	**0.0**	**7**	**0**	**4**	**1**	**+4**	....	....	....	....	....	....	....	....
	Capital District Islanders	AHL	67	10	10	20	....	....	....	65	....	....	....	....	....	....	....	....	....	....	....	....	....	....	....	....	....	....
1991-92	**New York Islanders**	**NHL**	**39**	**0**	**1**	**1**	**0**	**1**	**1**	**39**	**0**	**0**	**0**	**26**	**0.0**	**35**	**1**	**42**	**13**	**+5**	....	....	....	....	....	....	....	....
	Capital District Islanders	AHL	31	1	11	12	....	....	....	59	....	....	....	....	....	....	....	....	....	....	....	....	....	....	....	....	....	....
	United States	WC-A	6	0	0	0	....	....	....	6	....	....	....	....	....	....	....	....	....	....	....	....	....	....	....	....	....	....
1992-93	**New York Islanders**	**NHL**	**27**	**1**	**5**	**6**	**1**	**3**	**4**	**32**	**0**	**0**	**0**	**15**	**6.7**	**34**	**0**	**28**	**3**	**+9**	**18**	**0**	**6**	**6**	**14**	**0**	**0**	**0**
	Capital District Islanders	AHL	42	4	15	19	....	....	....	70	....	....	....	....	....	....	....	....	....	....	....	....	....	....	....	....	....	....
1993-94	**New York Islanders**	**NHL**	**65**	**2**	**11**	**13**	**2**	**8**	**10**	**76**	**0**	**0**	**0**	**71**	**2.8**	**71**	**5**	**67**	**22**	**+21**	**4**	**0**	**1**	**1**	**2**	**0**	**0**	**0**
1994-95	**New York Islanders**	**NHL**	**41**	**1**	**11**	**12**	**2**	**16**	**18**	**53**	**0**	**0**	**0**	**48**	**2.1**	**44**	**7**	**53**	**19**	**+3**	....	....	....	....	....	....	....	....
1995-96	**New York Islanders**	**NHL**	**19**	**1**	**6**	**7**	**1**	**5**	**6**	**21**	**1**	**0**	**1**	**19**	**5.3**	**10**	**0**	**30**	**13**	**–13**	....	....	....	....	....	....	....	....
1996-97	**New York Islanders**	**NHL**	**17**	**0**	**4**	**4**	**0**	**4**	**4**	**12**	**0**	**0**	**0**	**19**	**0.0**	**17**	**2**	**13**	**1**	**+3**	....	....	....	....	....	....	....	....
1997-98	**New York Islanders**	**NHL**	**19**	**0**	**3**	**3**	**0**	**3**	**3**	**12**	**0**	**0**	**0**	**16**	**0.0**	**18**	**3**	**16**	**3**	**+2**	....	....	....	....	....	....	....	....
	NHL Totals		**232**	**5**	**41**	**46**	**6**	**40**	**46**	**247**	**1**	**0**	**1**	**217**	**2.3**	**244**	**26**	**259**	**75**		**22**	**0**	**7**	**7**	**16**	**0**	**0**	**0**

• VASKO, ELMER

Elmer "Moose" Vasko D – L. 6'2", 200 lbs. b: Duparquet, Que., 12/11/1935.

Season	Club	League	GP	G	A	Pts	AG	AA	APts	PIM	PP	SH	GW	S	%	TGF	PGF	TGA	PGA	+/-	Playoffs GP	G	A	Pts	PIM	PP	SH	GW
1953-54	St. Catharines Teepees	OHA	59	5	17	22	....	....	....	25	....	....	....	....	....	....	....	....	....	....	15	0	2	2	10	....	....	....
1954-55	St. Catharines Teepees	OHA	49	16	20	36	....	....	....	75	....	....	....	....	....	....	....	....	....	....	11	2	3	5	17	....	....	....
1955-56	St. Catharines Teepees	OHA	47	9	31	40	....	....	....	90	....	....	....	....	....	....	....	....	....	....	6	2	3	5	8	....	....	....
	Buffalo Bisons	AHL	4	0	3	3	....	....	....	4	....	....	....	....	....	....	....	....	....	....	3	1	0	1	2	....	....	....
1956-57	**Chicago Black Hawks**	**NHL**	**64**	**3**	**12**	**15**	**4**	**14**	**18**	**31**	....	....	....	....	....	....	....	....	....	....	....	....	....	....	....	....	....	....
1957-58	**Chicago Black Hawks**	**NHL**	**59**	**6**	**20**	**26**	**8**	**22**	**30**	**51**	....	....	....	....	....	....	....	....	....	....	....	....	....	....	....	....	....	....
1958-59	**Chicago Black Hawks**	**NHL**	**63**	**6**	**10**	**16**	**8**	**11**	**19**	**52**	....	....	....	....	....	....	....	....	....	....	**6**	**0**	**1**	**1**	**4**	....	....	....
1959-60	**Chicago Black Hawks**	**NHL**	**69**	**3**	**27**	**30**	**4**	**28**	**32**	**110**	....	....	....	....	....	....	....	....	....	....	**4**	**0**	**0**	**0**	**0**	....	....	....
1960-61	**Chicago Black Hawks**	**NHL**	**63**	**4**	**18**	**22**	**5**	**18**	**23**	**40**	....	....	....	....	....	....	....	....	....	....	**12**	**1**	**1**	**2**	**23**	....	....	....
1961-62	**Chicago Black Hawks**	**NHL**	**64**	**2**	**22**	**24**	**2**	**22**	**24**	**87**	....	....	....	....	....	....	....	....	....	....	**12**	**0**	**0**	**0**	**4**	....	....	....
1962-63	**Chicago Black Hawks**	**NHL**	**64**	**4**	**9**	**13**	**5**	**9**	**14**	**70**	....	....	....	....	....	....	....	....	....	....	**6**	**0**	**1**	**1**	**8**	....	....	....
1963-64	**Chicago Black Hawks**	**NHL**	**70**	**2**	**18**	**20**	**3**	**20**	**23**	**65**	....	....	....	....	....	....	....	....	....	....	**7**	**0**	**0**	**0**	**4**	....	....	....
1964-65	**Chicago Black Hawks**	**NHL**	**69**	**1**	**10**	**11**	**1**	**11**	**12**	**56**	....	....	....	....	....	....	....	....	....	....	**14**	**1**	**2**	**3**	**20**	....	....	....
1965-66	**Chicago Black Hawks**	**NHL**	**56**	**1**	**7**	**8**	**1**	**7**	**8**	**44**	....	....	....	....	....	....	....	....	....	....	**3**	**0**	**0**	**0**	**4**	....	....	....
1966-67			DID NOT PLAY – RETIRED																									
1967-68	**Minnesota North Stars**	**NHL**	**70**	**1**	**6**	**7**	**1**	**6**	**7**	**45**	**0**	**0**	**0**	**23**	**4.3**	**49**	**3**	**88**	**6**	**–36**	**14**	**0**	**2**	**2**	**6**	**0**	**0**	**0**
1968-69	**Minnesota North Stars**	**NHL**	**72**	**1**	**7**	**8**	**1**	**7**	**8**	**68**	**0**	**0**	**0**	**52**	**1.9**	**70**	**2**	**109**	**23**	**–18**	....	....	....	....	....	....	....	....
1969-70	**Minnesota North Stars**	**NHL**	**3**	**0**	**0**	**0**	**0**	**0**	**0**	**0**	**0**	**0**	**0**	**3**	**0.0**	**1**	**0**	**3**	**1**	**–1**	....	....	....	....	....	....	....	....
	Salt Lake Golden Eagles	WHL	54	4	6	10	....	....	....	34	....	....	....	....	....	....	....	....	....	....	....	....	....	....	....	....	....	....
	NHL Totals		**786**	**34**	**166**	**200**	**43**	**175**	**218**	**719**	**0**	**0**	**0**	**78**	**43.6**	**120**	**5**	**200**	**30**		**78**	**2**	**7**	**9**	**73**	**0**	**0**	**0**

NHL Second All-Star Team (1963, 1964)
Played in NHL All-Star Game (1961, 1963, 1964, 1969)
Claimed by **Minnesota** from **Chicago** in Expansion Draft, June 6, 1967.

• VASKO, RICK

Rick "The Moose" Vasko D – L. 6', 185 lbs. b: St. Catharines, Ont., 1/12/1957. Detroit's 2nd choice, 37th overall, in 1977 Amateur Draft.

Season	Club	League	GP	G	A	Pts	AG	AA	APts	PIM	PP	SH	GW	S	%	TGF	PGF	TGA	PGA	+/-	Playoffs GP	G	A	Pts	PIM	PP	SH	GW
1975-76	Peterborough Petes	OHA	63	9	20	29	....	....	....	53	....	....	....	....	....	....	....	....	....	....	....	....	....	....	....	....	....	....
1976-77	Peterborough Petes	OHA	65	6	30	36	....	....	....	122	....	....	....	....	....	....	....	....	....	....	....	....	....	....	....	....	....	....
1977-78	**Detroit Red Wings**	**NHL**	**3**	**0**	**0**	**0**	**0**	**0**	**0**	**7**	**0**	**0**	**0**	**6**	**0.0**	**1**	**0**	**2**	**0**	**–1**	....	....	....	....	....	....	....	....
	Kansas City Red Wings	CHL	70	11	30	41	....	....	....	72	....	....	....	....	....	....	....	....	....	....	....	....	....	....	....	....	....	....
1978-79	Kansas City Red Wings	CHL	75	21	38	59	....	....	....	67	....	....	....	....	....	....	....	....	....	....	4	1	1	2	2	....	....	....
1979-80	**Detroit Red Wings**	**NHL**	**8**	**0**	**0**	**0**	**0**	**0**	**0**	**2**	**0**	**0**	**0**	**6**	**0.0**	**2**	**1**	**12**	**0**	**–11**	....	....	....	....	....	....	....	....
	Adirondack Red Wings	AHL	71	22	39	61	....	....	....	79	....	....	....	....	....	....	....	....	....	....	....	....	....	....	....	....	....	....
1980-81	**Detroit Red Wings**	**NHL**	**20**	**3**	**7**	**10**	**2**	**5**	**7**	**20**	**1**	**0**	**0**	**28**	**10.7**	**24**	**6**	**30**	**9**	**–3**	....	....	....	....	....	....	....	....
	Adirondack Red Wings	AHL	57	17	34	51	....	....	....	78	....	....	....	....	....	....	....	....	....	....	18	9	12	*21	31	....	....	....
1981-82	Oklahoma City Stars	CHL	68	9	32	41	....	....	....	92	....	....	....	....	....	....	....	....	....	....	4	1	1	2	4	....	....	....
	NHL Totals		**31**	**3**	**7**	**10**	**2**	**5**	**7**	**29**	**1**	**0**	**0**	**40**	**7.5**	**27**	**7**	**44**	**9**		....	....	....	....	....	....	....	....

AHL First All-Star Team (1980) • Won Eddie Shore Award (Outstanding Defenseman - AHL) (1980)
Traded to **Calgary** by **Detroit** to complete transaction that sent Brad Smith to Detroit (February 24, 1981), May 28, 1981.

• VAUTOUR, YVON

Yvon Vautour RW – R. 6', 200 lbs. b: St. John, N.B., 9/10/1956. NY Islanders' 6th choice, 104th overall, in 1976 Amateur Draft.

Season	Club	League	GP	G	A	Pts	AG	AA	APts	PIM	PP	SH	GW	S	%	TGF	PGF	TGA	PGA	+/-	Playoffs GP	G	A	Pts	PIM	PP	SH	GW
1971-72	Saint John Schooners	NBJHL	40	13	15	28	....	....	....	96	....	....	....	....	....	....	....	....	....	....	....	....	....	....	....	....	....	....
1972-73	Saint John Schooners	NBJHL	40	42	31	73	....	....	....	85	....	....	....	....	....	....	....	....	....	....	....	....	....	....	....	....	....	....
1973-74	Laval Nationale	QMJHL	61	38	39	77	....	....	....	118	....	....	....	....	....	....	....	....	....	....	....	....	....	....	....	....	....	....
1974-75	Laval Nationale	QMJHL	56	34	37	71	....	....	....	67	....	....	....	....	....	....	....	....	....	....	16	15	7	22	67	....	....	....
1975-76	Laval Nationale	QMJHL	72	43	60	103	....	....	....	61	....	....	....	....	....	....	....	....	....	....	....	....	....	....	....	....	....	....
1976-77	Muskegon Mohawks	IHL	76	43	47	90	....	....	....	52	....	....	....	....	....	....	....	....	....	....	7	3	4	7	2	....	....	....
	Fort Worth Texans	CHL	....	....	....	....	....	....	....	....	....	....	....	....	....	....	....	....	....	....	2	0	0	0	0	....	....	....
1977-78	Fort Worth Texans	CHL	64	14	21	35	....	....	....	84	....	....	....	....	....	....	....	....	....	....	14	2	6	8	16	....	....	....
1978-79	Fort Worth Texans	CHL	69	20	20	40	....	....	....	130	....	....	....	....	....	....	....	....	....	....	5	2	1	3	15	....	....	....
1979-80	**New York Islanders**	**NHL**	**17**	**3**	**1**	**4**	**3**	**1**	**4**	**24**	**0**	**0**	**1**	**16**	**18.8**	**5**	**0**	**12**	**1**	**–6**	....	....	....	....	....	....	....	....
	Indianapolis Checkers	CHL	59	27	28	55	....	....	....	140	....	....	....	....	....	....	....	....	....	....	7	2	5	7	11	....	....	....
1980-81	**Colorado Rockies**	**NHL**	**74**	**15**	**19**	**34**	**12**	**13**	**25**	**143**	**3**	**0**	**0**	**97**	**15.5**	**51**	**8**	**66**	**3**	**–20**	....	....	....	....	....	....	....	....
1981-82	**Colorado Rockies**	**NHL**	**14**	**1**	**2**	**3**	**1**	**1**	**2**	**18**	**1**	**0**	**0**	**21**	**4.8**	**7**	**1**	**12**	**0**	**–6**	....	....	....	....	....	....	....	....
1982-83	**New Jersey Devils**	**NHL**	**52**	**4**	**7**	**11**	**3**	**5**	**8**	**136**	**0**	**0**	**0**	**54**	**7.4**	**17**	**2**	**34**	**0**	**–19**	....	....	....	....	....	....	....	....
	Moncton Alpines	AHL	14	7	5	12	....	....	....	25	....	....	....	....	....	....	....	....	....	....	....	....	....	....	....	....	....	....
	Wichita Wind	CHL	4	3	0	3	....	....	....	0	....	....	....	....	....	....	....	....	....	....	....	....	....	....	....	....	....	....
1983-84	**New Jersey Devils**	**NHL**	**42**	**3**	**4**	**7**	**2**	**3**	**5**	**78**	**0**	**0**	**1**	**44**	**6.8**	**11**	**2**	**28**	**1**	**–18**	....	....	....	....	....	....	....	....
	Maine Mariners	AHL	24	8	12	20	....	....	....	117	....	....	....	....	....	....	....	....	....	....	....	....	....	....	....	....	....	....
1984-85	**Quebec Nordiques**	**NHL**	**5**	**0**	**0**	**0**	**0**	**0**	**0**	**2**	**0**	**0**	**0**	**1**	**0.0**	**0**	**0**	**0**	**0**	**0**	....	....	....	....	....	....	....	....
	Fredericton Express	AHL	68	7	20	27	....	....	....	222	....	....	....	....	....	....	....	....	....	....	4	1	1	2	26	....	....	....
1985-86			DID NOT PLAY – RETIRED																									
1986-87			DID NOT PLAY – RETIRED																									
1987-88	Saint John Schooners	NBSHL	28	17	11	28	....	....	....	98	....	....	....	....	....	....	....	....	....	....	....	....	....	....	....	....	....	....
1988-89	Saint John Vitos	NBSHL	27	17	25	42	....	....	....	118	....	....	....	....	....	....	....	....	....	....	....	4	11	15	....	....	....	....
1989-90	Saint John Vitos	NBSHL	26	5	11	16	....	....	....	*182	....	....	....	....	....	....	....	....	....	....	....	....	....	....	....	....	....	....
	NHL Totals		**204**	**26**	**33**	**59**	**21**	**23**	**44**	**401**	**4**	**0**	**2**	**233**	**11.2**	**91**	**13**	**152**	**5**		....	....	....	....	....	....	....	....

Claimed by **NY Islanders** as a fill-in during Expansion Draft, June 13, 1979. Claimed by **Colorado** from **NY Islanders** in Waiver Draft, October 8, 1980. Transferred to **New Jersey** after **Colorado** franchise relocated, June 30, 1982. Signed as a free agent by **Quebec**, October 18, 1984.

• VAYDIK, GREG

Greg Vaydik C – L. 6'1", 190 lbs. b: Yellowknife, N.W.T., 10/9/1955. Chicago's 1st choice, 7th overall, in 1975 Amateur Draft.

Season	Club	League	GP	G	A	Pts	AG	AA	APts	PIM	PP	SH	GW	S	%	TGF	PGF	TGA	PGA	+/-	Playoffs GP	G	A	Pts	PIM	PP	SH	GW
1971-72	Drumheller Falcons	AJHL	STATISTICS NOT AVAILABLE																									
1972-73	Medicine Hat Tigers	WCJHL	38	5	3	8	....	....	....	6	....	....	....	....	....	....	....	....	....	....	....	....	....	....	....	....	....	....
1973-74	Medicine Hat Tigers	WCJHL	68	33	41	74	....	....	....	24	....	....	....	....	....	....	....	....	....	....	....	....	....	....	....	....	....	....
1974-75	Medicine Hat Tigers	WCJHL	61	55	51	106	....	....	....	37	....	....	....	....	....	....	....	....	....	....	....	....	....	....	....	....	....	....
	Canada	WJC-A	3	0	1	1	....	....	....	0	....	....	....	....	....	....	....	....	....	....	....	....	....	....	....	....	....	....
1975-76	Dallas Black Hawks	CHL	17	5	5	10	....	....	....	2	....	....	....	....	....	....	....	....	....	....	....	....	....	....	....	....	....	....
1976-77	**Chicago Black Hawks**	**NHL**	**5**	**0**	**0**	**0**	**0**	**0**	**0**	**0**	**0**	**0**	**0**	**2**	**0.0**	**1**	**0**	**3**	**0**	**–2**	....	....	....	....	....	....	....	....
	Dallas Black Hawks	CHL	68	29	32	61	....	....	....	10	....	....	....	....	....	....	....	....	....	....	5	0	3	3	0	....	....	....
1977-78	Dallas Black Hawks	CHL	73	26	18	44	....	....	....	8	....	....	....	....	....	....	....	....	....	....	13	3	3	6	4	....	....	....
1978-79	Rochester Americans	AHL	80	16	25	41	....	....	....	10	....	....	....	....	....	....	....	....	....	....	....	....	....	....	....	....	....	....
1979-80	New Brunswick Hawks	AHL	60	12	19	31	....	....	....	0	....	....	....	....	....	....	....	....	....	....	....	....	....	....	....	....	....	....
1980-81	Dallas Black Hawks	CHL	26	6	5	11	....	....	....	6	....	....	....	....	....	....	....	....	....	....	....	....	....	....	....	....	....	....
1981-82	Dallas Black Hawks	CHL	65	20	30	50	....	....	....	20	....	....	....	....	....	....	....	....	....	....	16	3	6	9	8	....	....	....
	NHL Totals		**5**	**0**	**0**	**0**	**0**	**0**	**0**	**0**	**0**	**0**	**0**	**2**	**0.0**	**1**	**0**	**3**	**0**		....	....	....	....	....	....	....	....

• VEITCH, DARREN

Darren Veitch D – R. 5'11", 195 lbs. b: Saskatoon, Sask., 4/24/1960. Washington's 1st choice, 5th overall, in 1980 Entry Draft.

Season	Club	League	GP	G	A	Pts	AG	AA	APts	PIM	PP	SH	GW	S	%	TGF	PGF	TGA	PGA	+/-	Playoffs GP	G	A	Pts	PIM	PP	SH	GW
1976-77	Regina Blues	SJHL	60	15	21	36	....	....	....	121	....	....	....	....	....	....	....	....	....	....	....	....	....	....	....	....	....	....
	Regina Pats	WCJHL	1	0	0	0	....	....	....	0	....	....	....	....	....	....	....	....	....	....	....	....	....	....	....	....	....	....
1977-78	Regina Pats	WCJHL	71	13	32	45	....	....	....	135	....	....	....	....	....	....	....	....	....	....	9	0	2	2	4	....	....	....
1978-79	Regina Pats	WHL	51	11	36	47	....	....	....	80	....	....	....	....	....	....	....	....	....	....	....	....	....	....	....	....	....	....
1979-80	Regina Pats	WHL	71	29	*93	122	....	....	....	118	....	....	....	....	....	....	....	....	....	....	18	13	18	31	13	....	....	....
1980-81	**Washington Capitals**	**NHL**	**59**	**4**	**21**	**25**	**3**	**15**	**18**	**46**	**1**	**0**	**1**	**89**	**4.5**	**71**	**23**	**67**	**7**	**–12**	....	....	....	....	....	....	....	....
	Hershey Bears	AHL	26	6	22	28	....	....	....	12	....	....	....	....	....	....	....	....	....	....	10	6	3	9	15	....	....	....
1981-82	**Washington Capitals**	**NHL**	**67**	**9**	**44**	**53**	**7**	**29**	**36**	**54**	**5**	**0**	**1**	**203**	**4.4**	**128**	**60**	**101**	**16**	**–17**	....	....	....	....	....	....	....	....
	Hershey Bears	AHL	10	5	10	15	....	....	....	16	....	....	....	....	....	....	....	....	....	....	....	....	....	....	....	....	....	....
1982-83	**Washington Capitals**	**NHL**	**10**	**0**	**8**	**8**	**0**	**6**	**6**	**0**	**0**	**0**	**0**	**23**	**0.0**	**15**	**6**	**11**	**1**	**–1**	....	....	....	....	....	....	....	....
	Hershey Bears	AHL	5	0	1	1	....	....	....	2	....	....	....	....	....	....	....	....	....	....	....	....	....	....	....	....	....	....
1983-84	**Washington Capitals**	**NHL**	**46**	**6**	**18**	**24**	**5**	**12**	**17**	**17**	**4**	**0**	**0**	**120**	**5.0**	**65**	**28**	**43**	**6**	**0**	**5**	**0**	**1**	**1**	**15**	**0**	**0**	**0**
	Hershey Bears	AHL	11	1	6	7	....	....	....	4	....	....	....	....	....	....	....	....	....	....	....	....	....	....	....	....	....	....

Season	Club	League	GP	G	A	Pts	AG	AA	APts	PIM	PP	SH	GW	S	%	TGF	PGF	TGA	PGA	+/–	GP	G	A	Pts	PIM	PP	SH	GW
			REGULAR SEASON																		PLAYOFFS							
1984-85	Washington Capitals	NHL	75	3	18	21	2	12	14	37	2	0	0	126	2.4	101	22	81	33	+31	5	0	1	1	4	0	0	0
1985-86	Washington Capitals	NHL	62	3	9	12	2	6	8	27	0	0	0	82	3.7	58	1	57	21	+21	....	....	....	....	....	....	....	....
	Detroit Red Wings	NHL	13	0	5	5	0	3	3	2	0	0	0	22	0.0	16	4	24	3	–9	....	....	....	....	....	....	....	....
1986-87	Detroit Red Wings	NHL	77	13	45	58	11	33	44	52	7	1	2	164	7.9	120	46	85	25	+14	12	3	4	7	8	2	0	1
1987-88	Detroit Red Wings	NHL	63	7	33	40	6	23	29	45	4	0	1	156	4.5	102	31	69	9	+11	11	1	5	6	6	1	0	0
1988-89	Toronto Maple Leafs	NHL	37	3	7	10	3	5	8	16	1	0	0	69	4.3	31	10	48	10	–17	....	....	....	....	....	....	....	....
	Newmarket Saints	AHL	33	5	19	24	....	....	....	29	....	....	....	....	....	....	....	....	....	....	5	0	4	4	4	....	....	....
1989-90	Newmarket Saints	AHL	78	13	54	67	....	....	....	30	....	....	....	....	....	....	....	....	....	....	....	....	....	....	....	....	....	....
1990-91	Toronto Maple Leafs	NHL	2	0	1	1	0	1	1	0	0	0	0	2	0.0	3	1	6	0	–4	....	....	....	....	....	....	....	....
	Newmarket Saints	AHL	56	7	28	35	....	....	....	26	....	....	....	....	....	....	....	....	....	....	....	....	....	....	....	....	....	....
	Peoria Rivermen	IHL	18	2	14	16	....	....	....	10	....	....	....	....	....	....	....	....	....	....	19	4	12	16	10	....	....	....
1991-92	Moncton Hawks	AHL	61	6	23	29	....	....	....	47	....	....	....	....	....	....	....	....	....	....	11	0	6	6	2	....	....	....
	EV Landshut	Germany	14	2	4	6	....	....	....	4	....	....	....	....	....	....	....	....	....	....	....	....	....	....	....	....	....	....
1992-93	Peoria Rivermen	IHL	79	12	37	49	....	....	....	16	....	....	....	....	....	....	....	....	....	....	4	2	0	2	4	....	....	....
1993-94	Peoria Rivermen	IHL	76	21	54	75	....	....	....	16	....	....	....	....	....	....	....	....	....	....	6	1	1	2	0	....	....	....
1994-95	Peoria Rivermen	IHL	75	8	42	50	....	....	....	42	....	....	....	....	....	....	....	....	....	....	9	0	2	2	8	....	....	....
1995-96	Peoria Rivermen	IHL	15	1	9	10	....	....	....	8	....	....	....	....	....	....	....	....	....	....	....	....	....	....	....	....	....	....
	Phoenix Roadrunners	IHL	43	1	15	16	....	....	....	12	....	....	....	....	....	....	....	....	....	....	1	0	0	0	0	....	....	....
	NHL Totals		**511**	**48**	**209**	**257**	**39**	**145**	**184**	**296**	**24**	**1**	**5**	**1066**	**4.5**	**710**	**232**	**592**	**131**		**33**	**4**	**11**	**15**	**33**	**3**	**0**	**1**

WHL All-Star Team (1980) • Memorial Cup All-Star Team (1980) • AHL Second All-Star Team (1990) • Won Governors' Trophy (Top Defenseman - IHL) (1994)

Traded to **Detroit** by **Washington** for John Barrett and Greg Smith, March 10, 1986. Traded to **Toronto** by **Detroit** for Miroslav Frycer, June 10, 1988. Traded to **St. Louis** by **Toronto** with future considerations for Keith Osborne, March 5, 1991.

● VELISCHEK, RANDY

Randy Velischek D – L. 6′, 200 lbs. b: Montreal, Que., 2/10/1962. Minnesota's 3rd choice, 53rd overall, in 1980 Entry Draft.

Season	Club	League	GP	G	A	Pts	AG	AA	APts	PIM	PP	SH	GW	S	%	TGF	PGF	TGA	PGA	+/–	GP	G	A	Pts	PIM	PP	SH	GW
1979-80	Providence College	ECAC	31	5	5	10	....	....	....	20	....	....	....	....	....	....	....	....	....	....	....	....	....	....	....	....	....	....
1980-81	Providence College	ECAC	33	3	12	15	....	....	....	26	....	....	....	....	....	....	....	....	....	....	....	....	....	....	....	....	....	....
1981-82	Providence College	ECAC	33	1	14	15	....	....	....	38	....	....	....	....	....	....	....	....	....	....	....	....	....	....	....	....	....	....
1982-83	Providence College	ECAC	41	18	34	52	....	....	....	50	....	....	....	....	....	....	....	....	....	....	....	....	....	....	....	....	....	....
	Minnesota North Stars	NHL	3	0	0	0	0	0	0	2	0	0	0	4	0.0	1	0	8	3	–4	9	0	0	0	0	0	0	0
1983-84	Minnesota North Stars	NHL	33	2	2	4	2	1	3	10	0	0	0	15	13.3	24	0	34	4	–6	1	0	0	0	0	0	0	0
	Salt Lake Golden Eagles	CHL	43	7	21	28	....	....	....	54	....	....	....	....	....	....	....	....	....	....	5	0	3	3	2	....	....	....
1984-85	Minnesota North Stars	NHL	52	4	9	13	3	6	9	26	0	0	0	33	12.1	51	0	55	11	+7	9	2	3	5	8	0	0	0
	Springfield Indians	AHL	26	2	7	9	....	....	....	22	....	....	....	....	....	....	....	....	....	....	....	....	....	....	....	....	....	....
1985-86	New Jersey Devils	NHL	47	2	7	9	2	5	7	39	0	0	0	24	8.3	45	1	95	31	–20	....	....	....	....	....	....	....	....
	Maine Mariners	AHL	21	0	4	4	....	....	....	4	....	....	....	....	....	....	....	....	....	....	....	....	....	....	....	....	....	....
1986-87	New Jersey Devils	NHL	64	2	16	18	2	12	14	52	0	0	0	39	5.1	59	0	102	31	–12	....	....	....	....	....	....	....	....
1987-88	New Jersey Devils	NHL	51	3	9	12	3	6	9	66	0	1	0	39	7.7	25	1	56	19	–13	19	0	2	2	20	0	0	0
1988-89	New Jersey Devils	NHL	80	4	14	18	3	10	13	70	0	1	0	77	5.2	61	1	136	74	–2	....	....	....	....	....	....	....	....
1989-90	New Jersey Devils	NHL	62	0	6	6	0	4	4	72	0	0	0	34	0.0	44	0	56	16	+4	6	0	0	0	4	0	0	0
1990-91	Quebec Nordiques	NHL	79	2	10	12	2	8	10	42	0	0	0	47	4.3	59	1	139	62	–19	....	....	....	....	....	....	....	....
1991-92	Quebec Nordiques	NHL	38	2	3	5	2	2	4	22	0	0	0	23	8.7	23	1	42	17	–3	....	....	....	....	....	....	....	....
	Halifax Citadels	AHL	16	3	6	9	....	....	....	0	....	....	....	....	....	....	....	....	....	....	....	....	....	....	....	....	....	....
1992-93	Halifax Citadels	AHL	49	6	16	22	....	....	....	18	....	....	....	....	....	....	....	....	....	....	....	....	....	....	....	....	....	....
1993-94	Cornwall Aces	AHL	18	1	6	7	....	....	....	17	....	....	....	....	....	....	....	....	....	....	....	....	....	....	....	....	....	....
	Milwaukee Admirals	IHL	53	7	11	18	....	....	....	28	....	....	....	....	....	....	....	....	....	....	4	0	0	0	2	....	....	....
1994-95	Milwaukee Admirals	IHL	35	3	3	6	....	....	....	24	....	....	....	....	....	....	....	....	....	....	12	2	2	4	6	....	....	....
	NHL Totals		**509**	**21**	**76**	**97**	**19**	**54**	**73**	**401**	**0**	**2**	**0**	**335**	**6.3**	**392**	**5**	**723**	**268**		**44**	**2**	**5**	**7**	**32**	**0**	**0**	**0**

ECAC Second All-Star Team (1982) • ECAC First All-Star Team (1983) • NCAA East First All-American Team (1983)

Claimed by **New Jersey** from **Minnesota** in Waiver Draft, October 7, 1985. Traded to **Quebec** by **New Jersey** to complete transaction that sent Peter Stastny to New Jersey, August 13, 1990.

● VELLUCCI, MIKE

Mike Vellucci D – L. 6′1″, 180 lbs. b: Farmington, MI, 8/11/1966. Hartford's 3rd choice, 131st overall, in 1984 Entry Draft.

Season	Club	League	GP	G	A	Pts	AG	AA	APts	PIM	PP	SH	GW	S	%	TGF	PGF	TGA	PGA	+/–	GP	G	A	Pts	PIM	PP	SH	GW
1982-83	Detroit Compuware	NAJHL	70	23	20	43	....	....	....	98	....	....	....	....	....	....	....	....	....	....	....	....	....	....	....	....	....	....
1983-84	Belleville Bulls	OHL	67	2	20	22	....	....	....	83	....	....	....	....	....	....	....	....	....	....	3	1	0	1	6	....	....	....
1984-85	Belleville Bulls	OHL	DID NOT PLAY – INJURED																									
1985-86	Belleville Bulls	OHL	64	11	32	43	....	....	....	154	....	....	....	....	....	....	....	....	....	....	24	2	5	7	45	....	....	....
1986-87	Salt Lake Golden Eagles	IHL	60	5	30	35	....	....	....	94	....	....	....	....	....	....	....	....	....	....	....	....	....	....	....	....	....	....
1987-88	Hartford Whalers	NHL	2	0	0	0	0	0	0	11	0	0	0	2	0.0	0	0	1	0	–1	....	....	....	....	....	....	....	....
	Binghamton Whalers	AHL	3	0	0	0	....	....	....	2	....	....	....	....	....	....	....	....	....	....	....	....	....	....	....	....	....	....
	Milwaukee Admirals	IHL	66	7	10	25	....	....	....	202	....	....	....	....	....	....	....	....	....	....	....	....	....	....	....	....	....	....
1988-89	Binghamton Whalers	AHL	37	9	9	18	....	....	....	59	....	....	....	....	....	....	....	....	....	....	....	....	....	....	....	....	....	....
	Indianapolis Ice	IHL	12	1	2	3	....	....	....	43	....	....	....	....	....	....	....	....	....	....	....	....	....	....	....	....	....	....
1989-90	Erie Panthers	ECHL	22	7	20	29	....	....	....	57	....	....	....	....	....	....	....	....	....	....	7	1	4	5	6	....	....	....
	Winston-Salem Thunderbirds	ECHL	10	2	7	9	....	....	....	21	....	....	....	....	....	....	....	....	....	....	....	....	....	....	....	....	....	....
	Phoenix Roadrunners	IHL	4	0	0	0	....	....	....	5	....	....	....	....	....	....	....	....	....	....	....	....	....	....	....	....	....	....
	Whitley Warriors	Britain	5	1	5	6	....	....	....	41	....	....	....	....	....	....	....	....	....	....	....	....	....	....	....	....	....	....
1990-91			DID NOT PLAY																									
1991-92	Michigan Falcons	ColHL	56	17	33	50	....	....	....	103	....	....	....	....	....	....	....	....	....	....	....	....	....	....	....	....	....	....
	NHL Totals		**2**	**0**	**0**	**0**	**0**	**0**	**0**	**11**	**0**	**0**	**0**	**2**	**0.0**	**0**	**0**	**1**	**0**		....	....	....	....	....	....	....	....

● VENASKY, VIC

Vic Venasky C – R. 5′11″, 185 lbs. b: Thunder Bay, Ont., 6/3/1951. Los Angeles' 1st choice, 34th overall, in 1971 Amateur Draft.

Season	Club	League	GP	G	A	Pts	AG	AA	APts	PIM	PP	SH	GW	S	%	TGF	PGF	TGA	PGA	+/–	GP	G	A	Pts	PIM	PP	SH	GW
1969-70	Port Arthur Marrs	TBJHL	STATISTICS NOT AVAILABLE																									
1970-71	University of Denver	WCHA	36	20	36	56	....	....	....	12	....	....	....	....	....	....	....	....	....	....	....	....	....	....	....	....	....	....
1971-72	University of Denver	WCHA	17	16	17	23	....	....	....	....	....	....	....	....	....	....	....	....	....	....	....	....	....	....	....	....	....	....
1972-73	Los Angeles Kings	NHL	77	15	19	34	15	16	31	10	1	0	1	176	8.5	41	5	57	5	–16	....	....	....	....	....	....	....	....
1973-74	Los Angeles Kings	NHL	32	6	5	11	6	4	10	12	1	0	1	45	13.3	19	8	13	1	–1	....	....	....	....	....	....	....	....
	Springfield Kings	AHL	21	8	15	23	....	....	....	8	....	....	....	....	....	....	....	....	....	....	....	....	....	....	....	....	....	....
	Portland Buckaroos	WHL	10	1	11	12	....	....	....	4	....	....	....	....	....	....	....	....	....	....	9	*7	2	9	8	....	....	....
1974-75	Los Angeles Kings	NHL	17	1	2	3	1	2	3	0	1	0	0	17	5.9	6	2	2	1	+3	....	....	....	....	....	....	....	....
	Fort Worth Texans	CHL	14	5	11	16	....	....	....	6	....	....	....	....	....	....	....	....	....	....	....	....	....	....	....	....	....	....
	Springfield Indians	AHL	6	2	2	4	....	....	....	4	....	....	....	....	....	....	....	....	....	....	....	....	....	....	....	....	....	....
1975-76	Los Angeles Kings	NHL	80	18	26	44	17	20	37	12	4	0	5	103	17.5	57	11	57	5	–8	9	0	1	1	6	0	0	0
1976-77	Los Angeles Kings	NHL	80	14	26	40	13	21	34	18	1	1	2	120	11.7	56	7	56	9	+2	9	1	4	5	6	1	0	0
1977-78	Los Angeles Kings	NHL	71	3	10	13	3	8	11	6	0	0	3	53	5.7	16	0	19	4	+1	1	0	0	0	0	0	0	0
1978-79	Los Angeles Kings	NHL	73	4	13	17	4	10	14	8	0	0	1	47	8.5	23	1	28	6	0	2	0	0	0	0	0	0	0
1979-80	Binghamton Dusters	AHL	80	25	31	56	....	....	....	22	....	....	....	....	....	....	....	....	....	....	....	....	....	....	....	....	....	....
	NHL Totals		**430**	**61**	**101**	**162**	**59**	**81**	**140**	**66**	**8**	**1**	**13**	**561**	**10.9**	**218**	**34**	**232**	**31**		**21**	**1**	**5**	**6**	**12**	**1**	**0**	**0**

WCHA Second All-Star Team (1971) • NCAA West First All-American Team (1971)

● VENERUZZO, GARY

Gary Veneruzzo RW/LW – L. 5′8″, 165 lbs. b: Fort William, Ont., 6/28/1943.

Season	Club	League	GP	G	A	Pts	AG	AA	APts	PIM	PP	SH	GW	S	%	TGF	PGF	TGA	PGA	+/–	GP	G	A	Pts	PIM	PP	SH	GW
1963-64	Fort William Canadiens	TBJHL	STATISTICS NOT AVAILABLE																									
1964-65	Tulsa Oilers	CHL	60	11	17	28	....	....	....	29	....	....	....	....	....	....	....	....	....	....	10	1	4	5	8	....	....	....
1965-66	Tulsa Oilers	CHL	69	10	19	38	....	....	....	25	....	....	....	....	....	....	....	....	....	....	11	1	7	8	5	....	....	....
1966-67	Victoria Cougars	WHL	11	3	5	8	....	....	....	2	....	....	....	....	....	....	....	....	....	....	....	....	....	....	....	....	....	....
	Tulsa Oilers	CHL	59	21	25	46	....	....	....	38	....	....	....	....	....	....	....	....	....	....	....	....	....	....	....	....	....	....
1967-68	St. Louis Blues	NHL	5	1	1	2	1	1	2	0	0	0	0	8	12.5	2	0	1	0	+1	9	0	2	2	2	0	0	0
	Kansas City Blues	CHL	63	24	51	75	....	....	....	36	....	....	....	....	....	....	....	....	....	....	7	4	2	6	10	....	....	....
1968-69	Kansas City Blues	CHL	71	38	40	78	....	....	....	38	....	....	....	....	....	....	....	....	....	....	4	1	1	2	13	....	....	....
1969-70	Kansas City Blues	CHL	52	20	30	50	....	....	....	33	....	....	....	....	....	....	....	....	....	....	....	....	....	....	....	....	....	....
	Buffalo Bisons	AHL	21	8	11	19	....	....	....	2	....	....	....	....	....	....	....	....	....	....	14	6	5	11	9	....	....	....
1970-71	Kansas City Blues	CHL	2	2	0	2	....	....	....	2	....	....	....	....	....	....	....	....	....	....	....	....	....	....	....	....	....	....
	Seattle Totems	WHL	66	27	22	49	....	....	....	30	....	....	....	....	....	....	....	....	....	....	....	....	....	....	....	....	....	....

Season	Club	League	GP	G	A	Pts	AG	AA	APts	PIM	PP	SH	GW	S	%	TGF	PGF	TGA	PGA	+/-	Playoffs GP	G	A	Pts	PIM	PP	SH	GW
			REGULAR SEASON																		PLAYOFFS							
1971-72	St. Louis Blues	NHL	2	0	0	0	0	0	0	0	0	0	0	1	0.0	1	0	2	0	–1								
	Denver Spurs	WHL	72	*41	45	86				41											9	2	6	8	10			
1972-73	Los Angeles Sharks	WHA	78	43	30	73				34											6	3	0	3	4			
1973-74	Los Angeles Sharks	WHA	78	39	29	68				68																		
1974-75	Michigan-Baltimore	WHA	77	33	27	60				57																		
1975-76	Cincinnati Stingers	WHA	14	3	2	5				8																		
	Phoenix Roadrunners	WHA	61	19	24	43				27											5	2	0	2	7			
1976-77	San Diego Mariners	WHA	40	14	11	25				18											7	0	0	0	0			
1977-78	Thunder Bay Twins	CASH	14	2	4	6				20																		
	NHL Totals		7	1	1	2	1	1	2	0	0	0	0	9	11.1	3	0	3	0		9	0	2	2	2	0	0	0
	Other Major League Totals		348	151	123	274				212											18	5	0	5	11			

CHL Second All-Star Team (1968) • CHL First All-Star Team (1969) • WHL First All-Star Team (1972)

Claimed by **St. Louis** from **Toronto** in Expansion Draft, June 6, 1967. Selected by **LA Sharks** (WHA) in 1972 WHA General Player Draft, February 12, 1972. Transferred to **Michigan** (WHA) when **LA Sharks** (WHA) franchise relocated, April 11, 1974. Selected by **Cincinnati** (WHA) from **Baltimore-Michigan** (WHA) in WHA Dispersal Draft, June, 1975. Traded to **Phoenix** (WHA) by **Cincinnati** (WHA) for Ron Serafini, November, 1975. Traded to **San Diego** (WHA) by **Phoenix** (WHA) for future considerations, August, 1976.

• VERBEEK, PAT

Pat Verbeek RW/LW – R. 5'9", 192 lbs. b: Sarnia, Ont., 5/24/1964. New Jersey's 3rd choice, 43rd overall, in 1982 Entry Draft.

Season	Club	League	GP	G	A	Pts	AG	AA	APts	PIM	PP	SH	GW	S	%	TGF	PGF	TGA	PGA	+/-	Playoffs GP	G	A	Pts	PIM	PP	SH	GW
1980-81	Petrolia Jets	OJHL	42	44	44	88				155																		
1981-82	Sudbury Wolves	OHL	66	37	51	88				180																		
1982-83	Sudbury Wolves	OHL	61	40	67	107				184																		
	Canada	WJC-A	7	2	2	4				6																		
	New Jersey Devils	NHL	6	3	2	5	2	1	3	8	0	0	0	12	25.0	7	2	7	0	–2								
1983-84	New Jersey Devils	NHL	79	20	27	47	16	18	34	158	5	1	2	167	12.0	76	26	92	23	–19								
1984-85	New Jersey Devils	NHL	78	15	18	33	12	12	24	162	5	1	1	147	10.2	64	17	84	13	–24								
1985-86	New Jersey Devils	NHL	76	25	28	53	20	19	39	79	4	1	0	159	15.7	80	21	92	9	–24								
1986-87	New Jersey Devils	NHL	74	35	24	59	30	17	47	120	17	0	5	143	24.5	90	41	75	3	–23								
1987-88	New Jersey Devils	NHL	73	46	31	77	39	22	61	227	13	0	8	179	25.7	118	46	49	6	+29	20	4	8	12	51	2	0	1
1988-89	New Jersey Devils	NHL	77	26	21	47	22	15	37	189	9	0	1	175	14.9	69	24	63	0	–18								
	Canada	WEC-A	4	0	2	2				2																		
1989-90	Hartford Whalers	NHL	80	44	45	89	38	32	70	228	14	0	5	219	20.1	137	62	85	11	+1	7	2	2	4	26	1	0	1
1990-91	Hartford Whalers	NHL	80	43	39	82	40	30	70	246	15	0	5	247	17.4	121	54	76	9	0	6	3	2	5	40	2	0	0
1991-92	Hartford Whalers	NHL	76	22	35	57	20	26	46	243	10	0	3	163	13.5	90	44	67	5	–16	7	0	2	2	12	0	0	0
1992-93	Hartford Whalers	NHL	84	39	43	82	33	29	62	197	16	0	6	235	16.6	120	51	92	16	–7								
1993-94	Hartford Whalers	NHL	84	37	38	75	35	29	64	177	15	1	3	226	16.4	104	44	87	12	–15								
	Canada	WC-A	8	1	1	2				4																		
1994-95	Hartford Whalers	NHL	29	7	11	18	12	16	28	53	3	0	0	75	9.3	30	10	22	2	0								
	New York Rangers	NHL	19	10	5	15	18	7	25	18	4	0	2	56	17.9	28	14	16	0	–2	10	4	6	10	20	3	0	0
1995-96	New York Rangers	NHL	69	41	41	82	41	33	74	129	17	0	6	252	16.3	120	51	41	1	+29	11	3	6	9	12	1	0	0
1996-97	Canada	W Cup	1	0	0	0				0																		
	Dallas Stars	NHL	81	17	36	53	18	32	50	128	5	0	4	172	9.9	77	20	54	0	+3	7	1	3	4	16	1	0	0
1997-98	Dallas Stars	NHL	82	31	26	57	36	25	61	170	9	0	8	190	16.3	90	37	38	0	+15	17	3	2	5	26	2	0	1
	NHL Totals		1147	461	470	931	432	363	795	2532	161	4	59	2817	16.4	1421	564	1040	110		85	20	31	51	203	12	0	3

Played in NHL All-Star Game (1991, 1996)

Traded to **Hartford** by **New Jersey** for Sylvain Turgeon, June 17, 1989. Traded to **NY Rangers** by **Hartford** for Glen Featherstone, Michael Stewart, NY Rangers' 1st round choice (Jean-Sebastien Giguere) in 1995 Entry Draft and 4th round choice (Steve Wasylko) in 1996 Entry Draft, March 23, 1995. Signed as a free agent by **Dallas**, August 21, 1996.

• VERMETTE, MARK

Mark Vermette RW – R. 6'1", 203 lbs. b: Cochenour, Ont., 10/3/1967. Quebec's 8th choice, 134th overall, in 1986 Entry Draft.

Season	Club	League	GP	G	A	Pts	AG	AA	APts	PIM	PP	SH	GW	S	%	TGF	PGF	TGA	PGA	+/-	Playoffs GP	G	A	Pts	PIM	PP	SH	GW
1985-86	Lake Superior State University	CCHA	32	1	4	5				7																		
1986-87	Lake Superior State University	CCHA	38	19	17	36				59																		
1987-88	Lake Superior State University	CCHA	46	*45	30	75				154																		
1988-89	Quebec Nordiques	NHL	12	0	4	4	0	3	3	7	0	0	0	10	0.0	7	1	14	1	–7								
	Halifax Citadels	AHL	52	12	16	28				30											1	0	0	0	0			
1989-90	Quebec Nordiques	NHL	11	1	5	6	1	4	5	8	0	0	0	16	6.3	8	0	11	0	–3								
	Halifax Citadels	AHL	47	20	17	37				44											6	1	5	6	6			
1990-91	Quebec Nordiques	NHL	34	3	4	7	3	3	6	10	0	0	0	42	7.1	10	0	28	3	–15								
	Halifax Citadels	AHL	46	26	22	48				37																		
1991-92	Quebec Nordiques	NHL	10	1	0	1	1	0	1	8	0	0	0	12	8.3	3	1	10	2	–6								
	Halifax Citadels	AHL	44	21	18	39				39																		
1992-93	Halifax Citadels	AHL	67	42	37	79				32																		
1993-94	Las Vegas Thunder	IHL	77	22	38	60				61											4	0	0	0	2			
	NHL Totals		67	5	13	18	5	10	15	33	0	0	0	80	6.3	28	2	63	6									

NCAA West All-American Team (1988) • CCHA First All-Star Team (1988)

• VERRET, CLAUDE

Claude Verret C – L. 5'9", 165 lbs. b: Lachine, Que., 4/20/1963. Buffalo's 12th choice, 163rd overall, in 1982 Entry Draft.

Season	Club	League	GP	G	A	Pts	AG	AA	APts	PIM	PP	SH	GW	S	%	TGF	PGF	TGA	PGA	+/-	Playoffs GP	G	A	Pts	PIM	PP	SH	GW
1980-81	Trois-Rivieres Draveurs	QMJHL	68	39	73	112				4											19	13	24	37	7			
1981-82	Trois-Rivieres Draveurs	QMJHL	64	54	108	*162				14											23	13	*35	*48	4			
1982-83	Trois-Rivieres Draveurs	QMJHL	68	73	115	188				21											4	3	6	9	4			
1983-84	Buffalo Sabres	NHL	11	2	5	7	2	3	5	2	1	0	0	14	14.3	12	7	8	0	–3								
	Rochester Americans	AHL	65	39	51	90				4											18	5	9	14	4			
1984-85	Buffalo Sabres	NHL	3	0	0	0	0	0	0	0	0	0	0	5	0.0	1	1	2	0	–2								
	Rochester Americans	AHL	76	40	53	93				12											5	2	5	7	0			
1985-86	Rochester Americans	AHL	52	19	32	51				14																		
1986-87	EHC Kloten	Switz.	....	2	1	3															....	1	1	2	....			
	Rochester Americans	AHL	36	13	12	25				2											8	3	3	6	0			
1987-88	HC Rouen	France 2	STATISTICS NOT AVAILABLE																									
1988-89	HC Rouen	France	43	55	67	122				10																		
1989-90	HC Rouen	France 2	STATISTICS NOT AVAILABLE																									
1990-91	HC Rouen	France	28	19	37	56																						
1991-92	HC Rouen	France	STATISTICS NOT AVAILABLE																									
1992-93	HC Rouen	France	20	40	43	83																						
1993-94	Lausanne	Switz. 2	19	18	20	38				6											13	11	10	21	4			
1994-95	Lausanne	Switz. 2	36	44	45	89				6											11	10	20	30	6			
1995-96	Lausanne	Switz.	19	10	8	18				2																		
	NHL Totals		14	2	5	7	2	3	5	2	1	0	0	19	10.5	13	8	10	0									

QMJHL First All-Star Team (1982) • Won Dudley "Red" Garrett Memorial Award (Top Rookie - AHL) (1984) • AHL Second All-Star Team (1985)

• VERSTRAETE, LEIGH

Leigh Verstraete RW – R. 5'11", 185 lbs. b: Pincher Creek, Alta., 1/6/1962. Toronto's 13th choice, 192nd overall, in 1982 Entry Draft.

Season	Club	League	GP	G	A	Pts	AG	AA	APts	PIM	PP	SH	GW	S	%	TGF	PGF	TGA	PGA	+/-	Playoffs GP	G	A	Pts	PIM	PP	SH	GW
1978-79	Billings Bighorns	WHL	32	4	4	8				58											2	0	0	0	5			
1979-80	Billings Bighorns	WHL	10	1	0	1				47																		
	Calgary Wranglers	WHL	56	12	14	26				168											7	2	2	4	23			
1980-81	Calgary Wranglers	WHL	71	22	18	40				372											21	6	5	11	155			
1981-82	Calgary Wranglers	WHL	49	19	20	39				385											8	4	4	8	43			
1982-83	Toronto Maple Leafs	NHL	3	0	0	0	0	0	0	5	0	0	0	0	0.0	1	1	0	0	0								
	St. Catharines Saints	AHL	61	5	3	8				221																		
1983-84	St. Catharines Saints	AHL	51	0	7	7				183																		
	Muskegon Mohawks	IHL	19	5	5	10				123																		
1984-85	Toronto Maple Leafs	NHL	2	0	0	0	0	0	0	0	0	0	0	2	0.0	0	0	0	0	0								
	St. Catharines Saints	AHL	43	5	8	13				164																		
1985-86	St. Catharines Saints	AHL	75	8	12	20				300											11	2	3	5	14			

			REGULAR SEASON																		PLAYOFFS							
Season	Club	League	GP	G	A	Pts	AG	AA	APts	PIM	PP	SH	GW	S	%	TGF	PGF	TGA	PGA	+/–	GP	G	A	Pts	PIM	PP	SH	GW
1986-87	Newmarket Saints	AHL	57	9	7	16	....	....	....	179	....	....	....	....	....	....	....	....	....	....	....	....	....	....	....	....	....	....
1987-88	**Toronto Maple Leafs**	**NHL**	**3**	**0**	**1**	**1**	**0**	**1**	**1**	**9**	**0**	**0**	**0**	**0**	**0.0**	**1**	**0**	**3**	**0**	**–2**	....	....	....	....	....	....	....	....
	Newmarket Saints	AHL	12	4	3	7	....	....	....	38	....	....	....	....	....	....	....	....	....	....	....	....	....	....	....	....	....	....
	NHL Totals		**8**	**0**	**1**	**1**	**0**	**1**	**1**	**14**	**0**	**0**	**0**	**2**	**0.0**	**2**	**1**	**3**	**0**		....	....	....	....	....	....	....	....

• VERVERGAERT, DENNIS

Dennis Ververgaert RW – R. 6', 185 lbs. b: Hamilton, Ont., 3/30/1953. Vancouver's 1st choice, 3rd overall, in 1973 Amateur Draft.

Season	Club	League	GP	G	A	Pts	AG	AA	APts	PIM	PP	SH	GW	S	%	TGF	PGF	TGA	PGA	+/–	GP	G	A	Pts	PIM	PP	SH	GW
1970-71	London Knights	OHA	62	39	48	87	....	....	....	98	....	....	....	....	....	....	....	....	....	....	....	....	....	....	....	....	....	....
1971-72	London Knights	OHA	62	44	73	117	....	....	....	65	....	....	....	....	....	....	....	....	....	....	....	....	....	....	....	....	....	....
1972-73	London Knights	OHA	63	58	89	147	....	....	....	86	....	....	....	....	....	....	....	....	....	....	18	13	12	25	6	....	....	....
1973-74	**Vancouver Canucks**	**NHL**	**78**	**26**	**31**	**57**	**27**	**27**	**54**	**25**	**7**	**0**	**3**	**153**	**17.0**	**79**	**23**	**79**	**3**	**–20**	....	....	....	....	....	....	....	....
1974-75	**Vancouver Canucks**	**NHL**	**57**	**19**	**32**	**51**	**18**	**25**	**43**	**25**	**5**	**0**	**5**	**114**	**16.7**	**71**	**25**	**40**	**0**	**+6**	**1**	**0**	**0**	**0**	**0**	**0**	**0**	**0**
1975-76	**Vancouver Canucks**	**NHL**	**80**	**37**	**34**	**71**	**35**	**27**	**62**	**53**	**11**	**0**	**4**	**207**	**17.9**	**103**	**29**	**79**	**4**	**–1**	**2**	**1**	**0**	**1**	**4**	**1**	**0**	**0**
1976-77	**Vancouver Canucks**	**NHL**	**79**	**27**	**18**	**45**	**26**	**15**	**41**	**38**	**7**	**0**	**1**	**178**	**15.2**	**66**	**24**	**78**	**1**	**–35**	....	....	....	....	....	....	....	....
1977-78	**Vancouver Canucks**	**NHL**	**80**	**21**	**33**	**54**	**20**	**27**	**47**	**23**	**6**	**0**	**1**	**136**	**15.4**	**81**	**25**	**80**	**0**	**–24**	....	....	....	....	....	....	....	....
1978-79	**Vancouver Canucks**	**NHL**	**35**	**9**	**17**	**26**	**8**	**13**	**21**	**13**	**2**	**1**	**3**	**57**	**15.8**	**32**	**6**	**23**	**0**	**+3**	....	....	....	....	....	....	....	....
	Philadelphia Flyers	**NHL**	**37**	**9**	**7**	**16**	**8**	**5**	**13**	**6**	**2**	**0**	**1**	**54**	**16.7**	**28**	**5**	**28**	**1**	**–4**	**3**	**0**	**2**	**2**	**2**	**0**	**0**	**0**
1979-80	**Philadelphia Flyers**	**NHL**	**58**	**14**	**17**	**31**	**13**	**13**	**26**	**24**	**0**	**0**	**2**	**96**	**14.6**	**50**	**3**	**38**	**0**	**+9**	**2**	**0**	**0**	**0**	**0**	**0**	**0**	**0**
1980-81	**Washington Capitals**	**NHL**	**79**	**14**	**27**	**41**	**12**	**19**	**31**	**40**	**2**	**0**	**2**	**111**	**12.6**	**56**	**11**	**56**	**6**	**–5**	....	....	....	....	....	....	....	....
	NHL Totals		**583**	**176**	**216**	**392**	**167**	**171**	**338**	**247**	**42**	**1**	**22**	**1106**	**15.9**	**566**	**151**	**501**	**15**		**8**	**1**	**2**	**3**	**6**	**1**	**0**	**0**

OHA Second All-Star Team (1972) • OHA First All-Star Team (1973)

Played in NHL All-Star Game (1976, 1978)

Traded to **Philadelphia** by **Vancouver** for Drew Callander and Kevin McCarthy, December 31, 1978. Signed as a free agent by **Washington**, October 6, 1980.

• VESEY, JIM

Jim Vesey C/RW – R. 6'1", 202 lbs. b: Columbus, MA, 10/29/1965. St. Louis' 8th choice, 155th overall, in 1984 Entry Draft.

Season	Club	League	GP	G	A	Pts	AG	AA	APts	PIM	PP	SH	GW	S	%	TGF	PGF	TGA	PGA	+/–	GP	G	A	Pts	PIM	PP	SH	GW
1983-84	Columbus-Mass High School	H.S.	STATISTICS NOT AVAILABLE																									
1984-85	Merrimack College	ECAC II	33	19	11	30	....	....	....	28	....	....	....	....	....	....	....	....	....	....	....	....	....	....	....	....	....	....
1985-86	Merrimack College	ECAC II	32	29	32	61	....	....	....	67	....	....	....	....	....	....	....	....	....	....	....	....	....	....	....	....	....	....
1986-87	Merrimack College	ECAC II	35	22	36	58	....	....	....	57	....	....	....	....	....	....	....	....	....	....	....	....	....	....	....	....	....	....
1987-88	Merrimack College	ECAC II	33	33	50	83	....	....	....	....	....	....	....	....	....	....	....	....	....	....	....	....	....	....	....	....	....	....
1988-89	**St. Louis Blues**	**NHL**	**5**	**1**	**1**	**2**	**1**	**1**	**2**	**7**	**0**	**0**	**0**	**5**	**20.0**	**2**	**0**	**3**	**0**	**–1**	....	....	....	....	....	....	....	....
	Peoria Rivermen	IHL	76	47	46	93	....	....	....	137	....	....	....	....	....	....	....	....	....	....	4	1	2	3	6	....	....	....
1989-90	**St. Louis Blues**	**NHL**	**6**	**0**	**1**	**1**	**0**	**1**	**1**	**0**	**0**	**0**	**0**	**3**	**0.0**	**2**	**0**	**5**	**0**	**–3**	....	....	....	....	....	....	....	....
	Peoria Rivermen	IHL	60	47	44	91	....	....	....	75	....	....	....	....	....	....	....	....	....	....	5	1	3	4	21	....	....	....
1990-91	Peoria Rivermen	IHL	58	32	41	73	....	....	....	69	....	....	....	....	....	....	....	....	....	....	19	4	14	18	26	....	....	....
1991-92	**Boston Bruins**	**NHL**	**4**	**0**	**0**	**0**	**0**	**0**	**0**	**0**	**0**	**0**	**0**	**1**	**0.0**	**0**	**0**	**0**	**0**	**0**	....	....	....	....	....	....	....	....
	Maine Mariners	AHL	10	6	7	13	....	....	....	13	....	....	....	....	....	....	....	....	....	....	....	....	....	....	....	....	....	....
1992-93	Providence Bruins	AHL	71	38	39	77	....	....	....	42	....	....	....	....	....	....	....	....	....	....	6	2	5	7	4	....	....	....
1993-94	Phoenix Roadrunners	IHL	60	20	30	50	....	....	....	75	....	....	....	....	....	....	....	....	....	....	....	....	....	....	....	....	....	....
1994-95	Phoenix Roadrunners	IHL	41	10	10	20	....	....	....	62	....	....	....	....	....	....	....	....	....	....	....	....	....	....	....	....	....	....
	NHL Totals		**15**	**1**	**2**	**3**	**1**	**2**	**3**	**7**	**0**	**0**	**0**	**9**	**11.1**	**4**	**0**	**8**	**0**		....	....	....	....	....	....	....	....

NCAA (College Div.) East All-American Team (1986) • NCAA (College Div.) East Second All-American Team (1987) • IHL First All-Star Team (1989)

Traded to **Winnipeg** by **St. Louis** to complete transaction that sent Tom Draper to St. Louis (February 28, 1991), May 24, 1991. Traded to **Boston** by **Winnipeg** for future considerations, June 20, 1991.

• VEYSEY, SID

Sid Veysey C – L. 5'11", 175 lbs. b: Woodstock, N.B., 7/30/1955. Vancouver's 10th choice, 182nd overall, in 1975 Amateur Draft.

Season	Club	League	GP	G	A	Pts	AG	AA	APts	PIM	PP	SH	GW	S	%	TGF	PGF	TGA	PGA	+/–	GP	G	A	Pts	PIM	PP	SH	GW
1971-72	Riverview Reds	Jr. B.	26	22	23	45	....	....	....	62	....	....	....	....	....	....	....	....	....	....	....	....	....	....	....	....	....	....
	Moncton Beavers	NBJHL	15	15	13	28	....	....	....	52	....	....	....	....	....	....	....	....	....	....	....	....	....	....	....	....	....	....
1972-73	Moncton Beavers	NBJHL	....	31	*77	*108	....	....	....	69	....	....	....	....	....	....	....	....	....	....	[illegible]	7	4	11	41	....	....	....
1973-74	Sherbrooke Castors	QMJHL	[illegible]	[illegible]	44	[illegible]	....	....	....	[illegible]	....	....	....	....	....	....	....	....	....	....	....	....	....	....	....	....	....	....
1974-75	Sherbrooke Castors	QMJHL	48	37	53	90	....	....	....	65	....	....	....	....	....	....	....	....	....	....	....	....	....	....	....	....	....	....
1975-76	Tulsa Oilers	CHL	1	0	0	0	....	....	....	0	....	....	....	....	....	....	....	....	....	....	....	....	....	....	....	....	....	....
	Fort Wayne Komets	IHL	73	36	51	87	....	....	....	97	....	....	....	....	....	....	....	....	....	....	9	7	6	13	14	....	....	....
1976-77	Tulsa Oilers	CHL	76	29	51	80	....	....	....	66	....	....	....	....	....	....	....	....	....	....	9	1	3	4	4	....	....	....
1977-78	**Vancouver Canucks**	**NHL**	**1**	**0**	**0**	**0**	**0**	**0**	**0**	**0**	**0**	**0**	**0**	**0**	**0.0**	**0**	**0**	**1**	**0**	**–1**	....	....	....	....	....	....	....	....
	Tulsa Oilers	CHL	54	16	17	33	....	....	....	64	....	....	....	....	....	....	....	....	....	....	....	....	....	....	....	....	....	....
1978-79	Newcastle Northmen	NBSHL	STATISTICS NOT AVAILABLE																									
1979-80	University of New Brunswick	AUAA	27	25	28	53	....	....	....	46	....	....	....	....	....	....	....	....	....	....	....	....	....	....	....	....	....	....
1980-81	University of New Brunswick	AUAA	20	17	20	37	....	....	....	46	....	....	....	....	....	....	....	....	....	....	....	....	....	....	....	....	....	....
1981-82	Fredericton Express	AHL	17	2	10	12	....	....	....	17	....	....	....	....	....	....	....	....	....	....	2	0	5	5	2	....	....	....
1982-83	Saint John Gulls	NBSHL	24	17	19	36	....	....	....	39	....	....	....	....	....	....	....	....	....	....	11	4	11	15	18	....	....	....
	NHL Totals		**1**	**0**	**0**	**0**	**0**	**0**	**0**	**0**	**0**	**0**	**0**	**0**	**0.0**	**0**	**0**	**1**	**0**		....	....	....	....	....	....	....	....

QMJHL Second All-Star Team (1975) • Won Garry F. Longman Memorial Trophy (Top Rookie IHL) (1976)

• VIAL, DENNIS

Dennis Vial LW – L. 6'1", 220 lbs. b: Sault Ste. Marie, Ont., 4/10/1969. NY Rangers' 5th choice, 110th overall, in 1988 Entry Draft.

Season	Club	League	GP	G	A	Pts	AG	AA	APts	PIM	PP	SH	GW	S	%	TGF	PGF	TGA	PGA	+/–	GP	G	A	Pts	PIM	PP	SH	GW
1985-86	Hamilton Steelhawks	OHL	31	1	1	2	....	....	....	66	....	....	....	....	....	....	....	....	....	....	....	....	....	....	....	....	....	....
1986-87	Hamilton Steelhawks	OHL	53	1	8	9	....	....	....	194	....	....	....	....	....	....	....	....	....	....	8	0	0	0	8	....	....	....
1987-88	Hamilton Steelhawks	OHL	52	3	17	20	....	....	....	229	....	....	....	....	....	....	....	....	....	....	13	2	2	4	49	....	....	....
1988-89	Niagara Falls Thunder	OHL	50	10	27	37	....	....	....	227	....	....	....	....	....	....	....	....	....	....	15	1	7	8	44	....	....	....
1989-90	Flint Spirits	IHL	79	6	29	35	....	....	....	351	....	....	....	....	....	....	....	....	....	....	4	0	0	0	10	....	....	....
1990-91	**New York Rangers**	**NHL**	**21**	**0**	**0**	**0**	**0**	**0**	**0**	**61**	**0**	**0**	**0**	**5**	**0.0**	**6**	**0**	**10**	**0**	**–4**	....	....	....	....	....	....	....	....
	Binghamton Rangers	AHL	40	2	7	9	....	....	....	250	....	....	....	....	....	....	....	....	....	....	....	....	....	....	....	....	....	....
	Detroit Red Wings	**NHL**	**9**	**0**	**0**	**0**	**0**	**0**	**0**	**16**	**0**	**0**	**0**	**3**	**0.0**	**0**	**0**	**3**	**0**	**–3**	....	....	....	....	....	....	....	....
1991-92	**Detroit Red Wings**	**NHL**	**27**	**1**	**0**	**1**	**1**	**0**	**1**	**72**	**0**	**0**	**0**	**6**	**16.7**	**7**	**0**	**6**	**0**	**+1**	....	....	....	....	....	....	....	....
	Adirondack Red Wings	AHL	20	2	4	6	....	....	....	107	....	....	....	....	....	....	....	....	....	....	17	1	3	4	43	....	....	....
1992-93	**Detroit Red Wings**	**NHL**	**9**	**0**	**1**	**1**	**0**	**1**	**1**	**20**	**0**	**0**	**0**	**5**	**0.0**	**4**	**0**	**3**	**0**	**+1**	....	....	....	....	....	....	....	....
	Adirondack Red Wings	AHL	30	2	11	13	....	....	....	177	....	....	....	....	....	....	....	....	....	....	11	1	1	2	14	....	....	....
1993-94	**Ottawa Senators**	**NHL**	**55**	**2**	**5**	**7**	**2**	**4**	**6**	**214**	**0**	**0**	**0**	**37**	**5.4**	**25**	**1**	**46**	**13**	**–9**	....	....	....	....	....	....	....	....
1994-95	**Ottawa Senators**	**NHL**	**27**	**0**	**4**	**4**	**0**	**6**	**6**	**65**	**0**	**0**	**0**	**9**	**0.0**	**12**	**0**	**15**	**3**	**0**	....	....	....	....	....	....	....	....
1995-96	**Ottawa Senators**	**NHL**	**64**	**1**	**4**	**5**	**1**	**3**	**4**	**276**	**0**	**0**	**0**	**33**	**3.0**	**10**	**0**	**26**	**3**	**–13**	....	....	....	....	....	....	....	....
1996-97	**Ottawa Senators**	**NHL**	**11**	**0**	**1**	**1**	**0**	**1**	**1**	**25**	**0**	**0**	**0**	**4**	**0.0**	**2**	**1**	**1**	**0**	**0**	....	....	....	....	....	....	....	....
1997-98	**Ottawa Senators**	**NHL**	**19**	**0**	**0**	**0**	**0**	**0**	**0**	**45**	**0**	**0**	**0**	**9**	**0.0**	**1**	**0**	**1**	**0**	**0**	....	....	....	....	....	....	....	....
	Chicago Wolves	IHL	24	1	3	4	....	....	....	86	....	....	....	....	....	....	....	....	....	....	1	0	0	0	2	....	....	....
	NHL Totals		**242**	**4**	**15**	**19**	**4**	**15**	**19**	**794**	**0**	**0**	**0**	**111**	**3.6**	**67**	**2**	**111**	**19**		....	....	....	....	....	....	....	....

Traded to **Detroit** by **NY Rangers** with Kevin Miller and Jim Cummins for Joey Kocur and Per Djoos, March 5, 1991. Traded to **Quebec** by **Detroit** with Doug Crossman for cash, June 15, 1992. Traded to **Detroit** by **Quebec** for cash, September 9, 1992. Traded to **Tampa Bay** by **Detroit** for Steve Maltais, June 8, 1993. Claimed by **Anaheim** from **Tampa Bay** in Expansion Draft, June 24, 1993. Claimed by **Ottawa** from **Anaheim** in Phase II of Expansion Draft, June 25, 1993.

• VICKERS, STEVE

Steve "Sarge" Vickers LW – L. 6', 180 lbs. b: Toronto, Ont., 4/21/1951. NY Rangers' 1st choice, 10th overall, in 1971 Amateur Draft.

Season	Club	League	GP	G	A	Pts	AG	AA	APts	PIM	PP	SH	GW	S	%	TGF	PGF	TGA	PGA	+/–	GP	G	A	Pts	PIM	PP	SH	GW
1968-69	Markham Waxers	Jr. B	36	43	40	83	....	....	....	....	....	....	....	....	....	....	....	....	....	....	....	....	....	....	....	....	....	....
1969-70	Toronto Marlboros	OHA	52	28	38	66	....	....	....	23	....	....	....	....	....	....	....	....	....	....	....	....	....	....	....	....	....	....
1970-71	Toronto Marlboros	OHA	62	43	64	107	....	....	....	51	....	....	....	....	....	....	....	....	....	....	....	....	....	....	....	....	....	....
1971-72	Omaha Knights	CHL	70	36	23	59	....	....	....	45	....	....	....	....	....	....	....	....	....	....	....	....	....	....	....	....	....	....
1972-73	**New York Rangers**	**NHL**	**61**	**30**	**23**	**53**	**30**	**19**	**49**	**37**	**2**	**0**	**5**	**131**	**22.9**	**74**	**10**	**29**	**0**	**+35**	**10**	**5**	**4**	**9**	**4**	**0**	**0**	**0**
1973-74	**New York Rangers**	**NHL**	**75**	**34**	**24**	**58**	**35**	**21**	**56**	**18**	**5**	**0**	**5**	**168**	**20.2**	**82**	**20**	**58**	**2**	**+6**	**13**	**4**	**4**	**8**	**17**	**2**	**0**	**0**
1974-75	**New York Rangers**	**NHL**	**80**	**41**	**48**	**89**	**38**	**38**	**76**	**64**	**16**	**0**	**6**	**188**	**21.8**	**138**	**53**	**75**	**0**	**+10**	**3**	**2**	**4**	**6**	**6**	**0**	**0**	**0**
1975-76	**New York Rangers**	**NHL**	**80**	**30**	**53**	**83**	**28**	**42**	**70**	**40**	**10**	**0**	**4**	**202**	**14.9**	**128**	**46**	**99**	**0**	**–17**	....	....	....	....	....	....	....	....
1976-77	**New York Rangers**	**NHL**	**75**	**22**	**31**	**53**	**21**	**25**	**46**	**26**	**4**	**0**	**3**	**157**	**14.0**	**82**	**20**	**76**	**0**	**–14**	....	....	....	....	....	....	....	....
1977-78	**New York Rangers**	**NHL**	**79**	**19**	**44**	**63**	**18**	**36**	**54**	**30**	**9**	**0**	**2**	**113**	**16.8**	**101**	**38**	**54**	**1**	**+10**	**3**	**2**	**1**	**3**	**0**	**0**	**0**	**0**
1978-79	**New York Rangers**	**NHL**	**66**	**13**	**34**	**47**	**12**	**26**	**38**	**24**	**4**	**0**	**3**	**86**	**15.1**	**67**	**17**	**64**	**7**	**–7**	**18**	**5**	**3**	**8**	**13**	**1**	**0**	**1**

Season	Club	League	GP	G	A	Pts	AG	AA	APts	PIM	PP	SH	GW	S	%	TGF	PGF	TGA	PGA	+/-	GP	G	A	Pts	PIM	PP	SH	GW
1979-80	New York Rangers	NHL	75	29	33	62	26	25	51	38	12	0	2	98	29.6	95	32	44	1	+20	9	2	2	4	4	0	0	1
1980-81	New York Rangers	NHL	73	19	39	58	16	27	43	40	5	1	3	85	22.4	76	15	56	2	+7	12	4	7	11	14	1	0	0
1981-82	New York Rangers	NHL	34	9	11	20	7	7	14	13	2	0	2	48	18.8	35	10	21	0	+4	....							
	Springfield Indians	AHL	20	4	6	10				14																		
	NHL Totals		698	246	340	586	231	266	497	330	69	1	35	1276	19.3	878	261	576	13		68	24	25	49	58	4	0	2

OHA First All-Star Team (1971) • Won Calder Memorial Trophy (1973) • NHL Second All-Star Team (1975)
Played in NHL All-Star Game (1975, 1976)

● VIGNEAULT, ALAIN
Alain Vigneault D – R. 5'11", 195 lbs. b: Quebec City, Que., 5/14/1961. St. Louis' 7th choice, 167th overall, in 1981 Entry Draft.

Season	Club	League	GP	G	A	Pts	AG	AA	APts	PIM	PP	SH	GW	S	%	TGF	PGF	TGA	PGA	+/-	GP	G	A	Pts	PIM	PP	SH	GW
1979-80	Hull Olympiques	QMJHL	35	5	34	39				82											7	1	5	6	30			
	Trois-Rivieres Draveurs	QMJHL	28	6	19	25				93																		
1980-81	Trois-Rivieres Draveurs	QMJHL	67	7	55	62				181											19	4	6	10	53			
1981-82	**St. Louis Blues**	NHL	14	1	2	3	1	1	2	43	0	0	0	9	11.1	8	0	14	5	-1								
	Salt Lake Golden Eagles	CHL	64	2	10	12				266											7	1	1	2	37			
1982-83	**St. Louis Blues**	NHL	28	1	3	4	1	2	3	39	0	0	0	13	7.7	12	1	16	1	-4	4	0	1	1	26	0	0	0
	Salt Lake Golden Eagles	CHL	33	1	4	5				189																		
1983-84	Montana Magic	CHL	47	2	14	16				139																		
	Maine Mariners	AHL	11	0	1	1				46											1	0	0	0	4			
	NHL Totals		42	2	5	7	2	3	5	82	0	0	0	22	9.1	20	1	30	6		4	0	1	1	26	0	0	0

● VIITAKOSKI, VESA
Vesa Viitakoski LW – L. 6'3", 215 lbs. b: Lappeenranta, Finland, 2/13/1971. Calgary's 3rd choice, 32nd overall, in 1990 Entry Draft.

Season	Club	League	GP	G	A	Pts	AG	AA	APts	PIM	PP	SH	GW	S	%	TGF	PGF	TGA	PGA	+/-	GP	G	A	Pts	PIM	PP	SH	GW
1988-89	SaiPa Lappeenranta	Finland	11	4	1	5				6																		
1989-90	SaiPa Lappeenranta	Finland	44	24	10	34				8																		
	Finland	WJC-A	7	6	1	7				2																		
1990-91	Tappara Tampere	Finland	41	17	23	40				14											3	2	0	2	4			
	Finland	WJC-A	7	6	5	11				2																		
1991-92	Tappara Tampere	Finland	44	19	19	38				39																		
	Finland	WC-A	8	2	3	5				6																		
1992-93	Tappara Tampere	Finland	48	27	27	54				28																		
	Finland	WC-A	6	1	0	1				6																		
1993-94	**Calgary Flames**	NHL	8	1	2	3	1	2	3	0	1	0	0	15	6.7	7	3	4	0	0	5	1	2	3	2			
	Saint John Flames	AHL	67	28	39	67				24											4	0	1	1	2			
1994-95	Saint John Flames	AHL	56	17	26	43				8																		
	Calgary Flames	NHL	10	1	2	3	2	3	5	6	1	0	0	6	16.7	6	3	4	0	-1								
1995-96	**Calgary Flames**	NHL	5	0	0	0	0	0	0	2	0	0	0	7	0.0	0	0	1	0	-1								
	Saint John Flames	AHL	48	18	29	47				48											8	1	3	4	2			
	Cornwall Aces	AHL	10	7	6	13				4											5	1	1	2	2			
1996-97	HV-71 Jonkoping	Sweden	50	17	12	29				24											9	2	4	6	4			
1997-98	Ilves Tampere	Finland	47	11	19	30				12																		
	NHL Totals		23	2	4	6	3	5	8	8	2	0	0	28	7.1	13	6	9	0		....							

Finnish Rookie of the Year (1990)
Traded to **Colorado** by **Calgary** for Paxton Schulte, March 19, 1996.

● VILGRAIN, CLAUDE
Claude Vilgrain RW – R. 6'1", 205 lbs. b: Port-au-Prince, Haiti, 3/1/1963. Detroit's 6th choice, 107th overall, in 1982 Entry Draft.

Season	Club	League	GP	G	A	Pts	AG	AA	APts	PIM	PP	SH	GW	S	%	TGF	PGF	TGA	PGA	+/-	GP	G	A	Pts	PIM	PP	SH	GW
1980-81	Laval Titan	QMJHL	72	20	31	51				65											17	14	10	24	4			
1981-82	Laval Titan	QMJHL	58	26	29	55				64											12	10	4	14	4			
1982-83	Laval Titan	QMJHL	69	46	80	126				72																		
1983-84	University of Moncton	AUAA	20	11	20	31				8																		
1984-85	University of Moncton	AUAA	24	*35	28	63				20																		
1985-86	University of Moncton	AUAA	19	17	20	37				25																		
	Canada	Nat-Team	1	0	1	1				0																		
1986-87	Canada	Nat-Team	78	28	42	70				38																		
1987-88	Canada	Nat-Team	61	21	20	41				41																		
	Canada	Olympics	6	0	0	0				0																		
	Vancouver Canucks	NHL	6	1	1	2	1	1	2	0	0	0	0	7	14.3	4	1	6	0	-3								
1988-89	Milwaukee Admirals	IHL	23	9	13	22				26																		
	Utica Devils	AHL	55	23	30	53				41											5	0	2	2	2			
1989-90	**New Jersey Devils**	NHL	6	1	2	3	1	1	2	4	0	0	0	13	7.7	2	0	4	1	-1	4	0	0	0	0			
	Utica Devils	AHL	73	37	52	89				32																		
1990-91	Utica Devils	AHL	59	32	46	78				26																		
1991-92	**New Jersey Devils**	NHL	71	19	27	46	17	20	37	74	1	1	1	88	21.6	68	5	37	1	+27	7	1	1	2	17	0	0	0
1992-93	**New Jersey Devils**	NHL	4	0	2	2	0	1	1	0	0	0	0	2	0.0	2	0	5	0	-3	5	0	1	1	0			
	Utica Devils	AHL	22	6	8	14				4																		
	Cincinnati Cyclones	IHL	57	19	26	45				22																		
1993-94	**Philadelphia Flyers**	NHL	2	0	0	0	0	0	0	0	0	0	0	0	0.0	0	0	1	0	-1	11	1	6	7	2			
	Hershey Bears	AHL	76	30	53	83				45																		
1994-95	Canada	Nat-Team	10	5	11	16				6																		
1995-96	SC Herisau	Switz. B	36	27	41	68				44																		
	NHL Totals		89	21	32	53	19	23	42	78	1	1	1	110	19.1	76	6	53	2		11	1	1	2	17	0	0	0

QMJHL Second All-Star Team (1983)
Signed as a free agent by **Vancouver**, June 18, 1987. Traded to **New Jersey** by **Vancouver** for Tim Lenardon, March 7, 1989. Signed as a free agent by **Philadelphia**, August 3, 1993.

● VINCELETTE, DANIEL
Daniel Vincelette LW – L. 6'2", 202 lbs. b: Verdun, Que., 8/1/1967. Chicago's 3rd choice, 74th overall, in 1985 Entry Draft.

Season	Club	League	GP	G	A	Pts	AG	AA	APts	PIM	PP	SH	GW	S	%	TGF	PGF	TGA	PGA	+/-	GP	G	A	Pts	PIM	PP	SH	GW
1983-84	Magog Cantonniers	Midget	40	9	13	22				43											12	0	1	1	11			
1984-85	Drummondville Voltigeurs	QMJHL	64	11	24	35				124											22	11	14	25	40			
1985-86	Drummondville Voltigeurs	QMJHL	70	37	47	84				234											8	6	5	11	17			
1986-87	Drummondville Voltigeurs	QMJHL	50	34	35	69				288																		
	Chicago Blackhawks	NHL																			3	0	0	0	0			
1987-88	**Chicago Blackhawks**	NHL	69	6	11	17	5	8	13	109	2	0	0	67	9.0	37	10	46	4	-15	4	0	0	0	0	0	0	0
1988-89	**Chicago Blackhawks**	NHL	66	11	4	15	9	3	12	119	1	0	0	76	14.5	38	9	41	0	-9	5	0	0	0	4	0	0	0
	Saginaw Hawks	IHL	2	0	0	0				14																		
1989-90	**Chicago Blackhawks**	NHL	2	0	0	0	0	0	0	4	0	0	0	2	0.0	0	0	1	0	-1								
	Indianapolis Ice	IHL	49	16	13	29				262																		
	Quebec Nordiques	NHL	11	0	1	1	0	1	1	25	0	0	0	15	0.0	3	0	9	0	-6	2	0	0	0	0			
	Halifax Citadels	AHL																			2	0	0	0	4			
1990-91	**Quebec Nordiques**	NHL	16	0	1	1	0	1	1	38	0	0	0	16	0.0	2	0	12	0	-10								
	Halifax Citadels	AHL	24	4	9	13				85																		
	Indianapolis Ice	IHL	15	5	3	8				51											7	2	1	3	62			
1991-92	**Chicago Blackhawks**	NHL	29	3	5	8	3	4	7	56	0	0	0	28	10.7	18	2	24	2	-6								
	Indianapolis Ice	IHL	16	5	3	8				84																		
1992-93	Atlanta Knights	IHL	30	5	5	10				126																		
	San Diego Gulls	IHL	6	0	0	0				6																		

			REGULAR SEASON																		PLAYOFFS							
Season	Club	League	GP	G	A	Pts	AG	AA	APts	PIM	PP	SH	GW	S	%	TGF	PGF	TGA	PGA	+/–	GP	G	A	Pts	PIM	PP	SH	GW
1993-94	Durham Wasps	Britain	10	3	2	5	....	....	....	36	....	....	....	....	....	....	....	....	....	....	6	0	0	0	52	....	....	....
1994-95	DID NOT PLAY – RETIRED																											
1995-96	San Francisco Spiders	IHL	35	3	7	10	....	....	....	96	....	....	....	....	....	....	....	....	....	....	4	0	0	0	15	....	....	....
	NHL Totals		**193**	**20**	**22**	**42**	**17**	**17**	**34**	**351**	**3**	**0**	**0**	**204**	**9.8**	**98**	**21**	**133**	**9**		**12**	**0**	**0**	**0**	**4**	**0**	**0**	**0**

Traded to **Quebec** by **Chicago** with Mario Doyon and Everett Sanipass for Greg Millen, Michel Goulet and Quebec's 6th round choice (Kevin St. Jacques) in 1991 Entry Draft, March 5, 1990. Traded to **Chicago** by **Quebec** with Paul Gillis for Ryan McGill and Mike McNeil, March 5, 1991. Claimed by **Tampa Bay** from **Chicago** in Expansion Draft, June 18, 1992. Traded to **Philadelphia** by **Tampa Bay** for Steve Kasper, December 8, 1992.

• VIPOND, PETE

Pete Vipond LW – L. 5'10", 175 lbs. b: Oshawa, Ont., 12/8/1949. Oakland's 7th choice, 76th overall, in 1969 Amateur Draft.

Season	Club	League	GP	G	A	Pts	AG	AA	APts	PIM	PP	SH	GW	S	%	TGF	PGF	TGA	PGA	+/–	GP	G	A	Pts	PIM	PP	SH	GW
1967-68	Oshawa Generals	OHA	32	6	10	16	....	....	....	6	....	....	....	....	....	....	....	....	....	....	....	....	....	....	....	....	....	....
1968-69	Oshawa Generals	OHA	54	21	39	60	....	....	....	45	....	....	....	....	....	....	....	....	....	....	....	....	....	....	....	....	....	....
1969-70	Nelson Maple Leafs	WIHL	48	28	36	64	....	....	....	36	....	....	....	....	....	....	....	....	....	....	....	....	....	....	....	....	....	....
1970-71	Nelson Maple Leafs	WIHL	48	21	45	66	....	....	....	28	....	....	....	....	....	....	....	....	....	....	....	....	....	....	....	....	....	....
1971-72	Columbus Seals	IHL	66	23	39	62	....	....	....	24	....	....	....	....	....	....	....	....	....	....	....	....	....	....	....	....	....	....
1972-73	**California Golden Seals**	**NHL**	**3**	**0**	**0**	**0**	**0**	**0**	**0**	**0**	**0**	**0**	**0**	**2**	**0.0**	**0**	**0**	**0**	**0**	**0**	....	....	....	....	....	....	....	....
	Salt Lake Golden Eagles	WHL	66	33	24	57	....	....	....	17	....	....	....	....	....	....	....	....	....	....	9	1	3	4	2	....	....	....
1973-74	Tulsa Oilers	CHL	60	20	22	42	....	....	....	30	....	....	....	....	....	....	....	....	....	....	....	....	....	....	....	....	....	....
1974-75	Whitby Warriors	OHA Sr.	37	19	18	37	....	....	....	9	....	....	....	....	....	....	....	....	....	....	....	....	....	....	....	....	....	....
1975-76	Whitby Warriors	OHA Sr.	44	25	35	60	....	....	....	18	....	....	....	....	....	....	....	....	....	....	....	....	....	....	....	....	....	....
1976-77	Whitby Warriors	OHA Sr.	34	22	26	48	....	....	....	21	....	....	....	....	....	....	....	....	....	....	....	....	....	....	....	....	....	....
1977-78	Whitby Warriors	OHA Sr.	36	9	19	28	....	....	....	10	....	....	....	....	....	....	....	....	....	....	....	....	....	....	....	....	....	....
	NHL Totals		**3**	**0**	**0**	**0**	**0**	**0**	**0**	**0**	**0**	**0**	**0**	**2**	**0.0**	**0**	**0**	**0**	**0**		....	....	....	....	....	....	....	....

• VIRTA, HANNU

Hannu Virta D – L. 5'11", 183 lbs. b: Turku, Finland, 3/22/1963. Buffalo's 2nd choice, 38th overall, in 1981 Entry Draft.

Season	Club	League	GP	G	A	Pts	AG	AA	APts	PIM	PP	SH	GW	S	%	TGF	PGF	TGA	PGA	+/–	GP	G	A	Pts	PIM	PP	SH	GW
1980-81	TPS Turku	Finland	1	0	1	1	....	....	....	0	....	....	....	....	....	....	....	....	....	....	4	0	1	1	4	....	....	....
1981-82	TPS Turku	Finland	36	5	12	17	....	....	....	6	....	....	....	....	....	....	....	....	....	....	7	1	1	2	2	....	....	....
	Finland	WJC-A	7	1	7	8	....	....	....	4	....	....	....	....	....	....	....	....	....	....	....	....	....	....	....	....	....	....
	Buffalo Sabres	**NHL**	**3**	**0**	**1**	**1**	**0**	**1**	**1**	**4**	....	....	....	....	....	....	....	....	....	....	**4**	**0**	**1**	**1**	**0**	....	....	....
1982-83	**Buffalo Sabres**	**NHL**	**74**	**13**	**24**	**37**	**11**	**17**	**28**	**18**	**2**	**2**	**1**	**169**	**7.7**	**112**	**33**	**76**	**4**	**+7**	**10**	**1**	**2**	**3**	**4**	**0**	**0**	**0**
1983-84	**Buffalo Sabres**	**NHL**	**70**	**6**	**30**	**36**	**5**	**20**	**25**	**12**	**4**	**0**	**0**	**98**	**6.1**	**105**	**34**	**63**	**7**	**+15**	**3**	**0**	**0**	**0**	**2**	**0**	**0**	**0**
1984-85	**Buffalo Sabres**	**NHL**	**51**	**1**	**23**	**24**	**1**	**16**	**17**	**16**	**0**	**0**	**0**	**57**	**1.8**	**58**	**15**	**46**	**1**	**–2**	....	....	....	....	....	....	....	....
1985-86	**Buffalo Sabres**	**NHL**	**47**	**5**	**23**	**28**	**4**	**15**	**19**	**16**	**1**	**0**	**0**	**81**	**6.2**	**64**	**20**	**45**	**3**	**+2**	....	....	....	....	....	....	....	....
1986-87	TPS Turku	Finland	41	13	30	43	....	....	....	20	....	....	....	....	....	....	....	....	....	....	5	0	3	3	2	....	....	....
	Finland	WEC-A	8	0	4	4	....	....	....	4	....	....	....	....	....	....	....	....	....	....	....	....	....	....	....	....	....	....
1987-88	Finland	C Cup	5	0	1	1	....	....	....	0	....	....	....	....	....	....	....	....	....	....	....	....	....	....	....	....	....	....
	TPS Turku	Finland	44	10	28	38	....	....	....	20	....	....	....	....	....	....	....	....	....	....	....	....	....	....	....	....	....	....
1988-89	TPS Turku	Finland	43	7	25	32	....	....	....	30	....	....	....	....	....	....	....	....	....	....	10	1	7	8	0	....	....	....
	Finland	WEC-A	10	3	5	8	....	....	....	6	....	....	....	....	....	....	....	....	....	....	....	....	....	....	....	....	....	....
1989-90	TPS Turku	Finland	41	7	19	26	....	....	....	14	....	....	....	....	....	....	....	....	....	....	9	0	6	6	10	....	....	....
1990-91	TPS Turku	Finland	43	4	16	20	....	....	....	40	....	....	....	....	....	....	....	....	....	....	9	4	2	6	4	....	....	....
	Finland	WEC-A	7	0	2	2	....	....	....	4	....	....	....	....	....	....	....	....	....	....	....	....	....	....	....	....	....	....
1991-92	TPS Turku	Finland	43	6	22	28	....	....	....	32	....	....	....	....	....	....	....	....	....	....	3	1	4	5	0	....	....	....
1992-93	TPS Turku	Finland	39	1	18	19	....	....	....	18	....	....	....	....	....	....	....	....	....	....	12	2	2	4	14	....	....	....
1993-94	TPS Turku	Finland	47	3	17	20	....	....	....	18	....	....	....	....	....	....	....	....	....	....	....	....	....	....	....	....	....	....
	Finland	Olympics	8	2	1	3	....	....	....	2	....	....	....	....	....	....	....	....	....	....	....	....	....	....	....	....	....	....
	Finland	WC-A	8	1	4	5	....	....	....	6	....	....	....	....	....	....	....	....	....	....	....	....	....	....	....	....	....	....
1994-95	Zurich Grasshoppers	Switz. 2	36	12	18	30	....	....	....	14	....	....	....	....	....	....	....	....	....	....	12	5	9	14	2	....	....	....
	Finland	WC-A	7	1	1	2	....	....	....	8	....	....	....	....	....	....	....	....	....	....	....	....	....	....	....	....	....	....
1995-96	Zurich Grasshoppers	Switz. 2	35	12	26	38	....	....	....	10	....	....	....	....	....	....	....	....	....	....	11	1	7	8	0	....	....	....
	Finland	WC-A	6	0	6	6	....	....	....	4	....	....	....	....	....	....	....	....	....	....	....	....	....	....	....	....	....	....
1996-97	Finland	W Cup	4	1	0	1	....	....	....	6	....	....	....	....	....	....	....	....	....	....	....	....	....	....	....	....	....	....
	TPS Turku	Finland	48	7	14	21	....	....	....	24	....	....	....	....	....	....	....	....	....	....	12	0	1	1	6	....	....	....
	Finland	WC-A	8	0	3	3	....	....	....	4	....	....	....	....	....	....	....	....	....	....	....	....	....	....	....	....	....	....
1997-98	Zuricher SC	Switz.	38	3	20	23	....	....	....	0	....	....	....	....	....	....	....	....	....	....	....	....	....	....	....	....	....	....
	NHL Totals		**245**	**25**	**101**	**126**	**21**	**69**	**90**	**66**	**7**	**2**	**1**	**405**	**6.2**	**339**	**102**	**230**	**15**		**17**	**1**	**3**	**4**	**6**	**0**	**0**	**0**

EJC-A All-Star Team (1981) • Finnish Rookie of the Year (1982) • Finnish First All-Star Team (1987, 1989, 1990, 1991, 1992)
Named to All-Star Team, 1981 European Junior Championships • Named Rookie of the Year in Finnish National League (1982) • Finnish League First All-Star Team (1987)

• VISHEAU, MARK

Mark Visheau D – R. 6'6", 235 lbs. b: Burlington, Ont., 6/27/1973. Winnipeg's 4th choice, 84th overall, in 1992 Entry Draft.

Season	Club	League	GP	G	A	Pts	AG	AA	APts	PIM	PP	SH	GW	S	%	TGF	PGF	TGA	PGA	+/–	GP	G	A	Pts	PIM	PP	SH	GW
1990-91	London Knights	OHL	59	4	11	15	....	....	....	40	....	....	....	....	....	....	....	....	....	....	7	0	1	1	6	....	....	....
1991-92	London Knights	OHL	66	5	31	36	....	....	....	104	....	....	....	....	....	....	....	....	....	....	10	0	4	4	27	....	....	....
1992-93	London Knights	OHL	62	8	52	60	....	....	....	88	....	....	....	....	....	....	....	....	....	....	12	0	5	5	26	....	....	....
1993-94	**Winnipeg Jets**	**NHL**	**1**	**0**	**0**	**0**	**0**	**0**	**0**	**0**	**0**	**0**	**0**	**1**	**0.0**	**0**	**0**	**0**	**0**	**0**	....	....	....	....	....	....	....	....
	Moncton Hawks	AHL	48	4	5	9	....	....	....	58	....	....	....	....	....	....	....	....	....	....	....	....	....	....	....	....	....	....
1994-95	Springfield Falcons	AHL	35	0	4	4	....	....	....	94	....	....	....	....	....	....	....	....	....	....	....	....	....	....	....	....	....	....
1995-96	Cape Breton Oilers	AHL	8	0	0	0	....	....	....	30	....	....	....	....	....	....	....	....	....	....	....	....	....	....	....	....	....	....
	Minnesota Moose	IHL	10	0	0	0	....	....	....	25	....	....	....	....	....	....	....	....	....	....	....	....	....	....	....	....	....	....
	Wheeling Thunderbirds	ECHL	7	1	2	3	....	....	....	14	....	....	....	....	....	....	....	....	....	....	7	0	3	3	4	....	....	....
1996-97	Raleigh IceCaps	ECHL	15	1	5	6	....	....	....	61	....	....	....	....	....	....	....	....	....	....	....	....	....	....	....	....	....	....
	Quebec Rafales	IHL	64	3	10	13	....	....	....	173	....	....	....	....	....	....	....	....	....	....	9	1	1	2	11	....	....	....
1997-98	Milwaukee Admirals	IHL	72	4	12	16	....	....	....	227	....	....	....	....	....	....	....	....	....	....	....	....	....	....	....	....	....	....
	NHL Totals		**1**	**0**	**0**	**0**	**0**	**0**	**0**	**0**	**0**	**0**	**0**	**1**	**0.0**	**0**	**0**	**0**	**0**		....	....	....	....	....	....	....	....

Signed as a free agent by **LA Kings**, July 30, 1997.

• VITOLINSH, HARIJS

Harijs Vitolinsh C – L. 6'3", 212 lbs. b: Riga, Latvia, 4/30/1968. Winnipeg's 12th choice, 228th overall, in 1993 Entry Draft.

Season	Club	League	GP	G	A	Pts	AG	AA	APts	PIM	PP	SH	GW	S	%	TGF	PGF	TGA	PGA	+/–	GP	G	A	Pts	PIM	PP	SH	GW
1986-87	Dynamo Riga	USSR	17	1	1	2	....	....	....	8	....	....	....	....	....	....	....	....	....	....	....	....	....	....	....	....	....	....
1987-88	Dynamo Riga	USSR	30	3	3	6	....	....	....	24	....	....	....	....	....	....	....	....	....	....	....	....	....	....	....	....	....	....
	Soviet Union	WJC-A	7	2	0	2	....	....	....	6	....	....	....	....	....	....	....	....	....	....	....	....	....	....	....	....	....	....
1988-89	Dynamo Riga	USSR	36	3	2	5	....	....	....	16	....	....	....	....	....	....	....	....	....	....	....	....	....	....	....	....	....	....
	Dynamo Riga	Super S	7	1	0	1	....	....	....	2	....	....	....	....	....	....	....	....	....	....	....	....	....	....	....	....	....	....
1989-90	Dynamo Riga	FrTour	1	0	0	0	....	....	....	0	....	....	....	....	....	....	....	....	....	....	....	....	....	....	....	....	....	....
	Dynamo Riga	USSR	45	7	6	13	....	....	....	18	....	....	....	....	....	....	....	....	....	....	....	....	....	....	....	....	....	....
1990-91	Dynamo Riga	FrTour	1	0	0	0	....	....	....	0	....	....	....	....	....	....	....	....	....	....	....	....	....	....	....	....	....	....
	Dynamo Riga	USSR	46	12	19	31	....	....	....	22	....	....	....	....	....	....	....	....	....	....	....	....	....	....	....	....	....	....
1991-92	Dynamo Riga	CIS	30	12	5	17	....	....	....	10	....	....	....	....	....	....	....	....	....	....	....	....	....	....	....	....	....	....
1992-93	EHC Chur	Switz.	17	12	6	18	....	....	....	23	....	....	....	....	....	....	....	....	....	....	....	....	....	....	....	....	....	....
	Thunder Bay Thunder Hawks	ColHL	8	6	7	13	....	....	....	12	....	....	....	....	....	....	....	....	....	....	....	....	....	....	....	....	....	....
	New Haven Nighthawks	AHL	7	6	3	9	....	....	....	4	....	....	....	....	....	....	....	....	....	....	....	....	....	....	....	....	....	....
	Latvia	WC C	3	3	3	6	....	....	....	4	....	....	....	....	....	....	....	....	....	....	....	....	....	....	....	....	....	....
1993-94	**Winnipeg Jets**	**NHL**	**8**	**0**	**0**	**0**	**0**	**0**	**0**	**4**	**0**	**0**	**0**	**7**	**0.0**	**2**	**0**	**2**	**0**	**0**	....	....	....	....	....	....	....	....
	Moncton Hawks	AHL	70	28	34	62	....	....	....	41	....	....	....	....	....	....	....	....	....	....	20	1	3	4	4	....	....	....
1994-95	Rapperswil-Jona	Switz.	30	6	17	23	....	....	....	50	....	....	....	....	....	....	....	....	....	....	....	....	....	....	....	....	....	....
	Latvia	WC-B	7	3	4	7	....	....	....	16	....	....	....	....	....	....	....	....	....	....	....	....	....	....	....	....	....	....
1995-96	Rogle BK	Sweden	19	3	2	5	....	....	....	24	....	....	....	....	....	....	....	....	....	....	....	....	....	....	....	....	....	....
	Latvia	WC-B	7	3	6	9	....	....	....	2	....	....	....	....	....	....	....	....	....	....	....	....	....	....	....	....	....	....
1996-97	EHC Chur	Switz. 2	39	25	58	83	....	....	....	58	....	....	....	....	....	....	....	....	....	....	3	0	1	1	6	....	....	....
	Latvia	WC-A	8	4	5	9	....	....	....	4	....	....	....	....	....	....	....	....	....	....	....	....	....	....	....	....	....	....
	NHL Totals		**8**	**0**	**0**	**0**	**0**	**0**	**0**	**4**	**0**	**0**	**0**	**7**	**0.0**	**2**	**0**	**2**	**0**		....	....	....	....	....	....	....	....

WC-B All-Star Team (1990)
• Re-entered NHL draft. Originally Montreal's 10th choice, 188th overall, in 1988 Entry Draft.

			REGULAR SEASON																		PLAYOFFS							
Season	Club	League	GP	G	A	Pts	AG	AA	APts	PIM	PP	SH	GW	S	%	TGF	PGF	TGA	PGA	+/–	GP	G	A	Pts	PIM	PP	SH	GW

• VIVEIROS, EMANUEL

Emanuel Viveiros D – L. 6', 175 lbs. b: St. Albert, Alta., 1/8/1966. Edmonton's 6th choice, 106th overall, in 1984 Entry Draft.

1982-83	Prince Albert Raiders	WHL	59	6	26	32	....	....	....	55	....	....	....	....	....	....	....	....	....	....	....	....	....	....	....	....	....	....
1983-84	Prince Albert Raiders	WHL	67	15	94	109	....	....	....	48	....	....	....	....	....	....	....	....	....	....	2	0	3	3	6	....	....	....
1984-85	Prince Albert Raiders	WHL	68	17	71	88	....	....	....	94	....	....	....	....	....	....	....	....	....	....	13	2	9	11	14	....	....	....
1985-86	Prince Albert Raiders	WHL	57	22	70	92	....	....	....	30	....	....	....	....	....	....	....	....	....	....	20	4	24	28	4	....	....	....
	Canada	WJC-A	7	1	1	2	....	....	....	2	....	....	....	....	....	....	....	....	....	....	....	....	....	....	....	....	....	....
	Minnesota North Stars	**NHL**	**4**	**0**	**1**	**1**	**0**	**1**	**1**	**0**	**0**	**0**	**0**	**4**	**0.0**	**7**	**0**	**5**	**0**	**+2**	....	....	....	....	....	....	....	....
1986-87	**Minnesota North Stars**	**NHL**	**1**	**0**	**1**	**1**	**0**	**1**	**1**	**0**	**0**	**0**	**0**	**1**	**0.0**	**1**	**1**	**0**	**0**	**0**	....	....	....	....	....	....	....	....
	Springfield Indians	AHL	76	7	35	42	....	....	....	38	....	....	....	....	....	....	....	....	....	....	....	....	....	....	....	....	....	....
1987-88	**Minnesota North Stars**	**NHL**	**24**	**1**	**9**	**10**	**1**	**6**	**7**	**6**	**0**	**0**	**0**	**35**	**2.9**	**23**	**11**	**17**	**0**	**–5**	....	....	....	....	....	....	....	....
	Kalamazoo Wings	IHL	57	15	48	63	....	....	....	41	....	....	....	....	....	....	....	....	....	....	7	1	8	9	0	....	....	....
1988-89	Kalamazoo Wings	IHL	54	11	29	40	....	....	....	37	....	....	....	....	....	....	....	....	....	....	....	....	....	....	....	....	....	....
1989-90	Kaufberen Eagles	Germany	8	2	7	9	....	....	....	8	....	....	....	....	....	....	....	....	....	....	....	....	....	....	....	....	....	....
1990-91	Albany Choppers	IHL	14	3	7	10	....	....	....	6	....	....	....	....	....	....	....	....	....	....	....	....	....	....	....	....	....	....
	Springfield Indians	AHL	48	2	22	24	....	....	....	29	....	....	....	....	....	....	....	....	....	....	7	0	2	2	4	....	....	....
1991-92	VSV Villach	Austria	46	9	47	56	....	....	....	....	....	....	....	....	....	....	....	....	....	....	....	....	....	....	....	....	....	....
1992-93	VSV Villach	Austria	54	13	37	50	....	....	....	....	....	....	....	....	....	....	....	....	....	....	....	....	....	....	....	....	....	....
1993-94	VSV Villach	Austria	51	11	50	61	....	....	....	....	....	....	....	....	....	....	....	....	....	....	....	....	....	....	....	....	....	....
1994-95	VSV Villach	Austria	13	2	11	13	....	....	....	18	....	....	....	....	....	....	....	....	....	....	12	5	11	16	51	....	....	....
1995-96	Lustenau	Austria	33	10	23	33	....	....	....	36	....	....	....	....	....	....	....	....	....	....	....	....	....	....	....	....	....	....
1996-97	Schwenningen Wild Wings	Germany	44	8	16	24	....	....	....	34	....	....	....	....	....	....	....	....	....	....	5	0	2	2	31	....	....	....
1997-98	Schwenningen Wild Wings	Germany	51	5	11	16	....	....	....	36	....	....	....	....	....	....	....	....	....	....	....	....	....	....	....	....	....	....
	NHL Totals		**29**	**1**	**11**	**12**	**1**	**8**	**9**	**6**	**0**	**0**	**0**	**40**	**2.5**	**31**	**12**	**22**	**0**		....	....	....	....	....	....	....	....

WHL East Second All-Star Team (1985) • WHL East First All-Star Team (1986)

Traded to **Minnesota** by **Edmonton** with Marc Habscheid and Don Barber for Gord Sherven and Don Biggs, December 20, 1985. Signed as a free agent by **Hartford**, February 9, 1990.

• VOLCAN, MICKEY

Mickey Volcan D. 6', 190 lbs. b: Edmonton, Alta., 3/3/1962. Hartford's 3rd choice, 50th overall, in 1980 Entry Draft.

1977-78	St. Albert Saints	AJHL	60	28	40	68	....	....	....	106	....	....	....	....	....	....	....	....	....	....	....	....	....	....	....	....	....	....
1978-79	St. Albert Saints	AJHL	50	20	47	67	....	....	....	109	....	....	....	....	....	....	....	....	....	....	....	....	....	....	....	....	....	....
1979-80	University of North Dakota	WCHA	33	2	14	16	....	....	....	38	....	....	....	....	....	....	....	....	....	....	....	....	....	....	....	....	....	....
1980-81	**Hartford Whalers**	**NHL**	**49**	**2**	**11**	**13**	**2**	**8**	**10**	**26**	**0**	**0**	**0**	**49**	**4.1**	**47**	**2**	**63**	**6**	**–12**	....	....	....	....	....	....	....	....
	Binghamton Whalers	AHL	24	1	9	10	....	....	....	26	....	....	....	....	....	....	....	....	....	....	6	0	0	0	14	....	....	....
1981-82	**Hartford Whalers**	**NHL**	**26**	**1**	**5**	**6**	**1**	**3**	**4**	**29**	**1**	**0**	**0**	**45**	**2.2**	**19**	**2**	**41**	**7**	**–17**	....	....	....	....	....	....	....	....
	Binghamton Whalers	AHL	33	4	13	17	....	....	....	47	....	....	....	....	....	....	....	....	....	....	14	4	8	12	40	....	....	....
1982-83	**Hartford Whalers**	**NHL**	**68**	**4**	**13**	**17**	**3**	**9**	**12**	**73**	**0**	**0**	**0**	**72**	**5.6**	**56**	**6**	**96**	**16**	**–30**	....	....	....	....	....	....	....	....
1983-84	**Calgary Flames**	**NHL**	**19**	**1**	**4**	**5**	**1**	**3**	**4**	**18**	**0**	**0**	**1**	**13**	**7.7**	**19**	**0**	**24**	**3**	**–2**	....	....	....	....	....	....	....	....
	Colorado Flames	CHL	30	8	9	17	....	....	....	20	....	....	....	....	....	....	....	....	....	....	5	0	0	0	11	....	....	....
1984-85	Moncton Golden Flames	AHL	63	8	14	22	....	....	....	44	....	....	....	....	....	....	....	....	....	....	....	....	....	....	....	....	....	....
1985-86	Nova Scotia Oilers	AHL	66	12	36	48	....	....	....	114	....	....	....	....	....	....	....	....	....	....	....	....	....	....	....	....	....	....
1986-87	Baltimore Skipjacks	AHL	72	8	36	44	....	....	....	118	....	....	....	....	....	....	....	....	....	....	....	....	....	....	....	....	....	....
1987-88	JyP Jyraskyla	Finland	29	7	4	11	....	....	....	78	....	....	....	....	....	....	....	....	....	....	....	....	....	....	....	....	....	....
1988-89			DID NOT PLAY																									
1989-90			DID NOT PLAY																									
1990-91	Phoenix Roadrunners	IHL	59	13	29	42	....	....	....	103	....	....	....	....	....	....	....	....	....	....	11	0	6	6	11	....	....	....
	NHL Totals		**162**	**8**	**33**	**41**	**7**	**23**	**30**	**146**	**1**	**0**	**1**	**179**	**4.5**	**141**	**10**	**224**	**32**		....	....	....	....	....	....	....	....

Traded to **Calgary** by **Hartford** for Joel Quenneville and Richie Dunn, July 5, 1983.

• VOLEK, DAVID

David Volek LW/RW – L. 6', 185 lbs. b: Prague, Czech., 6/18/1966. NY Islanders' 11th choice, 208th overall, in 1984 Entry Draft.

1984-85	Sparta Praha	Czech.	32	5	5	10	....	....	....	14	....	....	....	....	....	....	....	....	....	....	....	....	....	....	....	....	....	....
1985-86	Sparta Praha	Czech.	35	10	7	17	....	....	....	....	....	....	....	....	....	....	....	....	....	....	....	....	....	....	....	....	....	....
	Czechoslovakia	WJC-A	7	4	3	7	....	....	....	6	....	....	....	....	....	....	....	....	....	....	....	....	....	....	....	....	....	....
1986-87	Sparta Praha	Czech.	39	27	25	52	....	....	....	38	....	....	....	....	....	....	....	....	....	....	....	....	....	....	....	....	....	....
	Czechoslovakia	WEC-A	10	3	1	4	....	....	....	2	....	....	....	....	....	....	....	....	....	....	....	....	....	....	....	....	....	....
1987-88	Czechoslovakia	C Cup	6	2	2	4	....	....	....	2	....	....	....	....	....	....	....	....	....	....	....	....	....	....	....	....	....	....
	Sparta Praha	Czech.	42	29	18	47	....	....	....	58	....	....	....	....	....	....	....	....	....	....	....	....	....	....	....	....	....	....
	Czechoslovakia	Olympics	7	1	2	3	....	....	....	2	....	....	....	....	....	....	....	....	....	....	....	....	....	....	....	....	....	....
1988-89	**New York Islanders**	**NHL**	**77**	**25**	**34**	**59**	**21**	**24**	**45**	**24**	**9**	**0**	**7**	**229**	**10.9**	**90**	**42**	**63**	**4**	**–11**	....	....	....	....	....	....	....	....
1989-90	**New York Islanders**	**NHL**	**80**	**17**	**22**	**39**	**15**	**16**	**31**	**41**	**6**	**0**	**0**	**181**	**9.4**	**69**	**27**	**52**	**8**	**–2**	**5**	**1**	**4**	**5**	**0**	**0**	**0**	**0**
1990-91	**New York Islanders**	**NHL**	**77**	**22**	**34**	**56**	**20**	**26**	**46**	**57**	**6**	**0**	**1**	**224**	**9.8**	**75**	**23**	**82**	**20**	**–10**	....	....	....	....	....	....	....	....
	Czechoslovakia	WEC-A	10	3	2	5	....	....	....	8	....	....	....	....	....	....	....	....	....	....	....	....	....	....	....	....	....	....
1991-92	**New York Islanders**	**NHL**	**74**	**18**	**42**	**60**	**16**	**32**	**48**	**35**	**4**	**1**	**2**	**167**	**10.8**	**87**	**26**	**86**	**25**	**0**	....	....	....	....	....	....	....	....
1992-93	**New York Islanders**	**NHL**	**56**	**8**	**13**	**21**	**7**	**9**	**16**	**34**	**2**	**0**	**1**	**118**	**6.8**	**38**	**5**	**41**	**7**	**–1**	**10**	**4**	**1**	**5**	**2**	**0**	**0**	**0**
1993-94	**New York Islanders**	**NHL**	**32**	**5**	**9**	**14**	**5**	**7**	**12**	**10**	**2**	**0**	**0**	**56**	**8.9**	**28**	**7**	**22**	**1**	**0**	....	....	....	....	....	....	....	....
1994-95			DID NOT PLAY – RETIRED																									
1995-96	Sparta Prava	Czech.	5	3	2	5	....	....	....	....	....	....	....	....	....	....	....	....	....	....	....	....	....	....	....	....	....	....
	NHL Totals		**396**	**95**	**154**	**249**	**84**	**114**	**198**	**201**	**29**	**1**	**11**	**975**	**9.7**	**387**	**130**	**346**	**65**		**15**	**5**	**5**	**10**	**2**	**0**	**0**	**0**

NHL All-Rookie Team (1989)

• VOLMAR, DOUG

Doug Volmar RW – R. 6'1", 215 lbs. b: Cleveland, OH, 1/9/1945.

1964-65	Michigan State Spartans	WCHA	....	27	9	36	....	....	....	....	....	....	....	....	....	....	....	....	....	....	....	....	....	....	....	....	....	....
1965-66	Michigan State Spartans	WCHA	29	26	28	54	....	....	....	57	....	....	....	....	....	....	....	....	....	....	....	....	....	....	....	....	....	....
1966-67	Michigan State Spartans	WCHA	32	21	12	33	....	....	....	100	....	....	....	....	....	....	....	....	....	....	....	....	....	....	....	....	....	....
1967-68	United States	Nat-Team	STATISTICS NOT AVAILABLE																									
	United States	Olympics	7	5	0	5	....	....	....	4	....	....	....	....	....	....	....	....	....	....	....	....	....	....	....	....	....	....
1968-69	Columbus Checkers	IHL	72	*63	28	91	....	....	....	74	....	....	....	....	....	....	....	....	....	....	3	2	1	3	0	....	....	....
1969-70	Fort Worth Wings	CHL	67	30	23	53	....	....	....	75	....	....	....	....	....	....	....	....	....	....	7	4	1	5	2	....	....	....
	Detroit Red Wings	**NHL**	....	....	....	....	....	....	....	....	....	....	....	....	....	....	....	....	....	....	**2**	**1**	**0**	**1**	**0**	....	....	....
	San Diego Gulls	WHL	....	....	....	....	....	....	....	....	....	....	....	....	....	....	....	....	....	....	2	0	3	3	0	....	....	....
1970-71	**Detroit Red Wings**	**NHL**	**2**	**0**	**1**	**1**	**0**	**1**	**1**	**2**	**0**	**0**	**0**	**0**	**0.0**	**1**	**1**	**0**	**0**	**0**	....	....	....	....	....	....	....	....
	Springfield Kings	AHL	69	*42	26	68	....	....	....	52	....	....	....	....	....	....	....	....	....	....	12	6	10	16	29	....	....	....
1971-72	**Detroit Red Wings**	**NHL**	**39**	**9**	**5**	**14**	**10**	**5**	**15**	**8**	**3**	**0**	**1**	**43**	**20.9**	**24**	**10**	**14**	**0**	**0**	....	....	....	....	....	....	....	....
	Tidewater Wings	AHL	20	8	8	16	....	....	....	8	....	....	....	....	....	....	....	....	....	....	....	....	....	....	....	....	....	....
1972-73	**Los Angeles Kings**	**NHL**	**21**	**4**	**2**	**6**	**4**	**2**	**6**	**16**	**0**	**0**	**1**	**33**	**12.1**	**12**	**0**	**14**	**0**	**–2**	....	....	....	....	....	....	....	....
1973-74	Portland Buckaroos	WHL	3	0	4	4	....	....	....	5	....	....	....	....	....	....	....	....	....	....	....	....	....	....	....	....	....	....
	Springfield Kings	AHL	25	11	5	16	....	....	....	20	....	....	....	....	....	....	....	....	....	....	....	....	....	....	....	....	....	....
	Richmond Robins	AHL	22	13	7	20	....	....	....	10	....	....	....	....	....	....	....	....	....	....	5	3	4	7	2	....	....	....
1974-75	San Diego Mariners	WHA	10	0	1	1	....	....	....	4	....	....	....	....	....	....	....	....	....	....	....	....	....	....	....	....	....	....
	Syracuse Blazers	NAHL	47	40	32	72	....	....	....	47	....	....	....	....	....	....	....	....	....	....	....	....	....	....	....	....	....	....
	NHL Totals		**62**	**13**	**8**	**21**	**14**	**8**	**22**	**26**	**3**	**0**	**2**	**76**	**17.1**	**37**	**11**	**28**	**0**		**2**	**1**	**0**	**1**	**0**	**0**	**0**	**0**
	Other Major League Totals		10	0	1	1	....	....	....	4	....	....	....	....	....	....	....	....	....	....	....	....	....	....	....	....	....	....

WCHA First All-Star Team (1966) • NCAA West First All-American Team (1966) • IHL Second All-Star Team (1969) • Won Garry F. Longman Memorial Trophy (Top Rookie - IHL) (1969)

Claimed by **San Diego** (WHL) from **Detroit** in Reverse Draft, June, 1969. Traded to **Detroit** by **San Diego** (WHL) for cash, July, 1969. Claimed by **LA Kings** from **Detroit** in Intra-League Draft, June 5, 1972. Traded to **Richmond** (AHL) by **Springfield** (AHL) for Roger Pelletier, February, 1974. Signed as a free agent by **San Diego** (WHA), June, 1974.

• VON STEFENELLI, PHIL

Phil Von Stefenelli D – L. 6'1", 200 lbs. b: Vancouver, B.C., 4/10/1969. Vancouver's 5th choice, 122nd overall, in 1988 Entry Draft.

1987-88	Boston University	H.E.	34	3	13	16	....	....	....	38	....	....	....	....	....	....	....	....	....	....	....	....	....	....	....	....	....	....
1988-89	Boston University	H.E.	33	2	6	8	....	....	....	34	....	....	....	....	....	....	....	....	....	....	....	....	....	....	....	....	....	....
1989-90	Boston University	H.E.	44	8	20	28	....	....	....	40	....	....	....	....	....	....	....	....	....	....	....	....	....	....	....	....	....	....
1990-91	Boston University	H.E.	41	7	23	30	....	....	....	32	....	....	....	....	....	....	....	....	....	....	....	....	....	....	....	....	....	....
1991-92	Milwaukee Admirals	IHL	80	2	34	36	....	....	....	40	....	....	....	....	....	....	....	....	....	....	5	1	2	3	2	....	....	....

			REGULAR SEASON																		PLAYOFFS							
Season	**Club**	**League**	**GP**	**G**	**A**	**Pts**	**AG**	**AA**	**APts**	**PIM**	**PP**	**SH**	**GW**	**S**	**%**	**TGF**	**PGF**	**TGA**	**PGA**	**+/–**	**GP**	**G**	**A**	**Pts**	**PIM**	**PP**	**SH**	**GW**
1992-93	Hamilton Canucks	AHL	78	11	20	31	....	....	....	75	....	....	....	....	....	....	....	....	....	....	....	....	....	....	....	....	....	....
1993-94	Hamilton Canucks	AHL	80	10	31	41	....	....	....	89	....	....	....	....	....	....	....	....	....	....	4	1	0	1	2	....	....	....
1994-95	Providence Bruins	AHL	75	6	13	19	....	....	....	93	....	....	....	....	....	....	....	....	....	....	13	2	4	6	6	....	....	....
1995-96	**Boston Bruins**	**NHL**	**37**	**0**	**4**	**4**	**0**	**3**	**3**	**16**	**0**	**0**	**0**	**20**	**0.0**	**15**	**5**	**11**	**3**	**+2**	....	....	....	....	....	....	....	....
	Providence Bruins	AHL	42	9	21	30	....	....	....	52	....	....	....	....	....	....	....	....	....	....	....	....	....	....	....	....	....	....
1996-97	**Ottawa Senators**	**NHL**	**6**	**0**	**1**	**1**	**0**	**1**	**1**	**7**	**0**	**0**	**0**	**2**	**0.0**	**3**	**2**	**5**	**1**	**–3**	....	....	....	....	....	....	....	....
	Detroit Vipers	IHL	67	14	26	40	....	....	....	86	....	....	....	....	....	....	....	....	....	....	21	2	4	6	20	....	....	....
	NHL Totals		**43**	**0**	**5**	**5**	**0**	**4**	**4**	**23**	**0**	**0**	**0**	**22**	**0.0**	**18**	**7**	**16**	**4**		....	....	....	....	....	....	....	....

Signed as a free agent by **Boston**, September 10, 1994. Signed as a free agent by **Ottawa**, July 17, 1996.

• VOPAT, JAN

Jan Vopat D – L. 6', 205 lbs. b: Most, Czech., 3/22/1973. Hartford's 3rd choice, 57th overall, in 1992 Entry Draft.

1990-91	CHZ Litvinov	Czech.	25	1	4	5	....	....	....	4	....	....	....	....	....	....	....	....	....	....	....	....	....	....	....	....	....	....
1991-92	CHZ Litvinov	Czech.	46	4	2	6	....	....	....	16	....	....	....	....	....	....	....	....	....	....	....	....	....	....	....	....	....	....
	Czechoslovakia	WJC-A	7	0	1	1	....	....	....	2	....	....	....	....	....	....	....	....	....	....	....	....	....	....	....	....	....	....
1992-93	CHZ Litvinov	Czech.	45	12	10	22	....	....	....	....	....	....	....	....	....	....	....	....	....	....	....	....	....	....	....	....	....	....
	Czech Republic	WJC-A	7	6	4	10	....	....	....	6	....	....	....	....	....	....	....	....	....	....	....	....	....	....	....	....	....	....
1993-94	CHZ Litvinov	Czech.	41	9	19	28	....	....	....	0	....	....	....	....	....	....	....	....	....	....	4	1	1	2	....	....	....	....
	Czech Republic	Olympics	8	0	1	1	....	....	....	8	....	....	....	....	....	....	....	....	....	....	....	....	....	....	....	....	....	....
1994-95	Chemopetrol Litvinov	Czech.	42	7	18	25	....	....	....	49	....	....	....	....	....	....	....	....	....	....	4	0	2	2	2	....	....	....
	Czech Republic	WC-A	8	0	1	1	....	....	....	6	....	....	....	....	....	....	....	....	....	....	....	....	....	....	....	....	....	....
1995-96	**Los Angeles Kings**	**NHL**	**11**	**1**	**4**	**5**	**1**	**3**	**4**	**4**	**0**	**0**	**0**	**13**	**7.7**	**15**	**6**	**7**	**1**	**+3**	....	....	....	....	....	....	....	....
	Phoenix Roadrunners	IHL	47	0	9	9	....	....	....	34	....	....	....	....	....	....	....	....	....	....	4	0	2	2	4	....	....	....
1996-97	**Los Angeles Kings**	**NHL**	**33**	**4**	**5**	**9**	**4**	**4**	**8**	**22**	**0**	**0**	**1**	**44**	**9.1**	**26**	**2**	**25**	**4**	**+3**	....	....	....	....	....	....	....	....
	Phoenix Roadrunners	IHL	4	0	6	6	....	....	....	6	....	....	....	....	....	....	....	....	....	....	....	....	....	....	....	....	....	....
1997-98	**Los Angeles Kings**	**NHL**	**21**	**1**	**5**	**6**	**1**	**5**	**6**	**10**	**0**	**0**	**1**	**13**	**7.7**	**18**	**1**	**13**	**4**	**+8**	**2**	**0**	**1**	**1**	**2**	**0**	**0**	**0**
	Utah Grizzlies	IHL	38	8	13	21	....	....	....	24	....	....	....	....	....	....	....	....	....	....	....	....	....	....	....	....	....	....
	NHL Totals		**65**	**6**	**14**	**20**	**6**	**12**	**18**	**36**	**0**	**0**	**2**	**70**	**8.6**	**59**	**9**	**45**	**9**		**2**	**0**	**1**	**1**	**2**	**0**	**0**	**0**

Rights traded to **LA Kings** by **Hartford** for LA Kings' 4th round choice (Ian MacNeil) in 1995 Entry Draft, May 31, 1995. Traded to **Nashville** by **LA Kings** with Kimmo Timonen for future considerations, June 26, 1998.

• VOPAT, ROMAN

Roman Vopat C – L. 6'3", 216 lbs. b: Litvinov, Czech., 4/21/1976. St. Louis' 4th choice, 172nd overall, in 1994 Entry Draft.

1993-94	Chemopetrol Litvinov	Czech.	7	0	0	0	....	....	....	0	....	....	....	....	....	....	....	....	....	....	....	....	....	....	....	....	....	....
1994-95	Moose Jaw Warriors	WHL	72	23	20	43	....	....	....	141	....	....	....	....	....	....	....	....	....	....	10	4	1	5	28	....	....	....
	Peoria Rivermen	IHL	....	....	....	....	....	....	....	....	....	....	....	....	....	....	....	....	....	....	6	0	2	2	2	....	....	....
1995-96	Moose Jaw Warriors	WHL	7	0	4	4	....	....	....	34	....	....	....	....	....	....	....	....	....	....	....	....	....	....	....	....	....	....
	Prince Albert Raiders	WHL	22	15	5	20	....	....	....	81	....	....	....	....	....	....	....	....	....	....	18	9	8	17	57	....	....	....
	St. Louis Blues	**NHL**	**25**	**2**	**3**	**5**	**2**	**2**	**4**	**48**	**1**	**0**	**1**	**33**	**6.1**	**6**	**1**	**14**	**1**	**–8**	....	....	....	....	....	....	....	....
	Worcester IceCats	AHL	5	2	0	2	....	....	....	14	....	....	....	....	....	....	....	....	....	....	....	....	....	....	....	....	....	....
1996-97	**Los Angeles Kings**	**NHL**	**29**	**4**	**5**	**9**	**4**	**4**	**8**	**60**	**1**	**0**	**2**	**54**	**7.4**	**16**	**1**	**23**	**1**	**–7**	....	....	....	....	....	....	....	....
	Phoenix Roadrunners	IHL	50	8	8	16	....	....	....	139	....	....	....	....	....	....	....	....	....	....	....	....	....	....	....	....	....	....
1997-98	**Los Angeles Kings**	**NHL**	**25**	**0**	**3**	**3**	**0**	**3**	**3**	**55**	**0**	**0**	**0**	**36**	**0.0**	**5**	**2**	**10**	**0**	**–7**	....	....	....	....	....	....	....	....
	Fredericton Canadiens	AHL	29	10	10	20	....	....	....	93	....	....	....	....	....	....	....	....	....	....	....	....	....	....	....	....	....	....
	NHL Totals		**79**	**6**	**11**	**17**	**6**	**9**	**15**	**163**	**2**	**0**	**3**	**123**	**4.9**	**27**	**4**	**47**	**2**		....	....	....	....	....	....	....	....

Traded to **LA Kings** by **St. Louis** with Craig Johnson, Patrice Tardif, St. Louis 5th round choice (Peter Hogan) in 1996 Entry Draft and 1st round choice (Matt Zultek) in 1997 Entry Draft for Wayne Gretzky, February 27, 1996.

• VOROBIEV, VLADIMIR

Vladimir Vorobiev LW – R. 6', 185 lbs. b: Cherepovets, USSR, 10/2/1972. NY Rangers' 10th choice, 240th overall, in 1992 Entry Draft

1992-93	Severstal Cherepovets	CIS	42	18	5	23	....	....	....	18	....	....	....	....	....	....	....	....	....	....	....	....	....	....	....	....	....	....
1993-94	Moscow Dynamo	CIS	11	3	1	4	....	....	....	2	....	....	....	....	....	....	....	....	....	....	....	....	....	....	....	....	....	....
1994-95	Moscow Dynamo	CIS	48	9	20	29	....	....	....	28	....	....	....	....	....	....	....	....	....	....	14	1	7	8	2	....	....	....
1995-96	Moscow Dynamo	CIS	42	19	9	28	....	....	....	49	....	....	....	....	....	....	....	....	....	....	9	2	8	10	2	....	....	....
1996-97	**New York Rangers**	**NHL**	**16**	**5**	**5**	**10**	**5**	**4**	**9**	**6**	**2**	**0**	**0**	**42**	**11.9**	**15**	**4**	**7**	**0**	**+4**	....	....	....	....	....	....	....	....
	Binghamton Rangers	AHL	61	22	27	49	....	....	....	6	....	....	....	....	....	....	....	....	....	....	4	1	1	2	2	....	....	....
1997-98	**New York Rangers**	**NHL**	**15**	**2**	**2**	**4**	**2**	**2**	**4**	**6**	**0**	**0**	**1**	**27**	**7.4**	**8**	**5**	**13**	**0**	**–10**	....	....	....	....	....	....	....	....
	Hartford Wolf Pack	AHL	56	20	28	48	....	....	....	18	....	....	....	....	....	....	....	....	....	....	15	11	8	19	4	....	....	....
	NHL Totals		**31**	**7**	**7**	**14**	**7**	**6**	**13**	**12**	**2**	**0**	**1**	**69**	**10.1**	**23**	**9**	**20**	**0**		....	....	....	....	....	....	....	....

• VUJTEK, VLADIMIR

Vladimir Vujtek LW – L. 6'1", 190 lbs. b: Ostrava, Czech., 2/17/1972. Montreal's 5th choice, 73rd overall, in 1991 Entry Draft.

1988-89	HC Vitkovice	Czech.	3	0	1	1	....	....	....	0	....	....	....	....	....	....	....	....	....	....	....	....	....	....	....	....	....	....
1989-90	HC Vitkovice	Czech.	29	7	7	14	....	....	....	....	....	....	....	....	....	....	....	....	....	....	....	....	....	....	....	....	....	....
1990-91	HC Vitkovice	Czech.	26	7	4	11	....	....	....	....	....	....	....	....	....	....	....	....	....	....	....	....	....	....	....	....	....	....
	Tri-City Americans	WHL	37	26	18	44	....	....	....	25	....	....	....	....	....	....	....	....	....	....	7	2	3	5	4	....	....	....
1991-92	Tri City Americans	WHL	53	41	61	102	....	....	....	114	....	....	....	....	....	....	....	....	....	....	....	....	....	....	....	....	....	....
	Montreal Canadiens	**NHL**	**2**	**0**	**0**	**0**	**0**	**0**	**0**	**0**	**0**	**0**	**0**	**1**	**0.0**	**0**	**0**	**1**	**0**	**–1**	....	....	....	....	....	....	....	....
1992-93	**Edmonton Oilers**	**NHL**	**30**	**1**	**10**	**11**	**1**	**7**	**8**	**8**	**0**	**0**	**0**	**49**	**2.0**	**16**	**4**	**13**	**0**	**–1**	....	....	....	....	....	....	....	....
	Cape Breton Oilers	AHL	20	10	9	19	....	....	....	14	....	....	....	....	....	....	....	....	....	....	1	0	0	0	0	....	....	....
1993-94	**Edmonton Oilers**	**NHL**	**40**	**4**	**15**	**19**	**4**	**12**	**16**	**14**	**1**	**0**	**0**	**66**	**6.1**	**25**	**4**	**28**	**0**	**–7**	....	....	....	....	....	....	....	....
1994-95	HC Vitkovice	Czech.	18	5	7	12	....	....	....	51	....	....	....	....	....	....	....	....	....	....	....	....	....	....	....	....	....	....
	Cape Breton Oilers	AHL	30	10	11	21	....	....	....	30	....	....	....	....	....	....	....	....	....	....	....	....	....	....	....	....	....	....
	Las Vegas Thunder	IHL	1	0	0	0	....	....	....	0	....	....	....	....	....	....	....	....	....	....	....	....	....	....	....	....	....	....
1995-96	HC Vitkovice	Czech.	26	6	7	13	....	....	....	....	....	....	....	....	....	....	....	....	....	....	4	1	1	2	....	....	....	....
1996-97	Assat Pori	Finland	50	27	31	58	....	....	....	48	....	....	....	....	....	....	....	....	....	....	4	1	2	3	2	....	....	....
	Czech Republic	WC-A	8	7	7	14	....	....	....	31	....	....	....	....	....	....	....	....	....	....	....	....	....	....	....	....	....	....
1997-98	**Tampa Bay Lightning**	**NHL**	**30**	**2**	**4**	**6**	**2**	**4**	**6**	**16**	**0**	**0**	**1**	**44**	**4.5**	**10**	**2**	**10**	**0**	**–2**	....	....	....	....	....	....	....	....
	Adirondack Red Wings	AHL	2	1	2	3	....	....	....	0	....	....	....	....	....	....	....	....	....	....	....	....	....	....	....	....	....	....
	NHL Totals		**102**	**7**	**29**	**36**	**7**	**23**	**30**	**38**	**1**	**0**	**1**	**160**	**4.4**	**51**	**10**	**52**	**0**		....	....	....	....	....	....	....	....

WHL West First All-Star Team (1992)
WC-A All-Star Team (1997)

Traded to **Edmonton** by **Montreal** with Shayne Corson and Brent Gilchrist for Vincent Damphousse and Edmonton's 4th round choice (Adam Wiesel) in 1993 Entry Draft, August 27, 1992.
Traded to **Tampa Bay** by **Edmonton** with Edmonton's 3rd round choice (Dmitri Afanasenkov) in 1998 Entry Draft for Brantt Myhres and a conditional draft choice, July 16, 1997.

• VUKOTA, MICK

Mick Vukota RW – R. 6'1", 225 lbs. b: Saskatoon, Sask., 9/14/1966.

1983-84	Winnipeg Warriors	WHL	3	1	1	2	....	....	....	10	....	....	....	....	....	....	....	....	....	....	....	....	....	....	....	....	....	....
1984-85	Kelowna Rockets	WHL	66	10	6	16	....	....	....	247	....	....	....	....	....	....	....	....	....	....	....	....	....	....	....	....	....	....
1985-86	Spokane Chiefs	WHL	64	19	14	33	....	....	....	369	....	....	....	....	....	....	....	....	....	....	9	6	4	10	68	....	....	....
1986-87	Spokane Chiefs	WHL	61	25	28	53	....	....	....	*337	....	....	....	....	....	....	....	....	....	....	4	0	0	0	40	....	....	....
1987-88	**New York Islanders**	**NHL**	**17**	**1**	**0**	**1**	**1**	**0**	**1**	**82**	**0**	**0**	**0**	**7**	**14.3**	**8**	**0**	**7**	**0**	**+1**	**2**	**0**	**0**	**0**	**23**	**0**	**0**	**0**
	Springfield Indians	AHL	52	7	9	16	....	....	....	375	....	....	....	....	....	....	....	....	....	....	....	....	....	....	....	....	....	....
1988-89	**New York Islanders**	**NHL**	**48**	**2**	**2**	**4**	**2**	**1**	**3**	**237**	**0**	**0**	**0**	**19**	**10.5**	**4**	**0**	**21**	**0**	**17**	....	....	....	....	....	....	....	....
	Springfield Indians	AHL	3	1	0	1	....	....	....	33	....	....	....	....	....	....	....	....	....	....	....	....	....	....	....	....	....	....
1989-90	**New York Islanders**	**NHL**	**76**	**4**	**8**	**12**	**3**	**6**	**9**	**290**	**0**	**0**	**0**	**55**	**7.3**	**24**	**0**	**15**	**1**	**+10**	**1**	**0**	**0**	**0**	**17**	**0**	**0**	**0**
1990-91	**New York Islanders**	**NHL**	**60**	**2**	**4**	**6**	**2**	**3**	**5**	**238**	**0**	**0**	**0**	**39**	**5.1**	**12**	**1**	**24**	**0**	**–13**	....	....	....	....	....	....	....	....
	Capital District Islanders	AHL	2	0	0	0	....	....	....	9	....	....	....	....	....	....	....	....	....	....	....	....	....	....	....	....	....	....
1991-92	**New York Islanders**	**NHL**	**74**	**0**	**6**	**6**	**0**	**4**	**4**	**293**	**0**	**0**	**0**	**34**	**0.0**	**15**	**0**	**21**	**0**	**–6**	....	....	....	....	....	....	....	....
1992-93	**New York Islanders**	**NHL**	**74**	**2**	**5**	**7**	**2**	**3**	**5**	**216**	**0**	**0**	**0**	**37**	**5.4**	**16**	**1**	**12**	**0**	**+3**	**15**	**0**	**0**	**0**	**16**	**0**	**0**	**0**
1993-94	**New York Islanders**	**NHL**	**72**	**3**	**1**	**4**	**3**	**1**	**4**	**237**	**0**	**0**	**0**	**26**	**11.5**	**8**	**1**	**12**	**0**	**–5**	**4**	**0**	**0**	**0**	**17**	**0**	**0**	**0**
1994-95	**New York Islanders**	**NHL**	**40**	**0**	**2**	**2**	**0**	**3**	**3**	**109**	**0**	**0**	**0**	**11**	**0.0**	**6**	**0**	**5**	**0**	**+1**	....	....	....	....	....	....	....	....
1995-96	**New York Islanders**	**NHL**	**32**	**1**	**1**	**2**	**1**	**1**	**2**	**106**	**0**	**0**	**0**	**11**	**9.1**	**2**	**0**	**5**	**0**	**–3**	....	....	....	....	....	....	....	....

Season	Club	League	GP	G	A	Pts	AG	AA	APts	PIM	PP	SH	GW	S	%	TGF	PGF	TGA	PGA	+/–	GP	G	A	Pts	PIM	PP	SH	GW
			REGULAR SEASON																		PLAYOFFS							
1996-97	**New York Islanders**	**NHL**	**17**	**1**	**0**	**1**	**1**	**0**	**1**	**71**	**0**	**0**	**0**	**7**	**14.3**	**1**	**0**	**3**	**0**	**–2**	....	....	....	....	....	....	....	....
	Utah Grizzlies	IHL	43	11	11	22	....	....	....	185	....	....	....	....	....	....	....	....	....	....	7	1	2	3	20	....	....	....
1997-98	**Tampa Bay Lightning**	**NHL**	**42**	**1**	**0**	**1**	**1**	**0**	**1**	**116**	**0**	**0**	**0**	**15**	**6.7**	**4**	**0**	**4**	**0**	**0**	....	....	....	....	....	....	....	....
	Montreal Canadiens	**NHL**	**22**	**0**	**0**	**0**	**0**	**0**	**0**	**76**	**0**	**0**	**0**	**8**	**0.0**	**0**	**0**	**4**	**0**	**–4**	**1**	**0**	**0**	**0**	**0**	**0**	**0**	**0**
	NHL Totals		**574**	**17**	**29**	**46**	**16**	**22**	**38**	**2071**	**0**	**0**	**0**	**269**	**6.3**	**100**	**3**	**133**	**1**		**23**	**0**	**0**	**0**	**73**	**0**	**0**	**0**

Signed as a free agent by **NY Islanders**, March 2, 1987. Claimed by **Tampa Bay** from **NY Islanders** in NHL Waiver Draft, September 28, 1997. Traded to **Montreal** by **Tampa Bay** with Patrick Poulin and Igor Ulanov for Stephane Richer, Darcy Tucker and David Wilkie, January 15, 1998.

• VYAZMIKIN, IGOR

Igor Vyazmikin RW/LW – L. 6'1", 194 lbs. b: Moscow, Soviet Union, 1/8/1966. Edmonton's 12th choice, 252nd overall, in 1987 Entry Draft.

Season	Club	League	GP	G	A	Pts	AG	AA	APts	PIM	PP	SH	GW	S	%	TGF	PGF	TGA	PGA	+/–	GP	G	A	Pts	PIM	PP	SH	GW
1983-84	CSKA Moscow	USSR	38	8	12	20	....	....	....	4	....	....	....	....	....	....	....	....	....	....	....	....	....	....	....	....	....	....
	Soviet Union	WJC-A	7	6	5	11	....	....	....	6	....	....	....	....	....	....	....	....	....	....	....	....	....	....	....	....	....	....
1984-85	CSKA Moscow	USSR	26	6	5	11	....	....	....	6	....	....	....	....	....	....	....	....	....	....	....	....	....	....	....	....	....	....
1985-86	CSKA Moscow	USSR	19	7	6	13	....	....	....	6	....	....	....	....	....	....	....	....	....	....	....	....	....	....	....	....	....	....
	Soviet Union	WJC-A	7	5	5	10	....	....	....	6	....	....	....	....	....	....	....	....	....	....	....	....	....	....	....	....	....	....
1986-87	CSKA Moscow	USSR	4	0	0	0	....	....	....	0	....	....	....	....	....	....	....	....	....	....	....	....	....	....	....	....	....	....
1987-88	CSKA Moscow	USSR	8	1	0	1	....	....	....	16	....	....	....	....	....	....	....	....	....	....	....	....	....	....	....	....	....	....
1988-89	CSKA Moscow	USSR	30	10	7	17	....	....	....	20	....	....	....	....	....	....	....	....	....	....	....	....	....	....	....	....	....	....
1989-90	Khimik Voskresensk	USSR	34	11	13	24	....	....	....	26	....	....	....	....	....	....	....	....	....	....	....	....	....	....	....	....	....	....
	Khimik Voskresensk	SuperS	6	1	6	7	....	....	....	0	....	....	....	....	....	....	....	....	....	....	....	....	....	....	....	....	....	....
1990-91	Khimik Voskresensk	FrTour	1	0	0	0	....	....	....	20	....	....	....	....	....	....	....	....	....	....	....	....	....	....	....	....	....	....
	Khimik Voskresensk	USSR	23	7	12	19	....	....	....	17	....	....	....	....	....	....	....	....	....	....	....	....	....	....	....	....	....	....
	Edmonton Oilers	**NHL**	**4**	**1**	**0**	**1**	**1**	**0**	**1**	**0**	**0**	**0**	**1**	**5**	**20.0**	**2**	**1**	**1**	**0**	**0**	....	....	....	....	....	....	....	....
	Cape Breton Oilers	AHL	33	12	19	31	....	....	....	21	....	....	....	....	....	....	....	....	....	....	4	3	2	5	10	....	....	....
1991-92	Milwaukee Admirals	IHL	8	3	5	8	....	....	....	2	....	....	....	....	....	....	....	....	....	....	....	....	....	....	....	....	....	....
	Phoenix Roadrunners	IHL	6	0	3	3	....	....	....	8	....	....	....	....	....	....	....	....	....	....	....	....	....	....	....	....	....	....
	NHL Totals		**4**	**1**	**0**	**1**	**1**	**0**	**1**	**0**	**0**	**0**	**1**	**5**	**20.0**	**2**	**1**	**1**	**0**		....	....	....	....	....	....	....	....

EJC-A All-Star Team (1983, 1984) • Named Best Forward at EJC-A (1983) • WJC-A All-Star Team (1986)

• WADDELL, DON

Don Waddell D – L. 5'10", 180 lbs. b: Detroit, MI, 8/19/1958. Los Angeles' 3rd choice, 111th overall, in 1978 Amateur Draft.

Season	Club	League	GP	G	A	Pts	AG	AA	APts	PIM	PP	SH	GW	S	%	TGF	PGF	TGA	PGA	+/–	GP	G	A	Pts	PIM	PP	SH	GW
1976-77	Northern Michigan University	CCHA	28	11	34	45	....	....	....	40	....	....	....	....	....	....	....	....	....	....	....	....	....	....	....	....	....	....
	United States	WJC-A	STATISTICS NOT AVAILABLE																									
1977-78	Northern Michigan University	CCHA	32	18	34	52	....	....	....	44	....	....	....	....	....	....	....	....	....	....	....	....	....	....	....	....	....	....
	United States	WJC-A	6	5	2	7	....	....	....	8	....	....	....	....	....	....	....	....	....	....	....	....	....	....	....	....	....	....
1978-79	Northern Michigan University	CCHA	23	5	20	25	....	....	....	24	....	....	....	....	....	....	....	....	....	....	....	....	....	....	....	....	....	....
1979-80	Northern Michigan University	CCHA	37	18	32	50	....	....	....	30	....	....	....	....	....	....	....	....	....	....	....	....	....	....	....	....	....	....
1980-81	**Los Angeles Kings**	**NHL**	**1**	**0**	**0**	**0**	**0**	**0**	**0**	**0**	**0**	**0**	**0**	**0**	**0.0**	**0**	**0**	**1**	**0**	**–1**	....	....	....	....	....	....	....	....
	Houston Apollos	CHL	31	4	5	9	....	....	....	23	....	....	....	....	....	....	....	....	....	....	....	....	....	....	....	....	....	....
	Saginaw Gears	IHL	40	4	18	22	....	....	....	33	....	....	....	....	....	....	....	....	....	....	13	2	4	6	6	....	....	....
1981-82	Saginaw Gears	IHL	77	26	69	95	....	....	....	61	....	....	....	....	....	....	....	....	....	....	14	1	*17	18	0	....	....	....
1982-83	Saginaw Gears	IHL	18	3	17	20	....	....	....	10	....	....	....	....	....	....	....	....	....	....	....	....	....	....	....	....	....	....
	New Haven Nighthawks	AHL	....	....	....	....	....	....	....	....	....	....	....	....	....	....	....	....	....	....	2	0	0	0	0	....	....	....
1983-84	Augsburg	Germany	8	6	5	11	....	....	....	10	....	....	....	....	....	....	....	....	....	....	....	....	....	....	....	....	....	....
1984-85	Flint Generals	IHL	35	3	14	17	....	....	....	10	....	....	....	....	....	....	....	....	....	....	....	....	....	....	....	....	....	....
	Toledo Goaldiggers	IHL	42	10	31	41	....	....	....	12	....	....	....	....	....	....	....	....	....	....	6	0	6	6	0	....	....	....
1985-86	Toledo Goaldiggers	IHL	63	19	50	69	....	....	....	113	....	....	....	....	....	....	....	....	....	....	....	....	....	....	....	....	....	....
	New Haven Nighthawks	AHL	6	1	4	5	....	....	....	9	....	....	....	....	....	....	....	....	....	....	5	1	2	3	4	....	....	....
1986-87	Flint Spirits	IHL	10	1	4	5	....	....	....	2	....	....	....	....	....	....	....	....	....	....	6	1	3	4	4	....	....	....
1987-88	Flint Spirits	IHL	71	17	58	75	....	....	....	61	....	....	....	....	....	....	....	....	....	....	15	5	10	15	6	....	....	....
	New Haven Nighthawks	AHL	2	1	2	3	....	....	....	0	....	....	....	....	....	....	....	....	....	....	....	....	....	....	....	....	....	....
	NHL Totals		**1**	**0**	**0**	**0**	**0**	**0**	**0**	**0**	**0**	**0**	**0**	**0**	**0.0**	**0**	**0**	**1**	**0**		....	....	....	....	....	....	....	....

CCHA First All-Star Team (1978, 1980) • IHL First All-Star Team (1982, 1986) • Won Governors' Trophy (Top Defenseman - IHL) (1982) • IHL Second All-Star Team (1988)

• WALKER, GORD

Gord Walker RW – L. 6', 175 lbs. b: Castlegar, B.C., 8/12/1965. NY Rangers' 4th choice, 54th overall, in 1983 Entry Draft.

Season	Club	League	GP	G	A	Pts	AG	AA	APts	PIM	PP	SH	GW	S	%	TGF	PGF	TGA	PGA	+/–	GP	G	A	Pts	PIM	PP	SH	GW
1981-82	Drumheller Miners	AJHL	60	35	44	79	....	....	....	90	....	....	....	....	....	....	....	....	....	....	....	....	....	....	....	....	....	....
1982-83	Portland Winter Hawks	WHL	66	24	30	54	....	....	....	95	....	....	....	....	....	....	....	....	....	....	14	5	8	13	12	....	....	....
1983-84	Portland Winter Hawks	WHL	58	28	41	69	....	....	....	65	....	....	....	....	....	....	....	....	....	....	14	8	11	19	18	....	....	....
1984-85	Kamloops Blazers	WHL	66	67	67	134	....	....	....	76	....	....	....	....	....	....	....	....	....	....	15	*13	14	27	34	....	....	....
1985-86	New Haven Nighthawks	AHL	46	11	28	39	....	....	....	66	....	....	....	....	....	....	....	....	....	....	....	....	....	....	....	....	....	....
1986-87	**New York Rangers**	**NHL**	**1**	**1**	**0**	**1**	**1**	**0**	**1**	**4**	**0**	**0**	**0**	**1**	**100.0**	**2**	**0**	**0**	**0**	**+2**	....	....	....	....	....	....	....	....
	New Haven Nighthawks	AHL	59	24	20	44	....	....	....	58	....	....	....	....	....	....	....	....	....	....	7	3	2	5	0	....	....	....
1987-88	**New York Rangers**	**NHL**	**18**	**1**	**4**	**5**	**1**	**3**	**4**	**17**	**0**	**0**	**0**	**23**	**4.3**	**6**	**1**	**14**	**1**	**–8**	....	....	....	....	....	....	....	....
	New Haven Nighthawks	AHL	14	10	9	19	....	....	....	17	....	....	....	....	....	....	....	....	....	....	....	....	....	....	....	....	....	....
	Colorado Rangers	IHL	16	4	9	13	....	....	....	4	....	....	....	....	....	....	....	....	....	....	....	....	....	....	....	....	....	....
1988-89	**Los Angeles Kings**	**NHL**	**11**	**1**	**0**	**1**	**1**	**0**	**1**	**2**	**0**	**0**	**0**	**13**	**7.7**	**2**	**0**	**4**	**0**	**–2**	....	....	....	....	....	....	....	....
	New Haven Nighthawks	AHL	60	21	25	46	....	....	....	50	....	....	....	....	....	....	....	....	....	....	17	7	8	15	23	....	....	....
1989-90	**Los Angeles Kings**	**NHL**	**1**	**0**	**0**	**0**	**0**	**0**	**0**	**0**	**0**	**0**	**0**	**0**	**0.0**	**0**	**0**	**0**	**0**	**0**	....	....	....	....	....	....	....	....
	New Haven Nighthawks	AHL	24	14	7	21	....	....	....	8	....	....	....	....	....	....	....	....	....	....	....	....	....	....	....	....	....	....
1990-91	Canada	Nat-Team	13	1	3	4	....	....	....	8	....	....	....	....	....	....	....	....	....	....	....	....	....	....	....	....	....	....
	San Diego Gulls	IHL	22	3	7	10	....	....	....	24	....	....	....	....	....	....	....	....	....	....	....	....	....	....	....	....	....	....
	NHL Totals		**31**	**3**	**4**	**7**	**3**	**3**	**6**	**23**	**0**	**0**	**0**	**37**	**8.1**	**10**	**1**	**18**	**1**		....	....	....	....	....	....	....	....

WHL West First All-Star Team (1985)

Traded to **LA Kings** by **NY Rangers** with Mike Siltala for Joe Paterson, January 21, 1988.

• WALKER, HOWARD

Howard Walker D – L. 6', 205 lbs. b: Grande Prairie, Alta., 8/5/1958.

Season	Club	League	GP	G	A	Pts	AG	AA	APts	PIM	PP	SH	GW	S	%	TGF	PGF	TGA	PGA	+/–	GP	G	A	Pts	PIM	PP	SH	GW
1978-79	University of North Dakota	WCHA	38	7	16	23	....	....	....	76	....	....	....	....	....	....	....	....	....	....	....	....	....	....	....	....	....	....
1979-80	University of North Dakota	WCHA	39	7	18	25	....	....	....	57	....	....	....	....	....	....	....	....	....	....	....	....	....	....	....	....	....	....
1980-81	**Washington Capitals**	**NHL**	**64**	**2**	**11**	**13**	**2**	**8**	**10**	**100**	**2**	**0**	**0**	**68**	**2.9**	**64**	**8**	**61**	**14**	**+9**	....	....	....	....	....	....	....	....
	Hershey Bears	AHL	7	1	0	1	....	....	....	24	....	....	....	....	....	....	....	....	....	....	....	....	....	....	....	....	....	....
1981-82	**Washington Capitals**	**NHL**	**16**	**0**	**2**	**2**	**0**	**1**	**1**	**26**	**0**	**0**	**0**	**18**	**0.0**	**9**	**1**	**18**	**1**	**–9**	....	....	....	....	....	....	....	....
	Hershey Bears	AHL	54	3	4	7	....	....	....	62	....	....	....	....	....	....	....	....	....	....	....	....	....	....	....	....	....	....
1982-83	**Calgary Flames**	**NHL**	**3**	**0**	**0**	**0**	**0**	**0**	**0**	**7**	**0**	**0**	**0**	**2**	**0.0**	**2**	**0**	**2**	**0**	**0**	....	....	....	....	....	....	....	....
	Colorado Flames	CHL	69	4	19	23	....	....	....	172	....	....	....	....	....	....	....	....	....	....	6	3	2	5	11	....	....	....
	NHL Totals		**83**	**2**	**13**	**15**	**2**	**9**	**11**	**133**	**2**	**0**	**0**	**88**	**2.3**	**75**	**9**	**81**	**15**		....	....	....	....	....	....	....	....

NCAA Championship All-Tournament Team (1979) • WCHA First All-Star Team (1980) • NCAA West First All-American Team (1980)

Signed as a free agent by **Washington**, June 5, 1980. Traded to **Calgary** by **Washington** with George White, Washington's 6th round choice (Mats Kihlstrom) in 1982 Entry Draft, 3rd round choice (Parry Berezan) in 1983 Entry Draft and 2nd round choice (Paul Ranheim) in 1984 Entry Draft for Pat Riggin and Ken Houston, June 7, 1982.

• WALKER, KURT

Kurt Walker D – R. 6'3", 200 lbs. b: Weymouth, MA, 6/10/1954.

Season	Club	League	GP	G	A	Pts	AG	AA	APts	PIM	PP	SH	GW	S	%	TGF	PGF	TGA	PGA	+/–	GP	G	A	Pts	PIM	PP	SH	GW
1973-74	Sherbrooke Castors	QMJHL	36	2	5	7	....	....	....	142	....	....	....	....	....	....	....	....	....	....	....	....	....	....	....	....	....	....
1974-75	Saginaw Gears	IHL	67	1	3	4	....	....	....	168	....	....	....	....	....	....	....	....	....	....	16	0	0	0	0	....	....	....
1975-76	**Toronto Maple Leafs**	**NHL**	**5**	**0**	**0**	**0**	**0**	**0**	**0**	**49**	**0**	**0**	**0**	**2**	**0.0**	**0**	**0**	**2**	**0**	**–2**	**6**	**0**	**0**	**0**	**24**	**0**	**0**	**0**
	Oklahoma City Blazers	CHL	59	4	5	9	....	....	....	184	....	....	....	....	....	....	....	....	....	....	....	....	....	....	....	....	....	....
1976-77	**Toronto Maple Leafs**	**NHL**	**26**	**2**	**3**	**5**	**2**	**2**	**4**	**24**	**0**	**0**	**0**	**6**	**33.3**	**10**	**0**	**5**	**0**	**+5**	....	....	....	....	....	....	....	....
	Dallas Black Hawks	CHL	6	3	0	3	....	....	....	50	....	....	....	....	....	....	....	....	....	....	....	....	....	....	....	....	....	....
1977-78	**Toronto Maple Leafs**	**NHL**	**40**	**2**	**2**	**4**	**2**	**2**	**4**	**69**	**0**	**0**	**0**	**12**	**16.7**	**5**	**1**	**9**	**0**	**–5**	**10**	**0**	**0**	**0**	**10**	**0**	**0**	**0**
	Dallas Black Hawks	CHL	20	3	3	6	....	....	....	53	....	....	....	....	....	....	....	....	....	....	2	1	0	1	2	....	....	....

			REGULAR SEASON																		PLAYOFFS							
Season	Club	League	GP	G	A	Pts	AG	AA	APts	PIM	PP	SH	GW	S	%	TGF	PGF	TGA	PGA	+/–	GP	G	A	Pts	PIM	PP	SH	GW
1978-79	Springfield Indians	AHL	11	0	1	1				22																		
	Tulsa Oilers	CHL	54	17	19	36				81																		
1979-80	Binghamton Dusters	AHL	6	0	0	0				4																		
	Syracuse Firebirds	AHL	11	1	4	5				18																		
	NHL Totals		**71**	**4**	**5**	**9**	**4**	**4**	**8**	**142**	**0**	**0**	**0**	**20**	**20.0**	**15**	**1**	**16**	**0**		**16**	**0**	**0**	**0**	**34**	**0**	**0**	**0**

Signed as a free agent by **Toronto**, September, 1975. Traded to **LA Kings** by **Toronto** with Scott Garland, Brian Glennie, Toronto's 2nd round choice (Mark Hardy) in 1979 Entry Draft and future considerations for Dave Hutchison and Lorne Stamler, June 14, 1978.

• WALKER, RUSS

Russ Walker RW – R. 6'2", 185 lbs. b: Red Deer, Alta., 5/24/1953. Los Angeles' 1st choice, 38th overall, in 1973 Amateur Draft.

Season	Club	League	GP	G	A	Pts	AG	AA	APts	PIM	PP	SH	GW	S	%	TGF	PGF	TGA	PGA	+/–	GP	G	A	Pts	PIM	PP	SH	GW
1969-70	Red Deer Rustlers	AJHL	1	0	0	0				0																		
	Lethbridge Silver Kings	AJHL	2	1	0	1				0																		
1970-71	Lethbridge Silver Kings	AJHL	STATISTICS NOT AVAILABLE																									
1971-72	Saskatoon Blades	WCJHL	68	24	28	52				218																		
1972-73	Saskatoon Blades	WCJHL	65	42	38	80				193																		
1973-74	Cleveland Crusaders	WHA	76	15	14	29				117											5	1	0	1	11			
1974-75	Cleveland Crusaders	WHA	66	14	11	25				80											5	1	0	1	17			
1975-76	Cleveland Crusaders	WHA	72	23	15	38				122											3	0	0	0	18			
1976-77	**Los Angeles Kings**	**NHL**	**16**	**1**	**0**	**1**	**1**	**0**	**1**	**35**	**0**	**0**	**0**	**12**	**8.3**	**6**	**0**	**8**	**0**	**–2**								
	Fort Worth Texans	CHL	53	23	17	40				106											5	1	2	3	9			
1977-78	**Los Angeles Kings**	**NHL**	**1**	**0**	**0**	**0**	**0**	**0**	**0**	**6**	**0**	**0**	**0**	**0**	**0.0**	**0**	**0**	**0**	**0**	**0**								
	Springfield Indians	AHL	77	30	36	66				79											4	2	0	2	0			
1978-79	Springfield Indians	AHL	61	23	19	42				88																		
	NHL Totals		**17**	**1**	**0**	**1**	**1**	**0**	**1**	**41**	**0**	**0**	**0**	**12**	**8.3**	**6**	**0**	**8**	**0**									
	Other Major League Totals		214	52	40	92				319											13	2	0	2	46			

Selected by **Cleveland** (WHA) in 1973 WHA Amateur Draft, June, 1973. Traded to **Cincinnati** (WHA) by **Cleveland** (WHA) for Bernie MacNeil, May, 1976.

• WALKER, SCOTT

Scott Walker C – R. 5'10", 189 lbs. b: Montreal, Que., 7/19/1973. Vancouver's 4th choice, 124th overall, in 1993 Entry Draft.

Season	Club	League	GP	G	A	Pts	AG	AA	APts	PIM	PP	SH	GW	S	%	TGF	PGF	TGA	PGA	+/–	GP	G	A	Pts	PIM	PP	SH	GW
1991-92	Owen Sound Platers	OHL	53	7	31	38				128											5	0	7	7	8			
1992-93	Owen Sound Platers	OHL	57	23	68	91				110											8	1	5	6	16			
	Canada	Nat-Team	2	3	0	3				0																		
1993-94	Hamilton Canucks	AHL	77	10	29	39				272											4	0	1	1	25			
1994-95	Syracuse Crunch	AHL	74	14	38	52				334																		
	Vancouver Canucks	**NHL**	**11**	**0**	**1**	**1**	**0**	**1**	**1**	**33**	**0**	**0**	**0**	**8**	**0.0**	**4**	**0**	**4**	**0**	**0**								
1995-96	**Vancouver Canucks**	**NHL**	**63**	**4**	**8**	**12**	**4**	**7**	**11**	**137**	**0**	**1**	**1**	**45**	**8.9**	**17**	**1**	**33**	**10**	**–7**								
	Syracuse Crunch	AHL	15	3	12	15				52											16	9	8	17	39			
1996-97	**Vancouver Canucks**	**NHL**	**64**	**3**	**15**	**18**	**3**	**13**	**16**	**132**	**0**	**0**	**0**	**55**	**5.5**	**27**	**0**	**29**	**4**	**+2**								
1997-98	**Vancouver Canucks**	**NHL**	**59**	**3**	**10**	**13**	**4**	**10**	**14**	**164**	**0**	**1**	**1**	**40**	**7.5**	**18**	**0**	**33**	**7**	**–8**								
	NHL Totals		**197**	**10**	**34**	**44**	**11**	**31**	**42**	**466**	**0**	**2**	**2**	**148**	**6.8**	**66**	**1**	**99**	**21**									

OHL Second All-Star Team (1993)

Claimed by **Nashville** from **Vancouver** in Expansion Draft, June 26, 1998.

• WALL, BOB

Bob Wall D – L. 5'10", 171 lbs. b: Richmond Hill, Ont., 12/1/1942.

Season	Club	League	GP	G	A	Pts	AG	AA	APts	PIM	PP	SH	GW	S	%	TGF	PGF	TGA	PGA	+/–	GP	G	A	Pts	PIM	PP	SH	GW
1959-60	Hamilton Tiger Cubs	OHA	48	3	11	14				44																		
1960-61	Hamilton Red Wings	OHA	48	2	8	10				30											12	1	3	4	29			
1961-62	Hamilton Red Wings	OHA	44	7	22	29				28											10	3	3	6	26			
1962-63	Hamilton Red Wings	OHA	36	5	30	35				27											5	0	6	6	2			
	Pittsburgh Hornets	AHL	3	0	2	2				2																		
	Edmonton Flyers	WHL	7	0	0	0				0																		
1963-64	Cincinnati Wings	CHL	59	10	20	30				16																		
	Quebec Aces	AHL	8	1	2	3				4																		
	Omaha Knights	CHL																			10	1	7	8	4			
1964-65	**Detroit Red Wings**	**NHL**	**1**	**0**	**0**	**0**	**0**	**0**	**0**	**0**											**1**	**0**	**0**	**0**	**0**			
	Memphis Wings	CHL	70	8	38	46				83																		
1965-66	**Detroit Red Wings**	**NHL**	**8**	**1**	**1**	**2**	**1**	**1**	**2**	**8**											**6**	**0**	**0**	**0**	**2**			
	Pittsburgh Hornets	AHL	63	10	35	45				26											3	0	1	1	8			
1966-67	**Detroit Red Wings**	**NHL**	**31**	**2**	**2**	**4**	**2**	**2**	**4**	**26**																		
	Pittsburgh Hornets	AHL	41	7	25	32				29											9	2	2	4	4			
1967-68	**Los Angeles Kings**	**NHL**	**71**	**5**	**18**	**23**	**6**	**19**	**25**	**66**	**1**	**0**	**2**	**148**	**3.4**	**77**	**14**	**94**	**22**	**–9**	**7**	**0**	**1**	**1**	**0**	**0**	**0**	**0**
1968-69	**Los Angeles Kings**	**NHL**	**71**	**13**	**13**	**26**	**15**	**12**	**27**	**16**	**1**	**1**	**1**	**147**	**8.8**	**38**	**6**	**51**	**13**	**–6**	**8**	**0**	**2**	**2**	**0**	**0**	**0**	**0**
1969-70	**Los Angeles Kings**	**NHL**	**70**	**5**	**13**	**18**	**6**	**13**	**19**	**26**	**5**	**0**	**1**	**116**	**4.3**	**54**	**25**	**65**	**10**	**–26**								
1970-71	**St. Louis Blues**	**NHL**	**25**	**2**	**4**	**6**	**2**	**4**	**6**	**4**	**1**	**0**	**0**	**29**	**6.9**	**12**	**1**	**15**	**3**	**–1**								
	Kansas City Blues	CHL	18	0	7	7				4																		
1971-72	**Detroit Red Wings**	**NHL**	**45**	**2**	**4**	**6**	**2**	**4**	**6**	**9**	**2**	**0**	**0**	**31**	**6.5**	**17**	**3**	**24**	**3**	**–7**								
	Tidewater Wings	AHL	17	2	4	6				12																		
1972-73	Alberta Oilers	WHA	78	16	29	45				20																		
1973-74	Edmonton Oilers	WHA	74	6	31	37				46											5	0	2	2	2			
1974-75	San Diego Mariners	WHA	33	0	9	9				15											10	0	3	3	2			
1975-76	San Diego Mariners	WHA	68	1	20	21				32											11	1	3	4	4			
	NHL Totals		**322**	**30**	**55**	**85**	**34**	**55**	**89**	**155**	**10**	**1**	**4**	**471**	**6.4**	**198**	**49**	**249**	**51**		**22**	**0**	**3**	**3**	**2**	**0**	**0**	**0**
	Other Major League Totals		253	23	89	112				113											26	1	8	9	8			

Claimed by **LA Kings** from **Detroit** in Expansion Draft, June 6, 1967. Traded to **St. Louis** by **LA Kings** for Ray Fortin, May 11, 1970. Traded to **Detroit** by **St. Louis** with Ab McDonald and Mike Lowe to complete transaction that sent Carl Brewer to Detroit (February 22, 1971), May 12, 1971. Selected by **Alberta** (WHA) in 1972 WHA General Player Draft, February 12, 1972. Traded to **San Diego** (WHA) by **Edmonton** (WHA) for Don Herriman, August, 1974.

• WALLIN, PETER

Peter Wallin RW – R. 5'9", 170 lbs. b: Stockholm, Sweden, 4/30/1957.

Season	Club	League	GP	G	A	Pts	AG	AA	APts	PIM	PP	SH	GW	S	%	TGF	PGF	TGA	PGA	+/–	GP	G	A	Pts	PIM	PP	SH	GW
1974-75	Djurgarden Stockholm	Sweden	1	0	0	0				2																		
1975-76	Djurgarden Stockholm	Sweden	12	3	4	7				0																		
1976-77	Djurgarden Stockholm	Sweden	STATISTICS NOT AVAILABLE																									
1977-78	Djurgarden Stockholm	Sweden	36	12	16	28				22																		
1978-79	Djurgarden Stockholm	Sweden	36	14	19	33				34											6	2	2	4	6			
	Sweden	WEC-A	8	1	3	4				2																		
1979-80	Djurgarden Stockholm	Sweden	30	11	15	26				66																		
	Sweden	Nat-Team	11	3	1	4																						
1980-81	Djurgarden Stockholm	Sweden	36	12	13	25				55																		
	Sweden	Nat-Team	6	1	1	2				0																		
	New York Rangers	**NHL**	**12**	**1**	**5**	**6**	**1**	**3**	**4**	**2**	**0**	**0**	**0**	**14**	**7.1**	**9**	**2**	**9**	**1**	**–1**	**14**	**2**	**6**	**8**	**6**	**0**	**0**	**0**
1981-82	**New York Rangers**	**NHL**	**40**	**2**	**9**	**11**	**2**	**6**	**8**	**12**	**0**	**0**	**1**	**50**	**4.0**	**21**	**3**	**17**	**0**	**+1**								
	Springfield Indians	AHL	16	4	10	14				8																		
1982-83	Tulsa Oilers	CHL	65	15	40	55				43																		
1983-84	Sodertalje SK	Sweden	28	12	13	25				38																		
1984-85	Sodertalje SK	Sweden	20	6	7	13				30											8	5	6	11	8			
1985-86	Sodertalje SK	Sweden	31	12	18	30				37											7	3	3	6	4			
	NHL Totals		**52**	**3**	**14**	**17**	**3**	**9**	**12**	**14**	**0**	**0**	**1**	**64**	**4.7**	**30**	**5**	**26**	**1**		**14**	**2**	**6**	**8**	**6**	**0**	**0**	**0**

Signed as a free agent by **NY Rangers**, March 8, 1981.

Season	Club	League	GP	G	A	Pts	AG	AA	APts	PIM	PP	SH	GW	S	%	TGF	PGF	TGA	PGA	+/–	GP	G	A	Pts	PIM	PP	SH	GW
			REGULAR SEASON																		PLAYOFFS							

• WALSH, JIM
Jim Walsh D – R. 6'1", 185 lbs. b: Norfolk, Virginia, 10/26/1956.

Season	Club	League	GP	G	A	Pts	AG	AA	APts	PIM	PP	SH	GW	S	%	TGF	PGF	TGA	PGA	+/–	GP	G	A	Pts	PIM	PP	SH	GW
1976-77	Northeastern University	ECAC	27	5	9	14	....	....	....	44	....	....	....	....	....	....	....	....	....	....	....	....	....	....	....	....	....	....
1977-78	Northeastern University	ECAC	27	3	26	29	....	....	....	69	....	....	....	....	....	....	....	....	....	....	....	....	....	....	....	....	....	....
1978-79	Northeastern University	ECAC	22	5	12	17	....	....	....	44	....	....	....	....	....	....	....	....	....	....	....	....	....	....	....	....	....	....
1979-80	Rochester Americans	AHL	33	2	4	6	....	....	....	64	....	....	....	....	....	....	....	....	....	....	....	....	....	....	....	....	....	....
1980-81	Rochester Americans	AHL	76	8	23	31	....	....	....	182	....	....	....	....	....	....	....	....	....	....	....	....	....	....	....	....	....	....
1981-82	**Buffalo Sabres**	**NHL**	**4**	**0**	**1**	**1**	**0**	**1**	**1**	**4**	....	....	....	....	....	....	....	....	....	....	....	....	....	....	....	....	....	....
	Rochester Americans	AHL	70	7	33	40	....	....	....	174	....	....	....	....	....	....	....	....	....	....	9	0	4	4	17	....	....	....
1982-83	Saginaw Gears	IHL	5	0	1	1	....	....	....	4	....	....	....	....	....	....	....	....	....	....	....	....	....	....	....	....	....	....
	Binghamton Whalers	AHL	49	1	13	14	....	....	....	93	....	....	....	....	....	....	....	....	....	....	....	....	....	....	....	....	....	....
1983-84	New Haven Nighthawks	AHL	13	0	5	5	....	....	....	14	....	....	....	....	....	....	....	....	....	....	....	....	....	....	....	....	....	....
	NHL Totals		**4**	**0**	**1**	**1**	**0**	**1**	**1**	**4**	**0**	**0**	**0**	**0**	**0.0**	**0**	**0**	**0**	**0**		....	....	....	....	....	....	....	....

Signed as a free agent by **Buffalo**, September 5, 1979.

• WALSH, MIKE
Mike Walsh LW – R. 6'2", 195 lbs. b: New York, NY, 4/3/1962.

Season	Club	League	GP	G	A	Pts	AG	AA	APts	PIM	PP	SH	GW	S	%	TGF	PGF	TGA	PGA	+/–	GP	G	A	Pts	PIM	PP	SH	GW
1980-81	Colgate University	ECAC	35	10	15	25	....	....	....	62	....	....	....	....	....	....	....	....	....	....	....	....	....	....	....	....	....	....
1981-82	Colgate University	ECAC	26	2	7	9	....	....	....	42	....	....	....	....	....	....	....	....	....	....	....	....	....	....	....	....	....	....
1982-83	Colgate University	ECAC	24	9	14	23	....	....	....	36	....	....	....	....	....	....	....	....	....	....	....	....	....	....	....	....	....	....
1983-84	Colgate University	ECAC	35	16	17	33	....	....	....	94	....	....	....	....	....	....	....	....	....	....	....	....	....	....	....	....	....	....
1984-85			DID NOT PLAY																									
1985-86	Malmo IF	Sweden	42	52	27	79	....	....	....	....	....	....	....	....	....	....	....	....	....	....	....	....	....	....	....	....	....	....
	Springfield Indians	AHL	2	1	0	1	....	....	....	0	....	....	....	....	....	....	....	....	....	....	....	....	....	....	....	....	....	....
1986-87	Springfield Indians	AHL	67	20	26	46	....	....	....	32	....	....	....	....	....	....	....	....	....	....	....	....	....	....	....	....	....	....
1987-88	**New York Islanders**	**NHL**	**1**	**0**	**0**	**0**	**0**	**0**	**0**	**0**	**0**	**0**	**0**	**2**	**0.0**	**0**	**0**	**0**	**0**	**0**	....	....	....	....	....	....	....	....
	Springfield Indians	AHL	77	27	23	50	....	....	....	48	....	....	....	....	....	....	....	....	....	....	....	....	....	....	....	....	....	....
1988-89	**New York Islanders**	**NHL**	**13**	**2**	**0**	**2**	**2**	**0**	**2**	**4**	**0**	**0**	**1**	**11**	**18.2**	**3**	**0**	**10**	**0**	**–7**	....	....	....	....	....	....	....	....
	Springfield Indians	AHL	68	31	34	65	....	....	....	73	....	....	....	....	....	....	....	....	....	....	....	....	....	....	....	....	....	....
1989-90	Springfield Indians	AHL	69	34	20	54	....	....	....	43	....	....	....	....	....	....	....	....	....	....	8	2	2	4	10	....	....	....
1990-91	SC Cortina	Italy	36	15	21	36	....	....	....	49	....	....	....	....	....	....	....	....	....	....	6	7	4	11	19	....	....	....
1991-92	Maine Mariners	AHL	76	27	24	51	....	....	....	42	....	....	....	....	....	....	....	....	....	....	....	....	....	....	....	....	....	....
1992-93	Providence Bruins	AHL	5	2	0	2	....	....	....	8	....	....	....	....	....	....	....	....	....	....	....	....	....	....	....	....	....	....
	NHL Totals		**14**	**2**	**0**	**2**	**2**	**0**	**2**	**4**	**0**	**0**	**1**	**13**	**15.4**	**3**	**0**	**10**	**0**		....	....	....	....	....	....	....	....

Signed as a free agent by **NY Islanders** , August, 1986.

• WALTER, RYAN
Ryan Walter C/LW – L. 6', 200 lbs. b: New Westminster, B.C., 4/23/1958. Washington's 1st choice, 2nd overall, in 1978 Amateur Draft.

Season	Club	League	GP	G	A	Pts	AG	AA	APts	PIM	PP	SH	GW	S	%	TGF	PGF	TGA	PGA	+/–	GP	G	A	Pts	PIM	PP	SH	GW
1973-74	Langley Lords	BCJHL	....	40	62	102	....	....	....	....	....	....	....	....	....	....	....	....	....	....	....	....	....	....	....	....	....	....
	Kamloops Chiefs	WCJHL	2	0	0	0	....	....	....	0	....	....	....	....	....	....	....	....	....	....	....	....	....	....	....	....	....	....
1974-75	Langley Lords	BCJHL	....	32	60	92	....	....	....	111	....	....	....	....	....	....	....	....	....	....	....	....	....	....	....	....	....	....
	Kamloops Chiefs	WCJHL	9	8	4	12	....	....	....	2	....	....	....	....	....	....	....	....	....	....	2	1	1	2	2	....	....	....
1975-76	Kamloops Chiefs	WHL	72	35	49	84	....	....	....	96	....	....	....	....	....	....	....	....	....	....	12	3	9	12	10	....	....	....
1976-77	Kamloops Chiefs	WCJHL	71	41	58	99	....	....	....	100	....	....	....	....	....	....	....	....	....	....	5	1	3	4	11	....	....	....
1977-78	Seattle Breakers	WCJHL	62	54	71	125	....	....	....	148	....	....	....	....	....	....	....	....	....	....	....	....	....	....	....	....	....	....
	Canada	WJC-A	6	5	3	8	....	....	....	4	....	....	....	....	....	....	....	....	....	....	....	....	....	....	....	....	....	....
1978-79	**Washington Capitals**	**NHL**	**69**	**28**	**28**	**56**	**25**	**21**	**46**	**70**	**6**	**0**	**1**	**156**	**17.9**	**87**	**25**	**83**	**20**	**–1**	....	....	....	....	....	....	....	....
	Canada	WEC-A	8	4	1	5	....	....	....	4	....	....	....	....	....	....	....	....	....	....	....	....	....	....	....	....	....	....
1979-80	**Washington Capitals**	**NHL**	**80**	**24**	**42**	**66**	**22**	**32**	**54**	**106**	**12**	**1**	**1**	**157**	**15.3**	**104**	**32**	**94**	**21**	**–1**	....	....	....	....	....	....	....	....
1980-81	**Washington Capitals**	**NHL**	**80**	**24**	**44**	**68**	**20**	**31**	**51**	**150**	**4**	**0**	**1**	**178**	**13.5**	**106**	**26**	**103**	**14**	**–9**	....	....	....	....	....	....	....	....
	Canada	WEC-A	8	0	1	1	....	....	....	2	....	....	....	....	....	....	....	....	....	....	....	....	....	....	....	....	....	....
1981-82	**Washington Capitals**	**NHL**	**78**	**38**	**49**	**87**	**30**	**32**	**62**	**142**	**19**	**1**	**3**	**183**	**20.8**	**141**	**58**	**103**	**17**	**–3**	....	....	....	....	....	....	....	....
	Canada	WEC-A	4	1	3	4	....	....	....	0	....	....	....	....	....	....	....	....	....	....	....	....	....	....	....	....	....	....
1982-83	**Montreal Canadiens**	**NHL**	**80**	**29**	**46**	**75**	**24**	**32**	**56**	**40**	**8**	**1**	**4**	**169**	**17.2**	**122**	**35**	**102**	**30**	**+15**	**3**	**0**	**0**	**0**	**11**	**0**	**0**	**0**
1983-84	**Montreal Canadiens**	**NHL**	**73**	**20**	**29**	**49**	**16**	**20**	**36**	**83**	**7**	**1**	**4**	**117**	**17.1**	**82**	**28**	**84**	**19**	**–11**	**15**	**2**	**1**	**3**	**4**	**1**	**0**	**1**
1984-85	**Montreal Canadiens**	**NHL**	**72**	**19**	**19**	**38**	**16**	**13**	**29**	**59**	**11**	**0**	**0**	**120**	**15.8**	**61**	**23**	**61**	**5**	**–18**	**12**	**2**	**7**	**9**	**13**	**0**	**0**	**0**
1985-86	**Montreal Canadiens**	**NHL**	**69**	**15**	**34**	**49**	**12**	**23**	**35**	**45**	**9**	**0**	**1**	**115**	**13.0**	**87**	**45**	**52**	**1**	**–9**	**5**	**0**	**1**	**1**	**2**	**0**	**0**	**0**
1986-87	**Montreal Canadiens**	**NHL**	**76**	**23**	**23**	**46**	**20**	**17**	**37**	**34**	**11**	**0**	**4**	**117**	**19.7**	**79**	**34**	**58**	**7**	**–6**	**17**	**7**	**12**	**19**	**10**	**2**	**1**	**1**
1987-88	**Montreal Canadiens**	**NHL**	**61**	**13**	**23**	**36**	**11**	**16**	**27**	**39**	**6**	**0**	**3**	**93**	**14.0**	**71**	**21**	**40**	**2**	**+12**	**11**	**2**	**4**	**6**	**6**	**2**	**0**	**1**
1988-89	**Montreal Canadiens**	**NHL**	**78**	**14**	**17**	**31**	**12**	**12**	**24**	**48**	**1**	**1**	**0**	**104**	**13.5**	**57**	**4**	**45**	**15**	**+23**	**21**	**3**	**5**	**8**	**6**	**0**	**1**	**2**
1989-90	**Montreal Canadiens**	**NHL**	**70**	**8**	**16**	**24**	**7**	**11**	**18**	**59**	**1**	**0**	**1**	**109**	**7.3**	**45**	**7**	**52**	**18**	**+4**	**11**	**0**	**2**	**2**	**0**	**0**	**0**	**0**
1990-91	Montreal Canadiens	FrTour	2	0	0	0	....	....	....	0	....	....	....	....	....	....	....	....	....	....	....	....	....	....	....	....	....	....
	Montreal Canadiens	**NHL**	**25**	**0**	**1**	**1**	**0**	**1**	**1**	**12**	**0**	**0**	**0**	**14**	**0.0**	**7**	**0**	**11**	**1**	**–3**	**5**	**0**	**0**	**0**	**2**	**0**	**0**	**0**
1991-92	**Vancouver Canucks**	**NHL**	**67**	**6**	**11**	**17**	**5**	**8**	**13**	**49**	**1**	**1**	**0**	**73**	**8.2**	**32**	**5**	**45**	**24**	**+6**	**13**	**0**	**3**	**3**	**8**	**0**	**0**	**0**
1992-93	**Vancouver Canucks**	**NHL**	**25**	**3**	**0**	**3**	**2**	**0**	**2**	**10**	**0**	**0**	**0**	**15**	**20.0**	**6**	**0**	**20**	**12**	**–2**	....	....	....	....	....	....	....	....
	NHL Totals		**1003**	**264**	**382**	**646**	**222**	**269**	**491**	**946**	**96**	**6**	**23**	**1720**	**15.3**	**1087**	**343**	**953**	**206**		**113**	**16**	**35**	**51**	**62**	**5**	**2**	**5**

WCJHL All-Star Team (1978) • Won Bud Man of the Year Award (1992)

Played in NHL All-Star Game (1983)

Traded to **Montreal** by **Washington** with Rick Green for Rod Langway, Brian Engblom, Doug Jarvis and Craig Laughlin, September 9, 1982. Signed as a free agent by **Vancouver**, July 26, 1991.

• WALTON, MIKE
Mike "Shaky" Walton C – L. 5'10", 175 lbs. b: Kirkland Lake, Ont., 1/3/1945.

Season	Club	League	GP	G	A	Pts	AG	AA	APts	PIM	PP	SH	GW	S	%	TGF	PGF	TGA	PGA	+/–	GP	G	A	Pts	PIM	PP	SH	GW
1961-62	St. Michael's Majors	Tor-Jr.	26	13	11	24	....	....	....	12	....	....	....	....	....	....	....	....	....	....	12	7	7	14	10	....	....	....
1962-63	Neil McNeil Maroons	Tor-Jr.	38	22	22	44	....	....	....	32	....	....	....	....	....	....	....	....	....	....	14	8	4	12	23	....	....	....
1963-64	Toronto Marlboros	OHA	53	41	51	92	....	....	....	62	....	....	....	....	....	....	....	....	....	....	9	6	9	15	6	....	....	....
	Rochester Americans	AHL	2	0	0	0	....	....	....	0	....	....	....	....	....	....	....	....	....	....	....	....	....	....	....	....	....	....
1964-65	Tulsa Oilers	CHL	68	40	44	84	....	....	....	86	....	....	....	....	....	....	....	....	....	....	12	7	6	13	16	....	....	....
1965-66	**Toronto Maple Leafs**	**NHL**	**6**	**1**	**3**	**4**	**1**	**3**	**4**	**0**	....	....	....	....	....	....	....	....	....	....	....	....	....	....	....	....	....	....
	Rochester Americans	AHL	68	35	51	86	....	....	....	67	....	....	....	....	....	....	....	....	....	....	12	*8	4	*12	*43	....	....	....
1966-67	**Toronto Maple Leafs**	**NHL**	**31**	**7**	**10**	**17**	**9**	**10**	**19**	**13**	....	....	....	....	....	....	....	....	....	....	**12**	**4**	**3**	**7**	**2**	....	....	....
	Rochester Americans	AHL	36	19	33	52	....	....	....	28	....	....	....	....	....	....	....	....	....	....	....	....	....	....	....	....	....	....
1967-68	**Toronto Maple Leafs**	**NHL**	**73**	**30**	**29**	**59**	**37**	**30**	**67**	**48**	**11**	**0**	**5**	**238**	**12.6**	**66**	**19**	**46**	**0**	**+1**	....	....	....	....	....	....	....	....
1968-69	**Toronto Maple Leafs**	**NHL**	**66**	**22**	**21**	**43**	**25**	**20**	**45**	**34**	**8**	**0**	**5**	**205**	**10.7**	**64**	**28**	**45**	**0**	**–9**	**4**	**0**	**0**	**0**	**4**	**0**	**0**	**0**
1969-70	**Toronto Maple Leafs**	**NHL**	**58**	**21**	**34**	**55**	**24**	**34**	**58**	**68**	**7**	**0**	**6**	**242**	**8.7**	**74**	**36**	**49**	**0**	**–11**	....	....	....	....	....	....	....	....
1970-71	**Toronto Maple Leafs**	**NHL**	**23**	**3**	**10**	**13**	**3**	**9**	**12**	**21**	**2**	**0**	**0**	**68**	**4.4**	**21**	**12**	**23**	**0**	**–14**	....	....	....	....	....	....	....	....
	Boston Bruins	**NHL**	**22**	**3**	**5**	**8**	**3**	**4**	**7**	**10**	**0**	**0**	**0**	**44**	**6.8**	**17**	**1**	**5**	**0**	**+11**	**5**	**2**	**0**	**2**	**19**	**1**	**0**	**0**
1971-72	**Boston Bruins**	**NHL**	**76**	**28**	**28**	**56**	**30**	**26**	**56**	**45**	**6**	**0**	**4**	**236**	**11.9**	**83**	**18**	**42**	**0**	**+23**	**15**	**6**	**6**	**12**	**13**	**1**	**0**	**2**
1972-73	**Boston Bruins**	**NHL**	**56**	**25**	**22**	**47**	**25**	**18**	**43**	**37**	**0**	**0**	**2**	**128**	**19.5**	**60**	**8**	**42**	**0**	**+10**	**5**	**1**	**1**	**2**	**2**	**0**	**0**	**0**
1973-74	Minnesota Fighting Saints	WHA	78	57	60	*117	....	....	....	88	....	....	....	....	....	....	....	....	....	....	11	*10	8	18	16	....	....	....
1974-75	Minnesota Fighting Saints	WHA	75	48	45	93	....	....	....	33	....	....	....	....	....	....	....	....	....	....	12	*10	7	17	10	....	....	....
1975-76	**Vancouver Canucks**	**NHL**	**10**	**8**	**8**	**16**	**7**	**6**	**13**	**9**	**2**	**0**	**2**	**27**	**29.6**	**17**	**8**	**4**	**0**	**+5**	**2**	**0**	**0**	**0**	**5**	**0**	**0**	**0**
1976-77	**Vancouver Canucks**	**NHL**	**40**	**7**	**24**	**31**	**7**	**19**	**26**	**32**	**2**	**0**	**1**	**75**	**9.3**	**42**	**12**	**46**	**1**	**–15**	....	....	....	....	....	....	....	....
1977-78	**Vancouver Canucks**	**NHL**	**65**	**29**	**37**	**66**	**28**	**30**	**58**	**30**	**14**	**0**	**4**	**115**	**25.2**	**87**	**44**	**69**	**0**	**–26**	....	....	....	....	....	....	....	....

			REGULAR SEASON																		PLAYOFFS							
Season	Club	League	GP	G	A	Pts	AG	AA	APts	PIM	PP	SH	GW	S	%	TGF	PGF	TGA	PGA	+/–	GP	G	A	Pts	PIM	PP	SH	GW
1978-79	**St. Louis Blues**	**NHL**	**22**	**7**	**11**	**18**	**6**	**8**	**14**	**6**	**3**	**0**	**0**	**41**	**17.1**	**25**	**12**	**27**	**1**	**–13**	....	....	....	....	....	....	....	....
	Boston Bruins	**NHL**	**14**	**4**	**2**	**6**	**4**	**2**	**6**	**0**	**0**	**0**	**1**	**15**	**26.7**	**7**	**0**	**9**	**1**	**–1**	....	....	....	....	....	....	....	....
	Rochester Americans	AHL	1	1	2	3	....	....	....	2	....	....	....	....	....	....	....	....	....	....	....	....	....	....	....	....	....	....
	Chicago Black Hawks	**NHL**	**26**	**6**	**3**	**9**	**5**	**2**	**7**	**4**	**3**	**0**	**1**	**37**	**16.2**	**15**	**8**	**11**	**0**	**–4**	**4**	**1**	**0**	**1**	**0**	**0**	**0**	**0**
	New Brunswick Hawks	AHL	7	1	5	6	....	....	....	6	....	....	....	....	....	....	....	....	....	....	....	....	....	....	....	....	....	....
	NHL Totals		**588**	**201**	**247**	**448**	**214**	**221**	**435**	**357**	**58**	**0**	**31**	**1471**	**13.7**	**578**	**206**	**418**	**3**		**47**	**14**	**10**	**24**	**45**	**2**	**0**	**2**
	Other Major League Totals		153	105	105	210	....	....	....	121	....	....	....	....	....	....	....	....	....	....	23	20	15	35	26	....	....	....

CHL First All-Star Team (1965) • Won Ken McKenzie Trophy (CHL's Rookie of the Year) (1965) • Won Dudley "Red" Garrett Memorial Award (Top Rookie - AHL) (1966) • WHA Second All-Star Team (1974) • Won W. D. (Bill) Hunter Trophy (WHA Scoring Leader) (1974)

Played in NHL All-Star Game (1968)

Traded to **Philadelphia** by **Toronto** with Bruce Gamble and Toronto's 1st round choice (Pierre Plante) in 1971 Amateur Draft for Bernie Parent and Philadelphia's 2nd round choice (Rick Kehoe) in 1971 Amateur Draft, February 1, 1971. Traded to **Boston** by **Philadelphia** for Danny Schock and Rick MacLeish, February 1, 1971. Selected by **LA Sharks** (WHA) in 1972 WHA General Player Draft, February 12, 1972. WHA rights traded to **Minnesota** (WHA) by **LA Sharks** (WHA) for cash, June, 1973. Traded to **Vancouver** by **Boston** with Chris Oddleifson and Fred O'Donnell for Bobby Schmautz, February 8, 1974. Traded to **St. Louis** by **Vancouver** for St. Louis' 4th round choice (Harold Luckner) in 1978 Amateur Draft and future considerations, June 12, 1978. Signed as a free agent by **Boston**, December 5, 1978. Signed as a free agent by **Chicago**, January 22, 1979.

• WALZ, WES

Wes Walz C – R. 5'10", 185 lbs. b: Calgary, Alta., 5/15/1970. Boston's 5th choice, 57th overall, in 1989 Entry Draft.

Season	Club	League	GP	G	A	Pts	AG	AA	APts	PIM	PP	SH	GW	S	%	TGF	PGF	TGA	PGA	+/–	GP	G	A	Pts	PIM	PP	SH	GW
1988-89	Lethbridge Hurricanes	WHL	63	29	75	104	....	....	....	32	....	....	....	....	....	....	....	....	....	....	8	1	5	6	6	....	....	....
1989-90	Lethbridge Hurricanes	WHL	56	54	86	140	....	....	....	69	....	....	....	....	....	....	....	....	....	....	19	13	*24	*37	33	....	....	....
	Canada	WJC-A	7	2	3	5	....	....	....	0	....	....	....	....	....	....	....	....	....	....	....	....	....	....	....	....	....	....
	Boston Bruins	**NHL**	**2**	**1**	**1**	**2**	**1**	**1**	**2**	**0**	**1**	**0**	**0**	**1**	**100.0**	**3**	**2**	**2**	**0**	**–1**	....	....	....	....	....	....	....	....
1990-91	**Boston Bruins**	**NHL**	**56**	**8**	**8**	**16**	**7**	**6**	**13**	**32**	**1**	**0**	**1**	**57**	**14.0**	**26**	**2**	**41**	**3**	**–14**	**2**	**0**	**0**	**0**	**0**	**0**	**0**	**0**
	Maine Mariners	AHL	20	8	12	20	....	....	....	19	....	....	....	....	....	....	....	....	....	....	2	0	0	0	21	....	....	....
1991-92	**Boston Bruins**	**NHL**	**15**	**0**	**3**	**3**	**0**	**2**	**2**	**12**	**0**	**0**	**0**	**17**	**0.0**	**4**	**0**	**8**	**1**	**–3**	....	....	....	....	....	....	....	....
	Maine Mariners	AHL	21	13	11	24	....	....	....	38	....	....	....	....	....	....	....	....	....	....	....	....	....	....	....	....	....	....
	Philadelphia Flyers	**NHL**	**2**	**1**	**0**	**1**	**1**	**0**	**1**	**0**	**0**	**0**	**1**	**2**	**50.0**	**1**	**0**	**0**	**0**	**+1**	....	....	....	....	....	....	....	....
	Hershey Bears	AHL	41	13	28	41	....	....	....	37	....	....	....	....	....	....	....	....	....	....	6	1	2	3	0	....	....	....
1992-93	Hershey Bears	AHL	78	35	45	80	....	....	....	106	....	....	....	....	....	....	....	....	....	....	....	....	....	....	....	....	....	....
1993-94	**Calgary Flames**	**NHL**	**53**	**11**	**27**	**38**	**10**	**21**	**31**	**16**	**1**	**0**	**0**	**79**	**13.9**	**55**	**15**	**21**	**1**	**+20**	**6**	**3**	**0**	**3**	**2**	**0**	**0**	**0**
	Saint John Flames	AHL	15	6	6	12	....	....	....	14	....	....	....	....	....	....	....	....	....	....	....	....	....	....	....	....	....	....
1994-95	**Calgary Flames**	**NHL**	**39**	**6**	**12**	**18**	**11**	**18**	**29**	**11**	**4**	**0**	**1**	**73**	**8.2**	**31**	**9**	**15**	**0**	**+7**	**1**	**0**	**0**	**0**	**0**	**0**	**0**	**0**
1995-96	**Detroit Red Wings**	**NHL**	**2**	**0**	**0**	**0**	**0**	**0**	**0**	**0**	**0**	**0**	**0**	**2**	**0.0**	**0**	**0**	**0**	**0**	**0**	....	....	....	....	....	....	....	....
	Adirondack Red Wings	AHL	38	20	35	55	....	....	....	58	....	....	....	....	....	....	....	....	....	....	....	....	....	....	....	....	....	....
1996-97	EV Zug	Switz.	41	24	22	46	....	....	....	67	....	....	....	....	....	....	....	....	....	....	9	5	1	6	39	....	....	....
1997-98	EV Zug	Switz.	38	18	34	52	....	....	....	32	....	....	....	....	....	....	....	....	....	....	20	16	12	28	18	....	....	....
	NHL Totals		**169**	**27**	**51**	**78**	**30**	**48**	**78**	**71**	**7**	**0**	**3**	**231**	**11.7**	**120**	**28**	**87**	**5**		**9**	**3**	**0**	**3**	**2**	**0**	**0**	**0**

WHL East First All-Star Team (1990)

Traded to **Philadelphia** by **Boston** with Garry Galley and Boston's 3rd round choice (Milos Holan) in 1993 Entry Draft for Gord Murphy, Brian Dobbin, Philadelphia's 3rd round choice (Sergei Zholtok) in 1992 Entry Draft and Philadelphia's 4th round choice (Charles Paquette) in 1993 Entry Draft, January 2, 1992. Signed as a free agent by **Calgary**, August 26, 1993. Signed as a free agent by **Detroit**, September 6, 1995.

• WAPPEL, GORD

Gord Wappel D – L. 6'2", 205 lbs. b: Regina, Sask., 7/26/1958. Atlanta's 4th choice, 80th overall, in 1978 Amateur Draft.

Season	Club	League	GP	G	A	Pts	AG	AA	APts	PIM	PP	SH	GW	S	%	TGF	PGF	TGA	PGA	+/–	GP	G	A	Pts	PIM	PP	SH	GW
1974-75	Regina Pats	WCJHL	20	0	3	3	....	....	....	9	....	....	....	....	....	....	....	....	....	....	5	0	0	0	4	....	....	....
1975-76	Regina Pats	WCJHL	72	5	28	33	....	....	....	76	....	....	....	....	....	....	....	....	....	....	6	0	2	2	28	....	....	....
1976-77	Regina Pats	WCJHL	54	4	28	32	....	....	....	137	....	....	....	....	....	....	....	....	....	....	....	....	....	....	....	....	....	....
1977-78	Regina Pats	WCJHL	72	10	30	40	....	....	....	177	....	....	....	....	....	....	....	....	....	....	13	5	5	10	20	....	....	....
1978-79	Tulsa Oilers	CHL	47	1	16	17	....	....	....	44	....	....	....	....	....	....	....	....	....	....	....	....	....	....	....	....	....	....
	Muskegon Mohawks	IHL	20	2	6	8	....	....	....	40	....	....	....	....	....	....	....	....	....	....	....	....	....	....	....	....	....	....
1979-80	**Atlanta Flames**	**NHL**	**2**	**0**	**0**	**0**	**0**	**0**	**0**	**0**	**0**	**0**	**0**	**2**	**0.0**	**2**	**0**	**1**	**0**	**+1**	**2**	**0**	**0**	**0**	**4**	**0**	**0**	**0**
	Birmingham Bulls	CHL	76	4	20	24	....	....	....	122	....	....	....	....	....	....	....	....	....	....	....	....	....	....	....	....	....	....
1980-81	**Calgary Flames**	**NHL**	**7**	**0**	**1**	**1**	**0**	**1**	**1**	**4**	**0**	**0**	**0**	**3**	**0.0**	**7**	**0**	**7**	**1**	**+1**	....	....	....	....	....	....	....	....
	Birmingham Bulls	CHL	44	6	19	25	....	....	....	89	....	....	....	....	....	....	....	....	....	....	....	....	....	....	....	....	....	....
	Nova Scotia Voyageurs	AHL	18	0	4	4	....	....	....	10	....	....	....	....	....	....	....	....	....	....	6	0	1	1	8	....	....	....
1981-82	**Calgary Flames**	**NHL**	**11**	**1**	**0**	**1**	**1**	**0**	**1**	**6**	**0**	**0**	**0**	**7**	**14.3**	**6**	**0**	**10**	**0**	**–4**	....	....	....	....	....	....	....	....
	Oklahoma City Stars	CHL	46	6	13	19	....	....	....	52	....	....	....	....	....	....	....	....	....	....	....	....	....	....	....	....	....	....
1982-83	Colorado Flames	CHL	70	10	34	44	....	....	....	110	....	....	....	....	....	....	....	....	....	....	6	0	8	8	2	....	....	....
	NHL Totals		**20**	**1**	**1**	**2**	**1**	**1**	**2**	**10**	**0**	**0**	**0**	**12**	**8.3**	**15**	**0**	**18**	**1**		**2**	**0**	**0**	**0**	**4**	**0**	**0**	**0**

Transferred to **Calgary** after **Atlanta** franchise relocated, June 24, 1980.

• WARD, AARON

Aaron Ward D – R. 6'2", 200 lbs. b: Windsor, Ont., 1/17/1973. Winnipeg's 7th choice, 5th overall, in 1991 Entry Draft.

Season	Club	League	GP	G	A	Pts	AG	AA	APts	PIM	PP	SH	GW	S	%	TGF	PGF	TGA	PGA	+/–	GP	G	A	Pts	PIM	PP	SH	GW
1989-90	Nepean Raiders	COJHL	52	6	33	39	....	....	....	85	....	....	....	....	....	....	....	....	....	....	....	....	....	....	....	....	....	....
1990-91	University of Michigan	CCHA	46	8	11	19	....	....	....	126	....	....	....	....	....	....	....	....	....	....	....	....	....	....	....	....	....	....
1991-92	University of Michigan	CCHA	42	7	12	19	....	....	....	64	....	....	....	....	....	....	....	....	....	....	....	....	....	....	....	....	....	....
1992-93	University of Michigan	CCHA	30	5	8	13	....	....	....	73	....	....	....	....	....	....	....	....	....	....	....	....	....	....	....	....	....	....
	Canada	Nat-Team	4	0	0	0	....	....	....	8	....	....	....	....	....	....	....	....	....	....	....	....	....	....	....	....	....	....
1993-94	**Detroit Red Wings**	**NHL**	**5**	**1**	**0**	**1**	**1**	**0**	**1**	**4**	**0**	**0**	**0**	**3**	**33.3**	**3**	**0**	**1**	**0**	**+2**	....	....	....	....	....	....	....	....
	Adirondack Red Wings	AHL	58	4	12	16	....	....	....	87	....	....	....	....	....	....	....	....	....	....	9	2	6	8	6	....	....	....
1994-95	Adirondack Red Wings	AHL	76	11	24	35	....	....	....	87	....	....	....	....	....	....	....	....	....	....	4	0	1	1	0	....	....	....
	Detroit Red Wings	**NHL**	**1**	**0**	**1**	**1**	**0**	**1**	**1**	**2**	**0**	**0**	**0**	**0**	**0.0**	**1**	**0**	**0**	**0**	**+1**	....	....	....	....	....	....	....	....
1995-96	Adirondack Red Wings	AHL	74	5	10	15	....	....	....	133	....	....	....	....	....	....	....	....	....	....	3	0	0	0	6	....	....	....
1996-97	**Detroit Red Wings**	**NHL**	**49**	**2**	**5**	**7**	**2**	**4**	**6**	**52**	**0**	**0**	**0**	**40**	**5.0**	**21**	**2**	**32**	**4**	**–9**	**19**	**0**	**0**	**0**	**17**	**0**	**0**	**0**
1997-98	**Detroit Red Wings**	**NHL**	**52**	**5**	**5**	**10**	**6**	**5**	**11**	**47**	**0**	**0**	**1**	**47**	**10.6**	**26**	**0**	**35**	**8**	**–1**	....	....	....	....	....	....	....	....
	NHL Totals		**107**	**8**	**11**	**19**	**9**	**10**	**19**	**105**	**0**	**0**	**1**	**90**	**8.9**	**51**	**2**	**68**	**12**		**19**	**0**	**0**	**0**	**17**	**0**	**0**	**0**

Traded to **Detroit** by **Winnipeg** with Toronto's 4th round choice (previously acquired by Winnipeg — later traded to Detroit — Detroit selected John Jakopin) in 1993 Entry Draft for Paul Ysebaert and future considerations (Alan Kerr, June 18, 1993), June 11, 1993.

• WARD, DIXON

Dixon Ward RW – R. 6', 200 lbs. b: Leduc, Alta., 9/23/1968. Vancouver's 6th choice, 128th overall, in 1988 Entry Draft.

Season	Club	League	GP	G	A	Pts	AG	AA	APts	PIM	PP	SH	GW	S	%	TGF	PGF	TGA	PGA	+/–	GP	G	A	Pts	PIM	PP	SH	GW
1987-88	Red Deer Rebels	AJHL	51	60	71	131	....	....	....	167	....	....	....	....	....	....	....	....	....	....	....	....	....	....	....	....	....	....
1988-89	University of North Dakota	WCHA	37	8	9	17	....	....	....	20	....	....	....	....	....	....	....	....	....	....	....	....	....	....	....	....	....	....
1989-90	University of North Dakota	WCHA	45	35	34	69	....	....	....	44	....	....	....	....	....	....	....	....	....	....	....	....	....	....	....	....	....	....
1990-91	University of North Dakota	WCHA	43	34	35	69	....	....	....	84	....	....	....	....	....	....	....	....	....	....	....	....	....	....	....	....	....	....
1991-92	University of North Dakota	WCHA	38	33	31	64	....	....	....	90	....	....	....	....	....	....	....	....	....	....	....	....	....	....	....	....	....	....
1992-93	**Vancouver Canucks**	**NHL**	**70**	**22**	**30**	**52**	**18**	**21**	**39**	**82**	**4**	**1**	**0**	**111**	**19.8**	**78**	**15**	**40**	**11**	**+34**	**9**	**2**	**3**	**5**	**0**	**2**	**0**	**0**
1993-94	**Vancouver Canucks**	**NHL**	**33**	**6**	**1**	**7**	**6**	**1**	**7**	**37**	**2**	**0**	**1**	**46**	**13.0**	**12**	**6**	**22**	**2**	**–14**	....	....	....	....	....	....	....	....
	Los Angeles Kings	**NHL**	**34**	**6**	**2**	**8**	**6**	**2**	**8**	**45**	**2**	**0**	**0**	**44**	**13.6**	**10**	**3**	**15**	**0**	**–8**	....	....	....	....	....	....	....	....
1994-95	**Toronto Maple Leafs**	**NHL**	**22**	**0**	**3**	**3**	**0**	**4**	**4**	**31**	**0**	**0**	**0**	**15**	**0.0**	**3**	**0**	**7**	**0**	**–4**	....	....	....	....	....	....	....	....
	St. John's Maple Leafs	AHL	6	3	3	6	....	....	....	19	....	....	....	....	....	....	....	....	....	....	....	....	....	....	....	....	....	....
	Detroit Vipers	IHL	7	3	6	9	....	....	....	7	....	....	....	....	....	....	....	....	....	....	5	3	0	3	7	....	....	....
1995-96	**Buffalo Sabres**	**NHL**	**8**	**2**	**2**	**4**	**2**	**2**	**4**	**6**	**0**	**0**	**1**	**12**	**16.7**	**5**	**1**	**3**	**0**	**+1**	....	....	....	....	....	....	....	....
	Rochester Americans	AHL	71	38	66	104	....	....	....	74	....	....	....	....	....	....	....	....	....	....	19	11	*24	*35	8	....	....	....
1996-97	**Buffalo Sabres**	**NHL**	**79**	**13**	**32**	**45**	**14**	**28**	**42**	**36**	**1**	**2**	**4**	**93**	**14.0**	**59**	**6**	**54**	**18**	**+17**	**12**	**2**	**3**	**5**	**6**	**0**	**0**	**0**
1997-98	**Buffalo Sabres**	**NHL**	**71**	**10**	**13**	**23**	**12**	**13**	**25**	**42**	**0**	**2**	**3**	**99**	**10.1**	**40**	**1**	**47**	**17**	**+9**	**15**	**3**	**8**	**11**	**6**	**0**	**0**	**0**
	NHL Totals		**317**	**59**	**83**	**142**	**58**	**71**	**129**	**279**	**9**	**5**	**9**	**420**	**14.0**	**207**	**32**	**188**	**48**		**36**	**7**	**14**	**21**	**12**	**2**	**0**	**0**

WCHA Second All-Star Team (1991, 1992) • Won Jack A. Butterfield Trophy (Playoff MVP - AHL) (1996)

Traded to **LA Kings** by **Vancouver** for Jimmy Carson, January 8, 1994. Traded to **Toronto** by **LA Kings** with Guy Leveque, Kelly Fairchild and Shayne Toporowski for Eric Lacroix, Chris Snell and Toronto's 4th round choice (Eric Belanger) in 1996 Entry draft, October 3, 1994. Signed as a free agent by **Buffalo**, September 20, 1995.

● WARD, ED Ed Ward RW – R. 6'3", 205 lbs. b: Edmonton, Alta., 11/10/1969. Quebec's 7th choice, 108th overall, in 1988 Entry Draft.

			REGULAR SEASON																		PLAYOFFS							
Season	Club	League	GP	G	A	Pts	AG	AA	APts	PIM	PP	SH	GW	S	%	TGF	PGF	TGA	PGA	+/–	GP	G	A	Pts	PIM	PP	SH	GW
1986-87	Sherwood Park Crusaders	AJHL	60	18	28	46				272																		
1987-88	Northern Michigan University	WCHA	25	0	2	2				40																		
1988-89	Northern Michigan University	WCHA	42	5	15	20				36																		
1989-90	Northern Michigan University	WCHA	39	5	11	16				77																		
1990-91	Northern Michigan University	WCHA	46	13	18	31				109																		
1991-92	Greensboro Monarchs	ECHL	12	4	8	12				21																		
	Halifax Citadels	AHL	51	7	11	18				65																		
1992-93	Halifax Citadels	AHL	70	13	19	32				56																		
1993-94	**Quebec Nordiques**	**NHL**	**7**	**1**	**0**	**1**	**1**	**0**	**1**	**5**	**0**	**0**	**0**	**3**	**33.3**	**2**	**0**	**2**	**0**	**0**								
	Cornwall Aces	AHL	60	12	30	42				65											12	1	3	4	14			
1994-95	Cornwall Aces	AHL	56	10	14	24				118																		
	Calgary Flames	**NHL**	**2**	**1**	**1**	**2**	**2**	**1**	**3**	**2**	**0**	**0**	**0**	**1**	**100.0**	**2**	**0**	**4**	**0**	**–2**								
	Saint John Flames	AHL	11	4	5	9				20											5	1	0	1	10			
1995-96	**Calgary Flames**	**NHL**	**41**	**3**	**5**	**8**	**3**	**4**	**7**	**44**	**0**	**0**	**0**	**33**	**9.1**	**12**	**1**	**13**	**0**	**–2**								
	Saint John Flames	AHL	12	1	2	3				45											16	4	4	8	27			
1996-97	**Calgary Flames**	**NHL**	**40**	**5**	**8**	**13**	**5**	**7**	**12**	**49**	**0**	**0**	**1**	**33**	**15.2**	**16**	**0**	**19**	**0**	**–3**								
	Saint John Flames	AHL	1	0	0	0				0																		
	Detroit Vipers	IHL	31	7	6	13				45																		
1997-98	**Calgary Flames**	**NHL**	**64**	**4**	**5**	**9**	**5**	**5**	**10**	**122**	**0**	**0**	**0**	**52**	**7.7**	**21**	**1**	**22**	**1**	**–1**								
	NHL Totals		**154**	**14**	**19**	**33**	**16**	**17**	**33**	**222**	**0**	**0**	**1**	**122**	**11.5**	**53**	**2**	**60**	**1**									

Traded to **Calgary** by **Quebec** for Francois Groleau, March 23, 1995.

● WARD, JOE Joe Ward C – L. 6', 180 lbs. b: Sarnia, Ont., 2/11/1961. Colorado's 2nd choice, 22nd overall, in 1980 Entry Draft.

Season	Club	League	GP	G	A	Pts	AG	AA	APts	PIM	PP	SH	GW	S	%	TGF	PGF	TGA	PGA	+/–	GP	G	A	Pts	PIM	PP	SH	GW
1978-79	Seattle Breakers	WHL	61	18	30	48				66																		
1979-80	Seattle Breakers	WHL	59	32	37	69				90																		
1980-81	Seattle Breakers	WHL	40	28	23	51				48																		
	Colorado Rockies	**NHL**	**4**	**0**	**0**	**0**	**0**	**0**	**0**	**2**	**0**	**0**	**0**	**2**	**0.0**	**1**	**0**	**3**	**0**	**–2**								
	Fort Worth Texans	CHL																			5	2	2	4	2			
1981-82	Fort Worth Texans	CHL	32	6	15	21				12																		
1982-83	Wichita Wind	CHL	7	0	2	2				2																		
	Muskegon Mohawks	IHL	53	34	25	59				4											4	1	2	3	4			
1983-84	Muskegon Mohawks	IHL	9	3	2	5				2																		
	NHL Totals		**4**	**0**	**0**	**0**	**0**	**0**	**0**	**2**	**0**	**0**	**0**	**2**	**0.0**	**1**	**0**	**3**	**0**									

● WARD, RON Ron Ward C – R. 5'11", 175 lbs. b: Cornwall, Ont., 9/12/1944.

Season	Club	League	GP	G	A	Pts	AG	AA	APts	PIM	PP	SH	GW	S	%	TGF	PGF	TGA	PGA	+/–	GP	G	A	Pts	PIM	PP	SH	GW
1964-65	Cornwall Royals	OJHL	36	29	31	60																						
1965-66	Tulsa Oilers	CHL	69	6	22	28				37											7	1	2	3	9			
1966-67	Tulsa Oilers	CHL	42	12	15	27				46																		
1967-68	Phoenix Roadrunners	WHL	1	0	1	1				0																		
	Tulsa Oilers	CHL	67	31	*54	*85				30											11	5	5	10	8			
1968-69	Rochester Americans	AHL	73	35	43	78				18																		
1969-70	**Toronto Maple Leafs**	**NHL**	**18**	**0**	**1**	**1**	**0**	**1**	**1**	**2**	**0**	**0**	**0**	**11**	**0.0**	**0**	**0**	**0**	**0**	**0**								
	Phoenix Roadrunners	WHL	22	7	9	16				12																		
	Tulsa Oilers	CHL	22	7	17	24				15																		
1970-71	Rochester Americans	AHL	69	23	16	39				33																		
1971-72	**Vancouver Canucks**	**NHL**	**71**	**2**	**4**	**6**	**2**	**4**	**6**	**4**	**0**	**1**	**0**	**45**	**4.4**	**9**	**0**	**54**	**43**	**–2**								
1972-73	New York Raiders	WHA	77	51	67	118				28																		
1973-74	Vancouver Blazers	WHA	7	0	2	2				2																		
	Los Angeles Sharks	WHA	40	14	19	33				16																		
	Cleveland Crusaders	WHA	23	19	7	26				7											5	3	0	3	2			
1974-75	Cleveland Crusaders	WHA	73	30	32	62				18											5	0	2	2	2			
1975-76	Cleveland Crusaders	WHA	75	32	50	82				24											3	0	2	2	0			
1976-77	Minnesota Fighting Saints	WHA	41	15	21	36				6																		
	Winnipeg Jets	WHA	14	4	7	11				2																		
	Calgary Cowboys	WHA	9	5	5	10				0																		
	NHL Totals		**89**	**2**	**5**	**7**	**2**	**5**	**7**	**6**	**0**	**1**	**0**	**56**	**3.6**	**9**	**0**	**54**	**43**									
	Other Major League Totals		359	170	210	380				103											13	3	4	7	4			

CHL Second All-Star Team (1968) • Won Dudley "Red" Garrett Memorial Award (Top Rookie - AHL) (1969) • WHA Second All-Star Team (1973)

Traded to **Toronto** by **Vancouver** (WHL) for the loan of Brad Selwood and Rene Robert, June, 1969. Claimed by **Vancouver** from **Toronto** in Expansion Draft, June 10, 1970. Selected by **NY Raiders** (WHA) in 1972 WHA General Player Draft, February 12, 1972. Traded to **Vancouver** (WHA) by **NY Golden Blades** (WHA) with Pete Donnelly for Andre Lacroix, Don Herriman and WHA rights to Bernie Parent, May, 1973. Traded to **LA Sharks** (WHA) by **Vancouver** (WHA) for George Gardner and future considerations (Ralph MacSweyn, November 5, 1973), October, 1973. Traded to **Cleveland** (WHA) by **LA Sharks** (WHA) for Bill Young and Ted Hodgson, February, 1974. Transferred to **Minnesota** (WHA) after **LA Sharks** (WHA) franchise relocated, April 11, 1974. Signed as a free agent by **Winnipeg** (WHA) after **Minnesota** (WHA) franchise folded, January 17, 1977. Traded to **Calgary** (WHA) by **Winnipeg** (WHA) with Veli-Pekka Ketola and Heikki Riihiranta for Dan Lawson, Mike Ford and future considerations, March, 1977.

● WARE, JEFF Jeff Ware D – L. 6'4", 220 lbs. b: Toronto, Ont., 5/19/1977. Toronto's 1st choice, 15th overall, in 1995 Entry Draft.

Season	Club	League	GP	G	A	Pts	AG	AA	APts	PIM	PP	SH	GW	S	%	TGF	PGF	TGA	PGA	+/–	GP	G	A	Pts	PIM	PP	SH	GW
1994-95	Oshawa Generals	OHL	55	2	11	13				86											7	1	1	2	6			
1995-96	Oshawa Generals	OHL	62	4	19	23				128											5	0	1	1	8			
	St. John's Maple Leafs	AHL	4	0	0	0				4											4	0	0	0	2			
1996-97	Oshawa Generals	OHL	24	1	10	11				38											13	0	3	3	34			
	Canada	WJC-A	7	0	0	0				6																		
	Toronto Maple Leafs	**NHL**	**13**	**0**	**0**	**0**	**0**	**0**	**0**	**6**	**0**	**0**	**0**	**4**	**0.0**	**5**	**0**	**3**	**0**	**+2**								
1997-98	**Toronto Maple Leafs**	**NHL**	**2**	**0**	**0**	**0**	**0**	**0**	**0**	**0**	**0**	**0**	**0**	**0**	**0.0**	**1**	**0**	**0**	**0**	**+1**								
	St. John's Maple Leafs	AHL	67	0	3	3				182											4	0	0	0	4			
	NHL Totals		**15**	**0**	**0**	**0**	**0**	**0**	**0**	**6**	**0**	**0**	**0**	**4**	**0.0**	**6**	**0**	**3**	**0**									

● WARE, MICHAEL Michael Ware RW – R. 6'5", 216 lbs. b: York, Ont., 3/22/1967. Edmonton's 3rd choice, 62nd overall, in 1985 Entry Draft.

Season	Club	League	GP	G	A	Pts	AG	AA	APts	PIM	PP	SH	GW	S	%	TGF	PGF	TGA	PGA	+/–	GP	G	A	Pts	PIM	PP	SH	GW
1983 84	Mississauga Reps	Jr. B	30	14	20	34				50																		
1984-85	Hamilton Steelhawks	OHL	57	4	14	18				225											12	0	1	1	29			
1985-86	Hamilton Steelhawks	OHL	44	8	11	19				155																		
1986-87	Cornwall Royals	OHL	50	5	19	24				173											5	0	1	1	10			
1987-88	Nova Scotia Oilers	AHL	52	0	8	8				253											3	0	0	0	16			
1988-89	**Edmonton Oilers**	**NHL**	**2**	**0**	**1**	**1**	**0**	**1**	**1**	**11**	**0**	**0**	**0**	**0**	**0.0**	**1**	**0**	**0**	**0**	**+1**								
	Cape Breton Oilers	AHL	48	1	11	12				317																		
1989-90	**Edmonton Oilers**	**NHL**	**3**	**0**	**0**	**0**	**0**	**0**	**0**	**4**	**0**	**0**	**0**	**1**	**0.0**	**0**	**0**	**1**	**0**	**–1**								
	Cape Breton Oilers	AHL	54	6	13	19				191											6	0	3	3	29			
1990-91	Cape Breton Oilers	AHL	43	4	8	12				176											3	0	0	0	4			
1991-92			DID NOT PLAY																									
1992-93	Murrayfield Racers	Britain	33	26	34	60				218											7	10	7	17	24			
1993-94	Murrayfield Racers	Britain	43	30	41	71				162											6	5	5	10	16			
1994-95	Murrayfield Racers	Britain	40	38	41	79				218											6	8	6	14	6			
1995-96	Cardiff Devils	Britain	32	16	30	46				169											6	0	1	1	37			
1996-97	Cardiff Devils	Britain	38	6	12	18				79											5	0	1	1	29			
1997-98	Sheffield Steelers	Britain	43	6	8	14				96											9	2	0	2	4			
	NHL Totals		**5**	**0**	**1**	**1**	**0**	**1**	**1**	**15**	**0**	**0**	**0**	**1**	**0.0**	**1**	**0**	**1**	**0**									

● **WARNER, BOB** Bob Warner D – L. 5'11", 180 lbs. b: Grimsby, Ont., 12/13/1950.

Season	Club	League	GP	G	A	Pts	AG	AA	APts	PIM	PP	SH	GW	S	%	TGF	PGF	TGA	PGA	+/–	GP	G	A	Pts	PIM	PP	SH	GW
			REGULAR SEASON																		PLAYOFFS							
1969-70	Ottawa 67's	OHA	7	0	0	0	....	....	....	2	....	....	....	....	....	....	....	....	....	....	....	....	....	....	....	....	....	....
1970-71	Johnstown Jets	IHL	71	20	24	44	....	....	....	139	....	....	....	....	....	....	....	....	....	....	10	5	5	10	18	....	....	....
1971-72	St. Mary's University	AUAA	18	5	10	15	....	....	....	33	....	....	....	....	....	....	....	....	....	....	....	....	....	....	....	....	....	....
1972-73	St. Mary's University	AUAA	21	6	15	21	....	....	....	66	....	....	....	....	....	....	....	....	....	....	....	....	....	....	....	....	....	....
1973-74	St. Mary's University	AUAA	17	4	11	15	....	....	....	15	....	....	....	....	....	....	....	....	....	....	....	....	....	....	....	....	....	....
1974-75	St. Mary's University	AUAA	18	4	19	23	....	....	....	48	....	....	....	....	....	....	....	....	....	....	....	....	....	....	....	....	....	....
1975-76	Oklahoma City Blazers	CHL	74	7	20	27	....	....	....	117	....	....	....	....	....	....	....	....	....	....	4	1	0	1	9	....	....	....
	Toronto Maple Leafs	**NHL**	....	....	....	....	....	....	....	....	....	....	....	....	....	....	....	....	....	....	**2**	**0**	**0**	**0**	**0**	....	....	....
1976-77	**Toronto Maple Leafs**	**NHL**	**10**	**1**	**1**	**2**	**1**	**1**	**2**	**4**	**0**	**0**	**0**	**9**	**11.1**	**5**	**0**	**1**	**0**	**+4**	**2**	**0**	**0**	**0**	**0**	**0**	**0**	**0**
	Dallas Black Hawks	CHL	69	26	19	45	....	....	....	75	....	....	....	....	....	....	....	....	....	....	5	2	0	2	0	....	....	....
1977-78	Dallas Black Hawks	CHL	61	5	14	19	....	....	....	62	....	....	....	....	....	....	....	....	....	....	13	2	2	4	18	....	....	....
1978-79	New Brunswick Hawks	AHL	80	10	14	24	....	....	....	52	....	....	....	....	....	....	....	....	....	....	5	0	0	0	2	....	....	....
1979-80	New Brunswick Hawks	AHL	61	8	6	14	....	....	....	35	....	....	....	....	....	....	....	....	....	....	4	0	0	0	2	....	....	....
1980-81			DID NOT PLAY																									
1981-82	Cap Pele Capitals	NBSHL	....	....	....	....	....	....	....	....	....	....	....	....	....	....	....	....	....	....	17	6	16	22	....	....	....	....
	NHL Totals		**10**	**1**	**1**	**2**	**1**	**1**	**2**	**4**	**0**	**0**	**0**	**9**	**11.1**	**5**	**0**	**1**	**0**		**4**	**0**	**0**	**0**	**0**	**0**	**0**	**0**

Signed as a free agent by **Toronto**, September 3, 1975.

● **WARNER, JIM** Jim Warner RW – R. 5'11", 180 lbs. b: Minneapolis, MN, 3/26/1954. NY Rangers' 23rd choice, 245th overall, in 1974 Amateur Draft.

Season	Club	League	GP	G	A	Pts	AG	AA	APts	PIM	PP	SH	GW	S	%	TGF	PGF	TGA	PGA	+/–	GP	G	A	Pts	PIM	PP	SH	GW
1972-73	Minnesota Jr. North Stars	CAJHL	....	21	17	38	....	....	....	22	....	....	....	....	....	....	....	....	....	....	....	....	....	....	....	....	....	....
1973-74	Minnesota Jr. North Stars	MWJHL	56	55	50	105	....	....	....	47	....	....	....	....	....	....	....	....	....	....	....	....	....	....	....	....	....	....
	United States	WJC-A	5	3	1	4	....	....	....	2	....	....	....	....	....	....	....	....	....	....	....	....	....	....	....	....	....	....
1974-75	Colorado College	WCHA	37	30	25	55	....	....	....	24	....	....	....	....	....	....	....	....	....	....	....	....	....	....	....	....	....	....
	United States	WEC-A	10	1	4	5	....	....	....	8	....	....	....	....	....	....	....	....	....	....	....	....	....	....	....	....	....	....
1975-76	Colorado College	WCHA	35	16	20	36	....	....	....	59	....	....	....	....	....	....	....	....	....	....	....	....	....	....	....	....	....	....
	United States	WEC-A	10	2	2	4	....	....	....	12	....	....	....	....	....	....	....	....	....	....	....	....	....	....	....	....	....	....
1976-77	Colorado College	WCHA	30	16	23	39	....	....	....	36	....	....	....	....	....	....	....	....	....	....	....	....	....	....	....	....	....	....
1977-78	Colorado College	WCHA	38	27	41	68	....	....	....	50	....	....	....	....	....	....	....	....	....	....	....	....	....	....	....	....	....	....
	United States	WEC-A	10	2	5	7	....	....	....	2	....	....	....	....	....	....	....	....	....	....	....	....	....	....	....	....	....	....
1978-79	New England Whalers	WHA	41	6	9	15	....	....	....	20	....	....	....	....	....	....	....	....	....	....	1	0	0	0	0	....	....	....
	Springfield Indians	AHL	40	17	7	24	....	....	....	15	....	....	....	....	....	....	....	....	....	....	....	....	....	....	....	....	....	....
1979-80	**Hartford Whalers**	**NHL**	**32**	**0**	**3**	**3**	**0**	**2**	**2**	**10**	**0**	**0**	**0**	**26**	**0.0**	**6**	**0**	**26**	**14**	**–6**	....	....	....	....	....	....	....	....
	Springfield Indians	AHL	45	14	19	33	....	....	....	22	....	....	....	....	....	....	....	....	....	....	....	....	....	....	....	....	....	....
	NHL Totals		**32**	**0**	**3**	**3**	**0**	**2**	**2**	**10**	**0**	**0**	**0**	**26**	**0.0**	**6**	**0**	**26**	**14**		....	....	....	....	....	....	....	....
	Other Major League Totals		41	6	9	15	....	....	....	20	....	....	....	....	....	....	....	....	....		1	0	0	0	0	....	....	....

WCHA Second All-Star Team (1975)

Signed as a free agent by **New England** (WHA), June, 1978. Rights retained by **Hartford** prior to Expansion Draft, June 9, 1979.

● **WARRENER, RHETT** Rhett Warrener D – L. 6'1", 209 lbs. b: Shaunavon, Sask., 1/27/1976. Florida's 2nd choice, 27th overall, in 1994 Entry Draft.

Season	Club	League	GP	G	A	Pts	AG	AA	APts	PIM	PP	SH	GW	S	%	TGF	PGF	TGA	PGA	+/–	GP	G	A	Pts	PIM	PP	SH	GW
1991-92	Saskatoon Blades	WHL	2	0	0	0	....	....	....	0	....	....	....	....	....	....	....	....	....	....	....	....	....	....	....	....	....	....
1992-93	Saskatoon Blades	WHL	68	2	17	19	....	....	....	100	....	....	....	....	....	....	....	....	....	....	9	0	0	0	14	....	....	....
1993-94	Saskatoon Blades	WHL	61	7	19	26	....	....	....	131	....	....	....	....	....	....	....	....	....	....	16	0	5	5	33	....	....	....
1994-95	Saskatoon Blades	WHL	66	13	26	39	....	....	....	137	....	....	....	....	....	....	....	....	....	....	10	0	3	3	6	....	....	....
1995-96	**Florida Panthers**	**NHL**	**28**	**0**	**3**	**3**	**0**	**2**	**2**	**46**	**0**	**0**	**0**	**19**	**0.0**	**16**	**0**	**16**	**4**	**+4**	**21**	**0**	**1**	**1**	**0**	**0**	**0**	**0**
	Canada	WJC-A	6	0	0	0	....	....	....	4	....	....	....	....	....	....	....	....	....	....	....	....	....	....	....	....	....	....
	Carolina Monarchs	AHL	9	0	0	0	....	....	....	4	....	....	....	....	....	....	....	....	....	....	....	....	....	....	....	....	....	....
1996-97	**Florida Panthers**	**NHL**	**62**	**4**	**9**	**13**	**4**	**8**	**12**	**88**	**1**	**0**	**1**	**58**	**6.9**	**52**	**5**	**42**	**15**	**+20**	**5**	**0**	**0**	**0**	**0**	**0**	**0**	**0**
1997-98	**Florida Panthers**	**NHL**	**79**	**0**	**4**	**4**	**0**	**4**	**4**	**99**	**0**	**0**	**0**	**66**	**0.0**	**33**	**1**	**77**	**29**	**–16**	....	....	....	....	....	....	....	....
	NHL Totals		**169**	**4**	**16**	**20**	**4**	**14**	**18**	**233**	**1**	**0**	**1**	**143**	**2.8**	**101**	**6**	**135**	**48**		**26**	**0**	**1**	**1**	**0**	**0**	**0**	**0**

● **WARRINER, TODD** Todd Warriner LW – L. 6'1", 188 lbs. b: Blenheim, Ont., 1/3/1974. Quebec's 1st choice, 4th overall, in 1992 Entry Draft.

Season	Club	League	GP	G	A	Pts	AG	AA	APts	PIM	PP	SH	GW	S	%	TGF	PGF	TGA	PGA	+/–	GP	G	A	Pts	PIM	PP	SH	GW
1990-91	Windsor Spitfires	OHL	57	36	28	64	....	....	....	26	....	....	....	....	....	....	....	....	....	....	11	5	6	11	12			
1991-92	Windsor Spitfires	OHL	50	41	41	82	....	....	....	64	....	....	....	....	....	....	....	....	....	....	7	5	4	9	6	....	....	....
1992-93	Windsor Spitfires	OHL	23	13	21	34	....	....	....	29	....	....	....	....	....	....	....	....	....	....	....	....	....	....	....	....	....	....
	Kitchener Rangers	OHL	32	19	24	43	....	....	....	35	....	....	....	....	....	....	....	....	....	....	7	5	14	19	14	....	....	....
1993-94	Canada	Nat-Team	50	11	20	31	....	....	....	33	....	....	....	....	....	....	....	....	....	....	....	....	....	....	....	....	....	....
	Canada	Olympics	4	1	1	2	....	....	....	0	....	....	....	....	....	....	....	....	....	....	....	....	....	....	....	....	....	....
	Kitchener Rangers	OHL	....	....	....	....	....	....	....	....	....	....	....	....	....	....	....	....	....	....	1	0	1	1	0	....	....	....
	Cornwall Aces	AHL	....	....	....	....	....	....	....	....	....	....	....	....	....	....	....	....	....	....	10	1	4	5	4	....	....	....
1994-95	St. John's Maple Leafs	AHL	46	8	10	18	....	....	....	22	....	....	....	....	....	....	....	....	....	....	4	1	0	1	2	....	....	....
	Toronto Maple Leafs	**NHL**	**5**	**0**	**0**	**0**	**0**	**0**	**0**	**0**	**0**	**0**	**0**	**1**	**0.0**	**0**	**0**	**3**	**0**	**–3**	....	....	....	....	....	....	....	....
1995-96	**Toronto Maple Leafs**	**NHL**	**57**	**7**	**8**	**15**	**7**	**7**	**14**	**26**	**1**	**0**	**0**	**79**	**8.9**	**27**	**7**	**31**	**0**	**–11**	**6**	**1**	**1**	**2**	**2**	**0**	**0**	**0**
	St. John's Maple Leafs	AHL	11	5	6	11	....	....	....	16	....	....	....	....	....	....	....	....	....	....	....	....	....	....	....	....	....	....
1996-97	**Toronto Maple Leafs**	**NHL**	**75**	**12**	**21**	**33**	**13**	**19**	**32**	**41**	**2**	**2**	**0**	**146**	**8.2**	**57**	**14**	**58**	**12**	**–3**	....	....	....	....	....	....	....	....
1997-98	**Toronto Maple Leafs**	**NHL**	**45**	**5**	**8**	**13**	**6**	**8**	**14**	**20**	**0**	**0**	**1**	**73**	**6.8**	**21**	**0**	**24**	**8**	**+5**	....	....	....	....	....	....	....	....
	NHL Totals		**182**	**24**	**37**	**61**	**26**	**34**	**60**	**87**	**3**	**2**	**1**	**299**	**8.0**	**105**	**21**	**116**	**20**		**6**	**1**	**1**	**2**	**2**	**0**	**0**	**0**

OHL First All-Star Team (1992)

Traded to **Toronto** by **Quebec** with Mats Sundin, Garth Butcher and Philadelphia's 1st round choice (previously acquired by Quebec — later traded to Washington — Washington selected Nolan Baumgartner) in 1994 Entry Draft for Wendel Clark, Sylvain Lefebvre, Landon Wilson and Toronto's 1st round choice (Jeffrey Kealty) in 1994 Entry Draft, June 28, 1994.

● **WASHBURN, STEVE** Steve Washburn C – L. 6'2", 191 lbs. b: Ottawa, Ont., 4/10/1975. Florida's 5th choice, 78th overall, in 1993 Entry Draft.

Season	Club	League	GP	G	A	Pts	AG	AA	APts	PIM	PP	SH	GW	S	%	TGF	PGF	TGA	PGA	+/–	GP	G	A	Pts	PIM	PP	SH	GW
1991-92	Ottawa Generals	OHL	59	5	17	22	....	....	....	10	....	....	....	....	....	....	....	....	....	....	11	2	3	5	4	....	....	....
1992-93	Ottawa Generals	OHL	66	20	38	58	....	....	....	54	....	....	....	....	....	....	....	....	....	....	....	....	....	....	....	....	....	....
1993-94	Ottawa Generals	OHL	65	30	50	80	....	....	....	88	....	....	....	....	....	....	....	....	....	....	17	7	16	23	10	....	....	....
1994-95	Ottawa Generals	OHL	63	43	63	106	....	....	....	72	....	....	....	....	....	....	....	....	....	....	....	....	....	....	....	....	....	....
	Cincinnati Cyclones	IHL	6	3	1	4	....	....	....	0	....	....	....	....	....	....	....	....	....	....	9	1	3	4	4	....	....	....
1995-96	**Florida Panthers**	**NHL**	**1**	**0**	**1**	**1**	**0**	**1**	**1**	**0**	**0**	**0**	**0**	**1**	**0.0**	**1**	**0**	**0**	**0**	**+1**	**1**	**0**	**1**	**1**	**0**	**0**	**0**	**0**
	Carolina Monarchs	AHL	78	29	54	83	....	....	....	45	....	....	....	....	....	....	....	....	....	....	....	....	....	....	....	....	....	....
1996-97	**Florida Panthers**	**NHL**	**18**	**3**	**6**	**9**	**3**	**5**	**8**	**4**	**1**	**0**	**0**	**21**	**14.3**	**14**	**2**	**10**	**0**	**+2**	....	....	....	....	....	....	....	....
	Carolina Monarchs	AHL	60	23	40	63	....	....	....	66	....	....	....	....	....	....	....	....	....	....	....	....	....	....	....	....	....	....
1997-98	**Florida Panthers**	**NHL**	**58**	**11**	**8**	**19**	**13**	**8**	**21**	**32**	**4**	**0**	**2**	**61**	**18.0**	**30**	**9**	**31**	**4**	**–6**	....	....	....	....	....	....	....	....
	Beast of New Haven	AHL	6	3	5	8	....	....	....	4	....	....	....	....	....	....	....	....	....	....	3	2	0	2	15	....	....	....
	NHL Totals		**77**	**14**	**15**	**29**	**16**	**14**	**30**	**36**	**5**	**0**	**2**	**83**	**16.9**	**45**	**11**	**41**	**4**		**1**	**0**	**1**	**1**	**0**	**0**	**0**	**0**

● **WATSON, BILL** Bill Watson RW – R. 6', 185 lbs. b: Pine Falls, Man., 3/30/1964. Chicago's 4th choice, 70th overall, in 1982 Entry Draft.

Season	Club	League	GP	G	A	Pts	AG	AA	APts	PIM	PP	SH	GW	S	%	TGF	PGF	TGA	PGA	+/–	GP	G	A	Pts	PIM	PP	SH	GW
1980-81	Prince Albert Raiders	AJHL	54	30	39	69	....	....	....	27	....	....	....	....	....	....	....	....	....	....	....	....	....	....	....	....	....	....
1981-82	Prince Albert Raiders	AJHL	47	43	41	84	....	....	....	37	....	....	....	....	....	....	....	....	....	....	....	....	....	....	....	....	....	....
1982-83	University of Minnesota-Duluth	WCHA	22	5	10	15	....	....	....	10	....	....	....	....	....	....	....	....	....	....	....	....	....	....	....	....	....	....
1983-84	University of Minnesota-Duluth	WCHA	40	35	51	86	....	....	....	12	....	....	....	....	....	....	....	....	....	....	....	....	....	....	....	....	....	....
1984-85	University of Minnesota-Duluth	WCHA	42	46	54	100	....	....	....	46	....	....	....	....	....	....	....	....	....	....	....	....	....	....	....	....	....	....
1985-86	**Chicago Black Hawks**	**NHL**	**52**	**8**	**16**	**24**	**6**	**11**	**17**	**2**	**2**	**0**	**0**	**67**	**11.9**	**36**	**9**	**31**	**0**	**–4**	**2**	**0**	**1**	**1**	**0**	**0**	**0**	**0**
1986-87	**Chicago Blackhawks**	**NHL**	**51**	**13**	**19**	**32**	**11**	**14**	**25**	**6**	**0**	**0**	**0**	**106**	**12.3**	**58**	**9**	**30**	**0**	**+19**	**4**	**0**	**1**	**1**	**0**	**0**	**0**	**0**

			REGULAR SEASON																		PLAYOFFS							
Season	Club	League	GP	G	A	Pts	AG	AA	APts	PIM	PP	SH	GW	S	%	TGF	PGF	TGA	PGA	+/–	GP	G	A	Pts	PIM	PP	SH	GW
1987-88	**Chicago Blackhawks**	**NHL**	**9**	**2**	**0**	**2**	**2**	**0**	**2**	**0**	**0**	**0**	**0**	**7**	**28.6**	**3**	**0**	**8**	**0**	**–5**	....	....	....	....	....	....	....	....
	Saginaw Hawks	IHL	35	15	20	35	....	....	....	10	....	....	....	....	....	....	....	....	....	....	....	....	....	....	....	....	....	....
1988-89	**Chicago Blackhawks**	**NHL**	**3**	**0**	**1**	**1**	**0**	**1**	**1**	**4**	**0**	**0**	**0**	**2**	**0.0**	**1**	**1**	**0**	**0**	**0**	....	....	....	....	....	....	....	....
	Saginaw Hawks	IHL	42	26	24	50	....	....	....	18	....	....	....	....	....	....	....	....	....	....	3	1	0	1	2	....	....	....
	NHL Totals		**115**	**23**	**36**	**59**	**19**	**26**	**45**	**12**	**2**	**0**	**0**	**182**	**12.6**	**98**	**19**	**69**	**0**		**6**	**0**	**2**	**2**	**0**	**0**	**0**	**0**

WCHA First All-Star Team (1984, 1985) • NCAA West First All-American Team (1984, 1985) • NCAA Championship All-Tournament Team (1985) • Won Hobey Baker Memorial Award (Top U.S. Collegiate Player) (1985)

• WATSON, BRYAN

Bryan "Bugsy" Watson D – R. 5'9", 175 lbs. b: Bancroft, Ont., 11/14/1942.

Season	Club	League	GP	G	A	Pts	AG	AA	APts	PIM	PP	SH	GW	S	%	TGF	PGF	TGA	PGA	+/–	GP	G	A	Pts	PIM	PP	SH	GW
1960-61	Peterborough Petes	OHA	18	0	1	1	....	....	....	4	....	....	....	....	....	....	....	....	....	....	....	....	....	....	....	....	....	....
1961-62	Peterborough Petes	OHA	50	3	16	19	....	....	....	129	....	....	....	....	....	....	....	....	....	....	....	....	....	....	....	....	....	....
1962-63	Peterborough Petes	OHA	49	9	22	31	....	....	....	80	....	....	....	....	....	....	....	....	....	....	6	0	3	3	10	....	....	....
	Hull-Ottawa Canadiens	EPHL	....	....	....	....	....	....	....	....	....	....	....	....	....	....	....	....	....	....	3	1	1	2	0	....	....	....
1963-64	**Montreal Canadiens**	**NHL**	**39**	**0**	**2**	**2**	**0**	**2**	**2**	**18**	....	....	....	....	....	....	....	....	....	....	**6**	**0**	**0**	**0**	**2**	....	....	....
	Omaha Knights	CHL	9	1	1	2	....	....	....	12	....	....	....	....	....	....	....	....	....	....	....	....	....	....	....	....	....	....
1964-65	**Montreal Canadiens**	**NHL**	**5**	**0**	**1**	**1**	**0**	**1**	**1**	**7**	....	....	....	....	....	....	....	....	....	....	....	....	....	....	....	....	....	....
	Quebec Aces	AHL	64	1	16	17	....	....	....	186	....	....	....	....	....	....	....	....	....	....	5	0	0	0	35	....	....	....
1965-66	**Detroit Red Wings**	**NHL**	**70**	**2**	**7**	**9**	**2**	**7**	**9**	**133**	....	....	....	....	....	....	....	....	....	....	**12**	**2**	**0**	**2**	**30**	....	....	....
1966-67	**Detroit Red Wings**	**NHL**	**48**	**0**	**1**	**1**	**0**	**1**	**1**	**66**	....	....	....	....	....	....	....	....	....	....	....	....	....	....	....	....	....	....
	Memphis Wings	CHL	16	1	3	4	....	....	....	76	....	....	....	....	....	....	....	....	....	....	....	....	....	....	....	....	....	....
1967-68	**Montreal Canadiens**	**NHL**	**12**	**0**	**1**	**1**	**0**	**1**	**1**	**9**	**0**	**0**	**0**	**6**	**0.0**	**2**	**0**	**6**	**1**	**–3**	....	....	....	....	....	....	....	....
	Cleveland Barons	AHL	12	2	4	6	....	....	....	22	....	....	....	....	....	....	....	....	....	....	....	....	....	....	....	....	....	....
	Houston Apollos	CHL	50	2	37	39	....	....	....	*293	....	....	....	....	....	....	....	....	....	....	....	....	....	....	....	....	....	....
1968-69	**Oakland Seals**	**NHL**	**50**	**2**	**3**	**5**	**2**	**3**	**5**	**97**	**0**	**0**	**1**	**39**	**5.1**	**23**	**3**	**57**	**21**	**–16**	....	....	....	....	....	....	....	....
	Pittsburgh Penguins	**NHL**	**18**	**0**	**4**	**4**	**0**	**4**	**4**	**35**	**0**	**0**	**0**	**34**	**0.0**	**11**	**2**	**25**	**5**	**–11**	....	....	....	....	....	....	....	....
1969-70	**Pittsburgh Penguins**	**NHL**	**61**	**1**	**9**	**10**	**1**	**9**	**10**	**189**	**0**	**0**	**0**	**61**	**1.6**	**48**	**0**	**74**	**25**	**–1**	**10**	**0**	**0**	**0**	**17**	**0**	**0**	**0**
	Baltimore Clippers	AHL	5	1	2	3	....	....	....	8	....	....	....	....	....	....	....	....	....	....	....	....	....	....	....	....	....	....
1970-71	**Pittsburgh Penguins**	**NHL**	**43**	**2**	**6**	**8**	**2**	**5**	**7**	**119**	**0**	**0**	**0**	**48**	**4.2**	**27**	**0**	**47**	**15**	**–5**	....	....	....	....	....	....	....	....
1971-72	**Pittsburgh Penguins**	**NHL**	**75**	**3**	**17**	**20**	**3**	**15**	**18**	***212**	**0**	**0**	**1**	**106**	**2.8**	**77**	**3**	**95**	**26**	**+5**	**4**	**0**	**0**	**0**	**21**	**0**	**0**	**0**
1972-73	**Pittsburgh Penguins**	**NHL**	**69**	**1**	**17**	**18**	**1**	**14**	**15**	**179**	**0**	**0**	**0**	**47**	**2.1**	**88**	**2**	**92**	**24**	**+18**	....	....	....	....	....	....	....	....
1973-74	**Pittsburgh Penguins**	**NHL**	**38**	**1**	**4**	**5**	**1**	**3**	**4**	**137**	**1**	**0**	**0**	**27**	**3.7**	**34**	**1**	**55**	**10**	**–12**	....	....	....	....	....	....	....	....
	St. Louis Blues	**NHL**	**11**	**0**	**1**	**1**	**0**	**1**	**1**	**19**	**0**	**0**	**0**	**10**	**0.0**	**11**	**0**	**13**	**2**	**0**	....	....	....	....	....	....	....	....
	Detroit Red Wings	**NHL**	**21**	**0**	**4**	**4**	**0**	**3**	**3**	**99**	**0**	**0**	**0**	**9**	**0.0**	**17**	**0**	**23**	**5**	**–1**	....	....	....	....	....	....	....	....
1974-75	**Detroit Red Wings**	**NHL**	**70**	**1**	**13**	**14**	**1**	**10**	**11**	**238**	**0**	**1**	**0**	**68**	**1.5**	**65**	**2**	**122**	**30**	**–29**	....	....	....	....	....	....	....	....
1975-76	**Detroit Red Wings**	**NHL**	**79**	**0**	**18**	**18**	**0**	**14**	**14**	**322**	**0**	**0**	**0**	**88**	**0.0**	**69**	**2**	**126**	**39**	**–20**	....	....	....	....	....	....	....	....
1976-77	**Detroit Red Wings**	**NHL**	**14**	**0**	**1**	**1**	**0**	**1**	**1**	**39**	**0**	**0**	**0**	**4**	**0.0**	**12**	**0**	**17**	**7**	**+2**	....	....	....	....	....	....	....	....
	Washington Capitals	**NHL**	**56**	**1**	**14**	**15**	**1**	**11**	**12**	**91**	**0**	**0**	**0**	**54**	**1.9**	**49**	**1**	**76**	**23**	**–5**	....	....	....	....	....	....	....	....
1977-78	**Washington Capitals**	**NHL**	**79**	**3**	**11**	**14**	**3**	**9**	**12**	**167**	**0**	**1**	**0**	**52**	**5.8**	**60**	**0**	**103**	**31**	**–12**	....	....	....	....	....	....	....	....
1978-79	**Washington Capitals**	**NHL**	**20**	**0**	**1**	**1**	**0**	**1**	**1**	**36**	**0**	**0**	**0**	**16**	**0.0**	**10**	**0**	**21**	**4**	**–7**	....	....	....	....	....	....	....	....
	Cincinnati Stingers	WHA	21	0	2	2	....	....	....	56	....	....	....	....	....	....	....	....	....	....	3	0	1	1	2	....	....	....
	NHL Totals		**878**	**17**	**135**	**152**	**17**	**115**	**132**	**2212**	**1**	**2**	**2**	**669**	**2.5**	**603**	**16**	**952**	**268**		**32**	**2**	**0**	**2**	**70**	**0**	**0**	**0**
	Other Major League Totals		21	0	2	2	....	....	....	56	....	....	....	....	....	....	....	....	....	....	3	0	1	1	2	....	....	....

CHL First All-Star Team (1968) • Named CHL's Top Defenseman (1968) • Won Tommy Ivan Trophy (CHL's MVP) (1968)

Traded to **Chicago** by **Montreal** for Don Johns, June 8, 1965. Claimed by **Detroit** from **Chicago** in Intra-League Draft, June 9, 1965. Claimed by **Minnesota** from **Detroit** in Expansion Draft, June 6, 1967. Traded to **Montreal** by **Minnesota** for Bill Plager and the rights to Leo Thiffault and Barrie Meissner, June 6, 1967. Traded to **Oakland** by **Montreal** with cash for Oakland's 1st round choice (Michel Larocque) in 1972 Amateur Draft, June 10, 1968. Traded to **Pittsburgh** by **Oakland** with George Swarbrick and Tracy Pratt for Earl Ingarfield, Gene Ubriaco and Dick Mattiussi, January 30, 1969. Selected by **LA Sharks** (WHA) in 1972 WHA General Player Draft, February 12, 1972. Traded to **St. Louis** by **Pittsburgh** with Greg Polis and Pittsburgh's 2nd round choice (Bob Hess) in 1974 Amateur Draft for Steve Durbano, Ab Demarco and Bob Kelly, January 17, 1974. Traded to **Detroit** by **St. Louis** with Chris Evans and Jean Hamel for Ted Harris, Bill Collins and Garnet Bailey, February 14, 1974. Traded to **Washington** by **Detroit** for Greg Joly, November 30, 1976. Signed as a free agent by **Cincinnati** (WHA) following release by **Washington**, March 2, 1979. Claimed by **Edmonton** from **Cincinnati** (WHA) in WHA Dispersal Draft, June 9, 1979.

• WATSON, DAVE

Dave Watson LW – L. 6'2", 190 lbs. b: Kirkland Lake, Ont., 5/19/1958. Colorado's 4th choice, 58th overall, in 1978 Amateur Draft.

Season	Club	League	GP	G	A	Pts	AG	AA	APts	PIM	PP	SH	GW	S	%	TGF	PGF	TGA	PGA	+/–	GP	G	A	Pts	PIM	PP	SH	GW
1976-77	Sudbury Wolves	OHA	39	12	13	25	....	....	....	34	....	....	....	....	....	....	....	....	....	....	....	....	....	....	....	....	....	....
	Sault Ste. Marie Greyhounds	OHA	26	11	9	20	....	....	....	18	....	....	....	....	....	....	....	....	....	....	....	....	....	....	....	....	....	....
1977-78	Sault Ste. Marie Greyhounds	OHA	65	21	30	51	....	....	....	112	....	....	....	....	....	....	....	....	....	....	....	....	....	....	....	....	....	....
1978-79			DID NOT PLAY – INJURED																									
1979-80	**Colorado Rockies**	**NHL**	**5**	**0**	**0**	**0**	**0**	**0**	**0**	**2**	**0**	**0**	**0**	**1**	**0.0**	**1**	**0**	**2**	**0**	**–1**	....	....	....	....	....	....	....	....
	Fort Worth Texans	CHL	68	19	22	41	....	....	....	124	....	....	....	....	....	....	....	....	....	....	14	4	6	10	14	....	....	....
1980-81	**Colorado Rockies**	**NHL**	**13**	**0**	**1**	**1**	**0**	**1**	**1**	**8**	**0**	**0**	**0**	**6**	**0.0**	**2**	**1**	**3**	**0**	**–2**	....	....	....	....	....	....	....	....
	Fort Worth Texans	CHL	50	16	20	36	....	....	....	115	....	....	....	....	....	....	....	....	....	....	....	....	....	....	....	....	....	....
1981-82	Fort Worth Texans	CHL	68	15	14	29	....	....	....	107	....	....	....	....	....	....	....	....	....	....	....	....	....	....	....	....	....	....
1982-83	Carolina Thunderbirds	ACHL	66	53	49	*102	....	....	....	101	....	....	....	....	....	....	....	....	....	....	8	6	8	*14	28	....	....	....
1983-84	Carolina Thunderbirds	ACHL	29	17	16	33	....	....	....	56	....	....	....	....	....	....	....	....	....	....	10	4	4	8	13	....	....	....
1984-85	Carolina Thunderbirds	ACHL	64	31	54	85	....	....	....	138	....	....	....	....	....	....	....	....	....	....	10	3	*14	17	26	....	....	....
1985-86	Carolina Thunderbirds	ACHL	9	3	3	6	....	....	....	21	....	....	....	....	....	....	....	....	....	....	....	....	....	....	....	....	....	....
	NHL Totals		**18**	**0**	**1**	**1**	**0**	**1**	**1**	**10**	**0**	**0**	**0**	**7**	**0.0**	**3**	**1**	**5**	**0**		....	....	....	....	....	....	....	....

• WATSON, JIM A.

Jim A. "Watty" Watson D – L. 6'2", 186 lbs. b: Malartic, Que., 6/28/1943.

Season	Club	League	GP	G	A	Pts	AG	AA	APts	PIM	PP	SH	GW	S	%	TGF	PGF	TGA	PGA	+/–	GP	G	A	Pts	PIM	PP	SH	GW
1961-62	Hamilton Red Wings	OHA	5	0	0	0	....	....	....	4	....	....	....	....	....	....	....	....	....	....	....	....	....	....	....	....	....	....
1962-63	Hamilton Red Wings	OHA	15	0	0	0	....	....	....	25	....	....	....	....	....	....	....	....	....	....	....	....	....	....	....	....	....	....
1963-64	**Detroit Red Wings**	**NHL**	**1**	**0**	**0**	**0**	**0**	**0**	**0**	**0**	....	....	....	....	....	....	....	....	....	....	....	....	....	....	....	....	....	....
	Cincinnati Wings	CHL	61	2	5	7	....	....	....	36	....	....	....	....	....	....	....	....	....	....	....	....	....	....	....	....	....	....
1964-65	**Detroit Red Wings**	**NHL**	**1**	**0**	**0**	**0**	**0**	**0**	**0**	**2**	....	....	....	....	....	....	....	....	....	....	....	....	....	....	....	....	....	....
	Pittsburgh Hornets	AHL	61	2	16	18	....	....	....	53	....	....	....	....	....	....	....	....	....	....	....	....	....	....	....	....	....	....
1965-66	**Detroit Red Wings**	**NHL**	**2**	**0**	**0**	**0**	**0**	**0**	**0**	**4**	....	....	....	....	....	....	....	....	....	....	....	....	....	....	....	....	....	....
	Memphis Wings	CHL	69	4	11	15	....	....	....	126	....	....	....	....	....	....	....	....	....	....	....	....	....	....	....	....	....	....
1966-67	San Diego Gulls	WHL	72	4	19	23	....	....	....	*158	....	....	....	....	....	....	....	....	....	....	....	....	....	....	....	....	....	....
1967-68	**Detroit Red Wings**	**NHL**	**61**	**0**	**3**	**3**	**0**	**3**	**3**	**87**	**0**	**0**	**0**	**55**	**0.0**	**34**	**0**	**57**	**3**	**–20**	....	....	....	....	....	....	....	....
1968-69	**Detroit Red Wings**	**NHL**	**8**	**0**	**1**	**1**	**0**	**1**	**1**	**4**	**0**	**0**	**0**	**5**	**0.0**	**3**	**0**	**6**	**0**	**–3**	....	....	....	....	....	....	....	....
	Baltimore Clippers	AHL	25	2	8	10	....	....	....	58	....	....	....	....	....	....	....	....	....	....	....	....	....	....	....	....	....	....
	Fort Worth Wings	CHL	21	1	8	9	....	....	....	54	....	....	....	....	....	....	....	....	....	....	....	....	....	....	....	....	....	....
1969-70	**Detroit Red Wings**	**NHL**	**4**	**0**	**0**	**0**	**0**	**0**	**0**	**0**	**0**	**0**	**0**	**6**	**0.0**	**0**	**0**	**0**	**0**	**0**	....	....	....	....	....	....	....	....
	Cleveland Barons	AHL	59	7	19	26	....	....	....	128	....	....	....	....	....	....	....	....	....	....	....	....	....	....	....	....	....	....
1970-71	**Buffalo Sabres**	**NHL**	**78**	**2**	**9**	**11**	**2**	**8**	**10**	**147**	**0**	**0**	**0**	**114**	**1.8**	**75**	**3**	**122**	**22**	**–28**	....	....	....	....	....	....	....	....
1971-72	**Buffalo Sabres**	**NHL**	**66**	**2**	**6**	**8**	**2**	**5**	**7**	**101**	**1**	**0**	**0**	**78**	**2.6**	**39**	**1**	**91**	**20**	**–33**	....	....	....	....	....	....	....	....
1972-73	Los Angeles Sharks	WHA	75	5	15	20	....	....	....	123	....	....	....	....	....	....	....	....	....	....	4	0	1	1	2	....	....	....
1973-74	Los Angeles Sharks	WHA	48	0	6	6	....	....	....	28	....	....	....	....	....	....	....	....	....	....	....	....	....	....	....	....	....	....
	Greensboro Generals	SHL	2	0	1	1	....	....	....	0	....	....	....	....	....	....	....	....	....	....	....	....	....	....	....	....	....	....
	Chicago Cougars	WHA	23	0	5	5	....	....	....	22	....	....	....	....	....	....	....	....	....	....	18	2	3	5	18	....	....	....
1974-75	Chicago Cougars	WHA	57	3	6	9	....	....	....	31	....	....	....	....	....	....	....	....	....	....	....	....	....	....	....	....	....	....
	Long Island Cougars	NAHL	4	0	1	1	....	....	....	6	....	....	....	....	....	....	....	....	....	....	....	....	....	....	....	....	....	....
1975-76	Quebec Nordiques	WHA	28	0	1	1	....	....	....	24	....	....	....	....	....	....	....	....	....	....	....	....	....	....	....	....	....	....
	NHL Totals		**221**	**4**	**19**	**23**	**4**	**17**	**21**	**345**	**1**	**0**	**0**	**258**	**1.6**	**151**	**4**	**276**	**45**		....	....	....	....	....	....	....	....
	Other Major League Totals		231	8	33	41	....	....	....	228	....	....	....	....	....	....	....	....	....	....	22	2	4	6	20	....	....	....

Claimed by **Buffalo** from **Detroit** in Expansion Draft, June 10, 1970. Selected by **LA Sharks** (WHA) in 1972 WHA General Player Draft, February 12, 1972. Traded to **Chicago Cougars** (WHA) by **LA Sharks** (WHA) with Don Gordon for Bob Whitlock, February, 1974. Claimed by **Quebec** (WHA) from **Chicago** (WHA) in WHA Dispersal Draft, June, 1975.

• WATSON, JIMMY

Jimmy Watson D – L. 6', 195 lbs. b: Smithers, B.C., 8/19/1952. Philadelphia's 3rd choice, 39th overall, in 1972 Amateur Draft.

Season	Club	League	GP	G	A	Pts	AG	AA	APts	PIM	PP	SH	GW	S	%	TGF	PGF	TGA	PGA	+/–	GP	G	A	Pts	PIM	PP	SH	GW
1968-69	Calgary Centennials	WCJHL	52	2	15	17	....	....	....	26	....	....	....	....	....	....	....	....	....	....	11	1	4	5	....	....	....	....
1969-70	Calgary Centennials	WCJHL	35	3	15	18	....	....	....	18	....	....	....	....	....	....	....	....	....	....	....	....	....	....	....	....	....	....
1970-71	Calgary Centennials	WCJHL	64	9	35	44	....	....	....	118	....	....	....	....	....	....	....	....	....	....	11	3	7	10	8	....	....	....

Season	Club	League	GP	G	A	Pts	AG	AA	APts	PIM	PP	SH	GW	S	%	TGF	PGF	TGA	PGA	+/–	GP	G	A	Pts	PIM	PP	SH	GW
			REGULAR SEASON																		PLAYOFFS							
1971-72	Calgary Centennials	WCJHL	66	13	52	65	....	....	....	50	....	....	....	....	....	....	....	....	....	....	13	3	9	12	6	....	....	....
1972-73	**Philadelphia Flyers**	**NHL**	**4**	**0**	**1**	**1**	**0**	**1**	**1**	**5**	**0**	**0**	**0**	**4**	**0.0**	**3**	**3**	**1**	**0**	**–1**	**2**	**0**	**0**	**0**	**0**	**0**	**0**	**0**
	Richmond Robins	AHL	73	5	33	38	....	....	....	83	....	....	....	....	....	....	....	....	....	....	4	1	2	3	6	....	....	....
1973-74	**Philadelphia Flyers**	**NHL**	**78**	**2**	**18**	**20**	**2**	**16**	**18**	**44**	**1**	**0**	**1**	**113**	**1.8**	**90**	**16**	**60**	**19**	**+33**	**17**	**1**	**2**	**3**	**41**	**1**	**0**	**0**
1974-75	**Philadelphia Flyers**	**NHL**	**68**	**7**	**18**	**25**	**6**	**14**	**20**	**72**	**1**	**0**	**2**	**113**	**6.2**	**83**	**10**	**61**	**29**	**+41**	**17**	**1**	**8**	**9**	**10**	**0**	**0**	**0**
1975-76	**Philadelphia Flyers**	**NHL**	**79**	**2**	**34**	**36**	**2**	**27**	**29**	**66**	**0**	**0**	**0**	**89**	**2.2**	**119**	**7**	**93**	**46**	**+65**	**16**	**1**	**8**	**9**	**6**	**0**	**0**	**0**
1976-77	Canada	C Cup	2	0	0	0	....	....	....	2	....	....	....	....	....	....	....	....	....	....	....	....	....	....	....	....	....	....
	Philadelphia Flyers	**NHL**	**71**	**3**	**23**	**26**	**3**	**19**	**22**	**35**	**0**	**0**	**0**	**72**	**4.2**	**88**	**4**	**70**	**20**	**+34**	**10**	**1**	**2**	**3**	**2**	**0**	**0**	**1**
1977-78	**Philadelphia Flyers**	**NHL**	**71**	**5**	**12**	**17**	**5**	**10**	**15**	**62**	**0**	**0**	**0**	**112**	**4.5**	**75**	**0**	**68**	**26**	**+33**	**12**	**1**	**7**	**8**	**6**	**0**	**0**	**0**
1978-79	**Philadelphia Flyers**	**NHL**	**77**	**9**	**13**	**22**	**8**	**10**	**18**	**52**	**0**	**2**	**0**	**112**	**8.0**	**73**	**2**	**91**	**31**	**+11**	**8**	**0**	**2**	**2**	**2**	**0**	**0**	**0**
1979-80	**Philadelphia Flyers**	**NHL**	**71**	**5**	**18**	**23**	**5**	**14**	**19**	**51**	**0**	**1**	**1**	**99**	**5.1**	**97**	**0**	**81**	**37**	**+53**	**15**	**0**	**4**	**4**	**20**	**0**	**0**	**0**
1980-81	**Philadelphia Flyers**	**NHL**	**18**	**2**	**2**	**4**	**2**	**1**	**3**	**6**	**1**	**0**	**0**	**14**	**14.3**	**21**	**1**	**11**	**5**	**+14**	....	....	....	....	....	....	....	....
1981-82	**Philadelphia Flyers**	**NHL**	**76**	**3**	**9**	**12**	**2**	**6**	**8**	**99**	**0**	**0**	**1**	**67**	**4.5**	**74**	**4**	**87**	**29**	**+12**	**4**	**0**	**1**	**1**	**2**	**0**	**0**	**0**
	NHL Totals		**613**	**38**	**148**	**186**	**35**	**118**	**153**	**492**	**3**	**3**	**5**	**795**	**4.8**	**723**	**47**	**623**	**242**		**101**	**5**	**34**	**39**	**89**	**1**	**0**	**1**

WCJHL All-Star Team (1972) • NHL Plus/Minus Leader (1980)

Played in NHL All-Star Game (1975, 1976, 1977, 1978, 1980)

• WATSON, JOE

Joe Watson D – R. 5'10", 185 lbs. b: Smithers, B.C., 7/6/1943.

Season	Club	League	GP	G	A	Pts	AG	AA	APts	PIM	PP	SH	GW	S	%	TGF	PGF	TGA	PGA	+/–	GP	G	A	Pts	PIM	PP	SH	GW
1962-63	Estevan Bruins	SJHL	53	5	24	29	....	....	....	74	....	....	....	....	....	....	....	....	....	....	11	2	10	12	14	....	....	....
1963-64	Minneapolis Bruins	CHL	71	0	20	20	....	....	....	55	....	....	....	....	....	....	....	....	....	....	5	0	0	0	2	....	....	....
1964-65	**Boston Bruins**	**NHL**	**4**	**0**	**1**	**1**	**0**	**1**	**1**	**0**	....	....	....	....	....	....	....	....	....	....	....	....	....	....	....	....	....	....
	Minneapolis Bruins	CHL	65	3	23	26	....	....	....	38	....	....	....	....	....	....	....	....	....	....	5	0	1	1	2	....	....	....
1965-66	Oklahoma City Blazers	CHL	69	8	24	32	....	....	....	58	....	....	....	....	....	....	....	....	....	....	9	1	3	4	6	....	....	....
1966-67	**Boston Bruins**	**NHL**	**69**	**2**	**13**	**15**	**2**	**13**	**15**	**38**	....	....	....	....	....	....	....	....	....	....	....	....	....	....	....	....	....	....
1967-68	**Philadelphia Flyers**	**NHL**	**73**	**5**	**14**	**19**	**6**	**15**	**21**	**56**	**1**	**0**	**1**	**91**	**5.5**	**80**	**6**	**95**	**33**	**+12**	**7**	**1**	**1**	**2**	**28**	**0**	**0**	**0**
1968-69	**Philadelphia Flyers**	**NHL**	**60**	**2**	**8**	**10**	**2**	**7**	**9**	**14**	**0**	**0**	**0**	**82**	**2.4**	**49**	**1**	**86**	**17**	**–21**	**4**	**0**	**0**	**0**	**0**	**0**	**0**	**0**
1969-70	**Philadelphia Flyers**	**NHL**	**54**	**3**	**11**	**14**	**3**	**11**	**14**	**28**	**1**	**0**	**0**	**102**	**2.9**	**46**	**3**	**61**	**18**	**0**	....	....	....	....	....	....	....	....
1970-71	**Philadelphia Flyers**	**NHL**	**57**	**3**	**7**	**10**	**3**	**6**	**9**	**50**	**0**	**0**	**0**	**61**	**4.9**	**43**	**1**	**39**	**6**	**+9**	**1**	**0**	**0**	**0**	**0**	**0**	**0**	**0**
1971-72	**Philadelphia Flyers**	**NHL**	**65**	**3**	**7**	**10**	**3**	**6**	**9**	**38**	**0**	**0**	**1**	**110**	**2.7**	**39**	**0**	**76**	**20**	**–17**	....	....	....	....	....	....	....	....
1972-73	**Philadelphia Flyers**	**NHL**	**63**	**2**	**24**	**26**	**2**	**20**	**22**	**46**	**0**	**0**	**1**	**72**	**2.8**	**87**	**8**	**77**	**28**	**+30**	**11**	**0**	**2**	**2**	**12**	**0**	**0**	**0**
1973-74	**Philadelphia Flyers**	**NHL**	**74**	**1**	**17**	**18**	**1**	**15**	**16**	**34**	**0**	**0**	**0**	**75**	**1.3**	**73**	**2**	**54**	**11**	**+28**	**17**	**1**	**4**	**5**	**24**	**0**	**0**	**0**
1974-75	**Philadelphia Flyers**	**NHL**	**80**	**6**	**17**	**23**	**6**	**13**	**19**	**42**	**0**	**0**	**0**	**115**	**5.2**	**92**	**6**	**84**	**40**	**+42**	**17**	**0**	**4**	**4**	**6**	**0**	**0**	**0**
1975-76	**Philadelphia Flyers**	**NHL**	**78**	**2**	**22**	**24**	**2**	**17**	**19**	**28**	**0**	**0**	**2**	**88**	**2.3**	**96**	**2**	**73**	**35**	**+56**	**16**	**1**	**1**	**2**	**10**	**0**	**0**	**0**
1976-77	**Philadelphia Flyers**	**NHL**	**77**	**4**	**26**	**30**	**4**	**21**	**25**	**39**	**0**	**0**	**1**	**101**	**4.0**	**87**	**1**	**82**	**25**	**+29**	**10**	**0**	**0**	**0**	**2**	**0**	**0**	**0**
1977-78	**Philadelphia Flyers**	**NHL**	**65**	**5**	**9**	**14**	**5**	**7**	**12**	**22**	**0**	**0**	**1**	**68**	**7.4**	**57**	**0**	**47**	**13**	**+23**	**1**	**0**	**0**	**0**	**0**	**0**	**0**	**0**
1978-79	**Colorado Rockies**	**NHL**	**16**	**0**	**2**	**2**	**0**	**2**	**2**	**12**	**0**	**0**	**0**	**20**	**0.0**	**13**	**1**	**30**	**5**	**–13**	....	....	....	....	....	....	....	....
	NHL Totals		**835**	**38**	**178**	**216**	**39**	**154**	**193**	**447**	**2**	**0**	**7**	**985**	**3.9**	**762**	**31**	**804**	**251**		**84**	**3**	**12**	**15**	**82**	**0**	**0**	**0**

CHL First All-Star Team (1966)

Played in NHL All-Star Game (1974, 1977)

Claimed by **Philadelphia** from **Boston** in Expansion Draft, June 6, 1967. Traded to **Colorado** by **Philadelphia** for cash, August 31, 1978.

• WATT, MIKE

Mike Watt LW – L. 6'2", 212 lbs. b: Seaforth, Ont., 3/31/1976. Edmonton's 3rd choice, 32nd overall, in 1994 Entry Draft.

Season	Club	League	GP	G	A	Pts	AG	AA	APts	PIM	PP	SH	GW	S	%	TGF	PGF	TGA	PGA	+/–	GP	G	A	Pts	PIM	PP	SH	GW
1994-95	Michigan State Spartans	CCHA	39	12	6	18	....	....	....	64	....	....	....	....	....	....	....	....	....	....	....	....	....	....	....	....	....	....
1995-96	Michigan State Spartans	CCHA	37	17	22	39	....	....	....	60	....	....	....	....	....	....	....	....	....	....	....	....	....	....	....	....	....	....
	Canada	WJC-A	6	1	2	3	....	....	....	6	....	....	....	....	....	....	....	....	....	....	....	....	....	....	....	....	....	....
1996-97	Michigan State Spartans	CCHA	39	24	17	41	....	....	....	109	....	....	....	....	....	....	....	....	....	....	....	....	....	....	....	....	....	....
1997-98	**Edmonton Oilers**	**NHL**	**14**	**1**	**2**	**3**	**1**	**2**	**3**	**4**	**0**	**0**	**1**	**14**	**7.1**	**6**	**3**	**7**	**0**	**–4**	....	....	....	....	....	....	....	....
	Hamilton Bulldogs	AHL	63	24	25	49	....	....	....	65	....	....	....	....	....	....	....	....	....	....	9	2	2	4	8	....	....	....
	NHL Totals		**14**	**1**	**2**	**3**	**1**	**2**	**3**	**4**	**0**	**0**	**1**	**14**	**7.1**	**6**	**3**	**7**	**0**		....	....	....	....	....	....	....	....

Traded to **NY Islanders** by **Edmonton** for Eric Fichaud, June 18, 1998.

• WATTERS, TIM

Tim "Muddy" Watters D – L. 5'11", 185 lbs. b: Kamloops, B.C., 7/25/1959. Winnipeg's 6th choice, 124th overall, in 1979 Entry Draft.

Season	Club	League	GP	G	A	Pts	AG	AA	APts	PIM	PP	SH	GW	S	%	TGF	PGF	TGA	PGA	+/–	GP	G	A	Pts	PIM	PP	SH	GW
1976-77	Kamloops Blazers	BCJHL	60	10	38	48	....	....	....	....	....	....	....	....	....	....	....	....	....	....	....	....	....	....	....	....	....	....
1977-78	Michigan Tech Huskies	WCHA	37	1	15	16	....	....	....	47	....	....	....	....	....	....	....	....	....	....	....	....	....	....	....	....	....	....
1978-79	Michigan Tech Huskies	WCHA	38	6	21	27	....	....	....	48	....	....	....	....	....	....	....	....	....	....	....	....	....	....	....	....	....	....
1979-80	Canada	Nat-Team	56	8	21	29	....	....	....	43	....	....	....	....	....	....	....	....	....	....	....	....	....	....	....	....	....	....
	Canada	Olympics	6	1	1	2	....	....	....	0	....	....	....	....	....	....	....	....	....	....	....	....	....	....	....	....	....	....
1980-81	Michigan Tech Huskies	WCHA	43	12	38	50	....	....	....	36	....	....	....	....	....	....	....	....	....	....	....	....	....	....	....	....	....	....
1981-82	**Winnipeg Jets**	**NHL**	**69**	**2**	**22**	**24**	**2**	**15**	**17**	**97**	**0**	**0**	**0**	**66**	**3.0**	**94**	**3**	**102**	**25**	**+14**	**4**	**0**	**1**	**1**	**8**	**0**	**0**	**0**
	Tulsa Oilers	CHL	5	1	2	3	....	....	....	0	....	....	....	....	....	....	....	....	....	....	....	....	....	....	....	....	....	....
1982-83	**Winnipeg Jets**	**NHL**	**77**	**5**	**18**	**23**	**4**	**12**	**16**	**98**	**2**	**0**	**1**	**57**	**8.8**	**85**	**5**	**125**	**35**	**–10**	**3**	**0**	**0**	**0**	**2**	**0**	**0**	**0**
	Canada	WEC-A	10	0	0	0	....	....	....	8	....	....	....	....	....	....	....	....	....	....	....	....	....	....	....	....	....	....
1983-84	**Winnipeg Jets**	**NHL**	**74**	**3**	**20**	**23**	**2**	**14**	**16**	**169**	**1**	**0**	**1**	**66**	**4.5**	**122**	**18**	**129**	**32**	**+7**	**3**	**1**	**0**	**1**	**2**	**0**	**0**	**0**
1984-85	**Winnipeg Jets**	**NHL**	**63**	**2**	**20**	**22**	**2**	**14**	**16**	**74**	**0**	**0**	**1**	**54**	**3.7**	**80**	**1**	**78**	**19**	**+20**	**8**	**0**	**1**	**1**	**16**	**0**	**0**	**0**
1985-86	**Winnipeg Jets**	**NHL**	**56**	**6**	**8**	**14**	**5**	**5**	**10**	**97**	**0**	**0**	**0**	**37**	**16.2**	**65**	**1**	**89**	**15**	**–10**	....	....	....	....	....	....	....	....
1986-87	**Winnipeg Jets**	**NHL**	**63**	**3**	**13**	**16**	**3**	**9**	**12**	**119**	**0**	**0**	**0**	**44**	**6.8**	**52**	**0**	**56**	**9**	**+5**	**10**	**0**	**0**	**0**	**21**	**0**	**0**	**0**
1987-88	Canada	Nat-Team	2	0	2	2	....	....	....	0	....	....	....	....	....	....	....	....	....	....	....	....	....	....	....	....	....	....
	Canada	Olympics	8	0	1	1	....	....	....	2	....	....	....	....	....	....	....	....	....	....	....	....	....	....	....	....	....	....
	Winnipeg Jets	**NHL**	**36**	**0**	**0**	**0**	**0**	**0**	**0**	**106**	**0**	**0**	**0**	**21**	**0.0**	**20**	**1**	**40**	**9**	**–12**	**4**	**0**	**0**	**0**	**4**	**0**	**0**	**0**
1988-89	**Los Angeles Kings**	**NHL**	**76**	**3**	**18**	**21**	**3**	**13**	**16**	**168**	**0**	**0**	**0**	**62**	**4.8**	**96**	**4**	**109**	**34**	**+17**	**11**	**0**	**1**	**1**	**6**	**0**	**0**	**0**
1989-90	**Los Angeles Kings**	**NHL**	**62**	**1**	**10**	**11**	**1**	**7**	**8**	**92**	**0**	**0**	**0**	**60**	**2.0**	**70**	**3**	**75**	**31**	**+23**	**4**	**0**	**0**	**0**	**6**	**0**	**0**	**0**
1990-91	**Los Angeles Kings**	**NHL**	**45**	**0**	**4**	**4**	**0**	**3**	**3**	**92**	**0**	**0**	**0**	**29**	**0.0**	**40**	**0**	**50**	**17**	**+7**	**7**	**0**	**0**	**0**	**12**	**0**	**0**	**0**
1991-92	**Los Angeles Kings**	**NHL**	**37**	**0**	**7**	**7**	**0**	**5**	**5**	**92**	**0**	**0**	**0**	**29**	**0.0**	**24**	**0**	**45**	**19**	**–2**	**6**	**0**	**0**	**0**	**8**	**0**	**0**	**0**
	Phoenix Roadrunners	IHL	5	0	3	3	....	....	....	6	....	....	....	....	....	....	....	....	....	....	....	....	....	....	....	....	....	....
1992-93	**Los Angeles Kings**	**NHL**	**22**	**0**	**2**	**2**	**0**	**1**	**1**	**18**	**0**	**0**	**0**	**8**	**0.0**	**16**	**0**	**31**	**12**	**–3**	**22**	**0**	**2**	**2**	**30**	**0**	**0**	**0**
	Phoenix Roadrunners	IHL	31	3	3	6	....	....	....	43	....	....	....	....	....	....	....	....	....	....	....	....	....	....	....	....	....	....
1993-94	**Los Angeles Kings**	**NHL**	**60**	**1**	**9**	**10**	**1**	**7**	**8**	**67**	**0**	**1**	**0**	**38**	**2.6**	**38**	**0**	**70**	**21**	**–11**	....	....	....	....	....	....	....	....
1994-95	**Los Angeles Kings**	**NHL**	**1**	**0**	**0**	**0**	**0**	**0**	**0**	**0**	**0**	**0**	**0**	**1**	**0.0**	**1**	**0**	**1**	**1**	**+1**	....	....	....	....	....	....	....	....
	Phoenix Roadrunners	IHL	36	1	8	9	....	....	....	58	....	....	....	....	....	....	....	....	....	....	7	0	1	1	10	....	....	....
	NHL Totals		**741**	**26**	**151**	**177**	**23**	**105**	**128**	**1209**	**3**	**1**	**3**	**562**	**4.6**	**803**	**36**	**1000**	**279**		**82**	**1**	**5**	**6**	**115**	**0**	**0**	**0**

WCHA First All-Star Team (1981) • NCAA West First All-American Team (1981) • NCAA Championship All-Tournament Team (1981)

Signed as a free agent by **LA Kings**, June 27, 1988.

• WATTS, BRIAN

Brian Watts LW – L. 6', 180 lbs. b: Hagersville, Ont., 9/10/1947. Detroit's 2nd choice, 7th overall, in 1964 Amateur Draft.

Season	Club	League	GP	G	A	Pts	AG	AA	APts	PIM	PP	SH	GW	S	%	TGF	PGF	TGA	PGA	+/–	GP	G	A	Pts	PIM	PP	SH	GW
1964-65	Hamilton Red Wings	OHA	49	5	8	13	....	....	....	31	....	....	....	....	....	....	....	....	....	....	....	....	....	....	....	....	....	....
1965-66	Hamilton Red Wings	OHA	48	9	15	24	....	....	....	51	....	....	....	....	....	....	....	....	....	....	5	0	2	2	0	....	....	....
1966-67	Michigan Tech Huskies	WCHA	DID NOT PLAY – FRESHMAN																									
1967-68	Michigan Tech Huskies	WCHA	32	14	17	31	....	....	....	39	....	....	....	....	....	....	....	....	....	....	....	....	....	....	....	....	....	....
1968-69	Michigan Tech Huskies	WCHA	31	7	15	22	....	....	....	38	....	....	....	....	....	....	....	....	....	....	....	....	....	....	....	....	....	....
1969-70	Michigan Tech Huskies	WCHA	31	16	20	36	....	....	....	60	....	....	....	....	....	....	....	....	....	....	....	....	....	....	....	....	....	....
1970-71	Port Huron Flags	IHL	44	9	14	23	....	....	....	25	....	....	....	....	....	....	....	....	....	....	....	....	....	....	....	....	....	....
1971-72	Fort Worth Wings	CHL	71	26	38	64	....	....	....	69	....	....	....	....	....	....	....	....	....	....	7	1	3	4	13	....	....	....
1972-73	Virginia Wings	AHL	72	20	25	45	....	....	....	43	....	....	....	....	....	....	....	....	....	....	13	4	4	8	16	....	....	....
1973-74	London Lions	Britain	70	34	30	64	....	....	....	30	....	....	....	....	....	....	....	....	....	....	....	....	....	....	....	....	....	....
1974-75	Virginia Wings	AHL	70	14	17	31	....	....	....	57	....	....	....	....	....	....	....	....	....	....	5	0	0	0	2	....	....	....
1975-76	**Detroit Red Wings**	**NHL**	**4**	**0**	**0**	**0**	**0**	**0**	**0**	**0**	**0**	**0**	**0**	**0**	**0.0**	**0**	**0**	**0**	**0**	**0**	....	....	....	....	....	....	....	....
	New Haven Nighthawks	CHL	57	8	9	17	....	....	....	14	....	....	....	....	....	....	....	....	....	....	....	....	....	....	....	....	....	....
1976-77	Bjorkloven Umea	Sweden	25	7	1	8	....	....	....	6	....	....	....	....	....	....	....	....	....	....	....	....	....	....	....	....	....	....
	NHL Totals		**4**	**0**	**0**	**0**	**0**	**0**	**0**	**0**	**0**	**0**	**0**	**0**	**0.0**	**0**	**0**	**0**	**0**		....	....	....	....	....	....	....	....

• WEBB, STEVE

Steve Webb RW – R. 6', 195 lbs. b: Peterborough, Ont., 4/20/1975. Buffalo's 8th choice, 176th overall, in 1994 Entry Draft.

			REGULAR SEASON																		PLAYOFFS							
Season	Club	League	GP	G	A	Pts	AG	AA	APts	PIM	PP	SH	GW	S	%	TGF	PGF	TGA	PGA	+/–	GP	G	A	Pts	PIM	PP	SH	GW
1992-93	Windsor Spitfires	OHL	60	14	25	39	....	....	....	190	....	....	....	....	....	....	....	....	....	....	....	....	....	....	....	....	....	....
1993-94	Peterborough Petes	OHL	35	6	16	22	....	....	....	126	....	....	....	....	....	....	....	....	....	....	6	1	1	2	10	....	....	....
1994-95	Peterborough Petes	OHL	42	8	16	24	....	....	....	109	....	....	....	....	....	....	....	....	....	....	11	3	3	6	22	....	....	....
1995-96	Muskegon Fury	ColHL	58	18	24	42	....	....	....	263	....	....	....	....	....	....	....	....	....	....	5	1	2	3	22	....	....	....
	Detroit Vipers	IHL	4	0	0	0	....	....	....	24	....	....	....	....	....	....	....	....	....	....	....	....	....	....	....	....	....	....
1996-97	**New York Islanders**	**NHL**	**41**	**1**	**4**	**5**	**1**	**4**	**5**	**144**	**1**	**0**	**0**	**21**	**4.8**	**10**	**2**	**18**	**0**	**–10**	....	....	....	....	....	....	....	....
	Kentucky Thoroughblades	AHL	25	6	6	12	....	....	....	103	....	....	....	....	....	....	....	....	....	....	2	0	0	0	19	....	....	....
1997-98	**New York Islanders**	**NHL**	**20**	**0**	**0**	**0**	**0**	**0**	**0**	**35**	**0**	**0**	**0**	**6**	**0.0**	**4**	**0**	**6**	**0**	**–2**	....	....	....	....	....	....	....	....
	Kentucky Thoroughblades	AHL	37	5	13	18	....	....	....	139	....	....	....	....	....	....	....	....	....	....	3	0	1	1	10	....	....	....
	NHL Totals		**61**	**1**	**4**	**5**	**1**	**4**	**5**	**179**	**1**	**0**	**0**	**27**	**3.7**	**14**	**2**	**24**	**0**		....	....	....	....	....	....	....	....

Signed as a free agent by **NY Islanders**, October 10, 1996.

• WEBSTER, TOM

Tom Webster RW – R. 5'10", 170 lbs. b: Kirkland Lake, Ont., 10/4/1948. Boston's 4th choice, 19th overall, in 1966 Amateur Draft.

Season	Club	League	GP	G	A	Pts	AG	AA	APts	PIM	PP	SH	GW	S	%	TGF	PGF	TGA	PGA	+/–	GP	G	A	Pts	PIM	PP	SH	GW
1965-66	Niagara Falls Flyers	OHA	43	16	27	43	....	....	....	16	....	....	....	....	....	....	....	....	....	....	6	2	3	5	0	....	....	....
1966-67	Niagara Falls Flyers	OHA	47	19	26	45	....	....	....	26	....	....	....	....	....	....	....	....	....	....	13	14	8	22	4	....	....	....
1967-68	Niagara Falls Flyers	OHA	54	50	64	*114	....	....	....	55	....	....	....	....	....	....	....	....	....	....	19	13	13	26	20	....	....	....
1968-69	**Boston Bruins**	**NHL**	**9**	**0**	**2**	**2**	**0**	**2**	**2**	**9**	**0**	**0**	**0**	**9**	**0.0**	**5**	**1**	**5**	**0**	**–1**	**1**	**0**	**0**	**0**	**0**	**0**	**0**	**0**
	Oklahoma City Blazers	CHL	44	29	42	71	....	....	....	31	....	....	....	....	....	....	....	....	....	....	12	*10	8	18	19	....	....	....
1969-70	**Boston Bruins**	**NHL**	**2**	**0**	**1**	**1**	**0**	**1**	**1**	**2**	**0**	**0**	**0**	**4**	**0.0**	**3**	**2**	**2**	**0**	**–1**	....	....	....	....	....	....	....	....
	Oklahoma City Blazers	CHL	49	29	35	64	....	....	....	49	....	....	....	....	....	....	....	....	....	....	....	....	....	....	....	....	....	....
1970-71	**Detroit Red Wings**	**NHL**	**78**	**30**	**37**	**67**	**31**	**33**	**64**	**40**	**7**	**0**	**5**	**183**	**16.4**	**85**	**29**	**104**	**1**	**–47**	....	....	....	....	....	....	....	....
1971-72	**Detroit Red Wings**	**NHL**	**5**	**1**	**1**	**2**	**1**	**1**	**2**	**4**	**1**	**0**	**0**	**7**	**14.3**	**5**	**3**	**7**	**0**	**–5**	....	....	....	....	....	....	....	....
	California Golden Seals	**NHL**	**7**	**2**	**1**	**3**	**2**	**1**	**3**	**6**	**0**	**0**	**0**	**6**	**33.3**	**6**	**3**	**3**	**1**	**+1**	....	....	....	....	....	....	....	....
1972-73	New England Whalers	WHA	77	53	50	103	....	....	....	89	....	....	....	....	....	....	....	....	....	....	15	12	14	26	6	....	....	....
1973-74	New England Whalers	WHA	64	43	27	70	....	....	....	28	....	....	....	....	....	....	....	....	....	....	3	5	0	5	7	....	....	....
1974-75	Canada	Summit	4	2	0	2	....	....	....	4	....	....	....	....	....	....	....	....	....	....	....	....	....	....	....	....	....	....
	New England Whalers	WHA	66	40	24	64	....	....	....	52	....	....	....	....	....	....	....	....	....	....	3	0	2	2	0	....	....	....
1975-76	New England Whalers	WHA	55	33	50	83	....	....	....	24	....	....	....	....	....	....	....	....	....	....	17	10	9	19	6	....	....	....
1976-77	New England Whalers	WHA	70	36	49	85	....	....	....	43	....	....	....	....	....	....	....	....	....	....	5	1	1	2	0	....	....	....
1977-78	New England Whalers	WHA	20	15	5	20	....	....	....	5	....	....	....	....	....	....	....	....	....	....	....	....	....	....	....	....	....	....
1978-79			DID NOT PLAY – INJURED																									
1979-80	**Detroit Red Wings**	**NHL**	**1**	**0**	**0**	**0**	**0**	**0**	**0**	**0**	**0**	**0**	**0**	**1**	**0.0**	**0**	**0**	**0**	**0**	**0**	....	....	....	....	....	....	....	....
	Adirondack Red Wings	AHL	12	4	5	9	....	....	....	2	....	....	....	....	....	....	....	....	....	....	....	....	....	....	....	....	....	....
	NHL Totals		**102**	**33**	**42**	**75**	**34**	**38**	**72**	**61**	**8**	**0**	**5**	**210**	**15.7**	**104**	**38**	**121**	**2**		**1**	**0**	**0**	**0**	**0**	**0**	**0**	**0**
	Other Major League Totals		352	220	205	425	....	....	....	241	....	....	....	....	....	....	....	....	....	....	43	28	26	54	19	....	....	....

OHA Second All-Star Team (1968) • WHA Second All-Star Team (1973)

Claimed by **Buffalo** from **Boston** in Expansion Draft, June 10, 1970. Traded to **Detroit** by **Buffalo** for Roger Crozier, June 10, 1970. Traded to **California** by **Detroit** for Ron Stackhouse, October 22, 1971. Selected by **New England** (WHA) in 1972 WHA General Player Draft, February 12, 1972. Signed as a free agent by **Detroit**, September 15, 1979.

• WEIGHT, DOUG

Doug Weight C – L. 5'11", 200 lbs. b: Warren, MI, 1/21/1971. NY Rangers' 2nd choice, 34th overall, in 1990 Entry Draft.

Season	Club	League	GP	G	A	Pts	AG	AA	APts	PIM	PP	SH	GW	S	%	TGF	PGF	TGA	PGA	+/–	GP	G	A	Pts	PIM	PP	SH	GW
1988-89	Bloomfield Jets	NAJHL	34	26	53	79	....	....	....	105	....	....	....	....	....	....	....	....	....	....	....	....	....	....	....	....	....	....
1989-90	Lake Superior State	CCHA	46	21	48	69	....	....	....	44	....	....	....	....	....	....	....	....	....	....	....	....	....	....	....	....	....	....
1990-91	Lake Superior State	CCHA	42	29	46	75	....	....	....	86	....	....	....	....	....	....	....	....	....	....	....	....	....	....	....	....	....	....
	New York Rangers	**NHL**	....	....	....	....	....	....	....	....	....	....	....	....	....	....	....	....	....	....	**1**	**0**	**0**	**0**	**0**	....	....	....
1991-92	**New York Rangers**	**NHL**	**53**	**8**	**22**	**30**	**7**	**17**	**24**	**23**	**0**	**0**	**2**	**72**	**11.1**	**45**	**17**	**34**	**3**	**–3**	**7**	**2**	**2**	**4**	**0**	**1**	**0**	**0**
	Binghamton Rangers	AHL	9	3	14	17	....	....	....	2	....	....	....	....	....	....	....	....	....	....	4	1	4	5	6	....	....	....
1992-93	**New York Rangers**	**NHL**	**65**	**15**	**25**	**40**	**12**	**17**	**29**	**55**	**3**	**0**	**1**	**90**	**16.7**	**58**	**18**	**36**	**0**	**+4**	....	....	....	....	....	....	....	....
	Edmonton Oilers	**NHL**	**13**	**2**	**6**	**8**	**2**	**4**	**6**	**10**	**0**	**0**	**0**	**35**	**5.7**	**8**	**2**	**14**	**6**	**–2**	....	....	....	....	....	....	....	....
	United States	WC-A	6	0	6	6	....	....	....	12	....	....	....	....	....	....	....	....	....	....	....	....	....	....	....	....	....	....
1993-94	**Edmonton Oilers**	**NHL**	**84**	**24**	**50**	**74**	**22**	**39**	**61**	**47**	**4**	**1**	**1**	**188**	**12.8**	**102**	**42**	**100**	**18**	**–22**	....	....	....	....	....	....	....	....
	United States	WC-A	8	0	4	4	....	....	....	16	....	....	....	....	....	....	....	....	....	....	....	....	....	....	....	....	....	....
1994-95	SB Rosenheim	Germany	8	2	3	5	....	....	....	18	....	....	....	....	....	....	....	....	....	....	....	....	....	....	....	....	....	....
	Edmonton Oilers	**NHL**	**48**	**7**	**33**	**40**	**12**	**49**	**61**	**69**	**1**	**0**	**1**	**104**	**6.7**	**53**	**27**	**45**	**2**	**–17**	....	....	....	....	....	....	....	....
1995-96	**Edmonton Oilers**	**NHL**	**82**	**25**	**79**	**104**	**25**	**65**	**90**	**95**	**9**	**0**	**2**	**204**	**12.3**	**129**	**59**	**94**	**5**	**–19**	....	....	....	....	....	....	....	....
1996-97	United States	W Cup	7	3	4	7	....	....	....	12	....	....	....	....	....	....	....	....	....	....	....	....	....	....	....	....	....	....
	Edmonton Oilers	**NHL**	**80**	**21**	**61**	**82**	**22**	**54**	**76**	**80**	**4**	**0**	**2**	**235**	**8.9**	**123**	**64**	**67**	**9**	**+1**	**12**	**3**	**8**	**11**	**8**	**0**	**0**	**0**
1997-98	**Edmonton Oilers**	**NHL**	**79**	**26**	**44**	**70**	**31**	**43**	**74**	**69**	**9**	**0**	**4**	**205**	**12.7**	**103**	**50**	**61**	**9**	**+1**	**12**	**2**	**7**	**9**	**14**	**2**	**0**	**1**
	United States	Olympics	4	0	2	2	....	....	....	2	....	....	....	....	....	....	....	....	....	....	....	....	....	....	....	....	....	....
	NHL Totals		**504**	**128**	**320**	**448**	**133**	**288**	**421**	**448**	**30**	**1**	**13**	**1133**	**11.3**	**621**	**279**	**451**	**52**		**32**	**7**	**17**	**24**	**22**	**3**	**0**	**1**

CCHA First All-Star Team (1991) • NCAA West Second All-American Team (1991)

Played in NHL All-Star Game (1996, 1998)

Traded to **Edmonton** by **NY Rangers** for Esa Tikkanen, March 17, 1993.

• WEINRICH, ERIC

Eric Weinrich D – L. 6'1", 210 lbs. b: Roanoke, VA, 12/19/1966. New Jersey's 3rd choice, 32nd overall, in 1985 Entry Draft.

Season	Club	League	GP	G	A	Pts	AG	AA	APts	PIM	PP	SH	GW	S	%	TGF	PGF	TGA	PGA	+/–	GP	G	A	Pts	PIM	PP	SH	GW
1984-85	North Yarmouth Academy	H.S.	20	6	21	27	....	....	....	....	....	....	....	....	....	....	....	....	....	....	....	....	....	....	....	....	....	....
	United States	WJC-A	7	1	1	2	....	....	....	8	....	....	....	....	....	....	....	....	....	....	....	....	....	....	....	....	....	....
1985-86	University of Maine	H.E.	34	0	14	14	....	....	....	26	....	....	....	....	....	....	....	....	....	....	....	....	....	....	....	....	....	....
	United States	WJC-A	7	1	0	1	....	....	....	4	....	....	....	....	....	....	....	....	....	....	....	....	....	....	....	....	....	....
1986-87	University of Maine	H.E.	41	12	32	44	....	....	....	59	....	....	....	....	....	....	....	....	....	....	....	....	....	....	....	....	....	....
1987-88	University of Maine	H.E.	8	4	7	11	....	....	....	22	....	....	....	....	....	....	....	....	....	....	....	....	....	....	....	....	....	....
	United States	Nat-Team	38	3	9	12	....	....	....	24	....	....	....	....	....	....	....	....	....	....	....	....	....	....	....	....	....	....
	United States	Olympics	3	0	0	0	....	....	....	0	....	....	....	....	....	....	....	....	....	....	....	....	....	....	....	....	....	....
1988-89	**New Jersey Devils**	**NHL**	**2**	**0**	**0**	**0**	**0**	**0**	**0**	**0**	**0**	**0**	**0**	**3**	**0.0**	**1**	**0**	**3**	**1**	**–1**	....	....	....	....	....	....	....	....
	Utica Devils	AHL	80	17	27	44	....	....	....	70	....	....	....	....	....	....	....	....	....	....	5	0	1	1	4	....	....	....
1989-90	**New Jersey Devils**	**NHL**	**19**	**2**	**7**	**9**	**2**	**5**	**7**	**11**	**1**	**0**	**1**	**16**	**12.5**	**25**	**9**	**15**	**0**	**+1**	**6**	**1**	**3**	**4**	**17**	**0**	**0**	**0**
	Utica Devils	AHL	57	12	48	60	....	....	....	38	....	....	....	....	....	....	....	....	....	....	....	....	....	....	....	....	....	....
1990-91	**New Jersey Devils**	**NHL**	**76**	**4**	**34**	**38**	**4**	**26**	**30**	**48**	**1**	**0**	**0**	**96**	**4.2**	**95**	**28**	**62**	**5**	**+10**	**7**	**1**	**2**	**3**	**6**	**1**	**0**	**0**
	United Statos	WEC-A	10	2	1	3	....	....	....	6	....	....	....	....	....	....	....	....	....	....	....	....	....	....	....	....	....	....
1991-92	United States	C Cup	8	0	0	0	....	....	....	2	....	....	....	....	....	....	....	....	....	....	....	....	....	....	....	....	....	....
	New Jersey Devils	**NHL**	**76**	**7**	**25**	**32**	**6**	**19**	**25**	**55**	**5**	**0**	**0**	**97**	**7.2**	**95**	**25**	**66**	**6**	**+10**	**7**	**0**	**2**	**2**	**4**	**0**	**0**	**0**
1992-93	**Hartford Whalers**	**NHL**	**79**	**7**	**29**	**36**	**6**	**20**	**26**	**76**	**0**	**2**	**2**	**104**	**6.7**	**114**	**27**	**129**	**31**	**–11**	....	....	....	....	....	....	....	....
	United States	WC-A	6	0	1	1	....	....	....	0	....	....	....	....	....	....	....	....	....	....	....	....	....	....	....	....	....	....
1993-94	**Hartford Whalers**	**NHL**	**8**	**1**	**1**	**2**	**1**	**1**	**2**	**2**	**1**	**0**	**0**	**10**	**10.0**	**5**	**3**	**15**	**8**	**–5**	....	....	....	....	....	....	....	....
	Chicago Blackhawks	**NHL**	**54**	**3**	**23**	**26**	**3**	**18**	**21**	**31**	**1**	**0**	**2**	**105**	**2.9**	**59**	**19**	**52**	**18**	**+6**	**6**	**0**	**2**	**2**	**6**	**0**	**0**	**0**
1994-95	**Chicago Blackhawks**	**NHL**	**48**	**3**	**10**	**13**	**5**	**15**	**20**	**33**	**1**	**0**	**2**	**50**	**6.0**	**39**	**10**	**42**	**14**	**+1**	**16**	**1**	**5**	**6**	**4**	**0**	**0**	**0**
1995-96	**Chicago Blackhawks**	**NHL**	**77**	**5**	**10**	**15**	**5**	**8**	**13**	**65**	**0**	**0**	**0**	**76**	**6.6**	**74**	**7**	**70**	**17**	**+14**	**10**	**1**	**4**	**5**	**10**	**1**	**0**	**0**
1996-97	United States	WC-A	6	0	4	4	....	....	....	2	....	....	....	....	....	....	....	....	....	....	....	....	....	....	....	....	....	....
	Chicago Blackhawks	**NHL**	**81**	**7**	**25**	**32**	**7**	**22**	**29**	**62**	**1**	**0**	**0**	**115**	**6.1**	**82**	**10**	**76**	**23**	**+19**	**6**	**0**	**1**	**1**	**4**	**0**	**0**	**0**
	United States	WC-A	6	0	2	2	....	....	....	16	....	....	....	....	....	....	....	....	....	....	....	....	....	....	....	....	....	....
1997-98	**Chicago Blackhawks**	**NHL**	**82**	**2**	**21**	**23**	**2**	**20**	**22**	**106**	**0**	**0**	**0**	**85**	**2.4**	**71**	**14**	**79**	**32**	**+10**	....	....	....	....	....	....	....	....
	NHL Totals		**602**	**41**	**185**	**226**	**41**	**154**	**195**	**489**	**11**	**2**	**7**	**757**	**5.4**	**660**	**152**	**609**	**155**		**58**	**4**	**19**	**23**	**51**	**2**	**0**	**0**

Hockey East First All-Star Team (1987) • NCAA East Second All-American Team (1987) • AHL First All-Star Team (1990) • Won Eddie Shore Plaque (Outstanding Defenseman - AHL) (1990) • NHL/Upper Deck All-Rookie Team (1991)

Traded to **Hartford** by **New Jersey** with Sean Burke for Bobby Holik, Hartford's 2nd round choice (Jay Pandolfo) in 1993 Entry Draft and future considerations, August 28, 1992. Traded to **Chicago** by **Hartford** with Patrick Poulin for Steve Larmer and Bryan Marchment, November 2, 1993.

• WEIR, STAN

Stan Weir C – L. 6'1", 180 lbs. b: Ponoka, Alta., 3/17/1952. California's 2nd choice, 28th overall, in 1972 Amateur Draft.

			REGULAR SEASON																		PLAYOFFS							
Season	Club	League	GP	G	A	Pts	AG	AA	APts	PIM	PP	SH	GW	S	%	TGF	PGF	TGA	PGA	+/–	GP	G	A	Pts	PIM	PP	SH	GW
1969-70	Ponoka Stampeders	Jr. B	42	35	26	*61	....	....	....	45	....	....	....	....	....	....	....	....	....	....	....	....	....	....	....	....	....	....
1970-71	Medicine Hat Tigers	WCJHL	66	52	59	111	....	....	....	88	....	....	....	....	....	....	....	....	....	....	....	....	....	....	....	....	....	....
1971-72	Medicine Hat Tigers	WCJHL	68	58	75	133	....	....	....	77	....	....	....	....	....	....	....	....	....	....	7	3	7	10	2	....	....	....
1972-73	**California Golden Seals**	**NHL**	**78**	**15**	**24**	**39**	**15**	**20**	**35**	**16**	**5**	**0**	**1**	**123**	**12.2**	**65**	**14**	**75**	**0**	**–24**	....	....	....	....	....	....	....	....
1973-74	**California Golden Seals**	**NHL**	**58**	**9**	**7**	**16**	**9**	**6**	**15**	**10**	**1**	**0**	**0**	**65**	**13.8**	**23**	**3**	**58**	**5**	**–33**	....	....	....	....	....	....	....	....
1974-75	**California Golden Seals**	**NHL**	**80**	**18**	**27**	**45**	**17**	**21**	**38**	**12**	**4**	**0**	**0**	**128**	**14.1**	**62**	**15**	**88**	**11**	**–30**	....	....	....	....	....	....	....	....
1975-76	**Toronto Maple Leafs**	**NHL**	**64**	**19**	**32**	**51**	**18**	**25**	**43**	**22**	**5**	**0**	**3**	**90**	**21.1**	**77**	**24**	**50**	**7**	**+10**	**9**	**1**	**3**	**4**	**0**	**1**	**0**	**1**
1976-77	**Toronto Maple Leafs**	**NHL**	**65**	**11**	**19**	**30**	**11**	**15**	**26**	**14**	**1**	**0**	**2**	**68**	**16.2**	**50**	**9**	**39**	**0**	**+2**	**7**	**2**	**1**	**3**	**0**	**1**	**0**	**1**
1977-78	**Toronto Maple Leafs**	**NHL**	**30**	**12**	**5**	**17**	**12**	**4**	**16**	**4**	**0**	**0**	**0**	**39**	**30.8**	**23**	**1**	**22**	**0**	**0**	**13**	**3**	**1**	**4**	**0**	**1**	**0**	**1**
	Tulsa Oilers	CHL	42	24	33	57	....	....	....	38	....	....	....	....	....	....	....	....	....	....	....	....	....	....	....	....	....	....
1978-79	Edmonton Oilers	WHA	68	31	30	61	....	....	....	20	....	....	....	....	....	....	....	....	....	....	13	2	5	7	2	....	....	....
1979-80	**Edmonton Oilers**	**NHL**	**79**	**33**	**33**	**66**	**30**	**25**	**55**	**40**	**3**	**2**	**2**	**129**	**25.6**	**92**	**16**	**113**	**39**	**+2**	**3**	**0**	**0**	**0**	**2**	**0**	**0**	**0**
1980-81	**Edmonton Oilers**	**NHL**	**70**	**12**	**20**	**32**	**10**	**14**	**24**	**40**	**1**	**0**	**2**	**84**	**14.3**	**45**	**4**	**92**	**44**	**–7**	**5**	**0**	**0**	**0**	**2**	**0**	**0**	**0**
1981-82	**Edmonton Oilers**	**NHL**	**51**	**3**	**13**	**16**	**2**	**9**	**11**	**13**	**1**	**0**	**1**	**29**	**10.3**	**23**	**2**	**45**	**24**	**0**	....	....	....	....	....	....	....	....
	Colorado Rockies	**NHL**	**10**	**2**	**3**	**5**	**2**	**2**	**4**	**10**	**0**	**0**	**1**	**12**	**16.7**	**6**	**0**	**17**	**4**	**–7**	....	....	....	....	....	....	....	....
1982-83	**Detroit Red Wings**	**NHL**	**57**	**5**	**24**	**29**	**4**	**17**	**21**	**2**	**1**	**0**	**1**	**59**	**8.5**	**50**	**8**	**47**	**5**	**0**	....	....	....	....	....	....	....	....
1983-84	Montana Magic	CHL	73	21	44	65	....	....	....	20	....	....	....	....	....	....	....	....	....	....	....	....	....	....	....	....	....	....
1984-85	Milwaukee Admirals	IHL	26	7	14	21	....	....	....	5	....	....	....	....	....	....	....	....	....	....	....	....	....	....	....	....	....	....
	NHL Totals		**642**	**139**	**207**	**346**	**130**	**158**	**288**	**183**	**22**	**2**	**13**	**826**	**16.8**	**516**	**96**	**646**	**139**		**37**	**6**	**5**	**11**	**4**	**3**	**0**	**3**
	Other Major League Totals		68	31	30	61	....	....	....	20	....	....	....	....	....	....	....	....	....	....	13	2	5	7	2	....	....	....

Selected by **Calgary-Cleveland** (WHA) in 1972 WHA General Player Draft, February 12, 1972. Traded to **Toronto** by **California** for Gary Sabourin, June 20, 1975. Signed as a free agent by **Edmonton** (WHA), June, 1978. Reclaimed by **Toronto** from **Edmonton** prior to Expansion Draft, June 9, 1979. Claimed on waivers by **Edmonton** from **Toronto**, July 4, 1979. Traded to **Colorado** by **Edmonton** for Ed Cooper, March 9, 1982. Traded to **Edmonton** by **Colorado** for Ed Cooper, July 2, 1982. Traded to **Detroit** by **Edmonton** for cash, September 14, 1982.

• WEIR, WALLY

Wally Weir D – R. 6'2", 200 lbs. b: Verdun, Que., 6/3/1954.

Season	Club	League	GP	G	A	Pts	AG	AA	APts	PIM	PP	SH	GW	S	%	TGF	PGF	TGA	PGA	+/–	GP	G	A	Pts	PIM	PP	SH	GW
1975-76	Beauce Jaros	NAHL	56	6	20	26	....	....	....	180	....	....	....	....	....	....	....	....	....	....	....	....	....	....	....	....	....	....
1976-77	Quebec Nordiques	WHA	69	3	17	20	....	....	....	197	....	....	....	....	....	....	....	....	....	....	17	1	5	6	13	....	....	....
1977-78	Quebec Nordiques	WHA	13	0	0	0	....	....	....	47	....	....	....	....	....	....	....	....	....	....	11	1	2	3	50	....	....	....
1978-79	Quebec Nordiques	WHA	68	2	7	9	....	....	....	166	....	....	....	....	....	....	....	....	....	....	4	0	1	1	4	....	....	....
1979-80	**Quebec Nordiques**	**NHL**	**73**	**3**	**12**	**15**	**3**	**9**	**12**	**133**	**0**	**0**	**0**	**91**	**3.3**	**56**	**1**	**86**	**13**	**–18**	....	....	....	....	....	....	....	....
1980-81	**Quebec Nordiques**	**NHL**	**54**	**6**	**8**	**14**	**5**	**6**	**11**	**77**	**0**	**0**	**0**	**50**	**12.0**	**30**	**3**	**32**	**5**	**0**	**3**	**0**	**0**	**0**	**15**	**0**	**0**	**0**
	Rochester Americans	AHL	7	1	1	2	....	....	....	79	....	....	....	....	....	....	....	....	....	....	....	....	....	....	....	....	....	....
1981-82	**Quebec Nordiques**	**NHL**	**62**	**3**	**5**	**8**	**2**	**3**	**5**	**173**	**0**	**0**	**0**	**44**	**6.8**	**25**	**1**	**53**	**13**	**–16**	**15**	**0**	**0**	**0**	**45**	**0**	**0**	**0**
1982-83	**Quebec Nordiques**	**NHL**	**58**	**5**	**11**	**16**	**4**	**8**	**12**	**135**	**1**	**0**	**0**	**50**	**10.0**	**37**	**2**	**28**	**4**	**+11**	**4**	**0**	**1**	**1**	**19**	**0**	**0**	**0**
1983-84	**Quebec Nordiques**	**NHL**	**25**	**2**	**3**	**5**	**2**	**2**	**4**	**17**	**0**	**0**	**1**	**15**	**13.3**	**12**	**0**	**7**	**0**	**+5**	**1**	**0**	**0**	**0**	**17**	**0**	**0**	**0**
	Fredericton Express	AHL	44	6	17	23	....	....	....	45	....	....	....	....	....	....	....	....	....	....	7	2	2	4	14	....	....	....
1984-85	**Hartford Whalers**	**NHL**	**34**	**2**	**3**	**5**	**2**	**2**	**4**	**56**	**0**	**0**	**0**	**24**	**8.3**	**15**	**0**	**26**	**4**	**–7**	....	....	....	....	....	....	....	....
	Pittsburgh Penguins	**NHL**	**14**	**0**	**3**	**3**	**0**	**2**	**2**	**34**	**0**	**0**	**0**	**8**	**0.0**	**8**	**0**	**8**	**1**	**+1**	....	....	....	....	....	....	....	....
1985-86	Baltimore Skipjacks	AHL	67	5	12	17	....	....	....	300	....	....	....	....	....	....	....	....	....	....	....	....	....	....	....	....	....	....
	NHL Totals		**320**	**21**	**45**	**66**	**18**	**32**	**50**	**625**	**1**	**0**	**1**	**282**	**7.4**	**183**	**7**	**240**	**40**		**23**	**0**	**1**	**1**	**96**	**0**	**0**	**0**
	Other Major League Totals		150	5	24	29	....	....	....	410	....	....	....	....	....	....	....	....	....	....	32	2	8	10	67	....	....	....

Signed as a free agent by **Quebec** (WHA), September, 1976. Claimed by **Hartford** from **Quebec** in Waiver Draft, October 9, 1981. Claimed on waivers by **Pittsburgh** from **Hartford**, March 1, 1985.

• WELLS, CHRIS

Chris Wells C – L. 6'6", 223 lbs. b: Calgary, Alta., 11/12/1975. Pittsburgh's 1st choice, 24th overall, in 1994 Entry Draft.

Season	Club	League	GP	G	A	Pts	AG	AA	APts	PIM	PP	SH	GW	S	%	TGF	PGF	TGA	PGA	+/–	GP	G	A	Pts	PIM	PP	SH	GW
1991-92	Seattle Thunderbirds	WHL	64	13	8	21	....	....	....	80	....	....	....	....	....	....	....	....	....	....	11	0	0	0	15	....	....	....
1992-93	Seattle Thunderbirds	WHL	63	18	37	55	....	....	....	111	....	....	....	....	....	....	....	....	....	....	5	2	3	5	4	....	....	....
1993-94	Seattle Thunderbirds	WHL	69	30	44	74	....	....	....	150	....	....	....	....	....	....	....	....	....	....	9	6	5	11	23	....	....	....
1994-95	Seattle Thunderbirds	WHL	69	45	63	108	....	....	....	148	....	....	....	....	....	....	....	....	....	....	3	0	1	1	4	....	....	....
	Cleveland Lumberjacks	IHL	3	0	1	1	....	....	....	2	....	....	....	....	....	....	....	....	....	....	....	....	....	....	....	....	....	....
1995-96	**Pittsburgh Penguins**	**NHL**	**54**	**2**	**2**	**4**	**2**	**2**	**4**	**59**	**0**	**1**	**0**	**25**	**8.0**	**9**	**0**	**18**	**3**	**–6**	....	....	....	....	....	....	....	....
1996-97	Cleveland Lumberjacks	IHL	15	4	6	10	....	....	....	9	....	....	....	....	....	....	....	....	....	....	....	....	....	....	....	....	....	....
	Florida Panthers	**NHL**	**47**	**2**	**6**	**8**	**2**	**5**	**7**	**42**	**0**	**0**	**0**	**29**	**6.9**	**17**	**0**	**12**	**0**	**+5**	**3**	**0**	**0**	**0**	**0**	**0**	**0**	**0**
1997-98	**Florida Panthers**	**NHL**	**61**	**5**	**10**	**15**	**6**	**10**	**16**	**47**	**0**	**1**	**0**	**57**	**8.8**	**21**	**1**	**29**	**13**	**+4**	....	....	....	....	....	....	....	....
	NHL Totals		**162**	**9**	**18**	**27**	**10**	**17**	**27**	**148**	**0**	**2**	**0**	**111**	**8.1**	**47**	**1**	**59**	**16**		**3**	**0**	**0**	**0**	**0**	**0**	**0**	**0**

WHL West First All-Star Team (1995)

Traded to **Florida** by **Pittsburgh** for Stu Barnes and Jason Woolley, November 19, 1996.

• WELLS, JAY

Jay Wells D – L. 6'1", 210 lbs. b: Paris, Ont., 5/18/1959. Los Angeles' 1st choice, 16th overall, in 1979 Entry Draft.

Season	Club	League	GP	G	A	Pts	AG	AA	APts	PIM	PP	SH	GW	S	%	TGF	PGF	TGA	PGA	+/–	GP	G	A	Pts	PIM	PP	SH	GW
1977-78	Kingston Canadians	OHA	68	9	13	22	....	....	....	195	....	....	....	....	....	....	....	....	....	....	5	1	2	3	6	....	....	....
1978-79	Kingston Canadians	OHA	48	6	21	27	....	....	....	100	....	....	....	....	....	....	....	....	....	....	11	2	7	9	29	....	....	....
1979-80	**Los Angeles Kings**	**NHL**	**43**	**0**	**0**	**0**	**0**	**0**	**0**	**113**	**0**	**0**	**0**	**22**	**0.0**	**15**	**0**	**42**	**5**	**–22**	**4**	**0**	**0**	**0**	**11**	**0**	**0**	**0**
	Binghamton Whalers	AHL	28	0	6	6	....	....	....	48	....	....	....	....	....	....	....	....	....	....	....	....	....	....	....	....	....	....
1980-81	**Los Angeles Kings**	**NHL**	**72**	**5**	**13**	**18**	**4**	**9**	**13**	**155**	**0**	**0**	**1**	**75**	**6.7**	**72**	**6**	**72**	**15**	**+9**	**4**	**0**	**0**	**0**	**27**	**0**	**0**	**0**
1981-82	**Los Angeles Kings**	**NHL**	**60**	**1**	**8**	**9**	**1**	**5**	**6**	**145**	**0**	**0**	**0**	**84**	**1.2**	**56**	**2**	**76**	**24**	**+2**	**10**	**1**	**3**	**4**	**41**	**0**	**0**	**0**
1982-83	**Los Angeles Kings**	**NHL**	**69**	**3**	**12**	**15**	**2**	**8**	**10**	**167**	**0**	**0**	**1**	**105**	**2.9**	**79**	**4**	**96**	**32**	**+11**	....	....	....	....	....	....	....	....
1983-84	**Los Angeles Kings**	**NHL**	**69**	**3**	**18**	**21**	**2**	**12**	**14**	**141**	**0**	**0**	**0**	**96**	**3.1**	**84**	**3**	**130**	**39**	**–10**	....	....	....	....	....	....	....	....
1984-85	**Los Angeles Kings**	**NHL**	**77**	**2**	**9**	**11**	**2**	**6**	**8**	**185**	**0**	**0**	**0**	**72**	**2.8**	**83**	**0**	**95**	**16**	**+4**	**3**	**0**	**1**	**1**	**0**	**0**	**0**	**0**
1985-86	**Los Angeles Kings**	**NHL**	**79**	**11**	**31**	**42**	**9**	**21**	**30**	**226**	**4**	**0**	**2**	**113**	**9.7**	**113**	**24**	**124**	**42**	**+7**	....	....	....	....	....	....	....	....
	Canada	WEC A	10	0	2	2	....	....	....	16	....	....	....	....	....	....	....	....	....	....	....	....	....	....	....	....	....	....
1986-87	**Los Angeles Kings**	**NHL**	**77**	**7**	**29**	**36**	**6**	**21**	**27**	**155**	**6**	**0**	**2**	**115**	**6.1**	**107**	**39**	**129**	**42**	**–19**	**5**	**1**	**2**	**3**	**10**	**1**	**0**	**0**
1987-88	**Los Angeles Kings**	**NHL**	**58**	**2**	**23**	**25**	**2**	**16**	**18**	**159**	**1**	**0**	**0**	**76**	**2.6**	**75**	**17**	**89**	**28**	**–3**	**5**	**1**	**2**	**3**	**21**	**0**	**0**	**0**
1988-89	**Philadelphia Flyers**	**NHL**	**67**	**2**	**19**	**21**	**2**	**13**	**15**	**184**	**0**	**0**	**0**	**67**	**3.0**	**78**	**25**	**73**	**17**	**–3**	**18**	**0**	**2**	**2**	**51**	**0**	**0**	**0**
1989-90	**Philadelphia Flyers**	**NHL**	**59**	**3**	**16**	**19**	**3**	**11**	**14**	**129**	**0**	**0**	**1**	**78**	**3.9**	**66**	**12**	**70**	**20**	**+4**	....	....	....	....	....	....	....	....
	Buffalo Sabres	**NHL**	**1**	**0**	**1**	**1**	**0**	**1**	**1**	**0**	**0**	**0**	**0**	**0**	**0.0**	**2**	**0**	**1**	**0**	**+1**	**6**	**0**	**0**	**0**	**12**	**0**	**0**	**0**
1990-91	**Buffalo Sabres**	**NHL**	**43**	**1**	**2**	**3**	**1**	**2**	**3**	**86**	**0**	**0**	**0**	**36**	**2.8**	**24**	**2**	**42**	**2**	**–18**	**1**	**0**	**1**	**1**	**0**	**0**	**0**	**0**
1991-92	**Buffalo Sabres**	**NHL**	**41**	**2**	**9**	**11**	**2**	**7**	**9**	**157**	**0**	**0**	**0**	**26**	**7.7**	**29**	**0**	**43**	**11**	**–3**	....	....	....	....	....	....	....	....
	New York Rangers	**NHL**	**11**	**0**	**0**	**0**	**0**	**0**	**0**	**24**	**0**	**0**	**0**	**4**	**0.0**	**3**	**0**	**1**	**0**	**+2**	**13**	**0**	**2**	**2**	**10**	**0**	**0**	**0**
1992-93	**New York Rangers**	**NHL**	**53**	**1**	**9**	**10**	**1**	**0**	**7**	**107**	**0**	**0**	**0**	**32**	**3.1**	**32**	**2**	**52**	**20**	**–2**	....	....	....	....	....	....	....	....
1993-94	**New York Rangers**	**NHL**	**79**	**2**	**7**	**9**	**2**	**5**	**7**	**110**	**0**	**0**	**0**	**64**	**3.1**	**35**	**2**	**37**	**8**	**+4**	**23**	**0**	**0**	**0**	**20**	**0**	**0**	**0**
1994-95	**New York Rangers**	**NHL**	**43**	**2**	**7**	**9**	**4**	**10**	**14**	**36**	**0**	**0**	**0**	**38**	**5.3**	**20**	**1**	**24**	**5**	**0**	**10**	**0**	**0**	**0**	**8**	**0**	**0**	**0**
1995-96	**St. Louis Blues**	**NHL**	**76**	**0**	**3**	**3**	**0**	**2**	**2**	**67**	**0**	**0**	**0**	**24**	**0.0**	**20**	**1**	**37**	**10**	**–8**	**12**	**0**	**1**	**1**	**2**	**0**	**0**	**0**
1996-97	**Tampa Bay Lightning**	**NHL**	**21**	**0**	**0**	**0**	**0**	**0**	**0**	**13**	**0**	**0**	**0**	**16**	**0.0**	**6**	**0**	**10**	**1**	**–3**	....	....	....	....	....	....	....	....
	NHL Totals		**1098**	**47**	**216**	**263**	**43**	**155**	**198**	**2359**	**11**	**0**	**7**	**1141**	**4.1**	**999**	**140**	**1243**	**337**		**114**	**3**	**14**	**17**	**213**	**1**	**0**	**0**

OHA First All-Star Team (1979)

Traded to **Philadelphia** by **LA Kings** for Doug Crossman, September 29, 1988. Traded to **Buffalo** by **Philadelphia** with Philadelphia's 4th round choice (Peter Ambroziak) in 1991 Entry Draft for Kevin Maguire and Buffalo's 2nd round choice (Mikael Renberg) in 1990 Entry Draft, March 5, 1990. Traded to **NY Rangers** by **Buffalo** for Randy Moller, March 9, 1992. Traded to **St. Louis** by **NY Rangers** for Doug Lidster, July 31, 1995. Signed as a free agent by **Tampa Bay**, August 3, 1996.

• WENSINK, JOHN

John Wensink LW – L. 6', 200 lbs. b: Cornwall, Ont., 4/1/1953. St. Louis' 6th choice, 104th overall, in 1973 Amateur Draft.

Season	Club	League	GP	G	A	Pts	AG	AA	APts	PIM	PP	SH	GW	S	%	TGF	PGF	TGA	PGA	+/–	GP	G	A	Pts	PIM	PP	SH	GW
1970-71	Cornwall Royals	QMJHL	57	11	6	17	....	....	....	151	....	....	....	....	....	....	....	....	....	....	....	....	....	....	....	....	....	....
1971-72	Cornwall Royals	QMJHL	60	10	22	32	....	....	....	69	....	....	....	....	....	....	....	....	....	....	15	2	2	4	64	....	....	....
1972-73	Cornwall Royals	QMJHL	52	9	26	35	....	....	....	242	....	....	....	....	....	....	....	....	....	....	16	1	6	7	55	....	....	....
1973-74	**St. Louis Blues**	**NHL**	**3**	**0**	**0**	**0**	**0**	**0**	**0**	**0**	**0**	**0**	**0**	**0**	**0.0**	**0**	**0**	**0**	**0**	**0**	....	....	....	....	....	....	....	....
	Rochester Americans	AHL	36	6	2	8	....	....	....	139	....	....	....	....	....	....	....	....	....	....	5	0	0	0	29	....	....	....
1974-75	Denver Spurs	CHL	21	3	8	11	....	....	....	75	....	....	....	....	....	....	....	....	....	....	....	....	....	....	....	....	....	....
1975-76			DID NOT PLAY – INJURED																									
1976-77	**Boston Bruins**	**NHL**	**23**	**4**	**6**	**10**	**4**	**5**	**9**	**32**	**0**	**0**	**0**	**24**	**16.7**	**13**	**0**	**9**	**1**	**+5**	**13**	**0**	**3**	**3**	**8**	**0**	**0**	**0**
	Rochester Americans	AHL	49	11	15	26	....	....	....	145	....	....	....	....	....	....	....	....	....	....	....	....	....	....	....	....	....	....

			REGULAR SEASON																		PLAYOFFS							
Season	Club	League	GP	G	A	Pts	AG	AA	APts	PIM	PP	SH	GW	S	%	TGF	PGF	TGA	PGA	+/–	GP	G	A	Pts	PIM	PP	SH	GW
1977-78	**Boston Bruins**	**NHL**	**80**	**16**	**20**	**36**	**15**	**16**	**31**	**181**	**1**	**0**	**3**	**131**	**12.2**	**65**	**2**	**40**	**0**	**+23**	**15**	**2**	**2**	**4**	**54**	**0**	**0**	**0**
1978-79	**Boston Bruins**	**NHL**	**76**	**28**	**18**	**46**	**25**	**14**	**39**	**106**	**0**	**0**	**4**	**131**	**21.4**	**77**	**6**	**51**	**0**	**+20**	**8**	**0**	**1**	**1**	**19**	**0**	**0**	**0**
1979-80	**Boston Bruins**	**NHL**	**69**	**9**	**11**	**20**	**8**	**8**	**16**	**110**	**0**	**0**	**2**	**71**	**12.7**	**36**	**0**	**29**	**0**	**+7**	**4**	**0**	**0**	**0**	**5**	**0**	**0**	**0**
1980-81	**Quebec Nordiques**	**NHL**	**53**	**6**	**3**	**9**	**5**	**2**	**7**	**124**	**0**	**0**	**1**	**55**	**10.9**	**16**	**1**	**29**	**0**	**–14**	**3**	**0**	**0**	**0**	**0**	**0**	**0**	**0**
1981-82	**Colorado Rockies**	**NHL**	**57**	**5**	**3**	**8**	**4**	**2**	**6**	**152**	**1**	**0**	**0**	**35**	**14.3**	**15**	**3**	**25**	**0**	**–13**	....	....	....	....	....	....	....	....
1982-83	**New Jersey Devils**	**NHL**	**42**	**2**	**7**	**9**	**2**	**5**	**7**	**135**	**1**	**0**	**0**	**30**	**6.7**	**15**	**4**	**19**	**0**	**–8**	....	....	....	....	....	....	....	....
	Wichita Wind	CHL	7	1	0	1	....	....	....	36	....	....	....	....	....	....	....	....	....	....	....	....	....	....	....	....	....	....
	NHL Totals		**403**	**70**	**68**	**138**	**63**	**52**	**115**	**840**	**3**	**0**	**10**	**477**	**14.7**	**237**	**16**	**202**	**1**		**43**	**2**	**6**	**8**	**86**	**0**	**0**	**0**

Signed as a free agent by **Boston**, October 12, 1976. Claimed by **Quebec** from **Boston** in Waiver Draft, October 10, 1980. Signed as a free agent by **Colorado**, September 21, 1981. Transferred to **New Jersey** after **Colorado** franchise relocated, June 30, 1982.

• WERENKA, BRAD

Brad Werenka D – L. 6'2", 210 lbs. b: Two Hills, Alta., 2/12/1969. Edmonton's 1st choice, 42nd overall, in 1987 Entry Draft.

Season	Club	League	GP	G	A	Pts	AG	AA	APts	PIM	PP	SH	GW	S	%	TGF	PGF	TGA	PGA	+/–	GP	G	A	Pts	PIM	PP	SH	GW
1986-87	Northern Michigan University	WCHA	30	4	4	8	....	....	....	35	....	....	....	....	....	....	....	....	....	....	....	....	....	....	....	....	....	....
1987-88	Northern Michigan University	WCHA	34	7	23	30	....	....	....	26	....	....	....	....	....	....	....	....	....	....	....	....	....	....	....	....	....	....
1988-89	Northern Michigan University	WCHA	28	7	13	20	....	....	....	16	....	....	....	....	....	....	....	....	....	....	....	....	....	....	....	....	....	....
1989-90	Northern Michigan University	WCHA	8	2	5	7	....	....	....	8	....	....	....	....	....	....	....	....	....	....	....	....	....	....	....	....	....	....
1990-91	Northern Michigan University	WCHA	47	20	43	63	....	....	....	36	....	....	....	....	....	....	....	....	....	....	....	....	....	....	....	....	....	....
	Cape Breton Oilers	AHL	66	6	21	27	....	....	....	95	....	....	....	....	....	....	....	....	....	....	5	0	3	3	6	....	....	....
1992-93	Canada	Nat-Team	18	3	7	10	....	....	....	10	....	....	....	....	....	....	....	....	....	....	....	....	....	....	....	....	....	....
	Edmonton Oilers	**NHL**	**27**	**5**	**4**	**9**	**4**	**3**	**7**	**24**	**0**	**1**	**1**	**38**	**13.2**	**32**	**9**	**25**	**3**	**+1**	....	....	....	....	....	....	....	....
	Cape Breton Oilers	AHL	4	1	1	2	....	....	....	4	....	....	....	....	....	....	....	....	....	....	16	4	17	21	12	....	....	....
1993-94	**Edmonton Oilers**	**NHL**	**15**	**0**	**4**	**4**	**0**	**3**	**3**	**14**	**0**	**0**	**0**	**11**	**0.0**	**12**	**4**	**12**	**3**	**–1**	....	....	....	....	....	....	....	....
	Cape Breton Oilers	AHL	25	6	17	23	....	....	....	19	....	....	....	....	....	....	....	....	....	....	....	....	....	....	....	....	....	....
	Canada	Olympics	8	2	2	4	....	....	....	8	....	....	....	....	....	....	....	....	....	....	....	....	....	....	....	....	....	....
	Quebec Nordiques	**NHL**	**11**	**0**	**7**	**7**	**0**	**5**	**5**	**8**	**0**	**0**	**0**	**17**	**0.0**	**15**	**5**	**7**	**1**	**+4**	....	....	....	....	....	....	....	....
	Cornwall Aces	AHL	....	....	....	....	....	....	....	....	....	....	....	....	....	....	....	....	....	....	12	2	10	12	22	....	....	....
1994-95	Milwaukee Admirals	IHL	80	8	45	53	....	....	....	161	....	....	....	....	....	....	....	....	....	....	15	3	10	13	36	....	....	....
1995-96	**Chicago Blackhawks**	**NHL**	**9**	**0**	**0**	**0**	**0**	**0**	**0**	**8**	**0**	**0**	**0**	**2**	**0.0**	**3**	**0**	**6**	**1**	**–2**	....	....	....	....	....	....	....	....
	Indianapolis Ice	IHL	73	15	42	57	....	....	....	85	....	....	....	....	....	....	....	....	....	....	5	1	3	4	8	....	....	....
1996-97	Indianapolis Ice	IHL	82	20	56	76	....	....	....	83	....	....	....	....	....	....	....	....	....	....	4	1	4	5	6	....	....	....
1997-98	**Pittsburgh Penguins**	**NHL**	**71**	**3**	**15**	**18**	**4**	**15**	**19**	**46**	**2**	**0**	**0**	**50**	**6.0**	**56**	**9**	**51**	**19**	**+15**	**6**	**1**	**0**	**1**	**8**	**0**	**1**	**0**
	NHL Totals		**133**	**8**	**30**	**38**	**8**	**26**	**34**	**100**	**2**	**1**	**1**	**118**	**6.8**	**118**	**27**	**101**	**27**		**6**	**1**	**0**	**1**	**8**	**0**	**1**	**0**

WCHA First All-Star Team (1991) • NCAA West First All-American Team (1991) • NCAA Championship All-Tournament Team (1991) • IHL First All-Star Team (1997) • Won Governors' Trophy (Top Defenseman - IHL) (1997)

Traded to **Quebec** by **Edmonton** for Steve Passmore, March 21, 1994. Signed as a free agent by **Chicago**, July 20, 1995. Signed as a free agent by **Pittsburgh**, July 31, 1997.

• WESLEY, BLAKE

Blake Wesley D – L. 6'1", 200 lbs. b: Red Deer, Alta., 7/10/1959. Philadelphia's 2nd choice, 22nd overall, in 1979 Entry Draft.

Season	Club	League	GP	G	A	Pts	AG	AA	APts	PIM	PP	SH	GW	S	%	TGF	PGF	TGA	PGA	+/–	GP	G	A	Pts	PIM	PP	SH	GW
1974-75	Red Deer Rustlers	AJHL	3	1	0	1	....	....	....	4	....	....	....	....	....	....	....	....	....	....	....	....	....	....	....	....	....	....
1975-76	Red Deer Rustlers	AJHL	55	19	41	60	....	....	....	199	....	....	....	....	....	....	....	....	....	....	....	....	....	....	....	....	....	....
1976-77	Portland Winter Hawks	WCJHL	63	8	25	33	....	....	....	111	....	....	....	....	....	....	....	....	....	....	10	0	5	5	32	....	....	....
1977-78	Portland Winter Hawks	WCJHL	67	7	37	44	....	....	....	190	....	....	....	....	....	....	....	....	....	....	8	1	2	3	20	....	....	....
1978-79	Portland Winter Hawks	WHL	69	10	42	52	....	....	....	292	....	....	....	....	....	....	....	....	....	....	25	3	8	11	70	....	....	....
1979-80	**Philadelphia Flyers**	**NHL**	**2**	**0**	**1**	**1**	**0**	**1**	**1**	**2**	**0**	**0**	**0**	**4**	**0.0**	**2**	**0**	**5**	**0**	**–3**	....	....	....	....	....	....	....	....
	Maine Mariners	AHL	62	12	22	34	....	....	....	76	....	....	....	....	....	....	....	....	....	....	12	2	5	7	62	....	....	....
1980-81	**Philadelphia Flyers**	**NHL**	**50**	**3**	**7**	**10**	**2**	**5**	**7**	**107**	**2**	**0**	**1**	**53**	**5.7**	**52**	**14**	**43**	**18**	**+13**	....	....	....	....	....	....	....	....
	Maine Mariners	AHL	24	6	10	16	....	....	....	20	....	....	....	....	....	....	....	....	....	....	9	1	8	9	53	....	....	....
1981-82	**Hartford Whalers**	**NHL**	**78**	**9**	**18**	**27**	**7**	**12**	**19**	**123**	**3**	**0**	**1**	**115**	**7.8**	**87**	**19**	**135**	**33**	**–34**	....	....	....	....	....	....	....	....
1982-83	**Hartford Whalers**	**NHL**	**22**	**0**	**1**	**1**	**0**	**1**	**1**	**46**	**0**	**0**	**0**	**12**	**0.0**	**13**	**1**	**34**	**6**	**–16**	....	....	....	....	....	....	....	....
	Quebec Nordiques	**NHL**	**52**	**4**	**8**	**12**	**3**	**6**	**9**	**84**	**2**	**0**	**1**	**59**	**6.8**	**53**	**7**	**68**	**18**	**–4**	**4**	**0**	**0**	**0**	**2**	**0**	**0**	**0**
1983-84	**Quebec Nordiques**	**NHL**	**46**	**2**	**8**	**10**	**2**	**5**	**7**	**75**	**0**	**0**	**0**	**40**	**5.0**	**47**	**1**	**40**	**8**	**+14**	**9**	**1**	**2**	**3**	**20**	**0**	**0**	**1**
1984-85	**Quebec Nordiques**	**NHL**	**21**	**0**	**2**	**2**	**0**	**1**	**1**	**28**	**0**	**0**	**0**	**11**	**0.0**	**7**	**0**	**11**	**2**	**–2**	**6**	**1**	**0**	**1**	**8**	**0**	**0**	**0**
	Fredericton Express	AHL	25	3	4	7	....	....	....	80	....	....	....	....	....	....	....	....	....	....	2	1	0	1	2	....	....	....
1985-86	**Toronto Maple Leafs**	**NHL**	**27**	**0**	**1**	**1**	**0**	**1**	**1**	**21**	**0**	**0**	**0**	**11**	**0.0**	**16**	**0**	**28**	**8**	**–4**	....	....	....	....	....	....	....	....
	St. Catharines Saints	AHL	37	3	4	7	....	....	....	56	....	....	....	....	....	....	....	....	....	....	13	0	3	3	41	....	....	....
1986-87	Newmarket Saints	AHL	79	1	12	13	....	....	....	170	....	....	....	....	....	....	....	....	....	....	....	....	....	....	....	....	....	....
1987-88	Maine Mariners	AHL	34	0	3	3	....	....	....	124	....	....	....	....	....	....	....	....	....	....	1	0	0	0	2	....	....	....
	NHL Totals		**298**	**18**	**46**	**64**	**14**	**32**	**46**	**486**	**7**	**0**	**3**	**305**	**5.9**	**277**	**42**	**364**	**93**		**19**	**2**	**2**	**4**	**30**	**0**	**0**	**1**

Traded to **Hartford** by **Philadelphia** with Rick MacLeish, Don Gillen and Philadelphia's 1st (Paul Lawless), 2nd (Mark Paterson) and 3rd (Kevin Dineen) round choices in 1982 Entry Draft for Ray Allison, Fred Arthur and Hartford's 1st (Ron Sutter), 2nd (later traded to Toronto — Toronto selected Peter Ihnacak) and 3rd (Miroslav Dvorak) round choices in 1982 Entry Draft, July 3, 1981. Traded to **Quebec** by **Hartford** for Pierre Lacroix, December 3, 1982. Signed as a free agent by **Toronto**, July 31, 1985.

• WESLEY, GLEN

Glen Wesley D – L. 6'1", 197 lbs. b: Red Deer, Alta., 10/2/1968. Boston's 2nd choice, 3rd overall, in 1987 Entry Draft.

Season	Club	League	GP	G	A	Pts	AG	AA	APts	PIM	PP	SH	GW	S	%	TGF	PGF	TGA	PGA	+/–	GP	G	A	Pts	PIM	PP	SH	GW
1983-84	Portland Winter Hawks	WHL	3	1	2	3	....	....	....	0	....	....	....	....	....	....	....	....	....	....	....	....	....	....	....	....	....	....
1984-85	Portland Winter Hawks	WHL	67	16	52	68	....	....	....	76	....	....	....	....	....	....	....	....	....	....	6	1	6	7	8	....	....	....
1985-86	Portland Winter Hawks	WHL	69	16	75	91	....	....	....	96	....	....	....	....	....	....	....	....	....	....	15	3	11	14	29	....	....	....
1986-87	Portland Winter Hawks	WHL	63	16	46	62	....	....	....	72	....	....	....	....	....	....	....	....	....	....	20	8	18	26	27	....	....	....
	Canada	WJC-A	6	2	1	3	....	....	....	4	....	....	....	....	....	....	....	....	....	....	....	....	....	....	....	....	....	....
1987-88	**Boston Bruins**	**NHL**	**79**	**7**	**30**	**37**	**6**	**21**	**27**	**69**	**1**	**2**	**0**	**158**	**4.4**	**111**	**26**	**91**	**27**	**+21**	**23**	**6**	**8**	**14**	**22**	**4**	**1**	**0**
1988-89	**Boston Bruins**	**NHL**	**77**	**19**	**35**	**54**	**16**	**25**	**41**	**61**	**8**	**1**	**1**	**181**	**10.5**	**136**	**48**	**92**	**27**	**+23**	**10**	**0**	**2**	**2**	**4**	**0**	**0**	**0**
1989-90	**Boston Bruins**	**NHL**	**78**	**9**	**27**	**36**	**8**	**19**	**27**	**48**	**5**	**0**	**4**	**166**	**5.4**	**122**	**55**	**82**	**21**	**+6**	**21**	**2**	**6**	**8**	**36**	**0**	**0**	**1**
1990-91	**Boston Bruins**	**NHL**	**80**	**11**	**32**	**43**	**10**	**24**	**34**	**78**	**5**	**1**	**1**	**199**	**5.5**	**135**	**53**	**109**	**27**	**0**	**19**	**2**	**9**	**11**	**19**	**2**	**0**	**0**
1991-92	**Boston Bruins**	**NHL**	**78**	**9**	**37**	**46**	**8**	**28**	**36**	**54**	**4**	**0**	**1**	**211**	**4.3**	**111**	**45**	**102**	**27**	**–9**	**15**	**2**	**4**	**6**	**16**	**0**	**0**	**0**
1992-93	**Boston Bruins**	**NHL**	**64**	**8**	**25**	**33**	**7**	**17**	**24**	**47**	**4**	**1**	**0**	**183**	**4.4**	**95**	**38**	**82**	**23**	**–2**	**4**	**0**	**0**	**0**	**0**	**0**	**0**	**0**
1993-94	**Boston Bruins**	**NHL**	**81**	**14**	**44**	**58**	**13**	**34**	**47**	**64**	**6**	**1**	**1**	**265**	**5.3**	**124**	**65**	**77**	**19**	**+1**	**13**	**3**	**3**	**6**	**12**	**1**	**0**	**0**
1994-95	**Hartford Whalers**	**NHL**	**48**	**2**	**14**	**16**	**4**	**21**	**25**	**50**	**1**	**0**	**1**	**125**	**1.6**	**57**	**23**	**56**	**16**	**–6**	....	....	....	....	....	....	....	....
1995-96	**Hartford Whalers**	**NHL**	**68**	**8**	**16**	**24**	**8**	**13**	**21**	**88**	**6**	**0**	**1**	**129**	**6.2**	**73**	**30**	**91**	**39**	**–9**	....	....	....	....	....	....	....	....
1996-97	**Hartford Whalers**	**NHL**	**68**	**6**	**26**	**32**	**6**	**23**	**29**	**40**	**3**	**1**	**0**	**126**	**4.8**	**75**	**19**	**72**	**16**	**0**	....	....	....	....	....	....	....	....
1997-98	**Carolina Hurricanes**	**NHL**	**82**	**6**	**19**	**25**	**7**	**19**	**26**	**36**	**1**	**0**	**1**	**121**	**5.0**	**66**	**13**	**61**	**15**	**+7**	....	....	....	....	....	....	....	....
	NHL Totals		**803**	**99**	**305**	**404**	**93**	**244**	**337**	**635**	**44**	**7**	**11**	**1864**	**5.3**	**1105**	**415**	**915**	**257**		**105**	**15**	**32**	**47**	**109**	**7**	**1**	**1**

WHL West All-Star Team (1986, 1987) • NHL All-Rookie Team (1988)

Played in NHL All-Star Game (1989)

Traded to **Hartford** by **Boston** for Hartford/Carolina's 1st round choices in 1995 (Kyle McLaren), 1996 (Jonathan Aitken) and 1997 (Sergei Samsonov) Entry Drafts, August 26, 1994. Transferred to **Carolina** after **Hartford** franchise relocated, June 25, 1997.

• WESTFALL, ED

Ed Westfall D/RW – R. 6'1", 197 lbs. b: Belleville, Ont., 9/19/1940.

Season	Club	League	GP	G	A	Pts	AG	AA	APts	PIM	PP	SH	GW	S	%	TGF	PGF	TGA	PGA	+/–	GP	G	A	Pts	PIM	PP	SH	GW
1957-58	Barrie Flyers	OHA	51	3	10	13	....	....	....	60	....	....	....	....	....	....	....	....	....	....	4	0	0	0	4	....	....	....
1958-59	Barrie Flyers	OHA	54	4	10	14	....	....	....	63	....	....	....	....	....	....	....	....	....	....	6	0	4	4	2	....	....	....
1959-60	Barrie Flyers	OHA	48	7	28	35	....	....	....	63	....	....	....	....	....	....	....	....	....	....	6	0	4	4	28	....	....	....
	Kingston Frontenacs	EPHL	1	0	0	0	....	....	....	2	....	....	....	....	....	....	....	....	....	....	....	....	....	....	....	....	....	....
1960-61	Niagara Falls Flyers	OHA	48	9	45	54	....	....	....	72	....	....	....	....	....	....	....	....	....	....	7	2	7	9	6	....	....	....
	Kingston Frontenacs	EPHL	2	0	0	0	....	....	....	0	....	....	....	....	....	....	....	....	....	....	....	....	....	....	....	....	....	....
1961-62	**Boston Bruins**	**NHL**	**63**	**2**	**9**	**11**	**2**	**9**	**11**	**53**	....	....	....	....	....	....	....	....	....	....	....	....	....	....	....	....	....	....
1962-63	**Boston Bruins**	**NHL**	**48**	**1**	**11**	**12**	**1**	**11**	**12**	**34**	....	....	....	....	....	....	....	....	....	....	....	....	....	....	....	....	....	....
	Kingston Frontenacs	EPHL	21	5	16	21	....	....	....	14	....	....	....	....	....	....	....	....	....	....	....	....	....	....	....	....	....	....
1963-64	**Boston Bruins**	**NHL**	**55**	**1**	**5**	**6**	**1**	**5**	**6**	**35**	....	....	....	....	....	....	....	....	....	....	....	....	....	....	....	....	....	....
	Providence Reds	AHL	13	1	3	4	....	....	....	8	....	....	....	....	....	....	....	....	....	....	3	0	0	0	4	....	....	....
1964-65	**Boston Bruins**	**NHL**	**68**	**12**	**15**	**27**	**15**	**16**	**31**	**65**	....	....	....	....	....	....	....	....	....	....	....	....	....	....	....	....	....	....
1965-66	**Boston Bruins**	**NHL**	**59**	**9**	**21**	**30**	**11**	**21**	**32**	**42**	....	....	....	....	....	....	....	....	....	....	....	....	....	....	....	....	....	....
1966-67	**Boston Bruins**	**NHL**	**70**	**12**	**24**	**36**	**15**	**25**	**40**	**26**	....	....	....	....	....	....	....	....	....	....	....	....	....	....	....	....	....	....
1967-68	**Boston Bruins**	**NHL**	**73**	**14**	**22**	**36**	**17**	**23**	**40**	**38**	**1**	**2**	**2**	**139**	**10.1**	**55**	**4**	**77**	**31**	**+5**	**4**	**2**	**0**	**2**	**2**	**0**	**0**	**0**

Season	Club	League	GP	G	A	Pts	AG	AA	APts	PIM	PP	SH	GW	S	%	TGF	PGF	TGA	PGA	+/-	GP	G	A	Pts	PIM	PP	SH	GW
1968-69	Boston Bruins	NHL	70	18	24	42	20	23	43	22	1	4	4	139	12.9	66	5	74	33	+20	10	3	7	10	11	0	0	2
1969-70	Boston Bruins	NHL	72	14	22	36	16	22	38	28	0	0	0	158	8.9	63	0	93	50	+20	14	3	5	8	4	0	1	1
1970-71	Boston Bruins	NHL	78	25	34	59	26	30	56	48	0	7	5	149	16.8	99	0	75	34	+58	7	1	2	3	2	0	1	0
1971-72	Boston Bruins	NHL	71	18	26	44	19	24	43	19	0	2	5	123	14.6	68	1	77	39	+29	15	4	3	7	10	0	2	1
1972-73	New York Islanders	NHL	67	15	31	46	15	26	41	25	4	0	1	160	9.4	76	25	121	28	-42	....							
1973-74	New York Islanders	NHL	68	19	23	42	19	20	39	28	6	0	0	177	10.7	65	17	90	37	-5	....							
1974-75	New York Islanders	NHL	73	22	33	55	20	26	46	28	6	1	1	170	12.9	81	20	77	35	+19	17	5	10	15	12	2	1	2
1975-76	New York Islanders	NHL	80	25	31	56	23	24	47	27	6	2	3	154	16.2	83	24	90	48	+17	8	2	3	5	0	1	0	0
1976-77	New York Islanders	NHL	79	14	33	47	13	27	40	8	1	3	0	118	11.9	69	8	75	35	+21	12	1	5	6	0	0	1	0
1977-78	New York Islanders	NHL	71	5	19	24	5	15	20	14	0	1	1	72	6.9	35	1	58	31	+7	2	0	0	0	0	0	0	0
1978-79	New York Islanders	NHL	55	5	11	16	5	8	13	4	0	1	1	51	9.8	25	0	50	25	0	6	1	2	3	0	0	0	0
NHL Totals			1220	231	394	625	243	355	598	544	25	23	23	1610	14.3	785	105	957	426		95	22	37	59	41	3	6	6

Won Bill Masterton Trophy (1977)

Played in NHL All-Star Game (1971, 1973, 1974, 1975)

Claimed by **NY Islanders** from **Boston** in Expansion Draft, June 6, 1972.

● **WHARRAM, KENNY**   Kenny Wharram   RW/C – R. 5'9", 160 lbs.   b: North Bay, Ont., 7/2/1933.

Season	Club	League	GP	G	A	Pts	AG	AA	APts	PIM	PP	SH	GW	S	%	TGF	PGF	TGA	PGA	+/-	GP	G	A	Pts	PIM	PP	SH	GW
1949-50	North Bay Black Hawks	EOSHL	2	0	1	1	....	....	....	0																		
1950-51	Galt Black Hawks	OHA	53	35	38	73	....	....	....	28											3	2	3	5	2			
1951-52	Galt Black Hawks	OHA	45	35	79	114	....	....	....	37																		
	Chicago Black Hawks	NHL	1	0	0	0	0	0	0	0																		
1952-53	Galt Black Hawks	OHA	54	34	40	74	....	....	....	42											11	9	*14	*23	2			
1953-54	Chicago Black Hawks	NHL	29	1	7	8	2	9	11	8																		
	Quebec Aces	QHL	29	7	10	17	....	....	....	8																		
1954-55	Buffalo Bisons	AHL	63	33	49	82	....	....	....	15											10	*9	7	*16	4			
1955-56	Chicago Black Hawks	NHL	3	0	0	0	0	0	0	0																		
	Buffalo Bisons	AHL	59	27	63	90	....	....	....	27											5	4	2	6	2			
1956-57	Buffalo Bisons	AHL	64	20	49	77	....	....	....	18																		
1957-58	Buffalo Bisons	AHL	58	31	26	57	....	....	....	14																		
1958-59	Chicago Black Hawks	NHL	66	10	9	19	13	10	23	14											6	0	2	2	2			
1959-60	Chicago Black Hawks	NHL	59	14	11	25	17	11	28	16											4	1	1	2	0			
1960-61	Chicago Black Hawks	NHL	64	16	29	45	20	30	50	12											12	3	5	8	12			
1961-62	Chicago Black Hawks	NHL	62	14	23	37	17	23	40	24											12	3	4	7	8			
1962-63	Chicago Black Hawks	NHL	55	20	18	38	25	19	44	17											6	1	5	6	0			
1963-64	Chicago Black Hawks	NHL	70	39	32	71	53	36	89	18											7	2	2	4	6			
1964-65	Chicago Black Hawks	NHL	68	24	20	44	31	22	53	27											12	2	3	5	4			
1965-66	Chicago Black Hawks	NHL	69	26	17	43	32	17	49	28											6	1	0	1	4			
1966-67	Chicago Black Hawks	NHL	70	31	34	65	39	35	74	21											6	2	2	4	2			
1967-68	Chicago Black Hawks	NHL	74	27	42	69	33	44	77	18	9	1	3	177	15.3	99	30	76	5	-2	9	1	3	4	0	0	0	0
1968-69	Chicago Black Hawks	NHL	76	30	39	69	34	37	71	19	5	0	4	167	18.0	107	31	60	2	+18								
NHL Totals			766	252	281	533	316	293	609	222	14	1	7	344	73.3	206	61	136	7		80	16	27	43	38	0	0	0

AHL Second All-Star Team (1955) • NHL First All-Star Team (1964, 1967) • Won Lady Byng Trophy (1964)

Played in NHL All-Star Game (1961, 1968)

Traded to **Buffalo** (AHL) by **Chicago** for cash, August, 1956. Traded to **Chicago** by **Buffalo** (AHL) for Wally Hergisimer and Frank Martin, May 5, 1958. • Suffered career-ending heart attack during training camp, October, 1969.

● **WHEELDON, SIMON**   Simon Wheeldon   C – L. 5'11", 170 lbs.   b: Vancouver, B.C., 8/30/1966.   Edmonton's 11th choice, 229th overall, in 1984 Entry Draft.

Season	Club	League	GP	G	A	Pts	AG	AA	APts	PIM	PP	SH	GW	S	%	TGF	PGF	TGA	PGA	+/-	GP	G	A	Pts	PIM	PP	SH	GW
1982-83	Kelowna Bucks	BCJHL	55	35	44	74	....	....	....	74											....							
1983-84	Victoria Cougars	WHL	56	14	24	38	....	....	....	43											....							
1984-85	Victoria Cougars	WHL	67	50	76	126	....	....	....	78											....							
	Nova Scotia Voyageurs	AHL	4	0	1	1	....	....	....	0											1	0	0	0	0			
1985-86	Victoria Cougars	WHL	70	61	96	157	....	....	....	85											....							
1986-87	Flint Spirits	IHL	41	17	53	70	....	....	....	20											....							
	New Haven Nighthawks	AHL	38	11	28	39	....	....	....	39											5	0	0	0	6			
1987-88	New York Rangers	NHL	5	0	1	1	0	1	1	4	0	0	0	2	0.0	1	0	3	0	-2	....							
	Colorado Rangers	IHL	69	45	54	99	....	....	....	80											13	8	11	19	12			
1988-89	New York Rangers	NHL	6	0	1	1	0	1	1	2	0	0	0	2	0.0	1	0	2	0	-1	....							
	Denver Rangers	IHL	74	50	56	106	....	....	....	77											4	0	2	2	6			
1989-90	Flint Spirits	IHL	76	34	49	83	....	....	....	61											4	1	2	3	2			
1990-91	Winnipeg Jets	NHL	4	0	0	0	0	0	0	4	0	0	0	4	0.0	2	0	0	0	+2	....							
	Moncton Hawks	AHL	66	30	38	68	....	....	....	38											8	4	3	7	2			
1991-92	Baltimore Skipjacks	AHL	78	38	53	91	....	....	....	62																		
1992-93	VEU Feldkirch	Austria	50	29	57	86																						
1993-94	VEU Feldkirch	Austria	55	*43	46	*89	....	....	....	24																		
1994-95	VEU Feldkirch	Austria	27	22	27	49	....	....	....	36											13	9	10	19	32			
1995-96	VEU Feldkirch	Austria	37	*35	*50	*85	....	....	....	32																		
	VEU Feldkirch	Alpenliga	8	13	11	24	....	....	....	6																		
1996-97	VEU Feldkirch	Austria	56	41	44	85	....	....	....	52																		
	Austria	WC-B	7	4	0	4				2																		
1997-98	VEU Feldkirch	EuroHL	10	6	6	12				8																		
	Austria	Olympics	4	0	1	1				8																		
	Austria	WC-A	3	1	0	1				2																		
NHL Totals			15	0	2	2	0	2	2	10	0	0	0	8	0.0	4	0	5	0									

WHL West Second All-Star Team (1985, 1986) • IHL Second All-Star Team (1988, 1989)

Signed as a free agent by **NY Rangers**, September 8, 1986. Traded to **Winnipeg** by **NY Rangers** for Brian McReynolds, July 9, 1990. Traded to **Washington** by **Winnipeg** with Craig Duncanson and Brent Hughes for Bob Joyce, Tyler Larter and Kent Paynter, May 21, 1991.

● **WHELDON, DONALD**   Donald Wheldon   D – R. 6'2", 185 lbs.   b: Falmouth, MA, 12/28/1954.   d: 6/3/1985.   St. Louis' 4th choice, 87th overall, in 1974 Amateur Draft.

Season	Club	League	GP	G	A	Pts	AG	AA	APts	PIM	PP	SH	GW	S	%	TGF	PGF	TGA	PGA	+/-	GP	G	A	Pts	PIM	PP	SH	GW
1971-72	Riverview Reds	NBJHL	24	6	11	17	....	....	....	59											....							
	Moncton Beavers	NBJHL	15	3	12	15	....	....	....	10											....							
1972-73	London Knights	OHA	65	2	7	9	....	....	....	70											....							
1973-74	London Knights	OHA	70	5	27	32	....	....	....	88											....							
1974-75	St. Louis Blues	NHL	2	0	0	0	0	0	0	0	0	0	0	0	0.0	0	0	1	1	0	....							
	Denver Spurs	CHL	8	0	1	1	....	....	....	8											....							
	Columbus Owls	IHL	43	6	12	18	....	....	....	28											5	2	1	3	2			
1975-76	Winston-Salem Polar Bears	SHL	70	11	28	39	....	....	....	52											4	1	0	1	4			
1976-77	Winston-Salem Polar Bears	SHL	37	9	13	22	....	....	....	14											....							
NHL Totals			2	0	0	0	0	0	0	0	0	0	0	0	0.0	0	0	1	1		....							

			REGULAR SEASON																		PLAYOFFS							
Season	Club	League	GP	G	A	Pts	AG	AA	APts	PIM	PP	SH	GW	S	%	TGF	PGF	TGA	PGA	+/–	GP	G	A	Pts	PIM	PP	SH	GW

• WHELTON, BILL

Bill Whelton D – L. 6'1", 180 lbs. b: Everett, MA, 8/28/1959. Winnipeg's 3rd choice, 61st overall, in 1979 Entry Draft.

Season	Club	League	GP	G	A	Pts	AG	AA	APts	PIM	PP	SH	GW	S	%	TGF	PGF	TGA	PGA	+/–	GP	G	A	Pts	PIM	PP	SH	GW
1978-79	Boston University	ECAC	30	2	5	7	....	....	....	20	....	....	....	....	....	....	....	....	....	....	....	....	....	....	....	....	....	....
1979-80	Boston University	ECAC	30	4	14	18	....	....	....	39	....	....	....	....	....	....	....	....	....	....	....	....	....	....	....	....	....	....
1980-81	Boston University	ECAC	29	4	18	22	....	....	....	42	....	....	....	....	....	....	....	....	....	....	....	....	....	....	....	....	....	....
	Winnipeg Jets	**NHL**	**2**	**0**	**0**	**0**	**0**	**0**	**0**	**0**	**0**	**0**	**0**	**1**	**0.0**	**0**	**0**	**1**	**0**	**–1**	....	....	....	....	....	....	....	....
1981-82	Tulsa Oilers	CHL	66	2	18	20	....	....	....	51	....	....	....	....	....	....	....	....	....	....	3	0	0	0	2	....	....	....
1982-83	Sherbrooke Jets	AHL	72	4	16	20	....	....	....	73	....	....	....	....	....	....	....	....	....	....	....	....	....	....	....	....	....	....
1983-84	Sherbrooke Jets	AHL	67	2	14	16	....	....	....	32	....	....	....	....	....	....	....	....	....	....	....	....	....	....	....	....	....	....
1984-85			DID NOT PLAY																									
1985-86	Brunico	Italy	35	12	21	33	....	....	....	61	....	....	....	....	....	....	....	....	....	....	5	1	4	5	4	....	....	....
	NHL Totals		**2**	**0**	**0**	**0**	**0**	**0**	**0**	**0**	**0**	**0**	**0**	**1**	**0.0**	**0**	**0**	**1**	**0**		....	....	....	....	....	....	....	....

• WHISTLE, ROB

Rob Whistle D – R. 6'2", 195 lbs. b: Thunder Bay, Ont., 4/4/1961.

Season	Club	League	GP	G	A	Pts	AG	AA	APts	PIM	PP	SH	GW	S	%	TGF	PGF	TGA	PGA	+/–	GP	G	A	Pts	PIM	PP	SH	GW
1976-77	Thunder Bay Flyers	Midget	28	10	21	31	....	....	....	....	....	....	....	....	....	....	....	....	....	....	....	....	....	....	....	....	....	....
1977-78	Thunder Bay Flyers	Midget	28	28	30	58	....	....	....	....	....	....	....	....	....	....	....	....	....	....	....	....	....	....	....	....	....	....
1978-79	Thunder Bay Flyers	Tier II	18	10	12	22	....	....	....	22	....	....	....	....	....	....	....	....	....	....	....	....	....	....	....	....	....	....
1979-80	Kitchener Rangers	OHA	55	2	5	7	....	....	....	68	....	....	....	....	....	....	....	....	....	....	....	....	....	....	....	....	....	....
1980-81	Kitchener Rangers	OHA	33	4	0	4	....	....	....	47	....	....	....	....	....	....	....	....	....	....	....	....	....	....	....	....	....	....
1981-82	Sir Wilfred Laurier University	OUAA	STATISTICS NOT AVAILABLE																									
1982-83	Sir Wilfred Laurier University	OUAA	24	6	14	20	....	....	....	12	....	....	....	....	....	....	....	....	....	....	....	....	....	....	....	....	....	....
1983-84	Sir Wilfred Laurier University	OUAA	24	9	15	24	....	....	....	42	....	....	....	....	....	....	....	....	....	....	....	....	....	....	....	....	....	....
1984-85	Sir Wilfred Laurier University	OUAA	24	5	22	27	....	....	....	31	....	....	....	....	....	....	....	....	....	....	....	....	....	....	....	....	....	....
1985-86	**New York Rangers**	**NHL**	**32**	**4**	**2**	**6**	**3**	**1**	**4**	**10**	**1**	**0**	**1**	**30**	**13.3**	**22**	**3**	**21**	**1**	**–1**	**3**	**0**	**0**	**0**	**2**	**0**	**0**	**0**
	New Haven Nighthawks	AHL	20	1	4	5	....	....	....	5	....	....	....	....	....	....	....	....	....	....	....	....	....	....	....	....	....	....
1986-87	New Haven Nighthawks	AHL	55	4	12	16	....	....	....	30	....	....	....	....	....	....	....	....	....	....	7	1	1	2	7	....	....	....
1987-88	**St. Louis Blues**	**NHL**	**19**	**3**	**3**	**6**	**3**	**2**	**5**	**6**	**0**	**0**	**1**	**17**	**17.6**	**19**	**0**	**23**	**4**	**0**	**1**	**0**	**0**	**0**	**0**	**0**	**0**	**0**
	Peoria Rivermen	IHL	39	5	21	26	....	....	....	21	....	....	....	....	....	....	....	....	....	....	....	....	....	....	....	....	....	....
1988-89	Baltimore Skipjacks	AHL	61	2	24	26	....	....	....	30	....	....	....	....	....	....	....	....	....	....	....	....	....	....	....	....	....	....
	Peoria Rivermen	IHL	4	0	1	1	....	....	....	4	....	....	....	....	....	....	....	....	....	....	....	....	....	....	....	....	....	....
	NHL Totals		**51**	**7**	**5**	**12**	**6**	**3**	**9**	**16**	**1**	**0**	**2**	**47**	**14.9**	**41**	**3**	**44**	**5**		**4**	**0**	**0**	**0**	**2**	**0**	**0**	**0**

Signed as a free agent by **NY Rangers**, August 13, 1985. Traded to **St. Louis** by **NY Rangers** for Bruce Bell and future considerations, May 28, 1987. Traded to **Washington** by **St. Louis** for Washington's 6th round choice (Derek Frenette) in 1989 Entry Draft, October 19, 1988.

• WHITE, BILL

Bill White D – R. 6'2", 195 lbs. b: Toronto, Ont., 8/26/1939.

Season	Club	League	GP	G	A	Pts	AG	AA	APts	PIM	PP	SH	GW	S	%	TGF	PGF	TGA	PGA	+/–	GP	G	A	Pts	PIM	PP	SH	GW
1956-57	Toronto Marlboros	OHA	2	0	0	0	....	....	....	4	....	....	....	....	....	....	....	....	....	....	....	....	....	....	....	....	....	....
1957-58	Toronto Marlboros	OHA	52	2	7	9	....	....	....	34	....	....	....	....	....	....	....	....	....	....	13	1	2	3	18	....	....	....
1958-59	Toronto Marlboros	OHA	54	3	17	20	....	....	....	63	....	....	....	....	....	....	....	....	....	....	5	3	0	3	2	....	....	....
1959-60	Toronto Marlboros	OHA	48	2	17	19	....	....	....	66	....	....	....	....	....	....	....	....	....	....	4	0	1	1	16	....	....	....
	Rochester Americans	AHL	1	0	0	0	....	....	....	0	....	....	....	....	....	....	....	....	....	....	....	....	....	....	....	....	....	....
1960-61	Sudbury Wolves	EPHL	21	1	2	3	....	....	....	20	....	....	....	....	....	....	....	....	....	....	....	....	....	....	....	....	....	....
	Rochester Americans	AHL	47	1	9	10	....	....	....	37	....	....	....	....	....	....	....	....	....	....	....	....	....	....	....	....	....	....
1961-62	Rochester Americans	AHL	67	5	21	26	....	....	....	58	....	....	....	....	....	....	....	....	....	....	2	0	1	1	2	....	....	....
1962-63	Springfield Indians	AHL	69	8	38	46	....	....	....	38	....	....	....	....	....	....	....	....	....	....	....	....	....	....	....	....	....	....
1963-64	Springfield Indians	AHL	72	7	31	38	....	....	....	76	....	....	....	....	....	....	....	....	....	....	....	....	....	....	....	....	....	....
1964-65	Springfield Indians	AHL	71	7	31	38	....	....	....	66	....	....	....	....	....	....	....	....	....	....	....	....	....	....	....	....	....	....
1965-66	Springfield Indians	AHL	68	5	14	19	....	....	....	42	....	....	....	....	....	....	....	....	....	....	6	0	2	2	6	....	....	....
1966-67	Springfield Indians	AHL	69	5	29	34	....	....	....	68	....	....	....	....	....	....	....	....	....	....	....	....	....	....	....	....	....	....
1967-68	**Los Angeles Kings**	**NHL**	**74**	**11**	**27**	**38**	**14**	**28**	**42**	**100**	**2**	**1**	**1**	**170**	**6.5**	**108**	**18**	**97**	**24**	**+17**	**7**	**2**	**2**	**4**	**4**	**0**	**0**	**1**
1968-69	**Los Angeles Kings**	**NHL**	**75**	**5**	**28**	**33**	**6**	**26**	**32**	**38**	**0**	**0**	**0**	**163**	**3.1**	**106**	**22**	**133**	**29**	**–20**	**11**	**1**	**4**	**5**	**8**	**0**	**0**	**0**
1969-70	**Los Angeles Kings**	**NHL**	**40**	**4**	**11**	**15**	**5**	**11**	**16**	**21**	**2**	**0**	**0**	**62**	**6.5**	**39**	**8**	**73**	**27**	**–15**	....	....	....	....	....	....	....	....
	Chicago Black Hawks	**NHL**	**21**	**0**	**5**	**5**	**0**	**5**	**5**	**18**	**0**	**0**	**0**	**32**	**0.0**	**24**	**3**	**25**	**7**	**+3**	**8**	**1**	**2**	**3**	**8**	**0**	**0**	**0**
1970-71	**Chicago Black Hawks**	**NHL**	**67**	**4**	**21**	**25**	**4**	**18**	**22**	**64**	**0**	**0**	**1**	**127**	**3.1**	**100**	**3**	**73**	**27**	**+51**	**18**	**1**	**4**	**5**	**20**	**0**	**0**	**1**
1971-72	**Chicago Black Hawks**	**NHL**	**76**	**7**	**22**	**29**	**7**	**20**	**27**	**58**	**0**	**0**	**0**	**122**	**5.7**	**107**	**5**	**86**	**26**	**+42**	**8**	**0**	**3**	**3**	**6**	**0**	**0**	**0**
1972-73	Canada	Summit	7	1	1	2	....	....	....	8	....	....	....	....	....	....	....	....	....	....	....	....	....	....	....	....	....	....
	Chicago Black Hawks	**NHL**	**72**	**9**	**38**	**47**	**9**	**32**	**41**	**80**	**1**	**0**	**2**	**176**	**5.1**	**151**	**40**	**115**	**34**	**+30**	**16**	**1**	**6**	**7**	**10**	**0**	**1**	**0**
1973-74	**Chicago Black Hawks**	**NHL**	**69**	**5**	**31**	**36**	**5**	**27**	**32**	**52**	**0**	**0**	**1**	**85**	**5.9**	**136**	**29**	**73**	**17**	**+51**	**11**	**1**	**7**	**8**	**14**	**1**	**0**	**0**
1974-75	**Chicago Black Hawks**	**NHL**	**51**	**4**	**23**	**27**	**4**	**18**	**22**	**20**	**2**	**0**	**0**	**83**	**4.8**	**93**	**26**	**77**	**19**	**+9**	**8**	**0**	**3**	**3**	**4**	**0**	**0**	**0**
1975-76	**Chicago Black Hawks**	**NHL**	**59**	**1**	**9**	**10**	**1**	**7**	**8**	**44**	**0**	**0**	**0**	**46**	**2.2**	**64**	**5**	**97**	**28**	**–10**	**4**	**0**	**1**	**1**	**2**	**0**	**0**	**0**
1976-77	**Chicago Black Hawks**	**NHL**	DID NOT PLAY – INJURED																									
1977-78	Oshawa Generals	OHA	DID NOT PLAY – COACHING																									
	NHL Totals		**604**	**50**	**215**	**265**	**55**	**192**	**247**	**495**	**7**	**1**	**5**	**1066**	**4.7**	**928**	**159**	**849**	**238**		**91**	**7**	**32**	**39**	**76**	**1**	**1**	**2**

NHL Second All-Star Team (1972, 1973, 1974)

Played in NHL All-Star Game (1969, 1970, 1971, 1972, 1973, 1974)

Traded to **Springfield** (AHL) by **Toronto** (Rochester - AHL) with Dick Mattiussi, Wally Boyer, Jim Wilcox and Roger Cote for Kent Douglas, June, 1962. NHL rights transferred to **LA Kings** after NHL club purchased **Springfield** (AHL) franchise, May, 1967. Traded to **Chicago** by **LA Kings** with Bryan Campbell and Gerry Desjardins for Gilles Marotte, Jim Stanfield and Denis Dejordy, February 20, 1970.

• WHITE, PETER

Peter White C – L. 5'11", 200 lbs. b: Montreal, Que., 3/15/1969. Edmonton's 4th choice, 92nd overall, in 1989 Entry Draft.

Season	Club	League	GP	G	A	Pts	AG	AA	APts	PIM	PP	SH	GW	S	%	TGF	PGF	TGA	PGA	+/–	GP	G	A	Pts	PIM	PP	SH	GW
1987-88	Pembroke Lumber Kings	OJHL	56	90	136	226	....	....	....	32	....	....	....	....	....	....	....	....	....	....	....	....	....	....	....	....	....	....
1988-89	Michigan State Spartans	CCHA	46	20	33	53	....	....	....	17	....	....	....	....	....	....	....	....	....	....	....	....	....	....	....	....	....	....
1989-90	Michigan State Spartans	CCHA	45	22	40	62	....	....	....	6	....	....	....	....	....	....	....	....	....	....	....	....	....	....	....	....	....	....
1990-91	Michigan State Spartans	CCHA	37	7	31	38	....	....	....	28	....	....	....	....	....	....	....	....	....	....	....	....	....	....	....	....	....	....
1991-92	Michigan State Spartans	CCHA	41	26	49	75	....	....	....	32	....	....	....	....	....	....	....	....	....	....	....	....	....	....	....	....	....	....
1992-93	Cape Breton Oilers	AHL	64	12	28	40	....	....	....	10	....	....	....	....	....	....	....	....	....	....	16	3	3	6	12	....	....	....
1993-94	**Edmonton Oilers**	**NHL**	**26**	**3**	**5**	**8**	**3**	**4**	**7**	**2**	**0**	**0**	**0**	**17**	**17.6**	**11**	**0**	**13**	**3**	**+1**	....	....	....	....	....	....	....	....
	Cape Breton Oilers	AHL	45	21	49	70	....	....	....	12	....	....	....	....	....	....	....	....	....	....	5	2	3	5	2	....	....	....
1994-95	Cape Breton Oilers	AHL	65	36	*69	*105	....	....	....	30	....	....	....	....	....	....	....	....	....	....	....	....	....	....	....	....	....	....
	Edmonton Oilers	**NHL**	**9**	**2**	**4**	**6**	**4**	**6**	**10**	**0**	**2**	**0**	**0**	**13**	**15.4**	**6**	**2**	**3**	**0**	**+1**	....	....	....	....	....	....	....	....
1995-96	**Edmonton Oilers**	**NHL**	**26**	**5**	**3**	**8**	**5**	**2**	**7**	**0**	**1**	**0**	**0**	**34**	**14.7**	**9**	**2**	**26**	**5**	**–14**	....	....	....	....	....	....	....	....
	Toronto Maple Leafs	**NHL**	**1**	**0**	**0**	**0**	**0**	**0**	**0**	**0**	**1**	**0**	**0**	**0**	**0.0**	**0**	**0**	**0**	**0**	**0**	....	....	....	....	....	....	....	....
	St. John's Maple Leafs	AHL	17	6	7	13	....	....	....	6	....	....	....	....	....	....	....	....	....	....	....	....	....	....	....	....	....	....
	Atlanta Knights	IHL	36	21	20	41	....	....	....	4	....	....	....	....	....	....	....	....	....	....	3	0	3	3	2	....	....	....
1996-97	Philadelphia Phantoms	AHL	80	*44	61	*105	....	....	....	28	....	....	....	....	....	....	....	....	....	....	10	6	8	14	6	....	....	....
1997-98	Philadelphia Phantoms	AHL	80	27	78	105	....	....	....	28	....	....	....	....	....	....	....	....	....	....	20	9	9	18	6	....	....	....
	NHL Totals		**62**	**10**	**12**	**22**	**12**	**12**	**24**	**2**	**4**	**0**	**0**	**64**	**15.6**	**26**	**4**	**42**	**8**		....	....	....	....	....	....	....	....

AHL Second All-Star Team (1995, 1997) • Won John B. Sollenberger Trophy (Top Scorer - AHL) (1995, 1997, 1998)

Traded to **Toronto** by **Edmonton** with Edmonton's 4th round choice (Jason Sessa) in 1996 Entry Draft for Kent Manderville, December 4, 1995. Signed as a free agent by **Philadelphia**, August 19, 1996.

• WHITE, TODD

Todd White C – L. 5'10", 180 lbs. b: Kanata, Ont., 5/21/1975.

			REGULAR SEASON																		PLAYOFFS							
Season	Club	League	GP	G	A	Pts	AG	AA	APts	PIM	PP	SH	GW	S	%	TGF	PGF	TGA	PGA	+/–	GP	G	A	Pts	PIM	PP	SH	GW
1993-94	Clarkson University	ECAC	33	10	12	22	....	....	....	28	....	....	....	....	....	....	....	....	....	....	....	....	....	....	....	....	....	....
1994-95	Clarkson University	ECAC	34	13	16	29	....	....	....	44	....	....	....	....	....	....	....	....	....	....	....	....	....	....	....	....	....	....
1995-96	Clarkson University	ECAC	38	29	43	72	....	....	....	36	....	....	....	....	....	....	....	....	....	....	....	....	....	....	....	....	....	....
1996-97	Clarkson University	ECAC	37	*38	*36	*74	....	....	....	22	....	....	....	....	....	....	....	....	....	....	....	....	....	....	....	....	....	....
1997-98	**Chicago Blackhawks**	**NHL**	**7**	**1**	**0**	**1**	**1**	**0**	**1**	**2**	**0**	**0**	**0**	**3**	**33.3**	**4**	**0**	**4**	**0**	**0**	....	....	....	....	....	....	....	....
	Indianapolis Ice	IHL	65	46	36	82	....	....	....	28	....	....	....	....	....	....	....	....	....	....	5	2	3	5	4	....	....	....
	NHL Totals		**7**	**1**	**0**	**1**	**1**	**0**	**1**	**2**	**0**	**0**	**0**	**3**	**33.3**	**4**	**0**	**4**	**0**		....	....	....	....	....	....	....	....

ECAC Second All-Star Team (1996) • NCAA East Second All-American Team (1996) • ECAC First All-Star Team (1997) • NCAA East First All-American Team (1997) • Won Garry F. Longman Memorial Trophy (Top Rookie - IHL) (1998)

Signed as a free agent by **Chicago**, August 27, 1997.

• WHITE, TONY

Tony White LW – L. 5'10", 175 lbs. b: Grand Falls, Nfld., 6/16/1954. Washington's 10th choice, 161st overall, in 1974 Amateur Draft.

Season	Club	League	GP	G	A	Pts	AG	AA	APts	PIM	PP	SH	GW	S	%	TGF	PGF	TGA	PGA	+/–	GP	G	A	Pts	PIM	PP	SH	GW
1972-73	Kitchener Rangers	OHA	60	20	33	53	....	....	....	65	....	....	....	....	....	....	....	....	....	....	....	....	....	....	....	....	....	....
1973-74	Kitchener Rangers	OHA	70	15	38	53	....	....	....	69	....	....	....	....	....	....	....	....	....	....	....	....	....	....	....	....	....	....
1974-75	**Washington Capitals**	**NHL**	**5**	**0**	**2**	**2**	**0**	**2**	**2**	**0**	**0**	**0**	**0**	**8**	**0.0**	**3**	**0**	**3**	**0**	**0**	....	....	....	....	....	....	....	....
	Dayton Gems	IHL	64	23	35	58	....	....	....	73	....	....	....	....	....	....	....	....	....	....	14	7	9	16	27	....	....	....
1975-76	**Washington Capitals**	**NHL**	**80**	**25**	**17**	**42**	**23**	**13**	**36**	**56**	**7**	**0**	**2**	**168**	**14.9**	**75**	**23**	**101**	**6**	**–43**	....	....	....	....	....	....	....	....
1976-77	**Washington Capitals**	**NHL**	**72**	**12**	**9**	**21**	**11**	**7**	**18**	**44**	**2**	**1**	**3**	**126**	**9.5**	**45**	**5**	**58**	**3**	**–15**	....	....	....	....	....	....	....	....
1977-78	**Washington Capitals**	**NHL**	**1**	**0**	**0**	**0**	**0**	**0**	**0**	**0**	**0**	**0**	**0**	**4**	**0.0**	**1**	**1**	**4**	**0**	**–4**	....	....	....	....	....	....	....	....
	Hershey Bears	AHL	68	24	29	53	....	....	....	28	....	....	....	....	....	....	....	....	....	....	....	....	....	....	....	....	....	....
1978-79	Springfield Indians	AHL	80	26	29	55	....	....	....	30	....	....	....	....	....	....	....	....	....	....	....	....	....	....	....	....	....	....
1979-80	**Minnesota North Stars**	**NHL**	**6**	**0**	**0**	**0**	**0**	**0**	**0**	**4**	**0**	**0**	**0**	**10**	**0.0**	**2**	**0**	**4**	**0**	**–2**	....	....	....	....	....	....	....	....
	Oklahoma City Stars	CHL	74	30	28	58	....	....	....	59	....	....	....	....	....	....	....	....	....	....	....	....	....	....	....	....	....	....
1980-81	Oklahoma City Stars	CHL	74	21	41	62	....	....	....	55	....	....	....	....	....	....	....	....	....	....	3	0	1	1	6	....	....	....
1981-82	EV Fussen	Germany	41	21	21	42	....	....	....	79	....	....	....	....	....	....	....	....	....	....	....	....	....	....	....	....	....	....
1982-83	EV Fussen	Germany	25	9	13	22	....	....	....	42	....	....	....	....	....	....	....	....	....	....	....	....	....	....	....	....	....	....
	NHL Totals		**164**	**37**	**28**	**65**	**34**	**22**	**56**	**104**	**9**	**1**	**5**	**316**	**11.7**	**126**	**29**	**170**	**9**		....	....	....	....	....	....	....	....

Signed as a free agent by **Minnesota**, September 17, 1979.

• WHITLOCK, BOB

Bob Whitlock C – R. 5'10", 175 lbs. b: Charlottetown, P.E.I., 7/16/1949.

Season	Club	League	GP	G	A	Pts	AG	AA	APts	PIM	PP	SH	GW	S	%	TGF	PGF	TGA	PGA	+/–	GP	G	A	Pts	PIM	PP	SH	GW
1966-67	Halifax Jr. Canadiens	NSJHL	48	52	70	122	....	....	....	52	....	....	....	....	....	....	....	....	....	....	18	14	18	32	18	....	....	....
1967-68	Halifax Jr. Canadians	NSJHL	38	53	42	95	....	....	....	4	....	....	....	....	....	....	....	....	....	....	11	*9	*11	*20	0	....	....	....
	Fredericton Jr. Red Wings	NBJHL	5	2	3	5	....	....	....	28	....	....	....	....	....	....	....	....	....	....	....	....	....	....	....	....	....	....
1968-69	Kitchener Rangers	OHA	22	9	15	24	....	....	....	51	....	....	....	....	....	....	....	....	....	....	....	....	....	....	....	....	....	....
	Edmonton Oil Kings	WCJHL	6	2	2	4	....	....	....	0	....	....	....	....	....	....	....	....	....	....	....	....	....	....	....	....	....	....
1969-70	**Minnesota North Stars**	**NHL**	**1**	**0**	**0**	**0**	**0**	**0**	**0**	**0**	**0**	**0**	**0**	**3**	**0.0**	**1**	**0**	**0**	**0**	**+1**	....	....	....	....	....	....	....	....
	Iowa Stars	CHL	63	26	28	54	....	....	....	58	....	....	....	....	....	....	....	....	....	....	11	4	3	7	4	....	....	....
1970-71	Cleveland Barons	AHL	68	19	15	34	....	....	....	30	....	....	....	....	....	....	....	....	....	....	8	1	2	3	4	....	....	....
1971-72	Phoenix Roadrunners	WHL	64	33	46	79	....	....	....	69	....	....	....	....	....	....	....	....	....	....	4	2	2	4	4	....	....	....
1972-73	Chicago Cougars	WHA	75	23	28	51	....	....	....	53	....	....	....	....	....	....	....	....	....	....	....	....	....	....	....	....	....	....
1973-74	Chicago Cougars	WHA	52	16	19	35	....	....	....	44	....	....	....	....	....	....	....	....	....	....	....	....	....	....	....	....	....	....
	Los Angeles Sharks	WHA	14	4	10	14	....	....	....	4	....	....	....	....	....	....	....	....	....	....	....	....	....	....	....	....	....	....
1974-75	Indianapolis Racers	WHA	73	31	26	57	....	....	....	56	....	....	....	....	....	....	....	....	....	....	....	....	....	....	....	....	....	....
1975-76	Indianapolis Racers	WHA	30	7	15	22	....	....	....	16	....	....	....	....	....	....	....	....	....	....	....	....	....	....	....	....	....	....
	Mohawk Valley Comets	NAHL	32	15	20	35	....	....	....	42	....	....	....	....	....	....	....	....	....	....	....	....	....	....	....	....	....	....
1976-77	Erie Blades	NAHL	15	7	7	14	....	....	....	8	....	....	....	....	....	....	....	....	....	....	....	....	....	....	....	....	....	....
	Johnstown Jets	NAHL	20	8	8	16	....	....	....	26	....	....	....	....	....	....	....	....	....	....	....	....	....	....	....	....	....	....
1977-78	Trail Smoke Eaters	WIHL	[illegible]	31	27	58	....	....	....	60	....	....	....	....	....	....	....	....	....	....	....	....	....	....	....	....	....	....
	NHL Totals		**1**	**0**	**0**	**0**	**0**	**0**	**0**	**0**	**0**	**0**	**0**	**3**	**0.0**	**1**	**0**	**0**	**0**		....	....	....	....	....	....	....	....
	Other Major League Totals		244	81	98	179	....	....	....	173	....	....	....	....	....	....	....	....	....		....	....	....	....	....	....	....	....

Won WIHL Rookie of the Year Award (1972)

Signed as a free agent by **Minnesota**, October 2, 1969. Selected by **LA Sharks** (WHA) in 1972 WHA General Player Draft, February 12, 1972. Traded to **Chicago** (WHA) by **LA Sharks** (WHA) for future considerations, August, 1972. Traded to **LA Sharks** (WHA) by **Chicago** (WHA) for Don Gordon and Jim Watson, February 20, 1974. Transferred to **Michigan** (WHA) after **LA Sharks** relocated, April 11, 1974. Claimed by **Indianapolis** (WHA) from **Michigan** (WHA) in WHA Expansion Draft, May, 1974.

• WHITNEY, RAY

Ray Whitney C – R. 5'9", 160 lbs. b: Fort Saskatchewan, Alta., 5/8/1972. San Jose's 2nd choice, 23rd overall, in 1991 Entry Draft.

Season	Club	League	GP	G	A	Pts	AG	AA	APts	PIM	PP	SH	GW	S	%	TGF	PGF	TGA	PGA	+/–	GP	G	A	Pts	PIM	PP	SH	GW
1988-89	Spokane Chiefs	WHL	71	17	33	50	....	....	....	16	....	....	....	....	....	....	....	....	....	....	....	....	....	....	....	....	....	....
1989-90	Spokane Chiefs	WHL	71	57	56	113	....	....	....	50	....	....	....	....	....	....	....	....	....	....	6	3	4	7	6	....	....	....
1990-91	Spokane Chiefs	WHL	72	67	118	*185	....	....	....	36	....	....	....	....	....	....	....	....	....	....	15	13	18	*31	12	....	....	....
1991-92	Kolner Haie	Germany	10	3	6	9	....	....	....	4	....	....	....	....	....	....	....	....	....	....	....	....	....	....	....	....	....	....
	Canada	Nat-Team	5	1	0	1	....	....	....	6	....	....	....	....	....	....	....	....	....	....	....	....	....	....	....	....	....	....
	San Jose Sharks	**NHL**	**2**	**0**	**3**	**3**	**0**	**2**	**2**	**0**	**0**	**0**	**0**	**4**	**0.0**	**3**	**2**	**2**	**0**	**–1**	....	....	....	....	....	....	....	....
	San Diego Gulls	IHL	63	36	54	90	....	....	....	12	....	....	....	....	....	....	....	....	....	....	4	0	0	0	0	....	....	....
1992-93	**San Jose Sharks**	**NHL**	**26**	**4**	**6**	**10**	**3**	**4**	**7**	**4**	**1**	**0**	**0**	**24**	**16.7**	**12**	**4**	**22**	**0**	**–14**	....	....	....	....	....	....	....	....
	Kansas City Blades	IHL	46	20	33	53	....	....	....	14	....	....	....	....	....	....	....	....	....	....	12	5	7	12	2	....	....	....
1993-94	**San Jose Sharks**	**NHL**	**61**	**14**	**26**	**40**	**13**	**20**	**33**	**14**	**1**	**0**	**0**	**82**	**17.1**	**56**	**18**	**38**	**2**	**+2**	**14**	**0**	**4**	**4**	**8**	**0**	**0**	**0**
1994-95	**San Jose Sharks**	**NHL**	**39**	**13**	**12**	**25**	**23**	**18**	**41**	**14**	**4**	**0**	**1**	**67**	**19.4**	**37**	**13**	**31**	**0**	**–7**	**11**	**4**	**4**	**8**	**2**	**0**	**0**	**1**
1995-96	**San Jose Sharks**	**NHL**	**60**	**17**	**24**	**41**	**17**	**20**	**37**	**16**	**4**	**2**	**2**	**106**	**16.0**	**58**	**17**	**74**	**10**	**–23**	....	....	....	....	....	....	....	....
1996-97	**San Jose Sharks**	**NHL**	**12**	**0**	**2**	**2**	**0**	**2**	**2**	**4**	**0**	**0**	**0**	**24**	**0.0**	**5**	**0**	**13**	**2**	**–6**	....	....	....	....	....	....	....	....
	Kentucky Thoroughblades	AHL	9	1	7	8	....	....	....	2	....	....	....	....	....	....	....	....	....	....	....	....	....	....	....	....	....	....
	Utah Grizzlies	IHL	43	13	35	48	....	....	....	34	....	....	....	....	....	....	....	....	....	....	7	3	1	4	6	....	....	....
1997-98	**Edmonton Oilers**	**NHL**	**9**	**1**	**3**	**4**	**1**	**3**	**4**	**0**	**0**	**0**	**0**	**19**	**5.3**	**6**	**4**	**3**	**0**	**–1**	....	....	....	....	....	....	....	....
	Florida Panthers	**NHL**	**68**	**32**	**29**	**61**	**38**	**28**	**66**	**28**	**12**	**0**	**2**	**156**	**20.5**	**77**	**34**	**33**	**0**	**+10**	....	....	....	....	....	....	....	....
	Canada	WC-A	6	4	2	6	....	....	....	4	....	....	....	....	....	....	....	....	....	....	....	....	....	....	....	....	....	....
	NHL Totals		**277**	**81**	**105**	**186**	**95**	**97**	**192**	**80**	**22**	**2**	**5**	**482**	**16.8**	**254**	**92**	**216**	**14**		**25**	**4**	**8**	**12**	**10**	**0**	**0**	**1**

WHL West First All-Star Team (1991) • Memorial Cup All-Star Team (1991) • Won George Parsons Trophy (Memorial Cup Tournament Most Sportsmanlike Player) (1991)

Claimed on waivers by **Florida** from **Edmonton**, November 6, 1997.

• WHYTE, SEAN

Sean Whyte RW – R. 6', 198 lbs. b: Sudbury, Ont., 5/4/1970. Los Angeles' 7th choice, 165th overall, in 1989 Entry Draft.

Season	Club	League	GP	G	A	Pts	AG	AA	APts	PIM	PP	SH	GW	S	%	TGF	PGF	TGA	PGA	+/–	GP	G	A	Pts	PIM	PP	SH	GW
1986-87	Guelph Platers	OHL	41	1	3	4	....	....	....	13	....	....	....	....	....	....	....	....	....	....	....	....	....	....	....	....	....	....
1987-88	Guelph Platers	OHL	62	6	22	28	....	....	....	71	....	....	....	....	....	....	....	....	....	....	....	....	....	....	....	....	....	....
1988-89	Guelph Platers	OHL	53	20	44	64	....	....	....	57	....	....	....	....	....	....	....	....	....	....	....	....	....	....	....	....	....	....
1989-90	Owen Sound Platers	OHL	54	23	30	53	....	....	....	90	....	....	....	....	....	....	....	....	....	....	3	0	1	1	10	....	....	....
1990-91	Phoenix Roadrunners	IHL	60	18	17	35	....	....	....	61	....	....	....	....	....	....	....	....	....	....	4	1	0	1	2	....	....	....
1991-92	**Los Angeles Kings**	**NHL**	**3**	**0**	**0**	**0**	**0**	**0**	**0**	**0**	**0**	**0**	**0**	**0**	**0.0**	**0**	**0**	**1**	**0**	**–1**	....	....	....	....	....	....	....	....
	Phoenix Roadrunners	IHL	72	24	30	54	....	....	....	113	....	....	....	....	....	....	....	....	....	....	....	....	....	....	....	....	....	....
1992-93	**Los Angeles Kings**	**NHL**	**18**	**0**	**2**	**2**	**0**	**1**	**1**	**12**	**0**	**0**	**0**	**7**	**0.0**	**6**	**0**	**5**	**0**	**+1**	....	....	....	....	....	....	....	....
	Phoenix Roadrunners	IHL	51	11	35	46	....	....	....	65	....	....	....	....	....	....	....	....	....	....	....	....	....	....	....	....	....	....
1993-94	Tulsa Oilers	CHL	50	42	29	71	....	....	....	93	....	....	....	....	....	....	....	....	....	....	....	....	....	....	....	....	....	....
	Cornwall Aces	AHL	18	6	9	15	....	....	....	16	....	....	....	....	....	....	....	....	....	....	9	1	2	3	2	....	....	....
1994-95	Worcester IceCats	AHL	59	13	8	21	....	....	....	76	....	....	....	....	....	....	....	....	....	....	....	....	....	....	....	....	....	....
1995-96	Fort Worth Fire	CHL	51	15	37	52	....	....	....	94	....	....	....	....	....	....	....	....	....	....	....	....	....	....	....	....	....	....
1996-97	El Paso Buzzards	WPHL	60	21	39	60	....	....	....	105	....	....	....	....	....	....	....	....	....	....	11	2	*14	16	36	....	....	....
1997-98	Phoenix Mustangs	WCHL	53	19	23	42	....	....	....	93	....	....	....	....	....	....	....	....	....	....	9	4	10	14	10	....	....	....
	NHL Totals		**21**	**0**	**2**	**2**	**0**	**1**	**1**	**12**	**0**	**0**	**0**	**7**	**0.0**	**6**	**0**	**6**	**0**		....	....	....	....	....	....	....	....

• WICKENHEISER, DOUG

Doug Wickenheiser C – L. 6'1", 200 lbs. b: Regina, Sask., 3/30/1961. Montreal's 1st choice, 1st overall, in 1980 Entry Draft.

Season	Club	League	GP	G	A	Pts	AG	AA	APts	PIM	PP	SH	GW	S	%	TGF	PGF	TGA	PGA	+/–	Playoffs GP	G	A	Pts	PIM	PP	SH	GW
1976-77	Regina Blues	SJHL	59	42	46	88	....	....	....	63	....	....	....	....	....	....	....	....	....	....	....	....	....	....	....	....	....	....
1977-78	Regina Pats	WCJHL	68	37	51	88	....	....	....	49	....	....	....	....	....	....	....	....	....	....	13	4	5	9	4	....	....	....
1978-79	Regina Pats	WHL	68	32	62	94	....	....	....	141	....	....	....	....	....	....	....	....	....	....	....	....	....	....	....	....	....	....
1979-80	Regina Pats	WHL	71	*89	81	*170	....	....	....	99	....	....	....	....	....	....	....	....	....	....	18	14	*26	*40	20	....	....	....
1980-81	**Montreal Canadiens**	**NHL**	**41**	**7**	**8**	**15**	**6**	**6**	**12**	**20**	**2**	**0**	**0**	**56**	**12.5**	**24**	**5**	**14**	**0**	**+5**	....	....	....	....	....	....	....	....
1981-82	**Montreal Canadiens**	**NHL**	**56**	**12**	**23**	**35**	**9**	**15**	**24**	**43**	**1**	**0**	**3**	**94**	**12.8**	**56**	**11**	**27**	**0**	**+18**	....	....	....	....	....	....	....	....
1982-83	**Montreal Canadiens**	**NHL**	**78**	**25**	**30**	**55**	**21**	**21**	**42**	**49**	**5**	**0**	**3**	**160**	**15.6**	**88**	**14**	**52**	**0**	**+22**	....	....	....	....	....	....	....	....
1983-84	**Montreal Canadiens**	**NHL**	**27**	**5**	**5**	**10**	**4**	**3**	**7**	**6**	**0**	**0**	**1**	**26**	**19.2**	**14**	**0**	**14**	**1**	**+1**	....	....	....	....	....	....	....	....
	St. Louis Blues	**NHL**	**46**	**7**	**21**	**28**	**6**	**14**	**20**	**19**	**2**	**0**	**1**	**118**	**5.9**	**43**	**10**	**45**	**22**	**+10**	**11**	**2**	**2**	**4**	**2**	**0**	**1**	**1**
1984-85	**St. Louis Blues**	**NHL**	**68**	**23**	**20**	**43**	**19**	**14**	**33**	**36**	**1**	**2**	**3**	**155**	**14.8**	**60**	**5**	**76**	**30**	**+9**	....	....	....	....	....	....	....	....
1985-86	**St. Louis Blues**	**NHL**	**36**	**8**	**11**	**19**	**6**	**7**	**13**	**16**	**0**	**0**	**2**	**53**	**15.1**	**30**	**1**	**30**	**12**	**+11**	**19**	**2**	**5**	**7**	**12**	**1**	**0**	**1**
1986-87	**St. Louis Blues**	**NHL**	**80**	**13**	**15**	**28**	**11**	**11**	**22**	**37**	**5**	**2**	**1**	**131**	**9.9**	**48**	**15**	**66**	**11**	**–22**	**6**	**0**	**0**	**0**	**2**	**0**	**0**	**0**
1987-88	**Vancouver Canucks**	**NHL**	**80**	**7**	**19**	**26**	**6**	**14**	**20**	**36**	**0**	**2**	**2**	**123**	**5.7**	**43**	**2**	**89**	**33**	**–15**	....	....	....	....	....	....	....	....
1988-89	**New York Rangers**	**NHL**	**1**	**1**	**0**	**1**	**1**	**0**	**1**	**0**	**0**	**0**	**0**	**4**	**25.0**	**1**	**0**	**0**	**0**	**+1**	....	....	....	....	....	....	....	....
	Flint Spirits	IHL	21	9	7	16	....	....	....	18	....	....	....	....	....	....	....	....	....	....	....	....	....	....	....	....	....	....
	Canada	Nat-Team	26	7	15	22	....	....	....	40	....	....	....	....	....	....	....	....	....	....	....	....	....	....	....	....	....	....
	Washington Capitals	**NHL**	**16**	**2**	**5**	**7**	**2**	**4**	**6**	**4**	**1**	**0**	**0**	**29**	**6.9**	**9**	**2**	**11**	**4**	**0**	**5**	**0**	**0**	**0**	**2**	**0**	**0**	**0**
	Baltimore Skipjacks	AHL	2	0	5	5	....	....	....	0	....	....	....	....	....	....	....	....	....	....	....	....	....	....	....	....	....	....
1989-90	Washington Capitals	FrTour	4	1	0	1	....	....	....	10	....	....	....	....	....	....	....	....	....	....	....	....	....	....	....	....	....	....
	Washington Capitals	**NHL**	**27**	**1**	**8**	**9**	**1**	**6**	**7**	**20**	**0**	**0**	**0**	**44**	**2.3**	**14**	**0**	**21**	**8**	**+1**	....	....	....	....	....	....	....	....
	Baltimore Skipjacks	AHL	35	9	19	28	....	....	....	22	....	....	....	....	....	....	....	....	....	....	12	2	5	7	22	....	....	....
1990-91	HC Asiago	Italy	35	25	32	57	....	....	....	9	....	....	....	....	....	....	....	....	....	....	....	....	....	....	....	....	....	....
1991-92	Klagenfurter AC	Austria	22	7	12	19	....	....	....	....	....	....	....	....	....	....	....	....	....	....	....	....	....	....	....	....	....	....
1992-93	Peoria Rivermen	IHL	80	30	45	75	....	....	....	30	....	....	....	....	....	....	....	....	....	....	4	0	2	2	2	....	....	....
1993-94	Fort Wayne Komets	IHL	73	22	37	59	....	....	....	22	....	....	....	....	....	....	....	....	....	....	14	2	2	4	4	....	....	....
	NHL Totals		**556**	**111**	**165**	**276**	**92**	**115**	**207**	**286**	**17**	**6**	**16**	**993**	**11.2**	**430**	**65**	**445**	**121**		**41**	**4**	**7**	**11**	**18**	**1**	**1**	**2**

WHL All-Star Team (1980) • Canadian Major Junior Player of the Year (1980)

Traded to **St. Louis** by **Montreal** with Gilbert Delorme and Greg Paslawski for Perry Turnbull, December 21, 1983. Claimed by **Hartford** from **St. Louis** in Waiver Draft, October 5, 1987. Claimed by **Vancouver** from **Hartford** in Waiver Draft, October 5, 1987. Signed as a free agent by **NY Rangers**, August 12, 1988. Signed as a free agent by **Washington**, February 28, 1989.

• WIDING, JUHA

Juha "Whitey" Widing C. 6', 180 lbs. b: Uleaborg, Sweden, 7/4/1947. Deceased.

Season	Club	League	GP	G	A	Pts	AG	AA	APts	PIM	PP	SH	GW	S	%	TGF	PGF	TGA	PGA	+/–	Playoffs GP	G	A	Pts	PIM	PP	SH	GW
1964-65	Brandon Wheat Kings	SJHL	45	23	15	38	....	....	....	26	....	....	....	....	....	....	....	....	....	....	9	3	5	8	6	....	....	....
1965-66	Brandon Wheat Kings	SJHL	50	*62	52	114	....	....	....	29	....	....	....	....	....	....	....	....	....	....	11	8	14	22	4	....	....	....
1966-67	Brandon Wheat Kings	MJHL	STATISTICS NOT AVAILABLE																									
1967-68	Omaha Knights	CHL	62	27	33	60	....	....	....	19	....	....	....	....	....	....	....	....	....	....	....	....	....	....	....	....	....	....
1968-69	Omaha Knights	CHL	72	*41	39	80	....	....	....	58	....	....	....	....	....	....	....	....	....	....	7	2	4	6	0	....	....	....
1969-70	**New York Rangers**	**NHL**	**44**	**7**	**7**	**14**	**8**	**7**	**15**	**10**	**2**	**0**	**0**	**90**	**7.8**	**22**	**2**	**18**	**0**	**+2**	....	....	....	....	....	....	....	....
	Los Angeles Kings	**NHL**	**4**	**0**	**2**	**2**	**0**	**2**	**2**	**2**	**0**	**0**	**0**	**12**	**0.0**	**3**	**1**	**5**	**2**	**–1**	....	....	....	....	....	....	....	....
1970-71	**Los Angeles Kings**	**NHL**	**78**	**25**	**40**	**65**	**26**	**35**	**61**	**24**	**5**	**0**	**4**	**202**	**12.4**	**87**	**16**	**83**	**1**	**–11**	....	....	....	....	....	....	....	....
1971-72	**Los Angeles Kings**	**NHL**	**78**	**27**	**28**	**55**	**29**	**26**	**55**	**26**	**3**	**0**	**3**	**192**	**14.1**	**64**	**16**	**86**	**2**	**–36**	....	....	....	....	....	....	....	....
1972-73	**Los Angeles Kings**	**NHL**	**77**	**16**	**54**	**70**	**16**	**45**	**61**	**30**	**0**	**0**	**3**	**189**	**8.5**	**97**	**32**	**79**	**0**	**–14**	....	....	....	....	....	....	....	....
1973-74	**Los Angeles Kings**	**NHL**	**71**	**27**	**30**	**57**	**28**	**26**	**54**	**26**	**5**	**0**	**4**	**175**	**15.4**	**74**	**17**	**62**	**1**	**–4**	**5**	**1**	**0**	**1**	**2**	**0**	**0**	**1**
1974-75	**Los Angeles Kings**	**NHL**	**80**	**26**	**34**	**60**	**24**	**27**	**51**	**46**	**7**	**0**	**3**	**186**	**14.0**	**83**	**29**	**36**	**0**	**+18**	**3**	**0**	**2**	**2**	**0**	**0**	**0**	**0**
1975-76	**Los Angeles Kings**	**NHL**	**67**	**7**	**15**	**22**	**7**	**12**	**19**	**26**	**1**	**0**	**2**	**84**	**8.3**	**35**	**7**	**40**	**0**	**–12**	....	....	....	....	....	....	....	....
1976-77	**Los Angeles Kings**	**NHL**	**47**	**3**	**8**	**11**	**3**	**6**	**9**	**8**	**0**	**0**	**1**	**69**	**4.3**	**15**	**1**	**30**	**0**	**–16**	....	....	....	....	....	....	....	....
1976-77	Sweden	C Cup	5	1	1	2	....	....	....	0	....	....	....	....	....	....	....	....	....	....	....	....	....	....	....	....	....	....
	Cleveland Barons	**NHL**	**29**	**6**	**8**	**14**	**6**	**6**	**12**	**10**	**1**	**0**	**1**	**39**	**15.4**	**18**	**3**	**22**	**0**	**–7**	....	....	....	....	....	....	....	....
1977-78	Edmonton Oilers	WHA	71	18	24	42	....	....	....	8	....	....	....	....	....	....	....	....	....	....	5	0	1	1	0	....	....	....
	NHL Totals		**575**	**144**	**226**	**370**	**147**	**192**	**339**	**208**	**24**	**0**	**21**	**1238**	**11.6**	**498**	**124**	**461**	**6**		**8**	**1**	**2**	**3**	**2**	**0**	**0**	**1**
	Other Major League Totals		71	18	24	42	....	....	....	8	....	....	....	....	....	....	....	....	....		5	0	1	1	0	....	....	....

CHL Second All-Star Team (1969)

Traded to **LA Kings** by **NY Rangers** with Real Lemieux for Ted Irvine, February 28, 1970. Selected by **Ontario-Ottawa** (WHA) in 1972 WHA General Player Draft, February 12, 1972. Traded to **Cleveland** by **LA Kings** with Gary Edwards for Jim Moxey and Gary Simmons, January 22, 1977. Signed as a free agent by **Edmonton** (WHA), June, 1979.

• WIDMER, JASON

Jason Widmer D – L. 6', 200 lbs. b: Calgary, Alta., 8/1/1973. NY Islanders' 8th choice, 176th overall, in 1992 Entry Draft.

Season	Club	League	GP	G	A	Pts	AG	AA	APts	PIM	PP	SH	GW	S	%	TGF	PGF	TGA	PGA	+/–	Playoffs GP	G	A	Pts	PIM	PP	SH	GW
1989-90	Moose Jaw Warriors	WHL	58	1	8	9	....	....	....	33	....	....	....	....	....	....	....	....	....	....	....	....	....	....	....	....	....	....
1990-91	Lethbridge Hurricanes	WHL	58	2	12	14	....	....	....	55	....	....	....	....	....	....	....	....	....	....	16	0	1	1	12	....	....	....
1991-92	Lethbridge Hurricanes	WHL	40	2	19	21	....	....	....	181	....	....	....	....	....	....	....	....	....	....	5	0	4	4	9	....	....	....
1992-93	Lethbridge Hurricanes	WHL	55	3	15	18	....	....	....	140	....	....	....	....	....	....	....	....	....	....	4	0	3	3	2	....	....	....
	Capital District Islanders	AHL	4	0	0	0	....	....	....	2	....	....	....	....	....	....	....	....	....	....	....	....	....	....	....	....	....	....
1993-94	Lethbridge Hurricanes	WHL	64	11	31	42	....	....	....	191	....	....	....	....	....	....	....	....	....	....	9	3	5	8	34	....	....	....
1994-95	Canada	Nat-Team	6	1	4	5	....	....	....	4	....	....	....	....	....	....	....	....	....	....	....	....	....	....	....	....	....	....
	New York Islanders	**NHL**	**1**	**0**	**0**	**0**	**0**	**0**	**0**	**0**	**0**	**0**	**0**	**0**	**0.0**	**0**	**0**	**1**	**0**	**–1**	....	....	....	....	....	....	....	....
	Worcester IceCats	AHL	73	8	26	34	....	....	....	136	....	....	....	....	....	....	....	....	....	....	....	....	....	....	....	....	....	....
1995-96	**New York Islanders**	**NHL**	**4**	**0**	**0**	**0**	**0**	**0**	**0**	**7**	**0**	**0**	**0**	**1**	**0.0**	**2**	**0**	**2**	**0**	**0**	....	....	....	....	....	....	....	....
	Worcester IceCats	AHL	76	6	21	27	....	....	....	129	....	....	....	....	....	....	....	....	....	....	4	2	0	2	9	....	....	....
1996-97	**San Jose Sharks**	**NHL**	**2**	**0**	**1**	**1**	**0**	**1**	**1**	**0**	**0**	**0**	**0**	**0**	**0.0**	**2**	**0**	**1**	**0**	**+1**	....	....	....	....	....	....	....	....
	Kentucky Thoroughblades	AHL	76	4	24	28	....	....	....	105	....	....	....	....	....	....	....	....	....	....	4	0	0	0	8	....	....	....
1997-98	Kentucky Thoroughblades	AHL	71	5	13	18	....	....	....	176	....	....	....	....	....	....	....	....	....	....	3	0	0	0	6	....	....	....
	NHL Totals		**7**	**0**	**1**	**1**	**0**	**1**	**1**	**7**	**0**	**0**	**0**	**1**	**0.0**	**4**	**0**	**4**	**0**		....	....	....	....	....	....	....	....

Signed as a free agent by **San Jose**, September 11, 1996.

• WIEMER, JASON

Jason Wiemer C – L. 6'2", 219 lbs. b: Kimberley, B.C., 4/14/1976. Tampa Bay's 1st choice, 8th overall, in 1994 Entry Draft.

Season	Club	League	GP	G	A	Pts	AG	AA	APts	PIM	PP	SH	GW	S	%	TGF	PGF	TGA	PGA	+/–	Playoffs GP	G	A	Pts	PIM	PP	SH	GW
1991-92	Portland Winter Hawks	WHL	2	0	1	1	....	....	....	0	....	....	....	....	....	....	....	....	....	....	....	....	....	....	....	....	....	....
1992-93	Portland Winter Hawks	WHL	68	18	34	52	....	....	....	159	....	....	....	....	....	....	....	....	....	....	16	7	3	10	27	....	....	....
1993-94	Portland Winter Hawks	WHL	72	45	51	96	....	....	....	236	....	....	....	....	....	....	....	....	....	....	10	4	4	8	32	....	....	....
1994-95	Portland Winter Hawks	WHL	16	10	14	24	....	....	....	63	....	....	....	....	....	....	....	....	....	....	....	....	....	....	....	....	....	....
	Tampa Bay Lightning	**NHL**	**36**	**1**	**4**	**5**	**2**	**6**	**8**	**44**	**0**	**0**	**0**	**10**	**10.0**	**9**	**0**	**11**	**0**	**–2**	....	....	....	....	....	....	....	....
1995-96	**Tampa Bay Lightning**	**NHL**	**66**	**9**	**9**	**18**	**9**	**7**	**16**	**81**	**4**	**0**	**1**	**89**	**10.1**	**41**	**24**	**33**	**7**	**–9**	**6**	**1**	**0**	**1**	**28**	**1**	**0**	**0**
1996-97	**Tampa Bay Lightning**	**NHL**	**63**	**9**	**5**	**14**	**10**	**4**	**14**	**134**	**2**	**0**	**0**	**103**	**8.7**	**29**	**4**	**42**	**4**	**–13**	....	....	....	....	....	....	....	....
	Adirondack Red Wings	AHL	4	1	0	1	....	....	....	7	....	....	....	....	....	....	....	....	....	....	....	....	....	....	....	....	....	....
1997-98	**Tampa Bay Lightning**	**NHL**	**67**	**8**	**9**	**17**	**9**	**9**	**18**	**132**	**2**	**0**	**0**	**106**	**7.5**	**30**	**4**	**42**	**7**	**–9**	....	....	....	....	....	....	....	....
	Calgary Flames	**NHL**	**12**	**4**	**1**	**5**	**5**	**1**	**6**	**28**	**1**	**0**	**2**	**16**	**25.0**	**10**	**4**	**7**	**0**	**–1**	....	....	....	....	....	....	....	....
	NHL Totals		**244**	**31**	**28**	**59**	**35**	**27**	**62**	**419**	**9**	**0**	**3**	**324**	**9.6**	**119**	**36**	**135**	**18**		**6**	**1**	**0**	**1**	**28**	**1**	**0**	**0**

Traded to **Calgary** by **Tampa Bay** for Sandy McCarthy and Calgary's 3rd (Brad Richards) and 5th (Curtis Rich) round choices in 1998 Entry Draft, March 24, 1998.

• WIEMER, JIM

Jim "Ripper" Wiemer D – L. 6'4", 216 lbs. b: Sudbury, Ont., 1/9/1961. Buffalo's 5th choice, 83rd overall, in 1980 Entry Draft.

Season	Club	League	GP	G	A	Pts	AG	AA	APts	PIM	PP	SH	GW	S	%	TGF	PGF	TGA	PGA	+/–	Playoffs GP	G	A	Pts	PIM	PP	SH	GW
1978-79	Peterborough Petes	OHA	61	15	12	27	....	....	....	50	....	....	....	....	....	....	....	....	....	....	18	4	4	8	15	....	....	....
1979-80	Peterborough Petes	OHA	53	17	32	49	....	....	....	63	....	....	....	....	....	....	....	....	....	....	14	6	9	15	19	....	....	....
	Canada	WJC-A	5	2	2	4	....	....	....	2	....	....	....	....	....	....	....	....	....	....	....	....	....	....	....	....	....	....
1980-81	Peterborough Petes	OHA	65	41	54	95	....	....	....	102	....	....	....	....	....	....	....	....	....	....	5	1	2	3	15	....	....	....
1981-82	Rochester Americans	AHL	74	19	26	45	....	....	....	57	....	....	....	....	....	....	....	....	....	....	9	0	4	4	2	....	....	....
1982-83	Rochester Americans	AHL	74	15	44	59	....	....	....	43	....	....	....	....	....	....	....	....	....	....	15	5	15	20	22	....	....	....
	Buffalo Sabres	**NHL**	....	....	....	....	....	....	....	....	....	....	....	....	....	....	....	....	....	....	**1**	**0**	**0**	**0**	**0**	....	....	....
1983-84	**Buffalo Sabres**	**NHL**	**64**	**5**	**15**	**20**	**4**	**10**	**14**	**48**	**0**	**1**	**0**	**91**	**5.5**	**63**	**7**	**61**	**6**	**+1**	....	....	....	....	....	....	....	....
	Rochester Americans	AHL	12	4	11	15	....	....	....	11	....	....	....	....	....	....	....	....	....	....	18	3	13	16	20	....	....	....

			REGULAR SEASON																		PLAYOFFS							
Season	Club	League	GP	G	A	Pts	AG	AA	APts	PIM	PP	SH	GW	S	%	TGF	PGF	TGA	PGA	+/-	GP	G	A	Pts	PIM	PP	SH	GW
1984-85	**Buffalo Sabres**	**NHL**	**10**	**3**	**2**	**5**	**2**	**1**	**3**	**4**	**2**	**0**	**0**	**22**	**13.6**	**10**	**6**	**9**	**0**	**–5**	....	....	....	....	....	....	....	....
	Rochester Americans	AHL	13	1	9	10	....	....	....	24	....	....	....	....	....	....	....	....	....	....	....	....	....	....	....	....	....	....
	New York Rangers	**NHL**	**22**	**4**	**3**	**7**	**3**	**2**	**5**	**30**	**2**	**0**	**0**	**51**	**7.8**	**19**	**8**	**24**	**3**	**–10**	**1**	**0**	**0**	**0**	**0**	**0**	**0**	**0**
	New Haven Nighthawks	AHL	33	9	27	36	....	....	....	39	....	....	....	....	....	....	....	....	....	....	....	....	....	....	....	....	....	....
1985-86	**New York Rangers**	**NHL**	**7**	**3**	**0**	**3**	**2**	**0**	**2**	**2**	**0**	**0**	**1**	**22**	**13.6**	**11**	**4**	**7**	**0**	**0**	**8**	**1**	**0**	**1**	**6**	**1**	**0**	**1**
	New Haven Nighthawks	AHL	73	24	49	73	....	....	....	108	....	....	....	....	....	....	....	....	....	....	....	....	....	....	....	....	....	....
1986-87	New Haven Nighthawks	AHL	6	0	7	7	....	....	....	6	....	....	....	....	....	....	....	....	....	....	....	....	....	....	....	....	....	....
	Nova Scotia Oilers	AHL	59	9	25	34	....	....	....	72	....	....	....	....	....	....	....	....	....	....	5	0	4	4	2	....	....	....
1987-88	**Edmonton Oilers**	**NHL**	**12**	**1**	**2**	**3**	**1**	**1**	**2**	**15**	**0**	**0**	**0**	**24**	**4.2**	**20**	**6**	**10**	**3**	**+7**	**2**	**0**	**0**	**0**	**2**	**0**	**0**	**0**
	Nova Scotia Oilers	AHL	57	11	32	43	....	....	....	99	....	....	....	....	....	....	....	....	....	....	5	1	1	2	14	....	....	....
1988-89	Cape Breton Oilers	AHL	51	12	29	41	....	....	....	80	....	....	....	....	....	....	....	....	....	....	....	....	....	....	....	....	....	....
	Los Angeles Kings	**NHL**	**9**	**2**	**3**	**5**	**2**	**2**	**4**	**20**	**0**	**1**	**1**	**17**	**11.8**	**5**	**1**	**2**	**0**	**+2**	**10**	**2**	**1**	**3**	**19**	**0**	**0**	**1**
	New Haven Nighthawks	AHL	3	1	1	2	....	....	....	2	....	....	....	....	....	....	....	....	....	....	7	2	3	5	2	....	....	....
1989-90	**Boston Bruins**	**NHL**	**61**	**5**	**14**	**19**	**4**	**10**	**14**	**63**	**0**	**0**	**1**	**90**	**5.6**	**50**	**8**	**33**	**2**	**+11**	**8**	**0**	**1**	**1**	**4**	**0**	**0**	**0**
	Maine Mariners	AHL	6	3	4	7	....	....	....	27	....	....	....	....	....	....	....	....	....	....	....	....	....	....	....	....	....	....
1990-91	**Boston Bruins**	**NHL**	**61**	**4**	**19**	**23**	**4**	**14**	**18**	**62**	**0**	**0**	**1**	**86**	**4.7**	**52**	**6**	**47**	**4**	**+3**	**16**	**1**	**3**	**4**	**14**	**1**	**0**	**0**
1991-92	**Boston Bruins**	**NHL**	**47**	**1**	**8**	**9**	**1**	**6**	**7**	**84**	**0**	**0**	**0**	**60**	**1.7**	**38**	**5**	**25**	**2**	**+10**	**15**	**1**	**3**	**4**	**14**	**0**	**0**	**1**
	Maine Mariners	AHL	3	0	1	1	....	....	....	4	....	....	....	....	....	....	....	....	....	....	....	....	....	....	....	....	....	....
1992-93	**Boston Bruins**	**NHL**	**28**	**1**	**6**	**7**	**1**	**4**	**5**	**48**	**0**	**0**	**0**	**39**	**2.6**	**24**	**4**	**21**	**2**	**+1**	**1**	**0**	**0**	**0**	**4**	**0**	**0**	**0**
	Providence Bruins	AHL	4	2	1	3	....	....	....	2	....	....	....	....	....	....	....	....	....	....	....	....	....	....	....	....	....	....
1993-94	**Boston Bruins**	**NHL**	**4**	**0**	**0**	**0**	**0**	**0**	**0**	**2**	**0**	**0**	**0**	**8**	**0.0**	**1**	**0**	**4**	**0**	**–3**	....	....	....	....	....	....	....	....
	Providence Bruins	AHL	35	5	12	17	....	....	....	81	....	....	....	....	....	....	....	....	....	....	....	....	....	....	....	....	....	....
1994-95	Rochester Americans	AHL	45	9	29	38	....	....	....	74	....	....	....	....	....	....	....	....	....	....	5	0	2	2	6	....	....	....
	NHL Totals		**325**	**29**	**72**	**101**	**24**	**50**	**74**	**378**	**4**	**2**	**4**	**510**	**5.7**	**293**	**55**	**243**	**22**		**62**	**5**	**8**	**13**	**63**	**2**	**0**	**3**

AHL First All-Star Team (1986) • Won Eddie Shore Award (Outstanding Defenseman - AHL) (1986)

Traded to **NY Rangers** by **Buffalo** with Steve Patrick for Dave Maloney and Chris Renaud, December 6, 1984. Traded to **Edmonton** by **NY Rangers** with Reijo Ruotsalainen. Clark Donatelli, Ville Kentala and future considerations (Stu Kulak, March 10, 1987) for Don Jackson, Mike Golden, Miloslav Horova and future considerations, October 23, 1986. Traded to **LA Kings** by **Edmonton** with Alan May for Brian Wilks and John English, March 7, 1989. Signed as a free agent by **Boston**, July 6, 1989.

• WILCOX, BARRY

Barry Wilcox RW – L. 6'1", 190 lbs. b: New Westminster, B.C., 4/23/1948.

1967-68	New Westminster Royals	BCJHL	28	25	25	50	....	....	....	....	....	....	....	....	....	....	....	....	....	....	....	....	....	....	....	....	....	....
1968-69	University of British Columbia	WCIAA	STATISTICS NOT AVAILABLE																									
1969-70	University of British Columbia	WCIAA	STATISTICS NOT AVAILABLE																									
1970-71	University of British Columbia	WCIAA	STATISTICS NOT AVAILABLE																									
1971-72	Rochester Americans	AHL	73	17	10	27	....	....	....	95	....	....	....	....	....	....	....	....	....	....	....	....	....	....	....	....	....	....
1972-73	**Vancouver Canucks**	**NHL**	**31**	**3**	**2**	**5**	**3**	**2**	**5**	**15**	**0**	**0**	**0**	**52**	**5.8**	**14**	**0**	**24**	**0**	**–10**	....	....	....	....	....	....	....	....
	Seattle Totems	WHL	47	19	22	41	....	....	....	38	....	....	....	....	....	....	....	....	....	....	....	....	....	....	....	....	....	....
1973-74	Seattle Totems	WHL	6	0	1	1	....	....	....	10	....	....	....	....	....	....	....	....	....	....	....	....	....	....	....	....	....	....
1974-75	**Vancouver Canucks**	**NHL**	**2**	**0**	**0**	**0**	**0**	**0**	**0**	**0**	**0**	**0**	**0**	**0**	**0.0**	**0**	**0**	**0**	**0**	**0**	....	....	....	....	....	....	....	....
	Seattle Totems	CHL	55	12	17	29	....	....	....	68	....	....	....	....	....	....	....	....	....	....	....	....	....	....	....	....	....	....
1975-76	Tulsa Oilers	CHL	44	8	8	16	....	....	....	36	....	....	....	....	....	....	....	....	....	....	....	....	....	....	....	....	....	....
	NHL Totals		**33**	**3**	**2**	**5**	**3**	**2**	**5**	**15**	**0**	**0**	**0**	**52**	**5.8**	**14**	**0**	**24**	**0**		....	....	....	....	....	....	....	....

Signed as a free agent by **Vancouver**, September, 1971.

• WILEY, JIM

Jim Wiley C – L. 6'2", 200 lbs. b: Sault Ste. Marie, Ont., 4/28/1950.

1968-69	Lake Superior State	CCHA	26	9	15	24	....	....	....	4	....	....	....	....	....	....	....	....	....	....	....	....	....	....	....	....	....	....
1969-70	Lake Superior State	CCHA	25	21	17	38	....	....	....	11	....	....	....	....	....	....	....	....	....	....	....	....	....	....	....	....	....	....
1970-71	Lake Superior State	CCHA	25	18	19	37	....	....	....	13	....	....	....	....	....	....	....	....	....	....	....	....	....	....	....	....	....	....
1971-72	Lake Superior State	CCHA	28	22	34	56	....	....	....	24	....	....	....	....	....	....	....	....	....	....	....	....	....	....	....	....	....	....
1972-73	**Pittsburgh Penguins**	**NHL**	**4**	**0**	**1**	**1**	**0**	**1**	**1**	**0**	**0**	**0**	**0**	**7**	**0.0**	**1**	**0**	**0**	**0**	**+1**	....	....	....	....	....	....	....	....
	Hershey Bears	AHL	71	30	45	75	....	....	....	30	....	....	....	....	....	....	....	....	....	....	7	1	1	2	5	....	....	....
1973-74	**Pittsburgh Penguins**	**NHL**	**22**	**0**	**3**	**3**	**0**	**3**	**3**	**2**	**0**	**0**	**0**	**12**	**0.0**	**6**	**0**	**10**	**0**	**–4**	....	....	....	....	....	....	....	....
	Hershey Bears	AHL	47	21	33	54	....	....	....	26	....	....	....	....	....	....	....	....	....	....	14	5	11	*16	15	....	....	....
1974-75	**Vancouver Canucks**	**NHL**	**1**	**0**	**0**	**0**	**0**	**0**	**0**	**0**	**0**	**0**	**0**	**0**	**0.0**	**0**	**0**	**0**	**0**	**0**	....	....	....	....	....	....	....	....
	Seattle Totems	CHL	51	10	25	35	....	....	....	24	....	....	....	....	....	....	....	....	....	....	....	....	....	....	....	....	....	....
1975-76	**Vancouver Canucks**	**NHL**	**2**	**0**	**0**	**0**	**0**	**0**	**0**	**2**	**0**	**0**	**0**	**1**	**0.0**	**0**	**0**	**1**	**0**	**–1**	....	....	....	....	....	....	....	....
	Tulsa Oilers	CHL	76	33	*63	*96	....	....	....	21	....	....	....	....	....	....	....	....	....	....	9	*5	4	9	38	....	....	....
1976-77	**Vancouver Canucks**	**NHL**	**34**	**4**	**6**	**10**	**4**	**5**	**9**	**4**	**0**	**0**	**0**	**37**	**10.8**	**13**	**0**	**28**	**0**	**–13**	....	....	....	....	....	....	....	....
	Tulsa Oilers	CHL	29	17	17	34	....	....	....	27	....	....	....	....	....	....	....	....	....	....	9	*4	4	8	4	....	....	....
1977-78			DID NOT PLAY																									
1978-79	Tulsa Oilers	CHL	73	23	45	68	....	....	....	29	....	....	....	....	....	....	....	....	....	....	....	....	....	....	....	....	....	....
1979-80	Tulsa Oilers	CHL	76	18	39	54	....	....	....	30	....	....	....	....	....	....	....	....	....	....	3	0	2	2	0	....	....	....
	NHL Totals		**63**	**4**	**10**	**14**	**4**	**9**	**13**	**8**	**0**	**0**	**0**	**57**	**7.0**	**20**	**0**	**37**	**0**		....	....	....	....	....	....	....	....

NCAA (College Div.) West All-American Team (1972) • CHL First All-Star Team (1975)

Signed as a free agent by **Pittsburgh**, June 25, 1972. Claimed by **Vancouver** from **Pittsburgh** in Intra-League Draft, June 10, 1974.

• WILKIE, BOB

Bob Wilkie D – R. 6'2", 215 lbs. b: Calgary, Alta., 2/11/1969. Detroit's 3rd choice, 41st overall, in 1987 Entry Draft.

1984-85	Calgary Buffaloes	AJHL	37	20	33	53	....	....	....	116	....	....	....	....	....	....	....	....	....	....	....	....	....	....	....	....	....	....
1985-86	Calgary Wranglers	WHL	63	8	19	27	....	....	....	56	....	....	....	....	....	....	....	....	....	....	....	....	....	....	....	....	....	....
1986-87	Swift Current Broncos	WHL	65	12	38	50	....	....	....	50	....	....	....	....	....	....	....	....	....	....	4	1	3	4	2	....	....	....
1987-88	Swift Current Broncos	WHL	67	12	68	80	....	....	....	124	....	....	....	....	....	....	....	....	....	....	10	4	12	16	8	....	....	....
1988-89	Swift Current Broncos	WHL	62	18	67	85	....	....	....	89	....	....	....	....	....	....	....	....	....	....	12	1	11	12	47	....	....	....
1989-90	Adirondack Red Wings	AHL	58	5	33	38	....	....	....	64	....	....	....	....	....	....	....	....	....	....	6	1	4	5	2	....	....	....
1990-91	**Detroit Red Wings**	**NHL**	**8**	**1**	**2**	**3**	**1**	**2**	**3**	**2**	**0**	**0**	**0**	**9**	**11.1**	**6**	**1**	**7**	**0**	**–2**	....	....	....	....	....	....	....	....
	Adirondack Red Wings	AHL	43	6	18	24	....	....	....	71	....	....	....	....	....	....	....	....	....	....	2	1	0	1	2	....	....	....
1991-92	Adirondack Red Wings	AHL	7	1	4	5	....	....	....	6	....	....	....	....	....	....	....	....	....	....	16	2	5	7	12	....	....	....
1992-93	Adirondack Red Wings	AHL	14	0	5	5	....	....	....	20	....	....	....	....	....	....	....	....	....	....	....	....	....	....	....	....	....	....
	Fort Wayne Komets	IHL	32	7	14	21	....	....	....	82	....	....	....	....	....	....	....	....	....	....	12	4	6	10	10	....	....	....
	Hershey Bears	AHL	28	7	25	32	....	....	....	18	....	....	....	....	....	....	....	....	....	....	....	....	....	....	....	....	....	....
1993-94	**Philadelphia Flyers**	**NHL**	**10**	**1**	**3**	**4**	**1**	**2**	**3**	**8**	**0**	**0**	**0**	**10**	**10.0**	**12**	**4**	**10**	**0**	**–2**	....	....	....	....	....	....	....	....
	Hershey Bears	AHL	69	8	53	61	....	....	....	100	....	....	....	....	....	....	....	....	....	....	9	1	4	5	8	....	....	....
1994-95	Hershey Bears	AHL	50	9	30	39	....	....	....	46	....	....	....	....	....	....	....	....	....	....	....	....	....	....	....	....	....	....
	Indianapolis Ice	IHL	29	5	22	27	....	....	....	30	....	....	....	....	....	....	....	....	....	....	....	....	....	....	....	....	....	....
1995-96	Augsburg Panthers	Germany	6	0	1	1	....	....	....	43	....	....	....	....	....	....	....	....	....	....	....	....	....	....	....	....	....	....
	Cincinnati Cyclones	IHL	22	4	6	10	....	....	....	32	....	....	....	....	....	....	....	....	....	....	....	....	....	....	....	....	....	....
1996-97			STATISTICS NOT AVAILABLE																									
1997-98	Fresno Fighting Falcons	WCHL	54	13	50	63	....	....	....	60	....	....	....	....	....	....	....	....	....	....	5	1	7	8	38	....	....	....
	Las Vegas Thunder	IHL	3	0	1	1	....	....	....	0	....	....	....	....	....	....	....	....	....	....	....	....	....	....	....	....	....	....
	NHL Totals		**18**	**2**	**5**	**7**	**2**	**4**	**6**	**10**	**0**	**0**	**0**	**19**	**10.5**	**18**	**5**	**17**	**0**		....	....	....	....	....	....	....	....

WCHL First All-Star Team (1998)

Traded to **Philadelphia** by **Detroit** for future considerations, February 2, 1993. Traded to **Chicago** by **Philadelphia** with future considerations for Karl Dykhuis, February 16, 1995.

• WILKIE, DAVID

David Wilkie D – R. 6'2", 210 lbs. b: Ellensburgh, WA, 5/30/1974. Montreal's 1st choice, 20th overall, in 1992 Entry Draft.

1990-91	Seattle Thunderbirds	WHL	25	1	1	2	....	....	....	22	....	....	....	....	....	....	....	....	....	....	....	....	....	....	....	....	....	....
1991-92	Kamloops Blazers	WHL	71	12	28	40	....	....	....	153	....	....	....	....	....	....	....	....	....	....	16	6	5	11	19	....	....	....
1992-93	Kamloops Blazers	WHL	53	11	26	37	....	....	....	109	....	....	....	....	....	....	....	....	....	....	6	4	2	6	2	....	....	....
	United States	WJC-A	7	0	2	2	....	....	....	2	....	....	....	....	....	....	....	....	....	....	....	....	....	....	....	....	....	....
1993-94	Kamloops Blazers	WHL	27	11	18	29	....	....	....	18	....	....	....	....	....	....	....	....	....	....	....	....	....	....	....	....	....	....
	United States	WJC-A	6	2	1	3	....	....	....	0	....	....	....	....	....	....	....	....	....	....	....	....	....	....	....	....	....	....
	Regina Pats	WHL	29	27	21	48	....	....	....	16	....	....	....	....	....	....	....	....	....	....	4	1	4	5	4	....	....	....

			REGULAR SEASON																		PLAYOFFS							
Season	**Club**	**League**	**GP**	**G**	**A**	**Pts**	**AG**	**AA**	**APts**	**PIM**	**PP**	**SH**	**GW**	**S**	**%**	**TGF**	**PGF**	**TGA**	**PGA**	**+/–**	**GP**	**G**	**A**	**Pts**	**PIM**	**PP**	**SH**	**GW**
1994-95	Fredericton Canadiens	AHL	70	10	43	53	....	....	....	34	....	....	....	....	....	....	....	....	....	....	1	0	0	0	0	....	....	....
	Montreal Canadiens	**NHL**	1	0	0	0	0	0	0	0	0	0	0	0	0.0	0	0	0	0	0	....	....	....	....	....	....	....	....
1995-96	**Montreal Canadiens**	**NHL**	24	1	5	6	1	4	5	10	1	0	0	39	2.6	21	8	29	6	–10	6	1	2	3	12	0	0	0
	Fredericton Canadiens	AHL	23	5	12	17	....	....	....	20	....	....	....	....	....	....	....	....	....	....	....	....	....	....	....	....	....	....
1996-97	**Montreal Canadiens**	**NHL**	61	6	9	15	6	8	14	63	3	0	0	65	9.2	46	9	49	3	–9	2	0	0	0	2	0	0	0
1997-98	**Montreal Canadiens**	**NHL**	5	1	0	1	1	0	1	4	0	0	1	2	50.0	1	0	2	0	–1	....	....	....	....	....	....	....	....
	Tampa Bay Lightning	**NHL**	29	1	5	6	1	5	6	17	0	0	0	46	2.2	17	6	33	1	–21	....	....	....	....	....	....	....	....
	NHL Totals		**120**	**9**	**19**	**28**	**9**	**17**	**26**	**94**	**4**	**0**	**1**	**152**	**5.9**	**85**	**23**	**113**	**10**		**8**	**1**	**2**	**3**	**14**	**0**	**0**	**0**

Traded to **Tampa Bay** by **Montreal** with Stephane Richer and Darcy Tucker for Patrick Poulin, Mick Vukota and Igor Ulanov, January 15, 1998.

• WILKINS, BARRY

Barry Wilkins D – L. 6′, 190 lbs. b: Toronto, Ont., 2/28/1947.

1963-64	Woodbridge Dodgers	Jr. B	STATISTICS NOT AVAILABLE																									
1964-65	Niagara Falls Flyers	OHA	51	2	12	14	....	....	....	45	....	....	....	....	....	....	....	....	....	....	9	0	0	0	2	....	....	....
1965-66	Oshawa Generals	OHA	47	8	11	19	....	....	....	128	....	....	....	....	....	....	....	....	....	....	17	3	7	10	36	....	....	....
1966-67	Oshawa Generals	OHA	40	8	21	29	....	....	....	69	....	....	....	....	....	....	....	....	....	....	....	....	....	....	....	....	....	....
	Boston Bruins	**NHL**	1	0	0	0	0	0	0	0	....	....	....	....	....	....	....	....	....	....	....	....	....	....	....	....	....	....
1967-68	Oklahoma City Blazers	CHL	69	6	27	33	....	....	....	146	....	....	....	....	....	....	....	....	....	....	7	1	0	1	12	....	....	....
1968-69	**Boston Bruins**	**NHL**	1	1	0	1	1	0	1	0	0	0	0	1	100.0	1	0	0	0	+1	....	....	....	....	....	....	....	....
	Oklahoma City Blazers	CHL	69	14	32	46	....	....	....	164	....	....	....	....	....	....	....	....	....	....	12	3	7	10	26	....	....	....
1969-70	**Boston Bruins**	**NHL**	6	0	0	0	0	0	0	2	0	0	0	2	0.0	1	0	2	0	–1	....	....	....	....	....	....	....	....
	Oklahoma City Blazers	CHL	61	11	41	52	....	....	....	204	....	....	....	....	....	....	....	....	....	....	....	....	....	....	....	....	....	....
1970-71	**Vancouver Canucks**	**NHL**	70	5	18	23	5	16	21	131	1	0	1	84	6.0	85	17	120	34	–18	....	....	....	....	....	....	....	....
1971-72	**Vancouver Canucks**	**NHL**	45	2	5	7	2	5	7	65	0	0	0	50	4.0	41	1	84	35	–9	....	....	....	....	....	....	....	....
1972-73	**Vancouver Canucks**	**NHL**	76	11	17	28	11	14	25	133	0	1	0	103	10.7	77	2	149	36	–38	....	....	....	....	....	....	....	....
1973-74	**Vancouver Canucks**	**NHL**	78	3	28	31	3	24	27	123	1	0	0	128	2.3	109	17	142	37	–13	....	....	....	....	....	....	....	....
1974-75	**Vancouver Canucks**	**NHL**	7	0	1	1	0	1	1	6	0	0	0	6	0.0	5	0	9	2	–2	....	....	....	....	....	....	....	....
	Pittsburgh Penguins	**NHL**	59	5	29	34	5	23	28	97	0	1	0	83	6.0	97	10	70	12	+29	3	0	0	0	0	0	0	0
1975-76	**Pittsburgh Penguins**	**NHL**	75	0	27	27	0	21	21	106	0	0	0	68	0.0	92	7	107	21	–1	3	0	1	1	4	0	0	0
1976-77	Edmonton Oilers	WHA	51	4	24	28	....	....	....	75	....	....	....	....	....	....	....	....	....	....	4	0	1	1	2	....	....	....
1977-78	Indianapolis Racers	WHA	79	2	21	23	....	....	....	79	....	....	....	....	....	....	....	....	....	....	....	....	....	....	....	....	....	....
1978-79	Philadelphia Firebirds	AHL	46	5	12	17	....	....	....	51	....	....	....	....	....	....	....	....	....	....	....	....	....	....	....	....	....	....
	NHL Totals		**418**	**27**	**125**	**152**	**27**	**104**	**131**	**663**	**2**	**2**	**1**	**525**	**5.1**	**508**	**54**	**683**	**177**		**6**	**0**	**1**	**1**	**4**	**0**	**0**	**0**
	Other Major League Totals		130	6	45	51	....	....	....	154	....	....	....	....	....	....	....	....	....		4	0	1	1	2	....	....	....

CHL First All-Star Team (1969) • CHL Second All-Star Team (1970)

Claimed by **Vancouver** from **Boston** in Expansion Draft, June 10, 1970. Selected by **Dayton-Houston** (WHA) in 1972 WHA General Player Draft, February 12, 1972. Traded to **Pittsburgh** by **Vancouver** for Ab Demarco Jr., November 4, 1974. WHA rights traded to **Edmonton** (WHA) by **Houston** (WHA) for future considerations, June, 1976. Traded to **Indianapolis** (WHA) by **Edmonton** (WHA) with Edgar Patenaude and Claude St. Sauveur for Blair MacDonald, Mike Zuke and Dave Inkpen, September, 1977.

• WILKINSON, NEIL

Neil Wilkinson D – R. 6′3″, 200 lbs. b: Selkirk, Man., 8/15/1967. Minnesota's 2nd choice, 30th overall, in 1986 Entry Draft.

1986-87	Michigan State Spartans	CCHA	19	3	4	7	....	....	....	18	....	....	....	....	....	....	....	....	....	....	....	....	....	....	....	....	....	....
1987-88	Medicine Hat Tigers	WHL	55	11	21	32	....	....	....	157	....	....	....	....	....	....	....	....	....	....	5	1	0	1	2	....	....	....
1988-89	Kalamazoo Wings	IHL	39	5	15	20	....	....	....	96	....	....	....	....	....	....	....	....	....	....	....	....	....	....	....	....	....	....
1989-90	**Minnesota North Stars**	**NHL**	36	0	5	5	0	4	4	100	0	0	0	36	0.0	29	3	35	8	–1	7	0	2	2	11	0	0	0
	Kalamazoo Wings	IHL	20	6	7	13	....	....	....	62	....	....	....	....	....	....	....	....	....	....	....	....	....	....	....	....	....	....
1990-91	Minnesota North Stars	FrTour	4	0	0	0	....	....	....	2	....	....	....	....	....	....	....	....	....	....	....	....	....	....	....	....	....	....
	Minnesota North Stars	**NHL**	50	2	9	11	2	7	9	117	0	0	0	55	3.6	37	7	49	14	–5	22	3	3	6	12	1	0	0
	Kalamazoo Wings	IHL	10	0	3	3	....	....	....	38	....	....	....	....	....	....	....	....	....	....	....	....	....	....	....	....	....	....
1991-92	**San Jose Sharks**	**NHL**	60	4	15	19	4	11	15	107	1	0	0	95	4.2	59	12	80	22	–11	....	....	....	....	....	....	....	....
1992-93	**San Jose Sharks**	**NHL**	59	1	7	8	1	5	6	96	0	1	0	51	2.0	31	2	104	25	–50	....	....	....	....	....	....	....	....
1993-94	**Chicago Blackhawks**	**NHL**	72	3	9	12	3	7	10	116	1	0	0	72	4.2	50	5	52	9	+2	4	0	0	0	0	0	0	0
1994-95	**Winnipeg Jets**	**NHL**	40	1	4	5	2	6	8	75	0	0	0	25	4.0	16	1	48	7	–26	....	....	....	....	....	....	....	....
1995-96	**Winnipeg Jets**	**NHL**	21	1	4	5	1	3	4	33	0	1	1	17	5.9	15	1	30	16	0	....	....	....	....	....	....	....	....
	Pittsburgh Penguins	**NHL**	41	2	10	12	2	8	10	87	0	0	0	42	4.8	48	0	52	16	+12	15	0	1	1	14	0	0	0
1996-97	**Pittsburgh Penguins**	**NHL**	23	0	0	0	0	0	0	36	0	0	0	16	0.0	8	0	24	4	–12	5	0	0	0	4	0	0	0
	Cleveland Lumberjacks	IHL	2	0	1	1	....	....	....	0	....	....	....	....	....	....	....	....	....	....	....	....	....	....	....	....	....	....
1997-98	**Pittsburgh Penguins**	**NHL**	34	2	4	6	2	4	6	24	1	0	0	19	10.5	17	3	19	5	0	....	....	....	....	....	....	....	....
	NHL Totals		**436**	**16**	**67**	**83**	**17**	**55**	**72**	**791**	**3**	**2**	**1**	**428**	**3.7**	**310**	**34**	**493**	**126**		**53**	**3**	**6**	**9**	**41**	**1**	**0**	**0**

Claimed by **San Jose** from **Minnesota** in Dispersal Draft, May 30, 1991. Traded to **Chicago** by **San Jose** to complete transaction that sent Jimmy Waite to San Jose (June 18, 1993), July 9, 1993. Traded to **Winnipeg** by **Chicago** for Chicago's 3rd round choice (previously acquired, Chicago selected Kevin McKay) in 1995 Entry Draft, June 3, 1994. Traded to **Pittsburgh** by **Winnipeg** for Norm Maciver, December 28, 1995.

• WILKS, BRIAN

Brian Wilks C – R. 5′11″, 175 lbs. b: North York, Ont., 2/27/1966. Los Angeles' 2nd choice, 24th overall, in 1984 Entry Draft.

1981-82	Toronto Marlboros	Midget	36	40	48	88	....	....	....	22	....	....	....	....	....	....	....	....	....	....	....	....	....	....	....	....	....	....
1982-83	Kitchener Rangers	OHL	69	6	17	23	....	....	....	25	....	....	....	....	....	....	....	....	....	....	1	0	0	0	0	....	....	....
1983-84	Kitchener Rangers	OHL	64	21	54	75	....	....	....	36	....	....	....	....	....	....	....	....	....	....	16	6	14	20	9	....	....	....
1984-85	Kitchener Rangers	OHL	58	30	63	93	....	....	....	52	....	....	....	....	....	....	....	....	....	....	4	2	4	6	2	....	....	....
	Los Angeles Kings	**NHL**	2	0	0	0	0	0	0	0	0	0	0	3	0.0	0	0	1	0	–1	....	....	....	....	....	....	....	....
1985-86	**Los Angeles Kings**	**NHL**	43	4	8	12	3	5	8	25	0	0	0	31	12.9	20	3	24	0	–7	....	....	....	....	....	....	....	....
1986-87	**Los Angeles Kings**	**NHL**	1	0	0	0	0	0	0	0	0	0	0	0	0.0	0	0	2	0	–2	....	....	....	....	....	....	....	....
	New Haven Nighthawks	AHL	43	16	20	36	....	....	....	23	....	....	....	....	....	....	....	....	....	....	7	1	3	4	7	....	....	....
1987-88	New Haven Nighthawks	AHL	18	4	8	12	....	....	....	26	....	....	....	....	....	....	....	....	....	....	....	....	....	....	....	....	....	....
1988-89	**Los Angeles Kings**	**NHL**	2	0	0	0	0	0	0	2	0	0	0	2	0.0	1	0	1	0	0	....	....	....	....	....	....	....	....
	New Haven Nighthawks	AHL	44	15	19	34	....	....	....	48	....	....	....	....	....	....	....	....	....	....	....	....	....	....	....	....	....	....
	Cape Breton Oilers	AHL	12	4	11	15	....	....	....	27	....	....	....	....	....	....	....	....	....	....	....	....	....	....	....	....	....	....
1989-90	Cape Breton Oilers	AHL	53	13	20	33	....	....	....	85	....	....	....	....	....	....	....	....	....	....	....	....	....	....	....	....	....	....
	Muskegon Lumberjacks	IHL	15	6	11	17	....	....	....	10	....	....	....	....	....	....	....	....	....	....	15	7	10	17	41	....	....	....
	NHL Totals		**48**	**4**	**8**	**12**	**3**	**5**	**8**	**27**	**0**	**0**	**0**	**36**	**11.1**	**21**	**3**	**28**	**0**		....	....	....	....	....	....	....	....

Won George Parsons Trophy (Memorial Cup Tournament Most Sportsmanlike Player) (1984)

Traded to **Edmonton** by **LA Kings** with John English for Jim Wiemer and Alan May, March 7, 1989. Traded to **Pittsburgh** by **Edmonton** for future considerations, March 6, 1990.

• WILLARD, ROD

Rod Willard LW – L. 6′, 190 lbs. b: New Liskeard, Ont., 5/1/1960.

1977-78	Cornwall Royals	QMJHL	66	12	29	41	....	....	....	27	....	....	....	....	....	....	....	....	....	....	9	1	6	7	21	....	....	....
1978-79	Cornwall Royals	QMJHL	72	38	57	95	....	....	....	69	....	....	....	....	....	....	....	....	....	....	7	3	3	6	15	....	....	....
1979-80	Cornwall Royals	QMJHL	55	29	50	79	....	....	....	84	....	....	....	....	....	....	....	....	....	....	18	6	8	14	18	....	....	....
1980-81	Tulsa Oilers	CHL	4	0	0	0	....	....	....	0	....	....	....	....	....	....	....	....	....	....	....	....	....	....	....	....	....	....
	Fort Wayne Komets	IHL	79	32	29	61	....	....	....	92	....	....	....	....	....	....	....	....	....	....	12	4	5	9	14	....	....	....
1981-82	New Brunswick Hawks	AHL	72	18	17	35	....	....	....	88	....	....	....	....	....	....	....	....	....	....	15	4	2	6	13	....	....	....
1982-83	**Toronto Maple Leafs**	**NHL**	1	0	0	0	0	0	0	0	0	0	0	2	0.0	0	0	1	0	–1	....	....	....	....	....	....	....	....
	St. Catharines Saints	AHL	46	6	11	17	....	....	....	22	....	....	....	....	....	....	....	....	....	....	....	....	....	....	....	....	....	....
	Springfield Indians	AHL	33	16	8	24	....	....	....	41	....	....	....	....	....	....	....	....	....	....	....	....	....	....	....	....	....	....
1983-84	Springfield Indians	AHL	76	17	19	36	....	....	....	76	....	....	....	....	....	....	....	....	....	....	....	....	....	....	....	....	....	....
1984-85	Fort Wayne Komets	IHL	18	2	8	10	....	....	....	19	....	....	....	....	....	....	....	....	....	....	....	....	....	....	....	....	....	....
	Kalamazoo Wings	IHL	10	2	1	3	....	....	....	0	....	....	....	....	....	....	....	....	....	....	....	....	....	....	....	....	....	....
	NHL Totals		**1**	**0**	**0**	**0**	**0**	**0**	**0**	**0**	**0**	**0**	**0**	**2**	**0.0**	**0**	**0**	**1**	**0**		....	....	....	....	....	....	....	....

Signed as a free agent by **Toronto**, September 14, 1982. Traded to **Chicago** by **Toronto** for Dave Snopek, January 23, 1983.

			REGULAR SEASON																		PLAYOFFS							
Season	**Club**	**League**	**GP**	**G**	**A**	**Pts**	**AG**	**AA**	**APts**	**PIM**	**PP**	**SH**	**GW**	**S**	**%**	**TGF**	**PGF**	**TGA**	**PGA**	**+/–**	**GP**	**G**	**A**	**Pts**	**PIM**	**PP**	**SH**	**GW**

• WILLIAMS, DARRYL

Darryl Williams LW – L. 5′11″, 185 lbs. b: Mt. Pearl, Nfld., 2/9/1968.

Season	Club	League	GP	G	A	Pts	AG	AA	APts	PIM	PP	SH	GW	S	%	TGF	PGF	TGA	PGA	+/–	GP	G	A	Pts	PIM	PP	SH	GW
1985-86	Victoria Cougars	WHL	38	3	2	5	....	....	....	66	....	....	....	....	....	....	....	....	....	....	....	....	....	....	....	....	....	....
1986-87	Hamilton Steelhawks	OHA	24	2	4	6	....	....	....	36	....	....	....	....	....	....	....	....	....	....	....	....	....	....	....	....	....	....
	Belleville Bulls	OHL	34	7	6	13	....	....	....	72	....	....	....	....	....	....	....	....	....	....	....	....	....	....	....	....	....	....
1987-88	Belleville Bulls	OHL	63	29	39	68	....	....	....	169	....	....	....	....	....	....	....	....	....	....	....	....	....	....	....	....	....	....
1988-89	Belleville Bulls	OHL	46	24	21	45	....	....	....	137	....	....	....	....	....	....	....	....	....	....	....	....	....	....	....	....	....	....
	New Haven Nighthawks	AHL	15	5	5	10	....	....	....	24	....	....	....	....	....	....	....	....	....	....	....	....	....	....	....	....	....	....
1989-90	New Haven Nighthawks	AHL	51	9	13	22	....	....	....	124	....	....	....	....	....	....	....	....	....	....	....	....	....	....	....	....	....	....
1990-91	New Haven Nighthawks	AHL	57	14	11	25	....	....	....	278	....	....	....	....	....	....	....	....	....	....	....	....	....	....	....	....	....	....
	Phoenix Roadrunners	IHL	12	1	2	3	....	....	....	53	....	....	....	....	....	....	....	....	....	....	7	1	0	1	12	....	....	....
1991-92	Phoenix Roadrunners	IHL	48	8	19	27	....	....	....	219	....	....	....	....	....	....	....	....	....	....	....	....	....	....	....	....	....	....
	New Haven Nighthawks	AHL	13	0	2	2	....	....	....	69	....	....	....	....	....	....	....	....	....	....	....	....	....	....	....	....	....	....
1992-93	**Los Angeles Kings**	**NHL**	**2**	**0**	**0**	**0**	**0**	**0**	**0**	**10**	**0**	**0**	**0**	**1**	**0.0**	**0**	**0**	**0**	**0**	**0**	....	....	....	....	....	....	....	....
	Phoenix Roadrunners	IHL	61	18	7	25	....	....	....	314	....	....	....	....	....	....	....	....	....	....	....	....	....	....	....	....	....	....
1993-94	Phoenix Roadrunners	IHL	52	11	18	29	....	....	....	237	....	....	....	....	....	....	....	....	....	....	....	....	....	....	....	....	....	....
1994-95	Detroit Vipers	IHL	66	10	12	22	....	....	....	268	....	....	....	....	....	....	....	....	....	....	4	0	0	0	14	....	....	....
1995-96	Detroit Vipers	IHL	72	8	19	27	....	....	....	294	....	....	....	....	....	....	....	....	....	....	12	0	3	3	30	....	....	....
1996-97	Long Beach Ice Dogs	IHL	82	13	17	30	....	....	....	215	....	....	....	....	....	....	....	....	....	....	14	2	2	4	26	....	....	....
1997-98	Long Beach Ice Dogs	IHL	82	16	17	33	....	....	....	184	....	....	....	....	....	....	....	....	....	....	17	6	6	12	52	....	....	....
	NHL Totals		**2**	**0**	**0**	**0**	**0**	**0**	**0**	**10**	**0**	**0**	**0**	**1**	**0.0**	**0**	**0**	**0**	**0**		....	....	....	....	....	....	....	....

Signed as a free agent by **LA Kings**, May 19, 1989.

• WILLIAMS, DAVE

Dave "Tiger" Williams LW – L. 5′11″, 190 lbs. b: Weyburn, Sask., 2/3/1954. Toronto's 2nd choice, 31st overall, in 1974 Amateur Draft.

Season	Club	League	GP	G	A	Pts	AG	AA	APts	PIM	PP	SH	GW	S	%	TGF	PGF	TGA	PGA	+/–	GP	G	A	Pts	PIM	PP	SH	GW
1971-72	Swift Current Broncos	WCJHL	68	12	22	34	....	....	....	278	....	....	....	....	....	....	....	....	....	....	....	....	....	....	....	....	....	....
1972-73	Swift Current Broncos	WCJHL	68	44	58	102	....	....	....	266	....	....	....	....	....	....	....	....	....	....	....	....	....	....	....	....	....	....
1973-74	Swift Current Broncos	WCJHL	68	52	56	108	....	....	....	310	....	....	....	....	....	....	....	....	....	....	12	14	10	24	23	....	....	....
1974-75	Oklahoma City Blazers	CHL	39	16	11	27	....	....	....	202	....	....	....	....	....	....	....	....	....	....	....	....	....	....	....	....	....	....
	Toronto Maple Leafs	**NHL**	**42**	**10**	**19**	**29**	**9**	**15**	**24**	**187**	**2**	**0**	**0**	**83**	**12.0**	**50**	**12**	**36**	**2**	**+4**	**7**	**1**	**3**	**4**	**25**	**1**	**0**	**0**
1975-76	**Toronto Maple Leafs**	**NHL**	**78**	**21**	**19**	**40**	**20**	**15**	**35**	**299**	**3**	**0**	**3**	**149**	**14.1**	**60**	**9**	**53**	**1**	**–1**	**10**	**0**	**0**	**0**	**75**	**0**	**0**	**0**
1976-77	**Toronto Maple Leafs**	**NHL**	**77**	**18**	**25**	**43**	**17**	**20**	**37**	***338**	**1**	**0**	**0**	**157**	**11.5**	**67**	**3**	**54**	**1**	**+11**	**9**	**3**	**6**	**9**	**29**	**0**	**0**	**1**
1977-78	**Toronto Maple Leafs**	**NHL**	**78**	**19**	**31**	**50**	**18**	**25**	**43**	**351**	**6**	**0**	**5**	**161**	**11.8**	**104**	**34**	**64**	**0**	**+6**	**12**	**1**	**2**	**3**	***63**	**0**	**0**	**0**
1978-79	**Toronto Maple Leafs**	**NHL**	**77**	**19**	**20**	**39**	**17**	**15**	**32**	***298**	**6**	**0**	**4**	**157**	**12.1**	**76**	**27**	**58**	**2**	**–7**	**6**	**0**	**0**	**0**	***48**	**0**	**0**	**0**
1979-80	**Toronto Maple Leafs**	**NHL**	**55**	**22**	**18**	**40**	**20**	**14**	**34**	**197**	**5**	**0**	**1**	**108**	**20.4**	**74**	**29**	**60**	**2**	**–13**	....	....	....	....	....	....	....	....
	Vancouver Canucks	**NHL**	**23**	**8**	**5**	**13**	**7**	**4**	**11**	**81**	**1**	**0**	**0**	**62**	**12.9**	**26**	**8**	**22**	**4**	**0**	**3**	**0**	**0**	**0**	**20**	**0**	**0**	**0**
1980-81	**Vancouver Canucks**	**NHL**	**77**	**35**	**27**	**62**	**29**	**19**	**48**	***343**	**11**	**1**	**4**	**186**	**18.8**	**102**	**38**	**88**	**28**	**+4**	**3**	**0**	**0**	**0**	**20**	**0**	**0**	**0**
1981-82	**Vancouver Canucks**	**NHL**	**77**	**17**	**21**	**38**	**13**	**14**	**27**	**341**	**5**	**1**	**1**	**138**	**12.3**	**69**	**18**	**65**	**8**	**–6**	**17**	**3**	**7**	**10**	***116**	**0**	**0**	**2**
1982-83	**Vancouver Canucks**	**NHL**	**68**	**8**	**13**	**21**	**7**	**9**	**16**	**265**	**0**	**0**	**1**	**78**	**10.3**	**43**	**2**	**49**	**1**	**–7**	**4**	**0**	**3**	**3**	**12**	**0**	**0**	**0**
1983-84	**Vancouver Canucks**	**NHL**	**67**	**15**	**16**	**31**	**12**	**11**	**23**	**294**	**2**	**0**	**1**	**119**	**12.6**	**60**	**9**	**64**	**2**	**–11**	**4**	**1**	**0**	**1**	**13**	**0**	**0**	**0**
1984-85	**Detroit Red Wings**	**NHL**	**55**	**3**	**8**	**11**	**2**	**5**	**7**	**158**	**0**	**0**	**0**	**34**	**8.8**	**22**	**2**	**47**	**11**	**–16**	....	....	....	....	....	....	....	....
	Adirondack Red Wings	AHL	8	5	2	7	....	....	....	4	....	....	....	....	....	....	....	....	....	....	....	....	....	....	....	....	....	....
	Los Angeles Kings	**NHL**	**12**	**4**	**3**	**7**	**3**	**2**	**5**	**43**	**0**	**0**	**0**	**19**	**21.1**	**10**	**1**	**9**	**0**	**0**	**3**	**0**	**0**	**0**	**4**	**0**	**0**	**0**
1985-86	**Los Angeles Kings**	**NHL**	**72**	**20**	**29**	**49**	**16**	**19**	**35**	**320**	**5**	**0**	**1**	**138**	**14.5**	**82**	**20**	**60**	**1**	**–6**	....	....	....	....	....	....	....	....
1986-87	**Los Angeles Kings**	**NHL**	**76**	**16**	**18**	**34**	**14**	**13**	**27**	***358**	**1**	**0**	**3**	**118**	**13.6**	**64**	**8**	**57**	**0**	**–1**	**5**	**3**	**2**	**5**	**30**	**0**	**0**	**1**
1987-88	**Los Angeles Kings**	**NHL**	**2**	**0**	**0**	**0**	**0**	**0**	**0**	**6**	**0**	**0**	**0**	**2**	**0.0**	**1**	**0**	**0**	**0**	**+1**	....	....	....	....	....	....	....	....
	Hartford Whalers	**NHL**	**26**	**6**	**0**	**6**	**5**	**0**	**5**	**87**	**1**	**0**	**1**	**31**	**19.4**	**12**	**2**	**8**	**0**	**+2**	....	....	....	....	....	....	....	....
	NHL Totals		**962**	**241**	**272**	**513**	**209**	**200**	**409**	**3966**	**49**	**2**	**25**	**1740**	**13.9**	**922**	**222**	**803**	**63**		**83**	**12**	**23**	**35**	**455**	**1**	**0**	**4**

Played in NHL All-Star Game (1981)

Traded to **Vancouver** by **Toronto** with Jerry Butler for Rick Vaive and Bill Derlago, February 18, 1980. Traded to **Detroit** by **Vancouver** for Rob McClanahan, August 8, 1984. Traded to **LA Kings** by **Detroit** for future considerations, March 12, 1985. Traded to **Hartford** by **LA Kings** for cash, October, 1987.

• WILLIAMS, DAVID

David Williams D – R. 6′2″, 195 lbs. b: Plainfield, NJ, 8/25/1967. New Jersey's 12th choice, 234th overall, in 1985 Entry Draft.

Season	Club	League	GP	G	A	Pts	AG	AA	APts	PIM	PP	SH	GW	S	%	TGF	PGF	TGA	PGA	+/–	GP	G	A	Pts	PIM	PP	SH	GW
1984-85	Choate Academy	H.S.	25	14	20	34	....	....	....	30	....	....	....	....	....	....	....	....	....	....	....	....	....	....	....	....	....	....
1985-86	Choate Academy	H.S.	STATISTICS NOT AVAILABLE																									
1986-87	Dartmouth College	ECAC	23	2	19	21	....	....	....	20	....	....	....	....	....	....	....	....	....	....	....	....	....	....	....	....	....	....
1987-88	Dartmouth College	ECAC	25	8	14	22	....	....	....	30	....	....	....	....	....	....	....	....	....	....	....	....	....	....	....	....	....	....
1988-89	Dartmouth College	ECAC	25	4	11	15	....	....	....	28	....	....	....	....	....	....	....	....	....	....	....	....	....	....	....	....	....	....
1989-90	Dartmouth College	ECAC	26	3	12	15	....	....	....	32	....	....	....	....	....	....	....	....	....	....	....	....	....	....	....	....	....	....
1990-91	Muskegon Lumberjacks	IHL	14	1	2	3	....	....	....	4	....	....	....	....	....	....	....	....	....	....	....	....	....	....	....	....	....	....
	Knoxville Cherokees	ECHL	38	12	15	27	....	....	....	40	....	....	....	....	....	....	....	....	....	....	3	0	0	0	4	....	....	....
	United States	WEC-A	9	0	2	2	....	....	....	8	....	....	....	....	....	....	....	....	....	....	....	....	....	....	....	....	....	....
1991-92	**San Jose Sharks**	**NHL**	**56**	**3**	**25**	**28**	**3**	**19**	**22**	**40**	**2**	**0**	**1**	**91**	**3.3**	**68**	**24**	**71**	**14**	**–13**	....	....	....	....	....	....	....	....
	Kansas City Blades	IHL	18	2	3	5	....	....	....	22	....	....	....	....	....	....	....	....	....	....	....	....	....	....	....	....	....	....
	United States	WC-A	6	0	1	1	....	....	....	8	....	....	....	....	....	....	....	....	....	....	....	....	....	....	....	....	....	....
1992-93	**San Jose Sharks**	**NHL**	**40**	**1**	**11**	**12**	**1**	**8**	**9**	**49**	**1**	**0**	**0**	**60**	**1.7**	**26**	**9**	**54**	**10**	**–27**	....	....	....	....	....	....	....	....
	Kansas City Blades	IHL	31	1	11	12	....	....	....	28	....	....	....	....	....	....	....	....	....	....	....	....	....	....	....	....	....	....
1993-94	**Anaheim Mighty Ducks**	**NHL**	**56**	**5**	**15**	**20**	**5**	**12**	**17**	**42**	**2**	**0**	**0**	**74**	**6.8**	**58**	**13**	**43**	**6**	**+8**	....	....	....	....	....	....	....	....
	San Diego Gulls	IHL	16	1	6	7	....	....	....	17	....	....	....	....	....	....	....	....	....	....	....	....	....	....	....	....	....	....
1994-95	**Anaheim Mighty Ducks**	**NHL**	**21**	**2**	**2**	**4**	**4**	**3**	**7**	**26**	**0**	**0**	**0**	**30**	**6.7**	**13**	**1**	**24**	**7**	**–5**	....	....	....	....	....	....	....	....
	San Diego Gulls	IHL	2	0	1	1	....	....	....	0	....	....	....	....	....	....	....	....	....	....	5	1	0	1	0	....	....	....
1995-96	Detroit Vipers	IHL	81	5	14	19	....	....	....	81	....	....	....	....	....	....	....	....	....	....	11	1	3	4	6	....	....	....
1996-97	Worcester IceCats	AHL	72	3	17	20	....	....	....	89	....	....	....	....	....	....	....	....	....	....	5	1	1	2	0	....	....	....
1997-98	Cincinnati Cyclones	IHL	80	3	15	18	....	....	....	78	....	....	....	....	....	....	....	....	....	....	8	0	2	2	8	....	....	....
	NHL Totals		**173**	**11**	**53**	**64**	**13**	**42**	**55**	**157**	**5**	**0**	**1**	**255**	**4.3**	**165**	**47**	**192**	**37**		....	....	....	....	....	....	....	....

ECAC First All-Star Team (1989)

Signed as a free agent by **San Jose**, August 9, 1991. Claimed by **Anaheim** from **San Jose** in Expansion Draft, June 24, 1993. Signed as a free agent by **Hartford**, August 25, 1995. Signed as a free agent by **St. Louis**, July 29, 1996.

• WILLIAMS, FRED

Fred "Fats" Williams C – L. 5′11″, 178 lbs. b: Saskatoon, Sask., 7/1/1956. Detroit's 1st choice, 4th overall, in 1976 Amateur Draft.

Season	Club	League	GP	G	A	Pts	AG	AA	APts	PIM	PP	SH	GW	S	%	TGF	PGF	TGA	PGA	+/–	GP	G	A	Pts	PIM	PP	SH	GW
1971-72	Saskatoon Blades	WCJHL	54	7	9	16	....	....	....	6	....	....	....	....	....	....	....	....	....	....	....	....	....	....	....	....	....	....
1972-73	Saskatoon Blades	WCJHL	67	7	18	25	....	....	....	24	....	....	....	....	....	....	....	....	....	....	....	....	....	....	....	....	....	....
1973-74	Saskatoon Blades	WCJHL	67	16	20	36	....	....	....	46	....	....	....	....	....	....	....	....	....	....	....	....	....	....	....	....	....	....
1974-75	Saskatoon Blades	WCJHL	59	21	49	70	....	....	....	61	....	....	....	....	....	....	....	....	....	....	....	....	....	....	....	....	....	....
1975-76	Saskatoon Blades	WHL	72	31	87	118	....	....	....	129	....	....	....	....	....	....	....	....	....	....	....	....	....	....	....	....	....	....
1976-77	**Detroit Red Wings**	**NHL**	**44**	**2**	**5**	**7**	**2**	**4**	**6**	**10**	**0**	**0**	**0**	**32**	**6.3**	**13**	**2**	**29**	**1**	**–17**	....	....	....	....	....	....	....	....
	Rhode Island Reds	AHL	34	7	19	26	....	....	....	24	....	....	....	....	....	....	....	....	....	....	....	....	....	....	....	....	....	....
1977-78	Kansas City Red Wings	CHL	32	0	6	6	....	....	....	12	....	....	....	....	....	....	....	....	....	....	....	....	....	....	....	....	....	....
	Philadelphia Firebirds	AHL	35	5	11	16	....	....	....	22	....	....	....	....	....	....	....	....	....	....	4	2	3	5	2	....	....	....
1978-79			DID NOT PLAY																									
1979-80	Maine Mariners	AHL	73	17	34	51	....	....	....	26	....	....	....	....	....	....	....	....	....	....	12	5	13	18	8	....	....	....
1980-81	Maine Mariners	AHL	79	21	34	55	....	....	....	78	....	....	....	....	....	....	....	....	....	....	20	8	8	16	20	....	....	....
1981-82	Maine Mariners	AHL	46	6	26	32	....	....	....	44	....	....	....	....	....	....	....	....	....	....	3	0	0	0	2	....	....	....
	NHL Totals		**44**	**2**	**5**	**7**	**2**	**4**	**6**	**10**	**0**	**0**	**0**	**32**	**6.3**	**13**	**2**	**29**	**1**		....	....	....	....	....	....	....	....

Signed as a free agent by **Philadelphia**, September 15, 1979.

• WILLIAMS, GORD

Gord Williams RW – R. 5′11″, 190 lbs. b: Saskatoon, Sask., 4/10/1960. Philadelphia's 7th choice, 119th overall, in 1979 Entry Draft.

			REGULAR SEASON																		PLAYOFFS							
Season	Club	League	GP	G	A	Pts	AG	AA	APts	PIM	PP	SH	GW	S	%	TGF	PGF	TGA	PGA	+/–	GP	G	A	Pts	PIM	PP	SH	GW
1976-77	Taber Golden Suns	AJHL	60	35	28	63	....	....	....	53	....	....	....	....	....	....	....	....	....	....	....	....	....	....	....	....	....	....
1977-78	Lethbridge Broncos	WCJHL	71	12	26	38	....	....	....	80	....	....	....	....	....	....	....	....	....	....	....	....	....	....	....	....	....	....
1978-79	Lethbridge Broncos	WHL	72	58	59	117	....	....	....	60	....	....	....	....	....	....	....	....	....	....	....	....	....	....	....	....	....	....
1979-80	Lethbridge Broncos	WHL	72	57	45	122	....	....	....	92	....	....	....	....	....	....	....	....	....	....	....	....	....	....	....	....	....	....
1980-81	Maine Mariners	AHL	65	14	12	26	....	....	....	62	....	....	....	....	....	....	....	....	....	....	12	3	5	8	4	....	....	....
1981-82	**Philadelphia Flyers**	**NHL**	**1**	**0**	**0**	**0**	**0**	**0**	**0**	**2**	**0**	**0**	**0**	**1**	**0.0**	**0**	**0**	**0**	**0**	**0**	....	....	....	....	....	....	....	....
	Maine Mariners	AHL	73	31	25	56	....	....	....	35	....	....	....	....	....	....	....	....	....	....	4	1	1	2	0	....	....	....
1982-83	**Philadelphia Flyers**	**NHL**	**1**	**0**	**0**	**0**	**0**	**0**	**0**	**0**	**0**	**0**	**0**	**1**	**0.0**	**0**	**0**	**0**	**0**	**0**	....	....	....	....	....	....	....	....
	Maine Mariners	AHL	56	26	37	63	....	....	....	34	....	....	....	....	....	....	....	....	....	....	8	2	4	6	4	....	....	....
	NHL Totals		**2**	**0**	**0**	**0**	**0**	**0**	**0**	**2**	**0**	**0**	**0**	**2**	**0.0**	**0**	**0**	**0**	**0**		....	....	....	....	....	....	....	....

• WILLIAMS, SEAN

Sean Williams C – L. 6′1″, 182 lbs. b: Oshawa, Ont., 1/28/1968. Chicago's 11th choice, 245th overall, in 1986 Entry Draft.

Season	Club	League	GP	G	A	Pts	AG	AA	APts	PIM	PP	SH	GW	S	%	TGF	PGF	TGA	PGA	+/–	GP	G	A	Pts	PIM	PP	SH	GW
1984-85	Oshawa Generals	OHL	40	6	7	13	....	....	....	28	....	....	....	....	....	....	....	....	....	....	5	1	0	1	0	....	....	....
1985-86	Oshawa Generals	OHL	55	15	23	38	....	....	....	23	....	....	....	....	....	....	....	....	....	....	6	2	3	5	4	....	....	....
1986-87	Oshawa Generals	OHL	62	21	23	44	....	....	....	32	....	....	....	....	....	....	....	....	....	....	25	7	5	12	19	....	....	....
1987-88	Oshawa Generals	OHL	65	*58	65	123	....	....	....	38	....	....	....	....	....	....	....	....	....	....	7	3	3	6	6	....	....	....
1988-89	Saginaw Hawks	IHL	77	32	27	59	....	....	....	75	....	....	....	....	....	....	....	....	....	....	6	0	3	3	0	....	....	....
1989-90	Indianapolis Ice	IHL	78	21	37	58	....	....	....	25	....	....	....	....	....	....	....	....	....	....	14	8	5	13	12	....	....	....
1990-91	Indianapolis Ice	IHL	82	46	52	98	....	....	....	59	....	....	....	....	....	....	....	....	....	....	7	1	2	3	12	....	....	....
1991-92	**Chicago Blackhawks**	**NHL**	**2**	**0**	**0**	**0**	**0**	**0**	**0**	**4**	**0**	**0**	**0**	**0**	**0.0**	**1**	**0**	**1**	**0**	**0**	....	....	....	....	....	....	....	....
	Indianapolis Ice	IHL	79	29	36	65	....	....	....	89	....	....	....	....	....	....	....	....	....	....	....	....	....	....	....	....	....	....
1992-93	Indianapolis Ice	IHL	81	28	37	65	....	....	....	66	....	....	....	....	....	....	....	....	....	....	5	0	1	1	4	....	....	....
1993-94	Val Gardena	Italy	22	20	23	43	....	....	....	4	....	....	....	....	....	....	....	....	....	....	....	....	....	....	....	....	....	....
	Val Gardena	Alpenliga	28	14	15	29	....	....	....	21	....	....	....	....	....	....	....	....	....	....	....	....	....	....	....	....	....	....
1994-95	Minnesota Moose	IHL	81	20	26	46	....	....	....	34	....	....	....	....	....	....	....	....	....	....	3	1	0	1	0	....	....	....
	NHL Totals		**2**	**0**	**0**	**0**	**0**	**0**	**0**	**4**	**0**	**0**	**0**	**0**	**0.0**	**1**	**0**	**1**	**0**		....	....	....	....	....	....	....	....

OHL First All-Star Team (1988)

• WILLIAMS, TOM

Tom (Thomas Charles) Williams LW – R. 5′11″, 187 lbs. b: Windsor, Ont., 2/7/1957. NY Rangers' 3rd choice, 27th overall, in 1971 Amateur Draft.

Season	Club	League	GP	G	A	Pts	AG	AA	APts	PIM	PP	SH	GW	S	%	TGF	PGF	TGA	PGA	+/–	GP	G	A	Pts	PIM	PP	SH	GW
1968-69	Hamilton Red Wings	OHA	54	21	29	50	....	....	....	18	....	....	....	....	....	....	....	....	....	....	5	0	1	1	0	....	....	....
1969-70	Hamilton Red Wings	OHA	54	23	27	50	....	....	....	17	....	....	....	....	....	....	....	....	....	....	....	....	....	....	....	....	....	....
1970-71	Hamilton Red Wings	OHA	59	43	26	69	....	....	....	8	....	....	....	....	....	....	....	....	....	....	....	....	....	....	....	....	....	....
1971-72	**New York Rangers**	**NHL**	**3**	**0**	**0**	**0**	**0**	**0**	**0**	**2**	**0**	**0**	**0**	**6**	**0.0**	**1**	**0**	**2**	**0**	**–1**	....	....	....	....	....	....	....	....
	Omaha Knights	CHL	67	30	34	64	....	....	....	4	....	....	....	....	....	....	....	....	....	....	....	....	....	....	....	....	....	....
1972-73	**New York Rangers**	**NHL**	**8**	**0**	**1**	**1**	**0**	**1**	**1**	**0**	**0**	**0**	**0**	**2**	**0.0**	**1**	**0**	**1**	**1**	**+1**	....	....	....	....	....	....	....	....
	Providence Reds	AHL	50	20	27	47	....	....	....	9	....	....	....	....	....	....	....	....	....	....	3	1	2	3	0	....	....	....
1973-74	**New York Rangers**	**NHL**	**14**	**1**	**2**	**3**	**1**	**2**	**3**	**4**	**0**	**0**	**0**	**18**	**5.6**	**4**	**1**	**5**	**0**	**–2**	....	....	....	....	....	....	....	....
	Los Angeles Kings	**NHL**	**46**	**11**	**17**	**28**	**11**	**15**	**26**	**6**	**2**	**0**	**2**	**113**	**9.7**	**42**	**16**	**23**	**0**	**+3**	**5**	**3**	**1**	**4**	**0**	**1**	**0**	**0**
1974-75	**Los Angeles Kings**	**NHL**	**74**	**24**	**22**	**46**	**22**	**17**	**39**	**16**	**6**	**0**	**3**	**188**	**12.8**	**66**	**23**	**29**	**0**	**+14**	**3**	**0**	**0**	**0**	**0**	**0**	**0**	**0**
1975-76	**Los Angeles Kings**	**NHL**	**70**	**19**	**20**	**39**	**18**	**16**	**34**	**14**	**4**	**0**	**2**	**157**	**12.1**	**65**	**16**	**49**	**0**	**0**	**9**	**2**	**2**	**4**	**2**	**0**	**0**	**0**
1976-77	**Los Angeles Kings**	**NHL**	**80**	**35**	**39**	**74**	**34**	**32**	**66**	**14**	**15**	**0**	**3**	**233**	**15.0**	**111**	**49**	**48**	**0**	**+14**	**9**	**3**	**4**	**7**	**2**	**1**	**0**	**0**
1977-78	**Los Angeles Kings**	**NHL**	**58**	**15**	**22**	**37**	**14**	**18**	**32**	**9**	**6**	**0**	**2**	**147**	**10.2**	**56**	**20**	**53**	**3**	**–14**	**2**	**0**	**0**	**0**	**0**	**0**	**0**	**0**
	Springfield Indians	AHL	7	6	3	9	....	....	....	13	....	....	....	....	....	....	....	....	....	....	....	....	....	....	....	....	....	....
1978-79	**Los Angeles Kings**	**NHL**	**44**	**10**	**15**	**25**	**9**	**11**	**20**	**8**	**3**	**0**	**2**	**84**	**11.9**	**37**	**13**	**31**	**0**	**–7**	**1**	**0**	**0**	**0**	**0**	**0**	**0**	**0**
1979-80	Salt Lake Golden Eagles	CHL	11	1	3	4	....	....	....	0	....	....	....	....	....	....	....	....	....	....	....	....	....	....	....	....	....	....
	NHL Totals		**397**	**115**	**138**	**253**	**109**	**112**	**221**	**73**	**36**	**0**	**14**	**948**	**12.1**	**383**	**138**	**241**	**4**		**29**	**8**	**7**	**15**	**4**	**2**	**0**	**0**

CHL Second All-Star Team (1972) • Won Ken McKenzie Trophy (CHL's Rookie of the Year) (1972)

Traded to **LA Kings** by **NY Rangers** with Mike Murphy and Sheldon Kannegiesser for Gilles Marotte and Real Lemieux, November 30, 1973. Traded to **St. Louis** by **LA Kings** to complete three-team transaction that sent Barry Gibbs to LA Kings (June 9, 1979) and Terry Richardson to LA Kings, August 16, 1979.

• WILLIAMS, TOMMY

Tommy (Thomas Mark) Williams RW – R. 5′11″, 180 lbs. b: Duluth, MN, 4/17/1940. Deceased. **USHOF**

Season	Club	League	GP	G	A	Pts	AG	AA	APts	PIM	PP	SH	GW	S	%	TGF	PGF	TGA	PGA	+/–	GP	G	A	Pts	PIM	PP	SH	GW
1958-59	United States	Nat-Team	50	21	12	33	....	....	....	22	....	....	....	....	....	....	....	....	....	....	5	1	1	2	0	....	....	....
	United States	WEC-A	8	7	0	....	....	....	....	....	....	....	....	....	....	....	....	....	....	....	....	....	....	....	....	....	....	....
1959-60	Fort William Hurricanes	NOHA	STATISTICS NOT AVAILABLE																									
	United States	Olympics	7	4	6	10	....	....	....	2	....	....	....	....	....	....	....	....	....	....	....	....	....	....	....	....	....	....
1960-61	Kingston Frontenacs	EPHL	51	16	26	42	....	....	....	18	....	....	....	....	....	....	....	....	....	....	5	0	2	2	0	....	....	....
1961-62	**Boston Bruins**	**NHL**	**26**	**6**	**6**	**12**	**7**	**6**	**13**	**2**	....	....	....	....	....	....	....	....	....	....	....	....	....	....	....	....	....	....
	Kingston Frontenacs	EPHL	36	10	18	28	....	....	....	35	....	....	....	....	....	....	....	....	....	....	....	....	....	....	....	....	....	....
1962-63	**Boston Bruins**	**NHL**	**69**	**23**	**20**	**43**	**28**	**21**	**49**	**11**	....	....	....	....	....	....	....	....	....	....	....	....	....	....	....	....	....	....
1963-64	**Boston Bruins**	**NHL**	**37**	**8**	**15**	**23**	**10**	**17**	**27**	**8**	....	....	....	....	....	....	....	....	....	....	....	....	....	....	....	....	....	....
1964-65	**Boston Bruins**	**NHL**	**65**	**13**	**21**	**34**	**17**	**23**	**40**	**28**	....	....	....	....	....	....	....	....	....	....	....	....	....	....	....	....	....	....
1965-66	**Boston Bruins**	**NHL**	**70**	**16**	**22**	**38**	**19**	**22**	**41**	**31**	....	....	....	....	....	....	....	....	....	....	....	....	....	....	....	....	....	....
1966-67	**Boston Bruins**	**NHL**	**29**	**8**	**13**	**21**	**10**	**13**	**23**	**2**	....	....	....	....	....	....	....	....	....	....	....	....	....	....	....	....	....	....
1967-68	**Boston Bruins**	**NHL**	**68**	**18**	**32**	**50**	**22**	**34**	**56**	**14**	**0**	**0**	**4**	**136**	**13.2**	**65**	**5**	**36**	**0**	**+24**	**4**	**1**	**0**	**1**	**2**	**0**	**0**	**0**
1968-69	**Boston Bruins**	**NHL**	**26**	**4**	**7**	**11**	**4**	**7**	**11**	**19**	**0**	**0**	**0**	**48**	**8.3**	**20**	**2**	**12**	**0**	**+6**	....	....	....	....	....	....	....	....
1969-70	**Minnesota North Stars**	**NHL**	**75**	**15**	**52**	**67**	**17**	**52**	**69**	**18**	**2**	**0**	**0**	**165**	**9.1**	**90**	**33**	**77**	**1**	**–19**	**6**	**1**	**5**	**6**	**0**	**0**	**0**	**0**
1970-71	**Minnesota North Stars**	**NHL**	**41**	**10**	**13**	**23**	**10**	**11**	**21**	**16**	**3**	**0**	**2**	**61**	**16.4**	**26**	**4**	**27**	**0**	**–5**	....	....	....	....	....	....	....	....
	California Golden Seals	**NHL**	**18**	**7**	**10**	**17**	**7**	**9**	**16**	**8**	**2**	**0**	**0**	**44**	**15.9**	**20**	**6**	**37**	**11**	**–12**	....	....	....	....	....	....	....	....
1971-72	**California Golden Seals**	**NHL**	**32**	**3**	**9**	**12**	**3**	**8**	**11**	**2**	**0**	**0**	**0**	**41**	**7.3**	**15**	**5**	**29**	**2**	**–17**	....	....	....	....	....	....	....	....
	Boston Braves	AHL	31	8	15	23	....	....	....	8	....	....	....	....	....	....	....	....	....	....	9	2	6	8	6	....	....	....
1972-73	New England Whalers	WHA	69	10	21	31	....	....	....	14	....	....	....	....	....	....	....	....	....	....	15	6	11	17	2	....	....	....
1973-74	New England Whalers	WHA	70	21	37	58	....	....	....	6	....	....	....	....	....	....	....	....	....	....	4	0	3	3	10	....	....	....
1974-75	**Washington Capitals**	**NHL**	**73**	**22**	**36**	**58**	**20**	**28**	**48**	**12**	**7**	**2**	**1**	**135**	**16.3**	**60**	**22**	**128**	**42**	**–48**	....	....	....	....	....	....	....	....
1975-76	**Washington Capitals**	**NHL**	**34**	**8**	**13**	**21**	**7**	**10**	**17**	**6**	**2**	**0**	**0**	**39**	**20.5**	**31**	**15**	**50**	**1**	**–33**	....	....	....	....	....	....	....	....
	New Haven Nighthawks	AHL	20	4	16	20	....	....	....	4	....	....	....	....	....	....	....	....	....	....	3	0	1	1	0	....	....	....
	NHL Totals		**663**	**161**	**269**	**430**	**181**	**261**	**442**	**177**	**16**	**2**	**7**	**669**	**24.1**	**327**	**92**	**396**	**57**		**10**	**2**	**5**	**7**	**2**	**0**	**0**	**0**
	Other Major League Totals		139	31	58	89	....	....	....	20	....	....	....	....	....	....	....	....	....	....	19	6	14	20	12	....	....	....

Traded to **Minnesota** by **Boston** with Barry Gibbs for Minnesota's 1st round choice (Don Tannahill) in 1969 Amateur Draft and Fred O'Donnell, May 17, 1969. Traded to **California** by **Minnesota** with Dick Redmond for Ted Hampson and Wayne Muloin, February 23, 1971. Selected by **New England** (WHA) in 1972 WHA General Player Draft, February 12, 1972. Traded to **Boston** by **California** for cash, March 5, 1972. Traded to **Washington** by **Boston** for cash, July 22, 1974.

• WILLIAMS, WARREN

Warren "Butch" Williams RW – R. 5′11″, 195 lbs. b: Duluth, MN, 9/11/1952.

Season	Club	League	GP	G	A	Pts	AG	AA	APts	PIM	PP	SH	GW	S	%	TGF	PGF	TGA	PGA	+/–	GP	G	A	Pts	PIM	PP	SH	GW
1970-71	Oshawa Generals	OHA	53	5	21	26	....	....	....	43	....	....	....	....	....	....	....	....	....	....	....	....	....	....	....	....	....	....
1971-72	Oshawa–Niagara Falls	OHA	47	13	18	31	....	....	....	101	....	....	....	....	....	....	....	....	....	....	....	....	....	....	....	....	....	....
1972-73	New England—Clinton	EHL	54	22	42	64	....	....	....	129	....	....	....	....	....	....	....	....	....	....	....	....	....	....	....	....	....	....
	Denver Spurs	WHL	13	2	5	7	....	....	....	15	....	....	....	....	....	....	....	....	....	....	5	1	2	3	2	....	....	....
1973-74	**St. Louis Blues**	**NHL**	**31**	**3**	**10**	**13**	**3**	**9**	**12**	**6**	**0**	**0**	**0**	**41**	**7.3**	**19**	**0**	**17**	**0**	**+2**	....	....	....	....	....	....	....	....
	Denver Spurs	WHL	35	13	11	24	....	....	....	86	....	....	....	....	....	....	....	....	....	....	....	....	....	....	....	....	....	....
1974-75	**California Golden Seals**	**NHL**	**63**	**11**	**21**	**32**	**10**	**17**	**27**	**118**	**2**	**0**	**0**	**109**	**10.1**	**53**	**14**	**56**	**1**	**–16**	....	....	....	....	....	....	....	....
	Denver Spurs	CHL	14	2	9	11	....	....	....	29	....	....	....	....	....	....	....	....	....	....	....	....	....	....	....	....	....	....
1975-76	**California Golden Seals**	**NHL**	**14**	**0**	**4**	**4**	**0**	**3**	**3**	**7**	**0**	**0**	**0**	**10**	**0.0**	**7**	**2**	**12**	**0**	**–7**	....	....	....	....	....	....	....	....
	Salt Lake City Golden Eagles	CHL	60	31	46	77	....	....	....	171	....	....	....	....	....	....	....	....	....	....	5	2	3	5	24	....	....	....

			REGULAR SEASON																		PLAYOFFS							
Season	Club	League	GP	G	A	Pts	AG	AA	APts	PIM	PP	SH	GW	S	%	TGF	PGF	TGA	PGA	+/–	GP	G	A	Pts	PIM	PP	SH	GW
1976-77	United States	C Cup	3	0	3	3	....	....	....	2	....	....	....	....	....	....	....	....	....	....	....	....	....	....	....	....	....	....
	Edmonton Oilers	WHA	29	3	10	13	....	....	....	16	....	....	....	....	....	....	....	....	....	....	....	....	....	....	....	....	....	....
	Rhode Island Reds	AHL	5	0	1	1	....	....	....	24	....	....	....	....	....	....	....	....	....	....	....	....	....	....	....	....	....	....
	United States	WEC-A	10	4	4	8	....	....	....	22	....	....	....	....	....	....	....	....	....	....	....	....	....	....	....	....	....	....
	NHL Totals		**108**	**14**	**35**	**49**	**13**	**29**	**42**	**131**	**2**	**0**	**0**	**160**	**8.8**	**79**	**16**	**85**	**1**		....	....	....	....	....	....	....	....
	Other Major League Totals		29	3	10	13	....	....	....	16	....	....	....	....	....	....	....	....	....		....	....	....	....	....	....	....	....

CHL First All-Star Team (1975)

Claimed by **Clinton** (EHL) after **New England** (EHL) franchise folded, December, 1972. Signed as a free agent by **St. Louis**, August, 1972. Traded to **California** by **St. Louis** with Dave Gardner for Craig Patrick and Stan Gilbertson, November 11, 1974. Signed as a free agent by **Edmonton** (WHA), September, 1976.

• WILSON, BEHN

Behn Wilson D – L. 6'3", 210 lbs. b: Toronto, Ont., 12/19/1958. Philadelphia's 1st choice, 6th overall, in 1978 Amateur Draft.

Season	Club	League	GP	G	A	Pts	AG	AA	APts	PIM	PP	SH	GW	S	%	TGF	PGF	TGA	PGA	+/–	GP	G	A	Pts	PIM	PP	SH	GW
1975-76	Ottawa 67's	OHA	63	5	16	21	....	....	....	131	....	....	....	....	....	....	....	....	....	....	12	3	2	5	46	....	....	....
1976-77	Ottawa 67's	OHA	31	8	29	37	....	....	....	115	....	....	....	....	....	....	....	....	....	....	....	....	....	....	....	....	....	....
	Windsor Spitfires	OHA	17	4	16	20	....	....	....	38	....	....	....	....	....	....	....	....	....	....	....	....	....	....	....	....	....	....
	Kalamazoo Wings	IHL	13	2	7	9	....	....	....	40	....	....	....	....	....	....	....	....	....	....	....	....	....	....	....	....	....	....
1977-78	Kingston Canadians	OHA	52	18	58	76	....	....	....	186	....	....	....	....	....	....	....	....	....	....	2	1	3	4	21	....	....	....
1978-79	**Philadelphia Flyers**	**NHL**	**80**	**13**	**36**	**49**	**12**	**28**	**40**	**197**	**6**	**0**	**2**	**174**	**7.5**	**128**	**34**	**110**	**29**	**+13**	**5**	**1**	**0**	**1**	**8**	**0**	**0**	**0**
1979-80	**Philadelphia Flyers**	**NHL**	**61**	**9**	**25**	**34**	**8**	**19**	**27**	**212**	**4**	**0**	**1**	**119**	**7.6**	**92**	**20**	**69**	**18**	**+21**	**19**	**4**	**9**	**13**	**66**	**0**	**0**	**2**
1980-81	**Philadelphia Flyers**	**NHL**	**77**	**16**	**47**	**63**	**13**	**33**	**46**	**237**	**2**	**2**	**2**	**216**	**7.4**	**144**	**37**	**99**	**31**	**+39**	**12**	**2**	**10**	**12**	**36**	**1**	**0**	**0**
1981-82	**Philadelphia Flyers**	**NHL**	**59**	**13**	**23**	**36**	**10**	**15**	**25**	**135**	**5**	**0**	**3**	**130**	**10.0**	**102**	**37**	**84**	**25**	**+6**	**4**	**1**	**4**	**5**	**10**	**1**	**0**	**0**
1982-83	**Philadelphia Flyers**	**NHL**	**62**	**8**	**24**	**32**	**7**	**17**	**24**	**92**	**3**	**0**	**2**	**117**	**6.8**	**53**	**14**	**38**	**2**	**+3**	**3**	**0**	**1**	**1**	**2**	**0**	**0**	**0**
1983-84	**Chicago Black Hawks**	**NHL**	**59**	**10**	**22**	**32**	**8**	**15**	**23**	**143**	**3**	**0**	**1**	**141**	**7.1**	**76**	**15**	**89**	**23**	**–5**	**4**	**0**	**0**	**0**	**0**	**0**	**0**	**0**
1984-85	**Chicago Black Hawks**	**NHL**	**76**	**10**	**23**	**33**	**8**	**16**	**24**	**185**	**2**	**0**	**1**	**106**	**9.4**	**94**	**12**	**100**	**23**	**+5**	**15**	**4**	**5**	**9**	**60**	**1**	**0**	**1**
1985-86	**Chicago Black Hawks**	**NHL**	**69**	**13**	**37**	**50**	**10**	**25**	**35**	**113**	**10**	**0**	**6**	**138**	**9.4**	**117**	**33**	**131**	**36**	**–11**	**2**	**0**	**0**	**0**	**2**	**0**	**0**	**0**
1986-87			DID NOT PLAY – INJURED																									
1987-88	**Chicago Blackhawks**	**NHL**	**58**	**6**	**23**	**29**	**5**	**16**	**21**	**166**	**3**	**0**	**0**	**103**	**5.8**	**72**	**25**	**88**	**22**	**–19**	**3**	**0**	**0**	**0**	**6**	**0**	**0**	**0**
	NHL Totals		**601**	**98**	**260**	**358**	**81**	**184**	**265**	**1480**	**38**	**2**	**18**	**1244**	**7.9**	**878**	**227**	**808**	**209**		**67**	**12**	**29**	**41**	**190**	**3**	**0**	**3**

Played in NHL All-Star Game (1981)

Traded to **Chicago** by **Philadelphia** for Doug Crossman and Philadelphia's 2nd round choice (Scott Mellanby) in 1984 Entry Draft, June, 1983. • Missed entire 1986-87 season due to back injury. Claimed by **Vancouver** from **Chicago** in Waiver Draft, October 3, 1988.

• WILSON, BERT

Bert Wilson LW – L. 6', 178 lbs. b: Orangeville, Ont., 10/17/1949. Deceased. NY Rangers' 3rd choice, 23rd overall, in 1969 Amateur Draft.

Season	Club	League	GP	G	A	Pts	AG	AA	APts	PIM	PP	SH	GW	S	%	TGF	PGF	TGA	PGA	+/–	GP	G	A	Pts	PIM	PP	SH	GW
1967-68	London Nationals	OHA	45	8	3	11	....	....	....	94	....	....	....	....	....	....	....	....	....	....	3	1	0	1	2	....	....	....
1968-69	London Knights	OHA	54	13	19	32	....	....	....	160	....	....	....	....	....	....	....	....	....	....	6	2	2	4	7	....	....	....
1969-70	Omaha Knights	CHL	32	7	6	13	....	....	....	103	....	....	....	....	....	....	....	....	....	....	12	3	2	5	15	....	....	....
	Buffalo Bisons	AHL	....	....	....	....	....	....	....	....	....	....	....	....	....	....	....	....	....	....	1	0	0	0	0	....	....	....
1970-71	Omaha Knights	CHL	69	13	15	28	....	....	....	164	....	....	....	....	....	....	....	....	....	....	11	0	4	4	29	....	....	....
1971-72	Providence Reds	AHL	59	11	12	23	....	....	....	105	....	....	....	....	....	....	....	....	....	....	5	0	2	2	16	....	....	....
1972-73	Providence Reds	AHL	72	15	24	39	....	....	....	131	....	....	....	....	....	....	....	....	....	....	4	2	0	2	15	....	....	....
1973-74	**New York Rangers**	**NHL**	**5**	**1**	**1**	**2**	**1**	**1**	**2**	**2**	**1**	**0**	**0**	**3**	**33.3**	**2**	**1**	**0**	**0**	**+1**	....	....	....	....	....	....	....	....
	Providence Reds	AHL	72	24	31	55	....	....	....	200	....	....	....	....	....	....	....	....	....	....	15	5	6	11	22	....	....	....
1974-75	**New York Rangers**	**NHL**	**61**	**5**	**1**	**6**	**5**	**1**	**6**	**66**	**1**	**0**	**1**	**38**	**13.2**	**17**	**3**	**17**	**3**	**0**	....	....	....	....	....	....	....	....
1975-76	**St. Louis Blues**	**NHL**	**45**	**2**	**3**	**5**	**2**	**2**	**4**	**47**	**0**	**0**	**1**	**25**	**8.0**	**8**	**0**	**16**	**2**	**–6**	....	....	....	....	....	....	....	....
	Los Angeles Kings	**NHL**	**13**	**0**	**0**	**0**	**0**	**0**	**0**	**17**	**0**	**0**	**0**	**5**	**0.0**	**1**	**0**	**1**	**0**	**0**	**8**	**0**	**0**	**0**	**24**	**0**	**0**	**0**
1976-77	**Los Angeles Kings**	**NHL**	**77**	**4**	**3**	**7**	**4**	**2**	**6**	**64**	**0**	**0**	**1**	**54**	**7.4**	**20**	**0**	**39**	**10**	**–9**	**8**	**0**	**2**	**2**	**12**	**0**	**0**	**0**
1977-78	**Los Angeles Kings**	**NHL**	**79**	**7**	**16**	**23**	**7**	**13**	**20**	**127**	**0**	**0**	**0**	**78**	**9.0**	**38**	**0**	**44**	**6**	**0**	**2**	**0**	**0**	**0**	**2**	**0**	**0**	**0**
1978-79	**Los Angeles Kings**	**NHL**	**73**	**9**	**10**	**19**	**8**	**8**	**16**	**138**	**0**	**0**	**2**	**72**	**12.5**	**30**	**1**	**37**	**3**	**–5**	....	....	....	....	....	....	....	....
1979-80	**Los Angeles Kings**	**NHL**	**75**	**4**	**3**	**7**	**4**	**2**	**6**	**91**	**1**	**1**	**0**	**56**	**7.1**	**17**	**2**	**40**	**6**	**–19**	**2**	**0**	**0**	**0**	**4**	**0**	**0**	**0**
1980-81	**Calgary Flames**	**NHL**	**50**	**5**	**7**	**12**	**4**	**5**	**9**	**94**	**0**	**0**	**1**	**34**	**14.7**	**19**	**0**	**30**	**5**	**–6**	**1**	**0**	**0**	**0**	**0**	**0**	**0**	**0**
1981-82	Salt Lake Golden Eagles	CHL	52	6	23	29	....	....	....	121	....	....	....	....	....	....	....	....	....	....	10	3	2	5	30	....	....	....
1982-83	Salt Lake Golden Eagles	CHL	69	11	13	24	....	....	....	114	....	....	....	....	....	....	....	....	....	....	6	1	2	3	2	....	....	....
	NHL Totals		**478**	**37**	**44**	**81**	**35**	**34**	**69**	**646**	**3**	**1**	**6**	**365**	**10.1**	**152**	**7**	**224**	**35**		**21**	**0**	**2**	**2**	**42**	**0**	**0**	**0**

Traded to **St. Louis** by **NY Rangers** with Ted Irvine and Jerry Butler for Bill Collins and John Davidson, June 18, 1975. Traded to **LA Kings** by **St. Louis** with rights to Curt Brackenbury for cash, March 6, 1976. Traded to **Calgary** by **LA Kings** with Randy Holt for Garry Unger, June 6, 1980.

• WILSON, CAREY

Carey Wilson C – R. 6'2", 195 lbs. b: Winnipeg, Man., 5/19/1962. Chicago's 8th choice, 67th overall, in 1980 Entry Draft.

Season	Club	League	GP	G	A	Pts	AG	AA	APts	PIM	PP	SH	GW	S	%	TGF	PGF	TGA	PGA	+/–	GP	G	A	Pts	PIM	PP	SH	GW
1978-79	Calgary Chinooks	AJHL	60	30	34	64	....	....	....	....	....	....	....	....	....	....	....	....	....	....	....	....	....	....	....	....	....	....
1979-80	Dartmouth College	ECAC	31	16	22	38	....	....	....	20	....	....	....	....	....	....	....	....	....	....	....	....	....	....	....	....	....	....
1980-81	Dartmouth College	ECAC	24	9	13	22	....	....	....	52	....	....	....	....	....	....	....	....	....	....	....	....	....	....	....	....	....	....
1981-82	HIFK Helsinki	Finland	29	15	17	32	....	....	....	58	....	....	....	....	....	....	....	....	....	....	7	1	4	5	6	....	....	....
	Canada	WJC-A	7	4	1	5	....	....	....	6	....	....	....	....	....	....	....	....	....	....	....	....	....	....	....	....	....	....
1982-83	HIFK Helsinki	Finland	36	16	24	40	....	....	....	62	....	....	....	....	....	....	....	....	....	....	9	1	3	4	12	....	....	....
1983-84	Canada	Nat-Team	56	19	24	43	....	....	....	34	....	....	....	....	....	....	....	....	....	....	....	....	....	....	....	....	....	....
	Canada	Olympics	7	3	3	6	....	....	....	6	....	....	....	....	....	....	....	....	....	....	....	....	....	....	....	....	....	....
	Calgary Flames	**NHL**	**15**	**2**	**5**	**7**	**2**	**3**	**5**	**2**	**0**	**0**	**0**	**11**	**18.2**	**10**	**1**	**10**	**0**	**–1**	**6**	**3**	**1**	**4**	**2**	**0**	**0**	**1**
1984-85	**Calgary Flames**	**NHL**	**74**	**24**	**48**	**72**	**20**	**33**	**53**	**27**	**4**	**0**	**3**	**128**	**18.8**	**97**	**17**	**56**	**0**	**+24**	**4**	**0**	**0**	**0**	**0**	**0**	**0**	**0**
1985-86	**Calgary Flames**	**NHL**	**76**	**29**	**29**	**58**	**23**	**19**	**42**	**24**	**5**	**0**	**2**	**149**	**19.5**	**84**	**22**	**82**	**1**	**+1**	**9**	**0**	**2**	**2**	**2**	**0**	**0**	**0**
1986-87	**Calgary Flames**	**NHL**	**80**	**20**	**36**	**56**	**17**	**26**	**43**	**42**	**3**	**1**	**2**	**140**	**14.3**	**78**	**16**	**75**	**11**	**–2**	**6**	**1**	**1**	**2**	**6**	**0**	**0**	**0**
1987-88	**Calgary Flames**	**NHL**	**34**	**9**	**21**	**30**	**8**	**15**	**23**	**18**	**3**	**0**	**3**	**61**	**14.8**	**43**	**12**	**39**	**10**	**+2**	....	....	....	....	....	....	....	....
	Hartford Whalers	**NHL**	**36**	**18**	**20**	**38**	**15**	**14**	**29**	**22**	**7**	**1**	**6**	**77**	**23.4**	**45**	**16**	**40**	**6**	**–5**	**6**	**2**	**4**	**6**	**2**	**1**	**0**	**1**
1988-89	**Hartford Whalers**	**NHL**	**34**	**11**	**11**	**22**	**9**	**8**	**17**	**14**	**4**	**0**	**2**	**56**	**19.6**	**28**	**10**	**36**	**6**	**–12**	....	....	....	....	....	....	....	....
	New York Rangers	**NHL**	**41**	**21**	**34**	**55**	**18**	**24**	**42**	**45**	**10**	**0**	**3**	**108**	**19.4**	**71**	**33**	**37**	**0**	**+1**	**4**	**1**	**2**	**3**	**2**	**0**	**0**	**0**
1989-90	**New York Rangers**	**NHL**	**41**	**9**	**17**	**26**	**8**	**12**	**20**	**57**	**4**	**0**	**1**	**64**	**14.1**	**48**	**26**	**19**	**1**	**+4**	**10**	**2**	**1**	**3**	**0**	**1**	**0**	**0**
1990-91	**Hartford Whalers**	**NHL**	**45**	**8**	**15**	**23**	**7**	**11**	**18**	**16**	**4**	**0**	**1**	**59**	**13.6**	**33**	**13**	**34**	**0**	**–14**	....	....	....	....	....	....	....	....
	Calgary Flames	**NHL**	**12**	**3**	**3**	**6**	**3**	**2**	**5**	**2**	**0**	**0**	**1**	**20**	**15.0**	**10**	**5**	**7**	**3**	**+1**	**7**	**2**	**2**	**4**	**0**	**1**	**0**	**0**
1991-92	**Calgary Flames**	**NHL**	**42**	**11**	**12**	**23**	**10**	**9**	**19**	**37**	**4**	**2**	**2**	**74**	**14.9**	**33**	**13**	**42**	**16**	**–6**	....	....	....	....	....	....	....	....
1992-93	**Calgary Flames**	**NHL**	**22**	**4**	**7**	**11**	**3**	**5**	**8**	**8**	**1**	**2**	**0**	**30**	**13.3**	**20**	**5**	**11**	**6**	**+10**	....	....	....	....	....	....	....	....
	NHL Totals		**552**	**169**	**258**	**427**	**143**	**181**	**324**	**314**	**49**	**6**	**26**	**977**	**17.3**	**600**	**189**	**468**	**60**		**52**	**11**	**13**	**24**	**14**	**3**	**0**	**2**

Rights traded to **Calgary** by **Chicago** for Denis Cyr, November 8, 1982. Traded to **Hartford** by **Calgary** with Neil Sheehy and rights to Lane MacDonald for Dana Murzyn and Shane Churla, January 3, 1988. Traded to **NY Rangers** by **Hartford** with Hartford's 5th round choice (Lubos Rob) in 1990 Entry Draft for Brian Lawton, Norm MacIver and Don Maloney, December 26, 1988. Traded to **Hartford** by **NY Rangers** with NY Rangers' 3rd round choice (Mikael Nylander) in 1991 Entry Draft for Jody Hull, July 9, 1990. Traded to **Calgary** by **Hartford** for Mark Hunter, March 5, 1991.

• WILSON, DOUG

Doug Wilson D – L. 6'1", 187 lbs. b: Ottawa, Ont., 7/5/1957. Chicago's 3rd choice, 6th overall, in 1977 Amateur Draft.

Season	Club	League	GP	G	A	Pts	AG	AA	APts	PIM	PP	SH	GW	S	%	TGF	PGF	TGA	PGA	+/–	GP	G	A	Pts	PIM	PP	SH	GW
1974-75	Ottawa 67's	OHA	55	29	58	87	....	....	....	75	....	....	....	....	....	....	....	....	....	....	....	....	....	....	....	....	....	....
1975-76	Ottawa 67's	OHA	58	26	62	88	....	....	....	142	....	....	....	....	....	....	....	....	....	....	12	5	10	15	24	....	....	....
1976-77	Ottawa 67's	OHA	43	25	54	79	....	....	....	85	....	....	....	....	....	....	....	....	....	....	19	4	20	24	34	....	....	....
1977-78	**Chicago Black Hawks**	**NHL**	**77**	**14**	**20**	**34**	**13**	**16**	**29**	**72**	**5**	**0**	**2**	**203**	**6.9**	**94**	**24**	**76**	**17**	**+11**	**4**	**0**	**0**	**0**	**0**	**0**	**0**	**0**
1978-79	**Chicago Black Hawks**	**NHL**	**56**	**5**	**21**	**26**	**5**	**16**	**21**	**37**	**2**	**1**	**0**	**136**	**3.7**	**67**	**17**	**61**	**15**	**+4**	....	....	....	....	....	....	....	....
1979-80	**Chicago Black Hawks**	**NHL**	**73**	**12**	**49**	**61**	**11**	**38**	**49**	**70**	**3**	**1**	**1**	**225**	**5.3**	**121**	**52**	**97**	**23**	**–5**	**7**	**2**	**8**	**10**	**6**	**0**	**0**	**0**
1980-81	**Chicago Black Hawks**	**NHL**	**76**	**12**	**39**	**51**	**10**	**27**	**37**	**80**	**3**	**0**	**1**	**245**	**4.9**	**130**	**49**	**99**	**24**	**+6**	**3**	**0**	**3**	**3**	**2**	**0**	**0**	**0**
1981-82	**Chicago Black Hawks**	**NHL**	**76**	**39**	**46**	**85**	**31**	**30**	**61**	**54**	**14**	**1**	**3**	**325**	**12.0**	**103**	**54**	**141**	**33**	**+1**	**15**	**3**	**10**	**13**	**32**	**0**	**1**	**1**
1982-83	**Chicago Black Hawks**	**NHL**	**74**	**18**	**51**	**69**	**15**	**35**	**50**	**58**	**3**	**0**	**3**	**260**	**6.9**	**153**	**59**	**105**	**33**	**+22**	**13**	**4**	**11**	**15**	**12**	**0**	**1**	**0**
1983-84	**Chicago Black Hawks**	**NHL**	**66**	**13**	**45**	**58**	**10**	**31**	**41**	**64**	**4**	**1**	**1**	**199**	**6.5**	**117**	**45**	**113**	**30**	**–11**	**5**	**0**	**3**	**3**	**2**	**0**	**0**	**0**
1984-85	Canada	C Cup	7	2	1	3	....	....	....	4	....	....	....	....	....	....	....	....	....	....	....	....	....	....	....	....	....	....
	Chicago Black Hawks	**NHL**	**78**	**22**	**54**	**76**	**18**	**37**	**55**	**44**	**7**	**0**	**2**	**236**	**9.3**	**151**	**46**	**129**	**47**	**+23**	**12**	**3**	**10**	**13**	**12**	**2**	**0**	**0**
1985-86	**Chicago Black Hawks**	**NHL**	**79**	**17**	**47**	**64**	**14**	**31**	**45**	**80**	**3**	**0**	**2**	**243**	**7.0**	**162**	**47**	**126**	**35**	**+24**	**3**	**1**	**1**	**2**	**2**	**0**	**0**	**0**
1986-87	**Chicago Blackhawks**	**NHL**	**69**	**16**	**32**	**48**	**14**	**23**	**37**	**36**	**7**	**1**	**1**	**249**	**6.4**	**123**	**40**	**106**	**38**	**+15**	**4**	**0**	**0**	**0**	**0**	**0**	**0**	**0**
	NHL All-Stars	RV'87	2	1	1	2	....	....	....	0	....	....	....	....	....	....	....	....	....	....	....	....	....	....	....	....	....	....
1987-88	**Chicago Blackhawks**	**NHL**	**27**	**8**	**24**	**32**	**7**	**17**	**24**	**28**	**6**	**1**	**1**	**87**	**9.2**	**53**	**34**	**47**	**11**	**–17**	....	....	....	....	....	....	....	....
1988-89	**Chicago Blackhawks**	**NHL**	**66**	**15**	**47**	**62**	**13**	**33**	**46**	**69**	**4**	**1**	**3**	**248**	**6.0**	**156**	**70**	**105**	**27**	**+8**	**4**	**1**	**2**	**3**	**0**	**1**	**0**	**0**

			REGULAR SEASON																		PLAYOFFS							
Season	Club	League	GP	G	A	Pts	AG	AA	APts	PIM	PP	SH	GW	S	%	TGF	PGF	TGA	PGA	+/–	GP	G	A	Pts	PIM	PP	SH	GW
1989-90	Chicago Blackhawks	NHL	70	23	50	73	20	36	56	40	13	1	2	242	9.5	155	55	117	30	+13	20	3	12	15	18	1	0	1
1990-91	Chicago Blackhawks	NHL	51	11	29	40	10	22	32	32	6	1	1	162	6.8	102	47	40	10	+25	5	2	1	3	2	2	0	0
1991-92	San Jose Sharks	NHL	44	9	19	28	8	14	22	26	4	0	0	123	7.3	50	24	85	21	–38	....	....	....	....	....	....	....	....
1992-93	San Jose Sharks	NHL	42	3	17	20	2	12	14	40	1	0	0	110	2.7	51	23	68	12	–28	....	....	....	....	....	....	....	....
	NHL Totals		1024	237	590	827	201	418	619	830	85	9	23	3293	7.2	1848	686	1515	406		95	19	61	80	88	6	2	2

OHA First All-Star Team (1977) • NHL First All-Star Team (1982) • Won James Norris Trophy (1982) • NHL Second All-Star Team (1985, 1990)

Played in NHL All-Star Game (1982, 1983, 1984, 1985, 1986, 1990, 1992)

Traded to **San Jose** by **Chicago** for Kerry Toporowski and San Jose's 2nd round choice (later traded to Winnipeg — Winnipeg selected Boris Mironov) in 1992 Entry Draft, September 6, 1991.

• WILSON, LANDON

Landon Wilson RW – R. 6'2", 216 lbs. b: St. Louis, MO, 3/13/1975. Toronto's 2nd choice, 19th overall, in 1993 Entry Draft.

Season	Club	League	GP	G	A	Pts	AG	AA	APts	PIM	PP	SH	GW	S	%	TGF	PGF	TGA	PGA	+/–	GP	G	A	Pts	PIM	PP	SH	GW
1992-93	Dubuque Fighting Saints	USHL	43	29	36	65	....	....	....	284	....	....	....	....	....	....	....	....	....	....	....	....	....	....	....	....	....	....
1993-94	University of North Dakota	WCHA	35	18	15	33	....	....	....	*147	....	....	....	....	....	....	....	....	....	....	....	....	....	....	....	....	....	....
1994-95	University of North Dakota	WCHA	31	7	16	23	....	....	....	141	....	....	....	....	....	....	....	....	....	....	....	....	....	....	....	....	....	....
	United States	WJC-A	7	3	2	5	....	....	....	37	....	....	....	....	....	....	....	....	....	....	....	....	....	....	....	....	....	....
	Cornwall Aces	AHL	8	4	4	8	....	....	....	25	....	....	....	....	....	....	....	....	....	....	13	3	4	7	68	....	....	....
1995-96	Colorado Avalanche	NHL	7	1	0	1	1	0	1	6	0	0	0	6	16.7	3	0	0	0	+3	....	....	....	....	....	....	....	....
	Cornwall Aces	AHL	53	21	13	34	....	....	....	154	....	....	....	....	....	....	....	....	....	....	8	1	3	4	22	....	....	....
1996-97	Colorado Avalanche	NHL	9	1	2	3	1	2	3	23	0	0	0	7	14.3	4	0	3	0	+1	....	....	....	....	....	....	....	....
	Boston Bruins	NHL	40	7	10	17	7	9	16	49	0	0	0	76	9.2	28	5	29	0	–6	....	....	....	....	....	....	....	....
	Providence Bruins	AHL	2	2	1	3	....	....	....	2	....	....	....	....	....	....	....	....	....	....	10	3	4	7	16	....	....	....
1997-98	Boston Bruins	NHL	28	1	5	6	1	5	6	7	0	0	0	26	3.8	8	2	3	0	+3	1	0	0	0	0	0	0	0
	Providence Bruins	AHL	42	18	10	28	....	....	....	146	....	....	....	....	....	....	....	....	....	....	....	....	....	....	....	....	....	....
	NHL Totals		84	10	17	27	10	16	26	85	0	0	0	115	8.7	43	7	35	0		1	0	0	0	0	0	0	0

Traded to **Quebec** by **Toronto** with Wendel Clark, Sylvain Lefebvre and Toronto's 1st round choice (Jeffrey Kealty) in 1994 Entry Draft for Mats Sundin, Garth Butcher, Todd Warriner and Philadelphia's 1st round choice (previously acquired by Quebec — later traded to Washington — Washington selected Nolan Baumgartner) in 1994 Entry Draft, June 28, 1994. Traded to **Boston** by **Colorado** with Anders Myrvold for Boston's 1st round choice (Robyn Regehr) in 1998 Entry Draft, November 22, 1996.

• WILSON, MIKE

Mike Wilson D – L. 6'6", 212 lbs. b: Brampton, Ont., 2/26/1975. Vancouver's 12th choice, 20th overall, in 1993 Entry Draft.

Season	Club	League	GP	G	A	Pts	AG	AA	APts	PIM	PP	SH	GW	S	%	TGF	PGF	TGA	PGA	+/–	GP	G	A	Pts	PIM	PP	SH	GW
1991-92	Georgetown Raiders	OJHL	41	9	13	22	....	....	....	65	....	....	....	....	....	....	....	....	....	....	....	....	....	....	....	....	....	....
1992-93	Sudbury Wolves	OHL	53	6	7	13	....	....	....	58	....	....	....	....	....	....	....	....	....	....	14	1	1	2	2	....	....	....
1993-94	Sudbury Wolves	OHL	60	4	22	26	....	....	....	62	....	....	....	....	....	....	....	....	....	....	9	1	3	4	8	....	....	....
1994-95	Sudbury Wolves	OHL	64	13	34	47	....	....	....	46	....	....	....	....	....	....	....	....	....	....	18	1	8	9	10	....	....	....
1995-96	Buffalo Sabres	NHL	58	4	8	12	4	7	11	41	1	0	1	52	7.7	54	2	59	20	+13	....	....	....	....	....	....	....	....
	Rochester Americans	AHL	15	0	5	5	....	....	....	38	....	....	....	....	....	....	....	....	....	....	....	....	....	....	....	....	....	....
1996-97	Buffalo Sabres	NHL	77	2	9	11	2	8	10	51	0	0	1	57	3.5	54	0	68	27	+13	10	0	1	1	2	0	0	0
1997-98	Buffalo Sabres	NHL	66	4	4	8	5	4	9	48	0	0	1	52	7.7	37	0	45	21	+13	15	0	1	1	13	0	0	0
	NHL Totals		201	10	21	31	11	19	30	140	1	0	3	161	6.2	145	2	172	68		25	0	2	2	15	0	0	0

Traded to **Buffalo** by **Vancouver** with Mike Peca and Vancouver's 1st round choice (Jay McKee) in 1995 Entry Draft for Alexander Mogilny and Buffalo's 5th round choice (Todd Norman) in 1995 Entry Draft, July 8, 1995.

• WILSON, MITCH

Mitch Wilson C – R. 5'8", 190 lbs. b: Kelowna B.C., 2/15/1962.

Season	Club	League	GP	G	A	Pts	AG	AA	APts	PIM	PP	SH	GW	S	%	TGF	PGF	TGA	PGA	+/–	GP	G	A	Pts	PIM	PP	SH	GW
1980-81	Seattle Breakers	WHL	64	8	23	31	....	....	....	253	....	....	....	....	....	....	....	....	....	....	5	3	0	3	31	....	....	....
1981-82	Seattle Breakers	WHL	60	18	17	35	....	....	....	436	....	....	....	....	....	....	....	....	....	....	10	3	7	10	55	....	....	....
1982-83	Wichita Wind	CHL	55	4	6	10	....	....	....	186	....	....	....	....	....	....	....	....	....	....	....	....	....	....	....	....	....	....
1983-84	Maine Mariners	AHL	71	6	8	14	....	....	....	349	....	....	....	....	....	....	....	....	....	....	17	3	6	9	98	....	....	....
1984-85	New Jersey Devils	NHL	9	0	2	2	0	1	1	21	0	0	0	7	0.0	4	0	3	0	+1	....	....	....	....	....	....	....	....
	Maine Mariners	AHL	51	6	3	9	....	....	....	220	....	....	....	....	....	....	....	....	....	....	2	0	0	0	32	....	....	....
1985-86	Maine Mariners	AHL	64	4	3	7	....	....	....	217	....	....	....	....	....	....	....	....	....	....	3	0	0	0	2	....	....	....
1986-87	Pittsburgh Penguins	NHL	17	2	1	3	2	1	3	83	0	0	0	7	28.6	3	0	6	0	–3	....	....	....	....	....	....	....	....
	Baltimore Skipjacks	AHL	58	8	9	17	....	....	....	*353	....	....	....	....	....	....	....	....	....	....	....	....	....	....	....	....	....	....
1987-88	Muskegon Lumberjacks	IHL	68	27	25	52	....	....	....	400	....	....	....	....	....	....	....	....	....	....	5	1	0	1	23	....	....	....
1988-89	Muskegon Lumberjacks	IHL	61	16	34	50	....	....	....	*382	....	....	....	....	....	....	....	....	....	....	11	4	5	9	83	....	....	....
1989-90	Muskegon Lumberjacks	IHL	63	13	24	37	....	....	....	283	....	....	....	....	....	....	....	....	....	....	15	1	4	5	97	....	....	....
1990-91	Muskegon Lumberjacks	IHL	78	14	19	33	....	....	....	387	....	....	....	....	....	....	....	....	....	....	4	1	2	3	34	....	....	....
1991-92	Louisville IceHawks	ECHL	25	9	11	20	....	....	....	144	....	....	....	....	....	....	....	....	....	....	....	....	....	....	....	....	....	....
	San Diego Gulls	IHL	12	0	0	0	....	....	....	55	....	....	....	....	....	....	....	....	....	....	....	....	....	....	....	....	....	....
	NHL Totals		26	2	3	5	2	2	4	104	0	0	0	14	14.3	7	0	9	0		....	....	....	....	....	....	....	....

Signed as a free agent by **New Jersey**, October 12, 1982. Signed as a free agent by **Pittsburgh**, July 24, 1986.

• WILSON, MURRAY

Murray Wilson LW – L. 6'1", 185 lbs. b: Toronto, Ont., 11/7/1951. Montreal's 3rd choice, 11th overall, in 1971 Amateur Draft.

Season	Club	League	GP	G	A	Pts	AG	AA	APts	PIM	PP	SH	GW	S	%	TGF	PGF	TGA	PGA	+/–	GP	G	A	Pts	PIM	PP	SH	GW
1968-69	Ottawa 67's	OHA	24	7	11	18	....	....	....	8	....	....	....	....	....	....	....	....	....	....	....	....	....	....	....	....	....	....
1969-70	Ottawa 67's	OHA	46	24	26	50	....	....	....	48	....	....	....	....	....	....	....	....	....	....	7	2	2	4	10	....	....	....
1970-71	Ottawa 67's	OHA	44	26	32	58	....	....	....	36	....	....	....	....	....	....	....	....	....	....	....	....	....	....	....	....	....	....
1971-72	Nova Scotia Voyageurs	AHL	65	11	21	32	....	....	....	30	....	....	....	....	....	....	....	....	....	....	15	2	7	9	11	....	....	....
1972-73	Montreal Canadiens	NHL	52	18	9	27	18	8	26	16	0	0	3	68	26.5	33	1	18	0	+14	16	2	4	6	6	0	0	1
1973-74	Montreal Canadiens	NHL	72	17	14	31	17	12	29	26	0	0	4	107	15.9	48	0	48	4	+4	5	1	0	1	2	0	0	0
1974-75	Montreal Canadiens	NHL	73	24	18	42	22	14	36	44	4	0	6	135	17.8	64	10	45	4	+13	5	0	3	3	4	0	0	0
1975-76	Montreal Canadiens	NHL	59	11	24	35	10	19	29	36	2	1	1	73	15.1	50	8	26	9	+25	12	1	1	2	6	0	0	0
1976-77	Montreal Canadiens	NHL	60	13	14	27	12	11	23	26	1	0	1	83	15.7	46	2	20	1	+25	14	1	6	7	14	0	0	0
1977-78	Montreal Canadiens	NHL	12	0	1	1	0	1	1	0	0	0	0	9	0.0	4	0	6	1	–1	....	....	....	....	....	....	....	....
1978-79	Los Angeles Kings	NHL	58	11	15	26	10	11	21	14	1	0	2	107	10.3	47	7	47	0	–7	1	0	0	0	0	0	0	0
	NHL Totals		386	94	95	189	89	76	165	162	8	1	17	582	16.2	292	28	210	19		53	5	14	19	32	0	0	1

Traded to **LA Kings** by **Montreal** with Montreal's 1st round choice (Jay Wells) in 1979 Entry Draft for LA King's 1st round choice (Gilbert Delorme) in 1981 Entry Draft, October 5, 1978.

• WILSON, RICK

Rick Wilson D – L. 6'1", 195 lbs. b: Prince Albert, Sask., 8/10/1950. Montreal's 6th choice, 66th overall, in 1970 Amateur Draft.

Season	Club	League	GP	G	A	Pts	AG	AA	APts	PIM	PP	SH	GW	S	%	TGF	PGF	TGA	PGA	+/–	GP	G	A	Pts	PIM	PP	SH	GW
1969-70	University of North Dakota	WCHA	30	2	9	11	....	....	....	32	....	....	....	....	....	....	....	....	....	....	....	....	....	....	....	....	....	....
1970-71	University of North Dakota	WCHA	33	6	9	15	....	....	....	113	....	....	....	....	....	....	....	....	....	....	....	....	....	....	....	....	....	....
1971-72	University of North Dakota	WCHA	25	7	19	26	....	....	....	38	....	....	....	....	....	....	....	....	....	....	....	....	....	....	....	....	....	....
1972-73	Nova Scotia Voyageurs	AHL	70	4	11	15	....	....	....	163	....	....	....	....	....	....	....	....	....	....	12	1	0	1	*56	....	....	....
1973-74	Montreal Canadiens	NHL	21	0	2	2	0	2	2	6	0	0	0	9	0.0	16	0	9	1	+8	....	....	....	....	....	....	....	....
	Nova Scotia Voyageurs	AHL	47	4	19	23	....	....	....	65	....	....	....	....	....	....	....	....	....	....	....	....	....	....	....	....	....	....
1974-75	St. Louis Blues	NHL	76	2	5	7	2	4	6	83	0	0	0	63	3.2	66	3	63	12	+12	2	0	0	0	0	0	0	0
1975-76	St. Louis Blues	NHL	65	1	6	7	1	5	6	20	1	0	0	44	2.3	36	2	63	19	–10	1	0	0	0	0	0	0	0
1976-77	Detroit Red Wings	NHL	77	3	13	16	3	11	14	56	0	0	0	60	5.0	66	6	109	29	–20	....	....	....	....	....	....	....	....
1977-78	Philadelphia Firebirds	AHL	75	4	28	32	....	....	....	101	....	....	....	....	....	....	....	....	....	....	4	0	1	1	2	....	....	....
	NHL Totals		239	6	26	32	6	22	28	165	1	0	0	176	3.4	184	11	244	61		3	0	0	0	0	0	0	0

WCHA Second All-Star Team (1972) • AHL First All-Star Team (1978)

Traded to **St. Louis** by **Montreal** with Montreal's 5th round choice (Don Wheldon) in 1974 Amateur Draft for St. Louis' 4th round choice (Barry Legge) in 1974 Amateur Draft and future considerations (Glen Sather, June 14, 1974), May 27, 1974. Traded to **Detroit** by **St. Louis** to complete transaction that sent Doug Grant to St. Louis (March 9, 1976), June 16, 1976.

• WILSON, RIK

Rik Wilson D – R. 6', 180 lbs. b: Long Beach, CA, 6/17/1962. St. Louis' 1st choice, 12th overall, in 1980 Entry Draft.

Season	Club	League	GP	G	A	Pts	AG	AA	APts	PIM	PP	SH	GW	S	%	TGF	PGF	TGA	PGA	+/–	GP	G	A	Pts	PIM	PP	SH	GW
1979-80	Kingston Canadians	OHA	67	15	38	53	....	....	....	75	....	....	....	....	....	....	....	....	....	....	....	....	....	....	....	....	....	....
1980-81	Kingston Canadians	OHA	68	30	70	100	....	....	....	108	....	....	....	....	....	....	....	....	....	....	13	1	9	10	18	....	....	....
	Salt Lake Golden Eagles	IHL	....	....	....	....	....	....	....	....	....	....	....	....	....	....	....	....	....	....	4	1	1	2	2	....	....	....
1981-82	Kingston Canadians	OHA	16	9	10	19	....	....	....	38	....	....	....	....	....	....	....	....	....	....	....	....	....	....	....	....	....	....
	St. Louis Blues	NHL	48	3	18	21	2	12	14	24	1	0	1	95	3.2	64	14	68	8	–10	9	0	3	3	14	0	0	0
1982-83	St. Louis Blues	NHL	56	3	11	14	2	8	10	50	1	0	1	77	3.9	44	8	51	5	–10	....	....	....	....	....	....	....	....
	Salt Lake Golden Eagles	CHL	4	0	0	0	....	....	....	0	....	....	....	....	....	....	....	....	....	....	....	....	....	....	....	....	....	....

			REGULAR SEASON																	PLAYOFFS							
Season	Club	League	GP	G	A	Pts	AG	AA	APts	PIM	PP	SH	GW	S	%	TGF	PGF	TGA	PGA	+/-	GP	G	A	Pts	PIM	PP	SH	GW
1983-84	St. Louis Blues	NHL	48	7	11	18	6	7	13	53	2	0	1	72	9.7	57	10	48	5	+4	11	0	0	0	9	0	0	0
	Montana Magic	CHL	6	0	3	3				2																		
1984-85	St. Louis Blues	NHL	51	8	16	24	7	11	18	39	3	0	0	85	9.4	62	15	36	3	+14	2	0	1	1	0	0	0	0
	Flint Generals	IHL	29	0	0	0				0											1	0	0	0	0			
	Salt Lake Golden Eagles	IHL	2	0	0	0				0																		
1985-86	St. Louis Blues	NHL	32	0	4	4	0	3	3	48	0	0	0	45	0.0	20	6	25	2	-9								
	Calgary Flames	NHL	2	0	0	0	0	0	0	0	0	0	0	3	0.0	3	0	1	0	+2								
	Nova Scotia Oilers	AHL	13	4	5	9				11																		
	Moncton Golden Flames	AHL	8	3	3	6				2																		
1986-87	Nova Scotia Oilers	AHL	45	8	13	21				109											5	1	3	4	20			
1987-88	Chicago Blackhawks	NHL	14	4	5	9	3	4	7	6	0	0	1	27	14.8	20	6	10	0	+4								
	Saginaw Hawks	IHL	33	4	5	9				105																		
1988-89	VSV Villach	Austria	45	17	43	60				110																		
1989-90	Peoria Rivermen	IHL	15	1	4	5				34																		
1990-91	VSV Villach	Austria	44	13	45	58																						
1991-92			DID NOT PLAY																									
1992-93	Fort Wayne Komets	IHL	2	0	0	0				4																		
	NHL Totals		251	25	65	90	20	45	65	220	7	0	4	404	6.2	270	59	239	23		22	0	4	4	23	0	0	0

OHA First All-Star Team (1981)

Traded to **Calgary** by **St. Louis** with Joe Mullen and Terry Johnson for Ed Beers, Charlie Bourgeois and Gino Cavallini, February 1, 1986. Traded to **Chicago** by **Calgary** for Tom McMurchy, March 11, 1986. Traded to **St. Louis** by **Chicago** for Craig Coxe, September 27, 1989.

● **WILSON, ROGER**   Roger Wilson   D – R. 5'11", 175 lbs.   b: Sudbury, Ont., 9/18/1946.

Season	Club	League	GP	G	A	Pts	AG	AA	APts	PIM	PP	SH	GW	S	%	TGF	PGF	TGA	PGA	+/-	GP	G	A	Pts	PIM	PP	SH	GW
1965-66	Sudbury Wolves	NOHA		10	33	43																						
1966-67	Sudbury Wolves	NOHA						STATISTICS NOT AVAILABLE																				
	Columbus Checkers	IHL	3	0	0	0				9																		
1967-68	Greensboro Generals	EHL	71	9	31	40				182											11	3	4	7	21			
1968-69	Dallas Black Hawks	CHL	4	0	0	0				13																		
	Greensboro Generals	EHL	70	9	28	37				128											8	1	2	3	10			
1969-70	Dallas Black Hawks	CHL	3	0	0	0				0																		
	Greensboro Generals	EHL	69	13	26	39				205											16	2	2	4	8			
1970-71	Greensboro Generals	EHL	71	21	49	70				285											9	4	5	9	12			
1971-72	Dallas Black Hawks	CHL	72	4	20	24				173											12	1	4	5	20			
1972-73	Dallas Black Hawks	CHL	65	7	27	34				120											7	0	1	1	12			
1973-74	Dallas Black Hawks	CHL	61	9	21	30				124											10	1	5	6	19			
1974-75	Chicago Black Hawks	NHL	7	0	2	2	0	2	2	6	0	0	0	10	0.0	5	0	4	0	+1								
	Dallas Black Hawks	CHL	52	6	27	33				71											10	1	1	2	16			
	NHL Totals		7	0	2	2	0	2	2	6	0	0	0	10	0.0	5	0	4	0									

EHL South First All-Star Team (1971)

● **WILSON, RON**   Ron Wilson   C – L. 5'9", 180 lbs.   b: Toronto, Ont., 5/13/1956.   Montreal's 7th choice, 133rd overall, in 1976 Amateur Draft.

Season	Club	League	GP	G	A	Pts	AG	AA	APts	PIM	PP	SH	GW	S	%	TGF	PGF	TGA	PGA	+/-	GP	G	A	Pts	PIM	PP	SH	GW
1974-75	Toronto Marlboros	OHA	16	6	12	18				6											23	9	17	26	6			
1975-76	St. Catharines Fincups	OHA	64	37	62	99				44											4	1	6	7	7			
1976-77	Nova Scotia Voyageurs	AHL	67	15	21	36				18											6	0	0	0	0			
1977-78	Nova Scotia Voyageurs	AHL	59	15	25	40				17											11	4	4	8	9			
1978-79	Nova Scotia Voyageurs	AHL	77	33	42	75				91											10	5	6	11	14			
1979-80	Winnipeg Jets	NHL	79	21	36	57	19	28	47	28	6	0	3	176	11.9	84	24	83	11	-12								
1980-81	Winnipeg Jets	NHL	77	18	33	51	15	23	38	55	4	1	0	192	9.4	79	23	106	16	-34								
1981-82	Winnipeg Jets	NHL	39	3	13	16	2	9	11	49	0	0	0	53	5.7	24	1	40	14	-3								
	Tulsa Oilers	CHL	41	20	38	58				22											3	1	0	1	2			
1982-83	Winnipeg Jets	NHL	12	6	3	9	5	2	7	4	2	0	0	20	30.0	12	1	6	2	+7	3	2	2	4	2	0	0	0
	Sherbrooke Jets	AHL	65	30	55	85				71																		
1983-84	Winnipeg Jets	NHL	51	3	12	15	2	8	10	12	0	0	1	52	5.8	21	0	43	19	-3								
	Sherbrooke Jets	AHL	22	10	30	40				16																		
1984-85	Winnipeg Jets	NHL	76	10	9	19	8	6	14	31	1	1	1	85	15.4	23	1	54	24	-8	8	4	2	6	2	0	0	1
1985-86	Winnipeg Jets	NHL	54	6	7	13	5	5	10	16	0	0	2	64	9.4	20	1	42	21	-2	1	0	0	0	0	0	0	0
	Sherbrooke Canadiens	AHL	10	9	8	17				9																		
1986-87	Winnipeg Jets	NHL	80	3	13	16	3	9	12	13	0	0	0	76	3.9	24	0	46	32	+10	10	1	2	3	0	0	0	0
1987-88	Winnipeg Jets	NHL	69	5	8	13	4	6	10	28	0	2	0	80	6.3	21	0	69	47	-1	1	0	0	0	0	0	0	0
1988-89	Moncton Hawks	AHL	80	31	61	92				110											8	1	4	5	20			
1989-90	Moncton Hawks	AHL	47	16	37	53				39																		
	St. Louis Blues	NHL	33	3	17	20	3	12	15	23	1	0	1	40	7.5	36	11	28	8	+5	12	3	5	8	18	2	0	0
1990-91	St. Louis Blues	NHL	73	10	27	37	9	20	29	54	1	2	1	101	9.9	49	4	71	25	-1	7	0	0	0	28	0	0	0
1991-92	St. Louis Blues	NHL	64	12	17	29	11	13	24	46	5	2	2	100	12.0	47	14	51	28	+10	6	0	1	1	0	0	0	0
1992-93	St. Louis Blues	NHL	78	8	11	19	7	8	15	44	0	3	1	75	10.7	29	1	51	31	-8	11	0	0	0	12	0	0	0
1993-94	Montreal Canadiens	NHL	48	2	10	12	2	8	10	12	0	0	0	39	5.1	15	0	34	17	-2	4	0	0	0	0	0	0	0
1994-95	Detroit Vipers	IHL	12	6	9	15				10																		
	San Diego Gulls	IHL	58	8	25	33				60											5	2	0	2	8			
1995-96	Wheeling Thunderbirds	ECHL	46	12	30	42				72											2	0	3	3	6			
	NHL Totals		832	110	216	326	95	157	252	415	20	13	10	1133	9.7	484	81	740	295		63	10	12	22	64	2	0	1

AHL Second All-Star Team (1989)

Traded to **Winnipeg** by **Montreal** for cash, October 4, 1979. Traded to **St. Louis** by **Winnipeg** for Doug Evans, January 22, 1990. Signed as a free agent by **Montreal**, August 20, 1993.

● **WILSON, RON**   Ron Wilson   D – R. 5'10", 170 lbs.   b: Windsor, Ont., 5/28/1955.   Toronto's 7th choice, 132nd overall, in 1975 Amateur Draft.

Season	Club	League	GP	G	A	Pts	AG	AA	APts	PIM	PP	SH	GW	S	%	TGF	PGF	TGA	PGA	+/-	GP	G	A	Pts	PIM	PP	SH	GW
1973-74	Providence College	ECAC	26	16	22	38				6																		
1974-75	Providence College	ECAC	27	26	*61	*87				12																		
	United States	WEC-A	10	1	2	3				4																		
1975-76	Providence College	ECAC	28	19	47	66				44																		
1976-77	Providence College	ECAC	30	17	42	69				62																		
	Dallas Black Hawks	CHL	4	1	0	1				2																		
1977-78	Toronto Maple Leafs	NHL	13	2	1	3	2	1	3	0	1	0	0	11	18.2	3	2	6	0	-5								
	Dallas Black Hawks	CHL	67	31	38	69				18																		
1978-79	Toronto Maple Leafs	NHL	46	5	12	17	5	9	14	4	4	0	0	58	8.6	36	28	19	1	-10	3	0	1	1	0	0	0	0
	New Brunswick Hawks	AHL	31	11	21	32				13																		
1979-80	Toronto Maple Leafs	NHL	5	0	2	2	0	2	2	2	0	0	0	6	0.0	6	3	6	1	-2	3	1	2	3	2	1	0	0
	New Brunswick Hawks	AHL	43	20	43	63				10											14	3	2	5	2			
1980-81	EHC Kloten	Switz.	38	22	23	45																						
	United States	WEC-A	8	3	4	7				2																		
1981-82	HC Davos	Switz.	38	24	23	47																						
1982-83	HC Davos	Switz.	36	32	32	64																						
1983-84	HC Davos	Switz.	36	33	39	72																						
1984-85	HC Davos	Switz.	38	39	62	101																						
	Minnesota North Stars	NHL	13	4	8	12	3	5	8	2	0	0	0	27	14.8	21	7	15	0	-1	9	1	6	7	2	1	0	0
1985-86	HC Davos	Switz.	27	20	41	69															6	2	6		2			
	Minnesota North Stars	NHL	11	1	3	4	1	2	3	8	1	0	0	21	4.8	20	11	12	1	-2	5	2	4	6	4	1	0	0

Season	Club	League	GP	G	A	Pts	AG	AA	APts	PIM	PP	SH	GW	S	%	TGF	PGF	TGA	PGA	+/–	GP	G	A	Pts	PIM	PP	SH	GW
			REGULAR SEASON																		PLAYOFFS							
1986-87	**Minnesota North Stars**	**NHL**	65	12	29	41	10	21	31	36	6	0	2	138	8.7	107	53	65	2	–9	....	....	....	....	....	....	....	....
	United States	WEC-A	10	1	3	4	....	....	....	12	....	....	....	....	....	....	....	....	....	....	....	....	....	....	....	....	....	....
1987-88	**Minnesota North Stars**	**NHL**	24	2	12	14	2	9	11	16	1	0	0	40	5.0	39	21	22	0	–4	....	....	....	....	....	....	....	....
	NHL Totals		177	26	67	93	23	49	72	68	13	0	2	301	8.6	232	125	145	5		20	4	13	17	8	3	0	0

ECAC First All-Star Team (1975, 1976) • NCAA East First All-American Team (1975, 1976) • ECAC Second All-Star Team (1977) • CHL First All-Star Team (1978) • WEC-B All-Star Team (1983)

Signed as a free agent by **Minnesota**, March 7, 1985.

• WING, MURRAY

Murray Wing D – R. 5'11", 180 lbs. b: Thunder Bay, Ont., 10/14/1950. Boston's 9th choice, 83rd overall, in 1970 Amateur Draft.

1969-70	University of North Dakota	WCHA	DID NOT PLAY – FRESHMAN																									
1970-71	University of North Dakota	WCHA	29	3	10	13	....	....	....	18	....	....	....	....	....	....	....	....	....	....	....	....	....	....	....	....	....	....
1971-72	Oklahoma City Blazers	CHL	71	12	15	27	....	....	....	79	....	....	....	....	....	....	....	....	....	....	6	0	0	0	14	....	....	....
1972-73	Boston Braves	AHL	57	2	10	12	....	....	....	37	....	....	....	....	....	....	....	....	....	....	10	2	6	8	2	....	....	....
	San Diego Gulls	WHL	6	0	0	0	....	....	....	2	....	....	....	....	....	....	....	....	....	....	....	....	....	....	....	....	....	....
1973-74	**Detroit Red Wings**	**NHL**	1	0	1	1	0	1	1	0	0	0	0	0	0.0	1	0	3	0	–2	....	....	....	....	....	....	....	....
	London Lions	Britain	71	21	21	42	....	....	....	24	....	....	....	....	....	....	....	....	....	....	....	....	....	....	....	....	....	....
1974-75	Thunder Bay Twins	USHL	44	16	35	51	....	....	....	23	....	....	....	....	....	....	....	....	....	....	....	....	....	....	....	....	....	....
1975-76	Thunder Bay Twins	OHA Sr.	22	3	15	18	....	....	....	8	....	....	....	....	....	....	....	....	....	....	....	....	....	....	....	....	....	....
1976-77	Thunder Bay Twins	OHA Sr.	12	2	11	13	....	....	....	2	....	....	....	....	....	....	....	....	....	....	....	....	....	....	....	....	....	....
	NHL Totals		1	0	1	1	0	1	1	0	0	0	0	0	0.0	1	0	3	0		....	....	....	....	....	....	....	....

Traded to **Detroit** by **Boston** to complete transaction that sent Garnet Bailey to Detroit (March 1, 1973), June 4, 1973.

• WINNES, CHRIS

Chris Winnes RW – R. 6', 201 lbs. b: Ridgefield, CT, 2/12/1968. Boston's 9th choice, 161st overall, in 1987 Entry Draft.

1985-86	Ridgefield High School	H.S.	24	40	30	70	....	....	....	....	....	....	....	....	....	....	....	....	....	....	....	....	....	....	....	....	....	....
1986-87	Northwood Prep School	H.S.	27	25	25	50	....	....	....	....	....	....	....	....	....	....	....	....	....	....	....	....	....	....	....	....	....	....
1987-88	University of New Hampshire	H.E.	30	17	19	36	....	....	....	28	....	....	....	....	....	....	....	....	....	....	....	....	....	....	....	....	....	....
1988-89	University of New Hampshire	H.E.	30	11	20	31	....	....	....	22	....	....	....	....	....	....	....	....	....	....	....	....	....	....	....	....	....	....
1989-90	University of New Hampshire	H.E.	24	10	13	23	....	....	....	12	....	....	....	....	....	....	....	....	....	....	....	....	....	....	....	....	....	....
1990-91	University of New Hampshire	H.E.	33	15	16	31	....	....	....	24	....	....	....	....	....	....	....	....	....	....	....	....	....	....	....	....	....	....
	Maine Mariners	AHL	7	3	1	4	....	....	....	0	....	....	....	....	....	....	....	....	....	....	1	0	2	2	0	....	....	....
	Boston Bruins	**NHL**	....	....	....	....	....	....	....	....	....	....	....	....	....	....	....	....	....	....	1	0	0	0	0	....	....	....
1991-92	**Boston Bruins**	**NHL**	24	1	3	4	1	2	3	6	0	0	0	20	5.0	7	3	10	0	–6	....	....	....	....	....	....	....	....
	Maine Mariners	AHL	45	12	35	47	....	....	....	30	....	....	....	....	....	....	....	....	....	....	....	....	....	....	....	....	....	....
	United States	WC-A	6	3	2	5	....	....	....	4	....	....	....	....	....	....	....	....	....	....	....	....	....	....	....	....	....	....
1992-93	**Boston Bruins**	**NHL**	5	0	1	1	0	1	1	0	0	0	0	2	0.0	1	0	0	0	+1	....	....	....	....	....	....	....	....
	Providence Bruins	AHL	64	23	36	59	....	....	....	34	....	....	....	....	....	....	....	....	....	....	4	0	2	2	5	....	....	....
1993-94	**Philadelphia Flyers**	**NHL**	4	0	2	2	0	2	2	0	0	0	0	4	0.0	3	0	2	0	+1	....	....	....	....	....	....	....	....
	Hershey Bears	AHL	70	29	21	50	....	....	....	20	....	....	....	....	....	....	....	....	....	....	7	1	3	4	0	....	....	....
1994-95	Hershey Bears	AHL	78	26	40	66	....	....	....	39	....	....	....	....	....	....	....	....	....	....	6	2	2	4	17	....	....	....
1995-96	Michigan K-Wings	IHL	27	6	13	19	....	....	....	14	....	....	....	....	....	....	....	....	....	....	....	....	....	....	....	....	....	....
	Fort Wayne Komets	IHL	39	6	7	13	....	....	....	12	....	....	....	....	....	....	....	....	....	....	2	0	0	0	0	....	....	....
1996-97	Utah Grizzlies	IHL	5	0	0	0	....	....	....	0	....	....	....	....	....	....	....	....	....	....	....	....	....	....	....	....	....	....
	HC Merano	Italy	12	11	5	16	....	....	....	10	....	....	....	....	....	....	....	....	....	....	....	....	....	....	....	....	....	....
1997-98	San Antonio Dragons	IHL	3	0	0	0	....	....	....	0	....	....	....	....	....	....	....	....	....	....	....	....	....	....	....	....	....	....
	Hartford Wolf Pack	AHL	64	17	23	40	....	....	....	16	....	....	....	....	....	....	....	....	....	....	13	1	4	5	2	....	....	....
	NHL Totals		33	1	6	7	1	5	6	6	0	0	0	26	3.8	11	3	12	0		1	0	0	0	0	0	0	0

Signed as a free agent by **Philadelphia**, August 4, 1993. Signed as a free agent by **NY Rangers**, July 21, 1998.

• WISEMAN, BRIAN

Brian Wiseman C – L. 5'8", 175 lbs. b: Chatham, Ont., 7/13/1971. NY Rangers' 11th choice, 257th overall, in 1991 Entry Draft.

1990-91	University of Michigan	CCHA	47	25	33	58	....	....	....	58	....	....	....	....	....	....	....	....	....	....	....	....	....	....	....	....	....	....
1991-92	University of Michigan	CCHA	44	27	44	71	....	....	....	38	....	....	....	....	....	....	....	....	....	....	....	....	....	....	....	....	....	....
1992-93	University of Michigan	CCHA	35	13	37	50	....	....	....	40	....	....	....	....	....	....	....	....	....	....	....	....	....	....	....	....	....	....
1993-94	University of Michigan	CCHA	40	19	50	69	....	....	....	44	....	....	....	....	....	....	....	....	....	....	....	....	....	....	....	....	....	....
1994-95	Chicago Wolves	IHL	75	17	55	72	....	....	....	52	....	....	....	....	....	....	....	....	....	....	3	1	1	2	4	....	....	....
1995-96	Chicago Wolves	IHL	73	33	55	88	....	....	....	117	....	....	....	....	....	....	....	....	....	....	....	....	....	....	....	....	....	....
1996-97	**Toronto Maple Leafs**	**NHL**	3	0	0	0	0	0	0	0	0	0	0	1	0.0	0	0	0	0	0	....	....	....	....	....	....	....	....
	St. John's Maple Leafs	AHL	71	33	62	95	....	....	....	83	....	....	....	....	....	....	....	....	....	....	7	5	4	9	8	....	....	....
1997-98	Houston Aeros	IHL	78	26	72	98	....	....	....	86	....	....	....	....	....	....	....	....	....	....	4	0	3	3	8	....	....	....
	NHL Totals		3	0	0	0	0	0	0	0	0	0	0	1	0.0	0	0	0	0		....	....	....	....	....	....	....	....

CCHA First All-Star Team (1994) • NCAA West First All-American Team (1994) • IHL First All-Star Team (1998)

Signed as a free agent by **Toronto**, August 14, 1996.

• WISTE, JIM

Jim Wiste C – L. 5'10", 185 lbs. b: Moose Jaw, Sask., 2/18/1946.

1962-63	Moose Jaw Canucks	SJHL	47	22	20	42	....	....	....	47	....	....	....	....	....	....	....	....	....	....	5	2	7	9	6	....	....	....
1963-64	Moose Jaw Canucks	SJHL	61	37	60	97	....	....	....	124	....	....	....	....	....	....	....	....	....	....	5	1	5	6	15	....	....	....
1964-65	University of Denver	WCHA	DID NOT PLAY – FRESHMAN																									
1965-66	University of Denver	WCHA	32	16	14	30	....	....	....	36	....	....	....	....	....	....	....	....	....	....	....	....	....	....	....	....	....	....
1966-67	University of Denver	WCHA	30	24	28	52	....	....	....	35	....	....	....	....	....	....	....	....	....	....	....	....	....	....	....	....	....	....
1967-68	University of Denver	WCHA	34	21	36	57	....	....	....	25	....	....	....	....	....	....	....	....	....	....	....	....	....	....	....	....	....	....
1968-69	**Chicago Black Hawks**	**NHL**	3	0	0	0	0	0	0	0	0	0	0	3	0.0	1	0	0	0	+1	....	....	....	....	....	....	....	....
	Dallas Black Hawks	CHL	68	32	44	76	....	....	....	77	....	....	....	....	....	....	....	....	....	....	10	7	6	13	6	....	....	....
1969-70	**Chicago Black Hawks**	**NHL**	26	0	8	8	0	8	8	8	0	0	0	11	0.0	12	2	12	2	0	....	....	....	....	....	....	....	....
	Dallas Black Hawks	CHL	11	6	9	15	....	....	....	27	....	....	....	....	....	....	....	....	....	....	....	....	....	....	....	....	....	....
1970-71	**Vancouver Canucks**	**NHL**	23	1	2	3	1	2	3	0	0	0	0	9	11.1	5	2	11	0	–8	....	....	....	....	....	....	....	....
	Seattle Totems	WHL	29	11	13	24	....	....	....	32	....	....	....	....	....	....	....	....	....	....	....	....	....	....	....	....	....	....
	Rochester Americans	AHL	....	....	....	....	....	....	....	....	....	....	....	....	....	....	....	....	....	....	10	2	8	10	35	....	....	....
1971-72	Seattle Totems	WHL	4	0	0	0	....	....	....	0	....	....	....	....	....	....	....	....	....	....	....	....	....	....	....	....	....	....
	Rochester Americans	AHL	13	4	8	12	....	....	....	2	....	....	....	....	....	....	....	....	....	....	....	....	....	....	....	....	....	....
	Providence Reds	AHL	53	12	26	38	....	....	....	35	....	....	....	....	....	....	....	....	....	....	3	0	1	1	0	....	....	....
1972-73	Cleveland Crusaders	WHA	70	28	43	71	....	....	....	24	....	....	....	....	....	....	....	....	....	....	9	3	8	11	13	....	....	....
1973-74	Cleveland Crusaders	WHA	76	23	35	58	....	....	....	26	....	....	....	....	....	....	....	....	....	....	5	0	1	1	0	....	....	....
1974-75	Indianapolis Racers	WHA	75	13	28	41	....	....	....	30	....	....	....	....	....	....	....	....	....	....	....	....	....	....	....	....	....	....
1975-76	Indianapolis Racers	WHA	7	0	2	2	....	....	....	0	....	....	....	....	....	....	....	....	....	....	....	....	....	....	....	....	....	....
	Mohawk Valley Comets	NAHL	5	0	1	1	....	....	....	0	....	....	....	....	....	....	....	....	....	....	....	....	....	....	....	....	....	....
	NHL Totals		52	1	10	11	1	10	11	8	0	0	0	23	4.3	18	4	23	2		....	....	....	....	....	....	....	....
	Other Major League Totals		228	64	108	172	....	....	....	80	....	....	....	....	....	....	....	....	....	....	14	3	9	12	13	....	....	....

WCHA First All-Star Team (1967, 1968) • NCAA West First All-American Team (1967, 1968)

Signed as a free agent by **Chicago**, September 27, 1968. Claimed by **Vancouver** from **Chicago** in Expansion Draft, June 10, 1970. Traded to **NY Rangers** by **Vancouver** with Gary Doak for Dave Balon, Wayne Connelly and Ron Stewart, November 16, 1971. Selected by **NY Raiders** (WHA) in 1972 WHA General Player Draft, February 12, 1972. Signed as a free agent by **Cleveland** (WHA) after securing release from **NY Raiders**, August, 1972. Claimed by **Indianapolis** (WHA) from **Cleveland** (WHA) in WHA Expansion Draft, May, 1974.

• WITHERSPOON, JIM
Jim Witherspoon D – R. 6'3", 205 lbs. b: Toronto, Ont., 10/3/1951.

			REGULAR SEASON																		PLAYOFFS							
Season	Club	League	GP	G	A	Pts	AG	AA	APts	PIM	PP	SH	GW	S	%	TGF	PGF	TGA	PGA	+/–	GP	G	A	Pts	PIM	PP	SH	GW
1970-71	Ohio State Buckeyes	CCHA	29	4	10	14	....	....	....	107	....	....	....	....	....	....	....	....	....	....	....	....	....	....	....	....	....	....
1971-72	Ohio State Buckeyes	CCHA	29	3	22	25	....	....	....	64	....	....	....	....	....	....	....	....	....	....	....	....	....	....	....	....	....	....
1972-73	Ohio State Buckeyes	CCHA	25	6	23	29	....	....	....	80	....	....	....	....	....	....	....	....	....	....	....	....	....	....	....	....	....	....
1973-74	Ohio State Buckeyes	CCHA	31	7	26	33	....	....	....	52	....	....	....	....	....	....	....	....	....	....	....	....	....	....	....	....	....	....
1974-75	Springfield Indians	AHL	61	3	9	12	....	....	....	33	....	....	....	....	....	....	....	....	....	....	16	0	1	1	4	....	....	....
1975-76	**Los Angeles Kings**	**NHL**	**2**	**0**	**0**	**0**	**0**	**0**	**0**	**2**	**0**	**0**	**0**	**0**	**0.0**	**0**	**0**	**1**	**0**	**–1**	....	....	....	....	....	....	....	....
	Fort Worth Texans	CHL	61	0	13	13	....	....	....	102	....	....	....	....	....	....	....	....	....	....	....	....	....	....	....	....	....	....
1976-77	Fort Worth Texans	CHL	30	1	4	5	....	....	....	69	....	....	....	....	....	....	....	....	....	....	....	....	....	....	....	....	....	....
1977-78	Springfield Indians	AHL	13	0	3	3	....	....	....	27	....	....	....	....	....	....	....	....	....	....	....	....	....	....	....	....	....	....
	NHL Totals		**2**	**0**	**0**	**0**	**0**	**0**	**0**	**2**	**0**	**0**	**0**	**0**	**0.0**	**0**	**0**	**1**	**0**		....	....	....	....	....	....	....	....

CCHA Second All-Star Team (1973)

Signed as a free agent by **LA Kings**, August, 1974.

• WITT, BRENDAN
Brendan Witt D – L. 6'1", 205 lbs. b: Humbolt, Sask., 2/20/1975. Washington's 1st choice, 11th overall, in 1993 Entry Draft.

Season	Club	League	GP	G	A	Pts	AG	AA	APts	PIM	PP	SH	GW	S	%	TGF	PGF	TGA	PGA	+/–	GP	G	A	Pts	PIM	PP	SH	GW
1991-92	Seattle Thunderbirds	WHL	67	3	9	12	....	....	....	212	....	....	....	....	....	....	....	....	....	....	15	1	1	2	84	....	....	....
1992-93	Seattle Thunderbirds	WHL	70	2	26	28	....	....	....	239	....	....	....	....	....	....	....	....	....	....	5	1	2	3	30	....	....	....
1993-94	Seattle Thunderbirds	WHL	56	8	31	39	....	....	....	235	....	....	....	....	....	....	....	....	....	....	9	3	8	11	23	....	....	....
	Canada	WJC-A	7	0	0	0	....	....	....	6	....	....	....	....	....	....	....	....	....	....	....	....	....	....	....	....	....	....
1994-95			DID NOT PLAY																									
1995-96	**Washington Capitals**	**NHL**	**48**	**2**	**3**	**5**	**2**	**2**	**4**	**85**	**0**	**0**	**1**	**44**	**4.5**	**20**	**0**	**27**	**3**	**–4**	....	....	....	....	....	....	....	....
1996-97	**Washington Capitals**	**NHL**	**44**	**3**	**2**	**5**	**3**	**2**	**5**	**88**	**0**	**0**	**0**	**41**	**7.3**	**17**	**0**	**39**	**2**	**–20**	....	....	....	....	....	....	....	....
	Portland Pirates	AHL	30	2	4	6	....	....	....	56	....	....	....	....	....	....	....	....	....	....	5	1	0	1	30	....	....	....
1997-98	**Washington Capitals**	**NHL**	**64**	**1**	**7**	**8**	**1**	**7**	**8**	**112**	**0**	**0**	**0**	**68**	**1.5**	**37**	**1**	**57**	**10**	**–11**	**16**	**1**	**0**	**1**	**14**	**0**	**0**	**0**
	NHL Totals		**156**	**6**	**12**	**18**	**6**	**11**	**17**	**285**	**0**	**0**	**1**	**153**	**3.9**	**74**	**1**	**123**	**15**		**16**	**1**	**0**	**1**	**14**	**0**	**0**	**0**

WHL West First All-Star Team (1993, 1994) • Canadian Major Junior First All-Star Team (1994)

• Sat out entire 1994-95 season after failing to come to contract terms with Washington.

• WOLANIN, CRAIG
Craig Wolanin D – L. 6'4", 215 lbs. b: Grosse Pointe, MI, 7/27/1967. New Jersey's 1st choice, 3rd overall, in 1985 Entry Draft.

Season	Club	League	GP	G	A	Pts	AG	AA	APts	PIM	PP	SH	GW	S	%	TGF	PGF	TGA	PGA	+/–	GP	G	A	Pts	PIM	PP	SH	GW
1983-84	Detroit Compuware	NAJHL	69	8	42	50	....	....	....	86	....	....	....	....	....	....	....	....	....	....	....	....	....	....	....	....	....	....
1984-85	Kitchener Rangers	OHL	60	5	16	21	....	....	....	95	....	....	....	....	....	....	....	....	....	....	4	1	1	2	2	....	....	....
1985-86	**New Jersey Devils**	**NHL**	**44**	**2**	**16**	**18**	**2**	**11**	**13**	**74**	**0**	**0**	**1**	**45**	**4.4**	**48**	**6**	**63**	**14**	**–7**	....	....	....	....	....	....	....	....
1986-87	**New Jersey Devils**	**NHL**	**68**	**4**	**6**	**10**	**3**	**4**	**7**	**109**	**0**	**0**	**0**	**68**	**5.9**	**46**	**2**	**95**	**20**	**–31**	....	....	....	....	....	....	....	....
	United States	WEC-A	9	0	0	0	....	....	....	32	....	....	....	....	....	....	....	....	....	....	....	....	....	....	....	....	....	....
1987-88	**New Jersey Devils**	**NHL**	**78**	**6**	**25**	**31**	**5**	**18**	**23**	**170**	**1**	**1**	**3**	**113**	**5.3**	**79**	**18**	**89**	**28**	**0**	**18**	**2**	**5**	**7**	**51**	**1**	**0**	**0**
1988-89	**New Jersey Devils**	**NHL**	**56**	**3**	**8**	**11**	**3**	**6**	**9**	**69**	**0**	**0**	**0**	**70**	**4.3**	**40**	**3**	**59**	**13**	**–9**	....	....	....	....	....	....	....	....
1989-90	**New Jersey Devils**	**NHL**	**37**	**1**	**7**	**8**	**1**	**5**	**6**	**47**	**0**	**0**	**0**	**35**	**2.9**	**28**	**1**	**41**	**1**	**–13**	....	....	....	....	....	....	....	....
	Utica Devils	AHL	6	2	4	6	....	....	....	2	....	....	....	....	....	....	....	....	....	....	....	....	....	....	....	....	....	....
	Quebec Nordiques	**NHL**	**13**	**0**	**3**	**3**	**0**	**2**	**2**	**10**	**0**	**0**	**0**	**25**	**0.0**	**15**	**0**	**30**	**17**	**+2**	....	....	....	....	....	....	....	....
1990-91	**Quebec Nordiques**	**NHL**	**80**	**5**	**13**	**18**	**5**	**10**	**15**	**89**	**0**	**1**	**0**	**109**	**4.6**	**74**	**1**	**133**	**47**	**–13**	....	....	....	....	....	....	....	....
	United States	WEC-A	10	2	2	4	....	....	....	22	....	....	....	....	....	....	....	....	....	....	....	....	....	....	....	....	....	....
1991-92	United States	C Cup	8	0	2	2	....	....	....	2	....	....	....	....	....	....	....	....	....	....	....	....	....	....	....	....	....	....
	Quebec Nordiques	**NHL**	**69**	**2**	**11**	**13**	**2**	**8**	**10**	**80**	**0**	**0**	**0**	**71**	**2.8**	**57**	**0**	**98**	**29**	**–12**	....	....	....	....	....	....	....	....
1992-93	**Quebec Nordiques**	**NHL**	**24**	**1**	**4**	**5**	**1**	**3**	**4**	**49**	**0**	**0**	**0**	**17**	**5.9**	**26**	**0**	**24**	**7**	**+9**	**4**	**0**	**0**	**0**	**4**	**0**	**0**	**0**
1993-94	**Quebec Nordiques**	**NHL**	**63**	**6**	**10**	**16**	**6**	**8**	**14**	**80**	**0**	**0**	**0**	**78**	**7.7**	**63**	**4**	**70**	**27**	**+16**	....	....	....	....	....	....	....	....
	United States	WC-A	8	2	1	3	....	....	....	4	....	....	....	....	....	....	....	....	....	....	....	....	....	....	....	....	....	....
1994-95	**Quebec Nordiques**	**NHL**	**40**	**3**	**6**	**9**	**5**	**9**	**14**	**40**	**0**	**0**	**0**	**36**	**8.3**	**37**	**2**	**36**	**13**	**+12**	**6**	**1**	**1**	**2**	**4**	**0**	**0**	**0**
1995-96	**Colorado Avalanche**	**NHL**	**75**	**7**	**20**	**27**	**7**	**16**	**23**	**50**	**0**	**3**	**0**	**73**	**9.6**	**80**	**2**	**81**	**28**	**+25**	**7**	**1**	**0**	**1**	**8**	**0**	**0**	**1**
1996-97	**Tampa Bay Lightning**	**NHL**	**15**	**0**	**0**	**0**	**0**	**0**	**0**	**8**	**0**	**0**	**0**	**12**	**0.0**	**5**	**0**	**15**	**1**	**–9**	....	....	....	....	....	....	....	....
	Toronto Maple Leafs	**NHL**	**23**	**0**	**4**	**4**	**0**	**4**	**4**	**13**	**0**	**0**	**0**	**31**	**0.0**	**15**	**0**	**15**	**3**	**+3**	....	....	....	....	....	....	....	....
1997-98	**Toronto Maple Leafs**	**NHL**	**10**	**0**	**0**	**0**	**0**	**0**	**0**	**6**	**0**	**0**	**0**	**5**	**0.0**	**1**	**0**	**10**	**0**	**–9**	....	....	....	....	....	....	....	....
	NHL Totals		**695**	**40**	**133**	**173**	**40**	**104**	**144**	**894**	**1**	**5**	**4**	**788**	**5.1**	**614**	**39**	**859**	**248**		**35**	**4**	**6**	**10**	**67**	**1**	**0**	**1**

Traded to **Quebec** by **New Jersey** with future considerations (Randy Velischek, August 13, 1990) for Peter Stastny, March 6, 1990. Transferred to **Colorado** after **Quebec** franchise relocated, July 1, 1995. Traded to **Tampa Bay** by **Colorado** for Tampa Bay's 2nd round choice (Ramzi Abid) in 1998 Entry Draft, July 29, 1996. Traded to **Toronto** by **Tampa Bay** for Toronto's 3rd round choice (later traded to Edmonton — Edmonton Selected Alex Henry) in 1998 Entry Draft, January 31, 1997.

• WOLF, BENNETT
Bennett Wolf D – R. 6'3", 205 lbs. b: Kitchener, Ont., 10/23/1959. Pittsburgh's 2nd choice, 52nd overall, in 1979 Entry Draft.

Season	Club	League	GP	G	A	Pts	AG	AA	APts	PIM	PP	SH	GW	S	%	TGF	PGF	TGA	PGA	+/–	GP	G	A	Pts	PIM	PP	SH	GW
1976-77	Kitchener Rangers	OHA	7	0	1	1	....	....	....	16	....	....	....	....	....	....	....	....	....	....	....	....	....	....	....	....	....	....
1976-77	Kitchener Rangers	OHA	7	0	1	1	....	....	....	16	....	....	....	....	....	....	....	....	....	....	....	....	....	....	....	....	....	....
1977-78	Toronto Marlboros	OHA	66	3	13	16	....	....	....	334	....	....	....	....	....	....	....	....	....	....	5	0	1	1	37	....	....	....
1978-79	Toronto Marlboros	OHA	18	0	3	3	....	....	....	48	....	....	....	....	....	....	....	....	....	....	....	....	....	....	....	....	....	....
	Kitchener Rangers	OHA	47	3	18	21	....	....	....	279	....	....	....	....	....	....	....	....	....	....	10	0	4	4	73	....	....	....
1979-80	Grand Rapids Owls	IHL	51	3	14	17	....	....	....	408	....	....	....	....	....	....	....	....	....	....	....	....	....	....	....	....	....	....
	Syracuse Firebirds	AHL	....	....	....	....	....	....	....	....	....	....	....	....	....	....	....	....	....	....	4	0	0	0	39	....	....	....
1980-81	**Pittsburgh Penguins**	**NHL**	**24**	**0**	**1**	**1**	**0**	**1**	**1**	**94**	**0**	**0**	**0**	**14**	**0.0**	**7**	**0**	**11**	**3**	**–1**	....	....	....	....	....	....	....	....
	Binghamton Whalers	AHL	14	2	2	4	....	....	....	106	....	....	....	....	....	....	....	....	....	....	....	....	....	....	....	....	....	....
1981-82	**Pittsburgh Penguins**	**NHL**	**1**	**0**	**0**	**0**	**0**	**0**	**0**	**2**	....	....	....	....	....	....	....	....	....	....	....	....	....	....	....	....	....	....
	Erie Blades	AHL	45	0	4	4	....	....	....	153	....	....	....	....	....	....	....	....	....	....	....	....	....	....	....	....	....	....
1982-83	**Pittsburgh Penguins**	**NHL**	**5**	**0**	**0**	**0**	**0**	**0**	**0**	**37**	**0**	**0**	**0**	**1**	**0.0**	**1**	**0**	**5**	**2**	**–2**	....	....	....	....	....	....	....	....
	Baltimore Skipjacks	AHL	61	1	10	11	....	....	....	223	....	....	....	....	....	....	....	....	....	....	....	....	....	....	....	....	....	....
1983-84	Baltimore Skipjacks	AHL	63	3	13	16	....	....	....	349	....	....	....	....	....	....	....	....	....	....	10	0	2	2	24	....	....	....
1984-85	Baltimore Skipjacks	AHL	55	0	8	8	....	....	....	285	....	....	....	....	....	....	....	....	....	....	13	0	2	2	89	....	....	....
	NHL Totals		**30**	**0**	**1**	**1**	**0**	**1**	**1**	**133**	**0**	**0**	**0**	**15**	**0.0**	**8**	**0**	**16**	**5**		....	....	....	....	....	....	....	....

• WONG, MIKE
Mike Wong C – L. 6'3", 204 lbs. b: Minneapolis, MN, 1/14/1955. Detroit's 7th choice, 77th overall, in 1975 Amateur Draft.

Season	Club	League	GP	G	A	Pts	AG	AA	APts	PIM	PP	SH	GW	S	%	TGF	PGF	TGA	PGA	+/–	GP	G	A	Pts	PIM	PP	SH	GW
1973-74	Minnesota Jr. Stars	MWJHL	57	24	32	56	....	....	....	128	....	....	....	....	....	....	....	....	....	....	....	....	....	....	....	....	....	....
	United States	WJC-A	5	0	0	0	....	....	....	4	....	....	....	....	....	....	....	....	....	....	....	....	....	....	....	....	....	....
1974-75	Montreal Jr. Canadiens	QMJHL	67	27	41	68	....	....	....	130	....	....	....	....	....	....	....	....	....	....	....	....	....	....	....	....	....	....
1975-76	**Detroit Red Wings**	**NHL**	**22**	**1**	**1**	**2**	**1**	**1**	**2**	**12**	**0**	**0**	**0**	**9**	**11.1**	**3**	**2**	**12**	**0**	**–11**	....	....	....	....	....	....	....	....
	Kalamazoo Wings	IHL	39	20	22	42	....	....	....	81	....	....	....	....	....	....	....	....	....	....	....	....	....	....	....	....	....	....
1976-77	Kalamazoo Wings	IHL	24	12	10	22	....	....	....	22	....	....	....	....	....	....	....	....	....	....	....	....	....	....	....	....	....	....
	Rhode Island Reds	AHL	18	3	5	8	....	....	....	6	....	....	....	....	....	....	....	....	....	....	....	....	....	....	....	....	....	....
1977-78	Kalamazoo Wings	IHL	8	0	1	1	....	....	....	0	....	....	....	....	....	....	....	....	....	....	....	....	....	....	....	....	....	....
	Muskegon Mohawks	IHL	58	23	18	41	....	....	....	63	....	....	....	....	....	....	....	....	....	....	4	1	0	1	18	....	....	....
1978-79	Kalamazoo Wings	IHL	6	2	2	4	....	....	....	21	....	....	....	....	....	....	....	....	....	....	....	....	....	....	....	....	....	....
	Johnstown Wings	NEHL	53	18	26	44	....	....	....	81	....	....	....	....	....	....	....	....	....	....	....	....	....	....	....	....	....	....
	NHL Totals		**22**	**1**	**1**	**2**	**1**	**1**	**2**	**12**	**0**	**0**	**0**	**9**	**11.1**	**3**	**2**	**12**	**0**		....	....	....	....	....	....	....	....

• WOOD, DODY
Dody Wood C – L. 6', 200 lbs. b: Chetwynd, B.C., 3/18/1972. San Jose's 4th choice, 45th overall, in 1991 Entry Draft.

Season	Club	League	GP	G	A	Pts	AG	AA	APts	PIM	PP	SH	GW	S	%	TGF	PGF	TGA	PGA	+/–	GP	G	A	Pts	PIM	PP	SH	GW
1989-90	Fort St. John Traders	PCJHL	44	51	73	124	....	....	....	270	....	....	....	....	....	....	....	....	....	....	....	....	....	....	....	....	....	....
	Seattle Thunderbirds	WHL	....	....	....	....	....	....	....	....	....	....	....	....	....	....	....	....	....	....	5	0	0	0	2	....	....	....
1990-91	Seattle Thunderbirds	WHL	69	28	37	65	....	....	....	272	....	....	....	....	....	....	....	....	....	....	6	0	1	1	2	....	....	....
1991-92	Seattle Thunderbirds	WHL	37	13	19	32	....	....	....	232	....	....	....	....	....	....	....	....	....	....	....	....	....	....	....	....	....	....
	Swift Current Broncos	WHL	3	0	2	2	....	....	....	14	....	....	....	....	....	....	....	....	....	....	7	2	1	3	37	....	....	....
1992-93	**San Jose Sharks**	**NHL**	**13**	**1**	**1**	**2**	**1**	**1**	**2**	**71**	**0**	**0**	**0**	**10**	**10.0**	**3**	**0**	**9**	**1**	**–5**	....	....	....	....	....	....	....	....
	Kansas City Blades	IHL	36	3	2	5	....	....	....	216	....	....	....	....	....	....	....	....	....	....	6	0	1	1	15	....	....	....
1993-94	Kansas City Blades	IHL	48	5	15	20	....	....	....	320	....	....	....	....	....	....	....	....	....	....	....	....	....	....	....	....	....	....
1994-95	Kansas City Blades	IHL	44	5	13	18	....	....	....	255	....	....	....	....	....	....	....	....	....	....	21	7	10	17	87	....	....	....
	San Jose Sharks	**NHL**	**9**	**1**	**1**	**2**	**2**	**1**	**3**	**29**	**0**	**0**	**0**	**5**	**20.0**	**2**	**0**	**2**	**0**	**0**	....	....	....	....	....	....	....	....

			REGULAR SEASON																		PLAYOFFS							
Season	Club	League	GP	G	A	Pts	AG	AA	APts	PIM	PP	SH	GW	S	%	TGF	PGF	TGA	PGA	+/–	GP	G	A	Pts	PIM	PP	SH	GW
1995-96	**San Jose Sharks**	**NHL**	**32**	**3**	**6**	**9**	**3**	**5**	**8**	**138**	**0**	**1**	**0**	**33**	**9.1**	**13**	**0**	**19**	**6**	**0**	....	....	....	....	....	....	....	....
1996-97	**San Jose Sharks**	**NHL**	**44**	**3**	**2**	**5**	**3**	**2**	**5**	**193**	**0**	**0**	**0**	**43**	**7.0**	**8**	**0**	**11**	**0**	**–3**	....	....	....	....	....	....	....	....
	Kansas City Blades	IHL	6	3	6	9	....	....	....	35	....	....	....	....	....	....	....	....	....	....	....	....	....	....	....	....	....	....
1997-98	**San Jose Sharks**	**NHL**	**8**	**0**	**0**	**0**	**0**	**0**	**0**	**40**	**0**	**0**	**0**	**4**	**0.0**	**1**	**0**	**4**	**0**	**–3**	....	....	....	....	....	....	....	....
	Kansas City Blades	IHL	2	0	1	1	....	....	....	31	....	....	....	....	....	....	....	....	....	....	....	....	....	....	....	....	....	....
	Albany River Rats	AHL	34	4	13	17	....	....	....	185	....	....	....	....	....	....	....	....	....	....	13	2	0	2	55	....	....	....
	NHL Totals		**106**	**8**	**10**	**18**	**9**	**9**	**18**	**471**	**0**	**1**	**0**	**95**	**8.4**	**27**	**0**	**45**	**7**		....	....	....	....	....	....	....	....

Traded to **New Jersey** by **San Jose** with Doug Bodger for John MacLean and Ken Sutton, December 7, 1997.

• WOOD, RANDY

Randy Wood LW/C – L. 6′, 195 lbs. b: Princeton, NJ, 10/12/1963.

Season	Club	League	GP	G	A	Pts	AG	AA	APts	PIM	PP	SH	GW	S	%	TGF	PGF	TGA	PGA	+/–	GP	G	A	Pts	PIM	PP	SH	GW
1982-83	Yale University	ECAC	26	5	14	19	....	....	....	10	....	....	....	....	....	....	....	....	....	....	....	....	....	....	....	....	....	....
1983-84	Yale University	ECAC	18	7	7	14	....	....	....	10	....	....	....	....	....	....	....	....	....	....	....	....	....	....	....	....	....	....
1984-85	Yale University	ECAC	32	25	28	53	....	....	....	23	....	....	....	....	....	....	....	....	....	....	....	....	....	....	....	....	....	....
1985-86	Yale University	ECAC	31	25	30	55	....	....	....	26	....	....	....	....	....	....	....	....	....	....	....	....	....	....	....	....	....	....
	United States	WEC-A	4	0	0	0	....	....	....	4	....	....	....	....	....	....	....	....	....	....	....	....	....	....	....	....	....	....
1986-87	**New York Islanders**	**NHL**	**6**	**1**	**0**	**1**	**1**	**0**	**1**	**4**	**0**	**0**	**0**	**4**	**25.0**	**1**	**0**	**2**	**0**	**–1**	**13**	**1**	**3**	**4**	**14**	**0**	**0**	**1**
	Springfield Indians	AHL	75	23	24	47	....	....	....	57	....	....	....	....	....	....	....	....	....	....	....	....	....	....	....	....	....	....
1987-88	**New York Islanders**	**NHL**	**75**	**22**	**16**	**38**	**19**	**11**	**30**	**80**	**0**	**1**	**2**	**106**	**20.8**	**46**	**1**	**57**	**10**	**–2**	**5**	**1**	**0**	**1**	**6**	**0**	**0**	**0**
	Springfield Indians	AHL	1	0	1	1	....	....	....	0	....	....	....	....	....	....	....	....	....	....	....	....	....	....	....	....	....	....
1988-89	**New York Islanders**	**NHL**	**77**	**15**	**13**	**28**	**13**	**9**	**22**	**44**	**0**	**0**	**0**	**115**	**13.0**	**38**	**0**	**88**	**32**	**–18**	....	....	....	....	....	....	....	....
	Springfield Indians	AHL	1	1	1	2	....	....	....	0	....	....	....	....	....	....	....	....	....	....	....	....	....	....	....	....	....	....
	United States	WEC-A	10	1	1	2	....	....	....	6	....	....	....	....	....	....	....	....	....	....	....	....	....	....	....	....	....	....
1989-90	**New York Islanders**	**NHL**	**74**	**24**	**24**	**48**	**21**	**17**	**38**	**39**	**6**	**1**	**3**	**185**	**13.0**	**76**	**22**	**84**	**20**	**–10**	**5**	**1**	**1**	**2**	**4**	**0**	**0**	**0**
1990-91	**New York Islanders**	**NHL**	**76**	**24**	**18**	**42**	**22**	**14**	**36**	**45**	**6**	**1**	**3**	**186**	**12.9**	**62**	**10**	**78**	**14**	**–12**	....	....	....	....	....	....	....	....
1991-92	United States	C Cup	3	0	2	2	....	....	....	0	....	....	....	....	....	....	....	....	....	....	....	....	....	....	....	....	....	....
	New York Islanders	**NHL**	**8**	**2**	**2**	**4**	**2**	**1**	**3**	**21**	**0**	**0**	**0**	**30**	**6.7**	**6**	**1**	**8**	**0**	**–3**	....	....	....	....	....	....	....	....
	Buffalo Sabres	**NHL**	**70**	**20**	**16**	**36**	**18**	**12**	**30**	**65**	**7**	**1**	**3**	**185**	**10.8**	**63**	**16**	**83**	**27**	**–9**	**7**	**2**	**1**	**3**	**6**	**0**	**0**	**0**
1992-93	**Buffalo Sabres**	**NHL**	**82**	**18**	**25**	**43**	**15**	**17**	**32**	**77**	**3**	**2**	**2**	**176**	**10.2**	**67**	**14**	**55**	**8**	**+6**	**8**	**1**	**4**	**5**	**4**	**1**	**0**	**0**
1993-94	**Buffalo Sabres**	**NHL**	**84**	**22**	**16**	**38**	**21**	**12**	**33**	**71**	**2**	**2**	**5**	**161**	**13.7**	**53**	**4**	**54**	**16**	**+11**	**6**	**0**	**0**	**0**	**0**	**0**	**0**	**0**
1994-95	**Toronto Maple Leafs**	**NHL**	**48**	**13**	**11**	**24**	**23**	**16**	**39**	**34**	**1**	**1**	**2**	**125**	**10.4**	**43**	**7**	**39**	**10**	**+7**	**7**	**2**	**0**	**2**	**6**	**1**	**0**	**1**
1995-96	**Toronto Maple Leafs**	**NHL**	**46**	**7**	**9**	**16**	**7**	**7**	**14**	**36**	**1**	**0**	**0**	**101**	**6.9**	**24**	**1**	**40**	**13**	**–4**	....	....	....	....	....	....	....	....
	Dallas Stars	**NHL**	**30**	**1**	**4**	**5**	**1**	**3**	**4**	**26**	**0**	**0**	**0**	**58**	**1.7**	**9**	**0**	**30**	**10**	**–11**	....	....	....	....	....	....	....	....
1996-97	**New York Islanders**	**NHL**	**65**	**6**	**5**	**11**	**6**	**4**	**10**	**61**	**0**	**1**	**2**	**96**	**6.3**	**17**	**0**	**40**	**16**	**–7**	....	....	....	....	....	....	....	....
	NHL Totals		**741**	**175**	**159**	**334**	**169**	**123**	**292**	**603**	**26**	**10**	**22**	**1528**	**11.5**	**505**	**76**	**658**	**176**		**51**	**8**	**9**	**17**	**40**	**2**	**0**	**2**

ECAC Second All-Star Team (1985) • ECAC First All-Star Team (1986) • NCAA East Second All-Star Team (1986)

Signed as a free agent by **NY Islanders**, September 17, 1986. Traded to **Buffalo** by **NY Islanders** with Pat Lafontaine, Randy Hillier and NY Islanders' 4th round choice (Dean Melanson) in 1992 Entry Draft for Pierre Turgeon, Uwe Krupp, Benoit Hogue and Dave McLlwain, October 25, 1991. Claimed by **Toronto** from **Buffalo** in NHL Waiver Draft, January 18, 1995. Traded to **Dallas** by **Toronto** with Benoit Hogue for Dave Gagner and Dallas' 6th round choice (Dmitriy Yakushin) in 1996 Entry Draft, January 29, 1996. Signed as a free agent by **NY Islanders**, October 2, 1996.

• WOODLEY, DAN

Dan Woodley RW – R. 5′11″, 185 lbs. b: Oklahoma City, OK, 12/29/1967. Vancouver's 1st choice, 7th overall, in 1986 Entry Draft.

Season	Club	League	GP	G	A	Pts	AG	AA	APts	PIM	PP	SH	GW	S	%	TGF	PGF	TGA	PGA	+/–	GP	G	A	Pts	PIM	PP	SH	GW
1983-84	Portland Winter Hawks	WHL	6	1	2	3	....	....	....	2	....	....	....	....	....	....	....	....	....	....	8	1	3	4	4	....	....	....
1983-84	Summerland Buckaroos	BCJHL	53	17	34	51	....	....	....	100	....	....	....	....	....	....	....	....	....	....	....	....	....	....	....	....	....	....
1984-85	Portland Winter Hawks	WHL	63	21	36	57	....	....	....	108	....	....	....	....	....	....	....	....	....	....	1	0	0	0	0	....	....	....
1985-86	Portland Winter Hawks	WHL	62	45	47	92	....	....	....	100	....	....	....	....	....	....	....	....	....	....	12	0	8	8	31	....	....	....
1986-87	Portland Winter Hawks	WHL	47	30	50	80	....	....	....	81	....	....	....	....	....	....	....	....	....	....	19	*19	17	*36	52	....	....	....
1987-88	**Vancouver Canucks**	**NHL**	**5**	**2**	**0**	**2**	**2**	**0**	**2**	**17**	**0**	**0**	**0**	**3**	**66.7**	**3**	**1**	**1**	**0**	**+1**	....	....	....	....	....	....	....	....
	Flint Spirits	IHL	69	29	37	66	....	....	....	104	....	....	....	....	....	....	....	....	....	....	9	1	3	4	26	....	....	....
1988-89	Milwaukee Admirals	IHL	30	9	12	21	....	....	....	48	....	....	....	....	....	....	....	....	....	....	....	....	....	....	....	....	....	....
	Sherbrooke Canadiens	AHL	30	9	16	25	....	....	....	69	....	....	....	....	....	....	....	....	....	....	4	1	6	7	5	....	....	....
1989-90	Sherbrooke Canadiens	AHL	65	18	40	58	....	....	....	144	....	....	....	....	....	....	....	....	....	....	10	1	6	7	58	....	....	....
1990-91	Fredericton Canadiens	AHL	4	0	0	0	....	....	....	4	....	....	....	....	....	....	....	....	....	....	....	....	....	....	....	....	....	....
	Kansas City Blades	IHL	20	6	4	10	....	....	....	30	....	....	....	....	....	....	....	....	....	....	....	....	....	....	....	....	....	....
	Albany Choppers	IHL	31	8	17	25	....	....	....	36	....	....	....	....	....	....	....	....	....	....	....	....	....	....	....	....	....	....
1991-92	Winston-Salem Thunderbirds	ECHL	57	24	42	66	....	....	....	102	....	....	....	....	....	....	....	....	....	....	5	3	3	6	2	....	....	....
1992-93	Flint Bulldogs	ColHL	39	20	36	56	....	....	....	112	....	....	....	....	....	....	....	....	....	....	6	4	7	11	21	....	....	....
1993-94	Muskegon Fury	ColHL	58	43	58	101	....	....	....	217	....	....	....	....	....	....	....	....	....	....	1	0	0	0	0	....	....	....
1994-95	Muskegon Mohawks	ColHL	43	25	26	51	....	....	....	87	....	....	....	....	....	....	....	....	....	....	....	....	....	....	....	....	....	....
	Saginaw Wheels	ColHL	11	11	4	15	....	....	....	18	....	....	....	....	....	....	....	....	....	....	2	1	1	2	24	....	....	....
	NHL Totals		**5**	**2**	**0**	**2**	**2**	**0**	**2**	**17**	**0**	**0**	**0**	**3**	**66.7**	**3**	**1**	**1**	**0**		....	....	....	....	....	....	....	....

Traded to **Montreal** by **Vancouver** for Jose Charbonneau, January 25, 1989.

• WOODS, PAUL

Paul "Woodsy" Woods LW – L. 5′10″, 175 lbs. b: Hespeler, Ont., 4/12/1955. Montreal's 5th choice, 51st overall, in 1975 Amateur Draft.

Season	Club	League	GP	G	A	Pts	AG	AA	APts	PIM	PP	SH	GW	S	%	TGF	PGF	TGA	PGA	+/–	GP	G	A	Pts	PIM	PP	SH	GW
1972-73	Sault Ste. Marie Greyhounds	OHA	60	30	34	64	....	....	....	65	....	....	....	....	....	....	....	....	....	....	....	....	....	....	....	....	....	....
1973-74	Sault Ste. Marie Greyhounds	OHA	48	17	32	49	....	....	....	91	....	....	....	....	....	....	....	....	....	....	....	....	....	....	....	....	....	....
1974-75	Sault Ste. Marie Greyhounds	OHA	62	38	81	119	....	....	....	116	....	....	....	....	....	....	....	....	....	....	....	....	....	....	....	....	....	....
1975-76	Nova Scotia Voyageurs	AHL	67	17	21	38	....	....	....	38	....	....	....	....	....	....	....	....	....	....	9	2	1	3	0	....	....	....
1976-77	Nova Scotia Voyageurs	AHL	45	20	18	38	....	....	....	51	....	....	....	....	....	....	....	....	....	....	12	1	3	4	6	....	....	....
1977-78	**Detroit Red Wings**	**NHL**	**80**	**19**	**23**	**42**	**18**	**19**	**37**	**52**	**3**	**2**	**3**	**107**	**17.8**	**83**	**13**	**83**	**31**	**+18**	**7**	**0**	**5**	**5**	**4**	**0**	**0**	**0**
1978-79	**Detroit Red Wings**	**NHL**	**80**	**14**	**23**	**37**	**13**	**18**	**31**	**59**	**1**	**3**	**1**	**127**	**11.0**	**60**	**12**	**110**	**36**	**–26**	....	....	....	....	....	....	....	....
	Canada	WEC-A	8	0	0	0	....	....	....	2	....	....	....	....	....	....	....	....	....	....	....	....	....	....	....	....	....	....
1979-80	**Detroit Red Wings**	**NHL**	**79**	**6**	**20**	**26**	**5**	**15**	**20**	**24**	**0**	**0**	**0**	**114**	**5.3**	**46**	**6**	**89**	**30**	**–19**	....	....	....	....	....	....	....	....
1980-81	**Detroit Red Wings**	**NHL**	**67**	**8**	**16**	**24**	**7**	**11**	**18**	**45**	**1**	**1**	**1**	**74**	**10.8**	**42**	**4**	**79**	**31**	**–10**	....	....	....	....	....	....	....	....
1981-82	**Detroit Red Wings**	**NHL**	**75**	**10**	**17**	**27**	**8**	**11**	**19**	**48**	**0**	**1**	**1**	**68**	**14.7**	**48**	**1**	**83**	**31**	**–5**	....	....	....	....	....	....	....	....
1982-83	**Detroit Red Wings**	**NHL**	**63**	**13**	**20**	**33**	**11**	**14**	**25**	**30**	**0**	**1**	**3**	**82**	**15.9**	**44**	**0**	**67**	**21**	**–2**	....	....	....	....	....	....	....	....
1983-84	**Detroit Red Wings**	**NHL**	**57**	**2**	**5**	**7**	**2**	**3**	**5**	**18**	**0**	**0**	**0**	**33**	**6.1**	**19**	**1**	**50**	**16**	**–16**	....	....	....	....	....	....	....	....
1984-85	Adirondack Red Wings	AHL	26	2	11	13	....	....	....	8	....	....	....	....	....	....	....	....	....	....	....	....	....	....	....	....	....	....
	NHL Totals		**501**	**72**	**124**	**196**	**64**	**91**	**155**	**276**	**5**	**8**	**9**	**605**	**11.9**	**342**	**37**	**561**	**196**		**7**	**0**	**5**	**5**	**4**	**0**	**0**	**0**

Claimed by **Detroit** from **Montreal** in Waiver Draft, October 10, 1977.

• WOOLLEY, JASON

Jason Woolley D – L. 6′, 188 lbs. b: Toronto, Ont., 7/27/1969. Washington's 4th choice, 61st overall, in 1989 Entry Draft.

Season	Club	League	GP	G	A	Pts	AG	AA	APts	PIM	PP	SH	GW	S	%	TGF	PGF	TGA	PGA	+/–	GP	G	A	Pts	PIM	PP	SH	GW
1987-88	St. Michael's Buzzers	Metro-Jr.	31	19	37	56	....	....	....	22	....	....	....	....	....	....	....	....	....	....	....	....	....	....	....	....	....	....
1988-89	Michigan State Spartans	CCHA	47	12	25	37	....	....	....	26	....	....	....	....	....	....	....	....	....	....	....	....	....	....	....	....	....	....
1989-90	Michigan State Spartans	CCHA	45	10	38	48	....	....	....	26	....	....	....	....	....	....	....	....	....	....	....	....	....	....	....	....	....	....
1990-91	Michigan State Spartans	CCHA	40	15	44	59	....	....	....	24	....	....	....	....	....	....	....	....	....	....	....	....	....	....	....	....	....	....
1991-92	Canada	Nat-Team	60	14	30	44	....	....	....	36	....	....	....	....	....	....	....	....	....	....	....	....	....	....	....	....	....	....
	Canada	Olympics	8	0	5	5	....	....	....	4	....	....	....	....	....	....	....	....	....	....	....	....	....	....	....	....	....	....
	Washington Capitals	**NHL**	**1**	**0**	**0**	**0**	**0**	**0**	**0**	**0**	**0**	**0**	**0**	**2**	**0.0**	**1**	**0**	**0**	**0**	**+1**	....	....	....	....	....	....	....	....
	Baltimore Skipjacks	AHL	15	1	10	11	....	....	....	6	....	....	....	....	....	....	....	....	....	....	....	....	....	....	....	....	....	....
	Canada	WC-A	6	1	2	3	....	....	....	2	....	....	....	....	....	....	....	....	....	....	....	....	....	....	....	....	....	....
1992-93	**Washington Capitals**	**NHL**	**26**	**0**	**2**	**2**	**0**	**1**	**1**	**10**	**0**	**0**	**0**	**11**	**0.0**	**18**	**3**	**13**	**1**	**+3**	....	....	....	....	....	....	....	....
	Baltimore Skipjacks	AHL	29	14	27	41	....	....	....	22	....	....	....	....	....	....	....	....	....	....	1	0	2	2	0	....	....	....
1993-94	**Washington Capitals**	**NHL**	**10**	**1**	**2**	**3**	**1**	**2**	**3**	**4**	**0**	**0**	**0**	**15**	**6.7**	**9**	**3**	**4**	**0**	**+2**	**4**	**1**	**0**	**1**	**4**	**0**	**0**	**1**
	Portland Pirates	AHL	41	12	29	41	....	....	....	14	....	....	....	....	....	....	....	....	....	....	9	2	2	4	4	....	....	....
1994-95	Detroit Vipers	IHL	48	8	28	36	....	....	....	38	....	....	....	....	....	....	....	....	....	....	....	....	....	....	....	....	....	....
	Florida Panthers	**NHL**	**34**	**4**	**9**	**13**	**7**	**13**	**20**	**18**	**1**	**0**	**0**	**76**	**5.3**	**31**	**11**	**21**	**0**	**–1**	....	....	....	....	....	....	....	....
1995-96	**Florida Panthers**	**NHL**	**52**	**6**	**28**	**34**	**6**	**23**	**29**	**32**	**3**	**0**	**0**	**98**	**6.1**	**72**	**44**	**40**	**3**	**–9**	**13**	**2**	**6**	**8**	**14**	**1**	**0**	**1**

Season	Club	League	REGULAR SEASON																		PLAYOFFS							
			GP	G	A	Pts	AG	AA	APts	PIM	PP	SH	GW	S	%	TGF	PGF	TGA	PGA	+/–	GP	G	A	Pts	PIM	PP	SH	GW
1996-97	**Florida Panthers**	**NHL**	**3**	**0**	**0**	**0**	**0**	**0**	**0**	**2**	**0**	**0**	**0**	**7**	**0.0**	**3**	**1**	**1**	**0**	**+1**	....	....	....	....	....	....	....	....
	Pittsburgh Penguins	**NHL**	**57**	**6**	**30**	**36**	**6**	**27**	**33**	**28**	**2**	**0**	**1**	**79**	**7.6**	**82**	**29**	**51**	**1**	**+3**	**5**	**0**	**3**	**3**	**0**	**0**	**0**	**0**
1997-98	**Buffalo Sabres**	**NHL**	**71**	**9**	**26**	**35**	**11**	**25**	**36**	**35**	**3**	**0**	**2**	**129**	**7.0**	**72**	**34**	**30**	**0**	**+8**	**15**	**2**	**9**	**11**	**12**	**1**	**0**	**1**
	NHL Totals		**254**	**26**	**97**	**123**	**31**	**91**	**122**	**129**	**9**	**0**	**3**	**417**	**6.2**	**288**	**125**	**160**	**5**		**37**	**5**	**18**	**23**	**30**	**2**	**0**	**3**

CCHA First All-Star Team (1991) • NCAA West First All-American Team (1991)

Signed as a free agent by **Florida**, February 15, 1995. Traded to **Pittsburgh** by **Florida** with Stu Barnes for Chris Wells, November 19, 1996. Traded to **Buffalo** by **Pittsburgh** for Buffalo's 5th round choice (Robert Scuderi) in 1998 Entry Draft, September 24, 1997.

• WORRELL, PETER

Peter Worrell LW – L. 6'6", 249 lbs. b: Pierre Fonds, Que., 8/18/1977. Florida's 7th choice, 166th overall, in 1995 Entry Draft.

Season	Club	League	GP	G	A	Pts	AG	AA	APts	PIM	PP	SH	GW	S	%	TGF	PGF	TGA	PGA	+/–	GP	G	A	Pts	PIM	PP	SH	GW
1994-95	Hull Olympiques	QMJHL	56	1	8	9	....	....	....	243	....	....	....	....	....	....	....	....	....	....	21	0	1	1	91	....	....	....
1995-96	Hull Olympiques	QMJHL	63	23	36	59	....	....	....	464	....	....	....	....	....	....	....	....	....	....	18	11	8	19	81	....	....	....
1996-97	Hull Olympiques	QMJHL	62	17	46	63	....	....	....	437	....	....	....	....	....	....	....	....	....	....	14	3	13	16	83	....	....	....
1997-98	**Florida Panthers**	**NHL**	**19**	**0**	**0**	**0**	**0**	**0**	**0**	**153**	**0**	**0**	**0**	**15**	**0.0**	**0**	**0**	**4**	**0**	**–4**	....	....	....	....	....	....	....	....
	Beast of New Haven	AHL	50	15	12	27	....	....	....	309	....	....	....	....	....	....	....	....	....	....	1	0	1	1	6	....	....	....
	NHL Totals		**19**	**0**	**0**	**0**	**0**	**0**	**0**	**153**	**0**	**0**	**0**	**15**	**0.0**	**0**	**0**	**4**	**0**		....	....	....	....	....	....	....	....

• WORTMAN, KEVIN

Kevin Wortman D – R. 6', 200 lbs. b: Sagus, MA, 2/22/1969. Calgary's 9th choice, 168th overall, in 1989 Entry Draft.

Season	Club	League	GP	G	A	Pts	AG	AA	APts	PIM	PP	SH	GW	S	%	TGF	PGF	TGA	PGA	+/–	GP	G	A	Pts	PIM	PP	SH	GW
1990-91	American International U.	NCAA	28	21	25	46	....	....	....	6	....	....	....	....	....	....	....	....	....	....	....	....	....	....	....	....	....	....
1991-92	Salt Lake Golden Eagles	IHL	82	12	34	46	....	....	....	34	....	....	....	....	....	....	....	....	....	....	5	1	0	1	0	....	....	....
1992-93	Salt Lake Golden Eagles	IHL	82	13	50	63	....	....	....	24	....	....	....	....	....	....	....	....	....	....	....	....	....	....	....	....	....	....
1993-94	**Calgary Flames**	**NHL**	**5**	**0**	**0**	**0**	**0**	**0**	**0**	**2**	**0**	**0**	**0**	**2**	**0.0**	**5**	**1**	**3**	**0**	**+1**	....	....	....	....	....	....	....	....
	Saint John Flames	AHL	72	17	32	49	....	....	....	32	....	....	....	....	....	....	....	....	....	....	7	1	5	6	16	....	....	....
1994-95	Kansas City Blades	IHL	80	6	28	34	....	....	....	22	....	....	....	....	....	....	....	....	....	....	21	1	1	2	4	....	....	....
1995-96	Fort Wayne Komets	IHL	82	12	21	33	....	....	....	26	....	....	....	....	....	....	....	....	....	....	5	2	4	6	4	....	....	....
1996-97	JyP HT Jvaskyla	Finland	49	8	15	23	....	....	....	26	....	....	....	....	....	....	....	....	....	....	4	1	2	3	0	....	....	....
1997-98	JyP HT Jyvaskyla	Finland	48	10	16	26	....	....	....	28	....	....	....	....	....	....	....	....	....	....	....	....	....	....	....	....	....	....
	NHL Totals		**5**	**0**	**0**	**0**	**0**	**0**	**0**	**2**	**0**	**0**	**0**	**2**	**0.0**	**5**	**1**	**3**	**0**		....	....	....	....	....	....	....	....

IHL Second All-Star Team (1993)

Signed as a free agent by **San Jose**, August 25, 1994.

• WOTTON, MARK

Mark Wotton D – L. 5'11", 187 lbs. b: Foxwarren, Man., 11/16/1973. Vancouver's 11th choice, 237th overall, in 1992 Entry Draft.

Season	Club	League	GP	G	A	Pts	AG	AA	APts	PIM	PP	SH	GW	S	%	TGF	PGF	TGA	PGA	+/–	GP	G	A	Pts	PIM	PP	SH	GW
1990-91	Saskatoon Blades	WHL	45	4	11	15	....	....	....	37	....	....	....	....	....	....	....	....	....	....	....	....	....	....	....	....	....	....
1991-92	Saskatoon Blades	WHL	64	11	25	36	....	....	....	92	....	....	....	....	....	....	....	....	....	....	....	....	....	....	....	....	....	....
1992-93	Saskatoon Blades	WHL	71	15	51	66	....	....	....	90	....	....	....	....	....	....	....	....	....	....	9	6	5	11	18	....	....	....
1993-94	Saskatoon Blades	WHL	65	12	34	46	....	....	....	108	....	....	....	....	....	....	....	....	....	....	16	3	12	15	32	....	....	....
1994-95	Syracuse Crunch	AHL	75	12	29	41	....	....	....	50	....	....	....	....	....	....	....	....	....	....	....	....	....	....	....	....	....	....
	Vancouver Canucks	**NHL**	**1**	**0**	**0**	**0**	**0**	**0**	**0**	**0**	**0**	**0**	**0**	**2**	**0.0**	**1**	**0**	**0**	**0**	**+1**	**5**	**0**	**0**	**0**	**4**	**0**	**0**	**0**
1995-96	Syracuse Crunch	AHL	80	10	35	45	....	....	....	96	....	....	....	....	....	....	....	....	....	....	15	1	12	13	20	....	....	....
1996-97	**Vancouver Canucks**	**NHL**	**36**	**3**	**6**	**9**	**3**	**5**	**8**	**19**	**0**	**1**	**0**	**41**	**7.3**	**32**	**0**	**34**	**10**	**+8**	....	....	....	....	....	....	....	....
	Syracuse Crunch	AHL	27	2	8	10	....	....	....	25	....	....	....	....	....	....	....	....	....	....	2	0	0	0	4	....	....	....
1997-98	**Vancouver Canucks**	**NHL**	**5**	**0**	**0**	**0**	**0**	**0**	**0**	**6**	**0**	**0**	**0**	**3**	**0.0**	**2**	**0**	**4**	**0**	**–2**	....	....	....	....	....	....	....	....
	Syracuse Crunch	AHL	56	12	21	33	....	....	....	80	....	....	....	....	....	....	....	....	....	....	5	0	0	0	12	....	....	....
	NHL Totals		**42**	**3**	**6**	**9**	**3**	**5**	**8**	**25**	**0**	**1**	**0**	**46**	**6.5**	**35**	**0**	**38**	**10**		**5**	**0**	**0**	**0**	**4**	**0**	**0**	**0**

WHL East Second All-Star Team (1994)

• WOYTOWICH, BOB

Bob "Augie" Woytowich D – R. 6', 185 lbs. b: Winnipeg, Man., 8/18/1941. d: 7/30/1988.

Season	Club	League	GP	G	A	Pts	AG	AA	APts	PIM	PP	SH	GW	S	%	TGF	PGF	TGA	PGA	+/–	GP	G	A	Pts	PIM	PP	SH	GW
1958-59	Transcona Rangers	MJHL	28	7	3	10	....	....	....	34	....	....	....	....	....	....	....	....	....	....	4	0	1	1	4	....	....	....
1959-60	Winnipeg Rangers	MJHL	27	7	16	23	....	....	....	68	....	....	....	....	....	....	....	....	....	....	12	6	2	8	34	....	....	....
1960-61	Winnipeg Rangers	MJHL	30	8	21	29	....	....	....	82	....	....	....	....	....	....	....	....	....	....	9	3	7	10	6	....	....	....
	Seattle Totems	WHL	2	0	0	0	....	....	....	0	....	....	....	....	....	....	....	....	....	....	....	....	....	....	....	....	....	....
1961-62	Winnipeg Rangers	MJHL	40	9	18	27	....	....	....	65	....	....	....	....	....	....	....	....	....	....	3	0	3	3	12	....	....	....
	Brandon Wheat Kings	MJHL	....	....	....	....	....	....	....	....	....	....	....	....	....	....	....	....	....	....	7	1	3	4	14	....	....	....
1962-63	Sudbury Wolves	EPHL	71	17	27	44	....	....	....	69	....	....	....	....	....	....	....	....	....	....	8	0	3	3	8	....	....	....
1963-64	St. Paul Rangers	CHL	68	9	31	40	....	....	....	101	....	....	....	....	....	....	....	....	....	....	11	2	4	6	8	....	....	....
1964-65	**Boston Bruins**	**NHL**	**21**	**2**	**10**	**12**	**3**	**11**	**14**	**16**	....	....	....	....	....	....	....	....	....	....	....	....	....	....	....	....	....	....
	Hershey Bears	AHL	48	5	21	26	....	....	....	56	....	....	....	....	....	....	....	....	....	....	....	....	....	....	....	....	....	....
1965-66	**Boston Bruins**	**NHL**	**68**	**2**	**17**	**19**	**2**	**17**	**19**	**75**	....	....	....	....	....	....	....	....	....	....	....	....	....	....	....	....	....	....
1966-67	**Boston Bruins**	**NHL**	**64**	**2**	**7**	**9**	**2**	**7**	**9**	**43**	....	....	....	....	....	....	....	....	....	....	....	....	....	....	....	....	....	....
1967-68	**Minnesota North Stars**	**NHL**	**66**	**4**	**17**	**21**	**5**	**18**	**23**	**63**	**2**	**0**	**0**	**86**	**4.7**	**72**	**18**	**81**	**4**	**–23**	**14**	**0**	**1**	**1**	**18**	**0**	**0**	**0**
1968-69	**Pittsburgh Penguins**	**NHL**	**71**	**9**	**20**	**29**	**10**	**19**	**29**	**62**	**1**	**2**	**0**	**127**	**7.1**	**88**	**28**	**101**	**15**	**–26**	....	....	....	....	....	....	....	....
1969-70	**Pittsburgh Penguins**	**NHL**	**68**	**8**	**25**	**33**	**9**	**25**	**34**	**49**	**16**	**0**	**0**	**155**	**5.2**	**85**	**31**	**89**	**23**	**–12**	**10**	**1**	**2**	**3**	**2**	**0**	**0**	**0**
1970-71	**Pittsburgh Penguins**	**NHL**	**78**	**4**	**22**	**26**	**4**	**19**	**23**	**30**	**2**	**0**	**0**	**149**	**2.7**	**90**	**24**	**77**	**19**	**+8**	....	....	....	....	....	....	....	....
1971-72	**Pittsburgh Penguins**	**NHL**	**31**	**1**	**4**	**5**	**1**	**4**	**5**	**8**	**1**	**0**	**0**	**36**	**2.8**	**19**	**7**	**38**	**7**	**–19**	....	....	....	....	....	....	....	....
	Los Angeles Kings	**NHL**	**36**	**0**	**4**	**4**	**0**	**4**	**4**	**6**	**0**	**0**	**0**	**19**	**0.0**	**31**	**9**	**40**	**10**	**–8**	....	....	....	....	....	....	....	....
1972-73	Winnipeg Jets	WHA	62	2	4	6	....	....	....	47	....	....	....	....	....	....	....	....	....	....	14	1	1	2	4	....	....	....
1973-74	Winnipeg Jets	WHA	72	6	28	34	....	....	....	43	....	....	....	....	....	....	....	....	....	....	4	0	0	0	0	....	....	....
1974-75	Winnipeg Jets	WHA	24	0	4	4	....	....	....	8	....	....	....	....	....	....	....	....	....	....	....	....	....	....	....	....	....	....
	Indianapolis Racers	WHA	42	0	8	8	....	....	....	28	....	....	....	....	....	....	....	....	....	....	....	....	....	....	....	....	....	....
1975-76	Indianapolis Racers	WHA	42	1	7	8	....	....	....	14	....	....	....	....	....	....	....	....	....	....	....	....	....	....	....	....	....	....
1976-77	Mohawk Valley Comets	NAHL	37	0	10	10	....	....	....	4	....	....	....	....	....	....	....	....	....	....	....	....	....	....	....	....	....	....
1977-78	Steinbach Stallions	MHL Sr.	....	0	1	1	....	....	....	7	....	....	....	....	....	....	....	....	....	....	....	....	....	....	....	....	....	....
	NHL Totals		**503**	**32**	**126**	**158**	**36**	**124**	**160**	**352**	**22**	**2**	**0**	**572**	**5.6**	**385**	**117**	**426**	**78**		**24**	**1**	**3**	**4**	**20**	**0**	**0**	**0**
	Other Major League Totals		242	9	51	60	....	....	....	140	....	....	....	....	....	....	....	....	....	....	18	1	1	2	4	....	....	....

CHL First All-Star Team (1964)

Played in NHL All-Star Game (1970)

Claimed by **Boston** from **NY Rangers** in Intra-League Draft, June 10, 1964. Claimed by **Minnesota** from **Boston** in Expansion Draft, June 6, 1967. Traded to **Pittsburgh** by **Minnesota** for Pittsburgh's 1st round choice (later traded to Montreal — Montreal selected Dave Gardner) in 1972 Amateur Draft, October 1, 1968. Traded to **LA Kings** by **Pittsburgh** for Al McDonaugh, January 11, 1972. Selected by **Winnipeg** (WHA) in 1972 WHA General Player Draft, February 12, 1972. Traded to **Indianapolis** (WHA) by **Winnipeg** (WHA) for cash, December, 1974.

• WREN, BOB

Bob Wren LW – L. 5'10", 185 lbs. b: Preston, Ont., 9/16/1974. Los Angeles' 3rd choice, 94th overall, in 1993 Entry Draft.

Season	Club	League	GP	G	A	Pts	AG	AA	APts	PIM	PP	SH	GW	S	%	TGF	PGF	TGA	PGA	+/–	GP	G	A	Pts	PIM	PP	SH	GW
1991-92	Detroit Ambassadors	OHL	62	13	36	49	....	....	....	58	....	....	....	....	....	....	....	....	....	....	7	3	4	7	19	....	....	....
1992-93	Detroit Jr. Red Wings	OHL	63	57	88	145	....	....	....	91	....	....	....	....	....	....	....	....	....	....	15	4	11	15	20	....	....	....
1993-94	Detroit Jr. Red Wings	OHL	57	45	64	109	....	....	....	81	....	....	....	....	....	....	....	....	....	....	17	12	18	30	20	....	....	....
1994-95	Springfield Falcons	AHL	61	16	15	31	....	....	....	118	....	....	....	....	....	....	....	....	....	....	....	....	....	....	....	....	....	....
	Richmond Renegades	ECHL	2	0	1	1	....	....	....	0	....	....	....	....	....	....	....	....	....	....	....	....	....	....	....	....	....	....
1995-96	Knoxville Cherokees	ECHL	50	21	35	56	....	....	....	257	....	....	....	....	....	....	....	....	....	....	8	4	11	15	32	....	....	....
	Detroit Vipers	IHL	1	0	0	0	....	....	....	0	....	....	....	....	....	....	....	....	....	....	....	....	....	....	....	....	....	....
1996-97	Baltimore Bandits	AHL	72	23	36	59	....	....	....	97	....	....	....	....	....	....	....	....	....	....	3	1	1	2	0	....	....	....
1997-98	**Anaheim Mighty Ducks**	**NHL**	**3**	**0**	**0**	**0**	**0**	**0**	**0**	**0**	**0**	**0**	**0**	**4**	**0.0**	**1**	**0**	**1**	**0**	**0**	....	....	....	....	....	....	....	....
	Cincinnati Mighty Ducks	AHL	77	42	58	100	....	....	....	151	....	....	....	....	....	....	....	....	....	....	....	....	....	....	....	....	....	....
	NHL Totals		**3**	**0**	**0**	**0**	**0**	**0**	**0**	**0**	**0**	**0**	**0**	**4**	**0.0**	**1**	**0**	**1**	**0**		....	....	....	....	....	....	....	....

OHL Second All-Star Team (1993, 1994)

Signed as a free agent by **Hartford**, September 6, 1994. Signed as a free agent by **Anaheim**, August 1, 1997.

• WRIGHT, JAMIE

Jamie Wright LW – L. 6', 172 lbs. b: Kitchener, Ont., 5/13/1976. Dallas' 3rd choice, 98th overall, in 1994 Entry Draft.

			REGULAR SEASON																		PLAYOFFS							
Season	Club	League	GP	G	A	Pts	AG	AA	APts	PIM	PP	SH	GW	S	%	TGF	PGF	TGA	PGA	+/–	GP	G	A	Pts	PIM	PP	SH	GW
1993-94	Guelph Platers	OHL	65	17	15	32	....	....	....	34	....	....	....	....	....	....	....	....	....	....	8	2	1	3	10	....	....	....
1994-95	Guelph Platers	OHL	65	43	39	82	....	....	....	36	....	....	....	....	....	....	....	....	....	....	14	6	8	14	6	....	....	....
1995-96	Guelph Platers	OHL	55	30	36	66	....	....	....	45	....	....	....	....	....	....	....	....	....	....	16	10	12	22	35	....	....	....
	Canada	WJC-A	6	1	2	3	....	....	....	2	....	....	....	....	....	....	....	....	....	....	....	....	....	....	....	....	....	....
1996-97	Michigan K-Wings	IHL	60	6	8	14	....	....	....	34	....	....	....	....	....	....	....	....	....	....	1	0	0	0	0	....	....	....
1997-98	**Dallas Stars**	**NHL**	**21**	**4**	**2**	**6**	**5**	**2**	**7**	**2**	**0**	**0**	**2**	**15**	**26.7**	**11**	**0**	**3**	**0**	**+8**	**5**	**0**	**0**	**0**	**0**	**0**	**0**	**0**
	Michigan K-Wings	IHL	53	15	11	26	....	....	....	31	....	....	....	....	....	....	....	....	....	....	....	....	....	....	....	....	....	....
	NHL Totals		**21**	**4**	**2**	**6**	**5**	**2**	**7**	**2**	**0**	**0**	**2**	**15**	**26.7**	**11**	**0**	**3**	**0**		**5**	**0**	**0**	**0**	**0**	**0**	**0**	**0**

• WRIGHT, JOHN

John Wright C – R. 5'11", 175 lbs. b: Toronto, Ont., 11/9/1948. Toronto's 1st choice, 4th overall, in 1966 Amateur Draft.

Season	Club	League	GP	G	A	Pts	AG	AA	APts	PIM	PP	SH	GW	S	%	TGF	PGF	TGA	PGA	+/–	GP	G	A	Pts	PIM	PP	SH	GW
1965-66	York Steel	Jr. B	....	26	18	44	....	....	....	....	....	....	....	....	....	....	....	....	....	....	....	....	....	....	....	....	....	....
1966-67	Toronto Marlboros	OHA	48	9	27	36	....	....	....	18	....	....	....	....	....	....	....	....	....	....	17	0	4	4	6	....	....	....
1967-68	Toronto Marlboros	OHA	54	22	42	64	....	....	....	31	....	....	....	....	....	....	....	....	....	....	5	1	3	4	2	....	....	....
	Toronto Marlboros	OHA Sr.	1	1	0	1	....	....	....	2	....	....	....	....	....	....	....	....	....	....	....	....	....	....	....	....	....	....
1968-69	University of Toronto	OUAA	15	18	19	37	....	....	....	....	....	....	....	....	....	....	....	....	....	....	....	....	....	....	....	....	....	....
1969-70	University of Toronto	OUAA	15	21	19	40	....	....	....	....	....	....	....	....	....	....	....	....	....	....	....	....	....	....	....	....	....	....
1970-71	University of Toronto	OUAA	31	32	23	55	....	....	....	....	....	....	....	....	....	....	....	....	....	....	....	....	....	....	....	....	....	....
1971-72	University of Toronto	OUAA	38	26	41	67	....	....	....	....	....	....	....	....	....	....	....	....	....	....	....	....	....	....	....	....	....	....
1972-73	**Vancouver Canucks**	**NHL**	**71**	**10**	**27**	**37**	**10**	**23**	**33**	**32**	**0**	**0**	**1**	**121**	**8.3**	**47**	**2**	**90**	**29**	**–16**	....	....	....	....	....	....	....	....
1973-74	**Vancouver Canucks**	**NHL**	**20**	**3**	**3**	**6**	**3**	**3**	**6**	**11**	**1**	**0**	**0**	**24**	**12.5**	**8**	**2**	**10**	**2**	**–2**	....	....	....	....	....	....	....	....
	St. Louis Blues	**NHL**	**32**	**3**	**6**	**9**	**3**	**5**	**8**	**22**	**0**	**0**	**0**	**43**	**7.0**	**11**	**0**	**14**	**2**	**–1**	....	....	....	....	....	....	....	....
1974-75	**Kansas City Scouts**	**NHL**	**4**	**0**	**0**	**0**	**0**	**0**	**0**	**2**	**0**	**0**	**0**	**5**	**0.0**	**0**	**0**	**3**	**0**	**–3**	....	....	....	....	....	....	....	....
	Providence Reds	AHL	68	30	40	70	....	....	....	47	....	....	....	....	....	....	....	....	....	....	6	0	0	0	4	....	....	....
	NHL Totals		**127**	**16**	**36**	**52**	**16**	**31**	**47**	**67**	**1**	**0**	**1**	**193**	**8.3**	**66**	**4**	**117**	**33**		....	....	....	....	....	....	....	....

Claimed by **Vancouver** (WHL) from **Toronto** in Reverse Draft, June, 1970. NHL rights transferred to **Vancouver** when owners of **Vancouver** (WHL) club awarded NHL expansion team, May 20, 1970. Traded to **St. Louis** by **Vancouver** for Mike Lampman, December, 1973. Claimed by **Kansas City** from **St. Louis** in Expansion Draft, June, 1974.

• WRIGHT, KEITH

Keith Wright LW – L. 6', 180 lbs. b: Aurora, Ont., 4/13/1944.

Season	Club	League	GP	G	A	Pts	AG	AA	APts	PIM	PP	SH	GW	S	%	TGF	PGF	TGA	PGA	+/–	GP	G	A	Pts	PIM	PP	SH	GW
1960-61	Peterborough Petes	OHA	48	5	10	15	....	....	....	50	....	....	....	....	....	....	....	....	....	....	5	0	1	1	2	....	....	....
1961-62	Peterborough Petes	OHA	50	13	22	35	....	....	....	67	....	....	....	....	....	....	....	....	....	....	....	....	....	....	....	....	....	....
1962-63	Peterborough Petes	OHA	50	21	23	44	....	....	....	59	....	....	....	....	....	....	....	....	....	....	6	0	2	2	0	....	....	....
1963-64	Peterborough Petes	OHA	5	2	3	5	....	....	....	6	....	....	....	....	....	....	....	....	....	....	3	1	0	1	4	....	....	....
1964-65	Omaha Knights	CHL	55	21	14	35	....	....	....	49	....	....	....	....	....	....	....	....	....	....	....	....	....	....	....	....	....	....
1965-66	Oklahoma City Blazers	CHL	68	16	22	38	....	....	....	66	....	....	....	....	....	....	....	....	....	....	9	2	3	5	7	....	....	....
1966-67	Oklahoma City Blazers	CHL	10	0	3	3	....	....	....	2	....	....	....	....	....	....	....	....	....	....	....	....	....	....	....	....	....	....
	California Seals	WHL	36	2	17	19	....	....	....	19	....	....	....	....	....	....	....	....	....	....	5	0	1	1	0	....	....	....
1967-68	**Philadelphia Flyers**	**NHL**	**1**	**0**	**0**	**0**	**0**	**0**	**0**	**0**	**0**	**0**	**0**	**1**	**0.0**	**1**	**0**	**0**	**0**	**+1**	....	....	....	....	....	....	....	....
	Quebec Aces	AHL	72	20	23	43	....	....	....	42	....	....	....	....	....	....	....	....	....	....	15	6	6	12	4	....	....	....
1968-69			DID NOT PLAY – RETIRED																									
1969-70			DID NOT PLAY – RETIRED																									
1970-71	Quebec Aces	AHL	39	0	14	14	....	....	....	22	....	....	....	....	....	....	....	....	....	....	....	....	....	....	....	....	....	....
	Oklahoma City Blazers	CHL	14	1	2	3	....	....	....	2	....	....	....	....	....	....	....	....	....	....	5	0	0	0	0	....	....	....
1971-72			DID NOT PLAY – RETIRED																									
1972-73	Orillia Terriers	OHA Sr.	37	13	20	33	....	....	....	52	....	....	....	....	....	....	....	....	....	....	....	....	....	....	....	....	....	....
	NHL Totals		**1**	**0**	**0**	**0**	**0**	**0**	**0**	**0**	**0**	**0**	**0**	**1**	**0.0**	**1**	**0**	**0**	**0**		....	....	....	....	....	....	....	....

Claimed by **NY Rangers** from **Montreal** in Reverse Draft, June, 1964. Claimed by **Boston** from **NY Rangers** in Intra-League Draft, June, 1965. Claimed by **Philadelphia** from **Boston** in Expansion Draft, June 6, 1967. Traded to **Quebec** (AHL) by **Philadelphia** for cash, December, 1968.

• WRIGHT, LARRY

Larry Wright C – L. 6'2", 180 lbs. b: Regina, Sask., 10/8/1951. Philadelphia's 1st choice, 8th overall, in 1971 Amateur Draft.

Season	Club	League	GP	G	A	Pts	AG	AA	APts	PIM	PP	SH	GW	S	%	TGF	PGF	TGA	PGA	+/–	GP	G	A	Pts	PIM	PP	SH	GW
1967-68	Regina Pats	WCJHL	60	20	47	67	....	....	....	10	....	....	....	....	....	....	....	....	....	....	....	....	....	....	....	....	....	....
1968-69	University of Minnesota	WCHA	DID NOT PLAY – FRESHMAN																									
1969-70	University of Minnesota	WCHA	24	11	11	22	....	....	....	8	....	....	....	....	....	....	....	....	....	....	....	....	....	....	....	....	....	....
1970-71	Regina Pats	WCJHL	59	24	60	84	....	....	....	43	....	....	....	....	....	....	....	....	....	....	....	....	....	....	....	....	....	....
1971-72	**Philadelphia Flyers**	**NHL**	**27**	**0**	**1**	**1**	**0**	**1**	**1**	**2**	**0**	**0**	**0**	**21**	**0.0**	**3**	**1**	**9**	**1**	**–6**	....	....	....	....	....	....	....	....
	Richmond Robins	AHL	44	10	12	22	....	....	....	10	....	....	....	....	....	....	....	....	....	....	....	....	....	....	....	....	....	....
1972-73	**Philadelphia Flyers**	**NHL**	**9**	**0**	**1**	**1**	**0**	**1**	**1**	**4**	**0**	**0**	**0**	**6**	**0.0**	**2**	**1**	**4**	**0**	**–3**	....	....	....	....	....	....	....	....
	Richmond Robins	AHL	61	26	25	51	....	....	....	29	....	....	....	....	....	....	....	....	....	....	4	1	3	4	2	....	....	....
1973-74	Richmond Robins	AHL	52	18	25	43	....	....	....	23	....	....	....	....	....	....	....	....	....	....	....	....	....	....	....	....	....	....
1974-75	**California Golden Seals**	**NHL**	**2**	**0**	**0**	**0**	**0**	**0**	**0**	**0**	**0**	**0**	**0**	**1**	**0.0**	**0**	**0**	**2**	**0**	**–2**	....	....	....	....	....	....	....	....
	Salt Lake Golden Eagles	CHL	14	0	3	3	....	....	....	9	....	....	....	....	....	....	....	....	....	....	11	1	4	5	2	....	....	....
1975-76	**Philadelphia Flyers**	**NHL**	**2**	**1**	**0**	**1**	**1**	**0**	**1**	**0**	**0**	**0**	**0**	**3**	**33.3**	**1**	**0**	**0**	**0**	**+1**	....	....	....	....	....	....	....	....
	Richmond Robins	AHL	72	28	35	63	....	....	....	38	....	....	....	....	....	....	....	....	....	....	6	2	3	5	0	....	....	....
1976-77	Dusseldorf	Germany	43	30	36	66	....	....	....	....	....	....	....	....	....	....	....	....	....	....	....	....	....	....	....	....	....	....
1977-78	**Detroit Red Wings**	**NHL**	**66**	**3**	**6**	**9**	**3**	**5**	**8**	**13**	**0**	**0**	**0**	**46**	**6.5**	**27**	**8**	**31**	**0**	**–12**	....	....	....	....	....	....	....	....
1978-79	Kansas City Red Wings	CHL	51	6	24	30	....	....	....	17	....	....	....	....	....	....	....	....	....	....	1	0	1	1	7	....	....	....
	NHL Totals		**106**	**4**	**8**	**12**	**4**	**7**	**11**	**19**	**0**	**0**	**0**	**77**	**5.2**	**33**	**10**	**46**	**1**		....	....	....	....	....	....	....	....

Traded to **California** by **Philadelphia** with Al MacAdam and Philadelphia's 1st round choice (Ron Chipperfield) in 1974 Amateur Draft for Reggie Leach, May 24, 1974. Signed as a free agent by **Detroit**, October 22, 1977.

• WRIGHT, TYLER

Tyler Wright C – R. 5'11", 185 lbs. b: Canora, Sask., 4/6/1973. Edmonton's 1st choice, 12th overall, in 1991 Entry Draft.

Season	Club	League	GP	G	A	Pts	AG	AA	APts	PIM	PP	SH	GW	S	%	TGF	PGF	TGA	PGA	+/–	GP	G	A	Pts	PIM	PP	SH	GW
1989-90	Swift Current Broncos	WHL	67	14	18	32	....	....	....	139	....	....	....	....	....	....	....	....	....	....	4	0	0	0	12	....	....	....
1990-91	Swift Current Broncos	WHL	66	41	51	92	....	....	....	157	....	....	....	....	....	....	....	....	....	....	3	0	0	0	6	....	....	....
1991-92	Swift Current Broncos	WHL	63	36	46	82	....	....	....	295	....	....	....	....	....	....	....	....	....	....	8	2	5	7	16	....	....	....
	Canada	WJC-A	7	1	0	1	....	....	....	16	....	....	....	....	....	....	....	....	....	....	....	....	....	....	....	....	....	....
1992-93	Swift Current Broncos	WHL	37	24	41	65	....	....	....	76	....	....	....	....	....	....	....	....	....	....	17	9	17	26	*49	....	....	....
	Canada	WJC-A	7	3	3	6	....	....	....	6	....	....	....	....	....	....	....	....	....	....	....	....	....	....	....	....	....	....
	Edmonton Oilers	**NHL**	**7**	**1**	**1**	**2**	**1**	**1**	**2**	**19**	**0**	**0**	**0**	**7**	**14.3**	**3**	**0**	**8**	**1**	**–4**	....	....	....	....	....	....	....	....
1993-94	**Edmonton Oilers**	**NHL**	**5**	**0**	**0**	**0**	**0**	**0**	**0**	**4**	**0**	**0**	**0**	**2**	**0.0**	**0**	**0**	**3**	**0**	**–3**	....	....	....	....	....	....	....	....
	Cape Breton Oilers	AHL	65	14	27	41	....	....	....	160	....	....	....	....	....	....	....	....	....	....	5	2	0	2	11	....	....	....
1994-95	Cape Breton Oilers	AHL	70	16	15	31	....	....	....	184	....	....	....	....	....	....	....	....	....	....	....	....	....	....	....	....	....	....
	Edmonton Oilers	**NHL**	**6**	**1**	**0**	**1**	**2**	**0**	**2**	**14**	**0**	**0**	**0**	**6**	**16.7**	**3**	**0**	**2**	**0**	**+1**	....	....	....	....	....	....	....	....
1995-96	**Edmonton Oilers**	**NHL**	**23**	**1**	**0**	**1**	**1**	**0**	**1**	**33**	**0**	**0**	**0**	**18**	**5.6**	**4**	**0**	**11**	**0**	**–7**	....	....	....	....	....	....	....	....
	Cape Breton Oilers	AHL	31	6	12	18	....	....	....	158	....	....	....	....	....	....	....	....	....	....	....	....	....	....	....	....	....	....
1996-97	**Pittsburgh Penguins**	**NHL**	**45**	**2**	**2**	**4**	**2**	**2**	**4**	**70**	**0**	**0**	**2**	**30**	**6.7**	**4**	**0**	**17**	**6**	**–7**	....	....	....	....	....	....	....	....
	Cleveland Lumberjacks	IHL	10	4	3	7	....	....	....	34	....	....	....	....	....	....	....	....	....	....	14	4	2	6	44	....	....	....
1997-98	**Pittsburgh Penguins**	**NHL**	**82**	**3**	**4**	**7**	**4**	**4**	**8**	**112**	**1**	**0**	**0**	**46**	**6.5**	**15**	**2**	**26**	**10**	**–3**	**6**	**0**	**1**	**1**	**4**	**0**	**0**	**0**
	NHL Totals		**168**	**8**	**7**	**15**	**10**	**7**	**17**	**252**	**1**	**0**	**2**	**109**	**7.3**	**29**	**2**	**67**	**17**		**6**	**0**	**1**	**1**	**4**	**0**	**0**	**0**

Traded to **Pittsburgh** by **Edmonton** for Pittsburgh's 7th round choice (Brandon Lafrance) in 1996 Entry Draft, June 22, 1996.

• WYLIE, DUANE

Duane Wylie C – L. 5'8", 170 lbs. b: Spokane, WA, 11/10/1950. NY Rangers' 6th choice, 81st overall, in 1970 Amateur Draft.

Season	Club	League	GP	G	A	Pts	AG	AA	APts	PIM	PP	SH	GW	S	%	TGF	PGF	TGA	PGA	+/–	GP	G	A	Pts	PIM	PP	SH	GW
1967-68	Moose Jaw Canucks	WCJHL	29	4	7	11	....	....	....	24	....	....	....	....	....	....	....	....	....	....	....	....	....	....	....	....	....	....
1968-69			DID NOT PLAY																									
1969-70	St. Catharines Black Hawks	OHA	53	18	23	41	....	....	....	54	....	....	....	....	....	....	....	....	....	....	....	....	....	....	....	....	....	....
1970-71	Flint Generals	IHL	64	15	26	41	....	....	....	31	....	....	....	....	....	....	....	....	....	....	7	2	1	3	2	....	....	....
1971-72	Flint Generals	IHL	72	26	39	65	....	....	....	43	....	....	....	....	....	....	....	....	....	....	4	0	1	1	2	....	....	....
1972-73	Dallas Black Hawks	CHL	61	11	19	30	....	....	....	46	....	....	....	....	....	....	....	....	....	....	7	1	2	3	8	....	....	....
1973-74	Dallas Black Hawks	CHL	72	30	27	57	....	....	....	39	....	....	....	....	....	....	....	....	....	....	10	*6	2	8	4	....	....	....

Season	Club	League	GP	G	A	Pts	AG	AA	APts	PIM	PP	SH	GW	S	%	TGF	PGF	TGA	PGA	+/–	Playoffs GP	G	A	Pts	PIM	PP	SH	GW
1974-75	**Chicago Black Hawks**	**NHL**	**6**	**1**	**3**	**4**	**1**	**2**	**3**	**2**	**0**	**0**	**0**	**7**	**14.3**	**4**	**0**	**7**	**2**	**–1**								
	Dallas Black Hawks	CHL	73	24	37	61				62											10	3	1	4	6			
1975-76	Dallas Black Hawks	CHL	74	30	40	70				28											10	2	6	8	2			
1976-77	**Chicago Black Hawks**	**NHL**	**8**	**2**	**0**	**2**	**2**	**0**	**2**	**0**	**1**	**0**	**0**	**12**	**16.7**	**2**	**1**	**6**	**1**	**–4**								
	Dallas Black Hawks	CHL	71	23	32	55				20											5	2	0	2	0			
1977-78	Dallas Black Hawks	CHL	77	17	29	46				24											13	4	5	9	2			
	NHL Totals		**14**	**3**	**3**	**6**	**3**	**2**	**5**	**2**	**1**	**0**	**0**	**19**	**15.8**	**6**	**1**	**13**	**3**									

Signed as a free agent by **Chicago**, October 12, 1972.

• WYROZUB, RANDY

Randy Wyrozub C – L. 5′11″, 180 lbs. b: Lacombe, Alta., 4/8/1950. Buffalo's 4th choice, 43rd overall, in 1970 Amateur Draft.

Season	Club	League	GP	G	A	Pts	AG	AA	APts	PIM	PP	SH	GW	S	%	TGF	PGF	TGA	PGA	+/–	Playoffs GP	G	A	Pts	PIM	PP	SH	GW
1868-69	Ponoka Stampeders	AJHL	STATISTICS NOT AVAILABLE																									
1969-70	Edmonton Oil Kings	WCJHL	58	24	34	58				23																		
1970-71	**Buffalo Sabres**	**NHL**	**16**	**2**	**2**	**4**	**2**	**2**	**4**	**6**	**1**	**0**	**0**	**22**	**9.1**	**4**	**1**	**12**	**0**	**–9**								
	Salt Lake Golden Eagles	WHL	23	7	4	11				2																		
1971-72	**Buffalo Sabres**	**NHL**	**34**	**3**	**4**	**7**	**3**	**4**	**7**	**0**	**0**	**0**	**0**	**36**	**8.3**	**12**	**1**	**13**	**0**	**–2**								
	Cincinnati Swords	AHL	35	14	14	28				10																		
1972-73	**Buffalo Sabres**	**NHL**	**45**	**3**	**3**	**6**	**3**	**2**	**5**	**4**	**0**	**0**	**2**	**23**	**13.0**	**8**	**0**	**9**	**0**	**–1**								
1973-74	**Buffalo Sabres**	**NHL**	**5**	**0**	**1**	**1**	**0**	**1**	**1**	**0**	**0**	**0**	**0**	**4**	**0.0**	**1**	**0**	**3**	**1**	**–1**								
	Cincinnati Swords	AHL	69	22	35	57				17											5	0	3	3	0			
1974-75	Richmond Robins	AHL	71	21	32	53				31											7	2	3	5	6			
1975-76	Indianapolis Racers	WHA	55	11	14	25				8																		
	Mohawk Valley Comets	NAHL	11	6	7	13				0											4	1	2	3	2			
1976-77	Mohawk Valley Comets	NAHL	73	26	57	83				18											5	4	2	6	2			
1977-78	San Francisco Shamrocks	PHL	42	27	33	60				12																		
1978-79	Tucson Rustlers	PHL	29	15	20	35				0																		
	Erie Blades	NEHL	19	6	10	16				6																		
	NHL Totals		**100**	**8**	**10**	**18**	**8**	**9**	**17**	**10**	**1**	**0**	**2**	**85**	**9.4**	**25**	**2**	**37**	**1**									
	Other Major League Totals		55	11	14	25				8																		

Selected by **Alberta** (WHA) in 1972 WHA General Player Draft, February 12, 1972. Claimed by **Washington** from **Buffalo** in Expansion Draft, June 12, 1974. WHA rights traded to **Edmonton** (WHA) by **Indianapolis** (WHA) for future considerations, September, 1975.

• YACHMENEV, VITALI

Vitali Yachmenev RW – L. 5′9″, 180 lbs. b: Chelyabinsk, USSR, 1/8/1975. Los Angeles' 3rd choice, 59th overall, in 1994 Entry Draft.

Season	Club	League	GP	G	A	Pts	AG	AA	APts	PIM	PP	SH	GW	S	%	TGF	PGF	TGA	PGA	+/–	Playoffs GP	G	A	Pts	PIM	PP	SH	GW
1992-93	Traktor Chelyabinsk	CIS 2	51	23	20	43				12																		
1993-94	North Bay Centennials	OHL	66	*61	52	113				18											18	13	19	32	12			
1994-95	North Bay Centennials	OHL	59	53	52	105				8											6	1	8	9	2			
	Russia	WJC-A	7	3	4	7				2																		
	Phoenix Roadrunners	IHL																			4	1	0	1	0			
1995-96	**Los Angeles Kings**	**NHL**	**80**	**19**	**34**	**53**	**19**	**28**	**47**	**16**	**6**	**1**	**2**	**133**	**14.3**	**91**	**41**	**58**	**5**	**–3**								
1996-97	**Los Angeles Kings**	**NHL**	**65**	**10**	**22**	**32**	**11**	**19**	**30**	**10**	**2**	**0**	**2**	**97**	**10.3**	**46**	**10**	**55**	**10**	**–9**								
1997-98	**Los Angeles Kings**	**NHL**	**4**	**0**	**1**	**1**	**0**	**1**	**1**	**4**	**0**	**0**	**0**	**4**	**0.0**	**2**	**0**	**1**	**0**	**+1**								
	Long Beach Ice Dogs	IHL	59	23	28	51				14											17	8	9	17	4			
	NHL Totals		**149**	**29**	**57**	**86**	**30**	**48**	**78**	**30**	**8**	**1**	**4**	**234**	**12.4**	**139**	**51**	**114**	**15**									

Canadian Major Junior Rookie of the Year (1994)

• YAKE, TERRY

Terry Yake RW – R. 5′11″, 190 lbs. b: New Westminster, B.C., 10/22/1968. Hartford's 3rd choice, 81st overall, in 1987 Entry Draft.

Season	Club	League	GP	G	A	Pts	AG	AA	APts	PIM	PP	SH	GW	S	%	TGF	PGF	TGA	PGA	+/–	Playoffs GP	G	A	Pts	PIM	PP	SH	GW
1984-85	Brandon Wheat Kings	WHL	11	1	1	2				0																		
1985-86	Brandon Wheat Kings	WHL	72	26	26	52				49																		
1986-87	Brandon Wheat Kings	WHL	71	44	58	102				64																		
1987-88	Brandon Wheat Kings	WHL	72	55	85	140				59											3	4	2	6	7			
1988-89	**Hartford Whalers**	**NHL**	**2**	**0**	**0**	**0**	**0**	**0**	**0**	**0**	**0**	**0**	**0**	**0**	**0.0**	**2**	**1**	**0**	**0**	**+1**								
	Binghamton Whalers	AHL	75	39	56	95				57																		
1989-90	**Hartford Whalers**	**NHL**	**2**	**0**	**1**	**1**	**0**	**1**	**1**	**0**	**0**	**0**	**0**	**2**	**0.0**	**1**	**0**	**2**	**0**	**–1**								
	Binghamton Whalers	AHL	77	13	42	55				37																		
1990-91	**Hartford Whalers**	**NHL**	**19**	**1**	**4**	**5**	**1**	**3**	**4**	**10**	**0**	**0**	**1**	**19**	**5.3**	**8**	**1**	**16**	**6**	**–3**	**6**	**1**	**1**	**2**	**16**	**0**	**1**	**0**
	Springfield Indians	AHL	60	35	42	77				56											15	9	9	18	10			
1991-92	**Hartford Whalers**	**NHL**	**15**	**1**	**1**	**2**	**1**	**1**	**2**	**4**	**0**	**0**	**0**	**12**	**8.3**	**3**	**0**	**8**	**3**	**–2**								
	Springfield Indians	AHL	53	21	34	55				63											8	3	4	7	2			
1992-93	**Hartford Whalers**	**NHL**	**66**	**22**	**31**	**53**	**18**	**21**	**39**	**46**	**4**	**1**	**2**	**98**	**22.4**	**74**	**17**	**71**	**17**	**+3**								
	Springfield Indians	AHL	16	8	14	22				27																		
1993-94	**Anaheim Mighty Ducks**	**NHL**	**82**	**21**	**31**	**52**	**20**	**24**	**44**	**44**	**5**	**0**	**2**	**188**	**11.2**	**80**	**27**	**60**	**9**	**+2**								
1994-95	**Toronto Maple Leafs**	**NHL**	**19**	**3**	**2**	**5**	**5**	**3**	**8**	**2**	**1**	**0**	**2**	**26**	**11.5**	**9**	**3**	**5**	**0**	**+1**								
	Denver Grizzlies	IHL	2	0	3	3				2											17	4	11	15	16			
1995-96	Milwaukee Admirals	IHL	70	32	56	88				70											5	3	6	9	4			
1996-97	Rochester Americans	AHL	78	34	*67	101				77											10	8	8	16	2			
1997-98	**St. Louis Blues**	**NHL**	**65**	**10**	**15**	**25**	**12**	**15**	**27**	**38**	**3**	**1**	**4**	**60**	**16.7**	**42**	**11**	**35**	**5**	**+1**	**10**	**2**	**1**	**3**	**6**	**2**	**0**	**1**
	NHL Totals		**270**	**58**	**85**	**143**	**57**	**68**	**125**	**144**	**13**	**2**	**11**	**405**	**14.3**	**219**	**60**	**197**	**40**		**16**	**3**	**2**	**5**	**22**	**2**	**1**	**1**

Claimed by **Anaheim** from **Hartford** in Expansion Draft, June 24, 1993. Traded to **Toronto** by **Anaheim** for David Sacco, September 28, 1994. Signed as a free agent by **Buffalo**, September 17, 1996. Signed as a free agent by **St. Louis**, July 24, 1997.

• YAREMCHUK, GARY

Gary "Weasel" Yaremchuk C – L. 6′, 185 lbs. b: Edmonton, Alta., 8/15/1961. Toronto's 2nd choice, 24th overall, in 1981 Entry Draft.

Season	Club	League	GP	G	A	Pts	AG	AA	APts	PIM	PP	SH	GW	S	%	TGF	PGF	TGA	PGA	+/–	Playoffs GP	G	A	Pts	PIM	PP	SH	GW
1979-80	Fort Saskatchewan Traders	AJHL	27	27	44	71				61																		
	Portland Winter Hawks	WHL	41	21	34	55				23											6	1	4	5	2			
1980-81	Portland Winter Hawks	WHL	72	56	79	135				121																		
1981-82	**Toronto Maple Leafs**	**NHL**	**18**	**0**	**3**	**3**	**0**	**2**	**2**	**10**	**0**	**0**	**0**	**6**	**0.0**	**6**	**0**	**14**	**1**	**–7**								
	Cincinnati Tigers	CHL	53	21	35	56				101											4	0	2	2	4			
1982-83	**Toronto Maple Leafs**	**NHL**	**3**	**0**	**0**	**0**	**0**	**0**	**0**	**2**	**0**	**0**	**0**	**3**	**0.0**	**0**	**0**	**1**	**0**	**–1**								
	St. Catharines Saints	AHL	61	17	28	45				72																		
1983-84	**Toronto Maple Leafs**	**NHL**	**1**	**0**	**0**	**0**	**0**	**0**	**0**	**0**	**0**	**0**	**0**	**1**	**0.0**	**1**	**1**	**1**	**0**	**–1**								
	St. Catharines Saints	AHL	73	24	37	61				84											7	5	1	6	2			
1984-85	**Toronto Maple Leafs**	**NHL**	**12**	**1**	**1**	**2**	**1**	**1**	**2**	**16**	**0**	**0**	**0**	**7**	**14.3**	**3**	**0**	**10**	**0**	**–7**								
	St. Catharines Saints	AHL	66	17	47	64				75																		
1985-86	Adirondack Red Wings	AHL	60	12	32	44				90											1	1	0	1	0			
1986-87	Jokerit Helsinki	Finland	20	7	21	28				116																		
1987-88	Karpat Oulu	Finland	36	16	27	43				92																		
1988-89	Kookoo	Finland	44	12	27	39				50																		
1989-90	Kookoo	Finland	42	16	19	35				81																		
1990-91			STATISTICS NOT AVAILABLE																									
1991-92	Amiens SC	France	17	15	18	33																						
1992-93	HC Val Gardena	Italy	18	9	21	30				14																		
1993-94	Durham Wasps	Britain	40	53	93	146				57																		
	NHL Totals		**34**	**1**	**4**	**5**	**1**	**3**	**4**	**28**	**0**	**0**	**0**	**17**	**5.9**	**10**	**1**	**26**	**1**									

Signed as a free agent by **Detroit**, August 13, 1985.

• YAREMCHUK, KEN

Ken Yaremchuk C – R. 5′11″, 185 lbs. b: Edmonton, Alta., 1/1/1964. Chicago's 2nd choice, 7th overall, in 1982 Entry Draft.

Season	Club	League	GP	G	A	Pts	AG	AA	APts	PIM	PP	SH	GW	S	%	TGF	PGF	TGA	PGA	+/–	Playoffs GP	G	A	Pts	PIM	PP	SH	GW
1979-80	Fort Saskatchewan Traders	AJHL	59	40	72	112				39																		
1980-81	Portland Winter Hawks	WHL	72	35	72	107				105											9	2	8	10	24			
1981-82	Portland Winter Hawks	WHL	72	58	99	157				181											15	10	21	31	12			
1982-83	Portland Winter Hawks	WHL	66	51	*109	160				76											14	11	15	26	12			
1983-84	**Chicago Black Hawks**	**NHL**	**47**	**6**	**7**	**13**	**5**	**5**	**10**	**19**	**0**	**0**	**0**	**49**	**12.2**	**19**	**1**	**25**	**0**	**–7**	**1**	**0**	**0**	**0**	**0**	**0**	**0**	**0**

Season	Club	League	GP	G	A	Pts	AG	AA	APts	PIM	PP	SH	GW	S	%	TGF	PGF	TGA	PGA	+/–	GP	G	A	Pts	PIM	PP	SH	GW
1984-85	**Chicago Black Hawks**	NHL	63	10	16	26	8	11	19	16	2	0	0	72	13.9	39	8	37	0	–6	15	5	5	10	37	0	0	1
	Milwaukee Admirals	IHL	7	4	6	10				9																		
1985-86	**Chicago Black Hawks**	NHL	78	14	20	34	11	13	24	43	0	0	2	82	17.1	53	2	68	0	–17	3	1	1	2	2	0	0	0
1986-87	**Toronto Maple Leafs**	NHL	20	3	8	11	3	6	9	16	0	0	0	33	9.1	13	2	11	0	0	6	0	0	0	0	0	0	0
	Newmarket Saints	AHL	14	2	4	6				21																		
1987-88	Canada	Nat-Team	38	15	18	33				63																		
	Canada	Olympics	8	3	3	6				2																		
	Toronto Maple Leafs	NHL	16	2	5	7	2	4	6	10	0	0	0	14	14.3	7	2	14	2	–7	6	0	2	2	10	0	0	0
1988-89	**Toronto Maple Leafs**	NHL	11	1	0	1	1	0	1	2	0	0	0	13	7.7	1	0	6	0	–5								
	Newmarket Saints	AHL	55	25	33	58				145											5	7	7	14	12			
1989-90	HC Asiago	Italy	34	37	76	113				32											6	5	6	11	8			
1990-91	EV Zug	Switz.	26	17	14	31																						
1991-92	EV Zug	Switz.	36	29	25	45				65																		
1992-93	EV Zug	Switz.	36	27	32	59				57											5	0	1	1	18			
1993-94	EV Zug	Switz.	36	17	39	56				19											2	1	0	1	0			
1994-95	EV Zug	Switz.	36	26	45	71				55											12	5	12	17	24			
1995-96	EV Zug	Switz.	26	16	30	46				69											6	1	4	5	6			
1996-97	HC Davos	Switz.	46	31	38	69				60											5	2	2	4	16			
1997-98	HC Davos	Switz.	39	20	22	42				76											18	11	14	25	34			
	NHL Totals		235	36	56	92	30	39	69	106	2	0	2	263	13.7	132	15	161	2		31	6	8	14	49	0	0	1

WHL First All-Star Team (1982) • WHL Second All-Star Team (1983) • Memorial Cup All-Star Team (1983)

Transferred to **Toronto** by Chicago with Jerome Dupont and Chicago's 4th round choice (Joe Sacco) in 1987 Entry Draft as compensation for Chicago's signing of free agent Gary Nylund, September 6, 1986.

● YASHIN, ALEXEI Alexei Yashin C – R. 6'3", 215 lbs. b: Sverdlovsk, USSR, 11/5/1973. Ottawa's 1st choice, 2nd overall, in 1992 Entry Draft.

Season	Club	League	GP	G	A	Pts	AG	AA	APts	PIM	PP	SH	GW	S	%	TGF	PGF	TGA	PGA	+/–	GP	G	A	Pts	PIM	PP	SH	GW
1990-91	Sverdlovsk	USSR	26	2	1	3				10																		
1991-92	Moscow Dynamo	CIS	35	7	5	12				19																		
	Russia	WJC-A	7	4	2	6				2																		
1992-93	Moscow Dynamo	CIS	27	10	12	22				18											10	7	3	10	18			
	Russia	WJC-A	3	1	0	1				4																		
	Russia	WC-A	8	2	1	3				5																		
1993-94	**Ottawa Senators**	NHL	83	30	49	79	28	38	66	22	11	2	3	232	12.9	94	39	126	22	–49								
	Russia	WC-A	5	1	2	3				8																		
1994-95	Las Vegas Thunder	IHL	24	15	20	35				32																		
	Ottawa Senators	NHL	47	21	23	44	37	34	71	20	11	0	1	154	13.6	59	25	55	1	–20								
1995-96	CSKA Moscow	CIS	4	2	2	4				4																		
	Ottawa Senators	NHL	46	15	24	39	15	20	35	28	8	0	1	143	10.5	51	22	44	0	–15								
	Russia	WC-A	8	4	5	9				4																		
1996-97	Russia	W Cup	5	0	2	2				6																		
	Ottawa Senators	NHL	82	35	40	75	37	35	72	44	10	0	5	291	12.0	100	35	82	10	–7	7	1	5	6	2	1	0	0
	Russia	WC-A	5	3	0	3				12																		
1997-98	**Ottawa Senators**	NHL	82	33	39	72	39	38	77	24	5	0	6	291	11.3	97	32	63	4	+6	11	5	3	8	8	3	0	2
	Russia	Olympics	6	3	3	6				0																		
	NHL Totals		340	134	175	309	156	165	321	138	45	2	16	1111	12.1	401	153	370	37		18	6	8	14	10	4	0	2

CIS First All-Star Team (1993)

Played in NHL All-Star Game (1994)

● YATES, ROSS Ross Yates C – R. 5'11", 170 lbs. b: Montreal, Que., 6/18/1959.

Season	Club	League	GP	G	A	Pts	AG	AA	APts	PIM	PP	SH	GW	S	%	TGF	PGF	TGA	PGA	+/–	GP	G	A	Pts	PIM	PP	SH	GW
1976-77	Mount Allison University	AUAA	20	7	7	14				18																		
1977-78	Mount Allison University	AUAA	20	8	21	29				38																		
1978-79	Mount Allison University	AUAA	20	*21	26	*47				34																		
1979-80	Mount Allison University	AUAA	27	23	*54	77				14																		
1980-81	Mount Allison University	AUAA	21	16	*56	*72				12																		
	Binghamton Whalers	AHL	14	4	1	5				2											5	0	0	0				
1981-82	Binghamton Whalers	AHL	80	22	23	45				53											15	6	5	11	10			
1982-83	Binghamton Whalers	AHL	77	41	*84	*125				28											5	0	6	6	2			
1983-84	**Hartford Whalers**	NHL	7	1	1	2	1	1	2	4	0	0	0	6	16.7	3	1	2	0	0								
	Binghamton Whalers	AHL	69	35	*73	108				82																		
1984-85	Mannheimer ERC	Germany	35	31	39	70				45											9	9	8	*17	6			
	Fredericton Express	AHL																			5	0	2	2	4			
1985-86	Mannheimer ERC	Germany	39	21	44	65				38											4	0	0	0				
	Rochester Americans	AHL	22	4	8	12				4																		
1986-87	EHC Kloten	Switz.	36	35	30	65															4	0	0	0				
1987-88	EHC Kloten	Switz.	36	31	36	67															7	0	*8	8				
1988-89	EHC Kloten	Switz. 2	36	34	*37	71															6	2	5	7				
	NHL Totals		7	1	1	2	1	1	2	4	0	0	0	6	16.7	3	1	2	0									

AHL First All-Star Team (1983) • Won Fred T. Hunt Memorial Trophy (Sportsmanship - AHL) (1983) • Won John B. Sollenberger Trophy (Top Scorer - AHL) (1983) • Won Les Cunningham Award (MVP - AHL) (1983)

Signed as a free agent by **Hartford**, August 6, 1981.

● YAWNEY, TRENT Trent Yawney D – L. 6'3", 195 lbs. b: Hudson Bay, Sask., 9/29/1965. Chicago's 2nd choice, 45th overall, in 1984 Entry Draft.

Season	Club	League	GP	G	A	Pts	AG	AA	APts	PIM	PP	SH	GW	S	%	TGF	PGF	TGA	PGA	+/–	GP	G	A	Pts	PIM	PP	SH	GW
1982-83	Saskatoon Blades	WHL	59	6	31	37				44											6	0	2	2	0			
1983-84	Saskatoon Blades	WHL	73	13	46	59				81																		
1984-85	Saskatoon Blades	WHL	72	16	51	67				158											3	1	6	7	7			
1985-86	Canada	Nat-Team	73	6	15	21				60																		
1986-87	Canada	Nat-Team	51	4	15	19				37																		
1987-88	Canada	Nat-Team	60	4	12	16				81																		
	Canada	Olympics	8	1	1	2				6																		
	Chicago Blackhawks	NHL	15	2	8	10	2	6	8	15	2	0	0	26	7.7	25	11	22	9	+1	5	0	4	4	8	0	0	0
1988-89	**Chicago Blackhawks**	NHL	69	5	19	24	4	13	17	116	3	1	0	75	6.7	82	20	110	43	–5	15	3	6	9	20	0	1	0
1989-90	**Chicago Blackhawks**	NHL	70	5	15	20	4	11	15	82	1	0	0	58	8.6	76	21	79	18	–6	20	3	5	8	27	3	0	1
1990-91	**Chicago Blackhawks**	NHL	61	3	13	16	3	10	13	77	3	0	0	52	5.8	55	18	49	18	+6	1	0	0	0	0	0	0	0
	Canada	WEC-A	10	2	4	6				4																		
1991-92	**Calgary Flames**	NHL	47	4	9	13	4	7	11	45	1	0	0	33	12.1	51	14	61	19	–5								
	Indianapolis Ice	IHL	9	2	3	5				12																		
	Canada	WC-A	6	0	1	1				4																		
1992-93	**Calgary Flames**	NHL	63	1	16	17	1	11	12	67	0	0	0	61	1.6	63	9	68	23	+9	6	3	2	5	6	1	0	0
1993-94	**Calgary Flames**	NHL	58	6	15	21	6	12	18	60	1	1	1	62	9.7	64	13	46	16	+21	7	0	0	0	16	0	0	0
1994-95	**Calgary Flames**	NHL	37	0	2	2	0	3	3	108	0	0	0	20	0.0	16	0	29	6	–4	2	0	0	0	2	0	0	0
1995-96	**Calgary Flames**	NHL	69	0	3	3	0	2	2	88	0	0	0	51	0.0	37	2	60	24	–1	4	0	0	0	0	0	0	0
1996-97	**St. Louis Blues**	NHL	39	0	2	2	0	2	2	17	0	0	0	8	0.0	15	2	15	2	+2								
1997-98	**Chicago Blackhawks**	NHL	45	1	0	1	1	0	1	76	0	0	0	19	5.3	13	0	21	3	–5								
	NHL Totals		573	27	102	129	25	77	102	751	11	2	2	465	5.8	497	108	560	184		60	9	17	26	81	4	1	1

Traded to **Calgary** by Chicago for Stephane Matteau, December 16, 1991. Signed as a free agent by **St. Louis**, July 31, 1996. Signed as a free agent by **Chicago**, September 25, 1997.

• YEGOROV, ALEXEI Alexei Yegorov C – L. 5'11", 195 lbs. b: St. Petersburg, USSR, 5/21/1975. San Jose's 3rd choice, 66th overall, in 1994 Entry Draft.

			REGULAR SEASON																		PLAYOFFS							
Season	Club	League	GP	G	A	Pts	AG	AA	APts	PIM	PP	SH	GW	S	%	TGF	PGF	TGA	PGA	+/–	GP	G	A	Pts	PIM	PP	SH	GW
1992-93	SKA St. Peterburg	CIS	17	1	2	3	....	....	....	10	....	....	....	....	....	....	....	....	....	....	6	3	1	4	6	....	....	....
1993-94	SKA St. Peterburg	CIS	23	5	3	8	....	....	....	18	....	....	....	....	....	....	....	....	....	....	6	0	0	0	4	....	....	....
1994-95	SKA St. Peterburg	CIS	10	2	1	3	....	....	....	10	....	....	....	....	....	....	....	....	....	....	....	....	....	....	....	....	....	....
	Fort Worth Fire	CHL	18	4	10	14	....	....	....	15	....	....	....	....	....	....	....	....	....	....	....	....	....	....	....	....	....	....
1995-96	**San Jose Sharks**	**NHL**	**9**	**3**	**2**	**5**	**3**	**2**	**5**	**2**	**2**	**0**	**0**	**10**	**30.0**	**6**	**3**	**8**	**0**	**–5**	....	....	....	....	....	....	....	....
	Kansas City Blades	IHL	65	31	25	56	....	....	....	84	....	....	....	....	....	....	....	....	....	....	5	2	0	2	8	....	....	....
1996-97	**San Jose Sharks**	**NHL**	**2**	**0**	**1**	**1**	**0**	**1**	**1**	**0**	**0**	**0**	**0**	**0**	**0.0**	**1**	**0**	**0**	**0**	**+1**	....	....	....	....	....	....	....	....
	Kentucky Thoroughblades	AHL	75	26	32	58	....	....	....	59	....	....	....	....	....	....	....	....	....	....	4	0	1	1	2	....	....	....
1997-98	Kentucky Thoroughblades	AHL	79	32	52	84	....	....	....	56	....	....	....	....	....	....	....	....	....	....	3	2	0	2	0	....	....	....
	NHL Totals		**11**	**3**	**3**	**6**	**3**	**3**	**6**	**2**	**2**	**0**	**0**	**10**	**30.0**	**7**	**3**	**8**	**0**		....	....	....	....	....	....	....	....

• YELLE, STEPHANE Stephane Yelle C – L. 6'1", 162 lbs. b: Ottawa, Ont., 5/9/1974. New Jersey's 9th choice, 186th overall, in 1992 Entry Draft.

Season	Club	League	GP	G	A	Pts	AG	AA	APts	PIM	PP	SH	GW	S	%	TGF	PGF	TGA	PGA	+/–	GP	G	A	Pts	PIM	PP	SH	GW
1991-92	Oshawa Generals	OHL	55	12	14	26	....	....	....	20	....	....	....	....	....	....	....	....	....	....	7	2	0	2	1	....	....	....
1992-93	Oshawa Generals	OHL	66	24	50	74	....	....	....	20	....	....	....	....	....	....	....	....	....	....	10	2	4	6	4	....	....	....
1993-94	Oshawa Generals	OHL	66	35	69	104	....	....	....	22	....	....	....	....	....	....	....	....	....	....	5	1	7	8	2	....	....	....
1994-95	Cornwall Aces	AHL	40	18	15	33	....	....	....	22	....	....	....	....	....	....	....	....	....	....	13	7	7	14	8	....	....	....
1995-96	**Colorado Avalanche**	**NHL**	**71**	**13**	**14**	**27**	**13**	**11**	**24**	**30**	**0**	**2**	**1**	**93**	**14.0**	**42**	**4**	**38**	**15**	**+15**	**22**	**1**	**4**	**5**	**8**	**0**	**1**	**0**
1996-97	**Colorado Avalanche**	**NHL**	**79**	**9**	**17**	**26**	**10**	**15**	**25**	**38**	**0**	**1**	**1**	**89**	**10.1**	**37**	**0**	**55**	**19**	**+1**	**12**	**1**	**6**	**7**	**2**	**0**	**0**	**0**
1997-98	**Colorado Avalanche**	**NHL**	**81**	**7**	**15**	**22**	**8**	**15**	**23**	**48**	**0**	**1**	**0**	**93**	**7.5**	**29**	**0**	**65**	**26**	**–10**	**7**	**1**	**0**	**1**	**12**	**0**	**0**	**0**
	NHL Totals		**231**	**29**	**46**	**75**	**31**	**41**	**72**	**116**	**0**	**4**	**2**	**275**	**10.5**	**108**	**4**	**158**	**60**		**41**	**3**	**10**	**13**	**22**	**0**	**1**	**0**

Traded to **Quebec** by **New Jersey** with New Jersey's 11th round choice (Steven Low) in 1994 Entry Draft for Quebec's 11th round choice (Mike Hansen) in 1994 Entry Draft, June 1, 1994. Transferred to **Colorado** after **Quebec** franchise relocated, June 21, 1995.

• YLONEN, YUHA Yuha Ylonen C – L. 6', 180 lbs. b: Helsinki, Finland, 2/13/1972. Winnipeg's 3rd choice, 91st overall, in 1991 Entry Draft.

Season	Club	League	GP	G	A	Pts	AG	AA	APts	PIM	PP	SH	GW	S	%	TGF	PGF	TGA	PGA	+/–	GP	G	A	Pts	PIM	PP	SH	GW
1990-91	K-Espoo	Finland 2	40	12	21	33	....	....	....	4	....	....	....	....	....	....	....	....	....	....	....	....	....	....	....	....	....	....
	Finland	WJC-A	6	1	1	2	....	....	....	2	....	....	....	....	....	....	....	....	....	....	....	....	....	....	....	....	....	....
1991-92	HPK Hameenlinna	Finland	43	7	11	18	....	....	....	8	....	....	....	....	....	....	....	....	....	....	....	....	....	....	....	....	....	....
	Finland	WJC-A	7	1	5	6	....	....	....	0	....	....	....	....	....	....	....	....	....	....	....	....	....	....	....	....	....	....
1992-93	HPK Hameenlinna	Finland	48	8	18	26	....	....	....	22	....	....	....	....	....	....	....	....	....	....	12	3	5	8	2	....	....	....
	Finland	WC-A	1	0	0	0	....	....	....	0	....	....	....	....	....	....	....	....	....	....	....	....	....	....	....	....	....	....
1993-94	Jokerit Helsinki	Finland	37	5	11	16	....	....	....	2	....	....	....	....	....	....	....	....	....	....	12	1	3	4	8	....	....	....
1994-95	Jokerit Helsinki	Finland	50	13	15	28	....	....	....	10	....	....	....	....	....	....	....	....	....	....	11	3	2	5	0	....	....	....
	Finland	WC-A	8	1	3	4	....	....	....	2	....	....	....	....	....	....	....	....	....	....	....	....	....	....	....	....	....	....
1995-96	Jokerit Helsinki	Finland	24	3	13	16	....	....	....	20	....	....	....	....	....	....	....	....	....	....	11	4	5	9	4	....	....	....
	Finland	WC-A	6	0	2	2	....	....	....	4	....	....	....	....	....	....	....	....	....	....	....	....	....	....	....	....	....	....
1996-97	Finland	W Cup	4	1	3	4	....	....	....	0	....	....	....	....	....	....	....	....	....	....	....	....	....	....	....	....	....	....
	Phoenix Coyotes	**NHL**	**2**	**0**	**0**	**0**	**0**	**0**	**0**	**0**	**0**	**0**	**0**	**2**	**0.0**	**0**	**0**	**0**	**0**	**0**	....	....	....	....	....	....	....	....
	Springfield Falcons	AHL	70	20	41	61	....	....	....	6	....	....	....	....	....	....	....	....	....	....	17	5	*10	21	4	....	....	....
1997-98	**Phoenix Coyotes**	**NHL**	**55**	**1**	**11**	**12**	**1**	**11**	**12**	**10**	**0**	**1**	**0**	**60**	**1.7**	**18**	**0**	**36**	**15**	**–3**	....	....	....	....	....	....	....	....
	Finland	Olympics	6	0	0	0	....	....	....	8	....	....	....	....	....	....	....	....	....	....	....	....	....	....	....	....	....	....
	NHL Totals		**57**	**1**	**11**	**12**	**1**	**11**	**12**	**10**	**0**	**1**	**0**	**62**	**1.6**	**18**	**0**	**36**	**15**		....	....	....	....	....	....	....	....

• YORK, HARRY Harry York C – L. 6'2", 215 lbs. b: Panoka, Alta., 4/16/1974.

Season	Club	League	GP	G	A	Pts	AG	AA	APts	PIM	PP	SH	GW	S	%	TGF	PGF	TGA	PGA	+/–	GP	G	A	Pts	PIM	PP	SH	GW
1994-95	Fort McMurray Oil Barons	AJHL	54	35	73	108	....	....	....	....	....	....	....	....	....	....	....	....	....	....	....	....	....	....	....	....	....	....
1995-96	Nashville Knights	ECHL	64	33	50	83	....	....	....	122	....	....	....	....	....	....	....	....	....	....	....	....	....	....	....	....	....	....
	Atlanta Knights	IHL	2	0	0	0	....	....	....	15	....	....	....	....	....	....	....	....	....	....	....	....	....	....	....	....	....	....
	Worcester IceCats	AHL	13	8	5	13	....	....	....	2	....	....	....	....	....	....	....	....	....	....	4	0	4	4	4	....	....	....
1996-97	**St. Louis Blues**	**NHL**	**74**	**14**	**18**	**32**	**15**	**16**	**31**	**24**	**3**	**1**	**3**	**86**	**16.3**	**55**	**12**	**46**	**4**	**+1**	**5**	**0**	**0**	**0**	**2**	**0**	**0**	**0**
1997-98	**St. Louis Blues**	**NHL**	**58**	**4**	**6**	**10**	**5**	**6**	**11**	**31**	**0**	**0**	**0**	**42**	**9.5**	**25**	**3**	**22**	**0**	**0**	....	....	....	....	....	....	....	....
	New York Rangers	**NHL**	**2**	**0**	**0**	**0**	**0**	**0**	**0**	**0**	**0**	**0**	**0**	**2**	**0.0**	**0**	**0**	**1**	**0**	**–1**	....	....	....	....	....	....	....	....
	NHL Totals		**134**	**18**	**24**	**42**	**20**	**22**	**42**	**55**	**3**	**1**	**3**	**130**	**13.8**	**80**	**15**	**69**	**4**		**5**	**0**	**0**	**0**	**2**	**0**	**0**	**0**

Signed as a free agent by **St. Louis**, May 1, 1996. Traded to **NY Rangers** by **St. Louis** for Mike Eastwood, March 24, 1998.

• YORK, JASON Jason York D – R. 6'2", 198 lbs. b: Nepean, Ont., 5/20/1970. Detroit's 6th choice, 120th overall, in 1990 Entry Draft.

Season	Club	League	GP	G	A	Pts	AG	AA	APts	PIM	PP	SH	GW	S	%	TGF	PGF	TGA	PGA	+/–	GP	G	A	Pts	PIM	PP	SH	GW
1989-90	Windsor Spitfires	OHL	39	9	30	39	....	....	....	38	....	....	....	....	....	....	....	....	....	....	....	....	....	....	....	....	....	....
	Kitchener Rangers	OHL	25	11	25	36	....	....	....	17	....	....	....	....	....	....	....	....	....	....	17	3	19	22	10	....	....	....
1990-91	Windsor Spitfires	OHL	66	13	80	93	....	....	....	40	....	....	....	....	....	....	....	....	....	....	11	3	10	13	12	....	....	....
1991-92	Adirondack Red Wings	AHL	49	4	20	24	....	....	....	32	....	....	....	....	....	....	....	....	....	....	5	0	1	1	0	....	....	....
1992-93	**Detroit Red Wings**	**NHL**	**2**	**0**	**0**	**0**	**0**	**0**	**0**	**0**	**0**	**0**	**0**	**1**	**0.0**	**1**	**0**	**1**	**0**	**0**	....	....	....	....	....	....	....	....
	Adirondack Red Wings	AHL	77	15	40	55	....	....	....	86	....	....	....	....	....	....	....	....	....	....	11	0	3	3	18	....	....	....
1993-94	**Detroit Red Wings**	**NHL**	**7**	**1**	**2**	**3**	**1**	**2**	**3**	**2**	**0**	**0**	**0**	**9**	**11.1**	**5**	**3**	**2**	**0**	**0**	....	....	....	....	....	....	....	....
	Adirondack Red Wings	AHL	74	10	56	66	....	....	....	98	....	....	....	....	....	....	....	....	....	....	12	3	11	14	22	....	....	....
1994-95	**Detroit Red Wings**	**NHL**	**10**	**1**	**2**	**3**	**2**	**3**	**5**	**2**	**0**	**0**	**0**	**6**	**16.7**	**3**	**1**	**2**	**0**	**0**	....	....	....	....	....	....	....	....
	Adirondack Red Wings	AHL	5	1	3	4	....	....	....	4	....	....	....	....	....	....	....	....	....	....	....	....	....	....	....	....	....	....
	Anaheim Mighty Ducks	**NHL**	**15**	**0**	**8**	**8**	**0**	**12**	**12**	**12**	**0**	**0**	**0**	**22**	**0.0**	**18**	**5**	**12**	**3**	**+4**	....	....	....	....	....	....	....	....
1995-96	**Anaheim Mighty Ducks**	**NHL**	**79**	**3**	**21**	**24**	**3**	**17**	**20**	**88**	**0**	**0**	**0**	**106**	**2.8**	**68**	**16**	**90**	**31**	**–7**	....	....	....	....	....	....	....	....
1996-97	**Ottawa Senators**	**NHL**	**75**	**4**	**17**	**21**	**4**	**15**	**19**	**67**	**1**	**0**	**0**	**121**	**3.3**	**78**	**20**	**77**	**11**	**–8**	**7**	**0**	**0**	**0**	**4**	**0**	**0**	**0**
1997-98	**Ottawa Senators**	**NHL**	**73**	**3**	**13**	**16**	**4**	**13**	**17**	**62**	**0**	**0**	**0**	**109**	**2.8**	**66**	**14**	**61**	**17**	**+8**	**7**	**1**	**1**	**2**	**7**	**1**	**0**	**0**
	NHL Totals		**261**	**12**	**63**	**75**	**14**	**62**	**76**	**233**	**1**	**0**	**0**	**374**	**3.2**	**239**	**59**	**245**	**62**		**14**	**1**	**1**	**2**	**11**	**1**	**0**	**0**

AHL First All-Star Team (1994)

Traded to **Anaheim** by **Detroit** with Mike Sillinger for Stu Grimson, Mark Ferner and Anaheim's 6th round choice (Magnus Nilsson) in 1996 Entry Draft, April 4, 1995. Traded to **Ottawa** by **Anaheim** with Shaun Van Allen for Ted Drury and the rights to Marc Moro, October 1, 1996.

• YOUNG, BRIAN Brian Young D – R. 6'1", 183 lbs. b: Jasper, Alta., 10/2/1958. Chicago's 4th choice, 63rd overall, in 1978 Amateur Draft.

Season	Club	League	GP	G	A	Pts	AG	AA	APts	PIM	PP	SH	GW	S	%	TGF	PGF	TGA	PGA	+/–	GP	G	A	Pts	PIM	PP	SH	GW
1974-75	Estevan Bruins	SJHL	STATISTICS NOT AVAILABLE																									
1975-76	New Westminster Bruins	WCJHL	72	4	32	36	....	....	....	77	....	....	....	....	....	....	....	....	....	....	17	0	13	13	36	....	....	....
1976-77	New Westminster Bruins	WCHL	69	7	34	41	....	....	....	75	....	....	....	....	....	....	....	....	....	....	12	0	5	5	26	....	....	....
1977-78	New Westminster Bruins	WCJHL	63	14	43	57	....	....	....	70	....	....	....	....	....	....	....	....	....	....	21	7	18	25	10	....	....	....
	Canada	WJC-A	6	0	2	2	....	....	....	2	....	....	....	....	....	....	....	....	....	....	....	....	....	....	....	....	....	....
1978-79	New Brunswick Hawks	AHL	79	10	16	26	....	....	....	35	....	....	....	....	....	....	....	....	....	....	5	0	2	2	2	....	....	....
1979-80	New Brunswick Hawks	AHL	73	18	30	48	....	....	....	82	....	....	....	....	....	....	....	....	....	....	17	2	11	13	20	....	....	....
1980-81	**Chicago Black Hawks**	**NHL**	**8**	**0**	**2**	**2**	**0**	**1**	**1**	**6**	**0**	**0**	**0**	**5**	**0.0**	**3**	**1**	**9**	**3**	**–4**	....	....	....	....	....	....	....	....
	Dallas Black Hawks	CHL	53	7	16	23	....	....	....	43	....	....	....	....	....	....	....	....	....	....	6	1	2	3	11	....	....	....
1981-82	New Brunswick Hawks	AHL	3	0	0	0	....	....	....	0	....	....	....	....	....	....	....	....	....	....	14	0	1	1	7	....	....	....
	Schwenninger ERC	Germany	44	11	17	28	....	....	....	102	....	....	....	....	....	....	....	....	....	....	....	....	....	....	....	....	....	....
1982-83	Schwenninger ERC	Germany	35	6	16	22	....	....	....	86	....	....	....	....	....	....	....	....	....	....	....	....	....	....	....	....	....	....
1983-84	Schwenninger ERC	Germany	35	5	9	14	....	....	....	52	....	....	....	....	....	....	....	....	....	....	....	....	....	....	....	....	....	....
1984-85	Schwenninger ERC	Germany	38	8	22	30	....	....	....	62	....	....	....	....	....	....	....	....	....	....	....	....	....	....	....	....	....	....
1985-86	Kolner EC	Germany	35	12	21	33	....	....	....	63	....	....	....	....	....	....	....	....	....	....	....	....	....	....	....	....	....	....
1986-87	Kolner EC	Germany	16	1	12	13	....	....	....	32	....	....	....	....	....	....	....	....	....	....	....	....	....	....	....	....	....	....
	NHL Totals		**8**	**0**	**2**	**2**	**0**	**1**	**1**	**6**	**0**	**0**	**0**	**5**	**0.0**	**3**	**1**	**9**	**3**		....	....	....	....	....	....	....	....

Memorial Cup All-Star Team (1978) • AHL Second All-Star Team (1980)

• YOUNG, C.J. C.J. (Carl Joshua) Young RW – R. 5'10", 180 lbs. b: Waban, MA, 1/1/1968. New Jersey's 1st choice, 5th overall, in 1989 Supplemental Draft.

Season	Club	League	GP	G	A	Pts	AG	AA	APts	PIM	PP	SH	GW	S	%	TGF	PGF	TGA	PGA	+/–	GP	G	A	Pts	PIM	PP	SH	GW
1986-87	Harvard University	ECAC	34	17	12	29	....	....	....	30	....	....	....	....	....	....	....	....	....	....	....	....	....	....	....	....	....	....
1987-88	Harvard University	ECAC	28	13	16	29	....	....	....	40	....	....	....	....	....	....	....	....	....	....	....	....	....	....	....	....	....	....
	United States	WJC-A	7	2	1	3	....	....	....	8	....	....	....	....	....	....	....	....	....	....	....	....	....	....	....	....	....	....

			REGULAR SEASON																		PLAYOFFS							
Season	Club	League	GP	G	A	Pts	AG	AA	APts	PIM	PP	SH	GW	S	%	TGF	PGF	TGA	PGA	+/–	GP	G	A	Pts	PIM	PP	SH	GW
1988-89	Harvard University	ECAC	36	20	31	51				36																		
1989-90	Harvard University	ECAC	28	21	28	49				32																		
1990-91	Salt Lake Golden Eagles	IHL	80	31	36	67				43											4	1	2	3	2			
1991-92	United States	Nat-Team	49	17	17	34				38																		
	Salt Lake Golden Eagles	IHL	9	2	2	4				2											5	0	1	1	4			
1992-93	**Calgary Flames**	**NHL**	**28**	**3**	**2**	**5**	**2**	**1**	**3**	**20**	**1**	**0**	**0**	**21**	**14.3**	**9**	**3**	**20**	**7**	**–7**								
	Boston Bruins	**NHL**	**15**	**4**	**5**	**9**	**3**	**3**	**6**	**12**	**0**	**0**	**1**	**22**	**18.2**	**11**	**0**	**10**	**0**	**+1**								
	Providence Bruins	AHL	7	4	3	7				26											6	1	0	1	16			
	NHL Totals		**43**	**7**	**7**	**14**	**5**	**4**	**9**	**32**	**1**	**0**	**1**	**43**	**16.3**	**20**	**3**	**30**	**7**									

ECAC Second All-Star Team (1989) • ECAC First All-Star Team (1990)

Signed as a free agent by **Calgary**, October 5, 1990. Traded to **Boston** by **Calgary** for Brent Ashton, February 1, 1993.

• YOUNG, HOWIE Howie "Wild Thing" Young RW – R. 5'11", 175 lbs. b: Toronto, Ont., 8/2/1937.

Season	Club	League	GP	G	A	Pts	AG	AA	APts	PIM	PP	SH	GW	S	%	TGF	PGF	TGA	PGA	+/–	GP	G	A	Pts	PIM	PP	SH	GW
1954-55	Kitchener Canucks	OHA	49	6	7	13				155																		
1955-56	Kitchener Canucks	OHA	28	2	5	7				40																		
1956-57	Hamilton Tiger Cubs	OHA	52	5	15	20				*228											4	0	1	1	28			
1957-58	Hamilton Tiger Cubs	OHA	40	3	7	10				163																		
1958-59	New Westminster Royals	WHL	4	0	1	1				26																		
	Chicoutimi Sagueneens	QHL	50	4	16	20				*180																		
1959-60	Rochester Americans	AHL	68	7	7	14				170																		
1960-61	**Detroit Red Wings**	**NHL**	**29**	**0**	**8**	**8**	**0**	**8**	**8**	**108**											**11**	**2**	**2**	**4**	***30**			
	Hershey Bears	AHL	33	1	5	6				160																		
1961-62	**Detroit Red Wings**	**NHL**	**30**	**0**	**2**	**2**	**0**	**2**	**2**	**67**																		
	Edmonton Flyers	WHL	24	3	15	18				97											12	3	10	13	*49			
1962-63	**Detroit Red Wings**	**NHL**	**64**	**4**	**5**	**9**	**5**	**5**	**10**	***273**											**8**	**0**	**2**	**2**	**16**			
1963-64	**Chicago Black Hawks**	**NHL**	**39**	**0**	**7**	**7**	**0**	**8**	**8**	**99**																		
	Los Angeles Blades	WHL	13	2	4	6				40											4	0	2	2	21			
1964-65	Los Angeles Blades	WHL	65	10	20	30				*227																		
1965-66	Los Angeles Blades	WHL	44	5	11	16				*170																		
1966-67	Los Angeles Blades	WHL	29	5	17	22				43																		
	Detroit Red Wings	**NHL**	**44**	**3**	**14**	**17**	**4**	**14**	**18**	**100**																		
1967-68	**Detroit Red Wings**	**NHL**	**62**	**2**	**17**	**19**	**2**	**18**	**20**	**112**	**0**	**0**	**0**	**87**	**2.3**	**71**	**3**	**68**	**16**	**+16**								
	Fort Worth Wings	CHL	5	1	2	3				12																		
1968-69	**Chicago Black Hawks**	**NHL**	**57**	**3**	**7**	**10**	**3**	**7**	**10**	**67**	**0**	**0**	**0**	**64**	**4.7**	**23**	**1**	**37**	**2**	**–13**								
1969-70	Rochester Americans	AHL	56	17	20	37				75																		
	Vancouver Canucks	WHL	16	0	3	3				44																		
1970-71	**Vancouver Canucks**	**NHL**	**11**	**0**	**2**	**2**	**0**	**2**	**2**	**25**	**0**	**0**	**0**	**18**	**0.0**	**6**	**2**	**13**	**2**	**–7**								
	Phoenix Roadrunners	WHL	57	11	32	43				136											10	0	3	3	21			
1971-72			DID NOT PLAY																									
1972-73	Phoenix Roadrunners	WHL	71	20	38	58				223											10	1	5	6	31			
1973-74	Phoenix Roadrunners	WHL	71	37	32	69				124											9	3	3	6	6			
1974-75	Phoenix Roadrunners	WHA	30	3	12	15				44																		
	Winnipeg Jets	WHA	42	13	10	23				42																		
1976-77	Phoenix Roadrunners	WHA	26	1	3	4				23																		
	Oklahoma City Blazers	CHL	4	0	0	0				8																		
1977-78	Phoenix Roadrunners	PHL	39	4	11	15				63																		
1978-79	Los Angeles Blades	PHL	14	0	2	2				22																		
1979-1985			DID NOT PLAY – RETIRED																									
1985-86	Flint Generals	IHL	4	0	1	1				2																		
	New York Slapshots	NAHL	7	0	1	1				18																		
	NHL Totals		**336**	**12**	**62**	**74**	**14**	**64**	**78**	**851**	**0**	**0**	**0**	**169**	**7.1**	**100**	**6**	**118**	**20**		**19**	**2**	**4**	**6**	**46**	**0**	**0**	**0**
	Other Major League Totals		98	17	25	42				109																		

WHL First All-Star Team (1974)

Traded to **Hershey** (AHL) by **Toronto** (Rochester - AHL) for cash, August, 1960. Traded to **Detroit** by **Hershey** (AHL) for Jack McIntyre, Marc Reaume and Pete Conacher, January, 1961. Traded to Chicago for Ron Ingram and Roger Crozier, June 5, 1963. Traded to **LA Blades** (WHL) by **Chicago** for cash and future considerations (Wayne Smith) February 11, 1964. Traded to **Detroit** by **Chicago** (LA Blades-WHL) for Al Lebrun, Murray Hall and Rick Morris, December 20, 1966. Traded to **Oakland** by **Detroit** with Gary Jarrett, Doug Roberts and Chris Worthy for Bob Baun and Ron Harris, May 27, 1968. Claimed on waivers by **Chicago** from **Oakland**, October 2, 1968. Traded to **Vancouver** (WHL) by **Chicago** for cash, October, 1969. Loaned to **Phoenix** (WHL) by **Vancouver** for remainder of 1970-71 season, November, 1970. Claimed by **San Diego** (WHL) from **Vancouver** in Reverse Draft, June, 1971. • Suspended by **San Diego** (WHL) for refusing to report to team for 1971-72 season, September, 1971. Traded to **Phoenix** (WHL) by **San Diego** (WHL) for cash, August, 1972. WHA rights transferred to **Phoenix** (WHA) after owners of **Phoenix** (WHL) franchise granted WHA expansion team, September 14, 1973. Traded to **Winnipeg** (WHA) by **Phoenix** (WHA) for cash, January, 1975. Signed as a free agent by **Phoenix** (WHA), February 12, 1977.

• YOUNG, SCOTT Scott Young RW – R. 6', 190 lbs. b: Clinton, MA, 10/1/1967. Hartford's 1st choice, 11th overall, in 1986 Entry Draft.

Season	Club	League	GP	G	A	Pts	AG	AA	APts	PIM	PP	SH	GW	S	%	TGF	PGF	TGA	PGA	+/–	GP	G	A	Pts	PIM	PP	SH	GW
1984-85	St. Marks-Mass High School	H.S.	23	28	41	69																						
	United States	WJC-A	7	1	2	3				4																		
1985-86	Boston University	H.E.	38	16	13	29				31																		
	United States	WJC-A	7	1	3	4				8																		
1986-87	Boston University	H.E.	33	15	21	36				24																		
	United States	WJC-A	7	7	2	9				2																		
	United States	WEC-A	4	0	1	1				2																		
1987-88	United States	Nat-Team	56	11	47	58				31																		
	United States	Olympics	6	2	6	8				4																		
	Hartford Whalers	**NHL**	**7**	**0**	**0**	**0**	**0**	**0**	**0**	**2**	**0**	**0**	**0**	**6**	**0.0**	**1**	**0**	**7**	**0**	**–6**	**4**	**1**	**0**	**1**	**0**	**0**	**0**	**0**
1988-89	**Hartford Whalers**	**NHL**	**76**	**19**	**40**	**59**	**16**	**28**	**44**	**27**	**6**	**0**	**2**	**203**	**9.4**	**106**	**60**	**67**	**0**	**–21**	**4**	**2**	**0**	**2**	**4**	**0**	**0**	**0**
	United States	WEC-A	10	0	7	7				6																		
1989-90	**Hartford Whalers**	**NHL**	**80**	**24**	**40**	**64**	**21**	**29**	**50**	**47**	**10**	**2**	**5**	**239**	**10.0**	**111**	**62**	**84**	**11**	**–24**	**7**	**2**	**0**	**2**	**2**	**0**	**0**	**0**
1990-91	**Hartford Whalers**	**NHL**	**34**	**6**	**9**	**15**	**5**	**7**	**12**	**8**	**3**	**1**	**2**	**94**	**6.4**	**38**	**18**	**33**	**4**	**–9**								
	Pittsburgh Penguins	**NHL**	**43**	**11**	**16**	**27**	**10**	**12**	**22**	**33**	**3**	**1**	**3**	**116**	**9.5**	**43**	**14**	**37**	**11**	**+3**	**17**	**1**	**6**	**7**	**2**	**1**	**0**	**0**
1991-92	HC Bolzano	Italy	18	22	17	39				6											5	4	3	7	7			
	United States	Nat-Team	10	2	4	6				21																		
	United States	Olympics	8	2	1	3				2																		
1992-93	**Quebec Nordiques**	**NHL**	**82**	**30**	**30**	**60**	**25**	**21**	**46**	**20**	**9**	**6**	**5**	**225**	**13.3**	**115**	**49**	**82**	**21**	**+5**	**6**	**4**	**1**	**5**	**0**	**0**	**0**	**2**
1993-94	**Quebec Nordiques**	**NHL**	**76**	**26**	**25**	**51**	**24**	**19**	**43**	**14**	**6**	**1**	**1**	**236**	**11.0**	**73**	**26**	**75**	**24**	**–4**								
	United States	WC-A	8	3	1	4				4																		
1994-95	EV Landshut	Germany	4	6	1	7				6																		
	Frankfurt Lions	Germany	1	1	0	1				0																		
	Quebec Nordiques	**NHL**	**48**	**18**	**21**	**39**	**32**	**31**	**63**	**14**	**3**	**3**	**0**	**167**	**10.8**	**57**	**24**	**31**	**7**	**+9**	**6**	**3**	**3**	**6**	**2**	**0**	**1**	**0**
1995-96	**Colorado Avalanche**	**NHL**	**81**	**21**	**39**	**60**	**21**	**32**	**53**	**50**	**7**	**0**	**5**	**229**	**9.2**	**86**	**31**	**62**	**9**	**+2**	**22**	**3**	**12**	**15**	**10**	**0**	**0**	**0**
1996-97	United States	W Cup	7	2	2	4				4																		
	Colorado Avalanche	**NHL**	**72**	**18**	**19**	**37**	**19**	**17**	**36**	**14**	**7**	**0**	**0**	**164**	**11.0**	**58**	**32**	**35**	**4**	**–5**	**17**	**4**	**2**	**6**	**14**	**2**	**0**	**0**
1997-98	**Anaheim Mighty Ducks**	**NHL**	**73**	**13**	**20**	**33**	**15**	**19**	**34**	**22**	**4**	**2**	**1**	**187**	**7.0**	**50**	**21**	**71**	**29**	**–13**								
	NHL Totals		**672**	**186**	**259**	**445**	**188**	**215**	**403**	**251**	**58**	**16**	**24**	**1866**	**10.0**	**738**	**337**	**584**	**120**		**83**	**20**	**24**	**44**	**34**	**3**	**1**	**2**

WJC-A All-Star Team (1987) • ECAC First All-Star Team (1989)

Traded to **Pittsburgh** by **Hartford** for Rob Brown, December 21, 1990. Traded to **Quebec** by **Pittsburgh** for Bryan Fogarty, March 10, 1992. Transferred to **Colorado** after **Quebec** franchise relocated, June 21, 1995. Traded to **Anaheim** by **Colorado** for Anaheim's 3rd round choice (later traded to Florida - Florida selected Lance Ward) in 1998 Entry Draft, September 17, 1997

• YOUNG, TIM Tim "Blade" Young C – R. 6'1", 190 lbs. b: Scarborough, Ont., 2/22/1955. Los Angeles' 1st choice, 16th overall, in 1975 Amateur Draft.

Season	Club	League	GP	G	A	Pts	AG	AA	APts	PIM	PP	SH	GW	S	%	TGF	PGF	TGA	PGA	+/–	GP	G	A	Pts	PIM	PP	SH	GW
1972-73	Pembroke Centennials	CJHL	55	41	40	81				148																		
1973-74	Ottawa 67's	OHA	69	45	61	106				161																		
1974-75	Ottawa 67's	OHA	70	56	*107	163				127											5	3	4	7	8			
1975-76	**Minnesota North Stars**	**NHL**	**63**	**18**	**33**	**51**	**17**	**26**	**43**	**71**	**5**	**0**	**2**	**127**	**14.2**	**60**	**17**	**54**	**1**	**–10**								
	New Haven Nighthawks	AHL	13	7	13	20				6																		

			REGULAR SEASON																		PLAYOFFS							
Season	Club	League	GP	G	A	Pts	AG	AA	APts	PIM	PP	SH	GW	S	%	TGF	PGF	TGA	PGA	+/–	GP	G	A	Pts	PIM	PP	SH	GW
1976-77	Minnesota North Stars	NHL	80	29	66	95	28	54	82	58	10	0	2	223	13.0	115	49	98	0	–32	2	1	1	2	2	0	0	0
1977-78	Minnesota North Stars	NHL	78	23	35	58	22	29	51	64	5	0	2	217	10.6	78	23	92	0	–37	....	....	....	....	....	....	....	....
1978-79	Minnesota North Stars	NHL	73	24	32	56	22	24	46	46	8	0	5	147	16.3	78	31	61	2	–12	....	....	....	....	....	....	....	....
1979-80	Minnesota North Stars	NHL	77	31	43	74	28	33	61	24	5	2	5	220	14.1	101	25	73	11	+14	15	2	5	7	4	1	1	0
1980-81	Minnesota North Stars	NHL	74	25	41	66	21	29	50	40	10	0	4	214	11.7	107	53	63	15	+6	12	3	14	17	9	0	0	1
1981-82	Minnesota North Stars	NHL	49	10	31	41	8	20	28	67	1	0	1	125	8.0	62	19	50	7	0	4	1	1	2	10	0	0	0
1982-83	Minnesota North Stars	NHL	70	18	35	53	15	24	39	31	6	2	2	152	11.8	76	33	71	27	–1	2	0	2	2	2	0	0	0
1983-84	Winnipeg Jets	NHL	44	15	19	34	12	13	25	25	3	0	0	77	19.5	50	17	56	12	–11	1	0	1	1	0	0	0	0
1984-85	Philadelphia Flyers	NHL	20	2	6	8	2	4	6	12	0	0	1	25	8.0	16	2	13	1	+2	....	....	....	....	....	....	....	....
	Hershey Bears	AHL	49	19	29	48	....	....	....	56	....	....	....	....	....	....	....	....	....	....	....	....	....	....	....	....	....	....
	NHL Totals		628	195	341	536	175	256	431	438	53	4	24	1527	12.8	743	269	631	76		36	7	24	31	27	1	1	1

Played in NHL All-Star Game (1977)

Traded to **Minnesota** by **LA Kings** for Minnesota's 2nd round choice (Steve Clippingdale) in 1976 Amateur Draft, August 15, 1975. Traded to **Winnipeg** by **Minnesota** for Craig Levie and Tom Ward, August 3, 1983. Traded to **Philadelphia** by **Winnipeg** for future considerations, October 16, 1984.

• YOUNG, WARREN

Warren Young C – L. 6'3", 195 lbs. b: Toronto, Ont., 1/11/1956. California's 4th choice, 59th overall, in 1976 Amateur Draft.

Season	Club	League	GP	G	A	Pts	AG	AA	APts	PIM	PP	SH	GW	S	%	TGF	PGF	TGA	PGA	+/–	GP	G	A	Pts	PIM	PP	SH	GW
1974-75	Dixie Beehives	OJHL	44	32	25	57	....	....	....	50	....	....	....	....	....	....	....	....	....	....	....	....	....	....	....	....	....	....
1975-76	Michigan Tech Huskies	WCHA	42	16	15	31	....	....	....	48	....	....	....	....	....	....	....	....	....	....	....	....	....	....	....	....	....	....
1976-77	Michigan Tech Huskies	WCHA	37	19	26	45	....	....	....	86	....	....	....	....	....	....	....	....	....	....	....	....	....	....	....	....	....	....
1977-78	Michigan Tech Huskies	WCHA	32	14	16	30	....	....	....	54	....	....	....	....	....	....	....	....	....	....	....	....	....	....	....	....	....	....
1978-79	Michigan Tech Huskies	CCHA	26	11	7	18	....	....	....	45	....	....	....	....	....	....	....	....	....	....	....	....	....	....	....	....	....	....
	Oklahoma City Stars	CHL	4	0	1	1	....	....	....	2	....	....	....	....	....	....	....	....	....	....	....	....	....	....	....	....	....	....
1979-80	Baltimore Clippers	EHL	65	*53	53	106	....	....	....	75	....	....	....	....	....	....	....	....	....	....	....	....	....	....	....	....	....	....
	Oklahoma City Stars	CHL	13	4	8	12	....	....	....	9	....	....	....	....	....	....	....	....	....	....	....	....	....	....	....	....	....	....
1980-81	Oklahoma City Stars	CHL	77	26	33	59	....	....	....	42	....	....	....	....	....	....	....	....	....	....	3	1	1	2	7	....	....	....
1981-82	Minnesota North Stars	NHL	1	0	0	0	0	0	0	0	0	0	0	0	0.0	0	0	3	0	–3	....	....	....	....	....	....	....	....
	Nashville South Stars	CHL	60	31	28	59	....	....	....	154	....	....	....	....	....	....	....	....	....	....	....	....	....	....	....	....	....	....
1982-83	Minnesota North Stars	NHL	4	1	1	2	1	1	2	0	0	0	0	2	50.0	2	0	2	0	0	....	....	....	....	....	....	....	....
	Birmingham South Stars	CHL	75	26	58	84	....	....	....	144	....	....	....	....	....	....	....	....	....	....	13	3	3	6	57	....	....	....
1983-84	Pittsburgh Penguins	NHL	15	1	7	8	1	5	6	19	0	0	0	12	8.3	13	1	14	0	–2	....	....	....	....	....	....	....	....
	Baltimore Skipjacks	AHL	59	25	38	63	....	....	....	142	....	....	....	....	....	....	....	....	....	....	10	2	6	8	18	....	....	....
1984-85	Pittsburgh Penguins	NHL	80	40	32	72	33	22	55	174	9	0	3	130	30.8	113	39	94	0	–20	....	....	....	....	....	....	....	....
1985-86	Detroit Red Wings	NHL	79	22	24	46	18	16	34	161	9	0	1	95	23.2	75	32	77	0	–34	....	....	....	....	....	....	....	....
1986-87	Pittsburgh Penguins	NHL	50	8	13	21	7	9	16	103	3	0	1	52	15.4	34	9	31	1	–5	....	....	....	....	....	....	....	....
	Baltimore Skipjacks	AHL	22	8	7	15	....	....	....	95	....	....	....	....	....	....	....	....	....	....	....	....	....	....	....	....	....	....
1987-88	Pittsburgh Penguins	NHL	7	0	0	0	0	0	0	15	0	0	0	3	0.0	1	0	5	0	–4	....	....	....	....	....	....	....	....
	Muskegon Lumberjacks	IHL	60	25	26	51	....	....	....	325	....	....	....	....	....	....	....	....	....	....	4	0	0	0	42	....	....	....
	NHL Totals		236	72	77	149	60	53	113	472	21	0	5	294	24.5	238	81	226	1		....	....	....	....	....	....	....	....

CHL Second All-Star Team (1983) • NHL All-Rookie Team (1985)

Signed as a free agent by **Minnesota**, October 22, 1981. Signed as a free agent by **Pittsburgh**, August 12, 1983. Signed as a free agent by **Detroit**, July 10, 1985. Traded to **Pittsburgh** by **Detroit** for cash, October 8, 1986.

• YOUNGHANS, TOM

Tom Younghans RW – R. 5'11", 175 lbs. b: St. Paul, MN, 1/22/1953

Season	Club	League	GP	G	A	Pts	AG	AA	APts	PIM	PP	SH	GW	S	%	TGF	PGF	TGA	PGA	+/–	GP	G	A	Pts	PIM	PP	SH	GW
1974-75	University of Minnesota	WCHA	22	13	15	28	....	....	....	22	....	....	....	....	....	....	....	....	....	....	....	....	....	....	....	....	....	....
1975-76	University of Minnesota	CCHA	44	19	24	43	....	....	....	94	....	....	....	....	....	....	....	....	....	....	....	....	....	....	....	....	....	....
	United States	WEC-A	10	2	2	4	....	....	....	8	....	....	....	....	....	....	....	....	....	....	....	....	....	....	....	....	....	....
1976-77	Minnesota North Stars	NHL	78	8	6	14	8	5	13	35	1	3	0	54	14.8	21	1	70	39	–11	2	0	0	0	0	0	0	0
	United States	WEC-A	10	0	4	4	....	....	....	8	....	....	....	....	....	....	....	....	....	....	....	....	....	....	....	....	....	....
1977-78	Minnesota North Stars	NHL	72	10	8	18	10	7	17	100	1	0	0	71	14.1	29	2	57	20	–10	....	....	....	....	....	....	....	....
	Fort Worth Texans	CHL	6	3	2	5	....	....	....	2	....	....	....	....	....	....	....	....	....	....	....	....	....	....	....	....	....	....
	United States	WEC-A	10	2	1	3	....	....	....	6	....	....	....	....	....	....	....	....	....	....	....	....	....	....	....	....	....	....
1978-79	Minnesota North Stars	NHL	76	8	10	18	7	8	15	50	0	0	1	70	11.4	25	0	69	21	–23	....	....	....	....	....	....	....	....
1979-80	Minnesota North Stars	NHL	79	10	6	16	9	5	14	92	0	1	0	79	12.7	30	0	67	24	–3	15	2	1	3	17	0	2	0
1980-81	Minnesota North Stars	NHL	74	4	6	10	3	4	7	79	1	1	2	55	7.3	18	1	60	35	–8	5	0	0	0	4	0	0	0
1981-82	United States	C Cup	4	0	0	0	....	....	....	0	....	....	....	....	....	....	....	....	....	....	....	....	....	....	....	....	....	....
	Minnesota North Stars	NHL	3	1	0	1	1	0	1	0	0	1	0	2	50.0	1	0	1	1	+1	....	....	....	....	....	....	....	....
	Nashville South Stars	CHL	5	5	3	8	....	....	....	2	....	....	....	....	....	....	....	....	....	....	....	....	....	....	....	....	....	....
	New York Rangers	NHL	47	3	5	8	2	3	5	17	0	0	0	37	8.1	14	0	32	18	0	2	0	0	0	0	0	0	0
	Springfield Indians	AHL	7	4	0	4	....	....	....	16	....	....	....	....	....	....	....	....	....	....	....	....	....	....	....	....	....	....
	NHL Totals		429	44	41	85	40	32	72	373	3	6	3	368	12.0	138	4	346	158		24	2	1	3	21	0	2	0

Signed as a free agent by **Minnesota**, September 14, 1979. Traded to **NY Rangers** by **Minnesota** for cash, October 30, 1981.

• YSEBAERT, PAUL

Paul Ysebaert C – L. 6'1", 194 lbs. b: Sarnia, Ont., 5/15/1966. New Jersey's 4th choice, 74th overall, in 1984 Entry Draft.

Season	Club	League	GP	G	A	Pts	AG	AA	APts	PIM	PP	SH	GW	S	%	TGF	PGF	TGA	PGA	+/–	GP	G	A	Pts	PIM	PP	SH	GW
1984-85	Bowling Green University	CCHA	42	23	32	55	....	....	....	54	....	....	....	....	....	....	....	....	....	....	....	....	....	....	....	....	....	....
1985-86	Bowling Green University	CCHA	42	23	45	68	....	....	....	50	....	....	....	....	....	....	....	....	....	....	....	....	....	....	....	....	....	....
1986-87	Bowling Green University	CCHA	45	27	58	85	....	....	....	44	....	....	....	....	....	....	....	....	....	....	....	....	....	....	....	....	....	....
	Canada	Nat-Team	5	1	0	1	....	....	....	4	....	....	....	....	....	....	....	....	....	....	....	....	....	....	....	....	....	....
1987-88	Utica Devils	AHL	78	30	49	79	....	....	....	60	....	....	....	....	....	....	....	....	....	....	....	....	....	....	....	....	....	....
1988-89	New Jersey Devils	NHL	5	0	4	4	0	3	3	0	0	0	0	4	0.0	6	2	2	0	+2	....	....	....	....	....	....	....	....
	Utica Devils	AHL	56	36	44	80	....	....	....	22	....	....	....	....	....	....	....	....	....	....	5	0	1	1	4	....	....	....
1989-90	New Jersey Devils	NHL	5	1	2	3	1	1	2	0	0	0	0	6	16.7	4	1	3	0	0	....	....	....	....	....	....	....	....
	Utica Devils	AHL	74	53	52	*105	....	....	....	61	....	....	....	....	....	....	....	....	....	....	5	2	4	6	0	....	....	....
1990-91	New Jersey Devils	NHL	11	4	3	7	4	2	6	6	1	0	0	14	28.6	8	2	5	0	+1	....	....	....	....	....	....	....	....
	Detroit Red Wings	NHL	51	15	18	33	14	14	28	16	5	0	1	114	13.2	49	16	46	5	–8	2	0	2	2	0	0	0	0
1991-92	Detroit Red Wings	NHL	79	35	40	75	32	30	62	55	3	4	3	211	16.6	114	29	56	15	+44	10	1	0	1	10	0	0	0
1992-93	Detroit Red Wings	NHL	80	34	28	62	28	19	47	42	3	3	8	186	18.3	91	20	64	12	+19	7	3	1	4	2	0	1	1
1993-94	Winnipeg Jets	NHL	60	9	18	27	8	14	22	18	1	0	0	120	7.5	39	13	39	5	–8	....	....	....	....	....	....	....	....
	Chicago Blackhawks	NHL	11	5	3	8	5	2	7	8	2	0	1	31	16.1	14	7	6	0	+1	6	0	0	0	8	0	0	0
1994-95	Chicago Blackhawks	NHL	15	4	5	9	7	7	14	6	0	0	1	23	17.4	14	2	8	0	+4	....	....	....	....	....	....	....	....
	Tampa Bay Lightning	NHL	29	8	11	19	14	16	30	12	0	0	0	70	11.4	33	7	29	2	–1	....	....	....	....	....	....	....	....
1995-96	Tampa Bay Lightning	NHL	55	16	15	31	16	12	28	16	4	1	1	135	11.9	57	27	53	4	–19	5	0	0	0	0	0	0	0
1996-97	Tampa Bay Lightning	NHL	39	5	12	17	5	11	16	4	2	0	0	91	5.5	26	6	23	4	+1	....	....	....	....	....	....	....	....
1997-98	Tampa Bay Lightning	NHL	82	13	27	40	15	26	41	32	2	1	0	145	9.0	56	23	89	13	–43	....	....	....	....	....	....	....	....
	NHL Totals		522	149	186	335	149	157	306	215	23	9	15	1150	13.0	511	155	423	60		30	4	3	7	20	0	1	1

CCHA Second All-Star Team (1986, 1987) • AHL First All-Star Team (1990) • Won John B. Sollenberger Trophy (Top Scorer - AHL) (1990) • Won Les Cunningham Plaque (MVP - AHL) (1990) • Won Alka-Seltzer Plus Award (1992)

Traded to **Detroit** by **New Jersey** for Lee Norwood and Detroit's 4th round choice (Scott McCabe) in 1992 Entry Draft, November 27, 1990. Traded to **Winnipeg** by **Detroit** with future considerations (Alan Kerr, June 18, 1993) for Aaron Ward and Toronto's 4th round choice (previously acquired by Winnipeg — later traded to Detroit — Detroit selected John Jakopin) in 1993 Entry Draft, June 11, 1993. Traded to **Chicago** by **Winnipeg** for Chicago's 3rd round choice (later traded back to Chicago — Chicago selected Kevin McKay) in 1995 Entry Draft, March 21, 1994. Traded to **Tampa Bay** by **Chicago** with Rich Sutter for Jim Cummins, Tom Tilley and Jeff Buchanan, February 22, 1995.

• YUSHKEVICH, DIMITRI

Dimitri Yushkevich D – R. 5'11", 208 lbs. b: Yaroslavl, USSR, 11/19/1971. Philadelphia's 6th choice, 122nd overall, in 1991 Entry Draft.

Season	Club	League	GP	G	A	Pts	AG	AA	APts	PIM	PP	SH	GW	S	%	TGF	PGF	TGA	PGA	+/–	GP	G	A	Pts	PIM	PP	SH	GW
1988-89	Torpedo Yaroslavl	USSR	23	2	1	3	....	....	....	8	....	....	....	....	....	....	....	....	....	....	....	....	....	....	....	....	....	....
1989-90	Torpedo Yaroslavl	USSR	41	2	3	5	....	....	....	39	....	....	....	....	....	....	....	....	....	....	....	....	....	....	....	....	....	....
1990-91	Torpedo Yaroslavl	USSR	41	10	4	14	....	....	....	22	....	....	....	....	....	....	....	....	....	....	....	....	....	....	....	....	....	....
1991-92	Moscow Dynamo	CIS	35	5	7	12	....	....	....	14	....	....	....	....	....	....	....	....	....	....	....	....	....	....	....	....	....	....
	Russia	Olympics	8	1	2	3	....	....	....	4	....	....	....	....	....	....	....	....	....	....	....	....	....	....	....	....	....	....
	Russia	WC-A	6	1	1	2	....	....	....	4	....	....	....	....	....	....	....	....	....	....	....	....	....	....	....	....	....	....
1992-93	Philadelphia Flyers	NHL	82	5	27	32	4	18	22	71	1	0	1	155	3.2	109	13	122	38	+12	....	....	....	....	....	....	....	....
	Russia	WC-A	7	1	4	5	....	....	....	10	....	....	....	....	....	....	....	....	....	....	....	....	....	....	....	....	....	....

			REGULAR SEASON																		PLAYOFFS							
Season	Club	League	GP	G	A	Pts	AG	AA	APts	PIM	PP	SH	GW	S	%	TGF	PGF	TGA	PGA	+/–	GP	G	A	Pts	PIM	PP	SH	GW
1993-94	Philadelphia Flyers	NHL	75	5	25	30	5	19	24	86	1	0	2	136	3.7	86	9	113	28	–8	....	....	....	....	....	....	....	....
	Russia	WC-A	6	1	2	3	....	....	....	12	....	....	....	....	....	....	....	....	....	....	....	....	....	....	....	....	....	....
1994-95	Torpedo Yaroslavl	CIS	10	3	4	7	....	....	....	8	....	....	....	....	....	....	....	....	....	....	....	....	....	....	....	....	....	....
	Philadelphia Flyers	NHL	40	5	9	14	9	13	22	47	3	1	1	80	6.3	45	15	44	10	–4	15	1	5	6	12	0	0	0
1995-96	Toronto Maple Leafs	NHL	69	1	10	11	1	8	9	54	1	0	0	96	1.0	48	10	81	29	–14	4	0	0	0	0	0	0	0
1996-97	Russia	W Cup	5	1	1	2	....	....	....	2	....	....	....	....	....	....	....	....	....	....	....	....	....	....	....	....	....	....
	Toronto Maple Leafs	NHL	74	4	10	14	4	9	13	56	1	1	1	99	4.0	58	5	105	28	–24	....	....	....	....	....	....	....	....
1997-98	Toronto Maple Leafs	NHL	72	0	12	12	0	12	12	78	0	0	0	92	0.0	58	6	82	17	–13	....	....	....	....	....	....	....	....
	NHL Totals		412	20	93	113	23	79	102	392	7	2	5	658	3.0	404	58	547	150		19	1	5	6	12	0	0	0

Named Best Defenseman at WC-A (1993)

Traded to **Toronto** by **Philadelphia** with Philadelphia's 2nd round choice (Francis Larivee) in 1996 Entry Draft for Toronto's 1st round choice (Dainius Zubrus) in 1996 Entry Draft, 2nd round choice (Jean-Marc Pelletier) in 1997 Entry Draft and LA Kings' 4th round choice (previously acquired by Toronto — later traded to LA Kings — LA Kings selected Mikael Simons) in 1996 Entry Draft, August 30, 1995.

• YZERMAN, STEVE

Steve Yzerman C – R. 5'11", 185 lbs. b: Cranbrook, B.C., 5/9/1965. Detroit's 1st choice, 4th overall, in 1983 Entry Draft.

Season	Club	League	GP	G	A	Pts	AG	AA	APts	PIM	PP	SH	GW	S	%	TGF	PGF	TGA	PGA	+/–	GP	G	A	Pts	PIM	PP	SH	GW
1981-82	Peterborough Petes	OHL	58	21	43	64	....	....	....	65	....	....	....	....	....	....	....	....	....	....	6	0	1	1	16	....	....	....
1982-83	Peterborough Petes	OHL	56	42	49	91	....	....	....	33	....	....	....	....	....	....	....	....	....	....	4	1	4	5	0	....	....	....
	Canada	WJC-A	7	2	3	5	....	....	....	2	....	....	....	....	....	....	....	....	....	....	....	....	....	....	....	....	....	....
1983-84	Detroit Red Wings	NHL	80	39	48	87	31	33	64	33	13	0	2	177	22.0	133	62	91	3	–17	4	3	3	6	0	1	0	1
1984-85	Canada	C Cup	4	0	0	0	....	....	....	0	....	....	....	....	....	....	....	....	....	....	....	....	....	....	....	....	....	....
	Detroit Red Wings	NHL	80	30	59	89	25	40	65	58	9	0	3	231	13.0	138	53	104	2	–17	3	2	1	3	2	0	0	0
	Canada	WEC-A	10	3	4	7	....	....	....	6	....	....	....	....	....	....	....	....	....	....	....	....	....	....	....	....	....	....
1985-86	Detroit Red Wings	NHL	51	14	28	42	11	19	30	16	3	0	3	132	10.6	72	31	74	9	–24	....	....	....	....	....	....	....	....
1986-87	Detroit Red Wings	NHL	80	31	59	90	27	43	70	43	9	1	2	217	14.3	125	53	87	14	–1	16	5	13	18	8	1	0	0
1987-88	Detroit Red Wings	NHL	64	50	52	102	43	37	80	44	10	6	6	242	20.7	132	42	75	15	+30	3	1	3	4	6	0	0	0
1988-89	Detroit Red Wings	NHL	80	65	90	155	56	64	120	61	17	3	7	388	16.8	189	65	152	45	+17	6	5	5	10	2	2	0	0
	Canada	WEC-A	8	5	7	12	....	....	....	2	....	....	....	....	....	....	....	....	....	....	....	....	....	....	....	....	....	....
1989-90	Detroit Red Wings	NHL	79	62	65	127	54	47	101	79	16	7	8	332	18.7	162	52	166	50	–6	....	....	....	....	....	....	....	....
	Canada	WEC-A	10	10	10	20	....	....	....	8	....	....	....	....	....	....	....	....	....	....	....	....	....	....	....	....	....	....
1990-91	Detroit Red Wings	NHL	80	51	57	108	47	43	90	34	12	6	4	326	15.6	141	51	141	49	–2	7	3	3	6	4	1	0	0
1991-92	Detroit Red Wings	NHL	79	45	58	103	41	44	85	64	9	8	9	295	15.3	143	51	102	36	+26	11	3	5	8	12	0	1	1
1992-93	Detroit Red Wings	NHL	84	58	79	137	49	54	103	44	13	7	6	307	18.9	174	61	114	34	+33	7	4	3	7	4	1	1	1
1993-94	Detroit Red Wings	NHL	58	24	58	82	22	45	67	36	7	3	3	217	11.1	103	30	81	19	+11	3	1	3	4	0	0	0	0
1994-95	Detroit Red Wings	NHL	47	12	26	38	21	38	59	40	4	0	1	134	9.0	67	34	36	9	+6	15	4	8	12	0	2	0	1
1995-96	Detroit Red Wings	NHL	80	36	59	95	36	48	84	64	16	2	8	220	16.4	130	61	63	23	+29	18	8	12	20	4	4	0	1
1996-97	Canada	W Cup	6	2	1	3	....	....	....	0	....	....	....	....	....	....	....	....	....	....	....	....	....	....	....	....	....	....
	Detroit Red Wings	NHL	81	22	63	85	23	56	79	78	8	0	3	232	9.5	123	49	72	20	+22	20	7	6	13	4	3	0	2
1997-98	Detroit Red Wings	NHL	75	24	45	69	28	44	72	46	6	2	0	188	12.8	96	41	67	15	+3	22	6	18	24	22	3	1	0
	Canada	Olympics	6	1	1	2	....	....	....	10	....	....	....	....	....	....	....	....	....	....	....	....	....	....	....	....	....	....
	NHL Totals		1098	563	846	1409	514	655	1169	740	152	45	65	3638	15.5	1928	736	1425	343		135	52	83	135	68	18	3	7

NHL All-Rookie Team (1984) • Won Lester B. Pearson Award (1989) • WEC-A All-Star Team (1989, 1990) • Named Best Forward at WEC-A (1990) • Won Conn Smythe Trophy (1998)

Played in NHL All-Star Game (1984, 1988, 1989, 1990, 1991, 1992, 1993, 1997)

• ZABRANSKY, LIBOR

Libor Zabransky D – L. 6'3", 196 lbs. b: Brno, Czech., 11/25/1973. St. Louis' 8th choice, 209th overall, in 1995 Entry Draft.

Season	Club	League	GP	G	A	Pts	AG	AA	APts	PIM	PP	SH	GW	S	%	TGF	PGF	TGA	PGA	+/–	GP	G	A	Pts	PIM	PP	SH	GW
1994-95	HC Ceske Budejovice	Czech.	44	2	6	8	....	....	....	54	....	....	....	....	....	....	....	....	....	....	9	0	4	4	6	....	....	....
1995-96	HC Ceske Budejovice	Czech.	40	4	7	11	....	....	....	....	....	....	....	....	....	....	....	....	....	....	10	0	1	1	....	....	....	....
1996-97	St. Louis Blues	NHL	34	1	5	6	1	4	5	44	0	0	1	26	3.8	23	3	31	10	–1	....	....	....	....	....	....	....	....
	Worcester IceCats	AHL	23	3	6	9	....	....	....	24	....	....	....	....	....	....	....	....	....	....	5	2	5	7	6	....	....	....
1997-98	St. Louis Blues	NHL	6	0	1	1	0	1	1	6	0	0	0	2	0.0	1	1	3	0	–3	....	....	....	....	....	....	....	....
	Worcester IceCats	AHL	54	2	17	19	....	....	....	61	....	....	....	....	....	....	....	....	....	....	6	1	1	2	8	....	....	....
	NHL Totals		40	1	6	7	1	5	6	50	0	0	1	28	3.6	24	4	34	10		....	....	....	....	....	....	....	....

• ZAHARKO, MILES

Miles Zaharko D – L. 6', 197 lbs. b: Mannville, Alta., 4/30/1957. Atlanta's 2nd choice, 20th overall, in 1977 Amateur Draft.

Season	Club	League	GP	G	A	Pts	AG	AA	APts	PIM	PP	SH	GW	S	%	TGF	PGF	TGA	PGA	+/–	GP	G	A	Pts	PIM	PP	SH	GW
1974-75	Vermilion Bruins	AJHL	60	40	44	84	....	....	....	110	....	....	....	....	....	....	....	....	....	....	....	....	....	....	....	....	....	....
1975-76	New Westminster Bruins	WCJHL	70	10	44	54	....	....	....	45	....	....	....	....	....	....	....	....	....	....	17	2	5	7	20	....	....	....
1976-77	New Westminster Bruins	WCJHL	72	14	48	62	....	....	....	68	....	....	....	....	....	....	....	....	....	....	14	1	10	11	20	....	....	....
1977-78	Atlanta Flames	NHL	71	1	19	20	1	15	16	26	0	0	0	54	1.9	57	2	77	9	–13	1	0	0	0	0	0	0	0
	Nova Scotia Voyageurs	AHL	8	0	3	3	....	....	....	6	....	....	....	....	....	....	....	....	....	....	....	....	....	....	....	....	....	....
1978-79	Chicago Black Hawks	NHL	1	0	0	0	0	0	0	0	0	0	0	0	0.0	0	0	0	0	0	....	....	....	....	....	....	....	....
	Tulsa Oilers	CHL	54	2	20	22	....	....	....	28	....	....	....	....	....	....	....	....	....	....	....	....	....	....	....	....	....	....
	New Brunswick Hawks	AHL	13	1	6	7	....	....	....	2	....	....	....	....	....	....	....	....	....	....	5	1	4	5	2	....	....	....
1979-80	New Brunswick Hawks	AHL	77	2	20	22	....	....	....	34	....	....	....	....	....	....	....	....	....	....	17	2	14	16	16	....	....	....
1980-81	Chicago Black Hawks	NHL	42	3	11	14	2	8	10	40	0	0	1	58	5.2	58	4	52	20	+22	2	0	0	0	0	0	0	0
	New Brunswick Hawks	AHL	33	7	18	25	....	....	....	27	....	....	....	....	....	....	....	....	....	....	....	....	....	....	....	....	....	....
1981-82	Chicago Black Hawks	NHL	15	1	2	3	1	1	2	18	0	0	0	20	5.0	11	0	17	5	–1	....	....	....	....	....	....	....	....
	New Brunswick Hawks	AHL	52	6	12	18	....	....	....	50	....	....	....	....	....	....	....	....	....	....	15	0	9	9	4	....	....	....
1982-83	Springfield Indians	AHL	54	6	18	24	....	....	....	20	....	....	....	....	....	....	....	....	....	....	....	....	....	....	....	....	....	....
1983-84	Duisburg	Germany	12	4	3	7	....	....	....	22	....	....	....	....	....	....	....	....	....	....	....	....	....	....	....	....	....	....
	NHL Totals		129	5	32	37	4	24	28	84	0	0	1	132	3.8	126	6	146	34		3	0	0	0	0	0	0	0

AHL Second All-Star Team (1982)

Traded to **Chicago** by **Atlanta** with Tom Lysiak, Pat Ribble, Greg Fox and Harold Phillipoff for Ivan Bolderiv, Phil Russell and Darcy Roya, March 13, 1979. Claimed by Chicago as fill in Expansion Draft, June 13, 1979.

• ZAINE, ROD

Rod "Zainer" Zaine C – L. 5'10", 180 lbs. b: Ottawa, Ont., 5/18/1946.

Season	Club	League	GP	G	A	Pts	AG	AA	APts	PIM	PP	SH	GW	S	%	TGF	PGF	TGA	PGA	+/–	GP	G	A	Pts	PIM	PP	SH	GW
1963-64	Oshawa Generals	OHA	55	6	11	17	....	....	....	32	....	....	....	....	....	....	....	....	....	....	2	0	0	0	0	....	....	....
1964-65	Ottawa Montagnards	City Sr.	24	18	31	49	....	....	....	56	....	....	....	....	....	....	....	....	....	....	....	....	....	....	....	....	....	....
1965-66	Smith's Falls Bears	City Jr.	34	35	56	91	....	....	....	46	....	....	....	....	....	....	....	....	....	....	....	....	....	....	....	....	....	....
1966-67	Clinton Comets	EHL	72	13	23	36	....	....	....	16	....	....	....	....	....	....	....	....	....	....	9	1	3	4	0	....	....	....
1967-68	Clinton Comets	EHL	72	24	53	77	....	....	....	68	....	....	....	....	....	....	....	....	....	....	14	5	7	12	5	....	....	....
1968-69	Ottawa Nationals	OHA Sr.	6	3	1	4	....	....	....	4	....	....	....	....	....	....	....	....	....	....	....	....	....	....	....	....	....	....
1969-70	Baltimore Clippers	AHL	53	19	23	42	....	....	....	36	....	....	....	....	....	....	....	....	....	....	5	1	2	3	4	....	....	....
1970-71	Pittsburgh Penguins	NHL	37	8	5	13	8	4	12	21	2	0	0	34	23.5	20	3	25	0	–8	....	....	....	....	....	....	....	....
	Baltimore Clippers	AHL	8	1	2	3	....	....	....	4	....	....	....	....	....	....	....	....	....	....	....	....	....	....	....	....	....	....
	Amarillo Wranglers	CHL	27	4	11	15	....	....	....	20	....	....	....	....	....	....	....	....	....	....	....	....	....	....	....	....	....	....
1971-72	Buffalo Sabres	NHL	24	2	1	3	2	1	3	4	0	0	1	23	8.7	8	0	23	1	–14	....	....	....	....	....	....	....	....
	Cincinnati Swords	AHL	32	8	15	23	....	....	....	6	....	....	....	....	....	....	....	....	....	....	10	5	5	10	10	....	....	....
1972-73	Chicago Cougars	WHA	74	3	14	17	....	....	....	25	....	....	....	....	....	....	....	....	....	....	....	....	....	....	....	....	....	....
1973-74	Chicago Cougars	WHA	78	5	13	18	....	....	....	17	....	....	....	....	....	....	....	....	....	....	18	2	1	3	2	....	....	....
1974-75	Chicago Cougars	WHA	68	3	6	9	....	....	....	16	....	....	....	....	....	....	....	....	....	....	....	....	....	....	....	....	....	....
	NHL Totals		61	10	6	16	10	5	15	25	2	0	1	57	17.5	28	3	48	1		....	....	....	....	....	....	....	....
	Other Major League Totals		220	11	33	44	....	....	....	58	....	....	....	....	....	....	....	....	....	....	18	2	1	3	2	....	....	....

Claimed by **Buffalo** from **Pittsburgh** in Intra-League Draft, June 8, 1971. Claimed by **Atlanta** from **Buffalo** in Expansion Draft, June 6, 1972. Selected by **Chicago** (WHA) in 1972 WHA General Player Draft, February 12, 1972.

• ZALAPSKI, ZARLEY

Zarley Zalapski D – L. 6'1", 215 lbs. b: Edmonton, Alta., 4/22/1968. Pittsburgh's 1st choice, 4th overall, in 1986 Entry Draft.

Season	Club	League	GP	G	A	Pts	AG	AA	APts	PIM	PP	SH	GW	S	%	TGF	PGF	TGA	PGA	+/–	GP	G	A	Pts	PIM	PP	SH	GW
1984-85	Fort Saskatchewan Traders	AJHL	23	17	30	47	....	....	....	14	....	....	....	....	....	....	....	....	....	....	....	....	....	....	....	....	....	....
1985-86	Fort Saskatchewan Traders	AJHL	27	20	33	53	....	....	....	46	....	....	....	....	....	....	....	....	....	....	....	....	....	....	....	....	....	....
	Canada	Nat-Team	32	2	4	6	....	....	....	10	....	....	....	....	....	....	....	....	....	....	....	....	....	....	....	....	....	....

			REGULAR SEASON																		PLAYOFFS							
Season	Club	League	GP	G	A	Pts	AG	AA	APts	PIM	PP	SH	GW	S	%	TGF	PGF	TGA	PGA	+/–	GP	G	A	Pts	PIM	PP	SH	GW
1986-87	Canada	Nat-Team	74	11	29	40	....	....	....	28	....	....	....	....	....	....	....	....	....	....	....	....	....	....	....	....	....	....
	Canada	WEC-A	10	0	3	3	....	....	....	2	....	....	....	....	....	....	....	....	....	....	....	....	....	....	....	....	....	....
1987-88	Canada	Nat-Team	47	3	13	16	....	....	....	32	....	....	....	....	....	....	....	....	....	....	....	....	....	....	....	....	....	....
	Canada	Olympics	8	1	3	4	....	....	....	2	....	....	....	....	....	....	....	....	....	....	....	....	....	....	....	....	....	....
	Pittsburgh Penguins	**NHL**	**15**	**3**	**8**	**11**	**3**	**6**	**9**	**7**	**0**	**0**	**0**	**31**	**9.7**	**29**	**6**	**21**	**8**	**+10**	....	....	....	....	....	....	....	....
1988-89	**Pittsburgh Penguins**	**NHL**	**58**	**12**	**33**	**45**	**10**	**23**	**33**	**57**	**5**	**1**	**2**	**95**	**12.6**	**120**	**61**	**72**	**22**	**+9**	**11**	**1**	**8**	**9**	**13**	**1**	**0**	**0**
1989-90	**Pittsburgh Penguins**	**NHL**	**51**	**6**	**25**	**31**	**5**	**18**	**23**	**37**	**5**	**0**	**2**	**85**	**7.1**	**74**	**36**	**74**	**22**	**–14**	....	....	....	....	....	....	....	....
1990-91	**Pittsburgh Penguins**	**NHL**	**66**	**12**	**36**	**48**	**11**	**27**	**38**	**59**	**5**	**1**	**1**	**135**	**8.9**	**103**	**35**	**84**	**31**	**+15**	....	....	....	....	....	....	....	....
	Hartford Whalers	**NHL**	**11**	**3**	**3**	**6**	**3**	**2**	**5**	**6**	**3**	**0**	**0**	**21**	**14.3**	**14**	**8**	**13**	**0**	**–7**	**6**	**1**	**3**	**4**	**8**	**0**	**0**	**1**
1991-92	**Hartford Whalers**	**NHL**	**79**	**20**	**37**	**57**	**18**	**28**	**46**	**120**	**4**	**0**	**3**	**230**	**8.7**	**132**	**52**	**112**	**25**	**–7**	**7**	**2**	**3**	**5**	**6**	**0**	**0**	**0**
1992-93	**Hartford Whalers**	**NHL**	**83**	**14**	**51**	**65**	**12**	**35**	**47**	**94**	**8**	**1**	**0**	**192**	**7.3**	**134**	**66**	**157**	**55**	**–34**	....	....	....	....	....	....	....	....
1993-94	**Hartford Whalers**	**NHL**	**56**	**7**	**30**	**37**	**7**	**23**	**30**	**56**	**0**	**0**	**0**	**121**	**5.8**	**76**	**31**	**68**	**17**	**–6**	....	....	....	....	....	....	....	....
	Calgary Flames	**NHL**	**13**	**3**	**7**	**10**	**3**	**5**	**8**	**18**	**1**	**0**	**1**	**35**	**8.6**	**22**	**14**	**12**	**4**	**0**	**7**	**0**	**3**	**3**	**2**	**0**	**0**	**0**
1994-95	**Calgary Flames**	**NHL**	**48**	**4**	**24**	**28**	**7**	**35**	**42**	**46**	**1**	**0**	**1**	**76**	**5.3**	**61**	**12**	**51**	**11**	**+9**	**7**	**0**	**4**	**4**	**4**	**0**	**0**	**0**
1995-96	**Calgary Flames**	**NHL**	**80**	**12**	**17**	**29**	**12**	**14**	**26**	**115**	**5**	**0**	**1**	**145**	**8.3**	**107**	**30**	**105**	**39**	**+11**	**4**	**0**	**1**	**1**	**10**	**0**	**0**	**0**
1996-97	**Calgary Flames**	**NHL**	**2**	**0**	**0**	**0**	**0**	**0**	**0**	**0**	**0**	**0**	**0**	**7**	**0.0**	**1**	**0**	**3**	**1**	**–1**	....	....	....	....	....	....	....	....
1997-98	**Calgary Flames**	**NHL**	**35**	**2**	**7**	**9**	**2**	**7**	**9**	**41**	**2**	**0**	**1**	**46**	**4.3**	**31**	**11**	**37**	**5**	**–12**	....	....	....	....	....	....	....	....
	Montreal Canadiens	**NHL**	**28**	**1**	**5**	**6**	**1**	**5**	**6**	**22**	**0**	**1**	**0**	**27**	**3.7**	**15**	**2**	**21**	**7**	**–1**	**6**	**0**	**1**	**1**	**4**	**0**	**0**	**0**
	NHL Totals		**625**	**99**	**283**	**382**	**94**	**228**	**322**	**678**	**39**	**4**	**12**	**1246**	**7.9**	**919**	**364**	**830**	**247**		**48**	**4**	**23**	**27**	**47**	**1**	**0**	**1**

NHL All-Rookie Team (1989)

Played in NHL All-Star Game (1993)

Traded to **Hartford** by **Pittsburgh** with John Cullen and Jeff Parker for Ron Francis, Grant Jennings and Ulf Samuelsson, March 4, 1991. Traded to **Calgary** by **Hartford** with James Patrick and Michael Nylander for Gary Suter, Paul Ranheim and Ted Drury, March 10, 1994. Traded to **Montreal** by **Calgary** with Jonas Hoglund for Valeri Bure and Montreal's 4th round choice (Shaun Sutter) in 1998 Entry Draft, February 1, 1998.

• ZAMUNER, ROB

Rob Zamuner LW – L. 6'2", 206 lbs. b: Oakville, Ont., 9/17/1969. NY Rangers' 3rd choice, 45th overall, in 1989 Entry Draft.

Season	Club	League	GP	G	A	Pts	AG	AA	APts	PIM	PP	SH	GW	S	%	TGF	PGF	TGA	PGA	+/–	GP	G	A	Pts	PIM	PP	SH	GW
1986-87	Guelph Platers	OHL	62	6	15	21	....	....	....	8	....	....	....	....	....	....	....	....	....	....	....	....	....	....	....	....	....	....
1987-88	Guelph Platers	OHL	58	20	41	61	....	....	....	18	....	....	....	....	....	....	....	....	....	....	....	....	....	....	....	....	....	....
1988-89	Guelph Platers	OHL	66	46	65	111	....	....	....	38	....	....	....	....	....	....	....	....	....	....	7	5	5	10	9	....	....	....
1989-90	Flint Spirits	IHL	77	44	35	79	....	....	....	32	....	....	....	....	....	....	....	....	....	....	4	1	0	1	6	....	....	....
1990-91	Binghamton Rangers	AHL	80	25	58	83	....	....	....	50	....	....	....	....	....	....	....	....	....	....	9	7	6	13	35	....	....	....
1991-92	**New York Rangers**	**NHL**	**9**	**1**	**2**	**3**	**1**	**1**	**2**	**2**	**0**	**0**	**0**	**11**	**9.1**	**3**	**0**	**3**	**0**	**0**	....	....	....	....	....	....	....	....
	Binghamton Rangers	AHL	61	19	53	72	....	....	....	42	....	....	....	....	....	....	....	....	....	....	11	8	9	17	8	....	....	....
1992-93	**Tampa Bay Lightning**	**NHL**	**84**	**15**	**28**	**43**	**12**	**19**	**31**	**74**	**1**	**0**	**0**	**183**	**8.2**	**64**	**21**	**79**	**11**	**–25**	....	....	....	....	....	....	....	....
1993-94	**Tampa Bay Lightning**	**NHL**	**59**	**6**	**6**	**12**	**6**	**5**	**11**	**42**	**0**	**0**	**1**	**109**	**5.5**	**18**	**1**	**34**	**8**	**–9**	....	....	....	....	....	....	....	....
1994-95	**Tampa Bay Lightning**	**NHL**	**43**	**9**	**6**	**15**	**16**	**9**	**25**	**24**	**0**	**3**	**1**	**74**	**12.2**	**23**	**2**	**33**	**9**	**–3**	....	....	....	....	....	....	....	....
1995-96	**Tampa Bay Lightning**	**NHL**	**72**	**15**	**20**	**35**	**15**	**16**	**31**	**62**	**0**	**3**	**4**	**152**	**9.9**	**50**	**4**	**63**	**28**	**+11**	**6**	**2**	**3**	**5**	**10**	**0**	**1**	**0**
1996-97	**Tampa Bay Lightning**	**NHL**	**82**	**17**	**33**	**50**	**18**	**29**	**47**	**56**	**0**	**4**	**3**	**216**	**7.9**	**62**	**0**	**91**	**32**	**+3**	....	....	....	....	....	....	....	....
	Canada	WC-A	11	4	2	6	....	....	....	16	....	....	....	....	....	....	....	....	....	....	....	....	....	....	....	....	....	....
1997-98	**Tampa Bay Lightning**	**NHL**	**77**	**14**	**12**	**26**	**16**	**12**	**28**	**41**	**0**	**3**	**4**	**126**	**11.1**	**42**	**10**	**88**	**25**	**–31**	....	....	....	....	....	....	....	....
	Canada	Olympics	6	1	0	1	....	....	....	8	....	....	....	....	....	....	....	....	....	....	....	....	....	....	....	....	....	....
	Canada	WC-A	5	0	2	2	....	....	....	4	....	....	....	....	....	....	....	....	....	....	....	....	....	....	....	....	....	....
	NHL Totals		**426**	**77**	**107**	**184**	**84**	**91**	**175**	**301**	**1**	**13**	**13**	**871**	**8.8**	**262**	**38**	**391**	**113**		**6**	**2**	**3**	**5**	**10**	**0**	**1**	**0**

Signed as a free agent by **Tampa Bay**, July 13, 1992.

• ZANUSSI, JOE

Joe Zanussi D – R. 5'10", 180 lbs. b: Rossland, B.C., 9/25/1947.

Season	Club	League	GP	G	A	Pts	AG	AA	APts	PIM	PP	SH	GW	S	%	TGF	PGF	TGA	PGA	+/–	GP	G	A	Pts	PIM	PP	SH	GW
1966-67	Edmonton Oil Kings	WCJHL	42	11	17	28	....	....	....	33	....	....	....	....	....	....	....	....	....	....	9	2	2	4	6	....	....	....
1967-68	Swift Current Broncos	WCJHL	57	17	48	65	....	....	....	46	....	....	....	....	....	....	....	....	....	....	....	....	....	....	....	....	....	....
1968-69	Johnstown Jets	EHL	72	20	30	56	....	....	....	107	....	....	....	....	....	....	....	....	....	....	3	2	1	3	12	....	....	....
1969-70	Fort Worth Wings	CHL	56	4	9	13	....	....	....	65	....	....	....	....	....	....	....	....	....	....	7	1	0	1	16	....	....	....
1970-71	Fort Worth Wings	CHL	72	13	19	32	....	....	....	172	....	....	....	....	....	....	....	....	....	....	3	0	1	1	4	....	....	....
1971-72	Fort Worth Wings	CHL	48	4	24	28	....	....	....	69	....	....	....	....	....	....	....	....	....	....	7	0	1	1	18	....	....	....
1972-73	Winnipeg Jets	WHA	73	4	21	25	....	....	....	53	....	....	....	....	....	....	....	....	....	....	14	2	5	7	6	....	....	....
1973-74	Winnipeg Jets	WHA	76	3	22	25	....	....	....	53	....	....	....	....	....	....	....	....	....	....	4	0	0	0	0	....	....	....
1974-75	**New York Rangers**	**NHL**	**8**	**0**	**2**	**2**	**0**	**2**	**2**	**4**	**0**	**0**	**0**	**8**	**0.0**	**7**	**1**	**2**	**1**	**+5**	....	....	....	....	....	....	....	....
	Providence Reds	AHL	64	22	36	58	....	....	....	76	....	....	....	....	....	....	....	....	....	....	3	1	0	1	4	....	....	....
1975-76	**Boston Bruins**	**NHL**	**60**	**1**	**7**	**8**	**1**	**5**	**6**	**30**	**0**	**0**	**0**	**77**	**1.3**	**32**	**2**	**38**	**10**	**+2**	**4**	**0**	**1**	**1**	**2**	**0**	**0**	**0**
	Providence Reds	AHL	11	8	11	19	....	....	....	29	....	....	....	....	....	....	....	....	....	....	....	....	....	....	....	....	....	....
	Rochester Americans	AHL	2	0	1	1	....	....	....	2	....	....	....	....	....	....	....	....	....	....	....	....	....	....	....	....	....	....
1976-77	**Boston Bruins**	**NHL**	**8**	**0**	**1**	**1**	**0**	**1**	**1**	**8**	**0**	**0**	**0**	**12**	**0.0**	**8**	**0**	**8**	**1**	**+1**	....	....	....	....	....	....	....	....
	Rochester Americans	AHL	17	1	9	10	....	....	....	18	....	....	....	....	....	....	....	....	....	....	....	....	....	....	....	....	....	....
	St. Louis Blues	**NHL**	**11**	**0**	**3**	**3**	**0**	**2**	**2**	**4**	**0**	**0**	**0**	**11**	**0.0**	**5**	**2**	**10**	**1**	**–6**	....	....	....	....	....	....	....	....
	Kansas City Blues	CHL	30	4	14	18	....	....	....	26	....	....	....	....	....	....	....	....	....	....	10	2	2	4	14	....	....	....
1977-78	Salt Lake Golden Eagles	CHL	71	10	24	34	....	....	....	74	....	....	....	....	....	....	....	....	....	....	6	1	4	5	2	....	....	....
	NHL Totals		**87**	**1**	**13**	**14**	**1**	**10**	**11**	**46**	**0**	**0**	**0**	**108**	**0.9**	**52**	**5**	**58**	**13**		**4**	**0**	**1**	**1**	**2**	**0**	**0**	**0**
	Other Major League Totals		149	7	43	50	....	....	....	106	....	....	....	....	....	....	....	....	....		18	2	5	7	6	....	....	....

CHL Second All-Star Team (1971) • Shared Tommy Ivan Trophy (CHL's MVP) with Andre Dupont, Gerry Ouellette & Peter McDuffe (1971) • AHL First All-Star Team (1975) • Won Eddie Shore Award (Outstanding Defenseman - AHL) (1975) • CHL First All-Star Team (1978)

Traded to **NY Rangers** by **Detroit** with Detroit's 1st round choice (Al Blanchard) in 1972 Amateur Draft for Gary Doak and Rick Newell, May 24, 1972. Selected by **Winnipeg** (WHA) in 1972 WHA General Player Draft, February 12, 1972. Traded to **Boston** by **NY Rangers** with Brad Park and Jean Ratelle for Phil Esposito and Carol Vadnais, November 7, 1975. Traded to **St. Louis** by **Boston** for Rick Smith, December 20, 1976.

• ZANUSSI, RON

Ron Zanussi RW – R. 5'11", 180 lbs. b: Toronto, Ont., 8/31/1956. Minnesota's 4th choice, 51st overall, in 1976 Amateur Draft.

Season	Club	League	GP	G	A	Pts	AG	AA	APts	PIM	PP	SH	GW	S	%	TGF	PGF	TGA	PGA	+/–	GP	G	A	Pts	PIM	PP	SH	GW
1973-74	London Knights	OHA	65	21	20	41	....	....	....	110	....	....	....	....	....	....	....	....	....	....	....	....	....	....	....	....	....	....
1974-75	London Knights	OHA	69	34	52	86	....	....	....	123	....	....	....	....	....	....	....	....	....	....	....	....	....	....	....	....	....	....
1975-76	London Knights	OHA	40	17	19	36	....	....	....	55	....	....	....	....	....	....	....	....	....	....	5	2	1	3	8	....	....	....
1976-77	Fort Wayne Komets	IHL	77	53	33	86	....	....	....	138	....	....	....	....	....	....	....	....	....	....	9	9	6	15	20	....	....	....
1977-78	**Minnesota North Stars**	**NHL**	**68**	**15**	**17**	**32**	**14**	**14**	**28**	**89**	**4**	**0**	**2**	**97**	**15.5**	**51**	**13**	**60**	**2**	**–20**	....	....	....	....	....	....	....	....
	Fort Worth Texans	CHL	6	2	1	3	....	....	....	5	....	....	....	....	....	....	....	....	....	....	....	....	....	....	....	....	....	....
1978-79	**Minnesota North Stars**	**NHL**	**63**	**14**	**16**	**30**	**13**	**12**	**25**	**82**	**3**	**0**	**0**	**98**	**14.3**	**66**	**12**	**43**	**4**	**+5**	....	....	....	....	....	....	....	....
	Oklahoma City Stars	CHL	4	3	1	4	....	....	....	6	....	....	....	....	....	....	....	....	....	....	....	....	....	....	....	....	....	....
1979-80	**Minnesota North Stars**	**NHL**	**72**	**14**	**31**	**45**	**13**	**24**	**37**	**93**	**2**	**0**	**3**	**129**	**10.9**	**76**	**15**	**57**	**0**	**+4**	**14**	**0**	**4**	**4**	**17**	**0**	**0**	**0**
1980-81	**Minnesota North Stars**	**NHL**	**41**	**6**	**11**	**17**	**5**	**8**	**13**	**89**	**0**	**0**	**0**	**43**	**14.0**	**31**	**3**	**25**	**0**	**+3**	....	....	....	....	....	....	....	....
	Oklahoma City Stars	CHL	3	3	2	5	....	....	....	5	....	....	....	....	....	....	....	....	....	....	....	....	....	....	....	....	....	....
	Toronto Maple Leafs	**NHL**	**12**	**3**	**0**	**3**	**2**	**0**	**2**	**6**	**0**	**0**	**0**	**15**	**20.0**	**4**	**0**	**15**	**4**	**–7**	**3**	**0**	**0**	**0**	**0**	**0**	**0**	**0**
1981-82	**Toronto Maple Leafs**	**NHL**	**43**	**0**	**8**	**8**	**0**	**5**	**5**	**14**	**0**	**0**	**0**	**25**	**0.0**	**16**	**1**	**40**	**21**	**–4**	....	....	....	....	....	....	....	....
	Cincinnati Tigers	CHL	21	12	9	21	....	....	....	32	....	....	....	....	....	....	....	....	....	....	4	0	2	2	4	....	....	....
1982-83	Sherbrooke Jets	AHL	72	9	21	30	....	....	....	53	....	....	....	....	....	....	....	....	....	....	....	....	....	....	....	....	....	....
1983-84	St. Catharines Saints	AHL	54	4	15	19	....	....	....	59	....	....	....	....	....	....	....	....	....	....	....	....	....	....	....	....	....	....
	NHL Totals		**299**	**52**	**83**	**135**	**47**	**63**	**110**	**373**	**9**	**0**	**5**	**407**	**12.8**	**234**	**44**	**240**	**31**		**17**	**0**	**4**	**4**	**17**	**0**	**0**	**0**

Won Garry F. Longman Memorial Trophy (Top Rookie - IHL) (Tied with Garth MacGuigan) (1977)

Claimed by **Minnesota** as a fill-in during **Cleveland-Minnesota** Dispersal Draft, June 15, 1978. Traded to **Toronto** by **Minnesota** with Minnesota's 3rd round choice (Ernie Godden) in 1981 Entry Draft for Toronto's 2nd round choice (Dave Donnelly) in 1981 Entry Draft, March 10, 1981.

• ZAVISHA, BRAD

Brad Zavisha LW – L. 6'2", 205 lbs. b: Hines Creek, Alta., 1/4/1972. Quebec's 3rd choice, 43rd overall, in 1990 Entry Draft.

Season	Club	League	GP	G	A	Pts	AG	AA	APts	PIM	PP	SH	GW	S	%	TGF	PGF	TGA	PGA	+/–	GP	G	A	Pts	PIM	PP	SH	GW
1988-89	Seattle Thunderbirds	WHL	52	8	13	21	....	....	....	43	....	....	....	....	....	....	....	....	....	....	....	....	....	....	....	....	....	....
1989-90	Seattle Thunderbirds	WHL	69	22	38	60	....	....	....	124	....	....	....	....	....	....	....	....	....	....	13	1	6	7	16	....	....	....
1990-91	Seattle Thunderbirds	WHL	24	15	12	27	....	....	....	40	....	....	....	....	....	....	....	....	....	....	....	....	....	....	....	....	....	....
	Portland Winter Hawks	WHL	48	25	22	47	....	....	....	41	....	....	....	....	....	....	....	....	....	....	....	....	....	....	....	....	....	....

			REGULAR SEASON																		PLAYOFFS							
Season	Club	League	GP	G	A	Pts	AG	AA	APts	PIM	PP	SH	GW	S	%	TGF	PGF	TGA	PGA	+/–	GP	G	A	Pts	PIM	PP	SH	GW
1991-92	Portland Winter Hawks	WHL	11	7	4	11	....	....	....	18	....	....	....	....	....	....	....	....	....	....	....	....	....	....	....	....	....	....
	Lethbridge Broncos	WHL	59	44	40	84	....	....	....	160	....	....	....	....	....	....	....	....	....	....	5	3	1	4	18	....	....	....
1992-93			DID NOT PLAY – INJURED																									
1993-94	**Edmonton Oilers**	**NHL**	**2**	**0**	**0**	**0**	**0**	**0**	**0**	**0**	**0**	**0**	**0**	**1**	**0.0**	**0**	**0**	**2**	**0**	**–2**	....	....	....	....	....	....	....	....
	Cape Breton Oilers	AHL	58	19	15	34	....	....	....	114	....	....	....	....	....	....	....	....	....	....	2	0	0	0	2	....	....	....
1994-95	Cape Breton Oilers	AHL	62	13	20	33	....	....	....	55	....	....	....	....	....	....	....	....	....	....	....	....	....	....	....	....	....	....
	Hershey Bears	AHL	9	3	0	3	....	....	....	12	....	....	....	....	....	....	....	....	....	....	....	....	....	....	....	....	....	....
1995-96	Hershey Bears	AHL	5	1	0	1	....	....	....	2	....	....	....	....	....	....	....	....	....	....	....	....	....	....	....	....	....	....
	Michigan K-Wings	IHL	5	1	0	1	....	....	....	2	....	....	....	....	....	....	....	....	....	....	....	....	....	....	....	....	....	....
1996-97	Manchester Storm	Britain	40	10	13	23	....	....	....	18	....	....	....	....	....	....	....	....	....	....	6	1	0	1	0	....	....	....
	NHL Totals		**2**	**0**	**0**	**0**	**0**	**0**	**0**	**0**	**0**	**0**	**0**	**1**	**0.0**	**0**	**0**	**2**	**0**		....	....	....	....	....	....	....	....

WHL East First All-Star Team (1992)

Traded to **Edmonton** by **Quebec** with Ron Tugnutt for Martin Rucinsky, March 10, 1992. • Missed entire 1992-93 season with knee injury. Traded to **Philadelphia** by **Edmonton** with Edmonton's 6th round choice (Jamie Sokolosky) in 1995 Entry Draft for Ryan McGill, March 13, 1995.

• ZEDNIK, RICHARD

Richard Zednik LW – L. 5'11", 172 lbs. b: Bystrica, Czech., 1/6/1976. Washington's 10th choice, 249th overall, in 1994 Entry Draft.

1993-94	B. Bystrica	Slov. 2	25	3	6	9	....	....	....	....	....	....	....	....	....	....	....	....	....	....	....	....	....	....	....	....	....	....
1994-95	Portland Winter Hawks	WHL	65	35	51	86	....	....	....	89	....	....	....	....	....	....	....	....	....	....	9	5	5	10	20	....	....	....
1995-96	Portland Winter Hawks	WHL	61	44	37	81	....	....	....	154	....	....	....	....	....	....	....	....	....	....	7	8	4	12	23	....	....	....
	Slovakia	WJC-A	6	5	2	7	....	....	....	10	....	....	....	....	....	....	....	....	....	....	....	....	....	....	....	....	....	....
	Washington Capitals	**NHL**	**1**	**0**	**0**	**0**	**0**	**0**	**0**	**0**	**0**	**0**	**0**	**0**	**0.0**	**0**	**0**	**0**	**0**	**0**	....	....	....	....	....	....	....	....
	Portland Pirates	AHL	1	1	1	2	....	....	....	0	....	....	....	....	....	....	....	....	....	....	21	4	5	9	26	....	....	....
1996-97	Slovakia	W Cup	3	0	0	0	....	....	....	0	....	....	....	....	....	....	....	....	....	....	....	....	....	....	....	....	....	....
	Washington Capitals	**NHL**	**11**	**2**	**1**	**3**	**2**	**1**	**3**	**4**	**1**	**0**	**0**	**21**	**9.5**	**5**	**2**	**8**	**0**	**–5**	....	....	....	....	....	....	....	....
	Portland Pirates	AHL	56	15	20	35	....	....	....	70	....	....	....	....	....	....	....	....	....	....	5	1	0	1	6	....	....	....
1997-98	**Washington Capitals**	**NHL**	**65**	**17**	**9**	**26**	**20**	**9**	**29**	**28**	**2**	**0**	**2**	**148**	**11.5**	**37**	**5**	**34**	**0**	**–2**	**17**	**7**	**3**	**10**	**16**	**2**	**0**	**0**
	NHL Totals		**77**	**19**	**10**	**29**	**22**	**10**	**32**	**32**	**3**	**0**	**2**	**169**	**11.2**	**42**	**7**	**42**	**0**		**17**	**7**	**3**	**10**	**16**	**2**	**0**	**0**

WHL West Second All-Star Team (1996)

• ZEIDEL, LARRY

Larry "The Rock" Zeidel D – L. 5'11", 185 lbs. b: Montreal, Que., 6/1/1928.

1944-45	Porcupine Combines	NOHA	....	2	1	3	....	....	....	2	....	....	....	....	....	....	....	....	....	....	....	....	....	....	....	....	....	....
1945-46	Verdun Maple Leafs	QJHL	17	2	7	9	....	....	....	34	....	....	....	....	....	....	....	....	....	....	3	1	1	2	2	....	....	....
1946-47	Barrie Flyers	OHA	28	7	13	20	....	....	....	48	....	....	....	....	....	....	....	....	....	....	5	2	0	2	0	....	....	....
1947-48	Quebec Aces	QSHL	48	7	20	27	....	....	....	82	....	....	....	....	....	....	....	....	....	....	10	1	3	4	13	....	....	....
1948-49	Quebec Aces	QSHL	52	4	18	22	....	....	....	92	....	....	....	....	....	....	....	....	....	....	....	....	....	....	....	....	....	....
1949-50	Quebec Aces	QSHL	55	7	19	26	....	....	....	*176	....	....	....	....	....	....	....	....	....	....	13	1	4	5	*49	....	....	....
1950-51	Saskatoon Quakers	SSHL	58	5	27	32	....	....	....	*169	....	....	....	....	....	....	....	....	....	....	12	3	3	6	*38	....	....	....
1951-52	**Detroit Red Wings**	**NHL**	**19**	**1**	**0**	**1**	**1**	**0**	**1**	**14**	....	....	....	....	....	....	....	....	....	....	**5**	**0**	**0**	**0**	**0**	....	....	....
	Indianapolis Capitals	AHL	43	6	17	23	....	....	....	99	....	....	....	....	....	....	....	....	....	....	....	....	....	....	....	....	....	....
1952-53	**Detroit Red Wings**	**NHL**	**9**	**0**	**0**	**0**	**0**	**0**	**0**	**8**	....	....	....	....	....	....	....	....	....	....	....	....	....	....	....	....	....	....
	Edmonton Flyers	WHL	59	4	22	26	....	....	....	114	....	....	....	....	....	....	....	....	....	....	15	2	6	8	*26	....	....	....
1953-54	**Chicago Black Hawks**	**NHL**	**64**	**1**	**6**	**7**	**2**	**8**	**10**	**102**	....	....	....	....	....	....	....	....	....	....	....	....	....	....	....	....	....	....
1954-55	Edmonton Flyers	WHL	70	10	40	50	....	....	....	142	....	....	....	....	....	....	....	....	....	....	9	2	5	7	2	....	....	....
1955-56	Hershey Bears	AHL	56	5	27	32	....	....	....	128	....	....	....	....	....	....	....	....	....	....	....	....	....	....	....	....	....	....
1956-57	Hershey Bears	AHL	64	9	19	28	....	....	....	*211	....	....	....	....	....	....	....	....	....	....	7	0	5	5	21	....	....	....
1957-58	Hershey Bears	AHL	58	2	16	18	....	....	....	152	....	....	....	....	....	....	....	....	....	....	11	0	6	6	20	....	....	....
1958-59	Hershey Bears	AHL	67	8	24	32	....	....	....	129	....	....	....	....	....	....	....	....	....	....	13	4	6	10	*59	....	....	....
1959-60	Hershey Bears	AHL	66	5	19	24	....	....	....	*293	....	....	....	....	....	....	....	....	....	....	....	....	....	....	....	....	....	....
1960-61	Hershey Bears	AHL	70	4	25	29	....	....	....	149	....	....	....	....	....	....	....	....	....	....	8	0	2	2	8	....	....	....
1961-62	Hershey Bears	AHL	70	3	19	22	....	....	....	146	....	....	....	....	....	....	....	....	....	....	7	0	1	1	20	....	....	....
1962-63	Hershey Bears	AHL	66	4	29	33	....	....	....	127	....	....	....	....	....	....	....	....	....	....	14	1	6	7	*51	....	....	....
1963-64	Seattle Totems	WHL	66	5	19	24	....	....	....	163	....	....	....	....	....	....	....	....	....	....	....	....	....	....	....	....	....	....
	Cleveland Barons	AHL	2	0	1	1	....	....	....	2	....	....	....	....	....	....	....	....	....	....	9	0	4	4	12	....	....	....
1964-65	Seattle Totems	WHL	64	2	12	14	....	....	....	202	....	....	....	....	....	....	....	....	....	....	7	1	2	3	2	....	....	....
1965-66	Cleveland Barons	AHL	72	3	12	15	....	....	....	*162	....	....	....	....	....	....	....	....	....	....	12	1	3	4	14	....	....	....
1966-67	Cleveland Barons	AHL	72	5	24	29	....	....	....	124	....	....	....	....	....	....	....	....	....	....	....	....	....	....	....	....	....	....
1967-68	**Philadelphia Flyers**	**NHL**	**57**	**1**	**10**	**11**	**1**	**10**	**11**	**68**	**0**	**0**	**1**	**33**	**3.0**	**50**	**4**	**54**	**20**	**+12**	**7**	**0**	**1**	**1**	**12**	**0**	**0**	**0**
1968-69	**Philadelphia Flyers**	**NHL**	**9**	**0**	**0**	**0**	**0**	**0**	**0**	**6**	**0**	**0**	**0**	**4**	**0.0**	**0**	**0**	**3**	**0**	**–3**	....	....	....	....	....	....	....	....
	NHL Totals		**158**	**3**	**16**	**19**	**4**	**18**	**22**	**198**	**0**	**0**	**1**	**37**	**8.1**	**50**	**4**	**57**	**20**		**12**	**0**	**1**	**1**	**12**	**0**	**0**	**0**

WHL First All-Star Team (1955) • AHL Second All-Star Team (1959)

Traded to **Chicago** by **Detroit** for cash, August, 1953. Traded to **Detroit** by **Chicago** for cash, June, 1954. Traded to **Montreal** by **Seattle** (WHL) for cash, June, 1965. Traded to **Cleveland** (AHL) by **Montreal** for cash, June, 1965. Traded to **Philadelphia** by **Cleveland** (AHL) for cash, October 23, 1967.

• ZELEPUKIN, VALERI

Valeri Zelepukin LW – L. 6', 200 lbs. b: Voskresensk, USSR, 9/17/1968. New Jersey's 13th choice, 221st overall, in 1990 Entry Draft.

1984-85	Khimik Voskresensk	USSR	5	0	0	0	....	....	....	2	....	....	....	....	....	....	....	....	....	....	....	....	....	....	....	....	....	....
1985-86	Khimik Voskresensk	USSR	33	2	2	4	....	....	....	10	....	....	....	....	....	....	....	....	....	....	....	....	....	....	....	....	....	....
1986-87	Khimik Voskresensk	USSR	19	1	0	1	....	....	....	4	....	....	....	....	....	....	....	....	....	....	....	....	....	....	....	....	....	....
1987-88	CSKA Moscow	USSR	19	3	1	4	....	....	....	8	....	....	....	....	....	....	....	....	....	....	....	....	....	....	....	....	....	....
	Soviet Union	WJC-A	7	6	1	7	....	....	....	4	....	....	....	....	....	....	....	....	....	....	....	....	....	....	....	....	....	....
1988-89	CSKA Moscow	USSR	17	2	3	5	....	....	....	2	....	....	....	....	....	....	....	....	....	....	....	....	....	....	....	....	....	....
	CSKA Moscow	SuperS	7	2	1	3	....	....	....	0	....	....	....	....	....	....	....	....	....	....	....	....	....	....	....	....	....	....
1989-90	Khimik Voskresensk	FrTour	1	0	1	1	....	....	....	0	....	....	....	....	....	....	....	....	....	....	....	....	....	....	....	....	....	....
	Khimik Voskresensk	USSR	46	17	14	31	....	....	....	26	....	....	....	....	....	....	....	....	....	....	....	....	....	....	....	....	....	....
	Khimik Voskresensk	SuperS	6	3	1	4	....	....	....	0	....	....	....	....	....	....	....	....	....	....	....	....	....	....	....	....	....	....
1990-91	Khimik Voskresensk	USSR	34	11	6	17	....	....	....	38	....	....	....	....	....	....	....	....	....	....	....	....	....	....	....	....	....	....
	Khimik Vosresensk	SuperS	7	4	4	8	....	....	....	2	....	....	....	....	....	....	....	....	....	....	....	....	....	....	....	....	....	....
	Soviet Union	WEC-A	9	0	4	4	....	....	....	5	....	....	....	....	....	....	....	....	....	....	....	....	....	....	....	....	....	....
1991-92	**New Jersey Devils**	**NHL**	**44**	**13**	**18**	**31**	**12**	**14**	**26**	**28**	**3**	**0**	**3**	**94**	**13.8**	**49**	**10**	**28**	**0**	**+11**	**4**	**1**	**1**	**2**	**2**	**0**	**0**	**0**
	Utica Devils	AHL	22	20	9	29	....	....	....	8	....	....	....	....	....	....	....	....	....	....	....	....	....	....	....	....	....	....
1992-93	**New Jersey Devils**	**NHL**	**78**	**23**	**41**	**64**	**19**	**28**	**47**	**70**	**5**	**1**	**2**	**174**	**13.2**	**93**	**20**	**55**	**1**	**+19**	**5**	**0**	**2**	**2**	**0**	**0**	**0**	**0**
1993-94	**New Jersey Devils**	**NHL**	**82**	**26**	**31**	**57**	**24**	**24**	**48**	**70**	**8**	**0**	**0**	**155**	**16.8**	**101**	**29**	**36**	**0**	**+36**	**20**	**5**	**2**	**7**	**14**	**1**	**0**	**0**
1994-95	**New Jersey Devils**	**NHL**	**4**	**1**	**2**	**3**	**2**	**3**	**5**	**6**	**0**	**0**	**0**	**6**	**16.7**	**4**	**1**	**0**	**0**	**+3**	**18**	**1**	**2**	**3**	**12**	**0**	**0**	**1**
1995-96	**New Jersey Devils**	**NHL**	**61**	**6**	**9**	**15**	**6**	**7**	**13**	**107**	**3**	**0**	**1**	**86**	**7.0**	**22**	**6**	**29**	**3**	**–10**	....	....	....	....	....	....	....	....
1996-97	Russia	W Cup	3	0	0	0	....	....	....	20	....	....	....	....	....	....	....	....	....	....	....	....	....	....	....	....	....	....
	New Jersey Devils	**NHL**	**71**	**14**	**24**	**38**	**15**	**21**	**36**	**36**	**3**	**0**	**2**	**111**	**12.6**	**47**	**7**	**51**	**1**	**–10**	**8**	**3**	**2**	**5**	**2**	**1**	**0**	**1**
1997-98	**New Jersey Devils**	**NHL**	**35**	**2**	**8**	**10**	**2**	**8**	**10**	**32**	**0**	**0**	**0**	**54**	**3.7**	**17**	**4**	**13**	**0**	**0**	....	....	....	....	....	....	....	....
	Edmonton Oilers	**NHL**	**33**	**2**	**10**	**12**	**2**	**10**	**12**	**57**	**0**	**0**	**0**	**47**	**4.3**	**19**	**8**	**14**	**1**	**–2**	**8**	**1**	**2**	**3**	**2**	**0**	**0**	**0**
	Russia	Olympics	6	1	2	3	....	....	....	0	....	....	....	....	....	....	....	....	....	....	....	....	....	....	....	....	....	....
	NHL Totals		**408**	**87**	**143**	**230**	**82**	**115**	**197**	**406**	**22**	**1**	**8**	**727**	**12.0**	**352**	**85**	**226**	**6**		**63**	**11**	**11**	**22**	**32**	**2**	**0**	**2**

Traded to **Edmonton** by **New Jersey** with Bill Guerin for Jason Arnott and Bryan Muir, January 4, 1998.

• ZEMLAK, RICHARD

Richard Zemlak RW – R. 6'2", 190 lbs. b: Wynard, Sask., 3/3/1963. St. Louis' 9th choice, 209th overall, in 1981 Entry Draft.

1979-80	Regina Blues	SJHL	30	4	7	11	....	....	....	80	....	....	....	....	....	....	....	....	....	....	....	....	....	....	....	....	....	....
1980-81	Spokane Flyers	WHL	72	19	19	38	....	....	....	132	....	....	....	....	....	....	....	....	....	....	4	1	1	2	6	....	....	....
1981-82	Spokane Flyers	WHL	26	9	20	29	....	....	....	113	....	....	....	....	....	....	....	....	....	....	....	....	....	....	....	....	....	....
	Winnipeg Clubs	WHL	2	1	2	3	....	....	....	0	....	....	....	....	....	....	....	....	....	....	....	....	....	....	....	....	....	....
	Medicine Hat Tigers	WHL	41	11	20	31	....	....	....	70	....	....	....	....	....	....	....	....	....	....	....	....	....	....	....	....	....	....
	Salt Lake Golden Eagles	CHL	6	0	0	0	....	....	....	2	....	....	....	....	....	....	....	....	....	....	1	0	0	0	0	....	....	....
1982-83	Medicine Hat Tigers	WHL	51	20	17	37	....	....	....	119	....	....	....	....	....	....	....	....	....	....	....	....	....	....	....	....	....	....
	Nanaimo Islanders	WHL	18	2	8	10	....	....	....	50	....	....	....	....	....	....	....	....	....	....	....	....	....	....	....	....	....	....

			REGULAR SEASON																		PLAYOFFS							
Season	Club	League	GP	G	A	Pts	AG	AA	APts	PIM	PP	SH	GW	S	%	TGF	PGF	TGA	PGA	+/–	GP	G	A	Pts	PIM	PP	SH	GW
1983-84	Montana Magic	CHL	14	2	2	4	....	....	....	17	....	....	....	....	....	....	....	....	....	....	....	....	....	....	....	....	....	....
	Toledo Goaldiggers	IHL	45	8	19	27	....	....	....	101	....	....	....	....	....	....	....	....	....	....	....	....	....	....	....	....	....	....
1984-85	Muskegon Mohawks	IHL	64	19	18	37	....	....	....	223	....	....	....	....	....	....	....	....	....	....	17	5	4	9	68	....	....	....
	Fredericton Express	AHL	16	3	4	7	....	....	....	59	....	....	....	....	....	....	....	....	....	....	....	....	....	....	....	....	....	....
1985-86	Fredericton Express	AHL	58	6	5	11	....	....	....	305	....	....	....	....	....	....	....	....	....	....	3	0	0	0	49	....	....	....
	Muskegon Lumberjacks	IHL	3	1	2	3	....	....	....	36	....	....	....	....	....	....	....	....	....	....	....	....	....	....	....	....	....	....
1986-87	**Quebec Nordiques**	**NHL**	**20**	**0**	**2**	**2**	**0**	**1**	**1**	**47**	**0**	**0**	**0**	**2**	**0.0**	**2**	**0**	**2**	**0**	**0**	....	....	....	....	....	....	....	....
	Fredericton Express	AHL	29	9	6	15	....	....	....	201	....	....	....	....	....	....	....	....	....	....	....	....	....	....	....	....	....	....
1987-88	**Minnesota North Stars**	**NHL**	**54**	**1**	**4**	**5**	**1**	**3**	**4**	**307**	**0**	**0**	**0**	**19**	**5.3**	**7**	**0**	**22**	**0**	**–15**	....	....	....	....	....	....	....	....
1988-89	**Minnesota North Stars**	**NHL**	**3**	**0**	**0**	**0**	**0**	**0**	**0**	**13**	**0**	**0**	**0**	**1**	**0.0**	**1**	**0**	**0**	**0**	**+1**	....	....	....	....	....	....	....	....
	Kalamazoo Wings	IHL	2	1	3	4	....	....	....	22	....	....	....	....	....	....	....	....	....	....	....	....	....	....	....	....	....	....
	Pittsburgh Penguins	**NHL**	**31**	**0**	**0**	**0**	**0**	**0**	**0**	**135**	**0**	**0**	**0**	**2**	**0.0**	**0**	**0**	**4**	**0**	**–4**	**1**	**0**	**0**	**0**	**10**	**0**	**0**	**0**
	Muskegon Lumberjacks	IHL	18	5	4	9	....	....	....	55	....	....	....	....	....	....	....	....	....	....	8	1	1	2	35	....	....	....
1989-90	**Pittsburgh Penguins**	**NHL**	**19**	**1**	**5**	**6**	**1**	**4**	**5**	**43**	**1**	**0**	**0**	**11**	**9.1**	**7**	**1**	**13**	**1**	**–6**	....	....	....	....	....	....	....	....
	Muskegon Lumberjacks	IHL	61	17	39	56	....	....	....	263	....	....	....	....	....	....	....	....	....	....	14	3	4	7	*105	....	....	....
1990-91	Salt Lake Golden Eagles	IHL	59	14	20	34	....	....	....	194	....	....	....	....	....	....	....	....	....	....	3	0	1	1	14	....	....	....
1991-92	**Calgary Flames**	**NHL**	**5**	**0**	**1**	**1**	**0**	**1**	**1**	**42**	**0**	**0**	**0**	**4**	**0.0**	**1**	**0**	**3**	**0**	**–2**	....	....	....	....	....	....	....	....
	Salt Lake Golden Eagles	IHL	60	5	14	19	....	....	....	204	....	....	....	....	....	....	....	....	....	....	3	0	0	0	0	....	....	....
1992-93	Milwaukee Admirals	IHL	62	3	9	12	....	....	....	301	....	....	....	....	....	....	....	....	....	....	2	1	1	2	6	....	....	....
1993-94	Milwaukee Admirals	IHL	61	3	8	11	....	....	....	243	....	....	....	....	....	....	....	....	....	....	2	0	0	0	16	....	....	....
	NHL Totals		**132**	**2**	**12**	**14**	**2**	**9**	**11**	**587**	**1**	**0**	**0**	**39**	**5.1**	**18**	**1**	**44**	**1**		**1**	**0**	**0**	**0**	**10**	**0**	**0**	**0**

Rights traded to **Quebec** by **St. Louis** with rights to Dan Wood and Roger Hagglund for cash, June 22, 1984. Claimed by **Minnesota** from **Quebec** in Waiver Draft, October 5, 1987. Traded to **Pittsburgh** by **Minnesota** for rights to Rob Gaudreau, November 1, 1988. Signed as a free agent by **Calgary**, November 8, 1990.

• ZENT, JASON

Jason Zent LW – L. 5′11″, 204 lbs. b: Buffalo, NY, 4/15/1971. NY Islanders' 3rd choice, 44th overall, in 1989 Entry Draft.

Season	Club	League	GP	G	A	Pts	AG	AA	APts	PIM	PP	SH	GW	S	%	TGF	PGF	TGA	PGA	+/–	GP	G	A	Pts	PIM	PP	SH	GW
1987-88	Nichols High School	H.S.	21	20	16	36	....	....	....	28	....	....	....	....	....	....	....	....	....	....	....	....	....	....	....	....	....	....
1988-89	Nichols High School	H.S.	29	49	32	81	....	....	....	26	....	....	....	....	....	....	....	....	....	....	....	....	....	....	....	....	....	....
1989-90	Nichols High School	H.S.	STATISTICS NOT AVAILABLE																									
	United States	WJC-A	7	1	0	1	....	....	....	4	....	....	....	....	....	....	....	....	....	....	....	....	....	....	....	....	....	....
1990-91	University of Wisconsin	WCHA	39	19	18	37	....	....	....	51	....	....	....	....	....	....	....	....	....	....	....	....	....	....	....	....	....	....
1991-92	University of Wisconsin	WCHA	39	22	17	39	....	....	....	128	....	....	....	....	....	....	....	....	....	....	....	....	....	....	....	....	....	....
1992-93	University of Wisconsin	WCHA	40	26	12	38	....	....	....	92	....	....	....	....	....	....	....	....	....	....	....	....	....	....	....	....	....	....
1993-94	University of Wisconsin	WCHA	42	20	21	41	....	....	....	120	....	....	....	....	....	....	....	....	....	....	....	....	....	....	....	....	....	....
1994-95	P.E.I. Senators	AHL	55	15	11	26	....	....	....	46	....	....	....	....	....	....	....	....	....	....	9	6	1	7	6	....	....	....
1995-96	P.E.I. Senators	AHL	68	14	5	19	....	....	....	61	....	....	....	....	....	....	....	....	....	....	5	2	1	3	4	....	....	....
1996-97	**Ottawa Senators**	**NHL**	**22**	**3**	**3**	**6**	**3**	**3**	**6**	**9**	**0**	**0**	**0**	**20**	**15.0**	**7**	**0**	**2**	**0**	**+5**	....	....	....	....	....	....	....	....
	Worcester IceCats	AHL	45	14	10	24	....	....	....	45	....	....	....	....	....	....	....	....	....	....	5	3	3	6	4	....	....	....
1997-98	**Ottawa Senators**	**NHL**	**3**	**0**	**0**	**0**	**0**	**0**	**0**	**4**	**0**	**0**	**0**	**1**	**0.0**	**0**	**0**	**0**	**0**	**0**	....	....	....	....	....	....	....	....
	Detroit Vipers	IHL	4	1	0	1	....	....	....	0	....	....	....	....	....	....	....	....	....	....	....	....	....	....	....	....	....	....
	Worcester IceCats	AHL	66	25	17	42	....	....	....	67	....	....	....	....	....	....	....	....	....	....	11	2	0	2	6	....	....	....
	NHL Totals		**25**	**3**	**3**	**6**	**3**	**3**	**6**	**13**	**0**	**0**	**0**	**21**	**14.3**	**7**	**0**	**2**	**0**		....	....	....	....	....	....	....	....

NCAA Championship All-Tournament Team (1992)

Traded to **Ottawa** by **NY Islanders** for Ottawa's 5th round choice (Andy Berenzweig) in 1996 Entry Draft, October 15, 1994.

• ZETTERSTROM, LARS

Lars Zetterstrom D – L. 6′1″, 100 lbs. b: Stockholm, Sweden, 11/6/1953.

Season	Club	League	GP	G	A	Pts	AG	AA	APts	PIM	PP	SH	GW	S	%	TGF	PGF	TGA	PGA	+/–	GP	G	A	Pts	PIM	PP	SH	GW
1972-73	Farjestad BK Karlstad	Sweden	14	2	4	6	....	....	....	2	....	....	....	....	....	....	....	....	....	....	13	1	4	5	0	....	....	....
1973-74	Farjestad BK Karlstad	Sweden	STATISTICS NOT AVAILABLE																									
1974-75	Farjestad BK Karlstad	Sweden	28	10	9	19	....	....	....	24	....	....	....	....	....	....	....	....	....	....	....	....	....	....	....	....	....	....
1975-76	Farjestad BK Karlstad	Sweden	35	9	6	15	....	....	....	25	....	....	....	....	....	....	....	....	....	....	....	1	0	1	2	....	....	....
1976-77	Farjestad BK Karlstad	Sweden	33	5	3	8	....	....	....	14	....	....	....	....	....	....	....	....	....	....	5	1	1	2	4	....	....	....
	Sweden	WEC-A	10	1	1	2	....	....	....	16	....	....	....	....	....	....	....	....	....	....	....	....	....	....	....	....	....	....
1977-78	Farjestad BK Karlstad	Sweden	36	6	6	12	....	....	....	42	....	....	....	....	....	....	....	....	....	....	....	....	....	....	....	....	....	....
	Sweden	WEC-A	9	0	5	5	....	....	....	4	....	....	....	....	....	....	....	....	....	....	....	....	....	....	....	....	....	....
1978-79	**Vancouver Canucks**	**NHL**	**14**	**0**	**1**	**1**	**0**	**1**	**1**	**2**	**0**	**0**	**0**	**12**	**0.0**	**3**	**1**	**13**	**1**	**–10**	....	....	....	....	....	....	....	....
	Dallas Black Hawks	CHL	58	1	33	34	....	....	....	33	....	....	....	....	....	....	....	....	....	....	9	2	4	6	6	....	....	....
1979-80	Cincinnati Stingers	CHL	27	3	14	17	....	....	....	14	....	....	....	....	....	....	....	....	....	....	....	....	....	....	....	....	....	....
1980-81	Farjestad BK Karlstad	Sweden	35	4	6	10	....	....	....	40	....	....	....	....	....	....	....	....	....	....	7	0	3	3	6	....	....	....
1981-82	Farjestad BK Karlstad	Sweden	31	5	4	9	....	....	....	45	....	....	....	....	....	....	....	....	....	....	2	0	0	0	2	....	....	....
1982-83	Farjestad BK Karlstad	Sweden	32	2	3	5	....	....	....	28	....	....	....	....	....	....	....	....	....	....	8	1	0	1	8	....	....	....
	NHL Totals		**14**	**0**	**1**	**1**	**0**	**1**	**1**	**2**	**0**	**0**	**0**	**12**	**0.0**	**3**	**1**	**13**	**1**		....	....	....	....	....	....	....	....

Signed as a free agent by **Vancouver**, June 5, 1978. Claimed by **Quebec** from **Vancouver** in Expansion Draft, June 13, 1979.

• ZETTLER, ROB

Rob Zettler D – L. 6′3″, 200 lbs. b: Sept Iles, Que., 3/8/1968. Minnesota's 5th choice, 55th overall, in 1986 Entry Draft.

Season	Club	League	GP	G	A	Pts	AG	AA	APts	PIM	PP	SH	GW	S	%	TGF	PGF	TGA	PGA	+/–	GP	G	A	Pts	PIM	PP	SH	GW
1984-85	Sault Ste. Marie Greyhounds	OHL	60	2	14	16	....	....	....	37	....	....	....	....	....	....	....	....	....	....	....	....	....	....	....	....	....	....
1985-86	Sault Ste. Marie Greyhounds	OHL	57	5	23	28	....	....	....	92	....	....	....	....	....	....	....	....	....	....	....	....	....	....	....	....	....	....
1986-87	Sault Ste. Marie Greyhounds	OHL	64	13	22	35	....	....	....	89	....	....	....	....	....	....	....	....	....	....	4	0	0	0	0	....	....	....
1987-88	Kalamazoo Wings	IHL	2	0	1	1	....	....	....	0	....	....	....	....	....	....	....	....	....	....	7	0	2	2	2	....	....	....
	Sault Ste. Marie Greyhounds	OHL	64	7	41	48	....	....	....	77	....	....	....	....	....	....	....	....	....	....	6	2	2	4	9	....	....	....
1988-89	**Minnesota North Stars**	**NHL**	**2**	**0**	**0**	**0**	**0**	**0**	**0**	**0**	**0**	**0**	**0**	**0**	**0.0**	**0**	**0**	**1**	**0**	**–1**	....	....	....	....	....	....	....	....
	Kalamazoo Wings	IHL	80	5	21	26	....	....	....	79	....	....	....	....	....	....	....	....	....	....	6	0	1	1	26	....	....	....
1989-90	**Minnesota North Stars**	**NHL**	**31**	**0**	**8**	**8**	**0**	**6**	**6**	**45**	**0**	**0**	**0**	**21**	**0.0**	**26**	**2**	**42**	**11**	**–7**	....	....	....	....	....	....	....	....
	Kalamazoo Wings	IHL	41	6	10	16	....	....	....	64	....	....	....	....	....	....	....	....	....	....	7	0	0	0	6	....	....	....
1990-91	**Minnesota North Stars**	**NHL**	**47**	**1**	**4**	**5**	**1**	**3**	**4**	**119**	**0**	**0**	**0**	**30**	**3.3**	**30**	**1**	**64**	**25**	**–10**	....	....	....	....	....	....	....	....
	Kalamazoo Wings	IHL	1	0	0	0	....	....	....	2	....	....	....	....	....	....	....	....	....	....	....	....	....	....	....	....	....	....
1991-92	**San Jose Sharks**	**NHL**	**74**	**1**	**8**	**9**	**1**	**6**	**7**	**99**	**0**	**0**	**0**	**72**	**1.4**	**59**	**2**	**112**	**32**	**–23**	....	....	....	....	....	....	....	....
1992-93	**San Jose Sharks**	**NHL**	**80**	**0**	**7**	**7**	**0**	**5**	**5**	**150**	**0**	**0**	**0**	**60**	**0.0**	**43**	**1**	**130**	**38**	**–50**	....	....	....	....	....	....	....	....
1993-94	**San Jose Sharks**	**NHL**	**42**	**0**	**3**	**3**	**0**	**2**	**2**	**65**	**0**	**0**	**0**	**28**	**0.0**	**21**	**2**	**43**	**17**	**–7**	....	....	....	....	....	....	....	....
	Philadelphia Flyers	**NHL**	**33**	**0**	**4**	**4**	**0**	**3**	**3**	**69**	**0**	**0**	**0**	**27**	**0.0**	**24**	**1**	**51**	**9**	**–19**	....	....	....	....	....	....	....	....
1994-95	**Philadelphia Flyers**	**NHL**	**32**	**0**	**1**	**1**	**0**	**1**	**1**	**34**	**0**	**0**	**0**	**17**	**0.0**	**14**	**0**	**28**	**11**	**–3**	**1**	**0**	**0**	**0**	**2**	**0**	**0**	**0**
1995-96	**Toronto Maple Leafs**	**NHL**	**29**	**0**	**1**	**1**	**0**	**1**	**1**	**48**	**0**	**0**	**0**	**11**	**0.0**	**8**	**0**	**14**	**5**	**–1**	**2**	**0**	**0**	**0**	**0**	**0**	**0**	**0**
1996-97	**Toronto Maple Leafs**	**NHL**	**48**	**2**	**12**	**14**	**2**	**11**	**13**	**51**	**0**	**0**	**0**	**31**	**6.5**	**37**	**0**	**39**	**10**	**+8**	....	....	....	....	....	....	....	....
	Utah Grizzlies	IHL	30	0	10	10	....	....	....	60	....	....	....	....	....	....	....	....	....	....	....	....	....	....	....	....	....	....
1997-98	**Toronto Maple Leafs**	**NHL**	**59**	**0**	**7**	**7**	**0**	**7**	**7**	**108**	**0**	**0**	**0**	**28**	**0.0**	**30**	**2**	**44**	**8**	**–8**	....	....	....	....	....	....	....	....
	NHL Totals		**477**	**4**	**55**	**59**	**4**	**45**	**49**	**788**	**0**	**0**	**0**	**325**	**1.2**	**292**	**11**	**568**	**166**		**3**	**0**	**0**	**0**	**2**	**0**	**0**	**0**

Claimed by **San Jose** from **Minnesota** in Dispersal Draft, May 30, 1991. Traded to **Philadelphia** by **San Jose** for Viacheslav Butsayev, February 1, 1994. Traded to **Toronto** by **Philadelphia** for Toronto's 5th round choice (Per-Ragna Bergqvist) in 1996 Entry Draft, July 8, 1995. Claimed by **Nashville** from **Toronto** in Expansion Draft, June 26, 1998.

• ZEZEL, PETER

Peter Zezel C – L. 5′11″, 200 lbs. b: Toronto, Ont., 4/22/1965. Philadelphia's 1st choice, 41st overall, in 1983 Entry Draft.

Season	Club	League	GP	G	A	Pts	AG	AA	APts	PIM	PP	SH	GW	S	%	TGF	PGF	TGA	PGA	+/–	GP	G	A	Pts	PIM	PP	SH	GW
1982-83	Toronto Marlboros	OHL	66	35	39	74	....	....	....	28	....	....	....	....	....	....	....	....	....	....	4	2	4	6	0	....	....	....
1983-84	Toronto Marlboros	OHL	68	47	86	133	....	....	....	31	....	....	....	....	....	....	....	....	....	....	9	7	5	12	4	....	....	....
1984-85	**Philadelphia Flyers**	**NHL**	**65**	**15**	**46**	**61**	**12**	**31**	**43**	**26**	**8**	**0**	**2**	**91**	**16.5**	**90**	**36**	**33**	**1**	**+22**	**19**	**1**	**8**	**9**	**28**	**1**	**0**	**0**
1985-86	**Philadelphia Flyers**	**NHL**	**79**	**17**	**37**	**54**	**14**	**25**	**39**	**76**	**4**	**0**	**4**	**144**	**11.8**	**78**	**18**	**42**	**9**	**+27**	**5**	**3**	**1**	**4**	**4**	**1**	**0**	**1**
1986-87	**Philadelphia Flyers**	**NHL**	**71**	**33**	**39**	**72**	**29**	**28**	**57**	**71**	**6**	**2**	**7**	**181**	**18.2**	**92**	**20**	**58**	**15**	**+21**	**25**	**3**	**10**	**13**	**10**	**1**	**1**	**1**
1987-88	**Philadelphia Flyers**	**NHL**	**60**	**22**	**35**	**57**	**19**	**25**	**44**	**42**	**14**	**0**	**1**	**133**	**16.5**	**80**	**37**	**49**	**13**	**+7**	**7**	**3**	**2**	**5**	**7**	**0**	**0**	**0**
1988-89	**Philadelphia Flyers**	**NHL**	**26**	**4**	**13**	**17**	**3**	**9**	**12**	**15**	**0**	**0**	**0**	**34**	**11.8**	**21**	**6**	**30**	**2**	**–13**	....	....	....	....	....	....	....	....
	St. Louis Blues	**NHL**	**52**	**17**	**36**	**53**	**14**	**25**	**39**	**27**	**5**	**1**	**4**	**115**	**14.8**	**75**	**28**	**68**	**20**	**–1**	**10**	**6**	**6**	**12**	**4**	**1**	**1**	**1**
1989-90	**St. Louis Blues**	**NHL**	**73**	**25**	**47**	**72**	**22**	**34**	**56**	**30**	**7**	**0**	**3**	**158**	**15.8**	**101**	**47**	**72**	**9**	**–9**	**12**	**1**	**7**	**8**	**4**	**1**	**0**	**0**
1990-91	**Washington Capitals**	**NHL**	**20**	**7**	**5**	**12**	**6**	**4**	**10**	**10**	**6**	**0**	**0**	**21**	**33.3**	**14**	**8**	**20**	**1**	**–13**	....	....	....	....	....	....	....	....
	Toronto Maple Leafs	**NHL**	**32**	**14**	**14**	**28**	**13**	**11**	**24**	**4**	**6**	**0**	**5**	**69**	**20.3**	**37**	**16**	**33**	**5**	**–7**	....	....	....	....	....	....	....	....
1991-92	**Toronto Maple Leafs**	**NHL**	**64**	**16**	**33**	**49**	**15**	**25**	**40**	**26**	**4**	**0**	**1**	**125**	**12.8**	**65**	**20**	**79**	**12**	**–22**	....	....	....	....	....	....	....	....
1992-93	**Toronto Maple Leafs**	**NHL**	**70**	**12**	**23**	**35**	**10**	**16**	**26**	**24**	**0**	**0**	**4**	**102**	**11.8**	**44**	**5**	**48**	**9**	**0**	**20**	**2**	**1**	**3**	**6**	**0**	**0**	**0**

Season	Club	League	GP	G	A	Pts	AG	AA	APts	PIM	PP	SH	GW	S	%	TGF	PGF	TGA	PGA	+/-	GP	G	A	Pts	PIM	PP	SH	GW
			REGULAR SEASON																		PLAYOFFS							
1993-94	Toronto Maple Leafs	NHL	41	8	8	16	7	6	13	19	0	0	0	47	17.0	21	0	34	18	+5	18	2	4	6	8	0	0	1
1994-95	Dallas Stars	NHL	30	6	5	11	11	7	18	19	0	0	1	47	12.8	13	1	28	10	–6	3	1	0	1	0	0	0	0
	Kalamazoo Wings	IHL	2	0	0	0	....	....	....	0	....	....	....	....	....	....	....	....	....	....	....	....	....	....	....	....	....	....
1995-96	St. Louis Blues	NHL	57	8	13	21	8	11	19	12	2	0	1	87	9.2	32	12	32	10	–2	10	3	0	3	2	0	1	0
1996-97	St. Louis Blues	NHL	35	4	9	13	4	8	12	12	0	0	1	49	8.2	21	2	21	8	+6	....	....	....	....	....	....	....	....
	New Jersey Devils	NHL	18	0	3	3	0	3	3	4	0	0	0	13	0.0	8	0	4	0	+4	2	0	0	0	10	0	0	0
1997-98	New Jersey Devils	NHL	5	0	3	3	0	3	3	0	0	0	0	3	0.0	3	0	2	1	+2	....	....	....	....	....	....	....	....
	Albany River Rats	AHL	35	13	37	50	....	....	....	18	....	....	....	....	....	....	....	....	....	....	....	....	....	....	....	....	....	....
	Vancouver Canucks	NHL	25	5	12	17	6	12	18	2	2	0	1	37	13.5	29	5	16	5	+13	....	....	....	....	....	....	....	....
	NHL Totals		832	213	381	594	193	283	476	419	64	3	35	1456	14.6	824	269	669	148		131	25	39	64	83	5	3	4

Traded to **St. Louis** by **Philadelphia** for Mike Bullard, November 29, 1988. Traded to **Washington** by **St. Louis** with Mike Lalor for Geoff Courtnall, July 13, 1990. Traded to **Toronto** by **Washington** with Bob Rouse for Al Iafrate, January 16, 1991. Transferred to **Dallas** by **Toronto** with Grant Marshall as compensation for Toronto's signing of free agent Mike Craig, August 10, 1994. Signed as a free agent by **St. Louis**, October 19, 1995. Traded to **New Jersey** by **St. Louis** for Chris McAlpine and New Jersey's 9th round choice in 1999 Entry Draft, February 11, 1997. Traded to **Vancouver** by **New Jersey** for Vancouver's 5th round choice (Anton But) in 1998 Entry Draft, February 5, 1998.

• ZHAMNOV, ALEXEI

Alexei Zhamnov C – L. 6'1", 195 lbs. b: Moscow, USSR, 10/1/1970. Winnipeg's 5th choice, 77th overall, in 1990 Entry Draft.

Season	Club	League	GP	G	A	Pts	AG	AA	APts	PIM	PP	SH	GW	S	%	TGF	PGF	TGA	PGA	+/-	GP	G	A	Pts	PIM	PP	SH	GW
1988-89	Moscow Dynamo	USSR	4	0	0	0	....	....	....	0	....	....	....	....	....	....	....	....	....	....	....	....	....	....	....	....	....	....
1989-90	Moscow Dynamo	FrTour	1	0	1	1	....	....	....	2	....	....	....	....	....	....	....	....	....	....	....	....	....	....	....	....	....	....
	Moscow Dynamo	USSR	43	11	6	17	....	....	....	21	....	....	....	....	....	....	....	....	....	....	....	....	....	....	....	....	....	....
	Soviet Union	WJC-A	7	6	1	7	....	....	....	6	....	....	....	....	....	....	....	....	....	....	....	....	....	....	....	....	....	....
1990-91	Moscow Dynamo	FrTour	1	0	0	0	....	....	....	0	....	....	....	....	....	....	....	....	....	....	....	....	....	....	....	....	....	....
	Moscow Dnyamo	USSR	46	16	12	28	....	....	....	24	....	....	....	....	....	....	....	....	....	....	....	....	....	....	....	....	....	....
	Moscow Dynamo	SuperS	7	1	1	2	....	....	....	0	....	....	....	....	....	....	....	....	....	....	....	....	....	....	....	....	....	....
	Soviet Union	WEC-A	10	4	5	9	....	....	....	12	....	....	....	....	....	....	....	....	....	....	....	....	....	....	....	....	....	....
1991-92	Soviet Union	C Cup	5	3	0	3	....	....	....	2	....	....	....	....	....	....	....	....	....	....	....	....	....	....	....	....	....	....
	Moscow Dynamo	CIS	39	15	21	36	....	....	....	28	....	....	....	....	....	....	....	....	....	....	....	....	....	....	....	....	....	....
	Russia	Olympics	8	0	3	3	....	....	....	8	....	....	....	....	....	....	....	....	....	....	....	....	....	....	....	....	....	....
	Russia	WC-A	6	0	0	0	....	....	....	29	....	....	....	....	....	....	....	....	....	....	....	....	....	....	....	....	....	....
1992-93	Winnipeg Jets	NHL	68	25	47	72	21	32	53	58	6	1	4	163	15.3	121	42	79	7	+7	6	0	2	2	2	0	0	0
1993-94	Winnipeg Jets	NHL	61	26	45	71	24	35	59	62	7	0	1	196	13.3	102	44	80	2	–20	....	....	....	....	....	....	....	....
1994-95	Winnipeg Jets	NHL	48	30	35	65	53	52	105	20	9	0	4	155	19.4	82	32	48	3	+5	....	....	....	....	....	....	....	....
1995-96	Winnipeg Jets	NHL	58	22	37	59	22	30	52	65	5	0	2	199	11.1	97	49	57	5	–4	6	2	1	3	8	0	0	0
1996-97	Russia	W Cup	4	0	2	2	....	....	....	6	....	....	....	....	....	....	....	....	....	....	....	....	....	....	....	....	....	....
	Chicago Blackhawks	NHL	74	20	42	62	21	37	58	56	6	1	2	208	9.6	85	28	56	17	+18	....	....	....	....	....	....	....	....
1997-98	Chicago Blackhawks	NHL	70	21	28	49	25	27	52	61	6	2	3	193	10.9	76	26	50	16	+16	....	....	....	....	....	....	....	....
	Russia	Olympics	6	2	1	3	....	....	....	2	....	....	....	....	....	....	....	....	....	....	....	....	....	....	....	....	....	....
	NHL Totals		379	144	234	378	166	213	379	322	39	4	16	1114	12.9	563	221	370	50		12	2	3	5	10	0	0	0

NHL Second All-Star Team (1995)

Traded to **Chicago** by **Phoenix** with Craig Mills and Phoenix's 1st round choice (Ty Jones) in 1997 Entry Draft for Jeremy Roenick, August 16, 1996.

• ZHITNIK, ALEXEI

Alexei Zhitnik D – L. 5'11", 204 lbs. b: Kiev, USSR, 10/10/1972. Los Angeles' 3rd choice, 81st overall, in 1991 Entry Draft.

Season	Club	League	GP	G	A	Pts	AG	AA	APts	PIM	PP	SH	GW	S	%	TGF	PGF	TGA	PGA	+/-	GP	G	A	Pts	PIM	PP	SH	GW
1989-90	Sokol Kiev	USSR	31	3	4	7	....	....	....	16	....	....	....	....	....	....	....	....	....	....	....	....	....	....	....	....	....	....
1990-91	Sokol Liev	FrTour	1	0	0	0	....	....	....	0	....	....	....	....	....	....	....	....	....	....	....	....	....	....	....	....	....	....
	Sokol Kiev	USSR	46	1	4	5	....	....	....	46	....	....	....	....	....	....	....	....	....	....	....	....	....	....	....	....	....	....
1991-92	Soviet Union	C Cup	5	0	0	0	....	....	....	4	....	....	....	....	....	....	....	....	....	....	....	....	....	....	....	....	....	....
	CSKA Moscow	CIS	44	2	7	9	....	....	....	52	....	....	....	....	....	....	....	....	....	....	....	....	....	....	....	....	....	....
	Russia	WJC-A	7	1	1	2	....	....	....	2	....	....	....	....	....	....	....	....	....	....	....	....	....	....	....	....	....	....
	Russia	Olympics	8	1	0	1	....	....	....	0	....	....	....	....	....	....	....	....	....	....	....	....	....	....	....	....	....	....
	Russia	WC-A	6	0	2	2	....	....	....	6	....	....	....	....	....	....	....	....	....	....	....	....	....	....	....	....	....	....
1992-93	Los Angeles Kings	NHL	78	12	36	48	10	25	35	80	5	0	2	136	8.8	104	42	77	12	–3	24	3	9	12	26	2	0	1
1993-94	Los Angeles Kings	NHL	81	12	40	52	11	31	42	101	11	0	1	227	5.3	128	59	99	19	–11	....	....	....	....	....	....	....	....
	Russia	WC-A	6	1	0	1	....	....	....	8	....	....	....	....	....	....	....	....	....	....	....	....	....	....	....	....	....	....
1994-95	Los Angeles Kings	NHL	11	2	5	7	4	7	11	27	2	0	0	33	6.1	19	8	14	0	–3	....	....	....	....	....	....	....	....
	Buffalo Sabres	NHL	21	2	5	7	4	7	11	34	1	0	0	33	6.1	23	11	15	0	–3	5	0	1	1	14	0	0	0
1995-96	Buffalo Sabres	NHL	80	6	30	36	6	24	30	58	5	0	0	193	3.1	109	50	112	28	–25	....	....	....	....	....	....	....	....
	Russia	WC-A	8	1	1	2	....	....	....	6	....	....	....	....	....	....	....	....	....	....	....	....	....	....	....	....	....	....
1996-97	Russia	W Cup	3	0	1	1	....	....	....	2	....	....	....	....	....	....	....	....	....	....	....	....	....	....	....	....	....	....
	Buffalo Sabres	NHL	80	7	28	35	7	25	32	95	3	1	0	170	4.1	92	22	86	26	+10	12	1	0	1	16	0	0	0
1997-98	Buffalo Sabres	NHL	78	15	30	45	18	29	47	102	2	3	3	191	7.9	103	31	80	27	+19	15	0	3	3	36	0	0	0
	Russia	Olympics	6	0	2	2	....	....	....	2	....	....	....	....	....	....	....	....	....	....	....	....	....	....	....	....	....	....
	NHL Totals		429	56	174	230	60	148	208	497	29	4	6	983	5.7	578	223	483	112		56	4	13	17	92	2	0	1

WC-A All-Star Team (1996) • Named Best Defenseman at WC-A (1996)

Traded to **Buffalo** by **LA Kings** with Robb Stauber, Charlie Huddy and LA Kings' 5th round choice (Marian Menhart) in 1995 Entry Draft for Philippe Boucher, Denis Tsygurov and Grant Fuhr, February 14, 1995.

• ZHOLTOK, SERGEI

Sergei Zholtok C – R. 6', 190 lbs. b: Riga, Latvia, 12/2/1972. Boston's 2nd choice, 55th overall, in 1992 Entry Draft.

Season	Club	League	GP	G	A	Pts	AG	AA	APts	PIM	PP	SH	GW	S	%	TGF	PGF	TGA	PGA	+/-	GP	G	A	Pts	PIM	PP	SH	GW
1990-91	Dynamo Riga	FrTour	1	0	0	0	....	....	....	0	....	....	....	....	....	....	....	....	....	....	....	....	....	....	....	....	....	....
	Dynamo Riga	USSR	39	4	0	4	....	....	....	16	....	....	....	....	....	....	....	....	....	....	....	....	....	....	....	....	....	....
1991-92	HC Riga	CIS	27	6	3	9	....	....	....	6	....	....	....	....	....	....	....	....	....	....	....	....	....	....	....	....	....	....
	Russia	WJC-A	7	2	4	6	....	....	....	6	....	....	....	....	....	....	....	....	....	....	....	....	....	....	....	....	....	....
1992-93	Boston Bruins	NHL	1	0	1	1	0	1	1	0	0	0	0	2	0.0	1	0	0	0	+1	....	....	....	....	....	....	....	....
	Providence Bruins	AHL	64	31	35	66	....	....	....	57	....	....	....	....	....	....	....	....	....	....	6	3	5	8	4	....	....	....
1993-94	Boston Bruins	NHL	24	2	1	3	2	1	3	2	1	0	0	25	8.0	3	1	10	1	–7	....	....	....	....	....	....	....	....
	Providence Bruins	AHL	54	29	33	62	....	....	....	16	....	....	....	....	....	....	....	....	....	....	....	....	....	....	....	....	....	....
	Latvia	WC-B	4	6	1	7	....	....	....	4	....	....	....	....	....	....	....	....	....	....	....	....	....	....	....	....	....	....
1994-95	Providence Bruins	AHL	78	23	35	58	....	....	....	42	....	....	....	....	....	....	....	....	....	....	13	8	5	13	6	....	....	....
1995-96	Las Vegas Thunder	IHL	82	51	50	101	....	....	....	30	....	....	....	....	....	....	....	....	....	....	15	7	13	20	6	....	....	....
1996-97	Ottawa Senators	NHL	57	12	16	28	13	14	27	19	5	0	0	96	12.5	42	15	25	0	+2	7	1	1	2	0	1	0	0
	Las Vegas Thunder	IHL	19	13	14	27	....	....	....	20	....	....	....	....	....	....	....	....	....	....	....	....	....	....	....	....	....	....
	Latvia	WC-A	5	3	3	6	....	....	....	2	....	....	....	....	....	....	....	....	....	....	....	....	....	....	....	....	....	....
1997-98	Ottawa Senators	NHL	78	10	13	23	12	13	25	16	7	0	1	127	7.9	34	17	24	0	–7	11	0	2	2	0	0	0	0
	NHL Totals		160	24	31	55	27	29	56	37	13	0	1	250	9.6	80	33	59	1		18	1	3	4	0	1	0	0

EJC-A All-Star Team (1990)

Signed as a free agent by **Ottawa**, July 10, 1996.

• ZMOLEK, DOUG

Doug Zmolek D – L. 6'2", 220 lbs. b: Rochester, MN, 11/3/1970. Minnesota's 1st choice, 7th overall, in 1989 Entry Draft.

Season	Club	League	GP	G	A	Pts	AG	AA	APts	PIM	PP	SH	GW	S	%	TGF	PGF	TGA	PGA	+/-	GP	G	A	Pts	PIM	PP	SH	GW
1988-89	John Marshall High School	H.S.	29	17	41	58	....	....	....	....	....	....	....	....	....	....	....	....	....	....	....	....	....	....	....	....	....	....
1989-90	University of Minnesota	WCHA	40	1	10	11	....	....	....	52	....	....	....	....	....	....	....	....	....	....	....	....	....	....	....	....	....	....
	United States	WJC-A	7	0	1	1	....	....	....	2	....	....	....	....	....	....	....	....	....	....	....	....	....	....	....	....	....	....
1990-91	University of Minnesota	WCHA	34	11	6	17	....	....	....	38	....	....	....	....	....	....	....	....	....	....	....	....	....	....	....	....	....	....
1991-92	University of Minnesota	WCHA	41	6	20	26	....	....	....	84	....	....	....	....	....	....	....	....	....	....	....	....	....	....	....	....	....	....
1992-93	San Jose Sharks	NHL	84	5	10	15	4	7	11	229	2	0	0	94	5.3	64	12	142	40	–50	....	....	....	....	....	....	....	....
1993-94	San Jose Sharks	NHL	68	0	4	4	0	3	3	122	0	0	0	29	0.0	35	0	69	25	–9	....	....	....	....	....	....	....	....
	Dallas Stars	NHL	7	1	0	1	1	0	1	11	0	0	0	3	33.3	6	0	5	0	+1	7	0	1	1	4	0	0	0
1994-95	Dallas Stars	NHL	42	0	5	5	0	7	7	67	0	0	0	28	0.0	22	2	39	13	–6	5	0	0	0	10	0	0	0

			REGULAR SEASON																		PLAYOFFS							
Season	Club	League	GP	G	A	Pts	AG	AA	APts	PIM	PP	SH	GW	S	%	TGF	PGF	TGA	PGA	+/–	GP	G	A	Pts	PIM	PP	SH	GW
1995-96	Dallas Stars	NHL	42	1	5	6	1	4	5	65	0	0	0	26	3.8	36	6	45	16	+1	....	....	....	....	....	....	....	....
	Los Angeles Kings	NHL	16	1	0	1	1	0	1	22	0	0	0	10	10.0	8	0	21	7	–6	....	....	....	....	....	....	....	....
1996-97	Los Angeles Kings	NHL	57	1	0	1	1	0	1	116	0	0	0	28	3.6	21	0	56	13	–22	....	....	....	....	....	....	....	....
1997-98	Los Angeles Kings	NHL	46	0	8	8	0	8	8	111	0	0	0	23	0.0	22	0	31	9	0	2	0	0	0	2	0	0	0
	NHL Totals		362	9	32	41	8	29	37	743	2	0	0	241	3.7	214	20	408	123		14	0	1	1	16	0	0	0

WCHA Second All-Star Team (1992) • NCAA West Second All-American Team (1992)

Claimed by **San Jose** from **Minnesota** in Dispersal Draft, May 30, 1991. Traded to **Dallas** by **San Jose** with Mike Lalor and cash for Ulf Dahlen and Dallas' 7th round choice (Brad Mehalko) in 1995 Entry Draft, March 19, 1994. Traded to **LA Kings** by **Dallas** with Shane Churla for Darryl Sydor and LA Kings' 5th round choice (Ryan Christie) in 1996 Entry Draft, February 17, 1996.

• ZOMBO, RICK

Rick Zombo D – R. 6'1", 202 lbs. b: Des Plaines, IL, 5/8/1963. Detroit's 6th choice, 149th overall, in 1981 Entry Draft.

1980-81	Austin Mavericks	USHL	43	10	26	36	....	....	....	73	....	....	....	....	....	....	....	....	....	....	....	....	....	....	....	....	....	....
1981-82	University of North Dakota	WCHA	45	1	15	16	....	....	....	31	....	....	....	....	....	....	....	....	....	....	....	....	....	....	....	....	....	....
1982-83	University of North Dakota	WCHA	35	5	11	16	....	....	....	41	....	....	....	....	....	....	....	....	....	....	....	....	....	....	....	....	....	....
	United States	WJC-A	7	0	0	0	....	....	....	0	....	....	....	....	....	....	....	....	....	....	....	....	....	....	....	....	....	....
1983-84	University of North Dakota	WCHA	34	7	24	31	....	....	....	40	....	....	....	....	....	....	....	....	....	....	....	....	....	....	....	....	....	....
1984-85	**Detroit Red Wings**	**NHL**	1	0	0	0	0	0	0	0	0	0	0	0	0.0	0	0	3	0	–3	....	....	....	....	....	....	....	....
	Adirondack Red Wings	AHL	56	3	32	35	....	....	....	70	....	....	....	....	....	....	....	....	....	....	....	....	....	....	....	....	....	....
1985-86	**Detroit Red Wings**	**NHL**	14	0	1	1	0	1	1	16	0	0	0	8	0.0	3	0	16	3	–10	....	....	....	....	....	....	....	....
	Adirondack Red Wings	AHL	69	7	34	41	....	....	....	94	....	....	....	....	....	....	....	....	....	....	17	0	4	4	40	....	....	....
1986-87	**Detroit Red Wings**	**NHL**	44	1	4	5	1	3	4	59	0	0	0	28	3.6	33	6	44	11	–6	7	0	1	1	9	0	0	0
	Adirondack Red Wings	AHL	25	0	6	6	....	....	....	22	....	....	....	....	....	....	....	....	....	....	....	....	....	....	....	....	....	....
1987-88	**Detroit Red Wings**	**NHL**	62	3	14	17	3	10	13	96	0	0	2	48	6.3	74	3	69	22	+24	16	0	6	6	55	0	0	0
1988-89	**Detroit Red Wings**	**NHL**	75	1	20	21	1	14	15	106	1	0	0	64	1.6	94	3	105	36	+22	6	0	1	1	16	0	0	0
1989-90	**Detroit Red Wings**	**NHL**	77	5	20	25	4	14	18	95	0	0	0	62	8.1	98	9	125	49	+13	....	....	....	....	....	....	....	....
1990-91	**Detroit Red Wings**	**NHL**	77	4	19	23	4	14	18	55	0	0	0	68	5.9	69	1	119	49	–2	7	1	0	1	10	0	0	0
1991-92	**Detroit Red Wings**	**NHL**	3	0	0	0	0	0	0	15	0	0	0	1	0.0	1	0	5	1	–3	....	....	....	....	....	....	....	....
	St. Louis Blues	**NHL**	64	3	15	18	3	11	14	46	0	0	0	47	6.4	55	2	74	25	+4	6	0	2	2	12	0	0	0
1992-93	**St. Louis Blues**	**NHL**	71	0	15	15	0	10	10	78	0	0	0	43	0.0	49	2	73	24	–2	11	0	1	1	12	0	0	0
1993-94	**St. Louis Blues**	**NHL**	74	2	8	10	2	6	8	85	0	0	0	53	3.8	59	6	93	25	–15	4	0	0	0	11	0	0	0
1994-95	**St. Louis Blues**	**NHL**	23	1	4	5	2	6	8	24	0	0	1	18	5.6	19	0	20	8	+7	3	0	0	0	2	0	0	0
1995-96	**Boston Bruins**	**NHL**	67	4	10	14	4	8	12	53	0	0	1	68	5.9	60	4	80	17	–7	....	....	....	....	....	....	....	....
1996-97	Phoenix Roadrunners	IHL	23	0	6	6	....	....	....	22	....	....	....	....	....	....	....	....	....	....	....	....	....	....	....	....	....	....
	NHL Totals		652	24	130	154	24	97	121	728	1	0	4	508	4.7	614	36	826	270		60	1	11	12	127	0	0	0

WCHA Second All-Star Team (1984)

Traded to **St. Louis** by **Detroit** for Vincent Riendeau, October 18, 1991. Traded to **Boston** by **St. Louis** for Fred Knipscheer, October 2, 1995. Signed as a free agent by **LA Kings**, December 13, 1996.

• ZUBOV, SERGEI

Sergei Zubov D – R. 6'1", 200 lbs. b: Moscow, USSR, 7/22/1970. NY Rangers' 6th choice, 85th overall, in 1990 Entry Draft.

1988-89	CSKA Moscow	USSR	29	1	4	5	....	....	....	10	....	....	....	....	....	....	....	....	....	....	....	....	....	....	....	....	....	....
	Soviet Union	WJC-A	7	0	5	5	....	....	....	4	....	....	....	....	....	....	....	....	....	....	....	....	....	....	....	....	....	....
1989-90	CSKA Moscow	FrTour	1	0	0	0	....	....	....	0	....	....	....	....	....	....	....	....	....	....	....	....	....	....	....	....	....	....
	CSKA Moscow	USSR	48	6	2	8	....	....	....	16	....	....	....	....	....	....	....	....	....	....	....	....	....	....	....	....	....	....
	Soviet Union	WJC-A	7	1	3	4	....	....	....	14	....	....	....	....	....	....	....	....	....	....	....	....	....	....	....	....	....	....
1990-91	CSKA Moscow	FrTour	1	1	0	1	....	....	....	25	....	....	....	....	....	....	....	....	....	....	....	....	....	....	....	....	....	....
	CSKA Moscow	USSR	41	6	5	11	....	....	....	12	....	....	....	....	....	....	....	....	....	....	....	....	....	....	....	....	....	....
	CSKA Moscow	SuperS	7	0	1	1	....	....	....	0	....	....	....	....	....	....	....	....	....	....	....	....	....	....	....	....	....	....
1991-92	CSKA Moscow	CIS	44	4	7	11	....	....	....	8	....	....	....	....	....	....	....	....	....	....	....	....	....	....	....	....	....	....
	Russia	Olympics	8	0	1	1				0	....	....	....	....	....	....	....	....	....	....	....	....	....	....	....	....	....	....
	Russia	WC-A	6	2	2	4	....	....	....	10	....	....	....	....	....	....	....	....	....	....	....	....	....	....	....	....	....	....
1992-93	CSKA Moscow	CIS	1	0	1	1	....	....	....	0	....	....	....	....	....	....	....	....	....	....	....	....	....	....	....	....	....	....
	New York Rangers	**NHL**	49	8	23	31	7	16	23	4	3	0	0	93	8.6	78	22	67	10	–1	....	....	....	....	....	....	....	....
	Binghamton Rangers	AHL	30	7	29	36	....	....	....	14	....	....	....	....	....	....	....	....	....	....	11	5	5	10	2	....	....	....
1993-94	**New York Rangers**	**NHL**	78	12	77	89	11	60	71	39	9	0	1	222	5.4	163	78	73	8	+20	22	5	14	19	0	2	0	0
	Binghamton Rangers	AHL	2	1	2	3	....	....	....	0	....	....	....	....	....	....	....	....	....	....	....	....	....	....	....	....	....	....
1994-95	**New York Rangers**	**NHL**	38	10	26	36	18	38	56	18	6	0	0	116	8.6	67	33	42	6	–2	10	3	8	11	2	1	0	0
1995-96	**Pittsburgh Penguins**	**NHL**	64	11	55	66	11	45	56	22	3	2	1	141	7.8	151	60	79	16	+28	18	1	14	15	26	1	0	0
1996-97	Russia	W Cup	4	1	1	2	....	....	....	0	....	....	....	....	....	....	....	....	....	....	....	....	....	....	....	....	....	....
	Dallas Stars	**NHL**	78	13	30	43	14	27	41	24	1	0	3	133	9.8	111	32	69	9	+19	7	0	3	3	2	0	0	0
1997-98	**Dallas Stars**	**NHL**	73	10	47	57	12	46	58	16	5	1	2	148	6.8	122	61	58	13	+16	17	4	5	9	2	3	0	1
	NHL Totals		380	64	258	322	73	232	305	123	27	3	7	853	7.5	692	286	388	62		74	13	44	57	32	7	0	1

EJC-A All-Star Team (1988) • Named Best Defenseman at EJC-A (1988)

Played in NHL All-Star Game (1998)

Traded to **Pittsburgh** by **NY Rangers** with Petr Nedved for Luc Robitaille and Ulf Samuelsson, August 31, 1995. Traded to **Dallas** by **Pittsburgh** for Kevin Hatcher, June 22, 1996.

• ZUBRUS, DAINIUS

Dainius Zubrus RW – L. 6'3", 215 lbs. b: Elektrenai, USSR, 6/16/1978. Philadelphia's 1st choice, 15th overall, in 1996 Entry Draft.

1995-96	Pembroke Lumber Kings	OJHL	28	19	13	32	....	....	....	73	....	....	....	....	....	....	....	....	....	....	....	....	....	....	....	....	....	....
	Caledon Canadians	OJHL	7	3	7	10	....	....	....	2	....	....	....	....	....	....	....	....	....	....	17	11	12	23	4	....	....	....
1996-97	**Philadelphia Flyers**	**NHL**	68	8	13	21	8	11	19	22	1	0	2	71	11.3	31	4	24	0	+3	19	5	4	9	12	1	0	1
1997-98	**Philadelphia Flyers**	**NHL**	69	8	25	33	9	24	33	42	1	0	5	101	7.9	64	10	25	0	+29	5	0	1	1	2	0	0	0
	NHL Totals		137	16	38	54	17	35	52	64	2	0	7	172	9.3	95	14	49	0		24	5	5	10	14	1	0	1

• ZUKE, MIKE

Mike Zuke C – R. 6', 180 lbs. b: Sault Ste. Marie, Ont., 4/16/1954. St. Louis' 3rd choice, 79th overall, in 1974 Amateur Draft.

1971-72	Sault Ste. Marie Greyhounds	NOHA	48	34	*63	*96	....	....	....	23	....	....	....	....	....	....	....	....	....	....	....	....	....	....	....	....	....	....
1972-73	Michigan Tech Huskies	CCHA	38	23	30	53	....	....	....	20	....	....	....	....	....	....	....	....	....	....	....	....	....	....	....	....	....	....
1973-74	Michigan Tech Huskies	CCHA	40	28	47	75	....	....	....	38	....	....	....	....	....	....	....	....	....	....	....	....	....	....	....	....	....	....
1974-75	Michigan Tech Huskies	CCHA	42	35	43	78	....	....	....	20	....	....	....	....	....	....	....	....	....	....	....	....	....	....	....	....	....	....
1975-76	Michigan Tech Huskies	CCHA	43	47	*57	104	....	....	....	42	....	....	....	....	....	....	....	....	....	....	....	....	....	....	....	....	....	....
1976-77	Mohawk Valley Comets	NAHL	48	42	29	71	....	....	....	33	....	....	....	....	....	....	....	....	....	....	....	....	....	....	....	....	....	....
	Indianapolis Racers	WHA	15	3	4	7	....	....	....	2	....	....	....	....	....	....	....	....	....	....	....	....	....	....	....	....	....	....
1977-78	Edmonton Oilers	WHA	71	23	34	57	....	....	....	47	....	....	....	....	....	....	....	....	....	....	5	2	3	5	0	....	....	....
1978-79	**St. Louis Blues**	**NHL**	34	9	17	26	8	13	21	18	3	0	0	80	11.3	41	18	39	8	–8	....	....	....	....	....	....	....	....
	Salt Lake Golden Eagles	CHL	29	9	13	22	....	....	....	4	....	....	....	....	....	....	....	....	....	....	....	....	....	....	....	....	....	....
1979-80	**St. Louis Blues**	**NHL**	69	22	42	64	20	32	52	30	6	1	1	172	12.8	86	37	57	6	–2	3	0	0	0	2	0	0	0
1980-81	**St. Louis Blues**	**NHL**	74	24	44	68	20	31	51	57	10	1	1	145	16.6	100	46	59	20	+15	11	4	5	9	4	3	0	0
1981-82	**St. Louis Blues**	**NHL**	76	13	40	53	10	26	36	41	1	1	2	159	8.2	86	38	91	25	–18	8	1	1	2	2	0	0	0
1982-83	**St. Louis Blues**	**NHL**	43	8	16	24	7	11	18	14	0	0	1	58	13.8	30	3	35	5	–3	4	1	0	1	4	0	0	1
	Salt Lake Golden Eagles	CHL	13	7	8	15	....	....	....	0	....	....	....	....	....	....	....	....	....	....	....	....	....	....	....	....	....	....
1983-84	**Hartford Whalers**	**NHL**	75	6	23	29	5	16	21	36	1	0	0	84	7.1	43	22	78	39	–18	....	....	....	....	....	....	....	....
1984-85	**Hartford Whalers**	**NHL**	67	4	12	16	3	8	11	12	0	0	1	54	7.4	27	0	56	25	–4	....	....	....	....	....	....	....	....
1985-86	**Hartford Whalers**	**NHL**	17	0	2	2	0	1	1	12	0	0	0	2	0.0	4	0	15	9	–2	....	....	....	....	....	....	....	....
	NHL Totals		455	86	196	282	73	138	211	220	21	3	6	754	11.4	417	164	430	137		26	6	6	12	12	3	0	1
	Other Major League Totals		86	26	38	64	....	....	....	49	....	....	....	....	....	....	....	....	....	....	5	2	3	5	0	....	....	....

WCHA First All-Star Team (1974, 1976) • NCAA West First All-American Team (1974) • WCHA Second All-Star Team (1975) • NCAA West First All-American Team (1976)

Selected by **Indianapolis** (WHA) in 1974 WHA Amateur Draft, May, 1974. Traded to **Edmonton** (WHA) by **Indianapolis** (WHA) with Blair MacDonald and Dave Inkpen for Barry Wilkins, Edgar Patenaude and Claude St. Sauveur, September, 1977. Signed as a free agent by **St. Louis**, September 29, 1978. Claimed by **Hartford** from **St. Louis** in Waiver Draft, October 3, 1983.

			REGULAR SEASON																				PLAYOFFS							
Season	Club	League	GP	G	A	Pts	AG	AA	APts	PIM	PP	SH	GW	S	%	TGF	PGF	TGA	PGA	+/−	GP	G	A	Pts	PIM	PP	SH	GW
● **ZYUZIN, ANDREI**	Andrei Zyuzin		D – L. 6′1″, 187 lbs.				b: Ufa, USSR, 1/21/1978.			San Jose's 1st choice, 2nd overall, in 1996 Entry Draft.																		
1994-95	Ufa Salavat............................	CIS	30	3	0	3	....	....	....	16	....	....	....	....	....	....	....	....	....	....	....	....	....	....	....	....	....	....
1995-96	Ufa Salavat............................	CIS	41	6	3	9	....	....	....	24	....	....	....	....	....	....	....	....	....	....	....	....	....	....	....	....	....	....
	Russia	WJC-A	7	1	4	5	....	....	....	2	....	....	....	....	....	....	....	....	....	....	7	1	1	2	4	....	....	....
1996-97	Ufa Salavat............................	Rus.	32	7	10	17	....	....	....	28	....	....	....	....	....	....	....	....	....	....	....	....	....	....	....	....	....	....
	Russia	WJC-A	6	1	1	2	....	....	....	6	....	....	....	....	....	....	....	....	....	....	....	....	....	....	....	....	....	....
1997-98	**San Jose Sharks**.................	**NHL**	56	6	7	13	7	7	14	66	2	0	2	72	8.3	47	16	25	2	+8	6	1	0	1	14	0	0	1
	Kentucky Thoroughblades	AHL	17	4	5	9				28																		
	NHL Totals		56	6	7	13	7	7	14	66	2	0	2	72	8.3	47	16	25	2		6	1	0	1	14	0	0	1

EJC-A All-Star Team (1996) • Named Best Defenseman at EJC-A (1996)

CHAPTER 74

Using the Goaltender Register

Ralph Dinger

THE GOALTENDER REGISTER begins on page 1602. It contains the complete statistical history of every goaltender who has played in the National Hockey League.

Here are notes on the various statistical categories used in the Goaltender Register:

Biographical – This field contains the goaltender's name, and given names (if these names are different than the name by which he is commonly known. For example, Gump Worsley's given names are Lorne John, Al Rollins' given names were Elwin Ira), nicknames, position (**G** – goaltender) and catching glove side (**R** – right, **L** – left). Additional items in a goaltender's biographical data are identical to those used for players. *See page 646.*

Season – From 1917–18 to the present day, the hockey season started in the fall and ended the following spring and is represented in the Goaltender Register as, for example, 1997–98. For players who retired or did not play for three or more seasons but later returned to the game, those years are represented as two four-digit dates, for example, 1964–1967.

Club – *See page 646.*

League – *See page 646.* A full list of the leagues found in *Total Hockey* and their abbreviations can be found on page 1878.

GP – Games Played – *See page 646.*

W – Wins – The goaltender in net when his team scores the game-winning goal is credited with the win. If a goaltender enters a game with his team leading 4–0 and his team eventually wins the game 5–4, that goaltender still receives credit for the victory.

L – Losses – The goaltender who allows the game-winning goal is charged with the loss. If a goaltender enters a game with his team losing 4–0 and his team eventually loses the game 5–4, that goaltender is still charged with the loss. A goaltender removed for an extra attacker in a tie game is charged with the loss if his teams surrenders an empty-net game-winning goal. For example, on April 1, 1989, the Toronto Maple Leafs needed a win over the St. Louis Blues to stay in contention for a playoff spot. With the game tied 3–3 in overtime, the Leafs pulled goaltender Allan Bester for an extra attacker. The Blues scored the winning goal into the empty net, but Bester was still charged with the loss. Until 1941–42, goaltenders were required to serve their own penalties. If the goalie's replacement allowed the winning goal, the penalized goaltender was still charged with the loss.

T – Ties – The goaltender in net when a tying goal is scored is credited with a tie. If a goaltender enters a game with his team winning 4–0 and the game ends 4–4, that goaltender is still credited with a tie. The NHL has not had a playoff game end in a tie since March 23, 1935 when the Black Hawks and Maroons played to a 0–0 tie in the first game of a two-game total goals series.

Since 1935, two playoff games were suspended with tie scores: Game two of the 1951 semifinals between Toronto and Boston was suspended at 11:45 p.m. with the score tied 1–1 due to Toronto's Sunday curfew laws. A game in the 1988 Stanley Cup finals was suspended with the score tied 3–3 when a power failure at the old Boston Garden stopped play late in the second period. These games would have been replayed if a seventh game was required to determine a series winner. Individual statistics recorded in these suspended games (including minutes played for goaltenders) are accepted as official.

Mins – Minutes played – Playing time for each goaltender, rounded off to the nearest minute. Goaltenders must play at least 30 seconds of each minute to receive credit for playing the full minute. For instance, a goaltender who leaves the game at the 4:29 mark of the second period is credited with playing 24 minutes of that game. His replacement would be credited with playing 36 minutes if he finished the game. Those goalies who play less than 30 seconds in an entire game are credited with one minute of playing time. The goaltender (or goaltenders) who played the rest of the game is still credited with playing the full 60 minutes. A note of explanation is included to explain this discrepancy. Although goaltenders have been removed from the net for an extra attacker since the 1930s, that time was not removed from a goaltender's minutes played until the 1980s.

GA – goals against – Goals scored against the goaltender. Previous to 1963–64, empty-nets goals were charged against the goaltender who had been removed. Since 1963–64, goals scored into an empty net are counted against the team, but not against the goaltender who had been removed.

SO – Shutouts – Games played without allowing a goal. To register a

shutout, the goaltender must play the entire game without allowing a goal. If two or more goaltenders play in a game in which their team does not allow a goal, they are considered to have shared the shutout, but no credit is given in the two goalies' statistical data panels.

Avg – Goals-against average – Goals allowed per 60 minutes of play. The goals-against average (**Avg**) is calculated by dividing goals against (**GA**) by minutes played (**Mins**) and multiplying the results by 60. For example, a goaltender who allows 117 goals in 2475 minutes of playing time has a goals-against average (**Avg**) of 2.84. Note that some modern minor leagues and college conferences calculate goaltender Mins down to the second. These fractional totals are reflected in their goaltender averages. In addition, some U.S. high school leagues play 40 or 45-minute games. The USAHA (1918 to 1926) also played 45-minute games. Goaltender averages for these leagues reflect these shorter game lengths.

AAvg – Adjusted average – A new goaltending statistic similar to *Total Hockey's* Adjusted Goals, Adjusted Points and Adjusted Points. (*See page 626*). Adjusted Average (**AAvg**) factors the league-wide goals-against average for the season in question against 3.13, the average of the NHL's goals-against average each season since 1917–18. This factor is multiplied by an individual goaltender's Avg. to determine his Adjusted Average. For example, let us consider goaltenders Smith and Jones with identical averages of 3.00. Smith played in 1953–54 when the league-wide average was a stingy 2.40 goals-against. Dividing the all-time NHL average of 3.13 by the 1952–53 mark of 2.40, yields a factor of 1.30. Smith's 3.00, multiplied by the factor of 1.30, adjusts to 3.90. Jones played in the 1981–82 season when the league-wide average had grown to 4.00. Dividing the all-time average of 3.13 by the 1981–82 mark of 4.00, yields a factor of 0.78. Smith's 3.00 adjusts to 2.34. (In this example, all figures have been rounded off to two decimal places.)

To further remove bias from our formula, we harness the power of the computer to remove each goaltender's individual goals against (**GA**) from the calculation of the league-wide Avg in the season being adjusted.

Eff – Goaltender's Efficiency – Combines shots against (**SA**) with **Avg.**, rewarding goaltenders who face a higher number of shots. To calculate **Eff**: (Avg x **GA**) divided by (**SA** divided by 10). An example: Martin Brodeur'n Avg in 1997–98 was 1.89. He allowed 130 **GA** on 1569 **SA**. His **Eff** is 1.57. Dominik Hasek's Avg. was 2.09. He allowed 147 **GA** in 2149 **SA**. His **Eff** is 1.43. Like conventional **Avg**, a lower **Eff** is better.

SA – Shots against – The number of shots-on-goal faced by each goaltender. Although shots-on-goal have been tabulated for many years, shots faced by goaltenders has only been an official statistic since 1982–83.

S% – Save percentage – Percentage of saves per 100 shots. The Save percentage (**S%**) is calculated by subtracting goals against (**GA**) from shots against (**SA**) and dividing that total by shots against (**SA**). For example, if a goaltender allows 147 goals on 2149 shots, his save percentage is .932, meaning he stops 93.2% of the shots he faces. Calculated since 1982–83.

SAPG – Shots against per game – The average shots faced per 60 minutes of play. The shots against per game (**SAPG**) average is calculated by dividing 60 by minutes played (**Mins**) and multiplying by shots against (**SA**). For example, a goaltender facing 177 shots in 305 minutes of playing time faces an average of 34.8 shots-per-game.

NHL Totals – Total of all primary NHL statistics found in the data panel.

Other Major League Totals – This field includes the total of all the other major leagues an NHL goaltender performed in from 1893 to date. (*See Chapter 68, page 642*) To be categorized as major a league must fall into one of the following three categories: it must have been professional, challenged for the Stanley Cup and/or competed with other major leagues to sign the top hockey talent of the day. (*For a complete list of other major leagues, see page 646.*)

Award and All-Star Notes – *See page 646.*

Trade Notes – This field contains details on NHL trades, drafts (Waiver, Reverse, Intra-League, Inter-League, Expansion and Dispersal) and free agent signings. WHA trade notes, draft information and free agent signings are included for every goaltender who played in both the WHA and the NHL. Trade notes and free agent signings for every goaltender who played in the NHL and the PCHA, WCHL and the WHL from 1917–18 to 1926–27 have also been included.

Special notes concerning injuries and other oddities and curiosities are indicated by a bullet (•).

CHAPTER 75

Goaltender Register

Career Records for All NHL Goaltenders

			REGULAR SEASON												PLAYOFFS									
Season	Club	League	GP	W	L	T	Mins	GA	SO	Avg	AAvg	Eff	SA	S%	SAPG	GP	W	L	T	Mins	GA	SO	Avg	Eff	SA	S%	SAPG

● ABBOTT, GEORGE George "Preacher" Abbott G – L. 5'7", 153 lbs. b: Synenham, Ont., 8/3/1911.

| 1943-44 | Boston Bruins | NHL | 1 | 0 | 1 | 0 | 60 | 7 | 0 | 7.00 | 5.31 | .... | .... | .... | .... | .... | .... | .... | .... | .... | .... | .... | .... | .... | .... | .... | .... |
| | NHL Totals | | 1 | 0 | 1 | 0 | 60 | 7 | 0 | 7.00 | | .... | .... | .... | .... | | | | | | | | | | | | |

• **Toronto's** practice goaltender loaned to **Boston** to replace injured Bert Gardiner, November 27, 1943. (Toronto 7, Boston 4)

● ADAMS, JOHN John Adams G – L. 6', 200 lbs. b: Port Arthur, Ont., 7/27/1946.

1966-67	Port Arthur Marrs	TBJHL	STATISTICS NOT AVAILABLE													4				240	21	0	5.25				
1967-68	Dayton Gems	IHL	45	....	....	....	2570	148	2	3.46						6				365	15	1	*2.47				
1968-69	Dayton Gems	IHL	32	....	....	....	1900	91	2	2.87																	
1969-70	Oklahoma City Blazers	CHL	51	18	26	7	3027	176	*5	3.49																	
1970-71	Oklahoma City Blazers	CHL	*57	25	22	10	3417	195	3	3.42						5	1	4	0	280	21	0	4.50				
1971-72	Oklahoma City Blazers	CHL	43	15	15	3	2168	129	2	3.57																	
1972-73	**Boston Bruins**	NHL	14	9	3	1	780	39	1	3.00	2.82																
	Boston Braves	AHL	23	....	....	....	1179	65	1	3.31						8	4	4	0	420	34	0	4.86				
1973-74	San Diego Gulls	WHL	*69	*38	26	4	*4094	223	1	3.27						4	0	4	0	261	19	0	4.37				
1974-75	**Washington Capitals**	NHL	8	0	7	0	400	46	0	6.90	6.25																
	Richmond Robins	AHL	28	7	13	3	1424	105	1	4.42																	
1975-76	Thunder Bay Twins	OHA Sr.	12	....	....	....	720	33	*3	2.75																	
	NHL Totals		22	9	10	1	1180	85	1	4.32		....	....	....	....												

Shared James Norris Memorial Trophy (fewest goals against - IHL) with Pat Rupp (1969) • CHL First All-Star Team (1972) • WHL Second All-Star Team (1974)
Traded to **San Diego** (WHL) by **Boston** to complete transaction that sent Ken Broderick to Boston (March 10, 1973), June 12, 1973. Traded to **Washington** by **San Diego** (WHL) for cash, July 11, 1974.

● AIKEN, JOHN John Aiken G – L. 5'11", 165 lbs. b: Arlington, MA, 1/1/1932.

1952-53	United States Military Academy	NCAA	STATISTICS NOT AVAILABLE																								
1953-54			DID NOT PLAY – TRANSFERRED COLLEGES																								
1954-1957	Boston University	NCAA	STATISTICS NOT AVAILABLE																								
1957-58	**Montreal Canadiens**	NHL	1	0	1	0	34	6	0	10.59	11.73																
	NHL Totals		1	0	1	0	34	6	0	10.59		....	....	....	....												

• **Boston's** practice goaltender loaned to **Montreal** to replace injured Jacques Plante in 2nd period, March 13, 1958. (Boston 7, Montreal 3) • At the time of his appearance with Montreal, he was employed as a mathematician with the U.S. Air Force.

● AIKENHEAD, ANDY Andy Aikenhead G – L. 5'9", 145 lbs. b: Glasgow, Scotland, 3/6/1904. d: 1968.

1922-23	University of Saskatchewan	City Sr.	STATISTICS NOT AVAILABLE													2	1	0	1	120	3	0	1.50				
	Saskatoon Quakers	SJHL														4	1	2	1	240	12	0	*3.00				
1923-24	Saskatoon Nationals	SSHL	5	*4	0	1	350	5	*1	*0.86																	
1924-25	Yorkton Terriers	SSHL	STATISTICS NOT AVAILABLE													2	0	1	1	140	9	0	3.86				
1925-26	Saskatoon Empires	SSHL	4	*4	0	0	240	12	*1	*3.00						4	1	3	0	240	7	0	1.75				
1926-27	Saskatoon Sheiks	PrHL	32	14	15	3	1920	94	*5	2.94																	
1927-28	Saskatoon Sheiks	PrHL	28	*18	5	5	1680	41	*7	*1.46																	
1928-29	Springfield Indians	Can-Am	40	13	13	13	2550	58	6	1.36						4	1	3	0	240	8	0	2.00				
1929-30	Portland Buckaroos	PCHL	36	*20	10	6	2160	34	*16	*0.94																	
1930-31	Portland Buckaroos	PCHL	35	12	15	8	2100	61	6	1.74						4	0	1	1	130	5	0	2.31				
1931-32	Bronx Tigers	Can-Am	33	16	13	4	2040	74	4	2.18						8	*6	1	1	488	13	*2	1.60				
1932-33	**New York Rangers**	NHL	*48	23	17	8	2970	107	3	2.16	2.91					2	0	1	1	120	2	1	1.00				
1933-34	**New York Rangers**	NHL	*48	21	19	8	2990	113	7	2.27	2.89																
1934-35	**New York Rangers**	NHL	10	3	7	0	610	37	1	3.64	4.51																
	Philadelphia Arrows	Can-Am	1	1	0	0	60	2	0	2.00						3	1	2	0	180	4	1	*1.33				
	Portland Buckaroos	NWHL	21	11	4	6	1260	40	5	*1.90						3	1	2	0	180	5	0	*1.67				
1935-36	Portland Buckaroos	NWHL	40	18	14	8	2400	68	5	*1.70						3	3	0	0	180	3	0	*1.00				
1936-37	Portland Buckaroos	PCHL	40	22	13	5	2400	72	*7	*1.80																	
	Spokane Clippers	PCHL	1	1	0	0	60	0	1	0.00						2	1	1	0	120	4	0	2.00				
1937-38	Portland Buckaroos	PCHL	42	16	18	8	2520	85	5	*2.02						5	*4	1	0	300	10	*1	*2.00				
1938-39	Portland Buckaroos	PCHL	48	*31	9	8	2880	114	*9	*2.38																	
	Seattle Seahawks	PCHL	1				60	3	0	3.00						5	1	4	0	300	17	0	3.40				
1939-40	Portland Buckaroos	PCHL	40	17	18	5	2400	98	4	*2.45																	
1940-41	Portland Buckaroos	PCHL	1				60	2	0	2.00																	
	NHL Totals		106	47	43	16	6570	257	11	2.35		....	....	....	....	10	6	2	2	608	15	3	1.48	....	....	....	....

● ALMAS, RED Red (Ralph Clayton) Almas G – R. 5'9", 160 lbs. b: Saskatoon, Sask., 4/26/1924.

1941-42	Saskatoon Quakers	SJHL	8	6	2	0	480	22	0	*2.75						9	4	3	2	550	34	0	3.71				
1942-43	Windsor Chrysler	City Sr.	2				120	8	0	4.00																	
1943-44	Saskatoon Navy	SSHL	17				1020	65	0	*3.82						4	1	3	0	240	21	0	5.25				
1944-45			MILITARY SERVICE																								
1945-46	Saskatoon Elks	WCSHL	35	14	19	2	2100	147	1	4.20						3	0	3	0	180	14	0	4.67				
1946-47	Indianapolis Capitols	AHL	64	33	18	13	3840	215	3	3.36						5	1	3	....	263	13	0	2.97				
	Detroit Red Wings	NHL	1	0	1	0	60	5	0	5.00	4.89																
1947-48	Indianapolis Capitols	AHL	65	30	28	6	3890	246	1	3.78																	
1948-49	St. Louis Flyers	AHL	66	39	18	9	3920	189	5	2.86						7	3	4	0	465	22	0	2.84				
1949-50	St. Louis Flyers	AHL	55	29	21	5	3300	182	4	3.31						2	0	2	0	120	10	0	5.00				
1950-51	St. Louis Flyers	AHL	70	32	34	4	4280	251	3	3.52																	
	Chicago Black Hawks	NHL	1	0	1	0	60	5	0	5.00	5.70																
1951-52	St. Louis Flyers	AHL	68	28	39	1	4100	262	2	3.83																	
1952-53	St. Louis Flyers	AHL	53	23	29	1	3200	200	1	3.75																	
	Detroit Red Wings	NHL	1	0	0	1	60	3	0	3.00	3.87																

Season	Club	League	GP	W	L	T	Mins	GA	SO	Avg	AAvg	Eff	SA	S%	SAPG	GP	W	L	T	Mins	GA	SO	Avg	Eff	SA	S%	SAPG
			REGULAR SEASON													PLAYOFFS											
1953-54	Buffalo Bisons	AHL	9	4	5	0	540	45	0	5.00	....	....	....	....	....	....	....	....	....	....	....	....	....	....	....	....	....
	Victoria Cougars	WHL	56	20	26	10	3360	174	2	3.10	....	....	....	....	....	....	....	....	....	....	....	....	....	....	....	....	....
1954-55	Calgary Stampeders	WHL	2	1	0	1	120	9	0	4.50	....	....	....	....	....	....	....	....	....	....	....	....	....	....	....	....	....
	NHL Totals		**3**	**0**	**2**	**1**	**180**	**13**	**0**	**4.33**	....	....	....	....	....	**5**	**1**	**3**	....	**263**	**13**	**0**	**2.97**	....	....	....	....

AHL Second All-Star Team (1949)

Traded to **St. Louis** (AHL) by **Detroit** with Barry Sullivan, Lloyd Doran, Tony Licari and Thain Simon for Hec Highton and Joe Lund, September 9, 1948. Traded to **Detroit** by **Chicago** with Guyle Fielder and Steve Hrymnak for cash, September 23, 1952.

• ANDERSON, LORNE

Lorne Anderson G – L. 5'11", 166 lbs. b: Renfrew, Ont., 7/26/1931. d: 3/20/1984.

Season	Club	League	GP	W	L	T	Mins	GA	SO	Avg	AAvg	Eff	SA	S%	SAPG	GP	W	L	T	Mins	GA	SO	Avg	Eff	SA	S%	SAPG
1947-48	Renfrew Kings	Jr. B	STATISTICS NOT AVAILABLE																								
	Atlantic City Sea Gulls	EHL	2	....	....	....	120	15	0	7.50	....	....	....	....	....	....	....	....	....	....	....	....	....	....	....	....	....
1948-49	Renfrew Kings	Jr. B	10	8	2	0	610	38	1	3.74	....	....	....	....	....	19	15	4	0	1160	72	1	3.72	....	....	....	....
1949-50	Renfrew Kings	Jr. B	12	....	....	....	720	46	0	3.80	....	....	....	....	....	6	....	....	....	360	23	0	3.83	....	....	....	....
	Pembroke Lumber Kings	Jr. B	....	....	....	....	....	....	....	....	....	....	....	....	....	2	1	1	0	120	11	0	5.50	....	....	....	....
1950-51	Atlantic City Sea Gulls	EHL	52	....	....	....	3120	213	0	4.09	....	....	....	....	....	....	....	....	....	....	....	....	....	....	....	....	....
1951-52	New York Rovers	EHL	61	25	34	2	3685	231	1	3.76	....	....	....	....	....	....	....	....	....	....	....	....	....	....	....	....	....
	Boston Olympics	EHL	2	0	2	0	120	6	0	3.00	....	....	....	....	....	....	....	....	....	....	....	....	....	....	....	....	....
	New York Rangers	**NHL**	**3**	**1**	**2**	**0**	**180**	**18**	**0**	**6.00**	**7.20**	....	....	....	....	....	....	....	....	....	....	....	....	....	....	....	....
	New Haven Ramblers	EHL	....	....	....	....	....	....	....	....	....	....	....	....	....	2	....	....	....	120	7	0	3.50	....	....	....	....
1952-53	Sudbury Wolves	NOHA	48	31	15	2	2880	165	0	*3.44	....	....	....	....	....	7	3	4	0	430	28	0	3.91	....	....	....	....
1953-54	Sudbury Wolves	NOHA	31	....	....	....	1860	92	1	*2.97	....	....	....	....	....	7	3	4	0	420	19	*1	2.71	....	....	....	....
1954-55	Sudbury Wolves	NOHA	57	....	....	....	3420	215	2	3.77	....	....	....	....	....	....	....	....	....	....	....	....	....	....	....	....	....
1955-56	North Bay Trappers	NOHA	52	....	....	....	3120	169	3	3.25	....	....	....	....	....	7	....	....	....	420	25	0	3.57	....	....	....	....
1956-57	Pembroke Lumber Kings	EOHL	32	....	....	....	1920	140	1	4.37	....	....	....	....	....	....	....	....	....	....	....	....	....	....	....	....	....
1957-58	Renfrew Kings	Ott-Sr.	DID NOT PLAY – INJURED																								
1958-59	Renfrew Kings	Ott-Sr.	17	4	13	0	1020	112	0	6.59	....	....	....	....	....	....	....	....	....	....	....	....	....	....	....	....	....
	Pembroke Lumber Kings	Ott-Sr.	....	....	....	....	....	....	....	....	....	....	....	....	....	9	6	3	0	540	36	0	4.00	....	....	....	....
1959-60	Pembroke Lumber Kings	Ott-Sr.	9	7	2	0	540	24	2	2.67	....	....	....	....	....	6	2	4	0	360	25	0	4.16	....	....	....	....
1960-61	Pembroke Lumber Kings	Ott-Sr.	28	8	15	5	1680	145	0	5.18	....	....	....	....	....	7	3	4	0	440	39	0	5.32	....	....	....	....
	NHL Totals		**3**	**1**	**2**	**0**	**180**	**18**	**0**	**6.00**	....	....	....	....	....	....	....	....	....	....	....	....	....	....	....	....	....

• ASKEY, TOM

Tom Askey G – L. 6'2", 185 lbs. b: Kenmore, NY, 10/4/1974. Anaheim's 8th choice, 186th overall, in 1993 Entry Draft.

Season	Club	League	GP	W	L	T	Mins	GA	SO	Avg	AAvg	Eff	SA	S%	SAPG	GP	W	L	T	Mins	GA	SO	Avg	Eff	SA	S%	SAPG
1992-93	Ohio State University	CCHA	25	2	19	0	1235	125	1	6.07	....	....	....	....	....	....	....	....	....	....	....	....	....	....	....	....	....
1993-94	Ohio State University	CCHA	27	3	19	4	1488	103	1	4.15	....	....	....	....	....	....	....	....	....	....	....	....	....	....	....	....	....
1994-95	Ohio State University	CCHA	26	4	19	2	1387	121	0	5.23	....	....	....	....	....	....	....	....	....	....	....	....	....	....	....	....	....
1995-96	Ohio State University	CCHA	26	8	11	4	1340	68	1	3.05	....	....	....	....	....	....	....	....	....	....	....	....	....	....	....	....	....
1996-97	Baltimore Bandits	AHL	40	17	18	2	2239	140	1	3.75	....	....	....	....	....	3	0	3	....	138	11	0	4.79	....	....	....	....
	United States	WC-A	1	....	....	....	60	4	0	4.00	....	....	....	....	....	....	....	....	....	....	....	....	....	....	....	....	....
1997-98	**Anaheim Mighty Ducks**	**NHL**	**7**	**0**	**1**	**2**	**273**	**12**	**0**	**2.64**	**3.09**	**2.80**	**113**	**.894**	**24.8**	....	....	....	....	....	....	....	....	....	....	....	....
	Cincinnati Mighty Ducks	AHL	32	10	16	4	1752	104	3	3.56	....	....	....	....	....	....	....	....	....	....	....	....	....	....	....	....	....
	NHL Totals		**7**	**0**	**1**	**2**	**273**	**12**	**0**	**2.64**	....	....	**113**	**.894**	....	....	....	....	....	....	....	....	....	....	....	....	....

CCHA Second All-Star Team (1996)

• ASTROM, HARDY

Hardy Astrom G – L. 6', 170 lbs. b: Skelleftea, Sweden, 3/29/1951.

Season	Club	League	GP	W	L	T	Mins	GA	SO	Avg	AAvg	Eff	SA	S%	SAPG	GP	W	L	T	Mins	GA	SO	Avg	Eff	SA	S%	SAPG
1974-75	Skelleftea	Sweden	30	....	....	....	1800	96	0	3.20	....	....	....	....	....	5	....	....	....	307	19	....	3.71	....	....	....	....
1975-76	Skelleftea	Sweden	36	....	....	....	2160	149	1	4.14	....	....	....	....	....	....	....	....	....	....	....	....	....	....	....	....	....
1976-77	Sweden	C Cup	4	....	....	....	240	17	....	4.00	....	....	....	....	....	....	....	....	....	....	....	....	....	....	....	....	....
	Skelleftea	Sweden	35	....	....	....	2092	142	0	4.07	....	....	....	....	....	....	....	....	....	....	....	....	....	....	....	....	....
	Sweden	WEC-A	4	....	....	....	188	10	0	3.19	....	....	....	....	....	....	....	....	....	....	....	....	....	....	....	....	....
1977-78	**New York Rangers**	**NHL**	**4**	**2**	**2**	**0**	**240**	**14**	**0**	**3.50**	**3.28**	....	....	....	....	....	....	....	....	....	....	....	....	....	....	....	....
	New Haven Nighthawks	AHL	27	17	5	3	1572	69	*5	*2.63	....	....	....	....	....	....	....	....	....	....	....	....	....	....	....	....	....
	Sweden	WEC-A	4	....	....	....	208	15	....	4.33	....	....	....	....	....	....	....	....	....	....	....	....	....	....	....	....	....
1978-79	Skelleftea	Sweden	26	....	....	....	1515	101	0	4.00	....	....	....	....	....	....	....	....	....	....	....	....	....	....	....	....	....
1979-80	**Colorado Rockies**	**NHL**	**49**	**9**	**27**	**6**	**2574**	**161**	**0**	**3.75**	**3.30**	....	....	....	....	....	....	....	....	....	....	....	....	....	....	....	....
1980-81	**Colorado Rockies**	**NHL**	**30**	**6**	**15**	**6**	**1642**	**103**	**0**	**3.76**	**3.01**	....	....	....	....	....	....	....	....	....	....	....	....	....	....	....	....
	Fort Worth Texans	CHL	7	1	5	0	345	21	0	3.65	....	....	....	....	....	1	0	0	0	20	3	0	9.00	....	....	....	....
1981-82	Oklahoma City Stars	CHL	35	12	18	1	1911	154	0	4.84	....	....	....	....	....	2	0	1	0	61	8	0	7.87	....	....	....	....
1982-83	MoDo Ornskoldsvik	Sweden	DID NOT PLAY – INJURED																								
1983-84	MoDo Ornskoldsvik	Sweden	36	....	....	....	1083	39	....	2.16	....	....	....	....	....	....	....	....	....	....	....	....	....	....	....	....	....
1984-85	Sodertalje SK	Sweden	27	....	....	....	1508	85	*3	3.38	....	....	....	....	....	8	*5	3	0	495	26	*1	*3.15	....	....	....	....
1985-86	Sodertalje SK	Sweden	28	....	....	....	1650	87	0	3.16	....	....	....	....	....	7	4	3	0	420	23	0	3.29	....	....	....	....
	NHL Totals		**83**	**17**	**44**	**12**	**4456**	**278**	**0**	**3.74**	....	....	....	....	....	....	....	....	....	....	....	....	....	....	....	....	....

Signed as a free agent by **NY Rangers**, March 15, 1977. Rights traded to **Colorado** by **NY Rangers** for Bill Lochead, July 2, 1979.

• BAILEY, SCOTT

Scott Bailey G – L. 6', 195 lbs. b: Calgary, Alta., 5/2/1972. Boston's 3rd choice, 112th overall, in 1992 Entry Draft.

Season	Club	League	GP	W	L	T	Mins	GA	SO	Avg	AAvg	Eff	SA	S%	SAPG	GP	W	L	T	Mins	GA	SO	Avg	Eff	SA	S%	SAPG
1990-91	Spokane Chiefs	WHL	46	33	11	0	2537	157	*4	3.71	....	....	....	....	....	....	....	....	....	....	....	....	....	....	....	....	....
1991-92	Spokane Chiefs	WHL	65	34	23	5	3798	206	1	3.30	....	....	....	....	....	10	5	5	....	605	43	0	4.26	....	....	....	....
1992-93	Johnstown Chiefs	ECHL	36	13	15	3	1750	112	1	3.84	....	....	....	....	....	....	....	....	....	....	....	....	....	....	....	....	....
1993-94	Providence Bruins	AHL	7	2	2	2	377	24	0	3.82	....	....	....	....	....	....	....	....	....	....	....	....	....	....	....	....	....
	Charlotte Checkers	ECHL	36	22	11	3	2180	130	1	3.58	....	....	....	....	....	3	1	2	....	187	12	0	3.83	....	....	....	....
1994-95	Providence Bruins	AHL	52	25	16	9	2936	147	2	3.00	....	....	....	....	....	9	4	4	....	504	31	*2	3.69	....	....	....	....
1995-96	**Boston Bruins**	**NHL**	**11**	**5**	**1**	**2**	**571**	**31**	**0**	**3.26**	**3.20**	**3.83**	**264**	**.883**	**27.7**	....	....	....	....	....	....	....	....	....	....	....	....
	Providence Bruins	AHL	37	15	19	3	2210	120	1	3.26	....	....	....	....	....	2	1	1	....	119	6	0	3.03	....	....	....	....
1996-97	**Boston Bruins**	**NHL**	**8**	**1**	**5**	**0**	**394**	**24**	**0**	**3.65**	**3.87**	**4.84**	**181**	**.867**	**27.6**	....	....	....	....	....	....	....	....	....	....	....	....
	Providence Bruins	AHL	31	11	17	2	1735	112	0	3.87	....	....	....	....	....	7	3	4	....	453	23	0	3.05	....	....	....	....
1997-98	San Antonio Dragons	IHL	37	11	17	3	1898	118	1	3.73	....	....	....	....	....	....	....	....	....	....	....	....	....	....	....	....	....
	NHL Totals		**19**	**6**	**6**	**2**	**965**	**55**	**0**	**3.42**	....	....	**445**	**.876**	....	....	....	....	....	....	....	....	....	....	....	....	....

WHL West Second All-Star Team (1991, 1992)

• BAKER, STEVE

Steve Baker G – L. 6'3", 200 lbs. b: Boston, MA, 5/6/1957. NY Rangers' 4th choice, 44th overall, in 1977 Amateur Draft.

Season	Club	League	GP	W	L	T	Mins	GA	SO	Avg	AAvg	Eff	SA	S%	SAPG	GP	W	L	T	Mins	GA	SO	Avg	Eff	SA	S%	SAPG
1975-76	Union College	ECAC	9	....	....	....	480	21	0	2.62	....	....	....	....	....	....	....	....	....	....	....	....	....	....	....	....	....
1976-77	Union College	ECAC	19	16	3	0	1117	67	0	3.60	....	....	....	....	....	2	1	1	0	120	10	0	5.00	....	....	....	....
1977-78	Union College	ECAC	6	....	....	....	[illegible]	20	0	5.60	....	....	....	....	....	....	....	....	....	....	....	....	....	....	....	....	....
	Toledo Goaldiggers	IHL	10	....	....	....	544	46	0	5.07	....	....	....	....	....	....	....	....	....	....	....	....	....	....	....	....	....
1978-79	New Haven Nighthawks	AHL	24	15	5	4	1435	82	1	3.43	....	....	....	....	....	5	2	3	0	297	17	0	3.43	....	....	....	....
1979-80	**New York Rangers**	**NHL**	**27**	**9**	**8**	**6**	**1391**	**79**	**1**	**3.41**	**2.99**	....	....	....	....	....	....	....	....	....	....	....	....	....	....	....	....
	New Haven Nighthawks	AHL	9	6	1	1	492	29	0	3.54	....	....	....	....	....	....	....	....	....	....	....	....	....	....	....	....	....
1980-81	New Haven Nighthawks	AHL	25	10	11	4	1497	90	1	3.57	....	....	....	....	....	....	....	....	....	....	....	....	....	....	....	....	....
	New York Rangers	**NHL**	**21**	**10**	**6**	**5**	**1260**	**73**	**2**	**3.48**	**2.79**	....	....	....	....	**14**	**7**	**7**	....	**826**	**55**	**0**	**4.00**	....	....	....	....
1981-82	United States	C Cup	1	0	0	1	60	4	0	4.00	....	....	....	....	....	....	....	....	....	....	....	....	....	....	....	....	....
	Springfield Indians	AHL	11	2	7	1	503	42	0	5.01	....	....	....	....	....	....	....	....	....	....	....	....	....	....	....	....	....
	New York Rangers	**NHL**	**6**	**1**	**5**	**0**	**328**	**33**	**0**	**6.04**	**4.66**	....	....	....	....	....	....	....	....	....	....	....	....	....	....	....	....
1982-83	**New York Rangers**	**NHL**	**3**	**0**	**1**	**0**	**102**	**5**	**0**	**2.94**	**2.35**	**3.34**	**44**	**.886**	**25.9**	....	....	....	....	....	....	....	....	....	....	....	....
	Tulsa Oilers	CHL	*49	22	27	0	*2901	186	0	3.85	....	....	....	....	....	....	....	....	....	....	....	....	....	....	....	....	....
1983-84	Binghamton Whalers	AHL	6	0	4	1	345	35	0	6.09	....	....	....	....	....	....	....	....	....	....	....	....	....	....	....	....	....
	Maine Mariners	AHL	13	5	5	2	744	41	0	3.31	....	....	....	....	....	6	3	3	0	353	23	0	3.91	....	....	....	....
	NHL Totals		**57**	**20**	**20**	**11**	**3081**	**190**	**3**	**3.70**	....	....	....	....	....	**14**	**7**	**7**	....	**826**	**55**	**0**	**4.00**	....	....	....	....

• BALES, MIKE

Mike Bales G – L. 6'1", 180 lbs. b: Prince Albert, Sask., 8/6/1971. Boston's 6th choice, 105th overall, in 1990 Entry Draft.

			REGULAR SEASON													PLAYOFFS											
Season	Club	League	GP	W	L	T	Mins	GA	SO	Avg	AAvg	Eff	SA	S%	SAPG	GP	W	L	T	Mins	GA	SO	Avg	Eff	SA	S%	SAPG
1989-90	Ohio State University	CCHA	21	6	13	2	1117	95	0	5.11	....	....	....	....	....	....	....	....	....	....	....	....	....	....	....	....	....
1990-91	Ohio State University	CCHA	*39	11	24	3	*2180	184	0	5.06	....	....	....	....	....	....	....	....	....	....	....	....	....	....	....	....	....
1991-92	Ohio State University	CCHA	36	11	20	5	2060	180	0	5.24	....	....	....	....	....	....	....	....	....	....	....	....	....	....	....	....	....
1992-93	**Boston Bruins**	**NHL**	**1**	**0**	**0**	**0**	**25**	**1**	**0**	**2.40**	**2.04**	**2.40**	**10**	**.900**	**24.0**	....	....	....	....	....	....	....	....	....	....	....	....
	Providence Bruins	AHL	44	22	17	0	2363	166	1	4.21	....	....	....	....	....	2	0	2	....	118	8	0	4.07	....	....	....	....
1993-94	Providence Bruins	AHL	33	9	15	4	1757	130	0	4.44	....	....	....	....	....	....	....	....	....	....	....	....	....	....	....	....	....
1994-95	P.E.I. Senators	AHL	45	25	16	3	2649	160	2	3.62	....	....	....	....	....	9	6	3	....	530	24	*2	2.72	....	....	....	....
	Ottawa Senators	**NHL**	**1**	**0**	**0**	**0**	**3**	**0**	**0**	**0.00**	**0.00**	**0.00**	**1**	**1.000**	**20.0**	....	....	....	....	....	....	....	....	....	....	....	....
1995-96	**Ottawa Senators**	**NHL**	**20**	**2**	**14**	**1**	**1040**	**72**	**0**	**4.15**	**4.09**	**5.34**	**560**	**.871**	**32.3**	....	....	....	....	....	....	....	....	....	....	....	....
	P.E.I. Senators	AHL	2	0	2	0	118	11	0	5.58	....	....	....	....	....	....	....	....	....	....	....	....	....	....	....	....	....
1996-97	**Ottawa Senators**	**NHL**	**1**	**0**	**1**	**0**	**52**	**4**	**0**	**4.62**	**4.89**	**10.27**	**18**	**.778**	**20.8**	....	....	....	....	....	....	....	....	....	....	....	....
	Baltimore Bandits	AHL	46	13	21	8	2544	130	3	3.07	....	....	....	....	....	....	....	....	....	....	....	....	....	....	....	....	....
1997-98	Rochester Americans	AHL	39	13	19	5	2229	127	0	3.42	....	....	....	....	....	....	....	....	....	....	....	....	....	....	....	....	....
	NHL Totals		**23**	**2**	**15**	**1**	**1120**	**77**	**0**	**4.12**	....	....	**589**	**.869**	....	....	....	....	....	....	....	....	....	....	....	....	....

Signed as a free agent by **Ottawa**, July 4, 1994. Signed as a free agent by **Buffalo**, September 9, 1997.

• BANNERMAN, MURRAY

Murray Bannerman G – L. 5'11", 185 lbs. b: Fort Frances, Ont., 4/27/1957. Vancouver's 5th choice, 58th overall, in 1977 Amateur Draft.

1972-73	St. James Canadians	MJHL	31	....	....	....	1778	104	*1	*3.51	....	....	....	....	....	....	....	....	....	....	....	....	....	....	....	....	....
1973-74	St. James Canadians	MJHL	17	....	....	....	930	69	0	4.45	....	....	....	....	....	....	....	....	....	....	....	....	....	....	....	....	....
	Winnipeg Clubs	WCJHL	6	....	....	....	258	29	0	6.74	....	....	....	....	....	....	....	....	....	....	....	....	....	....	....	....	....
1974-75	Winnipeg Clubs	WCJHL	28	3	12	5	1351	113	0	5.02	....	....	....	....	....	....	....	....	....	....	....	....	....	....	....	....	....
1975-76	Victoria Cougars	WCJHL	44	....	....	....	2450	178	1	4.36	....	....	....	....	....	*15	....	....	....	*878	50	0	3.42	....	....	....	....
1976-77	Victoria Cougars	WHL	67	....	....	....	3893	262	2	4.04	....	....	....	....	....	4	....	....	....	234	20	0	5.13	....	....	....	....
1977-78	Fort Wayne Komets	IHL	44	....	....	....	2435	133	1	3.28	....	....	....	....	....	6	....	....	....	335	26	0	4.66	....	....	....	....
	Vancouver Canucks	**NHL**	**1**	**0**	**0**	**0**	**20**	**0**	**0**	**0.00**	**0.00**					....	....	....	....	....	....	....	....	....	....	....	....
1978-79	New Brunswick Hawks	AHL	47	22	14	5	2557	152	0	3.57	....	....	....	....	....	3	1	1	0	122	10	0	4.92	....	....	....	....
1979-80	New Brunswick Hawks	AHL	*61	32	20	5	3361	186	*3	3.32	....	....	....	....	....	*17	*10	6	0	*1049	51	0	2.92	....	....	....	....
1980-81	**Chicago Black Hawks**	**NHL**	**15**	**2**	**10**	**2**	**865**	**62**	**0**	**4.30**	**3.45**					....	....	....	....	....	....	....	....	....	....	....	....
1981-82	**Chicago Black Hawks**	**NHL**	**29**	**11**	**12**	**4**	**1671**	**116**	**1**	**4.17**	**3.22**	....	....	....	....	**10**	**5**	**4**	....	**555**	**35**	**0**	**3.78**	....	....	....	....
1982-83	**Chicago Black Hawks**	**NHL**	**41**	**24**	**12**	**5**	**2460**	**127**	**4**	**3.10**	**2.46**	**3.07**	**1283**	**.901**	**31.3**	**8**	**4**	**4**	....	**480**	**32**	**0**	**4.00**	....	....	....	....
1983-84	**Chicago Black Hawks**	**NHL**	**56**	**23**	**29**	**4**	**3335**	**188**	**2**	**3.38**	**2.63**	**3.81**	**1667**	**.887**	**30.0**	**5**	**2**	**3**	....	**300**	**17**	**0**	**3.40**	**3.38**	**171**	**.901**	**34.2**
1984-85	**Chicago Black Hawks**	**NHL**	**60**	**27**	**25**	**4**	**3371**	**215**	**0**	**3.83**	**3.04**	**4.46**	**1847**	**.884**	**32.9**	**15**	**9**	**6**	....	**906**	**72**	**0**	**4.77**	**6.28**	**547**	**.868**	**36.2**
1985-86	**Chicago Black Hawks**	**NHL**	**48**	**20**	**19**	**6**	**2689**	**201**	**1**	**4.48**	**3.50**	**5.85**	**1538**	**.869**	**34.3**	**2**	**0**	**1**	....	**81**	**9**	**0**	**6.67**	**15.01**	**40**	**.775**	**29.6**
1986-87	**Chicago Blackhawks**	**NHL**	**39**	**9**	**18**	**8**	**2059**	**142**	**0**	**4.14**	**3.49**	**5.24**	**1122**	**.873**	**32.7**	....	....	....	....	....	....	....	....	....	....	....	....
1987-88	Baltimore Skipjacks	AHL	41	6	21	5	2014	154	0	4.59	....	....	....	....	....	....	....	....	....	....	....	....	....	....	....	....	....
	Saginaw Hawks	IHL	3	0	2	0	140	15	0	6.43	....	....	....	....	....	....	....	....	....	....	....	....	....	....	....	....	....
	NHL Totals		**289**	**116**	**125**	**33**	**16470**	**1051**	**8**	**3.83**	....	....	....	....	....	**40**	**20**	**18**	....	**2322**	**165**	**0**	**4.26**	....	....	....	....

IHL First All-Star Team (1978) • AHL Second All-Star Team (1980)

Played in NHL All-Star Game (1983, 1984)

Traded to **Chicago** by **Vancouver** to complete transaction that sent Pit Martin to Vancouver (November 4, 1977), May 27, 1978.

• BARON, MARCO

Marco Baron G – L. 5'11", 180 lbs. b: Montreal, Que., 4/8/1959. Boston's 6th choice, 99th overall, in 1979 Entry Draft.

1975-76	Montreal Jr. Canadiens	QMJHL	23	....	....	....	1376	81	2	3.53	....	....	....	....	....	....	....	....	....	....	....	....	....	....	....	....	....
1976-77	Montreal Jr. Canadiens	QMJHL	41	....	....	....	2006	182	1	5.44	....	....	....	....	....	....	....	....	....	....	....	....	....	....	....	....	....
1977-78	Verdun Eperviers	QMJHL	61	....	....	....	3395	251	0	4.44	....	....	....	....	....	13	....	....	....	780	51	0	3.92	....	....	....	....
1978-79	Verdun Eperviers	QMJHL	67	....	....	....	3630	230	4	3.80	....	....	....	....	....	11	....	....	....	610	46	0	4.52	....	....	....	....
1979-80	**Boston Bruins**	**NHL**	**1**	**0**	**1**	**0**	**40**	**2**	**0**	**3.00**	**2.64**	....	....	....	....	....	....	....	....	....	....	....	....	....	....	....	....
	Binghamton Whalers	AHL	6	0	5	0	265	26	0	5.89	....	....	....	....	....	....	....	....	....	....	....	....	....	....	....	....	....
	Grand Rapids Owls	IHL	35	....	....	....	1995	135	0	4.06	....	....	....	....	....	....	....	....	....	....	....	....	....	....	....	....	....
1980-81	Springfield Indians	AHL	23	12	11	0	1300	79	1	3.45	....	....	....	....	....	....	....	....	....	....	....	....	....	....	....	....	....
	Boston Bruins	**NHL**	**10**	**3**	**4**	**1**	**507**	**24**	**0**	**2.84**	**2.27**	....	....	....	....	**1**	**0**	**1**	....	**20**	**3**	**0**	**9.00**	....	....	....	....
1981-82	Erie Blades	AHL	2	1	1	0	119	8	0	4.04	....	....	....	....	....	....	....	....	....	....	....	....	....	....	....	....	....
	Boston Bruins	**NHL**	**44**	**22**	**16**	**4**	**2515**	**144**	**1**	**3.44**	**2.64**	....	....	....	....	....	....	....	....	....	....	....	....	....	....	....	....
1982-83	**Boston Bruins**	**NHL**	**9**	**6**	**3**	**0**	**516**	**33**	**0**	**3.84**	**3.07**	**5.44**	**233**	**.858**	**27.1**	....	....	....	....	....	....	....	....	....	....	....	....
	Baltimore Skipjacks	AHL	22	8	11	1	1260	97	0	4.62	....	....	....	....	....	....	....	....	....	....	....	....	....	....	....	....	....
1983-84	Moncton Alpines	AHL	16	6	7	3	858	45	0	3.15	....	....	....	....	....	....	....	....	....	....	....	....	....	....	....	....	....
	Los Angeles Kings	**NHL**	**21**	**3**	**14**	**4**	**1211**	**87**	**0**	**4.31**	**3.38**	**5.92**	**633**	**.863**	**31.4**	....	....	....	....	....	....	....	....	....	....	....	....
1984-85	Nova Scotia Oilers	AHL	17	8	7	1	1010	45	0	2.67	....	....	....	....	....	6	2	4	0	406	25	0	3.69	....	....	....	....
	Sherbrooke Canadiens	AHL	1	0	0	0	32	5	0	9.37	....	....	....	....	....	....	....	....	....	....	....	....	....	....	....	....	....
	Edmonton Oilers	**NHL**	**1**	**0**	**1**	**0**	**33**	**2**	**0**	**3.64**	**2.89**	**8.09**	**9**	**.778**	**16.4**	....	....	....	....	....	....	....	....	....	....	....	....
	NHL Totals		**86**	**34**	**39**	**9**	**4822**	**292**	**1**	**3.63**	....	....	....	....	....	**1**	**0**	**1**	....	**20**	**3**	**0**	**9.00**	....	....	....	....

QMJHL Second All-Star Team (1978)

Traded to **LA Kings** by **Boston** for Bob LaForest, January 3, 1984. Signed as a free agent by **Edmonton**, February 21, 1985.

• BARRASSO, TOM

Tom Barrasso G – R. 6'3", 211 lbs. b: Boston, MA, 3/31/1965. Buffalo's 1st choice, 5th overall, in 1983 Entry Draft.

1982-83	Acton-Boxboro	H.S.	23	....	....	....	1035	17	10	0.74	....	....	....	....	....	....	....	....	....	....	....	....	....	....	....	....	....
	United States	WJC-A	3	....	....	....	140	12	....	5.14	....	....	....	....	....	....	....	....	....	....	....	....	....	....	....	....	....
1983-84	**Buffalo Sabres**	**NHL**	**42**	**26**	**12**	**3**	**2475**	**117**	**2**	**2.84**	**2.21**	**3.03**	**1098**	**.893**	**26.6**	**3**	**0**	**2**	....	**139**	**8**	**0**	**3.45**	**4.68**	**59**	**.864**	**25.5**
1984-85	United States	C Cup	5	2	2	1	252	13	0	3.00	....	....	....	....	....	....	....	....	....	....	....	....	....	....	....	....	....
	Buffalo Sabres	**NHL**	**54**	**25**	**18**	**10**	**3248**	**144**	***5**	***2.66**	**2.09**	**3.01**	**1274**	**.887**	**23.5**	**5**	**2**	**3**	....	**300**	**22**	**0**	**4.40**	**6.41**	**151**	**.854**	**30.2**
	Rochester Americans	AHL	5	3	1	1	267	6	1	1.35	....	....	....	....	....	....	....	....	....	....	....	....	....	....	....	....	....
1985-86	**Buffalo Sabres**	**NHL**	**60**	**29**	**24**	**5**	**3561**	**214**	**2**	**3.61**	**2.80**	**4.34**	**1778**	**.880**	**30.0**	....	....	....	....	....	....	....	....	....	....	....	....
	United States	WEC-A	5	....	....	....	260	18	....	4.15	....	....	....	....	....	....	....	....	....	....	....	....	....	....	....	....	....
1986-87	**Buffalo Sabres**	**NHL**	**46**	**17**	**23**	**2**	**2501**	**152**	**2**	**3.65**	**3.07**	**4.62**	**1202**	**.874**	**28.8**	....	....	....	....	....	....	....	....	....	....	....	....
1987-88	United States	C Cup	1	0	1	0	60	5	0	5.00	....	....	....	....	....	....	....	....	....	....	....	....	....	....	....	....	....
	Buffalo Sabres	**NHL**	**54**	**25**	**18**	**8**	**3133**	**173**	**2**	**3.31**	**2.74**	**3.45**	**1658**	**.896**	**31.8**	**4**	**1**	**3**	....	**224**	**16**	**0**	**4.29**	**5.72**	**120**	**.867**	**32.1**
1988-89	**Buffalo Sabres**	**NHL**	**10**	**2**	**7**	**0**	**545**	**45**	**0**	**4.95**	**4.09**	**7.82**	**285**	**.842**	**31.4**	....	....	....	....	....	....	....	....	....	....	....	....
	Pittsburgh Penguins	**NHL**	**44**	**18**	**15**	**7**	**2406**	**162**	**0**	**4.04**	**3.34**	**4.53**	**1445**	**.888**	**36.0**	**11**	**7**	**4**	....	**631**	**40**	**0**	**3.80**	**3.91**	**389**	**.897**	**37.0**
1989-90	**Pittsburgh Penguins**	**NHL**	**24**	**7**	**12**	**3**	**1294**	**101**	**0**	**4.68**	**3.93**	**6.32**	**748**	**.865**	**34.7**	....	....	....	....	....	....	....	....	....	....	....	....
1990-91	**Pittsburgh Penguins**	**NHL**	**48**	**27**	**16**	**3**	**2754**	**165**	**1**	**3.59**	**3.21**	**3.75**	**1579**	**.896**	**34.4**	**20**	**12**	**7**	....	**1175**	**51**	***1**	***2.60**	**2.11**	**629**	**.919**	**32.1**
1991-92	**Pittsburgh Penguins**	**NHL**	**57**	**25**	**22**	**9**	**3329**	**196**	**1**	**3.53**	**3.13**	**4.07**	**1702**	**.885**	**30.7**	***21**	***16**	**5**	....	***1233**	**58**	**1**	**2.82**	**2.63**	**622**	**.907**	**30.3**
1992-93	**Pittsburgh Penguins**	**NHL**	**63**	***43**	**14**	**5**	**3702**	**186**	**4**	**3.01**	**2.55**	**2.97**	**1885**	**.901**	**30.6**	**12**	**7**	**5**	....	**722**	**35**	***2**	**2.91**	**2.75**	**370**	**.905**	**30.7**
1993-94	**Pittsburgh Penguins**	**NHL**	**44**	**22**	**15**	**5**	**2482**	**139**	**2**	**3.36**	**3.20**	**3.58**	**1304**	**.893**	**31.5**	**6**	**2**	**4**	....	**356**	**17**	**0**	**2.87**	**3.01**	**162**	**.895**	**27.3**
1994-95	**Pittsburgh Penguins**	**NHL**	**2**	**0**	**1**	**1**	**125**	**8**	**0**	**3.84**	**3.97**	**4.10**	**75**	**.893**	**36.0**	**2**	**0**	**1**	....	**80**	**8**	**0**	**6.00**	**11.71**	**41**	**.805**	**30.8**
1995-96	**Pittsburgh Penguins**	**NHL**	**49**	**29**	**16**	**2**	**2799**	**160**	**2**	**3.43**	**3.38**	**3.38**	**1626**	**.902**	**34.9**	**10**	**4**	**5**	....	**558**	**26**	**1**	**2.80**	**2.16**	**337**	**.923**	**36.2**
1996-97	**Pittsburgh Penguins**	**NHL**	**5**	**0**	**5**	**0**	**270**	**26**	**0**	**5.78**	**6.13**	**8.08**	**186**	**.860**	**41.3**	....	....	....	....	....	....	....	....	....	....	....	....
1997-98	**Pittsburgh Penguins**	**NHL**	**63**	**31**	**14**	**13**	**3542**	**122**	**7**	**2.07**	**2.41**	**1.62**	**1556**	**.922**	**26.4**	**6**	**2**	**4**	....	**376**	**17**	**0**	**2.71**	**2.69**	**171**	**.901**	**27.3**
	NHL Totals		**665**	**326**	**232**	**76**	**38166**	**2110**	**30**	**3.32**	....	....	**19401**	**.891**	....	**100**	**53**	**43**	....	**5794**	**298**	**5**	**3.09**	....	....	....	....

NHL All-Rookie Team (1984) • NHL First All-Star Team (1984) • Won Calder Memorial Trophy (1984) • Won Vezina Trophy (1984) • NHL Second All-Star Team (1985, 1993) • Shared William Jennings Trophy with Bob Sauve (1985)

Played in NHL All-Star Game (1985)

Traded to **Pittsburgh** by **Buffalo** with Buffalo's 3rd round choice (Joe Dziedzic) in 1990 Entry Draft for Doug Bodger and Darrin Shannon, November 12, 1988.

• BASSEN, HANK

Hank (Henry) "Red" Bassen G – L. 5'10", 180 lbs. b: Calgary, Alta., 12/6/1932.

1949-50	Calgary Buffaloes	WCJHL	30	11	18	1	1750	131	0	4.49	....	....	....	....	....	....	....	....	....	....	....	....	....	....	....	....	....
1950-51	Calgary Buffaloes	WCJHL	37	8	27	2	2280	176	*2	4.63	....	....	....	....	....	....	....	....	....	....	....	....	....	....	....	....	....
	Medicine Hat Tigers	WCJHL	1	0	1	0	60	10	0	10.00	....	....	....	....	....	....	....	....	....	....	....	....	....	....	....	....	....

			REGULAR SEASON													PLAYOFFS											
Season	Club	League	GP	W	L	T	Mins	GA	SO	Avg	AAvg	Eff	SA	S%	SAPG	GP	W	L	T	Mins	GA	SO	Avg	Eff	SA	S%	SAPG
1951-52	Calgary Buffaloes	WCJHL	42	21	17	4	2580	132	1	3.07	....	....	....	....	....	3	0	3	0	180	13	0	4.33	....	....	....	....
1952-53	Calgary Buffaloes	WCJHL	30	14	13	3	1860	145	0	4.68	....	....	....	....	....	3	0	3	0	180	11	0	3.67	....	....	....	....
1953-54	Chatham Maroons	OHA Sr.	55	22	30	3	3300	205	2	3.73	....	....	....	....	....	6	2	4	0	360	25	*1	4.17	....	....	....	....
1954-55	Buffalo Bisons	AHL	37	13	19	5	2220	121	3	3.27	....	....	....	....	....	....	....	....	....	....	....	....	....	....	....	....	....
	Chicago Black Hawks	**NHL**	**21**	**4**	**9**	**8**	**1260**	**63**	**0**	**3.00**	**3.71**	....	....	....	....	....	....	....	....	....	....	....	....	....	....	....	....
1955-56	Buffalo Bisons	AHL	55	26	23	4	3300	201	0	3.80	....	....	....	....	....	5	2	3	0	299	20	0	4.01	....	....	....	....
	Chicago Black Hawks	**NHL**	**12**	**2**	**9**	**1**	**720**	**42**	**1**	**3.50**	**4.31**	....	....	....	....	....	....	....	....	....	....	....	....	....	....	....	....
1956-57	Calgary Stampeders	WHL	68	29	35	4	4125	223	5	3.24	....	....	....	....	....	3	1	2	0	180	12	0	4.00	....	....	....	....
1957-58	Seattle Totems	WHL	60	27	27	6	3600	184	3	3.06	....	....	....	....	....	9	5	4	0	557	21	0	*2.26	....	....	....	....
1958-59	Springfield Indians	AHL	29	13	14	2	1740	102	1	3.52	....	....	....	....	....	....	....	....	....	....	....	....	....	....	....	....	....
1959-60	Vancouver Canucks	WHL	*70	*44	19	6	4220	172	*5	*2.45	....	....	....	....	....	*11	*9	2	0	*696	22	0	*1.90	....	....	....	....
1960-61	**Detroit Red Wings**	**NHL**	**35**	**13**	**13**	**8**	**2050**	**102**	**0**	**2.97**	**3.05**	....	....	....	....	**4**	**1**	**2**	....	**220**	**9**	**0**	**2.45**	....	....	....	....
1961-62	**Detroit Red Wings**	**NHL**	**27**	**9**	**12**	**6**	**1620**	**76**	**3**	**2.81**	**2.87**	....	....	....	....	....	....	....	....	....	....	....	....	....	....	....	....
	Edmonton Flyers	WHL	9	4	4	1	557	30	0	3.23	....	....	....	....	....	....	....	....	....	....	....	....	....	....	....	....	....
	Sudbury Wolves	EPHL	3	1	2	0	180	14	0	4.67	....	....	....	....	....	....	....	....	....	....	....	....	....	....	....	....	....
1962-63	**Detroit Red Wings**	**NHL**	**17**	**6**	**5**	**5**	**980**	**53**	**0**	**3.24**	**3.37**	....	....	....	....	....	....	....	....	....	....	....	....	....	....	....	....
	Pittsburgh Hornets	AHL	40	15	23	2	2400	134	2	3.35	....	....	....	....	....	....	....	....	....	....	....	....	....	....	....	....	....
1963-64	Cincinnati Wings	CHL	7	0	6	1	420	39	0	5.57	....	....	....	....	....	....	....	....	....	....	....	....	....	....	....	....	....
	Detroit Red Wings	**NHL**	**1**	**0**	**1**	**0**	**60**	**4**	**0**	**4.00**	**4.45**	....	....	....	....	....	....	....	....	....	....	....	....	....	....	....	....
	Pittsburgh Hornets	AHL	26	9	15	2	1560	82	1	3.15	....	....	....	....	....	1	0	1	0	60	4	0	4.00	....	....	....	....
1964-65	Pittsburgh Hornets	AHL	57	24	25	7	3430	182	2	3.18	....	....	....	....	....	4	1	3	0	240	15	0	3.75	....	....	....	....
1965-66	**Detroit Red Wings**	**NHL**	**11**	**3**	**3**	**0**	**406**	**17**	**0**	**2.51**	**2.54**	....	....	....	....	**1**	**0**	**1**	....	**54**	**2**	**0**	**2.22**	....	....	....	....
1966-67	**Detroit Red Wings**	**NHL**	**8**	**2**	**4**	**0**	**384**	**22**	**0**	**3.44**	**3.57**	....	....	....	....	....	....	....	....	....	....	....	....	....	....	....	....
	Pittsburgh Hornets	AHL	10	6	3	1	570	18	3	1.89	....	....	....	....	....	9	*8	1	0	541	15	1	*1.66	....	....	....	....
1967-68	**Pittsburgh Penguins**	**NHL**	**25**	**7**	**10**	**3**	**1299**	**62**	**1**	**2.86**	**3.17**	....	....	....	....	....	....	....	....	....	....	....	....	....	....	....	....
	NHL Totals		**157**	**46**	**66**	**31**	**8779**	**441**	**5**	**3.01**	....	....	....	....	....	**5**	**1**	**3**	....	**274**	**11**	**0**	**2.41**	....	....	....	....

WHL First All-Star Team (1960) • Won WHL Leading Goaltender Award (1960) • Won Leader Cup (WHL - MVP) (tied with Guyle Fielder) (1960)

Traded to **Detroit** by **Chicago** with John Wilson, Forbes Kennedy and William Preston for Ted Lindsay and Glenn Hall, July, 1957. Traded to **Springfield** (AHL) by **Detroit** with Dennis Olson and Bill McCreary for Gerry Ehman, April, 1958. Traded to **Vancouver** (WHL) by **Springfield** (AHL) for Colin Kilburn and $7,500, July, 1959. Claimed by **Detroit** from **Vancouver** (WHL) in Inter-League Draft, June, 1960. Traded to **Pittsburgh** by **Detroit** for Roy Edwards, September 7, 1967.

• BASTIEN, BAZ

Baz (Aldege) Bastien G – L. 5'7", 160 lbs. b: Timmins, Ont., 8/29/1919. d: 3/15/1983.

Season	Club	League	GP	W	L	T	Mins	GA	SO	Avg	AAvg	Eff	SA	S%	SAPG	GP	W	L	T	Mins	GA	SO	Avg	Eff	SA	S%	SAPG
1939-40	Port Colburne Sailors	OHA Sr.	17	....	....	....	1020	47	*2	2.76	....	....	....	....	....	4	1	3	0	240	23	0	5.75	....	....	....	....
	Atlantic City Seagulls	EHL	2	....	....	....	90	4	0	2.67	....	....	....	....	....	2	1	1	0	120	9	0	4.50	....	....	....	....
1940-41	Toronto Marlboros	OHA Sr.	15	....	....	....	880	35	1	2.39	....	....	....	....	....	18	11	7	0	1090	36	2	1.98	....	....	....	....
1941-42	Toronto Marlboros	OHA Sr.	30	14	12	4	1800	75	1	2.50	....	....	....	....	....	6	2	4	0	360	18	0	*3.00	....	....	....	....
1942-43	Cornwall Flyers	QSHL	30	....	....	....	1760	97	*4	*3.31	....	....	....	....	....	6	2	4	0	360	22	0	3.61	....	....	....	....
1943-44			MILITARY SERVICE																								
1944-45			MILITARY SERVICE																								
1945-46	**Toronto Maple Leafs**	**NHL**	**5**	**0**	**4**	**1**	**300**	**20**	**0**	**4.00**	**3.70**	....	....	....	....	....	....	....	....	....	....	....	....	....	....	....	....
	Pittsburgh Hornets	AHL	38	16	15	7	2280	144	1	3.79	....	....	....	....	....	6	3	3	0	385	20	0	3.12	....	....	....	....
1946-47	Pittsburgh Hornets	AHL	40	23	12	5	2400	104	*7	*2.60	....	....	....	....	....	12	7	5	0	720	29	1	2.42	....	....	....	....
	Hollywood Wolves	PCHL	22	....	....	....	1320	33	5	*1.50	....	....	....	....	....	....	....	....	....	....	....	....	....	....	....	....	....
1947-48	Pittsburgh Hornets	AHL	68	38	18	12	4080	170	*5	*2.50	....	....	....	....	....	2	0	2	0	130	6	0	2.77	....	....	....	....
1948-49	Pittsburgh Hornets	AHL	68	39	19	10	4080	175	6	*2.57	....	....	....	....	....	....	....	....	....	....	....	....	....	....	....	....	....
	NHL Totals		**5**	**0**	**4**	**1**	**300**	**20**	**0**	**4.00**	....	....	....	....	....	....	....	....	....	....	....	....	....	....	....	....	....

AHL First All-Star Team (1947, 1948, 1949) • Won Harry "Hap" Holmes Memorial Award (fewest goals against - AHL) (1948, 1949)

• Suffered career-ending eye injury on 1st day of training camp, September 30, 1949.

• BAUMAN, GARY

Gary Bauman G – L. 5'11", 175 lbs. b: Innisfail, Alta., 7/21/1940.

Season	Club	League	GP	W	L	T	Mins	GA	SO	Avg	AAvg	Eff	SA	S%	SAPG	GP	W	L	T	Mins	GA	SO	Avg	Eff	SA	S%	SAPG
1958-59	Prince Albert Mintos	SJHL	22	....	....	....	1310	90	0	4.12	....	....	....	....	....	4	....	....	....	240	10	0	*2.50	....	....	....	....
1959-60	Prince Albert Mintos	SJHL	55	....	....	....	3300	203	4	3.69	....	....	....	....	....	7	....	....		420	20	0	4.00	....	....	....	....
1960-61	Michigan Tech Huskies	WCHA		DID NOT PLAY			FRESHMAN																				
1961-62	Michigan Tech Huskies	WCHA	25	....	....	....	1500	61	0	2.44	....	....	....	....	....												
1962-63	Michigan Tech Huskies	WCHA	26	....	....	....	1500	70	3	2.80	....	....	....	....	....	....					....	....	....			....	....
1963-64	Michigan Tech Huskies	NCAA	24	....	....	....	1440	67	3	2.79	....	....	....	....	....	....	....	....	....	....	....	....	....	....	....	....	....
1964-65	Omaha Knights	CHL	43	22	16	5	2580	159	1	3.70	....	....	....	....	....	6	2	4	0	360	19	*1	3.17	....	....	....	....
1965-66	Quebec Aces	AHL	52	*38	11	4	3142	154	4	2.94	....	....	....	....	....	6	2	4	0	360	25	0	4.17	....	....	....	....
1966-67	**Montreal Canadiens**	**NHL**	**2**	**1**	**1**	**0**	**120**	**5**	**0**	**2.50**	**2.59**	....	....	....	....	....	....	....	....	....	....	....	....	....	....	....	....
	Quebec Aces	AHL	40	21	15	4	2330	128	2	3.30	....	....	....	....	....	5	2	3	0	300	18	0	3.60	....	....	....	....
1967-68	Rochester Americans	AHL	3	0	2	0	140	10	0	4.29	....	....	....	....	....	....	....	....	....	....	....	....	....	....	....	....	....
	Minnesota North Stars	**NHL**	**26**	**5**	**13**	**5**	**1294**	**75**	**0**	**3.48**	**3.88**	....	....	....	....	....	....	....	....	....	....	....	....	....	....	....	....
1968-69	**Minnesota North Stars**	**NHL**	**7**	**0**	**4**	**1**	**304**	**22**	**0**	**4.34**	**4.51**	....	....	....	....	....	....	....	....	....	....	....	....	....	....	....	....
	Memphis South Stars	CHL	6	....	....	....	360	30	0	5.00	....	....	....	....	....	....	....	....	....	....	....	....	....	....	....	....	....
	NHL Totals		**35**	**6**	**18**	**6**	**1718**	**102**	**0**	**3.56**	....	....	....	....	....	....	....	....	....	....	....	....	....	....	....	....	....

WCHA First All-Star Team (1962, 1963, 1964) • NCAA West First All-American Team (1963, 1964)

Played in NHL All-Star Game (1967)

Signed as a free agent by **Montreal**, September 20, 1964. Claimed by **Minnesota** from **Montreal** in Expansion Draft, June 6, 1967. Claimed by **Vancouver** (WHL) from **Minnesota** in Reverse Draft, June 12, 1969.

• BEAUPRE, DON

Don Beaupre G – L. 5'10", 172 lbs. b. Waterloo, Ont., 9/19/1961. Minnesota's 2nd choice, 37th overall, in 1980 Entry Draft.

Season	Club	League	GP	W	L	T	Mins	GA	SO	Avg	AAvg	Eff	SA	S%	SAPG	GP	W	L	T	Mins	GA	SO	Avg	Eff	SA	S%	SAPG
1978-79	Sudbury Wolves	OHA	54	....	....	....	3248	260	2	4.78	....	....	....	....	....	10	....	....	....	600	44	0	4.40	....	....	....	....
1979-80	Sudbury Wolves	OHA	59	28	29	2	3447	248	0	4.32	....	....	....	....	....	9	5	4	....	552	38	0	4.13	....	....	....	....
1980-81	**Minnesota North Stars**	**NHL**	**44**	**18**	**14**	**11**	**2585**	**138**	**0**	**3.20**	**2.55**	**3.36**	**1313**	**.895**	**30.5**	**6**	**4**	**2**	....	**360**	**26**	**0**	**4.33**	....	....	....	....
1981-82	**Minnesota North Stars**	**NHL**	**29**	**11**	**8**	**9**	**1634**	**101**	**0**	**3.71**	**2.86**	**4.12**	**909**	**.889**	**33.4**	**2**	**0**	**1**	....	**60**	**4**	**0**	**4.00**	....	....	....	....
	Nashville South Stars	CHL	5	2	3	0	299	25	0	5.02	....	....	....	....	....	....	....	....	....	....	....	....	....	....	....	....	....
1982-83	**Minnesota North Stars**	**NHL**	**36**	**19**	**10**	**5**	**2011**	**120**	**0**	**3.58**	**2.85**	**4.10**	**1048**	**.885**	**31.3**	**4**	**2**	**2**	....	**245**	**20**	**0**	**4.90**	....	....	....	....
	Birmingham South Stars	CHL	10	8	2	0	599	31	0	3.11	....	....	....	....	....	....	....	....	....	....	....	....	....	....	....	....	....
1983-84	**Minnesota North Stars**	**NHL**	**33**	**16**	**13**	**2**	**1791**	**123**	**0**	**4.12**	**3.23**	**5.22**	**971**	**.873**	**32.5**	**13**	**6**	**7**	....	**782**	**40**	**1**	**3.07**	**3.23**	**380**	**.895**	**29.2**
	Salt Lake Golden Eagles	CHL	7	2	5	0	419	30	0	4.30	....	....	....	....	....	....	....	....	....	....	....	....	....	....	....	....	....
1984-85	**Minnesota North Stars**	**NHL**	**31**	**10**	**17**	**3**	**1770**	**109**	**1**	**3.69**	**2.93**	**4.31**	**934**	**.883**	**31.7**	**4**	**1**	**1**	....	**184**	**12**	**0**	**3.91**	**5.87**	**80**	**.850**	**26.1**
1985-86	**Minnesota North Stars**	**NHL**	**52**	**25**	**20**	**6**	**3073**	**182**	**1**	**3.55**	**2.75**	**3.82**	**1690**	**.892**	**33.0**	**5**	**2**	**3**	....	**300**	**17**	**0**	**3.40**	**3.66**	**158**	**.892**	**31.6**
1986-87	**Minnesota North Stars**	**NHL**	**47**	**17**	**20**	**6**	**2622**	**174**	**1**	**3.98**	**3.35**	**4.81**	**1439**	**.879**	**32.9**	....	....	....	....	....	....	....	....	....	....	....	....
1987-88	**Minnesota North Stars**	**NHL**	**43**	**10**	**22**	**3**	**2288**	**161**	**0**	**4.22**	**3.52**	**5.41**	**1257**	**.872**	**33.0**	....	....	....	....	....	....	....	....	....	....	....	....
1988-89	**Minnesota North Stars**	**NHL**	**1**	**0**	**1**	**0**	**59**	**3**	**0**	**3.05**	**2.52**	**3.52**	**26**	**.885**	**26.4**	....	....	....	....	....	....	....	....	....	....	....	....
	Kalamazoo Wings	IHL	3	1	2	0	179	9	1	3.02	....	....	....	....	....	....	....	....	....	....	....	....	....	....	....	....	....
	Washington Capitals	**NHL**	**11**	**5**	**4**	**0**	**578**	**28**	**1**	**2.91**	**2.40**	**3.03**	**269**	**.896**	**27.9**	....	....	....	....	....	....	....	....	....	....	....	....
	Baltimore Skipjacks	AHL	30	14	12	2	1715	102	0	3.57	....	....	....	....	....	....	....	....	....	....	....	....	....	....	....	....	....
1989-90	Washington Capitals	FrTour	2	....	....	....	91	8	....	5.27	....	....	....	....	....	....	....	....	....	....	....	....	....	....	....	....	....
	Washington Capitals	**NHL**	**48**	**23**	**18**	**5**	**2793**	**150**	**2**	**3.22**	**2.69**	**3.55**	**1362**	**.890**	**29.3**	**8**	**4**	**3**	....	**401**	**18**	**0**	**2.69**	**2.59**	**187**	**.904**	**28.0**
1990-91	**Washington Capitals**	**NHL**	**45**	**20**	**18**	**3**	**2572**	**113**	***5**	**2.64**	**2.34**	**2.72**	**1095**	**.897**	**25.5**	**11**	**5**	**5**	....	**624**	**29**	***1**	**2.79**	**2.75**	**294**	**.901**	**28.3**
	Baltimore Skipjacks	AHL	2	2	0	0	120	3	0	1.50	....	....	....	....	....	....	....	....	....	....	....	....	....	....	....	....	....
1991-92	**Washington Capitals**	**NHL**	**54**	**29**	**17**	**6**	**3108**	**166**	**1**	**3.20**	**2.83**	**3.70**	**1435**	**.884**	**27.7**	**7**	**3**	**4**	....	**419**	**22**	**0**	**3.15**	**3.27**	**212**	**.896**	**30.4**
	Baltimore Skipjacks	AHL	3	1	1	1	184	10	0	3.26	....	....	....	....	....	....	....	....	....	....	....	....	....	....	....	....	....
1992-93	**Washington Capitals**	**NHL**	**58**	**27**	**23**	**5**	**3282**	**181**	**1**	**3.31**	**2.81**	**3.92**	**1530**	**.882**	**28.0**	**2**	**1**	**1**	....	**119**	**9**	**0**	**4.54**	**6.29**	**65**	**.862**	**32.8**
1993-94	**Washington Capitals**	**NHL**	**53**	**24**	**16**	**8**	**2853**	**135**	**2**	**2.84**	**2.70**	**3.42**	**1122**	**.880**	**23.6**	**8**	**5**	**2**	....	**429**	**21**	**1**	**2.94**	**3.23**	**191**	**.890**	**26.7**
1994-95	**Ottawa Senators**	**NHL**	**38**	**8**	**25**	**3**	**2161**	**121**	**1**	**3.36**	**3.49**	**3.48**	**1167**	**.896**	**32.4**	....	....	....	....	....	....	....	....	....	....	....	....
1995-96	**Ottawa Senators**	**NHL**	**33**	**6**	**23**	**0**	**1770**	**110**	**1**	**3.73**	**3.67**	**4.60**	**892**	**.877**	**30.2**	....	....	....	....	....	....	....	....	....	....	....	....
	Toronto Maple Leafs	**NHL**	**8**	**0**	**5**	**0**	[illegible]	**20**	**0**	**4.84**	**4.56**	**7.10**	**170**	**.847**	**30.4**	**2**	**0**	**0**	....	**20**	**2**	**0**	**6.00**	**9.23**	**13**	**.846**	**39.0**

Season	Club	League	REGULAR SEASON GP	W	L	T	Mins	GA	SO	Avg	AAvg	Eff	SA	S%	SAPG	PLAYOFFS GP	W	L	T	Mins	GA	SO	Avg	Eff	SA	S%	SAPG
1996-97	**Toronto Maple Leafs**	**NHL**	**3**	**0**	**3**	**0**	**110**	**10**	**0**	**5.45**	**5.77**	**9.08**	**60**	**.833**	**32.7**	....	....	....	....	....	....	....	....	....	....	....	....
	St. John's Maple Leafs	AHL	47	24	16	4	2623	128	3	2.93	....	....	....	....	....	....	....	....	....	....	....	....	....	....	....	....	....
	Utah Grizzlies	IHL	4	2	2	0	238	13	0	3.27	....	....	....	....	....	7	3	4	....	438	17	1	2.32	....	....	....	....
	NHL Totals		**667**	**268**	**277**	**75**	**37396**	**2151**	**17**	**3.45**	....	....	**18689**	**.885**	....	**72**	**33**	**31**	....	**3943**	**220**	**3**	**3.35**	....	....	....	....

OHA First All-Star Team (1980)

Played in NHL All-Star Game (1981, 1992)

Traded to **Washington** by **Minnesota** for rights to Claudio Scremin, November 1, 1988. Traded to **Ottawa** by **Washington** for Ottawa's 5th round choice (Benoit Gratton) in 1995 Entry Draft, January 18, 1995. Traded to **NY Islanders** by **Ottawa** with Martin Straka and Bryan Berard for Damian Rhodes and Wade Redden, January 23, 1996. Traded to **Toronto** by **NY Islanders** with Kirk Muller for future considerations, January 23, 1996.

• BEAUREGARD, STEPHANE

Stephane Beauregard G – R. 5'11", 190 lbs. b: Cowansville, Que., 1/10/1968. Winnipeg's 3rd choice, 52nd overall, in 1988 Entry Draft.

Season	Club	League	GP	W	L	T	Mins	GA	SO	Avg	AAvg	Eff	SA	S%	SAPG	GP	W	L	T	Mins	GA	SO	Avg	Eff	SA	S%	SAPG
1986-87	St-Jean Castors	QMJHL	13	6	7	0	785	58	0	4.43	....	....	....	....	....	5	1	3	....	260	26	0	6.00	....	....	....	....
1987-88	St-Jean Castors	QMJHL	66	38	20	3	3766	229	2	3.65	....	....	....	....	....	7	3	4	....	423	34	0	4.82	....	....	....	....
1988-89	Moncton Hawks	AHL	15	4	8	2	824	62	0	4.51	....	....	....	....	....	....	....	....	....	....	....	....	....	....	....	....	....
	Fort Wayne Komets	IHL	16	9	5	0	830	43	0	3.10	....	....	....	....	....	9	4	4	....	484	21	*1	*2.60	....	....	....	....
1989-90	**Winnipeg Jets**	**NHL**	**19**	**7**	**8**	**3**	**1079**	**59**	**0**	**3.28**	**2.74**	**3.40**	**570**	**.896**	**31.7**	**4**	**1**	**3**	....	**238**	**12**	**0**	**3.03**	**3.46**	**105**	**.886**	**26.5**
	Fort Wayne Komets	IHL	33	20	8	3	1949	115	0	3.54	....	....	....	....	....	....	....	....	....	....	....	....	....	....	....	....	....
1990-91	**Winnipeg Jets**	**NHL**	**16**	**3**	**10**	**1**	**836**	**55**	**0**	**3.95**	**3.53**	**5.14**	**423**	**.870**	**30.4**	....	....	....	....	....	....	....	....	....	....	....	....
	Moncton Hawks	AHL	9	3	4	1	504	20	1	2.38	....	....	....	....	....	1	1	0	....	60	1	0	1.00	....	....	....	....
	Fort Wayne Komets	IHL	32	14	13	2	1761	109	0	3.71	....	....	....	....	....	*19	*10	9	....	*1158	57	0	2.95	....	....	....	....
1991-92	**Winnipeg Jets**	**NHL**	**26**	**6**	**8**	**6**	**1267**	**61**	**2**	**2.89**	**2.56**	**2.89**	**611**	**.900**	**28.9**	....	....	....	....	....	....	....	....	....	....	....	....
1992-93	**Philadelphia Flyers**	**NHL**	**16**	**3**	**9**	**0**	**802**	**59**	**0**	**4.41**	**3.76**	**6.42**	**405**	**.854**	**30.3**	....	....	....	....	....	....	....	....	....	....	....	....
	Hershey Bears	AHL	13	5	5	3	794	48	0	3.63	....	....	....	....	....	....	....	....	....	....	....	....	....	....	....	....	....
1993-94	**Winnipeg Jets**	**NHL**	**13**	**0**	**4**	**1**	**418**	**34**	**0**	**4.88**	**4.65**	**7.86**	**211**	**.839**	**30.3**	....	....	....	....	....	....	....	....	....	....	....	....
	Moncton Hawks	AHL	37	18	11	6	2082	121	1	3.49	....	....	....	....	....	*21	*12	9	....	*1305	57	*2	2.62	....	....	....	....
1994-95	Springfield Falcons	AHL	24	10	11	3	1381	73	2	3.17	....	....	....	....	....	....	....	....	....	....	....	....	....	....	....	....	....
1995-96	San Francisco Spiders	IHL	*69	*36	24	8	*4022	207	1	3.09	....	....	....	....	....	4	1	3	....	241	10	0	2.49	....	....	....	....
1996-97	Quebec Rafales	IHL	67	35	20	11	3945	174	4	2.65	....	....	....	....	....	9	5	3	....	498	19	0	2.29	....	....	....	....
1997-98	Chicago Wolves	IHL	18	10	6	0	917	49	1	3.20	....	....	....	....	....	14	10	4	....	820	36	1	2.63	....	....	....	....
	NHL Totals		**90**	**19**	**39**	**11**	**4402**	**268**	**2**	**3.65**	....	....	**2220**	**.879**	....	**4**	**1**	**3**	....	**238**	**12**	**0**	**3.03**	....	....	....	....

QMJHL First All-Star Team (1988) • Canadian Major Junior Goaltender of the year (1988) • IHL First All-Star Team (1996) • Won James Gatschene Memorial Trophy (MVP - IHL) (1996)

Traded to **Buffalo** by **Winnipeg** for Christian Ruuttu and future considerations, June 15, 1992. Traded to **Chicago** by **Buffalo** with Buffalo's 4th round choice (Eric Daze) in 1993 Entry Draft for Dominik Hasek, August 7, 1992. Traded to **Winnipeg** by **Chicago** for Christian Ruuttu, August 10, 1992. Traded to **Philadelphia** by **Winnipeg** for future considerations, October 1, 1992. Traded to **Winnipeg** by **Philadelphia** for future considerations, June 11, 1993. Signed as a free agent by **Washington**, August 20, 1997.

• BEDARD, JIM

Jim Bedard G – L. 5'10", 181 lbs. b: Niagara Falls, Ont., 11/14/1956. Washington's 6th choice, 91st overall, in 1976 Amateur Draft.

Season	Club	League	GP	W	L	T	Mins	GA	SO	Avg	AAvg	Eff	SA	S%	SAPG	GP	W	L	T	Mins	GA	SO	Avg	Eff	SA	S%	SAPG
1973-74	Sudbury Wolves	OHA	28	....	....	....	1635	117	0	4.29	....	....	....	....	....	....	....	....	....	....	....	....	....	....	....	....	....
1974-75	Sudbury Wolves	OHA	51	....	....	....	3060	187	0	3.67	....	....	....	....	....	....	....	....	....	....	....	....	....	....	....	....	....
1975-76	Sudbury Wolves	OHA	58	....	....	....	3328	177	1	3.15	....	....	....	....	....	....	....	....	....	....	....	....	....	....	....	....	....
1976-77	Dayton Gems	IHL	48	....	....	....	2693	168	0	3.74	....	....	....	....	....	2	....	....	....	120	9	0	4.50	....	....	....	....
1977-78	**Washington Capitals**	**NHL**	**43**	**11**	**23**	**7**	**2492**	**152**	**1**	**3.66**	**3.44**	....	....	....	....	....	....	....	....	....	....	....	....	....	....	....	....
	Hershey Bears	AHL	14	6	7	1	766	39	0	3.05	....	....	....	....	....	....	....	....	....	....	....	....	....	....	....	....	....
1978-79	**Washington Capitals**	**NHL**	**30**	**6**	**17**	**6**	**1740**	**126**	**0**	**4.34**	**3.85**	....	....	....	....	....	....	....	....	....	....	....	....	....	....	....	....
	Hershey Bears	AHL	26	9	11	2	1404	88	0	3.76	....	....	....	....	....	....	....	....	....	....	....	....	....	....	....	....	....
1979-80	Hershey Bears	AHL	2	....	....	....	60	9	0	9.00	....	....	....	....	....	....	....	....	....	....	....	....	....	....	....	....	....
	Cincinnati Stingers	CHL	8	3	4	0	385	32	0	4.99	....	....	....	....	....	....	....	....	....	....	....	....	....	....	....	....	....
	Rochester Americans	AHL	6	....	....	....	339	20	0	3.54	....	....	....	....	....	....	....	....	....	....	....	....	....	....	....	....	....
	Tulsa Oilers	CHL	3	0	3	0	177	10	0	3.39	....	....	....	....	....	....	....	....	....	....	....	....	....	....	....	....	....
	Dayton Gems	IHL	16	....	....	....	858	55	0	3.85	....	....	....	....	....	....	....	....	....	....	....	....	....	....	....	....	....
1980-81	TPS Turku	Finland	29	....	....	....	....	112	0	3.90	....	....	....	....	....	....	....	....	....	....	....	....	....	....	....	....	....
1981-82	TPS Turku	Finland	27	....	....	....	1620	95	1	3.52	....	....	....	....	....	....	....	....	....	....	....	....	....	....	....	....	....
	NHL Totals		**73**	**17**	**40**	**13**	**4232**	**278**	**1**	**3.94**	....	....	....	....	....	....	....	....	....	....	....	....	....	....	....	....	....

OHA First All-Star Team (1976)

• Played professional hockey in Finland's 2nd division from 1982-83 through 1987-88.

• BEHREND, MARC

Marc Behrend G – L. 6'1", 180 lbs. b: Madison, WI, 1/11/1961. Winnipeg's 5th choice, 85th overall, in 1981 Entry Draft.

Season	Club	League	GP	W	L	T	Mins	GA	SO	Avg	AAvg	Eff	SA	S%	SAPG	GP	W	L	T	Mins	GA	SO	Avg	Eff	SA	S%	SAPG
1980-81	University of Wisconsin	WCHA	16	11	4	1	913	50	0	3.29	....	....	....	....	....	....	....	....	....	....	....	....	....	....	....	....	....
1981-82	University of Wisconsin	WCHA	25	21	3	1	1502	65	2	2.60	....	....	....	....	....	....	....	....	....	....	....	....	....	....	....	....	....
1982-83	University of Wisconsin	WCHA	19	17	1	1	1315	49	2	*2.24	....	....	....	....	....	....	....	....	....	....	....	....	....	....	....	....	....
1983-84	United States	Nat-Team	33	....	....	....	1898	100	....	3.16	....	....	....	....	....	....	....	....	....	....	....	....	....	....	....	....	....
	United States	Olympics	4	....	....	....	200	11	....	3.30	....	....	....	....	....	....	....	....	....	....	....	....	....	....	....	....	....
	Winnipeg Jets	**NHL**	**6**	**2**	**4**	**0**	**351**	**32**	**0**	**5.47**	**4.29**	**9.51**	**184**	**.826**	**31.5**	**2**	**0**	**2**	**0**	**121**	**9**	**0**	**4.46**	**4.41**	**91**	**.901**	**45.1**
1984-85	**Winnipeg Jets**	**NHL**	**24**	**8**	**10**	**3**	**1218**	**87**	**1**	**4.45**	**3.54**	**6.20**	**624**	**.861**	**30.7**	**4**	**1**	**1**	**0**	**179**	**10**	**0**	**3.35**	**3.42**	**98**	**.898**	**32.8**
	Sherbrooke Canadiens	AHL	7	2	3	2	427	25	0	3.51	....	....	....	....	....	....	....	....	....	....	....	....	....	....	....	....	....
1985-86	**Winnipeg Jets**	**NHL**	**9**	**2**	**5**	**0**	**422**	**41**	**0**	**5.83**	**4.54**	**10.87**	**220**	**.814**	**31.3**	**1**	**0**	**0**	**0**	**12**	**0**	**0**	**0.00**	**0.00**	**7**	**1.000**	**35.0**
	Sherbrooke Canadiens	AHL	35	16	5	2	2028	132	1	3.91	....	....	....	....	....	....	....	....	....	....	....	....	....	....	....	....	....
1986-87	Sherbrooke Canadiens	AHL	19	8	5	0	1124	62	0	3.31	....	....	....	....	....	1	0	1	0	59	3	0	3.05	....	....	....	....
	NHL Totals		**39**	**12**	**19**	**3**	**1991**	**160**	**1**	**4.82**	....	....	**1028**	**.844**	....	**7**	**1**	**3**	**0**	**312**	**19**	**0**	**3.65**	....	....	....	....

NCAA Championship All-Tournament Team (1981, 1983) • NCAA Championship Tournament MVP (1981, 1983) • WCHA Second All-Star Team (1982)

• BELANGER, YVES

Yves Belanger G – L. 5'11", 170 lbs. b: Baie Comeau, Que., 9/30/1952.

Season	Club	League	GP	W	L	T	Mins	GA	SO	Avg	AAvg	Eff	SA	S%	SAPG	GP	W	L	T	Mins	GA	SO	Avg	Eff	SA	S%	SAPG
1969-70	Sherbrooke Castors	QJHL	47	....	....	....	2780	225	0	4.86	....	....	....	....	....	....	....	....	....	....	....	....	....	....	....	....	....
1970-71	Sherbrooke Castors	QJHL	39	....	....	....	2340	182	0	4.67	....	....	....	....	....	8	....	....	....	460	50	0	6.52	....	....	....	....
1971-72	Sherbrooke Castors	QMJHL	38	....	....	....	2280	188	2	4.95	....	....	....	....	....	1	....	....	....	39	4	0	6.15	....	....	....	....
1972-73	Syracuse Blazers	EHL	38	....	....	....	2255	90	*5	2.39	....	....	....	....	....	7	7	0	0	436	11	1	1.51	....	....	....	....
1973-74	Jacksonville Barons	AHL	54	17	27	4	2878	199	0	4.15	....	....	....	....	....	....	....	....	....	....	....	....	....	....	....	....	....
1974-75	**St. Louis Blues**	**NHL**	**11**	**6**	**3**	**2**	**640**	**29**	**1**	**2.72**	**2.45**	....	....	....	....	....	....	....	....	....	....	....	....	....	....	....	....
	Denver Spurs	CHL	36	19	13	3	2060	105	0	3.06	....	....	....	....	....	....	....	....	....	....	....	....	....	....	....	....	....
1975-76	**St. Louis Blues**	**NHL**	**31**	**11**	**17**	**1**	**1763**	**113**	**0**	**3.85**	**3.49**	....	....	....	....	....	....	....	....	....	....	....	....	....	....	....	....
	Providence Reds	AHL	10	3	4	3	620	37	0	3.58	....	....	....	....	....	2	0	2	0	120	8	0	4.00	....	....	....	....
1976-77	**St. Louis Blues**	**NHL**	**3**	**2**	**0**	**0**	**140**	**7**	**0**	**3.00**	**2.79**	....	....	....	....	....	....	....	....	....	....	....	....	....	....	....	....
	Kansas City Blues	CHL	31	21	4	4	1826	83	1	2.73	....	....	....	....	....	....	....	....	....	....	....	....	....	....	....	....	....
1977-78	**St. Louis Blues**	**NHL**	**3**	**0**	**3**	**0**	**144**	**15**	**0**	**6.25**	**5.86**	....	....	....	....	....	....	....	....	....	....	....	....	....	....	....	....
	Atlanta Flames	**NHL**	**17**	**7**	**8**	**0**	**937**	**55**	**1**	**3.52**	**3.30**	....	....	....	....	....	....	....	....	....	....	....	....	....	....	....	....
	Salt Lake Golden Eagles	CHL	9	5	3	0	492	20	1	2.44	....	....	....	....	....	....	....	....	....	....	....	....	....	....	....	....	....
1978-79	**Atlanta Flames**	**NHL**	**5**	**1**	**2**	**0**	**182**	**21**	**0**	**6.92**	**6.12**	....	....	....	....	....	....	....	....	....	....	....	....	....	....	....	....
	Philadelphia Firebirds	AHL	22	4	14	1	1235	108	0	5.25	....	....	....	....	....	....	....	....	....	....	....	....	....	....	....	....	....
1979-80	**Boston Bruins**	**NHL**	**8**	**2**	**0**	**3**	**328**	**19**	**0**	**3.48**	**3.06**	....	....	....	....	....	....	....	....	....	....	....	....	....	....	....	....
	Binghamton Whalers	AHL	25	7	13	1	1334	95	0	4.27	....	....	....	....	....	....	....	....	....	....	....	....	....	....	....	....	....
1980-81	Charlottetown Islanders	NBIHL	STATISTICS NOT AVAILABLE																								
1981-82	Cap Pele Caps	NBIHL	22	....	....	....	1296	69	*1	*3.19	....	....	....	....	....	....	....	....	....	....	....	....	....	....	....	....	....
1982-83	Cap Pele Caps	NBIHL	21	....	....	....	1226	81	0	*3.96	....	....	....	....	....	7	3	4	0	420	19	0	2.72	....	....	....	....
	NHL Totals		**78**	**29**	**33**	**6**	**4134**	**259**	**2**	**3.76**	....	....	....	....	....	....	....	....	....	....	....	....	....	....	....	....	....

EHL South First All-Star Team (1973) • Won George L. Davis Jr. Trophy (fewest goals against - EHL) (1973) • CHL First All-Star Team (1977) • Shared Terry Sawchuk Trophy (fewest goals against - CHL) with Gord McRae (1977)

Signed as a free agent by **Cleveland** (WHA), August, 1972. Traded to **St. Louis** by **Cleveland** (WHA) for cash, August, 1974. Traded to **Atlanta** by **St. Louis** with Bob MacMillan, Dick Redmond and St. Louis' 2nd round choice (Mike Perkovich) in 1979 Entry Draft for Phil Myre, Curt Bennett and Barry Gibbs, December 12, 1977. Signed as a free agent by **Boston**, October 8, 1979.

			REGULAR SEASON													PLAYOFFS											
Season	Club	League	GP	W	L	T	Mins	GA	SO	Avg	AAvg	Eff	SA	S%	SAPG	GP	W	L	T	Mins	GA	SO	Avg	Eff	SA	S%	SAPG

• BELFOUR, ED

Ed "The Eagle" Belfour G – L. 5'11", 182 lbs. b: Carman, Man., 4/21/1965.

1986-87	University of North Dakota	WCHA	34	29	4	0	2049	81	3	2.43						....	....	....	....	....	....	....	....	....	....	....	....
1987-88	Saginaw Hawks	IHL	61	32	25	0	*3446	183	3	3.19	....	....	....	....	....	9	4	5	....	561	33	0	3.53	....	....	....	....
1988-89	**Chicago Blackhawks**	**NHL**	**23**	**4**	**12**	**3**	**1148**	**74**	**0**	**3.87**	**3.19**	**4.73**	**605**	**.878**	**31.6**	....	....	....	....	....	....	....	....	....	....	....	....
	Saginaw Hawks	IHL	29	12	10	0	1760	92	0	3.10	....	....	....	....	....	5	2	3	....	298	14	0	2.82	....	....	....	....
1989-90	Canada	Nat-Team	33	13	12	6	1808	93	0	3.08	....	....	....	....	....	....	....	....	....	....	....	....	....	....	....	....	....
	Chicago Blackhawks	**NHL**	....	....	....	....	....	....	....	....	....	....	....	....	....	**9**	**4**	**2**	....	**409**	**17**	**0**	**2.49**	**2.12**	**200**	**.915**	**29.3**
1990-91	**Chicago Blackhawks**	**NHL**	***74**	***43**	**19**	**7**	***4127**	**170**	**4**	***2.47**	**2.18**	**2.23**	**1883**	**.910**	**27.4**	**6**	**2**	**4**	....	**295**	**20**	**0**	**4.07**	**4.45**	**183**	**.891**	**37.2**
1991-92	Canada	C Cup	DID NOT PLAY – SPARE GOALTENDER																								
	Chicago Blackhawks	**NHL**	**52**	**21**	**18**	**10**	**2928**	**132**	***5**	**2.70**	**2.38**	**2.87**	**1241**	**.894**	**25.4**	**18**	**12**	**4**	....	**949**	**39**	**1**	***2.47**	**2.42**	**398**	**.902**	**25.2**
1992-93	**Chicago Blackhawks**	**NHL**	***71**	**41**	**18**	**11**	***4106**	**177**	***7**	**2.59**	**2.18**	**2.44**	**1880**	**.906**	**27.5**	**4**	**0**	**4**	....	**249**	**13**	**0**	**3.13**	**4.19**	**97**	**.866**	**23.4**
1993-94	**Chicago Blackhawks**	**NHL**	**70**	**37**	**24**	**6**	**3998**	**178**	***7**	**2.67**	**2.53**	**2.51**	**1892**	**.906**	**28.4**	**6**	**2**	**4**	....	**360**	**15**	**0**	**2.50**	**1.96**	**191**	**.921**	**31.8**
1994-95	**Chicago Blackhawks**	**NHL**	**42**	**22**	**15**	**3**	**2450**	**93**	***5**	**2.28**	**2.34**	**2.14**	**990**	**.906**	**24.2**	**16**	**9**	**7**	....	**1014**	**37**	**1**	**2.19**	**1.69**	**479**	**.923**	**28.3**
1995-96	**Chicago Blackhawks**	**NHL**	**50**	**22**	**17**	**10**	**2956**	**135**	**1**	**2.74**	**2.68**	**2.69**	**1373**	**.902**	**27.9**	**9**	**6**	**3**	....	**666**	**23**	**1**	**2.07**	**1.47**	**323**	**.929**	**29.1**
1996-97	**Chicago Blackhawks**	**NHL**	**33**	**11**	**15**	**6**	**1966**	**88**	**1**	**2.69**	**2.84**	**2.50**	**946**	**.907**	**28.9**	....	....	....	....	....	....	....	....	....	....	....	....
	San Jose Sharks	**NHL**	**13**	**3**	**9**	**0**	**757**	**43**	**1**	**3.41**	**3.61**	**3.95**	**371**	**.884**	**29.4**	....	....	....	....	....	....	....	....	....	....	....	....
1997-98	**Dallas Stars**	**NHL**	**61**	**37**	**12**	**10**	**3581**	**112**	**9**	***1.88**	**2.18**	**1.58**	**1335**	**.916**	**22.4**	**17**	**10**	**7**	....	**1039**	**31**	**1**	***1.79**	**1.39**	**399**	**.922**	**23.0**
	NHL Totals		**489**	**241**	**159**	**66**	**28017**	**1202**	**40**	**2.57**	....	....	**12516**	**.904**	....	**85**	**46**	**35**	....	**4981**	**195**	**4**	**2.35**	....	....	....	....

WCHA First All-Star Team (1987) • NCAA Championship All-Tournament Team (1987) • IHL First All-Star Team (1988) • Shared Garry F. Longman Memorial Trophy (Top Rookie - IHL) with John Cullen (1988) • NHL/Upper Deck All-Rookie Team (1991) • NHL First All-Star Team (1991, 1993) • Won Calder Memorial Trophy (1991) • Won William M. Jennings Trophy (1991, 1993, 1995) • Won Trico Goaltender Award (1991) • Won Vezina Trophy (1991, 1993) • NHL Second All-Star Team (1995)

Played in NHL All-Star Game (1992, 1993, 1996, 1998)

Signed as a free agent by **Chicago**, September 25, 1987. Traded to **San Jose** by **Chicago** for Chris Terreri, Ulf Dahlen and Michal Sykora, January 25, 1997. Signed as a free agent by **Dallas**, July 2, 1997.

• BELHUMEUR, MICHEL

Michel Belhumeur G – L. 5'10", 160 lbs. b: Sorel, Que., 9/2/1949. Philadelphia's 4th choice, 40th overall, in 1969 Amateur Draft.

1968-69	Drummondville Rangers	QJHL	34	....	....	....	2105	135	3	3.85	....	....	....	....	....	....	....	....	....	....	....	....	....	....	....	....	....
1969-70	Quebec Aces	AHL	2	....	....	....	100	10	0	6.00	....	....	....	....	....	....	....	....	....	....	....	....	....	....	....	....	....
	Charlotte Checkers	EHL	14	....	....	....	840	42	1	3.00	....	....	....	....	....	....	....	....	....	....	....	....	....	....	....	....	....
1970-71	Quebec Aces	AHL	37	12	15	8	2083	110	2	3.17	....	....	....	....	....	1	0	1	0	60	4	0	4.00	....	....	....	....
1971-72	Richmond Robins	AHL	45	20	17	8	2645	122	1	2.77	....	....	....	....	....	....	....	....	....	....	....	....	....	....	....	....	....
1972-73	Richmond Robins	AHL	12	....	....	....	671	49	0	4.38	....	....	....	....	....	....	....	....	....	....	....	....	....	....	....	....	....
	Philadelphia Flyers	**NHL**	**23**	**9**	**7**	**3**	**1117**	**60**	**0**	**3.22**	**3.03**	....	....	....	....	**1**	**0**	**0**	....	**10**	**1**	**0**	**6.00**	....	....	....	....
1973-74	Richmond Robins	AHL	45	13	23	7	2567	179	0	4.18	....	....	....	....	....	3	1	2	0	191	13	*1	4.08	....	....	....	....
1974-75	**Washington Capitals**	**NHL**	**35**	**0**	**24**	**3**	**1812**	**162**	**0**	**5.36**	**4.89**	....	....	....	....	....	....	....	....	....	....	....	....	....	....	....	....
1975-76	**Washington Capitals**	**NHL**	**7**	**0**	**5**	**1**	**377**	**32**	**0**	**5.09**	**4.61**	....	....	....	....	....	....	....	....	....	....	....	....	....	....	....	....
	Richmond Robins	AHL	45	19	24	2	2679	159	3	3.56	....	....	....	....	....	4	2	1	0	194	7	0	2.16	....	....	....	....
1976-77	Tulsa Oilers	CHL	34	17	12	3	1966	131	1	4.00	....	....	....	....	....	1	0	1	0	70	4	0	3.43	....	....	....	....
1977-78	Tulsa Oilers	CHL	24	8	14	0	1319	96	0	4.37	....	....	....	....	....	5	2	3	0	305	15	0	2.95	....	....	....	....
1978-79	Utica Mohawks	NEHL	24	....	....	....	1308	89	2	4.08	....	....	....	....	....	....	....	....	....	....	....	....	....	....	....	....	....
	Jersey-Hampton Aces	NEHL	11	....	....	....	665	37	1	3.34	....	....	....	....	....	....	....	....	....	....	....	....	....	....	....	....	....
	NHL Totals		**65**	**9**	**38**	**7**	**3306**	**254**	**0**	**4.61**	....	....	....	....	....	**1**	**0**	**0**		**10**	**1**	**0**	**6.00**	....	....	....	....

AHL Second All-Star Team (1972)

Claimed by **Washington** from **Philadelphia** in Expansion Draft, June 12, 1974. Signed as a free agent by **Atlanta**, October 7, 1976.

• BELL, GORDIE

Gordie Bell G – L. 5'10", 164 lbs. b: Portage la Prairie, Man., 3/13/1925. d: 11/3/1980.

1941-42	Portage Terriers	MJHL	17	*14	2	0	980	79	0	*4.84	....	....	....	....	....	15	14	1	0	900	74	0	4.93	....	....	....	....
1942-43	Buffalo Bisons	AHL	52	28	17	7	3120	125	*9	*2.40	....	....	....	....	....	9	*7	2	0	540	16	*1	*1.77	....	....	....	....
1943-44	Cornwallis Navy	City Sr.	2	2	0	0	120	6	0	3.00	....	....	....	....	....	5	4	1	0	300	15	0	3.00	....	....	....	....
	Winnipeg Navy	City Sr.	10	....	....	....	600	35	0	3.50	....	....	....	....	....	....	....	....	....	....	....	....	....	....	....	....	....
1944-45	Cornwallis Navy	City Sr.	5	....	....	....	250	24	0	5.76	....	....	....	....	....	....	....	....	....	....	....	....	....	....	....	....	....
1945-46	**Toronto Maple Leafs**	**NHL**	**8**	**3**	**5**	**0**	**480**	**31**	**0**	**3.88**	**3.60**	....	....	....	....	....	....	....	....	....	....	....	....	....	....	....	....
	Providence Reds	AHL	37	14	19	4	2220	152	1	4.10	....	....	....	....	....	2	0	2	0	120	7	0	3.50	....	....	....	....
1946-47	Pittsburgh Hornets	AHL	23	11	7	5	1380	80	1	3.48	....	....	....	....	....	....	....	....	....	....	....	....	....	....	....	....	....
	Hollywood Wolves	PCHL	26	....	....	....	1560	67	1	2.58	....	....	....	....	....	7	4	3	0	420	17	1	2.43	....	....	....	....
1947-48	Washington Lions	AHL	64	14	42	6	3840	332	1	5.19	....	....	....	....	....	....	....	....	....	....	....	....	....	....	....	....	....
1948-49	Fort Worth Rangers	USHL	13	5	5	3	780	57	0	4.38	....	....	....	....	....	....	....	....	....	....	....	....	....	....	....	....	....
	Springfield Indians	AHL	4	1	3	0	240	16	0	4.00	....	....	....	....	....	....	....	....	....	....	....	....	....	....	....	....	....
	Omaha Knights	USHL	36	21	7	7	2160	84	0	2.33	....	....	....	....	....	4	2	2	0	254	18	0	4.25	....	....	....	....
1949-50	Louisville Blades	USHL	29	13	13	3	1740	121	0	4.17	....	....	....	....	....	....	....	....	....	....	....	....	....	....	....	....	....
	Buffalo Bisons	AHL	36	17	14	5	2160	114	2	3.17	....	....	....	....	....	3	1	2	0	188	14	0	4.47	....	....	....	....
1950-51	Buffalo Bisons	AHL	7	5	2	0	420	23	0	3.29	....	....	....	....	....	....	....	....	....	....	....	....	....	....	....	....	....
	Springfield Indians	AHL	51	20	29	2	3120	186	2	3.58	....	....	....	....	....	2	0	2	0	120	15	0	7.50	....	....	....	....
1951-52	Syracuse Warriors	AHL	63	24	38	1	3820	244	0	3.83	....	....	....	....	....	....	....	....	....	....	....	....	....	....	....	....	....
1952-53	Syracuse Warriors	AHL	64	31	31	2	3870	200	*6	3.10	....	....	....	....	....	4	1	3	0	239	8	0	2.01	....	....	....	....
1953-54	Syracuse Warriors	AHL	49	21	25	3	2940	176	0	3.59	....	....	....	....	....	....	....	....	....	....	....	....	....	....	....	....	....
1954-55	Springfield Indians	AHL	10	2	8	0	600	47	0	4.70	....	....	....	....	....	....	....	....	....	....	....	....	....	....	....	....	....
1955-56	Springfield Indians	AHL	11	2	9	0	660	57	0	5.18	....	....	....	....	....	....	....	....	....	....	....	....	....	....	....	....	....
	Trois-Rivieres Lions	QHL	14	6	8	0	852	48	1	3.38	....	....	....	....	....	....	....	....	....	....	....	....	....	....	....	....	....
	New York Rangers	**NHL**	....	....	....	....	....	....	....	....	....	....	....	....	....	**2**	**1**	**1**	....	**120**	**9**	**0**	**4.50**	....	....	....	....
1956-57	Trois-Rivieres Lions	QHL	4	2	1	1	250	10	0	2.40	....	....	....	....	....	....	....	....	....	....	....	....	....	....	....	....	....
	Belleville McFarlands	EOHL	41	19	17	5	2460	154	0	3.75	....	....	....	....	....	9	4	5	0	540	30	*2	3.33	....	....	....	....
1957-58	Belleville McFarlands	EOHL	49	*29	17	3	2940	176	*4	3.59	....	....	....	....	....	30	21	8	1	1817	81	3	2.67	....	....	....	....
1958-59	Belleville McFarlands	EOHL	46	....	....	....	2760	156	*2	3.39	....	....	....	....	....	....	....	....	....	....	....	....	....	....	....	....	....
	Canada	WEC-A	6	5	1	0	360	9	2	1.50	....	....	....	....	....	....	....	....	....	....	....	....	....	....	....	....	....
1959-60	Belleville McFarlands	OHA Sr.	9	....	....	....	500	34	0	4.08	....	....	....	....	....	....	....	....	....	....	....	....	....	....	....	....	....
	NHL Totals		**8**	**3**	**5**	**0**	**480**	**31**	**0**	**3.88**	....	....	....	....	....	**2**	**1**	**1**	....	**120**	**9**	**0**	**4.50**	....	....	....	....

AHL First All-Star Team (1943) • USHL Second All-Star Team (1949)

Traded to **Springfield** (AHL) by **Toronto** with Armand Lemieux, Leo Curick and Rod Roy for Eldie Kobussen, April, 1948. Traded to **Montreal** (Buffalo - AHL) by **Springfield** (AHL) with Sid McNabney for Hub Macey, December 21, 1948. Signed as a free agent by **NY Rangers**, March 22, 1956.

• BENEDICT, CLINT

Clint Benedict G – L. b: Ottawa, Ont., 9/26/1892. d: 11/12/1976. **HHOF**

1910-11	Ottawa New Edinburghs	City Sr.	5	*5	0	0	300	14	0	2.80	....	....	....	....	....	3	3	0	0	180	13	0	4.25	....	....	....	....
1911-12			STATISTICS NOT AVAILABLE																								
1912-13	Ottawa Senators	NHA	10	7	2	1	275	16	1	3.49	....	....	....	....	....	....	....	....	....	....	....	....	....	....	....	....	....
1913-14	Ottawa Senators	NHA	9	5	3	0	474	29	0	3.67	....	....	....	....	....	....	....	....	....	....	....	....	....	....	....	....	....
1914-15	Ottawa Senators	NHA	20	14	6	0	1243	65	0	3.14	....	....	....	....	....	2	1	1	0	120	2	1	0.50	....	....	....	....
1915-16	Ottawa Senators	NHA	24	13	11	0	1447	72	1	2.99	....	....	....	....	....	....	....	....	....	....	....	....	....	....	....	....	....
1916-17	Ottawa Senators	NHA	18	14	4	0	1103	50	1	2.72	....	....	....	....	....	2	1	1	0	120	7	0	3.50	....	....	....	....
1917-18	**Ottawa Senators**	**NHL**	***22**	**9**	**13**	**0**	***1337**	**114**	***1**	**5.12**	**3.46**	....	....	....	....	....	....	....	....	....	....	....	....	....	....	....	....
1918-19	**Ottawa Senators**	**NHL**	***18**	***12**	**6**	**0**	***1152**	**53**	***2**	***2.86**	**1.80**	....	....	....	....	**5**	**1**	**4**	**0**	**300**	**26**	**0**	**5.20**	....	....	....	....
1919-20	**Ottawa Senators**	**NHL**	***24**	***19**	**5**	**0**	**1443**	**64**	***5**	***2.66**	**1.51**	....	....	....	....	***5**	***3**	**2**	**0**	***300**	**11**	***1**	***2.20**	....	....	....	....
1920-21	**Ottawa Senators**	**NHL**	***24**	***14**	**10**	**0**	***1457**	**75**	***2**	***3.09**	**2.07**	....	....	....	....	***7**	***5**	**2**	**0**	***420**	**12**	***2**	***1.71**	....	....	....	....
1921-22	**Ottawa Senators**	**NHL**	***24**	***14**	**8**	**2**	***1508**	**84**	***2**	***3.34**	**2.47**	....	....	....	....	**2**	**0**	**1**	**1**	**120**	**5**	**1**	**2.50**	....	....	....	....
1922-23	**Ottawa Senators**	**NHL**	***24**	***14**	**9**	**1**	**1486**	**54**	***4**	***2.18**	**1.85**	....	....	....	....	***8**	***6**	**2**	**0**	***480**	**10**	***3**	***1.25**	....	....	....	....
1923-24	**Ottawa Senators**	**NHL**	**22**	***16**	**6**	**0**	**1356**	**45**	***3**	**1.99**	**2.15**	....	....	....	....	**2**	**0**	**2**	**0**	**120**	**5**	**0**	**2.50**	....	....	....	....
1924-25	**Montreal Maroons**	**NHL**	***30**	**9**	**19**	**2**	**1843**	**65**	**2**	**2.12**	**2.54**	....	....	....	....	....	....	....	....	....	....	....	....	....	....	....	....
1925-26	**Montreal Maroons**	**NHL**	***36**	**20**	**11**	**5**	***2288**	**73**	**6**	**1.91**	**2.48**	....	....	....	....	***8**	***5**	**1**	**2**	**480**	**8**	***4**	***1.00**	....	....	....	....
1926-27	**Montreal Maroons**	**NHL**	**43**	**20**	**19**	**4**	**2748**	**65**	**13**	***1.42**	**2.12**	....	....	....	....	**2**	**0**	**1**	**1**	**132**	**2**	**0**	**0.91**	....	....	....	....
1927-28	**Montreal Maroons**	**NHL**	***44**	**24**	**14**	**6**	**2690**	**76**	**7**	**1.70**	**2.73**	....	....	....	....	***9**	***5**	**3**	**1**	***555**	**8**	***4**	***0.86**	....	....	....	....

			REGULAR SEASON													PLAYOFFS											
Season	Club	League	GP	W	L	T	Mins	GA	SO	Avg	AAvg	Eff	SA	S%	SAPG	GP	W	L	T	Mins	GA	SO	Avg	Eff	SA	S%	SAPG
1928-29	**Montreal Maroons**	**NHL**	**37**	**14**	**16**	**7**	**2300**	**57**	**11**	**1.49**	**3.17**	....	....	....	....	....	....	....	....	....	....	....	....	....	....	....	....
1929-30	**Montreal Maroons**	**NHL**	**14**	**6**	**6**	**1**	**752**	**33**	**0**	**2.63**	**2.74**	....	....	....	....	....	....	....	....	....	....	....	....	....	....	....	....
1930-31	Windsor Bulldogs	IAHL	40	20	15	5	2478	92	1	2.23	....	....	....	....	....	....	....	....	....	....	....	....	....	....	....	....	....
	NHL Totals		**362**	**191**	**142**	**28**	**22360**	**858**	**58**	**2.30**	**0.00**	**0.00**	....	....	**0.0**	**48**	**25**	**18**	**5**	**2907**	**87**	***15**	**1.80**	....	....	....	....
	Other Major League Totals		81	53	26	1	4542	232	3	3.06	....	....	....	....	....	4	2	2	0	240	9	1	2.25	....	....	....	....

Rights retained by **Ottawa** after NHA folded, November 26, 1917. Traded to **Montreal Maroons** by **Ottawa** with Punch Broadbent for cash, October 20, 1924.

● BENNETT, HARVEY

Harvey Bennett G – L. 6′, 175 lbs. b: Edington, Sask., 7/23/1925.

Season	Club	League	GP	W	L	T	Mins	GA	SO	Avg	AAvg	Eff	SA	S%	SAPG	GP	W	L	T	Mins	GA	SO	Avg	Eff	SA	S%	SAPG
1941-42	Regina Abbotts	SJHL	11	7	3	1	660	25	0	*2.27	....	....	....	....	....	5	....	....	....	300	16	0	3.20	....	....	....	....
1942-43	Oshawa Generals	OHA	14	12	2	0	840	42	*3	*3.00	....	....	....	....	....	7	6	1	0	420	20	*1	*2.86	....	....	....	....
1943-44	Oshawa Generals	OHA	26	*23	3	0	1540	69	*3	*2.69	....	....	....	....	....	11	*8	3	0	660	31	*1	*2.82	....	....	....	....
1944-45	**Boston Bruins**	**NHL**	**25**	**10**	**12**	**2**	**1470**	**103**	**0**	**4.20**	**3.52**	....	....	....	....	....	....	....	....	....	....	....	....	....	....	....	....
	Boston Olympics	EHL	13	10	2	1	780	35	1	2.69	....	....	....	....	....	4	4	0	0	240	5	0	*1.25	....	....	....	....
1945-46	Boston Olympics	EHL	45	*27	11	7	2700	145	2	*3.22	....	....	....	....	....	12	....	....	....	720	30	0	*2.50	....	....	....	....
1946-47	Hershey Bears	AHL	60	*34	15	11	3600	161	5	2.68	....	....	....	....	....	....	....	....	....	....	....	....	....	....	....	....	....
1947-48	Providence Reds	AHL	63	*40	19	4	3780	242	0	3.84	....	....	....	....	....	5	1	4	0	300	23	0	4.60	....	....	....	....
1948-49	Providence Reds	AHL	67	*43	18	6	4020	212	3	3.16	....	....	....	....	....	14	*8	6	0	900	41	1	2.73	....	....	....	....
1949-50	Providence Reds	AHL	60	31	26	3	3600	219	0	3.65	....	....	....	....	....	4	2	2	0	240	16	0	4.00	....	....	....	....
1950-51	Providence Reds	AHL	57	19	33	5	3480	218	2	3.76	....	....	....	....	....	....	....	....	....	....	....	....	....	....	....	....	....
1951-52	Providence Reds	AHL	47	24	19	3	2780	160	1	3.45	....	....	....	....	....	14	*8	6	0	885	31	1	2.10	....	....	....	....
1952-53	Providence Reds	AHL	58	27	31	1	3520	224	1	3.82	....	....	....	....	....	....	....	....	....	....	....	....	....	....	....	....	....
1953-54	Providence Reds	AHL	59	23	33	3	3540	230	2	3.90	....	....	....	....	....	....	....	....	....	....	....	....	....	....	....	....	....
1954-55	Providence Reds	AHL	48	14	29	5	2880	192	0	4.00	....	....	....	....	....	....	....	....	....	....	....	....	....	....	....	....	....
1955-56	Providence Reds	AHL	3	0	3	0	180	17	0	5.67	....	....	....	....	....	....	....	....	....	....	....	....	....	....	....	....	....
	Chatham Maroons	OHA Sr.	9	....	....	....	540	44	0	4.88	....	....	....	....	....	....	....	....	....	....	....	....	....	....	....	....	....
1956-57	Providence Reds	AHL	7	4	3	0	420	29	0	4.14	....	....	....	....	....	....	....	....	....	....	....	....	....	....	....	....	....
1957-58	Providence Reds	AHL	1	0	1	0	70	2	0	1.71	....	....	....	....	....	....	....	....	....	....	....	....	....	....	....	....	....
	Trois-Rivieres Lions	QHL	1	0	1	0	60	6	0	6.00	....	....	....	....	....	....	....	....	....	....	....	....	....	....	....	....	....
1958-59	Washington Presidents	EHL	3	1	2	0	180	18	0	6.00	....	....	....	....	....	....	....	....	....	....	....	....	....	....	....	....	....
	Providence Reds	AHL	10	1	9	0	600	39	1	3.90	....	....	....	....	....	....	....	....	....	....	....	....	....	....	....	....	....
	NHL Totals		**25**	**10**	**12**	**2**	**1470**	**103**	**0**	**4.20**	....	....	....	....	....	....	....	....	....	....	....	....	....	....	....	....	....

EHL First All-Star Team (1946) • Won George L. Davis Jr. Trophy (fewest goals against - EHL) (1946) • AHL Second All-Star Team (1947)

● BERGERON, JEAN-CLAUDE

Jean-Claude Bergeron G – L. 6′2″, 192 lbs. b: Hauterive, Que., 10/14/1968. Montreal's 6th choice, 104th overall, in 1988 Entry Draft.

Season	Club	League	GP	W	L	T	Mins	GA	SO	Avg	AAvg	Eff	SA	S%	SAPG	GP	W	L	T	Mins	GA	SO	Avg	Eff	SA	S%	SAPG
1987-88	Verdun Jr. Canadiens	QMJHL	49	13	31	3	2715	265	0	5.86	....	....	....	....	....	....	....	....	....	....	....	....	....	....	....	....	....
1988-89	Verdun Jr. Canadiens	QMJHL	44	8	34	1	2417	199	0	4.94	....	....	....	....	....	....	....	....	....	....	....	....	....	....	....	....	....
	Sherbrooke Canadiens	AHL	5	4	1	0	302	18	0	3.58	....	....	....	....	....	....	....	....	....	....	....	....	....	....	....	....	....
1989-90	Sherbrooke Canadiens	AHL	40	21	8	7	2254	103	2	*2.74	....	....	....	....	....	9	6	2	....	497	28	0	3.38	....	....	....	....
1990-91	Montreal Canadiens	FrTour	2	....	....	....	59	2	0	2.03	....	....	....	....	....	....	....	....	....	....	....	....	....	....	....	....	....
	Montreal Canadiens	**NHL**	**18**	**7**	**6**	**2**	**941**	**59**	**0**	**3.76**	**3.36**	**5.21**	**426**	**.862**	**27.2**	....	....	....	....	....	....	....	....	....	....	....	....
	Fredericton Canadiens	AHL	18	12	6	0	1083	59	1	3.27	....	....	....	....	....	10	5	5	....	546	32	0	3.52	....	....	....	....
1991-92	Fredericton Canadiens	AHL	13	5	7	1	791	57	0	4.32	....	....	....	....	....	....	....	....	....	....	....	....	....	....	....	....	....
	Peoria Rivermen	IHL	27	14	9	3	1632	96	1	3.53	....	....	....	....	....	6	3	3	....	352	24	0	4.09	....	....	....	....
1992-93	**Tampa Bay Lightning**	**NHL**	**21**	**8**	**10**	**1**	**1163**	**71**	**0**	**3.66**	**3.12**	**4.53**	**574**	**.876**	**29.6**	....	....	....	....	....	....	....	....	....	....	....	....
	Atlanta Knights	IHL	31	21	7	1	1722	92	1	3.21	....	....	....	....	....	6	3	3	....	368	19	0	3.10	....	....	....	....
1993-94	**Tampa Bay Lightning**	**NHL**	**3**	**1**	**1**	**1**	**134**	**7**	**0**	**3.13**	**2.98**	**3.18**	**69**	**.899**	**30.9**	....	....	....	....	....	....	....	....	....	....	....	....
	Atlanta Knights	IHL	48	27	11	7	2755	141	0	3.07	....	....	....	....	....	2	1	1	....	153	6	0	2.34	....	....	....	....
1994-95	Atlanta Knights	IHL	6	3	3	0	324	24	0	4.44	....	....	....	....	....	....	....	....	....	....	....	....	....	....	....	....	....
	Tampa Bay Lightning	**NHL**	**17**	**3**	**9**	**1**	**883**	**49**	**1**	**3.33**	**3.45**	**4.36**	**374**	**.869**	**25.4**	....	....	....	....	....	....	....	....	....	....	....	....
1995-96	**Tampa Bay Lightning**	**NHL**	**12**	**2**	**6**	**2**	**595**	**42**	**0**	**4.24**	**4.17**	**7.12**	**250**	**.832**	**25.2**	....	....	....	....	....	....	....	....	....	....	....	....
	Atlanta Knights	IHL	25	9	10	3	1326	92	0	4.16	....	....	....	....	....	....	....	....	....	....	....	....	....	....	....	....	....
1996-97	**Los Angeles Kings**	**NHL**	**1**	**0**	**1**	**0**	**56**	**4**	**0**	**4.29**	**4.54**	**4.90**	**35**	**.886**	**37.5**	....	....	....	....	....	....	....	....	....	....	....	....
	Phoenix Roadrunners	IHL	42	11	19	7	2296	127	0	3.32	....	....	....	....	....	....	....	....	....	....	....	....	....	....	....	....	....
	NHL Totals		**72**	**21**	**33**	**7**	**3772**	**232**	**1**	**3.69**	....	....	**1728**	**.866**	....	....	....	....	....	....	....	....	....	....	....	....	....

AHL First All-Star Team (1990) • Shared Harry "Hap" Holmes Trophy (fewest goals-against - AHL) with Andre Racicot (1990) • Won Baz Bastien Memorial Trophy (Top Goaltender - AHL) (1990) • Shared James Norris Memorial Trophy (fewest goals-against - IHL) with Mike Greenlay (1994)

Traded to **Tampa Bay** by **Montreal** for Frederic Chabot, June 19, 1992. Signed as a free agent by **Los Angeles**, August 28, 1996.

● BERNHARDT, TIM

Tim Bernhardt G – L. 5′9″, 160 lbs. b: Sarnia, Ont., 1/17/1958. Atlanta's 2nd choice, 47th overall, in 1978 Amateur Draft.

Season	Club	League	GP	W	L	T	Mins	GA	SO	Avg	AAvg	Eff	SA	S%	SAPG	GP	W	L	T	Mins	GA	SO	Avg	Eff	SA	S%	SAPG
1975-76	Cornwall Royals	QMJHL	51	....	....	....	2985	195	2	3.92	....	....	....	....	....	8	4	4	0	488	30	0	3.69	....	....	....	....
1976-77	Cornwall Royals	QMJHL	44	....	....	....	2497	151	0	*3.63	....	....	....	....	....	12	4	5	3	720	47	0	3.92	....	....	....	....
1977-78	Cornwall Royals	QMJHL	54	....	....	....	3165	179	2	3.39	....	....	....	....	....	9	5	4	0	540	27	2	3.00	....	....	....	....
	Canada	WJC-A	3	....	....	....	180	6	....	2.00	....	....	....	....	....	....	....	....	....	....	....	....	....	....	....	....	....
1978-79	Tulsa Oilers	CHL	46	15	26	3	2705	191	0	4.24	....	....	....	....	....	....	....	....	....	....	....	....	....	....	....	....	....
1979-80	Birmingham Bulls	CHL	34	15	16	1	1933	122	1	3.79	....	....	....	....	....	3	1	2	0	160	17	0	6.38	....	....	....	....
1980-81	Birmingham Bulls	CHL	29	11	13	2	1598	106	1	3.98	....	....	....	....	....	....	....	....	....	....	....	....	....	....	....	....	....
1981-82	Oklahoma City Stars	CHL	10	1	8	0	526	45	0	5.13	....	....	....	....	....	....	....	....	....	....	....	....	....	....	....	....	....
	Rochester Americans	AHL	29	15	10	2	1586	95	0	3.59	....	....	....	....	....	9	4	3	0	527	29	0	3.30	....	....	....	....
1982-83	**Calgary Flames**	**NHL**	**6**	**0**	**5**	**0**	**280**	**21**	**0**	**4.50**	**3.60**	**6.43**	**147**	**.857**	**31.5**	....	....	....	....	....	....	....	....	....	....	....	....
	Colorado Flames	CHL	34	19	11	1	1896	122	0	3.86	....	....	....	....	....	5	2	3	0	304	19	0	3.75	....	....	....	....
1983-84	St. Catharines Saints	AHL	42	25	13	4	2461	154	0	3.75	....	....	....	....	....	5	2	3	0	288	17	0	3.54	....	....	....	....
1984-85	**Toronto Maple Leafs**	**NHL**	**37**	**13**	**19**	**4**	**2182**	**136**	**0**	**3.74**	**2.97**	**4.60**	**1106**	**.877**	**30.4**	....	....	....	....	....	....	....	....	....	....	....	....
	St. Catharines Saints	AHL	14	5	7	2	801	55	0	4.12	....	....	....	....	....	....	....	....	....	....	....	....	....	....	....	....	....
1985-86	**Toronto Maple Leafs**	**NHL**	**23**	**4**	**12**	**3**	**1266**	**107**	**0**	**5.07**	**3.96**	**7.46**	**727**	**.853**	**34.5**	....	....	....	....	....	....	....	....	....	....	....	....
	St. Catharines Saints	AHL	14	6	4	2	776	38	1	2.94	....	....	....	....	....	3	0	3	0	140	12	0	5.14	....	....	....	....
1986-87	**Toronto Maple Leafs**	**NHL**	**1**	**0**	**0**	**0**	**20**	**3**	**0**	**9.00**	**7.57**	**38.57**	**7**	**.571**	**21.0**	....	....	....	....	....	....	....	....	....	....	....	....
	Newmarket Saints	AHL	31	6	17	0	1705	117	1	4.12	....	....	....	....	....	....	....	....	....	....	....	....	....	....	....	....	....
1987-88	Newmarket Saints	AHL	49	22	19	4	2704	166	0	3.68	....	....	....	....	....	....	....	....	....	....	....	....	....	....	....	....	....
1988-89	Newmarket Saints	AHL	37	17	16	2	2004	145	1	4.34	....	....	....	....	....	....	....	....	....	....	....	....	....	....	....	....	....
1989-90	Newmarket Saints	AHL	14	4	7	1	755	51	0	4.71	....	....	....	....	....	....	....	....	....	....	....	....	....	....	....	....	....
	NHL Totals		**67**	**17**	**36**	**7**	**3748**	**267**	**0**	**4.27**	....	....	**1987**	**.866**	....	....	....	....	....	....	....	....	....	....	....	....	....

QMJHL West Second All-Star Team (1976) • QMJHL First All-Star Team (1977, 1978) • AHL Second All-Star Team (1984)

Transferred to **Calgary** after **Atlanta** franchise relocated, June 24, 1980. Signed as a free agent by **Toronto**, December 5, 1984.

● BERTHIAUME, DANIEL

Daniel "The Bandit" Berthiaume G – L. 5′9″, 155 lbs. b: Longueuil, Que., 1/26/1966. Winnipeg's 3rd choice, 60th overall, in 1985 Entry Draft.

Season	Club	League	GP	W	L	T	Mins	GA	SO	Avg	AAvg	Eff	SA	S%	SAPG	GP	W	L	T	Mins	GA	SO	Avg	Eff	SA	S%	SAPG
1983-84	Drummondville Voltigeurs	QMJHL	28	....	....	....	1562	131	0	5.03	....	....	....	....	....	3	....	....	....	154	16	0	6.23	....	....	....	....
1984-85	Drummondville Voltigeurs	QMJHL	3	....	....	....	179	17	0	5.70	....	....	....	....	....	....	....	....	....	....	....	....	....	....	....	....	....
	Chicoutimi Sagueneens	QMJHL	56	....	....	....	3168	198	2	3.75	....	....	....	....	....	14	8	6	0	770	51	0	3.97	....	....	....	....
1985-86	Chicoutimi Sagueneens	QMJHL	66	34	29	3	3718	286	1	4.62	....	....	....	....	....	9	4	5	0	580	37	0	3.83	....	....	....	....
	Winnipeg Jets	**NHL**	....	....	....	....	....	....	....	....	....	....	....	....	....	**1**	**0**	**1**	....	**68**	**4**	**0**	**3.53**	**3.28**	**43**	**.907**	**37.9**
1986-87	**Winnipeg Jets**	**NHL**	**31**	**18**	**7**	**3**	**1758**	**93**	**1**	**3.17**	**2.66**	**3.64**	**810**	**.885**	**27.6**	**8**	**4**	**4**	....	**439**	**21**	**0**	**2.87**	**2.87**	**210**	**.900**	**28.7**
	Sherbrooke Canadiens	AHL	7	4	3	0	420	23	0	3.29	....	....	....	....	....	....	....	....	....	....	....	....	....	....	....	....	....
1987-88	**Winnipeg Jets**	**NHL**	**56**	**22**	**19**	**7**	**3010**	**176**	**2**	**3.51**	**2.91**	**4.15**	**1489**	**.882**	**29.7**	**5**	**1**	**4**	....	**300**	**25**	**0**	**5.00**	**8.12**	**154**	**.838**	**30.8**
1988-89	**Winnipeg Jets**	**NHL**	**9**	**0**	**8**	**0**	**443**	**44**	**0**	**5.96**	**4.93**	**10.28**	**255**	**.827**	**34.5**	....	....	....	....	....	....	....	....	....	....	....	....
	Moncton Hawks	AHL	21	6	9	2	1083	76	0	4.21	....	....	....	....	....	3	1	2	0	180	11	0	3.67	....	....	....	....
1989-90	**Winnipeg Jets**	**NHL**	**24**	**10**	**11**	**3**	**1387**	**86**	**1**	**3.72**	**3.12**	**4.80**	**667**	**.871**	**28.9**	....	....	....	....	....	....	....	....	....	....	....	....
	Minnesota North Stars	**NHL**	**5**	**1**	**3**	**0**	**240**	**14**	**0**	**3.50**	**2.93**	**4.71**	**104**	**.865**	**26.0**	....	....	....	....	....	....	....	....	....	....	....	....
1990-91	**Los Angeles Kings**	**NHL**	**37**	**20**	**11**	**4**	**2119**	**117**	**1**	**3.31**	**2.95**	**3.57**	**1086**	**.892**	**30.8**	....	....	....	....	....	....	....	....	....	....	....	....
1991-92	**Los Angeles Kings**	**NHL**	**19**	**7**	**10**	**1**	**979**	**66**	**0**	**4.04**	**3.59**	**4.93**	**541**	**.878**	**33.2**	....	....	....	....	....	....	....	....	....	....	....	....
	Boston Bruins	**NHL**	**8**	**1**	**4**	**2**	**399**	**21**	**0**	**3.16**	**2.80**	**4.25**	**156**	**.865**	**23.5**	....	....	....	....	....	....	....	....	....	....	....	....

			REGULAR SEASON													PLAYOFFS											
Season	Club	League	GP	W	L	T	Mins	GA	SO	Avg	AAvg	Eff	SA	S%	SAPG	GP	W	L	T	Mins	GA	SO	Avg	Eff	SA	S%	SAPG
1992-93	EC Graz	Alpenliga	28	....	....	....	....	110	0	4.07	....	....	....	....	....	....	....	....	....	....	....	....	....	....	....	....	....
	Ottawa Senators	NHL	25	2	17	1	1326	95	0	4.30	3.67	5.53	739	.871	33.4	....	....	....	....	....	....	....	....	....	....	....	....
1993-94	Ottawa Senators	NHL	1	0	0	0	1	2	0	120.00	114.26	1200.0	2	.00	120.0	....	....	....	....	....	....	....	....	....	....	....	....
	P.E.I. Senators	AHL	30	8	16	3	1640	130	0	4.76	....	....	....	....	....	....	....	....	....	....	....	....	....	....	....	....	....
	Adirondack Red Wings	AHL	11	7	2	0	552	35	0	3.80	....	....	....	....	....	11	6	4	0	632	30	0	2.85	....	....	....	....
1994-95	Providence Bruins	AHL	2	0	1	1	126	7	0	3.32	....	....	....	....	....	....	....	....	....	....	....	....	....	....	....	....	....
	Wheeling Thunderbirds	ECHL	10	6	1	1	600	41	0	4.10	....	....	....	....	....	....	....	....	....	....	....	....	....	....	....	....	....
	Roanoke Express	ECHL	21	15	4	2	1196	47	0	2.36	....	....	....	....	....	8	4	4	0	464	23	1	2.97	....	....	....	....
	Detroit Vipers	IHL	....	....	....	....	....	....	....	....	....	....	....	....	....	5	2	3	0	331	14	0	2.53	....	....	....	....
1995-96	Detroit Vipers	IHL	7	4	3	0	401	19	2	2.84	....	....	....	....	....	....	....	....	....	....	....	....	....	....	....	....	....
	Roanoke Express	ECHL	39	22	13	3	2109	112	*2	3.19	....	....	....	....	....	2	0	2	0	116	6	0	3.09	....	....	....	....
1996-97	Central Texas Stampede	WPHL	*54	30	20	0	*3034	171	*2	*3.38	....	....	....	....	....	*11	5	6	0	*678	43	*1	3.80	....	....	....	....
1997-98	Roanoke Express	ECHL	30	17	8	3	1711	74	2	*2.59	....	....	....	....	....	2	2	0	....	120	4	0	2.00	....	....	....	....
	NHL Totals		215	81	90	21	11662	714	5	3.67	....	....	5849	.878	....	14	5	9	....	807	50	0	3.72	....	....	....	....

QMJHL First All-Star Team (1985) • WPHL First All-Star Team (1997) • Named WPHL's Top Goaltender (1997)

Traded to **Minnesota** by **Winnipeg** for future considerations, January 22, 1990. Traded to **LA Kings** by **Minnesota** for Craig Duncanson, September 6, 1990. Traded to **Boston** by **LA Kings** for future considerations, January 18, 1992. Traded to **Winnipeg** by **Boston** for Doug Evans, June 10, 1992. Signed as a free agent by **Ottawa**, December 15, 1992. Traded to **Detroit** by **Ottawa** for Steve Konroyd, March 21, 1994.

• BESTER, ALLAN

Allan "Ernie" Bester G – L. 5'7", 155 lbs. b: Hamilton, Ont., 3/26/1964. Toronto's 3rd choice, 49th overall, in 1983 Entry Draft.

1981-82	Brantford Alexanders	OHL	19	4	11	0	970	68	0	4.21	....	....	....	....	....	....	....	....	....	....	....	....	....	....	....	....	....
1982-83	Brantford Alexanders	OHL	56	29	21	3	3210	188	0	3.51	....	....	....	....	....	8	3	3	....	480	20	*1	*2.50	....	....	....	....
1983-84	Toronto Maple Leafs	NHL	32	11	16	4	1848	134	0	4.35	3.41	5.10	1144	.883	37.1	....	....	....	....	....	....	....	....	....	....	....	....
	Brantford Alexanders	OHL	23	12	9	1	1271	71	1	3.35	....	....	....	....	....	1	0	1	....	60	5	0	5.00	....	....	....	....
1984-85	Toronto Maple Leafs	NHL	15	3	9	1	767	54	1	4.22	3.35	5.30	430	.874	33.6	....	....	....	....	....	....	....	....	....	....	....	....
	St. Catharines Saints	AHL	30	9	18	1	1669	133	0	4.78	....	....	....	....	....	....	....	....	....	....	....	....	....	....	....	....	....
1985-86	Toronto Maple Leafs	NHL	1	0	0	0	20	2	0	6.00	4.67	24.00	5	.600	15.0	....	....	....	....	....	....	....	....	....	....	....	....
	St. Catharines Saints	AHL	50	23	23	3	2855	173	1	3.64	....	....	....	....	....	11	7	3	....	637	27	0	2.54	....	....	....	....
1986-87	Toronto Maple Leafs	NHL	36	10	14	3	1808	110	2	3.65	3.07	4.05	991	.889	32.9	1	0	0	....	39	1	0	1.54	0.91	17	.941	26.2
	Newmarket Saints	AHL	3	1	0	0	190	6	0	1.89	....	....	....	....	....	....	....	....	....	....	....	....	....	....	....	....	....
1987-88	Toronto Maple Leafs	NHL	30	8	12	5	1607	102	2	3.81	3.17	4.42	879	.884	32.8	5	2	3	....	253	21	0	4.98	7.75	135	.844	32.0
1988-89	Toronto Maple Leafs	NHL	43	17	20	3	2460	156	2	3.80	3.14	4.17	1420	.890	34.6	....	....	....	....	....	....	....	....	....	....	....	....
1989-90	Toronto Maple Leafs	NHL	42	20	16	0	2206	165	0	4.49	3.78	5.72	1296	.873	35.2	4	0	3	....	196	14	0	4.29	5.01	120	.883	36.7
	Newmarket Saints	AHL	5	2	1	1	264	18	0	4.09	....	....	....	....	....	....	....	....	....	....	....	....	....	....	....	....	....
1990-91	Toronto Maple Leafs	NHL	6	0	4	0	247	18	0	4.37	3.91	6.10	129	.860	31.3	....	....	....	....	....	....	....	....	....	....	....	....
	Newmarket Saints	AHL	19	7	8	4	1157	58	1	3.01	....	....	....	....	....	....	....	....	....	....	....	....	....	....	....	....	....
	Detroit Red Wings	NHL	3	0	3	0	178	13	0	4.38	3.91	5.75	99	.869	33.4	1	0	0	....	20	1	0	3.00	2.50	12	.917	36.0
1991-92	Detroit Red Wings	NHL	1	0	0	0	31	2	0	3.87	3.43	8.60	9	.778	17.4	....	....	....	....	....	....	....	....	....	....	....	....
	Adirondack Red Wings	AHL	22	13	8	0	1268	78	0	3.69	....	....	....	....	....	*19	*14	5	....	1174	50	*1	*2.56	....	....	....	....
1992-93	Adirondack Red Wings	AHL	41	16	15	5	2268	133	1	3.52	....	....	....	....	....	10	7	3	....	633	26	*1	2.46	....	....	....	....
1993-94	San Diego Gulls	IHL	46	22	14	6	2543	150	1	3.54	....	....	....	....	....	8	4	4	....	419	28	0	4.00	....	....	....	....
1994-95	San Diego Gulls	IHL	58	28	23	5	3250	183	1	3.38	....	....	....	....	....	4	2	2	....	272	13	0	2.86	....	....	....	....
1995-96	Orlando Solar Bears	IHL	51	32	16	2	2947	176	1	3.58	....	....	....	....	....	*23	11	12	....	*1343	65	2	2.90	....	....	....	....
	Dallas Stars	NHL	10	4	5	1	601	30	0	3.00	2.95	3.03	297	.899	29.7	....	....	....	....	....	....	....	....	....	....	....	....
1996-97	Orlando Solar Bears	IHL	61	37	13	3	3115	132	2	2.54	....	....	....	....	....	10	4	4	....	512	27	0	3.16	....	....	....	....
1997-98	Orlando Solar Bears	IHL	26	13	8	1	1330	66	1	2.98	....	....	....	....	....	2	1	0	....	76	6	0	4.68	....	....	....	....
	NHL Totals		219	73	99	17	11773	786	7	4.01	....	....	6699	.883	....	11	2	6	....	508	37	0	4.37	....	....	....	....

OHL First All-Star Team (1983) • Won Jack Butterfield Trophy (Playoff MVP - AHL) (1992)

Traded to **Detroit** by **Toronto** for Detroit's 6th round choice (Alexander Kuzminsky) in 1991 Entry Draft, March 5, 1991. Signed as a free agent by **Anaheim**, September 9, 1993. Signed as a free agent by **Dallas**, January 21, 1996.

• BEVERIDGE, BILL

Bill Beveridge G – L. 5'8", 170 lbs. b: Ottawa, Ont., 7/1/1909. d: 2/13/1995.

1924-25	Ottawa Shamrocks	City Jr.	5	2	3	0	300	12	0	2.40	....	....	....	....	....	....	....	....	....	....	....	....	....	....	....	....	....
	Ottawa Shamrocks	City Sr.	6	3	3	0	400	23	0	3.45	....	....	....	....	....	....	....	....	....	....	....	....	....	....	....	....	....
1925-26	Ottawa Shamrocks	City Sr.	15	5	10	0	900	41	2	2.73	....	....	....	....	....	....	....	....	....	....	....	....	....	....	....	....	....
1926-27	Ottawa New Edinburghs	City Sr.	....	....	....	....	....	....	....	....	....	....	....	....	....	5	*3	2	0	300	4	*2	*0.80	....	....	....	....
1927-28	Ottawa New Edinburghs	City Sr.	15	10	4	1	900	27	....	1.80	....	....	....	....	....	6	3	3	0	360	9	2	1.50	....	....	....	....
1928-29	Ottawa New Edinburghs	City Sr.	15	9	6	0	900	17	*7	*1.13	....	....	....	....	....	2	2	0	0	120	6	0	3.00	....	....	....	....
1929-30	Ottawa New Edinburghs	City Sr.	1	0	1	0	60	3	0	3.00	....	....	....	....	....	....	....	....	....	....	....	....	....	....	....	....	....
	Detroit Cougars	NHL	39	14	20	5	2410	109	2	2.71	2.81	....	....	....	....	....	....	....	....	....	....	....	....	....	....	....	....
1930-31	Ottawa Senators	NHL	9	0	8	0	520	32	0	3.69	4.81	....	....	....	....	....	....	....	....	....	....	....	....	....	....	....	....
1931-32	Providence Reds	Can-Am	40	*23	11	6	2510	108	5	2.58	....	....	....	....	....	5	*5	0	0	310	6	1	*1.16	....	....	....	....
1932-33	Ottawa Senators	NHL	35	7	19	8	2195	95	5	2.60	3.57	....	....	....	....	....	....	....	....	....	....	....	....	....	....	....	....
	Providence Reds	Can-Am	5	2	3	0	300	10	1	2.00	....	....	....	....	....	....	....	....	....	....	....	....	....	....	....	....	....
1933-34	Ottawa Senators	NHL	*48	13	29	6	3000	143	3	2.86	3.76	....	....	....	....	....	....	....	....	....	....	....	....	....	....	....	....
1934-35	St. Louis Eagles	NHL	*48	11	31	6	2990	144	3	2.89	3.61	....	....	....	....	....	....	....	....	....	....	....	....	....	....	....	....
1935-36	Montreal Maroons	NHL	32	14	13	5	1970	71	1	2.16	3.08	....	....	....	....	....	....	....	....	....	....	....	....	....	....	....	....
1936-37	Montreal Maroons	NHL	21	12	6	3	1290	47	1	2.19	2.73	....	....	....	....	5	2	3	....	300	11	0	2.20	....	....	....	....
1937-38	Montreal Maroons	NHL	*48	12	30	6	2980	149	2	3.00	3.76	....	....	....	....	....	....	....	....	....	....	....	....	....	....	....	....
1938-39	Syracuse Stars	AHL	4	3	1	0	240	11	1	2.75	....	....	....	....	....	....	....	....	....	....	....	....	....	....	....	....	....
	New Haven Eagles	AHL	50	13	25	10	3000	144	5	2.88	....	....	....	....	....	....	....	....	....	....	....	....	....	....	....	....	....
	Providence Reds	AHL	2	0	2	0	120	9	0	4.50	....	....	....	....	....	5	2	3	0	300	15	1	2.50	....	....	....	....
1939-40	Syracuse Stars	AHL	*56	20	27	9	3450	169	3	2.94	....	....	....	....	....	....	....	....	....	....	....	....	....	....	....	....	....
1940-41	Buffalo Bisons	AHL	55	19	27	9	3470	172	3	2.97	....	....	....	....	....	....	....	....	....	....	....	....	....	....	....	....	....
1941-42	Cleveland Barons	AHL	31	16	12	2	1870	73	7	2.34	....	....	....	....	....	5	3	2	0	310	12	0	2.32	....	....	....	....
1942-43	Cleveland Barons	AHL	33	13	15	5	1980	109	1	3.21	....	....	....	....	....	....	....	....	....	....	....	....	....	....	....	....	....
	New York Rangers	NHL	17	4	10	3	1020	89	1	5.24	4.69	....	....	....	....	....	....	....	....	....	....	....	....	....	....	....	....
1943-44	Ottawa Commandos	QSHL	1	0	1	0	60	12	0	12.00	....	....	....	....	....	....	....	....	....	....	....	....	....	....	....	....	....
1944-45	Ottawa Commandos	QSHL	3	....	....	....	180	16	0	5.33	....	....	....	....	....	....	....	....	....	....	....	....	....	....	....	....	....
	NHL Totals		297	87	166	42	18375	879	18	2.87	....	....	....	....	....	5	2	3	....	300	11	0	2.20	....	....	....	....

Loaned to **Detroit Cougars** by **Ottawa** for 1929-30 season for cash, November 27, 1929. Transferred to **St. Louis** after **Ottawa** franchise relocated, September 22, 1934. Claimed by **Montreal Canadiens** from **St. Louis** in Dispersal Draft, October 15, 1935. Traded to **Montreal Maroons** by **Montreal Canadiens** for cash, October, 1935. Loaned to **NY Rangers** by **Cleveland** (AHL) to replace injured Jimmy Franks, January 26, 1943.

• BIBEAULT, PAUL

Paul Bibeault G – L. 5'9", 160 lbs. b: Montreal, Que., 4/13/1919. d: 8/2/1970.

1938-39	Verdun Jr. Maple Leafs	QJHL	11	*9	0	2	660	23	1	*2.09	....	....	....	....	....	10	6	4	0	600	29	0	2.90	....	....	....	....
	Verdun Maple Leafs	QSHL	....	....	....	....	....	....	....	....	....	....	....	....	....	1	0	1	0	60	4	0	4.00	....	....	....	....
1939-40	Verdun Maple Leafs	QSHL	30	11	11	8	1800	112	0	3.73	....	....	....	....	....	8	3	5	0	480	26	*1	*3.25	....	....	....	....
1940-41	Montreal Canadiens	NHL	4	1	2	0	210	15	0	4.29	4.97	....	....	....	....	....	....	....	....	....	....	....	....	....	....	....	....
	Montreal Canadiens	QSHL	34	....	....	....	2040	121	0	3.56	....	....	....	....	....	....	....	....	....	....	....	....	....	....	....	....	....
1941-42	Washington Lions	AHL	13	3	7	3	820	39	0	2.85	....	....	....	....	....	....	....	....	....	....	....	....	....	....	....	....	....
	Montreal Canadiens	NHL	38	17	19	2	2380	131	1	3.30	3.29	....	....	....	....	3	1	2	....	180	8	*1	2.67	....	....	....	....
1942-43	Montreal Canadiens	NHL	*50	19	19	12	3010	191	1	3.81	3.28	....	....	....	....	5	1	4	....	320	18	1	3.38	....	....	....	....
1943-44	Toronto Maple Leafs	NHL	29	13	14	2	1740	87	*5	3.00	2.21	....	....	....	....	5	1	4	....	300	23	0	4.60	....	....	....	....
1944-45	Boston Bruins	NHL	26	6	18	2	1530	116	0	4.55	3.85	....	....	....	....	7	3	4	....	437	22	0	3.02	....	....	....	....
1945-46	Boston Bruins	NHL	16	8	4	4	960	45	2	2.81	2.57	....	....	....	....	....	....	....	....	....	....	....	....	....	....	....	....
	Montreal Canadiens	NHL	10	4	6	0	600	30	0	3.00	2.76	....	....	....	....	....	....	....	....	....	....	....	....	....	....	....	....
1946-47	Chicago Black Hawks	NHL	41	13	25	3	2460	170	1	4.15	4.22	....	....	....	....	....	....	....	....	....	....	....	....	....	....	....	....
	Fort Worth Rangers	USHL	11	....	....	....	660	30	1	2.73	....	....	....	....	....	9	4	*5	0	540	30	*1	3.33	....	....	....	....
1947-48	Buffalo Bisons	AHL	25	15	8	2	1500	83	0	3.32	....	....	....	....	....	....	....	....	....	....	....	....	....	....	....	....	....
1948-49	Dallas Texans	USHL	65	24	26	15	3900	246	2	3.78	....	....	....	....	....	4	2	2	0	240	11	*1	*2.75	....	....	....	....

			REGULAR SEASON													PLAYOFFS											
Season	Club	League	GP	W	L	T	Mins	GA	SO	Avg	AAvg	Eff	SA	S%	SAPG	GP	W	L	T	Mins	GA	SO	Avg	Eff	SA	S%	SAPG
1949-50	Cincinnati Mohawks	AHL	15	7	7	1	900	51	0	3.40	....	....	....	....	....	....	....	....	....	....	....	....	....	....	....	....	....
1950-51	Cincinnati Mohawks	AHL	18	8	8	1	1099	58	0	3.17	....	....	....	....	....	....	....	....	....	....	....	....	....	....	....	....	....
1951-52	Cincinnati Mohawks	AHL	16	5	10	1	980	60	0	3.67	....	....	....	....	....	1	1	0	0	94	1	0	0.64	....	....	....	....
1952-53			DID NOT PLAY																								
1953-54	Cincinnati Mohawks	IHL	3	....	....	....	180	8	0	2.67	....	....	....	....	....	....	....	....	....	....	....	....	....	....	....	....	....
1954-55	Cincinnati Mohawks	IHL	2	....	....	....	120	5	0	2.50	....	....	....	....	....	....	....	....	....	....	....	....	....	....	....	....	....
	NHL Totals		**214**	**81**	**107**	**25**	**12890**	**785**	**10**	**3.65**	....	....	....	....	....	**20**	**6**	**14**	....	**1237**	**71**	**2**	**3.44**	....	....	....	....

NHL Second All-Star Team (1944) • USHL First All-Star Team (1949) • Won Charles Gardiner Memorial Trophy (USHL - Top Goaltender) (1949) • Won Herman W. Paterson Cup (USHL - MVP) (1949)

Signed as a free agent by **Montreal**, March 6, 1941. Loaned to **Toronto** by **Montreal** for remainder of 1943-44 season, December 22, 1943. Loaned to **Boston** by **Montreal** as a war-time replacement for Frank Brimsek, December 27, 1944. Returned to **Montreal** by **Boston** as an injury replacement for Bill Durnan, January 6, 1946. Mike McMahon was loaned to **Boston** on January 8, 1946 as compensation for recalling Bibeault. Traded to **Chicago** by **Montreal** for George Allen with both teams holding right of recall, September 23, 1946. Players returned to original teams, June 2, 1947.

• BIERK, ZAC

Zac Bierk G – L. 6′4″, 186 lbs. b: Peterborough, Ont., 9/17/1976. Tampa Bay's 8th choice, 212th overall, in 1995 Entry Draft.

Season	Club	League	GP	W	L	T	Mins	GA	SO	Avg	AAvg	Eff	SA	S%	SAPG	GP	W	L	T	Mins	GA	SO	Avg	Eff	SA	S%	SAPG
1993-94	Peterborough Petes	OHL	9	0	4	2	423	37	0	5.22	....	....	....	....	....	1	0	0	....	33	7	0	12.70	....	....	....	....
1994-95	Peterborough Petes	OHL	35	11	15	5	1779	117	0	3.95	....	....	....	....	....	6	2	3	....	301	24	0	4.78	....	....	....	....
1995-96	Peterborough Petes	OHL	58	31	16	6	3292	174	2	3.17	....	....	....	....	....	*22	*14	7	....	*1383	83	0	3.60	....	....	....	....
1996-97	Peterborough Petes	OHL	49	*28	16	0	2744	151	2	3.30	....	....	....	....	....	11	6	5	....	666	35	0	3.15	....	....	....	....
1997-98	**Tampa Bay Lightning**	**NHL**	**13**	**1**	**4**	**1**	**433**	**30**	**0**	**4.16**	**4.88**	**5.94**	**210**	**.857**	**29.1**	....	....	....	....	....	....	....	....	....	....	....	....
	Adirondack Red Wings	AHL	12	1	6	1	557	36	0	3.87	....	....	....	....	....	....	....	....	....	....	....	....	....	....	....	....	....
	NHL Totals		**13**	**1**	**4**	**1**	**433**	**30**	**0**	**4.16**	....	....	**210**	**.857**	....	....	....	....	....	....	....	....	....	....	....	....	....

OHL First All-Star Team (1997)

• BILLINGTON, CRAIG

Craig Billington G – L. 5′10″, 170 lbs. b: London, Ont., 9/11/1966. New Jersey's 2nd choice, 23rd overall, in 1984 Entry Draft.

Season	Club	League	GP	W	L	T	Mins	GA	SO	Avg	AAvg	Eff	SA	S%	SAPG	GP	W	L	T	Mins	GA	SO	Avg	Eff	SA	S%	SAPG
1983-84	Belleville Bulls	OHL	44	20	19	0	2335	162	1	4.16	....	....	....	....	....	1	0	0	....	30	3	0	6.00	....	....	....	....
1984-85	Belleville Bulls	OHL	47	26	19	0	2544	180	1	4.25	....	....	....	....	....	14	7	5	....	761	47	1	3.71	....	....	....	....
	Canada	WJC-A	5	....	....	....	300	13	....	2.60	....	....	....	....	....	....	....	....	....	....	....	....	....	....	....	....	....
1985-86	**New Jersey Devils**	**NHL**	**18**	**4**	**9**	**1**	**901**	**77**	**0**	**5.13**	**4.00**	**8.20**	**482**	**.840**	**32.1**	....	....	....	....	....	....	....	....	....	....	....	....
	Canada	WJC-A	5	....	....	....	300	14	....	2.80	....	....	....	....	....	....	....	....	....	....	....	....	....	....	....	....	....
	Belleville Bulls	OHL	3	2	1	0	180	11	0	3.67	....	....	....	....	....	20	9	6	....	1133	68	0	3.60	....	....	....	....
1986-87	**New Jersey Devils**	**NHL**	**22**	**4**	**13**	**2**	**1114**	**89**	**0**	**4.79**	**4.04**	**7.49**	**569**	**.844**	**30.6**	....	....	....	....	....	....	....	....	....	....	....	....
	Maine Mariners	AHL	20	9	8	2	1151	70	0	3.65	....	....	....	....	....	....	....	....	....	....	....	....	....	....	....	....	....
1987-88	Utica Devils	AHL	*59	22	27	8	*3404	208	1	3.67	....	....	....	....	....	....	....	....	....	....	....	....	....	....	....	....	....
1988-89	**New Jersey Devils**	**NHL**	**3**	**1**	**1**	**0**	**140**	**11**	**0**	**4.71**	**3.89**	**7.97**	**65**	**.831**	**27.9**	....	....	....	....	....	....	....	....	....	....	....	....
	Utica Devils	AHL	41	17	18	6	2432	150	2	3.70	....	....	....	....	....	4	1	3	....	220	18	0	4.91	....	....	....	....
1989-90	Utica Devils	AHL	38	20	13	1	2087	138	0	3.97	....	....	....	....	....	....	....	....	....	....	....	....	....	....	....	....	....
1990-91	Canada	Nat-Team	34	17	14	2	1879	110	2	3.51	....	....	....	....	....	....	....	....	....	....	....	....	....	....	....	....	....
	Canada	WEC-A	3	....	....	....	46	3	0	3.91	....	....	....	....	....	....	....	....	....	....	....	....	....	....	....	....	....
1991-92	**New Jersey Devils**	**NHL**	**26**	**13**	**7**	**1**	**1363**	**69**	**2**	**3.04**	**2.69**	**3.29**	**637**	**.892**	**28.0**	....	....	....	....	....	....	....	....	....	....	....	....
1992-93	**New Jersey Devils**	**NHL**	**42**	**21**	**16**	**4**	**2389**	**146**	**2**	**3.67**	**3.12**	**4.55**	**1178**	**.876**	**29.6**	**2**	**0**	**1**	....	**78**	**5**	**0**	**3.85**	**4.94**	**39**	**.872**	**30.0**
1993-94	**Ottawa Senators**	**NHL**	**63**	**11**	**41**	**4**	**3319**	**254**	**0**	**4.59**	**4.42**	**6.47**	**1801**	**.859**	**32.6**	....	....	....	....	....	....	....	....	....	....	....	....
1994-95	**Ottawa Senators**	**NHL**	**9**	**0**	**6**	**2**	**472**	**32**	**0**	**4.07**	**4.22**	**5.43**	**240**	**.867**	**30.5**	....	....	....	....	....	....	....	....	....	....	....	....
	Boston Bruins	**NHL**	**8**	**5**	**1**	**0**	**373**	**19**	**0**	**3.06**	**3.16**	**4.15**	**140**	**.864**	**22.5**	**1**	**0**	**0**	....	**25**	**1**	**0**	**2.40**	**2.40**	**10**	**.900**	**24.0**
1995-96	**Boston Bruins**	**NHL**	**27**	**10**	**13**	**3**	**1380**	**79**	**1**	**3.43**	**3.37**	**4.56**	**594**	**.867**	**25.8**	**1**	**0**	**1**	....	**60**	**6**	**0**	**6.00**	**12.86**	**28**	**.786**	**28.0**
1996-97	**Colorado Avalanche**	**NHL**	**23**	**11**	**8**	**2**	**1200**	**53**	**1**	**2.65**	**2.80**	**2.40**	**584**	**.909**	**29.2**	**1**	**0**	**0**	....	**20**	**1**	**0**	**3.00**	**2.31**	**13**	**.923**	**39.0**
1997-98	**Colorado Avalanche**	**NHL**	**23**	**8**	**7**	**4**	**1162**	**45**	**1**	**2.32**	**2.71**	**1.78**	**588**	**.923**	**30.4**	**1**	**0**	**0**	....	**1**	**0**	**0**	**0.00**	**0.00**	**0**	**.00**	**0.0**
	NHL Totals		**264**	**88**	**122**	**23**	**13813**	**874**	**7**	**3.80**	....	....	**6878**	**.873**	....	**6**	**0**	**2**	....	**184**	**13**	**0**	**4.24**	....	....	....	....

Named Best Goaltender at WJC-A (1985) • OHL First All-Star Team (1985)

Played in NHL All-Star Game (1993)

Traded to **Ottawa** by **New Jersey** with Troy Mallette and New Jersey's 4th round choice (Cosmo Dupaul) in 1993 Entry Draft for Peter Sidorkiewicz and future considerations (Mike Peluso, June 26, 1993), June 20, 1993. Traded to **Boston** by **Ottawa** for NY Islanders' 8th round choice (previously acquired, Ottawa selected Ray Schultz) in 1995 Entry Draft, April 7, 1995. Signed as a free agent by **Florida**, September 5, 1996. Claimed by **Colorado** from **Florida** in NHL Waiver Draft, September 30, 1996.

• BINETTE, ANDRE

Andre Binette G – L. 5′8″, 140 lbs. b: Montreal, Que., 12/2/1933.

Season	Club	League	GP	W	L	T	Mins	GA	SO	Avg	AAvg	Eff	SA	S%	SAPG	GP	W	L	T	Mins	GA	SO	Avg	Eff	SA	S%	SAPG
1953-54	Trois-Rivieres Flambeaux	QJHL	48	24	22	2	2850	180	1	3.79	....	....	....	....	....	3	....	....	....	180	22	0	7.33	....	....	....	....
1954-55	**Montreal Canadiens**	**NHL**	**1**	**1**	**0**	**0**	**60**	**4**	**0**	**4.00**	**4.90**	....	....	....	....	....	....	....	....	....	....	....	....	....	....	....	....
	Shawinigan Cataracts	QHL	4	2	2	0	240	16	0	4.00	....	....	....	....	....	1	0	1	0	60	4	0	4.00	....	....	....	....
1955-56	Cornwall Colts	EOHL	2	0	2	0	120	16	0	8.00	....	....	....	....	....	....	....	....	....	....	....	....	....	....	....	....	....
1956-57	Troy Bruins	IHL	20	....	....	....	1200	75	1	3.75	....	....	....	....	....	....	....	....	....	....	....	....	....	....	....	....	....
	Clinton Comets	EHL	38	....	....	....	2280	181	0	4.76	....	....	....	....	....	....	....	....	....	....	....	....	....	....	....	....	....
1957-58	Chatham Maroons	NOHA	1	1	0	0	60	2	0	2.00	....	....	....	....	....	....	....	....	....	....	....	....	....	....	....	....	....
	Toledo Mercurys	IHL	46	....	....	....	2740	174	3	3.81	....	....	....	....	....	....	....	....	....	....	....	....	....	....	....	....	....
	NHL Totals		**1**	**1**	**0**	**0**	**60**	**4**	**0**	**4.00**	....	....	....	....	....	....	....	....	....	....	....	....	....	....	....	....	....

• Promoted to **Montreal** from **Montreal Royals** (QHL) to replace injured Jacques Plante, November 11, 1954. (Montreal 7, Chicago 4)

• BINKLEY, LES

Les Binkley G – R. 6′, 175 lbs. b: Owen Sound, Ont., 6/6/1936.

Season	Club	League	GP	W	L	T	Mins	GA	SO	Avg	AAvg	Eff	SA	S%	SAPG	GP	W	L	T	Mins	GA	SO	Avg	Eff	SA	S%	SAPG
1951-52	Galt Black Hawks	OHA	47	31	13	2	2780	178	*4	3.84	....	....	....	....	....	3	0	3	0	190	16	0	5.05	....	....	....	....
1952-53	Galt Black Hawks	OHA	55	....	....	....	3300	213	1	3.87	....	....	....	....	....	11	....	....	....	660	51	0	4.64	....	....	....	....
1953-54	Galt Black Hawks	OHA	54	20	33	1	3240	250	0	4.63	....	....	....	....	....	....	....	....	....	....	....	....	....	....	....	....	....
	Kitchener Greenshirts	OHA	4	2	2	0	240	17	0	4.25	....	....	....	....	....	4	1	3	0	240	16	0	4.00	....	....	....	....
1954-55	Walkerton Capitols	Sr. B	STATISTICS NOT AVAILABLE																								
	Kitchener-Waterloo Dutchmen	OHA Sr.	3	....	....	....	180	12	0	4.00	....	....	....	....	....	....	....	....	....	....	....	....	....	....	....	....	....
1955-56	Fort Wayne Komets	IHL	3	1	2	0	180	13	0	4.33	....	....	....	....	....	....	....	....	....	....	....	....	....	....	....	....	....
	Baltimore-Charlotte Clippers	EHL	59	21	37	1	3540	302	0	5.11	....	....	....	....	....	....	....	....	....	....	....	....	....	....	....	....	....
1956-57	Charlotte Clippers	EHL	64	*50	13	1	3840	239	0	3.79	....	....	....	....	....	13	*8	5	0	780	35	*2	*2.69	....	....	....	....
1957-58	Charlotte Clippers	EHL	64	*38	25	1	3840	237	0	3.70	....	....	....	....	....	12	5	7	0	720	46	*1	3.83	....	....	....	....
1958-59	Toledo Mercurys	IHL	52	....	....	....	3100	205	1	3.97	....	....	....	....	....	....	....	....	....	....	....	....	....	....	....	....	....
	Cleveland Barons	AHL	1	0	1	0	60	3	0	3.00	....	....	....	....	....	....	....	....	....	....	....	....	....	....	....	....	....
1959-60	Toledo-St. Louis Mercurys	IHL	67	28	35	4	4020	294	2	4.39	....	....	....	....	....	....	....	....	....	....	....	....	....	....	....	....	....
1960-61	Toledo Mercurys	IHL	1	1	0	0	60	0	1	0.00	....	....	....	....	....	....	....	....	....	....	....	....	....	....	....	....	....
	Cleveland Barons	AHL	8	4	1	1	450	11	0	1.47	....	....	....	....	....	4	0	4	0	240	18	0	4.50	....	....	....	....
1961-62	Cleveland Barons	AHL	60	31	26	3	3600	181	5	3.02	....	....	....	....	....	3	1	2	0	201	10	0	2.99	....	....	....	....
1962-63	Cleveland Barons	AHL	63	28	27	7	3780	203	4	3.22	....	....	....	....	....	7	*4	3	0	420	22	1	3.14	....	....	....	....
1963-64	Cleveland Barons	AHL	65	34	27	3	3885	180	3	2.77	....	....	....	....	....	....	....	....	....	....	....	....	....	....	....	....	....
1964-65	Cleveland Barons	AHL	40	14	23	2	2330	152	0	3.91	....	....	....	....	....	....	....	....	....	....	....	....	....	....	....	....	....
1965-66	Cleveland Barons	AHL	*66	34	30	2	*3932	192	2	2.93	....	....	....	....	....	*12	*8	4	0	*696	27	1	2.33	....	....	....	....
1966-67	San Diego Gulls	WHL	55	15	36	2	3200	190	1	3.56	....	....	....	....	....	....	....	....	....	....	....	....	....	....	....	....	....
1967-68	**Pittsburgh Penguins**	**NHL**	**54**	**20**	**24**	**10**	**3141**	**151**	**6**	**2.88**	**3.19**	....	....	....	....	....	....	....	....	....	....	....	....	....	....	....	....
1968-69	**Pittsburgh Penguins**	**NHL**	**50**	**10**	**31**	**8**	**2885**	**158**	**0**	**3.29**	**3.43**	....	....	....	....	....	....	....	....	....	....	....	....	....	....	....	....
1969-70	**Pittsburgh Penguins**	**NHL**	**27**	**10**	**13**	**1**	**1477**	**79**	**3**	**3.21**	**3.42**	....	....	....	....	**7**	**5**	**2**	....	**428**	**15**	**0**	**2.10**	....	....	....	....
1970-71	**Pittsburgh Penguins**	**NHL**	**34**	**11**	**11**	**10**	**1870**	**89**	**2**	**2.86**	**2.82**	....	....	....	....	....	....	....	....	....	....	....	....	....	....	....	....
1971-72	**Pittsburgh Penguins**	**NHL**	**31**	**7**	**15**	**5**	**1673**	**98**	**0**	**3.51**	**3.55**	....	....	....	....	....	....	....	....	....	....	....	....	....	....	....	....
1972-73	Ottawa Nationals	WHA	30	10	17	1	1709	106	0	3.72	....	....	....	....	....	4	1	3	0	223	17	0	4.57	....	....	....	....
1973-74	Toronto Toros	WHA	27	14	9	1	1412	77	1	3.27	....	....	....	....	....	5	2	2	0	182	17	0	5.60	....	....	....	....

			REGULAR SEASON													PLAYOFFS											
Season	Club	League	GP	W	L	T	Mins	GA	SO	Avg	AAvg	Eff	SA	S%	SAPG	GP	W	L	T	Mins	GA	SO	Avg	Eff	SA	S%	SAPG
1974-75	Toronto Toros	WHA	17	6	4	0	772	47	0	3.65	....	....	....	....	....	1	0	1	0	59	5	0	5.08	....	....	....	....
1975-76	Toronto Toros	WHA	7	0	6	0	335	32	0	5.73	....	....	....	....	....	....	....	....	....	....	....	....	....	....	....	....	....
	Buffalo Norsemen	NAHL	24	....	....	....	1194	85	0	4.27	....	....	....	....	....	....	....	....	....	....	....	....	....	....	....	....	....
	NHL Totals		**196**	**58**	**94**	**34**	**11046**	**575**	**11**	**3.12**	....	....	....	....	....	**7**	**5**	**2**	....	**428**	**15**	**0**	**2.10**	....	....	....	....
	Other Major League Totals		81	30	36	2	4228	262	1	3.72	....	....	....	....	....	10	3	6	0	464	39	0	5.04	....	....	....	....

EHL Second All-Star Team (1957) • Won Dudley "Red" Garrett Memorial Award (Top Rookie - AHL) (1962) • AHL Second All-Star Team (1964, 1966) • Won Harry "Hap" Holmes Memorial Award (fewest goals against - AHL) (1966) • WHL Second All-Star Team (1967)

Signed by **Cleveland** (AHL) as assistant trainer and practice goaltender, September, 1957. Traded to **Detroit** (Pittsburgh - AHL) by **Cleveland** (AHL) for cash, August, 1966. Traded to **Pittsburgh** by **Detroit** for cash, June 14, 1967. Selected by **Ontario-Ottawa** (WHA) in 1972 WHA General Player Draft, February 12, 1972. Transferred to **Toronto** (WHA) after **Ottawa** (WHA) franchise relocated, May, 1973.

• BIRON, MARTIN

Martin Biron G – L. 6'1", 154 lbs. b: Lac St. Charles, Que., 8/15/1977. Buffalo's 2nd choice, 16th overall, in 1995 Entry Draft.

Season	Club	League	GP	W	L	T	Mins	GA	SO	Avg	AAvg	Eff	SA	S%	SAPG	GP	W	L	T	Mins	GA	SO	Avg	Eff	SA	S%	SAPG
1994-95	Beauport Harfangs	QMJHL	56	29	16	9	3193	132	3	*2.48	....	....	....	....	....	16	8	7	....	900	37	*4	2.47	....	....	....	....
1995-96	**Buffalo Sabres**	**NHL**	**3**	**0**	**2**	**0**	**119**	**10**	**0**	**5.04**	**4.95**	**7.88**	**64**	**.844**	**32.3**	....	....	....	....	....	....	....	....	....	....	....	....
	Beauport Harfangs	QMJHL	55	29	17	7	3201	152	1	2.85	....	....	....	....	....	*19	*12	7	....	1134	64	0	3.39	....	....	....	....
1996-97	Beauport Harfangs	QMJHL	18	6	9	1	928	61	1	3.94	....	....	....	....	....	....	....	....	....	....	....	....	....	....	....	....	....
	Canada	WJC-A	1	....	....	....	1	0	0	0.00	....	....	....	....	....	....	....	....	....	....	....	....	....	....	....	....	....
	Hull Olympiques	QMJHL	16	11	4	1	974	43	2	2.65	....	....	....	....	....	6	3	1	....	325	19	0	3.51	....	....	....	....
1997-98	Rochester Americans	AHL	41	14	18	6	2312	113	*5	2.93	....	....	....	....	....	4	1	3	....	239	16	0	4.01	....	....	....	....
	South Carolina Stingrays	ECHL	2	0	1	1	86	3	0	2.09	....	....	....	....	....	....	....	....	....	....	....	....	....	....	....	....	....
	NHL Totals		**3**	**0**	**2**	**0**	**119**	**10**	**0**	**5.04**	....	....	**64**	**.844**	....	....	....	....	....	....	....	....	....	....	....	....	....

Canadian Major Junior First All-Star Team (1995) • Canadian Major Junior Goaltender of the Year (1995)

• BITTNER, RICHARD

Richard Bittner G – L. 6', 170 lbs. b: New Haven, CT, 1/12/1922.

Season	Club	League	GP	W	L	T	Mins	GA	SO	Avg	AAvg	Eff	SA	S%	SAPG	GP	W	L	T	Mins	GA	SO	Avg	Eff	SA	S%	SAPG
1943-44	New Haven Eagles	EHL	12	1	11	0	700	68	0	5.83	....	....	....	....	....	....	....	....	....	....	....	....	....	....	....	....	....
	Brooklyn Crescents	EHL	4	0	4	0	240	28	0	7.25	....	....	....	....	....	11	1	*10	0	660	87	0	7.91	....	....	....	....
1944-45	Washington Lions	EHL	12	3	8	1	720	53	0	4.42	....	....	....	....	....	4	0	4	0	240	29	0	7.11	....	....	....	....
1945-46	Washington Lions	EHL	9	1	6	2	540	46	0	5.11	....	....	....	....	....	6	2	4	0	360	26	0	4.33	....	....	....	....
1946-47	New Haven All-Stars	Sr. B	STATISTICS NOT AVAILABLE																								
	San Francisco Shamrocks	PCHL	1	0	1	0	60	7	0	7.00	....	....	....	....	....	....	....	....	....	....	....	....	....	....	....	....	....
1947-48	Washington Lions	AHL	6	....	....	....	360	37	0	6.17	....	....	....	....	....	....	....	....	....	....	....	....	....	....	....	....	....
	Atlantic City Sea Gulls	EHL	3	1	2	0	180	16	0	5.33	....	....	....	....	....	....	....	....	....	....	....	....	....	....	....	....	....
1948-49	New Haven All-Stars	Sr. B	STATISTICS NOT AVAILABLE																								
	United States	WEC	STATISTICS NOT AVAILABLE																								
1949-50	Boston Olympics	EHL	36	14	17	5	2160	145	1	4.03	....	....	....	....	....	5	1	2	2	300	14	0	2.80	....	....	....	....
	Boston Bruins	**NHL**	**1**	**0**	**0**	**1**	**60**	**3**	**0**	**3.00**	**3.39**	....	....	....	....	....	....	....	....	....	....	....	....	....	....	....	....
1950-51	Boston Olympics	EHL	....	....	....	....	....	....	....	....	....	....	....	....	....	....	....	....	....	....	....	....	....	....	....	....	....
1951-52	Boston Olympics	EHL	2	1	1	0	120	9	0	4.50	....	....	....	....	....	....	....	....	....	....	....	....	....	....	....	....	....
	Atlantic City Sea Gulls	EHL	2	0	2	0	120	9	0	4.50	....	....	....	....	....	1	1	0	0	60	1	0	1.00	....	....	....	....
1952-53	Springfield Indians	EHL	2	0	2	0	120	10	0	5.00	....	....	....	....	....	....	....	....	....	....	....	....	....	....	....	....	....
	Troy Uncle Sam Trojans	EHL	1	....	....	....	60	4	0	4.00	....	....	....	....	....	....	....	....	....	....	....	....	....	....	....	....	....
1953-54			DID NOT PLAY																								
1954-55	New Haven Blades	EHL	45	22	21	2	2700	196	1	4.36	....	....	....	....	....	4	0	4	0	240	27	0	6.75	....	....	....	....
1955-1961			DID NOT PLAY – REFEREE																								
1961-62	Minneapolis Millers	IHL	1	1	0	0	60	0	1	0.00	....	....	....	....	....	....	....	....	....	....	....	....	....	....	....	....	....
1962-63	St. Paul Saints	IHL	1	0	1	0	60	12	0	12.00	....	....	....	....	....	....	....	....	....	....	....	....	....	....	....	....	....
	NHL Totals		**1**	**0**	**0**	**1**	**60**	**3**	**0**	**3.00**	....	....	....	....	....	....	....	....	....	....	....	....	....	....	....	....	....

• Promoted to **Boston** from **Boston Olympics** (EHL) to replace injured Jack Gelineau, February 12, 1950. (Montreal 3, Boston 3)

• BLAKE, MIKE

Mike Blake G – L. 6', 185 lbs. b: Kitchener, Ont., 4/6/1956.

Season	Club	League	GP	W	L	T	Mins	GA	SO	Avg	AAvg	Eff	SA	S%	SAPG	GP	W	L	T	Mins	GA	SO	Avg	Eff	SA	S%	SAPG
1977-78	Ohio State University	CCHA	18	....	....	....	980	71	0	4.35	....	....	....	....	....	....	....	....	....	....	....	....	....	....	....	....	....
1978-79	Ohio State University	CCHA	21	....	....	....	1000	78	0	4.33	....	....	....	....	....	....	....	....	....	....	....	....	....	....	....	....	....
1979-80	Ohio State University	CCHA	15	8	4	1	775	48	0	3.72	....	....	....	....	....	....	....	....	....	....	....	....	....	....	....	....	....
1980-81	Ohio State University	CCHA	37	22	9	3	2098	125	2	3.57	....	....	....	....	....	....	....	....	....	....	....	....	....	....	....	....	....
1981-82	**Los Angeles Kings**	**NHL**	**2**	**0**	**0**	**0**	**51**	**2**	**0**	**2.35**	**1.81**	....	....	....	....	....	....	....	....	....	....	....	....	....	....	....	....
	Saginaw Gears	IHL	36	....	....	....	1984	151	0	4.57	....	....	....	....	....	10	....	....	....	621	37	0	3.57	....	....	....	....
1982-83	**Los Angeles Kings**	**NHL**	**9**	**4**	**4**	**0**	**432**	**30**	**0**	**4.17**	**3.33**	**5.93**	**211**	**.858**	**29.3**	....	....	....	....	....	....	....	....	....	....	....	....
	New Haven Nighthawks	AHL	20	8	7	4	1178	72	1	3.67	....	....	....	....	....	7	5	2	0	428	16	0	*2.24	....	....	....	....
1983-84	**Los Angeles Kings**	**NHL**	**29**	**9**	**11**	**5**	**1634**	**118**	**0**	**4.33**	**3.39**	**5.73**	**891**	**.868**	**32.7**	....	....	....	....	....	....	....	....	....	....	....	....
	New Haven Nighthawks	AHL	16	7	8	0	864	64	0	4.44	....	....	....	....	....	....	....	....	....	....	....	....	....	....	....	....	....
1984-85	New Haven Nighthawks	AHL	42	17	19	4	2425	168	1	4.16	....	....	....	....	....	....	....	....	....	....	....	....	....	....	....	....	....
	NHL Totals		**40**	**13**	**15**	**5**	**2117**	**150**	**0**	**4.25**	....	....	....	....	....	....	....	....	....	....	....	....	....	....	....	....	....

CCHA First All-Star Team (1981)

Signed as a free agent by **LA Kings**, January 5, 1982.

• BLUE, JOHN

John Blue G – L. 5'10", 185 lbs. b: Huntington Beach, CA, 2/19/1966. Winnipeg's 9th choice, 197th overall, in 1986 Entry Draft.

Season	Club	League	GP	W	L	T	Mins	GA	SO	Avg	AAvg	Eff	SA	S%	SAPG	GP	W	L	T	Mins	GA	SO	Avg	Eff	SA	S%	SAPG
1984-85	University of Minnesota	WCHA	34	23	10	0	1964	111	2	3.39	....	....	....	....	....	....	....	....	....	....	....	....	....	....	....	....	....
1985-86	University of Minnesota	WCHA	29	20	6	0	1588	80	2	3.02	....	....	....	....	....	....	....	....	....	....	....	....	....	....	....	....	....
1986-87	University of Minnesota	WCHA	33	21	9	1	1889	99	3	3.14	....	....	....	....	....	....	....	....	....	....	....	....	....	....	....	....	....
1987-88	Kalamazoo Wings	IHL	15	3	8	4	847	65	0	4.60	....	....	....	....	....	1	0	1	0	40	6	0	9.00	....	....	....	....
	United States	Nat-Team	13	3	4	1	508	33	0	3.37	....	....	....	....	....	....	....	....	....	....	....	....	....	....	....	....	....
	United States	Olympics	DID NOT PLAY – SPARE GOALTENDER																								
1988-89	Kalamazoo Wings	IHL	17	8	6	0	970	69	0	4.27	....	....	....	....	....	....	....	....	....	....	....	....	....	....	....	....	....
	Virginia Lancers	ECHL	10	....	....	....	570	38	0	4.00	....	....	....	....	....	....	....	....	....	....	....	....	....	....	....	....	....
1989-90	Phoenix Roadrunners	IHL	19	5	10	3	986	92	0	5.65	....	....	....	....	....	....	....	....	....	....	....	....	....	....	....	....	....
	Knoxville Cherokees	ECHL	19	6	10	1	1000	85	0	5.15	....	....	....	....	....	....	....	....	....	....	....	....	....	....	....	....	....
	Kalamazoo Wings	IHL	4	2	1	1	232	18	0	4.65	....	....	....	....	....	....	....	....	....	....	....	....	....	....	....	....	....
	United States	WEC-A	5	....	....	....	204	17	....	4.99	....	....	....	....	....	....	....	....	....	....	....	....	....	....	....	....	....
1990-91	Maine Mariners	AHL	10	3	4	2	545	22	0	2.42	....	....	....	....	....	1	0	1	0	40	7	0	10.50	....	....	....	....
	Albany Choppers	IHL	19	11	6	0	1077	71	0	3.96	....	....	....	....	....	....	....	....	....	....	....	....	....	....	....	....	....
	Kalamazoo Wings	IHL	1	1	0	0	64	2	0	1.88	....	....	....	....	....	....	....	....	....	....	....	....	....	....	....	....	....
	Peoria Rivermen	IHL	4	4	0	0	240	12	0	3.00	....	....	....	....	....	....	....	....	....	....	....	....	....	....	....	....	....
	Knoxville Cherokees	ECHL	3	1	1	0	149	13	0	5.23	....	....	....	....	....	....	....	....	....	....	....	....	....	....	....	....	....
1991-92	Maine Mariners	AHL	43	11	23	6	2168	165	1	4.57	....	....	....	....	....	....	....	....	....	....	....	....	....	....	....	....	....
	United States	WC-A	DID NOT PLAY – SPARE GOALTENDER																								
1992-93	**Boston Bruins**	**NHL**	**23**	**9**	**8**	**4**	**1322**	**64**	**1**	**2.90**	**2.46**	**3.11**	**597**	**.893**	**27.1**	**2**	**0**	**1**	....	**96**	**5**	**0**	**3.13**	**3.19**	**49**	**.898**	**30.6**
	Providence Bruins	AHL	19	14	4	1	1159	67	0	3.47	....	....	....	....	....	....	....	....	....	....	....	....	....	....	....	....	....
1993-94	**Boston Bruins**	**NHL**	**18**	**5**	**8**	**3**	**944**	**47**	**0**	**2.99**	**2.84**	**3.45**	**407**	**.885**	**25.9**	....	....	....	....	....	....	....	....	....	....	....	....
	Providence Bruins	AHL	24	7	11	4	1298	76	1	3.51	....	....	....	....	....	....	....	....	....	....	....	....	....	....	....	....	....
1994-95	Providence Bruins	AHL	10	6	3	0	577	30	0	3.11	....	....	....	....	....	4	1	3	0	219	19	0	5.19	....	....	....	....

			REGULAR SEASON													PLAYOFFS											
Season	**Club**	**League**	**GP**	**W**	**L**	**T**	**Mins**	**GA**	**SO**	**Avg**	**AAvg**	**Eff**	**SA**	**S%**	**SAPG**	**GP**	**W**	**L**	**T**	**Mins**	**GA**	**SO**	**Avg**	**Eff**	**SA**	**S%**	**SAPG**
1995-96	Phoenix Roadrunners	IHL	8	1	5	0	309	21	0	4.07	....	....	....	....	....	....	....	....	....	....	....	....	....	....	....	....	....
	Fort Wayne Komets	IHL	5	1	2	2	249	19	0	4.58	....	....	....	....	....	....	....	....	....	....	....	....	....	....	....	....	....
	Buffalo Sabres	**NHL**	**5**	**2**	**2**	**0**	**255**	**15**	**0**	**3.53**	**3.47**	**3.86**	**137**	**.891**	**32.2**	....	....	....	....	....	....	....	....	....	....	....	....
	Rochester Americans	AHL	14	4	6	1	672	41	0	3.66	....	....	....	....	....	1	0	1	0	27	1	0	2.24	....	....	....	....
1996-97	Austin Ice-Bats	WPHL	33	17	11	5	1955	113	1	3.47	....	....	....	....	....	2	0	2	0	97	11	0	6.82	....	....	....	....
	United States	WC-A	1	1	0	0	60	1	0	1.00	....	....	....	....	....	....	....	....	....	....	....	....	....	....	....	....	....
	NHL Totals		**46**	**16**	**18**	**7**	**2521**	**126**	**1**	**3.00**	....	....	**1141**	**.890**	....	**2**	**0**	**1**	....	**96**	**5**	**0**	**3.13**	....	....	....	....

WCHA Second All-Star Team (1985) • WCHA First All-Star Team (1986)

Traded to **Minnesota** by **Winnipeg** for Winnipeg's 7th round choice (Markus Akerblom) in 1988 Entry Draft, March 7, 1988. Signed as a free agent by **Boston**, August 1, 1991. Signed as a free agent by **Buffalo**, December 28, 1995.

• BOISVERT, GILLES

Gilles Boisvert G – L. 5'8", 152 lbs. b: Trois Rivieres, Que., 2/15/1933.

1952-53	Barrie – Kitchener	OHA	51	....	....	....	3060	217	0	4.25	....	....	....	....	....	....	....	....	....	....	....	....	....	....	....	....	....
1953-54	Sydney Millionaires	MMHL	9	....	....	....	543	21	3	2.32	....	....	....	....	....	3	2	1	0	180	4	1	1.33	....	....	....	....
	Amherst Meteors	NBSHL	40	18	19	2	2410	152	0	3.78	....	....	....	....	....	7	2	5	0	436	27	1	3.72	....	....	....	....
1954-55	Montreal Royals	QHL	7	3	3	0	393	21	0	3.21	....	....	....	....	....	14	7	7	0	*840	41	*2	2.93	....	....	....	....
	Hershey Bears	AHL	5	4	1	0	300	11	1	2.20	....	....	....	....	....	....	....	....	....	....	....	....	....	....	....	....	....
1955-56	Edmonton Flyers	WHL	60	30	28	2	3669	214	2	3.50	....	....	....	....	....	....	....	....	....	....	....	....	....	....	....	....	....
1956-57	Hull-Ottawa Jr. Canadiens	QHL	10	5	3	1	574	23	0	2.40	....	....	....	....	....	....	....	....	....	....	....	....	....	....	....	....	....
	Rochester Americans	AHL	1	1	0	0	60	1	0	1.00	....	....	....	....	....	....	....	....	....	....	....	....	....	....	....	....	....
	Hull-Ottawa Canadiens	EOHL	17	....	....	....	1000	54	1	3.24	....	....	....	....	....	....	....	....	....	....	....	....	....	....	....	....	....
1957-58	Chicoutimi Sagueneens	QHL	51	*31	16	4	3060	150	*5	*2.94	....	....	....	....	....	6	2	4	0	373	13	1	*2.09	....	....	....	....
1958-59	Chicoutimi Sagueneens	QHL	51	23	27	1	3060	190	1	3.73	....	....	....	....	....	....	....	....	....	....	....	....	....	....	....	....	....
1959-60	Sudbury Wolves	EPHL	12	5	5	1	690	47	0	4.09	....	....	....	....	....	....	....	....	....	....	....	....	....	....	....	....	....
	Cleveland Barons	AHL	24	13	6	5	1440	67	2	2.79	....	....	....	....	....	....	....	....	....	....	....	....	....	....	....	....	....
	Detroit Red Wings	**NHL**	**3**	**0**	**3**	**0**	**180**	**9**	**0**	**3.00**	**3.14**	....	....	....	....	....	....	....	....	....	....	....	....	....	....	....	....
	Edmonton Flyers	WHL	11	7	4	0	660	39	0	3.55	....	....	....	....	....	....	....	....	....	....	....	....	....	....	....	....	....
1960-61	Ottawa Sr. Senators	City Sr.	17	....	....	....	1020	54	2	3.17	....	....	....	....	....	....	....	....	....	....	....	....	....	....	....	....	....
	Spokane Comets	WHL	36	16	19	0	2113	137	2	3.89	....	....	....	....	....	....	....	....	....	....	....	....	....	....	....	....	....
	Calgary Stampeders	WHL	3	1	2	0	180	12	0	4.00	....	....	....	....	....	....	....	....	....	....	....	....	....	....	....	....	....
1961-62	Hershey Bears	AHL	4	1	2	0	200	12	0	3.60	....	....	....	....	....	....	....	....	....	....	....	....	....	....	....	....	....
	Sudbury Wolves	EPHL	5	1	2	2	300	23	0	4.60	....	....	....	....	....	....	....	....	....	....	....	....	....	....	....	....	....
	Edmonton Flyers	WHL	44	23	18	3	2659	157	2	3.54	....	....	....	....	....	12	8	4	0	722	43	0	3.57	....	....	....	....
1962-63	Pittsburgh Hornets	AHL	12	3	8	1	720	58	1	4.83	....	....	....	....	....	....	....	....	....	....	....	....	....	....	....	....	....
	Edmonton Flyers	WHL	47	21	26	0	2820	174	0	3.70	....	....	....	....	....	3	1	2	0	182	9	0	*2.97	....	....	....	....
1963-64	St. Paul Rangers	CHL	3	0	3	0	180	15	0	5.00	....	....	....	....	....	....	....	....	....	....	....	....	....	....	....	....	....
	Baltimore Clippers	AHL	7	1	4	1	420	27	0	3.86	....	....	....	....	....	....	....	....	....	....	....	....	....	....	....	....	....
1964-65	Vancouver Canucks	WHL	10	5	5	0	600	28	1	2.80	....	....	....	....	....	....	....	....	....	....	....	....	....	....	....	....	....
	Baltimore Clippers	AHL	26	15	8	3	1570	89	0	3.40	....	....	....	....	....	....	....	....	....	....	....	....	....	....	....	....	....
1965-66	Baltimore Clippers	AHL	28	9	17	0	1601	100	0	3.75	....	....	....	....	....	....	....	....	....	....	....	....	....	....	....	....	....
1966-67	Baltimore Clippers	AHL	3	1	0	1	140	6	1	2.57	....	....	....	....	....	1	0	0	0	15	2	0	8.00	....	....	....	....
1967-68	Baltimore Clippers	AHL	18	5	9	2	1030	59	2	3.44	....	....	....	....	....	....	....	....	....	....	....	....	....	....	....	....	....
1968-69	Baltimore Clippers	AHL	16	9	5	2	956	49	2	3.08	....	....	....	....	....	1	0	0	0	40	2	0	3.00	....	....	....	....
1969-70	Baltimore Clippers	AHL	3	....	....	....	90	4	0	2.67	....	....	....	....	....	....	....	....	....	....	....	....	....	....	....	....	....
	NHL Totals		**3**	**0**	**3**	**0**	**180**	**9**	**0**	**3.00**	....	....	....	....	....	....	....	....	....	....	....	....	....	....	....	....	....

QHL Second All-Star Team (1958) • Won Vezina Memorial Trophy (Top Goaltender - QHL) (1958)

Claimed by **Boston** (Hershey - AHL) from **Montreal Royals** (QHL) in Inter-League Draft, June, 1955. Traded to **Detroit** by **Boston** with Real Chevrefils, Norm Corcoran, Warren Godfrey and Ed Sandford for Terry Sawchuk, Marcel Bonin, Lorne Davis and Vic Stasiuk, June 3, 1955. Traded to **Baltimore** (AHL) by **Detroit** for cash, August 15, 1965.

• BOUCHARD, DAN

Dan Bouchard G – L. 6', 190 lbs. b: Val d'Or, Que., 12/12/1950. Boston's 5th choice, 27th overall, in 1970 Amateur Draft.

1968-69	Sorel Eperviers	QJHL	STATISTICS NOT AVAILABLE																								
1969-70	London Knights	OHA	41	....	....	....	2452	159	2	3.89	....	....	....	....	....	....	....	....	....	....	....	....	....	....	....	....	....
1970-71	Hershey Bears	AHL	36	12	16	2	2029	106	1	3.13	....	....	....	....	....	....	....	....	....	....	....	....	....	....	....	....	....
1971-72	Boston Braves	AHL	50	*27	13	7	*2915	122	*4	2.51	....	....	....	....	....	6	2	3	0	311	14	0	2.70	....	....	....	....
	Oklahoma City Blazers	CHL	1	1	0	0	60	3	0	3.00	....	....	....	....	....	....	....	....	....	....	....	....	....	....	....	....	....
1972-73	**Atlanta Flames**	**NHL**	**34**	**9**	**15**	**10**	**1944**	**100**	**2**	**3.09**	**2.91**	....	....	....	....	....	....	....	....	....	....	....	....	....	....	....	....
1973-74	**Atlanta Flames**	**NHL**	**46**	**19**	**18**	**8**	**2660**	**123**	**5**	**2.77**	**2.66**	....	....	....	....	**1**	**0**	**1**	....	**60**	**4**	**0**	**4.00**	....	....	....	....
1974-75	**Atlanta Flames**	**NHL**	**40**	**20**	**15**	**5**	**2400**	**111**	**3**	**2.78**	**2.49**	....	....	....	....	....	....	....	....	....	....	....	....	....	....	....	....
1975-76	**Atlanta Flames**	**NHL**	**47**	**19**	**17**	**8**	**2671**	**113**	**2**	**2.54**	**2.28**	....	....	....	....	**2**	**0**	**2**	....	**120**	**3**	**0**	**1.50**	....	....	....	....
1976-77	**Atlanta Flames**	**NHL**	**42**	**17**	**17**	**5**	**2378**	**139**	**1**	**3.51**	**3.27**	....	....	....	....	**1**	**0**	**1**	....	**60**	**5**	**0**	**5.00**	....	....	....	....
1977-78	**Atlanta Flames**	**NHL**	**58**	**25**	**12**	**19**	**3340**	**153**	**2**	**2.75**	**2.56**	....	....	....	....	**2**	**0**	**2**	....	**120**	**7**	**0**	**3.50**	....	....	....	....
1978-79	**Atlanta Flames**	**NHL**	***64**	***32**	**21**	**7**	**3624**	**201**	**3**	**3.33**	**2.93**	....	....	....	....	**2**	**0**	**2**	....	**100**	**9**	**0**	**5.40**	....	....	....	....
1979-80	**Atlanta Flames**	**NHL**	**53**	**23**	**19**	**10**	**3076**	**163**	**2**	**3.18**	**2.79**	....	....	....	....	**4**	**1**	**3**	....	**241**	**14**	**0**	**3.49**	....	....	....	....
1980-81	**Calgary Flames**	**NHL**	**14**	**4**	**5**	**3**	**760**	**51**	**0**	**4.03**	**3.23**	....	....	....	....	....	....	....	....	....	....	....	....	....	....	....	....
	Quebec Nordiques	**NHL**	**29**	**19**	**5**	**5**	**1740**	**92**	**2**	**3.17**	**2.53**	....	....	....	....	**5**	**2**	**3**	....	**286**	**19**	***1**	**3.99**	....	....	....	....
1981-82	**Quebec Nordiques**	**NHL**	**60**	**27**	**22**	**11**	**3572**	**230**	**1**	**3.86**	**2.97**	....	....	....	....	**11**	**4**	**7**	....	**677**	**38**	**0**	**3.37**	....	....	....	....
1982-83	**Quebec Nordiques**	**NHL**	**50**	**20**	**21**	**8**	**2947**	**197**	**1**	**4.01**	**3.21**	**5.00**	**1579**	**.875**	**32.1**	**4**	**1**	**3**	....	**242**	**11**	**0**	**2.73**	....	....	....	....
1983-84	**Quebec Nordiques**	**NHL**	**57**	**29**	**18**	**8**	**3373**	**180**	**1**	**3.20**	**2.49**	**3.78**	**1523**	**.882**	**27.1**	**9**	**5**	**4**	....	**543**	**25**	**0**	**2.76**	**3.08**	**224**	**.888**	**24.8**
1984-85	**Quebec Nordiques**	**NHL**	**29**	**12**	**13**	**4**	**1738**	**101**	**0**	**3.49**	**2.77**	**4.28**	**824**	**.877**	**28.4**	**1**	**0**	**1**	....	**60**	**7**	**0**	**7.00**	**20.42**	**24**	**.708**	**24.0**
1985-86	**Winnipeg Jets**	**NHL**	**32**	**11**	**14**	**2**	**1696**	**107**	**2**	**3.79**	**2.95**	**5.13**	**790**	**.865**	**27.9**	**1**	**0**	**1**	....	**40**	**5**	**0**	**7.50**	**17.05**	**22**	**.773**	**33.0**
	NHL Totals		**655**	**286**	**232**	**113**	**37919**	**2061**	**27**	**3.26**	....	....	....	....	....	**43**	**13**	**30**	....	**2549**	**147**	**1**	**3.46**	....	....	....	....

AHL First All-Star Team (1972) • Shared Harry "Hap" Holmes Memorial Award (fewest goals against - AHL) with Ross Brooks (1972)

Claimed by **Atlanta** from **Boston** in Expansion Draft, June 6, 1972. Transferred to **Calgary** after **Atlanta** franchise relocated, June 24, 1980. Traded to **Quebec** by **Calgary** for Jamie Hislop, January 30, 1981. Traded to **Winnipeg** by **Quebec** for Winnipeg's 7th round choice (Mark Vermette) in 1986 Entry Draft, October 14, 1985.

• BOURQUE, CLAUDE

Claude Bourque G – L. 5'6", 140 lbs. b: Oxford, N.S., 3/31/1915. Deceased.

1928-29	Moncton St. Mary's	City Jr.	6	3	2	1	360	8	*2	1.33	....	....	....	....	....	....	....	....	....	....	....	....	....	....	....	....	....
1929-30	Moncton St. Mary's	City Jr.	6	3	2	1	280	11	0	2.36	....	....	....	....	....	....	....	....	....	....	....	....	....	....	....	....	....
1930-31	Moncton CCJA	City Jr.	4	3	1	0	240	2	*3	*0.50	....	....	....	....	....	....	....	....	....	....	....	....	....	....	....	....	....
	Moncton CNRC	City Jr.	2	1	1	0	120	4	0	2.00	....	....	....	....	....	....	....	....	....	....	....	....	....	....	....	....	....
	Moncton Aberdeen	H.S.	4	*4	0	0	240	5	*2	*1.25	....	....	....	....	....	1	0	1	0	60	3	0	3.00	....	....	....	....
1931-32	Moncton CCJA	City Jr.	6	*6	0	0	360	13	2	*2.11	....	....	....	....	....	3	*2	1	0	180	10	0	*3.33	....	....	....	....
1932-33	Moncton Red Indians	City Jr.	5	*4	0	1	330	8	*2	*1.46	....	....	....	....	....	2	*2	0	0	120	5	0	*2.50	....	....	....	....
1933-34	Montreal Jr. Canadiens	City Jr.	8	....	....	....	480	14	1	*1.75	....	....	....	....	....	2	....	....	....	120	5	0	*2.50	....	....	....	....
1934-35	Montreal Jr. Canadiens	City Jr.	10	....	....	....	600	46	0	4.60	....	....	....	....	....	1	....	....	....	60	5	0	5.00	....	....	....	....
1935-36	Montreal Canadiens	QSHL	21	....	....	....	1260	73	1	3.56	....	....	....	....	....	....	....	....	....	....	....	....	....	....	....	....	....
1936-37	Montreal Royals	QSHL	19	....	....	....	1140	44	2	2.32	....	....	....	....	....	5	....	....	....	300	13	0	2.60	....	....	....	....
1937-38	Verdun Maple Leafs	QSHL	18	....	....	....	1080	52	1	2.89	....	....	....	....	....	8	....	....	....	480	26	0	3.25	....	....	....	....
1938-39	**Montreal Canadiens**	**NHL**	**25**	**7**	**13**	**5**	**1560**	**69**	**2**	**2.65**	**3.24**	....	....	....	....	**3**	**1**	**2**	....	**188**	**8**	**1**	**2.55**	....	....	....	....
	Verdun Maple Leafs	QSHL	2	....	....	....	120	4	0	2.00	....	....	....	....	....	....	....	....	....	....	....	....	....	....	....	....	....
	Kansas City Greyhounds	AHA	3	0	3	0	214	15	0	4.21	....	....	....	....	....	....	....	....	....	....	....	....	....	....	....	....	....
1939-40	**Montreal Canadiens**	**NHL**	**36**	**9**	**24**	**3**	**2210**	**121**	**2**	**3.29**	**4.25**	....	....	....	....	....	....	....	....	....	....	....	....	....	....	....	....
	Detroit Red Wings	**NHL**	**1**	**0**	**1**	**0**	**60**	**3**	**0**	**3.00**	**3.72**	....	....	....	....	....	....	....	....	....	....	....	....	....	....	....	....
	New Haven Eagles	AHL	6	1	5	0	360	26	0	4.33	....	....	....	....	....	....	....	....	....	....	....	....	....	....	....	....	....

Season	Club	League	GP	W	L	T	Mins	GA	SO	Avg	AAvg	Eff	SA	S%	SAPG	GP	W	L	T	Mins	GA	SO	Avg	Eff	SA	S%	SAPG
			REGULAR SEASON													PLAYOFFS											
1940-41	Philadelphia Rockets	AHL	*56	25	25	6	*3470	167	1	2.89	....	....	....	....	....	....	....	....	....	....	....	....	....	....	....	....	....
1941-42	Buffalo Bisons	AHL	54	24	24	5	3350	150	4	2.69	....	....	....	....	....	....	....	....	....	....	....	....	....	....	....	....	....
1942-43	Lachine RCAF	Mtl-Sr.	34	....	....	....	2040	142	1	4.18	....	....	....	....	....	12	....	....	....	720	24	0	2.83	....	....	....	....
	NHL Totals		**62**	**16**	**38**	**8**	**3830**	**193**	**4**	**3.02**	....	....	....	....	....	**3**	**1**	**2**	....	**188**	**8**	**1**	**2.55**	....	....	....	....

AHL Second All-Star Team (1942)

Loaned to **Detroit** by **Montreal** to replace injured Tiny Thompson, February 15, 1940. (NY Rangers 3, Detroit 1). Traded to **NY Rangers** by **Montreal** for cash, April 26, 1940.

• BOUTIN, ROLLIE

Rollie Boutin G – L. 5'9", 179 lbs. b: Westlock, Alta., 11/6/1957. Washington's 7th choice, 111th overall, in 1977 Amateur Draft.

Season	Club	League	GP	W	L	T	Mins	GA	SO	Avg	AAvg	Eff	SA	S%	SAPG	GP	W	L	T	Mins	GA	SO	Avg	Eff	SA	S%	SAPG
1973-74	Prince Albert Raiders	SJHL	32	....	....	....	1920	119	1	3.89	....	....	....	....	....	....	....	....	....	....	....	....	....	....	....	....	....
	Swift Current Broncos	WCJHL	1	....	....	....	60	3	0	3.00	....	....	....	....	....	....	....	....	....	....	....	....	....	....	....	....	....
1974-75	Lethbridge Broncos	WCJHL	39	....	....	....	2196	162	1	4.43	....	....	....	....	....	3	0	3	0	180	11	0	3.49	....	....	....	....
1975-76	Lethbridge Broncos	WCJHL	61	....	....	....	3430	259	0	4.53	....	....	....	....	....	7	....	....	....	420	37	0	5.29	....	....	....	....
1976-77	Lethbridge Broncos	WCJHL	59	....	....	....	3296	246	1	4.45	....	....	....	....	....	15	....	....	....	855	63	0	4.42	....	....	....	....
1977-78	Port Huron Flags	IHL	58	....	....	....	3192	205	1	3.85	....	....	....	....	....	17	11	6	0	1002	68	0	4.07	....	....	....	....
1978-79	**Washington Capitals**	**NHL**	**2**	**0**	**1**	**0**	**90**	**10**	**0**	**6.67**	**5.89**	....	....	....	....	....	....	....	....	....	....	....	....	....	....	....	....
	Hershey Bears	AHL	30	13	8	5	1624	105	0	3.88	....	....	....	....	....	4	1	3	0	240	16	0	4.00	....	....	....	....
	Port Huron Flags	IHL	9	....	....	....	464	24	0	3.10	....	....	....	....	....	3	1	1	0	138	9	0	3.91	....	....	....	....
1979-80	**Washington Capitals**	**NHL**	**18**	**7**	**7**	**1**	**927**	**54**	**0**	**3.50**	**3.08**	....	....	....	....	....	....	....	....	....	....	....	....	....	....	....	....
	Hershey Bears	AHL	15	11	2	0	821	34	0	2.48	....	....	....	....	....	....	....	....	....	....	....	....	....	....	....	....	....
1980-81	**Washington Capitals**	**NHL**	**2**	**0**	**2**	**0**	**120**	**11**	**0**	**5.50**	**4.41**	....	....	....	....	....	....	....	....	....	....	....	....	....	....	....	....
	Hershey Bears	AHL	53	32	15	5	3056	182	*3	3.57	....	....	....	....	....	7	5	2	0	420	20	*1	2.88	....	....	....	....
1981-82	Hershey Bears	AHL	*62	27	27	4	*3459	238	1	4.13	....	....	....	....	....	3	0	2	0	107	13	0	7.30	....	....	....	....
1982-83	Birmingham South Stars	CHL	11	1	8	1	619	48	0	4.65	....	....	....	....	....	....	....	....	....	....	....	....	....	....	....	....	....
	Salt Lake Golden Eagles	CHL	14	8	4	1	807	43	1	3.20	....	....	....	....	....	5	2	2	0	251	21	0	5.02	....	....	....	....
1983-84	Binghamton Whalers	AHL	45	23	20	1	2623	188	3	4.30	....	....	....	....	....	....	....	....	....	....	....	....	....	....	....	....	....
	NHL Totals		**22**	**7**	**10**	**1**	**1137**	**75**	**0**	**3.96**	....	....	....	....	....	....	....	....	....	....	....	....	....	....	....	....	....

AHL Second All-Star Team (1981)

Traded to **Minnesota** by **Washington** with Wes Jarvis for Robbie Moore and Minnesota's 11th round choice (Anders Huss) in 1983 Entry Draft, August 4, 1982. Signed as a free agent by **Hartford**, December 8, 1983.

• BOUVRETTE, LIONEL

Lionel Bouvrette G – L. 5'9", 165 lbs. b: Hawksbury, Ont., 6/10/1914.

Season	Club	League	GP	W	L	T	Mins	GA	SO	Avg	AAvg	Eff	SA	S%	SAPG	GP	W	L	T	Mins	GA	SO	Avg	Eff	SA	S%	SAPG
1931-32	Montreal St-Francis Xavier	City Jr.	10	....	....	....	600	16	3	1.60	....	....	....	....	....	2	2	0	0	120	3	0	1.50	....	....	....	....
1932-33	Montreal St-Francis Xavier	City Jr.	11	....	....	....	660	29	1	2.64	....	....	....	....	....	2	2	0	0	120	3	0	1.50	....	....	....	....
1933-34	Montreal St-Francis Xavier	City Jr.	8	....	....	....	480	23	1	2.87	....	....	....	....	....	....	....	....	....	....	....	....	....	....	....	....	....
	Montreal St-Francis Xavier	City Sr.	1	0	1	0	60	5	0	5.00	....	....	....	....	....	....	....	....	....	....	....	....	....	....	....	....	....
1934-35	Montreal Lafontaine	City Sr.	STATISTICS NOT AVAILABLE																								
1935-36	Montreal Lafontaine	City Sr.	4	....	....	....	240	26	0	6.50	....	....	....	....	....	....	....	....	....	....	....	....	....	....	....	....	....
1936-37	Montreal Lafontaine	City Sr.	STATISTICS NOT AVAILABLE																								
1937-38	Montreal Lafontaine	City Sr.	STATISTICS NOT AVAILABLE																								
1938-39	Montreal Concordia	QSHL	5	....	....	....	300	12	1	2.40	....	....	....	....	....	3	....	....	....	180	9	0	3.00	....	....	....	....
1939-40	Montreal Concordia	QSHL	30	....	....	....	1800	106	1	3.53	....	....	....	....	....	5	....	....	....	300	17	*1	3.40	....	....	....	....
1940-41	Montreal Concordia	QSHL	36	....	....	....	2100	174	0	4.97	....	....	....	....	....	....	....	....	....	....	....	....	....	....	....	....	....
1941-42	Quebec Aces	QSHL	33	....	....	....	1980	92	*5	2.79	....	....	....	....	....	6	....	....	....	360	16	0	2.67	....	....	....	....
1942-43	Quebec Aces	QSHL	33	....	....	....	1980	123	1	3.73	....	....	....	....	....	4	....	....	....	240	12	0	3.00	....	....	....	....
	New York Rangers	**NHL**	**1**	**0**	**1**	**0**	**60**	**6**	**0**	**6.00**	**5.13**	....	....	....	....	....	....	....	....	....	....	....	....	....	....	....	....
1943-44	Quebec Aces	QSHL	24	....	....	....	1440	65	*3	*2.71	....	....	....	....	....	6	....	....	....	360	21	0	3.50	....	....	....	....
1944-45	Quebec Aces	QSHL	24	....	....	....	1440	89	*2	*3.71	....	....	....	....	....	7	....	....	....	420	17	0	*2.43	....	....	....	....
1945-46	Quebec Aces	QSHL	31	....	....	....	1860	115	1	3.71	....	....	....	....	....	....	....	....	....	....	....	....	....	....	....	....	....
1946-47	Quebec Aces	QSHL	8	....	....	....	480	39	0	4.88	....	....	....	....	....	4	....	....	....	240	19	0	4.75	....	....	....	....
	NHL Totals		**1**	**0**	**1**	**0**	**60**	**6**	**0**	**6.00**	....	....	....	....	....	....	....	....	....	....	....	....	....	....	....	....	....

Won Vimy Trophy (MVP - QSHL) (1944)

Loaned to **NY Rangers** by **Montreal** (Quebec-QSHL) to replace injured Jimmy Franks, March 18, 1943. (Montreal 6, NY Rangers 3)

• BOWER, JOHNNY

Johnny "The China Wall" Bower G – L. 5'11", 189 lbs. b: Prince Albert, Sask., 11/8/1924. **HHOF**

Season	Club	League	GP	W	L	T	Mins	GA	SO	Avg	AAvg	Eff	SA	S%	SAPG	GP	W	L	T	Mins	GA	SO	Avg	Eff	SA	S%	SAPG
1944-45	Prince Albert Black Hawks	SJHL	10	5	4	1	630	27	0	*2.57	....	....	....	....	....	3	0	3	0	180	23	0	7.67	....	....	....	....
1945-46	Cleveland Barons	AHL	41	18	17	6	2460	160	4	3.90	....	....	....	....	....	....	....	....	....	....	....	....	....	....	....	....	....
	Providence Reds	AHL	1	0	1	0	48	4	0	5.00	....	....	....	....	....	....	....	....	....	....	....	....	....	....	....	....	....
1946-47	Cleveland Barons	AHL	40	22	11	7	2400	124	3	3.10	....	....	....	....	....	....	....	....	....	....	....	....	....	....	....	....	....
1947-48	Cleveland Barons	AHL	31	18	6	6	1880	83	1	2.65	....	....	....	....	....	....	....	....	....	....	....	....	....	....	....	....	....
1948-49	Cleveland Barons	AHL	37	23	9	5	2200	127	3	3.43	....	....	....	....	....	5	2	3	0	329	23	0	4.19	....	....	....	....
1949-50	Cleveland Barons	AHL	61	*38	15	8	3660	201	*5	3.30	....	....	....	....	....	9	4	5	0	548	27	0	2.96	....	....	....	....
1950-51	Cleveland Barons	AHL	70	*44	21	5	4280	213	5	2.99	....	....	....	....	....	11	8	3	0	703	32	0	2.73	....	....	....	....
1951-52	Cleveland Barons	AHL	68	44	19	5	4110	165	3	2.41	....	....	....	....	....	5	2	3	0	300	17	0	3.40	....	....	....	....
1952-53	Cleveland Barons	AHL	61	*40	19	2	3680	155	*6	2.53	....	....	....	....	....	*11	*7	4	0	*745	21	*4	*1.69	....	....	....	....
1953-54	**New York Rangers**	**NHL**	***70**	**29**	**31**	**10**	***4200**	**182**	**5**	**2.60**	**3.40**	....	....	....	....	....	....	....	....	....	....	....	....	....	....	....	....
1954-55	Vancouver Canucks	WHL	63	30	25	8	3780	171	*7	*2.71	....	....	....	....	....	5	1	4	0	300	16	0	3.20	....	....	....	....
	New York Rangers	**NHL**	**5**	**2**	**2**	**1**	**300**	**13**	**0**	**2.60**	**3.18**	....	....	....	....	....	....	....	....	....	....	....	....	....	....	....	....
1955-56	Providence Reds	AHL	61	*45	14	2	3710	174	3	2.81	....	....	....	....	....	*9	*7	2	0	540	23	0	*2.56	....	....	....	....
1956-57	Providence Reds	AHL	57	30	19	8	3501	138	4	*2.37	....	....	....	....	....	5	1	4	0	300	15	0	3.00	....	....	....	....
	New York Rangers	**NHL**	**2**	**0**	**2**	**0**	**120**	**7**	**0**	**3.50**	**4.02**	....	....	....	....	....	....	....	....	....	....	....	....	....	....	....	....
1957-58	Cleveland Barons	AHL	64	37	23	3	3870	140	*8	*2.17	....	....	....	....	....	....	....	....	....	....	....	....	....	....	....	....	....
1958-59	**Toronto Maple Leafs**	**NHL**	**39**	**15**	**17**	**7**	**2340**	**107**	**3**	**2.74**	**2.90**	....	....	....	....	***12**	**5**	**7**	....	***746**	**39**	**0**	**3.14**	....	....	....	....
1959-60	**Toronto Maple Leafs**	**NHL**	**66**	**34**	**24**	**8**	**3960**	**180**	**5**	**2.73**	**2.82**	....	....	....	....	***10**	**4**	**6**	....	***645**	**31**	**0**	**2.88**	....	....	....	....
1960-61	**Toronto Maple Leafs**	**NHL**	**58**	***33**	**15**	**10**	**3480**	**145**	**2**	***2.50**	**2.50**	....	....	....	....	**3**	**0**	**3**	....	**180**	**9**	**0**	**3.00**	....	....	....	....
1961-62	**Toronto Maple Leafs**	**NHL**	**59**	**31**	**18**	**10**	**3540**	**152**	**2**	**2.58**	**2.59**	....	....	....	....	**10**	***6**	**3**	....	**579**	**22**	**0**	***2.28**	....	....	....	....
1962-63	**Toronto Maple Leafs**	**NHL**	**42**	**20**	**15**	**7**	**2520**	**110**	**1**	**2.62**	**2.68**	....	....	....	....	**10**	***8**	**2**	....	**600**	**16**	***2**	***1.60**	....	....	....	....
1963-64	**Toronto Maple Leafs**	**NHL**	**51**	**24**	**16**	**11**	**3009**	**106**	**5**	***2.11**	**2.27**	....	....	....	....	***14**	***8**	**6**	....	***850**	**30**	***2**	***2.12**	....	....	....	....
1964-65	**Toronto Maple Leafs**	**NHL**	**34**	**13**	**13**	**8**	**2040**	**81**	**3**	***2.38**	**2.52**	....	....	....	....	**6**	**2**	**3**	....	**321**	**13**	**0**	**2.43**	....	....	....	....
1965-66	**Toronto Maple Leafs**	**NHL**	**35**	**18**	**10**	**5**	**1998**	**75**	**3**	***2.25**	**2.23**	....	....	....	....	**2**	**0**	**2**	....	**120**	**8**	**0**	**4.00**	....	....	....	....
1966-67	**Toronto Maple Leafs**	**NHL**	**27**	**12**	**9**	**3**	**1431**	**63**	**2**	**2.64**	**2.71**	....	....	....	....	**4**	**2**	**0**	....	**183**	**5**	***1**	**1.64**	....	....	....	....
1967-68	**Toronto Maple Leafs**	**NHL**	**43**	**14**	**18**	**7**	**2239**	**84**	**4**	**2.25**	**2.47**	....	....	....	....	....	....	....	....	....	....	....	....	....	....	....	....
1968-69	**Toronto Maple Leafs**	**NHL**	**20**	**5**	**4**	**3**	**779**	**37**	**2**	**2.85**	**2.95**	....	....	....	....	**4**	**0**	**2**	....	**154**	**11**	**0**	**4.29**	....	....	....	....
1969-70	**Toronto Maple Leafs**	**NHL**	**1**	**0**	**1**	**0**	**60**	**5**	**0**	**5.00**	**5.32**	....	....	....	....	....	....	....	....	....	....	....	....	....	....	....	....
	NHL Totals		**552**	**250**	**195**	**90**	**32016**	**1347**	**37**	**2.52**	....	....	....	....	....	**74**	**35**	**34**	....	**4378**	**184**	**5**	**2.52**	....	....	....	....

AHL Second All-Star Team (1951) • AHL First All-Star Team (1952, 1953, 1956, 1957 1958) • Won Harry "Hap" Holmes Memorial Award (fewest goals against - AHL) (1952, 1957, 1958) • Won WHL Leading Goaltender Award (1955) • Won Les Cunningham Award (MVP - AHL) (1956, 1957, 1958) • NHL First All-Star Team (1961) • Won Vezina Trophy (1961) • Shared Vezina Trophy with Terry Sawchuk (1965)

Played in NHL All-Star Game (1961, 1962, 1963, 1964)

Traded to **NY Rangers** by **Cleveland** (AHL) for Emile Francis and Neil Strain, June, 1953. Traded to **Cleveland** (AHL) by **NY Rangers** for Ed MacQueen and cash, July, 1957. Claimed by **Toronto** from **Cleveland** (AHL) in Inter-League Draft, June 3, 1958.

• BRANIGAN, ANDY

Andy Branigan G – L. 5'11", 190 lbs. b: Winnipeg, Man., 4/11/1922. d: 4/13/1995.

Season	Club	League	GP	W	L	T	Mins	GA	SO	Avg	AAvg	Eff	SA	S%	SAPG	GP	W	L	T	Mins	GA	SO	Avg	Eff	SA	S%	SAPG
1940-41	**New York Americans**	**NHL**	**1**	**0**	**0**	**0**	**7**	**0**	**0**	**0.00**	**0.00**	....	....	....	....	....	....	....	....	....	....	....	....	....	....	....	....
	NHL Totals		**1**	**0**	**0**	**0**	**7**	**0**	**0**	**0.00**	....	....	....	....	....	....	....	....	....	....	....	....	....	....	....	....	....

• NY Americans defenseman replaced injured Chuck Rayner in 3rd period, February 28, 1941. (Detroit 5, NY Americans 4)

• BRATHWAITE, FRED
Fred Brathwaite G – L. 5'7", 170 lbs. b: Ottawa, Ont., 11/24/1972.

			REGULAR SEASON													PLAYOFFS											
Season	Club	League	GP	W	L	T	Mins	GA	SO	Avg	AAvg	Eff	SA	S%	SAPG	GP	W	L	T	Mins	GA	SO	Avg	Eff	SA	S%	SAPG
1989-90	Oshawa Generals	OHL	20	11	2	1	886	43	1	2.91	....	....	....	....	....	10	4	2	....	451	22	0	*2.93	....	....	....	....
1990-91	Oshawa Generals	OHL	39	25	6	3	1986	112	1	3.38	....	....	....	....	....	13	*9	2	....	677	43	0	3.81	....	....	....	....
1991-92	Oshawa Generals	OHL	24	12	7	2	1248	81	0	3.89	....	....	....	....	....	....	....	....	....	....	....	....	....	....	....	....	....
	London Knights	OHL	23	15	6	2	1325	61	*4	2.76	....	....	....	....	....	10	5	5	....	615	36	0	3.51	....	....	....	....
1992-93	Detroit Jr. Red Wings	OHL	37	23	10	4	2192	134	0	3.67	....	....	....	....	....	15	9	6	....	858	48	1	3.36	....	....	....	....
1993-94	**Edmonton Oilers**	**NHL**	**19**	**3**	**10**	**3**	**982**	**58**	**0**	**3.54**	**3.37**	**3.93**	**523**	**.889**	**32.0**	....	....	....	....	....	....	....	....	....	....	....	....
	Cape Breton Oilers	AHL	2	1	1	0	119	6	0	3.04	....	....	....	....	....	....	....	....	....	....	....	....	....	....	....	....	....
1994-95	**Edmonton Oilers**	**NHL**	**14**	**2**	**5**	**1**	**601**	**40**	**0**	**3.99**	**4.13**	**5.47**	**292**	**.863**	**29.2**	....	....	....	....	....	....	....	....	....	....	....	....
1995-96	**Edmonton Oilers**	**NHL**	**7**	**0**	**2**	**0**	**293**	**12**	**0**	**2.46**	**2.41**	**2.11**	**140**	**.914**	**28.7**	....	....	....	....	....	....	....	....	....	....	....	....
	Cape Breton Oilers	AHL	31	12	16	0	1699	110	1	3.88	....	....	....	....	....	....	....	....	....	....	....	....	....	....	....	....	....
1996-97	Manitoba Moose	IHL	58	22	22	5	2945	167	1	3.40	....	....	....	....	....	....	....	....	....	....	....	....	....	....	....	....	....
1997-98	Manitoba Moose	IHL	51	23	18	4	2736	138	1	3.03	....	....	....	....	....	2	0	1	....	72	4	0	3.30	....	....	....	....
	NHL Totals		**40**	**5**	**17**	**4**	**1876**	**110**	**0**	**3.52**	....	....	**955**	**.885**	....	....	....	....	....	....	....	....	....	....	....	....	....

• Scored a goal while with Detroit (OHL), April 20, 1993. • Scored a goal while with Manitoba (IHL), November 9, 1996.

Signed as a free agent by **Edmonton**, October 6, 1993.

• BRIMSEK, FRANK
Frank "Mr. Zero" Brimsek G – L. 5'9", 170 lbs. b: Eveleth, MN, 9/26/1915. **HHOF, USHOF**

Season	Club	League	GP	W	L	T	Mins	GA	SO	Avg	AAvg	Eff	SA	S%	SAPG	GP	W	L	T	Mins	GA	SO	Avg	Eff	SA	S%	SAPG
1934-35	Eveleth Rangers	USAHA	STATISTICS NOT AVAILABLE																								
	Pittsburgh Yellowjackets	USAHA	16	14	2	0	960	39	1	2.44	....	....	....	....	....	....	....	....	....	....	....	....	....	....	....	....	....
1935-36	Pittsburgh Yellowjackets	EHL	38	*20	16	2	2280	74	*8	1.95	....	....	....	....	....	8	4	3	1	480	19	2	2.36	....	....	....	....
1936-37	Pittsburgh Yellowjackets	EHL	47	19	23	5	2820	142	3	3.02	....	....	....	....	....	....	....	....	....	....	....	....	....	....	....	....	....
1937-38	Providence Reds	AHL	*48	25	16	7	2950	86	5	*1.75	....	....	....	....	....	7	*5	2	0	515	16	0	1.86	....	....	....	....
	New Haven Eagles	AHL	....	....	....	....	....	....	....	....	....	....	....	....	....	1	0	1	0	93	3	0	1.94	....	....	....	....
1938-39	**Boston Bruins**	**NHL**	**43**	***33**	**9**	**1**	**2610**	**68**	***10**	***1.56**	**1.80**	....	....	....	....	***12**	***8**	**4**	....	***863**	**18**	**1**	***1.25**	....	....	....	....
	Providence Reds	AHL	9	5	2	2	570	18	0	1.89	....	....	....	....	....	....	....	....	....	....	....	....	....	....	....	....	....
1939-40	**Boston Bruins**	**NHL**	***48**	***31**	**12**	**5**	**2950**	**98**	**6**	**1.99**	**2.39**	....	....	....	....	**6**	**2**	**4**	....	**360**	**15**	**0**	**2.50**	....	....	....	....
1940-41	**Boston Bruins**	**NHL**	***48**	**27**	**8**	**13**	***3040**	**102**	***6**	**2.01**	**2.22**	....	....	....	....	***11**	***8**	**3**	....	***678**	**23**	***1**	***2.04**	....	....	....	....
1941-42	**Boston Bruins**	**NHL**	**47**	**24**	**17**	**6**	**2930**	**115**	**3**	***2.35**	**2.24**	....	....	....	....	**5**	**2**	**3**	....	**307**	**16**	**0**	**3.13**	....	....	....	....
1942-43	**Boston Bruins**	**NHL**	***50**	**24**	**17**	**9**	**3000**	**176**	**1**	**3.52**	**2.98**	....	....	....	....	**9**	**4**	**5**	....	**560**	**33**	**0**	**3.54**	....	....	....	....
1943-44	Coast Guard Cutters	....	27	19	6	2	1620	83	1	3.07	....	....	....	....	....	5	4	0	0	300	4	1	0.80	....	....	....	....
1944-45			MILITARY SERVICE																								
1945-46	**Boston Bruins**	**NHL**	**34**	**16**	**14**	**4**	**2040**	**111**	**2**	**3.26**	**3.00**	....	....	....	....	***10**	**5**	**5**	....	***650**	**29**	**0**	**2.68**	....	....	....	....
1946-47	**Boston Bruins**	**NHL**	***60**	**26**	**23**	**11**	***3600**	**175**	**3**	**2.92**	**2.81**	....	....	....	....	**5**	**1**	**4**	....	**343**	**16**	**0**	**2.80**	....	....	....	....
1947-48	**Boston Bruins**	**NHL**	***60**	**23**	**24**	**13**	***3600**	**168**	**3**	**2.80**	**2.93**	....	....	....	....	**5**	**1**	**4**	....	**317**	**20**	**0**	**3.79**	....	....	....	....
1948-49	**Boston Bruins**	**NHL**	**54**	**26**	**20**	**8**	**3240**	**147**	**1**	**2.72**	**3.09**	....	....	....	....	**5**	**1**	**4**	....	**316**	**16**	**0**	**3.04**	....	....	....	....
1949-50	**Chicago Black Hawks**	**NHL**	***70**	**22**	**38**	**10**	***4200**	**244**	**5**	**3.49**	**4.17**	....	....	....	....	....	....	....	....	....	....	....	....	....	....	....	....
	NHL Totals		**514**	**252**	**182**	**80**	**31210**	**1404**	**40**	**2.70**	....	....	....	....	....	**68**	**32**	**36**	....	**4394**	**186**	**2**	**2.54**	....	....	....	....

EHL Second All-Star Team (1936) • Won George L. Davis Jr. Trophy (fewest goals against - EHL) (1936) • AHL First All-Star Team (1938) • NHL First All-Star Team (1939, 1942) • Won Calder Trophy (1939) • Won Vezina Trophy (1939, 1942) • NHL Second All-Star Team (1940, 1941, 1943, 1946, 1947, 1948)

Played in NHL All-Star Game (1939, 1947, 1948)

Signed as a free agent by **Boston**, October 27, 1938. • **Coast Guard Cutters** played exhibition season only in 1943-44. Traded to **Chicago** by **Boston** for cash, September 8, 1949.

• BRODA, TURK
Turk (Walter) Broda G – L. 5'9", 180 lbs. b: Brandon, Man., 5/15/1914. d: 10/17/1972. **HHOF**

Season	Club	League	GP	W	L	T	Mins	GA	SO	Avg	AAvg	Eff	SA	S%	SAPG	GP	W	L	T	Mins	GA	SO	Avg	Eff	SA	S%	SAPG
1933-34	Winnipeg Monarchs	MJHL	12	1	11	0	720	51	0	4.25	....	....	....	....	....	3	1	2	0	180	12	0	4.00	....	....	....	....
	Winnipeg Monarchs	MSHL	1	0	1	0	60	6	0	6.00	....	....	....	....	....	....	....	....	....	....	....	....	....	....	....	....	....
1934-35	Detroit Farm Crest	Sr.	2	1	1	0	120	4	0	2.00	....	....	....	....	....	....	....	....	....	....	....	....	....	....	....	....	....
1935-36	Detroit Olympics	IAHL	47	*26	18	3	2820	101	6	2.14	....	....	....	....	....	6	*6	0	0	360	8	1	1.33	....	....	....	....
1936-37	**Toronto Maple Leafs**	**NHL**	**45**	**22**	**19**	**4**	**2770**	**106**	**3**	**2.30**	**2.86**	....	....	....	....	**2**	**0**	**2**	....	**133**	**5**	**0**	**2.26**	....	....	....	....
1937-38	**Toronto Maple Leafs**	**NHL**	***48**	**24**	**15**	**9**	**2980**	**127**	**6**	**2.56**	**3.12**	....	....	....	....	**7**	**4**	**3**	....	**452**	**13**	**1**	**1.73**	....	....	....	....
1938-39	**Toronto Maple Leafs**	**NHL**	***48**	**19**	**20**	**9**	***2990**	**107**	**8**	**2.15**	**2.55**	....	....	....	....	**10**	**5**	**5**	....	**617**	**20**	***2**	**1.94**	....	....	....	....
1939-40	**Toronto Maple Leafs**	**NHL**	**47**	**25**	**17**	**5**	**2900**	**108**	**4**	**2.23**	**2.72**	....	....	....	....	**10**	**6**	**4**	....	**657**	**19**	**1**	**1.74**	....	....	....	....
1940-41	**Toronto Maple Leafs**	**NHL**	***48**	***28**	**14**	**6**	**2970**	**99**	**5**	***2.00**	**2.21**	....	....	....	....	**7**	**3**	**4**	....	**438**	**15**	**0**	**2.05**	....	....	....	....
1941-42	**Toronto Maple Leafs**	**NHL**	***48**	**27**	**18**	**3**	***2960**	**136**	***6**	**2.76**	**2.68**	....	....	....	....	***13**	***8**	**5**	....	***780**	**31**	***1**	**2.38**	....	....	....	....
1942-43	**Toronto Maple Leafs**	**NHL**	***50**	**22**	**19**	**9**	**3000**	**159**	**1**	**3.18**	**2.65**	....	....	....	....	**6**	**2**	**4**	....	**439**	**20**	**0**	**2.73**	....	....	....	....
1943-44			MILITARY SERVICE																								
1944-45			MILITARY SERVICE																								
1945-46	**Toronto Maple Leafs**	**NHL**	**15**	**6**	**6**	**3**	**900**	**53**	**0**	**3.53**	**3.27**	....	....	....	....	....	....	....	....	....	....	....	....	....	....	....	....
1946-47	**Toronto Maple Leafs**	**NHL**	***60**	**31**	**19**	**10**	***3600**	**172**	**4**	**2.87**	**2.75**	....	....	....	....	***11**	***8**	**3**	....	**680**	**27**	***1**	**2.38**	....	....	....	....
1947-48	**Toronto Maple Leafs**	**NHL**	***60**	***32**	**15**	**13**	***3600**	**143**	**5**	***2.38**	**2.42**	....	....	....	....	**9**	***8**	**1**	....	**557**	**20**	***1**	***2.15**	....	....	....	....
1948-49	**Toronto Maple Leafs**	**NHL**	***60**	**22**	**25**	**13**	***3600**	**161**	**5**	**2.68**	**3.04**	....	....	....	....	**9**	***8**	**1**	....	**574**	**15**	***1**	***1.57**	....	....	....	....
1949-50	**Toronto Maple Leafs**	**NHL**	**68**	**30**	**25**	**12**	**4040**	**167**	***9**	**2.48**	**2.75**	....	....	....	....	**7**	**3**	**4**	....	**450**	**10**	***3**	***1.33**	....	....	....	....
1950-51	**Toronto Maple Leafs**	**NHL**	**31**	**14**	**11**	**5**	**1827**	**68**	**6**	**2.23**	**2.50**	....	....	....	....	**8**	***5**	**1**	....	**492**	**9**	***2**	**1.10**	....	....	....	....
1951-52	**Toronto Maple Leafs**	**NHL**	**1**	**0**	**1**	**0**	**30**	**3**	**0**	**6.00**	**7.15**	....	....	....	....	**2**	**0**	**2**	....	**120**	**7**	**0**	**3.50**	....	....	....	....
	NHL Totals		**629**	**302**	**224**	**101**	**38167**	**1609**	**62**	**2.53**	....	....	....	....	....	**101**	**60**	**39**	....	**6389**	**211**	**13**	**1.98**	....	....	....	....

NHL First All-Star Team (1941, 1948) • Won Vezina Trophy (1941, 1948) • NHL Second All-Star Team (1942)

Played in NHL All-Star Game (1947, 1948, 1949, 1950)

Traded to **Toronto** by **Detroit** (Detroit-IAHL) for $7,500, May, 1936.

• BRODERICK, KEN
Ken Broderick G – R. 5'10", 178 lbs. b: Toronto, Ont., 2/16/1942.

Season	Club	League	GP	W	L	T	Mins	GA	SO	Avg	AAvg	Eff	SA	S%	SAPG	GP	W	L	T	Mins	GA	SO	Avg	Eff	SA	S%	SAPG
1959-60	Toronto Marlboros	OHA	48	*28	17	3	2880	180	4	3.75	....	....	....	....	....	4	0	4	0	240	17	0	4.25	....	....	....	....
1960-61	Toronto Marlboros	OHA	45	9	27	9	2700	187	0	4.15	....	....	....	....	....	....	....	....	....	....	....	....	....	....	....	....	....
1961-62	Brampton 7-Ups	OHA	31	....	....	....	1860	155	1	5.00	....	....	....	....	....	5	1	4	0	300	37	0	7.40	....	....	....	....
1962-63	Univ. of British Columbia	WCIAA	STATISTICS NOT AVAILABLE																								
1963-64	Canada	Nat-Team	STATISTICS NOT AVAILABLE																								
	Canada	Olympics	6	1	1	0	173	12	....	4.16	....	....	....	....	....	....	....	....	....	....	....	....	....	....	....	....	....
1964-65	Canada	Nat-Team	STATISTICS NOT AVAILABLE																								
	Canada	WEC-A	5	4	1	0	300	11	2	2.20	....	....	....	....	....	....	....	....	....	....	....	....	....	....	....	....	....
1965-66	Vancouver Canucks	WHL	3	1	1	1	190	8	0	2.53	....	....	....	....	....	....	....	....	....	....	....	....	....	....	....	....	....
	Canada	WEC-A	3	2	1	0	180	4	2	1.33	....	....	....	....	....	....	....	....	....	....	....	....	....	....	....	....	....
1966-67	Canada	Nat-Team	STATISTICS NOT AVAILABLE																								
1967-68	Winnipeg Nats	WCSHL	9	....	....	....	540	23	1	2.77	....	....	....	....	....	....	....	....	....	....	....	....	....	....	....	....	....
	Canada	Olympics	5	3	2	0	280	12	1	2.57	....	....	....	....	....	....	....	....	....	....	....	....	....	....	....	....	....
1968-69	Phoenix Roadrunners	WHL	34	9	17	5	1904	115	2	3.62	....	....	....	....	....	....	....	....	....	....	....	....	....	....	....	....	....
1969-70	Iowa Stars	CHL	16	9	5	2	930	44	2	2.84	....	....	....	....	....	....	....	....	....	....	....	....	....	....	....	....	....
	Minnesota North Stars	**NHL**	**7**	**2**	**4**	**0**	**360**	**26**	**0**	**4.33**	**4.62**	....	....	....	....	....	....	....	....	....	....	....	....	....	....	....	....
	Phoenix Roadrunners	WHL	8	3	2	1	440	23	1	3.14	....	....	....	....	....	....	....	....	....	....	....	....	....	....	....	....	....
1970-71	Oakville Oaks	OHA Sr.	STATISTICS NOT AVAILABLE																								
	Galt Hornets	OHA Sr.	STATISTICS NOT AVAILABLE																								
1971-72	San Diego Gulls	WHL	42	18	15	7	2359	128	*3	3.26	....	....	....	....	....	2	0	2	0	119	6	0	3.03	....	....	....	....
1972-73	San Diego Gulls	WHL	51	*24	20	6	*2977	146	*3	*2.94	....	....	....	....	....	3	0	3	0	145	17	0	7.02	....	....	....	....
1973-74	**Boston Bruins**	**NHL**	**5**	**2**	**2**	**1**	**300**	**16**	**0**	**3.20**	**3.09**	....	....	....	....	....	....	....	....	....	....	....	....	....	....	....	....
	Boston Braves	AHL	6	1	4	0	318	18	0	3.39	....	....	....	....	....	....	....	....	....	....	....	....	....	....	....	....	....
	San Diego Gulls	WHL	4	1	3	0	220	19	0	5.18	....	....	....	....	....	....	....	....	....	....	....	....	....	....	....	....	....
1974-75	**Boston Bruins**	**NHL**	**15**	**7**	**6**	**0**	**804**	**32**	**1**	**2.39**	**2.15**	....	....	....	....	....	....	....	....	....	....	....	....	....	....	....	....
	Rochester Americans	AHL	3	1	2	0	180	15	0	5.00	....	....	....	....	....	....	....	....	....	....	....	....	....	....	....	....	....
	Binghamton Dusters	NAHL	2	0	2	0	120	10	0	5.00	....	....	....	....	....	....	....	....	....	....	....	....	....	....	....	....	....
1975-76	Rochester Americans	AHL	42	22	13	7	2541	36	2	3.21	....	....	....	....	....	3	1	2	0	180	12	0	4.00	....	....	....	....

			REGULAR SEASON													PLAYOFFS											
Season	Club	League	GP	W	L	T	Mins	GA	SO	Avg	AAvg	Eff	SA	S%	SAPG	GP	W	L	T	Mins	GA	SO	Avg	Eff	SA	S%	SAPG
1976-77	Edmonton Oilers	WHA	40	18	18	1	2301	134	*4	3.49	....	....	....	....	....	3	1	2	0	179	10	0	3.35	....	....	....	....
1977-78	Edmonton Oilers	WHA	9	2	5	0	497	42	0	5.07	....	....	....	....	....	....	....	....	....	....	....	....	....	....	....	....	....
	Quebec Nordiques	WHA	24	9	8	1	1140	83	0	4.37	....	....	....	....	....	2	0	1	0	48	2	0	2.50	....	....	....	....
	NHL Totals		**27**	**11**	**12**	**1**	**1464**	**74**	**1**	**3.03**	....	....	....	....	....	....	....	....	....	....	....	....	....	....	....	....	....
	Other Major League Totals		73	29	31	2	3938	259	4	3.95	....	....	....	....	....	5	1	3	0	227	12	0	3.17	....	....	....	....

WHL First All-Star Team (1973) • Won WHL Leading Goaltender Award (1973) • Won Leader Cup (WHL - MVP) (1973)

Rights traded to **Minnesota** by **Toronto** for cash, June 6, 1967. Signed as a free agent by **San Diego** (WHL), June 12, 1971. Traded to **Boston** by **San Diego** (WHL) for cash and future considerations (John Adams, June 12, 1973), March 10, 1973. Signed as a free agent by **Edmonton** (WHA), September 28, 1976. Traded to **Quebec** (WHA) by **Edmonton** (WHA) with Dave Inkpen, Warren Miller and Rick Morris for Pierre Guite and Don McLeod, December, 1977.

• BRODERICK, LEN

Len Broderick G – L. 5'11", 175 lbs. b: Toronto, Ont., 10/11/1938.

Season	Club	League	GP	W	L	T	Mins	GA	SO	Avg	AAvg	Eff	SA	S%	SAPG	GP	W	L	T	Mins	GA	SO	Avg	Eff	SA	S%	SAPG
1955-56	Toronto Marlboros	OHA	5	4	1	0	300	8	1	1.60	....	....	....	....	....	11	8	2	1	660	26	1	*2.36	....	....	....	....
1956-57	Toronto Marlboros	OHA	42	28	11	3	2520	104	*8	*2.48	....	....	....	....	....	9	5	4	0	540	27	1	3.00	....	....	....	....
1957-58	Toronto Marlboros	OHA	40	16	15	9	2400	131	1	*3.28	....	....	....	....	....	18	9	7	2	1062	62	0	3.50	....	....	....	....
	Montreal Canadiens	**NHL**	**1**	**1**	**0**	**0**	**60**	**2**	**0**	**2.00**	**2.20**	....	....	....	....	....	....	....	....	....	....	....	....	....	....	....	....
1958-59	Toronto Marlboros	OHA	23	....	....	....	1380	72	1	3.13	....	....	....	....	....	5	1	4	0	300	24	0	4.80	....	....	....	....
1959-60	Oakville Oaks	OHA Sr.	STATISTICS NOT AVAILABLE																								
	St. Paul Saints	IHL	3	....	....	....	180	16	0	5.33	....	....	....	....	....	....	....	....	....	....	....	....	....	....	....	....	....
	NHL Totals		**1**	**1**	**0**	**0**	**60**	**2**	**0**	**2.00**	....	....	....	....	....	....	....	....	....	....	....	....	....	....	....	....	....

Loaned to **Montreal** by **Toronto Marlboros** (OHA) to replace Jacques Plante, October 30, 1957. (Montreal 6, Toronto 2)

• BRODEUR, MARTIN

Martin Brodeur G – L. 6'1", 205 lbs. b: Montreal, Que., 5/6/1972. New Jersey's 1st choice, 20th overall, in 1990 Entry Draft.

Season	Club	League	GP	W	L	T	Mins	GA	SO	Avg	AAvg	Eff	SA	S%	SAPG	GP	W	L	T	Mins	GA	SO	Avg	Eff	SA	S%	SAPG
1989-90	St-Hyacinthe Laser	QMJHL	42	23	13	2	2333	156	0	4.01	....	....	....	....	....	12	5	7	....	678	46	0	4.07	....	....	....	....
1990-91	St-Hyacinthe Laser	QMJHL	52	22	24	4	2946	162	2	3.30	....	....	....	....	....	4	0	4	....	232	16	0	4.14	....	....	....	....
1991-92	**New Jersey Devils**	**NHL**	**4**	**2**	**1**	**0**	**179**	**10**	**0**	**3.35**	**2.97**	**3.94**	**85**	**.882**	**28.5**	**1**	**0**	**1**	....	**32**	**3**	**0**	**5.63**	**11.26**	**15**	**.800**	**28.1**
	St-Hyacinthe Laser	QMJHL	48	27	16	4	2846	161	2	3.39	....	....	....	....	....	5	2	3	....	317	14	0	2.65	....	....	....	....
1992-93	Utica Devils	AHL	32	14	13	5	1952	131	0	4.03	....	....	....	....	....	4	1	3	....	258	18	0	4.19	....	....	....	....
1993-94	**New Jersey Devils**	**NHL**	**47**	**27**	**11**	**8**	**2625**	**105**	**3**	**2.40**	**2.27**	**2.04**	**1238**	**.915**	**28.3**	**17**	**8**	**9**	....	**1171**	**38**	**1**	**1.95**	**1.40**	**531**	**.928**	**27.2**
1994-95	**New Jersey Devils**	**NHL**	**40**	**19**	**11**	**6**	**2184**	**89**	**3**	**2.45**	**2.52**	**2.40**	**908**	**.902**	**24.9**	***20**	***16**	**4**	....	***1222**	**34**	***3**	***1.67**	**1.23**	**463**	**.927**	**22.7**
1995-96	**New Jersey Devils**	**NHL**	**77**	**34**	**30**	**12**	***4433**	**173**	**6**	**2.34**	**2.28**	**2.07**	**1954**	**.911**	**26.4**	....	....	....	....	....	....	....	....	....	....	....	....
1996-97	Canada	W Cup	2	0	1	0	60	4	0	4.00	....	....	....	....	....	....	....	....	....	....	....	....	....	....	....	....	....
	New Jersey Devils	**NHL**	**67**	**37**	**14**	**13**	**3838**	**120**	***10**	***1.88**	**1.97**	**1.38**	**1633**	**.927**	**25.5**	**10**	**5**	**5**	....	**659**	**19**	**2**	***1.73**	**1.23**	**268**	**.929**	**24.4**
1997-98	**New Jersey Devils**	**NHL**	**70**	***43**	**17**	**8**	**4128**	**130**	**10**	**1.89**	**2.19**	**1.57**	**1569**	**.917**	**22.8**	**6**	**2**	**4**	....	**366**	**12**	**0**	**1.97**	**1.44**	**164**	**.927**	**26.9**
	Canada	Olympics	DID NOT PLAY – SPARE GOALTENDER																								
	NHL Totals		**305**	**162**	**84**	**47**	**17387**	**627**	**32**	**2.16**	....	....	**7387**	**.915**	....	**54**	**31**	**23**	....	**3450**	**106**	**6**	**1.84**	....	....	....	....

QMJHL Second All-Star Team (1992) • NHL/Upper Deck All-Rookie Team (1994) • Won Calder Memorial Trophy (1994) • NHL Second All-Star Team (1997, 1998) • Shared William M. Jennings Trophy with Mike Dunham (1997) • Won William M. Jennings Trophy (1998)

Played in NHL All-Star Game (1996, 1997, 1998)

• Scored a goal in playoffs vs. Montreal, April 17, 1997.

• BRODEUR, RICHARD

Richard "King Richard" Brodeur G – L. 5'7", 160 lbs. b: Longueuil, Que., 9/15/1952. NY Islanders' 7th choice, 97th overall, in 1972 Amateur Draft.

Season	Club	League	GP	W	L	T	Mins	GA	SO	Avg	AAvg	Eff	SA	S%	SAPG	GP	W	L	T	Mins	GA	SO	Avg	Eff	SA	S%	SAPG
1970-71	Verdun Maple Leafs	QJHL	6	1	4	1	360	47	0	7.83	....	....	....	....	....	....	....	....	....	....	....	....	....	....	....	....	....
	Cornwall Royals	QJHL	35	....	....	....	2100	144	0	4.11	....	....	....	....	....	....	....	....	....	....	....	....	....	....	....	....	....
1971-72	Cornwall Royals	QMJHL	58	*40	17	1	3481	170	*5	*2.93	....	....	....	....	....	*16	*12	3	1	960	44	0	2.75	....	....	....	....
1972-73	Quebec Nordiques	WHA	24	5	14	2	1288	102	0	4.75	....	....	....	....	....	....	....	....	....	....	....	....	....	....	....	....	....
1973-74	Quebec Nordiques	WHA	30	15	12	1	1607	89	1	3.32	....	....	....	....	....	....	....	....	....	....	....	....	....	....	....	....	....
	Maine Nordiques	NAHL	16	10	5	1	927	47	0	3.04	....	....	....	....	....	....	....	....	....	....	....	....	....	....	....	....	....
1974-75	Quebec Nordiques	WHA	51	29	21	0	2938	188	0	3.84	....	....	....	....	....	*15	8	7	0	*906	48	1	3.18	....	....	....	....
1975-76	Quebec Nordiques	WHA	*69	*44	21	2	*3967	244	2	3.69	....	....	....	....	....	5	1	4	0	299	22	0	4.41	....	....	....	....
1976-77	Quebec Nordiques	WHA	53	29	18	2	2906	167	2	3.45	....	....	....	....	....	17	*12	5	0	1007	55	*1	3.28	....	....	....	....
1977-78	Quebec Nordiques	WHA	36	18	15	2	1962	121	0	3.70	....	....	....	....	....	11	5	5	0	622	38	*1	3.67	....	....	....	....
1978-79	Quebec Nordiques	WHA	42	25	13	3	2433	126	*3	3.11	....	....	....	....	....	3	0	2	0	114	14	0	7.37	....	....	....	....
1979-80	**New York Islanders**	**NHL**	**2**	**1**	**1**	**0**	**80**	**6**	**0**	**4.50**	**3.95**	....	....	....	....	....	....	....	....	....	....	....	....	....	....	....	....
	Indianapolis Checkers	CHL	46	22	19	5	2722	131	*4	*2.88	....	....	....	....	....	6	3	3	0	357	12	*1	*2.02	....	....	....	....
1980-81	**Vancouver Canucks**	**NHL**	**52**	**17**	**18**	**16**	**3024**	**177**	**0**	**3.51**	**2.81**	....	....	....	....	**3**	**0**	**3**	....	**185**	**13**	**0**	**4.22**	....	....	....	....
1981-82	**Vancouver Canucks**	**NHL**	**52**	**20**	**18**	**12**	**3010**	**168**	**2**	**3.35**	**2.57**	....	....	....	....	**17**	**11**	**6**	....	**1089**	**49**	**0**	**2.70**	....	....	....	....
1982-83	**Vancouver Canucks**	**NHL**	**58**	**21**	**26**	**8**	**3291**	**208**	**0**	**3.79**	**3.02**	**4.80**	**1641**	**.873**	**29.9**	**3**	**0**	**3**	....	**193**	**13**	**0**	**4.04**	....	....	....	....
1983-84	**Vancouver Canucks**	**NHL**	**36**	**10**	**21**	**5**	**2110**	**141**	**1**	**4.01**	**3.14**	**5.30**	**1067**	**.868**	**30.3**	**4**	**1**	**3**	....	**222**	**12**	**1**	**3.24**	**3.38**	**115**	**.896**	**31.1**
1984-85	**Vancouver Canucks**	**NHL**	**51**	**16**	**27**	**6**	**2930**	**228**	**0**	**4.67**	**3.73**	**6.76**	**1574**	**.855**	**32.2**	....	....	....	....	....	....	....	....	....	....	....	....
	Fredericton Express	AHL	4	3	0	1	249	13	0	3.13	....	....	....	....	....	....	....	....	....	....	....	....	....	....	....	....	....
1985-86	**Vancouver Canucks**	**NHL**	***64**	**19**	**32**	**8**	***3541**	**240**	**2**	**4.07**	**3.17**	**5.67**	**1724**	**.861**	**29.2**	**2**	**0**	**2**	....	**120**	**12**	**0**	**6.00**	**9.11**	**79**	**.848**	**39.5**
1986-87	**Vancouver Canucks**	**NHL**	**53**	**20**	**25**	**5**	**2972**	**178**	**1**	**3.59**	**3.02**	**4.59**	**1391**	**.872**	**28.1**	....	....	....	....	....	....	....	....	....	....	....	....
1987-88	**Vancouver Canucks**	**NHL**	**11**	**3**	**6**	**2**	**670**	**49**	**0**	**4.39**	**3.65**	**6.20**	**347**	**.859**	**31.1**	....	....	....	....	....	....	....	....	....	....	....	....
	Fredericton Express	AHL	2	0	1	0	99	8	0	4.85	....	....	....	....	....	....	....	....	....	....	....	....	....	....	....	....	....
	Hartford Whalers	**NHL**	**6**	**4**	**2**	**0**	**340**	**15**	**0**	**2.65**	**2.20**	**2.80**	**142**	**.894**	**25.1**	**4**	**1**	**3**	....	**200**	**12**	**0**	**3.60**	**4.97**	**87**	**.862**	**26.1**
1988-89	Binghamton Whalers	AHL	6	1	2	0	222	21	0	5.68	....	....	....	....	....	....	....	....	....	....	....	....	....	....	....	....	....
	NHL Totals		**385**	**131**	**176**	**62**	**21968**	**1410**	**6**	**3.85**	....	....	....	....	....	**33**	**13**	**20**	....	**2009**	**111**	**1**	**3.32**	....	....	....	....
	Other Major League Totals		305	165	114	12	17101	1037	8	3.64	....	....	....	....	....	51	26	23	0	2948	177	3	3.60	....	....	....	....

QMJHL First All-Star Team (1972) • Won Stafford Smythe Memorial Trophy (Memorial Cup Tournament MVP) (1972) • WHA Second All-Star Team (1979) • CHL First All-Star Team (1980) • Shared Terry Sawchuk Trophy (fewest goals against - CHL) with Jim Park (1980)

Selected by **Quebec** (WHA) in 1972 WHA General Player Draft, February 12, 1972. Reclaimed by **NY Islanders** from **Quebec** prior to Expansion Draft, June 9, 1979. Claimed as a priority selection by **Quebec**, June 9, 1979. Traded to **NY Islanders** by **Quebec** for Goran Hogasta, August, 1979. Traded to **Vancouver** by **NY Islanders** with NY Islanders' 5th round choice (Moe Lemay) in 1981 Entry Draft for Vancouver's 5th round choice (Jacques Sylvestre) in 1981 Entry Draft, October 6, 1980. Traded to **Hartford** by **Vancouver** for Steve Weeks, March 8, 1988.

• BROMLEY, GARY

Gary Bromley G – L. 5'10", 160 lbs. b: Edmonton, Alta., 1/19/1950.

Season	Club	League	GP	W	L	T	Mins	GA	SO	Avg	AAvg	Eff	SA	S%	SAPG	GP	W	L	T	Mins	GA	SO	Avg	Eff	SA	S%	SAPG
1969-70	Regina Pats	SJHL	34	....	....	....	2002	119	0	3.57	....	....	....	....	....	....	....	....	....	....	....	....	....	....	....	....	....
1970-71	Regina Pats	WCJHL	42	....	....	....	2457	152	2	3.71	....	....	....	....	....	6	....	....	....	340	24	0	4.24	....	....	....	....
1971-72	Charlotte Checkers	EHL	27	....	....	....	1620	73	4	2.70	....	....	....	....	....	1	0	1	0	60	7	0	7.00	....	....	....	....
	Cincinnati Swords	AHL	3	1	1	1	180	6	1	2.00	....	....	....	....	....	....	....	....	....	....	....	....	....	....	....	....	....
1972-73	Cincinnati Swords	AHL	31	....	....	....	1711	76	0	2.66	....	....	....	....	....	3	3	0	0	180	5	*1	1.67	....	....	....	....
1973-74	**Buffalo Sabres**	**NHL**	**12**	**3**	**5**	**3**	**598**	**33**	**0**	**3.31**	**3.20**	....	....	....	....	....	....	....	....	....	....	....	....	....	....	....	....
	Cincinnati Swords	AHL	34	19	11	3	1906	89	1	2.80	....	....	....	....	....	5	1	4	0	302	17	0	3.37	....	....	....	....
1974-75	**Buffalo Sabres**	**NHL**	**50**	**26**	**11**	**11**	**2787**	**144**	**4**	**3.10**	**2.78**	....	....	....	....	....	....	....	....	....	....	....	....	....	....	....	....
1975-76	**Buffalo Sabres**	**NHL**	**1**	**0**	**1**	**0**	**60**	**7**	**0**	**7.00**	**6.34**	....	....	....	....	....	....	....	....	....	....	....	....	....	....	....	....
	Providence Reds	AHL	7	4	1	1	405	30	0	4.44	....	....	....	....	....	....	....	....	....	....	....	....	....	....	....	....	....
1976-77	Calgary Cowboys	WHA	28	6	9	2	1237	79	0	3.83	....	....	....	....	....	....	....	....	....	....	....	....	....	....	....	....	....
1977-78	Winnipeg Jets	WHA	39	25	12	1	2250	124	1	3.31	....	....	....	....	....	5	4	0	0	268	7	0	*1.57	....	....	....	....
1978-79	Dallas Black Hawks	CHL	4	2	1	1	250	6	1	1.44	....	....	....	....	....	....	....	....	....	....	....	....	....	....	....	....	....
	Vancouver Canucks	**NHL**	**38**	**11**	**19**	**6**	**2144**	**136**	**2**	**3.81**	**3.37**	....	....	....	....	**3**	**1**	**2**	....	**180**	**14**	**0**	**4.67**	....	....	....	....
1979-80	Dallas Black Hawks	CHL	21	8	9	3	1289	88	0	4.10	....	....	....	....	....	....	....	....	....	....	....	....	....	....	....	....	....
	Vancouver Canucks	**NHL**	**15**	**8**	**2**	**4**	**860**	**43**	**1**	**3.00**	**2.83**	....	....	....	....	**4**	**1**	**3**	....	**180**	**11**	**0**	**3.67**	....	....	....	....

			REGULAR SEASON													PLAYOFFS											
Season	Club	League	GP	W	L	T	Mins	GA	SO	Avg	AAvg	Eff	SA	S%	SAPG	GP	W	L	T	Mins	GA	SO	Avg	Eff	SA	S%	SAPG
1980-81	**Vancouver Canucks**	**NHL**	**20**	**6**	**6**	**4**	**978**	**62**	**0**	**3.80**	**3.04**	....	....	....	....	....	....	....	....	....	....	....	....	....	....	....	....
	Dallas Black Hawks	CHL	2	1	1	0	127	8	0	3.78	....	....	....	....	....	....	....	....	....	....	....	....	....	....	....	....	....
1981-82	New Haven Nighthawks	AHL	44	....	....	....	2538	148	3	3.50	....	....	....	....	....	3	1	1	0	208	10	0	2.88	....	....	....	....
	NHL Totals		**136**	**54**	**44**	**28**	**7427**	**425**	**7**	**3.43**	....	....	....	....	....	**7**	**2**	**5**	....	**360**	**25**	**0**	**4.17**	....	....	....	....
	Other Major League Totals		67	31	21	3	3487	203	1	3.49	....	....	....	....	....	5	4	0	0	268	7	0	1.57	....	....	....	....

Signed as a free agent by **Buffalo**, September 29, 1971. Selected by **NY Raiders** (WHA) in 1972 WHA General Player Draft, February 12, 1972. WHA rights traded to **Calgary** (WHA) by **San Diego** (WHA), August, 1976. Signed as a free agent by **Winnipeg** (WHA) after **Calgary** (WHA) franchise folded, May 31, 1977. Signed as a free agent by **Vancouver**, May 23, 1978. Traded to **LA Kings** by **Vancouver** to complete transaction that sent Doug Halward to Vancouver (March 8, 1981), May 12, 1981.

• BROOKS, ARTHUR

Arthur Brooks G b: Guelph, Ont., 1892. Deceased.

1908-09	Pittsburgh Duquesne	WPHL	4	0	3	1	250	19	0	4.56	....	....	....	....	....	....	....	....	....	....	....	....	....	....	....	....	....
1909-10	Owen Sound Seniors	OHA Sr.	STATISTICS NOT AVAILABLE																								
1910-11	Owen Sound Seniors	OHA Sr.	STATISTICS NOT AVAILABLE																								
1911-12	Guelph Maple Leafs	OHA Sr.	STATISTICS NOT AVAILABLE																								
1912-13	Owen Sound Seniors	OHA Sr.	STATISTICS NOT AVAILABLE																								
1913-14			STATISTICS NOT AVAILABLE																								
1914-15			MILITARY SERVICE																								
1915-16			MILITARY SERVICE																								
1916-17	Toronto Arenas	NHA	4	2	2	0	238	16	0	4.03	....	....	....	....	....	....	....	....	....	....	....	....	....	....	....	....	....
1917-18	**Toronto Arenas**	**NHL**	**4**	**2**	**2**	**0**	**220**	**23**	**0**	**6.27**	**4.16**	....	....	....	....	....	....	....	....	....	....	....	....	....	....	....	....
	NHL Totals		**4**	**2**	**2**	**0**	**220**	**23**	**0**	**6.27**	....	....	....	....	....	....	....	....	....	....	....	....	....	....	....	....	....
	Other Major League Totals		4	2	2	0	238	16	0	4.03	....	....	....	....	....	....	....	....	....	....	....	....	....	....	....	....	....

Signed as a free agent by **Toronto Arenas**, December 5, 1917.

• BROOKS, ROSS

Ross Brooks G – L. 5'8", 173 lbs. b: Toronto, Ont., 10/17/1937.

1954-55	Barrie Flyers	OHA	11	....	....	....	660	69	0	6.27	....	....	....	....	....	....	....	....	....	....	....	....	....	....	....	....	....
1955-56	Lakeshore Bruins	NOHA	STATISTICS NOT AVAILABLE																								
1956-57	Barrie Flyers	OHA	43	11	31	1	2580	182	4	4.23	....	....	....	....	....	2	0	2	0	120	9	0	4.50	....	....	....	....
1957-58	Barrie Flyers	OHA	23	....	....	....	1380	110	1	4.78	....	....	....	....	....	3	1	2	0	180	16	0	5.33	....	....	....	....
1958-59	North Bay-Windsor-Kitchener	NOHA	12	....	....	....	720	63	0	5.25	....	....	....	....	....	....	....	....	....	....	....	....	....	....	....	....	....
	Washington Presidents	EHL	26	....	....	....	1560	118	1	4.54	....	....	....	....	....	....	....	....	....	....	....	....	....	....	....	....	....
1959-60	Philadelphia Ramblers	EHL	....	....	....	....	....	....	....	....	....	....	....	....	....	2	1	1	0	120	5	0	2.50	....	....	....	....
1960-61	Philadelphia Ramblers	EHL	64	32	28	4	3840	278	0	4.34	....	....	....	....	....	3	0	3	0	180	13	0	4.33	....	....	....	....
	Jersey Devils	EHL	1	1	0	0	60	3	0	3.00	....	....	....	....	....	....	....	....	....	....	....	....	....	....	....	....	....
	Providence Reds	AHL	2	....	....	....	20	3	0	9.00	....	....	....	....	....	....	....	....	....	....	....	....	....	....	....	....	....
1961-62	Philadelphia Ramblers	EHL	68	28	38	2	4080	337	0	4.96	....	....	....	....	....	3	....	....	....	180	12	0	4.00	....	....	....	....
	Long Island Ducks	EHL	3	0	3	0	180	23	0	7.67	....	....	....	....	....	....	....	....	....	....	....	....	....	....	....	....	....
1962-63	Philadelphia Ramblers	EHL	63	27	33	3	3780	272	3	4.32	....	....	....	....	....	3	0	3	0	180	13	0	4.33	....	....	....	....
1963-64	EHL Roving Goaltender	EHL	16	....	....	....	960	68	1	4.25	....	....	....	....	....	....	....	....	....	....	....	....	....	....	....	....	....
	Providence Reds	AHL	3	2	1	0	180	6	0	2.00	....	....	....	....	....	....	....	....	....	....	....	....	....	....	....	....	....
1964-65	Providence Reds	AHL	12	1	10	0	725	70	1	5.79	....	....	....	....	....	....	....	....	....	....	....	....	....	....	....	....	....
1965-66	Providence Reds	AHL	13	3	9	1	770	66	0	5.14	....	....	....	....	....	....	....	....	....	....	....	....	....	....	....	....	....
1966-67	Providence Reds	AHL	32	9	16	6	1849	137	0	4.45	....	....	....	....	....	....	....	....	....	....	....	....	....	....	....	....	....
1967-68	Providence Reds	AHL	19	7	10	1	1120	82	0	4.39	....	....	....	....	....	1	0	0	0	20	1	0	3.00	....	....	....	....
1968-69	Providence Reds	AHL	22	7	10	0	1097	80	0	4.38	....	....	....	....	....	....	....	....	....	....	....	....	....	....	....	....	....
1969-70	Providence Reds	AHL	13	....	....	....	612	43	0	4.22	....	....	....	....	....	....	....	....	....	....	....	....	....	....	....	....	....
1970-71	Providence Reds	AHL	12	1	7	3	657	40	1	3.65	....	....	....	....	....	....	....	....	....	....	....	....	....	....	....	....	....
	Phoenix Roadrunners	WHL	1	0	1	0	60	5	0	5.00	....	....	....	....	....	....	....	....	....	....	....	....	....	....	....	....	....
	Oklahoma City Blazers	CHL	9	....	....	....	530	44	0	4.99	....	....	....	....	....	1	0	1	0	20	5	0	15.00	....	....	....	....
1971-72	Boston Braves	AHL	30	14	8	7	1639	65	1	*2.38	....	....	....	....	....	5	2	2	0	248	12	0	2.90	....	....	....	....
1972-73	Boston Braves	AHL	7	....	....	....	379	16	0	2.52	....	....	....	....	....	....	....	....	....	....	....	....	....	....	....	....	....
	Boston Bruins	**NHL**	**16**	**11**	**1**	**3**	**910**	**40**	**1**	**2.64**	**2.48**	....	....	....	....	**1**	**0**	**0**	....	**20**	**3**	**0**	**9.00**	....	....	....	....
1973-74	**Boston Bruins**	**NHL**	**21**	**16**	**3**	**0**	**1170**	**46**	**3**	**2.36**	**2.27**	....	....	....	....	....	....	....	....	....	....	....	....	....	....	....	....
	Boston Braves	AHL	5	3	0	1	280	15	0	3.21	....	....	....	....	....	....	....	....	....	....	....	....	....	....	....	....	....
1974-75	**Boston Bruins**	**NHL**	**17**	**10**	**3**	**3**	**967**	**48**	**0**	**2.98**	**2.68**	....	....	....	....	....	....	....	....	....	....	....	....	....	....	....	....
1975-76	Rochester Americans	AHL	34	20	12	2	2056	103	2	3.00	....	....	....	....	....	4	2	2	0	239	17	0	4.27	....	....	....	....
	NHL Totals		**54**	**37**	**7**	**6**	**3047**	**134**	**4**	**2.64**	....	....	....	....	....	**1**	**0**	**0**	....	**20**	**3**	**0**	**9.00**	....	....	....	....

Shared Harry "Hap" Holmes Memorial Award (fewest goals against - AHL) with Dan Bouchard (1972)

Signed as an emergency injury replacement goaltender by **EHL** for 1963-64 season. Signed as a free agent by **Boston**, October 2, 1971.

• BROPHY, FRANK

Frank Brophy G – L. 5'6", 150 lbs. b: Quebec City, Quebec, 1900. Deceased.

1916-17	Quebec St. Pats	City Sr.	5	2	3	0	300	19	0	3.80	....	....	....	....	....	....	....	....	....	....	....	....	....	....	....	....	....
1917-18	Montreal St. Anns	City Sr.	9	6	2	1	540	19	2	2.11	....	....	....	....	....	2	1	1	0	120	5	0	2.50	....	....	....	....
	Montreal Westmount	City Sr.	STATISTICS NOT AVAILABLE																								
1918-19	Montreal Vickers	City Sr.	STATISTICS NOT AVAILABLE																								
1919-20	**Quebec Bulldogs**	**NHL**	**21**	**3**	**18**	**0**	**1249**	**148**	**0**	**7.11**	**5.36**	....	....	....	....	....	....	....	....	....	....	....	....	....	....	....	....
	Quebec Crescents	City Sr.	1	1	0	0	60	2	0	2.00	....	....	....	....	....	....	....	....	....	....	....	....	....	....	....	....	....
1920-21	Quebec Telegraph	City Sr.	STATISTICS NOT AVAILABLE																								
	NHL Totals		**21**	**3**	**18**	**0**	**1249**	**148**	**0**	**7.11**	....	....	....	....	....	....	....	....	....	....	....	....	....	....	....	....	....

Signed as a free agent by **Quebec**, November 25, 1919.

• BROWN, ANDY

Andy Brown G – L. 6', 185 lbs. b: Hamilton, Ont., 2/15/1944.

1962-63	Guelph Royals	OHA	20	....	....	....	1200	100	1	5.00	....	....	....	....	....	....	....	....	....	....	....	....	....	....	....	....	....
	Brampton 7-Ups	OHA	20	....	....	....	1175	109	0	5.54	....	....	....	....	....	....	....	....	....	....	....	....	....	....	....	....	....
1963-64			DID NOT PLAY – INJURED																								
1964-65	Gander Flyers	Nfld.	STATISTICS NOT AVAILABLE																								
1965-66	Baltimore Clippers	AHL	1	0	0	0	14	3	0	12.86	....	....	....	....	....	....	....	....	....	....	....	....	....	....	....	....	....
	Johnstown Jets	EHL	70	39	29	2	4200	253	0	3.61	....	....	....	....	....	3	0	3	0	180	14	0	4.67	....	....	....	....
1966-67	Long Island Ducks	EHL	46	....	....	....	2736	142	3	3.09	....	....	....	....	....	3	0	3	0	180	15	0	5.00	....	....	....	....
1967-68	Johnstown Jets	EHL	72	38	25	9	4320	273	4	3.79	....	....	....	....	....	2	0	2	0	....	13	0	8.33	....	....	....	....
1968-69	Baltimore Clippers	AHL	41	16	19	3	2211	134	2	3.64	....	....	....	....	....	....	....	....	....	....	....	....	....	....	....	....	....
1969-70	Baltimore Clippers	AHL	40	....	....	....	2082	125	1	3.60	....	....	....	....	....	....	....	....	....	....	....	....	....	....	....	....	....
1970-71	Baltimore Clippers	AHL	50	*28	13	8	*2954	141	4	2.86	....	....	....	....	....	6	2	4	0	360	18	*1	3.00	....	....	....	....
1971-72	Fort Worth Wings	CHL	16	9	4	3	960	52	0	3.25	....	....	....	....	....	....	....	....	....	....	....	....	....	....	....	....	....
	Tidewater Wings	AHL	23	4	16	1	1278	86	0	4.04	....	....	....	....	....	....	....	....	....	....	....	....	....	....	....	....	....
	Detroit Red Wings	**NHL**	**10**	**4**	**5**	**1**	**560**	**37**	**0**	**3.96**	**4.00**	....	....	....	....	....	....	....	....	....	....	....	....	....	....	....	....
1972-73	**Detroit Red Wings**	**NHL**	**7**	**2**	**1**	**2**	**337**	**20**	**0**	**3.56**	**3.36**	....	....	....	....	....	....	....	....	....	....	....	....	....	....	....	....
	Fort Worth Wings	CHL	22	....	....	....	1300	86	2	3.97	....	....	....	....	....	....	....	....	....	....	....	....	....	....	....	....	....
	Pittsburgh Penguins	**NHL**	**9**	**3**	**4**	**2**	**520**	**41**	**0**	**4.73**	**4.47**	....	....	....	....	....	....	....	....	....	....	....	....	....	....	....	....
1973-74	**Pittsburgh Penguins**	**NHL**	**36**	**13**	**16**	**4**	**1956**	**115**	**1**	**3.53**	**3.42**	....	....	....	....	....	....	....	....	....	....	....	....	....	....	....	....
1974-75	Indianapolis Racers	WHA	52	15	35	0	2979	206	2	4.15	....	....	....	....	....	....	....	....	....	....	....	....	....	....	....	....	....
1975-76	Indianapolis Racers	WHA	24	9	11	2	1368	82	1	3.60	....	....	....	....	....	....	....	....	....	....	....	....	....	....	....	....	....
1976-77	Indianapolis Racers	WHA	10	1	4	1	430	26	0	3.63	....	....	....	....	....	....	....	....	....	....	....	....	....	....	....	....	....
	NHL Totals		**62**	**22**	**26**	**9**	**3373**	**213**	**1**	**3.79**	....	....	....	....	....	....	....	....	....	....	....	....	....	....	....	....	....
	Other Major League Totals		86	25	50	3	4777	314	3	3.94	....	....	....	....	....	....	....	....	....	....	....	....	....	....	....	....	....

EHL North Second All-Star Team (1966) • AHL First All-Star Team (1971)

Claimed by **Detroit** from **Baltimore** (AHL) in Inter-League Draft, June 7, 1971. Selected by **Minnesota** (WHA) in 1972 WHA General Player Draft, February 12, 1972. Traded to **Pittsburgh** by **Detroit** for Pittsburgh's 3rd round choice (Nelson Pyatt) in 1973 Amateur Draft and cash, February 25, 1973. WHA rights traded to **Indianapolis** (WHA) by **Minnesota** (WHA) for future considerations, July, 1974. • Last NHL goaltender to play without a facemask, 1973-74.

● BROWN, KEN

Ken Brown G – L. 5'11", 175 lbs. b: Port Arthur, Ont., 12/19/1948.

			REGULAR SEASON													PLAYOFFS											
Season	Club	League	GP	W	L	T	Mins	GA	SO	Avg	AAvg	Eff	SA	S%	SAPG	GP	W	L	T	Mins	GA	SO	Avg	Eff	SA	S%	SAPG
1964-65	Moose Jaw Canucks	SJHL	13	....	....	....	780	60	1	4.61	....	....	....	....	....	....	....	....	....	....	....	....	....	....	....	....	....
1965-66	Moose Jaw Canucks	SJHL	14	....	....	....	830	60	0	4.34	....	....	....	....	....	....	....	....	....	....	....	....	....	....	....	....	....
	Estevan Bruins	SJHL	20	....	....	....	1190	46	1	2.32	....	....	....	....	....	3	....	....	....	180	13	0	4.33	....	....	....	....
1966-67	Moose Jaw Canucks	CMJHL	54	24	18	12	3240	174	*3	*3.22	....	....	....	....	....	14	7	3	4	840	55	0	3.93	....	....	....	....
1967-68	Moose Jaw Canucks	WCJHL	58	30	23	5	3480	236	0	4.07	....	....	....	....	....	10	4	5	1	600	56	1	5.60	....	....	....	....
1968-69	Dallas Black Hawks	CHL	23	....	....	....	1320	79	0	3.59	....	....	....	....	....	....	....	....	....	....	....	....	....	....	....	....	....
1969-70	Dallas Black Hawks	CHL	46	22	19	4	2720	142	4	3.13	....	....	....	....	....	....	....	....	....	....	....	....	....	....	....	....	....
1970-71	Dallas Black Hawks	CHL	26	....	....	....	1528	92	0	3.61	....	....	....	....	....	1	1	0	0	60	2	0	2.00	....	....	....	....
	Chicago Black Hawks	**NHL**	**1**	**0**	**0**	**0**	**18**	**1**	**0**	**3.33**	**3.29**	....	....	....	....	....	....	....	....	....	....	....	....	....	....	....	....
1971-72	Dallas Black Hawks	CHL	31	13	10	2	1683	90	2	3.20	....	....	....	....	....	*11	*7	3	0	*650	29	0	2.67	....	....	....	....
1972-73	Alberta Oilers	WHA	20	10	8	0	1034	63	1	3.66	....	....	....	....	....	....	....	....	....	....	....	....	....	....	....	....	....
1973-74	Winston-Salem Polar Bears	SHL	29	10	17	0	1575	145	0	5.53	....	....	....	....	....	5	3	2	0	285	12	0	*2.53	....	....	....	....
1974-75	Edmonton Oilers	WHA	32	11	11	0	1466	86	2	3.52	....	....	....	....	....	....	....	....	....	....	....	....	....	....	....	....	....
	NHL Totals		**1**	**0**	**0**	**0**	**18**	**1**	**0**	**3.33**	....	....	....	....	....	....	....	....	....	....	....	....	....	....	....	....	....
	Other Major League Totals		52	21	19	0	2500	149	3	3.58	....	....	....	....	....	....	....	....	....	....	....	....	....	....	....	....	....

Selected by **Calgary-Cleveland** (WHA) in 1972 WHA General Player Draft, February 12, 1972. WHA rights traded to **Alberta** (WHA) by **Cleveland** (WHA) for cash, July, 1972.

● BRUNETTA, MARIO

Mario Brunetta G – L. 6'3", 180 lbs. b: Quebec City, Que., 1/25/1967. Quebec's 9th choice, 162nd overall, in 1985 Entry Draft.

			REGULAR SEASON													PLAYOFFS											
Season	Club	League	GP	W	L	T	Mins	GA	SO	Avg	AAvg	Eff	SA	S%	SAPG	GP	W	L	T	Mins	GA	SO	Avg	Eff	SA	S%	SAPG
1984-85	Quebec Remparts	QMJHL	45	20	21	1	2255	192	0	5.11	....	....	....	....	....	2	0	2	0	120	13	0	6.50	....	....	....	....
1985-86	Laval Titans	QMJHL	63	30	25	1	3383	279	0	4.95	....	....	....	....	....	14	9	5	0	834	60	0	4.32	....	....	....	....
1986-87	Laval Titans	QMJHL	59	27	25	4	3469	261	1	4.51	....	....	....	....	....	14	8	6	0	820	63	0	4.61	....	....	....	....
1987-88	**Quebec Nordiques**	**NHL**	**29**	**10**	**12**	**1**	**1550**	**96**	**0**	**3.72**	**3.09**	**4.59**	**778**	**.877**	**30.1**	....	....	....	....	....	....	....	....	....	....	....	....
	Fredericton Express	AHL	5	4	1	0	300	24	0	4.80	....	....	....	....	....	....	....	....	....	....	....	....	....	....	....	....	....
1988-89	**Quebec Nordiques**	**NHL**	**5**	**1**	**3**	**0**	**226**	**19**	**0**	**5.04**	**4.16**	**8.18**	**117**	**.838**	**31.1**	....	....	....	....	....	....	....	....	....	....	....	....
	Halifax Citadels	AHL	36	14	14	5	1898	124	0	3.92	....	....	....	....	....	3	0	2	0	142	12	0	5.07	....	....	....	....
1989-90	**Quebec Nordiques**	**NHL**	**6**	**1**	**2**	**0**	**191**	**13**	**0**	**4.08**	**3.42**	**5.36**	**99**	**.869**	**31.1**	....	....	....	....	....	....	....	....	....	....	....	....
	Halifax Citadels	AHL	24	8	14	2	1444	99	0	4.11	....	....	....	....	....	....	....	....	....	....	....	....	....	....	....	....	....
1990-91	HC Asiago	Italy	42	....	....	....	2446	160	3	3.92	....	....	....	....	....	....	....	....	....	....	....	....	....	....	....	....	....
1991-92	HC Asiago	Italy	29	....	....	....	1746	116	1	3.98	....	....	....	....	....	11	....	....	....	668	43	1	3.86	....	....	....	....
1992-93	HC Asiago	Italy	22	....	....	....	1320	94	....	4.27	....	....	....	....	....	....	....	....	....	....	....	....	....	....	....	....	....
1993-94	Milano Devils	Italy	29	....	....	....	1551	81	....	3.13	....	....	....	....	....	....	....	....	....	....	....	....	....	....	....	....	....
1994-95	Milano Devils	Italy	STATISTICS NOT AVAILABLE																								
	Italy	WC-A	3	....	....	....	167	13	....	4.67	....	....	....	....	....	....	....	....	....	....	....	....	....	....	....	....	....
1995-96	Varese HC	Italy	40	....	....	....	1555	69	....	2.66	....	....	....	....	....	....	....	....	....	....	....	....	....	....	....	....	....
1996-97	Eisbaren Berlin	Germany	46	....	....	....	2729	144	0	3.17	....	....	....	....	....	8	....	....	....	493	24	*1	2.92	....	....	....	....
1997-98	Eisbaren Berlin	Germany	40	....	....	....	2277	101	2	2.66	....	....	....	....	....	*10	*7	3	....	*607	29	*1	3.00	....	....	....	....
	Italy	Olympics	1	0	1	0	23	4	0	10.17	....	....	....	....	....	....	....	....	....	....	....	....	....	....	....	....	....
	Italy	WC-A	1	0	1	0	60	5	0	5.00	....	....	....	....	....	....	....	....	....	....	....	....	....	....	....	....	....
	NHL Totals		**40**	**12**	**17**	**1**	**1967**	**128**	**0**	**3.90**	....	....	**994**	**.871**	....	....	....	....	....	....	....	....	....	....	....	....	....

● BULLOCK, BRUCE

Bruce Bullock G – R. 5'7", 160 lbs. b: Toronto, Ont., 5/9/1949.

			REGULAR SEASON													PLAYOFFS											
Season	Club	League	GP	W	L	T	Mins	GA	SO	Avg	AAvg	Eff	SA	S%	SAPG	GP	W	L	T	Mins	GA	SO	Avg	Eff	SA	S%	SAPG
1968-69	Clarkson University	ECAC	26	17	7	2	....	....	....	3.46	....	....	....	....	....	....	....	....	....	....	....	....	....	....	....	....	....
1969-70	Clarkson University	ECAC	27	19	8	0	1550	79	4	3.06	....	....	....	....	....	....	....	....	....	....	....	....	....	....	....	....	....
1970-71	Clarkson University	ECAC	30	25	4	1	1800	71	1	2.37	....	....	....	....	....	....	....	....	....	....	....	....	....	....	....	....	....
1971-72	Dallas Black Hawks	CHL	5	0	2	1	220	15	0	3.75	....	....	....	....	....	....	....	....	....	....	....	....	....	....	....	....	....
	Seattle Totems	WHL	10	3	7	0	564	43	0	4.57	....	....	....	....	....	....	....	....	....	....	....	....	....	....	....	....	....
1972-73	**Vancouver Canucks**	**NHL**	**14**	**3**	**8**	**3**	**840**	**67**	**0**	**4.79**	**4.54**	....	....	....	....	....	....	....	....	....	....	....	....	....	....	....	....
	Seattle Totems	WHL	13	7	6	0	750	45	0	3.60	....	....	....	....	....	....	....	....	....	....	....	....	....	....	....	....	....
1973-74	Seattle Totems	WHL	46	22	20	3	2703	165	2	3.66	....	....	....	....	....	....	....	....	....	....	....	....	....	....	....	....	....
1974-75	**Vancouver Canucks**	**NHL**	**1**	**0**	**1**	**0**	**60**	**4**	**0**	**4.00**	**3.60**	....	....	....	....	....	....	....	....	....	....	....	....	....	....	....	....
	Seattle Totems	CHL	48	14	20	7	2580	168	1	3.91	....	....	....	....	....	....	....	....	....	....	....	....	....	....	....	....	....
1975-76	Beauce Jaros	NAHL	18	....	....	....	1067	60	2	3.37	....	....	....	....	....	....	....	....	....	....	....	....	....	....	....	....	....
	Tulsa Oilers	CHL	17	13	3	0	958	39	1	2.44	....	....	....	....	....	6	*6	0	0	360	10	*1	*1.67	....	....	....	....
1976-77	**Vancouver Canucks**	**NHL**	**1**	**0**	**0**	**0**	**27**	**3**	**0**	**6.67**	**6.20**	....	....	....	....	....	....	....	....	....	....	....	....	....	....	....	....
	Tulsa Oilers	CHL	40	20	14	6	2347	135	1	3.45	....	....	....	....	....	8	4	4	0	480	21	0	2.63	....	....	....	....
1977-78	Phoenix Roadrunners	PHI	31	....	....	....	1747	104	*1	3.57	....	....	....	....	....	....	....	....	....	....	....	....	....	....	....	....	....
1978-79	Phoenix Roadrunners	PHI	31	....	....	....	1872	100	*1	3.21	....	....	....	....	....	....	....	....	....	....	....	....	....	....	....	....	....
	NHL Totals		**16**	**3**	**9**	**3**	**927**	**74**	**0**	**4.79**	....	....	....	....	....	....	....	....	....	....	....	....	....	....	....	....	....

NCAA East First All-American Team (1970, 1971) • NCAA Championship All-Tournament Team (1970) • ECAC First All-Star Team (1971)

Traded to **Vancouver** (Seattle-WHL) by **Chicago** (Dallas-CHL) for cash, February 26, 1972.

● BURKE, SEAN

Sean Burke G – L. 6'4", 208 lbs. b: Windsor, Ont., 1/29/1967. New Jersey's 2nd choice, 24th overall, in 1985 Entry Draft.

			REGULAR SEASON													PLAYOFFS											
Season	Club	League	GP	W	L	T	Mins	GA	SO	Avg	AAvg	Eff	SA	S%	SAPG	GP	W	L	T	Mins	GA	SO	Avg	Eff	SA	S%	SAPG
1984-85	Toronto Marlboros	OHL	49	25	21	3	2987	211	0	4.24	....	....	....	....	....	5	1	3	....	266	25	0	5.64	....	....	....	....
1985-86	Toronto Marlboros	OHL	47	16	27	3	2840	233	0	4.92	....	....	....	....	....	4	0	4	....	238	24	0	6.05	....	....	....	....
	Canada	WJC-A	2	1	1	0	120	7	0	3.50	....	....	....	....	....	....	....	....	....	....	....	....	....	....	....	....	....
1986-87	Canada	Nat-Team	42	27	13	2	2550	130	0	3.05	....	....	....	....	....	....	....	....	....	....	....	....	....	....	....	....	....
	Canada	WEC-A	5	....	....	....	300	12	....	2.40	....	....	....	....	....	....	....	....	....	....	....	....	....	....	....	....	....
1987-88	Canada	Nat-Team	37	19	9	2	1962	92	1	2.81	....	....	....	....	....	....	....	....	....	....	....	....	....	....	....	....	....
	Canada	Olympics	4	1	2	1	238	12	....	3.02	....	....	....	....	....	....	....	....	....	....	....	....	....	....	....	....	....
	New Jersey Devils	**NHL**	**13**	**10**	**1**	**0**	**689**	**35**	**1**	**3.05**	**2.53**	**3.56**	**300**	**.883**	**26.1**	**17**	**9**	**8**	....	**1001**	**57**	***1**	**3.42**	**3.79**	**515**	**.889**	**30.9**
1988-89	**New Jersey Devils**	**NHL**	**62**	**22**	**31**	**9**	**3590**	**230**	**3**	**3.84**	**3.17**	**4.84**	**1823**	**.874**	**30.5**	....	....	....	....	....	....	....	....	....	....	....	....
	Canada	WEC-A	5	....	....	....	275	10	....	2.18	....	....	....	....	....	....	....	....	....	....	....	....	....	....	....	....	....
1989-90	**New Jersey Devils**	**NHL**	**52**	**22**	**22**	**6**	**2914**	**175**	**0**	**3.60**	**3.01**	**4.34**	**1453**	**.880**	**29.9**	**2**	**0**	**2**	....	**125**	**8**	**0**	**3.84**	**5.39**	**57**	**.860**	**27.4**
1990-91	**New Jersey Devils**	**NHL**	**35**	**8**	**12**	**8**	**1870**	**112**	**0**	**3.59**	**3.21**	**4.60**	**875**	**.872**	**28.1**	....	....	....	....	....	....	....	....	....	....	....	....
	Canada	WEC-A	8	....	....	....	479	21	....	2.63	....	....	....	....	....	....	....	....	....	....	....	....	....	....	....	....	....
1991-92	Canada	C Cup	DID NOT PLAY – SPARE GOALTENDER																								
	Canada	Nat-Team	31	18	6	4	1721	75	1	2.61	....	....	....	....	....	....	....	....	....	....	....	....	....	....	....	....	....
	Canada	Olympics	7	5	2	0	429	17	0	2.37	....	....	....	....	....	....	....	....	....	....	....	....	....	....	....	....	....
	San Diego Gulls	IHL	7	4	2	1	424	17	0	2.41	....	....	....	....	....	3	0	3	....	160	13	0	4.88	....	....	....	....
1992-93	**Hartford Whalers**	**NHL**	**50**	**16**	**27**	**3**	**2656**	**184**	**0**	**4.16**	**3.55**	**5.15**	**1485**	**.876**	**33.5**	....	....	....	....	....	....	....	....	....	....	....	....
1993-94	**Hartford Whalers**	**NHL**	**47**	**17**	**24**	**5**	**2750**	**137**	**2**	**2.99**	**2.84**	**2.81**	**1458**	**.906**	**31.8**	....	....	....	....	....	....	....	....	....	....	....	....
1994-95	**Hartford Whalers**	**NHL**	**42**	**17**	**19**	**4**	**2418**	**108**	**0**	**2.68**	**2.76**	**2.35**	**1233**	**.912**	**30.6**	....	....	....	....	....	....	....	....	....	....	....	....
1995-96	**Hartford Whalers**	**NHL**	**66**	**28**	**28**	**6**	**3669**	**190**	**4**	**3.11**	**3.05**	**2.91**	**2034**	**.907**	**33.3**	....	....	....	....	....	....	....	....	....	....	....	....
1996-97	**Hartford Whalers**	**NHL**	**51**	**22**	**22**	**6**	**2985**	**134**	**4**	**2.69**	**2.84**	**2.31**	**1560**	**.914**	**31.4**	....	....	....	....	....	....	....	....	....	....	....	....
	Canada	WC-A	11	7	1	3	608	22	3	2.17	....	....	....	....	....	....	....	....	....	....	....	....	....	....	....	....	....
1997-98	**Carolina Hurricanes**	**NHL**	**25**	**7**	**11**	**5**	**1415**	**66**	**1**	**2.80**	**3.28**	**2.82**	**655**	**.899**	**27.8**	....	....	....	....	....	....	....	....	....	....	....	....
	Vancouver Canucks	**NHL**	**16**	**2**	**9**	**4**	**838**	**49**	**0**	**3.51**	**4.12**	**4.34**	**396**	**.876**	**28.4**	....	....	....	....	....	....	....	....	....	....	....	....
	Philadelphia Flyers	**NHL**	**11**	**7**	**3**	**0**	**632**	**27**	**1**	**2.56**	**2.99**	**2.22**	**311**	**.913**	**29.5**	**5**	**1**	**4**	....	**283**	**17**	**0**	**3.60**	**5.06**	**121**	**.860**	**25.7**
	NHL Totals		**470**	**178**	**209**	**58**	**26426**	**1447**	**16**	**3.29**	....	....	**13583**	**.893**	....	**24**	**10**	**14**		**1409**	**82**	**1**	**3.40**	....	....	....	....

WEC-A All-Star Team (1991)

Played in NHL All-Star Game (1989)

Traded to **Hartford** by **New Jersey** with Eric Weinrich for Bobby Holik, Hartford's 2nd round choice (Jay Pandolfo) in 1993 Entry Draft and future considerations, August 28, 1992. Transferred to **Carolina** after **Hartford** franchise relocated, June 25, 1997. Traded to **Vancouver** by **Carolina** with Geoff Sanderson and Enrico Ciccone for Kirk McLean and Martin Gelinas, January 3, 1998. Traded to **Philadelphia** by **Vancouver** for Garth Snow, March 4, 1998.

• BUZINSKI, STEVE

Steve "The Puck Goes Inski" Buzinski G – L. 5'8", 140 lbs. b: Dunblane, Sask., 10/15/1917.

			REGULAR SEASON													PLAYOFFS											
Season	Club	League	GP	W	L	T	Mins	GA	SO	Avg	AAvg	Eff	SA	S%	SAPG	GP	W	L	T	Mins	GA	SO	Avg	Eff	SA	S%	SAPG
1941-42	Swift Current Indians	SSHL	....	....	....	....	....	....	....	....	....	....	....	....	....	8	6	1	1	480	16	0	2.00	....	....	....	....
1942-43	**New York Rangers**	**NHL**	**9**	**2**	**6**	**1**	**560**	**55**	**0**	**5.89**	**5.12**	....	....	....	....	....	....	....	....	....	....	....	....	....	....	....	....
	Swift Current Indians	SSHL	STATISTICS NOT AVAILABLE																								
	NHL Totals		**9**	**2**	**6**	**1**	**560**	**55**	**0**	**5.89**	....	....	....	....	....	....	....	....	....	....	....	....	....	....	....	....	....

Signed as free agent by **NY Rangers** as a war-time replacement for Jim Henry, October, 1942.

• CALEY, DON

Don Caley G – L. 5'10", 160 lbs. b: Dauphin, Man., 10/9/1945.

Season	Club	League	GP	W	L	T	Mins	GA	SO	Avg	AAvg	Eff	SA	S%	SAPG	GP	W	L	T	Mins	GA	SO	Avg	Eff	SA	S%	SAPG
1963-64	Weyburn Red Wings	SJHL	18	....	....	....	1080	75	0	4.16	....	....	....	....	....	5	1	4	0	300	29	0	5.80	....	....	....	....
1964-65	Weyburn Red Wings	SJHL	54	36	15	3	3240	188	*2	3.49	....	....	....	....	....	15	....	....	....	900	45	*1	*3.00	....	....	....	....
	Peterborough Petes	OHA	1	1	0	0	60	1	0	1.00	....	....	....	....	....	....	....	....	....	....	....	....	....	....	....	....	....
1965-66	Weyburn Red Wings	SJHL	56	36	14	6	3360	165	*4	2.95	....	....	....	....	....	12	....	....	....	720	29	1	2.42	....	....	....	....
1966-67	Pittsburgh Hornets	AHL	20	6	11	2	1122	71	2	3.80	....	....	....	....	....	....	....	....	....	....	....	....	....	....	....	....	....
1967-68	**St. Louis Blues**	**NHL**	**1**	**0**	**0**	**0**	**30**	**3**	**0**	**6.00**	**6.65**	....	....	....	....	....	....	....	....	....	....	....	....	....	....	....	....
	Kansas City Blues	CHL	55	*26	23	5	3203	176	1	3.30	....	....	....	....	....	7	4	3	0	420	22	*1	3.14	....	....	....	....
1968-69	Buffalo Bisons	AHL	1	0	1	0	60	5	0	5.00	....	....	....	....	....	....	....	....	....	....	....	....	....	....	....	....	....
	Omaha Knights	CHL	34	....	....	....	1899	102	1	3.23	....	....	....	....	....	6	3	3	0	316	14	*1	2.66	....	....	....	....
1969-70	Phoenix Roadrunners	WHL	28	8	11	7	1578	83	0	3.16	....	....	....	....	....	....	....	....	....	....	....	....	....	....	....	....	....
1970-71	Phoenix Roadrunners	WHL	24	9	9	3	1306	67	2	3.08	....	....	....	....	....	4	2	2	0	207	10	0	2.90	....	....	....	....
1971-72	Phoenix Roadrunners	WHL	44	21	16	2	2425	129	2	3.19	....	....	....	....	....	3	1	2	0	199	13	0	3.91	....	....	....	....
1972-73	Phoenix Roadrunners	WHL	39	19	11	7	2236	128	2	3.43	....	....	....	....	....	*8	*7	1	0	*435	23	*1	3.17	....	....	....	....
1973-74	Phoenix Roadrunners	WHL	7	4	3	0	427	26	0	3.68	....	....	....	....	....	....	....	....	....	....	....	....	....	....	....	....	....
	NHL Totals		**1**	**0**	**0**	**0**	**30**	**3**	**0**	**6.00**	....	....	....	....	....	....	....	....	....	....	....	....	....	....	....	....	....

WHL First All-Star Team (1972) • WHL Second All-Star Team (1973)

Claimed by **St. Louis** from **Detroit** in Expansion Draft, June 6, 1967. Traded to **NY Rangers** by **St. Louis** with Wayne Rivers for Camille Henry, Bill Plager and Robbie Irons, June 13, 1968. Traded to **Phoenix** (WHL) by **NY Rangers** with Sandy Snow for Peter McDuffe, July, 1969.

• CAPRICE, FRANK

Frank Caprice G – L. 5'9", 150 lbs. b: Hamilton, Ont., 5/2/1962. Vancouver's 8th choice, 178th overall, in 1981 Entry Draft.

Season	Club	League	GP	W	L	T	Mins	GA	SO	Avg	AAvg	Eff	SA	S%	SAPG	GP	W	L	T	Mins	GA	SO	Avg	Eff	SA	S%	SAPG
1979-80	London Knights	OHA	18	3	7	3	919	74	1	4.84	....	....	....	....	....	3	1	1	0	94	10	0	6.38	....	....	....	....
1980-81	London Knights	OHA	42	11	26	0	2171	190	0	5.25	....	....	....	....	....	....	....	....	....	....	....	....	....	....	....	....	....
1981-82	London Knights	OHL	45	24	17	2	2614	196	0	4.50	....	....	....	....	....	4	1	3	0	240	18	0	4.50	....	....	....	....
	Canada	WJC-A	3	3	0	0	180	7	0	2.33	....	....	....	....	....	....	....	....	....	....	....	....	....	....	....	....	....
	Dallas Black Hawks	CHL	3	0	3	0	178	19	0	6.40	....	....	....	....	....	....	....	....	....	....	....	....	....	....	....	....	....
1982-83	**Vancouver Canucks**	**NHL**	**1**	**0**	**0**	**0**	**20**	**3**	**0**	**9.00**	**7.19**	**33.75**	**8**	**.625**	**24.0**	....	....	....	....	....	....	....	....	....	....	....	....
	Fredericton Express	AHL	14	5	8	1	819	50	0	3.67	....	....	....	....	....	....	....	....	....	....	....	....	....	....	....	....	....
1983-84	**Vancouver Canucks**	**NHL**	**19**	**8**	**8**	**2**	**1098**	**62**	**1**	**3.39**	**2.65**	**4.00**	**525**	**.882**	**28.7**	....	....	....	....	....	....	....	....	....	....	....	....
	Fredericton Express	AHL	18	11	5	2	1089	49	2	2.70	....	....	....	....	....	....	....	....	....	....	....	....	....	....	....	....	....
1984-85	**Vancouver Canucks**	**NHL**	**28**	**8**	**14**	**3**	**1523**	**122**	**0**	**4.81**	**3.83**	**7.17**	**818**	**.851**	**32.2**	....	....	....	....	....	....	....	....	....	....	....	....
1985-86	**Vancouver Canucks**	**NHL**	**7**	**0**	**3**	**2**	**308**	**28**	**0**	**5.45**	**4.24**	**9.85**	**155**	**.819**	**30.2**	....	....	....	....	....	....	....	....	....	....	....	....
	Fredericton Express	AHL	26	12	11	2	1526	109	0	4.29	....	....	....	....	....	6	2	4	0	333	22	0	3.96	....	....	....	....
1986-87	**Vancouver Canucks**	**NHL**	**25**	**8**	**11**	**2**	**1390**	**89**	**0**	**3.84**	**3.23**	**5.32**	**643**	**.862**	**27.8**	....	....	....	....	....	....	....	....	....	....	....	....
	Fredericton Express	AHL	12	5	5	0	686	47	0	4.11	....	....	....	....	....	....	....	....	....	....	....	....	....	....	....	....	....
1987-88	**Vancouver Canucks**	**NHL**	**22**	**7**	**10**	**2**	**1250**	**87**	**0**	**4.18**	**3.48**	**5.81**	**626**	**.861**	**30.0**	....	....	....	....	....	....	....	....	....	....	....	....
1988-89	Milwaukee Admirals	IHL	39	24	12	0	2204	143	2	3.89	....	....	....	....	....	2	0	1	0	91	5	0	3.30	....	....	....	....
1989-90	Maine Mariners	AHL	10	2	6	1	550	46	0	5.02	....	....	....	....	....	....	....	....	....	....	....	....	....	....	....	....	....
	Milwaukee Admirals	IHL	20	8	6	3	1098	78	0	4.26	....	....	....	....	....	3	0	2	0	142	10	0	4.23	....	....	....	....
1990-91			STATISTICS NOT AVAILABLE																								
1991-92			STATISTICS NOT AVAILABLE																								
1992-93	Val Gardena	Italy	19	....	....	....	1140	93	....	4.89	....	....	....	....	....	....	....	....	....	....	....	....	....	....	....	....	....
1993-94	Val Gardena	Italy	22	....	....	....	1204	100	....	4.98	....	....	....	....	....	....	....	....	....	....	....	....	....	....	....	....	....
1994-95	Val Gardena	Italy	STATISTICS NOT AVAILABLE																								
1995-96	Val Gardena	Italy	36	....	....	....	1678	100	....	3.58	....	....	....	....	....	....	....	....	....	....	....	....	....	....	....	....	....
1996-97	Cardiff Devils	Britain	12	....	....	....	705	38	....	3.23	....	....	....	....	....	1	....	....	....	60	3	0	3.00	....	....	....	....
1997-98	Cardiff Devils	Britain	21	....	....	....	1242	61	....	2.95	....	....	....	....	....	2	....	....	....	120	4	....	2.00	....	....	....	....
	NHL Totals		**102**	**31**	**46**	**11**	**5589**	**391**	**1**	**4.20**	....	....	**2775**	**.859**	....	....	....	....	....	....	....	....	....	....	....	....	....

• CAREY, JIM

Jim Carey G – L. 6'2", 205 lbs. b: Dorchester, MA, 5/31/1974. Washington's 2nd choice, 32nd overall, in 1992 Entry Draft.

Season	Club	League	GP	W	L	T	Mins	GA	SO	Avg	AAvg	Eff	SA	S%	SAPG	GP	W	L	T	Mins	GA	SO	Avg	Eff	SA	S%	SAPG
1991-92	Catholic Memorial	H.S.	21	....	....	....	940	34	8	1.63	....	....	....	....	....	....	....	....	....	....	....	....	....	....	....	....	....
1992-93	University of Wisconsin	WCHA	26	15	8	1	1525	78	1	3.07	....	....	....	....	....	....	....	....	....	....	....	....	....	....	....	....	....
	United States	WJC-A	4	....	....	....	240	14	....	3.50	....	....	....	....	....	....	....	....	....	....	....	....	....	....	....	....	....
1993-94	University of Wisconsin	WCHA	*40	*24	13	1	*2247	114	*1	*3.04	....	....	....	....	....	....	....	....	....	....	....	....	....	....	....	....	....
1994-95	Portland Pirates	AHL	55	30	14	11	3281	151	*6	2.76	....	....	....	....	....	....	....	....	....	....	....	....	....	....	....	....	....
	Washington Capitals	**NHL**	**28**	**18**	**6**	**3**	**1604**	**57**	**4**	**2.13**	**2.19**	**1.86**	**654**	**.913**	**24.5**	**7**	**2**	**4**	....	**358**	**25**	**0**	**4.19**	**6.94**	**151**	**.834**	**25.3**
1995-96	**Washington Capitals**	**NHL**	**71**	**35**	**24**	**9**	**4069**	**153**	***9**	**2.26**	**2.20**	**2.12**	**1631**	**.906**	**24.1**	**3**	**0**	**1**	....	**97**	**10**	**0**	**6.19**	**15.87**	**39**	**.744**	**24.1**
1996-97	United States	W Cup	DID NOT PLAY – SPARE GOALTENDER																								
	Washington Capitals	**NHL**	**40**	**17**	**18**	**3**	**2293**	**105**	**1**	**2.75**	**2.91**	**2.93**	**984**	**.893**	**25.7**	....	....	....	....	....	....	....	....	....	....	....	....
	Boston Bruins	**NHL**	**19**	**5**	**13**	**0**	**1004**	**64**	**0**	**3.82**	**4.05**	**4.93**	**496**	**.871**	**29.6**	....	....	....	....	....	....	....	....	....	....	....	....
1997-98	**Boston Bruins**	**NHL**	**10**	**3**	**2**	**1**	**496**	**24**	**2**	**2.90**	**3.39**	**3.09**	**225**	**.893**	**27.2**	....	....	....	....	....	....	....	....	....	....	....	....
	Providence Bruins	AHL	10	2	7	1	604	40	0	3.97	....	....	....	....	....	....	....	....	....	....	....	....	....	....	....	....	....
	NHL Totals		**168**	**78**	**63**	**16**	**9466**	**403**	**16**	**2.55**	....	....	**3990**	**.899**	....	**10**	**2**	**5**	....	**455**	**35**	**0**	**4.62**	....	....	....	....

WCHA Second All-Star Team (1993) • AHL First All-Star Team (1995) • Won Baz Bastien Memorial Trophy (Top Goaltender - AHL) (1995) • Won Dudley "Red" Garrett Memorial Trophy (Top Rookie - AHL) (1995) • NHL/Upper Deck All-Rookie Team (1995) • NHL First All-Star Team (1996) • Won Vezina Trophy (1996)

Traded to **Boston** by **Washington** with Anson Carter, Jason Allison and Washington's 3rd round choice (Lee Goren) in 1997 Entry Draft for Bill Ranford, Adam Oates and Rick Tocchet, March 1, 1997.

• CARON, JACQUES

Jacques Caron G – L. 6'2", 185 lbs. b: Noranda, Que., 4/21/1940.

Season	Club	League	GP	W	L	T	Mins	GA	SO	Avg	AAvg	Eff	SA	S%	SAPG	GP	W	L	T	Mins	GA	SO	Avg	Eff	SA	S%	SAPG
1956-57	Toronto Marlboros	OHA	10	....	....	....	600	29	2	2.90	....	....	....	....	....	....	....	....	....	....	....	....	....	....	....	....	....
1957-58	Peterborough Petes	OHA	31	....	....	....	1840	113	1	3.68	....	....	....	....	....	4	....	....	....	240	14	0	3.50	....	....	....	....
1958-59	Peterborough Petes	OHA	43	24	14	4	2580	129	2	*3.00	....	....	....	....	....	13	9	3	1	780	35	2	2.69	....	....	....	....
1959-60	Washington Presidents	EHL	55	....	....	....	3300	218	3	3.97	....	....	....	....	....	....	....	....	....	....	....	....	....	....	....	....	....
1960-61	Rouyn-Noranda Alouettes	NOHA	STATISTICS NOT AVAILABLE																								
1961-62	Springfield Indians	AHL	5	3	2	0	300	17	1	3.40	....	....	....	....	....	....	....	....	....	....	....	....	....	....	....	....	....
	Charlotte Clippers	EHL	5	....	....	....	300	26	0	5.20	....	....	....	....	....	....	....	....	....	....	....	....	....	....	....	....	....
1962-63	Springfield Indians	AHL	38	13	16	4	2180	112	2	3.08	....	....	....	....	....	....	....	....	....	....	....	....	....	....	....	....	....
1963-64	Springfield Indians	AHL	31	12	14	1	1780	110	0	3.71	....	....	....	....	....	....	....	....	....	....	....	....	....	....	....	....	....
1964-65	Springfield Indians	AHL	55	21	29	4	3321	195	2	3.52	....	....	....	....	....	....	....	....	....	....	....	....	....	....	....	....	....
1965-66	Springfield Indians	AHL	33	15	15	1	1832	80	2	2.62	....	....	....	....	....	6	3	3	0	360	14	0	2.33	....	....	....	....
1966-67	Springfield Indians	AHL	35	11	17	5	1866	136	1	4.37	....	....	....	....	....	....	....	....	....	....	....	....	....	....	....	....	....
1967-68	Springfield Kings	AHL	42	19	18	4	2393	151	0	3.79	....	....	....	....	....	....	....	....	....	....	....	....	....	....	....	....	....
	Los Angeles Kings	**NHL**	**1**	**0**	**1**	**0**	**60**	**4**	**0**	**4.00**	**4.43**	....	....	....	....	....	....	....	....	....	....	....	....	....	....	....	....
1968-69	Denver Spurs	WHL	31	7	21	3	1764	122	2	4.15	....	....	....	....	....	....	....	....	....	....	....	....	....	....	....	....	....
	Los Angeles Kings	**NHL**	**3**	**0**	**1**	**0**	**140**	**9**	**0**	**3.86**	**4.00**	....	....	....	....	....	....	....	....	....	....	....	....	....	....	....	....
1969-70	Denver Spurs	WHL	31	8	16	4	1548	120	0	4.65	....	....	....	....	....	....	....	....	....	....	....	....	....	....	....	....	....
1970-71	Denver Spurs	WHL	30	10	13	4	1668	109	2	3.92	....	....	....	....	....	2	0	2	0	120	9	0	4.50	....	....	....	....
1971-72	Denver Spurs	WHL	20	15	3	0	1160	45	0	2.32	....	....	....	....	....	....	....	....	....	....	....	....	....	....	....	....	....
	St. Louis Blues	**NHL**	**28**	**14**	**8**	**5**	**1619**	**68**	**1**	**2.52**	**2.53**	....	....	....	....	**9**	**4**	**5**	....	**499**	**26**	**0**	**3.13**	....	....	....	....
1972-73	**St. Louis Blues**	**NHL**	**30**	**8**	**14**	**5**	**1562**	**92**	**1**	**3.53**	**3.33**	....	....	....	....	**3**	**0**	**2**	....	**140**	**8**	**0**	**3.43**	....	....	....	....
1973-74	**Vancouver Canucks**	**NHL**	**10**	**2**	**5**	**1**	**465**	**38**	**0**	**4.90**	**4.75**	....	....	....	....	....	....	....	....	....	....	....	....	....	....	....	....
1974-75	Syracuse Eagles	AHL	50	16	21	9	2755	170	0	3.70	....	....	....	....	....	1	0	1	0	60	8	0	8.00	....	....	....	....

			REGULAR SEASON													PLAYOFFS											
Season	Club	League	GP	W	L	T	Mins	GA	SO	Avg	AAvg	Eff	SA	S%	SAPG	GP	W	L	T	Mins	GA	SO	Avg	Eff	SA	S%	SAPG
1975-76	Syracuse Blazers	NAHL	32	....	....	....	1725	90	3	3.10	....	....	....	....	....	....	....	....	....	....	....	....	....	....	....	....	....
	Cleveland Crusaders	WHA	2	1	0	1	130	8	0	3.69	....	....	....	....	....	....	....	....	....	....	....	....	....	....	....	....	....
1976-77	Syracuse Blazers	NAHL	22	....	....	....	1307	83	1	3.63	....	....	....	....	....	....	....	....	....	....	....	....	....	....	....	....	....
	Cincinnati Stingers	WHA	24	13	6	2	1292	61	3	2.83	....	....	....	....	....	1	0	1	0	14	3	0	12.86	....	....	....	....
1977-78	Binghamton Whalers	AHL	1	0	0	0	1	0	0	0.00	....	....	....	....	....	....	....	....	....	....	....	....	....	....	....	....	....
1978-79				DID NOT PLAY																							
1979-80				DID NOT PLAY																							
1980-81	Binghamton Whalers	AHL	1	0	0	0	19	1	0	3.16	....	....	....	....	....	....	....	....	....	....	....	....	....	....	....	....	....
	NHL Totals		**72**	**24**	**29**	**11**	**3846**	**211**	**2**	**3.29**	....	....	....	....	....	**12**	**4**	**7**	....	**639**	**34**	**0**	**3.19**	....	....	....	....
	Other Major League Totals		26	14	6	3	1422	69	3	2.91	....	....	....	....	....	1	0	1	0	14	3	0	12.86	....	....	....	....

NAHL First All-Star Team (1976)

Rights transferred to **LA Kings** when NHL club purchased **Springfield** (AHL) franchise, May, 1967. Claimed by **St. Louis** (Denver-WHL) from **LA Kings** in Reverse Draft, June 12, 1969. Selected by **Dayton-Houston** (WHA) in 1972 WHA General Player Draft, February 12, 1972. Claimed by **Vancouver** (Seattle-WHL) from **St. Louis** in Reverse Draft, June 15, 1973. Traded to **Buffalo** by **Vancouver** for future considerations, September 15, 1974. WHA rights traded to **Cleveland** (WHA) by **Houston** (WHA) for future considerations, February, 1976. Signed as a free agent by **Cincinnati** (WHA) after **Cleveland** (WHA) franchise folded, July, 1976.

• CARTER, LYLE

Lyle Carter G – L. 6'1", 185 lbs. b: Truro, N.S., 4/29/1945.

Season	Club	League	GP	W	L	T	Mins	GA	SO	Avg	AAvg	Eff	SA	S%	SAPG	GP	W	L	T	Mins	GA	SO	Avg	Eff	SA	S%	SAPG
1962-63	Windsor Maple Leafs	NSSHL	12	....	....	....	720	77	0	6.24	....	....	....	....	....	....	....	....	....	....	....	....	....	....	....	....	....
	Brampton 7-Ups	OHA	11	....	....	....	640	52	0	4.88	....	....	....	....	....	....	....	....	....	....	....	....	....	....	....	....	....
1963-64				DID NOT PLAY – INJURED																							
1964-65	New Glasgow Rangers	NSSHL	45	....	....	....	2700	172	0	*3.76	....	....	....	....	....	....	....	....	....	....	....	....	....	....	....	....	....
1965-66	Orillia Travelways	Sr. B		STATISTICS NOT AVAILABLE																							
1966-67	Gander Flyers	Nfld.		STATISTICS NOT AVAILABLE																							
1967-68	Cleveland Barons	AHL	2	....	....	....	120	12	0	6.00	....	....	....	....	....	....	....	....	....	....	....	....	....	....	....	....	....
	Toledo Blades	IHL	1	1	0	0	60	4	0	4.00	....	....	....	....	....	....	....	....	....	....	....	....	....	....	....	....	....
1968-69	Clinton Comets	EHL	72	*44	18	10	4320	169	*13	*2.35	....	....	....	....	....	15	8	7	0	900	40	0	*2.67	....	....	....	....
1969-70	Montreal Voyageurs	AHL	5	....	....	....	154	8	0	3.12	....	....	....	....	....	....	....	....	....	....	....	....	....	....	....	....	....
	Clinton Comets	EHL	5	....	....	....	300	11	3	2.20	....	....	....	....	....	....	....	....	....	....	....	....	....	....	....	....	....
1970-71	Montreal Voyageurs	AHL	1	0	1	0	40	5	0	7.50	....	....	....	....	....	....	....	....	....	....	....	....	....	....	....	....	....
	Muskegon Mohawks	IHL	50	30	15	4	2958	120	*6	*2.44	....	....	....	....	....	6	2	4	0	360	20	0	3.33	....	....	....	....
1971-72	Baltimore Clippers	AHL	6	1	2	1	237	15	0	3.79	....	....	....	....	....	....	....	....	....	....	....	....	....	....	....	....	....
	Salt Lake Golden Eagles	WHL	9	4	3	2	538	26	0	2.89	....	....	....	....	....	....	....	....	....	....	....	....	....	....	....	....	....
	California Golden Seals	**NHL**	**15**	**4**	**7**	**0**	**721**	**50**	**0**	**4.16**	**4.20**	....	....	....	....	....	....	....	....	....	....	....	....	....	....	....	....
	Oklahoma City Blazers	CHL	....	....	....	....	....	....	....	....	....	....	....	....	....	5	2	3	0	279	18	0	3.87	....	....	....	....
1972-73	Salt Lake Golden Eagles	WHL	35	17	14	4	2009	120	1	3.58	....	....	....	....	....	2	2	0	0	120	7	0	3.50	....	....	....	....
1973-74	New Haven Nighthawks	AHL	37	17	11	6	2034	101	1	2.97	....	....	....	....	....	10	4	6	0	636	33	0	3.11	....	....	....	....
1974-75	Syracuse Eagles	AHL	32	5	20	1	1561	133	0	5.11	....	....	....	....	....	....	....	....	....	....	....	....	....	....	....	....	....
	Greensboro Generals	SHL	4	....	....	....	216	17	0	4.72	....	....	....	....	....	....	....	....	....	....	....	....	....	....	....	....	....
	NHL Totals		**15**	**4**	**7**	**0**	**721**	**50**	**0**	**4.16**	....	....	....	....	....	....	....	....	....	....	....	....	....	....	....	....	....

EHL North First All-Star Team (1969) • Won George L. Davis Jr. Trophy (fewest goals against - EHL) (1969) • IHL First All-Star Team (1971) • Won James Norris Memorial Trophy (fewest goals against - IHL) (1971) • Won James Gatschene Memorial Trophy (MVP - IHL) (1971)

Signed as a free agent by **Montreal** (Cleveland - AHL), March 30, 1968. Traded to **California** by **Montreal** with John French for Randy Rota, October, 1971. Claimed by **Minnesota** (Jacksonville - AHL) from **California** in Reverse Draft, June 10, 1973. Traded to **Syracuse** (AHL) by **Minnesota** for cash, August, 1974.

• CASEY, JON

Jon Casey G – L. 5'10", 155 lbs. b: Grand Rapids, MN, 3/29/1962.

Season	Club	League	GP	W	L	T	Mins	GA	SO	Avg	AAvg	Eff	SA	S%	SAPG	GP	W	L	T	Mins	GA	SO	Avg	Eff	SA	S%	SAPG
1980-81	University of North Dakota	WCHA	5	3	1	0	300	19	0	3.80	....	....	....	....	....	....	....	....	....	....	....	....	....	....	....	....	....
1981-82	University of North Dakota	WCHA	18	15	3	0	1038	48	1	2.77	....	....	....	....	....	....	....	....	....	....	....	....	....	....	....	....	....
	United States	WJC-A	5	1	2	0	219	15	0	4.11	....	....	....	....	....	....	....	....	....	....	....	....	....	....	....	....	....
1982-83	University of North Dakota	WCHA	17	9	6	2	1020	42	0	2.51	....	....	....	....	....	....	....	....	....	....	....	....	....	....	....	....	....
1983-84	University of North Dakota	WCHA	37	25	10	2	2180	115	2	3.13	....	....	....	....	....	....	....	....	....	....	....	....	....	....	....	....	....
	Minnesota North Stars	**NHL**	**2**	**1**	**0**	**0**	**84**	**6**	**0**	**4.29**	**3.36**	**4.36**	**59**	**.898**	**42.1**	....	....	....	....	....	....	....	....	....	....	....	....
1984-85	Baltimore Skipjacks	AHL	46	30	11	4	2646	116	*4	*2.63	....	....	....	....	....	*13	8	3	....	689	38	0	3.31	....	....	....	....
1985-86	**Minnesota North Stars**	**NHL**	**26**	**11**	**11**	**1**	**1402**	**91**	**0**	**3.89**	**3.02**	**4.49**	**789**	**.885**	**33.8**	....	....	....	....	....	....	....	....	....	....	....	....
	Springfield Indians	AHL	9	4	3	1	464	30	0	3.88	....	....	....	....	....	....	....	....	....	....	....	....	....	....	....	....	....
1986-87	Springfield Indians	AHL	13	1	8	0	770	56	0	4.36	....	....	....	....	....	....	....	....	....	....	....	....	....	....	....	....	....
	Indianapolis Checkers	IHL	31	14	15	0	1794	133	0	4.45	....	....	....	....	....	....	....	....	....	....	....	....	....	....	....	....	....
1987-88	**Minnesota North Stars**	**NHL**	**14**	**1**	**7**	**4**	**663**	**41**	**0**	**3.71**	**3.08**	**4.37**	**348**	**.882**	**31.5**	....	....	....	....	....	....	....	....	....	....	....	....
	Kalamazoo Wings	IHL	42	24	13	5	2541	154	2	3.64	....	....	....	....	....	7	3	3	....	382	26	0	4.08	....	....	....	....
1988-89	**Minnesota North Stars**	**NHL**	**55**	**18**	**17**	**12**	**2961**	**151**	**1**	**3.06**	**2.51**	**3.06**	**1509**	**.900**	**30.6**	**4**	**1**	**3**	....	**211**	**16**	**0**	**4.55**	**6.02**	**121**	**.868**	**34.4**
1989-90	**Minnesota North Stars**	**NHL**	**61**	***31**	**22**	**4**	**3407**	**183**	**3**	**3.22**	**2.69**	**3.35**	**1757**	**.896**	**30.9**	**7**	**3**	**4**	....	**415**	**21**	**1**	**3.04**	**2.92**	**219**	**.904**	**31.7**
	United States	WEC-A	6	....	....	....	334	15	....	2.69	....	....	....	....	....	....	....	....	....	....	....	....	....	....	....	....	....
1990-91	Minnesota North Stars	FrTour	3	....	....	....	111	9	....	4.86	....	....	....	....	....	....	....	....	....	....	....	....	....	....	....	....	....
	Minnesota North Stars	**NHL**	**55**	**21**	**20**	**11**	**3185**	**158**	**3**	**2.98**	**2.65**	**3.25**	**1450**	**.891**	**27.3**	***23**	***14**	**7**	....	***1205**	**61**	***1**	**3.04**	**3.25**	**571**	**.893**	**28.4**
1991-92	**Minnesota North Stars**	**NHL**	**52**	**19**	**23**	**5**	**2911**	**165**	**2**	**3.40**	**3.01**	**4.00**	**1401**	**.882**	**28.9**	**7**	**3**	**4**	....	**437**	**22**	**0**	**3.02**	**2.95**	**225**	**.902**	**30.9**
	Kalamazoo Wings	IHL	4	2	1	1	250	11	0	2.64	....	....	....	....	....	....	....	....	....	....	....	....	....	....	....	....	....
1992-93	**Minnesota North Stars**	**NHL**	**60**	**26**	**26**	**5**	**3476**	**193**	**3**	**3.33**	**2.83**	**3.82**	**1683**	**.885**	**29.1**	....	....	....	....	....	....	....	....	....	....	....	....
1993-94	**Boston Bruins**	**NHL**	**57**	**30**	**15**	**9**	**3192**	**153**	**4**	**2.88**	**2.73**	**3.42**	**1289**	**.881**	**24.2**	**11**	**5**	**6**	....	**698**	**34**	**0**	**2.92**	**3.22**	**308**	**.890**	**26.5**
1994-95	**St. Louis Blues**	**NHL**	**19**	**7**	**5**	**4**	**872**	**40**	**0**	**2.75**	**2.84**	**2.75**	**400**	**.900**	**27.5**	**2**	**0**	**1**	....	**30**	**2**	**0**	**4.00**	**8.00**	**10**	**.800**	**20.0**
1995-96	**St. Louis Blues**	**NHL**	**9**	**2**	**3**	**0**	**395**	**25**	**0**	**3.80**	**3.73**	**5.28**	**180**	**.861**	**27.3**	**12**	**6**	**6**	....	**747**	**36**	**1**	**2.89**	**2.75**	**378**	**.905**	**30.4**
	Peoria Rivermen	IHL	43	21	19	2	2514	128	3	3.05	....	....	....	....	....	....	....	....	....	....	....	....	....	....	....	....	....
1996-97	**St. Louis Blues**	**NHL**	**15**	**3**	**8**	**0**	**707**	**40**	**0**	**3.39**	**3.59**	**4.54**	**299**	**.866**	**25.4**	....	....	....	....	....	....	....	....	....	....	....	....
	Worcester IceCats	AHL	4	2	1	1	245	10	0	2.45	....	....	....	....	....	....	....	....	....	....	....	....	....	....	....	....	....
1997-98	Kansas City Blades	IHL	24	9	13	2	1340	62	2	2.78	....	....	....	....	....	....	....	....	....	....	....	....	....	....	....	....	....
	NHL Totals		**425**	**170**	**157**	**55**	**23255**	**1246**	**16**	**3.21**	....	....	**11164**	**.888**	....	**66**	**32**	**31**	....	**3743**	**192**	**3**	**3.08**	....	....	....	....

WCHA First All-Star Team (1982, 1984) • WCHA Second All-Star Team (1983) • NCAA West First All-American Team (1984) • AHL First All-Star Team (1985) • Won Harry "Hap" Holmes Memorial Trophy (fewest goals against - AHL) (1985) • Won Baz Bastien Memorial Trophy (Top Goaltender - AHL) (1985)

Played in NHL All-Star Game (1993)

Signed as a free agent by **Minnesota**, April 1, 1984. Transferred to **Dallas** after **Minnesota** franchise relocated, June 9, 1993. Traded to **Boston** by **Dallas** for Andy Moog and (Gord Murphy, June 20, 1993), June 25, 1993. Signed as a free agent by **St. Louis**, June 29, 1994.

• CHABOT, FREDERIC

Frederic Chabot G – L. 5'11", 175 lbs. b: Hebertville-Station, Que., 2/12/1968. New Jersey's 10th choice, 192nd overall, in 1986 Entry Draft.

Season	Club	League	GP	W	L	T	Mins	GA	SO	Avg	AAvg	Eff	SA	S%	SAPG	GP	W	L	T	Mins	GA	SO	Avg	Eff	SA	S%	SAPG
1986-87	Drummondville Voltigeurs	QMJHL	62	31	29	0	3508	293	1	5.01	....	....	....	....	....	8	2	6	....	481	40	0	4.99	....	....	....	....
1987-88	Drummondville Voltigeurs	QMJHL	58	27	24	4	3276	237	1	4.34	....	....	....	....	....	16	10	6	....	1019	56	*1	*3.30	....	....	....	....
1988-89	Prince Albert Raiders	WHL	54	21	29	0	2957	202	2	4.10	....	....	....	....	....	4	1	1	....	199	16	0	4.82	....	....	....	....
1989-90	Sherbrooke Canadiens	AHL	2	1	1	0	119	8	0	4.03	....	....	....	....	....	....	....	....	....	....	....	....	....	....	....	....	....
	Fort Wayne Komets	IHL	23	6	13	3	1208	87	1	4.32	....	....	....	....	....	....	....	....	....	....	....	....	....	....	....	....	....
1990-91	**Montreal Canadiens**	**NHL**	**3**	**0**	**0**	**1**	**108**	**6**	**0**	**3.33**	**2.97**	**4.44**	**45**	**.867**	**25.0**	....	....	....	....	....	....	....	....	....	....	....	....
	Fredericton Canadiens	AHL	35	9	15	5	1800	122	0	4.07	....	....	....	....	....	....	....	....	....	....	....	....	....	....	....	....	....
1991-92	Fredericton Canadiens	AHL	30	17	9	4	1761	79	2	*2.69	....	....	....	....	....	7	3	4	....	457	20	0	2.63	....	....	....	....
	Winston-Salem Thunderbirds	ECHL	24	15	7	2	1449	71	0	*2.94	....	....	....	....	....	....	....	....	....	....	....	....	....	....	....	....	....
1992-93	**Montreal Canadiens**	**NHL**	**1**	**0**	**0**	**0**	**40**	**1**	**0**	**1.50**	**1.20**	**0.79**	**19**	**.947**	**28.5**	....	....	....	....	....	....	....	....	....	....	....	....
	Fredericton Canadiens	AHL	45	22	17	4	2544	141	0	3.33	....	....	....	....	....	4	1	3	....	261	16	0	3.68	....	....	....	....
1993-94	**Montreal Canadiens**	**NHL**	**1**	**0**	**1**	**0**	**60**	**5**	**0**	**5.00**	**4.76**	**10.42**	**24**	**.792**	**24.0**	....	....	....	....	....	....	....	....	....	....	....	....
	Fredericton Canadiens	AHL	3	0	1	1	143	12	0	5.03	....	....	....	....	....	....	....	....	....	....	....	....	....	....	....	....	....
	Las Vegas Thunder	IHL	2	1	1	0	110	5	0	2.72	....	....	....	....	....	....	....	....	....	....	....	....	....	....	....	....	....
	Philadelphia Flyers	**NHL**	**4**	**0**	**1**	**1**	**70**	**5**	**0**	**4.29**	**4.08**	**5.36**	**40**	**.875**	**34.3**	....	....	....	....	....	....	....	....	....	....	....	....
	Hershey Bears	AHL	28	13	5	6	1464	63	2	*2.58	....	....	....	....	....	11	7	4	....	665	32	0	2.89	....	....	....	....
1994-95	Cincinnati Cyclones	IHL	48	25	12	7	2622	128	1	2.93	....	....	....	....	....	5	3	2	....	326	16	0	2.94	....	....	....	....
1995-96	Cincinnati Cyclones	IHL	38	23	9	4	2147	88	3	*2.46	....	....	....	....	....	14	9	5	....	854	37	1	2.60	....	....	....	....

			REGULAR SEASON													PLAYOFFS											
Season	Club	League	GP	W	L	T	Mins	GA	SO	Avg	AAvg	Eff	SA	S%	SAPG	GP	W	L	T	Mins	GA	SO	Avg	Eff	SA	S%	SAPG
1996-97	Houston Aeros	IHL	*72	*39	26	7	*4265	180	*7	2.53	....	....	....	....	....	13	8	5	....	777	34	*2	2.63	....	....	....	....
1997-98	**Los Angeles Kings**	**NHL**	**12**	**3**	**3**	**2**	**554**	**29**	**0**	**3.14**	**3.68**	**3.41**	**267**	**.891**	**28.9**	....	....	....	....	....	....	....	....	....	....	....	....
	Houston Aeros	IHL	22	12	7	2	1237	46	1	2.23	....	....	....	....	....	4	1	3	....	238	11	0	2.77	....	....	....	....
	NHL Totals		**21**	**3**	**5**	**4**	**832**	**46**	**0**	**3.32**	....	....	**395**	**.884**	....	....	....	....	....	....	....	....	....	....	....	....	....

WHL East All-Star Team (1989) • Won Baz Bastien Award (Top Goaltender - AHL) (1994) • IHL Second All-Star Team (1996) • IHL First All-Star Team (1997) • Won James Gatschene Memorial Trophy (MVP - IHL) (1997)

Signed as a free agent by **Montreal**, January 16, 1990. Claimed by **Tampa Bay** from **Montreal** in Expansion Draft, June 18, 1992. Traded to **Montreal** by **Tampa Bay** for J.C. Bergeron, June 19, 1992. Traded to **Philadelphia** by **Montreal** for cash, February 21, 1994. Signed as a free agent by **Florida**, August 11, 1994. Signed as a free agent by **LA Kings**, September 3, 1997. Claimed by **Nashville** from **LA Kings** in Expansion Draft, June 26, 1998. Claimed on waivers by **LA Kings** from Nashville, July 20, 1998.

• CHABOT, LORNE

Lorne "Chabotsky" Chabot G – L. 6′1″, 185 lbs. b: Montreal, Que., 10/5/1900. d: 10/10/1946.

Season	Club	League	GP	W	L	T	Mins	GA	SO	Avg	AAvg	Eff	SA	S%	SAPG	GP	W	L	T	Mins	GA	SO	Avg	Eff	SA	S%	SAPG
1920-21	Brandon Wheat Kings	MHL Sr.	1	....	....	....	60	3	0	3.00	....	....	....	....	....	....	....	....	....	....	....	....	....	....	....	....	....
1921-22	Brandon Wheat Kings	MHL Sr.	STATISTICS NOT AVAILABLE																								
1922-23	Port Arthur Ports	MHL Sr.	16	11	5	0	960	57	0	3.56	....	....	....	....	....	2	1	1	0	120	3	*1	1.50	....	....	....	....
1923-24	Port Arthur Ports	MHL Sr.	15	11	4	0	900	37	1	2.46	....	....	....	....	....	2	0	1	1	120	6	0	3.00	....	....	....	....
1924-25	Port Arthur Bearcats	MHL Sr.	20	12	8	0	1200	51	*3	2.55	....	....	....	....	....	2	2	0	0	120	4	0	2.00	....	....	....	....
1925-26	Port Arthur Bearcats	TBSHL	20	*14	6	0	1200	42	2	2.10	....	....	....	....	....	6	5	1	0	300	13	1	2.16	....	....	....	....
1926-27	**New York Rangers**	**NHL**	**36**	**22**	**9**	**5**	**2307**	**56**	**10**	**1.46**	**2.20**	....	....	....	....	**2**	**0**	**1**	**1**	**120**	**3**	**1**	**1.50**	....	....	....	....
	Springfield Indians	Can-Am	1	1	0	0	60	2	0	2.00	....	....	....	....	....	....	....	....	....	....	....	....	....	....	....	....	....
1927-28	**New York Rangers**	**NHL**	***44**	**19**	**16**	**9**	**2730**	**79**	**11**	**1.74**	**2.80**	....	....	....	....	**6**	**2**	**2**	**1**	**321**	**8**	**1**	**1.50**	....	....	....	....
1928-29	**Toronto Maple Leafs**	**NHL**	**43**	**20**	**18**	**5**	**2458**	**66**	**12**	**1.61**	**3.46**	....	....	....	....	**4**	**2**	**2**	**0**	**242**	**5**	**0**	**1.24**	....	....	....	....
1929-30	**Toronto Maple Leafs**	**NHL**	**42**	**16**	**20**	**6**	**2620**	**113**	**6**	**2.59**	**2.67**	....	....	....	....	....	....	....	....	....	....	....	....	....	....	....	....
1930-31	**Toronto Maple Leafs**	**NHL**	**37**	**21**	**8**	**8**	**2300**	**80**	**6**	**2.09**	**2.66**	....	....	....	....	**2**	**0**	**1**	**1**	**139**	**4**	**0**	**1.73**	....	....	....	....
1931-32	**Toronto Maple Leafs**	**NHL**	**44**	**22**	**16**	**6**	**2698**	**106**	**4**	**2.36**	**2.88**	....	....	....	....	***7**	***5**	**1**	**1**	**438**	**15**	**0**	**2.05**	....	....	....	....
1932-33	**Toronto Maple Leafs**	**NHL**	***48**	**24**	**18**	**6**	**2946**	**111**	**5**	**2.26**	**3.06**	....	....	....	....	***9**	**4**	**5**	**0**	***686**	**18**	***2**	**1.57**	....	....	....	....
1933-34	**Montreal Canadiens**	**NHL**	**47**	**21**	**20**	**6**	**2928**	**101**	**8**	**2.07**	**2.61**	....	....	....	....	**2**	**0**	**1**	**1**	**131**	**4**	**0**	**1.83**	....	....	....	....
1934-35	**Chicago Black Hawks**	**NHL**	***48**	**26**	**17**	**5**	**2940**	**88**	**8**	***1.80**	**2.13**	....	....	....	....	**2**	**0**	**1**	**1**	**124**	**1**	**1**	**0.48**	....	....	....	....
1935-36	**Montreal Maroons**	**NHL**	**16**	**8**	**3**	**5**	**1010**	**35**	**2**	**2.08**	**2.96**	....	....	....	....	**3**	**0**	**3**	**0**	**297**	**6**	**0**	***1.21**	....	....	....	....
1936-37	**New York Americans**	**NHL**	**6**	**2**	**3**	**1**	**370**	**25**	**1**	**4.05**	**5.13**	....	....	....	....	....	....	....	....	....	....	....	....	....	....	....	....
	NHL Totals		**411**	**201**	**148**	**62**	**25307**	**860**	**73**	**2.04**	....	....	....	....	....	**37**	**13**	**17**	**6**	**2498**	**64**	**5**	**1.54**	....	....	....	....

NHL First All-Star Team (1935) • Won Vezina Trophy (1935)

Signed as a free agent by **NY Rangers**, September 2, 1926. Traded to **Toronto** by **NY Rangers** with Alex Gray and $10,000 for John Roach and Butch Keeling, October 18, 1928. Traded to **Montreal Canadiens** by **Toronto** for George Hainsworth, October 1, 1933. Traded to **Chicago** by **Montreal Canadiens** with Howie Morenz and Marty Burke for Lionel Conacher, Roger Jenkins and Leroy Goldsworthy, October 3, 1934. Traded to **Montreal Canadiens** by **Chicago** for cash, February 8, 1936. Traded to **Montreal Maroons** by **Montreal Canadiens** for Bill Miller, Toe Blake and the rights to Ken Grivel, February 13, 1936. Traded to **NY Americans** by **Montreal Maroons** for cash, October 22, 1936.

• CHADWICK, ED

Ed "Chad" Chadwick G – L. 5′11″, 184 lbs. b: Fergus, Ont., 5/8/1933.

Season	Club	League	GP	W	L	T	Mins	GA	SO	Avg	AAvg	Eff	SA	S%	SAPG	GP	W	L	T	Mins	GA	SO	Avg	Eff	SA	S%	SAPG
1950-51	St. Michael's Majors	OHA	40	....	....	....	2350	148	2	3.78	....	....	....	....	....	....	....	....	....	....	....	....	....	....	....	....	....
1951-52	St. Michael's Majors	OHA	49	28	17	3	2900	168	0	3.48	....	....	....	....	....	8	5	3	0	490	31	*1	3.80	....	....	....	....
1952-53	St. Michael's Majors	OHA	46	....	....	....	2760	151	3	3.28	....	....	....	....	....	16	8	8	0	960	59	0	3.69	....	....	....	....
	Pittsburgh Hornets	AHL	1	1	0	0	60	1	0	1.00	....	....	....	....	....	....	....	....	....	....	....	....	....	....	....	....	....
1953-54	Stratford Indians	OHA Sr.	4	....	....	....	210	17	0	4.86	....	....	....	....	....	....	....	....	....	....	....	....	....	....	....	....	....
	Pittsburgh Hornets	AHL	2	1	1	0	120	9	0	4.50	....	....	....	....	....	....	....	....	....	....	....	....	....	....	....	....	....
1954-55	Sault Ste. Marie Greyhounds	NOHA	38	....	....	....	2240	96	3	*2.57	....	....	....	....	....	14	....	....	....	840	34	*2	*2.43	....	....	....	....
	Buffalo Bisons	AHL	2	1	1	0	120	10	0	5.00	....	....	....	....	....	....	....	....	....	....	....	....	....	....	....	....	....
1955-56	Winnipeg Warriors	WHL	68	*39	27	2	4129	204	2	2.96	....	....	....	....	....	20	*16	4	0	1232	52	*1	2.53	....	....	....	....
	Toronto Maple Leafs	**NHL**	**5**	**2**	**0**	**3**	**300**	**3**	**2**	**0.60**	**0.72**	....	....	....	....	....	....	....	....	....	....	....	....	....	....	....	....
1956-57	**Toronto Maple Leafs**	**NHL**	***70**	**21**	**34**	**15**	***4200**	**192**	**5**	**2.74**	**3.16**	....	....	....	....	....	....	....	....	....	....	....	....	....	....	....	....
1957-58	**Toronto Maple Leafs**	**NHL**	***70**	**21**	**38**	**11**	***4200**	**226**	**4**	**3.23**	**3.68**	....	....	....	....	....	....	....	....	....	....	....	....	....	....	....	....
1958-59	**Toronto Maple Leafs**	**NHL**	**31**	**12**	**15**	**4**	**1860**	**93**	**3**	**3.00**	**3.20**	....	....	....	....	....	....	....	....	....	....	....	....	....	....	....	....
1959-60	Rochester Americans	AHL	67	*39	24	4	4020	184	4	*2.75	....	....	....	....	....	*12	5	7	0	*720	35	0	*2.92	....	....	....	....
	Toronto Maple Leafs	**NHL**	**4**	**1**	**2**	**1**	**240**	**15**	**0**	**3.75**	**3.94**	....	....	....	....	....	....	....	....	....	....	....	....	....	....	....	....
1960-61	Rochester Americans	AHL	*71	32	35	4	*4300	236	2	3.29	....	....	....	....	....	....	....	....	....	....	....	....	....	....	....	....	....
1961-62	Kingston Frontenacs	EPHL	67	36	23	8	4020	214	2	3.19	....	....	....	....	....	11	6	5	0	671	36	*1	3.22	....	....	....	....
	Boston Bruins	**NHL**	**4**	**0**	**3**	**1**	**240**	**22**	**0**	**5.50**	**5.68**	....	....	....	....	....	....	....	....	....	....	....	....	....	....	....	....
1962-63	Hershey Bears	AHL	*68	34	26	7	*4080	219	*6	3.22	....	....	....	....	....	*15	*8	7	0	*922	42	*1	2.73	....	....	....	....
1963-64	Hershey Bears	AHL	57	31	22	3	3340	189	2	3.40	....	....	....	....	....	6	3	3	0	360	29	0	4.84	....	....	....	....
1964-65	Buffalo Bisons	AHL	61	33	21	6	3696	186	*5	3.02	....	....	....	....	....	9	5	4	0	542	18	*2	*1.99	....	....	....	....
1965-66	Buffalo Bisons	AHL	34	14	18	1	1983	102	3	3.09	....	....	....	....	....	....	....	....	....	....	....	....	....	....	....	....	....
1966-67	Buffalo Bisons	AHL	36	5	23	2	1829	158	0	5.18	....	....	....	....	....	....	....	....	....	....	....	....	....	....	....	....	....
1967-68	Buffalo Bisons	AHL	18	5	8	1	881	55	1	3.75	....	....	....	....	....	1	0	0	0	53	5	0	5.66	....	....	....	....
	NHL Totals		**184**	**57**	**92**	**35**	**11040**	**551**	**14**	**2.99**	....	....	....	....	....	....	....	....	....	....	....	....	....	....	....	....	....

AHL First All-Star Team (1960) • Won Harry "Hap" Holmes Memorial Award (fewest goals against - AHL) (1960) • AHL Second All-Star Team (1961, 1965)

Traded to **Boston** by **Toronto** for Don Simmons, January 31, 1961. Traded to **Hershey** (AHL) by **Boston** with Barry Ashbee for Bob Perreault, June, 1962. Traded to **Chicago** by **Hershey** (AHL) for cash, August, 1964.

• CHAMPOUX, BOB

Bob Champoux G – L. 5′10″, 175 lbs. b: St. Hilaire, Que., 12/2/1942.

Season	Club	League	GP	W	L	T	Mins	GA	SO	Avg	AAvg	Eff	SA	S%	SAPG	GP	W	L	T	Mins	GA	SO	Avg	Eff	SA	S%	SAPG
1961-62	Montreal Jr. Canadiens	OHA	8	....	....	....	480	25	0	3.13	....	....	....	....	....	....	....	....	....	....	....	....	....	....	....	....	....
1962-63	St. Jerome Alouettes	QJHL	STATISTICS NOT AVAILABLE																								
1963-64	Cincinnati Wings	CHL	60	10	44	5	3610	337	1	5.60	....	....	....	....	....	....	....	....	....	....	....	....	....	....	....	....	....
	Detroit Red Wings	**NHL**	....	....	....	....	....	....	....	....	....	....	....	....	....	**1**	**1**	**0**	....	**55**	**4**	**0**	**4.36**	....	....	....	....
1964-65	Memphis Wings	CHL	4	1	3	0	240	16	0	4.00	....	....	....	....	....	....	....	....	....	....	....	....	....	....	....	....	....
	Minneapolis Bruins	CHL	1	1	0	0	60	0	1	0.00	....	....	....	....	....	....	....	....	....	....	....	....	....	....	....	....	....
	Pittsburgh Hornets	AHL	13	4	8	0	740	50	1	4.05	....	....	....	....	....	....	....	....	....	....	....	....	....	....	....	....	....
1965-66	Pittsburgh Hornets	AHL	8	4	3	0	412	21	1	3.06	....	....	....	....	....	....	....	....	....	....	....	....	....	....	....	....	....
	Memphis Wings	CHL	1	0	1	0	60	6	0	6.00	....	....	....	....	....	....	....	....	....	....	....	....	....	....	....	....	....
1966-67	San Diego Gulls	WHL	20	7	11	1	1140	72	0	3.86	....	....	....	....	....	....	....	....	....	....	....	....	....	....	....	....	....
1967-68	San Diego Gulls	WHL	33	15	16	2	1957	111	0	3.40	....	....	....	....	....	5	3	2	0	306	12	0	2.35	....	....	....	....
1968-69	San Diego Gulls	WHl	37	13	15	6	2048	123	*3	3.60	....	....	....	....	....	7	3	4	0	399	21	0	3.16	....	....	....	....
1969-70	San Diego Gulls	WHL	1	0	1	0	60	4	0	4.00	....	....	....	....	....	....	....	....	....	....	....	....	....	....	....	....	....
	Kansas City Blues	CHL	2	2	0	0	120	10	0	5.00	....	....	....	....	....	....	....	....	....	....	....	....	....	....	....	....	....
	Dallas Black Hawks	CHL	25	8	16	1	1460	89	2	3.66	....	....	....	....	....	....	....	....	....	....	....	....	....	....	....	....	....
1970-71	San Diego Gulls	WHL	2	0	1	1	120	6	0	3.00	....	....	....	....	....	....	....	....	....	....	....	....	....	....	....	....	....
	Jacksonville Rockets	EHL	21	....	....	....	1260	112	0	5.33	....	....	....	....	....	....	....	....	....	....	....	....	....	....	....	....	....
1971-72			DID NOT PLAY																								
1972-73	San Diego Gulls	WHL	24	8	9	5	1339	74	1	3.31	....	....	....	....	....	4	2	1	0	214	10	*1	2.80	....	....	....	....
1973-74	San Diego Gulls	WHL	2	0	2	0	120	8	0	4.00	....	....	....	....	....	....	....	....	....	....	....	....	....	....	....	....	....
	California Golden Seals	**NHL**	**17**	**2**	**11**	**3**	**923**	**80**	**0**	**5.20**	**5.06**	....	....	....	....	....	....	....	....	....	....	....	....	....	....	....	....
	Salt Lake Golden Eagles	WHL	44	23	16	3	2586	139	2	3.23	....	....	....	....	....	3	1	1	0	140	10	0	4.29	....	....	....	....
1974-75	Winston-Salem Polar Bears	SHL	22	....	....	....	1287	91	0	4.24	....	....	....	....	....	7	3	4	0	422	30	0	4.27	....	....	....	....
	Syracuse Blazers	NAHL	3	2	1	0	171	8	1	2.80	....	....	....	....	....	....	....	....	....	....	....	....	....	....	....	....	....
1975-76	Winston-Salem Polar Bears	SHL	47	18	20	9	2770	161	0	3.49	....	....	....	....	....	4	0	4	0	214	18	0	5.05	....	....	....	....
1976-77	Winston-Salem Polar Bears	SHL	23	....	....	....	1269	78	1	3.69	....	....	....	....	....	....	....	....	....	....	....	....	....	....	....	....	....
	NHL Totals		**17**	**2**	**11**	**3**	**923**	**80**	**0**	**5.20**	....	....	....	....	....	**1**	**1**	**0**	....	**55**	**4**	**0**	**4.36**	....	....	....	....

Traded to **San Diego** (WHL) by **Detroit** for cash, October, 1966. Loaned to **Kansas City** (CHL) by **San Diego** (WHL) for loan of Gary Edwards, November, 1969. Signed as a free agent by **California** (Salt Lake-CHL) after securing release from San Diego (WHL), November, 1973.

Season	Club	League	REGULAR SEASON GP	W	L	T	Mins	GA	SO	Avg	AAvg	Eff	SA	S%	SAPG	PLAYOFFS GP	W	L	T	Mins	GA	SO	Avg	Eff	SA	S%	SAPG

• CHEEVERS, GERRY

Gerry "Cheesy" Cheevers G – L. 5'11", 185 lbs. b: St. Catharines, Ont., 12/7/1940. **HHOF**

Season	Club	League	GP	W	L	T	Mins	GA	SO	Avg	AAvg	Eff	SA	S%	SAPG	GP	W	L	T	Mins	GA	SO	Avg	Eff	SA	S%	SAPG
1956-57	St. Michael's Majors	OHA	1	....	....	....	60	4	0	4.00	....	....	....	....	....	....	....	....	....	....	....	....	....	....	....	....	....
1957-58	St. Michael's Majors	OHA	1	1	0	0	60	3	0	3.00	....	....	....	....	....	....	....	....	....	....	....	....	....	....	....	....	....
1958-59	St. Michael's Majors	OHA	6	....	....	....	360	28	0	4.67	....	....	....	....	....	....	....	....	....	....	....	....	....	....	....	....	....
1959-60	St. Michael's Majors	OHA	36	18	13	5	2160	111	*5	*3.08	....	....	....	....	....	....	....	....	....	....	....	....	....	....	....	....	....
1960-61	St. Michael's Majors	OHA	30	12	20	5	1775	94	2	3.18	....	....	....	....	....	....	....	....	....	....	....	....	....	....	....	....	....
1961-62	Pittsburgh Hornets	AHL	5	2	2	1	300	21	0	4.20	....	....	....	....	....	....	....	....	....	....	....	....	....	....	....	....	....
	Rochester Americans	AHL	19	9	9	1	1140	69	1	3.63	....	....	....	....	....	2	2	0	0	120	8	0	4.00	....	....	....	....
	Sault Ste. Marie Thunderbirds	EPHL	29	13	13	3	1740	103	1	3.55	....	....	....	....	....	....	....	....	....	....	....	....	....	....	....	....	....
	Toronto Maple Leafs	**NHL**	**2**	**1**	**1**	**0**	**120**	**7**	**0**	**3.50**	**3.59**	....	....	....	....	....	....	....	....	....	....	....	....	....	....	....	....
1962-63	Rochester Americans	AHL	19	7	9	3	1140	75	1	3.95	....	....	....	....	....	....	....	....	....	....	....	....	....	....	....	....	....
	Sudbury Wolves	EPHL	51	17	24	10	3060	212	4	4.15	....	....	....	....	....	*8	*4	4	0	485	29	*1	3.59	....	....	....	....
1963-64	Rochester Americans	AHL	66	*38	25	2	3960	187	3	2.84	....	....	....	....	....	2	0	2	0	120	8	0	4.00	....	....	....	....
1964-65	Rochester Americans	AHL	*72	*48	21	3	*4359	195	*5	*2.68	....	....	....	....	....	10	*8	2	0	615	24	0	2.34	....	....	....	....
1965-66	**Boston Bruins**	**NHL**	**7**	**0**	**4**	**1**	**340**	**34**	**0**	**6.00**	**6.17**	....	....	....	....	....	....	....	....	....	....	....	....	....	....	....	....
	Oklahoma City Blazers	CHL	30	16	9	5	1760	73	3	*2.49	....	....	....	....	....	9	*8	1	0	540	19	0	*2.11	....	....	....	....
1966-67	**Boston Bruins**	**NHL**	**22**	**5**	**10**	**6**	**1298**	**72**	**1**	**3.33**	**3.47**	....	....	....	....	....	....	....	....	....	....	....	....	....	....	....	....
	Oklahoma City Blazers	CHL	26	14	6	5	1520	71	1	*2.80	....	....	....	....	....	11	*8	3	0	677	29	*1	*2.57	....	....	....	....
1967-68	**Boston Bruins**	**NHL**	**47**	**23**	**17**	**5**	**2646**	**125**	**3**	**2.83**	**3.14**	....	....	....	....	**4**	**0**	**4**	....	**240**	**15**	**0**	**3.75**	....	....	....	....
1968-69	**Boston Bruins**	**NHL**	**52**	**28**	**12**	**12**	**3112**	**145**	**3**	**2.80**	**2.89**	....	....	....	....	**9**	**6**	**3**	....	**572**	**16**	***3**	**1.68**	....	....	....	....
1969-70	**Boston Bruins**	**NHL**	**41**	**24**	**8**	**8**	**2384**	**108**	**4**	**2.72**	**2.88**	....	....	....	....	***13**	***12**	**1**	....	***781**	**29**	**0**	**2.23**	....	....	....	....
1970-71	**Boston Bruins**	**NHL**	**40**	**27**	**8**	**5**	**2400**	**109**	**3**	**2.73**	**2.69**	....	....	....	....	**6**	**3**	**3**	....	**360**	**21**	**0**	**3.50**	....	....	....	....
1971-72	**Boston Bruins**	**NHL**	**41**	**27**	**5**	**8**	**2420**	**101**	**2**	**2.50**	**2.50**	....	....	....	....	**8**	***6**	**2**	....	**483**	**21**	***2**	**2.61**	....	....	....	....
1972-73	Cleveland Crusaders	WHA	52	32	20	0	3144	149	*5	*2.84	....	....	....	....	....	9	5	4	0	548	22	0	*2.41	....	....	....	....
1973-74	Cleveland Crusaders	WHA	*59	30	20	6	*3562	180	*4	3.03	....	....	....	....	....	5	1	4	0	303	18	0	3.56	....	....	....	....
1974-75	Canada	Summit	7	....	....	....	420	24	....	3.43	....	....	....	....	....	....	....	....	....	....	....	....	....	....	....	....	....
	Cleveland Crusaders	WHA	52	26	24	2	3076	167	*4	3.26	....	....	....	....	....	5	1	4	0	300	23	0	4.60	....	....	....	....
1975-76	Cleveland Crusaders	WHA	28	11	14	1	1570	95	1	*3.63	....	....	....	....	....	....	....	....	....	....	....	....	....	....	....	....	....
	Boston Bruins	**NHL**	**15**	**8**	**2**	**5**	**900**	**41**	**1**	**2.73**	**2.46**	....	....	....	....	**6**	**2**	**4**	....	**392**	**14**	**1**	**2.14**	....	....	....	....
1976-77	Canada	C Cup	DID NOT PLAY – SPARE GOALTENDER																								
	Boston Bruins	**NHL**	**45**	**30**	**10**	**5**	**2700**	**137**	**3**	**3.04**	**2.82**	....	....	....	....	***14**	**8**	**5**	....	***858**	**44**	**1**	**3.08**	....	....	....	....
1977-78	**Boston Bruins**	**NHL**	**21**	**10**	**5**	**2**	**1086**	**48**	**1**	**2.65**	**2.47**	....	....	....	....	**12**	**8**	**4**	....	**731**	**35**	**1**	**2.87**	....	....	....	....
1978-79	**Boston Bruins**	**NHL**	**43**	**23**	**9**	**10**	**2509**	**132**	**1**	**3.16**	**2.78**	....	....	....	....	**6**	**4**	**2**	....	**360**	**15**	**0**	**2.50**	....	....	....	....
	NHL All-Stars	Chal Cup	1	0	1	0	60	6	0	6.00	....	....	....	....	....	....	....	....	....	....	....	....	....	....	....	....	....
1979-80	**Boston Bruins**	**NHL**	**42**	**24**	**11**	**7**	**2479**	**116**	**4**	**2.81**	**2.46**	....	....	....	....	**10**	**4**	**6**	....	**619**	**32**	**0**	**3.10**	....	....	....	....
	NHL Totals		**418**	**230**	**102**	**74**	**24394**	**1175**	**26**	**2.89**	....	....	....	....	....	**88**	**53**	**34**	....	**5396**	**242**	**8**	**2.69**	....	....	....	....
	Other Major League Totals		191	99	78	9	11352	591	14	3.12	....	....	....	....	....	19	7	12	0	1151	63	0	3.28	....	....	....	....

AHL First All-Star Team (1965) • Won Harry "Hap" Holmes Memorial Award (fewest goals against - AHL) (1965) • Won Terry Sawchuk Trophy (fewest goals against - CHL) (1967) • WHA First All-Star Team (1973) • Won Ben Hatskin Trophy (WHA Top Goaltender) (1973) • WHA Second All-Star Team (1974, 1975)

Played in NHL All-Star Game (1969)

Claimed by **Boston** from **Toronto** in Intra-League Draft, June 9, 1965. Selected by **New England** (WHA) in 1972 WHA General Player Draft, February 12, 1972. WHA rights traded to **Cleveland** (WHA) by **New England** (WHA) for cash, June, 1972. • Suspended by **Cleveland** (WHA) for refusing to play, January 25, 1976. Signed as a free agent by **Boston** after securing his release from **Cleveland** (WHA), January 27, 1976.

• CHEVELDAE, TIM

Tim Cheveldae G – L. 5'10", 195 lbs. b: Melville, Sask., 2/15/1968. Detroit's 4th choice, 64th overall, in 1986 Entry Draft.

Season	Club	League	GP	W	L	T	Mins	GA	SO	Avg	AAvg	Eff	SA	S%	SAPG	GP	W	L	T	Mins	GA	SO	Avg	Eff	SA	S%	SAPG
1985-86	Saskatoon Blades	WHL	36	21	10	3	2030	165	0	4.88	....	....	....	....	....	8	6	2	....	480	29	0	3.63	....	....	....	....
1986-87	Saskatoon Blades	WHL	33	20	11	0	1909	133	2	4.18	....	....	....	....	....	5	4	1	....	308	20	0	3.90	....	....	....	....
1987-88	Saskatoon Blades	WHL	66	44	19	3	3798	235	1	3.71	....	....	....	....	....	6	4	2	....	364	27	0	4.45	....	....	....	....
1988-89	**Detroit Red Wings**	**NHL**	**2**	**0**	**2**	**0**	**122**	**9**	**0**	**4.43**	**3.65**	**5.39**	**74**	**.878**	**36.4**	....	....	....	....	....	....	....	....	....	....	....	....
	Adirondack Red Wings	AHL	30	20	8	0	1694	98	1	3.47	....	....	....	....	....	2	1	0	....	99	9	0	5.45	....	....	....	....
1989-90	**Detroit Red Wings**	**NHL**	**28**	**10**	**9**	**8**	**1600**	**101**	**0**	**3.79**	**3.18**	**4.48**	**854**	**.882**	**32.0**	....	....	....	....	....	....	....	....	....	....	....	....
	Adirondack Red Wings	AHL	31	17	8	6	1848	116	0	3.77	....	....	....	....	....	....	....	....	....	....	....	....	....	....	....	....	....
1990-91	**Detroit Red Wings**	**NHL**	**65**	**30**	**26**	**5**	**3615**	**214**	**2**	**3.55**	**3.17**	**4.43**	**1716**	**.875**	**28.5**	**7**	**3**	**4**	....	**398**	**22**	**0**	**3.32**	**3.51**	**208**	**.894**	**31.4**
1991-92	**Detroit Red Wings**	**NHL**	***72**	***38**	**23**	**9**	***4236**	**226**	**2**	**3.20**	**2.83**	**3.66**	**1978**	**.886**	**28.0**	**11**	**3**	**7**	....	**597**	**25**	***2**	**2.51**	**2.27**	**277**	**.910**	**27.8**
1992-93	**Detroit Red Wings**	**NHL**	**67**	**34**	**24**	**7**	**3880**	**210**	**4**	**3.25**	**2.76**	**3.60**	**1897**	**.889**	**29.3**	**7**	**3**	**4**	....	**423**	**24**	**0**	**3.40**	**4.08**	**200**	**.880**	**28.4**
1993-94	**Detroit Red Wings**	**NHL**	**30**	**16**	**9**	**1**	**1572**	**91**	**1**	**3.47**	**3.31**	**4.34**	**727**	**.875**	**27.7**	....	....	....	....	....	....	....	....	....	....	....	....
	Adirondack Red Wings	AHL	2	1	0	1	125	7	0	3.36	....	....	....	....	....	....	....	....	....	....	....	....	....	....	....	....	....
	Winnipeg Jets	**NHL**	**14**	**5**	**8**	**1**	**788**	**52**	**1**	**3.96**	**3.77**	**4.25**	**485**	**.893**	**36.9**	....	....	....	....	....	....	....	....	....	....	....	....
1994-95	**Winnipeg Jets**	**NHL**	**30**	**8**	**16**	**3**	**1571**	**97**	**0**	**3.70**	**3.84**	**4.39**	**818**	**.881**	**31.2**	....	....	....	....	....	....	....	....	....	....	....	....
1995-96	**Winnipeg Jets**	**NHL**	**30**	**8**	**18**	**3**	**1695**	**111**	**0**	**3.93**	**3.87**	**4.60**	**948**	**.883**	**33.6**	....	....	....	....	....	....	....	....	....	....	....	....
	Hershey Bears	AHL	8	4	3	0	457	31	0	4.07	....	....	....	....	....	4	2	2	....	250	14	0	3.36	....	....	....	....
1996-97	**Boston Bruins**	**NHL**	**2**	**0**	**1**	**0**	**93**	**5**	**0**	**3.23**	**3.42**	**4.89**	**33**	**.848**	**21.3**	....	....	....	....	....	....	....	....	....	....	....	....
	Fort Wayne Komets	IHL	21	6	9	4	1137	75	0	3.96	....	....	....	....	....	....	....	....	....	....	....	....	....	....	....	....	....
1997-98	Las Vegas Thunder	IHL	38	9	17	5	1942	128	0	3.95	....	....	....	....	....	....	....	....	....	....	....	....	....	....	....	....	....
	NHL Totals		**340**	**149**	**136**	**37**	**19172**	**1116**	**10**	**3.49**	....	....	**9530**	**.883**	....	**25**	**9**	**15**	....	**1418**	**71**	**2**	**3.00**	....	....	....	....

WHL East All-Star Team (1988)

Played in NHL All-Star Game (1992)

Traded to **Winnipeg** by **Detroit** with Dallas Drake for Bob Essensa and Sergei Bautin, March 8, 1994. Traded to **Philadelphia** by **Winnipeg** with Winnipeg's 3rd round choice (Chester Gallant) in 1996 Entry Draft for Dominic Roussel, February 27, 1996. Signed as a free agent by **Boston**, August 27, 1996.

• CHEVRIER, ALAIN

Alain Chevrier G – L. 5'8", 180 lbs. b: Cornwall, Ont., 4/23/1961.

Season	Club	League	GP	W	L	T	Mins	GA	SO	Avg	AAvg	Eff	SA	S%	SAPG	GP	W	L	T	Mins	GA	SO	Avg	Eff	SA	S%	SAPG
1980-81	University of Miami-Ohio	NCAA	16	....	....	....	778	44	0	3.39	....	....	....	....	....	....	....	....	....	....	....	....	....	....	....	....	....
1981-82	University of Miami-Ohio	CCHA	19	8	10	1	1053	73	0	4.16	....	....	....	....	....	....	....	....	....	....	....	....	....	....	....	....	....
1982-83	University of Miami-Ohio	CCHA	33	15	16	1	1894	125	....	3.96	....	....	....	....	....	....	....	....	....	....	....	....	....	....	....	....	....
1983-84	University of Miami-Ohio	CCHA	32	9	19	1	1509	123	....	4.89	....	....	....			....	....	....	....	....	....	....	....	....	....	....	....
1984-85	Fort Wayne Komets	IHL	56	26	21	7	3219	194	0	3.62	....	....	....	....	....	9	5	4	0	556	28	0	3.02	....	....	....	....
1985-86	**New Jersey Devils**	**NHL**	**37**	**11**	**18**	**2**	**1862**	**143**	**0**	**4.61**	**3.60**	**6.93**	**951**	**.850**	**30.6**	....	....	....	....	....	....	....	....	....	....	....	....
1986-87	**New Jersey Devils**	**NHL**	**58**	**24**	**26**	**2**	**3153**	**227**	**0**	**4.32**	**3.65**	**5.47**	**1793**	**.873**	**34.1**	....	....	....	....	....	....	....	....	....	....	....	....
1987-88	**New Jersey Devils**	**NHL**	**45**	**18**	**19**	**3**	**2354**	**148**	**1**	**3.77**	**3.14**	**5.00**	**1117**	**.868**	**28.5**	....	....	....	....	....	....	....	....	....	....	....	....
1988-89	**Winnipeg Jets**	**NHL**	**22**	**8**	**8**	**2**	**1092**	**78**	**1**	**4.29**	**3.54**	**6.04**	**554**	**.859**	**30.4**	....	....	....	....	....	....	....	....	....	....	....	....
	Chicago Blackhawks	**NHL**	**27**	**13**	**11**	**2**	**1573**	**92**	**0**	**3.51**	**2.89**	**4.36**	**740**	**.876**	**28.2**	**16**	**9**	**7**	....	**1013**	**44**	**0**	**2.61**	**2.37**	**484**	**.909**	**28.7**
1989-90	**Chicago Blackhawks**	**NHL**	**39**	**16**	**14**	**3**	**1894**	**132**	**0**	**4.18**	**3.51**	**6.14**	**898**	**.853**	**28.4**	....	....	....	....	....	....	....	....	....	....	....	....
	Pittsburgh Penguins	**NHL**	**3**	**1**	**2**	**0**	**166**	**14**	**0**	**5.06**	**4.24**	**7.96**	**89**	**.843**	**32.2**	....	....	....	....	....	....	....	....	....	....	....	....
1990-91	**Detroit Red Wings**	**NHL**	**3**	**0**	**2**	**0**	**108**	**11**	**0**	**6.11**	**5.46**	**12.22**	**55**	**.800**	**30.6**	....	....	....	....	....	....	....	....	....	....	....	....
	San Diego Gulls	IHL	32	10	16	1	1689	124	0	4.40	....	....	....	....	....	....	....	....	....	....	....	....	....	....	....	....	....
	NHL Totals		**234**	**91**	**100**	**14**	**12202**	**845**	**2**	**4.16**	....	....	**6197**	**.864**	....	**16**	**9**	**7**	....	**1013**	**44**	**0**	**2.61**	....	....	....	....

Signed as a free agent by **New Jersey**, May 31, 1985. Traded to **Winnipeg** by **New Jersey** with New Jersey's 7th round choice (Doug Evans) in 1989 Entry Draft for Steve Rooney and Winnipeg's 3rd round choice (Brad Bombardir) in 1990 Entry Draft, July 19, 1988. Traded to **Chicago** by **Winnipeg** for Chicago's 4th round choice (Allain Roy) in 1989 Entry Draft, January 19, 1989. Traded to **Pittsburgh** by **Chicago** for future considerations, March 6, 1990. Signed as a free agent by **Detroit**, July 5, 1990.

• CLANCY, KING

King (Francis Michael) Clancy G – L. 5'9", 184 lbs. b: Ottawa, Ont., 2/25/1903. d: 11/8/1986. **HHOF**

Season	Club	League	GP	W	L	T	Mins	GA	SO	Avg	AAvg	Eff	SA	S%	SAPG	GP	W	L	T	Mins	GA	SO	Avg	Eff	SA	S%	SAPG
1924-25	**Ottawa Senators**	**NHL**	**1**	**0**	**0**	**0**	**2**	**0**	**0**	**0.00**	**0.00**	....	....	....	....	....	....	....	....	....	....	....	....	....	....	....	....
1931-32	**Toronto Maple Leafs**	**NHL**	**1**	**0**	**0**	**0**	**1**	**1**	**0**	**60.00**	**73.84**	....	....	....	....	....	....	....	....	....	....	....	....	....	....	....	....
	NHL Totals		**2**	**0**	**0**	**0**	**3**	**1**	**0**	**20.00**	....	....	....	....	....	....	....	....	....	....	....	....	....	....	....	....	....

• Ottawa defenseman replaced penalized Alex Connell, December 27, 1924. (Ottawa 4, Toronto 3) • Toronto defenseman replaced penalized Lorne Chabot, March 15, 1932. (Detroit 6, Toronto 2).

			REGULAR SEASON												PLAYOFFS								
Season	Club	League	GP	W	L	T	Mins	GA	SO	Avg	AAvg	Eff	SA	S%	SAPG	GP	W	L	T	Mins	GA	SO	Avg	Eff	SA	S%	SAPG

● CLEGHORN, ODIE — Odie (Ogilvie James) Cleghorn G – R. 5'9", 195 lbs. b: Montreal, Que..

Season	Club	League	GP	W	L	T	Mins	GA	SO	Avg	AAvg
1925-26	Pittsburgh Pirates	NHL	1	1	0	0	60	2	0	2.00	2.68
	NHL Totals		1	1	0	0	60	2	0	2.00	....

• Pittsburgh playing coach replaced Roy Worters, February 23, 1926. (Pittsburgh 3, Montreal Canadiens 2)

● CLEGHORN, SPRAGUE — Sprague Cleghorn G – L. 5'10", 190 lbs. b: Montreal, Que., 3/11/1990. d: 7/11/1956.   HHOF

Season	Club	League	GP	W	L	T	Mins	GA	SO	Avg	AAvg
1918-19	Ottawa Senators	NHL	1	0	0	0	3	0	0	0.00	0.00
1921-22	Montreal Canadiens	NHL	1	0	0	0	2	0	0	0.00	0.00
	NHL Totals		2	0	0	0	5	0	0	0.00	....

• Ottawa defenseman replaced penalized Clint Benedict, February 18, 1919. (Ottawa 4, Toronto 3) • Montreal defenseman replaced penalized Georges Vezina, February 1, 1922. (Ottawa 4, Montreal 2)

● CLIFFORD, CHRIS — Chris Clifford G – L. 5'9", 167 lbs. b: Kingston, Ont., 5/26/1966. Chicago's 6th choice, 111th overall, in 1984 Entry Draft.

Season	Club	League	GP	W	L	T	Mins	GA	SO	Avg	AAvg	Eff	SA	S%	SAPG	GP	W	L	T	Mins	GA	SO	Avg
1983-84	Kingston Canadians	OHL	50	16	28	0	2808	229	2	4.89													
1984-85	Kingston Canadians	OHL	52	15	34	0	2768	241	0	5.22													
	Chicago Black Hawks	NHL	1	0	0	0	20	0	0	0.00	0.00	0.00	8	1.000	24.0								
1985-86	Kingston Canadians	OHL	50	26	21	3	2988	178	1	3.57							10	5	5	0	564	31	1	3.30
1986-87	Kingston Raiders	OHL	44	18	25	0	2576	188	1	4.38							12	6	6	0	730	42	0	3.45
1987-88	Saginaw Hawks	IHL	22	9	7	2	1146	80	0	4.19														
1988-89	**Chicago Blackhawks**	NHL	1	0	0	0	4	0	0	0.00	0.00	0.00	0	.00	0.0								
	Saginaw Hawks	IHL	7	4	2	0	321	23	0	4.30														
1989-90	Muskegon Lumberjacks	IHL	23	17	4	1	1352	77	0	3.42							6	3	3	0	360	24	0	4.01
	Virginia Lancers	ECHL	10	7	1	0	547	16	0	1.75														
1990-91	Muskegon Lumberjacks	IHL	*56	24	26	4	*3247	215	1	3.97							5	1	4	0	299	20	0	4.01
1991-92	Fort Wayne Komets	IHL	2	2	0	0	120	4	0	2.00														
	Louisville IceHawks	ECHL	*56	29	19	6	*3151	223	0	4.25							13	7	6	0	780	53	0	4.08
	NHL Totals		2	0	0	0	24	0	0	0.00	....	....	8	1.000									

• Scored a goal while with Kingston (OHL), January 7, 1987.
Signed as a free agent by **Pittsburgh**, September 6, 1989.

● CLOUTIER, DAN — Dan Cloutier G – L. 6'1", 182 lbs. b: Mont-Laurier, Que., 4/22/1976. NY Rangers' 1st choice, 26th overall, in 1994 Entry Draft.

Season	Club	League	GP	W	L	T	Mins	GA	SO	Avg	AAvg	Eff	SA	S%	SAPG	GP	W	L	T	Mins	GA	SO	Avg
1992-93	Sault Ste. Marie Greyhounds	OHL	12	4	6	0	572	44	0	4.62							4	1	2		231	12	0	3.12
1993-94	Sault Ste. Marie Greyhounds	OHL	55	28	14	6	2934	174	*2	3.56							14	*10	4		833	52	0	3.75
1994-95	Sault Ste. Marie Greyhounds	OHL	45	15	26	2	2518	185	1	4.41														
	Canada	WJC-A	3	3	0	0	180	8	0	2.67														
1995-96	Sault Ste. Marie Greyhounds	OHL	13	9	3	0	641	43	0	4.02														
	Guelph Storm	OHL	17	12	2	2	1004	35	2	2.09							16	11	5		993	52	*2	3.14
1996-97	Binghamton Rangers	AHL	60	23	28	8	3367	199	3	3.55							4	1	3		236	13	0	3.31
1997-98	**New York Rangers**	NHL	12	4	5	1	551	23	0	2.50	2.92	2.32	248	.907	27.0								
	Hartford Wolf Pack	AHL	24	12	8	3	1417	62	0	2.63							8	5	3		478	24	0	3.01
	NHL Totals		12	4	5	1	551	23	0	2.50	....	....	248	.907									

OHL Second All-Star Team (1996)

● CLOUTIER, JACQUES — Jacques Cloutier G – L. 5'7", 168 lbs. b: Noranda, Que., 1/3/1960. Buffalo's 13th choice, 55th overall, in 1979 Entry Draft.

Season	Club	League	GP	W	L	T	Mins	GA	SO	Avg	AAvg	Eff	SA	S%	SAPG	GP	W	L	T	Mins	GA	SO	Avg	Eff	SA	S%	SAPG
1976-77	Trois-Rivières Draveurs	QMJHL	24				1109	93	0	5.03																		
1977-78	Trois-Rivières Draveurs	QMJHL	71	*46	17	7	4134	240	*4	3.48							13				779	40	1	3.08				
1978-79	Trois-Rivières Draveurs	QMJHL	72	*58	8	6	4168	218	*4	3.14							13				780	36	0	*2.77				
1979-80	Trois-Rivières Draveurs	QMJHL	55	27	20	7	3222	231	*2	4.30							7	3	4	0	420	33	0	4.71				
1980-81	Rochester Americans	AHL	*61	27	27	6	*3478	209	1	3.61																		
1981-82	**Buffalo Sabres**	NHL	7	5	1	0	311	13	0	2.51	1.93	2.09	156	.917	30.1												
	Rochester Americans	AHL	23	14	7	2	1366	64	0	2.81																		
1982-83	**Buffalo Sabres**	NHL	25	10	7	6	1390	81	0	3.50	2.79	4.96	572	.858	24.7												
	Rochester Americans	AHL	13	7	3	1	634	42	0	3.97							16	*12	4	0	992	47	0	2.84				
1983-84	Rochester Americans	AHL	*51	26	22	1	*2841	172	1	3.63							*18	9	9	0	*1145	68	0	3.56				
1984-85	**Buffalo Sabres**	NHL	1	0	0	1	65	4	0	3.69	2.93	3.99	37	.892	34.2												
	Rochester Americans	AHL	14	10	2	1	803	36	0	2.69																		
1985-86	**Buffalo Sabres**	NHL	15	5	9	1	872	49	1	3.37	2.62	3.86	428	.886	29.4												
	Rochester Americans	AHL	14	10	2	2	835	38	1	2.73																		
	Canada	WEC-A	5				298	15		3.02																		
1986-87	**Buffalo Sabres**	NHL	40	11	19	5	2167	137	0	3.79	3.19	5.02	1035	.868	28.7												
1987-88	**Buffalo Sabres**	NHL	20	4	8	2	851	67	0	4.72	3.93	7.03	450	.851	31.7												
1988-89	**Buffalo Sabres**	NHL	36	15	14	0	1786	108	0	3.63	2.99	4.57	857	.874	28.8	4	1	3		238	10	1	2.52	2.33	108	.907	27.2
	Rochester Americans	AHL	11	2	7	0	527	41	0	4.67																		
1989-90	**Chicago Blackhawks**	NHL	43	18	15	2	2178	112	2	3.09	2.58	3.72	931	.880	25.6	4	0	2		175	8	0	2.74	2.92	75	.893	25.7
1990-91	**Chicago Blackhawks**	NHL	10	2	3	0	403	24	0	3.57	3.19	4.90	175	.863	26.1												
	Quebec Nordiques	NHL	15	3	8	2	829	61	0	4.41	3.95	5.11	526	.884	38.1												
1991-92	**Quebec Nordiques**	NHL	26	6	14	3	1345	88	0	3.93	3.49	4.86	712	.876	31.8												
1992-93	**Quebec Nordiques**	NHL	3	0	2	1	154	10	0	3.90	3.32	6.00	65	.846	25.3												
1993-94	**Quebec Nordiques**	NHL	14	3	2	1	475	24	0	3.03	2.88	3.13	232	.897	29.3												
	NHL Totals		255	82	102	24	12826	778	3	3.64	....	....	6176	.874		8	1	5		413	18	1	2.62				

QMJHL First All-Star Team (1978, 1979)

Traded to **Chicago** by Buffalo for future considerations, September 28, 1989. Traded to **Quebec** by Chicago for Tony McKegney, January 29, 1991.

● COLVIN, LES — Les Colvin G – L. 5'6", 150 lbs. b: Oshawa, Ont., 2/8/1921.

Season	Club	League	GP	W	L	T	Mins	GA	SO	Avg	AAvg	Eff	SA	S%	SAPG	GP	W	L	T	Mins	GA	SO	Avg
1936-37	Oshawa Generals	OHA	1				60	4	0	4.00														
1937-38	Oshawa Generals	OHA	4				240	20	1	5.00														
1938-39	Oshawa Generals	OHA	7				420	8	1	*1.14							4	4	0	0	240	7	*1	*1.75
1939-40	Washington Eagles	EHL	23				1380	79	0	3.43							3	1	2	0	180	11	0	3.67
1940-41	Washington Eagles	EHL	27				1620	74	0	2.74							1				60	3	0	3.00
	New York Rovers	EHL					180	11	0	3.67														
1941-42				MILITARY SERVICE																				
1942-43	Toronto Army Daggers	City Sr.	1	0	1	0	60	8	0	8.00														
1943-44				MILITARY SERVICE																				
1944-45				MILITARY SERVICE																				
1945-46				DID NOT PLAY – INJURED																				
1946-47	Shawinigan Cataracts	QSHL	10				600	51	0	5.10							4				240	22	0	5.40
1947-48	Vancouver Canucks	PCHL	50	25	23	2	3000	197	1	3.94														
	Los Angeles Monarchs	PCHL	4	1	3	0	240	21	0	4.20														
	Portland Penguins	PCHL	1	1	0	0	60	3	0	3.00														
1948-49	Shawinigan Cataracts	QSHL	36				2307	56	10	1.46														
	Boston Bruins	NHL	1	0	1	0	60	4	0	4.00	4.55													
1949-50	Moncton Hawks	NBSHL	70	31	32	7	4200	270	1	3.87							4	0	4	0	250	22	0	5.28

Season	Club	League	REGULAR SEASON														PLAYOFFS											
			GP	W	L	T	Mins	GA	SO	Avg	AAvg	Eff	SA	S%	SAPG	GP	W	L	T	Mins	GA	SO	Avg	Eff	SA	S%	SAPG
1950-51	Moncton Hawks	MMHL	69	16	*45	5	4060	312	0	4.61	....	....	....	....	....	6	1	5	0	360	22	0	3.67	....	....	....	....
1951-52	North Bay Trappers	NOHA	18	....	....	....	1080	81	1	4.50	....	....	....	....	....	11	....	....	....	660	42	0	3.82	....	....	....	....
1952-53	North Bay Trappers	NOHA	47	21	23	2	2820	203	1	4.32	....	....	....	....	....	7	....	....	....	420	28	0	4.00	....	....	....	....
	NHL Totals		**1**	**0**	**1**	**0**	**60**	**4**	**0**	**4.00**	....	....	....	....	....	....	....	....	....	....	....	....	....	....	....	....	....

EHL Second All-Star Team (1941)

Loaned to **Boston** by **Shawinigan** (QSHL) to replace Frank Brimsek, January 22, 1949. (Montreal 4, Boston 2)

• CONACHER, CHARLIE

Charlie "The Big Bomber" Conacher G – L. 6'1", 195 lbs. b: Toronto, Ont., 12/20/1910. Deceased. **HHOF**

Season	Club	League	GP	W	L	T	Mins	GA	SO	Avg	AAvg	Eff	SA	S%	SAPG	GP	W	L	T	Mins	GA	SO	Avg	Eff	SA	S%	SAPG
1932-33	**Toronto Maple Leafs**	**NHL**	**2**	**0**	**0**	**0**	**4**	**0**	**0**	**0.00**	**0.00**	....	....	....	....	....	....	....	....	....	....	....	....	....	....	....	....
1934-35	**Toronto Maple Leafs**	**NHL**	**1**	**0**	**0**	**0**	**3**	**0**	**0**	**0.00**	**0.00**	....	....	....	....	....	....	....	....	....	....	....	....	....	....	....	....
1938-39	**Detroit Red Wings**	**NHL**	**1**	**0**	**0**	**0**	**3**	**0**	**0**	**0.00**	**0.00**	....	....	....	....	....	....	....	....	....	....	....	....	....	....	....	....
	NHL Totals		**4**	**0**	**0**	**0**	**10**	**0**	**0**	**0.00**	....	....	....	....	....	....	....	....	....	....	....	....	....	....	....	....	....

• Toronto right winger replaced penalized Lorne Chabot, November 20, 1932. (NY Rangers 7, Toronto 0) • Toronto right winger replaced penalized Lorne Chabot, March 16, 1933. (Detroit 1, Toronto 0) • Toronto right winger replaced injured George Hainsworth in 3rd period, March 16, 1935. (Toronto 5, Montreal Canadiens 3) • Detroit right winger replaced injured Tiny Thompson, February 21, 1939. (NY Rangers 7, Detroit 3)

• CONNELL, ALEX

Alex "The Ottawa Fireman" Connell G – R. 5'9", 150 lbs. b: Ottawa, Ont., 2/8/1902. d: 5/10/1958. **HHOF**

Season	Club	League	GP	W	L	T	Mins	GA	SO	Avg	AAvg	Eff	SA	S%	SAPG	GP	W	L	T	Mins	GA	SO	Avg	Eff	SA	S%	SAPG
1917-18	Kingston Frontenacs	OHA	4	*4	0	0	240	11	0	*2.75	....	....	....	....	....	4	3	1	0	240	18	0	4.50	....	....	....	....
1918-19	Kingston Frontenacs	OHA	5	3	2	0	305	24	0	4.72	....	....	....	....	....	4	0	1	3	240	20	0	5.00	....	....	....	....
1919-20	Ottawa Cliffsides	City Sr.	7	4	3	0	430	8	2	1.12	....	....	....	....	....	....	....	....	....	....	....	....	....	....	....	....	....
1920-21	Ottawa St. Brigids	City Sr.	11	*8	2	1	660	12	*2	*1.09	....	....	....	....	....	8	6	1	1	520	14	1	1.62	....	....	....	....
1921-22	Ottawa Gunners	City Sr.	14	*10	3	1	860	18	*5	*1.26	....	....	....	....	....	6	5	1	0	360	17	0	2.83	....	....	....	....
1922-23	Ottawa St. Brigids	City Sr.	17	8	8	1	1090	26	*4	1.43	....	....	....	....	....	....	....	....	....	....	....	....	....	....	....	....	....
1923-24	Ottawa St. Brigids	City Sr.	12	8	4	0	740	14	5	1.14	....	....	....	....	....	....	....	....	....	....	....	....	....	....	....	....	....
1924-25	**Ottawa Senators**	**NHL**	***30**	**17**	**12**	**1**	**1852**	**66**	***7**	**2.14**	**2.57**	....	....	....	....	....	....	....	....	....	....	....	....	....	....	....	....
1925-26	**Ottawa Senators**	**NHL**	***36**	***24**	**8**	**4**	**2251**	**42**	***15**	***1.12**	**1.38**	....	....	....	....	**2**	**0**	**1**	**1**	**120**	**2**	**0**	***1.00**	....	....	....	....
1926-27	**Ottawa Senators**	**NHL**	***44**	***30**	**10**	**4**	**2782**	**69**	**13**	**1.49**	**2.24**	....	....	....	....	**6**	***3**	**0**	**3**	**400**	**4**	***2**	***0.60**	....	....	....	....
1927-28	**Ottawa Senators**	**NHL**	***44**	**20**	**14**	**10**	**2760**	**57**	***15**	**1.24**	**1.94**	....	....	....	....	**2**	**0**	**2**	**0**	**120**	**3**	**0**	**1.50**	....	....	....	....
1928-29	**Ottawa Senators**	**NHL**	***44**	**14**	**17**	**13**	***2820**	**67**	**7**	**1.43**	**3.03**	....	....	....	....	....	....	....	....	....	....	....	....	....	....	....	....
1929-30	**Ottawa Senators**	**NHL**	***44**	**21**	**15**	**8**	**2780**	**118**	**3**	**2.55**	**2.63**	....	....	....	....	**2**	**0**	**1**	**1**	**120**	**6**	**0**	**3.00**	....	....	....	....
1930-31	**Ottawa Senators**	**NHL**	**36**	**10**	**22**	**4**	**2190**	**110**	**3**	**3.01**	**3.97**	....	....	....	....	....	....	....	....	....	....	....	....	....	....	....	....
1931-32	**Detroit Falcons**	**NHL**	***48**	**18**	**20**	**10**	***3050**	**108**	**6**	**2.12**	**2.55**	....	....	....	....	**2**	**0**	**1**	**1**	**120**	**3**	**0**	**1.50**	....	....	....	....
1932-33	**Ottawa Senators**	**NHL**	**15**	**4**	**8**	**2**	**845**	**36**	**1**	**2.56**	**3.49**	....	....	....	....	....	....	....	....	....	....	....	....	....	....	....	....
1933-34	**New York Americans**	**NHL**	**1**	**1**	**0**	**0**	**40**	**2**	**0**	**3.00**	**3.85**	....	....	....	....	....	....	....	....	....	....	....	....	....	....	....	....
1934-35	**Montreal Maroons**	**NHL**	***48**	**24**	**19**	**5**	**2970**	**92**	***9**	**1.86**	**2.21**	....	....	....	....	***7**	***5**	**0**	**2**	**429**	**8**	***2**	***1.12**	....	....	....	....
1935-36				DID NOT PLAY																							
1936-37	**Montreal Maroons**	**NHL**	**27**	**10**	**11**	**6**	**1710**	**63**	**2**	**2.21**	**2.75**	....	....	....	....	....	....	....	....	....	....	....	....	....	....	....	....
	NHL Totals		**417**	**193**	**156**	**67**	**26050**	**830**	**81**	**1.91**	....	....	....	....	....	**21**	**8**	**5**	**8**	**1309**	**26**	**4**	**1.19**	....	....	....	....

Signed as a free agent by **Ottawa**, November 18, 1924. Claimed by **Detroit Falcons** from **Ottawa** in Dispersal Draft for 1931-32 season, September 26, 1931. Loaned to **NY Americans** by **Ottawa** to replace injured Roy Worters, March 15, 1934. (NY Americans 3, Ottawa 2). Traded to **Montreal Maroons** by **Ottawa** for future considerations (Glenn Brydson, October 22, 1934), October 2, 1934.

• CORSI, JIM

Jim Corsi G – L. 5'10", 180 lbs. b: Montreal, Que., 6/19/1954.

Season	Club	League	GP	W	L	T	Mins	GA	SO	Avg	AAvg	Eff	SA	S%	SAPG	GP	W	L	T	Mins	GA	SO	Avg	Eff	SA	S%	SAPG
1975-76	Concordia University	QUAA		STATISTICS NOT AVAILABLE																							
1976-77	Maine Nordiques	NAHL	54	....	....	....	2988	181	1	3.57	....	....	....	....	....	12	7	5	0	714	46	*1	3.87	....	....	....	....
1977-78	Quebec Nordiques	WHA	23	10	7	0	1089	82	0	4.52	....	....	....	....	....	....	....	....	....	....	....	....	....	....	....	....	....
1978-79	Binghamton Whalers	AHL	4	1	2	0	211	7	0	1.99	....	....	....	....	....	....	....	....	....	....	....	....	....	....	....	....	....
	Quebec Nordiques	WHA	40	16	20	1	2291	126	*3	3.30	....	....	....	....	....	2	0	1	0	66	7	0	6.36	....	....	....	....
1979-80	**Edmonton Oilers**	**NHL**	**26**	**8**	**14**	**3**	**1366**	**83**	**0**	**3.65**	**3.21**	....	....	....	....	....	....	....	....	....	....	....	....	....	....	....	....
	Houston Apollos	CHL	17	8	5	2	959	57	0	3.57	....	....	....	....	....	....	....	....	....	....	....	....	....	....	....	....	....
	Oklahoma City Stars	CHL	11	5	6	0	645	28	1	2.60	....	....	....	....	....	....	....	....	....	....	....	....	....	....	....	....	....
1980-81	Italy	WEC-B	7	....	....	....	420	18	....	2.57	....	....	....	....	....	....	....	....	....	....	....	....	....	....	....	....	....
1981-82	Italy	WEC-A	7	....	....	....	390	38	....	5.84	....	....	....	....	....	....	....	....	....	....	....	....	....	....	....	....	....
1982-83	Italy	WEC-A	10	....	....	....	568	50	....	5.28	....	....	....	....	....	....	....	....	....	....	....	....	....	....	....	....	....
1984-85	Italy	WEC-B	7	....	....	....	420	22	....	3.14	....	....	....	....	....	....	....	....	....	....	....	....	....	....	....	....	....
1985-86	Italy	WEC-B	7	....	....	....	420	16	....	2.29	....	....	....	....	....	....	....	....	....	....	....	....	....	....	....	....	....
1986-87	Italy	WEC-B	7	....	....	....	420	29	....	4.14	....	....	....	....	....	....	....	....	....	....	....	....	....	....	....	....	....
1988-89	Italy	WEC-B	7	....	....	....	420	16	....	2.29	....	....	....	....	....	....	....	....	....	....	....	....	....	....	....	....	....
1989-90	Italy	WEC-B	5	....	....	....	299	14	....	2.81	....	....	....	....	....	....	....	....	....	....	....	....	....	....	....	....	....
	NHL Totals		**26**	**8**	**14**	**3**	**1366**	**83**	**0**	**3.65**	....	....	....	....	....	....	....	....	....	....	....	....	....	....	....	....	....
	Other Major League Totals		63	26	27	1	3380	208	3	3.69	....	....	....	....	....	2	0	1	0	66	7	0	6.36	....	....	....	....

WEC-B All-Star Team (1981, 1987) • Named Best Goaltender at WEC-B (1986)

• Played professional soccer with Montreal Olympics of the NASL, 1971-72. Signed as a free agent by **Quebec** (WHA), September, 1976. Signed as a free agent by **Edmonton**, October 4, 1979. Traded to **Minnesota** by **Edmonton** for future considerations, March 11, 1980. • Played professional hockey in Italy from 1980-81 through 1991-92.

• COURTEAU, MAURICE

Maurice Courteau G – L. 5'8", 162 lbs. b: Quebec City, Que., 2/18/1920.

Season	Club	League	GP	W	L	T	Mins	GA	SO	Avg	AAvg	Eff	SA	S%	SAPG	GP	W	L	T	Mins	GA	SO	Avg	Eff	SA	S%	SAPG
1937-38	Noranda Silver Kings	NOHA	16	1	13	2	960	86	0	5.37	....	....	....	....	....	....	....	....	....	....	....	....	....	....	....	....	....
1938-39	Atlantic City Seagulls	EHL	53	22	*25	6	3180	184	2	3.47	....	....	....	....	....	....	....	....	....	....	....	....	....	....	....	....	....
1939-40	Shawinigan Cataracts	QPHL	40	....	....	....	2400	155	1	3.88	....	....	....	....	....	....	....	....	....	....	....	....	....	....	....	....	....
1940-41	Quebec Royal Rifles	QSHL	33	17	11	5	1980	117	0	3.54	....	....	....	....	....	4	....	....	....	240	14	*1	3.50	....	....	....	....
1941-42	Quebec Aces	QSHL	7	....	....	....	420	15	1	2.14	....	....	....	....	....	1	0	1	0	60	5	0	5.00	....	....	....	....
1942-43	Philadelphia Falcons	EHL	26	....	....	....	1560	88	2	*3.39	....	....	....	....	....	....	....	....	....	....	....	....	....	....	....	....	....
1943-44	Providence Reds	AHL	1	0	0	1	60	2	0	2.00	....	....	....	....	....	....	....	....	....	....	....	....	....	....	....	....	....
	Boston Bruins	**NHL**	**6**	**2**	**4**	**0**	**360**	**33**	**0**	**5.50**	**4.19**	....	....	....	....	....	....	....	....	....	....	....	....	....	....	....	....
	Boston Olympics	EHL	36	*34	1	1	2160	79	4	*2.19	....	....	....	....	....	10	4	6	0	600	42	0	4.20	....	....	....	....
1944-45	Boston Olympics	EHL	33	22	9	2	1980	129	1	3.91	....	....	....	....	....	8	*7	0	1	480	26	0	3.25	....	....	....	....
1945-46	Sherbrooke Randies	QPHL	11	....	....	....	660	38	0	3.45	....	....	....	....	....	....	....	....	....	....	....	....	....	....	....	....	....
1946-47	Philadelphia Rockets	AHL	7	0	6	0	380	49	0	7.74	....	....	....	....	....	....	....	....	....	....	....	....	....	....	....	....	....
	San Francisco Shamrocks	PCHL	24	....	....	....	1440	145	0	6.04	....	....	....	....	....	....	....	....	....	....	....	....	....	....	....	....	....
1947-48	Philadelphia Rockets	AHL	30	8	21	1	1800	144	1	4.80	....	....	....	....	....	....	....	....	....	....	....	....	....	....	....	....	....
1948-49				DID NOT PLAY																							
1949-50	Magog Volanats	QPHL	19	....	....	....	1140	82	*2	4.32	....	....	....	....	....	....	....	....	....	....	....	....	....	....	....	....	....
	NHL Totals		**6**	**2**	**4**	**0**	**360**	**33**	**0**	**5.50**	....	....	....	....	....	....	....	....	....	....	....	....	....	....	....	....	....

EHL Second All-Star Team (1943, 1945) • EHL First All-Star Team (1944) • Won George L. Davis Jr. Trophy (fewest goals against - EHL) (1944)

Season	Club	League	REGULAR SEASON GP	W	L	T	Mins	GA	SO	Avg	AAvg	Eff	SA	S%	SAPG	PLAYOFFS GP	W	L	T	Mins	GA	SO	Avg	Eff	SA	S%	SAPG

• COUSINEAU, MARCEL

Marcel Cousineau G – L. 5'9", 180 lbs. b: Delson, Que., 4/30/1973. Boston's 3rd choice, 62nd overall, in 1991 Entry Draft.

Season	Club	League	GP	W	L	T	Mins	GA	SO	Avg	AAvg	Eff	SA	S%	SAPG	GP	W	L	T	Mins	GA	SO	Avg	Eff	SA	S%	SAPG
1990-91	Beauport Harfangs	QMJHL	49	13	29	3	2739	196	1	4.29	....	....	....	....	....	....	....	....	....	....	....	....	....	....	....	....	....
1991-92	Beauport Harfangs	QMJHL	*67	26	32	5	*3673	241	0	3.94	....	....	....	....	....	....	....	....	....	....	....	....	....	....	....	....	....
1992-93	Drummondville Voltigeurs	QMJHL	60	20	32	2	3298	225	0	4.09	....	....	....	....	....	9	3	6	....	498	37	*1	4.45	....	....	....	....
1993-94	St. John's Maple Leafs	AHL	37	13	11	9	2015	118	0	3.51	....	....	....	....	....	....	....	....	....	....	....	....	....	....	....	....	....
1994-95	St. John's Maple Leafs	AHL	58	22	27	6	3342	171	4	3.07	....	....	....	....	....	3	0	3	....	179	9	0	3.01	....	....	....	....
1995-96	St. John's Maple Leafs	AHL	62	21	26	13	3629	192	1	3.17	....	....	....	....	....	4	1	3	....	258	11	0	2.56	....	....	....	....
1996-97	**Toronto Maple Leafs**	**NHL**	**13**	**3**	**5**	**1**	**566**	**31**	**1**	**3.29**	**3.48**	**3.22**	**317**	**.902**	**33.6**	....	....	....	....	....	....	....	....	....	....	....	....
	St. John's Maple Leafs	AHL	19	7	8	3	1053	58	0	3.30	....	....	....	....	....	11	6	5	....	658	28	0	2.55	....	....	....	....
1997-98	**Toronto Maple Leafs**	**NHL**	**2**	**0**	**0**	**0**	**17**	**0**	**0**	**0.00**	**0.00**	**0.00**	**9**	**1.000**	**31.8**	....	....	....	....	....	....	....	....	....	....	....	....
	St. John's Maple Leafs	AHL	57	17	25	13	3306	167	1	3.03	....	....	....	....	....	4	1	3	....	254	10	0	2.36	....	....	....	....
	NHL Totals		**15**	**3**	**5**	**1**	**583**	**31**	**1**	**3.19**	....	....	**326**	**.905**	....	....	....	....	....	....	....	....	....	....	....	....	....

Signed as a free agent by **Toronto**, November 13, 1993. Signed as a free agent by **NY Islanders**, July 14, 1998.

• COWLEY, WAYNE

Wayne Cowley G – L. 6', 185 lbs. b: Scarborough, Ont., 12/4/1964.

Season	Club	League	GP	W	L	T	Mins	GA	SO	Avg	AAvg	Eff	SA	S%	SAPG	GP	W	L	T	Mins	GA	SO	Avg	Eff	SA	S%	SAPG
1985-86	Colgate University	ECAC	7	2	2	0	313	23	1	4.42	....	....	....	....	....	....	....	....	....	....	....	....	....	....	....	....	....
1986-87	Colgate University	ECAC	31	21	8	1	1805	106	0	3.52	....	....	....	....	....	....	....	....	....	....	....	....	....	....	....	....	....
1987-88	Colgate University	ECAC	20	11	7	1	1162	58	1	2.99	....	....	....	....	....	....	....	....	....	....	....	....	....	....	....	....	....
1988-89	Salt Lake Golden Eagles	IHL	29	17	7	1	1423	94	0	3.96	....	....	....	....	....	2	1	0	0	69	6	0	5.22	....	....	....	....
1989-90	Salt Lake Golden Eagles	IHL	36	15	12	5	2009	124	1	3.70	....	....	....	....	....	3	0	0	0	118	6	0	3.05	....	....	....	....
1990-91	Salt Lake Golden Eagles	IHL	7	3	4	0	377	23	1	3.66	....	....	....	....	....	....	....	....	....	....	....	....	....	....	....	....	....
	Cincinnati Cyclones	ECHL	30	19	9	2	1680	108	1	3.85	....	....	....	....	....	4	1	3	0	249	13	*1	3.13	....	....	....	....
1991-92	Blackburn Blackhawks	Britain	2	....	....	....	115	7	....	3.65	....	....	....	....	....	....	....	....	....	....	....	....	....	....	....	....	....
	Raleigh IceCaps	ECHL	38	16	18	2	2213	137	0	3.71	....	....	....	....	....	....	....	....	....	....	....	....	....	....	....	....	....
	Cape Breton Oilers	AHL	11	6	5	0	644	42	0	3.91	....	....	....	....	....	1	0	1	0	61	3	0	2.95	....	....	....	....
	Solihull Barons	Britain	....	....	....	....	....	....	....	....	....	....	....	....	....	8	....	....	....	463	48	....	6.22	....	....	....	....
1992-93	Cape Breton Oilers	AHL	42	14	17	6	2334	152	1	3.91	....	....	....	....	....	16	*14	2	0	1014	47	*1	2.78	....	....	....	....
	Wheeling Thunderbirds	ECHL	1	1	0	0	60	3	0	3.00	....	....	....	....	....	....	....	....	....	....	....	....	....	....	....	....	....
1993-94	**Edmonton Oilers**	**NHL**	**1**	**0**	**1**	**0**	**57**	**3**	**0**	**3.16**	**3.01**	**2.71**	**35**	**.914**	**36.8**	....	....	....	....	....	....	....	....	....	....	....	....
	Cape Breton Oilers	AHL	44	20	17	5	2486	150	0	3.62	....	....	....	....	....	5	1	4	0	0	20	0	4.66	....	....	....	....
1994-95	Worcester IceCats	AHL	45	11	25	6	2597	153	1	3.53	....	....	....	....	....	....	....	....	....	....	....	....	....	....	....	....	....
	Milwaukee Admirals	IHL	2	0	0	1	79	4	0	3.04	....	....	....	....	....	....	....	....	....	....	....	....	....	....	....	....	....
1995-96	Sheffield Steelers	Britain	20	....	....	....	1160	62	....	*3.21	....	....	....	....	....	7	....	....	....	420	17	*2	*2.43	....	....	....	....
1996-97	Wedemark Scorpions	Germany	43	....	....	....	2324	175	1	4.51	....	....	....	....	....	7	....	....	....	410	30	0	4.39	....	....	....	....
1997-98	Newcastle Cobras	Britain	28	....	....	....	1612	94	....	3.50	....	....	....	....	....	6	....	....	....	367	20	....	3.27	....	....	....	....
	NHL Totals		**1**	**0**	**1**	**0**	**57**	**3**	**0**	**3.16**	....	....	**35**	**.914**	....	....	....	....	....	....	....	....	....	....	....	....	....

ECHL Second All-Star Team (1991)

Signed as a free agent by **Calgary**, May 1, 1988. Signed as a free agent by **Edmonton**, September 13, 1993.

• COX, ABBIE

Abbie Cox G – L. 5'6", 140 lbs. b: London, Ontario, 7/19/1904.

Season	Club	League	GP	W	L	T	Mins	GA	SO	Avg	AAvg	Eff	SA	S%	SAPG	GP	W	L	T	Mins	GA	SO	Avg	Eff	SA	S%	SAPG
1921-22	Ottawa Munitions	City Sr.	12	4	7	2	720	42	1	3.50	....	....	....	....	....	2	0	2	0	120	11	0	5.50	....	....	....	....
1922-23	Iroquois Falls Papermakers	NOHA	STATISTICS NOT AVAILABLE																								
1923-24	New Haven Bears	USAHA	12	*6	6	0	730	21	2	1.73	....	....	....	....	....	....	....	....	....	....	....	....	....	....	....	....	....
1924-25	Boston Maples	USAHA	21	6	15	0	995	58	0	2.21	....	....	....	....	....	....	....	....	....	....	....	....	....	....	....	....	....
1925-26	New York Knicks	USAHA	DID NOT PLAY – SUSPENDED																								
1926-27	Springfield Indians	Can-Am	31	14	12	5	1950	51	6	1.57	....	....	....	....	....	6	*3	1	2	360	6	*2	*1.00	....	....	....	....
1927-28	Springfield Indians	Can-Am	40	*24	13	3	2450	71	12	1.74	....	....	....	....	....	4	2	2	0	240	7	*1	*1.75	....	....	....	....
1928-29	Windsor Bulldogs	Can-Pro	34	....	....	....	2040	64	7	1.88	....	....	....	....	....	8	*5	3	0	530	7	*3	*0.79	....	....	....	....
1929-30	Windsor Bulldogs	IAHL	41	20	13	8	2440	89	3	2.19	....	....	....	....	....	....	....	....	....	....	....	....	....	....	....	....	....
	Montreal Maroons	**NHL**	**1**	**1**	**0**	**0**	**60**	**2**	**0**	**2.00**	**2.09**	....	....	....	....	....	....	....	....	....	....	....	....	....	....	....	....
1930-31	Windsor Bulldogs	IAHL	1	0	0	1	70	4	0	3.43	....	....	....	....	....	....	....	....	....	....	....	....	....	....	....	....	....
	Detroit Olympics	IAHL	39	19	11	9	2470	78	8	1.89	....	....	....	....	....	6	0	6	0	370	19	0	3.08	....	....	....	....
1931-32	Pittsburgh Yellowjackets	IAHL	32	....	....	....	1920	86	5	2.75	....	....	....	....	....	....	....	....	....	....	....	....	....	....	....	....	....
1932-33	Detroit Olympics	IAHL	13	....	....	....	780	51	2	3.92	....	....	....	....	....	....	....	....	....	....	....	....	....	....	....	....	....
	Windsor Bulldogs	IAHL	2	2	0	0	120	2	0	1.00	....	....	....	....	....	....	....	....	....	....	....	....	....	....	....	....	....
1933-34	Detroit Olympics	IAHL	38	....	....	....	2280	80	5	2.11	....	....	....	....	....	6	3	3	0	360	17	0	2.83	....	....	....	....
	New York Americans	**NHL**	**1**	**0**	**1**	**0**	**24**	**3**	**0**	**7.50**	**9.63**	....	....	....	....	....	....	....	....	....	....	....	....	....	....	....	....
	Detroit Red Wings	**NHL**	**2**	**0**	**0**	**1**	**109**	**5**	**0**	**2.75**	**3.53**	....	....	....	....	....	....	....	....	....	....	....	....	....	....	....	....
	Cleveland Indians	IAHL	1	0	1	0	60	4	0	4.00	....	....	....	....	....	....	....	....	....	....	....	....	....	....	....	....	....
1934-35	Quebec Castors	Can-Am	43	19	18	6	2660	114	*5	2.57	....	....	....	....	....	3	1	2	0	180	6	*1	2.00	....	....	....	....
1935-36	Springfield Indians	Can-Am	38	15	20	3	2320	108	*6	2.79	....	....	....	....	....	....	....	....	....	....	....	....	....	....	....	....	....
	Montreal Canadiens	**NHL**	**1**	**0**	**0**	**1**	**70**	**1**	**0**	**0.86**	**1.22**	....	....	....	....	....	....	....	....	....	....	....	....	....	....	....	....
	Philadelphia Ramblers	Can-Am	1	....	....	....	60	4	0	4.00	....	....	....	....	....	....	....	....	....	....	....	....	....	....	....	....	....
1936-37	Kansas City Greyhounds	AHA	10	0	8	2	646	31	0	2.88	....	....	....	....	....	....	....	....	....	....	....	....	....	....	....	....	....
	NHL Totals		**5**	**1**	**1**	**2**	**263**	**11**	**0**	**2.51**	....	....	....	....	....	....	....	....	....	....	....	....	....	....	....	....	....

Signed as a free agent by **NY Rangers**, November 9, 1926. Traded to **Windsor** (Can-Pro) by **NY Rangers** for cash, September, 1928. Loaned to **Montreal Maroons** by **Windsor** (IAHL) to replace injured Clint Benedict and Flat Walsh, February 1, 1930. (Montreal Maroons 7, NY Americans 2). Loaned to **Detroit** (IAHL) by **Windsor** (IAHL) for cash, November 21, 1930. Loaned to **NY Americans** by **Windsor** (IAHL) to replace injured Roy Worters, November 12, 1933. (Detroit 5, NY Americans 2). Loaned to **Detroit** by **Windsor** (IAHL) to replace injured John Ross Roach, December 10, 1933. (Detroit 4, Montreal Maroons 1). Loaned to **Detroit** by **Windsor** (IAHL) to replace injured John Ross Roach, December 17, 1933. (NY Americans 4, Detroit 4). Loaned to **Montreal Canadiens** by **Springfield** (Can-Am) to replace injured Wilf Cude, February 16, 1936. (Montreal Canadiens 1, NY Rangers 1)

• CRAIG, JIM

Jim Craig G – L. 6'1", 190 lbs. b: North Easton, MA, 5/31/1957. Atlanta's 5th choice, 72nd overall, in 1977 Amateur Draft.

Season	Club	League	GP	W	L	T	Mins	GA	SO	Avg	AAvg	Eff	SA	S%	SAPG	GP	W	L	T	Mins	GA	SO	Avg	Eff	SA	S%	SAPG
1976-77	Boston University	ECAC	DID NOT PLAY – FRESHMAN																								
1977-78	Boston University	ECAC	16	16	0	0	967	60	0	3.72	....	....	....	....	....	5	5	0	0	305	17	0	3.34	....	....	....	....
1978-79	Boston University	ECAC	19	13	4	2	1009	60	1	3.57	....	....	....	....	....	2	1	1	0	120	8	0	4.00	....	....	....	....
	United States	WEC-A	5	....	....	....	280	10	....	2.14	....	....	....	....	....	....	....	....	....	....	....	....	....	....	....	....	....
1979-80	United States	Nat-Team	48	....	....	....	2790	110	0	2.37	....	....	....	....	....	....	....	....	....	....	....	....	....	....	....	....	....
	United States	Olympics	7	6	0	1	420	15	....	2.14	....	....	....	....	....	....	....	....	....	....	....	....	....	....	....	....	....
	Atlanta Flames	**NHL**	**4**	**1**	**2**	**1**	**206**	**13**	**0**	**3.79**	**3.33**	....	....	....	....	....	....	....	....	....	....	....	....	....	....	....	....
1980-81	**Boston Bruins**	**NHL**	**23**	**9**	**7**	**6**	**1272**	**78**	**0**	**3.68**	**2.95**	....	....	....	....	....	....	....	....	....	....	....	....	....	....	....	....
1981-82	Erie Blades	AHL	13	3	9	1	742	57	0	4.61	....	....	....	....	....	....	....	....	....	....	....	....	....	....	....	....	....
1982-83	United States	Nat-Team	26	....	....	....	1385	61	2	2.64	....	....	....	....	....	....	....	....	....	....	....	....	....	....	....	....	....
1983-84	**Minnesota North Stars**	**NHL**	**3**	**1**	**1**	**0**	**110**	**9**	**0**	**4.91**	**3.84**	**7.89**	**56**	**.839**	**30.5**	....	....	....	....	....	....	....	....	....	....	....	....
	Salt Lake Golden Eagles	CHL	27	....	....	....	1532	108	1	4.23	....	....	....	....	....	3	....	....	....	177	12	0	4.07	....	....	....	....
	NHL Totals		**30**	**11**	**10**	**7**	**1588**	**100**	**0**	**3.78**	....	....	....	....	....	....	....	....	....	....	....	....	....	....	....	....	....

ECAC First All-Star Team (1979) • NCAA East First All-American Team (1979) • WEC-B All-Star Team (1983)

Traded to **Boston** by **Atlanta** for Boston's 2nd round choice (Steve Konroyd) in 1980 Entry Draft and 3rd round choice (Mike Vernon) in 1981 Entry Draft, June 2, 1980. Signed as a free agent by **Minnesota**, March 2, 1983.

• CRHA, JIRI

Jiri "George" Crha G – L. 5'11", 170 lbs. b: Pardubice, Czechoslovakia, 4/13/1950.

Season	Club	League	GP	W	L	T	Mins	GA	SO	Avg	AAvg	Eff	SA	S%	SAPG	GP	W	L	T	Mins	GA	SO	Avg	Eff	SA	S%	SAPG
1972-73	Czechoslovakia	WEC-A	2	....	....	....	120	3	....	1.50	....	....	....	....	....	....	....	....	....	....	....	....	....	....	....	....	....
1973-74	Czechoslovakia	WEC-A	5	....	....	....	260	10	....	2.31	....	....	....	....	....	....	....	....	....	....	....	....	....	....	....	....	....
1974-75	Czechoslovakia	WEC-A	2	....	....	....	75	5	....	4.00	....	....	....	....	....	....	....	....	....	....	....	....	....	....	....	....	....
1975-76	Czechoslovakia	Olympics	2	....	....	....	37	1	....	1.62	....	....	....	....	....	....	....	....	....	....	....	....	....	....	....	....	....
1977-78	Pardubice	Czech.	44	....	....	....	2595	128	....	2.96	....	....	....	....	....	....	....	....	....	....	....	....	....	....	....	....	....
	Czechoslovakia	WEC-A	1	....	....	....	60	2	0	2.00	....	....	....	....	....	....	....	....	....	....	....	....	....	....	....	....	....
1978-79	Pardubice	Czech.	37	....	....	....	2220	117	....	3.16	....	....	....	....	....	....	....	....	....	....	....	....	....	....	....	....	....
1979-80	New Brunswick Hawks	AHL	7	4	1	2	404	15	1	2.23	....	....	....	....	....	....	....	....	....	....	....	....	....	....	....	....	....
	Toronto Maple Leafs	**NHL**	**15**	**8**	**7**	**0**	**830**	**50**	**0**	**3.61**	**3.17**	....	....	....	....	**2**	**0**	**2**	....	**121**	**10**	**0**	**4.96**	....	....	....	....

			REGULAR SEASON													PLAYOFFS											
Season	Club	League	GP	W	L	T	Mins	GA	SO	Avg	AAvg	Eff	SA	S%	SAPG	GP	W	L	T	Mins	GA	SO	Avg	Eff	SA	S%	SAPG
1980-81	**Toronto Maple Leafs**	**NHL**	**54**	**20**	**20**	**11**	**3112**	**211**	**0**	**4.07**	**3.27**	....	....	....	....	**3**	**0**	**2**	....	**65**	**11**	**0**	**10.15**	....	....	....	....
1981-82	Cincinnati Tigers	CHL	2	1	0	0	81	11	0	8.15	....	....	....	....	....	....	....	....	....	....	....	....	....	....	....	....	....
1982-83	St. Catharines Saints	AHL	1	....	....	....	60	6	0	6.00	....	....	....	....	....	....	....	....	....	....	....	....	....	....	....	....	....
	NHL Totals		**69**	**28**	**27**	**11**	**3942**	**261**	**0**	**3.97**	....	....	....	....	....	**5**	**0**	**4**	....	**186**	**21**	**0**	**6.77**	....	....	....	....

EJC-A All-Star Team (1968) • Named Best Goaltender at EJC-A (1968, 1969)

• Played in Czechoslovakia's top division from 1968-69 through 1976-77. Signed as a free agent by **Toronto**, February 4, 1980. • Played professional hockey in Germany from 1983-84 through 1990-91.

• CROZIER, ROGER

Roger Crozier G – R. 5'8", 165 lbs. b: Bracebridge, Ont., 3/16/1942. d: 1/11/1996.

Season	Club	League	GP	W	L	T	Mins	GA	SO	Avg	AAvg	Eff	SA	S%	SAPG	GP	W	L	T	Mins	GA	SO	Avg	Eff	SA	S%	SAPG
1959-60	St. Catharines Teepees	OHA	48	25	19	4	2880	191	1	3.98	....	....	....	....	....	17	....	....	....	1020	52	0	*3.06	....	....	....	....
1960-61	St. Catharines Teepees	OHA	48	18	24	6	2880	204	0	4.25	....	....	....	....	....	6	....	....	....	360	21	0	3.50	....	....	....	....
	Buffalo Bisons	AHL	3	2	0	0	130	5	0	2.31	....	....	....	....	....	....	....	....	....	....	....	....	....	....	....	....	....
1961-62	St. Catharines Teepees	OHA	45	....	....	....	2670	174	1	3.91	....	....	....	....	....	6	....	....	....	360	19	0	3.17	....	....	....	....
	Sault Ste. Marie Thunderbirds	EPHL	3	0	1	2	180	12	0	4.00	....	....	....	....	....	....	....	....	....	....	....	....	....	....	....	....	....
	Buffalo Bisons	AHL	1	0	1	0	60	4	0	4.00	....	....	....	....	....	....	....	....	....	....	....	....	....	....	....	....	....
1962-63	Buffalo Bisons	AHL	4	3	1	0	240	10	0	2.50	....	....	....	....	....	....	....	....	....	....	....	....	....	....	....	....	....
	St. Louis Braves	EPHL	*70	26	35	9	*4200	299	1	4.27	....	....	....	....	....	....	....	....	....	....	....	....	....	....	....	....	....
1963-64	Pittsburgh Hornets	AHL	44	30	13	1	2640	103	4	*2.34	....	....	....	....	....	3	1	2	0	184	9	0	2.93	....	....	....	....
	Detroit Red Wings	**NHL**	**15**	**5**	**6**	**4**	**900**	**51**	**2**	**3.40**	**3.81**	....	....	....	....	**3**	**0**	**2**	....	**126**	**5**	**0**	**2.38**	....	....	....	....
1964-65	**Detroit Red Wings**	**NHL**	***70**	***40**	**22**	**7**	***4168**	**168**	***6**	**2.42**	**2.52**	....	....	....	....	**7**	**3**	**4**	....	**420**	**23**	**0**	**3.29**	....	....	....	....
1965-66	**Detroit Red Wings**	**NHL**	***64**	**27**	**24**	**12**	**3734**	**173**	***7**	**2.78**	**2.78**	....	....	....	....	***12**	**6**	**5**	....	***668**	**26**	***1**	**2.34**	....	....	....	....
1966-67	**Detroit Red Wings**	**NHL**	**58**	**22**	**29**	**4**	**3256**	**182**	**4**	**3.35**	**3.53**	....	....	....	....	....	....	....	....	....	....	....	....	....	....	....	....
1967-68	Fort Worth Wings	CHL	5	3	2	0	265	12	0	2.49	....	....	....	....	....	....	....	....	....	....	....	....	....	....	....	....	....
	Detroit Red Wings	**NHL**	**34**	**9**	**18**	**2**	**1729**	**95**	**1**	**3.30**	**3.67**	....	....	....	....	....	....	....	....	....	....	....	....	....	....	....	....
1968-69	**Detroit Red Wings**	**NHL**	**38**	**12**	**16**	**3**	**1820**	**101**	**0**	**3.33**	**3.46**	....	....	....	....	....	....	....	....	....	....	....	....	....	....	....	....
1969-70	**Detroit Red Wings**	**NHL**	**34**	**16**	**6**	**9**	**1877**	**83**	**0**	**2.65**	**2.81**	....	....	....	....	**1**	**0**	**1**	....	**34**	**3**	**0**	**5.29**	....	....	....	....
1970-71	**Buffalo Sabres**	**NHL**	**44**	**9**	**20**	**7**	**2198**	**135**	**1**	**3.69**	**3.67**	....	....	....	....	....	....	....	....	....	....	....	....	....	....	....	....
1971-72	**Buffalo Sabres**	**NHL**	**63**	**13**	**34**	**14**	**3654**	**214**	**2**	**3.51**	**3.56**	....	....	....	....	....	....	....	....	....	....	....	....	....	....	....	....
1972-73	**Buffalo Sabres**	**NHL**	**49**	**23**	**13**	**7**	**2633**	**121**	**3**	**2.76**	**2.59**	....	....	....	....	**4**	**2**	**2**	....	**249**	**11**	**0**	**2.65**	....	....	....	....
1973-74	**Buffalo Sabres**	**NHL**	**12**	**4**	**5**	**0**	**615**	**39**	**0**	**3.80**	**3.67**	....	....	....	....	....	....	....	....	....	....	....	....	....	....	....	....
1974-75	**Buffalo Sabres**	**NHL**	**23**	**17**	**2**	**1**	**1260**	**55**	**3**	**2.62**	**2.35**	....	....	....	....	**5**	**3**	**2**	....	**292**	**14**	**0**	**2.88**	....	....	....	....
1975-76	**Buffalo Sabres**	**NHL**	**11**	**8**	**2**	**0**	**620**	**27**	**1**	**2.61**	**2.36**	....	....	....	....	....	....	....	....	....	....	....	....	....	....	....	....
1976-77	**Washington Capitals**	**NHL**	**3**	**1**	**0**	**0**	**103**	**2**	**0**	**1.17**	**1.09**	....	....	....	....	....	....	....	....	....	....	....	....	....	....	....	....
	NHL Totals		**518**	**206**	**197**	**70**	**28567**	**1446**	**30**	**3.04**	....	....	....	....	....	**32**	**14**	**16**	....	**1789**	**82**	**1**	**2.75**	....	....	....	....

AHL Second All-Star Team (1964) • Won Harry "Hap" Holmes Memorial Award (fewest goals against - AHL) (1964) • Won Dudley "Red" Garrett Memorial Award (Top Rookie - AHL) (1964) • NHL First All-Star Team (1965) • Won Calder Memorial Trophy (1965) • Won Conn Smythe Trophy (1966)

Traded to **Detroit** by **Chicago** with Ron Ingram for Howie Young, June 5, 1963. Traded to **Buffalo** by **Detroit** for Tom Webster, June 10, 1970. Traded to **Washington** by **Buffalo** for cash, March 3, 1977.

• CUDE, WILF

Wilf Cude G – L. 5'9", 146 lbs. b: Barry, South Wales, 7/4/1910. d: 5/5/1968.

Season	Club	League	GP	W	L	T	Mins	GA	SO	Avg	AAvg	Eff	SA	S%	SAPG	GP	W	L	T	Mins	GA	SO	Avg	Eff	SA	S%	SAPG
1928-29	Winnipeg Wellingtons	City Sr.	STATISTICS NOT AVAILABLE																								
1929-30	Melville Millionaires	ASHL	20	13	6	1	1200	40	3	2.00	....	....	....	....	....	2	1	1	0	120	3	*1	1.50	....	....	....	....
1930-31	**Philadelphia Quakers**	**NHL**	**30**	**2**	**25**	**3**	**1850**	**130**	**1**	**4.22**	**5.77**	....	....	....	....	....	....	....	....	....	....	....	....	....	....	....	....
1931-32	**Boston Bruins**	**NHL**	**2**	**1**	**1**	**0**	**120**	**6**	**1**	**3.00**	**3.69**	....	....	....	....	....	....	....	....	....	....	....	....	....	....	....	....
	Chicago Black Hawks	**NHL**	**1**	**0**	**0**	**0**	**41**	**9**	**0**	**13.17**	**16.31**	....	....	....	....	....	....	....	....	....	....	....	....	....	....	....	....
	Syracuse Stars	IAHL	1	1	0	0	60	1	0	1.00	....	....	....	....	....	....	....	....	....	....	....	....	....	....	....	....	....
	Boston Cubs	Can-Am	15	7	7	1	900	46	1	3.00	....	....	....	....	....	....	....	....	....	....	....	....	....	....	....	....	....
1932-33	Philadelphia Arrows	Can-Am	32	21	9	2	1950	64	*4	*1.97	....	....	....	....	....	5	2	*3	0	300	15	*1	3.00	....	....	....	....
1933-34	Syracuse Stars	IAHL	19	....	....	....	1140	39	3	2.05	....	....	....	....	....	....	....	....	....	....	....	....	....	....	....	....	....
	Montreal Canadiens	**NHL**	**1**	**1**	**0**	**0**	**60**	**0**	**1**	***0.00**	**0.00**	....	....	....	....	....	....	....	....	....	....	....	....	....	....	....	....
	Detroit Red Wings	**NHL**	**29**	**15**	**6**	**8**	**1860**	**47**	**4**	***1.52**	**1.89**	....	....	....	....	***9**	**4**	**5**	**0**	***593**	**21**	**1**	**2.12**	....	....	....	....
1934-35	**Montreal Canadiens**	**NHL**	***48**	**19**	**23**	**6**	**2960**	**145**	**1**	**2.94**	**3.69**	....	....	....	....	**2**	**0**	**1**	**1**	**120**	**6**	**0**	**3.00**	....	....	....	....
1935-36	**Montreal Canadiens**	**NHL**	**47**	**11**	**26**	**10**	**2940**	**122**	**6**	**2.49**	**3.83**	....	....	....	....	....	....	....	....	....	....	....	....	....	....	....	....
1936-37	**Montreal Canadiens**	**NHL**	**44**	**22**	**17**	**5**	**2730**	**99**	**5**	**2.18**	**2.69**	....	....	....	....	**5**	**2**	**3**	....	**352**	**13**	**0**	**2.22**	....	....	....	....
1937-38	**Montreal Canadiens**	**NHL**	**47**	**18**	**17**	**12**	**2990**	**120**	**3**	**2.53**	**3.08**	....	....	....	....	**3**	**1**	**2**	....	**192**	**11**	**0**	**3.44**	....	....	....	....
1938-39	**Montreal Canadiens**	**NHL**	**23**	**8**	**11**	**4**	**1440**	**77**	**2**	**3.21**	**3.99**	....	....	....	....	....	....	....	....	....	....	....	....	....	....	....	....
1939-40	**Montreal Canadiens**	**NHL**	**7**	**1**	**5**	**1**	**415**	**24**	**0**	**3.47**	**4.34**	....	....	....	....	....	....	....	....	....	....	....	....	....	....	....	....
	New Haven Eagles	AHL	44	23	18	3	2690	146	3	3.26	....	....	....	....	....	3	1	2	0	180	11	0	3.44	....	....	....	....
1940-41	**Montreal Canadiens**	**NHL**	**3**	**2**	**1**	**0**	**180**	**13**	**0**	**4.33**	**5.02**	....	....	....	....	....	....	....	....	....	....	....	....	....	....	....	....
	NHL Totals		**282**	**100**	**132**	**49**	**17586**	**798**	**24**	**2.72**	....	....	....	....	....	**19**	**7**	**11**	**1**	**1257**	**51**	**1**	**2.43**	....	....	....	....

NHL Second All-Star Team (1936, 1937)

Played in NHL All-Star Game (1937, 1939)

Signed as a free agent by **Pittsburgh**, February 18, 1930. Transferred to **Philadelphia** after **Pittsburgh** franchise relocated, October 18, 1930. • Signed as a utility back-up goaltender by **NHL** for 1931-32 season after **Philadelphia** franchise folded, September 27, 1931. Traded to **Montreal Canadiens** by **Philadelphia** for cash, October 19, 1933. Loaned to **Detroit Red Wings** by **Montreal Canadiens** for balance of 1933-34 season for cash, January 2, 1934.

• CUTTS, DON

Don Cutts G – L. 6'3", 190 lbs. b: Edmonton, Alta., 2/24/1953. NY Islanders' 6th choice, 97th overall, in 1973 Amateur Draft.

Season	Club	League	GP	W	L	T	Mins	GA	SO	Avg	AAvg	Eff	SA	S%	SAPG	GP	W	L	T	Mins	GA	SO	Avg	Eff	SA	S%	SAPG
1970-71	RPI Engineers	ECAC	8	....	....	....	480	20	....	2.73	....	....	....	....	....	....	....	....	....	....	....	....	....	....	....	....	....
1971-72	RPI Engineers	ECAC	21	....	....	....	1260	72	1	3.43	....	....	....	....	....	....	....	....	....	....	....	....	....	....	....	....	....
1972-73	RPI Engineers	ECAC	30	....	....	....	1800	109	1	3.54	....	....	....	....	....	....	....	....	....	....	....	....	....	....	....	....	....
1973-74	RPI Engineers	ECAC	30	14	15	1	1800	137	0	4.57	....	....	....	....	....	....	....	....	....	....	....	....	....	....	....	....	....
1974-75	Fort Worth Texans	CHL	15	2	10	0	773	58	0	4.50	....	....	....	....	....	....	....	....	....	....	....	....	....	....	....	....	....
	Muskegon Mohawks	IHL	9	....	....	....	550	24	2	2.62	....	....	....	....	....	1	0	1	0	54	5	0	5.55	....	....	....	....
1975-76	Muskegon Mohawks	IHL	58	....	....	....	3356	158	5	2.82	....	....	....	....	....	4	1	3	0	240	19	0	4.75	....	....	....	....
1976-77	Fort Worth Texans	CHL	34	12	14	7	1957	111	2	3.40	....	....	....	....	....	....	....	....	....	....	....	....	....	....	....	....	....
	Kalamazoo Wings	IHL	1	....	....	....	60	3	0	3.00	....	....	....	....	....	....	....	....	....	....	....	....	....	....	....	....	....
1977-78	Fort Worth Texans	CHL	44	23	13	2	2358	113	2	*2.88	....	....	....	....	....	6	3	2	0	350	15	0	*2.57	....	....	....	....
1978-79	Fort Wayne Komets	IHL	27	....	....	....	1368	100	0	4.37	....	....	....	....	....	....	....	....	....	....	....	....	....	....	....	....	....
	Fort Worth Texans	CHL	7	1	3	0	283	17	0	3.60	....	....	....	....	....	3	0	2	0	151	7	0	2.78	....	....	....	....
1979-80	**Edmonton Oilers**	**NHL**	**6**	**1**	**2**	**1**	**269**	**16**	**0**	**3.57**	**3.14**	....	....	....	....	....	....	....	....	....	....	....	....	....	....	....	....
	Muskegon Mohawks	IHL	25	....	....	....	1379	72	4	3.13	....	....	....	....	....	....	....	....	....	....	....	....	....	....	....	....	....
	Houston Apollos	CHL	28	11	13	3	1636	83	2	3.04	....	....	....	....	....	5	1	3	0	274	20	0	4.38	....	....	....	....
1980-81	Oklahoma City Stars	CHL	2	1	1	0	120	12	0	6.00	....	....	....	....	....	3	0	2	0	134	8	0	3.58	....	....	....	....
	Reipas Lahti	Finland	26	....	....	....	1560	97	1	3.72	....	....	....	....	....	....	....	....	....	....	....	....	....	....	....	....	....
1981-82	Muskegon Mohawks	IHL	24	....	....	....	1315	117	0	5.34	....	....	....	....	....	....	....	....	....	....	....	....	....	....	....	....	....
	NHL Totals		**6**	**1**	**2**	**1**	**269**	**16**	**0**	**3.57**	....	....	....	....	....	....	....	....	....	....	....	....	....	....	....	....	....

ECAC Second All-Star Team (1972, 1973) • IHL First All-Star Team (1976) • Won James Norris Memorial Trophy (fewest goals against - IHL) (1976)

Signed as a free agent by **Edmonton**, January 12, 1980.

• CYR, CLAUDE

Claude Cyr G – L. 5'10", 180 lbs. b: Montreal, Quebec, 3/27/1939. Deceased.

Season	Club	League	GP	W	L	T	Mins	GA	SO	Avg	AAvg	Eff	SA	S%	SAPG	GP	W	L	T	Mins	GA	SO	Avg	Eff	SA	S%	SAPG
1956-57	Montreal Lakeshore	QJHL	36		....	....	2160	113	3	3.14	....	....	....	....	....	....	....	....	....	....	....	....	....	....	....	....	....
1957-58	Hull-Ottawa Jr. Canadiens	Ott-Jr.	13	....	....	....	780	57	0	4.38	....	....	....	....	....	....	....	....	....	....	....	....	....	....	....	....	....
	Hull-Ottawa Canadiens	EOHL	11	....	....	....	660	59	1	5.36	....	....	....	....	....	....	....	....	....	....	....	....	....	....	....	....	....
1958-59	Hull-Ottawa Canadiens	EOHL	26	....	....	....	1560	114	0	4.38	....	....	....	....	....	1	....	....	....	60	4	0	4.00	....	....	....	....
	Montreal Canadiens	**NHL**	**1**	**0**	**0**	**0**	**20**	**1**	**0**	**3.00**	**3.20**	....	....	....	....	....	....	....	....	....	....	....	....	....	....	....	....
1959-60	Hull-Ottawa Canadiens	EPHL	6	2	4	0	360	22	0	3.67	....	....	....	....	....	....	....	....	....	....	....	....	....	....	....	....	....
	Montreal Royals	EPHL	7	2	4	1	420	27	0	3.86	....	....	....	....	....	....	....	....	....	....	....	....	....	....	....	....	....
	Cleveland Barons	AHL	2	0	2	0	120	7	0	3.50	....	....	....	....	....	....	....	....	....	....	....	....	....	....	....	....	....
	Calgary Stampeders	WHL	4	1	3	0	240	15	0	3.75	....	....	....	....	....	....	....	....	....	....	....	....	....	....	....	....	....

			REGULAR SEASON													PLAYOFFS											
Season	Club	League	GP	W	L	T	Mins	GA	SO	Avg	AAvg	Eff	SA	S%	SAPG	GP	W	L	T	Mins	GA	SO	Avg	Eff	SA	S%	SAPG
1960-61	Montreal Royals	EPHL	13	3	6	4	780	41	0	3.15	....	....	....	....	....	....	....	....	....	....	....	....	....	....	....	....	....
	Trail Smoke Eaters	WHL	7	6	1	0	420	19	0	2.71	....	....	....	....	....	2	1	0	0	74	4	0	3.24	....	....	....	....
	Canada	WEC-A	3	2	0	0	134	5	0	2.24	....	....	....	....	....	....	....	....	....	....	....	....	....	....	....	....	....
1961-62	Knoxville Knights	EHL	61	....	....	....	3660	211	3	3.46	....	....	....	....	....	8	4	4	0	480	17	1	*2.12	....	....	....	....
1962-63	Philadelphia–Knoxville	EHL	36	....	....	....	2160	118	5	3.28	....	....	....	....	....	....	....	....	....	....	....	....	....	....	....	....	....
1963-64	Verdun Pirates	QSHL	STATISTICS NOT AVAILABLE																								
1964-65	Sherbrooke Beavers	QSHL	STATISTICS NOT AVAILABLE																								
1965-66	Victoriaville Tigers	QSHL	16	....	....	....	960	82	*1	5.13	....	....	....	....	....	....	....	....	....	....	....	....	....	....	....	....	....
1966-67	Drummondville Eagles	QSHL	27	....	....	....	1620	96	2	3.50	....	....	....	....	....	20	18	2	0	1217	42	3	2.07	....	....	....	....
	NHL Totals		**1**	**0**	**0**	**0**	**20**	**1**	**0**	**3.00**	....	....	....	....	....	....	....	....	....	....	....	....	....	....	....	....	....

Loaned to **Montreal** by **Hull-Ottawa Canadiens** (EOHL) and replaced Claude Pronovost at start of 3rd period, March 19, 1959. (Toronto 6, Montreal 3)

• DADSWELL, DOUG

Doug Dadswell G – L. 5′10″, 180 lbs. b: Scarborough, Ont., 2/7/1964.

1984-85	Cornell University	ECAC	28	17	10	1	1654	97	0	3.52	....	....	....	....	....	....	....	....	....	....	....	....	....	....	....	....	....
1985-86	Cornell University	ECAC	30	20	7	3	1815	92	1	3.04	....	....	....	....	....	....	....	....	....	....	....	....	....	....	....	....	....
1986-87	**Calgary Flames**	**NHL**	**2**	**0**	**1**	**1**	**125**	**10**	**0**	**4.80**	**4.04**	**6.58**	**73**	**.863**	**35.0**	....	....	....	....	....	....	....	....	....	....	....	....
	Moncton Golden Flames	AHL	42	23	12	0	2276	138	1	3.64	....	....	....	....	....	6	2	4	0	326	23	0	4.20	....	....	....	....
1987-88	**Calgary Flames**	**NHL**	**25**	**8**	**7**	**2**	**1221**	**89**	**0**	**4.37**	**3.64**	**6.19**	**628**	**.858**	**30.9**	....	....	....	....	....	....	....	....	....	....	....	....
1988-89	Salt Lake Golden Eagles	IHL	32	15	10	0	1723	110	0	3.83	....	....	....	....	....	....	....	....	....	....	....	....	....	....	....	....	....
	Indianapolis Ice	IHL	24	4	15	0	1207	122	0	6.06	....	....	....	....	....	....	....	....	....	....	....	....	....	....	....	....	....
1989-90			DID NOT PLAY																								
1990-91	Canada	Nat-Team	28	16	6	1	1599	78	0	2.92	....	....	....	....	....	....	....	....	....	....	....	....	....	....	....	....	....
1991-92	Cincinnati Cyclones	ECHL	24	14	9	1	1361	89	0	3.92	....	....	....	....	....	....	....	....	....	....	....	....	....	....	....	....	....
	Utica Devils	AHL	22	7	9	2	1168	67	0	3.44	....	....	....	....	....	2	0	2	0	119	8	0	4.03	....	....	....	....
1992-93	Cincinnati Cyclones	IHL	17	5	11	1	1006	63	1	3.76	....	....	....	....	....	....	....	....	....	....	....	....	....	....	....	....	....
	Birmingham Bulls	ECHL	8	3	3	0	401	36	0	5.39	....	....	....	....	....	....	....	....	....	....	....	....	....	....	....	....	....
	NHL Totals		**27**	**8**	**8**	**3**	**1346**	**99**	**0**	**4.41**	....	....	**701**	**.859**	....	....	....	....	....	....	....	....	....	....	....	....	....

ECAC Second All-Star Team (1986) • NCAA East First All-American Team (1986)

Signed as a free agent by **Calgary**, August 6, 1986.

• DAFOE, BYRON

Byron Dafoe G – L. 5′11″, 175 lbs. b: Sussex, England, 2/25/1971. Washington's 2nd choice, 35th overall, in 1989 Entry Draft.

1988-89	Portland Winter Hawks	WHL	59	29	24	3	3279	291	1	5.32	....	....	....	....	....	*18	10	8	....	*1091	81	*1	4.45	....	....	....	....
1989-90	Washington Capitals	FrTour	2	....	....	....	60	3	0	3.00	....	....	....	....	....	....	....	....	....	....	....	....	....	....	....	....	....
	Portland Winter Hawks	WHL	40	14	21	3	2265	193	0	5.11	....	....	....	....	....	....	....	....	....	....	....	....	....	....	....	....	....
1990-91	Portland Winter Hawks	WHL	8	1	5	1	414	41	0	5.94	....	....	....	....	....	....	....	....	....	....	....	....	....	....	....	....	....
	Prince Albert Raiders	WHL	32	13	12	4	1839	124	0	4.05	....	....	....	....	....	....	....	....	....	....	....	....	....	....	....	....	....
1991-92	Baltimore Skipjacks	AHL	33	12	16	4	1847	119	0	3.87	....	....	....	....	....	....	....	....	....	....	....	....	....	....	....	....	....
	New Haven Nighthawks	AHL	7	3	2	1	364	22	0	3.63	....	....	....	....	....	....	....	....	....	....	....	....	....	....	....	....	....
	Hampton Roads Admirals	ECHL	10	6	4	0	562	26	0	2.78	....	....	....	....	....	....	....	....	....	....	....	....	....	....	....	....	....
1992-93	**Washington Capitals**	**NHL**	**1**	**0**	**0**	**0**	**1**	**0**	**0**	**0.00**	**0.00**	**0.00**	**0**	**.00**	**0.0**	....	....	....	....	....	....	....	....	....	....	....	....
	Baltimore Skipjacks	AHL	48	16	20	7	2617	191	1	4.38	....	....	....	....	....	5	2	3	....	241	22	0	5.48	....	....	....	....
1993-94	**Washington Capitals**	**NHL**	**5**	**2**	**2**	**0**	**230**	**13**	**0**	**3.39**	**3.23**	**4.36**	**101**	**.871**	**26.3**	**2**	**0**	**2**	....	**118**	**5**	**0**	**2.54**	**3.26**	**39**	**.872**	**19.8**
	Portland Pirates	AHL	47	24	16	4	2661	148	1	3.34	....	....	....	....	....	1	0	0	....	9	1	0	6.79	....	....	....	....
1994-95	Phoenix Roadrunners	IHL	49	25	16	6	2743	169	2	3.70	....	....	....	....	....	....	....	....	....	....	....	....	....	....	....	....	....
	Washington Capitals	**NHL**	**4**	**1**	**1**	**1**	**187**	**11**	**0**	**3.53**	**3.65**	**4.85**	**80**	**.863**	**25.7**	**1**	**0**	**0**	....	**20**	**1**	**0**	**3.00**	**10.00**	**3**	**.667**	**9.0**
	Portland Pirates	AHL	6	5	0	0	330	16	0	2.91	....	....	....	....	....	7	3	4	....	416	29	0	4.18	....	....	....	....
1995-96	**Los Angeles Kings**	**NHL**	**47**	**14**	**24**	**8**	**2666**	**172**	**1**	**3.87**	**3.82**	**4.33**	**1539**	**.888**	**34.6**	....	....	....	....	....	....	....	....	....	....	....	....
1996-97	**Los Angeles Kings**	**NHL**	**40**	**13**	**17**	**5**	**2162**	**112**	**0**	**3.11**	**3.30**	**2.96**	**1178**	**.905**	**32.7**	....	....	....	....	....	....	....	....	....	....	....	....
1997-98	**Boston Bruins**	**NHL**	**65**	**30**	**25**	**9**	**3693**	**138**	**6**	**2.24**	**2.61**	**1.93**	**1602**	**.914**	**26.0**	**6**	**2**	**4**	....	**422**	**14**	**1**	**1.99**	**1.75**	**159**	**.912**	**22.6**
	NHL Totals		**162**	**60**	**69**	**23**	**8939**	**446**	**7**	**2.99**	....	....	**4500**	**.901**	....	**9**	**2**	**6**	....	**560**	**20**	**1**	**2.14**	....	....	....	....

AHL First All-Star Team (1994) • Shared Harry "Hap" Holmes Trophy (fewest goals-against - AHL) with Olaf Kolzig (1994)

Traded to **Los Angeles** by **Washington** with Dimitri Khristich for Los Angeles' 1st round choice (Alexander Volchkov) and Dallas' 4th round choice (previously acquired, Washington selected Justin Davis) in 1996 Entry Draft, July 8, 1995. Traded to **Boston** by **Los Angeles** with Dimitri Khristich for Jozef Stumpel, Sandy Moger and Boston's 4th round choice (later traded to New Jersey - New Jersey selected Pierre Dagenais) in 1998 Entry Draft, August 29, 1997.

• D'ALESSIO, CORRIE

Corrie D'Alessio G – L. 5′11″, 155 lbs. b: Cornwall, Ont., 9/9/1969. Vancouver's 4th choice, 107th overall, in 1988 Entry Draft.

1987-88	Cornell University	ECAC	25	17	8	0	1457	67	0	2.76	....	....	....	....	....	....	....	....	....	....	....	....	....	....	....	....	....
1988-89	Cornell University	ECAC	29	15	13	1	1684	96	1	3.42	....	....	....	....	....	....	....	....	....	....	....	....	....	....	....	....	....
1989-90	Cornell University	ECAC	16	6	7	2	887	50	0	3.38	....	....	....	....	....	....	....	....	....	....	....	....	....	....	....	....	....
1990-91	Cornell University	ECAC	24	10	8	3	1160	67	0	3.47	....	....	....	....	....	....	....	....	....	....	....	....	....	....	....	....	....
1991-92	Milwaukee Admirals	IHL	27	9	14	2	1435	96	0	4.01	....	....	....	....	....	2	0	2	0	119	12	0	6.05	....	....	....	....
1992-93	**Hartford Whalers**	**NHL**	**1**	**0**	**0**	**0**	**11**	**0**	**0**	**0.00**	**0.00**	**0.00**	**3**	**1.000**	**16.4**	....	....	....	....	....	....	....	....	....	....	....	....
	Springfield Indians	AHL	23	3	13	2	1120	77	0	4.13	....	....	....	....	....	4	1	0	0	75	3	0	2.40	....	....	....	....
1993-94	Las Vegas Thunder	IHL	1	1	0	0	35	1	0	1.70	....	....	....	....	....	....	....	....	....	....	....	....	....	....	....	....	....
	NHL Totals		**1**	**0**	**0**	**0**	**11**	**0**	**0**	**0.00**	....	....	**3**	**1.000**	....	....	....	....	....	....	....	....	....	....	....	....	....

Traded to **Hartford** by **Vancouver** with future considerations for Kay Whitmore, October 1, 1992.

• DALEY, JOE

Joe "The Holy Goalie" Daley G – L. 5′10″, 170 lbs. b: Winnipeg, Man., 2/20/1943.

1961-62	Weyburn Red Wings	SJHL	53	17	29	7	3180	177	2	3.34	....	....	....	....	....	....	....	....	....	....	....	....	....	....	....	....	....
	Sudbury Wolves	EPHL	1	0	1	0	60	6	0	6.00	....	....	....	....	....	....	....	....	....	....	....	....	....	....	....	....	....
1962-63	Weyburn Red Wings	SJHL	51	28	17	6	3060	152	3	2.98	....	....	....	....	....	8	....	....	....	480	23	1	3.19	....	....	....	....
1963-64	Johnstown Jets	EHL	66	40	22	4	3960	221	4	3.35	....	....	....	....	....	10	5	5	0	600	27	1	2.70	....	....	....	....
	Cincinnati Wings	CHL	1	0	1	0	60	3	0	3.00	....	....	....	....	....	....	....	....	....	....	....	....	....	....	....	....	....
	Pittsburgh Hornets	AHL	2	1	1	0	120	7	0	3.50	....	....	....	....	....	2	0	1	0	60	6	0	6.00	....	....	....	....
1964-65	Johnstown Jets	EHL	*72	41	31	0	*4320	292	2	4.06	....	....	....	....	....	5	2	3	0	300	19	1	3.80	....	....	....	....
1965-66	Memphis Wings	CHL	68	25	31	12	4040	212	2	3.15	....	....	....	....	....	....	....	....	....	....	....	....	....	....	....	....	....
	San Francisco Seals	WHL	8	5	2	1	426	17	2	2.39	....	....	....	....	....	....	....	....	....	....	....	....	....	....	....	....	....
1966-67	Pittsburgh Hornets	AHL	16	11	1	3	948	43	0	2.72	....	....	....	....	....	....	....	....	....	....	....	....	....	....	....	....	....
	Memphis Wings	CHL	50	23	21	5	2960	169	0	3.42	....	....	....	....	....	7	3	4	0	433	27	0	3.74	....	....	....	....
1967-68	Baltimore Clippers	AHL	56	23	25	8	3300	192	2	3.49	....	....	....	....	....	....	....	....	....	....	....	....	....	....	....	....	....
1968-69	**Pittsburgh Penguins**	**NHL**	**29**	**10**	**13**	**3**	**1615**	**87**	**2**	**3.23**	**3.35**	....	....	....	....	....	....	....	....	....	....	....	....	....	....	....	....
1969-70	**Pittsburgh Penguins**	**NHL**	**9**	**1**	**5**	**3**	**528**	**26**	**0**	**2.95**	**3.14**	....	....	....	....	....	....	....	....	....	....	....	....	....	....	....	....
	Baltimore Clippers	AHL	34	....	....	....	1867	107	0	3.44	....	....	....	....	....	5	1	4	0	315	25	0	4.76	....	....	....	....
1970-71	**Buffalo Sabres**	**NHL**	**38**	**12**	**16**	**8**	**2073**	**128**	**1**	**3.70**	**3.68**	....	....	....	....	....	....	....	....	....	....	....	....	....	....	....	....
1971-72	**Detroit Red Wings**	**NHL**	**29**	**11**	**10**	**5**	**1620**	**85**	**0**	**3.15**	**3.17**	....	....	....	....	....	....	....	....	....	....	....	....	....	....	....	....
1972-73	Winnipeg Jets	WHA	29	17	10	1	1718	83	2	2.90	....	....	....	....	....	7	5	2	0	422	25	0	3.55	....	....	....	....
1973-74	Winnipeg Jets	WHA	41	19	20	1	2454	163	0	3.99	....	....	....	....	....	2	0	2	0	119	8	0	4.03	....	....	....	....
1974-75	Winnipeg Jets	WHA	51	23	21	4	2902	175	1	3.62	....	....	....	....	....	....	....	....	....	....	....	....	....	....	....	....	....
1975-76	Winnipeg Jets	WHA	62	41	17	1	3612	171	*5	2.84	....	....	....	....	....	12	*10	1	0	671	29	1	2.59	....	....	....	....
1976-77	Winnipeg Jets	WHA	65	*39	23	2	*3818	206	3	3.24	....	....	....	....	....	*20	11	9	0	*1186	71	*1	3.59	....	....	....	....
1977-78	Winnipeg Jets	WHA	37	21	11	1	2075	114	1	3.30	....	....	....	....	....	5	4	1	0	271	13	0	2.88	....	....	....	....
1978-79	Winnipeg Jets	WHA	23	7	11	3	1256	90	0	4.30	....	....	....	....	....	3	0	0	0	37	3	0	4.86	....	....	....	....
	NHL Totals		**105**	**34**	**44**	**19**	**5836**	**326**	**3**	**3.35**	....	....	....	....	....	....	....	....	....	....	....	....	....	....	....	....	....
	Other Major League Totals		308	167	113	13	17835	1002	12	3.37	....	....	....	....	....	49	30	15	0	2706	149	2	3.30	....	....	....	....

EHL Rookie of the Year (1964) • WHA First All-Star Team (1976) • WHA Second All-Star Team (1977)

Claimed by **Pittsburgh** from **Detroit** in Expansion Draft, June 6, 1967. Claimed on waivers by **Buffalo** from **Pittsburgh**, June 9, 1970. Traded to **Detroit** by **Buffalo** for Don Luce and Mike Robitaille, May 25, 1971. Selected by **Winnipeg** (WHA) in 1972 WHA General Player Draft, February 12, 1972. Claimed by **Cleveland** (AHL) from **Detroit** in Reverse Draft, June, 1972.

			REGULAR SEASON													PLAYOFFS								
Season	Club	League	GP	W	L	T	Mins	GA	SO	Avg	AAvg	Eff	SA	S%	SAPG	GP	W	L	T	Mins	GA	SO	Avg	Eff	SA	S%	SAPG

● DAMORE, NICK Nick Damore G – L. 5'6", 160 lbs. b: Niagara Falls, Ont., 7/10/1916.

Season	Club	League	GP	W	L	T	Mins	GA	SO	Avg	AAvg	GP	W	L	T	Mins	GA	SO	Avg
1933-34	Niagara Falls Cataracts	OHA	STATISTICS NOT AVAILABLE																
1934-35	Hershey B'ars	EHL	21	10	9	2	1260	56	3	2.67	....	6	3	3	0	360	22	0	3.67
1935-36	Hershey B'ars	EHL	22	16	5	1	1320	42	*5	*1.91	....	5	....	....	....	300	15	0	3.00
	Baltimore Orioles	EHL	1	0	1	0	60	5	0	5.00	....								
1936-37	Hershey B'ars	EHL	34	18	9	7	2040	61	1	*1.79	....	4	*3	1	0	250	9	*1	2.16
1937-38	Hershey B'ars	EHL	57	*31	15	11	3420	135	*7	*2.36	....								
1938-39	Providence Reds	AHL	43	16	18	9	2700	126	6	2.80	....								
	Hershey Bears	AHL										2	1	1	0	120	8	0	4.00
1939-40	Hershey Bears	AHL	42	21	18	3	2580	109	4	2.53	....	6	3	3	0	360	15	1	2.50
1940-41	Hershey Bears	AHL	*56	24	23	9	*3470	189	3	3.27	....	*10	*6	4	0	640	20	*2	*1.88
1941-42	Hershey Bears	AHL	56	33	17	6	3450	169	4	2.94	....	10	6	4	0	620	27	1	2.61
	Boston Bruins	**NHL**	1	1	0	0	60	3	0	3.00	2.97								
1942-43	Hershey Bears	AHL	54	*34	13	7	3240	161	2	2.98	....	6	2	4	0	360	23	1	3.83
1943-44	Hershey Bears	AHL	54	*30	16	8	3240	133	6	*2.46	....	7	3	4	0	425	18	0	2.54
1944-45	Hershey Bears	AHL	57	28	22	7	3420	176	7	3.09	....	11	6	5	0	660	29	0	2.63
1945-46	Hershey Bears	AHL	46	20	21	5	2760	160	3	3.48	....								
1946-47	Philadelphia Rockets	AHL	56	5	44	7	3360	342	1	6.11	....								
1947-1950			DID NOT PLAY																
1950-51	Johnstown Jets	EHL	23	....	....	....	1380	91	*2	3.95	....	6	2	4	0	360	27	0	4.50
1951-52	Washington Lions	EHL	12	2	9	1	720	57	0	4.75	....								
	NHL Totals		1	1	0	0	60	3	0	3.00									

EHL Second All-Star Team (1935) • EHL First All-Star Team (1936, 1937, 1938) • Won George L. Davis Jr. Trophy (fewest goals against - EHL) (1937, 1938) • AHL First All-Star Team (1944, 1945, 1946)

• Promoted to **Boston** from **Hershey** (AHL) to replace injured Frank Brimsek, January 25, 1942. (Boston 7, Montreal 3).

● D'AMOUR, MARC Marc D'Amour G – L. 5'9", 190 lbs. b: Sudbury, Ont., 5/29/1961.

Season	Club	League	GP	W	L	T	Mins	GA	SO	Avg	AAvg	Eff	SA	S%	SAPG	GP	W	L	T	Mins	GA	SO	Avg
1978-79	Sault Ste. Marie Greyhounds	OHA	30	....	....	....	1501	149	0	5.96	....												
1979-80	Sault Ste. Marie Greyhounds	OHA	33	6	15	0	1429	117	0	4.91	....												
1980-81	Sault Ste. Marie Greyhounds	OHA	16	7	1	1	653	38	0	3.49	....					14	5	4	0	683	41	0	3.60
1981-82	Sault Ste. Marie Greyhounds	OHL	46	28	12	1	2384	130	1	*3.27	....					10	3	2	0	504	30	0	3.57
1982-83	Colorado Flames	CHL	42	16	21	2	2373	153	1	3.87	....					1	0	1	0	59	4	0	4.08
1983-84	Colorado Flames	CHL	36	18	12	1	1917	131	0	4.10	....					1	0	0	0	20	0	0	0.00
1984-85	Moncton Golden Flames	AHL	37	18	14	2	2051	115	0	3.36	....												
	Salt Lake Golden Eagles	IHL	12	7	2	2	694	33	0	2.85	....												
1985-86	**Calgary Flames**	**NHL**	15	2	4	2	560	32	0	3.43	2.67	3.54	310	.897	33.2								
	Moncton Golden Flames	AHL	21	6	9	3	1129	72	0	3.83	....					5	1	4	0	296	20	0	4.05
1986-87	Binghamton Whalers	AHL	8	5	3	0	461	30	0	3.90	....												
	Salt Lake Golden Eagles	IHL	10	3	6	0	523	37	0	4.24	....												
	Canada	Nat-Team	1	0	0	0	30	4	0	8.00	....												
1987-88	Salt Lake Golden Eagles	IHL	*62	26	19	5	3245	177	0	3.27	....					*19	*12	7	0	*1123	67	0	3.58
1988-89	**Philadelphia Flyers**	**NHL**	1	0	0	0	19	0	0	0.00	0.00	0.00	14	1.000	44.2								
	Hershey Bears	AHL	39	19	13	3	2174	127	0	3.51	....												
	Indianapolis Ice	IHL	6	2	3	0	324	20	0	3.70	....												
1989-90	Hershey Bears	AHL	43	15	20	6	2505	148	2	3.54	....												
1990-91	Hershey Bears	AHL	28	10	8	4	1331	80	0	3.61	....					2	0	1	0	80	5	0	3.75
	Fort Wayne Komets	IHL	3	1	0	0	136	9	0	3.97	....												
1991-92	Hershey Bears	AHL	21	9	8	2	1073	79	0	4.42	....												
	NHL Totals		16	2	4	2	579	32	0	3.32			324	.901									

Signed as a free agent by **Calgary**, June 7, 1982. Signed as a free agent by **Philadelphia**, September 30, 1988.

● DARRAGH, JACK Jack Darragh G – L. 5'10", 168 lbs. b: Ottawa, Ont., 12/4/1890. d: 6/25/1924.

Season	Club	League	GP	W	L	T	Mins	GA	SO	Avg	AAvg
1919-20	**Ottawa Senators**	**NHL**	1	0	0	0	2	0	0	0.00	0.00
	NHL Totals		1	0	0	0	2	0	0	0.00	

Ottawa right winger replaced penalized Clint Benedict, January 24, 1920. (Toronto 5, Ottawa 3)

● DASKALAKIS, CLEON Cleon Daskalakis G – L. 5'9", 175 lbs. b: Boston, MA, 9/29/1962.

Season	Club	League	GP	W	L	T	Mins	GA	SO	Avg	AAvg	Eff	SA	S%	SAPG	GP	W	L	T	Mins	GA	SO	Avg
1980-81	Boston University	ECAC	8	4	2	0	399	24	0	3.61	....												
1981-82	Boston University	ECAC	20	9	6	3	1101	59	3	3.22	....												
1982-83	Boston University	ECAC	24	15	7	1	1398	78	1	3.35	....												
1983-84	Boston University	ECAC	35	25	10	0	1972	96	1	2.92	....												
1984-85	**Boston Bruins**	**NHL**	8	1	2	1	289	24	0	4.98	3.96	8.48	141	.830	29.3								
	Hershey Bears	AHL	30	9	13	4	1614	119	0	4.42	....												
1985-86	**Boston Bruins**	**NHL**	2	0	2	0	120	10	0	5.00	3.89	7.94	63	.841	31.5								
	Moncton Golden Flames	AHL	41	19	14	6	2343	141	0	3.61	....					6	4	1	0	372	13	0	*2.10
1986-87	**Boston Bruins**	**NHL**	2	2	0	0	97	7	0	4.33	3.64	5.94	51	.863	31.5								
	Moncton Golden Flames	AHL	27	8	14	0	1452	118	0	4.88	....					1	0	0	0	36	2	0	3.33
1987-88	Hershey Bears	AHL	3	1	1	0	122	9	0	4.43	....												
	Binghamton Whalers	AHL	6	2	1	0	344	27	0	4.71	....												
	Rochester Americans	AHL	8	4	3	0	382	22	0	3.46	....												
	Milwaukee Admirals	IHL	9	1	5	3	483	47	0	5.04	....												
1988-89	United States	Nat-Team	1	0	0	0	20	1	0	3.00	....												
	United States	WEC-A	DID NOT PLAY – SPARE GOALTENDER																				
	NHL Totals		12	3	4	1	506	41	0	4.86			255	.839									

ECAC Second All-Star Team (1983) • ECAC First All-Star Team (1984) • NCAA East First All-American Team (1984)
Signed as a free agent by **Boston**, June 1, 1984.

● DAVIDSON, JOHN John Davidson G – L. 6'3", 205 lbs. b: Ottawa, Ont., 2/27/1953. St. Louis' 1st choice, 5th overall, in 1973 Amateur Draft.

Season	Club	League	GP	W	L	T	Mins	GA	SO	Avg	AAvg	GP	W	L	T	Mins	GA	SO	Avg
1970-71	Lethbridge Native Sons	AJHL	46	....	....	....	2760	142	*3	*3.09	....								
	Calgary Centennials	WCJHL										1	....	....	....	19	1	0	3.16
1971-72	Calgary Centennials	WCJHL	66	....	....	....	3970	157	*8	*2.37	....	13	6	6	1	780	39	0	3.00
1972-73	Calgary Centennials	WCJHL	63	....	....	....	3735	201	2	3.30	....								
1973-74	**St. Louis Blues**	**NHL**	39	13	19	7	2300	118	0	3.08	2.97								
1974-75	Denver Spurs	CHL	7	4	2	1	420	27	0	3.86	....								
	St. Louis Blues	**NHL**	40	17	15	7	2360	144	0	3.66	3.30	1	0	1	0	60	4	0	4.00
1975-76	**New York Rangers**	**NHL**	56	22	28	5	3207	212	3	3.97	3.61								
1976-77	New Haven Nighthawks	AHL	2	....	....	....	119	5	0	2.52	....								
	New York Rangers	**NHL**	39	14	14	6	2116	125	1	3.54	3.29								
1977-78	**New York Rangers**	**NHL**	34	14	13	4	1848	98	1	3.18	2.97	2	1	1	0	122	7	0	3.44
1978-79	**New York Rangers**	**NHL**	39	20	15	2	2232	131	0	3.52	3.11	*18	11	7	....	*1106	42	*1	2.28
1979-80	New Haven Nighthawks	AHL	4	1	3	0	238	16	0	4.02	....								
	New York Rangers	**NHL**	41	20	15	4	2306	122	2	3.17	2.78	9	4	5	....	541	21	0	2.33
1980-81	**New York Rangers**	**NHL**	10	1	7	1	560	48	0	5.14	4.13								

			REGULAR SEASON												PLAYOFFS									
Season	Club	League	GP	W	L	T	Mins	GA	SO	Avg	AAvg	Eff	SA	S%	SAPG	GP	W	L	T	Mins	GA	SO	Avg	Eff	SA	S%	SAPG
1981-82	Springfield Indians	AHL	8	3	4	0	437	24	0	3.30	....	....	....	....	....	....	....	....	....	....	....	....	....	....
	New York Rangers	NHL	1	1	0	0	60	1	0	1.00	0.77	....	....	....	1	0	0		33	3	0	5.45
1982-83	New York Rangers	NHL	2	1	1	0	120	5	0	2.50	2.00	2.27	55	.909	27.5
	NHL Totals		301	123	124	39	17109	1004	7	3.52	....					31	16	14		1862	77	1	2.48

WCJHL All-Star Team (1972, 1973)

Traded to **NY Rangers** by **St. Louis** with Bill Collins for Jerry Butler, Ted Irvine and Bert Wilson, June 18, 1975.

● **DECOURCY, ROBERT**   Robert Decourcy   G – R. 5'11", 160 lbs.   b: Toronto, Ont., 6/12/1927.

Season	Club	League	GP	W	L	T	Mins	GA	SO	Avg	AAvg					GP	W	L	T	Mins	GA	SO	Avg
1945-46	St. Michael's Majors	OHA	1	0	0	0	20	0	0	0.00
1946-47	Hamilton Szabos	OHA	20				1200	176	0	8.80													
	New York Rovers	EHL	2	0	2	0	120	9	0	4.50						6	3	2	1	360	22	0	3.67
1947-48	New York Rovers	EHL	14				840	92	0	6.57
	New York Rangers	**NHL**	1	0	1	0	29	6	0	12.41	13.14
	New York Rovers	QSHL	10				600	55	0	5.50
	St. Paul Saints	USHL	8				480	21	2	2.62
1948-49	Kansas City Pla-Mors	USHL	2	0	1	1	120	6	0	3.00
	Omaha Knights	USHL	9	3	5	1	540	32	0	3.56
1949-50	St. Paul Saints	USHL	13	3	10	0	780	69	0	5.30
1950-51	St. Michael's Monarchs	OHA Sr.	1				60	5	0	5.00
	NHL Totals		1	0	1	0	29	6	0	12.41

● NY Rangers' spare goaltender replaced injured Claude Rayner in 2nd period, November 12, 1947. (Boston 8, NY Rangers 2).

● **DEFELICE, NORMAN**   Norman Defelice   G – L. 5'10", 150 lbs.   b: Schumacher, Ont., 1/19/1933.

Season	Club	League	GP	W	L	T	Mins	GA	SO	Avg	AAvg					GP	W	L	T	Mins	GA	SO	Avg
1951-52	Waterloo Hurricanes	OHA	18				1050	138	0	7.89
1952-53	St. Catharines Teepees	OHA	20				1200	55	2	2.75						2				120	8	0	4.00
1953-54	Sydney Millionaires	MMHL	69	35	30	3	4182	236	*7	*3.39						12	5	7	0	730	35	1	2.88
	Hershey Bears	AHL	1	0	1	0	60	4	0	4.00
1954-55	Johnstown Jets	IHL	37				2220	122	0	3.30
	Hershey Bears	AHL	21	9	11	1	1260	82	1	3.90
	Toledo Mercurys	IHL	4				240	21	0	5.25
	Washington Lions	EHL	1				60	5	0	5.00
1955-56	Hershey Bears	AHL	22	7	13	2	1320	91	0	4.14
	Washington Lions	EHL	4				240	12	0	3.00
1956-57	Hershey Bears	AHL	8	6	1	1	490	21	2	2.57
	Boston Bruins	**NHL**	10	3	5	2	600	30	0	3.00	3.45
	Springfield Indians	AHL	8	1	6	1	500	38	0	4.56
1957-58	Clinton Comets	EHL	45				2700	162	1	3.60
	Trois-Rivieres Lions	QHL	2	0	2	0	120	10	0	5.00
	Charlotte Clippers	EHL	1	0	1	0	60	8	0	8.00
	Washington Presidents	EHL														12	*8	4	0	720	32	*1	*2.67
1958-59	Clinton Comets	EHL	63	*41	20	2	3780	177	3	*2.82						8	*8	0	0	480	18	*1	*2.25
1959-60	Clinton Comets	EHL	37				2220	97	4	*2.62						8	3	5	0	480	23	0	2.88
	Greensboro Generals	EHL	1	1	0	0	60	4	0	4.00
1960-61	Clinton Comets	EHL	60	29	29	2	3600	220	*6	3.49						4	1	3	0	240	15	0	3.75
1961-62	Clinton Comets	EHL	68	*45	22	1	4080	193	*5	*2.99						6	1	5	0	360	22	0	3.65
1962-63	Clinton Comets	EHL	63	36	21	6	3780	163	*8	*2.59						13	8	5	0	780	45	0	3.23
1963-64	Clinton Comets	EHL	66	35	24	7	3960	193	*8	*2.92						12	7	5	0	730	45	1	3.70
1964-65	Clinton Comets	EHL	69				4140	*164	*15	*2.38						11	5	6	0	670	32	0	2.86
1965-66	New Jersey Devils	EHL	62				3720	239	1	3.85
1966-67	New Jersey Devils	EHL	52				3120	146	0	2.81						9	5	4	0	540	29	0	3.22
1967-68	Galt Hornets	OHA Sr.	29				1740	62	*5	*2.14
1968-69	Long Island Ducks	EHL	23				1380	75	1	3.26
1969-70	Galt Hornets	OHA Sr.	13				780	32	1	2.46
	NHL Totals		10	3	5	2	600	30	0	3.00

EHL First All-Star Team (1959, 1962, 1963) ● Won George L. Davis Jr. Trophy (fewest goals against - EHL) (1959, 1960, 1962, 1963, 1964, 1965) ● EHL Second All-Star Team (1961, 1964) ● EHL North First All-Star Team (1965) ● EHL North Second All-Star Team (1967)

● Promoted to **Boston** from **Hershey** (AHL) to replace Terry Sawchuk who was hospitalized for nervous exhaustion, December 13, 1956. Traded to **Springfield** (AHL) by **Boston** with Jack Bionda for Don Simmons, January, 1957.

● **DEJORDY, DENIS**   Denis DeJordy   G – L. 5'9", 185 lbs.   b: St. Hyacinthe, Que., 11/12/1938.

Season	Club	League	GP	W	L	T	Mins	GA	SO	Avg	AAvg					GP	W	L	T	Mins	GA	SO	Avg
1957-58	St. Catharines Teepees	OHA	52	*32	14	6	3120	174	1	3.35						8	3	4	1	480	36	0	4.50
	Buffalo Bisons	AHL	1	0	1	0	60	5	0	5.00
1958-59	St. Catharines Teepees	OHA	53	*40	10	3	3180	169	1	3.19						7	2	4	1	420	18	0	2.57
1959-60	Sault Ste. Marie Thunderbirds	EPHL	69	27	31	11	4140	258	1	3.74
1960-61	Sault Ste. Marie Thunderbirds	EPHL	33	16	14	3	1980	115	2	3.48
	Buffalo Bisons	AHL	40	20	18	2	2400	127	3	3.18						4	0	4	0	264	18	0	4.09
1961-62	Buffalo Bisons	AHL	*69	*36	30	3	*4170	210	*8	3.02						*11	6	5	0	706	20	*2	1.70
1962-63	Buffalo Bisons	AHL	67	*37	23	7	4020	187	*6	2.79						13	*8	5	0	802	28	1	*2.09
	Chicago Black Hawks	**NHL**	5	2	1	2	290	12	0	2.48	2.57
1963-64	**Chicago Black Hawks**	**NHL**	6	2	3	1	340	19	0	3.35	3.73					1	0	0		20	2	0	6.00
	St. Louis Braves	CHL	1	0	1	0	60	5	0	5.00
1964-65	Buffalo Bisons	AHL	7	3	4	0	450	20	1	2.67
	Chicago Black Hawks	**NHL**	30	16	11	3	1760	74	3	2.52	2.68					2	0	1	0	80	9	0	6.75
1965-66	St. Louis Braves	CHL	*70	30	31	9	*4200	217	4	3.10						5	1	4	0	300	18	0	3.60
1966-67	**Chicago Black Hawks**	**NHL**	44	22	12	7	2536	104	4	2.46	2.50					4	1	2		184	10	0	3.26
1967-68	**Chicago Black Hawks**	**NHL**	50	23	15	11	2838	128	4	2.71	2.99					11	5	6		662	34	0	3.08
1968-69	**Chicago Black Hawks**	**NHL**	53	22	22	7	2981	156	2	3.14	3.26
	Dallas Black Hawks	CHL	15	8	4	3	899	41	1	2.74
1969-70	**Chicago Black Hawks**	**NHL**	10	3	5	1	557	25	0	2.69	2.86
	Los Angeles Kings	**NHL**	21	5	11	4	1147	62	0	3.24	3.45
1970-71	**Los Angeles Kings**	**NHL**	60	18	29	11	3375	214	1	3.80	3.80
1971-72	**Los Angeles Kings**	**NHL**	5	0	5	0	291	23	0	4.74	4.78
	Montreal Canadiens	**NHL**	7	3	2	1	332	25	0	4.52	4.56
1972-73	Fort Worth Wings	CHL	10				560	41	0	4.39
	Detroit Red Wings	**NHL**	24	8	11	3	1331	83	1	3.74	3.53
1973-74	**Detroit Red Wings**	**NHL**	1	0	1	0	20	4	0	12.00	11.60
	Baltimore Clippers	AHL	42	21	13	6	2428	131	1	3.23						4	1	3	0	252	22	0	5.23
	NHL Totals		316	124	128	51	17798	929	15	3.13						18	6	9		946	55	0	3.49

AHL First All-Star Team (1963) ● Won Harry "Hap" Holmes Memorial Award (fewest goals against - AHL) (1963) ● Won Les Cunningham Award (MVP - AHL) (1963) ● CHL First All-Star Team (1966) ● Shared Vezina Trophy with Glenn Hall (1967) ● AHL Second All-Star Team (1974)

Traded to **LA Kings** by **Chicago** with Gilles Marotte and Jim Stanfield for Bill White, Bryan Campbell and Gerry Desjardins, February 20, 1970. Traded to **Montreal** by **LA Kings** with Dale Hoganson, Noel Price and Doug Robinson for Rogie Vachon, November 4, 1971. Traded to **NY Islanders** by **Montreal** with Glenn Resch, Germain Gagnon, Tony Featherstone, Murray Anderson and Alex Campbell for cash, June 26, 1972. Traded to **Detroit** by **NY Islanders** with Don McLaughlin for Arnie Brown and Gerry Gray, October 4, 1972.

● **DELGUIDICE, MATT**   Matt DelGuidice   G – R. 5'9", 170 lbs.   b: West Haven, CT, 3/5/1967.   Boston's 5th choice, 77th overall, in 1987 Entry Draft.

Season	Club	League	GP	W	L	T	Mins	GA	SO	Avg	AAvg					GP	W	L	T	Mins	GA	SO	Avg
1986-87	St. Anselm College	NCAA				STATISTICS NOT AVAILABLE																		
1987-88	University of Maine	H.E.				DID NOT PLAY – FRESHMAN																		
1988-89	University of Maine	H.E.	20	16	4	0	1090	57	1	*3.14						4	3	1	0	254	16	0	3.78
1989-90	University of Maine	H.E.	23	16	4	0	1257	68	0	3.25						5	3	1	0	244	15	0	3.69

			REGULAR SEASON													PLAYOFFS											
Season	Club	League	GP	W	L	T	Mins	GA	SO	Avg	AAvg	Eff	SA	S%	SAPG	GP	W	L	T	Mins	GA	SO	Avg	Eff	SA	S%	SAPG
1990-91	**Boston Bruins**	**NHL**	**1**	**0**	**0**	**0**	**10**	**0**	**0**	**0.00**	**0.00**	**0.00**	**7**	**1.000**	**42.0**	....	....	....	....	....	....	....	....	....	....	....	....
	Maine Mariners	AHL	52	23	18	9	2893	160	2	3.32	....	....	....	....	....	2	1	1	0	82	5	0	3.66	....	....	....	....
1991-92	**Boston Bruins**	**NHL**	**10**	**2**	**5**	**1**	**424**	**28**	**0**	**3.96**	**3.51**	**4.64**	**239**	**.883**	**33.8**	....	....	....	....	....	....	....	....	....	....	....	....
	Maine Mariners	AHL	25	5	15	0	1369	101	0	4.43	....	....	....	....	....	....	....	....	....	....	....	....	....	....	....	....	....
1992-93	Providence Bruins	AHL	9	0	7	1	478	58	0	7.28	....	....	....	....	....	....	....	....	....	....	....	....	....	....	....	....	....
	San Diego Gulls	IHL	1	0	0	0	20	2	0	6.00	....	....	....	....	....	....	....	....	....	....	....	....	....	....	....	....	....
1993-94	Albany River Rats	AHL	5	1	2	2	309	19	0	3.68	....	....	....	....	....	....	....	....	....	....	....	....	....	....	....	....	....
	Springfield Indians	AHL	1	0	0	1	65	3	0	2.77	....	....	....	....	....	....	....	....	....	....	....	....	....	....	....	....	....
	Raleigh IceCaps	ECHL	31	18	9	4	1877	92	1	*2.94	....	....	....	....	....	12	6	6	0	706	37	0	3.14	....	....	....	....
1994-95	Charlotte Checkers	ECHL	5	2	2	1	303	15	0	2.97	....	....	....	....	....	....	....	....	....	....	....	....	....	....	....	....	....
	Nashville Knights	ECHL	18	7	8	2	1009	81	0	4.82	....	....	....	....	....	2	0	1	0	74	6	0	4.84	....	....	....	....
	Atlanta Knights	IHL	1	0	0	0	52	5	0	5.70	....	....	....	....	....	....	....	....	....	....	....	....	....	....	....	....	....
1995-96	Roanoke Express	ECHL	35	13	10	3	1738	103	3	3.56	....	....	....	....	....	2	0	1	0	60	3	0	2.98	....	....	....	....
1996-97	Amarillo Rattlers	WPHL	49	13	26	7	2620	193	0	4.42	....	....	....	....	....	....	....	....	....	....	....	....	....	....	....	....	....
1997-98	Amarillo Rattlers	WPHL	31	7	17	4	1598	124	0	4.65	....	....	....	....	....	....	....	....	....	....	....	....	....	....	....	....	....
	Monroe Moccasins	WPHL	16	9	7	0	922	48	2	3.12	....	....	....	....	....	....	....	....	....	....	....	....	....	....	....	....	....
	NHL Totals		**11**	**2**	**5**	**1**	**434**	**28**	**0**	**3.87**	....	....	**246**	**.886**	....	....	....	....	....	....	....	....	....	....	....	....	....

NCAA (College Div.) East Second All-American Team (1987)

• DENIS, MARC

Marc Denis G – L. 6′, 188 lbs. b: Montreal, Que., 8/1/1977. Colorado's 1st choice, 25th overall, in 1995 Entry Draft.

Season	Club	League	GP	W	L	T	Mins	GA	SO	Avg	AAvg	Eff	SA	S%	SAPG	GP	W	L	T	Mins	GA	SO	Avg	Eff	SA	S%	SAPG
1994-95	Chicoutimi Sagueneens	QMJHL	32	17	9	1	1688	98	0	3.48	....	....	....	....	....	6	4	2	....	372	19	1	3.06	....	....	....	....
1995-96	Chicoutimi Sagueneens	QMJHL	51	23	21	4	2951	157	2	3.19	....	....	....	....	....	16	8	8	....	957	69	0	4.33	....	....	....	....
	Canada	WJC-A	2	2	0	0	120	2	....	1.00	....	....	....	....	....	....	....	....	....	....	....	....	....	....	....	....	....
1996-97	**Colorado Avalanche**	**NHL**	**1**	**0**	**1**	**0**	**60**	**3**	**0**	**3.00**	**3.18**	**3.46**	**26**	**.885**	**26.0**	....	....	....	....	....	....	....	....	....	....	....	....
	Chicoutimi Sagueneens	QMJHL	41	22	15	2	2323	104	4	*2.69	....	....	....	....	....	*21	*11	10	....	*1229	70	*1	3.42	....	....	....	....
	Canada	WJC-A	7	5	0	2	419	13	....	1.86	....	....	....	....	....	....	....	....	....	....	....	....	....	....	....	....	....
	Hershey Bears	AHL	....	....	....	....	....	....	....	....	....	....	....	....	....	4	1	0	....	56	1	0	1.08	....	....	....	....
1997-98	Hershey Bears	AHL	47	17	23	4	2588	125	1	2.90	....	....	....	....	....	6	3	3	....	346	15	0	2.59	....	....	....	....
	NHL Totals		**1**	**0**	**1**	**0**	**60**	**3**	**0**	**3.00**	....	....	**26**	**.885**	....	....	....	....	....	....	....	....	....	....	....	....	....

Named Best Goaltender at WJC-A (1997) • QMJHL First All-Star Team (1997) • Canadian Major Junior First All-Star Team (1997) • Canadian Major Junior Goaltender of the Year (1997)

• DeROUVILLE, PHILIPPE

Philippe DeRouville G – L. 6′1″, 185 lbs. b: Victoriaville, Que., 8/7/1974. Pittsburgh's 5th choice, 115th overall, in 1992 Entry Draft.

Season	Club	League	GP	W	L	T	Mins	GA	SO	Avg	AAvg	Eff	SA	S%	SAPG	GP	W	L	T	Mins	GA	SO	Avg	Eff	SA	S%	SAPG
1990-91	Longueuil College Francais	QMJHL	20	13	6	0	1030	50	0	2.91	....	....	....	....	....	....	....	....	....	....	....	....	....	....	....	....	....
1991-92	Verdun College Francais	QMJHL	34	20	6	3	1854	99	2	3.20	....	....	....	....	....	11	7	3	....	593	28	1	2.83	....	....	....	....
1992-93	Verdun College Francais	QMJHL	61	30	27	2	3491	210	1	3.61	....	....	....	....	....	4	0	4	....	256	18	0	3.61	....	....	....	....
	Canada	WJC-A	1	....	....	....	60	7	0	7.00	....	....	....	....	....	....	....	....	....	....	....	....	....	....	....	....	....
1993-94	Verdun College Francais	QMJHL	51	28	22	0	2845	145	1	*3.06	....	....	....	....	....	4	0	4	....	210	14	0	4.00	....	....	....	....
1994-95	Cleveland Lumberjacks	IHL	41	24	10	5	2369	131	1	3.32	....	....	....	....	....	4	1	3	....	263	18	0	4.09	....	....	....	....
	Pittsburgh Penguins	**NHL**	**1**	**1**	**0**	**0**	**60**	**3**	**0**	**3.00**	**3.10**	**3.33**	**27**	**.889**	**27.0**	....	....	....	....	....	....	....	....	....	....	....	....
1995-96	Cleveland Lumberjacks	IHL	38	19	11	3	2008	129	1	3.86	....	....	....	....	....	....	....	....	....	....	....	....	....	....	....	....	....
1996-97	**Pittsburgh Penguins**	**NHL**	**2**	**0**	**2**	**0**	**111**	**6**	**0**	**3.24**	**3.43**	**2.95**	**66**	**.909**	**35.7**	....	....	....	....	....	....	....	....	....	....	....	....
	Kansas City Blades	IHL	26	11	11	4	1470	69	2	2.82	....	....	....	....	....	2	0	1	....	32	4	0	7.35	....	....	....	....
1997-98	Louisville RiverFrogs	ECHL	8	5	2	1	480	27	0	3.38	....	....	....	....	....	....	....	....	....	....	....	....	....	....	....	....	....
	Utah Grizzlies	IHL	30	18	9	1	1524	65	3	2.56	....	....	....	....	....	2	1	1	....	129	7	0	3.25	....	....	....	....
	Hartford Wolf Pack	AHL	3	0	2	1	184	10	0	3.26	....	....	....	....	....	....	....	....	....	....	....	....	....	....	....	....	....
	NHL Totals		**3**	**1**	**2**	**0**	**171**	**9**	**0**	**3.16**	....	....	**93**	**.903**	....	....	....	....	....	....	....	....	....	....	....	....	....

QMJHL Second All-Star Team (1993, 1994)

• DESJARDINS, GERRY

Gerry Desjardins G – L. 5′11″, 190 lbs. b: Sudbury, Ont., 7/22/1944.

Season	Club	League	GP	W	L	T	Mins	GA	SO	Avg	AAvg	Eff	SA	S%	SAPG	GP	W	L	T	Mins	GA	SO	Avg	Eff	SA	S%	SAPG
1962-63	Toronto Marlboros	OHA	30	....	....	....	1780	97	2	3.27	....	....	....	....	....	....	....	....	....	....	....	....	....	....	....	....	....
1963-64	Garson Native Sons	NOHA	STATISTICS NOT AVAILABLE																								
	London Nationals	Jr. B	STATISTICS NOT AVAILABLE																								
1964-65	Toronto Marlboros	OHA	53	32	14	7	3180	202	1	3.81	....	....	....	....	....	....	....	....	....	....	....	....	....	....	....	....	....
1965-66	Houston Apollos	CHL	20	6	8	5	1160	73	0	3.78	....	....	....	....	....	....	....	....	....	....	....	....	....	....	....	....	....
1966-67	Houston Apollos	CHL	36	15	18	5	2160	130	1	3.61	....	....	....	....	....	6	2	4	0	328	18	0	3.29	....	....	....	....
1967-68	Cleveland Barons	AHL	*66	26	26	14	*3934	226	3	3.45	....	....	....	....	....	....	....	....	....	....	....	....	....	....	....	....	....
1968-69	**Los Angeles Kings**	**NHL**	**60**	**18**	**34**	**6**	**3499**	**190**	**4**	**3.26**	**3.40**	....	....	....	....	**9**	**3**	**4**	....	**431**	**28**	**0**	**3.90**	....	....	....	....
1969-70	**Los Angeles Kings**	**NHL**	**43**	**7**	**29**	**5**	**2453**	**159**	**3**	**3.89**	**4.20**	....	....	....	....	....	....	....	....	....	....	....	....	....	....	....	....
	Chicago Black Hawks	**NHL**	**4**	**4**	**0**	**0**	**240**	**8**	**0**	**2.00**	**2.12**	....	....	....	....	....	....	....	....	....	....	....	....	....	....	....	....
1970-71	**Chicago Black Hawks**	**NHL**	**22**	**12**	**6**	**3**	**1217**	**49**	**0**	**2.42**	**2.38**	....	....	....	....	....	....	....	....	....	....	....	....	....	....	....	....
1971-72	**Chicago Black Hawks**	**NHL**	**6**	**1**	**2**	**3**	**360**	**21**	**0**	**3.50**	**3.53**	....	....	....	....	**1**	**1**	**0**	....	**60**	**5**	**0**	**5.00**	....	....	....	....
1972-73	**New York Islanders**	**NHL**	**44**	**5**	**35**	**3**	**2498**	**195**	**0**	**4.68**	**4.47**	....	....	....	....	....	....	....	....	....	....	....	....	....	....	....	....
1973-74	**New York Islanders**	**NHL**	**36**	**9**	**17**	**6**	**1945**	**101**	**0**	**3.12**	**3.01**	....	....	....	....	....	....	....	....	....	....	....	....	....	....	....	....
1974-75	Michigan – Baltimore	WHA	41	9	28	1	2282	162	0	4.26	....	....	....	....	....	....	....	....	....	....	....	....	....	....	....	....	....
	Buffalo Sabres	**NHL**	**9**	**6**	**2**	**1**	**540**	**25**	**0**	**2.78**	**2.50**	....	....	....	....	***15**	**7**	**5**	....	**760**	**43**	**0**	**3.39**	....	....	....	....
1975-76	**Buffalo Sabres**	**NHL**	**55**	**29**	**15**	**11**	**3280**	**161**	**2**	**2.95**	**2.65**	....	....	....	....	**9**	**4**	**5**	....	**563**	**28**	**0**	**2.98**	....	....	....	....
1976-77	**Buffalo Sabres**	**NHL**	**49**	**31**	**12**	**6**	**2871**	**126**	**3**	**2.63**	**2.43**	....	....	....	....	**1**	**0**	**1**	....	**60**	**4**	**0**	**4.00**	....	....	....	....
1977-78	**Buffalo Sabres**	**NHL**	**3**	**0**	**1**	**0**	**111**	**7**	**0**	**3.78**	**3.54**	....	....	....	....	....	....	....	....	....	....	....	....	....	....	....	....
	NHL Totals		**331**	**122**	**153**	**44**	**19014**	**1042**	**12**	**3.29**	....	....	....	....	....	**35**	**15**	**15**	....	**1874**	**108**	**0**	**3.46**	....	....	....	....
	Other Major League Totals		41	9	28	1	2282	162	0	4.26	....	....	....	....	....	....	....	....	....	....	....	....	....	....	....	....	....

AHL First All-Star Team (1968) • Won Dudley "Red" Garrett Memorial Award (Top Rookie - AHL) (1968)

Played in NHL All-Star Game (1977)

Traded to **LA Kings** by **Montreal** for LA Kings' 1st round choices in 1969 (later traded to Minnesota — Minnesota selected Dick Redmond) and 1972 (Steve Shutt) Amateur Drafts, June 11, 1968. Traded to **Chicago** by **LA Kings** with Bill White and Bryan Campbell for Denis Dejordy, Gilles Marotte and Jim Stanfield, February 20, 1970. Traded to **California** by **Chicago** with Kerry Bond and Gerry Pinder for Gary Smith, September 9, 1971. Traded to **Chicago** by **California** for Paul Shmyr and Gilles Meloche, October 18, 1971. Selected by **NY Raiders** (WHA) in 1972 WHA General Player Draft, February 12, 1972. Claimed by **NY Islanders** from **Chicago** in Expansion Draft, June 6, 1972. WHA rights traded to **Michigan** (WHA) by **New York-New Jersey** (WHA) for cash, May, 1974. Rights traded to **Buffalo** by **NY Islanders** for the rights to Garry Lariviere, March 3, 1975.

• DICKIE, BILL

Bill Dickie G – R. 5′8″, 185 lbs. b: Campbellton, N.B., 2/20/1916. Deceased.

Season	Club	League	GP	W	L	T	Mins	GA	SO	Avg	AAvg	Eff	SA	S%	SAPG	GP	W	L	T	Mins	GA	SO	Avg	Eff	SA	S%	SAPG
1933-34	Mount Allison University	MIAA	4	*3	1	0	240	3	*2	*0.75	....	....	....	....	....	6	3	2	1	420	20	0	2.86	....	....	....	....
	Mount Allison University	NBSHL	7	*7	0	0	430	11	1	*1.53	....	....	....	....	....	8	5	2	1	540	23	0	2.56	....	....	....	....
1934-35	Mount Allison University	MIAA	4	*3	0	1	250	10	0	*2.40	....	....	....	....	....	....	....	....	....	....	....	....	....	....	....	....	....
	Mount Allison University	NBSHL	6	4	2	0	370	15	0	2.43	....	....	....	....	....	2	1	1	0	120	6	0	3.00	....	....	....	....
1935-36	Mount Allison University	MIAA	1	0	1	0	60	2	0	2.00	....	....	....	....	....	....	....	....	....	....	....	....	....	....	....	....	....
1936-37	Mount Allison University	MIAA	4	3	0	1	240	3	2	*0.75	....	....	....	....	....	1	0	1	0	60	6	0	6.00	....	....	....	....
1937-38	Saint John Beavers	NBSHL	29	16	11	1	1780	69	4	*2.33	....	....	....	....	....	4	1	3	0	195	11	0	3.39	....	....	....	....
1938-39	Saint John Beavers	NBSHL	34	20	9	5	2050	85	4	2.49	....	....	....	....	....	13	8	4	1	809	38	1	2.82	....	....	....	....
1939-40	Sydney Millionaires	CBSHL	35	*26	8	1	2100	85	*5	*2.43	....	....	....	....	....	4	3	1	0	240	13	0	*3.25	....	....	....	....
1940-41	Sydney Millionaires	CBSHL	40	*24	15	1	2400	125	3	*3.12	....	....	....	....	....	21	11	8	2	1160	64	1	3.31	....	....	....	....
1941-42	Montreal Pats	QSHL	40	10	21	0	2400	136	2	3.40	....	....	....	....	....	....	....	....	....	....	....	....	....	....	....	....	....
	Chicago Black Hawks	**NHL**	**1**	**1**	**0**	**0**	**60**	**3**	**0**	**3.00**	**2.97**	....	....	....	....	....	....	....	....	....	....	....	....	....	....	....	....
1942-1945			MILITARY SERVICE																								
	NHL Totals		**1**	**1**	**0**	**0**	**60**	**3**	**0**	**3.00**	....	....	....	....	....	....	....	....	....	....	....	....	....	....	....	....	....

Promoted to **Chicago** from **Montreal Pats** (QSHL) to replace injured Sam LoPresti, February 5, 1942. (Chicago 4, Montreal 3).

• DION, CONNIE

Connie Dion G – R. 5′4″, 140 lbs. b: St. Remi de Ringwick, Que., 8/11/1918.

Season	Club	League	GP	W	L	T	Mins	GA	SO	Avg	AAvg	Eff	SA	S%	SAPG	GP	W	L	T	Mins	GA	SO	Avg	Eff	SA	S%	SAPG
1937-38	Verdun Jr. Maple Leafs	QJHL	12	....	....	....	720	22	*2	1.83	....	....	....	....	....	4	....	....	....	240	11	0	*2.75	....	....	....	....
	Verdun Maple Leafs	QSHL	1	1	0	0	60	2	0	2.00	....	....	....	....	....	....	....	....	....	....	....	....	....	....	....	....	....
1938-39	Lachine Rapides	QPHL	38	....	....	....	2280	126	2	3.32	....	....	....	....	....	6	....	....	....	360	20	0	3.33	....	....	....	....

			REGULAR SEASON													PLAYOFFS											
Season	Club	League	GP	W	L	T	Mins	GA	SO	Avg	AAvg	Eff	SA	S%	SAPG	GP	W	L	T	Mins	GA	SO	Avg	Eff	SA	S%	SAPG
1939-40	Sherbrooke Red Raiders	QPHL	41	....	....	....	2460	130	*4	3.17	....	....	....	....	....	10	....	....	....	600	38	1	3.80	....	....	....	....
1940-41	Cornwall Flyers	QSHL	34	....	....	....	2040	122	1	3.68	....	....	....	....	....	4	....	....	....	240	14	0	3.50	....	....	....	....
1941-42	Cornwall Flyers	QSHL	37	20	14	3	2220	122	1	3.30	....	....	....	....	....	5	2	3	0	310	19	0	3.68	....	....	....	....
1942-43	Cornwall Flyers	QSHL	5	....	....	....	280	14	0	3.00	....	....	....	....	....	....	....	....	....	....	....	....	....	....	....	....	....
1943-44	Detroit Red Wings	NHL	26	17	7	2	1560	80	1	3.08	2.28	....	....	....	....	5	1	4	....	300	17	0	3.40	....	....	....	....
1944-45	Detroit Red Wings	NHL	12	6	4	2	720	39	0	3.25	2.68	....	....	....	....	....	....	....	....	....	....	....	....	....	....	....	....
	Indianapolis Capitols	AHL	39	14	19	6	2340	121	3	3.10	....	....	....	....	....	5	1	4	0	300	18	0	3.60	....	....	....	....
1945-46	St. Louis Flyers	AHL	8	1	6	1	480	40	0	5.00	....	....	....	....	....	....	....	....	....	....	....	....	....	....	....	....	....
	Buffalo Bisons	AHL	34	24	6	4	2040	84	1	2.47	....	....	....	....	....	12	*8	4	0	730	35	*1	*2.88	....	....	....	....
1946-47	Buffalo Bisons	AHL	61	....	....	....	3660	166	6	2.72	....	....	....	....	....	4	2	2	0	240	13	0	3.25	....	....	....	....
1947-48	Buffalo Bisons	AHL	43	26	15	2	2580	155	2	3.60	....	....	....	....	....	8	4	4	0	480	28	0	3.50	....	....	....	....
	Houston Huskies	USHL	7	4	3	0	420	30	0	4.28	....	....	....	....	....	....	....	....	....	....	....	....	....	....	....	....	....
1948-49	Buffalo Bisons	AHL	*68	33	27	8	*4080	213	4	3.13	....	....	....	....	....	....	....	....	....	....	....	....	....	....	....	....	....
	New York Rovers	QSHL	1	1	0	0	60	2	0	2.00	....	....	....	....	....	....	....	....	....	....	....	....	....	....	....	....	....
1949-50	Buffalo Bisons	AHL	34	15	15	4	2040	92	3	*2.71	....	....	....	....	....	2	0	2	0	120	11	0	5.50	....	....	....	....
	Louisville Blades	USHL	4	0	4	0	240	27	0	6.75	....	....	....	....	....	....	....	....	....	....	....	....	....	....	....	....	....
1950-51	Buffalo Bisons	AHL	63	35	24	4	3840	259	1	4.05	....	....	....	....	....	4	0	4	0	273	19	0	4.18	....	....	....	....
1951-52				DID NOT PLAY																							
1952-53	Sherbrooke Saints	QSHL	13	3	7	3	820	38	1	2.78	....	....	....	....	....	7	3	4	0	430	21	0	2.93	....	....	....	....
1953-54	Glace Bay Miners	MMHL	18	7	9	1	1079	85	0	4.73	....	....	....	....	....	....	....	....	....	....	....	....	....	....	....	....	....
	NHL Totals		38	23	11	4	2280	119	1	3.13	....	....	....	....	....	5	1	4	....	300	17	0	3.40	....	....	....	....

AHL Second All-Star Team (1945, 1946, 1950) • Won Harry "Hap" Holmes Memorial Award (fewest goals against - AHL) (1950)

Signed as a free agent by **Detroit**, January 25, 1944.

• DION, MICHEL

Michel Dion G – L. 5′10″, 185 lbs. b: Granby, Que., 2/11/1954.

			REGULAR SEASON													PLAYOFFS											
Season	Club	League	GP	W	L	T	Mins	GA	SO	Avg	AAvg	Eff	SA	S%	SAPG	GP	W	L	T	Mins	GA	SO	Avg	Eff	SA	S%	SAPG
1972-73	Montreal Jr. Canadiens	QMJHL	8	....	....	....	480	39	0	4.88	....	....	....	....	....	....	....	....	....	....	....	....	....	....	....	....	....
1973-74	Montreal Jr. Canadiens	QMJHL	31	....	....	....	1840	135	0	4.40	....	....	....	....	....	1	....	....	....	60	4	0	4.00	....	....	....	....
1974-75	Indianapolis Racers	WHA	1	0	1	0	59	4	0	4.07	....	....	....	....	....	....	....	....	....	....	....	....	....	....	....	....	....
	Mohawk Valley Comets	NAHL	28	10	12	2	1476	96	0	3.90	....	....	....	....	....	3	....	....	....	189	9	0	3.00	....	....	....	....
1975-76	Mohawk Valley Comets	NAHL	22	....	....	....	1295	83	0	3.84	....	....	....	....	....	....	....	....	....	....	....	....	....	....	....	....	....
	Indianapolis Racers	WHA	31	14	15	1	1860	85	0	*2.74	....	....	....	....	....	3	0	2	0	126	5	0	2.38	....	....	....	....
1976-77	Indianapolis Racers	WHA	42	17	19	3	2286	128	1	3.36	....	....	....	....	....	4	2	2	0	245	17	0	4.16	....	....	....	....
1977-78	Cincinnati Stingers	WHA	45	21	17	1	2356	140	*4	3.57		....	....	....	....	....	....	....	....	....	....	....	....	....	....	....	....
1978-79	Cincinnati Stingers	WHA	30	10	14	2	1681	93	0	3.32	....	....	....	....	....	....	....	....	....	....	....	....	....	....	....	....	....
1979-80	Quebec Nordiques	NHL	50	15	25	6	2773	171	2	3.70	3.26	....	....	....	....	....	....	....	....	....	....	....	....	....	....	....	....
1980-81	Indianapolis Checkers	CHL	6	2	3	0	364	19	0	3.13	....	....	....	....	....	....	....	....	....	....	....	....	....	....	....	....	....
	Quebec Nordiques	NHL	12	0	8	3	688	61	0	5.32	4.27	....	....	....	....	....	....	....	....	....	....	....	....	....	....	....	....
	Winnipeg Jets	NHL	14	3	6	3	757	61	0	4.83	3.88	....	....	....	....	....	....	....	....	....	....	....	....	....	....	....	....
1981-82	Pittsburgh Penguins	NHL	62	25	24	12	3580	226	0	3.79	2.92	....	....	....	....	5	2	3	....	304	22	0	4.34	....	....	....	....
1982-83	Pittsburgh Penguins	NHL	49	12	30	4	2791	198	0	4.26	3.41	5.58	1511	.869	32.5	....	....	....	....	....	....	....	....	....	....	....	....
1983-84	Pittsburgh Penguins	NHL	30	2	19	4	1553	138	0	5.33	4.19	7.85	937	.853	36.2	....	....	....	....	....	....	....	....	....	....	....	....
1984-85	Pittsburgh Penguins	NHL	10	3	6	0	553	43	0	4.67	3.71	6.35	316	.864	34.3	....	....	....	....	....	....	....	....	....	....	....	....
	Baltimore Skipjacks	AHL	21	10	6	2	1118	65	0	3.49	....	....	....	....	....	5	2	2	0	229	9	0	2.36	....	....	....	....
	NHL Totals		227	60	118	32	12695	898	2	4.24	....	....	....	....	....	5	2	3	....	304	22	0	4.34	....	....	....	....
	Other Major League Totals		149	62	66	7	8242	450	5	3.28	....	....	....	....	....	7	2	4	0	371	22	0	3.56	....	....	....	....

Won Ben Hatskin Trophy (WHA Top Goaltender) (1976)

Played in NHL All-Star Game (1982)

Selected by **Indianapolis** (WHA) in 1974 WHA Amateur Draft, May, 1974. Signed as a free agent by **Cincinnati** (WHA), October 12, 1977. Claimed by **Quebec** from **Cincinnati** (WHA) in WHA Dispersal Draft, June 9, 1979. Traded to **Winnipeg** by **Quebec** for cash, February 10, 1981. Signed as a free agent by **Pittsburgh**, June 30, 1981.

• DOLSON, DOLLY

Dolly (Clarence) Dolson G – L. 5′7″, 160 lbs. b: Hespeler, Ontario, 5/23/1897.

			REGULAR SEASON													PLAYOFFS											
Season	Club	League	GP	W	L	T	Mins	GA	SO	Avg	AAvg	Eff	SA	S%	SAPG	GP	W	L	T	Mins	GA	SO	Avg	Eff	SA	S%	SAPG
1923-24	Stratford Indians	OHA Sr.	12	*9	2	1	730	28	*2	*2.30	....	....	....	....	....	4	3	1	0	240	7	1	1.75	....	....	....	....
1924-25	Stratford Indians	OHA Sr.	20	12	8	0	1230	63	*2	3.07	....	....	....	....	....	2	1	1	0	120	6	1	3.00	....	....	....	....
1925-26	Stratford Indians	OHA Sr.	20	6	13	1	1280	66	0	3.09	....	....	....	....	....	....	....	....	....	....	....	....	....	....	....	....	....
1926-27	Stratford Nationals	Can-Pro	30	....	....	....	1800	76	2	2.53	....	....	....	....	....	2	0	2	0	120	4	0	2.00	....	....	....	....
1927-28	Stratford Nationals	Can-Pro	41	*25	11	5	2460	51	*11	*1.24	....	....	....	....	....	5	*4	0	1	300	3	*2	*0.60	....	....	....	....
1928-29	Detroit Cougars	NHL	*44	19	16	9	2750	63	10	1.37	2.89	....	....	....	....	2	0	2	0	120	7	0	3.50	....	....	....	....
1929-30	Detroit Cougars	NHL	5	0	4	1	320	24	0	4.50	4.74	....	....	....	....	....	....	....	....	....	....	....	....	....	....	....	....
	London Panthers	IAHL	31	....	....	....	1860	60	5	1.94	....	....	....	....	....	2	0	2	0	120	4	0	2.00	....	....	....	....
1930-31	Detroit Falcons	NHL	*44	16	21	7	2750	105	6	2.29	2.94	....	....	....	....	....	....	....	....	....	....	....	....	....	....	....	....
1931-32	Cleveland Indians	IAHL	14	....	....	....	840	54	0	3.86	....	....	....	....	....	....	....	....	....	....	....	....	....	....	....	....	....
1932-33	Cleveland Indians	IAHL	10	....	....	....	600	36	0	3.60	....	....	....	....	....	....	....	....	....	....	....	....	....	....	....	....	....
	NHL Totals		93	35	41	17	5820	192	16	1.98	....	....	....	....	....	2	0	2	0	120	7	0	3.50	....	....	....	....

Signed as a free agent by **Stratford** (Can-Pro), September 12, 1926. Signed as a free agent by **Detroit Cougars**, November 15, 1928.

• DOPSON, ROBERT

Robert Dopson G – L. 6′, 200 lbs. b: Smiths Falls, Ont., 8/21/1967.

			REGULAR SEASON													PLAYOFFS											
Season	Club	League	GP	W	L	T	Mins	GA	SO	Avg	AAvg	Eff	SA	S%	SAPG	GP	W	L	T	Mins	GA	SO	Avg	Eff	SA	S%	SAPG
1984-85	Kitchener Rangers	OHL	2	1	1	0	100	8	0	4.80	....	....	....	....	....	....	....	....	....	....	....	....	....	....	....	....	....
1985-86	Kitchener Rangers	OHL	8	5	2	0	403	32	0	4.76	....	....	....	....	....	....	....	....	....	....	....	....	....	....	....	....	....
1986-1989	Wilfred Laurier University	OUAA		STATISTICS NOT AVAILABLE																							
1989-90	Wilfred Laurier University	OUAA	22	....	....	....	1319	57	0	2.59	....	....	....	....	....	....	....	....	....	....	....	....	....	....	....	....	....
1990-91	Muskegon Lumberjacks	IHL	24	10	10	0	1243	90	0	4.34	....	....	....	....	....	....	....	....	....	....	....	....	....	....	....	....	....
	Louisville IceHawks	ECHL	3	3	0	0	180	12	0	4.00	....	....	....	....	....	5	3	1	0	270	16	0	3.55	....	....	....	....
1991-92	Muskegon Lumberjacks	IHL	29	13	12	2	1655	90	*4	3.26	....	....	....	....	....	12	8	4	0	697	40	0	3.44	....	....	....	....
1992-93	Cleveland Lumberjacks	IHL	50	26	15	3	2825	167	1	3.55	....	....	....	....	....	4	0	4	0	203	20	0	5.91	....	....	....	....
1993-94	Pittsburgh Penguins	NHL	2	0	0	0	45	3	0	4.00	3.81	5.22	23	.870	30.7	....	....	....	....	....	....	....	....	....	....	....	....
	Cleveland Lumberjacks	IHL	32	9	10	8	1681	109	0	3.89	....	....	....	....	....	....	....	....	....	....	....	....	....	....	....	....	....
1994-95	Houston Aeros	IHL	41	17	16	2	2102	119	0	3.40	....	....	....	....	....	1	0	0	0	40	6	0	9.00	....	....	....	....
1995-96	Louisiana Ice Gators	ECHL	2	1	0	1	120	4	0	2.00	....	....	....	....	....	....	....	....	....	....	....	....	....	....	....	....	....
	Kansas City Blades	IHL	5	1	0	1	183	10	0	3.28	....	....	....	....	....	....	....	....	....	....	....	....	....	....	....	....	....
	Houston Aeros	IHL	33	9	13	2	1518	96	0	3.79	....	....	....	....	....	....	....	....	....	....	....	....	....	....	....	....	....
1996-97	Houston Aeros	IHL	12	5	4	1	637	36	0	3.39	....	....	....	....	....	....	....	....	....	....	....	....	....	....	....	....	....
1997-98	Ayr Scottish Eagles	Britain	29	....	....	....	2274	70	....	1.85	....	....	....	....	....	9	....	....	....	567	19	....	2.01	....	....	....	....
	NHL Totals		2	0	0	0	45	3	0	4.00	....	....	23	.870	....	....	....	....	....	....	....	....	....	....	....	....	....

Signed as a free agent by **Pittsburgh**, July 6, 1991.

• DOWIE, BRUCE

Bruce Dowie G – L. 5′10″, 170 lbs. b: Oakville, Ont., 12/9/1962.

			REGULAR SEASON													PLAYOFFS											
Season	Club	League	GP	W	L	T	Mins	GA	SO	Avg	AAvg	Eff	SA	S%	SAPG	GP	W	L	T	Mins	GA	SO	Avg	Eff	SA	S%	SAPG
1979-80	Toronto Marlboros	OHA	60	31	24	3	3513	247	0	4.22	....	....	....	....	....	4	0	4	0	253	19	0	4.51	....	....	....	....
1980-81	Toronto Marlboros	OHA	57	28	26	0	3215	253	0	4.73	....	....	....	....	....	5	2	2	0	272	23	0	5.07	....	....	....	....
1981-82	Toronto Marlboros	OHL	37	16	17	0	2022	150	1	4.45	....	....	....	....	....	2	0	2	0	120	10	0	5.00	....	....	....	....
1982-83	Toronto Marlboros	OHL	30	19	8	3	1830	123	0	4.03	....	....	....	....	....	2	....	....	....	120	10	0	5.00	....	....	....	....
	St. Catharines Saints	AHL	8	2	3	1	424	35	0	4.95	....	....	....	....	....	....	....	....	....	....	....	....	....	....	....	....	....
1983-84	Muskegon Mohawks	IHL	25	....	....	....	1306	100	2	4.59	....	....	....	....	....	....	....	....	....	....	....	....	....	....	....	....	....
	Toronto Maple Leafs	NHL	2	0	1	0	72	4	0	3.33	2.61	3.10	43	.907	35.8	....	....	....	....	....	....	....	....	....	....	....	....
	St. Catharines Saints	AHL	9	2	2	1	410	41	0	6.00	....	....	....	....	....	....	....	....	....	....	....	....	....	....	....	....	....

			REGULAR SEASON													PLAYOFFS											
Season	Club	League	GP	W	L	T	Mins	GA	SO	Avg	AAvg	Eff	SA	S%	SAPG	GP	W	L	T	Mins	GA	SO	Avg	Eff	SA	S%	SAPG
1984-85	St. Catharines Saints	AHL	10	2	7	1	596	55	0	5.54	....	....	....	....	....	....	....	....	....	....	....	....	....	....	....	....	....
	Toledo Goaldiggers	IHL	5	2	1	2	310	20	0	3.87	....	....	....	....	....	....	....	....	....	....	....	....	....	....	....	....	....
1985-86	St. Catharines Saints	AHL	5	1	1	0	139	14	0	6.04	....	....	....	....	....	....	....	....	....	....	....	....	....	....	....	....	....
1986-87	Newmarket Saints	AHL	4	0	2	0	155	13	0	5.03	....	....	....	....	....	....	....	....	....	....	....	....	....	....	....	....	....
	NHL Totals		**2**	**0**	**1**	**0**	**72**	**4**	**0**	**3.33**	....	....	**43**	**.907**	....	....	....	....	....	....	....	....	....	....	....	....	....

Signed as a free agent by **Toronto**, May 6, 1983.

• DRAPER, TOM

Tom Draper G – L. 5'11", 185 lbs. b: Outremont, Que., 11/20/1966. Winnipeg's 8th choice, 105th overall, in 1985 Entry Draft.

Season	Club	League	GP	W	L	T	Mins	GA	SO	Avg	AAvg	Eff	SA	S%	SAPG	GP	W	L	T	Mins	GA	SO	Avg	Eff	SA	S%	SAPG
1983-84	University of Vermont	ECAC	20	8	12	0	1205	82	0	4.08	....	....	....	....	....	....	....	....	....	....	....	....	....	....	....	....	....
1984-85	University of Vermont	ECAC	24	5	17	0	1316	90	0	4.11	....	....	....	....	....	....	....	....	....	....	....	....	....	....	....	....	....
1985-86	University of Vermont	ECAC	29	15	12	1	1697	87	1	3.08	....	....	....	....	....	....	....	....	....	....	....	....	....	....	....	....	....
1986-87	University of Vermont	ECAC	29	16	13	0	1662	96	2	3.47	....	....	....	....	....	....	....	....	....	....	....	....	....	....	....	....	....
1987-88	Tappara Tampere	Finland	28	16	3	9	1619	87	0	3.22	....	....	....	....	....	....	....	....	....	....	....	....	....	....	....	....	....
1988-89	**Winnipeg Jets**	**NHL**	**2**	**1**	**1**	**0**	**120**	**12**	**0**	**6.00**	**4.95**	**10.91**	**66**	**.818**	**33.0**	....	....	....	....	....	....	....	....	....	....	....	....
	Moncton Hawks	AHL	*54	27	17	5	*2962	171	2	3.46	....	....	....	....	....	7	5	2	....	419	24	0	3.44	....	....	....	....
1989-90	**Winnipeg Jets**	**NHL**	**6**	**2**	**4**	**0**	**359**	**26**	**0**	**4.35**	**3.65**	**7.39**	**153**	**.830**	**25.6**	....	....	....	....	....	....	....	....	....	....	....	....
	Moncton Hawks	AHL	51	20	24	3	2844	167	1	3.52	....	....	....	....	....	....	....	....	....	....	....	....	....	....	....	....	....
1990-91	Moncton Hawks	AHL	30	15	13	2	1779	95	1	3.20	....	....	....	....	....	....	....	....	....	....	....	....	....	....	....	....	....
	Fort Wayne Komets	IHL	10	5	3	1	564	32	0	3.40	....	....	....	....	....	....	....	....	....	....	....	....	....	....	....	....	....
	Peoria Rivermen	IHL	10	6	3	1	584	36	0	3.70	....	....	....	....	....	4	2	1	....	214	10	0	2.80	....	....	....	....
1991-92	**Buffalo Sabres**	**NHL**	**26**	**10**	**9**	**5**	**1403**	**75**	**1**	**3.21**	**2.84**	**3.38**	**712**	**.895**	**30.4**	**7**	**3**	**4**	....	**433**	**19**	**1**	**2.63**	**2.49**	**201**	**.905**	**27.9**
	Rochester Americans	AHL	9	4	3	2	531	28	0	3.16	....	....	....	....	....	....	....	....	....	....	....	....	....	....	....	....	....
1992-93	**Buffalo Sabres**	**NHL**	**11**	**5**	**6**	**0**	**664**	**41**	**0**	**3.70**	**3.15**	**4.41**	**344**	**.881**	**31.1**	....	....	....	....	....	....	....	....	....	....	....	....
	Rochester Americans	AHL	5	3	2	0	303	22	0	4.36	....	....	....	....	....	....	....	....	....	....	....	....	....	....	....	....	....
1993-94	**New York Islanders**	**NHL**	**7**	**1**	**3**	**0**	**227**	**16**	**0**	**4.23**	**4.03**	**5.74**	**118**	**.864**	**31.2**	....	....	....	....	....	....	....	....	....	....	....	....
	Salt Lake Golden Eagles	IHL	35	7	23	3	1933	140	0	4.34	....	....	....	....	....	....	....	....	....	....	....	....	....	....	....	....	....
1994-95	Minnesota Moose	IHL	59	25	20	6	3063	187	1	3.66	....	....	....	....	....	2	0	2	....	118	10	0	5.07	....	....	....	....
1995-96	**Winnipeg Jets**	**NHL**	**1**	**0**	**0**	**0**	**34**	**3**	**0**	**5.29**	**5.20**	**11.34**	**14**	**.786**	**24.7**	....	....	....	....	....	....	....	....	....	....	....	....
	Milwaukee Admirals	IHL	31	14	12	3	1793	101	1	3.38	....	....	....	....	....	....	....	....	....	....	....	....	....	....	....	....	....
1996-97	Long Beach Ice Dogs	IHL	39	28	7	3	2267	87	2	2.30	....	....	....	....	....	*18	*13	5	....	*1096	41	*2	2.24	....	....	....	....
1997-98	Quebec Rafales	IHL	43	15	22	4	2418	131	2	3.25	....	....	....	....	....	....	....	....	....	....	....	....	....	....	....	....	....
	Cleveland Lumberjacks	IHL	9	4	2	2	497	20	0	2.41	....	....	....	....	....	10	5	5	....	582	32	0	3.30	....	....	....	....
	NHL Totals		**53**	**19**	**23**	**5**	**2807**	**173**	**1**	**3.70**	....	....	**1407**	**.877**	....	**7**	**3**	**4**	....	**433**	**19**	**1**	**2.63**	....	....	....	....

ECAC First All-Star Team (1987) • AHL Second All-Star Team (1989)

Traded to **St. Louis** by **Winnipeg** for future considerations (Jim Vesey, May 24, 1991), February 28, 1991. Traded to **Winnipeg** by **St. Louis** for future considerations, May 24, 1991. Traded to **Buffalo** by **Winnipeg** for Buffalo's 7th round choice (Artur Oktyabrev) in 1992 Entry Draft, June 22, 1991. Traded to **NY Islanders** by **Buffalo** for NY Islanders' 7th round choice (Steve Plouffe) in 1994 Entry Draft, September 30, 1993. Signed as a free agent by **Winnipeg**, December 14, 1995.

• DRYDEN, DAVE

Dave Dryden G – L. 6'1", 186 lbs. b: Hamilton, Ont., 9/5/1941.

Season	Club	League	GP	W	L	T	Mins	GA	SO	Avg	AAvg	Eff	SA	S%	SAPG	GP	W	L	T	Mins	GA	SO	Avg	Eff	SA	S%	SAPG
1959-60	St. Michael's Majors	OHA	12	5	6	1	720	39	1	3.25	....	....	....	....	....	1	0	0	0	20	2	0	6.00	....	....	....	....
1960-61	St. Michael's Majors	OHA	18	....	....	....	1080	66	1	3.67	....	....	....	....	....	....	....	....	....	....	....	....	....	....	....	....	....
1961-62	Toronto Marlboros	Tor-Jr.	32	17	8	6	1880	99	*3	3.16	....	....	....	....	....	12	7	5	0	720	49	0	4.08	....	....	....	....
	Rochester Americans	AHL	1	0	0	0	20	2	0	6.00	....	....	....	....	....	....	....	....	....	....	....	....	....	....	....	....	....
	New York Rangers	**NHL**	**1**	**0**	**1**	**0**	**40**	**3**	**0**	**4.50**	**4.62**	....	....	....	....	....	....	....	....	....	....	....	....	....	....	....	....
1962-63	Galt Terriers	OHA Sr.	40	....	....	....	2400	174	2	4.35	....	....	....	....	....	4	....	....	....	240	27	0	6.75	....	....	....	....
1963-64	Galt Terriers	OHA Sr.	39	....	....	....	2340	141	0	*3.62	....	....	....	....	....	11	6	5	0	660	36	*1	3.27	....	....	....	....
1964-65	Galt Hornets	OHA Sr.	35	....	....	....	2040	106	1	3.10	....	....	....	....	....	1	0	1	0	60	6	0	6.00	....	....	....	....
	Buffalo Bisons	AHL	4	4	0	0	240	6	1	1.50	....	....	....	....	....	....	....	....	....	....	....	....	....	....	....	....	....
1965-66	**Chicago Black Hawks**	**NHL**	**11**	**3**	**4**	**1**	**453**	**23**	**0**	**3.05**	**3.10**	....	....	....	....	**1**	**0**	**0**	....	**13**	**0**	**0**	**0.00**	....	....	....	....
1966-67	St. Louis Braves	CHL	48	17	17	14	2880	158	2	3.29	....	....	....	....	....	....	....	....	....	....	....	....	....	....	....	....	....
1967-68	**Chicago Black Hawks**	**NHL**	**27**	**7**	**8**	**5**	**1268**	**69**	**1**	**3.26**	**3.62**	....	....	....	....	....	....	....	....	....	....	....	....	....	....	....	....
1968-69	**Chicago Black Hawks**	**NHL**	**30**	**11**	**11**	**2**	**1479**	**79**	**3**	**3.20**	**3.02**	....	....	....	....	....	....	....	....	....	....	....	....	....	....	....	....
1969-70	Dallas Black Hawks	CHL	2	0	2	0	120	6	0	3.00	....	....	....	....	....	....	....	....	....	....	....	....	....	....	....	....	....
1970-71	Salt Lake Golden Eagles	WHL	8	1	6	0	364	34	0	5.60	....	....	....	....	....	....	....	....	....	....	....	....	....	....	....	....	....
	Buffalo Sabres	**NHL**	**10**	**3**	**3**	**0**	**409**	**23**	**1**	**3.37**	**3.33**	....	....	....	....	....	....	....	....	....	....	....	....	....	....	....	....
1971-72	**Buffalo Sabres**	**NHL**	**20**	**3**	**9**	**5**	**1026**	**68**	**0**	**3.98**	**4.03**	....	....	....	....	....	....	....	....	....	....	....	....	....	....	....	....
1972-73	**Buffalo Sabres**	**NHL**	**37**	**14**	**13**	**7**	**2018**	**89**	**3**	**2.65**	**2.48**	....	....	....	....	**2**	**0**	**2**	....	**120**	**9**	**0**	**4.50**	....	....	....	....
1973-74	**Buffalo Sabres**	**NHL**	**53**	**23**	**20**	**8**	**2987**	**148**	**1**	**2.97**	**2.86**	....	....	....	....	....	....	....	....	....	....	....	....	....	....	....	....
1974-75	Chicago Cougars	WHA	45	18	26	1	2728	176	1	3.87	....	....	....	....	....	....	....	....	....	....	....	....	....	....	....	....	....
1975-76	Edmonton Oilers	WHA	62	22	34	5	3567	235	1	3.95	....	....	....	....	....	3	0	3	0	180	15	0	5.00	....	....	....	....
1976-77	Edmonton Oilers	WHA	24	10	13	0	1416	77	1	3.26	....	....	....	....	....	....	....	....	....	....	....	....	....	....	....	....	....
1977-78	Edmonton Oilers	WHA	48	21	23	2	2578	150	2	3.49	....	....	....	....	....	2	0	1	0	91	6	0	3.96	....	....	....	....
1978-79	Edmonton Oilers	WHA	*63	*41	17	2	*3531	170	*3	*2.89	....	....	....	....	....	*13	6	7	0	*687	42	0	3.67	....	....	....	....
1979-80	**Edmonton Oilers**	**NHL**	**14**	**2**	**7**	**3**	**744**	**53**	**0**	**4.27**	**3.76**	....	....	....	....	....	....	....	....	....	....	....	....	....	....	....	....
	NHL Totals		**203**	**66**	**76**	**31**	**10424**	**555**	**9**	**3.19**	....	....	....	....	....	**3**	**0**	**2**	....	**133**	**9**	**0**	**4.06**	....	....	....	....
	Other Major League Totals		242	112	113	10	13820	808	8	3.51	....	....	....	....	....	18	6	11	0	958	63	0	3.95	....	....	....	....

CHL Second All-Star Team (1967) • WHA First All-Star Team (1979) • Won Ben Hatskin Trophy (WHA Top Goaltender) (1979) • Won Gary Davidson Trophy (WHA MVP) (1979)

Played in NHL All-Star Game (1974)

• Loaned to **NY Rangers** by **Toronto Marlboros** (OHA) to replace injured Gump Worsley in 2nd period, February 3, 1962. (Toronto 4, NY Rangers 1). Signed as a free agent by **Chicago** (Buffalo - AHL), March 12, 1965. • Suspended by **Chicago** (Dallas-CHL) after refusing assignment to minors, October, 1969. Traded to **Pittsburgh** by **Chicago** for cash, June 10, 1970. Traded to **Buffalo** by **Pittsburgh** for cash, October 9, 1970. Selected by **New England** (WHA) in 1972 WHA General Player Draft, February 12, 1972. WHA rights traded to **Chicago** (WHA) by **New England** (WHA) for future considerations, June, 1974. Claimed by **Edmonton** (WHA) from **Chicago** (WHA) in 1975 WHA Dispersal Draft, June, 1975. Traded to **New England** (WHA) by **Edmonton** (WHA) with Jack Carlson, Steve Carlson, Dave Keon and John McKenzie for future considerations (Dave Debol, June, 1977), Dan Arndt and cash, January, 1977. • Suspended by **New England** (WHA) for refusing to report to WHA club, January, 1977. Traded to **Edmonton** (WHA) by **New England** (WHA) with Brett Callighen and future considerations for Jean-Louis Levasseur, September, 1977. Reclaimed by **Buffalo** from **Edmonton** prior to Expansion Draft, June 9, 1979. Claimed as a priority selection by **Edmonton**, June 9, 1979.

• DRYDEN, KEN

Ken Dryden G – L. 6'4", 205 lbs. b: Hamilton, Ont., 8/8/1947. Boston's 3rd choice, 14th overall, in 1964 Amateur Draft. **HHOF**

Season	Club	League	GP	W	L	T	Mins	GA	SO	Avg	AAvg	Eff	SA	S%	SAPG	GP	W	L	T	Mins	GA	SO	Avg	Eff	SA	S%	SAPG
1966-67	Cornell University	ECAC	27	26	0	1	....	40	....	1.46	....	....	....	....	....	....	....	....	....	....	....	....	....	....	....	....	....
1967-68	Cornell University	ECAC	29	25	2	0	1620	41	....	1.52	....	....	....	....	....	....	....	....	....	....	....	....	....	....	....	....	....
1968-69	Cornell University	ECAC	27	25	2	0	....	47	3	1.79	....	....	....	....	....	....	....	....	....	....	....	....	....	....	....	....	....
	Canada	WEC-A	2	1	1	0	120	4	1	2.00	....	....	....	....	....	....	....	....	....	....	....	....	....	....	....	....	....
1969-70	Canada	Nat-Team	STATISTICS NOT AVAILABLE																								
1970-71	Montreal Voyageurs	AHL	33	16	7	8	1899	84	3	2.68	....	....	....	....	....	....	....	....	....	....	....	....	....	....	....	....	....
	Montreal Canadiens	**NHL**	**6**	**6**	**0**	**0**	**327**	**9**	**0**	**1.65**	**1.63**	....	....	....	....	***20**	***12**	**8**	....	***1221**	**61**	**0**	**3.00**	....	....	....	....
1971-72	**Montreal Canadiens**	**NHL**	***64**	***39**	**8**	**15**	***3800**	**142**	**8**	**2.24**	**2.22**	....	....	....	....	**6**	**2**	**4**	....	**360**	**17**	**0**	**2.83**	....	....	....	....
1972-73	Canada	Summit	4	....	....	....	240	19	0	4.75	....	....	....	....	....	....	....	....	....	....	....	....	....	....	....	....	....
	Montreal Canadiens	**NHL**	**54**	***33**	**7**	**13**	**3165**	**119**	***6**	***2.26**	**2.10**	....	....	....	....	***17**	***12**	**5**	....	***1039**	**50**	**1**	**2.89**	....	....	....	....
1973-74			DID NOT PLAY																								
1974-75	**Montreal Canadiens**	**NHL**	**56**	**30**	**9**	**16**	**3320**	**149**	**4**	**2.69**	**2.40**	....	....	....	....	**11**	**6**	**5**	....	**688**	**29**	**2**	**2.53**	....	....	....	....
1975-76	**Montreal Canadiens**	**NHL**	**62**	***42**	**10**	**8**	**3580**	**121**	***8**	***2.03**	**1.81**	....	....	....	....	***13**	***12**	**1**	....	***780**	**25**	**1**	***1.92**	....	....	....	....
1976-77	**Montreal Canadiens**	**NHL**	**56**	***41**	**8**	**8**	**3275**	**117**	***10**	**2.14**	**1.96**	....	....	....	....	***14**	***12**	**2**	....	**849**	**22**	***4**	***1.55**	....	....	....	....

			REGULAR SEASON													PLAYOFFS											
Season	Club	League	GP	W	L	T	Mins	GA	SO	Avg	AAvg	Eff	SA	S%	SAPG	GP	W	L	T	Mins	GA	SO	Avg	Eff	SA	S%	SAPG
1977-78	**Montreal Canadiens**	**NHL**	**52**	**37**	**7**	**7**	**3071**	**105**	**5**	***2.05**	**1.89**	....	....	....	....	***15**	***12**	**3**	....	***919**	**29**	***2**	***1.89**	....	....	....	....
1978-79	**Montreal Canadiens**	**NHL**	**47**	**30**	**10**	**7**	**2814**	**108**	***5**	***2.30**	**2.01**	....	....	....	....	**16**	***12**	**4**	....	**990**	**41**	**0**	**2.48**	....	....	....	....
	NHL All-Stars	Chal Cup	2	....	....	....	120	7	....	3.50	....	....	....	....	....	....	....	....	....	....	....	....	....	....	....	....	....
	NHL Totals		**397**	**258**	**57**	**74**	**23352**	**870**	**46**	**2.24**	....	....	....	....	....	**112**	**80**	**32**	....	**6846**	**274**	**10**	**2.40**	....	....	....	....

ECAC First All-Star Team (1967, 1968, 1969) • NCAA East First All-American Team (1967, 1968, 1969) • NCAA Championship All-Tournament Team (1967) • Won Conn Smythe Trophy (1971) • NHL Second All-Star Team (1972) • Won Calder Memorial Trophy (1972) • NHL First All-Star Team (1973, 1976, 1977, 1978, 1979) • Won Vezina Trophy (1973, 1976) • Shared Vezina Trophy with Michel Larocque (1977, 1978, 1979)

Played in NHL All-Star Game (1972, 1975, 1976, 1977, 1978)

Rights traded to **Montreal** by **Boston** with Alex Campbell for Guy Allen and Paul Reid, June, 1964. • Sat out 1973-74 season. Worked for a law firm.

• DUFFUS, PARRIS

Parris Duffus G – L. 6'2", 192 lbs. b: Denver, CO, 1/27/1970. St. Louis' 6th choice, 180th overall, in 1990 Entry Draft.

Season	Club	League	GP	W	L	T	Mins	GA	SO	Avg	AAvg	Eff	SA	S%	SAPG	GP	W	L	T	Mins	GA	SO	Avg	Eff	SA	S%	SAPG
1989-90	Melfort Mustangs	Jr. A	51	....	....	....	2828	226	....	4.79	....	....	....	....	....	....	....	....	....	....	....	....	....	....	....	....	....
1990-91	Cornell University	ECAC	4	0	0	0	37	3	0	4.86	....	....	....	....	....	....	....	....	....	....	....	....	....	....	....	....	....
1991-92	Cornell University	ECAC	28	14	11	3	1677	74	1	2.65	....	....	....	....	....	....	....	....	....	....	....	....	....	....	....	....	....
1992-93	Hampton Roads Admirals	ECHL	4	3	1	0	245	13	0	3.18	....	....	....	....	....	....	....	....	....	....	....	....	....	....	....	....	....
	Peoria Rivermen	IHL	37	16	15	4	2149	142	0	3.96	....	....	....	....	....	1	0	1	....	59	5	0	5.08	....	....	....	....
1993-94	Peoria Rivermen	IHL	36	19	10	3	1845	141	0	4.58	....	....	....	....	....	2	0	1	....	92	6	0	3.88	....	....	....	....
1994-95	Peoria Rivermen	IHL	29	17	7	3	1581	71	*3	2.69	....	....	....	....	....	7	4	2	....	409	17	0	2.49	....	....	....	....
1995-96	Minnesota Moose	IHL	35	10	17	2	1812	100	1	3.31	....	....	....	....	....	....	....	....	....	....	....	....	....	....	....	....	....
	United States	WC-A	7	4	3	0	425	18	1	2.54	....	....	....	....	....	....	....	....	....	....	....	....	....	....	....	....	....
1996-97	**Phoenix Coyotes**	**NHL**	**1**	**0**	**0**	**0**	**29**	**1**	**0**	**2.07**	**2.19**	**2.59**	**8**	**.875**	**16.6**	....	....	....	....	....	....	....	....	....	....	....	....
	Las Vegas Thunder	IHL	58	28	19	6	3266	176	3	3.23	....	....	....	....	....	3	0	3	....	175	8	0	2.73	....	....	....	....
1997-98	HPK Hameenlinna	Fin.	31	11	13	0	1436	79	0	3.30	....	....	....	....	....	....	....	....	....	....	....	....	....	....	....	....	....
	Cincinnati Cyclones	IHL	17	10	5	0	916	47	0	3.08	....	....	....	....	....	5	1	3	....	252	12	0	2.85	....	....	....	....
	NHL Totals		**1**	**0**	**0**	**0**	**29**	**1**	**0**	**2.07**	....	....	**8**	**.875**	....	....	....	....	....	....	....	....	....	....	....	....	....

ECAC Second All-Star Team (1992) • NCAA East First All-American Team (1992)

Signed as a free agent by **Winnipeg**, August 4, 1995. Transferred to **Phoenix** after **Winnipeg** franchise relocated, July 1, 1996.

• DUMAS, MICHEL

Michel Dumas G – L. 5'9", 180 lbs. b: St. Antoine-de-Pontbriand, Que, 7/8/1949.

Season	Club	League	GP	W	L	T	Mins	GA	SO	Avg	AAvg	Eff	SA	S%	SAPG	GP	W	L	T	Mins	GA	SO	Avg	Eff	SA	S%	SAPG
1968-69	Thetford Mines Canadiens	QJHL	STATISTICS NOT AVAILABLE																								
1969-70	Oklahoma City Blazers	CHL	2	0	1	0	80	9	0	6.75	....	....	....	....	....	....	....	....	....	....	....	....	....	....	....	....	....
	Dayton Gems	IHL	54	....	....	....	3000	180	3	3.60	....	....	....	....	....	13	8	5	0	746	36	0	2.90	....	....	....	....
1970-71	Dayton Gems	IHL	49	....	....	....	2811	167	1	3.56	....	....	....	....	....	5	....	....	....	300	19	0	3.80	....	....	....	....
1971-72	Dallas Black Hawks	CHL	*44	*30	10	4	2415	124	*3	*3.08	....	....	....	....	....	2	1	1	0	111	9	0	4.86	....	....	....	....
1972-73	Dallas Black Hawks	CHL	37	....	....	....	2160	108	1	3.00	....	....	....	....	....	4	....	....	....	200	16	0	4.80	....	....	....	....
1973-74	Dallas Black Hawks	CHL	*67	*26	23	16	*3896	194	*3	2.98	....	....	....	....	....	*10	*8	2	0	*580	15	*1	*1.55	....	....	....	....
1974-75	Dallas Black Hawks	CHL	52	26	20	6	3093	160	*4	3.10	....	....	....	....	....	....	....	....	....	....	....	....	....	....	....	....	....
	Chicago Black Hawks	**NHL**	**3**	**2**	**0**	**0**	**121**	**7**	**0**	**3.47**	**3.13**	....	....	....	....	**1**	**0**	**0**	....	**19**	**1**	**0**	**3.16**	....	....	....	....
1975-76	**Chicago Black Hawks**	**NHL**	DID NOT PLAY – SPARE GOALTENDER																								
1976-77	**Chicago Black Hawks**	**NHL**	**5**	**0**	**1**	**2**	**241**	**17**	**0**	**4.23**	**3.93**	....	....	....	....	....	....	....	....	....	....	....	....	....	....	....	....
	NHL Totals		**8**	**2**	**1**	**2**	**362**	**24**	**0**	**3.98**	....	....	....	....	....	**1**	**0**	**0**	....	**19**	**1**	**0**	**3.16**	....	....	....	....

CHL Second All-Star Team (1972, 1974) • Won Terry Sawchuk Trophy (fewest goals against - CHL) (1972)

Signed as a free agent by **Chicago**, October 7, 1971.

• DUNHAM, MICHAEL

Michael Dunham G – L. 6'3", 200 lbs. b: Johnson City, NY, 6/1/1972. New Jersey's 4th choice, 53rd overall, in 1990 Entry Draft.

Season	Club	League	GP	W	L	T	Mins	GA	SO	Avg	AAvg	Eff	SA	S%	SAPG	GP	W	L	T	Mins	GA	SO	Avg	Eff	SA	S%	SAPG
1989-90	Canterbury-Conn High	H.S.	32	....	....	....	1558	68	3	1.96	....	....	....	....	....	....	....	....	....	....	....	....	....	....	....	....	....
1990-91	University of Maine	H.E.	23	14	5	2	1275	63	0	*2.96	....	....	....	....	....	....	....	....	....	....	....	....	....	....	....	....	....
	United States	WJC-A	3	....	....	....	180	11	....	3.67	....	....	....	....	....	....	....	....	....	....	....	....	....	....	....	....	....
1991-92	University of Maine	H.E.	7	6	0	0	382	14	1	2.20	....	....	....	....	....	....	....	....	....	....	....	....	....	....	....	....	....
	United States	WJC-A	6	5	0	1	360	14	....	2.33	....	....	....	....	....	....	....	....	....	....	....	....	....	....	....	....	....
	United States	Nat-Team	3	0	1	1	157	10	0	3.82	....	....	....	....	....	....	....	....	....	....	....	....	....	....	....	....	....
	United States	Olympics	DID NOT PLAY – SPARE GOALTENDER																								
	United States	WC-A	3	0	1	0	107	7	....	3.92	....	....	....	....	....	....	....	....	....	....	....	....	....	....	....	....	....
1992-93	University of Maine	H.E.	25	*21	1	1	1429	63	0	2.65	....	....	....	....	....	....	....	....	....	....	....	....	....	....	....	....	....
	United States	WC-A	1	1	0	0	60	1	0	1.00	....	....	....	....	....	....	....	....	....	....	....	....	....	....	....	....	....
1993-94	United States	Nat-Team	33	22	9	2	1983	125	2	3.78	....	....	....	....	....	....	....	....	....	....	....	....	....	....	....	....	....
	United States	Olympics	3	0	1	2	180	15	0	5.00	....	....	....	....	....	....	....	....	....	....	....	....	....	....	....	....	....
	Albany River Rats	AHL	5	2	2	1	304	26	0	5.12	....	....	....	....	....	....	....	....	....	....	....	....	....	....	....	....	....
1994-95	Albany River Rats	AHL	35	20	7	8	2120	99	1	2.80	....	....	....	....	....	7	6	1	....	419	20	1	2.86	....	....	....	....
1995-96	Albany River Rats	AHL	44	30	10	2	2592	109	1	2.52	....	....	....	....	....	3	1	2	....	182	5	1	1.65	....	....	....	....
1996-97	**New Jersey Devils**	**NHL**	**26**	**8**	**7**	**1**	**1013**	**43**	**2**	**2.55**	**2.70**	**2.40**	**456**	**.906**	**27.0**	....	....	....	....	....	....	....	....	....	....	....	....
	Albany River Rats	AHL	3	1	1	1	184	12	0	3.91	....	....	....	....	....	....	....	....	....	....	....	....	....	....	....	....	....
1997-98	**New Jersey Devils**	**NHL**	**15**	**5**	**5**	**3**	**773**	**29**	**1**	**2.25**	**2.63**	**1.97**	**332**	**.913**	**25.8**	....	....	....	....	....	....	....	....	....	....	....	....
	United States	WC-A	2	0	1	0	40	4	0	6.00	....	....	....	....	....	....	....	....	....	....	....	....	....	....	....	....	....
	NHL Totals		**41**	**13**	**12**	**4**	**1786**	**72**	**3**	**2.42**	....	....	**788**	**.909**	....	....	....	....	....	....	....	....	....	....	....	....	....

WJC-A All-Star Team (1992) • Named Best Goaltender at WJC-A (1992) • Hockey East First All-Star Team (1993) • NCAA East First All-American Team (1993) • Shared Harry "Hap" Holmes Memorial Trophy (fewest goals against - AHL) with Corey Schwab (1995) • Shared Jack A. Butterfield Trophy (Playoff MVP - AHL) with Corey Schwab (1995) • AHL Second All-Star Team (1996) • Shared William M. Jennings Trophy with Martin Brodeur (1997)

Claimed by **Nashville** from **New Jersey** in Expansion Draft, June 26, 1998.

• DUPUIS, BOB

Bob Dupuis G – L. 5'11", 167 lbs. b: North Bay, Ont., 8/26/1952.

Season	Club	League	GP	W	L	T	Mins	GA	SO	Avg	AAvg	Eff	SA	S%	SAPG	GP	W	L	T	Mins	GA	SO	Avg	Eff	SA	S%	SAPG
1969-70	North Bay Trappers	NOHA	30	....	....	....	1786	134	0	5.16	....	....	....	....	....	....	....	....	....	....	....	....	....	....	....	....	....
1970-71	University of Waterloo	OUAA	STATISTICS NOT AVAILABLE																								
1971-72	University of Waterloo	OUAA	STATISTICS NOT AVAILABLE																								
1972-73	University of Waterloo	OUAA	14	....	....	....	820	52	0	3.80	....	....	....	....	....	....	....	....	....	....	....	....	....	....	....	....	....
	Cape Cod Cubs	EHL	14	....	....	....	840	102	0	4.79	....	....	....	....	....	....	....	....	....	....	....	....	....	....	....	....	....
1973-74	University of Waterloo	OUAA	12	....	....	....	665	40	0	3.61	....	....	....	....	....	....	....	....	....	....	....	....	....	....	....	....	....
	Macon Whoopees	SHL	19	....	....	....	842	79	1	5.63	....	....	....	....	....	....	....	....	....	....	....	....	....	....	....	....	....
1974-75	Cambridge Hornets	OHA Sr.	27	....	....	....	1620	114	1	4.22	....	....	....	....	....	....	....	....	....	....	....	....	....	....	....	....	....
1975-76	Cambridge Hornets	OHA Sr.	21	....	....	....	1260	81	1	3.83	....	....	....	....	....	....	....	....	....	....	....	....	....	....	....	....	....
1976-77	Cambridge Hornets	OHA Sr.	21	....	....	....	1260	81	*3	3.62	....	....	....	....	....	....	....	....	....	....	....	....	....	....	....	....	....
1977-78	Cambridge Hornets	OHA Sr.	20	....	....	....	1200	77	*1	3.91	....	....	....	....	....	....	....	....	....	....	....	....	....	....	....	....	....
1978-79	Cambridge Hornets	OHA Sr.	STATISTICS NOT AVAILABLE																								
1979-80	Canada	Olympics	3	1	2	0	122	7	0	3.44	....	....	....	....	....	....	....	....	....	....	....	....	....	....	....	....	....
	Edmonton Oilers	**NHL**	**1**	**0**	**1**	**0**	**60**	**4**	**0**	**4.00**	**3.51**	....	....	....	....	....	....	....	....	....	....	....	....	....	....	....	....
	Houston Apollos	CHL	4	1	1	0	123	13	0	6.34	....	....	....	....	....	....	....	....	....	....	....	....	....	....	....	....	....
1980-81	Milwaukee Admirals	IHL	17	....	....	....	959	78	0	4.88	....	....	....	....	....	....	....	....	....	....	....	....	....	....	....	....	....
	Hampton Aces	EHL	15	....	....	....	716	72	0	6.03	....	....	....	....	....	....	....	....	....	....	....	....	....	....	....	....	....
	NHL Totals		**1**	**0**	**1**	**0**	**60**	**4**	**0**	**4.00**	....	....	....	....	....	....	....	....	....	....	....	....	....	....	....	....	....

Signed as a free agent by **Edmonton**, March, 1980.

• DURNAN, BILL

Bill Durnan G – R. 6', 190 lbs. b: Toronto, Ont., 1/22/1916. d: 10/31/1972. **HHOF**

Season	Club	League	GP	W	L	T	Mins	GA	SO	Avg	AAvg	Eff	SA	S%	SAPG	GP	W	L	T	Mins	GA	SO	Avg	Eff	SA	S%	SAPG
1931-32	North Toronto Juniors	City Jr.	8	....	....	....	480	17	1	2.12	....	....	....	....	....	4	....	....	....	240	10	1	2.50	....	....	....	....
1932-33	Sudbury Wolves	NOHA	6	....	....	....	360	6	2	1.00	....	....	....	....	....	2	....	....	....	120	4	0	2.00	....	....	....	....
1933-34	Toronto Torontos	City Jr.	11	....	....	....	660	21	4	1.91	....	....	....	....	....	1	0	1	0	60	5	0	5.00	....	....	....	....
1934-35	Toronto All-Stars	City Sr.	2	....	....	....	120	9	0	4.50	....	....	....	....	....	....	....	....	....	....	....	....	....	....	....	....	....
	Toronto McColl	City Sr.	15	....	....	....	900	62	0	4.13	....	....	....	....	....	....	....	....	....	....	....	....	....	....	....	....	....
1935-36	Toronto Dominions	City Sr.	1	0	1	0	60	6	0	6.00	....	....	....	....	....	....	....	....	....	....	....	....	....	....	....	....	....

			REGULAR SEASON													PLAYOFFS											
Season	Club	League	GP	W	L	T	Mins	GA	SO	Avg	AAvg	Eff	SA	S%	SAPG	GP	W	L	T	Mins	GA	SO	Avg	Eff	SA	S%	SAPG
1936-37	Kirkland Lake Blue Devils	NOHA	4	4	0	0	240	5	0	1.25	....	....	....	....	....	4	1	0	3	240	8	1	2.00	....	....	....	....
1937-38	Kirkland Lake Blue Devils	NOHA	11	*8	1	1	610	27	1	2.66	....	....	....	....	....	4	2	2	0	240	13	1	3.25	....	....	....	....
1938-39	Kirkland Lake Blue Devils	NOHA	7	*7	0	0	420	7	*3	*1.00	....	....	....	....	....	7	5	2	0	419	15	*3	2.15	....	....	....	....
1939-40	Kirkland Lake Blue Devils	NOHA	6	....	....	....	360	12	1	2.00	....	....	....	....	....	17	14	1	2	1080	35	1	2.02	....	....	....	....
1940-41	Montreal Royals	QSHL	34	....	....	....	2000	100	1	3.00	....	....	....	....	....	22	16	5	1	1330	73	2	3.29	....	....	....	....
1941-42	Montreal Royals	QSHL	39	....	....	....	2340	143	0	3.67	....	....	....	....	....	....	....	....	....	....	....	....	....	....	....	....	....
1942-43	Montreal Royals	QSHL	31	....	....	....	1860	130	0	4.19	....	....	....	....	....	4	....	....	....	240	11	0	2.75	....	....	....	....
1943-44	**Montreal Canadiens**	**NHL**	***50**	***38**	**5**	**7**	***3000**	**109**	**2**	***2.18**	**1.51**	....	....	....	....	***9**	***8**	**1**	....	***549**	**14**	***1**	***1.53**	....	....	....	....
1944-45	**Montreal Canadiens**	**NHL**	***50**	***38**	**8**	**4**	***3000**	**121**	**1**	***2.42**	**1.88**	....	....	....	....	**6**	**2**	**4**	....	**373**	**15**	**0**	**2.41**	....	....	....	....
1945-46	**Montreal Canadiens**	**NHL**	**40**	***24**	**11**	**5**	**2400**	**104**	***4**	***2.60**	**2.32**	....	....	....	....	**9**	***8**	**1**	....	**581**	**20**	**0**	***2.07**	....	....	....	....
1946-47	**Montreal Canadiens**	**NHL**	***60**	***34**	**16**	**10**	***3600**	**138**	**4**	***2.30**	**2.13**	....	....	....	....	***11**	**6**	**5**	....	***720**	**23**	***1**	***1.92**	....	....	....	....
1947-48	**Montreal Canadiens**	**NHL**	**59**	**20**	**28**	**10**	**3505**	**162**	**5**	**2.77**	**2.89**	....	....	....	....	....	....	....	....	....	....	....	....	....	....	....	....
1948-49	**Montreal Canadiens**	**NHL**	***60**	**28**	**23**	**9**	***3600**	**126**	***10**	***2.10**	**2.28**	....	....	....	....	**7**	**3**	**4**	....	**468**	**17**	**0**	**2.18**	....	....	....	....
1949-50	**Montreal Canadiens**	**NHL**	**64**	**26**	**21**	**17**	**3840**	**141**	**8**	***2.20**	**2.40**	....	....	....	....	**3**	**0**	**3**	....	**180**	**10**	**0**	**3.33**	....	....	....	....
	NHL Totals		**383**	**208**	**112**	**62**	**22945**	**901**	**34**	**2.36**	....	....	....	....	....	**45**	**27**	**18**	....	**2871**	**99**	**2**	**2.07**	....	....	....	....

NHL First All-Star Team (1944, 1945, 1946, 1947, 1949, 1950) • Won Vezina Trophy (1944, 1945, 1946, 1947, 1949, 1950)

Played in NHL All-Star Game (1947, 1948, 1949)

Signed as a free agent by **Montreal**, October 30, 1943.

• DYCK, ED

Ed Dyck G – L. 5'11", 160 lbs. b: Warman, Sask., 10/29/1950. Vancouver's 3rd choice, 30th overall, in 1970 Amateur Draft.

Season	Club	League	GP	W	L	T	Mins	GA	SO	Avg	AAvg	Eff	SA	S%	SAPG	GP	W	L	T	Mins	GA	SO	Avg	Eff	SA	S%	SAPG
1967-68	Estevan Bruins	WCJHL	4	....	....	....	240	12	0	3.00	....	....	....	....	....	2	2	0	0	120	5	0	2.50	....	....	....	....
1968-69	Estevan-Calgary	WCJHL	36	....	....	....	2111	120	1	3.41	....	....	....	....	....	....	....	....	....	....	....	....	....	....	....	....	....
1969-70	Calgary Centennials	WCJHL	*60	....	....	....	3599	193	3	3.22	....	....	....	....	....	16	7	7	2	960	45	*1	*2.81	....	....	....	....
1970-71	Calgary Centennials	WCJHL	66	....	....	....	4069	172	4	*2.53	....	....	....	....	....	11	5	4	2	641	29	0	2.71	....	....	....	....
1971-72	Rochester Americans	AHL	10	4	3	2	554	43	1	4.66	....	....	....	....	....	....	....	....	....	....	....	....	....	....	....	....	....
	Vancouver Canucks	**NHL**	**12**	**1**	**6**	**2**	**573**	**35**	**0**	**3.66**	**3.69**	....	....	....	....	....	....	....	....	....	....	....	....	....	....	....	....
	Seattle Totems	WHL	6	1	5	0	360	31	0	5.17	....	....	....	....	....	....	....	....	....	....	....	....	....	....	....	....	....
1972-73	**Vancouver Canucks**	**NHL**	**25**	**5**	**17**	**1**	**1297**	**98**	**1**	**4.53**	**4.30**	....	....	....	....	....	....	....	....	....	....	....	....	....	....	....	....
	Seattle Totems	WHL	13	3	6	3	617	50	0	4.86	....	....	....	....	....	....	....	....	....	....	....	....	....	....	....	....	....
1973-74	**Vancouver Canucks**	**NHL**	**12**	**2**	**5**	**2**	**583**	**45**	**0**	**4.63**	**4.49**	....	....	....	....	....	....	....	....	....	....	....	....	....	....	....	....
	Seattle Totems	WHL	4	2	1	1	173	10	1	3.47	....	....	....	....	....	....	....	....	....	....	....	....	....	....	....	....	....
1974-75	Indianapolis Racers	WHA	32	3	21	3	1692	123	0	4.36	....	....	....	....	....	....	....	....	....	....	....	....	....	....	....	....	....
1975-76	HC Boden	Sweden	STATISTICS NOT AVAILABLE																								
	NHL Totals		**49**	**8**	**28**	**5**	**2453**	**178**	**1**	**4.35**	....	....	....	....	....	....	....	....	....	....	....	....	....	....	....	....	....
	Other Major League Totals		32	3	21	3	1692	123	0	4.36	....	....	....	....	....	....	....	....	....	....	....	....	....	....	....	....	....

WCJHL All-Star Team (1971)

Selected by **Calgary-Cleveland** (WHA) in 1972 WHA General Player Draft, February 12, 1972. WHA rights traded to **Indianapolis** (WHA) by **Cleveland** (WHA) for future considerations, April, 1974. Loaned to **Boden** (Sweden) by **Indianapolis** (WHA) for 1975-76 season as compensation for Indianapolis' signing of free agent Leif Holmqvist, June, 1974.

• EDWARDS, DON

Don "Dart" Edwards G – L. 5'9", 160 lbs. b: Hamilton, Ont., 9/28/1955. Buffalo's 7th choice, 89th overall, in 1975 Amateur Draft.

Season	Club	League	GP	W	L	T	Mins	GA	SO	Avg	AAvg	Eff	SA	S%	SAPG	GP	W	L	T	Mins	GA	SO	Avg	Eff	SA	S%	SAPG
1973-74	Kitchener Rangers	OHA	35	....	....	....	2089	95	*3	*2.73	....	....	....	....	....	....	....	....	....	....	....	....	....	....	....	....	....
1974-75	Kitchener Rangers	OHA	55	....	....	....	3204	258	1	4.70	....	....	....	....	....	....	....	....	....	....	....	....	....	....	....	....	....
1975-76	Hershey Bears	AHL	39	23	12	2	2253	128	3	3.41	....	....	....	....	....	5	1	3	0	293	18	0	3.68	....	....	....	....
1976-77	Hershey Bears	AHL	47	26	15	6	2797	136	*5	2.91	....	....	....	....	....	....	....	....	....	....	....	....	....	....	....	....	....
	Buffalo Sabres	**NHL**	**25**	**16**	**7**	**2**	**1480**	**62**	**2**	**2.51**	**2.32**	....	....	....	....	**5**	**2**	**3**	....	**300**	**15**	**0**	**3.00**	....	....	....	....
1977-78	**Buffalo Sabres**	**NHL**	***72**	***38**	**16**	**17**	***4209**	**185**	**5**	**2.64**	**2.45**	....	....	....	....	**8**	**3**	**5**	....	**482**	**22**	**0**	**2.74**	....	....	....	....
1978-79	**Buffalo Sabres**	**NHL**	**54**	**26**	**18**	**9**	**3160**	**159**	**2**	**3.02**	**2.65**	....	....	....	....	....	....	....	....	....	....	....	....	....	....	....	....
1979-80	**Buffalo Sabres**	**NHL**	**49**	**27**	**9**	**12**	**2920**	**125**	**2**	**2.57**	**2.24**	....	....	....	....	**6**	**3**	**3**	....	**360**	**17**	**1**	**2.83**	....	....	....	....
1980-81	**Buffalo Sabres**	**NHL**	**45**	**23**	**10**	**12**	**2700**	**133**	***3**	**2.96**	**2.36**	....	....	....	....	**8**	**4**	**4**	....	**503**	**28**	**0**	**3.34**	....	....	....	....
1981-82	Canada	C Cup	1	....	....	....	60	3	0	3.00	....	....	....	....	....	....	....	....	....	....	....	....	....	....	....	....	....
	Buffalo Sabres	**NHL**	**62**	**26**	**23**	**9**	**3500**	**205**	**0**	**3.51**	**2.69**	....	....	....	....	**4**	**1**	**3**	....	**214**	**16**	**0**	**4.49**	....	....	....	....
1982-83	**Calgary Flames**	**NHL**	**39**	**16**	**15**	**6**	**2209**	**148**	**1**	**4.02**	**3.21**	**4.74**	**1255**	**.882**	**34.1**	**5**	**1**	**2**	....	**226**	**22**	**0**	**5.84**	....	....	....	....
1983-84	**Calgary Flames**	**NHL**	**41**	**13**	**19**	**5**	**2303**	**157**	**0**	**4.09**	**3.20**	**5.28**	**1217**	**.871**	**31.7**	**6**	**2**	**1**	....	**217**	**12**	**0**	**3.32**	**3.00**	**133**	**.910**	**36.8**
1984-85	**Calgary Flames**	**NHL**	**34**	**11**	**15**	**2**	**1691**	**115**	**1**	**4.00**	**3.24**	**5.47**	**858**	**.866**	**30.4**	....	....	....	....	....	....	....	....	....	....	....	....
1985-86	**Toronto Maple Leafs**	**NHL**	**38**	**12**	**23**	**0**	**2009**	**160**	**0**	**4.78**	**3.73**	**6.71**	**1140**	**.860**	**34.0**	....	....	....	....	....	....	....	....	....	....	....	....
1986-87	Brantford Mott's Clamatos	Sr.	STATISTICS NOT AVAILABLE																								
1987-88	Nova Scotia Oilers	AHL	3	....	....	....	180	18	0	6.00	....	....	....	....	....	....	....	....	....	....	....	....	....	....	....	....	....
	NHL Totals		**459**	**208**	**155**	**74**	**26181**	**1449**	**16**	**3.32**	....	....	....	....	....	**42**	**16**	**21**	....	**2302**	**132**	**1**	**3.44**	....	....	....	....

OHA First All-Star Team (1974, 1975) • AHL Second All-Star Team (1976) • NHL Second All-Star Team (1978, 1980) • Shared Vezina Trophy with Bob Sauve (1980)

Played in NHL All-Star Game (1980, 1982)

Traded to **Calgary** by **Buffalo** with Richie Dunn, Buffalo's 2nd round choice (Richard Kromm) in 1982 Entry Draft and 1st round choice (Dan Quinn) in 1983 Entry Draft for Calgary's 1st (Paul Cyr) and 2nd (Jens Johansson) round choices in 1982 Entry Draft and 1st (Normand Lacombe) and 2nd (John Tucker) round choices in 1987 Entry Draft, May 29, 1982. Traded to **Toronto** by **Calgary** for Toronto's 4th round choice (Tim Harris) in 1987 Entry Draft, May 29, 1985.

• EDWARDS, GARY

Gary Edwards G – L. 5'9", 165 lbs. b: Toronto, Ont., 10/5/1947. St. Louis' 1st choice, 6th overall, in 1968 Amateur Draft.

Season	Club	League	GP	W	L	T	Mins	GA	SO	Avg	AAvg	Eff	SA	S%	SAPG	GP	W	L	T	Mins	GA	SO	Avg	Eff	SA	S%	SAPG
1966-67	Toronto Marlboros	OHA	8	....	....	....	480	37	0	4.62	....	....	....	....	....	....	....	....	....	....	....	....	....	....	....	....	....
1967-68	Toronto Marlboros	OHA	38	....	....	....	2250	120	2	3.20	....	....	....	....	....	5	....	....	....	290	18	0	3.72	....	....	....	....
1968-69	**St. Louis Blues**	**NHL**	**1**	**0**	**0**	**0**	**4**	**0**	**0**	**0.00**	**0.00**	....	....	....	....	....	....	....	....	....	....	....	....	....	....	....	....
	Kansas City Blues	CHL	32	....	....	....	1760	92	*4	3.00	....	....	....	....	....	4	1	3	0	240	18	0	4.50	....	....	....	....
1969-70	**St. Louis Blues**	**NHL**	**1**	**0**	**1**	**0**	**60**	**4**	**0**	**4.00**	**4.25**	....	....	....	....	....	....	....	....	....	....	....	....	....	....	....	....
	San Diego Gulls	WHL	3	2	0	1	180	3	1	1.00	....	....	....	....	....	....	....	....	....	....	....	....	....	....	....	....	....
	Kansas City Blues	CHL	34	11	17	6	2040	115	2	3.38	....	....	....	....	....	....	....	....	....	....	....	....	....	....	....	....	....
1970-71	San Diego Gulls	WHL	4	4	0	0	240	12	0	3.00	....	....	....	....	....	....	....	....	....	....	....	....	....	....	....	....	....
	Kansas City Blues	CHL	35	....	....	....	1980	85	2	2.58	....	....	....	....	....	....	....	....	....	....	....	....	....	....	....	....	....
1971-72	**Los Angeles Kings**	**NHL**	**44**	**13**	**23**	**5**	**2503**	**150**	**2**	**3.60**	**3.65**	....	....	....	....	....	....	....	....	....	....	....	....	....	....	....	....
1972-73	**Los Angeles Kings**	**NHL**	**27**	**9**	**16**	**1**	**1560**	**94**	**1**	**3.62**	**3.42**	....	....	....	....	....	....	....	....	....	....	....	....	....	....	....	....
1973-74	**Los Angeles Kings**	**NHL**	**18**	**5**	**7**	**2**	**929**	**50**	**1**	**3.23**	**3.12**	....	....	....	....	**1**	**1**	**0**	....	**60**	**1**	**0**	**1.00**	....	....	....	....
1974-75	**Los Angeles Kings**	**NHL**	**27**	**15**	**3**	**8**	**1561**	**61**	**3**	**2.34**	**2.10**	....	....	....	....	....	....	....	....	....	....	....	....	....	....	....	....
1975-76	**Los Angeles Kings**	**NHL**	**29**	**12**	**13**	**4**	**1740**	**103**	**0**	**3.55**	**3.21**	....	....	....	....	**2**	**1**	**1**	....	**120**	**9**	**0**	**4.50**	....	....	....	....
1976-77	**Los Angeles Kings**	**NHL**	**10**	**0**	**6**	**2**	**501**	**39**	**0**	**4.67**	**4.35**	....	....	....	....	....	....	....	....	....	....	....	....	....	....	....	....
	Cleveland Barons	**NHL**	**17**	**4**	**10**	**3**	**999**	**68**	**2**	**4.08**	**3.80**	....	....	....	....	....	....	....	....	....	....	....	....	....	....	....	....
1977-78	**Cleveland Barons**	**NHL**	**30**	**6**	**18**	**5**	**1700**	**128**	**0**	**4.52**	**4.26**	....	....	....	....	....	....	....	....	....	....	....	....	....	....	....	....
1978-79	**Minnesota North Stars**	**NHL**	**25**	**6**	**11**	**5**	**1337**	**83**	**0**	**3.72**	**3.29**	....	....	....	....	....	....	....	....	....	....	....	....	....	....	....	....
1979-80	**Minnesota North Stars**	**NHL**	**26**	**9**	**7**	**10**	**1539**	**82**	**0**	**3.20**	**2.81**	....	....	....	....	**7**	**3**	**3**	....	**337**	**22**	**0**	**3.92**	....	....	....	....
1980-81	**Edmonton Oilers**	**NHL**	**15**	**5**	**3**	**4**	**729**	**44**	**0**	**3.62**	**2.90**	....	....	....	....	**1**	**0**	**0**	....	**20**	**2**	**0**	**6.00**	....	....	....	....
1981-82	**St. Louis Blues**	**NHL**	**10**	**1**	**5**	**1**	**480**	**45**	**1**	**5.63**	**4.35**	....	....	....	....	....	....	....	....	....	....	....	....	....	....	....	....
	Pittsburgh Penguins	**NHL**	**6**	**3**	**2**	**1**	**360**	**22**	**1**	**3.67**	**2.83**	....	....	....	....	....	....	....	....	....	....	....	....	....	....	....	....
	NHL Totals		**286**	**88**	**125**	**51**	**16002**	**973**	**11**	**3.65**	....	....	....	....	....	**11**	**5**	**4**	....	**537**	**34**	**0**	**3.80**	....	....	....	....

Claimed by **Buffalo** from **St. Louis** in Expansion Draft, June 10, 1970. Claimed by **LA Kings** from **Buffalo** in Intra-League Draft, June 8, 1971. Traded to **Cleveland** by **LA Kings** with Juha Widing for Gary Simmons and Jim Moxey, January 22, 1977. Placed on **Minnesota** reserve list after Cleveland-Minnesota Dispersal Draft, June 15, 1978. Traded to **Edmonton** by **Minnesota** for future considerations, February 2, 1981. Claimed by **St. Louis** from **Edmonton** in Waiver Draft, October 8, 1981. Claimed on waivers by **Pittsburgh** from **St. Louis**, February 14, 1982.

• EDWARDS, MARV

Marv Edwards G – L. 5'8", 155 lbs. b: St. Catharines, Ont., 8/15/1935.

Season	Club	League	GP	W	L	T	Mins	GA	SO	Avg	AAvg	Eff	SA	S%	SAPG	GP	W	L	T	Mins	GA	SO	Avg	Eff	SA	S%	SAPG
1950-51	St. Catharines Teepees	OHA	1	0	1	0	60	11	0	11.00	....	....	....	....	....	....	....	....	....	....	....	....	....	....	....	....	....
1951-52	St. Catharines Teepees	OHA	48	....	....	....	2880	198	2	4.13	....	....	....	....	....	13	7	6	0	780	47	0	3.62	....	....	....	....
1952-53	St. Catharines Teepees	OHA	36	....	....	....	2160	149	2	4.14	....	....	....	....	....	1	....	....	....	60	5	0	5.00	....	....	....	....
	Barrie Flyers	OHA	....	....	....	....	....	....	....	....	....	....	....	....	....	3	....	....	....	180	10	0	3.33	....	....	....	....
1953-54	St. Catharines Teepees	OHA	49	....	....	....	2940	182	*4	3.71	....	....	....	....	....	15	....	....	....	900	55	*1	3.67	....	....	....	....

			REGULAR SEASON													PLAYOFFS											
Season	Club	League	GP	W	L	T	Mins	GA	SO	Avg	AAvg	Eff	SA	S%	SAPG	GP	W	L	T	Mins	GA	SO	Avg	Eff	SA	S%	SAPG
1954-55	St. Catharines Teepees	OHA	47	*32	13	2	2820	162	1	3.45	....	....	....	....	....	6	....	....	....	360	20	0	3.33	....	....	....	....
	Buffalo Bisons	AHL	2	1	1	0	120	6	0	3.00	....	....	....	....	....	....	....	....	....	....	....	....	....	....	....	....	....
1955-56	Chatham–Windsor	OHA Sr.	34	....	....	....	2040	158	0	4.72	....	....	....	....	....	11	....	....	....	660	38	0	3.45	....	....	....	....
1956-57	Chatham Maroons	OHA Sr.	52	28	22	2	3120	183	5	3.52	....	....	....	....	....	6	2	4	0	360	14	0	*2.33	....	....	....	....
	Calgary Stampeders	WHL	2	0	2	0	119	5	0	2.52	....	....	....	....	....	....	....	....	....	....	....	....	....	....	....	....	....
	Buffalo Bisons	AHL	1	0	1	0	60	4	0	4.00	....	....	....	....	....	....	....	....	....	....	....	....	....	....	....	....	....
1957-58	Windsor Bulldogs	NOHA	57	25	30	2	3420	213	1	3.73	....	....	....	....	....	13	....	....	....	780	42	1	3.23	....	....	....	....
	Buffalo Bisons	AHL	2	0	2	0	120	10	0	5.00	....	....	....	....	....	....	....	....	....	....	....	....	....	....	....	....	....
1958-59	North Bay Trappers	NOHA	35	....	....	....	2100	180	0	5.14	....	....	....	....	....	....	....	....	....	....	....	....	....	....	....	....	....
	Canada	WEC-A	2	2	0	0	120	0	2	0.00	....	....	....	....	....	....	....	....	....	....	....	....	....	....	....	....	....
1959-60	Milwaukee Falcons	IHL	64	24	39	1	3840	296	3	4.62	....	....	....	....	....	....	....	....	....	....	....	....	....	....	....	....	....
	Minneapolis Millers	IHL	....	....	....	....	....	....	....	....	....	....	....	....	....	6	2	4	0	360	17	1	2.83	....	....	....	....
1960-61	Johnstown Jets	EHL	64	40	22	2	3840	215	4	3.36	....	....	....	....	....	12	*10	2	0	720	18	*4	*1.50	....	....	....	....
	New Haven Blades	EHL	1	....	....	....	60	3	0	3.00	....	....	....	....	....	....	....	....	....	....	....	....	....	....	....	....	....
1961-62	Johnstown Jets	EHL	55	....	....	....	3300	193	3	3.51	....	....	....	....	....	....	....	....	....	....	....	....	....	....	....	....	....
1962-63	Knoxville Knights	EHL	1	1	0	0	60	1	0	1.00	....	....	....	....	....	....	....	....	....	....	....	....	....	....	....	....	....
	Nashville Dixie Flyers	EHL	68	16	48	4	4080	262	1	3.85	....	....	....	....	....	3	0	3	0	180	18	0	6.00	....	....	....	....
1963-64	Nashville Dixie Flyers	EHL	70	37	29	4	4200	230	5	3.29	....	....	....	....	....	3	0	3	0	180	14	0	4.67	....	....	....	....
	Clinton Comets	EHL	....	....	....	....	....	....	....	....	....	....	....	....	....	3	2	1	0	180	9	0	3.00	....	....	....	....
1964-65	Nashville Dixie Flyers	EHL	71	*54	17	0	4260	193	7	2.72	....	....	....	....	....	13	8	5	0	780	34	1	2.62	....	....	....	....
1965-66	Nashville Dixie Flyers	EHL	71	42	22	7	4260	174	*7	*2.45	....	....	....	....	....	11	*11	0	0	660	13	*2	*1.18	....	....	....	....
1966-67	Nashville Dixie Flyers	EHL	72	*51	19	2	4320	168	*6	*2.33	....	....	....	....	....	14	*11	3	0	840	14	*1	2.00	....	....	....	....
1967-68	Portland Buckaroos	WHL	40	21	16	2	2366	93	4	*2.36	....	....	....	....	....	5	1	4	0	328	16	1	2.93	....	....	....	....
1968-69	**Pittsburgh Penguins**	**NHL**	**1**	**0**	**1**	**0**	**60**	**3**	**0**	**3.00**	**3.11**	....	....	....	....	....	....	....	....	....	....	....	....	....	....	....	....
	Amarillo Wranglers	CHL	39	....	....	....	2190	116	1	3.18	....	....	....	....	....	....	....	....	....	....	....	....	....	....	....	....	....
	Baltimore Clippers	AHL	14	6	7	1	839	42	2	3.00	....	....	....	....	....	4	1	3	0	200	13	0	3.90	....	....	....	....
1969-70	**Toronto Maple Leafs**	**NHL**	**25**	**10**	**9**	**4**	**1420**	**77**	**1**	**3.25**	**3.46**	....	....	....	....	....	....	....	....	....	....	....	....	....	....	....	....
1970-71	Phoenix Roadrunners	WHL	53	27	17	6	2949	157	2	3.19	....	....	....	....	....	7	3	4	0	410	24	0	3.51	....	....	....	....
1971-72	Phoenix Roadrunners	WHL	35	19	11	3	1891	103	1	3.26	....	....	....	....	....	3	1	2	0	186	11	0	3.55	....	....	....	....
1972-73	**California Golden Seals**	**NHL**	**21**	**4**	**14**	**2**	**1207**	**87**	**1**	**4.32**	**4.09**	....	....	....	....	....	....	....	....	....	....	....	....	....	....	....	....
1973-74	**California Golden Seals**	**NHL**	**14**	**1**	**10**	**1**	**780**	**51**	**0**	**3.92**	**3.79**	....	....	....	....	....	....	....	....	....	....	....	....	....	....	....	....
	NHL Totals		**61**	**15**	**34**	**7**	**3467**	**218**	**2**	**3.77**	....	....	....	....	....	....	....	....	....	....	....	....	....	....	....	....	....

Won George L. Davis Jr. Trophy (fewest goals against - EHL) (1961, 1966, 1967) • EHL First All-Star Team (1964) • EHL South First All-Star Team (1965, 1966, 1967) • Shared WHL Leading Goaltender Award with Jim McLeod (1968) • CHL First All-Star Team (1969)

Signed as a free agent by **Pittsburgh**, September, 1967. Claimed by **Toronto** from **Pittsburgh** in Intra-League Draft, June 11, 1969. Claimed by **California** (Salt Lake-WHL) from **Toronto** in Reverse Draft, June 8, 1972.

• EDWARDS, ROY

Roy Edwards G – R. 5'8", 165 lbs. b: Seneca Township, Ont., 3/12/1937.

Season	Club	League	GP	W	L	T	Mins	GA	SO	Avg	AAvg	Eff	SA	S%	SAPG	GP	W	L	T	Mins	GA	SO	Avg	Eff	SA	S%	SAPG
1955-56	St. Catharines Teepees	OHA	41	26	12	3	2460	160	1	3.90	....	....	....	....	....	6	....	....	....	360	26	0	4.33	....	....	....	....
1956-57	St. Catharines Teepees	OHA	49	24	23	2	2940	179	3	3.65	....	....	....	....	....	14	....	....	....	840	55	1	3.93	....	....	....	....
1957-58	Whitby Dunlops	EOHL	7	....	....	....	420	21	0	3.00	....	....	....	....	....	....	....	....	....	....	....	....	....	....	....	....	....
	Fort Wayne Komets	IHL	25	....	....	....	1500	84	0	3.36	....	....	....	....	....	....	....	....	....	....	....	....	....	....	....	....	....
	Canada	WEC-A	7	*7	0	0	420	6	3	0.86	....	....	....	....	....	....	....	....	....	....	....	....	....	....	....	....	....
1958-59	Calgary Stampeders	WHL	63	*42	20	1	3780	192	2	3.05	....	....	....	....	....	8	4	4	0	480	27	0	3.37	....	....	....	....
1959-60	Buffalo Bisons	AHL	*72	33	35	4	*4360	267	4	3.67	....	....	....	....	....	....	....	....	....	....	....	....	....	....	....	....	....
1960-61	Buffalo Bisons	AHL	30	12	16	1	1800	128	1	4.27	....	....	....	....	....	....	....	....	....	....	....	....	....	....	....	....	....
	Sault Ste. Marie Thunderbirds	EPHL	37	16	15	6	2220	119	3	3.22	....	....	....	....	....	12	7	5	0	739	34	0	2.76	....	....	....	....
1961-62	Sault Ste. Marie Thunderbirds	EPHL	36	4	26	6	2160	157	1	4.36	....	....	....	....	....	....	....	....	....	....	....	....	....	....	....	....	....
	Pittsburgh Hornets	AHL	10	1	8	1	600	52	0	5.20	....	....	....	....	....	....	....	....	....	....	....	....	....	....	....	....	....
	Portland Buckeroos	WHL	8	3	5	0	480	32	0	4.00	....	....	....	....	....	....	....	....	....	....	....	....	....	....	....	....	....
1962-63	Calgary Stampeders	WHL	*70	23	44	2	4140	274	0	3.97	....	....	....	....	....	....	....	....	....	....	....	....	....	....	....	....	....
	Spokane Comets	WHL	1	0	1	0	60	3	0	3.00	....	....	....	....	....	....	....	....	....	....	....	....	....	....	....	....	....
1963-64	Buffalo Bisons	AHL	47	14	27	6	2820	155	2	3.30	....	....	....	....	....	....	....	....	....	....	....	....	....	....	....	....	....
	St. Louis Braves	CHL	3	1	1	1	180	8	0	2.66	....	....	....	....	....	....	....	....	....	....	....	....	....	....	....	....	....
1964-65	St. Louis Braves	CHL	65	12	47	6	3900	302	1	4.65	....	....	....	....	....	....	....	....	....	....	....	....	....	....	....	....	....
1965-66	Buffalo Bisons	AHL	40	15	22	2	2389	140	3	3.52	....	....	....	....	....	....	....	....	....	....	....	....	....	....	....	....	....
1966-67	Buffalo Bisons	AHL	39	9	24	5	2235	189	0	5.07	....	....	....	....	....	....	....	....	....	....	....	....	....	....	....	....	....
1967-68	Fort Worth Wings	CHL	9	8	0	1	540	12	4	1.33	....	....	....	....	....	....	....	....	....	....	....	....	....	....	....	....	....
	Detroit Red Wings	**NHL**	**41**	**15**	**15**	**8**	**2177**	**127**	**0**	**3.50**	**3.92**	....	....	....	....	....	....	....	....	....	....	....	....	....	....	....	....
1968-69	Fort Worth Wings	CHL	10	4	2	3	560	28	0	3.00	....	....	....	....	....	....	....	....	....	....	....	....	....	....	....	....	....
	Detroit Red Wings	**NHL**	**40**	**18**	**11**	**6**	**2099**	**89**	**4**	**2.54**	**2.62**	....	....	....	....	....	....	....	....	....	....	....	....	....	....	....	....
1969-70	**Detroit Red Wings**	**NHL**	**47**	**24**	**15**	**6**	**2683**	**116**	**2**	**2.59**	**2.74**	....	....	....	....	**4**	**0**	**3**	....	**206**	**11**	**0**	**3.20**	....	....	....	....
1970-71	**Detroit Red Wings**	**NHL**	**37**	**11**	**19**	**7**	**2104**	**119**	**0**	**3.39**	**3.36**	....	....	....	....	....	....	....	....	....	....	....	....	....	....	....	....
1971-72	**Pittsburgh Penguins**	**NHL**	**15**	**2**	**8**	**4**	**847**	**36**	**0**	**2.55**	**2.56**	....	....	....	....	....	....	....	....	....	....	....	....	....	....	....	....
1972-73	**Detroit Red Wings**	**NHL**	**52**	**27**	**17**	**7**	**3012**	**132**	***6**	**2.63**	**2.46**	....	....	....	....	....	....	....	....	....	....	....	....	....	....	....	....
1973-74	**Detroit Red Wings**	**NHL**	**4**	**0**	**3**	**0**	**187**	**18**	**0**	**5.78**	**5.59**	....	....	....	....	....	....	....	....	....	....	....	....	....	....	....	....
	NHL Totals		**236**	**97**	**88**	**38**	**13109**	**637**	**12**	**2.92**	....	....	....	....	....	**4**	**0**	**3**	....	**206**	**11**	**0**	**3.20**	....	....	....	....

WHL Prairie Division First All-Star Team (1959) • Won WHL Prairie Division Rookie of the Year Award (1959)

Claimed by **Pittsburgh** from **Chicago** in Expansion Draft, June 6, 1967. Traded to **Detroit** by **Pittsburgh** for Hank Bassen, September 7, 1967. Claimed on waivers by **Pittsburgh** from **Detroit**, June 7, 1971. Traded to **Detroit** by **Pittsburgh** for cash, October 6, 1972 . Claimed on waivers by **Buffalo** from **Detroit**, May 20, 1974.

• ELIOT, DARREN

Darren Eliot G – R. 6'1", 175 lbs. b: Hamilton, Ont., 11/26/1961. Los Angeles' 8th choice, 115th overall, in 1980 Entry Draft.

Season	Club	League	GP	W	L	T	Mins	GA	SO	Avg	AAvg	Eff	SA	S%	SAPG	GP	W	L	T	Mins	GA	SO	Avg	Eff	SA	S%	SAPG
1979-80	Cornell University	ECAC	26	14	8	0	1362	94	0	4.14	....	....	....	....	....	5	3	2	0	300	20	0	4.00	....	....	....	....
1980-81	Cornell University	ECAC	18	8	7	0	912	52	1	3.42	....	....	....	....	....	3	1	1	0	119	7	0	2.33	....	....	....	....
1981-82	Cornell University	ECAC	7	1	3	0	338	25	0	4.44	....	....	....	....	....	....	....	....	....	....	....	....	....	....	....	....	....
1982-83	Cornell University	ECAC	26	13	10	3	1606	100	1	3.74	....	....	....	....	....	....	....	....	....	....	....	....	....	....	....	....	....
1983-84	Canada	Nat-Team	31	....	....	....	1676	111	0	3.97	....	....	....	....	....	....	....	....	....	....	....	....	....	....	....	....	....
	Canada	Olympics	2	0	0	0	40	2	0	3.00	....	....	....	....	....	....	....	....	....	....	....	....	....	....	....	....	....
	New Haven Nighthawks	AHL	7	4	1	0	365	30	0	4.93	....	....	....	....	....	....	....	....	....	....	....	....	....	....	....	....	....
1984-85	**Los Angeles Kings**	**NHL**	**33**	**12**	**11**	**6**	**1882**	**137**	**0**	**4.37**	**3.48**	**6.34**	**944**	**.855**	**30.1**	....	....	....	....	....	....	....	....	....	....	....	....
1985-86	**Los Angeles Kings**	**NHL**	**27**	**5**	**17**	**3**	**1481**	**121**	**0**	**4.90**	**3.82**	**7.40**	**801**	**.849**	**32.5**	....	....	....	....	....	....	....	....	....	....	....	....
	New Haven Nighthawks	AHL	3	1	2	1	180	19	0	6.33	....	....	....	....	....	1	0	1	0	60	4	0	4.00	....	....	....	....
1986-87	**Los Angeles Kings**	**NHL**	**24**	**8**	**13**	**2**	**1404**	**103**	**1**	**4.40**	**3.71**	**6.55**	**692**	**.851**	**29.6**	**1**	**0**	**0**	....	**40**	**7**	**0**	**10.50**	**25.34**	**29**	**.759**	**43.5**
	New Haven Nighthawks	AHL	4	2	2	0	239	15	0	3.77	....	....	....	....	....	....	....	....	....	....	....	....	....	....	....	....	....
1987-88	**Detroit Red Wings**	**NHL**	**3**	**0**	**0**	**1**	**97**	**9**	**0**	**5.57**	**4.63**	**8.95**	**56**	**.839**	**34.6**	....	....	....	....	....	....	....	....	....	....	....	....
	Adirondack Red Wings	AHL	43	23	11	7	2445	136	0	3.34	....	....	....	....	....	10	4	6	0	614	45	0	4.40	....	....	....	....
1988-89	Rochester Americans	AHL	23	8	6	2	969	59	0	3.65	....	....	....	....	....	....	....	....	....	....	....	....	....	....	....	....	....
	Buffalo Sabres	**NHL**	**2**	**0**	**0**	**0**	**67**	**7**	**0**	**6.27**	**5.17**	**10.21**	**43**	**.837**	**38.5**	....	....	....	....	....	....	....	....	....	....	....	....
	NHL Totals		**89**	**25**	**41**	**12**	**4931**	**377**	**1**	**4.59**	....	....	**2536**	**.851**	....	**1**	**0**	**0**	....	**40**	**7**	**0**	**10.50**	....	....	....	....

ECAC First All-Star Team (1983) • NCAA East First All-American Team (1983)

Signed as a free agent by **Detroit**, June 30, 1987. Signed as a free agent by **Buffalo**, February 27, 1989.

• ELLACOTT, KEN

Ken Ellacott G – L. 5'8", 160 lbs. b: Paris, Ont., 3/3/1959. Vancouver's 3rd choice, 47th overall, in 1979 Entry Draft.

Season	Club	League	GP	W	L	T	Mins	GA	SO	Avg	AAvg	Eff	SA	S%	SAPG	GP	W	L	T	Mins	GA	SO	Avg	Eff	SA	S%	SAPG
			REGULAR SEASON													PLAYOFFS											
1977-78	Peterborough Petes	OHA	55				3270	200	0	3.65						21				1260	74	1	3.42				
1978-79	Peterborough Petes	OHA	48				2856	169	3	3.53						19				1140	61	1	3.21				
1979-80	Dallas Black Hawks	CHL	*54	19	28	5	*3155	198	*4	3.77																	
1980-81	Dallas Black Hawks	CHL	40	27	7	5	2336	119	1	3.06						4				180	13	0	4.33				
1981-82	Dallas Black Hawks	CHL	*68	31	25	5	*3742	282	1	4.52						*16	9	7	0	*1015	62	0	3.66				
1982-83	**Vancouver Canucks**	**NHL**	**12**	**2**	**3**	**4**	**555**	**41**	**0**	**4.43**	**3.54**	**5.88**	**309**	**.867**	**33.4**												
	Fredericton Express	AHL	17	11	6	0	998	63	0	3.79						12	6	6	0	743	41	0	3.31				
1983-84	Montana Magic	CHL	41				2441	208	1	5.11																	
	NHL Totals		**12**	**2**	**3**	**4**	**555**	**41**	**0**	**4.43**			**309**	**.867**													

Memorial Cup All-Star Team (1978) • Won Hap Emms Memorial Trophy (Memorial Cup Tournament Top Goaltender) (1978) • OHA First All-Star Team (1979) • Shared Terry Sawchuk Trophy (fewest goals against - CHL) with Paul Harrison (1981)

• ERICKSON, CHAD

Chad Erickson G – R. 5'10", 175 lbs. b: Minneapolis, MN, 8/21/1970. New Jersey's 8th choice, 138th overall, in 1988 Entry Draft.

Season	Club	League	GP	W	L	T	Mins	GA	SO	Avg	AAvg	Eff	SA	S%	SAPG	GP	W	L	T	Mins	GA	SO	Avg	Eff	SA	S%	SAPG
1987-88	Warroad	H.S.	24				1080	33	7	1.83																	
1988-89	U. of Minnesota-Duluth	WCHA	15	5	7	1	821	49	0	3.58																	
1989-90	U. of Minnesota-Duluth	WCHA	39	19	19	1	2301	141	0	3.68																	
1990-91	U. of Minnesota-Duluth	WCHA	40	14	19	7	2393	159	0	3.99																	
1991-92	**New Jersey Devils**	**NHL**	**2**	**1**	**1**	**0**	**120**	**9**	**0**	**4.50**	**3.99**	**7.36**	**55**	**.836**	**27.5**												
	Utica Devils	AHL	43	18	19	3	2341	147	2	3.77						2	0	2	0	127	11	0	5.20				
1992-93	Utica Devils	AHL	9	1	7	1	505	47	0	5.58																	
	Cincinnati Cyclones	IHL	10	2	6	1	516	42	0	4.88																	
	Birmingham Bulls	ECHL	14	6	6	2	856	54	0	3.79																	
1993-94	Albany River Rats	AHL	4	2	1	0	183	13	0	4.25																	
	Raleigh IceCaps	ECHL	32	19	9	3	1883	101	0	3.22						6	3	1	0	286	21	0	4.40				
1994-95	Albany River Rats	AHL	1	1	0	0	60	2	0	2.00																	
	Providence Bruins	AHL	7	1	6	0	351	33	0	5.64																	
	Springfield Falcons	AHL	1	0	0	0	23	3	0	7.78																	
	Raleigh IceCaps	ECHL	11	1	8	1	587	45	0	4.60																	
1995-96	Birmingham Bulls	ECHL	44	16	20	4	2410	201	0	5.00																	
1996-97	Austin Ice-Bats	WPHL	32	18	11	2	1875	122	0	3.90						5	2	2	0	281	19	0	4.06				
1997-98	Austin Ice-Bats	WPHL	51	26	13	10	2987	172	0	3.45																	
	NHL Totals		**2**	**1**	**1**	**0**	**120**	**9**	**0**	**4.50**			**55**	**.836**													

WCHA Second All-Star Team (1990) • NCAA West First All-American Team (1990)

• ESPOSITO, TONY

Tony "Tony 0" Esposito G – R. 5'11", 185 lbs. b: Sault Ste. Marie, Ont., 4/23/1943. **HHOF**

Season	Club	League	GP	W	L	T	Mins	GA	SO	Avg	AAvg	Eff	SA	S%	SAPG	GP	W	L	T	Mins	GA	SO	Avg	Eff	SA	S%	SAPG
1964-65	Michigan Tech Huskies	WCHA	17				1020	40	1	2.35																	
1965-66	Michigan Tech Huskies	WCHA	19				1140	51	1	2.68																	
1966-67	Michigan Tech Huskies	WCHA	15				900	39	0	2.60																	
1967-68	Vancouver Canucks	WHL	*63	*25	*33	4	*3734	199	*4	3.20																	
1968-69	**Montreal Canadiens**	**NHL**	**13**	**5**	**4**	**4**	**746**	**34**	**2**	**2.73**	**2.82**																
	Houston Apollos	CHL	19				1139	46	1	2.42						1	0	1	0	59	3	0	3.05				
1969-70	**Chicago Black Hawks**	**NHL**	**63**	***38**	**17**	**8**	**3763**	**136**	***15**	**2.17**	**2.26**					**8**	**4**	**4**		**480**	**27**	**0**	**3.38**				
1970-71	**Chicago Black Hawks**	**NHL**	**57**	***35**	**14**	**7**	**3325**	**126**	**6**	**2.27**	**2.21**					**18**	**11**	**7**		**1151**	**42**	***2**	***2.19**				
1971-72	**Chicago Black Hawks**	**NHL**	**48**	**31**	**10**	**6**	**2780**	**82**	***9**	***1.77**	**1.75**					**5**	**2**	**3**		**300**	**16**	**0**	**3.20**				
1972-73	Canada	Summit	4				240	13	0	3.25																	
	Chicago Black Hawks	**NHL**	**56**	**32**	**17**	**7**	**3340**	**140**	**4**	**2.51**	**2.34**					**15**	**10**	**5**		**895**	**46**	**1**	**3.08**				
1973-74	**Chicago Black Hawks**	**NHL**	**70**	**34**	**14**	**21**	**4143**	**141**	**10**	**2.04**	**1.93**					**10**	**6**	**4**		**584**	**28**	***2**	**2.88**				
1974-75	**Chicago Black Hawks**	**NHL**	**71**	**34**	**30**	**7**	***4219**	**193**	**6**	**2.74**	**2.44**					**8**	**3**	**5**		**472**	**34**	**0**	**4.32**				
1975-76	**Chicago Black Hawks**	**NHL**	***68**	**30**	**23**	**13**	***4003**	**198**	**4**	**2.97**	**2.67**					**4**	**0**	**4**		**240**	**13**	**0**	**3.25**				
1976-77	**Chicago Black Hawks**	**NHL**	***69**	**25**	**36**	**8**	***4067**	**234**	**2**	**3.45**	**3.21**					**2**	**0**	**2**		**120**	**6**	**0**	**3.00**				
	Canada	WEC-A	9				510	27		3.17																	
1977-78	**Chicago Black Hawks**	**NHL**	**64**	**28**	**22**	**14**	**3840**	**168**	**5**	**2.63**	**2.44**					**4**	**0**	**4**		**252**	**19**	**0**	**4.52**				
1978-79	**Chicago Black Hawks**	**NHL**	**63**	**24**	**28**	**11**	***3780**	**206**	**4**	**3.27**	**2.88**					**4**	**0**	**4**		**243**	**14**	**0**	**3.46**				
	NHL All-Stars	Chal Cup	DID NOT PLAY – SPARE GOALTENDER																								
1979-80	**Chicago Black Hawks**	**NHL**	***69**	**31**	**22**	**16**	***4140**	**205**	***6**	**2.97**	**2.59**					**6**	**3**	**3**		**373**	**14**	**0**	**2.25**				
1980-81	**Chicago Black Hawks**	**NHL**	***66**	**29**	**23**	**14**	***3935**	**246**	**0**	**3.75**	**3.00**					**3**	**0**	**3**		**215**	**15**	**0**	**4.19**				
1981-82	United States	C Cup	5	2	3	0	300	20	0	4.00																	
	Chicago Black Hawks	**NHL**	**52**	**19**	**25**	**8**	**3069**	**231**	**1**	**4.52**	**3.50**					**7**	**3**	**3**		**381**	**16**	***1**	**2.52**				
1982-83	**Chicago Black Hawks**	**NHL**	**39**	**23**	**11**	**5**	**2340**	**135**	**1**	**3.46**	**2.76**	**3.88**	**1203**	**.888**	**30.8**	**5**	**3**	**2**		**311**	**18**	**0**	**3.47**				
1983-84	**Chicago Black Hawks**	**NHL**	**18**	**5**	**10**	**3**	**1095**	**88**	**1**	**4.82**	**3.78**	**6.82**	**622**	**.859**	**34.1**												
	NHL Totals		**886**	**423**	**306**	**152**	**52585**	**2563**	**76**	**2.92**						**99**	**45**	**53**		**6017**	**308**	**6**	**3.07**				

WCHA First All-Star Team (1965, 1966, 1967) • NCAA West First All-American Team (1965, 1966, 1967) • NCAA Championship All-Tournament Team (1965) • NHL First All-Star Team (1970, 1972, 1980) • Won Calder Memorial Trophy (1970) • Won Vezina Trophy (1970) • Shared Vezina Trophy with Gary Smith (1972) • NHL Second All-Star Team (1973, 1974) • Won Vezina Trophy (tied with Bernie Parent) (1974)

Played in NHL All-Star Game (1970, 1971, 1972, 1973, 1974, 1980)

Signed as a free agent by **Montreal** (Cleveland - AHL), September 29, 1967. Claimed by **Chicago** from **Montreal** in Intra-League Draft, June 11, 1969.

• ESSENSA, BOB

Bob Essensa G – L. 6', 185 lbs. b: Toronto, Ont., 1/14/1965. Winnipeg's 5th choice, 71st overall, in 1983 Entry Draft.

Season	Club	League	GP	W	L	T	Mins	GA	SO	Avg	AAvg	Eff	SA	S%	SAPG	GP	W	L	T	Mins	GA	SO	Avg	Eff	SA	S%	SAPG
1982-83	Henry Carr Crusaders	H.S.	STATISTICS NOT AVAILABLE																								
1983-84	Michigan State Spartans	CCHA	17	11	4	0	946	44	2	2.79																	
1984-85	Michigan State Spartans	CCHA	18	15	2	0	1059	29	2	1.64																	
1985-86	Michigan State Spartans	CCHA	23	17	4	1	1333	74	1	3.33																	
1986-87	Michigan State Spartans	CCHA	25	19	3	1	1383	64	2	2.78																	
1987-88	Moncton Hawks	AHL	27	7	11	1	1287	100	1	4.66																	
1988-89	**Winnipeg Jets**	**NHL**	**20**	**6**	**8**	**3**	**1102**	**68**	**1**	**3.70**	**3.05**	**4.38**	**574**	**.882**	**31.3**												
	Fort Wayne Komets	IHL	22	14	7	0	1287	70	0	3.26																	
1989-90	**Winnipeg Jets**	**NHL**	**36**	**18**	**9**	**5**	**2035**	**107**	**1**	**3.15**	**2.63**	**3.41**	**988**	**.892**	**29.1**	**4**	**2**	**1**		**206**	**12**	**0**	**3.50**	**4.20**	**100**	**.880**	**29.1**
	Moncton Hawks	AHL	6	3	3	0	358	15	0	2.51																	
	Canada	WEC-A	4				101	5	0	2.97																	
1990-91	**Winnipeg Jets**	**NHL**	**55**	**19**	**24**	**6**	**2916**	**153**	**4**	**3.15**	**2.81**	**3.22**	**1496**	**.898**	**30.8**												
	Moncton Hawks	AHL	2	1	0	1	125	6	0	2.88																	
1991-92	**Winnipeg Jets**	**NHL**	**47**	**21**	**17**	**6**	**2627**	**126**	***5**	**2.88**	**2.54**	**2.58**	**1407**	**.910**	**32.1**	**1**	**0**	**0**		**33**	**3**	**0**	**5.45**	**9.62**	**17**	**.824**	**30.9**
1992-93	**Winnipeg Jets**	**NHL**	**67**	**33**	**26**	**6**	**3855**	**227**	**2**	**3.53**	**3.00**	**3.78**	**2119**	**.893**	**33.0**	**6**	**2**	**4**		**367**	**20**	**0**	**3.27**	**3.57**	**183**	**.891**	**29.9**
1993-94	**Winnipeg Jets**	**NHL**	**56**	**19**	**30**	**6**	**3136**	**201**	**1**	**3.85**	**3.68**	**4.51**	**1714**	**.883**	**32.8**												
	Detroit Red Wings	**NHL**	**13**	**4**	**7**	**2**	**778**	**34**	**1**	**2.62**	**2.49**	**2.64**	**337**	**.899**	**26.0**	**2**	**0**	**2**		**109**	**9**	**0**	**4.95**	**10.36**	**43**	**.791**	**23.7**
1994-95	San Diego Gulls	IHL	16	6	8	1	919	52	0	3.39						1	0	1		59	3	0	3.05				
1995-96	Adirondack Red Wings	AHL	3	1	2	0	179	11	0	3.69																	
	Fort Wayne Komets	IHL	45	24	14	5	2529	122	1	2.89						5	2	3		299	12	0	2.41				
1996-97	**Edmonton Oilers**	**NHL**	**19**	**4**	**8**	**0**	**868**	**41**	**1**	**2.83**	**3.00**	**2.86**	**406**	**.899**	**28.1**												
1997-98	**Edmonton Oilers**	**NHL**	**16**	**6**	**6**	**1**	**825**	**35**	**0**	**2.55**	**2.98**	**2.21**	**404**	**.913**	**29.4**	**1**	**0**	**0**		**27**	**1**	**0**	**2.22**	**2.02**	**11**	**.909**	**24.4**
	NHL Totals		**329**	**130**	**135**	**35**	**18142**	**992**	**16**	**3.28**			**9445**	**.895**		**14**	**4**	**7**		**742**	**45**	**0**	**3.64**				

CCHA First All-Star Team (1985) • CCHA Second All-Star Team (1986) • NHL All-Rookie Team (1990)

Traded to **Detroit** by **Winnipeg** with Sergei Bautin for Tim Cheveldae and Dallas Drake, March 8, 1994. Traded to **Edmonton** by **Detroit** for future considerations, June 14, 1996.

• EVANS, CLAUDE

Claude Evans G5'8", 165 lbs. b: Longueuil, Que., 4/28/1933. Deceased.

Season	Club	League	GP	W	L	T	Mins	GA	SO	Avg	AAvg	Eff	SA	S%	SAPG	GP	W	L	T	Mins	GA	SO	Avg	Eff	SA	S%	SAPG
1949-50	Montreal Nationale	QJHL	1	1	0	0	60	1	0	1.00																	
1950-51	Montreal Nationale	QJHL	44	25	10	0	2670	100	0	4.18						3	1	2	0	180	14	0	4.67				
1951-52	Montreal Nationale	QJHL	50	28	21	1	3000	198	1	3.96						9	4	5	0	544	33	0	3.64				

			REGULAR SEASON													PLAYOFFS											
Season	**Club**	**League**	**GP**	**W**	**L**	**T**	**Mins**	**GA**	**SO**	**Avg**	**AAvg**	**Eff**	**SA**	**S%**	**SAPG**	**GP**	**W**	**L**	**T**	**Mins**	**GA**	**SO**	**Avg**	**Eff**	**SA**	**S%**	**SAPG**
1952-53	Cincinnati Mohawks	IHL	*60	*43	13	4	*3600	152	*5	*2.53	....	....	....	....	....	9	*8	1	0	540	19	*1	*2.11	....	....	....	....
1953-54	Montreal Royals	QHL	14	6	5	3	870	43	2	2.97	....	....	....	....	....	2	1	1	0	120	5	0	2.50	....	....	....	....
	Valleyfield Braves	QHL	8	3	5	0	480	31	0	3.88	....	....	....	....	....	....	....	....	....	....	....	....	....	....	....	....	....
	Providence Reds	AHL	3	0	3	0	180	14	0	4.67	....	....	....	....	....	....	....	....	....	....	....	....	....	....	....	....	....
	Victoria Cougars	WHL	14	7	6	1	840	46	0	3.28	....	....	....	....	....	5	1	4	0	300	28	0	5.60	....	....	....	....
1954-55	Montreal Royals	QHL	21	10	8	3	1270	73	0	3.45	....	....	....	....	....	....	....	....	....	....	....	....	....	....	....	....	....
	Montreal Canadiens	**NHL**	**4**	**2**	**2**	**0**	**220**	**12**	**0**	**3.27**	**4.01**	....	....	....	....	....	....	....	....	....	....	....	....	....	....	....	....
	Quebec Aces	QHL	13	9	3	1	750	40	2	3.20	....	....	....	....	....	4	2	2	0	240	11	1	2.75	....	....	....	....
	Chicoutimi Sagueneens	QHL	4	2	2	0	240	15	0	3.75	....	....	....	....	....	....	....	....	....	....	....	....	....	....	....	....	....
1955-56	Quebec Aces	QHL	57	21	33	8	3410	199	2	3.50	....	....	....	....	....	....	....	....	....	....	....	....	....	....	....	....	....
1956-57	Springfield Indians	AHL	32	8	23	0	1960	143	1	4.47	....	....	....	....	....	....	....	....	....	....	....	....	....	....	....	....	....
1957-58	Springfield Indians	AHL	53	27	21	5	3252	173	1	3.19	....	....	....	....	....	*13	6	7	0	*783	40	*3	3.07	....	....	....	....
	Boston Bruins	**NHL**	**1**	**0**	**0**	**1**	**60**	**4**	**0**	**4.00**	**4.42**	....	....	....	....	....	....	....	....	....	....	....	....	....	....	....	....
1958-59	Springfield Indians	AHL	21	9	11	0	1220	84	2	4.13	....	....	....	....	....	....	....	....	....	....	....	....	....	....	....	....	....
	Trois-Rivieres Lions	QHL	38	*21	16	1	2280	116	*3	3.05	....	....	....	....	....	*8	*3	5	0	*484	26	0	3.22	....	....	....	....
1959-60	Trois-Rivieres Lions	EPHL	62	28	25	9	3720	207	4	3.34	....	....	....	....	....	7	3	4	0	422	15	0	*2.13	....	....	....	....
1960-61	Kitchener-Waterloo Beavers	EPHL	17	6	7	4	1020	69	0	4.06	....	....	....	....	....	....	....	....	....	....	....	....	....	....	....	....	....
	Vancouver Canucks	WHL	53	27	23	3	3180	147	6	2.77	....	....	....	....	....	9	4	5	0	575	24	0	2.50	....	....	....	....
1961-62	Vancouver Canucks	WHL	40	11	26	3	2427	165	2	4.08	....	....	....	....	....	....	....	....	....	....	....	....	....	....	....	....	....
	Pittsburgh Hornets	AHL	19	2	17	0	1140	132	0	6.95	....	....	....	....	....	....	....	....	....	....	....	....	....	....	....	....	....
	NHL Totals		**5**	**2**	**2**	**1**	**280**	**16**	**0**	**3.43**	....	....	....	....	....	....	....	....	....	....	....	....	....	....	....	....	....

IHL Second All-Star Team (1953) • QHL Second All-Star Team (1959)

Signed as a free agent by **Boston**, March 6, 1958.

• EXELBY, RANDY

Randy Exelby G – L. 5′9″, 170 lbs. b: Toronto, Ont., 8/13/1965. Montreal's 1st choice, 20th overall, in 1986 Supplemental Draft.

Season	Club	League	GP	W	L	T	Mins	GA	SO	Avg	AAvg	Eff	SA	S%	SAPG	GP	W	L	T	Mins	GA	SO	Avg	Eff	SA	S%	SAPG
1983-84	Lake Superior State	CCHA	21	6	10	0	905	75	0	4.97	....	....	....	....	....	....	....	....	....	....	....	....	....	....	....	....	....
1984-85	Lake Superior State	CCHA	36	22	11	1	1999	112	0	3.36	....	....	....	....	....	....	....	....	....	....	....	....	....	....	....	....	....
1985-86	Lake Superior State	CCHA	28	14	11	1	1625	98	0	3.62	....	....	....	....	....	....	....	....	....	....	....	....	....	....	....	....	....
1986-87	Lake Superior State	CCHA	28	12	9	1	1357	91	0	4.02	....	....	....	....	....	....	....	....	....	....	....	....	....	....	....	....	....
1987-88	Sherbrooke Canadiens	AHL	19	7	10	0	1050	49	0	2.80	....	....	....	....	....	4	2	2	0	212	13	0	3.68	....	....	....	....
1988-89	**Montreal Canadiens**	**NHL**	**1**	**0**	**0**	**0**	**3**	**0**	**0**	**0.00**	**0.00**	**0.00**	**1**	**1.000**	**20.0**	....	....	....	....	....	....	....	....	....	....	....	....
	Sherbrooke Canadiens	AHL	52	31	13	6	2935	146	6	2.98	....	....	....	....	....	6	1	4	0	329	24	0	4.38	....	....	....	....
1989-90	**Edmonton Oilers**	**NHL**	**1**	**0**	**1**	**0**	**60**	**5**	**0**	**5.00**	**4.19**	**8.33**	**30**	**.833**	**30.0**	....	....	....	....	....	....	....	....	....	....	....	....
	Phoenix Roadrunners	IHL	41	11	18	5	2146	163	0	4.56	....	....	....	....	....	....	....	....	....	....	....	....	....	....	....	....	....
1990-91	Springfield Indians	AHL	4	1	2	1	245	20	0	4.90	....	....	....	....	....	....	....	....	....	....	....	....	....	....	....	....	....
	Kansas City Blades	IHL	16	0	13	0	785	65	0	4.97	....	....	....	....	....	....	....	....	....	....	....	....	....	....	....	....	....
	Louisville IceHawks	ECHL	13	6	5	1	743	60	0	4.84	....	....	....	....	....	....	....	....	....	....	....	....	....	....	....	....	....
	NHL Totals		**2**	**0**	**1**	**0**	**63**	**5**	**0**	**4.76**	....	....	**31**	**.839**	....	....	....	....	....	....	....	....	....	....	....	....	....

AHL First All-Star Team (1989) • Shared Harry "Hap" Holmes Memorial Award (fewest goals against - AHL) with Francois Gravel (1989) • Won Aldege "Baz" Bastien Memorial Award (Top Goaltender - AHL) (1989)

Traded to **Edmonton** by **Montreal** for future considerations, October 2, 1989.

• FARR, ROCKY

Rocky (Norman Richard) Farr G – R. 5′10″, 175 lbs. b: Toronto, Ont., 4/7/1947.

Season	Club	League	GP	W	L	T	Mins	GA	SO	Avg	AAvg	Eff	SA	S%	SAPG	GP	W	L	T	Mins	GA	SO	Avg	Eff	SA	S%	SAPG
1963-64	Notre Dame de Grace Monarchs	Mtl-Jr.	2	....	....	....	120	7	0	3.50	....	....	....	....	....	....	....	....	....	....	....	....	....	....	....	....	....
	Montreal Jr. Canadiens	OHA	11	....	....	....	660	33	2	3.00	....	....	....	....	....	2	....	....	....	100	9	0	5.40	....	....	....	....
1964-65	Montreal Jr. Canadiens	OHA	10	....	....	....	600	40	0	4.00	....	....	....	....	....	....	....	....	....	....	....	....	....	....	....	....	....
1965-66	London Nationals	OHA	47	11	29	7	2820	232	0	4.94	....	....	....	....	....	....	....	....	....	....	....	....	....	....	....	....	....
1966-67	London–Oshawa	OHA	24	....	....	....	1440	112	0	4.63	....	....	....	....	....	4	....	....	....	240	17	0	4.86	....	....	....	....
1967-68	Houston Apollos	CHL	18	4	10	1	888	53	1	3.58	....	....	....	....	....	....	....	....	....	....	....	....	....	....	....	....	....
	Cleveland Barons	AHL	5	2	2	0	270	17	0	3.78	....	....	....	....	....	....	....	....	....	....	....	....	....	....	....	....	....
1968-69	Denver Spurs	WHL	46	16	23	4	2667	180	2	4.05	....	....	....	....	....	....	....	....	....	....	....	....	....	....	....	....	....
	Cleveland Barons	AHL	3	2	0	1	180	3	1	1.00	....	....	....	....	....	....	....	....	....	....	....	....	....	....	....	....	....
1969-70	Denver Spurs	WHL	47	16	21	7	2769	188	1	4.07	....	....	....	....	....	....	....	....	....	....	....	....	....	....	....	....	....
1970-71	Springfield Kings	AHL	4	0	3	1	166	18	0	6.50	....	....	....	....	....	....	....	....	....	....	....	....	....	....	....	....	....
	Salt Lake Golden Eagles	WHL	25	6	15	0	1276	83	3	3.91	....	....	....	....	....	....	....	....	....	....	....	....	....	....	....	....	....
	Fort Worth Wings	CHL	1	0	0	0	15	0	0	0.00	....	....	....	....	....	1	0	1	0	60	4	0	4.00	....	....	....	....
1971-72	Cincinnati Swords	AHL	*52	20	16	10	2843	145	2	3.06	....	....	....	....	....	9	4	3	0	472	21	0	2.66	....	....	....	....
1972-73	**Buffalo Sabres**	**NHL**	**1**	**0**	**1**	**0**	**29**	**3**	**0**	**6.21**	**5.85**	....	....	....	....	....	....	....	....	....	....	....	....	....	....	....	....
	Cincinnati Swords	AHL	48	....	....	....	2746	121	3	2.64	....	....	....	....	....	12	....	....	....	720	35	0	2.91	....	....	....	....
1973-74	**Buffalo Sabres**	**NHL**	**11**	**2**	**4**	**1**	**480**	**25**	**0**	**3.13**	**3.02**	....	....	....	....	....	....	....	....	....	....	....	....	....	....	....	....
	Cincinnati Swords	AHL	16	7	3	2	812	47	1	3.47	....	....	....	....	....	....	....	....	....	....	....	....	....	....	....	....	....
1974-75	**Buffalo Sabres**	**NHL**	**7**	**0**	**1**	**2**	**213**	**14**	**0**	**3.94**	**3.55**	....	....	....	....	....	....	....	....	....	....	....	....	....	....	....	....
1975-76	Springfield Indians	AHL	6	0	3	1	222	30	0	8.11	....	....	....	....	....	....	....	....	....	....	....	....	....	....	....	....	....
	Johnstown Jets	NAHL	1	....	....	....	60	8	0	8.00	....	....	....	....	....	....	....	....	....	....	....	....	....	....	....	....	....
	NHL Totals		**19**	**2**	**6**	**3**	**722**	**42**	**0**	**3.49**	....	....	....	....	....	....	....	....	....	....	....	....	....	....	....	....	....

Claimed by **Cleveland** (AHL) from **Montreal** in Reverse Draft, June 13, 1968. Claimed by **Buffalo** from **Montreal** in Expansion Draft, June 10, 1970. Traded to **Kansas City** by **Buffalo** for cash, October 1, 1975.

• FAVELL, DOUG

Doug Favell G – L. 5′10″, 172 lbs. b: St. Catharines, Ont., 4/5/1945.

Season	Club	League	GP	W	L	T	Mins	GA	SO	Avg	AAvg	Eff	SA	S%	SAPG	GP	W	L	T	Mins	GA	SO	Avg	Eff	SA	S%	SAPG
1962-63	St. Catharines Black Hawks	OHA	1	....	....	....	60	2	0	2.00	....	....	....	....	....	....	....	....	....	....	....	....	....	....	....	....	....
1963-64	Niagara Falls Flyers	OHA	28	....	....	....	....	98	3	3.36	....	....	....	....	....	....	....	....	....	....	....	....	....	....	....	....	....
1964-65	Niagara Falls Flyers	OHA	22	....	....	....	1320	79	0	3.59	....	....	....	....	....	3	....	....	....	180	9	0	3.00	....	....	....	....
	Minneapolis Bruins	CHL	1	1	0	0	60	3	0	3.00	....	....	....	....	....	....	....	....	....	....	....	....	....	....	....	....	....
1965-66	Oklahoma City Blazers	CHL	18	4	8	5	1060	59	0	3.34	....	....	....	....	....	....	....	....	....	....	....	....	....	....	....	....	....
	San Francisco Seals	WHL	2	1	1	0	120	6	0	3.00	....	....	....	....	....	2	0	2	0	113	10	0	5.31	....	....	....	....
1966-67	Oklahoma City Blazers	CHL	33	14	13	4	1860	88	1	2.83	....	....	....	....	....	....	....	....	....	....	....	....	....	....	....	....	....
1967-68	**Philadelphia Flyers**	**NHL**	**37**	**15**	**15**	**6**	**2192**	**83**	**4**	**2.27**	**2.49**	....	....	....	....	**2**	**0**	**2**	....	**120**	**8**	**0**	**4.00**	....	....	....	....
1968-69	Quebec Aces	AHL	4	0	4	0	199	16	0	4.82	....	....	....	....	....	....	....	....	....	....	....	....	....	....	....	....	....
	Philadelphia Flyers	**NHL**	**21**	**3**	**12**	**5**	**1195**	**71**	**1**	**3.56**	**3.70**	....	....	....	....	**1**	**0**	**1**	....	**60**	**5**	**0**	**5.00**	....	....	....	....
1969-70	**Philadelphia Flyers**	**NHL**	**15**	**4**	**5**	**4**	**820**	**43**	**1**	**3.15**	**3.35**	....	....	....	....	....	....	....	....	....	....	....	....	....	....	....	....
1970-71	**Philadelphia Flyers**	**NHL**	**44**	**16**	**15**	**9**	**2434**	**108**	**2**	**2.66**	**2.62**	....	....	....	....	**2**	**0**	**2**	....	**120**	**8**	**0**	**4.00**	....	....	....	....
1971-72	**Philadelphia Flyers**	**NHL**	**54**	**18**	**25**	**9**	**2993**	**140**	**5**	**2.81**	**2.82**	....	....	....	....	....	....	....	....	....	....	....	....	....	....	....	....
1972-73	**Philadelphia Flyers**	**NHL**	**44**	**20**	**15**	**4**	**2419**	**114**	**3**	**2.83**	**2.65**	....	....	....	....	**11**	**5**	**6**	....	**669**	**29**	**1**	**2.60**	....	....	....	....
1973-74	**Toronto Maple Leafs**	**NHL**	**32**	**14**	**7**	**9**	**1752**	**79**	**0**	**2.71**	**2.61**	....	....	....	....	**3**	**0**	**3**	....	**181**	**10**	**0**	**3.31**	....	....	....	....
1974-75	**Toronto Maple Leafs**	**NHL**	**39**	**12**	**17**	**6**	**2149**	**145**	**1**	**4.05**	**3.67**	....	....	....	....	....	....	....	....	....	....	....	....	....	....	....	....
1975-76	Oklahoma City Blazers	CHL	4	3	1	0	240	12	0	3.00	....	....	....	....	....	....	....	....	....	....	....	....	....	....	....	....	....
	Toronto Maple Leafs	**NHL**	**3**	**0**	**2**	**1**	**160**	**15**	**0**	**5.63**	**5.10**	....	....	....	....	....	....	....	....	....	....	....	....	....	....	....	....
1976-77	**Colorado Rockies**	**NHL**	**30**	**8**	**15**	**3**	**1614**	**105**	**0**	**3.90**	**3.64**	....	....	....	....	....	....	....	....	....	....	....	....	....	....	....	....
1977-78	**Colorado Rockies**	**NHL**	**47**	**13**	**20**	**11**	**2663**	**159**	**1**	**3.58**	**3.36**	....	....	....	....	**2**	**0**	**2**	....	**120**	**6**	**0**	**3.00**	....	....	....	....
1978-79	**Colorado Rockies**	**NHL**	**7**	**0**	**5**	**2**	**380**	**34**	**0**	**5.37**	**4.75**	....	....	....	....	....	....	....	....	....	....	....	....	....	....	....	....
	Philadelphia Firebirds	AHL	32	12	15	4	1834	137	1	4.48	....	....	....	....	....	....	....	....	....	....	....	....	....	....	....	....	....
	NHL Totals		**373**	**123**	**153**	**69**	**20771**	**1096**	**18**	**3.17**	....	....	....	....	....	**21**	**5**	**16**	....	**1270**	**66**	**1**	**3.12**	....	....	....	....

Claimed by **Philadelphia** from **Boston** in Expansion Draft, June 6, 1967. Traded to **Toronto** by **Philadelphia** to complete transaction that sent Bernie Parent and Toronto's 2nd round choice (Larry Goodenough) in 1973 Amateur Draft to Philadelphia for Philadelphia's 1st round choice (Bob Neely) in 1973 Amateur Draft (May 15, 1973), July 27, 1973. Traded to **Colorado** by **Toronto** for cash, September 15, 1976. Claimed by **Edmonton** from **Colorado** in Expansion Draft, June 13, 1979. • Only player to be claimed in both the 1967 and 1979 Expansion Drafts.

Season	Club	League	REGULAR SEASON														PLAYOFFS											
			GP	W	L	T	Mins	GA	SO	Avg	AAvg	Eff	SA	S%	SAPG	GP	W	L	T	Mins	GA	SO	Avg	Eff	SA	S%	SAPG

• FERNANDEZ, EMMANUEL

Emmanuel "Manny" Fernandez G – L. 6', 185 lbs. b: Etobicoke, Ont., 8/27/1974. Quebec's 4th choice, 52nd overall, in 1992 Entry Draft.

Season	Club	League	GP	W	L	T	Mins	GA	SO	Avg	AAvg	Eff	SA	S%	SAPG	GP	W	L	T	Mins	GA	SO	Avg	Eff	SA	S%	SAPG
1991-92	Laval Titan	QMJHL	31	14	13	2	1593	99	1	3.73	....	....	....	....	....	9	3	5	....	468	39	0	5.00	....	....	....	....
1992-93	Laval Titan	QMJHL	43	26	14	2	2347	141	1	3.60	....	....	....	....	....	13	*12	1	....	818	42	0	3.08	....	....	....	....
1993-94	Laval Titan	QMJHL	51	29	14	1	2776	143	*5	3.09	....	....	....	....	....	19	14	5	....	1116	49	*1	*2.63	....	....	....	....
1994-95	Kalamazoo Wings	IHL	46	21	10	9	2470	115	2	2.79	....	....	....	....	....	14	10	2	....	753	34	1	2.71	....	....	....	....
	Dallas Stars	**NHL**	**1**	**0**	**1**	**0**	**59**	**3**	**0**	**3.05**	**3.15**	**3.39**	**27**	**.889**	**27.5**	....	....	....	....	....	....	....	....	....	....	....	....
1995-96	**Dallas Stars**	**NHL**	**5**	**0**	**1**	**1**	**249**	**19**	**0**	**4.58**	**4.50**	**7.19**	**121**	**.843**	**29.2**	....	....	....	....	....	....	....	....	....	....	....	....
	Michigan K-Wings	IHL	47	22	15	9	2664	133	*4	3.00	....	....	....	....	....	6	5	1	....	372	14	0	*2.26	....	....	....	....
1996-97	Michigan K-Wings	IHL	48	20	24	2	2720	142	2	3.13	....	....	....	....	....	4	1	3	....	277	15	0	3.25	....	....	....	....
1997-98	**Dallas Stars**	**NHL**	**2**	**1**	**0**	**0**	**69**	**2**	**0**	**1.74**	**2.04**	**0.99**	**35**	**.943**	**30.4**	**1**	**0**	**0**	....	**2**	**0**	**0**	**0.00**	**0.00**	**0**	**.00**	**0.0**
	Michigan K-Wings	IHL	55	27	17	5	3022	139	5	2.76	....	....	....	....	....	2	0	2	....	88	7	0	4.73	....	....	....	....
	NHL Totals		**8**	**1**	**2**	**1**	**377**	**24**	**0**	**3.82**	....	....	**183**	**.869**	....	**1**	**0**	**0**	....	**2**	**0**	**0**	**0.00**	....	....	....	....

QMJHL First All-Star Team (1994) • IHL Second All-Star Team (1995)

Rights traded to **Dallas** by **Quebec** for Tommy Sjodin and Dallas' 3rd round choice (Chris Drury) in 1994 Entry Draft, February 13, 1994.

• FICHAUD, ERIC

Eric Fichaud G – L. 5'11", 171 lbs. b: Anjou, Que., 11/4/1975. Toronto's 1st choice, 16th overall, in 1994 Entry Draft.

Season	Club	League	GP	W	L	T	Mins	GA	SO	Avg	AAvg	Eff	SA	S%	SAPG	GP	W	L	T	Mins	GA	SO	Avg	Eff	SA	S%	SAPG
1992-93	Chicoutimi Sagueneens	QMJHL	43	18	13	1	2039	149	0	4.38	....	....	....	....	....	....	....	....	....	....	....	....	....	....	....	....	....
1993-94	Chicoutimi Sagueneens	QMJHL	*63	*37	21	3	*3493	192	4	3.30	....	....	....	....	....	*26	*16	10	....	*1560	86	*1	3.31	....	....	....	....
1994-95	Chicoutimi Sagueneens	QMJHL	46	21	19	4	2637	151	4	3.44	....	....	....	....	....	7	2	5	....	428	20	0	2.80	....	....	....	....
1995-96	**New York Islanders**	**NHL**	**24**	**7**	**12**	**2**	**1234**	**68**	**1**	**3.31**	**3.25**	**3.42**	**659**	**.897**	**32.0**	....	....	....	....	....	....	....	....	....	....	....	....
	Worcester IceCats	AHL	34	13	15	6	1989	97	1	2.93	....	....	....	....	....	2	1	1	....	127	7	0	3.30	....	....	....	....
1996-97	**New York Islanders**	**NHL**	**34**	**9**	**14**	**4**	**1759**	**91**	**0**	**3.10**	**3.28**	**3.14**	**897**	**.899**	**30.6**	....	....	....	....	....	....	....	....	....	....	....	....
	Canada	WC-A	DID NOT PLAY – SPARE GOALTENDER																								
1997-98	**New York Islanders**	**NHL**	**17**	**3**	**8**	**3**	**807**	**40**	**0**	**2.97**	**3.48**	**2.82**	**422**	**.905**	**31.4**	....	....	....	....	....	....	....	....	....	....	....	....
	Utah Grizzlies	IHL	1	0	0	0	40	3	0	4.45	....	....	....	....	....	....	....	....	....	....	....	....	....	....	....	....	....
	NHL Totals		**75**	**19**	**34**	**9**	**3800**	**199**	**1**	**3.14**	....	....	**1978**	**.899**	....	....	....	....	....	....	....	....	....	....	....	....	....

Canadian Major Junior Second All-Star Team (1994) • Memorial Cup All-Star Team (1994) • Won Hap Emms Memorial Trophy (Memorial Cup Tournament Top Goaltender) (1994) • QMJHL First All-Star Team (1995)

Traded to **NY Islanders** by **Toronto** for Benoit Hogue, NY Islanders' 3rd round choice (Ryan Pepperall) in 1995 Entry Draft and 5th round choice (Brandon Sugden) in 1996 Entry Draft, April 6, 1995. Traded to **Edmonton** by **NY Islanders** for Mike Watt, June 14, 1998.

• FISET, STEPHANE

Stephane Fiset G – L. 6'1", 195 lbs. b: Montreal, Que., 6/17/1970. Quebec's 3rd choice, 24th overall, in 1988 Entry Draft.

Season	Club	League	GP	W	L	T	Mins	GA	SO	Avg	AAvg	Eff	SA	S%	SAPG	GP	W	L	T	Mins	GA	SO	Avg	Eff	SA	S%	SAPG
1987-88	Victoriaville Tigres	QMJHL	40	15	17	4	2221	146	1	3.94	....	....	....	....	....	2	0	2	....	163	10	0	3.68	....	....	....	....
1988-89	Victoriaville Tigres	QMJHL	43	25	14	0	2401	138	1	*3.45	....	....	....	....	....	12	*9	2	....	711	33	0	*2.78	....	....	....	....
	Canada	WJC-A	6	....	....	....	329	18	....	3.28	....	....	....	....	....	....	....	....	....	....	....	....	....	....	....	....	....
1989-90	**Quebec Nordiques**	**NHL**	**6**	**0**	**5**	**1**	**342**	**34**	**0**	**5.96**	**5.00**	**10.18**	**199**	**.829**	**34.9**	....	....	....	....	....	....	....	....	....	....	....	....
	Victoriaville Tigres	QMJHL	24	14	6	3	1383	63	1	*2.73	....	....	....	....	....	*14	7	6	....	*790	49	0	3.72	....	....	....	....
	Canada	WJC-A	7	....	....	....	420	18	....	2.57	....	....	....	....	....	....	....	....	....	....	....	....	....	....	....	....	....
1990-91	**Quebec Nordiques**	**NHL**	**3**	**0**	**2**	**1**	**186**	**12**	**0**	**3.87**	**3.46**	**3.78**	**123**	**.902**	**39.7**	....	....	....	....	....	....	....	....	....	....	....	....
	Halifax Citadels	AHL	36	10	15	8	1902	131	0	4.13	....	....	....	....	....	....	....	....	....	....	....	....	....	....	....	....	....
1991-92	**Quebec Nordiques**	**NHL**	**23**	**7**	**10**	**2**	**1133**	**71**	**1**	**3.76**	**3.34**	**4.13**	**646**	**.890**	**34.2**	....	....	....	....	....	....	....	....	....	....	....	....
	Halifax Citadels	AHL	29	8	14	6	1675	110	*3	3.94	....	....	....	....	....	....	....	....	....	....	....	....	....	....	....	....	....
1992-93	**Quebec Nordiques**	**NHL**	**37**	**18**	**9**	**4**	**1939**	**110**	**0**	**3.40**	**2.89**	**3.96**	**945**	**.884**	**29.2**	**1**	**0**	**0**	....	**21**	**1**	**0**	**2.86**	**2.38**	**12**	**.917**	**34.3**
	Halifax Citadels	AHL	3	2	1	0	180	11	0	3.67	....	....	....	....	....	....	....	....	....	....	....	....	....	....	....	....	....
1993-94	**Quebec Nordiques**	**NHL**	**50**	**20**	**25**	**4**	**2798**	**158**	**2**	**3.39**	**3.23**	**3.74**	**1434**	**.890**	**30.8**	....	....	....	....	....	....	....	....	....	....	....	....
	Cornwall Aces	AHL	1	0	1	0	60	4	0	4.00	....	....	....	....	....	....	....	....	....	....	....	....	....	....	....	....	....
	Canada	WC-A	2	2	0	0	120	3	0	1.50	....	....	....	....	....	....	....	....	....	....	....	....	....	....	....	....	....
1994-95	**Quebec Nordiques**	**NHL**	**32**	**17**	**10**	**3**	**1879**	**87**	**2**	**2.78**	**2.87**	**2.50**	**968**	**.910**	**30.9**	**4**	**1**	**2**	....	**209**	**16**	**0**	**4.59**	**6.39**	**115**	**.861**	**33.0**
1995-96	**Colorado Avalanche**	**NHL**	**37**	**22**	**6**	**7**	**2107**	**103**	**1**	**2.93**	**2.87**	**2.98**	**1012**	**.898**	**28.8**	**1**	**0**	**0**	....	**1**	**0**	**0**	**0.00**	**0.00**	**0**	**.00**	**0.0**
1996-97	**Los Angeles Kings**	**NHL**	**44**	**13**	**24**	**5**	**2482**	**132**	**4**	**3.19**	**3.38**	**2.99**	**1410**	**.906**	**34.1**	....	....	....	....	....	....	....	....	....	....	....	....
1997-98	**Los Angeles Kings**	**NHL**	**60**	**26**	**25**	**8**	**3497**	**158**	**2**	**2.71**	**3.17**	**2.48**	**1728**	**.909**	**29.6**	**2**	**0**	**2**	....	**93**	**7**	**0**	**4.52**	**5.19**	**81**	[illegible]	**30.4**
	NHL Totals		**292**	**123**	**116**	**35**	**16363**	**865**	**12**	**3.17**	....	....	**8465**	**.898**	....	**8**	**1**	**4**	....	**324**	**24**	**0**	**4.44**	....	....	....	....

QMJHL First All-Star Team (1989) • Canadian Major Junior Goaltender of the Year (1989) • WJC-A All-Star Team (1990) • Named Best Goaltender at WJC-A (1990)

Transferred to **Colorado** after **Quebec** franchise relocated, June 21, 1995. Traded to **Los Angeles** by **Colorado** with Colorado's 1st round choice (Mathieu Biron) in 1998 Entry Draft for Eric Lacroix and Los Angeles' 1st round choice (Martin Skoula) in 1998 Entry Draft, June 20, 1996.

• FITZPATRICK, MARK

Mark Fitzpatrick G – L. 6'2", 198 lbs. b: Toronto, Ont., 11/13/1968. Los Angeles' 2nd choice, 27th overall, in 1987 Entry Draft.

Season	Club	League	GP	W	L	T	Mins	GA	SO	Avg	AAvg	Eff	SA	S%	SAPG	GP	W	L	T	Mins	GA	SO	Avg	Eff	SA	S%	SAPG
1984-85	Medicine Hat Tigers	WHL	3	1	2	0	180	9	0	3.00	....	....	....	....	....	1	0	0	0	20	2	0	6.00	....	....	....	....
1985-86	Medicine Hat Tigers	WHL	41	26	6	1	2074	99	1	*2.86	....	....	....	....	....	*19	*11	5	....	*986	58	0	3.53	....	....	....	....
1986-87	Medicine Hat Tigers	WHL	50	31	11	4	2844	159	4	3.35	....	....	....	....	....	20	12	8	....	1224	71	1	3.48	....	....	....	....
1987-88	Medicine Hat Tigers	WHL	63	36	15	6	3600	194	2	3.23	....	....	....	....	....	16	12	4	....	959	52	*1	*3.25	....	....	....	....
1988-89	**Los Angeles Kings**	**NHL**	**17**	**6**	**7**	**3**	**957**	**64**	**0**	**4.01**	**3.31**	**4.53**	**566**	**.887**	**35.5**	....	....	....	....	....	....	....	....	....	....	....	....
	New Haven Nighthawks	AHL	18	10	5	1	980	54	1	3.31	....	....	....	....	....	....	....	....	....	....	....	....	....	....	....	....	....
	New York Islanders	**NHL**	**11**	**3**	**5**	**2**	**627**	**41**	**0**	**3.92**	**3.23**	**5.13**	**313**	**.869**	**30.0**	....	....	....	....	....	....	....	....	....	....	....	....
1989-90	**New York Islanders**	**NHL**	**47**	**19**	**19**	**5**	**2653**	**150**	**3**	**3.39**	**2.83**	**3.45**	**1472**	**.898**	**33.3**	**4**	**0**	**2**	....	**152**	**13**	**0**	**5.13**	**9.39**	**71**	**.817**	**28.0**
1990-91	**New York Islanders**	**NHL**	**2**	**1**	**1**	**0**	**120**	**6**	**0**	**3.00**	**2.68**	**3.00**	**60**	**.900**	**30.0**	....	....	....	....	....	....	....	....	....	....	....	....
	Capital District Islanders	AHL	12	3	7	2	734	47	0	3.84	....	....	....	....	....	....	....	....	....	....	....	....	....	....	....	....	....
1991-92	**New York Islanders**	**NHL**	**30**	**11**	**13**	**5**	**1743**	**93**	**0**	**3.20**	**2.84**	**3.14**	**949**	**.902**	**32.7**	....	....	....	....	....	....	....	....	....	....	....	....
	Capital District Islanders	AHL	14	6	5	1	782	39	0	2.99	....	....	....	....	....	....	....	....	....	....	....	....	....	....	....	....	....
1992-93	**New York Islanders**	**NHL**	**39**	**17**	**15**	**5**	**2253**	**130**	**0**	**3.46**	**2.94**	**4.22**	**1066**	**.878**	**28.4**	**3**	**0**	**1**	....	**77**	**4**	**0**	**3.12**	**5.43**	**23**	**.826**	**17.9**
	Capital District Islanders	AHL	5	1	3	1	284	18	0	3.80	....	....	....	....	....	....	....	....	....	....	....	....	....	....	....	....	....
1993-94	**Florida Panthers**	**NHL**	**28**	**12**	**8**	**6**	**1603**	**73**	**1**	**2.73**	**2.59**	**2.36**	**844**	**.914**	**31.6**	....	....	....	....	....	....	....	....	....	....	....	....
1994-95	**Florida Panthers**	**NHL**	**15**	**6**	**7**	**2**	**819**	**36**	**2**	**2.64**	**2.72**	**2.63**	**361**	**.900**	**26.4**	....	....	....	....	....	....	....	....	....	....	....	....
1995-96	**Florida Panthers**	**NHL**	**34**	**15**	**11**	**3**	**1786**	**88**	**0**	**2.96**	**2.90**	**3.22**	**810**	**.891**	**27.2**	**2**	**0**	**0**	....	**60**	**6**	**0**	**6.00**	**12.00**	**30**	**.800**	**30.0**
1996-97	**Florida Panthers**	**NHL**	**30**	**8**	**9**	**9**	**1680**	**66**	**0**	**2.36**	**2.49**	**2.02**	**771**	**.914**	**27.5**	....	....	....	....	....	....	....	....	....	....	....	....
1997-98	**Florida Panthers**	**NHL**	**12**	**2**	**7**	**2**	**640**	**32**	**1**	**3.00**	**3.51**	**3.62**	**265**	**.879**	**24.8**	....	....	....	....	....	....	....	....	....	....	....	....
	Fort Wayne Komets	IHL	2	1	1	0	119	8	0	4.03	....	....	....	....	....	....	....	....	....	....	....	....	....	....	....	....	....
	Tampa Bay Lightning	**NHL**	**34**	**7**	**24**	**1**	**1938**	**102**	**1**	**3.16**	**3.71**	**3.31**	**975**	**.895**	**30.2**	....	....	....	....	....	....	....	....	....	....	....	....
	NHL Totals		**299**	**107**	**126**	**43**	**16819**	**881**	**8**	**3.14**	....	....	**8452**	**.896**	....	**9**	**0**	**3**	....	**289**	**23**	**0**	**4.78**	....	....	....	....

WHL East Second All-Star Team (1986, 1988) • Won Hap Emms Memorial Trophy (Memorial Cup Tournament Top Goaltender) (1987, 1988) • Won Bill Masterton Memorial Trophy (1992)

Traded to **NY Islanders** by **Los Angeles** with Wayne McBean and future considerations (Doug Crossman, May 23, 1989) for Kelly Hrudey, February 22, 1989. Traded to **Quebec** by **NY Islanders** with NY Islanders' 1st round choice (Adam Deadmarsh) in 1993 Entry Draft for Ron Hextall and Quebec's 1st round choice (Todd Bertuzzi) in 1993 Entry Draft, June 20, 1993. Claimed by **Florida** from **Quebec** in Expansion Draft, June 24, 1993. Traded to **Tampa Bay** by **Florida** with Jody Hull for Dino Ciccarelli and Jeff Norton, January 15, 1998.

• FLAHERTY, WADE

Wade Flaherty G – L. 6', 170 lbs. b: Terrace, B.C., 1/11/1968. Buffalo's 10th choice, 181st overall, in 1988 Entry Draft.

Season	Club	League	GP	W	L	T	Mins	GA	SO	Avg	AAvg	Eff	SA	S%	SAPG	GP	W	L	T	Mins	GA	SO	Avg	Eff	SA	S%	SAPG
1984-85	Kelowna Wings	WHL	1	0	0	0	55	5	0	5.45	....	....	....	....	....	....	....	....	....	....	....	....	....	....	....	....	....
1985-86	Seattle Thunderbirds	WHL	9	1	3	0	271	36	0	7.97	....	....	....	....	....	....	....	....	....	....	....	....	....	....	....	....	....
	Spokane Chiefs	WHL	5	0	3	0	161	21	0	7.83	....	....	....	....	....	....	....	....	....	....	....	....	....	....	....	....	....
1986-87	Victoria Cougars	WHL	3	0	2	0	127	16	0	7.56	....	....	....	....	....	....	....	....	....	....	....	....	....	....	....	....	....
1987-88	Victoria Cougars	WHL	36	20	15	0	2052	135	0	3.95	....	....	....	....	....	5	2	3	0	300	18	0	3.60	....	....	....	....
1988-89	Victoria Cougars	WHL	42	21	19	0	2408	180	4	4.49	....	....	....	....	....	....	....	....	....	....	....	....	....	....	....	....	....
1989-90	Greensboro Monarchs	ECHL	27	12	10	0	1308	96	0	4.40	....	....	....	....	....	....	....	....	....	....	....	....	....	....	....	....	....
1990-91	Kansas City Blades	IHL	*56	16	31	4	2990	224	0	4.49	....	....	....	....	....	....	....	....	....	....	....	....	....	....	....	....	....
1991-92	**San Jose Sharks**	**NHL**	**3**	**0**	**3**	**0**	**178**	**13**	**0**	**4.38**	**3.89**	**4.75**	**120**	**.892**	**40.4**	....	....	....	....	....	....	....	....	....	....	....	....
	Kansas City Blades	IHL	43	26	14	3	2603	140	1	3.23	....	....	....	....	....	1	0	0	....	1	0	0	0.00	....	....	....	....
1992-93	**San Jose Sharks**	**NHL**	**1**	**0**	**1**	**0**	**60**	**5**	**0**	**5.00**	**4.26**	**5.43**	**46**	**.891**	**46.0**	....	....	....	....	....	....	....	....	....	....	....	....
	Kansas City Blades	IHL	*61	*34	19	7	*3642	195	2	3.21	....	....	....	....	....	*12	6	6	....	733	34	*1	2.78	....	....	....	....
1993-94	Kansas City Blades	IHL	*60	32	19	9	*3564	202	0	3.40	....	....	....	....	....	....	....	....	....	....	....	....	....	....	....	....	....

			REGULAR SEASON													PLAYOFFS											
Season	**Club**	**League**	**GP**	**W**	**L**	**T**	**Mins**	**GA**	**SO**	**Avg**	**AAvg**	**Eff**	**SA**	**S%**	**SAPG**	**GP**	**W**	**L**	**T**	**Mins**	**GA**	**SO**	**Avg**	**Eff**	**SA**	**S%**	**SAPG**
1994-95	**San Jose Sharks**	**NHL**	**18**	**5**	**6**	**1**	**852**	**44**	**1**	**3.10**	**3.21**	**3.00**	**455**	**.903**	**32.0**	**7**	**2**	**3**	....	**377**	**31**	**0**	**4.93**	**6.92**	**221**	**.860**	**35.2**
1995-96	**San Jose Sharks**	**NHL**	**24**	**3**	**12**	**1**	**1137**	**92**	**0**	**4.85**	**4.79**	**6.48**	**689**	**.866**	**36.4**	....	....	....	....	....	....	....	....	....	....	....	....
1996-97	**San Jose Sharks**	**NHL**	**7**	**2**	**4**	**0**	**359**	**31**	**0**	**5.18**	**5.50**	**7.95**	**202**	**.847**	**33.8**	....	....	....	....	....	....	....	....	....	....	....	....
	Kentucky Thoroughblades	AHL	19	8	6	2	1032	54	1	3.14	....	....	....	....	....	3	1	2	....	200	11	0	3.30	....	....	....	....
1997-98	**New York Islanders**	**NHL**	**16**	**4**	**4**	**3**	**694**	**23**	**3**	**1.99**	**2.33**	**1.48**	**309**	**.926**	**26.7**	....	....	....	....	....	....	....	....	....	....	....	....
	Utah Grizzlies	IHL	24	16	5	3	1341	40	3	1.79	....	....	....	....	....	....	....	....	....	....	....	....	....	....	....	....	....
	NHL Totals		**69**	**14**	**30**	**5**	**3280**	**208**	**4**	**3.80**	....	....	**1821**	**.886**	....	**7**	**2**	**3**	....	**377**	**31**	**0**	**4.93**	....	....	....	....

WHL West Second All-Star Team (1988) • Playoff MVP - ECHL (1990) • Shared James Norris Memorial Trophy (fewest goals against - IHL) with Arturs Irbe (1992) • IHL Second All-Star Team (1993, 1994)

Signed as a free agent by **San Jose**, September 3, 1991. Signed as a free agent by **NY Islanders**, July 22, 1997.

• FORBES, JAKE

Jake (Vernon) "Jumpin' Jackie" Forbes G – L. 5'6", 140 lbs. b: Toronto, Ont., 7/4/1897. Deceased.

Season	**Club**	**League**	**GP**	**W**	**L**	**T**	**Mins**	**GA**	**SO**	**Avg**	**AAvg**	**Eff**	**SA**	**S%**	**SAPG**	**GP**	**W**	**L**	**T**	**Mins**	**GA**	**SO**	**Avg**	**Eff**	**SA**	**S%**	**SAPG**
1916-17	Toronto Aura Lee	OHA	6	*6	0	0	360	14	0	2.33	....	....	....	....	....	6	4	2	0	360	18	0	3.00	....	....	....	....
1917-18	Toronto Aura Lee	OHA	4	3	1	0	240	13	0	3.25	....	....	....	....	....	....	....	....	....	....	....	....	....	....	....	....	....
1918-19	Toronto Goodyears	City Sr.	STATISTICS NOT AVAILABLE																								
1919-20	Toronto Aura Lee	OHA Sr.	6	2	4	0	360	27	0	4.50	....	....	....	....	....	....	....	....	....	....	....	....	....	....	....	....	....
	Toronto Goodyears	City Sr.	STATISTICS NOT AVAILABLE																								
	Toronto St. Pats	**NHL**	**5**	**2**	**3**	**0**	**300**	**21**	**0**	**4.20**	**2.72**	....	....	....	....	....	....	....	....	....	....	....	....	....	....	....	....
1920-21	**Toronto St. Pats**	**NHL**	**20**	**13**	**7**	**0**	**1221**	**78**	**0**	**3.83**	**2.73**	....	....	....	....	**2**	**0**	**2**	**0**	**120**	**7**	**0**	**3.50**	....	....	....	....
1921-22			DID NOT PLAY – SUSPENDED																								
1922-23	**Hamilton Tigers**	**NHL**	***24**	**6**	**18**	**0**	**1469**	**110**	**0**	**4.49**	**4.87**	....	....	....	....	....	....	....	....	....	....	....	....	....	....	....	....
1923-24	**Hamilton Tigers**	**NHL**	***24**	**9**	**15**	**0**	**1483**	**68**	**1**	**2.75**	**3.23**	....	....	....	....	....	....	....	....	....	....	....	....	....	....	....	....
1924-25	**Hamilton Tigers**	**NHL**	***30**	***19**	**10**	**1**	**1833**	**60**	**6**	**1.96**	**2.32**	....	....	....	....	....	....	....	....	....	....	....	....	....	....	....	....
1925-26	**New York Americans**	**NHL**	***36**	**12**	**19**	**4**	**2241**	**86**	**2**	**2.30**	**3.08**	....	....	....	....	....	....	....	....	....	....	....	....	....	....	....	....
1926-27	**New York Americans**	**NHL**	***44**	**17**	**25**	**2**	**2715**	**91**	**8**	**2.01**	**3.11**	....	....	....	....	....	....	....	....	....	....	....	....	....	....	....	....
1927-28	**New York Americans**	**NHL**	**16**	**3**	**11**	**2**	**980**	**51**	**2**	**3.12**	**5.20**	....	....	....	....	....	....	....	....	....	....	....	....	....	....	....	....
	Providence Reds	Can-Am	13	....	....	....	780	20	2	1.46	....	....	....	....	....	....	....	....	....	....	....	....	....	....	....	....	....
	Niagara Falls Cataracts	CPHL	8	....	....	....	480	16	1	2.00	....	....	....	....	....	....	....	....	....	....	....	....	....	....	....	....	....
1928-29	**New York Americans**	**NHL**	**1**	**1**	**0**	**0**	**60**	**3**	**0**	**3.00**	**6.39**	....	....	....	....	....	....	....	....	....	....	....	....	....	....	....	....
	New Haven Eagles	Can-Am	26	....	....	....	1560	29	9	*1.06	....	....	....	....	....	2	1	1	0	123	4	0	1.95	....	....	....	....
1929-30	**New York Americans**	**NHL**	**1**	**0**	**0**	**1**	**70**	**1**	**0**	**0.86**	**0.90**	....	....	....	....	....	....	....	....	....	....	....	....	....	....	....	....
	New Haven Eagles	Can-Am	40	....	....	....	2400	101	3	2.44	....	....	....	....	....	....	....	....	....	....	....	....	....	....	....	....	....
1930-31	New Haven Eagles	Can-Am	40	....	....	....	2400	140	3	3.37	....	....	....	....	....	....	....	....	....	....	....	....	....	....	....	....	....
	Philadelphia Quakers	**NHL**	**2**	**0**	**2**	**0**	**120**	**7**	**0**	**3.50**	**4.52**	....	....	....	....	....	....	....	....	....	....	....	....	....	....	....	....
1931-32	**New York Americans**	**NHL**	**6**	**3**	**3**	**0**	**360**	**16**	**0**	**2.67**	**3.29**	....	....	....	....	....	....	....	....	....	....	....	....	....	....	....	....
	Springfield Indians	Can-Am	3	....	....	....	180	16	0	5.05	....	....	....	....	....	....	....	....	....	....	....	....	....	....	....	....	....
	Bronx Tigers	Can-Am	7	....	....	....	420	16	0	2.09	....	....	....	....	....	....	....	....	....	....	....	....	....	....	....	....	....
1932-33	**New York Americans**	**NHL**	**1**	**0**	**0**	**1**	**70**	**2**	**0**	**1.71**	**2.32**	....	....	....	....	....	....	....	....	....	....	....	....	....	....	....	....
	New Haven Eagles	Can-Am	5	....	....	....	300	15	0	3.11	....	....	....	....	....	....	....	....	....	....	....	....	....	....	....	....	....
1933-34	Windsor Bulldogs	IAHL	36	....	....	....	2160	89	6	2.41	....	....	....	....	....	....	....	....	....	....	....	....	....	....	....	....	....
1934-35	Syracuse Stars	IAHL	8	....	....	....	480	20	0	2.50	....	....	....	....	....	....	....	....	....	....	....	....	....	....	....	....	....
	London Tecumsehs	IAHL	8	....	....	....	480	21	0	2.63	....	....	....	....	....	5	2	3	0	319	12	1	2.26	....	....	....	....
1935-36	Syracuse/Rochester	IAHL	11	....	....	....	660	37	0	3.36	....	....	....	....	....	....	....	....	....	....	....	....	....	....	....	....	....
	NHL Totals		**210**	**85**	**113**	**11**	**12922**	**594**	**19**	**2.76**	....	....	....	....	....	**2**	**0**	**2**	**0**	**120**	**7**	**0**	**3.50**	....	....	....	....

Signed as a free agent by **Toronto St. Pats**, February 28, 1920. • Suspended by Toronto St. Pats for entire 1921-22 season for refusing to accept contract terms, December 12, 1921. Traded to **Hamilton** by **Toronto St. Pats** for cash, May 27, 1922. Rights transferred to **NY Americans** after NHL club purchased **Hamilton** franchise, November 7, 1925. Loaned to **Philadelphia** by **NY Americans** (New Haven - AHL) to replace injured Wilf Cude, January 13, 1931 (Montreal Canadiens 2, Philadelphia 1) and January 17, 1931. (Detroit 5, Philadelphia 2)

• FORD, BRIAN

Brian Ford G – L. 5'10", 170 lbs. b: Edmonton, Alta., 9/22/1961.

Season	**Club**	**League**	**GP**	**W**	**L**	**T**	**Mins**	**GA**	**SO**	**Avg**	**AAvg**	**Eff**	**SA**	**S%**	**SAPG**	**GP**	**W**	**L**	**T**	**Mins**	**GA**	**SO**	**Avg**	**Eff**	**SA**	**S%**	**SAPG**
1980-81	Billings Bighorns	WHL	44	14	26	0	2435	204	0	5.03	....	....	....	....	....	3	....	....	....	193	15	0	4.66	....	....	....	....
1981-82	Billings Bighorns	WHL	53	19	26	1	2791	256	0	5.50	....	....	....	....	....	5	1	4	0	226	26	0	6.90	....	....	....	....
1982-83	Fredericton Express	AHL	27	14	7	2	1443	84	0	3.49	....	....	....	....	....	1	0	0	0	11	1	0	5.56	....	....	....	....
	Carolina Thunderbirds	ACHL	4	....	....	....	203	7	0	2.07	....	....	....	....	....	....	....	....	....	....	....	....	....	....	....	....	....
1983-84	**Quebec Nordiques**	**NHL**	**3**	**1**	**1**	**0**	**123**	**13**	**0**	**6.34**	**4.96**	**11.77**	**70**	**.814**	**34.1**	....	....	....	....	....	....	....	....	....	....	....	....
	Fredericton Express	AHL	36	17	17	1	2132	105	2	*2.96	....	....	....	....	....	4	1	3	0	223	18	0	4.84	....	....	....	....
1984-85	Muskegon Mohawks	IHL	22	17	5	0	1321	59	1	2.68	....	....	....	....	....	....	....	....	....	....	....	....	....	....	....	....	....
	Pittsburgh Penguins	**NHL**	**8**	**2**	**6**	**0**	**457**	**48**	**0**	**6.30**	**5.02**	**10.36**	**292**	**.836**	**38.3**	....	....	....	....	....	....	....	....	....	....	....	....
	Baltimore Skipjacks	AHL	6	3	3	0	363	21	0	3.47	....	....	....	....	....	....	....	....	....	....	....	....	....	....	....	....	....
1985-86	Baltimore Skipjacks	AHL	39	12	20	4	2230	136	1	3.66	....	....	....	....	....	....	....	....	....	....	....	....	....	....	....	....	....
	Muskegon Lumberjacks	IHL	9	4	4	0	513	33	0	3.06	....	....	....	....	....	13	*12	1	0	793	41	0	*3.10	....	....	....	....
1986-87	Baltimore Skipjacks	AHL	32	10	11	0	1541	99	0	3.85	....	....	....	....	....	....	....	....	....	....	....	....	....	....	....	....	....
1987-88	Springfield Indians	AHL	35	12	15	4	1898	118	0	3.73	....	....	....	....	....	....	....	....	....	....	....	....	....	....	....	....	....
1988-89	Fredericton Capitals	NBSHL	30	....	....	....	1378	100	0	4.35	....	....	....	....	....	....	....	....	....	....	....	....	....	....	....	....	....
	Rochester Americans	AHL	19	12	4	1	1075	60	2	3.35	....	....	....	....	....	....	....	....	....	....	....	....	....	....	....	....	....
1989-90	Rochester Americans	AHL	19	7	6	4	1076	69	0	3.85	....	....	....	....	....	....	....	....	....	....	....	....	....	....	....	....	....
1990-91	Saint John Vitos	NBSHL	22	....	....	....	1320	101	*1	4.59	....	....	....	....	....	....	....	....	....	....	....	....	....	....	....	....	....
	Moncton Hawks	AHL	1	0	1	0	60	5	0	5.00	....	....	....	....	....	1	0	0	0	1	1	0	60.00	....	....	....	....
	NHL Totals		**11**	**3**	**7**	**0**	**580**	**61**	**0**	**6.31**	....	....	**362**	**.831**	....	....	....	....	....	....	....	....	....	....	....	....	....

Shared Harry "Hap" Holmes Memorial Award (fewest goals against - AHL) with Clint Malarchuk (1983) • AHL First All-Star Team (1984) • Won Harry "Hap" Holmes Memorial Award (fewest goals against - AHL) (1984) • Won Aldege "Baz" Bastien Memorial Award (Top Goaltender - AHL) (1984)

Signed as a free agent by **Quebec**, August 1, 1982. Traded to **Pittsburgh** by **Quebec** for Tom Thornbury, December 6, 1984.

• FOSTER, NORM

Norm Foster G – L. 5'9", 175 lbs. b: Vancouver, B.C., 2/10/1965. Boston's 11th choice, 231st overall, in 1983 Entry Draft.

Season	**Club**	**League**	**GP**	**W**	**L**	**T**	**Mins**	**GA**	**SO**	**Avg**	**AAvg**	**Eff**	**SA**	**S%**	**SAPG**	**GP**	**W**	**L**	**T**	**Mins**	**GA**	**SO**	**Avg**	**Eff**	**SA**	**S%**	**SAPG**
1982-83	Penticton Knights	BCJHL	33	....	....	....	1999	156	0	4.68	....	....	....	....	....	....	....	....	....	....	....	....	....	....	....	....	....
1983-84	Michigan State Spartans	CCHA	32	23	8	0	1815	83	1	2.74	....	....	....	....	....	....	....	....	....	....	....	....	....	....	....	....	....
1984-85	Michigan State Spartans	CCHA	26	22	4	0	1531	67	0	2.63	....	....	....	....	....	....	....	....	....	....	....	....	....	....	....	....	....
	Canada	WJC-A	2	....	....	....	120	1	1	0.50	....	....	....	....	....	....	....	....	....	....	....	....	....	....	....	....	....
1985-86	Michigan State Spartans	CCHA	24	17	5	1	1414	87	0	3.69	....	....	....	....	....	....	....	....	....	....	....	....	....	....	....	....	....
1986-87	Michigan State Spartans	CCHA	24	14	7	1	1383	90	1	3.90	....	....	....	....	....	....	....	....	....	....	....	....	....	....	....	....	....
1987-88	Milwaukee Admirals	IHL	38	10	22	1	2001	170	0	5.10	....	....	....	....	....	....	....	....	....	....	....	....	....	....	....	....	....
1988-89	Maine Mariners	AHL	47	16	17	6	2411	156	1	3.88	....	....	....	....	....	....	....	....	....	....	....	....	....	....	....	....	....
1989-90	Maine Mariners	AHL	*64	23	28	10	*3664	217	3	3.55	....	....	....	....	....	....	....	....	....	....	....	....	....	....	....	....	....
1990-91	**Boston Bruins**	**NHL**	**3**	**2**	**1**	**0**	**184**	**14**	**0**	**4.57**	**4.08**	**7.80**	**82**	**.829**	**26.7**	....	....	....	....	....	....	....	....	....	....	....	....
	Maine Mariners	AHL	2	1	1	0	122	7	0	3.44	....	....	....	....	....	....	....	....	....	....	....	....	....	....	....	....	....
	Cape Breton Oilers	AHL	40	15	14	7	2207	135	1	3.67	....	....	....	....	....	2	0	2	0	128	8	0	3.75	....	....	....	....
1991-92	**Edmonton Oilers**	**NHL**	**10**	**5**	**3**	**0**	**439**	**20**	**0**	**2.73**	**2.42**	**2.98**	**183**	**.891**	**25.0**	....	....	....	....	....	....	....	....	....	....	....	....
	Cape Breton Oilers	AHL	29	15	13	1	1699	119	0	4.20	....	....	....	....	....	3	1	2	0	193	14	0	4.35	....	....	....	....
1992-93	Cape Breton Oilers	AHL	10	5	5	0	560	53	0	5.68	....	....	....	....	....	....	....	....	....	....	....	....	....	....	....	....	....
	Kansas City Blades	IHL	8	6	1	1	489	28	0	3.44	....	....	....	....	....	1	0	0	0	16	0	0	0.00	....	....	....	....
1993-94	Hershey Bears	AHL	17	5	9	1	775	58	0	4.49	....	....	....	....	....	....	....	....	....	....	....	....	....	....	....	....	....
1994-95	Detroit Vipers	IHL	18	9	5	1	797	59	0	4.44	....	....	....	....	....	....	....	....	....	....	....	....	....	....	....	....	....
	Las Vegas Thunder	IHL	14	8	3	1	677	35	0	3.10	....	....	....	....	....	....	....	....	....	....	....	....	....	....	....	....	....
	NHL Totals		**13**	**7**	**4**	**0**	**623**	**34**	**0**	**3.27**	....	....	**265**	**.872**	....	....	....	....	....	....	....	....	....	....	....	....	....

CCHA Second All-Star Team (1984) • NCAA Championship All-Tournament Team (1985)

Traded to **Edmonton** by **Boston** for Edmonton's 6th round choice (Jiri Dopita) in 1992 Entry Draft, September 11, 1991. Signed as a free agent by **Philadelphia**, August 4, 1993.

			REGULAR SEASON												PLAYOFFS								
Season	Club	League	GP	W	L	T	Mins	GA	SO	Avg	AAvg	Eff	SA	S%	SAPG	GP	W	L	T	Mins	GA	SO	Avg	Eff	SA	S%	SAPG

● FOUNTAIN, MIKE   Mike Fountain   G – L. 6'1", 176 lbs.   b: North York, Ont., 1/26/1972.   Vancouver's 3rd choice, 45th overall, in 1992 Entry Draft.

Season	Club	League	GP	W	L	T	Mins	GA	SO	Avg	AAvg	Eff	SA	S%	SAPG	GP	W	L	T	Mins	GA	SO	Avg
1990-91	Sault Ste. Marie Greyhounds	OHL	7	5	2	0	380	19	0	3.00	....	....	....	....	....								
	Oshawa Generals	OHL	30	17	5	1	1483	84	0	3.40	....	....	....	....	....	8	1	4	....	292	26	0	5.34
1991-92	Oshawa Generals	OHL	40	18	13	6	2260	149	1	3.96	....	....	....	....	....	7	3	4	....	429	26	0	3.64
	Canada	WJC-A	DID NOT PLAY – SPARE GOALTENDER																				
1992-93	Canada	Nat-Team	13	7	5	1	745	37	1	2.98													
	Hamilton Canucks	AHL	12	2	8	0	618	46	0	4.47													
1993-94	Hamilton Canucks	AHL	*70	*34	28	6	*4005	241	*4	3.61						3	0	2	....	146	12	0	4.92
1994-95	Syracuse Crunch	AHL	61	25	29	7	3618	225	2	3.73													
1995-96	Syracuse Crunch	AHL	54	21	27	3	3060	184	1	3.61						15	8	7		915	57	*2	3.74
1996-97	**Vancouver Canucks**	**NHL**	6	2	2	0	245	14	1	3.43	3.63	3.56	135	.896	33.1								
	Syracuse Crunch	AHL	25	8	14	2	1462	78	1	3.20						2	0	2		120	12	0	6.02
1997-98	**Carolina Hurricanes**	**NHL**	3	0	3	0	163	10	0	3.68	4.31	5.41	68	.853	25.0								
	Beast of New Haven	AHL	50	25	19	5	2922	139	3	2.85													
	NHL Totals		9	2	5	0	408	24	1	3.53	....		203	.882									

OHL First All-Star Team (1992) • AHL Second All-Star Team (1994)

Signed as a free agent by **Carolina**, August 19, 1997.

● FOWLER, HEC   Hec (Norman) Fowler   G – L. 5'11", 190 lbs.   b: Saskatoon, Sask., 10/14/1892.

Season	Club	League	GP	W	L	T	Mins	GA	SO	Avg	AAvg	Eff	SA	S%	SAPG	GP	W	L	T	Mins	GA	SO	Avg
1915-16	Saskatoon Pilgrims	SSHL														2	0	2	0	120	10	0	5.00
1916-17	Spokane Canaries	PCHA	23	8	15	0	1383	143	0	6.20													
1917-18	Seattle Metropolitans	PCHA	18	*11	7	0	1168	65	*1	3.34						2	1	1	0	120	3	0	1.50
1918-19			MILITARY SERVICE																				
1919-20	Victoria Cougars	PCHA	22	10	12	0	1327	71	1	3.21													
1920-21	Victoria Cougars	PCHA	24	10	13	1	1541	88	*3	3.43													
1921-22	Victoria Cougars	PCHA	24	11	12	1	1468	70	1	2.86													
1922-23	Victoria Cougars	PCHA	*30	*16	14	0	*1846	85	4	2.76						2	1	1	0	120	5	0	2.50
1923-24	Victoria Cougars	PCHA	*30	11	18	I	1843	104	0	3.39													
1924-25	**Boston Bruins**	**NHL**	7	1	6	0	420	43	0	6.14	8.05												
	Edmonton Eskimos	WCHL	8	5	3	0	480	29	1	3.63													
1925-26			DID NOT PLAY																				
1926-27	Edmonton Eskimos	PrHL	32	12	18	2	1920	127	0	3.97													
1927-28			DID NOT PLAY																				
1928-29	Oakland Sheiks	Cal-Pro	STATISTICS NOT AVAILABLE																				
1929-30	Oakland Sheiks	Cal-Pro	42	*24	12	6	2520	72	....	*1.71						4	*3	0	1	250	5	1	*1.20
1930-31	Oakland Sheiks	Cal-Pro														4	*2	1	1	254	11	0	*2.60
	NHL Totals		7	1	6	0	420	43	0	6.14													
	Other Major League Totals		179	82	94	3	11056	655	11	3.55	....					4	2	2	0	240	8	0	2.00

PCHA First All-Star Team (1917) • PCHA Second All-Star Team (1918)

Signed as a free agent by **Victoria** (PCHA), December 14, 1919. Traded to **Boston** by Victoria (PCHA) for cash, October 29, 1924. Signed as a free agent by **Edmonton** (WCHL), January 28, 1925.

● FRANCIS, EMILE   Emile "Cat" Francis   G – L. 5'6", 145 lbs.   b: North Battleford, Sask., 9/13/1926.   HHOF

Season	Club	League	GP	W	L	T	Mins	GA	SO	Avg	AAvg	Eff	SA	S%	SAPG	GP	W	L	T	Mins	GA	SO	Avg
1941-42	North Battleford Beavers	SJHL	4	....	....	....	240	34	0	8.50													
1942-43	North Battleford Beavers	SJHL	8	....	....	....	480	59	0	7.37													
1943-44	Philadelphia Falcons	EHL	14	....	....	....	840	78	0	5.57													
1944-45	Washington Lions	EHL	36	....	....	....		243	0	6.75						8	1	6	1	57	0	7.12	
1945-46	Moose Jaw Canucks	SJHL	18	....	....	....	1080	55	0	*3.06						4	....	....	....	240	8	*1	*2.00
	Regina Capitals	WCSHL	1	....	....	....	60	5	0	5.00													
1946-47	**Chicago Black Hawks**	**NHL**	19	6	12	1	1140	104	0	5.47	5.56												
	Regina Capitals	WCSHL	32	....	....	....	1920	148	0	4.63													
1947-48	**Chicago Black Hawks**	**NHL**	54	18	31	5	3240	183	1	3.39	3.67												
	Kansas City Pla-Mors	USHL	7	3	2	2	420	24	1	3.42													
1948-49	New Haven Ramblers	AHL	40	15	27	7	2940	203	4	4.14													
	New York Rangers	**NHL**	2	2	0	0	120	4	0	2.00	2.27												
1949-50	New Haven Ramblers	AHL	68	22	36	10	4080	246	1	3.62													
	New York Rangers	**NHL**	1	0	1	0	60	8	0	8.00	9.07												
1950-51	Cincinnati Mohawks	AHL	53	20	26	7	3280	167	2	3.05													
	New York Rangers	**NHL**	5	1	1	2	260	14	0	3.23	3.68					6				18	0	3.00	
1951-52	Cincinnati Mohawks	AHL	51	24	22	5	3160	162	4	3.08													
	New York Rangers	**NHL**	14	4	7	3	840	42	0	3.00	3.59												
1952-53	Vancouver Canucks	WHL	70	*32	28	10	4200	216	5	*3.08						9	4	5	0	550	30	0	3.27
1953-54	Cleveland Barons	AHL	65	*37	28	0	3900	204	*5	3.14						9	*7	2	0	540	28	0	3.11
1954-55	Cleveland Barons	AHL	57	28	26	3	3420	204	2	3.58						3	1	2	0	158	12	0	4.56
1955-56	Saskatoon Quakers	WHL	68	27	33	8	4185	239	5	3.43						3	0	3	0	180	17	0	5.67
1956-57	Seattle Americans	WHL	68	35	27	6	4167	214	5	3.08						6	2	4	0	358	20	0	3.35
1957-58	Victoria Cougars	WHL	67	18	47	2	4040	294	2	4.37													
1958-59	Spokane Spokes	WHL	68	25	37	6	4150	269	1	3.89						4	1	3	0	240	16	0	4.00
1959-60	Spokane Spokes	WHL	68	19	46	3	4080	300	0	4.41													
	Seattle Totems	WHL	1	1	0	0	60	2	0	2.00													
	NHL Totals		95	31	52	11	5660	355	1	3.76													

WHL First All-Star Team (1953) • Won WHL Leading Goaltender Award (1953) • Won Leader Cup (WHL - MVP) (1953) • AHL Second All-Star Team (1954) • WHL Coast Division Second All-Star Team (1957) • Won Lester Patrick Trophy (1982)

Traded to **NY Rangers** by Chicago with Alex Kaleta for Jim Henry, October 7, 1948. Traded to **Cleveland** (AHL) by **NY Rangers** with Neil Strain for Johnny Bower, June, 1953.

● FRANKS, JIM   Jim Franks   G – L. 5'11", 156 lbs.   b: Melville, Sask., 11/8/1914.   Deceased.

Season	Club	League	GP	W	L	T	Mins	GA	SO	Avg	AAvg	Eff	SA	S%	SAPG	GP	W	L	T	Mins	GA	SO	Avg
1932-33	Regina Pats	SJHL	2	....	....	....	120	3	0	1.50						15	9	3	3	960	10	2	0.63
1933-34	Regina Pats	SJHL	STATISTICS NOT AVAILABLE																				
1934-35	Regina Pats	SJHL	STATISTICS NOT AVAILABLE																				
1935-36	Prince Albert Mintos	SSHL	18	11	6	1	1110	70	1	3.78						10	7	3	0	620	24	0	2.32
1936-37	Pittsburgh Hornets	AHL	20	8	9	3	1230	57	1	2.78						1	0	1		60	1	0	1.00
	Detroit Red Wings	**NHL**															1	0	1		30	2	0	4.00
1937-38	**Detroit Red Wings**	**NHL**	1	1	0	0	60	3	0	3.00	3.66												
	Pittsburgh Hornets	AHL	9	3	4	2	560	24	1	2.57													
1938-39	Pittsburgh Hornets	AHL	33	16	14	3	2030	103	1	3.04													
	Syracuse Stars	AHL	1	0	0	1	70	3	0	2.57													
	Kansas City Greyhounds	AHA	4	3	1	0	240	10	1	2.50													
1939-40	Indianapolis Capitols	AHL	29	16	7	6	1830	68	2	2.23													
1940-41	Indianapolis Capitols	AHL	*56	17	28	11	*3500	168	1	2.88													
1941-42	Omaha Knights	AHA	39	19	14	6	2307	116	1	2.90						8	*8	0	0	497	16	0	*1.93
1942-43	**New York Rangers**	**NHL**	23	5	14	4	1380	103	0	4.48	3.90												
	Pittsburgh Hornets	AHL	4	1	3	0	240	19	0	4.45													

			REGULAR SEASON													PLAYOFFS											
Season	Club	League	GP	W	L	T	Mins	GA	SO	Avg	AAvg	Eff	SA	S%	SAPG	GP	W	L	T	Mins	GA	SO	Avg	Eff	SA	S%	SAPG
1943-44	**Detroit Red Wings**	**NHL**	**17**	**6**	**8**	**3**	**1020**	**69**	**1**	**4.06**	**3.07**	....	....	....	....	....	....	....	....	....	....	....	....	....	....	....	....
	Boston Bruins	**NHL**	**1**	**0**	**1**	**0**	**60**	**6**	**0**	**6.00**	**4.55**	....	....	....	....	....	....	....	....	....	....	....	....	....	....	....	....
	Buffalo Bisons	AHL	1	1	0	0	60	1	0	1.00	....	....	....	....	....	....	....	....	....	....	....	....	....	....	....	....	....
1944-45	Buffalo Bisons	AHL	1	0	0	1	60	2	0	2.00	....	....	....	....	....	....	....	....	....	....	....	....	....	....	....	....	....
	St. Louis Flyers	AHL	29	5	21	3	1740	115	1	3.97	....	....	....	....	....	....	....	....	....	....	....	....	....	....	....	....	....
	NHL Totals		**42**	**12**	**23**	**7**	**2520**	**181**	**1**	**4.31**	....	....	....	....	....	**1**	**0**	**1**	....	**30**	**2**	**0**	**4.00**	....	....	....	....

Loaned to **NY Rangers** by **Detroit** for 1942-43 season as a war-time replacement for Jim Henry, October, 1942. • Suspended by Detroit for refusing assignment to Indianapolis (AHL), October, 1943. Suspension lifted after Franks agreed to play "road games only" for club, December, 1943. Loaned to **Boston** by **Detroit** to replace injured Bert Gardiner, January 29, 1944. (Detroit 6, Boston 1).

• FREDERICK, RAY

Ray Frederick G – L. 6′, 154 lbs. b: Fort Francis, Ont., 7/31/1929.

Season	Club	League	GP	W	L	T	Mins	GA	SO	Avg	AAvg	Eff	SA	S%	SAPG	GP	W	L	T	Mins	GA	SO	Avg	Eff	SA	S%	SAPG
1944-45	Fort Francis West Enders	TBSHL	5	....	....	....	270	41	0	9.11	....	....	....	....	....	....	....	....	....	....	....	....	....	....	....	....	....
1945-46	Hamilton Lloyds	OHA	12	....	....	....	720	94	0	7.83	....	....	....	....	....	....	....	....	....	....	....	....	....	....	....	....	....
1946-47	Fort Francis West Enders	TBJHL	STATISTICS NOT AVAILABLE																								
1947-48	Brandon Wheat Kings	MJHL	24	*15	9	0	1440	102	*2	4.25	....	....	....	....	....	5	....	....	....	300	29	0	5.80	....	....	....	....
1948-49	Brandon Wheat Kings	MJHL	30	*27	3	0	1800	78	*2	*2.60	....	....	....	....	....	18	*11	6	0	1090	49	1	2.70	....	....	....	....
1949-50	Edmonton Flyers	WCSHL	47	....	....	....	2820	159	0	3.38	....	....	....	....	....	6	2	4	0	360	23	0	3.83	....	....	....	....
1950-51	Edmonton Flyers	WCSHL	60	....	....	....	3600	198	2	3.30	....	....	....	....	....	8	....	....	....	480	27	*1	3.37	....	....	....	....
1951-52	Chicoutimi Sagueneens	QSHL	14	5	6	3	870	40	0	2.76	....	....	....	....	....	....	....	....	....	....	....	....	....	....	....	....	....
	Charlottetown Islanders	MMHL	54	26	22	6	3216	193	2	3.60	....	....	....	....	....	4	0	4	0	264	15	0	3.41	....	....	....	....
1952-53	Ottawa Senators	QSHL	*60	27	26	7	*3720	191	5	3.08	....	....	....	....	....	11	5	6	0	726	33	1	2.73	....	....	....	....
1953-54	Ottawa Senators	QHL	60	28	27	5	3656	172	*9	2.82	....	....	....	....	....	22	*12	10	0	1364	48	0	2.11	....	....	....	....
1954-55	Ottawa Senators	QHL	27	10	17	0	1626	90	1	3.32	....	....	....	....	....	....	....	....	....	....	....	....	....	....	....	....	....
	Chicago Black Hawks	**NHL**	**5**	**0**	**4**	**1**	**300**	**22**	**0**	**4.40**	**5.43**	....	....	....	....	....	....	....	....	....	....	....	....	....	....	....	....
	Buffalo Bisons	AHL	22	15	7	0	1320	83	0	3.77	....	....	....	....	....	10	5	5	0	639	32	*1	3.00	....	....	....	....
1955-56	Calgary Stampeders	WHL	60	34	26	0	3627	203	6	3.36	....	....	....	....	....	8	4	4	0	505	35	0	4.16	....	....	....	....
1956-57	Chicoutimi Sagueneens	QHL	64	32	28	4	3886	190	4	2.93	....	....	....	....	....	*10	6	4	0	605	26	*1	*2.59	....	....	....	....
1957-58	Cornwall Chevies	EOHL	38	....	....	....	2280	180	1	4.74	....	....	....	....	....	7	....	....	....	420	23	1	3.28	....	....	....	....
1958-59	Sudbury Wolves	NOHA	53	....	....	....	3180	207	1	3.91	....	....	....	....	....	5	....	....	....	300	19	0	3.80	....	....	....	....
	NHL Totals		**5**	**0**	**4**	**1**	**300**	**22**	**0**	**4.40**	....	....	....	....	....	....	....	....	....	....	....	....	....	....	....	....	....

QSHL Second All-Star Team (1953) • QHL Second All-Star Team (1954)

• FRIESEN, KARL

Karl Friesen G – L. 6′, 185 lbs. b: Winnipeg, Man., 6/30/1958.

Season	Club	League	GP	W	L	T	Mins	GA	SO	Avg	AAvg	Eff	SA	S%	SAPG	GP	W	L	T	Mins	GA	SO	Avg	Eff	SA	S%	SAPG
1977-78	Kildonan Northstars	MJHL	38	....	....	....	2091	164	0	4.71	....	....	....	....	....	18	12	6	0	1042	71	1	4.08	....	....	....	....
1978-79	Winnipeg Maroons	CASH	STATISTICS NOT AVAILABLE																								
1979-80			STATISTICS NOT AVAILABLE																								
1980-81	SB Rosenheim	Germany	44	....	....	....	2592	140	....	3.24	....	....	....	....	....	3	....	....	....	180	8	....	2.67	....	....	....	....
	West Germany	WEC-A	4	....	....	....	240	20	....	5.00	....	....	....	....	....	....	....	....	....	....	....	....	....	....	....	....	....
1981-82	SB Rosenheim	Germany	42	....	....	....	2469	147	....	3.57	....	....	....	....	....	7	....	....	....	420	15	....	2.14	....	....	....	....
	West Germany	WEC-A	7	....	....	....	420	30	....	4.28	....	....	....	....	....	....	....	....	....	....	....	....	....	....	....	....	....
1982-83	SB Rosenheim	Germany	36	....	....	....	2160	103	....	2.86	....	....	....	....	....	9	....	....	....	480	36	....	4.50	....	....	....	....
	West Germany	WEC-A	5	....	....	....	300	21	....	4.20	....	....	....	....	....	....	....	....	....	....	....	....	....	....	....	....	....
1983-84	SB Rosenheim	Germany	42	....	....	....	2490	136	....	3.28	....	....	....	....	....	4	....	....	....	240	10	....	2.50	....	....	....	....
	West Germany	Olympics	5	....	....	....	300	16	....	3.20	....	....	....	....	....	....	....	....	....	....	....	....	....	....	....	....	....
1984-85	West Germany	C Cup	4	....	....	....	240	21	....	5.25	....	....	....	....	....	....	....	....	....	....	....	....	....	....	....	....	....
	SB Rosenheim	Germany	35	....	....	....	2100	99	....	2.83	....	....	....	....	....	9	....	....	....	547	22	....	2.41	....	....	....	....
	West Germany	WEC-A	9	....	....	....	580	34	....	3.51	....	....	....	....	....	....	....	....	....	....	....	....	....	....	....	....	....
1985-86	Maine Mariners	AHL	35	16	11	5	1983	115	2	3.48	....	....	....	....	....	5	1	4	0	340	14	0	2.47	....	....	....	....
1986-87	**New Jersey Devils**	**NHL**	**4**	**0**	**2**	**1**	**130**	**16**	**0**	**7.38**	**6.21**	**14.76**	**80**	**.800**	**36.9**	....	....	....	....	....	....	....	....	....	....	....	....
	SB Rosenheim	Germany	15	....	....	....	840	39	....	2.79	....	....	....	....	....	9	....	....	....	424	18	....	2.55	....	....	....	....
	West Germany	WEC-A	5	....	....	....	300	19	....	3.80	....	....	....	....	....	....	....	....	....	....	....	....	....	....	....	....	....
1987-88	SB Rosenheim	Germany	35	....	....	....	1980	85	....	2.58	....	....	....	....	....	14	....	....	....	840	33	....	2.36	....	....	....	....
	West Germany	Olympics	6	....	....	....	328	17	....	3.11	....	....	....	....	....	....	....	....	....	....	....	....	....	....	....	....	....
1988-89	SB Rosenheim	Germany	36	19	8	9	2160	98	....	2.72	....	....	....	....	....	11	....	....	....	655	27	....	2.47	....	....	....	....
	West Germany	WEC-A	8	....	....	....	480	31	....	3.87	....	....	....	....	....	....	....	....	....	....	....	....	....	....	....	....	....
1989-90	SB Rosenheim	Germany	19	....	....	....	1060	43	....	2.43	....	....	....	....	....	11	....	....	....	526	37	....	4.22	....	....	....	....
1990-91	SB Rosenheim	Germany	40	....	....	....	2340	105	....	2.69	....	....	....	....	....	11	....	....	....	612	36	....	3.53	....	....	....	....
1991-92	SB Rosenheim	Germany	44	....	....	....	2447	133	....	3.26	....	....	....	....	....	9	....	....	....	547	27	....	2.96	....	....	....	....
	Germany	Olympics	1	....	....	....	60	5	0	5.00	....	....	....	....	....	....	....	....	....	....	....	....	....	....	....	....	....
1992-93	EC Hedos Munich	Germany	44	21	15	8	2640	111	....	2.52	....	....	....	....	....	4	....	....	....	240	14	....	3.50	....	....	....	....
1993-94	EC Hedos Munich	Germany	44	....	....	....	2172	81	....	2.24	....	....	....	....	....	10	....	....	....	600	25	....	2.50	....	....	....	....
1994-95	EC Hedos Munich	Germany	26	....	....	....	1409	71	....	3.02	....	....	....	....	....	....	....	....	....	....	....	....	....	....	....	....	....
1995-96	Star Bulls Rosenheim	Germany	28	....	....	....	1571	81	....	3.09	....	....	....	....	....	4	....	....	....	240	18	....	4.50	....	....	....	....
	NHL Totals		**4**	**0**	**2**	**1**	**130**	**16**	**0**	**7.38**	....	....	**80**	**.800**	....	....	....	....	....	....	....	....	....	....	....	....	....

German Player of the Year (1982, 1988, 1989, 1990) • Shared Harry "Hap" Holmes Memorial Award (fewest goals against - AHL) with Sam St. Laurent (1986)

Signed as a free agent by **New Jersey**, April 24, 1985.

• FROESE, BOB

Bob Froese G – L. 5′11″, 176 lbs. b: St. Catharines, Ont., 6/30/1958. St. Louis' 11th choice, 160th overall, in 1978 Amateur Draft.

Season	Club	League	GP	W	L	T	Mins	GA	SO	Avg	AAvg	Eff	SA	S%	SAPG	GP	W	L	T	Mins	GA	SO	Avg	Eff	SA	S%	SAPG
1974-75	St. Catharines Black Hawks	OHA	15	....	....	....	871	71	0	4.89	....	....	....	....	....	....	....	....	....	....	....	....	....	....	....	....	....
1975-76	St. Catharines Black Hawks	OHA	39	....	....	....	1976	193	0	5.86	....	....	....	....	....	4	....	....	....	240	20	0	5.00	....	....	....	....
1976-77	Oshawa Generals	OHA	39	....	....	....	2063	161	*2	4.68	....	....	....	....	....	....	....	....	....	....	....	....	....	....	....	....	....
1977-78	Niagara Falls Flyers	OHA	53	....	....	....	3128	246	0	4.72	....	....	....	....	....	3	....	....	....	236	17	0	4.36	....	....	....	....
1978-79	Saginaw Gears	IHL	21	....	....	....	1050	58	0	3.31	....	....	....	....	....	....	....	....	....	....	....	....	....	....	....	....	....
	Milwaukee Admirals	IHL	14	....	....	....	715	42	1	3.52	....	....	....	....	....	7	....	....	....	334	23	0	4.14	....	....	....	....
1979-80	Maine Mariners	AHL	1	0	1	0	60	5	0	5.00	....	....	....	....	....	....	....	....	....	....	....	....	....	....	....	....	....
	Saginaw Gears	IHL	52	....	....	....	2827	178	0	3.78	....	....	....	....	....	4	....	....	....	213	13	0	3.66	....	....	....	....
1980-81	Saginaw Gears	IHL	43	....	....	....	2298	114	3	2.98	....	....	....	....	....	*13	*12	1	0	*806	29	*2	*2.16	....	....	....	....
1981-82	Maine Mariners	AHL	33	16	11	4	1900	104	2	3.28	....	....	....	....	....	....	....	....	....	....	....	....	....	....	....	....	....
1982-83	**Philadelphia Flyers**	**NHL**	**25**	**17**	**4**	**2**	**1407**	**59**	**4**	**2.52**	**2.00**	**2.61**	**569**	**.896**	**24.3**	....	....	....	....	....	....	....	....	....	....	....	....
	Maine Mariners	AHL	33	18	11	3	1966	110	2	3.36	....	....	....	....	....	....	....	....	....	....	....	....	....	....	....	....	....
1983-84	**Philadelphia Flyers**	**NHL**	**48**	**28**	**13**	**7**	**2863**	**150**	**2**	**3.14**	**2.44**	**3.55**	**1326**	**.887**	**27.8**	**3**	**0**	**2**	....	**154**	**11**	**0**	**4.29**	**6.13**	**77**	**.857**	**30.0**
1984-85	**Philadelphia Flyers**	**NHL**	**17**	**13**	**2**	**0**	**923**	**37**	**1**	**2.41**	**1.91**	**2.09**	**427**	**.913**	**27.8**	**4**	**0**	**1**	....	**146**	**11**	**0**	**4.52**	**7.00**	**71**	**.845**	**29.2**
	Hershey Bears	AHL	4	1	2	1	245	15	0	3.67	....	....	....	....	....	....	....	....	....	....	....	....	....	....	....	....	....
1985-86	**Philadelphia Flyers**	**NHL**	**51**	***31**	**10**	**3**	**2728**	**116**	***5**	***2.55**	**1.96**	**2.33**	**1270**	**.909**	**27.9**	**5**	**2**	**3**	....	**293**	**15**	**0**	**3.07**	**3.68**	**125**	**.880**	**25.6**
1986-87	**Philadelphia Flyers**	**NHL**	**3**	**3**	**0**	**0**	**180**	**8**	**0**	**2.67**	**2.24**	**2.43**	**88**	**.909**	**29.3**	....	....	....	....	....	....	....	....	....	....	....	....
	New York Rangers	**NHL**	**28**	**14**	**11**	**0**	**1474**	**92**	**0**	**3.74**	**3.15**	**4.39**	**784**	**.883**	**31.9**	**4**	**1**	**1**	....	**165**	**10**	**0**	**3.64**	**3.79**	**96**	**.896**	**34.9**
	Canada	WEC-A	5	....	....	....	300	18	....	3.60	....	....	....	....	....	....	....	....	....	....	....	....	....	....	....	....	....
1987-88	**New York Rangers**	**NHL**	**25**	**8**	**11**	**3**	**1443**	**85**	**0**	**3.53**	**2.93**	**4.30**	**697**	**.878**	**29.0**	....	....	....	....	....	....	....	....	....	....	....	....
1988-89	**New York Rangers**	**NHL**	**30**	**9**	**14**	**4**	**1621**	**102**	**1**	**3.78**	**3.12**	**4.87**	**791**	**.871**	**29.3**	**2**	**0**	**2**	....	**72**	**8**	**0**	**6.67**	**10.46**	**51**	**.843**	**42.5**
1989-90	**New York Rangers**	**NHL**	**15**	**5**	**7**	**1**	**812**	**45**	**0**	**3.33**	**2.79**	**4.22**	**355**	**.873**	**26.2**	....	....	....	....	....	....	....	....	....	....	....	....
	NHL Totals		**242**	**128**	**72**	**20**	**13451**	**694**	**13**	**3.10**	....	....	**6307**	**.890**	....	**18**	**3**	**9**	....	**830**	**55**	**0**	**3.98**	....	....	....	....

NHL Second All-Star Team (1986) • Shared William M. Jennings Trophy with Darren Jensen (1986)

Played in NHL All-Star Game (1986)

Signed as a free agent by **Philadelphia**, June 18, 1981. Traded to **NY Rangers** by **Philadelphia** for Kjell Samuelsson and NY Rangers' 2nd round choice (Patrik Juhlin) in 1989 Entry Draft, December 18, 1986.

• FUHR, GRANT

Grant Fuhr G – R. 5′9″, 190 lbs. b: Spruce Grove, Alta., 9/28/1962. Edmonton's 1st choice, 8th overall, in 1981 Entry Draft.

Season	Club	League	GP	W	L	T	Mins	GA	SO	Avg	AAvg	Eff	SA	S%	SAPG	GP	W	L	T	Mins	GA	SO	Avg	Eff	SA	S%	SAPG
1979-80	Victoria Cougars	WHL	43	30	12	0	2488	130	2	3.14	....	....	....	....	....	8	5	3	....	465	22	0	2.84	....	....	....	....
1980-81	Victoria Cougars	WHL	59	48	9	1	3448	160	*4	*2.78	....	....	....	....	....	15	12	3	....	899	45	*1	*3.00	....	....	....	....
1981-82	**Edmonton Oilers**	**NHL**	**48**	**28**	**5**	**14**	**2847**	**157**	**0**	**3.31**	**2.54**	**3.39**	**1532**	**.898**	**32.3**	**5**	**2**	**3**	....	**309**	**26**	**0**	**5.05**	....	....	....	....

Season	Club	League	REGULAR SEASON													PLAYOFFS											
			GP	W	L	T	Mins	GA	SO	Avg	AAvg	Eff	SA	S%	SAPG	GP	W	L	T	Mins	GA	SO	Avg	Eff	SA	S%	SAPG
1982-83	Edmonton Oilers	NHL	32	13	12	5	1803	129	0	4.29	3.43	5.68	974	.868	32.4	1	0	0	....	11	0	0	0.00	....	....	....	....
	Moncton Alpines	AHL	10	4	5	1	604	40	0	3.98	....	....	....	....	....	....	....	....	....	....	....	....	....	....	....	....	....
1983-84	Edmonton Oilers	NHL	45	30	10	4	2625	171	1	3.91	3.06	4.57	1463	.883	33.4	16	11	4	....	883	44	1	2.99	2.68	491	.910	33.4
1984-85	Canada	C Cup	2	1	0	1	120	6	0	3.00	....	....	....	....	....	....	....	....	....	....	....	....	....	....	....	....	....
	Edmonton Oilers	NHL	46	26	8	7	2559	165	1	3.87	3.07	4.48	1426	.884	33.4	*18	*15	3	....	1064	55	0	3.10	3.27	522	.895	29.4
1985-86	Edmonton Oilers	NHL	40	29	8	0	2184	143	0	3.93	3.06	4.34	1296	.890	35.6	9	5	4	....	541	28	0	3.11	3.19	273	.897	30.3
1986-87	Edmonton Oilers	NHL	44	22	13	3	2388	137	0	3.44	2.89	4.10	1149	.881	28.9	19	14	5	....	1148	47	0	2.46	2.26	511	.908	26.7
	NHL All-Stars	RV '87	2	1	1	0	120	8	0	4.00	....	....	....	....	....	....	....	....	....	....	....	....	....	....	....	....	....
1987-88	Canada	C Cup	9	6	1	2	575	32	0	3.00	....	....	....	....	....	....	....	....	....	....	....	....	....	....	....	....	....
	Edmonton Oilers	NHL	*75	*40	24	9	*4304	246	*4	3.43	2.84	4.08	2066	.881	28.8	*19	*16	2	....	*1136	55	0	2.90	3.39	471	.883	24.9
1988-89	Edmonton Oilers	NHL	59	23	26	6	3341	213	1	3.83	3.16	4.76	1714	.876	30.8	7	3	4	....	417	24	1	3.45	3.65	227	.894	32.7
	Canada	WEC-A	5	....	....	....	298	18	....	3.62	....	....	....	....	....	....	....	....	....	....	....	....	....	....	....	....	....
1989-90	Edmonton Oilers	NHL	21	9	7	3	1081	70	1	3.89	3.26	5.12	532	.868	29.5	....	....	....	....	....	....	....	....	....	....	....	....
	Cape Breton Oilers	AHL	2	2	0	0	120	6	0	3.01	....	....	....	....	....	....	....	....	....	....	....	....	....	....	....	....	....
1990-91	Edmonton Oilers	NHL	13	6	4	3	778	39	1	3.01	2.69	3.09	380	.897	29.3	17	8	7	....	1019	51	0	3.00	3.14	488	.895	28.7
	Cape Breton Oilers	AHL	4	2	2	0	240	17	0	4.25	....	....	....	....	....	....	....	....	....	....	....	....	....	....	....	....	....
1991-92	Toronto Maple Leafs	NHL	66	25	33	5	3774	230	2	3.66	3.25	4.35	1933	.881	30.7	....	....	....	....	....	....	....	....	....	....	....	....
1992-93	Toronto Maple Leafs	NHL	29	13	9	4	1665	87	1	3.14	2.67	3.31	826	.895	29.8	....	....	....	....	....	....	....	....	....	....	....	....
	Buffalo Sabres	NHL	29	11	15	2	1694	98	0	3.47	2.95	3.77	903	.891	32.0	8	3	4	....	474	27	1	3.42	4.28	216	.875	27.3
1993-94	Buffalo Sabres	NHL	32	13	12	3	1726	106	2	3.68	3.51	4.30	907	.883	31.5	....	....	....	....	....	....	....	....	....	....	....	....
	Rochester Americans	AHL	5	3	0	2	310	10	0	1.94	....	....	....	....	....	....	....	....	....	....	....	....	....	....	....	....	....
1994-95	Buffalo Sabres	NHL	3	1	2	0	180	12	0	4.00	4.14	5.65	85	.859	28.3	....	....	....	....	....	....	....	....	....	....	....	....
	Los Angeles Kings	NHL	14	1	7	3	698	47	0	4.04	4.19	5.01	379	.876	32.6	....	....	....	....	....	....	....	....	....	....	....	....
1995-96	St. Louis Blues	NHL	*79	30	28	16	4365	209	3	2.87	2.81	2.78	2157	.903	29.6	2	1	0	....	69	1	0	0.87	0.19	45	.978	39.1
1996-97	St. Louis Blues	NHL	73	33	27	11	4261	193	3	2.72	2.87	2.71	1940	.901	27.3	6	2	4	....	357	13	2	2.18	1.55	183	.929	30.8
1997-98	St. Louis Blues	NHL	58	29	21	6	3274	138	3	2.53	2.96	2.58	1354	.898	24.8	10	6	4	....	616	28	0	2.73	2.57	297	.906	28.9
	NHL Totals		806	382	271	104	45547	2590	23	3.41	....	....	23016	.887	....	137	86	44	....	8044	399	5	2.98	....	....	....	....

WHL First All-Star Team (1980, 1981) • NHL Second All-Star Team (1982) • Canada Cup All-Star Team (1987) • NHL First All-Star Team (1988) • Won Vezina Trophy (1988) • Shared William M. Jennings Trophy with Dominik Hasek (1994)

Played in NHL All-Star Game (1982, 1984, 1985, 1986, 1988, 1989)

• Statistics (Mins., GA) for suspended game on May 24, 1988 are included in playoff record.

Traded to **Toronto** by **Edmonton** with Glenn Anderson and Craig Berube for Vincent Damphousse, Peter Ing, Scott Thornton, Luke Richardson, future considerations and cash, September 19, 1991. Traded to **Buffalo** by **Toronto** with Toronto's 5th round choice (Kevin Popp) in 1995 Entry Draft for Dave Andreychuk, Daren Puppa and Buffalo's 1st round choice (Kenny Jonsson) in 1993 Entry Draft, February 2, 1993. Traded to **Los Angeles** by **Buffalo** with Philippe Boucher and Denis Tsygurov for Alexei Zhitnik, Robb Stauber, Charlie Huddy and Los Angeles' 5th round choice (Marian Menhart) in 1995 Entry Draft, February 14, 1995. Signed as a free agent by **St. Louis**, July 14, 1995.

• GAGE, JOAQUIN

Joaquin Gage G – L. 6', 200 lbs. b: Vancouver, B.C., 10/19/1973. Edmonton's 6th choice, 109th overall, in 1992 Entry Draft.

Season	Club	League	GP	W	L	T	Mins	GA	SO	Avg	AAvg	Eff	SA	S%	SAPG	GP	W	L	T	Mins	GA	SO	Avg	Eff	SA	S%	SAPG
1990-91	Portland Winter Hawks	WHL	3	0	3	0	180	17	0	5.70	....	....	....	....	....	....	....	....	....	....	....	....	....	....	....	....	....
1991-92	Portland Winter Hawks	WHL	63	27	30	4	3635	269	2	4.44	....	....	....	....	....	6	2	4	....	366	28	0	4.59	....	....	....	....
1992-93	Portland Winter Hawks	WHL	38	21	16	1	2302	153	2	3.99	....	....	....	....	....	8	5	2	....	427	30	0	4.22	....	....	....	....
1993-94	Prince Albert Raiders	WHL	53	24	25	3	3041	212	1	4.18	....	....	....	....	....	....	....	....	....	....	....	....	....	....	....	....	....
1994-95	Cape Breton Oilers	AHL	54	17	28	5	3010	207	0	4.13	....	....	....	....	....	....	....	....	....	....	....	....	....	....	....	....	....
	Edmonton Oilers	**NHL**	**2**	**0**	**2**	**0**	**99**	**7**	**0**	**4.24**	**4.38**	**7.42**	**40**	**.825**	**24.2**	....	....	....	....	....	....	....	....	....	....	....	....
1995-96	**Edmonton Oilers**	**NHL**	**16**	**2**	**8**	**1**	**717**	**45**	**0**	**3.77**	**3.71**	**4.85**	**360**	**.871**	**29.3**	....	....	....	....	....	....	....	....	....	....	....	....
	Cape Breton Oilers	AHL	21	8	11	0	1162	80	0	4.13	....	....	....	....	....	....	....	....	....	....	....	....	....	....	....	....	....
1996-97	Hamilton Bulldogs	AHL	29	7	14	4	1558	91	0	3.50	....	....	....	....	....	....	....	....	....	....	....	....	....	....	....	....	....
	Wheeling Nailers	ECHL	3	1	0	0	120	8	0	4.00	....	....	....	....	....	....	....	....	....	....	....	....	....	....	....	....	....
1997-98	Raleigh IceCaps	ECHL	39	19	14	3	2173	116	1	3.20	....	....	....	....	....	....	....	....	....	....	....	....	....	....	....	....	....
	Syracuse Crunch	AHL	2	1	1	0	120	7	0	3.50	....	....	....	....	....	....	....	....	....	....	....	....	....	....	....	....	....
	NHL Totals		**18**	**2**	**10**	**1**	**816**	**52**	**0**	**3.82**	....	....	**390**	**.867**	....	....	....	....	....	....	....	....	....	....	....	....	....

• GAGNON, DAVID

David Gagnon G – L. 6', 185 lbs. b: Windsor, Ont., 10/31/1967.

Season	Club	League	GP	W	L	T	Mins	GA	SO	Avg	AAvg	Eff	SA	S%	SAPG	GP	W	L	T	Mins	GA	SO	Avg	Eff	SA	S%	SAPG
1987-88	Colgate University	ECAC	13	6	4	2	743	43	1	3.47	....	....	....	....	....	....	....	....	....	....	....	....	....	....	....	....	....
1988-89	Colgate University	ECAC	28	17	9	2	1622	102	0	3.77	....	....	....	....	....	....	....	....	....	....	....	....	....	....	....	....	....
1989-90	Colgate University	ECAC	33	28	3	1	1986	93	0	2.81	....	....	....	....	....	....	....	....	....	....	....	....	....	....	....	....	....
1990-91	**Detroit Red Wings**	**NHL**	**2**	**0**	**1**	**0**	**35**	**6**	**0**	**10.29**	**9.20**	**22.05**	**28**	**.786**	**48.0**	....	....	....	....	....	....	....	....	....	....	....	....
	Adirondack Red Wings	AHL	24	8	8	5	1356	94	0	4.16	....	....	....	....	....	....	....	....	....	....	....	....	....	....	....	....	....
	Hampton Roads Admirals	ECHL	10	7	1	2	606	26	2	2.57	....	....	....	....	....	11	*10	1	0	606	27	0	*2.32	....	....	....	....
1991-92	Fort Wayne Komets	IHL	2	2	0	0	125	7	0	3.36	....	....	....	....	....	....	....	....	....	....	....	....	....	....	....	....	....
	Toledo Storm	ECHL	7	4	2	0	354	18	0	3.05	....	....	....	....	....	....	....	....	....	....	....	....	....	....	....	....	....
1992-93	Adirondack Red Wings	AHL	1	0	1	0	60	5	0	5.00	....	....	....	....	....	....	....	....	....	....	....	....	....	....	....	....	....
	Fort Wayne Komets	IHL	31	15	11	2	1771	116	0	3.93	....	....	....	....	....	1	0	0	0	6	0	0	0.00	....	....	....	....
1993-94	Fort Wayne Komets	IHL	19	7	6	3	1026	58	0	3.39	....	....	....	....	....	....	....	....	....	....	....	....	....	....	....	....	....
	Toledo Storm	ECHL	20	13	5	0	1122	65	1	3.48	....	....	....	....	....	*14	*12	2	0	*909	41	0	*2.70	....	....	....	....
1994-95	Roanoke Express	ECHL	29	17	7	5	1738	82	1	2.83	....	....	....	....	....	....	....	....	....	....	....	....	....	....	....	....	....
	Minnesota Moose	IHL	16	5	4	2	767	55	0	4.30	....	....	....	....	....	1	0	1	0	60	9	0	9.00	....	....	....	....
1995-96	Minnesota Moose	IHL	52	18	25	4	2721	188	0	4.14	....	....	....	....	....	....	....	....	....	....	....	....	....	....	....	....	....
1996-97	Roanoke Express	ECHL	60	34	18	6	3386	181	3	3.21	....	....	....	....	....	3	1	2	0	219	10	0	2.73	....	....	....	....
1997-98	Roanoke Express	ECHL	43	25	13	4	2466	119	2	2.89	....	....	....	....	....	7	3	4	....	441	15	1	2.04	....	....	....	....
	NHL Totals		**2**	**0**	**1**	**0**	**35**	**6**	**0**	**10.29**	....	....	**28**	**.786**	....	....	....	....	....	....	....	....	....	....	....	....	....

ECAC First All-Star Team (1990) • Shared Playoff MVP with Dave Flanagan - ECHL (1991) • Playoff MVP - ECHL (1994) • ECHL Second All-Star Team (1995)

Signed as a free agent by **Detroit**, June 11, 1990.

• GAMBLE, BRUCE

Bruce "Paladin" Gamble G – L. 5'9", 200 lbs. b: Port Arthur, Ont., 5/24/1938. d: 12/29/1982.

Season	Club	League	GP	W	L	T	Mins	GA	SO	Avg	AAvg	Eff	SA	S%	SAPG	GP	W	L	T	Mins	GA	SO	Avg	Eff	SA	S%	SAPG
1952-53	Port Arthur West End Bruins	TBJHL	11	....	....	....	660	82	0	7.45	....	....	....	....	....	....	....	....	....	....	....	....	....	....	....	....	....
1953-54	Port Arthur Bruins	TBJHL	30	20	15	1	2160	150	0	4.17	....	....	....	....	....	9	....	....	....	540	42	0	4.67	....	....	....	....
1954-55	Port Arthur Bruins	TBJHL	STATISTICS NOT AVAILABLE																								
1955-56	Port Arthur North Stars	TBJHL	31	19	10	2	1860	97	0	*3.13	....	....	....	....	....	9	....	....	....	540	27	0	*3.00	....	....	....	....
1956-57	Guelph Biltmores	OHA	40	....	....	....	2360	102	6	2.59	....	....	....	....	....	10	....	....	....	600	34	0	3.40	....	....	....	....
1957-58	Guelph Biltmores	OHA	50	13	32	5	3000	205	1	4.10	....	....	....	....	....	....	....	....	....	....	....	....	....	....	....	....	....
	Providence Reds	AHL	1	1	0	0	60	1	0	1.00	....	....	....	....	....	....	....	....	....	....	....	....	....	....	....	....	....
	Hull-Ottawa Jr. Canadiens	OHA	STATISTICS NOT AVAILABLE																								
1958-59	Vancouver Canucks	WHL	65	29	26	10	3900	199	*7	3.06	....	....	....	....	....	5	2	3	0	300	11	*2	2.20	....	....	....	....
	New York Rangers	**NHL**	**2**	**0**	**2**	**0**	**120**	**6**	**0**	**3.00**	**3.20**	....	....	....	....	....	....	....	....	....	....	....	....	....	....	....	....
1959-60	Providence Reds	AHL	71	37	32	2	4280	231	4	3.24	....	....	....	....	....	5	1	4	0	328	19	0	3.48	....	....	....	....
1960-61	Providence Reds	AHL	19	6	13	0	1140	85	0	4.47	....	....	....	....	....	....	....	....	....	....	....	....	....	....	....	....	....
	Boston Bruins	**NHL**	**52**	**12**	**33**	**7**	**3120**	**195**	**0**	**3.75**	**3.99**	....	....	....	....	....	....	....	....	....	....	....	....	....	....	....	....
1961-62	Portland Buckeroos	WHL	41	28	11	2	2476	108	2	*2.62	....	....	....	....	....	....	....	....	....	....	....	....	....	....	....	....	....
	Boston Bruins	**NHL**	**28**	**6**	**18**	**4**	**1680**	**123**	**1**	**4.39**	**4.65**	....	....	....	....	....	....	....	....	....	....	....	....	....	....	....	....
1962-63	Kingston Frontenacs	EPHL	68	*39	18	11	4080	220	1	3.23	....	....	....	....	....	5	*4	1	0	300	13	*1	*2.60	....	....	....	....
1963-64	Springfield Indians	AHL	21	5	12	3	1230	80	0	3.90	....	....	....	....	....	....	....	....	....	....	....	....	....	....	....	....	....
1964-65			DID NOT PLAY																								
1965-66	Tulsa Oilers	CHL	54	21	24	9	3240	166	4	2.07	....	....	....	....	....	....	....	....	....	....	....	....	....	....	....	....	....
	Toronto Maple Leafs	**NHL**	**10**	**5**	**2**	**3**	**501**	**21**	**4**	**2.51**	**2.54**	....	....	....	....	....	....	....	....	....	....	....	....	....	....	....	....
1966-67	**Toronto Maple Leafs**	**NHL**	**23**	**5**	**10**	**4**	**1185**	**67**	**0**	**3.39**	**3.53**	....	....	....	....	....	....	....	....	....	....	....	....	....	....	....	....
	Tulsa Oilers	CHL	7	2	4	1	420	24	0	3.43	....	....	....	....	....	....	....	....	....	....	....	....	....	....	....	....	....
	Rochester Americans	AHL	5	2	3	0	300	25	0	5.00	....	....	....	....	....	1	0	0	0	40	4	0	6.00	....	....	....	....
1967-68	**Toronto Maple Leafs**	**NHL**	**41**	**19**	**13**	**3**	**2201**	**85**	**5**	**2.32**	**2.66**	....	....	....	....	....	....	....	....	....	....	....	....	....	....	....	....
1968-69	**Toronto Maple Leafs**	**NHL**	**61**	**28**	**20**	**11**	**3446**	**161**	**3**	**2.80**	**2.89**	....	....	....	....	**3**	**0**	**2**	....	**86**	**13**	**0**	**9.07**	....	....	....	....
1969-70	**Toronto Maple Leafs**	**NHL**	**52**	**19**	**24**	**9**	**3057**	**156**	**5**	**3.06**	**3.26**	....	....	....	....	....	....	....	....	....	....	....	....	....	....	....	....

			REGULAR SEASON													PLAYOFFS											
Season	Club	League	GP	W	L	T	Mins	GA	SO	Avg	AAvg	Eff	SA	S%	SAPG	GP	W	L	T	Mins	GA	SO	Avg	Eff	SA	S%	SAPG
1970-71	**Toronto Maple Leafs**	**NHL**	**23**	**6**	**14**	**1**	**1286**	**83**	**2**	**3.87**	**3.84**	....	....	....	....	....	....	....	....	....	....	....	....	....	....	....	....
	Philadelphia Flyers	**NHL**	**11**	**3**	**6**	**2**	**660**	**37**	**0**	**3.36**	**3.32**	....	....	....	....	**2**	**0**	**2**	....	**120**	**12**	**0**	**6.00**	....	....	....	....
1971-72	**Philadelphia Flyers**	**NHL**	**24**	**7**	**8**	**2**	**1186**	**58**	**2**	**2.93**	**2.95**	....	....	....	....	....	....	....	....	....	....	....	....	....	....	....	....
	NHL Totals		**327**	**110**	**150**	**46**	**18442**	**992**	**22**	**3.23**	....	....	....	....	....	**5**	**0**	**4**	....	**206**	**25**	**0**	**7.28**	....	....	....	....

WHL Coast Division Second All-Star Team (1959) • Won WHL Coast Division Rookie of the Year Award (1959)

Played in NHL All-Star Game (1968)

Claimed by **Boston** from **NY Rangers** in Intra-League Draft, June, 1959. Traded to **Springfield** (AHL) by **Boston** with Terry Gray, Randy Miller and Dale Rolfe for Bob McCord, June, 1963. Traded to **Toronto** by **Springfield** (AHL) for Larry Johnston and Bill Smith, September, 1965. Traded to **Philadelphia** by **Toronto** with Mike Walton and Toronto's 1st round choice (Pierre Plante) in 1971 Amateur Draft for Bernie Parent and Philadelphia's 2nd round choice (Rick Kehoe) in 1971 Amateur Draft, February 1, 1971. • Suffered career-ending heart attack during game vs. Vancouver, February 9, 1972.

• GAMBLE, TROY

Troy Gamble G – L. 5′11″, 195 lbs. b: New Glasgow, N.S., 4/7/1967. Vancouver's 2nd choice, 25th overall, in 1985 Entry Draft.

Season	Club	League	GP	W	L	T	Mins	GA	SO	Avg	AAvg	Eff	SA	S%	SAPG	GP	W	L	T	Mins	GA	SO	Avg	Eff	SA	S%	SAPG
1984-85	Medicine Hat Tigers	WHL	37	27	6	2	2095	100	*3	*2.86	....	....	....	....	....	2	1	1	0	120	9	0	4.50	....	....	....	....
1985-86	Medicine Hat Tigers	WHL	45	28	11	0	2264	142	0	3.76	....	....	....	....	....	11	5	4	0	530	31	0	3.51	....	....	....	....
1986-87	**Vancouver Canucks**	**NHL**	**1**	**0**	**1**	**0**	**60**	**4**	**0**	**4.00**	**3.36**	**6.96**	**23**	**.826**	**23.0**	....	....	....	....	....	....	....	....	....	....	....	....
	Medicine Hat Tigers	WHL	11	7	3	0	646	46	0	4.27	....	....	....	....	....	....	....	....	....	....	....	....	....	....	....	....	....
	Spokane Chiefs	WHL	38	17	17	1	2155	163	0	4.54	....	....	....	....	....	5	0	5	0	298	35	0	7.05	....	....	....	....
1987-88	Spokane Chiefs	WHL	67	36	26	1	3824	235	0	3.69	....	....	....	....	....	15	7	8	0	875	56	1	3.84	....	....	....	....
1988-89	**Vancouver Canucks**	**NHL**	**5**	**2**	**3**	**0**	**302**	**12**	**0**	**2.38**	**1.96**	**2.04**	**140**	**.914**	**27.8**	....	....	....	....	....	....	....	....	....	....	....	....
	Milwaukee Admirals	IHL	42	23	9	0	2198	138	0	3.77	....	....	....	....	....	11	5	5	0	640	35	0	3.28	....	....	....	....
1989-90	Milwaukee Admirals	IHL	*56	22	21	4	2779	160	2	4.21	....	....	....	....	....	5	2	2	0	216	19	0	5.28	....	....	....	....
1990-91	**Vancouver Canucks**	**NHL**	**47**	**16**	**16**	**6**	**2433**	**140**	**1**	**3.45**	**3.08**	**4.18**	**1156**	**.879**	**28.5**	**4**	**1**	**3**	....	**249**	**16**	**0**	**3.86**	**4.64**	**133**	**.880**	**32.0**
1991-92	**Vancouver Canucks**	**NHL**	**19**	**4**	**9**	**3**	**1009**	**73**	**0**	**4.34**	**3.86**	**6.12**	**518**	**.859**	**30.8**	....	....	....	....	....	....	....	....	....	....	....	....
	Milwaukee Admirals	IHL	9	2	4	2	521	31	0	3.57	....	....	....	....	....	....	....	....	....	....	....	....	....	....	....	....	....
1992-93	Hamilton Canucks	AHL	14	1	10	2	769	62	0	4.84	....	....	....	....	....	....	....	....	....	....	....	....	....	....	....	....	....
	Cincinnati Cyclones	IHL	33	11	18	2	1762	134	0	4.56	....	....	....	....	....	....	....	....	....	....	....	....	....	....	....	....	....
1993-94	Kalamazoo Wings	IHL	48	25	13	5	2607	146	*2	3.36	....	....	....	....	....	2	0	1	0	80	7	0	5.25	....	....	....	....
1994-95	Houston Aeros	IHL	43	18	17	5	2421	132	1	3.27	....	....	....	....	....	4	1	3	0	203	16	0	4.72	....	....	....	....
1995-96	Houston Aeros	IHL	52	16	25	5	2722	174	0	3.83	....	....	....	....	....	....	....	....	....	....	....	....	....	....	....	....	....
	NHL Totals		**72**	**22**	**29**	**9**	**3804**	**229**	**1**	**3.61**	....	....	**1837**	**.875**	....	**4**	**1**	**3**	....	**249**	**16**	**0**	**3.86**	....	....	....	....

WHL East First All-Star Team (1985) • WHL West First All-Star Team (1988)

Signed as a free agent by **Dallas**, August 28, 1993.

• GARDINER, BERT

Bert Gardiner G – L. 5′11″, 160 lbs. b: Saskatoon, Sask., 3/25/1913.

Season	Club	League	GP	W	L	T	Mins	GA	SO	Avg	AAvg	Eff	SA	S%	SAPG	GP	W	L	T	Mins	GA	SO	Avg	Eff	SA	S%	SAPG
1931-32	Calgary K of C	City Jr.	2	2	0	0	120	2	0	*1.00	....	....	....	....	....	3	3	0	0	180	1	*2	*0.33	....	....	....	....
1932-33	Calgary K of C	City Jr.	2	2	0	0	120	2	0	1.00	....	....	....	....	....	....	....	....	....	....	....	....	....	....	....	....	....
1933-34	Saskatoon Quakers	SSHL	14	6	7	1	910	53	0	3.49	....	....	....	....	....	4	3	1	0	240	8	1	2.00	....	....	....	....
1934-35	Brooklyn Crescents	EHL	21	*15	5	1	1260	35	*6	*1.67	....	....	....	....	....	8	*7	1	0	560	13	*1	*1.39	....	....	....	....
1935-36	**New York Rangers**	**NHL**	**1**	**1**	**0**	**0**	**60**	**1**	**0**	**1.00**	**1.42**	....	....	....	....	....	....	....	....	....	....	....	....	....	....	....	....
	Philadelphia Arrows	Can-Am	45	26	16	3	2760	94	5	*2.04	....	....	....	....	....	4	3	1	0	265	4	*1	0.91	....	....	....	....
1936-37	Philadelphia Ramblers	AHL	47	26	13	8	2900	105	4	*2.17	....	....	....	....	....	6	3	3	0	360	15	*2	2.50	....	....	....	....
1937-38	Philadelphia Ramblers	AHL	*48	*26	18	4	*2950	126	*8	2.56	....	....	....	....	....	5	3	2	0	369	10	*2	*1.63	....	....	....	....
1938-39	Philadelphia Ramblers	AHL	52	*32	16	4	3230	150	2	2.79	....	....	....	....	....	5	3	2	0	335	11	0	1.97	....	....	....	....
	New York Rangers	**NHL**	....	....	....	....	....	....	....	....	....	....	....	....	....	**6**	**3**	**3**	....	**433**	**12**	**0**	**1.66**	....	....	....	....
1939-40	Philadelphia Rockets	AHL	54	15	31	8	3350	170	4	3.04	....	....	....	....	....	....	....	....	....	....	....	....	....	....	....	....	....
	New Haven Eagles	AHL	3	3	0	0	180	4	1	1.67	....	....	....	....	....	....	....	....	....	....	....	....	....	....	....	....	....
1940-41	**Montreal Canadiens**	**NHL**	**42**	**13**	**23**	**6**	**2600**	**119**	**2**	**2.75**	**3.18**	....	....	....	....	**3**	**1**	**2**	....	**214**	**8**	**0**	**2.24**	....	....	....	....
1941-42	**Montreal Canadiens**	**NHL**	**10**	**1**	**8**	**1**	**620**	**42**	**0**	**4.06**	**4.06**	....	....	....	....	....	....	....	....	....	....	....	....	....	....	....	....
	Washington Lions	AHL	34	12	19	3	2080	99	4	2.86	....	....	....	....	....	2	0	2	0	120	7	0	3.50	....	....	....	....
1942-43	**Chicago Black Hawks**	**NHL**	***50**	**17**	**18**	**15**	***3020**	**180**	**1**	**3.58**	**3.04**	....	....	....	....	....	....	....	....	....	....	....	....	....	....	....	....
1943-44	**Boston Bruins**	**NHL**	**41**	**17**	**19**	**5**	**2460**	**212**	**1**	**5.17**	**4.08**	....	....	....	....	....	....	....	....	....	....	....	....	....	....	....	....
	NHL Totals		**144**	**49**	**68**	**27**	**8760**	**554**	**4**	**3.79**	....	....	....	....	....	**9**	**4**	**5**	....	**647**	**20**	**0**	**1.85**	....	....	....	....

EHL First All-Star Team (1935) • Won George L. Davis Jr. Trophy (fewest goals against - EHL) (1935) • Can-Am First All-Star Team (1936) • AHL First All-Star Team (1939) • AHL Second All-Star Team (1940)

Traded to **Montreal** by **NY Rangers** with cash for Claude Bourque, April 26, 1940. Traded to **Chicago** by **Montreal** for cash with Montreal holding rights of repurchase (exercised), October 14, 1942. Traded to **Boston** by **Montreal** for cash with Montreal holding rights of repurchase, October 30, 1943.

• GARDINER, CHUCK

Chuck (Charles) Gardiner G – R. 176 lbs. b: Edinburgh, Scotland, 12/31/1904. d: 6/13/1934. **HHOF**

Season	Club	League	GP	W	L	T	Mins	GA	SO	Avg	AAvg	Eff	SA	S%	SAPG	GP	W	L	T	Mins	GA	SO	Avg	Eff	SA	S%	SAPG
1923-24	Winnipeg Tigers	MHL Jr.	1	1	0	0	60	0	0	0.00	....	....	....	....	....	....	....	....	....	....	....	....	....	....	....	....	....
1924-25	Selkirk Fishermen	Wpg-Sr.	18	....	....	....	1080	33	2	1.83	....	....	....	....	....	2	0	2	0	120	6	0	3.00	....	....	....	....
1925-26	Winnipeg Maroons	USAHA	38	....	....	....	2280	82	6	2.16	....	....	....	....	....	5	....	....	....	300	10	1	2.00	....	....	....	....
1926-27	Winnipeg Maroons	AHA	36	17	14	5	2203	77	6	2.14	....	....	....	....	....	3	0	3	0	180	8	0	2.67	....	....	....	....
1927-28	**Chicago Black Hawks**	**NHL**	**40**	**6**	**32**	**2**	**2420**	**114**	**3**	**2.83**	**4.83**	....	....	....	....	....	....	....	....	....	....	....	....	....	....	....	....
1928-29	**Chicago Black Hawks**	**NHL**	***44**	**7**	**29**	**8**	**2758**	**85**	**5**	**1.85**	**4.06**	....	....	....	....	....	....	....	....	....	....	....	....	....	....	....	....
1929-30	**Chicago Black Hawks**	**NHL**	***44**	**21**	**18**	**5**	**2750**	**111**	**3**	**2.42**	**2.48**	....	....	....	....	**2**	**0**	**1**	**1**	**172**	**3**	**0**	**1.05**	....	....	....	....
1930-31	**Chicago Black Hawks**	**NHL**	***44**	**24**	**17**	**3**	**2710**	**78**	***12**	**1.73**	**2.16**	....	....	....	....	**9**	**5**	**3**	**1**	**638**	**14**	***2**	**1.32**	....	....	....	....
1931-32	**Chicago Black Hawks**	**NHL**	***48**	**18**	**19**	**11**	**2989**	**92**	**4**	***1.85**	**2.19**	....	....	....	....	**2**	**1**	**1**	**0**	**120**	**6**	***1**	**3.00**	....	....	....	....
1932-33	**Chicago Black Hawks**	**NHL**	***48**	**16**	**20**	**12**	***3010**	**101**	**5**	**2.01**	**2.69**	....	....	....	....	....	....	....	....	....	....	....	....	....	....	....	....
1933-34	**Chicago Black Hawks**	**NHL**	***48**	**20**	**17**	**11**	**3050**	**83**	***10**	**1.63**	**2.00**	....	....	....	....	**8**	***6**	**1**	**1**	**542**	**12**	***2**	***1.33**	....	....	....	....
	NHL Totals		**316**	**112**	**152**	**52**	**19687**	**664**	**42**	**2.02**	....	....	....	....	....	**21**	**12**	**6**	**3**	**1472**	**35**	**5**	**1.43**	....	....	....	....

NHL First All-Star Team (1931, 1932, 1934) • Won Vezina Trophy (1932, 1934) • NHL Second All-Star Team (1933)

Played in NHL All-Star Game (1934)

• GARDNER, GEORGE

George Gardner G – L. 5′8″, 165 lbs. b: Lachine, Que., 10/8/1942.

Season	Club	League	GP	W	L	T	Mins	GA	SO	Avg	AAvg	Eff	SA	S%	SAPG	GP	W	L	T	Mins	GA	SO	Avg	Eff	SA	S%	SAPG
1961-62	Victoriaville Bruins	QJHL	STATISTICS NOT AVAILABLE																								
1962-63	Niagara Falls Flyers	OHA	50	....	....	....	3000	146	3	2.92	....	....	....	....	....	24	....	....	....	1440	71	1	2.96	....	....	....	....
1963-64	Minneapolis Bruins	CHL	63	30	27	6	3780	235	1	3.63	....	....	....	....	....	5	1	4	0	300	21	0	4.20	....	....	....	....
1964-65	Memphis Wings	CHL	66	25	32	9	3960	229	1	3.47	....	....	....	....	....	....	....	....	....	....	....	....	....	....	....	....	....
1965-66	Pittsburgh Hornets	AHL	*66	34	30	1	*3932	196	*7	2.99	....	....	....	....	....	3	0	3	0	180	14	0	4.67	....	....	....	....
	Detroit Red Wings	**NHL**	**1**	**1**	**0**	**0**	**60**	**1**	**0**	**1.00**	**1.01**	....	....	....	....	....	....	....	....	....	....	....	....	....	....	....	....
1966-67	Pittsburgh Hornets	AHL	28	18	6	4	1680	76	2	*2.71	....	....	....	....	....	....	....	....	....	....	....	....	....	....	....	....	....
	Detroit Red Wings	**NHL**	**11**	**3**	**6**	**0**	**560**	**36**	**0**	**3.86**	**4.02**	....	....	....	....	....	....	....	....	....	....	....	....	....	....	....	....
	Memphis Wings	CHL	16	4	9	3	960	72	0	4.50	....	....	....	....	....	....	....	....	....	....	....	....	....	....	....	....	....
1967-68	**Detroit Red Wings**	**NHL**	**12**	**3**	**2**	**2**	**534**	**32**	**0**	**3.60**	**4.00**	....	....	....	....	....	....	....	....	....	....	....	....	....	....	....	....
	Fort Worth Wings	CHL	12	4	7	0	680	39	0	3.44	....	....	....	....	....	....	....	....	....	....	....	....	....	....	....	....	....
1968-69	Vancouver Canucks	WHL	*53	*25	18	9	*3073	154	2	3.01	....	....	....	....	....	....	....	....	....	....	....	....	....	....	....	....	....
1969-70	Vancouver Canucks	WHL	*62	*41	14	6	*3556	171	3	*2.89	....	....	....	....	....	*11	*8	3	0	*664	35	0	3.16	....	....	....	....
1970-71	Rochester Americans	AHL	4	0	1	3	240	13	0	3.25	....	....	....	....	....	....	....	....	....	....	....	....	....	....	....	....	....
	Vancouver Canucks	**NHL**	**18**	**6**	**8**	**1**	**922**	**52**	**0**	**3.38**	**3.35**	....	....	....	....	....	....	....	....	....	....	....	....	....	....	....	....
1971-72	**Vancouver Canucks**	**NHL**	**24**	**3**	**14**	**3**	**1237**	**86**	**0**	**4.17**	**4.23**	....	....	....	....	....	....	....	....	....	....	....	....	....	....	....	....
1972-73	Los Angeles Sharks	WHA	49	19	22	4	2713	149	1	3.30	....	....	....	....	....	3	1	2	0	116	11	0	5.69	....	....	....	....

			REGULAR SEASON													PLAYOFFS											
Season	Club	League	GP	W	L	T	Mins	GA	SO	Avg	AAvg	Eff	SA	S%	SAPG	GP	W	L	T	Mins	GA	SO	Avg	Eff	SA	S%	SAPG
1973-74	Los Angeles Sharks	WHA	2	0	2	0	120	13	0	6.50	....	....	....	....	....	....	....	....	....	....	....	....	....	....	....	....	....
	Vancouver Blazers	WHA	28	4	21	0	1590	125	0	4.72	....	....	....	....	....	....	....	....	....	....	....	....	....	....	....	....	....
	Roanoke Valley Rebels	SHL	4	....	....	....	245	18	0	4.41	....	....	....	....	....	....	....	....	....	....	....	....	....	....	....	....	....
	NHL Totals		**66**	**16**	**30**	**6**	**3313**	**207**	**0**	**3.75**	....	....	....	....	....	....	....	....	....	....	....	....	....	....	....	....	....
	Other Major League Totals		79	23	45	4	4423	287	1	3.89	....	....	....	....	....	3	1	2	0	116	11	0	5.69	....	....	....	....

AHL Second All-Star Team (1966) • WHL Second All-Star Team (1970) • Won WHL Leading Goaltender Award (1970)

Claimed by **Detroit** from **Boston** in Intra-League Draft, June 10, 1964. Claimed by **Vancouver** (Rochester - AHL) from **Detroit** in Reverse Draft, June 13, 1968. Selected by **LA Sharks** (WHA) in 1972 WHA General Player Draft, February 12, 1972. Traded to **Vancouver** (WHA) by **LA Sharks** (WHA) with Ralph MacSweyn for Ron Ward, October, 1973.

• GARRETT, JOHN

John Garrett G – L. 5'8", 175 lbs. b: Trenton, Ont., 6/17/1951. St. Louis' 2nd choice, 38th overall, in 1971 Amateur Draft.

			REGULAR SEASON													PLAYOFFS											
Season	Club	League	GP	W	L	T	Mins	GA	SO	Avg	AAvg	Eff	SA	S%	SAPG	GP	W	L	T	Mins	GA	SO	Avg	Eff	SA	S%	SAPG
1969-70	Peterborough Petes	OHA	48	....	....	....	2850	142	*3	*2.99	....	....	....	....	....	....	....	....	....	....	....	....	....	....	....	....	....
1970-71	Peterborough Petes	OHA	51	....	....	....	3062	151	5	*2.96	....	....	....	....	....	....	....	....	....	....	....	....	....	....	....	....	....
1971-72	Kansas City Blues	CHL	35	13	14	7	2041	121	*3	3.55	....	....	....	....	....	....	....	....	....	....	....	....	....	....	....	....	....
1972-73	Portland Buckaroos	WHL	17	6	8	2	951	52	2	3.28	....	....	....	....	....	....	....	....	....	....	....	....	....	....	....	....	....
	Richmond Robins	AHL	37	....	....	....	2138	117	0	3.26	....	....	....	....	....	3	0	3	0	123	17	0	8.29	....	....	....	....
1973-74	Minnesota Fighting Saints	WHA	40	21	18	0	2290	137	1	3.59	....	....	....	....	....	7	4	2	0	372	25	0	4.03	....	....	....	....
1974-75	Minnesota Fighting Saints	WHA	58	30	23	2	3294	180	2	3.28	....	....	....	....	....	12	6	6	0	726	41	1	3.39	....	....	....	....
1975-76	Minnesota Fighting Saints	WHA	52	26	22	4	3179	177	2	3.34	....	....	....	....	....	....	....	....	....	....	....	....	....	....	....	....	....
	Toronto Toros	WHA	9	3	6	0	551	33	1	3.59	....	....	....	....	....	....	....	....	....	....	....	....	....	....	....	....	....
1976-77	Birmingham Bulls	WHA	65	24	34	4	3803	224	*4	3.53	....	....	....	....	....	....	....	....	....	....	....	....	....	....	....	....	....
1977-78	Birmingham Bulls	WHA	*58	24	31	1	3306	210	2	3.81	....	....	....	....	....	5	1	4	0	271	26	0	5.76	....	....	....	....
1978-79	New England Whalers	WHA	41	20	17	4	2496	149	2	3.58	....	....	....	....	....	8	4	3	0	447	32	0	4.30	....	....	....	....
1979-80	**Hartford Whalers**	**NHL**	**52**	**16**	**24**	**11**	**3046**	**202**	**0**	**3.98**	**3.51**	....	....	....	....	**1**	**0**	**1**	....	**60**	**8**	**0**	**8.00**	....	....	....	....
1980-81	**Hartford Whalers**	**NHL**	**54**	**15**	**27**	**12**	**3152**	**241**	**0**	**4.59**	**3.70**	....	....	....	....	....	....	....	....	....	....	....	....	....	....	....	....
	Canada	WEC-A	3	....	....	....	120	8	....	4.00	....	....	....	....	....	....	....	....	....	....	....	....	....	....	....	....	....
1981-82	**Hartford Whalers**	**NHL**	**16**	**5**	**6**	**4**	**898**	**63**	**0**	**4.21**	**3.25**	....	....	....	....	....	....	....	....	....	....	....	....	....	....	....	....
	Quebec Nordiques	**NHL**	**12**	**4**	**5**	**3**	**720**	**62**	**0**	**5.17**	**3.99**	....	....	....	....	**5**	**3**	**2**	....	**323**	**21**	**0**	**3.90**	....	....	....	....
1982-83	**Quebec Nordiques**	**NHL**	**17**	**6**	**8**	**2**	**953**	**64**	**0**	**4.03**	**3.22**	**5.09**	**507**	**.874**	**31.9**	....	....	....	....	....	....	....	....	....	....	....	....
	Vancouver Canucks	**NHL**	**17**	**7**	**6**	**3**	**934**	**48**	**1**	**3.08**	**2.45**	**2.92**	**506**	**.905**	**32.5**	**1**	**1**	**0**	....	**60**	**4**	**0**	**4.00**	....	....	....	....
1983-84	**Vancouver Canucks**	**NHL**	**29**	**14**	**10**	**2**	**1653**	**113**	**0**	**4.10**	**3.21**	**6.11**	**758**	**.851**	**27.5**	**2**	**0**	**0**	....	**18**	**0**	**0**	**0.00**	**0.00**	**5**	**1.000**	**16.7**
1984-85	**Vancouver Canucks**	**NHL**	**10**	**1**	**5**	**0**	**407**	**44**	**0**	**6.49**	**5.17**	**11.75**	**243**	**.819**	**35.8**	....	....	....	....	....	....	....	....	....	....	....	....
1985-86	Fredericton Express	AHL	3	2	1	0	179	9	0	3.02	....	....	....	....	....	....	....	....	....	....	....	....	....	....	....	....	....
	NHL Totals		**207**	**68**	**91**	**37**	**11763**	**837**	**1**	**4.27**	....	....	....	....	....	**9**	**4**	**3**	....	**461**	**33**	**0**	**4.30**	....	....	....	....
	Other Major League Totals		323	148	151	15	18919	1110	14	3.52	....	....	....	....	....	32	15	15	0	1816	124	1	4.10	....	....	....	....

OHA Second All-Star Team (1970) • OHA First All-Star Team (1971) • WHA First All-Star Team (1977)

Played in NHL All-Star Game (1983)

Rights traded to **Chicago** by **St. Louis** for Christian Bordeleau, September 19, 1972. Selected by **Minnesota** (WHA) in 1973 WHA Professional Player Draft, June, 1973. Signed as a free agent by **Toronto** (WHA) after **Minnesota** (WHA) franchise folded, March, 1976. Transferred to **Birmingham** (WHA) after **Toronto** (WHA) franchise relocated, June 30, 1976. Traded to **New England** (WHA) by **Birmingham** (WHA) for future considerations, September, 1978. Reclaimed by **Chicago** from **Hartford** prior to Expansion Draft, June 9, 1979. Claimed by **Hartford** as a priority selection, June 9, 1979. Traded to **Quebec** by **Hartford** for Michel Plasse and Quebec's 4th round choice (Ron Chyzowski) in 1983 Entry Draft, January 12, 1982. Traded to **Vancouver** by **Quebec** for Anders Eldebrink, February 4, 1983.

• GATHERUM, DAVE

Dave Gatherum G – L. 5'8", 170 lbs. b: Fort William, Ont., 3/28/1932.

			REGULAR SEASON													PLAYOFFS											
Season	Club	League	GP	W	L	T	Mins	GA	SO	Avg	AAvg	Eff	SA	S%	SAPG	GP	W	L	T	Mins	GA	SO	Avg	Eff	SA	S%	SAPG
1948-49	Fort William Hurricanes	TBJHL	12	3	8	1	720	67	*1	5.58	....	....	....	....	....	1	0	1	0	60	8	0	8.00	....	....	....	....
1949-50	Fort William Hurricanes	TBJHL	17	10	6	1	1020	82	0	4.24	....	....	....	....	....	5	....	....	....	300	17	*1	3.40	....	....	....	....
1950-51	Fort William Hurricanes	TBJHL	21	11	10	0	1260	84	0	4.00	....	....	....	....	....	12	....	....	....	720	52	0	4.33	....	....	....	....
1951-52	Fort William Hurricanes	TBJHL	30	15	14	1	1800	128	0	4.27	....	....	....	....	....	12	0	5	0	760	36	0	2.84	....	....	....	....
1952-53	Shawinigan Cataracts	QSHL	30	6	21	3	1830	112	0	3.67	....	....	....	....	....	....	....	....	....	....	....	....	....	....	....	....	....
	Edmonton Flyers	WHL	6	3	1	2	360	14	0	2.30	....	....	....	....	....	....	....	....	....	....	....	....	....	....	....	....	....
	St. Louis Flyers	AHL	11	3	8	0	660	55	0	5.00	....	....	....	....	....	....	....	....	....	....	....	....	....	....	....	....	....
1953-54	Sherbrooke Saints	QHL	53	24	24	5	3240	176	4	3.26	....	....	....	....	....	4	1	3	0	240	13	0	3.25	....	....	....	....
	Detroit Red Wings	**NHL**	**3**	**2**	**0**	**1**	**180**	**3**	**1**	**1.00**	**1.28**	....	....	....	....	....	....	....	....	....	....	....	....	....	....	....	....
1954-55	Quebec Aces	QHL	20	9	10	0	1174	74	1	3.78	....	....	....	....	....	....	....	....	....	....	....	....	....	....	....	....	....
	Edmonton Flyers	WHL	4	1	2	1	240	15	0	3.75	....	....	....	....	....	....	....	....	....	....	....	....	....	....	....	....	....
	New Westminster Royals	WHL	4	1	1	2	240	10	0	2.50	....	....	....	....	....	....	....	....	....	....	....	....	....	....	....	....	....
1955-56	Kelowna Packers	OSHL	52	....	....	....	3120	221	1	4.20	....	....	....	....	....	....	....	....	....	....	....	....	....	....	....	....	....
	New Westminster Royals	WHL	7	1	6	0	422	32	0	4.55	....	....	....	....	....	....	....	....	....	....	....	....	....	....	....	....	....
1956-57	Kelowna Packers	OSHL	49	....	....	....	2940	213	1	4.34	....	....	....	....	....	7	2	5	0	420	30	0	4.29	....	....	....	....
1957-58	Kelowna Packers	OSHL	51	....	....	....	3060	183	0	*3.61	....	....	....	....	....	12	*8	3	1	720	32	1	*2.67	....	....	....	....
1958-59	Kelowna Packers	OSHL	53	....	....	....	3180	189	*2	*3.57	....	....	....	....	....	....	....	....	....	....	....	....	....	....	....	....	....
	NHL Totals		**3**	**2**	**0**	**1**	**180**	**3**	**1**	**1.00**	....	....	....	....	....	....	....	....	....	....	....	....	....	....	....	....	....

• GAUTHIER, PAUL

Paul Gauthier G – R. 5'5", 125 lbs. b: Winnipeg, Man., 3/6/1915.

			REGULAR SEASON													PLAYOFFS											
Season	Club	League	GP	W	L	T	Mins	GA	SO	Avg	AAvg	Eff	SA	S%	SAPG	GP	W	L	T	Mins	GA	SO	Avg	Eff	SA	S%	SAPG
1932-33	Winnipeg Monarchs	MJHL	1	1	0	0	60	1	0	1.00	....	....	....	....	....	....	....	....	....	....	....	....	....	....	....	....	....
1933-34	Winnipeg Monarchs	MJHL	STATISTICS NOT AVAILABLE																								
1934-35	Winnipeg Monarchs	MJHL	7	....	....	....	420	15	0	*2.14	....	....	....	....	....	4	4	0	0	240	12	0	3.00	....	....	....	....
1935-36	Montreal Canadiens	QSHL	1	0	1	0	30	3	0	6.00	....	....	....	....	....	....	....	....	....	....	....	....	....	....	....	....	....
	Pittsburgh Shamrocks	IAHL	16	....	....	....	960	56	0	3.50	....	....	....	....	....	....	....	....	....	....	....	....	....	....	....	....	....
1936-37	Minneapolis Millers	AHA	48	23	21	4	2880	105	6	2.19	....	....	....	....	....	6	*6	0	0	408	8	*1	*1.18	....	....	....	....
1937-38	New Haven Eagles	AHL	47	13	27	7	2910	126	5	2.60	....	....	....	....	....	1	0	1	0	60	2	0	2.00	....	....	....	....
	Montreal Canadiens	**NHL**	**1**	**0**	**0**	**1**	**70**	**2**	**0**	**1.71**	**2.08**	....	....	....	....	....	....	....	....	....	....	....	....	....	....	....	....
1938-39	Spokane Clippers	PCHL	34	....	....	....	2040	105	3	3.09	....	....	....	....	....	....	....	....	....	....	....	....	....	....	....	....	....
	New Haven Eagles	AHL	6	1	5	0	370	30	0	4.86	....	....	....	....	....	....	....	....	....	....	....	....	....	....	....	....	....
1939-40	Kansas City Greyhounds	AHA	47	20	27	0	2871	163	6	3.41	....	....	....	....	....	....	....	....	....	....	....	....	....	....	....	....	....
1940-41	Seattle Olympics	PCHL	41	....	....	....	2460	131	1	3.20	....	....	....	....	....	2	1	1	0	120	5	0	2.50	....	....	....	....
1941-42	Washington Lions	AHL	9	5	4	0	540	34	0	3.78	....	....	....	....	....	....	....	....	....	....	....	....	....	....	....	....	....
	New Haven Eagles	AHL	1	0	1	0	60	8	0	8.00	....	....	....	....	....	....	....	....	....	....	....	....	....	....	....	....	....
1942-43	Washington Lions	AHL	41	10	26	5	2460	203	0	4.95	....	....	....	....	....	....	....	....	....	....	....	....	....	....	....	....	....
1943-44	Buffalo Bisons	AHL	1	1	0	0	60	3	0	3.00	....	....	....	....	....	....	....	....	....	....	....	....	....	....	....	....	....
	Cleveland Barons	AHL	46	29	10	7	2760	139	4	3.02	....	....	....	....	....	4	1	3	0	240	25	0	6.25	....	....	....	....
1944-45	Cleveland Barons	AHL	4	3	0	1	240	15	0	3.75	....	....	....	....	....	....	....	....	....	....	....	....	....	....	....	....	....
1945-46	Petawawa Army	Ott-Sr.	STATISTICS NOT AVAILABLE																								
1946-47	Houston Huskies	USHL	16	4	10	2	960	69	1	4.31	....	....	....	....	....	....	....	....	....	....	....	....	....	....	....	....	....
	Philadelphia Rockets	AHL	1	0	1	0	60	9	0	9.00	....	....	....	....	....	....	....	....	....	....	....	....	....	....	....	....	....
	Buffalo Bisons	AHL	3	3	0	0	180	7	0	2.33	....	....	....	....	....	....	....	....	....	....	....	....	....	....	....	....	....
	San Francisco Shamrocks	PCHL	5	....	....	....	300	19	0	3.80	....	....	....	....	....	....	....	....	....	....	....	....	....	....	....	....	....
1947-48	Houston Huskies	USHL	27	16	9	1	1640	112	1	4.10	....	....	....	....	....	7	5	2	0	423	19	0	2.70	....	....	....	....
	Omaha Knights	USHL	5	1	3	1	310	29	0	5.61	....	....	....	....	....	....	....	....	....	....	....	....	....	....	....	....	....
1948-49	Washington Lions	AHL	13	1	9	0	716	72	0	6.03	....	....	....	....	....	....	....	....	....	....	....	....	....	....	....	....	....
	NHL Totals		**1**	**0**	**0**	**1**	**70**	**2**	**0**	**1.71**	....	....	....	....	....	....	....	....	....	....	....	....	....	....	....	....	....

Loaned to **Montreal Canadiens** by **New Haven** (AHL) to replace injured Wilf Cude, January 13, 1938. (Montreal Canadiens 2, Chicago 2)

• GELINEAU, JACK

Jack Gelineau G – L. 6', 180 lbs. b: Toronto, Ont., 11/11/1924.

			REGULAR SEASON													PLAYOFFS											
Season	Club	League	GP	W	L	T	Mins	GA	SO	Avg	AAvg	Eff	SA	S%	SAPG	GP	W	L	T	Mins	GA	SO	Avg	Eff	SA	S%	SAPG
1943-44	Toronto Young Rangers	OHA	11	....	....	....	660	58	1	5.27	....	....	....	....	....	....	....	....	....	....	....	....	....	....	....	....	....
1944-45	Montreal RCAF	City Sr.	8	....	....	....	480	24	0	3.00	....	....	....	....	....	5	....	....	....	300	28	0	5.60	....	....	....	....
	Montreal Royals	QJHL	5	2	3	0	300	19	3	3.80	....	....	....	....	....	9	2	7	0	528	43	0	4.96	....	....	....	....
1945-46	McGill University	OQAA	15	13	2	0	900	52	1	3.47	....	....	....	....	....	....	....	....	....	....	....	....	....	....	....	....	....
1946-47	McGill University	OQAA	16	10	5	1	960	46	1	2.01	....	....	....	....	....	....	....	....	....	....	....	....	....	....	....	....	....
1947-48	McGill University	OQAA	20	14	6	0	1200	62	1	3.10	....	....	....	....	....	....	....	....	....	....	....	....	....	....	....	....	....

Season	Club	League	REGULAR SEASON													PLAYOFFS											
			GP	W	L	T	Mins	GA	SO	Avg	AAvg	Eff	SA	S%	SAPG	GP	W	L	T	Mins	GA	SO	Avg	Eff	SA	S%	SAPG
1948-49	McGill University	OQAA	6	3	3	0	360	20	0	3.33	....	....	....	....	....	....	....	....	....	....	....	....	....	....	....	....	....
	Boston Bruins	**NHL**	**4**	**2**	**2**	**0**	**240**	**12**	**0**	**3.00**	**3.41**	....	....	....	....	....	....	....	....	....	....	....	....	....	....	....	....
1949-50	**Boston Bruins**	**NHL**	**67**	**22**	**30**	**15**	**4020**	**220**	**3**	**3.28**	**3.85**	....	....	....	....	....	....	....	....	....	....	....	....	....	....	....	....
1950-51	**Boston Bruins**	**NHL**	***70**	**22**	**30**	**18**	***4200**	**197**	**4**	**2.81**	**3.22**	....	....	....	....	**4**	**1**	**2**	....	**260**	**7**	**1**	**1.62**	....	....	....	....
1951-52	Quebec Aces	QSHL	12	6	4	2	740	42	0	3.41	....	....	....	....	....	12	8	4	0	739	28	1	2.27	....	....	....	....
1952-53	Quebec Aces	QSHL	21	8	9	4	1300	59	1	2.72	....	....	....	....	....	21	*13	8	0	1303	51	1	*2.35	....	....	....	....
1953-54	Quebec Aces	QHL	57	24	27	6	3466	158	5	2.74	....	....	....	....	....	17	10	7	0	1059	40	4	2.27	....	....	....	....
	Chicago Black Hawks	**NHL**	**2**	**0**	**2**	**0**	**120**	**18**	**0**	**9.00**	**11.71**	....	....	....	....	....	....	....	....	....	....	....	....	....	....	....	....
1954-55	Quebec Aces	QHL	11	4	7	0	640	38	1	3.56	....	....	....	....	....	4	1	3	0	240	14	0	3.50	....	....	....	....
	NHL Totals		**143**	**46**	**64**	**33**	**8580**	**447**	**7**	**3.13**	....	....	....	....	....	**4**	**1**	**2**	....	**260**	**7**	**1**	**1.62**	....	....	....	....

Won Calder Memorial Trophy (1950)
Traded to **Chicago** by **Boston** for cash, November 28, 1953.

● GIACOMIN, ED

Ed Giacomin G – L. 5′11″, 180 lbs. b: Sudbury, Ont., 6/6/1939. **HHOF**

1958-59	Sudbury Bell Telephone	Sr.	STATISTICS NOT AVAILABLE																								
	Washington–Clinton	EHL	4	....	....	....	240	13	0	3.25	....	....	....	....	....	....	....	....	....	....	....	....	....	....	....	....	....
1959-60	Clinton–NY Rovers	EHL	51	....	....	....	3060	206	3	4.04	....	....	....	....	....	....	....	....	....	....	....	....	....	....	....	....	....
	Providence Reds	AHL	1	1	0	0	60	4	0	4.00	....	....	....	....	....	....	....	....	....	....	....	....	....	....	....	....	....
1960-61	Providence Reds	AHL	43	17	24	0	2510	183	0	4.37	....	....	....	....	....	....	....	....	....	....	....	....	....	....	....	....	....
1961-62	Providence Reds	AHL	40	20	19	1	2400	144	2	3.60	....	....	....	....	....	....	....	....	....	....	....	....	....	....	....	....	....
	New York Rovers	EHL	12	....	....	....	720	54	0	4.50	....	....	....	....	....	....	....	....	....	....	....	....	....	....	....	....	....
1962-63	Providence Reds	AHL	39	22	14	2	2340	102	4	*2.62	....	....	....	....	....	6	2	4	0	359	31	0	5.18	....	....	....	....
1963-64	Providence Reds	AHL	*69	30	34	5	*4140	232	*6	3.37	....	....	....	....	....	3	1	2	0	120	12	0	4.00	....	....	....	....
1964-65	Providence Reds	AHL	59	19	38	2	3527	226	0	3.84	....	....	....	....	....	....	....	....	....	....	....	....	....	....	....	....	....
1965-66	**New York Rangers**	**NHL**	**36**	**8**	**19**	**7**	**2096**	**128**	**0**	**3.66**	**3.78**	....	....	....	....	....	....	....	....	....	....	....	....	....	....	....	....
	Baltimore Clippers	AHL	7	3	4	0	420	21	0	3.00	....	....	....	....	....	....	....	....	....	....	....	....	....	....	....	....	....
1966-67	**New York Rangers**	**NHL**	***68**	***30**	**27**	**11**	***3981**	**173**	***9**	**2.61**	**2.64**	....	....	....	....	**4**	**0**	**4**	....	**246**	**14**	**0**	**3.41**	....	....	....	....
1967-68	**New York Rangers**	**NHL**	***66**	***36**	**20**	**10**	***3940**	**160**	***8**	**2.44**	**2.67**	....	....	....	....	**6**	**2**	**4**	....	**360**	**18**	**0**	**3.00**	....	....	....	....
1968-69	**New York Rangers**	**NHL**	***70**	***37**	**23**	**7**	***4114**	**175**	**7**	**2.55**	**2.61**	....	....	....	....	**3**	**0**	**3**	....	**180**	**10**	**0**	**3.33**	....	....	....	....
1969-70	**New York Rangers**	**NHL**	***70**	**35**	**21**	**14**	***4148**	**163**	**6**	**2.36**	**2.47**	....	....	....	....	**5**	**2**	**3**	....	**276**	**19**	**0**	**4.13**	....	....	....	....
1970-71	**New York Rangers**	**NHL**	**45**	**27**	**10**	**7**	**2641**	**95**	***8**	**2.16**	**2.11**	....	....	....	....	**12**	**7**	**5**	....	**759**	**28**	**0**	**2.21**	....	....	....	....
1971-72	**New York Rangers**	**NHL**	**44**	**24**	**10**	**9**	**2551**	**115**	**1**	**2.70**	**2.71**	....	....	....	....	***10**	***6**	**4**	....	***600**	**27**	**0**	**2.70**	....	....	....	....
1972-73	**New York Rangers**	**NHL**	**43**	**26**	**11**	**6**	**2580**	**125**	**4**	**2.91**	**2.73**	....	....	....	....	**10**	**5**	**4**	....	**539**	**23**	**1**	**2.56**	....	....	....	....
1973-74	**New York Rangers**	**NHL**	**56**	**30**	**15**	**10**	**3286**	**168**	**5**	**3.07**	**2.96**	....	....	....	....	**13**	**7**	**6**	....	**788**	**37**	**0**	**2.82**	....	....	....	....
1974-75	**New York Rangers**	**NHL**	**37**	**13**	**12**	**8**	**2069**	**120**	**1**	**3.48**	**3.14**	....	....	....	....	**2**	**0**	**2**	....	**86**	**4**	**0**	**2.79**	....	....	....	....
1975-76	**New York Rangers**	**NHL**	**4**	**0**	**3**	**1**	**240**	**19**	**0**	**4.75**	**4.30**	....	....	....	....	....	....	....	....	....	....	....	....	....	....	....	....
	Detroit Red Wings	**NHL**	**29**	**12**	**14**	**3**	**1740**	**100**	**2**	**3.45**	**3.12**	....	....	....	....	....	....	....	....	....	....	....	....	....	....	....	....
1976-77	**Detroit Red Wings**	**NHL**	**33**	**8**	**18**	**3**	**1791**	**107**	**3**	**3.58**	**3.33**	....	....	....	....	....	....	....	....	....	....	....	....	....	....	....	....
1977-78	**Detroit Red Wings**	**NHL**	**9**	**3**	**5**	**1**	**516**	**27**	**0**	**3.14**	**2.94**	....	....	....	....	....	....	....	....	....	....	....	....	....	....	....	....
	NHL Totals		**610**	**289**	**208**	**97**	**35693**	**1675**	**54**	**2.82**	....	....	....	....	....	**65**	**29**	**35**	....	**3834**	**180**	**1**	**2.82**	....	....	....	....

NHL First All-Star Team (1967, 1971) • NHL Second All-Star Team (1968, 1969, 1970) • Shared Vezina Trophy with Gilles Villemure (1971)
Played in NHL All-Star Game (1967, 1968, 1969, 1970, 1971, 1973)
Traded to **NY Rangers** by **Providence** (AHL) for Marcel Paille, Aldo Guidolin, Don McGregor and Jim Mikol, May 18, 1965. Claimed on waivers by **Detroit** from **NY Rangers**, October 31, 1975.

● GIGUERE, JEAN-SEBASTIEN

Jean-Sebastien Giguere G – L. 6′, 175 lbs. b: Montreal, Que., 5/16/1977. Hartford's 1st choice, 13th overall, in 1995 Entry Draft.

1993-94	Verdun College-Francais	QMJHL	25	13	5	2	1234	66	1	3.21	....	....	....	....	....	....	....	....	....	....	....	....	....	....	....	....	....
1994-95	Halifax Mooseheads	QMJHL	47	14	27	5	2755	181	2	3.94	....	....	....	....	....	7	3	4	....	417	17	1	*2.45	....	....	....	....
1995-96	Halifax Mooseheads	QMJHL	55	26	23	2	3230	185	1	3.44	....	....	....	....	....	6	1	5	....	354	24	0	4.07	....	....	....	....
1996-97	**Hartford Whalers**	**NHL**	**8**	**1**	**4**	**0**	**394**	**24**	**0**	**3.65**	**3.87**	**4.36**	**201**	**.881**	**30.6**	....	....	....	....	....	....	....	....	....	....	....	....
	Halifax Mooseheads	QMJHL	50	28	19	3	3014	170	2	3.38	....	....	....	....	....	16	9	7	....	954	58	0	3.65	....	....	....	....
1997-98	Saint John Flames	AHL	31	16	10	3	1758	72	2	2.46	....	....	....	....	....	10	5	3	....	536	27	0	3.02	....	....	....	....
	NHL Totals		**8**	**1**	**4**	**0**	**394**	**24**	**0**	**3.65**	....	....	**201**	**.881**	....	....	....	....	....	....	....	....	....	....	....	....	....

QMJHL Second All-Star Team (1997) • Shared Harry "Hap" Holmes Memorial Trophy (fewest goals against - AHL) with Tyler Moss (1998)
Transferred to **Carolina** after **Hartford** franchise relocated, June 25, 1997. Traded to **Calgary** by **Carolina** with Andrew Cassels for Gary Roberts and Trevor Kidd, August 25, 1997.

● GILBERT, GILLES

Gilles Gilbert G – L. 6′1″, 175 lbs. b: St. Esprit, Que., 3/31/1949. Minnesota's 3rd choice, 25th overall, in 1969 Amateur Draft.

1968-69	London Knights	OHA	37	....	....	....	2200	167	1	4.55	....	....	....	....	....	....	....	....	....	....	....	....	....	....	....	....	....
1969-70	Iowa Stars	CHL	39	17	16	5	2340	127	2	3.26	....	....	....	....	....	4	2	2	0	245	14	0	3.43	....	....	....	....
	Minnesota North Stars	**NHL**	**1**	**0**	**1**	**0**	**60**	**6**	**0**	**6.00**	**6.38**	....	....	....	....	....	....	....	....	....	....	....	....	....	....	....	....
1970-71	**Minnesota North Stars**	**NHL**	**17**	**5**	**9**	**2**	**931**	**59**	**0**	**3.80**	**3.77**	....	....	....	....	....	....	....	....	....	....	....	....	....	....	....	....
1971-72	**Minnesota North Stars**	**NHL**	**4**	**1**	**2**	**1**	**218**	**11**	**0**	**3.03**	**3.05**	....	....	....	....	....	....	....	....	....	....	....	....	....	....	....	....
	Cleveland Barons	AHL	41	20	15	5	2319	140	2	3.62	....	....	....	....	....	4	1	2	0	187	18	0	5.78	....	....	....	....
1972-73	**Minnesota North Stars**	**NHL**	**22**	**10**	**10**	**2**	**1320**	**67**	**2**	**3.05**	**2.87**	....	....	....	....	**1**	**0**	**1**	....	**60**	**4**	**0**	**4.00**	....	....	....	....
1973-74	**Boston Bruins**	**NHL**	**54**	**34**	**12**	**8**	**3210**	**158**	**6**	**2.95**	**2.84**	....	....	....	....	**16**	**10**	**6**	....	**977**	**43**	**1**	**2.64**	....	....	....	....
1974-75	**Boston Bruins**	**NHL**	**53**	**23**	**17**	**11**	**3029**	**158**	**3**	**3.13**	**2.81**	....	....	....	....	**3**	**1**	**2**	....	**188**	**12**	**0**	**3.83**	....	....	....	....
1975-76	**Boston Bruins**	**NHL**	**55**	**33**	**8**	**10**	**3123**	**151**	**3**	**2.90**	**2.61**	....	....	....	....	**6**	**3**	**3**	....	**360**	**19**	***2**	**3.17**	....	....	....	....
1976-77	**Boston Bruins**	**NHL**	**34**	**18**	**13**	**3**	**2040**	**97**	**1**	**2.85**	**2.64**	....	....	....	....	**1**	**0**	**1**	....	**20**	**3**	**0**	**9.00**	....	....	....	....
1977-78	**Boston Bruins**	**NHL**	**25**	**15**	**6**	**2**	**1326**	**56**	**2**	**2.53**	**2.36**	....	....	....	....	....	....	....	....	....	....	....	....	....	....	....	....
1978-79	**Boston Bruins**	**NHL**	**23**	**12**	**8**	**2**	**1254**	**74**	**0**	**3.54**	**3.12**	....	....	....	....	**5**	**3**	**2**	....	**314**	**16**	**0**	**3.06**	....	....	....	....
1979-80	**Boston Bruins**	**NHL**	**33**	**20**	**9**	**3**	**1933**	**88**	**1**	**2.73**	**2.39**	....	....	....	....	....	....	....	....	....	....	....	....	....	....	....	....
1980-81	**Detroit Red Wings**	**NHL**	**48**	**11**	**24**	**9**	**2618**	**175**	**0**	**4.01**	**3.22**	....	....	....	....	....	....	....	....	....	....	....	....	....	....	....	....
1981-82	**Detroit Red Wings**	**NHL**	**27**	**6**	**10**	**6**	**1478**	**105**	**0**	**4.26**	**3.29**	....	....	....	....	....	....	....	....	....	....	....	....	....	....	....	....
1982-83	**Detroit Red Wings**	**NHL**	**20**	**4**	**14**	**1**	**1137**	**85**	**0**	**4.49**	**3.59**	**6.75**	**565**	**.850**	**29.8**	....	....	....	....	....	....	....	....	....	....	....	....
	NHL Totals		**416**	**192**	**143**	**60**	**23677**	**1290**	**18**	**3.27**	....	....	....	....	....	**32**	**17**	**15**	....	**1919**	**97**	**3**	**3.03**	....	....	....	....

Played in NHL All-Star Game (1974)
Traded to **Boston** by **Minnesota** for Fred Stanfield, May 22, 1973. Traded to **Detroit** by **Boston** for Rogie Vachon, July 15, 1980.

● GILL, ANDRE

Andre Gill G – L. 5′7″, 145 lbs. b: Sorel, Que., 9/19/1941.

1961-62	Sorel Royals	QJHL	STATISTICS NOT AVAILABLE																								
1962-63	Hershey Bears	AHL	4	2	2	0	240	12	0	3.00	....	....	....	....	....	....	....	....	....	....	....	....	....	....	....	....	....
1963-64	Minneapolis Bruins	CHL	5	4	1	0	300	16	0	3.20	....	....	....	....	....	....	....	....	....	....	....	....	....	....	....	....	....
	Hershey Bears	AHL	19	5	9	2	1000	60	0	3.60	....	....	....	....	....	....	....	....	....	....	....	....	....	....	....	....	....
1964-65	Hershey Bears	AHL	7	2	4	0	369	25	0	4.07	....	....	....	....	....	....	....	....	....	....	....	....	....	....	....	....	....
1965-66	Hershey Bears	AHL	18	6	9	0	966	55	1	3.42	....	....	....	....	....	....	....	....	....	....	....	....	....	....	....	....	....
1966-67	Hershey Bears	AHL	56	28	18	10	3334	161	*4	2.90	....	....	....	....	....	....	....	....	....	....	....	....	....	....	....	....	....
1967-68	Hershey Bears	AHL	46	23	17	5	2564	134	0	3.14	....	....	....	....	....	5	1	4	0	307	15	0	2.93	....	....	....	....
	Boston Bruins	**NHL**	**5**	**3**	**2**	**0**	**270**	**13**	**1**	**2.89**	**3.20**	....	....	....	....	....	....	....	....	....	....	....	....	....	....	....	....
1968-69	Hershey Bears	AHL	27	15	10	2	1548	83	0	3.22	....	....	....	....	....	....	....	....	....	....	....	....	....	....	....	....	....
1969-70	Hershey Bears	AHL	52	....	....	....	3043	161	1	3.17	....	....	....	....	....	7	3	4	0	441	20	0	2.72	....	....	....	....
1970-71	Hershey Bears	AHL	40	18	14	8	2284	102	4	*2.67	....	....	....	....	....	4	1	3	0	240	16	0	4.00	....	....	....	....
1971-72	Hershey Bears	AHL	40	17	13	9	2310	114	2	2.96	....	....	....	....	....	3	0	3	0	194	13	0	4.02	....	....	....	....
1972-73	Chicago Cougars	WHA	33	4	24	0	1709	118	0	4.14	....	....	....	....	....	....	....	....	....	....	....	....	....	....	....	....	....
1973-74	Chicago Cougars	WHA	13	4	7	2	803	46	0	3.44	....	....	....	....	....	11	6	5	0	614	38	0	3.71	....	....	....	....
	Long Island Cougars	NAHL	18	....	....	....	1137	50	0	2.63	....	....	....	....	....	5	....	....	....	286	13	0	2.73	....	....	....	....

Season	Club	League	GP	W	L	T	Mins	GA	SO	Avg	AAvg	Eff	SA	S%	SAPG	GP	W	L	T	Mins	GA	SO	Avg	Eff	SA	S%	SAPG
			REGULAR SEASON													PLAYOFFS											
1974-75	Hampton Gulls	SHL	24	....	....	....	1406	70	1	*2.99	....	....	....	....	....	11	....	....	....	660	39	1	3.55	....	....	....	....
1975-76			DID NOT PLAY																								
1976-77	Richmond Wildcats	SHL	17	....	....	....	884	53	0	3.60	....	....	....	....	....	....	....	....	....	....	....	....	....	....	....	....	....
	NHL Totals		**5**	**3**	**2**	**0**	**270**	**13**	**1**	**2.89**	....	....	....	....	....	....	....	....	....	....	....	....	....	....	....	....	....
	Other Major League Totals		46	8	31	2	2512	164	0	3.92	....	....	....	....	....	11	6	5	0	614	38	0	3.71	....	....	....	....

AHL First All-Star Team (1967) • Won Harry "Hap" Holmes Memorial Award (fewest goals against - AHL) (1967) • SHL Second All-Star Team (1975)

Traded to **Boston** by **Hershey** (AHL) for cash, December, 1967. Selected by **Dayton-Houston** (WHA) in 1972 WHA General Player Draft, February 12, 1972. WHA rights traded to **Chicago** (WHA) by **Houston** (WHA) for cash, September, 1972.

• GOODMAN, PAUL

Paul Goodman G – L. 5'10", 165 lbs. b: Selkirk, Man., 2/25/1905. d: 11/4/1959.

Season	Club	League	GP	W	L	T	Mins	GA	SO	Avg	AAvg	Eff	SA	S%	SAPG	GP	W	L	T	Mins	GA	SO	Avg	Eff	SA	S%	SAPG
1931-32	Selkirk Fishermen	MSHL	12	....	....	....	720	17	4	1.92	....	....	....	....	....	2	....	....	....	120	3	0	1.50	....	....	....	....
1932-33	Selkirk Fishermen	MSHL	16	....	....	....	960	26	1	1.63	....	....	....	....	....	4	....	....	....	240	4	*1	*1.00	....	....	....	....
1933-34	Selkirk Fishermen	MSHL	16	....	....	....	960	30	*2	1.88	....	....	....	....	....	4	....	....	....	240	12	0	3.00	....	....	....	....
1934-35	Selkirk Fishermen	MSHL	10	....	....	....	600	29	0	2.90	....	....	....	....	....	2	....	....	....	120	12	0	3.00	....	....	....	....
1935-36	Wichita Skyhawks	AHA	48	16	32	0	2880	114	7	2.90	....	....	....	....	....	....	....	....	....	....	....	....	....	....	....	....	....
1936-37	Wichita Skyhawks	AHA	48	18	*27	3	2880	87	9	1.77	....	....	....	....	....	....	....	....	....	....	....	....	....	....	....	....	....
1937-38	Wichita Skyhawks	AHA	47	23	20	4	2820	130	1	2.69	....	....	....	....	....	4	1	3	0	240	15	1	3.75	....	....	....	....
	Chicago Black Hawks	**NHL**	....	....	....	....	....	....	....	....	....	....	....	....	....	**1**	**0**	**1**	....	**60**	**5**	**0**	**5.00**	....	....	....	....
1938-39	Wichita Skyhawks	AHA	45	13	*32	0	2737	156	0	3.42	....	....	....	....	....	3	0	3	0	182	19	0	6.26	....	....	....	....
1939-40	**Chicago Black Hawks**	**NHL**	**31**	**16**	**10**	**5**	**1920**	**62**	**4**	**1.94**	**2.35**	....	....	....	....	**2**	**0**	**2**	....	**127**	**5**	**0**	**2.36**	....	....	....	....
	Providence Reds	AHL	21	10	9	2	1300	58	2	2.68	....	....	....	....	....	....	....	....	....	....	....	....	....	....	....	....	....
1940-41	**Chicago Black Hawks**	**NHL**	**21**	**7**	**10**	**4**	**1320**	**55**	**2**	**2.50**	**2.87**	....	....	....	....	....	....	....	....	....	....	....	....	....	....	....	....
	NHL Totals		**52**	**23**	**20**	**9**	**3240**	**117**	**6**	**2.17**	....	....	....	....	....	**3**	**0**	**3**	....	**187**	**10**	**0**	**3.21**	....	....	....	....

• GORDON, SCOTT

Scott Gordon G – L. 5'10", 175 lbs. b: Brockton, MA, 2/6/1963.

Season	Club	League	GP	W	L	T	Mins	GA	SO	Avg	AAvg	Eff	SA	S%	SAPG	GP	W	L	T	Mins	GA	SO	Avg	Eff	SA	S%	SAPG
1982-83	Boston College	ECAC	9	3	3	0	371	15	0	2.43	....	....	....	....	....	....	....	....	....	....	....	....	....	....	....	....	....
1983-84	Boston College	ECAC	35	21	13	0	2034	127	1	3.75	....	....	....	....	....	....	....	....	....	....	....	....	....	....	....	....	....
1984-85	Boston College	H.E.	36	23	11	2	2179	131	1	3.61	....	....	....	....	....	....	....	....	....	....	....	....	....	....	....	....	....
1985-86	Boston College	H.E.	32	17	8	1	1852	112	2	3.63	....	....	....	....	....	....	....	....	....	....	....	....	....	....	....	....	....
1986-87	Fredericton Express	AHL	32	9	12	2	1616	120	0	4.46	....	....	....	....	....	....	....	....	....	....	....	....	....	....	....	....	....
1987-88	Baltimore Skipjacks	AHL	34	7	17	3	1638	145	0	5.31	....	....	....	....	....	....	....	....	....	....	....	....	....	....	....	....	....
1988-89	Halifax Citadels	AHL	2	0	2	0	116	10	0	5.17	....	....	....	....	....	....	....	....	....	....	....	....	....	....	....	....	....
	Johnstown Chiefs	ECHL	31	18	9	3	1839	117	*2	*3.82	....	....	....	....	....	11	7	4	0	647	36	0	3.34	....	....	....	....
1989-90	**Quebec Nordiques**	**NHL**	**10**	**2**	**8**	**0**	**597**	**53**	**0**	**5.33**	**4.48**	**7.68**	**368**	**.856**	**37.0**	....	....	....	....	....	....	....	....	....	....	....	....
	Halifax Citadels	AHL	48	28	16	3	2851	158	0	3.33	....	....	....	....	....	6	2	4	0	340	28	0	4.94	....	....	....	....
1990-91	**Quebec Nordiques**	**NHL**	**13**	**0**	**8**	**0**	**485**	**48**	**0**	**5.94**	**5.32**	**12.67**	**225**	**.787**	**27.8**	....	....	....	....	....	....	....	....	....	....	....	....
	Halifax Citadels	AHL	24	12	10	2	1410	87	2	3.70	....	....	....	....	....	....	....	....	....	....	....	....	....	....	....	....	....
	United States	WEC-A	2	....	....	....	72	9	0	7.50	....	....	....	....	....	....	....	....	....	....	....	....	....	....	....	....	....
1991-92	United States	Nat-Team	29	13	12	3	1666	112	0	4.03	....	....	....	....	....	....	....	....	....	....	....	....	....	....	....	....	....
	United States	Olympics	1	0	0	0	17	2	0	3.53	....	....	....	....	....	....	....	....	....	....	....	....	....	....	....	....	....
	Halifax Citadels	AHL	7	3	3	1	424	27	0	3.82	....	....	....	....	....	....	....	....	....	....	....	....	....	....	....	....	....
	New Haven Nighthawks	AHL	4	3	1	0	239	11	0	2.76	....	....	....	....	....	2	0	2	0	119	9	0	4.54	....	....	....	....
1992-93	Nashville Knights	ECHL	23	13	9	1	1380	99	0	4.30	....	....	....	....	....	9	5	4	0	548	40	0	4.38	....	....	....	....
1993-94	Knoxville Cherokees	ECHL	26	15	10	1	1517	98	0	3.87	....	....	....	....	....	....	....	....	....	....	....	....	....	....	....	....	....
	Atlanta Knights	IHL	5	0	1	3	233	13	0	3.34	....	....	....	....	....	....	....	....	....	....	....	....	....	....	....	....	....
	NHL Totals		**23**	**2**	**16**	**0**	**1082**	**101**	**0**	**5.60**	....	....	**593**	**.830**	....	....	....	....	....	....	....	....	....	....	....	....	....

Hockey East First All-Star Team (1986) • ECHL First All-Star Team (1989)

Signed as a free agent by **Quebec**, October 2, 1986.

• GOSSELIN, MARIO

Mario "Goose" Gosselin G – L. 5'8", 160 lbs. b: Thetford Mines, Que., 6/15/1963. Quebec's 3rd choice, 55th overall, in 1982 Entry Draft.

Season	Club	League	GP	W	L	T	Mins	GA	SO	Avg	AAvg	Eff	SA	S%	SAPG	GP	W	L	T	Mins	GA	SO	Avg	Eff	SA	S%	SAPG
1980-81	Shawinigan Cataracts	QMJHL	21	4	0	0	907	75	0	4.96	....	....	....	....	....	1	0	0	0	20	2	0	6.00	....	....	....	....
1981-82	Shawinigan Cataracts	QMJHL	*60	33	25	2	*3404	230	0	4.05	....	....	....	....	....	14	7	7	0	788	58	0	4.42	....	....	....	....
1982-83	Shawinigan Cataracts	QMJHL	46	32	9	1	2556	133	*3	*3.12	....	....	....	....	....	8	5	3	0	457	29	0	3.81	....	....	....	....
	Canada	WJC-A	DID NOT PLAY – SPARE GOALTENDER																								
1983-84	Canada	Nat-Team	36	....	....	....	2007	126	0	3.77	....	....	....	....	....	....	....	....	....	....	....	....	....	....	....	....	....
	Canada	Olympics	7	4	3	0	380	14	....	2.21	....	....	....	....	....	....	....	....	....	....	....	....	....	....	....	....	....
	Quebec Nordiques	**NHL**	**3**	**2**	**0**	**0**	**148**	**3**	**1**	**1.22**	**0.95**	**0.56**	**67**	**.955**	**27.2**	....	....	....	....	....	....	....	....	....	....	....	....
1984-85	**Quebec Nordiques**	**NHL**	**35**	**19**	**11**	**3**	**1960**	**109**	**1**	**3.34**	**2.64**	**4.10**	**887**	**.877**	**27.2**	**17**	**9**	**8**	**0**	**1059**	**54**	**0**	**3.06**	**3.49**	**473**	**.886**	**26.8**
1985-86	**Quebec Nordiques**	**NHL**	**31**	**14**	**14**	**1**	**1726**	**111**	**2**	**3.86**	**3.00**	**5.38**	**796**	**.861**	**27.7**	**1**	**0**	**1**	**0**	**40**	**5**	**0**	**7.50**	**17.05**	**22**	**.773**	**33.0**
	Fredericton Express	AHL	5	2	2	1	304	15	0	2.96	....	....	....	....	....	....	....	....	....	....	....	....	....	....	....	....	....
1986-87	**Quebec Nordiques**	**NHL**	**30**	**13**	**11**	**1**	**1625**	**86**	**0**	**3.18**	**2.67**	**3.61**	**758**	**.887**	**28.0**	**11**	**7**	**4**	**0**	**654**	**37**	**0**	**3.39**	**3.85**	**326**	**.887**	**29.9**
1987-88	**Quebec Nordiques**	**NHL**	**54**	**20**	**28**	**4**	**3002**	**189**	**2**	**3.78**	**3.14**	**5.02**	**1422**	**.867**	**28.4**	....	....	....	....	....	....	....	....	....	....	....	....
1988-89	**Quebec Nordiques**	**NHL**	**39**	**11**	**19**	**3**	**2064**	**146**	**0**	**4.24**	**3.51**	**5.60**	**1105**	**.868**	**32.1**	....	....	....	....	....	....	....	....	....	....	....	....
	Halifax Citadels	AHL	3	3	0	0	183	9	0	2.95	....	....	....	....	....	....	....	....	....	....	....	....	....	....	....	....	....
1989-90	**Los Angeles Kings**	**NHL**	**26**	**7**	**11**	**1**	**1226**	**79**	**0**	**3.87**	**3.24**	**5.21**	**587**	**.865**	**28.7**	**3**	**0**	**2**	**0**	**63**	**3**	**0**	**2.90**	**3.78**	**23**	**.870**	**21.9**
1990-91	Phoenix Roadrunners	IHL	46	24	15	4	2673	172	1	3.86	....	....	....	....	....	11	7	4	0	670	43	0	3.85	....	....	....	....
1991-92	Springfield Indians	AHL	47	28	11	5	2606	142	0	3.27	....	....	....	....	....	6	1	4	0	319	18	0	3.39	....	....	....	....
1992-93	**Hartford Whalers**	**NHL**	**16**	**5**	**9**	**1**	**867**	**57**	**0**	**3.94**	**3.36**	**4.50**	**499**	**.886**	**34.5**	....	....	....	....	....	....	....	....	....	....	....	....
	Springfield Indians	AHL	23	8	7	7	1345	75	0	3.35	....	....	....	....	....	....	....	....	....	....	....	....	....	....	....	....	....
1993-94	**Hartford Whalers**	**NHL**	**7**	**0**	**4**	**0**	**239**	**21**	**0**	**5.27**	**5.02**	**10.34**	**107**	**.804**	**26.9**	....	....	....	....	....	....	....	....	....	....	....	....
	Springfield Indians	AHL	2	2	0	0	120	5	0	2.50	....	....	....	....	....	....	....	....	....	....	....	....	....	....	....	....	....
	NHL Totals		**241**	**91**	**107**	**14**	**12857**	**801**	**6**	**3.74**	....	....	**6228**	**.871**	....	**32**	**16**	**15**	**0**	**1816**	**99**	**0**	**3.27**	....	....	....	....

QMJHL Second All-Star Team (1982) • QMJHL First All-Star Team (1983)

Played in NHL All-Star Game (1986)

Signed as a free agent by **LA Kings**, June 14, 1989. Signed as a free agent by **Hartford**, September 4, 1991.

• GOVERDE, DAVID

David Goverde G – R. 6', 210 lbs. b: Toronto, Ont., 4/9/1970. Los Angeles' 4th choice, 91st overall, in 1990 Entry Draft.

Season	Club	League	GP	W	L	T	Mins	GA	SO	Avg	AAvg	Eff	SA	S%	SAPG	GP	W	L	T	Mins	GA	SO	Avg	Eff	SA	S%	SAPG
1987-88	Windsor Spitfires	OHL	10	5	3	1	471	28	0	3.57	....	....	....	....	....	....	....	....	....	....	....	....	....	....	....	....	....
1988-89	Windsor Spitfires	OHL	5	0	3	0	221	24	0	6.52	....	....	....	....	....	....	....	....	....	....	....	....	....	....	....	....	....
	Sudbury Wolves	OHL	39	16	15	4	2189	156	0	4.28	....	....	....	....	....	....	....	....	....	....	....	....	....	....	....	....	....
1989-90	Sudbury Wolves	OHL	52	28	12	7	2941	182	0	3.71	....	....	....	....	....	7	3	3	....	394	25	0	3.81	....	....	....	....
1990-91	Phoenix Roadrunners	IHL	40	11	19	5	2007	137	0	4.10	....	....	....	....	....	....	....	....	....	....	....	....	....	....	....	....	....
1991-92	**Los Angeles Kings**	**NHL**	**2**	**1**	**1**	**0**	**120**	**9**	**0**	**4.50**	**3.99**	**6.43**	**63**	**.857**	**31.5**	....	....	....	....	....	....	....	....	....	....	....	....
	Phoenix Roadrunners	IHL	36	11	19	3	1951	129	1	3.97	....	....	....	....	....	....	....	....	....	....	....	....	....	....	....	....	....
	New Haven Nighthawks	AHL	5	1	3	0	248	17	0	4.11	....	....	....	....	....	....	....	....	....	....	....	....	....	....	....	....	....
1992-93	**Los Angeles Kings**	**NHL**	**2**	**0**	**2**	**0**	**98**	**13**	**0**	**7.96**	**6.78**	**20.29**	**51**	**.745**	**31.2**	....	....	....	....	....	....	....	....	....	....	....	....
	Phoenix Roadrunners	IHL	45	18	21	3	2569	173	1	4.04	....	....	....	....	....	....	....	....	....	....	....	....	....	....	....	....	....
1993-94	**Los Angeles Kings**	**NHL**	**1**	**0**	**1**	**0**	**60**	**7**	**0**	**7.00**	**6.67**	**13.24**	**37**	**.811**	**37.0**	....	....	....	....	....	....	....	....	....	....	....	....
	Phoenix Roadrunners	IHL	30	15	13	1	1716	93	0	3.25	....	....	....	....	....	....	....	....	....	....	....	....	....	....	....	....	....
	Portland Pirates	AHL	1	0	1	0	59	4	0	4.01	....	....	....	....	....	....	....	....	....	....	....	....	....	....	....	....	....
	Peoria Rivermen	IHL	5	4	1	0	299	13	0	2.61	....	....	....	....	....	1	0	1	....	59	7	0	7.05	....	....	....	....
1994-95	Detroit Falcons	ColHL	4	4	0	0	240	10	0	2.50	....	....	....	....	....	....	....	....	....	....	....	....	....	....	....	....	....
	Phoenix Roadrunners	IHL	2	0	2	0	76	5	0	3.95	....	....	....	....	....	....	....	....	....	....	....	....	....	....	....	....	....
	Detroit Vipers	IHL	15	8	5	0	814	49	0	3.61	....	....	....	....	....	....	....	....	....	....	....	....	....	....	....	....	....
1995-96	Saint John Flames	AHL	1	0	0	0	47	9	0	11.40	....	....	....	....	....	....	....	....	....	....	....	....	....	....	....	....	....
	Louisville IceHawks	ECHL	12	5	5	1	697	46	*1	3.96	....	....	....	....	....	....	....	....	....	....	....	....	....	....	....	....	....
	Toledo Storm	ECHL	31	23	3	4	1817	79	*1	2.61	....	....	....	....	....	11	8	3	....	666	32	0	2.88	....	....	....	....

			REGULAR SEASON													PLAYOFFS											
Season	Club	League	GP	W	L	T	Mins	GA	SO	Avg	AAvg	Eff	SA	S%	SAPG	GP	W	L	T	Mins	GA	SO	Avg	Eff	SA	S%	SAPG
1996-97	Toledo Storm	ECHL	44	23	14	6	2554	126	*5	2.96	....	....	....	....	....	5	2	3	....	346	15	0	*2.59	....	....	....	....
	Fort Wayne Komets	IHL	1	0	1	0	60	7	0	7.00	....	....	....	....	....	....	....	....	....	....	....	....	....	....	....	....	....
1997-98	Phoenix Mustangs	WCHL	53	30	21	2	3149	178	2	3.39	....	....	....	....	....	9	3	5	....	492	38	0	4.63	....	....	....	....
	NHL Totals		**5**	**1**	**4**	**0**	**278**	**29**	**0**	**6.26**	....	....	**151**	**.808**	....	....	....	....	....	....	....	....	....	....	....	....	....

ECHL Second All-Star Team (1997) • WCHL Second All-Star Team (1998)

• GRAHAME, RON

Ron Grahame G – L. 5'11", 175 lbs. b: Victoria, B.C., 6/7/1950.

Season	Club	League	GP	W	L	T	Mins	GA	SO	Avg	AAvg	Eff	SA	S%	SAPG	GP	W	L	T	Mins	GA	SO	Avg	Eff	SA	S%	SAPG
1969-70	University of Denver	WCHA	30	19	10	1	1800	103	1	3.43	....	....	....	....	....	....	....	....	....	....	....	....	....	....	....	....	....
1970-71	University of Denver	WCHA	17	9	7	1	1020	70	1	4.12	....	....	....	....	....	....	....	....	....	....	....	....	....	....	....	....	....
1971-72	University of Denver	WCHA	37	26	11	0	2200	132	0	3.60	....	....	....	....	....	....	....	....	....	....	....	....	....	....	....	....	....
1972-73	University of Denver	WCHA	35	27	7	1	2094	102	2	*2.92	....	....	....	....	....	....	....	....	....	....	....	....	....	....	....	....	....
1973-74	Macon Whoopees	SHL	46	....	....	....	2588	178	0	4.13	....	....	....	....	....	....	....	....	....	....	....	....	....	....	....	....	....
	Houston Aeros	WHA	4	3	0	1	250	5	1	1.20	....	....	....	....	....	....	....	....	....	....	....	....	....	....	....	....	....
1974-75	Houston Aeros	WHA	43	*33	10	0	2590	131	*4	*3.03	....	....	....	....	....	13	*12	1	0	780	26	*3	*2.00	....	....	....	....
1975-76	Houston Aeros	WHA	57	39	17	0	3343	182	3	3.27	....	....	....	....	....	*14	6	8	0	817	54	1	3.97	....	....	....	....
1976-77	Houston Aeros	WHA	39	27	10	2	2345	107	*4	*2.74	....	....	....	....	....	9	4	5	0	561	36	0	3.85	....	....	....	....
1977-78	**Boston Bruins**	**NHL**	**40**	**26**	**6**	**7**	**2328**	**107**	**3**	**2.76**	**2.57**	....	....	....	....	**4**	**2**	**1**	....	**202**	**7**	**0**	**2.08**	....	....	....	....
1978-79	**Los Angeles Kings**	**NHL**	**34**	**11**	**19**	**2**	**1940**	**136**	**0**	**4.21**	**3.73**	....	....	....	....	....	....	....	....	....	....	....	....	....	....	....	....
1979-80	**Los Angeles Kings**	**NHL**	**26**	**9**	**11**	**4**	**1405**	**98**	**2**	**4.19**	**3.69**	....	....	....	....	....	....	....	....	....	....	....	....	....	....	....	....
1980-81	**Los Angeles Kings**	**NHL**	**6**	**3**	**2**	**1**	**360**	**28**	**0**	**4.67**	**3.75**	....	....	....	....	....	....	....	....	....	....	....	....	....	....	....	....
	Quebec Nordiques	**NHL**	**8**	**1**	**5**	**1**	**439**	**40**	**0**	**5.47**	**4.39**	....	....	....	....	....	....	....	....	....	....	....	....	....	....	....	....
	Binghamton Whalers	AHL	22	....	....	....	1240	72	0	3.48	....	....	....	....	....	5	....	....	....	289	22	0	4.57	....	....	....	....
	NHL Totals		**114**	**50**	**43**	**15**	**6472**	**409**	**5**	**3.79**	....	....	....	....	....	**4**	**2**	**1**	....	**202**	**7**	**0**	**2.08**	....	....	....	....
	Other Major League Totals		143	102	37	3	8528	425	12	2.99	....	....	....	....	....	36	22	14	0	2158	116	4	3.23	....	....	....	....

WCHA First All-Star Team (1973) • NCAA West First All-American Team (1973) • WHA First All-Star Team (1975) • Won Ben Hatskin Trophy (WHA Top Goaltender) (1975, 1977) • Won WHA Playoff MVP Trophy (1975) • WHA Second All-Star Team (1976)

Selected by **NY Raiders** (WHA) in 1972 WHA General Player Draft, February 12, 1972. WHA rights traded to **Houston** (WHA) by **NY Raiders** (WHA) for Ray Larose, June, 1973. Signed as a free agent by **Boston**, October 13, 1977. Traded to **LA Kings** by **Boston** for LA Kings' 1st round choice (Ray Bourque) in 1979 Entry Draft, October 9, 1978. Sold to **Quebec** by **LA Kings** for cash, December 12, 1980.

• GRANT, BEN

Ben Grant G – L. 5'11", 160 lbs. b: Owen Sound, Ont., 7/14/1908. d: 7/30/1991.

Season	Club	League	GP	W	L	T	Mins	GA	SO	Avg	AAvg	Eff	SA	S%	SAPG	GP	W	L	T	Mins	GA	SO	Avg	Eff	SA	S%	SAPG
1924-25	Owen Sound Greys	OHA	1	0	0	0	20	0	0	0.00	....	....	....	....	....	....	....	....	....	....	....	....	....	....	....	....	....
1925-26	Owen Sound Greys	OHA	3	2	1	0	150	4	1	1.60	....	....	....	....	....	....	....	....	....	....	....	....	....	....	....	....	....
1926-27	Owen Sound Greys	OHA	16	12	3	1	960	35	2	2.19	....	....	....	....	....	....	....	....	....	....	....	....	....	....	....	....	....
1927-28	London Panthers	Can-Pro	3	....	....	....	140	14	0	6.00	....	....	....	....	....	....	....	....	....	....	....	....	....	....	....	....	....
1928-29	**Toronto Maple Leafs**	**NHL**	**3**	**1**	**0**	**0**	**110**	**3**	**0**	**1.64**	**3.49**	....	....	....	....	....	....	....	....	....	....	....	....	....	....	....	....
1929-30	**Toronto Maple Leafs**	**NHL**	**2**	**1**	**1**	**0**	**130**	**11**	**0**	**5.08**	**5.33**	....	....	....	....	....	....	....	....	....	....	....	....	....	....	....	....
	Minneapolis Millers	AHA	21	....	....	....	1260	36	3	1.71	....	....	....	....	....	....	....	....	....	....	....	....	....	....	....	....	....
	New York Americans	**NHL**	**7**	**3**	**4**	**0**	**420**	**25**	**0**	**3.57**	**3.75**	....	....	....	....	....	....	....	....	....	....	....	....	....	....	....	....
1930-31	**Toronto Maple Leafs**	**NHL**	**7**	**1**	**5**	**1**	**430**	**19**	**2**	**2.65**	**3.42**	....	....	....	....	....	....	....	....	....	....	....	....	....	....	....	....
	Boston Tigers	Can-Am	26	10	12	4	1609	69	1	2.57	....	....	....	....	....	9	*3	4	2	712	23	0	*1.94	....	....	....	....
1931-32	**Toronto Maple Leafs**	**NHL**	**5**	**1**	**2**	**1**	**320**	**18**	**1**	**3.38**	**4.18**	....	....	....	....	....	....	....	....	....	....	....	....	....	....	....	....
	Syracuse Stars	IAHL	27	....	....	....	1260	66	4	2.45	....	....	....	....	....	....	....	....	....	....	....	....	....	....	....	....	....
1932-33	Syracuse Stars	IAHL	44	23	15	6	2640	119	2	2.70	....	....	....	....	....	6	2	3	1	360	10	0	*1.60	....	....	....	....
1933-34	**New York Americans**	**NHL**	**5**	**1**	**4**	**0**	**320**	**18**	**1**	**3.38**	**4.35**	....	....	....	....	....	....	....	....	....	....	....	....	....	....	....	....
	Syracuse/Windsor	IAHL	9	....	....	....	500	26	0	3.12	....	....	....	....	....	....	....	....	....	....	....	....	....	....	....	....	....
1934-35	Boston Cubs	Can-Am	10	5	3	1	590	20	1	2.03	....	....	....	....	....	....	....	....	....	....	....	....	....	....	....	....	....
	Philadelphia Arrows	Can-Am	32	10	21	1	1930	114	1	3.54	....	....	....	....	....	....	....	....	....	....	....	....	....	....	....	....	....
1935-36	New Haven Eagles	Can-Am	28	11	15	2	1740	93	2	3.21	....	....	....	....	....	....	....	....	....	....	....	....	....	....	....	....	....
	Springfield Indians	Can-Am	8	6	1	1	490	14	3	1.71	....	....	....	....	....	3	0	2	1	180	9	0	3.00	....	....	....	....
1936-37	Springfield Indians	AHL	*48	22	17	9	*2970	127	*7	2.57	....	....	....	....	....	5	2	3	0	300	14	1	2.60	....	....	....	....
1937-38	Springfield Indians	AHL	45	9	28	7	2790	132	3	2.84	....	....	....	....	....	....	....	....	....	....	....	....	....	....	....	....	....
1938-39	Springfield Indians	AHL	52	15	28	9	3240	171	5	3.17	....	....	....	....	....	3	1	2	0	180	7	1	2.33	....	....	....	....
1939-40	Springfield Indians	AHL	54	24	24	6	*3330	149	3	2.68	....	....	....	....	....	3	1	2	0	180	10	0	3.33	....	....	....	....
1940-41	St. Paul Saints	AHA	48	25	23	0	2991	116	*7	2.33	....	....	....	....	....	4	1	3	0	262	10	0	2.29	....	....	....	....
1941-42	St. Paul Saints	AHA	50	28	17	5	3060	99	10	*1.94	....	....	....	....	....	2	0	2	0	120	7	0	3.50	....	....	....	....
1942-43			DID NOT PLAY																								
1943-44	**Toronto Maple Leafs**	**NHL**	**20**	**9**	**9**	**2**	**1200**	**83**	**0**	**4.15**	**3.14**	....	....	....	....	....	....	....	....	....	....	....	....	....	....	....	....
	Boston Bruins	**NHL**	**1**	**0**	**1**	**0**	**60**	**10**	**0**	**10.00**	**7.60**	....	....	....	....	....	....	....	....	....	....	....	....	....	....	....	....
	NHL Totals		**50**	**17**	**26**	**4**	**2990**	**187**	**4**	**3.75**	....	....	....	....	....	....	....	....	....	....	....	....	....	....	....	....	....

AHA First All-Star Team (1942)

Traded to **Toronto** by **London** (Can-Pro) for cash, January, 1928. Loaned to **NY Americans** by **Toronto** for cash, December 18, 1929. Loaned to **NY Americans** by **Toronto** to replace injured Moe Roberts, December 9, 1933. (Boston 4, NY Americans 2). Signed as a free agent by **Toronto** as a war-time replacement for Turk Broda, October, 1942. Loaned to **Boston** by **Toronto** to replace Maurice Courteau, March 18, 1944. (Toronto 10, Boston 2)

• GRANT, DOUG

Doug Grant G – L. 6'1", 200 lbs. b: Corner Brook, Nfld., 7/27/1948.

Season	Club	League	GP	W	L	T	Mins	GA	SO	Avg	AAvg	Eff	SA	S%	SAPG	GP	W	L	T	Mins	GA	SO	Avg	Eff	SA	S%	SAPG
1967-68	Corner Brook Royals	Nfld.	40	19	16	5	2400	174	0	4.35	....	....	....	....	....	....	....	....	....	....	....	....	....	....	....	....	....
1968-69	Corner Brook Royals	Nfld.	STATISTICS NOT AVAILABLE																								
1969-70	Corner Brook Royals	Nfld.	STATISTICS NOT AVAILABLE																								
1970-71	Corner Brook Royals	Nfld.	35	....	....	....	2100	150	*2	4.29	....	....	....	....	....	12	3	9	0	720	72	0	6.00	....	....	....	....
1971-72	Memorial University	AUAA	14	....	....	....	850	29	*2	*2.05	....	....	....	....	....	....	....	....	....	....	....	....	....	....	....	....	....
	Fort Worth Wings	CHL	3	2	1	0	180	9	0	3.00	....	....	....	....	....	....	....	....	....	....	....	....	....	....	....	....	....
1972-73	Virginia Wings	AHL	51	....	....	....	3037	129	*6	2.54	....	....	....	....	....	12	6	6	0	717	42	*1	3.51	....	....	....	....
1973-74	**Detroit Red Wings**	**NHL**	**37**	**15**	**16**	**2**	**2018**	**140**	**1**	**4.16**	**4.05**	....	....	....	....	....	....	....	....	....	....	....	....	....	....	....	....
	Virginia Wings	AHL	6	1	3	2	359	20	1	3.34	....	....	....	....	....	....	....	....	....	....	....	....	....	....	....	....	....
1974-75	**Detroit Red Wings**	**NHL**	**7**	**1**	**5**	**0**	**380**	**34**	**0**	**5.37**	**4.85**	....	....	....	....	....	....	....	....	....	....	....	....	....	....	....	....
	Virginia Wings	AHL	35	14	11	8	1978	106	1	3.21	....	....	....	....	....	3	2	1	0	180	16	0	5.33	....	....	....	....
1975-76	**Detroit Red Wings**	**NHL**	**2**	**1**	**1**	**0**	**120**	**8**	**0**	**4.00**	**3.62**	....	....	....	....	....	....	....	....	....	....	....	....	....	....	....	....
	New Haven Nighthawks	AHL	23	8	13	2	1392	95	0	4.10	....	....	....	....	....	....	....	....	....	....	....	....	....	....	....	....	....
1976-77	**St. Louis Blues**	**NHL**	**17**	**7**	**7**	**3**	**960**	**50**	**1**	**3.13**	**2.91**	....	....	....	....	....	....	....	....	....	....	....	....	....	....	....	....
	Kansas City Blues	CHL	20	10	6	4	1199	57	*3	2.85	....	....	....	....	....	....	....	....	....	....	....	....	....	....	....	....	....
1977-78	**St. Louis Blues**	**NHL**	**9**	**3**	**3**	**2**	**500**	**24**	**0**	**2.88**	**2.69**	....	....	....	....	....	....	....	....	....	....	....	....	....	....	....	....
	Salt Lake Golden Eagles	CHL	35	17	13	3	2068	107	1	3.10	....	....	....	....	....	....	....	....	....	....	....	....	....	....	....	....	....
1978-79	**St. Louis Blues**	**NHL**	**4**	**0**	**2**	**1**	**190**	**23**	**0**	**7.26**	**6.42**	....	....	....	....	....	....	....	....	....	....	....	....	....	....	....	....
	Salt Lake Golden Eagles	CHL	31	15	12	3	1871	91	3	2.92	....	....	....	....	....	4	1	2	0	198	15	0	4.54	....	....	....	....
1979-80	**St. Louis Blues**	**NHL**	**1**	**0**	**0**	**0**	**31**	**1**	**0**	**1.94**	**1.70**	....	....	....	....	....	....	....	....	....	....	....	....	....	....	....	....
	Salt Lake Golden Eagles	CHL	38	24	12	2	2283	130	1	3.42	....	....	....	....	....	9	7	2	0	483	27	0	3.35	....	....	....	....
1980-81	Salt Lake Golden Eagles	CHL	5	3	1	0	260	14	1	3.23	....	....	....	....	....	....	....	....	....	....	....	....	....	....	....	....	....
1981-82	Salt Lake Golden Eagles	CHL	7	2	3	0	354	34	0	5.76	....	....	....	....	....	....	....	....	....	....	....	....	....	....	....	....	....
	NHL Totals		**77**	**27**	**34**	**8**	**4199**	**280**	**2**	**4.00**	....	....	....	....	....	....	....	....	....	....	....	....	....	....	....	....	....

AHL First All-Star Team (1973) • CHL Second All-Star Team (1978) • Shared Terry Sawchuk Trophy (fewest goals against - CHL) with Ed Staniowski (1978) • Shared Terry Sawchuk Trophy (fewest goals against - CHL) with Terry Richardson (1979)

Signed as a free agent by **Detroit**, March 1, 1972. Traded to **St. Louis** by **Detroit** for future considerations (Rick Wilson, June 16, 1976), March 9, 1976.

● GRATTON, GILLES

Gilles "Grattony the Loony" Gratton   G – L. 5'11", 160 lbs.   b: LaSalle, Que., 7/28/1952.   Buffalo's 5th choice, 69th overall, in 1972 Amateur Draft.

Season	Club	League	GP	W	L	T	Mins	GA	SO	Avg	AAvg	Eff	SA	S%	SAPG	GP	W	L	T	Mins	GA	SO	Avg	Eff	SA	S%	SAPG
1969-70	Oshawa Generals	OHA	26				1550	129	0	4.99																	
1970-71	Oshawa Generals	OHA	47				2808	234	0	5.00																	
1971-72	Oshawa Generals	OHA	50			3	3000	178	3	3.55																	
1972-73	Ottawa Nationals	WHA	51	25	22	3	3021	187	0	3.71						2	0	1	0	87	7	0	4.83				
1973-74	Toronto Toros	WHA	57	26	24	3	3200	188	2	3.53						10	5	3	0	539	25	*1	2.78				
1974-75	Canada	Summit	1				2	0		0.00																	
	Toronto Toros	WHA	53	30	20	1	2881	185	2	3.85						1	0	1	0	36	5	0	8.33				
1975-76	**St. Louis Blues**	**NHL**	6	2	0	2	265	11	0	2.49	2.25																
1976-77	**New York Rangers**	**NHL**	41	11	18	7	2034	143	0	4.22	3.95																
1977-78	New Haven Nighthawks	AHL	1	0	1	0	60	6	0	6.00																	
	NHL Totals		47	13	18	9	2299	154	0	4.02																	
	Other Major League Totals		161	81	66	7	9102	560	4	3.69						13	5	5	0	662	37	1	3.35				

OHA Second All-Star Team (1972)

Selected by **Edmonton** (WHA) in 1972 WHA General Player Draft, February 12, 1972. WHA rights traded to **Ottawa** (WHA) by **Edmonton** (WHA) for cash, September, 1972. Transferred to **Toronto** (WHA) after **Ottawa** (WHA) franchise relocated, May, 1973. Rights traded to **St. Louis** by **Buffalo** for cash, July 3, 1975. ● Placed on "voluntary retired" list after walking out on the team following game vs. NY Islanders, November 28, 1975. St. Louis refused to place Gratton on waivers, blocking his attempt to sign with Toronto (WHA). Signed as a free agent by **NY Rangers** after securing release from **St. Louis**, March 24, 1976.

● GRAY, GERRY

Gerry Gray   G – L. 6', 165 lbs.   b: Brantford, Ont., 1/28/1948.

Season	Club	League	GP	W	L	T	Mins	GA	SO	Avg	AAvg	Eff	SA	S%	SAPG	GP	W	L	T	Mins	GA	SO	Avg	Eff	SA	S%	SAPG
1965-66	Hamilton Red Wings	OHA	32				1920	151	0	4.72						1	0	0	0	20	0	0	0.00				
1966-67	Hamilton Red Wings	OHA	44				2600	142	1	3.28						17				1020	59	0	3.47				
1967-68	Hamilton Red Wings	OHA	45				2680	138	0	3.09						11				641	45	0	4.21				
1968-69	Fort Worth Wings	CHL	40				2125	127	2	3.59																	
1969-70	Cleveland Barons	AHL	35				1997	131	1	3.94																	
1970-71	**Detroit Red Wings**	**NHL**	7	1	4	1	380	30	0	4.74	4.70																
	Fort Worth Wings	CHL	33				1940	90	2	2.78																	
1971-72	Tidewater Wings	AHL	18	7	7	2	1009	45	2	2.68																	
	Fort Worth Wings	CHL	32	14	11	6	1633	95	0	3.49						7				444	30	0	4.05				
1972-73	**New York Islanders**	**NHL**	1	0	1	0	60	5	0	5.00	4.71																
	New Haven Nighthawks	AHL	36				2071	156	0	4.51																	
1973-74	Jacksonville Barons	AHL	30	5	16	4	1464	113	0	4.63																	
1974-75	Brantford Foresters	OHA Sr.	6				360	27	0	4.56																	
1975-76	Cambridge Hornets	OHA Sr.	22				1320	82	0	3.76																	
1976-77	Brantford Alexanders	OHA Sr.	19				1140	89	1	4.60																	
1977-78	Brantford Alexanders	OHA Sr.	15				900	84	0	5.57																	
	NHL Totals		8	1	5	1	440	35	0	4.77																	

OHA First All-Star Team (1968) ● Shared Terry Sawchuk Trophy (fewest goals against - CHL) with Don McLeod (1971)
Traded to **NY Islanders** by **Detroit** with Arnie Brown for Denis Dejordy and Don McLaughlin, October 4, 1972.

● GRAY, HARRISON

Harrison Gray   G 5'11", 165 lbs.   b: Calgary, Alta., 9/5/1941.

Season	Club	League	GP	W	L	T	Mins	GA	SO	Avg	AAvg	Eff	SA	S%	SAPG	GP	W	L	T	Mins	GA	SO	Avg	Eff	SA	S%	SAPG
1961-62	Edmonton Oil Kings	AJHL			STATISTICS NOT AVAILABLE																						
	Edmonton Flyers	WHL	1	0	0	0	20	0	0	0.00																	
1962-63	Edmonton Flyers	WHL	14	0	13	0	840	87	0	6.21																	
1963-64	**Detroit Red Wings**	**NHL**	1	0	1	0	40	5	0	7.50	8.36																
	Cincinnati Wings	CHL	3	1	1	1	180	10	0	3.33																	
1964-65	Knoxville Knights	EHL	55				3300	208	2	3.78						10	5	5	0	600	37	0	3.70				
1965-66	Knoxville Knights	EHL	28	14	14	0	1080	118	0	4.21						3	0	3	0	180	15	0	5.00				
	New Haven Blades	EHL	37				2220	170	1	4.59																	
1966-67	Florida Rockets	EHL	72	27	43	2	4320	314	2	4.36																	
1967-68	Florida Rockets	EHL	72	30	34	8	4320	286	3	3.97						5	2	3	0	300	20	0	4.00				
1968-69	Jacksonville Rockets	EHL	54				3240	226	0	4.18						1	1	0	0	60	2	0	2.00				
1969-70	Drumheller Miners	ASHL	17				1020	72	1	4.24																	
	NHL Totals		1	0	1	0	40	5	0	7.50																	

● Detroit's spare goaltender replaced injured Terry Sawchuk at start of 2nd period, November 28, 1963. (Montreal 7, Detroit 3).

● GREENLAY, MIKE

Mike Greenlay   G – L. 6'3", 200 lbs.   b: Vitoria, Brazil, 9/15/1968.   Edmonton's 9th choice, 189th overall, in 1986 Entry Draft.

Season	Club	League	GP	W	L	T	Mins	GA	SO	Avg	AAvg	Eff	SA	S%	SAPG	GP	W	L	T	Mins	GA	SO	Avg	Eff	SA	S%	SAPG
1985-86	Calgary	Midget			STATISTICS NOT AVAILABLE																						
1986-87	Lake Superior State	CCHA	17	7	5	0	744	44	0	3.54																	
1987-88	Lake Superior State	CCHA	19	10	3	3	1023	57	0	3.34																	
1988-89	Lake Superior State	CCHA	2	1	1	0	85	6	0	4.23																	
	Saskatoon Blades	WHL	20	10	8	1	1128	86	0	4.57						6	2	0	0	174	16	0	5.52				
1989-90	**Edmonton Oilers**	**NHL**	2	0	0	0	20	4	0	12.00	10.06	28.24	17	.765	51.0												
	Cape Breton Oilers	AHL	46	19	18	5	2595	146	2	3.38						5	1	3	0	306	26	0	5.09				
1990-91	Cape Breton Oilers	AHL	11	5	2	0	493	33	0	4.02																	
	Knoxville Cherokees	ECHL	29	17	9	2	1725	108	2	3.75																	
1991-92	Cape Breton Oilers	AHL	3	1	1	0	144	12	0	5.00																	
	Knoxville Cherokees	ECHL	27	8	12	2	1415	113	0	4.79																	
1992-93	Louisville IceHawks	ECHL	27	12	11	2	1437	96	1	4.01																	
	Atlanta Knights	IHL	12	5	3	0	637	40	0	3.77																	
1993-94	Atlanta Knights	IHL	34	16	10	4	1741	104	0	3.58						13	*11	1	0	749	29	*1	*2.32				
1994-95	Atlanta Knights	IHL	20	7	10	0	1059	72	0	4.08																	
	Hershey Bears	AHL	16	5	5	2	704	46	0	3.92						5	2	3	0	270	12	0	2.66				
1995-96	Houston Aeros	IHL	1	0	1	0	17	2	0	6.86																	
	NHL Totals		2	0	0	0	20	4	0	12.00			17	.765													

Memorial Cup All-Star Team (1989) ● Won Hap Emms Memorial Trophy (Memorial Cup Tournament Top Goaltender) (1989) ● Shared James Norris Memorial Trophy (fewest goals against - IHL) with J.C. Bergeron (1994)
Signed as a free agent by **Tampa Bay**, July 29, 1992. Traded to **Philadelphia** by **Tampa Bay** for Scott LaGrand, February 2, 1995.

● GUENETTE, STEVE

Steve Guenette   G – L. 5'10", 175 lbs.   b: Gloucester, Ont., 11/13/1965.

Season	Club	League	GP	W	L	T	Mins	GA	SO	Avg	AAvg	Eff	SA	S%	SAPG	GP	W	L	T	Mins	GA	SO	Avg	Eff	SA	S%	SAPG
1983-84	Guelph Platers	OHL	38	9	20	1	1808	155	0	5.14																	
1984-85	Guelph Platers	OHL	47	16	22	4	2593	200	1	4.63																	
1985-86	Guelph Platers	OHL	50	26	20	1	2910	165	*3	3.40						20	15	3	0	1167	54	1	2.77				
1986-87	**Pittsburgh Penguins**	**NHL**	2	0	2	0	113	8	0	4.25	3.57	6.30	54	.852	28.7												
	Baltimore Skipjacks	AHL	54	21	23	0	3035	157	5	3.10																	
1987-88	**Pittsburgh Penguins**	**NHL**	19	12	7	0	1092	61	1	3.35	2.78	3.51	582	.895	32.0												
	Muskegon Lumberjacks	IHL	33	23	4	5	1943	91	*4	2.81																	
1988-89	**Pittsburgh Penguins**	**NHL**	11	5	6	0	574	41	0	4.29	3.54	5.71	308	.867	32.2												
	Muskegon Lumberjacks	IHL	10	6	4	0	597	39	0	3.92																	
	Salt Lake Golden Eagles	IHL	30	24	5	0	1810	82	2	2.72						*13	*8	5	0	*782	44	0	3.38				
1989-90	Calgary Flames	FrTour	1				27	0	0	0.00																	
	Calgary Flames	**NHL**	2	1	1	0	119	8	0	4.03	3.38	6.45	50	.840	25.2												
	Salt Lake Golden Eagles	IHL	47	22	21	4	2779	160	0	3.45						*10	4	4	0	545	35	*1	3.85				

			REGULAR SEASON													PLAYOFFS											
Season	Club	League	GP	W	L	T	Mins	GA	SO	Avg	AAvg	Eff	SA	S%	SAPG	GP	W	L	T	Mins	GA	SO	Avg	Eff	SA	S%	SAPG
1990-91	Calgary Flames	NHL	1	1	0	0	60	4	0	4.00	3.57	5.33	30	.867	30.0	....	....	....	....	....	....	....	....	....	....	....	....
	Salt Lake Golden Eagles	IHL	43	*26	13	4	2521	137	2	3.26	....	....	....	....	....	2	0	1	0	59	9	0	9.15	....	....	....	....
1991-92	Kalamazoo Wings	IHL	21	7	9	3	1094	70	1	3.84	....	....	....	....	....	....	....	....	....	....	....	....	....	....	....	....	....
	NHL Totals		35	19	16	0	1958	122	1	3.74	....	....	1024	.881	....	....	....	....	....	....	....	....	....	....	....	....	....

OHL Second All-Star Team (1986) • Memorial Cup All-Star Team (1986) • Won Hap Emms Memorial Trophy (Memorial Cup Tournament Top Goaltender) (1986) • IHL Second All-Star Team (1988, 1989) • Won James Norris Memorial Trophy (fewest goals against - IHL) (1988)

Signed as a free agent by **Pittsburgh**, April 6, 1985. Traded to **Calgary** by **Pittsburgh** for Calgary's 6th round choice (Mike Needham) in 1989 Entry Draft, January 9, 1989. Traded to **Minnesota** by **Calgary** for Minnesota's 7th round choice (Matt Hoffman) in 1991 Entry Draft, May 30, 1991.

• HACKETT, JEFF

Jeff Hackett G – L. 6'1", 195 lbs. b: London, Ont., 6/1/1968. NY Islanders' 2nd choice, 34th overall, in 1987 Entry Draft.

Season	Club	League	GP	W	L	T	Mins	GA	SO	Avg	AAvg	Eff	SA	S%	SAPG	GP	W	L	T	Mins	GA	SO	Avg	Eff	SA	S%	SAPG
1986-87	Oshawa Generals	OHL	31	18	9	2	1672	85	2	3.05	....	....	....	....	....	15	8	7	....	895	40	0	2.68	....	....	....	....
1987-88	Oshawa Generals	OHL	53	30	21	2	3165	205	0	3.89	....	....	....	....	....	7	3	4	....	438	31	0	4.25	....	....	....	....
	Canada	WJC-A	DID NOT PLAY – SPARE GOALTENDER																								
1988-89	New York Islanders	NHL	13	4	7	0	662	39	0	3.53	2.91	4.18	329	.881	29.8	....	....	....	....	....	....	....	....	....	....	....	....
	Springfield Indians	AHL	29	12	14	2	1677	116	0	4.15	....	....	....	....	....	....	....	....	....	....	....	....	....	....	....	....	....
1989-90	Springfield Indians	AHL	54	24	25	3	3045	187	1	3.68	....	....	....	....	....	*17	*10	5	....	934	60	0	3.85	....	....	....	....
1990-91	New York Islanders	NHL	30	5	18	1	1508	91	0	3.62	3.24	4.45	741	.877	29.5	....	....	....	....	....	....	....	....	....	....	....	....
1991-92	San Jose Sharks	NHL	42	11	27	1	2314	148	0	3.84	3.41	4.16	1366	.892	35.4	....	....	....	....	....	....	....	....	....	....	....	....
1992-93	San Jose Sharks	NHL	36	2	30	1	2000	176	0	5.28	4.53	7.62	1220	.856	36.6	....	....	....	....	....	....	....	....	....	....	....	....
1993-94	Chicago Blackhawks	NHL	22	2	12	3	1084	62	0	3.43	3.27	3.76	566	.890	31.3	....	....	....	....	....	....	....	....	....	....	....	....
1994-95	Chicago Blackhawks	NHL	7	1	3	2	328	13	0	2.38	2.46	2.06	150	.913	27.4	2	0	0	....	26	1	0	2.31	2.10	11	.909	25.4
1995-96	Chicago Blackhawks	NHL	35	18	11	4	2000	80	4	2.40	2.35	2.03	948	.916	28.4	1	0	1	....	60	5	0	5.00	7.81	32	.844	32.0
1996-97	Chicago Blackhawks	NHL	41	19	18	4	2473	89	2	2.16	2.27	1.59	1212	.927	29.4	6	2	4	....	345	25	0	4.35	5.72	190	.868	33.0
1997-98	Chicago Blackhawks	NHL	58	21	25	11	3441	126	8	2.20	2.56	1.82	1520	.917	26.5	....	....	....	....	....	....	....	....	....	....	....	....
	Canada	WC-A	2	0	1	1	120	9	0	4.50	....	....	....	....	....	....	....	....	....	....	....	....	....	....	....	....	....
	NHL Totals		284	83	151	27	15810	824	14	3.13	....	....	8052	.898	....	9	2	5	....	431	31	0	4.32	....	....	....	....

Won Jack A. Butterfield Trophy (Playoff MVP - AHL) (1990)

Claimed by **San Jose** from **NY Islanders** in Expansion Draft, May 30, 1991. Traded to **Chicago** by **San Jose** for Chicago's 3rd round choice (Alexei Yegorov) in 1994 Entry Draft, July 13, 1993.

• HAINSWORTH, GEORGE

George Hainsworth G – R. 5'6", 150 lbs. b: Toronto, Ont., 6/26/1895. d: 10/9/1950. **HHOF**

Season	Club	League	GP	W	L	T	Mins	GA	SO	Avg	AAvg	Eff	SA	S%	SAPG	GP	W	L	T	Mins	GA	SO	Avg	Eff	SA	S%	SAPG
1911-12	Berlin Union Jacks	OHA	4	*3	1	0	240	13	0	3.25	....	....	....	....	....	6	2	3	1	360	30	0	5.00	....	....	....	....
1912-13	Berlin City Seniors	OHA Sr.	4	*3	1	0	240	12	1	3.00	....	....	....	....	....	8	4	3	1	480	35	1	4.38	....	....	....	....
1913-14	Berlin City Seniors	OHA Sr.	7	*7	0	0	420	11	0	*1.57	....	....	....	....	....	9	7	1	1	590	31	1	3.15	....	....	....	....
1914-15	Berlin City Seniors	OHA Sr.	5	*5	0	0	300	9	1	*1.80	....	....	....	....	....	4	2	1	1	240	19	1	4.75	....	....	....	....
1915-16	Berlin City Seniors	OHA Sr.	8	*8	0	0	480	18	*1	2.85	....	....	....	....	....	4	2	2	0	280	18	0	3.86	....	....	....	....
1916-17	Toronto Kew Beach	City Sr.	STATISTICS NOT AVAILABLE																								
1917-18	Kitchener Greenshirts	OHA Sr.	9	*9	0	0	540	31	0	*3.44	....	....	....	....	....	5	3	1	1	298	10	1	2.01	....	....	....	....
1918-19	Kitchener Greenshirts	OHA Sr.	9	5	3	1	570	28	0	2.95	....	....	....	....	....	....	....	....	....	....	....	....	....	....	....	....	....
1919-20	Kitchener Greenshirts	OHA Sr.	8	*6	2	0	480	16	*1	*2.00	....	....	....	....	....	2	0	1	1	150	6	0	2.40	....	....	....	....
1920-21	Kitchener Greenshirts	OHA Sr.	10	7	3	0	600	22	*3	2.20	....	....	....	....	....	1	0	1	0	60	6	0	6.00	....	....	....	....
1921-22	Kitchener Greenshirts	OHA Sr.	10	3	7	0	600	38	*1	3.80	....	....	....	....	....	....	....	....	....	....	....	....	....	....	....	....	....
1922-23	Kitchener Greenshirts	OHA Sr.	12	8	4	0	720	32	1	2.67	....	....	....	....	....	....	....	....	....	....	....	....	....	....	....	....	....
1923-24	Saskatoon Crescents	WCHL	*30	15	12	3	*1871	73	*4	2.34	....	....	....	....	....	....	....	....	....	....	....	....	....	....	....	....	....
1924-25	Saskatoon Crescents	WCHL	*28	16	11	1	*1698	75	2	2.65	....	....	....	....	....	2	0	1	1	120	6	0	3.00	....	....	....	....
1925-26	Saskatoon Crescents	WHL	*30	17	12	1	1821	64	4	2.11	....	....	....	....	....	2	0	1	1	129	4	0	1.86	....	....	....	....
1926-27	Montreal Canadiens	NHL	*44	28	14	2	2732	67	*14	1.47	2.20	....	....	....	....	4	1	1	2	252	6	1	1.43	....	....	....	....
1927-28	Montreal Canadiens	NHL	*44	26	11	7	2730	48	13	*1.05	1.62	....	....	....	....	2	0	1	1	128	3	0	1.41	....	....	....	....
1928-29	Montreal Canadiens	NHL	*44	22	7	15	2800	43	*22	*0.92	1.87	....	....	....	....	3	0	3	0	180	5	0	1.67	....	....	....	....
1929-30	Montreal Canadiens	NHL	42	20	13	9	3008	108	*4	2.15	2.17	....	....	....	....	*6	*5	0	1	*481	6	*3	*0.75	....	....	....	....
1930-31	Montreal Canadiens	NHL	*44	26	10	8	2740	89	8	1.95	2.46	....	....	....	....	*10	*6	4	0	*722	21	*2	1.75	....	....	....	....
1931-32	Montreal Canadiens	NHL	*48	*25	16	7	2998	110	6	2.20	2.66	....	....	....	....	4	1	3	0	300	13	0	2.60	....	....	....	....
1932-33	Montreal Canadiens	NHL	*48	18	25	5	2980	115	8	2.32	3.15	....	....	....	....	2	0	1	1	120	8	0	4.00	....	....	....	....
1933-34	Toronto Maple Leafs	NHL	*48	*26	13	9	*3010	119	3	2.37	3.03	....	....	....	....	5	2	3	0	302	11	0	2.19	....	....	....	....
1934-35	Toronto Maple Leafs	NHL	*48	*30	14	4	2957	111	8	2.25	2.72	....	....	....	....	*7	3	4	0	*460	12	*2	1.57	....	....	....	....
1935-36	Toronto Maple Leafs	NHL	*48	23	19	6	3000	106	8	2.12	3.01	....	....	....	....	*9	4	5	0	*541	27	0	2.99	....	....	....	....
1936-37	Toronto Maple Leafs	NHL	3	0	2	1	190	9	0	2.84	3.56	....	....	....	....	....	....	....	....	....	....	....	....	....	....	....	....
	Montreal Canadiens	NHL	4	2	1	1	270	12	0	2.67	3.35	....	....	....	....	....	....	....	....	....	....	....	....	....	....	....	....
	NHL Totals		465	246	145	74	29415	937	94	1.91	....	....	....	....	....	52	22	25	5	3486	112	8	1.93	....	....	....	....
	Other Major League Totals		88	48	35	5	5390	212	10	2.36	....	....	....	....	....	4	0	2	2	249	10	0	2.41	....	....	....	....

WHL All-Star Team (1926) • Won Vezina Trophy (1927, 1928, 1929)

Played in NHL All-Star Game (1934)

Signed as a free agent by **Saskatoon** (WCHL), October 11, 1923. Traded to **Montreal Canadiens** by **Saskatoon** (WHL) for cash, August 23, 1926. Traded to **Toronto** by **Montreal Canadiens** for Lorne Chabot, October 1, 1933. Signed as a free agent by **Montreal Canadiens**, November 24, 1936.

• HALL, GLENN

Glenn "Mr. Goalie" Hall G – L. 5'11", 180 lbs. b: Humboldt, Sask., 10/3/1931.

Season	Club	League	GP	W	L	T	Mins	GA	SO	Avg	AAvg	Eff	SA	S%	SAPG	GP	W	L	T	Mins	GA	SO	Avg	Eff	SA	S%	SAPG
1947-48	Humboldt Indians	SJHL	5	....	....	....	300	17	0	3.40	....	....	....	....	....	2	0	2	0	120	15	0	7.50	....	....	....	....
1948-49	Humboldt Indians	SJHL	24	13	9	2	1440	99	1	4.13	....	....	....	....	....	7	3	4	0	420	36	0	5.14	....	....	....	....
1949-50	Windsor Spitfires	OHA	43	31	11	1	2580	152	0	3.53	....	....	....	....	....	11	6	5	0	660	37	0	3.36	....	....	....	....
1950-51	Windsor Spitfires	OHA	54	32	18	4	3240	167	*6	3.09	....	....	....	....	....	8	....	....	....	480	30	0	3.75	....	....	....	....
1951-52	Indianapolis Capitols	AHL	*68	22	40	6	*4190	272	0	3.89	....	....	....	....	....	....	....	....	....	....	....	....	....	....	....	....	....
1952-53	Edmonton Flyers	WHL	63	27	27	9	3780	207	2	3.29	....	....	....	....	....	15	*10	5	0	905	53	0	3.51	....	....	....	....
	Detroit Red Wings	NHL	6	4	1	1	360	10	1	1.67	2.14	....	....	....	....	....	....	....	....	....	....	....	....	....	....	....	....
1953-54	Edmonton Flyers	WHL	*70	29	30	11	*4200	259	0	3.70	....	....	....	....	....	13	7	6	0	783	44	*2	3.37	....	....	....	....
1954-55	Edmonton Flyers	WHL	66	*38	18	10	3960	187	5	2.83	....	....	....	....	....	16	11	5	0	1000	43	1	2.58	....	....	....	....
	Detroit Red Wings	NHL	2	2	0	0	120	2	0	1.00	1.22	....	....	....	....	....	....	....	....	....	....	....	....	....	....	....	....
1955-56	Detroit Red Wings	NHL	*70	30	24	16	*4200	148	*12	2.11	2.49	....	....	....	....	*10	5	5	....	*604	28	0	2.78	....	....	....	....
1956-57	Detroit Red Wings	NHL	*70	*38	20	12	*4200	157	4	2.24	2.49	....	....	....	....	5	1	4	....	300	15	0	3.00	....	....	....	....
1957-58	Chicago Black Hawks	NHL	*70	24	39	7	*4200	202	7	2.89	3.21	....	....	....	....	....	....	....	....	....	....	....	....	....	....	....	....
1958-59	Chicago Black Hawks	NHL	*70	28	29	13	*4200	208	1	2.97	3.18	....	....	....	....	6	2	4	....	360	21	0	3.50	....	....	....	....
1959-60	Chicago Black Hawks	NHL	*70	28	29	13	*4200	180	*6	2.57	2.62	....	....	....	....	4	0	4	....	249	14	0	3.37	....	....	....	....
1960-61	Chicago Black Hawks	NHL	*70	29	24	17	*4200	180	*6	2.57	2.57	....	....	....	....	*12	*8	4	....	*772	27	*2	*2.10	....	....	....	....
1961-62	Chicago Black Hawks	NHL	*70	31	26	13	*4200	186	*9	2.66	2.67	....	....	....	....	*12	*6	6	....	*720	31	*2	2.58	....	....	....	....
1962-63	Chicago Black Hawks	NHL	66	30	20	15	3910	166	*5	2.55	2.58	....	....	....	....	6	2	4	....	360	25	0	4.17	....	....	....	....
1963-64	Chicago Black Hawks	NHL	65	*34	19	11	3860	148	7	2.30	2.48	....	....	....	....	7	3	4	....	408	22	0	3.24	....	....	....	....
1964-65	Chicago Black Hawks	NHL	41	18	17	5	2440	99	4	2.43	2.57	....	....	....	....	*13	*7	6	....	*760	28	1	2.21	....	....	....	....
1965-66	Chicago Black Hawks	NHL	*64	*34	21	7	*3747	164	4	2.63	2.61	....	....	....	....	6	2	4	....	347	22	0	3.80	....	....	....	....
1966-67	Chicago Black Hawks	NHL	32	19	5	5	1664	66	2	*2.38	2.43	....	....	....	....	3	1	2	....	176	8	0	2.73	....	....	....	....
1967-68	St. Louis Blues	NHL	49	19	21	9	2858	118	5	2.48	2.73	....	....	....	....	*18	8	10	....	*1111	45	*1	2.43	....	....	....	....
1968-69	St. Louis Blues	NHL	41	19	12	8	2354	85	*8	2.17	2.22	....	....	....	....	3	0	2	....	131	5	0	2.29	....	....	....	....
1969-70	St. Louis Blues	NHL	18	7	8	3	1010	49	1	2.91	3.09	....	....	....	....	7	4	3	....	421	21	0	2.99	....	....	....	....
1970-71	St. Louis Blues	NHL	32	13	11	8	1761	71	2	2.42	2.38	....	....	....	....	3	0	3	....	180	9	0	3.00	....	....	....	....
	NHL Totals		906	407	326	163	53484	2239	84	2.51	....	....	....	....	....	115	49	65	....	6899	321	6	2.79	....	....	....	....

WHL First All-Star Team (1955) • NHL Second All-Star Team (1956, 1961, 1962, 1967) • Won Calder Memorial Trophy (1956) • NHL First All-Star Team (1957, 1958, 1960, 1963, 1964, 1966, 1969) • Won Vezina Trophy (1963) • Shared Vezina Trophy with Denis Dejordy (1967) • Won Conn Smythe Trophy (1968) • Shared Vezina Trophy with Jacques Plante (1969)

Played in NHL All-Star Game (1955, 1956, 1957, 1958, 1960, 1961, 1962, 1963, 1964, 1965, 1967, 1968, 1969)

Traded to **Chicago** by **Detroit** with Ted Lindsay for John Wilson, Forbes Kennedy, William Preston and Hank Bassen, July, 1957. Claimed by **St. Louis** from **Chicago** in Expansion Draft, June 6, 1967.

● **HAMEL, PIERRE** Pierre Hamel G – L. 5'9", 170 lbs. b: Montreal, Que., 9/16/1952.

			REGULAR SEASON													PLAYOFFS											
Season	Club	League	GP	W	L	T	Mins	GA	SO	Avg	AAvg	Eff	SA	S%	SAPG	GP	W	L	T	Mins	GA	SO	Avg	Eff	SA	S%	SAPG
1969-70	Verdun Maple Leafs	QJHL	12	....	....	....	680	79	0	6.97	....	....	....	....	....	1	0	0	0	6	1	0	10.00	....	....	....	....
1970-71	Verdun Maple Leafs	QJHL	43	....	....	....	2580	200	0	4.65	....	....	....	....	....	1	0	1	0	30	7	0	14.00	....	....	....	....
1971-72	Laval Titans	QMJHL	15	....	....	....	870	86	0	5.93	....	....	....	....	....	....	....	....	....	....	....	....	....	....	....	....	....
	Drummondville Rangers	QMJHL	34	....	....	....	2000	120	1	3.60	....	....	....	....	....	8	....	....	....	450	28	0	3.73	....	....	....	....
1972-73	Trail Smoke Eaters	WHL	STATISTICS NOT AVAILABLE													....	....	....	....	....	....	....	....	....	....	....	....
1973-74	Trail Smoke Eaters	WHL	30	....	....	....	1800	105	1	3.50	....	....	....	....	....	....	....	....	....	....	....	....	....	....	....	....	....
	Salt Lake Golden Eagles	WHL	1	0	1	0	60	4	0	4.00	....	....	....	....	....	....	....	....	....	....	....	....	....	....	....	....	....
1974-75	**Toronto Maple Leafs**	**NHL**	**4**	**1**	**2**	**0**	**195**	**18**	**0**	**5.54**	**5.00**	....	....	....	....	....	....	....	....	....	....	....	....	....	....	....	....
	Oklahoma City Blazers	CHL	44	22	12	6	2349	125	3	3.19	....	....	....	....	....	1	0	0	0	22	2	0	5.45	....	....	....	....
1975-76	Oklahoma City Blazers	CHL	39	14	12	6	2038	107	2	3.15	....	....	....	....	....	2	0	2	0	82	8	0	5.85	....	....	....	....
1976-77	Oklahoma City Blazers	CHL	33	5	19	4	1696	162	0	5.73	....	....	....	....	....	....	....	....	....	....	....	....	....	....	....	....	....
1977-78	Dallas Black Hawks	CHL	36	15	16	1	1982	126	0	3.81	....	....	....	....	....	1	0	0	0	20	2	0	6.00	....	....	....	....
1978-79	**Toronto Maple Leafs**	**NHL**	**1**	**0**	**0**	**0**	**1**	**0**	**0**	**0.00**	**0.00**	....	....	....	....	....	....	....	....	....	....	....	....	....	....	....	....
	New Brunswick Hawks	AHL	37	18	12	5	2068	119	0	2.45	....	....	....	....	....	3	1	2	0	187	13	0	4.17	....	....	....	....
1979-80	**Winnipeg Jets**	**NHL**	**35**	**9**	**19**	**3**	**1947**	**130**	**0**	**4.01**	**3.53**	....	....	....	....	....	....	....	....	....	....	....	....	....	....	....	....
1980-81	**Winnipeg Jets**	**NHL**	**29**	**3**	**20**	**4**	**1623**	**128**	**0**	**4.73**	**3.80**	....	....	....	....	....	....	....	....	....	....	....	....	....	....	....	....
	Tulsa Oilers	CHL	9	2	5	1	478	3	0	4.14	....	....	....	....	....	....	....	....	....	....	....	....	....	....	....	....	....
1981-82	Tulsa Oilers	CHL	5	3	1	0	247	14	0	3.40	....	....	....	....	....	....	....	....	....	....	....	....	....	....	....	....	....
	Fredericton Express	AHL	29	5	15	3	1571	114	1	4.35	....	....	....	....	....	....	....	....	....	....	....	....	....	....	....	....	....
1982-83	Sherbrooke Jets	AHL	2	1	1	0	119	6	0	3.02	....	....	....	....	....	....	....	....	....	....	....	....	....	....	....	....	....
1983-84	Carolina Thunderbirds	ACHL	38	....	....	....	2192	151	*2	4.13	....	....	....	....	....	8	....	....	....	500	26	0	3.12	....	....	....	....
1984-85	Carolina Thunderbirds	ACHL	36	....	....	....	1909	109	*1	3.42	....	....	....	....	....	8	....	....	....	452	27	0	3.58	....	....	....	....
	NHL Totals		**69**	**13**	**41**	**7**	**3766**	**276**	**0**	**4.40**	....	....	....	....	....	....	....	....	....	....	....	....	....	....	....	....	....

CHL Second All-Star Team (1976)

Signed as a free agent by **Toronto**, September 27, 1974. Claimed by **Winnipeg** from **Toronto** in Expansion Draft, June 13, 1979.

● **HANLON, GLEN** Glen "Red" Hanlon G – R. 6', 185 lbs. b: Brandon, Man., 2/20/1957. Vancouver's 3rd choice, 40th overall, in 1977 Amateur Draft.

Season	Club	League	GP	W	L	T	Mins	GA	SO	Avg	AAvg	Eff	SA	S%	SAPG	GP	W	L	T	Mins	GA	SO	Avg	Eff	SA	S%	SAPG
1974-75	Brandon Wheat Kings	WCJHL	43	....	....	....	2498	176	0	4.22	....	....	....	....	....	5	....	....	....	284	29	0	6.13	....	....	....	....
1975-76	Brandon Wheat Kings	WCJHL	*64	....	....	....	*3523	234	*4	3.99	....	....	....	....	....	5	....	....	....	300	33	0	6.60	....	....	....	....
1976-77	Brandon Wheat Kings	WCJHL	65	....	....	....	3784	195	*4	*3.09	....	....	....	....	....	*16	....	....	....	*913	53	0	3.48	....	....	....	....
1977-78	**Vancouver Canucks**	**NHL**	**4**	**1**	**2**	**1**	**200**	**9**	**0**	**2.70**	**2.53**	....	....	....	....	....	....	....	....	....	....	....	....	....	....	....	....
	Tulsa Oilers	CHL	53	25	23	3	3123	160	*3	3.07	....	....	....	....	....	2	1	1	0	120	5	0	2.50	....	....	....	....
1978-79	**Vancouver Canucks**	**NHL**	**31**	**12**	**13**	**5**	**1821**	**94**	**3**	**3.10**	**2.73**	....	....	....	....	....	....	....	....	....	....	....	....	....	....	....	....
1979-80	**Vancouver Canucks**	**NHL**	**57**	**17**	**29**	**10**	**3341**	**193**	**0**	**3.47**	**3.05**	....	....	....	....	**2**	**0**	**0**	....	**60**	**3**	**0**	**3.00**	....	....	....	....
1980-81	**Vancouver Canucks**	**NHL**	**17**	**5**	**8**	**0**	**798**	**59**	**1**	**4.44**	**3.56**	....	....	....	....	....	....	....	....	....	....	....	....	....	....	....	....
	Dallas Black Hawks	CHL	4	3	1	0	239	8	1	2.01	....	....	....	....	....	....	....	....	....	....	....	....	....	....	....	....	....
1981-82	**Vancouver Canucks**	**NHL**	**28**	**8**	**14**	**5**	**1610**	**106**	**1**	**3.95**	**3.04**	....	....	....	....	....	....	....	....	....	....	....	....	....	....	....	....
	St. Louis Blues	**NHL**	**2**	**0**	**1**	**0**	**76**	**8**	**0**	**6.32**	**4.87**	....	....	....	....	**3**	**0**	**2**	....	**109**	**9**	**0**	**4.95**	....	....	....	....
1982-83	**St. Louis Blues**	**NHL**	**14**	**3**	**8**	**1**	**671**	**50**	**0**	**4.47**	**3.57**	**5.40**	**414**	**.879**	**37.0**	....	....	....	....	....	....	....	....	....	....	....	....
	New York Rangers	**NHL**	**21**	**9**	**10**	**1**	**1173**	**67**	**0**	**3.43**	**2.74**	**3.62**	**635**	**.894**	**32.5**	**1**	**0**	**1**	....	**60**	**5**	**0**	**5.00**	....	....	....	....
1983-84	**New York Rangers**	**NHL**	**50**	**28**	**14**	**4**	**2837**	**166**	**1**	**3.51**	**2.74**	**3.86**	**1508**	**.890**	**31.9**	**5**	**2**	**3**	....	**308**	**13**	**1**	**2.53**	**1.98**	**166**	**.922**	**32.3**
1984-85	**New York Rangers**	**NHL**	**44**	**14**	**20**	**7**	**2510**	**175**	**0**	**4.18**	**3.33**	**6.08**	**1409**	**.876**	**34.4**	**3**	**0**	**3**	....	**168**	**14**	**0**	**5.00**	**7.07**	**99**	**.859**	**35.4**
1985-86	**New York Rangers**	**NHL**	**23**	**5**	**12**	**1**	**1170**	**65**	**0**	**3.33**	**2.58**	**3.56**	**608**	**.893**	**31.2**	**3**	**0**	**0**	....	**75**	**6**	**0**	**4.80**	**9.00**	**32**	**.813**	**25.6**
	Adirondack Red Wings	AHL	10	5	4	1	605	33	0	3.27	....	....	....	....	....	....	....	....	....	....	....	....	....	....	....	....	....
	New Haven Nighthawks	AHL	5	3	2	0	279	22	0	4.73	....	....	....	....	....	....	....	....	....	....	....	....	....	....	....	....	....
1986-87	**Detroit Red Wings**	**NHL**	**36**	**11**	**16**	**5**	**1963**	**104**	**1**	**3.18**	**2.67**	**3.39**	**975**	**.893**	**29.8**	**8**	**5**	**2**	....	**467**	**13**	***2**	***1.67**	**0.96**	**227**	**.943**	**29.2**
1987-88	**Detroit Red Wings**	**NHL**	**47**	**22**	**17**	**5**	**2623**	**141**	***4**	**3.23**	**2.68**	**3.53**	**1292**	**.891**	**29.6**	**8**	**4**	**3**	....	**431**	**22**	***1**	**3.06**	**3.94**	**171**	**.871**	**23.8**
1988-89	**Detroit Red Wings**	**NHL**	**39**	**13**	**14**	**8**	**2092**	**124**	**1**	**3.56**	**2.93**	**4.18**	**1055**	**.882**	**30.3**	**2**	**0**	**1**	....	**78**	**7**	**0**	**5.38**	**8.01**	**47**	**.851**	**36.2**
1989-90	**Detroit Red Wings**	**NHL**	**45**	**15**	**18**	**5**	**2290**	**154**	**1**	**4.03**	**3.38**	**5.35**	**1159**	**.867**	**30.4**	....	....	....	....	....	....	....	....	....	....	....	....
1990-91	**Detroit Red Wings**	**NHL**	**19**	**4**	**6**	**3**	**862**	**46**	**0**	**3.20**	**2.86**	**3.36**	**438**	**.895**	**30.5**	....	....	....	....	....	....	....	....	....	....	....	....
	San Diego Gulls	IHL	11	6	4	0	603	39	0	3.88	....	....	....	....	....	....	....	....	....	....	....	....	....	....	....	....	....
	NHL Totals		**477**	**167**	**202**	**61**	**26037**	**1561**	**13**	**3.60**	....	....	....	....	....	**35**	**11**	**15**	....	**1756**	**92**	**4**	**3.14**	....	....	....	....

WCJHL All-Star Team (1976, 1977) • CHL First All-Star Team (1978) • Won Ken McKenzie Trophy (CHL's Rookie of the Year) (1978)

Traded to **St. Louis** by **Vancouver** for Rick Heinz, Tony Currie, Jim Nill and St. Louis' 4th round choice (Shawn Kilroy) in 1982 Entry Draft, March 9, 1982. Traded to **NY Rangers** by **St. Louis** with Vaclav Nedomansky for Andre Dore, January 4, 1983. Traded to **Detroit** by **NY Rangers** with NY Rangers' 3rd round choices in 1987 (Dennis Holland) and 1988 (Guy Dupuis) Entry Drafts for Kelly Kisio, Lane Lambert and Jim Leavins, July 29, 1986.

● **HARRISON, PAUL** Paul Harrison G – L. 6'1", 196 lbs. b: Timmins, Ont., 2/11/1955. Minnesota's 2nd choice, 40th overall, in 1975 Amateur Draft.

Season	Club	League	GP	W	L	T	Mins	GA	SO	Avg	AAvg	Eff	SA	S%	SAPG	GP	W	L	T	Mins	GA	SO	Avg	Eff	SA	S%	SAPG
1973-74	Oshawa Generals	OHA	33	....	....	....	1968	131	1	3.99	....	....	....	....	....	....	....	....	....	....	....	....	....	....	....	....	....
1974-75	Oshawa Generals	OHA	34	....	....	....	2040	153	2	4.50	....	....	....	....	....	4	....	....	....	240	17	0	4.25	....	....	....	....
1975-76	**Minnesota North Stars**	**NHL**	**6**	**0**	**4**	**1**	**307**	**28**	**0**	**5.47**	**4.96**	....	....	....	....	....	....	....	....	....	....	....	....	....	....	....	....
	Providence Reds	AHL	3	1	1	1	145	13	0	5.38	....	....	....	....	....	....	....	....	....	....	....	....	....	....	....	....	....
1976-77	**Minnesota North Stars**	**NHL**	**2**	**0**	**2**	**0**	**120**	**11**	**0**	**5.50**	**5.12**	....	....	....	....	....	....	....	....	....	....	....	....	....	....	....	....
	New Haven Nighthawks	AHL	*55	*32	17	6	*3265	172	2	3.16	....	....	....	....	....	6	2	4	0	363	25	0	4.13	....	....	....	....
1977-78	**Minnesota North Stars**	**NHL**	**27**	**6**	**16**	**2**	**1555**	**99**	**1**	**3.82**	**3.59**	....	....	....	....	....	....	....	....	....	....	....	....	....	....	....	....
1978-79	**Toronto Maple Leafs**	**NHL**	**25**	**8**	**12**	**3**	**1403**	**82**	**1**	**3.51**	**3.10**	....	....	....	....	**2**	**0**	**1**	....	**91**	**7**	**0**	**4.62**	....	....	....	....
1979-80	**Toronto Maple Leafs**	**NHL**	**30**	**9**	**17**	**2**	**1492**	**110**	**0**	**4.42**	**3.90**	....	....	....	....	....	....	....	....	....	....	....	....	....	....	....	....
	New Brunswick Hawks	AHL	9	4	3	1	485	30	0	3.71	....	....	....	....	....	....	....	....	....	....	....	....	....	....	....	....	....
1980-81	Dallas Black Hawks	CHL	37	24	7	2	2047	92	*4	2.70	....	....	....	....	....	4	....	....	....	179	16	0	5.33	....	....	....	....
	Toronto Maple Leafs	**NHL**	....	....	....	....	....	....	....	....	....	....	....	....	....	**1**	**0**	**0**	....	**40**	**1**	**0**	**1.50**	....	....	....	....
1981-82	**Pittsburgh Penguins**	**NHL**	**13**	**3**	**7**	**0**	**700**	**64**	**0**	**5.49**	**4.24**	....	....	....	....	....	....	....	....	....	....	....	....	....	....	....	....
	Buffalo Sabres	**NHL**	**6**	**2**	**1**	**1**	**229**	**14**	**0**	**3.67**	**2.83**	....	....	....	....	**1**	**0**	**0**	....	**26**	**1**	**0**	**2.31**	....	....	....	....
	NHL Totals		**109**	**28**	**59**	**9**	**5806**	**408**	**2**	**4.22**	....	....	....	....	....	**4**	**0**	**1**	....	**157**	**9**	**0**	**3.44**	....	....	....	....

AHL Second All-Star Team (1977) • CHL Second All-Star Team (1981) • Shared Terry Sawchuk Trophy (fewest goals against - CHL) with Ken Ellacott (1981)

Traded to **Toronto** by **Minnesota** for Toronto's 4th round choice (Terry Tait) in 1981 Entry Draft, June 14, 1978. Traded to **Pittsburgh** by **Toronto** for future considerations, September 11, 1981. Claimed on waivers by **Buffalo** from **Pittsburgh**, February 8, 1982.

● **HASEK, DOMINIK** Dominik "The Dominator" Hasek G – L. 5'11", 168 lbs. b: Pardubice, Czech., 1/29/1965. Chicago's 11th choice, 207th overall, in 1983 Entry Draft.

Season	Club	League	GP	W	L	T	Mins	GA	SO	Avg	AAvg	Eff	SA	S%	SAPG	GP	W	L	T	Mins	GA	SO	Avg	Eff	SA	S%	SAPG
1981-82	HC Pardubice	Czech.	12	....	....	....	661	34	....	3.09	....	....	....	....	....	....	....	....	....	....	....	....	....	....	....	....	....
	Czechoslovakia	EJC-A	5	....	....	....	20	1	....	3.00	....	....	....	....	....	....	....	....	....	....	....	....	....	....	....	....	....
1982-83	HC Pardubice	Czech.	42	....	....	....	2358	105	....	2.67	....	....	....	....	....	....	....	....	....	....	....	....	....	....	....	....	....
	Czechoslovakia	WEC-A	2	1	1	0	120	5	....	2.50	....	....	....	....	....	....	....	....	....	....	....	....	....	....	....	....	....
1983-84	HC Pardubice	Czech.	40	....	....	....	2304	108	....	2.81	....	....	....	....	....	....	....	....	....	....	....	....	....	....	....	....	....
1984-85	Czechoslovakia	C Cup	4	0	3	1	188	12	....	4.00	....	....	....	....	....	....	....	....	....	....	....	....	....	....	....	....	....
	HC Pardubice	Czech.	42	....	....	....	2419	131	....	3.25	....	....	....	....	....	....	....	....	....	....	....	....	....	....	....	....	....
	Czechoslovakia	WJC-A	7	....	....	....	380	10	....	1.89	....	....	....	....	....	....	....	....	....	....	....	....	....	....	....	....	....
1985-86	HC Pardubice	Czech.	45	....	....	....	2689	138	....	3.08	....	....	....	....	....	....	....	....	....	....	....	....	....	....	....	....	....
	Czechoslovakia	WEC-A	9	....	....	....	538	19	....	2.12	....	....	....	....	....	....	....	....	....	....	....	....	....	....	....	....	....
1986-87	HC Pardubice	Czech.	43	....	....	....	2515	103	....	2.46	....	....	....	....	....	....	....	....	....	....	....	....	....	....	....	....	....
	Czechoslovakia	WEC-A	9	5	2	2	520	19	....	2.19	....	....	....	....	....	....	....	....	....	....	....	....	....	....	....	....	....
1987-88	Czechoslovakia	C Cup	6	2	3	1	300	20	....	3.00	....	....	....	....	....	....	....	....	....	....	....	....	....	....	....	....	....
	HC Pardubice	Czech.	31	....	....	....	1862	93	....	3.00	....	....	....	....	....	....	....	....	....	....	....	....	....	....	....	....	....
	Czechoslovakia	Olympics	5	....	....	....	217	18	....	4.98	....	....	....	....	....	....	....	....	....	....	....	....	....	....	....	....	....
1988-89	HC Pardubice	Czech.	42	....	....	....	2507	114	....	2.73	....	....	....	....	....	....	....	....	....	....	....	....	....	....	....	....	....
	Czechoslovakia	WEC-A	10	4	4	2	600	21	....	2.10	....	....	....	....	....	....	....	....	....	....	....	....	....	....	....	....	....
1989-90	Dukla Jihlava	Czech.	40	....	....	....	2251	80	....	2.13	....	....	....	....	....	....	....	....	....	....	....	....	....	....	....	....	....
	Czechoslovakia	WEC-A	8	5	3	0	480	20	....	2.50	....	....	....	....	....	....	....	....	....	....	....	....	....	....	....	....	....
1990-91	**Chicago Blackhawks**	**NHL**	**5**	**3**	**0**	**1**	**195**	**8**	**0**	**2.46**	**2.20**	**2.12**	**93**	**.914**	**28.6**	**3**	**0**	**0**	....	**69**	**3**	**0**	**2.61**	**2.01**	**39**	**.923**	**33.9**
	Indianapolis Ice	IHL	33	20	11	1	1903	80	*5	*2.52	....	....	....	....	....	1	1	0	....	60	3	0	3.00	....	....	....	....

			REGULAR SEASON													PLAYOFFS											
Season	Club	League	GP	W	L	T	Mins	GA	SO	Avg	AAvg	Eff	SA	S%	SAPG	GP	W	L	T	Mins	GA	SO	Avg	Eff	SA	S%	SAPG
1991-92	Czechoslovakia	C Cup	5	1	4	0	300	18	....	4.00	....	....	....	....	....	....	....	....	....	....	....	....	....	....	....	....	....
	Chicago Blackhawks	**NHL**	**20**	**10**	**4**	**1**	**1014**	**44**	**1**	**2.60**	**2.30**	**2.77**	**413**	**.893**	**24.4**	**3**	**0**	**2**	....	**158**	**8**	**0**	**3.04**	**3.47**	**70**	**.886**	**26.6**
	Indianapolis Ice	IHL	20	7	10	3	1162	69	1	3.56	....	....	....	....	....	....	....	....	....	....	....	....	....	....	....	....	....
1992-93	**Buffalo Sabres**	**NHL**	**28**	**11**	**10**	**4**	**1429**	**75**	**0**	**3.15**	**2.68**	**3.28**	**720**	**.896**	**30.2**	**1**	**1**	**0**	....	**45**	**1**	**0**	**1.33**	**0.55**	**24**	**.958**	**32.0**
1993-94	**Buffalo Sabres**	**NHL**	**58**	**30**	**20**	**6**	**3358**	**109**	***7**	***1.95**	**1.84**	**1.37**	**1552**	**.930**	**27.7**	**7**	**3**	**4**	....	**484**	**13**	**2**	***1.61**	**0.80**	**261**	**.950**	**32.4**
1994-95	HC Pardubice	Czech.	2	....	....	....	124	6	0	2.90	....	....	....	....	....	....	....	....	....	....	....	....	....	....	....	....	....
	Buffalo Sabres	**NHL**	**41**	**19**	**14**	**7**	**2416**	**85**	***5**	***2.11**	**2.16**	**1.47**	**1221**	**.930**	**30.3**	**5**	**1**	**4**	....	**309**	**18**	**0**	**3.50**	**4.81**	**131**	**.863**	**25.4**
1995-96	**Buffalo Sabres**	**NHL**	**59**	**22**	**30**	**6**	**3417**	**161**	**2**	**2.83**	**2.77**	**2.27**	**2011**	**.920**	**35.3**	....	....	....	....	....	....	....	....	....	....	....	....
1996-97	**Buffalo Sabres**	**NHL**	**67**	**37**	**20**	**10**	**4037**	**153**	**5**	**2.27**	**2.39**	**1.60**	**2177**	**.930**	**32.4**	**3**	**1**	**1**	....	**153**	**5**	**0**	**1.96**	**1.44**	**68**	**.926**	**26.7**
1997-98	**Buffalo Sabres**	**NHL**	***72**	**33**	**23**	**13**	***4220**	**147**	***13**	**2.09**	**2.43**	**1.43**	**2149**	**.932**	**30.6**	**15**	**10**	**5**	....	**948**	**32**	**1**	**2.03**	**1.26**	**514**	**.938**	**32.5**
	Czech Republic	Olympics	6	5	1	0	369	6	2	0.97	....	....	....	....	....	....	....	....	....	....	....	....	....	....	....	....	....
	NHL Totals		**350**	**165**	**121**	**48**	**20086**	**782**	**33**	**2.34**	....	....	**10336**	**.924**	....	**37**	**16**	**16**	....	**2166**	**80**	**3**	**2.22**	....	....	....	....

EJC-A All-Star Team (1982) • Named Best Goaltender at EJC-A (1982) • WJC-A All-Star Team (1983) • Czechoslovakian Goaltender-of-the-Year (1986, 1987, 1988, 1989, 1990) • Czechoslovakian Player-of-the-Year (1987, 1989, 1990) • WEC-A All-Star Team (1987, 1989, 1990) • Named Best Goaltender at WEC-A (1987, 1989) • Czechoslovakian First All-Star Team (1988, 1989, 1990) • IHL First All-Star Team (1991) • NHL/Upper Deck All-Rookie Team (1992) • NHL First All-Star Team (1994, 1995, 1997, 1998) • Shared William M. Jennings Trophy with Grant Fuhr (1994) • Won Vezina Trophy (1994, 1995, 1997, 1998) • Won Lester B. Pearson Award (1997, 1998) • Won Hart Trophy (1997, 1998) • Named Best Goaltender at Olympic Games (1998)

Played in NHL All-Star Game (1996, 1997, 1998)

Traded to **Buffalo** by **Chicago** for Stephane Beauregard and Buffalo's 4th round choice (Eric Daze) in 1993 Entry Draft, August 7, 1992.

• HAYWARD, BRIAN

Brian Hayward G – L. 5′10″, 180 lbs. b: Toronto, Ont., 6/25/1960.

Season	Club	League	GP	W	L	T	Mins	GA	SO	Avg	AAvg	Eff	SA	S%	SAPG	GP	W	L	T	Mins	GA	SO	Avg	Eff	SA	S%	SAPG
1978-79	Cornell University	ECAC	25	18	6	0	1469	95	0	3.88	....	....	....	....	....	3	2	1	0	179	14	0	4.66	....	....	....	....
1979-80	Cornell University	ECAC	12	2	7	0	508	52	0	6.02	....	....	....	....	....	....	....	....	....	....	....	....	....	....	....	....	....
1980-81	Cornell University	ECAC	19	11	4	1	967	58	1	3.54	....	....	....	....	....	4	2	1	0	181	18	0	4.50	....	....	....	....
1981-82	Cornell University	ECAC	22	11	10	1	1249	66	0	3.17	....	....	....	....	....	....	....	....	....	....	....	....	....	....	....	....	....
1982-83	**Winnipeg Jets**	**NHL**	**24**	**10**	**12**	**2**	**1440**	**89**	**1**	**3.71**	**2.96**	**4.20**	**786**	**.887**	**32.8**	**3**	**0**	**3**	....	**160**	**14**	**0**	**5.25**	....	....	....	....
	Sherbrooke Jets	AHL	22	6	11	3	1208	89	1	4.42	....	....	....	....	....	....	....	....	....	....	....	....	....	....	....	....	....
1983-84	**Winnipeg Jets**	**NHL**	**28**	**7**	**18**	**2**	**1530**	**124**	**0**	**4.86**	**3.82**	**7.01**	**860**	**.856**	**33.7**	....	....	....	....	....	....	....	....	....	....	....	....
	Sherbrooke Jets	AHL	15	4	8	0	781	69	0	5.30	....	....	....	....	....	....	....	....	....	....	....	....	....	....	....	....	....
1984-85	**Winnipeg Jets**	**NHL**	**61**	**33**	**17**	**7**	**3436**	**220**	**0**	**3.84**	**3.05**	**4.66**	**1814**	**.879**	**31.7**	**6**	**2**	**4**	....	**309**	**23**	**0**	**4.47**	**6.59**	**156**	**.853**	**30.3**
1985-86	**Winnipeg Jets**	**NHL**	**52**	**13**	**28**	**5**	**2721**	**217**	**0**	**4.79**	**3.75**	**7.57**	**1373**	**.842**	**30.3**	**2**	**0**	**1**	....	**68**	**6**	**0**	**5.29**	**10.24**	**31**	**.806**	**27.4**
	Sherbrooke Canadiens	AHL	3	2	0	1	185	5	0	1.62	....	....	....	....	....	....	....	....	....	....	....	....	....	....	....	....	....
1986-87	**Montreal Canadiens**	**NHL**	**37**	**19**	**13**	**4**	**2178**	**102**	**1**	***2.81**	**2.35**	**2.99**	**959**	**.894**	**26.4**	**13**	**6**	**5**	....	**708**	**32**	**0**	**2.71**	**2.82**	**308**	**.896**	**26.1**
1987-88	**Montreal Canadiens**	**NHL**	**39**	**22**	**10**	**4**	**2247**	**107**	**2**	**2.86**	**2.37**	**2.97**	**1032**	**.896**	**27.6**	**4**	**2**	**2**	....	**230**	**9**	**0**	**2.35**	**2.49**	**85**	**.894**	**22.2**
1988-89	**Montreal Canadiens**	**NHL**	**36**	**20**	**13**	**3**	**2091**	**101**	**1**	**2.90**	**2.38**	**3.28**	**894**	**.887**	**25.7**	**2**	**1**	**1**	....	**124**	**7**	**0**	**3.39**	**4.39**	**54**	**.870**	**26.1**
1989-90	**Montreal Canadiens**	**NHL**	**29**	**10**	**12**	**6**	**1674**	**94**	**1**	**3.37**	**2.82**	**4.11**	**770**	**.878**	**27.6**	**1**	**0**	**0**	....	**33**	**2**	**0**	**3.64**	**4.04**	**18**	**.889**	**32.7**
1990-91	Montreal Canadiens	FrTour	2	....	....	....	64	2	....	1.87	....	....	....	....	....	....	....	....	....	....	....	....	....	....	....	....	....
	Kalamazoo Wings	IHL	2	2	0	0	120	5	0	2.50	....	....	....	....	....	....	....	....	....	....	....	....	....	....	....	....	....
	Minnesota North Stars	**NHL**	**26**	**6**	**15**	**3**	**1473**	**77**	**2**	**3.14**	**2.80**	**3.59**	**674**	**.886**	**27.5**	**6**	**0**	**2**	....	**171**	**11**	**0**	**3.86**	**5.66**	**75**	**.853**	**26.3**
1991-92	**San Jose Sharks**	**NHL**	**7**	**1**	**4**	**0**	**305**	**25**	**0**	**4.92**	**4.37**	**6.95**	**177**	**.859**	**34.8**	....	....	....	....	....	....	....	....	....	....	....	....
	Kansas City Blades	IHL	2	1	1	0	119	3	1	1.51	....	....	....	....	....	....	....	....	....	....	....	....	....	....	....	....	....
1992-93	**San Jose Sharks**	**NHL**	**18**	**2**	**14**	**1**	**930**	**86**	**0**	**5.55**	**4.74**	**8.54**	**559**	**.846**	**36.1**	....	....	....	....	....	....	....	....	....	....	....	....
	NHL Totals		**357**	**143**	**156**	**37**	**20025**	**1242**	**8**	**3.72**	....	....	**9898**	**.875**	....	**37**	**11**	**18**	....	**1803**	**104**	**0**	**3.46**	....	....	....	....

ECAC First All-Star Team (1982) • NCAA East First All-American Team (1982) • Shared William M. Jennings Trophy with Patrick Roy (1987, 1988, 1989)

Signed as a free agent by **Winnipeg**, May 5, 1982. Traded to **Montreal** by **Winnipeg** for Steve Penney and the rights to Jan Ingman, August 19, 1986. Traded to **Minnesota** by **Montreal** for Jayson Moore, November 7, 1990. Claimed by **San Jose** from **Minnesota** in Dispersal Draft, May 30, 1991.

• HEAD, DON

Don Head G – L. 5′10″, 200 lbs. b: Mt. Dennis, Ont., 6/30/1933.

Season	Club	League	GP	W	L	T	Mins	GA	SO	Avg	AAvg	Eff	SA	S%	SAPG	GP	W	L	T	Mins	GA	SO	Avg	Eff	SA	S%	SAPG
1951-52	Toronto Marlboros	OHA	37	....	....	....	2220	107	*4	*2.87	....	....	....	....	....	....	....	....	....	....	....	....	....	....	....	....	....
1952-53			STATISTICS NOT AVAILABLE																								
1953-54	Stratford Indians	OHA Sr.	14	....	....	....	840	53	1	3.79	....	....	....	....	....	....	....	....	....	....	....	....	....	....	....	....	....
1954-55	Stratford Indians	OHA Sr.	13	....	....	....	780	49	0	3.77	....	....	....	....	....	....	....	....	....	....	....	....	....	....	....	....	....
1955-56	Stratford Indians	OHA Sr.	47	....	....	....	2820	186	*3	3.96	....	....	....	....	....	6	....	....	....	360	25	0	4.17	....	....	....	....
1956-57	Windsor Bulldogs	OHA Sr.	50	30	17	3	3000	144	*6	*2.88	....	....	....	....	....	12	....	....	....	720	50	0	4.17	....	....	....	....
1957-58	Chatham Maroons	NOHA	49	....	....	....	2940	168	3	3.43	....	....	....	....	....	....	....	....	....	....	....	....	....	....	....	....	....
1958-59	Chatham Maroons	NOHA	54	37	15	2	3240	183	*6	3.39	....	....	....	....	....	10	....	....	....	600	27	*1	2.70	....	....	....	....
1959-60	Windsor Bulldogs	OHA Sr.	48	....	....	....	2860	138	*3	*2.90	....	....	....	....	....	17	....	....	....	1020	47	*3	*2.76	....	....	....	....
	Canada	Olympics	7	5	1	0	385	12	*2	1.87	....	....	....	....	....	....	....	....	....	....	....	....	....	....	....	....	....
1960-61	Portland Buckaroos	WHL	*70	*38	23	9	*4290	192	*7	*2.69	....	....	....	....	....	*14	*10	4	0	*846	30	*2	*2.13	....	....	....	....
1961-62	**Boston Bruins**	**NHL**	**38**	**9**	**26**	**3**	**2280**	**161**	**2**	**4.24**	**4.53**	....	....	....	....	....	....	....	....	....	....	....	....	....	....	....	....
	Portland Buckaroos	WHL	5	3	1	1	300	16	0	3.20	....	....	....	....	....	....	....	....	....	....	....	....	....	....	....	....	....
1962-63	Portland Buckaroos	WHL	*70	*43	21	6	*4200	178	4	*2.54	....	....	....	....	....	7	3	4	0	423	22	0	3.12	....	....	....	....
1963-64	Portland Buckaroos	WHL	16	6	9	1	940	57	0	3.64	....	....	....	....	....	....	....	....	....	....	....	....	....	....	....	....	....
1964-65	Portland Buckaroos	WHL	51	26	20	4	3055	153	3	3.00	....	....	....	....	....	9	*8	1	0	554	13	*3	*1.41	....	....	....	....
1965-66	Portland Buckaroos	WHL	36	20	12	3	2154	100	4	*2.79	....	....	....	....	....	....	....	....	....	....	....	....	....	....	....	....	....
1966-67	Portland Buckaroos	WHL	44	26	13	5	2714	120	3	2.65	....	....	....	....	....	4	0	3	0	225	10	0	2.67	....	....	....	....
1967-68	Seattle Totems	WHL	46	23	19	4	2717	114	3	2.52	....	....	....	....	....	*9	*8	1	0	*556	20	*2	*2.17	....	....	....	....
1968-69	Seattle Totems	WHL	44	22	13	4	2377	120	1	3.03	....	....	....	....	....	4	0	4	0	245	19	0	4.65	....	....	....	....
1969-70	Seattle Totems	WHL	20	8	10	2	1200	71	0	3.55	....	....	....	....	....	....	....	....	....	....	....	....	....	....	....	....	....
1970-71	Seattle Totems	WHL	16	4	7	3	769	45	0	3.51	....	....	....	....	....	....	....	....	....	....	....	....	....	....	....	....	....
	NHL Totals		**38**	**9**	**26**	**3**	**2280**	**161**	**2**	**4.24**	....	....	....	....	....	....	....	....	....	....	....	....	....	....	....	....	....

WHL First All-Star Team (1961, 1963, 1968) • Won WHL Rookie of the Year Award (1961) • Won WHL Leading Goaltender Award (1961, 1963) • WHL Second All-Star Team (1965, 1966) • Shared WHL Leading Goaltender Award with Dave Kelly (1966)

Traded to **Boston** by **Portland** (WHL) for Jack Bionda and future considerations, May, 1961. Traded to **Portland** (WHL) by **Boston** for cash, June 10, 1962.

• HEALY, GLENN

Glenn Healy G – L. 5′10″, 185 lbs. b: Pickering, Ont., 8/23/1962.

Season	Club	League	GP	W	L	T	Mins	GA	SO	Avg	AAvg	Eff	SA	S%	SAPG	GP	W	L	T	Mins	GA	SO	Avg	Eff	SA	S%	SAPG
1981-82	Western Michigan University	CCHA	27	7	19	1	1569	116	0	4.44	....	....	....	....	....	....	....	....	....	....	....	....	....	....	....	....	....
1982-83	Western Michigan University	CCHA	30	8	19	2	1732	116	0	4.01	....	....	....	....	....	....	....	....	....	....	....	....	....	....	....	....	....
1983-84	Western Michigan University	CCHA	38	19	16	3	2241	146	0	3.90	....	....	....	....	....	....	....	....	....	....	....	....	....	....	....	....	....
1984-85	Western Michigan University	CCHA	37	21	14	2	2171	118	0	3.26	....	....	....	....	....	....	....	....	....	....	....	....	....	....	....	....	....
1985-86	**Los Angeles Kings**	**NHL**	**1**	**0**	**0**	**0**	**51**	**6**	**0**	**7.06**	**5.49**	**12.10**	**35**	**.829**	**41.2**	....	....	....	....	....	....	....	....	....	....	....	....
	New Haven Nighthawks	AHL	43	21	15	4	2410	160	0	3.98	....	....	....	....	....	2	0	2	....	49	11	0	5.55	....	....	....	....
1986-87	New Haven Nighthawks	AHL	47	21	15	0	2828	173	1	3.67	....	....	....	....	....	7	3	4	....	427	19	0	2.67	....	....	....	....
1987-88	**Los Angeles Kings**	**NHL**	**34**	**12**	**18**	**1**	**1869**	**135**	**1**	**4.33**	**3.61**	**5.82**	**1005**	**.866**	**32.3**	**4**	**1**	**3**	....	**240**	**20**	**0**	**5.00**	**7.81**	**128**	**.844**	**32.0**
1988-89	**Los Angeles Kings**	**NHL**	**48**	**25**	**19**	**2**	**2699**	**192**	**0**	**4.27**	**3.53**	**5.43**	**1509**	**.873**	**33.5**	**3**	**0**	**1**	....	**97**	**6**	**0**	**3.71**	**3.77**	**59**	**.898**	**36.5**
1989-90	**New York Islanders**	**NHL**	**39**	**12**	**19**	**6**	**2197**	**128**	**2**	**3.50**	**2.93**	**3.70**	**1210**	**.894**	**33.0**	**4**	**1**	**2**	....	**166**	**9**	**0**	**3.25**	**3.70**	**79**	**.886**	**28.6**
1990-91	**New York Islanders**	**NHL**	**53**	**18**	**24**	**9**	**2999**	**166**	**0**	**3.32**	**2.96**	**3.54**	**1557**	**.893**	**31.2**	....	....	....	....	....	....	....	....	....	....	....	....
1991-92	**New York Islanders**	**NHL**	**37**	**14**	**16**	**4**	**1960**	**124**	**1**	**3.80**	**3.38**	**4.51**	**1045**	**.881**	**32.0**	....	....	....	....	....	....	....	....	....	....	....	....
1992-93	**New York Islanders**	**NHL**	**47**	**22**	**20**	**2**	**2655**	**146**	**1**	**3.30**	**2.80**	**3.66**	**1316**	**.889**	**29.7**	**18**	**9**	**8**	....	**1109**	**59**	**0**	**3.19**	**3.59**	**524**	**.887**	**28.4**
1993-94	**New York Rangers**	**NHL**	**29**	**10**	**12**	**2**	**1368**	**69**	**2**	**3.03**	**2.88**	**3.69**	**567**	**.878**	**24.9**	**2**	**0**	**0**	....	**68**	**1**	**0**	**0.88**	**0.52**	**17**	**.941**	**15.0**
1994-95	**New York Rangers**	**NHL**	**17**	**8**	**6**	**1**	**888**	**35**	**1**	**2.36**	**2.43**	**2.19**	**377**	**.907**	**25.5**	**5**	**2**	**1**	....	**230**	**13**	**0**	**3.39**	**4.74**	**93**	**.860**	**24.3**
1995-96	**New York Rangers**	**NHL**	**44**	**17**	**14**	**11**	**2564**	**124**	**2**	**2.90**	**2.84**	**2.91**	**1237**	**.900**	**28.9**	....	....	....	....	....	....	....	....	....	....	....	....
1996-97	**New York Rangers**	**NHL**	**23**	**5**	**12**	**4**	**1357**	**59**	**1**	**2.61**	**2.76**	**2.44**	**632**	**.907**	**27.9**	....	....	....	....	....	....	....	....	....	....	....	....
1997-98	**Toronto Maple Leafs**	**NHL**	**21**	**4**	**10**	**2**	**1068**	**53**	**0**	**2.98**	**3.49**	**3.49**	**453**	**.883**	**25.4**	....	....	....	....	....	....	....	....	....	....	....	....
	NHL Totals		**393**	**147**	**170**	**44**	**21675**	**1237**	**11**	**3.42**	....	....	**10943**	**.887**	....	**36**	**13**	**15**	....	**1910**	**108**	**0**	**3.39**	....	....	....	....

CCHA Second All-Star Team (1985) • NCAA West Second All-American Team (1985)

Signed as a free agent by **Los Angeles**, June 13, 1985. Signed as a free agent by **NY Islanders**, August 16, 1989. Claimed by **Anaheim** from **NY Islanders** in Expansion Draft, June 24, 1993. Claimed by **Tampa Bay** from **Anaheim** in Phase II of Expansion Draft, June 25, 1993. Traded to **NY Rangers** by **Tampa Bay** for Tampa Bay's 3rd round choice (previously acquired, Tampa Bay selected Allan Egeland) in 1993 Entry Draft, June 25, 1993. Signed as a free agent by **Toronto**, August 8, 1997.

			REGULAR SEASON													PLAYOFFS											
Season	Club	League	GP	W	L	T	Mins	GA	SO	Avg	AAvg	Eff	SA	S%	SAPG	GP	W	L	T	Mins	GA	SO	Avg	Eff	SA	S%	SAPG

• HEBERT, GUY

Guy Hebert G – L. 5'11", 185 lbs. b: Troy, NY, 1/7/1967. St. Louis' 8th choice, 159th overall, in 1987 Entry Draft.

Season	Club	League	GP	W	L	T	Mins	GA	SO	Avg	AAvg	Eff	SA	S%	SAPG	GP	W	L	T	Mins	GA	SO	Avg	Eff	SA	S%	SAPG
1985-86	Hamilton College	NCAA	18	4	12	2	1011	69	2	4.09	....	....	....	....	....	....	....	....	....	....	....	....	....	....	....	....	....
1986-87	Hamilton College	NCAA	18	12	5	0	1070	40	3	2.19	....	....	....	....	....	2	1	1	....	134	6	0	2.69	....	....	....	....
1987-88	Hamilton College	NCAA	9	5	3	0	510	22	1	2.58	....	....	....	....	....	1	0	1	....	60	3	0	3.00	....	....	....	....
1988-89	Hamilton College	NCAA	25	18	7	0	1454	62	2	2.56	....	....	....	....	....	2	1	1	....	126	4	0	1.90	....	....	....	....
1989-90	Peoria Rivermen	IHL	30	7	13	7	1706	124	1	4.36	....	....	....	....	....	2	0	1	....	76	5	0	3.95	....	....	....	....
1990-91	Peoria Rivermen	IHL	36	24	10	1	2093	100	2	2.87	....	....	....	....	....	8	3	4	....	458	32	0	4.19	....	....	....	....
1991-92	**St. Louis Blues**	**NHL**	**13**	**5**	**5**	**1**	**738**	**36**	**0**	**2.93**	**2.60**	**2.68**	**393**	**.908**	**32.0**	....	....	....	....	....	....	....	....	....	....	....	....
	Peoria Rivermen	IHL	29	20	9	0	1731	98	0	3.40	....	....	....	....	....	4	3	1	....	239	9	0	2.26	....	....	....	....
1992-93	**St. Louis Blues**	**NHL**	**24**	**8**	**8**	**2**	**1210**	**74**	**1**	**3.67**	**3.12**	**4.31**	**630**	**.883**	**31.2**	**1**	**0**	**0**	....	**2**	**0**	**0**	**0.00**	**0.00**	**1**	**1.000**	**30.0**
1993-94	**Anaheim Mighty Ducks**	**NHL**	**52**	**20**	**27**	**3**	**2991**	**141**	**2**	**2.83**	**2.69**	**2.64**	**1513**	**.907**	**30.4**	....	....	....	....	....	....	....	....	....	....	....	....
	United States	WC-A	6	4	2	0	300	18	....	3.60	....	....	....	....	....	....	....	....	....	....	....	....	....	....	....	....	....
1994-95	**Anaheim Mighty Ducks**	**NHL**	**39**	**12**	**20**	**4**	**2092**	**109**	**2**	**3.13**	**3.24**	**3.01**	**1132**	**.904**	**32.5**	....	....	....	....	....	....	....	....	....	....	....	....
1995-96	**Anaheim Mighty Ducks**	**NHL**	**59**	**28**	**23**	**5**	**3326**	**157**	**4**	**2.83**	**2.77**	**2.44**	**1820**	**.914**	**32.8**	....	....	....	....	....	....	....	....	....	....	....	....
1996-97	United States	W Cup	1	....	....	....	60	3	0	3.00	....	....	....	....	....	....	....	....	....	....	....	....	....	....	....	....	....
	Anaheim Mighty Ducks	**NHL**	**67**	**29**	**25**	**12**	**3863**	**172**	**4**	**2.67**	**2.82**	**2.15**	**2133**	**.919**	**33.1**	**9**	**4**	**4**	....	**534**	**18**	**1**	**2.02**	**1.43**	**255**	**.929**	**28.7**
1997-98	**Anaheim Mighty Ducks**	**NHL**	**46**	**13**	**24**	**6**	**2660**	**130**	**3**	**2.93**	**3.44**	**2.84**	**1339**	**.903**	**30.2**	....	....	....	....	....	....	....	....	....	....	....	....
	NHL Totals		**300**	**115**	**132**	**33**	**16880**	**819**	**16**	**2.91**	....	....	**8960**	**.909**	....	**10**	**4**	**4**	....	**536**	**18**	**1**	**2.01**	....	....	....	....

Shared James Norris Memorial Trophy (fewest goals against - IHL) with Pat Jablonski (1991) • IHL Second All-Star Team (1991)

Played in NHL All-Star Game (1997)

Claimed by **Anaheim** from **St. Louis** in Expansion Draft, June 24, 1993.

• HEBERT, SAMMY

Sammy Hebert G – R. 5'10", 145 lbs. b: Ottawa, Ontario, 3/31/1894. d: 7/23/1965.

Season	Club	League	GP	W	L	T	Mins	GA	SO	Avg	AAvg	Eff	SA	S%	SAPG	GP	W	L	T	Mins	GA	SO	Avg	Eff	SA	S%	SAPG
1913-14	Toronto Blueshirts	NHA	19	4	15	0	1160	108	0	5.59	....	....	....	....	....	....	....	....	....	....	....	....	....	....	....	....	....
1914-15	Ottawa Senators	NHA	2	0	0	0	23	1	0	2.61	....	....	....	....	....	....	....	....	....	....	....	....	....	....	....	....	....
	Ottawa New Edinburghs	City Sr.	STATISTICS NOT AVAILABLE																								
1915-16			MILITARY SERVICE																								
1916-17	Ottawa Senators	NHA	1	0	1	0	60	8	0	8.00	....	....	....	....	....	....	....	....	....	....	....	....	....	....	....	....	....
	Quebec Bulldogs	NHA	15	8	5	2	780	92	0	7.08	....	....	....	....	....	....	....	....	....	....	....	....	....	....	....	....	....
1917-18	**Toronto Arenas**	**NHL**	**2**	**1**	**0**	**0**	**80**	**10**	**0**	**7.50**	**4.94**	....	....	....	....	....	....	....	....	....	....	....	....	....	....	....	....
1918-19	Ottawa City Cedar	City Sr.	DID NOT PLAY																								
1919-20	Ottawa City Cedar	City Sr.	STATISTICS NOT AVAILABLE																								
1920-21	Ottawa City Cedar	City Sr.	STATISTICS NOT AVAILABLE																								
1921-22	Saskatoon Sheiks	WCHL	23	5	18	0	1380	131	0	5.70	....	....	....	....	....	....	....	....	....	....	....	....	....	....	....	....	....
1922-23	Saskatoon Sheiks	WCHL	19	4	13	2	1219	79	0	3.89	....	....	....	....	....	....	....	....	....	....	....	....	....	....	....	....	....
1923-24	**Ottawa Senators**	**NHL**	**2**	**0**	**2**	**0**	**120**	**9**	**0**	**4.50**	**5.31**	....	....	....	....	....	....	....	....	....	....	....	....	....	....	....	....
	NHL Totals		**4**	**1**	**2**	**0**	**200**	**19**	**0**	**5.70**	....	....	....	....	....	....	....	....	....	....	....	....	....	....	....	....	....
	Other Major League Totals		79	21	52	4	4622	419	0	5.44	....	....	....	....	....	....	....	....	....	....	....	....	....	....	....	....	....

Signed as a free agent by **Ottawa** (NHA), December 1, 1916. Loaned to **Quebec** (NHA) by **Ottawa** (NHA) for cash, December, 1916. Traded to **Toronto** (NHA) by **Ottawa** (NHA) with $750.00 for Cy Denneny, January, 1917. Signed as a free agent by **Toronto Arenas**, December 5, 1917. Traded to **Ottawa** by **Toronto Arenas** for cash, February 11, 1918. Signed as a free agent by **Saskatoon** (WCHL), December 2, 1921. Signed as a free agent by **Ottawa**, February 29, 1924.

• HEINZ, RICK

Rick Heinz G – L. 5'10", 165 lbs. b: Essex, Ont., 5/30/1955.

Season	Club	League	GP	W	L	T	Mins	GA	SO	Avg	AAvg	Eff	SA	S%	SAPG	GP	W	L	T	Mins	GA	SO	Avg	Eff	SA	S%	SAPG
1974-75	Univ. of Minnesota-Duluth	WCHA	20	6	11	2	1187	94	0	4.75	....	....	....	....	....	....	....	....	....	....	....	....	....	....	....	....	....
1975-76	Univ. of Minnesota-Duluth	WCHA	34	14	20	0	2029	162	0	4.79	....	....	....	....	....	....	....	....	....	....	....	....	....	....	....	....	....
1976-77	Univ. of Minnesota-Duluth	WCHA	23	6	15	2	1332	123	0	5.54	....	....	....	....	....	....	....	....	....	....	....	....	....	....	....	....	....
1977-78	Univ. of Minnesota-Duluth	WCHA	33	13	18	1	1961	157	0	4.80	....	....	....	....	....	....	....	....	....	....	....	....	....	....	....	....	....
1978-79	Port Huron Flags	IHL	54	....	....	....	2800	157	5	3.36	....	....	....	....	....	6	....	....	....	281	18	1	3.84	....	....	....	....
	Salt Lake Golden Eagles	CHL	1	0	1	0	59	3	0	3.05	....	....	....	....	....	....	....	....	....	....	....	....	....	....	....	....	....
1979-80	Salt Lake Golden Eagles	CHL	39	22	11	5	2353	119	0	3.03	....	....	....	....	....	5	1	3	0	324	16	0	2.96	....	....	....	....
1980-81	**St. Louis Blues**	**NHL**	**4**	**2**	**1**	**1**	**220**	**8**	**0**	**2.18**	**1.75**	....	....	....	....	....	....	....	....	....	....	....	....	....	....	....	....
	Salt Lake Golden Eagles	CHL	36	19	14	3	2210	128	3	3.48	....	....	....	....	....	*14	*10	4	0	*859	39	0	*2.72	....	....	....	....
1981-82	Salt Lake Golden Eagles	CHL	19	14	3	2	433	35	0	3.65	....	....	....	....	....	....	....	....	....	....	....	....	....	....	....	....	....
	St. Louis Blues	**NHL**	**9**	**2**	**5**	**0**	**400**	**35**	**0**	**4.85**	**3.74**	....	....	....	....	....	....	....	....	....	....	....	....	....	....	....	....
	Vancouver Canucks	**NHL**	**3**	**2**	**1**	**0**	**180**	**9**	**1**	**3.00**	**2.31**	....	....	....	....	....	....	....	....	....	....	....	....	....	....	....	....
1982-83	**St. Louis Blues**	**NHL**	**9**	**1**	**5**	**1**	**335**	**24**	**1**	**4.30**	**3.43**	**6.41**	**161**	**.851**	**28.8**	....	....	....	....	....	....	....	....	....	....	....	....
	Salt Lake Golden Eagles	CHL	17	9	8	0	1031	58	1	3.38	....	....	....	....	....	....	....	....	....	....	....	....	....	....	....	....	....
1983-84	**St. Louis Blues**	**NHL**	**22**	**7**	**7**	**3**	**1118**	**80**	**0**	**4.29**	**3.36**	**6.37**	**539**	**.852**	**28.9**	**1**	**0**	**0**	....	**8**	**1**	**0**	**7.50**	....	....	....	....
1984-85	**St. Louis Blues**	**NHL**	**2**	**0**	**0**	**0**	**70**	**3**	**0**	**2.57**	**2.04**	**2.97**	**26**	**.885**	**22.3**	....	....	....	....	....	....	....	....	....	....	....	....
	Peoria Rivermen	IHL	43	24	12	4	2443	129	2	3.17	....	....	....	....	....	10	6	4	0	607	31	1	3.06	....	....	....	....
1985-86	Binghamton Whalers	AHL	1	0	1	0	60	9	0	9.00	....	....	....	....	....	....	....	....	....	....	....	....	....	....	....	....	....
	Salt Lake Golden Eagles	IHL	52	22	20	0	3000	185	1	3.70	....	....	....	....	....	5	1	4	0	299	26	0	5.22	....	....	....	....
1986-87	Salt Lake Golden Eagles	IHL	51	29	20	0	3026	201	1	3.99	....	....	....	....	....	16	12	4	0	912	57	0	3.75	....	....	....	....
	NHL Totals		**49**	**14**	**19**	**5**	**2356**	**159**	**2**	**4.05**	....	....	....	....	....	**1**	**0**	**0**	....	**8**	**1**	**0**	**7.50**	....	....	....	....

IHL Second All-Star Team (1979) • CHL Second All-Star Team (1980) • IHL First All-Star Team (1985) • Won James Norris Memorial Trophy (fewest goals against - IHL) (1985)

Signed as a free agent by **St. Louis**, April 16, 1979. Traded to **Vancouver** by **St. Louis** with Tony Currie, Jim Nill and St. Louis' 4th round choice (Shawn Kilroy) in 1982 Entry Draft for Glen Hanlon, March 9, 1982. Traded to **St. Louis** by **Vancouver** for cash, June 3, 1982.

• HENDERSON, JOHN

John "Long John" Henderson G – L. 6'1", 174 lbs. b: Toronto, Ont., 3/25/1933.

Season	Club	League	GP	W	L	T	Mins	GA	SO	Avg	AAvg	Eff	SA	S%	SAPG	GP	W	L	T	Mins	GA	SO	Avg	Eff	SA	S%	SAPG
1950-51	Toronto Marlboros	OHA	12	....	....	....	720	39	1	3.25	....	....	....	....	....	....	....	....	....	....	....	....	....	....	....	....	....
1951-52	Toronto Marlboros	OHA	16	....	....	....	960	39	1	2.44	....	....	....	....	....	6	2	4	0	360	26	0	4.33	....	....	....	....
1952-53	Toronto Marlboros	OHA	50	....	....	....	3000	128	3	*2.56	....	....	....	....	....	7	....	....	....	420	23	0	3.29	....	....	....	....
	Pittsburgh Hornets	AHL	1	0	1	0	60	1	0	1.00	....	....	....	....	....	....	....	....	....	....	....	....	....	....	....	....	....
1953-54	Springfield Indians	QHL	22	8	11	3	1357	93	0	4.11	....	....	....	....	....	....	....	....	....	....	....	....	....	....	....	....	....
	Syracuse Warriors	AHL	21	3	17	1	1260	141	0	6.71	....	....	....	....	....	....	....	....	....	....	....	....	....	....	....	....	....
1954-55	Hershey Bears	AHL	15	7	5	3	900	46	0	3.07	....	....	....	....	....	....	....	....	....	....	....	....	....	....	....	....	....
	Boston Bruins	**NHL**	**45**	**15**	**14**	**15**	**2628**	**109**	**5**	**2.49**	**3.04**	....	....	....	....	**2**	**0**	**2**	....	**120**	**8**	**0**	**4.00**	....	....	....	....
1955-56	Hershey Bears	AHL	42	12	26	4	2400	175	0	4.17	....	....	....	....	....	....	....	....	....	....	....	....	....	....	....	....	....
	Boston Bruins	**NHL**	**1**	**0**	**1**	**0**	**60**	**4**	**0**	**4.00**	**4.00**	....	....	....	....	....	....	....	....	....	....	....	....	....	....	....	....
	Whitby Dunlops	EOHL	23	....	....	....	1380	76	1	*3.30	....	....	....	....	....	....	....	....	....	....	....	....	....	....	....	....	....
1956-57	Whitby Dunlops	EOHL	16	....	....	....	960	38	*2	2.37	....	....	....	....	....	8	....	....	....	480	17	1	*2.12	....	....	....	....
1957-58	Whitby Dunlops	EOHL	22	....	....	....	1320	70	1	*3.18	....	....	....	....	....	....	....	....	....	....	....	....	....	....	....	....	....
	Hull-Ottawa Canadiens	EOHL	1	0	1	0	60	6	0	6.00	....	....	....	....	....	....	....	....	....	....	....	....	....	....	....	....	....
	Canada	WEC-A	DID NOT PLAY – SPARE GOALTENDER																								
1958-59	Whitby Dunlops	EOHL	50	....	....	....	3000	145	2	*2.90	....	....	....	....	....	10	....	....	....	600	24	*2	*2.40	....	....	....	....
1959-60	Whitby Dunlops	OHA Sr.	53	....	....	....	3180	191	*3	3.67	....	....	....	....	....	11	....	....	....	660	47	0	4.27	....	....	....	....
	Cleveland Barons	AHL	1	1	0	0	60	3	0	3.00	....	....	....	....	....	....	....	....	....	....	....	....	....	....	....	....	....
1960-61	Kingston Frontenacs	EPHL	39	15	17	7	2340	145	1	3.72	....	....	....	....	....	5	1	4	0	303	14	0	2.77	....	....	....	....
1961-1965			DID NOT PLAY																								
1965-66	Oklahoma City Blazers	CHL	2	1	1	0	120	7	0	3.60	....	....	....	....	....	....	....	....	....	....	....	....	....	....	....	....	....
	San Francisco Seals	WHL	10	3	6	1	613	40	0	3.92	....	....	....	....	....	....	....	....	....	....	....	....	....	....	....	....	....
	Victoria Cougars	WHL	14	8	6	0	844	51	1	3.63	....	....	....	....	....	*14	*8	6	0	*890	42	0	2.83	....	....	....	....
1966-67	Hershey Bears	AHL	16	9	5	0	866	46	3	3.19	....	....	....	....	....	5	1	4	0	300	15	0	3.00	....	....	....	....
	California Seals	WHL	3	2	1	0	180	9	0	3.00	....	....	....	....	....	....	....	....	....	....	....	....	....	....	....	....	....
1967-68	Hershey Bears	AHL	32	11	13	3	1756	112	0	3.83	....	....	....	....	....	....	....	....	....	....	....	....	....	....	....	....	....
1968-69	Hershey Bears	AHL	41	23	14	3	2252	109	2	2.90	....	....	....	....	....	11	*8	3	0	660	32	*2	2.91	....	....	....	....
1969-70	Hershey Bears	AHL	6	....	....	....	306	24	0	4.71	....	....	....	....	....	....	....	....	....	....	....	....	....	....	....	....	....
	NHL Totals		**46**	**15**	**15**	**15**	**2688**	**113**	**5**	**2.52**	....	....	....	....	....	**2**	**0**	**2**	....	**120**	**8**	**0**	**4.00**	....	....	....	....

Traded to **Boston** by **Toronto** for Ray Gariepy, September, 1954.

• HENRY, GORD

Gord Henry G – L. 6', 185 lbs. b: Owen Sound, Ont., 8/17/1926. d: 10/3/1972.

			REGULAR SEASON													PLAYOFFS											
Season	Club	League	GP	W	L	T	Mins	GA	SO	Avg	AAvg	Eff	SA	S%	SAPG	GP	W	L	T	Mins	GA	SO	Avg	Eff	SA	S%	SAPG
1943-44	Philadelphia Falcons	EHL	28	....	....	....	1680	129	1	4.61	....	....	....	....	....	12	6	6	0	720	52	0	4.33	....	....	....	....
1944-45	Hershey Bears	AHL	3	0	2	1	180	10	0	3.33	....	....	....	....	....	....	....	....	....	....	....	....	....	....	....	....	....
	Philadelphia Falcons	EHL	35	....	....	....	2100	160	*3	4.57	....	....	....	....	....	12	....	....	....	720	47	*1	3.92	....	....	....	....
1945-46	Hershey Bears	AHL	16	6	5	5	960	61	0	3.81	....	....	....	....	....	3	1	2	0	180	10	1	3.33	....	....	....	....
	Baltimore Clippers	EHL	4	....	....	....	240	27	0	5.50	....	....	....	....	....	....	....	....	....	....	....	....	....	....	....	....	....
	Philadelphia Falcons	EHL	1	....	....	....	60	3	0	3.00	....	....	....	....	....	....	....	....	....	....	....	....	....	....	....	....	....
	New York Rovers	EHL	1	1	0	0	60	0	1	0.00	....	....	....	....	....	....	....	....	....	....	....	....	....	....	....	....	....
1946-47	Boston Olympics	EHL	43	21	17	5	2580	201	1	4.67	....	....	....	....	....	....	....	....	....	....	....	....	....	....	....	....	....
	Hershey Bears	AHL	5	2	1	1	260	13	0	3.00	....	....	....	....	....	11	*8	3	0	660	16	*5	*1.45	....	....	....	....
1947-48	Hershey Bears	AHL	*68	25	30	13	*4080	273	1	4.01	....	....	....	....	....	1	0	1	0	20	2	0	6.00	....	....	....	....
1948-49	Hershey Bears	AHL	66	28	33	5	3960	249	3	3.71	....	....	....	....	....	11	7	4	0	694	26	*1	*2.25	....	....	....	....
	Boston Bruins	**NHL**	**1**	**1**	**0**	**0**	**60**	**0**	**1**	**0.00**	**0.00**	....	....	....	....	....	....	....	....	....	....	....	....	....	....	....	....
1949-50	Hershey Bears	AHL	64	19	35	10	3840	270	1	4.22	....	....	....	....	....	....	....	....	....	....	....	....	....	....	....	....	....
	Boston Bruins	**NHL**	**2**	**0**	**2**	**0**	**120**	**5**	**0**	**2.50**	**2.82**	....	....	....	....	....	....	....	....	....	....	....	....	....	....	....	....
1950-51	Hershey Bears	AHL	*70	38	28	4	*4278	242	3	3.39	....	....	....	....	....	6	3	3	0	415	17	0	2.46	....	....	....	....
	Boston Bruins	**NHL**	....	....	....	....	....	....	....	....	....	....	....	....	....	**2**	**0**	**2**	....	**120**	**10**	**0**	**5.00**	....	....	....	....
1951-52	Hershey Bears	AHL	*68	35	28	5	*4120	211	4	3.07	....	....	....	....	....	5	1	4	0	348	14	0	2.42	....	....	....	....
1952-53	Hershey Bears	AHL	*64	31	32	1	3870	214	5	3.32	....	....	....	....	....	3	0	3	0	189	12	0	3.81	....	....	....	....
	Boston Bruins	**NHL**	....	....	....	....	....	....	....	....	....	....	....	....	....	**3**	**0**	**2**	....	**163**	**11**	**0**	**4.05**	....	....	....	....
1953-54	Hershey Bears	AHL	63	33	26	4	3780	211	1	3.35	....	....	....	....	....	9	4	5	0	570	24	*1	2.53	....	....	....	....
1954-55	Hershey Bears	AHL	23	9	11	3	1380	85	0	3.70	....	....	....	....	....	....	....	....	....	....	....	....	....	....	....	....	....
1955-56	Owen Sound Mercurys	OHA Sr.	22	....	....	....	1280	77	1	3.61	....	....	....	....	....	3	....	....	....	180	11	0	3.67	....	....	....	....
1956-57	Philadelphia Ramblers	EHL	1	0	1	0	60	6	0	6.00	....	....	....	....	....	....	....	....	....	....	....	....	....	....	....	....	....
	NHL Totals		**3**	**1**	**2**	**0**	**180**	**5**	**1**	**1.67**	....	....	....	....	....	**5**	**0**	**4**	....	**283**	**21**	**0**	**4.45**	....	....	....	....

EHL Second All-Star Team (1944) • AHL Second All-Star Team (1952)

• HENRY, JIM

Jim "Sugar Jim" Henry G – L. 5'9", 165 lbs. b: Winnipeg, Man., 10/23/1920.

Season	Club	League	GP	W	L	T	Mins	GA	SO	Avg	AAvg	Eff	SA	S%	SAPG	GP	W	L	T	Mins	GA	SO	Avg	Eff	SA	S%	SAPG
1938-39	Brandon Elks	MJHL	15	....	....	....	900	44	*1	2.96	....	....	....	....	....	13	9	4	0	780	56	1	4.31	....	....	....	....
1939-40	Brandon Elks	MJHL	23	....	....	....	1380	82	0	3.57	....	....	....	....	....	3	3	0	0	180	6	*1	*2.00	....	....	....	....
1940-41	Regina Rangers	SJHL	29	....	....	....	1740	87	*2	*3.00	....	....	....	....	....	8	....	....	....	480	22	1	2.75	....	....	....	....
1941-42	**New York Rangers**	**NHL**	***48**	***29**	**17**	**2**	***2960**	**143**	**1**	**2.90**	**2.84**	....	....	....	....	**6**	**2**	**4**	....	**360**	**13**	***1**	***2.17**	....	....	....	....
1942-43	Ottawa Commandos	QSHL	23	....	....	....	1380	84	1	3.65	....	....	....	....	....	12	9	2	1	740	35	2	2.84	....	....	....	....
	Ottawa Staff Clerks	City Sr.	8	....	....	....	480	53	0	6.63	....	....	....	....	....	....	....	....	....	....	....	....	....	....	....	....	....
1943-44	Red Deer Army	Cgy-Sr.	16	....	....	....	960	52	0	3.25	....	....	....	....	....	5	....	....	....	300	19	0	3.80	....	....	....	....
1944-45	Calgary Navy	City Sr.	15	....	....	....	900	92	0	6.13	....	....	....	....	....	....	....	....	....	....	....	....	....	....	....	....	....
1945-46	New Haven Eagles	AHL	25	8	15	2	1500	96	1	3.84	....	....	....	....	....	....	....	....	....	....	....	....	....	....	....	....	....
	New York Rangers	**NHL**	**11**	**1**	**7**	**2**	**623**	**42**	**1**	**4.04**	**3.76**	....	....	....	....	....	....	....	....	....	....	....	....	....	....	....	....
1946-47	New Haven Ramblers	AHL	58	20	28	10	3480	197	5	3.40	....	....	....	....	....	3	1	2	0	180	11	0	3.67	....	....	....	....
	New York Rangers	**NHL**	**2**	**0**	**2**	**0**	**120**	**9**	**0**	**4.50**	**4.40**	....	....	....	....	....	....	....	....	....	....	....	....	....	....	....	....
1947-48	New Haven Ramblers	AHL	13	6	6	1	780	40	1	3.08	....	....	....	....	....	....	....	....	....	....	....	....	....	....	....	....	....
	New York Rangers	**NHL**	**48**	**17**	**18**	**13**	**2880**	**153**	**2**	**3.19**	**3.41**	....	....	....	....	....	....	....	....	....	....	....	....	....	....	....	....
1948-49	**Chicago Black Hawks**	**NHL**	***60**	**21**	**31**	**8**	***3600**	**211**	**0**	**3.52**	**4.25**	....	....	....	....	....	....	....	....	....	....	....	....	....	....	....	....
1949-50	Kansas City Pla-Mors	USHL	68	29	27	12	4080	255	*3	3.75	....	....	....	....	....	3	0	3	0	180	20	0	6.67	....	....	....	....
1950-51	Omaha Knights	USHL	7	5	2	0	420	18	1	2.57	....	....	....	....	....	....	....	....	....	....	....	....	....	....	....	....	....
	Indianapolis Capitols	AHL	58	37	19	2	3520	202	0	3.44	....	....	....	....	....	3	0	3	0	190	11	0	3.47	....	....	....	....
1951-52	**Boston Bruins**	**NHL**	***70**	**25**	**29**	**16**	***4200**	**176**	**7**	**2.51**	**2.97**	....	....	....	....	**7**	**3**	**4**	....	**448**	**18**	**1**	**2.41**	....	....	....	....
1952-53	**Boston Bruins**	**NHL**	***70**	**28**	**29**	**13**	***4200**	**172**	**7**	**2.46**	**3.19**	....	....	....	....	***9**	**5**	**4**	....	***510**	**26**	**0**	**3.06**	....	....	....	....
1953-54	**Boston Bruins**	**NHL**	***70**	**32**	**28**	**10**	***4200**	**181**	**8**	**2.59**	**3.38**	....	....	....	....	**4**	**0**	**4**	....	**240**	**16**	**0**	**4.00**	....	....	....	....
1954-55	**Boston Bruins**	**NHL**	**27**	**8**	**12**	**6**	**1572**	**79**	**1**	**3.02**	**3.74**	....	....	....	....	**3**	**1**	**2**	....	**183**	**8**	**0**	**2.62**	....	....	....	....
1955-56	Sault Ste. Marie Greyhounds	NOHA	STATISTICS NOT AVAILABLE																								
1956-57			DID NOT PLAY																								
1957-58			DID NOT PLAY																								
1958-59	Warroad Lakers	MHL Sr.	14	....	....	....	840	41	0	*2.92	....	....	....	....	....	....	....	....	....	....	....	....	....	....	....	....	....
1959-60	St. Paul Saints	IHL	9	....	....	....	540	35	0	3.89	....	....	....	....	....	....	....	....	....	....	....	....	....	....	....	....	....
	NHL Totals		**406**	**161**	**173**	**70**	**24355**	**1166**	**27**	**2.87**	....	....	....	....	....	**29**	**11**	**18**	....	**1741**	**81**	**2**	**2.79**	....	....	....	....

USHL First All-Star Team (1950) • Won Charles Gardiner Memorial Trophy (USHL - Top Goaltender) (1950) • NHL Second All-Star Team (1952)

Played in NHL All-Star Game (1952)

Traded to **Chicago** by **NY Rangers** for Emile Francis and Alex Kaleta, October, 1948. Traded to **Detroit** by **Chicago** with Metro Prystai, Gaye Stewart and Bob Goldham for Harry Lumley, Jack Stewart, Al Dewsbury, Pete Babando and Don Morrison, July, 1950. Traded to **Boston** by **Detroit** for cash, September 28, 1951.

• HERRON, DENIS

Denis Herron G – L. 5'11", 165 lbs. b: Chambly, Que., 6/18/1952. Pittsburgh's 3rd choice, 40th overall, in 1972 Amateur Draft.

Season	Club	League	GP	W	L	T	Mins	GA	SO	Avg	AAvg	Eff	SA	S%	SAPG	GP	W	L	T	Mins	GA	SO	Avg	Eff	SA	S%	SAPG
1969-70	Trois Rivieres Draveurs	QJHL	2	0	1	0	96	10	0	6.25	....	....	....	....	....	....	....	....	....	....	....	....	....	....	....	....	....
1970-71	Trois Rivieres Draveurs	QJHL	33	....	....	....	1980	136	0	4.12	....	....	....	....	....	7	....	....	....	420	23	1	3.29	....	....	....	....
1971-72	Trois Rivieres Draveurs	QMJHL	40	....	....	....	2400	160	2	4.00	....	....	....	....	....	4	....	....	....	200	19	0	5.70	....	....	....	....
1972-73	**Pittsburgh Penguins**	**NHL**	**18**	**6**	**7**	**2**	**967**	**55**	**2**	**3.41**	**3.21**	....	....	....	....	....	....	....	....	....	....	....	....	....	....	....	....
	Hershey Bears	AHL	21	....	....	....	1185	63	0	3.19	....	....	....	....	....	4	....	....	....	240	16	0	4.00	....	....	....	....
1973-74	**Pittsburgh Penguins**	**NHL**	**5**	**1**	**3**	**0**	**260**	**18**	**0**	**4.15**	**4.01**	....	....	....	....	....	....	....	....	....	....	....	....	....	....	....	....
	Salt Lake Golden Eagles	WHL	9	6	2	1	530	32	0	3.62	....	....	....	....	....	....	....	....	....	....	....	....	....	....	....	....	....
	Hershey Bears	AHL	17	10	4	1	967	52	0	3.22	....	....	....	....	....	4	4	0	0	242	7	0	*1.73	....	....	....	....
1974-75	Hershey Bears	AHL	12	2	7	2	615	45	0	4.39	....	....	....	....	....	....	....	....	....	....	....	....	....	....	....	....	....
	Pittsburgh Penguins	**NHL**	**3**	**1**	**1**	**0**	**108**	**11**	**0**	**6.11**	**5.51**	....	....	....	....	....	....	....	....	....	....	....	....	....	....	....	....
	Kansas City Scouts	**NHL**	**22**	**4**	**13**	**4**	**1280**	**80**	**0**	**3.75**	**3.38**	....	....	....	....	....	....	....	....	....	....	....	....	....	....	....	....
1975-76	**Kansas City Scouts**	**NHL**	**64**	**11**	**39**	**11**	**3620**	**243**	**0**	**4.03**	**3.67**	....	....	....	....	....	....	....	....	....	....	....	....	....	....	....	....
1976-77	**Pittsburgh Penguins**	**NHL**	**34**	**15**	**11**	**5**	**1920**	**94**	**1**	**2.94**	**2.72**	....	....	....	....	**3**	**1**	**2**	....	**180**	**11**	**0**	**3.67**	....	....	....	....
1977-78	**Pittsburgh Penguins**	**NHL**	**60**	**20**	**25**	**15**	**3534**	**210**	**0**	**3.57**	**3.35**	....	....	....	....	....	....	....	....	....	....	....	....	....	....	....	....
1978-79	**Pittsburgh Penguins**	**NHL**	**56**	**22**	**19**	**12**	**3208**	**180**	**0**	**3.37**	**2.97**	....	....	....	....	**7**	**2**	**5**	....	**421**	**24**	**0**	**3.42**	....	....	....	....
1979-80	**Montreal Canadiens**	**NHL**	**34**	**25**	**3**	**3**	**1909**	**80**	**0**	**2.51**	**2.19**	....	....	....	....	**5**	**2**	**3**	....	**300**	**15**	**0**	**3.00**	....	....	....	....
1980-81	**Montreal Canadiens**	**NHL**	**25**	**6**	**9**	**6**	**1147**	**67**	**1**	**3.50**	**2.80**	....	....	....	....	....	....	....	....	....	....	....	....	....	....	....	....
1981-82	**Montreal Canadiens**	**NHL**	**27**	**12**	**6**	**8**	**1547**	**68**	***3**	***2.64**	**2.02**	....	....	....	....	....	....	....	....	....	....	....	....	....	....	....	....
1982-83	**Pittsburgh Penguins**	**NHL**	**31**	**5**	**18**	**5**	**1707**	**151**	**1**	**5.31**	**4.27**	**8.61**	**931**	**.838**	**32.7**	....	....	....	....	....	....	....	....	....	....	....	....
1983-84	**Pittsburgh Penguins**	**NHL**	**38**	**8**	**24**	**2**	**2028**	**138**	**1**	**4.08**	**3.19**	**4.69**	**1200**	**.885**	**35.5**	....	....	....	....	....	....	....	....	....	....	....	....
1984-85	**Pittsburgh Penguins**	**NHL**	**42**	**10**	**22**	**3**	**2193**	**170**	**1**	**4.65**	**3.71**	**5.80**	**1362**	**.875**	**37.3**	....	....	....	....	....	....	....	....	....	....	....	....
1985-86	**Pittsburgh Penguins**	**NHL**	**3**	**0**	**3**	**0**	**180**	**14**	**0**	**4.67**	**3.63**	**7.11**	**92**	**.848**	**30.7**	....	....	....	....	....	....	....	....	....	....	....	....
	Baltimore Clippers	AHL	27	10	11	4	1510	86	0	3.42	....	....	....	....	....	....	....	....	....	....	....	....	....	....	....	....	....
	NHL Totals		**462**	**146**	**203**	**76**	**25608**	**1579**	**10**	**3.70**	....	....	....	....	....	**15**	**5**	**10**	....	**901**	**50**	**0**	**3.33**	....	....	....	....

QMJHL Second All-Star Team (1972) • Shared Vezina Trophy with Richard Sevigny and Michel Larocque (1981) • Shared William M. Jennings Trophy with Rick Walmsley (1982)

Traded to **Kansas City** by **Pittsburgh** with Jean-Guy Lagace for Michel Plasse, January 10, 1975. Signed as a free agent by **Pittsburgh**, August 7, 1976. Traded to **Montreal** by **Pittsburgh** with Pittsburgh's 2nd round choice (Jocelyn Gauvreau) in 1982 Entry Draft for Pat Hughes and Robbie Holland, August 30, 1979. Traded to **Pittsburgh** by **Montreal** for Pittsburgh's 3rd round choice (later traded to St. Louis - St. Louis selected Nelson Emerson) in 1985 Entry Draft, September 15, 1982.

• HEXTALL, RON

Ron Hextall G – L. 6'3", 192 lbs. b: Brandon, Man., 5/3/1964. Philadelphia's 6th choice, 119th overall, in 1982 Entry Draft.

Season	Club	League	GP	W	L	T	Mins	GA	SO	Avg	AAvg	Eff	SA	S%	SAPG	GP	W	L	T	Mins	GA	SO	Avg	Eff	SA	S%	SAPG
1981-82	Brandon Wheat Kings	WHL	30	12	11	0	1398	133	0	5.71	....	....	....	....	....	3	0	2	....	103	16	0	9.32	....	....	....	....
1982-83	Brandon Wheat Kings	WHL	44	13	30	0	2589	249	0	5.77	....	....	....	....	....	....	....	....	....	....	....	....	....	....	....	....	....
1983-84	Brandon Wheat Kings	WHL	46	29	13	2	2670	190	0	4.27	....	....	....	....	....	10	5	5	....	592	37	0	3.75	....	....	....	....
1984-85	Hershey Bears	AHL	11	4	6	0	555	34	0	3.68	....	....	....	....	....	....	....	....	....	....	....	....	....	....	....	....	....
	Kalamazoo Wings	IHL	19	6	11	1	1103	80	0	4.35	....	....	....	....	....	....	....	....	....	....	....	....	....	....	....	....	....
1985-86	Hershey Bears	AHL	*53	30	19	2	*3061	174	*5	3.41	....	....	....	....	....	13	5	7	....	780	42	*1	3.23	....	....	....	....
1986-87	**Philadelphia Flyers**	**NHL**	***66**	**37**	**21**	**6**	***3799**	**190**	**1**	**3.00**	**2.51**	**2.95**	**1933**	**.902**	**30.5**	***26**	**15**	**11**	....	***1540**	**71**	***2**	**2.77**	**2.56**	**769**	**.908**	**30.0**
	NHL All-Stars	RV87	DID NOT PLAY – SPARE GOALTENDER																								

Season	Club	League	GP	W	L	T	Mins	GA	SO	Avg	AAvg	Eff	SA	S%	SAPG	GP	W	L	T	Mins	GA	SO	Avg	Eff	SA	S%	SAPG
			REGULAR SEASON													PLAYOFFS											
1987-88	Canada	C Cup	DID NOT PLAY – SPARE GOALTENDER																								
	Philadelphia Flyers	**NHL**	**62**	**30**	**22**	**7**	**3561**	**208**	**0**	**3.50**	**2.90**	**4.01**	**1817**	**.886**	**30.6**	**7**	**2**	**4**	....	**379**	**30**	**0**	**4.75**	**7.27**	**196**	**.847**	**31.0**
1988-89	**Philadelphia Flyers**	**NHL**	**64**	**30**	**28**	**6**	**3756**	**202**	**0**	**3.23**	**2.65**	**3.51**	**1860**	**.891**	**29.7**	**15**	**8**	**7**	....	**886**	**49**	**0**	**3.32**	**3.66**	**445**	**.890**	**30.1**
1989-90	**Philadelphia Flyers**	**NHL**	**8**	**4**	**2**	**1**	**419**	**29**	**0**	**4.15**	**3.48**	**5.50**	**219**	**.868**	**31.4**	....	....	....	....	....	....	....	....	....	....	....	....
	Hershey Bears	AHL	1	1	0	0	49	3	0	3.67	....	....	....	....	....	....	....	....	....	....	....	....	....	....	....	....	....
1990-91	**Philadelphia Flyers**	**NHL**	**36**	**13**	**16**	**5**	**2035**	**106**	**0**	**3.13**	**2.79**	**3.38**	**982**	**.892**	**29.0**	....	....	....	....	....	....	....	....	....	....	....	....
1991-92	**Philadelphia Flyers**	**NHL**	**45**	**16**	**21**	**6**	**2668**	**151**	**3**	**3.40**	**3.01**	**3.97**	**1294**	**.883**	**29.1**	....	....	....	....	....	....	....	....	....	....	....	....
	Canada	WC-A	5	1	2	1	273	13	0	2.86	....	....	....	....	....	....	....	....	....	....	....	....	....	....	....	....	....
1992-93	**Quebec Nordiques**	**NHL**	**54**	**29**	**16**	**5**	**2988**	**172**	**0**	**3.45**	**2.93**	**3.88**	**1529**	**.888**	**30.7**	**6**	**2**	**4**	....	**372**	**18**	**0**	**2.90**	**2.47**	**211**	**.915**	**34.0**
1993-94	**New York Islanders**	**NHL**	**65**	**27**	**26**	**6**	**3581**	**184**	**5**	**3.08**	**2.93**	**3.15**	**1801**	**.898**	**30.2**	**3**	**0**	**3**	....	**158**	**16**	**0**	**6.08**	**12.16**	**80**	**.800**	**30.4**
1994-95	**Philadelphia Flyers**	**NHL**	**31**	**17**	**9**	**4**	**1824**	**88**	**1**	**2.89**	**2.98**	**3.18**	**801**	**.890**	**26.3**	**15**	**10**	**5**	....	**897**	**42**	**0**	**2.81**	**2.70**	**437**	**.904**	**29.2**
1995-96	**Philadelphia Flyers**	**NHL**	**53**	**31**	**13**	**7**	**3102**	**112**	**4**	***2.17**	**2.11**	**1.88**	**1292**	**.913**	**25.0**	**12**	**6**	**6**	....	**760**	**27**	**0**	**2.13**	**1.80**	**319**	**.915**	**25.2**
1996-97	**Philadelphia Flyers**	**NHL**	**55**	**31**	**16**	**5**	**3094**	**132**	**5**	**2.56**	**2.70**	**2.63**	**1285**	**.897**	**24.9**	**8**	**4**	**3**	....	**444**	**22**	**0**	**2.97**	**3.22**	**203**	**.892**	**27.4**
1997-98	**Philadelphia Flyers**	**NHL**	**46**	**21**	**17**	**7**	**2688**	**97**	**4**	**2.17**	**2.53**	**1.93**	**1089**	**.911**	**24.3**	**1**	**0**	**0**	....	**20**	**1**	**0**	**3.00**	**3.75**	**8**	**.875**	**24.0**
	NHL Totals		**585**	**286**	**207**	**65**	**33515**	**1671**	**23**	**2.99**	....	....	**15902**	**.895**	....	**93**	**47**	**43**	....	**5456**	**276**	**2**	**3.04**	....	....	....	....

AHL First All-Star Team (1986) • Won Dudley "Red" Garrett Memorial Trophy (Top Rookie - AHL) (1986) • NHL All-Rookie Team (1987) • NHL First All-Star Team (1987) • Won Vezina Trophy (1987) • Won Conn Smythe Trophy (1987)

• Scored a goal vs. Boston, December 8, 1987 • Scored a goal in playoffs vs. Washington, April 11, 1989.

Played in NHL All-Star Game (1988)

Traded to **Quebec** by **Philadelphia** with Peter Forsberg, Steve Duchesne, Kerry Huffman, Mike Ricci, Chris Simon, Philadelphia's 1st round choice in the 1993 (Jocelyn Thibault) and 1994 (later traded to Toronto — later traded to Washington — Washington selected Nolan Baumgartner) Entry Drafts and cash for Eric Lindros, June 30, 1992. Traded to **NY Islanders** by **Quebec** with Quebec's 1st round choice (Todd Bertuzzi) in 1993 Entry Draft for Mark Fitzpatrick and NY Islanders' 1st round choice (Adam Deadmarsh) in 1993 Entry Draft, June 20, 1993. Traded to **Philadelphia** by **NY Islanders** with NY Islanders' 6th round choice (Dimitri Tertyshny) in 1995 Entry Draft for Tommy Soderstrom, September 22, 1994

• HIGHTON, HEC

Hec Highton G – R. 6', 175 lbs. b: Medicine Hat, Alta., 12/10/1923.

Season	Club	League	GP	W	L	T	Mins	GA	SO	Avg	AAvg	Eff	SA	S%	SAPG	GP	W	L	T	Mins	GA	SO	Avg	Eff	SA	S%	SAPG
1941-42			MILITARY SERVICE																								
1942-43	New Westminster Spitfires	PCHL	10	....	....	....	600	33	*1	3.30	....	....	....	....	....	3	1	2	0	190	18	0	5.68	....	....	....	....
1943-44	**Chicago Black Hawks**	**NHL**	**24**	**10**	**14**	**0**	**1440**	**108**	**0**	**4.50**	**3.43**	....	....	....	....	....	....	....	....	....	....	....	....	....	....	....	....
	Providence Reds	AHL	27	5	21	1	1620	125	0	4.62	....	....	....	....	....	....	....	....	....	....	....	....	....	....	....	....	....
1944-45	St. Louis Flyers	AHL	26	7	15	4	1560	118	0	4.54	....	....	....	....	....	....	....	....	....	....	....	....	....	....	....	....	....
	Providence Reds	AHL	4	0	4	0	240	29	0	7.25	....	....	....	....	....	....	....	....	....	....	....	....	....	....	....	....	....
1945-46	St. Louis Flyers	AHL	52	20	24	8	3120	215	1	4.13	....	....	....	....	....	....	....	....	....	....	....	....	....	....	....	....	....
1946-47	St. Louis Flyers	AHL	59	16	32	11	3540	257	0	4.36	....	....	....	....	....	....	....	....	....	....	....	....	....	....	....	....	....
1947-48	St. Louis Flyers	AHL	65	21	34	10	3900	278	0	4.28	....	....	....	....	....	....	....	....	....	....	....	....	....	....	....	....	....
1948-49	Los Angeles Monarchs	PCHL	70	28	33	9	4200	271	1	3.87	....	....	....	....	....	7	4	3	0	434	25	0	3.46	....	....	....	....
1949-50	Los Angeles Monarchs	PCHL	62	26	28	8	3720	209	3	3.37	....	....	....	....	....	17	10	7	0	1032	50	3	2.91	....	....	....	....
1950-51	Victoria Cougars	PCHL	19	7	8	4	1140	68	0	3.58	....	....	....	....	....	....	....	....	....	....	....	....	....	....	....	....	....
	Vancouver Canucks	PCHL	48	13	21	13	2860	173	3	3.63	....	....	....	....	....	....	....	....	....	....	....	....	....	....	....	....	....
	Portland Eagles	PCHL	....	....	....	....	....	....	....	....	....	....	....	....	....	7	3	4	0	480	20	1	2.50	....	....	....	....
	NHL Totals		**24**	**10**	**14**	**0**	**1440**	**108**	**0**	**4.50**	....	....	....	....	....	....	....	....	....	....	....	....	....	....	....	....	....

Traded to **Providence** (AHL) by **Chicago** with Gord Buttrey and $10,000 for Mike Karakas, January 7, 1944. Traded to **Detroit** by **St. Louis (AHL)** with Joe Lund for Red Almas, Lloyd Doran, Tony Licari, Barry Sullivan and Thain Simon, September 9, 1948.

• HIMES, NORMIE

Normie Himes G – R. 5'9", 145 lbs. b: Galt, Ont., 4/13/1903. d: 9/14/1958.

Season	Club	League	GP	W	L	T	Mins	GA	SO	Avg	AAvg	Eff	SA	S%	SAPG	GP	W	L	T	Mins	GA	SO	Avg	Eff	SA	S%	SAPG
1927-28	**New York Americans**	**NHL**	**1**	**0**	**0**	**0**	**19**	**0**	**0**	**0.00**	**0.00**	....	....	....	....	....	....	....	....	....	....	....	....	....	....	....	....
1928-29	**New York Americans**	**NHL**	**1**	**0**	**1**	**0**	**60**	**3**	**0**	**3.00**	**6.39**	....	....	....	....	....	....	....	....	....	....	....	....	....	....	....	....
	NHL Totals		**2**	**0**	**1**	**0**	**79**	**3**	**0**	**2.28**	....	....	....	....	....	....	....	....	....	....	....	....	....	....	....	....	....

• NY Americans' center replaced injured Joe Miller in 3rd period, December 5, 1927. (NY Americans 0, Pittsburgh 0) • NY Americans' center replaced Jake Forbes, December 1, 1928. (Toronto 3, NY Americans 0)

• HIRSCH, COREY

Corey Hirsch G – L. 5'10", 160 lbs. b: Medicine Hat, Alta., 7/1/1972. NY Rangers' 7th choice, 169th overall, in 1991 Entry Draft.

Season	Club	League	GP	W	L	T	Mins	GA	SO	Avg	AAvg	Eff	SA	S%	SAPG	GP	W	L	T	Mins	GA	SO	Avg	Eff	SA	S%	SAPG
1988-89	Kamloops Blazers	WHL	32	11	12	2	1516	106	2	4.20	....	....	....	....	....	5	3	2	....	245	19	0	4.65	....	....	....	....
1989-90	Kamloops Blazers	WHL	*63	*48	13	0	3608	230	*3	3.82	....	....	....	....	....	*17	*14	3	....	*1043	60	0	*3.45	....	....	....	....
1990-91	Kamloops Blazers	WHL	38	26	7	1	1970	100	3	*3.05	....	....	....	....	....	11	5	6	....	623	42	0	4.04	....	....	....	....
1991-92	Kamloops Blazers	WHL	48	35	10	2	2732	124	*5	*2.72	....	....	....	....	....	*16	*11	5	....	954	35	*2	*2.20	....	....	....	....
1992-93	**New York Rangers**	**NHL**	**4**	**1**	**2**	**1**	**224**	**14**	**0**	**3.75**	**3.19**	**4.53**	**116**	**.879**	**31.1**	....	....	....	....	....	....	....	....	....	....	....	....
	Binghamton Rangers	AHL	46	*35	4	5	2692	125	1	*2.79	....	....	....	....	....	14	7	7	....	831	46	0	3.32	....	....	....	....
1993-94	Canada	Nat-Team	45	24	17	3	2653	124	0	2.80	....	....	....	....	....	....	....	....	....	....	....	....	....	....	....	....	....
	Canada	Olympics	8	5	2	1	495	18	....	2.18	....	....	....	....	....	....	....	....	....	....	....	....	....	....	....	....	....
	Binghamton Rangers	AHL	10	5	4	1	610	38	0	3.73	....	....	....	....	....	....	....	....	....	....	....	....	....	....	....	....	....
1994-95	Binghamton Rangers	AHL	57	31	20	5	3371	175	0	3.11	....	....	....	....	....	....	....	....	....	....	....	....	....	....	....	....	....
	Canada	WC-A	8	....	....	....	488	21	....	2.58	....	....	....	....	....	....	....	....	....	....	....	....	....	....	....	....	....
1995-96	**Vancouver Canucks**	**NHL**	**41**	**17**	**14**	**6**	**2338**	**114**	**1**	**2.93**	**2.87**	**2.85**	**1173**	**.903**	**30.1**	**6**	**2**	**3**	....	**338**	**21**	**0**	**3.73**	**4.72**	**166**	**.873**	**29.5**
1996-97	**Vancouver Canucks**	**NHL**	**39**	**12**	**20**	**4**	**2127**	**116**	**2**	**3.27**	**3.47**	**3.48**	**1090**	**.894**	**30.7**	....	....	....	....	....	....	....	....	....	....	....	....
1997-98	**Vancouver Canucks**	**NHL**	**1**	**0**	**0**	**0**	**50**	**5**	**0**	**6.00**	**7.02**	**8.82**	**34**	**.853**	**40.8**	....	....	....	....	....	....	....	....	....	....	....	....
	Syracuse Crunch	AHL	60	30	22	6	3512	187	1	3.19	....	....	....	....	....	5	2	3	....	297	10	1	*2.02	....	....	....	....
	NHL Totals		**85**	**30**	**36**	**11**	**4739**	**249**	**3**	**3.15**	....	....	**2413**	**.897**	....	**6**	**2**	**3**	....	**338**	**21**	**0**	**3.73**	....	....	....	....

WHL West Second All-Star Team (1990) • WHL West First All-Star Team (1991, 1992) • Canadian Major Junior Goaltender of the Year (1992) • Memorial Cup All-Star Team (1992) • Memorial Cup Tournament Top Goaltender (1992) • AHL First All-Star Team (1993) • Won Dudley "Red" Garrett Memorial Trophy (AHL Rookie of the Year) (1993) • Shared Harry "Hap" Holmes Memorial Trophy (fewest goals-against - AHL) with Boris Rousson (1993) • NHL All-Rookie Team (1996)

Traded to **Vancouver** by **NY Rangers** for Nathan Lafayette, April 7, 1995.

• HODGE, CHARLIE

Charlie Hodge G – L. 5'6", 150 lbs. b: Lachine, Que., 7/28/1933.

Season	Club	League	GP	W	L	T	Mins	GA	SO	Avg	AAvg	Eff	SA	S%	SAPG	GP	W	L	T	Mins	GA	SO	Avg	Eff	SA	S%	SAPG
1950-51	Montreal Jr. Canadiens	QJHL	23	14	8	0	1320	57	1	*2.59	....	....	....	....	....	9	4	5	0	564	31	0	3.30	....	....	....	....
1951-52	Montreal Jr. Canadiens	QJHL	45	32	10	3	2700	100	3	*2.22	....	....	....	....	....	19	13	6	0	1149	51	1	2.66	....	....	....	....
	Montreal Royals	QSHL	1	0	0	0	40	3	0	4.50	....	....	....	....	....	....	....	....	....	....	....	....	....	....	....	....	....
1952-53	Montreal Jr. Canadiens	QJHL	44	*35	9	0	2640	100	*5	*2.27	....	....	....	....	....	7	....	....	....	560	18	0	2.57	....	....	....	....
	Montreal Royals	QSHL	1	0	1	0	60	4	0	4.00	....	....	....	....	....	....	....	....	....	....	....	....	....	....	....	....	....
1953-54	Cincinnati Mohawks	IHL	62	....	....	....	3720	145	*10	*2.34	....	....	....	....	....	11	*8	3	0	660	19	*2	*1.73	....	....	....	....
	Buffalo Bisons	AHL	3	2	1	0	180	10	0	3.33	....	....	....	....	....	....	....	....	....	....	....	....	....	....	....	....	....
1954-55	Providence Reds	AHL	5	3	2	0	300	18	1	3.60	....	....	....	....	....	....	....	....	....	....	....	....	....	....	....	....	....
	Montreal Canadiens	**NHL**	**14**	**7**	**3**	**4**	**840**	**31**	**1**	**2.21**	**2.69**	....	....	....	....	**4**	**1**	**1**	....	**83**	**6**	**0**	**4.34**	....	....	....	....
	Montreal Royals	QHL	35	17	17	1	2100	113	2	3.23	....	....	....	....	....	....	....	....	....	....	....	....	....	....	....	....	....
1955-56	Seattle Americans	WHL	70	31	37	2	4246	239	0	3.38	....	....	....	....	....	....	....	....	....	....	....	....	....	....	....	....	....
1956-57	Rochester Americans	AHL	41	18	18	4	2460	132	2	3.22	....	....	....	....	....	....	....	....	....	....	....	....	....	....	....	....	....
	Shawinigan Cataracts	QHL	14	7	5	2	859	39	2	2.72	....	....	....	....	....	....	....	....	....	....	....	....	....	....	....	....	....
1957-58	**Montreal Canadiens**	**NHL**	**12**	**8**	**2**	**2**	**720**	**31**	**1**	**2.58**	**2.84**	....	....	....	....	....	....	....	....	....	....	....	....	....	....	....	....
	Montreal Royals	QHL	48	23	21	4	2880	153	4	3.19	....	....	....	....	....	7	2	4	0	380	25	1	3.95	....	....	....	....
1958-59	Montreal Royals	QHL	24	15	8	1	1440	67	1	2.79	....	....	....	....	....	2	2	0	0	120	4	0	*2.00	....	....	....	....
	Rochester Americans	AHL	4	0	4	0	240	12	0	3.00	....	....	....	....	....	....	....	....	....	....	....	....	....	....	....	....	....
	Montreal Canadiens	**NHL**	**2**	**1**	**1**	**0**	**120**	**6**	**0**	**3.00**	**3.20**	....	....	....	....	....	....	....	....	....	....	....	....	....	....	....	....
1959-60	Montreal Royals	EPHL	33	15	12	6	1980	96	*5	2.91	....	....	....	....	....	....	....	....	....	....	....	....	....	....	....	....	....
	Hull-Ottawa Canadiens	EPHL	26	15	6	5	1560	74	*2	2.85	....	....	....	....	....	7	3	4	0	430	24	0	3.35	....	....	....	....
	Montreal Canadiens	**NHL**	**1**	**0**	**1**	**0**	**60**	**3**	**0**	**3.00**	**3.14**	....	....	....	....	....	....	....	....	....	....	....	....	....	....	....	....
1960-61	Montreal Royals	EPHL	22	5	13	4	1320	74	0	3.36	....	....	....	....	....	....	....	....	....	....	....	....	....	....	....	....	....
	Montreal Canadiens	**NHL**	**30**	**19**	**8**	**3**	**1800**	**76**	**4**	**2.53**	**2.57**	....	....	....	....	....	....	....	....	....	....	....	....	....	....	....	....
1961-62	Quebec Aces	AHL	65	28	33	4	3900	185	5	2.85	....	....	....	....	....	....	....	....	....	....	....	....	....	....	....	....	....
1962-63	Quebec Aces	AHL	67	31	25	11	4020	190	4	2.84	....	....	....	....	....	....	....	....	....	....	....	....	....	....	....	....	....

Season	Club	League	REGULAR SEASON GP	W	L	T	Mins	GA	SO	Avg	AAvg	Eff	SA	S%	SAPG	PLAYOFFS GP	W	L	T	Mins	GA	SO	Avg	Eff	SA	S%	SAPG
1963-64	Quebec Aces	AHL	10	4	6	0	600	32	1	3.20	....	....	....	....	....	....	....	....	....	....	....	....	....	....	....	....	....
	Montreal Canadiens	**NHL**	**62**	**33**	**18**	**11**	**3720**	**140**	***8**	**2.26**	**2.43**	....	....	....	....	**7**	**3**	**4**	....	**420**	**16**	**1**	**2.29**	....	....	....	....
1964-65	**Montreal Canadiens**	**NHL**	**53**	**26**	**16**	**10**	**3180**	**135**	**3**	**2.55**	**2.69**	....	....	....	....	**5**	**3**	**2**	....	**300**	**10**	**1**	**2.00**	....	....	....	....
1965-66	**Montreal Canadiens**	**NHL**	**26**	**12**	**7**	**2**	**1301**	**56**	**1**	**2.58**	**2.60**	....	....	....	....	....	....	....	....	....	....	....	....	....	....	....	....
1966-67	**Montreal Canadiens**	**NHL**	**37**	**11**	**15**	**7**	**2055**	**88**	**3**	**2.57**	**2.63**	....	....	....	....	....	....	....	....	....	....	....	....	....	....	....	....
1967-68	**Oakland Seals**	**NHL**	**58**	**13**	**29**	**13**	**3311**	**158**	**3**	**2.86**	**3.17**	....	....	....	....	....	....	....	....	....	....	....	....	....	....	....	....
1968-69	**Oakland Seals**	**NHL**	**14**	**4**	**6**	**1**	**781**	**48**	**0**	**3.69**	**3.83**	....	....	....	....	....	....	....	....	....	....	....	....	....	....	....	....
	Vancouver Canucks	WHL	13	7	2	4	779	32	0	2.54	....	....	....	....	....	8	*8	0	0	*497	12	*1	*1.45	....	....	....	....
1969-70	**Oakland Seals**	**NHL**	**14**	**3**	**5**	**2**	**738**	**43**	**0**	**3.50**	**3.73**	....	....	....	....	....	....	....	....	....	....	....	....	....	....	....	....
1970-71	**Vancouver Canucks**	**NHL**	**35**	**15**	**13**	**5**	**1967**	**112**	**0**	**3.42**	**3.39**	....	....	....	....	....	....	....	....	....	....	....	....	....	....	....	....
	NHL Totals		**358**	**152**	**124**	**60**	**20593**	**927**	**24**	**2.70**	....	....	....	....	....	**16**	**7**	**7**	....	**803**	**32**	**2**	**2.39**	....	....	....	....

IHL Second All-Star Team (1954) • QHL Second All-Star Team (1955) • QHL First All-Star Team (1958) • AHL Second All-Star Team (1963) • NHL Second All-Star Team (1964, 1965) • Won Vezina Trophy (1964) • Shared Vezina Trophy with Gump Worsley (1966)

Played in NHL All-Star Game (1964, 1965, 1967)

Claimed by **California** from **Montreal** in Expansion Draft, June 6, 1967. Claimed by **Vancouver** from **Oakland** in Expansion Draft, June 10, 1970.

• HODSON, KEVIN

Kevin Hodson G – L. 6′, 182 lbs. b: Winnipeg, Man., 3/27/1972.

Season	Club	League	GP	W	L	T	Mins	GA	SO	Avg	AAvg	Eff	SA	S%	SAPG	GP	W	L	T	Mins	GA	SO	Avg	Eff	SA	S%	SAPG
1990-91	Sault Ste. Marie Greyhounds	OHL	30	18	11	0	1638	88	*2	*3.22	....	....	....	....	....	10	*9	1	....	581	28	0	*2.89	....	....	....	....
1991-92	Sault Ste. Marie Greyhounds	OHL	50	28	12	4	2722	151	0	3.33	....	....	....	....	....	18	12	6	....	1116	54	1	2.90	....	....	....	....
1992-93	Sault Ste. Marie Greyhounds	OHL	26	18	5	2	1470	76	1	*3.10	....	....	....	....	....	14	11	2	....	755	34	0	2.70	....	....	....	....
	Indianapolis Ice	IHL	14	5	9	0	777	53	0	4.09	....	....	....	....	....	....	....	....	....	....	....	....	....	....	....	....	....
1993-94	Adirondack Red Wings	AHL	37	20	10	5	2082	102	2	2.94	....	....	....	....	....	3	0	2	....	89	10	0	6.77	....	....	....	....
1994-95	Adirondack Red Wings	AHL	51	19	22	8	2731	161	1	3.54	....	....	....	....	....	4	0	4	....	237	14	0	3.53	....	....	....	....
1995-96	**Detroit Red Wings**	**NHL**	**4**	**2**	**0**	**0**	**163**	**3**	**1**	**1.10**	**1.08**	**0.49**	**67**	**.955**	**24.7**	....	....	....	....	....	....	....	....	....	....	....	....
	Adirondack Red Wings	AHL	32	13	13	2	1654	87	0	3.16	....	....	....	....	....	3	0	2	....	150	8	0	3.21	....	....	....	....
1996-97	**Detroit Red Wings**	**NHL**	**6**	**2**	**2**	**1**	**294**	**8**	**1**	**1.63**	**1.72**	**1.14**	**114**	**.930**	**23.3**	....	....	....	....	....	....	....	....	....	....	....	....
	Quebec Rafales	IHL	2	1	1	0	118	7	0	3.54	....	....	....	....	....	....	....	....	....	....	....	....	....	....	....	....	....
1997-98	**Detroit Red Wings**	**NHL**	**21**	**9**	**3**	**3**	**988**	**44**	**2**	**2.67**	**3.12**	**2.65**	**444**	**.901**	**27.0**	**1**	**0**	**0**	....	**1**	**0**	**0**	**0.00**	**0.00**	**0**	**.00**	**0.0**
	NHL Totals		**31**	**13**	**5**	**4**	**1445**	**55**	**4**	**2.28**	....	....	**625**	**.912**	....	**1**	**0**	**0**	....	**1**	**0**	**0**	**0.00**	....	....	....	....

Memorial Cup All-Star Team (1993) • Won Hap Emms Memorial Trophy (Memorial Cup Tournament Top Goaltender) (1993)

Signed as a free agent by **Chicago**, August 17, 1992. Signed as a free agent by **Detroit**, June 16, 1993. • Played 16 seconds in playoff game vs. Chicago, May 17, 1998.

• HOFFORT, BRUCE

Bruce Hoffort G – L. 5′10″, 185 lbs. b: North Battleford, Sask., 7/30/1966.

Season	Club	League	GP	W	L	T	Mins	GA	SO	Avg	AAvg	Eff	SA	S%	SAPG	GP	W	L	T	Mins	GA	SO	Avg	Eff	SA	S%	SAPG
1987-88	Lake Superior State Univ.	CCHA	31	23	4	3	1787	79	2	2.65	....	....	....	....	....	....	....	....	....	....	....	....	....	....	....	....	....
1988-89	Lake Superior State Univ.	CCHA	44	27	10	5	2595	117	0	2.71	....	....	....	....	....	....	....	....	....	....	....	....	....	....	....	....	....
1989-90	**Philadelphia Flyers**	**NHL**	**7**	**3**	**0**	**2**	**329**	**19**	**0**	**3.47**	**2.91**	**4.15**	**159**	**.881**	**29.0**	....	....	....	....	....	....	....	....	....	....	....	....
	Hershey Bears	AHL	40	16	18	4	2284	139	1	3.65	....	....	....	....	....	....	....	....	....	....	....	....	....	....	....	....	....
1990-91	**Philadelphia Flyers**	**NHL**	**2**	**1**	**0**	**1**	**39**	**3**	**0**	**4.62**	**4.13**	**6.93**	**20**	**.850**	**30.8**	....	....	....	....	....	....	....	....	....	....	....	....
	Hershey Bears	AHL	18	3	12	1	913	74	0	4.86	....	....	....	....	....	....	....	....	....	....	....	....	....	....	....	....	....
	Kansas City Blades	IHL	18	6	7	0	883	68	0	4.62	....	....	....	....	....	....	....	....	....	....	....	....	....	....	....	....	....
1991-92	San Diego Gulls	IHL	26	11	9	4	1474	89	0	3.62	....	....	....	....	....	....	....	....	....	....	....	....	....	....	....	....	....
	NHL Totals		**9**	**4**	**0**	**3**	**368**	**22**	**0**	**3.59**	....	....	**179**	**.877**	....	....	....	....	....	....	....	....	....	....	....	....	....

CCHA First All-Star Team (1988, 1989) • NCAA Championship All-Tournament Team (1988) • NCAA Championship Tournament MVP (1988) • NCAA West First All-American Team (1989)

Signed as a free agent by **Philadelphia**, June 30, 1989.

• HOGANSON, PAUL

Paul Hoganson G – R. 5′11″, 175 lbs. b: Toronto, Ont., 11/12/1949. Pittsburgh's 5th choice, 62nd overall, in 1969 Amateur Draft.

Season	Club	League	GP	W	L	T	Mins	GA	SO	Avg	AAvg	Eff	SA	S%	SAPG	GP	W	L	T	Mins	GA	SO	Avg	Eff	SA	S%	SAPG
1966-67	Hamilton Red Wings	OHA	5	....	....	....	290	19	0	3.93	....	....	....	....	....	....	....	....	....	....	....	....	....	....	....	....	....
1967-68	Quebec Remparts	QJHL	STATISTICS NOT AVAILABLE																								
	Hamilton Red Wings	OHA	1	....	....	....	60	5	0	5.00	....	....	....	....	....	....	....	....	....	....	....	....	....	....	....	....	....
1968-69	Hamilton Red Wings	OHA	1	....	....	....	60	3	0	3.00	....	....	....	....	....	....	....	....	....	....	....	....	....	....	....	....	....
	Kitchener Rangers	OHA	22	....	....	....	1320	125	0	5.68	....	....	....	....	....	....	....	....	....	....	....	....	....	....	....	....	....
	Toronto Marlboros	OHA	22	....	....	....	1310	84	0	3.84	....	....	....	....	....	6	....	....	....	360	28	0	4.67	....	....	....	....
1969-70	Fort Wayne Komets	IHL	37	....	....	....	2101	121	3	3.46	....	....	....	....	....	3	0	3	0	180	14	0	4.67	....	....	....	....
	Baltimore Clippers	AHL	3	....	....	....	100	5	0	3.00	....	....	....	....	....	....	....	....	....	....	....	....	....	....	....	....	....
1970-71	**Pittsburgh Penguins**	**NHL**	**2**	**0**	**1**	**0**	**57**	**7**	**0**	**7.37**	**7.29**	....	....	....	....	....	....	....	....	....	....	....	....	....	....	....	....
	Amarillo Wranglers	CHL	48	....	....	....	2828	203	0	4.37	....	....	....	....	....	....	....	....	....	....	....	....	....	....	....	....	....
1971-72	Fort Wayne Komets	IHL	52	....	....	....	3074	161	2	3.14	....	....	....	....	....	8	4	4	0	480	25	0	3.12	....	....	....	....
1972-73	Hershey Bears	AHL	41	....	....	....	2251	110	3	2.98	....	....	....	....	....	3	....	....	....	179	14	0	4.69	....	....	....	....
1973-74	Los Angeles Sharks	WHA	27	6	16	0	1308	102	0	4.68	....	....	....	....	....	....	....	....	....	....	....	....	....	....	....	....	....
	Greensboro Generals	SHL	3	....	....	....	180	12	0	4.00	....	....	....	....	....	....	....	....	....	....	....	....	....	....	....	....	....
1974-75	Baltimore-Michigan	WHA	32	9	19	2	1776	121	2	4.09	....	....	....	....	....	....	....	....	....	....	....	....	....	....	....	....	....
	Tulsa Oilers	CHL	6	3	3	0	320	19	0	3.56	....	....	....	....	....	....	....	....	....	....	....	....	....	....	....	....	....
1975-76	New England Whalers	WHA	4	1	2	0	224	16	0	4.29	....	....	....	....	....	....	....	....	....	....	....	....	....	....	....	....	....
	Cincinnati Stingers	WHA	45	19	24	0	2392	145	2	3.64	....	....	....	....	....	....	....	....	....	....	....	....	....	....	....	....	....
1976-77	Binghamton Dusters	NAHL	8	....	....	....	480	440	0	5.05	....	....	....	....	....	....	....	....	....	....	....	....	....	....	....	....	....
	Cincinnati Stingers	WHA	17	5	6	1	823	64	1	4.67	....	....	....	....	....	....	....	....	....	....	....	....	....	....	....	....	....
	Indianapolis Racers	WHA	11	3	2	0	395	24	0	3.65	....	....	....	....	....	5	3	2	0	348	17	*1	*2.93	....	....	....	....
1977-78	Cincinnati Stingers	WHA	7	1	2	1	326	24	0	4.42	....	....	....	....	....	....	....	....	....	....	....	....	....	....	....	....	....
	Hampton Gulls	AHL	3	1	1	1	155	11	0	4.26	....	....	....	....	....	....	....	....	....	....	....	....	....	....	....	....	....
	San Francisco Shamrocks	PHL	11	....	....	....	660	614	0	3.90	....	....	....	....	....	....	....	....	....	....	....	....	....	....	....	....	....
1978-79	Tucson Rustlers	PHL	37	....	....	....	2058	170	1	4.96	....	....	....	....	....	....	....	....	....	....	....	....	....	....	....	....	....
	NHL Totals		**2**	**0**	**1**	**0**	**57**	**7**	**0**	**7.37**	....	....	....	....	....	....	....	....	....	....	....	....	....	....	....	....	....
	Other Major League Totals		143	44	71	4	7244	496	5	4.11	....	....	....	....	....	5	3	2	0	348	17	1	2.93	....	....	....	....

OHA Second All-Star Team (1969) • IHL Second All-Star Team (1972)

Selected by **LA Sharks** (WHA) in 1972 WHA General Player Draft, February 12, 1972. Transferred to **Michigan** (WHA) after **LA Sharks** (WHA) franchise relocated, April 11, 1974. Selected by **New England** (WHA) from **Michigan-Baltimore** (WHA) in WHA Dispersal Draft, June, 1975. Signed as a free agent by **Cincinnati** (WHA) after securing release from **New England** (WHA), November, 1975. Traded to **Indianapolis** (WHA) by **Cincinnati** (WHA) for cash, February, 1976. Signed as a free agent by **Cincinnati** (WHA) after **Indianapolis** (WHA) franchise folded, February, 1978.

• HOGOSTA, GORAN

Goran Hogosta G – L. 6′1″, 179 lbs. b: Appelbo, Sweden, 4/15/1954.

Season	Club	League	GP	W	L	T	Mins	GA	SO	Avg	AAvg	Eff	SA	S%	SAPG	GP	W	L	T	Mins	GA	SO	Avg	Eff	SA	S%	SAPG
1971-72	Tunabro	Sweden	11	....	....	....	660	64	0	5.82	....	....	....	....	....	....	....	....	....	....	....	....	....	....	....	....	....
	Sweden	EJC-A	2	....	....	....	70	2	....	1.71	....	....	....	....	....	....	....	....	....	....	....	....	....	....	....	....	....
1972-73	Tunabro	Sweden	10	....	....	....	600	59	0	5.90	....	....	....	....	....	6	3	0	3	360	21	0	3.50	....	....	....	....
	Sweden	EJC-A	4	....	....	....	210	11	....	3.14	....	....	....	....	....	....	....	....	....	....	....	....	....	....	....	....	....
1973-74	Tunabro	Sweden	STATISTICS NOT AVAILABLE													5				304	15	0	2.96				
1974-75	Leksands IF	Sweden	30	....	....	....	1800	80	0	2.67	....	....	....	....	....	5	....	....	....	304	15	0	2.96	....	....	....	....
	Sweden	WEC-A	4	....	....	....	220	12	....	3.27	....	....	....	....	....	....	....	....	....	....	....	....	....	....	....	....	....
1975-76	Leksands IF	Sweden	27	....	....	....	1620	118	0	4.37	....	....	....	....	....	....	....	....	....	....	....	....	....	....	....	....	....
	Sweden	WEC-A	6	....	....	....	360	20	....	3.33	....	....	....	....	....	....	....	....	....	....	....	....	....	....	....	....	....
1976-77	Sweden	C Cup	1	....	....	....	60	1	0	1.00	....	....	....	....	....	....	....	....	....	....	....	....	....	....	....	....	....
	Leksands IF	Sweden	33	....	....	....	1921	126	0	3.94	....	....	....	....	....	4	....	....	....	245	16	0	3.92	....	....	....	....
	Sweden	WEC-A	7	....	....	....	412	9	....	1.31	....	....	....	....	....	....	....	....	....	....	....	....	....	....	....	....	....
1977-78	**New York Islanders**	**NHL**	**1**	**0**	**0**	**0**	**9**	**0**	**0**	**0.00**	**0.00**	....	....	....	....	....	....	....	....	....	....	....	....	....	....	....	....
	Fort Worth Texans	CHL	5	3	2	0	297	19	0	3.84	....	....	....	....	....	....	....	....	....	....	....	....	....	....	....	....	....
	Hershey Bears	AHL	23	6	13	2	1254	82	1	3.92	....	....	....	....	....	....	....	....	....	....	....	....	....	....	....	....	....
	Sweden	WEC-A	7	....	....	....	392	22	....	3.37	....	....	....	....	....	....	....	....	....	....	....	....	....	....	....	....	....
1978-79	Fort Worth Texans	CHL	61	25	29	4	3332	195	2	3.51	....	....	....	....	....	3	1	2	0	167	9	0	3.23	....	....	....	....
1979-80	**Quebec Nordiques**	**NHL**	**21**	**5**	**12**	**3**	**1199**	**83**	**1**	**4.15**	**3.65**	....	....	....	....	....	....	....	....	....	....	....	....	....	....	....	....
	Syracuse Firebirds	AHL	17	4	9	4	1037	69	0	3.99	....	....	....	....	....	....	....	....	....	....	....	....	....	....	....	....	....

Season	Club	League	REGULAR SEASON													PLAYOFFS											
			GP	W	L	T	Mins	GA	SO	Avg	AAvg	Eff	SA	S%	SAPG	GP	W	L	T	Mins	GA	SO	Avg	Eff	SA	S%	SAPG
1980-81	Vastra Frolunda	Sweden	18	....	....	....	1078	76	0	4.23	....	....	....	....	....	1	0	1	0	60	6	0	6.00	....	....	....	....
1981-82	Vastra Frolunda	Sweden	28	....	....	....	1582	89	0	3.38	....	....	....	....	....	....	....	....	....	....	....	....	....	....	....	....	....
1982-83	Vastra Frolunda	Sweden	34	....	....	....	1980	140	1	4.24	....	....	....	....	....	....	....	....	....	....	....	....	....	....	....	....	....
1983-84	Vastra Frolunda	Sweden	36	....	....	....	1093	151	1	8.29	....	....	....	....	....	....	....	....	....	....	....	....	....	....	....	....	....
	NHL Totals		**22**	**5**	**12**	**3**	**1208**	**83**	**1**	**4.12**	....	....	....	....	....	....	....	....	....	....	....	....	....	....	....	....	....

Named Best Goaltender at EJC-A (1973) • WEC-A All-Star Team (1977) • Named Best Goaltender at WEC-A (1977)

Signed as a free agent by **NY Islanders**, June 18, 1977. Traded to **Quebec** by **NY Islanders** for Richard Brodeur, August, 1979.

• HOLDEN, MARK

Mark Holden G – L. 5'10", 165 lbs. b: Weymouth, MA, 6/12/1957. Montreal's 16th choice, 160th overall, in 1977 Amateur Draft.

Season	Club	League	GP	W	L	T	Mins	GA	SO	Avg	AAvg	Eff	SA	S%	SAPG	GP	W	L	T	Mins	GA	SO	Avg	Eff	SA	S%	SAPG
1976-77	Brown University	ECAC	5	0	0	0	82	5	0	3.68	....	....	....	....	....	....	....	....	....	....	....	....	....	....	....	....	....
1977-78	Brown University	ECAC	10	4	6	0	590	33	1	3.36	....	....	....	....	....	....	....	....	....	....	....	....	....	....	....	....	....
1978-79	Brown University	ECAC	13	7	6	0	755	49	0	3.90	....	....	....	....	....	....	....	....	....	....	....	....	....	....	....	....	....
1979-80	Brown University	ECAC	26	10	14	2	1508	93	0	3.70	....	....	....	....	....	....	....	....	....	....	....	....	....	....	....	....	....
1980-81	Nova Scotia Voyageurs	AHL	42	20	17	1	2223	127	2	3.43	....	....	....	....	....	3	0	3	0	159	12	0	4.53	....	....	....	....
1981-82	**Montreal Canadiens**	**NHL**	**1**	**0**	**0**	**0**	**20**	**0**	**0**	**0.00**	**0.00**	....	....	....	....	....	....	....	....	....	....	....	....	....	....	....	....
	Nova Scotia Voyageurs	AHL	44	19	19	5	2534	142	0	3.36	....	....	....	....	....	7	2	5	0	435	21	0	2.90	....	....	....	....
1982-83	**Montreal Canadiens**	**NHL**	**2**	**0**	**1**	**1**	**87**	**6**	**0**	**4.14**	**3.31**	**5.91**	**42**	**.857**	**29.0**	....	....	....	....	....	....	....	....	....	....	....	....
	Nova Scotia Voyageurs	AHL	41	21	16	1	2369	160	0	4.05	....	....	....	....	....	6	3	2	0	319	13	0	2.44	....	....	....	....
1983-84	**Montreal Canadiens**	**NHL**	**1**	**0**	**1**	**0**	**52**	**4**	**0**	**4.62**	**3.61**	**10.87**	**17**	**.765**	**19.6**	....	....	....	....	....	....	....	....	....	....	....	....
	Nova Scotia Voyageurs	AHL	47	19	8	7	2739	153	0	3.35	....	....	....	....	....	10	4	6	0	534	40	0	4.49	....	....	....	....
1984-85	**Winnipeg Jets**	**NHL**	**4**	**2**	**0**	**0**	**213**	**15**	**0**	**4.23**	**3.36**	**6.10**	**104**	**.856**	**29.3**	....	....	....	....	....	....	....	....	....	....	....	....
	Nova Scotia Oilers	AHL	22	8	12	1	1261	87	1	4.14	....	....	....	....	....	....	....	....	....	....	....	....	....	....	....	....	....
1985-86	Sherbrooke Canadiens	AHL	12	5	7	0	696	52	0	4.48	....	....	....	....	....	....	....	....	....	....	....	....	....	....	....	....	....
	Fort Wayne Komets	IHL	9	3	3	0	496	26	1	3.14	....	....	....	....	....	....	....	....	....	....	....	....	....	....	....	....	....
	NHL Totals		**8**	**2**	**2**	**1**	**372**	**25**	**0**	**4.03**	....	....	....	....	....	....	....	....	....	....	....	....	....	....	....	....	....

NCAA East First All-American Team (1980)

Traded to **Winnipeg** by **Montreal** for Doug Soetaert, October 9, 1984.

• HOLLAND, KEN

Ken Holland G – L. 5'8", 160 lbs. b: Vernon, B.C., 11/10/1955. Toronto's 13th choice, 188th overall, in 1975 Amateur Draft.

Season	Club	League	GP	W	L	T	Mins	GA	SO	Avg	AAvg	Eff	SA	S%	SAPG	GP	W	L	T	Mins	GA	SO	Avg	Eff	SA	S%	SAPG
1974-75	Medicine Hat Tigers	WCJHL	37	....	....	....	2114	138	1	3.91	....	....	....	....	....	4	....	....	....	230	16	0	4.17	....	....	....	....
1975-76	Medicine Hat Tigers	WCJHL	41	....	....	....	2152	150	2	4.18	....	....	....	....	....	9	....	....	....	528	30	0	3.41	....	....	....	....
1976-77	Binghamton Dusters	NAHL	48	....	....	....	2620	165	0	3.78	....	....	....	....	....	6	....	....	....	320	22	0	4.13	....	....	....	....
1977-78	Binghamton Dusters	AHL	39	12	19	3	2057	147	0	4.28	....	....	....	....	....	....	....	....	....	....	....	....	....	....	....	....	....
1978-79	Binghamton Dusters	AHL	41	19	17	3	2315	151	0	3.91	....	....	....	....	....	*10	5	5	0	*572	39	*1	4.09	....	....	....	....
1979-80	Springfield Indians	AHL	37	15	14	5	2092	129	2	3.70	....	....	....	....	....	....	....	....	....	....	....	....	....	....	....	....	....
1980-81	**Hartford Whalers**	**NHL**	**1**	**0**	**1**	**0**	**60**	**7**	**0**	**7.00**	**5.61**	....	....	....	....	....	....	....	....	....	....	....	....	....	....	....	....
	Binghamton Whalers	AHL	47	15	25	4	2543	168	2	3.96	....	....	....	....	....	2	0	2	0	79	3	0	2.28	....	....	....	....
1981-82	Binghamton Whalers	AHL	46	27	13	4	2733	133	2	2.92	....	....	....	....	....	*15	8	7	0	*888	57	0	3.85	....	....	....	....
1982-83	Binghamton Whalers	AHL	*48	23	18	5	2700	196	0	4.36	....	....	....	....	....	3	1	2	0	180	16	0	5.33	....	....	....	....
1983-84	**Detroit Red Wings**	**NHL**	**3**	**0**	**1**	**1**	**146**	**10**	**0**	**4.11**	**3.22**	**7.75**	**53**	**.811**	**21.8**	....	....	....	....	....	....	....	....	....	....	....	....
	Adirondack Red Wings	AHL	42	19	15	6	2495	154	0	3.70	....	....	....	....	....	7	3	4	0	416	25	0	3.61	....	....	....	....
1984-85	Adirondack Red Wings	AHL	43	13	22	6	2478	176	0	4.26	....	....	....	....	....	....	....	....	....	....	....	....	....	....	....	....	....
	NHL Totals		**4**	**0**	**2**	**1**	**206**	**17**	**0**	**4.95**	....	....	....	....	....	....	....	....	....	....	....	....	....	....	....	....	....

NAHL Second All-Star Team (1977) • AHL Second All-Star Team (1982)

Signed as a free agent by **Hartford**, July 17, 1980. Signed as a free agent by **Detroit**, July 6, 1983.

• HOLLAND, ROBBIE

Robbie Holland G – L. 6'1", 180 lbs. b: Montreal, Que., 9/10/1957. Montreal's 8th choice, 64th overall, in 1977 Amateur Draft.

Season	Club	League	GP	W	L	T	Mins	GA	SO	Avg	AAvg	Eff	SA	S%	SAPG	GP	W	L	T	Mins	GA	SO	Avg	Eff	SA	S%	SAPG
1975-76	Montreal Jr. Canadiens	QMJHL	37	....	....	....	1995	147	0	4.42	....	....	....	....	....	6	....	....	....	360	21	0	3.50	....	....	....	....
1976-77	Montreal Jr. Canadiens	QMJHL	45	....	....	....	2314	184	0	4.77	....	....	....	....	....	13	....	....	....	780	64	0	4.92	....	....	....	....
1977-78	Nova Scotia Voyageurs	AHL	38	13	14	11	2270	120	1	3.17	....	....	....	....	....	5	3	2	0	299	14	0	2.81	....	....	....	....
1978-79	Nova Scotia Voyageurs	AHL	43	10	19	2	2377	154	*2	3.89	....	....	....	....	....	1	0	1	0	60	7	0	7.00	....	....	....	....
1979-80	**Pittsburgh Penguins**	**NHL**	**34**	**10**	**17**	**6**	**1974**	**126**	**1**	**3.83**	**3.37**	....	....	....	....	....	....	....	....	....	....	....	....	....	....	....	....
1980-81	**Pittsburgh Penguins**	**NHL**	**10**	**1**	**5**	**3**	**539**	**45**	**0**	**5.01**	**4.02**	....	....	....	....	....	....	....	....	....	....	....	....	....	....	....	....
	Binghamton Whalers	AHL	7	1	4	0	354	28	0	4.75	....	....	....	....	....	....	....	....	....	....	....	....	....	....	....	....	....
	Indianapolis Checkers	CHL	15	6	6	2	845	41	1	2.91	....	....	....	....	....	3	....	....	....	179	13	0	4.36	....	....	....	....
1981-82	Indianapolis Checkers	CHL	30	15	11	1	1672	95	0	3.41	....	....	....	....	....	....	....	....	....	....	....	....	....	....	....	....	....
	Toledo Goaldiggers	IHL	7	....	....		423	25	0	3.55	....	....	....	....	....	....	....	....	....	....	....	....	....	....	....	....	....
1982-83	Indianapolis Checkers	CHL	37	24	11	1	2111	101	*4	*2.87	....	....	....	....	....	3	2	1	0	200	13	0	3.90	....	....	....	....
1983-84	Indianapolis Checkers	CHL	39	....	....	....	2149	131	0	3.66	....	....	....	....	....	7	....	....	....	379	22	0	3.48	....	....	....	....
1984-85	Indianapolis Checkers	IHL	57	....	....	....	3344	184	*4	3.28	....	....	....	....	....	6	....	....	....	359	21	*1	3.51	....	....	....	....
1985-86	Springfield Indians	AHL	8	6	2	0	478	23	0	2.88	....	....	....	....	....	....	....	....	....	....	....	....	....	....	....	....	....
	Indianapolis Checkers	IHL	44	....	....	....	2246	146	0	3.90	....	....	....	....	....	4	....	....	....	182	15	0	4.94	....	....	....	....
1986-87	Milwaukee Admirals	IHL	66	....	....	....	3915	268	1	4.11	....	....	....	....	....	6	....	....	....	360	30	0	5.00	....	....	....	....
	NHL Totals		**44**	**11**	**22**	**9**	**2513**	**171**	**1**	**4.08**	....	....	....	....	....	....	....	....	....	....	....	....	....	....	....	....	....

Shared Harry "Hap" Holmes Memorial Award (fewest goals against - AHL) with Maurice Barrett (1978) • Shared Terry Sawchuk Trophy (fewest goals against - CHL) with Kelly Hrudey (1982, 1983) • CHL Second All-Star Team (1983)

Traded to **Pittsburgh** by **Montreal** with Pat Hughes for Denis Herron and Pittsburgh's 2nd round choice (Jocelyn Gauvreau) in 1982 Entry Draft, August 30, 1979. Rights traded to **NY Islanders** by **Pittsburgh** for future considerations, September 28, 1981.

• HOLMES, HARRY

Harry "Hap" Holmes G – L. 5'10", 170 lbs. b: Aurora, Ont., 2/21/1892. d: 1940. **HHOF**

Season	Club	League	GP	W	L	T	Mins	GA	SO	Avg	AAvg	Eff	SA	S%	SAPG	GP	W	L	T	Mins	GA	SO	Avg	Eff	SA	S%	SAPG
1909-10	Toronto Canoe Club	OHA Sr.	4	2	2	0	240	26	0	6.50	....	....	....	....	....	....	....	....	....	....	....	....	....	....	....	....	....
1910-11	Toronto Parkdale Canoe Club	OHA Sr.	4	*3	1	0	240	12	0	3.00	....	....	....	....	....	2	0	1	1	120	9	0	4.50	....	....	....	....
1911-12	Toronto Tecumsehs	Sr.	1	1	0	0	60	3	0	3.00	....	....	....	....	....	....	....	....	....	....	....	....	....	....	....	....	....
1912-13	Toronto Blueshirts	NHA	15	6	7	0	779	58	*1	4.47	....	....	....	....	....	....	....	....	....	....	....	....	....	....	....	....	....
1913-14	Toronto Blueshirts	NHA	20	*13	7	0	1204	65	*1	3.24	....	....	....	....	....	5	4	1	0	315	10	2	1.90	....	....	....	....
1914-15	Toronto Blueshirts	NHA	20	8	12	0	1218	84	0	4.18	....	....	....	....	....	....	....	....	....	....	....	....	....	....	....	....	....
1915-16	Toronto Blueshirts	NHA	1	0	1	0	60	6	0	6.00	....	....	....	....	....	....	....	....	....	....	....	....	....	....	....	....	....
	Seattle Metropolitans	PCHA	18	9	9	0	1080	66	0	3.67	....	....	....	....	....	....	....	....	....	....	....	....	....	....	....	....	....
1916-17	Seattle Metropolitans	PCHA	24	*16	8	0	1465	80	*2	*3.28	....	....	....	....	....	4	*3	1	0	140	11	0	2.75	....	....	....	....
1917-18	**Toronto Arenas**	**NHL**	**16**	**9**	**7**	**0**	**965**	**76**	**0**	**4.73**	**3.08**	....	....	....	....	***7**	***4**	**3**	**0**	***420**	**28**	**0**	***4.00**	....	....	....	....
1918-19	**Toronto Arenas**	**NHL**	**2**	**0**	**2**	**0**	**120**	**9**	**0**	**4.50**	**3.36**	....	....	....	....	....	....	....	....	....	....	....	....	....	....	....	....
	Seattle Metropolitans	PCHA	20	11	9	0	1225	46	0	*2.25	....	....	....	....	....	7	3	3	1	456	15	2	1.97	....	....	....	....
1919-20	Seattle Metropolitans	PCHA	22	12	10	0	1340	55	*4	*2.46	....	....	....	....	....	7	3	4	0	420	18	1	2.57	....	....	....	....
1920-21	Seattle Metropolitans	PCHA	24	12	11	1	1551	68	0	*2.63	....	....	....	....	....	2	0	2	0	120	13	0	6.50	....	....	....	....
1921-22	Seattle Metropolitans	PCHA	24	*12	11	1	1479	64	*4	*2.60	....	....	....	....	....	2	0	2	0	120	2	0	1.00	....	....	....	....
1922-23	Seattle Metropolitans	PCHA	*30	15	15	0	1844	106	2	3.45	....	....	....	....	....	....	....	....	....	....	....	....	....	....	....	....	....
1923-24	Seattle Metropolitans	PCHA	*30	*14	16	0	1824	99	*2	3.26	....	....	....	....	....	2	0	1	1	134	4	0	1.79	....	....	....	....
1924-25	Victoria Cougars	WCHL	*28	16	12	0	1683	63	*3	*2.25	....	....	....	....	....	*8	*5	1	2	480	13	1	1.63	....	....	....	....
1925-26	Victoria Cougars	WHL	*30	15	11	4	*1894	53	4	*1.68	....	....	....	....	....	4	*2	0	2	248	6	1	*1.45	....	....	....	....
1926-27	**Detroit Cougars**	**NHL**	**41**	**11**	**26**	**4**	**2685**	**100**	**6**	**2.23**	**3.49**	....	....	....	....	....	....	....	....	....	....	....	....	....	....	....	....
1927-28	**Detroit Cougars**	**NHL**	***44**	**19**	**19**	**6**	**2740**	**79**	**11**	**1.73**	**2.78**	....	....	....	....	....	....	....	....	....	....	....	....	....	....	....	....
	NHL Totals		**103**	**39**	**54**	**10**	**6510**	**264**	**17**	**2.43**	....	....	....	....	....	**7**	**4**	**3**	**0**	**420**	**28**	**0**	**4.00**	....	....	....	....
	Other Major League Totals		306	159	139	6	18646	913	23	2.94	....	....	....	....	....	41	20	15	6	2433	92	7	2.27	....	....	....	....

PCHA Second All-Star Team (1916, 1917, 1919, 1920, 1921, 1922, 1923) • WCHL All-Star Team (1925)

Loaned to **Toronto Arenas** by **Seattle** (PCHA), January 4, 1918. Signed as a free agent by **Victoria** (WCHL), November 7, 1924. Rights transferred to **Detroit Cougars** after NHL club purchased **Victoria** (WHL) franchise, May 26, 1926.

• HORNER, RED

Red (Reginald) Horner G – R. 6', 190 lbs. b: Lynden, Ont., 5/28/1909.

Season	Club	League	GP	W	L	T	Mins	GA	SO	Avg	AAvg	Eff	SA	S%	SAPG	GP	W	L	T	Mins	GA	SO	Avg	Eff	SA	S%	SAPG
			REGULAR SEASON													PLAYOFFS											
1931-32	**Toronto Maple Leafs**	**NHL**	**1**	**0**	**0**	**0**	**1**	**1**	**0**	**60.00**	**73.84**	....	....	....	....	....	....	....	....	....	....	....	....	....	....	....	....
	NHL Totals		**1**	**0**	**0**	**0**	**1**	**1**	**0**	**60.00**	....	....	....	....	....	....	....	....	....	....	....	....	....	....	....	....	....

• Toronto defenseman replaced penalized Lorne Chabot, March 15, 1932. (Detroit 6, Toronto 2)

• HRIVNAK, JIM

Jim Hrivnak G – L. 6'2", 195 lbs. b: Montreal, Que., 5/28/1968. Washington's 4th choice, 61st overall, in 1986 Entry Draft.

Season	Club	League	GP	W	L	T	Mins	GA	SO	Avg	AAvg	Eff	SA	S%	SAPG	GP	W	L	T	Mins	GA	SO	Avg	Eff	SA	S%	SAPG
1985-86	Merrimack College	NCAA	21	12	6	2	1230	75	0	3.66	....	....	....	....	....	....	....	....	....	....	....	....	....	....	....	....	....
1986-87	Merrimack College	NCAA	34	27	7	0	1950	80	3	2.46	....	....	....	....	....	....	....	....	....	....	....	....	....	....	....	....	....
1987-88	Merrimack College	NCAA	37	31	6	0	2119	84	4	2.38	....	....	....	....	....	....	....	....	....	....	....	....	....	....	....	....	....
1988-89	Merrimack College	NCAA	22	18	4	0	1295	52	4	2.41	....	....	....	....	....	....	....	....	....	....	....	....	....	....	....	....	....
	Baltimore Skipjacks	AHL	10	1	8	0	502	55	0	6.57	....	....	....	....	....	....	....	....	....	....	....	....	....	....	....	....	....
1989-90	**Washington Capitals**	**NHL**	**11**	**5**	**5**	**0**	**609**	**36**	**0**	**3.55**	**2.97**	**4.36**	**293**	**.877**	**28.9**	....	....	....	....	....	....	....	....	....	....	....	....
	Baltimore Skipjacks	AHL	47	24	19	2	2722	139	*4	3.06	....	....	....	....	....	6	4	2	0	360	19	0	3.17	....	....	....	....
1990-91	**Washington Capitals**	**NHL**	**9**	**4**	**2**	**1**	**432**	**26**	**0**	**3.61**	**3.22**	**4.15**	**226**	**.885**	**31.4**	....	....	....	....	....	....	....	....	....	....	....	....
	Baltimore Skipjacks	AHL	42	20	16	6	2481	134	1	3.24	....	....	....	....	....	6	2	3	0	324	21	0	3.89	....	....	....	....
1991-92	**Washington Capitals**	**NHL**	**12**	**6**	**3**	**0**	**605**	**35**	**0**	**3.47**	**3.08**	**4.43**	**274**	**.872**	**27.2**	....	....	....	....	....	....	....	....	....	....	....	....
	Baltimore Skipjacks	AHL	22	10	8	3	1303	73	0	3.36	....	....	....	....	....	....	....	....	....	....	....	....	....	....	....	....	....
1992-93	**Washington Capitals**	**NHL**	**27**	**13**	**9**	**2**	**1421**	**83**	**0**	**3.50**	**2.98**	**4.29**	**677**	**.877**	**28.6**	....	....	....	....	....	....	....	....	....	....	....	....
	Winnipeg Jets	**NHL**	**3**	**2**	**1**	**0**	**180**	**13**	**0**	**4.33**	**3.69**	**5.86**	**96**	**.865**	**32.0**	....	....	....	....	....	....	....	....	....	....	....	....
1993-94	**St. Louis Blues**	**NHL**	**23**	**4**	**10**	**0**	**970**	**69**	**0**	**4.27**	**4.07**	**5.23**	**563**	**.877**	**34.8**	....	....	....	....	....	....	....	....	....	....	....	....
1994-95	Milwaukee Admirals	IHL	28	17	10	1	1634	106	0	3.89	....	....	....	....	....	....	....	....	....	....	....	....	....	....	....	....	....
	Kansas City Blades	IHL	10	3	5	2	550	35	0	3.81	....	....	....	....	....	2	0	2	0	118	7	0	3.55	....	....	....	....
1995-96	Carolina Monarchs	AHL	11	1	4	1	458	27	0	3.54	....	....	....	....	....	....	....	....	....	....	....	....	....	....	....	....	....
	Las Vegas Thunder	IHL	13	10	1	1	713	34	0	2.86	....	....	....	....	....	....	....	....	....	....	....	....	....	....	....	....	....
	Kansas City Blades	IHL	4	1	1	0	154	11	0	4.29	....	....	....	....	....	....	....	....	....	....	....	....	....	....	....	....	....
1996-97	Kolner Haie	Germany	21	....	....	....	1144	53	1	2.78	....	....	....	....	....	2	....	....	....	121	7	0	3.47	....	....	....	....
	Kolner Haie	EuroHL	2	....	....	....	120	3	....	1.50	....	....	....	....	....	....	....	....	....	....	....	....	....	....	....	....	....
1997-98	Manchester Storm	Britain	24	....	....	....	1487	62	....	2.50	....	....	....	....	....	....	....	....	....	....	....	....	....	....	....	....	....
	NHL Totals		**85**	**34**	**30**	**3**	**4217**	**262**	**0**	**3.73**	....	....	**2129**	**.877**	....	....	....	....	....	....	....	....	....	....	....	....	....

NCAA (College Div.) East First All-American Team (1987)

Traded to **Winnipeg** by **Washington** with Washington's 2nd round choice (Alexei Budayev) in 1993 Entry Draft for Rick Tabaracci, March 22, 1993. Traded to **St. Louis** by **Winnipeg** for St. Louis' 7th round choice (later traded to Florida — later traded to Edmonton — later traded to Winnipeg — Winnipeg selected Chris Kibermanis) in 1994 Entry Draft and future considerations, July 29, 1993.

• HRUDEY, KELLY

Kelly Hrudey G – L. 5'10", 189 lbs. b: Edmonton, Alta., 1/13/1961. NY Islanders' 2nd choice, 38th overall, in 1980 Entry Draft.

Season	Club	League	GP	W	L	T	Mins	GA	SO	Avg	AAvg	Eff	SA	S%	SAPG	GP	W	L	T	Mins	GA	SO	Avg	Eff	SA	S%	SAPG
1978-79	Medicine Hat Tigers	WHL	57	12	34	7	3093	318	0	6.17	....	....	....	....	....	....	....	....	....	....	....	....	....	....	....	....	....
1979-80	Medicine Hat Tigers	WHL	57	25	23	4	3049	212	1	4.17	....	....	....	....	....	13	6	6	....	638	48	0	4.51	....	....	....	....
1980-81	Medicine Hat Tigers	WHL	55	32	19	1	3023	200	4	3.97	....	....	....	....	....	4	1	3	....	244	17	0	4.18	....	....	....	....
	Indianapolis Checkers	CHL	....	....	....	....	....	....	....	....	....	....	....	....	....	2	....	....	....	135	8	0	3.56	....	....	....	....
1981-82	Indianapolis Checkers	CHL	51	27	19	4	3033	149	1	*2.95	....	....	....	....	....	13	11	2	....	842	34	*1	*2.42	....	....	....	....
1982-83	Indianapolis Checkers	CHL	47	*26	17	1	2744	139	2	3.04	....	....	....	....	....	10	*7	3	....	*637	28	0	*2.64	....	....	....	....
1983-84	**New York Islanders**	**NHL**	**12**	**7**	**2**	**0**	**535**	**28**	**0**	**3.14**	**2.45**	**3.04**	**289**	**.903**	**32.4**	....	....	....	....	....	....	....	....	....	....	....	....
	Indianapolis Checkers	CHL	6	3	2	1	370	21	0	3.40	....	....	....	....	....	....	....	....	....	....	....	....	....	....	....	....	....
1984-85	**New York Islanders**	**NHL**	**41**	**19**	**17**	**3**	**2335**	**141**	**2**	**3.62**	**2.87**	**4.14**	**1234**	**.886**	**31.7**	**5**	**1**	**3**	....	**281**	**8**	**0**	**1.71**	**0.92**	**149**	**.946**	**31.8**
1985-86	**New York Islanders**	**NHL**	**45**	**19**	**15**	**8**	**2563**	**137**	**1**	**3.21**	**2.48**	**3.02**	**1455**	**.906**	**34.1**	**2**	**0**	**2**	....	**120**	**6**	**0**	**3.00**	**3.05**	**59**	**.898**	**29.5**
	Canada	WEC-A	5	....	....	....	299	22	....	4.41	....	....	....	....	....	....	....	....	....	....	....	....	....	....	....	....	....
1986-87	**New York Islanders**	**NHL**	**46**	**21**	**15**	**7**	**2634**	**145**	**0**	**3.30**	**2.77**	**3.93**	**1219**	**.881**	**27.8**	**14**	**7**	**7**	....	**842**	**38**	**0**	**2.71**	**2.22**	**464**	**.918**	**33.1**
1987-88	Canada	C Cup	DID NOT PLAY – SPARE GOALTENDER																								
	New York Islanders	**NHL**	**47**	**22**	**17**	**5**	**2751**	**153**	**3**	**3.34**	**2.77**	**3.48**	**1467**	**.896**	**32.0**	**6**	**2**	**4**	....	**381**	**23**	**0**	**3.62**	**5.41**	**154**	**.851**	**24.3**
1988-89	**New York Islanders**	**NHL**	***50**	**18**	**24**	**3**	***2800**	**183**	**0**	**3.92**	**3.24**	**4.92**	**1457**	**.874**	**31.2**	....	....	....	....	....	....	....	....	....	....	....	....
	Los Angeles Kings	**NHL**	***16**	**10**	**4**	**2**	***974**	**47**	**1**	**2.90**	**2.39**	**2.78**	**491**	**.904**	**30.2**	**10**	**4**	**6**	....	**566**	**35**	**0**	**3.71**	**4.43**	**293**	**.881**	**31.1**
1989-90	**Los Angeles Kings**	**NHL**	**52**	**22**	**21**	**6**	**2860**	**194**	**2**	**4.07**	**3.42**	**5.15**	**1532**	**.873**	**32.1**	**9**	**4**	**4**	....	**539**	**39**	**0**	**4.34**	**6.39**	**265**	**.853**	**29.5**
1990-91	**Los Angeles Kings**	**NHL**	**47**	**26**	**13**	**6**	**2730**	**132**	**3**	**2.90**	**2.58**	**2.90**	**1321**	**.900**	**29.0**	**12**	**6**	**6**	....	**798**	**37**	**0**	**2.78**	**2.69**	**382**	**.903**	**28.7**
1991-92	**Los Angeles Kings**	**NHL**	**60**	**26**	**17**	**13**	**3509**	**197**	**1**	**3.37**	**2.99**	**3.46**	**1916**	**.897**	**32.8**	**6**	**2**	**4**	....	**355**	**22**	**0**	**3.72**	**4.57**	**179**	**.877**	**30.3**
1992-93	**Los Angeles Kings**	**NHL**	**50**	**18**	**21**	**6**	**2718**	**175**	**2**	**3.86**	**3.29**	**4.35**	**1552**	**.887**	**34.3**	**20**	**10**	**10**	....	**1261**	**74**	**0**	**3.52**	**3.97**	**656**	**.887**	**31.2**
1993-94	**Los Angeles Kings**	**NHL**	**64**	**22**	**31**	**7**	**3713**	**228**	**1**	**3.68**	**3.52**	**3.78**	**2219**	**.897**	**35.9**	....	....	....	....	....	....	....	....	....	....	....	....
1994-95	**Los Angeles Kings**	**NHL**	**35**	**14**	**13**	**5**	**1894**	**99**	**0**	**3.14**	**3.25**	**2.83**	**1099**	**.910**	**34.8**	....	....	....	....	....	....	....	....	....	....	....	....
1995-96	**Los Angeles Kings**	**NHL**	**36**	**7**	**15**	**10**	**2077**	**113**	**0**	**3.26**	**3.20**	**3.03**	**1214**	**.907**	**35.1**	....	....	....	....	....	....	....	....	....	....	....	....
	Phoenix Roadrunners	IHL	1	0	1	0	50	5	0	5.95	....	....	....	....	....	....	....	....	....	....	....	....	....	....	....	....	....
1996-97	**San Jose Sharks**	**NHL**	**48**	**16**	**24**	**5**	**2631**	**140**	**0**	**3.19**	**3.38**	**3.54**	**1263**	**.889**	**28.8**	....	....	....	....	....	....	....	....	....	....	....	....
1997-98	**San Jose Sharks**	**NHL**	**28**	**4**	**16**	**2**	**1360**	**62**	**1**	**2.74**	**3.21**	**2.83**	**600**	**.897**	**26.5**	**1**	**0**	**0**	....	**20**	**1**	**0**	**3.00**	**5.00**	**6**	**.833**	**18.0**
	NHL Totals		**677**	**271**	**265**	**88**	**38084**	**2174**	**17**	**3.43**	....	....	**20328**	**.893**	....	**85**	**36**	**46**	....	**5163**	**283**	**0**	**3.29**	....	....	....	....

WHL Second All-Star Team (1981) • CHL First All-Star Team (1982, 1983) • Shared Terry Sawchuk Trophy (fewest goals against - CHL) with Rob Holland (1982, 1983) • Won Tommy Ivan Trophy (CHL's MVP) (1983)

Traded to **LA Kings** by **NY Islanders** for Mark Fitzpatrick, Wayne McBean and future considerations (Doug Crossman, May 23, 1989) February 22, 1989. Signed as a free agent by **San Jose**, August 18, 1996.

• ING, PETER

Peter Ing G – L. 6'2", 170 lbs. b: Toronto, Ont., 4/28/1969. Toronto's 3rd choice, 48th overall, in 1988 Entry Draft.

Season	Club	League	GP	W	L	T	Mins	GA	SO	Avg	AAvg	Eff	SA	S%	SAPG	GP	W	L	T	Mins	GA	SO	Avg	Eff	SA	S%	SAPG
1986-87	Windsor Compuware Spitfires	OHL	28	13	11	3	1615	105	0	3.90	....	....	....	....	....	5	4	0	0	161	9	0	3.35	....	....	....	....
1987-88	Windsor Compuware Spitfires	OHL	43	30	7	1	2422	125	2	3.10	....	....	....	....	....	3	2	0	0	225	7	0	1.87	....	....	....	....
1988-89	Windsor Compuware Spitfires	OHL	19	7	7	3	1043	76	*1	4.37	....	....	....	....	....	....	....	....	....	....	....	....	....	....	....	....	....
	London Knights	OHL	32	18	11	2	1848	104	*2	3.38	....	....	....	....	....	21	11	9	0	1093	82	0	4.50	....	....	....	....
1989-90	**Toronto Maple Leafs**	**NHL**	**3**	**0**	**2**	**1**	**182**	**18**	**0**	**5.93**	**4.97**	**9.98**	**107**	**.832**	**35.3**	....	....	....	....	....	....	....	....	....	....	....	....
	Newmarket Saints	AHL	48	16	19	12	2829	184	0	3.90	....	....	....	....	....	....	....	....	....	....	....	....	....	....	....	....	....
	Canada	Nat-Team	10	2	2	4	460	29	....	3.78	....	....	....	....	....	....	....	....	....	....	....	....	....	....	....	....	....
	London Knights	OHL	8	6	2	0	480	27	0	3.38	....	....	....	....	....	....	....	....	....	....	....	....	....	....	....	....	....
1990-91	**Toronto Maple Leafs**	**NHL**	**56**	**16**	**29**	**8**	**3126**	**200**	**1**	**3.84**	**3.44**	**4.48**	**1716**	**.883**	**32.9**	....	....	....	....	....	....	....	....	....	....	....	....
1991-92	**Edmonton Oilers**	**NHL**	**12**	**3**	**4**	**0**	**463**	**33**	**0**	**4.28**	**3.80**	**5.60**	**252**	**.869**	**32.7**	....	....	....	....	....	....	....	....	....	....	....	....
	Cape Breton Oilers	AHL	24	9	10	4	1411	92	0	3.91	....	....	....	....	....	1	0	1	0	60	9	0	9.00	....	....	....	....
1992-93	Detroit Falcons	ColHL	3	2	1	0	136	6	0	2.65	....	....	....	....	....	....	....	....	....	....	....	....	....	....	....	....	....
	San Diego Gulls	IHL	17	11	4	1	882	53	0	3.61	....	....	....	....	....	4	2	2	0	183	13	0	4.26	....	....	....	....
1993-94	**Detroit Red Wings**	**NHL**	**3**	**1**	**2**	**0**	**170**	**15**	**0**	**5.29**	**5.04**	**7.78**	**102**	**.853**	**36.0**	....	....	....	....	....	....	....	....	....	....	....	....
	Adirondack Red Wings	AHL	7	3	3	1	425	26	1	3.67	....	....	....	....	....	....	....	....	....	....	....	....	....	....	....	....	....
	Las Vegas Thunder	IHL	30	16	7	4	1627	91	0	3.36	....	....	....	....	....	2	0	1	0	40	4	0	5.87	....	....	....	....
1994-95	Fort Wayne Komets	IHL	36	15	18	2	2018	119	2	3.54	....	....	....	....	....	2	0	1	0	94	5	0	3.19	....	....	....	....
1995-96	Fort Wayne Komets	IHL	31	12	16	0	1674	109	2	3.91	....	....	....	....	....	....	....	....	....	....	....	....	....	....	....	....	....
	Cincinnati Cyclones	IHL	1	0	1	0	60	8	0	8.00	....	....	....	....	....	....	....	....	....	....	....	....	....	....	....	....	....
	NHL Totals		**74**	**20**	**37**	**9**	**3941**	**266**	**1**	**4.05**	....	....	**2177**	**.878**	....	....	....	....	....	....	....	....	....	....	....	....	....

Traded to **Edmonton** by **Toronto** with Vincent Damphousse, Scott Thornton, Luke Richardson, future considerations and cash for Grant Fuhr, Glenn Anderson and Craig Berube, September 19, 1991. Traded to **Detroit** by **Edmonton** for Detroit's 7th round choice (Chris Wickenheiser) in 1994 Entry Draft and future considerations, August 30, 1993.

• INNESS, GARY

Gary Inness G – L. 6', 195 lbs. b: Toronto, Ont., 5/28/1949.

Season	Club	League	GP	W	L	T	Mins	GA	SO	Avg	AAvg	Eff	SA	S%	SAPG	GP	W	L	T	Mins	GA	SO	Avg	Eff	SA	S%	SAPG
1970-71	McMaster University	OQAA	16	....	....	....	888	70	0	4.73	....	....	....	....	....	....	....	....	....	....	....	....	....	....	....	....	....
1971-72	McMaster University	OUAA	18	....	....	....	1060	59	0	3.44	....	....	....	....	....	....	....	....	....	....	....	....	....	....	....	....	....
1972-73	University of Toronto	OUAA	9	....	....	....	540	24	0	2.67	....	....	....	....	....	....	....	....	....	....	....	....	....	....	....	....	....
1973-74	**Pittsburgh Penguins**	**NHL**	**20**	**7**	**10**	**1**	**1032**	**56**	**0**	**3.26**	**3.15**	....	....	....	....	....	....	....	....	....	....	....	....	....	....	....	....
	Hershey Bears	AHL	20	11	4	4	1160	56	1	2.89	....	....	....	....	....	....	....	....	....	....	....	....	....	....	....	....	....
1974-75	**Pittsburgh Penguins**	**NHL**	**57**	**24**	**18**	**10**	**3122**	**161**	**2**	**3.09**	**2.77**	....	....	....	....	**9**	**5**	**4**	....	**540**	**24**	**0**	**2.67**	....	....	....	....

Season	Club	League	REGULAR SEASON													PLAYOFFS											
			GP	W	L	T	Mins	GA	SO	Avg	AAvg	Eff	SA	S%	SAPG	GP	W	L	T	Mins	GA	SO	Avg	Eff	SA	S%	SAPG
1975-76	Hershey Bears	AHL	2	0	2	0	119	9	0	4.54	....	....	....	....	....	....	....	....	....	....	....	....	....	....	....	....	....
	Pittsburgh Penguins	**NHL**	**23**	**8**	**9**	**2**	**1212**	**82**	**0**	**4.06**	**3.68**	....	....	....	....	....	....	....	....	....	....	....	....	....	....	....	....
	Philadelphia Flyers	**NHL**	**2**	**2**	**0**	**0**	**120**	**3**	**0**	**1.50**	**1.36**	....	....	....	....	....	....	....	....	....	....	....	....	....	....	....	....
1976-77	**Philadelphia Flyers**	**NHL**	**6**	**1**	**0**	**2**	**210**	**9**	**0**	**2.57**	**2.39**	....	....	....	....	....	....	....	....	....	....	....	....	....	....	....	....
1977-78	Indianapolis Racers	WHA	52	14	30	4	2850	200	0	4.21	....	....	....	....	....	....	....	....	....	....	....	....	....	....	....	....	....
1978-79	Indianapolis Racers	WHA	11	3	6	0	609	51	0	5.02	....	....	....	....	....	....	....	....	....	....	....	....	....	....	....	....	....
	Washington Capitals	**NHL**	**37**	**14**	**14**	**8**	**2107**	**130**	**0**	**3.70**	**3.27**	....	....	....	....	....	....	....	....	....	....	....	....	....	....	....	....
1979-80	**Washington Capitals**	**NHL**	**14**	**2**	**9**	**2**	**727**	**44**	**0**	**3.63**	**3.19**	....	....	....	....	....	....	....	....	....	....	....	....	....	....	....	....
	Hershey Bears	AHL	11	4	4	3	673	44	0	3.92	....	....	....	....	....	8	7	1	0	531	25	0	2.82	....	....	....	....
1980-81	**Washington Capitals**	**NHL**	**3**	**0**	**1**	**2**	**180**	**9**	**0**	**3.00**	**2.40**	....	....	....	....	....	....	....	....	....	....	....	....	....	....	....	....
	Hershey Bears	AHL	10	4	2	2	529	31	1	3.52	....	....	....	....	....	4	0	3	0	198	12	0	3.64	....	....	....	....
	NHL Totals		**162**	**58**	**61**	**27**	**8710**	**494**	**2**	**3.40**	....	....	....	....	....	**9**	**5**	**4**	....	**540**	**24**	**0**	**2.67**	....	....	....	....
	Other Major League Totals		63	17	36	4	3459	251	0	4.35	....	....	....	....	....	....	....	....	....	....	....	....	....	....	....	....	....

Signed as a free agent by **Pittsburgh**, June, 1973. Traded to **Philadelphia** by **Pittsburgh** with future considerations for Bobby Taylor and Ed Van Impe, March 9, 1976. Signed as a free agent by **Indianapolis** (WHA), September, 1977. Signed as a free agent by **Washington**, December 19, 1978.

• IRBE, ARTURS

Arturs Irbe G – L. 5'8", 175 lbs. b: Riga, Latvia, 2/2/1967. Minnesota's 11th choice, 196th overall, in 1989 Entry Draft.

Season	Club	League	GP	W	L	T	Mins	GA	SO	Avg	AAvg	Eff	SA	S%	SAPG	GP	W	L	T	Mins	GA	SO	Avg	Eff	SA	S%	SAPG
1984-85	Soviet Union	EJC-A	5	....	....	....	300	5	....	1.00	....	....	....	....	....	....	....	....	....	....	....	....	....	....	....	....	....
1986-87	Dynamo Riga	USSR	2	....	....	....	27	1	0	2.22	....	....	....	....	....	....	....	....	....	....	....	....	....	....	....	....	....
1987-88	Dynamo Riga	USSR	34	....	....	....	1870	86	4	2.69	....	....	....	....	....	....	....	....	....	....	....	....	....	....	....	....	....
1988-89	Dynamo Riga	USSR	40	....	....	....	2460	116	4	2.85	....	....	....	....	....	....	....	....	....	....	....	....	....	....	....	....	....
	Dynamo Riga	SuperS	7	....	....	....	425	23	....	3.25	....	....	....	....	....	....	....	....	....	....	....	....	....	....	....	....	....
1989-90	Dynamo Riga	FrTour	1	....	....	....	63	2	0	1.90	....	....	....	....	....	....	....	....	....	....	....	....	....	....	....	....	....
	Dynamo Riga	USSR	48	....	....	....	2880	115	2	2.42	....	....	....	....	....	....	....	....	....	....	....	....	....	....	....	....	....
	CSKA Moscow	SuperS	4	....	....	....	240	10	....	2.50	....	....	....	....	....	....	....	....	....	....	....	....	....	....	....	....	....
	Soviet Union	WEC-A	6	....	....	....	315	5	....	0.95	....	....	....	....	....	....	....	....	....	....	....	....	....	....	....	....	....
1990-91	Dynamo Riga	FrTour	1	....	....	....	60	4	0	4.00	....	....	....	....	....	....	....	....	....	....	....	....	....	....	....	....	....
	Dynamo Riga	USSR	46	....	....	....	2713	133	5	2.94	....	....	....	....	....	....	....	....	....	....	....	....	....	....	....	....	....
1991-92	**San Jose Sharks**	**NHL**	**13**	**2**	**6**	**3**	**645**	**40**	**0**	**4.47**	**3.97**	**5.88**	**365**	**.868**	**34.0**	....	....	....	....	....	....	....	....	....	....	....	....
	Kansas City Blades	IHL	32	24	7	1	1955	80	0	*2.46	....	....	....	....	....	*15	*12	3	....	914	44	0	*2.89	....	....	....	....
1992-93	**San Jose Sharks**	**NHL**	**36**	**7**	**26**	**0**	**2074**	**142**	**1**	**4.11**	**3.51**	**4.67**	**1250**	**.886**	**36.2**	....	....	....	....	....	....	....	....	....	....	....	....
	Kansas City Blades	IHL	6	3	3	0	364	20	0	3.30	....	....	....	....	....	....	....	....	....	....	....	....	....	....	....	....	....
1993-94	**San Jose Sharks**	**NHL**	***74**	**30**	**28**	**16**	***4412**	**209**	**3**	**2.84**	**2.69**	**2.88**	**2064**	**.899**	**28.1**	**14**	**7**	**7**	....	**806**	**50**	**0**	**3.72**	**4.66**	**399**	**.875**	**29.7**
1994-95	**San Jose Sharks**	**NHL**	**38**	**14**	**19**	**3**	**2043**	**111**	**4**	**3.26**	**3.38**	**3.43**	**1056**	**.895**	**31.0**	**6**	**2**	**4**	....	**316**	**27**	**0**	**5.13**	**7.53**	**184**	**.853**	**34.9**
1995-96	**San Jose Sharks**	**NHL**	**22**	**4**	**12**	**4**	**1112**	**85**	**0**	**4.59**	**4.53**	**6.43**	**607**	**.860**	**32.8**	....	....	....	....	....	....	....	....	....	....	....	....
	Kansas City Blades	IHL	4	1	2	1	226	16	0	4.24	....	....	....	....	....	....	....	....	....	....	....	....	....	....	....	....	....
	Latvia	WC-B	4	....	....	....	....	7	....	1.75	....	....	....	....	....	....	....	....	....	....	....	....	....	....	....	....	....
1996-97	**Dallas Stars**	**NHL**	**35**	**17**	**12**	**3**	**1965**	**88**	**3**	**2.69**	**2.84**	**2.87**	**825**	**.893**	**25.2**	**1**	**0**	**0**	....	**13**	**0**	**0**	**0.00**	**0.00**	**4**	**1.000**	**18.5**
	Latvia	WC-A	5	4	0	1	300	10	....	2.00	....	....	....	....	....	....	....	....	....	....	....	....	....	....	....	....	....
1997-98	**Vancouver Canucks**	**NHL**	**41**	**14**	**11**	**6**	**1999**	**91**	**2**	**2.73**	**3.20**	**2.53**	**982**	**.907**	**29.5**	....	....	....	....	....	....	....	....	....	....	....	....
	Latvia	WC-A	6	3	2	1	358	17	1	2.85	....	....	....	....	....	....	....	....	....	....	....	....	....	....	....	....	....
	NHL Totals		**259**	**88**	**114**	**35**	**14250**	**774**	**13**	**3.26**	....	....	**7149**	**.892**	....	**21**	**9**	**11**	....	**1135**	**77**	**0**	**4.07**	....	....	....	....

Named Best Goaltender at EJC-A (1985) • USSR Rookie-of-the-Year (1988) • Named Best Goaltender at WEC A (1990) • IHL First All-Star Team (1992) • Shared James Norris Memorial Trophy (fewest goals against - IHL) with Wade Flaherty (1992)

Played in NHL All-Star Game (1994)

Claimed by **San Jose** from **Minnesota** in Dispersal Draft, May 30, 1991. Signed as a free agent by **Dallas**, August 19, 1996. Signed as a free agent by **Vancouver**, August 25, 1997.

• IRELAND, RANDY

Randy Ireland G – L. 6', 165 lbs. b: Rosetown, Sask., 4/5/1957. Buffalo's 3rd choice, 82nd overall, in 1978 Amateur Draft.

Season	Club	League	GP	W	L	T	Mins	GA	SO	Avg	AAvg	Eff	SA	S%	SAPG	GP	W	L	T	Mins	GA	SO	Avg	Eff	SA	S%	SAPG
1973-74	Saskatoon Blades	WCJHL	35	....	....	....	1883	124	0	3.06	....	....	....	....	....	1	0	1	0	60	9	0	9.00	....	....	....	....
1974-75	Saskatoon Blades	WCJHL	28	....	....	....	1654	114	1	4.14	....	....	....	....	....	7	....	....	....	420	16	1	2.77	....	....	....	....
1975-76	Saskatoon Blades	WCJHL	40	....	....	....	2218	140	0	4.00	....	....	....	....	....	15	....	....	....	785	60	0	3.82	....	....	....	....
1976-77	Saskatoon Blades	WCJHL	1	0	1	0	60	7	0	7.00	....	....	....	....	....	....	....	....	....	....	....	....	....	....	....	....	....
	Portland Winter Hawks	WCJHL	46	....	....	....	2589	162	3	3.76	....	....	....	....	....	10	....	....	....	611	27	*1	*2.65	....	....	....	....
1977-78	Flint Generals	IHL	45	....	....	....	2617	205	0	4.70	....	....	....	....	....	3	....	....	....	119	8	0	4.03	....	....	....	....
1978-79	**Buffalo Sabres**	**NHL**	**2**	**0**	**0**	**0**	**30**	**3**	**0**	**6.00**	**5.30**	....	....	....	....	....	....	....	....	....	....	....	....	....	....	....	....
	Hershey Bears	AHL	29	9	16	1	1477	113	0	4.60	....	....	....	....	....	....	....	....	....	....	....	....	....	....	....	....	....
1979-80	Rochester Americans	AHL	29	9	10	5	1559	94	0	3.62	....	....	....	....	....	1	0	1	0	60	6	0	6.00	....	....	....	....
1980-81	Oklahoma City Stars	CHL	2	2	0	0	120	8	0	4.00	....	....	....	....	....	....	....	....	....	....	....	....	....	....	....	....	....
	Baltimore Clippers	EHL	33	....	....	....	1776	105	2	3.55	....	....	....	....	....	....	....	....	....	....	....	....	....	....	....	....	....
	Richmond Rifles	EHL	13	....	....	....	770	48	0	3.74	....	....	....	....	....	4	....	....	....	240	23	0	5.75	....	....	....	....
1981-82	Mohawk Valley Stars	ACHL	25	....	....	....	1234	89	0	4.33	....	....	....	....	....	8	....	....	....	467	29	0	3.73	....	....	....	....
1982-83	Mohawk Valley Stars	ACHL	38	....	....	....	2044	148	1	4.39	....	....	....	....	....	9	....	....	....	*544	33	0	3.63	....	....	....	....
	NHL Totals		**2**	**0**	**0**	**0**	**30**	**3**	**0**	**6.00**	....	....	....	....	....	....	....	....	....	....	....	....	....	....	....	....	....

• Re-entered NHL draft. Originally Chicago's 3rd choice, 60th overall, in 1977 Amateur Draft.

• IRONS, ROBBIE

Robbie Irons G – L. 5'8", 150 lbs. b: Toronto, Ont., 11/19/1946.

Season	Club	League	GP	W	L	T	Mins	GA	SO	Avg	AAvg	Eff	SA	S%	SAPG	GP	W	L	T	Mins	GA	SO	Avg	Eff	SA	S%	SAPG
1966-67	Kitchener Rangers	OHA	33	....	....	....	1940	95	*3	2.94	....	....	....	....	....	13	....	....	....	780	49	0	3.77	....	....	....	....
1967-68	Fort Wayne Komets	IHL	43	....	....	....	2398	134	1	3.35	....	....	....	....	....	5	1	3	0	262	19	0	4.35	....	....	....	....
1968-69	Kansas City Blues	CHL	24	....	....	....	1309	83	0	3.80	....	....	....	....	....	....	....	....	....	....	....	....	....	....	....	....	....
	St. Louis Blues	**NHL**	**1**	**0**	**0**	**0**	**3**	**0**	**0**	**0.00**	**0.00**	....	....	....	....	....	....	....	....	....	....	....	....	....	....	....	....
1969-70	Kansas City Blues	CHL	30	10	16	4	1800	104	2	3.47	....	....	....	....	....	....	....	....	....	....	....	....	....	....	....	....	....
1970-71	Kansas City Blues	CHL	6	....	....	....	300	23	0	3.83	....	....	....	....	....	....	....	....	....	....	....	....	....	....	....	....	....
	Fort Wayne Komets	IHL	31	....	....	....	1811	80	1	2.25	....	....	....	....	....	4	0	4	0	240	22	0	5.50	....	....	....	....
1971-72	Fort Wayne Komets	IHL	21	....	....	....	1251	83	1	4.00	....	....	....	....	....	....	....	....	....	....	....	....	....	....	....	....	....
1972-73	Fort Wayne Komets	IHL	46	....	....	....	2737	132	2	2.89	....	....	....	....	....	1	1	0	0	60	0	1	0.00	....	....	....	....
1973-74	Fort Wayne Komets	IHL	47	....	....	....	2701	148	2	3.29	....	....	....	....	....	....	....	....	....	....	....	....	....	....	....	....	....
1974-75	Fort Wayne Komets	IHL	46	....	....	....	2713	146	2	3.27	....	....	....	....	....	....	....	....	....	....	....	....	....	....	....	....	....
1975-76	Fort Wayne Komets	IHL	63	....	....	....	3321	199	1	3.60	....	....	....	....	....	9	5	4	0	530	39	0	5.44	....	....	....	....
1976-77	Fort Wayne Komets	IHL	41	....	....	....	2248	141	1	3.70	....	....	....	....	....	....	....	....	....	....	....	....	....	....	....	....	....
1977-78	Fort Wayne Komets	IHL	39	....	....	....	2152	129	0	3.60	....	....	....	....	....	7	....	....	....	319	20	0	3.70	....	....	....	....
1978-79	Fort Wayne Komets	IHL	54	....	....	....	2490	193	1	3.90	....	....	....	....	....	13	7	6	0	780	56	0	4.29	....	....	....	....
1979-80	Fort Wayne Komets	IHL	41	....	....	....	2188	147	1	4.03	....	....	....	....	....	14	....	....	....	806	44	1	3.28	....	....	....	....
1980-81	Fort Wayne Komets	IHL	51	....	....	....	2719	168	0	3.71	....	....	....	....	....	11	....	....	....	633	47	0	4.45	....	....	....	....
	NHL Totals		**1**	**0**	**0**	**0**	**3**	**0**	**0**	**0.00**	....	....	....	....	....	....	....	....	....	....	....	....	....	....	....	....	....

Shared James Norris Memorial Trophy (fewest goals against - IHL) with Don Atchison (1973) • IHL Second All-Star Team (1981)

Traded to **St. Louis** by **NY Rangers** with Camille Henry and Bill Plager for Don Caley and Wayne Rivers, June 13, 1968. • Replaced Glenn Hall in 1st period vs. NY Rangers after Hall was given a game misconduct, November 13, 1968. Irons holds record for having shortest career (three minutes) in NHL history.

• IRONSTONE, JOE

Joe "Kelly" Ironstone G – R. 5'6", 180 lbs. b: Sudbury, Ontario, 6/28/1898. d: 1972.

Season	Club	League	GP	W	L	T	Mins	GA	SO	Avg	AAvg	Eff	SA	S%	SAPG	GP	W	L	T	Mins	GA	SO	Avg	Eff	SA	S%	SAPG
1921-22	Sudbury Wolves	NOHA	6	3	2	0	350	12	0	2.06	....	....	....	....	....	....	....	....	....	....	....	....	....	....	....	....	....
	Sudbury Legion	City Sr.	3	*3	0	0	180	4	0	1.33	....	....	....	....	....	....	....	....	....	....	....	....	....	....	....	....	....
1922-23	Sudbury Wolves	NOHA	8	4	4	0	478	23	*2	2.89	....	....	....	....	....	....	....	....	....	....	....	....	....	....	....	....	....
1923-24	Sudbury Wolves	NOHA	STATISTICS NOT AVAILABLE																								
1924-25	**Ottawa Senators**	**NHL**	DID NOT PLAY – SPARE GOALTENDER																								
1925-26	**New York Americans**	**NHL**	**1**	**0**	**0**	**0**	**40**	**3**	**0**	**4.50**	**6.04**	....	....	....	....	....	....	....	....	....	....	....	....	....	....	....	....
1926-27	Niagara Falls Cataracts	CPHL	23	....	....	....	1380	64	1	2.82	....	....	....	....	....	....	....	....	....	....	....	....	....	....	....	....	....
1927-28	Niagara Falls Cataracts	CPHL	14	....	....	....	840	33	1	2.36	....	....	....	....	....	....	....	....	....	....	....	....	....	....	....	....	....
	Toronto Ravinas	CPHL	26	....	....	....	1560	46	7	1.77	....	....	....	....	....	2	0	2	0	120	11	0	5.50	....	....	....	....
	Toronto Maple Leafs	**NHL**	**1**	**0**	**0**	**1**	**70**	**0**	**1**	**0.00**	**0.00**	....	....	....	....	....	....	....	....	....	....	....	....	....	....	....	....
1928-29	London Panthers	CPHL	42	16	22	4	2520	109	3	2.60	....	....	....	....	....	....	....	....	....	....	....	....	....	....	....	....	....

			REGULAR SEASON													PLAYOFFS											
Season	Club	League	GP	W	L	T	Mins	GA	SO	Avg	AAvg	Eff	SA	S%	SAPG	GP	W	L	T	Mins	GA	SO	Avg	Eff	SA	S%	SAPG
1929-30	London Panthers	IAHL	10	....	....	....	350	35	0	3.76	....	....	....	....	....	....	....	....	....	....	....	....	....	....	....	....	....
	Kitchener Flying Dutchmen	CPHL	15	7	8	0	910	39	*2	*2.57	....	....	....	....	....	....	....	....	....	....	....	....	....	....	....	....	....
1930-31	Guelph Maple Leafs	OPHL	19	....	....	....	1140	53	1	2.79	....	....	....	....	....	....	....	....	....	....	....	....	....	....	....	....	....
	Marquette Iron Rangers	NMHL	STATISTICS NOT AVAILABLE																								
	Syracuse Stars	IAHL	13	1	10	2	830	51	1	3.69	....	....	....	....	....	....	....	....	....	....	....	....	....	....	....	....	....
1931-32			DID NOT PLAY – INJURED																								
1932-33			DID NOT PLAY																								
1933-34	Sudbury Legion	City Sr.	STATISTICS NOT AVAILABLE																								
1934-35	Sudbury Legion	City Sr.	10	....	....	....	600	42	0	4.20	....	....	....	....	....	....	....	....	....	....	....	....	....	....	....	....	....
1935-36	Falconbridge Falcons	NOHA	6	....	....	....	360	12	*1	*2.00	....	....	....	....	....	3	....	....	....	180	9	0	*3.00	....	....	....	....
	Sudbury Wolves	NOHA	1	0	1	0	60	6	0	6.00	....	....	....	....	....	....	....	....	....	....	....	....	....	....	....	....	....
	NHL Totals		**2**	**0**	**0**	**1**	**110**	**3**	**1**	**1.64**	....	....	....	....	....	....	....	....	....	....	....	....	....	....	....	....	....

Signed as a free agent by **Ottawa**, October 30, 1924. Signed as a free agent by **NY Americans**, October 30, 1925. Loaned to **Toronto** by **Toronto Ravinas** (CPHL) to replace injured John Ross Roach, March 3, 1928. (Toronto 0, NY Americans 0).

● JABLONSKI, PAT

Pat Jablonski G – R. 6′, 180 lbs. b: Toledo, OH, 6/20/1967. St. Louis' 6th choice, 138th overall, in 1985 Entry Draft.

Season	Club	League	GP	W	L	T	Mins	GA	SO	Avg	AAvg	Eff	SA	S%	SAPG	GP	W	L	T	Mins	GA	SO	Avg	Eff	SA	S%	SAPG
1984-85	Detroit Compuware	NAJHL	STATISTICS NOT AVAILABLE																								
1985-86	Windsor Spitfires	OHL	29	6	16	4	1600	119	1	4.46	....	....	....	....	....	6	0	3	....	263	20	0	4.56	....	....	....	....
1986-87	Windsor Spitfires	OHL	41	22	14	2	2328	128	*3	3.30	....	....	....	....	....	12	8	4	....	710	38	0	3.21	....	....	....	....
	United States	WJC-A	4	....	....	....	200	13	....	3.90	....	....	....	....	....	....	....	....	....	....	....	....	....	....	....	....	....
1987-88	Peoria Rivermen	IHL	5	2	2	1	285	17	0	3.58	....	....	....	....	....	....	....	....	....	....	....	....	....	....	....	....	....
	Windsor Spitfires	OHL	18	14	3	0	994	48	2	2.90	....	....	....	....	....	9	*8	0	....	537	28	0	3.13	....	....	....	....
1988-89	Peoria Rivermen	IHL	35	11	20	0	2051	163	1	4.77	....	....	....	....	....	3	0	2	....	130	13	0	6.00	....	....	....	....
1989-90	**St. Louis Blues**	**NHL**	**4**	**0**	**3**	**0**	**208**	**17**	**0**	**4.90**	**4.11**	**8.50**	**98**	**.827**	**28.3**	....	....	....	....	....	....	....	....	....	....	....	....
	Peoria Rivermen	IHL	36	14	17	4	2023	165	0	4.89	....	....	....	....	....	4	1	3	....	223	19	0	5.11	....	....	....	....
1990-91	**St. Louis Blues**	**NHL**	**8**	**2**	**3**	**3**	**492**	**25**	**0**	**3.05**	**2.72**	**3.34**	**228**	**.890**	**27.8**	**3**	**0**	**0**	....	**90**	**5**	**0**	**3.33**	**4.76**	**35**	**.857**	**23.3**
	Peoria Rivermen	IHL	29	23	3	2	1738	87	0	3.00	....	....	....	....	....	10	7	2	....	532	23	0	2.59	....	....	....	....
1991-92	United States	C Cup	DID NOT PLAY – SPARE GOALTENDER																								
	St. Louis Blues	**NHL**	**10**	**3**	**6**	**0**	**468**	**38**	**0**	**4.87**	**4.33**	**7.15**	**259**	**.853**	**33.2**	....	....	....	....	....	....	....	....	....	....	....	....
	Peoria Rivermen	IHL	8	6	1	1	493	29	1	3.53	....	....	....	....	....	....	....	....	....	....	....	....	....	....	....	....	....
1992-93	**Tampa Bay Lightning**	**NHL**	**43**	**8**	**24**	**4**	**2268**	**150**	**1**	**3.97**	**3.38**	**4.99**	**1194**	**.874**	**31.6**	....	....	....	....	....	....	....	....	....	....	....	....
	United States	WC-A	2	....	....	....	62	1	....	0.96	....	....	....	....	....	....	....	....	....	....	....	....	....	....	....	....	....
1993-94	**Tampa Bay Lightning**	**NHL**	**15**	**5**	**6**	**3**	**834**	**54**	**0**	**3.88**	**3.70**	**5.60**	**374**	**.856**	**26.9**	....	....	....	....	....	....	....	....	....	....	....	....
	St. John's Maple Leafs	AHL	16	12	3	1	962	49	1	3.05	....	....	....	....	....	11	6	5	....	676	36	0	3.19	....	....	....	....
1994-95	Chicago Wolves	IHL	4	0	4	0	216	17	0	4.71	....	....	....	....	....	....	....	....	....	....	....	....	....	....	....	....	....
	Houston Aeros	IHL	3	1	1	1	179	9	0	3.01	....	....	....	....	....	....	....	....	....	....	....	....	....	....	....	....	....
	United States	WC-A	6	....	....	....	360	15	....	2.50	....	....	....	....	....	....	....	....	....	....	....	....	....	....	....	....	....
1995-96	**St. Louis Blues**	**NHL**	**1**	**0**	**0**	**0**	**8**	**1**	**0**	**7.50**	**7.37**	**15.00**	**5**	**.800**	**37.5**	....	....	....	....	....	....	....	....	....	....	....	....
	Montreal Canadiens	**NHL**	**23**	**5**	**9**	**6**	**1264**	**62**	**0**	**2.94**	**2.89**	**2.70**	**676**	**.908**	**32.1**	**1**	**0**	**0**	....	**49**	**1**	**0**	**1.22**	**0.72**	**17**	**.941**	**20.8**
1996-97	**Montreal Canadiens**	**NHL**	**17**	**4**	**6**	**2**	**754**	**50**	**0**	**3.98**	**4.22**	**4.54**	**438**	**.886**	**34.9**	....	....	....	....	....	....	....	....	....	....	....	....
	Phoenix Coyotes	**NHL**	**2**	**0**	**1**	**0**	**59**	**2**	**0**	**2.03**	**2.15**	**1.69**	**24**	**.917**	**24.4**	....	....	....	....	....	....	....	....	....	....	....	....
1997-98	**Carolina Hurricanes**	**NHL**	**5**	**1**	**4**	**0**	**279**	**14**	**0**	**3.01**	**3.52**	**3.66**	**115**	**.878**	**24.7**	....	....	....	....	....	....	....	....	....	....	....	....
	Cleveland Lumberjacks	IHL	34	13	13	6	1950	98	0	3.01	....	....	....	....	....	....	....	....	....	....	....	....	....	....	....	....	....
	Quebec Rafales	IHL	7	3	3	0	368	21	0	3.42	....	....	....	....	....	....	....	....	....	....	....	....	....	....	....	....	....
	NHL Totals		**128**	**28**	**62**	**18**	**6634**	**413**	**1**	**3.74**	....	....	**3411**	**.879**	....	**4**	**0**	**0**	....	**139**	**6**	**0**	**2.59**	....	....	....	....

Shared James Norris Memorial Trophy (fewest goals against - IHL) with Guy Hebert (1991)

Traded to **Tampa Bay** by **St. Louis** with Steve Tuttle and Darin Kimble for future considerations, June 19, 1992. Traded to **Toronto** by **Tampa Bay** for cash, February 21, 1994. Claimed by **St. Louis** from **Toronto** in NHL Waiver Draft, October 2, 1995. Traded to **Montreal** by **St. Louis** for J.J. Daigneault, November 7, 1995. Traded to **Phoenix** by **Montreal** for Steve Cheredaryk, March 18, 1997. Signed as a free agent by **Carolina**, August 12, 1997.

● JACKSON, DOUG

Doug Jackson G – L. 5′10″, 150 lbs. b: Winnipeg, Man., 12/12/1924.

Season	Club	League	GP	W	L	T	Mins	GA	SO	Avg	AAvg	Eff	SA	S%	SAPG	GP	W	L	T	Mins	GA	SO	Avg	Eff	SA	S%	SAPG
1941-42	Winnipeg Rangers	MJHL	2	....	....	....	120	13	0	6.50	....	....	....	....	....	....	....	....	....	....	....	....	....	....	....	....	....
1942-43	Winnipeg Rangers	MJHL	13	....	....	....	780	51	0	*3.92	....	....	....	....	....	6	....	....	....	360	23	0	3.83	....	....	....	....
1943-44			MILITARY SERVICE																								
1944-45			MILITARY SERVICE																								
1945-46	Kansas City Pla-Mors	USHL	52	....	....	....	3120	169	2	3.25	....	....	....	....	....	12	8	4	0	720	33	....	2.75	....	....	....	....
1946-47	Kansas City Pla-Mors	USHL	54	26	17	11	3240	177	3	3.27	....	....	....	....	....	12	10	2	0	720	21	*1	*1.75	....	....	....	....
1947-48	Kansas City Pla-Mors	USHL	59	32	25	2	3540	220	*4	3.72	....	....	....	....	....	7	3	4	0	434	23	0	3.18	....	....	....	....
	Chicago Black Hawks	**NHL**	**6**	**2**	**3**	**1**	**360**	**42**	**0**	**7.00**	**7.55**	....	....	....	....	....	....	....	....	....	....	....	....	....	....	....	....
1948-49	Vancouver Canucks	PCHL	66	31	29	6	3960	241	1	3.65	....	....	....	....	....	3	0	3	0	203	14	0	4.14	....	....	....	....
1949-50	Los Angeles Monarchs	PCHL	8	4	2	2	480	38	0	4.75	....	....	....	....	....	....	....	....	....	....	....	....	....	....	....	....	....
	San Francisco Shamrocks	PCHL	5	1	2	2	300	20	0	4.00	....	....	....	....	....	....	....	....	....	....	....	....	....	....	....	....	....
	Victoria Cougars	PCHL	1	0	1	0	60	11	0	11.00	....	....	....	....	....	....	....	....	....	....	....	....	....	....	....	....	....
1950-51			STATISTICS NOT AVAILABLE																								
1951-52	Nanaimo Clippers	PCSHL	41	....	....	....	2460	147	1	3.65	....	....	....	....	....	6	4	2	0	360	19	0	3.17	....	....	....	....
	NHL Totals		**6**	**2**	**3**	**1**	**360**	**42**	**0**	**7.00**	....	....	....	....	....	....	....	....	....	....	....	....	....	....	....	....	....

USHL Second All-Star Team (1946)

● JACKSON, PERCY

Percy Jackson G – L. 5′9″, 165 lbs. b: Canmore, Alta., 9/21/1907.

Season	Club	League	GP	W	L	T	Mins	GA	SO	Avg	AAvg	Eff	SA	S%	SAPG	GP	W	L	T	Mins	GA	SO	Avg	Eff	SA	S%	SAPG
1927-28	Trail Smoke Eaters	WKHL	STATISTICS NOT AVAILABLE																								
1928-29	Vancouver Lions	PCHL	35	*25	7	3	2100	51	*11	*1.46	....	....	....	....	....	3	*3	0	0	180	3	1	*1.00	....	....	....	....
1929-30	Vancouver Lions	PCHL	36	*20	8	8	2160	46	10	1.28	....	....	....	....	....	4	*3	1	0	240	6	0	*1.50	....	....	....	....
1930-31	Vancouver Lions	PCHL	34	14	12	8	2040	56	7	1.65	....	....	....	....	....	4	*3	1	0	240	7	*2	1.75	....	....	....	....
1931-32	**Boston Bruins**	**NHL**	**4**	**1**	**1**	**1**	**232**	**8**	**0**	**2.07**	**2.54**	....	....	....	....	....	....	....	....	....	....	....	....	....	....	....	....
	Boston Cubs	Can-Am	25	14	9	2	1540	62	2	2.42	....	....	....	....	....	5	1	4	0	300	15	0	3.00	....	....	....	....
1932-33	Boston Cubs	Can-Am	45	21	16	8	2800	105	2	2.25	....	....	....	....	....	7	*5	2	0	420	14	0	*2.00	....	....	....	....
1933-34	Boston Cubs	Can-Am	41	18	16	7	2560	104	4	2.44	....	....	....	....	....	5	2	3	0	300	13	0	2.60	....	....	....	....
	New York Americans	**NHL**	**1**	**0**	**1**	**0**	**60**	**9**	**0**	**9.00**	**11.61**	....	....	....	....	....	....	....	....	....	....	....	....	....	....	....	....
1934-35	**New York Rangers**	**NHL**	**1**	**0**	**1**	**0**	**60**	**8**	**0**	**8.00**	**9.86**	....	....	....	....	....	....	....	....	....	....	....	....	....	....	....	....
	Providence Reds	Can-Am	1	....	....	....	60	2	0	2.00	....	....	....	....	....	....	....	....	....	....	....	....	....	....	....	....	....
	Boston Cubs	Can-Am	39	24	10	5	2340	105	1	2.69	....	....	....	....	....	3	*3	0	0	180	2	*1	*0.67	....	....	....	....
1935-36	**Boston Bruins**	**NHL**	**1**	**0**	**0**	**0**	**40**	**1**	**0**	**1.50**	**2.14**	....	....	....	....	....	....	....	....	....	....	....	....	....	....	....	....
	Boston Cubs	Can-Am	46	20	22	4	2840	129	0	2.73	....	....	....	....	....	....	....	....	....	....	....	....	....	....	....	....	....
	Philadelphia Ramblers	Can-Am	1	0	1	0	60	6	0	6.00	....	....	....	....	....	....	....	....	....	....	....	....	....	....	....	....	....
1936-37	Vancouver Lions	PCHL	40	....	....	....	2400	105	3	2.62	....	....	....	....	....	3	1	2	0	180	6	0	2.00	....	....	....	....
1937-38	Vancouver Lions	PCHL	42	19	18	5	2520	91	5	2.17	....	....	....	....	....	6	*4	2	0	480	8	*2	*1.33	....	....	....	....
1938-39	Vancouver Lions	PCHL	48	15	24	9	2880	195	0	4.06	....	....	....	....	....	2	0	2	0	120	10	0	5.00	....	....	....	....
1939-40	Vancouver Lions	PCHL	40	*22	16	2	2400	125	1	3.12	....	....	....	....	....	5	*4	1	0	300	12	0	*2.40	....	....	....	....
1940-41	Portland Buckaroos	PCHL	1	1	0	0	60	1	0	1.00	....	....	....	....	....	....	....	....	....	....	....	....	....	....	....	....	....
	Vancouver Lions	PCHL	48	22	21	5	2880	145	3	3.02	....	....	....	....	....	6	*5	1	0	360	11	*1	1.83	....	....	....	....
1941-42	Tulsa Oilers	AHA	50	13	34	3	3010	188	1	3.75	....	....	....	....	....	2	0	2	0	120	9	0	4.50	....	....	....	....
1942-43	Vancouver St. Regis	PCHL	3	....	....	....	180	14	0	4.67	....	....	....	....	....	5	....	....	....	300	18	0	*3.60	....	....	....	....
1943-44	Vancouver St. Regis	PCHL	24	....	....	....	1440	142	0	5.92	....	....	....	....	....	3	0	3	0	180	24	0	8.00	....	....	....	....
	Vancouver RCAF Seahawks	City Sr.	3	2	1	0	180	19	0	6.33	....	....	....	....	....	....	....	....	....	....	....	....	....	....	....	....	....
	Vancouver Maple Leafs	City Sr.	2	1	1	0	120	12	0	6.00	....	....	....	....	....	4	*3	1	0	240	22	0	5.50	....	....	....	....
	NHL Totals		**7**	**1**	**3**	**1**	**392**	**26**	**0**	**3.98**	....	....	....	....	....	....	....	....	....	....	....	....	....	....	....	....	....

Loaned to **NY Americans** by **Boston** to replace injured Roy Worters, March 18, 1934. (NY Americans 9, Boston 5). Traded to **NY Rangers** by **Boston** for Jean Pusie, November 1, 1934. Traded to **Boston** by **NY Rangers** for cash, November 18, 1934.

• JAKS, PAULI
Pauli Jaks G – L. 6', 194 lbs. b: Schaffhausen, Switz., 1/25/1972. Los Angeles' 4th choice, 108th overall, in 1991 Entry Draft.

			REGULAR SEASON													PLAYOFFS											
Season	Club	League	GP	W	L	T	Mins	GA	SO	Avg	AAvg	Eff	SA	S%	SAPG	GP	W	L	T	Mins	GA	SO	Avg	Eff	SA	S%	SAPG
1990-91	Ambri-Piotta	Switz.	22	....	....	....	1247	100	0	4.81	....	....	....	....	....	....	....	....	....	....	....	....	....	....	....	....	....
	Switzerland	WJC-A	5	....	....	....	300	30	....	6.00	....	....	....	....	....	....	....	....	....	....	....	....	....	....	....	....	....
1991-92	Ambri-Piotta	Switz.	33	25	7	1	1890	97	2	2.93	....	....	....	....	....	....	....	....	....	....	....	....	....	....	....	....	....
	Switzerland	WJC-A	5	....	....	....	300	31	....	6.20	....	....	....	....	....	....	....	....	....	....	....	....	....	....	....	....	....
1992 93	Ambri-Piotta	Switz.	29	....	....	....	1740	92	....	3.17	....	....	....	....	....	....	....	....	....	....	....	....	....	....	....	....	....
1993-94	Phoenix Roadrunners	IHL	33	16	13	1	1712	101	0	3.54	....	....	....	....	....	....	....	....	....	....	....	....	....	....	....	....	....
1994-95	Phoenix Roadrunners	IHL	15	2	4	4	635	44	0	4.15	....	....	....	....	....	....	....	....	....	....	....	....	....	....	....	....	....
	Los Angeles Kings	**NHL**	**1**	**0**	**0**	**0**	**40**	**2**	**0**	**3.00**	**3.10**	**2.40**	**25**	**.920**	**37.5**	....	....	....	....	....	....	....	....	....	....	....	....
1995-96	Ambri-Piotta	Switz.	30	....	....	....	1799	106	....	3.53	....	....	....	....	....	....	....	....	....	....	....	....	....	....	....	....	....
	Switzerland	WC-B	1	....	....	....	60	1	0	1.00	....	....	....	....	....	....	....	....	....	....	....	....	....	....	....	....	....
1996-97	Ambri-Piotta	Switz.	42	....	....	....	2486	143	....	3.45	....	....	....	....	....	....	....	....	....	....	....	....	....	....	....	....	....
1997-98	Ambri-Piotta	Switz.	28	....	....	....	1645	81	....	2.95	....	....	....	....	....	3	....	....	....	169	12	....	4.26	....	....	....	....
	NHL Totals		**1**	**0**	**0**	**0**	**40**	**2**	**0**	**3.00**	....	....	**25**	**.920**	....	....	....	....	....	....	....	....	....	....	....	....	....

WJC-A All-Star Team (1991) • Named Best Goaltender at WJC-A (1991)

• JANASZAK, STEVE
Steve Janaszak G – R. 6'1", 210 lbs. b: St. Paul, MN, 1/7/1957.

Season	Club	League	GP	W	L	T	Mins	GA	SO	Avg	AAvg	Eff	SA	S%	SAPG	GP	W	L	T	Mins	GA	SO	Avg	Eff	SA	S%	SAPG
1975-76	University of Minnesota	WCHA	4	1	2	0	240	21	0	5.25	....	....	....	....	....	....	....	....	....	....	....	....	....	....	....	....	....
1976-77	University of Minnesota	WCHA	17	6	9	2	1100	86	0	4.69	....	....	....	....	....	....	....	....	....	....	....	....	....	....	....	....	....
1977-78	University of Minnesota	WCHA	28	14	10	2	1653	106	3	3.85	....	....	....	....	....	....	....	....	....	....	....	....	....	....	....	....	....
1978-79	University of Minnesota	WCHA	41	29	11	1	2428	131	1	3.23	....	....	....	....	....	....	....	....	....	....	....	....	....	....	....	....	....
1979-80	United States	Nat-Team	17	....	....	....	894	47	2	3.15	....	....	....	....	....	....	....	....	....	....	....	....	....	....	....	....	....
	United States	Olympics	DID NOT PLAY – SPARE GOALTENDER																								
	Minnesota North Stars	**NHL**	**1**	**0**	**0**	**1**	**60**	**2**	**0**	**2.00**	**1.76**	....	....	....	....	....	....	....	....	....	....	....	....	....	....	....	....
	Oklahoma City Stars	CHL	1	1	0	0	60	2	0	2.00	....	....	....	....	....	....	....	....	....	....	....	....	....	....	....	....	....
	Tulsa Oilers	CHL	1	0	1	0	59	6	0	6.10	....	....	....	....	....	....	....	....	....	....	....	....	....	....	....	....	....
	Baltimore Clippers	EHL	4	....	....	....	219	19	0	5.21	....	....	....	....	....	....	....	....	....	....	....	....	....	....	....	....	....
1980-81	Fort Worth Texans	CHL	6	0	6	0	357	26	0	4.37	....	....	....	....	....	....	....	....	....	....	....	....	....	....	....	....	....
	Fort Wayne Komets	IHL	42	....	....	....	2196	130	0	3.55	....	....	....	....	....	3	....	....	....	104	7	0	4.04	....	....	....	....
1981-82	Fort Worth Texans	CHL	37	8	24	0	1962	152	2	4.65	....	....	....	....	....	....	....	....	....	....	....	....	....	....	....	....	....
	Colorado Rockies	**NHL**	**2**	**0**	**1**	**0**	**100**	**13**	**0**	**7.80**	**6.02**	....	....	....	....	....	....	....	....	....	....	....	....	....	....	....	....
	United States	WEC-A	3	....	....	....	180	17	....	5.66	....	....	....	....	....	....	....	....	....	....	....	....	....	....	....	....	....
1982-83	Wichita Wind	CHL	35	13	18	1	1996	147	0	4.42	....	....	....	....	....	....	....	....	....	....	....	....	....	....	....	....	....
	NHL Totals		**3**	**0**	**1**	**1**	**160**	**15**	**0**	**5.62**	....	....	....	....	....	....	....	....	....	....	....	....	....	....	....	....	....

NCAA Championship All-Tournament Team (1979) • NCAA Championship Tournament MVP (1979)

Signed as a free agent by **Minnesota**, March, 1980. Signed as a free agent by **Colorado**, April 14, 1980. Traded to **Calgary** by **Colorado** for future considerations, September 18, 1982.

• JANECYK, BOB
Bob Janecyk G – L. 6'1", 180 lbs. b: Chicago, IL, 5/18/1957.

Season	Club	League	GP	W	L	T	Mins	GA	SO	Avg	AAvg	Eff	SA	S%	SAPG	GP	W	L	T	Mins	GA	SO	Avg	Eff	SA	S%	SAPG
1975-1979	Chicago State University	NCAA	STATISTICS NOT AVAILABLE																								
1979-80	Flint Generals	IHL	2	....	....	....	119	5	0	2.53	....	....	....	....	....	....	....	....	....	....	....	....	....	....	....	....	....
	Fort Wayne Komets	IHL	40	....	....	....	2208	128	1	3.48	....	....	....	....	....	3	....	....	....	89	4	0	2.70	....	....	....	....
1980-81	New Brunswick Hawks	AHL	34	11	18	1	1915	131	0	4.10	....	....	....	....	....	....	....	....	....	....	....	....	....	....	....	....	....
1981-82	New Brunswick Hawks	AHL	53	32	13	7	3224	153	2	2.85	....	....	....	....	....	14	*11	2	0	818	32	*1	*2.35	....	....	....	....
1982-83	Springfield Indians	AHL	47	19	24	4	*2754	167	*3	3.64	....	....	....	....	....	....	....	....	....	....	....	....	....	....	....	....	....
1983-84	**Chicago Black Hawks**	**NHL**	**8**	**2**	**3**	**1**	**412**	**28**	**0**	**4.08**	**3.19**	**4.82**	**237**	**.882**	**34.5**	....	....	....	....	....	....	....	....	....	....	....	....
	Springfield Indians	AHL	30	14	11	4	1664	94	0	3.39	....	....	....	....	....	....	....	....	....	....	....	....	....	....	....	....	....
1984-85	**Los Angeles Kings**	**NHL**	**51**	**22**	**21**	**8**	**3002**	**183**	**2**	**3.66**	**2.90**	**4.62**	**1483**	**.877**	**29.6**	**3**	**0**	**3**	....	**184**	**10**	**0**	**3.26**	**3.26**	**100**	**.900**	**32.6**
1985-86	**Los Angeles Kings**	**NHL**	**38**	**14**	**16**	**4**	**2083**	**162**	**0**	**4.67**	**3.65**	**6.70**	**1130**	**.857**	**32.5**	....	....	....	....	....	....	....	....	....	....	....	....
1986-87	**Los Angeles Kings**	**NHL**	**7**	**4**	**3**	**0**	**420**	**34**	**0**	**4.86**	**4.09**	**7.44**	**222**	**.847**	**31.7**	....	....	....	....	....	....	....	....	....	....	....	....
1987-88	**Los Angeles Kings**	**NHL**	**5**	**1**	**4**	**0**	**303**	**23**	**0**	**4.55**	**3.79**	**6.34**	**165**	**.861**	**32.7**	....	....	....	....	....	....	....	....	....	....	....	....
	New Haven Nighthawks	AHL	37	19	13	3	2162	125	1	3.47	....	....	....	....	....	....	....	....	....	....	....	....	....	....	....	....	....
1988-89	**Los Angeles Kings**	**NHL**	**1**	**0**	**0**	**0**	**30**	**2**	**0**	**4.00**	**3.30**	**3.64**	**22**	**.909**	**44.0**	....	....	....	....	....	....	....	....	....	....	....	....
	New Haven Nighthawks	AHL	34	14	13	6	1992	131	1	3.95	....	....	....	....	....	....	....	....	....	....	....	....	....	....	....	....	....
	NHL Totals		**110**	**43**	**47**	**13**	**6250**	**432**	**2**	**4.15**	....	....	**3259**	**.867**	....	**3**	**0**	**3**		**184**	**10**	**0**	**3.26**	....	....	....	....

NCAA (College Div.) West All-American Team (1976, 1977, 1978) • IHL Second All-Star Team (1980) • AHL First All-Star Team (1982, 1983) • Shared Harry "Hap" Holmes Memorial Award (fewest goals against - AHL) with Warren Skorodenski (1982)

Signed as a free agent by **Chicago**, June 3, 1980. Traded to **LA Kings** by **Chicago** with Chicago's 1st (Craig Redmond), 3rd (John English) and 4th (Tom Glavine) round choices in 1984 Entry Draft for LA Kings' 1st (Ed Olczyk) and 4th (Tommy Eriksson) round choices in 1984 Entry Draft, June 9, 1984.

• JENKINS, ROGER
Roger Jenkins G – R. 5'11", 173 lbs. b: Appleton, WI, 11/18/1911.

Season	Club	League	GP	W	L	T	Mins	GA	SO	Avg	AAvg	Eff	SA	S%	SAPG	GP	W	L	T	Mins	GA	SO	Avg	Eff	SA	S%	SAPG
1938-39	**New York Americans**	**NHL**	**1**	**0**	**1**	**0**	**30**	**7**	**0**	**14.00**	**17.15**	....	....	....	....	....	....	....	....	....	....	....	....	....	....	....	....
	NHL Totals		**1**	**0**	**1**	**0**	**30**	**7**	**0**	**14.00**	....	....	....	....	....	....	....	....	....	....	....	....	....	....	....	....	....

• NY Americans' defenseman replaced injured Earl Robertson in 2nd period, March 18, 1939. (NY Rangers 11, NY Americans 5)

• JENSEN, AL
Al Jensen G – L. 5'10", 180 lbs. b: Hamilton, Ont., 11/27/1958. Detroit's 4th choice, 31st overall, in 1978 Amateur Draft.

Season	Club	League	GP	W	L	T	Mins	GA	SO	Avg	AAvg	Eff	SA	S%	SAPG	GP	W	L	T	Mins	GA	SO	Avg	Eff	SA	S%	SAPG
1975-76	Hamilton Fincups	OHA	28	....	....	....	1451	97	0	3.97	....	....	....	....	....	....	....	....	....	....	....	....	....	....	....	....	....
1976-77	St. Catharines Fincups	OHA	48	....	....	....	2727	168	*2	3.70	....	....	....	....	....	13	....	....	....	707	36	1	2.97	....	....	....	....
	Canada	WJC-A	7	....	....	....	400	19	....	2.85	....	....	....	....	....	....	....	....	....	....	....	....	....	....	....	....	....
1977-78	Hamilton Fincups	OHA	43	....	....	....	2582	146	*3	*3.35	....	....	....	....	....	17	....	....	....	967	43	1	2.54	....	....	....	....
	Canada	WJC-A	3	....	....	....	180	12	....	4.00	....	....	....	....	....	....	....	....	....	....	....	....	....	....	....	....	....
1978 79	Kalamazoo Wings	IHL	47	....	....	....	2596	156	2	3.61	....	....	....	....	....	12	....	....	....	718	34	0	2.84	....	....	....	....
1979-80	Adirondack Red Wings	AHL	57	27	24	5	*3406	199	2	3.51	....	....	....	....	....	4	0	4	0	212	15	0	4.25	....	....	....	....
1980-81	**Detroit Red Wings**	**NHL**	**1**	**0**	**1**	**0**	**60**	**7**	**0**	**7.00**	**5.61**	....	....	....	....	....	....	....	....	....	....	....	....	....	....	....	....
	Adirondack Red Wings	AHL	60	27	21	3	3169	203	*3	3.84	....	....	....	....	....	11	7	4	0	626	46	0	4.41	....	....	....	....
1981-82	**Washington Capitals**	**NHL**	**26**	**8**	**8**	**4**	**1274**	**81**	**0**	**3.81**	**2.93**	....	....	....	....	....	....	....	....	....	....	....	....	....	....	....	....
	Hershey Bears	AHL	8	4	1	1	407	24	0	3.54	....	....	....	....	....	3	2	1	0	162	9	0	3.33	....	....	....	....
1982-83	**Washington Capitals**	**NHL**	**40**	**22**	**12**	**6**	**2358**	**135**	**1**	**3.44**	**2.74**	**4.07**	**1140**	**.882**	**29.0**	**3**	**1**	**2**	....	**139**	**10**	**0**	**4.32**	....	....	....	....
	Hershey Bears	AHL	6	....	....	....	316	14	1	2.66	....	....	....	....	....	....	....	....	....	....	....	....	....	....	....	....	....
1983-84	Hershey Bears	AHL	3	1	2	0	180	16	0	5.33	....	....	....	....	....	....	....	....	....	....	....	....	....	....	....	....	....
	Washington Capitals	**NHL**	**43**	**25**	**13**	**3**	**2414**	**117**	**4**	**2.91**	**2.26**	**3.42**	**995**	**.882**	**24.7**	**6**	**3**	**1**	....	**258**	**14**	**0**	**3.26**	**3.80**	**120**	**.883**	**27.9**
1984-85	**Washington Capitals**	**NHL**	**14**	**10**	**3**	**1**	**803**	**34**	**1**	**2.54**	**2.01**	**2.93**	**295**	**.885**	**22.0**	**3**	**1**	**2**	....	**201**	**8**	**0**	**2.39**	**2.22**	**86**	**.907**	**25.7**
	Binghamton Whalers	AHL	3	2	1	0	180	9	0	3.00	....	....	....	....	....	....	....	....	....	....	....	....	....	....	....	....	....
1985-86	**Washington Capitals**	**NHL**	**44**	**28**	**9**	**3**	**2437**	**129**	**2**	**3.18**	**2.46**	**3.51**	**1168**	**.890**	**28.8**	....	....	....	....	....	....	....	....	....	....	....	....
1986-87	**Washington Capitals**	**NHL**	**6**	**1**	**3**	**1**	**328**	**27**	**0**	**4.94**	**4.16**	**7.25**	**184**	**.853**	**33.7**	....	....	....	....	....	....	....	....	....	....	....	....
	Binghamton Whalers	AHL	13	5	6	0	684	42	0	3.68	....	....	....	....	....	....	....	....	....	....	....	....	....	....	....	....	....
	Los Angeles Kings	**NHL**	**5**	**1**	**4**	**0**	**300**	**27**	**0**	**5.40**	**4.55**	**9.47**	**154**	**.825**	**30.8**	....	....	....	....	....	....	....	....	....	....	....	....
1987-88	New Haven Nighthawks	AHL	20	5	12	3	1129	84	0	4.46	....	....	....	....	....	....	....	....	....	....	....	....	....	....	....	....	....
	NHL Totals		**179**	**95**	**53**	**18**	**9974**	**557**	**8**	**3.35**	....	....	....	....	....	**12**	**5**	**5**	....	**598**	**32**	**0**	**3.21**	....	....	....	....

OHA Second All-Star Team (1077) • OHA First All-Star Team (1978) • Shared William M. Jennings Trophy with Pat Riggin (1984)

Traded to **Washington** by **Detroit** for Mark Lofthouse, July 23, 1981. Traded to **LA Kings** by **Washington** for Garry Galley, February 14, 1987.

• JENSEN, DARREN
Darren Jensen G – L. 5'9", 165 lbs. b: Creston, B.C., 5/27/1960. Hartford's 5th choice, 92nd overall, in 1980 Entry Draft.

Season	Club	League	GP	W	L	T	Mins	GA	SO	Avg	AAvg	Eff	SA	S%	SAPG	GP	W	L	T	Mins	GA	SO	Avg	Eff	SA	S%	SAPG
1979-80	University of North Dakota	WCHA	15	....	....	....	890	33	1	2.22	....	....	....	....	....	....	....	....	....	....	....	....	....	....	....	....	....
1980-81	University of North Dakota	WCHA	25	....	....	....	1510	110	0	4.37	....	....	....	....	....	....	....	....	....	....	....	....	....	....	....	....	....
1981-82	University of North Dakota	WCHA	16	....	....	....	910	45	1	2.97	....	....	....	....	....	....	....	....	....	....	....	....	....	....	....	....	....
1982-83	University of North Dakota	WCHA	16				905	46	0	3.05	....	....	....	....	....	....	....	....	....	....	....	....	....	....	....	....	....
1983-84	Fort Wayne Komets	IHL	56	40	12	3	3325	162	*4	*2.92	....	....	....	....	....	6	2	4	0	358	21	0	3.52	....	....	....	....

			REGULAR SEASON													PLAYOFFS											
Season	Club	League	GP	W	L	T	Mins	GA	SO	Avg	AAvg	Eff	SA	S%	SAPG	GP	W	L	T	Mins	GA	SO	Avg	Eff	SA	S%	SAPG
1984-85	**Philadelphia Flyers**	**NHL**	**1**	**0**	**1**	**0**	**60**	**7**	**0**	**7.00**	**5.56**	**16.33**	**30**	**.767**	**30.0**												
	Hershey Bears	AHL	39	12	20	6	2263	150	1	3.98																	
1985-86	**Philadelphia Flyers**	**NHL**	**29**	**15**	**9**	**1**	**1436**	**88**	**2**	**3.68**	**2.86**	**4.28**	**756**	**.884**	**31.6**												
	Hershey Bears	AHL	14	11	1	1	795	38	1	2.87						7	5	1	0	365	19	0	3.12				
1986-87	Hershey Bears	AHL	60	26	26	0	3429	215	0	3.76						4	1	2	0	203	15	0	4.43				
1987-88	Fredericton Express	AHL	42	18	19	4	2459	158	0	3.86						12	7	5	0	715	40	0	3.36				
1988-89	Milwaukee Admirals	IHL	11	7	2	0	555	36	0	3.89																	
	NHL Totals		**30**	**15**	**10**	**1**	**1496**	**95**	**2**	**3.81**			**786**	**.879**													

NCAA Championship All-Tournament Team (1982) • IHL First All-Star Team (1984) • Won James Norris Memorial Trophy (fewest goals against - IHL) (1984) • Won Garry F. Longman Memorial Trophy (Top Rookie - IHL) (1984) • Won James Gatschene Memorial Trophy (MVP - IHL) (1984) • Shared William M. Jennings Trophy with Bob Froese (1986)

Signed as a free agent by **Philadelphia**, May 1, 1984. Traded to **Vancouver** by **Philadelphia** with Daryl Stanley for Wendell Young and Vancouver's 3rd round choice (Kimbi Daniels) in 1990 Entry Draft, August 28, 1987.

• JOHNSON, BOB

Bob Johnson G – L. 6′1″, 185 lbs. b: Farmington, MI, 11/12/1948.

Season	Club	League	GP	W	L	T	Mins	GA	SO	Avg	AAvg	Eff	SA	S%	SAPG	GP	W	L	T	Mins	GA	SO	Avg	Eff	SA	S%	SAPG
1967-68	Michigan State Spartans	WCHA	17				1020	69	0	4.06																	
1968-69	Michigan State Spartans	WCHA	13				760	49	0	3.87																	
1969-70	Michigan State Spartans	WCHA	5				280	23	0	4.93																	
1970-71	Toledo Hornets	IHL	44				2478	176	0	4.26																	
	Fort Worth Wings	CHL	1				60	3	0	3.00																	
1971-72	Denver Spurs	WHL	37	19	10	6	2030	96	1	*2.83						5	4	1	0	299	5	*2	*1.00				
1972-73	**St. Louis Blues**	**NHL**	**12**	**6**	**5**	**0**	**583**	**26**	**0**	**2.68**	**2.52**																
	Denver Spurs	WHL	30	11	10	6	1589	91	2	3.44						4	1	3	0	245	16	0	3.92				
1973-74	Hershey Bears	AHL	43	18	15	9	2426	131	0	3.23						10	8	2	0	608	31	*1	3.05				
1974-75	**Pittsburgh Penguins**	**NHL**	**12**	**3**	**4**	**1**	**476**	**40**	**0**	**5.04**	**4.55**																
	Hershey Bears	AHL	31	11	13	5	1750	106	1	3.63																	
1975-76	Denver–Ottawa	WHA	24	8	14	1	1334	88	0	3.96																	
	Cleveland Crusaders	WHA	18	9	8	0	1043	56	1	3.22						2	0	2	0	120	8	0	4.00				
1976-77	Rhode Island Reds	AHL	10	2	8	0	568	43	0	4.54																	
	Hampton Gulls	SHL	3				180	8	0	2.67																	
	Binghamton Dusters	NAHL	5				275	22	0	4.78																	
	NHL Totals		**24**	**9**	**9**	**1**	**1059**	**66**	**0**	**3.74**																	
	Other Major League Totals		42	17	22	1	2377	144	1	3.63						2	0	2	0	120	8	0	4.00				

WHL Second All-Star Team (1969) • Shared WHL Leading Goaltender Award with Peter McDuffe (1972)

Signed as a free agent by **Detroit**, September 29, 1970. Traded to **St. Louis** (Denver-WHL) by **Detroit** for cash, October 1, 1971. Traded to **Pittsburgh** by **St. Louis** for Nick Harbaruk, October 4, 1973. Signed as a free agent by **Denver** (WHA), September, 1975. Signed as a free agent by **Cleveland** (WHA) after **Denver/Ottawa** (WHA) franchise folded, January 17, 1976.

• JOHNSTON, EDDIE

Eddie Johnston G – L. 6′, 190 lbs. b: Montreal, Que., 11/24/1935.

Season	Club	League	GP	W	L	T	Mins	GA	SO	Avg	AAvg	Eff	SA	S%	SAPG	GP	W	L	T	Mins	GA	SO	Avg	Eff	SA	S%	SAPG
1953-54	Montreal Jr. Royals	QJHL	35					226	0	6.46						4	0	4	0	240	32	0	8.00				
1954-55	Trois-Rivieres Flambeaux	QJHL	46	20	24	2	2760	169	1	3.67						10	3	7	0	613	29	*1	2.84				
1955-56	Montreal Jr. Canadiens	QJHL	STATISTICS NOT AVAILABLE																								
	Chatham Maroons	OHA Sr.	7				420	31	0	4.29																	
	Amherst Ramblers	MSHL	1	1	0	0	60	2	0	2.00																	
	Chicoutimi Sagueneens	QHL	1	0	0	0	20	1	0	3.00																	
1956-57	Winnipeg Warriors	WHL	50	17	32	1	3040	192	2	3.79																	
1957-58	Shawinigan Cataracts	QHL	*63	*31	27	5	*3760	230	*5	3.65						*14	*8	6	0	*880	49	1	3.34				
1958-59	Edmonton Flyers	WHL	49	26	21	2	2960	163	1	3.30						3	0	3	0	180	12	0	4.00				
1959-60	Johnstown Jets	EHL	63				3780	169	4	2.69						13	9	4	0	780	25	*2	*1.92				
1960-61	Hull-Ottawa Canadiens	EPHL	*70	*41	20	9	*4200	187	*11	*2.67						*14	*8	6	0	*857	27	0	*1.89				
1961-62	Spokane Comets	WHL	*70	*37	28	5	*4310	237	3	3.30						*16	*9	7	0	*972	58	*1	3.58				
1962-63	**Boston Bruins**	**NHL**	**50**	**11**	**27**	**11**	**2913**	**196**	**1**	**4.04**	**4.40**																
1963-64	**Boston Bruins**	**NHL**	***70**	**18**	**40**	**12**	***4200**	**211**	**6**	**3.01**	**3.40**																
1964-65	**Boston Bruins**	**NHL**	**47**	**11**	**32**	**4**	**2820**	**163**	**3**	**3.47**	**3.82**																
1965-66	**Boston Bruins**	**NHL**	**33**	**10**	**19**	**2**	**1744**	**108**	**1**	**3.72**	**3.84**																
	Los Angeles Blades	WHL	5	2	2	0	260	10	1	2.31																	
1966-67	**Boston Bruins**	**NHL**	**34**	**8**	**21**	**2**	**1880**	**116**	**0**	**3.70**	**3.91**																
1967-68	**Boston Bruins**	**NHL**	**28**	**11**	**8**	**5**	**1524**	**73**	**0**	**2.87**	**3.18**																
1968-69	**Boston Bruins**	**NHL**	**24**	**14**	**6**	**4**	**1440**	**74**	**2**	**3.08**	**3.19**					**1**	**0**	**1**		**65**	**4**	**0**	**3.69**				
1969-70	**Boston Bruins**	**NHL**	**37**	**16**	**9**	**11**	**2176**	**108**	**3**	**2.98**	**3.17**					**1**	**0**	**1**		**60**	**4**	**0**	**4.00**				
1970-71	**Boston Bruins**	**NHL**	**38**	**30**	**6**	**2**	**2280**	**96**	**4**	**2.53**	**2.48**					**1**	**0**	**1**		**60**	**7**	**0**	**7.00**				
1971-72	**Boston Bruins**	**NHL**	**38**	**27**	**8**	**3**	**2260**	**102**	**2**	**2.71**	**2.72**					**7**	***6**	**1**		**420**	**13**	**1**	***1.86**				
1972-73	Canada	Summit	DID NOT PLAY – SPARE GOALTENDER																								
	Boston Bruins	**NHL**	**45**	**24**	**17**	**1**	**2510**	**137**	**5**	**3.27**	**3.08**					**3**	**1**	**2**		**160**	**9**	**0**	**3.38**				
1973-74	**Toronto Maple Leafs**	**NHL**	**26**	**12**	**9**	**4**	**1516**	**78**	**1**	**3.09**	**2.98**					**1**	**0**	**1**		**60**	**6**	**0**	**6.00**				
1974-75	**St. Louis Blues**	**NHL**	**30**	**12**	**13**	**5**	**1800**	**93**	**2**	**3.10**	**2.79**					**1**	**0**	**1**		**60**	**5**	**0**	**5.00**				
1975-76	**St. Louis Blues**	**NHL**	**38**	**11**	**17**	**9**	**2152**	**130**	**1**	**3.62**	**3.28**																
1976-77	**St. Louis Blues**	**NHL**	**38**	**13**	**16**	**5**	**2111**	**108**	**1**	**3.07**	**2.85**					**3**	**0**	**2**		**138**	**9**	**0**	**3.91**				
1977-78	**St. Louis Blues**	**NHL**	**12**	**5**	**6**	**1**	**650**	**45**	**0**	**4.15**	**3.89**																
	Chicago Black Hawks	**NHL**	**4**	**1**	**3**	**0**	**240**	**17**	**0**	**4.25**	**3.98**																
	NHL Totals		**592**	**234**	**257**	**81**	**34216**	**1855**	**32**	**3.25**						**18**	**7**	**10**		**1023**	**57**	**1**	**3.34**				

EHL First All-Star Team (1960) • WHL Second All-Star Team (1962)

Claimed by **Boston** from **Spokane** (WHL) in Inter-League Draft, June, 1962. Traded to **Toronto** by **Boston** to complete transaction that sent Jacques Plante to Boston (March 3, 1973), May 22, 1973. Traded to **St. Louis** by **Toronto** for Gary Sabourin, May 27, 1974. Traded to **Chicago** by **St. Louis** for cash, January 27, 1978.

• JOSEPH, CURTIS

Curtis "Cujo" Joseph G – L. 5′10″, 185 lbs. b: Keswick, Ont., 4/29/1967.

Season	Club	League	GP	W	L	T	Mins	GA	SO	Avg	AAvg	Eff	SA	S%	SAPG	GP	W	L	T	Mins	GA	SO	Avg	Eff	SA	S%	SAPG
1988-89	University of Wisconsin	WCHA	38	21	11	5	2267	94	1	2.49																	
1989-90	**St. Louis Blues**	**NHL**	**15**	**9**	**5**	**1**	**852**	**48**	**0**	**3.38**	**2.83**	**3.73**	**435**	**.890**	**30.6**	**6**	**4**	**1**		**327**	**18**	**0**	**3.30**	**3.56**	**167**	**.892**	**30.6**
	Peoria Rivermen	IHL	23	10	8	2	1241	80	0	3.87																	
1990-91	**St. Louis Blues**	**NHL**	**30**	**16**	**10**	**2**	**1710**	**89**	**0**	**3.12**	**2.78**	**3.18**	**874**	**.898**	**30.7**												
1991-92	**St. Louis Blues**	**NHL**	**60**	**27**	**20**	**10**	**3494**	**175**	**2**	**3.01**	**2.66**	**2.70**	**1953**	**.910**	**33.5**	**6**	**2**	**4**		**379**	**23**	**0**	**3.64**	**3.86**	**217**	**.894**	**34.4**
1992-93	**St. Louis Blues**	**NHL**	**68**	**29**	**28**	**9**	**3890**	**196**	**1**	**3.02**	**2.56**	**2.69**	**2202**	**.911**	**34.0**	**11**	**7**	**4**		**715**	**27**	***2**	**2.27**	**1.40**	**438**	**.938**	**36.8**
1993-94	**St. Louis Blues**	**NHL**	**71**	**36**	**23**	**11**	**4127**	**213**	**1**	**3.10**	**2.95**	**2.77**	**2382**	**.911**	**34.6**	**4**	**0**	**4**		**246**	**15**	**0**	**3.66**	**3.47**	**158**	**.905**	**38.5**
1994-95	**St. Louis Blues**	**NHL**	**36**	**20**	**10**	**1**	**1914**	**89**	**1**	**2.79**	**2.88**	**2.75**	**904**	**.902**	**28.3**	**7**	**3**	**3**		**392**	**24**	**0**	**3.67**	**4.95**	**178**	**.865**	**27.2**
1995-96	Las Vegas Thunder	IHL	15	12	2	1	874	29	1	1.99																	
	Edmonton Oilers	**NHL**	**34**	**15**	**16**	**2**	**1936**	**111**	**0**	**3.44**	**3.38**	**3.93**	**971**	**.886**	**30.1**												
	Canada	WC-A	8				409	12		1.94																	
1996-97	Canada	W Cup	7	5	2	0	468	18	1	2.00																	
	Edmonton Oilers	**NHL**	**72**	**32**	**29**	**9**	**4100**	**200**	**6**	**2.93**	**3.10**	**2.73**	**2144**	**.907**	**31.4**	**12**	**5**	**7**		**767**	**36**	**2**	**2.82**	**2.51**	**405**	**.911**	**31.7**
1997-98	**Edmonton Oilers**	**NHL**	**71**	**29**	**31**	**9**	**4132**	**181**	**8**	**2.63**	**3.08**	**2.50**	**1901**	**.905**	**27.6**	**12**	**5**	**7**		**716**	**23**	**3**	**1.93**				
	Canada	Olympics	DID NOT PLAY – SPARE GOALTENDER																								
	NHL Totals		**457**	**213**	**172**	**54**	**26155**	**1302**	**19**	**2.99**			**13766**	**.905**		**58**	**26**	**30**		**3542**	**166**	**7**	**2.81**				

WCHA First All-Star Team (1989) • NCAA West Second All-American Team (1989)

Played in NHL All-Star Game (1994)

Signed as a free agent by **St. Louis**, June 16, 1989. Traded to **Edmonton** by **St. Louis** with the rights to Michael Grier for St. Louis' 1st round choices (previously acquired) in 1996 (St. Louis selected Marty Reasoner) and 1997 (later traded to Los Angeles — Los Angeles selected Matt Zultek) Entry Drafts, August 4, 1995. Signed as a free agent by **Toronto**, July 15, 1998.

Season	Club	League	GP	W	L	T	Mins	GA	SO	Avg	AAvg	Eff	SA	S%	SAPG	GP	W	L	T	Mins	GA	SO	Avg	Eff	SA	S%	SAPG
			REGULAR SEASON													PLAYOFFS											

• JUNKIN, JOE

Joe Junkin G – L. 5'11", 180 lbs. b: Lindsay, Ont., 9/8/1946.

Season	Club	League	GP	W	L	T	Mins	GA	SO	Avg	AAvg	Eff	SA	S%	SAPG	GP	W	L	T	Mins	GA	SO	Avg	Eff	SA	S%	SAPG
1966-67	Bobcaygeon Bobcats	Jr. B	STATISTICS NOT AVAILABLE																								
1967-68	Belleville Mohawks	OHA Sr.	24	....	....	....	1410	100	0	4.26	....	....	....	....	....	....	....	....	....	....	....	....	....	....	....	....	....
1968-69	Oklahoma City Blazers	CHL	27	....	....	....	1420	78	0	3.30	....	....	....	....	....	5	0	4	0	230	19	0	4.96	....	....	....	....
	Boston Bruins	**NHL**	**1**	**0**	**0**	**0**	**8**	**0**	**0**	**0.00**	**0.00**	....	....	....	....	....	....	....	....	....	....	....	....	....	....	....	....
1969-70	Oklahoma City Blazers	CHL	9	4	4	0	500	38	1	4.56	....	....	....	....	....	....	....	....	....	....	....	....	....	....	....	....	....
	Hershey Bears	AHL	17	....	....	....	969	63	0	3.90	....	....	....	....	....	....	....	....	....	....	....	....	....	....	....	....	....
1970-71			DID NOT PLAY – INJURED																								
1971-72	Fenelon Falls Flyers	OVSHL	STATISTICS NOT AVAILABLE																								
1972-73	Long Island Ducks	EHL	2	....	....	....	80	12	0	9.23	....	....	....	....	....	....	....	....	....	....	....	....	....	....	....	....	....
	Syracuse Blazers	EHL	34	....	....	....	2071	90	*5	2.60	....	....	....	....	....	7	3	3	0	399	17	*1	2.57	....	....	....	....
1973-74	New York–New Jersey	WHA	53	21	25	4	3122	197	1	3.79	....	....	....	....	....	....	....	....	....	....	....	....	....	....	....	....	....
1974-75	San Diego Mariners	WHA	16	6	7	0	839	46	1	3.29	....	....	....	....	....	....	....	....	....	....	....	....	....	....	....	....	....
	Syracuse Blazers	NAHL	20	11	8	0	1183	72	0	3.65	....	....	....	....	....	6	....	....	....	360	21	*1	3.50	....	....	....	....
1975-76	Tidewater Sharks	SHL	7	1	5	1	390	30	0	4.62	....	....	....	....	....	....	....	....	....	....	....	....	....	....	....	....	....
	Roanoke Valley Rebels	SHL	29	12	13	3	1686	97	1	3.45	....	....	....	....	....	....	....	....	....	....	....	....	....	....	....	....	....
	NHL Totals		**1**	**0**	**0**	**0**	**8**	**0**	**0**	**0.00**	....	....	....	....	....	....	....	....	....	....	....	....	....	....	....	....	....
	Other Major League Totals		69	27	32	4	3961	243	2	3.68	....	....	....	....	....	....	....	....	....	....	....	....	....	....	....	....	....

EHL North First All-Star Team (1973)

Signed as a free agent by **Boston**, September 12, 1968. • Missed entire 1970-71 season after ungoing retina-reattachment surgery, July, 1970. Signed as a free agent by **NY Raiders** (WHA), September, 1972. Transferred to **San Diego** (WHA) after **New York-New Jersey** (WHA) franchise relocated, April 30, 1974. Traded to **Cincinnati** (WHA) by **San Diego** (WHA) for Cincinnati's 3rd round choice (Mark Suzor) in 1976 WHA Amateur Draft, June, 1975.

• KAARELA, JARI

Jari Kaarela G – L. 5'10", 165 lbs. b: Tampere, Finland, 8/8/1958.

Season	Club	League	GP	W	L	T	Mins	GA	SO	Avg	AAvg	Eff	SA	S%	SAPG	GP	W	L	T	Mins	GA	SO	Avg	Eff	SA	S%	SAPG
1979-80	SaiPa Lapeenranta	Finland 2	STATISTICS NOT AVAILABLE																								
1980-81	Fort Worth Texans	CHL	36	13	20	2	2093	133	1	3.81	....	....	....	....	....	....	....	....	....	....	....	....	....	....	....	....	....
	Colorado Rockies	**NHL**	**5**	**2**	**2**	**0**	**220**	**22**	**0**	**6.00**	**4.81**	....	....	....	....	....	....	....	....	....	....	....	....	....	....	....	....
	Indianapolis Checkers	CHL	2	2	0	0	120	4	1	2.00	....	....	....	....	....	....	....	....	....	....	....	....	....	....	....	....	....
1981-82	Muskegon Mohawks	IHL	49	....	....	....	2682	219	1	4.90	....	....	....	....	....	....	....	....	....	....	....	....	....	....	....	....	....
	Fort Worth Texans	CHL	2	0	2	0	120	13	0	6.50	....	....	....	....	....	....	....	....	....	....	....	....	....	....	....	....	....
	NHL Totals		**5**	**2**	**2**	**0**	**220**	**22**	**0**	**6.00**	....	....	....	....	....	....	....	....	....	....	....	....	....	....	....	....	....

Signed as a free agent by **Colorado**, February 9, 1981. Traded to **NY Islanders** by **Colorado** with Mike McEwen for Glenn Resch and Steve Tambellini, March 10, 1981. • Played professional hockey in Finland from 1982-83 through 1985-86.

• KAMPURRI, HANNU

Hannu Kampurri G – R. 6', 175 lbs. b: Helsinki, Finland, 6/1/1957.

Season	Club	League	GP	W	L	T	Mins	GA	SO	Avg	AAvg	Eff	SA	S%	SAPG	GP	W	L	T	Mins	GA	SO	Avg	Eff	SA	S%	SAPG
1977-78	Jokerit Helsinki	Finland	36	....	....	....	1456	177	....	7.29	....	....	....	....	....	....	....	....	....	....	....	....	....	....	....	....	....
1978-79	Jokerit Helsinki	Finland	36	....	....	....	2160	161	0	4.47	....	....	....	....	....	....	....	....	....	....	....	....	....	....	....	....	....
	Edmonton Oilers	WHA	2	0	1	0	90	10	0	6.67	....	....	....	....	....	....	....	....	....	....	....	....	....	....	....	....	....
1979-80	Houston Apollos	CHL	19	6	11	2	1119	88	0	4.72	....	....	....	....	....	2	....	....	....	103	9	0	5.24	....	....	....	....
	Baltimore Clippers	EHL	3	....	....	....	....	4	1	1.33	....	....	....	....	....	....	....	....	....	....	....	....	....	....	....	....	....
1980-81	Tappara Tampere	Finland	36	....	....	....	2160	118	0	3.27	....	....	....	....	....	....	....	....	....	....	....	....	....	....	....	....	....
1981-82	Tappara Tampere	Finland	36	....	....	....	2160	118	0	3.67	....	....	....	....	....	....	....	....	....	....	....	....	....	....	....	....	....
1982-83	Tappara Tampere	Finland	36	....	....	....	2160	121	0	3.36	....	....	....	....	....	....	....	....	....	....	....	....	....	....	....	....	....
1983-84	Tappara Tampere	Finland	37	....	....	....	2220	102	0	2.77	....	....	....	....	....	....	....	....	....	....	....	....	....	....	....	....	....
1984-85	**New Jersey Devils**	**NHL**	**13**	**1**	**10**	**1**	**645**	**54**	**0**	**5.02**	**3.99**	**7.72**	**351**	**.846**	**32.7**	....	....	....	....	....	....	....	....	....	....	....	....
	Maine Mariners	AHL	7	4	2	0	340	19	0	3.35	....	....	....	....	....	....	....	....	....	....	....	....	....	....	....	....	....
	Fort Wayne Komets	IHL	1	0	1	0	60	4	0	4.00	....	....	....	....	....	....	....	....	....	....	....	....	....	....	....	....	....
1985-86	Saipa Lappeenranta	Finland	34	....	....	....	2109	147		4.18	....	....	....	....	....	....	....	....	....	....	....	....	....	....	....	....	....
1986-87	Karpat Oulu	Finland	44	....	....	....	2666	159	0	*3.58	....	....	....	....	....	9	4	5	0	540	27	0	3.00	....	....	....	....
1987-88	Karpat Oulu	Finland	STATISTICS NOT AVAILABLE																								
1988-89	Koo Koo Kouvola	Finland	41	....	....	....	2403	171	0	4.27	....	....	....	....	....	....	....	....	....	....	....	....	....	....	....	....	....
	NHL Totals		**13**	**1**	**10**	**1**	**645**	**54**	**0**	**5.02**	....	....	**351**	**.846**	....	....	....	....	....	....	....	....	....	....	....	....	....
	Other Major League Totals		2	0	1	0	90	10	0	6.67	....	....	....	....	....	....	....	....	....	....	....	....	....	....	....	....	....

Signed as a free agent by **Edmonton** (WHA), March, 1978. Signed as a free agent by **New Jersey**, August 1, 1984.

• KARAKAS, MIKE

Mike Karakas G – L. 5'11", 147 lbs. b: Aurora, MN, 12/12/1911. Deceased. USHOF

Season	Club	League	GP	W	L	T	Mins	GA	SO	Avg	AAvg	Eff	SA	S%	SAPG	GP	W	L	T	Mins	GA	SO	Avg	Eff	SA	S%	SAPG
1929-30	Eveleth Rangers	CHL	STATISTICS NOT AVAILABLE																								
1930-31	Chicago Shamrocks	AHA	8	5	2	0	435	16	0	2.21	....	....	....	....	....	....	....	....	....	....	....	....	....	....	....	....	....
1931-32	Chicago Shamrocks	AHA	45	*29	11	5	2624	65	9	1.59	....	....	....	....	....	4	*3	1	0	242	10	0	2.48	....	....	....	....
1932-33	St. Louis Flyers	AHA	43	23	19	1	2702	85	*5	1.89	....	....	....	....	....	4	2	2	0	284	6	*1	1.27	....	....	....	....
1933-34	Tulsa Oilers	AHA	48	23	25	0	2918	110	7	2.26	....	....	....	....	....	4	2	2	0	260	7	*1	1.62	....	....	....	....
1934-35	Tulsa Oilers	AHA	41	20	17	4	2640	77	4	*1.52	....	....	....	....	....	2	0	2	0	130	8	0	3.69	....	....	....	....
1935-36	**Chicago Black Hawks**	**NHL**	***48**	**21**	**19**	**8**	**2990**	**92**	**9**	**1.85**	**2.58**	....	....	....	....	**2**	**1**	**1**	**0**	**120**	**7**	**0**	**3.50**	....	....	....	....
1936-37	**Chicago Black Hawks**	**NHL**	***48**	**14**	**27**	**7**	**2978**	**131**	**5**	**2.64**	**3.34**	....	....	....	....	....	....	....	....	....	....	....	....	....	....	....	....
1937-38	**Chicago Black Hawks**	**NHL**	***48**	**14**	**25**	**9**	**2980**	**139**	**1**	**2.80**	**3.46**	....	....	....	....	***8**	***6**	**2**	....	***525**	**15**	***2**	**1.71**	....	....	....	....
1938-39	**Chicago Black Hawks**	**NHL**	***48**	**12**	**28**	**8**	**2988**	**132**	**5**	**2.65**	**3.25**	....	....	....	....	....	....	....	....	....	....	....	....	....	....	....	....
1939-40	**Chicago Black Hawks**	**NHL**	**17**	**7**	**9**	**1**	**1050**	**58**	**0**	**3.31**	**4.18**	....	....	....	....	....	....	....	....	....	....	....	....	....	....	....	....
	Providence Reds	AHL	14	7	5	2	860	43	1	3.00	....	....	....	....	....	8	*6	2	0	545	21	*2	2.31	....	....	....	....
	Montreal Canadiens	**NHL**	**5**	**0**	**4**	**1**	**310**	**18**	**0**	**3.48**	**4.34**	....	....	....	....	....	....	....	....	....	....	....	....	....	....	....	....
1940-41	Providence Reds	AHL	*56	*31	21	4	*3450	171	0	2.97	....	....	....	....	....	4	1	3	0	279	13	0	2.60	....	....	....	....
1941-42	Providence Reds	AHL	*56	17	32	7	*3470	237	1	4.10	....	....	....	....	....	....	....	....	....	....	....	....	....	....	....	....	....
	New Haven Eagles	AHL	1	0	1	0	60	7	0	7.00	....	....	....	....	....	....	....	....	....	....	....	....	....	....	....	....	....
	Springfield Indians	AHL	....	....	....	....	....	....	....	....	....	....	....	....	....	3	0	2	0	160	7	0	2.63	....	....	....	....
1942-43	Providence Reds	AHL	*56	27	27	2	*3360	216	2	3.86	....	....	....	....	....	2	0	2	0	120	7	0	3.50	....	....	....	....
1943-44	Providence Reds	AHL	24	6	15	3	1440	67	0	3.63	....	....	....	....	....	....	....	....	....	....	....	....	....	....	....	....	....
	Chicago Black Hawks	**NHL**	**26**	**12**	**9**	**5**	**1560**	**79**	**3**	**3.04**	**2.25**	....	....	....	....	***9**	**4**	**5**	....	***549**	**24**	***1**	**2.62**	....	....	....	....
1944-45	**Chicago Black Hawks**	**NHL**	**48**	**12**	**29**	**7**	**2880**	**187**	***4**	**3.90**	**3.26**	....	....	....	....	....	....	....	....	....	....	....	....	....	....	....	....
1945-46	**Chicago Black Hawks**	**NHL**	**48**	**22**	**19**	**7**	**2880**	**166**	**1**	**3.46**	**3.21**	....	....	....	....	**4**	**0**	**4**	....	**240**	**26**	**0**	**6.50**	....	....	....	....
1946-47	Providence Reds	AHL	62	21	31	10	3720	206	0	4.29	....	....	....	....	....	....	....	....	....	....	....	....	....	....	....	....	....
1947-48	Providence Reds	AHL	2	1	1	0	120	7	0	3.50	....	....	....	....	....	....	....	....	....	....	....	....	....	....	....	....	....
	NHL Totals		**336**	**114**	**169**	**53**	**20616**	**1002**	**28**	**2.92**	....	....	....	....	....	**23**	**11**	**12**	**0**	**1434**	**72**	**3**	**3.01**	....	....	....	....

AHA First All-Star Team (1935) • NHL Rookie of the Year (1936) • AHL First All-Star Team (1941) • AHL Second All-Star Team (1943) • NHL Second All-Star Team (1945)

• Suspended by **Chicago** for remainder of 1939-40 season after refusing assignment to **Providence** (AHL), December 30, 1939. • Suspension lifted by NHL President Frank Calder and rights loaned to **Montreal** for remainder of 1939-40 season after Montreal goaltender Wilf Cude suffered season-ending shoulder injury, February 23, 1940. Traded to **Chicago** by **Providence** (AHL) for Hec Highton, Gord Buttrey and $10,000, January 7, 1944.

• KEANS, DOUG

Doug Keans G – L. 5'7", 185 lbs. b: Pembroke, Ont., 1/7/1958. Los Angeles' 2nd choice, 94th overall, in 1978 Amateur Draft.

Season	Club	League	GP	W	L	T	Mins	GA	SO	Avg	AAvg	Eff	SA	S%	SAPG	GP	W	L	T	Mins	GA	SO	Avg	Eff	SA	S%	SAPG
1976-77	Oshawa Generals	OHA	48	....	....	....	2632	291	0	6.63	....	....	....	....	....	....	....	....	....	....	....	....	....	....	....	....	....
1977-78	Oshawa Generals	OHA	42	....	....	....	2500	172	1	4.13	....	....	....	....	....	5	....	....	....	299	23	0	4.63	....	....	....	....
1978-79	Saginaw Gears	IHL	59	....	....	....	3207	217	0	4.06	....	....	....	....	....	2	....	....	....	120	10	0	5.05	....	....	....	....
1979-80	Saginaw Gears	IHL	22	....	....	....	1070	67	1	3.76	....	....	....	....	....	....	....	....	....	....	....	....	....	....	....	....	....
	Binghamton Dusters	AHL	7	3	3	2	429	25	0	3.50	....	....	....	....	....	....	....	....	....	....	....	....	....	....	....	....	....
	Los Angeles Kings	**NHL**	**10**	**3**	**3**	**3**	**559**	**23**	**0**	**2.47**	**2.17**	....	....	....	....	**1**	**0**	**1**	....	**40**	**7**	**0**	**10.50**	....	....	....	....
1980-81	**Los Angeles Kings**	**NHL**	**9**	**2**	**3**	**1**	**454**	**37**	**0**	**4.89**	**3.92**	....	....	....	....	....	....	....	....	....	....	....	....	....	....	....	....
	Houston Apollos	CHL	11	3	4	4	699	27	0	2.32	....	....	....	....	....	....	....	....	....	....	....	....	....	....	....	....	....
	Oklahoma City Stars	CHL	9	3	5	0	492	32	1	3.90	....	....	....	....	....	....	....	....	....	....	....	....	....	....	....	....	....
1981-82	New Haven Nighthawks	AHL	13	5	5	1	686	33	2	2.89	....	....	....	....	....	....	....	....	....	....	....	....	....	....	....	....	....
	Los Angeles Kings	**NHL**	**31**	**8**	**10**	**7**	**1436**	**103**	**0**	**4.30**	**3.32**	....	....	....	....	**2**	**0**	**1**	....	**32**	**1**	**0**	**1.88**	....	....	....	....

			REGULAR SEASON													PLAYOFFS											
Season	Club	League	GP	W	L	T	Mins	GA	SO	Avg	AAvg	Eff	SA	S%	SAPG	GP	W	L	T	Mins	GA	SO	Avg	Eff	SA	S%	SAPG
1982-83	Los Angeles Kings	NHL	6	0	2	2	304	24	0	4.74	3.79	8.24	138	.826	27.2	....	....	....	....	....	....	....	....	....	....	....	....
	New Haven Nighthawks	AHL	30	13	13	2	1724	125	0	4.35	....	....	....	....	....	....	....	....	....	....	....	....	....	....	....	....	....
1983-84	Boston Bruins	NHL	33	19	8	3	1779	92	2	3.10	2.42	3.61	791	.884	26.7	....	....	....	....	....	....	....	....	....	....	....	....
1984-85	Boston Bruins	NHL	25	16	6	3	1497	82	1	3.29	2.61	4.03	669	.877	26.8	4	2	2	....	240	15	0	3.75	5.11	110	.864	27.5
1985-86	Boston Bruins	NHL	30	14	13	3	1757	107	0	3.65	2.83	4.99	782	.863	26.7	....	....	....	....	....	....	....	....	....	....	....	....
1986-87	Boston Bruins	NHL	36	18	8	4	1942	108	0	3.34	2.80	3.97	909	.881	28.1	2	0	2	....	120	11	0	5.50	10.43	58	.810	29.0
1987-88	Boston Bruins	NHL	30	16	11	0	1660	90	1	3.25	2.70	3.89	751	.880	27.1	....	....	....	....	....	....	....	....	....	....	....	....
	Maine Mariners	AHL	10	8	2	0	600	34	0	3.40	....	....	....	....	....	10	5	5	0	617	42	0	4.08	....	....	....	....
1988-89	Baltimore Skipjacks	AHL	4	1	3	0	239	17	0	4.27	....	....	....	....	....	....	....	....	....	....	....	....	....	....	....	....	....
	Springfield Indians	AHL	32	11	16	2	1737	124	0	4.28	....	....	....	....	....	....	....	....	....	....	....	....	....	....	....	....	....
	NHL Totals		210	96	64	26	11388	666	4	3.51	....	....	....	....	....	9	2	6	....	432	34	0	4.72	....	....	....	....

Claimed on waivers by **Boston** from **LA Kings**, May 24, 1983.

• KEENAN, DON Don Keenan G – L. 6', 170 lbs. b: Toronto, Ontario, 8/8/1938.

Season	Club	League	GP	W	L	T	Mins	GA	SO	Avg	AAvg	Eff	SA	S%	SAPG	GP	W	L	T	Mins	GA	SO	Avg	Eff	SA	S%	SAPG
1955-56	St. Michael's Majors	OHA	2	....	....	....	120	10	0	5.00	....	....	....	....	....	....	....	....	....	....	....	....	....	....	....	....	....
	St. Francis Xavier X-Men	AUAA	STATISTICS NOT AVAILABLE																								
1956-57	St. Francis Xavier X-Men	AUAA	10	*8	0	2	600	24	2	2.40	....	....	....	....	....	*4	*3	0	1	*240	10	0	*2.50	....	....	....	....
1957-58	St. Francis Xavier X-Men	AUAA	STATISTICS NOT AVAILABLE																								
1958-59	Boston Bruins	NHL	1	0	1	0	60	4	0	4.00	4.26	....	....	....	....	....	....	....	....	....	....	....	....	....	....	....	....
1959-60	University of Toronto	OQAA	STATISTICS NOT AVAILABLE																								
	NHL Totals		1	0	1	0	60	4	0	4.00	....	....	....	....	....	....	....	....	....	....	....	....	....	....	....	....	....

Loaned to **Boston** by **St. Michael's** (OHA) to replace Harry Lumley, March 7, 1959. (Toronto 4, Boston 1).

• KERR, DAVE Dave Kerr G – R. 5'10", 160 lbs. b: Toronto, Ont., 1/11/1910. d: 5/11/1978.

Season	Club	League	GP	W	L	T	Mins	GA	SO	Avg	AAvg	Eff	SA	S%	SAPG	GP	W	L	T	Mins	GA	SO	Avg	Eff	SA	S%	SAPG
1924-25	Toronto Canoe Club	OHA	3	2	0	0	140	5	0	2.14	....	....	....	....	....	2	0	2	0	120	7	0	3.50	....	....	....	....
1925-26	Toronto Canoe Club	OHA	7	3	3	0	380	22	0	3.47	....	....	....	....	....	....	....	....	....	....	....	....	....	....	....	....	....
1926-27	Iroquois Falls Papermakers	NOHA	STATISTICS NOT AVAILABLE																								
1927-28	Iroquois Falls Papermakers	NOHA	STATISTICS NOT AVAILABLE																								
1928-29	Iroquois Falls Papermakers	NOHA	STATISTICS NOT AVAILABLE																								
1929-30	Montreal AAA	City Sr.	9	*8	0	1	540	6	4	*0.67	....	....	....	....	....	11	8	1	2	760	7	*6	*0.55	....	....	....	....
	Montreal CPR	City Sr.	9	3	2	4	540	10	3	1.11	....	....	....	....	....	2	0	1	0	120	4	0	2.00	....	....	....	....
1930-31	Montreal Maroons	NHL	29	13	11	4	1769	70	1	2.37	3.05	....	....	....	....	2	0	2	0	120	8	0	4.00	....	....	....	....
1931-32	Windsor Bulldogs	IAHL	34	....	....	....	2040	70	6	2.56	....	....	....	....	....	....	....	....	....	....	....	....	....	....	....	....	....
	New York Americans	NHL	1	0	1	0	60	6	0	6.00	7.40	....	....	....	....	....	....	....	....	....	....	....	....	....	....	....	....
1932-33	Montreal Maroons	NHL	25	14	8	3	1520	58	4	2.29	3.11	....	....	....	....	2	0	2	0	120	5	0	2.50	....	....	....	....
	Philadelphia Arrows	Can-Am	16	8	3	5	1020	31	2	1.82	....	....	....	....	....	....	....	....	....	....	....	....	....	....	....	....	....
1933-34	Montreal Maroons	NHL	*48	19	18	11	3060	122	6	2.39	3.06	....	....	....	....	4	1	2	1	240	7	1	1.75	....	....	....	....
1934-35	New York Rangers	NHL	37	19	12	6	2290	94	4	2.46	3.01	....	....	....	....	4	1	1	2	240	10	0	2.50	....	....	....	....
1935-36	New York Rangers	NHL	47	18	17	12	2980	95	8	1.91	2.68	....	....	....	....	....	....	....	....	....	....	....	....	....	....	....	....
1936-37	New York Rangers	NHL	*48	19	20	9	3020	106	4	2.11	2.59	....	....	....	....	*9	*6	3	....	*553	10	*4	*1.08	....	....	....	....
1937-38	New York Rangers	NHL	*48	27	15	6	2960	96	*8	1.95	2.30	....	....	....	....	3	1	2	....	262	8	0	1.83	....	....	....	....
1938-39	New York Rangers	NHL	*48	26	16	6	2970	105	6	2.12	2.51	....	....	....	....	1	0	1	....	119	2	0	1.01	....	....	....	....
1939-40	New York Rangers	NHL	*48	27	11	10	3000	77	*8	*1.54	1.79	....	....	....	....	*12	*8	4	....	*770	20	*3	*1.56	....	....	....	....
1940-41	New York Rangers	NHL	*48	21	19	8	3010	125	2	2.49	2.83	....	....	....	....	3	1	2	....	192	6	0	1.88	....	....	....	....
	NHL Totals		427	203	148	75	26639	954	51	2.15	....	....	....	....	....	40	18	19	3	2616	76	8	1.74	....	....	....	....

NHL Second All-Star Team (1938) • NHL First All-Star Team (1940) • Won Vezina Trophy (1940)

Signed as a free agent by **Montreal Maroons**, September 2, 1930. Loaned to **NY Americans** by **Montreal Maroons** to replace injured Roy Worters, March 8, 1932. (Montreal Canadiens 6, NY Americans 1). Traded to **NY Rangers** by **Montreal Maroons** for cash, December 14, 1934.

• KHABIBULIN, NIKOLAI Nikolai "Bulin Wall" Khabibulin G – L. 6'1", 176 lbs. b: Sverdlovsk, USSR, 1/13/1973. Winnipeg's 8th choice, 204th overall, in 1992 Entry Draft.

Season	Club	League	GP	W	L	T	Mins	GA	SO	Avg	AAvg	Eff	SA	S%	SAPG	GP	W	L	T	Mins	GA	SO	Avg	Eff	SA	S%	SAPG
1988-89	Sverdlovsk	USSR	1	....	....	....	3	0	0	0.00	....	....	....	....	....	....	....	....	....	....	....	....	....	....	....	....	....
1989-90	Sverdlovsk Jrs.	USSR	STATISTICS NOT AVAILABLE																								
1990-91	Sputnik	USSR 3	STATISTICS NOT AVAILABLE																								
	Soviet Union	EJC-A	5	....	....	....	242	11	....	2.73	....	....	....	....	....	....	....	....	....	....	....	....	....	....	....	....	....
1991-92	CSKA Moscow	CIS	2	....	....	....	34	2	0	3.52	....	....	....	....	....	....	....	....	....	....	....	....	....	....	....	....	....
	Russia	Olympics	DID NOT PLAY – SPARE GOALTENDER																								
	Russia	WJC-A	6	6	0	0	289	7	....	1.45	....	....	....	....	....	....	....	....	....	....	....	....	....	....	....	....	....
1992-93	CSKA Moscow	CIS	13	....	....	....	491	27	....	3.29	....	....	....	....	....	....	....	....	....	....	....	....	....	....	....	....	....
1993-94	CSKA Moscow	CIS	46	....	....	....	2625	116	....	2.65	....	....	....	....	....	3	....	....	....	193	11	....	3.42	....	....	....	....
	Russian Penguins	IHL	12	2	7	2	639	47	0	4.41	....	....	....	....	....	....	....	....	....	....	....	....	....	....	....	....	....
1994-95	Springfield Falcons	AHL	23	9	9	3	1240	80	0	3.87	....	....	....	....	....	....	....	....	....	....	....	....	....	....	....	....	....
	Winnipeg Jets	NHL	26	8	9	4	1339	76	0	3.41	3.53	3.58	723	.895	32.4	....	....	....	....	....	....	....	....	....	....	....	....
1995-96	Winnipeg Jets	NHL	53	26	20	3	2914	152	2	3.13	3.07	2.87	1656	.908	34.1	6	2	4	....	359	19	0	3.18	2.82	214	.911	35.8
1996-97	Russia	W Cup	2	0	2	0	100	10	0	6.00	....	....	....	....	....	....	....	....	....	....	....	....	....	....	....	....	....
	Phoenix Coyotes	NHL	72	30	33	6	4091	193	7	2.83	2.99	2.61	2094	.908	30.7	7	3	4	....	426	15	1	2.11	1.43	222	.932	31.3
1997-98	Phoenix Coyotes	NHL	70	30	28	10	4026	184	4	2.74	3.21	2.75	1835	.900	27.3	4	2	1	....	185	13	0	4.22	5.18	106	.877	34.4
	NHL Totals		221	94	90	23	12370	605	13	2.93	....	....	6308	.904	....	17	7	9	....	970	47	1	2.91	....	....	....	....

Played in NHL All-Star Game (1998)

Transferred to **Phoenix** after **Winnipeg** franchise relocated, July 1, 1996.

• KIDD, TREVOR Trevor Kidd G – L. 6'2", 190 lbs. b: Dugald, Man., 3/29/1972. Calgary's 1st choice, 11th overall, in 1990 Entry Draft.

Season	Club	League	GP	W	L	T	Mins	GA	SO	Avg	AAvg	Eff	SA	S%	SAPG	GP	W	L	T	Mins	GA	SO	Avg	Eff	SA	S%	SAPG
1988-89	Brandon Wheat Kings	WHL	32	11	13	1	1509	102	0	4.06	....	....	....	....	....	....	....	....	....	....	....	....	....	....	....	....	....
1989-90	Brandon Wheat Kings	WHL	*63	24	32	2	*3676	254	2	4.15	....	....	....	....	....	....	....	....	....	....	....	....	....	....	....	....	....
	Canada	WJC-A	DID NOT PLAY – SPARE GOALTENDER																								
1990-91	Brandon Wheat Kings	WHL	30	10	19	1	1730	117	0	4.06	....	....	....	....	....	....	....	....	....	....	....	....	....	....	....	....	....
	Canada	WJC-A	6	....	....	....	340	15	....	2.65	....	....	....	....	....	....	....	....	....	....	....	....	....	....	....	....	....
	Spokane Chiefs	WHL	14	8	3	0	749	44	0	3.52	....	....	....	....	....	15	*14	1	....	926	32	2	*2.07	....	....	....	....
1991-92	Canada	Nat-Team	28	18	4	4	1349	79	2	3.51	....	....	....	....	....	....	....	....	....	....	....	....	....	....	....	....	....
	Canada	WJC-A	7	2	3	2	420	29	0	4.14	....	....	....	....	....	....	....	....	....	....	....	....	....	....	....	....	....
	Canada	Olympics	1	1	0	0	60	0	1	0.00	....	....	....	....	....	....	....	....	....	....	....	....	....	....	....	....	....
	Calgary Flames	NHL	2	1	1	0	120	8	0	4.00	3.55	5.71	56	.857	28.0	....	....	....	....	....	....	....	....	....	....	....	....
	Canada	WC-A	1	1	0	0	60	3	0	3.00	....	....	....	....	....	....	....	....	....	....	....	....	....	....	....	....	....
1992-93	Salt Lake Golden Eagles	IHL	29	10	16	1	1696	111	1	3.93	....	....	....	....	....	....	....	....	....	....	....	....	....	....	....	....	....
1993-94	Calgary Flames	NHL	31	13	7	6	1614	85	0	3.16	3.01	3.57	752	.887	28.0	....	....	....	....	....	....	....	....	....	....	....	....
1994-95	Calgary Flames	NHL	*43	22	14	6	*2463	107	3	2.61	2.69	2.39	1170	.909	28.5	7	3	4	....	434	26	1	3.59	5.16	181	.856	25.0
1995-96	Calgary Flames	NHL	47	15	21	8	2570	119	3	2.78	2.72	2.93	1130	.895	26.4	2	0	1	....	83	9	0	6.51	14.65	40	.775	28.9
1996-97	Calgary Flames	NHL	55	21	23	6	2979	141	4	2.84	3.00	2.83	1416	.900	28.5	....	....	....	....	....	....	....	....	....	....	....	....
1997-98	Carolina Hurricanes	NHL	47	21	21	3	2685	97	3	2.17	2.53	1.70	1237	.922	27.6	....	....	....	....	....	....	....	....	....	....	....	....
	NHL Totals		225	93	87	29	12431	557	13	2.69	....	....	5761	.903	....	9	3	5	....	517	35	1	4.06	....	....	....	....

WHL East First All-Star Team (1990) • Canadian Major Junior Goaltender of the Year (1990)

Traded to **Carolina** by **Calgary** with Gary Roberts for Andrew Cassels and Jean-Sebastien Giguere, August 25, 1997.

• KING, SCOTT Scott King G – L. 6'1", 185 lbs. b: Thunder Bay, Ont., 6/25/1967. Detroit's 10th choice, 190th overall, in 1986 Entry Draft.

Season	Club	League	GP	W	L	T	Mins	GA	SO	Avg	AAvg	Eff	SA	S%	SAPG	GP	W	L	T	Mins	GA	SO	Avg	Eff	SA	S%	SAPG
1985-86	Vernon Lakers	BCJHL	29	17	9	0	1718	133	0	4.64	....	....	....	....	....	....	....	....	....	....	....	....	....	....	....	....	....
1986-87	University of Maine	H.E.	21	11	6	1	1111	58	0	3.13	....	....	....	....	....	2	1	1	0	115	7	0	3.65	....	....	....	....
1987-88	University of Maine	H.E.	33	25	5	1	1762	91	0	3.10	....	....	....	....	....	6	4	2	0	340	20	0	3.53	....	....	....	....
1988-89	University of Maine	H.E.	27	13	8	0	1394	83	0	3.57	....	....	....	....	....	3	1	2	0	189	17	0	5.40	....	....	....	....
1989-90	University of Maine	H.E.	29	17	7	2	1526	67	1	2.63	....	....	....	....	....	4	2	2	0	240	9	1	2.25	....	....	....	....

Season	Club	League	GP	W	L	T	Mins	GA	SO	Avg	AAvg	Eff	SA	S%	SAPG	GP	W	L	T	Mins	GA	SO	Avg	Eff	SA	S%	SAPG
			REGULAR SEASON													PLAYOFFS											
1990-91	**Detroit Red Wings**	**NHL**	**1**	**0**	**0**	**0**	**45**	**2**	**0**	**2.67**	**2.38**	**4.85**	**11**	**.818**	**14.7**												
	Adirondack Red Wings	AHL	24	8	10	2	1287	91	0	4.24						1	0	0	0	32	4	0	7.50				
	Hampton Roads Admirals	ECHL	15	8	4	1	819	57	0	4.17																	
1991-92	**Detroit Red Wings**	**NHL**	**1**	**0**	**0**	**0**	**16**	**1**	**0**	**3.75**	**3.33**	**7.50**	**5**	**.800**	**18.8**												
	Adirondack Red Wings	AHL	33	14	14	3	1904	112	0	3.53																	
	Toledo Storm	ECHL	7	4	2	1	424	25	0	3.54																	
1992-93	Adirondack Red Wings	AHL	1	1	0	0	60	1	0	1.00																	
	Toledo Storm	ECHL	*45	*26	11	7	*2602	153	2	3.53						*14	*10	3	0	*823	52	0	3.79				
	NHL Totals		**2**	**0**	**0**	**0**	**61**	**3**	**0**	**2.95**			**16**	**.813**													

Hockey East First All-Star Team (1988, 1990) • Hockey East Second All-Star Team (1989) • ECHL Second All-Star Team (1993)

• KLEISINGER, TERRY

Terry Kleisinger G – R. 6', 190 lbs. b: Regina, Sask., 10/10/1960.

Season	Club	League	GP	W	L	T	Mins	GA	SO	Avg	AAvg	Eff	SA	S%	SAPG	GP	W	L	T	Mins	GA	SO	Avg	Eff	SA	S%	SAPG
1980-81	University of Wisconsin	WCHA	16	11	5	0	1011	61	2	3.62						1	0	1	0	34	7	0	12.36				
1981-82	University of Wisconsin	WCHA	22	14	8	0	1337	59	4	2.65						5	3	2	0	300	10	2	2.00				
1982-83	University of Wisconsin	WCHA	18	11	6	1	1021	48	3	2.82						1	1	0	0	60	1	0	1.00				
1983-84	University of Wisconsin	WCHA	24	11	11	1	1406	96	0	4.10						2	0	2	0	109	12	0	6.63				
1984-85			DID NOT PLAY																								
1985-86	Flint Spirits	IHL	4	0	3	0	200	25	0	7.50																	
	Toledo Goaldiggers	IHL	14	1	10	0	786	76	0	5.80																	
	New Haven Nighthawks	AHL	10	2	5	2	497	34	0	4.10																	
	New York Rangers	**NHL**	**4**	**0**	**2**	**0**	**191**	**14**	**0**	**4.40**	**3.42**	**5.65**	**109**	**.872**	**34.2**												
1986-87	New Haven Nighthawks	AHL	1	0	1	0	40	4	0	6.00																	
	Flint Spirits	IHL	2	0	0	0	53	5	0	5.66																	
	Indianapolis Checkers	IHL	4	0	4	0	240	25	0	6.25																	
	NHL Totals		**4**	**0**	**2**	**0**	**191**	**14**	**0**	**4.40**			**109**	**.872**													

• Missed entire 1984-85 season due to illness. Signed as a free agent by **NY Rangers**, October 8, 1985.

• KLYMKIW, JULIAN

Julian Klymkiw G – R. 5'11", 180 lbs. b: Winnipeg, Man., 7/16/1933.

Season	Club	League	GP	W	L	T	Mins	GA	SO	Avg	AAvg	Eff	SA	S%	SAPG	GP	W	L	T	Mins	GA	SO	Avg	Eff	SA	S%	SAPG
1951-52	Brandon Wheat Kings	MJHL	16	8	8	0	960	66	0	4.13																	
1952-53	Brandon Wheat Kings	MJHL	36	*23	11	1	2160	123	*1	3.36						4				240	18	0	4.50				
1953-54	Troy-Louisville-Grand Rapids	IHL	57				3420	239	1	4.19																	
1954-55	Brandon Wheat Kings	MSHL	24				1440	95	*2	*3.96																	
1955-56			STATISTICS NOT AVAILABLE																								
1956-57	Winnipeg Warriors	WHL	4	2	2	0	240	20	0	5.00																	
	Sault Ste. Marie Greyhounds	NOHA	33				1980	133	1	4.03																	
1957-58	Winnipeg Warriors	WHL	3	0	2	1	180	8	0	2.67																	
1958-59	**New York Rangers**	**NHL**	**1**	**0**	**0**	**0**	**19**	**2**	**0**	**6.32**	**6.74**																
	NHL Totals		**1**	**0**	**0**	**0**	**19**	**2**	**0**	**6.32**																	

Detroit's assistant trainer/practice goaltender loaned to **NY Rangers** to replace injured Gump Worsley in 3rd period, October 12, 1958. (Detroit 3, NY Rangers 0).

• KNICKLE, RICK

Rick Knickle G – L. 5'10", 175 lbs. b: Chatham, N.B., 2/26/1960. Buffalo's 7th choice, 116th overall, in 1979 Entry Draft.

Season	Club	League	GP	W	L	T	Mins	GA	SO	Avg	AAvg	Eff	SA	S%	SAPG	GP	W	L	T	Mins	GA	SO	Avg	Eff	SA	S%	SAPG
1977-78	Brandon Wheat Kings	WCJHL	49	34	5	7	2806	182	0	3.89						0	4	4		450	36	0	4.82				
1978-79	Brandon Wheat Kings	WHL	38	26	3	8	2240	118	1	*3.16						16	12	3		886	41	*1	*2.78				
1979-80	Brandon Wheat Kings	WHL	33	11	14	1	1604	125	0	4.68																	
	Muskegon Mohawks	IHL	16				829	52	0	3.76						3				156	17	0	6.54				
1980-81	Erie Blades	EHL	43				2347	125	1	*3.20						8				446	14	0	*1.88				
1981-82	Rochester Americans	AHL	31	10	12	5	1753	108	1	3.70						3	0	2		125	7	0	3.37				
1982-83	Flint Generals	IHL	27				1638	92	2	3.37						3				193	10	0	3.11				
	Rochester Americans	AHL	4	0	3	0	143	11	0	4.64																	
1983-84	Flint Generals	IHL	60	32	21	5	3518	203	3	3.46						8	8	0		480	24	0	3.00				
1984-85	Sherbrooke Canadiens	AHL	14	7	6	0	780	53	0	4.08																	
	Flint Generals	IHL	36	18	11	3	2018	115	2	3.42						7	3	4		401	27	0	4.04				
1985-86	Saginaw Generals	IHL	39	16	15	0	2235	135	2	3.62						3	2	1		193	12	0	3.73				
1986-87	Saginaw Generals	IHL	26	9	13	0	1413	113	0	4.80						5	1	4		329	21	0	3.83				
1987-88	Flint Spirits	IHL	1	0	1	0	60	4	0	4.00																	
	Peoria Rivermen	IHL	13	2	8	1	705	58	0	4.94						6	3	3		294	20		4.08				
1988-89	Fort Wayne Komets	IHL	47	22	16	0	2716	141	1	*3.11						4	1	2		173	15	0	5.20				
1989-90	Flint Spirits	IHL	55	26	24	1	2998	210	1	4.20						2	0	2		101	13	0	7.72				
1990-91	Albany Choppers	IHL	14	4	6	2	679	52	0	4.59																	
	Springfield Indians	AHL	9	6	0	2	509	28	0	3.30																	
1991-92	San Diego Gulls	IHL	46	*28	13	4	2686	155	0	3.46						2	0	1		78	3	0	2.31				
1992-93	San Diego Gulls	IHL	41	33	4	4	2437	88	*4	*2.17																	
	Los Angeles Kings	**NHL**	**10**	**6**	**4**	**0**	**532**	**35**	**0**	**3.95**	**3.36**	**4.73**	**292**	**.880**	**32.9**												
1993-94	**Los Angeles Kings**	**NHL**	**4**	**1**	**2**	**0**	**174**	**9**	**0**	**3.10**	**2.95**	**3.93**	**71**	**.873**	**24.5**												
	Phoenix Roadrunners	IHL	25	8	9	3	1292	89	1	4.13																	
1994-95	Detroit Vipers	IHL	49	24	15	5	2725	134	*3	2.95																	
1995-96	Detroit Vipers	IHL	18	9	5	1	872	50	0	3.44																	
	Las Vegas Thunder	IHL	7	6	1	0	420	27	0	3.86						4	1	0		126	7	0	3.33				
1996-97	Milwaukee Admirals	IHL	19	5	9	1	940	60	0	3.83																	
	NHL Totals		**14**	**7**	**6**	**0**	**706**	**44**	**0**	**3.74**			**363**	**.879**													

WHL First All-Star Team (1979) • EHL First All-Star Team (1981) • IHL Second All-Star Team (1984, 1992) • IHL First All-Star Team (1989, 1993) • Won James Norris Memorial Trophy (fewest goals against - IHL) (1989) • Shared James Norris Memorial Trophy (fewest goals against - IHL) with Clint Malarchuk (1993)

Signed as a free agent by **Montreal**, February 8, 1985. Signed as a free agent by **Los Angeles**, February 16, 1993.

• KOLZIG, OLAF

Olaf "Godzilla" Kolzig G – L. 6'3", 225 lbs. b: Johannesburg, South Africa, 4/9/1970. Washington's 1st choice, 19th overall, in 1989 Entry Draft.

Season	Club	League	GP	W	L	T	Mins	GA	SO	Avg	AAvg	Eff	SA	S%	SAPG	GP	W	L	T	Mins	GA	SO	Avg	Eff	SA	S%	SAPG
1987-88	New Westminster Bruins	WHL	15	6	5	0	650	48	1	4.43						3	0	3		149	11	0	4.43				
1988-89	Tri-City Americans	WHL	30	16	10	2	1671	97	1	*3.48																	
1989-90	Washington Capitals	FrTour	2				65	4		3.69																	
	Washington Capitals	**NHL**	**2**	**0**	**2**	**0**	**120**	**12**	**0**	**6.00**	**5.03**	**11.43**	**63**	**.810**	**31.5**												
	Tri-City Americans	WHL	48	27	27	3	2504	250	1	4.38						6	4	0		318	27	0	5.09				
1990-91	Baltimore Skipjacks	AHL	26	10	12	1	1367	72	0	3.16																	
	Hampton Roads Admirals	ECHL	21	11	9	1	1248	71	2	3.41						3	1	2		180	14	0	4.66				
1991-92	Baltimore Skipjacks	AHL	28	5	17	2	1503	105	1	4.19																	
	Hampton Roads Admirals	ECHL	14	11	3	0	847	41	0	2.90																	
1992-93	**Washington Capitals**	**NHL**	**1**	**0**	**0**	**0**	**20**	**2**	**0**	**6.00**	**5.11**	**17.14**	**7**	**.714**	**21.0**												
	Rochester Americans	AHL	49	25	16	4	2737	168	0	3.68						*17	9	8		*1040	61	0	3.52				
1993-94	**Washington Capitals**	**NHL**	**7**	**0**	**3**	**0**	**224**	**20**	**0**	**5.36**	**5.11**	**8.38**	**128**	**.844**	**34.3**												
	Portland Pirates	AHL	29	16	8	5	1725	88	3	3.06						17	*12	5		1035	44	0	*2.55				
1994-95	**Washington Capitals**	**NHL**	**14**	**2**	**8**	**2**	**724**	**30**	**0**	**2.49**	**2.57**	**2.45**	**305**	**.902**	**25.3**	**2**	**1**	**0**		**44**	**1**	**0**	**1.36**	**0.65**	**21**	**.952**	**28.6**
	Portland Pirates	AHL	2	1	0	1	125	3	0	1.44																	
1995-96	**Washington Capitals**	**NHL**	**18**	**4**	**8**	**2**	**897**	**46**	**0**	**3.08**	**3.02**	**3.49**	**406**	**.887**	**27.2**	**5**	**2**	**3**		**341**	**11**	**0**	***1.94**	**1.28**	**167**	**.934**	**29.4**
	Portland Pirates	AHL	5	5	0	0	300	7	1	1.40																	

			REGULAR SEASON													PLAYOFFS											
Season	Club	League	GP	W	L	T	Mins	GA	SO	Avg	AAvg	Eff	SA	S%	SAPG	GP	W	L	T	Mins	GA	SO	Avg	Eff	SA	S%	SAPG
1996-97	Germany	W Cup	1	....	....	....	45	5	0	6.67	....	....	....	....	....	....	....	....	....	....	....	....	....	....	....	....	....
	Washington Capitals	**NHL**	**29**	**8**	**15**	**4**	**1645**	**71**	**2**	**2.59**	**2.74**	**2.43**	**758**	**.906**	**27.6**	....	....	....	....	....	....	....	....	....	....	....	....
	Germany	WC-A	4	0	3	0	199	13	0	3.92	....	....	....	....	....	....	....	....	....	....	....	....	....	....	....	....	....
1997-98	**Washington Capitals**	**NHL**	**64**	**33**	**18**	**10**	**3788**	**139**	**5**	**2.20**	**2.56**	**1.77**	**1729**	**.920**	**27.4**	**21**	**12**	**9**	....	**1351**	**44**	***4**	**1.95**	**1.16**	**740**	**.941**	**32.9**
	Germany	Olympics	2	2	0	0	120	2	1	1.00	....	....	....	....	....	....	....	....	....	....	....	....	....	....	....	....	....
	NHL Totals		**135**	**47**	**54**	**18**	**7418**	**320**	**7**	**2.59**	....	....	**3396**	**.906**	....	**28**	**15**	**12**	....	**1736**	**56**	**4**	**1.94**	....	....	....	....

WHL West Second All-Star Team (1989) • Shared Harry "Hap" Holmes Trophy (fewest goals-against - AHL) with Byron Dafoe (1994) • Won Jack Butterfield Trophy (Playoff MVP - IHL) (1994)
Played in NHL All-Star Game (1998)
• Scored a goal while with Tri-City (WHL), November 29, 1989.

• KUNTAR, LES

Les Kuntar G – L. 6'2", 195 lbs. b: Elma, NY, 7/28/1969. Montreal's 8th choice, 122nd overall, in 1987 Entry Draft.

Season	Club	League	GP	W	L	T	Mins	GA	SO	Avg	AAvg	Eff	SA	S%	SAPG	GP	W	L	T	Mins	GA	SO	Avg	Eff	SA	S%	SAPG
1986-87	Nicholls-NY High School	H.S.	STATISTICS NOT AVAILABLE																								
1987-88	St. Lawrence University	ECAC	10	6	1	0	488	27	0	3.32	....	....	....	....	....	....	....	....	....	....	....	....	....	....	....	....	....
1988-89	St. Lawrence University	ECAC	14	11	2	0	786	31	0	2.37	....	....	....	....	....	....	....	....	....	....	....	....	....	....	....	....	....
1989-90	St. Lawrence University	ECAC	20	7	11	1	1136	80	0	4.23	....	....	....	....	....	....	....	....	....	....	....	....	....	....	....	....	....
1990-91	St. Lawrence University	ECAC	*33	*19	11	1	*1797	97	*1	*3.24	....	....	....	....	....	....	....	....	....	....	....	....	....	....	....	....	....
1991-92	Fredericton Canadiens	AHL	11	7	3	0	638	26	0	2.45	....	....	....	....	....	....	....	....	....	....	....	....	....	....	....	....	....
	United States	Nat-Team	13	3	5	3	725	57	0	4.72	....	....	....	....	....	....	....	....	....	....	....	....	....	....	....	....	....
1992-93	Fredericton Canadiens	AHL	42	16	14	7	2315	130	0	3.37	....	....	....	....	....	1	0	1	0	64	6	0	5.63	....	....	....	....
1993-94	**Montreal Canadiens**	**NHL**	**6**	**2**	**2**	**0**	**302**	**16**	**0**	**3.18**	**3.03**	**3.91**	**130**	**.877**	**25.8**	....	....	....	....	....	....	....	....	....	....	....	....
	Fredericton Canadiens	AHL	34	10	17	3	1804	109	1	3.62	....	....	....	....	....	....	....	....	....	....	....	....	....	....	....	....	....
	United States	WC-A	4	....	....	....	135	11	....	4.89	....	....	....	....	....	....	....	....	....	....	....	....	....	....	....	....	....
1994-95	Worcester IceCats	AHL	24	6	10	5	1241	77	2	3.72	....	....	....	....	....	....	....	....	....	....	....	....	....	....	....	....	....
	Hershey Bears	AHL	32	15	13	2	1802	89	0	2.96	....	....	....	....	....	2	0	1	0	70	5	0	4.28	....	....	....	....
1995-96	Hershey Bears	AHL	20	7	8	2	1020	71	0	4.18	....	....	....	....	....	....	....	....	....	....	....	....	....	....	....	....	....
	Fort Wayne Komets	IHL	8	2	3	1	387	26	1	4.03	....	....	....	....	....	....	....	....	....	....	....	....	....	....	....	....	....
1996-97	Rochester Americans	AHL	21	6	9	3	1052	60	0	3.42	....	....	....	....	....	....	....	....	....	....	....	....	....	....	....	....	....
	Pensacola Ice Pilots	ECHL	4	2	2	0	220	13	0	3.55	....	....	....	....	....	....	....	....	....	....	....	....	....	....	....	....	....
	Cleveland Lumberjacks	IHL	1	1	0	0	60	4	0	4.00	....	....	....	....	....	....	....	....	....	....	....	....	....	....	....	....	....
	Utah Grizzlies	IHL	3	1	0	0	87	1	0	0.69	....	....	....	....	....	....	....	....	....	....	....	....	....	....	....	....	....
	NHL Totals		**6**	**2**	**2**	**0**	**302**	**16**	**0**	**3.18**	....	....	**130**	**.877**	....	....	....	....	....	....	....	....	....	....	....	....	....

ECAC First All-Star Team (1991)
Signed as a free agent by **Philadelphia**, June 30, 1995.

• KURT, GARY

Gary Kurt G – L. 6'3", 205 lbs. b: Kitchener, Ont., 3/9/1947.

Season	Club	League	GP	W	L	T	Mins	GA	SO	Avg	AAvg	Eff	SA	S%	SAPG	GP	W	L	T	Mins	GA	SO	Avg	Eff	SA	S%	SAPG
1963-64	Kitchener Rangers	OHA	11	....	....	....	620	49	0	4.74	....	....	....	....	....	....	....	....	....	....	....	....	....	....	....	....	....
1964-65	Kitchener Rangers	OHA	21	....	....	....	1240	103	0	4.98	....	....	....	....	....	....	....	....	....	....	....	....	....	....	....	....	....
1965-66	Kitchener Rangers	OHA	9	....	....	....	540	33	1	3.67	....	....	....	....	....	17	....	....	....	1020	67	1	3.94	....	....	....	....
1966-67	Kitchener Rangers	OHA	16	....	....	....	940	69	0	4.40	....	....	....	....	....	....	....	....	....	....	....	....	....	....	....	....	....
1967-68	Omaha Knights	CHL	34	5	21	3	1842	124	0	4.04	....	....	....	....	....	....	....	....	....	....	....	....	....	....	....	....	....
1968-69	Omaha Knights	CHL	35	....	....	....	1940	108	1	3.34	....	....	....	....	....	3	1	0	0	104	5	0	2.88	....	....	....	....
1969-70	Cleveland Barons	AHL	40	....	....	....	2320	121	2	3.13	....	....	....	....	....	....	....	....	....	....	....	....	....	....	....	....	....
1970-71	Cleveland Barons	AHL	42	24	12	3	2263	101	3	*2.67	....	....	....	....	....	7	4	3	0	420	20	0	2.85	....	....	....	....
1971-72	Baltimore Clippers	AHL	17	12	4	1	1020	47	1	2.76	....	....	....	....	....	....	....	....	....	....	....	....	....	....	....	....	....
	California Golden Seals	**NHL**	**16**	**1**	**7**	**5**	**838**	**60**	**0**	**4.30**	**4.35**					....	....	....	....	....	....	....	....	....	....	....	....
1972-73	New York Raiders	WHA	36	10	21	0	1881	150	0	4.78	....	....	....	....	....	....	....	....	....	....	....	....	....	....	....	....	....
1973-74	New York/Jersey	WHA	20	8	10	0	1089	75	0	4.13	....	....	....	....	....	....	....	....	....	....	....	....	....	....	....	....	....
	Syracuse Blazers	NAHL	24	....	....	....	1357	66	0	2.92	....	....	....	....	....	....	....	....	....	....	....	....	....	....	....	....	....
1974-75	Phoenix Roadrunners	WHA	47	25	16	4	2841	156	2	3.29	....	....	....	....	....	4	1	2	0	207	12	0	3.48	....	....	....	....
1975-76	Phoenix Roadrunners	WHA	40	18	20	2	2369	147	1	3.72	....	....	....	....	....	....	....	....	....	....	....	....	....	....	....	....	....
1976-77	Phoenix Roadrunners	WHA	33	11	19	1	1752	162	0	5.55	....	....	....	....	....	....	....	....	....	....	....	....	....	....	....	....	....
	Oklahoma City Blazers	CHL	3	....	....	....	180	15	0	5.00	....	....	....	....	....	....	....	....	....	....	....	....	....	....	....	....	....
	NHL Totals		**16**	**1**	**7**	**5**	**838**	**60**	**0**	**4.30**	....	....	....	....	....	....	....	....	....	....	....	....	....	....	....	....	....
	Other Major League Totals		176	72	86	7	9932	690	3	4.17	....	....	....	....	....	4	1	2	0	207	12	0	3.48	....	....	....	....

AHL Second All-Star Team (1971) • Won Harry "Hap" Holmes Memorial Award (fewest goals against - AHL) (1971) • NAHL First All-Star Team (1974)
Claimed by **Cleveland** (AHL) from **NY Rangers** in Reverse Draft, June 12, 1969. Claimed by **California** from **Cleveland** (AHL) in Inter-League Draft, June 7, 1971. Selected by **NY Raiders** (WHA) in 1972 WHA General Player Draft, February 12, 1972. Claimed by **Phoenix** (WHA) from **New York-New Jersey** (WHA) in 1974 WHA Expansion Draft, June, 1974.

• LABRECQUE, PATRICK

Patrick Labrecque G – L. 6', 190 lbs. b: Laval, Que., 3/6/1971. Quebec's 5th choice, 90th overall, in 1991 Entry Draft.

Season	Club	League	GP	W	L	T	Mins	GA	SO	Avg	AAvg	Eff	SA	S%	SAPG	GP	W	L	T	Mins	GA	SO	Avg	Eff	SA	S%	SAPG
1990-91	St-Jean Lynx	QMJHL	59	17	34	6	3375	216	1	3.84	....	....	....	....	....	....	....	....	....	....	....	....	....	....	....	....	....
1991-92	Halifax Citadels	AHL	29	5	12	8	1570	114	0	4.36	....	....	....	....	....	....	....	....	....	....	....	....	....	....	....	....	....
1992-93	Greensboro Monarchs	ECHL	11	6	3	2	650	31	0	2.86	....	....	....	....	....	1	0	1	....	59	5	0	5.08	....	....	....	....
	Halifax Citadels	AHL	20	3	12	2	914	76	0	4.99	....	....	....	....	....	....	....	....	....	....	....	....	....	....	....	....	....
1993-94	Cornwall Aces	AHL	4	1	2	0	198	8	1	2.42	....	....	....	....	....	....	....	....	....	....	....	....	....	....	....	....	....
	Greensboro Monarchs	ECHL	29	17	8	2	1609	89	0	3.32	....	....	....	....	....	1	0	0	....	22	4	0	10.80	....	....	....	....
1994-95	Fredericton Canadiens	AHL	35	15	17	1	1913	104	1	3.26	....	....	....	....	....	*16	*10	6	....	*967	40	1	2.48	....	....	....	....
	Wheeling Thunderbirds	ECHL	5	2	3	0	281	22	0	4.69	....	....	....	....	....	....	....	....	....	....	....	....	....	....	....	....	....
1995-96	**Montreal Canadiens**	**NHL**	**2**	**0**	**1**	**0**	**98**	**7**	**0**	**4.29**	**4.21**	**6.39**	**47**	**.851**	**28.8**	....	....	....	....	....	....	....	....	....	....	....	....
	Fredericton Canadiens	AHL	48	23	18	6	2686	153	3	3.42	....	....	....	....	....	7	3	3	....	405	31	0	4.59	....	....	....	....
1996-97	Fredericton Canadiens	AHL	12	1	7	1	602	31	0	3.09	....	....	....	....	....	....	....	....	....	....	....	....	....	....	....	....	....
	Quebec Rafales	IHL	9	2	6	0	482	29	0	3.61	....	....	....	....	....	....	....	....	....	....	....	....	....	....	....	....	....
1997-98	Baton Rouge Kingfish	ECHL	34	17	13	4	1935	107	0	3.32	....	....	....	....	....	....	....	....	....	....	....	....	....	....	....	....	....
	Hershey Bears	AHL	....	....	....	....	....	....	....	....	....	....	....	....	....	1	0	0	....	10	0	0	0.00	....	....	....	....
	NHL Totals		**2**	**0**	**1**	**0**	**98**	**7**	**0**	**4.29**	....	....	**47**	**.851**	....	....	....	....	....	....	....	....	....	....	....	....	....

Signed as a free agent by **Montreal**, June 21, 1994.

• LACHER, BLAINE

Blaine Lacher G – L. 6'1", 205 lbs. b: Medicine Hat, Alta., 9/5/1970.

Season	Club	League	GP	W	L	T	Mins	GA	SO	Avg	AAvg	Eff	SA	S%	SAPG	GP	W	L	T	Mins	GA	SO	Avg	Eff	SA	S%	SAPG
1991-92	Lake Superior State	CCHA	9	5	3	0	410	22	0	3.22	....	....	....	....	....	....	....	....	....	....	....	....	....	....	....	....	....
1992-93	Lake Superior State	CCHA	34	24	5	3	1915	86	2	2.70	....	....	....	....	....	....	....	....	....	....	....	....	....	....	....	....	....
1993-94	Lake Superior State	CCHA	30	20	5	4	1785	59	6	*1.98	....	....	....	....	....	....	....	....	....	....	....	....	....	....	....	....	....
1994-95	**Boston Bruins**	**NHL**	**35**	**19**	**11**	**2**	**1965**	**79**	**4**	**2.41**	**2.48**	**2.37**	**805**	**.902**	**24.6**	**5**	**1**	**4**	....	**283**	**12**	**0**	**2.54**	**2.44**	**125**	**.904**	**26.5**
	Providence Bruins	AHL	1	0	1	0	59	3	0	3.03	....	....	....	....	....	....	....	....	....	....	....	....	....	....	....	....	....
1995-96	**Boston Bruins**	**NHL**	**12**	**3**	**5**	**2**	**671**	**44**	**0**	**3.93**	**3.86**	**6.09**	**284**	**.845**	**25.4**	....	....	....	....	....	....	....	....	....	....	....	....
	Providence Bruins	AHL	9	3	5	0	462	30	0	3.90	....	....	....	....	....	....	....	....	....	....	....	....	....	....	....	....	....
	Cleveland Lumberjacks	IHL	8	3	4	1	478	28	0	3.51	....	....	....	....	....	3	0	3	....	191	10	0	3.14	....	....	....	....
1996-97	Grand Rapids Griffins	IHL	11	1	8	1	510	32	0	3.76	....	....	....	....	....	....	....	....	....	....	....	....	....	....	....	....	....
	NHL Totals		**47**	**22**	**16**	**4**	**2636**	**123**	**4**	**2.80**	....	....	**1089**	**.887**	....	**5**	**1**	**4**	....	**283**	**12**	**0**	**2.54**	....	....	....	....

NCAA Championship All-Tournament Team (1994)
Signed as a free agent by **Boston**, June 2, 1994.

• LACROIX, ALBERT

Albert "Frenchy" Lacroix G – L. 5'7", 136 lbs. b: Newton, MA, 10/21/1897.

Season	Club	League	GP	W	L	T	Mins	GA	SO	Avg	AAvg	Eff	SA	S%	SAPG	GP	W	L	T	Mins	GA	SO	Avg	Eff	SA	S%	SAPG
1914-15	Newton-Mass High School	H.S.	7	5	1	1	294	15	0	2.04	....	....	....	....	....	1	1	0	0	40	1	0	1.00	....	....	....	....
1915-16	Newton-Mass High School	H.S.	7	5	2	0	280	9	2	1.29	....	....	....	....	....	....	....	....	....	....	....	....	....	....	....	....	....
1916-17	Newton-Mass High School	H.S.	8	7	0	1	320	10	4	1.25	....	....	....	....	....	....	....	....	....	....	....	....	....	....	....	....	....
1917-18	Boston Navy Yard	City Sr.	11	7	4	0	455	22	*3	*1.93	....	....	....	....	....	....	....	....	....	....	....	....	....	....	....	....	....
1918-19	Boston Navy Yard	City Sr.	STATISTICS NOT AVAILABLE													....	....	....	....	....	....	....	....	....	....	....	....
1919-20	Boston AA Unicorns	City Sr.	3	2	1	0	135	8	0	2.67						....	....	....	....	....	....	....	....	....	....	....	....
1920-21	Boston AA Unicorns	USAHA	DID NOT PLAY – SPARE GOALTENDER																								

			REGULAR SEASON													PLAYOFFS											
Season	Club	League	GP	W	L	T	Mins	GA	SO	Avg	AAvg	Eff	SA	S%	SAPG	GP	W	L	T	Mins	GA	SO	Avg	Eff	SA	S%	SAPG
1921-22	Boston AA Unicorns	USAHA	1	1	0	0	45	2	0	2.00	....	....	....	....	....	....	....	....	....	....	....	....	....	....	....	....	....
1922-23	Boston AA Unicorns	USAHA	9	*9	0	0	405	10	*4	*1.11	....	....	....	....	....	4	*3	1	0	180	4	*1	*1.00	....	....	....	....
1923-24	Boston AA Unicorns	USAHA	6	3	3	0	270	10	1	1.67	....	....	....	....	....	3	1	2	0	180	8	0	2.67	....	....	....	....
	United States	Olympics	5	4	1	0	225	6	4	1.20	....	....	....	....	....	....	....	....	....	....	....	....	....	....	....	....	....
1924-25	Boston AA Unicorns	USAHA	21	15	6	0	955	40	*4	1.88	....	....	....	....	....	4	1	3	0	150	10	*1	3.00	....	....	....	....
1925-26	**Montreal Canadiens**	**NHL**	**5**	**1**	**4**	**0**	**280**	**15**	**0**	**3.21**	**4.33**	....	....	....	....	....	....	....	....	....	....	....	....	....	....	....	....
1926-27	**Montreal Canadiens**	**NHL**	DID NOT PLAY – SPARE GOALTENDER																								
1927-28	Providence Reds	Can-Am	4	1	3	0	250	12	0	2.88	....	....	....	....	....	....	....	....	....	....	....	....	....	....	....	....	....
	Lewiston St. Doms	NEHL	22	8	12	2	1350	42	5	1.87	....	....	....	....	....	5	....	....	....	305	16	0	3.15	....	....	....	....
1928-29	Lewiston St. Doms	NEHL	4	3	1	0	240	9	0	2.25	....	....	....	....	....	3	2	1	0	240	8	*1	*2.67	....	....	....	....
1929-30	Providence Reds	Can-Am	1	1	0	0	60	2	0	2.00	....	....	....	....	....	....	....	....	....	....	....	....	....	....	....	....	....
1930-31	Boston Tigers	Can-Am	4	1	3	0	240	13	0	3.25	....	....	....	....	....	....	....	....	....	....	....	....	....	....	....	....	....
	NHL Totals		**5**	**1**	**4**	**0**	**280**	**15**	**0**	**3.21**	....	....	....	....	....	....	....	....	....	....	....	....	....	....	....	....	....

Signed as a free agent by **Montreal Canadiens**, November 10, 1925.

• LAFERRIERE, RICK

Rick LaFerriere G – L. 5'8", 165 lbs. b: Hawkesbury, Ont., 1/3/1961. Colorado's 3rd choice, 64th overall, in 1980 Entry Draft.

Season	Club	League	GP	W	L	T	Mins	GA	SO	Avg	AAvg	Eff	SA	S%	SAPG	GP	W	L	T	Mins	GA	SO	Avg	Eff	SA	S%	SAPG
1978-79	Peterborough Petes	OHA	21	....	....	....	1279	76	1	3.56	....	....	....	....	....	....	....	....	....	....	....	....	....	....	....	....	....
1979-80	Peterborough Petes	OHA	55	....	....	....	3118	170	2	*3.27	....	....	....	....	....	14	....	....	....	863	38	0	2.64	....	....	....	....
	Canada	WJC-A	4	2	2	0	240	13	0	3.25	....	....	....	....	....	....	....	....	....	....	....	....	....	....	....	....	....
1980-81	Peterborough Petes	OHA	34	15	15	2	1959	144	0	4.41	....	....	....	....	....	....	....	....	....	....	....	....	....	....	....	....	....
	Brantford Alexanders	OHA	20	11	8	0	1155	93	0	4.83	....	....	....	....	....	....	....	....	....	....	....	....	....	....	....	....	....
1981-82	Fort Worth Texans	CHL	37	8	26	2	2155	189	1	5.26	....	....	....	....	....	....	....	....	....	....	....	....	....	....	....	....	....
	Colorado Rockies	**NHL**	**1**	**0**	**0**	**0**	**20**	**1**	**0**	**3.00**	**2.31**	....	....	....	....	....	....	....	....	....	....	....	....	....	....	....	....
	Brantford Alexanders	OHL	20	....	....	....	1155	92	0	4.83	....	....	....	....	....	4	....	....	....	194	19	0	5.90	....	....	....	....
1982-83	Muskegon Mohawks	IHL	44	....	....	....	2578	186	0	4.33	....	....	....	....	....	2	....	....	....	120	8	0	4.00	....	....	....	....
1983-84	Muskegon Mohawks	IHL	16	....	....	....	817	83	0	6.09	....	....	....	....	....	....	....	....	....	....	....	....	....	....	....	....	....
	Tulsa Oilers	CHL	2	....	....	....	79	4	0	3.03	....	....	....	....	....	1	0	0	0	20	2	0	6.00	....	....	....	....
	NHL Totals		**1**	**0**	**0**	**0**	**20**	**1**	**0**	**3.00**	....	....	....	....	....	....	....	....	....	....	....	....	....	....	....	....	....

OHA Second All-Star Team (1980) • Memorial Cup All-Star Team (1980) • Won Hap Emms Memorial Trophy (Memorial Cup Tournament Top Goaltender) (1980)

• LaFOREST, MARK

Mark "Trees" LaForest G – L. 5'11", 190 lbs. b: Welland, Ont., 7/10/1962.

Season	Club	League	GP	W	L	T	Mins	GA	SO	Avg	AAvg	Eff	SA	S%	SAPG	GP	W	L	T	Mins	GA	SO	Avg	Eff	SA	S%	SAPG
1981-82	Niagara Falls Flyers	OHL	24	10	13	1	1365	105	1	4.62	....	....	....	....	....	5	1	2	....	300	19	0	3.80	....	....	....	....
1982-83	North Bay Centennials	OHL	54	34	17	1	3140	195	0	3.73	....	....	....	....	....	8	4	4	....	474	31	0	3.92	....	....	....	....
1983-84	Adirondack Red Wings	AHL	7	3	3	1	351	29	0	4.96	....	....	....	....	....	....	....	....	....	....	....	....	....	....	....	....	....
	Kalamazoo Wings	IHL	13	4	5	2	718	48	1	4.01	....	....	....	....	....	....	....	....	....	....	....	....	....	....	....	....	....
1984-85	Adirondack Red Wings	AHL	11	2	3	1	430	35	0	4.88	....	....	....	....	....	....	....	....	....	....	....	....	....	....	....	....	....
1985-86	**Detroit Red Wings**	**NHL**	**28**	**4**	**21**	**0**	**1383**	**114**	**1**	**4.95**	**3.86**	**7.61**	**742**	**.846**	**32.2**	....	....	....	....	....	....	....	....	....	....	....	....
	Adirondack Red Wings	AHL	19	13	5	1	1142	57	0	2.99	....	....	....	....	....	*17	*12	5	....	*1075	58	0	3.24	....	....	....	....
1986-87	**Detroit Red Wings**	**NHL**	**5**	**2**	**1**	**0**	**219**	**12**	**0**	**3.29**	**2.77**	**3.56**	**111**	**.892**	**30.4**	....	....	....	....	....	....	....	....	....	....	....	....
	Adirondack Red Wings	AHL	37	23	8	0	2229	105	*3	2.83	....	....	....	....	....	....	....	....	....	....	....	....	....	....	....	....	....
1987-88	**Philadelphia Flyers**	**NHL**	**21**	**5**	**9**	**2**	**972**	**60**	**1**	**3.70**	**3.08**	**4.64**	**478**	**.874**	**29.5**	**2**	**1**	**0**	....	**48**	**1**	**0**	**1.25**	**1.04**	**12**	**.917**	**15.0**
	Hershey Bears	AHL	5	2	1	2	309	13	0	2.52	....	....	....	....	....	....	....	....	....	....	....	....	....	....	....	....	....
1988-89	**Philadelphia Flyers**	**NHL**	**17**	**5**	**7**	**2**	**933**	**64**	**0**	**4.12**	**3.40**	**5.31**	**497**	**.871**	**32.0**	....	....	....	....	....	....	....	....	....	....	....	....
	Hershey Bears	AHL	3	2	0	0	185	9	0	2.92	....	....	....	....	....	12	7	5	....	744	27	1	2.18	....	....	....	....
1989-90	**Toronto Maple Leafs**	**NHL**	**27**	**9**	**14**	**0**	**1343**	**87**	**0**	**3.89**	**3.26**	**4.42**	**765**	**.886**	**34.2**	....	....	....	....	....	....	....	....	....	....	....	....
	Newmarket Saints	AHL	10	6	4	0	604	33	1	3.28	....	....	....	....	....	....	....	....	....	....	....	....	....	....	....	....	....
1990-91	Binghamton Rangers	AHL	45	25	14	2	2452	129	0	3.16	....	....	....	....	....	9	3	4	....	442	28	1	3.80	....	....	....	....
1991-92	Binghamton Rangers	AHL	43	25	15	3	2559	146	1	3.42	....	....	....	....	....	11	7	4	....	662	34	0	3.08	....	....	....	....
1992-93	New Haven Nighthawks	AHL	30	10	18	1	1688	121	1	4.30	....	....	....	....	....	....	....	....	....	....	....	....	....	....	....	....	....
	Brantford Smoke	ColHL	10	5	3	1	565	35	1	3.72	....	....	....	....	....	....	....	....	....	....	....	....	....	....	....	....	....
1993-94	**Ottawa Senators**	**NHL**	**5**	**0**	**2**	**0**	**182**	**17**	**0**	**5.60**	**5.34**	**9.92**	**96**	**.823**	**31.6**	....	....	....	....	....	....	....	....	....	....	....	....
	P.E.I. Senators	AHL	43	9	25	5	2359	161	0	4.09	....	....	....	....	....	....	....	....	....	....	....	....	....	....	....	....	....
1994-95	Milwaukee Admirals	IHL	42	19	13	7	2325	123	2	3.17	....	....	....	....	....	15	8	7	....	937	40	*2	2.56	....	....	....	....
1995-96	Milwaukee Admirals	IHL	53	26	20	7	3079	191	0	3.72	....	....	....	....	....	5	2	3	....	315	18	0	3.42	....	....	....	....
1996-97	Binghamton Rangers	AHL	9	0	4	1	393	26	0	3.97	....	....	....	....	....	....	....	....	....	....	....	....	....	....	....	....	....
	Utica Blizzard	ColHL	6	1	2	2	312	31	0	5.96	....	....	....	....	....	....	....	....	....	....	....	....	....	....	....	....	....
	NHL Totals		**103**	**25**	**54**	**4**	**5032**	**354**	**2**	**4.22**	....	....	**2689**	**.868**	....	**2**	**1**	**0**	....	**48**	**1**	**0**	**1.25**	....	....	....	....

Won Baz Bastien Memorial Trophy (Top Goaltender - AHL) (1987, 1991) • AHL Second All-Star Team (1991)

Signed as a free agent by **Detroit**, April 29, 1983. Traded to **Philadelphia** by **Detroit** for Philadelphia's 2nd round choice (Bob Wilkie) in 1987 Entry Draft, June 13, 1987. Traded to **Toronto** by **Philadelphia** for Toronto's 5th round choice (later traded to Winnipeg — Winnipeg selected Juha Ylonen) in 1991 Entry Draft and Philadelphia's 7th round choice (previously acquired, Philadelphia selected Andrei Lomakin) in 1991 Entry Draft, September 8, 1989. Traded to **NY Rangers** by **Toronto** with Tie Domi for Greg Johnston, June 28, 1990. Claimed by **Ottawa** from **NY Rangers** in Expansion Draft, June 18, 1992.

• LALIME, PATRICK

Patrick Lalime G – L. 6'2", 170 lbs. b: St. Bonaventure, Que., 7/7/1974. Pittsburgh's 6th choice, 156th overall, in 1993 Entry Draft.

Season	Club	League	GP	W	L	T	Mins	GA	SO	Avg	AAvg	Eff	SA	S%	SAPG	GP	W	L	T	Mins	GA	SO	Avg	Eff	SA	S%	SAPG
1992-93	Shawinigan Cataracts	QMJHL	44	10	24	4	2467	192	0	4.67	....	....	....	....	....	....	....	....	....	....	....	....	....	....	....	....	....
1993-94	Shawinigan Cataracts	QMJHL	48	22	20	0	2733	192	1	4.22	....	....	....	....	....	5	1	3	....	223	25	0	6.73	....	....	....	....
1994-95	Hampton Roads Admirals	ECHL	26	15	7	3	1470	82	2	3.35	....	....	....	....	....	....	....	....	....	....	....	....	....	....	....	....	....
	Cleveland Lumberjacks	IHL	23	7	10	4	1230	91	0	4.44	....	....	....	....	....	....	....	....	....	....	....	....	....	....	....	....	....
1995-96	Cleveland Lumberjacks	IHL	41	20	12	7	2314	149	0	3.86	....	....	....	....	....	....	....	....	....	....	....	....	....	....	....	....	....
1996-97	**Pittsburgh Penguins**	**NHL**	**39**	**21**	**12**	**2**	**2058**	**101**	**3**	**2.94**	**3.11**	**2.55**	**1166**	**.913**	**34.0**	....	....	....	....	....	....	....	....	....	....	....	....
	Cleveland Lumberjacks	IHL	14	6	6	2	834	45	1	3.24	....	....	....	....	....	....	....	....	....	....	....	....	....	....	....	....	....
1997-98	Grand Rapids Griffins	IHL	31	10	10	9	1749	76	2	2.61	....	....	....	....	....	1	0	1	....	77	4	0	3.11	....	....	....	....
	NHL Totals		**39**	**21**	**12**	**2**	**2058**	**101**	**3**	**2.94**	....	....	**1166**	**.913**	....	....	....	....	....	....	....	....	....	....	....	....	....

NHL All-Rookie Team (1997)

Rights traded to **Anaheim** by **Pittsburgh** for Sean Pronger, March 24, 1998.

• LANGKOW, SCOTT

Scott Langkow G – L. 5'11", 190 lbs. b: Sherwood Park, Alta., 4/21/1975. Winnipeg's 2nd choice, 31st overall, in 1993 Entry Draft.

Season	Club	League	GP	W	L	T	Mins	GA	SO	Avg	AAvg	Eff	SA	S%	SAPG	GP	W	L	T	Mins	GA	SO	Avg	Eff	SA	S%	SAPG
1991-92	Portland Winter Hawks	WHL	1	0	0	0	33	2	0	3.46	....	....	....	....	....	....	....	....	....	....	....	....	....	....	....	....	....
1992-93	Portland Winter Hawks	WHL	34	24	8	2	2064	110	2	3.40	....	....	....	....	....	9	6	3	....	535	31	0	3.48	....	....	....	....
1993-94	Portland Winter Hawks	WHL	39	27	9	1	2302	121	2	3.15	....	....	....	....	....	10	6	4	....	600	34	0	3.40	....	....	....	....
1994-95	Portland Winter Hawks	WHL	63	20	36	5	*3638	240	1	3.96	....	....	....	....	....	8	3	5	....	510	30	0	3.53	....	....	....	....
1995-96	**Winnipeg Jets**	**NHL**	**1**	**0**	**0**	**0**	**6**	**0**	**0**	**0.00**	**0.00**	**0.00**	**2**	**1.000**	**20.0**	....	....	....	....	....	....	....	....	....	....	....	....
	Springfield Falcons	AHL	39	18	15	6	2329	116	3	2.99	....	....	....	....	....	7	4	2	....	393	23	0	3.51	....	....	....	....
1996-97	Springfield Falcons	AHL	33	15	9	7	1929	85	0	2.64	....	....	....	....	....	....	....	....	....	....	....	....	....	....	....	....	....
1997-98	**Phoenix Coyotes**	**NHL**	**3**	**0**	**1**	**1**	**137**	**10**	**0**	**4.38**	**5.13**	**7.30**	**60**	**.833**	**26.3**	....	....	....	....	....	....	....	....	....	....	....	....
	Springfield Falcons	AHL	51	30	13	5	2874	128	3	2.67	....	....	....	....	....	4	1	3	....	216	14	0	3.88	....	....	....	....
	NHL Totals		**4**	**0**	**1**	**1**	**143**	**10**	**0**	**4.20**	....	....	**62**	**.839**	....	....	....	....	....	....	....	....	....	....	....	....	....

WHL West Second All-Star Team (1994, 1995) • Shared Harry "Hap" Holmes Memorial Trophy (fewest goals against - AHL) with Manny Legace (1996) • AHL First All-Star Team (1998) • Won Baz Bastien Memorial Trophy (Top Goaltender - AHL) (1998)

Transferred to **Phoenix** after **Winnipeg** franchise relocated, July 1, 1996.

• LAROCQUE, MICHEL

Michel "Bunny" Larocque G – L. 5'10", 185 lbs. b: Hull, Que., 4/6/1952. Deceased. Montreal's 2nd choice, 6th overall, in 1972 Amateur Draft.

Season	Club	League	GP	W	L	T	Mins	GA	SO	Avg	AAvg	Eff	SA	S%	SAPG	GP	W	L	T	Mins	GA	SO	Avg	Eff	SA	S%	SAPG
1967-68	Ottawa 67's	OHA	4	....	....	....	210	32	0	9.14	....	....	....	....	....	....	....	....	....	....	....	....	....	....	....	....	....
1968-69	Ottawa 67's	OHA	4	....	....	....	190	24	0	7.58	....	....	....	....	....	....	....	....	....	....	....	....	....	....	....	....	....
1969-70	Ottawa 67's	OHA	*51	....	....	....	*3060	185	*3	*3.63	....	....	....	....	....	....	....	....	....	....	....	....	....	....	....	....	....
1970-71	Ottawa 67's	OHA	56	....	....	....	3345	189	*5	3.39	....	....	....	....	....	....	....	....	....	....	....	....	....	....	....	....	....
1971-72	Ottawa 67's	OHA	55	....	....	....	3207	109	*4	*3.45	....	....	....	....	....	....	....	....	....	....	....	....	....	....	....	....	....
1972-73	Nova Scotia Voyageurs	AHL	47	....	....	....	2705	113	1	*2.50	....	....	....	....	....	*13	....	....	....	*760	36	0	2.84	....	....	....	....

			REGULAR SEASON													PLAYOFFS											
Season	Club	League	GP	W	L	T	Mins	GA	SO	Avg	AAvg	Eff	SA	S%	SAPG	GP	W	L	T	Mins	GA	SO	Avg	Eff	SA	S%	SAPG
1973-74	Montreal Canadiens	NHL	27	15	8	2	1431	69	0	2.89	2.79	....	....	....	....	6	2	4	....	364	18	0	2.97	....	....	....	....
1974-75	Montreal Canadiens	NHL	25	17	5	3	1480	74	3	3.00	2.70	....	....	....	....	....	....	....	....	....	....	....	....	....	....	....	....
1975-76	Montreal Canadiens	NHL	22	16	1	3	1220	50	2	2.46	2.22	....	....	....	....	....	....	....	....	....	....	....	....	....	....	....	....
1976-77	Montreal Canadiens	NHL	26	19	2	4	1525	53	4	*2.09	1.93	....	....	....	....	....	....	....	....	....	....	....	....	....	....	....	....
1977-78	Montreal Canadiens	NHL	30	22	3	4	1729	77	1	2.67	2.49	....	....	....	....	....	....	....	....	....	....	....	....	....	....	....	....
1978-79	Montreal Canadiens	NHL	34	22	7	4	1986	94	3	2.84	2.49	....	....	....	....	1	0	0	....	20	0	0	0.00	....	....	....	....
1979-80	Montreal Canadiens	NHL	39	17	13	8	2259	125	3	3.32	2.91	....	....	....	....	5	4	1	....	300	11	1	2.20	....	....	....	....
1980-81	Montreal Canadiens	NHL	28	16	9	3	1623	82	1	3.03	2.42	....	....	....	....	....	....	....	....	....	....	....	....	....	....	....	....
	Toronto Maple Leafs	NHL	8	3	3	2	460	40	0	5.22	4.19	....	....	....	....	2	0	1	....	75	8	0	6.40	....	....	....	....
1981-82	Toronto Maple Leafs	NHL	50	10	24	8	2647	207	0	4.69	3.63	....	....	....	....	....	....	....	....	....	....	....	....	....	....	....	....
1982-83	Toronto Maple Leafs	NHL	16	3	8	3	835	68	0	4.89	3.91	7.32	454	.850	32.6	....	....	....	....	....	....	....	....	....	....	....	....
	Philadelphia Flyers	NHL	2	0	1	1	120	8	0	4.00	3.19	5.71	56	.857	28.0	....	....	....	....	....	....	....	....	....	....	....	....
1983-84	Springfield Indians	AHL	5	3	2	0	301	21	0	4.18	....	....	....	....	....	....	....	....	....	....	....	....	....	....	....	....	....
	St. Louis Blues	NHL	5	0	5	0	300	31	0	6.20	4.86	11.72	164	.811	32.8	....	....	....	....	....	....	....	....	....	....	....	....
1984-85	Peoria Rivermen	IHL	13	7	3	3	786	41	0	3.13	....	....	....	....	....	....	....	....	....	....	....	....	....	....	....	....	....
	NHL Totals		312	160	89	45	17615	978	17	3.33	....	....	....	....	....	14	6	6	....	759	37	1	2.92	....	....	....	....

OHA Second All-Star Team (1971) • OHA First All-Star Team (1972) • AHL Second All-Star Team (1973) • Shared Harry "Hap" Holmes Memorial Award (fewest goals against - AHL) with Michel Deguise (1973) • Shared Vezina Trophy with Ken Dryden (1977, 1978, 1979) • Shared Vezina Trophy with Denis Herron and Richard Sevigny (1981)

Traded to **Toronto** by **Montreal** for Robert Picard, March 10, 1981. Traded to **Philadelphia** by **Toronto** for Rick St. Croix, January 11, 1983. Traded to **St. Louis** by **Philadelphia** for cash, January 5, 1984.

• LASKOWSKI, GARY

Gary Laskowski G – L. 6'1", 175 lbs. b: Ottawa, Ont., 6/6/1959.

Season	Club	League	GP	W	L	T	Mins	GA	SO	Avg	AAvg	Eff	SA	S%	SAPG	GP	W	L	T	Mins	GA	SO	Avg	Eff	SA	S%	SAPG
1978-79	St. Lawrence University	ECAC	21	5	15	0	1130	93	0	4.94	....	....	....	....	....	....	....	....	....	....	....	....	....	....	....	....	....
1979-80	St. Lawrence University	ECAC	17	3	13	0	904	72	0	4.78	....	....	....	....	....	....	....	....	....	....	....	....	....	....	....	....	....
1980-81	St. Lawrence University	ECAC	21	10	10	1	1196	64	0	3.21	....	....	....	....	....	....	....	....	....	....	....	....	....	....	....	....	....
1981-82	St. Lawrence University	ECAC	15	7	7	0	851	50	0	3.53	....	....	....	....	....	....	....	....	....	....	....	....	....	....	....	....	....
1982-83	Los Angeles Kings	NHL	46	15	20	4	2277	173	0	4.56	3.66	6.51	1212	.857	31.9	....	....	....	....	....	....	....	....	....	....	....	....
1983-84	Los Angeles Kings	NHL	13	4	7	1	665	55	0	4.96	3.89	8.50	321	.829	29.0	....	....	....	....	....	....	....	....	....	....	....	....
	New Haven Nighthawks	AHL	22	....	....	....	1179	97	0	4.94	....	....	....	....	....	....	....	....	....	....	....	....	....	....	....	....	....
	NHL Totals		59	19	27	5	2942	228	0	4.65	....	....	1533	.851	....	....	....	....	....	....	....	....	....	....	....	....	....

Signed as a free agent by **LA Kings**, October 22, 1982.

• LAXTON, GORD

Gord Laxton G – L. 5'10", 195 lbs. b: Montreal, Que., 3/16/1955. Pittsburgh's 1st choice, 13th overall, in 1975 Amateur Draft.

Season	Club	League	GP	W	L	T	Mins	GA	SO	Avg	AAvg	Eff	SA	S%	SAPG	GP	W	L	T	Mins	GA	SO	Avg	Eff	SA	S%	SAPG
1973-74	New Westminster Bruins	WCJHL	25	....	....	....	1350	75	0	3.33	....	....	....	....	....	4	....	....	....	126	14	0	6.67	....	....	....	....
1974-75	New Westminster Bruins	WCJHL	70	....	....	....	3980	239	3	3.60	....	....	....	....	....	18	....	....	....	1081	67	0	3.71	....	....	....	....
1975-76	Pittsburgh Penguins	NHL	8	3	4	0	414	31	0	4.49	4.07	....	....	....	....	....	....	....	....	....	....	....	....	....	....	....	....
	Hershey Bears	AHL	31	16	11	4	1857	104	0	3.36	....	....	....	....	....	*6	4	2	0	*309	19	0	3.69	....	....	....	....
1976-77	Pittsburgh Penguins	NHL	6	1	3	0	253	26	0	6.17	5.75	....	....	....	....	....	....	....	....	....	....	....	....	....	....	....	....
	Hershey Bears	AHL	18	4	11	0	958	80	0	5.01	....	....	....	....	....	....	....	....	....	....	....	....	....	....	....	....	....
1977-78	Pittsburgh Penguins	NHL	2	0	1	0	73	9	0	7.40	6.94	....	....	....	....	....	....	....	....	....	....	....	....	....	....	....	....
	Grand Rapids Owls	IHL	45	....	....	....	2651	183	0	4.14	....	....	....	....	....	....	....	....	....	....	....	....	....	....	....	....	....
1978-79	Pittsburgh Penguins	NHL	1	0	1	0	60	8	0	8.00	7.07	....	....	....	....	....	....	....	....	....	....	....	....	....	....	....	....
	Grand Rapids Owls	IHL	63	....	....	....	3742	192	3	3.08	....	....	....	....	....	19	10	9	0	1178	81	1	4.13	....	....	....	....
1979-80	Syracuse Firebirds	AHL	2	0	1	0	69	11	0	9.56	....	....	....	....	....	....	....	....	....	....	....	....	....	....	....	....	....
	Grand Rapids Owls	IHL	20	....	....	....	1197	90	0	4.51	....	....	....	....	....	....	....	....	....	....	....	....	....	....	....	....	....
1980-81	Binghamton Whalers	AHL	2	0	2	0	118	12	0	6.10	....	....	....	....	....	....	....	....	....	....	....	....	....	....	....	....	....
	Port Huron Flags	IHL	52	....	....	....	2923	207	0	4.25	....	....	....	....	....	3	0	3	0	191	12	0	3.77	....	....	....	....
1981-82	Erie Blades	AHL	31	2	23	1	1672	172	0	6.17	....	....	....	....	....	....	....	....	....	....	....	....	....	....	....	....	....
	Muskegon Mohawks	IHL	3	....	....	....	175	11	0	3.71	....	....	....	....	....	....	....	....	....	....	....	....	....	....	....	....	....
1982-83	Muskegon Mohawks	IHL	40	....	....	....	2326	158	1	4.08	....	....	....	....	....	2	1	1	0	120	8	0	4.00	....	....	....	....
	NHL Totals		17	4	9	0	800	74	0	5.55	....	....	....	....	....	....	....	....	....	....	....	....	....	....	....	....	....

IHL First All-Star Team (1979) • Won James Norris Memorial Trophy (fewest goals against - IHL) (1979)

• LEBLANC, RAYMOND

Raymond LeBlanc G – R. 5'10", 170 lbs. b: Fitchburg, MA, 10/24/1964.

Season	Club	League	GP	W	L	T	Mins	GA	SO	Avg	AAvg	Eff	SA	S%	SAPG	GP	W	L	T	Mins	GA	SO	Avg	Eff	SA	S%	SAPG
1983-84	Kitchener Rangers	OHL	*54	*39	7	1	2965	185	1	3.74	....	....	....	....	....	....	....	....	....	....	....	....	....	....	....	....	....
1984-85	Pinebridge Bucks	ACHL	40	....	....	....	2178	150	0	4.13	....	....	....	....	....	....	....	....	....	....	....	....	....	....	....	....	....
1985-86	Carolina Thunderbirds	ACHL	42	....	....	....	2505	133	3	3.19	....	....	....	....	....	....	....	....	....	....	....	....	....	....	....	....	....
1986-87	Flint Spirits	IHL	64	33	23	1	3417	222	0	3.90	....	....	....	....	....	4	1	3	....	233	17	0	4.38	....	....	....	....
1987-88	Flint Spirits	IHL	62	27	19	8	3269	239	1	4.39	....	....	....	....	....	16	10	6	....	925	55	1	3.57	....	....	....	....
1988-89	Flint Spirits	IHL	15	5	9	0	852	67	0	4.72	....	....	....	....	....	....	....	....	....	....	....	....	....	....	....	....	....
	New Haven Nighthawks	AHL	1	0	0	0	20	3	0	9.00	....	....	....	....	....	....	....	....	....	....	....	....	....	....	....	....	....
	Saginaw Hawks	IHL	29	19	7	2	1655	99	0	3.59	....	....	....	....	....	1	0	1	....	5	9	0	3.05	....	....	....	....
1989-90	Indianapolis Ice	IHL	23	15	6	2	1334	71	2	3.19	....	....	....	....	....	....	....	....	....	....	....	....	....	....	....	....	....
	Fort Wayne Komets	IHL	15	3	3	3	680	44	0	3.88	....	....	....	....	....	3	0	2	....	139	11	0	4.75	....	....	....	....
1990-91	Fort Wayne Komets	IHL	21	10	8	0	1072	69	0	3.86	....	....	....	....	....	....	....	....	....	....	....	....	....	....	....	....	....
	Indianapolis Ice	IHL	3	2	0	0	145	7	0	2.90	....	....	....	....	....	1	0	0	....	19	1	0	3.20	....	....	....	....
1991-92	United States	Nat-Team	17	5	10	1	891	54	0	3.63	....	....	....	....	....	....	....	....	....	....	....	....	....	....	....	....	....
	Chicago Blackhawks	NHL	1	1	0	0	60	1	0	1.00	0.89	0.45	22	.955	22.0	....	....	....	....	....	....	....	....	....	....	....	....
	Indianapolis Ice	IHL	25	14	9	2	1468	84	2	3.43	....	....	....	....	....	....	....	....	....	....	....	....	....	....	....	....	....
1992-93	Indianapolis Ice	IHL	56	23	22	7	3201	206	0	3.86	....	....	....	....	....	5	1	4	....	276	23	0	5.00	....	....	....	....
1993-94	Indianapolis Ice	IHL	2	0	1	0	112	8	0	4.25	....	....	....	....	....	....	....	....	....	....	....	....	....	....	....	....	....
	Cincinnati Cyclones	IHL	34	17	9	3	1779	104	1	3.51	....	....	....	....	....	5	0	3	....	159	9	0	3.39	....	....	....	....
1994-95	Chicago Wolves	IHL	44	19	14	6	2375	129	1	3.26	....	....	....	....	....	3	0	3	....	177	14	0	4.73	....	....	....	....
1995-96	Chicago Wolves	IHL	31	10	14	2	1614	97	0	3.61	....	....	....	....	....	....	....	....	....	....	....	....	....	....	....	....	....
1996-97	Chicago Wolves	IHL	38	15	14	2	1911	103	2	3.23	....	....	....	....	....	....	....	....	....	....	....	....	....	....	....	....	....
1997-98	Chicago Wolves	IHL	14	9	3	0	728	34	0	2.80	....	....	....	....	....	....	....	....	....	....	....	....	....	....	....	....	....
	Flint Generals	UHL	29	12	4	5	1303	79	2	3.64	....	....	....	....	....	....	....	....	....	....	....	....	....	....	....	....	....
	NHL Totals		1	1	0	0	60	1	0	1.00	....	....	22	.955	....	....	....	....	....	....	....	....	....	....	....	....	....

IHL Second All-Star Team (1987)

Signed as a free agent by **Chicago**, July 5, 1989.

• LEDUC, ALBERT

Albert "Battleship" LeDuc G – R. 5'9", 180 lbs. b: Valleyfield, Que., 11/22/1902.

Season	Club	League	GP	W	L	T	Mins	GA	SO	Avg	AAvg	Eff	SA	S%	SAPG	GP	W	L	T	Mins	GA	SO	Avg	Eff	SA	S%	SAPG
1931-32	Montreal Canadiens	NHL	1	0	0	0	2	1	0	30.00	36.92	....	....	....	....	....	....	....	....	....	....	....	....	....	....	....	....
	NHL Totals		1	0	0	0	2	1	0	30.00	....	....	....	....	....	....	....	....	....	....	....	....	....	....	....	....	....

• Montreal Canadiens' defenseman replaced penalized George Hainsworth, December 2, 1931. (Chicago 2, Montreal Canadiens 1)

• LEGRIS, CLAUDE

Claude Legris G – L. 5'9", 160 lbs. b: Verdun, Que., 11/6/1956. Detroit's 8th choice, 120th overall, in 1976 Amateur Draft.

Season	Club	League	GP	W	L	T	Mins	GA	SO	Avg	AAvg	Eff	SA	S%	SAPG	GP	W	L	T	Mins	GA	SO	Avg	Eff	SA	S%	SAPG
1972-73	Sorel Eperviers	QMJHL	26	....	....	....	1530	156	0	6.12	....	....	....	....	....	5	....	....	....	300	36	0	7.20	....	....	....	....
1973-74	Sorel Eperviers	QMJHL	48	....	....	....	2880	216	*2	4.50	....	....	....	....	....	12	....	....	....	680	53	0	4.68	....	....	....	....
1974-75	Sorel Eperviers	QMJHL	47	....	....	....	2513	231	0	5.52	....	....	....	....	....	....	....	....	....	....	....	....	....	....	....	....	....
1975-76	Sorel Eperviers	QMJHL	67	....	....	....	3862	301	0	4.68	....	....	....	....	....	5	....	....	....	300	23	0	4.60	....	....	....	....
1976-77	Campbellton Tigers	NNBHL	STATISTICS NOT AVAILABLE																								
1977-78	Campbellton Tigers	NNBSL	1	1	0	0	60	1	0	1.00	....	....	....	....	....	4	....	....	....	232	13	0	3.36	....	....	....	....
	Bathurst Alpines	NNBSL	....	....	....	....	....	....	....	....	....	....	....	....	....	1	....	....	....	60	1	0	1.00	....	....	....	....
1978-79	Kalamazoo Wings	IHL	16	....	....	....	730	55	0	4.52	....	....	....	....	....	....	....	....	....	....	....	....	....	....	....	....	....
1979-80	Adirondack Red Wings	AHL	17	3	6	5	898	64	0	4.27	....	....	....	....	....	....	....	....	....	....	....	....	....	....	....	....	....
	Johnstown Red Wings	EHL	1	....	....	....	33	4	0	7.27	....	....	....	....	....	....	....	....	....	....	....	....	....	....	....	....	....

Season	Club	League	GP	W	L	T	Mins	GA	SO	Avg	AAvg	Eff	SA	S%	SAPG	GP	W	L	T	Mins	GA	SO	Avg	Eff	SA	S%	SAPG
			REGULAR SEASON													PLAYOFFS											
1980-81	**Detroit Red Wings**	**NHL**	**3**	**0**	**1**	**0**	**63**	**4**	**0**	**3.81**	**3.05**	....	....	....	....	....	....	....	....	....	....	....	....	....	....	....	....
	Adirondack Red Wings	AHL	2	1	1	0	120	7	0	3.50	....	....	....	....	....	....	....	....	....	....	....	....	....	....	....	....	....
	Kalamazoo Wings	IHL	52	....	....	....	3010	154	5	3.07	....	....	....	....	....	6	2	2	0	251	17	1	4.06	....	....	....	....
1981-82	**Detroit Red Wings**	**NHL**	**1**	**0**	**0**	**1**	**28**	**0**	**0**	**0.00**	**0.00**	....	....	....	....	....	....	....	....	....	....	....	....	....	....	....	....
	Springfield Indians	AHL	18	7	9	1	1002	71	0	4.25	....	....	....	....	....	....	....	....	....	....	....	....	....	....	....	....	....
	Kalamazoo Wings	IHL	7	....	....	....	396	28	0	4.24	....	....	....	....	....	....	....	....	....	....	....	....	....	....	....	....	....
1982-83	Adirondack Red Wings	AHL	32	11	12	2	1680	118	0	4.21	....	....	....	....	....	....	....	....	....	....	....	....	....	....	....	....	....
	NHL Totals		**4**	**0**	**1**	**1**	**91**	**4**	**0**	**2.64**	....	....	....	....	....	....	....	....	....	....	....	....	....	....	....	....	....

QMJHL East Division Second All-Star Team (1976) • IHL First All-Star Team (1981) • Shared James Norris Memorial Trophy (fewest goals against - IHL) with Georges Gagnon (1981)

• LEHMAN, HUGH

Hugh Lehman G – L. 5'8", 168 lbs. b: Pembroke, Ont., 10/27/1885. d: 4/8/1961.

Season	Club	League	GP	W	L	T	Mins	GA	SO	Avg	AAvg	Eff	SA	S%	SAPG	GP	W	L	T	Mins	GA	SO	Avg	Eff	SA	S%	SAPG
1903-04	Pembroke Lumber Kings	Ott-Sr.	5	1	4	0	300	22	0	....	....	....	....	....	....	....	....	....	....	....	....	....	....	....	....	....	....
1904-05	Pembroke Lumber Kings	Ott-Sr.		STATISTICS NOT AVAILABLE																							
1905-06	Pembroke Lumber Kings	Ott-Sr.	8	*8	0	0	480	13	*1	*1.67	....	....	....	....	....	1	1	0	0	60	0	1	0.00	....	....	....	....
1906-07	Canadian Soo	IHL	24	13	11	0	1440	123	0	5.13	....	....	....	....	....	....	....	....	....	....	....	....	....	....	....	....	....
1907-08	Pembroke Lumber Kings	OVHL		STATISTICS NOT AVAILABLE																							
1908-09	Berlin Professionals	OPHL	15	9	6	0	890	72	0	4.85	....	....	....	....	....	....	....	....	....	....	....	....	....	....	....	....	....
1909-10	Berlin Professionals	OPHL	17	*11	6	0	1020	74	1	*4.35	....	....	....	....	....	1	0	1	0	60	7	0	7.00	....	....	....	....
	Galt Professionals	OPHL	....	....	....	....	....	....	....	....	....	....	....	....	....	2	0	2	0	120	15	0	7.50	....	....	....	....
1910-11	Berlin Professionals	OPHL	15	7	8	0	900	87	0	5.80	....	....	....	....	....	....	....	....	....	....	....	....	....	....	....	....	....
1911-12	New Westminster Royals	PCHA	15	*9	6	0	911	77	0	*5.07	....	....	....	....	....	....	....	....	....	....	....	....	....	....	....	....	....
1912-13	New Westminster Royals	PCHA	12	4	8	0	739	51	0	4.14	....	....	....	....	....	....	....	....	....	....	....	....	....	....	....	....	....
1913-14	New Westminster Royals	PCHA	16	7	9	0	997	81	0	4.87	....	....	....	....	....	....	....	....	....	....	....	....	....	....	....	....	....
1914-15	Vancouver Millionaires	PCHA	17	*14	3	0	1043	71	*1	*4.08	....	....	....	....	....	3	*3	0	0	180	8	0	2.67	....	....	....	....
1915-16	Vancouver Millionaires	PCHA	18	9	9	0	1091	69	0	3.79	....	....	....	....	....	....	....	....	....	....	....	....	....	....	....	....	....
1916-17	Vancouver Millionaires	PCHA	23	14	9	0	1404	124	0	5.30	....	....	....	....	....	....	....	....	....	....	....	....	....	....	....	....	....
1917-18	Vancouver Millionaires	PCHA	18	9	9	0	1179	60	*1	*3.05	....	....	....	....	....	7	3	3	1	420	14	1	2.86	....	....	....	....
1918-19	Vancouver Millionaires	PCHA	20	*12	8	0	1277	55	1	2.58	....	....	....	....	....	2	1	1	0	120	7	0	3.50	....	....	....	....
1919-20	Vancouver Millionaires	PCHA	22	11	11	0	1334	65	1	2.92	....	....	....	....	....	2	1	1	0	120	7	0	3.50	....	....	....	....
1920-21	Vancouver Millionaires	PCHA	24	13	11	0	1449	79	*3	3.27	....	....	....	....	....	7	4	3	0	420	14	1	2.00	....	....	....	....
1921-22	Vancouver Millionaires	PCHA	22	*12	10	0	1318	62	*4	2.82	....	....	....	....	....	9	5	4	0	545	18	4	1.98	....	....	....	....
1922-23	Vancouver Maroons	PCHA	25	*16	8	1	1571	61	*5	*2.33	....	....	....	....	....	6	2	4	0	360	13	1	2.17	....	....	....	....
1923-24	Vancouver Maroons	PCHA	*30	13	16	1	*1846	81	1	*2.63	....	....	....	....	....	7	2	4	1	434	18	0	2.49	....	....	....	....
1924-25	Vancouver Maroons	WCHL	11	7	4	0	663	29	0	2.62	....	....	....	....	....	....	....	....	....	....	....	....	....	....	....	....	....
1925-26	Vancouver Maroons	WHL	*30	10	18	2	1839	89	3	2.90	....	....	....	....	....	....	....	....	....	....	....	....	....	....	....	....	....
1926-27	**Chicago Black Hawks**	**NHL**	***44**	**19**	**22**	**3**	***2797**	**116**	**5**	**2.49**	**3.96**	....	....	....	....	**2**	**0**	**1**	**1**	**120**	**10**	**0**	**5.00**	....	....	....	....
1927-28	**Chicago Black Hawks**	**NHL**	**4**	**1**	**2**	**1**	**250**	**20**	**1**	**4.80**	**7.91**	....	....	....	....	....	....	....	....	....	....	....	....	....	....	....	....
	NHL Totals		**48**	**20**	**24**	**4**	**3047**	**136**	**6**	**2.68**	....	....	....	....	....	**2**	**0**	**1**	**1**	**120**	**10**	**0**	**5.00**	....	....	....	....
	Other Major League Totals		374	200	170	4	22911	1410	21	3.69	....	....	....	....	....	46	21	23	2	2779	121	7	2.61	....	....	....	....

PCHA All-Star Team (1912 , 1914, 1915, 1924) • PCHA First All-Star Team (1916, 1918, 1919, 1920, 1921, 1922, 1923)

Traded to **Chicago** by **Vancouver** (WHL) for cash, October 9, 1926.

• LEMELIN, REGGIE

Reggie Lemelin G – L. 5'11", 170 lbs. b: Quebec City, Que., 11/19/1954. Philadelphia's 6th choice, 125th overall, in 1974 Amateur Draft.

Season	Club	League	GP	W	L	T	Mins	GA	SO	Avg	AAvg	Eff	SA	S%	SAPG	GP	W	L	T	Mins	GA	SO	Avg	Eff	SA	S%	SAPG
1972-73	Sherbrooke Castors	QMJHL	28	....	....	....	1600	140	0	5.28	....	....	....	....	....	2	....	....	....	120	12	0	6.00	....	....	....	....
1973-74	Sherbrooke Castors	QMJHL	35	....	....	....	2060	158	0	4.60	....	....	....	....	....	1	....	....	....	60	3	0	3.00	....	....	....	....
1974-75	Philadelphia Firebirds	NAHL	43	21	16	2	2277	131	3	3.45	....	....	....	....	....	....	....	....	....	....	....	....	....	....	....	....	....
1975-76	Richmond Robins	AHL	7	....	....	....	402	30	0	4.48	....	....	....	....	....	....	....	....	....	....	....	....	....	....	....	....	....
	Philadelphia Firebirds	NAHL	29	....	....	....	1601	97	1	3.63	....	....	....	....	....	3	....	....	....	171	15	0	5.26	....	....	....	....
1976-77	Springfield Indians	AHL	3	2	1	0	180	10	0	3.33	....	....	....	....	....	....	....	....	....	....	....	....	....	....	....	....	....
	Philadelphia Firebirds	NAHL	51	26	19	1	2763	170	1	3.61	....	....	....	....	....	3	....	....	....	191	14	0	4.40	....	....	....	....
1977-78	Philadelphia Firebirds	AHL	*60	31	21	7	*3585	177	4	2.90	....	....	....	....	....	2	0	2	0	119	12	0	6.05	....	....	....	....
1978-79	**Atlanta Flames**	**NHL**	**18**	**8**	**8**	**1**	**994**	**55**	**0**	**3.32**	**2.93**	....	....	....	....	**1**	**0**	**0**	....	**20**	**0**	**0**	**0.00**	....	....	....	....
	Philadelphia Firebirds	AHL	13	3	9	1	780	36	0	2.77	....	....	....	....	....	....	....	....	....	....	....	....	....	....	....	....	....
1979-80	**Atlanta Flames**	**NHL**	**3**	**0**	**2**	**0**	**150**	**15**	**0**	**6.00**	**5.28**	....	....	....	....	....	....	....	....	....	....	....	....	....	....	....	....
	Birmingham Bulls	CHL	38	13	21	2	2188	137	0	3.76	....	....	....	....	....	2	0	1	0	79	5	0	3.80	....	....	....	....
1980-81	**Calgary Flames**	**NHL**	**29**	**14**	**6**	**7**	**1629**	**88**	**2**	**3.24**	**2.59**	....	....	....	....	**6**	**3**	**3**	....	**366**	**22**	**0**	**3.61**	....	....	....	....
	Birmingham Bulls	CHL	13	3	8	2	757	56	0	4.44	....	....	....	....	....	....	....	....	....	....	....	....	....	....	....	....	....
1981-82	**Calgary Flames**	**NHL**	**34**	**10**	**15**	**6**	**1866**	**135**	**0**	**4.34**	**3.35**	....	....	....	....	....	....	....	....	....	....	....	....	....	....	....	....
1982-83	**Calgary Flames**	**NHL**	**39**	**16**	**12**	**8**	**2211**	**133**	**0**	**3.61**	**2.80**	**4.03**	**1192**	**.888**	**32.3**	**7**	**3**	**3**	....	**327**	**27**	**0**	**4.95**	....	....	....	....
1983-84	**Calgary Flames**	**NHL**	**51**	**21**	**12**	**9**	**2568**	**150**	**0**	**3.50**	**2.73**	**3.74**	**1405**	**.893**	**32.8**	**8**	**4**	**4**	....	**448**	**32**	**0**	**4.29**	**4.73**	**290**	**.890**	**38.8**
1984-85	**Calgary Flames**	**NHL**	**56**	**30**	**12**	**10**	**3176**	**183**	**1**	**3.46**	**2.74**	**3.87**	**1638**	**.888**	**30.9**	**4**	**1**	**3**	....	**248**	**15**	**1**	**3.63**	**4.25**	**128**	**.883**	**31.0**
1985-86	**Calgary Flames**	**NHL**	**60**	**29**	**24**	**4**	**3369**	**229**	**1**	**4.08**	**3.18**	**5.23**	**1787**	**.872**	**31.8**	**3**	**0**	**1**	....	**109**	**7**	**0**	**3.85**	**5.61**	**48**	**.854**	**26.4**
1986-87	**Calgary Flames**	**NHL**	**34**	**16**	**9**	**1**	**1735**	**94**	**2**	**3.25**	**2.73**	**3.70**	**825**	**.886**	**28.5**	**2**	**0**	**1**	....	**101**	**6**	**0**	**3.56**	**4.54**	**47**	**.872**	**27.9**
1987-88	**Boston Bruins**	**NHL**	**49**	**24**	**17**	**6**	**2828**	**138**	**3**	**2.93**	**2.42**	**3.25**	**1244**	**.889**	**26.4**	**17**	**11**	**6**	....	**1027**	**45**	***1**	***2.63**	**2.75**	**430**	**.895**	**25.1**
1988-89	**Boston Bruins**	**NHL**	**40**	**19**	**15**	**6**	**2392**	**120**	**0**	**3.01**	**2.47**	**3.40**	**1061**	**.887**	**26.6**	**4**	**1**	**3**	....	**252**	**16**	**0**	**3.81**	**5.44**	**112**	**.857**	**26.7**
1989-90	**Boston Bruins**	**NHL**	**43**	**22**	**15**	**2**	**2310**	**108**	**2**	**2.81**	**2.34**	**3.03**	**1002**	**.892**	**26.0**	**3**	**0**	**1**	....	**135**	**13**	**0**	**5.78**	**13.18**	**57**	**.772**	**25.3**
1990-91	**Boston Bruins**	**NHL**	**33**	**17**	**10**	**3**	**1829**	**111**	**1**	**3.64**	**3.25**	**4.80**	**841**	**.868**	**27.6**	**2**	**0**	**0**	....	**32**	**0**	**0**	**0.00**	**0.00**	**18**	**1.000**	**33.8**
1991-92	**Boston Bruins**	**NHL**	**8**	**5**	**1**	**0**	**407**	**23**	**0**	**3.39**	**3.01**	**3.71**	**210**	**.890**	**31.0**	**2**	**0**	**0**	....	**54**	**3**	**0**	**3.33**	**4.34**	**23**	**.870**	**25.6**
1992-93	**Boston Bruins**	**NHL**	**10**	**5**	**4**	**0**	**542**	**31**	**0**	**3.43**	**2.92**	**4.73**	**225**	**.862**	**24.9**	....	....	....	....	....	....	....	....	....	....	....	....
	NHL Totals		**507**	**236**	**162**	**63**	**28006**	**1613**	**12**	**3.46**	....	....	....	....	....	**59**	**23**	**25**	....	**3119**	**186**	**2**	**3.58**	....	....	....	....

AHL First All-Star Team (1978) • Shared William M. Jennings Trophy with Andy Moog (1990)

Played in NHL All-Star Game (1989)

Signed as a free agent by **Atlanta**, August 17, 1978. Transferred to **Calgary** after **Atlanta** franchise relocated, June 24, 1980. Signed as a free agent by **Boston**, August 13, 1987.

• LENARDUZZI, MIKE

Mike Lenarduzzi G – L. 6'1", 165 lbs. b: London, Ont., 9/14/1972. Hartford's 3rd choice, 57th overall, in 1990 Entry Draft.

Season	Club	League	GP	W	L	T	Mins	GA	SO	Avg	AAvg	Eff	SA	S%	SAPG	GP	W	L	T	Mins	GA	SO	Avg	Eff	SA	S%	SAPG
1988-89	Oshawa Generals	OHL	6	0	0	2	166	9	0	3.25	....	....	....	....	....	....	....	....	....	....	....	....	....	....	....	....	....
1989-90	Oshawa Generals	OHL	12	6	3	1	444	32	0	4.32	....	....	....	....	....	....	....	....	....	....	....	....	....	....	....	....	....
	Sault Ste. Marie Greyhounds	OHL	20	8	8	2	1117	66	0	3.55	....	....	....	....	....	....	....	....	....	....	....	....	....	....	....	....	....
1990-91	Sault Ste. Marie Greyhounds	OHL	35	19	8	3	1966	107	0	3.27	....	....	....	....	....	5	3	1	....	268	13	*1	2.91	....	....	....	....
1991-92	Sault Ste. Marie Greyhounds	OHL	9	5	3	0	486	33	0	4.07	....	....	....	....	....	....	....	....	....	....	....	....	....	....	....	....	....
	Ottawa 67's	OHL	18	5	12	1	986	60	1	3.65	....	....	....	....	....	....	....	....	....	....	....	....	....	....	....	....	....
	Sudbury Wolves	OHL	22	11	5	4	1201	84	2	4.20	....	....	....	....	....	11	4	7	....	651	38	0	3.50	....	....	....	....
	Springfield Indians	AHL	....	....	....	....	....	....	....	....	....	....	....	....	....	1	0	0	....	39	2	0	3.08	....	....	....	....
1992-93	**Hartford Whalers**	**NHL**	**3**	**1**	**1**	**1**	**168**	**9**	**0**	**3.21**	**2.73**	**3.32**	**87**	**.897**	**31.1**	....	....	....	....	....	....	....	....	....	....	....	....
	Springfield Indians	AHL	36	10	17	5	1945	142	0	4.38	....	....	....	....	....	2	1	0	....	100	5	0	3.00	....	....	....	....
1993-94	**Hartford Whalers**	**NHL**	**1**	**0**	**0**	**0**	**21**	**1**	**0**	**2.86**	**2.72**	**2.00**	**12**	**.917**	**34.3**	....	....	....	....	....	....	....	....	....	....	....	....
	Springfield Indians	AHL	22	5	7	2	984	73	0	4.45	....	....	....	....	....	....	....	....	....	....	....	....	....	....	....	....	....
	Salt Lake Golden Eagles	IHL	4	0	4	0	211	22	0	6.25	....	....	....	....	....	....	....	....	....	....	....	....	....	....	....	....	....
1994-95	London Wildcats	ColHL	43	19	16	0	2198	172	0	4.69	....	....	....	....	....	5	1	2	....	274	20	0	4.37	....	....	....	....
1995-96	Saginaw Wheels	ColHL	43	14	15	3	2153	155	0	4.32	....	....	....	....	....	5	1	4	....	299	19	0	3.82	....	....	....	....
1996-97	Hershey Bears	AHL	2	0	0	0	13	0	0	0.00	....	....	....	....	....	....	....	....	....	....	....	....	....	....	....	....	....
	Mobile Mystics	ECHL	37	15	10	8	1032	110	1	3.66	....	....	....	....	....	1	0	1	....	60	4	0	4.00	....	....	....	....
1997-98	Mobile Mystics	ECHL	44	21	13	2	2201	122	2	3.32	....	....	....	....	....	3	0	2	....	133	11	0	4.96	....	....	....	....
	NHL Totals		**4**	**1**	**1**	**1**	**189**	**10**	**0**	**3.17**	....	....	**99**	**.899**	....	....	....	....	....	....	....	....	....	....	....	....	....

• LESSARD, MARIO

Mario Lessard G – L. 5'9", 190 lbs. b: East Broughton, Que., 6/25/1954. Los Angeles' 7th choice, 154th overall, in 1974 Amateur Draft.

Season	Club	League	GP	W	L	T	Mins	GA	SO	Avg	AAvg	Eff	SA	S%	SAPG	GP	W	L	T	Mins	GA	SO	Avg	Eff	SA	S%	SAPG
1971-72	Sherbrooke Castors	QMJHL	17	....	....	....	1020	72	2	4.24	....	....	....	....	....	3	0	2	0	133	24	0	10.83	....	....	....	....
1972-73	Sherbrooke Castors	QMJHL	37	....	....	....	2180	161	0	4.43	....	....	....	....	....	6	....	....	....	360	24	0	4.00	....	....	....	....
1973-74	Sherbrooke Castors	QMJHL	36	....	....	....	2140	180	0	5.05	....	....	....	....	....	4	....	....	....	240	24	0	6.00	....	....	....	....
1974-75	Saginaw Gears	IHL	59	....	....	....	3186	171	4	3.22	....	....	....	....	....	17	10	7	0	1016	64	2	3.78	....	....	....	....

Season	Club	League	GP	W	L	T	Mins	GA	SO	Avg	AAvg	Eff	SA	S%	SAPG	GP	W	L	T	Mins	GA	SO	Avg	Eff	SA	S%	SAPG
			REGULAR SEASON													PLAYOFFS											
1975-76	Saginaw Gears	IHL	62	....	....	....	3323	187	3	3.38	....	....	....	....	....	12	7	5	0	722	31	1	2.58	....	....	....	....
1976-77	Fort Worth Texans	CHL	4	1	3	0	192	11	0	3.44	....	....	....	....	....	....	....	....	....	....	....	....	....	....	....	....	....
	Saginaw Gears	IHL	44	....	....	....	2489	144	0	3.47	....	....	....	....	....	18	12	6	0	1059	52	1	2.95	....	....	....	....
1977-78	Springfield Indians	AHL	57	30	19	6	3295	204	1	3.71	....	....	....	....	....	4	1	3	0	239	10	*1	2.51	....	....	....	....
1978-79	**Los Angeles Kings**	**NHL**	**49**	**23**	**15**	**10**	**2860**	**148**	**4**	**3.10**	**2.72**	....	....	....	....	**2**	**0**	**2**	....	**126**	**8**	**0**	**3.81**	....	....	....	....
1979-80	**Los Angeles Kings**	**NHL**	**50**	**18**	**22**	**7**	**2836**	**185**	**0**	**3.91**	**3.45**	....	....	....	....	**4**	**1**	**2**	....	**207**	**14**	**0**	**4.06**	....	....	....	....
1980-81	**Los Angeles Kings**	**NHL**	**64**	***35**	**18**	**11**	**3746**	**203**	**2**	**3.25**	**2.59**	....	....	....	....	**4**	**1**	**3**	....	**220**	**20**	**0**	**5.45**	....	....	....	....
1981-82	**Los Angeles Kings**	**NHL**	**52**	**13**	**28**	**8**	**2933**	**213**	**2**	**4.36**	**3.37**	....	....	....	....	**10**	**4**	**5**	....	**583**	**41**	**0**	**4.22**	....	....	....	....
1982-83	**Los Angeles Kings**	**NHL**	**19**	**3**	**10**	**2**	**888**	**68**	**1**	**4.59**	**3.67**	**7.23**	**432**	**.843**	**29.2**	....	....	....	....	....	....	....	....	....	....	....	....
	Birmingham South Stars	CHL	8	4	2	0	405	28	0	4.15	....	....	....	....	....	*11	6	3	0	*637	35	0	3.30	....	....	....	....
1983-84	**Los Angeles Kings**	**NHL**	**6**	**0**	**4**	**1**	**266**	**26**	**0**	**5.86**	**4.59**	**9.52**	**160**	**.838**	**36.1**	....	....	....	....	....	....	....	....	....	....	....	....
	New Haven Nighthawks	AHL	5	1	3	1	281	27	0	5.77	....	....	....	....	....	....	....	....	....	....	....	....	....	....	....	....	....
	NHL Totals		**240**	**92**	**97**	**39**	**13529**	**843**	**9**	**3.74**	....	....	....	....	....	**20**	**6**	**12**	....	**1136**	**83**	**0**	**4.38**	....	....	....	....

IHL First All-Star Team (1977) • AHL Second All-Star Team (1978) • NHL Second All-Star Team (1981)

Played in NHL All-Star Game (1981)

• LEVASSEUR, JEAN-LOUIS

Jean-Louis Levasseur G – L. 5′10″, 160 lbs. b: Noranda, Que., 6/16/1949.

Season	Club	League	GP	W	L	T	Mins	GA	SO	Avg	AAvg	Eff	SA	S%	SAPG	GP	W	L	T	Mins	GA	SO	Avg	Eff	SA	S%	SAPG
1972-73	Orillia Terriers	OHA Sr.	35	....	....	....	2100	114	1	3.26	....	....	....	....	....	....	....	....	....	....	....	....	....	....	....	....	....
	Tulsa Oilers	CHL	4	....	....	....	169	13	1	4.62	....	....	....	....	....	....	....	....	....	....	....	....	....	....	....	....	....
1973-74	Orillia Terriers	OHA Sr.	14	....	....	....	840	48	1	3.43	....	....	....	....	....	....	....	....	....	....	....	....	....	....	....	....	....
1974-75	Johnstown Jets	NAHL	28	....	....	....	1504	79	1	3.15	....	....	....	....	....	12	8	4	0	654	29	0	2.66	....	....	....	....
1975-76	Johnstown Jets	NAHL	30	....	....	....	1757	89	1	3.04	....	....	....	....	....	5	....	....	....	264	19	0	4.32	....	....	....	....
	Minnesota Fighting Saints	WHA	4	2	1	0	193	10	0	3.11	....	....	....	....	....	....	....	....	....	....	....	....	....	....	....	....	....
1976-77	Minnesota Fighting Saints	WHA	30	15	11	2	1715	78	2	2.73	....	....	....	....	....	....	....	....	....	....	....	....	....	....	....	....	....
	Edmonton Oilers	WHA	21	6	12	3	1213	88	0	4.35	....	....	....	....	....	2	0	2	0	133	10	0	4.51	....	....	....	....
1977-78	New England Whalers	WHA	27	14	11	2	1655	91	3	3.30	....	....	....	....	....	*12	*8	4	0	*719	31	0	2.59	....	....	....	....
1978-79	Binghamton Whalers	AHL	25	10	12	2	1463	92	0	3.77	....	....	....	....	....	....	....	....	....	....	....	....	....	....	....	....	....
	Springfield Indians	AHL	9	4	3	0	480	30	0	3.75	....	....	....	....	....	....	....	....	....	....	....	....	....	....	....	....	....
	Quebec Nordiques	WHA	3	0	1	0	140	14	0	6.00	....	....	....	....	....	1	0	1	0	59	8	0	8.14	....	....	....	....
1979-80	**Minnesota North Stars**	**NHL**	**1**	**0**	**1**	**0**	**60**	**7**	**0**	**7.00**	**6.15**	....	....	....	....	....	....	....	....	....	....	....	....	....	....	....	....
	Oklahoma City Stars	CHL	37	19	14	3	2225	107	*4	2.89	....	....	....	....	....	....	....	....	....	....	....	....	....	....	....	....	....
1980-81	Oklahoma City Stars	CHL	21	9	8	1	1120	72	0	3.86	....	....	....	....	....	....	....	....	....	....	....	....	....	....	....	....	....
	NHL Totals		**1**	**0**	**1**	**0**	**60**	**7**	**0**	**7.00**	....	....	....	....	....	....	....	....	....	....	....	....	....	....	....	....	....
	Other Major League Totals		85	37	36	7	4916	281	5	3.43	....	....	....	....	....	15	8	7	0	911	49	0	3.23	....	....	....	....

Signed as a free agent by **Minnesota** (WHA), September, 1974. Traded to **Edmonton** (WHA) by **Minnesota** (WHA) with Mike Antonovich, Bill Butters, Dave Keon, Jack Carlson, Steve Carlson and John McKenzie for cash, January, 1977. Traded to **New England** (WHA) by **Edmonton** (WHA) for Brett Callighen, Dave Dryden and future considerations, September, 1977. Traded to **Quebec** (WHA) by **New England** (WHA) for Warren Miller, September, 1978. Signed as a free agent by **Minnesota**, October 2, 1979.

• LEVINSKY, ALEX

Alex "Mine-Boy" Levinsky G – L. 5′10″, 184 lbs. b: Syracuse, NY, 2/2/1910. Deceased.

Season	Club	League	GP	W	L	T	Mins	GA	SO	Avg	AAvg	Eff	SA	S%	SAPG	GP	W	L	T	Mins	GA	SO	Avg	Eff	SA	S%	SAPG
1931-32	**Toronto Maple Leafs**	**NHL**	**1**	**0**	**0**	**0**	**1**	**1**	**0**	**60.00**	**73.84**	....	....	....	....	....	....	....	....	....	....	....	....	....	....	....	....
	NHL Totals		**1**	**0**	**0**	**0**	**1**	**1**	**0**	**60.00**	....	....	....	....	....	....	....	....	....	....	....	....	....	....	....	....	....

• Toronto defenseman replaced penalized Lorne Chabot, March 15, 1932. (Detroit 6, Toronto 2)

• LINDBERGH, PELLE

Pelle Lindbergh G – L. 5′9″, 165 lbs. b: Stockholm, Sweden, 5/24/1959. d: 11/10/1985. Philadelphia's 3rd choice, 35th overall, in 1979 Entry Draft.

Season	Club	League	GP	W	L	T	Mins	GA	SO	Avg	AAvg	Eff	SA	S%	SAPG	GP	W	L	T	Mins	GA	SO	Avg	Eff	SA	S%	SAPG
1975-76	Sweden	EJC-A	3	....	....	....	180	4	....	1.33	....	....	....	....	....	....	....	....	....	....	....	....	....	....	....	....	....
1976-77	Sweden	EJC-A	3	....	....	....	180	3	....	1.00	....	....	....	....	....	....	....	....	....	....	....	....	....	....	....	....	....
1978-79	AIK Solna	Sweden	6	....	....	....	360	38	0	6.33	....	....	....	....	....	....	....	....	....	....	....	....	....	....	....	....	....
	Sweden	WEC-A	6	....	....	....	360	38	....	6.33	....	....	....	....	....	....	....	....	....	....	....	....	....	....	....	....	....
1979-80	AIK Solna	Sweden	32	....	....	....	1866	106	1	3.41	....	....	....	....	....	....	....	....	....	....	....	....	....	....	....	....	....
	Sweden	Olympics	5	....	....	....	300	18	....	3.60	....	....	....	....	....	....	....	....	....	....	....	....	....	....	....	....	....
1980-81	Maine Mariners	AHL	51	31	14	5	3035	165	1	3.26	....	....	....	....	....	*20	*10	7	0	*1120	66	0	3.54	....	....	....	....
1981-82	Sweden	C Cup	2	0	0	0	92	9	0	6.00	....	....	....	....	....	....	....	....	....	....	....	....	....	....	....	....	....
	Philadelphia Flyers	**NHL**	**8**	**2**	**4**	**2**	**480**	**35**	**0**	**4.38**	**3.38**	....	....	....	....	....	....	....	....	....	....	....	....	....	....	....	....
	Maine Mariners	AHL	25	17	7	2	1505	83	0	3.31	....	....	....	....	....	....	....	....	....	....	....	....	....	....	....	....	....
1982-83	**Philadelphia Flyers**	**NHL**	**40**	**23**	**13**	**3**	**2334**	**116**	**3**	**2.98**	**2.37**	**3.26**	**1060**	**.891**	**27.2**	**3**	**0**	**3**	....	**180**	**18**	**0**	**6.00**	....	....	....	....
	Sweden	WEC-A	9	....	....	....	540	27	....	3.00	....	....	....	....	....	....	....	....	....	....	....	....	....	....	....	....	....
1983-84	Springfield Indians	AHL	4	4	0	0	240	12	0	3.00	....	....	....	....	....	....	....	....	....	....	....	....	....	....	....	....	....
	Philadelphia Flyers	**NHL**	**36**	**16**	**13**	**3**	**1999**	**135**	**1**	**4.05**	**3.17**	**5.66**	**966**	**.860**	**29.0**	**2**	**0**	**1**	....	**26**	**3**	**0**	**6.92**	**15.97**	**13**	**.769**	**30.0**
1984-85	**Philadelphia Flyers**	**NHL**	***65**	***40**	**17**	**7**	***3858**	**194**	**2**	**3.02**	**2.38**	**3.04**	**1929**	**.899**	**30.0**	***18**	**12**	**6**	....	**1008**	**42**	***3**	**2.50**	**2.14**	**490**	**.914**	**29.2**
1985-86	**Philadelphia Flyers**	**NHL**	**8**	**6**	**2**	**0**	**480**	**23**	**1**	**2.88**	**2.24**	**3.33**	**199**	**.884**	**24.9**	....	....	....	....	....	....	....	....	....	....	....	....
	NHL Totals		**157**	**87**	**49**	**15**	**9151**	**503**	**7**	**3.30**	....	....	....	....	....	**23**	**12**	**10**	....	**1214**	**63**	**3**	**3.11**	....	....	....	....

Named Best Goaltender at EJC-A (1976, 1977) • WJC-A All-Star Team (1979) • Named Best Goaltender at WJC-A (1979) • Swedish World All-Star Team (1979, 1980, 1983) • AHL First All-Star Team (1981) • Shared Harry "Hap" Holmes Memorial Award (fewest goals against - AHL) with Robbie Moore (1981) • Won Dudley "Red" Garrett Memorial Award (Top Rookie - AHL) (1981) • Won Les Cunningham Award (MVP - AHL) (1981) • NHL All-Rookie Team (1983) • NHL First All-Star Team (1985) • Won Vezina Trophy (1985)

Played in NHL All-Star Game (1983, 1985)

• LINDSAY, BERT

Bert Lindsay G5′70″, 160 lbs. b: Garafraxa County, Ont.,, 7/23/1881. d: 11/11/1960.

Season	Club	League	GP	W	L	T	Mins	GA	SO	Avg	AAvg	Eff	SA	S%	SAPG	GP	W	L	T	Mins	GA	SO	Avg	Eff	SA	S%	SAPG
1904-05	McGill University	Mtl-Sr.	STATISTICS NOT AVAILABLE																								
1905-06	Toronto Rowing Club	City Sr.	STATISTICS NOT AVAILABLE																								
1906-07	Renfrew Riversides	OVSHL	STATISTICS NOT AVAILABLE																								
1907-08	Renfrew Creamery Kings	OVSHL	4	*4	0	0	240	16	0	4.00	....	....	....	....	....	....	....	....	....	....	....	....	....	....	....	....	....
1908-09	Renfrew Creamery Kings	FAHL	STATISTICS NOT AVAILABLE																								
	Edmonton AAA	City Sr.	STATISTICS NOT AVAILABLE													2	0	2	0	120	13	0	6.50				
1909-10	Renfrew Creamery Kings	NHA	12	8	3	1	730	54	0	4.44	....	....	....	....	....	....	....	....	....	....	....	....	....	....	....	....	....
1910-11	Renfrew Millionaires	NHA	16	8	8	0	960	101	0	6.31	....	....	....	....	....	....	....	....	....	....	....	....	....	....	....	....	....
1911-12	Victoria Aristocrats	PCHA	16	7	9	0	*975	90	0	5.54	....	....	....	....	....	....	....	....	....	....	....	....	....	....	....	....	....
1912-13	Victoria Aristocrats	PCHA	*15	*10	5	0	*927	56	*1	*3.62	....	....	....	....	....	3	2	1	0	180	12	0	4.00	....	....	....	....
1913-14	Victoria Aristocrats	PCHA	16	*10	6	0	1005	80	0	4.78	....	....	....	....	....	3	0	3	0	195	13	0	4.00	....	....	....	....
1914-15	Victoria Aristocrats	PCHA	17	4	13	0	1054	116	0	6.60	....	....	....	....	....	....	....	....	....	....	....	....	....	....	....	....	....
1915-16	Montreal Wanderers	NHA	23	10	13	0	1380	110	*1	4.78	....	....	....	....	....	....	....	....	....	....	....	....	....	....	....	....	....
1916-17	Montreal Wanderers	NHA	15	5	10	0	903	96	0	6.03	....	....	....	....	....	....	....	....	....	....	....	....	....	....	....	....	....
1917-18	**Montreal Wanderers**	**NHL**	**4**	**1**	**3**	**0**	**240**	**35**	**0**	**8.75**	**6.00**	....	....	....	....	....	....	....	....	....	....	....	....	....	....	....	....
1918-19	**Toronto Arenas**	**NHL**	**16**	**5**	**11**	**0**	**998**	**83**	**0**	**4.99**	**4.08**	....	....	....	....	....	....	....	....	....	....	....	....	....	....	....	....
	NHL Totals		**20**	**6**	**14**	**0**	**1238**	**118**	**0**	**5.72**	....	....	....	....	....	....	....	....	....	....	....	....	....	....	....	....	....
	Other Major League Totals		130	62	67	1	7934	703	2	5.32	....	....	....	....	....	6	2	4	0	375	25	0	4.00	....	....	....	....

PCHA All-Star Team (1913)

Signed as a free agent by **Toronto Arenas**, December 28, 1918.

• LITTMAN, DAVID

David Littman G – L. 6′, 183 lbs. b: Cranston, RI, 6/13/1967. Buffalo's 12th choice, 211th overall, in 1987 Entry Draft.

Season	Club	League	GP	W	L	T	Mins	GA	SO	Avg	AAvg	Eff	SA	S%	SAPG	GP	W	L	T	Mins	GA	SO	Avg	Eff	SA	S%	SAPG
1985-86	Boston College	H.E.	7	4	0	1	312	18	0	3.46	....	....	....	....	....	....	....	....	....	....	....	....	....	....	....	....	....
1986-87	Boston College	H.E.	21	15	5	0	1182	68	0	3.45	....	....	....	....	....	....	....	....	....	....	....	....	....	....	....	....	....
1987-88	Boston College	H.E.	30	11	16	2	1726	116	0	4.03	....	....	....	....	....	....	....	....	....	....	....	....	....	....	....	....	....
1988-89	Boston College	H.E.	*32	19	9	4	*1945	107	0	3.30	....	....	....	....	....	....	....	....	....	....	....	....	....	....	....	....	....
1989-90	Rochester Americans	AHL	14	5	6	1	681	37	0	3.26	....	....	....	....	....	....	....	....	....	....	....	....	....	....	....	....	....
	Phoenix Roadrunners	IHL	18	8	7	2	1047	64	0	3.67	....	....	....	....	....	....	....	....	....	....	....	....	....	....	....	....	....
1990-91	**Buffalo Sabres**	**NHL**	**1**	**0**	**0**	**0**	**36**	**3**	**0**	**5.00**	**4.47**	**8.33**	**18**	**.833**	**30.0**	....	....	....	....	....	....	....	....	....	....	....	....
	Rochester Americans	AHL	*56	*33	13	5	*3155	160	3	3.04	....	....	....	....	....	8	4	2	....	378	16	0	2.54	....	....	....	....

Season	Club	League	GP	W	L	T	Mins	GA	SO	Avg	AAvg	Eff	SA	S%	SAPG	GP	W	L	T	Mins	GA	SO	Avg	Eff	SA	S%	SAPG
			REGULAR SEASON													PLAYOFFS											
1991-92	**Buffalo Sabres**	**NHL**	**1**	**0**	**1**	**0**	**60**	**4**	**0**	**4.00**	**3.55**	**5.52**	**29**	**.862**	**29.0**	....	....	....	....	....	....	....	....	....	....	....	....
	Rochester Americans	AHL	*61	*29	20	9	*3558	174	*3	2.93	....	....	....	....	....	15	8	7	....	879	43	*1	2.94	....	....	....	....
1992-93	**Tampa Bay Lightning**	**NHL**	**1**	**0**	**1**	**0**	**45**	**7**	**0**	**9.33**	**7.94**	**31.10**	**21**	**.667**	**28.0**	....	....	....	....	....	....	....	....	....	....	....	....
	Atlanta Knights	IHL	44	23	12	4	2390	134	0	3.36	....	....	....	....	....	3	1	2	....	178	8	0	2.70	....	....	....	....
1993-94	Fredericton Canadiens	AHL	16	8	7	0	872	63	0	4.33	....	....	....	....	....	....	....	....	....	....	....	....	....	....	....	....	....
	Providence Bruins	AHL	25	10	11	3	1385	83	0	3.60	....	....	....	....	....	....	....	....	....	....	....	....	....	....	....	....	....
	United States	WC-A	1	....	....	....	45	6	0	8.00	....	....	....	....	....	....	....	....	....	....	....	....	....	....	....	....	....
1994-95	Richmond Renegades	ECHL	8	4	2	0	346	13	1	2.25	....	....	....	....	....	*17	*12	4	....	*953	37	*3	*2.33	....	....	....	....
1995-96	Los Angeles Ice Dogs	IHL	43	17	16	5	2245	145	1	3.88	....	....	....	....	....	....	....	....	....	....	....	....	....	....	....	....	....
1996-97	San Antonio Dragons	IHL	45	20	16	5	2437	138	2	3.40	....	....	....	....	....	4	1	3	....	230	11	0	2.87	....	....	....	....
1997-98	Orlando Solar Bears	IHL	44	21	13	6	2303	102	0	2.66	....	....	....	....	....	16	8	8	....	966	48	1	2.98	....	....	....	....
	NHL Totals		**3**	**0**	**2**	**0**	**141**	**14**	**0**	**5.96**	....	....	**68**	**.794**	....	....	....	....	....	....	....	....	....	....	....	....	....

Hockey East Second All-Star Team (1988) • Hockey East First All-Star Team (1989) • NCAA East Second All-American Team (1989) • Shared Harry "Hap" Holmes Memorial Trophy (fewest goals against - AHL) with Darcy Wakaluk (1991) • AHL First All-Star Team (1991) • AHL Second All-Star Team (1992) • Won Harry "Hap" Holmes Memorial Trophy (fewest goals against - AHL) (1992)

Signed as a free agent by **Tampa Bay**, August 27, 1992. Signed as a free agent by **Boston**, August 6, 1993.

• LIUT, MIKE

Mike Liut G – L. 6'2", 195 lbs. b: Weston, Ont., 1/7/1956. St. Louis' 5th choice, 56th overall, in 1976 Amateur Draft.

Season	Club	League	GP	W	L	T	Mins	GA	SO	Avg	AAvg	Eff	SA	S%	SAPG	GP	W	L	T	Mins	GA	SO	Avg	Eff	SA	S%	SAPG
1973-74	Bowling Green University	CCHA	24	10	12	0	1272	88	1	4.15	....	....	....	....	....	....	....	....	....	....	....	....	....	....	....	....	....
1974-75	Bowling Green University	CCHA	20	12	6	1	1174	78	0	3.99	....	....	....	....	....	....	....	....	....	....	....	....	....	....	....	....	....
1975-76	Bowling Green University	CCHA	21	13	5	0	1171	50	2	2.56	....	....	....	....	....	....	....	....	....	....	....	....	....	....	....	....	....
1976-77	Bowling Green University	CCHA	24	18	4	0	1346	61	2	2.72	....	....	....	....	....	....	....	....	....	....	....	....	....	....	....	....	....
1977-78	Cincinnati Stingers	WHA	27	8	12	0	1215	86	0	4.25	....	....	....	....	....	....	....	....	....	....	....	....	....	....	....	....	....
1978-79	Cincinnati Stingers	WHA	54	23	27	4	3181	184	*3	3.47	....	....	....	....	....	3	1	2	0	179	10	0	3.35	....	....	....	....
1979-80	**St. Louis Blues**	**NHL**	**64**	***33**	**23**	**9**	**3661**	**194**	**2**	**3.18**	**2.78**	....	....	....	....	**3**	**0**	**3**	....	**193**	**12**	**0**	**3.73**	....	....	....	....
1980-81	**St. Louis Blues**	**NHL**	**61**	**33**	**14**	**13**	**3570**	**199**	**1**	**3.34**	**2.66**	....	....	....	....	**11**	**5**	**6**	....	**685**	**50**	**0**	**4.38**	....	....	....	....
1981-82	Canada	C Cup	6	4	1	1	360	19	1	3.17	....	....	....	....	....	....	....	....	....	....	....	....	....	....	....	....	....
	St. Louis Blues	**NHL**	***64**	**28**	**28**	**7**	***3691**	**250**	**2**	**4.06**	**3.13**	....	....	....	....	**10**	**5**	**3**	....	**494**	**27**	**0**	**3.28**	....	....	....	....
1982-83	**St. Louis Blues**	**NHL**	***68**	**21**	**27**	**13**	***3794**	**235**	**1**	**3.72**	**2.97**	**4.56**	**1919**	**.878**	**30.3**	**4**	**1**	**3**	....	**240**	**15**	**0**	**3.75**	....	....	....	....
1983-84	**St. Louis Blues**	**NHL**	**58**	**25**	**29**	**4**	**3425**	**197**	**3**	**3.45**	**2.69**	**4.01**	**1697**	**.884**	**29.7**	**11**	**6**	**5**	....	**714**	**29**	**1**	**2.44**	**1.95**	**362**	**.920**	**30.4**
1984-85	**St. Louis Blues**	**NHL**	**32**	**12**	**12**	**6**	**1869**	**119**	**1**	**3.82**	**3.03**	**4.58**	**992**	**.880**	**31.8**	....	....	....	....	....	....	....	....	....	....	....	....
	Hartford Whalers	**NHL**	**12**	**4**	**7**	**1**	**731**	**36**	**1**	**2.95**	**2.34**	**2.53**	**419**	**.914**	**34.4**	....	....	....	....	....	....	....	....	....	....	....	....
1985-86	**Hartford Whalers**	**NHL**	**57**	**27**	**23**	**4**	**3282**	**198**	**2**	**3.62**	**2.81**	**4.55**	**1574**	**.874**	**28.8**	**8**	**5**	**2**	....	**441**	**14**	***1**	***1.90**	**1.18**	**226**	**.938**	**30.7**
1986-87	**Hartford Whalers**	**NHL**	**59**	**31**	**22**	**5**	**3476**	**187**	***4**	**3.23**	**2.71**	**3.72**	**1625**	**.885**	**28.0**	**6**	**2**	**4**	....	**332**	**25**	**0**	**4.52**	**7.11**	**159**	**.843**	**28.7**
1987-88	**Hartford Whalers**	**NHL**	**60**	**25**	**28**	**5**	**3532**	**187**	**2**	**3.18**	**2.63**	**3.67**	**1620**	**.885**	**27.5**	**3**	**1**	**1**	....	**160**	**11**	**0**	**4.13**	**5.54**	**82**	**.866**	**30.8**
1988-89	**Hartford Whalers**	**NHL**	**35**	**13**	**19**	**1**	**2006**	**142**	**1**	**4.25**	**3.51**	**5.88**	**1027**	**.862**	**30.7**	....	....	....	....	....	....	....	....	....	....	....	....
1989-90	**Hartford Whalers**	**NHL**	**29**	**15**	**12**	**1**	**1683**	**74**	***3**	***2.64**	**2.20**	**2.62**	**745**	**.901**	**26.6**	....	....	....	....	....	....	....	....	....	....	....	....
	Washington Capitals	**NHL**	**8**	**4**	**4**	**0**	**478**	**17**	***1**	***2.13**	**1.78**	**1.67**	**217**	**.922**	**27.2**	**9**	**4**	**4**	....	**507**	**28**	**0**	**3.31**	**4.16**	**223**	**.874**	**26.4**
1990-91	**Washington Capitals**	**NHL**	**35**	**13**	**16**	**3**	**1834**	**114**	**0**	**3.73**	**3.34**	**5.41**	**786**	**.855**	**25.7**	**2**	**0**	**1**	....	**48**	**4**	**0**	**5.00**	**6.67**	**30**	**.867**	**37.5**
1991-92	**Washington Capitals**	**NHL**	**21**	**10**	**7**	**2**	**1123**	**70**	**1**	**3.74**	**3.32**	**4.69**	**558**	**.875**	**29.8**	....	....	....	....	....	....	....	....	....	....	....	....
	NHL Totals		**663**	**294**	**271**	**74**	**38155**	**2219**	**25**	**3.49**	....	....	....	....	....	**67**	**29**	**32**	....	**3814**	**215**	**2**	**3.38**	....	....	....	....
	Other Major League Totals		81	31	39	4	4396	270	3	3.69	....	....	....	....	....	3	1	2	0	179	10	0	3.35	....	....	....	....

CCHA First All-Star Team (1975, 1977) • CCHA Second All-Star Team (1976) • NHL First All-Star Team (1981) • Won Lester B. Pearson Award (1981) • NHL Second All-Star Team (1987)

Played in NHL All-Star Game (1981)

Selected by **New England** (WHA) in 1976 WHA Amateur Draft, May, 1976. WHA rights traded to **Cincinnati** (WHA) by **New England** (WHA) with future considerations for Greg Carroll and Bryan Maxwell, May, 1975. Reclaimed by **St. Louis** from **Cincinnati** (WHA) prior to Expansion Draft, June 9, 1979. Traded to **Hartford** by **St. Louis** with Jorgen Pettersson for Mark Johnson and Greg Millen, February 21, 1985. Traded to **Washington** by **Hartford** for Yvon Corriveau, March 6, 1990.

• LOCKETT, KEN

Ken Lockett G – L. 6', 160 lbs. b: Toronto, Ont., 8/30/1947.

Season	Club	League	GP	W	L	T	Mins	GA	SO	Avg	AAvg	Eff	SA	S%	SAPG	GP	W	L	T	Mins	GA	SO	Avg	Eff	SA	S%	SAPG
1967-68	North York Rangers	Jr. B	STATISTICS NOT AVAILABLE																								
1968-69	Fort Wayne Komets	IHL	6	....	....	....	300	28	0	5.60	....	....	....	....	....	....	....	....	....	....	....	....	....	....	....	....	....
1969-70	Fort Wayne Komets	IHL	2	....	....	....	120	10	0	5.00	....	....	....	....	....	....	....	....	....	....	....	....	....	....	....	....	....
	Owen Sound Mercurys	OHA Sr.	9	....	....	....	520	45	0	5.19	....	....	....	....	....	....	....	....	....	....	....	....	....	....	....	....	....
1970-71	University of Guelph	OQAA	15	....	....	....	900	54	0	3.60	....	....	....	....	....	....	....	....	....	....	....	....	....	....	....	....	....
1971-72	University of Guelph	OUAA	17	....	....	....	1020	64	0	3.76	....	....	....	....	....	....	....	....	....	....	....	....	....	....	....	....	....
1972-73	Baltimore Clippers	AHL	32	....	....	....	1009	139	0	4.57	....	....	....	....	....	....	....	....	....	....	....	....	....	....	....	....	....
1973-74	Baltimore Clippers	AHL	37	21	11	4	2128	99	2	2.79	....	....	....	....	....	5	3	2	0	300	18	0	3.60	....	....	....	....
1974-75	**Vancouver Canucks**	**NHL**	**25**	**6**	**7**	**1**	**912**	**48**	**2**	**3.16**	**2.85**	....	....	....	....	**1**	**0**	**1**	....	**60**	**6**	**0**	**6.00**	....	....	....	....
1975-76	**Vancouver Canucks**	**NHL**	**30**	**7**	**8**	**7**	**1436**	**83**	**0**	**3.47**	**3.14**	....	....	....	....	....	....	....	....	....	....	....	....	....	....	....	....
1976-77	San Diego Mariners	WHA	45	18	19	1	2397	148	1	3.70	....	....	....	....	....	5	1	3	0	260	19	0	4.38	....	....	....	....
	NHL Totals		**55**	**13**	**15**	**8**	**2348**	**131**	**2**	**3.35**	....	....	....	....	....	**1**	**0**	**1**	....	**60**	**6**	**0**	**6.00**	....	....	....	....
	Other Major League Totals		45	18	19	1	2397	148	1	3.70	....	....	....	....	....	5	1	3	0	260	19	0	4.38	....	....	....	....

Traded to **Vancouver** by **Baltimore** (AHL), August, 1974. Signed as a free agent by **San Diego** (WHA), September, 1976.

• LOCKHART, HOWARD

Howard "Holes" Lockhart G – L. 5'8", 180 lbs. b: North Bay, Ontario, 1895. Deceased.

Season	Club	League	GP	W	L	T	Mins	GA	SO	Avg	AAvg	Eff	SA	S%	SAPG	GP	W	L	T	Mins	GA	SO	Avg	Eff	SA	S%	SAPG
1912-13	North Bay Seniors	NOHA	8	5	3	0	480	36	0	4.50	....	....	....	....	....	2	1	1	0	120	16	0	8.00	....	....	....	....
1913-1916	North Bay Intermediates	Inter-Sr.	STATISTICS NOT AVAILABLE																								
1916-17	Toronto 228th Battalion	NHA	12	6	6	0	720	69	*1	5.75	....	....	....	....	....	....	....	....	....	....	....	....	....	....	....	....	....
1917-18			MILITARY SERVICE																								
1918-19			MILITARY SERVICE																								
1919-20	**Toronto St. Pats**	**NHL**	**7**	**4**	**2**	**0**	**310**	**25**	**0**	**4.04**	**3.16**	....	....	....	....	....	....	....	....	....	....	....	....	....	....	....	....
	Quebec Bulldogs	**NHL**	**1**	**0**	**1**	**0**	**60**	**11**	**0**	**11.00**	**7.26**	....	....	....	....	....	....	....	....	....	....	....	....	....	....	....	....
1920-21	**Hamilton Tigers**	**NHL**	***24**	**6**	**18**	**0**	**1454**	**132**	**1**	**5.45**	**4.40**	....	....	....	....	....	....	....	....	....	....	....	....	....	....	....	....
1921-22	**Hamilton Tigers**	**NHL**	***24**	**6**	**17**	**0**	**1409**	**103**	**0**	**4.39**	**3.54**	....	....	....	....	....	....	....	....	....	....	....	....	....	....	....	....
1922-23			DID NOT PLAY																								
1923-24	**Toronto St. Pats**	**NHL**	**1**	**0**	**1**	**0**	**60**	**5**	**0**	**5.00**	**5.00**	....	....	....	....	....	....	....	....	....	....	....	....	....	....	....	....
1924-25	**Boston Bruins**	**NHL**	**2**	**0**	**2**	**0**	**120**	**11**	**0**	**5.50**	**6.88**	....	....	....	....	....	....	....	....	....	....	....	....	....	....	....	....
1925-26			DID NOT PLAY																								
1926-27	Hamilton Tigers	CPHL	19	....	....	....	1140	51	0	2.79	....	....	....	....	....	....	....	....	....	....	....	....	....	....	....	....	....
	NHL Totals		**59**	**16**	**41**	**0**	**3413**	**287**	**1**	**5.05**	....	....	....	....	....	....	....	....	....	....	....	....	....	....	....	....	....
	Other Major League Totals		12	6	6	0	720	69	1	5.75	....	....	....	....	....	....	....	....	....	....	....	....	....	....	....	....	....

Signed as a free agent by **Toronto St. Pats**, December 15, 1919. Loaned to **Quebec** by **Toronto St. Pats**, March 6, 1920. (Toronto 11, Quebec 2). Traded to **Hamilton** by **Toronto St. Pats** for cash, December 16, 1920. Signed as a free agent by **Toronto St. Pats**, December 18, 1923. Traded to **Boston** by **Toronto St. Pats** for cash, December 24, 1924.

• LOPRESTI, PETE

Pete LoPresti G – L. 6'1", 195 lbs. b: Virginia, MN, 5/23/1954. Minnesota's 3rd choice, 42nd overall, in 1974 Amateur Draft.

Season	Club	League	GP	W	L	T	Mins	GA	SO	Avg	AAvg	Eff	SA	S%	SAPG	GP	W	L	T	Mins	GA	SO	Avg	Eff	SA	S%	SAPG
1972-73	University of Denver	WCHA	4	2	2	0	240	13	0	3.25	....	....	....	....	....	....	....	....	....	....	....	....	....	....	....	....	....
1973-74	University of Denver	WCHA	38	22	13	3	2280	155	1	4.10	....	....	....	....	....	4	2	1	1	240	9	0	2.25	....	....	....	....
1974-75	New Haven Nighthawks	AHL	11	4	4	3	658	36	0	3.28	....	....	....	....	....	....	....	....	....	....	....	....	....	....	....	....	....
	Minnesota North Stars	**NHL**	**35**	**9**	**20**	**3**	**1964**	**137**	**1**	**4.19**	**3.79**	....	....	....	....	....	....	....	....	....	....	....	....	....	....	....	....
1975-76	**Minnesota North Stars**	**NHL**	**34**	**7**	**22**	**1**	**1789**	**123**	**1**	**4.13**	**3.75**	....	....	....	....	....	....	....	....	....	....	....	....	....	....	....	....
	United States	WEC-A	5	....	....	....	300	27	....	5.40	....	....	....	....	....	....	....	....	....	....	....	....	....	....	....	....	....
1976-77	United States	C Cup	2	1	1	0	120	6	0	3.00	....	....	....	....	....	....	....	....	....	....	....	....	....	....	....	....	....
	Minnesota North Stars	**NHL**	**44**	**13**	**20**	**10**	**2590**	**156**	**1**	**3.61**	**3.36**	....	....	....	....	**2**	**0**	**2**	....	**77**	**6**	**0**	**4.68**	....	....	....	....
1977-78	**Minnesota North Stars**	**NHL**	**53**	**12**	**35**	**6**	**3065**	**216**	**2**	**4.23**	**4.00**	....	....	....	....	....	....	....	....	....	....	....	....	....	....	....	....
	United States	WEC-A	9	....	....	....	540	50	....	5.56	....	....	....	....	....	....	....	....	....	....	....	....	....	....	....	....	....
1978-79	**Minnesota North Stars**	**NHL**	**7**	**2**	**4**	**0**	**345**	**28**	**0**	**4.87**	**4.30**	....	....	....	....	....	....	....	....	....	....	....	....	....	....	....	....
	Oklahoma City Stars	CHL	33	16	15	0	1928	129	0	4.01	....	....	....	....	....	....	....	....	....	....	....	....	....	....	....	....	....

			REGULAR SEASON												PLAYOFFS										
Season	Club	League	GP	W	L	T	Mins	GA	SO	Avg	AAvg	Eff	SA	S%	SAPG	GP	W	L	T	Mins	GA	SO	Avg	Eff	SA	S%	SAPG
1979-80			DID NOT PLAY																							
1980-81	Wichita Wind	CHL	36	9	25	0	2029	161	1	4.76	....	....	....	....	....	....	....	....	....	....	....	....	....	....	....	....
	Edmonton Oilers	NHL	2	0	1	0	105	8	0	4.57	3.66															
	NHL Totals		175	43	102	20	9858	668	5	4.07	....		....		....	2	0	2		77	6	0	4.68		....		....

Claimed by **Edmonton** from **Minnesota** in Expansion Draft, June 13, 1979.

● **LOPRESTI, SAM**   Sam LoPresti   G – L. 5'11", 200 lbs.   b: Eveleth, MN, 1/30/1917.   Deceased.   **USHOF**

Season	Club	League	GP	W	L	T	Mins	GA	SO	Avg	AAvg	Eff	SA	S%	SAPG	GP	W	L	T	Mins	GA	SO	Avg	Eff	SA	S%	SAPG
1936-37	Eveleth Rangers	TBSHL	2	....	....	....	120	9	0	4.50																
1937-38	St. Paul Saints	AHA	48	10	36	2	2952	178	2	3.62																
1938-39	St. Paul Saints	AHA	44	23	21	0	2684	122	1	2.73						3	0	3	0	180	11	0	3.67				
1939-40	St. Paul Saints	AHA	47	29	18	0	2848	121	4	2.55						7	*6	1	0	420	9	*2	*1.29				
1940-41	Kansas City Americans	AHA	18	9	9	0	1142	61	0	3.21																	
	Chicago Black Hawks	NHL	27	9	15	3	1670	84	1	3.02	3.52					5	2	3		343	12	0	2.10				
1941-42	Chicago Black Hawks	NHL	47	21	23	3	2860	152	3	3.19	3.17					3	1	2	....	187	5	*1	1.60				
1942-43			MILITARY SERVICE																							
1943-44			MILITARY SERVICE																							
1944-45	San Diego Skyhawks	PCHL	STATISTICS NOT AVAILABLE																							
1945-46			DID NOT PLAY																							
1946-47	Duluth Coolerators	TBSHL	4	....	....	....	240	30	0	7.50																	
1947-48			DID NOT PLAY																							
1948-49	Duluth Steelers	NAHL	STATISTICS NOT AVAILABLE																							
1949-50	Eveleth Rangers	NAHL	30	17	13	0	1800	114	0	3.79																	
1950-51	Eveleth Rangers	NAHL	20	....	....	....	1200	99	0	4.98																	
	NHL Totals		74	30	38	6	4530	236	4	3.13						8	3	5		530	17	1	1.92		....		....

AHA Second All-Star Team (1940)

● **LORENZ, DANNY**   Danny Lorenz   G – L. 5'10", 187 lbs.   b: Murrayville, B.C., 12/12/1969.   NY Islanders' 4th choice, 58th overall, in 1988 Entry Draft.

Season	Club	League	GP	W	L	T	Mins	GA	SO	Avg	AAvg	Eff	SA	S%	SAPG	GP	W	L	T	Mins	GA	SO	Avg	Eff	SA	S%	SAPG
1986-87	Seattle Thunderbirds	WHL	38	12	21	2	2103	199	0	5.68																	
1987-88	Seattle Thunderbirds	WHL	62	20	37	2	3302	314	0	5.71																	
1988-89	Springfield Indians	AHL	4	2	1	0	210	12	0	3.43																	
	Seattle Thunderbirds	WHL	*68	31	33	4	*4003	240	*3	3.60						13	6	7		751	40	0	3.21				
1989-90	Seattle Thunderbirds	WHL	56	37	15	2	3226	221	0	4.11																	
1990-91	New York Islanders	NHL	2	0	1	0	80	5	0	3.75	3.35	5.21	36	.861	27.0												
	Capital District Islanders	AHL	17	5	9	2	940	70	0	4.47																	
	Richmond Renegades	ECHL	20	6	9	2	1020	75	0	4.41																	
1991-92	New York Islanders	NHL	2	0	2	0	120	10	0	5.00	4.44	8.33	60	.833	30.0												
	Capital District Islanders	AHL	53	22	22	7	3050	181	2	3.56						7	3	4		442	25	0	3.39				
1992-93	New York Islanders	NHL	4	1	2	0	157	10	0	3.82	3.25	4.90	78	.872	29.8												
	Capital District Islanders	AHL	44	16	17	5	2412	146	1	3.63						4	0	3		219	12	0	3.29				
1993-94	Salt Lake Golden Eagles	IHL	20	4	12	0	982	91	0	5.56						2	0	0		35	0	0	0.00				
	Springfield Indians	AHL	14	5	7	1	801	59	0	4.42																	
1994-95	Cincinnati Cyclones	IHL	41	24	10	3	2222	126	0	3.40						5	2	3		308	16	0	3.12				
1995-96	Cincinnati Cyclones	IHL	46	28	12	5	2694	139	1	3.10						5	1	2		199	11	0	3.31				
1996-97	Milwaukee Admirals	IHL	67	33	27	6	3903	221	0	3.40						3	0	3		187	11	0	3.53				
1997-98	Milwaukee Admirals	IHL	54	28	18	4	2718	140	0	3.09						10	5	5		622	31	1	2.99				
	NHL Totals		8	1	5	0	357	25	0	4.20			174	.856													

WHL West First All-Star Team (1989, 1990)

Signed as a free agent by **Florida**, June 14, 1994.

● **LOUSTEL, RON**   Ron Loustel   G – L. 5'11", 185 lbs.   b: Winnipeg, Man., 3/7/1962.   Winnipeg's 6th choice, 107th overall, in 1980 Entry Draft.

Season	Club	League	GP	W	L	T	Mins	GA	SO	Avg	AAvg	Eff	SA	S%	SAPG	GP	W	L	T	Mins	GA	SO	Avg	Eff	SA	S%	SAPG
1978-79	Kelowna Rockets	BCJHL	44	....	....	....	2493	203	0	4.88																	
1979-80	Saskatoon Blades	WHL	41	....	....	....	2203	181	0	4.92																	
1980-81	Saskatoon Blades	WHL	55	....	....	....	2932	278	0	5.60																	
	Winnipeg Jets	NHL	1	0	1	0	60	10	0	10.00	8.02																
	Tulsa Oilers	CHL	1	0	0	0	29	5	0	10.34																	
1981-82	Saskatoon Blades	WHL	42	....	....	....	2280	172	0	4.53																	
1982-83	Brandon Wheat Kings	WHL	28	7	20	0	1627	192	0	7.08																	
	Fort Wayne Komets	IHL	1	....	....	....	33	3	0	5.45																	
	NHL Totals		1	0	1	0	60	10	0	10.00																	

● **LOW, RON**   Ron Low   G – L. 6'1", 205 lbs.   b: Birtle, Man., 6/21/1950.   Toronto's 8th choice, 103rd overall, in 1970 Amateur Draft.

Season	Club	League	GP	W	L	T	Mins	GA	SO	Avg	AAvg	Eff	SA	S%	SAPG	GP	W	L	T	Mins	GA	SO	Avg	Eff	SA	S%	SAPG
1969-70	Dauphin Kings	MJHL	*33	....	....	....	2001	119	0	3.57																	
1970-71	Jacksonville Rockets	EHL	49	....	....	....	2940	293	1	5.98																	
	Tulsa Oilers	CHL	4	....	....	....	192	11	0	5.11																	
1971-72	Richmond Robins	AHL	1	1	0	0	60	2	0	2.00																	
	Tulsa Oilers	CHL	43	21	18	2	*2428	135	1	3.33						8				474	15	*1	*1.89				
1972-73	**Toronto Maple Leafs**	NHL	42	12	24	4	2343	152	1	3.89	3.69																
1973-74	Tulsa Oilers	CHL	56	23	23	8	3213	169	1	3.16																	
1974-75	**Washington Capitals**	NHL	48	8	36	2	2588	235	1	5.45	5.00																
1975-76	**Washington Capitals**	NHL	43	6	31	2	2289	208	0	5.45	5.01																
1976-77	**Washington Capitals**	NHL	54	16	27	5	2918	188	0	3.87	3.62																
1977-78	**Detroit Red Wings**	NHL	32	9	12	9	1816	102	1	3.37	3.16					4	1	3		240	17	0	4.25				
1978-79	Kansas City Red Wings	CHL	*63	*33	28	2	*3795	244	0	3.86						5	1	4	0	237	15	0	3.80				
1979-80	Syracuse Firebirds	AHL	15	5	9	1	905	70	0	4.64																	
	Quebec Nordiques	NHL	15	5	7	2	828	51	0	3.70	3.25																
	Edmonton Oilers	NHL	11	8	2	1	650	37	0	3.42	3.00					3	0	3		212	12	0	3.40				
1980-81	Edmonton Oilers	NHL	24	5	13	3	1260	93	0	4.43	3.56																
	Wichita Wind	CHL	2	0	2	0	120	10	0	5.00																	
1981-82	Edmonton Oilers	NHL	29	17	7	1	1554	100	0	3.86	2.97																
1982-83	Edmonton Oilers	NHL	3	0	1	0	104	10	0	5.77	4.61	10.49	55	.818	31.7												
	New Jersey Devils	NHL	11	2	7	1	608	41	0	4.05	3.23	4.83	344	.881	33.9												
1983-84	New Jersey Devils	NHL	44	8	25	4	2218	161	0	4.36	3.42	6.20	1133	.858	30.6												
1984-85	New Jersey Devils	NHL	26	6	11	4	1326	85	1	3.85	3.06	5.21	628	.865	28.4												
1985-86	Nova Scotia Oilers	AHL	6	1	5	0	299	24	0	4.82																	
	NHL Totals		382	102	203	38	20502	1463	4	4.28						7	1	6		452	29	0	3.85		....		....

EHL South Rookie of the Year (1971) • CHL Second All-Star Team (1974) • CHL First All-Star Team (1979) • Won Tommy Ivan Trophy (CHL's MVP) (1979)

Claimed by **Washington** from **Toronto** in Expansion Draft, June 12, 1974. Signed as a free agent by **Detroit**, August 17, 1977. Claimed by **Quebec** from **Detroit** in Expansion Draft, June 13, 1979. Traded to **Edmonton** by **Quebec** for Ron Chipperfield, March 11, 1980. Traded to **New Jersey** by **Edmonton** with Jim McTaggart for Lindsay Middlebrook and Paul Miller, February 19, 1983.

● **LOZINSKI, LARRY** Larry Lozinski G – R. 5'11", 175 lbs. b: Hudson Bay, Sask., 3/11/1958. Detroit's 16th choice, 219th overall, in 1978 Amateur Draft.

Season	Club	League	GP	W	L	T	Mins	GA	SO	Avg	AAvg	Eff	SA	S%	SAPG	GP	W	L	T	Mins	GA	SO	Avg	Eff	SA	S%	SAPG
			REGULAR SEASON													PLAYOFFS											
1977-78	Flin Flon Bombers	WCJHL	37	14	17	5	1939	178	0	5.51	....	....	....	....	....	16	....	....	....	941	86	0	5.48	....	....	....	....
1978-79	Kansas City Red Wings	CHL	13	4	6	1	688	45	0	3.92	....	....	....	....	....	....	....	....	....	....	....	....	....	....	....	....	....
1979-80	Kalamazoo Wings	IHL	69	....	....	....	4000	232	5	3.48	....	....	....	....	....	10	....	....	....	597	24	1	2.41	....	....	....	....
1980-81	**Detroit Red Wings**	**NHL**	**30**	**6**	**11**	**7**	**1459**	**105**	**0**	**4.32**	**3.47**	....	....	....	....	....	....	....	....	....	....	....	....	....	....	....	....
	Adirondack Red Wings	AHL	16	4	9	1	789	53	0	4.03	....	....	....	....	....	....	....	....	....	....	....	....	....	....	....	....	....
1981-82	Adirondack Red Wings	AHL	55	25	23	4	3207	175	1	3.27	....	....	....	....	....	5	....	....	....	280	22	0	4.71	....	....	....	....
1982-83	Adirondack Red Wings	AHL	32	....	....	....	1709	128	*3	4.49	....	....	....	....	....	6	2	4	0	390	22	0	3.38	....	....	....	....
	Kalamazoo K-Wings	IHL	12	....	....	....	674	51	0	4.54	....	....	....	....	....	....	....	....	....	....	....	....	....	....	....	....	....
	NHL Totals		**30**	**6**	**11**	**7**	**1459**	**105**	**0**	**4.32**	....	....	....	....	....	....	....	....	....	....	....	....	....	....	....	....	....

IHL First All-Star Team (1980) • Won James Norris Memorial Trophy (fewest goals against - IHL) (1980)

● **LUMLEY, HARRY** Harry "Apple Cheeks" Lumley G – L. 6', 195 lbs. b: Owen Sound, Ont., 11/11/1926. HHOF

Season	Club	League	GP	W	L	T	Mins	GA	SO	Avg	AAvg	Eff	SA	S%	SAPG	GP	W	L	T	Mins	GA	SO	Avg	Eff	SA	S%	SAPG
1942-43	Barrie Colts	OHA	STATISTICS NOT AVAILABLE																								
1943-44	Indianapolis Capitols	AHL	52	19	18	15	3120	147	0	2.84	....	....	....	....	....	5	1	4	0	300	18	0	3.60	....	....	....	....
	Detroit Red Wings	**NHL**	**2**	**0**	**2**	**0**	**120**	**13**	**0**	**6.50**	**4.94**	....	....	....	....	....	....	....	....	....	....	....	....	....	....	....	....
	New York Rangers	**NHL**	**1**	**0**	**0**	**0**	**20**	**0**	**0**	**0.00**	**0.00**	....	....	....	....	....	....	....	....	....	....	....	....	....	....	....	....
1944-45	Indianapolis Capitols	AHL	21	11	5	5	1260	46	2	2.14	....	....	....	....	....	....	....	....	....	....	....	....	....	....	....	....	....
	Detroit Red Wings	**NHL**	**37**	**24**	**10**	**3**	**2220**	**119**	**1**	**3.22**	**2.62**	....	....	....	....	***14**	**7**	**7**	....	***871**	**31**	**2**	***2.14**	....	....	....	....
1945-46	**Detroit Red Wings**	**NHL**	***50**	**20**	**20**	**10**	***3000**	**159**	**2**	**3.18**	**2.91**	....	....	....	....	**5**	**1**	**4**	....	**309**	**16**	***1**	**3.11**	....	....	....	....
1946-47	**Detroit Red Wings**	**NHL**	**52**	**22**	**20**	**10**	**3120**	**159**	**3**	**3.06**	**2.97**	....	....	....	....	....	....	....	....	....	....	....	....	....	....	....	....
1947-48	**Detroit Red Wings**	**NHL**	***60**	**30**	**18**	**12**	**3592**	**147**	***7**	**2.46**	**2.51**	....	....	....	....	***10**	**4**	**6**	....	***600**	**30**	**0**	**3.00**	....	....	....	....
1948-49	**Detroit Red Wings**	**NHL**	***60**	***34**	**19**	**7**	***3600**	**145**	**6**	**2.42**	**2.69**	....	....	....	....	***11**	**4**	**7**	....	***726**	**26**	**0**	**2.15**	....	....	....	....
1949-50	**Detroit Red Wings**	**NHL**	**63**	***33**	**16**	**14**	**3780**	**148**	**7**	**2.35**	**2.59**	....	....	....	....	***14**	***8**	**6**	....	**910**	**28**	***3**	**1.85**	....	....	....	....
1950-51	**Chicago Black Hawks**	**NHL**	**64**	**12**	**41**	**10**	**3785**	**246**	**3**	**3.90**	**4.81**	....	....	....	....	....	....	....	....	....	....	....	....	....	....	....	....
1951-52	**Chicago Black Hawks**	**NHL**	***70**	**17**	**44**	**9**	**4180**	**241**	**2**	**3.46**	**4.40**	....	....	....	....	....	....	....	....	....	....	....	....	....	....	....	....
1952-53	**Toronto Maple Leafs**	**NHL**	***70**	**27**	**30**	**13**	***4200**	**167**	***10**	**2.39**	**3.08**	....	....	....	....	....	....	....	....	....	....	....	....	....	....	....	....
1953-54	**Toronto Maple Leafs**	**NHL**	**69**	**32**	**24**	**13**	**4140**	**128**	***13**	***1.86**	**2.29**	....	....	....	....	**5**	**1**	**4**	....	**321**	**15**	**0**	**2.80**	....	....	....	....
1954-55	**Toronto Maple Leafs**	**NHL**	***69**	**23**	**24**	**22**	***4140**	**134**	**8**	**1.94**	**2.27**	....	....	....	....	**4**	**0**	**4**	....	**240**	**14**	**0**	**3.50**	....	....	....	....
1955-56	**Toronto Maple Leafs**	**NHL**	**59**	**21**	**28**	**10**	**3527**	**159**	**3**	**2.70**	**3.33**	....	....	....	....	**5**	**1**	**4**	....	**304**	**14**	**1**	**2.76**	....	....	....	....
1956-57	Buffalo Bisons	AHL	*63	25	36	2	*3780	264	0	4.19	....	....	....	....	....	....	....	....	....	....	....	....	....	....	....	....	....
1957-58	Buffalo Bisons	AHL	17	7	9	1	1029	63	1	3.67	....	....	....	....	....	....	....	....	....	....	....	....	....	....	....	....	....
	Boston Bruins	**NHL**	**25**	**11**	**10**	**4**	**1500**	**71**	**3**	**2.84**	**3.14**	....	....	....	....	**1**	**0**	**1**	....	**60**	**5**	**0**	**5.00**	....	....	....	....
1958-59	Providence Reds	AHL	58	27	29	2	3480	208	4	3.59	....	....	....	....	....	....	....	....	....	....	....	....	....	....	....	....	....
	Boston Bruins	**NHL**	**11**	**8**	**2**	**1**	**660**	**27**	**1**	**2.45**	**2.60**	....	....	....	....	**7**	**3**	**4**	....	**436**	**20**	**0**	**2.75**	....	....	....	....
1959-60	**Boston Bruins**	**NHL**	**42**	**16**	**21**	**5**	**2520**	**147**	**2**	**3.50**	**3.74**	....	....	....	....	....	....	....	....	....	....	....	....	....	....	....	....
1960-61	Kingston Frontenacs	EPHL	2	1	1	0	120	7	0	3.50	....	....	....	....	....	....	....	....	....	....	....	....	....	....	....	....	....
	Winnipeg Warriors	WHL	61	17	40	4	3660	213	0	3.49	....	....	....	....	....	....	....	....	....	....	....	....	....	....	....	....	....
	NHL Totals		**804**	**330**	**329**	**143**	**48104**	**2210**	**71**	**2.76**	....	....	....	....	....	**76**	**29**	**47**	....	**4777**	**199**	**7**	**2.50**	....	....	....	....

NHL First All-Star Team (1954, 1955) • Won Vezina Trophy (1954) • AHL Second All-Star Team (1957)

Played in NHL All-Star Game (1951, 1954, 1955)

Loaned to **NY Rangers** by **Detroit** to replace injured Ken McAuley, December 23, 1943. (Detroit 5, NY Rangers 3). Traded to **Chicago** by **Detroit** with Jack Stewart, Al Dewsbury, Pete Babando and Don Morrison for Metro Prystai, Gaye Stewart, Bob Goldham and Jim Henry, July, 1950. Traded to **Toronto** by **Chicago** for Al Rollins, Gus Mortson, Cal Gardner and Ray Hannigan, September 11, 1952. Traded to **Chicago** by **Toronto** with Eric Nesterenko for cash, May, 1956. Traded to **Boston** by **Chicago** for cash, January, 1958.

● **MACKENZIE, SHAWN** Shawn MacKenzie G – L. 5'10", 175 lbs. b: Bedford, N.S., 8/22/1962. Colorado's 8th choice, 169th overall, in 1980 Entry Draft.

Season	Club	League	GP	W	L	T	Mins	GA	SO	Avg	AAvg	Eff	SA	S%	SAPG	GP	W	L	T	Mins	GA	SO	Avg	Eff	SA	S%	SAPG
1979-80	Windsor Spitfires	OHA	41	17	14	1	1964	158	0	4.83	....	....	....	....	....	13	6	6	0	600	45	0	3.97	....	....	....	....
1980-81	Windsor Spitfires	OHA	*60	30	27	2	*3540	282	1	4.78	....	....	....	....	....	11	3	4	0	622	47	0	4.53	....	....	....	....
1981-82	Windsor Spitfires	OHL	17	6	11	0	1001	77	0	4.62	....	....	....	....	....	....	....	....	....	....	....	....	....	....	....	....	....
	Oshawa Generals	OHL	32	20	12	0	1934	124	1	3.85	....	....	....	....	....	12	7	5	0	707	53	0	4.50	....	....	....	....
1982-83	**New Jersey Devils**	**NHL**	**4**	**0**	**1**	**0**	**130**	**15**	**0**	**6.92**	**5.53**	**15.26**	**68**	**.779**	**31.4**	....	....	....	....	....	....	....	....	....	....	....	....
	Wichita Wind	CHL	36	10	23	2	2083	140	1	4.26	....	....	....	....	....	....	....	....	....	....	....	....	....	....	....	....	....
1983-84	Maine Mariners	AHL	34	14	13	5	1946	113	0	3.48	....	....	....	....	....	1	0	0	0	0	0	0	0.00	....	....	....	....
1984-85	Maine Mariners	AHL	24	8	8	3	1254	70	3	3.35	....	....	....	....	....	2	0	1	0	[illegible]	9	0	7.03	....	....	....	....
1985-86	Hershey Bears	AHL	10	5	3	0	521	36	0	4.15	....	....	....	....	....	....	....	....	....	....	....	....	....	....	....	....	....
	Kalamazoo Wings	IHL	6	4	2	0	362	27	0	4.40	....	....	....	....	....	....	....	....	....	....	....	....	....	....	....	....	....
1986-87	Maine Mariners	AHL	6	3	2	0	321	19	1	3.55	....	....	....	....	....	....	....	....	....	....	....	....	....	....	....	....	....
	NHL Totals		**4**	**0**	**1**	**0**	**130**	**15**	**0**	**6.92**	....	....	**68**	**.779**	....	....	....	....	....	....	....	....	....	....	....	....	....

Transferred to **New Jersey** after **Colorado** franchise relocated, June 30, 1982.

● **MADELEY, DARRIN** Darrin Madeley G – L. 5'11", 170 lbs. b: Holland Landing, Ont., 2/25/1968.

Season	Club	League	GP	W	L	T	Mins	GA	SO	Avg	AAvg	Eff	SA	S%	SAPG	GP	W	L	T	Mins	GA	SO	Avg	Eff	SA	S%	SAPG
1989-90	Lake Superior State	CCHA	30	21	7	1	1683	68	1	2.42	....	....	....	....	....	....	....	....	....	....	....	....	....	....	....	....	....
1990-91	Lake Superior State	CCHA	36	*29	3	3	2137	93	1	*2.61	....	....	....	....	....	....	....	....	....	....	....	....	....	....	....	....	....
1991-92	Lake Superior State	CCHA	36	23	6	4	2144	69	2	*2.05	....	....	....	....	....	....	....	....	....	....	....	....	....	....	....	....	....
1992-93	**Ottawa Senators**	**NHL**	**2**	**0**	**2**	**0**	**90**	**10**	**0**	**6.67**	**5.68**	**15.16**	**44**	**.773**	**29.3**	....	....	....	....	....	....	....	....	....	....	....	....
	New Haven Nighthawks	AHL	41	10	16	9	2295	127	0	3.32	....	....	....	....	....	....	....	....	....	....	....	....	....	....	....	....	....
1993-94	**Ottawa Senators**	**NHL**	**32**	**3**	**18**	**5**	**1583**	**115**	**0**	**4.36**	**4.17**	**5.78**	**868**	**.868**	**32.9**	....	....	....	....	....	....	....	....	....	....	....	....
	P.E.I. Senators	AHL	6	0	4	0	270	26	0	5.77	....	....	....	....	....	....	....	....	....	....	....	....	....	....	....	....	....
1994-95	**Ottawa Senators**	**NHL**	**5**	**1**	**3**	**0**	**255**	**15**	**0**	**3.53**	**3.65**	**3.60**	**147**	**.898**	**34.6**	....	....	....	....	....	....	....	....	....	....	....	....
	P.E.I. Senators	AHL	3	1	1	1	185	8	0	2.59	....	....	....	....	....	....	....	....	....	....	....	....	....	....	....	....	....
	Detroit Vipers	IHL	9	7	2	0	498	20	1	2.41	....	....	....	....	....	....	....	....	....	....	....	....	....	....	....	....	....
1995-96	P.E.I. Senators	AHL	1	1	0	0	60	4	0	4.00	....	....	....	....	....	....	....	....	....	....	....	....	....	....	....	....	....
	Detroit Vipers	IHL	40	16	14	4	2047	108	0	3.17	....	....	....	....	....	7	3	3	....	355	23	0	3.89	....	....	....	....
1996-97	Detroit Vipers	IHL	4	2	0	0	177	11	0	3.72	....	....	....	....	....	....	....	....	....	....	....	....	....	....	....	....	....
	Saint John Flames	AHL	46	11	18	11	2316	124	0	3.21	....	....	....	....	....	2	0	0	....	58	0	0	0.00	....	....	....	....
1997-98	TPS Turku	Finland	2	1	0	0	85	2	0	1.41	....	....	....	....	....	....	....	....	....	....	....	....	....	....	....	....	....
	Richmond Renegades	ECHL	5	1	1	0	137	8	0	3.49	....	....	....	....	....	....	....	....	....	....	....	....	....	....	....	....	....
	NHL Totals		**39**	**4**	**23**	**5**	**1928**	**140**	**0**	**4.36**	....	....	**1059**	**.868**	....	....	....	....	....	....	....	....	....	....	....	....	....

CCHA Second All-Star Team (1990) • CCHA First All-Star Team (1991, 1992) • NCAA West First All-American Team (1991, 1992) • NCAA Championship All-Tournament Team (1991, 1992) • AHL Second All-Star Team (1993)

Signed as a free agent by **Ottawa**, June 20, 1992. Signed as a free agent by **San Jose**, October 22, 1996.

● **MALARCHUK, CLINT** Clint Malarchuk G – L. 6', 185 lbs. b: Grande Prairie, Alta., 5/1/1961. Quebec's 3rd choice, 74th overall, in 1981 Entry Draft.

Season	Club	League	GP	W	L	T	Mins	GA	SO	Avg	AAvg	Eff	SA	S%	SAPG	GP	W	L	T	Mins	GA	SO	Avg	Eff	SA	S%	SAPG
1978-79	Portland Winter Hawks	WHL	2	2	0	0	120	4	0	2.00	....	....	....	....	....	....	....	....	....	....	....	....	....	....	....	....	....
1979-80	Portland Winter Hawks	WHL	37	21	10	0	1948	147	0	4.53	....	....	....	....	....	1	0	0	0	40	3	0	4.50	....	....	....	....
1980-81	Portland Winter Hawks	WHL	38	28	8	0	2235	142	3	3.81	....	....	....	....	....	5	3	2	0	307	21	0	4.10	....	....	....	....
1981-82	**Quebec Nordiques**	**NHL**	**2**	**0**	**1**	**1**	**120**	**14**	**0**	**7.00**	**5.40**	**14.85**	**66**	**.788**	**33.0**	....	....	....	....	....	....	....	....	....	....	....	....
	Fredericton Express	AHL	51	15	34	2	2906	247	0	5.10	....	....	....	....	....	....	....	....	....	....	....	....	....	....	....	....	....
1982-83	**Quebec Nordiques**	**NHL**	**15**	**8**	**5**	**2**	**900**	**71**	**0**	**4.73**	**3.78**	**6.50**	**517**	**.863**	**34.5**	....	....	....	....	....	....	....	....	....	....	....	....
	Fredericton Express	AHL	25	14	6	5	1506	78	0	*3.11	....	....	....	....	....	....	....	....	....	....	....	....	....	....	....	....	....
1983-84	**Quebec Nordiques**	**NHL**	**23**	**10**	**9**	**2**	**1215**	**80**	**0**	**3.95**	**3.09**	**5.35**	**591**	**.865**	**29.2**	....	....	....	....	....	....	....	....	....	....	....	....
	Fredericton Express	AHL	11	5	5	1	663	40	0	3.62	....	....	....	....	....	....	....	....	....	....	....	....	....	....	....	....	....
1984-85	Fredericton Express	AHL	*56	26	25	4	*3347	198	2	3.55	....	....	....	....	....	6	2	4	0	379	20	0	3.17	....	....	....	....
1985-86	**Quebec Nordiques**	**NHL**	**46**	**26**	**12**	**4**	**2657**	**142**	**4**	**3.21**	**2.48**	**3.36**	**1358**	**.895**	**30.7**	**3**	**0**	**2**	....	**143**	**11**	**0**	**4.62**	**6.27**	**81**	**.864**	**34.0**
1986-87	**Quebec Nordiques**	**NHL**	**54**	**18**	**26**	**9**	**3092**	**175**	**1**	**3.40**	**2.85**	**3.94**	**1512**	**.884**	**29.3**	**3**	**0**	**2**	....	**140**	**8**	**0**	**3.43**	**4.90**	**56**	**.857**	**24.0**
	NHL All-Stars	RV87	DID NOT PLAY – SPARE GOALTENDER																								
1987-88	**Washington Capitals**	**NHL**	**54**	**24**	**20**	**4**	**2926**	**154**	***4**	**3.16**	**2.62**	**3.63**	**1340**	**.885**	**27.5**	**4**	**0**	**2**	....	**193**	**15**	**0**	**4.66**	**7.36**	**95**	**.842**	**29.5**
1988-89	**Washington Capitals**	**NHL**	**42**	**16**	**18**	**7**	**2428**	**141**	**1**	**3.48**	**2.87**	**4.29**	**1145**	**.877**	**28.3**	....	....	....	....	....	....	....	....	....	....	....	....
	Buffalo Sabres	**NHL**	**7**	**3**	**1**	**1**	**326**	**13**	**1**	**2.39**	**1.97**	**2.19**	**142**	**.908**	**26.1**	**1**	**0**	**1**	**0**	**59**	**5**	**0**	**5.08**	**7.94**	**32**	**.844**	**32.5**

Season	Club	League	REGULAR SEASON GP	W	L	T	Mins	GA	SO	Avg	AAvg	Eff	SA	S%	SAPG	PLAYOFFS GP	W	L	T	Mins	GA	SO	Avg	Eff	SA	S%	SAPG
1989-90	**Buffalo Sabres**	**NHL**	**29**	**14**	**11**	**2**	**1596**	**89**	**0**	**3.35**	**2.80**	**3.26**	**914**	**.903**	**34.4**	....	....	....	....	....	....	....	....	....	....	....	....
1990-91	**Buffalo Sabres**	**NHL**	**37**	**12**	**14**	**10**	**2131**	**119**	**1**	**3.35**	**2.99**	**3.66**	**1090**	**.891**	**30.7**	**4**	**2**	**2**	....	**246**	**17**	**0**	**4.15**	**6.08**	**116**	**.853**	**28.3**
1991-92	**Buffalo Sabres**	**NHL**	**29**	**10**	**13**	**3**	**1639**	**102**	**0**	**3.73**	**3.31**	**4.21**	**903**	**.887**	**33.1**	....	....	....	....	....	....	....	....	....	....	....	....
	Rochester Americans	AHL	2	2	0	0	120	3	1	1.50	....	....	....	....	....	....	....	....	....	....	....	....	....	....	....	....	....
1992-93	San Diego Gulls	IHL	27	17	3	3	1516	72	3	2.85	....	....	....	....	....	*12	6	4	0	668	34	0	3.05	....	....	....	....
1993-94	Las Vegas Thunder	IHL	55	*34	10	7	3076	172	1	3.35	....	....	....	....	....	5	1	3	0	257	16	0	3.74	....	....	....	....
1994-95	Las Vegas Thunder	IHL	38	15	13	3	2039	127	0	3.74	....	....	....	....	....	2	0	0	0	32	2	0	3.70	....	....	....	....
1995-96	Las Vegas Thunder	IHL	1	0	0	0	4	0	0	0.00	....	....	....	....	....	....	....	....	....	....	....	....	....	....	....	....	....
1996-97	Las Vegas Thunder	IHL	3	1	1	0	63	6	0	5.63	....	....	....	....	....	....	....	....	....	....	....	....	....	....	....	....	....
	NHL Totals		**338**	**141**	**130**	**45**	**19030**	**1100**	**12**	**3.47**	....	....	**9578**	**.885**	....	**15**	**2**	**9**	**0**	**781**	**56**	**0**	**4.30**	....	....	....	....

Shared Harry "Hap" Holmes Memorial Award (fewest goals against - AHL) with Brian Ford (1983) • Shared James Norris Memorial Trophy (fewest goals against - IHL) with Rick Knickle (1993)

Traded to **Washington** by **Quebec** with Dale Hunter for Gaetan Duchesne, Alan Haworth and Washington's 1st round choice (Joe Sakic) in 1987 Entry Draft, June 13, 1987. Traded to **Buffalo** by **Washington** with Grant Ledyard and Washington's 6th round choice (Brian Holzinger) in 1991 Entry Draft for Calle Johansson and Buffalo's 2nd round choice (Byron Dafoe) in 1989 Entry Draft, March 7, 1989.

• MANELUK, GEORGE

George Maneluk G – L. 5'11", 185 lbs. b: Winnipeg, Man., 7/25/1967. NY Islanders' 4th choice, 76th overall, in 1987 Entry Draft.

Season	Club	League	GP	W	L	T	Mins	GA	SO	Avg	AAvg	Eff	SA	S%	SAPG	GP	W	L	T	Mins	GA	SO	Avg	Eff	SA	S%	SAPG
1985-86	University of Manitoba	CWUAA	2	1	1	0	120	14	0	7.00	....	....	....	....	....	....	....	....	....	....	....	....	....	....	....	....	....
1986-87	Brandon Wheat Kings	WHL	58	16	35	4	3258	315	0	5.80	....	....	....	....	....	....	....	....	....	....	....	....	....	....	....	....	....
1987-88	Brandon Wheat Kings	WHL	64	24	33	3	3651	297	0	4.88	....	....	....	....	....	4	1	3	0	271	22	0	4.87	....	....	....	....
	Springfield Indians	AHL	2	0	1	1	125	9	0	4.32	....	....	....	....	....	....	....	....	....	....	....	....	....	....	....	....	....
	Peoria Rivermen	IHL	3	1	2	0	148	14	0	5.68	....	....	....	....	....	1	0	1	0	60	5	0	5.00	....	....	....	....
1988-89	Springfield Indians	AHL	24	7	13	0	1202	84	0	4.19	....	....	....	....	....	....	....	....	....	....	....	....	....	....	....	....	....
1989-90	Springfield Indians	AHL	27	11	9	1	1382	94	1	4.08	....	....	....	....	....	4	2	1	0	174	9	0	3.10	....	....	....	....
	Winston-Salem Thunderbirds	ECHL	3	2	0	0	140	11	0	4.71	....	....	....	....	....	....	....	....	....	....	....	....	....	....	....	....	....
1990-91	**New York Islanders**	**NHL**	**4**	**1**	**1**	**0**	**140**	**15**	**0**	**6.43**	**5.75**	**10.26**	**94**	**.840**	**40.3**	....	....	....	....	....	....	....	....	....	....	....	....
	Capital District Islanders	AHL	29	10	14	1	1524	103	1	4.06	....	....	....	....	....	....	....	....	....	....	....	....	....	....	....	....	....
1991-92	New Haven Nighthawks	AHL	54	25	22	0	2863	175	1	3.67	....	....	....	....	....	3	1	2	0	216	13	0	3.61	....	....	....	....
1992-93	Springfield Indians	AHL	7	4	3	0	343	23	0	4.02	....	....	....	....	....	14	6	7	0	778	53	0	4.09	....	....	....	....
	Phoenix Roadrunners	IHL	2	1	1	0	120	10	0	5.00	....	....	....	....	....	....	....	....	....	....	....	....	....	....	....	....	....
	Muskegon Fury	ColHL	27	....	....	....	1494	113	*1	4.54	....	....	....	....	....	1	0	1	0	59	6	0	6.10	....	....	....	....
1993-94	Springfield Indians	AHL	31	8	14	6	1515	107	0	4.24	....	....	....	....	....	....	....	....	....	....	....	....	....	....	....	....	....
1994-95	Wichita Thunder	CHL	44	27	10	2	2439	153	2	3.76	....	....	....	....	....	9	6	3	0	476	37	0	4.65	....	....	....	....
1995-96	Louisiana Ice Gators	ECHL	36	18	13	2	1969	129	0	3.93	....	....	....	....	....	3	0	2	0	160	14	0	5.25	....	....	....	....
	Los Angeles Ice Dogs	IHL	1	0	0	0	9	0	0	0.00	....	....	....	....	....	....	....	....	....	....	....	....	....	....	....	....	....
	NHL Totals		**4**	**1**	**1**	**0**	**140**	**15**	**0**	**6.43**	....	....	**94**	**.840**	....	....	....	....	....	....	....	....	....	....	....	....	....

CHL Second All-Star Team (1995)

• MANIAGO, CESARE

Cesare "Hail Cesare" Maniago G – L. 6'3", 195 lbs. b: Trail, B.C., 1/13/1939.

Season	Club	League	GP	W	L	T	Mins	GA	SO	Avg	AAvg	Eff	SA	S%	SAPG	GP	W	L	T	Mins	GA	SO	Avg	Eff	SA	S%	SAPG
1957-58	St. Michael's Majors	OHA	48	21	19	7	2880	173	*2	3.60	....	....	....	....	....	....	....	....	....	....	....	....	....	....	....	....	....
1958-59	St. Michael's Majors	OHA	42	....	....	....	2520	131	*4	3.12	....	....	....	....	....	....	....	....	....	....	....	....	....	....	....	....	....
1959-60	Kitchener-Waterloo Dutchmen	OHA Sr.	38	....	....	....	2240	149	0	3.99	....	....	....	....	....	....	....	....	....	....	....	....	....	....	....	....	....
1960-61	Vancouver Canucks	WHL	2	2	0	0	120	5	0	2.50	....	....	....	....	....	....	....	....	....	....	....	....	....	....	....	....	....
	Spokane Comets	WHL	30	17	10	3	1800	90	1	3.00	....	....	....	....	....	4	1	3	0	240	19	0	4.75	....	....	....	....
	Toronto Maple Leafs	**NHL**	**7**	**4**	**2**	**1**	**420**	**18**	**0**	**2.57**	**2.64**	....	....	....	....	**2**	**1**	**1**	....	**145**	**6**	**0**	**2.48**	....	....	....	....
	Sudbury Wolves	EPHL	11	7	3	1	660	19	3	1.73	....	....	....	....	....	....	....	....	....	....	....	....	....	....	....	....	....
1961-62	Hull-Ottawa Canadiens	EPHL	68	*37	21	10	4080	168	3	*2.47	....	....	....	....	....	*13	*8	5	0	*823	32	0	*2.33	....	....	....	....
1962-63	**Montreal Canadiens**	**NHL**	**14**	**5**	**5**	**4**	**820**	**42**	**0**	**3.07**	**3.19**	....	....	....	....	....	....	....	....	....	....	....	....	....	....	....	....
	Quebec Aces	AHL	5	2	3	0	300	19	0	3.80	....	....	....	....	....	....	....	....	....	....	....	....	....	....	....	....	....
	Spokane Comets	WHL	1	0	1	0	60	4	0	4.00	....	....	....	....	....	....	....	....	....	....	....	....	....	....	....	....	....
	Hull-Ottawa Canadiens	EPHL	28	13	11	4	1680	86	1	3.07	....	....	....	....	....	3	0	3	0	185	9	0	2.92	....	....	....	....
1963-64	Buffalo Bisons	AHL	27	11	13	1	1630	103	0	3.82	....	....	....	....	....	....	....	....	....	....	....	....	....	....	....	....	....
	Omaha Knights	CHL	6	2	2	2	360	23	0	3.83	....	....	....	....	....	....	....	....	....	....	....	....	....	....	....	....	....
1964-65	Minneapolis Bruins	CHL	67	34	26	7	4020	184	*6	*2.75	....	....	....	....	....	5	1	4	0	300	19	*1	3.80	....	....	....	....
1965-66	Baltimore Clippers	AHL	27	11	16	0	1572	83	1	3.17	....	....	....	....	....	....	....	....	....	....	....	....	....	....	....	....	....
	New York Rangers	**NHL**	**28**	**9**	**16**	**3**	**1613**	**94**	**2**	**3.50**	**3.59**	....	....	....	....	....	....	....	....	....	....	....	....	....	....	....	....
1966-67	**New York Rangers**	**NHL**	**6**	**0**	**1**	**1**	**219**	**14**	**0**	**3.84**	**3.99**	....	....	....	....	....	....	....	....	....	....	....	....	....	....	....	....
1967-68	**Minnesota North Stars**	**NHL**	**52**	**21**	**17**	**9**	**2877**	**133**	**6**	**2.77**	**3.07**	....	....	....	....	**14**	**7**	**7**	....	**893**	**39**	**0**	**2.62**	....	....	....	....
1968-69	**Minnesota North Stars**	**NHL**	**64**	**18**	**33**	**10**	**3599**	**198**	**1**	**3.30**	**3.44**	....	....	....	....	....	....	....	....	....	....	....	....	....	....	....	....
1969-70	**Minnesota North Stars**	**NHL**	**50**	**9**	**24**	**16**	**2887**	**163**	**2**	**3.39**	**3.64**	....	....	....	....	**3**	**1**	**2**	....	**180**	**6**	***1**	**2.00**	....	....	....	....
1970-71	**Minnesota North Stars**	**NHL**	**40**	**19**	**15**	**6**	**2380**	**107**	**5**	**2.70**	**2.66**	....	....	....	....	**8**	**3**	**5**	....	**480**	**28**	**0**	**3.50**	....	....	....	....
1971-72	**Minnesota North Stars**	**NHL**	**43**	**20**	**17**	**4**	**2539**	**112**	**3**	**2.65**	**2.65**	....	....	....	....	**4**	**1**	**3**	....	**238**	**12**	**0**	**3.03**	....	....	....	....
1972-73	**Minnesota North Stars**	**NHL**	**47**	**21**	**18**	**6**	**2736**	**132**	**5**	**2.89**	**2.71**	....	....	....	....	**5**	**2**	**3**	....	**309**	**9**	***2**	***1.75**	....	....	....	....
1973-74	**Minnesota North Stars**	**NHL**	**40**	**12**	**18**	**10**	**2378**	**138**	**1**	**3.48**	**3.37**	....	....	....	....	....	....	....	....	....	....	....	....	....	....	....	....
1974-75	**Minnesota North Stars**	**NHL**	**37**	**11**	**21**	**4**	**2129**	**149**	**1**	**4.20**	**3.81**	....	....	....	....	....	....	....	....	....	....	....	....	....	....	....	....
1975-76	**Minnesota North Stars**	**NHL**	**47**	**13**	**27**	**5**	**2704**	**151**	**2**	**3.35**	**3.03**	....	....	....	....	....	....	....	....	....	....	....	....	....	....	....	....
1976-77	**Vancouver Canucks**	**NHL**	**47**	**17**	**21**	**9**	**2699**	**151**	**1**	**3.36**	**3.12**	....	....	....	....	....	....	....	....	....	....	....	....	....	....	....	....
1977-78	**Vancouver Canucks**	**NHL**	**46**	**10**	**24**	**8**	**2570**	**172**	**1**	**4.02**	**3.79**	....	....	....	....	....	....	....	....	....	....	....	....	....	....	....	....
	NHL Totals		**568**	**189**	**259**	**96**	**32570**	**1774**	**30**	**3.27**	....	....	....	....	....	**36**	**15**	**21**	....	**2245**	**100**	**3**	**2.67**	....	....	....	....

CHL First All-Star Team (1965) • Won Terry Sawchuk Trophy (fewest goals against - CHL) (1965) • Won Tommy Ivan Trophy (CHL's MVP) (1965)

Claimed by **Montreal** from **Toronto** (Spokane - WHL) in Intra-League Draft, June 12, 1961. Traded to **NY Rangers** by **Montreal** with Garry Peters for Noel Price, Earl Ingarfield, Gord Labossiere, Dave McComb and cash, June 8, 1965. Claimed by **Minnesota** from **NY Rangers** in Expansion Draft, June 6, 1967. Traded to **Vancouver** by **Minnesota** for Gary Smith, August 23, 1976.

• MARACLE, NORM

Norm Maracle G – L. 5'9", 175 lbs. b: Belleville, Ont., 10/2/1974. Detroit's 6th choice, 126th overall, in 1993 Entry Draft.

Season	Club	League	GP	W	L	T	Mins	GA	SO	Avg	AAvg	Eff	SA	S%	SAPG	GP	W	L	T	Mins	GA	SO	Avg	Eff	SA	S%	SAPG
1991-92	Saskatoon Blades	WHL	29	13	6	3	1529	87	1	3.41	....	....	....	....	....	15	9	5	....	860	37	0	3.38	....	....	....	....
1992-93	Saskatoon Blades	WHL	53	27	18	3	1939	160	1	3.27	....	....	....	....	....	9	4	5	....	569	33	0	3.48	....	....	....	....
1993-94	Saskatoon Blades	WHL	56	*41	13	1	3219	148	2	2.76	....	....	....	....	....	16	*11	5	....	940	48	*1	3.06	....	....	....	....
1994-95	Adirondack Red Wings	AHL	39	12	15	2	1997	119	0	3.57	....	....	....	....	....	....	....	....	....	....	....	....	....	....	....	....	....
1995-96	Adirondack Red Wings	AHL	54	24	18	6	2949	135	2	2.75	....	....	....	....	....	1	0	1	....	30	4	0	8.11	....	....	....	....
1996-97	Adirondack Red Wings	AHL	*68	*34	22	9	*3843	173	5	2.70	....	....	....	....	....	4	1	3	....	192	10	1	3.13	....	....	....	....
1997-98	**Detroit Red Wings**	**NHL**	**4**	**2**	**0**	**1**	**178**	**6**	**0**	**2.02**	**2.36**	**1.92**	**63**	**.905**	**21.2**	....	....	....	....	....	....	....	....	....	....	....	....
	Adirondack Red Wings	AHL	*66	27	29	8	*3709	190	1	3.07	....	....	....	....	....	3	0	3	....	180	10	0	3.33	....	....	....	....
	NHL Totals		**4**	**2**	**0**	**1**	**178**	**6**	**0**	**2.02**	....	....	**63**	**.905**	....	....	....	....	....	....	....	....	....	....	....	....	....

WHL East Second All-Star Team (1993) • WHL East First All-Star Team (1994) • Canadian Major Junior First All-Star Team (1994) • Canadian Major Junior Goaltender of the Year (1994) • AHL Second All-Star Team (1997, 1998)

• MAROIS, JEAN

Jean Marois G – L. 5'8", 155 lbs. b: Quebec City, Que., 5/11/1924.

Season	Club	League	GP	W	L	T	Mins	GA	SO	Avg	AAvg	Eff	SA	S%	SAPG	GP	W	L	T	Mins	GA	SO	Avg	Eff	SA	S%	SAPG
1941-42	St. Michael's Majors	OHA	4	....	....	....	240	22	0	5.50	....	....	....	....	....	1	1	0	0	60	3	0	3.00	....	....	....	....
1942-43	St. Michael's Majors	OHA	20	....	....	....	1200	99	0	4.95	....	....	....	....	....	6	....	....	....	360	35	*1	5.95	....	....	....	....
1943-44	St. Michael's Majors	OHA	14	....	....	....	840	44	1	3.14	....	....	....	....	....	6	....	....	....	360	20	0	3.38	....	....	....	....
	Toronto Maple Leafs	**NHL**	**1**	**1**	**0**	**0**	**60**	**4**	**0**	**4.00**	**3.03**	....	....	....	....	....	....	....	....	....	....	....	....	....	....	....	....
1944-45	St. Michael's Majors	OHA	STATISTICS NOT AVAILABLE																								
1945-46	Quebec Aces	QSHL	7	....	....	....	420	38	0	5.43	....	....	....	....	....	6	2	4	0	360	28	0	4.67	....	....	....	....
1946-47	Quebec Aces	QSHL	32	....	....	....	1920	119	0	3.72	....	....	....	....	....	....	....	....	....	....	....	....	....	....	....	....	....
1947-48	Quebec Aces	QSHL	35	....	....	....	2080	120	0	3.46	....	....	....	....	....	10	....	....	....	600	30	1	3.00	....	....	....	....
1948-49	Quebec Aces	QSHL	59	22	31	6	3540	205	4	3.47	....	....	....	....	....	3	0	3	0	180	18	0	6.00	....	....	....	....
1949-50	Shawinigan Cataracts	QSHL	46	....	....	....	2760	204	3	3.43	....	....	....	....	....	....	....	....	....	....	....	....	....	....	....	....	....
1950-51	Quebec Aces	QSHL	60	31	22	7	3600	192	*3	3.20	....	....	....	....	....	19	*12	7	0	1140	55	1	2.89	....	....	....	....
1951-52	Quebec Aces	QSHL	48	*31	12	5	2950	126	*6	*2.56	....	....	....	....	....	8	6	2	0	519	18	1	2.08	....	....	....	....
1952-53	Quebec Aces	QSHL	36	13	14	8	2220	118	1	3.19	....	....	....	....	....	1	0	1	0	60	6	0	6.00	....	....	....	....

			REGULAR SEASON													PLAYOFFS											
Season	Club	League	GP	W	L	T	Mins	GA	SO	Avg	AAvg	Eff	SA	S%	SAPG	GP	W	L	T	Mins	GA	SO	Avg	Eff	SA	S%	SAPG
1953-54	Quebec Aces	QHL	15	6	7	2	927	54	0	3.50	....	....	....	....	....	5	1	4	0	300	20	1	4.00	....	....	....	....
	Hershey Bears	AHL	6	4	2	0	360	16	0	2.67	....	....	....	....	....	....	....	....	....	....	....	....	....	....	....	....	....
	Providence Reds	AHL	3	2	1	0	180	11	0	3.67	....	....	....	....	....	....	....	....	....	....	....	....	....	....	....	....	....
	Chicago Black Hawks	**NHL**	**2**	**0**	**2**	**0**	**120**	**11**	**0**	**5.50**	**7.11**	....	....	....	....	....	....	....	....	....	....	....	....	....	....	....	....
1954-55	Providence Reds	AHL	11	4	6	1	660	47	0	4.27	....	....	....	....	....	....	....	....	....	....	....	....	....	....	....	....	....
	Quebec Aces	QHL	17	9	7	1	1013	56	1	3.32	....	....	....	....	....	....	....	....	....	....	....	....	....	....	....	....	....
	NHL Totals		**3**	**1**	**2**	**0**	**180**	**15**	**0**	**5.00**	....	....	....	....	....	....	....	....	....	....	....	....	....	....	....	....	....

• Promoted to **Toronto** from **St. Michael's** (OHA) to replace injured Benny Grant, November 18, 1943. (Montreal 5, Toronto 2). Signed as a free agent by **Chicago**, November 21, 1953.

• MARTIN, SETH

Seth Martin G – L. 5'11", 180 lbs. b: Rossland, B.C., 5/4/1933.

Season	Club	League	GP	W	L	T	Mins	GA	SO	Avg	AAvg	Eff	SA	S%	SAPG	GP	W	L	T	Mins	GA	SO	Avg	Eff	SA	S%	SAPG
1950-51	Lethbridge Native Sons	WJHL	30	....	....	....	1800	98	0	3.27	....	....	....	....	....	2	....	....	....	80	3	0	*2.25	....	....	....	....
1951-52	Lethbridge Native Sons	WJHL	36	23	12	1	2160	138	1	3.84	....	....	....	....	....	4	0	4	0	240	30	0	7.50	....	....	....	....
1952-53	Lethbridge Native Sons	WJHL	27	17	6	4	1620	115	0	4.26	....	....	....	....	....	25	16	7	2	1540	96	2	3.74	....	....	....	....
1953-54	Trail Smoke Eaters	WIHL	28	....	....	....	1680	139	0	4.96	....	....	....	....	....	4	1	3	0	240	21	0	5.20	....	....	....	....
	Kelowna Packers	OSHL	3	....	....	....	180	7	0	2.33	....	....	....	....	....	....	....	....	....	....	....	....	....	....	....	....	....
1954-55	Trail Smoke Eaters	WIHL	28	....	....	....	1680	134	*1	4.78	....	....	....	....	....	4	....	....	....	240	13	0	*3.25	....	....	....	....
1955-56	Trail Smoke Eaters	WIHL	39	....	....	....	2340	183	0	4.69	....	....	....	....	....	10	5	5	0	600	35	1	3.50	....	....	....	....
1956-57	Trail Smoke Eaters	WIHL	26				1560	80	0	*3.12	....	....	....	....	....	9	....	....	....	540	42	0	4.67	....	....	....	....
1957-58	Trail Smoke Eaters	WIHL	47	....	....	....	2820	211	1	4.49	....	....	....	....	....	7	3	4	0	420	29	0	4.14	....	....	....	....
1958-59	Trail Smoke Eaters	WIHL	39	17	20	2	2340	165	*4	4.23	....	....	....	....	....	7	3	4	0	379	29	0	4.60	....	....	....	....
1959-60	Trail Smoke Eaters	WIHL	37	....	....	....	2220	185	0	5.00	....	....	....	....	....	11	*9	2	0	660	45	1	4.09	....	....	....	....
	Spokane Spokes	WHL	2	0	2	0	120	8	0	4.00	....	....	....	....	....	....	....	....	....	....	....	....	....	....	....	....	....
	Vancouver Canucks	WHL	1	....	....	....	40	4	0	6.00	....	....	....	....	....	....	....	....	....	....	....	....	....	....	....	....	....
1960-61	Trail Smoke Eaters	WIHL	37	*34	3	0	2220	111	0	3.00	....	....	....	....	....	13	11	1	0	780	30	0	2.31	....	....	....	....
	Canada	WEC-A	4	3	0	1	226	5	0	1.33	....	....	....	....	....	....	....	....	....	....	....	....	....	....	....	....	....
1961-62	Portland Buckeroos	WHL	1	....	....	....	60	1	0	1.00	....	....	....	....	....	....	....	....	....	....	....	....	....	....	....	....	....
	Trail Smoke Eaters	WIHL	31	....	....	....	1860	112	*2	*3.70	....	....	....	....	....	....	....	....	....	....	....	....	....	....	....	....	....
1962-63	Canada	Nat-Team	STATISTICS NOT AVAILABLE																								
	Canada	WEC-A	7	4	2	1	420	23	1	3.29	....	....	....	....	....	....	....	....	....	....	....	....	....	....	....	....	....
1963-64	Canada	Nat-Team	STATISTICS NOT AVAILABLE																								
	Canada	Olympics	6	4	1	0	247	5	....	1.21	....	....	....	....	....	....	....	....	....	....	....	....	....	....	....	....	....
1964-65	Rossland Warriors	WIHL	41	....	....	....	2460	192	0	4.68	....	....	....	....	....	....	....	....	....	....	....	....	....	....	....	....	....
1965-66	Rossland Warriors	WIHL	23	....	....	....	1380	107	0	4.65	....	....	....	....	....	....	....	....	....	....	....	....	....	....	....	....	....
	Canada	WEC-A	4	1	3	0	240	11	0	2.75	....	....	....	....	....	....	....	....	....	....	....	....	....	....	....	....	....
1966-67	Rossland Warriors	WIHL	33	....	....	....	1980	158	0	4.79	....	....	....	....	....	....	....	....	....	....	....	....	....	....	....	....	....
	Canada	WEC-A	6	3	2	1	360	14	0	2.33	....	....	....	....	....	....	....	....	....	....	....	....	....	....	....	....	....
1967-68	**St. Louis Blues**	**NHL**	**30**	**8**	**10**	**7**	**1552**	**67**	**1**	**2.59**	**2.86**	....	....	....	....	**2**	**0**	**0**	....	**73**	**5**	**0**	**4.11**	....	....	....	....
1968-69	Trail Smoke Eaters	WIHL	17	....	....	....	1020	67	1	3.94	....	....	....	....	....	....	....	....	....	....	....	....	....	....	....	....	....
1969-70	Spokane Jets	WIHL	24	....	....	....	1440	56	*3	*2.33	....	....	....	....	....	....	....	....	....	....	....	....	....	....	....	....	....
1970-71			DID NOT PLAY													....	....	....	....	....	....	....	....	....	....	....	....
1971-72	Spokane Jets	WIHL	3	....	....	....	180	14	0	4.66	....	....	....	....	....	....	....	....	....	....	....	....	....	....	....	....	....
1972-73	Portland Buckaroos	WHL	2	0	2	0	100	11	0	6.59	....	....	....	....	....	....	....	....	....	....	....	....	....	....	....	....	....
	NHL Totals		**30**	**8**	**10**	**7**	**1552**	**67**	**1**	**2.59**	....	....	....	....	....	**2**	**0**	**0**	....	**73**	**5**	**0**	**4.11**	....	....	....	....

WEC-A All-Star Team (1961, 1966) • Named Best Goaltender at WEC-A (1961, 1963, 1966)

Signed as a free agent by **St. Louis**, June 6, 1967. Claimed by **Buffalo** (AHL) from **St. Louis** in Reverse Draft, June 13, 1968. Traded to **St. Louis** by **Buffalo** (AHL) for cash, June 27, 1968.

• MASON, BOB

Bob Mason G – R. 6'1", 180 lbs. b: International Falls, MN, 4/22/1961.

Season	Club	League	GP	W	L	T	Mins	GA	SO	Avg	AAvg	Eff	SA	S%	SAPG	GP	W	L	T	Mins	GA	SO	Avg	Eff	SA	S%	SAPG
1981-82	Univ. of Minnesota-Duluth	WCHA	27	9	15	3	1401	115	0	4.45	....	....	....	....	....	....	....	....	....	....	....	....	....	....	....	....	....
1982-83	Univ. of Minnesota-Duluth	WCHA	43	26	16	1	2594	151	1	3.49	....	....	....	....	....	....	....	....	....	....	....	....	....	....	....	....	....
1983-84	United States	Nat-Team	33	17	10	5	1895	89	0	2.82	....	....	....	....	....	....	....	....	....	....	....	....	....	....	....	....	....
	United States	Olympics	3	1	0	1	160	10	0	3.75	....	....	....	....	....	....	....	....	....	....	....	....	....	....	....	....	....
	Washington Capitals	**NHL**	**2**	**2**	**0**	**0**	**120**	**3**	**0**	**1.50**	**1.17**	**0.98**	**46**	**.935**	**23.0**	....	....	....	....	....	....	....	....	....	....	....	....
	Hershey Bears	AHL	5	1	4	0	282	26	0	5.53	....	....	....	....	....	....	....	....	....	....	....	....	....	....	....	....	....
1984-85	**Washington Capitals**	**NHL**	**12**	**8**	**2**	**1**	**661**	**31**	**1**	**2.81**	**2.23**	**2.99**	**291**	**.893**	**26.4**	....	....	....	....	....	....	....	....	....	....	....	....
	Binghamton Whalers	AHL	20	10	6	1	1052	58	1	3.31	....	....	....	....	....	....	....	....	....	....	....	....	....	....	....	....	....
1985-86	**Washington Capitals**	**NHL**	**1**	**1**	**0**	**0**	**16**	**0**	**0**	**0.00**	**0.00**	**0.00**	**5**	**1.000**	**18.8**	....	....	....	....	....	....	....	....	....	....	....	....
	Binghamton Whalers	AHL	34	20	11	2	1940	126	0	3.90	....	....	....	....	....	3	1	1	0	124	9	0	4.35	....	....	....	....
1986-87	**Washington Capitals**	**NHL**	**45**	**20**	**18**	**5**	**2536**	**137**	**0**	**3.24**	**2.72**	**3.56**	**1247**	**.890**	**29.5**	**4**	**2**	**2**	....	**309**	**9**	**1**	**1.75**	**1.10**	**143**	**.937**	**27.8**
	Binghamton Whalers	AHL	2	1	1	0	119	4	0	2.02	....	....	....	....	....	....	....	....	....	....	....	....	....	....	....	....	....
1987-88	United States	C Cup	DID NOT PLAY – SPARE GOALTENDER																								
	Chicago Blackhawks	**NHL**	**41**	**13**	**18**	**8**	**2312**	**160**	**0**	**4.15**	**3.46**	**4.91**	**1353**	**.882**	**35.1**	**1**	**0**	**1**	....	**60**	**3**	**0**	**3.00**	**2.90**	**31**	**.903**	**31.0**
1988-89	**Quebec Nordiques**	**NHL**	**22**	**5**	**14**	**1**	**1168**	**92**	**0**	**4.73**	**3.91**	**6.94**	**627**	**.853**	**32.2**	....	....	....	....	....	....	....	....	....	....	....	....
	Halifax Citadels	AHL	23	11	7	1	1278	73	1	3.43	....	....	....	....	....	2	0	2	0	97	9	0	5.57	....	....	....	....
1989-90	Washington Capitals	Fr-Tour	1	....	....	....	30	4	0	8.00	....	....	....	....	....	....	....	....	....	....	....	....	....	....	....	....	....
	Washington Capitals	**NHL**	**16**	**4**	**9**	**1**	**822**	**48**	**0**	**3.50**	**2.93**	**4.32**	**389**	**.877**	**28.4**	....	....	....	....	....	....	....	....	....	....	....	....
	Baltimore Skipjacks	AHL	13	9	2	2	770	44	0	3.43	....	....	....	....	....	6	2	4	0	373	20	0	3.22	....	....	....	....
1990-91	**Vancouver Canucks**	**NHL**	**6**	**2**	**4**	**0**	**353**	**29**	**0**	**4.93**	**4.41**	**7.60**	**188**	**.846**	**32.0**	....	....	....	....	....	....	....	....	....	....	....	....
	Milwaukee Admirals	IHL	22	8	12	1	1199	82	0	4.10	....	....	....	....	....	....	....	....	....	....	....	....	....	....	....	....	....
1991-92	Milwaukee Admirals	IHL	51	27	18	4	3024	171	1	3.39	....	....	....	....	....	3	1	2	0	179	15	0	5.03	....	....	....	....
1992-93	Hamilton Canucks	AHL	44	20	19	3	2601	159	0	3.67	....	....	....	....	....	....	....	....	....	....	....	....	....	....	....	....	....
1993-94	Milwaukee Admirals	IHL	40	21	9	8	2206	132	0	3.59	....	....	....	....	....	3	0	1	0	141	9	0	3.83	....	....	....	....
1994-95	Fort Wayne Komets	IHL	1	0	1	0	60	5	0	5.00	....	....	....	....	....	....	....	....	....	....	....	....	....	....	....	....	....
	Milwaukee Admirals	IHL	13	7	4	1	745	50	0	4.03	....	....	....	....	....	....	....	....	....	....	....	....	....	....	....	....	....
	NHL Totals		**145**	**55**	**65**	**16**	**7988**	**500**	**1**	**3.76**	....	....	**4146**	**.879**	....	**5**	**2**	**3**	....	**369**	**12**	**1**	**1.95**	....	....	....	....

WCHA First All-Star Team (1983)

Signed as a free agent by **Washington**, February 21, 1984. Signed as a free agent by **Chicago**, June 12, 1987. Traded to **Quebec** by **Chicago** for Mike Eagles, July 5, 1988. Traded to **Washington** by **Quebec** for future considerations, June 17, 1989. Signed as a free agent by **Vancouver**, December 1, 1990.

• MATTSSON, MARKUS

Markus Mattsson G – R. 6', 180 lbs. b: Suoneiemi, Finland, 7/30/1957. NY Islanders' 6th choice, 87th overall, in 1977 Amateur Draft.

Season	Club	League	GP	W	L	T	Mins	GA	SO	Avg	AAvg	Eff	SA	S%	SAPG	GP	W	L	T	Mins	GA	SO	Avg	Eff	SA	S%	SAPG
1974-75	Finland	EJC-A	3	....	....	....	180	9	....	3.00	....	....	....	....	....	....	....	....	....	....	....	....	....	....	....	....	....
	Finland	WJC-A	5	....	....	....	300	14	....	2.80	....	....	....	....	....	....	....	....	....	....	....	....	....	....	....	....	....
1975-76	Finland	EJC-A	4	....	....	....	240	16	....	4.00	....	....	....	....	....	....	....	....	....	....	....	....	....	....	....	....	....
1976-77	Finland	C Cup	2	1	1	0	80	14	0	11.00	....	....	....	....	....	....	....	....	....	....	....	....	....	....	....	....	....
1977-78	Tulsa Oilers	CHL	2	1	1	0	92	6	0	3.91	....	....	....	....	....	....	....	....	....	....	....	....	....	....	....	....	....
	Quebec Nordiques	WHA	6	1	3	0	266	30	0	6.77	....	....	....	....	....	....	....	....	....	....	....	....	....	....	....	....	....
	Winnipeg Jets	WHA	10	4	5	0	511	30	0	3.52	....	....	....	....	....	....	....	....	....	....	....	....	....	....	....	....	....
1978-79	Winnipeg Jets	WHA	52	25	21	3	2990	181	0	3.63	....	....	....	....	....	....	....	....	....	....	....	....	....	....	....	....	....
1979-80	**Winnipeg Jets**	**NHL**	**21**	**5**	**11**	**4**	**1200**	**65**	**2**	**3.25**	**2.85**	....	....	....	....	....	....	....	....	....	....	....	....	....	....	....	....
	Tulsa Oilers	CHL	20	10	7	2	1196	56	2	2.81	....	....	....	....	....	....	....	....	....	....	....	....	....	....	....	....	....
1980-81	**Winnipeg Jets**	**NHL**	**31**	**3**	**21**	**4**	**1707**	**128**	**1**	**4.50**	**3.62**	....	....	....	....	....	....	....	....	....	....	....	....	....	....	....	....
	Tulsa Oilers	CHL	5	3	2	0	299	10	1	2.01	....	....	....	....	....	....	....	....	....	....	....	....	....	....	....	....	....
1981-82	Finland	C Cup	2	0	2	0	120	15	0	7.50	....	....	....	....	....	....	....	....	....	....	....	....	....	....	....	....	....
	Tulsa Oilers	CHL	50	20	23	0	2963	195	0	3.95	....	....	....	....	....	1	0	1	0	60	7	0	7.00	....	....	....	....

			REGULAR SEASON													PLAYOFFS											
Season	Club	League	GP	W	L	T	Mins	GA	SO	Avg	AAvg	Eff	SA	S%	SAPG	GP	W	L	T	Mins	GA	SO	Avg	Eff	SA	S%	SAPG
1982-83	Birmingham South Stars	CHL	28	17	10	0	1614	89	1	3.31	....	....	....	....	....	....	....	....	....	....	....	....	....	....	....	....	....
	Minnesota North Stars	**NHL**	**2**	**1**	**1**	**0**	**100**	**6**	**1**	**3.60**	**2.87**	**3.09**	**70**	**.914**	**42.0**	....	....	....	....	....	....	....	....	....	....	....	....
	Los Angeles Kings	**NHL**	**19**	**5**	**5**	**4**	**899**	**65**	**1**	**4.34**	**3.47**	**6.21**	**454**	**.857**	**30.3**	....	....	....	....	....	....	....	....	....	....	....	....
1983-84	**Los Angeles Kings**	**NHL**	**19**	**7**	**8**	**2**	**1101**	**79**	**1**	**4.31**	**3.38**	**6.42**	**530**	**.851**	**28.9**	....	....	....	....	....	....	....	....	....	....	....	....
	New Haven Nighthawks	AHL	31	16	10	1	1701	110	0	3.88	....	....	....	....	....	....	....	....	....	....	....	....	....	....	....	....	....
	NHL Totals		**92**	**21**	**46**	**14**	**5007**	**343**	**6**	**4.11**	....	....	....	....	....	....	....	....	....	....	....	....	....	....	....	....	....
	Other Major League Totals		68	30	29	3	3767	241	0	3.84	....	....	....	....	....	....	....	....	....	....	....	....	....	....	....	....	....

Finnish Rookie of the Year (1975) • Finnish First All-Star Team (1986)

• Played professional hockey in Finland from 1974-75 through 1976-77. Selected by **Houston** (WHA) in 1977 WHA Amateur Draft, May, 1977. WHA rights traded to **Winnipeg** (WHA) by **Houston** (WHA) for future considerations, June, 1977. Traded to **Quebec** (WHA) by **Winnipeg** (WHA) for future considerations, February, 1978. Traded to **Winnipeg** (WHA) by **Quebec** (WHA) for future considerations, March, 1978. Reclaimed by **NY Islanders** from **Winnipeg** prior to Expansion Draft, June 9, 1979. Claimed as a priority selection by **Winnipeg**, June 9, 1979. Signed as a free agent by **Minnesota**, September 24, 1982. Traded to **LA Kings** by **Minnesota** for LA Kings' 3rd round choice (Stephane Roy) in 1985 Entry Draft, February 1, 1983. • Played professional hockey in Finland from 1984-85 through 1985-86.

• MAY, DARRELL

Darrell May G – L. 6', 175 lbs. b: Edmonton, Alta., 3/6/1962. Vancouver's 4th choice, 91st overall, in 1980 Entry Draft.

1978-79	Portland Winter Hawks	WHL	21	12	2	2	1113	64	0	3.45	....	....	....	....	....	2	1	0	0	80	7	0	5.25	....	....	....	....
1979-80	Portland Winter Hawks	WHL	43	32	8	1	2416	143	1	3.55	....	....	....	....	....	8	3	5	0	439	27	0	3.69	....	....	....	....
1980-81	Portland Winter Hawks	WHL	36	28	7	1	2128	122	3	3.44	....	....	....	....	....	4	....	....	....	243	21	0	5.19	....	....	....	....
1981-82	Portland Winter Hawks	WHL	53	31	20	2	3097	226	0	4.38	....	....	....	....	....	15	....	....	....	851	59	0	4.16	....	....	....	....
1982-83	Fort Wayne Komets	IHL	46	....	....	....	2584	177	0	4.11	....	....	....	....	....	2	....	....	....	120	13	0	6.50	....	....	....	....
1983-84	Erie Golden Blades	ACHL	43	21	16	2	2404	163	1	4.07	....	....	....	....	....	7	....	....	....	461	16	*1	*2.08	....	....	....	....
1984-85	Peoria Rivermen	IHL	19	13	4	2	1133	56	1	2.97	....	....	....	....	....	10	6	4	0	609	33	0	3.25	....	....	....	....
	Erie Golden Blades	ACHL	43	....	....	....	2580	170	*1	3.95	....	....	....	....	....	....	....	....	....	....	....	....	....	....	....	....	....
1985-86	**St. Louis Blues**	**NHL**	**3**	**1**	**2**	**0**	**184**	**13**	**0**	**4.24**	**3.30**	**6.41**	**86**	**.849**	**28.0**	....	....	....	....	....	....	....	....	....	....	....	....
	Peoria Rivermen	IHL	56	33	21	0	3321	179	1	3.23	....	....	....	....	....	11	6	5	0	634	38	1	3.60	....	....	....	....
1986-87	Peoria Rivermen	IHL	58	26	31	1	3420	214	2	3.75	....	....	....	....	....	....	....	....	....	....	....	....	....	....	....	....	....
1987-88	**St. Louis Blues**	**NHL**	**3**	**0**	**3**	**0**	**180**	**18**	**0**	**6.00**	**4.99**	**10.09**	**107**	**.832**	**35.7**	....	....	....	....	....	....	....	....	....	....	....	....
	Peoria Rivermen	IHL	48	22	19	5	2754	162	1	3.53	....	....	....	....	....	....	....	....	....	....	....	....	....	....	....	....	....
1988-89	Peoria Rivermen	IHL	52	20	22	0	2908	202	0	4.17	....	....	....	....	....	2	0	2	0	137	13	0	5.69	....	....	....	....
	NHL Totals		**6**	**1**	**5**	**0**	**364**	**31**	**0**	**5.11**	....	....	**193**	**.839**	....	....	....	....	....	....	....	....	....	....	....	....	....

IHL First All-Star Team (1986, 1987) • Won James Gatschene Memorial Trophy (MVP - IHL) (1986)

Signed as a free agent by **St. Louis**, October 9, 1985. Traded to **Montreal** by **St. Louis** with Jocelyn Lemieux and St. Louis' 2nd round choice (Patrice Brisebois) in 1989 Entry Draft for Sergio Momesso and Vincent Riendeau, August 9, 1988.

• MAYER, GILLES

Gilles "The Needle" Mayer G – L. 5'6", 135 lbs. b: Ottawa, Ont., 8/24/1930.

1944-45	Hull Volants	Ott-Jr.	7	....	....	....	420	15	*1	*2.14	....	....	....	....	....	4	2	2	0	240	18	0	4.50	....	....	....	....
1945-46	Hull Volants	Ott-Jr.	5	....	....	....	300	35	0	6.99	....	....	....	....	....	....	....	....	....	....	....	....	....	....	....	....	....
1946-47	Lake Placid Roamers	NYJHL	STATISTICS NOT AVAILABLE																								
1947-48	Barrie Flyers	OHA	19	....	....	....	1140	59	3	3.11	....	....	....	....	....	10	....	....	....	600	36	0	3.60	....	....	....	....
1948-49	Barrie Flyers	OHA	46	*26	16	4	2760	134	*5	*2.91	....	....	....	....	....	15	11	4	0	910	41	2	2.70	....	....	....	....
1949-50	Pittsburgh Hornets	AHL	50	20	19	11	3000	142	4	2.84	....	....	....	....	....	....	....	....	....	....	....	....	....	....	....	....	....
	Toronto Maple Leafs	**NHL**	**1**	**0**	**1**	**0**	**60**	**2**	**0**	**2.00**	**2.26**	....	....	....	....	....	....	....	....	....	....	....	....	....	....	....	....
1950-51	Pittsburgh Hornets	AHL	71	31	33	7	*4350	174	*6	*2.40	....	....	....	....	....	*13	*9	4	0	835	26	*2	*1.87	....	....	....	....
1951-52	Pittsburgh Hornets	AHL	*68	*46	19	3	*4120	175	*5	2.55	....	....	....	....	....	11	*8	3	0	753	24	*1	*1.91	....	....	....	....
1952-53	Pittsburgh Hornets	AHL	62	36	20	6	3760	146	*6	*2.33	....	....	....	....	....	10	6	4	0	695	20	0	1.73	....	....	....	....
1953-54	Pittsburgh Hornets	AHL	68	33	30	5	4080	212	3	3.12	....	....	....	....	....	5	2	3	0	330	13	*1	*2.36	....	....	....	....
	Toronto Maple Leafs	**NHL**	**1**	**0**	**0**	**1**	**60**	**3**	**0**	**3.00**	**3.86**	....	....	....	....	....	....	....	....	....	....	....	....	....	....	....	....
1954-55	Pittsburgh Hornets	AHL	*64	31	25	8	*3840	179	*3	*2.80	....	....	....	....	....	*10	*7	3	0	639	28	*1	*2.63	....	....	....	....
	Toronto Maple Leafs	**NHL**	**1**	**1**	**0**	**0**	**60**	**1**	**0**	**1.00**	**1.22**	....	....	....	....	....	....	....	....	....	....	....	....	....	....	....	....
1955-56	Pittsburgh Hornets	AHL	56	40	12	4	3360	151	*5	*2.70	....	....	....	....	....	4	1	3	0	312	14	0	2.69	....	....	....	....
	Toronto Maple Leafs	**NHL**	**6**	**1**	**5**	**0**	**360**	**19**	**0**	**3.17**	**3.88**	....	....	....	....	....	....	....	....	....	....	....	....	....	....	....	....
1956-57	Hershey Bears	AHL	29	14	12	3	1740	103	1	3.55	....	....	....	....	....	....	....	....	....	....	....	....	....	....	....	....	....
1957-58	Hershey Bears	AHL	22	12	7	3	1358	62	0	2.74	....	....	....	....	....	....	....	....	....	....	....	....	....	....	....	....	....
1958-59	Hershey Bears	AHL	STATISTICS NOT AVAILABLE																								
1959-60	Cleveland Barons	AHL	41	19	19	3	2460	126	3	3.07	....	....	....	....	....	7	3	4	0	420	22	*1	3.14	....	....	....	....
1960-61	Cleveland Barons	AHL	66	32	34	0	3960	222	3	3.36	....	....	....	....	....	....	....	....	....	....	....	....	....	....	....	....	....
1961-62	Providence Reds	AHL	30	16	13	1	1800	122	1	4.07	....	....	....	....	....	3	1	2	0	185	11	0	3.57	....	....	....	....
1962-63	Providence Reds	AHL	34	16	15	3	2040	99	1	2.91	....	....	....	....	....	....	....	....	....	....	....	....	....	....	....	....	....
	NHL Totals		**9**	**2**	**6**	**1**	**540**	**25**	**0**	**2.78**	....	....	....	....	....	....	....	....	....	....	....	....	....	....	....	....	....

AHL First All-Star Team (1951, 1954, 1955) • Won Harry "Hap" Holmes Memorial Award (fewest goals against - AHL) (1951, 1953, 1954, 1955, 1956) • AHL Second All-Star Team (1953, 1956)

Traded to **Hershey** (AHL) by **Pittsburgh** (AHL) with Jack Price, Willie Marshall, Bob Hassard, Bob Solinger and Ray Gariepy for cash, June, 1956. Traded to **Cleveland** (AHL) by **Hershey** (AHL) for Gord Hollingworth and Claude Dufour, June, 1959.

• McAULEY, KEN

Ken McAuley G – R. 5'10", 190 lbs. b: Edmonton, Alta., 1/9/1921. Deceased.

1938-39	Edmonton Maple Leafs	City Jr.	11	....	....	....	660	38	0	3.45	....	....	....	....	....	....	....	....	....	....	....	....	....	....	....	....	....
1939-40	Edmonton Maple Leafs	City Jr.	STATISTICS NOT AVAILABLE																								
1940-41	Edmonton Maple Leafs	City Jr.	STATISTICS NOT AVAILABLE																								
1941-42	Regina Rangers	SSHL	32	....	....	....	1920	110	2	3.44	....	....	....	....	....	3	....	....	....	180	15	0	5.00	....	....	....	....
1942-43			MILITARY SERVICE																								
1943-44	**New York Rangers**	**NHL**	***50**	**6**	**39**	**5**	**2980**	**310**	**0**	**6.24**	**5.27**	....	....	....	....	....	....	....	....	....	....	....	....	....	....	....	....
1944-45	**New York Rangers**	**NHL**	**46**	**11**	**25**	**10**	**2760**	**227**	**1**	**4.93**	**4.34**	....	....	....	....	....	....	....	....	....	....	....	....	....	....	....	....
1945-46	Edmonton Flyers	WCSHL	36	24	10	2	2160	130	0	3.61	....	....	....	....	....	8	4	4	0	480	31	0	3.75	....	....	....	....
1946-47	Edmonton Flyers	WCSHL	40	....	....	....	2400	138	1	3.45	....	....	....	....	....	1	....	....	....	60	5	0	5.00	....	....	....	....
1947-48	Saskatoon Quakers	WCSHL	48	....	....	....	2860	235	0	4.93	....	....	....	....	....	....	....	....	....	....	....	....	....	....	....	....	....
1948-49	Saskatoon Quakers	WCSHL	6	....	....	....	360	42	0	7.00	....	....	....	....	....	....	....	....	....	....	....	....	....	....	....	....	....
1949-50	Kimberley Dynamiters	Kootenay	1	1	0	0	60	2	0	2.00	....	....	....	....	....	....	....	....	....	....	....	....	....	....	....	....	....
	NHL Totals		**96**	**17**	**64**	**15**	**5740**	**537**	**1**	**5.61**	....	....	....	....	....	....	....	....	....	....	....	....	....	....	....	....	....

• McCARTAN, JACK

Jack McCartan G6'1", 195 lbs. b: St. Paul, MN, 8/5/1935. **USHOF**

1955-56	University of Minnesota	WIHL	24	....	....	....	1440	67	0	2.79	....	....	....	....	....	....	....	....	....	....	....	....	....	....	....	....	....
1956-57	University of Minnesota	WCHA	15	....	....	....	900	43	0	2.87	....	....	....	....	....	....	....	....	....	....	....	....	....	....	....	....	....
1957-58	University of Minnesota	WCHA	28	....	....	....	1680	89	1	3.18	....	....	....	....	....	....	....	....	....	....	....	....	....	....	....	....	....
1958-59	United States	Nat-Team	29	....	....	....	1740	104	0	3.65	....	....	....	....	....	3	....	....	....	180	12	0	4.00	....	....	....	....
1959-60	Minneapolis Rangers	CMHL	5	....	....	....	300	17	1	3.40	....	....	....	....	....	....	....	....	....	....	....	....	....	....	....	....	....
	United States	Olympics	5	*5	0	0	300	11	0	*2.20	....	....	....	....	....	....	....	....	....	....	....	....	....	....	....	....	....
	New York Rangers	**NHL**	**4**	**1**	**1**	**2**	**240**	**7**	**0**	**1.75**	**1.83**	....	....	....	....	....	....	....	....	....	....	....	....	....	....	....	....
1960-61	**New York Rangers**	**NHL**	**8**	**1**	**6**	**1**	**440**	**36**	**1**	**4.91**	**5.10**	....	....	....	....	....	....	....	....	....	....	....	....	....	....	....	....
	Kitchener-Waterloo Beavers	EPHL	52	25	21	6	3120	145	2	2.79	....	....	....	....	....	7	3	4	0	421	20	*2	2.85	....	....	....	....
1961-62	Kitchener-Waterloo Beavers	EPHL	*70	36	24	10	*4200	217	*5	3.10	....	....	....	....	....	7	3	4	0	451	20	0	2.66	....	....	....	....
1962-63	Los Angeles Blades	WHL	60	31	27	2	3600	187	4	3.12	....	....	....	....	....	3	1	2	0	181	9	0	2.98	....	....	....	....
1963-64	St. Louis Braves	CHL	*67	31	30	6	*4020	262	3	3.91	....	....	....	....	....	6	2	4	0	361	27	0	4.49	....	....	....	....
1964-65	St. Louis Braves	CHL	5	1	4	0	300	27	0	5.40	....	....	....	....	....	....	....	....	....	....	....	....	....	....	....	....	....
	Los Angeles Blades	WHL	32	8	22	2	1948	122	1	3.76	....	....	....	....	....	....	....	....	....	....	....	....	....	....	....	....	....
1965-66	San Francisco Seals	WHL	53	23	27	3	3229	183	2	3.40	....	....	....	....	....	....	....	....	....	....	....	....	....	....	....	....	....
1966-67	California Seals	WHL	61	25	26	10	3784	200	1	3.17	....	....	....	....	....	5	2	3	0	300	13	0	2.60	....	....	....	....
1967-68	Omaha Knights	CHL	43	9	25	7	2380	148	1	3.77	....	....	....	....	....	....	....	....	....	....	....	....	....	....	....	....	....
1968-69	San Diego Gulls	WHL	43	20	14	6	2380	134	0	3.38	....	....	....	....	....	1	0	0	0	20	2	0	6.00	....	....	....	....
1969-70	San Diego Gulls	WHL	52	21	20	9	3025	162	3	3.21	....	....	....	....	....	4	0	3	0	199	19	0	5.73	....	....	....	....
1970-71	San Diego Gulls	WHL	*55	24	20	11	*3239	161	3	2.98	....	....	....	....	....	6	2	4	0	379	24	0	3.80	....	....	....	....
1971-72	San Diego Gulls	WHL	36	14	16	2	1955	112	0	3.44	....	....	....	....	....	2	0	2	0	118	6	0	3.05	....	....	....	....

			REGULAR SEASON													PLAYOFFS											
Season	Club	League	GP	W	L	T	Mins	GA	SO	Avg	AAvg	Eff	SA	S%	SAPG	GP	W	L	T	Mins	GA	SO	Avg	Eff	SA	S%	SAPG
1972-73	Minnesota Fighting Saints	WHA	38	15	19	1	2160	129	1	3.58	....	....	....	....	....	4	1	2	0	213	14	0	3.94	....	....	....	....
1973-74	Minnesota Fighting Saints	WHA	2	0	0	0	42	5	0	7.14	....	....	....	....	....	....	....	....	....	....	....	....	....	....	....	....	....
	Suncoast Suns	SHL	6	....	....	....	323	26	0	4.83	....	....	....	....	....	....	....	....	....	....	....	....	....	....	....	....	....
1974-75	Minnesota Fighting Saints	WHA	2	1	0	0	61	5	0	4.92	....	....	....	....	....	....	....	....	....	....	....	....	....	....	....	....	....
	NHL Totals		**12**	**2**	**7**	**3**	**680**	**43**	**1**	**3.79**	....	....	....	....	....	....	....	....	....	....	....	....	....	....	....	....	....
	Other Major League Totals		42	16	19	1	2263	139	1	3.69	....	....	....	....	....	4	1	2	0	213	14	0	3.94	....	....	....	....

WCHA First All-Star Team (1957, 1958) • NCAA West First All-American Team (1958) • WHL Second All-Star Team (1969) • WHL First All-Star Team (1970, 1971)

Signed to a five-game amateur tryout contract by **NY Rangers** following 1960 Winter Olympic Games, March 2, 1960. Claimed by **Chicago** from **NY Rangers** in Intra-League Draft, June, 1963. Traded to **LA Blades** (WHL) by **Chicago** for cash, January, 1965. Traded to **San Francisco** (WHL) by **LA Blades** (WHL) for Paul Jackson, June, 1965. NHL rights transferred to **California** after owners of **San Francisco** (WHL) franchise granted expansion team, April 6, 1966. Claimed by **San Diego** (WHL) from **Oakland** in Reverse Draft, June 13, 1968. Selected by **Minnesota** (WHA) in 1972 WHA General Player Draft, February 12, 1972.

• McCOOL, FRANK

Frank "Ulcers" McCool G – L. 6', 170 lbs. b: Calgary, Alta., 10/27/1918. d: 5/20/1973.

Season	Club	League	GP	W	L	T	Mins	GA	SO	Avg	AAvg	Eff	SA	S%	SAPG	GP	W	L	T	Mins	GA	SO	Avg	Eff	SA	S%	SAPG
1936-37	Calgary Bronks	ASHL	2	....	....	....	120	9	0	4.50	....	....	....	....	....	....	....	....	....	....	....	....	....	....	....	....	....
	Calgary Canadians	City Jr.	1	....	....	....	60	3	0	3.00	....	....	....	....	....	....	....	....	....	....	....	....	....	....	....	....	....
1937-38	Calgary Columbus Club	City Sr.	12	....	....	....	720	47	*1	3.92	....	....	....	....	....	3	....	....	....	180	8	0	2.67	....	....	....	....
1938-39	Calgary Columbus Club	City Sr.	STATISTICS NOT AVAILABLE																								
1939-40	Spokane Gonzaga University	Kootenay	8	....	....	....	480	46	0	5.75	....	....	....	....	....	....	....	....	....	....	....	....	....	....	....	....	....
1940-41			DID NOT PLAY – INJURED																								
1941-42			DID NOT PLAY – INJURED																								
1942-43	Calgary Currie Army	ASHL	24	....	....	....	1440	81	*1	*3.37	....	....	....	....	....	10	5	5	0	600	40	0	4.00	....	....	....	....
1943-44			STATISTICS NOT AVAILABLE																								
1944-45	**Toronto Maple Leafs**	**NHL**	***50**	**24**	**22**	**4**	***3000**	**161**	***4**	**3.22**	**2.60**	....	....	....	....	**13**	***8**	**5**	....	**807**	**30**	***4**	**2.23**	....	....	....	....
1945-46	**Toronto Maple Leafs**	**NHL**	**22**	**10**	**9**	**3**	**1320**	**81**	**0**	**3.68**	**3.42**	....	....	....	....	....	....	....	....	....	....	....	....	....	....	....	....
	NHL Totals		**72**	**34**	**31**	**7**	**4320**	**242**	**4**	**3.36**	....	....	....	....	....	**13**	**8**	**5**	....	**807**	**30**	**4**	**2.23**	....	....	....	....

Won Calder Memorial Trophy (1945)

Signed as a free agent by **Toronto**, October 25, 1944.

• McDUFFE, PETE

Pete McDuffe G – L. 5'9", 180 lbs. b: Milton, Ont., 2/16/1948.

Season	Club	League	GP	W	L	T	Mins	GA	SO	Avg	AAvg	Eff	SA	S%	SAPG	GP	W	L	T	Mins	GA	SO	Avg	Eff	SA	S%	SAPG
1964-65	St. Catharines Black Hawks	OHA	2	0	1	0	80	9	0	6.92	....	....	....	....	....	....	....	....	....	....	....	....	....	....	....	....	....
1965-66	St. Catharines Black Hawks	OHA	21	....	....	....	1260	112	0	5.33	....	....	....	....	....	....	....	....	....	....	....	....	....	....	....	....	....
1966-67	St. Catharines Black Hawks	OHA	30	....	....	....	1840	90	2	*2.93	....	....	....	....	....	6	....	....	....	360	26	0	4.33	....	....	....	....
	Buffalo Bisons	AHL	2	0	2	0	120	13	0	6.50	....	....	....	....	....	....	....	....	....	....	....	....	....	....	....	....	....
1967-68	St. Catharines Black Hawks	OHA	50	....	....	....	3036	192	0	3.79	....	....	....	....	....	5	....	....	....	300	34	0	6.80	....	....	....	....
1968-69	Greensboro Generals	EHL	65	....	....	....	3900	246	4	3.78	....	....	....	....	....	8	....	....	....	480	28	0	3.50	....	....	....	....
1969-70	Omaha Rangers	CHL	*59	*26	24	9	*3500	174	2	2.98	....	....	....	....	....	*12	*8	4	0	*720	31	*1	*2.58	....	....	....	....
1970-71	Omaha Rangers	CHL	*57	....	....	....	*3420	57	3	2.77	....	....	....	....	....	*11	*8	3	0	*692	26	*2	*2.36	....	....	....	....
1971-72	Denver Spurs	WHL	21	10	7	2	1126	65	1	3.46	....	....	....	....	....	4	4	0	0	240	6	1	1.50	....	....	....	....
	St. Louis Blues	**NHL**	**10**	**0**	**6**	**0**	**467**	**29**	**0**	**3.73**	**3.76**	....	....	....	....	**1**	**0**	**1**	....	**60**	**7**	**0**	**7.00**	....	....	....	....
1972-73	**New York Rangers**	**NHL**	**1**	**1**	**0**	**0**	**60**	**1**	**0**	**1.00**	**0.94**	....	....	....	....	....	....	....	....	....	....	....	....	....	....	....	....
1973-74	**New York Rangers**	**NHL**	**6**	**3**	**2**	**1**	**340**	**18**	**0**	**3.18**	**3.07**	....	....	....	....	....	....	....	....	....	....	....	....	....	....	....	....
	Providence Reds	AHL	36	17	12	6	2098	123	0	3.51	....	....	....	....	....	*14	8	6	0	*883	45	*1	3.05	....	....	....	....
1974-75	**Kansas City Scouts**	**NHL**	**36**	**7**	**25**	**4**	**2100**	**148**	**0**	**4.23**	**3.83**	....	....	....	....	....	....	....	....	....	....	....	....	....	....	....	....
1975-76	**Detroit Red Wings**	**NHL**	**4**	**0**	**3**	**1**	**240**	**22**	**0**	**5.50**	**4.98**	....	....	....	....	....	....	....	....	....	....	....	....	....	....	....	....
	New Haven Nighthawks	AHL	21	8	9	3	1245	85	0	4.10	....	....	....	....	....	1	0	1	0	60	4	0	4.00	....	....	....	....
1976-77	Rhode Island Reds	AHL	11	....	....	....	621	46	0	4.44	....	....	....	....	....	....	....	....	....	....	....	....	....	....	....	....	....
	New Haven Nighthawks	AHL	6	....	....	....	323	32	0	5.94	....	....	....	....	....	....	....	....	....	....	....	....	....	....	....	....	....
1977-78	Indianapolis Racers	WHA	12	1	6	1	539	39	0	4.34	....	....	....	....	....	....	....	....	....	....	....	....	....	....	....	....	....
	NHL Totals		**57**	**11**	**36**	**6**	**3207**	**218**	**0**	**4.08**	....	....	....	....	....	**1**	**0**	**1**		**60**	**7**	**0**	**7.00**	....	....	....	....
	Other Major League Totals		12	1	6	1	539	39	0	4.34	....	....	....	....	....	....	....	....	....	....	....	....	....	....	....	....	....

EHL South First All-Star Team (1969) • EHL South Rookie of the Year (1969) • CHL Second All-Star Team (1970) • CHL First All-Star Team (1971) • Shared Tommy Ivan Trophy (CHL's MVP) with Andre Dupont, Gerry Ouellette & Joe Zanussi (1971) • Shared WHL Leading Goaltender Award with Bob Johnson (1972)

Claimed by **Phoenix** (WHL) from **Chicago** in Reverse Draft, June 12, 1969. Traded to **NY Rangers** by **Phoenix** (WHL) for Don Caley and Sandy Snow, July, 1969. Traded to **St. Louis** by **NY Rangers** for St. Louis' 1st round choice (Steve Vickers) in 1971 Amateur Draft, May 25, 1971. Selected by **NY Raiders** (WHA) in 1972 WHA General Player Draft, February 12, 1972. Traded to **NY Rangers** by **St. Louis** with Curt Bennett to complete transaction that sent Steve Durbano to St. Louis (May 24, 1972), June 7, 1972. Claimed by **Kansas City** from **NY Rangers** in Expansion Draft, June 12, 1974. Traded to **Detroit** by **Kansas City** with Glen Burdon for Gary Bergman and Bill McKenzie, August 22, 1975. Signed as a free agent by **Indianapolis** (WHA), September, 1977.

• McGRATTAN, TOM

Tom McGrattan G – L. 6'2", 170 lbs. b: Brantford, Ont., 10/19/1927.

Season	Club	League	GP	W	L	T	Mins	GA	SO	Avg	AAvg	Eff	SA	S%	SAPG	GP	W	L	T	Mins	GA	SO	Avg	Eff	SA	S%	SAPG
1945-46	Galt Red Wings	OHA	21	....	....	....	1260	66	2	3.14	....	....	....	....	....	3	....	....	....	180	14	0	4.67	....	....	....	....
1946-47	Windsor Spitfires	OHA	16	....	....	....	960	62	0	3.87	....	....	....	....	....	....	....	....	....	....	....	....	....	....	....	....	....
	Windsor Spitfires	IHL	3	....	....	....	180	17	0	5.67	....	....	....	....	....	....	....	....	....	....	....	....	....	....	....	....	....
	Stratford Kroehlers	OHA	....	....	....	....	....	....	....	....	....	....	....	....	....	2	0	2	0	120	10	0	5.00	....	....	....	....
1947-48	Detroit Bright's Goodyears	IHL	15	....	....	....	900	75	1	5.00	....	....	....	....	....	2	....	....	....	120	11	0	5.50	....	....	....	....
	Detroit Red Wings	**NHL**	**1**	**0**	**0**	**0**	**8**	**0**	**0**	**0.00**	**0.00**	....	....	....	....	....	....	....	....	....	....	....	....	....	....	....	....
1948-49	Owen Sound Mercurys	OHA Sr.	25	....	....	....	1500	125	0	5.00	....	....	....	....	....	4	....	....	....	240	26	0	6.50	....	....	....	....
	NHL Totals		**1**	**0**	**0**	**0**	**8**	**0**	**0**	**0.00**	....	....	....	....	....	....	....	....	....	....	....	....	....	....	....	....	....

• **Detroit's** spare goaltender replaced injured Harry Lumley in 3rd period, November 9, 1947. (Toronto 6, Detroit 0)

• McKAY, ROSS

Ross McKay G – R. 5'11", 175 lbs. b: Edmonton, Alta., 3/3/1964.

Season	Club	League	GP	W	L	T	Mins	GA	SO	Avg	AAvg	Eff	SA	S%	SAPG	GP	W	L	T	Mins	GA	SO	Avg	Eff	SA	S%	SAPG
1981-82	Calgary Wranglers	WHL	1	....	....	....	53	1	0	1.13	....	....	....	....	....	....	....	....	....	....	....	....	....	....	....	....	....
1982-83	Calgary Wranglers	WHL	29	14	6	0	1404	91	0	3.89	....	....	....	....	....	2	....	....	....	35	5	0	8.57	....	....	....	....
1983-84	Calgary Wranglers	WHL	42	....	....	....	2342	175	0	4.48	....	....	....	....	....	1	0	1	0	60	9	0	9.00	....	....	....	....
1984-85	University of Saskatchewan	CWUAA	18	....	....	....	1099	59	*2	3.22	....	....	....	....	....	....	....	....	....	....	....	....	....	....	....	....	....
1985-86	University of Saskatchewan	CWUAA	15	....	....	....	887	59	*2	3.99	....	....	....	....	....	....	....	....	....	....	....	....	....	....	....	....	....
1986-87	University of Saskatchewan	CWUAA	18	....	....	....	996	58	0	3.49	....	....	....	....	....	....	....	....	....	....	....	....	....	....	....	....	....
1987-88	University of Saskatchewan	CWUAA	16	*12	3	0	920	42	1	*2.74	....	....	....	....	....	2	1	1	0	148	11	0	4.46	....	....	....	....
1988-89	Binghamton Whalers	AHL	19	5	9	2	938	81	1	5.18	....	....	....	....	....	....	....	....	....	....	....	....	....	....	....	....	....
	Indianapolis Ice	IHL	5	1	3	0	187	18	0	5.78	....	....	....	....	....	....	....	....	....	....	....	....	....	....	....	....	....
1989-90	Binghamton Whalers	AHL	18	0	10	1	713	58	0	4.88	....	....	....	....	....	....	....	....	....	....	....	....	....	....	....	....	....
	Knoxville Cherokees	ECHL	8	4	2	1	426	20	0	2.81	....	....	....	....	....	....	....	....	....	....	....	....	....	....	....	....	....
1990-91	**Hartford Whalers**	**NHL**	**1**	**0**	**0**	**0**	**35**	**3**	**0**	**5.14**	**4.59**	**10.28**	**15**	**.800**	**25.7**	....	....	....	....	....	....	....	....	....	....	....	....
	Springfield Indians	AHL	23	7	10	3	1275	75	0	3.53	....	....	....	....	....	3	1	2	0	191	11	0	3.46	....	....	....	....
	NHL Totals		**1**	**0**	**0**	**0**	**35**	**3**	**0**	**5.14**	....	....	**15**	**.800**	....	....	....	....	....	....	....	....	....	....	....	....	....

Signed as a free agent by **Hartford**, May 2, 1988.

• McKENZIE, BILL

Bill McKenzie G – R. 5'11", 180 lbs. b: St. Thomas, Ont., 3/12/1949.

Season	Club	League	GP	W	L	T	Mins	GA	SO	Avg	AAvg	Eff	SA	S%	SAPG	GP	W	L	T	Mins	GA	SO	Avg	Eff	SA	S%	SAPG
1969-70	Ohio State University	CCHA	25	....	....	....	1500	79	4	3.16	....	....	....	....	....	....	....	....	....	....	....	....	....	....	....	....	....
1970-71	Ohio State University	CCHA	24	....	....	....	1420	65	2	2.74	....	....	....	....	....	....	....	....	....	....	....	....	....	....	....	....	....
1971-72	Ohio State University	CCHA	22	....	....	....	1280	48	2	2.25	....	....	....	....	....	....	....	....	....	....	....	....	....	....	....	....	....
1972-73	Port Huron Wings	IHL	45	....	....	....	2532	120	2	2.84	....	....	....	....	....	5	3	2	0	280	6	*2	*1.29	....	....	....	....
1973-74	**Detroit Red Wings**	**NHL**	**13**	**4**	**4**	**4**	**720**	**43**	**1**	**3.58**	**3.46**	....	....	....	....	....	....	....	....	....	....	....	....	....	....	....	....
	Virginia Wings	AHL	29	8	13	2	1470	99	1	4.04	....	....	....	....	....	....	....	....	....	....	....	....	....	....	....	....	....
	London Lions	Britain	2	....	....	....	120	6	0	3.00	....	....	....	....	....	....	....	....	....	....	....	....	....	....	....	....	....
1974-75	**Detroit Red Wings**	**NHL**	**13**	**1**	**9**	**2**	**740**	**58**	**0**	**4.70**	**4.25**	....	....	....	....	....	....	....	....	....	....	....	....	....	....	....	....
	Virginia Wings	AHL	14	8	6	0	700	33	1	2.82	....	....	....	....	....	....	....	....	....	....	....	....	....	....	....	....	....
1975-76	**Kansas City Scouts**	**NHL**	**22**	**1**	**16**	**1**	**1120**	**97**	**0**	**5.20**	**4.74**	....	....	....	....	....	....	....	....	....	....	....	....	....	....	....	....

			REGULAR SEASON													PLAYOFFS											
Season	Club	League	GP	W	L	T	Mins	GA	SO	Avg	AAvg	Eff	SA	S%	SAPG	GP	W	L	T	Mins	GA	SO	Avg	Eff	SA	S%	SAPG
1976-77	Rhode Island Reds	AHL	2	0	1	1	125	10	0	4.80	....	....	....	....	....	....	....	....	....	....	....	....	....	....	....	....	....
	Colorado Rockies	NHL	5	0	2	1	200	8	0	2.40	2.23	....	....	....	....	....	....	....	....	....	....	....	....	....	....	....	....
	Oklahoma City Blazers	CHL	6	2	3	1	358	24	0	4.02	....	....	....	....	....	....	....	....	....	....	....	....	....	....	....	....	....
	Kansas City Blues	CHL	10	7	2	1	513	25	0	2.92	....	....	....	....	....	*10	*8	2	0	*634	23	*2	*2.18	....	....	....	....
1977-78	Colorado Rockies	NHL	12	3	6	2	654	42	0	3.85	3.61	....	....	....	....	....	....	....	....	....	....	....	....	....	....	....	....
	Hampton Gulls	AHL	12	7	4	0	645	38	1	3.53	....	....	....	....	....	....	....	....	....	....	....	....	....	....	....	....	....
	Philadelphia Firebirds	AHL	5	1	4	0	305	22	1	4.33	....	....	....	....	....	....	....	....	....	....	....	....	....	....	....	....	....
1978-79	Tulsa Oilers	CHL	35	6	25	1	1935	164	0	5.09	....	....	....	....	....	....	....	....	....	....	....	....	....	....	....	....	....
1979-80	Colorado Rockies	NHL	26	9	12	3	1342	78	1	3.49	3.07	....	....	....	....	....	....	....	....	....	....	....	....	....	....	....	....
	Fort Worth Texans	CHL	9	2	5	1	521	29	1	3.34	....	....	....	....	....	....	....	....	....	....	....	....	....	....	....	....	....
	NHL Totals		91	18	49	13	4776	326	2	4.10	....	....	....	....	....	....	....	....	....	....	....	....	....	....	....	....	....

IHL First All-Star Team (1973)

Signed as a free agent by **Detroit**, October 4, 1972. Traded to **Kansas City** by **Detroit** with Gary Bergman for Peter McDuffe and Glen Burdon, August 22, 1975. Transferred to **Colorado** after **Kansas City** franchise relocated, July 15, 1976.

• McKICHAN, STEVE

Steve McKichan G – L. 5′11″, 180 lbs. b: Strathroy, Ont., 5/29/1967. Vancouver's 2nd choice, 7th overall, in 1988 Supplemental Draft.

Season	Club	League	GP	W	L	T	Mins	GA	SO	Avg	AAvg	Eff	SA	S%	SAPG	GP	W	L	T	Mins	GA	SO	Avg	Eff	SA	S%	SAPG
1986-87	University of Miami-Ohio	CCHA	28	3	19	0	1351	130	0	5.77	....	....	....	....	....	....	....	....	....	....	....	....	....	....	....	....	....
1987-88	University of Miami-Ohio	CCHA	34	12	17	1	1767	140	1	4.75	....	....	....	....	....	....	....	....	....	....	....	....	....	....	....	....	....
1988-89	University of Miami-Ohio	CCHA	21	4	15	0	1014	85	0	5.03	....	....	....	....	....	....	....	....	....	....	....	....	....	....	....	....	....
1989-90	Virginia Lancers	ECHL	28	16	11	2	1445	97	0	4.02	....	....	....	....	....	3	1	2	0	209	11	0	3.16	....	....	....	....
	Milwaukee Admirals	IHL	1	1	0	0	40	2	0	3.00	....	....	....	....	....	....	....	....	....	....	....	....	....	....	....	....	....
1990-91	Vancouver Canucks	NHL	1	0	0	0	20	2	0	6.00	5.36	15.00	8	.750	24.0	....	....	....	....	....	....	....	....	....	....	....	....
	Milwaukee Admirals	IHL	30	12	10	2	1571	87	2	3.32	....	....	....	....	....	4	1	2	0	212	13	0	3.68	....	....	....	....
	NHL Totals		1	0	0	0	20	2	0	6.00	....	....	8	.750	....	....	....	....	....	....	....	....	....	....	....	....	....

• McLACHLAN, MURRAY

Murray McLachlan G – L. 6′, 195 lbs. b: London, Ont., 10/20/1948.

Season	Club	League	GP	W	L	T	Mins	GA	SO	Avg	AAvg	Eff	SA	S%	SAPG	GP	W	L	T	Mins	GA	SO	Avg	Eff	SA	S%	SAPG
1967-68	University of Minnesota	WCHA	22	13	9	0	1320	71	2	3.23	....	....	....	....	....	....	....	....	....	....	....	....	....	....	....	....	....
1968-69	University of Minnesota	WCHA	24	12	7	2	1178	53	1	2.70	....	....	....	....	....	....	....	....	....	....	....	....	....	....	....	....	....
1969-70	University of Minnesota	WCHA	25	*18	7	0	1500	81	*2	*3.24	....	....	....	....	....	....	....	....	....	....	....	....	....	....	....	....	....
1970-71	Tulsa Oilers	CHL	38	17	17	4	2271	144	0	3.84	....	....	....	....	....	....	....	....	....	....	....	....	....	....	....	....	....
	Toronto Maple Leafs	NHL	2	0	1	0	25	4	0	9.60	9.50	....	....	....	....	....	....	....	....	....	....	....	....	....	....	....	....
1971-72	Tulsa Oilers	CHL	15	8	7	0	892	49	1	3.29	....	....	....	....	....	....	....	....	....	....	....	....	....	....	....	....	....
	NHL Totals		2	0	1	0	25	4	0	9.60	....	....	....	....	....	....	....	....	....	....	....	....	....	....	....	....	....

WCHA First All-Star Team (1969, 1970) • NCAA West First All-American Team (1970)

Signed as a free agent by **Toronto**, October 1, 1970.

• McLEAN, KIRK

Kirk McLean G – L. 6′, 195 lbs. b: Willowdale, Ont., 6/26/1966. New Jersey's 6th choice, 107th overall, in 1984 Entry Draft.

Season	Club	League	GP	W	L	T	Mins	GA	SO	Avg	AAvg	Eff	SA	S%	SAPG	GP	W	L	T	Mins	GA	SO	Avg	Eff	SA	S%	SAPG
1983-84	Oshawa Generals	OHL	17	5	9	0	940	67	0	4.28	....	....	....	....	....	....	....	....	....	....	....	....	....	....	....	....	....
1984-85	Oshawa Generals	OHL	47	23	17	2	2581	143	1	*3.32	....	....	....	....	....	5	1	3	....	271	21	0	4.65	....	....	....	....
1985-86	New Jersey Devils	NHL	2	1	1	0	111	11	0	5.95	4.63	11.09	59	.814	31.9	....	....	....	....	....	....	....	....	....	....	....	....
	Oshawa Generals	OHL	51	24	21	2	2830	169	1	3.58	....	....	....	....	....	4	1	2	....	201	18	0	5.37	....	....	....	....
1986-87	New Jersey Devils	NHL	4	1	1	0	160	10	0	3.75	3.15	5.14	73	.863	27.4	....	....	....	....	....	....	....	....	....	....	....	....
	Maine Mariners	AHL	45	15	23	4	2606	140	1	3.22	....	....	....	....	....	....	....	....	....	....	....	....	....	....	....	....	....
1987-88	Vancouver Canucks	NHL	41	11	27	3	2380	147	1	3.71	3.08	4.63	1178	.875	29.7	....	....	....	....	....	....	....	....	....	....	....	....
1988-89	Vancouver Canucks	NHL	42	20	17	3	2477	127	4	3.08	2.53	3.35	1169	.891	28.3	5	2	3	....	302	18	0	3.58	3.86	167	.892	33.2
1989-90	Vancouver Canucks	NHL	*63	21	30	10	*3739	216	0	3.47	2.90	4.15	1804	.880	28.9	....	....	....	....	....	....	....	....	....	....	....	....
	Canada	WEC-A	10	....	....	....	457	27	....	3.54	....	....	....	....	....	....	....	....	....	....	....	....	....	....	....	....	....
1990-91	Vancouver Canucks	NHL	41	10	22	3	1969	131	0	3.99	3.57	5.32	983	.867	30.0	2	1	1	....	123	7	0	3.41	3.62	66	.894	32.2
1991-92	Vancouver Canucks	NHL	65	*38	17	9	3852	176	*5	2.74	2.41	2.71	1780	.901	27.7	13	6	7	....	785	33	*2	2.52	2.28	364	.909	27.8
1992-93	Vancouver Canucks	NHL	54	28	21	5	3261	184	3	3.39	2.88	3.86	1615	.886	29.7	12	6	6	....	754	42	0	3.34	3.80	369	.886	29.4
1993-94	Vancouver Canucks	NHL	52	23	26	3	3128	156	3	2.99	2.84	3.26	1430	.891	27.4	*24	15	9	....	*1544	59	*4	2.29	1.65	820	.928	31.9
1994-95	Vancouver Canucks	NHL	40	18	12	10	2374	109	1	2.75	2.83	2.63	1140	.904	28.8	11	4	7	....	660	36	0	3.27	3.50	336	.893	30.5
1995-96	Vancouver Canucks	NHL	45	15	21	9	2645	156	2	3.54	3.49	4.27	1292	.879	29.3	1	0	1	....	21	3	0	8.57	21.43	12	.750	34.3
1996-97	Vancouver Canucks	NHL	44	21	18	3	2581	138	0	3.21	3.40	3.55	1247	.889	29.0	....	....	....	....	....	....	....	....	....	....	....	....
1997-98	Vancouver Canucks	NHL	29	6	17	4	1583	97	1	3.68	4.33	4.46	800	.879	30.3	....	....	....	....	....	....	....	....	....	....	....	....
	Carolina Hurricanes	NHL	8	4	2	0	401	22	0	3.29	3.85	4.00	181	.878	27.1	....	....	....	....	....	....	....	....	....	....	....	....
	Florida Panthers	NHL	7	4	2	1	406	22	0	3.25	3.81	3.45	207	.894	30.6	....	....	....	....	....	....	....	....	....	....	....	....
	NHL Totals		537	221	234	63	31067	1702	20	3.29	....	....	14958	.886	....	68	34	34	....	4189	198	6	2.84	....	....	....	....

NHL Second All-Star Team (1992)

Played in NHL All-Star Game (1990, 1992)

Traded to **Vancouver** by **New Jersey** with Greg Adams for Patrik Sundstrom and Vancouver's 4th round choice (Matt Ruchty) in 1988 Entry Draft, September 15, 1987. Traded to **Carolina** by **Vancouver** with Martin Gelinas for Sean Burke, Geoff Sanderson and Enrico Ciccone, January 3, 1998. Traded to **Florida** by **Carolina** for Ray Sheppard, March 24, 1998.

• McLELLAND, DAVE

Dave McLelland G – L. 5′9″, 165 lbs. b: Penticton, B.C., 11/20/1952. Vancouver's 6th choice, 83rd overall, in 1972 Amateur Draft.

Season	Club	League	GP	W	L	T	Mins	GA	SO	Avg	AAvg	Eff	SA	S%	SAPG	GP	W	L	T	Mins	GA	SO	Avg	Eff	SA	S%	SAPG
1971-72	Brandon Wheat Kings	WCJHL	65	....	....	....	3778	285	1	4.53	....	....	....	....	....	11	....	....	....	662	54	0	4.89	....	....	....	....
1972-73	Des Moines Capitols	IHL	2	0	1	0	84	13	0	9.28	....	....	....	....	....	....	....	....	....	....	....	....	....	....	....	....	....
	Vancouver Canucks	NHL	2	1	1	0	120	10	0	5.00	4.71	....	....	....	....	....	....	....	....	....	....	....	....	....	....	....	....
	Seattle Totems	WHL	6	0	1	0	141	11	0	4.68	....	....	....	....	....	....	....	....	....	....	....	....	....	....	....	....	....
1973-74	Des Moines Capitols	IHL	55	....	....	....	3071	146	1	2.85	....	....	....	....	....	9	8	1	0	540	14	*2	*1.55	....	....	....	....
1974-75	Des Moines Capitols	IHL	32	....	....	....	1705	94	1	3.31	....	....	....	....	....	2	0	2	0	120	9	0	4.50	....	....	....	....
	NHL Totals		2	1	1	0	120	10	0	5.00	....	....	....	....	....	....	....	....	....	....	....	....	....	....	....	....	....

• McLENNAN, JAMIE

Jamie McLennan G – L. 6′, 190 lbs. b: Edmonton, Alta., 6/30/1971. NY Islanders' 3rd choice, 48th overall, in 1991 Entry Draft.

Season	Club	League	GP	W	L	T	Mins	GA	SO	Avg	AAvg	Eff	SA	S%	SAPG	GP	W	L	T	Mins	GA	SO	Avg	Eff	SA	S%	SAPG
1989-90	Lethbridge Hurricanes	WHL	34	20	4	2	1690	110	1	3.91	....	....	....	....	....	13	6	5	....	677	44	0	3.90	....	....	....	....
1990-91	Lethbridge Hurricanes	WHL	56	32	18	4	3230	205	0	3.81	....	....	....	....	....	*16	8	8	....	*970	56	0	3.46	....	....	....	....
1991-92	Capital District Islanders	AHL	18	4	10	2	952	60	1	3.78	....	....	....	....	....	....	....	....	....	....	....	....	....	....	....	....	....
	Richmond Renegades	ECHL	32	16	12	2	1837	114	0	3.72	....	....	....	....	....	....	....	....	....	....	....	....	....	....	....	....	....
1992-93	Capital District Islanders	AHL	38	17	14	6	2171	117	1	3.23	....	....	....	....	....	1	0	1	....	20	5	0	15.00	....	....	....	....
1993-94	New York Islanders	NHL	22	8	7	6	1287	61	0	2.84	2.70	2.71	639	.905	29.8	2	0	1	....	82	6	0	4.39	5.60	47	.872	34.4
	Salt Lake Golden Eagles	IHL	24	8	12	2	1320	80	0	3.64	....	....	....	....	....	....	....	....	....	....	....	....	....	....	....	....	....
1994-95	New York Islanders	NHL	21	6	11	2	1185	67	0	3.39	3.51	4.21	539	.876	27.3	....	....	....	....	....	....	....	....	....	....	....	....
	Denver Grizzlies	IHL	4	3	0	1	239	12	0	3.00	....	....	....	....	....	11	8	2	....	640	23	1	*2.15	....	....	....	....
1995-96	New York Islanders	NHL	13	3	9	1	636	39	0	3.68	3.62	4.20	342	.886	32.3	....	....	....	....	....	....	....	....	....	....	....	....
	Utah Grizzlies	IHL	14	9	2	2	728	29	0	2.39	....	....	....	....	....	....	....	....	....	....	....	....	....	....	....	....	....
	Worcester IceCats	AHL	22	14	7	1	1216	57	0	2.81	....	....	....	....	....	2	0	2	....	119	8	0	4.04	....	....	....	....
1996-97	Worcester IceCats	AHL	39	18	13	4	2152	100	2	2.79	....	....	....	....	....	4	2	2	....	262	16	0	3.67	....	....	....	....
1997-98	St. Louis Blues	NHL	30	16	8	2	1658	60	2	2.17	2.53	2.11	618	.903	22.4	1	0	0	....	14	1	0	4.29	10.73	4	.750	17.1
	NHL Totals		86	33	35	11	4766	227	2	2.86	....	....	2138	.894	....	3	0	1	....	96	7	0	4.38	....	....	....	....

WHL East First All-Star Team (1991) • Won Bill Masterton Memorial Trophy (1998)

Signed as a free agent by **St. Louis**, July 15, 1996.

• McLEOD, DON

Don McLeod G – L. 6′, 190 lbs. b: Trail, B.C., 8/24/1946. Pittsburgh's 11th choice, 164th overall, in 1973 Amateur Draft.

Season	Club	League	GP	W	L	T	Mins	GA	SO	Avg	AAvg	Eff	SA	S%	SAPG	GP	W	L	T	Mins	GA	SO	Avg	Eff	SA	S%	SAPG
1965-66	Edmonton Oil Kings	WCJHL	29	....	....	....	1740	115	0	3.97	....	....	....	....	....	....	....	....	....	....	....	....	....	....	....	....	....
1966-67	Edmonton Oil Kings	WCJHL	38	....	....	....	2280	126	1	3.32	....	....	....	....	....	9	2	3	4	522	34	*2	3.91	....	....	....	....
1967-68	Quebec Aces	AHL	2	0	1	0	80	10	0	7.50	....	....	....	....	....	....	....	....	....	....	....	....	....	....	....	....	....
	Springfield Kings	AHL	9	6	2	1	540	27	0	3.00	....	....	....	....	....	4	1	3	0	240	13	0	3.25	....	....	....	....
	Fort Worth Wings	CHL	17	5	6	5	1020	51	0	3.00	....	....	....	....	....	....	....	....	....	....	....	....	....	....	....	....	....

Season	Club	League	GP	W	L	T	Mins	GA	SO	Avg	AAvg	Eff	SA	S%	SAPG	GP	W	L	T	Mins	GA	SO	Avg	Eff	SA	S%	SAPG
			REGULAR SEASON													PLAYOFFS											
1968-69	Baltimore Clippers	AHL	7	2	3	1	379	28	0	4.43	....	....	....	....	....	....	....	....	....	....	....	....	....	....	....	....	....
	Springfield Kings	AHL	34	15	13	2	1833	105	0	3.44	....	....	....	....	....	....	....	....	....	....	....	....	....	....	....	....	....
1969-70	Fort Worth Wings	CHL	37	18	11	8	2200	109	1	2.97	....	....	....	....	....	3	0	3	0	176	11	0	3.75	....	....	....	....
1970-71	**Detroit Red Wings**	**NHL**	**14**	**3**	**7**	**0**	**698**	**60**	**0**	**5.16**	**5.14**	....	....	....	....	....	....	....	....	....	....	....	....	....	....	....	....
	Fort Worth Wings	CHL	36	....	....	....	2124	90	2	*2.57	....	....	....	....	....	3	....	....	....	207	15	0	4.35	....	....	....	....
1971-72	**Philadelphia Flyers**	**NHL**	**4**	**0**	**3**	**1**	**181**	**14**	**0**	**4.64**	**4.68**	....	....	....	....	....	....	....	....	....	....	....	....	....	....	....	....
	Richmond Robins	AHL	5	1	3	1	300	14	0	2.80	....	....	....	....	....	....	....	....	....	....	....	....	....	....	....	....	....
	Providence Reds	AHL	19	6	8	4	1083	66	0	2.73	....	....	....	....	....	....	....	....	....	....	....	....	....	....	....	....	....
1972-73	Houston Aeros	WHA	41	19	20	1	2410	145	1	3.61	....	....	....	....	....	3	0	3	0	178	8	0	2.70	....	....	....	....
1973-74	Houston Aeros	WHA	49	*33	13	3	2971	127	3	*2.56	....	....	....	....	....	*14	*12	2	0	*842	35	0	*2.49	....	....	....	....
1974-75	Canada	Summit	1	0	1	0	58	8	0	8.28	....	....	....	....	....	....	....	....	....	....	....	....	....	....	....	....	....
	Vancouver Blazers	WHA	*72	*33	35	2	*4184	233	1	3.34	....	....	....	....	....	....	....	....	....	....	....	....	....	....	....	....	....
1975-76	Calgary Cowboys	WHA	63	30	27	3	3534	206	1	3.50	....	....	....	....	....	10	5	5	0	559	37	0	3.97	....	....	....	....
1976-77	Calgary Cowboys	WHA	*67	25	34	5	3701	210	3	3.40	....	....	....	....	....	....	....	....	....	....	....	....	....	....	....	....	....
1977-78	Quebec Nordiques	WHA	7	2	4	0	403	28	0	4.17	....	....	....	....	....	....	....	....	....	....	....	....	....	....	....	....	....
	Edmonton Oilers	WHA	33	15	10	1	1723	102	2	3.55	....	....	....	....	....	4	1	3	0	207	16	1	4.64	....	....	....	....
	NHL Totals		**18**	**3**	**10**	**1**	**879**	**74**	**0**	**5.05**	....	....	....	....	....	....	....	....	....	....	....	....	....	....	....	....	....
	Other Major League Totals		332	157	143	15	18926	1051	11	3.33	....	....	....	....	....	31	18	13	0	1786	96	1	3.23	....	....	....	....

Shared Terry Sawchuk Trophy (fewest goals against - CHL) with Gerry Gray (1971) • WHA First All-Star Team (1974) • Won Ben Hatskin Trophy (WHA Top Goaltender) (1974)

Claimed by **Philadelphia** (Quebec - AHL) from **Detroit** in Reverse Draft, June, 1971. Selected by **Houston** (WHA) in 1972 WHA General Player Draft, February 12, 1972. Signed as a free agent by **Vancouver** (WHA) after securing release from **Houston** (WHA), August 15, 1974. Transferred to **Calgary** (WHA) after **Vancouver** (WHA) franchise relocated, May 7, 1975. Claimed by **Quebec** (WHA) from **Calgary** (WHA) in WHA Dispersal Auction, August, 1977. Traded to **Edmonton** (WHA) by **Quebec** (WHA) with Pierre Guite for Dave Inkpen, Ken Broderick, Warren Miller and Rick Miller, December, 1977.

• McLEOD, JIM

Jim McLeod G – L. 5'8", 170 lbs. b: Port Arthur, Ont., 4/7/1937.

Season	Club	League	GP	W	L	T	Mins	GA	SO	Avg	AAvg	Eff	SA	S%	SAPG	GP	W	L	T	Mins	GA	SO	Avg	Eff	SA	S%	SAPG
1956-57	Vernon Canadians	OSHL	4	....	....	....	240	15	0	3.75	....	....	....	....	....	....	....	....	....	....	....	....	....	....	....	....	....
1957-58	Vernon Canadians	OSHL	2	....	....	....	120	12	0	6.00	....	....	....	....	....	....	....	....	....	....	....	....	....	....	....	....	....
1958-59	Vernon Canadians	OSHL	6	....	....	....	360	30	1	5.00	....	....	....	....	....	....	....	....	....	....	....	....	....	....	....	....	....
1959-60	Vernon Canadians	OSHL	44	....	....	....	2640	148	2	*3.36	....	....	....	....	....	13	7	5	1	780	44	1	3.38	....	....	....	....
1960-61	Muskegon Zephyrs	IHL	62	....	....	....	3720	269	1	4.34	....	....	....	....	....	13	5	8	0	780	48	0	3.38	....	....	....	....
	Seattle Totems	WHL	7	5	2	0	428	24	0	3.36	....	....	....	....	....	....	....	....	....	....	....	....	....	....	....	....	....
1961-62	Muskegon Zephyrs	IHL	47	....	....	....	2820	157	1	3.34	....	....	....	....	....	9	8	1	0	540	28	0	3.11	....	....	....	....
	Seattle Totems	WHL	12	6	6	0	720	37	0	3.08	....	....	....	....	....	....	....	....	....	....	....	....	....	....	....	....	....
1962-63	San Francisco Seals	WHL	67	*43	23	1	4090	202	4	3.01	....	....	....	....	....	*17	*10	7	0	1054	56	*3	3.19	....	....	....	....
1963-64	Los Angeles Blades	WHL	39	18	15	6	2340	127	*4	3.26	....	....	....	....	....	5	2	2	0	260	14	0	*3.23	....	....	....	....
1964-65	Seattle Totems	WHL	65	*35	27	3	3970	181	*5	2.74	....	....	....	....	....	7	3	4	0	420	19	1	2.71	....	....	....	....
1965-66	Seattle Totems	WHL	46	20	23	2	2751	167	2	3.64	....	....	....	....	....	....	....	....	....	....	....	....	....	....	....	....	....
1966-67	Seattle Totems	WHL	42	26	11	4	2528	101	4	*2.40	....	....	....	....	....	*8	*6	2	0	*480	15	*1	1.88	....	....	....	....
1967-68	Portland Buckaroos	WHL	33	18	10	4	1961	73	4	2.23	....	....	....	....	....	7	4	3	0	407	17	1	2.51	....	....	....	....
1968-69	Portland Buckaroos	WHL	42	23	9	8	2363	90	*3	*2.29	....	....	....	....	....	8	4	3	0	433	27	0	3.74	....	....	....	....
1969-70	Portland Buckaroos	WHL	33	21	9	0	1794	103	0	3.44	....	....	....	....	....	9	5	4	0	539	25	*2	*2.78	....	....	....	....
1970-71	Portland Buckaroos	WHL	47	*32	10	3	2710	122	*5	*2.70	....	....	....	....	....	*11	*8	3	0	*678	23	*1	*2.03	....	....	....	....
1971-72	**St. Louis Blues**	**NHL**	**16**	**6**	**6**	**4**	**880**	**44**	**0**	**3.00**	**3.02**	....	....	....	....	....	....	....	....	....	....	....	....	....	....	....	....
	Portland Buckaroos	WHL	13	9	3	0	735	34	0	2.78	....			....	....	*11	*6	6	0	*650	39	0	3.55	....	....	....	....
1972-73	Chicago Cougars	WHA	54	22	25	2	2996	166	1	3.32	....	....	....	....	....	....	....	....	....	....	....	....	....	....	....	....	....
1973-74	New York - New Jersey	WHA	10	3	7	0	517	36	0	4.18	....	....	....	....	....	....	....	....	....	....	....	....	....	....	....	....	....
	Los Angeles Sharks	WHA	17	4	13	0	969	69	1	4.27	....	....	....	....	....	....	....	....	....	....	....	....	....	....	....	....	....
1974-75	Michigan - Baltimore	WHA	16	3	6	1	694	53	0	4.58	....	....	....	....	....	....	....	....	....	....	....	....	....	....	....	....	....
	Syracuse Blazers	NAHL	3	3	0	0	180	5	0	1.67	....	....	....	....	....	....	....	....	....	....	....	....	....	....	....	....	....
	Greensboro Generals	SHL	2	....	....	....	120	8	0	4.00	....	....	....	....	....	....	....	....	....	....	....	....	....	....	....	....	....
	NHL Totals		**16**	**6**	**6**	**4**	**880**	**44**	**0**	**3.00**		....	....	....	....	....	....	....	....	....	....	....	....	....	....	....	....
	Other Major League Totals		97	32	51	3	5176	324	2	3.76	....	....	....	....	....	....	....	....	....	....	....	....	....	....	....	....	....

WHL First All-Star Team (1965, 1969) • Won WHL Leading Goaltender Award (1965, 1967, 1971) • WHL Second All-Star Team (1968, 1971) • Shared WHL Leading Goaltender Award with Marv Edwards (1968) • Shared WHL Leading Goaltender Award with Dave Kelly (1969)

Claimed by **St. Louis** from **Portland** (WHL) in Inter-League Draft, June 7, 1971. Selected by **Chicago** (WHA) in 1972 WHA General Player Draft, February 12, 1972. Traded to **NY Raiders** (WHA) by **Chicago** (WHA) for cash, July, 1973. Traded to **LA Sharks** (WHA) by **New York-New Jersey** (WHA) for Earl Heiskala and Russ Gillow, January, 1974. Transferred to **Michigan** (WHA) after **New York-New Jersey** (WHA) franchise relocated, April 1974.

• McNAMARA, GERRY

Gerry McNamara G – L. 6'2", 190 lbs. b: Turgeon Falls, Ont., 9/22/1934.

Season	Club	League	GP	W	L	T	Mins	GA	SO	Avg	AAvg	Eff	SA	S%	SAPG	GP	W	L	T	Mins	GA	SO	Avg	Eff	SA	S%	SAPG
1951-52	St. Michael's Majors	OHA	5	2	3	0	280	20	0	4.29	....	....	....	....	....	....	....	....	....	....	....	....	....	....	....	....	....
1952-53	St. Michael's Majors	OHA	10	....	....	....	600	30	0	3.00	....	....	....	....	....	1	....	....	....	60	4	0	4.00	....	....	....	....
1953-54	St. Michael's Majors	OHA	57	....	....	....	3420	205	2	3.59	....	....	....	....	....	8	....	....	....	480	41	0	5.12	....	....	....	....
1954-55	St. Michael's Majors	OHA	46	25	18	3	2750	149	2	3.24	....	....	....	....	....	2	....	....	....	120	8	0	4.00	....	....	....	....
1955-56	Pittsburgh Hornets	AHL	5	1	4	0	300	19	0	3.80	....	....	....	....	....	....	....	....	....	....	....	....	....	....	....	....	....
1956-57	Winnipeg Warriors	WHL	16	4	11	1	965	60	0	3.73	....	....	....	....	....	....	....	....	....	....	....	....	....	....	....	....	....
	Hershey Bears	AHL	22	10	12	0	1320	92	0	4.18	....	....	....	....	....	7	3	4	0	430	16	*2	*2.23	....	....	....	....
1957-58	Buffalo Bisons	AHL	37	14	21	2	2245	149	0	3.98	....	....	....	....	....	....	....	....	....	....	....	....	....	....	....	....	....
1958-59	Cleveland Barons	AHL	49	29	18	2	2940	155	3	3.16	....	....	....	....	....	7	3	4	0	420	18	*1	2.57	....	....	....	....
1959-60	Sudbury Wolves	EPHL	59	31	21	7	3520	236	2	4.02	....	....	....	....	....	*14	7	7	0	850	41	*1	2.89	....	....	....	....
	Rochester Americans	AHL	2	0	2	0	120	13	0	6.50	....	....	....	....	....	....	....	....	....	....	....	....	....	....	....	....	....
1960-61	Sudbury Wolves	EPHL	52	....	....	....	3120	210	3	4.04	....	....	....	....	....	....	....	....	....	....	....	....	....	....	....	....	....
	Rochester Americans	AHL	1	0	1	0	60	5	0	5.00	....	....	....	....	....	....	....	....	....	....	....	....	....	....	....	....	....
	Toronto Maple Leafs	**NHL**	**5**	**2**	**2**	**1**	**300**	**13**	**0**	**2.60**	**2.67**	....	....	....	....	....	....	....	....	....	....	....	....	....	....	....	....
1961-62	Pittsburgh Hornets	AHL	35	5	30	0	2100	140	0	4.23	....	....	....	....	....	....	....	....	....	....	....	....	....	....	....	....	....
	Portland Buckeroos	WHL	6	1	3	2	380	25	0	3.95	....	....	....	....	....	....	....	....	....	....	....	....	....	....	....	....	....
1962-63	Rochester Americans	AHL	32	10	18	3	1920	123	1	3.84	....	....	....	....	....	....	....	....	....	....	....	....	....	....	....	....	....
1963-64	Charlotte Checkers	EHL	29	....	....	....	1740	109	1	3.76	....	....	....	....	....	....	....	....	....	....	....	....	....	....	....	....	....
1964-65			DID NOT PLAY																								
1965-66			DID NOT PLAY																								
1966-67	Toronto Grads	OHA Sr.	31	....	....	....	1830	112	2	3.67	....	....	....	....	....	....	....	....	....	....	....	....	....	....	....	....	....
1967-68	Toronto Marlboros	OHA Sr.	37	....	....	....	2210	111	0	3.01	....	....	....	....	....	....	....	....	....	....			....	....	....	....	....
1968-69	Orillia Terriers	OHA Sr.	20	....	....	....	1097	105	1	3.71	....	....	....	....	....	....	....	....	....	....	....	....	....	....	....	....	....
1969-70	**Toronto Maple Leafs**	**NHL**	**2**	**0**	**0**	**0**	**23**	**2**	**0**	**5.22**	**5.55**	....	....	....	....	....	....	....	....	....	....	....	....	....	....	....	....
	Orillia Terriers	OHA Sr.	25	....	....	....	1500	61	*3	*2.44	....	....	....	....	....	....	....	....	....	....	....	....	....	....	....	....	....
1970-71			DID NOT PLAY – INJURED																								
1971-72	Orillia Terriers	OHA Sr.	31	....	....	....	1817	112	*3	3.70	....	....	....	....	....	....	....	....	....	....	....	....	....	....	....	....	....
	NHL Totals		**7**	**2**	**2**	**1**	**323**	**15**	**0**	**2.79**	....	....	....	....	....	....	....	....	....	....	....	....	....	....	....	....	....

• McNEIL, GERRY

Gerry McNeil G – L. 5'7", 155 lbs. b: Quebec City, Que., 4/17/1926.

Season	Club	League	GP	W	L	T	Mins	GA	SO	Avg	AAvg	Eff	SA	S%	SAPG	GP	W	L	T	Mins	GA	SO	Avg	Eff	SA	S%	SAPG
1943-44	Montreal Royals	QJHL	3	....	....	....	180	10	0	3.33	....	....	....	....	....	....	....	....	....	....	....	....	....	....	....	....	....
	Montreal Royals	QSHL	21	....	....	....	1260	110	1	5.24	....	....	....	....	....	7	....	....	....	420	30	0	4.29	....	....	....	....
1944-45	Montreal Royals	QSHL	23	....	....	....	1350	90	0	4.00	....	....	....	....	....	7	....	....	....	420	30	*1	4.29	....	....	....	....
1945-46	Montreal Royals	QSHL	26	....	....	....	1560	87	1	*3.35	....	....	....	....	....	11	....	....	....	660	31	0	*2.82	....	....	....	....
1946-47	Montreal Royals	QSHL	40	....	....	....	2400	124	*2	*3.10	....	....	....	....	....	11	....	....	....	660	22	0	*2.00	....	....	....	....
1947-48	**Montreal Canadiens**	**NHL**	**2**	**0**	**1**	**1**	**95**	**7**	**0**	**4.42**	**4.67**	....	....	....	....	....	....	....	....	....	....	....	....	....	....	....	....
	Montreal Royals	QSHL	47	....	....	....	2820	156	*3	3.32	....	....	....	....	....	3	0	3	0	180	9	0	3.00	....	....	....	....
1948-49	Montreal Royals	QSHL	59	35	19	5	3540	178	*5	3.02	....	....	....	....	....	9	3	4	0	540	25	1	2.78	....	....	....	....
1949-50	Cincinnati Mohawks	AHL	55	12	30	13	3300	201	3	3.65	....	....	....	....	....	....	....	....	....	....	....	....	....	....	....	....	....
	Montreal Canadiens	**NHL**	**6**	**3**	**1**	**2**	**360**	**9**	**1**	**1.50**	**1.68**	....	....	....	....	**2**	**1**	**1**	....	**135**	**5**	**0**	**2.22**	....	....	....	....
1950-51	**Montreal Canadiens**	**NHL**	***70**	**25**	**30**	**15**	***4200**	**184**	**6**	**2.63**	**2.97**	....	....	....	....	***11**	***5**	**6**	....	***785**	**25**	**1**	**1.91**	....	....	....	....
1951-52	**Montreal Canadiens**	**NHL**	***70**	**34**	**26**	**10**	***4200**	**164**	**5**	**2.34**	**2.73**	....	....	....	....	***11**	**4**	**7**	....	***688**	**23**	**1**	**2.01**	....	....	....	....
1952-53	**Montreal Canadiens**	**NHL**	**66**	**25**	**23**	**18**	**3960**	**140**	***10**	**2.12**	**2.68**	....	....	....	....	**8**	***5**	**3**	....	**486**	**16**	***2**	**1.98**	....	....	....	....

			REGULAR SEASON													PLAYOFFS											
Season	Club	League	GP	W	L	T	Mins	GA	SO	Avg	AAvg	Eff	SA	S%	SAPG	GP	W	L	T	Mins	GA	SO	Avg	Eff	SA	S%	SAPG
1953-54	**Montreal Canadiens**	**NHL**	53	28	19	6	3180	114	6	2.15	2.72	....	....	....	....	3	2	1	....	190	3	1	0.95	....	....	....	....
1954-55				DID NOT PLAY																							
1955-56	Montreal Royals	QHL	54	30	17	7	3330	128	*5	*2.31	....	....	....	....	....	19	9	10	0	1161	63	1	3.26	....	....	....	....
1956-57	Montreal Royals	QHL	59	26	28	4	3610	175	3	2.91	....	....	....	....	....	4	0	4	0	245	11	0	2.69	....	....	....	....
	Montreal Canadiens	**NHL**	9	4	5	0	540	32	0	3.56	4.11	....	....	....	....	....	....	....	....	....	....	....	....	....	....	....	....
1957-58	Rochester Americans	AHL	*68	28	34	6	*4158	229	5	3.30	....	....	....	....	....	....	....	....	....	....	....	....	....	....	....	....	....
1958-59	Rochester Americans	AHL	66	31	30	5	4010	199	2	2.98	....	....	....	....	....	5	1	4	0	304	12	0	*2.37	....	....	....	....
1959-60	Montreal Royals	EPHL	28	13	9	6	1680	67	5	*2.39	....	....	....	....	....	*14	*8	6	0	842	34	*1	2.42	....	....	....	....
1960-61	Quebec Aces	AHL	50	21	27	1	2933	176	3	3.60	....	....	....	....	....	....	....	....	....	....	....	....	....	....	....	....	....
	NHL Totals		276	119	105	52	16535	650	28	2.36	....	....	....	....	....	35	17	18	....	2284	72	5	1.89	....	....	....	....

Won Vimy Trophy (MVP - QSHL) (1947) • NHL Second All-Star Team (1953) • QHL First All-Star Team (1956) • Won Vezina Memorial Trophy (Top Goaltender - QHL) (1956) • AHL Second All-Star Team (1958)

Played in NHL All-Star Game (1951, 1952, 1953)

• McRAE, GORD

Gord "The Bird" McRae G – L. 6′, 180 lbs. b: Sherbrooke, Que., 4/12/1948.

1967-68	Michigan Tech Huskies	WCHA	12	....	....	....	720	25	2	2.08	....	....	....	....	....	....	....	....	....	....	....	....	....	....	....	....	....
1968-69	Michigan Tech Huskies	WCHA	28	....	....	....	1680	84	1	3.00	....	....	....	....	....	....	....	....	....	....	....	....	....	....	....	....	....
1969-70	Michigan Tech Huskies	WCHA	31	....	....	....	1860	112	1	3.61	....	....	....	....	....	....	....	....	....	....	....	....	....	....	....	....	....
1970-71	Charlotte–Jersey–J'ville	EHL	24	....	....	....	1440	69	3	2.88	....	....	....	....	....	7	7	0	0	420	8	*3	*1.14	....	....	....	....
1971-72	Providence Reds	AHL	3	2	1	0	140	8	0	3.42	....	....	....	....	....	....	....	....	....	....	....	....	....	....	....	....	....
	Tulsa Oilers	CHL	17	5	5	6	879	54	0	3.68	....	....	....	....	....	7	3	4	0	372	28	0	4.51	....	....	....	....
	Orillia Terriers	OHA Sr.	2	....	....	....	120	11	0	5.50	....	....	....	....	....	....	....	....	....	....	....	....	....	....	....	....	....
1972-73	**Toronto Maple Leafs**	**NHL**	11	7	3	0	620	39	0	3.77	3.56	....	....	....	....	....	....	....	....	....	....	....	....	....	....	....	....
	Tulsa Oilers	CHL	*43	18	19	6	*2459	154	3	3.75	....	....	....	....	....	....	....	....	....	....	....	....	....	....	....	....	....
1973-74	Oklahoma City Blazers	CHL	39	20	14	4	2222	119	2	3.21	....	....	....	....	....	8	....	....	....	460	17	*1	2.21	....	....	....	....
1974-75	Oklahoma City Blazers	CHL	29	4	16	4	1483	99	0	4.01	....	....	....	....	....	....	....	....	....	....	....	....	....	....	....	....	....
	Toronto Maple Leafs	**NHL**	20	10	3	6	1063	57	0	3.22	2.90	....	....	....	....	7	2	5	....	441	21	0	2.86	....	....	....	....
1975-76	**Toronto Maple Leafs**	**NHL**	20	6	5	2	956	59	0	3.70	3.35	....	....	....	....	1	0	0	....	13	1	0	4.62	....	....	....	....
1976-77	**Toronto Maple Leafs**	**NHL**	2	0	1	1	120	9	0	4.50	4.18	....	....	....	....	....	....	....	....	....	....	....	....	....	....	....	....
	Dallas Black Hawks	CHL	30	17	6	7	1796	81	1	*2.71	....	....	....	....	....	3	1	2	0	179	10	0	3.35	....	....	....	....
1977-78	**Toronto Maple Leafs**	**NHL**	18	7	10	1	1040	57	1	3.29	3.08	....	....	....	....	....	....	....	....	....	....	....	....	....	....	....	....
	NHL Totals		71	30	22	10	3799	221	1	3.49	....	....	....	....	....	8	2	5	....	454	22	0	2.91	....	....	....	....

CHL First All-Star Team (1977) • Shared Terry Sawchuk Trophy (fewest goals against - CHL) with Yves Belanger (1977)

Signed as a free agent by **Toronto** (Tulsa-CHL), December 18, 1971.

• MELANSON, ROLLIE

Rollie "Rollie the Goalie" Melanson G – L. 5′10″, 185 lbs. b: Moncton, N.B., 6/28/1960. NY Islanders' 4th choice, 59th overall, in 1979 Entry Draft.

1977-78	Windsor Spitfires	OHA	44	....	....	....	2592	195	1	4.51	....	....	....	....	....	....	....	....	....	....	....	....	....	....	....	....	....
1978-79	Windsor Spitfires	OHA	*62	....	....	....	*3461	254	1	4.40	....	....	....	....	....	7	....	....	....	392	31	0	4.74	....	....	....	....
1979-80	Windsor Spitfires	OHA	22	11	8	0	1099	90	0	4.91	....	....	....	....	....	....	....	....	....	....	....	....	....	....	....	....	....
	Oshawa Generals	OHA	38	26	12	0	2240	136	*3	3.64	....	....	....	....	....	7	3	4	0	420	32	0	4.57	....	....	....	....
1980-81	**New York Islanders**	**NHL**	11	8	1	1	620	32	0	3.10	2.48	....	....	....	....	3	1	0	....	92	6	0	3.91	....	....	....	....
	Indianapolis Checkers	CHL	*52	31	16	3	*3056	131	2	*2.57	....	....	....	....	....	....	....	....	....	....	....	....	....	....	....	....	....
1981-82	**New York Islanders**	**NHL**	36	22	7	6	2115	114	0	3.23	2.48	....	....	....	....	3	0	1	....	64	5	0	4.69	....	....	....	....
1982-83	**New York Islanders**	**NHL**	44	24	12	5	2460	109	1	2.66	2.11	2.40	1206	.910	29.4	5	2	2	....	238	10	0	2.52	....	....	....	....
1983-84	**New York Islanders**	**NHL**	37	20	11	2	2019	110	0	3.27	2.55	3.19	1129	.903	33.6	6	0	1	....	87	5	0	3.45	5.39	32	.844	22.1
1984-85	**New York Islanders**	**NHL**	8	3	3	0	425	35	0	4.94	3.93	6.73	257	.864	36.3	....	....	....	....	....	....	....	....	....	....	....	....
	Minnesota North Stars	**NHL**	20	5	10	3	1142	78	0	4.10	3.26	5.45	587	.867	30.8	....	....	....	....	....	....	....	....	....	....	....	....
1985-86	**Minnesota North Stars**	**NHL**	6	2	1	2	325	24	0	4.43	3.45	6.08	175	.863	32.3	....	....	....	....	....	....	....	....	....	....	....	....
	Los Angeles Kings	**NHL**	22	4	16	1	1246	87	0	4.19	3.26	5.57	654	.867	31.5	....	....	....	....	....	....	....	....	....	....	....	....
	New Haven Nighthawks	AHL	3	1	2	0	179	13	0	4.36	....	....	....	....	....	....	....	....	....	....	....	....	....	....	....	....	....
1986-87	**Los Angeles Kings**	**NHL**	46	18	21	6	2734	168	1	3.69	3.10	4.37	1420	.882	31.2	5	1	4	....	260	24	0	5.54	8.63	154	.844	35.5
1987-88	**Los Angeles Kings**	**NHL**	47	17	20	7	2676	195	2	4.37	3.65	6.09	1399	.861	31.4	1	0	1	....	60	9	0	9.00	16.20	50	.820	50.0
1988-89	**Los Angeles Kings**	**NHL**	4	1	1	0	178	19	0	6.40	5.28	11.16	109	.826	36.7	....	....	....	....	....	....	....	....	....	....	....	....
	New Haven Nighthawks	AHL	29	11	15	3	1734	106	1	3.67	....	....	....	....	....	*17	9	8	0	*1019	74	1	4.36	....	....	....	....
1989-90	Utica Devils	AHL	48	24	19	3	2737	167	1	3.66	....	....	....	....	....	5	1	4	0	298	20	0	4.03	....	....	....	....
1990-91	**New Jersey Devils**	**NHL**	1	0	0	0	20	2	0	6.00	5.36	17.14	7	.714	21.0	....	....	....	....	....	....	....	....	....	....	....	....
	Utica Devils	AHL	54	23	28	1	3058	208	0	4.08	....	....	....	....	....	....	....	....	....	....	....	....	....	....	....	....	....
1991-92	**Montreal Canadiens**	**NHL**	9	5	3	0	492	22	2	2.68	2.37	3.02	195	.887	23.8	....	....	....	....	....	....	....	....	....	....	....	....
1992-93	Brantford Smoke	ColHL	14	....	....	....	811	54	*1	4.00	....	....	....	....	....	15	*11	3	0	844	50	0	3.55	....	....	....	....
1993-94	Saint John Flames	AHL	7	1	2	0	270	20	0	4.44	....	....	....	....	....	....	....	....	....	....	....	....	....	....	....	....	....
	NHL Totals		291	129	106	33	16452	995	6	3.63	....	....	....	....	....	23	4	9	....	801	59	0	4.42	....	....	....	....

OHA Second All-Star Team (1979) • CHL First All-Star Team (1981) • Won Ken McKenzie Trophy (CHL's Rookie of the Year) (1981) • NHL Second All-Star Team (1983) • Shared William M. Jennings Trophy with Billy Smith (1983)

Traded to **Minnesota** by **NY Islanders** for Minnesota's 1st round choice (Brad Dalgarno) in 1985 Entry Draft, November 19, 1984. Traded to **NY Rangers** by **Minnesota** for NY Rangers' 2nd round choice (Neil Wilkinson) in 1986 Entry Draft and 4th round choice (John Weisbrod) in 1987 Entry Draft, December 9, 1985. Traded to **LA Kings** by **NY Rangers** with Grant Ledyard for Brian MacLellan and LA Kings' 4th round choice (Michael Sullivan) in 1987 Entry Draft, December 9, 1985. Signed as a free agent by **New Jersey**, August 10, 1989. Traded to **Montreal** by **New Jersey** with Kirk Muller for Stephane Richer and Tom Chorske, September 20, 1991.

• MELOCHE, GILLES

Gilles Meloche G – L. 5′9″, 185 lbs. b: Montreal, Que., 7/12/1950. Chicago's 5th choice, 70th overall, in 1970 Amateur Draft.

1969-70	Verdun Jr. Maple Leafs	QJHL	45	....	....	....	2679	221	*1	4.95	....	....	....	....	....	11	5	6	0	654	34	0	3.12	....	....	....	....
1970-71	Flint Generals	IHL	33	....	....	....	1866	104	2	3.34	....	....	....	....	....	3	....	....	....	183	11	0	3.61	....	....	....	....
	Chicago Black Hawks	**NHL**	2	2	0	0	120	6	0	3.00	2.97	....	....	....	....	....	....	....	....	....	....	....	....	....	....	....	....
1971-72	**California Golden Seals**	**NHL**	56	16	25	13	3121	173	4	3.33	3.37	....	....	....	....	....	....	....	....	....	....	....	....	....	....	....	....
1972-73	**California Golden Seals**	**NHL**	*59	12	32	14	*3473	235	1	4.06	3.87	....	....	....	....	....	....	....	....	....	....	....	....	....	....	....	....
1973-74	**California Golden Seals**	**NHL**	47	9	33	5	2800	198	1	4.24	4.15	....	....	....	....	....	....	....	....	....	....	....	....	....	....	....	....
1974-75	**California Golden Seals**	**NHL**	47	9	27	10	2771	186	1	4.03	3.65	....	....	....	....	....	....	....	....	....	....	....	....	....	....	....	....
1975-76	**California Golden Seals**	**NHL**	41	12	23	6	2440	140	1	3.44	3.11	....	....	....	....	....	....	....	....	....	....	....	....	....	....	....	....
1976-77	**Cleveland Barons**	**NHL**	51	19	24	6	2961	171	2	3.47	3.23	....	....	....	....	....	....	....	....	....	....	....	....	....	....	....	....
1977-78	**Cleveland Barons**	**NHL**	54	16	27	8	3100	195	1	3.77	3.55	....	....	....	....	....	....	....	....	....	....	....	....	....	....	....	....
1978-79	**Minnesota North Stars**	**NHL**	53	20	25	7	3118	173	2	3.33	2.93	....	....	....	....	....	....	....	....	....	....	....	....	....	....	....	....
1979-80	**Minnesota North Stars**	**NHL**	54	27	20	5	3141	160	1	3.06	2.68	....	....	....	....	11	5	4	....	564	34	1	3.62	....	....	....	....
1980-81	**Minnesota North Stars**	**NHL**	38	17	14	6	2215	120	2	3.25	2.60	....	....	....	....	13	8	5	....	802	47	0	3.52	....	....	....	....
1981-82	**Minnesota North Stars**	**NHL**	51	26	15	9	3026	175	1	3.47	2.66	....	....	....	....	4	1	2	....	184	8	0	2.61	....	....	....	....
	Canada	WEC-A	5	3	2	0	299	16	1	3.21	....	....	....	....	....	....	....	....	....	....	....	....	....	....	....	....	....
1982-83	**Minnesota North Stars**	**NHL**	47	20	13	11	2689	160	1	3.57	2.84	4.05	1411	.887	31.5	5	2	3	....	319	18	0	3.39	....	....	....	....
1983-84	**Minnesota North Stars**	**NHL**	52	21	17	8	2883	201	2	4.18	3.28	5.51	1524	.868	31.7	4	1	2	....	200	11	0	3.30	4.13	88	.875	26.4
1984-85	**Minnesota North Stars**	**NHL**	32	10	13	6	1817	115	0	3.80	3.02	4.60	949	.879	31.3	8	4	3	....	395	25	1	3.80	3.71	256	.902	38.9
1985-86	**Pittsburgh Penguins**	**NHL**	34	13	15	5	1989	119	0	3.59	2.79	4.26	1003	.881	30.3	....	....	....	....	....	....	....	....	....	....	....	....
1986-87	**Pittsburgh Penguins**	**NHL**	43	13	19	7	2343	134	0	3.43	2.88	4.09	1123	.881	28.8	....	....	....	....	....	....	....	....	....	....	....	....
1987-88	**Pittsburgh Penguins**	**NHL**	27	8	9	5	1394	95	0	4.09	3.41	5.38	722	.868	31.1	....	....	....	....	....	....	....	....	....	....	....	....
	NHL Totals		788	270	351	131	45401	2756	20	3.64	....	....	....	....	....	45	21	19	....	2464	143	2	3.48	....	....	....	....

QJHL First All-Star Team (1970)

Played in NHL All-Star Game (1980, 1982)

Traded to **California** by **Chicago** with Paul Shmyr for Gerry Desjardins, October 18, 1971. Transferred to **Cleveland** after **California** franchise relocated, August 26, 1976. Protected by **Minnesota** prior to Cleveland - Minnesota Dispersal Draft, June 15, 1978. Traded to **Edmonton** by **Minnesota** for Paul Houck, May 31, 1985. Traded to **Pittsburgh** by **Edmonton** for Marty McSorley, Tim Hrynewich and future considerations (Craig Muni, October 6, 1986), September 11, 1985.

			REGULAR SEASON													PLAYOFFS											
Season	Club	League	GP	W	L	T	Mins	GA	SO	Avg	AAvg	Eff	SA	S%	SAPG	GP	W	L	T	Mins	GA	SO	Avg	Eff	SA	S%	SAPG

• MICALEF, CORRADO

Corrado Micalef G – R. 5'8", 172 lbs. b: Montreal, Que., 4/20/1961. Detroit's 2nd choice, 44th overall, in 1981 Entry Draft.

Season	Club	League	GP	W	L	T	Mins	GA	SO	Avg	AAvg	Eff	SA	S%	SAPG	GP	W	L	T	Mins	GA	SO	Avg	Eff	SA	S%	SAPG
1978-79	Sherbrooke Castors	QMJHL	42	....	....	....	2045	142	1	4.17	....	....	....	....	....	4	....	....	....	38	2	0	3.16	....	....	....	....
1979-80	Sherbrooke Castors	QMJHL	64	37	17	7	3598	252	1	*4.20	....	....	....	....	....	15	10	5	0	842	52	0	3.71	....	....	....	....
1980-81	Sherbrooke Castors	QMJHL	64	35	26	3	3764	280	*2	4.46	....	....	....	....	....	14	7	7	0	842	46	*1	*3.28	....	....	....	....
	Canada	WJC-A	5	....	....	....	207	20	....	5.79	....	....	....	....	....	....	....	....	....	....	....	....	....	....	....	....	....
1981-82	**Detroit Red Wings**	**NHL**	**18**	**4**	**10**	**1**	**809**	**63**	**0**	**4.67**	**3.60**	....	....	....	....	....	....	....	....	....	....	....	....	....	....	....	....
	Adirondack Red Wings	AHL	1	0	0	0	10	0	0	0.00	....	....	....	....	....	....	....	....	....	....	....	....	....	....	....	....	....
	Kalamazoo Wings	IHL	20	....	....	....	1146	91	1	4.76	....	....	....	....	....	1	....	....	....	25	5	0	11.90	....	....	....	....
1982-83	**Detroit Red Wings**	**NHL**	**34**	**11**	**13**	**5**	**1756**	**106**	**2**	**3.62**	**2.89**	**5.01**	**766**	**.862**	**26.2**	....	....	....	....	....	....	....	....	....	....	....	....
	Adirondack Red Wings	AHL	11	6	5	0	660	37	0	3.36	....	....	....	....	....	....	....	....	....	....	....	....	....	....	....	....	....
1983-84	**Detroit Red Wings**	**NHL**	**14**	**5**	**8**	**1**	**808**	**52**	**0**	**3.86**	**3.02**	**5.56**	**361**	**.856**	**26.8**	**1**	**0**	**0**	....	**7**	**2**	**0**	**17.14**	**68.56**	**5**	**.600**	**42.9**
	Adirondack Red Wings	AHL	29	14	10	5	1767	132	0	4.48	....	....	....	....	....	1	0	0	0	1	0	0	0.00	....	....	....	....
1984-85	**Detroit Red Wings**	**NHL**	**36**	**5**	**19**	**7**	**1856**	**136**	**0**	**4.40**	**3.50**	**6.07**	**986**	**.862**	**31.9**	**2**	**0**	**0**	....	**42**	**6**	**0**	**8.57**	**28.57**	**18**	**.667**	**25.7**
	Adirondack Red Wings	AHL	1	1	0	0	60	2	0	2.00	....	....	....	....	....	....	....	....	....	....	....	....	....	....	....	....	....
1985-86	**Detroit Red Wings**	**NHL**	**11**	**1**	**9**	**1**	**565**	**52**	**0**	**5.52**	**4.30**	**8.39**	**342**	**.848**	**36.3**	....	....	....	....	....	....	....	....	....	....	....	....
	Kalamazoo Wings	IHL	7	....	....	....	398	29	0	4.37	....	....	....	....	....	....	....	....	....	....	....	....	....	....	....	....	....
	Adirondack Red Wings	AHL	25	12	9	2	1436	93	0	3.89	....	....	....	....	....	....	....	....	....	....	....	....	....	....	....	....	....
	Canada	WEC-A	DID NOT PLAY – SPARE GOALTENDER																								
1986-87	Adirondack Red Wings	AHL	1	0	1	0	59	5	0	5.08	....	....	....	....	....	....	....	....	....	....	....	....	....	....	....	....	....
		Switz.	STATISTICS NOT AVAILABLE																								
1987-88			DID NOT PLAY																								
1988-89	CS Villard-de-Lans	France	STATISTICS NOT AVAILABLE																								
1989-90	CS Villard-de-Lans	France	STATISTICS NOT AVAILABLE																								
1990-91	CS Villard-de-Lans	France	STATISTICS NOT AVAILABLE																								
1991-92	HC Briancon	France	19	....	....	....	1093	54	1	2.96	....	....	....	....	....	....	....	....	....	....	....	....	....	....	....	....	....
1992-93	Varese HC	Italy	19	....	....	....	1077	84	0	4.68	....	....	....	....	....	....	....	....	....	....	....	....	....	....	....	....	....
1993-94	HC Courmaosta	Italy	26	....	....	....	1433	95	0	3.98	....	....	....	....	....	....	....	....	....	....	....	....	....	....	....	....	....
1994-95	HC Courmaosta	Italy	STATISTICS NOT AVAILABLE																								
1995-96	San Francisco Spiders	IHL	18	4	8	2	851	56	0	3.95	....	....	....	....	....	....	....	....	....	....	....	....	....	....	....	....	....
	NHL Totals		**113**	**26**	**59**	**15**	**5794**	**409**	**2**	**4.24**	....	....	....	....	....	**3**	**0**	**0**	....	**49**	**8**	**0**	**9.80**	....	....	....	....

QMJHL Second All-Star Team (1980) • QMJHL First All-Star Team (1981) • Memorial Cup All-Star Team (1981) • Won Hap Emms Memorial Trophy (Memorial Cup Tournament Top Goaltender) (1981)

• MIDDLEBROOK, LINDSAY

Lindsay Middlebrook G – R. 5'7", 160 lbs. b: Collingwood, Ont., 9/7/1955.

Season	Club	League	GP	W	L	T	Mins	GA	SO	Avg	AAvg	Eff	SA	S%	SAPG	GP	W	L	T	Mins	GA	SO	Avg	Eff	SA	S%	SAPG
1973-74	St. Louis University	CCHA	2	0	1	0	41	6	0	8.82	....	....	....	....	....	....	....	....	....	....	....	....	....	....	....	....	....
1974-75	St. Louis University	CCHA	24	....	....	....	1459	71	1	2.98	....	....	....	....	....	....	....	....	....	....	....	....	....	....	....	....	....
1975-76	St. Louis University	CCHA	30	....	....	....	1767	88	0	2.99	....	....	....	....	....	....	....	....	....	....	....	....	....	....	....	....	....
1976-77	St. Louis University	CCHA	18	....	....	....	1058	54	1	3.07	....	....	....	....	....	....	....	....	....	....	....	....	....	....	....	....	....
1977-78	New Haven Nighthawks	AHL	17	5	9	3	968	71	0	4.40	....	....	....	....	....	....	....	....	....	....	....	....	....	....	....	....	....
	Toledo Goaldiggers	IHL	16	....	....	....	949	45	*2	2.85	....	....	....	....	....	13	....	....	....	739	32	0	2.60	....	....	....	....
1978-79	New Haven Nighthawks	AHL	*54	*29	19	5	*3221	173	1	3.22	....	....	....	....	....	5	2	3	0	301	16	0	3.19	....	....	....	....
1979-80	**Winnipeg Jets**	**NHL**	**10**	**2**	**8**	**0**	**580**	**40**	**0**	**4.14**	**3.64**	....	....	....	....	....	....	....	....	....	....	....	....	....	....	....	....
	Tulsa Oilers	CHL	37	16	15	3	2073	102	0	2.95	....	....	....	....	....	2	0	2	0	119	8	0	4.03	....	....	....	....
1980-81	**Winnipeg Jets**	**NHL**	**14**	**0**	**9**	**3**	**653**	**65**	**0**	**5.97**	**4.80**	....	....	....	....	....	....	....	....	....	....	....	....	....	....	....	....
	Tulsa Oilers	CHL	36	17	16	2	2115	120	2	3.63	....	....	....	....	....	8	4	4	0	479	33	0	4.13	....	....	....	....
1981-82	**Minnesota North Stars**	**NHL**	**3**	**0**	**0**	**2**	**140**	**7**	**0**	**3.00**	**2.31**	....	....	....	....	....	....	....	....	....	....	....	....	....	....	....	....
	Nashville South Stars	CHL	31	17	11	2	1868	93	*3	2.99	....	....	....	....	....	3	0	3	0	179	11	0	3.69	....	....	....	....
1982-83	**New Jersey Devils**	**NHL**	**9**	**0**	**6**	**1**	**412**	**37**	**0**	**5.39**	**4.31**	**9.07**	**220**	**.832**	**32.0**	....	....	....	....	....	....	....	....	....	....	....	....
	Wichita Wind	CHL	13	6	7	0	779	46	0	3.54	....	....	....	....	....	....	....	....	....	....	....	....	....	....	....	....	....
	Edmonton Oilers	**NHL**	**1**	**1**	**0**	**0**	**60**	**3**	**0**	**3.00**	**2.40**	**2.73**	**33**	**.909**	**33.0**	....	....	....	....	....	....	....	....	....	....	....	....
	Moncton Alpines	AHL	11	6	4	1	669	42	0	3.77	....	....	....	....	....	....	....	....	....	....	....	....	....	....	....	....	....
1983-84	Montana Magic	CHL	36	10	22	3	2104	162	0	4.62	....	....	....	....	....	....	....	....	....	....	....	....	....	....	....	....	....
1984-85	Toledo Goaldiggers	IHL	50	18	25	3	2791	183	0	3.93	....	....	....	....	....	6	2	4	0	339	24	0	4.25	....	....	....	....
1985-86	Milwaukee Admirals	IHL	56	33	10	0	3318	191	*3	3.45	....	....	....	....	....	5	1	4	0	298	18	1	3.62	....	....	....	....
	NHL Totals		**37**	**3**	**23**	**6**	**1845**	**152**	**0**	**4.94**	....	....	....	....	....	....	....	....	....	....	....	....	....	....	....	....	....

CCHA First All-Star Team (1975) • AHL First All-Star Team (1979) • CHL Second All-Star Team (1981)

Signed as a free agent by **NY Rangers**, October 12, 1977. Claimed by **Winnipeg** from **NY Rangers** in Expansion Draft, June 13, 1979. Traded to **Minnesota** by **Winnipeg** for cash, July 31, 1981. Signed as a free agent by **New Jersey**, September 25, 1982. Traded to **Edmonton** by **New Jersey** with Paul Miller for Ron Low and Jim McTaggart, February 19, 1983.

• MILLAR, AL

Al Millar G – L. 5'11", 175 lbs. b: Winnipeg, Man., 9/18/1929. Deceased.

Season	Club	League	GP	W	L	T	Mins	GA	SO	Avg	AAvg	Eff	SA	S%	SAPG	GP	W	L	T	Mins	GA	SO	Avg	Eff	SA	S%	SAPG
1947-48	Winnipeg Canadiens	MJHL	16	10	4	2	960	64	0	*4.00	....	....	....	....	....	5	....	....	....	280	29	0	6.17	....	....	....	....
1948-49	St. Hyacinthe Flyers	QJHL	28	14	12	1	1680	85	1	3.04	....	....	....	....	....	....	....	....	....	....	....	....	....	....	....	....	....
	Montreal Nationale	QJHL	2	1	1	0	120	11	1	5.50	....	....	....	....	....	....	....	....	....	....	....	....	....	....	....	....	....
	Montreal Jr. Canadiens	QJHL	....	....	....	....	....	....	....	....	....	....	....	....	....	1	0	1	0	60	4	0	4.00	....	....	....	....
1949-50	Quebec Aces	QSHL	37	....	....	....	2220	109	2	2.95	....	....	....	....	....	13	6	7	0	780	32	*2	2.38	....	....	....	....
1950-51	New Haven Ramblers	AHL	19	3	16	0	1160	105	1	5.43	....	....	....	....	....	....	....	....	....	....	....	....	....	....	....	....	....
	Kansas City Royals	USHL	4	2	2	0	240	15	1	3.75	....	....	....	....	....	....	....	....	....	....	....	....	....	....	....	....	....
	Portland Eagles	PCHL	28	15	10	3	1680	95	0	3.39	....	....	....	....	....	....	....	....	....	....	....	....	....	....	....	....	....
1951-52	Shawinigan Cataracts	QSHL	60	19	34	7	3680	200	5	3.26	....	....	....	....	....	....	....	....	....	....	....	....	....	....	....	....	....
1952-53	Quebec Aces	QSHL	4	1	3	0	240	22	0	5.50	....	....	....	....	....	....	....	....	....	....	....	....	....	....	....	....	....
	Charlottetown Islanders	MMHL	67	37	26	4	4038	200	6	*3.01	....	....	....	....	....	18	9	9	0	1142	61	1	3.20	....	....	....	....
1953-54	Sudbury Wolves	NOHA	32	....	....	....	1920	120	2	3.75	....	....	....	....	....	4	....	....	....	240	8	0	2.00	....	....	....	....
1954-55	Sault Ste. Marie Indians	NOHA	60	27	27	6	3600	190	*5	3.17	....	....	....	....	....	7	....	....	....	400	18	1	2.70	....	....	....	....
1955-56	Sault Ste. Marie Indians	NOHA	60	26	29	5	3600	207	3	3.45	....	....	....	....	....	7	....	....	....	420	22	0	3.14	....	....	....	....
	Quebec Aces	QHL	3	2	1	0	180	8	1	2.67	....	....	....	....	....	7	3	4	0	426	20	0	2.82	....	....	....	....
1956-57	Quebec Aces	QHL	*65	38	20	7	*3988	165	*5	*2.48	....	....	....	....	....	16	*13	3	0	960	48	*1	3.00	....	....	....	....
1957-58	Springfield Indians	AHL	14	2	9	3	873	56	1	3.85	....	....	....	....	....	....	....	....	....	....	....	....	....	....	....	....	....
	Quebec Aces	QHL	25	9	15	1	1500	97	0	3.88	....	....	....	....	....	13	7	6	0	827	28	*2	*2.03	....	....	....	....
	Boston Bruins	**NHL**	**6**	**1**	**4**	**1**	**360**	**25**	**0**	**4.17**	**4.63**	....	....	....	....	....	....	....	....	....	....	....	....	....	....	....	....
	Buffalo Bisons	AHL	5	2	3	0	300	19	0	3.80	....	....	....	....	....	....	....	....	....	....	....	....	....	....	....	....	....
	Chicoutimi Sagueneens	QHL	1	0	1	0	60	7	0	7.00	....	....	....	....	....	....	....	....	....	....	....	....	....	....	....	....	....
1958-59	Quebec Aces	QHL	*62	31	30	0	3809	232	1	3.65	....	....	....	....	....	....	....	....	....	....	....	....	....	....	....	....	....
1959-60	Quebec Aces	AHL	61	16	42	2	3660	273	2	4.48	....	....	....	....	....	....	....	....	....	....	....	....	....	....	....	....	....
1960-61	Hershey Bears	AHL	32	14	16	1	1894	90	2	2.85	....	....	....	....	....	....	....	....	....	....	....	....	....	....	....	....	....
	Sudbury Wolves	EPHL	2	2	0	0	120	7	0	3.50	....	....	....	....	....	....	....	....	....	....	....	....	....	....	....	....	....
1961-62	Seattle Totems	WHL	58	30	23	5	3540	182	3	3.08	....	....	....	....	....	2	0	2	0	119	6	0	3.03	....	....	....	....
1962-63	Seattle Totems	WHL	*70	35	33	2	4200	232	0	3.31	....	....	....	....	....	*17	9	8	0	*1061	56	0	3.17	....	....	....	....
1963-64	Denver Invaders	WHL	*70	*44	23	3	4230	198	*4	*2.81	....	....	....	....	....	3	1	2	0	179	13	0	4.36	....	....	....	....
1964-65	Victoria Cougars	WHL	64	31	31	2	3835	208	4	3.25	....	....	....	....	....	*10	5	5	0	*600	25	0	2.50	....	....	....	....
1965-66	Victoria Cougars	WHL	51	29	18	4	3100	160	0	3.10	....	....	....	....	....	....	....	....	....	....	....	....	....	....	....	....	....
	Tulsa Oilers	CHL	16	8	5	3	960	43	1	2.69	....	....	....	....	....	*11	4	7	0	*694	47	*1	4.06	....	....	....	....
1966-67	Tulsa Oilers	CHL	62	12	36	14	3732	241	1	3.87	....	....	....	....	....	....	....	....	....	....	....	....	....	....	....	....	....

			REGULAR SEASON													PLAYOFFS											
Season	Club	League	GP	W	L	T	Mins	GA	SO	Avg	AAvg	Eff	SA	S%	SAPG	GP	W	L	T	Mins	GA	SO	Avg	Eff	SA	S%	SAPG
1967-68	Quebec Aces	AHL	33	15	12	4	1771	100	1	3.39	....	....	....	....	....	6	....	....	....	298	18	0	3.62	....	....	....	....
1968-69	Vancouver Canucks	WHL	12	4	4	1	580	34	0	3.52	....	....	....	....	....	....	....	....	....	....	....	....	....	....	....	....	....
1969-70	Rochester Americans	AHL	11	....	....	....	577	52	0	5.41	....	....	....	....	....	....	....	....	....	....	....	....	....	....	....	....	....
	NHL Totals		**6**	**1**	**4**	**1**	**360**	**25**	**0**	**4.17**	....	....	....	....	....	....	....	....	....	....	....	....	....	....	....	....	....

QHL First All-Star Team (1957) • Won Vezina Memorial Trophy (Top Goaltender - QHL) (1957) • WHL First All-Star Team (1962, 1964) • Won WHL Leading Goaltender Award (1962, 1964)

• Promoted to **Boston** from **Quebec** (AHL) to replace injured Don Simmons, December 31, 1957. Traded to **Detroit** (Hershey - AHL) by **Boston** (Quebec - AHL) with Myron Stankiewicz for Claude Dufour, June, 1961. Transferred to **Seattle** (WHL) by **Detroit** as compensation for the loss of Les Hunt and Marc Boileau, November 5, 1961. Traded to **Toronto** (Denver-WHL) by **Seattle** (WHL) for cash, September, 1967. Traded to **Philadelphia** by **Toronto** for cash, September, 1967. Traded to **Vancouver** (WHL) by **Philadelphia** for cash, October, 1968.

• MILLEN, GREG

Greg Millen G – R. 5'9", 175 lbs. b: Toronto, Ont., 6/25/1957. Pittsburgh's 4th choice, 102nd overall, in 1977 Amateur Draft.

Season	Club	League	GP	W	L	T	Mins	GA	SO	Avg	AAvg	Eff	SA	S%	SAPG	GP	W	L	T	Mins	GA	SO	Avg	Eff	SA	S%	SAPG
1974-75	Peterborough Petes	OHA	27	....	....	....	1584	90	2	*3.41	....	....	....	....	....	....	....	....	....	....	....	....	....	....	....	....	....
1975-76	Peterborough Petes	OHA	58	....	....	....	3282	233	0	4.26	....	....	....	....	....	....	....	....	....	....	....	....	....	....	....	....	....
1976-77	Peterborough Petes	OHA	59	....	....	....	3457	244	0	4.23	....	....	....	....	....	4	....	....	....	240	23	0	5.75	....	....	....	....
	Sault Ste. Marie Greyhounds	OHA	25	....	....	....	1469	105	1	4.29	....	....	....	....	....	13	....	....	....	774	61	0	4.73	....	....	....	....
	Kalamazoo Wings	IHL	3	....	....	....	180	14	0	4.67	....	....	....	....	....	....	....	....	....	....	....	....	....	....	....	....	....
1978-79	**Pittsburgh Penguins**	**NHL**	**28**	**14**	**11**	**1**	**1532**	**86**	**2**	**3.37**	**2.97**	....	....	....	....	....	....	....	....	....	....	....	....	....	....	....	....
1979-80	**Pittsburgh Penguins**	**NHL**	**44**	**18**	**18**	**7**	**2586**	**157**	**2**	**3.64**	**3.20**	....	....	....	....	**5**	**2**	**3**	....	**300**	**21**	**0**	**4.20**	....	....	....	....
1980-81	**Pittsburgh Penguins**	**NHL**	**63**	**25**	**27**	**10**	**3721**	**258**	**0**	**4.16**	**3.34**	....	....	....	....	**5**	**2**	**3**	....	**325**	**19**	**0**	**3.51**	....	....	....	....
1981-82	**Hartford Whalers**	**NHL**	**55**	**11**	**30**	**12**	**3201**	**229**	**0**	**4.29**	**3.31**	....	....	....	....	....	....	....	....	....	....	....	....	....	....	....	....
	Canada	WEC-A	5	2	1	2	300	14	1	2.80	....	....	....	....	....	....	....	....	....	....	....	....	....	....	....	....	....
1982-83	**Hartford Whalers**	**NHL**	**60**	**14**	**38**	**6**	**3520**	**282**	**1**	**4.81**	**3.87**	**6.60**	**2056**	**.863**	**35.0**	....	....	....	....	....	....	....	....	....	....	....	....
1983-84	**Hartford Whalers**	**NHL**	***60**	**21**	**30**	**9**	***3583**	**221**	**2**	**3.70**	**2.89**	**4.50**	**1817**	**.878**	**30.4**	....	....	....	....	....	....	....	....	....	....	....	....
1984-85	**Hartford Whalers**	**NHL**	**44**	**16**	**22**	**6**	**2659**	**187**	**1**	**4.22**	**3.36**	**6.13**	**1288**	**.855**	**29.1**	....	....	....	....	....	....	....	....	....	....	....	....
	St. Louis Blues	**NHL**	**10**	**2**	**7**	**1**	**607**	**35**	**0**	**3.46**	**2.75**	**4.47**	**271**	**.871**	**26.8**	**1**	**0**	**1**	....	**60**	**2**	**0**	**2.00**	**1.14**	**35**	**.943**	**35.0**
1985-86	**St. Louis Blues**	**NHL**	**36**	**14**	**16**	**6**	**2168**	**129**	**1**	**3.57**	**2.77**	**4.04**	**1140**	**.887**	**31.5**	**10**	**6**	**3**	....	**586**	**29**	**0**	**2.97**	**2.61**	**330**	**.912**	**33.8**
1986-87	**St. Louis Blues**	**NHL**	**42**	**15**	**18**	**9**	**2482**	**146**	**0**	**3.53**	**2.97**	**4.47**	**1152**	**.873**	**27.8**	**4**	**1**	**3**	....	**250**	**10**	**0**	**2.40**	**1.97**	**122**	**.918**	**29.3**
1987-88	**St. Louis Blues**	**NHL**	**48**	**21**	**19**	**7**	**2854**	**167**	**1**	**3.51**	**2.91**	**4.20**	**1396**	**.880**	**29.3**	**10**	**5**	**5**	....	**600**	**38**	**0**	**3.80**	**5.73**	**252**	**.849**	**25.2**
1988-89	**St. Louis Blues**	**NHL**	**52**	**22**	**20**	**7**	**3019**	**170**	***6**	**3.38**	**2.78**	**4.07**	**1411**	**.880**	**28.0**	**10**	**5**	**5**	....	**649**	**34**	**0**	**3.14**	**3.47**	**308**	**.890**	**28.5**
1989-90	**St. Louis Blues**	**NHL**	**21**	**11**	**7**	**3**	**1245**	**61**	**1**	**2.94**	**2.46**	**3.23**	**556**	**.890**	**26.8**	....	....	....	....	....	....	....	....	....	....	....	....
	Quebec Nordiques	**NHL**	**18**	**3**	**14**	**1**	**1080**	**95**	**0**	**5.28**	**4.44**	**7.74**	**648**	**.853**	**36.0**	....	....	....	....	....	....	....	....	....	....	....	....
	Chicago Blackhawks	**NHL**	**10**	**5**	**4**	**1**	**575**	**32**	**0**	**3.34**	**2.80**	**4.00**	**267**	**.880**	**27.9**	**14**	**6**	**6**	....	**613**	**40**	**0**	**3.92**	**5.23**	**300**	**.867**	**29.4**
1990-91	**Chicago Blackhawks**	**NHL**	**3**	**0**	**1**	**0**	**58**	**4**	**0**	**4.14**	**3.70**	**5.18**	**32**	**.875**	**33.1**	....	....	....	....	....	....	....	....	....	....	....	....
1991-92	Maine Mariners	AHL	11	2	5	2	599	37	0	3.71	....	....	....	....	....	....	....	....	....	....	....	....	....	....	....	....	....
	Detroit Red Wings	**NHL**	**10**	**3**	**2**	**3**	**487**	**22**	**0**	**2.71**	**2.40**	**2.81**	**212**	**.896**	**26.1**	....	....	....	....	....	....	....	....	....	....	....	....
	San Diego Gulls	IHL	5	2	3	0	296	20	0	4.05	....	....	....	....	....	....	....	....	....	....	....	....	....	....	....	....	....
	NHL Totals		**604**	**215**	**284**	**89**	**35377**	**2281**	**17**	**3.87**	....	....	....	....	....	**59**	**27**	**29**	....	**3383**	**193**	**0**	**3.42**	....	....	....	....

Signed as a free agent by **Hartford**, June 15, 1981. Traded to **St. Louis** by **Hartford** with Mark Johnson for Mike Liut and Jorgen Pettersson, February 21, 1985. Traded to **Quebec** by **St. Louis** with Tony Hrkac for Jeff Brown, December 13, 1989. Traded to **Chicago** by **Quebec** with Michel Goulet and Quebec's 6th round choice (Kevin St. Jacques) in 1991 Entry Draft for Mario Doyon, Everett Sanipass and Dan Vincelette, March 5, 1990. Traded to **NY Rangers** by **Chicago** for future considerations, September 24, 1991. Traded to **Detroit** by **NY Rangers** for future considerations, December 26, 1991.

• MILLER, JOE

Joe Miller G5'9", 170 lbs. b: Morrisburg, Ont., 10/6/1900. d: 1963.

Season	Club	League	GP	W	L	T	Mins	GA	SO	Avg	AAvg	Eff	SA	S%	SAPG	GP	W	L	T	Mins	GA	SO	Avg	Eff	SA	S%	SAPG
1916-17	Pittsburgh AA	USAHA	40	37	3	0	2447	63	5	1.54	....	....	....	....	....	....	....	....	....	....	....	....	....	....	....	....	....
1917-18	Renfrew Creamery Kings	Ott-Sr.	7	4	3	0	432	16	0	2.22	....	....	....	....	....	....	....	....	....	....	....	....	....	....	....	....	....
1918-19	Ottawa New Edinburghs	City Sr.	4	3	1	0	240	5	2	1.25	....	....	....	....	....	....	....	....	....	....	....	....	....	....	....	....	....
1919-20	Ottawa New Edinburghs	City Sr.	7	4	2	0	400	10	1	1.50	....	....	....	....	....	....	....	....	....	....	....	....	....	....	....	....	....
1920-21	Ottawa New Edinburghs	City Sr.	11	4	6	1	675	25	0	2.22	....	....	....	....	....	....	....	....	....	....	....	....	....	....	....	....	....
1921-22	Ottawa New Edinburghs	City Sr.	13	4	7	2	780	30	2	2.31	....	....	....	....	....	....	....	....	....	....	....	....	....	....	....	....	....
1922-23	Ottawa New Edinburghs	City Sr.	18	10	6	2	1200	43	2	2.15	....	....	....	....	....	3	1	1	1	222	3	1	*0.81	....	....	....	....
1923-24	Ottawa New Edinburghs	City Sr.	12	*9	3	0	720	18	1	1.50	....	....	....	....	....	2	0	2	0	120	5	0	2.50	....	....	....	....
1924-25	Fort Pitt Hornets	USAHA	22	*17	5	0	1020	39	*1	*1.72	....	....	....	....	....	4	3	1	0	180	3	*1	*0.75	....	....	....	....
1925-26	St. Paul Saints	USAHA	38	....	....	....	2280	70	6	1.84	....	....	....	....	....	....	....	....	....	....	....	....	....	....	....	....	....
1926-27	St. Paul Saints	AHA	30	13	12	5	1850	54	*10	1.75	....	....	....	....	....	....	....	....	....	....	....	....	....	....	....	....	....
1927-28	**New York Americans**	**NHL**	**28**	**8**	**16**	**4**	**1721**	**77**	**5**	**2.68**	**4.48**	....	....	....	....	....	....	....	....	....	....	....	....	....	....	....	....
	Niagara Falls Cataracts	CPHL	13	....	....	....	780	30	2	2.31	....	....	....	....	....	....	....	....	....	....	....	....	....	....	....	....	....
	New York Rangers	**NHL**	....	....	....	....	....	....	....	....	....	....	....	....	....	**3**	**2**	**1**	**0**	**180**	**3**	**1**	**1.00**	....	....	....	....
1928-29	**Pittsburgh Pirates**	**NHL**	***44**	**9**	**27**	**8**	**2780**	**80**	**11**	**1.73**	**3.76**	....	....	....	....	....	....	....	....	....	....	....	....	....	....	....	....
1929-30	**Pittsburgh Pirates**	**NHL**	**43**	**5**	**35**	**3**	**2630**	**179**	**0**	**4.08**	**4.46**	....	....	....	....	....	....	....	....	....	....	....	....	....	....	....	....
1930-31	**Philadelphia Quakers**	**NHL**	**12**	**2**	**9**	**1**	**740**	**47**	**0**	**3.81**	**5.00**	....	....	....	....	....	....	....	....	....	....	....	....	....	....	....	....
1931-32	Syracuse Stars	IAHL	20	....	....	....	1200	51	3	2.55	....	....	....	....	....	....	....	....	....	....	....	....	....	....	....	....	....
	NHL Totals		**127**	**24**	**87**	**16**	**7871**	**383**	**16**	**2.92**	....	....	....	....	....	**3**	**2**	**1**	**0**	**180**	**3**	**1**	**1.00**	....	....	....	....

Signed as a free agent by **NY Americans**, September 19, 1927. Loaned to **NY Rangers** by **NY Americans** to replace injured Lorne Chabot for remainder of Stanley Cup Finals, April 10, 1928. Traded to **Pittsburgh** by **NY Americans** with $20,000 for Roy Worters, November 1, 1928. Transferred to **Philadelphia** after **Pittsburgh** franchise relocated, October 26, 1930.

• MIO, EDDIE

Eddie Mio G – L. 5'10", 180 lbs. b: Windsor, Ont., 1/31/1954. Chicago's 7th choice, 124th overall, in 1974 Amateur Draft.

Season	Club	League	GP	W	L	T	Mins	GA	SO	Avg	AAvg	Eff	SA	S%	SAPG	GP	W	L	T	Mins	GA	SO	Avg	Eff	SA	S%	SAPG
1972-73	Colorado College	WCHA	23	6	17	0	1322	119	0	5.40	....	....	....	....	....	....	....	....	....	....	....	....	....	....	....	....	....
1973-74	Colorado College	WCHA	13	4	7	2	698	57	0	4.90	....	....	....	....	....	....	....	....	....	....	....	....	....	....	....	....	....
1974-75	Colorado College	WCHA	21	....	....	....	1260	83	0	3.95	....	....	....	....	....	....	....	....	....	....	....	....	....	....	....	....	....
1975-76	Colorado College	WCHA	34	15	18	1	2038	144	0	4.24	....	....	....	....	....	....	....	....	....	....	....	....	....	....	....	....	....
1976-77	Tidewater Sharks	SHL	19	....	....	....	1123	66	1	3.53	....	....	....	....	....	....	....	....	....	....	....	....	....	....	....	....	....
	Erie Blades	NAHL	17	....	....	....	771	42	0	3.27	....	....	....	....	....	2	0	1	0	80	8	0	6.00	....	....	....	....
1977-78	Hampton Gulls	AHL	19	5	9	0	949	53	2	3.35	....	....	....	....	....	....	....	....	....	....	....	....	....	....	....	....	....
	Indianapolis Racers	WHA	17	6	8	0	900	64	0	4.27	....	....	....	....	....	....	....	....	....	....	....	....	....	....	....	....	....
1978-79	Dallas Black Hawks	CHL	7	4	3	0	424	25	0	3.54	....	....	....	....	....	....	....	....	....	....	....	....	....	....	....	....	....
	Indianapolis Racers	WHA	5	2	2	1	242	13	1	3.22	....	....	....	....	....	....	....	....	....	....	....	....	....	....	....	....	....
	Edmonton Oilers	WHA	22	7	10	0	1068	71	1	3.99	....	....	....	....	....	3	0	0	0	90	6	0	4.00	....	....	....	....
1979-80	**Edmonton Oilers**	**NHL**	**34**	**9**	**13**	**5**	**1711**	**120**	**1**	**4.21**	**3.71**	....	....	....	....	....	....	....	....	....	....	....	....	....	....	....	....
1980-81	**Edmonton Oilers**	**NHL**	**43**	**16**	**15**	**9**	**2393**	**155**	**0**	**3.89**	**3.12**	....	....	....	....	....	....	....	....	....	....	....	....	....	....	....	....
1981-82	Wichita Wind	CHL	11	3	8	0	657	46	0	4.20	....	....	....	....	....	....	....	....	....	....	....	....	....	....	....	....	....
	New York Rangers	**NHL**	**25**	**13**	**6**	**5**	**1500**	**89**	**0**	**3.56**	**2.74**	....	....	....	....	**8**	**4**	**3**	....	**443**	**28**	**0**	**3.79**	....	....	....	....
1982-83	**New York Rangers**	**NHL**	**41**	**16**	**18**	**6**	**2365**	**136**	**2**	**3.45**	**2.75**	**4.05**	**1159**	**.883**	**29.4**	**8**	**5**	**3**	....	**480**	**32**	**0**	**4.00**	....	....	....	....
1983-84	Adirondack Red Wings	AHL	4	1	1	2	250	11	0	2.64	....	....	....	....	....	....	....	....	....	....	....	....	....	....	....	....	....
	Detroit Red Wings	**NHL**	**24**	**7**	**11**	**3**	**1295**	**95**	**1**	**4.40**	**3.45**	**6.17**	**677**	**.860**	**31.4**	**1**	**0**	**1**	....	**63**	**3**	**0**	**2.86**	**3.58**	**24**	**.875**	**22.9**
1984-85	**Detroit Red Wings**	**NHL**	**7**	**1**	**3**	**2**	**376**	**27**	**0**	**4.31**	**3.42**	**6.69**	**174**	**.845**	**27.8**	....	....	....	....	....	....	....	....	....	....	....	....
	Adirondack Red Wings	AHL	33	19	12	1	1871	871	2	3.75	....	....	....	....	....	....	....	....	....	....	....	....	....	....	....	....	....
1985-86	**Detroit Red Wings**	**NHL**	**18**	**2**	**7**	**0**	**788**	**83**	**0**	**6.32**	**4.94**	**11.58**	**453**	**.817**	**34.5**	....	....	....	....	....	....	....	....	....	....	....	....
	Adirondack Red Wings	AHL	8	4	1	3	487	32	0	3.94	....	....	....	....	....	....	....	....	....	....	....	....	....	....	....	....	....
	NHL Totals		**192**	**64**	**73**	**30**	**10428**	**705**	**4**	**4.06**	....	....	....	....	....	**17**	**9**	**7**	....	**986**	**63**	**0**	**3.83**	....	....	....	....
	Other Major League Totals		44	15	20	1	2210	148	2	4.02	....	....	....	....	....	3	0	0	0	90	6	0	4.00	....	....	....	....

WCHA Second All-Star Team (1975) • NCAA West First All-American Team (1975, 1976) • WCHA First All-Star Team (1976)

Selected by **Vancouver** (WHA) in 1974 WHA Amateur Draft, May, 1974. Signed as a free agent by **Birmingham** (WHA) after **Calgary** (WHA) franchise folded, May 31, 1977. Traded to **Indianapolis** (WHA) by **Birmingham** (WHA) for cash, February, 1978. NHL rights traded to **Minnesota** by **Chicago** with future considerations (Pierre Plante, May 4, 1978) for Doug Hicks and Minnesota's 3rd round choice (Marcel Frere) in 1980 Entry Draft, March 14, 1978. Traded to **Edmonton** (WHA) by **Indianapolis** (WHA) with Wayne Gretzky and Peter Driscoll for cash, November 1978. Reclaimed by **Minnesota from Edmonton** prior to Expansion Draft, June 9, 1979. Claimed as priority selection by **Edmonton**, June 9, 1979. Traded to **NY Rangers** by **Edmonton** for Lance Nethery, December 11, 1981. Traded to **Detroit** by **NY Rangers** with Ron Duguay and Eddie Johnstone for Willie Huber, Mike Blaisdell and Mark Osborne, June 15, 1983.

• MITCHELL, IVAN

Ivan "Mike" Mitchell G b: 1896. Deceased.

Season	Club	League	GP	W	L	T	Mins	GA	SO	Avg	AAvg	Eff	SA	S%	SAPG	GP	W	L	T	Mins	GA	SO	Avg	Eff	SA	S%	SAPG
			REGULAR SEASON													PLAYOFFS											
1913-14	Toronto Canoe Club	OHA	4	1	3	0	240	21	0	5.25	....	....	....	....	....	....	....	....	....	....	....	....	....	....	....	....	....
1914-15	Toronto R & AA	OHA	6	5	1	0	370	23	0	3.73	....	....	....	....	....	1	0	1	0	60	14	0	14.00	....	....	....	....
1915-16	Toronto R & AA	OHA Sr.	4	0	4	0	240	32	0	8.00	....	....	....	....	....	....	....	....	....	....	....	....	....	....	....	....	....
1916-17			MILITARY SERVICE																								
1917-18	New York Wanderers	USAHA	STATISTICS NOT AVAILABLE																								
1918-19	Toronto Veterans	OHA Sr.	2	0	2	0	120	22	0	11.00	....	....	....	....	....	....	....	....	....	....	....	....	....	....	....	....	....
1919-20	Toronto Granites	OHA Sr.	1	1	0	0	60	3	0	3.00	....	....	....	....	....	....	....	....	....	....	....	....	....	....	....	....	....
	Toronto St. Pats	**NHL**	**16**	**6**	**7**	**0**	**830**	**60**	**0**	**4.34**	**2.79**	....	....	....	....	....	....	....	....	....	....	....	....	....	....	....	....
1920-21	**Toronto St. Pats**	**NHL**	**4**	**2**	**2**	**0**	**240**	**22**	**0**	**5.50**	**4.07**	....	....	....	....	....	....	....	....	....	....	....	....	....	....	....	....
1921-22	**Toronto St. Pats**	**NHL**	**2**	**2**	**0**	**0**	**120**	**6**	**0**	**3.00**	**2.33**	....	....	....	....	....	....	....	....	....	....	....	....	....	....	....	....
	NHL Totals		**22**	**10**	**9**	**0**	**1190**	**88**	**0**	**4.44**	....	....	....	....	....	....	....	....	....	....	....	....	....	....	....	....	....
	Other Major League Totals		6	5	1	0	370	23	0	3.73	....	....	....	....	....	1	0	1	0	60	14	0	14.00	....	....	....	....

Signed as a free agent by **Toronto St. Pats**, December 15, 1919. Traded to **Hamilton** by **Toronto St. Pats** for cash, December 5, 1921. Loaned to **Toronto St. Pats** by **Hamilton** to replace injured John Ross Roach, December 13, 1921.

• MOFFAT, MIKE

Mike Moffat G – L. 5'10", 165 lbs. b: Galt, Ont., 2/4/1962. Boston's 7th choice, 165th overall, in 1980 Entry Draft.

Season	Club	League	GP	W	L	T	Mins	GA	SO	Avg	AAvg	Eff	SA	S%	SAPG	GP	W	L	T	Mins	GA	SO	Avg	Eff	SA	S%	SAPG
1979-80	Kingston Canadians	OHA	21	7	7	1	968	71	0	4.40	....	....	....	....	....	2	1	0	0	104	8	0	4.62	....	....	....	....
1980-81	Kingston Canadians	OHA	57	33	21	3	3442	211	0	3.68	....	....	....	....	....	14	6	6	0	814	56	0	4.13	....	....	....	....
1981-82	Kingston Canadians	OHL	46	19	21	4	2666	184	1	4.15	....	....	....	....	....	4	0	1	0	199	17	0	5.13	....	....	....	....
	Canada	WJC-A	4	3	0	1	240	7	1	1.75	....	....	....	....	....	....	....	....	....	....	....	....	....	....	....	....	....
	Boston Bruins	**NHL**	**2**	**2**	**0**	**0**	**120**	**6**	**0**	**3.00**	**2.31**	....	....	....	....	**11**	**6**	**5**	....	**663**	**38**	**0**	**3.44**	....	....	....	....
1982-83	**Boston Bruins**	**NHL**	**13**	**4**	**6**	**1**	**673**	**49**	**0**	**4.37**	**3.49**	**7.90**	**271**	**.819**	**24.2**	....	....	....	....	....	....	....	....	....	....	....	....
	Baltimore Skipjacks	AHL	17	5	8	3	937	78	0	4.99	....	....	....	....	....	....	....	....	....	....	....	....	....	....	....	....	....
1983-84	**Boston Bruins**	**NHL**	**4**	**1**	**1**	**1**	**186**	**15**	**0**	**4.84**	**3.79**	**8.96**	**81**	**.815**	**26.1**	....	....	....	....	....	....	....	....	....	....	....	....
	Hershey Bears	AHL	30	8	13	4	1592	124	0	4.67	....	....	....	....	....	....	....	....	....	....	....	....	....	....	....	....	....
1984-85	Nova Scotia Oilers	AHL	1	0	1	0	60	9	0	9.00	....	....	....	....	....	....	....	....	....	....	....	....	....	....	....	....	....
1985-86			DID NOT PLAY																								
1986-87	Canada	Nat-Team	6	2	3	1	333	18	0	3.24	....	....	....	....	....	....	....	....	....	....	....	....	....	....	....	....	....
	NHL Totals		**19**	**7**	**7**	**2**	**979**	**70**	**0**	**4.29**	....	....	....	....	....	**11**	**6**	**5**	....	**663**	**38**	**0**	**3.44**	....	....	....	....

OHA Second All-Star Team (1981) • WJC-A All-Star Team (1982) • Named Best Goaltender at WJC-A (1982)

• MOOG, ANDY

Andy Moog G – L. 5'8", 175 lbs. b: Penticton, B.C., 2/18/1960. Edmonton's 6th choice, 132nd overall, in 1980 Entry Draft.

Season	Club	League	GP	W	L	T	Mins	GA	SO	Avg	AAvg	Eff	SA	S%	SAPG	GP	W	L	T	Mins	GA	SO	Avg	Eff	SA	S%	SAPG
1978-79	Billings Bighorns	WHL	26	13	5	4	1306	90	4	4.13	....	....	....	....	....	5	1	3	....	229	21	0	5.50	....	....	....	....
1979-80	Billings Bighorns	WHL	46	23	14	1	2435	149	1	3.67	....	....	....	....	....	3	2	1	....	190	10	0	3.16	....	....	....	....
1980-81	**Edmonton Oilers**	**NHL**	**7**	**3**	**3**	**0**	**313**	**20**	**0**	**3.83**	**3.07**	**4.51**	**170**	**.882**	**32.6**	**9**	**5**	**4**	....	**526**	**32**	**0**	**3.65**	....	....	....	....
	Wichita Wind	CHL	29	14	13	1	1602	89	0	3.33	....	....	....	....	....	5	3	2	....	300	16	0	3.20	....	....	....	....
1981-82	**Edmonton Oilers**	**NHL**	**8**	**3**	**5**	**0**	**399**	**32**	**0**	**4.81**	**3.71**	**7.58**	**203**	**.842**	**30.5**	....	....	....	....	....	....	....	....	....	....	....	....
	Wichita Wind	CHL	40	23	13	3	2391	119	1	2.99	....	....	....	....	....	7	3	4	....	434	23	0	3.18	....	....	....	....
1982-83	**Edmonton Oilers**	**NHL**	**50**	**33**	**8**	**7**	**2833**	**167**	**1**	**3.54**	**2.82**	**3.86**	**1531**	**.891**	**32.4**	**16**	**11**	**5**	....	**949**	**48**	**0**	**3.03**	....	....	....	....
1983-84	**Edmonton Oilers**	**NHL**	**38**	**27**	**8**	**1**	**2212**	**139**	**1**	**3.77**	**2.95**	**4.44**	**1179**	**.882**	**32.0**	**7**	**4**	**0**	....	**263**	**12**	**0**	**2.74**	**2.99**	**110**	**.891**	**25.1**
1984-85	**Edmonton Oilers**	**NHL**	**39**	**22**	**9**	**3**	**2019**	**111**	**1**	**3.30**	**2.61**	**3.49**	**1050**	**.894**	**31.2**	**2**	**0**	**0**	....	**20**	**0**	**0**	**0.00**	**0.00**	**3**	**1.000**	**9.0**
1985-86	**Edmonton Oilers**	**NHL**	**47**	**27**	**9**	**7**	**2664**	**104**	**1**	**3.69**	**2.86**	**4.09**	**1480**	**.889**	**33.3**	**1**	**1**	**0**	....	**60**	**1**	**0**	**1.00**	**0.37**	**27**	**.963**	**27.0**
1986-87	**Edmonton Oilers**	**NHL**	**46**	**28**	**11**	**3**	**2461**	**144**	**0**	**3.51**	**2.95**	**4.15**	**1218**	**.882**	**29.7**	**2**	**2**	**0**	....	**120**	**8**	**0**	**4.00**	**8.65**	**37**	**.784**	**18.5**
1987-88	Canada	Nat-Team	27	10	7	5	1438	86	0	3.58	....	....	....	....	....	....	....	....	....	....	....	....	....	....	....	....	....
	Canada	Olympics	4	4	0	0	240	9	1	2.25	....	....	....	....	....	....	....	....	....	....	....	....	....	....	....	....	....
	Boston Bruins	**NHL**	**6**	**4**	**2**	**0**	**360**	**17**	**1**	**2.83**	**2.35**	**2.66**	**181**	**.906**	**30.2**	**7**	**1**	**4**	....	**354**	**25**	**0**	**4.24**	**6.39**	**166**	**.849**	**28.1**
1988-89	**Boston Bruins**	**NHL**	**41**	**18**	**14**	**8**	**2482**	**133**	**1**	**3.22**	**2.65**	**3.97**	**1079**	**.877**	**26.1**	**6**	**4**	**2**	....	**359**	**14**	**0**	**2.34**	**2.41**	**136**	**.897**	**22.7**
1989-90	**Boston Bruins**	**NHL**	**46**	**24**	**10**	**7**	**2536**	**122**	**3**	**2.89**	**2.41**	**3.08**	**1145**	**.893**	**27.1**	**20**	**13**	**7**	....	**1195**	**44**	***2**	***2.21**	**2.00**	**486**	**.909**	**24.4**
1990-91	**Boston Bruins**	**NHL**	**51**	**25**	**13**	**9**	**2844**	**136**	**4**	**2.87**	**2.55**	**2.99**	**1307**	**.896**	**27.6**	**19**	**10**	**9**	....	**1133**	**60**	**0**	**3.18**	**3.35**	**569**	**.895**	**30.1**
1991-92	**Boston Bruins**	**NHL**	**62**	**28**	**22**	**9**	**3640**	**196**	**1**	**3.23**	**2.86**	**3.67**	**1727**	**.887**	**28.5**	**15**	**8**	**7**	....	**866**	**46**	**1**	**3.19**	**3.81**	**385**	**.881**	**26.7**
1992-93	**Boston Bruins**	**NHL**	**55**	**37**	**14**	**3**	**3194**	**168**	**3**	**3.16**	**2.68**	**3.91**	**1357**	**.876**	**25.5**	**3**	**0**	**3**	....	**161**	**14**	**0**	**5.22**	**10.91**	**67**	**.791**	**25.0**
1993-94	**Dallas Stars**	**NHL**	**55**	**24**	**20**	**7**	**3121**	**170**	**2**	**3.27**	**3.11**	**3.47**	**1604**	**.894**	**30.8**	**4**	**1**	**3**	....	**246**	**12**	**0**	**2.93**	**2.91**	**121**	**.901**	**29.5**
1994-95	**Dallas Stars**	**NHL**	**31**	**10**	**12**	**7**	**1770**	**72**	**2**	**2.44**	**2.51**	**2.08**	**846**	**.915**	**28.7**	**5**	**1**	**4**	....	**277**	**16**	**0**	**3.47**	**3.29**	**169**	**.905**	**26.6**
1995-96	**Dallas Stars**	**NHL**	**41**	**13**	**19**	**7**	**2228**	**111**	**1**	**2.99**	**2.93**	**3.00**	**1106**	**.900**	**29.8**	....	....	....	....	....	....	....	....	....	....	....	....
1996-97	**Dallas Stars**	**NHL**	**48**	**28**	**13**	**5**	**2738**	**98**	**3**	**2.15**	**2.26**	**1.88**	**1121**	**.913**	**24.6**	**7**	**3**	**4**	....	**449**	**21**	**0**	**2.81**	**2.76**	**214**	**.902**	**28.6**
1997-98	**Montreal Canadiens**	**NHL**	**42**	**18**	**17**	**5**	**2337**	**97**	**3**	**2.49**	**2.91**	**2.36**	**1024**	**.905**	**26.3**	**9**	**4**	**5**	....	**474**	**24**	**1**	**3.04**	**3.58**	**204**	**.882**	**25.8**
	NHL Totals		**713**	**372**	**209**	**88**	**40151**	**2097**	**28**	**3.13**	....	....	**19328**	**.892**	....	**132**	**68**	**57**	....	**7452**	**377**	**4**	**3.04**	....	....	....	....

WHL Second All-Star Team (1980) • CHL Second All-Star Team (1982) • Shared William Jennings Trophy with Rejean Lemelin (1990)

Played in NHL All-Star Game (1985, 1986, 1991, 1997)

• Statistics (Mins., GA) for suspended game on May 24, 1988 are included in playoff record.

Traded to **Boston** by **Edmonton** for Geoff Courtnall, Bill Ranford and Boston's 2nd round choice (Petro Koivunen) in 1988 Entry Draft, March 8, 1988. Traded to **Dallas** by **Boston** with (Gord Murphy, June 20, 1993) for Jon Casey, June 25, 1993. Signed as a free agent by **Montreal**, July 17, 1997.

• MOORE, ALFIE

Alfie Moore G – R. 5'11", 155 lbs. b: Toronto, Ont., 12/1/1905.

Season	Club	League	GP	W	L	T	Mins	GA	SO	Avg	AAvg	Eff	SA	S%	SAPG	GP	W	L	T	Mins	GA	SO	Avg	Eff	SA	S%	SAPG
1920-21	Toronto Canoe Club	OHA	3	3	0	0	180	2	*1	*0.67	....	....	....	....	....	....	....	....	....	....	....	....	....	....	....	....	....
1921-22	Toronto Aura Lee	OHA	3	*3	0	0	180	4	0	*1.33	....	....	....	....	....	....	....	....	....	....	....	....	....	....	....	....	....
1922-23	Toronto Aura Lee	OHA	1	0	1	0	60	3	0	3.00	....	....	....	....	....	....	....	....	....	....	....	....	....	....	....	....	....
1923-24	Toronto Aura Lee	OHA	4	2	1	1	290	7	1	*1.45	....	....	....	....	....	....	....	....	....	....	....	....	....	....	....	....	....
	Toronto Aura Lee	OHA Sr.	3	0	2	0	160	11	0	4.13	....	....	....	....	....	....	....	....	....	....	....	....	....	....	....	....	....
1924-25	Toronto Aura Lee	OHA Sr.	9	2	6	0	520	31	0	3.58	....	....	....	....	....	....	....	....	....	....	....	....	....	....	....	....	....
1925-26	London Ravens	OHA Sr.	20	*14	5	1	1300	51	0	2.35	....	....	....	....	....	4	1	1	2	240	13	0	3.25	....	....	....	....
1926-27	Chicago Cardinals	AHA	12	4	7	1	720	22	3	1.83	....	....	....	....	....	....	....	....	....	....	....	....	....	....	....	....	....
	London Ravens	OHA Sr.	STATISTICS NOT AVAILABLE																								
1927-28	Chicago Cardinals	AHA	STATISTICS NOT AVAILABLE																								
	Kitchener Millionaires	Can-Pro	1	....	....	....	60	3	0	3.00	....	....	....	....	....	....	....	....	....	....	....	....	....	....	....	....	....
1928-29	Kitchener Flying Dutchmen	Can-Pro	42	19	19	4	2520	113	7	2.67	....	....	....	....	....	3	....	....	....	230	6	1	1.57	....	....	....	....
1929-30	Cleveland Indians	IAHL	42	*24	9	9	2610	78	*8	1.79	....	....	....	....	....	6	*5	1	0	390	9	*2	*1.38	....	....	....	....
1930-31	Springfield Indians	Can-Am	40	*29	2	2	2459	99	2	2.42	....	....	....	....	....	7	*3	2	0	570	19	0	2.00	....	....	....	....
1931-32	Springfield Indians	Can-Am	22	5	13	4	1350	64	0	2.84	....	....	....	....	....	....	....	....	....	....	....	....	....	....	....	....	....
1932-33	Cleveland Indians	IAHL	24	....	....	....	1440	78	3	3.24	....	....	....	....	....	....	....	....	....	....	....	....	....	....	....	....	....
	Springfield Indians	Can-Am	13	6	5	2	810	30	1	2.22	....	....	....	....	....	....	....	....	....	....	....	....	....	....	....	....	....
1933-34	New Haven Eagles	Can-Am	41	12	*25	4	2530	107	4	2.54	....	....	....	....	....	....	....	....	....	....	....	....	....	....	....	....	....
1934-35	New Haven Eagles	Can-Am	48	16	*23	9	3000	145	2	2.90	....	....	....	....	....	....	....	....	....	....	....	....	....	....	....	....	....
	Philadelphia Arrows	Can-Am	1	0	1	0	60	1	0	1.00	....	....	....	....	....	....	....	....	....	....	....	....	....	....	....	....	....
1935-36	New Haven Eagles	Can-Am	20	8	10	2	1240	56	3	2.71	....	....	....	....	....	....	....	....	....	....	....	....	....	....	....	....	....
	Springfield Indians	Can-Am	1	0	0	1	70	2	0	1.71	....	....	....	....	....	....	....	....	....	....	....	....	....	....	....	....	....
	Providence Reds	Can-Am	6	4	2	0	360	16	1	2.67	....	....	....	....	....	....	....	....	....	....	....	....	....	....	....	....	....
	Boston Cubs	Can-Am	1	0	1	0	60	3	0	3.00	....	....	....	....	....	....	....	....	....	....	....	....	....	....	....	....	....
1936-37	New Haven Eagles	AHL	28	8	14	6	1730	75	3	2.60	....	....	....	....	....	....	....	....	....	....	....	....	....	....	....	....	....
	New York Americans	**NHL**	**18**	**7**	**11**	**0**	**1110**	**64**	**1**	**3.46**	**4.42**	....	....	....	....	....	....	....	....	....	....	....	....	....	....	....	....
1937-38	Pittsburgh Hornets	AHL	39	19	14	6	2430	80	7	1.98	....	....	....	....	....	2	0	2	0	130	8	0	3.69	....	....	....	....
	Chicago Black Hawks	**NHL**	....	....	....	....	....	....	....	....	....	....	....	....	....	**1**	**1**	**0**	....	**60**	**1**	**0**	**1.00**	....	....	....	....
1938-39	**New York Americans**	**NHL**	**2**	**0**	**2**	**0**	**120**	**14**	**0**	**7.00**	**8.61**	....	....	....	....	**2**	**0**	**2**	....	**120**	**6**	**0**	**3.00**	....	....	....	....
	Hershey Bears	AHL	53	*31	18	4	3260	105	7	*1.93	....	....	....	....	....	3	1	2	0	180	8	0	2.66	....	....	....	....
1939-40	**Detroit Red Wings**	**NHL**	**1**	**0**	**1**	**0**	**60**	**3**	**0**	**3.00**	**3.72**	....	....	....	....	....	....	....	....	....	....	....	....	....	....	....	....
	Hershey Bears	AHL	13	6	5	2	810	45	1	3.33	....	....	....	....	....	....	....	....	....	....	....	....	....	....	....	....	....
	Indianapolis Capitols	AHL	27	10	13	4	1670	76	4	2.73	....	....	....	....	....	5	2	3	0	342	12	0	*2.11	....	....	....	....

			REGULAR SEASON													PLAYOFFS											
Season	Club	League	GP	W	L	T	Mins	GA	SO	Avg	AAvg	Eff	SA	S%	SAPG	GP	W	L	T	Mins	GA	SO	Avg	Eff	SA	S%	SAPG
1940-41	Springfield Indians	AHL	8	4	3	1	500	24	1	2.88	....	....	....	....	....	....	....	....	....	....	....	....	....	....	....	....	....
	New Haven Eagles	AHL	3	1	0	2	200	11	0	3.30	....	....	....	....	....	....	....	....	....	....	....	....	....	....	....	....	....
	Cleveland Barons	AHL	8	3	4	1	490	27	0	3.31	....	....	....	....	....	6	4	2	0	360	16	0	2.67	....	....	....	....
1941-42	Philadelphia Rockets	AHL	19	6	11	2	1160	79	1	4.09	....	....	....	....	....	....	....	....	....	....	....	....	....	....	....	....	....
	Buffalo Bisons	AHL	2	0	1	1	130	7	0	3.23	....	....	....	....	....	....	....	....	....	....	....	....	....	....	....	....	....
	NHL Totals		**21**	**7**	**14**	**0**	**1290**	**81**	**1**	**3.77**	....	....	....	....	....	**3**	**1**	**2**	....	**180**	**7**	**0**	**2.33**	....	....	....	....

AHL Second All-Star Team (1939)

Claimed by **NY Rangers** from **Cleveland** (IAHL) in Inter-League Draft, April 15, 1930. Traded to **NY Americans** by **New Haven** (AHL) for Lloyd Jackson and cash, January, 1937. Loaned to **Chicago** by **NY Americans** (Pittsburgh - AHL) to replace injured Mike Karakas for game one of the 1938 Stanley Cup Finals, April 5, 1938. Traded to **Detroit** by **NY Americans** for cash, November 7, 1939. Promoted to **Detroit** by **Indianapolis** to replace injured Tiny Thompson, January 9, 1940. (Boston 3, Detroit 1)

• MOORE, ROBBIE

Robbie Moore G – R. 5′5″, 155 lbs. b: Sarnia, Ont., 5/3/1954.

1972-73	University of Michigan	WCHA	31	....	....	....	1840	176	0	5.74	....	....	....	....	....	....	....	....	....	....	....	....	....	....	....	....	....
1973-74	University of Michigan	WCHA	36	....	....	....	2000	144	0	4.32	....	....	....	....	....	....	....	....	....	....	....	....	....	....	....	....	....
1974-75	University of Michigan	WCHA	24	....	....	....	1420	94	0	3.97	....	....	....	....	....	....	....	....	....	....	....	....	....	....	....	....	....
1975-76	University of Michigan	WCHA	37	....	....	....	2137	157	1	4.41	....	....	....	....	....	....	....	....	....	....	....	....	....	....	....	....	....
1976-77	University of Western Ontario	OUAA	30	....	....	....	770	52	0	4.05	....	....	....	....	....	....	....	....	....	....	....	....	....	....	....	....	....
1978-79	Maine Mariners	AHL	26	12	6	6	1489	84	1	3.38	....	....	....	....	....	4	1	2	0	163	9	0	3.31	....	....	....	....
	Philadelphia Flyers	**NHL**	**5**	**3**	**0**	**1**	**237**	**7**	**2**	**1.77**	**1.56**	....	....	....	....	**5**	**3**	**2**	....	**268**	**18**	**0**	**4.03**	....	....	....	....
1979-80	Maine Mariners	AHL	32	14	11	4	1830	106	1	3.48	....	....	....	....	....	7	5	2	0	448	21	*1	*2.81	....	....	....	....
1980-81	Maine Mariners	AHL	25	11	11	2	1431	92	1	3.86	....	....	....	....	....	4	0	3	0	139	14	0	6.04	....	....	....	....
1981-82	Nashville South Stars	CHL	39	18	17	1	2204	159	0	4.33	....	....	....	....	....	....	....	....	....	....	....	....	....	....	....	....	....
1982-83	**Washington Capitals**	**NHL**	**1**	**0**	**1**	**0**	**20**	**1**	**0**	**3.00**	**2.40**	**3.75**	**8**	**.875**	**24.0**	....	....	....	....	....	....	....	....	....	....	....	....
	Hershey Bears	AHL	35	15	14	1	1798	115	0	3.84	....	....	....	....	....	1	0	1	0	87	3	0	2.07	....	....	....	....
1983-84	Milwaukee Admirals	IHL	49	....	....	....	2788	195	0	4.20	....	....	....	....	....	4	....	....	....	206	13	0	3.79	....	....	....	....
	NHL Totals		**6**	**3**	**1**	**1**	**257**	**8**	**2**	**1.87**	....	....	....	....	....	**5**	**3**	**2**	....	**268**	**18**	**0**	**4.03**	....	....	....	....

NCAA West First All-American Team (1974) • WCHA Second All-Star Team (1976) • Shared Harry "Hap" Holmes Memorial Award (fewest goals against - AHL) with Pete Peters (1979) • Shared Harry "Hap" Holmes Memorial Award (fewest goals against - AHL) with Rick St. Croix (1980) • Shared Harry "Hap" Holmes Memorial Award (fewest goals against - AHL) with Pelle Lindbergh (1981)

Signed as a free agent by **Philadelphia**, November 7, 1978. Signed as a free agent by **Minnesota**, July 27, 1981. Traded to **Washington** by **Minnesota** with Minnesota's 11th round choice (Anders Huss) in 1983 Entry Draft for Wes Jarvis and Rollie Boutin, August 4, 1982.

• MORISSETTE, JEAN-GUY

Jean-Guy Morissette G – L. 5′6″, 140 lbs. b: Causapscal, N.B., 12/16/1937.

1955-56	Jonquiere Aces	QJHL	STATISTICS NOT AVAILABLE																								
	Chicoutimi Sagueneens	QHL	1	....	....	....	60	3	0	3.00	....	....	....	....	....	....	....	....	....	....	....	....	....	....	....	....	....
1956-1961	Jonquiere Aces	QPHL	STATISTICS NOT AVAILABLE																								
1961-62	Amherst Ramblers	NSSHL	7	....	....	....	420	20	1	2.86	....	....	....	....	....	9	*8	1	0	540	26	*2	*2.89	....	....	....	....
1962-63	Amherst/Moncton	NSSHL	55	....	....	....	3300	228	*1	*4.15	....	....	....	....	....	26	*18	8	0	1570	82	0	3.13	....	....	....	....
1963-64	Omaha Knights	CHL	7	4	1	2	420	22	0	3.14	....	....	....	....	....	....	....	....	....	....	....	....	....	....	....	....	....
	Montreal Canadiens	**NHL**	**1**	**0**	**1**	**0**	**36**	**4**	**0**	**6.67**	**7.43**	....	....	....	....	....	....	....	....	....	....	....	....	....	....	....	....
	Cleveland Barons	AHL	5	2	2	1	310	14	1	2.71	....	....	....	....	....	*9	*9	0	0	540	17	0	*1.89	....	....	....	....
	Quebec Aces	AHL	1	1	0	0	60	2	0	2.00	....	....	....	....	....	....	....	....	....	....	....	....	....	....	....	....	....
1964-65	Cleveland Barons	AHL	11	4	6	1	670	38	0	3.40	....	....	....	....	....	....	....	....	....	....	....	....	....	....	....	....	....
	Baltimore Clippers	AHL	20	9	10	0	1173	70	1	3.58	....	....	....	....	....	....	....	....	....	....	....	....	....	....	....	....	....
	Omaha Knights	CHL	12	4	6	2	720	39	3	3.25	....	....	....	....	....	....	....	....	....	....	....	....	....	....	....	....	....
	Victoria Cougars	WHL	....	....	....	....	....	....	....	....	....	....	....	....	....	2	1	1	0	125	6	0	2.88	....	....	....	....
1965-66	Cleveland Barons	AHL	8	4	2	0	398	24	0	3.62	....	....	....	....	....	1	0	0	0	24	1	0	2.50	....	....	....	....
1966-67	California Seals	WHL	8	5	2	0	440	21	1	2.86	....	....	....	....	....	....	....	....	....	....	....	....	....	....	....	....	....
	Quebec Aces	AHL	9	3	2	1	409	19	0	2.79	....	....	....	....	....	....	....	....	....	....	....	....	....	....	....	....	....
1967-68	Vancouver Canucks	WHL	11	1	8	1	638	58	0	5.45	....	....	....	....	....	....	....	....	....	....	....	....	....	....	....	....	....
1968-69			DID NOT PLAY																								
1969-70	Victoriaville Tigers	QSHL	STATISTICS NOT AVAILABLE																								
1970-71	Grand Falls Cataracts	Nfld.	35	14	16	5	2100	144	1	4.11	....	....	....	....	....	17	*11	6	0	1020	50	....	*2.94	....	....	....	....
	NHL Totals		**1**	**0**	**1**	**0**	**36**	**4**	**0**	**6.67**	....	....	....	....	....	....	....	....	....	....	....	....	....	....	....	....	....

Montreal's spare goaltender replaced injured Gump Worsley in 2nd period, October 30, 1963. (Toronto 6, Montreal 3). Traded to **NY Rangers** by **Montreal** with Bill Hicke for Dick Duff and Dave McComb, December 21, 1964.

• MOSS, TYLER

Tyler Moss G – R. 6′, 184 lbs. b: Ottawa, Ont., 6/29/1975. Tampa Bay's 2nd choice, 29th overall, in 1993 Entry Draft.

1992-93	Kingston Frontenacs	OHL	31	13	7	5	1537	97	0	3.79	....	....	....	....	....	6	1	2	....	228	19	0	5.00	....	....	....	....
1993-94	Kingston Frontenacs	OHL	13	6	4	3	795	42	1	3.17	....	....	....	....	....	3	0	2	....	136	8	0	3.53	....	....	....	....
1994-95	Kingston Frontenacs	OHL	*57	33	17	5	*3249	164	1	3.03	....	....	....	....	....	6	2	4	....	333	27	0	4.86	....	....	....	....
1995-96	Atlanta Knights	IHL	40	11	19	4	2030	138	1	4.08	....	....	....	....	....	3	0	3	....	213	11	0	3.10	....	....	....	....
1996-97	Adirondack Red Wings	AHL	11	1	5	2	507	42	1	4.97	....	....	....	....	....	....	....	....	....	....	....	....	....	....	....	....	....
	Grand Rapids Griffins	IHL	15	5	6	1	715	35	0	2.94	....	....	....	....	....	....	....	....	....	....	....	....	....	....	....	....	....
	Muskegon Fury	ColHL	2	1	1	0	119	5	0	2.51	....	....	....	....	....	....	....	....	....	....	....	....	....	....	....	....	....
	Saint John Flames	AHL	9	6	1	1	534	17	0	1.91	....	....	....	....	....	5	2	3	....	242	15	0	3.72	....	....	....	....
1997-98	**Calgary Flames**	**NHL**	**6**	**2**	**3**	**1**	**367**	**20**	**0**	**3.27**	**3.83**	**3.52**	**186**	**.892**	**30.4**	....	....	....	....	....	....	....	....	....	....	....	....
	Saint John Flames	AHL	39	19	10	7	2194	91	0	2.49	....	....	....	....	....	15	8	5	....	761	37	0	2.91	....	....	....	....
	NHL Totals		**6**	**2**	**3**	**1**	**367**	**20**	**0**	**3.27**	....	....	**186**	**.892**	....	....	....	....	....	....	....	....	....	....	....	....	....

OHL First All-Star Team (1995) • Shared Harry "Hap" Holmes Memorial Trophy (fewest goals against - AHL) with Jean-Sebastien Giguere (1998)

Traded to **Calgary** by **Tampa Bay** for Jamie Huscroft, March 18, 1997.

• MOWERS, JOHNNY

Johnny "Mum" Mowers G – L. 5′11″, 185 lbs. b: Niagara Falls, Ont., 10/29/1916. d: 1995.

1936-37	Niagara Falls Cataracts	OHA Sr.	18	....	....	....	1080	54	0	*3.00	....	....	....	....	....	9	....	....	....	540	30	0	3.33	....	....	....	....
1937-38	Niagara Falls Cataracts	OHA Sr.	16	....	....	....	960	50	0	3.12	....	....	....	....	....	2	2	0	0	120	2	*1	*1.00	....	....	....	....
1938-39	Niagara Falls Cataracts	OHA Sr.	20	....	....	....	1200	63	4	3.15	....	....	....	....	....	....	....	....	....	....	....	....	....	....	....	....	....
1939-40	Detroit Pontiacs	MOHL	20	....	....	....	1200	84	0	4.20	....	....	....	....	....	....	....	....	....	....	....	....	....	....	....	....	....
	Omaha Knights	AHA	21	16	5	0	1272	41	3	1.93	....	....	....	....	....	9	4	*5	0	610	21	1	2.07	....	....	....	....
1940-41	**Detroit Red Wings**	**NHL**	***48**	**21**	**16**	**11**	***3040**	**102**	**4**	**2.01**	**2.22**	....	....	....	....	**9**	**4**	**5**	....	**561**	**20**	**0**	**2.14**	....	....	....	....
1941-42	**Detroit Red Wings**	**NHL**	**47**	**19**	**25**	**3**	**2880**	**144**	**5**	**3.00**	**2.95**	....	....	....	....	**12**	**7**	**5**	....	**720**	**38**	**0**	**3.17**	....	....	....	....
1942-43	**Detroit Red Wings**	**NHL**	***50**	***25**	**14**	**11**	**3010**	**124**	***6**	***2.47**	**1.98**	....	....	....	....	***10**	***8**	**2**	....	***679**	**22**	***2**	***1.94**	....	....	....	....
1943-44	Toronto RCAF	City Sr.	9	....	....	....	540	53	0	5.89	....	....	....	....	....	....	....	....	....	....	....	....	....	....	....	....	....
1944-45			MILITARY SERVICE																								
1945-46			MILITARY SERVICE																								
1946-47	**Detroit Red Wings**	**NHL**	**7**	**0**	**6**	**1**	**420**	**29**	**0**	**4.14**	**4.07**	....	....	....	....	**1**	**0**	**1**	....	**40**	**5**	**0**	**7.50**	....	....	....	....
1947-48	Indianapolis Capitols	AHL	2	1	1	0	120	7	0	3.50	....	....	....	....	....	....	....	....	....	....	....	....	....	....	....	....	....
	NHL Totals		**152**	**65**	**61**	**26**	**9350**	**399**	**15**	**2.56**	....	....	....	....	....	**32**	**19**	**13**	....	**2000**	**85**	**2**	**2.55**	....	....	....	....

NHL First All-Star Team (1943) • Won Vezina Trophy (1943)

• MRAZEK, JEROME

Jerome Mrazek G – L. 5′9″, 160 lbs. b: Prince Albert, Sask., 10/15/1951. Philadelphia's 8th choice, 106th overall, in 1971 Amateur Draft.

1970-71	U. of Minnesota-Duluth	WCHA	4	2	1	0	200	17	0	5.10	....	....	....	....	....	....	....	....	....	....	....	....	....	....	....	....	....
1971-72	U. of Minnesota-Duluth	WCHA	27	12	13	1	1590	114	0	4.30	....	....	....	....	....	....	....	....	....	....	....	....	....	....	....	....	....
1972-73	U. of Minnesota-Duluth	WCHA	27	14	13	0	1608	119	0	4.44	....	....	....	....	....	....	....	....	....	....	....	....	....	....	....	....	....
1973-74	U. of Minnesota-Duluth	WCHA	29	17	12	0	1729	115	1	3.99	....	....	....	....	....	....	....	....	....	....	....	....	....	....	....	....	....
1974-75	Des Moines Capitols	IHL	50	....	....	....	2787	154	2	3.32	....	....	....	....	....	5	2	3	0	311	13	0	*2.51	....	....	....	....
1975-76	**Philadelphia Flyers**	**NHL**	**1**	**0**	**0**	**0**	**6**	**1**	**0**	**10.00**	**9.05**	....	....	....	....	....	....	....	....	....	....	....	....	....	....	....	....
	Richmond Robins	AHL	20	5	9	4	1135	72	2	3.81	....	....	....	....	....	5	3	2	0	289	14	0	2.91	....	....	....	....

Season	Club	League	GP	W	L	T	Mins	GA	SO	Avg	AAvg	Eff	SA	S%	SAPG	GP	W	L	T	Mins	GA	SO	Avg	Eff	SA	S%	SAPG
								REGULAR SEASON													**PLAYOFFS**						
1976-77	Springfield Indians	AHL	33	....	....	....	1685	151	0	5.38					....	....	....	....	....	....	....	....	....			....	....
	Hershey Bears	AHL	10	....	....	....	537	38	0	4.24					....	6	2	4	0	358	21	0	3.52			....	....
1977-78	Maine Mariners	AHL	27	12	10	4	1488	80	3	3.33					....	....	....	....	....	....	....	....	....			....	....
	Hershey Bears	AHL	14	2	10	1	831	67	0	4.84					....	....	....	....	....	....	....	....	....			....	....
	NHL Totals		**1**	**0**	**0**	**0**	**6**	**1**	**0**	**10.00**																	

● MUMMERY, HARRY   Harry "Mum" Mummery   G – L. 5'11", 220 lbs.   b: Chicago, IL, 8/25/1889.   d: 12/7/1945.

Season	Club	League	GP	W	L	T	Mins	GA	SO	Avg	AAvg															
1919-20	**Quebec Bulldogs**	**NHL**	3	1	1	0	142	18	0	7.61	5.03
1921-22	**Hamilton Tigers**	**NHL**	1	1	0	0	49	2	0	2.45	1.90
	NHL Totals		**4**	**2**	**1**	**0**	**191**	**20**	**0**	**6.28**	

● Quebec defenseman replaced injured Frank Brophy, February 4, March 8 and 10, 1920. Hamilton defenseman replaced injured Howard Lockhart in 1st period, January 21, 1922. (Hamilton 7, Ottawa 6)

● MUNRO, DUNC   Dunc Munro   G – L. 5'8", 190 lbs.   b: Moray, Scotland, 1/19/1901.   d: 1/3/1958.

Season	Club	League	GP	W	L	T	Mins	GA	SO	Avg	AAvg
1924-25	**Montreal Maroons**	**NHL**	1	0	0	0	2	0	0	0.00	0.00
	NHL Totals		**1**	**0**	**0**	**0**	**2**	**0**	**0**	**0.00**	

● Montreal Maroons' defenseman replaced penalized Clint Benedict, December 20, 1924. (Hamilton 3, Montreal Maroons 1)

● MURPHY, HAL   Hal Murphy   G – R. 5'9", 140 lbs.   b: Montreal, Que., 7/6/1927.   Deceased.

Season	Club	League	GP	W	L	T	Mins	GA	SO	Avg	AAvg
1952-53	Montreal Royals	QSHL	3	2	1	0	180	6	0	2.00	
	Montreal Canadiens	**NHL**	1	1	0	0	60	4	0	4.00	5.16
1953-54	Sir George Williams University	QUAA		STATISTICS NOT AVAILABLE							
	Ottawa Senators	QHL	3	2	1	0	180	11	0	3.67	
	NHL Totals		**1**	**1**	**0**	**0**	**60**	**4**	**0**	**4.00**	

Promoted to **Montreal** from **Montreal Royals** (QSHL) to replace injured Gerry McNeil, November 8, 1952. (Montreal 6, Chicago 4)

● MURRAY, MICKEY   Mickey Murray   G – R. 5'10",   b: Peterbourgh, Ont., 10/14/1898.

Season	Club	League	GP	W	L	T	Mins	GA	SO	Avg	AAvg	GP	W	L	T	Mins	GA	SO	Avg
1916-17	Peterborough Hockey Club	OHA	3	2	1	0	180	15	0	5.00		2	0	2	0	120	21	0	10.50
1917-18	Peterborough Hockey Club	OHA	3	*3	0	0	180	7	0	2.33		4	1	3	0	240	37	0	9.25
1918-19				STATISTICS NOT AVAILABLE															
1919-20	Peterborough Seniors	OHA Sr.	....	....	....	....	....	....	....	....		5	3	2	0	300	24	0	4.80
1920-21	Peterborough Seniors	OHA Sr.	4	1	3	0	240	22	0	5.50									
1921-22				STATISTICS NOT AVAILABLE															
1922-23	North Toronto Rangers	OHA Sr.		STATISTICS NOT AVAILABLE															
1923-24	North Toronto Rangers	OHA Sr.		STATISTICS NOT AVAILABLE															
1924-25	Galt Terriers	OHA Sr.	20	7	12	1	1200	48	1	*2.48									
1925-26	Galt Terriers	OHA Sr.	20	*14	4	2	1200	33	3	*1.65		2	0	1	1	120	8	0	4.00
1926-27	Galt Terriers	OHA Sr.	10	4	6	0	600	30	0	3.00									
1927-28	Philadelphia Arrows	Can-Am	3	1	2	0	200	4	1	1.20									
	Providence Reds	Can-Am	21	6	10	5	1310	42	1	1.92									
1928-29	Providence Reds	Can-Am	40	18	12	6	2540	58	*12	1.37		6	1	3	2	363	14	1	2.31
1929-30	Providence Reds	Can-Am	39	*23	11	5	2394	96	*6	*2.41		3	*3	0	0	180	4	0	*1.33
	Montreal Canadiens	**NHL**	1	0	1	0	60	4	0	4.00	4.19								
1930-31	Providence Reds	Can-Am	40	23	11	6	2470	96	*4	*2.33		2	1	1	0	142	7	0	2.96
1931-32	Philadelphia Arrows	Can-Am	38	13	*20	5	2352	97	3	2.48									
1932-33				DID NOT PLAY															
1933-34	St. Louis Flyers	AHA	48	*26	18	4	3050	84	7	*1.65		7	2	4	1	460	12	1	1.57
1934-35	St. Louis Flyers	AHA	46	*29	14	3	2920	97	6	1.99		6	3	3	0	370	18	0	2.92
1935-36	St. Louis Flyers	AHA	47	27	16	4	2941	87	*9	1.78		1	0	0	0	80	1	0	0.75
1936-37	Kansas City Greyhounds	AHA	36	21	13	2	2189	54	*11	*1.48		3	0	3	0	180	10	3	3.33
1937-38	Kansas City Greyhounds	AHA	48	21	22	5	3005	120	0	2.40									
1938-39	St. Paul Saints	AHA	4	1	3	0	240	20	1	5.00									
	NHL Totals		**1**	**0**	**1**	**0**	**60**	**4**	**0**	**4.00**									

AHA Second All-Star Team (1935, 1936, 1938)

Promoted to **Montreal Canadiens** from **Providence** (Can-Am) to replace injured Georges Hainsworth, February 25, 1930. (NY Americans 4, Montreal Canadiens 2)

● MUZZATTI, JASON   Jason Muzzatti   G – L. 6'2", 210 lbs.   b: Toronto, Ont., 2/3/1970.   Calgary's 1st choice, 21st overall, in 1988 Entry Draft.

Season	Club	League	GP	W	L	T	Mins	GA	SO	Avg	AAvg	Eff	SA	S%	SAPG	GP	W	L	T	Mins	GA	SO	Avg
1987-88	Michigan State Spartans	CCHA	33	19	9	3	1915	109	0	3.41														
1988-89	Michigan State Spartans	CCHA	42	32	9	0	2515	127	3	*3.03														
1989-90	Michigan State Spartans	CCHA	33	*24	6	0	1976	99	0	3.01														
1990-91	Michigan State Spartans	CCHA	22	8	10	2	1204	75	1	3.74														
1991-92	Salt Lake Golden Eagles	IHL	52	24	22	5	3033	167	2	3.30						4	1	3		247	18	0	4.37
1992-93	Canada	Nat-Team	16	6	9	0	880	53	0	3.84													
	Indianapolis Ice	IHL	12	5	6	1	707	48	0	4.07													
	Salt Lake Golden Eagles	IHL	13	5	6	1	747	52	0	4.18													
1993-94	**Calgary Flames**	**NHL**	1	0	1	0	60	8	0	8.00	7.62	18.29	35	.771	35.0								
	Saint John Flames	AHL	51	26	21	3	2939	183	2	3.74						7	3	4		415	19	0	2.75
1994-95	Saint John Flames	AHL	31	10	14	4	1741	101	2	3.48													
	Calgary Flames	**NHL**	1	0	0	0	10	0	0	0.00	0.00	0.00	8	1.000	48.0								
1995-96	**Hartford Whalers**	**NHL**	22	4	8	3	1013	49	1	2.90	2.85	2.58	551	.911	32.6								
	Springfield Falcons	AHL	5	4	0	1	300	12	1	2.40													
1996-97	**Hartford Whalers**	**NHL**	31	9	13	5	1591	91	0	3.43	3.64	3.83	815	.888	30.7								
1997-98	**New York Rangers**	**NHL**	6	0	3	2	313	17	0	3.26	3.82	3.55	156	.891	29.9								
	Hartford Wolf Pack	AHL	17	11	5	1	999	57	0	3.42													
	San Jose Sharks	**NHL**	1	0	0	0	27	2	0	4.44	5.20	6.83	13	.846	28.9								
	Kentucky Thoroughblades	AHL	7	2	3	2	430	25	0	3.49						3	0	3		153	13	0	5.07
	NHL Totals		**62**	**13**	**25**	**10**	**3014**	**167**	**1**	**3.32**			**1578**	**.894**									

CCHA Second All-Star Team (1988) ● CCHA First All-Star Team (1990) ● NCAA West Second All-American Team (1990)

Claimed on waivers by **Hartford** from **Calgary**, October 6, 1995. Transferred to **Carolina** after **Hartford** franchise relocated, June 25, 1997. Traded to **NY Rangers** by **Carolina** for NY Rangers' 4th round choice (Tommy Westlund) in 1998 Entry Draft, August 8, 1997. Traded to **San Jose** by **NY Rangers** for Rich Brennan, March 24, 1998.

● MYLLYS, JARMO   Jarmo Myllys   G – L. 5'8", 160 lbs.   b: Savonlinna, Finland, 5/29/1965.   Minnesota's 9th choice, 172nd overall, in 1987 Entry Draft.

Season	Club	League	GP	W	L	T	Mins	GA	SO	Avg	AAvg	Eff	SA	S%	SAPG	GP	W	L	T	Mins	GA	SO	Avg
1984-85	Finland	WJC-A	1				60	2	0	2.00													
1985-86	Lukko Rauma	Finland		STATISTICS NOT AVAILABLE																			
1986-87	Lukko Rauma	Finland	43	....	....	....	2542	160	0	3.78													
	Finland	WEC-A	8	....	....	....	464	27	....	3.49													
1987-88	Finland	C Cup	1				20	1	0	3.00													
	Lukko Rauma	Finland	43	....	....	....	2468	160	0	3.72						8				480			
	Finland	Olympics	6				360	11		1.83													
1988-89	**Minnesota North Stars**	**NHL**	6	1	4	0	230	22	0	5.55	4.58	8.85	138	.841	34.8								
	Kalamazoo Wings	IHL	28	13	8	4	1523	93	0	3.66						6	2	4	0	419	22	0	3.15
1989-90	**Minnesota North Stars**	**NHL**	4	0	3	0	156	16	0	6.15	5.16	11.86	83	.807	31.9								
	Kalamazoo Wings	IHL	49	31	9	3	2/15	159	1	3.51						7	2	4	0	356	22	0	3.71
1990-91	Minnesota North Stars	FrTour	3				85	4	0	2.82													
	Minnesota North Stars	**NHL**	2	0	2	0	78	8	0	6.15	5.50	8.63	57	.860	43.8								
	Kalamazoo Wings	IHL	38	24	13	1	2278	144	1	3.79						10	0	4	0	600	26	0	*2.60
1991-92	**San Jose Sharks**	**NHL**	27	3	18	1	1374	115	0	5.02	4.48	6.70	862	.867	37.6								
	Kansas City Blades	IHL	5	5	0	0	307	15	0	2.93													

			REGULAR SEASON													PLAYOFFS											
Season	**Club**	**League**	**GP**	**W**	**L**	**T**	**Mins**	**GA**	**SO**	**Avg**	**AAvg**	**Eff**	**SA**	**S%**	**SAPG**	**GP**	**W**	**L**	**T**	**Mins**	**GA**	**SO**	**Avg**	**Eff**	**SA**	**S%**	**SAPG**
1992-93	Koo Koo Kouvola	Finland 2	39				2310	120		3.11						6				359	24		4.01				
1993-94	Lukko Rauma	Finland	46				2762	131	2	*2.05																	
	Finland	Olympics	5				300	3		0.60																	
	Finland	WC-A	7				400	10		1.35																	
1994-95	Lulea HF	Sweden	37				2220	106	*4	2.86						9				540	28	0	3.11				
	Finland	WC-A	7				420	12		1.71																	
1995-96	Lulea HF	Sweden	39				2340	104	1	2.67						7				780	29	0	*2.23				
	Finland	WC-A	4				238	12		3.02																	
1996-97	Finland	W Cup	2				120	8		4.00																	
	Lulea HF	Sweden	37				2158	80	*5	*2.22						10				612	25	*1	2.45				
	Lulea HF	Euro	4				240	9		2.25																	
	Finland	WC-A	6				357	10		1.68																	
1997-98	Lulea HF	Sweden	43				2534	111		2.63						3				180	10		3.33				
	Finland	Olympics	4	1	3	0	237	14	0	3.54																	
	Finland	WC-A	2	1	1	0	119	4		2.02																	
	NHL Totals		**39**	**4**	**27**	**1**	**1846**	**161**	**0**	**5.23**			**1140**	**.859**													

EJC-A All-Star Team (1983) • Named Best Goaltender at EJC-A (1983) • Finnish First All-Star Team (1988, 1994) • Finnish Player of the Year (1988) • IHL Second All-Star Team (1990, 1991) • Named Best Goaltender at WC-A (1995)

• Played professional hockey in Finland from 1982-83 through 1985-86. Claimed by **San Jose** from **Minnesota** in Dispersal Draft, May 30, 1991. Traded to **Toronto** by **San Jose** for cash, June 15, 1992.

• MYLNIKOV, SERGEI

Sergei Mylnikov G – L. 5'10", 176 lbs. b: Chelyabinsk, Soviet Union, 10/6/1958. Quebec's 8th choice, 127th overall, in 1989 Entry Draft.

Season	Club	League	GP	W	L	T	Mins	GA	SO	Avg	AAvg	Eff	SA	S%	SAPG	GP	W	L	T	Mins	GA	SO	Avg	Eff	SA	S%	SAPG
1976-77	Traktor Chelyabinsk	USSR	2				120	2		1.00																	
	Soviet Union	WJC-A	2				80	4		3.00																	
1977-78	Traktor Chelyabinsk	USSR	22				1320	71		3.22																	
	Soviet Union	WJC-A	3				110	3		1.63																	
1978-79	Traktor Chelyabinsk	USSR	32				1862	90		2.90																	
1979-80	Traktor Chelyabinsk	USSR	17				1023	58		3.40																	
1980-81	SKA Leningrad	USSR	40				2415	157		3.90																	
1981-82	SKA Leningrad	USSR	42				2310	132		3.42																	
1982-83	Traktor Chelyabinsk	USSR	37				1954	124		3.80																	
1983-84	Traktor Chelyabinsk	USSR	37				2173	91		2.51																	
1984-85	Traktor Chelyabinsk	USSR	28				1360	74		3.26																	
	Soviet Union	WEC-A	1	0	0	0	20	3	0	9.00																	
1985-86	Traktor Chelyabinsk	USSR	37				2126	96		2.70																	
	CSKA Moscow	SuperS	6				364	16		2.64																	
	Soviet Union	WEC-A	3				180	4		1.33																	
1986-87	Traktor Chelyabinsk	USSR	36				2059	103		3.00																	
	Soviet Union	RV '87	DID NOT PLAY – SPARE GOALTENDER																								
	Soviet Union	WEC-A	DID NOT PLAY – SPARE GOALTENDER																								
1987-88	Soviet Union	C Cup	6	5	1	0	365	18	1	3.00																	
	Traktor Chelyabinsk	USSR	28				1559	69		2.65																	
	Soviet Union	Olympics	8				480	13		1.62																	
1988-89	Traktor Chelyabinsk	USSR	33				1980	85		2.58																	
	CSKA Moscow	SuperS	6				327	16		2.93																	
	Soviet Union	WEC-A	7				420	11		1.57																	
1989-90	**Quebec Nordiques**	**NHL**	**10**	**1**	**7**	**2**	**568**	**47**	**0**	**4.96**	**4.16**	**7.06**	**330**	**.858**	**34.9**												
	Soviet Union	WEC-A	5				280	8		1.71																	
	NHL Totals		**10**	**1**	**7**	**2**	**568**	**47**	**0**	**4.96**			**330**	**.858**													

USSR First All-Star Team (1988)

• MYRE, PHIL

Phil Myre G – L. 6'1", 185 lbs. b: Ste-Anne-de-Bellevue, Que., 11/1/1948. Montreal's 1st choice, 5th overall, in 1966 Amateur Draft.

Season	Club	League	GP	W	L	T	Mins	GA	SO	Avg	AAvg	Eff	SA	S%	SAPG	GP	W	L	T	Mins	GA	SO	Avg	Eff	SA	S%	SAPG
1965-66	Shawinigan Bruins	QJHL	STATISTICS NOT AVAILABLE																								
1966-67	Niagara Falls Flyers	OHA	34				2010	135	1	4.03						9				540	44	0	4.89				
1967-68	Niagara Falls Flyers	OHA	50				2970	153	4	3.09						19				1140	72	0	3.79				
1968-69	Houston Apollos	CHL	*53				*3150	150	2	2.83						2	0	2	0	119	7	0	3.53				
1969-70	Montreal Voyageurs	AHL	15				900	37	0	2.47																	
	Montreal Canadiens	**NHL**	**10**	**4**	**3**	**2**	**503**	**19**	**0**	**2.27**	**2.41**																
1970-71	**Montreal Canadiens**	**NHL**	**30**	**13**	**11**	**4**	**1677**	**87**	**1**	**3.11**	**3.07**																
1971-72	**Montreal Canadiens**	**NHL**	**9**	**4**	**5**	**0**	**528**	**32**	**0**	**3.64**	**3.67**																
1972-73	**Atlanta Flames**	**NHL**	**46**	**16**	**23**	**5**	**2736**	**138**	**2**	**3.03**	**2.85**																
1973-74	**Atlanta Flames**	**NHL**	**36**	**11**	**16**	**6**	**2020**	**112**	**0**	**3.33**	**3.22**					**3**	**0**	**3**		**186**	**13**	**0**	**4.19**				
1974-75	**Atlanta Flames**	**NHL**	**40**	**14**	**16**	**10**	**2400**	**114**	**5**	**2.85**	**2.56**																
1975-76	**Atlanta Flames**	**NHL**	**37**	**16**	**16**	**4**	**2129**	**123**	**1**	**3.47**	**3.14**																
1976-77	**Atlanta Flames**	**NHL**	**43**	**17**	**17**	**7**	**2422**	**124**	**3**	**3.07**	**2.85**					**2**	**1**	**1**		**120**	**5**	**0**	**2.50**				
1977-78	**Atlanta Flames**	**NHL**	**9**	**2**	**7**	**0**	**523**	**43**	**0**	**4.93**	**4.63**																
	St. Louis Blues	**NHL**	**44**	**11**	**25**	**8**	**2620**	**159**	**1**	**3.64**	**3.42**																
1978-79	**St. Louis Blues**	**NHL**	**39**	**9**	**22**	**8**	**2259**	**163**	**1**	**4.33**	**3.85**																
1979-80	**Philadelphia Flyers**	**NHL**	**41**	**18**	**7**	**15**	**2367**	**141**	**0**	**3.57**	**3.14**					**6**	**5**	**1**		**384**	**16**	**1**	**2.50**				
1980-81	**Philadelphia Flyers**	**NHL**	**16**	**6**	**5**	**4**	**900**	**61**	**0**	**4.07**	**3.26**																
	Colorado Rockies	**NHL**	**10**	**3**	**6**	**1**	**580**	**33**	**0**	**3.41**	**2.73**																
	Canada	WEC-A	7				359	26		4.34																	
1981-82	Fort Worth Texans	CHL	10	4	5	1	615	40	0	3.90																	
	Colorado Rockies	**NHL**	**24**	**2**	**17**	**2**	**1256**	**112**	**0**	**5.35**	**4.14**																
1982-83	Rochester Americans	AHL	43	28	8	5	2541	156	0	3.68																	
	Buffalo Sabres	**NHL**	**5**	**3**	**2**	**0**	**300**	**21**	**0**	**4.20**	**3.35**	**5.80**	**152**	**.862**	**30.4**	**1**	**0**	**0**		**57**	**7**	**0**	**7.37**				
1983-84	Rochester Americans	AHL	33	19	9	1	1803	104	4	3.46																	
	NHL Totals		**439**	**149**	**198**	**76**	**25220**	**1482**	**14**	**3.53**						**12**	**6**	**5**		**747**	**41**	**1**	**3.29**				

OHA Second All-Star Team (1968) • CHL Second All-Star Team (1969) • Won Terry Sawchuk Trophy (fewest goals against - CHL) (1969)

Claimed by **Atlanta** from **Montreal** in Expansion Draft, June 6, 1972. Traded to **St. Louis** by **Atlanta** with Curt Bennett and Barry Gibbs for Yves Belanger, Dick Redmond, Bob MacMillan and St. Louis' 2nd round choice (Mike Perovich) in 1979 Entry Draft, December 12, 1977. Traded to **Philadelphia** by **St. Louis** for Blake Dunlop and Rick Lapointe, June 7, 1979. Traded to **Colorado** by **Philadelphia** for cash, February 26, 1981. Signed as a free agent by **Buffalo**, September 11, 1982.

• NEWTON, CAM

Cam Newton G – L. 5'11", 170 lbs. b: Peterborough, Ont., 2/25/1950. Pittsburgh's 8th choice, 102nd overall, in 1970 Amateur Draft.

Season	Club	League	GP	W	L	T	Mins	GA	SO	Avg	AAvg	Eff	SA	S%	SAPG	GP	W	L	T	Mins	GA	SO	Avg	Eff	SA	S%	SAPG
1966-67	Toronto Marlboros	OHA	18				1044	59	0	3.39						10				600	32	0	3.20				
1967-68	Toronto Marlboros	OHA	18				1030	60	0	3.50						1	0	0	0	10	0	0	0.00				
1968-69	Toronto Marlboros	OHA	27				1600	129	0	4.84																	
	Kitchener Rangers	OHA	24				1440	135	0	5.63																	
1969-70	Kitchener Rangers	OHA	42				2520	179	1	4.26																	
1970-71	**Pittsburgh Penguins**	**NHL**	**5**	**1**	**3**	**1**	**281**	**16**	**0**	**3.42**	**3.38**																
	Amarillo Wranglers	CHL	15				873	68	0	4.74																	
1971-72	Hershey Bears	AHL	35	13	17	4	2065	131	0	3.80						1	0	1	0	60	7	0	7.00				
1972-73	**Pittsburgh Penguins**	**NHL**	**11**	**3**	**4**	**0**	**533**	**35**	**0**	**3.94**	**3.72**																
	Hershey Bears	AHL	19				1121	53	2	2.83																	
1973-74	Chicago Cougars	WHA	45	25	18	2	2732	143	1	3.14						10	2	5	0	486	34	0	4.20				
1974-75	Chicago Cougars	WHA	32	12	20	0	1905	126	0	3.97																	

			REGULAR SEASON													PLAYOFFS											
Season	Club	League	GP	W	L	T	Mins	GA	SO	Avg	AAvg	Eff	SA	S%	SAPG	GP	W	L	T	Mins	GA	SO	Avg	Eff	SA	S%	SAPG
1975-76	Denver - Ottawa	WHA	10	4	6	0	573	35	1	3.66	....	....	....	....	....	....	....	....	....	....	....	....	....	....	....	....	....
	Cleveland Crusaders	WHA	15	7	7	1	896	48	0	3.21	....	....	....	....	....	1	0	1	0	60	6	0	6.00	....	....	....	....
1976-77	Erie Blades	NAHL	4	....	....	....	122	5	1	1.96	....	....	....	....	....	....	....	....	....	....	....	....	....	....	....	....	....
	NHL Totals		**16**	**4**	**7**	**1**	**814**	**51**	**0**	**3.76**	....	....	....	....	....	....	....	....	....	....	....	....	....	....	....	....	....
	Other Major League Totals		102	48	51	3	6106	352	2	3.46	....	....	....	....	....	11	2	6	0	546	40	0	4.40	....	....	....	....

Signed as a free agent by **Chicago** (WHA), May, 1973. Claimed by **Denver** (WHA) from **Chicago** (WHA) in 1975 WHA Expansion Draft, May, 1975. Signed as a free agent by **Cleveland** (WHA) after **Denver-Ottawa** (WHA) franchise folded, January 17, 1976.

• NORRIS, JACK

Jack Norris G – L. 5'10", 185 lbs. b: Saskatoon, Sask., 8/5/1942.

Season	Club	League	GP	W	L	T	Mins	GA	SO	Avg	AAvg	Eff	SA	S%	SAPG	GP	W	L	T	Mins	GA	SO	Avg	Eff	SA	S%	SAPG
1959-60	Estevan Bruins	SJHL	20	....	....	....	1200	86	1	4.30	....	....	....	....	....	....	....	....	....	....	....	....	....	....	....	....	....
1960-61	Estevan Bruins	SJHL	50	....	....	....	2980	154	3	3.10	....	....	....	....	....	7	....	....	....	380	20	0	3.16	....	....	....	....
1961-62	Estevan Bruins	SJHL	43	....	....	....	2580	87	*7	*2.02	....	....	....	....	....	....	....	....	....	....	....	....	....	....	....	....	....
1962-63	Estevan Bruins	SJHL	54	....	....	....	3240	139	5	*2.57	....	....	....	....	....	11	....	....	....	660	23	0	*2.09	....	....	....	....
1963-64	Los Angeles Blades	WHL	31	13	16	2	1836	115	2	3.71	....	....	....	....	....	8	4	4	0	491	31	0	3.79	....	....	....	....
	Minneapolis Bruins	CHL	4	2	1	1	240	19	0	4.75	....	....	....	....	....	....	....	....	....	....	....	....	....	....	....	....	....
1964-65	Los Angeles Blades	WHL	38	18	19	1	2307	146	1	3.80	....	....	....	....	....	....	....	....	....	....	....	....	....	....	....	....	....
	Boston Bruins	**NHL**	**23**	**10**	**11**	**2**	**1380**	**85**	**1**	**3.70**	**4.04**	....	....	....	....	....	....	....	....	....	....	....	....	....	....	....	....
1965-66	Los Angeles Blades	WHL	20	5	15	0	1200	117	0	5.85	....	....	....	....	....	....	....	....	....	....	....	....	....	....	....	....	....
	Oklahoma City Blazers	CHL	18	9	7	2	1040	51	1	2.94	....	....	....	....	....	....	....	....	....	....	....	....	....	....	....	....	....
1966-67	Los Angeles Blades	WHL	35	14	17	3	2102	133	2	3.80	....	....	....	....	....	....	....	....	....	....	....	....	....	....	....	....	....
1967-68	**Chicago Black Hawks**	**NHL**	**7**	**2**	**3**	**0**	**334**	**22**	**1**	**3.95**	**4.38**	....	....	....	....	....	....	....	....	....	....	....	....	....	....	....	....
	Dallas Black Hawks	CHL	39	13	15	10	2423	132	0	3.27	....	....	....	....	....	....	....	....	....	....	....	....	....	....	....	....	....
1968-69	**Chicago Black Hawks**	**NHL**	**3**	**1**	**0**	**0**	**100**	**10**	**0**	**6.00**	**6.22**	....	....	....	....	....	....	....	....	....	....	....	....	....	....	....	....
	Dallas Black Hawks	CHL	36	....	....	....	2099	98	*4	*2.80	....	....	....	....	....	*11	*10	1	0	*660	26	0	*2.36	....	....	....	....
1969-70	Montreal Voyageurs	AHL	55	....	....	....	3265	149	4	2.74	....	....	....	....	....	8	4	4	0	495	24	*1	2.91	....	....	....	....
1970-71	**Los Angeles Kings**	**NHL**	**25**	**7**	**11**	**2**	**1305**	**85**	**0**	**3.91**	**3.89**	....	....	....	....	....	....	....	....	....	....	....	....	....	....	....	....
1971-72	Seattle Totems	WHL	38	5	28	5	2219	152	2	4.14	....	....	....	....	....	....	....	....	....	....	....	....	....	....	....	....	....
	Springfield Kings	AHL	10	5	4	1	569	36	0	3.80	....	....	....	....	....	2	0	2	0	108	14	0	7.78	....	....	....	....
1972-73	Alberta Oilers	WHA	*64	28	29	3	*3702	189	1	3.06	....	....	....	....	....	....	....	....	....	....	....	....	....	....	....	....	....
1973-74	Edmonton Oilers	WHA	53	23	24	1	2954	150	2	3.21	....	....	....	....	....	3	0	2	0	111	9	0	4.86	....	....	....	....
1974-75	Phoenix Roadrunners	WHA	33	14	15	4	1962	107	1	3.27	....	....	....	....	....	2	0	2	0	100	10	0	6.00	....	....	....	....
1975-76	Phoenix Roadrunners	WHA	41	21	14	4	2412	128	1	3.18	....	....	....	....	....	5	2	3	0	298	17	0	3.42	....	....	....	....
	NHL Totals		**58**	**20**	**25**	**4**	**3119**	**202**	**2**	**3.89**	....	....	....	....	....	....	....	....	....	....	....	....	....	....	....	....	....
	Other Major League Totals		191	86	82	12	11030	582	5	3.17	....	....	....	....	....	10	2	7	0	509	36	0	4.24	....	....	....	....

AHL Second All-Star Team (1970)

Traded to **Chicago** by **Boston** with Gilles Marotte and Pit Martin for Phil Esposito, Ken Hodge and Fred Stanfield, May 15, 1967. Claimed by **Montreal** from **Chicago** in Intra-League Draft, June 11, 1969. Traded to **LA Kings** by **Montreal** with Larry Mickey and Lucien Grenier for Leon Rochefort, Greg Boddy and Wayne Thomas, May 22, 1970. Claimed by **Seattle** (WHL) from **LA Kings** in Reverse Draft, June, 1971. Selected by **Calgary-Cleveland** (WHA) in 1972 WHA General Player Draft, February 12, 1972. WHA rights traded to **Alberta** (WHA) by **Cleveland** (WHA) for cash, June, 1972. Traded to **Indianapolis** (WHA) by **Edmonton** (WHA) for future considerations, June, 1974. Traded to **Phoenix** (WHA) by **Indianapolis** (WHA) for Ray Reeson, September, 1974.

• OLESCHUK, BILL

Bill Oleschuk G – L. 6'3", 194 lbs. b: Edmonton, Alta., 7/20/1955. Kansas City's 7th choice, 110th overall, in 1975 Amateur Draft.

Season	Club	League	GP	W	L	T	Mins	GA	SO	Avg	AAvg	Eff	SA	S%	SAPG	GP	W	L	T	Mins	GA	SO	Avg	Eff	SA	S%	SAPG
1971-72	Edmonton Mets	AJHL	22	....	....	....	1320	99	0	4.58	....	....	....	....	....	....	....	....	....	....	....	....	....	....	....	....	....
1972-73	Edmonton Mets	AJHL	STATISTICS NOT AVAILABLE																								
	Winnipeg Jets	WCJHL	1	....	....	....	20	2	0	6.00	....	....	....	....	....	....	....	....	....	....	....	....	....	....	....	....	....
1973-74	Prince Albert Raiders	SJHL	10	....	....	....	2280	38	0	3.85	....	....	....	....	....	....	....	....	....	....	....	....	....	....	....	....	....
	Swift Current Broncos	WCJHL	11	....	....	....	518	36	0	4.17	....	....	....	....	....	....	....	....	....	....	....	....	....	....	....	....	....
1974-75	Lethbridge Broncos	WCJHL	2	....	....	....	80	8	0	6.00	....	....	....	....	....	....	....	....	....	....	....	....	....	....	....	....	....
	Saskatoon Blades	WCJHL	43	....	....	....	2499	129	*4	3.09	....	....	....	....	....	12	....	....	....	720	37	0	3.30	....	....	....	....
1975-76	**Kansas City Scouts**	**NHL**	**1**	**0**	**1**	**0**	**60**	**4**	**0**	**4.00**	**3.62**	....	....	....	....	....	....	....	....	....	....	....	....	....	....	....	....
	Port Huron Flags	IHL	44	....	....	....	2417	145	0	3.60	....	....	....	....	....	9	....	....	....	443	24	0	3.25	....	....	....	....
1976-77	Baltimore Clippers	SHL	30	....	....	....	1780	97	1	3.27	....	....	....	....	....	....	....	....	....	....	....	....	....	....	....	....	....
	Oklahoma City Blazers	CHL	3	0	3	0	159	15	0	5.66	....	....	....	....	....	....	....	....	....	....	....	....	....	....	....	....	....
1977-78	**Colorado Rockies**	**NHL**	**2**	**0**	**2**	**0**	**100**	**9**	**0**	**5.40**	**5.08**	....	....	....	....	....	....	....	....	....	....	....	....	....	....	....	....
	Phoenix Roadrunners	CHL	9	2	6	1	549	45	0	4.92	....	....	....	....	....	....	....	....	....	....	....	....	....	....	....	....	....
	Hampton Gulls	AHL	11	1	9	1	616	40	0	3.90	....	....	....	....	....	....	....	....	....	....	....	....	....	....	....	....	....
	Philadelphia Firebirds	AHL	2	0	1	0	65	9	0	8.30	....	....	....	....	....	....	....	....	....	....	....	....	....	....	....	....	....
	Flint Generals	IHL	13	....	....	....	702	57	0	4.87	....	....	....	....	....	4	....	....	....	204	10	0	2.94	....	....	....	....
1978-79	**Colorado Rockies**	**NHL**	**40**	**6**	**19**	**8**	**2118**	**136**	**1**	**3.85**	**3.41**	....	....	....	....	....	....	....	....	....	....	....	....	....	....	....	....
1979-80	**Colorado Rockies**	**NHL**	**12**	**1**	**6**	**2**	**557**	**39**	**0**	**4.20**	**3.69**	....	....	....	....	....	....	....	....	....	....	....	....	....	....	....	....
	Fort Worth Texans	CHL	43	24	14	5	2478	134	1	3.24	....	....	....	....	....	2	1	1	0	72	8	0	6.67	....	....	....	....
1980-81	Fort Worth Texans	CHL	36	10	22	1	2054	122	0	3.56	....	....	....	....	....	5	....	....	....	300	14	0	2.80	....	....	....	....
1981-82	Dallas Black Hawks	CHL	7	2	4	0	322	26	0	4.84	....	....	....	....	....	....	....	....	....	....	....	....	....	....	....	....	....
1982-83	Peoria Prancers	IHL	29	....	....	....	1448	147	1	6.09	....	....	....	....	....	....	....	....	....	....	....	....	....	....	....	....	....
1983-84	Fort Wayne Komets	IHL	1	....	....	....	60	7	0	7.00	....	....	....	....	....	....	....	....	....	....	....	....	....	....	....	....	....
	NHL Totals		**55**	**7**	**28**	**10**	**2835**	**188**	**1**	**3.98**	....	....	....	....	....	....	....	....	....	....	....	....	....	....	....	....	....

Transferred to **Colorado** after **Kansas City** franchise relocated, July 15, 1976.

• OLESEVICH, DAN

Dan Olesevich G – R. 6', 170 lbs. b: Port Colborne, Ont., 9/16/1937. d: 7/15/1983.

Season	Club	League	GP	W	L	T	Mins	GA	SO	Avg	AAvg	Eff	SA	S%	SAPG	GP	W	L	T	Mins	GA	SO	Avg	Eff	SA	S%	SAPG
1953-54	Hamilton Tiger Cubs	OHA	5	....	....	....	300	23	0	4.60	....	....	....	....	....	....	....	....	....	....	....	....	....	....	....	....	....
1954-55	Hamilton Tiger Cubs	OHA	DID NOT PLAY – SPARE GOALTENDER																								
1955-56	Hamilton Tiger Cubs	OHA	1	0	1	0	60	6	0	6.00	....	....	....	....	....	....	....	....	....	....	....	....	....	....	....	....	....
1956-57	Hamilton Tiger Cubs	OHA	2	0	2	0	120	12	0	6.00	....	....	....	....	....	....	....	....	....	....	....	....	....	....	....	....	....
1957-58	Edmonton Flyers	WHL	1	1	0	0	60	1	0	1.00	....	....	....	....	....	....	....	....	....	....	....	....	....	....	....	....	....
1958-59	Charlotte – Johnstown	EHL	30	....	....	....	1800	121	2	4.03	....	....	....	....	....	....	....	....	....	....	....	....	....	....	....	....	....
	Windsor Bulldogs	NOHA	26	....	....	....	1560	90	1	3.46	....	....	....	....	....	....	....	....	....	....	....	....	....	....	....	....	....
1961-62	**New York Rangers**	**NHL**	**1**	**0**	**0**	**1**	**29**	**2**	**0**	**4.14**	**4.25**	....	....	....	....	....	....	....	....	....	....	....	....	....	....	....	....
	NHL Totals		**1**	**0**	**0**	**1**	**29**	**2**	**0**	**4.14**	....	....	....	....	....	....	....	....	....	....	....	....	....	....	....	....	....

• Retired after 1958-59 season and hired as Detroit's assistant trainer/practice goaltender. Loaned to **NY Rangers** by **Detroit** to replace injured Gump Worsley in 2nd period, October 21, 1961. (NY Rangers 4, Detroit 4)

• O'NEILL, MIKE

Mike O'Neill G – L. 5'7", 160 lbs. b: LaSalle, Que., 11/3/1967. Winnipeg's 1st choice, 15th overall, in 1988 Supplemental Draft.

Season	Club	League	GP	W	L	T	Mins	GA	SO	Avg	AAvg	Eff	SA	S%	SAPG	GP	W	L	T	Mins	GA	SO	Avg	Eff	SA	S%	SAPG
1985-86	Yale University	ECAC	6	3	1	0	389	17	0	3.53	....	....	....	....	....	....	....	....	....	....	....	....	....	....	....	....	....
1986-87	Yale University	ECAC	16	9	6	1	964	55	2	3.42	....	....	....	....	....	....	....	....	....	....	....	....	....	....	....	....	....
1987-88	Yale University	ECAC	24	6	17	0	1385	101	0	4.37	....	....	....	....	....	....	....	....	....	....	....	....	....	....	....	....	....
1988-89	Yale University	ECAC	25	10	14	1	1490	93	0	3.74	....	....	....	....	....	....	....	....	....	....	....	....	....	....	....	....	....
1989-90	Tappara Tampere	Finland	41	23	13	5	2369	127	2	3.22	....	....	....	....	....	....	....	....	....	....	....	....	....	....	....	....	....
1990-91	Fort Wayne Komets	IHL	8	5	2	1	490	31	0	3.80	....	....	....	....	....	....	....	....	....	....	....	....	....	....	....	....	....
	Moncton Hawks	AHL	30	13	7	6	1613	84	0	3.12	....	....	....	....	....	8	3	4	....	435	29	0	4.00	....	....	....	....
1991-92	**Winnipeg Jets**	**NHL**	**1**	**0**	**0**	**0**	**13**	**1**	**0**	**4.62**	**4.10**	**6.60**	**7**	**.857**	**32.3**	....	....	....	....	....	....	....	....	....	....	....	....
	Moncton Hawks	AHL	32	14	16	2	1902	108	1	3.41	....	....	....	....	....	11	4	7	....	670	43	*1	3.85	....	....	....	....
	Fort Wayne Komets	IHL	33	22	6	3	1858	97	*4	3.13	....	....	....	....	....	....	....	....	....	....	....	....	....	....	....	....	....
1992-93	**Winnipeg Jets**	**NHL**	**2**	**0**	**0**	**1**	**73**	**6**	**0**	**4.93**	**4.20**	**8.70**	**34**	**.824**	**27.9**	....	....	....	....	....	....	....	....	....	....	....	....
	Moncton Hawks	AHL	30	13	10	4	1649	88	1	3.20	....	....	....	....	....	....	....	....	....	....	....	....	....	....	....	....	....
1993-94	**Winnipeg Jets**	**NHL**	**17**	**0**	**9**	**1**	**738**	**51**	**0**	**4.15**	**3.96**	**5.54**	**382**	**.866**	**31.1**	....	....	....	....	....	....	....	....	....	....	....	....
	Moncton Hawks	AHL	12	8	4	0	716	33	1	2.76	....	....	....	....	....	....	....	....	....	....	....	....	....	....	....	....	....
	Fort Wayne Komets	IHL	11	4	4	3	642	38	0	3.55	....	....	....	....	....	....	....	....	....	....	....	....	....	....	....	....	....
1994-95	Fort Wayne Komets	IHL	28	11	12	4	1603	109	0	4.08	....	....	....	....	....	....	....	....	....	....	....	....	....	....	....	....	....
	Phoenix Roadrunners	IHL	21	13	4	4	1256	64	1	3.06	....	....	....	....	....	9	4	5	....	535	33	0	3.70	....	....	....	....
1995-96	Baltimore Bandits	AHL	*74	31	31	7	*4250	250	2	3.53	....	....	....	....	....	12	6	6	....	689	43	0	3.75	....	....	....	....

			REGULAR SEASON													PLAYOFFS											
Season	Club	League	GP	W	L	T	Mins	GA	SO	Avg	AAvg	Eff	SA	S%	SAPG	GP	W	L	T	Mins	GA	SO	Avg	Eff	SA	S%	SAPG
1996-97	**Anaheim Mighty Ducks**	**NHL**	**1**	**0**	**0**	**0**	**31**	**3**	**0**	**5.81**	**6.15**	**17.43**	**10**	**.700**	**19.4**	....	....	....	....	....	....	....	....	....	....	....	....
	Long Beach Ice Dogs	IHL	45	26	12	6	2644	145	1	3.29	....	....	....	....	....	1	0	0	....	7	0	0	0.00	....	....	....	....
1997-98	Portland Pirates	AHL	47	16	18	10	2640	135	1	3.07	....	....	....	....	....	6	2	3	....	305	16	0	3.15	....	....	....	....
	NHL Totals		**21**	**0**	**9**	**2**	**855**	**61**	**0**	**4.28**	....	....	**433**	**.859**	....	....	....	....	....	....	....	....	....	....	....	....	....

ECAC First All-Star Team (1987, 1989) • NCAA East First All-American Team (1989)

Signed as a free agent by **Anaheim**, July 14, 1995. Signed as a free agent by **Washington**, August 20, 1997.

• OSGOOD, CHRIS

Chris Osgood G – L. 5′10″, 160 lbs. b: Peace River, Alta., 11/26/1972. Detroit's 3rd choice, 54th overall, in 1991 Entry Draft.

Season	Club	League	GP	W	L	T	Mins	GA	SO	Avg	AAvg	Eff	SA	S%	SAPG	GP	W	L	T	Mins	GA	SO	Avg	Eff	SA	S%	SAPG
1989-90	Medicine Hat Tigers	WHL	57	24	28	2	3094	228	0	4.42	....	....	....	....	....	3	0	3	....	173	17	0	5.91	....	....	....	....
1990-91	Medicine Hat Tigers	WHL	46	23	18	3	2630	173	2	3.95	....	....	....	....	....	12	7	5	....	712	42	0	3.54	....	....	....	....
1991-92	Medicine Hat Tigers	WHL	15	10	3	0	819	44	0	3.22	....	....	....	....	....	....	....	....	....	....	....	....	....	....	....	....	....
	Brandon Wheat Kings	WHL	16	3	10	1	890	60	1	4.04	....	....	....	....	....	....	....	....	....	....	....	....	....	....	....	....	....
	Seattle Thunderbirds	WHL	21	12	7	1	1217	65	1	3.20	....	....	....	....	....	15	9	6	....	904	51	0	3.38	....	....	....	....
1992-93	Adirondack Red Wings	AHL	45	19	19	4	2438	159	0	3.91	....	....	....	....	....	1	0	1	....	59	2	0	2.03	....	....	....	....
1993-94	**Detroit Red Wings**	**NHL**	**41**	**23**	**8**	**5**	**2206**	**105**	**2**	**2.86**	**2.72**	**3.01**	**999**	**.895**	**27.2**	**6**	**3**	**2**	....	**307**	**12**	**1**	**2.35**	**2.56**	**110**	**.891**	**21.5**
	Adirondack Red Wings	AHL	4	3	1	0	239	13	0	3.26	....	....	....	....	....	....	....	....	....	....	....	....	....	....	....	....	....
1994-95	**Detroit Red Wings**	**NHL**	**19**	**14**	**5**	**0**	**1087**	**41**	**1**	**2.26**	**2.33**	**1.87**	**496**	**.917**	**27.4**	**2**	**0**	**0**	....	**68**	**2**	**0**	**1.76**	**1.41**	**25**	**.920**	**22.1**
	Adirondack Red Wings	AHL	2	1	1	0	120	6	0	3.00	....	....	....	....	....	....	....	....	....	....	....	....	....	....	....	....	....
1995-96	**Detroit Red Wings**	**NHL**	**50**	***39**	**6**	**5**	**2933**	**106**	**5**	**2.17**	**2.12**	**1.93**	**1190**	**.911**	**24.3**	**15**	**8**	**7**	....	**936**	**33**	**2**	**2.12**	**2.17**	**322**	**.898**	**20.6**
1996-97	**Detroit Red Wings**	**NHL**	**47**	**23**	**13**	**9**	**2769**	**106**	**6**	**2.30**	**2.42**	**2.07**	**1175**	**.910**	**25.5**	**2**	**0**	**0**	....	**47**	**2**	**0**	**2.55**	**2.43**	**21**	**.905**	**26.8**
1997-98	**Detroit Red Wings**	**NHL**	**64**	**33**	**20**	**11**	**3807**	**140**	**6**	**2.21**	**2.57**	**1.93**	**1605**	**.913**	**25.3**	***22**	***16**	**6**	....	***1361**	**48**	**2**	**2.12**	**1.73**	**588**	**.918**	**25.9**
	NHL Totals		**221**	**132**	**52**	**30**	**12802**	**498**	**20**	**2.33**	....	....	**5465**	**.909**	....	**47**	**27**	**15**	....	**2719**	**97**	**5**	**2.14**	....	....	....	....

WHL East Second All-Star Team (1991) • NHL Second All-Star Team (1996) • Shared William M. Jennings Trophy with Mike Vernon (1996)

Played in NHL All-Star Game (1996, 1997, 1998)

• Scored a goal while with Medicine Hat (WHL), January 3, 1991. • Scored a goal vs. Hartford, March 6, 1996.

• OUIMET, TED

Ted Ouimet G5′9″, 165 lbs. b: Noranda, Que., 7/6/1947.

Season	Club	League	GP	W	L	T	Mins	GA	SO	Avg	AAvg	Eff	SA	S%	SAPG	GP	W	L	T	Mins	GA	SO	Avg	Eff	SA	S%	SAPG
1964-65	Montreal Jr. Canadiens	OHA	5	....	....	....	300	20	0	4.00	....	....	....	....	....	1	....	....	....	20	0	0	0.00	....	....	....	....
1965-66	Montreal Jr. Canadiens	OHA	32	....	....	....	1920	88	*3	*2.75	....	....	....	....	....	10	....	....	....	600	28	1	2.80	....	....	....	....
1966-67	Montreal Jr. Canadiens	OHA	41	....	....	....	2450	177	2	4.33	....	....	....	....	....	6	....	....	....	320	27	0	5.09	....	....	....	....
1967-68	London Nationals	OHA	35	....	....	....	2093	166	0	4.76	....	....	....	....	....	2	....	....	....	120	7	0	3.50	....	....	....	....
1968-69	Kansas City Blues	CHL	22	....	....	....	....	64	2	3.07	....	....	....	....	....	....	....	....	....	....	....	....	....	....	....	....	....
	St. Louis Blues	**NHL**	**1**	**0**	**1**	**0**	**60**	**2**	**0**	**2.00**	**2.07**	....	....	....	....	....	....	....	....	....	....	....	....	....	....	....	....
1969-70	San Diego Gulls	WHL	18	10	8	0	1050	71	0	4.06	....	....	....	....	....	3	2	1	0	165	12	0	4.37	....	....	....	....
	Kansas City Blues	CHL	6	1	4	1	360	29	0	4.83	....	....	....	....	....	....	....	....	....	....	....	....	....	....	....	....	....
1970-71	Kansas City Blues	CHL	8	....	....	....	....	32	0	4.00	....	....	....	....	....	....	....	....	....	....	....	....	....	....	....	....	....
	Port Huron Flags	IHL	27	....	....	....	1588	104	1	3.93	....	....	....	....	....	3	....	....	....	140	14	0	6.00	....	....	....	....
1971-72	Port Huron Wings	IHL	1	....	....	....	60	5	0	5.00	....	....	....	....	....	....	....	....	....	....	....	....	....	....	....	....	....
	Jacksonville–Syracuse	EHL	35	....	....	....	2080	149	0	4.30	....	....	....	....	....	14	....	....	....	840	45	1	3.21	....	....	....	....
1972-73	Cleveland–Jacksonville	AHL	19	....	....	....	909	74	0	4.88	....	....	....	....	....	....	....	....	....	....	....	....	....	....	....	....	....
1973-74	Syracuse Blazers	NAHL	35	....	....	....	2119	105	0	2.97	....	....	....	....	....	6	....	....	....	341	12	0	*2.11	....	....	....	....
1974-75	New England Whalers	WHA	1	0	0	0	20	3	0	9.00	....	....	....	....	....	....	....	....	....	....	....	....	....	....	....	....	....
	Cape Cod Codders	NAHL	45	21	16	4	2551	161	2	3.79	....	....	....	....	....	4	....	....	....	240	14	0	3.50	....	....	....	....
	NHL Totals		**1**	**0**	**1**	**0**	**60**	**2**	**0**	**2.00**	....	....	....	....	....	....	....	....	....	....	....	....	....	....	....	....	....
	Other Major League Totals		1	0	0	0	20	3	0	9.00	....	....	....	....	....	....	....	....	....	....	....	....	....	....	....	....	....

NAHL First All-Star Team (1974)

Traded to **St. Louis** by **Montreal** for cash, June 11, 1968. Signed as a free agent by **Jacksonville** (EHL), October, 1971. Traded to **Syracuse** (EHL) by **Jacksonville** (EHL) for cash, December, 1971. Traded to **Cleveland** (WHA) by **Syracuse** (NAHL) for John Raynak and cash, October, 1974. Traded to **New England** (WHA) by **Cleveland** (WHA) for cash, December, 1974. Traded to **Cleveland** (WHA) by **New England** (WHA) for cash, January, 1976.

• PAGEAU, PAUL

Paul Pageau G – R. 5′9″, 160 lbs. b: Montreal, Que., 10/1/1959.

Season	Club	League	GP	W	L	T	Mins	GA	SO	Avg	AAvg	Eff	SA	S%	SAPG	GP	W	L	T	Mins	GA	SO	Avg	Eff	SA	S%	SAPG
1976-77	Quebec Remparts	QMJHL	19	....	....	....	955	56	0	3.52	....	....	....	....	....	....	....	....	....	....	....	....	....	....	....	....	....
1977-78	Quebec Remparts	QMJHL	33	....	....	....	1656	138	0	5.00	....	....	....	....	....	3	....	....	....	83	8	0	5.78	....	....	....	....
1978-79	Quebec Remparts	QMJHL	7	....	....	....	345	28	0	4.87	....	....	....	....	....	....	....	....	....	....	....	....	....	....	....	....	....
	Shawinigan Cataracts	QMJHL	43	....	....	....	2352	199	0	5.08	....	....	....	....	....	4	....	....	....	236	27	0	6.86	....	....	....	....
1979-80	Shawinigan Cataracts	QMJHL	43	19	18	4	2438	175	*2	4.31	....	....	....	....	....	7	3	4	0	421	34	0	4.85	....	....	....	....
	Canada	Nat-Team	10	....	....	....	506	16	1	1.89	....	....	....	....	....	....	....	....	....	....	....	....	....	....	....	....	....
	Canada	Olympics	4	2	1	0	238	11	1	2.77	....	....	....	....	....	....	....	....	....	....	....	....	....	....	....	....	....
1980-81	**Los Angeles Kings**	**NHL**	**1**	**0**	**1**	**0**	**60**	**8**	**0**	**8.00**	**6.42**	....	....	....	....	....	....	....	....	....	....	....	....	....	....	....	....
	Houston Apollos	CHL	21	9	9	3	1282	64	0	3.00	....	....	....	....	....	....	....	....	....	....	....	....	....	....	....	....	....
	Oklahoma City Stars	CHL	11	4	4	0	590	32	0	3.25	....	....	....	....	....	....	....	....	....	....	....	....	....	....	....	....	....
	Saginaw Gears	IHL	1	....	....	....	60	4	0	4.00	....	....	....	....	....	....	....	....	....	....	....	....	....	....	....	....	....
1981-82	Saginaw Gears	IHL	29	....	....	....	1621	140	0	5.18	....	....	....	....	....	4	....	....	....	249	18	0	4.34	....	....	....	....
1982-83	New Haven Nighthawks	AHL	37	17	14	2	1939	123	2	3.81	....	....	....	....	....	6	2	3	0	374	21	0	3.37	....	....	....	....
1983-84	Sherbrooke Jets	AHL	45	12	26	3	2432	205	0	5.06	....	....	....	....	....	....	....	....	....	....	....	....	....	....	....	....	....
1984-85	Sherbrooke Canadiens	AHL	20	8	11	0	1074	66	0	3.69	....	....	....	....	....	3	0	1	0	80	5	0	3.75	....	....	....	....
	Flint Generals	IHL	6	0	5	0	3331	37	0	6.71	....	....	....	....	....	....	....	....	....	....	....	....	....	....	....	....	....
	NHL Totals		**1**	**0**	**1**	**0**	**60**	**8**	**0**	**8.00**	....	....	....	....	....	....	....	....	....	....	....	....	....	....	....	....	....

QMJHL First All-Star Team (1980)

Signed as a free agent by **LA Kings**, May 6, 1980.

• PAILLE, MARCEL

Marcel Paille G – L. 5′8″, 175 lbs. b: Shawinigan Falls, Que., 12/8/1932.

Season	Club	League	GP	W	L	T	Mins	GA	SO	Avg	AAvg	Eff	SA	S%	SAPG	GP	W	L	T	Mins	GA	SO	Avg	Eff	SA	S%	SAPG
1949-50	Quebec Citadelle	QJHL	18	13	5	0	1080	60	3	3.33	....	....	....	....	....	15	9	5	1	926	50	0	*3.24	....	....	....	....
1950-51	Quebec Citadelle	QJHL	46	*33	13	0	2764	135	0	2.93	....	....	....	....	....	23	*15	8	0	1404	80	2	3.42	....	....	....	....
1951-52	Quebec Citadelle	QJHL	14	7	7	0	844	38	1	2.70	....	....	....	....	....	....	....	....	....	....	....	....	....	....	....	....	....
1952-53	Quebec Citadelle	QJHL	48	30	15	3	286	149	1	3.12	....	....	....	....	....	9	....	....	....	540	20	0	*2.22	....	....	....	....
1953-54	Matane Red Rocks	QPHL	65	....	....	....	3900	182	*5	*2.80	....	....	....	....	....	....	....	....	....	....	....	....	....	....	....	....	....
1954-55	North Bay Trappers	NOHA	59	24	25	10	3540	228	1	3.86	....	....	....	....	....	13	....	....	....	780	40	1	3.08	....	....	....	....
1955-56	Chicoutimi Sagueneens	QHL	*61	30	26	4	*3632	176	2	2.91	....	....	....	....	....	5	1	4	0	300	19	0	3.80	....	....	....	....
1956-57	Cleveland Barons	AHL	62	*34	25	3	3750	200	*7	3.20	....	....	....	....	....	*12	*8	4	0	*767	31	0	2.43	....	....	....	....
1957-58	Providence Reds	AHL	41	19	20	2	2491	124	4	2.99	....	....	....	....	....	5	1	4	0	300	17	1	3.40	....	....	....	....
	New York Rangers	**NHL**	**33**	**11**	**15**	**7**	**1980**	**102**	**1**	**3.09**	**3.44**	....	....	....	....	....	....	....	....	....	....	....	....	....	....	....	....
1958-59	**New York Rangers**	**NHL**	**1**	**0**	**0**	**1**	**60**	**4**	**0**	**4.00**	**4.26**	....	....	....	....	....	....	....	....	....	....	....	....	....	....	....	....
	Buffalo Bisons	AHL	*70	*38	27	4	*4200	195	3	2.79	....	....	....	....	....	11	*6	5	0	664	27	*1	2.44	....	....	....	....
1959-60	Springfield Indians	AHL	57	32	20	5	3420	183	2	3.21	....	....	....	....	....	10	*8	2	0	628	31	0	2.96	....	....	....	....
	New York Rangers	**NHL**	**17**	**6**	**9**	**2**	**1020**	**67**	**1**	**3.94**	**4.18**	....	....	....	....	....	....	....	....	....	....	....	....	....	....	....	....
1960-61	Springfield Indians	AHL	67	*47	19	1	4020	188	*8	*2.81	....	....	....	....	....	4	*4	0	....	226	5	0	*1.33	....	....	....	....
	New York Rangers	**NHL**	**4**	**1**	**2**	**1**	**240**	**16**	**0**	**4.00**	**4.12**	....	....	....	....	....	....	....	....	....	....	....	....	....	....	....	....
1961-62	Springfield Indians	AHL	45	28	15	2	2780	115	2	*2.56	....	....	....	....	....	*11	*8	3	0	*758	21	*2	*1.66	....	....	....	....
	New York Rangers	**NHL**	**10**	**4**	**4**	**2**	**600**	**28**	**0**	**2.80**	**2.87**	....	....	....	....	....	....	....	....	....	....	....	....	....	....	....	....
1962-63	Baltimore Clippers	AHL	41	18	20	3	2460	146	0	3.56	....	....	....	....	....	....	....	....	....	....	....	....	....	....	....	....	....
	New York Rangers	**NHL**	**3**	**0**	**1**	**2**	**180**	**10**	**0**	**3.33**	**3.46**	....	....	....	....	....	....	....	....	....	....	....	....	....	....	....	....
1963-64	Vancouver Canucks	WHL	*70	26	41	3	4230	254	2	3.60	....	....	....	....	....	....	....	....	....	....	....	....	....	....	....	....	....
	Denver Invaders	WHL	....	....	....	....	....	....	....	....	....	....	....	....	....	3	1	2	0	194	12	0	3.71	....	....	....	....
1964-65	**New York Rangers**	**NHL**	**39**	**10**	**21**	**7**	**2262**	**135**	**0**	**3.58**	**3.94**	....	....	....	....	....	....	....	....	....	....	....	....	....	....	....	....
1965-66	Providence Reds	AHL	60	17	40	2	3650	243	1	3.99	....	....	....	....	....	....	....	....	....	....	....	....	....	....	....	....	....
1966-67	Providence Reds	AHL	42	4	30	7	2471	188	0	4.56	....	....	....	....	....	....	....	....	....	....	....	....	....	....	....	....	....
1967-68	Providence Reds	AHL	54	23	23	8	3200	188	1	3.53	....	....	....	....	....	8	4	4	0	460	19	0	*2.48	....	....	....	....
1968-69	Providence Reds	AHL	58	25	26	6	3321	202	2	3.65	....	....	....	....	....	9	5	4	0	544	28	0	3.09	....	....	....	....

Season	Club	League	REGULAR SEASON GP	W	L	T	Mins	GA	SO	Avg	AAvg	Eff	SA	S%	SAPG	PLAYOFFS GP	W	L	T	Mins	GA	SO	Avg	Eff	SA	S%	SAPG
1969-70	Providence Reds	AHL	62	....	....	....	3565	211	2	3.55	....	....	....	....	....	....	....	....	....	....	....	....	....	....	....	....	....
1970-71	Providence Reds	AHL	51	24	17	9	2789	167	1	3.59	....	....	....	....	....	10	4	*6	0	599	32	*1	3.21	....	....	....	....
1971-72	Providence Reds	AHL	34	15	16	2	1981	110	3	3.33	....	....	....	....	....	5	1	4	0	303	18	0	3.56	....	....	....	....
1972-73	Philadelphia Blazers	WHA	15	2	8	0	611	49	0	4.81	....	....	....	....	....	....	....	....	....	....	....	....	....	....	....	....	....
1973-74	Richmond Robins	AHL	21	5	11	4	1201	85	0	4.24	....	....	....	....	....	2	0	2	0	119	9	0	4.54	....	....	....	....
	NHL Totals		**107**	**32**	**52**	**22**	**6342**	**362**	**2**	**3.42**	....	....	....	....	....	....	....	....	....	....	....	....	....	....	....	....	....
	Other Major League Totals		15	2	8	0	611	49	0	4.81	....	....	....	....	....	....	....	....	....	....	....	....	....	....	....	....	....

Won William Northey Trophy (Top Rookie - QHL) (1956) • AHL Second All-Star Team (1957, 1960) • AHL First All-Star Team (1959, 1961, 1962) • Won Harry "Hap" Holmes Memorial Award (fewest goals against - AHL) (1961, 1962) • WHL Second All-Star Team (1964)

Claimed by **NY Rangers** from **Chicoutimi** (QHL) in Inter-League Draft, June 5, 1956. Traded to **Providence** (AHL) by **NY Rangers** with Aldo Guidolin, Don McGregor and Jim Mikol for Ed Giacomin, May 18, 1965. Selected by **Chicago** (WHA) in 1972 WHA General Player Draft, February 12, 1972. WHA rights traded to **Philadelphia** (WHA) by **Chicago** (WHA) for future considerations, June, 1972.

• PALMATEER, MIKE

Mike "The Popcorn Kid" Palmateer G – R. 5'9", 170 lbs. b: Toronto, Ont., 1/13/1954. Toronto's 5th choice, 85th overall, in 1974 Amateur Draft.

Season	Club	League	GP	W	L	T	Mins	GA	SO	Avg	AAvg	Eff	SA	S%	SAPG	GP	W	L	T	Mins	GA	SO	Avg	Eff	SA	S%	SAPG
1972-73	Toronto Marlboros	OHA	31	....	....	....	1860	87	5	2.81	....	....	....	....	....	....	....	....	....	....	....	....	....	....	....	....	....
1973-74	Toronto Marlboros	OHA	32	....	....	....	1895	120	0	3.80	....	....	....	....	....	....	....	....	....	....	....	....	....	....	....	....	....
1974-75	Saginaw Gears	IHL	20	....	....	....	1095	70	2	3.84	....	....	....	....	....	....	....	....	....	....	....	....	....	....	....	....	....
	Oklahoma City Blazers	CHL	16	7	5	2	841	39	1	2.78	....	....	....	....	....	5	2	3	0	278	18	0	3.88	....	....	....	....
1975-76	Oklahoma City Blazers	CHL	42	15	21	4	2272	137	1	3.61	....	....	....	....	....	3	0	2	0	158	8	0	3.04	....	....	....	....
1976-77	Dallas Black Hawks	CHL	3	0	2	1	171	5	0	1.75	....	....	....	....	....	....	....	....	....	....	....	....	....	....	....	....	....
	Toronto Maple Leafs	**NHL**	**50**	**23**	**18**	**8**	**2877**	**154**	**4**	**3.21**	**2.98**	....	....	....	....	**6**	**3**	**3**	....	**360**	**16**	**0**	**2.67**	....	....	....	....
1977-78	**Toronto Maple Leafs**	**NHL**	**63**	**34**	**19**	**9**	**3760**	**172**	**5**	**2.74**	**2.55**	....	....	....	....	**13**	**6**	**7**	....	**795**	**32**	***2**	**2.42**	....	....	....	....
1978-79	**Toronto Maple Leafs**	**NHL**	**58**	**26**	**21**	**10**	**3396**	**167**	**4**	**2.95**	**2.59**	....	....	....	....	**5**	**2**	**3**	....	**298**	**17**	**0**	**3.42**	....	....	....	....
1979-80	**Toronto Maple Leafs**	**NHL**	**38**	**16**	**14**	**3**	**2039**	**125**	**2**	**3.68**	**3.24**	....	....	....	....	**1**	**0**	**1**	....	**60**	**7**	**0**	**7.00**	....	....	....	....
1980-81	**Washington Capitals**	**NHL**	**49**	**18**	**19**	**9**	**2679**	**172**	**2**	**3.85**	**3.09**	....	....	....	....	....	....	....	....	....	....	....	....	....	....	....	....
1981-82	**Washington Capitals**	**NHL**	**11**	**2**	**7**	**2**	**584**	**47**	**0**	**4.83**	**3.73**	....	....	....	....	....	....	....	....	....	....	....	....	....	....	....	....
1982-83	St. Catharines Saints	AHL	2	1	0	1	125	4	1	1.92	....	....	....	....	....	....	....	....	....	....	....	....	....	....	....	....	....
	Toronto Maple Leafs	**NHL**	**53**	**21**	**23**	**7**	**2965**	**197**	**0**	**3.99**	**3.19**	**5.12**	**1534**	**.872**	**31.0**	**4**	**1**	**3**	....	**252**	**17**	**0**	**4.05**	....	....	....	....
1983-84	**Toronto Maple Leafs**	**NHL**	**34**	**9**	**17**	**4**	**1831**	**149**	**0**	**4.88**	**3.83**	**7.37**	**986**	**.849**	**32.3**	....	....	....	....	....	....	....	....	....	....	....	....
	NHL Totals		**356**	**149**	**138**	**52**	**20131**	**1183**	**17**	**3.53**	....	....	....	....	....	**29**	**12**	**17**	....	**1765**	**89**	**2**	**3.03**	....	....	....	....

OHA First All-Star Team (1973)

Traded to **Washington** by **Toronto** with Toronto's 3rd round choice (Torrie Robertson) in 1980 Entry Draft for Robert Picard, Tim Coulis and Washington's 2nd round choice (Bob McGill) in 1980 Entry Draft, June 11, 1980. Traded to **Toronto** by **Washington** for cash, September 9, 1982.

• PANG, DARREN

Darren Pang G – L. 5'5", 155 lbs. b: Meaford, Ont., 2/17/1964.

Season	Club	League	GP	W	L	T	Mins	GA	SO	Avg	AAvg	Eff	SA	S%	SAPG	GP	W	L	T	Mins	GA	SO	Avg	Eff	SA	S%	SAPG
1981-82	Belleville Bulls	OHL	47	15	21	1	2234	173	0	4.65	....	....	....	....	....	....	....	....	....	....	....	....	....	....	....	....	....
1982-83	Belleville Bulls	OHL	12	3	8	0	570	44	0	4.63	....	....	....	....	....	....	....	....	....	....	....	....	....	....	....	....	....
	Ottawa 67's	OHL	47	28	14	3	2729	166	1	3.65	....	....	....	....	....	9	5	4	0	510	33	0	3.88	....	....	....	....
1983-84	Ottawa 67's	OHL	43	29	10	1	2318	117	2	3.03	....	....	....	....	....	13	....	....	....	726	41	*1	*3.31	....	....	....	....
1984-85	Milwaukee Admirals	IHL	53	19	29	3	3129	226	0	4.33	....	....	....	....	....	....	....	....	....	....	....	....	....	....	....	....	....
	Chicago Black Hawks	**NHL**	**1**	**0**	**1**	**0**	**60**	**4**	**0**	**4.00**	**3.18**	**7.27**	**22**	**.818**	**22.0**	....	....	....	....	....	....	....	....	....	....	....	....
1985-86	Saginaw Generals	IHL	44	21	21	0	2638	148	2	3.37	....	....	....	....	....	8	3	5	0	492	32	0	3.90	....	....	....	....
1986-87	Nova Scotia Oilers	AHL	7	4	2	0	389	21	0	3.24	....	....	....	....	....	3	1	2	0	200	11	0	3.30	....	....	....	....
	Saginaw Generals	IHL	44	25	16	0	2500	151	0	3.62	....	....	....	....	....	....	....	....	....	....	....	....	....	....	....	....	....
1987-88	**Chicago Blackhawks**	**NHL**	**45**	**17**	**23**	**1**	**2548**	**163**	**0**	**3.84**	**3.20**	**4.17**	**1501**	**.891**	**35.3**	**4**	**1**	**3**	....	**240**	**18**	**0**	**4.50**	**6.23**	**130**	**.862**	**32.5**
1988-89	**Chicago Blackhawks**	**NHL**	**35**	**10**	**11**	**6**	**1644**	**120**	**0**	**4.38**	**3.62**	**5.74**	**915**	**.869**	**33.4**	**2**	**0**	**0**	....	**10**	**0**	**0**	**0.00**	**0.00**	**4**	**1.000**	**24.0**
	Saginaw Hawks	IHL	2	1	0	0	89	6	0	4.04	....	....	....	....	....	....	....	....	....	....	....	....	....	....	....	....	....
1989-90	Indianapolis Ice	IHL	7	4	1	2	401	17	1	2.54	....	....	....	....	....	4	3	1	0	253	12	0	2.85	....	....	....	....
	NHL Totals		**81**	**27**	**35**	**7**	**4252**	**287**	**0**	**4.05**	....	....	**2438**	**.882**	....	**6**	**1**	**3**	....	**250**	**18**	**0**	**4.32**	....	....	....	....

OHL First All-Star Team (1984) • Memorial Cup All-Star Team (1984) • Won Hap Emms Memorial Trophy (Memorial Cup Tournament Top Goaltender) (1984) • IHL Second All-Star Team (1987) • NHL All-Rookie Team (1988)

Signed as a free agent by **Chicago**, August 15, 1984.

• PARENT, BERNIE

Bernie Parent G – L. 5'10", 180 lbs. b: Montreal, Que., 4/3/1945. **HHOF**

Season	Club	League	GP	W	L	T	Mins	GA	SO	Avg	AAvg	Eff	SA	S%	SAPG	GP	W	L	T	Mins	GA	SO	Avg	Eff	SA	S%	SAPG
1963-64	Niagara Falls Flyers	OHA	28	....	....	....	1680	80	4	*2.86	....	....	....	....	....	4	0	4	0	240	26	0	6.50	....	....	....	....
1964-65	Niagara Falls Flyers	OHA	34	....	....	....	2004	86	2	*2.58	....	....	....	....	....	8	*6	2	0	480	15	1	*1.86	....	....	....	....
1965-66	Oklahoma City Blazers	CHL	3	1	1	1	180	11	0	3.67	....	....	....	....	....	....	....	....	....	....	....	....	....	....	....	....	....
	Boston Bruins	**NHL**	**39**	**11**	**20**	**3**	**2083**	**128**	**1**	**3.69**	**3.82**	....	....	....	....	....	....	....	....	....	....	....	....	....	....	....	....
1966-67	**Boston Bruins**	**NHL**	**18**	**4**	**12**	**2**	**1022**	**62**	**0**	**3.64**	**3.80**	....	....	....	....	....	....	....	....	....	....	....	....	....	....	....	....
	Oklahoma City Blazers	CHL	14	10	4	0	820	37	*4	2.70	....	....	....	....	....	....	....	....	....	....	....	....	....	....	....	....	....
1967-68	**Philadelphia Flyers**	**NHL**	**38**	**16**	**17**	**5**	**2248**	**93**	**4**	**2.48**	**2.73**	....	....	....	....	**5**	**2**	**3**	....	**355**	**8**	**0**	***1.35**	....	....	....	....
1968-69	**Philadelphia Flyers**	**NHL**	**58**	**17**	**23**	**16**	**3365**	**151**	**1**	**2.69**	**2.77**	....	....	....	....	**3**	**0**	**3**	....	**180**	**12**	**0**	**4.00**	....	....	....	....
1969-70	**Philadelphia Flyers**	**NHL**	**62**	**13**	**29**	**20**	**3680**	**171**	**3**	**2.79**	**2.96**	....	....	....	....	....	....	....	....	....	....	....	....	....	....	....	....
1970-71	**Philadelphia Flyers**	**NHL**	**30**	**9**	**12**	**6**	**1586**	**73**	**2**	**2.76**	**2.72**	....	....	....	....	....	....	....	....	....	....	....	....	....	....	....	....
	Toronto Maple Leafs	**NHL**	**18**	**7**	**7**	**3**	**1040**	**46**	**0**	**2.65**	**2.61**	....	....	....	....	**4**	**2**	**2**	....	**235**	**9**	**0**	**2.30**	....	....	....	....
1971-72	**Toronto Maple Leafs**	**NHL**	**47**	**17**	**18**	**9**	**2715**	**116**	**3**	**2.56**	**2.56**	....	....	....	....	**4**	**1**	**3**	....	**243**	**13**	**0**	**3.21**	....	....	....	....
1972-73	Philadelphia Blazers	WHA	63	*33	28	0	3653	220	2	3.61	....	....	....	....	....	1	0	1	0	70	3	0	2.57	....	....	....	....
1973-74	**Philadelphia Flyers**	**NHL**	***73**	***47**	**13**	**12**	***4314**	**136**	***12**	***1.89**	**1.78**	....	....	....	....	***17**	***12**	**5**	....	***1042**	**35**	***2**	**2.02**	....	....	....	....
1974-75	**Philadelphia Flyers**	**NHL**	**68**	***44**	**14**	**10**	**4041**	**137**	***12**	***2.03**	**1.79**	....	....	....	....	***15**	***10**	**5**	....	***922**	**29**	***4**	***1.89**	....	....	....	....
1975-76	**Philadelphia Flyers**	**NHL**	**11**	**6**	**2**	**3**	**615**	**24**	**0**	**2.34**	**2.11**	....	....	....	....	**8**	**4**	**4**	....	**480**	**27**	**0**	**3.30**	....	....	....	....
1976-77	**Philadelphia Flyers**	**NHL**	**61**	**35**	**13**	**12**	**3525**	**159**	**5**	**2.71**	**2.50**	....	....	....	....	**3**	**0**	**3**	....	**123**	**8**	**0**	**3.90**	....	....	....	....
1977-78	**Philadelphia Flyers**	**NHL**	**49**	**29**	**6**	**13**	**2923**	**108**	***7**	**2.22**	**2.06**	....	....	....	....	**12**	**7**	**5**	....	**722**	**33**	**0**	**2.74**	....	....	....	....
1978-79	**Philadelphia Flyers**	**NHL**	**36**	**16**	**12**	**7**	**1979**	**89**	**4**	**2.70**	**2.37**	....	....	....	....	....	....	....	....	....	....	....	....	....	....	....	....
	NHL Totals		**608**	**271**	**198**	**121**	**35136**	**1493**	**54**	**2.55**	....	....	....	....	....	**71**	**38**	**33**	....	**4302**	**174**	**6**	**2.43**	....	....	....	....
	Other Major League Totals		63	33	28	0	3653	220	2	3.61	....	....	....	....	....	1	0	1	0	70	3	0	2.57	....	....	....	....

WHA Second All-Star Team (1973) • NHL First All-Star Team (1974, 1975) • Won Vezina Trophy (tied with Tony Esposito) (1974) • Won Conn Smythe Trophy (1974, 1975) • Won Vezina Trophy (1975)

Played in NHL All-Star Game (1969, 1970, 1974, 1975, 1977)

Claimed by **Philadelphia** from **Boston** in Expansion Draft, June 6, 1967. Traded to **Toronto** by **Philadelphia** with Philadelphia's 2nd round choice (Rick Kehoe) in 1971 Amateur Draft for Bruce Gamble, Mike Walton and Toronto's 1st round choice (Pierre Plante) in 1971 Amateur Draft, February 1, 1971. Selected by Miami-Philadelphia (WHA) in 1972 WHA General Player Draft, February 12, 1972. • Suspended by Philadelphia (WHA) after leaving team following game vs. Cleveland, April 4, 1973. WHA rights traded to **NY Raiders** (WHA) by **Philadelphia-Vancouver** (WHA) with Dan Herriman and Andre Lacroix for Ron Ward and Pete Donnelly, June, 1973. Traded to **Philadelphia** by **Toronto** with Toronto's 2nd round choice (Larry Goodenough) in 1973 Amateur Draft for Philadelphia's 1st round choice (Bob Neely) in 1973 Amateur Draft and future considerations (Doug Favell, July 27, 1973), May 15, 1973.

• PARENT, BOB

Bob Parent G – R. 5'9", 175 lbs. b: Windsor, Ont., 2/19/1958. Toronto's 3rd choice, 65th overall, in 1978 Amateur Draft.

Season	Club	League	GP	W	L	T	Mins	GA	SO	Avg	AAvg	Eff	SA	S%	SAPG	GP	W	L	T	Mins	GA	SO	Avg	Eff	SA	S%	SAPG
1975-76	Windsor Spitfires	OHA	9	5	4	0	377	53	0	8.44	....	....	....	....	....	....	....	....	....	....	....	....	....	....	....	....	....
1976-77	Windsor Spitfires	OHA	39	....	....	....	1689	161	0	5.73	....	....	....	....	....	....	....	....	....	....	....	....	....	....	....	....	....
1977-78	Windsor Spitfires	OHA	11	....	....	....	604	37	0	3.66	....	....	....	....	....	....	....	....	....	....	....	....	....	....	....	....	....
	Kitchener Rangers	OHA	48	....	....	....	2848	182	1	3.81	....	....	....	....	....	9	....	....	....	532	45	0	4.95	....	....	....	....
1978-79	Saginaw Gears	IHL	2	....	....	....	49	10	0	12.24	....	....	....	....	....	....	....	....	....	....	....	....	....	....	....	....	....
	Port Huron Flags	IHL	24	....	....	....	1177	73	0	3.72	....	....	....	....	....	....	....	....	....	....	....	....	....	....	....	....	....
1979-80	Port Huron Flags	IHL	37	....	....	....	2212	137	0	3.72	....	....	....	....	....	11	6	5	0	671	36	0	3.22	....	....	....	....
1980-81	Hampton Aces	EHL	46	....	....	....	2536	200	1	4.73	....	....	....	....	....	....	....	....	....	....	....	....	....	....	....	....	....
	New Brunswick Hawks	AHL	2	0	2	0	80	5	0	3.75	....	....	....	....	....	13	7	6	0	845	39	0	2.77	....	....	....	....
1981-82	**Toronto Maple Leafs**	**NHL**	**2**	**0**	**2**	**0**	**120**	**13**	**0**	**6.50**	**5.01**	....	....	....	....	....	....	....	....	....	....	....	....	....	....	....	....
	Cincinnati Tigers	CHL	65	*34	24	3	3680	252	2	4.11	....	....	....	....	....	3	1	2	0	180	13	0	4.33	....	....	....	....

			REGULAR SEASON													PLAYOFFS											
Season	Club	League	GP	W	L	T	Mins	GA	SO	Avg	AAvg	Eff	SA	S%	SAPG	GP	W	L	T	Mins	GA	SO	Avg	Eff	SA	S%	SAPG
1982-83	**Toronto Maple Leafs**	**NHL**	**1**	**0**	**0**	**0**	**40**	**2**	**0**	**3.00**	**2.40**	**2.73**	**22**	**.909**	**33.0**	....	....	....	....	....	....	....	....	....	....	....	....
	St. Catharines Saints	AHL	46	18	20	3	2485	180	1	4.35	....	....	....	....	....	....	....	....	....	....	....	....	....	....	....	....	....
1983-84	St. Catharines Saints	AHL	18	6	11	0	900	73	0	4.87	....	....	....	....	....	....	....	....	....	....	....	....	....	....	....	....	....
	Muskegon Mohawks	IHL	35	....	....	....	2063	185	0	5.38	....	....	....	....	....	....	....	....	....	....	....	....	....	....	....	....	....
	NHL Totals		**3**	**0**	**2**	**0**	**160**	**15**	**0**	**5.62**	....	....	....	....	....	....	....	....	....	....	....	....	....	....	....	....	....

• PARENT, RICH

Rich Parent G – L. 6'3", 195 lbs. b: Montreal, Que., 1/12/1973.

			REGULAR SEASON													PLAYOFFS											
Season	Club	League	GP	W	L	T	Mins	GA	SO	Avg	AAvg	Eff	SA	S%	SAPG	GP	W	L	T	Mins	GA	SO	Avg	Eff	SA	S%	SAPG
1994-95	Muskegon Fury	ColHL	35	17	11	3	1867	112	1	3.60	....	....	....	....	....	13	7	3	....	725	47	1	3.89	....	....	....	....
1995-96	Muskegon Fury	ColHL	36	23	7	4	2087	85	2	2.44	....	....	....	....	....	....	....	....	....	....	....	....	....	....	....	....	....
	Detroit Vipers	IHL	19	16	0	1	1040	48	2	2.77	....	....	....	....	....	7	3	3	....	363	22	0	3.64	....	....	....	....
1996-97	Detroit Vipers	IHL	53	31	13	4	2815	104	4	2.22	....	....	....	....	....	15	8	3	....	786	21	1	*1.60	....	....	....	....
1997-98	**St. Louis Blues**	**NHL**	**1**	**0**	**0**	**0**	**12**	**0**	**0**	**0.00**	**0.00**	**0.00**	**1**	**1.000**	**5.0**	....	....	....	....	....	....	....	....	....	....	....	....
	Manitoba Moose	IHL	26	8	12	2	1334	69	3	3.10	....	....	....	....	....	....	....	....	....	....	....	....	....	....	....	....	....
	Detroit Vipers	IHL	7	4	0	3	417	15	0	2.15	....	....	....	....	....	5	1	0	....	157	6	0	2.29	....	....	....	....
	NHL Totals		**1**	**0**	**0**	**0**	**12**	**0**	**0**	**0.00**	....	....	**1**	**1.000**	....	....	....	....	....	....	....	....	....	....	....	....	....

ColHL First All-Star Team (1996) • Named ColHL's Outstanding Goaltender (1996) • Shared James Norris Memorial Trophy (fewest goals against - IHL) with Jeff Reese (1997)

Signed as a free agent by **St. Louis**, July 31, 1997.

• PARRO, DAVE

Dave Parro G – L. 5'11", 165 lbs. b: Saskatoon, Sask., 4/30/1957. Boston's 2nd choice, 34th overall, in 1977 Amateur Draft.

			REGULAR SEASON													PLAYOFFS											
Season	Club	League	GP	W	L	T	Mins	GA	SO	Avg	AAvg	Eff	SA	S%	SAPG	GP	W	L	T	Mins	GA	SO	Avg	Eff	SA	S%	SAPG
1973-74	Saskatoon Olympics	SJHL	29	....	....	....	1740	137	0	4.21	....	....	....	....	....	....	....	....	....	....	....	....	....	....	....	....	....
1974-75	Saskatoon Olympics	SJHL	35	....	....	....	2100	136	0	4.34	....	....	....	....	....	....	....	....	....	....	....	....	....	....	....	....	....
	Saskatoon Blades	WCJHL	1	....	....	....	60	2	0	2.00	....	....	....	....	....	....	....	....	....	....	....	....	....	....	....	....	....
1975-76	Saskatoon Blades	WCJHL	36	....	....	....	2100	119	1	3.40	....	....	....	....	....	9	....	....	....	414	31	0	4.49	....	....	....	....
1976-77	Saskatoon Blades	WCJHL	69	....	....	....	3956	246	1	3.73	....	....	....	....	....	6	....	....	....	360	23	0	3.83	....	....	....	....
1977-78	Rochester Americans	AHL	46	25	16	3	2694	164	0	3.65	....	....	....	....	....	3	2	1	0	180	9	0	3.00	....	....	....	....
1978-79	Grand Rapids Owls	IHL	7	....	....	....	419	25	0	3.58	....	....	....	....	....	....	....	....	....	....	....	....	....	....	....	....	....
	Rochester Americans	AHL	36	12	15	5	2065	130	*2	3.78	....	....	....	....	....	....	....	....	....	....	....	....	....	....	....	....	....
1979-80	Hershey Bears	AHL	54	20	30	3	3159	172	0	3.27	....	....	....	....	....	8	5	3	0	479	34	0	4.26	....	....	....	....
1980-81	**Washington Capitals**	**NHL**	**18**	**4**	**7**	**2**	**811**	**49**	**1**	**3.63**	**2.91**	....	....	....	....	....	....	....	....	....	....	....	....	....	....	....	....
	Hershey Bears	AHL	14	7	6	1	834	60	0	4.32	....	....	....	....	....	....	....	....	....	....	....	....	....	....	....	....	....
1981-82	**Washington Capitals**	**NHL**	**52**	**16**	**26**	**7**	**2942**	**206**	**1**	**4.20**	**3.24**	....	....	....	....	....	....	....	....	....	....	....	....	....	....	....	....
1982-83	**Washington Capitals**	**NHL**	**6**	**1**	**3**	**1**	**261**	**19**	**0**	**4.37**	**3.49**	**6.54**	**127**	**.850**	**29.2**	....	....	....	....	....	....	....	....	....	....	....	....
	Hershey Bears	AHL	47	21	20	4	2714	175	1	3.87	....	....	....	....	....	4	1	3	0	240	15	0	3.75	....	....	....	....
1983-84	**Washington Capitals**	**NHL**	**1**	**0**	**0**	**0**	**1**	**0**	**0**	**0.00**	**0.00**	**0.00**	**0**	**.00**	**0.0**	....	....	....	....	....	....	....	....	....	....	....	....
	Hershey Bears	AHL	42	12	21	5	2277	190	1	5.01	....	....	....	....	....	....	....	....	....	....	....	....	....	....	....	....	....
1984-85	Salt Lake Golden Eagles	IHL	28	11	14	3	1672	102	0	3.66	....	....	....	....	....	....	....	....	....	....	....	....	....	....	....	....	....
1985-86	Flint Generals	IHL	46	10	34	0	2527	235	0	5.30	....	....	....	....	....	....	....	....	....	....	....	....	....	....	....	....	....
	Fort Wayne Komets	IHL	5	1	3	1	305	18	0	3.54	....	....	....	....	....	....	....	....	....	....	....	....	....	....	....	....	....
1986-87	Indianapolis Checkers	IHL	32	16	14	0	1780	124	*3	4.18	....	....	....	....	....	....	....	....	....	....	....	....	....	....	....	....	....
	NHL Totals		**77**	**21**	**36**	**10**	**4015**	**274**	**2**	**4.09**	....	....	....	....	....	....	....	....	....	....	....	....	....	....	....	....	....

AHL Second All-Star Team (1983)

Claimed by **Quebec** from **Boston** in Expansion Draft, June 13, 1979. Traded to **Washington** by **Quebec** for Nelson Burton, June 15, 1979.

• PATRICK, LESTER

Lester "The Silver Fox" Patrick G6'1", 180 lbs. b: Drummondville, Que., 12/30/1883. d: 6/1/1960. **HHOF**

			REGULAR SEASON													PLAYOFFS											
Season	Club	League	GP	W	L	T	Mins	GA	SO	Avg	AAvg	Eff	SA	S%	SAPG	GP	W	L	T	Mins	GA	SO	Avg	Eff	SA	S%	SAPG
1921-22	Victoria Aristocrats	PCHA	1	0	0	0	10	1	0	6.00	....	....	....	....	....	....	....	....	....	....	....	....	....	....	....	....	....
1927-28	**New York Rangers**	**NHL**	....	....	....	....	....	....	....	....	....	....	....	....	....	**1**	**1**	**0**	**0**	**46**	**1**	**0**	**1.30**	....	....	....	....
	NHL Totals		....	....	....	....	....	....	....	....	....	....	....	....	....	**1**	**1**	**0**	**0**	**46**	**1**	**0**	**1.30**	....	....	....	....
	Other Major League Totals		1	0	0	0	10	1	0	6.00	....	....	....	....	....	....	....	....	....	....	....	....	....	....	....	....	....

NY Rangers' coach/general manager replaced injured Lorne Chabot in 2nd period, April 7, 1928. (NY Rangers 2, Montreal Maroons 1)

• PEETERS, PETE

Pete Peeters G – L. 6'1", 195 lbs. b: Edmonton, Alta., 8/17/1957. Philadelphia's 9th choice, 135th overall, in 1977 Amateur Draft.

			REGULAR SEASON													PLAYOFFS											
Season	Club	League	GP	W	L	T	Mins	GA	SO	Avg	AAvg	Eff	SA	S%	SAPG	GP	W	L	T	Mins	GA	SO	Avg	Eff	SA	S%	SAPG
1975-76	Medicine Hat Tigers	WCJHL	37	....	....	....	2074	147	0	4.25	....	....	....	....	....	....	....	....	....	....	....	....	....	....	....	....	....
1976-77	Medicine Hat Tigers	WCJHL	62	....	....	....	3423	232	1	4.07	....	....	....	....	....	4	....	....	....	204	17	0	5.00	....	....	....	....
1977-78	Milwaukee Admirals	IHL	32	....	....	....	1698	93	1	3.29	....	....	....	....	....	....	....	....	....	....	....	....	....	....	....	....	....
	Maine Mariners	AHL	17	8	2	2	855	40	1	2.80	....	....	....	....	....	11	*8	3	0	562	25	*1	*2.67	....	....	....	....
1978-79	**Philadelphia Flyers**	**NHL**	**5**	**1**	**2**	**1**	**280**	**16**	**0**	**3.43**	**3.03**	....	....	....	....	....	....	....	....	....	....	....	....	....	....	....	....
	Maine Mariners	AHL	35	25	6	3	2067	100	*2	*2.90	....	....	....	....	....	6	5	0	0	329	15	0	*2.74	....	....	....	....
1979-80	**Philadelphia Flyers**	**NHL**	**40**	**29**	**5**	**5**	**2373**	**108**	**1**	**2.73**	**2.39**	....	....	....	....	**13**	**8**	**5**	....	**799**	**37**	**1**	**2.78**	....	....	....	....
1980-81	**Philadelphia Flyers**	**NHL**	**40**	**22**	**12**	**5**	**2333**	**115**	**2**	**2.96**	**2.36**	....	....	....	....	**3**	**2**	**1**	....	**180**	**12**	**0**	**4.00**	....	....	....	....
1981-82	**Philadelphia Flyers**	**NHL**	**44**	**23**	**18**	**3**	**2591**	**160**	**0**	**3.71**	**2.85**	....	....	....	....	**4**	**1**	**2**	....	**220**	**17**	**0**	**4.64**	....	....	....	....
1982-83	**Boston Bruins**	**NHL**	**62**	***40**	**11**	**9**	**3611**	**142**	***8**	***2.36**	**1.86**	**2.26**	**1482**	**.904**	**24.6**	***17**	**9**	**8**	....	***1024**	**61**	**1**	**3.57**	....	....	....	....
1983-84	**Boston Bruins**	**NHL**	**50**	**29**	**16**	**2**	**2868**	**151**	**0**	**3.16**	**2.46**	**3.90**	**1222**	**.876**	**25.6**	**3**	**0**	**3**	....	**180**	**10**	**0**	**3.33**	**4.90**	**68**	**.853**	**22.7**
1984-85	Canada	C Cup	4	3	1	0	234	13	....	3.00	....	....	....	....	....	....	....	....	....	....	....	....	....	....	....	....	....
	Boston Bruins	**NHL**	**51**	**19**	**26**	**4**	**2975**	**172**	**1**	**3.47**	**2.75**	**4.57**	**1307**	**.868**	**26.4**	**1**	**0**	**1**	....	**60**	**4**	**0**	**4.00**	**6.15**	**26**	**.846**	**26.0**
1985-86	**Boston Bruins**	**NHL**	**8**	**3**	**4**	**1**	**485**	**31**	**0**	**3.84**	**2.99**	**4.86**	**245**	**.873**	**30.3**	....	....	....	....	....	....	....	....	....	....	....	....
	Washington Capitals	**NHL**	**34**	**19**	**11**	**3**	**2021**	**113**	**1**	**3.35**	**2.60**	**4.16**	**910**	**.876**	**27.0**	**9**	**5**	**4**	....	**544**	**24**	**0**	**2.65**	**2.51**	**253**	**.905**	**27.9**
1986-87	**Washington Capitals**	**NHL**	**37**	**17**	**11**	**4**	**2002**	**107**	**0**	**3.21**	**2.69**	**3.69**	**930**	**.885**	**27.9**	**3**	**1**	**2**	....	**180**	**9**	**0**	**3.00**	**3.55**	**76**	**.882**	**25.3**
	Binghamton Whalers	AHL	4	3	0	0	245	4	1	0.98	....	....	....	....	....	....	....	....	....	....	....	....	....	....	....	....	....
1987-88	**Washington Capitals**	**NHL**	**35**	**14**	**12**	**5**	**1896**	**88**	**2**	***2.78**	**2.30**	**2.82**	**866**	**.898**	**27.4**	**12**	**7**	**5**	....	**654**	**34**	**0**	**3.12**	**3.25**	**326**	**.896**	**29.9**
1988-89	**Washington Capitals**	**NHL**	**33**	**20**	**7**	**3**	**1854**	**88**	**4**	**2.85**	**2.34**	**3.17**	**790**	**.889**	**25.6**	**6**	**2**	**4**	....	**359**	**24**	**0**	**4.01**	**5.87**	**164**	**.854**	**27.4**
1989-90	**Philadelphia Flyers**	**NHL**	**24**	**1**	**13**	**5**	**1140**	**72**	**1**	**3.79**	**3.18**	**4.50**	**606**	**.881**	**31.9**	....	....	....	....	....	....	....	....	....	....	....	....
1990-91	**Philadelphia Flyers**	**NHL**	**26**	**9**	**7**	**1**	**1270**	**61**	**1**	**2.88**	**2.57**	**2.82**	**623**	**.902**	**29.4**	....	....	....	....	....	....	....	....	....	....	....	....
	Hershey Bears	AHL	2	0	1	0	105	11	0	6.29	....	....	....	....	....	....	....	....	....	....	....	....	....	....	....	....	....
	NHL Totals		**489**	**246**	**155**	**51**	**27699**	**1424**	**21**	**3.08**	....	....	....	....	....	**71**	**35**	**35**	....	**4200**	**232**	**2**	**3.31**	....	....	....	....

AHL Second All-Star Team (1979) • Shared Harry "Hap" Holmes Memorial Award (fewest goals against - AHL) with Robbie Moore (1979) • NHL First All-Star Team (1983) • Won Vezina Trophy (1983)

Played in NHL All-Star Game (1980, 1981, 1983, 1984)

Traded to **Boston** by **Philadelphia** for Brad McCrimmon, June 9, 1982. Traded to **Washington** by **Boston** for Pat Riggin, November 14, 1985. Signed as a free agent by **Philadelphia**, June 17, 1989. Traded to **Winnipeg** by **Philadelphia** with Keith Acton for future considerations, September 28, 1989. Traded to **Philadelphia** by **Winnipeg** with Keith Acton for Toronto's 5th round choice (previously acquired, Winnipeg selected Juha Ylonen) in 1991 Entry Draft and the cancellation of future considerations owed Philadelphia from the trade for Shawn Cronin (July 21, 1989), October 3, 1989.

• PELLETIER, MARCEL

Marcel Pelletier G – R. 5'11", 180 lbs. b: Drummondville, Que., 12/6/1927.

			REGULAR SEASON													PLAYOFFS											
Season	Club	League	GP	W	L	T	Mins	GA	SO	Avg	AAvg	Eff	SA	S%	SAPG	GP	W	L	T	Mins	GA	SO	Avg	Eff	SA	S%	SAPG
1946-47	Verdun Jr. Maple Leafs	QJHL	24	11	9	4	1410	79	3	3.36	....	....	....	....	....	5	2	3	0	360	23	0	4.60	....	....	....	....
1947-48	Verdun Jr. Maple Leafs	QJHL	15	5	9	1	900	49	1	3.27	....	....	....	....	....	3	0	2	1	180	7	0	2.33	....	....	....	....
1948-49	Kitchener-Waterloo Dutchmen	OHA Sr.	40	....	....	....	2380	105	4	*2.65	....	....	....	....	....	12	....	....	....	720	31	*1	*2.58	....	....	....	....
1949-50	Quebec Aces	QSHL	23	....	....	....	1380	66	2	2.87	....	....	....	....	....	....	....	....	....	....	....	....	....	....	....	....	....
	Kansas City Mohawks	USHL	2	1	1	0	120	12	0	6.00	....	....	....	....	....	....	....	....	....	....	....	....	....	....	....	....	....
1950-51	Milwaukee Sea Gulls	USHL	41	13	23	5	2506	177	1	4.24	....	....	....	....	....	....	....	....	....	....	....	....	....	....	....	....	....
	Chicago Black Hawks	**NHL**	**6**	**1**	**5**	**0**	**355**	**29**	**0**	**4.90**	**5.64**	....	....	....	....	....	....	....	....	....	....	....	....	....	....	....	....
	Omaha Knights	USHL	1	0	0	1	70	5	0	4.29	....	....	....	....	....	....	....	....	....	....	....	....	....	....	....	....	....
1951-52	Chicoutimi Sagueneens	QSHL	46	21	19	6	2840	139	2	2.94	....	....	....	....	....	18	*11	7	0	1123	43	*3	2.30	....	....	....	....
1952-53	Chicoutimi Sagueneens	QSHL	59	*33	15	11	3680	149	*6	*2.43	....	....	....	....	....	20	11	9	0	1280	53	*3	2.46	....	....	....	....
1953-54	Seattle Bombers	WHL	68	22	39	7	4080	236	2	3.47	....	....	....	....	....	....	....	....	....	....	....	....	....	....	....	....	....
1954-55	Victoria Cougars	WHL	70	33	29	8	*4080	197	6	2.81	....	....	....	....	....	4	1	3	0	245	14	0	3.43	....	....	....	....
1955-56	Victoria Cougars	WHL	69	35	29	5	4216	191	*8	2.72	....	....	....	....	....	9	5	4	0	547	28	*1	3.07	....	....	....	....

			REGULAR SEASON													PLAYOFFS											
Season	Club	League	GP	W	L	T	Mins	GA	SO	Avg	AAvg	Eff	SA	S%	SAPG	GP	W	L	T	Mins	GA	SO	Avg	Eff	SA	S%	SAPG
1956-57	Victoria Cougars	WHL	69	29	33	7	4240	198	4	2.80	....	....	....	....	....	3	1	2	0	199	6	0	1.81	....	....	....	....
	Seattle Americans	WHL	1	1	0	0	60	2	0	2.00	....	....	....	....	....	....	....	....	....	....	....	....	....	....	....	....	....
	New Westminster Royals	WHL	....	....	....	....	....	....	....	....	....	....	....	....	....	2	0	2	0	119	7	0	3.53	....	....	....	....
1957-58	Vancouver Canucks	WHL	*70	*44	21	5	*4250	173	*8	*2.44	....	....	....	....	....	11	*8	3	0	738	31	0	2.52	....	....	....	....
1958-59	Victoria Cougars	WHL	69	30	35	4	4180	247	5	3.55	....	....	....	....	....	3	0	3	0	180	12	0	4.00	....	....	....	....
1959-60	Victoria Cougars	WHL	*70	37	29	4	4240	190	2	2.69	....	....	....	....	....	11	6	5	0	671	27	*2	2.41	....	....	....	....
1960-61	Victoria Cougars	WHL	*70	27	41	2	4220	263	1	3.74	....	....	....	....	....	5	2	3	0	335	12	0	2.15	....	....	....	....
1961-62	Los Angeles Blades	WHL	67	24	37	6	4080	281	0	4.13	....	....	....	....	....	....	....	....	....	....	....	....	....	....	....	....	....
1962-63	**New York Rangers**	**NHL**	**2**	**0**	**1**	**0**	**40**	**4**	**0**	**6.00**	**6.24**	....	....	....	....	....	....	....	....	....	....	....	....	....	....	....	....
	Baltimore Clippers	AHL	30	16	10	4	1800	91	1	3.03	....	....	....	....	....	3	1	2	0	180	12	0	4.00	....	....	....	....
1963-64	St. Paul Rangers	CHL	61	34	23	3	3660	181	*9	2.97	....	....	....	....	....	*11	5	6	0	661	48	0	4.36	....	....	....	....
1964-65	Baltimore Clippers	AHL	11	5	5	1	639	37	1	3.47	....	....	....	....	....	....	....	....	....	....	....	....	....	....	....	....	....
	St. Paul Rangers	CHL	32	19	7	5	1863	89	0	2.87	....	....	....	....	....	11	*8	3	0	660	27	0	*2.45	....	....	....	....
1965-66	Los Angeles Blades	WHL	48	15	31	2	2900	199	0	4.12	....	....	....	....	....	....	....	....	....	....	....	....	....	....	....	....	....
	San Francisco Seals	WHL	....	....	....	....	....	....	....	....	....	....	....	....	....	3	2	1	0	182	7	0	2.31	....	....	....	....
1966-67	New Jersey Devils	EHL	23	....	....	....	1380	63	1	2.74	....	....	....	....	....	7	....	....	....	420	14	*1	*2.00	....	....	....	....
1967-68	Rimouski Kades	QSHL	43	....	....	....	2580	143	*6	3.37	....	....	....	....	....	....	....	....	....	....	....	....	....	....	....	....	....
1968-69	New Jersey Devils	EHL	1	1	0	0	60	1	0	1.00	....	....	....	....	....	....	....	....	....	....	....	....	....	....	....	....	....
	NHL Totals		**8**	**1**	**6**	**0**	**395**	**33**	**0**	**5.01**	....	....	....	....	....	....	....	....	....	....	....	....	....	....	....	....	....

QSHL First All-Star Team (1953) • WHL First All-Star Team (1956) • WHL Coast Division First All-Star Team (1957) • WHL Coast Division Second All-Star Team (1958) • Won WHL Leading Goaltender Award (1958) • WHL Second All-Star Team (1961) • CHL First All-Star Team (1964)

Loaned to **Chicago** by **Milwaukee** (IHL) to replace injured Harry Lumley, January, 1951. • Signed as a free agent by **NY Rangers** organization to serve as a roving substitute goaltender, June, 1962.

• PENNEY, STEVE

Steve Penney G – L. 6'1", 190 lbs. b: Ste-Foy, Que., 2/2/1961. Montreal's 10th choice, 166th overall, in 1980 Entry Draft.

Season	Club	League	GP	W	L	T	Mins	GA	SO	Avg	AAvg	Eff	SA	S%	SAPG	GP	W	L	T	Mins	GA	SO	Avg	Eff	SA	S%	SAPG
1978-79	Shawinigan Cataracts	QMJHL	36	....	....	....	1631	180	0	6.62	....	....	....	....	....	1	0	0	0	4	0	0	0.00	....	....	....	....
1979-80	Shawinigan Cataracts	QMJHL	31	9	14	5	1682	143	0	5.10	....	....	....	....	....	....	....	....	....	....	....	....	....	....	....	....	....
1980-81	Shawinigan Cataracts	QMJHL	62	30	25	4	3456	244	0	4.24	....	....	....	....	....	5	1	4	0	279	21	0	4.52	....	....	....	....
1981-82	Nova Scotia Voyageurs	AHL	6	2	1	1	308	22	0	4.29	....	....	....	....	....	....	....	....	....	....	....	....	....	....	....	....	....
	Flint Generals	IHL	36	....	....	....	2040	147	1	4.32	....	....	....	....	....	4	0	4	0	222	17	0	4.59	....	....	....	....
1982-83	Flint Generals	IHL	48	....	....	....	2552	179	0	4.21	....	....	....	....	....	3	0	2	0	111	10	0	5.40	....	....	....	....
1983-84	Nova Scotia Voyageurs	AHL	27	11	12	4	1571	92	0	3.51	....	....	....	....	....	....	....	....	....	....	....	....	....	....	....	....	....
	Montreal Canadiens	**NHL**	**4**	**0**	**4**	**0**	**240**	**19**	**0**	**4.75**	**3.72**	**7.85**	**115**	**.835**	**28.8**	**15**	**9**	**6**	....	**871**	**32**	***3**	***2.20**	**1.99**	**354**	**.910**	**24.4**
1984-85	**Montreal Canadiens**	**NHL**	**54**	**26**	**18**	**8**	**3252**	**167**	**1**	**3.08**	**2.43**	**3.83**	**1344**	**.876**	**24.8**	**12**	**6**	**6**	....	**733**	**40**	**1**	**3.27**	**4.36**	**300**	**.867**	**24.6**
1985-86	**Montreal Canadiens**	**NHL**	**18**	**6**	**8**	**2**	**990**	**72**	**0**	**4.36**	**3.39**	**7.02**	**447**	**.839**	**27.1**	....	....	....	....	....	....	....	....	....	....	....	....
1986-87	**Winnipeg Jets**	**NHL**	**7**	**1**	**4**	**1**	**327**	**25**	**0**	**4.59**	**3.86**	**8.56**	**134**	**.813**	**24.6**	....	....	....	....	....	....	....	....	....	....	....	....
	Sherbrooke Canadiens	AHL	4	1	2	0	199	12	0	3.62	....	....	....	....	....	....	....	....	....	....	....	....	....	....	....	....	....
1987-88	**Winnipeg Jets**	**NHL**	**8**	**2**	**4**	**1**	**385**	**30**	**0**	**4.68**	**3.89**	**7.55**	**186**	**.839**	**29.0**	....	....	....	....	....	....	....	....	....	....	....	....
	Moncton Hawks	AHL	28	9	14	4	1541	107	0	4.17	....	....	....	....	....	....	....	....	....	....	....	....	....	....	....	....	....
	NHL Totals		**91**	**35**	**38**	**12**	**5194**	**313**	**1**	**3.62**	....	....	**2226**	**.859**	....	**27**	**15**	**12**	....	**1604**	**72**	**4**	**2.69**	....	....	....	....

NHL All-Rookie Team (1985)

Traded to **Winnipeg** by **Montreal** with the rights to Jan Ingman for Brian Hayward, August 19, 1988.

• PERREAULT, BOB

Bob (Robert) "Miche" Perreault G – L. 5'8", 170 lbs. b: Trois Rivieres, Que., 1/28/1931. Deceased.

Season	Club	League	GP	W	L	T	Mins	GA	SO	Avg	AAvg	Eff	SA	S%	SAPG	GP	W	L	T	Mins	GA	SO	Avg	Eff	SA	S%	SAPG
1948-49	Trois-Rivieres Flambeaux	QJHL	46	26	16	4	2830	142	6	3.01	....	....	....	....	....	8	4	4	0	490	29	0	3.55	....	....	....	....
1949-50	Trois-Rivieres Flambeaux	QJHL	36	22	12	2	2190	91	*4	2.49	....	....	....	....	....	9	4	5	0	549	30	0	3.28	....	....	....	....
1950-51	Trois-Rivieres Flambeaux	QJHL	35	25	10	0	2108	96	2	2.73	....	....	....	....	....	8	4	4	0	517	30	0	3.48	....	....	....	....
1951-52	Providence Reds	AHL	22	8	13	0	1250	95	0	4.56	....	....	....	....	....	1	0	1	0	60	7	0	7.00	....	....	....	....
1952-53	Providence Reds	AHL	6	1	5	0	360	26	0	4.33	....	....	....	....	....	....	....	....	....	....	....	....	....	....	....	....	....
	Sherbrooke Saints	QSHL	29	15	11	3	1780	84	1	2.83	....	....	....	....	....	....	....	....	....	....	....	....	....	....	....	....	....
1953-54	Montreal Royals	QHL	58	34	20	4	3528	160	4	2.72	....	....	....	....	....	9	5	4	0	544	22	2	2.43	....	....	....	....
1954-55	Shawinigan Cataracts	QHL	58	*37	18	3	3400	129	*10	*2.22	....	....	....	....	....	12	*9	3	0	720	31	1	*2.58	....	....	....	....
1955-56	Shawinigan Cataracts	QHL	57	*40	14	3	3450	146	4	2.54	....	....	....	....	....	11	6	5	0	665	24	*2	*2.17	....	....	....	....
	Montreal Canadiens	**NHL**	**6**	**3**	**3**	**0**	**360**	**12**	**1**	**2.00**	**2.43**	....	....	....	....	....	....	....	....	....	....	....	....	....	....	....	....
1956-57	Shawinigan Cataracts	QHL	41	12	22	7	2556	132	0	3.10	....	....	....	....	....	....	....	....	....	....	....	....	....	....	....	....	....
	Rochester Americans	AHL	24	15	7	1	1440	66	3	2.75	....	....	....	....	....	10	5	5	0	637	27	*2	2.54	....	....	....	....
1957-58	Hershey Bears	AHL	STATISTICS NOT AVAILABLE													11	*8	3	0	660	31	0	2.82				
1958-59	Hershey Bears	AHL	52	....	....	....	3000	134	*6	*2.68		....	....	....	....	*13	*8	5	0	*780	35	*1	2.69	....	....	....	....
	Detroit Red Wings	**NHL**	**3**	**2**	**1**	**0**	**180**	**9**	**1**	**3.00**	**3.20**	....	....	....	....	....	....	....	....	....	....	....	....	....	....	....	....
1959-60	Hershey Bears	AHL	66	26	33	7	3960	205	*5	3.11	....	....	....	....	....	....	....	....	....	....	....	....	....	....	....	....	....
1960-61	Hershey Bears	AHL	41	22	16	3	2460	116	3	2.83	....	....	....	....	....	*8	*4	4	0	*504	24	0	2.86	....	....	....	....
1961-62	Hershey Bears	AHL	66	*36	25	5	3960	189	4	2.86	....	....	....	....	....	7	3	4	0	451	17	0	2.26	....	....	....	....
1962-63	**Boston Bruins**	**NHL**	**22**	**3**	**12**	**6**	**1287**	**85**	**1**	**3.86**	**4.08**	....	....	....	....	....	....	....	....	....	....	....	....	....	....	....	....
	Rochester Americans	AHL	10	3	4	2	600	27	0	2.70	....	....	....	....	....	2	0	2	0	120	11	0	5.50	....	....	....	....
1963-64	San Francisco Seals	WHL	*70	32	35	3	4230	257	0	3.65	....	....	....	....	....	*11	*8	3	0	*677	41	0	3.63	....	....	....	....
1964-65	San Francisco Seals	WHL	*69	30	37	2	*4164	268	0	3.86	....	....	....	....	....	....	....	....	....	....	....	....	....	....	....	....	....
1965-66	Rochester Americans	AHL	41	26	10	1	2361	121	3	3.07	....	....	....	....	....	9	7	2	0	532	17	*2	*1.92	....	....	....	....
1966-67	Rochester Americans	AHL	54	30	17	5	3149	158	*4	3.01	....	....	....	....	....	*13	6	7	0	*785	38	*2	2.90	....	....	....	....
1967-68	Rochester Americans	AHL	57	*31	15	7	3101	149	*6	2.88	....	....	....	....	....	9	5	3	0	515	28	1	3.26	....	....	....	....
1968-69	Rochester Americans	AHL	19	5	10	1	913	63	0	4.14	....	....	....	....	....	....	....	....	....	....	....	....	....	....	....	....	....
1969-70	Des Moines Oak Leafs	IHL	27	....	....	....	1467	66	1	*2.70	....	....	....	....	....	....	....	....	....	....	....	....	....	....	....	....	....
1970-71	Des Moines Oak Leafs	IHL	19	....	....	....	1062	57	1	3.22	....	....	....	....	....	8	....	....	....	478	21	0	2.63	....	....	....	....
1971-72	Des Moines Oak Leafs	IHL	51	....	....	....	3139	176	1	3.36	....	....	....	....	....	3	0	3	0	180	15	0	5.00	....	....	....	....
1972-73	Los Angeles Sharks	WHA	1	1	0	0	60	2	0	2.00	....	....	....	....	....	....	....	....	....	....	....	....	....	....	....	....	....
1973-74	Greensboro Generals	SHL	16	....	....	....	930	62	0	4.01	....	....	....	....	....	....	....	....	....	....	....	....	....	....	....	....	....
	NHL Totals		**31**	**8**	**16**	**6**	**1827**	**106**	**3**	**3.48**	....	....	....	....	....	....	....	....	....	....	....	....	....	....	....	....	....
	Other Major League Totals		1	1	0	0	60	2	0	2.00	....	....	....	....	....	....	....	....	....	....	....	....	....	....	....	....	....

QHL First All-Star Team (1955) • Won Vezina Memorial Trophy (Top Goaltender - QHL) (1955) • QHL Second All-Star Team (1956) • AHL Second All-Star Team (1958, 1959, 1962, 1968) • Won Harry "Hap" Holmes Memorial Award (fewest goals against - AHL) (1959, 1968) • Shared James Norris Memorial Trophy (fewest goals against - IHL) with Gaye Cooley (1970)

Traded to **Montreal** by **Providence** (AHL) for cash, June 11, 1953. Claimed by **Detroit** (Hershey - AHL) from **Montreal** (Shawinigan-QHL) in Inter-League Draft, June, 1957. Traded to **Boston** by **Detroit** (Hershey - AHL) for Ed Chadwick and Barry Ashbee, June, 1962. Traded to **San Francisco** (WHL) by **Boston** for $25,000, June 4, 1963. Selected by **LA Sharks** (WHA) in 1972 WHA General Player Draft, February 12, 1972.

• PETTIE, JIM

Jim Pettie G – L. 6', 195 lbs. b: Toronto, Ont., 10/24/1953. Boston's 10th choice, 142nd overall, in 1973 Amateur Draft.

Season	Club	League	GP	W	L	T	Mins	GA	SO	Avg	AAvg	Eff	SA	S%	SAPG	GP	W	L	T	Mins	GA	SO	Avg	Eff	SA	S%	SAPG
1972-73	St. Catharines Black Hawks	OHA	31	....	....	....	1089	152	1	5.04	....	....	....	....	....	....	....	....	....	....	....	....	....	....	....	....	....
1973-74	Dayton Gems	IHL	40	....	....	....	2092	96	1	*2.75	....	....	....	....	....	4	1	3	0	197	15	0	4.57	....	....	....	....
1974-75	Dayton Gems	IHL	27	....	....	....	1310	73	0	3.34	....	....	....	....	....	13	6	7	0	197	30	0	*2.82	....	....	....	....
1975-76	Binghamton Dusters	NAHL	5	....	....	....	260	16	1	3.69	....	....	....	....	....	....	....	....	....	....	....	....	....	....	....	....	....
	Dayton Gems	IHL	51	....	....	....	2178	104	*5	2.86	....	....	....	....	....	15	12	3	0	921	43	1	2.80	....	....	....	....
1976-77	**Boston Bruins**	**NHL**	**1**	**1**	**0**	**0**	**60**	**3**	**0**	**3.00**	**2.79**	....	....	....	....	....	....	....	....	....	....	....	....	....	....	....	....
	Rochester Americans	AHL	43	26	15	1	2462	131	2	3.19	....	....	....	....	....	*11	6	5	0	*660	36	0	3.27	....	....	....	....
1977-78	**Boston Bruins**	**NHL**	**1**	**0**	**1**	**0**	**60**	**6**	**0**	**6.00**	**5.62**	....	....	....	....	....	....	....	....	....	....	....	....	....	....	....	....
	Rochester Americans	AHL	32	16	12	4	1897	107	2	3.38		....	....	....	....	3	0	3	0	188	8	0	2.55	....	....	....	....
1978-79	Rochester Americans	AHL	9	0	7	1	451	39	0	5.19	....	....	....	....	....	....	....	....	....	....	....	....	....	....	....	....	....
	Boston Bruins	**NHL**	**19**	**8**	**6**	**2**	**1037**	**62**	**1**	**3.59**	**3.17**	....	....	....	....	....	....	....	....	....	....	....	....	....	....	....	....
1979-80	New Haven Nighthawks	AHL	33	16	13	3	1975	131	2	4.00	....	....	....	....	....	2	1	1	0	120	11	0	5.00	....	....	....	....
1980-81	Birmingham Bulls	CHL	21	....	....	....	1189	109	0	5.50	....	....	....	....	....	....	....	....	....	....	....	....	....	....	....	....	....
	Richmond Rifles	EHL	1	0	1	0	62	7	0	6.77	....	....	....	....	....	....	....	....	....	....	....	....	....	....	....	....	....
	NHL Totals		**21**	**9**	**7**	**2**	**1157**	**71**	**1**	**3.68**	....	....	....	....	....	....	....	....	....	....	....	....	....	....	....	....	....

IHL Second All-Star Team (1976)

● PIETRANGELO, FRANK Frank Pietrangelo G – L. 5'10", 185 lbs. b: Niagara Falls, Ont., 12/17/1964. Pittsburgh's 4th choice, 64th overall, in 1983 Entry Draft.

			REGULAR SEASON													PLAYOFFS											
Season	Club	League	GP	W	L	T	Mins	GA	SO	Avg	AAvg	Eff	SA	S%	SAPG	GP	W	L	T	Mins	GA	SO	Avg	Eff	SA	S%	SAPG
1982-83	University of Minnesota	WCHA	25	15	6	1	1348	80	1	3.56	....	....	....	....	....	....	....	....	....	....	....	....	....	....	....	....	....
1983-84	University of Minnesota	WCHA	20	13	7	0	1141	66	0	3.47	....	....	....	....	....	....	....	....	....	....	....	....	....	....	....	....	....
1984-85	University of Minnesota	WCHA	17	8	3	3	912	52	0	3.42	....	....	....	....	....	....	....	....	....	....	....	....	....	....	....	....	....
1985-86	University of Minnesota	WCHA	23	15	7	0	1284	76	0	3.55	....	....	....	....	....	....	....	....	....	....	....	....	....	....	....	....	....
1986-87	Muskegon Lumberjacks	IHL	35	23	11	0	2090	119	2	3.42	....	....	....	....	....	15	10	4	0	923	46	0	2.99	....	....	....	....
1987-88	**Pittsburgh Penguins**	**NHL**	**21**	**9**	**11**	**0**	**1207**	**80**	**1**	**3.98**	**3.31**	**5.31**	**600**	**.867**	**29.8**	....	....	....	....	....	....	....	....	....	....	....	....
	Muskegon Lumberjacks	IHL	15	11	3	1	868	43	2	2.97	....	....	....	....	....	....	....	....	....	....	....	....	....	....	....	....	....
1988-89	**Pittsburgh Penguins**	**NHL**	**15**	**5**	**3**	**0**	**669**	**45**	**0**	**4.04**	**3.33**	**4.44**	**409**	**.890**	**36.7**	....	....	....	....	....	....	....	....	....	....	....	....
	Muskegon Lumberjacks	IHL	13	10	1	0	760	38	1	3.00	....	....	....	....	....	9	*8	1	0	566	29	0	3.07	....	....	....	....
1989-90	**Pittsburgh Penguins**	**NHL**	**21**	**8**	**6**	**2**	**1066**	**77**	**0**	**4.33**	**3.63**	**5.75**	**580**	**.867**	**32.6**	....	....	....	....	....	....	....	....	....	....	....	....
	Muskegon Lumberjacks	IHL	12	9	2	1	691	38	0	3.30	....	....	....	....	....	....	....	....	....	....	....	....	....	....	....	....	....
1990-91	**Pittsburgh Penguins**	**NHL**	**25**	**10**	**11**	**1**	**1311**	**86**	**0**	**3.94**	**3.53**	**4.75**	**714**	**.880**	**32.7**	**5**	**4**	**1**	....	**288**	**15**	***1**	**3.13**	**3.17**	**148**	**.899**	**30.8**
1991-92	**Pittsburgh Penguins**	**NHL**	**5**	**2**	**1**	**0**	**225**	**20**	**0**	**5.33**	**4.73**	**8.20**	**130**	**.846**	**34.7**	....	....	....	....	....	....	....	....	....	....	....	....
	Hartford Whalers	**NHL**	**5**	**3**	**1**	**1**	**306**	**12**	**0**	**2.35**	**2.08**	**1.81**	**156**	**.923**	**30.6**	**7**	**3**	**4**	....	**425**	**19**	**0**	**2.68**	**2.09**	**244**	**.922**	**34.4**
1992-93	**Hartford Whalers**	**NHL**	**30**	**4**	**15**	**1**	**1373**	**111**	**0**	**4.85**	**4.14**	**6.88**	**783**	**.858**	**34.2**	....	....	....	....	....	....	....	....	....	....	....	....
1993-94	**Hartford Whalers**	**NHL**	**19**	**5**	**11**	**1**	**984**	**59**	**0**	**3.60**	**3.43**	**4.49**	**473**	**.875**	**28.8**	....	....	....	....	....	....	....	....	....	....	....	....
	Springfield Indians	AHL	23	9	10	2	1314	73	0	3.33	....	....	....	....	....	6	2	4	0	324	23	0	4.26	....	....	....	....
1994-95	Minnesota Moose	IHL	15	3	8	1	756	52	0	4.12	....	....	....	....	....	....	....	....	....	....	....	....	....	....	....	....	....
	NHL Totals		**141**	**46**	**59**	**6**	**7141**	**490**	**1**	**4.12**	....	....	**3845**	**.873**	....	**12**	**7**	**5**	....	**713**	**34**	**1**	**2.86**	....	....	....	....

Traded to **Hartford** by **Pittsburgh** for Hartford's 3rd (Sven Butenschon) and 7th (Serge Aubin) round choices in 1994 Entry Draft, March 10, 1992. Signed as a free agent by **NY Islanders**, July 28, 1994.

● PLANTE, JACQUES Jacques "Jake the Snake" Plante G – L. 6', 175 lbs. b: Shawinigan Falls, Que., 1/17/1929. d: 2/26/1986. **HHOF**

Season	Club	League	GP	W	L	T	Mins	GA	SO	Avg	AAvg	Eff	SA	S%	SAPG	GP	W	L	T	Mins	GA	SO	Avg	Eff	SA	S%	SAPG
1947-48	Quebec Citadelle	QJHL	31	18	11	1	1840	87	2	2.84	....	....	....	....	....	9	4	5	0	545	28	2	3.08	....	....	....	....
	Montreal Jr. Canadiens	QJHL	2	0	0	2	120	5	0	2.50	....	....	....	....	....	....	....	....	....	....	....	....	....	....	....	....	....
1948-49	Quebec Citadelle	QJHL	47	35	8	4	2860	95	8	1.99	....	....	....	....	....	13	7	6	0	790	43	0	3.27	....	....	....	....
1949-50	Montreal Royals	QSHL	58	27	22	9	3480	180	0	3.10	....	....	....	....	....	6	....	....	....	360	20	0	3.33	....	....	....	....
1950-51	Montreal Royals	QSHL	60	28	29	3	3670	201	4	3.29	....	....	....	....	....	7	2	5	0	420	26	1	3.71	....	....	....	....
1951-52	Montreal Royals	QSHL	60	30	24	6	3560	201	4	3.39	....	....	....	....	....	7	3	4	0	420	21	1	3.00	....	....	....	....
1952-53	Montreal Royals	QSHL	29	20	8	1	1760	61	4	2.08	....	....	....	....	....	....	....	....	....	....	....	....	....	....	....	....	....
	Montreal Canadiens	**NHL**	**3**	**2**	**0**	**1**	**180**	**4**	**0**	**1.33**	**1.71**	....	....	....	....	**4**	**3**	**1**	....	**240**	**7**	**1**	***1.75**	....	....	....	....
	Buffalo Bisons	AHL	33	13	19	1	2000	114	2	3.42	....	....	....	....	....	....	....	....	....	....	....	....	....	....	....	....	....
1953-54	Buffalo Bisons	AHL	55	32	17	6	3370	148	3	*2.64	....	....	....	....	....	....	....	....	....	....	....	....	....	....	....	....	....
	Montreal Canadiens	**NHL**	**17**	**7**	**5**	**5**	**1020**	**27**	**5**	**1.59**	**2.01**	....	....	....	....	**8**	**5**	**3**	....	**480**	**15**	***2**	**1.88**	....	....	....	....
1954-55	**Montreal Canadiens**	**NHL**	**52**	**31**	**13**	**7**	**3080**	**110**	**5**	**2.14**	**2.57**	....	....	....	....	***12**	**6**	**4**	....	**640**	**30**	**0**	**2.81**	....	....	....	....
1955-56	**Montreal Canadiens**	**NHL**	**64**	***42**	**12**	**10**	**3840**	**119**	**7**	***1.86**	**2.16**	....	....	....	....	***10**	***8**	**2**	....	**600**	**18**	***2**	***1.80**	....	....	....	....
1956-57	**Montreal Canadiens**	**NHL**	**61**	**31**	**18**	**12**	**3660**	**123**	***9**	***2.02**	**2.22**	....	....	....	....	***10**	***8**	**2**	....	***616**	**18**	**1**	***1.75**	....	....	....	....
1957-58	**Montreal Canadiens**	**NHL**	**57**	***34**	**14**	**8**	**3386**	**119**	***9**	***2.11**	**2.24**	....	....	....	....	**10**	***8**	**2**	....	**618**	**20**	***1**	***1.94**	....	....	....	....
1958-59	**Montreal Canadiens**	**NHL**	**67**	***38**	**16**	**13**	**4000**	**144**	***9**	***2.16**	**2.20**	....	....	....	....	**11**	***8**	**3**	....	**670**	**28**	**0**	***2.51**	....	....	....	....
1959-60	**Montreal Canadiens**	**NHL**	**69**	***40**	**17**	**12**	**4140**	**175**	**3**	***2.54**	**2.59**	....	....	....	....	**8**	***8**	**0**	....	**489**	**11**	***3**	***1.35**	....	....	....	....
1960-61	Montreal Royals	EPHL	8	3	4	1	480	24	0	3.00	....	....	....	....	....	....	....	....	....	....	....	....	....	....	....	....	....
	Montreal Canadiens	**NHL**	**40**	**22**	**11**	**7**	**2400**	**112**	**2**	**2.80**	**2.86**	....	....	....	....	**6**	**2**	**4**	....	**412**	**16**	**0**	**2.33**	....	....	....	....
1961-62	**Montreal Canadiens**	**NHL**	***70**	***42**	**14**	**14**	***4200**	**166**	**4**	***2.37**	**2.33**	....	....	....	....	**6**	**2**	**4**	....	**360**	**19**	**0**	**3.17**	....	....	....	....
1962-63	**Montreal Canadiens**	**NHL**	**56**	**22**	**14**	**19**	**3320**	**138**	***5**	***2.49**	**2.52**	....	....	....	....	**5**	**1**	**4**	....	**300**	**14**	**0**	**2.80**	....	....	....	....
1963-64	**New York Rangers**	**NHL**	**65**	**22**	**36**	**7**	**3900**	**220**	**3**	**3.38**	**3.91**	....	....	....	....	....	....	....	....	....	....	....	....	....	....	....	....
1964-65	**New York Rangers**	**NHL**	**33**	**10**	**17**	**5**	**1938**	**109**	**2**	**3.37**	**3.67**	....	....	....	....	....	....	....	....	....	....	....	....	....	....	....	....
	Baltimore Clippers	AHL	17	6	9	1	1018	51	1	3.01	....	....	....	....	....	5	2	3	0	315	14	1	2.67	....	....	....	....
1965-1968			DID NOT PLAY – RETIRED																								
1968-69	**St. Louis Blues**	**NHL**	**37**	**18**	**12**	**6**	**2139**	**70**	**5**	***1.96**	**2.00**	....	....	....	....	***10**	***8**	**2**	....	***589**	**14**	***3**	**1.43**	....	....	....	....
1969-70	**St. Louis Blues**	**NHL**	**32**	**18**	**9**	**5**	**1839**	**67**	**5**	**2.19**	**2.31**	....	....	....	....	**6**	**4**	**1**	....	**324**	**8**	***1**	***1.48**	....	....	....	....
1970-71	**Toronto Maple Leafs**	**NHL**	**40**	**24**	**11**	**4**	**2329**	**73**	**4**	***1.88**	**1.83**	....	....	....	....	**3**	**0**	**2**	....	**134**	**7**	**0**	**3.13**	....	....	....	....
1971-72	**Toronto Maple Leafs**	**NHL**	**34**	**16**	**13**	**5**	**1965**	**86**	**2**	**2.63**	**2.64**	....	....	....	....	**1**	**0**	**1**	....	**60**	**5**	**0**	**5.00**	....	....	....	....
1972-73	**Toronto Maple Leafs**	**NHL**	**32**	**8**	**14**	**6**	**1717**	**87**	**1**	**3.04**	**2.86**	....	....	....	....	....	....	....	....	....	....	....	....	....	....	....	....
	Boston Bruins	**NHL**	**8**	**7**	**1**	**0**	**480**	**16**	**2**	**2.00**	**1.88**	....	....	....	....	**2**	**0**	**2**	....	**120**	**10**	**0**	**5.00**	....	....	....	....
1973-74			DID NOT PLAY – RETIRED																								
1974-75	Edmonton Oilers	WHA	31	15	14	1	1592	88	1	3.32	....	....	....	....	....	....	....	....	....	....	....	....	....	....	....	....	....
	NHL Totals		**837**	**434**	**247**	**146**	**49533**	**1965**	**82**	**2.38**	....	....	....	....	....	**112**	**71**	**37**	....	**6652**	**240**	**14**	**2.16**	....	....	....	....
	Other Major League Totals		31	15	14	1	1592	88	1	3.32	0.00	0.00	....	....	0.0	....	....	....	....	....	....	....	....	....	....	....	....

Won Vezina Memorial Trophy (Top Goaltender - QHL) (1953) • NHL First All-Star Team (1956, 1959, 1962) • Won Vezina Trophy (1956, 1957, 1958, 1959, 1960, 1962) • NHL Second All-Star Team (1957, 1958, 1960, 1971) • Won Hart Trophy (1962) • Shared Vezina Trophy with Glenn Hall (1969)

Played in NHL All-Star Game (1956, 1957, 1958, 1959, 1960, 1962, 1969, 1970)

Traded to **NY Rangers** by **Montreal** with Don Marshall and Phil Goyette for Gump Worsley, Dave Balon, Leon Rochefort and Len Ronson, June 4, 1963. •Signed to training camp try-out contract by **California**, September, 1967. •Plante left camp after it was confirmed his rights were still property of NY Rangers, September, 1967. Claimed by **St. Louis** from **NY Rangers** in Intra-League Draft, June 12, 1968. Traded to **Toronto** by **St. Louis** for cash, May 18, 1970. Selected by **Miami-Philadelphia** (WHA) in 1972 WHA General Player Draft, February 12, 1972. Traded to **Boston** by **Toronto** with Toronto's 3rd round choice (Doug Gibson) in 1973 Amateur Draft for Boston's 1st round choice (Ian Turnbull) in 1973 Amateur Draft and future considerations (Ed Johnston, May 22, 1973), March 3, 1973. Selected by **Edmonton** (WHA) in 1973 WHA Professional Player Draft, June, 1973. • Served as General Manager of Quebec Nordiques (WHA) in 1973-74.

● PLASSE, MICHEL Michel Plasse G – L. 5'11", 172 lbs. b: Montreal, Que., 6/1/1948. Montreal's 1st choice, 1st overall, in 1968 Amateur Draft.

Season	Club	League	GP	W	L	T	Mins	GA	SO	Avg	AAvg	Eff	SA	S%	SAPG	GP	W	L	T	Mins	GA	SO	Avg	Eff	SA	S%	SAPG
1967-68	Drummondville Rangers	QJHL	30	....	....	....	1800	63	3	*2.10	....	....	....	....	....	....	....	....	....	....	....	....	....	....	....	....	....
1968-69	Cleveland Barons	AHL	7	2	4	0	320	27	0	5.06	....	....	....	....	....	....	....	....	....	....	....	....	....	....	....	....	....
1969-70	Jacksonville Rockets	EHL	61	....	....	....	3660	297	0	4.87	....	....	....	....	....	4	0	4	0	240	35	0	8.75	....	....	....	....
1970-71	**St. Louis Blues**	**NHL**	**1**	**1**	**0**	**0**	**60**	**3**	**0**	**3.00**	**2.97**	....	....	....	....	....	....	....	....	....	....	....	....	....	....	....	....
	Kansas City Blues	CHL	16	....	....	....	960	42	0	2.63	....	....	....	....	....	....	....	....	....	....	....	....	....	....	....	....	....
1971-72	Nova Scotia Voyageurs	AHL	36	17	13	4	2036	94	1	2.77	....	....	....	....	....	15	*12	3	0	912	19	*3	*1.25	....	....	....	....
1972-73	**Montreal Canadiens**	**NHL**	**17**	**11**	**2**	**3**	**932**	**40**	**0**	**2.58**	**2.42**	....	....	....	....	....	....	....	....	....	....	....	....	....	....	....	....
1973-74	**Montreal Canadiens**	**NHL**	**15**	**7**	**4**	**2**	**839**	**57**	**0**	**4.08**	**3.95**	....	....	....	....	....	....	....	....	....	....	....	....	....	....	....	....
1974-75	**Kansas City Scouts**	**NHL**	**24**	**4**	**16**	**3**	**1420**	**96**	**0**	**4.06**	**3.67**	....	....	....	....	....	....	....	....	....	....	....	....	....	....	....	....
	Pittsburgh Penguins	**NHL**	**20**	**9**	**5**	**4**	**1094**	**73**	**0**	**4.0....**	....	....	....	....	....	....	....	....	....	....	....	....	....	....	....	....	....
1975-76	Hershey Bears	AHL	5	0	4	0	2/8	25	0	5.40	....	....	....	....	....	....	....	....	....	....	....	....	....	....	....	....	....
	Pittsburgh Penguins	**NHL**	**55**	**24**	**19**	**10**	**3096**	**178**	**2**	**3.45**	**3.12**	....	....	....	....	**3**	**1**	**2**	....	**180**	**8**	**1**	**2.67**	....	....	....	....
1976-77	**Colorado Rockies**	**NHL**	**54**	**12**	**29**	**10**	**2986**	**190**	**0**	**3.82**	**3.57**	....	....	....	....	....	....	....	....	....	....	....	....	....	....	....	....
1977-78	**Colorado Rockies**	**NHL**	**25**	**3**	**12**	**8**	**1383**	**90**	**0**	**3.90**	**3.66**	....	....	....	....	....	....	....	....	....	....	....	....	....	....	....	....
	Hampton Gulls	AHL	2	0	1	1	124	5	0	2.42	....	....	....	....	....	....	....	....	....	....	....	....	....	....	....	....	....
1978-79	Philadelphia Firebirds	AHL	7	0	6	1	423	31	0	4.39	....	....	....	....	....	....	....	....	....	....	....	....	....	....	....	....	....
	Colorado Rockies	**NHL**	**41**	**9**	**29**	**2**	**2302**	**152**	**0**	**3.96**	**3.51**	....	....	....	....	....	....	....	....	....	....	....	....	....	....	....	....
1979-80	**Colorado Rockies**	**NHL**	**6**	**0**	**3**	**2**	**327**	**26**	**0**	**4.77**	**4.20**	....	....	....	....	....	....	....	....	....	....	....	....	....	....	....	....
	Fort Worth Texans	CHL	32	9	13	3	1632	113	0	4.15	....	....	....	....	....	*14	*8	5	0	*827	41	*1	2.97	....	....	....	....
1980-81	**Quebec Nordiques**	**NHL**	**33**	**10**	**14**	**9**	**1933**	**118**	**0**	**3.66**	**2.93**	....	....	....	....	**1**	**0**	**0**	....	**15**	**1**	**0**	**4.00**	....	....	....	....
1981-82	**Quebec Nordiques**	**NHL**	**8**	**2**	**3**	**1**	**388**	**35**	**0**	**5.41**	**4.17**	....	....	....	....	....	....	....	....	....	....	....	....	....	....	....	....
	Binghamton Whalers	AHL	8	3	3	1	444	32	0	4.32	....	....	....	....	....	....	....	....	....	....	....	....	....	....	....	....	....
	NHL Totals		**299**	**92**	**136**	**54**	**16760**	**1058**	**2**	**3.79**	....	....	....	....	....	**4**	**1**	**2**	....	**195**	**9**	**1**	**2.77**	....	....	....	....

• Scored a goal while with Kansas City (CHL), February 21, 1971.

Traded to **St. Louis** by **Montreal** for cash, December 11, 1970. Traded to **Montreal** by **St. Louis** for cash, August 23, 1971. Claimed by **Kansas City** from **Montreal** in Expansion Draft, June 12, 1974. Traded to **Pittsburgh** by **Kansas City** with Jean-Guy Lagace for Denis Herron, January 10, 1975. Acquired by **Colorado** from **Pittsburgh** with Simon Nolet as compensation for Pittsburgh's signing of free agent Denis Herron, August 7, 1976. Signed as a free agent by **Quebec**, September 14, 1980. Traded to **Hartford** by **Quebec** with Quebec's 4th round choice (Ron Chyzowski) in 1983 Entry Draft for John Garrett, January 12, 1982.

• PLAXTON, HUGH

Hugh Plaxton G – L. 5'10", 184 lbs. b: Barrie, Ont., 5/16/1904.

Season	Club	League	REGULAR SEASON GP	W	L	T	Mins	GA	SO	Avg	AAvg	Eff	SA	S%	SAPG	PLAYOFFS GP	W	L	T	Mins	GA	SO	Avg	Eff	SA	S%	SAPG
1932-33	**Montreal Maroons**	**NHL**	**1**	**0**	**1**	**0**	**57**	**5**	**0**	**5.26**	**7.15**	....	....	....	....	....	....	....	....	....	....	....	....	....	....	....	....
	NHL Totals		**1**	**0**	**1**	**0**	**57**	**5**	**0**	**5.26**	....	....	....	....	....	....	....	....	....	....	....	....	....	....	....	....	....

• **Montreal Maroons'** left winger replaced injured Flat Walsh in 1st period, November 22, 1932. (NY Americans 5, Montreal Maroons 2)

• POTVIN, FELIX

Felix "The Cat" Potvin G – L. 6', 190 lbs. b: Anjou, Que., 6/23/1971. Toronto's 2nd choice, 31st overall, in 1990 Entry Draft.

Season	Club	League	GP	W	L	T	Mins	GA	SO	Avg	AAvg	Eff	SA	S%	SAPG	GP	W	L	T	Mins	GA	SO	Avg	Eff	SA	S%	SAPG
1988-89	Chicoutimi Sagueneens	QMJHL	*65	25	31	1	*3489	271	*2	4.66	....	....	....	....	....	....	....	....	....	....	....	....	....	....	....	....	....
1989-90	Chicoutimi Sagueneens	QMJHL	*62	*31	26	2	*3478	231	*2	3.99	....	....	....	....	....	....	....	....	....	....	....	....	....	....	....	....	....
1990-91	Chicoutimi Sagueneens	QMJHL	54	33	15	4	3216	145	*6	*2.70	....	....	....	....	....	*16	*11	5	....	*992	46	0	*2.78	....	....	....	....
	Canada	WJC-A	2	....	....	....	80	3	....	2.25	....	....	....	....	....	....	....	....	....	....	....	....	....	....	....	....	....
1991-92	**Toronto Maple Leafs**	**NHL**	**4**	**0**	**2**	**1**	**210**	**8**	**0**	**2.29**	**2.03**	**1.53**	**120**	**.933**	**34.3**	....	....	....	....	....	....	....	....	....	....	....	....
	St. John's Maple Leafs	AHL	35	18	10	6	2070	101	2	2.93	....	....	....	....	....	11	7	4	....	642	41	0	3.83	....	....	....	....
1992-93	**Toronto Maple Leafs**	**NHL**	**48**	**25**	**15**	**7**	**2781**	**116**	**2**	***2.50**	**2.11**	**2.26**	**1286**	**.910**	**27.7**	***21**	**11**	**10**	....	***1308**	**62**	**1**	**2.84**	**2.77**	**636**	**.903**	**29.2**
	St. John's Maple Leafs	AHL	5	3	0	2	309	18	0	3.50	....	....	....	....	....	....	....	....	....	....	....	....	....	....	....	....	....
1993-94	**Toronto Maple Leafs**	**NHL**	**66**	**34**	**22**	**9**	**3883**	**187**	**3**	**2.89**	**2.74**	**2.69**	**2010**	**.907**	**31.1**	**18**	**9**	**9**	....	**1124**	**46**	**3**	**2.46**	**2.18**	**520**	**.912**	**27.8**
1994-95	**Toronto Maple Leafs**	**NHL**	**36**	**15**	**13**	**7**	**2144**	**104**	**0**	**2.91**	**3.01**	**2.70**	**1120**	**.907**	**31.3**	**7**	**3**	**4**	....	**424**	**20**	**1**	**2.83**	**2.24**	**253**	**.921**	**35.8**
1995-96	**Toronto Maple Leafs**	**NHL**	**69**	**30**	**26**	**11**	**4009**	**192**	**2**	**2.87**	**2.81**	**2.58**	**2135**	**.910**	**32.0**	**6**	**2**	**4**	....	**350**	**19**	**0**	**3.26**	**3.13**	**198**	**.904**	**33.9**
1996-97	**Toronto Maple Leafs**	**NHL**	***74**	**27**	**36**	**7**	***4271**	**224**	**0**	**3.15**	**3.34**	**2.89**	**2438**	**.908**	**34.2**	....	....	....	....	....	....	....	....	....	....	....	....
1997-98	**Toronto Maple Leafs**	**NHL**	**67**	**26**	**33**	**7**	**3864**	**176**	**5**	**2.73**	**3.20**	**2.55**	**1882**	**.906**	**29.2**	....	....	....	....	....	....	....	....	....	....	....	....
	Canada	WC-A	4	3	0	1	240	8	0	2.00	....	....	....	....	....	....	....	....	....	....	....	....	....	....	....	....	....
	NHL Totals		**364**	**157**	**147**	**49**	**21162**	**1007**	**12**	**2.86**	....	....	**10991**	**.908**	....	**52**	**25**	**27**	....	**3206**	**147**	**5**	**2.75**	....	....	....	....

QMJHL Second All-Star Team (1990) • QMJHL First All-Star Team (1991) • Canadian Major Junior Goaltender of the Year (1991) • Memorial Cup All-Star Team (1991) • Won Hap Emms Memorial Trophy (Memorial Cup Top Goaltender) (1991) • AHL First All-Star Team (1992) • Won Baz Bastien Memorial Trophy (Top Goaltender - AHL) (1992) • Won Dudley "Red" Garrett Memorial Trophy (Top Rookie - AHL) (1992) • NHL/Upper Deck All-Rookie Team (1993)

Played in NHL All-Star Game (1994, 1996)

• PRONOVOST, CLAUDE

Claude Pronovost G – L. 5'9", b: Shawinigan Falls, Ont., 7/22/1935.

Season	Club	League	GP	W	L	T	Mins	GA	SO	Avg	AAvg	Eff	SA	S%	SAPG	GP	W	L	T	Mins	GA	SO	Avg	Eff	SA	S%	SAPG
1952-53	Shawinigan Cataracts	QSHL	2	0	2	0	120	5	0	2.50	....	....	....	....	....	....	....	....	....	....	....	....	....	....	....	....	....
1953-54	Montreal Royals	QJHL	21	....	....	....	1260	80	1	3.81	....	....	....	....	....	....	....	....	....	....	....	....	....	....	....	....	....
	Kitchener Greenshirts	OHA	33	....	....	....	1980	122	2	3.70	....	....	....	....	....	....	....	....	....	....	....	....	....	....	....	....	....
1954-55	Montreal Jr. Canadiens	QJHL	46	24	21	1	2760	143	2	3.10	....	....	....	....	....	5	1	4	0	315	23	0	4.38	....	....	....	....
	Chicoutimi Sagueneens	QHL	3	1	2	0	180	10	0	3.33	....	....	....	....	....	....	....	....	....	....	....	....	....	....	....	....	....
1955-56	Montreal Royals	QHL	9	4	5	0	540	31	0	3.44	....	....	....	....	....	....	....	....	....	....	....	....	....	....	....	....	....
	Boston Bruins	**NHL**	**1**	**1**	**0**	**0**	**60**	**0**	**1**	**0.00**	**0.00**	....	....	....	....	....	....	....	....	....	....	....	....	....	....	....	....
	Chicoutimi Sagueneens	QHL	2	0	2	0	108	7	0	3.89	....	....	....	....	....	....	....	....	....	....	....	....	....	....	....	....	....
1956-57	Chicoutimi Sagueneens	QHL	1	1	0	0	60	1	0	1.00	....	....	....	....	....	....	....	....	....	....	....	....	....	....	....	....	....
	Montreal Royals	QHL	9	2	6	1	554	36	0	3.90	....	....	....	....	....	....	....	....	....	....	....	....	....	....	....	....	....
	Shawinigan Cataracts	QHL	11	4	7	0	662	37	1	3.35	....	....	....	....	....	....	....	....	....	....	....	....	....	....	....	....	....
	Edmonton Flyers	WHL	3	1	2	0	190	10	0	3.16	....	....	....	....	....	....	....	....	....	....	....	....	....	....	....	....	....
1957-58	Montreal Royals	QHL	16	6	9	1	960	66	1	4.13	....	....	....	....	....	1	1	0	0	46	1	0	1.30	....	....	....	....
	Shawinigan Cataracts	QHL	1	0	1	0	60	5	0	5.00	....	....	....	....	....	....	....	....	....	....	....	....	....	....	....	....	....
1958-59	Montreal Royals	QHL	37	18	14	5	2220	91	2	*2.46	....	....	....	....	....	6	*0	3	0	364	15	*1	*2.47	....	....	....	....
	Montreal Canadiens	**NHL**	**2**	**0**	**1**	**0**	**60**	**7**	**0**	**7.00**	**7.48**	....	....	....	....	....	....	....	....	....	....	....	....	....	....	....	....
1959-60	Calgary Stampeders	WHL	37	15	21	1	2220	125	0	3.37	....	....	....	....	....	....	....	....	....	....	....	....	....	....	....	....	....
1960-61	Montreal Royals	EPHL	27	....	....	....	1620	85	1	3.15	....	....	....	....	....	....	....	....	....	....	....	....	....	....	....	....	....
1961-62	North Bay Trappers	EPHL	4	1	3	0	240	16	0	4.00	....	....	....	....	....	....	....	....	....	....	....	....	....	....	....	....	....
1962-63	Hull-Ottawa Canadiens	EPHL	1	0	1	0	60	5	0	5.00	....	....	....	....	....	....	....	....	....	....	....	....	....	....	....	....	....
	NHL Totals		**3**	**1**	**1**	**0**	**120**	**7**	**1**	**3.50**	....	....	....	....	....	....	....	....	....	....	....	....	....	....	....	....	....

QHL First All-Star Team (1959) • Won Vezina Memorial Trophy (Top Goaltender - QHL) (1959)

Loaned to **Boston** by **Montreal Royals** (QHL) to replace John Henderson, January 14, 1956. (Boston 2, Montreal 0)

• PUPPA, DAREN

Daren Puppa G – R. 6'4", 205 lbs. b: Kirkland Lake, Ont., 3/23/1965. Buffalo's 6th choice, 76th overall, in 1983 Entry Draft.

Season	Club	League	GP	W	L	T	Mins	GA	SO	Avg	AAvg	Eff	SA	S%	SAPG	GP	W	L	T	Mins	GA	SO	Avg	Eff	SA	S%	SAPG
1982-83	Kirkland Lake Intermediates	NOHA	STATISTICS NOT AVAILABLE																								
1983-84	RPI Engineers	ECAC	32	24	6	0	1816	89	0	2.94	....	....	....	....	....	....	....	....	....	....	....	....	....	....	....	....	....
1984-85	RPI Engineers	ECAC	32	31	1	0	1830	78	0	2.56	....	....	....	....	....	....	....	....	....	....	....	....	....	....	....	....	....
1985-86	**Buffalo Sabres**	**NHL**	**7**	**3**	**4**	**0**	**401**	**21**	**1**	**3.14**	**2.44**	**3.58**	**184**	**.886**	**27.5**	....	....	....	....	....	....	....	....	....	....	....	....
	Rochester Americans	AHL	20	8	11	0	1092	79	0	4.34	....	....	....	....	....	....	....	....	....	....	....	....	....	....	....	....	....
1986-87	**Buffalo Sabres**	**NHL**	**3**	**0**	**2**	**1**	**185**	**13**	**0**	**4.22**	**3.55**	**6.86**	**80**	**.838**	**25.9**	....	....	....	....	....	....	....	....	....	....	....	....
	Rochester Americans	AHL	57	*33	14	0	3129	146	1	2.80	....	....	....	....	....	*16	*10	6	....	*944	48	*1	3.05	....	....	....	....
1987-88	**Buffalo Sabres**	**NHL**	**17**	**8**	**6**	**1**	**874**	**61**	**0**	**4.19**	**3.49**	**5.45**	**469**	**.870**	**32.2**	**3**	**1**	**1**	....	**142**	**11**	**0**	**4.65**	**7.63**	**67**	**.836**	**28.3**
	Rochester Americans	AHL	26	14	8	2	1415	65	2	2.76	....	....	....	....	....	2	0	1	....	108	5	0	2.78	....	....	....	....
1988-89	**Buffalo Sabres**	**NHL**	**37**	**17**	**10**	**6**	**1908**	**107**	**1**	**3.36**	**2.77**	**3.74**	**961**	**.889**	**30.2**	....	....	....	....	....	....	....	....	....	....	....	....
1989-90	**Buffalo Sabres**	**NHL**	**56**	***31**	**16**	**6**	**3241**	**156**	**1**	**2.89**	**2.40**	**2.80**	**1610**	**.903**	**29.8**	**6**	**2**	**4**	....	**370**	**15**	**0**	**2.43**	**1.90**	**192**	**.922**	**31.1**
1990-91	**Buffalo Sabres**	**NHL**	**38**	**15**	**11**	**6**	**2092**	**118**	**2**	**3.38**	**3.02**	**3.88**	**1029**	**.885**	**29.5**	**2**	**0**	**1**	....	**81**	**10**	**0**	**7.41**	**16.11**	**46**	**.783**	**34.1**
1991-92	**Buffalo Sabres**	**NHL**	**33**	**11**	**14**	**4**	**1757**	**114**	**0**	**3.89**	**3.46**	**4.76**	**932**	**.878**	**31.8**	....	....	....	....	....	....	....	....	....	....	....	....
	Rochester Americans	AHL	2	0	2	0	119	9	0	4.54	....	....	....	....	....	....	....	....	....	....	....	....	....	....	....	....	....
1992-93	**Buffalo Sabres**	**NHL**	**24**	**11**	**5**	**4**	**1306**	**78**	**0**	**3.58**	**3.05**	**3.96**	**706**	**.890**	**32.4**	....	....	....	....	....	....	....	....	....	....	....	....
	Toronto Maple Leafs	**NHL**	**8**	**6**	**2**	**0**	**479**	**18**	**2**	**2.25**	**1.91**	**1.75**	**232**	**.922**	**29.1**	**1**	**0**	**0**	....	**20**	**1**	**0**	**3.00**	**4.29**	**7**	**.857**	**21.0**
1993-94	**Tampa Bay Lightning**	**NHL**	**63**	**22**	**33**	**6**	**3653**	**165**	**4**	**2.71**	**2.57**	**2.73**	**1637**	**.899**	**26.9**	....	....	....	....	....	....	....	....	....	....	....	....
1994-95	**Tampa Bay Lightning**	**NHL**	**36**	**14**	**19**	**2**	**2013**	**90**	**1**	**2.68**	**2.76**	**2.55**	**946**	**.905**	**28.2**	....	....	....	....	....	....	....	....	....	....	....	....
1995-96	**Tampa Bay Lightning**	**NHL**	**57**	**29**	**16**	**9**	**3189**	**131**	**5**	**2.46**	**2.40**	**2.01**	**1605**	**.918**	**30.2**	**4**	**1**	**3**	....	**173**	**14**	**0**	**4.86**	**7.91**	**86**	**.837**	**29.8**
1996-97	**Tampa Bay Lightning**	**NHL**	**6**	**1**	**1**	**2**	**325**	**14**	**0**	**2.58**	**2.73**	**2.41**	**150**	**.907**	**27.7**	....	....	....	....	....	....	....	....	....	....	....	....
	Adirondack Red Wings	AHL	1	1	0	0	62	3	0	2.90	....	....	....	....	....	....	....	....	....	....	....	....	....	....	....	....	....
1997-98	**Tampa Bay Lightning**	**NHL**	**26**	**5**	**14**	**6**	**1456**	**66**	**0**	**2.72**	**3.18**	**2.72**	**660**	**.900**	**27.2**	....	....	....	....	....	....	....	....	....	....	....	....
	NHL Totals		**411**	**173**	**153**	**53**	**22879**	**1152**	**17**	**3.02**	....	....	**11201**	**.897**	....	**16**	**4**	**9**	....	**786**	**51**	**0**	**3.89**	....	....	....	....

AHL First All-Star Team (1987) • NHL Second All-Star Team (1990)

Played in NHL All-Star Game (1990)

Traded to **Toronto** by **Buffalo** with Dave Andreychuk and Buffalo's 1st round choice (Kenny Jonsson) in 1993 Entry Draft for Grant Fuhr and Toronto's 5th round choice (Kevin Popp) in 1995 Entry Draft, February 2, 1993. Claimed by **Florida** from **Toronto** in Expansion Draft, June 24, 1993. Claimed by **Tampa Bay** from **Florida** in Phase II of Expansion Draft, June 25, 1993.

• PUSEY, CHRIS

Chris Pusey G – L. 6', 180 lbs. b: Brantford, Ont., 6/30/1965. Detroit's 7th choice, 109th overall, in 1983 Entry Draft.

Season	Club	League	GP	W	L	T	Mins	GA	SO	Avg	AAvg	Eff	SA	S%	SAPG	GP	W	L	T	Mins	GA	SO	Avg	Eff	SA	S%	SAPG
1982-83	London Knights	OHL	1	0	1	0	60	7	0	7.00	....	....	....	....	....	....	....	....	....	....	....	....	....	....	....	....	....
	Brantford Alexanders	OHL	20	5	11	0	991	85	0	5.15	....	....	....	....	....	....	....	....	....	....	....	....	....	....	....	....	....
1983-84	Brantford Alexanders	OHL	50	26	18	2	2858	158	2	3.32	....	....	....	....	....	5	0	1	0	300	17	0	3.40	....	....	....	....
1984-85	Hamilton Steelhawks	OHL	49	17	19	2	2450	179	1	4.38	....	....	....	....	....	15	7	6	0	824	73	0	5.32	....	....	....	....
1985-86	**Detroit Red Wings**	**NHL**	**1**	**0**	**0**	**0**	**40**	**3**	**0**	**4.50**	**3.50**	**11.25**	**12**	**.750**	**18.0**	....	....	....	....	....	....	....	....	....	....	....	....
	Adirondack Red Wings	AHL	22	7	12	1	1171	76	1	3.89	....	....	....	....	....	1	0	0	0	27	4	0	8.89	....	....	....	....
1986-87	Adirondack Red Wings	AHL	11	4	5	0	617	40	0	3.89	....	....	....	....	....	....	....	....	....	....	....	....	....	....	....	....	....
	Indianapolis Checkers	IHL	6	1	4	0	330	36	0	6.55	....	....	....	....	....	....	....	....	....	....	....	....	....	....	....	....	....
	Carolina Thunderbirds	ACHL	4	....	....	....	238	20	0	5.04	....	....	....	....	....	....	....	....	....	....	....	....	....	....	....	....	....
1987-88	Dundas Real McCoys	OHA Sr.	STATISTICS NOT AVAILABLE																								
1988-89	Carolina Thunderbirds	ECHL	3	2	1	0	180	13	0	4.33	....	....	....	....	....	....	....	....	....	....	....	....	....	....	....	....	....
	Saint John Vitos	NBSHL	18	....	....	....	824	48	*1	*3.49	....	....	....	....	....	5	....	....	....	320	20	0	3.75	....	....	....	....

Season	Club	League	GP	W	L	T	Mins	GA	SO	Avg	AAvg	Eff	SA	S%	SAPG	GP	W	L	T	Mins	GA	SO	Avg	Eff	SA	S%	SAPG
			REGULAR SEASON													PLAYOFFS											
1989-90			STATISTICS NOT AVAILABLE																								
1990-91			DID NOT PLAY																								
1991-92	Brantford Smoke	ColHL	2	0	2	0	100	11	0	6.60	....	....	....	....	....	....	....	....	....	....	....	....	....	....	....	....	....
	NHL Totals		**1**	**0**	**0**	**0**	**40**	**3**	**0**	**4.50**	....	....	**12**	**.750**	....	....	....	....	....	....	....	....	....	....	....	....	....

OHL Second All-Star Team (1984)

• RACICOT, ANDRE

Andre "Red Light" Racicot G – L. 5'11", 165 lbs. b: Rouyn-Noranda, Que., 6/9/1969. Montreal's 6th choice, 83rd overall, in 1989 Entry Draft.

Season	Club	League	GP	W	L	T	Mins	GA	SO	Avg	AAvg	Eff	SA	S%	SAPG	GP	W	L	T	Mins	GA	SO	Avg	Eff	SA	S%	SAPG
1986-87	Longueuil Chevaliers	QMJHL	3	1	2	0	180	19	0	6.33	....	....	....	....	....	....	....	....	....	....	....	....	....	....	....	....	....
1987-88	Granby Bisons	QMJHL	30	15	11	1	1547	105	1	4.07	....	....	....	....	....	5	1	4	....	298	23	0	4.63	....	....	....	....
1988-89	Granby Bisons	QMJHL	54	22	24	3	2944	198	0	4.04	....	....	....	....	....	4	0	4	....	218	18	0	4.95	....	....	....	....
1989-90	**Montreal Canadiens**	**NHL**	**1**	**0**	**0**	**0**	**13**	**3**	**0**	**13.85**	**11.61**	**69.25**	**6**	**.500**	**27.7**	....	....	....	....	....	....	....	....	....	....	....	....
	Sherbrooke Canadiens	AHL	33	19	11	2	1948	97	1	2.99	....	....	....	....	....	5	0	4	....	227	18	0	4.76	....	....	....	....
1990-91	Montreal Canadiens	FrTour	2	....	....	....	56	5	....	5.35	....	....	....	....	....	....	....	....	....	....	....	....	....	....	....	....	....
	Montreal Canadiens	**NHL**	**21**	**7**	**9**	**2**	**975**	**52**	**1**	**3.20**	**2.86**	**3.47**	**479**	**.891**	**29.5**	**2**	**0**	**1**	....	**12**	**2**	**0**	**10.00**	**14.29**	**14**	**.857**	**70.0**
	Fredericton Canadiens	AHL	22	13	8	1	1252	60	1	2.88	....	....	....	....	....	....	....	....	....	....	....	....	....	....	....	....	....
1991-92	**Montreal Canadiens**	**NHL**	**9**	**0**	**3**	**3**	**436**	**23**	**0**	**3.17**	**2.81**	**3.33**	**219**	**.895**	**30.1**	**1**	**0**	**0**	....	**1**	**0**	**0**	**0.00**	**0.00**	**1**	**1.000**	**60.0**
	Fredericton Canadiens	AHL	28	14	8	5	1666	86	0	3.10	....	....	....	....	....	....	....	....	....	....	....	....	....	....	....	....	....
1992-93	**Montreal Canadiens**	**NHL**	**26**	**17**	**5**	**1**	**1433**	**81**	**1**	**3.39**	**2.88**	**4.03**	**682**	**.881**	**28.6**	**1**	**0**	**0**	....	**18**	**2**	**0**	**6.67**	**14.82**	**9**	**.778**	**30.0**
1993-94	**Montreal Canadiens**	**NHL**	**11**	**2**	**6**	**2**	**500**	**37**	**0**	**4.44**	**4.23**	**6.68**	**246**	**.850**	**29.5**	....	....	....	....	....	....	....	....	....	....	....	....
	Fredericton Canadiens	AHL	6	1	4	0	292	16	0	3.28	....	....	....	....	....	....	....	....	....	....	....	....	....	....	....	....	....
1994-95	Portland Pirates	AHL	19	10	7	0	1080	53	1	2.94	....	....	....	....	....	....	....	....	....	....	....	....	....	....	....	....	....
	Phoenix Roadrunners	IHL	3	1	0	0	132	8	0	3.62	....	....	....	....	....	2	0	0	....	20	0	0	0.00	....	....	....	....
1995-96	Albany River Rats	AHL	2	2	0	0	120	4	0	2.00	....	....	....	....	....	....	....	....	....	....	....	....	....	....	....	....	....
	Columbus Chill	ECHL	1	1	0	0	60	2	0	2.00	....	....	....	....	....	....	....	....	....	....	....	....	....	....	....	....	....
	Indianapolis Ice	IHL	11	3	6	0	547	43	0	4.71	....	....	....	....	....	....	....	....	....	....	....	....	....	....	....	....	....
	Peoria Rivermen	IHL	4	2	1	1	240	14	0	3.50	....	....	....	....	....	11	6	5	....	654	34	1	3.12	....	....	....	....
1996-97	Indianapolis Ice	IHL	2	1	0	1	120	3	1	1.50	....	....	....	....	....	....	....	....	....	....	....	....	....	....	....	....	....
	Kansas City Blades	IHL	6	1	4	0	273	21	0	4.60	....	....	....	....	....	....	....	....	....	....	....	....	....	....	....	....	....
	Las Vegas Thunder	IHL	13	6	5	1	759	40	1	3.16	....	....	....	....	....	....	....	....	....	....	....	....	....	....	....	....	....
1997-98	Monroe Moccasins	WPHL	31	16	12	2	1789	80	1	*2.68	....	....	....	....	....	....	....	....	....	....	....	....	....	....	....	....	....
	Basingstoke Bison	Britain	3	....	....	....	186	11	....	3.55	....	....	....	....	....	5	....	....	....	303	21	....	4.16	....	....	....	....
	NHL Totals		**68**	**26**	**23**	**8**	**3357**	**196**	**2**	**3.50**	....	....	**1632**	**.880**	....	**4**	**0**	**1**	....	**31**	**4**	**0**	**7.74**	....	....	....	....

QMJHL Second All-Star Team (1989) • Shared Harry "Hap" Holmes Trophy (fewest goals-against - AHL) with J.C. Bergeron (1990)

Signed as a free agent by **Los Angeles**, September 22, 1994. Signed as a free agent by **Chicago**, August 25, 1995.

• RACINE, BRUCE

Bruce Racine G – L. 6', 170 lbs. b: Cornwall, Ont., 8/9/1966. Pittsburgh's 3rd choice, 58th overall, in 1985 Entry Draft.

Season	Club	League	GP	W	L	T	Mins	GA	SO	Avg	AAvg	Eff	SA	S%	SAPG	GP	W	L	T	Mins	GA	SO	Avg	Eff	SA	S%	SAPG
1984-85	Northeastern University	H.E.	26	11	14	1	1615	103	1	3.83	....	....	....	....	....	....	....	....	....	....	....	....	....	....	....	....	....
1985-86	Northeastern University	H.E.	32	17	14	1	1920	147	0	4.56	....	....	....	....	....	....	....	....	....	....	....	....	....	....	....	....	....
1986-87	Northeastern University	H.E.	33	12	18	3	1966	133	0	4.06	....	....	....	....	....	....	....	....	....	....	....	....	....	....	....	....	....
1987-88	Northeastern University	H.E.	30	15	11	4	1808	108	1	3.58	....	....	....	....	....	....	....	....	....	....	....	....	....	....	....	....	....
1988-89	Muskegon Lumberjacks	IHL	51	*37	11	0	*3039	184	*3	3.63	....	....	....	....	....	5	4	1	....	300	15	0	3.00	....	....	....	....
1989-90	Muskegon Lumberjacks	IHL	49	29	15	4	2911	182	1	3.75	....	....	....	....	....	9	5	4	....	566	32	1	3.34	....	....	....	....
1990-91	Albany Choppers	IHL	29	7	18	1	1567	104	0	3.98	....	....	....	....	....	....	....	....	....	....	....	....	....	....	....	....	....
	Muskegon Lumberjacks	IHL	9	4	4	1	516	40	0	4.65	....	....	....	....	....	....	....	....	....	....	....	....	....	....	....	....	....
1991-92	Muskegon Lumberjacks	IHL	27	13	10	3	1559	91	1	3.50	....	....	....	....	....	1	0	1	....	60	6	0	6.00	....	....	....	....
1992-93	Cleveland Lumberjacks	IHL	35	13	16	6	1949	140	1	4.31	....	....	....	....	....	2	0	0	....	37	2	0	3.24	....	....	....	....
1993-94	St. John's Maple Leafs	AHL	37	20	9	2	1875	116	0	3.71	....	....	....	....	....	1	0	0	....	20	1	0	0.00	....	....	....	....
1994-95	St. John's Maple Leafs	AHL	27	11	10	4	1492	85	1	3.42	....	....	....	....	....	2	1	1	....	119	3	0	1.51	....	....	....	....
1995-96	**St. Louis Blues**	**NHL**	**11**	**0**	**3**	**0**	**230**	**12**	**0**	**3.13**	**3.07**	**3.72**	**101**	**.881**	**26.3**	**1**	**0**	**0**	....	**1**	**0**	**0**	**0.00**	**0.00**	**0**	**.00**	**0.0**
	Peoria Rivermen	IHL	22	11	10	1	1228	69	1	3.37	....	....	....	....	....	1	0	1	....	59	3	0	3.05	....	....	....	....
1996-97	San Antonio Dragons	IHL	44	25	14	2	2426	122	6	3.02	....	....	....	....	....	6	3	2	....	325	17	0	3.13	....	....	....	....
1997-98	San Antonio Dragons	IHL	15	4	9	1	836	51	0	3.66	....	....	....	....	....	....	....	....	....	....	....	....	....	....	....	....	....
	Fort Wayne Komets	IHL	45	30	10	4	2605	109	1	2.51	....	....	....	....	....	3	1	2	....	152	10	0	3.95	....	....	....	....
	NHL Totals		**11**	**0**	**3**	**0**	**230**	**12**	**0**	**3.13**	....	....	**101**	**.881**	....	**1**	**0**	**0**	....	**1**	**0**	**0**	**0.00**	....	....	....	....

Hockey East Second All-Star Team (1985) • Hockey East First All-Star Team (1987) • NCAA East First All-American Team (1987, 1988) • IHL First All-Star Team (1998)

Signed as a free agent by **Toronto**, August 11, 1993. Signed as a free agent by **St. Louis**, August 10, 1995.

• RAM, JAMIE

Jamie Ram G – L. 5'11", 175 lbs. b: Scarborough, Ont., 1/18/1971. NY Rangers' 9th choice, 213th overall, in 1991 Entry Draft.

Season	Club	League	GP	W	L	T	Mins	GA	SO	Avg	AAvg	Eff	SA	S%	SAPG	GP	W	L	T	Mins	GA	SO	Avg	Eff	SA	S%	SAPG
1990-91	Michigan Tech Huskies	WCHA	14	5	9	0	826	57	0	4.14	....	....	....	....	....	....	....	....	....	....	....	....	....	....	....	....	....
1991-92	Michigan Tech Huskies	WCHA	23	9	9	1	1144	83	0	4.35	....	....	....	....	....	....	....	....	....	....	....	....	....	....	....	....	....
1992-93	Michigan Tech Huskies	WCHA	*36	16	14	5	*2078	115	0	3.32	....	....	....	....	....	....	....	....	....	....	....	....	....	....	....	....	....
1993-94	Michigan Tech Huskies	WCHA	39	12	20	5	2192	117	*1	3.20	....	....	....	....	....	....	....	....	....	....	....	....	....	....	....	....	....
1994-95	Binghamton Rangers	AHL	26	12	10	2	1472	81	1	3.30	....	....	....	....	....	11	6	5	....	663	29	1	2.62	....	....	....	....
1995-96	**New York Rangers**	**NHL**	**1**	**0**	**0**	**0**	**27**	**0**	**0**	**0.00**	**0.00**	**0.00**	**9**	**1.000**	**20.0**	....	....	....	....	....	....	....	....	....	....	....	....
	Binghamton Rangers	AHL	40	18	16	3	2262	151	1	4.01	....	....	....	....	....	1	0	0	....	34	1	0	1.75	....	....	....	....
1996-97	Kentucky Thoroughblades	AHL	50	25	19	5	2937	161	4	3.29	....	....	....	....	....	1	0	1	....	60	3	0	3.00	....	....	....	....
1997-98	Kentucky Thoroughblades	AHL	44	17	18	5	2553	124	3	2.91	....	....	....	....	....	....	....	....	....	....	....	....	....	....	....	....	....
	Utah Grizzlies	IHL	7	3	4	0	398	24	0	3.61	....	....	....	....	....	1	0	1	....	59	3	0	3.04	....	....	....	....
	NHL Totals		**1**	**0**	**0**	**0**	**27**	**0**	**0**	**0.00**	....	....	**9**	**1.000**	....	....	....	....	....	....	....	....	....	....	....	....	....

WCHA First All-Star Team (1993, 1994) • NCAA West First All-American Team (1993, 1994)

Signed as a free agent by **San Jose**, August 19, 1997. Signed as a free agent by **Anaheim**, July 22, 1998.

• RANFORD, BILL

Bill Ranford G – L. 5'11", 185 lbs. b: Brandon, Man., 12/14/1966. Boston's 2nd choice, 52nd overall, in 1985 Entry Draft.

Season	Club	League	GP	W	L	T	Mins	GA	SO	Avg	AAvg	Eff	SA	S%	SAPG	GP	W	L	T	Mins	GA	SO	Avg	Eff	SA	S%	SAPG
1983-84	New Westminster Bruins	WHL	27	10	14	0	1450	130	0	5.38	....	....	....	....	....	1	0	0	....	27	2	0	4.44	....	....	....	....
1984-85	New Westminster Bruins	WHL	38	19	17	0	2034	142	0	4.19	....	....	....	....	....	7	2	3	....	309	26	0	5.05	....	....	....	....
1985-86	**Boston Bruins**	**NHL**	**4**	**3**	**1**	**0**	**240**	**10**	**0**	**2.50**	**1.94**	**2.36**	**106**	**.906**	**26.5**	**2**	**0**	**2**	....	**120**	**7**	**0**	**3.50**	**5.57**	**44**	**.841**	**22.0**
	New Westminster Bruins	WHL	53	17	29	1	2791	225	1	4.84	....	....	....	....	....	....	....	....	....	....	....	....	....	....	....	....	....
1986-87	**Boston Bruins**	**NHL**	**41**	**16**	**20**	**2**	**2234**	**124**	**3**	**3.33**	**2.79**	**3.63**	**1137**	**.891**	**30.5**	**2**	**0**	**2**	....	**123**	**8**	**0**	**3.90**	**5.67**	**55**	**.855**	**26.8**
	Moncton Golden Flames	AHL	3	3	0	0	180	6	0	2.00	....	....	....	....	....	....	....	....	....	....	....	....	....	....	....	....	....
1987-88	Maine Mariners	AHL	51	27	16	6	2856	165	1	3.47	....	....	....	....	....	....	....	....	....	....	....	....	....	....	....	....	....
	Edmonton Oilers	**NHL**	**6**	**3**	**0**	**2**	**325**	**16**	**0**	**2.95**	**2.45**	**2.97**	**159**	**.899**	**29.4**	....	....	....	....	....	....	....	....	....	....	....	....
1988-89	**Edmonton Oilers**	**NHL**	**29**	**15**	**8**	**2**	**1509**	**88**	**1**	**3.50**	**2.88**	**4.29**	**718**	**.877**	**28.5**	....	....	....	....	....	....	....	....	....	....	....	....
1989-90	**Edmonton Oilers**	**NHL**	**56**	**24**	**16**	**9**	**3107**	**165**	**1**	**3.19**	**2.66**	**3.60**	**1463**	**.887**	**28.3**	***22**	***16**	**6**	....	***1401**	**59**	**1**	**2.53**	**2.22**	**672**	**.912**	**28.8**
1990-91	**Edmonton Oilers**	**NHL**	**60**	**27**	**27**	**3**	**3415**	**182**	**0**	**3.20**	**2.85**	**3.42**	**1705**	**.893**	**30.0**	**3**	**1**	**2**	....	**135**	**8**	**0**	**3.56**	**3.65**	**78**	**.897**	**34.7**
1991-92	Canada	C Cup	8	6	0	2	480	14	....	2.00	....	....	....	....	....	....	....	....	....	....	....	....	....	....	....	....	....
	Edmonton Oilers	**NHL**	**67**	**27**	**26**	**10**	**3822**	**228**	**1**	**3.58**	**3.18**	**4.14**	**1971**	**.884**	**30.9**	**16**	**8**	**8**	....	**909**	**51**	***2**	**3.37**	**3.55**	**484**	**.895**	**31.9**
1992-93	**Edmonton Oilers**	**NHL**	**67**	**17**	**38**	**6**	**3753**	**240**	**1**	**3.84**	**3.27**	**4.46**	**2065**	**.884**	**33.0**	....	....	....	....	....	....	....	....	....	....	....	....
	Canada	WC-A	6	5	1	0	354	11	....	1.86	....	....	....	....	....	....	....	....	....	....	....	....	....	....	....	....	....
1993-94	**Edmonton Oilers**	**NHL**	**71**	**22**	**34**	**11**	**4070**	**236**	**1**	**3.48**	**3.32**	**3.53**	**2325**	**.898**	**34.3**	....	....	....	....	....	....	....	....	....	....	....	....
	Canada	WC-A	6	6	0	0	360	7	1	1.17	....	....	....	....	....	....	....	....	....	....	....	....	....	....	....	....	....
1994-95	**Edmonton Oilers**	**NHL**	**40**	**15**	**20**	**3**	**2203**	**133**	**2**	**3.62**	**3.77**	**4.25**	**1134**	**.883**	**30.9**	....	....	....	....	....	....	....	....	....	....	....	....
1995-96	**Edmonton Oilers**	**NHL**	**37**	**13**	**18**	**5**	**2015**	**128**	**1**	**3.81**	**3.75**	**4.76**	**1024**	**.875**	**30.5**	....	....	....	....	....	....	....	....	....	....	....	....
	Boston Bruins	**NHL**	**40**	**21**	**12**	**4**	**2307**	**109**	**1**	**2.83**	**2.77**	**2.99**	**1030**	**.894**	**26.8**	**4**	**1**	**3**	....	**239**	**16**	**0**	**4.02**	**5.74**	**112**	**.857**	**28.1**

			REGULAR SEASON														PLAYOFFS								
Season	Club	League	GP	W	L	T	Mins	GA	SO	Avg	AAvg	Eff	SA	S%	SAPG	GP	W	L	T	Mins	GA	SO	Avg	Eff	SA	S%	SAPG

1996-97	Canada	W Cup	DID NOT PLAY – SPARE GOALTENDER																								
	Boston Bruins	NHL	37	12	16	8	2147	125	2	3.49	3.71	3.96	1102	.887	30.8												
	Washington Capitals	NHL	18	8	7	2	1009	46	0	2.74	2.90	3.06	412	.888	24.5												
1997-98	Washington Capitals	NHL	22	7	12	2	1183	55	0	2.79	3.27	2.76	555	.901	28.1												
	NHL Totals		595	230	255	69	33339	1885	14	3.39			16906	.889		49	26	23		2927	149	3	3.05				

WHL West Second All-Star Team (1986) • Won Conn Smythe Trophy (1990) • Canada Cup All-Star Team (1991) • WC-A All-Star Team (1994) • Named Best Goaltender at WC-A (1994)
Played in NHL All-Star Game (1991)

Traded to **Edmonton** by **Boston** with Geoff Courtnall and future considerations for Andy Moog, March 8, 1988. Traded to **Boston** by **Edmonton** for Mariusz Czerkawski, Sean Brown and Boston's 1st round choice (Matthieu Descoteaux) in 1996 Entry Draft, January 11, 1996. Traded to **Washington** by **Boston** with Adam Oates and Rick Tocchet for Jim Carey, Anson Carter, Jason Allison and Washington's 3rd round choice (Lee Goren) in 1997 Entry Draft, March 1, 1997. Traded to **Tampa Bay** by **Washington** for Tampa Bay's 3rd round choice (Todd Hornung) in 1998 Entry Draft and 2nd round choice in 1999 Entry Draft, June 18, 1998.

● RAYMOND, ALAIN   Alain Raymond   G – L. 5'10", 180 lbs.   b: Rimouski, Que., 6/24/1965.   Washington's 7th choice, 224th overall, in 1983 Entry Draft.

1982-83	Hull Olympiques	QMJHL	17				809	80	0	5.93																	
	Trois-Rivières Draveurs	QMJHL	22				1176	124	0	6.33						2				120	12	0	6.00				
1983-84	Trois-Rivières Draveurs	QMJHL	53	18	25	0	2725	223	*2	4.91																	
1984-85	Trois-Rivières Draveurs	QMJHL	58	29	26	1	3295	220	*2	4.01						7	3	4	0	438	32	0	4.38				
1985-86	Canada	Nat-Team	46	25	18	3	2571	151	4	3.52																	
1986-87	Fort Wayne Komets	IHL	45	23	16	0	2433	134	1	*3.30						6	2	3	0	320	23	0	4.31				
1987-88	**Washington Capitals**	**NHL**	1	0	1	0	40	2	0	3.00	2.49	3.00	20	.900	30.0												
	Fort Wayne Komets	IHL	40	20	15	3	2271	142	2	3.75						2	0	1	0	67	7	0	6.27				
1988-89	Baltimore Skipjacks	AHL	41	14	22	2	2301	162	0	4.22																	
1989-90	Baltimore Skipjacks	AHL	11	4	5	2	612	34	0	3.33																	
	Hampton Roads Admirals	ECHL	31	17	12	1	2048	123	0	3.60						5	2	3	0	302	24	0	4.77				
1990-91	Peoria Rivermen	IHL	5	1	3	1	304	22	0	4.34																	
	Nashville Knights	ECHL	43	21	18	3	2508	189	1	4.52																	
1991-92	Peoria Rivermen	IHL	6	1	3	2	370	27	0	4.38																	
	NHL Totals		1	0	1	0	40	2	0	3.00				20	.900													

QMJHL First All-Star Team (1984) • QMJHL Second All-Star Team (1985) • Shared James Norris Memorial Trophy (fewest goals against - IHL) with Michel Dufour (1987) • ECHL First All-Star Team (1990)
Signed as a free agent by **St. Louis**, September 12, 1990.

● RAYNER, CHUCK   Chuck (Claude Earl) "Bonnie Prince Charlie" Rayner   G – L. 5'11", 190 lbs.   b: Sutherland, Sask., 8/11/1920.   HHOF

1937-38	Kenora Thistles	MJHL	22				1320	103	0	4.68																	
1938-39	Kenora Thistles	MJHL	22				1320	64	0	2.91																	
1939-40	Kenora Thistles	MJHL	24				1440	66	*1	2.75						9				540	18	0	*2.00				
1940-41	Springfield Indians	AHL	37	17	13	6	2280	87	*6	*2.29																	
	New York Americans	NHL	12	2	7	3	773	44	0	3.42	3.98																
1941-42	Brooklyn Americans	NHL	36	13	21	2	2230	129	1	3.47	3.49																
	Springfield Indians	AHL	1	1	0	0	60	3	0	3.00																	
1942-43	Victoria Navy	City Sr.	12				720	39	*1	*3.25						6	4	2	0	370	29	0	4.70				
1943-44	Victoria Navy	PCI IL	18				1080	52	*1	*2.89						2	1	1	0	130	6	0	2.77				
1944-45			MILITARY SERVICE																							
1945-46	New York Rangers	NHL	40	12	21	7	2377	149	1	3.76	3.54																
1946-47	New York Rangers	NHL	58	22	30	6	3480	177	*5	3.05	2.96																
1947-48	New York Rangers	NHL	12	4	7	0	691	42	0	3.65	3.88						6	2	4		360	17	0	2.83				
	New Haven Ramblers	AHL	15	7	6	2	900	40	0	2.67																	
1948-49	New York Rangers	NHL	58	16	31	11	3480	168	7	2.90	3.34																
1949-50	New York Rangers	NHL	69	28	30	11	4140	181	6	2.62	2.94						12	7	5		773	29	1	2.25				
1950-51	New York Rangers	NHL	66	19	28	19	3940	187	2	2.85	2.57																
1951-52	New York Rangers	NHL	53	18	25	10	3180	159	2	3.00	3.65																
1952-53	New York Rangers	NHL	20	4	8	0	1200	58	1	2.90	3.70																
1953-54	Saskatoon Quakers	WHL	68	31	28	9	4045	204	6	3.03						6	2	4	0	360	23	1	3.83				
1954-55	Nelson Maple Leafs	WIHL	2				120	4	0	2.00						1	1	0	0	60	2	0	2.00				
1955-56	Nelson Maple Leafs	WIHL	6				360	18	0	3.00																	
	NHL Totals		424	138	208	77	25491	1294	25	3.05						18	9	9		1135	46	1	2.43				

AHL Second All-Star Team (1941) • NHL Second All-Star Team (1949, 1950, 1951) • Won Hart Trophy (1950)
Played in NHL All-Star Game (1949, 1950, 1951)
Signed as a free agent by **NY Rangers** after **Brooklyn** franchise folded, 1945.

● REAUGH, DARYL   Daryl Reaugh   G – L. 5'8", 175 lbs.   b: Prince George, B.C., 2/13/1965.   Edmonton's 2nd choice, 42nd overall, in 1984 Entry Draft.

1983-84	Kamloops Jr. Oilers	WHL	55				2748	199	1	4.34						17	*14	3	0	972	57	0	*3.52				
1984-85	Kamloops Blazers	WHL	49	*36	8	1	2749	170	2	3.71						*14				*787	56	0	4.27				
	Edmonton Oilers	NHL	1	0	1	0	60	5	0	5.00	3.97	7.14	35	.857	35.0												
1985-86	Nova Scotia Oilers	AHL	38	15	18	4	2205	156	0	4.24																	
1986-87	Nova Scotia Oilers	AHL	46	19	22	0	2637	163	1	3.71						2	0	2	0	120	13	0	6.50				
1987-88	**Edmonton Oilers**	**NHL**	6	1	1	0	176	14	0	4.77	3.97	5.86	114	.877	38.9												
	Nova Scotia Oilers	AHL	8	2	5	0	443	33	0	4.47																	
	Milwaukee Admirals	IHL	9	0	8	0	493	44	0	5.35																	
1988-89	Cape Breton Oilers	AHL	13	3	10	0	778	72	0	5.55																	
	Karpat Oulu	Finland	13	7	5	1	756	46	2	3.65																	
1989-90	Binghamton Whalers	AHL	52	8	31	6	2375	192	0	4.21																	
1990-91	**Hartford Whalers**	**NHL**	20	7	7	1	1010	53	1	3.15	2.81	3.49	479	.889	28.5												
	Springfield Indians	AHL	16	7	6	3	912	55	0	3.62																	
1991-92	Springfield Indians	AHL	22	3	12	2	1005	63	0	3.76						1	0	0	0	39	1	0	1.54				
1992-93	Hershey Bears	AHL	1	0	0	0	22	1	0	2.73																	
1993-94	Dayton Bombers	ECHL	4	1	3	0	160	17	0	6.38																	
	NHL Totals		27	8	9	1	1246	72	1	3.47				628	.885													

WHL West First All-Star Team (1985)
Signed as a free agent by **Hartford**, October 9, 1989.

● REDDICK, POKEY   Pokey (Eldon) Reddick   G – L. 5'8", 170 lbs.   b: Halifax, N.S., 10/6/1964.

1982-83	Nanaimo Islanders	WHL	*66	19	38	1	*3549	383	0	6.46																	
1983-84	New Westminster Bruins	WHL	50	24	22	2	2930	215	0	4.40						9	4	5		542	53	0	5.87				
1984-85	Brandon Wheat Kings	WHL	47	14	30	1	2585	243	0	5.64																	
1985-86	Fort Wayne Komets	IHL	29	15	11	0	1674	86	*3	3.08																	
1986-87	**Winnipeg Jets**	**NHL**	48	21	21	4	2762	149	0	3.24	2.72	3.84	1256	.881	27.3	3	0	2		166	10	0	3.61	4.88	74	.865	26.7
1987-88	**Winnipeg Jets**	**NHL**	28	9	13	3	1487	102	0	4.12	3.43	5.90	712	.857	28.7												
	Moncton Hawks	AHL	9	2	6	1	545	26	0	2.86																	
1988-89	**Winnipeg Jets**	**NHL**	41	11	17	7	2109	144	0	4.10	3.39	5.22	1132	.873	32.2												
1989-90	**Edmonton Oilers**	**NHL**	11	5	4	2	604	31	0	3.08	2.50	3.37	283	.890	28.1	1	0	0	0	2	0	0	0.00	0.00	1	1.000	30.0
	Cape Breton Oilers	AHL	15	9	4	1	821	54	0	3.95																	
	Phoenix Roadrunners	IHL	3	2	1	0	185	7	0	2.27																	
1990-91	**Edmonton Oilers**	**NHL**	2	0	2	0	120	9	0	4.50	4.02	6.86	59	.847	29.5												
	Cape Breton Oilers	AHL	31	19	10	0	1673	97	2	3.48						2	0	2		124	10	0	4.84				
1991-92	Cape Breton Oilers	AHL	16	5	3	3	765	45	0	3.53						7	3	4		369	18	0	2.93				
	Fort Wayne Komets	IHL	14	6	5	2	787	40	1	3.05																	
1992-93	Fort Wayne Komets	IHL	54	33	16	4	3043	156	3	3.08						*12	*12	0		723	18	0	*1.49				

			REGULAR SEASON													PLAYOFFS											
Season	Club	League	GP	W	L	T	Mins	GA	SO	Avg	AAvg	Eff	SA	S%	SAPG	GP	W	L	T	Mins	GA	SO	Avg	Eff	SA	S%	SAPG
1993-94	**Florida Panthers**	**NHL**	2	0	1	0	80	8	0	6.00	5.71	10.67	45	.822	33.8	....	....	....	....	....	....	....	....	....	....	....	....
	Cincinnati Cyclones	IHL	54	31	12	6	2894	147	*2	3.05	....	....	....	....	....	10	6	2	....	498	21	*1	2.53	....	....	....	....
1994-95	Las Vegas Thunder	IHL	40	23	13	1	2075	104	*3	3.01	....	....	....	....	....	10	4	6	....	592	31	0	3.14	....	....	....	....
1995-96	Las Vegas Thunder	IHL	47	27	12	4	2636	129	1	2.94	....	....	....	....	....	15	8	6	....	770	43	0	3.35	....	....	....	....
1996-97	Grand Rapids Griffins	IHL	61	30	14	10	3244	134	6	2.48	....	....	....	....	....	5	2	3	....	335	13	0	2.32	....	....	....	....
1997-98	Grand Rapids Griffens	IHL	10	5	5	0	575	33	0	3.44	....	....	....	....	....	....	....	....	....	....	....	....	....	....	....	....	....
	San Antonio Dragons	IHL	16	5	9	1	861	45	1	3.13	....	....	....	....	....	....	....	....	....	....	....	....	....	....	....	....	....
	Kansas City Blades	IHL	22	10	7	3	1255	55	1	2.63	....	....	....	....	....	4	2	1	....	203	14	0	4.14	....	....	....	....
	NHL Totals		132	46	58	16	7162	443	0	3.71	....	....	3487	.873	....	4	0	2	....	168	10	0	3.57	....	....	....	....

Shared James Norris Memorial Trophy (fewest goals against - IHL) with Rick St. Croix (1986) • Won "Bud" Poile Trophy (Playoff MVP - IHL) (1993)

Signed as a free agent by **Winnipeg**, September 27, 1985. Traded to **Edmonton** by **Winnipeg** for future considerations, September 28, 1989. Signed as a free agent by **Florida**, July 12, 1993.

• REDDING, GEORGE
George Redding G – L. 5'7", 145 lbs. b: Peterborough, Ont., 3/6/1903. Deceased.

1924-25	**Boston Bruins**	**NHL**	1	0	0	0	11	1	0	5.45	6.74	....	....	....	....	....	....	....	....	....	....	....	....	....	....	....	....
	NHL Totals		1	0	0	0	11	1	0	5.45	....	....	....	....	....	....	....	....	....	....	....	....	....	....	....	....	....

• Boston defenseman replaced Hec Fowler, December 22, 1924. (Toronto 10, Boston 1)

• REDQUEST, GREG
Greg Redquest G – L. 5'10", 190 lbs. b: Toronto, Ont., 7/30/1956. Pittsburgh's 5th choice, 65th overall, in 1976 Amateur Draft.

1973-74	Hamilton Red Wings	OHA	64	....	....	....	1226	111	1	5.43	....	....	....	....	....	....	....	....	....	....	....	....	....	....	....	....	....
1974-75	Hamilton Fincups	OHA	32	....	....	....	1920	123	1	3.82	....	....	....	....	....	....	....	....	....	....	....	....	....	....	....	....	....
1975-76	Hamilton Fincups	OHA	1	0	1	0	60	5	0	5.00	....	....	....	....	....	....	....	....	....	....	....	....	....	....	....	....	....
	Oshawa Generals	OHA	55	....	....	....	3053	217	1	3.95	....	....	....	....	....	....	....	....	....	....	....	....	....	....	....	....	....
1976-77	Columbus Owls	IHL	31	....	....	....	1596	105	1	3.95	....	....	....	....	....	3	....	....	....	95	6	0	3.79	....	....	....	....
1977-78	**Pittsburgh Penguins**	**NHL**	1	0	0	0	13	3	0	13.85	12.97	....	....	....	....	....	....	....	....	....	....	....	....	....	....	....	....
	New Jersey Devils	City Sr.	STATISTICS NOT AVAILABLE																								
	Flint Generals	IHL	1	1	0	0	60	3	0	3.00	....	....	....	....	....	....	....	....	....	....	....	....	....	....	....	....	....
1978-79	Jersey - Hampton Aces	NEHL	22	....	....	....	1150	90	0	4.70	....	....	....	....	....	....	....	....	....	....	....	....	....	....	....	....	....
	NHL Totals		1	0	0	0	13	3	0	13.85	....	....	....	....	....	....	....	....	....	....	....	....	....	....	....	....	....

OHA Second All-Star Team (1976)

• REECE, DAVE
Dave Reece G – R. 6'1", 190 lbs. b: Troy, NY, 9/13/1948.

1968-69	University of Vermont	ECAC II	25	13	12	0	1500	84	3	3.36	....	....	....	....	....	....	....	....	....	....	....	....	....	....	....	....	....
1969-70	University of Vermont	ECAC II	24	16	8	0	1440	65	*4	*2.71	....	....	....	....	....	....	....	....	....	....	....	....	....	....	....	....	....
1970-71	University of Vermont	ECAC II	26	17	9	0	1560	75	3	2.88	....	....	....	....	....	....	....	....	....	....	....	....	....	....	....	....	....
1971-72			DID NOT PLAY – INJURED																								
1972-73	Boston Braves	AHL	41	....	....	....	2183	112	3	3.07	....	....	....	....	....	....	....	....	....	....	....	....	....	....	....	....	....
1973-74	Boston Braves	AHL	*57	18	28	11	*3241	189	1	3.49	....	....	....	....	....	....	....	....	....	....	....	....	....	....	....	....	....
1974-75	Rochester Americans	AHL	42	19	16	7	2478	121	1	2.92	....	....	....	....	....	11	6	5	0	680	34	0	3.00	....	....	....	....
1975-76	**Boston Bruins**	**NHL**	14	7	5	2	777	43	2	3.32	3.00	....	....	....	....	....	....	....	....	....	....	....	....	....	....	....	....
	Springfield Indians	AHL	20	13	7	0	1202	78	0	3.89	....	....	....	....	....	....	....	....	....	....	....	....	....	....	....	....	....
1976-77	Rochester Americans	AHL	32	....	....	....	1891	111	1	3.52	....	....	....	....	....	....	....	....	....	....	....	....	....	....	....	....	....
	Rhode Island Reds	AHL	11	....	....	....	634	51	0	4.82	....	....	....	....	....	....	....	....	....	....	....	....	....	....	....	....	....
	United States	WEC-A	5	....	....	....	299	16	0	3.21	....	....	....	....	....	....	....	....	....	....	....	....	....	....	....	....	....
	NHL Totals		14	7	5	2	777	43	2	3.32	....	....	....	....	....	....	....	....	....	....	....	....	....	....	....	....	....

NCAA (College Div.) East All-American Team (1970, 1971) • AHL Second All-Star Team (1975)

Signed as a free agent by **Boston** (Boston - AHL), November 24, 1972.

• REESE, JEFF
Jeff Reese G – L. 5'9", 180 lbs. b: Brantford, Ont., 3/24/1966. Toronto's 3rd choice, 67th overall, in 1984 Entry Draft.

1983-84	London Knights	OHL	43	18	19	1	2308	173	0	4.50	....	....	....	....	....	6	3	3	....	327	27	0	4.95	....	....	....	....
1984-85	London Knights	OHL	50	31	15	1	2878	186	1	3.88	....	....	....	....	....	8	5	2	....	440	20	1	2.73	....	....	....	....
1985-86	London Knights	OHL	*57	25	26	3	*3281	215	0	3.93	....	....	....	....	....	5	0	4	....	299	25	0	5.02	....	....	....	....
1986-87	Newmarket Saints	AHL	50	11	29	0	2822	193	1	4.10	....	....	....	....	....	....	....	....	....	....	....	....	....	....	....	....	....
1987-88	**Toronto Maple Leafs**	**NHL**	5	1	2	1	249	17	0	4.10	3.41	5.45	128	.867	30.8	....	....	....	....	....	....	....	....	....	....	....	....
	Newmarket Saints	AHL	28	10	14	3	1587	103	0	3.89	....	....	....	....	....	....	....	....	....	....	....	....	....	....	....	....	....
1988-89	**Toronto Maple Leafs**	**NHL**	10	2	6	1	486	40	0	4.94	4.08	6.91	286	.860	35.3	....	....	....	....	....	....	....	....	....	....	....	....
	Newmarket Saints	AHL	37	17	14	3	2072	132	0	3.82	....	....	....	....	....	....	....	....	....	....	....	....	....	....	....	....	....
1989-90	**Toronto Maple Leafs**	**NHL**	21	9	6	3	1101	81	0	4.41	3.70	5.67	630	.871	34.3	2	1	1	....	108	6	0	3.33	4.00	50	.880	27.8
	Newmarket Saints	AHL	7	3	2	2	431	29	0	4.04	....	....	....	....	....	....	....	....	....	....	....	....	....	....	....	....	....
1990-91	**Toronto Maple Leafs**	**NHL**	30	6	13	3	1430	92	1	3.86	3.45	5.11	695	.868	29.2	....	....	....	....	....	....	....	....	....	....	....	....
	Newmarket Saints	AHL	3	2	1	0	180	7	0	2.33	....	....	....	....	....	....	....	....	....	....	....	....	....	....	....	....	....
1991-92	**Toronto Maple Leafs**	**NHL**	8	1	5	1	413	20	1	2.91	2.58	2.77	210	.905	30.5	....	....	....	....	....	....	....	....	....	....	....	....
	Calgary Flames	**NHL**	12	3	2	2	587	37	0	3.78	3.35	4.82	290	.872	29.6	....	....	....	....	....	....	....	....	....	....	....	....
1992-93	**Calgary Flames**	**NHL**	26	14	4	1	1311	70	1	3.20	2.72	3.56	629	.889	28.8	4	1	3	....	209	17	0	4.88	9.12	91	.813	26.1
1993-94	**Calgary Flames**	**NHL**	1	0	0	0	13	1	0	4.62	4.40	9.24	5	.800	23.1	....	....	....	....	....	....	....	....	....	....	....	....
	Hartford Whalers	**NHL**	19	5	9	3	1086	56	1	3.09	2.94	3.30	524	.893	29.0	....	....	....	....	....	....	....	....	....	....	....	....
1994-95	**Hartford Whalers**	**NHL**	11	2	5	1	477	26	0	3.27	3.38	3.63	234	.889	29.4	....	....	....	....	....	....	....	....	....	....	....	....
1995-96	**Hartford Whalers**	**NHL**	7	2	3	0	275	14	1	3.05	3.00	2.51	170	.918	37.1	....	....	....	....	....	....	....	....	....	....	....	....
	Tampa Bay Lightning	**NHL**	19	7	7	1	994	54	0	3.26	3.20	3.79	464	.884	28.0	5	1	1	....	198	12	0	3.64	4.37	100	.880	30.3
1996-97	**New Jersey Devils**	**NHL**	3	0	2	0	139	13	0	5.61	5.94	11.22	65	.800	28.1	....	....	....	....	....	....	....	....	....	....	....	....
	Detroit Vipers	IHL	32	23	4	3	1763	55	4	*1.87	....	....	....	....	....	11	7	3	....	518	22	0	2.55	....	....	....	....
1997-98	Detroit Vipers	IHL	46	27	9	8	2570	95	4	2.22	....	....	....	....	....	*22	*13	9	....	*1276	52	*2	2.44	....	....	....	....
	NHL Totals		172	52	64	17	8561	521	5	3.65	....	....	4330	.880	....	11	3	5	....	515	35	0	4.08	....	....	....	....

IHL Second All-Star Team (1997, 1998) • Shared James Norris Memorial Trophy (fewest goals against - IHL) with Rich Parent (1997)

Traded to **Calgary** by **Toronto** with Craig Berube, Alexander Godynyuk, Gary Leeman and Michel Petit for Doug Gilmour, Jamie Macoun, Ric Nattress, Rick Wamsley and Kent Manderville, January 2, 1992. Traded to **Hartford** by **Calgary** for Dan Keczmer, November 19, 1993. Traded to **Tampa Bay** by **Hartford** for Tampa Bay's 9th round choice (Ashhat Rakhmatullin) in 1996 Entry Draft, December 1, 1995. Traded to **New Jersey** by **Tampa Bay** with Chicago's 2nd round choice (previously acquired, New Jersey selected Pierre Dagenais) in 1996 Entry Draft and Tampa Bay's 8th round choice (Jason Bertsch) in 1996 Entry Draft for Corey Schwab, June 22, 1996.

• RESCH, GLENN
Glenn "Chico" Resch G – L. 5'9", 165 lbs. b: Moose Jaw, Sask., 7/10/1948.

1967-68	Univ. of Minnesota-Duluth	WCHA	DID NOT PLAY – FRESHMAN																								
1968-69	Univ. of Minnesota-Duluth	WCHA	24	5	19	0	1424	117	0	4.93	....	....	....	....	....	....	....	....	....	....	....	....	....	....	....	....	....
1969-70	Univ. of Minnesota-Duluth	WCHA	25	12	12	1	1500	97	1	3.88	....	....	....	....	....	....	....	....	....	....	....	....	....	....	....	....	....
1970-71	Univ. of Minnesota-Duluth	WCHA	26	11	14	1	1518	107	0	4.23	....	....	....	....	....	....	....	....	....	....	....	....	....	....	....	....	....
1971-72	Muskegon Mohawks	IHL	59	....	....	....	3488	180	*4	*3.09	....	....	....	....	....	11	....	....	....	617	29	0	2.82	....	....	....	....
1972-73	New Haven Nighthawks	AHL	43	....	....	....	2408	166	0	4.13	....	....	....	....	....	....	....	....	....	....	....	....	....	....	....	....	....
1973-74	**New York Islanders**	**NHL**	2	1	1	0	120	6	0	3.00	2.90	....	....	....	....	....	....	....	....	....	....	....	....	....	....	....	....
	Fort Worth Wings	CHL	55	24	20	11	3300	175	2	3.18	....	....	....	....	....	5	1	4	0	300	21	0	3.60	....	....	....	....
1974-75	**New York Islanders**	**NHL**	25	12	7	5	1432	59	3	2.47	2.22	....	....	....	....	12	8	4	....	692	25	1	2.17	....	....	....	....
1975-76	**New York Islanders**	**NHL**	44	23	11	8	2546	88	7	2.07	1.85	....	....	....	....	7	3	3	....	357	18	0	3.03	....	....	....	....
1976-77	Canada	C Cup	DID NOT PLAY – SPARE GOALTENDER																								
	New York Islanders	**NHL**	46	26	13	6	2711	103	4	2.28	2.10	....	....	....	....	3	1	1	....	144	5	0	2.08	....	....	....	....
1977-78	**New York Islanders**	**NHL**	45	28	9	7	2637	112	3	2.55	2.37	....	....	....	....	7	3	4	....	388	15	0	2.32	....	....	....	....
1978-79	**New York Islanders**	**NHL**	43	26	7	10	2539	106	2	2.50	2.19	....	....	....	....	5	2	3	....	300	11	*1	2.20	....	....	....	....
1979-80	**New York Islanders**	**NHL**	45	23	14	6	2606	132	3	3.04	2.66	....	....	....	....	4	0	2	....	120	9	0	4.50	....	....	....	....
1980-81	**New York Islanders**	**NHL**	32	18	7	5	1817	93	*3	3.07	2.45	....	....	....	....	....	....	....	....	....	....	....	....	....	....	....	....
	Colorado Rockies	**NHL**	8	2	4	2	449	28	0	3.74	3.00	....	....	....	....	....	....	....	....	....	....	....	....	....	....	....	....
1981-82	**Colorado Rockies**	**NHL**	61	16	31	11	3424	230	0	4.03	3.11	....	....	....	....	....	....	....	....	....	....	....	....	....	....	....	....
	United States	WEC-A	4	0	4	0	239	21	....	5.27	....	....	....	....	....	....	....	....	....	....	....	....	....	....	....	....	....

			REGULAR SEASON													PLAYOFFS											
Season	Club	League	GP	W	L	T	Mins	GA	SO	Avg	AAvg	Eff	SA	S%	SAPG	GP	W	L	T	Mins	GA	SO	Avg	Eff	SA	S%	SAPG
1982-83	**New Jersey Devils**	**NHL**	**65**	**15**	**35**	**12**	**3650**	**242**	**0**	**3.98**	**3.18**	**4.98**	**1933**	**.875**	**31.8**	....	....	....	....	....	....	....	....	....	....	....	....
1983-84	**New Jersey Devils**	**NHL**	**51**	**9**	**31**	**3**	**2641**	**184**	**1**	**4.18**	**3.28**	**5.39**	**1426**	**.871**	**32.4**	....	....	....	....	....	....	....	....	....	....	....	....
1984-85	United States	C Cup	2	0	1	1	108	9	0	5.00	....	....	....	....	....	....	....	....	....	....	....	....	....	....	....	....	....
	New Jersey Devils	**NHL**	**51**	**15**	**27**	**5**	**2884**	**200**	**0**	**4.16**	**3.31**	**5.94**	**1401**	**.857**	**29.1**	....	....	....	....	....	....	....	....	....	....	....	....
1985-86	**New Jersey Devils**	**NHL**	**31**	**10**	**20**	**0**	**1769**	**126**	**0**	**4.27**	**3.33**	**6.08**	**885**	**.858**	**30.0**	....	....	....	....	....	....	....	....	....	....	....	....
	Philadelphia Flyers	**NHL**	**5**	**1**	**2**	**0**	**187**	**10**	**0**	**3.21**	**2.60**	**3.82**	**84**	**.881**	**27.0**	**1**	**0**	**0**	....	**7**	**1**	**0**	**8.57**	**85.70**	**1**	**.00**	**8.6**
1986-87	**Philadelphia Flyers**	**NHL**	**17**	**6**	**5**	**2**	**867**	**42**	**0**	**2.91**	**2.44**	**2.80**	**436**	**.904**	**30.2**	**2**	**0**	**0**	....	**36**	**1**	**0**	**1.67**	**1.39**	**12**	**.917**	**20.0**
	NHL Totals		**571**	**231**	**224**	**82**	**32279**	**1761**	**26**	**3.27**	....	....	....	....	....	**41**	**17**	**17**	....	**2044**	**85**	**2**	**2.50**	....	....	....	....

WCHA Second All-Star Team (1971) • IHL First All-Star Team (1972) • Won James Norris Memorial Trophy (fewest goals against - IHL) (1972) • Won Garry F. Longman Memorial Trophy (Top Rookie - IHL) (1972) • CHL First All-Star Team (1974) • Won Tommy Ivan Trophy (CHL's MVP) (1974) • NHL Second All-Star Team (1976, 1979) • Won Bill Masterton Trophy (1982)

Played in NHL All-Star Game (1976, 1977, 1984)

Traded to **NY Islanders** by **Montreal** with Denis Dejordy, Germain Gagnon, Tony Featherstone, Murray Anderson and Alex Campbell for cash, June 26, 1972. Traded to **Colorado** by **NY Islanders** with Steve Tambellini for Mike McEwen and Jari Kaarela, March 10, 1981. Transferred to **New Jersey** after **Colorado** franchise relocated, June 30, 1982. Traded to **Philadelphia** by **New Jersey** for Philadelphia's 3rd round choice (Marc Laniel) in 1986 Entry Draft, March 11, 1986.

• RHEAUME, HERB

Herb Rheaume G – L. 6′, 200 lbs. b: Mason, Que., 1/12/1900.

Season	Club	League	GP	W	L	T	Mins	GA	SO	Avg	AAvg	Eff	SA	S%	SAPG	GP	W	L	T	Mins	GA	SO	Avg	Eff	SA	S%	SAPG
1915-16	Ottawa Grand Trunk	City Sr.	3	2	1	0	180	9	1	3.00	....	....	....	....	....	....	....	....	....	....	....	....	....	....	....	....	....
1916-17	Ottawa Grand Trunk	City Sr.	8	2	5	1	480	22	1	2.75	....	....	....	....	....	....	....	....	....	....	....	....	....	....	....	....	....
1917-18	Hull Canadians	Ott-Sr.	4	0	4	0	240	11	0	2.75	....	....	....	....	....	....	....	....	....	....	....	....	....	....	....	....	....
1918-19	Hamilton Tigers	OHA Sr.	8	*6	2	0	480	35	0	4.38	....	....	....	....	....	6	3	3	0	370	19	0	3.08	....	....	....	....
1919-20	Hamilton Tigers	OHA Sr.	6	*5	1	0	360	17	0	*2.83	....	....	....	....	....	2	1	1	0	120	6	0	3.00	....	....	....	....
1920-21	Hamilton Tigers	OHA Sr.	9	3	6	0	540	39	0	4.33	....	....	....	....	....	....	....	....	....	....	....	....	....	....	....	....	....
1921-22	Boston Westminsters	USAHA	STATISTICS NOT AVAILABLE													....	....	....	....	....	....	....	....	....	....	....	....
1922-23	New Haven Westminsters	USAHA	STATISTICS NOT AVAILABLE																								
1923-24	Trois-Rivieres Renards	ECHA	2	1	1	0	120	1	1	0.50	....	....	....	....	....	....	....	....	....	....	....	....	....	....	....	....	....
1924-25	Quebec Sons of Ireland	ECHA	8	4	4	0	480	23	0	2.88	....	....	....	....	....	....	....	....	....	....	....	....	....	....	....	....	....
1925-26	**Montreal Canadiens**	**NHL**	**31**	**10**	**20**	**1**	**1889**	**92**	**0**	**2.92**	**4.06**	....	....	....	....	....	....	....	....	....	....	....	....	....	....	....	....
1926-27	Boston Tigers	Can-Am	32	14	15	3	1980	46	5	*1.39	....	....	....	....	....	....	....	....	....	....	....	....	....	....	....	....	....
1927-28	Boston Tigers	Can-Am	40	21	14	5	2500	71	6	1.70	....	....	....	....	....	2	2	0	0	120	4	0	2.00	....	....	....	....
1928-29	Boston Tigers	Can-Am	40	*21	15	4	2474	56	*11	1.36	....	....	....	....	....	4	4	0	0	240	*4	*1	*1.00	....	....	....	....
1929-30	Boston Tigers	Can-Am	40	17	18	5	2471	129	1	3.13	....	....	....	....	....	3	2	1	0	180	7	1	2.33	....	....	....	....
1930-31	St. Louis Flyers	AHA	34	10	21	3	2043	101	3	2.97	....	....	....	....	....	....	....	....	....	....	....	....	....	....	....	....	....
1931-32	St. Louis Flyers	AHA	35	13	14	8	2159	62	7	1.70	....	....	....	....	....	....	....	....	....	....	....	....	....	....	....	....	....
1932-33	Regina-Vancouver Maroons	WCHL	30	15	13	2	1800	102	0	3.40	....	....	....	....	....	2	0	1	0	120	8	0	4.00	....	....	....	....
1933-34	Portland Buckaroos	NWHL	34	....	....	....	2040	118	1	3.47	....	....	....	....	....	....	....	....	....	....	....	....	....	....	....	....	....
1934-35	Edmonton Eskimos	NWHL	21	....	....	....	1260	79	1	3.76	....	....	....	....	....	....	....	....	....	....	....	....	....	....	....	....	....
1935-36	Vancouver Lions	NWHL	10	....	....	....	600	22	2	2.22	....	....	....	....	....	7	*5	2	0	420	19	*1	2.71	....	....	....	....
	NHL Totals		**31**	**10**	**20**	**1**	**1889**	**92**	**0**	**2.92**	....	....	....	....	....	....	....	....	....	....	....	....	....	....	....	....	....

Signed as a free agent by **Montreal Canadiens**, December 13, 1925.

• RHODES, DAMIAN

Damian "Dusty" Rhodes G – L. 6′, 180 lbs. b: St. Paul, MN, 5/28/1969. Toronto's 6th choice, 112th overall, in 1987 Entry Draft.

Season	Club	League	GP	W	L	T	Mins	GA	SO	Avg	AAvg	Eff	SA	S%	SAPG	GP	W	L	T	Mins	GA	SO	Avg	Eff	SA	S%	SAPG
1986-87	Richfield-Minn High School	H.S.	19	....	....	....	673	51	1	4.55	....	....	....	....	....	....	....	....	....	....	....	....	....	....	....	....	....
1987-88	Michigan Tech Huskies	WCHA	29	16	10	1	1626	114	0	4.20	....	....	....	....	....	....	....	....	....	....	....	....	....	....	....	....	....
	United States	WJC-A	5	....	....	....	204	20	....	5.88	....	....	....	....	....	....	....	....	....	....	....	....	....	....	....	....	....
1988-89	Michigan Tech Huskies	WCHA	37	15	22	0	2216	163	0	4.41	....	....	....	....	....	....	....	....	....	....	....	....	....	....	....	....	....
1989-90	Michigan Tech Huskies	WCHA	25	6	17	0	1358	119	0	6.26	....	....	....	....	....	....	....	....	....	....	....	....	....	....	....	....	....
1990-91	**Toronto Maple Leafs**	**NHL**	**1**	**1**	**0**	**0**	**60**	**1**	**0**	**1.00**	**0.89**	**0.38**	**26**	**.962**	**26.0**	....	....	....	....	....	....	....	....	....	....	....	....
	Newmarket Saints	AHL	38	8	24	3	2154	144	1	4.01	....	....	....	....	....	....	....	....	....	....	....	....	....	....	....	....	....
	United States	WEC-A	DID NOT PLAY – SPARE GOALTENDER													....	....	....	....	....	....	....	....	....	....	....	....
1991-92	St. John's Maple Leafs	AHL	43	20	16	5	2454	148	0	3.62	....	....	....	....	....	6	4	1	....	331	16	0	2.90	....	....	....	....
1992-93	St. John's Maple Leafs	AHL	*52	27	16	8	*3074	184	1	3.59	....	....	....	....	....	9	4	5	....	538	37	0	4.13	....	....	....	....
1993-94	**Toronto Maple Leafs**	**NHL**	**22**	**9**	**7**	**3**	**1213**	**53**	**0**	**2.62**	**2.49**	**2.57**	**541**	**.902**	**26.0**	**1**	**0**	**0**	....	**1**	**0**	**0**	**0.00**	**0.00**	**0**	**.00**	**0.0**
1994-95	**Toronto Maple Leafs**	**NHL**	**13**	**6**	**6**	**1**	**760**	**34**	**0**	**2.68**	**2.77**	**2.26**	**404**	**.916**	**31.9**	....	....	....	....	....	....	....	....	....	....	....	....
1995-96	**Toronto Maple Leafs**	**NHL**	**11**	**4**	**5**	**1**	**624**	**29**	**0**	**2.79**	**2.74**	**2.69**	**301**	**.904**	**28.9**	....	....	....	....	....	....	....	....	....	....	....	....
	Ottawa Senators	**NHL**	**36**	**10**	**22**	**4**	**2123**	**98**	**2**	**2.77**	**2.71**	**2.61**	**1041**	**.906**	**29.4**	....	....	....	....	....	....	....	....	....	....	....	....
1996-97	**Ottawa Senators**	**NHL**	**50**	**14**	**20**	**14**	**2934**	**133**	**1**	**2.72**	**2.87**	**2.98**	**1213**	**.890**	**24.8**	....	....	....	....	....	....	....	....	....	....	....	....
1997-98	**Ottawa Senators**	**NHL**	**50**	**19**	**19**	**7**	**2743**	**107**	**5**	**2.34**	**2.73**	**2.18**	**1148**	**.907**	**25.1**	**10**	**5**	**5**	....	**590**	**21**	**0**	**2.14**	**1.90**	**236**	**.911**	**24.0**
	NHL Totals		**183**	**63**	**79**	**30**	**10457**	**455**	**8**	**2.61**	....	....	**4674**	**.903**	....	**11**	**5**	**5**	....	**591**	**21**	**0**	**2.13**	....	....	....	....

• Credited with scoring a goal while with Michigan Tech (WCHA), January 21, 1989.

• Played 10 seconds in playoff game vs. San Jose, May 6, 1994. Traded to **NY Islanders** by **Toronto** with Ken Belanger for future considerations, January 23, 1996. Traded to **Ottawa** by **NY Islanders** with Wade Redden for Don Beaupre, Martin Straka and Bryan Berard, January 23, 1996.

• RICCI, NICK

Nick Ricci G – L. 5′10″, 160 lbs. b: Niagara Falls, Ont., 6/3/1959. Pittsburgh's 4th choice, 94th overall, in 1979 Entry Draft.

Season	Club	League	GP	W	L	T	Mins	GA	SO	Avg	AAvg	Eff	SA	S%	SAPG	GP	W	L	T	Mins	GA	SO	Avg	Eff	SA	S%	SAPG
1978-79	Niagara Falls Flyers	OHA	52	....	....	....	3129	183	3	3.49	....	....	....	....	....	20	....	....	....	1172	54	1	2.66	....	....	....	....
1979-80	**Pittsburgh Penguins**	**NHL**	**4**	**2**	**2**	**0**	**240**	**14**	**0**	**3.50**	**3.08**	....	....	....	....	....	....	....	....	....	....	....	....	....	....	....	....
	Grand Rapids Owls	IHL	29	....	....	....	1585	113	1	4.28	....	....	....	....	....	....	....	....	....	....	....	....	....	....	....	....	....
1980-81	**Pittsburgh Penguins**	**NHL**	**9**	**4**	**5**	**0**	**540**	**35**	**0**	**3.89**	**3.12**	....	....	....	....	....	....	....	....	....	....	....	....	....	....	....	....
	Binghamton Whalers	AHL	8	2	4	0	359	34	0	5.68	....	....	....	....	....	....	....	....	....	....	....	....	....	....	....	....	....
1981-82	**Pittsburgh Penguins**	**NHL**	**3**	**0**	**3**	**0**	**160**	**14**	**0**	**5.25**	**4.05**	....	....	....	....	....	....	....	....	....	....	....	....	....	....	....	....
	Erie Blades	AHL	40	16	19	4	2254	175	0	4.66	....	....	....	....	....	....	....	....	....	....	....	....	....	....	....	....	....
1982-83	**Pittsburgh Penguins**	**NHL**	**3**	**1**	**2**	**0**	**147**	**16**	**0**	**6.53**	**5.22**	**13.57**	**77**	**.792**	**31.4**	....	....	....	....	....	....	....	....	....	....	....	....
	Baltimore Skipjacks	AHL	9	3	3	2	486	41	0	5.06	....	....	....	....	....	....	....	....	....	....	....	....	....	....	....	....	....
1983-84	St. Catharines Saints	AHL	15	3	4	1	597	47	0	4.72	....	....	....	....	....	....	....	....	....	....	....	....	....	....	....	....	....
	Muskegon Mohawks	IHL	13	1	11	1	764	59	0	4.63	....	....	....	....	....	....	....	....	....	....	....	....	....	....	....	....	....
1984-85	Peoria Rivermen	IHL	7	4	3	0	423	30	0	4.26	....	....	....	....	....	....	....	....	....	....	....	....	....	....	....	....	....
	NHL Totals		**19**	**7**	**12**	**0**	**1087**	**79**	**0**	**4.36**	....	....	....	....	....	....	....	....	....	....	....	....	....	....	....	....	....

Traded to **Toronto** by **Pittsburgh** with Pat Graham for Vincent Tremblay and Rocky Saganiuk, August 15, 1983.

• RICHARDSON, TERRY

Terry Richardson G – R. 6′1″, 190 lbs. b: Powell River, B.C., 5/7/1953. Detroit's 1st choice, 11th overall, in 1973 Amateur Draft.

Season	Club	League	GP	W	L	T	Mins	GA	SO	Avg	AAvg	Eff	SA	S%	SAPG	GP	W	L	T	Mins	GA	SO	Avg	Eff	SA	S%	SAPG
1971-72	New Westminster Bruins	WCJHL	49	....	....	....	2737	140	3	3.07	....	....	....	....	....	5	1	4	0	300	19	0	3.80	....	....	....	....
1972-73	New Westminster Bruins	WCJHL	*68	31	22	15	3800	239	0	3.77	....	....	....	....	....	5	....	....	....	300	32	0	6.40	....	....	....	....
1973-74	**Detroit Red Wings**	**NHL**	**9**	**1**	**4**	**0**	**315**	**28**	**0**	**5.33**	**5.16**	....	....	....	....	....	....	....	....	....	....	....	....	....	....	....	....
	Virginia Wings	AHL	14	5	7	2	744	44	0	3.54	....	....	....	....	....	....	....	....	....	....	....	....	....	....	....	....	....
	London Lions	Britain	14	....	....	....	710	37	0	3.12	....	....	....	....	....	....	....	....	....	....	....	....	....	....	....	....	....
1974-75	**Detroit Red Wings**	**NHL**	**4**	**1**	**2**	**0**	**202**	**23**	**0**	**6.83**	**6.17**	....	....	....	....	....	....	....	....	....	....	....	....	....	....	....	....
	Virginia Wings	AHL	30	10	13	3	1612	96	1	3.57	....	....	....	....	....	2	0	2	0	119	7	0	3.52	....	....	....	....
1975-76	Springfield Indians	AHL	20	6	10	1	1080	77	0	4.28	....	....	....	....	....	....	....	....	....	....	....	....	....	....	....	....	....
	Detroit Red Wings	**NHL**	**1**	**0**	**1**	**0**	**60**	**7**	**0**	**7.00**	**6.34**	....	....	....	....	....	....	....	....	....	....	....	....	....	....	....	....
	New Haven Nighthawks	AHL	4	1	2	1	243	14	0	3.46	....	....	....	....	....	2	0	2	0	126	6	0	2.86	....	....	....	....
1976-77	**Detroit Red Wings**	**NHL**	**5**	**1**	**3**	**0**	**269**	**18**	**0**	**4.01**	**3.73**	....	....	....	....	....	....	....	....	....	....	....	....	....	....	....	....
	Kalamazoo Wings	IHL	65	....	....	....	3612	218	0	3.62	....	....	....	....	....	10	5	5	0	585	30	0	3.08	....	....	....	....
1977-78	Kansas City Red Wings	CHL	*63	*27	32	2	*3766	199	1	3.17	....	....	....	....	....	....	....	....	....	....	....	....	....	....	....	....	....

			REGULAR SEASON													PLAYOFFS											
Season	**Club**	**League**	**GP**	**W**	**L**	**T**	**Mins**	**GA**	**SO**	**Avg**	**AAvg**	**Eff**	**SA**	**S%**	**SAPG**	**GP**	**W**	**L**	**T**	**Mins**	**GA**	**SO**	**Avg**	**Eff**	**SA**	**S%**	**SAPG**
1978-79	**St. Louis Blues**	**NHL**	**1**	**0**	**1**	**0**	**60**	**9**	**0**	**9.00**	**7.95**	....	....	....	....	....	....	....	....	....	....	....	....	....	....	....	....
	Salt Lake Golden Eagles	CHL	40	30	7	3	2422	102	*5	*2.53	....	....	....	....	....	7	....	....	....	398	21	0	3.17	....	....	....	....
1979-80	Springfield Indians	AHL	46	15	22	7	2661	162	0	3.65	....	....	....	....	....	....	....	....	....	....	....	....	....	....	....	....	....
	NHL Totals		**20**	**3**	**11**	**0**	**906**	**85**	**0**	**5.63**	....	....	....	....	....	....	....	....	....	....	....	....	....	....	....	....	....

IHL Second All-Star Team (1977) • Won James Norris Memorial Trophy (fewest goals against - IHL) (1977) • CHL Second All-Star Team (1978, 1979) • Shared Terry Sawchuk Trophy (fewest goals against - CHL) with Doug Grant (1979)

Signed as a free agent by **St. Louis**, July 26, 1978. Traded to **NY Islanders** by **St. Louis** with Barry Gibbs for future considerations, June 9, 1979. Traded to **Hartford** by **NY Islanders** for Ralph Klassen, June 14, 1979.

• RICHTER, MIKE

Mike Richter G – L. 5'11", 187 lbs. b: Abington, PA, 9/22/1966. NY Rangers' 2nd choice, 28th overall, in 1985 Entry Draft.

Season	Club	League	GP	W	L	T	Mins	GA	SO	Avg	AAvg	Eff	SA	S%	SAPG	GP	W	L	T	Mins	GA	SO	Avg	Eff	SA	S%	SAPG
1984-85	Northwood Prep High School	H.S.	STATISTICS NOT AVAILABLE																								
	United States	WJC-A	3	....	....	....	43	6	0	8.37	....	....	....	....	....	....	....	....	....	....	....	....	....	....	....	....	....
1985-86	University of Wisconsin	WCHA	24	14	9	0	1394	92	1	3.96	....	....	....	....	....	....	....	....	....	....	....	....	....	....	....	....	....
	United States	WJC-A	4	....	....	....	208	9	....	2.60	....	....	....	....	....	....	....	....	....	....	....	....	....	....	....	....	....
	United States	WEC-A	1	0	0	0	53	5	0	5.66	....	....	....	....	....	....	....	....	....	....	....	....	....	....	....	....	....
1986-87	University of Wisconsin	WCHA	36	19	16	1	2136	126	0	3.54	....	....	....	....	....	....	....	....	....	....	....	....	....	....	....	....	....
	United States	WEC-A	2	0	2	0	80	8	0	6.00	....	....	....	....	....	....	....	....	....	....	....	....	....	....	....	....	....
1987-88	United States	Nat-Team	29	17	7	2	1559	86	0	3.31	....	....	....	....	....	....	....	....	....	....	....	....	....	....	....	....	....
	United States	Olympics	4	....	....	....	230	15	....	3.91	....	....	....	....	....	....	....	....	....	....	....	....	....	....	....	....	....
	Colorado Rangers	IHL	22	16	5	0	1298	68	1	3.14	....	....	....	....	....	10	5	3	....	536	35	0	3.92	....	....	....	....
1988-89	Denver Rangers	IHL	*57	23	26	0	3031	217	1	4.30	....	....	....	....	....	4	0	4	....	210	21	0	6.00	....	....	....	....
	New York Rangers	**NHL**	....	....	....	....	....	....	....	....	....	....	....	....	....	**1**	**0**	**1**	....	**58**	**4**	**0**	**4.14**	**5.52**	**30**	**.867**	**31.0**
1989-90	**New York Rangers**	**NHL**	**23**	**12**	**5**	**5**	**1320**	**66**	**0**	**3.00**	**2.51**	**2.89**	**686**	**.904**	**31.2**	**6**	**3**	**2**	....	**330**	**19**	**0**	**3.45**	**3.60**	**182**	**.896**	**33.1**
	Flint Spirits	IHL	13	7	4	2	782	49	0	3.76	....	....	....	....	....	....	....	....	....	....	....	....	....	....	....	....	....
1990-91	**New York Rangers**	**NHL**	**45**	**21**	**13**	**7**	**2596**	**135**	**0**	**3.12**	**2.78**	**3.03**	**1392**	**.903**	**32.2**	**6**	**2**	**4**	....	**313**	**14**	***1**	**2.68**	**2.06**	**182**	**.923**	**34.9**
1991-92	United States	C Cup	7	4	3	0	420	22	....	3.00	....	....	....	....	....	....	....	....	....	....	....	....	....	....	....	....	....
	New York Rangers	**NHL**	**41**	**23**	**12**	**2**	**2298**	**119**	**3**	**3.11**	**2.75**	**3.07**	**1205**	**.901**	**31.5**	**7**	**4**	**2**	....	**412**	**24**	**1**	**3.50**	**3.72**	**226**	**.894**	**32.9**
1992-93	**New York Rangers**	**NHL**	**38**	**13**	**19**	**3**	**2105**	**134**	**1**	**3.82**	**3.25**	**4.34**	**1180**	**.886**	**33.6**	....	....	....	....	....	....	....	....	....	....	....	....
	Binghamton Rangers	AHL	5	4	0	1	305	6	0	1.18	....	....	....	....	....	....	....	....	....	....	....	....	....	....	....	....	....
	United States	WC-A	4	1	1	2	237	13	....	3.29	....	....	....	....	....	....	....	....	....	....	....	....	....	....	....	....	....
1993-94	**New York Rangers**	**NHL**	**68**	***42**	**12**	**6**	**3710**	**159**	**5**	**2.57**	**2.43**	**2.32**	**1758**	**.910**	**28.4**	**23**	***16**	**7**	....	**1417**	**49**	***4**	**2.07**	**1.63**	**623**	**.921**	**26.4**
1994-95	**New York Rangers**	**NHL**	**35**	**14**	**17**	**2**	**1993**	**97**	**2**	**2.92**	**3.02**	**3.20**	**884**	**.890**	**26.6**	**7**	**2**	**5**	....	**384**	**23**	**0**	**3.59**	**4.37**	**189**	**.878**	**29.5**
1995-96	**New York Rangers**	**NHL**	**41**	**24**	**13**	**3**	**2396**	**107**	**3**	**2.68**	**2.62**	**2.35**	**1221**	**.912**	**30.6**	**11**	**5**	**6**	....	**661**	**36**	**0**	**3.27**	**3.82**	**308**	**.883**	**28.0**
1996-97	United States	W Cup	6	4	2	0	370	15	....	2.00	....	....	....	....	....	....	....	....	....	....	....	....	....	....	....	....	....
	New York Rangers	**NHL**	**61**	**33**	**22**	**6**	**3598**	**161**	**4**	**2.68**	**2.83**	**2.22**	**1945**	**.917**	**32.4**	**15**	**9**	**6**	....	**939**	**33**	***3**	**2.11**	**1.43**	**488**	**.932**	**31.2**
1997-98	**New York Rangers**	**NHL**	***72**	**21**	**31**	**15**	**4143**	**184**	**0**	**2.66**	**3.11**	**2.59**	**1888**	**.903**	**27.3**	....	....	....	....	....	....	....	....	....	....	....	....
	United States	Olympics	4	1	3	0	237	14	0	3.55	....	....	....	....	....	....	....	....	....	....	....	....	....	....	....	....	....
	NHL Totals		**424**	**203**	**144**	**49**	**24159**	**1162**	**18**	**2.89**	....	....	**12159**	**.904**	....	**76**	**41**	**33**	....	**4514**	**202**	**9**	**2.68**	....	....	....	....

WCHA Second All-Star Team (1987) • World Cup All-Star Team (1996) • Named World Cup MVP (1996)

Played in NHL All-Star Game (1992, 1994)

Claimed by **Nashville** from **NY Rangers** in Expansion Draft, June 26, 1998.

• RIDLEY, CURT

Curt Ridley G – L. 6', 190 lbs. b: Minnedosa, Man., 9/24/1951. Boston's 3rd choice, 28th overall, in 1971 Amateur Draft.

Season	Club	League	GP	W	L	T	Mins	GA	SO	Avg	AAvg	Eff	SA	S%	SAPG	GP	W	L	T	Mins	GA	SO	Avg	Eff	SA	S%	SAPG
1969-70	Portage Terriers	MJHL	23	....	....	....	....	90	0	3.86	....	....	....	....	....	....	....	....	....	....	....	....	....	....	....	....	....
1970-71	Portage Terriers	MJHL	45	....	....	....	2685	148	*5	*3.31	....	....	....	....	....	....	....	....	....	....	....	....	....	....	....	....	....
	Brandon Wheat Kings	WCJHL	5	....	....	....	299	14	0	2.81	....	....	....	....	....	....	....	....	....	....	....	....	....	....	....	....	....
1971-72	Oklahoma City Blazers	CHL	41	12	18	4	1869	127	1	4.07	....	....	....	....	....	1	0	1	0	42	5	0	7.14	....	....	....	....
1972-73	Dayton Gems	IHL	56	....	....	....	3217	145	2	*2.70	....	....	....	....	....	6	3	3	0	360	19	0	3.17	....	....	....	....
	Boston Braves	AHL	....	....	....	....	....	....	....	....	....	....	....	....	....	4	0	3	0	192	17	0	5.31	....	....	....	....
1973-74	Providence Reds	AHL	39	19	11	6	2234	107	1	2.87	....	....	....	....	....	1	1	0	0	60	4	0	4.00	....	....	....	....
1974-75	**New York Rangers**	**NHL**	**2**	**1**	**1**	**0**	**81**	**7**	**0**	**5.19**	**4.68**	....	....	....	....	....	....	....	....	....	....	....	....	....	....	....	....
	Providence Reds	AHL	*57	*32	14	9	*3311	181	1	3.27	....	....	....	....	....	6	2	4	0	373	24	0	3.86	....	....	....	....
1975-76	Tulsa Oilers	CHL	30	15	10	5	1779	79	2	*2.66	....	....	....	....	....	....	....	....	....	....	....	....	....	....	....	....	....
	Vancouver Canucks	**NHL**	**9**	**6**	**0**	**2**	**500**	**19**	**1**	**2.28**	**2.06**	....	....	....	....	**2**	**0**	**2**	....	**120**	**8**	**0**	**4.00**	....	....	....	....
1976-77	**Vancouver Canucks**	**NHL**	**37**	**8**	**21**	**4**	**2074**	**134**	**0**	**3.88**	**3.62**	....	....	....	....	....	....	....	....	....	....	....	....	....	....	....	....
1977-78	**Vancouver Canucks**	**NHL**	**40**	**9**	**17**	**8**	**2010**	**136**	**0**	**4.06**	**3.82**	....	....	....	....	....	....	....	....	....	....	....	....	....	....	....	....
1978-79	Dallas Black Hawks	CHL	33	22	10	0	1871	115	1	3.69	....	....	....	....	....	*9	*8	1	0	*520	26	0	*3.00	....	....	....	....
1979-80	**Vancouver Canucks**	**NHL**	**10**	**2**	**6**	**2**	**599**	**39**	**0**	**3.91**	**3.44**	....	....	....	....	....	....	....	....	....	....	....	....	....	....	....	....
	Toronto Maple Leafs	**NHL**	**3**	**0**	**1**	**0**	**110**	**8**	**0**	**4.36**	**3.83**	....	....	....	....	....	....	....	....	....	....	....	....	....	....	....	....
	Dallas Black Hawks	CHL	4	0	4	0	218	21	0	5.78	....	....	....	....	....	....	....	....	....	....	....	....	....	....	....	....	....
1980-81	**Toronto Maple Leafs**	**NHL**	**3**	**1**	**1**	**0**	**124**	**12**	**0**	**5.81**	**4.66**	....	....	....	....	....	....	....	....	....	....	....	....	....	....	....	....
	New Brunswick Hawks	AHL	2	1	1	0	120	7	0	3.50	....	....	....	....	....	....	....	....	....	....	....	....	....	....	....	....	....
1981-82	Cincinnati Tigers	CHL	22	10	6	1	1043	73	0	4.20	....	....	....	....	....	1	0	1	0	63	3	0	2.86	....	....	....	....
	NHL Totals		**104**	**27**	**47**	**16**	**5498**	**355**	**1**	**3.87**	....	....	....	....	....	**2**	**0**	**2**	....	**120**	**8**	**0**	**4.00**	....	....	....	....

Won Terry Sawchuk Trophy (fewest goals against - CHL) (1976)

Claimed by **NY Rangers** (Providence - AHL) from **Boston** in Reverse Draft, June 13, 1973. Traded to **Atlanta** by **NY Rangers** for Jerry Byers, September 9, 1975. Traded to **Vancouver** by **Atlanta** for Vancouver's 1st round choice (Dave Shand) in 1976 Amateur Draft, January 20, 1976. Traded to **Toronto** by **Vancouver** for cash, February 10, 1980.

• RIENDEAU, VINCENT

Vincent Riendeau G – L. 5'10", 185 lbs. b: St. Hyacinthe, Que., 4/20/1966.

Season	Club	League	GP	W	L	T	Mins	GA	SO	Avg	AAvg	Eff	SA	S%	SAPG	GP	W	L	T	Mins	GA	SO	Avg	Eff	SA	S%	SAPG
1985-86	Drummondville Voltigeurs	QMJHL	57	33	20	3	3336	215	2	3.87	....	....	....	....	....	23	10	13	....	1271	106	1	5.00	....	....	....	....
1986-87	Sherbrooke Canadiens	AHL	41	25	14	0	2363	114	2	2.89	....	....	....	....	....	13	8	5	....	742	47	0	3.80	....	....	....	....
1987-88	**Montreal Canadiens**	**NHL**	**1**	**0**	**0**	**0**	**36**	**5**	**0**	**8.33**	**6.93**	**18.93**	**22**	**.773**	**36.7**	....	....	....	....	....	....	....	....	....	....	....	....
	Sherbrooke Canadiens	AHL	44	27	13	3	2521	112	*4	*2.67	....	....	....	....	....	2	0	2	....	127	7	0	3.31	....	....	....	....
1988-89	**St. Louis Blues**	**NHL**	**32**	**11**	**15**	**5**	**1842**	**108**	**0**	**3.52**	**2.90**	**4.55**	**836**	**.871**	**27.2**	....	....	....	....	....	....	....	....	....	....	....	....
1989-90	**St. Louis Blues**	**NHL**	**43**	**17**	**19**	**5**	**2551**	**149**	**1**	**3.50**	**2.93**	**4.10**	**1271**	**.883**	**29.9**	**8**	**3**	**4**	....	**397**	**24**	**0**	**3.63**	**3.91**	**223**	**.892**	**33.7**
1990-91	**St. Louis Blues**	**NHL**	**44**	**29**	**9**	**6**	**2671**	**134**	**3**	**3.01**	**2.68**	**3.25**	**1241**	**.892**	**27.9**	**13**	**6**	**7**	....	**687**	**35**	***1**	**3.06**	**3.64**	**294**	**.881**	**25.7**
1991-92	**St. Louis Blues**	**NHL**	**3**	**1**	**2**	**0**	**157**	**11**	**0**	**4.20**	**3.73**	**4.81**	**96**	**.885**	**36.7**	....	....	....	....	....	....	....	....	....	....	....	....
	Detroit Red Wings	**NHL**	**2**	**2**	**0**	**0**	**87**	**2**	**0**	**1.38**	**1.22**	**0.89**	**31**	**.935**	**21.4**	**2**	**1**	**0**	....	**73**	**4**	**0**	**3.29**	**4.39**	**30**	**.867**	**24.7**
	Adirondack Red Wings	AHL	3	2	1	0	179	8	0	2.68	....	....	....	....	....	....	....	....	....	....	....	....	....	....	....	....	....
1992-93	**Detroit Red Wings**	**NHL**	**22**	**13**	**4**	**2**	**1193**	**64**	**0**	**3.22**	**2.74**	**3.95**	**522**	**.877**	**26.3**	....	....	....	....	....	....	....	....	....	....	....	....
1993-94	**Detroit Red Wings**	**NHL**	**8**	**2**	**4**	**0**	**345**	**23**	**0**	**4.00**	**3.81**	**7.02**	**131**	**.824**	**22.8**	....	....	....	....	....	....	....	....	....	....	....	....
	Adirondack Red Wings	AHL	10	6	3	0	582	30	0	3.09	....	....	....	....	....	....	....	....	....	....	....	....	....	....	....	....	....
	Boston Bruins	**NHL**	**18**	**7**	**6**	**1**	**976**	**50**	**1**	**3.07**	**2.92**	**3.70**	**415**	**.880**	**25.5**	**2**	**1**	**1**	....	**120**	**8**	**0**	**4.00**	**7.62**	**42**	**.810**	**21.0**
1994-95	**Boston Bruins**	**NHL**	**11**	**3**	**6**	**1**	**565**	**27**	**0**	**2.87**	**2.97**	**3.51**	**221**	**.878**	**23.5**	....	....	....	....	....	....	....	....	....	....	....	....
	Providence Bruins	AHL	0	0	0	0	0	0	0	0.00	....	....	....	....	....	1	1	0	....	60	3	0	3.00	....	....	....	....
1995-96	SC Riessersee	Germany	47	....	....	....	2776	184	....	4.00	....	....	....	....	....	3	....	....	....	189	20	0	6.35	....	....	....	....
1996-97	Manitoba Moose	IHL	41	10	18	5	1941	113	0	3.49	....	....	....	....	....	....	....	....	....	....	....	....	....	....	....	....	....
1997-98	ECR Revier Lowen	Germany	14	....	....	....	750	38	0	3.04	....	....	....	....	....	....	....	....	....	....	....	....	....	....	....	....	....
	NHL Totals		**184**	**85**	**65**	**20**	**10423**	**573**	**5**	**3.30**	....	....	**4786**	**.880**	....	**25**	**11**	**12**	....	**1277**	**71**	**1**	**3.34**	....	....	....	....

QMJHL Second All-Star Team (1986) • Won Harry "Hap" Holmes Memorial Trophy (fewest goals-against - AHL) (1987) • Shared Harry "Hap" Holmes Memorial Trophy (fewest goals-against - AHL) with Jocelyn Perreault (1988) • AHL Second All-Star Team (1988)

Signed as a free agent by **Montreal**, October 9, 1985. Traded to **St. Louis** by **Montreal** with Sergio Momesso for Jocelyn Lemieux, Darrell May and St. Louis' 2nd round choice (Patrice Brisebois) in 1989 Entry Draft, August 9, 1988. Traded to **Detroit** by **St. Louis** for Rick Zombo, October 18, 1991. Traded to **Boston** by **Detroit** for Boston's 5th round choice (Chad Wilchynski) in 1995 Entry Draft, January 17, 1994.

• RIGGIN, DENNIS

Dennis Riggin G – L. 5'11", 156 lbs. b: Kincardine, Ont., 4/11/1936.

			REGULAR SEASON													PLAYOFFS											
Season	Club	League	GP	W	L	T	Mins	GA	SO	Avg	AAvg	Eff	SA	S%	SAPG	GP	W	L	T	Mins	GA	SO	Avg	Eff	SA	S%	SAPG
1951-52	Windsor Spitfires	OHA	25				1480	163	0	6.61																	
1952-53	Windsor Spitfires	OHA	55				3300	177	4	3.21																	
1953-54	Hamilton Cubs	OHA	53	30	20	3	3180	176	3	*3.32						7				420	23	0	3.39				
	Hamilton Tigers	OHA Sr.	1	1	0	0	60	1	0	1.00																	
1954-55	Hamilton Tiger Cubs	OHA	49	21	23	5	2940	173	0	3.45						12				720	42	*2	3.50				
1955-56	Hamilton Tiger Cubs	OHA	47	13	29	5	2820	244	0	5.19																	
	Edmonton Flyers	WHL	8	3	5	0	480	29	0	3.63						3	0	3	0	188	13	0	4.15				
1956-57	Edmonton Flyers	WHL	67	38	25	4	4085	200	1	2.94						8	3	5	0	480	21	0	2.62				
1957-58	Edmonton Flyers	WHL	69	37	28	4	4190	222	5	3.18						5	2	3	0	300	13	*1	2.60				
1957-58	Calgary Stampeders	WHL	1	0	1	0	60	4	0	4.00																	
1958-59	Edmonton Flyers	WHL	13	7	5	1	800	27	3	2.03																	
1959-60	Edmonton Flyers	WHL	59	30	25	4	3580	200	3	3.35						4	0	4	0	274	13	0	2.85				
	Detroit Red Wings	NHL	9	2	6	1	540	32	1	3.56	3.74																
1960-61	Edmonton Flyers	WHL	69	26	*43	0	4140	289	0	4.19																	
1961-62	Edmonton Flyers	WHL	10	9	1	0	602	18	1	1.79																	
1962-63	Pittsburgh Hornets	AHL	19	1	16	1	1140	112	0	5.89																	
	Detroit Red Wings	NHL	9	4	4	1	445	22	0	2.97	3.08																
	Edmonton Flyers	WHL	8	3	4	1	480	34	0	4.25																	
	NHL Totals		18	6	10	2	985	54	1	3.29																	

WHL Prairie Division Second All-Star Team (1957) • Won WHL Prairie Division Rookie of the Year Award (1957) • WHL Prairie Division First All-Star Team (1958) • WHL Second All-Star Team (1960)

• RIGGIN, PAT

Pat Riggin G – R. 5'9", 170 lbs. b: Kincardine, Ont., 5/26/1959. Atlanta's 3rd choice, 33rd overall, in 1979 Entry Draft.

Season	Club	League	GP	W	L	T	Mins	GA	SO	Avg	AAvg	Eff	SA	S%	SAPG	GP	W	L	T	Mins	GA	SO	Avg	Eff	SA	S%	SAPG
1975-76	London Knights	OHA	29				1385	86	0	3.68																	
1976-77	London Knights	OHA	48				2809	138	*2	*2.95						20				1197	66	2	3.20				
1977-78	London Knights	OHA	38				2266	140	0	3.65						9				536	27	0	3.03				
1978-79	Birmingham Bulls	WHA	46	16	22	5	2511	158	1	3.78																	
1979-80	Atlanta Flames	NHL	25	11	9	2	1368	73	2	3.20	2.81																
	Birmingham Bulls	CHL	12	8	2	2	746	32	0	2.57																	
1980-81	Calgary Flames	NHL	42	21	16	4	2411	154	0	3.83	3.07					11	6	4		629	37	0	3.53				
1981-82	Calgary Flames	NHL	52	19	19	11	2934	207	2	4.23	3.27					3	0	3		194	10	0	3.09				
1982-83	Washington Capitals	NHL	38	16	9	9	2161	121	0	3.36	2.68	4.01	1015	.881	28.2	3	0	1		101	8	0	4.75				
1983-84	Hershey Bears	AHL	3	2	0	1	185	7	0	2.27																	
	Washington Capitals	NHL	41	21	14	2	2299	102	*4	*2.66	2.07	2.94	924	.890	24.1	5	1	3		230	9	0	2.35	2.61	81	.889	21.1
1984-85	Washington Capitals	NHL	57	28	20	7	3388	168	2	2.98	2.35	3.39	1478	.886	26.2	2	1	1		122	5	0	2.46	3.15	39	.872	19.2
	Canada	WEC-A	4				213	11		3.10																	
1985-86	Washington Capitals	NHL	7	2	3	1	369	23	0	3.74	2.91	6.47	133	.827	21.6												
	Boston Bruins	NHL	39	17	11	8	2272	127	1	3.35	2.60	4.37	973	.869	25.7	1	0	1		60	3	0	3.00	3.91	23	.870	23.0
1986-87	Boston Bruins	NHL	10	3	5	1	513	29	0	3.39	2.85	4.17	236	.877	27.6												
	Moncton Golden Flames	AHL	14	6	5	0	798	34	1	2.56																	
	Pittsburgh Penguins	NHL	17	8	6	3	988	55	0	3.34	2.81	3.95	465	.882	28.2												
	Canada	WEC-A	DID NOT PLAY – SPARE GOALTENDER																								
1987-88	Pittsburgh Penguins	NHL	22	7	8	4	1169	76	0	3.90	3.24	5.11	680	.888	29.8												
	Muskegon Lumberjacks	IHL	18	13	2	0	956	43	0	2.70						2	1	1		110	12	0	6.55				
	NHL Totals		350	153	120	52	19872	1135	11	3.43						25	8	13		1336	72	0	3.23				
	Other Major League Totals		46	16	22	5	2511	158	1	3.78																	

OHA First All-Star Team (1977) • Memorial Cup All-Star Team (1977) • Won Hap Emms Memorial Trophy (Memorial Cup Tournament Top Goaltender) (1977) • OHA Second All-Star Team (1978) • NHL Second All-Star Team (1984) • Shared William M. Jennings Trophy with Al Jensen (1984)

Signed as a free agent by **Birmingham** (WHA), July, 1978. Transferred to **Calgary** after **Atlanta** franchise relocated, June 24, 1980. Traded to **Washington** by **Calgary** with Ken Houston for Howard Walker, George White, Washington's 6th round choice (Mats Kihlstron) in 1982 Entry Draft, 3rd round choice (Perry Berezan) in 1983 Entry Draft and 2nd round choice (Paul Ranheim) in 1984 Entry Draft, June 9, 1982. Traded to **Boston** by **Washington** for Pete Peeters, November 14, 1985. Traded to **Pittsburgh** by **Boston** for Roberto Romano, February 6, 1987.

• RING, BOB

Bob Ring G b: 1946.

Season	Club	League	GP	W	L	T	Mins	GA	SO	Avg	AAvg	Eff	SA	S%	SAPG	GP	W	L	T	Mins	GA	SO	Avg	Eff	SA	S%	SAPG
1964-65	Niagara Falls Flyers	OHA	1	0	0	0	40	3	0	4.50																	
1965-66	Niagara Falls Flyers	OHA	22				1320	74	1	3.24																	
	Boston Bruins	NHL	1	0	0	0	33	4	0	7.27	7.39																
	Springfield Indians	AHL	1	0	0	0	20	3	0	9.00																	
1966-67	Acadia University	MIAA	STATISTICS NOT AVAILABLE																								
1967-68	Acadia University	MIAA	16	10	5	1	940	62	0	3.96																	
1968-69	Acadia University	AIAA	18	12	5	1	1080	56	0	3.11																	
1969-70	Acadia University	AIAA	10				600	43	0	4.30																	
	NHL Totals		1	0	0	0	33	4	0	7.27																	

• Replaced injured Ed Johnston in 2nd period, October 30, 1965. (NY Rangers 8, Boston 2)

• RIVARD, FERN

Fern Rivard G – L. 5'9", 160 lbs. b: Grand'Mere, Que., 1/18/1946.

Season	Club	League	GP	W	L	T	Mins	GA	SO	Avg	AAvg	Eff	SA	S%	SAPG	GP	W	L	T	Mins	GA	SO	Avg	Eff	SA	S%	SAPG
1963-64	Thetford Mines Canadiens	QJHL	STATISTICS NOT AVAILABLE																								
	Quebec Aces	AHL	1	1	0	0	60	2	0	2.00																	
1964-65	Montreal Jr. Canadiens	OHA	26				1560	92	1	3.54						7				400	30	0	4.50				
1965-66	Peterborough Petes	OHA	15				880	61	0	4.16						1	0	1	0	60	7	0	7.00				
1966-67	Muskegon Mohawks	IHL	68				4080	265	1	3.91																	
1967-68	Quebec Aces	AHL	46	19	16	7	2529	132	0	3.13						*11				*614	36	0	3.52				
1968-69	Minnesota North Stars	NHL	13	0	6	4	657	48	0	4.38	4.56																
	Memphis South Stars	CHL	29				1682	101	2	3.53																	
1969-70	Minnesota North Stars	NHL	14	3	5	5	800	42	1	3.15	3.35																
	Iowa Stars	CHL	18	9	5	4	1050	61	1	3.49						7	3	4	0	415	24	*1	3.47				
1970-71	Cleveland Barons	AHL	36	15	14	4	2047	102	2	2.98						1	0	1	0	60	6	0	6.00				
1971-72	Cleveland Barons	AHL	40	12	19	5	2199	118	1	3.21						4	1	2	0	173	11	0	3.82				
1972-73	Jacksonville Barons	AHL	*65				*3643	250	2	4.11																	
1973-74	Minnesota North Stars	NHL	13	3	6	2	701	50	1	4.28	4.15																
	New Haven Nighthawks	AHL	12	7	3	2	700	41	2	3.51																	
1974-75	Minnesota North Stars	NHL	15	3	9	0	707	50	0	4.24	3.83																
	New Haven Nighthawks	AHL	7	1	4	1	404	26	0	3.86																	
	NHL Totals		55	9	26	11	2865	190	2	3.98																	

Rights transferred to **Philadelphia** after NHL club purchased **Quebec** (AHL) franchise, May 8, 1967. Claimed by **Minnesota** from **Philadelphia** in Intra-League Draft, June 12, 1968.

• ROACH, JOHN ROSS

John Ross "Little Napolean" Roach G – L. 5'5", 130 lbs. b: Port Perry, Ont., 6/23/1900. d: 7/9/1973.

Season	Club	League	GP	W	L	T	Mins	GA	SO	Avg	AAvg	Eff	SA	S%	SAPG	GP	W	L	T	Mins	GA	SO	Avg	Eff	SA	S%	SAPG
1919-20	Toronto Aura Lee	OHA	6	4	2	0	360	31	0	5.17																	
1920-21	Toronto Granites	OHA Sr.	10	*8	2	0	566	12	3	*1.27						2	1	1	0	120	7	0	3.50				
1921-22	Toronto St. Pats	NHL	22	11	10	1	1340	91	0	4.07	3.20					*7	*4	2	1	*425	13	*2	*1.84				
1922-23	Toronto St. Pats	NHL	*24	13	10	1	1469	88	1	3.59	3.52																
1923-24	Toronto St. Pats	NHL	23	10	13	0	1380	80	1	3.48	4.48																
1924-25	Toronto St. Pats	NHL	*30	*19	11	0	1800	84	1	2.80	3.54					2	0	2	0	120	5	0	*2.50				
1925-26	Toronto St. Pats	NHL	*36	12	21	3	2231	114	2	3.07	4.36																
1926-27	Toronto Maple Leafs	NHL	*44	15	24	5	2764	94	4	2.04	3.16																
1927-28	Toronto Maple Leafs	NHL	43	18	18	7	2690	88	4	1.96	3.20																
1928-29	New York Rangers	NHL	*44	21	13	10	2760	65	13	1.41	2.99					*6	3	2	1	*392	5	*3	0.77				
1929-30	New York Rangers	NHL	*44	17	17	10	2770	143	1	3.10	3.26					4	1	2	1	309	7	0	1.36				
1930-31	New York Rangers	NHL	*44	19	16	9	*2760	87	7	1.89	2.38					4	2	2	0	240	4	1	*1.00				

			REGULAR SEASON													PLAYOFFS											
Season	Club	League	GP	W	L	T	Mins	GA	SO	Avg	AAvg	Eff	SA	S%	SAPG	GP	W	L	T	Mins	GA	SO	Avg	Eff	SA	S%	SAPG
1931-32	New York Rangers	NHL	*48	23	17	8	3020	112	*9	2.23	2.70	....	....	....	....	*7	3	4	0	*480	27	*1	3.38	....	....	....	....
	Springfield Indians	IAHL	1	1	0	0	60	1	0	1.00	....	....	....	....	....	....	....	....	....	....	....	....	....	....	....	....	....
1932-33	Detroit Red Wings	NHL	*48	*25	15	8	2970	93	10	1.88	2.49	....	....	....	....	4	2	2	0	240	8	1	2.00	....	....	....	....
1933-34	Detroit Red Wings	NHL	19	9	8	1	1030	45	1	2.62	3.37	....	....	....	....	....	....	....	....	....	....	....	....	....	....	....	....
	Syracuse Stars	IAHL	13	....	....	....	780	36	2	2.77	....	....	....	....	....	6	....	....	....	360	19	0	3.17	....	....	....	....
1934-35	Detroit Red Wings	NHL	23	7	11	5	1460	62	4	2.55	3.13	....	....	....	....	....	....	....	....	....	....	....	....	....	....	....	....
	Detroit Olympics	IAHL	9	....	....	....	540	15	1	1.67	....	....	....	....	....	....	....	....	....	....	....	....	....	....	....	....	....
	NHL Totals		492	219	204	68	30444	1246	58	2.46	....	....	....	....	....	34	15	16	3	2206	69	8	1.88	....	....	....	....

NHL First All-Star Team (1933)

Signed as a free agent by **Toronto St. Pats**, December 5, 1921. Traded to **NY Rangers** by **Toronto** with Butch Keeling for Lorne Chabot, Alex Gray and $10,000, October 18, 1928. Traded to **Detroit** by **NY Rangers** for cash, October 25, 1932.

• ROBERTS, MOE

Moe Roberts G – R. 5'9", 165 lbs. b: Waterbury, CT, 12/13/1905. d: 2/7/1975.

1923-24	Boston AA Unicorns	USAHA	STATISTICS NOT AVAILABLE																								
1924-25	Boston AA Unicorns	USAHA	....	....	....	....	....	....	....	....	....	....	....	....	....	1	0	0	0	30	1	0	1.50	....	....	....	....
1925-26	Boston Bruins	NHL	2	0	1	0	90	5	0	3.33	4.47	....	....	....	....	....	....	....	....	....	....	....	....	....	....	....	....
1926-27	New Haven Eagles	Can-Am	32	*18	14	0	1980	66	1	2.00	....	....	....	....	....	4	1	2	1	240	9	0	2.25	....	....	....	....
1927-28	New Haven Eagles	Can-Am	40	16	*20	4	2450	90	4	2.20	....	....	....	....	....	....	....	....	....	....	....	....	....	....	....	....	....
1928-29	Philadelphia Arrows	Can-Am	40	12	*21	7	2490	73	5	1.76	....	....	....	....	....	....	....	....	....	....	....	....	....	....	....	....	....
1929-30	Philadelphia Arrows	Can-Am	40	20	18	2	2470	121	3	2.94	....	....	....	....	....	1	....	....	....	120	5	0	2.50	....	....	....	....
1930-31	Philadelphia Arrows	Can-Am	40	12	22	6	2460	108	3	2.63	....	....	....	....	....	....	....	....	....	....	....	....	....	....	....	....	....
1931-32	New Haven Eagles	Can-Am	22	12	10	0	1370	48	2	2.10	....	....	....	....	....	2	0	2	0	120	8	0	4.00	....	....	....	....
	New York Americans	NHL	1	1	0	0	60	1	0	1.00	1.23	....	....	....	....	....	....	....	....	....	....	....	....	....	....	....	....
1932-33	New Haven Eagles	Can-Am	44	16	23	5	2680	123	*4	2.75	....	....	....	....	....	....	....	....	....	....	....	....	....	....	....	....	....
1933-34	New York Americans	NHL	6	1	4	0	336	25	0	4.46	5.78	....	....	....	....	....	....	....	....	....	....	....	....	....	....	....	....
	Cleveland Indians	IAHL	35	....	....	....	2100	98	3	2.80	....	....	....	....	....	....	....	....	....	....	....	....	....	....	....	....	....
1934-35	Cleveland Falcons	IAHL	44	20	23	1	2640	132	4	3.00	....	....	....	....	....	2	0	2	0	120	6	0	3.00	....	....	....	....
1935-36	Cleveland Falcons	IAHL	29	....	....	....	1740	59	5	2.03	....	....	....	....	....	2	1	1	0	120	3	1	1.50	....	....	....	....
1936-37	Cleveland Barons	AHL	45	13	24	8	2840	134	3	2.83	....	....	....	....	....	....	....	....	....	....	....	....	....	....	....	....	....
1937-38	Cleveland Barons	AHL	45	24	11	9	2810	103	5	2.20	....	....	....	....	....	2	0	2	0	183	9	0	2.95	....	....	....	....
1938-39	Cleveland Barons	AHL	*54	23	22	9	*3410	138	4	2.43	....	....	....	....	....	*9	*7	2	0	*635	12	*4	*1.13	....	....	....	....
1939-40	Cleveland Barons	AHL	*56	24	24	8	*3482	130	5	*2.24	....	....	....	....	....	....	....	....	....	....	....	....	....	....	....	....	....
1940-41	Cleveland Barons	AHL	43	20	15	7	2640	122	3	2.77	....	....	....	....	....	4	2	1	0	239	10	0	2.51	....	....	....	....
1941-42	Cleveland Barons	AHL	27	17	7	2	1560	79	2	3.04	....	....	....	....	....	....	....	....	....	....	....	....	....	....	....	....	....
	Pittsburgh Hornets	AHL	3	1	2	0	180	14	0	4.67	....	....	....	....	....	....	....	....	....	....	....	....	....	....	....	....	....
1942-1945			DID NOT PLAY – RETIRED																								
1945-46	Washington Lions	EHL	24	....	....	....	1440	97	2	4.04	....	....	....	....	....	6	....	....	....	360	22	*1	3.67	....	....	....	....
1946-1951			DID NOT PLAY – RETIRED																								
1951-52	Chicago Black Hawks	NHL	1	0	0	0	20	0	0	0.00	0.00	....	....	....	....	....	....	....	....	....	....	....	....	....	....	....	....
	NHL Totals		10	2	5	0	506	31	0	3.68	....	....	....	....	....	....	....	....	....	....	....	....	....	....	....	....	....

AHL Second All-Star Team (1938) • AHL First All-Star Team (1940)

Signed as a free agent by **Boston**, December 8, 1925. Promoted to **NY Americans** from **New Haven** (Can-Am) to replace injured Roy Worters, March 10, 1932. (NY Americans 5, NY Rangers 1). Signed as a free agent by **Chicago**, November 25, 1951.

• ROBERTSON, EARL

Earl Robertson G – L. 5'10", 165 lbs. b: Bengough, Sask., 11/24/1910. d: 1/19/1979.

1925-26	Regina Falcons	City Jr.	8	*4	3	1	490	15	0	*1.84	....	....	....	....	....	3	1	2	0	180	9	1	3.00	....	....	....	....
1926-27	Regina Falcons	SJHL	6	4	2	0	370	11	0	1.76	....	....	....	....	....	....	....	....	....	....	....	....	....	....	....	....	....
1927-28	Vancouver Monarchs	City Jr.	STATISTICS NOT AVAILABLE																								
1928-29	Victoria Cubs	PCHL	34	....	....	....	2040	86	1	2.53	....	....	....	....	....	....	....	....	....	....	....	....	....	....	....	....	....
1929-30	Victoria Cubs	PCHL	32	....	....	....	1920	112	1	3.50	....	....	....	....	....	....	....	....	....	....	....	....	....	....	....	....	....
1930-31	Tacoma Tigers	PCHL	10	....	....	....	600	24	2	2.40	....	....	....	....	....	....	....	....	....	....	....	....	....	....	....	....	....
	Oakland Sheiks	Cal-Pro	1	1	0	0	60	1	0	1.00	....	....	....	....	....	....	....	....	....	....	....	....	....	....	....	....	....
1931-32	Hollywood Stars	Cal-Pro	31	*20	7	4	1860	86	....	*2.77	....	....	....	....	....	7	*4	3	0	420	20	*1	*2.86	....	....	....	....
1932-33	Edmonton Eskimos	WCHL	27	....	....	....	1620	73	*6	2.70	....	....	....	....	....	8	....	....	....	480	15	*1	1.88	....	....	....	....
1933-34	Edmonton Eskimos	WCHL	33	....	....	....	1960	89	4	2.70	....	....	....	....	....	2	0	2	0	120	7	0	3.50	....	....	....	....
1934-35	Windsor Bulldogs	IAHL	40	....	....	....	2400	100	6	2.50	....	....	....	....	....	....	....	....	....	....	....	....	....	....	....	....	....
1935-36	Windsor Bulldogs	IAHL	46	18	19	11	2880	120	4	2.50	....	....	....	....	....	8	2	*4	2	480	18	*2	2.25	....	....	....	....
1936-37	Pittsburgh Hornets	AHL	29	14	14	0	1760	74	5	2.52	....	....	....	....	....	4	1	3	0	240	12	0	3.00	....	....	....	....
	Detroit Red Wings	NHL	....	....	....	....	....	....	....	....	....	....	....	....	....	6	3	2	....	340	8	2	1.41	....	....	....	....
1937-38	New York Americans	NHL	*48	19	18	11	*3000	111	6	2.22	2.66	....	....	....	....	6	3	3	....	475	12	0	*1.52	....	....	....	....
1938-39	New York Americans	NHL	46	17	18	10	2850	136	3	2.86	3.56	....	....	....	....	....	....	....	....	....	....	....	....	....	....	....	....
1939-40	New York Americans	NHL	*48	15	29	4	2960	140	6	2.84	3.61	....	....	....	....	3	1	2	....	180	9	0	3.00	....	....	....	....
1940-41	New York Americans	NHL	36	6	22	8	2260	142	1	3.77	4.58	....	....	....	....	....	....	....	....	....	....	....	....	....	....	....	....
	Springfield Indians	AHL	11	4	5	2	680	37	0	3.26	....	....	....	....	....	3	1	2	0	236	5	0	*1.27	....	....	....	....
1941-42	Brooklyn Americans	NHL	12	3	8	1	750	46	0	3.68	3.67	....	....	....	....	....	....	....	....	....	....	....	....	....	....	....	....
	Springfield Indians	AHL	41	24	14	3	2460	125	2	3.05	....	....	....	....	....	3	2	1	0	160	15	0	5.63	....	....	....	....
	NHL Totals		190	60	95	34	11820	575	16	2.92	....	....	....	....	....	15	7	7	....	995	29	2	1.75	....	....	....	....

IAHL Second All-Star Team (1936) • NHL Second All-Star Team (1939)

Traded to **Detroit** by **Windsor** (IAHL) for $1500, October 21, 1936. Traded to **NY Americans** by **Detroit** for Red Doran and $7,500, May 9, 1937.

• ROLLINS, AL

Al (Elwin Ira) "Ally" Rollins G – L. 6'2", 175 lbs. b: Vanguard, Sask., 10/9/1926. d: 7/27/1996.

1942-43	Moose Jaw Canucks	City Jr.	15	....	....	....	900	51	0	3.40	....	....	....	....	....	2	....	....	....	120	7	0	3.50	....	....	....	....
1943-44	New York Rovers	EHL	22	....	....	....	1290	120	0	5.58	....	....	....	....	....	....	....	....	....	....	....	....	....	....	....	....	....
1944-45	Seattle Ironmen	PCHL	STATISTICS NOT AVAILABLE																								
1945-46	Seattle Ironmen	PCHL	55	....	....	....	3300	210	*2	*3.65	....	....	....	....	....	3	....	....	....	180	12	0	4.00	....	....	....	....
1946-47	Vancouver Canucks	PCHL	54	27	26	1	3240	253	0	4.59	....	....	....	....	....	4	1	3	0	240	17	0	4.25	....	....	....	....
1947-48	Edmonton Flyers	WCSHL	45	....	....	....	2700	166	*1	*3.69	....	....	....	....	....	24	20	3	1	1440	59	4	2.46	....	....	....	....
1948-49	Kansas City Pla-Mors	USHL	60	29	21	10	3600	189	1	3.16	....	....	....	....	....	2	0	2	0	120	6	0	3.00	....	....	....	....
1949-50	Cleveland Barons	AHL	6	4	0	2	360	17	0	2.83	....	....	....	....	....	....	....	....	....	....	....	....	....	....	....	....	....
	Pittsburgh Hornets	AHL	20	9	7	4	1200	43	3	2.15	....	....	....	....	....	....	....	....	....	....	....	....	....	....	....	....	....
	Toronto Maple Leafs	NHL	2	1	1	0	100	4	1	2.40	2.71	....	....	....	....	....	....	....	....	....	....	....	....	....	....	....	....
1950-51	Toronto Maple Leafs	NHL	40	27	5	8	2373	70	5	*1.77	1.94	....	....	....	....	4	3	1	....	210	6	0	1.71	....	....	....	....
1951-52	Toronto Maple Leafs	NHL	*70	29	24	16	4170	154	5	2.20	2.54	....	....	....	....	2	0	2	....	120	6	0	3.00	....	....	....	....
1952-53	Chicago Black Hawks	NHL	*70	27	28	15	*4200	175	6	2.50	3.25	....	....	....	....	7	3	4	....	425	18	0	2.54	....	....	....	....
1953-54	Chicago Black Hawks	NHL	66	12	47	7	3960	213	5	3.23	4.43	....	....	....	....	....	....	....	....	....	....	....	....	....	....	....	....
1954-55	Chicago Black Hawks	NHL	44	9	27	8	2640	150	0	3.41	4.35	....	....	....	....	....	....	....	....	....	....	....	....	....	....	....	....
1955-56	Chicago Black Hawks	NHL	58	17	30	11	3480	174	3	3.00	3.76	....	....	....	....	....	....	....	....	....	....	....	....	....	....	....	....
	Buffalo Bisons	AHL	6	2	3	1	360	25	1	4.17	....	....	....	....	....	....	....	....	....	....	....	....	....	....	....	....	....
1956-57	Chicago Black Hawks	NHL	*70	16	39	15	*4200	225	3	3.21	3.83	....	....	....	....	....	....	....	....	....	....	....	....	....	....	....	....
1957-58	Calgary Stampeders	WHL	68	30	33	5	4130	214	3	3.11	....	....	....	....	....	*14	6	*8	0	*880	47	0	3.20	....	....	....	....
1958-59	Winnipeg Warriors	WHL	31	17	14	0	1860	99	3	3.19	....	....	....	....	....	7	3	4	0	420	22	0	3.14	....	....	....	....

			REGULAR SEASON													PLAYOFFS											
Season	Club	League	GP	W	L	T	Mins	GA	SO	Avg	AAvg	Eff	SA	S%	SAPG	GP	W	L	T	Mins	GA	SO	Avg	Eff	SA	S%	SAPG
1959-60	Winnipeg Warriors	WHL	55	22	31	2	3300	193	2	3.51	....	....	....	....	....	....	....	....	....	....	....	....	....	....	....	....	....
	New York Rangers	**NHL**	**10**	**3**	**4**	**3**	**600**	**31**	**0**	**3.10**	**3.25**	....	....	....	....	....	....	....	....	....	....	....	....	....	....	....	....
1960-61			STATISTICS NOT AVAILABLE																								
1961-62	Portland Buckaroos	WHL	8	5	3	0	480	18	1	2.25	....	....	....	....	....	7	3	4	0	432	18	0	*2.49	....	....	....	....
	NHL Totals		**430**	**141**	**205**	**83**	**25723**	**1196**	**28**	**2.79**	....	....	....	....	....	**13**	**6**	**7**	....	**755**	**30**	**0**	**2.38**	....	....	....	....

Won Vezina Trophy (1951) • Won Hart Trophy (1954)

Played in NHL All-Star Game (1954)

Traded to **Cleveland** (AHL) by **Kansas City** (USHL) for Doug Baldwin, Ralph Wycherley and cash, September 15, 1949. Traded to **Toronto** by **Cleveland** (AHL) for Bobby Dawes, $40,000 and future considerations, December, 1949. Traded to **Chicago** by **Toronto** with Gus Mortson, Cal Gardner and Ray Hannigan for Harry Lumley, September 11, 1952. Loaned to **NY Rangers** by **Chicago** (Winnipeg-WHL) for the loan of Ray Mikulan, future considerations and cash, February 20, 1960.

• ROLOSON, DWAYNE

Dwayne Roloson G – L. 6'1", 180 lbs. b: Simcoe, Ont., 10/12/1969.

			REGULAR SEASON													PLAYOFFS											
Season	Club	League	GP	W	L	T	Mins	GA	SO	Avg	AAvg	Eff	SA	S%	SAPG	GP	W	L	T	Mins	GA	SO	Avg	Eff	SA	S%	SAPG
1990-91	University of Mass.-Lowell	H.E.	15	5	9	0	823	63	0	4.59	....	....	....	....	....	....	....	....	....	....	....	....	....	....	....	....	....
1991-92	University of Mass.-Lowell	H.E.	12	3	8	0	660	52	0	4.73	....	....	....	....	....	....	....	....	....	....	....	....	....	....	....	....	....
1992-93	University of Mass.-Lowell	H.E.	*39	20	17	2	*2342	150	0	3.84	....	....	....	....	....	....	....	....	....	....	....	....	....	....	....	....	....
1993-94	University of Mass.-Lowell	H.E.	*40	*23	10	7	*2305	106	0	2.76	....	....	....	....	....	....	....	....	....	....	....	....	....	....	....	....	....
1994-95	Saint John Flames	AHL	46	16	21	8	2734	156	1	3.42	....	....	....	....	....	5	1	4	....	298	13	0	2.61	....	....	....	....
	Canada	WC-A	DID NOT PLAY – SPARE GOALTENDER																								
1995-96	Saint John Flames	AHL	67	*33	22	11	4026	190	1	2.83	....	....	....	....	....	16	10	6	....	1027	49	1	2.86	....	....	....	....
1996-97	**Calgary Flames**	**NHL**	**31**	**9**	**14**	**3**	**1618**	**78**	**1**	**2.89**	**3.06**	**2.97**	**760**	**.897**	**28.2**	....	....	....	....	....	....	....	....	....	....	....	....
	Saint John Flames	AHL	8	6	2	0	481	22	1	2.75	....	....	....	....	....	....	....	....	....	....	....	....	....	....	....	....	....
1997-98	**Calgary Flames**	**NHL**	**39**	**11**	**16**	**8**	**2205**	**110**	**0**	**2.99**	**3.51**	**3.30**	**997**	**.890**	**27.1**	....	....	....	....	....	....	....	....	....	....	....	....
	Saint John Flames	AHL	4	3	0	1	245	8	0	1.96	....	....	....	....	....	....	....	....	....	....	....	....	....	....	....	....	....
	NHL Totals		**70**	**20**	**30**	**11**	**3823**	**188**	**1**	**2.95**	....	....	**1757**	**.893**	....	....	....	....	....	....	....	....	....	....	....	....	....

Hockey East First All-Star Team (1994) • NCAA East First All-Ameircan Team (1994)

Signed as a free agent by **Calgary**, July 4, 1994.

• ROMANO, ROBERTO

Roberto Romano G – L. 5'6", 170 lbs. b: Montreal, Que., 10/10/1962.

			REGULAR SEASON													PLAYOFFS											
Season	Club	League	GP	W	L	T	Mins	GA	SO	Avg	AAvg	Eff	SA	S%	SAPG	GP	W	L	T	Mins	GA	SO	Avg	Eff	SA	S%	SAPG
1979-80	Quebec Remparts	QMJHL	52	21	17	3	2411	183	0	4.55	....	....	....	....	....	3	1	1	0	150	12	0	4.80	....	....	....	....
1980-81	Quebec Remparts	QMJHL	59	24	26	2	3174	233	0	4.40	....	....	....	....	....	4	1	2	0	164	18	0	6.59	....	....	....	....
1981-82	Quebec Remparts	QMJHL	1	....	....	....	60	4	0	4.00	....	....	....	....	....	....	....	....	....	....	....	....	....	....	....	....	....
	Hull Olympiques	QMJHL	56	....	....	....	3090	194	*1	3.77	....	....	....	....	....	13	....	....	....	760	50	0	3.95	....	....	....	....
1982-83	Baltimore Skipjacks	AHL	38	19	14	3	2163	146	0	4.05	....	....	....	....	....	....	....	....	....	....	....	....	....	....	....	....	....
	Pittsburgh Penguins	**NHL**	**3**	**0**	**3**	**0**	**155**	**18**	**0**	**6.97**	**5.57**	**13.07**	**96**	**.813**	**37.2**	....	....	....	....	....	....	....	....	....	....	....	....
1983-84	**Pittsburgh Penguins**	**NHL**	**18**	**6**	**11**	**0**	**1020**	**78**	**1**	**4.59**	**3.60**	**5.69**	**629**	**.876**	**37.0**	....	....	....	....	....	....	....	....	....	....	....	....
	Baltimore Skipjacks	AHL	31	23	6	1	1759	106	0	3.62	....	....	....	....	....	9	5	3	0	544	36	0	3.97	....	....	....	....
1984-85	**Pittsburgh Penguins**	**NHL**	**31**	**9**	**17**	**2**	**1629**	**120**	**1**	**4.42**	**3.52**	**5.45**	**974**	**.877**	**35.9**	....	....	....	....	....	....	....	....	....	....	....	....
	Baltimore Skipjacks	AHL	12	2	8	2	719	44	0	3.67	....	....	....	....	....	....	....	....	....	....	....	....	....	....	....	....	....
1985-86	**Pittsburgh Penguins**	**NHL**	**46**	**21**	**20**	**3**	**2684**	**159**	**2**	**3.55**	**2.75**	**4.05**	**1394**	**.886**	**31.2**	....	....	....	....	....	....	....	....	....	....	....	....
1986-87	**Pittsburgh Penguins**	**NHL**	**25**	**9**	**11**	**2**	**1438**	**87**	**0**	**3.63**	**3.05**	**4.43**	**713**	**.878**	**29.7**	....	....	....	....	....	....	....	....	....	....	....	....
	Baltimore Skipjacks	AHL	5	0	3	0	274	18	0	3.94	....	....	....	....	....	....	....	....	....	....	....	....	....	....	....	....	....
	Boston Bruins	**NHL**	**1**	**0**	**1**	**0**	**60**	**6**	**0**	**0.00**	**5.05**	**10.59**	**34**	**.824**	**34.0**	....	....	....	....	....	....	....	....	....	....	....	....
	Moncton Golden Flames	AHL	1	0	0	0	65	3	0	2.77	....	....	....	....	....	....	....	....	....	....	....	....	....	....	....	....	....
1987-88	Maine Mariners	AHL	16	5	8	1	875	52	0	3.57	....	....	....	....	....	....	....	....	....	....	....	....	....	....	....	....	....
1988-89	HC Merano	Italy	STATISTICS NOT AVAILABLE																								
1989-90	HC Bolzano	Italy	32	....	....	....	1778	105	0	3.54	....	....	....	....	....	....	....	....	....	....	....	....	....	....	....	....	....
1990-91	Milano Devils	Italy	10	....	....	....	538	31	0	3.45	....	....	....	....	....	....	....	....	....	....	....	....	....	....	....	....	....
1991-92	Milano Devils	Italy	29	....	....	....	1704	78	2	2.74	....	....	....	....	....	....	....	....	....	....	....	....	....	....	....	....	....
	Milano Devils	Alpenliga	17	....	....	....	973	42	1	2.68	....	....	....	....	....	2	....	....	....	120	2	1	1.00	....	....	....	....
	Italy	WC-A	3	....	....	....	151	11	....	4.37	....	....	....	....	....	....	....	....	....	....	....	....	....	....	....	....	....
1992-93	Milano Devils	Alpenliga	28	....	....	....	1540	73	0	2.02	....	....	....	....	....	....	....	....	....	....	....	....	....	....	....	....	....
1993-94	**Pittsburgh Penguins**	**NHL**	**2**	**1**	**0**	**1**	**125**	**3**	**0**	**1.44**	**1.37**	**0.77**	**56**	**.946**	**26.9**	....	....	....	....	....	....	....	....	....	....	....	....
	Cleveland Lumberjacks	IHL	11	2	7	2	642	45	1	4.20	....	....	....	....	....	....	....	....	....	....	....	....	....	....	....	....	....
	NHL Totals		**126**	**46**	**63**	**8**	**7111**	**471**	**4**	**3.97**			**2906**	**.870**	....	....	....	....	....	....	....	....	....	....	....	....	....

QMJHL First All-Star Team (1982)

Signed as a free agent by **Pittsburgh**, December 6, 1982. Traded to **Boston** by **Pittsburgh** for Pat Riggin, February 6, 1987. Signed as a free agent by **Pittsburgh**, October 7, 1993.

• ROUSSEL, DOMINIC

Dominic Roussel G – L. 6'1", 191 lbs. b: Hull, Que., 2/22/1970. Philadelphia's 4th choice, 63rd overall, in 1988 Entry Draft.

			REGULAR SEASON													PLAYOFFS											
Season	Club	League	GP	W	L	T	Mins	GA	SO	Avg	AAvg	Eff	SA	S%	SAPG	GP	W	L	T	Mins	GA	SO	Avg	Eff	SA	S%	SAPG
1987-88	Trois-Rivières Draveurs	QMJHL	51	18	25	4	2905	251	0	5.18	....	....	....	....	....	....	....	....	....	....	....	....	....	....	....	....	....
1988-89	Shawinigan Cataracts	QMJHL	46	24	15	2	2555	171	0	4.02	....	....	....	....	....	10	6	4	....	638	36	0	3.39	....	....	....	....
1989-90	Shawinigan Cataracts	QMJHL	37	20	14	1	1985	133	0	4.02	....	....	....	....	....	2	1	1	....	120	12	0	6.00	....	....	....	....
1990-91	Hershey Bears	AHL	45	20	14	7	2507	151	1	3.61	....	....	....	....	....	7	3	4	....	366	21	0	3.44	....	....	....	....
1991-92	**Philadelphia Flyers**	**NHL**	**17**	**7**	**8**	**2**	**922**	**40**	**1**	**2.60**	**2.30**	**2.38**	**437**	**.908**	**28.4**	....	....	....	....	....	....	....	....	....	....	....	....
	Hershey Bears	AHL	35	15	11	6	2040	121	1	3.56	....	....	....	....	....	....	....	....	....	....	....	....	....	....	....	....	....
1992-93	**Philadelphia Flyers**	**NHL**	**34**	**13**	**11**	**5**	**1769**	**111**	**1**	**3.76**	**3.20**	**4.47**	**933**	**.881**	**31.6**	....	....	....	....	....	....	....	....	....	....	....	....
	Hershey Bears	AHL	6	0	3	3	372	23	0	3.71	....	....	....	....	....	....	....	....	....	....	....	....	....	....	....	....	....
1993-94	**Philadelphia Flyers**	**NHL**	**60**	**29**	**20**	**5**	**3285**	**183**	**1**	**3.34**	**3.18**	**3.47**	**1762**	**.896**	**32.2**	....	....	....	....	....	....	....	....	....	....	....	....
1994-95	**Philadelphia Flyers**	**NHL**	**19**	**11**	**7**	**0**	**1075**	**42**	**1**	**2.34**	**2.41**	**2.02**	**486**	**.914**	**27.1**	**1**	**0**	**0**	....	**23**	**0**	**0**	**0.00**	**0.00**	**8**	**1.000**	**20.9**
	Hershey Bears	AHL	1	0	1	0	59	5	0	5.07	....	....	....	....	....	....	....	....	....	....	....	....	....	....	....	....	....
1995-96	**Philadelphia Flyers**	**NHL**	**9**	**2**	**3**	**2**	**456**	**22**	**1**	**2.89**	**2.84**	**3.67**	**170**	**.870**	**23.4**	....	....	....	....	....	....	....	....	....	....	....	....
	Hershey Bears	AHL	12	4	4	3	690	32	0	2.78	....	....	....	....	....	....	....	....	....	....	....	....	....	....	....	....	....
	Winnipeg Jets	**NHL**	**7**	**2**	**2**	**0**	**285**	**16**	**0**	**3.37**	**3.31**	**4.02**	**134**	**.881**	**28.2**	....	....	....	....	....	....	....	....	....	....	....	....
1996-97	Philadelphia Phantoms	AHL	36	18	9	3	1852	82	2	2.66	....	....	....	....	....	1	0	0	....	26	3	0	6.93	....	....	....	....
1997-98	Star Bulls Rosenheim	Germany	2	....	....	....	120	12	0	6.00	....	....	....	....	....	....	....	....	....	....	....	....	....	....	....	....	....
	NHL Totals		**146**	**64**	**51**	**14**	**7792**	**414**	**5**	**3.19**	....	....	**3930**	**.895**	....	**1**	**0**	**0**	....	**23**	**0**	**0**	**0.00**	....	....	....	....

Traded to **Winnipeg** by **Philadelphia** for Tim Cheveldae and Winnipeg's 3rd round choice (Chester Gallant) in 1996 Entry Draft, February 27, 1996. Signed as a free agent by **Philadelphia**, July 3, 1996. Traded to **Nashville** by **Philadelphia** with Jeff Staples for Nashville's 7th round choice (Cam Ondrik) in 1998 Entry Draft, June 26, 1998.

• ROY, PATRICK

Patrick Roy G – L. 6', 192 lbs. b: Quebec City, Que., 10/5/1965. Montreal's 4th choice, 51st overall, in 1984 Entry Draft.

			REGULAR SEASON													PLAYOFFS											
Season	Club	League	GP	W	L	T	Mins	GA	SO	Avg	AAvg	Eff	SA	S%	SAPG	GP	W	L	T	Mins	GA	SO	Avg	Eff	SA	S%	SAPG
1982-83	Granby Bisons	QMJHL	54	13	35	1	2808	293	0	6.26	....	....	....	....	....	....	....	....	....	....	....	....	....	....	....	....	....
1983-84	Granby Bisons	QMJHL	61	29	29	1	3585	265	0	4.44	....	....	....	....	....	4	0	4	....	244	22	0	5.41	....	....	....	....
1984-85	**Montreal Canadiens**	**NHL**	**1**	**1**	**0**	**0**	**20**	**0**	**0**	**0.00**	**0.00**	**0.00**	**2**	**1.000**	**6.0**	....	....	....	....	....	....	....	....	....	....	....	....
	Granby Bisons	QMJHL	44	16	25	1	2463	228	0	5.55	....	....	....	....	....	....	....	....	....	....	....	....	....	....	....	....	....
	Sherbrooke Canadiens	AHL	1	1	0	0	60	4	0	4.00	....	....	....	....	....	13	10	3	....	*769	37	0	*2.89	....	....	....	....
1985-86	**Montreal Canadiens**	**NHL**	**47**	**23**	**18**	**3**	**2651**	**148**	**1**	**3.35**	**2.59**	**4.18**	**1185**	**.875**	**26.8**	**20**	***15**	**5**	....	**1218**	**39**	***1**	**1.92**	**1.48**	**506**	**.923**	**24.9**
1986-87	**Montreal Canadiens**	**NHL**	**46**	**22**	**16**	**6**	**2686**	**131**	**1**	**2.93**	**2.45**	**3.17**	**1210**	**.892**	**27.0**	**6**	**4**	**2**	....	**330**	**22**	**0**	**4.00**	**5.09**	**173**	**.873**	**31.5**
1987-88	**Montreal Canadiens**	**NHL**	**45**	**23**	**12**	**9**	**2586**	**125**	**3**	**2.90**	**2.40**	**2.90**	**1248**	**.900**	**29.0**	**8**	**3**	**4**	....	**430**	**24**	**0**	**3.35**	**3.69**	**218**	**.890**	**30.4**
1988-89	**Montreal Canadiens**	**NHL**	**48**	**33**	**5**	**6**	**2744**	**113**	**4**	***2.47**	**2.02**	**2.27**	**1228**	**.908**	**26.9**	**19**	**13**	**6**	....	**1206**	**42**	**2**	***2.09**	**1.66**	**528**	**.920**	**26.3**
1989-90	**Montreal Canadiens**	**NHL**	**54**	***31**	**16**	**5**	**3173**	**134**	**3**	**2.53**	**2.10**	**2.22**	**1524**	**.912**	**28.8**	**11**	**5**	**6**	....	**641**	**26**	**1**	**2.43**	**2.16**	**292**	**.911**	**27.3**
1990-91	Montreal Canadiens	FrTour	2	....	....	....	62	3	....	2.90	....	....	....	....	....	....	....	....	....	....	....	....	....	....	....	....	....
	Montreal Canadiens	**NHL**	**48**	**25**	**15**	**0**	**2835**	**128**	**1**	**2.71**	**2.41**	**2.55**	**1362**	**.906**	**28.8**	**13**	**7**	**5**	....	**785**	**40**	**0**	**3.06**	**3.11**	**394**	**.898**	**30.1**
1991-92	**Montreal Canadiens**	**NHL**	**67**	**36**	**22**	**8**	**3935**	**155**	***5**	***2.36**	**2.07**	**2.03**	**1806**	**.914**	**27.5**	**11**	**4**	**7**	....	**686**	**30**	**1**	**2.62**	**2.52**	**312**	**.904**	**27.3**
1992-93	**Montreal Canadiens**	**NHL**	**62**	**31**	**25**	**5**	**3595**	**192**	**2**	**3.20**	**2.71**	**3.39**	**1814**	**.894**	**30.3**	**20**	***16**	**4**	....	**1293**	**46**	**0**	***2.13**	**1.51**	**647**	**.929**	**30.0**
1993-94	**Montreal Canadiens**	**NHL**	**68**	**35**	**17**	**11**	**3867**	**161**	***7**	**2.50**	**2.36**	**2.06**	**1956**	**.918**	**30.3**	**6**	**3**	**3**	....	**375**	**16**	**0**	**2.56**	**1.80**	**228**	**.930**	**36.5**
1994-95	**Montreal Canadiens**	**NHL**	**43**	**17**	**20**	**6**	**2566**	**127**	**1**	**2.97**	**3.07**	**2.78**	**1357**	**.906**	**31.7**	....	....	....	....	....	....	....	....	....	....	....	....
1995-96	**Montreal Canadiens**	**NHL**	**22**	**12**	**9**	**1**	**1260**	**62**	**1**	**2.95**	**2.90**	**2.74**	**667**	**.907**	**31.8**	....	....	....	....	....	....	....	....	....	....	....	....
	Colorado Avalanche	**NHL**	**39**	**22**	**15**	**1**	**2305**	**103**	**1**	**2.68**	**2.62**	**2.44**	**1130**	**.909**	**20.4**	***22**	***10**	**8**	....	***1454**	**51**	***3**	**2.10**	**1.65**	**649**	**.921**	**26.8**

			REGULAR SEASON													PLAYOFFS											
Season	Club	League	GP	W	L	T	Mins	GA	SO	Avg	AAvg	Eff	SA	S%	SAPG	GP	W	L	T	Mins	GA	SO	Avg	Eff	SA	S%	SAPG
1996-97	**Colorado Avalanche**	**NHL**	**62**	***38**	**15**	**7**	**3698**	**143**	**7**	**2.32**	**2.44**	**1.78**	**1861**	**.923**	**30.2**	**17**	**10**	**7**	....	**1034**	**38**	***3**	**2.21**	**1.50**	**559**	**.932**	**32.4**
1997-98	**Colorado Avalanche**	**NHL**	**65**	**31**	**19**	**13**	**3835**	**153**	**4**	**2.39**	**2.79**	**2.00**	**1825**	**.916**	**28.6**	**7**	**3**	**4**	....	**430**	**18**	**0**	**2.51**	**2.37**	**191**	**.906**	**26.7**
	Canada	Olympics	6	3	3	0	369	9	1	1.46	....	....	....	....	....	....	....	....	....	....	....	....	....	....	....	....	....
	NHL Totals		**717**	**380**	**224**	**87**	**41756**	**1875**	**41**	**2.69**	....	....	**20175**	**.907**	....	***160**	***99**	**59**	....	***9882**	**392**	**11**	**2.38**	....	....	....	....

NHL All-Rookie Team (1986) • Won Conn Smythe Trophy (1986, 1993) • Shared William Jennings Trophy with Brian Hayward (1987, 1988, 1989) • NHL Second All-Star Team (1988, 1991) • NHL First All-Star Team (1989, 1990, 1992) • Won Trico Goaltending Award (1989, 1990) • Won Vezina Trophy (1989, 1990, 1992) • Won William M. Jennings Award (1992)

Played in NHL All-Star Game (1988, 1990, 1991, 1992, 1993, 1994, 1997, 1998)

Traded to **Colorado** by **Montreal** with Mike Keane for Andrei Kovalenko, Martin Rucinsky and Jocelyn Thibault, December 6, 1995.

• RUPP, PAT

Pat Rupp G – L. 5′11″, 180 lbs. b: Detroit, MI, 8/12/1942.

Season	Club	League	GP	W	L	T	Mins	GA	SO	Avg	AAvg	Eff	SA	S%	SAPG	GP	W	L	T	Mins	GA	SO	Avg	Eff	SA	S%	SAPG
1961-62	Flin Flon Bombers	SJHL	51	....	....	....	3060	178	2	3.49	....	....	....	....	....	....	....	....	....	....	....	....	....	....	....	....	....
1962-63	Flin Flon Bombers	SJHL	52	....	....	....	3120	226	2	4.34	....	....	....	....	....	6	....	....	....	360	28	0	4.67	....	....	....	....
1963-64	Philadelphia Ramblers	EHL	38	....	....	....	2280	191	0	5.03	....	....	....	....	....	....	....	....	....	....	....	....	....	....	....	....	....
	Detroit Red Wings	**NHL**	**1**	**0**	**1**	**0**	**60**	**4**	**0**	**4.00**	**4.45**	....	....	....	....	....	....	....	....	....	....	....	....	....	....	....	....
1964-65	Dayton Gems	IHL	28	....	....	....	1680	160	0	5.75	....	....	....	....	....	....	....	....	....	....	....	....	....	....	....	....	....
	New Jersey Devils	EHL	41	....	....	....	2460	188	1	4.59	....	....	....	....	....	....	....	....	....	....	....	....	....	....	....	....	....
1965-66	Dayton Gems	IHL	69	33	34	2	4140	316	2	4.58	....	....	....	....	....	11	5	6	0	660	45	0	4.09	....	....	....	....
1966-67	Dayton Gems	IHL	71	44	24	3	4260	277	0	3.85	....	....	....	....	....	4	0	4	0	240	19	0	4.75	....	....	....	....
1968-69	Dayton Gems	IHL	41	....	....	....	2420	136	4	3.37	....	....	....	....	....	3	....	....	....	185	6	0	1.94	....	....	....	....
1969-70	Dayton Gems	IHL	28	....	....	....	1320	90	1	4.09	....	....	....	....	....	1	0	0	0	37	2	0	3.24	....	....	....	....
1970-71	Dayton Gems	IHL	27	....	....	....	1509	95	1	3.78	....	....	....	....	....	6	....	....	....	333	14	*1	*2.52	....	....	....	....
1971-72	Dayton Gems	IHL	49	....	....	....	2949	161	0	3.28	....	....	....	....	....	5	1	4	0	271	22	0	4.87	....	....	....	....
1972-1975				DID NOT PLAY																							
1975-76	Buffalo Norsemen	NAHL	4	....	....	....	148	13	0	5.25	....	....	....	....	....	....	....	....	....	....	....	....	....	....	....	....	....
	NHL Totals		**1**	**0**	**1**	**0**	**60**	**4**	**0**	**4.00**	....	....	....	....	....	....	....	....	....	....	....	....	....	....	....	....	....

Shared James Norris Memorial Trophy (fewest goals against - IHL) with John Adams (1969)

Loaned to **Detroit** by **Philadelphia** (EHL) to replace injured Terry Sawchuk, March 22, 1964. (Toronto 4, Detroit 1)

• RUTHERFORD, JIM

Jim Rutherford G – L. 5′8″, 168 lbs. b: Beeton, Ont., 2/17/1949. Detroit's 1st choice, 10th overall, in 1969 Amateur Draft.

Season	Club	League	GP	W	L	T	Mins	GA	SO	Avg	AAvg	Eff	SA	S%	SAPG	GP	W	L	T	Mins	GA	SO	Avg	Eff	SA	S%	SAPG
1966-67	Aurora Tigers	Jr. C	30	....	....	....	1800	63	....	2.10	....	....	....	....	....	....	....	....	....	....	....	....	....	....	....	....	....
1967-68	Hamilton Red Wings	OHA	9	....	....	....	510	19	0	2.24	....	....	....	....	....	1	0	0	0	20	0	0	0.00	....	....	....	....
1968-69	Hamilton Red Wings	OHA	45	....	....	....	2730	153	*3	3.36	....	....	....	....	....	5	....	....	....	300	27	0	5.40	....	....	....	....
1969-70	Fort Worth Wings	CHL	35	12	14	8	2060	92	1	2.68	....	....	....	....	....	4	3	1	0	244	12	0	2.95	....	....	....	....
1970-71	Fort Worth Wings	CHL	3	....	....	....	180	11	0	3.66	....	....	....	....	....	....	....	....	....	....	....	....	....	....	....	....	....
	Detroit Red Wings	**NHL**	**29**	**7**	**15**	**3**	**1498**	**94**	**1**	**3.77**	**3.74**	....	....	....	....	....	....	....	....	....	....	....	....	....	....	....	....
1971-72	Hershey Bears	AHL	3	3	0	0	180	7	0	2.33	....	....	....	....	....	....	....	....	....	....	....	....	....	....	....	....	....
	Pittsburgh Penguins	**NHL**	**40**	**17**	**15**	**5**	**2160**	**116**	**1**	**3.22**	**3.25**	....	....	....	....	**4**	**0**	**4**	....	**240**	**14**	**0**	**3.50**	....	....	....	....
1972-73	**Pittsburgh Penguins**	**NHL**	**49**	**20**	**22**	**5**	**2660**	**129**	**3**	**2.91**	**2.73**	....	....	....	....	....	....	....	....	....	....	....	....	....	....	....	....
1973-74	**Pittsburgh Penguins**	**NHL**	**26**	**7**	**12**	**4**	**1432**	**82**	**0**	**3.44**	**3.33**	....	....	....	....	....	....	....	....	....	....	....	....	....	....	....	....
	Detroit Red Wings	**NHL**	**25**	**9**	**11**	**4**	**1420**	**86**	**0**	**3.63**	**3.51**	....	....	....	....	....	....	....	....	....	....	....	....	....	....	....	....
1974-75	**Detroit Red Wings**	**NHL**	**59**	**20**	**29**	**10**	**3478**	**217**	**2**	**3.74**	**3.38**	....	....	....	....	....	....	....	....	....	....	....	....	....	....	....	....
1975-76	**Detroit Red Wings**	**NHL**	**44**	**13**	**25**	**6**	**2640**	**158**	**4**	**3.59**	**3.25**	....	....	....	....	....	....	....	....	....	....	....	....	....	....	....	....
1976-77	**Detroit Red Wings**	**NHL**	**48**	**7**	**34**	**6**	**2740**	**180**	**0**	**3.94**	**3.68**	....	....	....	....	....	....	....	....	....	....	....	....	....	....	....	....
	Canada	WEC-A	2	....	....	....	89	7	....	4.72	....	....	....	....	....	....	....	....	....	....	....	....	....	....	....	....	....
1977-78	**Detroit Red Wings**	**NHL**	**43**	**20**	**17**	**4**	**2468**	**134**	**1**	**3.26**	**3.05**	....	....	....	....	**3**	**2**	**1**	....	**180**	**12**	**0**	**4.00**	....	....	....	....
1978-79	**Detroit Red Wings**	**NHL**	**32**	**13**	**14**	**5**	**1892**	**103**	**1**	**3.27**	**2.88**	....	....	....	....	....	....	....	....	....	....	....	....	....	....	....	....
	Canada	WEC-A	6	1	5	0	320	24	0	4.50	....	....	....	....	....	....	....	....	....	....	....	....	....	....	....	....	....
1979-80	**Detroit Red Wings**	**NHL**	**23**	**6**	**13**	**3**	**1326**	**92**	**1**	**4.16**	**3.66**	....	....	....	....	....	....	....	....	....	....	....	....	....	....	....	....
1980-81	**Detroit Red Wings**	**NHL**	**10**	**2**	**6**	**2**	**600**	**43**	**0**	**4.30**	**3.45**	....	....	....	....	....	....	....	....	....	....	....	....	....	....	....	....
	Toronto Maple Leafs	**NHL**	**18**	**4**	**10**	**2**	**961**	**82**	**0**	**5.12**	**4.12**	....	....	....	....	....	....	....	....	....	....	....	....	....	....	....	....
	Los Angeles Kings	**NHL**	**3**	**3**	**0**	**0**	**180**	**10**	**0**	**3.33**	**2.67**	....	....	....	....	**1**	**0**	**0**	....	**20**	**2**	**0**	**6.00**	....	....	....	....
1981-82	**Los Angeles Kings**	**NHL**	**7**	**3**	**3**	**0**	**380**	**43**	**0**	**6.79**	**5.25**	....	....	....	....	....	....	....	....	....	....	....	....	....	....	....	....
	New Haven Nighthawks	AHL	29	12	11	4	1614	90	0	3.35	....	....	....	....	....	2	0	2	0	144	8	0	3.33	....	....	....	....
1982-83	**Detroit Red Wings**	**NHL**	**1**	**0**	**1**	**0**	**60**	**7**	**0**	**7.00**	**5.59**	**12.56**	**39**	**.821**	**39.0**	....	....	....	....	....	....	....	....	....	....	....	....
	Adirondack Red Wings	AHL	12	3	7	1	591	44	0	4.47	....	....	....	....	....	....	....	....	....	....	....	....	....	....	....	....	....
	NHL Totals		**457**	**151**	**227**	**59**	**25895**	**1576**	**14**	**3.65**	....	....	....	....	....	**8**	**2**	**5**	....	**440**	**28**	**0**	**3.82**	....	....	....	....

OHA First All-Star Team (1969)

Claimed by **Pittsburgh** from **Detroit** in Intra-League Draft, June 8, 1971. Traded to **Detroit** by **Pittsburgh** with Jack Lynch for Ron Stackhouse, January 18, 1974. Traded to **Toronto** by **Detroit** for Mark Kirton, December 4, 1980. Traded to **LA Kings** by **Toronto** for LA Kings' 5th round choice (Barry Brigley) in 1981 Entry Draft, March 10, 1981. Signed as a free agent by **Detroit**, September 13, 1982.

• RUTLEDGE, WAYNE

Wayne Rutledge G – L. 6′2″, 200 lbs. b: Barrie, Ont., 1/5/1942.

Season	Club	League	GP	W	L	T	Mins	GA	SO	Avg	AAvg	Eff	SA	S%	SAPG	GP	W	L	T	Mins	GA	SO	Avg	Eff	SA	S%	SAPG
1959-60	Barrie Flyers	OHA	48	24	17	6	2840	168	3	3.55	....	....	....	....	....	6	....	....	....	300	30	0	5.00	....	....	....	....
1960-61	Niagara Falls Flyers	OHA	47	22	20	5	2790	159	2	3.42	....	....	....	....	....	6	....	....	....	300	37	0	6.17	....	....	....	....
1961-62	Niagara Falls Flyers	OHA	43	....	....	....	2580	163	2	3.79	....	....	....	....	....	10	....	....	....	600	36	0	3.60	....	....	....	....
1962-63	Windsor Bulldogs	OHA Sr.	30	....	....	....	1800	95	2	3.17	....	....	....	....	....	11	....	....	....	660	22	*3	*2.00	....	....	....	....
	Clinton Comets	EHL	5	....	....	....	300	20	1	4.00	....	....	....	....	....	....	....	....	....	....	....	....	....	....	....	....	....
	Kingston Frontenacs	EPHL	4	3	1	0	240	9	0	2.25	....	....	....	....	....	....	....	....	....	....	....	....	....	....	....	....	....
1963-64	Windsor Bulldogs	IHL	65	....	....	....	3900	243	0	3.74	....	....	....	....	....	6	2	4	0	360	20	0	3.33	....	....	....	....
1964-65	St. Paul Rangers	CHL	39	22	16	1	2320	134	2	3.47	....	....	....	....	....	....	....	....	....	....	....	....	....	....	....	....	....
1965-66	Minnesota Rangers	CHL	*70	*34	25	11	*4200	197	*7	2.81	....	....	....	....	....	7	3	4	0	454	19	*1	2.51	....	....	....	....
1966-67	Omaha Knights	CHL	*70	*36	24	10	*4200	203	2	2.90	....	....	....	....	....	*12	5	7	0	*742	36	*1	2.91	....	....	....	....
1967-68	**Los Angeles Kings**	**NHL**	**45**	**20**	**18**	**4**	**2444**	**117**	**2**	**2.87**	**3.18**	....	....	....	....	**3**	**1**	**1**	....	**149**	**8**	**0**	**3.22**	....	....	....	....
1968-69	**Los Angeles Kings**	**NHL**	**17**	**6**	**7**	**4**	**921**	**56**	**0**	**3.65**	**3.79**	....	....	....	....	**5**	**1**	**3**	....	**229**	**12**	**0**	**3.14**	....	....	....	....
1969-70	Springfield Kings	AHL	6	....	....	....	340	23	0	4.06	....	....	....	....	....	....	....	....	....	....	....	....	....	....	....	....	....
	Los Angeles Kings	**NHL**	**20**	**2**	**12**	**1**	**960**	**68**	**0**	**4.25**	**4.55**	....	....	....	....	....	....	....	....	....	....	....	....	....	....	....	....
	Long Island Ducks	EHL	3	....	....	....	180	21	0	7.00	....	....	....	....	....	....	....	....	....	....	....	....	....	....	....	....	....
1970-71	Denver Spurs	WHL	47	15	18	12	2648	142	3	3.22	....	....	....	....	....	3	1	2	0	198	13	0	3.94	....	....	....	....
1971-72	Salt Lake Golden Eagles	WHL	*60	24	27	8	*3517	206	1	3.51	....	....	....	....	....	....	....	....	....	....	....	....	....	....	....	....	....
1972-73	Houston Aeros	WHA	36	20	14	2	2163	110	0	3.05	....	....	....	....	....	7	4	3	0	422	20	0	2.84	....	....	....	....
1973-74	Houston Aeros	WHA	25	12	12	1	1509	84	0	3.34	....	....	....	....	....	....	....	....	....	....	....	....	....	....	....	....	....
1974-75	Houston Aeros	WHA	35	20	15	0	2098	113	2	3.23	....	....	....	....	....	....	....	....	....	....	....	....	....	....	....	....	....
1975-76	Houston Aeros	WHA	25	14	10	0	1456	77	1	3.17	....	....	....	....	....	4	1	2	0	200	10	0	3.00	....	....	....	....
1976-77	Houston Aeros	WHA	42	23	14	4	2512	132	3	3.15	....	....	....	....	....	2	2	0	0	120	4	0	2.00	....	....	....	....
1977-78	Houston Aeros	WHA	12	4	7	0	634	47	0	4.45	....	....	....	....	....	3	1	2	0	131	8	0	3.66	....	....	....	....
	NHL Totals		**82**	**28**	**37**	**9**	**4325**	**241**	**2**	**3.34**	....	....	....	....	....	**8**	**2**	**4**	....	**378**	**20**	**0**	**3.17**	....	....	....	....
	Other Major League Totals		175	93	72	7	10372	563	6	3.26	....	....	....	....	....	16	8	7	0	873	42	0	2.89	....	....	....	....

CHL Second All-Star Team (1966) • Won Terry Sawchuk Trophy (fewest goals against - CHL) (1966) • CHL First All-Star Team (1967) • WHL Second All-Star Team (1972)

Claimed by **LA Kings** from **NY Rangers** in Expansion Draft, June 6, 1967. Claimed by **Salt Lake** (WHL) from **LA Kings** in Reverse Draft, June, 1971. Selected by **Houston** (WHA) in 1972 WHA General Player Draft, February 12, 1972.

• ST. CROIX, RICK

Rick St. Croix G – L. 5′10″, 160 lbs. b: Kenora, Ont., 1/3/1955. Philadelphia's 3rd choice, 72nd overall, in 1975 Amateur Draft.

Season	Club	League	GP	W	L	T	Mins	GA	SO	Avg	AAvg	Eff	SA	S%	SAPG	GP	W	L	T	Mins	GA	SO	Avg	Eff	SA	S%	SAPG
1970-71	Kenora Muskies	MJHL	23	....	....	....	1265	71	0	3.37	....	....	....	....	....	....	....	....	....	....	....	....	....	....	....	....	....
1971-72	Kenora Muskies	MJHL	43	....	....	....	2402	172	0	4.30	....	....	....	....	....	....	....	....	....	....	....	....	....	....	....	....	....
	Winnipeg Jets	WCJHL	3	....	....	....	160	13	0	4.88	....	....	....	....	....	....	....	....	....	....	....	....	....	....	....	....	....
1972-73	Oshawa Generals	OHA	52	....	....	....	3176	247	0	4.67	....	....	....	....	....	....	....	....	....	....	....	....	....	....	....	....	....
1973-74	Oshawa Generals	OHA	33	....	....	....	1932	130	1	4.04	....	....	....	....	....	....	....	....	....	....	....	....	....	....	....	....	....
1974-75	Oshawa Generals	OHA	32	....	....	....	1965	131	1	4.00	....	....	....	....	....	1	0	1	0	60	9	0	9.00	....	....	....	....
1975-76	Flint Generals	IHL	42	....	....	....	2201	118	0	3.22	....	....	....	....	....	....	....	....	....	....	....	....	....	....	....	....	....

			REGULAR SEASON													PLAYOFFS											
Season	Club	League	GP	W	L	T	Mins	GA	SO	Avg	AAvg	Eff	SA	S%	SAPG	GP	W	L	T	Mins	GA	SO	Avg	Eff	SA	S%	SAPG
1976-77	Springfield Indians	AHL	1	1	0	0	60	3	0	3.00	....	....	....	....	....	....	....	....	....	....	....	....	....	....	....	....	....
	Flint Generals	IHL	53	....	....	....	2956	179	3	3.63	....	....	....	....	....	5	1	4	0	337	30	0	5.34	....	....	....	....
1977-78	**Philadelphia Flyers**	NHL	7	2	4	1	395	20	0	3.04	2.85	....	....	....	....	....	....	....	....	....	....	....	....	....	....	....	....
	Maine Mariners	AHL	40	22	14	2	2266	116	2	3.07	....	....	....	....	....	4	1	3	0	174	18	0	6.21	....	....	....	....
1978-79	**Philadelphia Flyers**	NHL	2	0	1	1	117	6	0	3.08	2.72	....	....	....	....	....	....	....	....	....	....	....	....	....	....	....	....
	Philadelphia Firebirds	AHL	9	4	4	1	484	22	0	2.73	....	....	....	....	....	....	....	....	....	....	....	....	....	....	....	....	....
	Maine Mariners	AHL	22	10	9	3	1312	63	0	2.88	....	....	....	....	....	....	....	....	....	....	....	....	....	....	....	....	....
1979-80	**Philadelphia Flyers**	NHL	1	1	0	0	60	2	0	2.00	1.76	....	....	....	....	....	....	....	....	....	....	....	....	....	....	....	....
	Maine Mariners	AHL	46	25	14	7	2729	132	1	*2.90	....	....	....	....	....	5	1	4	0	311	16	0	3.09	....	....	....	....
1980-81	**Philadelphia Flyers**	NHL	27	13	7	6	1567	65	2	2.49	1.98	....	....	....	....	9	4	5	....	541	27	*1	2.99	....	....	....	....
1981-82	**Philadelphia Flyers**	NHL	29	13	9	6	1729	112	0	3.89	3.00	....	....	....	....	1	0	1	....	20	1	0	3.00	....	....	....	....
1982-83	**Philadelphia Flyers**	NHL	16	9	5	2	940	54	0	3.45	2.75	4.31	432	.875	27.6	....	....	....	....	....	....	....	....	....	....	....	....
	Toronto Maple Leafs	NHL	16	4	9	2	900	57	0	3.80	3.03	4.34	499	.886	33.3	1	0	0	....	1	1	0	60.00	....	....	....	....
1983-84	**Toronto Maple Leafs**	NHL	20	5	10	0	939	80	0	5.11	4.01	7.70	531	.849	33.9	....	....	....	....	....	....	....	....	....	....	....	....
	St. Catharines Saints	AHL	8	7	1	0	482	29	0	3.61	....	....	....	....	....	3	1	1	0	133	10	0	4.50	....	....	....	....
1984-85	**Toronto Maple Leafs**	NHL	11	2	9	0	628	54	0	5.16	4.11	8.87	314	.828	30.0	....	....	....	....	....	....	....	....	....	....	....	....
	St. Catharines Saints	AHL	18	6	10	1	1076	92	0	5.13	....	....	....	....	....	....	....	....	....	....	....	....	....	....	....	....	....
1985-86	Fort Wayne Komets	IHL	42	25	13	0	2474	132	2	3.20	....	....	....	....	....	8	3	4	0	411	30	0	4.38	....	....	....	....
	NHL Totals		129	49	54	18	7275	450	2	3.71	....	....	....	....	....	11	4	6	....	562	29	1	3.10	....	....	....	....

OHA Second All-Star Team (1973) • AHL First All Star Team (1980) • Shared Harry "Hap" Holmes Memorial Award (fewest goals against - AHL) with Robbie Moore (1980) • IHL Second All-Star Team (1986) • Shared James Norris Memorial Trophy (fewest goals against - IHL) with Eldon (Pokey) Reddick (1986)

Traded to **Toronto** by **Philadelphia** for Michel Larocque, January 11, 1983.

• ST. LAURENT, SAM

Sam St. Laurent G – L. 5'10", 190 lbs. b: Arvida, Que., 2/16/1959.

Season	Club	League	GP	W	L	T	Mins	GA	SO	Avg	AAvg	Eff	SA	S%	SAPG	GP	W	L	T	Mins	GA	SO	Avg	Eff	SA	S%	SAPG
1975-76	Chicoutimi Sagueneens	QMJHL	17	....	....	....	889	81	0	5.47	....	....	....	....	....	1	....	....	....	40	9	0	13.50	....	....	....	....
1976-77	Chicoutimi Sagueneens	QMJHL	21	....	....	....	901	81	0	5.39	....	....	....	....	....	4	....	....	....	200	19	0	5.70	....	....	....	....
1977-78	Chicoutimi Sagueneens	QMJHL	60	....	....	....	3251	351	0	6.48	....	....	....	....	....	....	....	....	....	....	....	....	....	....	....	....	....
1978-79	Chicoutimi Sagueneens	QMJHL	70	....	....	....	3806	290	0	4.57	....	....	....	....	....	1	....	....	....	47	8	0	10.21	....	....	....	....
1979-80	Maine Mariners	AHL	5	2	1	0	229	17	0	4.45	....	....	....	....	....	....	....	....	....	....	....	....	....	....	....	....	....
	Toledo Goaldiggers	IHL	38	....	....	....	2143	138	2	3.86	....	....	....	....	....	4	0	4	0	239	24	0	6.03	....	....	....	....
1980-81	Maine Mariners	AHL	7	3	3	0	363	28	0	4.63	....	....	....	....	....	....	....	....	....	....	....	....	....	....	....	....	....
	Toledo Goaldiggers	IHL	30	....	....	....	1614	113	1	4.20	....	....	....	....	....	....	....	....	....	....	....	....	....	....	....	....	....
1981-82	Toledo Goaldiggers	IHL	4	....	....	....	248	11	0	2.66	....	....	....	....	....	....	....	....	....	....	....	....	....	....	....	....	....
	Maine Mariners	AHL	25	15	7	1	1396	76	0	3.27	....	....	....	....	....	4	1	3	0	240	18	0	4.50	....	....	....	....
1982-83	Maine Mariners	AHL	30	12	12	4	1739	109	0	3.76	....	....	....	....	....	*17	8	9	0	*1012	54	0	3.20	....	....	....	....
1983-84	Maine Mariners	AHL	38	14	18	4	2158	145	0	4.03	....	....	....	....	....	12	9	2	0	708	32	*1	*2.71	....	....	....	....
1984-85	Maine Mariners	AHL	55	26	22	7	3245	168	4	3.11	....	....	....	....	....	10	5	5	0	656	45	0	4.12	....	....	....	....
1985-86	**New Jersey Devils**	NHL	4	2	1	0	188	13	1	4.15	3.23	4.86	111	.883	35.4	....	....	....	....	....	....	....	....	....	....	....	....
	Maine Mariners	AHL	50	24	20	4	2862	161	1	3.38	....	....	....	....	....	....	....	....	....	....	....	....	....	....	....	....	....
1986-87	**Detroit Red Wings**	NHL	6	1	2	2	342	16	0	2.81	2.36	3.33	135	.881	23.7	....	....	....	....	....	....	....	....	....	....	....	....
	Adirondack Red Wings	AHL	25	7	13	0	1397	98	1	4.21	....	....	....	....	....	3	0	2	0	105	10	0	5.71	....	....	....	....
1987-88	**Detroit Red Wings**	NHL	6	2	2	0	294	16	0	3.27	2.72	3.54	148	.892	30.2	1	0	0	....	10	1	0	6.00	8.57	7	.857	42.0
	Adirondack Red Wings	AHL	32	12	14	4	1826	104	2	3.42	....	....	....	....	....	1	0	1	0	59	6	0	6.10	....	....	....	....
1988-89	**Detroit Red Wings**	NHL	4	0	1	1	141	9	0	3.83	3.16	3.79	91	.901	38.7	....	....	....	....	....	....	....	....	....	....	....	....
	Adirondack Red Wings	AHL	34	20	11	3	2054	113	0	3.30	....	....	....	....	....	16	*11	5	0	956	47	*2	*2.95	....	....	....	....
1989-90	**Detroit Red Wings**	NHL	14	2	6	1	607	38	0	3.76	3.15	4.40	325	.883	32.1	....	....	....	....	....	....	....	....	....	....	....	....
	Adirondack Red Wings	AHL	13	10	2	1	785	40	0	3.06	....	....	....	....	....	....	....	....	....	....	....	....	....	....	....	....	....
1990-91	Binghamton Rangers	AHL	45	19	16	4	2379	138	1	3.48	....	....	....	....	....	3	1	2	0	160	11	0	4.13	....	....	....	....
1991-92	Canada	Nat-Team	1	0	1	0	60	3	0	3.00	....	....	....	....	....	....	....	....	....	....	....	....	....	....	....	....	....
	Canada	Olympics	DID NOT PLAY – SPARE GOALTENDER																								
	Binghamton Rangers	AHL	1	0	0	0	20	2	0	6.00	....	....	....	....	....	....	....	....	....	....	....	....	....	....	....	....	....
	NHL Totals		34	7	12	4	1572	92	1	3.51	....	....	810	.886	....	1	0	0	....	10	1	0	6.00	....	....	....	....

AHL Second All-Star Team (1985, 1986) • Shared Harry "Hap" Holmes Memorial Award (fewest goals against - AHL) with Karl Friesen (1986) • Won Aldege "Baz" Bastien Memorial Award (Top Goaltender - AHL) (1986) • Won Jack A. Butterfield Trophy (Playoff MVP - AHL) (1989)

Signed as a free agent by **Philadelphia**, October 10, 1979. Traded to **New Jersey** by **Philadelphia** for future considerations, September 27, 1984. Traded to **Detroit** by **New Jersey** for Steve Richmond, August 18, 1986. Traded to **NY Rangers** by **Detroit** for cash, June 26, 1990.

• SALO, TOMMY

Tommy Salo G – L. 5'11", 173 lbs. b: Surahammar, Sweden, 2/1/1971. NY Islanders' 5th choice, 118th overall, in 1993 Entry Draft.

Season	Club	League	GP	W	L	T	Mins	GA	SO	Avg	AAvg	Eff	SA	S%	SAPG	GP	W	L	T	Mins	GA	SO	Avg	Eff	SA	S%	SAPG
1990-91	Vasteras IK	Sweden	2	....	....	....	100	11	0	6.60	....	....	....	....	....	....	....	....	....	....	....	....	....	....	....	....	....
	Sweden	WJC-A	6	....	....	....	343	19	....	3.32	....	....	....	....	....	....	....	....	....	....	....	....	....	....	....	....	....
1991-92	Vasteras IK	Sweden	STATISTICS NOT AVAILABLE																								
1992-93	Vasteras IK	Sweden	24	....	....	....	1431	59	2	2.47	....	....	....	....	....	2	....	....	....	120	6	0	3.00	....	....	....	....
1993-94	Vasteras IK	Sweden	32	....	....	....	1896	106	0	3.35	....	....	....	....	....	....	....	....	....	....	....	....	....	....	....	....	....
	Sweden	Olympics	6	5	1	0	370	13	....	2.11	....	....	....	....	....	....	....	....	....	....	....	....	....	....	....	....	....
	Sweden	WC-A	3	1	1	1	180	10	....	3.33	....	....	....	....	....	....	....	....	....	....	....	....	....	....	....	....	....
1994-95	Denver Grizzlies	IHL	*65	*45	14	4	*3810	165	*3	*2.60	....	....	....	....	....	8	7	0	....	390	20	0	3.07	....	....	....	....
	New York Islanders	NHL	6	1	5	0	358	18	0	3.02	3.12	2.88	189	.905	31.7	....	....	....	....	....	....	....	....	....	....	....	....
1995-96	**New York Islanders**	NHL	10	1	7	1	523	35	0	4.02	3.95	5.63	250	.860	28.7	....	....	....	....	....	....	....	....	....	....	....	....
	Utah Grizzlies	IHL	45	28	15	2	2695	119	*4	2.65	....	....	....	....	....	22	*15	7	....	1342	51	*3	2.28	....	....	....	....
1996-97	Sweden	W Cup	2	1	1	0	160	4	....	2.00	....	....	....	....	....	....	....	....	....	....	....	....	....	....	....	....	....
	New York Islanders	NHL	58	20	27	8	3208	151	5	2.82	2.98	2.70	1576	.904	29.5	....	....	....	....	....	....	....	....	....	....	....	....
	Sweden	WC-A	10	6	3	1	597	20	....	2.01	....	....	....	....	....	....	....	....	....	....	....	....	....	....	....	....	....
1997-98	**New York Islanders**	NHL	62	23	29	5	3461	152	4	2.64	3.09	2.48	1617	.906	28.0	....	....	....	....	....	....	....	....	....	....	....	....
	Sweden	Olympics	4	2	2	0	238	9	0	2.27	....	....	....	....	....	....	....	....	....	....	....	....	....	....	....	....	....
	Sweden	WC-A	9	9	0	0	540	7	3	0.78	....	....	....	....	....	....	....	....	....	....	....	....	....	....	....	....	....
	NHL Totals		136	45	68	14	7550	356	9	2.83	....	....	3632	.902	....	....	....	....	....	....	....	....	....	....	....	....	....

IHL First All-Star Team (1995) • Won James Norris Memorial Trophy (Fewest goals against - IHL) (1995) • Won Garry F. Longman Memorial Trophy (Top Rookie - IHL) (1995) • Won James Gatschene Memorial Trophy (MVP - IHL) (1995) • Shared James Norris Memorial Trophy (fewest goals against - IHL) with Mark McArthur (1996) • Won "Bud" Poile Trophy (Playoff MVP - IHL) (1996) • WC-A All-Star Team (1997) • Named Best Goaltender at WC-A (1997)

• SANDS, CHARLIE

Charlie Sands G – R. 5'9", 160 lbs. b: Fort William, Ont., 3/23/1911.

Season	Club	League	GP	W	L	T	Mins	GA	SO	Avg	AAvg	Eff	SA	S%	SAPG	GP	W	L	T	Mins	GA	SO	Avg	Eff	SA	S%	SAPG
1939-40	**Montreal Canadiens**	NHL	1	0	0	0	25	5	0	12.00	14.96	....	....	....	....	....	....	....	....	....	....	....	....	....	....	....	....
	NHL Totals		1	0	0	0	25	5	0	12.00	....	....	....	....	....	....	....	....	....	....	....	....	....	....	....	....	....

• Montreal center replaced injured Wilf Cude in 2nd period, February 22, 1940. (Chicago 10, Montreal 1)

• SANDS, MIKE

Mike Sands G – L. 5'9", 170 lbs. b: Mississauga, Ont., 4/6/1963. Minnesota's 3rd choice, 31st overall, in 1981 Entry Draft.

Season	Club	League	GP	W	L	T	Mins	GA	SO	Avg	AAvg	Eff	SA	S%	SAPG	GP	W	L	T	Mins	GA	SO	Avg	Eff	SA	S%	SAPG
1980-81	Sudbury Wolves	OHA	50	15	28	2	2789	236	0	5.08	....	....	....	....	....	....	....	....	....	....	....	....	....	....	....	....	....
1981-82	Sudbury Wolves	OHL	53	13	33	1	2854	265	1	5.57	....	....	....	....	....	....	....	....	....	....	....	....	....	....	....	....	....
	Nashville South Stars	CHL	7	3	3	1	380	26	0	4.11	....	....	....	....	....	....	....	....	....	....	....	....	....	....	....	....	....
1982-83	Sudbury Wolves	OHL	43	11	27	0	2320	204	1	5.28	....	....	....	....	....	....	....	....	....	....	....	....	....	....	....	....	....
	Canada	WJC-A	5	....	....	....	240	13	....	3.25	....	....	....	....	....	....	....	....	....	....	....	....	....	....	....	....	....
	Birmingham South Stars	CHL	4	0	4	0	169	14	0	4.97	....	....	....	....	....	....	....	....	....	....	....	....	....	....	....	....	....
1983-84	Salt Lake Golden Eagles	CHL	23	7	12	1	1145	93	0	4.87	....	....	....	....	....	....	....	....	....	....	....	....	....	....	....	....	....
1984-85	**Minnesota North Stars**	NHL	3	0	3	0	139	14	0	6.04	4.80	9.61	88	.841	38.0	....	....	....	....	....	....	....	....	....	....	....	....
	Springfield Indians	AHL	46	23	17	3	2589	140	2	3.24	....	....	....	....	....	3	0	3	0	130	15	0	6.92	....	....	....	....
1985-86	Springfield Indians	AHL	27	8	15	1	1490	94	0	3.79	....	....	....	....	....	....	....	....	....	....	....	....	....	....	....	....	....
1986-87	**Minnesota North Stars**	NHL	3	0	2	0	163	12	0	4.42	3.72	5.10	104	.885	38.3	....	....	....	....	....	....	....	....	....	....	....	....
	Springfield Indians	AHL	19	4	10	0	1048	77	0	4.41	....	....	....	....	....	....	....	....	....	....	....	....	....	....	....	....	....

			REGULAR SEASON													PLAYOFFS											
Season	**Club**	**League**	**GP**	**W**	**L**	**T**	**Mins**	**GA**	**SO**	**Avg**	**AAvg**	**Eff**	**SA**	**S%**	**SAPG**	**GP**	**W**	**L**	**T**	**Mins**	**GA**	**SO**	**Avg**	**Eff**	**SA**	**S%**	**SAPG**
1987-88	Baltimore Skipjacks	AHL	4	0	4	0	185	22	0	7.14	....	....	....	....	....	....	....	....	....	....	....	....	....	....	....	....	....
	Kalamazoo Wings	IHL	3	0	2	1	184	16	0	5.22	....	....	....	....	....	....	....	....	....	....	....	....	....	....	....	....	....
1988-89	Canada	Nat-Team	21	6	13	1	1012	75	0	4.45	....	....	....	....	....	....	....	....	....	....	....	....	....	....	....	....	....
	NHL Totals		**6**	**0**	**5**	**0**	**302**	**26**	**0**	**5.17**	....	....	**192**	**.865**	....	....	....	....	....	....	....	....	....	....	....	....	....

● SARJEANT, GEOFF

Geoff Sarjeant G – L. 5'9", 180 lbs. b: Newmarket, Ont., 11/30/1969. St. Louis' 1st choice, 17th overall, in 1990 Supplemental Draft.

1988-89	Michigan Tech Huskies	WCHA	6	0	3	2	329	22	0	4.01	....	....	....	....	....	....	....	....	....	....	....	....	....	....	....	....	....
1989-90	Michigan Tech Huskies	WCHA	19	4	13	0	1043	94	0	5.41	....	....	....	....	....	....	....	....	....	....	....	....	....	....	....	....	....
1990-91	Michigan Tech Huskies	WCHA	23	5	15	3	1540	97	0	3.78	....	....	....	....	....	....	....	....	....	....	....	....	....	....	....	....	....
1991-92	Michigan Tech Huskies	WCHA	23	7	13	0	1201	90	1	4.50	....	....	....	....	....	....	....	....	....	....	....	....	....	....	....	....	....
1992-93	Peoria Rivermen	IHL	41	22	14	3	2356	130	0	3.31	....	....	....	....	....	3	0	3	....	179	13	0	4.36	....	....	....	....
1993-94	Peoria Rivermen	IHL	41	25	9	2	2275	93	*2	*2.45	....	....	....	....	....	4	2	2	....	211	13	0	3.69	....	....	....	....
1994-95	Peoria Rivermen	IHL	55	32	12	8	3146	158	0	3.01	....	....	....	....	....	4	0	3	....	206	20	0	5.81	....	....	....	....
	St. Louis Blues	**NHL**	**4**	**1**	**0**	**0**	**120**	**6**	**0**	**3.00**	**3.10**	**3.46**	**52**	**.885**	**26.0**	....	....	....	....	....	....	....	....	....	....	....	....
1995-96	**San Jose Sharks**	**NHL**	**4**	**0**	**2**	**1**	**171**	**14**	**0**	**4.91**	**4.83**	**7.90**	**87**	**.839**	**30.5**	....	....	....	....	....	....	....	....	....	....	....	....
	Kansas City Blades	IHL	41	18	18	1	2167	140	1	3.88	....	....	....	....	....	2	0	1	....	99	3	0	1.82	....	....	....	....
1996-97	Cincinnati Cyclones	IHL	59	32	20	5	3287	157	1	2.87	....	....	....	....	....	3	0	3	....	158	12	0	4.55	....	....	....	....
1997-98	Cincinnati Cyclones	IHL	54	25	19	9	3118	142	5	2.73	....	....	....	....	....	5	4	1	....	353	14	0	2.38	....	....	....	....
	NHL Totals		**8**	**1**	**2**	**1**	**291**	**20**	**0**	**4.12**	....	....	**139**	**.856**	....	....	....	....	....	....	....	....	....	....	....	....	....

IHL First All-Star Team (1994)

Signed as a free agent by **San Jose**, September 23, 1995.

● SAUVE, BOB

Bob Sauve G – L. 5'8", 175 lbs. b: Ste. Genevieve, Que., 6/17/1955. Buffalo's 1st choice, 17th overall, in 1975 Amateur Draft.

1971-72	Verdun Maple Leafs	QMJHL	34	....	....	....	2020	202	0	6.00	....	....	....	....	....	2	0	2	0	120	12	0	6.00	....	....	....	....
1972-73	Laval Titan	QMJHL	35	....	....	....	2100	224	0	6.40	....	....	....	....	....	3	....	....	....	160	20	0	7.50	....	....	....	....
1973-74	Laval Titan	QMJHL	61	....	....	....	3620	341	0	5.65	....	....	....	....	....	11	....	....	....	660	60	0	5.45	....	....	....	....
1974-75	Laval Titan	QMJHL	57	....	....	....	3403	287	0	5.06	....	....	....	....	....	16	....	....	....	960	81	0	5.06	....	....	....	....
1975-76	Providence Reds	AHL	14	5	8	1	848	44	0	3.11	....	....	....	....	....	....	....	....	....	....	....	....	....	....	....	....	....
	Charlotte Checkers	SHL	17	....	....	....	979	36	2	2.21	....	....	....	....	....	7	....	....	....	420	10	*2	*1.43	....	....	....	....
1976-77	Rhode Island Reds	AHL	25	....	....	....	1346	94	0	4.14	....	....	....	....	....	....	....	....	....	....	....	....	....	....	....	....	....
	Buffalo Sabres	**NHL**	**4**	**1**	**2**	**0**	**184**	**11**	**0**	**3.59**	**3.34**	....	....	....	....	....	....	....	....	....	....	....	....	....	....	....	....
	Hershey Bears	AHL	9	....	....	....	539	38	0	4.23	....	....	....	....	....	....	....	....	....	....	....	....	....	....	....	....	....
1977-78	**Buffalo Sabres**	**NHL**	**11**	**6**	**2**	**0**	**480**	**20**	**0**	**2.50**	**2.34**	....	....	....	....	....	....	....	....	....	....	....	....	....	....	....	....
	Hershey Bears	AHL	16	4	6	3	872	59	0	4.05	....	....	....	....	....	....	....	....	....	....	....	....	....	....	....	....	....
1978-79	Hershey Bears	AHL	5	3	2	0	278	14	0	3.02	....	....	....	....	....	....	....	....	....	....	....	....	....	....	....	....	....
	Buffalo Sabres	**NHL**	**29**	**10**	**10**	**7**	**1610**	**100**	**0**	**3.73**	**3.30**	....	....	....	....	**3**	**1**	**2**	....	**181**	**9**	**0**	**2.98**	....	....	....	....
1979-80	**Buffalo Sabres**	**NHL**	**32**	**20**	**8**	**4**	**1880**	**74**	**4**	***2.36**	**2.06**	....	....	....	....	**8**	**6**	**2**	....	**501**	**17**	***2**	***2.04**	....	....	....	....
1980-81	**Buffalo Sabres**	**NHL**	**35**	**16**	**10**	**9**	**2100**	**111**	**2**	**3.17**	**2.53**	....	....	....	....	....	....	....	....	....	....	....	....	....	....	....	....
1981-82	**Buffalo Sabres**	**NHL**	**14**	**6**	**1**	**5**	**760**	**35**	**0**	**2.76**	**2.12**	....	....	....	....	....	....	....	....	....	....	....	....	....	....	....	....
	Detroit Red Wings	**NHL**	**41**	**11**	**25**	**4**	**2365**	**165**	**0**	**4.19**	**3.23**	....	....	....	....	....	....	....	....	....	....	....	....	....	....	....	....
1982-83	**Buffalo Sabres**	**NHL**	**54**	**25**	**20**	**7**	**3110**	**179**	**1**	**3.45**	**2.75**	**4.43**	**1393**	**.872**	**26.9**	**10**	**6**	**4**	....	**545**	**28**	***2**	**3.08**	....	....	....	....
1983-84	**Buffalo Sabres**	**NHL**	**40**	**22**	**13**	**4**	**2375**	**138**	**0**	**3.49**	**2.72**	**4.59**	**1050**	**.869**	**26.5**	**2**	**0**	**1**	....	**41**	**5**	**0**	**7.32**	**26.14**	**14**	**.643**	**20.5**
1984-85	**Buffalo Sabres**	**NHL**	**27**	**13**	**10**	**3**	**1564**	**84**	**0**	**3.22**	**2.55**	**4.66**	**581**	**.855**	**22.3**	....	....	....	....	....	....	....	....	....	....	....	....
1985-86	**Chicago Black Hawks**	**NHL**	**38**	**19**	**13**	**2**	**2099**	**138**	**0**	**3.94**	**3.06**	**4.49**	**1210**	**.886**	**34.6**	**2**	**0**	**2**	....	**99**	**8**	**0**	**4.85**	**6.36**	**61**	**.869**	**37.0**
1986-87	**Chicago Blackhawks**	**NHL**	**46**	**19**	**19**	**5**	**2660**	**159**	**1**	**3.59**	**3.02**	**3.81**	**1497**	**.894**	**33.8**	**4**	**0**	**4**	....	**245**	**15**	**0**	**3.67**	**4.05**	**136**	**.890**	**33.3**
1987-88	**New Jersey Devils**	**NHL**	**34**	**10**	**16**	**3**	**1804**	**107**	**0**	**3.56**	**2.96**	**4.63**	**823**	**.870**	**27.4**	**5**	**2**	**1**	....	**238**	**13**	**0**	**3.28**	**3.61**	**118**	**.890**	**29.7**
1988-89	**New Jersey Devils**	**NHL**	**15**	**4**	**5**	**1**	**720**	**56**	**0**	**4.67**	**3.86**	**7.85**	**333**	**.832**	**27.8**	....	....	....	....	....	....	....	....	....	....	....	....
	NHL Totals		**420**	**182**	**154**	**54**	**23711**	**1377**	**8**	**3.48**	....	....	....	....	....	**34**	**15**	**16**	....	**1850**	**95**	**4**	**3.08**	....	....	....	....

QMJHL First All-Star Team (1974) • Shared Vezina Trophy with Don Edwards (1980) • Shared William M. Jennings Trophy with Tom Barrasso (1985)

Traded to **Detroit** by **Buffalo** for future considerations, December 2, 1981. Signed as a free agent by **Buffalo**, June 1, 1982. Traded to **Chicago** by **Buffalo** for Chicago's 3rd round choice (Kevin Kerr) in 1986 Entry Draft, October 15, 1985. Signed as a free agent by **New Jersey**, July 10, 1987.

● SAWCHUK, TERRY

Terry "Ukey" Sawchuk G – L. 5'11", 195 lbs. b: Winnipeg, Man., 12/28/1929. d: 5/31/1970. **HHOF**

1945-46	Winnipeg Monarchs	MJHL	10	....	....	....	600	58	0	5.80	....	....	....	....	....	2	0	2	0	120	12	0	6.00	....	....	....	....
1946-47	Galt Red Wings	OHA	30	....	....	....	1800	94	4	3.13	....	....	....	....	....	2	0	2	0	125	9	0	4.32	....	....	....	....
1947-48	Windsor Spitfires	OHA	4	....	....	....	240	11	0	2.75	....	....	....	....	....	....	....	....	....	....	....	....	....	....	....	....	....
	Windsor Hettche Spitfires	IHL	3	3	0	0	180	5	0	1.67	....	....	....	....	....	....	....	....	....	....	....	....	....	....	....	....	....
	Omaha Knights	USHL	54	30	18	5	3248	174	*4	3.21	....	....	....	....	....	3	1	2	0	180	9	0	3.00	....	....	....	....
1948-49	Indianapolis Capitols	AHL	67	....	....	....	4020	205	2	3.06	....	....	....	....	....	2	0	2	0	120	9	0	4.50	....	....	....	....
1949-50	Indianapolis Capitols	AHL	61	31	20	10	3660	188	3	3.08	....	....	....	....	....	8	*8	0	0	480	12	0	*1.50	....	....	....	....
	Detroit Red Wings	**NHL**	**7**	**4**	**3**	**0**	**420**	**16**	**1**	**2.29**	**2.58**	....	....	....	....	....	....	....	....	....	....	....	....	....	....	....	....
1950-51	**Detroit Red Wings**	**NHL**	***70**	***44**	**13**	**13**	***4200**	**139**	***11**	**1.99**	**2.15**	....	....	....	....	**6**	**2**	**4**	....	**463**	**13**	**1**	**1.68**	....	....	....	....
1951-52	**Detroit Red Wings**	**NHL**	***70**	***44**	**14**	**12**	***4200**	**133**	***12**	***1.90**	**2.15**	....	....	....	....	***8**	***8**	**0**	....	**480**	**5**	***4**	***0.63**	....	....	....	....
1952-53	**Detroit Red Wings**	**NHL**	**63**	***32**	**15**	**16**	**3780**	**120**	**9**	***1.90**	**2.36**	....	....	....	....	**6**	**2**	**4**	....	**372**	**21**	**1**	**3.39**	....	....	....	....
1953-54	**Detroit Red Wings**	**NHL**	**67**	***35**	**19**	**13**	**4004**	**129**	**12**	**1.93**	**2.39**	....	....	....	....	***12**	***8**	**4**	....	***751**	**20**	***2**	***1.60**	....	....	....	....
1954-55	**Detroit Red Wings**	**NHL**	**68**	***40**	**17**	**11**	**4080**	**132**	***12**	***1.94**	**2.27**	....	....	....	....	**11**	***8**	**3**	....	***660**	**26**	***1**	***2.36**	....	....	....	....
1955-56	**Boston Bruins**	**NHL**	**68**	**22**	**33**	**13**	**4080**	**181**	**9**	**2.66**	**3.27**	....	....	....	....	....	....	....	....	....	....	....	....	....	....	....	....
1956-57	**Boston Bruins**	**NHL**	**34**	**18**	**10**	**6**	**2040**	**81**	**2**	**2.38**	**2.70**	....	....	....	....	....	....	....	....	....	....	....	....	....	....	....	....
1957-58	**Detroit Red Wings**	**NHL**	***70**	**29**	**29**	**12**	***4200**	**207**	**3**	**2.96**	**3.30**	....	....	....	....	**4**	**0**	**4**	....	**252**	**19**	**0**	**4.52**	....	....	....	....
1958-59	**Detroit Red Wings**	**NHL**	**67**	**23**	**36**	**8**	**4020**	**209**	**5**	**3.12**	**3.37**	....	....	....	....	....	....	....	....	....	....	....	....	....	....	....	....
1959-60	**Detroit Red Wings**	**NHL**	**58**	**24**	**20**	**14**	**3480**	**156**	**5**	**2.69**	**2.78**	....	....	....	....	**6**	**2**	**4**	....	**405**	**20**	**0**	**2.96**	....	....	....	....
1960-61	**Detroit Red Wings**	**NHL**	**37**	**12**	**16**	**8**	**2150**	**113**	**2**	**3.17**	**3.27**	....	....	....	....	**8**	**5**	**3**	....	**465**	**18**	**1**	**2.32**	....	....	....	....
1961-62	**Detroit Red Wings**	**NHL**	**43**	**14**	**21**	**8**	**2580**	**143**	**5**	**3.33**	**3.46**	....	....	....	....	....	....	....	....	....	....	....	....	....	....	....	....
1962-63	**Detroit Red Wings**	**NHL**	**48**	**22**	**16**	**7**	**2775**	**119**	**3**	**2.57**	**2.62**	....	....	....	....	***11**	**5**	**6**	....	***660**	**36**	**0**	**3.27**	....	....	....	....
1963-64	**Detroit Red Wings**	**NHL**	**53**	**25**	**20**	**7**	**3140**	**138**	**5**	**2.64**	**2.91**	....	....	....	....	**13**	**6**	**5**	....	**677**	**31**	**1**	**2.75**	....	....	....	....
1964-65	**Toronto Maple Leafs**	**NHL**	**36**	**17**	**13**	**6**	**2160**	**92**	**1**	**2.56**	**2.72**	....	....	....	....	**1**	**0**	**1**	....	**60**	**3**	**0**	**3.00**	....	....	....	....
1965-66	**Toronto Maple Leafs**	**NHL**	**27**	**10**	**11**	**3**	**1521**	**80**	**1**	**3.16**	**3.22**	....	....	....	....	**2**	**0**	**2**	....	**120**	**6**	**0**	**3.00**	....	....	....	....
1966-67	**Toronto Maple Leafs**	**NHL**	**28**	**15**	**5**	**4**	**1409**	**66**	**2**	**2.81**	**2.90**	....	....	....	....	***10**	***6**	**4**	....	***565**	**25**	**0**	**2.65**	....	....	....	....
1967-68	**Los Angeles Kings**	**NHL**	**36**	**11**	**14**	**6**	**1936**	**99**	**2**	**3.07**	**3.41**	....	....	....	....	**5**	**2**	**3**	....	**280**	**18**	***1**	**3.86**	....	....	....	....
1968-69	**Detroit Red Wings**	**NHL**	**13**	**3**	**4**	**3**	**641**	**28**	**0**	**2.62**	**2.71**	....	....	....	....	....	....	....	....	....	....	....	....	....	....	....	....
1969-70	**New York Rangers**	**NHL**	**8**	**3**	**1**	**2**	**412**	**20**	**1**	**2.91**	**3.09**	....	....	....	....	**3**	**0**	**1**	....	**80**	**6**	**0**	**4.50**	....	....	....	....
	NHL Totals		***971**	***447**	**330**	**172**	***57228**	**2401**	***103**	**2.52**	....	....	....	....	....	**106**	**54**	**48**	....	**6290**	**267**	**12**	**2.55**	....	....	....	....

USHL Second All-Star Team (1948) • Won Outstanding Rookie Cup (Top Rookie - USHL) (1948) • Won Dudley "Red" Garrett Memorial Award (Top Rookie - AHL) (1949) • AHL First All-Star Team (1950) • NHL First All-Star Team (1951, 1952, 1953) • Won Calder Memorial Trophy (1951) • Won Vezina Trophy (1952, 1953, 1955) • NHL Second All-Star Team (1954, 1955, 1959, 1963) • Shared Vezina Trophy with Johnny Bower (1965) • Won Lester Patrick Trophy (1971)

Played in NHL All-Star Game (1950, 1951, 1952, 1953, 1954, 1955, 1956, 1959, 1963, 1964, 1968)

Traded to **Boston** by **Detroit** with Marcel Bonin, Lorne Davis and Vic Stasiuk for Gilles Boisvert, Real Chevrefils, Norm Corcoran, Warren Godfrey and Ed Sandford, June 3, 1955. Traded to **Detroit** by **Boston** for John Bucyk, June 10, 1957. Claimed by **Toronto** from **Detroit** in Intra-League Draft, June 10, 1964. Claimed by **LA Kings** from **Toronto** in Expansion Draft, June 6, 1967. Traded to **Detroit** by **LA Kings** for Jimmy Peters, October 15, 1968. Traded to **NY Rangers** by **Detroit** with Sandy Snow for Larry Jeffrey, June 17, 1969.

			REGULAR SEASON													PLAYOFFS											
Season	Club	League	GP	W	L	T	Mins	GA	SO	Avg	AAvg	Eff	SA	S%	SAPG	GP	W	L	T	Mins	GA	SO	Avg	Eff	SA	S%	SAPG

• SCHAEFER, JOE

Joe Schaefer G – L. 5'8", 165 lbs. b: Long Island, NY, 12/21/1924.

Season	Club	League	GP	W	L	T	Mins	GA	SO	Avg	AAvg	Eff	SA	S%	SAPG	GP	W	L	T	Mins	GA	SO	Avg	Eff	SA	S%	SAPG
1955-56	New Haven Blades	EHL	1				60	3	0	3.00																	
1956-57	Philadelphia Ramblers	EHL	2				120	9	0	4.50																	
1957-58	Buffalo Bisons	AHL	1	0	1	0	60	12	0	12.00																	
	Philadelphia Ramblers	EHL	1				60	5	0	5.00																	
1958-59	Johnstown Jets	EHL	1	0	1	0	60	11	0	11.00																	
1959-60	**New York Rangers**	**NHL**	**1**	**0**	**1**	**0**	**39**	**5**	**0**	**7.69**	**8.07**																
1960-61	**New York Rangers**	**NHL**	**1**	**0**	**1**	**0**	**47**	**3**	**0**	**3.83**	**3.94**																
	NHL Totals		**2**	**0**	**2**	**0**	**86**	**8**	**0**	**5.58**																	

• **NY Rangers'** assistant trainer/practice goaltender replaced injured Gump Worsley in 2nd period, February 17, 1960. (Chicago 5, NY Rangers 1). • **NY Rangers'** assistant trainer/practice goaltender replaced injured Gump Worsley in 1st period, March 8, 1961. (Chicago 4, NY Rangers 3)

• SCHAFER, PAXTON

Paxton Schafer G – L. 5'9", 164 lbs. b: Medicine Hat, Alta., 2/26/1976. Boston's 3rd choice, 47th overall, in 1995 Entry Draft.

Season	Club	League	GP	W	L	T	Mins	GA	SO	Avg	AAvg	Eff	SA	S%	SAPG	GP	W	L	T	Mins	GA	SO	Avg	Eff	SA	S%	SAPG
1993-94	Medicine Hat Tigers	WHL	19	6	9	1	909	67	0	4.42																	
1994-95	Medicine Hat Tigers	WHL	61	32	26	2	3519	185	0	3.15						5	1	4		339	18	0	3.19				
1995-96	Medicine Hat Tigers	WHL	60	24	30	3	3256	200	1	3.69						5	1	4		251	25	0	5.98				
1996-97	**Boston Bruins**	**NHL**	**3**	**0**	**0**	**0**	**77**	**6**	**0**	**4.68**	**4.96**	**11.23**	**25**	**.760**	**19.5**												
	Providence Bruins	AHL	22	9	10	0	1206	75	1	3.73																	
	Charlotte Checkers	ECHL	4	3	1	0	239	7	0	1.75																	
1997-98	Charlotte Checkers	ECHL	44	21	17	5	2538	131	1	3.10						7	3	4		428	21	0	2.94				
	Providence Bruins	AHL	3	1	1	0	158	11	0	4.16																	
	NHL Totals		**3**	**0**	**0**	**0**	**77**	**6**	**0**	**4.68**			**25**	**.760**													

WHL East First All-Star Team (1995)

• SCHWAB, COREY

Corey Schwab G – L. 6', 180 lbs. b: North Battleford, Sask., 11/4/1970. New Jersey's 12th choice, 200th overall, in 1990 Entry Draft.

Season	Club	League	GP	W	L	T	Mins	GA	SO	Avg	AAvg	Eff	SA	S%	SAPG	GP	W	L	T	Mins	GA	SO	Avg	Eff	SA	S%	SAPG
1988-89	Seattle Thunderbirds	WHL	10	2	2	0	386	31	0	4.82																	
1989-90	Seattle Thunderbirds	WHL	27	15	2	1	1150	69	1	3.60						3	0	0		49	2	0	2.45				
1990-91	Seattle Thunderbirds	WHL	*58	32	18	3	*3289	224	0	4.09						6	1	5		382	25	0	3.93				
1991-92	Utica Devils	AHL	24	9	12	1	1322	95	0	4.31																	
	Cincinnati Cyclones	ECHL	8	6	0	1	450	31	0	4.13						9	6	3		540	29	0	3.22				
1992-93	Utica Devils	AHL	40	18	16	5	2387	169	*2	4.25						1	0	1		59	6	0	6.10				
	Cincinnati Cyclones	IHL	3	1	2	0	185	17	0	5.51																	
1993-94	Albany River Rats	AHL	51	27	21	3	3058	184	0	3.61						5	1	4		298	20	0	4.02				
1994-95	Albany River Rats	AHL	45	25	10	9	2711	117	3	*2.59						7	6	1		425	19	0	2.68				
1995-96	**New Jersey Devils**	**NHL**	**10**	**0**	**3**	**0**	**331**	**12**	**0**	**2.18**	**2.14**	**2.20**	**119**	**.899**	**21.6**												
	Albany River Rats	AHL	5	3	2	0	299	13	0	2.61																	
1996-97	**Tampa Bay Lightning**	**NHL**	**31**	**11**	**12**	**1**	**1462**	**74**	**2**	**3.04**	**3.22**	**3.13**	**719**	**.897**	**29.5**												
1997-98	**Tampa Bay Lightning**	**NHL**	**16**	**2**	**9**	**1**	**821**	**40**	**1**	**2.92**	**3.42**	**3.16**	**370**	**.892**	**27.0**												
	NHL Totals		**57**	**13**	**24**	**2**	**2614**	**126**	**3**	**2.89**			**1208**	**.896**													

AHL Second All-Star Team (1995) • Shared Harry "Hap" Holmes Memorial Trophy (fewest goals against - AHL) with Mike Dunham (1995) • Shared Jack A. Butterfield Trophy (Playoff MVP - AHL) with Mike Dunham (1995)

Traded to **Tampa Bay** by **New Jersey** for Jeff Reese, Chicago's 2nd round choice (previously acquired, New Jersey selected Pierre Dagenais) in 1996 Entry Draft and Tampa Bay's 8th round choice (Jason Bertsch) in 1996 Entry Draft, June 22, 1996.

• SCOTT, RON

Ron Scott G – L. 5'8", 155 lbs. b: Guelph, Ont., 7/21/1960.

Season	Club	League	GP	W	L	T	Mins	GA	SO	Avg	AAvg	Eff	SA	S%	SAPG	GP	W	L	T	Mins	GA	SO	Avg	Eff	SA	S%	SAPG
1978-79	Cornwall Royals	QMJHL	56				2827	248	1	5.26						7				394	29	1	4.42				
1979-80	Cornwall Royals	QMJHL	41				2086	165	0	4.75						16				904	55	1	3.65				
1980-81	Michigan State Spartans	WCHA	33	11	21	1	1899	123	2	3.89																	
1981-82	Michigan State Spartans	CCHA	20	[illegible]	10	1	2298	109	2	2.85																	
1982-83	Michigan State Spartans	CCHA	40	29	9	1	2273	100	2	2.64																	
1983-84	**New York Rangers**	**NHL**	**9**	**2**	**3**	**3**	**485**	**29**	**0**	**3.59**	**2.81**	**4.10**	**254**	**.886**	**31.4**												
	Tulsa Oilers	CHL	29	13	13	3	1717	109	0	3.81						5				280	20	0	4.28				
1984-85	New Haven Nighthawks	AHL	36	13	18	4	2047	130	0	3.81																	
1985-86	**New York Rangers**	**NHL**	**4**	**0**	**3**	**0**	[illegible]	**11**	**0**	[illegible]	[illegible]	**8.31**	**56**	**.804**	**21.5**												
	New Haven Nighthawks	AHL	19	8	8	1	1069	66	1	3.70						2	1	1	0	143	8	0	3.36				
1986-87	**New York Rangers**	**NHL**	**1**	**0**	**0**	**1**	**65**	**5**	**0**	**4.62**	**3.89**	**6.60**	**35**	**.857**	**32.3**												
	New Haven Nighthawks	AHL	29	16	7	0	1744	107	2	3.68																	
1987-88	**New York Rangers**	**NHL**	**2**	**1**	**1**	**0**	**90**	**6**	**0**	**4.00**	**3.33**	**5.85**	**41**	**.854**	**27.3**												
	New Haven Nighthawks	AHL	17	8	7	1	963	49	0	3.05																	
	Colorado Rangers	IHL	8	3	4	0	395	33	0	5.01						5	1	4	0	259	16		3.71				
1988-89	Denver Rangers	IHL	18	7	11	0	990	79	0	4.79																	
1989-90	**Los Angeles Kings**	**NHL**	**12**	**5**	**6**	**0**	**654**	**40**	**0**	**3.67**	**3.07**	**4.57**	**321**	**.875**	**29.4**	**1**	**0**	**0**		**32**	**4**	**0**	**7.50**	**30.00**	**10**	**.600**	**18.8**
	New Haven Nighthawks	AHL	22	8	11	1	1224	79	1	3.87																	
1990-91	New Haven Nighthawks	AHL	29	5	15	4	1540	104	0	4.05																	
	NHL Totals		**28**	**8**	**13**	**4**	**1450**	**91**	**0**	**3.77**			**707**	**.871**		**1**	**0**	**0**		**32**	**4**	**0**	**7.50**				

WCHA First All-Star Team (1981) • CCHA First All-Star Team (1982, 1983) • NCAA West First All-American Team (1982, 1983) • Shared Terry Sawchuk Trophy (fewest goals against - CHL) with John Vanbiesbrouck (1984)

Signed as a free agent by **NY Rangers**, May 25, 1983. Signed as a free agent by **LA Kings**, January 12, 1990.

• SEVIGNY, RICHARD

Richard Sevigny G – L. 5'8", 172 lbs. b: Montreal, Que., 4/11/1957. Montreal's 11th choice, 124th overall, in 1977 Amateur Draft.

Season	Club	League	GP	W	L	T	Mins	GA	SO	Avg	AAvg	Eff	SA	S%	SAPG	GP	W	L	T	Mins	GA	SO	Avg	Eff	SA	S%	SAPG
1974-75	Granby Vics	Jr. A	50				2966	240	*2	4.85																	
	Sherbrooke Castors	QMJHL	2				62	4	0	3.87																	
1975-76	Sherbrooke Castors	QMJHL	55				3058	196	2	3.85						15				797	56	0	4.22				
	Canada	WJC	4				226	23		6.10																	
1976-77	Sherbrooke Castors	QMJHL	65				3656	248	*2	4.07						18				1058	60	2	3.40				
1977-78	Kalamazoo Wings	IHL	35				1897	95	1	3.01						7				296	12	0	*2.43				
1978-79	Springfield Indians	AHL	22	6	12	3	1302	77	0	3.55																	
	Nova Scotia Voyageurs	AHL	20	12	6	1	1169	57	1	2.93						10	5	5	0	607	37	0	3.66				
1979-80	**Montreal Canadiens**	**NHL**	**11**	**5**	**4**	**2**	**632**	**31**	**0**	**2.94**	**2.58**																
	Nova Scotia Voyageurs	AHL	35	17	12	4	2104	114	*3	3.25						4	1	3	0	239	15	0	3.77				
1980-81	**Montreal Canadiens**	**NHL**	**33**	**20**	**4**	**3**	**1777**	**71**	**2**	***2.40**	**1.91**					**3**	**0**	**3**		**180**	**13**	**0**	**4.33**				
1981-82	**Montreal Canadiens**	**NHL**	**19**	**11**	**4**	**2**	**1027**	**53**	**0**	**3.10**	**2.38**																
1982-83	**Montreal Canadiens**	**NHL**	**38**	**15**	**11**	**8**	**2130**	**122**	**1**	**3.44**	**2.74**	**4.02**	**1045**	**.883**	**29.4**	**1**	**0**	**0**		**28**	**0**	**0**	**0.00**				
1983-84	**Montreal Canadiens**	**NHL**	**40**	**16**	**18**	**2**	**2203**	**124**	**1**	**3.38**	**2.64**	**4.43**	**946**	**.869**	**25.8**												
1984-85	**Quebec Nordiques**	**NHL**	**20**	**10**	**6**	**2**	**1104**	**62**	**1**	**3.37**	**2.67**	**4.26**	**491**	**.874**	**26.7**												
1985-86	**Quebec Nordiques**	**NHL**	**11**	**3**	**5**	**1**	**468**	**33**	**0**	**4.23**	**3.29**	**5.77**	**242**	**.864**	**31.0**												
	Fredericton Express	AHL	6	3	3	0	362	21	0	3.48																	
1986-87	**Quebec Nordiques**	**NHL**	**4**	**0**	**2**	**0**	**144**	**11**	**0**	**4.58**	**3.85**	**9.00**	**56**	**.804**	**23.3**												
	Fredericton Express	AHL	16	4	10	0	884	62	0	4.21																	
1987-88	Fredericton Express	AHL	1	0	0	0	16	2	0	7.50																	
	NHL Totals		**176**	**80**	**54**	**20**	**9485**	**507**	**5**	**3.21**						**4**	**0**	**3**		**208**	**13**	**0**	**3.75**				

QMJHL West First All-Star Team (1976) • IHL Second All-Star Team (1978) • Shared Vezina Trophy with Denis Herron and Michel Larocque (1981)

Signed as a free agent by **Quebec**, July 4, 1984.

• SHARPLES, SCOTT

Scott (Warren) Sharples G – L. 6', 180 lbs. b: Montreal, Que., 3/1/1968. Calgary's 8th choice, 184th overall, in 1986 Entry Draft.

Season	Club	League	GP	W	L	T	Mins	GA	SO	Avg	AAvg	Eff	SA	S%	SAPG	GP	W	L	T	Mins	GA	SO	Avg	Eff	SA	S%	SAPG
1985-86	Penticton Broncos	BCJHL	28	20	6	0	1522	94	0	*3.71																	
1986-87	University of Michigan	CCHA	32	12	16	1	1728	140	1	5.14																	
1987-88	University of Michigan	CCHA	33	18	15	0	1930	132	0	4.10																	

Season	Club	League	REGULAR SEASON GP	W	L	T	Mins	GA	SO	Avg	AAvg	Eff	SA	S%	SAPG	PLAYOFFS GP	W	L	T	Mins	GA	SO	Avg	Eff	SA	S%	SAPG
1988-89	University of Michigan	CCHA	33	17	11	2	1887	116	0	3.69	....	....	....	....	....	....	....	....	....	....	....	....	....	....	....	....	....
1989-90	University of Michigan	CCHA	*39	20	10	6	*2165	117	0	3.24	....	....	....	....	....	....	....	....	....	....	....	....	....	....	....	....	....
	Salt Lake Golden Eagles	IHL	3	0	3	0	178	13	0	4.38	....	....	....	....	....	....	....	....	....	....	....	....	....	....	....	....	....
1990-91	Salt Lake Golden Eagles	IHL	37	21	11	1	2097	124	2	3.55	....	....	....	....	....	4	0	3	0	188	14	0	4.47	....	....	....	....
1991-92	**Calgary Flames**	**NHL**	**1**	**0**	**0**	**1**	**65**	**4**	**0**	**3.69**	**3.27**	**3.69**	**40**	**.900**	**36.9**	....	....	....	....	....	....	....	....	....	....	....	....
	Salt Lake Golden Eagles	IHL	35	9	18	4	1936	121	0	3.75	....	....	....	....	....	1	0	1	0	60	7	0	7.00	....	....	....	....
1992-93	St. John's Maple Leafs	AHL	25	9	8	3	1168	80	0	4.11	....	....	....	....	....	1	0	0	0	7	0	0	0.00	....	....	....	....
	Brantford Smoke	ColHL	7	5	1	0	400	27	0	4.05	....	....	....	....	....	....	....	....	....	....	....	....	....	....	....	....	....
	NHL Totals		**1**	**0**	**0**	**1**	**65**	**4**	**0**	**3.69**	....	....	**40**	**.900**	....	....	....	....	....	....	....	....	....	....	....	....	....

• SHIELDS, AL

Al Shields G – R. 6', 188 lbs. b: Ottawa, Ont., 5/10/1907.

Season	Club	League	GP	W	L	T	Mins	GA	SO	Avg	AAvg	Eff	SA	S%	SAPG	GP	W	L	T	Mins	GA	SO	Avg	Eff	SA	S%	SAPG
1931-32	**New York Americans**	**NHL**	**2**	**0**	**0**	**0**	**41**	**9**	**0**	**13.17**	**16.31**	....	....	....	....	....	....	....	....	....	....	....	....	....	....	....	....
	NHL Totals		**2**	**0**	**0**	**0**	**41**	**9**	**0**	**13.17**	....	....	....	....	....	....	....	....	....	....	....	....	....	....	....	....	....

• NY Americans' defenseman replaced injured Roy Worters in 3rd period, November 17, 1931. (NY Rangers 3, NY Americans 0) • Replaced injured Roy Worters in 2nd period, January 19, 1932. (Toronto 11, NY Americans 3)

• SHIELDS, STEVE

Steve Shields G – L. 6'3", 210 lbs. b: Toronto, Ont., 7/19/1972. Buffalo's 5th choice, 101st overall, in 1991 Entry Draft.

Season	Club	League	GP	W	L	T	Mins	GA	SO	Avg	AAvg	Eff	SA	S%	SAPG	GP	W	L	T	Mins	GA	SO	Avg	Eff	SA	S%	SAPG
1990-91	University of Michigan	CCHA	37	26	6	3	1963	106	0	3.24	....	....	....	....	....	....	....	....	....	....	....	....	....	....	....	....	....
1991-92	University of Michigan	CCHA	*37	*27	7	2	*2090	99	1	2.84	....	....	....	....	....	....	....	....	....	....	....	....	....	....	....	....	....
1992-93	University of Michigan	CCHA	*39	*30	6	2	2027	75	2	*2.22	....	....	....	....	....	....	....	....	....	....	....	....	....	....	....	....	....
1993-94	University of Michigan	CCHA	36	*28	6	1	1961	87	0	2.66	....	....	....	....	....	....	....	....	....	....	....	....	....	....	....	....	....
1994-95	Rochester Americans	AHL	13	3	8	0	673	53	0	4.72	....	....	....	....	....	1	0	0	....	20	3	0	9.00	....	....	....	....
	South Carolina Stingrays	ECHL	21	11	5	2	1158	52	2	2.69	....	....	....	....	....	3	0	2	....	144	11	0	4.58	....	....	....	....
1995-96	**Buffalo Sabres**	**NHL**	**2**	**1**	**0**	**0**	**75**	**4**	**0**	**3.20**	**3.14**	**4.00**	**32**	**.875**	**25.6**	....	....	....	....	....	....	....	....	....	....	....	....
	Rochester Americans	AHL	43	20	17	2	2357	140	1	3.56	....	....	....	....	....	*19	*15	3	....	*1127	47	1	2.50	....	....	....	....
1996-97	**Buffalo Sabres**	**NHL**	**13**	**3**	**8**	**2**	**789**	**39**	**0**	**2.97**	**3.14**	**2.59**	**447**	**.913**	**34.0**	**10**	**4**	**6**	....	**570**	**26**	**1**	**2.74**	**2.13**	**334**	**.922**	**35.2**
	Rochester Americans	AHL	23	14	6	2	1331	60	1	2.70	....	....	....	....	....	....	....	....	....	....	....	....	....	....	....	....	....
1997-98	**Buffalo Sabres**	**NHL**	**16**	**3**	**6**	**4**	**785**	**37**	**0**	**2.83**	**3.31**	**2.57**	**408**	**.909**	**31.2**	....	....	....	....	....	....	....	....	....	....	....	....
	Rochester Americans	AHL	1	0	1	0	59	3	0	3.04	....	....	....	....	....	....	....	....	....	....	....	....	....	....	....	....	....
	NHL Totals		**31**	**7**	**14**	**6**	**1649**	**80**	**0**	**2.91**	....	....	**887**	**.910**	....	**10**	**4**	**6**	....	**570**	**26**	**1**	**2.74**	....	....	....	....

CCHA First All-Star Team (1993, 1994) • NCAA West Second All-American Team (1993, 1994)

Traded to **San Jose** by **Buffalo** with Buffalo's 4th round choice (Miroskav Zalesak) in 1998 Entry Draft for Kay Whitmore, Colorado's 2nd round choice (previously acquired, Buffalo selected Jaroslav Kristek) in 1998 Entry Draft and San Jose's 5th round choice in 2000 Entry Draft, June 18, 1998.

• SHTALENKOV, MIKHAIL

Mikhail Shtalenkov G – L. 6'2", 185 lbs. b: Moscow, USSR, 10/20/1965. Anaheim's 5th choice, 108th overall, in 1993 Entry Draft.

Season	Club	League	GP	W	L	T	Mins	GA	SO	Avg	AAvg	Eff	SA	S%	SAPG	GP	W	L	T	Mins	GA	SO	Avg	Eff	SA	S%	SAPG
1986-87	Moscow Dynamo	USSR	17	....	....	....	893	36	1	2.41	....	....	....	....	....	....	....	....	....	....	....	....	....	....	....	....	....
1987-88	Moscow Dynamo	USSR	25	....	....	....	1302	72	1	3.31	....	....	....	....	....	....	....	....	....	....	....	....	....	....	....	....	....
1988-89	Moscow Dynamo	USSR	4	....	....	....	80	3	0	2.25	....	....	....	....	....	....	....	....	....	....	....	....	....	....	....	....	....
1989-90	Moscow Dynamo	FrTour	1	....	....	....	2	0	0	0.00	....	....	....	....	....	....	....	....	....	....	....	....	....	....	....	....	....
	Moscow Dynamo	USSR	6	....	....	....	20	1	0	3.00	....	....	....	....	....	....	....	....	....	....	....	....	....	....	....	....	....
1990-91	Moscow Dynamo	FrTour	1	....	....	....	60	1	0	1.00	....	....	....	....	....	....	....	....	....	....	....	....	....	....	....	....	....
	Moscow Dynamo	USSR	31	....	....	....	1568	56	2	2.14	....	....	....	....	....	....	....	....	....	....	....	....	....	....	....	....	....
	Moscow Dynamo	SuperS	3	....	....	....	160	11	....	4.13	....	....	....	....	....	....	....	....	....	....	....	....	....	....	....	....	....
1991-92	Soviet Union	C Cup	5	1	2	1	276	11	....	2.00	....	....	....	....	....	....	....	....	....	....	....	....	....	....	....	....	....
	Moscow Dynamo	CIS	27	....	....	....	1268	45	1	2.12	....	....	....	....	....	....	....	....	....	....	....	....	....	....	....	....	....
	Russia	Olympics	8	7	1	0	440	12	....	1.64	....	....	....	....	....	....	....	....	....	....	....	....	....	....	....	....	....
	Russia	WC-A	6	3	1	1	293	10	....	2.05	....	....	....	....	....	....	....	....	....	....	....	....	....	....	....	....	....
1992-93	Milwaukee Admirals	IHL	47	26	14	5	2669	135	2	3.03	....	....	....	....	....	3	1	2	....	209	11	0	3.16	....	....	....	....
1993-94	**Anaheim Mighty Ducks**	**NHL**	**10**	**3**	**4**	**1**	**543**	**24**	**0**	**2.65**	**2.52**	**2.40**	**265**	**.909**	**29.3**	....	....	....	....	....	....	....	....	....	....	....	....
	San Diego Gulls	IHL	28	15	11	2	1616	93	0	3.45	....	....	....	....	....	....	....	....	....	....	....	....	....	....	....	....	....
	Russia	WC-A	6	3	1	0	296	5	....	1.01	....	....	....	....	....	....	....	....	....	....	....	....	....	....	....	....	....
1994-95	**Anaheim Mighty Ducks**	**NHL**	**18**	**4**	**7**	**1**	**810**	**49**	**0**	**3.63**	**3.76**	**3.97**	**448**	**.891**	**33.2**	....	....	....	....	....	....	....	....	....	....	....	....
1995-96	**Anaheim Mighty Ducks**	**NHL**	**30**	**7**	**16**	**3**	**1637**	**85**	**0**	**3.12**	**3.06**	**3.26**	**814**	**.896**	**29.8**	....	....	....	....	....	....	....	....	....	....	....	....
	Russia	WC-A	3	2	1	0	185	10	....	3.24	....	....	....	....	....	....	....	....	....	....	....	....	....	....	....	....	....
1996-97	Russia	W Cup	DID NOT PLAY – SPARE GOALTENDER																								
	Anaheim Mighty Ducks	**NHL**	**24**	**7**	**8**	**1**	**1079**	**52**	**2**	**2.89**	**3.06**	**2.79**	**539**	**.904**	**30.0**	**4**	**0**	**3**	....	**211**	**10**	**0**	**2.84**	**1.75**	**162**	**.938**	**46.1**
1997-98	**Anaheim Mighty Ducks**	**NHL**	**40**	**13**	**18**	**5**	**2049**	**110**	**1**	**3.22**	**3.78**	**3.44**	**1031**	**.893**	**30.2**	....	....	....	....	....	....	....	....	....	....	....	....
	Russia	Olympics	5	4	1	0	290	8	0	1.65	....	....	....	....	....	....	....	....	....	....	....	....	....	....	....	....	....
	NHL Totals		**122**	**34**	**53**	**11**	**6118**	**320**	**3**	**3.14**	....	....	**3097**	**.897**	....	**4**	**0**	**3**	....	**211**	**10**	**0**	**2.84**	....	....	....	....

USSR Rookie of the Year (1987) • Won Garry F. Longman Memorial Trophy (Top Rookie - IHL) (1993)

Claimed by **Nashville** from **Anaheim** in Expansion Draft, June 26, 1998.

• SHULMISTRA, RICHARD

Richard Shulmistra G – R. 6'2", 185 lbs. b: Sudbury, Ont., 4/1/1971. Quebec's 1st choice, 4th overall, in 1992 Supplemental Draft.

Season	Club	League	GP	W	L	T	Mins	GA	SO	Avg	AAvg	Eff	SA	S%	SAPG	GP	W	L	T	Mins	GA	SO	Avg	Eff	SA	S%	SAPG
1990-91	University of Miami-Ohio	CCHA	20	2	12	2	920	80	0	5.21	....	....	....	....	....	....	....	....	....	....	....	....	....	....	....	....	....
1991-92	University of Miami-Ohio	CCHA	19	3	5	2	850	67	0	4.72	....	....	....	....	....	....	....	....	....	....	....	....	....	....	....	....	....
1992-93	University of Miami-Ohio	CCHA	33	22	6	4	1949	88	1	2.71	....	....	....	....	....	....	....	....	....	....	....	....	....	....	....	....	....
1993-94	University of Miami-Ohio	CCHA	27	13	12	1	1521	74	0	2.92	....	....	....	....	....	....	....	....	....	....	....	....	....	....	....	....	....
1994-95	Cornwall Aces	AHL	20	4	9	2	937	58	0	3.71	....	....	....	....	....	8	4	3	....	446	22	0	2.95	....	....	....	....
1995-96	Cornwall Aces	AHL	36	9	18	2	1844	100	0	3.25	....	....	....	....	....	1	0	0	....	9	1	0	6.76	....	....	....	....
1996-97	Albany River Rats	AHL	23	5	9	2	1062	43	2	2.43	....	....	....	....	....	2	1	0	....	77	2	0	1.56	....	....	....	....
1997-98	Fort Wayne Komets	IHL	11	3	8	0	656	34	1	3.11	....	....	....	....	....	....	....	....	....	....	....	....	....	....	....	....	....
	New Jersey Devils	**NHL**	**1**	**0**	**1**	**0**	**62**	**2**	**0**	**1.94**	**2.27**	**1.29**	**30**	**.933**	**29.0**	....	....	....	....	....	....	....	....	....	....	....	....
	Albany River Rats	AHL	35	20	8	4	2022	78	2	*2.31	....	....	....	....	....	13	8	3	....	696	32	1	2.76	....	....	....	....
	NHL Totals		**1**	**0**	**1**	**0**	**62**	**2**	**0**	**1.94**	....	....	**30**	**.933**		....	....	....	....	....	....	....	....	....	....	....	....

CCHA Second All-Star Team (1993) • AHL Second All-Star Team (1998)

Transferred to **Colorado** after **Quebec** franchise relocated, June 21, 1995. Signed as a free agent by **New Jersey**, December 31, 1997.

• SIDORKIEWICZ, PETER

Peter Sidorkiewicz G – L. 5'9", 180 lbs. b: Dabrowa Bialostocka, Pol., 6/29/1963. Washington's 5th choice, 91st overall, in 1981 Entry Draft.

Season	Club	League	GP	W	L	T	Mins	GA	SO	Avg	AAvg	Eff	SA	S%	SAPG	GP	W	L	T	Mins	GA	SO	Avg	Eff	SA	S%	SAPG
1980-81	Oshawa Generals	OHA	7	3	3	0	308	24	0	4.68	....	....	....	....	....	5	2	2	....	266	20	0	4.52	....	....	....	....
1981-82	Oshawa Generals	OHL	29	14	11	1	1553	123	*2	4.75	....	....	....	....	....	1	0	0	....	13	1	0	4.62	....	....	....	....
1982-83	Oshawa Generals	OHL	60	36	20	3	3536	213	0	3.61	....	....	....	....	....	17	15	1	....	1020	60	0	3.53	....	....	....	....
1983-84	Oshawa Generals	OHL	52	28	21	1	2966	250	1	4.15	....	....	....	....	....	7	3	4	....	420	27	*1	3.86	....	....	....	....
1984-85	Binghamton Whalers	AHL	45	31	9	5	2691	137	3	3.05	....	....	....	....	....	8	4	4	....	481	31	0	3.87	....	....	....	....
	Fort Wayne Komets	IHL	10	4	4	2	590	43	0	4.37	....	....	....	....	....	....	....	....	....	....	....	....	....	....	....	....	....
1985-86	Binghamton Whalers	AHL	49	21	22	3	2819	150	2	*3.19	....	....	....	....	....	4	1	3	....	235	12	0	3.06	....	....	....	....
1986-87	Binghamton Whalers	AHL	57	23	16	0	3304	161	4	2.92	....	....	....	....	....	13	6	7	....	794	36	0	*2.72	....	....	....	....
1987-88	**Hartford Whalers**	**NHL**	**1**	**0**	**1**	**0**	**60**	**6**	**0**	**6.00**	**4.99**	**10.00**	**36**	**.833**	**36.0**	....	....	....	....	....	....	....	....	....	....	....	....
	Binghamton Whalers	AHL	42	19	17	3	2345	144	0	3.68	....	....	....	....	....	3	0	2	....	147	8	0	3.27	....	....	....	....
1988-89	**Hartford Whalers**	**NHL**	**44**	**22**	**18**	**4**	**2635**	**133**	**4**	**3.03**	**2.49**	**3.34**	**1207**	**.890**	**27.5**	**2**	**0**	**2**	....	**124**	**8**	**0**	**3.87**	**6.88**	**45**	**.822**	**21.8**
	Canada	WEC-A	1	....	....	....	25	0	0	0.00	....	....	....	....	....	....	....	....	....	....	....	....	....	....	....	....	....
1989-90	**Hartford Whalers**	**NHL**	**46**	**19**	**19**	**7**	**2703**	**161**	**1**	**3.57**	**2.99**	**4.78**	**1203**	**.866**	**26.7**	**7**	**3**	**4**	....	**429**	**23**	**0**	**3.22**	**3.84**	**193**	**.881**	**27.0**
1990-91	**Hartford Whalers**	**NHL**	**52**	**21**	**22**	**7**	**2953**	**164**	**1**	**3.33**	**2.97**	**4.25**	**1284**	**.872**	**26.1**	**6**	**2**	**4**	....	**359**	**24**	**0**	**4.01**	**5.53**	**174**	**.862**	**29.1**
1991-92	**Hartford Whalers**	**NHL**	**35**	**9**	**19**	**6**	**1995**	**111**	**2**	**3.34**	**2.96**	**3.94**	**940**	**.882**	**28.3**	....	....	....	....	....	....	....	....	....	....	....	....
1992-93	**Ottawa Senators**	**NHL**	**64**	**8**	**46**	**3**	**3388**	**250**	**0**	**4.43**	**3.79**	**6.38**	**1737**	**.856**	**30.8**	....	....	....	....	....	....	....	....	....	....	....	....
1993-94	**New Jersey Devils**	**NHL**	**3**	**0**	**3**	**0**	**130**	**6**	**0**	**2.77**	**2.64**	**3.02**	**55**	**.891**	**25.4**	....	....	....	....	....	....	....	....	....	....	....	....
	Albany River Rats	AHL	15	6	7	2	907	60	0	3.97	....	....	....	....	....	....	....	....	....	....	....	....	....	....	....	....	....
	Fort Wayne Komets	IHL	11	6	3	0	591	27	*2	2.74	....	....	....	....	....	*18	10	8	....	*1054	59	*1	3.36	....	....	....	....
1994-95	Fort Wayne Komets	IHL	16	8	6	1	941	58	1	3.70	....	....	....	....	....	3	1	2	....	144	12	0	5.00	....	....	....	....
1995-96	Albany River Rats	AHL	32	19	7	5	1809	89	3	2.95	....	....	....	....	....	1	0	1	....	59	3	0	3.06	....	....	....	....

Season	Club	League	REGULAR SEASON													PLAYOFFS											
			GP	W	L	T	Mins	GA	SO	Avg	AAvg	Eff	SA	S%	SAPG	GP	W	L	T	Mins	GA	SO	Avg	Eff	SA	S%	SAPG
1996-97	Albany River Rats	AHL	62	31	23	6	3539	171	2	2.90	....	....	....	....	....	16	7	8	....	920	48	0	3.13	....	....	....	....
1997-98	**New Jersey Devils**	**NHL**	**1**	**0**	**0**	**0**	**20**	**1**	**0**	**3.00**	**3.51**	**3.75**	**8**	**.875**	**24.0**	....	....	....	....	....	....	....	....	....	....	....	....
	Albany River Rats	AHL	43	21	15	5	2422	115	3	2.85	....	....	....	....	....	2	1	1	....	89	6	0	4.01	....	....	....	....
	NHL Totals		**246**	**79**	**128**	**27**	**13884**	**832**	**8**	**3.60**	....	....	**6470**	**.871**	....	**15**	**5**	**10**	....	**912**	**55**	**0**	**3.62**	....	....	....	....

AHL Second All-Star Team (1987) • NHL All-Rookie Team (1989)

Played in NHL All-Star Game (1993)

Traded to **Hartford** by **Washington** with Dean Evason for David Jensen, March 12, 1985. Claimed by **Ottawa** from **Hartford** in Expansion Draft, June 18, 1992. Traded to **New Jersey** by **Ottawa** with future considerations (Mike Peluso, June 26, 1993) for Craig Billington, Troy Mallette and New Jersey's 4th round choice (Cosmo Dupaul) in 1993 Entry Draft, June 20, 1993.

• SIMMONS, DON

Don "Dippy" Simmons G – R. 5'10", 150 lbs. b: Port Colborne, Ont., 9/13/1931.

Season	Club	League	GP	W	L	T	Mins	GA	SO	Avg	AAvg	Eff	SA	S%	SAPG	GP	W	L	T	Mins	GA	SO	Avg	Eff	SA	S%	SAPG
1948-49	Galt Rockets	OHA	12	....	....	....	720	73	0	6.08	....	....	....	....	....	....	....	....	....	....	....	....	....	....	....	....	....
1949-50			STATISTICS NOT AVAILABLE																								
1950-51	St. Catharines Teepees	OHA	53	....	....	....	3180	181	3	3.41	....	....	....	....	....	6	....	....	....	360	19	1	3.17	....	....	....	....
1951-52	Springfield Indians	EHL	37	18	18	1	2270	121	0	3.20	....	....	....	....	....	3	0	3	0	180	19	0	6.33	....	....	....	....
1952-53	Springfield Indians	EHL	44	*31	11	2	2680	168	0	3.76	....	....	....	....	....	....	....	....	....	....	....	....	....	....	....	....	....
1953-54	Johnstown Jets	IHL	24	....	....	....	1440	66	2	2.75	....	....	....	....	....	10	6	4	0	600	21	1	2.10	....	....	....	....
1954-55	Springfield Indians	AHL	54	30	21	3	3240	185	2	3.43	....	....	....	....	....	4	1	3	0	258	16	0	3.72	....	....	....	....
1955-56	Springfield Indians	AHL	52	16	33	2	3120	233	0	4.48	....	....	....	....	....	....	....	....	....	....	....	....	....	....	....	....	....
1956-57	Springfield Indians	AHL	25	10	12	3	1300	84	0	3.36	....	....	....	....	....	....	....	....	....	....	....	....	....	....	....	....	....
	Boston Bruins	**NHL**	**26**	**13**	**9**	**4**	**1560**	**63**	**4**	**2.42**	**2.76**	....	....	....	....	***10**	**5**	**5**	....	**600**	**29**	***2**	**2.90**	....	....	....	....
1957-58	**Boston Bruins**	**NHL**	**38**	**15**	**14**	**8**	**2228**	**93**	**5**	**2.50**	**2.73**	....	....	....	....	***11**	**6**	**5**	....	***671**	**27**	***1**	**2.41**	....	....	....	....
1958-59	**Boston Bruins**	**NHL**	**58**	**24**	**26**	**8**	**3480**	**184**	**3**	**3.17**	**3.43**	....	....	....	....	....	....	....	....	....	....	....	....	....	....	....	....
1959-60	**Boston Bruins**	**NHL**	**28**	**12**	**13**	**3**	**1680**	**94**	**2**	**3.36**	**3.55**	....	....	....	....	....	....	....	....	....	....	....	....	....	....	....	....
1960-61	**Boston Bruins**	**NHL**	**18**	**3**	**9**	**6**	**1079**	**59**	**1**	**3.28**	**3.39**	....	....	....	....	....	....	....	....	....	....	....	....	....	....	....	....
	Providence Reds	AHL	10	3	7	0	590	51	0	5.19	....	....	....	....	....	....	....	....	....	....	....	....	....	....	....	....	....
1961-62	Rochester Americans	AHL	51	24	22	5	3060	169	0	3.31	....	....	....	....	....	....	....	....	....	....	....	....	....	....	....	....	....
	Toronto Maple Leafs	**NHL**	**9**	**5**	**3**	**1**	**540**	**21**	**1**	**2.33**	**2.38**	....	....	....	....	**3**	**2**	**1**	....	**165**	**8**	**0**	**2.91**	....	....	....	....
1962-63	**Toronto Maple Leafs**	**NHL**	**28**	**15**	**8**	**5**	**1680**	**70**	**1**	**2.50**	**2.57**	....	....	....	....	....	....	....	....	....	....	....	....	....	....	....	....
	Rochester Americans	AHL	9	4	5	0	540	27	1	3.00	....	....	....	....	....	....	....	....	....	....	....	....	....	....	....	....	....
1963-64	**Toronto Maple Leafs**	**NHL**	**21**	**9**	**9**	**1**	**1191**	**63**	**3**	**3.17**	**3.55**	....	....	....	....	....	....	....	....	....	....	....	....	....	....	....	....
1964-65	Tulsa Oilers	CHL	*69	*35	26	8	*3540	219	3	3.17	....	....	....	....	....	*12	6	6	0	*720	38	*1	3.17	....	....	....	....
1965-66	Baltimore Clippers	AHL	13	4	6	2	750	42	0	3.36	....	....	....	....	....	....	....	....	....	....	....	....	....	....	....	....	....
	New York Rangers	**NHL**	**11**	**1**	**6**	**1**	**491**	**37**	**0**	**4.52**	**4.63**	....	....	....	....	....	....	....	....	....	....	....	....	....	....	....	....
1966-67	Vancouver Canucks	WHL	*72	*38	32	2	*4326	213	*7	2.95	....	....	....	....	....	3	2	0	0	140	3	0	1.29	....	....	....	....
1967-68	**New York Rangers**	**NHL**	**5**	**2**	**1**	**2**	**300**	**13**	**0**	**2.60**	**2.88**	....	....	....	....	....	....	....	....	....	....	....	....	....	....	....	....
	Buffalo Bisons	AHL	22	9	7	5	1279	74	0	3.47	....	....	....	....	....	....	....	....	....	....	....	....	....	....	....	....	....
1968-69	**New York Rangers**	**NHL**	**5**	**2**	**2**	**1**	**206**	**8**	**0**	**2.33**	**2.41**	....	....	....	....	....	....	....	....	....	....	....	....	....	....	....	....
	Buffalo Bisons	AHL	5	2	3	0	259	14	1	3.24	....	....	....	....	....	....	....	....	....	....	....	....	....	....	....	....	....
	NHL Totals		**247**	**101**	**100**	**40**	**14435**	**705**	**20**	**2.93**	....	....	....	....	....	**24**	**13**	**11**	....	**1436**	**64**	**3**	**2.67**	....	....	....	....

EHL Second All-Star Team (1952, 1953) • AHL Second All-Star Team (1955) • WHL First All-Star Team (1967)

Played in NHL All-Star Game (1963)

Traded to **Boston** by **Springfield** (AHL) for Norm Defelice and Jack Bionda, January 22, 1957. Traded to **Toronto** by **Boston** for Ed Chadwick, January, 1961. Claimed by **NY Rangers** from **Toronto** (Tulsa - CHL) in Inter-League Draft, June 8, 1965.

• SIMMONS, GARY

Gary "The Snake" Simmons G – L. 6'2", 200 lbs. b: Charlottetown, P.E.I., 7/19/1944.

Season	Club	League	GP	W	L	T	Mins	GA	SO	Avg	AAvg	Eff	SA	S%	SAPG	GP	W	L	T	Mins	GA	SO	Avg	Eff	SA	S%	SAPG
1965-66	P. Huron–D. Moines–Toledo	IHL	21	....	....	....	1240	102	0	4.94	....	....	....	....	....	....	....	....	....	....	....	....	....	....	....	....	....
1966-67	Conception Bay Ceebees	Nfld.	37	23	14	0	2265	147	0	3.97	....	....	....	....	....	....	....	....	....	....	....	....	....	....	....	....	....
1967-68	Conception Bay Ceebees	Nfld.	40	20	17	3	2400	180	*2	4.50	....	....	....	....	....	....	....	....	....	....	....	....	....	....	....	....	....
1968-69	Calgary Stampeders	ASHL	STATISTICS NOT AVAILABLE																								
1969-70	Calgary Stampeders	ASHL	*38	*30	8	0	*2280	113	....	*2.97	....	....	....	....	....	....	....	....	....	....	....	....	....	....	....	....	....
1970-71	San Diego Gulls	WHL	14	5	6	0	717	41	0	3.43	....	....	....	....	....	....	....	....	....	....	....	....	....	....	....	....	....
1971-72	Calgary Stampeders	ASHL	21	....	....	....	1260	66	*2	*2.90	....	....	....	....	....	....	....	....	....	....	....	....	....	....	....	....	....
1972-73	Phoenix Roadrunners	WHL	36	18	16	2	2078	119	3	3.44	....	....	....	....	....	3	1	1	0	166	10	0	3.61	....	....	....	....
1973-74	Tulsa Oilers	CHL	1	0	1	0	60	7	0	7.00	....	....	....	....	....	....	....	....	....	....	....	....	....	....	....	....	....
	Phoenix Roadrunners	WHL	49	28	17	2	2861	142	0	[illegible]	....	....	....	....	....	*9	*8	1	0	*566	22	*2	2.33	....	....	....	....
1974-75	**California Golden Seals**	**NHL**	**34**	**10**	**21**	**3**	**2029**	**124**	**2**	**3.67**	**3.31**	....	....	....	....	....	....	....	....	....	....	....	....	....	....	....	....
1975-76	**California Golden Seals**	**NHL**	**40**	**15**	**19**	**5**	**2360**	**131**	**2**	**3.33**	**3.01**	....	....	....	....	....	....	....	....	....	....	....	....	....	....	....	....
1976-77	**Cleveland Barons**	**NHL**	**15**	**2**	**8**	**4**	**840**	**51**	**1**	**3.64**	**3.39**	....	....	....	....	....	....	....	....	....	....	....	....	....	....	....	....
	Los Angeles Kings	**NHL**	**4**	**1**	**2**	**1**	**240**	**16**	**0**	**4.00**	**3.72**	....	....	....	....	**1**	**0**	**0**	....	**20**	**1**	**0**	**3.00**	....	....	....	....
1977-78	**Los Angeles Kings**	**NHL**	**14**	**2**	**7**	**2**	**693**	**44**	**0**	**3.81**	**3.57**	....	....	....	....	....	....	....	....	....	....	....	....	....	....	....	....
1978-79	Springfield Indians	AHL	5	2	2	1	306	13	0	2.55	....	....	....	....	....	....	....	....	....	....	....	....	....	....	....	....	....
	NHL Totals		**107**	**30**	**57**	**15**	**6162**	**366**	**5**	**3.56**	....	....	....	....	....	**1**	**0**	**0**	....	**20**	**1**	**0**	**3.00**	....	....	....	....

Rights transferred to **Phoenix** (WHA) after owners of **Phoenix** (WHL) franchise granted WHA expansion team, September 14, 1973. Traded to **California** by **Phoenix** (WHA) for cash, October 1, 1974. Transferred to **Cleveland** after **California** franchise relocated, August 26, 1976. Traded to **LA Kings** by **Cleveland** with Jim Moxey for Gary Edwards and Juha Widing, January 22, 1977.

• SKIDMORE, PAUL

Paul Skidmore G – L. 6', 180 lbs. b: Smithtown, NY, 7/22/1956. St. Louis' 6th choice, 61st overall, in 1976 Amateur Draft.

Season	Club	League	GP	W	L	T	Mins	GA	SO	Avg	AAvg	Eff	SA	S%	SAPG	GP	W	L	T	Mins	GA	SO	Avg	Eff	SA	S%	SAPG
1971-72	Suffolk Ducks	NYJHL	30	....	....	....	1800	134	1	4.47	....	....	....	....	....	....	....	....	....	....	....	....	....	....	....	....	....
1972-73	Suffolk Ducks	NYJHL	37	....	....	....	2179	142	2	3.91	....	....	....	....	....	....	....	....	....	....	....	....	....	....	....	....	....
1973-74	Suffolk Ducks	NYJHL	12	....	....	....	819	46	3	3.37	....	....	....	....	....	....	....	....	....	....	....	....	....	....	....	....	....
1974-75	Suffolk Ducks	NYJHL	11	....	....	....	660	36	0	3.27	....	....	....	....	....	....	....	....	....	....	....	....	....	....	....	....	....
1975-76	Boston College	ECAC	27	13	10	1	1500	105	0	4.20	....	....	....	....	....	....	....	....	....	....	....	....	....	....	....	....	....
1976-77	Boston College	ECAC	25	15	9	1	1510	105	1	4.17	....	....	....	....	....	....	....	....	....	....	....	....	....	....	....	....	....
1977-78	Boston College	ECAC	25	18	7	0	1417	88	2	3.73	....	....	....	....	....	....	....	....	....	....	....	....	....	....	....	....	....
1978-79	Boston College	ECAC	18	8	9	0	1039	95	0	5.49	....	....	....	....	....	....	....	....	....	....	....	....	....	....	....	....	....
1979-80	Port Huron Flags	IHL	36	....	....	....	2138	131	2	3.68	....	....	....	....	....	1	0	0	0	31	5	0	9.62	....	....	....	....
1980-81	Salt Lake Golden Eagles	CHL	40	24	14	2	2414	150	1	3.73	....	....	....	....	....	4	1	2	0	179	15	0	5.03	....	....	....	....
1981-82	**St. Louis Blues**	**NHL**	**2**	**1**	**1**	**0**	**120**	**6**	**0**	**3.00**	**2.31**	....	....	....	....	....	....	....	....	....	....	....	....	....	....	....	....
	Salt Lake Golden Eagles	CHL	50	21	27	1	2996	192	*3	3.85	....	....	....	....	....	10	5	5	0	640	46	0	4.31	....	....	....	....
1982-83	Salt Lake Golden Eagles	CHL	40	21	19	0	2414	155	3	3.85	....	....	....	....	....	3	0	1	0	120	14	0	7.00	....	....	....	....
1983-84	Montana Magic	CHL	1	0	1	0	60	8	0	8.00	....	....	....	....	....	....	....	....	....	....	....	....	....	....	....	....	....
1984-85	Salt Lake Golden Eagles	IHL	1	0	1	0	40	5	0	7.50	....	....	....	....	....	....	....	....	....	....	....	....	....	....	....	....	....
	NHL Totals		**2**	**1**	**1**	**0**	**120**	**6**	**0**	**3.00**	....	....	....	....	....	....	....	....	....	....	....	....	....	....	....	....	....

ECAC Second All-Star Team (1976, 1977) • NCAA Championship All-Tournament Team (1978)

• SKORODENSKI, WARREN

Warren Skorodenski G – L. 5'8", 165 lbs. b: Winnipeg, Man., 3/22/1960.

Season	Club	League	GP	W	L	T	Mins	GA	SO	Avg	AAvg	Eff	SA	S%	SAPG	GP	W	L	T	Mins	GA	SO	Avg	Eff	SA	S%	SAPG
1977-78	Calgary Wranglers	WHL	53	8	22	10	2460	213	1	5.20	....	....	....	....	....	....	....	....	....	....	....	....	....	....	....	....	....
1978-79	Calgary Wranglers	WHL	*66	26	31	5	*3595	309	1	5.16	....	....	....	....	....	15	7	8	0	884	61	0	4.14	....	....	....	....
1979-80	Calgary Wranglers	WHL	66	39	23	2	3724	261	1	4.21	....	....	....	....	....	7	3	4	0	357	29	1	4.87	....	....	....	....
1980-81	New Brunswick Hawks	AHL	2	0	1	0	124	9	0	4.35	....	....	....	....	....	....	....	....	....	....	....	....	....	....	....	....	....
	Flint Generals	IHL	47	....	....	....	2602	189	2	4.36	....	....	....	....	....	6	2	4	0	301	18	0	3.58	....	....	....	....
1981-82	**Chicago Black Hawks**	**NHL**	**1**	**0**	**1**	**0**	**60**	**5**	**0**	**5.00**	**3.85**	....	....	....	....	....	....	....	....	....	....	....	....	....	....	....	....
	New Brunswick Hawks	AHL	28	16	8	4	1644	70	*3	*2.55	....	....	....	....	....	2	0	2	0	90	6	0	4.00	....	....	....	....
1982-83	Springfield Indians	AHL	13	3	6	0	592	49	0	4.97	....	....	....	....	....	....	....	....	....	....	....	....	....	....	....	....	....
	Birmingham South Stars	CHL	25	11	11	1	1450	81	1	3.35	....	....	....	....	....	5	0	4	0	195	19	0	5.85	....	....	....	....
1983-84	Sherbrooke Jets	AHL	19	5	10	2	1048	88	0	5.04	....	....	....	....	....	....	....	....	....	....	....	....	....	....	....	....	....
	Springfield Indians	AHL	14	3	11	0	756	67	0	5.32	....	....	....	....	....	2	0	2	0	124	3	0	6.28	....	....	....	....
1984-85	**Chicago Black Hawks**	**NHL**	**27**	**11**	**9**	**3**	**1396**	**75**	**2**	**3.22**	**2.55**	**3.12**	**775**	**.903**	**33.3**	**2**	**0**	**0**	....	**33**	**6**	**0**	**10.91**	**20.00**	**20**	**.700**	**36.4**
1985-86	**Chicago Black Hawks**	**NHL**	**1**	**0**	**1**	**0**	**60**	**6**	**0**	**6.00**	**4.07**	**8.00**	**45**	**.867**	**45.0**	....	....	....	....	....	....	....	....	....	....	....	....
	Nova Scotia Oilers	AHL	32	11	14	2	1716	109	0	3.81	....	....	....	....	....	....	....	....	....	....	....	....	....	....	....	....	....

Season	Club	League	REGULAR SEASON													PLAYOFFS											
			GP	W	L	T	Mins	GA	SO	Avg	AAvg	Eff	SA	S%	SAPG	GP	W	L	T	Mins	GA	SO	Avg	Eff	SA	S%	SAPG
1986-87	**Chicago Blackhawks**	**NHL**	**3**	**1**	**0**	**1**	**155**	**7**	**0**	**2.71**	**2.28**	**2.11**	**90**	**.922**	**34.8**	....	....	....	....	....	....	....	....	....	....	....	....
	Nova Scotia Oilers	AHL	32	10	15	0	1813	121	2	4.00	....	....	....	....	....	....	....	....	....	....	....	....	....	....	....	....	....
	Saginaw Generals	IHL	6	4	1	0	319	21	0	3.95	....	....	....	....	....	6	3	2	0	304	24	0	4.74	....	....	....	....
1987-88	**Edmonton Oilers**	**NHL**	**3**	**0**	**0**	**0**	**61**	**7**	**0**	**6.89**	**5.73**	**19.29**	**25**	**.720**	**24.6**	....	....	....	....	....	....	....	....	....	....	....	....
	Nova Scotia Oilers	AHL	46	25	15	5	2746	171	0	3.74	....	....	....	....	....	5	1	4	0	305	22	0	4.33	....	....	....	....
1988-89	Cape Breton Oilers	AHL	25	11	13	1	1497	111	0	4.45	....	....	....	....	....	....	....	....	....	....	....	....	....	....	....	....	....
	Canada	Nat-Team	22	8	9	1	1160	82	0	4.24	....	....	....	....	....	....	....	....	....	....	....	....	....	....	....	....	....
1989-90	Canada	Nat-Team	41	18	17	0	2182	140	0	3.85	....	....	....	....	....	....	....	....	....	....	....	....	....	....	....	....	....
1990-91	Canada	Nat-Team	2	2	0	0	120	5	0	2.50	....	....	....	....	....	....	....	....	....	....	....	....	....	....	....	....	....
	NHL Totals		**35**	**12**	**11**	**4**	**1732**	**100**	**2**	**3.46**	....	....	....	....	....	**2**	**0**	**0**	....	**33**	**6**	**0**	**10.91**	....	....	....	....

Shared Harry "Hap" Holmes Memorial Award (fewest goals against - AHL) with Bob Janecyk (1982)

Signed as a free agent by **Chicago**, August 12, 1979. Signed as a free agent by **Edmonton**, October 8, 1987.

• SKUDRA, PETER Peter Skudra G – L. 6′1″, 182 lbs. b: Riga, USSR, 4/24/1973.

Season	Club	League	GP	W	L	T	Mins	GA	SO	Avg	AAvg	Eff	SA	S%	SAPG	GP	W	L	T	Mins	GA	SO	Avg	Eff	SA	S%	SAPG
1992-93	Pardaugava Riga	CIS	27	....	....	....	1498	74	....	2.96	....	....	....	....	....	1	....	....	....	60	5	0	5.00	....	....	....	....
1993-94	Pardaugava Riga	CIS	14	....	....	....	783	42	....	3.22	....	....	....	....	....	1	....	....	....	55	4	0	4.36	....	....	....	....
1994-95	Greensboro Monarchs	ECHL	33	13	9	5	1612	113	0	4.20	....	....	....	....	....	6	2	2	....	341	28	0	4.92	....	....	....	....
	Memphis River Kings	CHL	2	0	1	0	60	8	0	6.01	....	....	....	....	....	....	....	....	....	....	....	....	....	....	....	....	....
1995-96	Erie Panthers	ECHL	12	3	8	1	681	47	0	4.14	....	....	....	....	....	....	....	....	....	....	....	....	....	....	....	....	....
	Johnstown Chiefs	ECHL	30	12	11	4	1657	98	0	3.55	....	....	....	....	....	....	....	....	....	....	....	....	....	....	....	....	....
1996-97	Hamilton Bulldogs	AHL	32	8	16	2	1615	101	0	3.75	....	....	....	....	....	....	....	....	....	....	....	....	....	....	....	....	....
	Johnstown Cheifs	ECHL	4	2	1	1	200	11	0	3.30	....	....	....	....	....	....	....	....	....	....	....	....	....	....	....	....	....
1997-98	**Pittsburgh Penguins**	**NHL**	**17**	**6**	**4**	**3**	**851**	**26**	**0**	**1.83**	**2.14**	....	....	....	....	....	....	....	....	....	....	....	....	....	....	....	....
	Houston Aeros	IHL	9	5	3	1	499	23	0	2.77	....	....	....	....	....	....	....	....	....	....	....	....	....	....	....	....	....
	Kansas City Blades	IHL	13	10	3	0	775	37	0	2.86	....	....	....	....	....	8	4	4	....	512	20	1	*2.34	....	....	....	....
	NHL Totals		**17**	**6**	**4**	**3**	**851**	**26**	**0**	**1.83**	....	....	....	....	....	....	....	....	....	....	....	....	....	....	....	....	....

Signed as a free agent by **Pittsburgh**, September 24, 1997.

• SMITH, AL Al "The Bear" Smith G – L. 6′1″, 200 lbs. b: Toronto, Ont., 11/10/1945.

Season	Club	League	GP	W	L	T	Mins	GA	SO	Avg	AAvg	Eff	SA	S%	SAPG	GP	W	L	T	Mins	GA	SO	Avg	Eff	SA	S%	SAPG
1964-65	Toronto Marlboros	OHA	3	....	....	....	180	20	0	6.67	....	....	....	....	....	....	....	....	....	....	....	....	....	....	....	....	....
1965-66	Toronto Marlboros	OHA	22	....	....	....	1320	92	0	4.15	....	....	....	....	....	14	....	....	....	840	37	0	2.61	....	....	....	....
	Toronto Maple Leafs	**NHL**	**2**	**1**	**0**	**0**	**62**	**2**	**0**	**1.94**	**1.97**	....	....	....	....	....	....	....	....	....	....	....	....	....	....	....	....
1966-67	**Toronto Maple Leafs**	**NHL**	**1**	**0**	**1**	**0**	**60**	**5**	**0**	**5.00**	**5.18**	....	....	....	....	....	....	....	....	....	....	....	....	....	....	....	....
	Victoria Cougars	WHL	56	24	26	5	3375	180	6	3.20	....	....	....	....	....	....	....	....	....	....	....	....	....	....	....	....	....
	Vancouver Canucks	WHL	....	....	....	....	....	....	....	....	....	....	....	....	....	6	1	4	0	345	15	*1	2.61	....	....	....	....
	California Seals	WHL	....	....	....	....	....	....	....	....	....	....	....	....	....	1	0	1	0	60	4	0	4.00	....	....	....	....
1967-68	Tulsa Oilers	CHL	40	23	12	5	2278	126	0	3.32	....	....	....	....	....	4	2	2	0	240	11	0	2.75	....	....	....	....
1968-69	**Toronto Maple Leafs**	**NHL**	**7**	**2**	**2**	**1**	**335**	**16**	**0**	**2.87**	**2.97**	....	....	....	....	....	....	....	....	....	....	....	....	....	....	....	....
	Tulsa Oilers	CHL	8	....	....	....	480	22	0	2.87	....	....	....	....	....	....	....	....	....	....	....	....	....	....	....	....	....
	Rochester Americans	AHL	34	13	12	7	1979	114	2	3.46	....	....	....	....	....	....	....	....	....	....	....	....	....	....	....	....	....
1969-70	Baltimore Clippers	AHL	3	....	....	....	180	8	0	2.67	....	....	....	....	....	....	....	....	....	....	....	....	....	....	....	....	....
	Pittsburgh Penguins	**NHL**	**46**	**15**	**20**	**8**	**2555**	**129**	**2**	**3.03**	**3.23**	....	....	....	....	**3**	**1**	**2**	....	**180**	**10**	**0**	**3.33**	....	....	....	....
1970-71	**Pittsburgh Penguins**	**NHL**	**46**	**9**	**22**	**9**	**2472**	**128**	**2**	**3.11**	**3.07**	....	....	....	....	....	....	....	....	....	....	....	....	....	....	....	....
1971-72	**Detroit Red Wings**	**NHL**	**43**	**18**	**20**	**4**	**2500**	**135**	**4**	**3.24**	**3.27**	....	....	....	....	....	....	....	....	....	....	....	....	....	....	....	....
1972-73	New England Whalers	WHA	51	31	19	1	3059	162	3	3.18	....	....	....	....	....	*15	*12	3	0	*909	49	0	3.23	....	....	....	....
1973-74	New England Whalers	WHA	55	30	21	2	3194	164	2	3.08	....	....	....	....	....	7	3	4	0	399	21	*1	3.16	....	....	....	....
1974-75	New England Whalers	WHA	59	*33	21	4	3494	202	2	3.47	....	....	....	....	....	6	2	4	0	366	28	0	4.59	....	....	....	....
1975-76	**Buffalo Sabres**	**NHL**	**14**	**9**	**3**	**2**	**840**	**43**	**0**	**3.07**	**2.77**	....	....	....	....	**1**	**0**	**0**	....	**17**	**1**	**0**	**3.53**	....	....	....	....
1976-77	**Buffalo Sabres**	**NHL**	**7**	**0**	**3**	**0**	**265**	**19**	**0**	**4.30**	**4.00**	....	....	....	....	....	....	....	....	....	....	....	....	....	....	....	....
1977-78	New England Whalers	WHA	55	*30	20	3	3246	174	2	*3.22	....	....	....	....	....	3	0	2	0	120	14	0	7.00	....	....	....	....
1978-79	New England Whalers	WHA	40	17	17	5	2396	132	1	3.31	....	....	....	....	....	4	1	2	0	153	12	0	4.71	....	....	....	....
1979-80	Springfield Indians	AHL	2	1	1	0	120	6	0	3.00	....	....	....	....	....	....	....	....	....	....	....	....	....	....	....	....	....
	Hartford Whalers	**NHL**	**30**	**11**	**10**	**8**	**1754**	**107**	**2**	**3.66**	**3.22**	....	....	....	....	**2**	**0**	**2**	....	**120**	**10**	**0**	**5.00**	....	....	....	....
1980-81	**Colorado Rockies**	**NHL**	**37**	**9**	**18**	**4**	**1909**	**151**	**0**	**4.75**	**3.82**	....	....	....	....	....	....	....	....	....	....	....	....	....	....	....	....
	NHL Totals		**233**	**74**	**99**	**36**	**12752**	**735**	**10**	**3.46**	....	....	....	....	....	**6**	**1**	**4**	....	**317**	**21**	**0**	**3.97**	....	....	....	....
	Other Major League Totals		260	141	98	15	15389	834	10	3.25	....	....	....	....	....	35	18	15	0	1947	124	1	3.82	....	....	....	....

WHA First All-Star Team (1978) • Won Ben Hatskin Trophy (WHA Top Goaltender) (1978)

Played in NHL All-Star Game (1968)

Claimed by **Pittsburgh** from **Toronto** in Intra-League Draft, June 11, 1969. Claimed by **Detroit** from **Pittsburgh** in Intra-League Draft, June 8, 1971. Selected by **New England** (WHA) in 1972 WHA General Player Draft, February 12, 1972. Traded to **Buffalo** by **Detroit** for future considerations, March 10, 1975. Signed as a free agent by **New England** (WHA), August 15, 1977. NHL rights retained by **Hartford** prior to Expansion Draft, June 9, 1979. Traded to **Colorado** by **Hartford** for cash, September 4, 1980.

• SMITH, BILLY Billy "Hatchet Man" Smith G – L. 5′10″, 185 lbs. b: Perth, Ont., 12/12/1950. Los Angeles' 6th choice, 59th overall, in 1970 Amateur Draft. HHOF

Season	Club	League	GP	W	L	T	Mins	GA	SO	Avg	AAvg	Eff	SA	S%	SAPG	GP	W	L	T	Mins	GA	SO	Avg	Eff	SA	S%	SAPG
1969-70	Cornwall Royals	QJHL	55	....	....	....	3300	249	1	4.53	....	....	....	....	....	6	....	....	....	360	14	1	2.33	....	....	....	....
1970-71	Springfield Kings	AHL	49	19	20	6	2728	160	2	3.51	....	....	....	....	....	11	*9	1	0	*682	29	*1	*2.56	....	....	....	....
1971-72	**Los Angeles Kings**	**NHL**	**5**	**1**	**3**	**1**	**300**	**23**	**0**	**4.60**	**4.64**	....	....	....	....	....	....	....	....	....	....	....	....	....	....	....	....
	Springfield Kings	AHL	28	13	10	5	1649	77	*4	2.80	....	....	....	....	....	4	1	2	0	192	13	0	4.06	....	....	....	....
1972-73	**New York Islanders**	**NHL**	**37**	**7**	**24**	**3**	**2122**	**147**	**0**	**4.16**	**3.95**	....	....	....	....	....	....	....	....	....	....	....	....	....	....	....	....
1973-74	**New York Islanders**	**NHL**	**46**	**9**	**23**	**12**	**2615**	**134**	**0**	**3.07**	**2.96**	....	....	....	....	....	....	....	....	....	....	....	....	....	....	....	....
1974-75	**New York Islanders**	**NHL**	**58**	**21**	**18**	**17**	**3368**	**156**	**3**	**2.78**	**2.49**	....	....	....	....	**6**	**1**	**4**	....	**333**	**23**	**0**	**4.14**	....	....	....	....
1975-76	**New York Islanders**	**NHL**	**39**	**19**	**10**	**9**	**2254**	**98**	**3**	**2.61**	**2.35**	....	....	....	....	**8**	**4**	**3**	....	**437**	**21**	**0**	**2.88**	....	....	....	....
1976-77	**New York Islanders**	**NHL**	**36**	**21**	**8**	**6**	**2089**	**87**	**2**	**2.50**	**2.31**	....	....	....	....	**10**	**7**	**3**	....	**580**	**27**	**0**	**2.79**	....	....	....	....
1977-78	**New York Islanders**	**NHL**	**38**	**20**	**8**	**8**	**2154**	**95**	**2**	**2.65**	**2.47**	....	....	....	....	**1**	**0**	**0**	....	**47**	**1**	**0**	**1.28**	....	....	....	....
1978-79	**New York Islanders**	**NHL**	**40**	**25**	**8**	**4**	**2261**	**108**	**1**	**2.87**	**2.52**	....	....	....	....	**5**	**4**	**1**	....	**315**	**10**	***1**	***1.90**	....	....	....	....
1979-80	**New York Islanders**	**NHL**	**38**	**15**	**14**	**7**	**2114**	**104**	**2**	**2.95**	**2.58**	....	....	....	....	***20**	***15**	**4**	....	***1198**	**56**	**1**	**2.80**	....	....	....	....
1980-81	**New York Islanders**	**NHL**	**41**	**22**	**10**	**8**	**2363**	**129**	**2**	**3.28**	**2.62**	....	....	....	....	***17**	***14**	**3**	....	***994**	**42**	**0**	***2.54**	....	....	....	....
1981-82	Canada	C Cup	DID NOT PLAY – SPARE GOALTENDER																								
	New York Islanders	**NHL**	**46**	***32**	**9**	**4**	**2685**	**133**	**0**	**2.97**	**2.27**	....	....	....	....	***18**	***15**	**3**	....	***1120**	**47**	***1**	**2.52**	....	....	....	....
1982-83	**New York Islanders**	**NHL**	**41**	**18**	**14**	**7**	**2340**	**112**	**1**	**2.87**	**2.28**	**2.69**	**1195**	**.906**	**30.6**	***17**	***13**	**3**	....	**962**	**43**	***2**	***2.68**	....	....	....	....
1983-84	**New York Islanders**	**NHL**	**42**	**23**	**13**	**2**	**2279**	**130**	**2**	**3.42**	**2.67**	**3.55**	**1252**	**.896**	**33.0**	***21**	***12**	**8**	....	***1190**	**54**	**0**	**2.72**	**2.59**	**567**	**.905**	**28.6**
1984-85	**New York Islanders**	**NHL**	**37**	**18**	**14**	**3**	**2090**	**133**	**0**	**3.82**	**3.03**	**4.62**	**1100**	**.879**	**31.6**	**6**	**3**	**3**	....	**342**	**19**	**0**	**3.33**	**3.48**	**182**	**.896**	**31.9**
1985-86	**New York Islanders**	**NHL**	**41**	**20**	**14**	**4**	**2308**	**143**	**1**	**3.72**	**2.89**	**4.42**	**1204**	**.881**	**31.3**	**1**	**0**	**1**	....	**60**	**4**	**0**	**4.00**	**4.71**	**34**	**.882**	**34.0**
1986-87	**New York Islanders**	**NHL**	**40**	**14**	**18**	**5**	**2252**	**132**	**1**	**3.52**	**2.96**	**4.61**	**1007**	**.869**	**26.8**	**2**	**0**	**0**	....	**67**	**1**	**0**	**0.90**	**0.41**	**22**	**.955**	**19.7**
1987-88	**New York Islanders**	**NHL**	**38**	**17**	**14**	**5**	**2107**	**113**	**2**	**3.22**	**2.67**	**3.43**	**1062**	**.894**	**30.2**	....	....	....	....	....	....	....	....	....	....	....	....
1988-89	**New York Islanders**	**NHL**	**17**	**3**	**11**	**0**	**730**	**54**	**0**	**4.44**	**3.67**	**6.59**	**364**	**.852**	**29.9**	....	....	....	....	....	....	....	....	....	....	....	....
	NHL Totals		**680**	**305**	**233**	**105**	**38431**	**2031**	**22**	**3.17**	....	....	....	....	....	**132**	**88**	**36**	....	**7645**	**348**	**5**	**2.73**	....	....	....	....

QJHL Second All-Star Team (1970) • NHL First All-Star Team (1982) • Won Vezina Trophy (1982) • Shared William M. Jennings Trophy with Roland Melanson (1983) • Won Conn Smythe Trophy (1983)

Played in NHL All-Star Game (1978)

• Credited with scoring a goal vs. Colorado, November 28, 1979.

Claimed by **NY Islanders** from **LA Kings** in Expansion Draft, June 6, 1972.

• SMITH, GARY Gary "Suitcase" Smith G – L. 6′4″, 215 lbs. b: Ottawa, Ont., 2/4/1944.

Season	Club	League	GP	W	L	T	Mins	GA	SO	Avg	AAvg	Eff	SA	S%	SAPG	GP	W	L	T	Mins	GA	SO	Avg	Eff	SA	S%	SAPG
1961-62	St. Michael's Majors	Tor-Jr.	31	*24	6	1	1860	83	*3	*2.68	....	....	....	....	....	12	....	....	....	720	36	0	*3.00	....	....	....	....
1962-63	Neil McNeil Maroons	Tor-Jr.	28	....	....	....	1660	65	*3	*2.35	....	....	....	....	....	16	10	6	0	960	67	0	4.19	....	....	....	....
1963-64	Toronto Marlboros	OHA	55	*40	8	7	3270	186	3	3.41	....	....	....	....	....	9	....	....	....	540	26	1	2.89	....	....	....	....
1964-65	Rochester Americans	AHL	1	0	0	0	2	0	0	0.00	....	....	....	....	....	....	....	....	....	....	....	....	....	....	....	....	....
	Tulsa Oilers	CHL	1	0	1	0	60	5	0	5.00	....	....	....	....	....	....	....	....	....	....	....	....	....	....	....	....	....
	Victoria Cougars	WHL	8	1	5	0	411	30	0	4.38	....	....	....	....	....	....	....	....	....	....	....	....	....	....	....	....	....

Season	Club	League	GP	W	L	T	Mins	GA	SO	Avg	AAvg	Eff	SA	S%	SAPG	GP	W	L	T	Mins	GA	SO	Avg	Eff	SA	S%	SAPG
			REGULAR SEASON													PLAYOFFS											
1965-66	Rochester Americans	AHL	37	20	11	4	2038	97	2	2.86	....	....	....	....	....	4	2	2	0	188	12	0	3.83	....	....	....	....
	Toronto Maple Leafs	**NHL**	**3**	**0**	**2**	**0**	**118**	**7**	**0**	**3.56**	**3.62**	....	....	....	....	....	....	....	....	....	....	....	....	....	....	....	....
1966-67	Rochester Americans	AHL	17	6	5	4	871	38	1	2.62	....	....	....	....	....	....	....	....	....	....	....	....	....	....	....	....	....
	Victoria Cougars	WHL	17	6	8	3	1029	51	2	2.97	....	....	....	....	....	....	....	....	....	....	....	....	....	....	....	....	....
	Toronto Maple Leafs	**NHL**	**2**	**0**	**2**	**0**	**115**	**7**	**0**	**3.65**	**3.78**	....	....	....	....	....	....	....	....	....	....	....	....	....	....	....	....
1967-68	**Oakland Seals**	**NHL**	**21**	**2**	**13**	**4**	**1129**	**60**	**1**	**3.19**	**3.54**	....	....	....	....	....	....	....	....	....	....	....	....	....	....	....	....
1968-69	**Oakland Seals**	**NHL**	**54**	**21**	**24**	**7**	**2993**	**148**	**4**	**2.97**	**3.07**	....	....	....	....	**7**	**3**	**4**	....	**420**	**23**	**0**	**3.29**	....	....	....	....
1969-70	**Oakland Seals**	**NHL**	**65**	**19**	**34**	**12**	**3762**	**195**	**2**	**3.11**	**3.32**	....	....	....	....	**4**	**0**	**4**	....	**248**	**13**	**0**	**3.15**	....	....	....	....
1970-71	**California Golden Seals**	**NHL**	***71**	**19**	**48**	**4**	***3975**	**256**	**2**	**3.86**	**3.87**	....	....	....	....	....	....	....	....	....	....	....	....	....	....	....	....
1971-72	**Chicago Black Hawks**	**NHL**	**28**	**14**	**5**	**6**	**1540**	**62**	**5**	**2.42**	**2.42**	....	....	....	....	**2**	**1**	**1**	....	**120**	**3**	**1**	**1.50**	....	....	....	....
1972-73	**Chicago Black Hawks**	**NHL**	**23**	**10**	**10**	**2**	**1340**	**79**	**0**	**3.54**	**3.34**	....	....	....	....	**2**	**0**	**1**	....	**65**	**5**	**0**	**4.62**	....	....	....	....
1973-74	**Vancouver Canucks**	**NHL**	**66**	**20**	**33**	**8**	**3632**	**208**	**3**	**3.44**	**3.33**	....	....	....	....	....	....	....	....	....	....	....	....	....	....	....	....
1974-75	**Vancouver Canucks**	**NHL**	***72**	**32**	**24**	**9**	**3828**	**197**	**6**	**3.09**	**2.77**	....	....	....	....	**4**	**1**	**3**	....	**257**	**14**	**0**	**3.27**	....	....	....	....
1975-76	**Vancouver Canucks**	**NHL**	**51**	**20**	**24**	**6**	**2864**	**167**	**2**	**3.50**	**3.17**	....	....	....	....	....	....	....	....	....	....	....	....	....	....	....	....
1976-77	**Minnesota North Stars**	**NHL**	**36**	**10**	**17**	**8**	**2090**	**139**	**1**	**3.99**	**3.73**	....	....	....	....	**1**	**0**	**0**	....	**43**	**4**	**0**	**5.58**	....	....	....	....
1977-78	**Washington Capitals**	**NHL**	**17**	**2**	**12**	**3**	**980**	**68**	**0**	**4.16**	**3.91**	....	....	....	....	....	....	....	....	....	....	....	....	....	....	....	....
	Hershey Bears	AHL	1	0	0	1	65	4	0	3.69	....	....	....	....	....	....	....	....	....	....	....	....	....	....	....	....	....
	Minnesota North Stars	**NHL**	**3**	**0**	**2**	**1**	**180**	**9**	**0**	**3.00**	**2.81**	....	....	....	....	....	....	....	....	....	....	....	....	....	....	....	....
	Fort Worth Texans	CHL	13	8	3	1	765	38	1	2.98	....	....	....	....	....	9	5	4	0	511	25	*1	2.94	....	....	....	....
1978-79	Indianapolis Racers	WHA	11	0	10	1	664	61	0	5.51	....	....	....	....	....	....	....	....	....	....	....	....	....	....	....	....	....
	Winnipeg Jets	WHA	11	7	3	0	626	31	0	2.97	....	....	....	....	....	10	*8	2	0	563	35	0	*3.73	....	....	....	....
1979-80	**Winnipeg Jets**	**NHL**	**20**	**4**	**11**	**4**	**1073**	**73**	**0**	**4.08**	**3.59**	....	....	....	....	....	....	....	....	....	....	....	....	....	....	....	....
	Tulsa Oilers	CHL	22	7	11	4	1324	73	0	3.31	....	....	....	....	....	1	0	1	0	60	6	0	6.00	....	....	....	....
	NHL Totals		**532**	**173**	**261**	**74**	**29619**	**1675**	**26**	**3.39**	....	....	....	....	....	**20**	**5**	**13**	....	**1153**	**62**	**1**	**3.23**	....	....	....	....
	Other Major League Totals		22	7	13	1	1290	92	0	4.28	....	....	....	....	....	10	8	2	0	563	35	0	3.73	....	....	....	....

Shared Vezina Trophy with Tony Esposito (1972)

Played in NHL All-Star Game (1975)

Claimed by **California** from **Toronto** in Expansion Draft, June 6, 1967. Traded to **Chicago** by **California** for Kerry Bond, Gerry Pinder and Gerry Desjardins, September 9, 1971. Selected by **Chicago** (WHA) in 1972 WHA General Player Draft, February 12, 1972. Traded to **Vanoouver** by **Chicago** with Jerry Korab for Dale Tallon, May 14, 1973. Traded to **Minnesota** by **Vancouver** for Cesare Maniago, August 23, 1976. Signed as a free agent by **Washington**, September 3, 1977. Traded to **Minnesota** by **Washington** for cash, February 19, 1978. Signed as a free agent by **Indianapolis**, September, 1978. Signed as a free agent by **Winnipeg** (WHA) after **Indianapolis** (WHA) franchise folded, December 17, 1978. NHL rights retained by **Winnipeg** prior to Expansion Draft, June 9, 1979.

• SMITH, NORMAN

Norman Smith G – L. 5'7", 165 lbs. b: Toronto, Ont., 3/18/1908. d: 2/2/1988.

Season	Club	League	GP	W	L	T	Mins	GA	SO	Avg	AAvg	Eff	SA	S%	SAPG	GP	W	L	T	Mins	GA	SO	Avg	Eff	SA	S%	SAPG
1930-31	Montreal AAA	City Sr.	STATISTICS NOT AVAILABLE																								
	Windsor Bulldogs	IAHL	7	5	1	1	430	16	1	2.23	....	....	....	....	....	6	*4	1	1	390	11	0	1.69	....	....	....	....
1931-32	**Montreal Maroons**	**NHL**	**21**	**5**	**12**	**4**	**1267**	**62**	**0**	**2.94**	**3.65**	....	....	....	....	....	....	....	....	....	....	....	....	....	....	....	....
	Windsor Bulldogs	IAHL	14	....	....	....	840	35	3	2.50	....	....	....	....	....	6	*4	1	1	360	8	*3	*1.33	....	....	....	....
1932-33	Windsor Bulldogs	IAHL	42	14	22	6	2520	120	2	2.86	....	....	....	....	....	6	2	4	0	360	18	0	3.00	....	....	....	....
1933-34	Quebec Castors	Can-Am	32	12	12	8	2009	64	3	*1.91	....	....	....	....	....	....	....	....	....	....	....	....	....	....	....	....	....
1934-35	**Detroit Red Wings**	**NHL**	**25**	**12**	**11**	**2**	**1550**	**52**	**2**	**2.01**	**2.43**	....	....	....	....	....	....	....	....	....	....	....	....	....	....	....	....
	Detroit Olympics	IAHL	27	....	....	....	1620	59	4	*2.19	....	....	....	....	....	10	7	3	0	639	19	2	1.78	....	....	....	....
	Windsor Bulldogs	IAHL	1	1	0	0	60	3	0	*3.00	....	....	....	....	....	....	....	....	....	....	....	....	....	....	....	....	....
1935-36	**Detroit Red Wings**	**NHL**	***48**	***24**	**16**	**8**	***3030**	**103**	**6**	**2.04**	**2.88**	....	....	....	....	**7**	***6**	**1**	**0**	**530**	**12**	***2**	**1.34**	....	....	....	....
1936-37	**Detroit Red Wings**	**NHL**	***48**	***25**	**14**	**9**	**2980**	**102**	***6**	***2.05**	**2.51**	....	....	....	....	**5**	**3**	**1**	....	**282**	**6**	**1**	**1.28**	....	....	....	....
1937-38	**Detroit Red Wings**	**NHL**	**47**	**11**	**25**	**11**	**2930**	**130**	**3**	**2.66**	**3.26**	....	....	....	....	....	....	....	....	....	....	....	....	....	....	....	....
1938-39	**Detroit Red Wings**	**NHL**	**4**	**0**	**4**	**0**	**240**	**12**	**0**	**3.00**	**3.66**	....	....	....	....	....	....	....	....	....	....	....	....	....	....	....	....
1939-1943			DID NOT PLAY – RETIRED																								
1943-44	**Detroit Red Wings**	**NHL**	**5**	**3**	**1**	**1**	**300**	**15**	**0**	**3.00**	**2.26**	....	....	....	....	....	....	....	....	....	....	....	....	....	....	....	....
1944-45	**Detroit Red Wings**	**NHL**	**1**	**1**	**0**	**0**	**60**	**3**	**0**	**3.00**	**2.49**	....	....	....	....	....	....	....	....	....	....	....	....	....	....	....	....
	NHL Totals		**199**	**81**	**83**	**35**	**12357**	**479**	**17**	**2.33**	....	....	....	....	....	**12**	**9**	**2**	**0**	**820**	**18**	**3**	**1.32**	....	....	....	....

NHL First All-Star Team (1937) • Won Vezina Trophy (1937)

Traded to **St. Louis** by **Montreal Maroons** for cash, Summer, 1934. Traded to **Detroit** by **St. Louis** for Burton Williams, October 21, 1934. • Suspended by Detroit for refusing to play following 2-0 loss to NY Rangers, November 15, 1938. Rights traded to **Boston** by **Detroit** with $15000 for Tiny Thompson, November 26, 1939. Smith refused to report and retired.

• SNEDDON, BOB

Bob Sneddon G – R. 6'2", 190 lbs. b: Montreal, Que., 5/31/1944.

Season	Club	League	GP	W	L	T	Mins	GA	SO	Avg	AAvg	Eff	SA	S%	SAPG	GP	W	L	T	Mins	GA	SO	Avg	Eff	SA	S%	SAPG
1963-64	St. Catharines Black Hawks	OHA	52	29	16	7	3080	184	4	3.58	....	....	....	....	....	11	....	....	....	660	45	1	4.09	....	....	....	....
1964-65	Port Huron–Muskegon	IHL	45	....	....	....	2700	230	0	4.89	....	....	....	....	....	....	....	....	....	....	....	....	....	....	....	....	....
1965-66	Port Huron Flags	IHL	67	....	....	....	3980	254	*5	3.83	....	....	....	....	....	9	8	1	0	540	27	0	*3.00	....	....	....	....
1966-67	St. Louis Braves	CHL	20	7	7	6	1200	66	1	3.30	....	....	....	....	....	....	....	....	....	....	....	....	....	....	....	....	....
1967-68	Dallas Black Hawks	CHL	36	17	14	1	1777	119	3	4.02	....	....	....	....	....	5	2	3	0	300	11	*1	*2.20	....	....	....	....
1968-69	Portland Buckaroos	WHL	2	0	0	1	80	7	0	5.26	....	....	....	....	....	....	....	....	....	....	....	....	....	....	....	....	....
	Quebec Aces	AHL	13	5	4	1	626	37	0	3.55	....	....	....	....	....	....	....	....	....	....	....	....	....	....	....	....	....
1969-70	Springfield Kings	AHL	27	....	....	....	1493	108	0	4.34	....	....	....	....	....	8	....	....	....	481	30	0	3.74	....	....	....	....
1970-71	**California Golden Seals**	**NHL**	**5**	**0**	**2**	**0**	**225**	**21**	**0**	**5.60**	**5.55**	....	....	....	....	....	....	....	....	....	....	....	....	....	....	....	....
	Providence Reds	AHL	16	7	6	1	807	55	1	4.19	....	....	....	....	....	....	....	....	....	....	....	....	....	....	....	....	....
1971-72	Tidewater Wings	AHL	5	1	3	0	213	14	0	3.94	....	....	....	....	....	....	....	....	....	....	....	....	....	....	....	....	....
	Seattle Totems	WHL	23	3	13	2	1174	104	0	5.31	....	....	....	....	....	....	....	....	....	....	....	....	....	....	....	....	....
1972-73	Springfield Kings	AHL	36	....	....	....	1936	133	0	4.12	....	....	....	....	....	....	....	....	....	....	....	....	....	....	....	....	....
1973-74	Rochester Americans	AHL	31	15	9	6	1807	114	1	3.78	....	....	....	....	....	2	0	2	0	120	10	0	5.00	....	....	....	....
1974-75	Rochester Americans	AHL	35	22	7	2	1924	101	0	3.14	....	....	....	....	....	1	0	1	0	60	6	0	6.00	....	....	....	....
1975-76	Baltimore Clippers	AHL	19	3	13	1	1049	91	0	5.20	....	....	....	....	....	....	....	....	....	....	....	....	....	....	....	....	....
1976-77	Binghamton Dusters	NAHL	16	8	6	1	901	70	0	4.53	....	....	....	....	....	....	....	....	....	....	....	....	....	....	....	....	....
	Johnstown Jets	NAHL	16	....	....	....	913	77	0	4.93	....	....	....	....	....	....	....	....	....	....	....	....	....	....	....	....	....
1977-78	Brantford Alexanders	OHA Sr.	24	....	....	....	1485	104	0	4.20	....	....	....	....	....	....	....	....	....	....	....	....	....	....	....	....	....
	NHL Totals		**5**	**0**	**2**	**0**	**225**	**21**	**0**	**5.60**	....	....	....	....	....	....	....	....	....	....	....	....	....	....	....	....	....

IHL First All-Star Team (1966) • Won James Norris Memorial Trophy (fewest goals against - IHL) (1966)

Traded to **Philadelphia** by **Chicago** for Brian Bradley, December, 1968. Claimed by **LA Kings** (Springfield - AHL) from **Philadelphia** in Reverse Draft, June 12, 1969. Claimed by **California** (Providence - AHL) from **Los Angeles** (Springfield - AHL) in Reverse Draft, June, 1970. Claimed by **Detroit** (Tidewater - AHL) from **California** (Cleveland - AHL) in Reverse Draft, June, 1971. Traded to **Seattle** (WHL) by **Detroit** for Art Stratton, November, 1971.

• SNOW, GARTH

Garth Snow G – L. 6'3", 200 lbs. b: Wrentham, MA, 7/28/1969. Quebec's 6th choice, 114th overall, in 1987 Entry Draft.

Season	Club	League	GP	W	L	T	Mins	GA	SO	Avg	AAvg	Eff	SA	S%	SAPG	GP	W	L	T	Mins	GA	SO	Avg	Eff	SA	S%	SAPG
1986-87	Mount St. Charles Academy	H.S.	30	....	....	....	1795	53	10	1.77	....	....	....	....	....	....	....	....	....	....	....	....	....	....	....	....	....
1987-88	Mount St. Charles Academy	H.S.	STATISTICS NOT AVAILABLE																								
1988-89	University of Maine	H.E.	5	2	2	0	241	14	1	3.49	....	....	....	....	....	....	....	....	....	....	....	....	....	....	....	....	....
1989-90			DID NOT PLAY																								
1990-91	University of Maine	H.E.	25	*18	4	0	1290	64	2	2.98	....	....	....	....	....	....	....	....	....	....	....	....	....	....	....	....	....
1991-92	University of Maine	H.E.	31	*25	4	2	1792	73	*2	*2.44	....	....	....	....	....	....	....	....	....	....	....	....	....	....	....	....	....
1992-93	University of Maine	H.E.	23	*21	0	1	1210	42	1	*2.08	....	....	....	....	....	....	....	....	....	....	....	....	....	....	....	....	....
1993-94	United States	Nat-Team	23	13	5	3	1324	71	1	3.22	....	....	....	....	....	....	....	....	....	....	....	....	....	....	....	....	....
	United States	Olympics	5	....	....	....	299	17	....	3.41	....	....	....	....	....	....	....	....	....	....	....	....	....	....	....	....	....
	Quebec Nordiques	**NHL**	**5**	**3**	**2**	**0**	**279**	**16**	**0**	**3.44**	**3.27**	**4.33**	**127**	**.874**	**27.3**	....	....	....	....	....	....	....	....	....	....	....	....
	Cornwall Aces	AHL	16	6	5	3	927	51	0	3.30	....	....	....	....	....	13	8	5	....	790	42	0	3.19	....	....	....	....
1994-95	Cornwall Aces	AHL	*62	*32	20	7	*3558	162	3	2.73	....	....	....	....	....	8	4	3	....	402	14	*2	*2.09	....	....	....	....
	Quebec Nordiques	**NHL**	**2**	**1**	**1**	**0**	**119**	**11**	**0**	**5.55**	**5.74**	**9.69**	**63**	**.825**	**31.8**	**1**	**0**	**0**	....	**9**	**1**	**0**	**6.67**	**22.23**	**3**	**.667**	**20.0**
1995-96	**Philadelphia Flyers**	**NHL**	**26**	**12**	**8**	**4**	**1437**	**69**	**0**	**2.88**	**2.83**	**3.07**	**648**	**.894**	**27.1**	**1**	**0**	**0**	....	**1**	**0**	**0**	**0.00**	**0.00**	**0**	**.00**	**0.0**
1996-97	**Philadelphia Flyers**	**NHL**	**35**	**14**	**8**	**8**	**1884**	**79**	**2**	**2.52**	**2.66**	**2.44**	**816**	**.903**	**26.0**	**12**	**8**	**4**	....	**699**	**33**	**0**	**2.83**	**3.06**	**305**	**.892**	**26.2**

			REGULAR SEASON													PLAYOFFS											
Season	Club	League	GP	W	L	T	Mins	GA	SO	Avg	AAvg	Eff	SA	S%	SAPG	GP	W	L	T	Mins	GA	SO	Avg	Eff	SA	S%	SAPG
1997-98	**Philadelphia Flyers**	**NHL**	**29**	**14**	**9**	**4**	**1651**	**67**	**1**	**2.43**	**2.84**	**2.39**	**682**	**.902**	**24.8**	....	....	....	....	....	....	....	....	....	....	....	....
	Vancouver Canucks	**NHL**	**12**	**3**	**6**	**0**	**504**	**26**	**0**	**3.10**	**3.63**	**3.08**	**262**	**.901**	**31.2**	....	....	....	....	....	....	....	....	....	....	....	....
	United States	WC-A	5	1	2	1	260	12	0	2.77	....	....	....	....	....	....	....	....	....	....	....	....	....	....	....	....	....
	NHL Totals		**109**	**47**	**34**	**16**	**5874**	**268**	**3**	**2.74**	....	....	**2598**	**.897**	....	**14**	**8**	**4**	....	**709**	**34**	**0**	**2.88**	....	....	....	....

Hockey East Second All-Star Team (1992, 1993) • NCAA Championship All-Tournament Team (1993)

Transferred to **Colorado** after **Quebec** franchise relocated, June 21, 1995. Traded to **Philadelphia** by **Colorado** for Philadelphia's 3rd (later traded to Washington — Washington selected Shawn McNeil) and 6th (Kai Fischer) round choices in 1996 Entry Draft, July 12, 1995. Traded to **Vancouver** by **Philadelphia** for Sean Burke, March 4, 1998.

• SODERSTROM, TOMMY

Tommy Soderstrom G – L. 5'7", 157 lbs. b: Stockholm, Sweden, 7/17/1969. Philadelphia's 14th choice, 214th overall, in 1990 Entry Draft.

Season	Club	League	GP	W	L	T	Mins	GA	SO	Avg	AAvg	Eff	SA	S%	SAPG	GP	W	L	T	Mins	GA	SO	Avg	Eff	SA	S%	SAPG
1986-87	Djurgarden IF Stockholm	Swe-Jr.	STATISTICS NOT AVAILABLE																								
	Sweden	EJC-A	5	....	....	....	300	4	....	0.80	....	....	....	....	....	....	....	....	....	....	....	....	....	....	....	....	....
1987-88	Djurgarden IF Stockholm	Swe-Jr.	STATISTICS NOT AVAILABLE																								
1988-89	Djurgarden IF Stockholm	Swe-Jr.	STATISTICS NOT AVAILABLE																								
	Sweden	WJC-A	3	....	....	....	180	7	....	2.33	....	....	....	....	....	....	....	....	....	....	....	....	....	....	....	....	....
1989-90	Djurgarden IF Stockholm	Sweden	4	....	....	....	240	14	0	3.50	....	....	....	....	....	....	....	....	....	....	....	....	....	....	....	....	....
1990-91	Djurgarden IF Stockholm	Sweden	39	....	....	....	2340	104	3	2.67	....	....	....	....	....	7	....	....	....	423	10	2	1.42	....	....	....	....
	Sweden	WEC-A	1	0	0	1	60	3	0	3.00	....	....	....	....	....	....	....	....	....	....	....	....	....	....	....	....	....
1991-92	Sweden	C Cup	4	2	2	0	240	12	....	3.00	....	....	....	....	....	....	....	....	....	....	....	....	....	....	....	....	....
	Djurgarden IF Stockholm	Sweden	39	15	8	11	2340	109	4	2.79	....	....	....	....	....	10	....	....	....	635	28	0	2.65	....	....	....	....
	Sweden	Olympics	5	3	1	1	298	13	....	2.62	....	....	....	....	....	....	....	....	....	....	....	....	....	....	....	....	....
	Sweden	WC-A	5	4	1	0	299	7	....	1.40	....	....	....	....	....	....	....	....	....	....	....	....	....	....	....	....	....
1992-93	**Philadelphia Flyers**	**NHL**	**44**	**20**	**17**	**6**	**2512**	**143**	**5**	**3.42**	**2.91**	**3.69**	**1327**	**.892**	**31.7**	....	....	....	....	....	....	....	....	....	....	....	....
	Hershey Bears	AHL	7	4	1	0	373	15	0	2.41	....	....	....	....	....	....	....	....	....	....	....	....	....	....	....	....	....
	Sweden	WC-A	7	4	3	0	386	20	....	3.10	....	....	....	....	....	....	....	....	....	....	....	....	....	....	....	....	....
1993-94	**Philadelphia Flyers**	**NHL**	**34**	**6**	**18**	**4**	**1736**	**116**	**2**	**4.01**	**3.83**	**5.47**	**851**	**.864**	**29.4**	....	....	....	....	....	....	....	....	....	....	....	....
	Hershey Bears	AHL	9	3	4	1	461	37	0	4.81	....	....	....	....	....	....	....	....	....	....	....	....	....	....	....	....	....
1994-95	**New York Islanders**	**NHL**	**26**	**8**	**12**	**3**	**1350**	**70**	**1**	**3.11**	**3.22**	**3.04**	**717**	**.902**	**31.9**	....	....	....	....	....	....	....	....	....	....	....	....
1995-96	**New York Islanders**	**NHL**	**51**	**11**	**22**	**6**	**2590**	**167**	**2**	**3.87**	**3.82**	**4.72**	**1370**	**.878**	**31.7**	....	....	....	....	....	....	....	....	....	....	....	....
1996-97	Sweden	W Cup	2	....	....	....	120	2	....	1.00	....	....	....	....	....	....	....	....	....	....	....	....	....	....	....	....	....
	New York Islanders	**NHL**	**1**	**0**	**0**	**0**	**1**	**0**	**0**	**0.00**	**0.00**	**0.00**	**0**	**.00**	**0.0**	....	....	....	....	....	....	....	....	....	....	....	....
	Rochester Americans	AHL	2	2	0	0	120	8	0	4.00	....	....	....	....	....	....	....	....	....	....	....	....	....	....	....	....	....
	Utah Grizzlies	IHL	26	12	11	0	1463	76	0	3.12	....	....	....	....	....	....	....	....	....	....	....	....	....	....	....	....	....
1997-98	Djurgarden IF Stockholm	Sweden	*46	....	....	....	*2760	103	....	*2.24	....	....	....	....	....	*15	....	....	....	*936	34	....	2.18	....	....	....	....
	Sweden	Olympics	DID NOT PLAY – SPARE GOALTENDER																								
	NHL Totals		**156**	**45**	**69**	**19**	**8189**	**496**	**10**	**3.63**	....	....	**4265**	**.884**	....	....	....	....	....	....	....	....	....	....	....	....	....

EJC-A All-Star Team (1987) • Named Best Goaltender at EJC-A (1987) • Swedish Rookie of the Year (1991) • Swedish World All-Star Team (1992) • Named Best Goaltender at WC-A (1992)

Traded to **NY Islanders** by **Philadelphia** for Ron Hextall and NY Islanders' 6th round choice (Dmitry Tertyshny) in 1995 Entry Draft, September 22, 1994. • Played 10 seconds in game on March 31, 1997.

• SOETAERT, DOUG

Doug "Soapy" Soetaert G – L. 6', 180 lbs. b: Edmonton, Alta., 4/21/1955. NY Rangers' 2nd choice, 30th overall, in 1975 Amateur Draft.

Season	Club	League	GP	W	L	T	Mins	GA	SO	Avg	AAvg	Eff	SA	S%	SAPG	GP	W	L	T	Mins	GA	SO	Avg	Eff	SA	S%	SAPG
1971-72	Edmonton Oil Kings	WCJHL	37	....	....	....	1738	105	3	3.62	....	....	....	....	....	6	....	....	....	267	13	0	2.92	....	....	....	....
1972-73	Edmonton Oil Kings	WCJHL	43	....	....	....	2111	129	1	3.67	....	....	....	....	....	6	....	....	....	339	33	0	5.84	....	....	....	....
1973-74	Edmonton Oil Kings	WCJHL	39	....	....	....	2190	163	1	4.47	....	....	....	....	....	3	....	....	....	141	9	0	3.83	....	....	....	....
1974-75	Edmonton Oil Kings	WCJHL	65	....	....	....	3706	273	1	4.42	....	....	....	....	....	....	....	....	....	....	....	....	....	....	....	....	....
	Canada	WJC-A	2	....	....	....	120	5	....	2.50	....	....	....	....	....	....	....	....	....	....	....	....	....	....	....	....	....
1975-76	**New York Rangers**	**NHL**	**8**	**2**	**2**	**0**	**273**	**24**	**0**	**5.27**	**4.78**	....	....	....	....	....	....	....	....	....	....	....	....	....	....	....	....
	Providence Reds	AHL	16	6	9	1	896	65	0	4.35	....	....	....	....	....	1	0	1	0	59	6	0	6.10	....	....	....	....
1976-77	**New York Rangers**	**NHL**	**12**	**3**	**4**	**1**	**570**	**28**	**1**	**2.95**	**2.74**	....	....	....	....	....	....	....	....	....	....	....	....	....	....	....	....
	New Haven Nighthawks	AHL	16	6	9	0	947	61	0	3.86	....	....	....	....	....	....	....	....	....	....	....	....	....	....	....	....	....
1977-78	**New York Rangers**	**NHL**	**6**	**2**	**2**	**2**	**360**	**20**	**0**	**3.33**	**3.12**	....	....	....	....	....	....	....	....	....	....	....	....	....	....	....	....
	New Haven Nighthawks	AHL	38	16	16	6	2252	141	0	3.75	....	....	....	....	....	*15	8	7	0	*916	53	0	3.47	....	....	....	....
1978-79	New Haven Nighthawks	AHL	3	2	1	0	180	11	1	3.67	....	....	....	....	....	....	....	....	....	....	....	....	....	....	....	....	....
	New York Rangers	**NHL**	**17**	**5**	**7**	**3**	**900**	**57**	**0**	**3.80**	**3.36**	....	....	....	....	....	....	....	....	....	....	....	....	....	....	....	....
1979-80	**New York Rangers**	**NHL**	**8**	**5**	**2**	**0**	**435**	**33**	**0**	**4.55**	**4.00**	....	....	....	....	....	....	....	....	....	....	....	....	....	....	....	....
	New Haven Nighthawks	AHL	32	17	18	5	1808	108	*3	3.58	....	....	....	....	....	8	5	3	0	478	24	0	3.01	....	....	....	....
1980-81	**New York Rangers**	**NHL**	**39**	**16**	**16**	**7**	**2320**	**152**	**0**	**3.93**	**3.15**	....	....	....	....	....	....	....	....	....	....	....	....	....	....	....	....
	New Haven Nighthawks	AHL	12	5	5	1	668	35	2	3.14	....	....	....	....	....	4	0	3	0	220	19	0	5.18	....	....	....	....
1981-82	**Winnipeg Jets**	**NHL**	**39**	**13**	**14**	**8**	**2157**	**155**	**2**	**4.31**	**3.33**	....	....	....	....	**2**	**1**	**1**	....	**120**	**8**	**0**	**4.00**	....	....	....	....
1982-83	**Winnipeg Jets**	**NHL**	**44**	**19**	**19**	**6**	**2533**	**174**	**0**	**4.12**	**3.30**	**5.40**	**1328**	**.869**	**31.5**	**1**	**0**	**0**	....	**20**	**0**	**0**	**0.00**	....	....	....	....
1983-84	**Winnipeg Jets**	**NHL**	**47**	**18**	**15**	**7**	**2539**	**182**	**0**	**4.30**	**3.37**	**5.65**	**1385**	**.869**	**32.7**	**1**	**0**	**1**	....	**20**	**5**	**0**	**15.00**	**39.47**	**19**	**.737**	**57.0**
1984-85	**Montreal Canadiens**	**NHL**	**28**	**14**	**9**	**4**	**1606**	**91**	**0**	**3.40**	**2.69**	**4.97**	**622**	**.854**	**23.2**	**1**	**0**	**0**	....	**20**	**1**	**0**	**3.00**	**3.33**	**9**	**.889**	**27.0**
1985-86	**Montreal Canadiens**	**NHL**	**23**	**11**	**7**	**2**	**1215**	**56**	**3**	**2.77**	**2.15**	**2.91**	**533**	**.895**	**26.3**	....	....	....	....	....	....	....	....	....	....	....	....
1986-87	**New York Rangers**	**NHL**	**13**	**2**	**7**	**2**	**675**	**58**	**0**	**5.16**	**4.35**	**8.13**	**368**	**.842**	**32.7**	....	....	....	....	....	....	....	....	....	....	....	....
	NHL Totals		**284**	**110**	**104**	**42**	**15583**	**1030**	**6**	**3.97**						**5**	**1**	**2**	....	**180**	**14**	**0**	**4.67**				

Traded to **Winnipeg** by **NY Rangers** for Winnipeg's 3rd round choice (Vesa Salo) in 1983 Entry Draft, September 8, 1981. Traded to **Montreal** by **Winnipeg** for Mark Holden, October 9, 1984. Signed as a free agent by **NY Rangers**, July 24, 1986.

• SOUCY, CHRISTIAN

Christian Soucy G – L. 5'11", 160 lbs. b: Gatineau, Que., 9/14/1970.

Season	Club	League	GP	W	L	T	Mins	GA	SO	Avg	AAvg	Eff	SA	S%	SAPG	GP	W	L	T	Mins	GA	SO	Avg	Eff	SA	S%	SAPG
1991-92	University of Vermont	ECAC	*30	15	11	3	*1783	81	0	2.83	....	....	....	....	....	....	....	....	....	....	....	....	....	....	....	....	....
1992-93	University of Vermont	ECAC	29	11	15	3	1708	90	1	3.16	....	....	....	....	....	....	....	....	....	....	....	....	....	....	....	....	....
1993-94	**Chicago Blackhawks**	**NHL**	**1**	**0**	**0**	**0**	**3**	**0**	**0**	**0.00**	**0.00**	**0.00**	**0**	**.00**	**0.0**	....	....	....	....	....	....	....	....	....	....	....	....
	Indianapolis Ice	IHL	46	14	25	1	2302	159	1	4.14	....	....	....	....	....	....	....	....	....	....	....	....	....	....	....	....	....
1994-95	Indianapolis Ice	IHL	42	15	17	5	2216	148	0	4.01	....	....	....	....	....	....	....	....	....	....	....	....	....	....	....	....	....
1995-96	Fort Worth Fire	CHL	5	3	2	0	300	19	0	3.80	....	....	....	....	....	....	....	....	....	....	....	....	....	....	....	....	....
	Jacksonville Lizard Kings	ECHL	3	2	1	0	179	11	0	3.68	....	....	....	....	....	....	....	....	....	....	....	....	....	....	....	....	....
	Indianapolis Ice	IHL	22	12	9	0	1198	62	0	3.11	....	....	....	....	....	....	....	....	....	....	....	....	....	....	....	....	....
1996-97	Kentucky Thoroughblades	AHL	3	0	2	0	138	11	0	4.77	....	....	....	....	....	....	....	....	....	....	....	....	....	....	....	....	....
	Baton Rouge Kingfish	ECHL	46	18	20	3	2421	128	3	3.17	....	....	....	....	....	....	....	....	....	....	....	....	....	....	....	....	....
1997-98	Austin Ice-Bats	WPHL	11	6	5	0	658	38	0	3.46	....	....	....	....	....	5	2	3	....	321	14	0	*2.61	....	....	....	....
	Houston Aeros	IHL	5	4	1	0	288	9	0	1.87	....	....	....	....	....	....	....	....	....	....	....	....	....	....	....	....	....
	NHL Totals		**1**	**0**	**0**	**0**	**3**	**0**	**0**	**0.00**	....	....	....	....	....	....	....	....	....	....	....	....	....	....	....	....	....

ECAC First All-Star Team (1992) • NCAA East Second All-American Team (1992) • ECAC Second All-Star Team (1993)

Signed as a free agent by **Chicago**, June 21, 1993.

• SPOONER, RED

Red (Andrew) Spooner G – L. 5'8", 170 lbs. b: Port Arthur, Ont., 8/24/1910. d: 5/7/1984.

Season	Club	League	GP	W	L	T	Mins	GA	SO	Avg	AAvg	Eff	SA	S%	SAPG	GP	W	L	T	Mins	GA	SO	Avg	Eff	SA	S%	SAPG
1927-28	Port Arthur Bearcats	TBSHL	1	1	0	0	60	2	0	2.00	....	....	....	....	....	....	....	....	....	....	....	....	....	....	....	....	....
1928-29	Fort William Forts	TBSHL	STATISTICS NOT AVAILABLE																								
1929-30	Fort William Forts	TBSHL	STATISTICS NOT AVAILABLE																								
	Pittsburgh Pirates	**NHL**	**1**	**0**	**1**	**0**	**60**	**6**	**0**	**6.00**	**6.29**	....	....	....	....	....	....	....	....	....	....	....	....	....	....	....	....
1930-31	Port Arthur Ports	TBSHL	STATISTICS NOT AVAILABLE																								
1931-32	Port Arthur Ports	TBSHL	STATISTICS NOT AVAILABLE																								
1932-33	Port Arthur Ports	TBSHL	6	....	....	....	360	10	2	1.67	....	....	....	....	....	1	....	....	....	60	3	0	3.00	....	....	....	....
	NHL Totals		**1**	**0**	**1**	**0**	**60**	**6**	**0**	**6.00**	....	....	....	....	....	....	....	....	....	....	....	....	....	....	....	....	....

Loaned to **Pittsburgh** by **Fort William Forts** (TBSHL) to replace injured Joe Miller, January 18, 1930. (NY Rangers 6, Pittsburgh 5)

• SPRING, JESSE

Jesse Spring G – L. 6', 185 lbs. b: Alba, PA, 1/18/1901. d: 3/25/1942.

Season	Club	League	GP	W	L	T	Mins	GA	SO	Avg	AAvg	Eff	SA	S%	SAPG	GP	W	L	T	Mins	GA	SO	Avg	Eff	SA	S%	SAPG
			REGULAR SEASON													PLAYOFFS											
1924-25	**Hamilton Tigers**	**NHL**	**1**	**0**	**0**	**0**	**2**	**0**	**0**	**0.00**	**0.00**	....	....	....	....	....	....	....	....	....	....	....	....	....	....	....	....
	NHL Totals		**1**	**0**	**0**	**0**	**2**	**0**	**0**	**0.00**	....	....	....	....	....	....	....	....	....	....	....	....	....	....	....	....	....

• Hamilton defenseman replaced penalized Jake Forbes, February 14, 1925. (Toronto 3, Hamilton 1)

• STANIOWSKI, ED

Ed Staniowski G – L. 5'9", 170 lbs. b: Moose Jaw, Sask., 7/7/1955. St. Louis' 1st choice, 27th overall, in 1975 Amateur Draft.

Season	Club	League	GP	W	L	T	Mins	GA	SO	Avg	AAvg	Eff	SA	S%	SAPG	GP	W	L	T	Mins	GA	SO	Avg	Eff	SA	S%	SAPG
1971-72	Regina Pats	WCJHL	15	....	....	....	777	41	2	3.17	....	....	....	....	....	1	....	....	....	60	6	0	6.00	....	....	....	....
1972-73	Regina Pats	WCJHL	64	....	....	....	3768	236	0	3.76	....	....	....	....	....	4	....	....	....	240	17	0	4.25	....	....	....	....
1973-74	Regina Pats	WCJHL	62	*39	12	9	3629	185	2	3.06	....	....	....	....	....	16	....	....	....	965	47	1	2.92	....	....	....	....
1974-75	Regina Pats	WCJHL	65	....	....	....	3898	255	2	3.95	....	....	....	....	....	11	....	....	....	673	39	0	3.48	....	....	....	....
	Canada	WJC-A	2	....	....	....	120	3	....	1.50	....	....	....	....	....	....	....	....	....	....	....	....	....	....	....	....	....
1975-76	Providence Reds	AHL	29	15	11	1	1709	108	0	3.79	....	....	....	....	....	....	....	....	....	....	....	....	....	....	....	....	....
	St. Louis Blues	**NHL**	**11**	**5**	**3**	**2**	**620**	**33**	**0**	**3.19**	**2.88**	....	....	....	....	**3**	**1**	**2**	....	**206**	**7**	**0**	**2.04**	....	....	....	....
1976-77	Kansas City Blues	CHL	17	8	9	0	1008	59	2	3.51	....	....	....	....	....	....	....	....	....	....	....	....	....	....	....	....	....
	St. Louis Blues	**NHL**	**29**	**10**	**16**	**1**	**1589**	**108**	**0**	**4.08**	**3.81**	....	....	....	....	**3**	**0**	**2**	....	**102**	**9**	**0**	**5.29**	....	....	....	....
1977-78	**St. Louis Blues**	**NHL**	**17**	**1**	**10**	**2**	**886**	**57**	**0**	**3.86**	**3.62**	....	....	....	....	....	....	....	....	....	....	....	....	....	....	....	....
	Salt Lake Golden Eagles	CHL	31	18	13	0	1805	96	0	3.19	....	....	....	....	....	6	2	4	0	402	22	0	3.28	....	....	....	....
1978-79	Salt Lake Golden Eagles	CHL	5	2	2	1	309	10	2	1.94	....	....	....	....	....	....	....	....	....	....	....	....	....	....	....	....	....
	St. Louis Blues	**NHL**	**39**	**9**	**25**	**3**	**2291**	**146**	**0**	**3.82**	**3.38**	....	....	....	....	....	....	....	....	....	....	....	....	....	....	....	....
	Canada	WEC-A	3	1	1	0	160	19	0	7.12	....	....	....	....	....	....	....	....	....	....	....	....	....	....	....	....	....
1979-80	**St. Louis Blues**	**NHL**	**22**	**2**	**11**	**3**	**1108**	**80**	**0**	**4.33**	**3.81**	....	....	....	....	....	....	....	....	....	....	....	....	....	....	....	....
	Salt Lake Golden Eagles	CHL	4	3	1	0	239	6	0	1.51	....	....	....	....	....	....	....	....	....	....	....	....	....	....	....	....	....
1980-81	**St. Louis Blues**	**NHL**	**19**	**10**	**3**	**3**	**1010**	**72**	**0**	**4.28**	**3.43**	....	....	....	....	....	....	....	....	....	....	....	....	....	....	....	....
1981-82	**Winnipeg Jets**	**NHL**	**45**	**20**	**19**	**6**	**2643**	**174**	**1**	**3.95**	**3.04**	....	....	....	....	**2**	**0**	**2**	....	**120**	**12**	**0**	**6.00**	....	....	....	....
1982-83	**Winnipeg Jets**	**NHL**	**17**	**4**	**8**	**0**	**827**	**65**	**1**	**4.72**	**3.78**	**7.36**	**417**	**.844**	**30.3**	....	....	....	....	....	....	....	....	....	....	....	....
	Sherbrooke Jets	AHL	10	1	7	0	573	48	0	5.03	....	....	....	....	....	....	....	....	....	....	....	....	....	....	....	....	....
1983-84	**Winnipeg Jets**	**NHL**	**1**	**0**	**0**	**0**	**40**	**8**	**0**	**12.00**	**9.40**	**48.00**	**20**	**.600**	**30.0**	....	....	....	....	....	....	....	....	....	....	....	....
	Hartford Whalers	**NHL**	**18**	**6**	**9**	**1**	**1041**	**74**	**0**	**4.27**	**3.34**	**5.68**	**556**	**.867**	**32.0**	....	....	....	....	....	....	....	....	....	....	....	....
1984-85	**Hartford Whalers**	**NHL**	**1**	**0**	**0**	**0**	**20**	**1**	**0**	**3.00**	**2.38**	**3.00**	**10**	**.900**	**30.0**	....	....	....	....	....	....	....	....	....	....	....	....
	Binghamton Whalers	AHL	10	4	4	2	612	44	0	4.31	....	....	....	....	....	....	....	....	....	....	....	....	....	....	....	....	....
	Salt Lake Golden Eagles	IHL	9	4	5	0	538	33	0	3.68	....	....	....	....	....	5	1	4	0	265	17	0	3.85	....	....	....	....
	NHL Totals		**219**	**67**	**104**	**21**	**12075**	**818**	**2**	**4.06**	....	....	....	....	....	**8**	**1**	**6**	....	**428**	**28**	**0**	**3.93**	....	....	....	....

WCJHL First All-Star Team (1975) • Canadian Major Junior Player of the Year (1975) • Shared Terry Sawchuk Trophy (fewest goals against - CHL) with Doug Grant (1978)

Traded to **Winnipeg** by **St. Louis** with Bryan Maxwell and Paul MacLean for Scott Campbell and John Markell, July 3, 1981. Traded to **Hartford** by **Winnipeg** for Mike Veisor, November 10, 1983.

• STARR, HAROLD

Harold Starr G – L. 5'11", 176 lbs. b: Ottawa, Ont., 7/6/1906.

Season	Club	League	GP	W	L	T	Mins	GA	SO	Avg	AAvg	Eff	SA	S%	SAPG	GP	W	L	T	Mins	GA	SO	Avg	Eff	SA	S%	SAPG
1931-32	**Montreal Maroons**	**NHL**	**1**	**0**	**0**	**0**	**3**	**0**	**0**	**0.00**	**0.00**	....	....	....	....	....	....	....	....	....	....	....	....	....	....	....	....
	NHL Totals		**1**	**0**	**0**	**0**	**3**	**0**	**0**	**0.00**	....	....	....	....	....	....	....	....	....	....	....	....	....	....	....	....	....

• **Montreal Maroons'** defenseman replaced injured Norm Smith in 3rd period, January 2, 1933. (Montreal Canadiens 5, Montreal Maroons 1)

• STAUBER, ROBB

Robb Stauber G – L. 5'11", 180 lbs. b: Duluth, MN, 11/25/1967. Los Angeles' 5th choice, 107th overall, in 1986 Entry Draft.

Season	Club	League	GP	W	L	T	Mins	GA	SO	Avg	AAvg	Eff	SA	S%	SAPG	GP	W	L	T	Mins	GA	SO	Avg	Eff	SA	S%	SAPG
1985-86	Duluth Denfield High	H.S.	27	....	....	....	1215	66	0	3.26	....	....	....	....	....	....	....	....	....	....	....	....	....	....	....	....	....
1986-87	University of Minnesota	WCHA	20	13	5	0	1072	63	0	3.53	....	....	....	....	....	....	....	....	....	....	....	....	....	....	....	....	....
	United States	WJC-A	4	....	....	....	220	17	....	4.64	....	....	....	....	....	....	....	....	....	....	....	....	....	....	....	....	....
1987-88	University of Minnesota	WCHA	44	34	10	0	2621	119	5	2.72	....	....	....	....	....	....	....	....	....	....	....	....	....	....	....	....	....
1988-89	University of Minnesota	WCHA	34	26	8	0	2024	82	0	2.43	....	....	....	....	....	....	....	....	....	....	....	....	....	....	....	....	....
	United States	WEC-A	6	....	....	....	313	19	....	3.64	....	....	....	....	....	....	....	....	....	....	....	....	....	....	....	....	....
1989-90	**Los Angeles Kings**	**NHL**	**2**	**0**	**1**	**0**	**83**	**11**	**0**	**7.95**	**6.67**	**20.34**	**43**	**.744**	**31.1**	....	....	....	....	....	....	....	....	....	....	....	....
	New Haven Nighthawks	AHL	14	6	6	2	851	43	0	3.03	....	....	....	....	....	5	2	3	....	302	24	0	4.77	....	....	....	....
1990-91	New Haven Nighthawks	AHL	33	13	16	4	1882	115	1	3.67	....	....	....	....	....	....	....	....	....	....	....	....	....	....	....	....	....
	Phoenix Roadrunners	IHL	4	1	2	0	160	11	0	4.13	....	....	....	....	....	....	....	....	....	....	....	....	....	....	....	....	....
1991-92	Phoenix Roadrunners	IHL	22	8	12	1	1242	80	0	3.86	....	....	....	....	....	....	....	....	....	....	....	....	....	....	....	....	....
1992-93	**Los Angeles Kings**	**NHL**	**31**	**15**	**8**	**4**	**1735**	**111**	**0**	**3.84**	**3.27**	**4.32**	**987**	**.888**	**34.1**	**4**	**3**	**1**	....	**240**	**16**	**0**	**4.00**	**4.08**	**157**	**.898**	**39.3**
1993-94	**Los Angeles Kings**	**NHL**	**22**	**4**	**11**	**5**	**1144**	**65**	**1**	**3.41**	**3.25**	**3.14**	**706**	**.908**	**37.0**	....	....	....	....	....	....	....	....	....	....	....	....
	Phoenix Roadrunners	IHL	3	1	1	0	121	13	0	6.42	....	....	....	....	....	....	....	....	....	....	....	....	....	....	....	....	....
1994-95	**Los Angeles Kings**	**NHL**	**1**	**0**	**0**	**0**	**16**	**2**	**0**	**7.50**	**7.75**	**25.00**	**6**	**.667**	**22.5**	....	....	....	....	....	....	....	....	....	....	....	....
	Buffalo Sabres	**NHL**	**6**	**2**	**3**	**0**	**317**	**20**	**0**	**3.79**	**3.92**	**5.05**	**150**	**.867**	**28.4**	....	....	....	....	....	....	....	....	....	....	....	....
1995-96	Rochester Americans	AHL	16	6	7	1	833	49	0	3.53	....	....	....	....	....	....	....	....	....	....	....	....	....	....	....	....	....
1996-97	Portland Pirates	AHL	30	13	13	2	1606	82	0	3.06	....	....	....	....	....	....	....	....	....	....	....	....	....	....	....	....	....
1997-98	Hartford Wolf Pack	AHL	39	20	10	6	2221	89	2	2.40	....	....	....	....	....	7	3	4	....	419	30	0	4.29	....	....	....	....
	NHL Totals		**62**	**21**	**23**	**9**	**3295**	**209**	**1**	**3.81**	....	....	**1892**	**.890**	....	**4**	**3**	**1**	....	**240**	**16**	**0**	**4.00**	....	....	....	....

WCHA First All-Star Team (1988) • NCAA West First All-American Team (1988) • Won Hobey Baker Memorial Award (Top U.S. Collegiate Player) (1988) • WCHA Second All-Star Team (1989)
• Scored a goal while with Rochester (AHL), October 9, 1995.

Traded to **Buffalo** by **Los Angeles** with Alexei Zhitnik, Charlie Huddy and Los Angeles' 5th round choice (Marian Menhart) in 1995 Entry Draft for Philippe Boucher, Denis Tsygurov and Grant Fuhr, February 14, 1995. Signed as a free agent by **Washington**, August 27, 1996. Signed as a free agent by **NY Rangers**, August, 1997.

• STEFAN, GREG

Greg Stefan G – L. 5'11", 180 lbs. b: Brantford, Ont., 2/11/1961. Detroit's 5th choice, 128th overall, in 1981 Entry Draft.

Season	Club	League	GP	W	L	T	Mins	GA	SO	Avg	AAvg	Eff	SA	S%	SAPG	GP	W	L	T	Mins	GA	SO	Avg	Eff	SA	S%	SAPG
1978-79	Oshawa Generals	OHA	33	....	....	....	1635	133	0	4.88	....	....	....	....	....	....	....	....	....	....	....	....	....	....	....	....	....
1979-80	Oshawa Generals	OHA	17	8	6	0	897	58	0	3.88	....	....	....	....	....	....	....	....	....	....	....	....	....	....	....	....	....
1980-81	Oshawa Generals	OHA	46	23	14	3	2407	174	0	4.34	....	....	....	....	....	6	2	3	0	298	20	0	4.02	....	....	....	....
1981-82	**Detroit Red Wings**	**NHL**	**2**	**0**	**2**	**0**	**120**	**10**	**0**	**5.00**	**3.85**	....	....	....	....	....	....	....	....	....	....	....	....	....	....	....	....
	Adirondack Red Wings	AHL	29	11	13	3	1571	99	2	3.78	....	....	....	....	....	1	0	0	0	20	0	0	0.00	....	....	....	....
1982-83	**Detroit Red Wings**	**NHL**	**35**	**6**	**16**	**9**	**1847**	**139**	**0**	**4.52**	**3.62**	**6.63**	**947**	**.853**	**30.8**	....	....	....	....	....	....	....	....	....	....	....	....
1983-84	**Detroit Red Wings**	**NHL**	**50**	**19**	**22**	**2**	**2600**	**152**	**2**	**3.51**	**2.74**	**4.36**	**1223**	**.876**	**28.2**	**3**	**1**	**2**	....	**210**	**8**	**0**	**2.29**	**2.13**	**86**	**.907**	**24.6**
1984-85	**Detroit Red Wings**	**NHL**	**46**	**21**	**19**	**3**	**2635**	**190**	**0**	**4.33**	**3.45**	**6.04**	**1361**	**.860**	**31.0**	**3**	**0**	**3**	....	**138**	**17**	**0**	**7.39**	**18.21**	**69**	**.754**	**30.0**
1985-86	**Detroit Red Wings**	**NHL**	**37**	**10**	**20**	**5**	**2068**	**155**	**1**	**4.50**	**3.51**	**6.46**	**1080**	**.856**	**31.3**	....	....	....	....	....	....	....	....	....	....	....	....
1986-87	**Detroit Red Wings**	**NHL**	**43**	**20**	**17**	**3**	**2351**	**135**	**1**	**3.45**	**2.00**	**4.30**	**1082**	**.875**	**27.8**	**9**	**4**	**5**	....	**508**	**24**	**0**	**2.83**	**2.70**	**252**	**.905**	**29.8**
1987-88	**Detroit Red Wings**	**NHL**	**33**	**17**	**9**	**5**	**1854**	**96**	**1**	**3.11**	**2.58**	**3.23**	**925**	**.896**	**29.9**	**10**	**5**	**4**	....	**531**	**32**	***1**	**3.62**	**4.91**	**236**	**.864**	**26.7**
1988-89	**Detroit Red Wings**	**NHL**	**46**	**21**	**17**	**3**	**2499**	**167**	**0**	**4.01**	**3.31**	**5.19**	**1290**	**.871**	**31.0**	**5**	**2**	**3**	....	**294**	**18**	**0**	**3.67**	**4.37**	**151**	**.881**	**30.8**
1989-90	**Detroit Red Wings**	**NHL**	**7**	**1**	**5**	**0**	**359**	**24**	**0**	**4.01**	**3.36**	**6.55**	**147**	**.837**	**24.6**	....	....	....	....	....	....	....	....	....	....	....	....
	Adirondack Red Wings	AHL	3	1	0	1	128	7	0	3.28	....	....	....	....	....	....	....	....	....	....	....	....	....	....	....	....	....
1990-91	Adirondack Red Wings	AHL	2	0	1	0	66	7	0	6.36	....	....	....	....	....	....	....	....	....	....	....	....	....	....	....	....	....
	NHL Totals		**299**	**115**	**127**	**30**	**16333**	**1068**	**5**	**3.92**	....	....	....	....	....	**30**	**12**	**17**	....	**1681**	**99**	**1**	**3.53**	....	....	....	....

• STEIN, PHIL

Phil Stein G – L. 5'11", b: Toronto, Ont., 9/13/1913.

Season	Club	League	GP	W	L	T	Mins	GA	SO	Avg	AAvg	Eff	SA	S%	SAPG	GP	W	L	T	Mins	GA	SO	Avg	Eff	SA	S%	SAPG
1930-31	Toronto Marlboros	OHA	7	....	....	....	420	18	0	2.57	....	....	....	....	....	2	....	....	....	120	5	0	2.50	....	....	....	....
1931-32	Toronto Marlboros	OHA	8	....	....	....	460	15	0	*1.96	....	....	....	....	....	4	....	....	....	240	4	1	1.00	....	....	....	....
1932-33	Toronto Marlboros	OHA	9	....	....	....	540	6	*2	1.56	....	....	....	....	....	3	....	....	....	180	6	*1	2.00	....	....	....	....
1933-34	Syracuse Stars	IAHL	23	....	....	....	1380	51	3	2.22	....	....	....	....	....	2	....	....	....	120	4	0	2.00	....	....	....	....
1934-35	Syracuse Stars	IAHL	36	....	....	....	2160	97	2	2.69	....	....	....	....	....	2	0	2	0	120	7	0	3.50	....	....	....	....
1935-36	Syracuse Stars	IAHL	40	....	....	....	2400	105	3	2.26	....	....	....	....	....	3	....	....	....	180	8	0	2.67	....	....	....	....
1936-37	Syracuse Stars	AHL	*48	*27	16	5	*2960	134	2	2.72	....	....	....	....	....	*9	*6	3	0	*540	15	*2	*1.66	....	....	....	....
1937-38	Syracuse Stars	AHL	*48	21	20	7	*2970	122	3	2.46	....	....	....	....	....	*8	*5	3	0	612	23	0	2.25	....	....	....	....
1938-39	Syracuse Stars	AHL	49	23	18	8	3030	109	6	2.16	....	....	....	....	....	3	1	2	0	180	6	0	2.00	....	....	....	....
1939-40	Omaha Knights	AHA	6	3	3	0	360	16	0	2.67	....	....	....	....	....	....	....	....	....	....	....	....	....	....	....	....	....
	Providence Reds	AHL	10	10	5	4	1190	56	1	2.82	....	....	....	....	....	....	....	....	....	....	....	....	....	....	....	....	....
	Toronto Maple Leafs	**NHL**	**1**	**0**	**0**	**1**	**70**	**2**	**0**	**1.71**	**2.12**	....	....	....	....	....	....	....	....	....	....	....	....	....	....	....	....

			REGULAR SEASON													PLAYOFFS											
Season	**Club**	**League**	**GP**	**W**	**L**	**T**	**Mins**	**GA**	**SO**	**Avg**	**AAvg**	**Eff**	**SA**	**S%**	**SAPG**	**GP**	**W**	**L**	**T**	**Mins**	**GA**	**SO**	**Avg**	**Eff**	**SA**	**S%**	**SAPG**
1940-41	New Haven Eagles	AHL	53	26	21	6	3270	142	4	2.61	....	....	....	....	....	2	0	2	0	130	3	0	1.38	....	....	....	....
1941-42	New Haven Eagles	AHL	54	26	24	4	3330	204	2	3.68	....	....	....	....	....	2	0	2	0	120	4	0	2.00	....	....	....	....
1942-43	Toronto Research Colonels	City Sr.	8	....	....	....	480	57	0	7.12	....	....	....	....	....	....	....	....	....	....	....	....	....	....	....	....	....
	NHL Totals		**1**	**0**	**0**	**1**	**70**	**2**	**0**	**1.71**	....	....	....	....	....	....	....	....	....	....	....	....	....	....	....	....	....

Loaned to **Toronto** by **Providence** (AHL) to replace injured Turk Broda, January 18, 1940. (NY Americans 2, Toronto 2)

• STEPHENSON, WAYNE

Wayne Stephenson G – L. 5'9", 175 lbs. b: Fort William, Ont., 1/29/1945.

Season	Club	League	GP	W	L	T	Mins	GA	SO	Avg	AAvg	Eff	SA	S%	SAPG	GP	W	L	T	Mins	GA	SO	Avg	Eff	SA	S%	SAPG
1963-64	Winnipeg Braves	MJHL	29	11	*15	3	1804	120	0	3.99	....	....	....	....	....	....	....	....	....	....	....	....	....	....	....	....	....
1964-65	Winnipeg Braves	MJHL	43	*26	12	5	2580	128	*2	*2.97	....	....	....	....	....	15	10	5	0	910	60	0	3.96	....	....	....	....
1965-66	Canada	Nat-Team	STATISTICS NOT AVAILABLE																								
1966-67	Canada	Nat-Team	STATISTICS NOT AVAILABLE																								
	Canada	WEC-A	1	1	0	0	60	1	0	1.00	....	....	....	....	....	....	....	....	....	....	....	....	....	....	....	....	....
1967-68	Winnipeg Nats	WCSHL	15	....	....	....	900	30	1	2.11	....	....	....	....	....	....	....	....	....	....	....	....	....	....	....	....	....
	Canada	Olympics	3	2	0	0	140	3	1	1.29	....	....	....	....	....	....	....	....	....	....	....	....	....	....	....	....	....
1968-69	Canada	Nat-Team	STATISTICS NOT AVAILABLE																								
	Canada	WEC-A	8	3	5	0	480	27	1	3.38	....	....	....	....	....	....	....	....	....	....	....	....	....	....	....	....	....
1969-70	Canada	Nat-Team	STATISTICS NOT AVAILABLE																								
1970-71	Canada	Nat-Team	STATISTICS NOT AVAILABLE																								
1971-72	Kansas City Blues	CHL	21	5	11	4	1210	80	0	3.93	....	....	....	....	....	....	....	....	....	....	....	....	....	....	....	....	....
	St. Louis Blues	**NHL**	**2**	**0**	**1**	**0**	**100**	**9**	**0**	**5.40**	**5.44**	....	....	....	....	....	....	....	....	....	....	....	....	....	....	....	....
1972-73	**St. Louis Blues**	**NHL**	**45**	**18**	**15**	**7**	**2535**	**128**	**1**	**3.03**	**2.85**	....	....	....	....	**3**	**1**	**2**	....	**160**	**14**	**0**	**5.25**	....	....	....	....
1973-74	**St. Louis Blues**	**NHL**	**40**	**13**	**21**	**5**	**2360**	**123**	**2**	**3.13**	**3.02**	....	....	....	....	....	....	....	....	....	....	....	....	....	....	....	....
1974-75	**Philadelphia Flyers**	**NHL**	**12**	**7**	**2**	**1**	**639**	**29**	**1**	**2.72**	**2.45**	....	....	....	....	**2**	**2**	**0**	....	**123**	**4**	**1**	**1.95**	....	....	....	....
1975-76	**Philadelphia Flyers**	**NHL**	**66**	**40**	**10**	**13**	**3819**	**164**	**1**	**2.58**	**2.31**	....	....	....	....	**8**	**4**	**4**	....	**494**	**22**	**0**	**2.67**	....	....	....	....
1976-77	**Philadelphia Flyers**	**NHL**	**21**	**12**	**3**	**2**	**1065**	**41**	**3**	**2.31**	**2.14**	....	....	....	....	**9**	**4**	**3**	....	**532**	**23**	**1**	**2.59**	....	....	....	....
1977-78	**Philadelphia Flyers**	**NHL**	**26**	**14**	**10**	**1**	**1482**	**68**	**3**	**2.75**	**2.57**	....	....	....	....	....	....	....	....	....	....	....	....	....	....	....	....
1978-79	**Philadelphia Flyers**	**NHL**	**40**	**20**	**10**	**5**	**2187**	**122**	**2**	**3.35**	**2.95**	....	....	....	....	**4**	**0**	**3**	....	**213**	**16**	**0**	**4.51**	....	....	....	....
1979-80	**Washington Capitals**	**NHL**	**56**	**18**	**24**	**10**	**3146**	**187**	**0**	**3.57**	**3.14**	....	....	....	....	....	....	....	....	....	....	....	....	....	....	....	....
1980-81	**Washington Capitals**	**NHL**	**20**	**4**	**7**	**5**	**1010**	**66**	**1**	**3.92**	**3.14**	....	....	....	....	....	....	....	....	....	....	....	....	....	....	....	....
	NHL Totals		**328**	**146**	**103**	**49**	**18343**	**937**	**14**	**3.06**	....	....	....	....	....	**26**	**11**	**12**	....	**1522**	**79**	**2**	**3.11**	....	....	....	....

Played in NHL All-Star Game (1976, 1978)

Signed as a free agent by **St. Louis**, January 2, 1972. Traded to **Philadelphia** by **St. Louis** for rights to Randy Andreachuk and Philadelphia's 2nd round choice (Jamie Masters) in 1975 Amateur Draft, September 16, 1974. Traded to **Washington** by **Philadelphia** for Washington's 3rd round choice (Barry Tabobondung) in 1981 Entry Draft, August 16, 1979.

• STEVENSON, DOUG

Doug Stevenson G – L. 5'8", 170 lbs. b: Regina, Sask., 4/6/1924.

Season	Club	League	GP	W	L	T	Mins	GA	SO	Avg	AAvg	Eff	SA	S%	SAPG	GP	W	L	T	Mins	GA	SO	Avg	Eff	SA	S%	SAPG
1941-42	Edmonton A.C.	City Jr.	STATISTICS NOT AVAILABLE																								
1942-43	**Chicago Black Hawks**	**NHL**	DID NOT PLAY – SPARE GOALTENDER																								
1943-44	Kingston Frontenacs	OHA Sr.	2	0	2	0	120	12	0	6.00	....	....	....	....	....	....	....	....	....	....	....	....	....	....	....	....	....
1944-45	**New York Rangers**	**NHL**	**4**	**0**	**4**	**0**	**240**	**20**	**0**	**5.00**	**4.16**	....	....	....	....	....	....	....	....	....	....	....	....	....	....	....	....
	New York Rovers	EHL	20	....	....	....	1200	99	0	4.95	....	....	....	....	....	6	....	....	....	360	31	0	5.17	....	....	....	....
	Chicago Black Hawks	**NHL**	**2**	**1**	**1**	**0**	**120**	**7**	**0**	**3.50**	**2.90**	....	....	....	....	....	....	....	....	....	....	....	....	....	....	....	....
1945-46	**Chicago Black Hawks**	**NHL**	**2**	**1**	**1**	**0**	**120**	**12**	**0**	**6.00**	**5.57**	....	....	....	....	....	....	....	....	....	....	....	....	....	....	....	....
	Kansas City Pla-Mors	USHL	52	....	....	....	3120	169	2	3.25	....	....	....	....	....	....	....	....	....	....	....	....	....	....	....	....	....
	St. Paul Saints	USHL	4	....	....	....	240	13	0	3.25	....	....	....	....	....	....	....	....	....	....	....	....	....	....	....	....	....
1946-47	St. Paul Saints	USHL	28	....	....	....	1680	114	2	4.07	....	....	....	....	....	....	....	....	....	....	....	....	....	....	....	....	....
	New Haven Ramblers	AHL	1	0	0	0	20	1	0	3.00	....	....	....	....	....	....	....	....	....	....	....	....	....	....	....	....	....
1947-48	St. Paul Saints	USHL	3	1	2	0	180	9	0	3.00	....	....	....	....	....	....	....	....	....	....	....	....	....	....	....	....	....
	New Haven Ramblers	AHL	39	18	17	4	2340	154	0	3.95	....	....	....	....	....	4	2	2	0	240	11	0	2.75	....	....	....	....
1948-49	Tacoma Rockets	PCHL	59	27	27	5	3540	216	0	3.66	....	....	....	....	....	6	3	3	0	384	21	1	3.28	....	....	....	....
1949-50	Tacoma Rockets	PCHL	70	*34	27	9	4200	238	4	3.40	....	....	....	....	....	5	2	3	0	310	12	0	2.32	....	....	....	....
1950-51	Tacoma Rockets	PCHL	70	27	26	17	4200	219	4	3.12	....	....	....	....	....	6	2	4	0	366	16	1	2.62	....	....	....	....
1951-52	Tacoma Rockets	PCHL	70	34	25	11	4200	236	1	3.37	....	....	....	....	....	7	3	4	0	452	28	0	3.72	....	....	....	....
1952-53	Tacoma Rockets	WHL	68	27	29	12	4080	231	4	3.40	....	....	....	....	....	....	....	....	....	....	....	....	....	....	....	....	....
	Seattle Bombers	WHL	....	....	....	....	....	....	....	....	....	....	....	....	....	1	0	1	0	60	6	0	6.00	....	....	....	....
1953-54	Seattle Bombers	WHL	2	0	2	0	120	7	0	3.50	....	....	....	....	....	....	....	....	....	....	....	....	....	....	....	....	....
	Kelowna Packers	OSHL	26	....	....	....	1560	91	0	3.50	....	....	....	....	....	8	4	4	0	480	31	0	3.87	....	....	....	....
1954-55	Vancouver Canucks	WHL	1	1	0	0	60	3	0	3.00	....	....	....	....	....	....	....	....	....	....	....	....	....	....	....	....	....
	Saskatoon Quakers	WHL	23	5	14	4	1380	85	2	3.70	....	....	....	....	....	....	....	....	....	....	....	....	....	....	....	....	....
	Calgary Stampeders	WHL	32	11	15	6	1920	121	0	3.78	....	....	....	....	....	9	4	5	0	546	25	*1	2.75	....	....	....	....
	Kamloops Chiefs	OSHL	8	....	....	....	480	29	0	3.62	....	....	....	....	....	....	....	....	....	....	....	....	....	....	....	....	....
1955-56	Brandon Regals	WHL	2	0	2	0	128	8	0	3.75	....	....	....	....	....	....	....	....	....	....	....	....	....	....	....	....	....
	Saskatoon Quakers	WHL	2	0	2	0	120	10	0	5.00	....	....	....	....	....	....	....	....	....	....	....	....	....	....	....	....	....
	Edmonton Flyers	WHL	2	0	1	1	130	9	0	4.15	....	....	....	....	....	....	....	....	....	....	....	....	....	....	....	....	....
	Calgary Stampeders	WHL	10	6	4	0	603	39	1	3.88	....	....	....	....	....	....	....	....	....	....	....	....	....	....	....	....	....
	NHL Totals		**8**	**2**	**6**	**0**	**480**	**39**	**0**	**4.88**	....	....	....	....	....	....	....	....	....	....	....	....	....	....	....	....	....

PCHL Northern Second All-Star Team (1950) • PCHL Second All-Star Team (1951)

Loaned to **Chicago** by **NY Rangers** to replace injured Mike Karakas, March 17, 1945. (Montreal 4, Chicago 3)

• STEWART, CHARLES

Charles "Doc" Stewart G – L. 5'7", 140 lbs. b: Carleton Place, Ont., 11/13/1895.

Season	Club	League	GP	W	L	T	Mins	GA	SO	Avg	AAvg	Eff	SA	S%	SAPG	GP	W	L	T	Mins	GA	SO	Avg	Eff	SA	S%	SAPG
1913-14	Kingston Collegiate Institute	OHA	6	4	2	0	360	40	0	6.67	....	....	....	....	....	....	....	....	....	....	....	....	....	....	....	....	....
1914-15	Kingston Frontenacs	OHA	STATISTICS NOT AVAILABLE																								
1915-16	Toronto Argonauts	OHA Sr.	3	2	1	0	180	8	0	2.67	....	....	....	....	....	2	0	1	1	112	7	0	3.75	....	....	....	....
1916-17	Toronto Dentals	OHA Sr.	10	*7	2	1	620	26	*2	*2.52	....	....	....	....	....	4	*4	0	0	280	8	0	*1.71	....	....	....	....
1917-18	Toronto Dentals	OHA Sr.	9	*9	0	0	540	35	0	*3.89	....	....	....	....	....	2	0	1	1	118	7	0	3.56	....	....	....	....
1918-19	Toronto Dentals	OHA Sr.	7	5	2	0	420	27	0	*3.86	....	....	....	....	....	2	1	1	0	120	6	0	*3.00	....	....	....	....
1919-20	Toronto Dentals	OHA Sr.	6	3	3	0	390	24	0	3.69	....	....	....	....	....	....	....	....	....	....	....	....	....	....	....	....	....
1920-21	Toronto Aura Lee	OHA Sr.	9	3	5	0	529	22	1	2.50	....	....	....	....	....	....	....	....	....	....	....	....	....	....	....	....	....
1921-22	Hamilton Tigers	OHA Sr.	9	4	4	1	570	34	0	3.56	....	....	....	....	....	....	....	....	....	....	....	....	....	....	....	....	....
1922-23	Hamilton Tigers	OHA Sr.	12	*9	2	0	699	28	1	2.40	....	....	....	....	....	2	0	1	1	120	6	0	3.00	....	....	....	....
1923-24	Hamilton Tigers	OHA Sr.	10	*9	1	0	620	26	0	*2.52	....	....	....	....	....	6	4	2	0	358	16	0	2.68	....	....	....	....
1924-25	**Boston Bruins**	**NHL**	**21**	**5**	**16**	**0**	**1266**	**65**	**2**	**3.08**	**3.92**	....	....	....	....	....	....	....	....	....	....	....	....	....	....	....	....
1925-26	**Boston Bruins**	**NHL**	**35**	**16**	**14**	**4**	**2173**	**80**	**6**	**2.21**	**2.94**	....	....	....	....	....	....	....	....	....	....	....	....	....	....	....	....
1926-27	**Boston Bruins**	**NHL**	**21**	**9**	**11**	**1**	**1303**	**49**	**2**	**2.26**	**3.51**	....	....	....	....	....	....	....	....	....	....	....	....	....	....	....	....
	Hamilton Tigers	Can-Pro	9	....	....	....	540	17	1	1.89	....	....	....	....	....	1	0	1	0	30	5	0	10.00	....	....	....	....
	NHL Totals		**77**	**30**	**41**	**5**	**4742**	**194**	**10**	**2.45**	....	....	....	....	....	....	....	....	....	....	....	....	....	....	....	....	....

Signed as a free agent by **Boston**, December 25, 1924.

• STEWART, JIM

Jim Stewart G – L. 5'11", 170 lbs. b: Cambridge, MA, 4/23/1957.

Season	Club	League	GP	W	L	T	Mins	GA	SO	Avg	AAvg	Eff	SA	S%	SAPG	GP	W	L	T	Mins	GA	SO	Avg	Eff	SA	S%	SAPG
1976-77	South Shore Whalers	NEJHL	44	....	....	....	2336	156	1	4.01	....	....	....	....	....	....	....	....	....	....	....	....	....	....	....	....	....
1977-78	College of the Holy Cross	ECAC 2	15	10	5	0	905	51	....	3.37	....	....	....	....	....	....	....	....	....	....	....	....	....	....	....	....	....
	Cape Cod Freedoms	NEHL	1	0	1	0	60	6	0	6.00	....	....	....	....	....	....	....	....	....	....	....	....	....	....	....	....	....
1978-79	College of the Holy Cross	ECAC 2	5	1	4	0	316	22	....	4.19	....	....	....	....	....	....	....	....	....	....	....	....	....	....	....	....	....
1979-80	**Boston Bruins**	**NHL**	**1**	**0**	**1**	**0**	**20**	**5**	**0**	**15.00**	**13.19**	....	....	....	....	....	....	....	....	....	....	....	....	....	....	....	....
	Binghamton Dusters	AHL	13	4	6	2	690	46	0	4.00	....	....	....	....	....	....	....	....	....	....	....	....	....	....	....	....	....
	Utica Mohawks	EHL	30	....	....	....	1673	122	3	4.38	....	....	....	....	....	2	0	1	0	80	12	0	9.00	....	....	....	....
1980-81	Springfield Indians	AHL	3	0	3	0	180	14	0	4.67	....	....	....	....	....	....	....	....	....	....	....	....	....	....	....	....	....
	Indianapolis Checkers	CHL	3	1	1	0	140	11	1	4.71	....	....	....	....	....	....	....	....	....	....	....	....	....	....	....	....	....
	Salem Raiders	EHL	16	....	....	....	892	69	0	4.64	....	....	....	....	....	....	....	....	....	....	....	....	....	....	....	....	....
	Saginaw Gears	IHL	3	....	....	....	153	16	0	6.27	....	....	....	....	....	....	....	....	....	....	....	....	....	....	....	....	....

Season	Club	League	GP	W	L	T	Mins	GA	SO	Avg	AAvg	Eff	SA	S%	SAPG	GP	W	L	T	Mins	GA	SO	Avg	Eff	SA	S%	SAPG
			REGULAR SEASON													PLAYOFFS											
1981-82	Binghamton Whalers	AHL	4	1	3	0	240	17	0	4.25	....	....	....	....	....	1	0	0	0	9	1	0	6.67	....	....	....	....
	Nashville South Stars	CHL	3	1	1	0	110	8	0	4.37	....	....	....	....	....	....	....	....	....	....	....	....	....	....	....	....	....
	Cape Cod Buccaneers	ACHL	26	....	....	....	1410	98	0	4.17	....	....	....	....	....	....	....	....	....	....	....	....	....	....	....	....	....
	Baltimore Skipjacks	ACHL	7	....	....	....	370	16	0	2.59	....	....	....	....	....	7	....	....	....	392	36	0	5.51	....	....	....	....
	NHL Totals		**1**	**0**	**1**	**0**	**20**	**5**	**0**	**15.00**	....	....	....	....	....	....	....	....	....	....	....	....	....	....	....	....	....

NCAA (College Div.) East All-American Team (1978)

Signed as a free agent by **Boston**, September, 1979.

• STORR, JAMIE

Jamie Storr G – L. 6', 170 lbs. b: Brampton, Ont., 12/28/1975. Los Angeles' 1st choice, 7th overall, in 1994 Entry Draft.

Season	Club	League	GP	W	L	T	Mins	GA	SO	Avg	AAvg	Eff	SA	S%	SAPG	GP	W	L	T	Mins	GA	SO	Avg	Eff	SA	S%	SAPG
1991-92	Owen Sound Platers	OHL	34	11	16	1	1732	128	0	4.43	....	....	....	....	....	5	1	4	....	299	28	0	5.62	....	....	....	....
1992-93	Owen Sound Platers	OHL	41	20	17	3	2362	180	0	4.57	....	....	....	....	....	8	4	4	....	454	35	0	4.63	....	....	....	....
1993-94	Owen Sound Platers	OHL	35	21	11	1	2004	120	1	3.59	....	....	....	....	....	9	4	5	....	547	44	0	4.83	....	....	....	....
	Canada	WJC-A	4	....	....	....	240	10	....	2.50	....	....	....	....	....	....	....	....	....	....	....	....	....	....	....	....	....
	Canada	WC-A	DID NOT PLAY – SPARE GOALTENDER																								
1994-95	Owen Sound Platers	OHL	17	5	9	2	977	64	0	3.93	....	....	....	....	....	....	....	....	....	....	....	....	....	....	....	....	....
	Canada	WJC-A	4	....	....	....	240	14	....	3.50	....	....	....	....	....	....	....	....	....	....	....	....	....	....	....	....	....
	Los Angeles Kings	**NHL**	**5**	**1**	**3**	**1**	**263**	**17**	**0**	**3.88**	**4.01**	**4.34**	**152**	**.888**	**34.7**	....	....	....	....	....	....	....	....	....	....	....	....
	Windsor Spitfires	OHL	4	3	1	0	241	8	1	1.99	....	....	....	....	....	10	6	3	....	520	34	1	3.92	....	....	....	....
1995-96	**Los Angeles Kings**	**NHL**	**5**	**3**	**1**	**0**	**262**	**12**	**0**	**2.75**	**2.70**	**2.24**	**147**	**.918**	**33.7**	....	....	....	....	....	....	....	....	....	....	....	....
	Phoenix Roadrunners	IHL	48	22	20	4	2711	139	2	3.08	....	....	....	....	....	2	1	1	....	118	4	1	2.03	....	....	....	....
1996-97	**Los Angeles Kings**	**NHL**	**5**	**2**	**1**	**1**	**265**	**11**	**0**	**2.49**	**2.63**	**1.86**	**147**	**.925**	**33.3**	....	....	....	....	....	....	....	....	....	....	....	....
	Phoenix Roadrunners	IHL	44	16	22	4	2441	147	0	3.61	....	....	....	....	....	....	....	....	....	....	....	....	....	....	....	....	....
1997-98	**Los Angeles Kings**	**NHL**	**17**	**9**	**5**	**1**	**920**	**34**	**2**	**2.22**	**2.59**	**1.57**	**482**	**.929**	**31.4**	**3**	**0**	**2**	....	**145**	**9**	**0**	**3.72**	**4.35**	**77**	**.883**	**31.9**
	Long Beach Ice Dogs	IHL	11	7	2	1	629	31	0	2.96	....	....	....	....	....	....	....	....	....	....	....	....	....	....	....	....	....
	NHL Totals		**32**	**15**	**10**	**3**	**1710**	**74**	**2**	**2.60**	....	....	**928**	**.920**	....	**3**	**0**	**2**	....	**145**	**9**	**0**	**3.72**	....	....	....	....

Named Best Goaltender at WJC-A (1994) • OHL First All-Star Team (1994) • NHL All-Rookie Team (1998)

• STUART, HERB

Herb Stuart G – L. 5'6", 175 lbs. b: Brantford, Ont., 3/30/1899.

Season	Club	League	GP	W	L	T	Mins	GA	SO	Avg	AAvg	Eff	SA	S%	SAPG	GP	W	L	T	Mins	GA	SO	Avg	Eff	SA	S%	SAPG
1916-17	Brantford Alexanders	OHA	4	3	1	0	240	15	0	3.75	....	....	....	....	....	2	0	1	1	120	7	0	3.50	....	....	....	....
1917-18	Paris AAA	OHA	5	*5	0	0	300	11	0	2.20	....	....	....	....	....	2	1	1	0	120	14	0	7.00	....	....	....	....
1918-19	Paris AAA	OHA	STATISTICS NOT AVAILABLE																								
1919-20	Brandon Elks	MHL Sr.	2	0	2	0	120	18	0	9.00	....	....	....	....	....	....	....	....	....	....	....	....	....	....	....	....	....
1920-21	Brandon Elks	MHL Sr.	11	7	4	0	660	47	0	4.27	....	....	....	....	....	....	....	....	....	....	....	....	....	....	....	....	....
1921-22	Brandon Elks	MHL Sr.	12	9	3	0	720	55	0	4.58	....	....	....	....	....	2	2	0	0	120	5	0	2.50	....	....	....	....
1922-23	Brandon Elks	MHL Sr.	16	9	7	0	960	57	0	3.56	....	....	....	....	....	....	....	....	....	....	....	....	....	....	....	....	....
1923-24	Brandon Elks	MHL Sr.	12	9	3	0	720	36	*1	3.00	....	....	....	....	....	4	1	2	1	240	7	1	1.75	....	....	....	....
1924-25	Edmonton Eskimos	WCHL	17	7	9	1	1060	68	1	3.85	....	....	....	....	....	....	....	....	....	....	....	....	....	....	....	....	....
1925-26	Edmonton Eskimos	WHL	*30	*19	11	0	1800	77	2	2.57	....	....	....	....	....	2	0	1	1	120	5	0	2.50	....	....	....	....
1926-27	**Detroit Cougars**	**NHL**	**3**	**1**	**2**	**0**	**180**	**5**	**0**	**1.67**	**2.58**	....	....	....	....	....	....	....	....	....	....	....	....	....	....	....	....
1927-28	Detroit Olympics	Can-Pro	42	....	....	....	2520	75	0	1.79	....	....	....	....	....	2	1	1	0	120	4	0	2.00	....	....	....	....
1928-29	Detroit Olympics	Can-Pro	42	*27	10	5	1520	67	*11	*1.59	....	....	....	....	....	7	4	3	0	420	14	2	1.83	....	....	....	....
1929-30	Detroit Olympics	IAHL	42	....	....	....	2520	74	7	1.76	....	....	....	....	....	3	....	....	....	180	7	0	2.33	....	....	....	....
1930-31	London Tecumsehs	IAHL	48	21	21	6	3010	83	12	1.65	....	....	....	....	....	....	....	....	....	....	....	....	....	....	....	....	....
1931-32	London Tecumsehs	IAHL	48	21	15	12	2880	70	*13	*1.46	....	....	....	....	....	6	1	2	3	360	10	*3	1.67	....	....	....	....
1932-33	London Tecumsehs	IAHL	44	*27	9	8	2640	66	*12	*1.46	....	....	....	....	....	6	2	3	1	360	11	1	1.83	....	....	....	....
1933-34	Syracuse Stars	IAHL	2	....	....	....	120	4	0	2.00	....	....	....	....	....	....	....	....	....	....	....	....	....	....	....	....	....
	London Tecumsehs	IAHL	44	18	17	9	2640	80	6	1.81	....	....	....	....	....	6	5	1	0	360	9	*1	*1.50	....	....	....	....
1934-35	London Tecumsehs	IAHL	36	....	....	....	2160	90	4	2.50	....	....	....	....	....	....	....	....	....	....	....	....	....	....	....	....	....
1935-36	London Tecumsehs	IAHL	48	23	22	5	2880	125	3	2.60	....	....	....	....	....	2	0	0	2	120	4	0	2.00	....	....	....	....
	NHL Totals		**3**	**1**	**2**	**0**	**180**	**5**	**0**	**1.67**	....	....	....	....	....	....	....	....	....	....	....	....	....	....	....	....	....
	Other Major League Totals		47	26	20	1	2860	145	3	3.04	....	....	....	....	....	2	0	1	1	120	5	0	2.50	....	....	....	....

Signed as a free agent by **Edmonton** (WCHL), November 13, 1924. Traded to **Detroit Cougars** by **Edmonton** (WHL) for cash, October 5, 1926. Traded to **London** (IAHL) by **Detroit Cougars** for John Sorrell, November 10, 1930.

• SYLVESTRI, DON

Don Sylvestri G – L. 6', 180 lbs. b: Sudbury, Ont., 6/2/1961. Boston's 8th choice, 182nd overall, in 1981 Entry Draft.

Season	Club	League	GP	W	L	T	Mins	GA	SO	Avg	AAvg	Eff	SA	S%	SAPG	GP	W	L	T	Mins	GA	SO	Avg	Eff	SA	S%	SAPG
1979-80	Oshawa Generals	OHA	16	5	4	0	621	49	0	4.73	....	....	....	....	....	....	....	....	....	....	....	....	....	....	....	....	....
1980-81	Clarkson University	ECAC	29	22	3	4	1740	84	1	2.90	....	....	....	....	....	....	....	....	....	....	....	....	....	....	....	....	....
1981-82	Clarkson University	ECAC	30	22	6	1	1800	87	2	2.90	....	....	....	....	....	....	....	....	....	....	....	....	....	....	....	....	....
1982-83	Clarkson University	ECAC	11	3	3	1	425	23	0	3.25	....	....	....	....	....	....	....	....	....	....	....	....	....	....	....	....	....
1983-84	Clarkson University	ECAC	16	5	4	0	611	31	1	3.04	....	....	....	....	....	....	....	....	....	....	....	....	....	....	....	....	....
1984-85	Indianapolis Checkers	IHL	14	5	7	0	676	57	0	5.06	....	....	....	....	....	....	....	....	....	....	....	....	....	....	....	....	....
	Boston Bruins	**NHL**	**3**	**0**	**0**	**2**	**102**	**6**	**0**	**3.53**	**2.80**	**4.07**	**52**	**.885**	**30.6**	....	....	....	....	....	....	....	....	....	....	....	....
	Pinebridge Bucks	ACHL	6	....	....	....	360	28	0	5.85	....	....	....	....	....	....	....	....	....	....	....	....	....	....	....	....	....
	NHL Totals		**3**	**0**	**0**	**2**	**102**	**6**	**0**	**3.53**	....	....	**52**	**.885**	....	....	....	....	....	....	....	....	....	....	....	....	....

ECAC First All-Star Team (1981) • NCAA East First All-American Team (1981)

• TABARACCI, RICK

Rick Tabaracci G – L. 6'1", 180 lbs. b: Toronto, Ont., 1/2/1969. Pittsburgh's 2nd choice, 26th overall, in 1987 Entry Draft.

Season	Club	League	GP	W	L	T	Mins	GA	SO	Avg	AAvg	Eff	SA	S%	SAPG	GP	W	L	T	Mins	GA	SO	Avg	Eff	SA	S%	SAPG
1986-87	Cornwall Royals	OHL	*59	23	32	3	*3347	290	1	5.20	....	....	....	....	....	5	1	4	....	303	26	0	3.17	....	....	....	....
1987-88	Cornwall Royals	OHL	58	*33	18	6	3448	200	*3	3.48	....	....	....	....	....	11	5	6	....	642	37	0	3.46	....	....	....	....
	Muskegon Lumberjacks	IHL	....	....	....	....	....	....	....	....	....	....	....	....	....	1	0	0	....	13	1	0	4.62	....	....	....	....
1988-89	**Pittsburgh Penguins**	**NHL**	**1**	**0**	**0**	**0**	**33**	**4**	**0**	**7.27**	**6.00**	**13.85**	**21**	**.810**	**38.2**	....	....	....	....	....	....	....	....	....	....	....	....
	Cornwall Royals	OHL	50	24	20	5	2974	210	1	4.24	....	....	....	....	....	18	10	8	....	1080	65	*1	3.61	....	....	....	....
1989-90	Moncton Hawks	AHL	27	10	15	2	1580	107	2	4.06	....	....	....	....	....	....	....	....	....	....	....	....	....	....	....	....	....
	Fort Wayne Komets	IHL	22	8	9	1	1064	73	0	4.12	....	....	....	....	....	3	1	2	....	159	19	0	7.17	....	....	....	....
1990-91	**Winnipeg Jets**	**NHL**	**24**	**4**	**9**	**4**	**1093**	**71**	**1**	**3.90**	**3.49**	**4.86**	**570**	**.875**	**31.3**	....	....	....	....	....	....	....	....	....	....	....	....
	Moncton Hawks	AHL	11	4	5	2	645	41	0	3.81	....	....	....	....	....	....	....	....	....	....	....	....	....	....	....	....	....
1991-92	**Winnipeg Jets**	**NHL**	**18**	**6**	**7**	**3**	**966**	**52**	**0**	**3.23**	**2.86**	**3.57**	**470**	**.889**	**29.2**	**7**	**3**	**4**	....	**387**	**26**	**0**	**4.03**	**4.94**	**212**	**.877**	**32.9**
	Moncton Hawks	AHL	23	10	11	1	1313	80	0	3.66	....	....	....	....	....	....	....	....	....	....	....	....	....	....	....	....	....
	Canada	WC-A	1	0	1	0	25	4	0	9.60	....	....	....	....	....	....	....	....	....	....	....	....	....	....	....	....	....
1992-93	**Winnipeg Jets**	**NHL**	**19**	**5**	**10**	**0**	**959**	**70**	**0**	**4.38**	**3.73**	**6.18**	**496**	**.859**	**31.0**	....	....	....	....	....	....	....	....	....	....	....	....
	Moncton Hawks	AHL	5	2	1	2	290	18	0	3.72	....	....	....	....	....	....	....	....	....	....	....	....	....	....	....	....	....
	Washington Capitals	**NHL**	**6**	**3**	**2**	**0**	**343**	**10**	**2**	**1.75**	**1.49**	**1.08**	**162**	**.938**	**28.3**	**4**	**1**	**3**	....	**304**	**14**	**0**	**2.76**	**2.42**	**160**	**.913**	**31.6**
1993-94	**Washington Capitals**	**NHL**	**32**	**13**	**14**	**2**	**1770**	**91**	**2**	**3.08**	**2.93**	**3.43**	**817**	**.889**	**27.7**	**2**	**0**	**2**	....	**111**	**6**	**0**	**3.24**	**3.89**	**50**	**.880**	**27.0**
	Portland Pirates	AHL	3	3	0	0	176	8	0	2.72	....	....	....	....	....	....	....	....	....	....	....	....	....	....	....	....	....
1994-95	**Washington Capitals**	**NHL**	**8**	**1**	**3**	**2**	**394**	**16**	**0**	**2.44**	**2.52**	**2.66**	**147**	**.891**	**22.4**	....	....	....	....	....	....	....	....	....	....	....	....
	Chicago Wolves	IHL	2	1	1	0	119	9	0	4.51	....	....	....	....	....	....	....	....	....	....	....	....	....	....	....	....	....
	Calgary Flames	**NHL**	**5**	**2**	**0**	**1**	**202**	**5**	**0**	**1.49**	**1.54**	**0.80**	**93**	**.946**	**27.6**	**1**	**0**	**0**	....	**19**	**0**	**0**	**0.00**	**0.00**	**9**	**1.000**	**28.4**
1995-96	**Calgary Flames**	**NHL**	**43**	**19**	**16**	**3**	**2391**	**117**	**3**	**2.94**	**2.88**	**3.16**	**1087**	**.892**	**27.3**	**3**	**0**	**3**	....	**204**	**7**	**0**	**2.06**	**1.72**	**84**	**.917**	**24.7**
1996-97	**Calgary Flames**	**NHL**	**7**	**2**	**4**	**0**	**361**	**14**	**1**	**2.33**	**2.47**	**2.10**	**155**	**.910**	**25.8**	....	....	....	....	....	....	....	....	....	....	....	....
	Tampa Bay Lightning	**NHL**	**55**	**20**	**25**	**6**	**3012**	**138**	**4**	**2.75**	**2.91**	**2.60**	**1415**	**.902**	**28.2**	....	....	....	....	....	....	....	....	....	....	....	....
	Canada	WC-A	3	0	0	0	50	0	0	0.00	....	....	....	....	....	....	....	....	....	....	....	....	....	....	....	....	....
1997-98	**Calgary Flames**	**NHL**	**42**	**13**	**22**	**6**	**2419**	**116**	**0**	**2.88**	**3.38**	**3.07**	**1087**	**.893**	**27.0**	....	....	....	....	....	....	....	....	....	....	....	....
	NHL Totals		**260**	**88**	**112**	**27**	**13943**	**704**	**13**	**3.03**	....	....	**6520**	**.892**	....	**17**	**4**	**12**	....	**1025**	**53**	**0**	**3.10**	....	....	....	....

OHL First All-Star Team (1988) • OHL Second All-Star Team (1989)

Traded to **Winnipeg** by **Pittsburgh** with Randy Cunneyworth and Dave McLlwain for Jim Kyte, Andrew McBain and Randy Gilhen, June 17, 1989. Traded to **Washington** by **Winnipeg** for Jim Hrivnak and Washington's 2nd round choice (Alexei Budayev) in 1993 Entry Draft, March 22, 1993. Traded to **Calgary** by **Washington** for Calgary's 5th round choice (Joel Cort) in 1995 Entry Draft, April 7, 1995. Traded to **Tampa Bay** by **Calgary** for Aaron Gavey, November 19, 1996. Traded to **Calgary** by **Tampa Bay** for Calgary's 4th round choice (Eric Beaudoin) in 1998 Entry Draft, June 21, 1997.

			REGULAR SEASON													PLAYOFFS											
Season	Club	League	GP	W	L	T	Mins	GA	SO	Avg	AAvg	Eff	SA	S%	SAPG	GP	W	L	T	Mins	GA	SO	Avg	Eff	SA	S%	SAPG

• TAKKO, KARI

Kari Takko G – L. 6'2", 189 lbs. b: Uusikaupunki, Finland, 6/23/1962. Minnesota's 8th choice, 97th overall, in 1984 Entry Draft.

Season	Club	League	GP	W	L	T	Mins	GA	SO	Avg	AAvg	Eff	SA	S%	SAPG	GP	W	L	T	Mins	GA	SO	Avg	Eff	SA	S%	SAPG
1978-79	Assat Pori	Finland	2	....	....	....	120	2	0	1.00	....	....	....	....	....	....	....	....	....	....	....	....	....	....	....	....	....
	Finland	EJC-A	4	....	....	....	240	8	....	2.00	....	....	....	....	....	....	....	....	....	....	....	....	....	....	....	....	....
1979-80	Assat Pori	Finland	2	....	....	....	120	8	....	4.00	....	....	....	....	....	....	....	....	....	....	....	....	....	....	....	....	....
1980-81	Assat Pori	Finland	4	....	....	....	240	16	....	4.00	....	....	....	....	....	....	....	....	....	....	....	....	....	....	....	....	....
	Finland	WJC-A	4	....	....	....	240	12	....	3.00	....	....	....	....	....	....	....	....	....	....	....	....	....	....	....	....	....
1981-82	Assat Pori	Finland	14	....	....	....	840	60	....	4.28	....	....	....	....	....	....	....	....	....	....	....	....	....	....	....	....	....
	Finland	WJC-A	7	5	2	0	420	29	0	4.14	....	....	....	....	....	....	....	....	....	....	....	....	....	....	....	....	....
1982-83	Assat Pori	Finland	21	....	....	....	1260	77	0	3.66	....	....	....	....	....	....	....	....	....	....	....	....	....	....	....	....	....
	Finland	WEC-A	6	....	....	....	360	25	....	4.17	....	....	....	....	....	....	....	....	....	....	....	....	....	....	....	....	....
1983-84	Assat Pori	Finland	32	....	....	....	1920	102	3	3.19	....	....	....	....	....	9	....	....	....	540	37	0	4.11	....	....	....	....
	Finland	Olympics	5	....	....	....	195	19	....	5.85	....	....	....	....	....	....	....	....	....	....	....	....	....	....	....	....	....
1984-85	Assat Pori	Finland	35	....	....	....	2100	123	3	3.51	....	....	....	....	....	8	....	....	....	480	32	0	4.00	....	....	....	....
	Finland	WEC-A	7	....	....	....	420	23	....	3.28	....	....	....	....	....	....	....	....	....	....	....	....	....	....	....	....	....
1985-86	Springfield Indians	AHL	43	18	19	3	2286	161	1	4.05	....	....	....	....	....	....	....	....	....	....	....	....	....	....	....	....	....
	Minnesota North Stars	**NHL**	**1**	**0**	**1**	**0**	**60**	**3**	**0**	**3.00**	**2.33**	**2.65**	**34**	**.912**	**34.0**	....	....	....	....	....	....	....	....	....	....	....	....
1986-87	**Minnesota North Stars**	**NHL**	**38**	**13**	**18**	**4**	**2075**	**119**	**0**	**3.44**	**2.89**	**3.86**	**1061**	**.888**	**30.7**	....	....	....	....	....	....	....	....	....	....	....	....
	Springfield Indians	AHL	5	3	2	0	300	16	1	3.20	....	....	....	....	....	....	....	....	....	....	....	....	....	....	....	....	....
1987-88	Finland	C Cup	5	0	5	0	280	22	....	5.00	....	....	....	....	....	....	....	....	....	....	....	....	....	....	....	....	....
	Minnesota North Stars	**NHL**	**37**	**8**	**19**	**6**	**1919**	**143**	**1**	**4.47**	**3.73**	**5.97**	**1070**	**.866**	**33.5**	....	....	....	....	....	....	....	....	....	....	....	....
1988-89	**Minnesota North Stars**	**NHL**	**32**	**8**	**15**	**4**	**1603**	**93**	**0**	**3.48**	**2.87**	**3.51**	**922**	**.899**	**34.5**	**3**	**0**	**1**	....	**105**	**7**	**0**	**4.00**	**5.09**	**55**	**.873**	**31.4**
1989-90	Kalamazoo Wings	IHL	1	0	1	0	59	5	0	5.08	....	....	....	....	....	....	....	....	....	....	....	....	....	....	....	....	....
	Minnesota North Stars	**NHL**	**21**	**4**	**12**	**0**	**1012**	**68**	**0**	**4.03**	**3.38**	**5.69**	**482**	**.859**	**28.6**	**1**	**0**	**0**	....	**4**	**0**	**0**	**0.00**	**0.00**	**0**	**.00**	**0.0**
1990-91	Minnesota North Stars	FrTour	2	....	....	....	49	4	0	4.89	....	....	....	....	....	....	....	....	....	....	....	....	....	....	....	....	....
	Minnesota North Stars	**NHL**	**2**	**0**	**2**	**0**	**119**	**12**	**0**	**6.05**	**5.41**	**9.81**	**74**	**.838**	**37.3**	....	....	....	....	....	....	....	....	....	....	....	....
	Kalamazoo Wings	IHL	5	4	1	0	300	10	1	2.00	....	....	....	....	....	....	....	....	....	....	....	....	....	....	....	....	....
	Edmonton Oilers	**NHL**	**11**	**4**	**4**	**0**	**529**	**37**	**0**	**4.20**	**3.76**	**5.57**	**279**	**.867**	**31.6**	....	....	....	....	....	....	....	....	....	....	....	....
	Finland	WEC-A	3	2	1	0	178	9	....	3.03	....	....	....	....	....	....	....	....	....	....	....	....	....	....	....	....	....
1991-92	Assat Pori	Finland	28	....	....	....	1628	98	1	3.61	....	....	....	....	....	6	....	....	....	359	17	1	2.84	....	....	....	....
1992-93	Assat Pori	Finland	45	....	....	....	2723	138	3	3.04	....	....	....	....	....	7	....	....	....	430	29	0	4.05	....	....	....	....
1993-94	Assat Pori	Finland	48	....	....	....	1420	145	3	2.92	....	....	....	....	....	....	....	....	....	....	....	....	....	....	....	....	....
1994-95	Assat Pori	Finland	49	....	....	....	2963	157	....	3.18	....	....	....	....	....	....	....	....	....	....	....	....	....	....	....	....	....
1995-96	Assat Pori	Finland	42	....	....	....	2510	128	2	3.06	....	....	....	....	....	3	....	....	....	178	12	....	4.05	....	....	....	....
1996-97	Finland	W Cup	2	....	....	....	119	7	....	3.53	....	....	....	....	....	....	....	....	....	....	....	....	....	....	....	....	....
	Assat Pori	Finland	42	16	16	9	2492	139	1	3.35	....	....	....	....	....	4	1	3	0	217	15	0	4.14	....	....	....	....
1997-98	HV-71 Jonkoping	Sweden	38	....	....	....	2280	119	1	3.13	....	....	....	....	....	5	....	....	....	314	11	....	2.10	....	....	....	....
	NHL Totals		**142**	**37**	**71**	**14**	**7317**	**475**	**1**	**3.90**	....	....	**3922**	**.879**	....	**4**	**0**	**1**	....	**109**	**7**	**0**	**3.85**	....	....	....	....

Finnish First All-Star Team (1985)

• Re-entered NHL draft. Originally Quebec's 8th choice, 200th overall, in 1981 Entry Draft. Traded to **Edmonton** by **Minnesota** for Bruce Bell, November 22, 1990.

• TALLAS, ROBBIE

Robbie Tallas G – L. 6', 163 lbs. b: Edmonton, Alta., 3/20/1973.

Season	Club	League	GP	W	L	T	Mins	GA	SO	Avg	AAvg	Eff	SA	S%	SAPG	GP	W	L	T	Mins	GA	SO	Avg	Eff	SA	S%	SAPG
1991-92	Seattle Thunderbirds	WHL	14	4	7	0	708	52	0	4.41	....	....	....	....	....	....	....	....	....	....	....	....	....	....	....	....	....
1992-93	Seattle Thunderbirds	WHL	58	24	23	3	3151	194	2	3.69	....	....	....	....	....	5	1	4	....	333	18	0	3.24	....	....	....	....
1993-94	Seattle Thunderbirds	WHL	51	23	21	3	2849	188	0	3.96	....	....	....	....	....	9	5	4	....	567	40	0	4.23	....	....	....	....
1994-95	Charlotte Checkers	ECHL	36	21	9	3	2011	114	0	3.40	....	....	....	....	....	....	....	....	....	....	....	....	....	....	....	....	....
	Providence Bruins	AHL	2	1	0	0	82	4	1	2.90	....	....	....	....	....	....	....	....	....	....	....	....	....	....	....	....	....
1995-96	**Boston Bruins**	**NHL**	**1**	**1**	**0**	**0**	**60**	**3**	**0**	**3.00**	**2.95**	**3.10**	**29**	**.897**	**29.0**	....	....	....	....	....	....	....	....	....	....	....	....
	Providence Bruins	AHL	37	12	16	7	2136	117	1	3.29	....	....	....	....	....	2	0	2	....	135	9	0	4.01	....	....	....	....
1996-97	**Boston Bruins**	**NHL**	**28**	**8**	**12**	**1**	**1244**	**69**	**1**	**3.33**	**3.53**	**3.91**	**587**	**.882**	**28.3**	....	....	....	....	....	....	....	....	....	....	....	....
	Providence Bruins	AHL	24	9	14	1	1424	83	0	3.50	....	....	....	....	....	....	....	....	....	....	....	....	....	....	....	....	....
1997-98	**Boston Bruins**	**NHL**	**14**	**6**	**3**	**3**	**788**	**24**	**1**	**1.83**	**2.14**	**1.35**	**326**	**.926**	**24.8**	....	....	....	....	....	....	....	....	....	....	....	....
	Providence Bruins	AHL	10	1	8	1	575	39	0	4.07	....	....	....	....	....	....	....	....	....	....	....	....	....	....	....	....	....
	NHL Totals		**43**	**15**	**15**	**4**	**2092**	**96**	**2**	**2.75**	....	....	**942**	**.898**	....	....	....	....	....	....	....	....	....	....	....	....	....

Signed as a free agent by **Boston**, September 13, 1995.

• TANNER, JOHN

John Tanner G – L. 6'3", 182 lbs. b: Cambridge, Ont., 3/17/1971. Quebec's 4th choice, 54th overall, in 1989 Entry Draft.

Season	Club	League	GP	W	L	T	Mins	GA	SO	Avg	AAvg	Eff	SA	S%	SAPG	GP	W	L	T	Mins	GA	SO	Avg	Eff	SA	S%	SAPG
1987-88	Peterborough Petes	OHL	26	18	4	3	1532	88	0	3.45	....	....	....	....	....	2	1	0	0	98	3	0	1.84	....	....	....	....
1988-89	Peterborough Petes	OHL	34	22	10	0	1923	107	2	*3.34	....	....	....	....	....	8	4	3	0	369	23	0	3.74	....	....	....	....
1989-90	**Quebec Nordiques**	**NHL**	**1**	**0**	**1**	**0**	**60**	**3**	**0**	**3.00**	**2.51**	**3.00**	**30**	**.900**	**30.0**	....	....	....	....	....	....	....	....	....	....	....	....
	Peterborough Petes	OHL	18	6	8	2	1037	70	0	4.05	....	....	....	....	....	....	....	....	....	....	....	....	....	....	....	....	....
	London Knights	OHL	19	12	5	1	1097	53	1	2.90	....	....	....	....	....	6	2	4	0	341	24	0	4.22	....	....	....	....
1990-91	**Quebec Nordiques**	**NHL**	**6**	**1**	**3**	**1**	**228**	**16**	**0**	**4.21**	**3.76**	**5.06**	**133**	**.880**	**35.0**	....	....	....	....	....	....	....	....	....	....	....	....
	London Knights	OHL	7	3	3	1	427	29	0	4.07	....	....	....	....	....	....	....	....	....	....	....	....	....	....	....	....	....
	Sudbury Wolves	OHL	19	10	8	0	1043	60	0	3.45	....	....	....	....	....	5	1	4	0	274	21	0	4.60	....	....	....	....
1991-92	**Quebec Nordiques**	**NHL**	**14**	**1**	**7**	**4**	**796**	**46**	**1**	**3.47**	**3.08**	**4.05**	**394**	**.883**	**29.7**	....	....	....	....	....	....	....	....	....	....	....	....
	New Haven Nighthawks	AHL	16	7	6	2	908	57	0	3.77	....	....	....	....	....	....	....	....	....	....	....	....	....	....	....	....	....
	Halifax Citadels	AHL	12	6	5	1	672	29	2	2.59	....	....	....	....	....	....	....	....	....	....	....	....	....	....	....	....	....
1992-93	Halifax Citadels	AHL	51	20	18	7	2852	199	0	4.19	....	....	....	....	....	....	....	....	....	....	....	....	....	....	....	....	....
1993-94	Cornwall Aces	AHL	38	14	15	4	2035	123	1	3.63	....	....	....	....	....	....	....	....	....	....	....	....	....	....	....	....	....
	San Diego Gulls	IHL	13	5	3	2	629	37	0	3.53	....	....	....	....	....	3	0	1	0	118	5	0	2.53	....	....	....	....
1994-95	Greensboro Monarchs	ECHL	6	0	4	1	342	27	0	4.73	....	....	....	....	....	....	....	....	....	....	....	....	....	....	....	....	....
	San Diego Gulls	IHL	8	1	3	1	344	28	0	4.87	....	....	....	....	....	....	....	....	....	....	....	....	....	....	....	....	....
1995-96	Detroit Falcons	ColHL	2	1	0	0	112	8	0	4.27	....	....	....	....	....	....	....	....	....	....	....	....	....	....	....	....	....
	Muskegon Fury	ColHL	2	0	2	0	89	8	0	5.38	....	....	....	....	....	....	....	....	....	....	....	....	....	....	....	....	....
	Rochester Americans	AHL	10	3	6	1	579	38	0	3.94	....	....	....	....	....	....	....	....	....	....	....	....	....	....	....	....	....
1996-97	Wheeling Nailers	ECHL	19	7	10	1	940	59	0	3.76	....	....	....	....	....	....	....	....	....	....	....	....	....	....	....	....	....
	NHL Totals		**21**	**2**	**11**	**5**	**1084**	**65**	**1**	**3.60**	....	....	**557**	**.883**		....	....	....	....	....	....	....	....	....	....	....	....

Traded to **Anaheim** by **Quebec** for Anaheim's 4th round choice (Tomi Kallio) in 1995 Entry Draft, February 20, 1994.

• TATARYN, DAVE

Dave Tataryn G – L. 5'9", 160 lbs. b: Sudbury, Ont., 7/17/1950. St. Louis' 8th choice, 104th overall, in 1970 Amateur Draft.

Season	Club	League	GP	W	L	T	Mins	GA	SO	Avg	AAvg	Eff	SA	S%	SAPG	GP	W	L	T	Mins	GA	SO	Avg	Eff	SA	S%	SAPG
1967-68	Niagara Falls Flyers	OHA	5	....	....	....	300	16	0	3.55	....	....	....	....	....	....	....	....	....	....	....	....	....	....	....	....	....
1968-69	Niagara Falls Flyers	OHA	49	....	....	....	2940	197	2	4.04	....	....	....	....	....	14	....	....	....	820	67	0	4.88	....	....	....	....
1969-70	Niagara Falls Flyers	OHA	38	....	....	....	2280	223	0	5.87	....	....	....	....	....	....	....	....	....	....	....	....	....	....	....	....	....
1970-71			DID NOT PLAY																								
1971-72	University of Toronto	OUAA	12	....	....	....	7200	21	0	1.75	....	....	....	....	....	....	....	....	....	....	....	....	....	....	....	....	....
1972-73	Laurentian University	OUAA	16	....	....	....	960	63	0	3.94	....	....	....	....	....	....	....	....	....	....	....	....	....	....	....	....	....
1973-74	Laurentian University	OUAA	17	....	....	....	1020	66	0	3.88	....	....	....	....	....	....	....	....	....	....	....	....	....	....	....	....	....
1974-75	Laurentian University	OUAA	14	....	....	....	800	48	0	3.60	....	....	....	....	....	....	....	....	....	....	....	....	....	....	....	....	....
1975-76	Toronto Toros	WHA	23	7	12	1	1261	100	0	4.76	....	....	....	....	....	....	....	....	....	....	....	....	....	....	....	....	....
	Columbus Owls	IHL	4	....	....	....	183	14	0	4.59	....	....	....	....	....	....	....	....	....	....	....	....	....	....	....	....	....
	Buffalo Norsemen	NAHL	2	2	0	0	120	7	0	3.50	....	....	....	....	....	....	....	....	....	....	....	....	....	....	....	....	....
	Whitby Warriors	OHA Sr.	2	2	0	0	120	4	0	2.00	....	....	....	....	....	....	....	....	....	....	....	....	....	....	....	....	....

			REGULAR SEASON													PLAYOFFS											
Season	Club	League	GP	W	L	T	Mins	GA	SO	Avg	AAvg	Eff	SA	S%	SAPG	GP	W	L	T	Mins	GA	SO	Avg	Eff	SA	S%	SAPG
1976-77	Charlotte Checkers	SHL	39	....	....	....	2284	114	1	2.99	....	....	....	....	....	....	....	....	....	....	....	....	....	....	....	....	....
	Mohawk Valley Comets	NAHL	1	0	1	0	60	7	0	7.00	....	....	....	....	....	....	....	....	....	....	....	....	....	....	....	....	....
	New Haven Nighthawks	AHL	3	2	1	0	179	11	0	3.69	....	....	....	....	....	....	....	....	....	....	....	....	....	....	....	....	....
	New York Rangers	**NHL**	**2**	**1**	**1**	**0**	**80**	**10**	**0**	**7.50**	**6.98**	....	....	....	....	....	....	....	....	....	....	....	....	....	....	....	....
1977-78	Cambridge Hornets	OHA Sr.	20	....	....	....	1250	73	*1	*3.50	....	....	....	....	....	....	....	....	....	....	....	....	....	....	....	....	....
	NHL Totals		**2**	**1**	**1**	**0**	**80**	**10**	**0**	**7.50**	....	....	....	....	....	....	....	....	....	....	....	....	....	....	....	....	....
	Other Major League Totals		23	7	12	1	1261	100	0	4.76	....	....	....	....	....	....	....	....	....	....	....	....	....	....	....	....	....

Signed as a free agent by **Toronto** (WHA), June, 1975. Signed as a free agent by **NY Rangers** (New Haven - AHL) after Southern Hockey League folded, January 30, 1977.

• TAYLOR, BOBBY

Bobby Taylor G – L. 6'1", 180 lbs. b: Calgary, Alta., 1/24/1945.

Season	Club	League	GP	W	L	T	Mins	GA	SO	Avg	AAvg	Eff	SA	S%	SAPG	GP	W	L	T	Mins	GA	SO	Avg	Eff	SA	S%	SAPG
1964-65	Edmonton Oil Kings	AJHL	STATISTICS NOT AVAILABLE																								
	St. Catharines Black Hawks	OHA	18	....	....	....	1060	85	0	4.81	....	....	....	....	....	....	....	....	....	....	....	....	....	....	....	....	....
1965-66			DID NOT PLAY – INJURED																								
1966-67	Calgary Spurs	WCSHL	16	....	....	....	960	40	0	*2.50	....	....	....	....	....	4	....	....	....	240	15	0	3.75	....	....	....	....
1967-68	Calgary Spurs	WCSHL	27	....	....	....	1620	133	0	5.02	....	....	....	....	....	3	1	2	0	140	13	0	5.69	....	....	....	....
1968-69	New Jersey Devils	EHL	70	25	38	7	4200	285	1	4.07	....	....	....	....	....	....	....	....	....	....	....	....	....	....	....	....	....
1969-70	Seattle Totems	WHL	5	....	....	....	240	14	0	3.50	....	....	....	....	....	....	....	....	....	....	....	....	....	....	....	....	....
	Quebec Aces	AHL	14	....	....	....	759	53	0	4.18	....	....	....	....	....	2	1	1	0	123	5	0	2.44	....	....	....	....
	New Jersey Devils	EHL	8	....	....	....	480	55	1	6.88	....	....	....	....	....	....	....	....	....	....	....	....	....	....	....	....	....
1970-71	Quebec Aces	AHL	39	13	15	8	2154	122	*5	3.39	....	....	....	....	....	....	....	....	....	....	....	....	....	....	....	....	....
1971-72	**Philadelphia Flyers**	**NHL**	**6**	**1**	**2**	**2**	**320**	**16**	**0**	**3.00**	**3.02**	....	....	....	....	....	....	....	....	....	....	....	....	....	....	....	....
	Richmond Robins	AHL	26	7	14	4	1538	78	1	3.04	....	....	....	....	....	....	....	....	....	....	....	....	....	....	....	....	....
1972-73	**Philadelphia Flyers**	**NHL**	**23**	**8**	**8**	**4**	**1144**	**78**	**0**	**4.09**	**3.87**	....	....	....	....	....	....	....	....	....	....	....	....	....	....	....	....
	Richmond Robins	AHL	6	....	....	....	337	23	0	4.09	....	....	....	....	....	....	....	....	....	....	....	....	....	....	....	....	....
1973-74	Richmond Robins	AHL	11	4	4	3	659	38	0	3.45	....	....	....	....	....	....	....	....	....	....	....	....	....	....	....	....	....
	Philadelphia Flyers	**NHL**	**8**	**3**	**3**	**0**	**366**	**26**	**0**	**4.26**	**4.12**	....	....	....	....	....	....	....	....	....	....	....	....	....	....	....	....
1974-75	Richmond Robins	AHL	5	3	1	1	303	18	0	3.56	....	....	....	....	....	....	....	....	....	....	....	....	....	....	....	....	....
	Philadelphia Flyers	**NHL**	**3**	**0**	**2**	**0**	**120**	**13**	**0**	**6.50**	**5.86**	....	....	....	....	....	....	....	....	....	....	....	....	....	....	....	....
1975-76	Richmond Robins	AHL	4	0	2	1	204	18	0	5.29	....	....	....	....	....	....	....	....	....	....	....	....	....	....	....	....	....
	Philadelphia Flyers	**NHL**	**4**	**3**	**1**	**0**	**240**	**15**	**0**	**3.75**	**3.39**	....	....	....	....	....	....	....	....	....	....	....	....	....	....	....	....
	Springfield Indians	AHL	23	7	14	0	1230	86	0	4.20	....	....	....	....	....	....	....	....	....	....	....	....	....	....	....	....	....
	Pittsburgh Penguins	**NHL**	**2**	**0**	**1**	**0**	**78**	**7**	**0**	**5.38**	**4.87**	....	....	....	....	....	....	....	....	....	....	....	....	....	....	....	....
	NHL Totals		**46**	**15**	**17**	**6**	**2268**	**155**	**0**	**4.10**	....	....	....	....	....	....	....	....	....	....	....	....	....	....	....	....	....

Signed as a free agent by **Philadelphia**, September, 1968. Traded to **Pittsburgh** by **Philadelphia** with Ed Van Impe for Gary Inness and future considerations, March 8, 1976.

• TENO, HARVEY

Harvey Teno G – L. 5'7", 175 lbs. b: Windsor, Ont., 2/15/1915. Deceased.

Season	Club	League	GP	W	L	T	Mins	GA	SO	Avg	AAvg	Eff	SA	S%	SAPG	GP	W	L	T	Mins	GA	SO	Avg	Eff	SA	S%	SAPG
1932-33	Windsor Wanderers	MOHL	16	....	....	....	1080	55	1	3.06	....	....	....	....	....	....	....	....	....	....	....	....	....	....	....	....	....
1933-34	St. Michael's Majors	OHA	11	....	....	....	660	30	1	2.73	....	....	....	....	....	3	....	....	....	180	9	0	*3.00	....	....	....	....
1934-35	St. Michael's Majors	OHA	11	....	....	....	660	34	1	3.09	....	....	....	....	....	3	....	....	....	180	8	*1	2.67	....	....	....	....
	Toronto Dominions	City Sr.	15	....	....	....	900	54	0	3.60	....	....	....	....	....	3	....	....	....	180	23	0	7.67	....	....	....	....
1935-36	Oakville Villans	OHA Sr.	17	....	....	....	1020	53	1	3.12	....	....	....	....	....	2	....	....	....	120	7	0	3.50	....	....	....	....
	Toronto McColl-Frontenacs	City Sr.	14	....	....	....	840	43	*1	3.07	....	....	....	....	....	4	....	....	....	240	17	0	4.25	....	....	....	....
1936-37	Atlantic City Seagulls	EHL	48	*27	19	2	2880	116	*4	2.43	....	....	....	....	....	4	1	3	0	240	10	0	2.40	....	....	....	....
1937-38	Atlantic City Seagulls	EHL	57	20	28	3	3420	168	3	2.94	....	....	....	....	....	....	....	....	....	....	....	....	....	....	....	....	....
1938-39	Pittsburgh Hornets	AHL	20	6	13	1	1200	58	0	2.90	....	....	....	....	....	....	....	....	....	....	....	....	....	....	....	....	....
	Philadelphia Ramblers	AHL	2	0	1	1	130	11	0	5.08	....	....	....	....	....	4	1	3	0	240	9	1	2.25	....	....	....	....
	Detroit Red Wings	**NHL**	**5**	**2**	**3**	**0**	**300**	**15**	**0**	**3.00**	**3.66**	....	....	....	....	....	....	....	....	....	....	....	....	....	....	....	....
	Hershey Bears	AHL	1	0	0	1	70	4	0	3.43	....	....	....	....	....	....	....	....	....	....	....	....	....	....	....	....	....
1939-40	Pittsburgh Hornets	AHL	*56	*25	22	9	3480	133	4	2.29	....	....	....	....	....	*9	4	5	0	*563	24	1	2.56	....	....	....	....
1940-41	Pittsburgh Hornets	AHL	24	9	12	2	1408	63	2	2.68	....	....	....	....	....	6	3	3	0	426	12	0	*1.69	....	....	....	....
	Cleveland Barons	AHL	6	3	2	1	370	13	0	2.11	....	....	....	....	....	....	....	....	....	....	....	....	....	....	....	....	....
	Buffalo Bisons	AHL	1	0	0	1	70	3	0	2.57	....	....	....	....	....	....	....	....	....	....	....	....	....	....	....	....	....
1941-42	Pittsburgh Hornets	AHL	53	22	26	5	3280	209	0	3.82	....	....	....	....	....	....	....	....	....	....	....	....	....	....	....	....	....
1942-43	Pittsburgh Hornets	AHL	52	26	21	6	3120	186	2	3.58	....	....	....	....	....	2	0	2	0	120	10	0	5.00	....	....	....	....
1943-44	Pittsburgh Hornets	AHL	6	1	4	1	360	19	0	3.17	....	....	....	....	....	....	....	....	....	....	....	....	....	....	....	....	....
1944-45	Cleveland Barons	AHL	56	*31	15	9	3300	178	4	3.23	....	....	....	....	....	12	*8	4	0	730	39	0	3.21	....	....	....	....
1945-46	Cleveland Barons	AHL	21	10	9	2	1260	94	1	4.48	....	....	....	....	....	12	7	5	0	755	50	1	3.97	....	....	....	....
1946-47	Minneapolis Millers	USHL	13	7	6	0	780	41	2	3.15	....	....	....	....	....	....	....	....	....	....	....	....	....	....	....	....	....
1947-48	Hershey Bears	AHL	....	....	....	....	....	....	....	....	....	....	....	....	....	2	0	2	0	100	6	0	3.60	....	....	....	....
	NHL Totals		**5**	**2**	**3**	**0**	**300**	**15**	**0**	**3.00**	....	....	....	....	....	....	....	....	....	....	....	....	....	....	....	....	....

EHL Second All-Star Team (1937, 1938)

Promoted to **Detroit** from **Pittsburgh** (AHL) to replace suspended Norman Smith, November 17, 1938. Loaned to **Boston** by **Detroit** for remainder of 1938-39 season, December 28, 1938.

• TERRERI, CHRIS

Chris Terreri G – L. 5'8", 160 lbs. b: Providence, RI, 11/15/1964. New Jersey's 3rd choice, 87th overall, in 1983 Entry Draft.

Season	Club	League	GP	W	L	T	Mins	GA	SO	Avg	AAvg	Eff	SA	S%	SAPG	GP	W	L	T	Mins	GA	SO	Avg	Eff	SA	S%	SAPG
1982-83	Providence College	ECAC	11	7	1	0	528	17	2	1.93	....	....	....	....	....	....	....	....	....	....	....	....	....	....	....	....	....
1983-84	Providence College	ECAC	10	4	2	0	391	20	0	3.07	....	....	....	....	....	....	....	....	....	....	....	....	....	....	....	....	....
1984-85	Providence College	H.E.	33	15	13	5	1956	116	1	3.35	....	....	....	....	....	....	....	....	....	....	....	....	....	....	....	....	....
	United States	WEC-A	3	....	....	....	111	12	....	6.48	....	....	....	....	....	....	....	....	....	....	....	....	....	....	....	....	....
1985-86	Providence College	H.E.	22	6	16	0	1320	84	0	3.74	....	....	....	....	....	....	....	....	....	....	....	....	....	....	....	....	....
	United States	WEC-A	5	....	....	....	286	20	....	4.20	....	....	....	....	....	....	....	....	....	....	....	....	....	....	....	....	....
1986-87	**New Jersey Devils**	**NHL**	**7**	**0**	**3**	**1**	**286**	**21**	**0**	**4.41**	**3.71**	**5.35**	**173**	**.879**	**36.3**	....	....	....	....	....	....	....	....	....	....	....	....
	Maine Mariners	AHL	14	4	9	1	765	57	0	4.47	....	....	....	....	....	....	....	....	....	....	....	....	....	....	....	....	....
	United States	WEC-A	2	....	....	....	100	12	....	7.20	....	....	....	....	....	....	....	....	....	....	....	....	....	....	....	....	....
1987-88	Utica Devils	AHL	7	5	1	0	399	18	0	2.71	....	....	....	....	....	....	....	....	....	....	....	....	....	....	....	....	....
	United States	Nat-Team	26	17	7	2	1430	81	0	3.40	....	....	....	....	....	....	....	....	....	....	....	....	....	....	....	....	....
	United States	Olympics	3	....	....	....	127	14	....	6.58	....	....	....	....	....	....	....	....	....	....	....	....	....	....	....	....	....
1988-89	**New Jersey Devils**	**NHL**	**8**	**0**	**4**	**2**	**402**	**18**	**0**	**2.69**	**2.22**	**2.85**	**170**	**.894**	**25.4**	....	....	....	....	....	....	....	....	....	....	....	....
	Utica Devils	AHL	39	20	15	3	2314	132	0	3.42	....	....	....	....	....	2	0	1	....	80	6	0	4.50	....	....	....	....
1989-90	**New Jersey Devils**	**NHL**	**35**	**15**	**12**	**3**	**1931**	**110**	**0**	**3.42**	**2.86**	**3.75**	**1004**	**.890**	**31.2**	**4**	**2**	**2**	....	**238**	**13**	**0**	**3.28**	**4.14**	**103**	**.874**	**26.0**
1990-91	**New Jersey Devils**	**NHL**	**53**	**24**	**21**	**7**	**2970**	**144**	**1**	**2.91**	**2.59**	**3.11**	**1348**	**.893**	**27.2**	**7**	**3**	**4**	....	**428**	**21**	**0**	**2.94**	**2.06**	**216**	**.903**	**30.3**
1991-92	**New Jersey Devils**	**NHL**	**54**	**22**	**22**	**10**	**3186**	**169**	**1**	**3.10**	**2.01**	**3.58**	**1511**	**.888**	**28.5**	**7**	**3**	**3**	....	**386**	**23**	**0**	**3.58**	**4.06**	**203**	**.887**	**31.6**
1992-93	**New Jersey Devils**	**NHL**	**48**	**19**	**21**	**3**	**2672**	**151**	**2**	**3.39**	**2.88**	**3.87**	**1324**	**.886**	**29.7**	**4**	**1**	**3**	....	**219**	**17**	**0**	**4.66**	**6.71**	**118**	**.856**	**32.3**
1993-94	**New Jersey Devils**	**NHL**	**44**	**20**	**11**	**4**	**2340**	**106**	**2**	**2.72**	**2.58**	**2.53**	**1141**	**.907**	**29.3**	**4**	**3**	**0**	....	**200**	**9**	**0**	**2.70**	**2.19**	**111**	**.919**	**33.3**
1994-95	**New Jersey Devils**	**NHL**	**15**	**3**	**7**	**2**	**734**	**31**	**0**	**2.53**	**2.61**	**2.54**	**309**	**.900**	**25.3**	**1**	**0**	**0**	....	**8**	**0**	**0**	**0.00**	**0.00**	**2**	**1.000**	**15.0**
1995-96	**New Jersey Devils**	**NHL**	**4**	**3**	**0**	**0**	**210**	**9**	**0**	**2.57**	**2.52**	**2.51**	**92**	**.902**	**26.3**	....	....	....	....	....	....	....	....	....	....	....	....
	San Jose Sharks	**NHL**	**46**	**13**	**29**	**1**	**2516**	**155**	**0**	**3.70**	**3.65**	**4.34**	**1322**	**.883**	**31.5**	....	....	....	....	....	....	....	....	....	....	....	....
1996-97	**San Jose Sharks**	**NHL**	**22**	**6**	**10**	**3**	**1200**	**55**	**0**	**2.75**	**2.91**	**2.74**	**553**	**.901**	**27.7**	....	....	....	....	....	....	....	....	....	....	....	....
	Chicago Blackhawks	**NHL**	**7**	**4**	**1**	**2**	**429**	**19**	**0**	**2.66**	**2.81**	**2.63**	**192**	**.901**	**26.9**	**2**	**0**	**0**	....	**44**	**3**	**0**	**4.09**	**4.38**	**28**	**.893**	**38.2**
	United States	WC-A	6	2	3	1	357	16	....	2.69	....	....	....	....	....	....	....	....	....	....	....	....	....	....	....	....	....
1997-98	**Chicago Blackhawks**	**NHL**	**21**	**8**	**10**	**2**	**1222**	**49**	**2**	**2.41**	**2.82**	**2.28**	**519**	**.906**	**25.5**	....	....	....	....	....	....	....	....	....	....	....	....
	Indianapolis Ice	IHL	3	2	0	1	180	3	1	1.00	....	....	....	....	....	....	....	....	....	....	....	....	....	....	....	....	....
	NHL Totals		**364**	**137**	**151**	**40**	**20098**	**1037**	**8**	**3.10**	....	....	**9658**	**.893**	....	**29**	**12**	**12**	....	**1523**	**86**	**0**	**3.39**	....	....	....	....

Hockey East First All-Star Team (1985) • NCAA East First All-American Team (1985) • NCAA Championship All Tournament Team (1985) • NCAA Championship Tournament MVP (1985)

Traded to **San Jose** by **New Jersey** for San Jose's 2nd round choice (later traded to Pittsburgh — Pittsburgh selected Pavel Skrbek) in 1996 Entry Draft, November 15, 1995. Traded to **Chicago** by **San Jose** with Ulf Dahlen and Michal Sykora for Ed Belfour, January 25, 1997.

• THEODORE, JOSE

Jose Theodore G – R. 5'11", 181 lbs. b: Laval, Que., 9/13/1976. Montreal's 2nd choice, 44th overall, in 1994 Entry Draft.

			REGULAR SEASON													PLAYOFFS											
Season	Club	League	GP	W	L	T	Mins	GA	SO	Avg	AAvg	Eff	SA	S%	SAPG	GP	W	L	T	Mins	GA	SO	Avg	Eff	SA	S%	SAPG
1992-93	St-Jean Lynx	QMJHL	34	12	16	2	1776	112	0	3.78	....	....	....	....	....	3	0	2	....	175	11	0	3.77	....	....	....	....
1993-94	St-Jean Lynx	QMJHL	57	20	29	6	3225	194	0	3.61	....	....	....	....	....	5	1	4	....	296	18	0	3.65	....	....	....	....
1994-95	Hull Olympiques	QMJHL	*58	*32	22	2	*3348	193	5	3.46	....	....	....	....	....	*21	*15	6	....	*1263	59	*1	2.80	....	....	....	....
	Fredericton Canadiens	AHL	....	....	....	....	....	....	....	....	....	....	....	....	....	1	0	1	....	60	3	0	3.00	....	....	....	....
1995-96	**Montreal Canadiens**	**NHL**	**1**	**0**	**0**	**0**	**9**	**1**	**0**	**6.67**	**6.55**	**33.35**	**2**	**.500**	**13.3**	....	....	....	....	....	....	....	....	....	....	....	....
	Hull Olympiques	QMJHL	48	33	11	2	2807	158	0	3.38	....	....	....	....	....	5	2	3	....	299	20	0	4.01	....	....	....	....
	Canada	WJC-A	4	4	0	0	240	6	0	1.50	....	....	....	....	....	....	....	....	....	....	....	....	....	....	....	....	....
1996-97	**Montreal Canadiens**	**NHL**	**16**	**5**	**6**	**2**	**821**	**53**	**0**	**3.87**	**4.11**	**4.04**	**508**	**.896**	**37.1**	**2**	**1**	**1**	....	**168**	**7**	**0**	**2.50**	**1.62**	**108**	**.935**	**38.6**
	Fredericton Canadiens	AHL	26	12	12	0	1469	87	0	3.55	....	....	....	....	....	....	....	....	....	....	....	....	....	....	....	....	....
1997-98	Fredericton Canadiens	AHL	53	20	23	8	3053	145	2	2.85	....	....	....	....	....	4	1	3	....	237	13	0	3.28	....	....	....	....
	Montreal Canadiens	**NHL**	....	....	....	....	....	....	....	....	....	....	....	....	....	**3**	**0**	**1**	....	**120**	**1**	**0**	**0.50**	**0.14**	**35**	**.971**	**17.5**
	NHL Totals		**17**	**5**	**6**	**2**	**830**	**54**	**0**	**3.90**	....	....	**510**	**.894**	....	**5**	**1**	**2**	....	**288**	**8**	**0**	**1.67**	....	....	....	....

QMJHL Second All-Star Team (1995, 1996) • WJC-A All-Star Team (1996) • Named Best Goaltender at WJC-A (1996)

• THIBAULT, JOCELYN

Jocelyn Thibault G – L. 5'11", 170 lbs. b: Montreal, Que., 1/12/1975. Quebec's 1st choice, 10th overall, in 1993 Entry Draft.

Season	Club	League	GP	W	L	T	Mins	GA	SO	Avg	AAvg	Eff	SA	S%	SAPG	GP	W	L	T	Mins	GA	SO	Avg	Eff	SA	S%	SAPG
1991-92	Trois Rivieres Draveurs	QMJHL	30	14	7	1	1496	77	0	3.09	....	....	....	....	....	3	1	1	....	110	4	0	2.19	....	....	....	....
1992-93	Sherbrooke Faucons	QMJHL	56	34	14	5	3190	159	3	2.99	....	....	....	....	....	15	9	6	....	882	57	0	3.87	....	....	....	....
1993-94	**Quebec Nordiques**	**NHL**	**29**	**8**	**13**	**3**	**1504**	**83**	**0**	**3.31**	**3.15**	**3.58**	**768**	**.892**	**30.6**	....	....	....	....	....	....	....	....	....	....	....	....
	Cornwall Aces	AHL	4	4	0	0	240	9	1	2.25	....	....	....	....	....	....	....	....	....	....	....	....	....	....	....	....	....
1994-95	Sherbrooke Faucons	QMJHL	13	6	6	1	776	38	1	2.94	....	....	....	....	....	....	....	....	....	....	....	....	....	....	....	....	....
	Quebec Nordiques	**NHL**	**18**	**12**	**2**	**2**	**898**	**35**	**1**	**2.34**	**2.41**	**1.94**	**423**	**.917**	**28.3**	**3**	**1**	**2**	....	**148**	**8**	**0**	**3.24**	**3.41**	**76**	**.895**	**30.8**
1995-96	**Colorado Avalanche**	**NHL**	**10**	**3**	**4**	**2**	**558**	**28**	**0**	**3.01**	**2.96**	**3.80**	**222**	**.874**	**23.9**	....	....	....	....	....	....	....	....	....	....	....	....
	Montreal Canadiens	**NHL**	**40**	**23**	**13**	**3**	**2334**	**110**	**3**	**2.83**	**2.77**	**2.47**	**1258**	**.913**	**32.3**	**6**	**2**	**4**	....	**311**	**18**	**0**	**3.47**	**3.32**	**188**	**.904**	**36.3**
1996-97	**Montreal Canadiens**	**NHL**	**61**	**22**	**24**	**11**	**3397**	**164**	**1**	**2.90**	**3.07**	**2.62**	**1815**	**.910**	**32.1**	**3**	**0**	**3**	....	**179**	**13**	**0**	**4.36**	**5.61**	**101**	**.871**	**33.9**
1997-98	**Montreal Canadiens**	**NHL**	**47**	**19**	**15**	**8**	**2652**	**109**	**2**	**2.47**	**2.89**	**2.43**	**1109**	**.902**	**25.1**	**2**	**0**	**0**	....	**43**	**4**	**0**	**5.58**	**13.95**	**16**	**.750**	**22.3**
	NHL Totals		**205**	**87**	**71**	**29**	**11343**	**529**	**7**	**2.80**	....	....	**5595**	**.905**	....	**14**	**3**	**9**	....	**681**	**43**	**0**	**3.79**	....	....	....	....

QMJHL First All-Star Team (1993) • Canadian Major Junior First All-Star Team (1993) • Canadian Major Junior Goaltender of the Year (1993)

Transferred to **Colorado** after **Quebec** franchise relocated, June 21, 1995. Traded to **Montreal** by **Colorado** with Andrei Kovalenko and Martin Rucinsky for Patrick Roy and Mike Keane, December 6, 1995.

• THOMAS, WAYNE

Wayne Thomas G – L. 6'2", 195 lbs. b: Ottawa, Ont., 10/9/1947.

Season	Club	League	GP	W	L	T	Mins	GA	SO	Avg	AAvg	Eff	SA	S%	SAPG	GP	W	L	T	Mins	GA	SO	Avg	Eff	SA	S%	SAPG
1968-69	University of Wisconsin	WCHA	16	9	6	1	943	44	2	2.80	....	....	....	....	....	....	....	....	....	....	....	....	....	....	....	....	....
1969-70	University of Wisconsin	WCHA	21	14	7	0	1250	60	1	2.88	....	....	....	....	....	4	3	1	0	240	10	0	2.50	....	....	....	....
1970-71	Montreal Voyageurs	AHL	33	8	17	6	1845	111	1	3.57	....	....	....	....	....	3	0	3	0	179	12	0	4.02	....	....	....	....
1971-72	Nova Scotia Voyageurs	AHL	41	22	8	10	2393	100	1	2.51	....	....	....	....	....	....	....	....	....	....	....	....	....	....	....	....	....
1972-73	Nova Scotia Voyageurs	AHL	6	....	....	....	300	8	1	1.60	....	....	....	....	....	....	....	....	....	....	....	....	....	....	....	....	....
	Montreal Canadiens	**NHL**	**10**	**8**	**1**	**0**	**583**	**23**	**1**	**2.37**	**2.23**	....	....	....	....	....	....	....	....	....	....	....	....	....	....	....	....
1973-74	**Montreal Canadiens**	**NHL**	**42**	**23**	**12**	**5**	**2410**	**111**	**1**	**2.76**	**2.65**	....	....	....	....	....	....	....	....	....	....	....	....	....	....	....	....
1974-75			DID NOT PLAY																								
1975-76	**Toronto Maple Leafs**	**NHL**	**64**	**28**	**24**	**12**	**3684**	**196**	**2**	**3.19**	**2.88**	....	....	....	....	**10**	**5**	**5**	....	**587**	**34**	**1**	**3.48**	....	....	....	....
1976-77	**Toronto Maple Leafs**	**NHL**	**33**	**10**	**13**	**6**	**1803**	**116**	**1**	**3.86**	**3.60**	....	....	....	....	**4**	**1**	**2**	....	**202**	**12**	**0**	**3.56**	....	....	....	....
1977-78	**New York Rangers**	**NHL**	**41**	**12**	**20**	**7**	**2352**	**141**	**4**	**3.60**	**3.38**	....	....	....	....	**1**	**0**	**1**	....	**60**	**4**	**0**	**4.00**	....	....	....	....
1978-79	**New York Rangers**	**NHL**	**31**	**15**	**10**	**3**	**1668**	**101**	**1**	**3.63**	**3.21**	....	....	....	....	....	....	....	....	....	....	....	....	....	....	....	....
1979-80	**New York Rangers**	**NHL**	**12**	**4**	**7**	**0**	**668**	**44**	**0**	**3.95**	**3.47**	....	....	....	....	....	....	....	....	....	....	....	....	....	....	....	....
	New Haven Nighthawks	AHL	5	5	0	0	280	11	0	2.36	....	....	....	....	....	....	....	....	....	....	....	....	....	....	....	....	....
1980-81	**New York Rangers**	**NHL**	**10**	**3**	**6**	**1**	**600**	**34**	**0**	**3.40**	**2.72**	....	....	....	....	....	....	....	....	....	....	....	....	....	....	....	....
	NHL Totals		**243**	**103**	**93**	**34**	**13768**	**766**	**10**	**3.34**	....	....	....	....	....	**15**	**6**	**8**	....	**849**	**50**	**1**	**3.53**	....	....	....	....

WCHA Second All-Star Team (1970)

Played in NHL All-Star Game (1976)

Traded to **LA Kings** by **Toronto** with Brian Murphy and Gary Croteau for Grant Moore and Lou Deveault, September, 1968. Traded to **Montreal** by **LA Kings** with Leon Rochefort and Greg Boddy for Jack Norris, Larry Mickey and Lucien Grenier, May 22, 1970. Traded to **Toronto** by **Montreal** for Toronto's 1st round choice (Peter Lee) in 1976 Amateur Draft, June 17, 1975. Claimed by **NY Rangers** from **Toronto** in Waiver Draft, October 10, 1977.

• THOMPSON, TINY

Tiny (Cecil) Thompson G – R. 5'10", 160 lbs. b: Sandon, Alta., 5/31/1905. d: 2/11/1981. **HHOF**

Season	Club	League	GP	W	L	T	Mins	GA	SO	Avg	AAvg	Eff	SA	S%	SAPG	GP	W	L	T	Mins	GA	SO	Avg	Eff	SA	S%	SAPG
1923-24	Bellevue Bulldogs	ASHL	STATISTICS NOT AVAILABLE																								
1924-25	Duluth Hornets	USAHA	40	17	20	3	1920	59	11	1.38	....	....	....	....	....	....	....	....	....	....	....	....	....	....	....	....	....
1925-26	Minneapolis Millers	USAHA	36	....	....	....	2160	59	10	1.64	....	....	....	....	....	3	3	0	0	180	1	2	0.33	....	....	....	....
1926-27	Minneapolis Millers	AHA	38	17	11	10	2253	51	9	1.42	....	....	....	....	....	6	3	3	0	361	8	1	1.33	....	....	....	....
1927-28	Minneapolis Millers	AHA	40	*28	7	5	2475	51	12	1.23	....	....	....	....	....	8	*4	0	4	520	3	*5	0.38	....	....	....	....
1928-29	**Boston Bruins**	**NHL**	***44**	***26**	**13**	**5**	**2710**	**52**	**12**	**1.15**	**2.39**	....	....	....	....	**5**	***5**	**0**	**0**	**300**	**3**	***3**	***0.60**	....	....	....	....
1929-30	**Boston Bruins**	**NHL**	***44**	***38**	**5**	**1**	**2680**	**98**	**3**	***2.19**	**2.23**	....	....	....	....	***6**	**3**	**3**	**0**	**432**	**12**	**0**	**1.67**	....	....	....	....
1930-31	**Boston Bruins**	**NHL**	***44**	***28**	**10**	**6**	**2730**	**90**	**3**	**1.98**	**2.50**	....	....	....	....	**5**	**2**	**3**	**0**	**343**	**13**	**0**	**2.27**	....	....	....	....
1931-32	**Boston Bruins**	**NHL**	**43**	**13**	**19**	**11**	**2698**	**103**	***9**	**2.29**	**2.78**	....	....	....	....	....	....	....	....	....	....	....	....	....	....	....	....
1932-33	**Boston Bruins**	**NHL**	***48**	***25**	**15**	**8**	**3000**	**88**	***11**	***1.76**	**2.32**	....	....	....	....	**5**	**2**	**3**	**0**	**438**	**9**	**0**	***1.23**	....	....	....	....
1933-34	**Boston Bruins**	**NHL**	***48**	**18**	**25**	**5**	**2980**	**130**	**5**	**2.62**	**3.40**	....	....	....	....	....	....	....	....	....	....	....	....	....	....	....	....
1934-35	**Boston Bruins**	**NHL**	***48**	**26**	**16**	**6**	**2970**	**112**	**8**	**2.26**	**2.74**	....	....	....	....	**4**	**1**	**3**	**0**	**273**	**7**	**1**	**1.54**	....	....	....	....
1935-36	**Boston Bruins**	**NHL**	***48**	**22**	**20**	**6**	**2930**	**82**	***10**	***1.68**	**2.32**	....	....	....	....	**2**	**1**	**1**	**0**	**120**	**8**	**1**	**4.00**	....	....	....	....
1936-37	**Boston Bruins**	**NHL**	***48**	**23**	**18**	**7**	**2970**	**110**	***6**	**2.22**	**2.74**	....	....	....	....	**3**	**1**	**2**	....	**180**	**8**	**1**	**2.67**	....	....	....	....
1937-38	**Boston Bruins**	**NHL**	***48**	***30**	**11**	**7**	**2970**	**89**	**7**	***1.80**	**2.10**	....	....	....	....	**3**	**0**	**3**	....	**212**	**6**	**0**	**1.70**	....	....	....	....
1938-39	**Boston Bruins**	**NHL**	**5**	**3**	**1**	**1**	**310**	**8**	**0**	**1.55**	**1.88**	....	....	....	....	....	....	....	....	....	....	....	....	....	....	....	....
	Detroit Red Wings	**NHL**	**39**	**16**	**17**	**6**	**2397**	**101**	**4**	**2.53**	**3.08**	....	....	....	....	**6**	**3**	**3**	....	**374**	**15**	**1**	**2.41**	....	....	....	....
1939-40	**Detroit Red Wings**	**NHL**	**46**	**16**	**24**	**6**	**2830**	**120**	**3**	**2.54**	**3.16**	....	....	....	....	**5**	**2**	**3**	....	**300**	**12**	**0**	**2.40**	....	....	....	....
1940-41	Buffalo Bisons	AHL	1	0	0	0	40	1	0	1.50	....	....	....	....	....	....	....	....	....	....	....	....	....	....	....	....	....
1941-42			DID NOT PLAY																								
1942-43	Calgary RCAF Mustangs	ASHL	....	....	....	....	....	....	....	....	....	....	....	....	....	4	....	....	....	....	11	0	3.00	....	....	....	....
	NHL Totals		**553**	**284**	**194**	**75**	**34175**	**1183**	**81**	**2.08**	....	....	....	....	....	**44**	**20**	**24**	**0**	**2972**	**93**	**7**	**1.88**	....	....	....	....

Won Vezina Trophy (1930, 1933, 1936, 1938) • NHL Second All-Star Team (1931, 1935) • NHL First All-Star Team (1936, 1938)

Played in NHL All-Star Game (1937)

Traded to **Detroit** by **Boston** for Norman Smith and $15000, November 16, 1938.

• TOPPAZZINI, JERRY

Jerry "Topper" Toppazzini G – L. 6', 180 lbs. b: Copper Cliff, Ont., 7/29/1930.

Season	Club	League	GP	W	L	T	Mins	GA	SO	Avg	AAvg	Eff	SA	S%	SAPG	GP	W	L	T	Mins	GA	SO	Avg	Eff	SA	S%	SAPG
1960-61	**Boston Bruins**	**NHL**	**1**	**0**	**0**	**0**	**1**	**0**	**0**	**0.00**	**0.00**	....	....	....	....	....	....	....	....	....	....	....	....	....	....	....	....
	NHL Totals		**1**	**0**	**0**	**0**	**1**	**0**	**0**	**0.00**	....	....	....	....	....	....	....	....	....	....	....	....	....	....	....	....	....

• Boston right winger replaced injured Don Simmons in 3rd period, October 16, 1960. (Chicago 5, Boston 2)

• TORCHIA, MIKE

Mike Torchia G – L. 5'11", 215 lbs. b: Toronto, Ont., 2/23/1972. Minnesota's 2nd choice, 74th overall, in 1991 Entry Draft.

Season	Club	League	GP	W	L	T	Mins	GA	SO	Avg	AAvg	Eff	SA	S%	SAPG	GP	W	L	T	Mins	GA	SO	Avg	Eff	SA	S%	SAPG
1988-89	Kitchener Rangers	OHL	30	14	9	4	1672	112	0	4.02	....	....	....	....	....	2	0	2	....	126	8	0	3.81	....	....	....	....
1989-90	Kitchener Rangers	OHL	40	25	11	2	2280	136	1	3.58	....	....	....	....	....	*17	*11	6	....	*1023	60	0	3.52	....	....	....	....
1990-91	Kitchener Rangers	OHL	57	25	24	7	*3317	219	0	3.96	....	....	....	....	....	6	2	4	....	382	30	0	4.71	....	....	....	....
1991-92	Kitchener Rangers	OHL	*55	25	24	3	*3042	203	1	4.00	....	....	....	....	....	14	7	7	....	900	47	0	3.13	....	....	....	....
1992-93	Canada	Nat-Team	5	5	0	0	300	11	1	2.20	....	....	....	....	....	....	....	....	....	....	....	....	....	....	....	....	....
	Kalamazoo Wings	IHL	48	19	17	9	2729	173	0	3.80	....	....	....	....	....	....	....	....	....	....	....	....	....	....	....	....	....
1993-94	Kalamazoo Wings	IHL	43	23	12	2	2168	133	0	3.68	....	....	....	....	....	4	1	3	....	221	14	*1	3.80	....	....	....	....
1994-95	Kalamazoo Wings	IHL	41	19	14	5	2140	106	*3	2.97	....	....	....	....	....	6	0	4	....	257	17	0	3.97	....	....	....	....
	Dallas Stars	**NHL**	**6**	**3**	**2**	**1**	**327**	**18**	**0**	**3.30**	**3.41**	**3.45**	**172**	**.895**	**31.6**	....	....	....	....	....	....	....	....	....	....	....	....

			REGULAR SEASON													PLAYOFFS											
Season	Club	League	GP	W	L	T	Mins	GA	SO	Avg	AAvg	Eff	SA	S%	SAPG	GP	W	L	T	Mins	GA	SO	Avg	Eff	SA	S%	SAPG
1995-96	Portland Pirates	AHL	12	2	6	2	577	46	0	4.79	....	....	....	....	....	....	....	....	....	....	....	....	....	....	....	....	....
	Hampton Roads Admirals	ECHL	5	2	2	0	260	17	0	3.92	....	....	....	....	....	....	....	....	....	....	....	....	....	....	....	....	....
	Michigan K-Wings	IHL	1	1	0	0	60	1	0	1.00	....	....	....	....	....	....	....	....	....	....	....	....	....	....	....	....	....
	Orlando Solar Bears	IHL	7	3	1	1	341	17	0	2.99	....	....	....	....	....	....	....	....	....	....	....	....	....	....	....	....	....
	Baltimore Bandits	AHL	5	2	1	1	256	18	0	4.21	....	....	....	....	....	1	0	0	....	40	0	0	0.00	....	....	....	....
1996-97	Fort Wayne Komets	IHL	57	20	31	3	2970	172	1	3.47	....	....	....	....	....	....	....	....	....	....	....	....	....	....	....	....	....
	Baltimore Bandits	AHL	....	....	....	....	....	....	....	....	....	....	....	....	....	1	0	0	....	40	4	0	6.00	....	....	....	....
1997-98	Milwaukee Admirals	IHL	34	13	14	1	1828	94	1	3.09	....	....	....	....	....	....	....	....	....	....	....	....	....	....	....	....	....
	Peoria Rivermen	ECHL	5	4	1	0	299	16	0	3.21	....	....	....	....	....	1	0	1	....	60	7	0	7.00	....	....	....	....
	San Antonio Dragons	IHL	2	0	2	0	118	12	0	6.07	....	....	....	....	....	....	....	....	....	....	....	....	....	....	....	....	....
	NHL Totals		**6**	**3**	**2**	**1**	**327**	**18**	**0**	**3.30**	....	....	**172**	**.895**	....	....	....	....	....	....	....	....	....	....	....	....	....

Memorial Cup All-Star Team (1990) • Won Hap Emms Memorial Memorial Trophy (Memorial Cup Tournament Top Goaltender) (1990) • OHL First All-Star Team (1991)

Transferred to **Dallas** after **Minnesota** franchise relocated, June 9, 1993. Traded to **Washington** by **Dallas** for cash, July 14, 1995. Traded to **Anaheim** by **Washington** for Todd Krygier, March 8, 1996.

• TREFILOV, ANDREI

Andrei Trefilov G – L. 6', 190 lbs. b: Kirovo-Chepetsk, USSR, 8/31/1969. Calgary's 14th choice, 261st overall, in 1991 Entry Draft.

Season	Club	League	GP	W	L	T	Mins	GA	SO	Avg	AAvg	Eff	SA	S%	SAPG	GP	W	L	T	Mins	GA	SO	Avg	Eff	SA	S%	SAPG
1990-91	Moscow Dynamo	USSR	20	....	....	....	1070	36	0	2.01	....	....	....	....	....	....	....	....	....	....	....	....	....	....	....	....	....
	Moscow Dynamo	SuperS	5	....	....	....	270	6	....	1.33	....	....	....	....	....	....	....	....	....	....	....	....	....	....	....	....	....
	Soviet Union	WEC-A	8	5	1	2	400	18	0	2.70	....	....	....	....	....	....	....	....	....	....	....	....	....	....	....	....	....
1991-92	Soviet Union	C Cup	1	0	0	0	4	0	0	0.00	....	....	....	....	....	....	....	....	....	....	....	....	....	....	....	....	....
	Moscow Dynamo	CIS	28	....	....	....	1326	35	0	1.58	....	....	....	....	....	....	....	....	....	....	....	....	....	....	....	....	....
	Russia	Olympics	4	0	0	0	39	2	0	3.08	....	....	....	....	....	....	....	....	....	....	....	....	....	....	....	....	....
	Russia	WC-A	2	1	0	0	66	2	0	1.82	....	....	....	....	....	....	....	....	....	....	....	....	....	....	....	....	....
1992-93	**Calgary Flames**	**NHL**	**1**	**0**	**0**	**1**	**65**	**5**	**0**	**4.62**	**3.93**	**5.92**	**39**	**.872**	**36.0**	....	....	....	....	....	....	....	....	....	....	....	....
	Salt Lake Golden Eagles	IHL	44	23	17	3	2536	135	0	3.19	....	....	....	....	....	....	....	....	....	....	....	....	....	....	....	....	....
	Russia	WC-A	6	4	2	0	360	14	0	2.33	....	....	....	....	....	....	....	....	....	....	....	....	....	....	....	....	....
1993-94	**Calgary Flames**	**NHL**	**11**	**3**	**4**	**2**	**623**	**26**	**2**	**2.50**	**2.38**	**2.13**	**305**	**.915**	**29.4**	....	....	....	....	....	....	....	....	....	....	....	....
	Saint John Flames	AHL	28	10	10	7	1629	93	0	3.42	....	....	....	....	....	....	....	....	....	....	....	....	....	....	....	....	....
1994-95	**Calgary Flames**	**NHL**	**6**	**0**	**3**	**0**	**236**	**16**	**0**	**4.07**	**4.21**	**5.01**	**130**	**.877**	**33.1**	....	....	....	....	....	....	....	....	....	....	....	....
	Saint John Flames	AHL	7	1	5	1	383	20	0	3.13	....	....	....	....	....	....	....	....	....	....	....	....	....	....	....	....	....
1995-96	**Buffalo Sabres**	**NHL**	**22**	**8**	**8**	**1**	**1094**	**64**	**0**	**3.51**	**3.45**	**3.40**	**660**	**.903**	**36.2**	....	....	....	....	....	....	....	....	....	....	....	....
	Rochester Americans	AHL	5	4	1	0	299	13	0	2.61	....	....	....	....	....	....	....	....	....	....	....	....	....	....	....	....	....
	Russia	WC-A	5	4	1	0	310	7	0	1.35	....	....	....	....	....	....	....	....	....	....	....	....	....	....	....	....	....
1996-97	Russia	W Cup	4	....	....	....	200	9	....	3.00	....	....	....	....	....	....	....	....	....	....	....	....	....	....	....	....	....
	Buffalo Sabres	**NHL**	**3**	**0**	**2**	**0**	**159**	**10**	**0**	**3.77**	**3.99**	**3.85**	**98**	**.898**	**37.0**	**1**	**0**	**0**	....	**5**	**0**	**0**	**0.00**	**0.00**	**4**	**1.000**	**48.0**
1997-98	Rochester Americans	AHL	3	1	0	1	138	6	0	2.60	....	....	....	....	....	....	....	....	....	....	....	....	....	....	....	....	....
	Chicago Blackhawks	**NHL**	**6**	**1**	**4**	**0**	**299**	**17**	**0**	**3.41**	**3.99**	**4.00**	**145**	**.883**	**29.1**	....	....	....	....	....	....	....	....	....	....	....	....
	Indianapolis Ice	IHL	1	0	1	0	59	3	0	3.03	....	....	....	....	....	....	....	....	....	....	....	....	....	....	....	....	....
	Russia	Olympics	2	1	0	0	69	4	0	3.45	....	....	....	....	....	....	....	....	....	....	....	....	....	....	....	....	....
	NHL Totals		**49**	**12**	**21**	**4**	**2476**	**138**	**2**	**3.34**	....	....	**1377**	**.900**	....	**1**	**0**	**0**	....	**5**	**0**	**0**	**0.00**	....	....	....	....

Signed as a free agent by **Buffalo**, July 11, 1995. Traded to **Chicago** by **Buffalo** for future considerations, November 12, 1997.

• TREMBLAY, VINCE

Vince Tremblay G – L. 6'1", 180 lbs. b: Quebec City, Que., 10/21/1959. Toronto's 3rd choice, 72nd overall, in 1979 Entry Draft.

Season	Club	League	GP	W	L	T	Mins	GA	SO	Avg	AAvg	Eff	SA	S%	SAPG	GP	W	L	T	Mins	GA	SO	Avg	Eff	SA	S%	SAPG
1977-78	Quebec Remparts	QMJHL	50	....	....	....	2664	201	0	4.53	....	....	....	....	....	3	0	3	0	157	18	0	6.88	....	....	....	....
1978-79	Quebec Remparts	QMJHL	66	....	....	....	3588	273	2	4.56	....	....	....	....	....	6	....	....	....	350	30	0	5.14	....	....	....	....
1979-80	**Toronto Maple Leafs**	**NHL**	**10**	**2**	**1**	**0**	**329**	**28**	**0**	**5.11**	**4.50**	....	....	....	....	....	....	....	....	....	....	....	....	....	....	....	....
	New Brunswick Hawks	AHL	13	4	3	0	510	35	0	4.12	....	....	....	....	....	1	0	1	0	42	4	0	5.71	....	....	....	....
1980-81	**Toronto Maple Leafs**	**NHL**	**3**	**0**	**3**	**0**	**143**	**16**	**0**	**6.71**	**5.38**	....	....	....	....	....	....	....	....	....	....	....	....	....	....	....	....
	New Brunswick Hawks	AHL	46	24	12	8	2613	141	2	*3.24	....	....	....	....	....	....	....	....	....	....	....	....	....	....	....	....	....
1981-82	**Toronto Maple Leafs**	**NHL**	**40**	**10**	**18**	**8**	**2033**	**153**	**1**	**4.52**	**3.49**	....	....	....	....	....	....	....	....	....	....	....	....	....	....	....	....
1982-83	**Toronto Maple Leafs**	**NHL**	**1**	**0**	**0**	**0**	**40**	**2**	**0**	**3.00**	**2.40**	**2.22**	**27**	**.926**	**40.5**	....	....	....	....	....	....	....	....	....	....	....	....
	St. Catharines Saints	AHL	34	....	....	....	1699	133	0	4.70	....	....	....	....	....	....	....	....	....	....	....	....	....	....	....	....	....
1983-84	**Pittsburgh Penguins**	**NHL**	**4**	**0**	**4**	**0**	**240**	**24**	**0**	**6.00**	**4.70**	**10.14**	**142**	**.831**	**35.5**	....	....	....	....	....	....	....	....	....	....	....	....
	Baltimore Skipjacks	AHL	28	10	8	7	1590	106	0	4.00	....	....	....	....	....	....	....	....	....	....	....	....	....	....	....	....	....
1984-85	Riverview Trappers	NBSHL	STATISTICS NOT AVAILABLE																								
	Rochester Americans	AHL	33	13	10	8	1811	115	0	3.81	....	....	....	....	....	3	1	1	0	121	46	0	5.45	....	....	....	....
	NHL Totals		**58**	**12**	**26**	**8**	**2785**	**223**	**1**	**4.80**	....	....	....	....	....	....	....	....	....	....	....	....	....	....	....	....	....

QMJHL Second All-Star Team (1979)

Traded to **Pittsburgh** by **Toronto** with Rocky Saganiuk for Nick Ricci and Pat Graham, August 15, 1983. Signed as a free agent by **Buffalo**, March 7, 1985.

• TUCKER, TED

Ted Tucker G – L. 5'11", 165 lbs. b: Fort William, Ont., 5/7/1949.

Season	Club	League	GP	W	L	T	Mins	GA	SO	Avg	AAvg	Eff	SA	S%	SAPG	GP	W	L	T	Mins	GA	SO	Avg	Eff	SA	S%	SAPG
1967-68	Montreal Jr. Canadiens	OHA	5	....	....	....	250	16	0	3.84	....	....	....	....	....	1	1	0	0	30	1	0	2.00	....	....	....	....
1968-69	Montreal Jr. Canadiens	OHA	27	....	....	....	1600	89	2	3.34	....	....	....	....	....	2	0	1	0	80	7	0	5.38	....	....	....	....
1969-70	Clinton Comets	EHL	69	....	....	....	4140	211	*6	3.06	....	....	....	....	....	*17	*12	5	0	....	47	2	2.77	....	....	....	....
1970-71	Clinton Comets	EHL	74	31	32	11	4440	231	4	3.12	....	....	....	....	....	5	1	4	0	300	20	0	4.00	....	....	....	....
	Syracuse Blazers	EHL	....	....	....	....	....	....	....	....	....	....	....	....	....	2	0	2	0	120	14	0	7.00	....	....	....	....
1971-72	Clinton Comets	EHL	43	....	....	....	2610	142	2	3.26	....	....	....	....	....	3	1	2	0	220	12	0	3.27	....	....	....	....
1972-73	Salt Lake Golden Eagles	WHL	33	14	7	10	1919	112	1	3.50	....	....	....	....	....	7	2	5	0	427	26	0	3.63	....	....	....	....
1973-74	**California Golden Seals**	**NHL**	**5**	**1**	**1**	**1**	**177**	**10**	**0**	**3.39**	**3.27**	....	....	....	....	....	....	....	....	....	....	....	....	....	....	....	....
	Salt Lake Golden Eagles	WHL	13	6	6	0	713	61	0	5.13	....	....	....	....	....	3	0	3	0	160	12	0	4.49	....	....	....	....
1974-75	Toledo Goaldiggers	IHL	39	....	....	....	2166	114	2	3.16	....	....	....	....	....	11	....	....	....	522	31	1	3.56	....	....	....	....
1975-76	Toledo/Port Huron	IHL	24	....	....	....	1044	73	0	4.20	....	....	....	....	....	1	0	1	0	60	5	0	5.00	....	....	....	....
1976-77	Toledo Goaldiggers	IHL	3	....	....	....	164	12	0	4.39	....	....	....	....	....	....	....	....	....	....	....	....	....	....	....	....	....
	Muskegon Mohawks	IHL	46	....	....	....	2478	154	2	3.73	....	....	....	....	....	3	....	....	....	179	10	0	3.35	....	....	....	....
1977-78	Port Huron–Toledo	IHL	41	....	....	....	2121	142	0	4.02	....	....	....	....	....	1	0	0	0	17	2	0	7.06	....	....	....	....
1978-79			DID NOT PLAY																								
1979-80	Dayton Gems	IHL	23	....	....	....	1189	91	0	4.59	....	....	....	....	....	....	....	....	....	....	....	....	....	....	....	....	....
	Saginaw Gears	IHL	12	....	....	....	691	33	0	2.87	....	....	....	....	....	4	....	....	....	205	11	0	3.22	....	....	....	....
1980-81	Saginaw Gears	IHL	40	....	....	....	2068	126	1	3.66	....	....	....	....	....	....	....	....	....	....	....	....	....	....	....	....	....
	NHL Totals		**5**	**1**	**1**	**1**	**177**	**10**	**0**	**3.39**	....	....	....	....	....	....	....	....	....	....	....	....	....	....	....	....	....

EHL North First All-Star Team (1970, 1971) • EHL North Rookie of the Year (1970)

Traded to **Atlanta** by **Montreal** for cash, June, 1972. Traded to **California** by **Atlanta** for cash, June 10, 1973.

• TUGNUTT, RON

Ron Tugnutt G – L. 5'11", 155 lbs. b: Scarborough, Ont., 10/22/1967. Quebec's 4th choice, 81st overall, in 1986 Entry Draft.

Season	Club	League	GP	W	L	T	Mins	GA	SO	Avg	AAvg	Eff	SA	S%	SAPG	GP	W	L	T	Mins	GA	SO	Avg	Eff	SA	S%	SAPG
1984-85	Peterborough Petes	OHL	18	7	4	2	938	59	0	3.77	....	....	....	....	....	....	....	....	....	....	....	....	....	....	....	....	....
1985-86	Peterborough Petes	OHL	26	18	7	0	1543	74	1	2.88	....	....	....	....	....	3	2	0	....	133	6	0	2.71	....	....	....	....
1986-87	Peterborough Petes	OHL	31	21	7	2	1891	88	2	*2.79	....	....	....	....	....	6	3	3	....	374	21	1	3.37	....	....	....	....
1987-88	**Quebec Nordiques**	**NHL**	**6**	**2**	**3**	**0**	**284**	**16**	**0**	**3.38**	**2.81**	**4.40**	**123**	**.870**	**26.0**	....	....	....	....	....	....	....	....	....	....	....	....
	Fredericton Express	AHL	34	20	9	4	1964	118	1	3.60	....	....	....	....	....	4	1	2	....	204	11	0	3.24	....	....	....	....
1988-89	**Quebec Nordiques**	**NHL**	**26**	**10**	**10**	**3**	**1367**	**82**	**0**	**3.60**	**2.97**	**3.90**	**756**	**.892**	**33.2**	....	....	....	....	....	....	....	....	....	....	....	....
	Halifax Citadels	AHL	24	14	7	2	1368	79	1	3.46	....	....	....	....	....	....	....	....	....	....	....	....	....	....	....	....	....
1989-90	**Quebec Nordiques**	**NHL**	**35**	**5**	**24**	**3**	**1978**	**152**	**0**	**4.61**	**3.88**	**6.49**	**1080**	**.859**	**32.8**	....	....	....	....	....	....	....	....	....	....	....	....
	Halifax Citadels	AHL	6	1	5	0	366	23	0	3.77	....	....	....	....	....	....	....	....	....	....	....	....	....	....	....	....	....
1990-91	**Quebec Nordiques**	**NHL**	**56**	**12**	**29**	**10**	**3144**	**212**	**0**	**4.05**	**3.64**	**4.64**	**1851**	**.885**	**35.3**	....	....	....	....	....	....	....	....	....	....	....	....
	Halifax Citadels	AHL	2	0	1	0	100	8	0	4.80	....	....	....	....	....	....	....	....	....	....	....	....	....	....	....	....	....
1991-92	**Quebec Nordiques**	**NHL**	**30**	**6**	**17**	**3**	**1583**	**106**	**1**	**4.02**	**3.57**	**5.45**	**782**	**.864**	**29.6**	....	....	....	....	....	....	....	....	....	....	....	....
	Halifax Citadels	AHL	8	3	3	1	447	30	0	4.03	....	....	....	....	....	....	....	....	....	....	....	....	....	....	....	....	....
	Edmonton Oilers	**NHL**	**3**	**1**	**1**	**0**	**124**	**10**	**0**	**4.04**	**4.30**	**6.63**	**73**	**.863**	**35.3**	**2**	**0**	**0**	....	**60**	**3**	**0**	**3.00**	**2.65**	**34**	**.912**	**34.0**
1992-93	**Edmonton Oilers**	**NHL**	**26**	**9**	**12**	**2**	**1338**	**93**	**0**	**4.17**	**3.55**	**5.06**	**767**	**.879**	**34.4**	....	....	....	....	....	....	....	....	....	....	....	....
	Canada	WC-A	4	....	....	....	125	6	....	2.87	....	....	....	....	....	....	....	....	....	....	....	....	....	....	....	....	....

			REGULAR SEASON													PLAYOFFS											
Season	Club	League	GP	W	L	T	Mins	GA	SO	Avg	AAvg	Eff	SA	S%	SAPG	GP	W	L	T	Mins	GA	SO	Avg	Eff	SA	S%	SAPG
1993-94	Anaheim Mighty Ducks	NHL	28	10	15	1	1520	76	1	3.00	2.85	2.75	828	.908	32.7	....	....	....	....	....	....	....	....	....	....	....	....
	Montreal Canadiens	NHL	8	2	3	1	378	24	0	3.81	3.63	5.32	172	.860	27.3	1	0	1	....	59	5	0	5.08	10.16	25	.800	25.4
1994-95	Montreal Canadiens	NHL	7	1	3	1	346	18	0	3.12	3.23	3.27	172	.895	29.8	....	....	....	....	....	....	....	....	....	....	....	....
1995-96	Portland Pirates	AHL	58	21	23	6	3068	171	2	3.34	....	....	....	....	....	13	7	6	....	782	36	1	2.76	....	....	....	....
1996-97	Ottawa Senators	NHL	37	17	15	1	1991	93	3	2.80	2.96	2.95	882	.895	26.6	7	3	4	....	425	14	1	1.98	1.64	169	.917	23.9
1997-98	Ottawa Senators	NHL	42	15	14	8	2236	84	3	2.25	2.63	2.14	882	.905	23.7	2	0	1	....	74	6	0	4.86	11.66	25	.760	20.3
	NHL Totals		304	90	146	33	16289	966	8	3.56	....	....	8368	.885	....	12	3	6	....	618	28	1	2.72	....	....	....	....

OHL First All-Star Team (1987)

Traded to **Edmonton** by **Quebec** with Brad Zavisha for Martin Rucinsky, March 10, 1992. Claimed by **Anaheim** from **Edmonton** in Expansion Draft, June 24, 1993. Traded to **Montreal** by **Anaheim** for Stephan Lebeau, February 20, 1994. Signed as a free agent by **Washington**, September 25, 1995. Signed as a free agent by **Ottawa**, August 14, 1996.

• TUREK, ROMAN

Roman Turek G – R. 6'3", 190 lbs. b: Pisek, Czech., 5/21/1970. Minnesota's 6th choice, 113th overall, in 1990 Entry Draft.

Season	Club	League	GP	W	L	T	Mins	GA	SO	Avg	AAvg	Eff	SA	S%	SAPG	GP	W	L	T	Mins	GA	SO	Avg	Eff	SA	S%	SAPG
1987-88	Czechoslovakia	EJC-A	5	....	....	....	273	9	....	1.98	....	....	....	....	....	....	....	....	....	....	....	....	....	....	....	....	....
1988-89	Czechoslovakia	WJC-A	7	....	....	....	390	16	....	2.46	....	....	....	....	....	....	....	....	....	....	....	....	....	....	....	....	....
1989-90	Czechoslovakia	WJC-A	6	....	....	....	326	14	....	2.57	....	....	....	....	....	....	....	....	....	....	....	....	....	....	....	....	....
1990-91	Ceske Budejovice	Czech.	26	....	....	....	1244	98	0	4.70	....	....	....	....	....	....	....	....	....	....	....	....	....	....	....	....	....
1991-92	Ceske Budejovice	Czech. 2		STATISTICS NOT AVAILABLE																							
1992-93	Ceske Budejovice	Czech.	43	....	....	....	2555	121	....	2.84	....	....	....	....	....	....	....	....	....	....	....	....	....	....	....	....	....
	Czech Republic	WC-A		DID NOT PLAY – SPARE GOALTENDER																							
1993-94	Ceske Budejovice	Czech.	44	....	....	....	2584	111	....	2.51	....	....	....	....	....	3	....	....	....	180	12	0	4.00	....	....	....	....
	Czech Republic	Olympics	2	....	....	....	120	3	....	1.50	....	....	....	....	....	....	....	....	....	....	....	....	....	....	....	....	....
	Czech Republic	WC-A	2	....	....	....	120	4	....	2.00	....	....	....	....	....	....	....	....	....	....	....	....	....	....	....	....	....
1994-95	Ceske Budejovice	Czech.	44	....	....	....	2587	119	....	2.76	....	....	....	....	....	9	....	....	....	498	25	....	3.01	....	....	....	....
	Czech Republic	WC-A	6	3	3	0	359	9	....	1.50	....	....	....	....	....	....	....	....	....	....	....	....	....	....	....	....	....
1995-96	Nurnberg Ice Tigers	Germany	48	....	....	....	2787	154	....	3.31	....	....	....	....	....	5	....	....	....	338	14	....	2.48	....	....	....	....
	Czech Republic	WC-A	8	7	0	1	480	15	....	1.88	....	....	....	....	....	....	....	....	....	....	....	....	....	....	....	....	....
1996-97	Czech Republic	W Cup	3	0	3	0	82	10	0	7.00	....	....	....	....	....	....	....	....	....	....	....	....	....	....	....	....	....
	Dallas Stars	NHL	6	3	1	0	263	9	0	2.05	2.17	1.43	129	.930	29.4	....	....	....	....	....	....	....	....	....	....	....	....
	Michigan K-Wings	IHL	29	8	13	4	1555	77	0	2.97	....	....	....	....	....	....	....	....	....	....	....	....	....	....	....	....	....
1997-98	Dallas Stars	NHL	23	11	10	1	1324	49	1	2.22	2.59	2.19	496	.901	22.5	....	....	....	....	....	....	....	....	....	....	....	....
	Michigan K-Wings	IHL	2	1	1	0	119	5	0	2.51	....	....	....	....	....	....	....	....	....	....	....	....	....	....	....	....	....
	NHL Totals		29	14	11	1	1587	58	1	2.19	....	....	625	.907	....	....	....	....	....	....	....	....	....	....	....	....	....

EJC-A All-Star Team (1988) • Czech Republic Player of the Year (1994) • WC-A All-Star Team (1995, 1996) • Named Best Goaltender at WC-A (1996)

Transferred to **Dallas** after **Minnesota** franchise relocated, June 9, 1993.

• TURNER, JOE

Joe Turner G – L. 5'10", 182 lbs. b: Windsor, Ont., 1919. d: 1945.

Season	Club	League	GP	W	L	T	Mins	GA	SO	Avg	AAvg	Eff	SA	S%	SAPG	GP	W	L	T	Mins	GA	SO	Avg	Eff	SA	S%	SAPG
1933-34	Toronto Canoe Club	OHA	9	....	....	....	540	24	0	*2.72	....	....	....	....	....	2	....	....	....	120	13	0	6.50	....	....	....	....
1934-35	Windsor Motors	MOHL	3	....	....	....	180	13	0	4.33	....	....	....	....	....	....	....	....	....	....	....	....	....	....	....	....	....
1935-36	Windsor Motors	MOHL		STATISTICS NOT AVAILABLE																							
1936-37	Windsor Bulldogs	MOHL	26	....	....	....	1560	91	0	3.50	....	....	....	....	....	5	1	2	2	300	13	0	2.68	....	....	....	....
1937-38	Stratford Midgets	OHA	14	....	....	....	840	33	0	*2.36	....	....	....	....	....	7	2	3	1	420	23	1	3.28	....	....	....	....
1938-39	Guelph Indians	OHA	14	....	....	....	840	38	*2	2.71	....	....	....	....	....	2	....	....	....	120	7	0	3.50	....	....	....	....
1939-40	Detroit Holzbaugh	MOHL	36	27	3	6	1620	76	*6	*2.11	....	....	....	....	....	12	9	3	0	730	27	2	2.22	....	....	....	....
	Windsor Chryslers	MOHL	1	1	0	0	60	1	0	1.00	....	....	....	....	....	....	....	....	....	....	....	....	....	....	....	....	....
	London Mohawks	OHA Sr.	1	1	0	0	60	1	0	1.00	....	....	....	....	....	....	....	....	....	....	....	....	....	....	....	....	....
1940-41	Detroit Holzbaugh	MOHL	27	13	10	4	1620	84	1	3.11	....	....	....	....	....	7	4	3	0	420	25	0	3.57	....	....	....	....
1941-42	Indianapolis Capitols	AHL	52	*34	10	7	3175	139	4	2.63	....	....	....	....	....	10	*7	3	0	630	34	0	3.24	....	....	....	....
	Detroit Red Wings	NHL	1	0	0	1	70	3	0	2.57	2.54	....	....	....	....	....	....	....	....	....	....	....	....	....	....	....	....
1942-1945				MILITARY SERVICE																							
	NHL Totals		1	0	0	1	70	3	0	2.57	....	....	....	....	....	....	....	....	....	....	....	....	....	....	....	....	....

AHL First All-Star Team (1942)

Promoted to **Detroit** from **Indianapolis** (AHL) to replace injured Johnny Mowers, February 5, 1942. (Toronto 3, Detroit 3). • Killed in action in Holland while serving with U.S. Marine Corps., January, 1945.

• VACHON, ROGIE

Rogie (Rogatien) Vachon G – L. 5'7", 170 lbs. b: Palmarolle, Que., 9/8/1945.

Season	Club	League	GP	W	L	T	Mins	GA	SO	Avg	AAvg	Eff	SA	S%	SAPG	GP	W	L	T	Mins	GA	SO	Avg	Eff	SA	S%	SAPG
1963-64	Notre Dame de Grace Monarchs	QJHL	29	....	....	....	1740	71	*4	2.45	....	....	....	....	....	....	....	....	....	....	....	....	....	....	....	....	....
	Montreal Jr. Canadiens	OHA	7	....	....	....	400	29	0	4.35	....	....	....	....	....	....	....	....	....	....	....	....	....	....	....	....	....
1964-65	Montreal Jr. Canadiens	OHA	14	....	....	....	840	58	0	4.14	....	....	....	....	....	....	....	....	....	....	....	....	....	....	....	....	....
1965-66	Thetford Mines Canadiens	QJHL		STATISTICS NOT AVAILABLE																							
	Quebec Aces	AHL	10	6	4	0	601	30	0	3.00	....	....	....	....	....	....	....	....	....	....	....	....	....	....	....	....	....
1966-67	Houston Apollos	CHL	34	17	12	5	2020	99	2	2.91	....	....	....	....	....	....	....	....	....	....	....	....	....	....	....	....	....
	Montreal Canadiens	NHL	19	11	3	4	1137	47	1	2.48	2.55	....	....	....	....	9	*6	3	....	555	22	0	*2.38	....	....	....	....
1967-68	Montreal Canadiens	NHL	39	23	13	2	2227	92	4	2.48	2.73	....	....	....	....	2	1	1	....	113	4	0	2.12	....	....	....	....
1968-69	Montreal Canadiens	NHL	36	22	9	3	2051	98	2	2.87	2.97	....	....	....	....	8	7	1	....	507	12	1	1.42	....	....	....	....
1969-70	Montreal Canadiens	NHL	64	31	18	12	3697	162	4	2.63	2.78	....	....	....	....	....	....	....	....	....	....	....	....	....	....	....	....
1970-71	Montreal Canadiens	NHL	47	23	12	9	2676	118	2	2.65	2.60	....	....	....	....	....	....	....	....	....	....	....	....	....	....	....	....
1971-72	Montreal Canadiens	NHL	1	0	1	0	20	4	0	12.00	12.09	....	....	....	....	....	....	....	....	....	....	....	....	....	....	....	....
	Los Angeles Kings	NHL	28	6	18	3	1586	107	0	4.05	4.11	....	....	....	....	....	....	....	....	....	....	....	....	....	....	....	....
1972-73	Los Angeles Kings	NHL	53	22	20	10	3120	148	4	2.85	2.67	....	....	....	....	....	....	....	....	....	....	....	....	....	....	....	....
1973-74	Los Angeles Kings	NHL	65	28	26	10	3751	175	5	2.80	2.69	....	....	....	....	4	0	4	....	240	7	0	1.75	....	....	....	....
1974-75	Los Angeles Kings	NHL	54	27	14	13	3239	121	6	2.24	1.99	....	....	....	....	3	1	2	....	199	7	0	2.11	....	....	....	....
1975-76	Los Angeles Kings	NHL	51	26	20	5	3060	160	5	3.14	2.83	....	....	....	....	7	4	3	....	438	17	1	2.33	....	....	....	....
1976-77	Canada	C Cup	7	6	1	0	432	10	2	1.39	....	....	....	....	....	....	....	....	....	....	....	....	....	....	....	....	....
	Los Angeles Kings	NHL	68	33	23	12	4059	184	8	2.72	2.51	....	....	....	....	9	4	5	....	520	36	0	4.15	....	....	....	....
1977-78	Los Angeles Kings	NHL	70	29	27	13	4107	196	4	2.86	2.66	....	....	....	....	2	0	2	....	120	11	0	5.50	....	....	....	....
1978-79	Detroit Red Wings	NHL	50	10	27	11	2908	189	0	3.90	3.46	....	....	....	....	....	....	....	....	....	....	....	....	....	....	....	....
1979-80	Detroit Red Wings	NHL	59	20	30	8	3474	209	4	3.61	3.18	....	....	....	....	....	....	....	....	....	....	....	....	....	....	....	....
1980-81	Boston Bruins	NHL	53	25	19	6	3021	168	1	3.34	2.67	....	....	....	....	3	0	2	....	164	16	0	5.85	....	....	....	....
1981-82	Boston Bruins	NHL	38	19	11	6	2165	132	1	3.66	2.82	....	....	....	....	1	0	0	....	20	1	0	3.00	....	....	....	....
	NHL Totals		795	355	291	127	46298	2310	51	2.99	....	....	....	....	....	48	23	23	....	2876	133	2	2.77	....	....	....	....

Shared Vezina Trophy with Gump Worsley (1968) • NHL Second All-Star Team (1975, 1977) • Canada Cup All-Star Team (1976)

Played in NHL All-Star Game (1973, 1975, 1978)

Traded to **LA Kings** by **Montreal** for Denis Dejordy, Dale Hoganson, Noel Price and Doug Robinson, November 4, 1971. Signed as a free agent by **Detroit**, August 8, 1978. Traded to **Boston** by **Detroit** for Gilles Gilbert, July 15, 1980.

• VANBIESBROUCK, JOHN

John "Beezer" Vanbiesbrouck G – L. 5'8", 176 lbs. b: Detroit, MI, 9/4/1963. NY Rangers' 5th choice, 72nd overall, in 1981 Entry Draft.

Season	Club	League	GP	W	L	T	Mins	GA	SO	Avg	AAvg	Eff	SA	S%	SAPG	GP	W	L	T	Mins	GA	SO	Avg	Eff	SA	S%	SAPG
1980-81	Sault Ste. Marie Greyhounds	OHA	56	31	16	1	2941	203	0	4.14	....	....	....	....	....	11	3	3	....	457	24	1	3.15	....	....	....	....
1981-82	New York Rangers	NHL	1	1	0	0	60	1	0	1.00	0.77	0.33	30	.967	30.0	....	....	....	....	....	....	....	....	....	....	....	....
	Sault Ste. Marie Greyhounds	OHL	31	12	12	2	1686	102	0	3.62	....	....	....	....	....	7	1	4	....	276	20	0	4.35	....	....	....	....
	United States	WJC-A	5	1	3	0	200	19	0	5.70	....	....	....	....	....	....	....	....	....	....	....	....	....	....	....	....	....
1982-83	Sault Ste. Marie Greyhounds	OHL	*62	39	21	1	3471	209	0	3.61	....	....	....	....	....	16	7	6	....	944	56	*1	3.56	....	....	....	....
	United States	WJC-A	5	....	....	....	280	17	....	3.64	....	....	....	....	....	....	....	....	....	....	....	....	....	....	....	....	....
1983-84	New York Rangers	NHL	3	2	1	0	180	10	0	3.33	2.60	3.92	85	.882	28.3	1	0	0	....	1	0	0	0.00	0.00	0	.00	0.0
	Tulsa Oilers	CHL	37	20	13	2	2153	124	*3	3.46	....	....	....	....	....	4	4	0	....	240	10	0	*2.50	....	....	....	....
1984-85	New York Rangers	NHL	42	12	24	3	2358	166	1	4.22	3.36	5.20	1346	.877	34.2	1	0	0	....	20	0	0	0.00	0.00	12	1.000	36.0
	United States	WEC-A	9	6	3	0	492	46	....	5.64	....	....	....	....	....	....	....	....	....	....	....	....	....	....	....	....	....
1985-86	New York Rangers	NHL	61	*31	21	5	3326	184	3	3.32	2.57	3.76	1625	.887	29.3	16	8	8	....	899	49	*1	3.27	3.36	477	.897	31.8
1986-87	New York Rangers	NHL	50	18	20	5	2656	161	0	3.64	3.06	4.28	1369	.882	30.9	4	1	3	....	195	11	1	3.38	3.38	110	.900	33.8
	United States	WEC-A	7	2	5	0	419	28	....	4.01	....	....	....	....	....	....	....	....	....	....	....	....	....	....	....	....	....

			REGULAR SEASON													PLAYOFFS											
Season	Club	League	GP	W	L	T	Mins	GA	SO	Avg	AAvg	Eff	SA	S%	SAPG	GP	W	L	T	Mins	GA	SO	Avg	Eff	SA	S%	SAPG
1987-88	United States	C Cup	4	2	2	0	240	9	....	2.00	....	....	....	....	....	....	....	....	....	....	....	....	....	....	....	....	....
	New York Rangers	NHL	56	27	22	7	3319	187	2	3.38	2.80	3.72	1700	.890	30.7	....	....	....	....	....	....	....	....	....	....	....	....
1988-89	New York Rangers	NHL	56	28	21	4	3207	197	0	3.69	3.04	4.36	1666	.882	31.2	2	0	1	....	107	6	0	3.36	3.67	55	.891	30.8
	United States	WEC-A	5	....	....	....	....	20	....	4.53	....	....	....	....	....	....	....	....	....	....	....	....	....	....	....	....	....
1989-90	New York Rangers	NHL	47	19	19	7	2734	154	1	3.38	2.82	3.82	1362	.887	29.9	6	2	3	....	298	15	0	3.02	2.96	153	.902	30.8
1990-91	New York Rangers	NHL	40	15	18	6	2257	126	3	3.35	2.99	3.66	1154	.891	30.7	1	0	0	....	52	1	0	1.15	0.62	22	.955	25.4
	United States	WEC-A	10	....	....	....	....	41	....	4.67	....	....	....	....	....	....	....	....	....	....	....	....	....	....	....	....	....
1991-92	United States	C Cup	1	1	0	0	60	3	0	3.00	....	....	....	....	....	....	....	....	....	....	....	....	....	....	....	....	....
	New York Rangers	NHL	45	27	13	3	2526	120	2	2.85	2.52	2.57	1331	.910	31.6	7	2	5	....	368	23	0	3.75	4.82	179	.872	29.2
1992-93	New York Rangers	NHL	48	20	18	7	2757	152	4	3.31	2.81	3.30	1525	.900	33.2	....	....	....	....	....	....	....	....	....	....	....	....
1993-94	Florida Panthers	NHL	57	21	25	11	3440	145	1	2.53	2.39	1.92	1912	.924	33.3	....	....	....	....	....	....	....	....	....	....	....	....
1994-95	Florida Panthers	NHL	37	14	15	4	2087	86	4	2.47	2.54	2.12	1000	.914	28.7	....	....	....	....	....	....	....	....	....	....	....	....
1995-96	Florida Panthers	NHL	57	26	20	7	3178	142	2	2.68	2.62	2.58	1473	.904	27.8	*22	12	10	....	1332	50	1	2.25	1.53	735	.932	33.1
1996-97	Florida Panthers	NHL	57	27	19	10	3347	128	2	2.29	2.41	1.85	1582	.919	28.4	5	1	4	....	328	13	1	2.38	1.68	184	.929	33.7
1997-98	Florida Panthers	NHL	60	18	29	11	3451	165	4	2.87	3.37	2.89	1638	.899	28.5	....	....	....	....	....	....	....	....	....	....	....	....
	United States	Olympics	1	0	0	0	1	0	0	0.00	....	....	....	....	....	....	....	....	....	....	....	....	....	....	....	....	....
	NHL Totals		717	306	285	90	40883	2124	29	3.12	....	....	20798	.898	....	65	26	34	....	3600	168	4	2.80	....	....	....	....

OHL Second All-Star Team (1983) • CHL First All-Star Team (1984) • Shared Terry Sawchuk Trophy (CHL's Leading Goaltender) with Ron Scott (1984) • Shared Tommy Ivan Trophy (CHL's MVP) with Bruce Affleck (1984) • NHL First All-Star Team (1986) • Won Vezina Trophy (1986) • NHL Second All-Star Team (1994)

Played in NHL All-Star Game (1994, 1996, 1997)

Traded to **Vancouver** by **NY Rangers** for future considerations (Doug Lidster, June 25, 1993), June 20, 1993. Claimed by **Florida** from **Vancouver** in Expansion Draft, June 24, 1993. Signed as a free agent by **Philadelphia**, July 7, 1998.

• VEISOR, MIKE

Mike Veisor G – L. 5'9", 160 lbs. b: Toronto, Ont., 8/25/1952. Chicago's 3rd choice, 45th overall, in 1972 Amateur Draft.

Season	Club	League	GP	W	L	T	Mins	GA	SO	Avg	AAvg	Eff	SA	S%	SAPG	GP	W	L	T	Mins	GA	SO	Avg	Eff	SA	S%	SAPG
1969-70	Hamilton Red Wings	OHA	43	....	....	....	2580	172	0	4.00	....	....	....	....	....	....	....	....	....	....	....	....	....	....	....	....	....
1970-71	Hamilton Red Wings	OHA	53	....	....	....	3177	266	0	5.02	....	....	....	....	....	....	....	....	....	....	....	....	....	....	....	....	....
1971-72	Peterborough Petes	OHA	49	....	....	....	2920	203	1	4.17	....	....	....	....	....	....	....	....	....	....	....	....	....	....	....	....	....
1972-73	Dallas Black Hawks	CHL	39	....	....	....	2160	99	*4	*2.75	....	....	....	....	....	4	....	....	....	219	14	0	3.83	....	....	....	....
1973-74	Chicago Black Hawks	NHL	10	7	0	2	537	20	1	2.23	2.15	....	....	....	....	2	0	1	....	80	5	0	3.75	....	....	....	....
1974-75	Chicago Black Hawks	NHL	9	1	5	1	460	36	0	4.70	4.24	....	....	....	....	....	....	....	....	....	....	....	....	....	....	....	....
	Dallas Black Hawks	CHL	16	11	5	0	958	52	0	3.26	....	....	....	....	....	*10	6	4	0	*656	28	*2	*2.56	....	....	....	....
1975-76	Dallas Black Hawks	CHL	*62	*28	22	9	*3561	174	*5	2.93	....	....	....	....	....	*9	5	4	0	*540	22	*1	2.44	....	....	....	....
1976-77	Chicago Black Hawks	NHL	3	1	2	0	180	13	0	4.33	4.03	....	....	....	....	....	....	....	....	....	....	....	....	....	....	....	....
	Dallas Black Hawks	CHL	40	17	15	6	2279	116	2	3.05	....	....	....	....	....	2	0	2	0	119	6	0	3.03	....	....	....	....
1977-78	Chicago Black Hawks	NHL	12	3	4	5	720	31	2	2.58	2.41	....	....	....	....	....	....	....	....	....	....	....	....	....	....	....	....
1978-79	Chicago Black Hawks	NHL	17	5	8	4	1020	60	0	3.53	3.12	....	....	....	....	....	....	....	....	....	....	....	....	....	....	....	....
1979-80	Chicago Black Hawks	NHL	11	3	5	3	660	37	0	3.36	2.95	....	....	....	....	1	0	1	....	60	6	0	6.00	....	....	....	....
1980-81	Hartford Whalers	NHL	29	6	13	6	1588	118	1	4.46	3.58	....	....	....	....	....	....	....	....	....	....	....	....	....	....	....	....
1981-82	Hartford Whalers	NHL	13	5	5	2	701	53	0	4.54	3.50	....	....	....	....	....	....	....	....	....	....	....	....	....	....	....	....
	Binghamton Whalers	AHL	22	13	8	1	1299	67	1	3.09	....	....	....	....	....	....	....	....	....	....	....	....	....	....	....	....	....
1982-83	Hartford Whalers	NHL	23	5	16	1	1280	118	1	5.53	4.44	8.01	815	.855	38.2	....	....	....	....	....	....	....	....	....	....	....	....
	Canada	WEC-A	DID NOT PLAY – SPARE GOALTENDER																								
1983-84	Hartford Whalers	NHL	4	1	3	0	240	20	0	5.00	3.91	8.77	114	.825	28.5	....	....	....	....	....	....	....	....	....	....	....	....
	Sherbrooke Jets	AHL	5	1	4	0	259	24	0	5.56	....	....	....	....	....	....	....	....	....	....	....	....	....	....	....	....	....
	Winnipeg Jets	NHL	8	4	1	2	420	26	0	3.71	2.90	5.61	172	.849	24.6	1	0	0	....	40	4	0	6.00	8.28	29	.862	43.5
	NHL Totals		139	41	62	26	7806	532	5	4.09	....	....	....	....	....	4	0	2	....	180	15	0	5.00	....	....	....	....

CHL First All-Star Team (1973, 1975) • Won Terry Sawchuk Trophy (fewest goals against - CHL) (1973) • Won Ken McKenzie Trophy (CHL's Rookie of the Year) (1973)

Traded to **Hartford** by **Chicago** for Hartford's 2nd round choice (Kevin Griffin) in 1981 Entry Draft, June 19, 1980. Traded to **Winnipeg** by **Hartford** for Ed Staniowski, November 10, 1983.

• VERNON, MIKE

Mike Vernon G – L. 5'9", 165 lbs. b: Calgary, Alta., 2/24/1963. Calgary's 2nd choice, 56th overall, in 1981 Entry Draft.

Season	Club	League	GP	W	L	T	Mins	GA	SO	Avg	AAvg	Eff	SA	S%	SAPG	GP	W	L	T	Mins	GA	SO	Avg	Eff	SA	S%	SAPG
1980-81	Calgary Wranglers	WHL	59	33	17	1	3154	198	1	3.77	....	....	....	....	....	22	14	8	....	1271	82	1	3.87	....	....	....	....
1981-82	Calgary Wranglers	WHL	42	22	14	2	2329	143	3	3.68	....	....	....	....	....	9	5	4	....	527	30	0	3.42	....	....	....	....
	Oklahoma City Stars	CHL	....	....	....	....	....	....	....	....	....	....	....	....	....	1	0	1	....	70	4	0	3.43	....	....	....	....
1982-83	Calgary Flames	NHL	2	0	2	0	100	11	0	6.59	5.27	15.76	46	.761	27.6	....	....	....	....	....	....	....	....	....	....	....	....
	Calgary Wranglers	WHL	50	29	18	[illegible]	2856	155	[illegible]	[illegible]	....	....	....	....	....	16	9	7	....	925	60	0	3.89	....	....	....	....
	Canada	WJC-A	4	3	0	0	180	10	0	3.33	....	....	....	....	....	....	....	....	....	....	....	....	....	....	....	....	....
1983-84	Calgary Flames	NHL	1	0	1	0	11	4	0	22.22	17.39	148.13	6	.333	32.7	....	....	....	....	....	....	....	....	....	....	....	....
	Colorado Flames	CHL	46	30	13	2	2648	148	1	*3.35	....	....	....	....	....	6	2	4	....	347	21	0	3.63	....	....	....	....
1984-85	Moncton Golden Flames	AHL	41	10	20	4	2050	134	0	3.92	....	....	....	....	....	....	....	....	....	....	....	....	....	....	....	....	....
1985-86	Calgary Flames	NHL	18	9	3	3	921	52	1	3.39	2.63	4.23	417	.875	27.2	*21	12	*9	....	*1229	60	0	2.93	3.02	583	.897	28.5
	Moncton Golden Flames	AHL	6	3	1	2	374	21	0	3.37	....	....	....	....	....	....	....	....	....	....	....	....	....	....	....	....	....
	Salt Lake Golden Eagles	IHL	10	6	4	0	600	34	1	3.40	....	....	....	....	....	....	....	....	....	....	....	....	....	....	....	....	....
1986-87	Calgary Flames	NHL	54	30	21	1	2957	178	1	3.61	3.03	4.21	1528	.884	31.0	5	2	3	....	263	16	0	3.65	4.29	136	.882	31.0
1987-88	Calgary Flames	NHL	64	39	16	7	3565	210	1	3.53	2.93	4.34	1708	.877	28.7	9	4	4	....	515	34	0	3.96	6.41	210	.838	24.5
1988-89	Calgary Flames	NHL	52	*37	6	5	2938	130	0	2.65	2.17	2.73	1263	.897	25.8	*22	*16	5	....	*1381	52	*3	2.26	2.14	550	.905	23.9
1989-90	Calgary Flames	FrTour	3	....	....	....	129	3	....	1.39	....	....	....	....	....	....	....	....	....	....	....	....	....	....	....	....	....
	Calgary Flames	NHL	47	23	14	9	2795	146	0	3.13	2.61	4.07	1122	.870	24.1	6	2	3	....	342	19	0	3.33	4.22	150	.873	26.3
1990-91	Calgary Flames	NHL	54	31	19	3	3121	172	1	3.31	2.95	4.05	1406	.878	27.0	7	3	4	....	427	21	0	2.95	3.04	204	.897	28.7
	Canada	WEC-A	2	0	1	0	73	6	0	4.93	....	....	....	....	....	....	....	....	....	....	....	....	....	....	....	....	....
1991-92	Calgary Flames	NHL	63	24	30	9	3640	217	0	3.58	3.18	4.19	1853	.883	30.5	....	....	....	....	....	....	....	....	....	....	....	....
1992-93	Calgary Flames	NHL	64	29	26	9	3732	203	2	3.26	2.77	3.67	1804	.887	29.0	4	1	1	....	150	15	0	6.00	11.11	81	.815	32.4
1993-94	Calgary Flames	NHL	48	26	17	5	2798	131	3	2.81	2.67	3.04	1209	.892	25.9	7	3	4	....	466	23	0	2.96	3.09	220	.895	28.3
1994-95	Detroit Red Wings	NHL	30	19	6	4	1807	76	1	2.52	2.59	2.70	710	.893	23.6	18	12	6	....	1063	41	1	2.31	2.56	370	.889	20.9
1995-96	Detroit Red Wings	NHL	32	21	7	2	1855	70	3	2.26	2.21	2.19	723	.903	23.4	4	2	2	....	243	11	0	2.72	3.69	81	.864	20.0
1996-97	Detroit Red Wings	NHL	33	13	11	8	1952	79	0	2.43	2.57	2.45	782	.899	24.0	*20	*16	4	....	*1229	36	1	1.76	1.28	494	.927	24.1
1997-98	San Jose Sharks	NHL	62	30	22	8	3564	146	5	2.46	2.87	2.56	1401	.896	23.6	6	2	4	....	348	14	1	2.41	2.44	138	.899	23.8
	NHL Totals		624	331	201	73	35756	1825	18	3.06	....	....	15978	.886	....	129	76	49	....	7656	342	6	2.68	....	....	....	....

WHL First All-Star Team (1982, 1983) • Won Hap Emms Memorial Trophy (Memorial Cup Tournament Top Goaltender) (1983) • CHL Second All-Star Team (1984) • NHL Second All-Star Team (1989) • Shared William M. Jennings Trophy with Chris Osgood (1996) • Won Conn Smythe Trophy (1997)

Played in NHL All-Star Game (1988, 1989, 1990, 1991, 1993)

Traded to **Detroit** by **Calgary** for Steve Chiasson, June 29, 1994. Traded to **San Jose** by **Detroit** with Detroit's 5th round choice in 1999 Entry Draft for San Jose's 2nd round choice (later traded to St. Louis - St. Louis selected Maxim Linnik) in 1998 Entry Draft and San Jose's 2nd round choice in 1999 Entry Draft, August 18, 1997.

• VEZINA, GEORGES

Georges "Chicoutimi Cucumber" Vezina G – L. 5'6", 185 lbs. b: Chicoutimi, Que., 1/21/1887. d: 3/27/1926. HHOF

Season	Club	League	GP	W	L	T	Mins	GA	SO	Avg	AAvg	Eff	SA	S%	SAPG	GP	W	L	T	Mins	GA	SO	Avg	Eff	SA	S%	SAPG
1909-10	Chicoutimi Sagueneens	Mtl-Sr.	STATISTICS NOT AVAILABLE																								
1910-11	Montreal Canadiens	NHA	16	8	8	0	980	62	0	3.80	....	....	....	....	....	....	....	....	....	....	....	....	....	....	....	....	....
1911-12	Montreal Canadiens	NHA	18	8	10	0	1109	66	0	3.57	....	....	....	....	....	....	....	....	....	....	....	....	....	....	....	....	....
1912-13	Montreal Canadiens	NHA	20	11	9	0	1217	81	1	3.99	....	....	....	....	....	....	....	....	....	....	....	....	....	....	....	....	....
1913-14	Montreal Canadiens	NHA	20	*13	7	0	1222	64	*1	*3.14	....	....	....	....	....	2	1	1	0	120	6	1	3.00	....	....	....	....
1914-15	Montreal Canadiens	NHA	20	6	14	0	1257	81	0	3.86	....	....	....	....	....	....	....	....	....	....	....	....	....	....	....	....	....
1915-16	Montreal Canadiens	NHA	24	*16	7	1	1482	76	0	3.08	....	....	....	....	....	5	*3	2	0	300	13	0	2.60	....	....	....	....
1916-17	Montreal Canadiens	NHA	20	10	10	0	1217	80	0	3.94	....	....	....	....	....	6	2	4	0	240	29	0	4.80	....	....	....	....
1917-18	Montreal Canadiens	NHL	21	*12	9	0	1282	84	*1	*3.93	2.39	....	....	....	....	2	1	1	0	120	10	0	5.00	....	....	....	....
1918-19	Montreal Canadiens	NHL	*18	10	8	0	1117	78	1	4.19	3.13	....	....	....	....	*10	*6	3	1	*636	37	*1	*3.49	....	....	....	....
1919-20	Montreal Canadiens	NHL	*24	13	11	0	*1456	113	0	4.66	3.02	....	....	....	....	....	....	....	....	....	....	....	....	....	....	....	....
1920-21	Montreal Canadiens	NHL	*24	13	11	0	1436	99	1	4.14	3.00	....	....	....	....	....	....	....	....	....	....	....	....	....	....	....	....
1921-22	Montreal Canadiens	NHL	*24	12	11	1	1468	94	0	3.84	2.96	....	....	....	....	....	....	....	....	....	....	....	....	....	....	....	....
1922-23	Montreal Canadiens	NHL	*24	13	9	2	1488	61	2	2.46	2.15	....	....	....	....	2	1	1	0	120	3	0	1.50	....	....	....	....

			REGULAR SEASON													PLAYOFFS											
Season	Club	League	GP	W	L	T	Mins	GA	SO	Avg	AAvg	Eff	SA	S%	SAPG	GP	W	L	T	Mins	GA	SO	Avg	Eff	SA	S%	SAPG
1923-24	Montreal Canadiens	NHL	*24	13	11	0	1459	48	*3	*1.97	2.11	....	....	....	....	*6	*6	0	0	*360	6	*2	*1.00	....	....	....	....
1924-25	Montreal Canadiens	NHL	*30	17	11	2	*1860	56	5	*1.81	2.11	....	....	....	....	*6	*3	3	0	*360	18	*1	3.00	....	....	....	....
1925-26	Montreal Canadiens	NHL	1	0	0	0	20	0	0	0.00	0.00	....	....	....	....	....	....	....	....	....	....	....	....	....	....	....	....
	NHL Totals		190	103	81	5	11586	633	13	3.28	....	....	....	....	....	26	17	8	1	1596	74	4	2.78	....	....	....	....
	Other Major League Totals		138	72	65	1	8484	510	2	3.61	....	....	....	....	....	13	6	7	0	660	48	1	4.36	....	....	....	....

Rights retained by **Montreal Canadiens** after NHA folded, November 26, 1917. • Forced to retire because of tuberculosis after appearing in 325 consecutive regular-season games for Montreal Canadiens, November 28, 1925.

• VILLEMURE, GILLES

Gilles Villemure G – R. 5′8″, 185 lbs. b: Trois-Rivieres, Que., 5/30/1940.

Season	Club	League	GP	W	L	T	Mins	GA	SO	Avg	AAvg	Eff	SA	S%	SAPG	GP	W	L	T	Mins	GA	SO	Avg	Eff	SA	S%	SAPG
1958-59	Troy Bruins	IHL	3	1	2	0	180	18	0	6.00	....	....	....	....	....	....	....	....	....	....	....	....	....	....	....	....	....
1959-60	Guelph Biltmores	OHA	35	....	....	....	1980	128	1	3.66	....	....	....	....	....	5	....	....	....	300	19	*1	3.80	....	....	....	....
1960-61	New York Rovers	EHL	51	....	....	....	3060	223	1	4.37	....	....	....	....	....	....	....	....	....	....	....	....	....	....	....	....	....
1961-62	L. Island–J'town–Charlotte	EHL	67	....	....	....	4020	251	3	3.75	....	....	....	....	....	....	....	....	....	....	....	....	....	....	....	....	....
1962-63	Vancouver Canucks	WHL	*70	35	31	4	*4200	228	*5	3.26	....	....	....	....	....	7	3	4	0	429	27	1	3.78	....	....	....	....
1963-64	Baltimore Clippers	AHL	66	31	33	2	3960	192	3	2.91	....	....	....	....	....	....	....	....	....	....	....	....	....	....	....	....	....
	New York Rangers	NHL	5	0	2	3	300	18	0	3.60	4.02	....	....	....	....	....	....	....	....	....	....	....	....	....	....	....	....
1964-65	Vancouver Canucks	WHL	60	27	26	6	3676	212	2	3.46	....	....	....	....	....	5	1	4	0	309	17	0	3.30	....	....	....	....
1965-66	Vancouver Canucks	WHL	*69	*32	34	3	*4178	223	*5	3.20	....	....	....	....	....	7	3	4	0	420	27	0	3.86	....	....	....	....
1966-67	Baltimore Clippers	AHL	*70	34	27	9	4180	238	*4	3.42	....	....	....	....	....	9	4	5	0	569	39	0	4.11	....	....	....	....
1967-68	New York Rangers	NHL	4	1	2	0	200	8	1	2.40	2.66	....	....	....	....	....	....	....	....	....	....	....	....	....	....	....	....
	Buffalo Bisons	AHL	37	18	13	6	2160	89	3	*2.47	....	....	....	....	....	5	1	3	0	247	15	0	3.64	....	....	....	....
1968-69	New York Rangers	NHL	4	2	1	1	240	9	0	2.25	2.33	....	....	....	....	1	0	1	....	60	4	0	4.00	....	....	....	....
	Buffalo Bisons	AHL	62	36	12	14	3674	148	*6	*2.42	....	....	....	....	....	6	2	4	0	360	19	1	3.17	....	....	....	....
1969-70	Buffalo Bisons	AHL	*65	....	....	....	*3714	156	*8	*2.52	....	....	....	....	....	*14	*11	3	0	*875	31	*1	*2.13	....	....	....	....
1970-71	New York Rangers	NHL	34	22	8	4	2039	78	4	2.30	2.25	....	....	....	....	2	0	1	....	80	6	0	4.50	....	....	....	....
1971-72	New York Rangers	NHL	37	24	7	4	2129	74	3	2.09	2.08	....	....	....	....	6	4	2	....	360	14	0	2.33	....	....	....	....
1972-73	New York Rangers	NHL	34	20	12	2	2040	78	3	2.29	2.14	....	....	....	....	2	0	1	....	61	2	0	1.97	....	....	....	....
1973-74	New York Rangers	NHL	21	7	7	3	1054	62	0	3.53	3.41	....	....	....	....	1	0	0	....	1	0	0	0.00	....	....	....	....
1974-75	New York Rangers	NHL	45	22	14	6	2470	130	2	3.16	2.84	....	....	....	....	2	1	0	....	94	6	0	3.83	....	....	....	....
1975-76	Chicago Black Hawks	NHL	15	2	7	5	797	57	0	4.29	3.89	....	....	....	....	....	....	....	....	....	....	....	....	....	....	....	....
1976-77	Chicago Black Hawks	NHL	6	0	4	1	312	28	0	5.38	5.01	....	....	....	....	....	....	....	....	....	....	....	....	....	....	....	....
	NHL Totals		205	100	64	29	11581	542	13	2.81	....	....	....	....	....	14	5	5	....	656	32	0	2.93	....	....	....	....

WHL Second All-Star Team (1963) • Won WHL Rookie of the Year Award (1963) • WHL First All-Star Team (1966) • AHL Second All-Star Team (1967) • AHL First All-Star Team (1969, 1970) • Won Harry "Hap" Holmes Memorial Award (fewest goals against - AHL) (1969, 1970) • Won Les Cunningham Award (MVP - AHL) (1969, 1970) • Shared Vezina Trophy with Ed Giacomin (1971)

Played in NHL All-Star Game (1971, 1972, 1973)

Traded to **Chicago** by **NY Rangers** for Doug Jarrett, October 28, 1975.

• VOKOUN, TOMAS

Tomas Vokoun G – R. 5′11″, 208 lbs. b: Karlovy Vary, Czech., 7/2/1976. Montreal's 11th choice, 226th overall, in 1994 Entry Draft.

Season	Club	League	GP	W	L	T	Mins	GA	SO	Avg	AAvg	Eff	SA	S%	SAPG	GP	W	L	T	Mins	GA	SO	Avg	Eff	SA	S%	SAPG
1993-94	Poldi Kladno	Czech.	1	0	0	0	20	2	0	6.01	....	....	....	....	....	....	....	....	....	....	....	....	....	....	....	....	....
	Czech Republic	EJC-A	5	....	....	....	300	11	....	2.20	....	....	....	....	....	....	....	....	....	....	....	....	....	....	....	....	....
1994-95	Poldi Kladno	Czech.	26	....	....	....	1368	70	....	3.07	....	....	....	....	....	5	....	....	....	240	19	....	4.75	....	....	....	....
1995-96	Wheeling Thunderbirds	ECHL	35	20	10	2	1912	117	0	3.67	....	....	....	....	....	7	4	3	....	436	19	0	2.61	....	....	....	....
	Czech Republic	WJC-A	6	....	....	....	356	21	....	3.54	....	....	....	....	....	....	....	....	....	....	....	....	....	....	....	....	....
	Fredericton Canadiens	AHL	....	....	....	....	....	....	....	....	....	....	....	....	....	1	0	1	....	59	4	0	4.09	....	....	....	....
1996-97	Montreal Canadiens	NHL	1	0	0	0	20	4	0	12.00	12.71	34.29	14	.714	42.0	....	....	....	....	....	....	....	....	....	....	....	....
	Fredericton Canadiens	AHL	47	12	26	7	2645	154	2	3.49	....	....	....	....	....	....	....	....	....	....	....	....	....	....	....	....	....
1997-98	Fredericton Canadiens	AHL	31	13	13	2	1735	90	0	3.11	....	....	....	....	....	....	....	....	....	....	....	....	....	....	....	....	....
	NHL Totals		1	0	0	0	20	4	0	12.00	....	....	14	.714	....	....	....	....	....	....	....	....	....	....	....	....	....

EJC-A All-Star Team (1994) • Named Best Goaltender at EJC-A (1994)

Claimed by **Nashville** from **Montreal** in Expansion Draft, June 26, 1998.

• WAITE, JIMMY

Jimmy Waite G – L. 6′1″, 180 lbs. b: Sherbrooke, Que., 4/15/1969. Chicago's 1st choice, 8th overall, in 1987 Entry Draft.

Season	Club	League	GP	W	L	T	Mins	GA	SO	Avg	AAvg	Eff	SA	S%	SAPG	GP	W	L	T	Mins	GA	SO	Avg	Eff	SA	S%	SAPG
1986-87	Chicoutimi Sagueneens	QMJHL	50	23	17	3	2569	209	2	4.48	....	....	....	....	....	11	4	6	....	576	54	1	5.63	....	....	....	....
	Canada	WJC-A	4	....	....	....	220	12	....	3.27	....	....	....	....	....	....	....	....	....	....	....	....	....	....	....	....	....
1987-88	Chicoutimi Sagueneens	QMJHL	36	17	16	1	2000	150	0	4.50	....	....	....	....	....	4	1	2	....	222	17	0	4.59	....	....	....	....
	Canada	WJC-A	7	6	1	0	419	16	....	2.29	....	....	....	....	....	....	....	....	....	....	....	....	....	....	....	....	....
1988-89	Chicago Blackhawks	NHL	11	0	7	1	494	43	0	5.22	4.31	8.87	253	.830	30.7	....	....	....	....	....	....	....	....	....	....	....	....
	Saginaw Hawks	IHL	5	3	1	0	304	10	0	1.97	....	....	....	....	....	....	....	....	....	....	....	....	....	....	....	....	....
1989-90	Chicago Blackhawks	NHL	4	2	0	0	183	14	0	4.59	3.85	6.98	92	.848	30.2	....	....	....	....	....	....	....	....	....	....	....	....
	Indianapolis Ice	IHL	54	*34	14	5	*3207	135	*5	*2.53	....	....	....	....	....	*10	*9	1	....	*602	19	*1	*1.89	....	....	....	....
1990-91	Chicago Blackhawks	NHL	1	1	0	0	60	2	0	2.00	1.79	1.43	28	.929	28.0	....	....	....	....	....	....	....	....	....	....	....	....
	Indianapolis Ice	IHL	49	*26	18	4	2888	167	3	3.47	....	....	....	....	....	6	2	4	....	369	20	0	3.25	....	....	....	....
1991-92	Chicago Blackhawks	NHL	17	4	7	4	877	54	0	3.69	3.28	5.74	347	.844	23.7	....	....	....	....	....	....	....	....	....	....	....	....
	Indianapolis Ice	IHL	13	4	7	1	702	53	0	4.53	....	....	....	....	....	....	....	....	....	....	....	....	....	....	....	....	....
	Hershey Bears	AHL	11	6	4	1	631	44	0	4.18	....	....	....	....	....	6	2	4	....	360	19	0	3.17	....	....	....	....
1992-93	Chicago Blackhawks	NHL	20	6	7	1	996	49	2	2.95	2.51	3.52	411	.881	24.8	....	....	....	....	....	....	....	....	....	....	....	....
1993-94	San Jose Sharks	NHL	15	3	7	0	697	50	0	4.30	4.10	6.74	319	.843	27.5	2	0	0	....	40	3	0	4.50	7.94	17	.824	25.5
1994-95	Chicago Blackhawks	NHL	2	1	1	0	119	5	0	2.52	2.60	2.47	51	.902	25.7	....	....	....	....	....	....	....	....	....	....	....	....
	Indianapolis Ice	IHL	4	2	1	1	239	13	0	3.25	....	....	....	....	....	....	....	....	....	....	....	....	....	....	....	....	....
1995-96	Chicago Blackhawks	NHL	1	0	0	0	31	0	0	0.00	0.00	0.00	8	1.000	15.5	....	....	....	....	....	....	....	....	....	....	....	....
	Indianapolis Ice	IHL	56	28	18	6	3157	179	0	3.40	....	....	....	....	....	5	2	3	....	298	15	1	3.02	....	....	....	....
1996-97	Chicago Blackhawks	NHL	2	0	1	1	105	7	0	4.00	4.24	4.83	58	.879	33.1	....	....	....	....	....	....	....	....	....	....	....	....
	Indianapolis Ice	IHL	41	22	15	4	2450	112	4	2.74	....	....	....	....	....	4	1	3	....	222	13	0	3.51	....	....	....	....
1997-98	Phoenix Coyotes	NHL	17	5	6	1	793	28	1	2.12	2.48	1.84	322	.913	24.4	4	0	3	....	171	11	0	3.86	4.38	97	.887	34.0
	NHL Totals		90	22	36	8	4355	252	3	3.47	....	....	1889	.867	....	6	0	3	....	211	14	0	3.98	....	....	....	....

QMJHL Second All-Star Team (1987) • WJC-A All-Start Team (1988) • Named Best Goaltender at WJC-A (1988) • IHL First All-Star Team (1990) • Won James Norris Memorial Trophy (fewest goals against - IHL) (1990)

Traded to **San Jose** by **Chicago** for future considerations (Neil Wilkinson, July 9, 1993), June 19, 1993. Traded to **Chicago** by **San Jose** for Chicago's 4th round choice (later traded to NY Rangers — NY Rangers selected Tomi Kallarsson) in 1997 Entry Draft, February 5, 1995. Claimed by **Phoenix** from **Chicago** in NHL Waiver Draft, September 28, 1997.

• WAKALUK, DARCY

Darcy Wakaluk G – L. 5′11″, 180 lbs. b: Pincher Creek, Alta., 3/14/1966. Buffalo's 7th choice, 144th overall, in 1984 Entry Draft.

Season	Club	League	GP	W	L	T	Mins	GA	SO	Avg	AAvg	Eff	SA	S%	SAPG	GP	W	L	T	Mins	GA	SO	Avg	Eff	SA	S%	SAPG
1983-84	Kelowna Wings	WHL	31	2	22	0	1555	163	0	6.29	....	....	....	....	....	....	....	....	....	....	....	....	....	....	....	....	....
1984-85	Kelowna Wings	WHL	54	19	30	4	3094	244	0	4.73	....	....	....	....	....	5	1	4	....	282	22	0	4.68	....	....	....	....
1985-86	Spokane Chiefs	WHL	47	21	22	1	2562	224	1	5.25	....	....	....	....	....	7	3	4	....	419	37	0	5.30	....	....	....	....
1986-87	Rochester Americans	AHL	11	2	2	0	545	26	0	2.86	....	....	....	....	....	5	2	0	....	141	11	0	4.68	....	....	....	....
1987-88	Rochester Americans	AHL	55	27	16	3	2763	159	0	3.45	....	....	....	....	....	6	3	3	....	328	22	0	4.02	....	....	....	....
1988-89	Buffalo Sabres	NHL	6	1	3	0	214	15	0	4.21	3.47	7.02	90	.833	25.2	....	....	....	....	....	....	....	....	....	....	....	....
	Rochester Americans	AHL	33	11	14	0	1566	97	1	3.72	....	....	....	....	....	....	....	....	....	....	....	....	....	....	....	....	....
1989-90	Rochester Americans	AHL	56	31	16	4	3095	173	2	3.35	....	....	....	....	....	*17	*10	6	....	*1001	50	0	*3.01	....	....	....	....
1990-91	Buffalo Sabres	NHL	16	4	5	3	630	35	0	3.33	2.97	3.99	292	.880	27.8	2	0	1	....	37	2	0	3.24	2.95	22	.909	35.7
	Rochester Americans	AHL	26	10	10	3	1363	68	4	*2.99	....	....	....	....	....	9	6	3	....	544	30	0	3.31	....	....	....	....
1991-92	Minnesota North Stars	NHL	36	13	19	1	1905	104	1	3.28	2.91	3.90	874	.881	27.5	....	....	....	....	....	....	....	....	....	....	....	....
	Kalamazoo Wings	IHL	1	1	0	0	60	7	0	7.00	....	....	....	....	....	....	....	....	....	....	....	....	....	....	....	....	....
1992-93	Minnesota Stars	NHL	29	10	12	5	1596	97	1	3.65	3.11	4.41	803	.879	30.2	....	....	....	....	....	....	....	....	....	....	....	....
1993-94	Dallas Stars	NHL	36	18	9	6	2000	88	3	2.64	2.51	2.38	978	.910	29.3	5	4	1	....	307	15	0	2.93	2.62	168	.911	32.8

Season	Club	League	GP	W	L	T	Mins	GA	SO	Avg	AAvg	Eff	SA	S%	SAPG	GP	W	L	T	Mins	GA	SO	Avg	Eff	SA	S%	SAPG
			REGULAR SEASON													PLAYOFFS											
1994-95	**Dallas Stars**	**NHL**	15	4	8	0	754	40	2	3.18	3.29	3.73	341	.883	27.1	1	0	0	....	20	1	0	3.00	3.33	9	.889	27.0
1995-96	**Dallas Stars**	**NHL**	37	9	16	5	1875	106	1	3.39	3.33	3.69	975	.891	31.2	....	....	....	....	....	....	....	....	....	....	....	....
1996-97	**Phoenix Coyotes**	**NHL**	16	8	3	1	782	39	1	2.99	3.17	3.02	386	.899	29.6	....	....	....	....	....	....	....	....	....	....	....	....
	NHL Totals		191	67	75	21	9756	524	9	3.22	....	....	4739	.889	....	8	4	2	....	364	18	0	2.97	....	....	....	....

Shared Harry "Hap" Holmes Memorial Trophy (fewest goals against - AHL) with David Littman (1991)

• Scored a goal while with Rochester (AHL), December 6, 1987.

Traded to **Minnesota** by **Buffalo** for Minnesota's 8th round choice (Jiri Kuntos) in 1991 Entry Draft and Minnesota's 5th round choice (later traded to Toronto — Toronto selected Chris Deruiter) in 1992 Entry Draft, May 26, 1991. Transferred to **Dallas** after **Minnesota** franchise relocated, June 9, 1993. Signed as a free agent by **Phoenix**, July 23, 1996.

• WAKELY, ERNIE

Ernie Wakely G – L. 5'11", 160 lbs. b: Flin Flon, Man., 11/27/1940.

Season	Club	League	GP	W	L	T	Mins	GA	SO	Avg	AAvg	Eff	SA	S%	SAPG	GP	W	L	T	Mins	GA	SO	Avg	Eff	SA	S%	SAPG
1957-58	Winnipeg Braves	MJHL	27	12	14	1	1640	121	*1	4.48	....	....	....	....	....	5	2	3	0	300	20	0	4.00	....	....	....	....
1958-59	Winnpeg Braves	MJHL	30	*22	7	1	1810	107	1	3.54	....	....	....	....	....	24	19	5	0	1410	67	2	2.85	....	....	....	....
1959-60	Winnipeg Braves	MJHL	STATISTICS NOT AVAILABLE																								
	Winnipeg Warriors	WHL	4	1	3	0	240	16	0	4.00	....	....	....	....	....	....	....	....	....	....	....	....	....	....	....	....	....
1960-61	Winnipeg Braves	MJHL	31	18	13	0	1860	111	*2	*3.57	....	....	....	....	....	3	0	3	0	210	14	0	4.00	....	....	....	....
	Winnipeg Warriors	WHL	9	4	5	0	540	43	0	4.77	....	....	....	....	....	....	....	....	....	....	....	....	....	....	....	....	....
1961-62	Hull-Ottawa Canadiens	EPHL	2	1	0	1	120	4	0	2.00	....	....	....	....	....	....	....	....	....	....	....	....	....	....	....	....	....
	Kingston Frontenacs	EPHL	3	2	1	0	180	10	0	3.33	....	....	....	....	....	....	....	....	....	....	....	....	....	....	....	....	....
	North Bay Trappers	EPHL	6	1	4	1	360	18	0	3.00	....	....	....	....	....	....	....	....	....	....	....	....	....	....	....	....	....
1962-63	**Montreal Canadiens**	**NHL**	1	1	0	0	60	3	0	3.00	3.11	....	....	....	....	....	....	....	....	....	....	....	....	....	....	....	....
	Hull-Ottawa Canadiens	EPHL	41	26	12	3	2460	122	*2	*2.97	....	....	....	....	....	....	....	....	....	....	....	....	....	....	....	....	....
	Spokane Comets	WHL	3	1	2	0	180	16	0	5.33	....	....	....	....	....	....	....	....	....	....	....	....	....	....	....	....	....
1963-64	Quebec Aces	AHL	8	3	5	0	480	33	0	4.12	....	....	....	....	....	....	....	....	....	....	....	....	....	....	....	....	....
	Omaha Knights	CHL	59	*38	16	5	3540	173	2	*2.93	....	....	....	....	....	10	*8	2	0	600	19	*3	*1.90	....	....	....	....
1964-65	Omaha Knights	CHL	15	11	3	1	900	40	0	2.67	....	....	....	....	....	....	....	....	....	....	....	....	....	....	....	....	....
	Cleveland Barons	AHL	10	2	8	0	600	49	0	4.90	....	....	....	....	....	....	....	....	....	....	....	....	....	....	....	....	....
	Quebec Aces	AHL	20	9	10	1	1228	77	1	3.76	....	....	....	....	....	4	1	3	0	240	17	0	4.25	....	....	....	....
1965-66	Cleveland Barons	AHL	1	0	0	0	20	1	0	3.00	....	....	....	....	....	....	....	....	....	....	....	....	....	....	....	....	....
	Quebec Aces	AHL	1	0	1	0	60	6	0	6.00	....	....	....	....	....	....	....	....	....	....	....	....	....	....	....	....	....
	Seattle Totems	WHL	27	12	14	1	1617	83	2	3.08	....	....	....	....	....	....	....	....	....	....	....	....	....	....	....	....	....
1966-67	Cleveland Barons	AHL	*70	*36	25	9	*4187	216	0	3.10	....	....	....	....	....	5	2	3	0	301	10	0	1.99	....	....	....	....
1967-68	Houston Apollos	CHL	*57	24	21	10	*3312	163	1	2.95	....	....	....	....	....	....	....	....	....	....	....	....	....	....	....	....	....
1968-69	**Montreal Canadiens**	**NHL**	1	0	1	0	60	4	0	4.00	4.14	....	....	....	....	....	....	....	....	....	....	....	....	....	....	....	....
	Cleveland Barons	AHL	*65	25	28	11	*3852	210	1	3.27	....	....	....	....	....	5	2	3	0	304	20	0	3.95	....	....	....	....
1969-70	**St. Louis Blues**	**NHL**	30	12	9	4	1651	58	4	*2.11	2.22	....	....	....	....	4	0	4	....	216	17	0	4.72	....	....	....	....
1970-71	**St. Louis Blues**	**NHL**	51	20	14	11	2859	133	3	2.79	2.75	....	....	....	....	3	2	1	....	180	7	1	2.33	....	....	....	....
1971-72	**St. Louis Blues**	**NHL**	30	8	18	2	1614	92	1	3.42	3.45	....	....	....	....	3	0	1	....	113	13	0	6.90	....	....	....	....
1972-73	Winnipeg Jets	WHA	49	26	19	3	2889	152	2	3.16	....	....	....	....	....	7	4	3	0	420	22	*2	3.14	....	....	....	....
1973-74	Winnipeg Jets	WHA	37	15	18	4	2254	123	3	3.27	....	....	....	....	....	....	....	....	....	....	....	....	....	....	....	....	....
1974-75	Winnipeg Jets	WHA	6	3	3	0	355	16	1	2.70	....	....	....	....	....	....	....	....	....	....	....	....	....	....	....	....	....
	San Diego Mariners	WHA	35	20	12	2	2062	115	2	3.35	....	....	....	....	....	10	4	6	0	520	39	0	4.50	....	....	....	....
1975-76	San Diego Mariners	WHA	67	35	27	4	3824	208	3	3.26	....	....	....	....	....	11	5	6	0	640	39	0	3.66	....	....	....	....
1976-77	San Diego Mariners	WHA	46	22	18	3	2506	129	3	3.09	....	....	....	....	....	3	2	1	0	160	9	0	3.38	....	....	....	....
1977-78	Cincinnati Stingers	WHA	6	0	5	0	*311	26	0	5.02	....	....	....	....	....	....	....	....	....	....	....	....	....	....	....	....	....
	Houston Aeros	WHA	51	28	18	4	*3070	166	2	3.24	....	....	....	....	....	....	....	....	....	....	....	....	....	....	....	....	....
1978-79	Birmingham Bulls	WHA	37	15	17	1	2060	129	0	3.76	....	....	....	....	....	....	....	....	....	....	....	....	....	....	....	....	....
	Phoenix Roadrunners	PHL	1	....	....	....	60	4	0	4.00	....	....	....	....	....	....	....	....	....	....	....	....	....	....	....	....	....
	NHL Totals		113	41	42	17	6244	290	8	2.79	....	....	....	....	....	10	2	6	....	509	37	1	4.36	....	....	....	....
	Other Major League Totals		334	164	137	21	19331	1064	16	3.30	....	....	....	....	....	31	15	16	0	1740	109	2	3.76	....	....	....	....

Won Terry Sawchuk Trophy (fewest goals against - CHL) (1964) • CHL Second All-Star Team (1968) • AHL Second All-Star Team (1969) • WHA Second All-Star Team (1978)

Played in NHL All-Star Game (1971)

Traded to **St. Louis** by **Montreal** for Norm Beaudin and Bob Schmautz, June 27, 1969. Selected by **Winnipeg** (WHA) in 1972 WHA General Player Draft, February 12, 1972. Traded to **San Diego** (WHA) by **Winnipeg** (WHA) for cash and future considerations, January, 1975. Claimed by **Cincinnati** (WHA) from **San Diego** in WHA Dispersal Auction, August, 1977. Traded to **Houston** (WHA) by **Cincinnati** (WHA) for future considerations, November, 1977. Signed as a free agent by **Birmingham** (WHA) after **Houston** (WHA) franchise folded, July 6, 1978

• WALSH, JAMES

James "Flat" Walsh G – L. 5'11", 180 lbs. b: Kingston, Ont., 3/23/1897. d: 1959.

Season	Club	League	GP	W	L	T	Mins	GA	SO	Avg	AAvg	Eff	SA	S%	SAPG	GP	W	L	T	Mins	GA	SO	Avg	Eff	SA	S%	SAPG
1914-15	Kingston Collegiate Inst.	OHA	4	3	1	0	260	14	0	3.23	....	....	....	....	....	3	1	1	1	180	13	0	4.33	....	....	....	....
1915-16	Kingston Frontenacs	OHA	1	0	1	0	60	7	0	7.00	....	....	....	....	....	....	....	....	....	....	....	....	....	....	....	....	....
	Kingston Frontenacs	OHA Sr.	STATISTICS NOT AVAILABLE																								
1916-17	Kingston Hockey Club	OHA	3	3	0	0	180	8	0	2.67	....	....	....	....	....	4	3	1	0	240	14	0	3.50	....	....	....	....
1917-18	Kingston Hockey Club	Inter-Sr.	STATISTICS NOT AVAILABLE																								
1918-19	Kingston Hockey Club	Inter-Sr.	4	3	1	0	240	11	1	2.75	....	....	....	....	....	8	4	4	0	480	26	0	3.25	....	....	....	....
1919-20	Canadian Soo Greyhounds	NOHA	5	1	3	1	330	23	0	4.18	....	....	....	....	....	....	....	....	....	....	....	....	....	....	....	....	....
	Canadian Soo Greyhounds	NMHL	14	9	3	2	930	26	2	1.68	....	....	....	....	....	....	....	....	....	....	....	....	....	....	....	....	....
1920-21	Canadian Soo Greyhounds	NOHA	9	7	1	1	570	14	*4	*1.47	....	....	....	....	....	5	3	2	0	300	24	0	4.80	....	....	....	....
	Canadian Soo Greyhounds	NMHL	16	13	3	0	970	26	6	1.61	....	....	....	....	....	....	....	....	....	....	....	....	....	....	....	....	....
1921-22	Canadian Soo Greyhounds	NOHA	8	*7	1	0	500	18	*1	*2.16	....	....	....	....	....	2	0	1	1	120	7	0	3.50	....	....	....	....
	Canadian Soo Greyhounds	NMHL	12	*11	1	0	720	16	1	*1.33	....	....	....	....	....	....	....	....	....	....	....	....	....	....	....	....	....
1922-23	Canadian Soo Greyhounds	NOHA	8	4	4	0	476	22	0	*2.77	....	....	....	....	....	7	5	1	1	420	21	0	3.00	....	....	....	....
1923-24	Canadian Soo Greyhounds	NOHA	7	*6	1	0	400	19	0	*2.85	....	....	....	....	....	7	5	2	0	420	11	2	1.57	....	....	....	....
1924-25	Canadian Soo Greyhounds	NOHA	STATISTICS NOT AVAILABLE																								
1925-26	Canadian Soo Greyhounds	USAHA	32	....			1920	100	1	3.13	....	....	....	....	....	....	....	....	....	....	....	....	....	....	....	....	....
1926-27	Detroit Greyhounds	AHA	6	0	6	0	360	23	0	3.83	....	....	....	....	....	....	....	....	....	....	....	....	....	....	....	....	....
	Montreal Maroons	**NHL**	1	0	1	0	60	3	0	3.00	4.64	....	....	....	....	....	....	....	....	....	....	....	....	....	....	....	....
1927-28	**Montreal Maroons**	**NHL**	1	0	0	0	40	1	0	1.50	2.44	....	....	....	....	....	....	....	....	....	....	....	....	....	....	....	....
1928-29	**New York Americans**	**NHL**	4	2	0	2	260	1	3	0.23	0.48	....	....	....	....	....	....	....	....	....	....	....	....	....	....	....	....
	Montreal Maroons	**NHL**	7	1	4	2	450	8	1	1.07	2.26	....	....	....	....	....	....	....	....	....	....	....	....	....	....	....	....
1929-30	**Montreal Maroons**	**NHL**	30	16	10	4	1898	74	2	2.34	2.41	....	....	....	....	4	1	3	0	312	11	1	2.12	....	....	....	....
1930-31	**Montreal Maroons**	**NHL**	16	7	7	2	961	36	2	2.25	2.90	....	....	....	....	....	....	....	....	....	....	....	....	....	....	....	....
1931-32	**Montreal Maroons**	**NHL**	27	14	10	3	1670	77	2	2.77	3.43	....	....	....	....	4	1	1	2	258	5	*1	*1.16	....	....	....	....
	New Haven Eagles	Can-Am	18	7	9	2	1110	27	*6	1.46	....	....	....	....	....	....	....	....	....	....	....	....	....	....	....	....	....
1932-33	**Montreal Maroons**	**NHL**	22	8	11	3	1303	56	2	2.58	3.52	....	....	....	....	....	....	....	....	....	....	....	....	....	....	....	....
	Quebec Castors	Can-Am	3	2	1	0	180	3	2	1.00	....	....	....	....	....	....	....	....	....	....	....	....	....	....	....	....	....
	NHL Totals		108	48	43	16	6642	256	12	2.31	....	....	....	....	....	8	2	4	2	570	16	2	1.68	....	....	....	....

Signed as a free agent by **Detroit** (AHA), June 23, 1926. Signed as a free agent by **Montreal Maroons** after **Detroit** (AHA) franchise folded, December, 1926. Loaned to **NY Americans** by **Montreal Maroons** until NHL and club resolved the status of Roy Worters' contract, November 15, 1928.

• WAMSLEY, RICK

Rick Wamsley G – L. 5'11", 185 lbs. b: Simcoe, Ont., 5/25/1959. Montreal's 5th choice, 58th overall, in 1979 Entry Draft.

Season	Club	League	GP	W	L	T	Mins	GA	SO	Avg	AAvg	Eff	SA	S%	SAPG	GP	W	L	T	Mins	GA	SO	Avg	Eff	SA	S%	SAPG
1976-77	St. Catharines Fincups	OHA	12	....	....	....	647	36	0	3.34	....	....	....	....	....	....	....	....	....	....	....	....	....	....	....	....	....
1977-78	Hamilton Fincups	OHA	25	....	....	....	1495	74	2	*2.97	....	....	....	....	....	....	....	....	....	....	....	....	....	....	....	....	....
1978-79	Brantford Alexanders	OHA	24	....	....	....	1444	128	0	5.32	....	....	....	....	....	....	....	....	....	....	....	....	....	....	....	....	....
1979-80	Nova Scotia Voyageurs	AHL	40	19	16	2	2305	125	2	3.25	....	....	....	....	....	3	1	1	0	143	12	0	5.03	....	....	....	....
1980-81	**Montreal Canadiens**	**NHL**	5	3	0	1	253	8	1	1.90	1.52	....	....	....	....	....	....	....	....	....	....	....	....	....	....	....	....
	Nova Scotia Voyageurs	AHL	43	17	19	3	2372	155	0	3.92	....	....	....	....	....	4	2	1	0	199	6	*1	1.81	....	....	....	....
1981-82	**Montreal Canadiens**	**NHL**	38	23	7	7	2206	101	2	2.75	2.10	....	....	....	....	5	2	3	....	300	11	0	*2.20	....	....	....	....
1982-83	**Montreal Canadiens**	**NHL**	46	27	12	5	2583	151	0	3.51	2.80	4.27	1240	.878	28.8	3	0	3	....	152	7	0	2.76	....	....	....	....
	Canada	WEC-A	10	....	....	....	600	30	....	3.00	....	....	....	....	....	....	....	....	....	....	....	....	....	....	....	....	....
1983-84	**Montreal Canadiens**	**NHL**	42	19	17	3	2333	144	2	3.70	2.89	5.45	977	.853	25.1	1	0	0	....	32	0	0	0.00	0.00	12	1.000	22.5
1984-85	**St. Louis Blues**	**NHL**	40	23	12	5	2319	126	0	3.26	2.58	3.75	1094	.885	28.3	2	0	2	....	120	7	0	3.50	4.38	56	.875	28.0
	Canada	WEC-A	2	....	....	....	120	11	0	5.50	....	....	....	....	....	....	....	....	....	....	....	....	....	....	....	....	....
1985-86	**St. Louis Blues**	**NHL**	42	22	16	3	2517	144	1	3.43	2.66	3.65	1354	.894	32.3	10	4	6	....	569	37	0	3.90	4.70	307	.879	32.4

			REGULAR SEASON													PLAYOFFS											
Season	Club	League	GP	W	L	T	Mins	GA	SO	Avg	AAvg	Eff	SA	S%	SAPG	GP	W	L	T	Mins	GA	SO	Avg	Eff	SA	S%	SAPG
1986-87	St. Louis Blues	NHL	41	17	15	6	2410	142	0	3.54	2.97	4.15	1212	.883	30.2	2	1	1	....	120	5	0	2.50	2.31	54	.907	27.0
1987-88	St. Louis Blues	NHL	31	13	16	1	1818	103	2	3.40	2.82	3.80	922	.888	30.4	....	....	....	....	....	....	....	....	....	....	....	....
	Calgary Flames	NHL	2	1	0	0	73	5	0	4.11	3.42	5.71	36	.861	29.6	1	0	1	....	33	2	0	3.64	9.10	8	.750	14.5
1988-89	Calgary Flames	NHL	35	17	11	4	1927	95	2	2.96	2.43	3.53	796	.881	24.8	1	0	1	....	20	2	0	6.00	12.00	10	.800	30.0
1989-90	Calgary Flames	FrTour	3	....	....	....	92	5	0	3.26	....	....	....	....	....	....	....	....	....	....	....	....	....	....	....	....	....
	Calgary Flames	NHL	36	18	8	6	1969	107	2	3.26	2.72	4.08	855	.875	26.1	1	0	1	....	49	9	0	11.02	43.12	23	.609	28.2
1990-91	Calgary Flames	NHL	29	14	7	5	1670	85	0	3.05	2.72	3.40	762	.888	27.4	1	0	0	....	2	1	0	30.00	150.00	2	.500	60.0
1991-92	Calgary Flames	NHL	9	3	4	0	457	34	0	4.46	3.96	6.71	226	.850	29.7	....	....	....	....	....	....	....	....	....	....	....	....
	Toronto Maple Leafs	NHL	8	4	3	0	428	27	0	3.79	3.36	4.69	218	.876	30.6	....	....	....	....	....	....	....	....	....	....	....	....
1992-93	Toronto Maple Leafs	NHL	3	0	3	0	160	15	0	5.63	4.79	9.28	91	.835	34.1	....	....	....	....	....	....	....	....	....	....	....	....
	St. John's Maple Leafs	AHL	2	0	1	0	112	8	0	4.29	....	....	....	....	....	....	....	....	....	....	....	....	....	....	....	....	....
	NHL Totals		407	204	131	46	23123	1287	12	3.34	....	....	....	....	....	27	7	18	....	1397	81	0	3.48	....	....	....	....

Shared William M. Jennings Trophy with Denis Herron (1982)

Traded to **St. Louis** by **Montreal** with Hartford's 2nd round choice (previously acquired, St. Louis selected Brian Benning) in 1984 Entry Draft, Montreal's 2nd (Tony Hrkac) and 3rd (Robert Dirk) round choices in 1984 Entry Draft for St. Louis' 1st (Shayne Corson) and 2nd (Stephane Richer) round choices in 1984 Entry Draft, June 9, 1984. Traded to **Calgary** by **St. Louis** with Rob Ramage for Brett Hull and Steve Bozek, March 7, 1988. Traded to **Toronto** by **Calgary** with Doug Gilmour, Jamie Macoun, Kent Manderville and Ric Nattress for Gary Leeman, Alexander Godynyuk, Jeff Reese, Michel Petit and Craig Berube, January 2, 1992.

• WATT, JIM

Jim Watt G – L. 5'11", 180 lbs. b: Duluth, MN, 5/11/1950.

Season	Club	League	GP	W	L	T	Mins	GA	SO	Avg	AAvg	Eff	SA	S%	SAPG	GP	W	L	T	Mins	GA	SO	Avg	Eff	SA	S%	SAPG
1969-70	Michigan State Spartans	WCHA	1	0	0	0	42	4	0	5.70	....	....	....	....	....	....	....	....	....	....	....	....	....	....	....	....	....
1970-71	Michigan State Spartans	WCHA	25	....	....	....	1480	101	0	4.09	....	....	....	....	....	....	....	....	....	....	....	....	....	....	....	....	....
1971-72	Michigan State Spartans	WCHA	36	20	16	0	2160	128	0	3.56	....	....	....	....	....	....	....	....	....	....	....	....	....	....	....	....	....
1972-73	Denver Spurs	WHL	15	4	8	0	791	53	0	4.02	....	....	....	....	....	....	....	....	....	....	....	....	....	....	....	....	....
	Fort Worth Wings	CHL	7	....	....	....	335	26	0	4.65	....	....	....	....	....	....	....	....	....	....	....	....	....	....	....	....	....
1973-74	St. Louis Blues	NHL	1	0	0	0	20	2	0	6.00	5.79	....	....	....	....	....	....	....	....	....	....	....	....	....	....	....	....
	Denver Spurs	WHL	31	14	15	0	1827	112	0	3.68	....	....	....	....	....	....	....	....	....	....	....	....	....	....	....	....	....
1974-75	Denver Spurs	CHL	30	10	10	9	1738	100	0	3.45	....	....	....	....	....	....	....	....	....	....	....	....	....	....	....	....	....
1975-76	Tidewater Sharks	SHL	55	19	23	11	3147	172	1	3.28	....	....	....	....	....	....	....	....	....	....	....	....	....	....	....	....	....
	Kalamazoo Wings	IHL	8	....	....	....	420	25	0	3.57	....	....	....	....	....	6	2	4	0	381	18	1	2.83	....	....	....	....
1976-77	Winston-Salem Polar Bears	SHL	3	....	....	....	149	16	0	6.44	....	....	....	....	....	....	....	....	....	....	....	....	....	....	....	....	....
	NHL Totals		1	0	0	0	20	2	0	6.00	....	....	....	....	....	....	....	....	....	....	....	....	....	....	....	....	....

WCHA First All-Star Team (1972) • NCAA West First All-American Team (1972)

Signed as a free agent by **St. Louis** (Fort Worth-CHL), October 1, 1972.

• WEEKES, KEVIN

Kevin Weekes G – L. 6', 158 lbs. b: Toronto, Ont., 4/4/1975. Florida's 2nd choice, 41st overall, in 1993 Entry Draft.

Season	Club	League	GP	W	L	T	Mins	GA	SO	Avg	AAvg	Eff	SA	S%	SAPG	GP	W	L	T	Mins	GA	SO	Avg	Eff	SA	S%	SAPG
1992-93	Owen Sound Platers	OHL	29	9	12	5	1645	143	0	5.22	....	....	....	....	....	1	0	0	....	26	5	0	11.50	....	....	....	....
1993-94	Owen Sound Platers	OHL	34	13	19	1	1974	158	0	4.80	....	....	....	....	....	....	....	....	....	....	....	....	....	....	....	....	....
1994-95	Ottawa 67's	OHL	41	13	23	4	2266	153	1	4.05	....	....	....	....	....	....	....	....	....	....	....	....	....	....	....	....	....
1995-96	Carolina Monarchs	AHL	60	24	25	8	3404	229	2	4.04	....	....	....	....	....	....	....	....	....	....	....	....	....	....	....	....	....
1996-97	Carolina Monarchs	AHL	51	17	28	4	2899	172	1	3.56	....	....	....	....	....	....	....	....	....	....	....	....	....	....	....	....	....
1997-98	Florida Panthers	NHL	11	0	5	1	485	32	0	3.96	4.64	5.13	247	.870	30.6	....	....	....	....	....	....	....	....	....	....	....	....
	Fort Wayne Komets	IHL	12	9	2	1	719	34	1	2.84	....	....	....	....	....	....	....	....	....	....	....	....	....	....	....	....	....
	NHL Totals		11	0	5	1	485	32	0	3.96	....	....	247	.870	....	....	....	....	....	....	....	....	....	....	....	....	....

• WEEKS, STEVE

Steve Weeks G – L. 5'11", 170 lbs. b: Scarborough, Ont., 6/30/1958. NY Rangers' 12th choice, 176th overall, in 1978 Amateur Draft.

Season	Club	League	GP	W	L	T	Mins	GA	SO	Avg	AAvg	Eff	SA	S%	SAPG	GP	W	L	T	Mins	GA	SO	Avg	Eff	SA	S%	SAPG
1976-77	Northern Michigan University	CCHA	16	7	7	0	811	58	0	4.29	....	....	....	....	....	1	0	1	0	60	6	0	6.00	....	....	....	....
1977-78	Northern Michigan University	CCHA	19	10	5	2	1015	56	1	3.31	....	....	....	....	....	....	....	....	....	....	....	....	....	....	....	....	....
1978-79	Northern Michigan University	CCHA	25	13	8	2	1437	82	0	3.42	....	....	....	....	....	2	0	1	0	151	10	0	3.97	....	....	....	....
1979-80	Northern Michigan University	CCHA	36	29	6	1	2133	105	1	*2.95	....	....	....	....	....	6	4	1	0	330	18	0	3.27	....	....	....	....
1980-81	New Haven Nighthawks	AHL	36	14	17	3	2065	142	1	4.04	....	....	....	....	....	....	....	....	....	....	....	....	....	....	....	....	....
	New York Rangers	NHL	1	0	1	0	60	2	0	2.00	1.60	....	....	....	....	1	0	0	....	14	1	0	4.29	....	....	....	....
1981-82	New York Rangers	NHL	49	23	16	9	2852	179	1	3.77	2.90	....	....	....	....	4	1	2	....	127	9	0	4.25	....	....	....	....
1982-83	New York Rangers	NHL	18	9	5	3	1040	68	0	3.92	3.13	5.43	491	.862	28.3	....	....	....	....	....	....	....	....	....	....	....	....
	Tulsa Oilers	CHL	19	8	10	0	1116	60	0	3.23	....	....	....	....	....	....	....	....	....	....	....	....	....	....	....	....	....
1983-84	New York Rangers	NHL	26	10	11	2	1361	90	0	3.97	3.11	5.36	667	.865	29.4	....	....	....	....	....	....	....	....	....	....	....	....
	Tulsa Oilers	CHL	3	3	0	0	180	7	0	2.33	....	....	....	....	....	....	....	....	....	....	....	....	....	....	....	....	....
1984-85	Hartford Whalers	NHL	23	9	12	2	1397	91	2	3.91	3.10	5.08	700	.870	30.1	....	....	....	....	....	....	....	....	....	....	....	....
	Binghamton Whalers	AHL	5	5	0	0	303	13	0	2.57	....	....	....	....	....	....	....	....	....	....	....	....	....	....	....	....	....
	Canada	WEC-A	5	....	....	....	265	9	....	2.04	....	....	....	....	....	....	....	....	....	....	....	....	....	....	....	....	....
1985-86	Hartford Whalers	NHL	27	13	13	0	1544	99	1	3.85	2.99	5.27	723	.863	28.1	3	1	2	....	169	8	0	2.84	3.55	64	.875	22.7
1986-87	Hartford Whalers	NHL	25	12	8	2	1367	78	1	3.42	2.87	4.34	615	.873	27.0	1	0	0	....	36	1	0	1.67	0.76	22	.955	36.7
1987-88	Hartford Whalers	NHL	18	6	7	2	918	55	0	3.59	2.98	5.09	388	.858	25.4	....	....	....	....	....	....	....	....	....	....	....	....
	Vancouver Canucks	NHL	9	4	3	2	550	31	0	3.38	2.81	3.66	286	.892	31.2	....	....	....	....	....	....	....	....	....	....	....	....
1988-89	Vancouver Canucks	NHL	35	11	19	5	2056	102	0	2.98	2.45	3.19	953	.893	27.8	3	1	1	....	140	8	0	3.43	3.47	79	.899	33.9
1989-90	Vancouver Canucks	NHL	21	4	11	4	1142	79	0	4.15	3.48	5.26	623	.873	32.7	....	....	....	....	....	....	....	....	....	....	....	....
1990-91	Vancouver Canucks	NHL	1	0	1	0	59	6	0	6.10	5.45	12.62	29	.793	29.5	....	....	....	....	....	....	....	....	....	....	....	....
	Milwaukee Admirals	IHL	37	16	19	0	2014	127	0	3.78	....	....	....	....	....	3	1	2	0	210	13	0	3.71	....	....	....	....
1991-92	New York Islanders	NHL	23	9	4	2	1032	62	0	3.60	3.19	3.94	566	.890	32.9	....	....	....	....	....	....	....	....	....	....	....	....
	Los Angeles Kings	NHL	7	1	3	0	252	17	0	4.05	3.59	5.06	136	.875	32.4	....	....	....	....	....	....	....	....	....	....	....	....
1992-93	Ottawa Senators	NHL	7	0	5	0	249	30	0	7.23	6.17	15.06	144	.792	34.7	....	....	....	....	....	....	....	....	....	....	....	....
	New Haven Senators	AHL	6	0	6	0	323	32	0	5.94	....	....	....	....	....	....	....	....	....	....	....	....	....	....	....	....	....
	NHL Totals		290	111	119	33	15879	989	5	3.74	....	....	....	....	....	12	3	5	....	486	27	0	3.33	....	....	....	....

CCHA Second All-Star Team (1979) • CCHA First All-Star Team (1980) • NCAA Championship All-Tournament Team (1980)

Traded to **Hartford** by **NY Rangers** for future considerations, September 5, 1984. Traded to **Vancouver** by **Hartford** for Richard Brodeur, March 8, 1988. Traded to **Buffalo** by **Vancouver** for future considerations, March 5, 1991. Signed as a free agent by **NY Islanders**, September 16, 1991. Traded to **LA Kings** by **NY Islanders** for LA Kings' 7th round choice (Steve O'Rourke) in 1992 Entry Draft, February 18, 1992. Signed as a free agent by **Washington**, June 16, 1992. Traded to **Ottawa** by **Washington** for future considerations, August 13, 1992.

• WETZEL, CARL

Carl Wetzel G – L. 6'1", 170 lbs. b: Detroit, MI, 12/12/1938.

Season	Club	League	GP	W	L	T	Mins	GA	SO	Avg	AAvg	Eff	SA	S%	SAPG	GP	W	L	T	Mins	GA	SO	Avg	Eff	SA	S%	SAPG
1956-57	Hamilton Tiger Cubs	OHA	48	24	22	2	2880	167	3	3.48	....	....	....	....	....	4	1	3	0	240	13	0	3.25	....	....	....	....
1957-58	Hamilton Tiger Cubs	OHA	50	26	17	7	2980	172	1	3.46	....	....	....	....	....	15	8	6	1	900	59	0	3.93	....	....	....	....
1958-59	Hamilton Tiger Cubs	OHA	25	....	....	....	1500	105	0	4.26	....	....	....	....	....	....	....	....	....	....	....	....	....	....	....	....	....
	Edmonton Flyers	WHL	1	0	1	0	60	7	0	7.00	....	....	....	....	....	....	....	....	....	....	....	....	....	....	....	....	....
1959-60	Omaha Knights	IHL	62	....	....	....	3720	271	1	4.37	....	....	....	....	....	....	....	....	....	....	....	....	....	....	....	....	....
1960-61	Spokane Comets	WHL	5	0	5	0	302	25	0	4.97	....	....	....	....	....	....	....	....	....	....	....	....	....	....	....	....	....
	Indianapolis Chiefs	IHL	52	....	....	....	3120	202	0	3.88	....	....	....	....	....	....	....	....	....	....	....	....	....	....	....	....	....
	Fort Wayne Komets	IHL	....	....	....	....	....	....	....	....	....	....	....	....	....	8	3	3	0	480	26	0	3.25	....	....	....	....
1961-62	Sudbury Wolves	EPHL	61	25	26	10	3660	228	0	3.74	....	....	....	....	....	5	1	4	0	300	30	0	6.00	....	....	....	....
1962-63			MILITARY SERVICE																								
1963-64			MILITARY SERVICE																								
1964-65	Detroit Red Wings	NHL	2	0	1	0	32	4	0	7.50	8.06	....	....	....	....	....	....	....	....	....	....	....	....	....	....	....	....
	Pittsburgh Hornets	AHL	4	1	3	0	241	21	0	5.23	....	....	....	....	....	....	....	....	....	....	....	....	....	....	....	....	....
1965-66	Houston Apollos	CHL	51	21	24	6	3040	171	4	3.38	....	....	....	....	....	....	....	....	....	....	....	....	....	....	....	....	....
	Quebec Aces	AHL	1	0	1	0	60	6	0	6.00	....	....	....	....	....	....	....	....	....	....	....	....	....	....	....	....	....
1966-67	United States	Nat-Team	12	....	....	....	720	38	0	3.17	....	....	....	....	....	....	....	....	....	....	....	....	....	....	....	....	....
	United States	WEC-A	7	....	....	....	420	23	....	3.29	....	....	....	....	....	....	....	....	....	....	....	....	....	....	....	....	....
1967-68	Minnesota North Stars	NHL	5	1	2	1	269	18	0	4.01	4.45	....	....	....	....	....	....	....	....	....	....	....	....	....	....	....	....
	Memphis South Stars	CHL	20	8	9	2	1095	61	0	3.34	....	....	....	....	....	....	....	....	....	....	....	....	....	....	....	....	....
	Rochester Americans	AHL	10	3	3	1	495	28	1	3.39	....	....	....	....	....	4	2	1	0	164	6	0	2.20	....	....	....	....
1968-69	Cleveland Barons	AHL	2	1	0	0	80	3	1	2.25	....	....	....	....	....	....	....	....	....	....	....	....	....	....	....	....	....
	Memphis South Stars	CHL	39	....	....	....	2276	170	0	4.48	....	....	....	....	....	....	....	....	....	....	....	....	....	....	....	....	....

Season	Club	League	GP	W	L	T	Mins	GA	SO	Avg	AAvg	Eff	SA	S%	SAPG	GP	W	L	T	Mins	GA	SO	Avg	Eff	SA	S%	SAPG
			REGULAR SEASON													PLAYOFFS											
1969-70	United States	Nat-Team	17	....	....	....	930	30	0	1.94	....	....	....	....	....	....	....	....	....	....	....	....	....	....	....	....	....
	Rochester Mustangs	USHL	4	....	....	....	240	15	0	3.75	....	....	....	....	....	....	....	....	....	....	....	....	....	....	....	....	....
1970-71	United States	Nat-Team	STATISTICS NOT AVAILABLE																								
	United States	WEC-A	8	....	....	....	400	38	....	5.70	....	....	....	....	....	....	....	....	....	....	....	....	....	....	....	....	....
1971-72	Kitzbuhel	Austria	44	....	....	....	2640	132	4	3.00	....	....	....	....	....	....	....	....	....	....	....	....	....	....	....	....	....
1972-73	Minnesota Fighting Saints	WHA	1	0	1	0	60	3	0	3.00	....	....	....	....	....	....	....	....	....	....	....	....	....	....	....	....	....
	NHL Totals		**7**	**1**	**3**	**1**	**301**	**22**	**0**	**4.39**	....	....	....	....	....	....	....	....	....	....	....	....	....	....	....	....	....
	Other Major League Totals		1	0	1	0	60	3	0	3.00	....	....	....	....	....	....	....	....	....	....	....	....	....	....	....	....	....

Claimed by **Montreal** (Quebec - AHL) from **Detroit** in Reverse Draft, June, 1965. Traded to **Minnesota** by **Montreal** for cash, June 14, 1967. Signed as a free agent by **Minnesota** (WHA), January 23, 1973.

• WHITMORE, KAY

Kay Whitmore G – L. 5'11", 175 lbs. b: Sudbury, Ont., 4/10/1967. Hartford's 2nd choice, 26th overall, in 1985 Entry Draft.

Season	Club	League	GP	W	L	T	Mins	GA	SO	Avg	AAvg	Eff	SA	S%	SAPG	GP	W	L	T	Mins	GA	SO	Avg	Eff	SA	S%	SAPG
1983-84	Peterborough Petes	OHL	29	17	8	0	1471	110	0	4.49	....	....	....	....	....	....	....	....	....	....	....	....	....	....	....	....	....
1984-85	Peterborough Petes	OHL	*53	*35	16	2	*3077	172	*2	3.35	....	....	....	....	....	17	10	4	....	1020	58	0	3.41	....	....	....	....
1985-86	Peterborough Petes	OHL	41	27	12	2	2467	114	*3	*2.77	....	....	....	....	....	14	8	5	....	837	40	0	2.87	....	....	....	....
1986-87	Peterborough Petes	OHL	36	14	17	5	2159	118	1	3.28	....	....	....	....	....	7	3	3	....	366	17	1	2.79	....	....	....	....
1987-88	Binghamton Whalers	AHL	38	17	15	4	2137	121	*3	3.40	....	....	....	....	....	2	0	2	....	118	10	0	5.08	....	....	....	....
1988-89	**Hartford Whalers**	**NHL**	**3**	**2**	**1**	**0**	**180**	**10**	**0**	**3.33**	**2.75**	**3.47**	**96**	**.896**	**32.0**	**2**	**0**	**2**	....	**135**	**10**	**0**	**4.44**	**6.08**	**73**	**.863**	**32.4**
	Binghamton Whalers	AHL	*56	21	29	4	*3200	241	1	4.52	....	....	....	....	....	....	....	....	....	....	....	....	....	....	....	....	....
1989-90	**Hartford Whalers**	**NHL**	**9**	**4**	**2**	**1**	**442**	**26**	**0**	**3.53**	**2.96**	**5.02**	**183**	**.858**	**24.8**	....	....	....	....	....	....	....	....	....	....	....	....
	Binghamton Whalers	AHL	24	3	19	2	1386	109	0	4.72	....	....	....	....	....	....	....	....	....	....	....	....	....	....	....	....	....
1990-91	**Hartford Whalers**	**NHL**	**18**	**3**	**9**	**3**	**850**	**52**	**0**	**3.67**	**3.28**	**5.04**	**379**	**.863**	**26.8**	....	....	....	....	....	....	....	....	....	....	....	....
	Springfield Indians	AHL	33	22	9	1	1916	98	1	3.07	....	....	....	....	....	*15	*11	4	....	*926	37	0	*2.40	....	....	....	....
1991-92	**Hartford Whalers**	**NHL**	**45**	**14**	**21**	**6**	**2567**	**155**	**3**	**3.62**	**3.21**	**4.34**	**1292**	**.880**	**30.2**	**1**	**0**	**0**	....	**19**	**1**	**0**	**3.16**	**6.32**	**5**	**.800**	**15.8**
1992-93	**Vancouver Canucks**	**NHL**	**31**	**18**	**8**	**4**	**1817**	**94**	**1**	**3.10**	**2.63**	**3.40**	**858**	**.890**	**28.3**	....	....	....	....	....	....	....	....	....	....	....	....
1993-94	**Vancouver Canucks**	**NHL**	**32**	**18**	**14**	**0**	**1921**	**113**	**0**	**3.53**	**3.36**	**4.70**	**848**	**.867**	**26.5**	....	....	....	....	....	....	....	....	....	....	....	....
1994-95	**Vancouver Canucks**	**NHL**	**11**	**0**	**6**	**2**	**558**	**37**	**0**	**3.98**	**4.12**	**5.28**	**279**	**.867**	**30.0**	**1**	**0**	**0**	....	**20**	**2**	**0**	**6.00**	**6.67**	**18**	**.889**	**54.0**
1995-96	Detroit Vipers	IHL	10	3	5	0	501	33	0	3.95	....	....	....	....	....	....	....	....	....	....	....	....	....	....	....	....	....
	Los Angeles Ice Dogs	IHL	30	10	9	7	1503	99	1	3.80	....	....	....	....	....	....	....	....	....	....	....	....	....	....	....	....	....
	Syracuse Crunch	AHL	11	6	4	1	663	37	0	3.35	....	....	....	....	....	....	....	....	....	....	....	....	....	....	....	....	....
	Binghamton Rangers	AHL	....	....	....	....	....	....	....	....	....	....	....	....	....	2	0	2	....	127	9	0	4.27	....	....	....	....
1996-97	Sodertalje SK	Sweden	25	....	....	....	1320	85	0	3.86	....	....	....	....	....	....	....	....	....	....	....	....	....	....	....	....	....
1997-98	Long Beach Ice Dogs	IHL	46	28	12	3	2516	109	3	2.60	....	....	....	....	....	14	9	5	....	838	43	0	3.08	....	....	....	....
	NHL Totals		**149**	**59**	**61**	**16**	**8335**	**487**	**4**	**3.51**	....	....	**3935**	**.876**	....	**4**	**0**	**2**	....	**174**	**13**	**0**	**4.48**	....	....	....	....

OHL First All-Star Team (1986) • Won Jack A. Butterfield Trophy (Playoff MVP - AHL) (1991) • Shared James Norris Memorial Trophy (fewest goals against - IHL) with Mike Buzak (1998)

Traded to **Vancouver** by **Hartford** for Corrie D'Alessio and future considerations, October 1, 1992. Traded to **NY Rangers** by **Vancouver** for Joe Kocur, March 20, 1996. Signed as a free agent by **San Jose**, September 10, 1997. Traded to **Buffalo** by **San Jose** with Colorado's 2nd round choice (previously acquired, Buffalo selected Jaroslav Kristek) in 1998 Entry Draft and San Jose's 5th round choice in 2000 Entry Draft for Steve Shields and Buffalo's 4th round choice (Miroslav Zalesak) in 1998 Entry Draft, June 18, 1998.

• WILKINSON, DEREK

Derek Wilkinson G – L. 6', 170 lbs. b: Ont., 7/29/1974. Tampa Bay's 7th choice, 145th overall, in 1992 Entry Draft.

Season	Club	League	GP	W	L	T	Mins	GA	SO	Avg	AAvg	Eff	SA	S%	SAPG	GP	W	L	T	Mins	GA	SO	Avg	Eff	SA	S%	SAPG
1991-92	Detroit Ambassadors	OHL	38	16	17	1	1943	138	1	4.26	....	....	....	....	....	7	3	2	....	313	28	0	5.37	....	....	....	....
1992-93	Detroit Jr. Red Wings	OHL	*4	1	2	1	*245	18	0	4.41	....	....	....	....	....	....	....	....	....	....	....	....	....	....	....	....	....
	Belleville Bulls	OHL	*50	21	24	11	*3070	237	0	4.22	....	....	....	....	....	7	3	4	....	434	29	0	4.01	....	....	....	....
1993-94	Belleville Bulls	OHL	*56	24	16	4	2860	179	*2	3.76	....	....	....	....	....	12	6	6	....	700	39	*1	3.34	....	....	....	....
1994-95	Atlanta Knights	IHL	46	22	17	2	2414	121	1	3.01	....	....	....	....	....	4	2	1	....	197	8	0	2.43	....	....	....	....
1995-96	**Tampa Bay Lightning**	**NHL**	**4**	**0**	**3**	**0**	**200**	**15**	**0**	**4.50**	**4.42**	**6.43**	**105**	**.857**	**31.5**	....	....	....	....	....	....	....	....	....	....	....	....
	Atlanta Knights	IHL	28	11	11	2	1433	98	1	4.10	....	....	....	....	....	....	....	....	....	....	....	....	....	....	....	....	....
1996-97	**Tampa Bay Lightning**	**NHL**	**5**	**0**	**2**	**1**	**169**	**12**	**0**	**4.26**	**4.51**	**7.10**	**72**	**.833**	**25.6**	....	....	....	....	....	....	....	....	....	....	....	....
	Cleveland Lumberjacks	IHL	46	20	17	6	2595	138	1	3.19	....	....	....	....	....	14	8	6	....	893	44	0	2.95	....	....	....	....
1997-98	**Tampa Bay Lightning**	**NHL**	**8**	**2**	**4**	**1**	**311**	**17**	**0**	**3.28**	**3.84**	**3.77**	**148**	**.885**	**28.6**	....	....	....	....	....	....	....	....	....	....	....	....
	Cleveland Lumberjacks	IHL	25	9	12	2	1295	63	1	2.92	....	....	....	....	....	1	0	0	....	27	1	0	2.19	....	....	....	....
	NHL Totals		**17**	**2**	**9**	**2**	**680**	**44**	**0**	**3.88**	....	....	**325**	**.865**	....	....	....	....	....	....	....	....	....	....	....	....	....

• WILLIS, JORDAN

Jordan Willis G – L. 5'9", 155 lbs. b: Kincardine, Ont., 2/28/1975. Dallas' 8th choice, 243rd overall, in 1993 Entry Draft.

Season	Club	League	GP	W	L	T	Mins	GA	SO	Avg	AAvg	Eff	SA	S%	SAPG	GP	W	L	T	Mins	GA	SO	Avg	Eff	SA	S%	SAPG
1992-93	London Knights	OHL	26	13	6	3	1428	101	1	4.24	....	....	....	....	....	7	2	4	....	355	19	0	3.21	....	....	....	....
1993-94	London Knights	OHL	44	20	19	2	2428	158	1	3.90	....	....	....	....	....	1	0	0	....	8	1	0	7.50	....	....	....	....
1994-95	London Knights	OHL	53	16	29	3	2824	202	0	4.29	....	....	....	....	....	3	0	3	....	165	15	0	5.45	....	....	....	....
1995-96	**Dallas Stars**	**NHL**	**1**	**0**	**1**	**0**	**19**	**1**	**0**	**3.16**	**3.10**	**2.26**	**14**	**.929**	**44.2**	....	....	....	....	....	....	....	....	....	....	....	....
	Michigan K-Wings	IHL	38	17	9	9	2184	118	1	3.24	....	....	....	....	....	4	1	3	....	238	17	0	4.29	....	....	....	....
1996-97	Canada	Nat-Team	15	7	4	2	804	42	....	3.13	....	....	....	....	....	....	....	....	....	....	....	....	....	....	....	....	....
	Daytona Bombers	ECHL	8	4	4	0	429	25	0	3.50	....	....	....	....	....	....	....	....	....	....	....	....	....	....	....	....	....
	Michigan K-Wings	IHL	2	0	2	0	102	8	0	4.70	....	....	....	....	....	....	....	....	....	....	....	....	....	....	....	....	....
1997-98	Michigan K-Wings	IHL	31	8	18	2	1584	93	1	3.52	....	....	....	....	....	....	....	....	....	....	....	....	....	....	....	....	....
	NHL Totals		**1**	**0**	**1**	**0**	**19**	**1**	**0**	**3.16**	....	....	**14**	**.929**	....	....	....	....	....	....	....	....	....	....	....	....	....

• WILSON, DUNC

Dunc Wilson G5'11", 175 lbs. b: Toronto, Ont., 3/22/1948.

Season	Club	League	GP	W	L	T	Mins	GA	SO	Avg	AAvg	Eff	SA	S%	SAPG	GP	W	L	T	Mins	GA	SO	Avg	Eff	SA	S%	SAPG
1964-65	Oshawa Generals	OHA	2	....	....	....	70	8	0	6.86	....	....	....	....	....	....	....	....	....	....	....	....	....	....	....	....	....
1965-66	Niagara Falls Flyers	OHA	22	....	....	....	137	82	1	3.59	....	....	....	....	....	4	1	2	1	240	17	0	4.25	....	....	....	....
1966-67	Niagara Falls Flyers	OHA	1	0	1	0	40	6	0	9.00	....	....	....	....	....	....	....	....	....	....	....	....	....	....	....	....	....
	Peterborough Petes	OHA	14	....	....	....	840	56	0	4.42	....	....	....	....	....	....	....	....	....	....	....	....	....	....	....	....	....
1967-68	Oshawa Generals	OHA	30	....	....	....	1800	159	1	5.30	....	....	....	....	....	....	....	....	....	....	....	....	....	....	....	....	....
1968-69	Quebec Aces	AHL	37	11	14	9	1814	98	0	3.24	....	....	....	....	....	*15	6	8	0	*835	38	0	*2.73	....	....	....	....
1969-70	**Philadelphia Flyers**	**NHL**	**1**	**0**	**1**	**0**	**60**	**3**	**0**	**3.00**	**3.19**	....	....	....	....	....	....	....	....	....	....	....	....	....	....	....	....
	Quebec Aces	AHL	57	....	....	....	3288	191	2	3.49	....	....	....	....	....	4	2	2	0	272	10	0	2.21	....	....	....	....
1970-71	**Vancouver Canucks**	**NHL**	**35**	**3**	**25**	**2**	**1791**	**128**	**0**	**4.29**	**4.29**	....	....	....	....	....	....	....	....	....	....	....	....	....	....	....	....
1971-72	**Vancouver Canucks**	**NHL**	**53**	**16**	**30**	**3**	**2870**	**173**	**1**	**3.62**	**3.67**	....	....	....	....	....	....	....	....	....	....	....	....	....	....	....	....
1972-73	**Vancouver Canucks**	**NHL**	**43**	**13**	**21**	**5**	**2423**	**159**	**1**	**3.94**	**3.74**	....	....	....	....	....	....	....	....	....	....	....	....	....	....	....	....
1973-74	**Toronto Maple Leafs**	**NHL**	**24**	**9**	**11**	**3**	**1412**	**68**	**1**	**2.89**	**2.79**	....	....	....	....	....	....	....	....	....	....	....	....	....	....	....	....
1974-75	**Toronto Maple Leafs**	**NHL**	**25**	**8**	**11**	**4**	**1393**	**86**	**0**	**3.70**	**3.34**	....	....	....	....	....	....	....	....	....	....	....	....	....	....	....	....
	New York Rangers	**NHL**	**3**	**1**	**2**	**0**	**180**	**13**	**0**	**4.33**	**3.90**	....	....	....	....	....	....	....	....	....	....	....	....	....	....	....	....
1975-76	**New York Rangers**	**NHL**	**20**	**5**	**9**	**3**	**1080**	**76**	**0**	**4.22**	**3.83**	....	....	....	....	....	....	....	....	....	....	....	....	....	....	....	....
	Baltimore Clippers	AHL	6	3	2	0	325	15	1	2.77	....	....	....	....	....	....	....	....	....	....	....	....	....	....	....	....	....
1976-77	**Pittsburgh Penguins**	**NHL**	**45**	**18**	**19**	**8**	**2627**	**129**	**5**	**2.95**	**2.73**	....	....	....	....	....	....	....	....	....	....	....	....	....	....	....	....
1977-78	**Pittsburgh Penguins**	**NHL**	**21**	**5**	**11**	**3**	**1180**	**95**	**0**	**4.83**	**4.55**	....	....	....	....	....	....	....	....	....	....	....	....	....	....	....	....
1978-79	**Vancouver Canucks**	**NHL**	**17**	**2**	**10**	**2**	**835**	**58**	**0**	**4.17**	**3.60**	....	....	....	....	....	....	....	....	....	....	....	....	....	....	....	....
	Binghamton Whalers	AHL	3	0	2	0	109	11	0	6.06	....	....	....	....	....	....	....	....	....	....	....	....	....	....	....	....	....
	Dallas Black Hawks	CHL	3	2	1	0	180	11	0	3.67	....	....	....	....	....	....	....	....	....	....	....	....	....	....	....	....	....
	NHL Totals		**287**	**80**	**150**	**33**	**15851**	**988**	**8**	**3.74**	....	....	....	....	....	....	....	....	....	....	....	....	....	....	....	....	....

Claimed by **Philadelphia** from **Boston** (Oshawa-OHA) in Special Internal Amateur Draft, June, 1968. Claimed by **Vancouver** from **Philadelphia** in Expansion Draft, June 10, 1970. Traded to **Toronto** by **Vancouver** for Larry McIntyre and Murray Heatley, May 29, 1973. Claimed on waivers by **NY Rangers** from **Toronto**, February 15, 1975. Traded to **Pittsburgh** by **NY Rangers** for Pittsburgh's 4th round choice (Dave Silk) in 1978 Amateur Draft, October 8, 1976. Traded to **Vancouver** by **Pittsburgh** for cash, November 17, 1978.

• WILSON, LEFTY

Lefty (Ross Ingram) Wilson G – L. 5'11", 178 lbs. b: Toronto, Ont., 10/15/1919.

Season	Club	League	GP	W	L	T	Mins	GA	SO	Avg	AAvg	Eff	SA	S%	SAPG	GP	W	L	T	Mins	GA	SO	Avg	Eff	SA	S%	SAPG
1937-38	Toronto Lions	OHA	11	....	....	....	660	72	0	6.55	....	....	....	....	....	....	....	....	....	....	....	....	....	....	....	....	....
1938-1943				DID NOT PLAY																							
1943-44	St. Catharines	Inter-Sr.		STATISTICS NOT AVAILABLE																							
1944-45	Toronto Navy	City Sr.		STATISTICS NOT AVAILABLE																							
1945-46	Omaha Knights	USHL	3	....	....	....	180	15	0	4.99	....	....	....	....	....	....	....	....	....	....	....	....	....	....	....	....	....
	St. Paul Saints	USHL	1	....	....	....	60	4	0	4.00	....	....	....	....	....	....	....	....	....	....	....	....	....	....	....	....	....
1946-47				DID NOT PLAY																							

			REGULAR SEASON													PLAYOFFS											
Season	Club	League	GP	W	L	T	Mins	GA	SO	Avg	AAvg	Eff	SA	S%	SAPG	GP	W	L	T	Mins	GA	SO	Avg	Eff	SA	S%	SAPG
1947-48	Indianapolis Capitols	AHL	2	1	1	0	80	7	0	5.25	....	....	....	....	....	....	....	....	....	....	....	....	....	....	....	....	....
1948-49	Indianapolis Capitols	AHL	2	1	0	0	80	4	0	3.00	....	....	....	....	....	....	....	....	....	....	....	....	....	....	....	....	....
1949-50	Indianapolis Capitols	AHL	3	2	1	0	180	12	0	4.00	....	....	....	....	....	....	....	....	....	....	....	....	....	....	....	....	....
1953-54	**Detroit Red Wings**	**NHL**	**1**	**0**	**0**	**0**	**16**	**0**	**0**	**0.00**	**0.00**	....	....	....	....	....	....	....	....	....	....	....	....	....	....	....	....
1955-56	**Toronto Maple Leafs**	**NHL**	**1**	**0**	**0**	**0**	**13**	**0**	**0**	**0.00**	**0.00**	....	....	....	....	....	....	....	....	....	....	....	....	....	....	....	....
1957-58	**Boston Bruins**	**NHL**	**1**	**0**	**0**	**1**	**52**	**1**	**0**	**1.15**	**1.27**	....	....	....	....	....	....	....	....	....	....	....	....	....	....	....	....
	NHL Totals		**3**	**0**	**0**	**1**	**81**	**1**	**0**	**0.74**	....	....	....	....	....	....	....	....	....	....	....	....	....	....	....	....	....

Detroit's assistant trainer/practice goaltender replaced injured Terry Sawchuk in 3rd period, October 10, 1953. (Montreal 4, Detroit 1). Loaned to **Toronto** by **Detroit** to replace injured Harry Lumley in 3rd period, January 22, 1956. (Detroit 4, Toronto 1). Loaned to **Boston** by **Detroit** to replace injured Don Simmons in 1st period, December 29, 1957. (Boston 2, Detroit 2)

• WINKLER, HAL

Hal Winkler G5′8″, 150 lbs. b: Gretna, Man., 3/20/1892. d: 5/29/1956.

Season	Club	League	GP	W	L	T	Mins	GA	SO	Avg	AAvg	Eff	SA	S%	SAPG	GP	W	L	T	Mins	GA	SO	Avg	Eff	SA	S%	SAPG
1913-14	Winnipeg Winnipegs	MHL Sr.	8	2	6	0	480	47	0	5.87	....	....	....	....	....	....	....	....	....	....	....	....	....	....	....	....	....
1914-15	Winnipeg Winnipegs	MHL Sr.	6	....	....	....	300	51	0	8.50	....	....	....	....	....	....	....	....	....	....	....	....	....	....	....	....	....
1915-16	Winnipeg 61st Battalion	MHL Sr.	1	1	0	0	60	4	0	4.00	....	....	....	....	....	....	....	....	....	....	....	....	....	....	....	....	....
1916-17	Winnipeg Monarchs	MHL Sr.	8	....	....	....	480	46	0	5.75	....	....	....	....	....	....	....	....	....	....	....	....	....	....	....	....	....
1917-18	Winnipeg Ypres	MHL Sr.	8	....	....	....	480	29	0	*3.63	....	....	....	....	....	5	4	1	0	300	9	2	1.80	....	....	....	....
1918-19	Brandon Elks	MHL Sr.	9	5	4	0	540	49	0	5.41	....	....	....	....	....	....	....	....	....	....	....	....	....	....	....	....	....
1919-20	Moose Jaw Maple Leafs	SSHL	12	*9	3	0	730	40	0	3.29	....	....	....	....	....	2	*2	0	0	120	4	0	*2.00	....	....	....	....
1920-21	Saskatoon Crescents	SSHL	16	*10	6	0	960	49	*2	3.06	....	....	....	....	....	4	2	2	0	240	14	0	3.50	....	....	....	....
1921-22	Edmonton Eskimos	WCHL	14	10	4	0	831	33	1	*2.38	....	....	....	....	....	2	0	1	1	120	3	0	1.50	....	....	....	....
1922-23	Edmonton Eskimos	WCHL	28	*17	10	1	*1738	87	1	3.00	....	....	....	....	....	4	1	2	1	272	6	1	1.32	....	....	....	....
1923-24	Edmonton Eskimos	WCHL	26	9	13	4	1655	69	1	2.50	....	....	....	....	....	....	....	....	....	....	....	....	....	....	....	....	....
1924-25	Calgary Tigers	WCHL	*28	*17	11	0	1680	80	2	2.86	....	....	....	....	....	2	0	1	1	120	3	0	1.50	....	....	....	....
1925-26	Calgary Tigers	WHL	*30	10	17	3	1874	80	*6	2.56	....	....	....	....	....	....	....	....	....	....	....	....	....	....	....	....	....
1926-27	**New York Rangers**	**NHL**	**8**	**3**	**4**	**1**	**514**	**16**	**2**	**1.87**	**2.89**	....	....	....	....	....	....	....	....	....	....	....	....	....	....	....	....
	Boston Bruins	**NHL**	**23**	**12**	**9**	**2**	**1445**	**40**	**4**	**1.66**	**2.54**	....	....	....	....	***8**	**2**	**2**	**4**	***520**	**13**	***2**	**1.50**	....	....	....	....
1927-28	**Boston Bruins**	**NHL**	***44**	**20**	**13**	**11**	***2780**	**70**	***15**	**1.51**	**2.40**	....	....	....	....	**2**	**0**	**1**	**1**	**120**	**5**	**0**	**2.50**	....	....	....	....
1928-29	Minneapolis Millers	AHA	34	17	7	10	2144	35	*14	*0.98	....	....	....	....	....	4	1	3	0	240	7	0	1.75	....	....	....	....
1929-30	Seattle Eskimos	PCHL	36	15	13	8	2160	58	9	1.61	....	....	....	....	....	....	....	....	....	....	....	....	....	....	....	....	....
1930-31	Boston Tigers	Can-Am	10	3	7	0	610	32	0	3.15	....	....	....	....	....	....	....	....	....	....	....	....	....	....	....	....	....
	NHL Totals		**75**	**35**	**26**	**14**	**4739**	**126**	**21**	**1.60**	....	....	....	....	....	**10**	**2**	**3**	**5**	**640**	**18**	**2**	**1.69**	....	....	....	....
	Other Major League Totals		126	63	55	8	7778	349	11	2.69	....	....	....	....	....	8	1	4	3	512	12	1	1.41	....	....	....	....

WCHL All-Star Team (1923)

Signed as a free agent by **Saskatoon** (SSHL), November 8, 1920. Traded to **Edmonton** (WCHL) by **Saskatoon** (WCHL) for cash, January 13, 1922. Traded to **Calgary** (WCHL) by **Edmonton** (WCHL) with Spunk Sparrow for cash, August 28, 1924. Sold to **NY Rangers** by **Calgary** (WHL) for cash, October 27, 1926. Traded to **Boston** by **NY Rangers** for $5,000, January 17, 1927.

• WOLFE, BERNIE

Bernie Wolfe G5′9″, 165 lbs. b: Montreal, Que., 12/18/1951.

Season	Club	League	GP	W	L	T	Mins	GA	SO	Avg	AAvg	Eff	SA	S%	SAPG	GP	W	L	T	Mins	GA	SO	Avg	Eff	SA	S%	SAPG
1973-74	Sir George Williams University	QUAA	18	10	4	4	1080	74	0	4.11	....	....	....	....	....	....	....	....	....	....	....	....	....	....	....	....	....
1974-75	Maine Nordiques	NAHL	37	19	17	1	2156	150	1	4.17	....	....	....	....	....	....	....	....	....	....	....	....	....	....	....	....	....
	Richmond Robins	AHL	17	6	7	2	918	142	2	2.74	....	....	....	....	....	7	3	4	0	427	26	0	3.65	....	....	....	....
1975-76	**Washington Capitals**	**NHL**	**40**	**5**	**23**	**7**	**2134**	**148**	**0**	**4.16**	**3.78**	....	....	....	....	....	....	....	....	....	....	....	....	....	....	....	....
	Richmond Robins	AHL	3	2	0	0	147	6	0	2.44	....	....	....	....	....	....	....	....	....	....	....	....	....	....	....	....	....
1976-77	**Washington Capitals**	**NHL**	**37**	**7**	**15**	**9**	**1779**	**114**	**1**	**3.84**	**3.58**	....	....	....	....	....	....	....	....	....	....	....	....	....	....	....	....
1977-78	**Washington Capitals**	**NHL**	**25**	**4**	**14**	**4**	**1328**	**94**	**0**	**4.25**	**4.00**	....	....	....	....	....	....	....	....	....	....	....	....	....	....	....	....
	Hershey Bears	AHL	3	3	0	0	180	4	1	1.33	....	....	....	....	....	....	....	....	....	....	....	....	....	....	....	....	....
1978-79	**Washington Capitals**	**NHL**	**18**	**4**	**9**	**1**	**863**	**68**	**0**	**4.73**	**4.19**	....	....	....	....	....	....	....	....	....	....	....	....	....	....	....	....
	NHL Totals		**120**	**20**	**61**	**21**	**6104**	**424**	**1**	**4.17**	....	....	....	....	....	....	....	....	....	....	....	....	....	....	....	....	....

Signed as a free agent by **Washington**, October 1, 1974.

• WOOD, ALEX

Alex Wood G – L. 5′11″, 165 lbs. b: Falkirk, Scotland, 1/15/1911.

Season	Club	League	GP	W	L	T	Mins	GA	SO	Avg	AAvg	Eff	SA	S%	SAPG	GP	W	L	T	Mins	GA	SO	Avg	Eff	SA	S%	SAPG
1928-29	Regina Pats	City Jr.	6	*6	0	0	310	8	*2	*1.55	....	....	....	....	....	7	4	1	0	420	15	0	2.14	....	....	....	....
1929-30	Ottawa New Edinburghs	City Sr.	3	1	2	0	180	9	0	3.00	....	....	....	....	....	....	....	....	....	....	....	....	....	....	....	....	....
	Regina Aces	SJHL	18	*15	1	2	1190	21	*6	*1.06	....	....	....	....	....	2	0	2	0	120	4	0	2.00	....	....	....	....
1930-31	Cleveland Indians	IAHL	19	12	4	3	1120	44	1	2.36	....	....	....	....	....	2	2	0	....	130	6	0	2.77	....	....	....	....
1931-32	Cleveland Indians	IAHL	30	....	....	....	1800	77	0	2.57	....	....	....	....	....	....	....	....	....	....	....	....	....	....	....	....	....
1932-33	Boston Cubs	Can-Am	3	0	2	1	190	14	0	4.67	....	....	....	....	....	....	....	....	....	....	....	....	....	....	....	....	....
	Quebec Castors	Can-Am	1	0	1	0	60	8	0	8.00	....	....	....	....	....	....	....	....	....	....	....	....	....	....	....	....	....
1933-34	Philadelphia Arrows	Can-Am	41	18	16	7	2540	101	2	2.39	....	....	....	....	....	2	0	2	0	120	6	0	3.00	....	....	....	....
1934-35	Philadelphia Arrows	Can-Am	13	4	7	2	800	40	2	3.00	....	....	....	....	....	....	....	....	....	....	....	....	....	....	....	....	....
	Providence Reds	Can-Am	3	0	2	1	190	13	0	4.11	....	....	....	....	....	....	....	....	....	....	....	....	....	....	....	....	....
1935-36	Rochester Cardinals	IAHL	4	....	....	....	240	8	0	2.00	....	....	....	....	....	....	....	....	....	....	....	....	....	....	....	....	....
	Buffalo Bisons	IAHL	48	22	20	6	2880	111	*13	2.31	....	....	....	....	....	5	2	3	0	300	6	1	*1.20	....	....	....	....
1936-37	New Haven Eagles	AHL	20	6	14	0	1210	70	0	3.47	....	....	....	....	....	....	....	....	....	....	....	....	....	....	....	....	....
	New York Americans	**NHL**	**1**	**0**	**1**	**0**	**70**	**3**	**0**	**2.57**	**3.22**	....	....	....	....	....	....	....	....	....	....	....	....	....	....	....	....
	Buffalo Bisons	AHL	11	3	8	0	660	30	1	2.73	....	....	....	....	....	....	....	....	....	....	....	....	....	....	....	....	....
	Cleveland Barons	AHL	3	0	3	0	180	18	0	6.00	....	....	....	....	....	....	....	....	....	....	....	....	....	....	....	....	....
1937-38	Minneapolis Millers	AHA	48	24	15	9	3065	100	9	1.96	....	....	....	....	....	7	3	4	0	425	9	1	1.27	....	....	....	....
1938-39	Minneapolis Millers	AHA	48	31	17	0	2977	139	4	2.81	....	....	....	....	....	4	2	2	0	255	8	*1	*1.88	....	....	....	....
1939-40	Minneapolis Millers	AHA	48	26	22	0	2931	140	3	2.87	....	....	....	....	....	3	0	3	0	180	14	0	4.67	....	....	....	....
1940-41	St. Louis Flyers	AHA	47	*31	16	0	2905	98	*7	2.02	....	....	....	....	....	7	*6	1	0	474	14	*1	*1.77	....	....	....	....
1941-42	St. Louis Flyers	AHA	50	*30	15	5	3060	103	*11	2.02	....	....	....	....	....	3	0	3	0	180	11	0	3.67	....	....	....	....
1942-43	New Haven Eagles	AHL	21	5	11	5	1260	77	0	3.67	....	....	....	....	....	....	....	....	....	....	....	....	....	....	....	....	....
	Hull Volants	Ott-Sr.	4	....	....	....	240	24	0	6.00	....	....	....	....	....	4	....	....	....	240	19	0	4.75	....	....	....	....
1943-44	Hull Volants	Ott-Sr.	14	*7	*6	1	840	58	0	4.14	....	....	....	....	....	12	7	3	1	740	50	1	4.05	....	....	....	....
1944-45	Hull Volants	QSHL	24	....	....	....	1440	176	0	7.33	....	....	....	....	....	2	....	....	....	120	8	0	4.00	....	....	....	....
	NHL Totals		**1**	**0**	**1**	**0**	**70**	**3**	**0**	**2.57**	....	....	....	....	....	....	....	....	....	....	....	....	....	....	....	....	....

IAHL First All-Star Team (1936) • AHA First All-Star Team (1938, 1941) • AHA Second All-Star Team (1942)

Loaned to **NY Americans** by **New Haven** (AHL) to replace Alfie Moore, January 31, 1937. (Montreal Maroons 3, NY Americans 2). Traded to **Chicago** by **St. Louis** (AHA) with Leo Carbol for cash, October 9, 1942.

• WORSLEY, GUMP

Gump (Lorne John) Worsley G – L. 5′7″, 180 lbs. b: Montreal, Que., 5/14/1929. **HHOF**

Season	Club	League	GP	W	L	T	Mins	GA	SO	Avg	AAvg	Eff	SA	S%	SAPG	GP	W	L	T	Mins	GA	SO	Avg	Eff	SA	S%	SAPG
1946-47	Verdun Cyclones	QJHL	25	6	18	1	1500	138	3	5.52	....	....	....	....	....	....	....	....	....	....	....	....	....	....	....	....	....
1947-48	Verdun Cyclones	QJHL	29	13	11	5	1740	95	1	3.28	....	....	....	....	....	5	1	4	0	317	21	0	3.97	....	....	....	....
1948-49	Montreal St-Francis Xavier	City Jr.	47	24	21	2	2840	122	7	2.58	....	....	....	....	....	5	2	3	0	310	16	0	3.10	....	....	....	....
	New York Rovers	QSHL	2	....	....	....	120	5	0	2.50	....	....	....	....	....	....	....	....	....	....	....	....	....	....	....	....	....
1949-50	New York Rovers	EHL	47	25	17	5	2830	133	*7	2.86	....	....	....	....	....	12	*8	2	0	720	27	*1	*2.25	....	....	....	....
	New Haven Ramblers	AHL	2	2	0	0	120	4	0	2.00	....	....	....	....	....	....	....	....	....	....	....	....	....	....	....	....	....
1950-51	St. Paul Saints	USHL	64	33	26	5	*3920	184	*3	*2.82	....	....	....	....	....	4	1	3	0	247	9	0	*2.19	....	....	....	....
1951-52	Saskatoon Quakers	PCHL	66	33	19	14	3960	206	*5	3.07	....	....	....	....	....	13	*10	3	0	818	31	*1	2.27	....	....	....	....
1952-53	Saskatoon Quakers	WHL	13	5	7	1	780	50	0	3.84	....	....	....	....	....	....	....	....	....	....	....	....	....	....	....	....	....
	Edmonton Flyers	WHL	1	1	0	0	60	2	0	2.00	....	....	....	....	....	....	....	....	....	....	....	....	....	....	....	....	....
	New York Rangers	**NHL**	**50**	**13**	**29**	**8**	**3000**	**153**	**2**	**3.06**	**4.09**	....	....	....	....	....	....	....	....	....	....	....	....	....	....	....	....
1953-54	Vancouver Canucks	WHL	70	*39	24	7	4200	168	4	*2.40	....	....	....	....	....	12	7	4	0	709	29	0	2.45	....	....	....	....
1954-55	**New York Rangers**	**NHL**	**65**	**15**	**33**	**17**	**3900**	**197**	**4**	**3.03**	**3.85**	....	....	....	....	....	....	....	....	....	....	....	....	....	....	....	....
1955-56	**New York Rangers**	**NHL**	***70**	**32**	**28**	**10**	***4200**	**203**	**4**	**2.90**	**3.64**	....	....	....	....	**3**	**0**	**3**	....	**180**	**15**	**0**	**5.00**	....	....	....	....
1956-57	**New York Rangers**	**NHL**	**68**	**26**	**28**	**14**	**4080**	**220**	**3**	**3.24**	**3.87**	....	....	....	....	**5**	**1**	**4**	....	**316**	**22**	**0**	**4.18**	....	....	....	....
1957-58	**New York Rangers**	**NHL**	**37**	**21**	**10**	**6**	**2220**	**86**	**4**	**2.32**	**2.52**	....	....	....	....	**6**	**2**	**4**	....	**365**	**28**	**0**	**4.60**	....	....	....	....
	Providence Reds	AHL	25	12	11	2	1528	83	0	3.26	....	....	....	....	....	....	....	....	....	....	....	....	....	....	....	....	....
1958-59	**New York Rangers**	**NHL**	**67**	**26**	**30**	**11**	**4001**	**205**	**2**	**3.07**	**3.31**	....	....	....	....	....	....	....	....	....	....	....	....	....	....	....	....

Season	Club	League	REGULAR SEASON GP	W	L	T	Mins	GA	SO	Avg	AAvg	Eff	SA	S%	SAPG	PLAYOFFS GP	W	L	T	Mins	GA	SO	Avg	Eff	SA	S%	SAPG
1959-60	**New York Rangers**	**NHL**	**39**	**7**	**23**	**8**	**2301**	**137**	**0**	**3.57**	**3.82**	....	....	....	....	....	....	....	....	....	....	....	....	....	....	....	....
	Springfield Indians	AHL	15	11	3	1	900	33	3	2.20	....	....	....	....	....	....	....	....	....	....	....	....	....	....	....	....	....
1960-61	**New York Rangers**	**NHL**	**59**	**20**	**29**	**8**	**3473**	**193**	**1**	**3.33**	**3.48**	....	....	....	....	....	....	....	....	....	....	....	....	....	....	....	....
1961-62	**New York Rangers**	**NHL**	**60**	**22**	**27**	**9**	**3531**	**174**	**2**	**2.96**	**3.03**	....	....	....	....	**6**	**2**	**4**	....	**384**	**22**	**0**	**3.44**	....	....	....	....
1962-63	**New York Rangers**	**NHL**	***67**	**22**	**34**	**10**	***3980**	**219**	**2**	**3.30**	**3.50**	....	....	....	....	....	....	....	....	....	....	....	....	....	....	....	....
1963-64	**Montreal Canadiens**	**NHL**	**8**	**3**	**2**	**2**	**444**	**22**	**1**	**2.97**	**3.31**	....	....	....	....	....	....	....	....	....	....	....	....	....	....	....	....
	Quebec Aces	AHL	47	30	16	1	2820	128	5	2.72	....	....	....	....	....	*9	4	5	0	*543	29	0	3.20	....	....	....	....
1964-65	Quebec Aces	AHL	37	24	12	1	2247	101	2	2.70	....	....	....	....	....	....	....	....	....	....	....	....	....	....	....	....	....
	Montreal Canadiens	**NHL**	**19**	**10**	**7**	**1**	**1020**	**50**	**1**	**2.94**	**3.16**	....	....	....	....	**8**	**5**	**3**	....	**501**	**14**	***2**	***1.68**	....	....	....	....
1965-66	**Montreal Canadiens**	**NHL**	**51**	**29**	**14**	**6**	**2899**	**114**	**2**	**2.36**	**2.33**	....	....	....	....	**10**	***8**	**2**	....	**602**	**20**	***1**	***1.99**	....	....	....	....
1966-67	**Montreal Canadiens**	**NHL**	**18**	**9**	**6**	**2**	**888**	**47**	**1**	**3.18**	**3.30**	....	....	....	....	**2**	**0**	**1**	....	**80**	**2**	**0**	**1.50**	....	....	....	....
1967-68	**Montreal Canadiens**	**NHL**	**40**	**19**	**9**	**8**	**2213**	**73**	**6**	***1.98**	**2.16**	....	....	....	....	**12**	***11**	**0**	....	**669**	**21**	***1**	**1.88**	....	....	....	....
1968-69	**Montreal Canadiens**	**NHL**	**30**	**19**	**5**	**4**	**1703**	**64**	**5**	**2.25**	**2.31**	....	....	....	....	**7**	**5**	**1**	....	**370**	**14**	**0**	**2.27**	....	....	....	....
1969-70	**Montreal Canadiens**	**NHL**	**6**	**3**	**1**	**2**	**360**	**14**	**0**	**2.33**	**2.47**	....	....	....	....	....	....	....	....	....	....	....	....	....	....	....	....
	Minnesota North Stars	**NHL**	**8**	**5**	**1**	**1**	**453**	**20**	**1**	**2.65**	**2.81**	....	....	....	....	**3**	**1**	**2**	....	**180**	**14**	**0**	**4.67**	....	....	....	....
1970-71	**Minnesota North Stars**	**NHL**	**24**	**4**	**10**	**8**	**1369**	**57**	**0**	**2.50**	**2.46**	....	....	....	....	**4**	**3**	**1**	....	**240**	**13**	**0**	**3.25**	....	....	....	....
1971-72	**Minnesota North Stars**	**NHL**	**34**	**16**	**10**	**7**	**1923**	**68**	**2**	**2.12**	**2.11**	....	....	....	....	**4**	**2**	**1**	....	**194**	**7**	**1**	**2.16**	....	....	....	....
1972-73	**Minnesota North Stars**	**NHL**	**12**	**6**	**2**	**3**	**624**	**30**	**0**	**2.88**	**2.71**	....	....	....	....	....	....	....	....	....	....	....	....	....	....	....	....
1973-74	**Minnesota North Stars**	**NHL**	**29**	**8**	**14**	**5**	**1601**	**86**	**0**	**3.22**	**3.11**	....	....	....	....	....	....	....	....	....	....	....	....	....	....	....	....
	NHL Totals		**861**	**335**	**352**	**150**	**50183**	**2432**	**43**	**2.91**	....	....	....	....	....	**70**	**40**	**26**	....	**4081**	**192**	**5**	**2.82**	....	....	....	....

EHL First All-Star Team (1950) • USHL First All-Star Team (1951) • Won Outstanding Rookie Cup (Top Rookie - USHL) (1951) • Won Charles Gardiner Memorial Trophy (USHL - Top Goaltender) (1951) • PCHL Second All-Star Team (1952) • Won Calder Memorial Trophy (1953) • WHL First All-Star Team (1954) • Won WHL Leading Goaltender Award (1954) • Won Leader Cup (WHL - MVP) (1954) • AHL First All-Star Team (1964) • NHL Second All-Star Team (1966) • Shared Vezina Trophy with Charlie Hodge (1966) • NHL First All-Star Team (1968) • Shared Vezina Trophy with Rogie Vachon (1968)

Played in NHL All-Star Game (1961, 1962, 1965, 1972)

Traded to **Montreal** by **NY Rangers** with Dave Balon, Leon Rochefort and Len Ronson for Jacques Plante, Don Marshall and Phil Goyette, June 4, 1963. Traded to **Minnesota** by **Montreal** for cash, February 27, 1970.

• WORTERS, ROY

Roy "Shrimp" Worters G – L. 5'3", 135 lbs. b: Toronto, Ont., 10/19/1900. d: 11/7/1957. **HHOF**

Season	Club	League	GP	W	L	T	Mins	GA	SO	Avg	AAvg	Eff	SA	S%	SAPG	GP	W	L	T	Mins	GA	SO	Avg	Eff	SA	S%	SAPG
1918-19	Toronto Parkdale Canoe Club	OHA	8	*7	1	0	480	22	0	2.75	....	....	....	....	....	2	1	1	0	120	6	0	3.00	....	....	....	....
1919-20	Toronto Canoe Club Paddlers	OHA	3	3	0	0	180	14	0	4.67	....	....	....	....	....	7	7	0	0	420	25	0	3.57	....	....	....	....
1920-21	Porcupine Miners	NOHA	10	7	2	1	630	27	0	2.57	....	....	....	....	....	2	0	2	0	120	10	0	5.00	....	....	....	....
1921-22			DID NOT PLAY – SUSPENDED																								
1922-23	Toronto Argonauts	City Sr.	10	....	....	....	558	37	0	3.98	....	....	....	....	....	....	....	....	....	....	....	....	....	....	....	....	....
1923-24	Pittsburgh Yellowjackets	USAHA	20	*15	5	0	1225	25	*7	*1.23	....	....	....	....	....	13	*9	3	1	840	12	*5	*0.86	....	....	....	....
1924-25	Pittsburgh Yellowjackets	USAHA	39	*25	10	4	1895	34	*17	*0.81	....	....	....	....	....	8	*6	1	1	400	8	1	*1.20	....	....	....	....
1925-26	**Pittsburgh Pirates**	**NHL**	**35**	**18**	**16**	**1**	**2145**	**68**	**7**	**1.90**	**2.47**	....	....	....	....	**2**	**0**	**1**	**1**	**120**	**6**	**0**	**3.00**	....	....	....	....
1926-27	**Pittsburgh Pirates**	**NHL**	***44**	**15**	**26**	**3**	**2711**	**108**	**4**	**2.39**	**3.78**	....	....	....	....	....	....	....	....	....	....	....	....	....	....	....	....
1927-28	**Pittsburgh Pirates**	**NHL**	***44**	**19**	**17**	**8**	**2740**	**76**	**10**	**1.66**	**2.66**	....	....	....	....	**2**	**1**	**1**	**0**	**120**	**6**	**0**	**3.00**	....	....	....	....
1928-29	**New York Americans**	**NHL**	**38**	**16**	**12**	**10**	**2390**	**46**	**13**	**1.15**	**2.40**	....	....	....	....	**2**	**0**	**1**	**1**	**150**	**1**	**1**	**0.40**	....	....	....	....
1929-30	**New York Americans**	**NHL**	**36**	**11**	**21**	**4**	**2270**	**135**	**2**	**3.57**	**3.81**	....	....	....	....	....	....	....	....	....	....	....	....	....	....	....	....
	Montreal Canadiens	**NHL**	**1**	**1**	**0**	**0**	**60**	**2**	**0**	**2.00**	**2.09**	....	....	....	....	....	....	....	....	....	....	....	....	....	....	....	....
1930-31	**New York Americans**	**NHL**	***44**	**18**	**16**	**10**	***2760**	**74**	**8**	***1.61**	**2.00**	....	....	....	....	....	....	....	....	....	....	....	....	....	....	....	....
1931-32	**New York Americans**	**NHL**	**40**	**12**	**20**	**8**	**2459**	**110**	**5**	**2.68**	**3.32**	....	....	....	....	....	....	....	....	....	....	....	....	....	....	....	....
1932-33	**New York Americans**	**NHL**	**47**	**15**	**22**	**10**	**2970**	**116**	**5**	**2.34**	**3.19**	....	....	....	....	....	....	....	....	....	....	....	....	....	....	....	....
	Quebec Castors	Can-Am	1	0	1	0	60	3	0	3.00	....	....	....	....	....	....	....	....	....	....	....	....	....	....	....	....	....
1933-34	**New York Americans**	**NHL**	**36**	**12**	**13**	**10**	**2240**	**75**	**4**	**2.01**	**2.54**	....	....	....	....	....	....	....	....	....	....	....	....	....	....	....	....
1934-35	**New York Americans**	**NHL**	***48**	**12**	**27**	**9**	***3000**	**142**	**3**	**2.84**	**3.54**	....	....	....	....	....	....	....	....	....	....	....	....	....	....	....	....
1935-36	**New York Americans**	**NHL**	***48**	**16**	**25**	**7**	**3000**	**122**	**3**	**2.44**	**3.55**	....	....	....	....	**5**	**2**	**3**	**0**	**300**	**11**	***2**	**2.20**	....	....	....	....
1936-37	**New York Americans**	**NHL**	**23**	**6**	**14**	**3**	**1430**	**69**	**2**	**2.90**	**3.68**	....	....	....	....	....	....	....	....	....	....	....	....	....	....	....	....
	NHL Totals		**484**	**171**	**229**	**83**	**30175**	**1143**	**66**	**2.27**	....	....	....	....	....	**11**	**3**	**6**	**2**	**690**	**24**	**3**	**2.09**	....	....	....	....

Won Hart Trophy (1929) • Won Vezina Trophy (1931) • NHL Second All-Star Team (1932, 1934)

Signed as a free agent by **Pittsburgh**, September 26, 1925. Traded to **NY Americans** by **Pittsburgh** for Joe Miller and $20,000, November 1, 1928. • Suspended by NHL President Frank Calder for refusing to report to **NY Americans**, November 12, 1928. • Was re-instated at a special Board of Govenors meeting in December, 1928. Loaned to **Montreal Canadiens** by **NY Americans** to replace George Hainsworth, February 27, 1930. (Montreal Canadiens 6, Toronto 2)

• WORTHY, CHRIS

Chris Worthy G – L. 6', 180 lbs. b: Bristol, England, 10/23/1947.

Season	Club	League	GP	W	L	T	Mins	GA	SO	Avg	AAvg	Eff	SA	S%	SAPG	GP	W	L	T	Mins	GA	SO	Avg	Eff	SA	S%	SAPG
1965-66	Flin Flon Bombers	SJHL	53	....	....	....	3180	410	0	7.74	....	....	....	....	....	....	....	....	....	....	....	....	....	....	....	....	....
1966-67	Flin Flon Bombers	WCJHL	STATISTICS NOT AVAILABLE																								
1967-68	Flin Flon Bombers	WCJHL	54	....	....	....	3240	129	*10	*2.39	....	....	....	....	....	13	8	4	1	780	35	1	2.69	....	....	....	....
1968-69	**Oakland Seals**	**NHL**	**14**	**4**	**6**	**3**	**786**	**54**	**0**	**4.12**	**4.29**	....	....	....	....	....	....	....	....	....	....	....	....	....	....	....	....
1969-70	**Oakland Seals**	**NHL**	**1**	**0**	**1**	**0**	**60**	**5**	**0**	**5.00**	**5.32**	....	....	....	....	....	....	....	....	....	....	....	....	....	....	....	....
	Seattle Totems	WHL	31	14	14	3	1836	110	0	3.59	....	....	....	....	....	2	0	1	0	100	10	0	5.98	....	....	....	....
	Providence Reds	AHL	3	....	....	....	140	12	0	5.14	....	....	....	....	....	....	....	....	....	....	....	....	....	....	....	....	....
1970-71	**California Golden Seals**	**NHL**	**11**	**1**	**3**	**1**	**480**	**39**	**0**	**4.88**	**4.84**	....	....	....	....	....	....	....	....	....	....	....	....	....	....	....	....
1971-72	Kansas City Blues	CHL	19	3	10	5	1069	73	0	4.09	....	....	....	....	....	....	....	....	....	....	....	....	....	....	....	....	....
1972-73	Denver Spurs	WHL	37	12	14	7	1929	131	0	4.07	....	....	....	....	....	1	0	1	0	59	5	0	5.10	....	....	....	....
1973-74	Edmonton Oilers	WHA	29	11	12	1	1452	92	0	3.80	....	....	....	....	....	3	1	1	0	146	8	0	3.29	....	....	....	....
1974-75	Edmonton Oilers	WHA	29	11	13	3	1660	99	1	3.58	....	....	....	....	....	....	....	....	....	....	....	....	....	....	....	....	....
1975-76	Edmonton Oilers	WHA	24	5	14	0	1256	98	1	4.68	....	....	....	....	....	1	0	1	0	60	7	0	7.00	....	....	....	....
	NHL Totals		**26**	**5**	**10**	**4**	**1326**	**98**	**0**	**4.43**		....	....	....	....	....	....	....	....	....	....	....	....	....			
	Other Major League Totals		82	27	39	4	4368	289	2	3.97	....	....	....	....	....	4	1	2	0	206	15	0	4.37	....	....	....	....

WCJHL All-Star Team (1968)

Traded to **Oakland** by **Detroit** with Gary Jarrett, Howie Young and Doug Roberts for Bob Baun and Ron Harris, May 27, 1968. Selected by Dayton-Houston (WHA) in 1972 WHA General Player Draft, February 12, 1972. Claimed by **Denver** (WHL) from **California** in Reverse Draft, June, 1972. Claimed by **Edmonton** (WHA) in 1973 WHA Professional Player Draft, June, 1973.

• WREGGET, KEN

Ken Wregget G – L. 6'1", 201 lbs. b: Brandon, Man., 3/25/1964. Toronto's 4th choice, 45th overall, in 1982 Entry Draft.

Season	Club	League	GP	W	L	T	Mins	GA	SO	Avg	AAvg	Eff	SA	S%	SAPG	GP	W	L	T	Mins	GA	SO	Avg	Eff	SA	S%	SAPG
1981-82	Lethbridge Broncos	WHL	36	19	12	0	1713	118	0	4.13	....	....	....	....	....	3	2	0	....	84	3	0	2.14	....	....	....	....
1982-83	Lethbridge Broncos	WHL	48	26	17	1	2696	157	1	3.49	....	....	....	....	....	*20	14	5	....	*1154	58	*1	*3.02	....	....	....	....
1983-84	**Toronto Maple Leafs**	**NHL**	**3**	**1**	**1**	**1**	**165**	**14**	**0**	**5.09**	**3.98**	**5.57**	**128**	**.891**	**46.5**	....	....	....	....	....	....	....	....	....	....	....	....
	Lethbridge Broncos	WHL	53	32	20	0	3053	161	0	*3.16	....	....	....	....	....	4	1	3	....	210	18	0	5.14	....	....	....	....
1984-85	**Toronto Maple Leafs**	**NHL**	**23**	**2**	**15**	**3**	**1278**	**103**	**0**	**4.84**	**3.85**	**6.63**	**752**	**.863**	**35.3**	....	....	....	....	....	....	....	....	....	....	....	....
	St. Catharines Saints	AHL	12	2	8	1	688	48	0	4.19	....	....	....	....	....	....	....	....	....	....	....	....	....	....	....	....	....
1985-86	**Toronto Maple Leafs**	**NHL**	**30**	**9**	**13**	**4**	**1566**	**113**	**0**	**4.33**	**3.37**	**5.43**	**901**	**.875**	**34.5**	**10**	**6**	**4**	....	**607**	**32**	***1**	**3.16**	**3.13**	**323**	**.901**	**31.9**
	St. Catharines Saints	AHL	18	8	9	0	1058	78	1	4.42	....	....	....	....	....	....	....	....	....	....	....	....	....	....	....	....	....
1986-87	**Toronto Maple Leafs**	**NHL**	**56**	**22**	**28**	**3**	**3026**	**200**	**0**	**3.97**	**3.35**	**4.97**	**1598**	**.875**	**31.7**	**13**	**7**	**6**	....	**761**	**29**	**1**	**2.29**	**1.80**	**368**	**.921**	**29.0**
1987-88	**Toronto Maple Leafs**	**NHL**	**56**	**12**	**35**	**4**	**3000**	**222**	**2**	**4.44**	**3.71**	**5.76**	**1712**	**.870**	**34.2**	**2**	**0**	**1**	....	**108**	**11**	**0**	**6.11**	**10.84**	**62**	**.823**	**34.4**
1988-89	**Toronto Maple Leafs**	**NHL**	**32**	**9**	**20**	**2**	**1888**	**139**	**0**	**4.42**	**3.66**	**5.92**	**1037**	**.866**	**33.0**	....	....	....	....	....	....	....	....	....	....	....	....
	Philadelphia Flyers	**NHL**	**3**	**1**	**1**	**0**	**130**	**13**	**0**	**6.00**	**4.95**	**10.68**	**73**	**.822**	**33.7**	**5**	**2**	**2**	....	**268**	**10**	**0**	**2.24**	**1.61**	**139**	**.928**	**31.1**
1989-90	**Philadelphia Flyers**	**NHL**	**51**	**22**	**24**	**3**	**2961**	**169**	**0**	**3.42**	**2.86**	**3.71**	**1560**	**.892**	**31.6**	....	....	....	....	....	....	....	....	....	....	....	....
	Canada	WLC-A	1	....	....	....	60	0	1	0.00	....	....	....	....	....	....	....	....	....	....	....	....	....	....	....	....	....
1990-91	**Philadelphia Flyers**	**NHL**	**30**	**10**	**14**	**3**	**1484**	**88**	**0**	**3.56**	**3.18**	**4.75**	**660**	**.867**	**26.7**	....	....	....	....	....	....	....	....	....	....	....	....
1991-92	**Philadelphia Flyers**	**NHL**	**23**	**9**	**8**	**3**	**1259**	**75**	**0**	**3.57**	**3.17**	**4.81**	**557**	**.865**	**26.5**	....	....	....	....	....	....	....	....	....	....	....	....
	Pittsburgh Penguins	**NHL**	**9**	**5**	**3**	**0**	**448**	**31**	**0**	**4.15**	**3.68**	**6.37**	**202**	**.847**	**27.1**	**1**	**0**	**0**	....	**40**	**4**	**0**	**6.00**	**15.00**	**16**	**.750**	**24.0**
1992-93	**Pittsburgh Penguins**	**NHL**	**25**	**13**	**7**	**2**	**1368**	**78**	**0**	**3.42**	**2.91**	**3.85**	**692**	**.887**	**30.4**	....	....	....	....	....	....	....	....	....	....	....	....
1993-94	**Pittsburgh Penguins**	**NHL**	**42**	**21**	**12**	**7**	**2456**	**138**	**1**	**3.37**	**3.21**	**3.60**	**1291**	**.893**	**31.5**	....	....	....	....	....	....	....	....	....	....	....	....
1994-95	**Pittsburgh Penguins**	**NHL**	**38**	***25**	**9**	**2**	**2208**	**118**	**0**	**3.21**	**3.32**	**3.11**	**1219**	**.903**	**33.1**	**11**	**5**	**6**	....	**661**	**33**	**1**	**3.00**	**2.84**	**349**	**.905**	**31.7**

			REGULAR SEASON												PLAYOFFS									
Season	Club	League	GP	W	L	T	Mins	GA	SO	Avg	AAvg	Eff	SA	S%	SAPG	GP	W	L	T	Mins	GA	SO	Avg	Eff	SA	S%	SAPG
1995-96	Pittsburgh Penguins	NHL	37	20	13	2	2132	115	3	3.24	3.18	3.09	1205	.905	33.9	9	7	2	....	599	23	0	2.30	1.61	328	.930	32.9
1996-97	Pittsburgh Penguins	NHL	46	17	17	6	2514	136	2	3.25	3.45	3.20	1383	.902	33.0	5	1	4	....	297	18	0	3.64	3.11	211	.915	42.6
1997-98	Pittsburgh Penguins	NHL	15	3	6	2	611	28	0	2.75	3.22	2.63	293	.904	28.8												
	NHL Totals		519	201	226	47	28494	1780	8	3.75	....	....	15263	.883	....	56	28	25	....	3341	160	3	2.87	....	....	....	....

WHL East First All-Star Team (1984)

Traded to **Philadelphia** by **Toronto** for Philadelphia's 1st round choice (Rob Pearson) and Calgary's 1st round choice (previously acquired, Toronto selected Steve Bancroft) in 1989 Entry Draft, March 6, 1989. Traded to **Pittsburgh** by **Philadelphia** with Rick Tocchet, Kjell Samuelsson and Philadelphia's 3rd round choice (Dave Roche) in 1993 Entry Draft for Mark Recchi, Brian Benning and Los Angeles' 1st round choice (previously acquired, Philadelphia selected Jason Bowen) in 1992 Entry Draft, February 19, 1992. Traded to **Calgary** by **Pittsburgh** with Dave Roche for German Titov and Todd Hlushko, June 17, 1998.

● **YOUNG, DOUG**   Doug "The Gleichen Cowboy" Young   G – R. 5'10", 190 lbs.   b: Medicine Hat, Alta., 10/1/1908.

1933-34	Detroit Red Wings	NHL	1	0	0	0	21	1	0	2.86	3.67	....	....	....	....	....	....	....	....	....	....	....	....	....	....	....	....
	NHL Totals		1	0	0	0	21	1	0	2.86	....	....	....	....	....	....	....	....	....	....	....	....	....	....	....	....	....

● **Detroit** defenseman replaced injured John Ross Roach in 2nd period, December 14, 1933. (Chicago 4, Detroit 0)

● **YOUNG, WENDELL**   Wendell Young   G – L. 5'9", 181 lbs.   b: Halifax, N.S., 8/1/1963.   Vancouver's 3rd choice, 73rd overall, in 1981 Entry Draft.

1980-81	Kitchener Rangers	OHA	42	19	15	0	2215	164	1	4.44	....	....	....	....	....	14	9	1	....	800	42	*1	3.15	....	....	....	....
1981-82	Kitchener Rangers	OHL	*60	*38	17	2	*3470	195	1	3.37	....	....	....	....	....	15	12	1	....	900	35	*1	*2.33	....	....	....	....
1982-83	Kitchener Rangers	OHL	61	*41	19	0	*3611	231	1	3.84	....	....	....	....	....	12	6	5	....	720	43	0	3.58	....	....	....	....
1983-84	Fredericton Express	AHL	11	7	3	0	569	39	1	4.11	....	....	....	....	....												
	Milwaukee Admirals	IHL	6	4	1	1	339	17	0	3.01	....	....	....	....	....												
	Salt Lake Golden Eagles	CHL	20	11	6	0	1094	80	0	4.39	....	....	....	....	....	4	0	2	....	122	11	0	5.42	....	....	....	....
1984-85	Fredericton Express	AHL	22	7	11	3	1242	83	0	4.01	....	....	....	....	....												
1985-86	Vancouver Canucks	NHL	22	4	9	3	1023	61	0	3.58	2.78	4.07	536	.886	31.4	1	0	1	....	60	5	0	5.00	7.81	32	.844	32.0
	Fredericton Express	AHL	24	12	8	4	1457	78	0	3.21	....	....	....	....	....												
1986-87	Vancouver Canucks	NHL	8	1	6	1	420	35	0	5.00	4.21	7.81	224	.844	32.0												
	Fredericton Express	AHL	30	11	16	0	1676	118	0	4.22	....	....	....	....	....												
1987-88	Philadelphia Flyers	NHL	6	3	2	0	320	20	0	3.75	3.12	5.03	149	.866	27.9												
	Hershey Bears	AHL	51	*33	15	1	2922	135	1	2.77	....	....	....	....	....	12	*12	0	....	*767	28	*1	*2.19	....	....	....	....
1988-89	Pittsburgh Penguins	NHL	22	12	9	0	1150	92	0	4.80	3.97	6.56	673	.863	35.1	1	0	0	....	39	1	0	1.54	1.40	11	.909	16.9
	Muskegon Lumberjacks	IHL	2	1	0	1	125	7	0	3.36	....	....	....	....	....												
1989-90	Pittsburgh Penguins	NHL	43	16	20	3	2318	161	1	4.17	3.50	5.30	1267	.873	32.8												
1990-91	Pittsburgh Penguins	NHL	18	4	6	2	773	52	0	4.04	3.61	4.91	428	.879	33.2												
1991-92	Pittsburgh Penguins	NHL	18	7	6	0	838	53	0	3.79	3.36	4.22	476	.889	34.1												
1992-93	Tampa Bay Lightning	NHL	31	7	19	2	1591	97	0	3.66	3.12	4.68	758	.872	28.6												
	Atlanta Knights	IHL	3	3	0	0	183	8	0	2.62	....	....	....	....	....												
1993-94	Tampa Bay Lightning	NHL	9	2	3	1	480	20	1	2.50	2.38	2.37	211	.905	26.4												
	Atlanta Knights	IHL	2	2	0	0	120	6	0	3.00	....	....	....	....	....												
1994-95	Chicago Wolves	IHL	37	14	11	7	1882	112	0	3.57	....	....	....	....	....												
	Pittsburgh Penguins	NHL	10	3	6	0	497	27	0	3.26	3.37	3.45	255	.894	30.8												
1995-96	Chicago Wolves	IHL	61	30	20	6	3285	199	1	3.63	....	....	....	....	....	9	4	5	....	540	30	0	3.33	....	....	....	....
1996-97	Chicago Wolves	IHL	52	35	12	1	2931	170	1	3.48	....	....	....	....	....	4	1	3	....	256	13	0	3.04	....	....	....	....
1997-98	Chicago Wolves	IHL	51	31	14	3	2912	149	2	3.07	....	....	....	....	....	9	5	3	....	515	24	1	2.79	....	....	....	....
	NHL Totals		187	59	86	12	9410	618	2	3.94	....	....	4977	.876	....	2	0	1	....	99	6	0	3.64	....	....	....	....

AHL First All-Star Team (1988) ● Won Baz Bastien Memorial Trophy (Top Goaltender - AHL) (1988) ● Won Jack Butterfield Trophy (Playoff MVP - AHL) (1988)

Traded to **Philadelphia** by **Vancouver** with Vancouver's 3rd round choice (Kimbi Daniels) in 1990 Entry Draft for Darren Jensen and Daryl Stanley, August 28, 1987. Traded to **Pittsburgh** by **Philadelphia** with Philadelphia's 7th round choice (Mika Valila) in 1990 Entry Draft for Pittsburgh's 3rd round choice (Chris Therien) in 1990 Entry Draft, September 1, 1988. Claimed by **Tampa Bay** from **Pittsburgh** in Expansion Draft, June 18, 1992. Traded to **Pittsburgh** by **Tampa Bay** for future considerations, February 16, 1995.

● **ZANIER, MIKE**   Mike Zanier   G – L. 5'11", 183 lbs.   b: Trail, B.C., 8/22/1962.

1980-81	New Westminster Bruins	WHL	49	11	27	1	2494	275	0	6.62	....	....	....	....	....												
1981-82	Spokane Flyers	WHL	9	1	7	0	476	55	0	6.93	....	....	....	....	....												
	Billings Bighorns	WHL	11	1	8	0	327	64	0	7.76	....	....	....	....	....												
	Medicine Hat Tigers	WHL	13	3	8	0	620	70	0	6.77	....	....	....	....	....												
	Calgary Wranglers	WHL	11	5	5	0	526	28	1	3.19	....	....	....	....	....	1	0	0	0	25	1	0	2.40	....	....	....	....
1982-83	Trail Smoke Eaters	WIHL	30				1734	116	0	4.01	....	....	....	....	....												
1983-84	Moncton Alpines	AHL	31	11	15	1	1743	96	0	3.30	....	....	....	....	....												
1984-85	Edmonton Oilers	NHL	3	1	1	1	185	12	0	3.89	3.09	4.67	100	.880	32.4												
	Nova Scotia Oilers	AHL	44	20	17	5	2484	143	0	3.45	....	....	....	....	....												
1985-86	Indianapolis Checkers	IHL	47	21	10	0	2727	151	0	3.32	....	....	....	....	....	2	1	1	0	120	9	0	4.50	....	....	....	....
1986-87	HC Salzburg	Austria	STATISTICS NOT AVAILABLE																								
	Indianapolis Checkers	IHL	14	6	8	0	807	60	0	4.46	....	....	....	....	....	6	2	4	0	359	21	0	3.51	....	....	....	....
1987-88	HC Bolzano	Italy	STATISTICS NOT AVAILABLE																								
1988-89	HC Bolzano	Italy	32				1920	114	0	3.56	....	....	....	....	....												
1989-90	HC Asiago	Italy	STATISTICS NOT AVAILABLE																								
1990-91	Milano Devils	Italy	45				2650	167	1	3.78	....	....	....	....	....												
1991-92	Milano Devils	Italy	24				1399	80	0	3.43	....	....	....	....	....												
	Milano Devils	Alpenliga	11				619	36	1	3.49	....	....	....	....	....												
	Italy	Olympics	3				155	14	0	5.42	....	....	....	....	....												
1992-93	Dallas Freeze	CHL	40	24	14	2	2384	150	1	3.78	....	....	....	....	....	7	2	4	0	424	33	0	4.67	....	....	....	....
1993-94	Milano Devils	Italy	20				1163	74	0	3.82	....	....	....	....	....												
	Milano Devils	Alpenliga	27				1589	92	0	3.47	....	....	....	....	....												
1994-95	Milano Devils	Italy	31				1755	108	0	3.69	....	....	....	....	....												
1995-96	Milano Devils	Italy	25				1496	79	2	3.17	....	....	....	....	....												
1996-97	Milano Devils	Alpenliga	28				1601	97	1	3.64	....	....	....	....	....												
	Milano Devils	EuroHL	6				184	26	0	8.48	....	....	....	....	....												
	Milano Devils	Italy	16				925	46	0	2.98	....	....	....	....	....												
	NHL Totals		3	1	1	1	185	12	0	3.89	....	....	100	.880	....	....	....	....	....	....	....	....	....	....	....	....	....

Signed as a free agent by **Edmonton**, October 4, 1983.

CHAPTER 76

Coaches Register

Complete NHL Coaching Records

THE COACHES REGISTER contains complete career NHL coaching records. Included are playing coaches such as Odie Cleghorn and Charlie Smith and interim coaches such as Mike Smith and Phil Esposito. If a coach has played in the NHL, the reader is directed to his career playing record in the Pre-Expansion Player, Modern Player or Goaltender registers.

Each coachís data panel includes his date of birth, place of birth and date of death. If only the birth year is known, it is included. If the death date is unknown, the coach is listed as Deceased. If the coach is a member of the Hockey Hall of Fame (**HHOF**) or the U.S. Hockey Hall of Fame (**USHOF**), this is noted here.

GC ñ games coached. **W–L–T** ñ a coach is credited with a result for every game his team wins, loses or ties while he is under contract as coach. If a coach is absent due to illness, suspension or family emergency, he is still credited with his teamís results.

W% ó Winning percentage is the percentage of available points gained in games coached. It is calculated as follows:

$$(W + W + T) \text{ divided by } (GC + GC)$$

Season	Club	League	REGULAR SEASON					PLAYOFFS				
			GC	W	L	T	W%	GC	W	L	T	W%
● ABEL, SID												HHOF
b: Melville, Sask., 2/22/1918.												
Played in NHL. See Pre-Expansion Player Register for career statistics.												
1952-53	Chicago	NHL	70	27	28	15	.493	7	3	4	0	.429
1953-54	Chicago	NHL	70	12	51	7	.221	....	....	....	....	....
1957-58	Detroit	NHL	33	16	12	5	.561	4	0	4	0	.000
1958-59	Detroit	NHL	70	25	37	8	.414	....	....	....	....	....
1959-60	Detroit	NHL	70	26	29	15	.479	6	2	4	0	.333
1960-61	Detroit	NHL	70	25	29	16	.471	11	6	5	0	.545
1961-62	Detroit	NHL	70	23	33	14	.429	....	....	....	....	....
1962-63	Detroit	NHL	70	32	25	13	.550	14	7	7	0	.500
1963-64	Detroit	NHL	70	30	29	11	.507	11	5	6	0	.455
1964-65	Detroit	NHL	70	40	23	7	.621	7	3	4	0	.429
1965-66	Detroit	NHL	70	31	27	12	.529	12	6	6	0	.500
1966-67	Detroit	NHL	70	27	39	4	.414	....	....	....	....	....
1967-68	Detroit	NHL	74	27	35	12	.446	....	....	....	....	....
1969-70	Detroit	NHL	74	38	21	15	.615	4	0	4	0	.000
1971-72	St. Louis	NHL	10	3	6	1	.350	....	....	....	....	....
1975-76	Kansas City	NHL	3	0	3	0	.000	....	....	....	....	....
	NHL Totals		**964**	**382**	**427**	**155**	**.477**	**76**	**32**	**44**	**0**	**.421**
● ADAMS, JACK												HHOF
b: Fort William, Ont., 6/14/1895. d: 5/1/1968.												
Played in NHL. See Pre-Expansion Player Register for career statistics.												
1922-23	Toronto	NHL	18	10	7	1	.583	....	....	....	....	....
1927-28	Detroit	NHL	44	19	19	6	.500	....	....	....	....	....
1928-29	Detroit	NHL	44	19	16	9	.534	2	0	2	0	.000
1929-30	Detroit	NHL	44	14	24	6	.386	....	....	....	....	....
1930-31	Detroit	NHL	44	16	21	7	.443	....	....	....	....	....
1931-32	Detroit	NHL	48	18	20	10	.479	2	0	1	1	.250
1932-33	Detroit	NHL	48	25	15	8	.604	4	2	2	0	.500
1933-34	Detroit	NHL	48	24	14	10	.604	9	4	5	0	.444
1934-35	Detroit	NHL	48	19	22	7	.469	....	....	....	....	....
1935-36	Detroit	NHL	48	24	16	8	.583	7	6	1	0	.857
1936-37	Detroit	NHL	48	25	14	9	.615	10	6	4	0	.600
1937-38	Detroit	NHL	48	12	25	11	.365	....	....	....	....	....
1938-39	Detroit	NHL	48	18	24	6	.438	6	3	3	0	.500
1939-40	Detroit	NHL	48	16	26	6	.396	5	2	3	0	.400
1940-41	Detroit	NHL	48	21	16	11	.552	9	4	5	0	.444
1941-42	Detroit	NHL	48	19	25	4	.438	12	7	5	0	.583
1942-43	Detroit	NHL	50	25	14	11	.610	10	8	2	0	.800
1943-44	Detroit	NHL	50	26	18	6	.580	5	1	4	0	.200
1944-45	Detroit	NHL	50	31	14	5	.670	14	7	7	0	.500
1945-46	Detroit	NHL	50	20	20	10	.500	5	1	4	0	.200
1946-47	Detroit	NHL	60	22	27	11	.458	5	1	4	0	.200
	NHL Totals		**982**	**423**	**397**	**162**	**.513**	**105**	**52**	**52**	**1**	**.500**
● ALLEN, KEITH												HHOF
b: Saskatoon, Sask., 8/21/1923.												
Played in NHL. See Pre-Expansion Player Register for career statistics.												
1967-68	Philadelphia	NHL	74	31	32	11	.493	7	3	4	0	.429
1968-69	Philadelphia	NHL	76	20	35	21	.401	4	0	4	0	.000
	NHL Totals		**150**	**51**	**67**	**32**	**.447**	**11**	**3**	**8**	**0**	**.273**
● ALLISON, DAVE												
b: Fort Frances, Ont., 4/14/1959.												
Played in NHL. See Modern Player Register for career statistics.												
1995-96	Ottawa	NHL	25	2	22	1	.100	....	....	....	....	....
	NHL Totals		**25**	**2**	**22**	**1**	**.100**	....	....	....	....	....

Season	Club	League	REGULAR SEASON					PLAYOFFS				
			GC	W	L	T	W%	GC	W	L	T	W%
● ANDERSON, JIM												
b: Pembroke, Ont., 12/1/1930.												
Played in NHL. See Modern Player Register for career statistics.												
1974-75	Washington	NHL	54	4	45	5	.120	....	....	....	....	....
	NHL Totals		**54**	**4**	**45**	**5**	**.120**	....	....	....	....	....
● ANGOTTI, LOU												
b: Toronto, Ont., 1/16/1938.												
Played in NHL. See Modern Player Register for career statistics.												
1973-74	St. Louis	NHL	23	4	15	4	.261	....	....	....	....	....
1974-75	St. Louis	NHL	9	2	5	2	.333	....	....	....	....	....
1983-84	Pittsburgh	NHL	80	16	58	6	.238	....	....	....	....	....
	NHL Totals		**112**	**22**	**78**	**12**	**.250**	....	....	....	....	....
● ARBOUR, AL												HHOF
b: Sudbury, Ont., 11/1/1932.												
Played in NHL. See Modern Player Register for career statistics.												
1970-71	St. Louis	NHL	50	21	15	14	.560	....	....	....	....	....
1971-72	St. Louis	NHL	44	19	19	6	.500	11	4	7	0	.364
1972-73	St. Louis	NHL	13	2	6	5	.346	....	....	....	....	....
1973-74	NY Islanders	NHL	70	19	41	10	.359	....	....	....	....	....
1974-75	NY Islanders	NHL	80	33	25	22	.550	17	9	8	0	.529
1975-76	NY Islanders	NHL	80	42	21	17	.631	13	7	6	0	.538
1976-77	NY Islanders	NHL	80	47	21	12	.663	12	8	4	0	.667
1977-78	NY Islanders	NHL	80	48	17	15	.694	7	3	4	0	.429
1978-79	NY Islanders	NHL	80	51	15	14	.725	10	6	4	0	.600
1979-80	NY Islanders	NHL	80	39	28	13	.569	21	15	6	0	.714
1980-81	NY Islanders	NHL	80	48	18	14	.688	18	15	3	0	.833
1981-82	NY Islanders	NHL	80	54	16	10	.738	19	15	4	0	.789
1982-83	NY Islanders	NHL	80	42	26	12	.600	20	15	5	0	.750
1983-84	NY Islanders	NHL	80	50	26	4	.650	21	12	9	0	.571
1984-85	NY Islanders	NHL	80	40	34	6	.538	10	4	6	0	.400
1985-86	NY Islanders	NHL	80	39	29	12	.563	3	0	3	0	.000
1988-89	NY Islanders	NHL	53	21	29	3	.425	....	....	....	....	....
1989-90	NY Islanders	NHL	80	31	38	11	.456	5	1	4	0	.200
1990-91	NY Islanders	NHL	80	25	45	10	.375	....	....	....	....	....
1991-92	NY Islanders	NHL	80	34	35	11	.494	....	....	....	....	....
1992-93	NY Islanders	NHL	84	40	37	7	.518	18	9	9	0	.500
1993-94	NY Islanders	NHL	84	36	36	12	.500	4	0	4	0	.000
	NHL Totals		**1606**	**781**	**577**	**248**	**.564**	**209**	**123**	**86**	**0**	**.589**
▪ Won Jack Adams Award (1979)												
● ARMSTRONG, GEORGE												HHOF
b: Skead, Ontario, 7/6/1930.												
Played in NHL. See Modern Player Register for career statistics.												
1988-89	Toronto	NHL	47	17	26	4	.404	....	....	....	....	....
	NHL Totals		**47**	**17**	**26**	**4**	**.404**	....	....	....	....	....
● BARKLEY, DOUG												
b: Lethbridge, Alta., 1/6/1937.												
Played in NHL. See Pre-Expansion Player Register for career statistics.												
1970-71	Detroit	NHL	40	10	23	7	.338	....	....	....	....	....
1971-72	Detroit	NHL	11	3	8	0	.273	....	....	....	....	....
1975-76	Detroit	NHL	26	7	15	4	.346	....	....	....	....	....
	NHL Totals		**77**	**20**	**46**	**11**	**.331**	....	....	....	....	....
● BEAULIEU, ANDRE												
b: unknown.												
1977-78	Minnesota	NHL	32	6	23	3	.234	....	....	....	....	....
	NHL Totals		**32**	**6**	**23**	**3**	**.234**	....	....	....	....	....

• BELISLE, DANNY

b: South Porcupine, Ont., 5/9/1937.
Played in NHL. See Pre-Expansion Player Register for career statistics.

1978-79	Washington	NHL	80	24	41	15	.394	....	....	....	....	....
1979-80	Washington	NHL	16	4	10	2	.313	....	....	....	....	....
	NHL Totals		**96**	**28**	**51**	**17**	**.380**	....	....	....	....	....

• BERENSON, RED

b: Regina, Sask., 12/8/1939.
Played in NHL. See Modern Player Register for career statistics.

1979-80	St. Louis	NHL	56	27	20	9	.563	3	0	3	0	.000
1980-81	St. Louis	NHL	80	45	18	17	.669	11	5	6	0	.455
1981-82	St. Louis	NHL	68	28	34	6	.456	....	....	....	....	....
	NHL Totals		**204**	**100**	**72**	**32**	**.569**	**14**	**5**	**9**	**0**	**.357**

• Won Jack Adams Award (1981)

• BERGERON, MICHEL

b: Chicoutimi, Que., 11/11/1954.

1980-81	Quebec	NHL	74	29	29	16	.500	5	2	3	0	.400
1981-82	Quebec	NHL	80	33	31	16	.513	16	7	9	0	.438
1982-83	Quebec	NHL	80	34	34	12	.500	4	1	3	0	.250
1983-84	Quebec	NHL	80	42	28	10	.588	9	5	4	0	.556
1984-85	Quebec	NHL	80	41	30	9	.569	18	9	9	0	.500
1985-86	Quebec	NHL	80	43	31	6	.575	3	0	3	0	.000
1986-87	Quebec	NHL	80	31	39	10	.450	13	7	6	0	.538
1987-88	NY Rangers	NHL	80	36	34	10	.513	....	....	....	....	....
1988-89	NY Rangers	NHL	78	37	33	8	.526	....	....	....	....	....
1989-90	Quebec	NHL	80	12	61	7	.194	....	....	....	....	....
	NHL Totals		**792**	**338**	**350**	**104**	**.492**	**68**	**31**	**37**	**0**	**.456**

• BERRY, BOB

b: Montreal, Que., 11/29/1943.
Played in NHL. See Modern Player Register for career statistics.

1978-79	Los Angeles	NHL	80	34	34	12	.500	2	0	2	0	.000
1979-80	Los Angeles	NHL	80	30	36	14	.463	4	1	3	0	.250
1980-81	Los Angeles	NHL	80	43	24	13	.619	4	1	3	0	.250
1981-82	Montreal	NHL	80	46	17	17	.681	5	2	3	0	.400
1982-83	Montreal	NHL	80	42	24	14	.613	3	0	3	0	.000
1983-84	Montreal	NHL	63	28	30	5	.484	....	....	....	....	....
1984-85	Pittsburgh	NHL	80	24	51	5	.331	....	....	....	....	....
1985-86	Pittsburgh	NHL	80	34	38	8	.475	....	....	....	....	....
1986-87	Pittsburgh	NHL	80	30	38	12	.450	....	....	....	....	....
1992-93	St. Louis	NHL	73	33	30	10	.521	11	7	4	0	.636
1993-94	St. Louis	NHL	84	40	33	11	.542	4	0	4	0	.000
	NHL Totals		**860**	**384**	**355**	**121**	**.517**	**33**	**11**	**22**	**0**	**.333**

• BEVERLEY, NICK

b: Toronto, Ont., 4/21/1947.
Played in NHL. See Modern Player Register for career statistics.

1995-96	Toronto	NHL	17	9	6	2	.588	6	2	4	0	.333
	NHL Totals		**17**	**9**	**6**	**2**	**.588**	**6**	**2**	**4**	**0**	**.333**

• BLACKBURN, DON

b: Kirkland Lake, Ont., 5/14/1938.
Played in NHL. See Modern Player Register for career statistics.

1979-80	Hartford	NHL	80	27	34	19	.456	3	0	3	0	.000
1980-81	Hartford	NHL	60	15	29	16	.383	....	....	....	....	....
	NHL Totals		**140**	**42**	**63**	**35**	**.425**	**3**	**0**	**3**	**0**	**.000**

• BLAIR, WREN

b: Lindsay, Ont., 10/2/1925.

1967-68	Minnesota	NHL	74	27	32	15	.466	14	7	7	0	.500
1968-69	Minnesota	NHL	41	12	20	9	.402	....	....	....	....	....
1969-70	Minnesota	NHL	32	9	13	10	.438	....	....	....	....	....
	NHL Totals		**147**	**48**	**65**	**34**	**.442**	**14**	**7**	**7**	**0**	**.500**

• BLAKE, TOE — HHOF

b: Victoria Mines, Ont., 8/21/1912. d: 5/17/1995.
Played in NHL. See Pre-Expansion Player Register for career statistics.

1955-56	Montreal	NHL	70	45	15	10	.714	10	8	2	0	.800
1956-57	Montreal	NHL	70	35	23	12	.586	10	8	2	0	.800
1957-58	Montreal	NHL	70	43	17	10	.686	10	8	2	0	.800
1958-59	Montreal	NHL	70	39	18	13	.650	11	8	3	0	.727
1959-60	Montreal	NHL	70	40	18	12	.657	8	8	0	0	1.000
1960-61	Montreal	NHL	70	41	19	10	.657	6	2	4	0	.333
1961-62	Montreal	NHL	70	42	14	14	.700	6	2	4	0	.333
1962-63	Montreal	NHL	70	28	19	23	.564	7	3	4	0	.429
1963-64	Montreal	NHL	70	36	21	13	.607	7	1	4	0	.200
1964-65	Montreal	NHL	70	36	23	11	.593	13	8	5	0	.615
1965-66	Montreal	NHL	70	41	21	8	.643	10	8	2	0	.800
1966-67	Montreal	NHL	70	32	25	13	.550	10	6	4	0	.600
1967-68	Montreal	NHL	74	42	22	10	.635	13	12	1	0	.923
	NHL Totals		**914**	**500**	**255**	**159**	**.634**	**119**	**82**	**37**	**0**	**.689**

• BOILEAU, MARC

b: Pointe Claire, Que., 9/3/1932.
Played in NHL. See Pre-Expansion Player Register for career statistics.

1973-74	Pittsburgh	NHL	28	14	10	4	.571	....	....	....	....	....
1974-75	Pittsburgh	NHL	80	37	28	15	.556	9	5	4	0	.556
1975-76	Pittsburgh	NHL	43	15	23	5	.407	....	....	....	....	....
	NHL Totals		**151**	**66**	**61**	**24**	**.517**	**9**	**5**	**4**	**0**	**.556**

• BOIVIN, LEO — HHOF

b: Prescott, Ont., 8/2/1932.
Played in NHL. See Modern Player Register for career statistics.

1975-76	St. Louis	NHL	43	17	17	9	.500	3	1	2	0	.333
1977-78	St. Louis	NHL	54	11	36	7	.269	....	....	....	....	....
	NHL Totals		**97**	**28**	**53**	**16**	**.371**	**3**	**1**	**2**	**0**	**.333**

• BOUCHER, FRANK — HHOF

b: Ottawa, Ont., 10/7/1901. d: 12/12/1977.
Played in NHL. See Pre-Expansion Player Register for career statistics.

1939-40	NY Rangers	NHL	48	27	11	10	.667	12	8	4	0	.667
1940-41	NY Rangers	NHL	48	21	19	8	.521	3	1	2	0	.333
1941-42	NY Rangers	NHL	48	29	17	2	.625	6	2	4	0	.333
1942-43	NY Rangers	NHL	50	11	31	8	.300	....	....	....	....	....
1943-44	NY Rangers	NHL	50	6	39	5	.170	....	....	....	....	....
1944-45	NY Rangers	NHL	50	11	29	10	.320	....	....	....	....	....
1945-46	NY Rangers	NHL	50	13	28	9	.350	....	....	....	....	....
1946-47	NY Rangers	NHL	60	22	32	6	.417	....	....	....	....	....
1947-48	NY Rangers	NHL	60	21	26	13	.458	6	2	4	0	.333
1948-49	NY Rangers	NHL	23	6	11	6	.391	....	....	....	....	....
1953-54	NY Rangers	NHL	40	14	20	6	.425	....	....	....	....	....
	NHL Totals		**527**	**181**	**263**	**83**	**.422**	**27**	**13**	**14**	**0**	**.481**

• BOUCHER, GEORGE — HHOF

b: Ottawa, Ont., 8/19/1896. d: 10/17/1960.
Played in NHL. See Pre-Expansion Player Register for career statistics.

1930-31	Mtl. Maroons	NHL	12	6	5	1	.542	2	0	2	0	.000
1933-34	Ottawa	NHL	48	13	29	6	.333	....	....	....	....	....
1934-35	St. Louis	NHL	35	9	20	6	.343	....	....	....	....	....
1949-50	Boston	NHL	70	22	32	16	.429	....	....	....	....	....
	NHL Totals		**165**	**50**	**86**	**29**	**.391**	**2**	**0**	**2**	**0**	**.000**

• BOWMAN, SCOTTY — HHOF

b: Montreal, Que., 9/18/1933.

1967-68	St. Louis	NHL	58	23	21	14	.517	18	8	10	0	.444
1968-69	St. Louis	NHL	76	37	25	14	.579	12	8	4	0	.667
1969-70	St. Louis	NHL	76	37	27	12	.566	16	8	8	0	.500
1970-71	St. Louis	NHL	28	13	10	5	.554	6	2	4	0	.333
1971-72	Montreal	NHL	78	46	16	16	.692	6	2	4	0	.333
1972-73	Montreal	NHL	78	52	10	16	.769	17	12	5	0	.706
1973-74	Montreal	NHL	78	45	24	9	.635	6	2	4	0	.333
1974-75	Montreal	NHL	80	47	14	19	.706	11	6	5	0	.545
1975-76	Montreal	NHL	80	58	11	11	.794	13	12	1	0	.923
1976-77	Montreal	NHL	80	60	8	12	.825	14	12	2	0	.857
1977-78	Montreal	NHL	80	59	10	11	.806	15	12	3	0	.800
1978-79	Montreal	NHL	80	52	17	11	.719	16	12	4	0	.750
1979-80	Buffalo	NHL	80	47	17	16	.688	14	9	5	0	.643
1981-82	Buffalo	NHL	35	18	10	7	.614	4	1	3	0	.250
1982-83	Buffalo	NHL	80	38	29	13	.556	10	6	4	0	.600
1983-84	Buffalo	NHL	80	48	25	7	.644	3	0	3	0	.000
1984-85	Buffalo	NHL	80	38	28	14	.563	5	2	3	0	.400
1985-86	Buffalo	NHL	37	18	18	1	.500	....	....	....	....	....
1986-87	Buffalo	NHL	12	3	7	2	.333	....	....	....	....	....
1991-92	Pittsburgh	NHL	80	39	32	9	.544	21	16	5	0	.762
1992-93	Pittsburgh	NHL	84	56	21	7	.708	12	7	5	0	.583
1993-94	Detroit	NHL	84	46	30	8	.595	7	3	4	0	.429
1994-95	Detroit	NHL	48	33	11	4	.729	18	12	6	0	.667
1995-96	Detroit	NHL	82	62	13	7	.799	19	10	9	0	.526
1996-97	Detroit	NHL	82	38	26	18	.573	20	16	4	0	.800
1997-98	Detroit	NHL	82	44	23	15	.628	22	16	6	0	.727
	NHL Totals		**1818**	**1057**	**483**	**278**	**.658**	**305**	**194**	**111**	**0**	**.636**

• Won Jack Adams Award (1977, 1996)

• BOWNESS, RICK

b: Moncton, N.B., 1/25/1955.
Played in NHL. See Modern Player Register for career statistics.

1988-89	Winnipeg	NHL	28	8	17	3	.339	....	....	....	....	....
1991-92	Boston	NHL	80	36	32	12	.525	15	8	7	0	.533
1992-93	Ottawa	NHL	84	10	70	4	.143	....	....	....	....	....
1993-94	Ottawa	NHL	84	14	61	9	.220	....	....	....	....	....
1994-95	Ottawa	NHL	48	9	34	5	.240	....	....	....	....	....
1995-96	Ottawa	NHL	19	6	13	0	.316	....	....	....	....	....
1996-97	NY Islanders	NHL	37	16	18	3	.473	....	....	....	....	....
1997-98	NY Islanders	NHL	63	22	32	9	.421	....	....	....	....	....
	NHL Totals		**443**	**121**	**277**	**45**	**.324**	**15**	**8**	**7**	**0**	**.533**

• BROOKS, HERB — USHOF

b: St. Paul, MN, 8/5/1937.

1981-82	NY Rangers	NHL	80	39	27	14	.575	10	5	5	0	.500
1982-83	NY Rangers	NHL	80	35	35	10	.500	9	5	4	0	.556
1983-84	NY Rangers	NHL	80	42	29	9	.581	5	2	3	0	.400
1984-85	NY Rangers	NHL	45	15	22	8	.422	....	....	....	....	....
1987-88	Minnesota	NHL	80	19	48	13	.319	....	....	....	....	....
1992-93	New Jersey	NHL	84	40	37	7	.518	5	1	4	0	.200
	NHL Totals		**449**	**190**	**198**	**61**	**.491**	**29**	**13**	**16**	**0**	**.448**

• BROPHY, JOHN

b: Antigonish, N.S., 1/20/1933.

1986-87	Toronto	NHL	80	32	42	6	.438	13	7	6	0	.538
1987-88	Toronto	NHL	80	21	49	10	.325	6	2	4	0	.333
1988-89	Toronto	NHL	33	11	20	2	.364	....	....	....	....	....
	NHL Totals		**193**	**64**	**111**	**18**	**.378**	**19**	**9**	**10**	**0**	**.474**

• BURNETT, GEORGE

b: Port Perry, Ont., 3/25/1962.

1994-95	Edmonton	NHL	35	12	20	3	.386	....	....	....	....	....
	NHL Totals		**35**	**12**	**20**	**3**	**.386**	....	....	....	....	....

• BURNS, CHARLIE
b: Detroit, MI, 2/14/1936.
Played in NHL. See Modern Player Register for career statistics.

Season	Club	League	GC	W	L	T	W%	GC	W	L	T	W%
			REGULAR SEASON					PLAYOFFS				
1969-70	Minnesota	NHL	44	10	22	12	.364	6	2	4	0	.333
1974-75	Minnesota	NHL	42	12	28	2	.310	....	....	....	....	....
	NHL Totals		**86**	**22**	**50**	**14**	**.337**	**6**	**2**	**4**	**0**	**.333**

• BURNS, PAT
b: St-Henri, Que., 4/4/1952.

Season	Club	League	GC	W	L	T	W%	GC	W	L	T	W%
1988-89	Montreal	NHL	80	53	18	9	.719	21	14	7	0	.667
1989-90	Montreal	NHL	80	41	28	11	.581	11	5	6	0	.455
1990-91	Montreal	NHL	80	39	30	11	.556	13	7	6	0	.538
1991-92	Montreal	NHL	80	41	28	11	.581	11	4	7	0	.364
1992-93	Toronto	NHL	84	44	29	11	.589	21	11	10	0	.524
1993-94	Toronto	NHL	84	43	29	12	.583	18	9	9	0	.500
1994-95	Toronto	NHL	48	21	19	8	.521	7	3	4	0	.429
1995-96	Toronto	NHL	65	25	30	10	.462	....	....	....	....	....
1997-98	Boston	NHL	82	39	30	13	.555	6	2	4	0	.333
	NHL Totals		**683**	**346**	**241**	**96**	**.577**	**108**	**55**	**53**	**0**	**.509**

• Won Jack Adams Award (1989, 1993, 1998)

• BUSH, EDDIE
b: Collingwood, Ont., 7/11/1918. d: 5/31/1984.
Played in NHL. See Pre-Expansion Player Register for career statistics.

Season	Club	League	GC	W	L	T	W%	GC	W	L	T	W%
1975-76	Kansas City	NHL	32	1	23	8	.156	....	....	....	....	....
	NHL Totals		**32**	**1**	**23**	**8**	**.156**	....	....	....	....	....

• CAMPBELL, COLIN
b: London, Ont., 1/28/1953.
Played in NHL. See Modern Player Register for career statistics.

Season	Club	League	GC	W	L	T	W%	GC	W	L	T	W%
1994-95	NY Rangers	NHL	48	22	23	3	.490	10	4	6	0	.400
1995-96	NY Rangers	NHL	82	41	27	14	.585	11	5	6	0	.455
1996-97	NY Rangers	NHL	82	38	34	10	.524	15	9	6	0	.600
1997-98	NY Rangers	NHL	57	17	24	16	.439	....	....	....	....	....
	NHL Totals		**269**	**118**	**108**	**43**	**.519**	**36**	**18**	**18**	**0**	**.500**

• CAROLL, DICK
b. Guelph, Ont., 1888. d: 1/21/1952.

Season	Club	League	GC	W	L	T	W%	GC	W	L	T	W%
1917-18	Toronto	NHL	22	13	9	0	.591	7	4	3	0	.571
1918-19	Toronto	NHL	18	5	13	0	.278	....	....	....	....	....
1920-21	Toronto	NHL	24	15	9	0	.625	2	0	2	0	.000
	NHL Totals		**64**	**33**	**31**	**0**	**.516**	**9**	**4**	**5**	**0**	**.444**

• CARPENTER, DOUG
b: Cornwall, Ont., 7/1/1942.

Season	Club	League	GC	W	L	T	W%	GC	W	L	T	W%
1984-85	New Jersey	NHL	80	22	48	10	.338	....	....	....	....	....
1985-86	New Jersey	NHL	80	28	49	3	.369	....	....	....	....	....
1986-87	New Jersey	NHL	80	29	45	6	.400	....	....	....	....	....
1987-88	New Jersey	NHL	50	21	24	5	.470	....	....	....	....	....
1989-90	Toronto	NHL	80	38	38	4	.500	5	1	4	0	.200
1990-91	Toronto	NHL	11	1	9	1	.136	....	....	....	....	....
	NHL Totals		**381**	**139**	**213**	**29**	**.403**	**5**	**1**	**4**	**0**	**.200**

• CASHMAN, WAYNE
b: Kingston, Ont., 6/24/1945.
Played in NHL. See Modern Player Register for career statistics.

Season	Club	League	GC	W	L	T	W%	GC	W	L	T	W%
1997-98	Philadelphia	NHL	61	32	20	9	.598	....	....	....	....	....
	NHL Totals		**61**	**32**	**20**	**9**	**.598**	....	....	....	....	....

• CHAMBERS, DAVE
b: Leaside, Ont., 5/7/1940.

Season	Club	League	GC	W	L	T	W%	GC	W	L	T	W%
1990-91	Quebec	NHL	80	16	50	14	.288	....	....	....	....	....
1991-92	Quebec	NHL	18	3	14	1	.194	....	....	....	....	....
	NHL Totals		**98**	**19**	**64**	**15**	**.270**	....	....	....	....	....

• CHARRON, GUY
b: Verdun, Que., 1/24/1949.
Played in NHL. See Modern Player Register for career statistics.

Season	Club	League	GC	W	L	T	W%	GC	W	L	T	W%
1991-92	Calgary	NHL	16	6	7	3	.469	....	....	....	....	....
	NHL Totals		**16**	**6**	**7**	**3**	**.469**	....	....	....	....	....

• CHEEVERS, GERRY HHOF
b: St. Catharines, Ont., 12/7/1940.
Played in NHL. See Goaltender Register for career statistics.

Season	Club	League	GC	W	L	T	W%	GC	W	L	T	W%
1980-81	Boston	NHL	80	37	30	13	.544	3	0	3	0	.000
1981-82	Boston	NHL	80	43	27	10	.600	11	6	5	0	.545
1982-83	Boston	NHL	80	50	20	10	.688	17	9	8	0	.529
1983-84	Boston	NHL	80	49	25	6	.650	3	0	3	0	.000
1984-85	Boston	NHL	56	25	24	7	.509	....	....	....	....	....
	NHL Totals		**376**	**204**	**126**	**46**	**.604**	**34**	**15**	**19**	**0**	**.441**

• CHERRY, DON
b: Kingston, Ont., 2/5/1934.
Played in NHL. See Pre-Expansion Player Register for career statistics.

Season	Club	League	GC	W	L	T	W%	GC	W	L	T	W%
1974-75	Boston	NHL	80	40	26	14	.588	3	1	2	0	.333
1975-76	Boston	NHL	80	48	15	17	.706	12	5	7	0	.417
1976-77	Boston	NHL	80	49	23	8	.663	14	8	6	0	.571
1977-78	Boston	NHL	80	51	18	11	.706	15	10	5	0	.667
1978-79	Boston	NHL	80	43	23	14	.625	11	7	4	0	.636
1979-80	Colorado	NHL	80	19	48	13	.319	....	....	....	....	....
	NHL Totals		**480**	**250**	**153**	**77**	**.601**	**55**	**31**	**24**	**0**	**.564**

• Won Jack Adams Award (1976)

• CLANCY, KING HHOF
b: Ottawa, Ont., 2/25/1903. d: 11/8/1986.
Played in NHL. See Pre-Expansion Player Register for career statistics.

Season	Club	League	GC	W	L	T	W%	GC	W	L	T	W%
1937-38	Mtl. Maroons	NHL	18	6	11	1	.361	....	....	....	....	....
1953-54	Toronto	NHL	70	32	24	14	.557	5	1	4	0	.200
1954-55	Toronto	NHL	70	24	24	22	.500	4	0	4	0	.000
1955-56	Toronto	NHL	70	24	33	13	.436	5	1	4	0	.200
1971-72	Toronto	NHL	15	9	3	3	.700	5	1	4	0	.200
	NHL Totals		**243**	**95**	**95**	**53**	**.500**	**19**	**3**	**16**	**0**	**.158**

• CLAPPER, DIT HHOF
b: Newmarket, Ont., 2/9/1907. d: 1/21/1978.
Played in NHL. See Pre-Expansion Player Register for career statistics.

Season	Club	League	GC	W	L	T	W%	GC	W	L	T	W%
1945-46	Boston	NHL	50	24	18	8	.560	10	5	5	0	.500
1946-47	Boston	NHL	60	26	23	11	.525	5	1	4	0	.200
1947-48	Boston	NHL	60	23	24	13	.492	5	1	4	0	.200
1948-49	Boston	NHL	60	29	23	8	.550	5	1	4	0	.200
	NHL Totals		**230**	**102**	**88**	**40**	**.530**	**25**	**8**	**17**	**0**	**.320**

• CLEGHORN, ODIE
b: Montreal, Que., 9/19/1891. d: 7/13/1956.
Played in NHL. See Pre-Expansion Player Register for career statistics.

Season	Club	League	GC	W	L	T	W%	GC	W	L	T	W%
1925-26	Pittsburgh	NHL	36	19	16	1	.542	2	0	1	1	.250
1926-27	Pittsburgh	NHL	44	15	26	3	.375	....	....	....	....	....
1927-28	Pittsburgh	NHL	44	19	17	8	.523	2	1	1	0	.500
1928-29	Pittsburgh	NHL	44	9	27	8	.295	....	....	....	....	....
	NHL Totals		**168**	**62**	**86**	**20**	**.429**	**4**	**1**	**2**	**1**	**.375**

• CLEGHORN, SPRAGUE HHOF
b: Montreal, Que., 3/11/1890. d: 7/11/1956.
Played in NHL. See Pre-Expansion Player Register for career statistics.

Season	Club	League	GC	W	L	T	W%	GC	W	L	T	W%
1931-32	Mtl. Maroons	NHL	48	19	22	7	.469	4	1	1	2	.500
	NHL Totals		**48**	**19**	**22**	**7**	**.469**	**4**	**1**	**1**	**2**	**.500**

• COLVILLE, NEIL HHOF
b: Edmonton, Alta., 8/4/1914. d: 12/26/1987.
Played in NHL. See Pre-Expansion Player Register for career statistics.

Season	Club	League	GC	W	L	T	W%	GC	W	L	T	W%
1950-51	NY Rangers	NHL	70	20	29	21	.436	....	....	....	....	....
1951-52	NY Rangers	NHL	23	6	12	5	.370	....	....	....	....	....
	NHL Totals		**93**	**26**	**41**	**26**	**.419**	....	....	....	....	....

• CONACHER, CHARLIE HHOF
b: Toronto, Ont., 12/20/1910. Deceased.
Played in NHL. See Pre-Expansion Player Register for career statistics.

Season	Club	League	GC	W	L	T	W%	GC	W	L	T	W%
1947-48	Chicago	NHL	32	13	15	4	.469	....	....	....	....	....
1948-49	Chicago	NHL	60	21	31	8	.417	....	....	....	....	....
1949-50	Chicago	NHL	70	22	38	10	.386	....	....	....	....	....
	NHL Totals		**162**	**56**	**84**	**22**	**.414**	....	....	....	....	....

• CONACHER, LIONEL HHOF
b: Toronto, Ont., 5/24/1901. d: 5/26/1954.
Played in NHL. See Pre-Expansion Player Register for career statistics.

Season	Club	League	GC	W	L	T	W%	GC	W	L	T	W%
1929-30	NY Americans	NHL	44	14	25	5	.375	....	....	....	....	....
	NHL Totals		**44**	**14**	**25**	**5**	**.375**	....	....	....	....	....

• CONSTANTINE, KEVIN
b: International Falls, MN, 12/27/1958.

Season	Club	League	GC	W	L	T	W%	GC	W	L	T	W%
1993-94	San Jose	NHL	84	33	35	16	.488	14	7	7	0	.500
1994-95	San Jose	NHL	48	19	25	4	.438	11	4	7	0	.364
1995-96	San Jose	NHL	25	3	18	4	.200	....	....	....	....	....
1997-98	Pittsburgh	NHL	82	40	24	18	.598	6	2	4	0	.333
	NHL Totals		**239**	**95**	**102**	**42**	**.485**	**31**	**13**	**18**	**0**	**.419**

• COOK, BILL HHOF
b: Brantford, Ont., 10/9/1896. d: 4/6/1986.
Played in NHL. See Pre-Expansion Player Register for career statistics.

Season	Club	League	GC	W	L	T	W%	GC	W	L	T	W%
1951-52	NY Rangers	NHL	47	17	22	8	.447	....	....	....	....	....
1952-53	NY Rangers	NHL	70	17	37	16	.357	....	....	....	....	....
	NHL Totals		**117**	**34**	**59**	**24**	**.393**	....	....	....	....	....

• CRAWFORD, MARC
b: Belleville, Ont., 2/13/1961.
Played in NHL. See Modern Player Register for career statistics.

Season	Club	League	GC	W	L	T	W%	GC	W	L	T	W%
1994-95	Quebec	NHL	48	30	13	5	.677	6	2	4	0	.333
1995-96	Colorado	NHL	82	47	25	10	.634	22	16	6	0	.727
1996-97	Colorado	NHL	82	49	24	9	.652	17	10	7	0	.588
1997-98	Colorado	NHL	82	39	26	17	.579	7	3	4	0	.429
	NHL Totals		**294**	**165**	**88**	**41**	**.631**	**52**	**31**	**21**	**0**	**.596**

Won Jack Adams Award (1995)

• CREAMER, PIERRE
b: Chomedy, Que, 7/6/1944.

Season	Club	League	GC	W	L	T	W%	GC	W	L	T	W%
1987-88	Pittsburgh	NHL	80	36	35	9	.506	....	....	....	....	....
	NHL Totals		**80**	**36**	**35**	**9**	**.506**	....	....	....	....	....

• CREIGHTON, FRED
b: Hamiota, Man., 7/14/1933.

Season	Club	League	REGULAR SEASON GC	W	L	T	W%	PLAYOFFS GC	W	L	T	W%
1974-75	Atlanta	NHL	28	12	11	5	.518	....	....	....	....	....
1975-76	Atlanta	NHL	80	35	33	12	.513	2	1	1	0	.500
1976-77	Atlanta	NHL	80	34	34	12	.500	3	1	2	0	.333
1977-78	Atlanta	NHL	80	34	27	19	.544	2	0	2	0	.000
1978-79	Atlanta	NHL	80	41	31	8	.563	2	0	2	0	.000
1979-80	Boston	NHL	73	40	20	13	.637	....	....	....	....	....
	NHL Totals		**421**	**196**	**156**	**69**	**.548**	**9**	**2**	**7**	**0**	**.222**

• CRISP, TERRY
b: Parry Sound, Ont., 5/28/1943.
Played in NHL. See Modern Player Register for career statistics.

Season	Club	League	REGULAR SEASON GC	W	L	T	W%	PLAYOFFS GC	W	L	T	W%
1987-88	Calgary	NHL	80	48	23	9	.656	9	4	5	0	.444
1988-89	Calgary	NHL	80	54	17	9	.731	22	16	6	0	.727
1989-90	Calgary	NHL	80	42	23	15	.619	6	2	4	0	.333
1992-93	Tampa Bay	NHL	84	23	54	7	.315	....	....	....	....	....
1993-94	Tampa Bay	NHL	84	30	43	11	.423	....	....	....	....	....
1994-95	Tampa Bay	NHL	48	17	28	3	.385	....	....	....	....	....
1995-96	Tampa Bay	NHL	82	38	32	12	.537	6	2	4	0	.333
1996-97	Tampa Bay	NHL	82	32	40	10	.451	....	....	....	....	....
1997-98	Tampa Bay	NHL	11	2	7	2	.273	....	....	....	....	....
	NHL Totals		**631**	**286**	**267**	**78**	**.515**	**43**	**24**	**19**	**0**	**.558**

• CROZIER, JOE
b: Winnipeg, Man., 2/19/1929.
Played in NHL. See Pre-Expansion Player Register for career statistics.

Season	Club	League	REGULAR SEASON GC	W	L	T	W%	PLAYOFFS GC	W	L	T	W%
1971-72	Buffalo	NHL	36	8	19	9	.347	....	....	....	....	....
1972-73	Buffalo	NHL	78	37	27	14	.564	6	2	4	0	.333
1973-74	Buffalo	NHL	78	32	34	12	.487	....	....	....	....	....
1980-81	Toronto	NHL	40	13	22	5	.388	....	....	....	....	....
	NHL Totals		**232**	**90**	**102**	**40**	**.474**	**6**	**2**	**4**	**0**	**.333**

• CROZIER, ROGER
b: Bracebridge, Ont., 3/16/1942. d: 1/11/1996.
Played in NHL. See Goaltender Register for career statistics.

Season	Club	League	REGULAR SEASON GC	W	L	T	W%	PLAYOFFS GC	W	L	T	W%
1981-82	Washington	NHL	1	0	1	0	.000	....	....	....	....	....
	NHL Totals		**1**	**0**	**1**	**0**	**.000**	....	....	....	....	....

• CUNNIFF, JOHN
b: South Boston, MA, 7/9/1943.

Season	Club	League	REGULAR SEASON GC	W	L	T	W%	PLAYOFFS GC	W	L	T	W%
1982-83	Hartford	NHL	13	3	9	1	.269	....	....	....	....	....
1989-90	New Jersey	NHL	66	31	28	7	.523	6	2	4	0	.333
1990-91	New Jersey	NHL	67	28	28	11	.500	....	....	....	....	....
	NHL Totals		**146**	**62**	**65**	**19**	**.490**	**6**	**2**	**4**	**0**	**.333**

• DANDURAND, LEO — HHOF
b: Bourbonnais, IL, 7/9/1889. d: 6/26/1964.

Season	Club	League	REGULAR SEASON GC	W	L	T	W%	PLAYOFFS GC	W	L	T	W%
1921-22	Montreal	NHL	17	10	6	1	.618	....	....	....	....	....
1922-23	Montreal	NHL	24	13	9	2	.583	2	1	1	0	.500
1923-24	Montreal	NHL	24	13	11	0	.542	6	6	0	0	1.000
1924-25	Montreal	NHL	30	17	11	2	.600	6	3	3	0	.500
1925-26	Montreal	NHL	36	11	24	1	.319	....	....	....	....	....
1934-35	Montreal	NHL	32	14	15	3	.484	2	0	2	0	.000
	NHL Totals		**163**	**78**	**76**	**9**	**.506**	**16**	**10**	**6**	**0**	**.625**

• DAY, HAP — HHOF
b: Owen Sound, Ont., 6/14/1901. d: 2/17/1990.
Played in NHL. See Pre-Expansion Player Register for career statistics.

Season	Club	League	REGULAR SEASON GC	W	L	T	W%	PLAYOFFS GC	W	L	T	W%
1940-41	Toronto	NHL	48	28	14	6	.646	7	3	4	0	.429
1941-42	Toronto	NHL	48	27	18	3	.594	13	8	5	0	.615
1942-43	Toronto	NHL	50	22	19	9	.530	6	2	4	0	.333
1943-44	Toronto	NHL	50	23	23	4	.500	5	1	4	0	.200
1944-45	Toronto	NHL	50	24	22	4	.520	13	8	5	0	.615
1945-46	Toronto	NHL	50	19	24	7	.450	....	....	....	....	....
1946-47	Toronto	NHL	60	31	19	10	.600	11	8	3	0	.727
1947-48	Toronto	NHL	60	32	15	13	.642	9	8	1	0	.889
1948-49	Toronto	NHL	60	22	25	13	.475	9	8	1	0	.889
1949-50	Toronto	NHL	70	31	27	12	.529	7	3	4	0	.429
	NHL Totals		**546**	**259**	**206**	**81**	**.549**	**80**	**49**	**31**	**0**	**.613**

• DEA, BILLY
b: Edmonton, Alta., 4/3/1933.
Played in NHL. See Modern Player Register for career statistics.

Season	Club	League	REGULAR SEASON GC	W	L	T	W%	PLAYOFFS GC	W	L	T	W%
1981-82	Detroit	NHL	11	3	8	0	.273	....	....	....	....	....
	NHL Totals		**11**	**3**	**8**	**0**	**.273**	....	....	....	....	....

• DELVECCHIO, ALEX — HHOF
b: Fort William, Ont., 12/4/1932.
Played in NHL. See Modern Player Register for career statistics.

Season	Club	League	REGULAR SEASON GC	W	L	T	W%	PLAYOFFS GC	W	L	T	W%
1973-74	Detroit	NHL	67	27	31	9	.470	....	....	....	....	....
1974-75	Detroit	NHL	80	23	45	12	.363	....	....	....	....	....
1975-76	Detroit	NHL	54	19	29	6	.407	....	....	....	....	....
1976-77	Detroit	NHL	44	13	26	5	.352	....	....	....	....	....
	NHL Totals		**245**	**82**	**131**	**32**	**.400**	....	....	....	....	....

• DEMERS, JACQUES
b: Montreal, Que., 8/25/1944.

Season	Club	League	REGULAR SEASON GC	W	L	T	W%	PLAYOFFS GC	W	L	T	W%
1979-80	Quebec	NHL	80	25	44	11	.381	....	....	....	....	....
1983-84	St. Louis	NHL	80	32	41	7	.444	11	6	5	0	.545
1984-85	St. Louis	NHL	80	37	31	12	.538	3	0	3	0	.000
1985-86	St. Louis	NHL	80	37	34	9	.519	19	10	9	0	.526
1986-87	Detroit	NHL	80	34	36	10	.488	16	9	7	0	.563
1987-88	Detroit	NHL	80	41	28	11	.581	16	9	7	0	.563
1988-89	Detroit	NHL	80	34	34	12	.500	6	2	4	0	.333
1989-90	Detroit	NHL	80	28	38	14	.438	....	....	....	....	....
1992-93	Montreal	NHL	84	48	30	6	.607	20	16	4	0	.800
1993-94	Montreal	NHL	84	41	29	14	.571	7	3	4	0	.429
1994-95	Montreal	NHL	48	18	23	7	.448	....	....	....	....	....
1995-96	Montreal	NHL	5	0	5	0	.000	....	....	....	....	....
1997-98	Tampa Bay	NHL	63	15	40	8	.302	....	....	....	....	....
	NHL Totals		**924**	**390**	**413**	**121**	**.488**	**98**	**55**	**43**	**0**	**.561**

• Won Jack Adams Award (1987, 1988)

• DENNENY, CY — HHOF
b: Farrow's Point, Ont., 12/23/1891. d: 10/12/1970.
Played in NHL. See Pre-Expansion Player Register for career statistics.

Season	Club	League	REGULAR SEASON GC	W	L	T	W%	PLAYOFFS GC	W	L	T	W%
1928-29	Boston	NHL	44	26	13	5	.648	5	5	0	0	1.000
1932-33	Ottawa	NHL	48	11	27	10	.333	....	....	....	....	....
	NHL Totals		**92**	**37**	**40**	**15**	**.484**	**5**	**5**	**0**	**0**	**1.000**

• DINEEN, BILL
b: Arvida, Que., 9/18/1932.
Played in NHL. See Pre-Expansion Player Register for career statistics.

Season	Club	League	REGULAR SEASON GC	W	L	T	W%	PLAYOFFS GC	W	L	T	W%
1991-92	Philadelphia	NHL	56	24	23	9	.509	....	....	....	....	....
1992-93	Philadelphia	NHL	84	36	37	11	.494	....	....	....	....	....
	NHL Totals		**140**	**60**	**60**	**20**	**.500**	....	....	....	....	....

• DUDLEY, RICK
b: Toronto, Ont., 1/31/1949.
Played in NHL. See Modern Player Register for career statistics.

Season	Club	League	REGULAR SEASON GC	W	L	T	W%	PLAYOFFS GC	W	L	T	W%
1989-90	Buffalo	NHL	80	45	27	8	.613	6	2	4	0	.333
1990-91	Buffalo	NHL	80	31	30	19	.506	6	2	4	0	.333
1991-92	Buffalo	NHL	28	9	15	4	.393	....	....	....	....	....
	NHL Totals		**188**	**85**	**72**	**31**	**.535**	**12**	**4**	**8**	**0**	**.333**

• DUFF, DICK
b: Kirkland Lake, Ont., 2/18/1936.
Played in NHL. See Modern Player Register for career statistics.

Season	Club	League	REGULAR SEASON GC	W	L	T	W%	PLAYOFFS GC	W	L	T	W%
1979-80	Toronto	NHL	2	0	2	0	.000	....	....	....	....	....
	NHL Totals		**2**	**0**	**2**	**0**	**.000**	....	....	....	....	....

• DUGAL, JULES
b: unknown. Deceased.

Season	Club	League	REGULAR SEASON GC	W	L	T	W%	PLAYOFFS GC	W	L	T	W%
1938-39	Montreal	NHL	18	9	6	3	.583	3	1	2	0	.333
	NHL Totals		**18**	**9**	**6**	**3**	**.583**	**3**	**1**	**2**	**0**	**.333**

• DUNCAN, ART
b: Sault Ste. Marie, Ont., 7/4/1894. d: 4/13/1975.
Played in NHL. See Pre-Expansion Player Register for career statistics.

Season	Club	League	REGULAR SEASON GC	W	L	T	W%	PLAYOFFS GC	W	L	T	W%
1926-27	Detroit	NHL	33	10	21	2	.333	....	....	....	....	....
1930-31	Toronto	NHL	42	21	13	8	.595	2	0	1	1	.250
1931-32	Toronto	NHL	5	0	3	2	.200	....	....	....	....	....
	NHL Totals		**80**	**31**	**37**	**12**	**.463**	**2**	**0**	**1**	**1**	**.250**

• DUTTON, RED — HHOF
b: Russell, Man., 7/23/1898. d: 3/15/1987.
Played in NHL. See Pre-Expansion Player Register for career statistics.

Season	Club	League	REGULAR SEASON GC	W	L	T	W%	PLAYOFFS GC	W	L	T	W%
1935-36	NY Americans	NHL	48	16	25	7	.406	5	2	3	0	.400
1936-37	NY Americans	NHL	48	15	29	4	.354	....	....	....	....	....
1937-38	NY Americans	NHL	48	19	18	11	.510	6	3	3	0	.500
1938-39	NY Americans	NHL	48	17	21	10	.458	2	0	2	0	.000
1939-40	NY Americans	NHL	48	15	29	4	.354	3	1	2	0	.333
1940-41	NY Americans	NHL	48	8	29	11	.281	....	....	....	....	....
1941-42	Brooklyn	NHL	48	16	29	3	.365	....	....	....	....	....
	NHL Totals		**336**	**106**	**180**	**50**	**.390**	**16**	**6**	**10**	**0**	**.375**

• EDDOLLS, FRANK
b: Lachine, Que., 7/5/1921. d: 8/13/1961.
Played in NHL. See Pre-Expansion Player Register for career statistics.

Season	Club	League	REGULAR SEASON GC	W	L	T	W%	PLAYOFFS GC	W	L	T	W%
1954-55	Chicago	NHL	70	13	40	17	.307	....	....	....	....	....
	NHL Totals		**70**	**13**	**40**	**17**	**.307**	....	....	....	....	....

• ESPOSITO, PHIL — HHOF
b: Sault Ste. Marie, Ont., 2/20/1942.
Played in NHL. See Modern Player Register for career statistics.

Season	Club	League	REGULAR SEASON GC	W	L	T	W%	PLAYOFFS GC	W	L	T	W%
1986-87	NY Rangers	NHL	43	24	19	0	.558	6	2	4	0	.333
1988-89	NY Rangers	NHL	2	0	2	0	.000	4	0	4	0	.000
	NHL Totals		**45**	**24**	**21**	**0**	**.533**	**10**	**2**	**8**	**0**	**.200**

• EVANS, JACK

b: Morriston, South Wales, 4/21/1928. d: 11/10/1996.
Played in NHL. See Pre-Expansion Player Register for career statistics.

Season	Club	League	Regular Season GC	W	L	T	W%	Playoffs GC	W	L	T	W%
1975-76	California	NHL	80	27	42	11	.406	....	....	....	....	....
1976-77	Cleveland	NHL	80	25	42	13	.394	....	....	....	....	....
1977-78	Cleveland	NHL	80	22	45	13	.356	....	....	....	....	....
1983-84	Hartford	NHL	80	28	42	10	.413	....	....	....	....	....
1984-85	Hartford	NHL	80	30	41	9	.431	....	....	....	....	....
1985-86	Hartford	NHL	80	40	36	4	.525	10	6	4	0	.600
1986-87	Hartford	NHL	80	43	30	7	.581	6	2	4	0	.333
1987-88	Hartford	NHL	54	22	25	7	.472	....	....	....	....	....
	NHL Totals		**614**	**237**	**303**	**74**	**.446**	**16**	**8**	**8**	**0**	**.500**

• FASHOWAY, GORDIE

b: Portage La Prairie, Man., 6/16/1926.
Played in NHL. See Pre-Expansion Player Register for career statistics.

Season	Club	League	Regular Season GC	W	L	T	W%	Playoffs GC	W	L	T	W%
1967-68	Oakland	NHL	10	4	5	1	.450	....	....	....	....	....
	NHL Totals		**10**	**4**	**5**	**1**	**.450**	....	....	....	....	....

• FERGUSON, JOHN

b: Vancouver, B.C., 9/5/1938.
Played in NHL. See Modern Player Register for career statistics.

Season	Club	League	Regular Season GC	W	L	T	W%	Playoffs GC	W	L	T	W%
1975-76	NY Rangers	NHL	41	14	22	5	.402	....	....	....	....	....
1976-77	NY Rangers	NHL	80	29	37	14	.450	....	....	....	....	....
1985-86	Winnipeg	NHL	14	7	6	1	.536	3	0	3	0	.000
	NHL Totals		**135**	**50**	**65**	**20**	**.444**	**3**	**0**	**3**	**0**	**.000**

• FILION, MAURICE

b: Montreal, Que., 2/12/1932.

Season	Club	League	Regular Season GC	W	L	T	W%	Playoffs GC	W	L	T	W%
1980-81	Quebec	NHL	6	1	3	2	.333	....	....	....	....	....
	NHL Totals		**6**	**1**	**3**	**2**	**.333**	....	....	....	....	....

• FRANCIS, EMILE — HHOF

b: North Battleford, Sask., 9/13/1926.
Played in NHL. See Goaltender Register for career statistics.

Season	Club	League	Regular Season GC	W	L	T	W%	Playoffs GC	W	L	T	W%
1965-66	NY Rangers	NHL	50	13	31	6	.320	....	....	....	....	....
1966-67	NY Rangers	NHL	70	30	28	12	.514	4	0	4	0	.000
1967-68	NY Rangers	NHL	74	39	23	12	.608	6	2	4	0	.333
1968-69	NY Rangers	NHL	33	19	8	6	.667	4	0	4	0	.000
1969-70	NY Rangers	NHL	76	38	22	16	.605	6	2	4	0	.333
1970-71	NY Rangers	NHL	78	49	18	11	.699	13	7	6	0	.538
1971-72	NY Rangers	NHL	78	48	17	13	.699	16	10	6	0	.625
1972-73	NY Rangers	NHL	78	47	23	8	.654	10	5	5	0	.500
1973-74	NY Rangers	NHL	37	22	10	5	.662	13	7	6	0	.538
1974-75	NY Rangers	NHL	80	37	29	14	.550	3	1	2	0	.333
1976-77	St. Louis	NHL	80	32	39	9	.456	4	0	4	0	.000
1981-82	St. Louis	NHL	12	4	6	2	.417	10	5	5	0	.500
1982-83	St. Louis	NHL	32	10	19	3	.359	....	....	....	....	....
	NHL Totals		**778**	**388**	**273**	**117**	**.574**	**89**	**39**	**50**	**0**	**.438**

• FREDRICKSON, FRANK — HHOF

b: Winnipeg, Man., 6/11/1895. d: 5/28/1979.
Played in NHL. See Pre-Expansion Player Register for career statistics.

Season	Club	League	Regular Season GC	W	L	T	W%	Playoffs GC	W	L	T	W%
1929-30	Pittsburgh	NHL	44	5	36	3	.148	....	....	....	....	....
	NHL Totals		**44**	**5**	**36**	**3**	**.148**	....	....	....	....	....

• FTOREK, ROBBIE — USHOF

b: Needham, MA, 1/2/1952.
Played In NHL. See Modern Player Register for career statistics.

Season	Club	League	Regular Season GC	W	L	T	W%	Playoffs GC	W	L	T	W%
1987-88	Los Angeles	NHL	52	23	25	4	.481	5	1	4	0	.200
1988-89	Los Angeles	NHL	80	42	31	7	.569	11	4	7	0	.364
	NHL Totals		**132**	**65**	**56**	**11**	**.534**	**16**	**5**	**11**	**0**	**.313**

• GADSBY, BILL — HHOF

b: Calgary, Alta., 8/8/1927.
Played in NHL. See Pre-Expansion Player Register for career statistics.

Season	Club	League	Regular Season GC	W	L	T	W%	Playoffs GC	W	L	T	W%
1968-69	Detroit	NHL	76	33	31	12	.513	....	....	....	....	....
1969-70	Detroit	NHL	2	2	0	0	1.000	....	....	....	....	....
	NHL Totals		**78**	**35**	**31**	**12**	**.526**	....	....	....	....	....

• GAINEY, BOB — HHOF

b: Peterborough, Ont., 12/13/1953.
Played in NHL. See Modern Player Register for career statistics.

Season	Club	League	Regular Season GC	W	L	T	W%	Playoffs GC	W	L	T	W%
1990-91	Minnesota	NHL	80	27	39	14	.425	23	14	9	0	.609
1991-92	Minnesota	NHL	80	32	42	6	.438	7	3	4	0	.429
1992-93	Minnesota	NHL	84	36	38	10	.488	....	....	....	....	....
1993-94	Dallas	NHL	84	42	29	13	.577	9	5	4	0	.556
1994-95	Dallas	NHL	48	17	23	8	.438	5	1	4	0	.200
1995-96	Dallas	NHL	39	11	19	9	.397	....	....	....	....	....
	NHL Totals		**415**	**165**	**190**	**60**	**.470**	**44**	**23**	**21**	**0**	**.523**

• GARDINER, HERB — HHOF

b: Winnipeg, Man., 5/8/1891. d: 1/11/1972.
Played in NHL. See Pre-Expansion Player Register for career statistics.

Season	Club	League	Regular Season GC	W	L	T	W%	Playoffs GC	W	L	T	W%
1928-29	Chicago	NHL	44	7	29	8	.250	....	....	....	....	....
	NHL Totals		**44**	**7**	**29**	**8**	**.250**	....	....	....	....	....

• GARDNER, JIMMY — HHOF

b: Montreal, Que., 11/18/1881. d: 11/7/1940.

Season	Club	League	Regular Season GC	W	L	T	W%	Playoffs GC	W	L	T	W%
1924-25	Hamilton	NHL	30	19	10	1	.650	....	....	....	....	....
	NHL Totals		**30**	**19**	**10**	**1**	**.650**	....	....	....	....	....

• GARVIN, TED

b: Sarnia, Ont., 8/20/1923.

Season	Club	League	Regular Season GC	W	L	T	W%	Playoffs GC	W	L	T	W%
1973-74	Detroit	NHL	11	2	8	1	.227	....	....	....	....	....
	NHL Totals		**11**	**2**	**8**	**1**	**.227**	....	....	....	....	....

• GEOFFRION, BERNIE — HHOF

b: Montreal, Que., 2/14/1931.
Played in NHL. See Modern Player Register for career statistics.

Season	Club	League	Regular Season GC	W	L	T	W%	Playoffs GC	W	L	T	W%
1968-69	NY Rangers	NHL	43	22	18	3	.547	....	....	....	....	....
1972-73	Atlanta	NHL	78	25	38	15	.417	....	....	....	....	....
1973-74	Atlanta	NHL	78	30	34	14	.474	4	0	4	0	.000
1974-75	Atlanta	NHL	52	22	20	10	.519	....	....	....	....	....
1979-80	Montreal	NHL	30	15	9	6	.600	....	....	....	....	....
	NHL Totals		**281**	**114**	**119**	**48**	**.491**	**4**	**0**	**4**	**0**	**.000**

• GERARD, EDDIE — HHOF

b: Ottawa, Ont., 2/22/1890. d: 12/7/1937.
Played in NHL. See Pre-Expansion Player Register for career statistics.

Season	Club	League	Regular Season GC	W	L	T	W%	Playoffs GC	W	L	T	W%
1917-18	Ottawa	NHL	22	9	13	0	.409	....	....	....	....	....
1924-25	Mtl. Maroons	NHL	30	9	19	2	.333	....	....	....	....	....
1925-26	Mtl. Maroons	NHL	36	20	11	5	.625	8	5	1	2	.750
1926-27	Mtl. Maroons	NHL	44	20	20	4	.500	2	0	1	1	.250
1927-28	Mtl. Maroons	NHL	44	24	14	6	.614	9	5	3	1	.611
1928-29	Mtl. Maroons	NHL	44	15	20	9	.443	....	....	....	....	....
1930-31	NY Americans	NHL	44	18	16	10	.523	....	....	....	....	....
1931-32	NY Americans	NHL	48	16	24	8	.417	....	....	....	....	....
1932-33	Mtl. Maroons	NHL	48	22	20	6	.521	2	0	2	0	.000
1933-34	Mtl. Maroons	NHL	48	19	18	11	.510	4	1	2	1	.375
1934-35	St. Louis	NHL	13	2	11	0	.154	....	....	....	....	....
	NHL Totals		**421**	**174**	**186**	**61**	**.486**	**25**	**11**	**9**	**5**	**.540**

• GILL, DAVID

b: unknown.

Season	Club	League	Regular Season GC	W	L	T	W%	Playoffs GC	W	L	T	W%
1926-27	Ottawa	NHL	44	30	10	4	.727	6	3	0	3	.750
1927-28	Ottawa	NHL	44	20	14	10	.568	2	0	2	0	.000
1928-29	Ottawa	NHL	44	14	17	13	.466	....	....	....	....	....
	NHL Totals		**132**	**64**	**41**	**27**	**.587**	**8**	**3**	**2**	**3**	**.563**

• GLOVER, FRED

b: Toronto, Ont., 1/5/1928.
Played in NHL. See Pre-Expansion Player Register for career statistics.

Season	Club	League	Regular Season GC	W	L	T	W%	Playoffs GC	W	L	T	W%
1968-69	Oakland	NHL	76	29	36	11	.454	7	3	4	0	.429
1969-70	Oakland	NHL	76	22	40	14	.382	4	0	4	0	.000
1970-71	California	NHL	78	20	53	5	.288	....	....	....	....	....
1971-72	California	NHL	3	0	1	2	.333	....	....	....	....	....
	Los Angeles	NHL	68	18	42	8	.324	....	....	....	....	....
1972-73	California	NHL	66	14	39	13	.311	....	....	....	....	....
1973-74	California	NHL	57	11	38	8	.263	....	....	....	....	....
	NHL Totals		**424**	**114**	**249**	**61**	**.341**	**11**	**3**	**8**	**0**	**.273**

• GOODFELLOW, EBBIE — HHOF

b: Ottawa, Ont., 4/9/1907. d: 9/10/1965.
Played in NHL. See Pre-Expansion Player Register for career statistics.

Season	Club	League	Regular Season GC	W	L	T	W%	Playoffs GC	W	L	T	W%
1950-51	Chicago	NHL	70	13	47	10	.257	....	....	....	....	....
1951-52	Chicago	NHL	70	17	44	9	.307	....	....	....	....	....
	NHL Totals		**140**	**30**	**91**	**19**	**.282**	....	....	....	....	....

• GORDON, JACKIE

b: Winnipeg, Man., 3/3/1928.
Played in NHL. See Pre-Expansion Player Register for career statistics.

Season	Club	League	Regular Season GC	W	L	T	W%	Playoffs GC	W	L	T	W%
1970-71	Minnesota	NHL	78	28	34	16	.462	12	6	6	0	.500
1971-72	Minnesota	NHL	78	37	29	12	.551	7	3	4	0	.429
1972-73	Minnesota	NHL	78	37	30	11	.545	6	2	4	0	.333
1973-74	Minnesota	NHL	17	3	8	6	.353	....	....	....	....	....
1974-75	Minnesota	NHL	38	11	22	5	.355	....	....	....	....	....
	NHL Totals		**289**	**116**	**123**	**50**	**.488**	**25**	**11**	**14**	**0**	**.440**

• GORING, BUTCH

b: St. Boniface, Man., 10/22/1949.
Played in NHL. See Modern Player Register for career statistics.

Season	Club	League	Regular Season GC	W	L	T	W%	Playoffs GC	W	L	T	W%
1985-86	Boston	NHL	80	37	31	12	.538	3	0	3	0	.000
1986-87	Boston	NHL	13	7	5	1	.577	....	....	....	....	....
	NHL Totals		**93**	**44**	**36**	**13**	**.543**	**3**	**0**	**3**	**0**	**.000**

• GORMAN, TOMMY — HHOF

b: Ottawa, Ont., 6/9/1886. d: 5/15/1961.

Season	Club	League	Regular Season GC	W	L	T	W%	Playoffs GC	W	L	T	W%
1925-26	NY Americans	NHL	36	12	20	4	.389	....	....	....	....	....
1928-29	NY Americans	NHL	44	19	13	12	.568	2	0	1	1	.250
1932-33	Chicago	NHL	25	8	11	6	.440	....	....	....	....	....
1933-34	Chicago	NHL	48	20	17	11	.531	8	6	1	1	.813
1934-35	Mtl. Maroons	NHL	48	24	19	5	.552	7	5	0	2	.857
1935-36	Mtl. Maroons	NHL	48	22	16	10	.563	3	0	3	0	.000
1936-37	Mtl. Maroons	NHL	48	22	17	9	.552	5	2	3	0	.400
1937-38	Mtl. Maroons	NHL	30	6	19	5	.283	....	....	....	....	....
	NHL Totals		**327**	**133**	**132**	**62**	**.502**	**25**	**13**	**8**	**4**	**.600**

• GOTTSELIG, JOHNNY

b: Odessa, Russia, 6/24/1905. d: 5/15/1986.
Played in NHL. See Pre-Expansion Player Register for career statistics.

Season	Club	League	Regular Season GC	W	L	T	W%	Playoffs GC	W	L	T	W%
1944-45	Chicago	NHL	49	13	29	7	.337	....	....	....	....	....
1945-46	Chicago	NHL	50	23	20	7	.530	4	0	4	0	.000
1946-47	Chicago	NHL	60	19	37	4	.350	....	....	....	....	....
1947-48	Chicago	NHL	28	7	19	2	.286	....	....	....	....	....
	NHL Totals		**187**	**62**	**105**	**20**	**.385**	**4**	**0**	**4**	**0**	**.000**

• GOYETTE, PHIL
b: Lachine, Que., 10/31/1933.
Played in NHL. See Modern Player Register for career statistics.

Season	Club	League	GC	W	L	T	W%	GC	W	L	T	W%
			REGULAR SEASON					**PLAYOFFS**				
1972-73	NY Islanders	NHL	48	6	38	4	.167	....	....	....	....	....
	NHL Totals		**48**	**6**	**38**	**4**	**.167**	....	....	....	....	....

• GREEN, GARY
b: Tillsonburg, Ont., 8/23/1953.

Season	Club	League	GC	W	L	T	W%	GC	W	L	T	W%
1979-80	Washington	NHL	64	23	30	11	.445	....	....	....	....	....
1980-81	Washington	NHL	80	26	36	18	.438	....	....	....	....	....
1981-82	Washington	NHL	13	1	12	0	.077	....	....	....	....	....
	NHL Totals		**157**	**50**	**78**	**29**	**.411**	....	....	....	....	....

• GREEN, PETE
b: unknown. Deceased.

Season	Club	League	GC	W	L	T	W%	GC	W	L	T	W%
1919-20	Ottawa	NHL	24	19	5	0	.792	5	3	2	0	.600
1920-21	Ottawa	NHL	24	14	10	0	.583	7	5	2	0	.714
1921-22	Ottawa	NHL	24	14	8	2	.625	2	0	1	1	.250
1922-23	Ottawa	NHL	24	14	9	1	.604	8	6	1	1	.813
1923-24	Ottawa	NHL	24	16	8	0	.667	2	0	2	0	.000
1924-25	Ottawa	NHL	30	17	12	1	.583	....	....	....	....	....
1925-26	Ottawa	NHL	36	24	8	4	.722	2	0	1	1	.250
	NHL Totals		**186**	**118**	**60**	**8**	**.656**	**26**	**14**	**9**	**3**	**.596**

• GREEN, SHORTY HHOF
b: Sudbury, Ont., 7/17/1896. d: 4/19/1960.
Played in NHL. See Pre-Expansion Player Register for career statistics.

Season	Club	League	GC	W	L	T	W%	GC	W	L	T	W%
1927-28	NY Americans	NHL	44	11	27	6	.318	....	....	....	....	....
	NHL Totals		**44**	**11**	**27**	**6**	**.318**	....	....	....	....	....

• GREEN, TED
b: Eriksdale, Man., 3/23/1940.
Played in NHL. See Modern Player Register for career statistics.

Season	Club	League	GC	W	L	T	W%	GC	W	L	T	W%
1991-92	Edmonton	NHL	80	36	34	10	.513	16	8	8	0	.500
1992-93	Edmonton	NHL	84	26	50	8	.357	....	....	....	....	....
1993-94	Edmonton	NHL	24	3	18	3	.188	....	....	....	....	....
	NHL Totals		**188**	**65**	**102**	**21**	**.402**	**16**	**8**	**8**	**0**	**.500**

• GUIDOLIN, ALDO
b: Forks of Credit, Ont., 6/6/1932.
Played in NHL. See Pre-Expansion Player Register for career statistics.

Season	Club	League	GC	W	L	T	W%	GC	W	L	T	W%
1978-79	Colorado	NHL	59	12	39	8	.271	....	....	....	....	....
	NHL Totals		**59**	**12**	**39**	**8**	**.271**	....	....	....	....	....

• GUIDOLIN, BEP
b: Thorold, Ont., 12/9/1925.
Played in NHL. See Pre-Expansion Player Register for career statistics.

Season	Club	League	GC	W	L	T	W%	GC	W	L	T	W%
1972-73	Boston	NHL	26	20	6	0	.769	5	1	4	0	.200
1973-74	Boston	NHL	78	52	17	9	.724	16	10	6	0	.625
1974-75	Kansas City	NHL	80	15	54	11	.256	....	....	....	....	....
1975-76	Kansas City	NHL	45	11	30	4	.289	....	....	....	....	....
	NHL Totals		**229**	**98**	**107**	**24**	**.480**	**21**	**11**	**10**	**0**	**.524**

• HARKNESS, NED
b: Ottawa, Ont., 9/19/1921.

Season	Club	League	GC	W	L	T	W%	GC	W	L	T	W%
1970-71	Detroit	NHL	38	12	22	4	.368	....	....	....	....	....
	NHL Totals		**38**	**12**	**22**	**4**	**.368**	....	....	....	....	....

• HARRIS, TED
b: Winnipeg, Man., 7/18/1936.
Played in NHL. See Modern Player Register for career statistics.

Season	Club	League	GC	W	L	T	W%	GC	W	L	T	W%
1975-76	Minnesota	NHL	80	20	53	7	.294	....	....	....	....	....
1976-77	Minnesota	NHL	80	23	39	18	.400	2	0	2	0	.000
1977-78	Minnesota	NHL	19	5	12	2	.316	....	....	....	....	....
	NHL Totals		**179**	**48**	**104**	**27**	**.344**	**2**	**0**	**2**	**0**	**.000**

• HART, CECIL
b: unknown. Deceased.

Season	Club	League	GC	W	L	T	W%	GC	W	L	T	W%
1926-27	Montreal	NHL	44	28	14	2	.659	4	1	1	2	.500
1927-28	Montreal	NHL	44	26	11	7	.670	2	0	1	1	.250
1928-29	Montreal	NHL	44	22	7	15	.670	3	0	3	0	.000
1929-30	Montreal	NHL	44	21	14	9	.580	6	5	0	1	.917
1930-31	Montreal	NHL	44	26	10	8	.682	10	6	4	0	.600
1931-32	Montreal	NHL	48	25	16	7	.594	4	1	3	0	.250
1936-37	Montreal	NHL	48	24	18	6	.563	5	2	3	0	.400
1937-38	Montreal	NHL	48	18	17	13	.510	3	1	2	0	.333
1938-39	Montreal	NHL	30	6	18	6	.300	....	....	....	....	....
	NHL Totals		**394**	**196**	**125**	**73**	**.590**	**37**	**16**	**17**	**4**	**.486**

• HARTSBURG, CRAIG
b: Stratford, Ont., 6/29/1959.
Played in NHL. See Modern Player Register for career statistics.

Season	Club	League	GC	W	L	T	W%	GC	W	L	T	W%
1995-96	Chicago	NHL	82	40	28	14	.573	10	6	4	0	.600
1996-97	Chicago	NHL	82	34	35	13	.494	6	2	4	0	.333
1997-98	Chicago	NHL	82	30	39	13	.445	....	....	....	....	....
	NHL Totals		**246**	**104**	**102**	**40**	**.504**	**16**	**8**	**8**	**0**	**.500**

• HARVEY, DOUG HHOF
b: Montreal, Que., 12/19/1924. d: 12/26/1989.
Played in NHL. See Modern Player Register for career statistics.

Season	Club	League	GC	W	L	T	W%	GC	W	L	T	W%
1961-62	NY Rangers	NHL	70	26	32	12	.457	6	2	4	0	.333
	NHL Totals		**70**	**26**	**32**	**12**	**.457**	**6**	**2**	**4**	**0**	**.333**

• HAY, DON
b: Kamloops, B.C., 2/13/1954.
Played in NHL. See Modern Player Register for career statistics.

Season	Club	League	GC	W	L	T	W%	GC	W	L	T	W%
1996-97	Phoenix	NHL	82	38	37	7	.506	7	3	4	0	.429
	NHL Totals		**82**	**38**	**37**	**7**	**.506**	**7**	**3**	**4**	**0**	**.429**

• HEFFERNAN, FRANK
b: Peterborough, Ontario. Deceased.
Played in NHL. See Pre-Expansion Player Register for career statistics.

Season	Club	League	GC	W	L	T	W%	GC	W	L	T	W%
1919-20	Toronto	NHL	12	5	7	0	.417	....	....	....	....	....
	NHL Totals		**12**	**5**	**7**	**0**	**.417**	....	....	....	....	....

• HENNING, LORNE
b: Melfort, Sask., 2/22/1952.
Played in NHL. See Modern Player Register for career statistics.

Season	Club	League	GC	W	L	T	W%	GC	W	L	T	W%
1985-86	Minnesota	NHL	80	38	33	9	.531	5	2	3	0	.400
1986-87	Minnesota	NHL	78	30	39	9	.442	....	....	....	....	....
1994-95	NY Islanders	NHL	48	15	28	5	.365	....	....	....	....	....
	NHL Totals		**206**	**83**	**100**	**23**	**.459**	**5**	**2**	**3**	**0**	**.400**

• HITCHCOCK, KEN
b: Edmonton, Alta., 12/17/1951.

Season	Club	League	GC	W	L	T	W%	GC	W	L	T	W%
1995-96	Dallas	NHL	43	15	23	5	.407	....	....	....	....	....
1996-97	Dallas	NHL	82	48	26	8	.634	7	3	4	0	.429
1997-98	Dallas	NHL	82	49	22	11	.665	17	10	7	0	.588
	NHL Totals		**207**	**112**	**71**	**24**	**.599**	**24**	**13**	**11**	**0**	**.542**

• HOLMGREN, PAUL
b: St. Paul, MN, 12/2/1955.
Played in NHL. See Modern Player Register for career statistics.

Season	Club	League	GC	W	L	T	W%	GC	W	L	T	W%
1988-89	Philadelphia	NHL	80	36	36	8	.500	19	10	9	0	.526
1989-90	Philadelphia	NHL	80	30	39	11	.444	....	....	....	....	....
1990-91	Philadelphia	NHL	80	33	37	10	.475	....	....	....	....	....
1991-92	Philadelphia	NHL	24	8	14	2	.375	....	....	....	....	....
1992-93	Hartford	NHL	84	26	52	6	.345	....	....	....	....	....
1993-94	Hartford	NHL	17	4	11	2	.294	....	....	....	....	....
1994-95	Hartford	NHL	48	19	24	5	.448	....	....	....	....	....
1995-96	Hartford	NHL	12	5	6	1	.458	....	....	....	....	....
	NHL Totals		**425**	**161**	**219**	**45**	**.432**	**19**	**10**	**9**	**0**	**.526**

• HOWELL, HARRY HHOF
b: Hamilton, Ont., 12/28/1932.
Played in NHL. See Modern Player Register for career statistics.

Season	Club	League	GC	W	L	T	W%	GC	W	L	T	W%
1978-79	Minnesota	NHL	11	3	6	2	.364	....	....	....	....	....
	NHL Totals		**11**	**3**	**6**	**2**	**.364**	....	....	....	....	....

• IMLACH, PUNCH HHOF
b: Toronto, Ont., 3/15/1918. d: 12/1/1987.

Season	Club	League	GC	W	L	T	W%	GC	W	L	T	W%
1958-59	Toronto	NHL	50	22	20	8	.520	12	5	7	0	.417
1959-60	Toronto	NHL	70	35	26	9	.564	10	4	6	0	.400
1960-61	Toronto	NHL	70	39	19	12	.643	5	1	4	0	.200
1961-62	Toronto	NHL	70	37	22	11	.607	12	8	4	0	.667
1962-63	Toronto	NHL	70	35	23	12	.586	14	8	6	0	.571
1963-64	Toronto	NHL	70	33	25	12	.557	10	8	2	0	.800
1964-65	Toronto	NHL	70	30	26	14	.529	6	2	4	0	.333
1965-66	Toronto	NHL	70	34	25	11	.564	4	0	4	0	.000
1966-67	Toronto	NHL	70	32	27	11	.536	12	8	4	0	.667
1967-68	Toronto	NHL	74	33	31	10	.514	....	....	....	....	....
1968-69	Toronto	NHL	76	35	26	15	.559	4	0	4	0	.000
1970-71	Buffalo	NHL	78	24	39	15	.404	....	....	....	....	....
1971-72	Buffalo	NHL	41	8	23	10	.317	....	....	....	....	....
1979-80	Toronto	NHL	10	5	5	0	.500	3	0	3	0	.000
	NHL Totals		**889**	**402**	**337**	**150**	**.537**	**92**	**44**	**48**	**0**	**.478**

• INGARFIELD, EARL
b: New York, NY, 1/30/1959.
Played in NHL. See Modern Player Register for career statistics.

Season	Club	League	GC	W	L	T	W%	GC	W	L	T	W%
1972-73	NY Islanders	NHL	30	6	22	2	.233	....	....	....	....	....
	NHL Totals		**30**	**6**	**22**	**2**	**.233**	....	....	....	....	....

• INGLIS, BILL
b: Ottawa, Ont., 5/11/1943.
Played in NHL. See Modern Player Register for career statistics.

Season	Club	League	GC	W	L	T	W%	GC	W	L	T	W%
1978-79	Buffalo	NHL	56	28	18	10	.589	3	1	2	0	.333
	NHL Totals		**56**	**28**	**18**	**10**	**.589**	**3**	**1**	**2**	**0**	**.333**

• IRVIN, DICK — HHOF

b: Hamilton, Ont., 7/19/1892. d: 3/16/1957.
Played in NHL. See Pre-Expansion Player Register for career statistics.

Season	Club	League	Reg. GC	W	L	T	W%	Playoffs GC	W	L	T	W%
1930-31	Chicago	NHL	44	24	17	3	.580	9	5	3	1	.611
1931-32	Toronto	NHL	43	23	15	5	.593	7	5	1	1	.786
	Chicago	NHL	5	3	1	1	.700	....	....	....	....	....
1932-33	Toronto	NHL	48	24	18	6	.563	9	4	5	0	.444
1933-34	Toronto	NHL	48	26	13	9	.635	5	2	3	0	.400
1934-35	Toronto	NHL	48	30	14	4	.667	7	3	4	0	.429
1935-36	Toronto	NHL	48	23	19	6	.542	9	4	5	0	.444
1936-37	Toronto	NHL	48	22	21	5	.510	2	0	2	0	.000
1937-38	Toronto	NHL	48	24	15	9	.594	7	4	3	0	.571
1938-39	Toronto	NHL	48	19	20	9	.490	10	5	5	0	.500
1939-40	Toronto	NHL	48	25	17	6	.583	10	6	4	0	.600
1940-41	Montreal	NHL	48	16	26	6	.396	3	1	2	0	.333
1941-42	Montreal	NHL	48	18	27	3	.406	3	1	2	0	.333
1942-43	Montreal	NHL	50	19	19	12	.500	5	1	4	0	.200
1943-44	Montreal	NHL	50	38	5	7	.830	9	8	1	0	.889
1944-45	Montreal	NHL	50	38	8	4	.800	6	2	4	0	.333
1945-46	Montreal	NHL	50	28	17	5	.610	9	8	1	0	.889
1946-47	Montreal	NHL	60	34	16	10	.650	11	6	5	0	.545
1947-48	Montreal	NHL	60	20	29	11	.425	....	....	....	....	....
1948-49	Montreal	NHL	60	28	23	9	.542	7	3	4	0	.429
1949-50	Montreal	NHL	70	29	22	19	.550	5	1	4	0	.200
1950-51	Montreal	NHL	70	25	30	15	.464	11	5	6	0	.455
1951-52	Montreal	NHL	70	34	26	10	.557	11	4	7	0	.364
1952-53	Montreal	NHL	70	28	23	19	.536	12	8	4	0	.667
1953-54	Montreal	NHL	70	35	24	11	.579	11	7	4	0	.636
1954-55	Montreal	NHL	70	41	18	11	.664	12	7	5	0	.583
1955-56	Chicago	NHL	70	19	39	12	.357	....	....	....	....	....
	NHL Totals		**1442**	**693**	**522**	**227**	**.559**	**190**	**100**	**88**	**2**	**.532**

• IVAN, TOMMY — HHOF

b: Toronto, Ont., 1/31/1911.

Season	Club	League	Reg. GC	W	L	T	W%	Playoffs GC	W	L	T	W%
1947-48	Detroit	NHL	60	30	18	12	.600	10	4	6	0	.400
1948-49	Detroit	NHL	60	34	19	7	.625	11	4	7	0	.364
1949-50	Detroit	NHL	70	37	19	14	.629	14	8	6	0	.571
1950-51	Detroit	NHL	70	44	13	13	.721	6	2	4	0	.333
1951-52	Detroit	NHL	70	44	14	12	.714	8	8	0	0	1.000
1952-53	Detroit	NHL	70	36	16	18	.643	6	2	4	0	.333
1953-54	Detroit	NHL	70	37	19	14	.629	12	8	4	0	.667
1956-57	Chicago	NHL	70	16	39	15	.336	....	....	....	....	....
1957-58	Chicago	NHL	33	10	17	6	.394	....	....	....	....	....
	NHL Totals		**573**	**288**	**174**	**111**	**.599**	**67**	**36**	**31**	**0**	**.537**

• IVERSON, EMIL

b: unknown. Deceased.

Season	Club	League	Reg. GC	W	L	T	W%	Playoffs GC	W	L	T	W%
1932-33	Chicago	NHL	21	8	7	6	.524	....	....	....	....	....
	NHL Totals		**21**	**8**	**7**	**6**	**.524**	....	....	....	....	....

• JOHNSON, BOB — HHOF, USHOF

b: Farmington, MI, 11/12/1948. d: 11/26/1991.

Season	Club	League	Reg. GC	W	L	T	W%	Playoffs GC	W	L	T	W%
1982-83	Calgary	NHL	80	32	34	14	.488	9	4	5	0	.444
1983-84	Calgary	NHL	80	34	32	14	.513	11	6	5	0	.545
1984-85	Calgary	NHL	80	41	27	12	.588	4	1	3	0	.250
1985-86	Calgary	NHL	80	40	31	9	.556	22	12	10	0	.545
1986-87	Calgary	NHL	80	46	31	3	.594	6	2	4	0	.333
1990-91	Pittsburgh	NHL	80	41	33	6	.550	24	16	8	0	.667
	NHL Totals		**480**	**234**	**188**	**58**	**.548**	**76**	**41**	**35**	**0**	**.539**

• JOHNSON, MARSHALL

b: Birch Hills, Sask., 6/6/1941.
Played in NHL. See Modern Player Register for career statistics.

Season	Club	League	Reg. GC	W	L	T	W%	Playoffs GC	W	L	T	W%
1981-82	Colorado	NHL	56	15	32	9	.348	....	....	....	....	....
	NHL Totals		**56**	**15**	**32**	**9**	**.348**	....	....	....	....	....

• JOHNSON, TOM — HHOF

b: Baldur, Man., 2/18/1928.
Played in NHL. See Pre-Expansion Player Register for career statistics.

Season	Club	League	Reg. GC	W	L	T	W%	Playoffs GC	W	L	T	W%
1970-71	Boston	NHL	78	57	14	7	.776	7	3	4	0	.429
1971-72	Boston	NHL	78	54	13	11	.763	15	12	3	0	.800
1972-73	Boston	NHL	52	31	16	5	.644	....	....	....	....	....
	NHL Totals		**208**	**142**	**43**	**23**	**.738**	**22**	**15**	**7**	**0**	**.682**

• JOHNSTON, EDDIE

b: Montreal, Que., 11/24/1935.
Played in NHL. See Goaltender Register for career statistics.

Season	Club	League	Reg. GC	W	L	T	W%	Playoffs GC	W	L	T	W%
1979-80	Chicago	NHL	80	34	27	19	.544	7	3	4	0	.429
1980-81	Pittsburgh	NHL	80	30	37	13	.456	5	2	3	0	.400
1981-82	Pittsburgh	NHL	80	31	36	13	.469	5	2	3	0	.400
1982-83	Pittsburgh	NHL	80	18	53	9	.281	....	....	....	....	....
1993-94	Pittsburgh	NHL	84	44	27	13	.601	6	2	4	0	.333
1994-95	Pittsburgh	NHL	48	29	16	3	.635	12	5	7	0	.417
1995-96	Pittsburgh	NHL	82	49	29	4	.622	18	11	7	0	.611
1996-97	Pittsburgh	NHL	62	31	26	5	.540	....	....	....	....	....
	NHL Totals		**596**	**266**	**251**	**79**	**.513**	**53**	**25**	**28**	**0**	**.472**

• JOHNSTON, MARSHALL

b: Birch Hills, Sask., 6/6/1941.
Played in NHL. See Modern Player Register for career statistics.

Season	Club	League	Reg. GC	W	L	T	W%	Playoffs GC	W	L	T	W%
1973-74	California	NHL	21	2	17	2	.143	....	....	....	....	....
1974-75	California	NHL	48	11	28	9	.323	....	....	....	....	....
	NHL Totals		**69**	**13**	**45**	**11**	**.268**	....	....	....	....	....

• KASPER, STEVE

b: Montreal, Que., 9/28/1961.
Played in NHL. See Modern Player Register for career statistics.

Season	Club	League	Reg. GC	W	L	T	W%	Playoffs GC	W	L	T	W%
1995-96	Boston	NHL	82	40	31	11	.555	5	1	4	0	.200
1996-97	Boston	NHL	82	26	47	9	.372	....	....	....	....	....
	NHL Totals		**164**	**66**	**78**	**20**	**.463**	**5**	**1**	**4**	**0**	**.200**

• KEATS, DUKE — HHOF

b: Montreal, Que., 3/1/1895. d: 1/16/1971.
Played in NHL. See Pre-Expansion Player Register for career statistics.

Season	Club	League	Reg. GC	W	L	T	W%	Playoffs GC	W	L	T	W%
1926-27	Detroit	NHL	11	2	7	2	.273	....	....	....	....	....
	NHL Totals		**11**	**2**	**7**	**2**	**.273**	....	....	....	....	....

• KEENAN, MIKE

b: Toronto, Ont., 10/21/1949.

Season	Club	League	Reg. GC	W	L	T	W%	Playoffs GC	W	L	T	W%
1984-85	Philadelphia	NHL	80	53	20	7	.706	19	12	7	0	.632
1985-86	Philadelphia	NHL	80	53	23	4	.688	5	2	3	0	.400
1986-87	Philadelphia	NHL	80	46	26	8	.625	26	15	11	0	.577
1987-88	Philadelphia	NHL	80	38	33	9	.531	7	3	4	0	.429
1988-89	Chicago	NHL	80	27	41	12	.413	16	9	7	0	.563
1989-90	Chicago	NHL	80	41	33	6	.550	20	10	10	0	.500
1990-91	Chicago	NHL	80	49	23	8	.663	6	2	4	0	.333
1991-92	Chicago	NHL	80	36	29	15	.544	18	12	6	0	.667
1993-94	NY Rangers	NHL	84	52	24	8	.667	23	16	7	0	.696
1994-95	St. Louis	NHL	48	28	15	5	.635	7	3	4	0	.429
1995-96	St. Louis	NHL	82	32	34	16	.488	13	7	6	0	.538
1996-97	St. Louis	NHL	33	15	17	1	.470	....	....	....	....	....
1997-98	Vancouver	NHL	63	21	30	12	.429	....	....	....	....	....
	NHL Totals		**950**	**491**	**348**	**111**	**.575**	**160**	**91**	**69**	**0**	**.569**

• Won Jack Adams Award (1985)

• KELLY, PAT

b: Sioux Lookout, Ont., 9/8/1935.

Season	Club	League	Reg. GC	W	L	T	W%	Playoffs GC	W	L	T	W%
1977-78	Colorado	NHL	80	19	40	21	.369	2	0	2	0	.000
1978-79	Colorado	NHL	21	3	14	4	.238	....	....	....	....	....
	NHL Totals		**101**	**22**	**54**	**25**	**.342**	**2**	**0**	**2**	**0**	**.000**

• KELLY, RED — HHOF

b: Simcoe, Ont., 7/9/1927.
Played in NHL. See Pre-Expansion Player Register for career statistics.

Season	Club	League	Reg. GC	W	L	T	W%	Playoffs GC	W	L	T	W%
1967-68	Los Angeles	NHL	74	31	33	10	.486	7	3	4	0	.429
1968-69	Los Angeles	NHL	76	24	42	10	.382	11	4	7	0	.364
1969-70	Pittsburgh	NHL	76	26	38	12	.421	10	6	4	0	.600
1970-71	Pittsburgh	NHL	78	21	37	20	.397	....	....	....	....	....
1971-72	Pittsburgh	NHL	78	26	38	14	.423	4	0	4	0	.000
1972-73	Pittsburgh	NHL	42	17	19	6	.476	....	....	....	....	....
1973-74	Toronto	NHL	78	35	27	16	.551	4	0	4	0	.000
1974-75	Toronto	NHL	80	31	33	16	.488	7	2	5	0	.286
1975-76	Toronto	NHL	80	34	31	15	.519	10	5	5	0	.500
1976-77	Toronto	NHL	80	33	32	15	.506	9	4	5	0	.444
	NHL Totals		**742**	**278**	**330**	**134**	**.465**	**62**	**24**	**38**	**0**	**.387**

• KING, DAVE

b: Saskatoon, Sask., 12/22/1947.

Season	Club	League	Reg. GC	W	L	T	W%	Playoffs GC	W	L	T	W%
1992-93	Calgary	NHL	84	43	30	11	.577	6	2	4	0	.333
1993-94	Calgary	NHL	84	42	29	13	.577	7	3	4	0	.429
1994-95	Calgary	NHL	48	24	17	7	.573	7	3	4	0	.429
	NHL Totals		**216**	**109**	**76**	**31**	**.576**	**20**	**8**	**12**	**0**	**.400**

• KINGSTON, GEORGE

b: Biggar, Sask., 8/20/1939.

Season	Club	League	Reg. GC	W	L	T	W%	Playoffs GC	W	L	T	W%
1991-92	San Jose	NHL	80	17	58	5	.244	....	....	....	....	....
1992-93	San Jose	NHL	84	11	71	2	.143	....	....	....	....	....
	NHL Totals		**164**	**28**	**129**	**7**	**.192**	....	....	....	....	....

• KISH, LARRY

b: Welland, Ont., 12/11/1941.

Season	Club	League	Reg. GC	W	L	T	W%	Playoffs GC	W	L	T	W%
1982-83	Hartford	NHL	49	12	32	5	.296	....	....	....	....	....
	NHL Totals		**49**	**12**	**32**	**5**	**.296**	....	....	....	....	....

• KROMM, BOBBY

b: Calgary, Alta., 6/8/1928.

Season	Club	League	Reg. GC	W	L	T	W%	Playoffs GC	W	L	T	W%
1977-78	Detroit	NHL	80	32	34	14	.488	7	3	4	0	.429
1978-79	Detroit	NHL	80	23	41	16	.388	....	....	....	....	....
1979-80	Detroit	NHL	71	24	36	11	.415	....	....	....	....	....
	NHL Totals		**231**	**79**	**111**	**41**	**.431**	**7**	**3**	**4**	**0**	**.429**

• Won Jack Adams Award (1978)

• KURTENBACH, ORLAND

b: Cudworth, Sask., 9/7/1936.
Played in NHL. See Modern Player Register for career statistics.

Season	Club	League	Reg. GC	W	L	T	W%	Playoffs GC	W	L	T	W%
1976-77	Vancouver	NHL	45	16	19	10	.467	....	....	....	....	....
1977-78	Vancouver	NHL	80	20	43	17	.356	....	....	....	....	....
	NHL Totals		**125**	**36**	**62**	**27**	**.396**	....	....	....	....	....

• LAFORGE, BILL

b: Edmonton, Alta., 9/2/1951.

Season	Club	League	Reg. GC	W	L	T	W%	Playoffs GC	W	L	T	W%
1984-85	Vancouver	NHL	20	4	14	2	.250	....	....	....	....	....
	NHL Totals		**20**	**4**	**14**	**2**	**.250**	....	....	....	....	....

• LALONDE, NEWSY HHOF

b: Cornwall, Ont., 10/31/1888. d: 11/21/1971.
Played in NHL. See Pre-Expansion Player Register for career statistics.

Season	Club	League	Regular Season GC	W	L	T	W%	Playoffs GC	W	L	T	W%
1917-18	Montreal	NHL	22	13	9	0	.591	2	1	1	0	.500
1918-19	Montreal	NHL	18	10	8	0	.556	10	6	3	1	.650
1919-20	Montreal	NHL	24	13	11	0	.542	....	....	....	....	....
1920-21	Montreal	NHL	24	13	11	0	.542	....	....	....	....	....
1921-22	Montreal	NHL	7	2	5	0	.286	....	....	....	....	....
1926-27	NY Americans	NHL	44	17	25	2	.409	....	....	....	....	....
1929-30	Ottawa	NHL	44	21	15	8	.568	2	0	1	1	.250
1930-31	Ottawa	NHL	44	10	30	4	.273	....	....	....	....	....
1932-33	Montreal	NHL	48	18	25	5	.427	2	0	1	1	.250
1933-34	Montreal	NHL	48	22	20	6	.521	2	0	1	1	.250
1934-35	Montreal	NHL	16	5	8	3	.406	....	....	....	....	....
	NHL Totals		**339**	**144**	**167**	**28**	**.466**	**18**	**7**	**7**	**4**	**.500**

• LAPOINTE, RON

b: Verdun, Que., 11/12/1949.

Season	Club	League	Regular Season GC	W	L	T	W%	Playoffs GC	W	L	T	W%
1987-88	Quebec	NHL	56	22	30	4	.429	....	....	....	....	....
1988-89	Quebec	NHL	33	11	20	2	.364	....	....	....	....	....
	NHL Totals		**89**	**33**	**50**	**6**	**.404**	....	....	....	....	....

• LAYCOE, HAL

b: Sutherland, Sask., 6/23/1922. d: 4/29/1997.
Played in NHL. See Pre-Expansion Player Register for career statistics.

Season	Club	League	Regular Season GC	W	L	T	W%	Playoffs GC	W	L	T	W%
1969-70	Los Angeles	NHL	24	5	18	1	.229	....	....	....	....	....
1970-71	Vancouver	NHL	78	24	46	8	.359	....	....	....	....	....
1971-72	Vancouver	NHL	78	20	50	8	.308	....	....	....	....	....
	NHL Totals		**180**	**49**	**114**	**17**	**.319**	....	....	....	....	....

• LEHMAN, HUGH HHOF

b: Pembroke, Ont., 10/27/1885. d: 4/8/1961.
Played in NHL. See Goaltender Register for career statistics.

Season	Club	League	Regular Season GC	W	L	T	W%	Playoffs GC	W	L	T	W%
1927-28	Chicago	NHL	21	3	17	1	.167	....	....	....	....	....
	NHL Totals		**21**	**3**	**17**	**1**	**.167**	....	....	....	....	....

• LEMAIRE, JACQUES HHOF

b: LaSalle, Que., 9/7/1945.
Played in NHL. See Modern Player Register for career statistics.

Season	Club	League	Regular Season GC	W	L	T	W%	Playoffs GC	W	L	T	W%
1983-84	Montreal	NHL	17	7	10	0	.412	15	9	6	0	.600
1984-85	Montreal	NHL	80	41	27	12	.588	12	6	6	0	.500
1993-94	New Jersey	NHL	84	47	25	12	.631	20	11	9	0	.550
1994-95	New Jersey	NHL	48	22	18	8	.542	20	16	4	0	.800
1995-96	New Jersey	NHL	82	37	33	12	.524	....	....	....	....	....
1996-97	New Jersey	NHL	82	45	23	14	.634	10	5	5	0	.500
1997-98	New Jersey	NHL	82	48	23	11	.652	6	2	4	0	.333
	NHL Totals		**475**	**247**	**159**	**69**	**.593**	**83**	**49**	**34**	**0**	**.590**

• LEPINE, PIT

b: St. Anne de Bellevue, Que., 7/30/1901. d: 8/2/1955.
Played in NHL. See Pre-Expansion Player Register for career statistics.

Season	Club	League	Regular Season GC	W	L	T	W%	Playoffs GC	W	L	T	W%
1939-40	Montreal	NHL	48	10	33	5	.260	....	....	....	....	....
	NHL Totals		**48**	**10**	**33**	**5**	**.260**	....	....	....	....	....

• LESUEUR, PERCY HHOF

b: Querbec City, Que., 11/18/1881. d: 1/27/1962.

Season	Club	League	Regular Season GC	W	L	T	W%	Playoffs GC	W	L	T	W%
1923-24	Hamilton	NHL	10	3	7	0	.300	....	....	....	....	....
	NHL Totals		**10**	**3**	**7**	**0**	**.300**	....	....	....	....	....

• LEY, RICK

b: Orillia, Ont., 11/2/1948.
Played in NHL. See Modern Player Register for career statistics.

Season	Club	League	Regular Season GC	W	L	T	W%	Playoffs GC	W	L	T	W%
1989-90	Hartford	NHL	80	38	33	9	.531	7	3	4	0	.429
1990-91	Hartford	NHL	80	31	38	11	.456	6	2	4	0	.333
1994-95	Vancouver	NHL	48	18	18	12	.500	11	4	7	0	.364
1995-96	Vancouver	NHL	76	29	32	15	.480	....	....	....	....	....
	NHL Totals		**284**	**116**	**121**	**47**	**.491**	**24**	**9**	**15**	**0**	**.375**

• LINDSAY, TED HHOF

b: Renfrew, Ont., 7/29/1925.
Played in NHL. See Pre-Expansion Player Register for career statistics.

Season	Club	League	Regular Season GC	W	L	T	W%	Playoffs GC	W	L	T	W%
1979-80	Detroit	NHL	9	2	7	0	.222	....	....	....	....	....
1980-81	Detroit	NHL	20	3	14	3	.225	....	....	....	....	....
	NHL Totals		**29**	**5**	**21**	**3**	**.224**	....	....	....	....	....

• LONG, BARRY

b: Brantford, Ont., 1/3/1949.
Played in NHL. See Modern Player Register for career statistics.

Season	Club	League	Regular Season GC	W	L	T	W%	Playoffs GC	W	L	T	W%
1983-84	Winnipeg	NHL	59	25	25	9	.500	3	0	3	0	.000
1984-85	Winnipeg	NHL	80	43	27	10	.600	8	3	5	0	.375
1985-86	Winnipeg	NHL	66	19	41	6	.333	....	....	....	....	....
	NHL Totals		**205**	**87**	**93**	**25**	**.485**	**11**	**3**	**8**	**0**	**.273**

• LOUGHLIN, CLEM

b: Carroll, Man., 11/15/1894. Deceased.
Played in NHL. See Pre-Expansion Player Register for career statistics.

Season	Club	League	Regular Season GC	W	L	T	W%	Playoffs GC	W	L	T	W%
1934-35	Chicago	NHL	48	26	17	5	.594	2	0	1	1	.250
1935-36	Chicago	NHL	48	21	19	8	.521	2	1	1	0	.500
1936-37	Chicago	NHL	48	14	27	7	.365	....	....	....	....	....
	NHL Totals		**144**	**61**	**63**	**20**	**.493**	**4**	**1**	**2**	**1**	**.375**

• LOW, RON

b: Birtle, Man., 6/21/1950.
Played in NHL. See Goaltender Register for career statistics.

Season	Club	League	Regular Season GC	W	L	T	W%	Playoffs GC	W	L	T	W%
1994-95	Edmonton	NHL	13	5	7	1	.423	....	....	....	....	....
1995-96	Edmonton	NHL	82	30	44	8	.415	....	....	....	....	....
1996-97	Edmonton	NHL	82	36	37	9	.494	12	5	7	0	.417
1997-98	Edmonton	NHL	82	35	37	10	.488	12	5	7	0	.417
	NHL Totals		**259**	**106**	**125**	**28**	**.463**	**24**	**10**	**14**	**0**	**.417**

• MacDONALD, PARKER

b: Sydney, N.S., 6/14/1933.
Played in NHL. See Modern Player Register for career statistics.

Season	Club	League	Regular Season GC	W	L	T	W%	Playoffs GC	W	L	T	W%
1973-74	Minnesota	NHL	61	20	30	11	.418	....	....	....	....	....
1981-82	Los Angeles	NHL	42	13	24	5	.369	....	....	....	....	....
	NHL Totals		**103**	**33**	**54**	**16**	**.398**	....	....	....	....	....

• MacLEAN, DOUG

b: unknown.

Season	Club	League	Regular Season GC	W	L	T	W%	Playoffs GC	W	L	T	W%
1995-96	Florida	NHL	82	41	31	10	.561	22	12	10	0	.545
1996-97	Florida	NHL	82	35	28	19	.543	5	1	4	0	.200
1997-98	Florida	NHL	23	7	12	4	.391	....	....	....	....	....
	NHL Totals		**187**	**83**	**71**	**33**	**.532**	**27**	**13**	**14**	**0**	**.481**

• MACMILLAN, BILL

b: Charlottetown, P.E.I., 3/7/1943.
Played in NHL. See Modern Player Register for career statistics.

Season	Club	League	Regular Season GC	W	L	T	W%	Playoffs GC	W	L	T	W%
1980-81	Colorado	NHL	80	22	45	13	.356	....	....	....	....	....
1982-83	New Jersey	NHL	80	17	49	14	.300	....	....	....	....	....
1983-84	New Jersey	NHL	20	2	18	0	.100	....	....	....	....	....
	NHL Totals		**180**	**41**	**112**	**27**	**.303**	....	....	....	....	....

• MACNEIL, AL

b: Sydney, N.S., 9/27/1935.
Played in NHL. See Modern Player Register for career statistics.

Season	Club	League	Regular Season GC	W	L	T	W%	Playoffs GC	W	L	T	W%
1970-71	Montreal	NHL	55	31	15	9	.645	20	12	8	0	.600
1979-80	Atlanta	NHL	80	35	32	13	.519	4	1	3	0	.250
1980-81	Calgary	NHL	80	39	27	14	.575	16	9	7	0	.563
1981-82	Calgary	NHL	80	29	34	17	.469	3	0	3	0	.000
	NHL Totals		**295**	**134**	**108**	**53**	**.544**	**43**	**22**	**21**	**0**	**.512**

• MAGNUSON, KEITH

b: Saskatoon, Sask., 4/27/1947.
Played in NHL. See Modern Player Register for career statistics.

Season	Club	League	Regular Season GC	W	L	T	W%	Playoffs GC	W	L	T	W%
1980-81	Chicago	NHL	80	31	33	16	.488	3	0	3	0	.000
1981-82	Chicago	NHL	52	18	24	10	.442	....	....	....	....	....
	NHL Totals		**132**	**49**	**57**	**26**	**.470**	**3**	**0**	**3**	**0**	**.000**

• MAGUIRE, PIERRE

b: unknown.

Season	Club	League	Regular Season GC	W	L	T	W%	Playoffs GC	W	L	T	W%
1993-94	Hartford	NHL	67	23	37	7	.396	....	....	....	....	....
	NHL Totals		**67**	**23**	**37**	**7**	**.396**	....	....	....	....	....

• MAHONEY, BILL

b: Peterborough, Ont., 6/23/1939.

Season	Club	League	Regular Season GC	W	L	T	W%	Playoffs GC	W	L	T	W%
1983-84	Minnesota	NHL	80	39	31	10	.550	16	7	9	0	.438
1984-85	Minnesota	NHL	13	3	8	2	.308	....	....	....	....	....
	NHL Totals		**93**	**42**	**39**	**12**	**.516**	**16**	**7**	**9**	**0**	**.438**

• MALONEY, DAN

b: Barrie, Ont., 9/24/1950.
Played in NHL. See Modern Player Register for career statistics.

Season	Club	League	Regular Season GC	W	L	T	W%	Playoffs GC	W	L	T	W%
1984-85	Toronto	NHL	80	20	52	8	.300	....	....	....	....	....
1985-86	Toronto	NHL	80	25	48	7	.356	10	6	4	0	.600
1986-87	Winnipeg	NHL	80	40	32	8	.550	10	4	6	0	.400
1987-88	Winnipeg	NHL	80	33	36	11	.481	5	1	4	0	.200
1988-89	Winnipeg	NHL	52	18	25	9	.433	....	....	....	....	....
	NHL Totals		**372**	**136**	**193**	**43**	**.423**	**25**	**11**	**14**	**0**	**.440**

• MALONEY, PHIL

b: Ottawa, Ont., 10/6/1927.
Played in NHL. See Pre-Expansion Player Register for career statistics.

Season	Club	League	Regular Season GC	W	L	T	W%	Playoffs GC	W	L	T	W%
1973-74	Vancouver	NHL	37	15	18	4	.459	....	....	....	....	....
1974-75	Vancouver	NHL	80	38	32	10	.538	5	1	4	0	.200
1975-76	Vancouver	NHL	80	33	32	15	.506	2	0	2	0	.000
1976-77	Vancouver	NHL	35	9	23	3	.300	....	....	....	....	....
	NHL Totals		**232**	**95**	**105**	**32**	**.478**	**7**	**1**	**6**	**0**	**.143**

• MANTHA, SYLVIO HHOF

b: Montreal, Que., 4/14/1902. d: 8/7/1974.
Played in NHL. See Pre-Expansion Player Register for career statistics.

Season	Club	League	Regular Season GC	W	L	T	W%	Playoffs GC	W	L	T	W%
1935-36	Montreal	NHL	48	11	26	11	.344	....	....	....	....	....
	NHL Totals		**48**	**11**	**26**	**11**	**.344**	....	....	....	....	....

• MARSHALL, BERT

b: Kamloops, B.C., 11/22/1943.
Played in NHL. See Modern Player Register for career statistics.

Season	Club	League	Regular Season GC	W	L	T	W%	Playoffs GC	W	L	T	W%
1981-82	Colorado	NHL	24	3	17	4	.208	....	....	....	....	....
	NHL Totals		**24**	**3**	**17**	**4**	**.208**	....	....	....	....	....

• MARTIN, JACQUES
b: St. Pascal, Ont., 10/1/1952.

Season	Club	League	GC	W	L	T	W%	GC	W	L	T	W%
			REGULAR SEASON					PLAYOFFS				
1986-87	St. Louis	NHL	80	32	33	15	.494	6	2	4	0	.333
1987-88	St. Louis	NHL	80	34	38	8	.475	10	5	5	0	.500
1995-96	Ottawa	NHL	38	10	24	4	.316	....	....	....	....	....
1996-97	Ottawa	NHL	82	31	36	15	.470	7	3	4	0	.429
1997-98	Ottawa	NHL	82	34	33	15	.506	11	5	6	0	.455
	NHL Totals		**362**	**141**	**164**	**57**	**.468**	**34**	**15**	**19**	**0**	**.441**

• MATHESON, GODFREY
b: unknown.

Season	Club	League	GC	W	L	T	W%	GC	W	L	T	W%
1932-33	Chicago	NHL	2	0	2	0	.000	....	....	....	....	....
	NHL Totals		**2**	**0**	**2**	**0**	**.000**	....	....	....	....	....

• MAURICE, PAUL
b: Sault Ste. Marie, Ont., 1/30/1967.
Played in NHL. See Modern Player Register for career statistics.

Season	Club	League	GC	W	L	T	W%	GC	W	L	T	W%
1995-96	Hartford	NHL	70	29	33	8	.471	....	....	....	....	....
1996-97	Hartford	NHL	82	32	39	11	.457	....	....	....	....	....
1997-98	Carolina	NHL	82	33	41	8	.451	....	....	....	....	....
	NHL Totals		**234**	**94**	**113**	**27**	**.459**	....	....	....	....	....

• MAXNER, WAYNE
b: Halifax, N.S., 9/27/1942.
Played in NHL. See Pre-Expansion Player Register for career statistics.

Season	Club	League	GC	W	L	T	W%	GC	W	L	T	W%
1980-81	Detroit	NHL	60	16	29	15	.392	....	....	....	....	....
1981-82	Detroit	NHL	69	18	39	12	.348	....	....	....	....	....
	NHL Totals		**129**	**34**	**68**	**27**	**.368**	....	....	....	....	....

• McCAMMON, BOB
b: Kenora, Ont., 4/14/1941.

Season	Club	League	GC	W	L	T	W%	GC	W	L	T	W%
1978-79	Philadelphia	NHL	50	22	17	11	.550	....	....	....	....	....
1981-82	Philadelphia	NHL	8	4	2	2	.625	4	1	3	0	.250
1982-83	Philadelphia	NHL	80	49	23	8	.663	3	0	3	0	.000
1983-84	Philadelphia	NHL	80	44	26	10	.613	3	0	3	0	.000
1987-88	Vancouver	NHL	80	25	46	9	.369	....	....	....	....	....
1988-89	Vancouver	NHL	80	33	39	8	.463	7	3	4	0	.429
1989-90	Vancouver	NHL	80	25	41	14	.400	....	....	....	....	....
1990-91	Vancouver	NHL	54	19	30	5	.398	....	....	....	....	....
	NHL Totals		**512**	**221**	**224**	**67**	**.497**	**17**	**4**	**13**	**0**	**.235**

• McCREARY, BILL
b: Springfield, MA, 4/15/1960.
Played in NHL. See Modern Player Register for career statistics.

Season	Club	League	GC	W	L	T	W%	GC	W	L	T	W%
1971-72	St. Louis	NHL	24	6	14	4	.333	....	....	....	....	....
1973-74	Vancouver	NHL	41	9	25	7	.305	....	....	....	....	....
1974-75	California	NHL	32	8	20	4	.313	....	....	....	....	....
	NHL Totals		**97**	**23**	**59**	**15**	**.314**	....	....	....	....	....

• McLELLAN, JOHN
b: South Porcupine, Ont., 8/6/1928. d: 10/27/1979.
Played in NHL. See Pre-Expansion Player Register for career statistics.

Season	Club	League	GC	W	L	T	W%	GC	W	L	T	W%
1969-70	Toronto	NHL	76	29	34	13	.467	....	....	....	....	....
1970-71	Toronto	NHL	78	37	33	8	.526	6	2	4	0	.333
1971-72	Toronto	NHL	63	24	28	11	.468	....	....	....	....	....
1972-73	Toronto	NHL	78	27	41	10	.410	....	....	....	....	....
	NHL Totals		**295**	**117**	**136**	**42**	**.468**	**6**	**2**	**4**	**0**	**.333**

• McVIE, TOM
b: Trail, B.C., 6/6/1935.

Season	Club	League	GC	W	L	T	W%	GC	W	L	T	W%
1975-76	Washington	NHL	44	8	31	5	.239	....	....	....	....	....
1976-77	Washington	NHL	80	24	42	14	.388	....	....	....	....	....
1977-78	Washington	NHL	80	17	49	14	.300	....	....	....	....	....
1979-80	Winnipeg	NHL	77	19	47	11	.318	....	....	....	....	....
1980-81	Winnipeg	NHL	28	1	20	7	.161	....	....	....	....	....
1983-84	New Jersey	NHL	60	15	38	7	.308	....	....	....	....	....
1990-91	New Jersey	NHL	13	4	5	4	.462	7	3	4	0	.429
1991-92	New Jersey	NHL	80	38	31	11	.544	7	3	4	0	.429
	NHL Totals		**462**	**126**	**263**	**73**	**.352**	**14**	**6**	**8**	**0**	**.429**

• MEEKER, HOWIE
b: Kitchener, Ont., 11/4/1924.
Played in NHL. See Pre-Expansion Player Register for career statistics.

Season	Club	League	GC	W	L	T	W%	GC	W	L	T	W%
1956-57	Toronto	NHL	70	21	34	15	.407	....	....	....	....	....
	NHL Totals		**70**	**21**	**34**	**15**	**.407**	....	....	....	....	....

• MELROSE, BARRY
b: Kelvington, Sask., 7/15/1956.
Played in NHL. See Modern Player Register for career statistics.

Season	Club	League	GC	W	L	T	W%	GC	W	L	T	W%
1992-93	Los Angeles	NHL	84	39	35	10	.524	24	13	11	0	.542
1993-94	Los Angeles	NHL	84	27	45	12	.393	....	....	....	....	....
1994-95	Los Angeles	NHL	41	13	21	7	.402	....	....	....	....	....
	NHL Totals		**209**	**79**	**101**	**29**	**.447**	**24**	**13**	**11**	**0**	**.542**

• MILBURY, MIKE
b: Brighton, MA, 6/17/1952.
Played in NHL. See Modern Player Register for career statistics.

Season	Club	League	GC	W	L	T	W%	GC	W	L	T	W%
1989-90	Boston	NHL	80	46	25	9	.631	21	13	8	0	.619
1990-91	Boston	NHL	80	44	24	12	.625	19	10	9	0	.526
1995-96	NY Islanders	NHL	82	22	50	10	.329	....	....	....	....	....
1996-97	NY Islanders	NHL	45	13	23	9	.389	....	....	....	....	....
1997-98	NY Islanders	NHL	19	8	9	2	.474	....	....	....	....	....
	NHL Totals		**306**	**133**	**131**	**42**	**.503**	**40**	**23**	**17**	**0**	**.575**

• MUCKLER, JOHN
b: Midland, Ont., 4/3/1934.

Season	Club	League	GC	W	L	T	W%	GC	W	L	T	W%
1968-69	Minnesota	NHL	35	6	23	6	.257	....	....	....	....	....
1989-90	Edmonton	NHL	80	38	28	14	.563	22	16	6	0	.727
1990-91	Edmonton	NHL	80	37	37	6	.500	18	9	9	0	.500
1991-92	Buffalo	NHL	52	22	22	8	.500	7	3	4	0	.429
1992-93	Buffalo	NHL	84	38	36	10	.512	8	4	4	0	.500
1993-94	Buffalo	NHL	84	43	32	9	.565	7	3	4	0	.429
1994-95	Buffalo	NHL	48	22	19	7	.531	5	1	4	0	.200
1997-98	NY Rangers	NHL	25	8	15	2	.360	....	....	....	....	....
	NHL Totals		**488**	**214**	**212**	**62**	**.502**	**67**	**36**	**31**	**0**	**.537**

• MULDOON, PETE
b: St. Mary, Ont., 1881. d: 3/13/2029.

Season	Club	League	GC	W	L	T	W%	GC	W	L	T	W%
1926-27	Chicago	NHL	44	19	22	3	.466	2	0	1	1	.250
	NHL Totals		**44**	**19**	**22**	**3**	**.466**	**2**	**0**	**1**	**1**	**.250**

• MUNRO, DUNC
b: Moray, Scotland, 1/19/1901. d: 1/3/1958.
Played in NHL. See Pre-Expansion Player Register for career statistics.

Season	Club	League	GC	W	L	T	W%	GC	W	L	T	W%
1929-30	Mtl. Maroons	NHL	44	23	16	5	.580	4	1	3	0	.250
1930-31	Mtl. Maroons	NHL	32	14	13	5	.516	....	....	....	....	....
	NHL Totals		**76**	**37**	**29**	**10**	**.553**	**4**	**1**	**3**	**0**	**.250**

• MURDOCH, BOB
b: Cranbrook, B.C., 1/29/1954.
Played in NHL. See Modern Player Register for career statistics.

Season	Club	League	GC	W	L	T	W%	GC	W	L	T	W%
1989-90	Winnipeg	NHL	80	37	32	11	.531	7	3	4	0	.429
1990-91	Winnipeg	NHL	80	26	43	11	.394	....	....	....	....	....
	NHL Totals		**160**	**63**	**75**	**22**	**.463**	**7**	**3**	**4**	**0**	**.429**

• Won Jack Adams Award (1990)

• MURPHY, MIKE
b: Toronto, Ont., 9/12/1950.
Played in NHL. See Modern Player Register for career statistics.

Season	Club	League	GC	W	L	T	W%	GC	W	L	T	W%
1986-87	Los Angeles	NHL	38	13	21	4	.395	5	1	4	0	.200
1987-88	Los Angeles	NHL	27	7	16	4	.333	....	....	....	....	....
1996-97	Toronto	NHL	82	30	44	8	.415	....	....	....	....	....
1997-98	Toronto	NHL	82	30	43	9	.421	....	....	....	....	....
	NHL Totals		**229**	**80**	**124**	**25**	**.404**	**5**	**1**	**4**	**0**	**.200**

• MURRAY, BRYAN
b: Shawville, Que., 12/5/1942.

Season	Club	League	GC	W	L	T	W%	GC	W	L	T	W%
1981-82	Washington	NHL	66	25	28	13	.477	....	....	....	....	....
1982-83	Washington	NHL	80	39	25	16	.588	4	1	3	0	.250
1983-84	Washington	NHL	80	48	27	5	.631	8	4	4	0	.500
1984-85	Washington	NHL	80	46	25	9	.631	5	2	3	0	.400
1985-86	Washington	NHL	80	50	23	7	.669	9	5	4	0	.556
1986-87	Washington	NHL	80	38	32	10	.538	7	3	4	0	.429
1987-88	Washington	NHL	80	38	33	9	.531	14	7	7	0	.500
1988-89	Washington	NHL	80	41	29	10	.575	6	2	4	0	.333
1989-90	Washington	NHL	46	18	24	4	.435	....	....	....	....	....
1990-91	Detroit	NHL	80	34	38	8	.475	7	3	4	0	.429
1991-92	Detroit	NHL	80	43	25	12	.613	11	4	7	0	.364
1992-93	Detroit	NHL	84	47	28	9	.613	7	3	4	0	.429
1997-98	Florida	NHL	59	17	31	11	.381	....	....	....	....	....
	NHL Totals		**975**	**484**	**368**	**123**	**.559**	**78**	**34**	**44**	**0**	**.436**

• Won Jack Adams Award (1984)

• MURRAY, TERRY
b: Shawville, Que., 7/20/1950.
Played in NHL. See Modern Player Register for career statistics.

Season	Club	League	GC	W	L	T	W%	GC	W	L	T	W%
1989-90	Washington	NHL	34	18	14	2	.559	15	8	7	0	.533
1990-91	Washington	NHL	80	37	36	7	.506	11	5	6	0	.455
1991-92	Washington	NHL	80	45	27	8	.613	7	3	4	0	.429
1992-93	Washington	NHL	84	43	34	7	.554	6	2	4	0	.333
1993-94	Washington	NHL	47	20	23	4	.468	....	....	....	....	....
1994-95	Philadelphia	NHL	48	28	16	4	.625	15	10	5	0	.667
1995-96	Philadelphia	NHL	82	45	24	13	.628	12	6	6	0	.500
1996-97	Philadelphia	NHL	82	45	24	13	.628	19	12	7	0	.632
	NHL Totals		**537**	**281**	**198**	**58**	**.577**	**85**	**46**	**39**	**0**	**.541**

• NANNE, LOU
b: Sault Ste. Marie, Ont., 6/2/1941.
Played in NHL. See Modern Player Register for career statistics.

Season	Club	League	GC	W	L	T	W%	GC	W	L	T	W%
1977-78	Minnesota	NHL	29	7	18	4	.310	....	....	....	....	....
	NHL Totals		**29**	**7**	**18**	**4**	**.310**	....	....	....	....	....

• NEALE, HARRY
b: Sarnia, Ont., 3/9/1937.

Season	Club	League	GC	W	L	T	W%	GC	W	L	T	W%
1978-79	Vancouver	NHL	80	25	42	13	.394	3	1	2	0	.333
1979-80	Vancouver	NHL	80	27	37	16	.438	4	1	3	0	.250
1980-81	Vancouver	NHL	80	28	32	20	.475	3	0	3	0	.000
1981-82	Vancouver	NHL	75	26	33	16	.453	....	....	....	....	....
1983-84	Vancouver	NHL	32	15	13	4	.531	4	1	3	0	.250
1984-85	Vancouver	NHL	60	21	32	7	.408	....	....	....	....	....
1985-86	Detroit	NHL	35	8	23	4	.286	....	....	....	....	....
	NHL Totals		**442**	**150**	**212**	**80**	**.430**	**14**	**3**	**11**	**0**	**.214**

• NEILSON, ROGER
b: Toronto, Ont., 6/16/1934.

Season	Club	League	GC	W	L	T	W%	GC	W	L	T	W%
			REGULAR SEASON					PLAYOFFS				
1977-78	Toronto	NHL	80	41	29	10	.575	13	6	7	0	.462
1978-79	Toronto	NHL	80	34	33	13	.506	6	2	4	0	.333
1980-81	Buffalo	NHL	80	39	20	21	.619	8	4	4	0	.500
1981-82	Vancouver	NHL	5	4	0	1	.900	17	11	6	0	.647
1982-83	Vancouver	NHL	80	30	35	15	.469	4	1	3	0	.250
1983-84	Vancouver	NHL	48	17	26	5	.406	....	....	....	....	....
	Los Angeles	NHL	28	8	17	3	.339	....	....	....	....	....
1989-90	NY Rangers	NHL	80	36	31	13	.531	10	5	5	0	.500
1990-91	NY Rangers	NHL	80	36	31	13	.531	6	2	4	0	.333
1991-92	NY Rangers	NHL	80	50	25	5	.656	13	6	7	0	.462
1992-93	NY Rangers	NHL	40	19	17	4	.525	....	....	....	....	....
1993-94	Florida	NHL	84	33	34	17	.494	....	....	....	....	....
1994-95	Florida	NHL	48	20	22	6	.479	....	....	....	....	....
1997-98	Philadelphia	NHL	21	10	9	2	.524	5	1	4	0	.200
	NHL Totals		**834**	**377**	**329**	**128**	**.529**	**82**	**38**	**44**	**0**	**.463**

• NOLAN, TED
b: Sault Ste. Marie, Ont., 4/7/1958.
Played in NHL. See Modern Player Register for career statistics.

Season	Club	League	GC	W	L	T	W%	GC	W	L	T	W%
1995-96	Buffalo	NHL	82	33	42	7	.445	....	....	....	....	....
1996-97	Buffalo	NHL	82	40	30	12	.561	12	5	7	0	.417
	NHL Totals		**164**	**73**	**72**	**19**	**.503**	**12**	**5**	**7**	**0**	**.417**

• Won Jack Adams Award (1997)

• NYKOLUK, MIKE
b: Toronto, Ont., 12/11/1934.
Played in NHL. See Pre-Expansion Player Register for career statistics.

Season	Club	League	GC	W	L	T	W%	GC	W	L	T	W%
1980-81	Toronto	NHL	40	15	15	10	.500	3	0	3	0	.000
1981-82	Toronto	NHL	80	20	44	16	.350	....	....	....	....	....
1982-83	Toronto	NHL	80	28	40	12	.425	4	1	3	0	.250
1983-84	Toronto	NHL	80	26	45	9	.381	....	....	....	....	....
	NHL Totals		**280**	**89**	**144**	**47**	**.402**	**7**	**1**	**6**	**0**	**.143**

• O'REILLY, TERRY
b: Niagara Falls, Ont., 6/7/1951.
Played in NHL. See Modern Player Register for career statistics.

Season	Club	League	GC	W	L	T	W%	GC	W	L	T	W%
1986-87	Boston	NHL	67	32	29	6	.522	4	0	4	0	.000
1987-88	Boston	NHL	80	44	30	6	.588	23	12	10	1	.543
1988-89	Boston	NHL	80	37	29	14	.550	10	5	5	0	.500
	NHL Totals		**227**	**113**	**88**	**26**	**.555**	**37**	**17**	**19**	**1**	**.473**

• OLIVER, MURRAY
b: Hamilton, Ont., 11/14/1937.
Played in NHL. See Modern Player Register for career statistics.

Season	Club	League	GC	W	L	T	W%	GC	W	L	T	W%
1981-82	Minnesota	NHL	4	3	0	1	.875	4	1	3	0	.250
1982-83	Minnesota	NHL	37	18	12	7	.581	9	4	5	0	.444
	NHL Totals		**41**	**21**	**12**	**8**	**.610**	**13**	**5**	**8**	**0**	**.385**

• OLMSTEAD, BERT — HHOF
b: Scepter, Sask., 9/4/1926.
Played in NHL. See Pre-Expansion Player Register for career statistics.

Season	Club	League	GC	W	L	T	W%	GC	W	L	T	W%
1967-68	Oakland	NHL	64	11	37	16	.297	....	....	....	....	....
	NHL Totals		**64**	**11**	**37**	**16**	**.297**	....	....	....	....	....

• PADDOCK, JOHN
b: Brandon, Man., 6/9/1954.
Played in NHL. See Modern Player Register for career statistics.

Season	Club	League	GC	W	L	T	W%	GC	W	L	T	W%
1991-92	Winnipeg	NHL	80	33	32	15	.506	7	3	4	0	.429
1992-93	Winnipeg	NHL	84	40	37	7	.518	6	2	4	0	.333
1993-94	Winnipeg	NHL	84	24	51	9	.339	....	....	....	....	....
1994-95	Winnipeg	NHL	33	9	18	6	.364	....	....	....	....	....
	NHL Totals		**281**	**106**	**138**	**37**	**.443**	**13**	**5**	**8**	**0**	**.385**

• PAGE, PIERRE
b: St-Hermas, Que., 4/30/1948.

Season	Club	League	GC	W	L	T	W%	GC	W	L	T	W%
1988-89	Minnesota	NHL	80	27	37	16	.438	5	1	4	0	.200
1989-90	Minnesota	NHL	80	36	40	4	.475	7	3	4	0	.429
1991-92	Quebec	NHL	62	17	34	11	.363	....	....	....	....	....
1992-93	Quebec	NHL	84	47	27	10	.619	6	2	4	0	.333
1993-94	Quebec	NHL	84	34	42	8	.452	....	....	....	....	....
1995-96	Calgary	NHL	82	34	37	11	.482	4	0	4	0	.000
1996-97	Calgary	NHL	82	32	41	9	.445	....	....	....	....	....
1997-98	Anaheim	NHL	82	26	43	13	.396	....	....	....	....	....
	NHL Totals		**636**	**253**	**301**	**82**	**.462**	**22**	**6**	**16**	**0**	**.273**

• PARK, BRAD — HHOF
b: Toronto, Ont., 7/6/1948.
Played in NHL. See Modern Player Register for career statistics.

Season	Club	League	GC	W	L	T	W%	GC	W	L	T	W%
1985-86	Detroit	NHL	45	9	34	2	.222	....	....	....	....	....
	NHL Totals		**45**	**9**	**34**	**2**	**.222**	....	....	....	....	....

• PATERSON, RICK
b: Kingston, Ont., 2/10/1958.
Played in NHL. See Modern Player Register for career statistics.

Season	Club	League	GC	W	L	T	W%	GC	W	L	T	W%
1997-98	Tampa Bay	NHL	8	0	8	0	.000	....	....	....	....	....
	NHL Totals		**8**	**0**	**8**	**0**	**.000**	....	....	....	....	....

• PATRICK, CRAIG — USHOF
b: Detroit, MI, 5/20/1946.
Played in NHL. See Modern Player Register for career statistics.

Season	Club	League	GC	W	L	T	W%	GC	W	L	T	W%
1980-81	NY Rangers	NHL	60	26	23	11	.525	14	7	7	0	.500
1984-85	NY Rangers	NHL	35	11	22	2	.343	3	0	3	0	.000
1989-90	Pittsburgh	NHL	54	22	26	6	.463	....	....	....	....	....
1996-97	Pittsburgh	NHL	20	7	10	3	.425	5	1	4	0	.200
	NHL Totals		**169**	**66**	**81**	**22**	**.456**	**22**	**8**	**14**	**0**	**.364**

• PATRICK, FRANK — HHOF
b: Ottawa, Ont., 12/21/1885. d: 6/29/1960.

Season	Club	League	GC	W	L	T	W%	GC	W	L	T	W%
1934-35	Boston	NHL	48	26	16	6	.604	4	1	3	0	.250
1935-36	Boston	NHL	48	22	20	6	.521	2	1	1	0	.500
	NHL Totals		**96**	**48**	**36**	**12**	**.563**	**6**	**2**	**4**	**0**	**.333**

• PATRICK, LESTER — HHOF
b: Drummondville, Que., 12/30/1883. Deceased.
Played in NHL. See Pre-Expansion Player Register for career statistics.

Season	Club	League	GC	W	L	T	W%	GC	W	L	T	W%
1926-27	NY Rangers	NHL	44	25	13	6	.636	2	0	1	1	.250
1927-28	NY Rangers	NHL	44	19	16	9	.534	9	5	3	1	.611
1928-29	NY Rangers	NHL	44	21	13	10	.591	6	3	2	1	.583
1929-30	NY Rangers	NHL	44	17	17	10	.500	4	1	2	1	.375
1930-31	NY Rangers	NHL	44	19	16	9	.534	4	2	2	0	.500
1931-32	NY Rangers	NHL	48	23	17	8	.563	7	3	4	0	.429
1932-33	NY Rangers	NHL	48	23	17	8	.563	8	6	1	1	.813
1933-34	NY Rangers	NHL	48	21	19	8	.521	2	0	1	1	.250
1934-35	NY Rangers	NHL	48	22	20	6	.521	4	2	1	1	.625
1935-36	NY Rangers	NHL	48	19	17	12	.521	....	....	....	....	....
1936-37	NY Rangers	NHL	48	19	20	9	.490	9	6	3	0	.667
1937-38	NY Rangers	NHL	48	27	15	6	.625	3	1	2	0	.333
1938-39	NY Rangers	NHL	48	26	16	6	.604	7	3	4	0	.429
	NHL Totals		**604**	**281**	**216**	**107**	**.554**	**65**	**32**	**26**	**7**	**.546**

• PATRICK, LYNN — HHOF
b: Victoria, B.C., 2/3/1912. Deceased.
Played in NHL. See Pre-Expansion Player Register for career statistics.

Season	Club	League	GC	W	L	T	W%	GC	W	L	T	W%
1948-49	NY Rangers	NHL	37	12	20	5	.392	....	....	....	....	....
1949-50	NY Rangers	NHL	70	28	31	11	.479	12	7	5	0	.583
1950-51	Boston	NHL	70	22	30	18	.443	6	1	4	1	.250
1951-52	Boston	NHL	70	25	29	16	.471	7	3	4	0	.429
1952-53	Boston	NHL	70	28	29	13	.493	11	5	6	0	.455
1953-54	Boston	NHL	70	32	28	10	.529	4	0	4	0	.000
1954-55	Boston	NHL	30	10	14	6	.433	....	....	....	....	....
1967-68	St. Louis	NHL	16	4	10	2	.313	....	....	....	....	....
1974-75	St. Louis	NHL	2	1	0	1	.750	....	....	....	....	....
1975-76	St. Louis	NHL	8	3	5	0	.375	....	....	....	....	....
	NHL Totals		**443**	**165**	**196**	**82**	**.465**	**40**	**16**	**23**	**1**	**.413**

• PATRICK, MUZZ
b: Victoria, B.C., 6/28/1915. d: 7/23/1998.
Played in NHL. See Pre-Expansion Player Register for career statistics.

Season	Club	League	GC	W	L	T	W%	GC	W	L	T	W%
1953-54	NY Rangers	NHL	30	15	11	4	.567	....	....	....	....	....
1954-55	NY Rangers	NHL	70	17	35	18	.371	....	....	....	....	....
1959-60	NY Rangers	NHL	2	0	1	1	.250	....	....	....	....	....
1962-63	NY Rangers	NHL	34	11	19	4	.382	....	....	....	....	....
	NHL Totals		**136**	**43**	**66**	**27**	**.415**	....	....	....	....	....

• PERRON, JEAN
b: St-Isidore d'Auckland, Que., 10/5/1946.

Season	Club	League	GC	W	L	T	W%	GC	W	L	T	W%
1985-86	Montreal	NHL	80	40	33	7	.544	20	15	5	0	.750
1986-87	Montreal	NHL	80	41	29	10	.575	17	10	7	0	.588
1987-88	Montreal	NHL	80	45	22	13	.644	11	5	6	0	.455
1988-89	Quebec	NHL	47	16	26	5	.394	....	....	....	....	....
	NHL Totals		**287**	**142**	**110**	**35**	**.556**	**48**	**30**	**18**	**0**	**.625**

• PERRY, DON
b: Edmonton, Alta., 3/16/1930.

Season	Club	League	GC	W	L	T	W%	GC	W	L	T	W%
1981-82	Los Angeles	NHL	38	11	17	10	.421	10	4	6	0	.400
1982-83	Los Angeles	NHL	80	27	41	12	.413	....	....	....	....	....
1983-84	Los Angeles	NHL	50	14	27	9	.370	....	....	....	....	....
	NHL Totals		**168**	**52**	**85**	**31**	**.402**	**10**	**4**	**6**	**0**	**.400**

• PIKE, ALF
b: Winnipeg, Man., 9/15/1917.
Played in NHL. See Pre-Expansion Player Register for career statistics.

Season	Club	League	GC	W	L	T	W%	GC	W	L	T	W%
1959-60	NY Rangers	NHL	53	14	28	11	.368	....	....	....	....	....
1960-61	NY Rangers	NHL	70	22	38	10	.386	....	....	....	....	....
	NHL Totals		**123**	**36**	**66**	**21**	**.378**	....	....	....	....	....

• PILOUS, RUDY
b: Winnipeg, Man., 8/11/1914. d: 12/11/1994.

Season	Club	League	GC	W	L	T	W%	GC	W	L	T	W%
1957-58	Chicago	NHL	37	14	22	1	.392	....	....	....	....	....
1958-59	Chicago	NHL	70	28	29	13	.493	6	2	4	0	.333
1959-60	Chicago	NHL	70	28	29	13	.493	4	0	4	0	.000
1960-61	Chicago	NHL	70	29	24	17	.536	12	8	4	0	.667
1961-62	Chicago	NHL	70	31	26	13	.536	12	6	6	0	.500
1962-63	Chicago	NHL	70	32	21	17	.579	7	3	4	0	.429
	NHL Totals		**387**	**162**	**151**	**74**	**.514**	**41**	**19**	**22**	**0**	**.463**

• PLAGER, BARCLAY
b: Kirkland Lake, Ont., 3/26/1941. d: 2/6/1988.
Played in NHL. See Modern Player Register for career statistics.

			REGULAR SEASON					PLAYOFFS				
Season	Club	League	GC	W	L	T	W%	GC	W	L	T	W%
1977-78	St. Louis	NHL	26	9	11	6	.462	....	....	....	....	....
1978-79	St. Louis	NHL	80	18	50	12	.300	....	....	....	....	....
1979-80	St. Louis	NHL	24	7	14	3	.354	....	....	....	....	....
1982-83	St. Louis	NHL	48	15	21	12	.438	4	1	3	0	.250
	NHL Totals		**178**	**49**	**96**	**33**	**.368**	**4**	**1**	**3**	**0**	**.250**

• PLAGER, BOB
b: Kirkland Lake, Ont., 3/11/1943.
Played in NHL. See Modern Player Register for career statistics.

Season	Club	League	GC	W	L	T	W%	GC	W	L	T	W%
1992-93	St. Louis	NHL	11	4	6	1	.409	....	....	....	....	....
	NHL Totals		**11**	**4**	**6**	**1**	**.409**	....	....	....	....	....

• PLEAU, LARRY
b: Lynn, MA, 1/29/1947.
Played in NHL. See Modern Player Register for career statistics.

Season	Club	League	GC	W	L	T	W%	GC	W	L	T	W%
1980-81	Hartford	NHL	20	6	12	2	.350	....	....	....	....	....
1981-82	Hartford	NHL	80	21	41	18	.375	....	....	....	....	....
1982-83	Hartford	NHL	18	4	13	1	.250	....	....	....	....	....
1987-88	Hartford	NHL	26	13	13	0	.500	6	2	4	0	.333
1988-89	Hartford	NHL	80	37	38	5	.494	4	0	4	0	.000
	NHL Totals		**224**	**81**	**117**	**26**	**.420**	**10**	**2**	**8**	**0**	**.200**

• POLANO, NICK
b: Sudbury, Ont., 3/25/1941.

Season	Club	League	GC	W	L	T	W%	GC	W	L	T	W%
1982-83	Detroit	NHL	80	21	44	15	.356	....	....	....	....	....
1983-84	Detroit	NHL	80	31	42	7	.431	4	1	3	0	.250
1984-85	Detroit	NHL	80	27	41	12	.413	3	0	3	0	.000
	NHL Totals		**240**	**79**	**127**	**34**	**.400**	**7**	**1**	**6**	**0**	**.143**

• POPEIN, LARRY
b: Yorkton, Sask., 8/11/1930.
Played in NHL. See Modern Player Register for career statistics.

Season	Club	League	GC	W	L	T	W%	GC	W	L	T	W%
1973-74	NY Rangers	NHL	41	18	14	9	.549	....	....	....	....	....
	NHL Totals		**41**	**18**	**14**	**9**	**.549**	....	....	....	....	....

• POWERS, EDDIE
b: Toronto, Ont.. d: 1/18/1943.

Season	Club	League	GC	W	L	T	W%	GC	W	L	T	W%
1921-22	Toronto	NHL	24	13	10	1	.563	7	4	2	1	.643
1923-24	Toronto	NHL	24	10	14	0	.417	....	....	....	....	....
1924-25	Toronto	NHL	30	19	11	0	.633	2	0	2	0	.000
1925-26	Toronto	NHL	36	12	21	3	.375	....	....	....	....	....
	NHL Totals		**114**	**54**	**56**	**4**	**.491**	**9**	**4**	**4**	**1**	**.500**

• PRIMEAU, JOE — HHOF
b: Lindsay, Ont., 1/29/1906. d: 5/14/1989.
Played in NHL. See Pre-Expansion Player Register for career statistics.

Season	Club	League	GC	W	L	T	W%	GC	W	L	T	W%
1950-51	Toronto	NHL	70	41	16	13	.679	11	8	2	1	.773
1951-52	Toronto	NHL	70	29	25	16	.529	4	0	4	0	.000
1952-53	Toronto	NHL	70	27	30	13	.479	....	....	....	....	....
	NHL Totals		**210**	**97**	**71**	**42**	**.562**	**15**	**8**	**6**	**1**	**.567**

• PRONOVOST, MARCEL — HHOF
b: Shawinigan Falls, Que., 6/15/1930.
Played in NHL. See Modern Player Register for career statistics.

Season	Club	League	GC	W	L	T	W%	GC	W	L	T	W%
1977-78	Buffalo	NHL	80	44	19	17	.656	8	3	5	0	.375
1978-79	Buffalo	NHL	24	8	10	6	.458	....	....	....	....	....
	NHL Totals		**104**	**52**	**29**	**23**	**.611**	**8**	**3**	**5**	**0**	**.375**

• PULFORD, BOB — HHOF
b: Newton Robinson, Ont., 3/31/1936.
Played in NHL. See Modern Player Register for career statistics.

Season	Club	League	GC	W	L	T	W%	GC	W	L	T	W%
1972-73	Los Angeles	NHL	78	31	36	11	.468	....	....	....	....	....
1973-74	Los Angeles	NHL	78	33	33	12	.500	5	1	4	0	.200
1974-75	Los Angeles	NHL	80	42	17	21	.656	3	1	2	0	.333
1975-76	Los Angeles	NHL	80	38	33	9	.531	9	4	5	0	.444
1976-77	Los Angeles	NHL	80	34	31	15	.519	9	4	5	0	.444
1977-78	Chicago	NHL	80	32	29	19	.519	4	0	4	0	.000
1978-79	Chicago	NHL	80	29	36	15	.456	4	0	4	0	.000
1981-82	Chicago	NHL	28	12	14	2	.464	15	8	7	0	.533
1984-85	Chicago	NHL	27	16	7	4	.667	15	9	6	0	.600
1985-86	Chicago	NHL	80	39	33	8	.538	3	0	3	0	.000
1986-87	Chicago	NHL	80	29	37	14	.450	4	0	4	0	.000
1987-88	Chicago	NHL	80	30	41	9	.431	5	1	4	0	.200
	NHL Totals		**851**	**365**	**347**	**139**	**.511**	**76**	**28**	**48**	**0**	**.368**

• Won Jack Adams Award (1975)

• QUENNEVILLE, JOEL
b: Windsor, Ont., 9/15/1958.
Played in NHL. See Modern Player Register for career statistics.

Season	Club	League	GC	W	L	T	W%	GC	W	L	T	W%
1996-97	St. Louis	NHL	40	18	15	7	.538	6	2	4	0	.333
1997-98	St. Louis	NHL	82	45	29	8	.598	10	6	4	0	.600
	NHL Totals		**122**	**63**	**44**	**15**	**.578**	**16**	**8**	**8**	**0**	**.500**

• QUERRIE, CHARLES
b: unknown. Deceased.

Season	Club	League	GC	W	L	T	W%	GC	W	L	T	W%
1922-23	Toronto	NHL	6	3	3	0	.500	....	....	....	....	....
	NHL Totals		**6**	**3**	**3**	**0**	**.500**	....	....	....	....	....

• QUINN, MIKE
b: unknown. Deceased.

Season	Club	League	GC	W	L	T	W%	GC	W	L	T	W%
1919-20	Quebec	NHL	24	4	20	0	.167	....	....	....	....	....
	NHL Totals		**24**	**4**	**20**	**0**	**.167**	....	....	....	....	....

• QUINN, PAT
b: Hamilton, Ont., 1/29/1943.
Played in NHL. See Modern Player Register for career statistics.

Season	Club	League	GC	W	L	T	W%	GC	W	L	T	W%
1978-79	Philadelphia	NHL	30	18	8	4	.667	8	3	5	0	.375
1979-80	Philadelphia	NHL	80	48	12	20	.725	19	13	6	0	.684
1980-81	Philadelphia	NHL	80	41	24	15	.606	12	6	6	0	.500
1981-82	Philadelphia	NHL	72	34	29	9	.535	....	....	....	....	....
1984-85	Los Angeles	NHL	80	34	32	14	.513	3	0	3	0	.000
1985-86	Los Angeles	NHL	80	23	49	8	.338	....	....	....	....	....
1986-87	Los Angeles	NHL	42	18	20	4	.476	....	....	....	....	....
1990-91	Vancouver	NHL	26	9	13	4	.423	6	2	4	0	.333
1991-92	Vancouver	NHL	80	42	26	12	.600	13	6	7	0	.462
1992-93	Vancouver	NHL	84	46	29	9	.601	12	6	6	0	.500
1993-94	Vancouver	NHL	84	41	40	3	.506	24	15	9	0	.625
1995-96	Vancouver	NHL	6	3	3	0	.500	6	2	4	0	.333
	NHL Totals		**744**	**357**	**285**	**102**	**.548**	**103**	**53**	**50**	**0**	**.515**

• Won Jack Adams Award (1980, 1992)

• RAMSAY, CRAIG
b: Weston, Ont., 3/17/1951.
Played in NHL. See Modern Player Register for career statistics.

Season	Club	League	GC	W	L	T	W%	GC	W	L	T	W%
1986-87	Buffalo	NHL	21	4	15	2	.238	....	....	....	....	....
	NHL Totals		**21**	**4**	**15**	**2**	**.238**	....	....	....	....	....

• RANDALL, KEN
b: Kingston, Ont.. Deceased.
Played in NHL. See Pre-Expansion Player Register for career statistics.

Season	Club	League	GC	W	L	T	W%	GC	W	L	T	W%
1923-24	Hamilton	NHL	14	6	8	0	.429	....	....	....	....	....
	NHL Totals		**14**	**6**	**8**	**0**	**.429**	....	....	....	....	....

• REAY, BILLY
b: Winnipeg, Man., 8/21/1918.
Played in NHL. See Pre-Expansion Player Register for career statistics.

Season	Club	League	GC	W	L	T	W%	GC	W	L	T	W%
1957-58	Toronto	NHL	70	21	38	11	.379	....	....	....	....	....
1958-59	Toronto	NHL	20	5	12	3	.325	....	....	....	....	....
1963-64	Chicago	NHL	70	36	22	12	.600	6	2	4	0	.333
1964-65	Chicago	NHL	70	34	28	8	.543	14	7	7	0	.500
1965-66	Chicago	NHL	70	37	25	8	.586	6	2	4	0	.333
1966-67	Chicago	NHL	70	41	17	12	.671	6	2	4	0	.333
1967-68	Chicago	NHL	74	32	26	16	.541	11	5	6	0	.455
1968-69	Chicago	NHL	76	34	33	9	.507	....	....	....	....	....
1969-70	Chicago	NHL	76	45	22	9	.651	8	4	4	0	.500
1970-71	Chicago	NHL	78	49	20	9	.686	18	11	7	0	.611
1971-72	Chicago	NHL	78	46	17	15	.686	8	4	4	0	.500
1972-73	Chicago	NHL	78	42	27	9	.596	16	10	6	0	.625
1973-74	Chicago	NHL	78	41	14	23	.673	11	6	5	0	.545
1974-75	Chicago	NHL	80	37	35	8	.513	8	3	5	0	.375
1975-76	Chicago	NHL	80	32	30	18	.513	4	0	4	0	.000
1976-77	Chicago	NHL	34	10	19	5	.368	....	....	....	....	....
	NHL Totals		**1102**	**542**	**385**	**175**	**.571**	**118**	**56**	**60**	**0**	**.483**

• REGAN, LARRY
b: North Bay, Ont., 8/9/1930.
Played in NHL. See Pre-Expansion Player Register for career statistics.

Season	Club	League	GC	W	L	T	W%	GC	W	L	T	W%
1970-71	Los Angeles	NHL	78	25	40	13	.404	....	....	....	....	....
1971-72	Los Angeles	NHL	10	2	7	1	.250	....	....	....	....	....
	NHL Totals		**88**	**27**	**47**	**14**	**.386**	....	....	....	....	....

• RENNEY, TOM
b: Cranbrooke, B.C., 3/1/1955.

Season	Club	League	GC	W	L	T	W%	GC	W	L	T	W%
1996-97	Vancouver	NHL	82	35	40	7	.470	....	....	....	....	....
1997-98	Vancouver	NHL	19	4	13	2	.263	....	....	....	....	....
	NHL Totals		**101**	**39**	**53**	**9**	**.431**	....	....	....	....	....

• RISEBROUGH, DOUG
b: Guelph, Ont., 1/29/1954.
Played in NHL. See Modern Player Register for career statistics.

Season	Club	League	GC	W	L	T	W%	GC	W	L	T	W%
1990-91	Calgary	NHL	80	46	26	8	.625	7	3	4	0	.429
1991-92	Calgary	NHL	64	25	30	9	.461	....	....	....	....	....
	NHL Totals		**144**	**71**	**56**	**17**	**.552**	**7**	**3**	**4**	**0**	**.429**

• ROBERTS, JIM
b: Toronto, Ont., 4/9/1940.
Played in NHL. See Modern Player Register for career statistics.

Season	Club	League	GC	W	L	T	W%	GC	W	L	T	W%
1981-82	Buffalo	NHL	45	21	16	8	.556	....	....	....	....	....
1991-92	Hartford	NHL	80	26	41	13	.406	7	3	4	0	.429
1996-97	St. Louis	NHL	9	3	3	3	.500	....	....	....	....	....
	NHL Totals		**134**	**50**	**60**	**24**	**.463**	**7**	**3**	**4**	**0**	**.429**

• ROBINSON, LARRY — HHOF
b: Winchester, Ont., 6/2/1951.
Played in NHL. See Modern Player Register for career statistics.

Season	Club	League	GC	W	L	T	W%	GC	W	L	T	W%
1995-96	Los Angeles	NHL	82	24	40	18	.402	....	....	....	....	....
1996-97	Los Angeles	NHL	82	28	43	11	.409	....	....	....	....	....
1997-98	Los Angeles	NHL	82	38	33	11	.530	4	0	4	0	.000
	NHL Totals		**246**	**90**	**116**	**40**	**.447**	**4**	**0**	**4**	**0**	**.000**

			REGULAR SEASON					PLAYOFFS				
Season	Club	League	GC	W	L	T	W%	GC	W	L	T	W%

● RODDEN, MIKE
b: 4/24/1891. d: 1/11/1978.

1926-27	Toronto	NHL	30	8	18	4	.333	....	....	....	....	....
	NHL Totals		**30**	**8**	**18**	**4**	**.333**	....	....	....	....	....

● ROMERIL, ALEX
b: unknown.

1926-27	Toronto	NHL	14	7	6	1	.536	....	....	....	....	....
	NHL Totals		**14**	**7**	**6**	**1**	**.536**	....	....	....	....	....

● ROSS, ART   HHOF
b: Naughton, Ont., 1/13/1886. d: 8/5/1964.
Played in NHL. See Pre-Expansion Player Register for career statistics.

1917-18	Mtl. Wanderers	NHL	6	1	5	0	.167	....	....	....	....	....
1922-23	Hamilton	NHL	24	6	18	0	.250	....	....	....	....	....
1924-25	Boston	NHL	30	6	24	0	.200	....	....	....	....	....
1925-26	Boston	NHL	36	17	15	4	.528	....	....	....	....	....
1926-27	Boston	NHL	44	21	20	3	.511	8	2	2	4	.500
1927-28	Boston	NHL	44	20	13	11	.580	2	0	1	1	.250
1929-30	Boston	NHL	44	38	5	1	.875	6	3	3	0	.500
1930-31	Boston	NHL	44	28	10	6	.705	5	2	3	0	.400
1931-32	Boston	NHL	48	15	21	12	.438	....	....	....	....	....
1932-33	Boston	NHL	48	25	15	8	.604	5	2	3	0	.400
1933-34	Boston	NHL	48	18	25	5	.427	....	....	....	....	....
1936-37	Boston	NHL	48	23	18	7	.552	3	1	2	0	.333
1937-38	Boston	NHL	48	30	11	7	.698	3	0	3	0	.000
1938-39	Boston	NHL	48	36	10	2	.771	12	8	4	0	.667
1941-42	Boston	NHL	48	25	17	6	.583	5	2	3	0	.400
1942-43	Boston	NHL	50	24	17	9	.570	9	4	5	0	.444
1943-44	Boston	NHL	50	19	26	5	.430	....	....	....	....	....
1944-45	Boston	NHL	50	16	30	4	.360	7	3	4	0	.429
	NHL Totals		**758**	**368**	**300**	**90**	**.545**	**65**	**27**	**33**	**5**	**.454**

● RUEL, CLAUDE
b: Sherbrooke, Que., 9/12/1938.

1968-69	Montreal	NHL	76	46	19	11	.678	14	12	2	0	.857
1969-70	Montreal	NHL	76	38	22	16	.605	....	....	....	....	....
1970-71	Montreal	NHL	23	11	8	4	.565	....	....	....	....	....
1979-80	Montreal	NHL	50	32	11	7	.710	10	6	4	0	.600
1980-81	Montreal	NHL	80	45	22	13	.644	3	0	3	0	.000
	NHL Totals		**305**	**172**	**82**	**51**	**.648**	**27**	**18**	**9**	**0**	**.667**

● RUFF, LINDY
b: Warburg, Alta., 2/17/1960.
Played in NHL. See Modern Player Register for career statistics.

1997-98	Buffalo	NHL	82	36	29	17	.543	15	10	5	0	.667
	NHL Totals		**82**	**36**	**29**	**17**	**.543**	**15**	**10**	**5**	**0**	**.667**

● SATHER, GLEN   HHOF
b: High River, Alta., 9/2/1943.
Played in NHL. See Modern Player Register for career statistics.

1979-80	Edmonton	NHL	80	28	39	13	.431	3	0	3	0	.000
1980-81	Edmonton	NHL	62	25	26	11	.492	9	5	4	0	.556
1981-82	Edmonton	NHL	80	48	17	15	.694	5	2	3	0	.400
1982-83	Edmonton	NHL	80	47	21	12	.663	16	11	5	0	.688
1983-84	Edmonton	NHL	80	57	18	5	.744	19	15	4	0	.789
1984-85	Edmonton	NHL	80	49	20	11	.681	18	15	3	0	.833
1985-86	Edmonton	NHL	80	56	17	7	.744	10	6	4	0	.600
1986-87	Edmonton	NHL	80	50	24	6	.663	21	16	5	0	.762
1987-88	Edmonton	NHL	80	44	25	11	.619	19	16	2	1	.868
1988-89	Edmonton	NHL	80	38	34	8	.525	7	3	4	0	.429
1993-94	Edmonton	NHL	60	22	27	11	.458	....	....	....	....	....
	NHL Totals		**842**	**464**	**268**	**110**	**.616**	**127**	**89**	**37**	**1**	**.705**

● Won Jack Adams Award (1986)

● SATOR, TED
b: Utica, NY, 11/18/1949.

1985-86	NY Rangers	NHL	80	36	38	6	.488	16	8	8	0	.500
1986-87	Buffalo	NHL	47	21	22	4	.489	....	....	....	....	....
1986-87	NY Rangers	NHL	19	5	10	4	.368	....	....	....	....	....
1987-88	Buffalo	NHL	80	37	32	11	.531	6	2	4	0	.333
1988-89	Buffalo	NHL	80	38	35	7	.519	5	1	4	0	.200
	NHL Totals		**306**	**137**	**137**	**32**	**.500**	**27**	**11**	**16**	**0**	**.407**

● SAVARD, ANDRE
b: Temiscamingue, Que., 2/9/1953.
Played in NHL. See Modern Player Register for career statistics.

1987-88	Quebec	NHL	24	10	13	1	.438	....	....	....	....	....
	NHL Totals		**24**	**10**	**13**	**1**	**.438**	....	....	....	....	....

● SCHINKEL, KEN
b: Jansen, Sask., 11/27/1932.
Played in NHL. See Modern Player Register for career statistics.

1972-73	Pittsburgh	NHL	36	15	18	3	.458	....	....	....	....	....
1973-74	Pittsburgh	NHL	50	14	31	5	.330	....	....	....	....	....
1975-76	Pittsburgh	NHL	37	20	10	7	.635	3	1	2	0	.333
1976-77	Pittsburgh	NHL	80	34	33	13	.506	3	1	2	0	.333
	NHL Totals		**203**	**83**	**92**	**28**	**.478**	**6**	**2**	**4**	**0**	**.333**

● SCHMIDT, MILT   HHOF
b: Kitchener, Ont., 3/5/1918.
Played in NHL. See Pre-Expansion Player Register for career statistics.

1954-55	Boston	NHL	40	13	12	15	.513	5	1	4	0	.200
1955-56	Boston	NHL	70	23	34	13	.421	....	....	....	....	....
1956-57	Boston	NHL	70	34	24	12	.571	10	5	5	0	.500
1957-58	Boston	NHL	70	27	28	15	.493	12	6	6	0	.500
1958-59	Boston	NHL	70	32	29	9	.521	7	3	4	0	.429
1959-60	Boston	NHL	70	28	34	8	.457	....	....	....	....	....
1960-61	Boston	NHL	70	15	42	13	.307	....	....	....	....	....
1962-63	Boston	NHL	56	13	31	12	.339	....	....	....	....	....
1963-64	Boston	NHL	70	18	40	12	.343	....	....	....	....	....
1964-65	Boston	NHL	70	21	43	6	.343	....	....	....	....	....
1965-66	Boston	NHL	70	21	43	6	.343	....	....	....	....	....
1974-75	Washington	NHL	8	2	6	0	.250	....	....	....	....	....
1975-76	Washington	NHL	36	3	28	5	.153	....	....	....	....	....
	NHL Totals		**770**	**250**	**394**	**126**	**.406**	**34**	**15**	**19**	**0**	**.441**

● SCHOENFELD, JIM
b: Galt, Ont., 9/4/1952.
Played in NHL. See Modern Player Register for career statistics.

1985-86	Buffalo	NHL	43	19	19	5	.500	....	....	....	....	....
1987-88	New Jersey	NHL	30	17	12	1	.583	20	11	9	0	.550
1988-89	New Jersey	NHL	80	27	41	12	.413	....	....	....	....	....
1989-90	New Jersey	NHL	14	6	6	2	.500	....	....	....	....	....
1993-94	Washington	NHL	37	19	12	6	.595	11	5	6	0	.455
1994-95	Washington	NHL	48	22	18	8	.542	7	3	4	0	.429
1995-96	Washington	NHL	82	39	32	11	.543	6	2	4	0	.333
1996-97	Washington	NHL	82	33	40	9	.457	....	....	....	....	....
1997-98	Phoenix	NHL	82	35	35	12	.500	6	2	4	0	.333
	NHL Totals		**498**	**217**	**215**	**66**	**.502**	**50**	**23**	**27**	**0**	**.460**

● SHAUGHNESSY, TOM
b: unknown. Deceased.

1929-30	Chicago	NHL	21	10	8	3	.548	....	....	....	....	....
	NHL Totals		**21**	**10**	**8**	**3**	**.548**	....	....	....	....	....

● SHERO, FRED
b: Winnipeg, Man., 10/23/1925. Deceased.
Played in NHL. See Pre-Expansion Player Register for career statistics.

1971-72	Philadelphia	NHL	78	26	38	14	.423	....	....	....	....	....
1972-73	Philadelphia	NHL	78	37	30	11	.545	11	5	6	0	.455
1973-74	Philadelphia	NHL	78	50	16	12	.718	17	12	5	0	.706
1974-75	Philadelphia	NHL	80	51	18	11	.706	17	12	5	0	.706
1975-76	Philadelphia	NHL	80	51	13	16	.738	16	8	8	0	.500
1976-77	Philadelphia	NHL	80	48	16	16	.700	10	4	6	0	.400
1977-78	Philadelphia	NHL	80	45	20	15	.656	12	7	5	0	.583
1978-79	NY Rangers	NHL	80	40	29	11	.569	18	11	7	0	.611
1979-80	NY Rangers	NHL	80	38	32	10	.538	9	4	5	0	.444
1980-81	NY Rangers	NHL	20	4	13	3	.275	....	....	....	....	....
	NHL Totals		**734**	**390**	**225**	**119**	**.612**	**110**	**63**	**47**	**0**	**.573**

● Won Jack Adams Award (1974)

● SIMPSON, JOE   HHOF
b: Selkirk, Man., 8/13/1893. d: 12/25/1973.
Played in NHL. See Pre-Expansion Player Register for career statistics.

1932-33	NY Americans	NHL	48	15	22	11	.427	....	....	....	....	....
1933-34	NY Americans	NHL	48	15	23	10	.417	....	....	....	....	....
1934-35	NY Americans	NHL	48	12	27	9	.344	....	....	....	....	....
	NHL Totals		**144**	**42**	**72**	**30**	**.396**	....	....	....	....	....

● SIMPSON, TERRY
b: Brantford, Ont., 8/30/1943.

1986-87	NY Islanders	NHL	80	35	33	12	.513	14	7	7	0	.500
1987-88	NY Islanders	NHL	80	39	31	10	.550	6	2	4	0	.333
1988-89	NY Islanders	NHL	27	7	18	2	.296	....	....	....	....	....
1993-94	Philadelphia	NHL	84	35	39	10	.476	....	....	....	....	....
1994-95	Winnipeg	NHL	15	7	7	1	.500	....	....	....	....	....
1995-96	Winnipeg	NHL	82	36	40	6	.476	6	2	4	0	.333
	NHL Totals		**368**	**159**	**168**	**41**	**.488**	**26**	**11**	**15**	**0**	**.423**

● SIMS, AL
b: Toronto, Ont., 4/18/1953.
Played in NHL. See Modern Player Register for career statistics.

1996-97	San Jose	NHL	82	27	47	8	.378	....	....	....	....	....
	NHL Totals		**82**	**27**	**47**	**8**	**.378**	....	....	....	....	....

● SINDEN, HARRY   HHOF
b: Collins Bay, Ont., 9/14/1932.

1966-67	Boston	NHL	70	17	43	10	.314	....	....	....	....	....
1967-68	Boston	NHL	74	37	27	10	.568	4	0	4	0	.000
1968-69	Boston	NHL	76	42	18	16	.658	10	6	4	0	.600
1969-70	Boston	NHL	76	40	17	19	.651	14	12	2	0	.857
1979-80	Boston	NHL	7	6	1	0	.857	10	4	6	0	.400
1984-85	Boston	NHL	24	11	10	3	.521	5	2	3	0	.400
	NHL Totals		**327**	**153**	**116**	**58**	**.557**	**43**	**24**	**19**	**0**	**.558**

● SKINNER, JIMMY
b: Selkirk, Man., 1/12/1918.

1954-55	Detroit	NHL	70	42	17	11	.679	11	8	3	0	.727
1955-56	Detroit	NHL	70	30	24	16	.543	10	5	5	0	.500
1956-57	Detroit	NHL	70	38	20	12	.629	5	1	4	0	.200
1957-58	Detroit	NHL	37	13	17	7	.446	....	....	....	....	....
	NHL Totals		**247**	**123**	**78**	**46**	**.591**	**26**	**14**	**12**	**0**	**.538**

			REGULAR SEASON					PLAYOFFS				
Season	Club	League	GC	W	L	T	W%	GC	W	L	T	W%

● SMEATON, COOPER   HHOF
b: Carleton Place, Ont., 7/22/1890.   d: 10/3/1978.

1930-31	Philadelphia	NHL	44	4	36	4	.136	....	....	....	....	....
	NHL Totals		**44**	**4**	**36**	**4**	**.136**	....	....	....	....	....

● SMITH, ALF   HHOF
b: Ottawa, Ont., 6/3/1873.   d: 8/21/1953.

1918-19	Ottawa	NHL	18	12	6	0	.667	5	1	4	0	.200
	NHL Totals		**18**	**12**	**6**	**0**	**.667**	**5**	**1**	**4**	**0**	**.200**

● SMITH, FLOYD
b: Perth, Ont., 5/16/1935.
Played in NHL. See Modern Player Register for career statistics.

1971-72	Buffalo	NHL	1	0	1	0	.000	....	....	....	....	....
1974-75	Buffalo	NHL	80	49	16	15	.706	17	10	7	0	.588
1975-76	Buffalo	NHL	80	46	21	13	.656	9	4	5	0	.444
1976-77	Buffalo	NHL	80	48	24	8	.650	6	2	4	0	.333
1979-80	Toronto	NHL	68	30	33	5	.478	....	....	....	....	....
	NHL Totals		**309**	**173**	**95**	**41**	**.626**	**32**	**16**	**16**	**0**	**.500**

● SMITH, MIKE
b: Potsdam, NY, 8/31/1945.

1980-81	Winnipeg	NHL	23	2	17	4	.174	....	....	....	....	....
	NHL Totals		**23**	**2**	**17**	**4**	**.174**	....	....	....	....	....

● SMITH, RON
b: Port Hope, Ont., 11/19/1952.
Played in NHL. See Modern Player Register for career statistics.

1992-93	NY Rangers	NHL	44	15	22	7	.420	....	....	....	....	....
	NHL Totals		**44**	**15**	**22**	**7**	**.420**	....	....	....	....	....

● SMYTHE, CONN   HHOF
b: Toronto, Ont., 2/1/1895.   d: 11/18/1980.

1927-28	Toronto	NHL	44	18	18	8	.500	....	....	....	....	....
1928-29	Toronto	NHL	44	21	18	5	.534	4	2	2	0	.500
1929-30	Toronto	NHL	44	17	21	6	.455	....	....	....	....	....
1930-31	Toronto	NHL	2	1	0	1	.750	....	....	....	....	....
	NHL Totals		**134**	**57**	**57**	**20**	**.500**	**4**	**2**	**2**	**0**	**.500**

● SONMOR, GLEN
b: Moose Jaw, Sask., 4/22/1929.
Played in NHL. See Pre-Expansion Player Register for career statistics.

1978-79	Minnesota	NHL	69	25	34	10	.435	....	....	....	....	....
1979-80	Minnesota	NHL	80	36	28	16	.500	15	8	7	0	.533
1980-81	Minnesota	NHL	80	35	28	17	.544	19	12	7	0	.632
1981-82	Minnesota	NHL	76	34	23	19	.572	....	....	....	....	....
1982-83	Minnesota	NHL	43	22	12	9	.616	....	....	....	....	....
1984-85	Minnesota	NHL	67	22	35	10	.403	9	5	4	0	.556
1986-87	Minnesota	NHL	2	0	1	1	.250	....	....	....	....	....
	NHL Totals		**417**	**174**	**161**	**82**	**.516**	**43**	**25**	**18**	**0**	**.581**

● SPROULE, HARRY
b: unknown.   Deceased.

1919-20	Toronto	NHL	12	7	5	0	.583	....	....	....	....	....
	NHL Totals		**12**	**7**	**5**	**0**	**.583**	....	....	....	....	....

● STANLEY, BARNEY   HHOF
b: Paisley, Ont., 1/1/1893.   d: 5/14/1971.
Played in NHL. See Pre-Expansion Player Register for career statistics.

1927-28	Chicago	NHL	23	4	17	2	.217	....	....	....	....	....
	NHL Totals		**23**	**4**	**17**	**2**	**.217**	....	....	....	....	....

● STASIUK, VIC
b: Lethbridge, Alta., 5/23/1929.
Played in NHL. See Pre-Expansion Player Register for career statistics.

1969-70	Philadelphia	NHL	76	17	35	24	.382	....	....	....	....	....
1970-71	Philadelphia	NHL	78	28	33	17	.468	4	0	4	0	.000
1971-72	California	NHL	75	21	38	16	.387	....	....	....	....	....
1972-73	Vancouver	NHL	78	22	47	9	.340	....	....	....	....	....
	NHL Totals		**307**	**88**	**153**	**66**	**.394**	**4**	**0**	**4**	**0**	**.000**

● STEWART, BILL   USHOF
b: Toronto, Ont., 10/6/1957.

1937-38	Chicago	NHL	48	14	25	9	.385	10	7	3	0	.700
1938-39	Chicago	NHL	21	8	10	3	.452	....	....	....	....	....
	NHL Totals		**69**	**22**	**35**	**12**	**.406**	**10**	**7**	**3**	**0**	**.700**

● STEWART, RON
b: Calgary, Alta., 7/11/1932.
Played in NHL. See Modern Player Register for career statistics.

1975-76	NY Rangers	NHL	39	15	20	4	.436	....	....	....	....	....
1977-78	Los Angeles	NHL	80	31	34	15	.481	2	0	2	0	.000
	NHL Totals		**119**	**46**	**54**	**19**	**.466**	**2**	**0**	**2**	**0**	**.000**

● SULLIVAN, RED
b: Peterborough, Ont., 12/24/1929.
Played in NHL. See Pre-Expansion Player Register for career statistics.

1962-63	NY Rangers	NHL	36	11	17	8	.417	....	....	....	....	....
1963-64	NY Rangers	NHL	70	22	38	10	.386	....	....	....	....	....
1964-65	NY Rangers	NHL	70	20	38	12	.371	....	....	....	....	....
1965-66	NY Rangers	NHL	20	5	10	5	.375	....	....	....	....	....
1967-68	Pittsburgh	NHL	74	27	34	13	.453	....	....	....	....	....
1968-69	Pittsburgh	NHL	76	20	45	11	.336	....	....	....	....	....
1974-75	Washington	NHL	18	2	16	0	.111	....	....	....	....	....
	NHL Totals		**364**	**107**	**198**	**59**	**.375**	....	....	....	....	....

● SUTHERLAND, BILL
b: Regina, Sask., 11/10/1934.
Played in NHL. See Modern Player Register for career statistics.

1979-80	Winnipeg	NHL	3	1	2	0	.333	....	....	....	....	....
1980-81	Winnipeg	NHL	29	6	20	3	.259	....	....	....	....	....
	NHL Totals		**32**	**7**	**22**	**3**	**.266**	....	....	....	....	....

● SUTTER, BRIAN
b: Viking, Alta., 10/7/1956.
Played in NHL. See Modern Player Register for career statistics.

1988-89	St. Louis	NHL	80	33	35	12	.488	10	5	5	0	.500
1989-90	St. Louis	NHL	80	37	34	9	.519	12	7	5	0	.583
1990-91	St. Louis	NHL	80	47	22	11	.656	13	6	7	0	.462
1991-92	St. Louis	NHL	80	36	33	11	.519	6	2	4	0	.333
1992-93	Boston	NHL	84	51	26	7	.649	4	0	4	0	.000
1993-94	Boston	NHL	84	42	29	13	.577	13	6	7	0	.462
1994-95	Boston	NHL	48	27	18	3	.594	5	1	4	0	.200
1997-98	Calgary	NHL	82	26	41	15	.409	....	....	....	....	....
	NHL Totals		**618**	**299**	**238**	**81**	**.549**	**63**	**27**	**36**	**0**	**.429**

• Won Jack Adams Award (1991)

● SUTTER, DARRYL
b: Viking, Alta., 8/19/1958.
Played in NHL. See Modern Player Register for career statistics.

1992-93	Chicago	NHL	84	47	25	12	.631	4	0	4	0	.000
1993-94	Chicago	NHL	84	39	36	9	.518	6	2	4	0	.333
1994-95	Chicago	NHL	48	24	19	5	.552	16	9	7	0	.563
1997-98	San Jose	NHL	82	34	38	10	.476	6	2	4	0	.333
	NHL Totals		**208**	**144**	**110**	**30**	**.544**	**32**	**13**	**19**	**0**	**.406**

● TALBOT, JEAN-GUY
b: Cap de La Madeliene, Que., 7/11/1932.
Played in NHL. See Modern Player Register for career statistics.

1972-73	St. Louis	NHL	65	30	28	7	.515	5	1	4	0	.200
1973-74	St. Louis	NHL	55	22	25	8	.473	....	....	....	....	....
1977-78	NY Rangers	NHL	80	30	37	13	.456	3	1	2	0	.333
	NHL Totals		**200**	**82**	**90**	**28**	**.480**	**8**	**2**	**6**	**0**	**.250**

● TESSIER, ORVAL
b: Cornwall, Ont., 6/30/1933.
Played in NHL. See Pre-Expansion Player Register for career statistics.

1982-83	Chicago	NHL	80	47	23	10	.650	13	7	6	0	.538
1983-84	Chicago	NHL	80	30	42	8	.425	5	2	3	0	.400
1984-85	Chicago	NHL	53	22	28	3	.443	....	....	....	....	....
	NHL Totals		**213**	**99**	**93**	**21**	**.514**	**18**	**9**	**9**	**0**	**.500**

• Won Jack Adams Award (1983)

● THOMPSON, PAUL
b: Calgary, Alta., 11/2/1906.   Deceased.
Played in NHL. See Pre-Expansion Player Register for career statistics.

1938-39	Chicago	NHL	27	4	18	5	.241	....	....	....	....	....
1939-40	Chicago	NHL	48	23	19	6	.542	2	0	2	0	.000
1940-41	Chicago	NHL	48	16	25	7	.406	5	2	3	0	.400
1941-42	Chicago	NHL	48	22	23	3	.490	3	1	2	0	.333
1942-43	Chicago	NHL	50	17	18	15	.490	....	....	....	....	....
1943-44	Chicago	NHL	50	22	23	5	.490	9	4	5	0	.444
1944-45	Chicago	NHL	1	0	1	0	.000	....	....	....	....	....
	NHL Totals		**272**	**104**	**127**	**41**	**.458**	**19**	**7**	**12**	**0**	**.368**

● THOMPSON, PERCY
b: unknown.   Deceased.

1920-21	Hamilton	NHL	24	6	18	0	.250	....	....	....	....	....
1921-22	Hamilton	NHL	24	7	17	0	.292	....	....	....	....	....
	NHL Totals		**48**	**13**	**35**	**0**	**.271**	....	....	....	....	....

● TOBIN, BILL
b: Ottawa, Ont., 5/20/1895.   d: 5/8/1963.

1929-30	Chicago	NHL	23	11	10	2	.522	2	0	1	1	.250
1931-32	Chicago	NHL	43	15	18	10	.465	2	1	1	0	.500
	NHL Totals		**66**	**26**	**28**	**12**	**.485**	**4**	**1**	**2**	**1**	**.375**

● TREMBLAY, MARIO
b: Montreal, Que., 2/9/1956.
Played in NHL. See Modern Player Register for career statistics.

1995-96	Montreal	NHL	77	40	27	10	.584	6	2	4	0	.333
1996-97	Montreal	NHL	82	31	36	15	.470	5	1	4	0	.200
	NHL Totals		**159**	**71**	**63**	**25**	**.525**	**11**	**3**	**8**	**0**	**.273**

Season	Club	League	GC	W	L	T	W%	GC	W	L	T	W%

● UBRIACO, GENE
b: Sault Ste. Marie, Ont., 12/26/1937.
Played in NHL. See Modern Player Register for career statistics.

1988-89	Pittsburgh	NHL	80	40	33	7	.544	11	7	4	0	.636
1989-90	Pittsburgh	NHL	26	10	14	2	.423	....				
	NHL Totals		106	50	47	9	.514	11	7	4	0	.636

● VACHON, ROGIE
b: Palmarolle, Que., 9/8/1945.
Played in NHL. See Goaltender Register for career statistics.

1983-84	Los Angeles	NHL	2	1	0	1	.750	....				
1987-88	Los Angeles	NHL	1	0	1	0	.000	....				
1994-95	Los Angeles	NHL	7	3	2	2	.571	....				
	NHL Totals		10	4	3	3	.550	....				

● VIGNEAULT, ALAIN
b: Quebec City, Que., 5/14/1961.
Played in NHL. See Modern Player Register for career statistics.

| 1997-98 | Montreal | NHL | 82 | 37 | 32 | 13 | .530 | 10 | 4 | 6 | 0 | .400 |
| | NHL Totals | | 82 | 37 | 32 | 13 | .530 | 10 | 4 | 6 | 0 | .400 |

● WATSON, BRYAN
b: Bancroft, Ont., 11/14/1942.
Played in NHL. See Modern Player Register for career statistics.

| 1980-81 | Edmonton | NHL | 18 | 4 | 9 | 5 | .361 | .... | | | | |
| | NHL Totals | | 18 | 4 | 9 | 5 | .361 | .... | | | | |

● WATSON, PHIL
b: Montreal, Que., 4/24/1914. Deceased.
Played in NHL. See Pre-Expansion Player Register for career statistics.

1955-56	NY Rangers	NHL	70	32	28	10	.529	5	1	4	0	.200
1956-57	NY Rangers	NHL	70	26	30	14	.471	5	1	4	0	.200
1957-58	NY Rangers	NHL	70	32	25	13	.550	6	2	4	0	.333
1958-59	NY Rangers	NHL	70	26	32	12	.457	....				
1959-60	NY Rangers	NHL	15	3	9	3	.300	....				
1961-62	Boston	NHL	70	15	47	8	.271	....				
1962-63	Boston	NHL	14	1	8	5	.250	....				
	NHL Totals		379	135	179	65	.442	16	4	12	0	.250

● WATT, TOM
b: Toronto, Ont., 6/17/1935.

1981-82	Winnipeg	NHL	80	33	33	14	.500	4	1	3	0	.250
1982-83	Winnipeg	NHL	80	33	39	8	.463	3	0	3	0	.000
1983-84	Winnipeg	NHL	21	6	13	2	.333	....				
1985-86	Vancouver	NHL	80	23	44	13	.369	3	0	3	0	.000
1986-87	Vancouver	NHL	80	29	43	8	.413	....				
1990-91	Toronto	NHL	69	22	37	10	.391	....				
1991-92	Toronto	NHL	80	30	43	7	.419	....				
	NHL Totals		490	176	252	62	.422	10	1	9	0	.100

● Won Jack Adams Award (1982)

● WEBSTER, TOM
b: Kirkland Lake, Ont., 10/4/1948.
Played in NHL. See Modern Player Register for career statistics.

1986-87	NY Rangers	NHL	18	5	9	4	.389	....				
1989-90	Los Angeles	NHL	80	34	39	7	.469	10	4	6	0	.400
1990-91	Los Angeles	NHL	80	46	24	10	.638	12	6	6	0	.500
1991-92	Los Angeles	NHL	80	35	31	14	.525	6	2	4	0	.333
	NHL Totals		258	120	103	35	.533	28	12	16	0	.429

● WEILAND, COONEY   HHOF
b: Seaforth (Edmondville), Ont., 11/5/1904. d: 7/3/1985.
Played in NHL. See Pre-Expansion Player Register for career statistics.

1939-40	Boston	NHL	48	31	12	5	.698	6	2	4	0	.333
1940-41	Boston	NHL	48	27	8	13	.698	11	8	3	0	.727
	NHL Totals		96	58	20	18	.698	17	10	7	0	.588

● WHITE, BILL
b: Toronto, Ont., 8/26/1939.
Played in NHL. See Modern Player Register for career statistics.

| 1976-77 | Chicago | NHL | 46 | 16 | 24 | 6 | .413 | 2 | 0 | 2 | 0 | .000 |
| | NHL Totals | | 46 | 16 | 24 | 6 | .413 | 2 | 0 | 2 | 0 | .000 |

● WILEY, JIM
b: Sault Ste. Marie, Ont., 4/28/1950.
Played in NHL. See Modern Player Register for career statistics.

| 1995-96 | San Jose | NHL | 57 | 17 | 37 | 3 | .325 | .... | | | | |
| | NHL Totals | | 57 | 17 | 37 | 3 | .325 | .... | | | | |

● WILSON, JOHNNY
b: Kincardine, Ont., 6/14/1929.
Played in NHL. See Pre-Expansion Player Register for career statistics.

1969-70	Los Angeles	NHL	52	9	34	9	.260	....				
1971-72	Detroit	NHL	67	30	27	10	.522	....				
1972-73	Detroit	NHL	78	37	29	12	.551	....				
1976-77	Colorado	NHL	80	20	46	14	.338	....				
1977-78	Pittsburgh	NHL	80	25	37	18	.425	....				
1978-79	Pittsburgh	NHL	80	36	31	13	.531	7	2	5	0	.286
1979-80	Pittsburgh	NHL	80	30	37	13	.456	5	2	3	0	.400
	NHL Totals		517	187	241	89	.448	12	4	8	0	.333

● WILSON, LARRY
b: Kincardine, Ont., 10/23/1930. d: 8/16/1979.
Played in NHL. See Pre-Expansion Player Register for career statistics.

| 1976-77 | Detroit | NHL | 36 | 3 | 29 | 4 | .139 | .... | | | | |
| | NHL Totals | | 36 | 3 | 29 | 4 | .139 | .... | | | | |

● WILSON, RON
b: Toronto, Ont., 5/13/1956.
Played in NHL. See Modern Player Register for career statistics.

1993-94	Anaheim	NHL	84	33	46	5	.423	....				
1994-95	Anaheim	NHL	48	16	27	5	.385	....				
1995-96	Anaheim	NHL	82	35	39	8	.476	....				
1996-97	Anaheim	NHL	82	36	33	13	.518	11	4	7	0	.364
1997-98	Washington	NHL	82	40	30	12	.561	21	12	9	0	.571
	NHL Totals		378	160	175	43	.480	32	16	16	0	.500

● YOUNG, GARRY
b: Toronto, Ont., 1/2/1936.

1972-73	California	NHL	12	2	7	3	.292	....				
1974-75	St. Louis	NHL	69	32	26	11	.543	2	0	2	0	.000
1975-76	St. Louis	NHL	29	9	15	5	.397	....				
	NHL Totals		110	43	48	19	.477	2	0	2	0	.000

CHAPTER 77

Biographical Registers

Eric Zweig and Igor Kuperman

*P*LAYERS, GOALTENDERS, *coaches, administrators, referees and linesmen are included in this complete biographical register of hockey. Every member of the Hockey Hall of Fame and the U.S. Hockey Hall of Fame can be found here along with an array of other contemporary and retired players. With the exception of Hall of Fame inductees and significant NHL players trained in Europe, biographies of international and Olympic hockey stars can be found beginning on page 1830, in Section 2 of this chapter. Biographies of top women's hockey players can be found beginning on page 1871, in Section 3.*

Section 1

NORTH AMERICAN BIOGRAPHICAL REGISTER

SID ABEL was the center of the Detroit Red Wings famed Production Line in the late 1940s and early 1950s. He made his NHL debut with a one-game appearance in 1938–39 and became a regular in 1940–41. He earned a berth on the Second All-Star Team in 1941–42 and was team captain when Detroit won the Stanley Cup in 1943. Abel missed the next two years due to military service, but returned to play briefly in 1945–46. He was first teamed with Gordie Howe and Ted Lindsay during the 1946–47 season.

It was during the 1948–49 season that the Abel-Lindsay-Howe combination was dubbed the Production Line, and Abel won the Hart Trophy that year after leading the Red Wings in scoring. Detroit finished first in the regular-season standings. Lindsay, Abel and Howe finished 1–2–3 respectively in the league scoring race in 1949–50, and Abel established career highs with 34 goals and 69 points. The Red Wings won the Stanley Cup that season, and again in 1952, before Abel left Detroit to become a playing coach with the Chicago Black Hawks. He gave up playing to concentrate solely on coaching in 1953–54, then returned to Detroit as a commentator on Red Wings television broadcasts. Midway through the 1957–58 season, Abel returned to coaching when the Wings' Jimmy Skinner was forced to resign due to illness.

Abel continued to coach the Red Wings through the 1967–68 season and also served as general manager from 1962–63 until being replaced in 1970–71. His teams reached the Stanley Cup finals in 1961, 1963, 1964 and 1966 and had the best record in the NHL in 1964–65. Abel was inducted into the Hockey Hall of Fame in 1969.

TAFFY ABEL For much of his career with the New York Rangers and Chicago Black Hawks, Clarence "Taffy" Abel was the only American-born player in the NHL. A native of Sault Ste. Marie, Michigan, Abel began his hockey career in his hometown but also played amateur hockey in Minnesota. He was on the U.S. Olympic team at the first Winter Games in Chamonix, France in 1924 and won a silver medal.

Abel was signed by the New York Rangers when they entered the NHL in 1926–27 and was paired on defense with Ching Johnson. At 6'1" and 225 pounds, Abel and his equally formidable partner formed one of the toughest defenses in the league—particularly in the days before forward passing in the offensive zone. Abel helped lead the Rangers to the American Division title in their first season and the Stanley Cup in 1928, earning particular fame during that season's finals for the brilliant defense he and Johnson provided when the team's manager-coach, Lester Patrick, took over in goal after Lorne Chabot was injured in game two of the series against the Montreal Maroons.

The Rangers traded Abel to the Chicago Black Hawks after the 1928–29 season. He played for five years with Chicago and retired when the team won its first Stanley Cup title in 1934. In 1973, Taffy Abel was one of the charter members in the United States Hockey Hall of Fame.

CHARLES ADAMS worked his way up from grocery store clerk to the head of a major United States chain. In 1924, he purchased the rights to the first American team in the NHL, hiring Art Ross to run his new Boston franchise. The name Bruins was chosen from the many selections offered by fans, the news media and club employees, and the team was clad in the brown and yellow colors of Adams' grocery store chain.

The Bruins struggled in their first two years until Adams made some key player purchases for the 1926–27 season from the recently defunct Western Hockey League. The most prominent new player was Eddie Shore, who helped the Bruins establish themselves as an NHL power. The following season, Adams guaranteed a sum of $500,000 over a five-year span to help fund construction of Boston Garden. He was elected to the Hockey Hall of Fame as a builder in 1960. His son Weston Adams, who succeeded him as Bruins president in 1936, was elected to the Hall of Fame in 1972.

JACK ADAMS became one of hockey's most famous coaches and executives over a long association with the Detroit Red Wings and after a Hall of Fame career as a player. He had played amateur hockey in Peterborough and Sarnia, Ontario before turning pro with Toronto in the first NHL season of 1917–18.

Adams was on a Stanley Cup winner his first year in Toronto, then spent a second season with the Arenas before joining the Vancouver Millionaires in 1919–20. It was while playing in the Pacific Coast Hockey Association that he emerged as a scoring star. In the Stanley Cup final of 1922, Adams had six goals in five games as Vancouver lost to the Toronto St. Pats. He then returned to the NHL with the St. Pats the following season. His playing career ended in 1926–27 when he helped the Ottawa Senators win the Stanley Cup.

Joining a team then known as the Cougars, Adams signed on with Detroit for the new franchise's second season of 1927–28. As the club's coach and general manager, Adams sold hockey in Detroit by developing a strong farm system and building winning teams. The Red Wings won 12 regular-season championships under Adams, including seven in a row from 1948–49 to 1954–55, and seven Stanley Cup titles. In his 35 years with the Red Wings, Detroit only missed the playoffs seven times. His greatest personal satisfaction came from the development of Gordie Howe into a superstar.

Adams was inducted into the Hockey Hall of Fame in 1959 and remained with the Red Wings until the end of the 1961–62 season. When the New York Rangers presented the Lester Patrick Trophy to the NHL in 1966 to recognize outstanding service to hockey in the United States, Adams was named the first winner. He had become president of the Central Hockey League following his departure from Detroit and died while at his desk on May 1, 1968.

WESTON ADAMS From November 1, 1924, when his father, Charles Adams, was awarded an NHL franchise, until his death on March 19, 1973, Weston W. Adams Sr. had a continuous association with the Boston Bruins. After graduating from Harvard University (where he played goal on the hockey team), Adams became a director of the Bruins. In 1932, he was named president of the Boston Tigers farm club. He succeeded his father as president of the Bruins in 1936.

When the United States entered World War II, Adams left Boston for a position in the U.S. navy. He served actively in the Pacific, retiring at the end of the war with the rank of Commander. At this time, the Bruins corporate structure was changed after a merger with the Boston Garden Arena Company, and Adams relinquished his role as president while remaining a majority stockholder at the Garden.

Adams became chairman of the board of the Boston Garden in 1956, and two years later he was elected chairman of the hockey club as well. By 1964, he was president of the Bruins again, holding the position for five years before he retired in favor of his son, Weston Adams Jr. In his two terms as president, the Bruins had won the Stanley Cup in 1939 and 1941, and he assembled the club executives and coaching staff that would lead Boston to the Stanley Cup again in 1970 and 1972. Weston Adams Sr. was elected to the Hockey Hall of Fame as a builder in 1972. His father had been inducted in 1960.

FRANK AHEARN had been involved in amateur hockey before turning to the pro game in the 1920s, in part to build a new arena in Ottawa. He helped run the Senators teams that won the Stanley Cup in 1920, 1921 and 1923, becoming sole owner of the club in 1924. The team he bought won a fourth Stanley Cup championship in 1926–27.

Ahearn, considered a generous owner, was well-liked by his players, but the Great Depression ended his benevolence. Ottawa was by far the smallest city with an NHL franchise at the time, and poor revenues soon forced Ahearn to

sell off many of his star players. Still, his personal losses were pegged at about $200,000 when he moved his team to St. Louis in 1934–35. He folded the franchise the following year. Ahearn was elected to the Hockey Hall of Fame as a builder in 1962.

BUNNY AHEARNE John Francis "Bunny" Ahearne became secretary of the British Ice Hockey Association in 1933 and retained the position for 40 years. He also served as Britain's delegate to the International Ice Hockey Federation from 1934 until the outbreak of World War II in 1939, and managed the British Nationals to a gold medal at the 1936 Winter Olympics. As an executive member of the IIHF after the War, Ahearne played a key role in negotiating the return of Canada and the United States to active membership in 1947.

Ahearne was elected vice president of the IIHF in 1955, became president two years later, and served in one of these two positions until retiring in 1975. During his tenure, the World Championships became a major international event. Ahearne saw the importance of television to the sport and negotiated lucrative broadcasting rights while also popularizing the idea of selling advertising space along the boards in arenas. Much of the money raised by these ventures helped finance the growth of international hockey. In 1977, Bunny Ahearne was inducted into the Hockey Hall of Fame as a builder.

DANIEL ALFREDSSON of the Ottawa Senators won the Calder Trophy as rookie of the year in 1995–96, leading all rookies with 26 goals, 35 assists and 61 points. He was also the only first-year player to lead his team in scoring. In 1996–97, he led Ottawa with 47 assists as the Senators made the playoffs for the first time in franchise history.

A native of Sweden, Alfredsson won a silver medal at the 1995 World Championships and represented his country again at the World Championships the following year. He also played for Sweden at the World Cup of Hockey in 1996 and was a member of the Swedish Olympic team at Nagano in 1998.

SIR H. MONTAGU ALLAN A member of a prominent Montreal family that made its fortune in shipping and railroads, Sir Hugh Montagu Allan donated a trophy in 1908 that would symbolize amateur hockey supremacy in Canada. William Northey, president of the Montreal Amateur Athletic Association, prevailed upon Allan to donate such a trophy because the Stanley Cup increasingly was becoming available only to professional teams.

For many years, the Allan Cup rivaled the Stanley Cup in terms of its importance as a hockey trophy in Canada, and the Allan Cup playoffs inspired fierce national rivalries. A board of trustees oversaw all Allan Cup competition until 1928, when the trophy was donated outright to the Canadian Amateur Hockey Association.

In addition to the family shipping business, Allan was the last president of the Merchants Bank of Canada, which was amalgamated into the Bank of Montreal in 1922. He was president of the Montreal Jockey Club and owned horses that won the Queen's Plate. Allan was also honorary lieutenant-colonel of the Black Watch (a Royal Highland regiment) and he lost a son to military action during World War I. Two of Allan's daughter's were killed in 1915 in the sinking of the Lusitania.

Sir H. Montagu Allan was inducted into the Hockey Hall of Fame, along with Lord Stanley of Preston and 10 players, when the first selections were made in 1945.

KEITH ALLEN joined the Philadelphia Flyers one year before the team's opening season and was the team's first coach in 1967–68, guiding the Flyers to a first-place finish in the West Division. On December 29, 1969, Allen was promoted to general manager in Philadelphia, and through shrewd trades and drafting, built the team that became back-to-back Stanley Cup champions in 1974 and 1975. Allen saw his team reach the Stanley Cup finals again in 1976 and 1980 while serving as g.m., a position he relinquished at the end of the 1982–83 season. He then became executive vice president of the Flyers, a position he continues to hold. Allen received the Lester Patrick Trophy for his contribution to hockey in the United States in 1988 and was elected to the Hockey Hall of Fame as a builder in 1992.

Prior to joining the Flyers, Allen had served as coach and general manager with Seattle of the Western Hockey League from 1956–57 until 1966–67. He also spent 13 years playing pro hockey, mostly with Springfield and Syracuse of the American Hockey League, and made brief appearances with the Detroit Red Wings in 1953–54 and 1954–55. He played on a Stanley Cup winner in Detroit in 1954.

OSCAR ALMQUIST hailed from the hockey hotbed of Eveleth, Minnesota and played goal for the Eveleth high school team from 1923 through 1927. He spent the next two years playing amateur hockey in Virginia before returning to Minnesota to attend St. Mary's College in Winona, where he played four years of varsity hockey and was named team captain in 1932–33. He also earned a selection to the all-American team that year. Almquist returned to Eveleth upon graduation and played pro hockey for a year there, then for three years with St. Paul in the American Hockey Association. He was named to the league all-star team in 1933–34 and 1935–36, then the coaching career for

which he would become famous began at Williams, Minnesota in 1937. That year, he coached the high school team to a second-place finish in the district.

Almquist moved to Roseau, Minnesota the following season and coached the high school B team until 1941. He was then promoted to head coach at Roseau High and held the position until 1967. During this time, Roseau became a perennial high school power, appearing in the state tournament 14 times and winning in 1946, 1958, 1959 and 1961. Almquist's Roseau teams also finished runner-up on four occasions, in third place once and won two consolation titles. When Almquist gave up coaching to become strictly principal and athletic director, he had posted a record of 404–148–21. In a stretch between 1957 and 1959, his teams went 49 games without a loss.

In recognition of his career achievements, Oscar Almquist was made an honorary life member of the American Hockey Coaches Association in 1969, elected to the Minnesota Hockey Coaches Hall of Fame in 1982 and inducted into the United States Hockey Hall of Fame in the coaches category in 1983.

TONY AMONTE starred at Boston University and signed his first professional contract with the New York Rangers on April 2, 1991—two days after BU lost the NCAA championship to Michigan in triple overtime. He made his NHL debut in game five of the Patrick Division semifinals that year and became a regular with the Rangers the following season.

Amonte scored 35 goals as a rookie in 1991–92 and was a finalist for the Calder Trophy that went to Pavel Bure that year. After a 33-goal season in 1992–93, Amonte struggled during the 1993–94 campaign and was traded to the Chicago Blackhawks on March 21, 1994. One month later, on April 23, he became just the second Blackhawks player (Denis Savard) ever to score four goals in one playoff game. In 1996–97, Amonte led Chicago in seven offensive categories including goals (41), points (77) and plus–minus (+35).

In international play, Amonte represented the United States at the World Junior Championships in 1989 and at the World Championships in 1991 and 1993. In 1996, he scored the series-winning goal in game three as the United States beat Canada in the World Cup of Hockey. He was also a member of the U.S. Olympic team at Nagano in 1998.

GLENN ANDERSON joined the Edmonton Oilers in 1980–81 after a season with the Canadian Olympic team and quickly developed into a dangerous scorer as the Oilers became the greatest offensive team in hockey history. He was a member of five Stanley Cup champions in Edmonton and earned a sixth title with the New York Rangers in 1994. He played for Team Canada at the Canada Cup in 1984 and 1987 and also took part in Rendez-Vous '87.

Anderson emerged as a star in just his second NHL season of 1981–82 when he cracked the top–10 in scoring with 105 points. He had another top–10 finish with 104 points the next season and recorded 54 goals in 1983–84 for a career high he would match two years later when he enjoyed his third 100-point season. Anderson's production declined after 1985–86, but his speed always made him a dangerous offensive player. He was a key offensive contributor in the playoffs on all five Oilers Stanley Cup teams.

Traded to the Toronto Maple Leafs in a blockbuster deal with Grant Fuhr on September 19, 1991, Anderson was among the top scorers in Toronto for two seasons before being dealt to the New York Rangers for Mike Gartner on March 21, 1994. He joined several ex-Oilers in New York to help the Rangers end a 54-year Stanley Cup drought.

Anderson never again saw regular duty in the NHL, playing for the Canadian national team, in Europe, with the St. Louis Blues, and the Oilers again through the 1996–97 season. His 498 career goals and 601 assists rank him among the all-time leaders in NHL history.

TOM ANDERSON is one of only two players (Al Rollins) to win the Hart Trophy as the NHL's most valuable player while playing on a last-place team. He won it in 1941–42 after being converted from left wing to defense and leading all NHL defensemen in scoring.

Anderson began his NHL career with the Detroit Red Wings in 1934–35 but failed to impress Jack Adams and was sold to the New York Americans during the 1935–36 season. He played left wing on a line with Eddie Wiseman and Carl Voss that year as the Americans made the playoffs for the first time since 1928–29.

The following season, Nels Stewart centered Anderson and Wiseman and the two wingers helped Stewart lead the NHL in goals. Sweeny Schriner of the American led the NHL in points, but a weak defense saw the team miss the playoffs. In 1937–38, the American reached the semifinals for the only time in franchise history and in 1938–39 Anderson had a career-high 13 goals and 40 points to finish second to Schriner on the team in scoring.

The Americans had long been struggling financially and after a bad season in 1940–41 the team became known as the Brooklyn Americans in 1941–42. This was the year that Anderson was moved to defense and yet he still collected a career-high 41 points that season. In addition to winning the Hart Trophy, Anderson was also named to the First All-Star Team.

The 1941–42 season proved to be the last in the NHL for both the Americans and Tommy Anderson. He spent the next three years in the Canadian Armed Forces, then played minor-league hockey after World War II.

DAVE ANDREYCHUK entered the NHL with the Buffalo Sabres in 1982–83 after collecting 57 goals and 100 points for the Oshawa Generals of the Ontario Hockey League the previous season. Andreychuk split the 1982–83 campaign between Buffalo and Oshawa before becoming a regular in 1983–84. He was the leading scorer on Team Canada and won a bronze medal at the World Junior Championships in 1983.

Andreychuk quickly demonstrated his scoring prowess in the NHL, leading the Sabres in goals during both of his first two full seasons with the team. He either led or shared the lead in goal-scoring four times in his nine-plus seasons in Buffalo and set a team record when he scored five goals on February 8, 1986. Andreychuk enjoyed his best year in 1991–92 when he had 41 goals and 50 assists, but on February 2, 1993, he was traded to the Toronto Maple Leafs. Teamed on a line with Doug Gilmour, Andreychuk scored 25 goals in just 31 games with Toronto, giving him a total of 54 that season. The following year, he had 53 goals to join Rick Vaive and Gary Leeman as the only players in Maple Leafs history to score 50 in a season. Andreychuk helped Toronto to reach the conference finals in both 1992–93 and 1993–94.

The Maple Leafs traded Andreychuk to the New Jersey Devils on March 13, 1996. Almost exactly a year later, on March 15, 1997, Andreychuk became the 26th player in NHL history to score 500 goals.

SYL APPS was the inspirational leader of the Toronto Maple Leafs in the late 1930s and 1940s, serving as team captain from 1940–41 to 1942–43, and again from 1945–46 until he retired after the 1947–48 season. In addition to his great hockey talent, Apps was an excellent football player at McMaster University in Hamilton. He also won the Canadian and British Empire championship in the pole vault in 1934 and finished sixth at the 1936 Berlin Olympics.

Apps entered the NHL with the Maple Leafs in 1936–37 and was named rookie of the year after finishing second in the league with 45 points. He was runner-up to linemate Gordie Drillon in the 1937–38 NHL scoring race and was rewarded with a selection to the Second All-Star Team at center. Apps was a Second Team All-Star again in 1940–41 and 1942–43, and earned First Team honors in 1938–39 and 1941–42. He also won the Lady Byng Trophy in 1941–42 and played on his first Stanley Cup champion that year.

After a two-year absence from hockey while he served in the Canadian army, Apps returned to the Maple Leafs in 1945–46. He set new career highs in goals with 24, 25 and 26 over each of the next three seasons and helped the Leafs win the Stanley Cup again in 1947 and 1948 before he retired. In 1961, Apps was elected to the Hockey Hall of Fame.

AL ARBOUR ranks among the greatest coaches in NHL history, trailing only Scotty Bowman for most games and most wins in both regular-season and playoff history. His four Stanley Cup championships with the New York Islanders are surpassed only by Toe Blake, Bowman and Hap Day. Arbour was also on three Stanley Cup winners as a player.

A defenseman who wore glasses on the ice, Arbour broke into the NHL with the Detroit Red Wings in 1953–54. He joined the Chicago Black Hawks in 1958–59 and helped them to win their first Stanley Cup title in 23 years in 1961. The following year, he won another Stanley Cup championship as a member of the Toronto Maple Leafs. Arbour remained with the Maple Leafs until 1967, but spent most of his time with their American Hockey League affiliate in Rochester until he was selected by the St. Louis Blues in the 1967 Expansion Draft.

Arbour began his coaching career with the Blues in 1970–71, but resigned during the season to continue playing. The following year, he became coach again. He joined the Islanders in their second season of 1973–74 and quickly developed the sad-sack expansion team into a powerhouse. The Islanders had more than 100 points four years in a row between 1975–76 and 1978–79, then won four consecutive Stanley Cup titles from 1980 until 1983.

Following the 1985–86 season, Arbour retired from coaching to become a vice president with the Islanders, but was back behind the bench in 1988. He guided the team again until 1994, then returned to a position in the club's front office. He was elected to the Hockey Hall of Fame as a builder in 1996.

GEORGE ARMSTRONG spent his entire NHL career with the Toronto Maple Leafs, playing a club record 1,187 games between 1949–50 and 1970–71. He captained the team from 1957–58 until 1967–68, a period that included Stanley Cup victories in 1962, 1963, 1964 and 1967. Armstrong also ranks in the top five in Maple Leafs history in goals, assists and points. He was known as "the Chief" in a tribute to his Native heritage.

Armstrong was sent to the Maple Leafs organization by scout Bob Wilson and was a standout junior in the Ontario Hockey Association with Stratford and the Toronto Marlboros. He won the Allan Cup as a member of the Marlboros senior team in 1949–50, the year in which he also made his NHL debut. After spending most of the next two seasons with Toronto's American Hockey League farm club in Pittsburgh, Armstrong became a regular with the Maple Leafs in 1952–53.

Armstrong played mostly right wing, but some center, during his lengthy career. Though never a great skater, he was an excellent two-way performer whose dedication to the game and leadership qualities enabled him to bring out the best in his teammates. After his playing days, he worked in the Toronto and Quebec Nordiques organizations, and briefly coached the Maple Leafs during the 1988–89 season. He currently serves as a scout for Toronto. Armstrong was elected to the Hockey Hall of Fame in 1975.

NEIL ARMSTRONG began working as a part-time NHL linesman during the 1957–58 season, officiating in 11 games that year. Over the next 20 seasons, he went on to work another 1,733 regular-season games, 208 playoff games (including 48 in the Stanley Cup finals) and 10 All-Star Games. Known as the "ironman" of NHL officials, Armstrong did not miss a single assignment over 16 years. After retiring as a linesman, he served as a scout for the Montreal Canadiens. Armstrong was elected to the Hockey Hall of Fame in 1991.

JOHN ASHLEY Between 1959–60 and 1971–72, John Ashley was one of the top referees in the NHL. He had played junior hockey with Galt, Toronto, Guelph and Stratford in the Ontario Hockey Association between 1947 and 1950 before playing professional with Pittsburgh and Syracuse of the American Hockey League from 1950–51 to 1952–53. Ashley then played senior amateur hockey in Stratford until 1958 and signed his first NHL contract as a referee in 1959.

During the next 12 seasons, Ashley worked 17 NHL games as a linesman and 605 as a referee. He also worked 59 postseason games, and in 1971 became the first man to referee in the seventh game of three different series in one playoff year. After retiring as a referee following the 1971–72 season, Ashley was hired by the NHL to scout young officials. He was elected to the Hockey Hall of Fame in 1981.

LARRY AURIE was signed by Jack Adams when he took over as coach and general manager of the Detroit Cougars in 1927–28. He went on to spend his entire 11-year career with the team that later became the Falcons, then the Detroit Red Wings.

Detroit struggled in the early years Aurie played for the team, but by 1933–34 the Red Wings were champions of the American Division. Aurie was playing on a line with future Hall of Famers Cooney Weiland and Herbie Lewis and was the team's leading scorer that season. The tiny-but-talented trio (the three only averaged 150 pounds) outplayed the Toronto Maple Leafs' famed Kid Line of Charlie Conacher, Joe Primeau and Busher Jackson in the playoffs to reach the Stanley Cup final, but Detroit was beaten by the Chicago Black Hawks.

Aurie again led the Red Wings in scoring in 1934–35 and was third in the NHL with 46 points in 48 games but Detroit missed the playoffs that year. Adams then acquired Marty Barry to center Aurie and Lewis and the three-some led the Red Wings to their first Stanley Cup title in 1935–36. In 1936–37, Aurie led the NHL with 23 goals and was named to the First All-Star Team. Unfortunately, a broken ankle kept him out of the playoffs but the Red Wings were still able to become the first American-based team to repeat as Stanley Cup champions.

Still feeling the effects of his injury, both Aurie and the Red Wings slumped in 1937–38. He played just one game in 1938–39 as his NHL career came to an end, though he played several more years with Pittsburgh of the American Hockey League, where he also served as coach.

RALPH BACKSTROM was a product of the strong Montreal Canadiens farm system who had two brief trials with the club before winning a spot in 1958–59. Though the Canadiens were already deep at center, Backstrom saw enough playing time to win the Calder Trophy as rookie of the year. He also helped the Canadiens win the Stanley Cup that season and cap their run of five in a row in 1959–60.

Backstrom had a career-high 27 goals in 1961–62 and led the Canadiens with 65 points. He followed up that season with 23 goals in 1962–62, then slumped badly before rebounding to top 20 goals again on Stanley Cup-winning Montreal teams in 1965 and 1966. Backstrom added fifth and sixth Stanley Cup victories in 1968 and 1969. Though he was a fine playmaker and a good back-checker, Backstrom was never more than the number-three center in Montreal behind Jean Beliveau and Henri Richard and was traded to the Los Angeles Kings on January 26, 1971.

Backstrom continued to perform well with the Kings, but was traded to the Chicago Black Hawks on February 26, 1973. The following season, he joined the Chicago Cougars of the World Hockey Association and established career highs with 33 goals and 50 assists for 83 points. He played three more seasons in the WHA before retiring.

ACE BAILEY Irvine "Ace" Bailey had his hockey career cut short tragically on December 12, 1933 when he was hit from behind by Eddie Shore of the Boston Bruins, suffering a fractured skull. But in the seven-and-a-half-seasons in which he played in the NHL, Bailey had established himself as a great scorer and then a top defensive forward.

Bailey played junior and senior hockey in Toronto and Peterborough, Ontario before signing professionally with the Toronto St. Pats in 1926–27. The team was renamed the Maple Leafs after being purchased by Conn

Smythe later that season, and Bailey and Hap Day became cornerstones of the new club. Bailey led the NHL in both goals and points in 1928–29, and he was the Leafs top scorer until the arrival of Charlie Conacher the following season. When the Kid Line of Conacher, Joe Primeau and Busher Jackson became the Leafs' top offensive unit, Bailey developed into a defensive specialist who helped Toronto win the Stanley Cup in 1932.

After his near-fatal accident in Boston, Bailey got into coaching and later joined the staff of off-ice officials at Maple Leaf Gardens, where he remained for many years. The NHL's first All-Star Game on February 14, 1934 was played to benefit Bailey and his family. He was elected to the Hockey Hall of Fame in 1975.

DAN BAIN was an exceptional sportsman who often is considered to be the greatest all-round athlete in the history of the province of Manitoba. A star at virtually everything he tried, Bain won championship honors in several sports over a span of more than 35 years.

Though born in Belleville, Ontario, Bain moved to Winnipeg with his family as a six-year-old in 1880, and by 17 he was the champion gymnast in his new city. He won titles in cycling, snowshoeing, speed skating, roller skating, lacrosse and golf right up until 1930, but his greatest fame came as captain of the Winnipeg Victorias hockey team.

Bain played center with the Victorias from 1895–96 to 1901–02. Winnipeg challenged for the Stanley Cup during six of those seasons and he helped the team win in 1896 and 1901. Bain's overtime goal on January 31, 1901 gave the Victorias a Stanley Cup victory over the Montreal Shamrocks. He was inducted into the Hockey Hall of Fame as one of the 12 original selections back in 1945.

HOBEY BAKER The name of Hobey Baker is legendary in United States college hockey history, where the Hobey Baker Award is presented annually to the outstanding player in the NCAA. He was the greatest player in American hockey before, during and after the three years he spent at Princeton University from 1910 to 1913.

Hobart Amery Hare Baker first came to prominence in hockey with the St. Paul's School in Concord, New Hampshire. He was a rover during the era of the seven-man game, and he was an exceptional skater and stickhandler. In addition to his hockey skills, Baker was also prominent in football, golf, track, swimming and gymnastics, captaining the football team for a year at Princeton in addition to his two years as hockey captain.

After leaving Princeton, Baker continued to play hockey with the St. Nicholas Club in New York until 1916. His playing days ended when he joined the famed United States flying unit, the Lafayette Esquadrille, in World War I. Baker survived the conflict, but he was killed in a tragic air accident shortly after the armistice was signed. He was one of the first 12 men selected to the Hockey Hall of Fame in 1945, and he later became an original inductee into the United States Hockey Hall of Fame in 1973.

HAROLD BALLARD In his youth, Harold Ballard was a champion speedskater and powerboat racer and was associated with his father in the manufacturing of ice skates that bore the family name. He soon was actively involved in hockey and served as coach and general manager of the Toronto National "Sea Fleas" when they won the Allan Cup in 1932 and a silver medal at the 1933 World Championships. He was also general manager of the West Toronto Nationals when they won the Memorial Cup in 1936. As the principal executive and financial backer of the Toronto Marlboros, Ballard was associated with another Allan Cup champion in 1950 and with Memorial Cup winners again in 1955, 1956, 1964, 1967, 1973 and 1975.

On November 21, 1961, Ballard became one of three principal owners of the Toronto Maple Leafs, along with John Bassett and Stafford Smythe, and added four Stanley Cup championships to his impressive trophy collection when the Maple Leafs won in 1962, 1963, 1964 and 1967. After Stafford Smythe's death on October 13, 1971, Ballard became the Leafs principal owner. Outspoken and often controversial, he was an active participant in NHL affairs, though the Maple Leafs suffered on the ice under his autocratic ownership. He had many detractors, but was a generous supporter of children's charities. Ballard was elected to the Hockey Hall of Fame as a builder in 1977.

In addition to his ownership of the Toronto Maple Leafs, Ballard bought the Hamilton Tiger-Cats of the Canadian Football League in 1977. He provided much-needed financial support to the team and the league and saw his Ticats win the Grey Cup in 1986.

BILL BARBER was a high-scoring junior with the Kitchener Rangers of the Ontario Hockey Association. He was drafted in the first round (seventh overall) by the Flyers in 1972 and spent just 11 games in the minors before being called up to Philadelphia that season. Barber spent 12 years in the NHL, all with the Flyers, and his 420 goals are the most in team history. He was inducted into the Hockey Hall of Fame in 1990.

Barber was a center in junior hockey but was converted to left wing in Philadelphia by coach Fred Shero. He scored 30 goals as a rookie playing alongside Bobby Clarke in 1972–73 and, as an all-around player, was a key

component on the Flyers Stanley Cup-winning teams of 1974 and 1975. Barber established career highs with 50 goals, 62 assists and 112 points in 1975–76 and was named to the First All-Star Team. He was a Second Team All-Star in 1978–79 and 1980–81, but was forced to retire after undergoing knee surgery in April of 1984.

Following his retirement, Barber spent three seasons as an assistant coach with the Flyers. He was briefly the head man with the club's American Hockey League affiliate in Hershey in 1984–85 before being named director of pro scouting in Philadelphia in 1988–89. He remained on the job until 1995–96, when he again took over at Hershey. Barber became head coach of the Flyers' Philadelphia Phantoms farm team in 1996–97.

BILL BARILKO was not known for his offensive talent, yet scored one of the most famous goals in NHL history. On April 21, 1951, Barilko lifted a shot past Gerry McNeil of the Montreal Canadiens for a goal at 2:53 of overtime that won the Stanley Cup for the Toronto Maple Leafs. In the off-season, Barilko was killed in a plane crash while on a fishing trip in Northern Ontario. It was 11 years before his body was found and 11 years before the Maple Leafs won the Stanley Cup again.

Barilko was thought to be on the verge of stardom at the time of his death. A sturdy defenseman and solid checker, he had been summoned from Hollywood of the Pacific Coast Hockey League late in the 1946–47 season and helped the Leafs win the Stanley Cup in each of his first three seasons. Barilko's goal in 1951 capped a Stanley Cup final in which each of the five games was decided in overtime.

TOM BARRASSO won both the Vezina Trophy and Calder Trophy in his first season in the NHL with the Buffalo Sabres in 1983–84. At the time, he joined Frank Brimsek and Tony Esposito as the only players to be honored as the best rookie and the top goaltender in the same season. Barrasso has gone on to become the winningest American-born goalie in NHL history. He surpassed Frank Brimsek's record of 252 victories on February 15, 1994 and on October 19, 1997, he become the first U.S.-born goalie to post 300 wins.

In addition to his other honors, Barrasso was named to the First All-Star Team in his rookie season of 1983–84. In 1984–85, he was a Second Team All-Star after sharing the Jennings Trophy with Bob Sauve and leading the league with five shutouts and a 2.66 goals-against average. Internationally, Barrasso represented the United States at the Canada Cup in 1984 and 1987. He also played at the World Junior Championships in 1983.

Barrasso remained with Buffalo until November 12, 1988, when he was dealt to Pittsburgh, where he has gone on to become the winningest goalie in Penguins history. His 2.60 goals-against average in the 1991 playoffs led all goaltenders as Pittsburgh won its first Stanley Cup title that year. Barrasso won a record-tying 11 games in a row to close out the playoffs in 1992 when the Penguins repeated as Stanley Cup champions. He led the NHL in victories with 43 in 1992–93 and was named to the Second All-Star Team.

Injuries caused Barrasso to miss virtually all of the 1994–95 and 1996–97 seasons but he displayed a remarkable return to form during the 1997–98 campaign, recording a career-best 2.07 goals-against average and receiving his fifth nomination for the Vezina Trophy.

MARTY BARRY was almost 24 years old before making the NHL to stay, but over the next 11 years he was one of the best players in hockey. After playing briefly with the New York Americans in 1927–28, Barry joined the Boston Bruins in 1929–30 as an effective second-line center on the powerhouse Boston club that led the NHL with a 38–5–1 record. By 1932–33, he had developed into the Bruins' top offensive threat and he led the team in scoring three years in a row.

In 1935, Jack Adams acquired Barry for the Detroit Red Wings, placing him on a line with Larry Aurie and Herbie Lewis. The trio was one of the most effective in the NHL, which enabled Barry to lead his new team in scoring on three occasions. He helped Detroit to win the Stanley Cup in 1936 and 1937, while also winning the Lady Byng Trophy and a First All-Star Team berth for the 1936–37 season. Barry ended his NHL career with the Montreal Canadiens in 1939–40, later turning to coaching. He was elected to the Hockey Hall of Fame in 1965.

EARL BARTHOLOME was born in North Dakota but raised in Minneapolis and learned to play hockey there as a boy. He later attended West High School and played on teams that won three consecutive high school championships between 1929 and 1931, then played with the Flour City amateur team before turning pro with the Minneapolis Millers in 1932–33. After three seasons, he moved on to Rochester and the International Hockey League and subsequently joined the Cleveland Barons in the American Hockey League in 1936–37.

Bartholome spent the next decade with the Barons and helped the team win the Calder Cup in 1939, 1941 and 1945. A center who could skate, shoot and stickhandle, he was also an excellent backchecker who was often used to kill penalties. He was named the Barons' most valuable player in 1941–42 and had his most productive offensive seasons in 1943–44 and 1944–45, when he finished sixth and fifth in AHL scoring with 67 and 81 points. With the Barons,

Bartholome became the first American pro hockey player ever to play more than 500 games with one club. He returned to Minneapolis in 1946–47, where he continued to play as a professional and then an amateur until 1952. He was inducted into the United States Hockey Hall of Fame in 1977.

ANDY BATHGATE was a strong skater, slick stickhandler, powerful shooter and skilled playmaker. He suffered a serious knee injury while playing in Guelph of the Ontario Hockey Association that required him to wear a special brace, but he overcame the handicap to become a star in the NHL.

After winning a Memorial Cup title with Guelph in 1952, Bathgate joined the New York Rangers in 1952–53 but spent most of his first two seasons in the minor leagues before becoming a regular in 1954–55. He had 20 goals and 20 assists that year, then led the Rangers in points each of the next eight seasons. Bathgate was third in the NHL in scoring in 1957–58 and earned a spot as the right winger on the Second All-Star Team. The following year, he established career highs with 40 goals and 88 points and won the Hart Trophy as the NHL's most valuable player. Bathgate was a First Team All-Star that year, as he would be again in 1961–62 when he tied Bobby Hull for the NHL scoring title with 84 points. (Hull was awarded the Art Ross Trophy because he had 54 goals to Bathgate's 28.) The Rangers star was named to the Second Team again in 1962–63, but on February 22, 1964, New York traded him to the Toronto Maple Leafs as part of a seven-player swap.

Bathgate won his only Stanley Cup championship with the Maple Leafs in the spring of 1964, but problems with his knee the following season limited him to just 55 games, and on May 20, 1965 he was dealt to the Detroit Red Wings. After helping the Red Wings reach the Stanley Cup finals in 1966, he was acquired by the Pittsburgh Penguins in the 1967 Expansion Draft. Bathgate played a year in Pittsburgh, then two seasons with Vancouver of the Western Hockey League (winning the MVP in 1969–70) before returning to the Penguins for a final NHL season in 1970–71.

After serving as a player-coach with Ambri-Piotta in Switzerland in 1971–72, Bathgate was out of hockey until returning to Vancouver in 1973–74 as a coach with the Blazers of the World Hockey Association. He made a brief comeback as a player when he took part in 11 games for Vancouver the following year. Bathgate was elected to the Hockey Hall of Fame in 1978.

BOBBY BAUER followed former Kitchener-Waterloo teammates Woody Dumart and Milt Schmidt to the Boston Bruins when he joined the team for the final game of the 1936–37 season and scored a goal. The following year, he became a regular in Boston, playing right wing alongside Schmidt and Dumart. The Kraut Line went on to become one of the most famous trios in hockey history.

Bauer led the Bruins with 20 goals in 1937–38 and was a key member of Boston's Stanley Cup champions the following year when he earned the first of three consecutive selections to the NHL's Second All-Star Team. In 1939–40, Schmidt, Dumart and Bauer finished 1–2–3 in the league scoring race and Bauer won the Lady Byng Trophy. He won the Lady Byng again in 1940–41 when Boston recaptured the Stanley Cup.

All three members of the Kraut Line left the Bruins midway through the 1942–43 season for service in the Royal Canadian Air Force during World War II. They were back for 1945–46, and though Bauer was contemplating retirement after that season, he returned for one more year and was named again to the Second All-Star Team in 1946–47. He also won the Lady Byng Trophy for the third time in his career. Bauer left Boston after that year and had his amateur status restored so that he could return to play hockey in Kitchener. He made a brief NHL comeback on March 18, 1952, when the Bruins held a night to honor his former linemates who were still active in Boston. Milt Schmidt scored his 200th career goal that night and Bauer also scored in a 4–0 Bruins victory over the Chicago Black Hawks.

In 1996, Bobby Bauer was elected to the Hockey Hall of Fame, joining fellow Kraut Line teammates Schmidt and Dumart and his brother, Father David Bauer, who had been elected in 1989.

FATHER DAVID BAUER was a member of a prominent sports family. His brother Bobby Bauer was part of the Boston Bruins' famous Kraut Line as the right winger alongside Milt Schmidt and Woody Dumart between 1935–36 and 1951–52. David Bauer played left wing at St. Michael's College in Toronto and was loaned to the Oshawa Generals, along with teammates Ted Lindsay and Gus Mortson, for a playoff run that saw them win the 1944 Memorial Cup. While Lindsay and Mortson went on to pursue NHL careers, Bauer became a Basilian priest.

Following his ordination in 1953, Father Bauer joined the teaching staff at St. Michael's College in Toronto and coached the school's Junior A team to a Memorial Cup victory in 1961. St. Mike's discontinued its hockey program after that season and in June of 1962 the Canadian Amateur Hockey Association granted permission for Father Bauer to pursue a plan to develop an amateur Canadian national team to take part in international tournaments.

Father Bauer's national team first represented Canada abroad at the 1964 Winter Olympics in Innsbruck, Austria, where a last-minute change in the tie-breaking procedure robbed the team of a bronze medal. The national team

moved its home base from Vancouver to Winnipeg in 1964–65 and finished a disappointing fourth at that year's World Championships under coach Gordon Simpson. With Jackie McLeod as the new player-coach and Father Bauer as general manager, bronze medals were achieved at the 1966 and 1967 World Championships and at the 1968 Winter Olympics in Grenoble, France, but the program was dropped after 1969. With the exception of exhibition tournaments like the 1972 Summit Series against the Soviets, Canada did not return to international competition until 1977. In 1989, Father David Bauer was inducted into the Hockey Hall of Fame as a builder.

BOB BAUN was a defensive defenseman over 17 NHL seasons between 1956–57 and 1972–73. Baun averaged only slightly more than two goals per year as a member of the Toronto Maple Leafs, Detroit Red Wings and Oakland Seals, and never scored more than eight in a single season, but he is remembered for scoring one of the most famous goals in NHL history.

On April 23, 1964, in game six of the Stanley Cup finals, Baun was felled by a slapshot during the third period and taken off the ice on a stretcher. In the Maple Leafs dressing room, Baun had his ankle frozen and taped and returned to the game for overtime. At 1:42 of the extra session, he fired a shot that deflected off Detroit Red Wings defenseman Bill Gadsby and past Terry Sawchuk for a 4–3 Toronto victory.

Inspired by Baun's heroics, the Maple Leafs were easy 4–0 winners in game seven and claimed their third consecutive Stanley Cup. Not until after the series was it disclosed that Baun had scored his overtime goal while playing on a fractured ankle.

ED BELFOUR signed as a free agent with the Dallas Stars on July 2, 1997 and led the NHL with a 1.88 goals-against average in 1997–98 while posting nine shutouts. For Belfour, it was a return to the form he had displayed with the Chicago Blackhawks earlier in his career. He won the Vezina Trophy twice in his first three full seasons in Chicago and won the William M. Jennings Trophy for lowest goals-against average three times.

Though he had played 23 games for the Blackhawks in 1988–89 and nine games in the playoffs the following year, Belfour was technically still a rookie when he became the top goalie in Chicago in 1990–91. He led the league with 74 games played, 43 wins and a 2.47 goals-against average that year, breaking Tony Esposito's club records for games and wins in a single season. Belfour also joined Esposito, Frank Brimsek and Tom Barrasso as the only goaltenders to be awarded the Vezina and Calder trophies in the same season. "the Eagle," as he is known, also won the Jennings Trophy and was a First Team All-Star that year.

In 1991–92, Belfour led the NHL with five shutouts and helped Chicago to reach the Stanley Cup finals. In 1992–93, he again won the Vezina and Jennings trophies and was a First Team All-Star. His 41 wins made Belfour just the fifth goalie in history to win 40-plus games more than once. His third Jennings Trophy and a selection to the Second All-Star Team came in 1994–95, a season that saw him lead the league in shutouts for the fourth straight time. On January 25, 1997, the Blackhawks dealt Belfour to San Jose for three players and a draft choice. He signed with Dallas after the season.

Prior to joining the NHL, Belfour had been an all-star with the 1986–87 NCAA champions from the University of North Dakota and was rookie of the year and an all-star with Saginaw of the International Hockey League in 1987–88. Belfour also played for the Canadian national team in 1989–90.

JEAN BELIVEAU was already a legend in Quebec before achieving greatness with the Montreal Canadiens. At 6'3" and 205 pounds, he was a rare blend of grace and power with a long, sweeping stride that gave him deceptive speed. Because of his size, he was difficult to check, but he was always a gentleman both on the ice and off.

After two stellar seasons in Victoriaville, Beliveau joined the Quebec Citadelles of the Quebec Junior Hockey League in 1949–50. The following year, he had a goal and an assist during a two-game trial with the Canadiens, but instead of signing with Montreal, Beliveau joined the Quebec Aces of the Quebec Senior Hockey League. He made another brief appearance with the Canadiens in 1952–53, scoring five goals in three games, and finally signed with Montreal the following year amid much fanfare.

Injuries plagued Beliveau during his rookie season of 1953–54, as they would throughout his career, but he blossomed into an NHL star during 1954–55, finishing third in league scoring with 73 points, one behind teammate Maurice Richard and two back of Montreal's Bernie Geoffrion. Beliveau was named to the First All-Star Team at center that year and would go on to be an All-Star eight more times. In 1955–56, Beliveau led the NHL in scoring with a career-high 47 goals and 88 points. He won the Hart Trophy in addition to the Art Ross that year, and played on a Stanley Cup champion for the first of 10 times. Beliveau led the league in goals again in 1958–59 when he fired 45 and added 46 assists for a career-high 91 points.

Beliveau was named captain of the Canadiens in 1961–62, and in 1963–64 he won his second Hart Trophy. In 1965, he was the first recipient of the Conn Smythe Trophy as most valuable player in the playoffs. On March 3, 1968, Beliveau joined Gordie Howe as the only players to that point in NHL history

to reach 1,000 career points. On February 11, 1971, he became just the fourth player in history to score 500 goals. Beliveau retired after the Canadiens upset the Chicago Black Hawks to win the Stanley Cup that spring. At the time, his 507 goals were the most ever scored by a center in the NHL. The traditional three-year waiting period was waived and Beliveau was elected to the Hockey Hall of Fame in 1972.

After his playing days, Beliveau moved into a front-office job with Montreal. His name was added to the Stanley Cup seven more times as an executive with the Canadiens before he retired in 1994. The Jean Beliveau Trophy is awarded annually to the top scorer in the Quebec Major Junior Hockey League.

BRIAN BELLOWS was a First Team All-Star in the the Ontario Hockey League in 1981–82 and helped the Kitchener Rangers to win the Memorial Cup that year. He was selected second overall by the Minnesota North Stars in the 1982 Entry Draft and went on to become the leading goal scorer in franchise history.

Bellows had 35 goals as a rookie in 1982–83 and scored 30 goals or more in eight of his 11 seasons in Minnesota. He established career highs with 55 goals and 99 points in 1989–90 and was named to the Second All-Star Team that year. In 1990–91, he led the North Stars with 19 assists and 29 points in the playoffs as Minnesota reached the Stanley Cup finals. By the time he was traded to the Montreal Canadiens for Russ Courtnall on August 31, 1992, Bellows was the North Stars' all-time leader with 342 goals and ranked second in both assists (380) and points (722).

In his first season with Montreal in 1992–93, Bellows led the team with 40 goals and helped the Canadiens to win the Stanley Cup. He played two more years in Montreal before another trade took him to the Tampa Bay Lightning. In 1996–97, Bellows helped the Mighty Ducks of Anaheim to reach the playoffs for the first time in franchise history. After playing in Germany during the 1997–98 season, Bellows returned to the NHL with the Washington Capitals late in the year.

CLINT BENEDICT is considered one of the greatest goaltenders of all-time, ranking ahead of even Georges Vezina in most estimates of the players of his era. His habit of "accidentally" falling to the ice to stop shots and cover loose pucks forced a change to the NHL rule that stated goaltenders must remain standing at all times.

After first playing the game as a six-year-old, Benedict showed rapid improvement. He had moved into senior hockey by the time he was 15. He joined the Ottawa Senators of the National Hockey Association in 1912–13 and continued with the team through the formation of the NHL before being traded to the Montreal Maroons prior to the 1924–25 season. Benedict won the Stanley Cup with Ottawa in 1920, 1921 and 1923, and he won a fourth title with the Maroons in 1926. He was also a member of the Senators team that lost the Stanley Cup finals to the Vancouver Millionaires in 1915. He led the NHL in goals-against average five years in a row between 1918–19 and 1922–23 and for a sixth time with a career-best 1.42 mark in 1926–27.

At age 37, Benedict's NHL career was ended by a series of injuries resulting from shots fired by Howie Morenz. Those injuries, suffered during the 1929–30 season, initially forced Benedict to try the first facemask ever worn by a goaltender in the NHL, but he claimed the nosepiece obscured his vision, and he stopped using it. He played a final season in the International-American Hockey League in 1930–31, then retired. Benedict was elected to the Hockey Hall of Fame in 1965.

DOUG BENTLEY was the first of the Bentley brothers to play in the NHL, breaking in with the Chicago Black Hawks in 1939–40. Max joined him in Chicago the following year. Doug Bentley possessed speed, stickhandling skill and scoring power in abundance, though he stood just 5'8" and weighed only 145 pounds.

Bentley began his hockey career in his hometown of Delisle, Saskatchewan and quickly advanced through the amateur ranks there. He later played in Regina and Moose Jaw before moving on to Drumheller, Alberta for the first of two seasons in 1937–38. The Drumheller team featured four Bentley brothers. When Max and Doug later joined forces in Chicago, both became stars. Doug led the NHL in goals and points in 1942–43 when his 73 points tied the NHL single-season record, and he was named to the First All-Star Team at left wing. He was a First Team All-Star again after leading the league in goals for a second straight year in 1943–44. He had 77 points that season, but lost the scoring title to the Boston Bruins' Herb Cain, who set a new single-season record with 82.

Bentley did not play during the 1944–45 season, but was back in 1945–46 when he and and his brother were teamed with Bill Mosienko on the Pony Line. The trio was among the best in the NHL, as Max Bentley won the scoring title two years in a row and Doug was again a First Team All-Star in 1946–47. The line was broken up the following year when Max was traded to the Toronto Maple Leafs, but Doug remained among the best scorers in the NHL over the next three seasons. In 1948–49, he finished second to linemate Roy Conacher in the scoring race and was named to the Second All-Star Team.

In 1950, Bentley was named the greatest player in Black Hawks history.

By 1950–51, Doug Bentley was slowing down. He played just eight games in Chicago the following year and finished out the season playing in Saskatoon. In 1953–54, he made a brief comeback when he joined Max with the New York Rangers. Bentley remained active as a player, coach and scout after leaving the NHL, last suiting up with Los Angeles of the Western Hockey League in 1961–62. In 1964, Doug Bentley was inducted into the Hockey Hall of Fame. Brother Max was elected two years later.

MAX BENTLEY Known as "the Dipsy-Doodle Dandy of Delisle" for his skating and stickhandling skill (and his hometown in Saskatchewan), Max Bentley stood just 5'8" and weighed only 158 pounds, but was one of the top players in the NHL during the 1940s and early 1950s. He joined his brother Doug with the Chicago Black Hawks during the 1940–41 season and by 1942–43 the Bentleys were among the most dangerous scorers in the NHL. Doug led the league in both goals and points that year, while Max finished third in scoring and won the Lady Byng Trophy.

Max Bentley missed the next two seasons due to military service in World War II, but was back with the Black Hawks in 1945–46. The Bentleys were teamed with Bill Mosienko that year, and the Pony Line became the most effective trio in the NHL. Max was the league's leading scorer in 1945–46 and 1946–47 and was selected to the all-star team after both seasons. Bentley was now at the height of his fame, but on November 4, 1947, the struggling Black Hawks traded him to the Toronto Maple Leafs, along with Cy Thomas, for Gus Bodnar, Bud Poile, Gaye Stewart, Bob Goldham and Ernie Dickens.

Bentley enjoyed an excellent season with the Maple Leafs in 1947–48 and helped Toronto repeat as Stanley Cup champions that year. He was with Stanley Cup winners in Toronto again in 1949 and in 1951, which proved to be his last great season. Injuries and a scoring slump saw Bentley return home to Saskatchewan during the 1952–53 season, and though he finished the year with the Maple Leafs, he was signed by the New York Rangers in 1953–54. Briefly reunited with Doug in New York, it would prove to be his last NHL season, though he would continue to play in Saskatoon for several years. Max Bentley was inducted into the Hockey Hall of Fame in 1966, two years after his brother Doug.

BRYAN BERARD was selected first overall by the New York Islanders in the 1995 Entry Draft, joining Brian Lawton and Mike Modano as just the third U.S.-born player ever picked first in the draft. He made his NHL debut in 1996–97 and immediately established himself among the best young defensemen in the game, winning the Calder Trophy and being named to the All-Rookie Team. After the season, he played for the United States at the World Championships. In 1998, Berard was a member of the U.S. Olympic team at Nagano.

Berard had been a highly touted prospect en route to the NHL. He played high school hockey at Mount St. Charles Academy in Rhode Island and led the team to three state championships, then played junior hockey with Detroit of the Ontario Hockey League in 1994–95 and 1995–96. Berard was both an OHL and Canadian major junior first team all-star each season and was named Canadian major junior rookie of the year in 1994–95 and defenseman of the year in 1995–96.

RED BERENSON Gordon "Red" Berenson was the first Canadian hockey player to go directly from American college hockey to the NHL, joining the Montreal Canadiens from the University of Michigan late in the 1961–62 season. He played just four games that year, scoring a goal that happened to give the Canadiens a new NHL record for goals scored in a single season. He would later become one of only seven players in the history of the National Hockey League to score six goals in a single game and the only player to accomplish the feat while playing on the road.

Berenson was with the Canadiens until 1966 when he was traded to the New York Rangers, but did not become a star until joining the St. Louis Blues after expansion. In 1968–69, he became the first player from an expansion team to crack the top–10 in scoring, with 82 points on 35 goals and 47 assists. It was during that season (November 7, 1968) that Berenson scored six times in an 8–0 win over the Philadelphia Flyers.

A top–10 scorer again in 1969–70, Berenson was traded to the Detroit Red Wings the following year but never again finished as one of the NHL's leading scorers. He returned to St. Louis in 1974–75 and finished his playing career there in 1978. Berenson then coached the Blues from 1979 to 1982. Since leaving St. Louis, Berenson has been the long-serving head coach at his alma mater in Ann Arbor.

AMO BESSONE spent 28 years as the hockey coach at Michigan State University and was one of the most prominent leaders in college hockey during an era when the sport was primarily organized, operated and regulated by its coaches. Still, his lifetime record of 367–427–20 does not accurately reflect the competitiveness of his teams, as most of the region's best hockey talent was usually recruited to more traditional hockey powers such as rival University of Michigan.

Bessone struggled to build up an MSU program that endured 18 losing seasons before rising above .500. During this time, Bessone's most memorable season was 1965–66, when the Spartans rose from a sixth-place 9–11–0 season in the Western Collegiate Hockey Association to a Cinderella playoff run that saw them become NCAA national champions. The following year, the school was 8–11–1 and finished fifth in the WCHA before going all the way to the NCAA final four.

But Bessone's colorful coaching career has obscured what was also an impressive playing record. Growing up in Springfield, Massachusetts, he played defense at West Springfield High School and at the Kents Hill and Hebron academies in Maine before going on to play at the University of Illinois. Bessone also had a brief professional career in the American Hockey League with Providence.

Bessone got into coaching after the war when he assisted with football and baseball at Westfield High School in Massachusetts. He started the hockey program at Michigan Tech in 1948 before moving to Michigan State in 1951, where he remained until 1979. Bessone was enshrined in the coaches category of the United States Hockey Hall of Fame in 1992, joining his brother Pete, who had been inducted as a player in 1978.

PETER BESSONE was a star in hockey, football and baseball at West Springfield (Massachusetts) High School who went on to a successful career in both international and professional hockey.

After his high school successes, Bessone played with the West Side Rangers in Springfield before he was lured to Europe in 1931, where he became known as "the Babe Ruth of Paris" because he was the biggest drawing card in French hockey. In 1934, Bessone was a late replacement on the United States national team and earned a silver medal at the World Championships in Italy when the Americans finished second to Canada. He returned to the U.S. for the 1936–37 hockey season and played amateur hockey with the Pittsburgh Yellow Jackets, where he was a teammate of Frank Brimsek. Bessone turned pro with the Pittsburgh Hornets the following year. He also made a brief NHL appearance in 1937–38 when he played six games with the Detroit Red Wings.

Bessone played the next nine years in the American Hockey League with the Hornets and Cleveland Barons where he was one of the toughest defensemen in the league, gaining over 100 penalty minutes in three different seasons. He twice saw his teams reach the AHL finals—with Pittsburgh in 1939–40 and the Barons in 1943–44—before Cleveland finally captured a Calder Cup championship title in 1944–45. He also helped Cleveland reach the finals again in 1945–46.

After the 1946–47 season, Bessone returned to international hockey and coached teams in Switzerland, Italy and France. He finished his playing career with four games for Springfield in the AHL in 1949–50. Bessone was inducted into the United States Hockey Hall of Fame in 1978. Brother Amo Bessone was inducted in 1992 after a legendary coaching career at Michigan State.

GARY BETTMAN was unanimously elected commissioner of the National Hockey League by the NHL's Board of Governors on December 11, 1992. A graduate of Cornell University (1974) and New York University of Law (1977), he practiced law in Manhattan before joining the National Basketball Association in 1981 as assistant general counsel. In 1984 he became the NBA's senior vice president and general counsel.

Since Bettman assumed office as NHL commissioner on February 1, 1993, the league has achieved its first national network television contract in the United States in 20 years and has expanded its presence on national cable outlets. The league has also successfully launched franchises in Florida, Dallas and Anaheim, returned to Denver, and is establishing NHL franchises in non-traditional hockey markets, including Nashville, Atlanta and Columbus.

The commissioner's economic policies have helped stabilize teams in Buffalo, Dallas, Edmonton, Florida, Long Island, Los Angeles, New Jersey and Tampa Bay and the league has signed significant corporate sponsorships.

Under Bettman's leadership the NHL reached a landmark agreement with the International Ice Hockey Federation in the summer of 1995 that resulted in the first World Cup of Hockey in 1996 and the NHL's participation in the Winter Olympics beginning in 1998.

In January 1995 Bettman concluded the negotiation of a new Collective Bargaining Agreement with the NHL Players' Association. Twice extended, this agreement remains in effect until September 15, 2004.

J.P. BICKELL John Paris Bickell was an industrialist, mining executive, financier and public servant who played an important behind-the-scenes role in professional hockey in Toronto. He was a silent partner with a $25,000 investment in the Toronto St. Pats, and he was convinced later to transfer his personal and financial interests after Conn Smythe bought the team and renamed it the Maple Leafs.

Bickell agreed with Smythe's view that a new arena was needed in Toronto and his financial knowledge and support helped Smythe build Maple Leaf Gardens during the height of the Great Depression. Bickell became the first president and chairman of the board at Maple Leaf Gardens when it opened in

1931, holding the position until his death on August 22, 1951. His memory is perpetuated by the Bickell Memorial Cup, which is awarded at the discretion of Maple Leaf Gardens directors to a member of the Leafs who performs with a very high standard of excellence. Bickell was inducted into the Hockey Hall of Fame as a builder in 1978.

CECIL BLACHFORD Though he played with many future Hall of Famers, including Lester Patrick, it was Cecil Blachford who captained the Montreal Wanderers when they were Stanley Cup champions in 1906, 1907, and 1908. He had been a member of the Montreal Amateur Athletic Association in 1902–03 and was one of several players who left the team when James Strachan organized the Wanderers in 1904. This precipitated a war in hockey circles that led to the formation of the Federal Amateur Hockey League.

The Wanderers were members of the Eastern Canada Amateur Hockey Association when they defeated Ottawa for the league championship and Stanley Cup in 1906. Except for a loss to the Kenora Thistles in January of 1907 that was quickly avenged, the Wanderers beat all challengers for the Stanley Cup over the next three seasons. Following a brief retirement, Blachford helped the Wanderers regain the Stanley Cup in 1910.

When Blachford first retired in 1909, he was given permanent possession of the Arena Cup, which the Wanderers had also won three successive years as champions of the ECAHA. The trophy now resides in the Hockey Hall of Fame.

TOM BLADON was the top offensive defenseman on the great Philadelphia Flyers teams of the mid 1970s, reaching double figures in goals during five of six seasons with the club. On December 11, 1977, he had four goals and four assists in a 10–1 win over the Cleveland Barons to break Bobby Orr's record of seven points in a game by a defenseman. (The record has since been equaled by Paul Coffey.) Bladon, who had 14 goals the year before, established career highs with 43 assists and 53 points that season.

BOB BLAKE was born in Ashland, Wisconsin, but moved to Hibbing, Minnesota with his family when he was four years old and grew up to become an outstanding high school athlete, earning four letters in hockey and three each in football and track.

Blake began his professional hockey career as a 17-year-old in 1933 when he joined the Duluth Miners of the Central Hockey League. He began playing regularly midway through the season and quickly developed into a top–10 scorer. Boston Bruins scout Perk Galbraith then signed Blake to a contract with the club's Boston Cubs farm team, where he played for two years—and helped win a league title in 1934–45—before joining the Minneapolis Millers for the 1936–37 season. With Blake in the lineup, the Millers took the league title that year. Blake was a popular player with Millers fans and earned a reputation as an ironman for his durability and consistent play.

In 1937, his contract was bought by the Cleveland Barons of the International-American Hockey League. He finished out the 1937–38 season in Minneapolis, then spent the next two seasons in Cleveland, where he was the Barons' fastest skater and helped the team win the league title in 1938–39.

In 1940–41, Blake joined the Buffalo Bisons. Injuries to the team's defensive corps saw him converted from a forward to a defenseman that year, and with his speed, durability and aggressive play, he adapted well to his new assignment. In 1941–42, he was named the Bisons' most valuable player. He also captained the team that season and led Buffalo to a Calder Cup title the following year. After his career was interrupted by two years of military service in the Pacific with the Army Air Corps, Blake rejoined the Bisons late in 1945–46 for another championship run. He remained in Buffalo until the 1947–48 season, when he joined Houston in the United States Hockey League and helped them win the Loudan Trophy. Blake was rated the best defenseman in the league by most critics that season. In 1985, he was enshrined in the United States Hockey Hall of Fame.

ROB BLAKE is considered one of the top defensemen in the game. He joined the Los Angeles Kings late in 1989–90 and played a full season in 1990–91 when he was named to the All-Rookie Team after leading all rookie defensemen in scoring. Blake was chosen as the Kings' best defenseman in each of his first four full seasons before injuries began to limit his play. Finally healthy again in 1997–98, Blake led all blueliners with 23 goals and was a key component in the resurgence of the Kings that season. His play earned him the Norris Trophy as the NHL's best defenseman and a spot on the First All-Star Team.

Blake was selected by Los Angeles in the 1988 Entry Draft but played two more seasons at Bowling Green University before making his NHL debut. He was a Central Collegiate Hockey Association all-star in each of those two years and an NCAA all American in 1989–90. In international hockey, Blake won a silver medal for Canada at the World Championships in 1991 and gold medals in 1994 and 1997. He was also a member of Team Canada at the 1996 World Cup of Hockey and played at the Olympics in Nagano in 1998, where he was named the best defenseman despite Canada's fourth-place finish.

TOE BLAKE Hector "Toe" Blake was a star player with the Montreal Canadiens during the 1930s and 1940s who later coached the team with great

success during the 1950s and 1960s. Known as "the Lamplighter" for his scoring skill, Blake first came to prominence as a hockey player in Sudbury, Ontario, where he led the Cub Wolves to the Memorial Cup in 1932. He played briefly with the Stanley Cup champion Montreal Maroons in 1934–35, but on February 13, 1936, was traded to the Montreal Canadiens as part of a deal for Lorne Chabot.

Blake became a regular with the Canadiens in 1936–37 and was named to the Second All-Star Team at left wing the following year. In 1938–39, he led the NHL in scoring, won the Hart Trophy as league MVP and was named a First Team All-Star. Blake was the leading scorer on a weak club in three of the next four seasons and was named captain in 1940–41. In 1943–44, he was teamed with Maurice Richard and Elmer Lach and the Punch Line was born. The Canadiens cruised to first place that year in the regular-season standings and Blake had 18 points in nine playoff games as Montreal won its first Stanley Cup title in 13 years.

In 1944–45, Lach, Richard and Blake finished 1–2–3 in league scoring and all three were named to the First All-Star Team. Blake was a Second Team All-Star and won the Lady Byng Trophy in 1945–46, when the Canadiens won another Stanley Cup championship. His NHL playing career came to an end when he broke his leg in a game against the New York Rangers on January 11, 1948. Blake finished the year as coach of the Houston Huskies in the United States Hockey League and led the team to the championship.

Blake was playing again in 1948–49 as a member of the Buffalo Bisons in the American Hockey League and took over as coach midway through the season. On February 10, 1949 he became the head coach with the Valleyfield Braves of the Quebec Senior Hockey League, where he remained until 1953–54. He was hired to coach the Montreal Canadiens for the 1955–56 season in the hope he would be able to harness the temper of his former linemate Maurice Richard. The Canadiens were Stanley Cup champions in Blake's first season as head coach and went on to win the Cup five years in a row.

Blake's teams continued to top the regular-season standings three times in four years between 1960–61 and 1963–64, then won the Stanley Cup again in 1965 and 1966. He retired after coaching his eighth Stanley Cup champion in 1968. Blake had been elected to the Hockey Hall of Fame two years before.

GUS BODNAR On October 30, 1943, rookie Gus Bodnar scored for the Toronto Maple Leafs just 15 seconds into the first game of the season, establishing a record that still stands for the fastest goal by a player in his first NHL game. Bodnar finished the season with 22 goals and established what were then also rookie records with 40 assists and 62 points. He was an easy winner of the Calder Trophy as the NHL's top rookie in 1943–44.

Bodnar was never able to match his rookie performance over a 12-year career. By the 1946–47 season, the Maple Leafs had sent him to the minors and on November 4, 1947 he was one of five players Toronto sent to the Chicago Black Hawks for Max Bentley. Bodnar remained in Chicago until a trade to Boston in 1953–54 and ended his career with the Bruins the following season.

LEO BOIVIN was a rugged defenseman who was considered the premier bodychecker of his era. Tim Horton, himself one of the most powerful players in hockey, rated Boivin as the toughest defenseman in the league to beat, while Lynn Patrick compared his style to that of Eddie Shore. Like Shore, Boivin sometimes would knock down opponents as they attempted to break up his rushes.

Boivin began his NHL career with a brief appearance for the Toronto Maple Leafs in 1951–52, and became a regular the following season. He was traded to the Boston Bruins in November of 1954, where he would remain there for 11 years. Boivin helped Boston reach the Stanley Cup finals in 1957 and 1958, losing to the Montreal Canadiens both times. The team fell on hard times in the early 1960s and had finished last in the six-team NHL three years in a row when Boivin was named captain in 1963–64. He retained the honor until February of 1966, when he was traded to the Detroit Red Wings. Boivin helped the Red Wings reach the Stanley Cup finals that year and spent one more season in Detroit before being selected by the Pittsburgh Penguins in the 1967 Expansion Draft.

Boivin played one-and-a-half seasons with Pittsburgh and the Minnesota North Stars before retiring as a player in 1970. His 1,150 games played ranked him among the leaders of his era. He remained associated with hockey as a coach and scout, serving behind the bench with the St. Louis Blues in 1975–76 and 1977–78. Boivin was elected to the Hockey Hall of Fame in 1986.

PETER BONDRA joined the Washington Capitals in 1990–91 and led all club rookies with 12 goals and 28 points that year. By the 1992–93 season, he was the team's leading scorer with 37 goals and 85 points. On February 5, 1994, Bondra became just the second player in Washington history (Bengt-Ake Gustafsson was the first) to score five goals in a single game. In 1994–95, he was the first Capitals player ever to lead the NHL in goals when he scored 34 in 47 games during the lockout-shortened, 48-game season. In 1995–96, Bondra topped 50 goals for the first time with 52. He had 52 goals again (and tied Teemu Selanne for the NHL lead) in 1997–98. He is known as one of the fastest skaters in the NHL.

Bondra was born in the Ukraine but raised in the former Czechoslovakia and has held Slovakian citizenship since 1995. He helped the Slovakian team qualify for the 1994 Olympics and was the country's leading scorer at the World Cup of Hockey in 1996. Bondra was also a member of the Slovakian team at the Nagano Olympics in 1998.

DICKIE BOON moved up the ranks in Montreal to become a member of the Montreal Amateur Athletic Association hockey team by the turn of the century. In 1902, he helped the team win the Stanley Cup in a thrilling three-game series with the Winnipeg Victorias. Boon starred on defense in a 2–1 victory in the final game that earned the team the nickname "Little Men of Iron" for the tenacious way they hung on to win.

When the Montreal Wanderers were formed for the 1903–04 season, Boon was one of several AAA players who were recruited to fill the roster. The player raid forced the Wanderers to form the new Federal Amateur Hockey League in order to escape repercussions from the Canadian Amateur Hockey League. Boon was both player and manager with the Wanderers in 1903–04 and 1904–05 before retiring as a player to coach the team. He led the Wanderers to Stanley Cup titles in 1906, 1907 and 1908, and he was manager of the team when the Wanderers entered the National Hockey Association in 1910 and won another Stanley Cup championship. Boon still was serving in that capacity when the team entered the NHL for the inaugural season of 1917–18 before withdrawing when fire destroyed the Montreal Arena on January 2, 1918.

During his playing days, Boon was a fast, wiry defenseman who weighed only about 130 pounds. He is considered to be the first man to use the poke check to steal pucks from opposing players. Boon was elected to the Hockey Hall of Fame in 1952.

MIKE BOSSY After four high-scoring seasons as a junior with Laval of the Quebec Junior Hockey League, Mike Bossy was selected 15th in the NHL Amateur Draft by the New York Islanders in 1977. He won the Calder Trophy in 1977–78 after setting a rookie scoring record with 53 goals, and went on to top 50 goals for a record nine consecutive seasons. Bossy fell short only in his final season of 1986–87 when injuries limited him to 38 goals in 63 games.

Bossy topped 60 goals five times in his career and led the NHL in goal-scoring with 69 in 1978–79 and 68 in 1980–81. In the latter year, he equaled Maurice Richard's legendary achievement of 50 goals in 50 games. Bossy went on to become the first Islanders player to reach 500 goals and 1,000 points, ending his career with 573 goals and 553 assists for 1,126 points. He had 85 goals and 160 points in postseason play and was a key member of all four Islanders Stanley Cup-winning teams between 1980 and 1983. Bossy scored the Cup-winning goal in both 1982 and 1983 and won the Conn Smythe Trophy in 1982. He also won the Lady Byng Trophy in 1982–83, 1983–84 and 1985–86.

For the first eight seasons of his career, Bossy was selected as an NHL All-Star at right wing, earning five berths on the First Team. He played for Team Canada at the Canada Cup in 1981 and 1984, winning in 1984 after scoring in overtime to eliminate the Soviet Union in the semifinals. A chronic back ailment forced Bossy to retire after the 1986–87 season. He was inducted into the Hockey Hall of Fame in 1991.

HENRY BOUCHA has been called the most electrifying and colorful player in the history of Minnesota hockey. The powerfully built Ojibwa from Warroad, Minnesota was also skilled at football and baseball and starred for five years at both defense and center for the Warroad High School hockey team, leading the school to the 1969 state tournament where they were beaten 5–4 in overtime by Edina in the final game.

Boucha played briefly for the famed Warroad Lakers and was a member of the U.S. national team at the World Championships in 1971. He was with the surprising silver medal-winning American team at the Sapporo Olympics as a 19-year-old in 1972, then signed with the Detroit Red Wings and scored a goal in his first NHL game on February 22, 1972. Almost a year later (January 28, 1973), Boucha set what was then an NHL record when he scored six seconds into a game against the Montreal Canadiens.

On August 27, 1974, Boucha came home to Minnesota when he was acquired by the North Stars in a trade for Danny Grant. However, he suffered an eye injury on January 4, 1975 and his career never rebounded. He played briefly with the Minnesota Fighting Saints in the World Hockey Association in 1975–76 and also with the Kansas City Scouts in the NHL that season, then retired after playing only nine games with the Colorado Rockies in 1976–77. He was elected to the United States Hockey Hall of Fame in 1995.

BUTCH BOUCHARD Emile "Butch" Bouchard was a powerful defenseman who starred for 15 seasons with the Montreal Canadiens. The 6'2", 205-pounder reportedly rode a bicycle 50 miles in order to attend his first training camp in 1941. Though his talents were still raw, Bouchard made the team. He became a regular in 1942–43 after Ken Reardon left the team for military service.

By 1943–44, the Canadiens were the top team in hockey and Bouchard was one of the NHL's best defensemen. Montreal won the Stanley Cup that season

and Bouchard was named to the Second All-Star Team. He was a First Team All-Star each of the next three seasons and played on another Stanley Cup winner in 1946. After injuries forced Toe Blake to retire from the Canadiens in 1947–48, Bouchard was named to succeed him as team captain. He led the Canadiens to another Stanley Cup victory in 1952–53, and though injuries had slowed him down by the 1955–56 season, he made a final appearance in the dying moments of that year's Stanley Cup finals as the Canadiens were again champions.

During his time in Montreal, Bouchard was paired with such greats as Ken Reardon, Doug Harvey and Tom Johnson. He was one of the strongest men in the game and a well-respected team leader. After retiring from the NHL, he remained active in junior hockey, and the Emile "Butch" Bouchard Trophy is presented annually to the top defenseman in the Quebec Major Junior Hockey League. He was elected to the Hockey Hall of Fame in 1966. Son Pierre Bouchard played in the NHL with the Canadiens and Washington Capitals between 1970–71 and 1981–82.

FRANK BOUCHER was considered the best playmaker in hockey and the game's most sportsmanlike player during his days with the New York Rangers. He won the Lady Byng Trophy seven times in eight years between 1927–28 and 1934–35, and he was given permanent possession of the original trophy.

Boucher was a member of a prominent hockey-playing family in Ottawa. He and his brother George are both members of the Hall of Fame, while brothers Bob and Billy also spent time in the NHL. Frank Boucher entered the NHL as a part-time player with the Ottawa Senators in 1921–22, spending the next four seasons with the Vancouver Maroons before returning to the NHL with the original New York Rangers team in 1926–27.

With the Rangers, Boucher centered a line with brothers Bill and Bun Cook that was the most productive unit in the NHL. With his precise passing, he ranked consistently among the NHL scoring leaders, leading the league in assists three times while helping the Rangers win the Stanley Cup in 1928 and 1933. He also earned selections to the First or Second All-Star Team on four occasions.

Boucher retired as a player to take over from Lester Patrick as coach of the Rangers in 1938–39. He led the team to a Stanley Cup victory the following year. He remained as coach until 1948–49 (including a brief comeback as a player in 1943–44), and he also succeeded Lester Patrick as general manager in 1946–47, staying with that job until 1954–55. In 1958, Frank Boucher was elected to the Hockey Hall of Fame.

GEORGE BOUCHER George "Buck" Boucher was part of a great hockey family. Brothers Billy and Bob both saw action in the NHL during the 1920s, while George and his brother Frank Boucher were both star players who later became honored members of the Hall of Fame.

George Boucher played football with the Ottawa Rough Riders prior to turning pro in hockey with the Ottawa Senators for the 1915–16 season. He spent two years in the National Hockey Association before the Senators became part of the NHL, and he was one of the highest-scoring defenseman of his era over a lengthy career. Boucher played on four Stanley Cup winners in Ottawa between 1919–20 and 1926–27, but he was sold to the Montreal Maroons by the financially strapped Senators during the 1928–29 season. After two-and-a-half years with the Maroons, including a brief stint as coach in 1930–31, he ended his NHL playing career with Chicago in 1931–32.

Boucher returned to coaching after his playing days, guiding the Ottawa Senators/St. Louis Eagles during the final two years of the franchise's existence. He later helped select and train the Ottawa RCAF team that won the Olympic championship in 1948. Boucher also brought the Allan Cup to Ottawa the following year while coaching the amateur Senators. He later guided Boston's farm club in the old Canadian-American League before coaching the Bruins in the 1949–50 NHL season. Boucher was elected to the Hockey Hall of Fame in 1960.

RAYMOND BOURQUE of the Boston Bruins established himself as one of the best defenseman in hockey in his rookie season of 1979–80 when he won the Calder Trophy and was also named to the First All-Star Team. Bourque was the first non-goaltender to achieve that double honor. He was named to either the First or Second All-Star Team in each of his first 17 seasons, breaking Gordie Howe's record for consecutive All-Star berths. As a five-time winner of the Norris Trophy, he trails only Bobby Orr (eight) and Doug Harvey (seven) in the number of times he has been named the NHL's best defenseman.

Bourque has spent his entire professional career in Boston and is the club's all-time leader in assists and points. He surpassed Bobby Orr as the Bruins' all-time goal-scoring leader among defenseman with his 265th on January 22, 1992 and became the third defenseman in history (after Denis Potvin and Paul Coffey) to top 300 career goals. Bourque has led the Bruins in scoring five times and has ranked consistently among the top-scoring defenseman in the league. He ranks high among the NHL's all-time leaders in both assists and points, and when he collected his 1,000th assist on March 27, 1997, he became just the fifth player ever to reach that milestone, joining Wayne Gretzky, Gordie Howe, Marcel Dionne and Paul Coffey.

Bourque has been captain of the Bruins since 1988–89, and switched his uniform number from seven to 77 that season when the Bruins honored Phil Esposito by retiring his number on December 3, 1988. Though the Bruins have ranked among the best teams in the NHL for most of his career, reaching the Stanley Cup finals in 1988 and 1990, Bourque never has played for a Stanley Cup winner. He was a member of Team Canada at the Canada Cup in 1981, 1984 and 1987, but chose not to participate in 1991 or at the World Cup of Hockey in 1996. He was a member of Canada's Olympic team at the 1998 Games in Nagano.

JOHNNY BOWER Though his exact age was always a matter for debate, official records list Johnny Bower's date of birth as November 8, 1924. He began playing hockey in his hometown of Prince Albert, Saskatchewan and, after serving in the Canadian armed forces in World War II, started his lengthy professional career in the American Hockey League in 1945–46.

Bower spent eight seasons with the Cleveland Barons of the AHL (winning the Hap Holmes Memorial Trophy as outstanding goalie in 1951–52) before he got his first opportunity to play in the NHL. He played all 70 games for the Rangers in 1953–54 and posted a respectable 2.60 goals-against average on a fifth-place team, but was back in the minors with Vancouver of the Western Hockey League (where he was again named the top goalie) in 1954–55. Bower spent the next three years in the AHL with Cleveland and Providence and won the Les Cunningham Plaque as the league's MVP all three seasons.

Finally, in 1958, Bower made the NHL to stay after Punch Imlach drafted him for the Maple Leafs. Bower split the netminding duties with Ed Chadwick in 1958–59 before emerging as the starting goaltender the following year. In 1960–61, he won the Vezina Trophy for the first time and was named to the NHL's First All-Star Team. In each of the next three seasons, his play helped the Maple Leafs win the Stanley Cup. In 1964–65, Toronto acquired Terry Sawchuk and he and Bower shared the Vezina Trophy that season. In 1967, the duo of Bower and Sawchuk led the Maple Leafs to another Stanley Cup title.

Bower continued to see regular duty with the Maple Leafs after NHL expansion in 1967–68 and played his final game during the 1969–70 season. He was elected to the Hockey Hall of Fame in 1976.

RUSSELL BOWIE Russell "Dubbie" Bowie was the greatest goal scorer of his era, rivaled only by the legendary Frank McGee, whose career was much shorter. Bowie spent 10 seasons with the Montreal Victorias from 1898–99 to 1907–08, playing 80 regular-season games during that time and scoring the astounding total of 234 goals—an average of almost three per game.

Though professionalism came to hockey during this period, Bowie remained an amateur throughout his career, and he is said to have turned down an offer of a grand piano to leave the Victorias for the rival Montreal Wanderers. Considered a great stickhandler, Bowie played both center and rover during hockey's seven-man era and he led his league in scoring five times in 10 seasons. He was runner-up on four other occasions and he never finished lower than third. His greatest individual total came in 1906–07, when he had 38 goals in 10 games. Though he was his era's greatest star, Bowie was only a member of a Stanley Cup champion during his rookie year. The Victorias won a challenge match during February of 1899, but surrendered their title by season's end.

Bowie retired as a player after the 1907–08 season, but he was continually pursued by professional teams until he suffered a broken collar bone in 1910. He never played again, but he did serve as a referee in the National Hockey Association. In 1945, Bowie was one of the first 12 men inducted into the Hockey Hall of Fame.

SCOTTY BOWMAN William Scott Bowman has coached and won more games in both the regular season and playoffs than any man in NHL history. His eighth Stanley Cup coaching victory in 1998 tied him with the legendary Toe Blake for the most Cup championships ever. He had already been inducted into the Hall of Fame as a builder in 1991.

Bowman was a protege of Sam Pollock and became a coach with junior teams in the Montreal Canadiens organization after a head injury on March 7, 1952 forced him to cut short his playing career two years later. He also scouted for the Canadiens before making his NHL debut as coach of the St. Louis Blues in 1967–68. He was named general manager the following year and guided the Blues to the Stanley Cup finals in each of the team's first three seasons in the NHL.

In 1971–72, Pollock persuaded Bowman to return to Montreal. He won his first Stanley Cup title the following year and soon was coaching one of the greatest dynasties in NHL history. The Canadiens won the Stanley Cup four years in a row from 1975–76 until 1978–79 while posting some of the best regular-season win totals in NHL history. Bowman's Canadiens were 60–8–12 in 1977–78, setting a record for wins and points with 132. After eight years and five Stanley Cup titles with Montreal (plus a Canada Cup victory in 1976), Bowman left the Canadiens following the 1978–79 season to become coach, general manager and director of hockey operations with the Buffalo Sabres.

Bowman won a division title his first year in Buffalo and spent seven seasons with the Sabres. He was fired during the 1986–87 campaign and became a television analyst with Hockey Night in Canada the following season. He left

that position in June of 1990 to become director of player development with the Pittsburgh Penguins. Bowman helped to assemble the Penguins team that won the Stanley Cup in 1991, then took over as coach during the illness of Bob Johnson and won another Stanley Cup in 1992.

Bowman left the Penguins to become coach of the Red Wings in 1992–93. In his first three years in Detroit, his teams had excellent regular-season records, only to come up short in the playoffs. The Red Wings were swept by New Jersey in the 1995 Stanley Cup finals, then went on to set a record with 62 wins (62–13–7) in 1995–96. However, they lost to the eventual Stanley Cup champion Colorado Avalanche in the semifinals that year. In 1996–97, Bowman led the Red Wings to their first Stanley Cup victory in 42 years with a four-game sweep of the Philadelphia Flyers in the finals. Detroit made it two in a row in 1998 with a victory over the Washington Capitals.

CARL BREWER was a member of the Toronto Marlboros of the Ontario Hockey Association in 1957–58 when he played his first two NHL games with the Toronto Maple Leafs. He became a regular the following year. Brewer was strong-willed and a free-spirit who often clashed with Maple Leafs coach Punch Imlach, but was one of the best defenseman in the NHL.

Brewer was a mainstay on the Toronto defense with Tim Horton, Allan Stanley and Bob Baun, when the Maple Leafs won the Stanley Cup three years in a row between 1960–61 and 1962–63. He was named to the all-star team three times in his career, earning a First-Team selection in 1962–63 and Second-Team berths in 1961–62 and 1964–65.

Brewer was a fast skater and an excellent stickhandler who was also adept at baiting and needling opposition forwards and would cut the palms out of his gloves in order to grab a player's sweater without being detected. As a result of his tactics, Brewer was involved in plenty of altercations and led the league in penalty minutes in 1959–60 and 1964–65.

Brewer's feud with Punch Imlach resulted in his holding out from the Maple Leafs prior to the 1963–64 season. At the time, he announced his plans to further his education and enrolled at McMaster University in Hamilton. He even went out for the football team, but he was quickly re-signed by the Maple Leafs after a picture of him in his football uniform was shown in the Toronto papers. However, Brewer's relationship with Imlach did not improve and led to his retirement after the 1964–65 season.

After leaving the Maple Leafs, Brewer fought to have his amateur status reinstated and played for the Canadian national team in 1966–67. Brewer played in Finland 1967–68 and returned to the NHL with the Detroit Red Wings in 1969–70. (His rights had been traded by the Maple Leafs as part of the deal that sent Frank Mahovlich to Detroit.) Brewer played one season in Detroit and two years with the St. Louis Blues, then joined the Toronto Toros of the World Hockey Association in 1973–74 before retiring once again. He served as an assistant coach with the Finnish team at the first Canada Cup tournament in September of 1976, but had not been active as a player in six years when he made a comeback with the Maple Leafs in 1979–80. Brewer played 20 games with the team that year.

Alan Eagleson had been instrumental in helping Brewer regain his amateur status when he first left the Maple Leafs, but after his career was finally over Brewer began investigating the many irregularities in Eagleson's conduct. Brewer's work eventually helped in bringing charges against Eagleson that resulted in the former Players' Association director being sent to jail in January of 1998.

FRANK BRIMSEK was a rookie sensation with the Boston Bruins after replacing the legendary Tiny Thompson in goal early in the 1938–39 season. Brimsek earned the nickname "Mr. Zero" after twice recording streaks of three straight shutouts during his first month in Boston. He went on to lead the league with 10 shutouts and a 1.56 goals-against average that season. He won the Calder Trophy, the Vezina Trophy, a selection to the First All-Star Team, and he helped the Bruins to win the Stanley Cup.

Brimsek was a product of Eveleth High School in Minnesota, graduating to play amateur hockey with the famed Pittsburgh Yellow Jackets before beginning his pro career in New Haven and Providence en route to the NHL. After his brilliant rookie season, Brimsek was a Second Team All-Star in 1939–40 and in 1940–41 when Boston won another Stanley Cup title. He won the Vezina Trophy, earning a First Team All-Star selection again in 1941–42 for almost single-handedly leading Boston into the playoffs after the entire Kraut Line of Milt Schmidt, Bobby Bauer and Woody Dumart reported to the Canadian armed forces. Brimsek himself joined the United States Coast Guard after the 1942–43 season.

Returning to Boston after his military service, Brimsek continued to play in the NHL from 1945–46 until 1949–50, though his last season was spent with the Chicago Black Hawks. He was inducted into the Hockey Hall of Fame in 1966. He is also a member of the United States Hockey Hall of Fame.

ROD BRIND'AMOUR was drafted ninth overall by the St. Louis Blues in 1988 after helping the Notre Dame Hounds to win the Saskatchewan Junior Hockey League title in 1987–88. He spent the 1988–89 season at Michigan State, where he was named Central Collegiate Hockey Association freshman

of the year, and made his NHL debut with the Blues in the playoffs on April 11, 1989. Brind'Amour scored his first NHL goal on his very first shot.

In 1989–90, Brind'Amour was named to the NHL All-Rookie Team after finishing in a fourth-place tie among rookie scorers with 26 goals. Following his trade to Philadelphia on September 22, 1991, Brind'Amour recorded three straight 30-goal seasons. He won the Bobby Clarke Trophy as the Flyers MVP in 1991–92, scored a career-high 37 goals in 1992–93 and had a career-best 97 points in 1993–94. The Flyers missed the playoffs in each of those seasons, so Brind'Amour was added to the roster of the Canadian team at the World Championships three years in a row. In 1994, he played for the Canadian team that won the world title for the first time since 1961. Brind'Amour also played for Team Canada at the 1996 World Cup of Hockey and was a member of the 1998 Olympic team in Nagano.

An alternate captain with the Flyers since the 1994–95 season, Brind'Amour tied Claude Lemieux for the playoff lead with 13 goals when the Flyers reached the Stanley Cup finals in 1997.

PUNCH BROADBENT Harry "Punch" Broadbent led the NHL in scoring with 32 goals and 14 assists in 1921–22. That season, he set a record which still stands when he scored in 16 consecutive games, totalling 25 goals during the streak. Broadbent was a star player who was as talented battling opponents with his elbows as he was scoring goals.

A native of Ottawa, Broadbent spent most of his career there, working his way up through the amateur ranks before joining the Senators of the National Hockey Association in 1912–13. He led his team in scoring and he finished among the league leaders in two of the next three years before leaving to serve in the Canadian armed forces. Returning from World War I with the Military Medal, Broadbent resumed his hockey career with Ottawa (which was now in the NHL) during the 1918–19 season. He spent the next six seasons with the Senators, helping the team win the Stanley Cup in 1920, 1921 and 1923.

Prior to the 1924–25 season, Ottawa sold Broadbent and goalie Clint Benedict to the expansion Montreal Maroons. Though considered to be past his prime, Broadbent scored five goals in a game on January 7, 1925 and he and Benedict helped the Maroons win the Stanley Cup in 1926 after just their second season in the NHL. Broadbent returned to the Senators for the 1927–28 season, then spent the following year with the New York Americans before retiring in the wake of the stock market crash of 1929. He was elected to the Hockey Hall of Fame in 1962.

TURK BRODA Walter "Turk" Broda never appeared to let the rigors of goaltending affect his cheerful personality. Always able to maintain his cool, Broda posted a lifetime 2.53 goals-against average, but was at his best in the postseason where his average was an incredible 1.98. He helped the Toronto Maple Leafs win the Stanley Cup five times and his 13 postseason shutouts were a modern NHL record until surpassed by Jacques Plante in 1970.

Broda had been playing in the Detroit Red Wings organization when Conn Smythe purchased him for $8,000 to replace aging veteran George Hainsworth in 1936–37. He would remain a Maple Leaf for the next 16 seasons, with two years lost to military duty in World War II. Toronto reached the Stanley Cup finals in each of Broda's first three seasons, and in 1940–41 he won the Vezina Trophy and was named to the NHL's First All-Star Team. The following season, Broda and the Maple Leafs won the Stanley Cup. The 1942–43 campaign was his last before a two-year hitch in the military. He announced his retirement from hockey after the war, but was back with the Maple Leafs for the final 15 games of 1945–46.

With Broda back in goal full-time by 1946–47, the Leafs embarked on the most successful run in team history, winning the Stanley Cup three years in a row from 1947 to 1949, and adding a fourth championship in 1950–51. Broda was at his best during the 1947–48 campaign, when he again won the Vezina Trophy and a First Team All-Star berth. By 1950–51, he was sharing the Maple Leafs goaltending job with Al Rollins. He played just one game during the 1951–52 season and retired after the playoffs. Broda got into coaching after his playing career and guided the Toronto Marlboros to back-to-back Memorial Cup championships in 1955 and 1956. He was inducted into the Hockey Hall of Fame in 1967.

MARTIN BRODEUR made his NHL debut playing four games for the New Jersey Devils in 1991–92. His first full season was 1993–94 and he won the Calder Trophy as rookie of the year. In his second season of 1994–95, Brodeur helped the Devils to win the Stanley Cup for the first time in franchise history. He was the NHL's playoff leader that year in games, wins, minutes, shutouts and goals-against average. All three of Brodeur's playoff shutouts came in the second round against the Boston Bruins, making him just the fifth goalie in history (Dave Kerr, 1940; Frank McCool, 1945; Turk Broda 1950; Felix Potvin, 1994) to record three shutouts in one playoff series.

Brodeur starred again during the 1995–96 season, setting an NHL record for minutes played with 4,433 and posting a 2.34 goals-against average, though the defending Stanley Cup champion Devils missed the playoffs that year. In 1996–97, Brodeur led the NHL with 10 shutouts and a 1.88 goals-against average but finished second behind Dominik Hasek in voting for the

Vezina Trophy, earning a place on the Second All-Star Team. His 10 shutouts made him the first goalie to reach double digits since Ken Dryden in 1976–77 and his goals-against average was the lowest since Tony Esposito's 1.77 in 1971–72. Brodeur shared the Jennings Trophy with Devils teammate Mike Dunham in 1996–97. He also scored a goal against the Montreal Canadiens in the playoffs that year, shooting the puck into an empty net on April 17, 1997. He led the NHL with 43 wins in 1997–98, posting 10 shutouts again and a 1.89 goals-against average. Brodeur earned the Jennings Trophy himself that season, but once again lost the Vezina Trophy to Hasek.

Brodeur is a product of an athletic family. His brother Claude was a pitcher in the Montreal Expos system before an arm injury ended his career, and his father Denis (a long-time photographer for the Montreal Canadiens and Montreal Expos) won a bronze medal as a goalie with Canada on the 1956 Olympic team. Martin was a member of the Canadian team at the World Cup of Hockey in 1996 and the Canadian Olympic team at Nagano in 1998.

RICHARD BRODEUR was dubbed "King Richard" by the fans in Vancouver while leading the Canucks to the Stanley Cup finals against the New York Islanders in 1982. Though he gained fame during Vancouver's surprising playoff run, he never again enjoyed the same success during his NHL career.

Brodeur had been one of the top goalies in the World Hockey Association before joining the NHL. He signed with the Quebec Nordiques right out of junior hockey in 1972 and went on to post 165 wins over the seven-year history of the WHA, second all-time to Joe Daley's 167. Brodeur set a record with 44 wins in 1975–76 and led Quebec to the Avco Cup championship the following year.

When four WHA teams were admitted into the NHL in 1979–80, Brodeur joined the New York Islanders (who had drafted him back in 1972) before being traded to the Canucks on October 6, 1980. He spent seven full seasons in Vancouver before ending his NHL career with the Hartford Whalers. Brodeur was the last man from the inaugural season of the WHA to still be active as a player.

HERB BROOKS gained fame as the coach of the United States Olympic hockey team that won the gold medal at Lake Placid in the "Miracle on Ice" of 1980. Two decades before that, he had been the last player cut from the 1960 squad that won the gold medal in hockey at the 1960 Winter Olympics in Squaw Valley. He did later play on U.S. Olympic teams in 1964 and 1968 and U.S. national teams in 1962, 1965, 1967 and 1970.

Brooks was a collegiate player at the University of Minnesota from 1955 to 1959. He became coach there in 1972, and had transformed the last-place Gophers into NCAA champions by 1974 (and again in 1976 and 1979) before going on to guide the U.S. gold medal team. After Lake Placid, there was immediate speculation that Brooks would be hired by the New York Rangers, but he wound up in Switzerland for a year before joining his former Olympic assistant, Craig Patrick, in New York. His Rangers team had a 92-point season in 1981–82 and bettered that with 93 points two years later. Brooks recorded 100 wins faster than any other Rangers coach and is one of just six men in the team's history to reach that mark.

When the Rangers fired Brooks during the 1984–85 season, he coached St. Cloud State to third place in the national small-college tournament before moving them up to Division I status. He resurfaced in the NHL with the Minnesota North Stars for a dismal 19–48–13 season in 1987–88, then spent a few seasons as a color commentator on television before retiring to a business career. He came back to coaching with New Jersey's Utica farm club in 1991–92 and coached the Devils the following year. He rejoined Craig Patrick when he became a scout with the Pittsburgh Penguins in 1995. In 1998, Brooks coached the Olympic hockey team from France at the Nagano Games. He was elected to the United States Hockey Hall of Fame in the coaches category in 1990.

FRED BROPHY For over 80 years, until Ron Hextall performed the feat in December of 1987, Fred Brophy was the only goaltender in hockey history to shoot a puck that scored a goal in a regulation game at the sport's highest level. On February 18, 1905, while playing for Westmount in a Canadian Amateur Hockey League game against Quebec, Brophy rushed the length of the ice and scored on future Hall of Famer Paddy Moran. Unfortunately, 17 pucks got past Brophy that night as Westmount suffered a resounding 17–5 defeat.

A little more than a year later, Brophy scored again. Now a member of Montreal in the Eastern Canada Amateur Hockey Association, Brophy beat Nathan Frye of the Victorias on March 7, 1906. Even with his goal, Brophy was on the wrong end of a 14–6 score.

NEAL BROTEN was a member of the "Miracle on Ice" U.S. Olympic team that won the gold medal in Lake Placid in 1980. He went on to become the highest scoring American-born player in the history of the NHL until being surpassed by Joe Mullen. Broten added a Stanley Cup victory to his Olympic gold medal as a member of the New Jersey Devils in 1994–95. Brothers Paul and Aaron also played in the NHL.

A native of Roseau, Minnesota, and a product of the University of

Minnesota, Broten won the Hobey Baker Award in 1980–81 as the top player in the NCAA and made his NHL debut with the North Stars on March 31, 1981. Minnesota reached the Stanley Cup finals that year and Broten became a regular with the team the following season. The 38 goals he scored as a rookie would prove to be the highest single-season total of his career, though he would remain a productive player over the next 11 years in Minnesota.

Broten established career highs with 76 assists and 105 points in 1985–86 when he became the first American player to top 100 points in the NHL.

Broten reached the Stanley Cup finals for a second time in Minnesota in 1992. He moved to Dallas with the North Stars franchise in 1993–94 and was traded to the New Jersey Devils on February 27, 1995. He ranks first all-time in Minnesota/Dallas history in games played, points and assists.

GEORGE BROWN was a pioneer of hockey in the United States. When the old Boston Arena was built in 1910, Brown organized a hockey team on behalf of the Boston Athletic Association and became the driving force behind this team, which played top amateur clubs in the eastern United States as well as Canadian college and club teams. After the Boston Arena was destroyed by fire in 1918, Brown formed the corporation that built a new one. He then managed both the Arena and the BAA hockey team, which formed the basis of the U.S. Olympic team that won a silver medal in 1924.

It was also in 1924 that Boston became the first American city in the NHL. Brown was not originally part of the professional scene, but after the Bruins left the Boston Arena for the Boston Garden in 1928, he helped to organize the Canada-American League and entered a team called the Boston Tigers. (This league was the forerunner of the American Hockey League.)

In 1934, Brown became general manager of both the Boston Arena and the Boston Garden, and he continued to boost the local game at all levels. He and his son, Walter Brown, are both members of the Hockey Hall of Fame and the United States Hockey Hall of Fame.

WALTER BROWN Like his father, George Brown, Walter Brown was prominent in amateur hockey in Boston before becoming involved in the pro game. At the time of his death on September 7, 1964, Brown was president of the Boston Garden, chairman of the Basketball Hall of Fame, a member of the Hockey Hall of Fame governing committee, past president of the International Ice Hockey Federation and president of two important franchises, hockey's Boston Bruins and basketball's Boston Celtics.

Brown coached the Boston Olympics amateur hockey team from 1930 to 1940, winning five American championships and a world championship in 1933 while representing the United States in Prague, Czechoslovakia. As chairman of the U.S. Olympic Ice Hockey Committee in 1960, he played a significant role in selecting the American team that won a gold medal at Squaw Valley, California. In 1962, Brown was elected to the Hockey Hall of Fame as a builder, one year after his father had been so honored. In 1973, both George and Walter Brown were among the first inductees into the United States Hockey Hall of Fame.

MUD BRUNETEAU Modere "Mud" Bruneteau was a rookie right winger with the Detroit Red Wings when he scored the goal that ended the longest game in NHL history. Bruneteau's goal after 116:30 of the overtime gave Detroit a 1–0 victory over the Montreal Maroons in the first game of the 1936 playoffs. The Red Wings went on to sweep the Maroons, then beat the Toronto Maple Leafs to win the Stanley Cup.

Bruneteau won another Stanley Cup title with the Red Wings in 1937, but did not peak as a player until Detroit won again in 1942–43. That season, he led the team with 23 goals and scored a hat trick against the Boston Bruins in the first game of the Stanley Cup final. In 1943–44, Bruneteau had a career-high 35 goals in just 39 games.

He had another good year with 23 goals in 1944–45, but was out of the NHL by the end of the 1945–46 season. He spent the 1946–47 and 1947–48 seasons with Omaha of the United States Hockey League, then became the club's coach. He guided the team to a league title in 1950–51. Bruneteau's brother Eddie also played with the Red Wings.

FRANK BUCKLAND's first involvement in amateur hockey came in Toronto, but upon graduation from university a job offer took him to Peterborough, Ontario, where he coached both junior and senior teams from 1932 to 1940. He was elected to the executive of the Ontario Hockey Association and became president for a two-year term beginning in 1955. In 1961, Buckland was elected treasurer of the OHA.

The Canadian Amateur Hockey Association recognized Buckland's outstanding service in 1965 when it presented him with the CAHA Meritorious Award. That same year, he was presented with the OHA's Golden Stick Award and in 1973 he was named a Life Member of the OHA. In 1974, the Province of Ontario presented Buckland with its Sports Achievement Award. In 1975, he was elected to the Hockey Hall of Fame as a builder.

JOHN BUCYK stood six feet tall and weighed 215 pounds, which made him the biggest left winger in hockey during his career. Still, he was a remarkably

fast and agile skater. Though often overshadowed by bigger stars, when Bucyk retired in 1978, he had 556 goals and 813 assists for 1,369 points—a total surpassed by only Gordie Howe, Phil Esposito and Stan Mikita at the time.

Bucyk played hockey in his hometown of Edmonton before breaking into the NHL with the Red Wings in 1955–56. He played two years in Detroit and was then traded to the Boston Bruins in a deal that returned Terry Sawchuk to the Motor City. Bucyk was teamed with Vic Stasiuk and Bronco Horvath in Boston, and the high-scoring Uke Line (short for Ukrainian) helped the Bruins reach the Stanley Cup finals in 1958 and 1959. The Bruins fell on hard times in 1959–60 and missed the playoffs eight years in a row. During that span, Bucyk led the team in goals three times and points on four occasions. He was named team captain in 1966–67.

The Bruins fortunes made a quick recovery after the NHL expanded in 1967. With Bobby Orr and Phil Esposito now on board, Boston became a powerhouse. Bucyk was a Second Team All-Star in 1967–68 and played on his first Stanley Cup champion in 1970. In 1970–71, he became just the fifth man in NHL history to score 50 goals in a season, when he had 51 at age 35 and was named to the First All-Star Team. Boston won another Stanley Cup title in 1972, and in 1973–74 Bucyk was again named captain of the team. Individual honors in his career also include the Lady Byng Trophy in 1971 and 1974. He was elected to the Hockey Hall of Fame in 1981.

BILLY BURCH was born in Yonkers, New York, but he grew up in Canada, playing amateur hockey in Toronto before joining the NHL with the Hamilton Tigers during the 1922–23 season. The following year, he was joined by brothers Red and Shorty Green, and the three formed a high-scoring forward line that soon transformed the Tigers from perennial losers to first-place finishers.

Burch led the Tigers in scoring in 1923–24 and 1924–25, earning the Hart Trophy for leading Hamilton to the top of the NHL standings during the 1924–25 campaign. The NHL season had been increased to 30 games that year, and the Hamilton players refused to take part in the postseason unless they received an additional $200 each as compensation for the extra games. As a result, the Tigers were suspended from the playoffs and Burch likely lost his best chance at the Stanley Cup.

The following season, the Hamilton club was sold and it became the New York Americans. Burch led the club in scoring once again in 1925–26, taking the Lady Byng Trophy for sportsmanlike conduct. He led the Americans in scoring once more in 1926–27. A knee injury limited his play during the 1927–28 season, but Burch remained in New York until 1932 when he was sold to Boston. He split his final season between the Bruins and the Chicago Black Hawks in 1932–33 before retiring. Burch was elected to the Hockey Hall of Fame in 1974.

PAVEL BURE Known as "the Russian Rocket," Pavel Bure was selected 113th overall by the Vancouver Canucks in the 1989 NHL Entry Draft. He then was declared draft-ineligible by NHL president John Ziegler on May 21, 1990, but the decision was reversed on June 14 and Bure was reinstated as Canucks property. He made his debut in Vancouver in 1991–92 and set a club rookie record with 34 goals. Bure became the first Canucks player to receive a major postseason award when he won the Calder Trophy as the NHL's rookie of the year that season.

In 1992–93, Bure became the first Vancouver player to top 50 goals and 100 points in a season when he scored 60 times and added 50 assists. He led the league when he scored 60 goals again in 1993–94, then led all playoff scorers with 16 goals as the Canucks reached the Stanley Cup finals before losing to the New York Rangers in seven games. Bure was named to the First All-Star Team at right wing that season. He was the Canucks scoring leader for the third year in a row in 1994–95, but injuries limited his play over the next two seasons. Healthy again in 1997–98, Bure returned to his position among the top scorers in the game with 51 goals. His brother Valeri spent three-and-a-half seasons with the Montreal Canadiens but was traded to the Calgary Flames on February 1, 1998.

Bure had established himself as a star in the Soviet Union before his arrival in the NHL. He made the Central Red Army team as a 17-year-old in 1988–89 and starred on a line with Sergei Fedorov and Alexander Mogilny on the Soviet team that won the World Junior Championship that season. Bure was selected as the tournament's top forward. He won a silver medal at the World Junior tournament in 1990 and 1991. He played for the Soviet national team at the World Championships in 1991 and 1992, winning gold and bronze.

Bure was a member of the Russian team at the World Cup of Hockey in 1996, though an injury kept him out of the tournament. He played for Russia at the Nagano Olympics in 1998 and was named the best forward at the Olympics after topping the tournament with nine goals and leading his team to a silver medal.

PAT BURNS When Pat Burns was named coach of the Boston Bruins on May 21, 1997, he joined Dick Irvin as the only men in history to coach three of the NHL's so-called "Original Six" teams. Burns began his NHL coaching career with the Montreal Canadiens in 1988–89 and guided the Toronto Maple Leafs from 1992–93 until he was fired on March 5, 1996.

Formerly an undercover police officer, Burns began his coaching career in 1983–84 with the Hull Olympiques of the Quebec Major Junior Hockey League. He coached the team for four years, reaching the Memorial Cup finals in 1986. That year, he was also an assistant coach with Team Canada, which won a silver medal at the World Junior Championships. In 1986–87, Burns moved up to the pro ranks with Montreal's American Hockey League affiliate in Sherbrooke. He was promoted to the Canadiens on June 1, 1988.

Burns set a Canadiens record for a rookie coach by guiding his team to 53 wins in 1988–89 as Montreal collected 115 points and won the Adams Division with the second-best record in the NHL. The Canadiens lost the Stanley Cup finals to the Calgary Flames, who had been first overall with 117 points, but Burns won the Jack Adams Award as coach of the year that season. He went on to be the winningest coach in hockey over his four years in Montreal with a record of 174–104–42.

On May 29, 1992, Maple Leafs president Cliff Fletcher hired Burns in Toronto and he led the team to its biggest one-season turnaround in club history. The Maple Leafs went from 67 points in 1991–92 to a club record 44 wins and 99 points in 1992–93. Toronto reached the Conference Championship that year and Burns was rewarded with his second Jack Adams Award, joining Pat Quinn as the only men ever to be named coach of the year with two different teams. Toronto reached the Conference finals again under Burns in 1993–94. His record over three-plus seasons in Toronto was 133–107–41.

Burns coached the Boston Bruins in 1997–98, directing a young club to 91 points and a fifth-place finish in the Eastern Conference. By leading his team to a 30-point improvement, Burns became the first man to win the Jack Adams Award three times.

WALTER BUSH First he brought pro hockey back to Minnesota in the form of the minor-league Minneapolis Bruins, and then Walter Bush Jr. became the driving force in landing an NHL team for the state when he, Bob McNulty and Gordon Ritz were awarded the Minnesota North Stars franchise as part of 1967 expansion. Control of the North Stars was taken over by George and Gordon Gund following the merger with the Cleveland Barons in 1978–79. Bush was chosen as vice president of the amalgamated franchise. He also served as either the North Stars' governor or alternate governor on the NHL's Board of Governors every year from 1967–68 until 1982–83.

Bush's interest in hockey began at the Breck School in Minneapolis and continued at Dartmouth College. He was working towards his law degree at the University of Minnesota when he helped organize the U.S. Central Hockey League (which became the United States Hockey League). He managed the U.S. national team in 1959 and the U.S. Olympic team in 1964, served on the United States Olympic Committee in 1963 and subsequently spent a four-year term with the USOC's hockey section and was also president and vice president of the Minnesota Amateur Hockey Association and a director of the Amateur Hockey Association of the United States.

In 1973, Walter Bush received the Lester Patrick Trophy for his contributions to hockey in the United States and was inducted into the United States Hockey Hall of Fame as an administrator in 1980.

JACK BUTTERFIELD A long-time executive of the Springfield Indians, Jack Butterfield became president of the American Hockey League in 1966. He ushered the league through a difficult era of NHL expansion and the rise of the World Hockey Association, which threatened to kill minor pro hockey. He is credited as being the man most responsible for keeping the game alive at that level. Butterfield stayed on as AHL president until 1994–95, watching his league flourish before his promotion to chairman of the board. No one in league history has served a longer term as president.

In his youth, Butterfield had been a hockey player until an injury cut short his career. He served in the Royal Canadian Air Force from 1940 to 1945 and later worked for teams owned and/or operated by his uncle, Eddie Shore, in New Haven of the AHL, Fort Worth of the United States Hockey League and Oakland of the Western Hockey League. With Shore's Springfield Indians, he worked in a variety of roles, including coach and general manager. He was general manager of the Springfield club that won the Calder Cup three years in a row between 1960 and 1962, making him the only g.m. in AHL history to win three consecutive championships.

Butterfield was elected to the Hockey Hall of Fame as a builder in 1980. A trophy bearing his name has been presented to the most valuable player in the AHL playoffs since 1983–84. He won the Lester Patrick Trophy for outstanding service to hockey in the United States in 1985.

HERB CAIN set an NHL record for points in a single season when he led the league with 82 in 1943–44. Cain's record was accomplished when the NHL played a 50-game regular-season schedule and was not surpassed until Gordie Howe had 86 points in 70 games in 1950–51.

Cain made his NHL debut with the Montreal Maroons in 1933–34. The following season, he led the Maroons with 20 goals (making him one of only 11 players in the NHL to score 20 or more goals that season) as the Montreal team won the Stanley Cup. When financial problems forced the Maroons to fold

after the 1937–38 season, Cain joined the Montreal Canadiens in 1938–39 but was traded to the Boston Bruins for the 1939–40 campaign.

Cain played on a line with Bill Cowley and Mel Hill with Boston and the trio proved to be an effective combination though they played second fiddle to the Bruins' great Kraut Line of Milt Schmidt, Woody Dumart and Bobby Bauer who finished 1–2–3 in the NHL scoring race that season. In 1940–41, Cowley won the scoring title and the Bruins won the Stanley Cup.

By the 1943–44 season, Cain was playing on a line with Cowley and Art Jackson. The Bruins had been weakened by the loss of the Kraut Line and goalie Frank Brimsek to military service and finished out of the playoffs that year despite Cain's record-breaking offensive totals. Even though he won the scoring title that year, Cain was only named to the Second All-Star Team at left wing while Doug Bentley (who had finished second to Cain with 77 points) earned the First-Team selection.

Cain followed up his 36-goal, 46-assist season of 1943–44 with a team leading 35 goals in 1944–45 but his point total dropped to 45. He played just one more year in Boston but at the time he left the NHL after the 1945–46 season he was one of only 20 players who had played in the league since 1927 to score 200 career goals (206). Cain continued to play with the Hershey Bears of the American Hockey League for four more seasons.

FRANK CALDER had been the secretary of the National Hockey Association before that league disbanded, and he was elected as the first president when the old association was re-formed as the National Hockey League in November of 1917. From the hectic formative years of the NHL through many rule changes and disputes, Calder sat at the head of the league as its guiding light.

Calder presided over the NHL's growth from four teams in 1917–18 to a high of 10 teams by 1930–31 before the Great Depression saw the league cut back to what would become known as the "Original Six" in 1942–43. It was Calder who announced on September 28, 1942, that the governments of Canada and the United States wanted the NHL to remain operating through the war years in the interest of public morale. On February 4, 1943, Calder died after suffering a heart attack.

Since 1936–37, Frank Calder had been buying a trophy each season to present to the player voted as rookie of the year. In his honor, the Calder Memorial Trophy was donated by the NHL after his death. In 1947, he was elected to the Hockey Hall of Fame.

ANGUS CAMPBELL played on championship teams in hockey and lacrosse while attending the University of Toronto. He also played professional hockey with the Cobalt Silver Kings, where he took part in the 1909–10 inaugural season of the National Hockey Association. In 1911, Campbell returned to play hockey in the northern Ontario silver mining town upon graduation from U of T with a Bachelor of Science degree in mining engineering. He was active as a player there until 1919–20.

After his hockey career, Campbell played an important part in the development of amateur hockey in northern Ontario. He became the first president of the Northern Ontario Hockey Association when the league was founded in 1919, later becoming an executive of the Ontario Hockey Association. Campbell was elected to the Hockey Hall of Fame as a builder in 1964.

CLARENCE CAMPBELL served as president of the National Hockey League from 1946 until 1971. A Rhodes Scholar at Oxford, Campbell had distinguished himself as a lawyer, then as a Canadian military officer in World War II. He commanded the 4th Canadian Armed Division headquarters throughout operations in Europe and joined the Canadian War Crimes Unit in 1945. He was again practicing law in Montreal when he was chosen to succeed Red Dutton as NHL president. Campbell had worked as a sports administrator and had been a referee in lacrosse and in the NHL prior to the war.

Campbell governed the NHL through much of the six-team era and successfully guided the league through expansion in 1967. By the time he retired in 1977, the NHL had grown to 18 teams. He also had helped pioneer the NHL Pension Society in 1946. In 1966, Campbell was elected to the Hockey Hall of Fame as a builder. The playoff champion in the NHL's Western Conference is presented with the Clarence Campbell Bowl.

HARRY CAMERON No defenseman in the history of Stanley Cup competition prior to 1926 scored more goals than Harry Cameron. He almost invariably topped his fellow defensive players in scoring, often ranking among the league leaders in the NHL. Cameron was reputed to have the ability to curve his shots without making modifications to his stick.

Feuds with management occasionally caused him to be traded, but after making his pro debut with Toronto in 1912–13, Cameron almost always found his way back to that city. He was with the Toronto Blueshirts when they won the Stanley Cup in 1914, he was a member of the team known as the Toronto Arenas when they won in 1918, and he played for the Toronto St. Patricks Stanley Cup team of 1922. Cameron finally left Toronto for good in November of 1923 when he was sent to the Saskatoon Sheiks (who became the Saskatoon Crescents that season) of the Western Canada Hockey League.

After professional hockey collapsed in the west in 1926, Cameron continued to play in the minor leagues, later coaching in Saskatoon. He was elected to the Hockey Hall of Fame in 1962.

WAYNE CASHMAN was a fierce competitor over a 17-year NHL playing career spent entirely in Boston. A tough and gritty forward, he embodied the image of "the Big Bad Bruins." Cashman played on Stanley Cup winners in 1970 and 1972 and had eight seasons with more than 20 goals, often playing alongside Phil Esposito and Ken Hodge on the team's top line. His best year was 1973–74 when he had 30 goals and 59 assists to finish fourth in scoring in the NHL behind Esposito, Bobby Orr, and Hodge. Cashman was selected to the Second All-Star Team that year. He was captain of the Bruins from 1977–78 until his retirement in 1983.

In 1986, Cashman joined the New York Rangers as a scout then spent the next five seasons as an assistant coach. From 1992–93 to 1995–96, he worked with Terry Crisp as an assistant coach for the Tampa Bay Lightning. He was an assistant with the San Jose Sharks in 1996–97 and was on the staff of Canada's winning entry at the World Hockey Championships that spring. Cashman finally got a head coaching job when he was hired to run the Philadelphia Flyers on July 7, 1997, but midway through the season (March 9, 1998) he was demoted to assistant coach after the Flyers hired Roger Neilson.

JOSEPH CATTARINICH excelled at lacrosse while playing hockey as a goaltender. He was a member of the original Montreal Canadiens in the first season of the National Hockey Association in 1909–10, but after seeing Georges Vezina in action during a game against Chicoutimi, Cattarinich convinced the Canadiens to sign the future star for the 1910–11 season.

On November 3, 1921, Cattarinich, Leo Dandurand and Louis Letourneau purchased the Canadiens for $11,000, later acquiring such stars at Aurel Joliat and Howie Morenz. The Canadiens won the Stanley Cup in 1924, 1930 and 1931 before Letourneau retired. Cattarinich and Dandurand kept the team until 1935, when Depression-era economics forced them to sell it for $165,000. In 1977, Cattarinich was inducted into the Hockey Hall of Fame as a builder.

JOE CAVANAGH was one of the greatest prep school hockey players in New England history. He was raised in a family of eight in Warwick, Rhode Island, and starred with the Cranston Thunderbolts in his high school years. A talented forward known for his hard work on the ice, he led the state in scoring in 1964, 1965 and 1966, was named all-State three times and was chosen Rhode Island's most valuable high school player in 1965 and 1966.

Cavanagh carried on his career as a star player at Harvard for three seasons. Freshmen were not allowed to participate in varsity athletics at the time, but he made a big impression during his sophomore season of 1968–69: He was named a First Team all-American as well as first team all-East, first team all-Ivy League and first team all-New England; he won the Walter Brown Award as the best American-born player in the East; and he was named MVP at the annual Beanpot Tournament (a Boston area event involving Boston University, Boston College, Northeastern and Harvard) after Harvard defeated Boston University for the coveted trophy. Then he repeated all of his First Team honors in both his junior and senior seasons, won the John Tudor Memorial Cup as Harvard's most valuable player both years and added another Walter Brown Award after his senior year. He set a school record with 50 assists in his senior season and was the school's leading scorer all three years that he played. Cavanagh is still one of Harvard's all-time leading scorers with 187 points on 60 goals and 127 assists and was named to the Eastern Collegiate Athletic Conference's all-decade first all-star team.

Now an attorney in the Warwick area, Cavanagh has continued his interest in hockey through youth leagues in his community. He was enshrined in the United States Hockey Hall of Fame in 1994.

LEN CEGLARSKI became the winningest coach in NCAA history with 673 victories over a 34-year career at Clarkson College and Boston College. He was also the first coach ever to have more than 250 victories at two schools, posting a 254–97–10 record in 14 years at Clarkson and 419–242–27 in 20 years with Boston College.

Ceglarski had been a star player at Boston College prior to his coaching career. He was an all-American as a junior and captained the Eagles hockey team in his senior year. Ceglarski ranked fourth on the school's all-time scoring list with 108 points on 49 goals and 59 assists despite playing only 52 games. In 1949, he scored the tying goal as Boston College went on to defeat Dartmouth 4–3 for the NCAA championships. Ceglarski also was a fine baseball player, earning his letter three times in that sport.

Ceglarski was a member of the silver medal-winning U.S. Olympic hockey team in Oslo in 1952, then served in the Marine Corps before returning to the Boston area to begin his coaching career. He coached high school hockey at Norwood and Walpole and won the New England championship with Walpole in 1957–58. That fall, he became head coach at Clarkson.

In 14 seasons at Clarkson, Ceglarski's teams topped 20 wins six times and set a school record for victories with a 28–4–0 record in 1970–71. His Knights made 11 consecutive trips to the Eastern Collegiate Athletic Conference tour-

nament and won the championship once. Clarkson also played in the NCAA tournament four times and reached the title game in 1962, 1966 and 1970.

Ceglarski returned to his alma mater in 1972 to replace his old coach, Snooks Kelley, who had been the first college coach ever to win 500 games. Ceglarski carried on the winning tradition as his school won the ECAC tournament in 1972–73 and reached the NCAA final four. Ceglarski received his first of three Spencer Penrose Awards as the nation's top college coach that year. His team won the ECAC title again in 1977–78, and when Hockey East began in 1984–85, the Eagles won six of the first seven league championships.

Boston College made nine more trips to the NCAA tournament and set a school record with a 31–8–0 mark in 1986–87, but Ceglarski was never able to win the NCAA championship as a coach. He was elected to the United States Hockey Hall of Fame in the coaches category in 1992.

LORNE CHABOT At 6'1" and 185 pounds, Lorne Chabot was a large man in an era of small goaltenders. He was a star at Port Arthur, leading the Bearcats to Allan Cup championships in 1924–25 and 1925–26 and was signed by Conn Smythe for the New York Rangers after beating Smythe's University of Toronto team in the Allan Cup playoffs. When Smythe was fired, Lester Patrick rotated Chabot with Hal Winkler in the Rangers goal before Chabot won the job outright. In his second year, he helped the Rangers win the Stanley Cup, though it was during the final series in 1928 that he had to be replaced after a serious cut above his eye.

Chabot was traded to the Toronto Maple Leafs prior to the 1928–29 campaign and posted career bests with 12 shutouts and a 1.56 goals-against average that season. He helped the Leafs win their first Stanley Cup title in 1931–32, but was traded to the Montreal Canadiens for George Hainsworth following the 1932–33 season. After another excellent year, Chabot was packaged with Howie Morenz and Marty Burke and traded to the Chicago Black Hawks for Lionel Conacher, Roger Jenkins and Leroy Goldsworthy.

In Chicago, Chabot replaced Charlie Gardner, who had won the Vezina Trophy and led Chicago to the Stanley Cup in 1934 before dying of a brian tumor. He proved worthy of the challenge, leading the league with a 1.83 goals-against average, winning the Vezina Trophy, and being named to the First All-Star Team. However, Chabot lost his job to Mike Karakas the following season. After refusing a demotion to the minors, he eventually finished the year with the Montreal Maroons. Chabot saw limited action with the New York Americans in 1936–37, then retired.

Lorne Chabot's total of 73 shutouts are exceeded by only seven goalies in NHL history, and his career goals-against average of 2.04 ranks among the greatest ever. He also played in the two longest games in NHL history, earning a shutout in Toronto's 1–0 win over Boston at 104:46 of overtime in 1933, and losing 1–0 to the Detroit Red Wings after 116:30 of overtime with the Maroons in 1936.

BILL CHADWICK joined the NHL as a linesman in 1939–40. The following year, he became a referee and was one of the best in hockey until his retirement in 1955. He is credited with devising the system of hand signals by which referees identify the type of penalty that has been called.

Chadwick's association with hockey began in his hometown of New York, where he played with the Stock Exchange team in the local Metropolitan League. His play earned him a promotion to the New York Rovers of the Eastern Amateur Hockey League, where, while sitting out with injuries, he was asked to substitute for a referee who had failed to appear. In 1964, he was inducted into the Hockey Hall of Fame. Ten years later, Chadwick was the first referee inducted into the United States Hockey Hall of Fame.

RAY CHAISSON centered one of the greatest lines in the history of American college hockey with wingers Al Dumon and John Pryor during their days at Boston College. Chaisson led all scorers in the East in 1939–40 and 1940–41, when he had 67 and 59 points respectively. He had five goals in a game against Cornell during the 1939–40 season and 33 goals in just 18 games that year. His 29 goals in 14 games in 1940–41 give him an average of 2.07 goals per game, which is the best in his college's history. His eight hat tricks also set a school record.

Service in the United States Navy during World War II cut short Chaisson's college career after just two seasons, though he continued to play with the Boston Olympics, New York Rovers and Philadelphia Falcons in the Eastern Amateur Hockey League until 1943–44. After the war, Chaisson played senior amateur hockey with the Los Angeles Monarchs in the Pacific Coast Hockey League in 1946–47 and 1947–48. He was inducted into the U.S. Hockey Hall of Fame in 1974.

JOHN CHASE began his formal hockey career at Milton Academy in his hometown of Milton, Massachusetts in 1922–23. He transferred to Exeter Academy the following year, then enrolled at Harvard in the fall of 1924. A center, he was taking a regular shift in his freshman season, then became a first-line player on the varsity club for the next three years. He captained the team as a senior. In addition to starring in hockey at Harvard, Chase also excelled at baseball, which he later played in top amateur leagues.

Chase was highly sought by professional teams after graduating in 1928 but chose to pursue a career in business instead. He did continue playing amateur hockey, however, with such teams as the Boston Athletic Association, Boston University Club and the Brac Burn Hockey Club. In 1932, he captained the silver medal-winning United States team at the Lake Placid Olympics.

After his playing career, Chase returned to Harvard and coached the varsity team from 1942 through 1950. He became a charter member of the United States Hockey Hall of Fame in 1973.

GERRY CHEEVERS was at his best in big games. He was perhaps the greatest clutch goaltender in the NHL during the 1970s, helping the Boston Bruins to win the Stanley Cup in both 1970 and 1972 and to reach the Stanley Cup finals in 1976 and 1977. Cheevers played a scrambling style, ranging far from his crease to handle the puck, pass to his defenseman and challenge opposing shooters. He was also one of the first goalies to decorate his mask, painting stitches to represent the injuries he might have suffered without it.

Cheevers was a product of the Maple Leafs system who played just two games in Toronto (in 1961–62) before being drafted by Boston in 1965. By 1967–68, Cheevers was the top goalie in Boston, sharing the load with Ed Johnston as the Bruins emerged from a terrible decade in the 1960s to become an NHL powerhouse during the 1970s. In 1971–72, Cheevers set an NHL record by going undefeated in 32 games (24 wins and eight ties) but, at the height of his career, he left Boston in 1972–73 to join the World Hockey Association. Cheevers spent three-and-a-half years as one of the top goaltenders in the WHA with the Cleveland Crusaders before returning to Boston during the 1975–76 season.

Problems with his knees forced Cheevers to retire after the 1979–80 season and he was named coach of the Bruins in July of 1980. His teams were successful for four years, but Cheevers was fired in February of 1985, midway through a subpar season. He was inducted into the Hockey Hall of Fame later that same year.

CHRIS CHELIOS became the first American-born defenseman to win the Norris Trophy when he received the award as a member of the Montreal Canadiens in 1988–89. Chelios was also the Norris Trophy winner with the Chicago Blackhawks in 1992–93 and 1995–96. The 1995–96 season also saw him tie his own club record for a defenseman with 58 assists and become the first blueliner in Blackhawks history to lead the team in scoring.

A native of Chicago who played NCAA hockey at the University of Wisconsin, Chelios entered the NHL with the Canadiens in 1983–84 and was named to the All-Rookie Team. He was a member of Montreal's Stanley Cup-winning team of 1986 and played four more years with the club before being traded for Denis Savard on June 29, 1990. Combining both good offensive skills and an aggressive defensive game, Chelios' reputation as one of the best players at his position was established firmly after his arrival in Chicago.

Internationally, Chelios represented the United States at the World Junior Championships in 1982 and played for both the U.S. National and Olympic team in 1983–84. He was a member of the American squad at the 1991 Canada Cup and a key contributor to the U.S. team that beat Canada at the World Cup of Hockey in 1996. Chelios also played for the U.S. Olympic team in Nagano in 1998.

DON CHERRY was a much-traveled minor-league defenseman who saw action in just one NHL game during a pro career that stretched from 1954 to 1972. He came to prominence in the mid 1970s as the flamboyant coach of the Boston Bruins and later gained fame as a colorful television commentator.

Cherry was signed by Boston in 1952 and assigned to the club's junior franchise in Barrie of the Ontario Hockey Association. He won the Memorial Cup with Barrie in 1952–53 before turning professional with the Bruins' American Hockey League affiliate in Hershey in 1954. On March 31, 1955, he made his NHL debut in a 5–1 Boston playoff loss to the Montreal Canadiens. Cherry would later be property of the Detroit Red Wings, Canadiens, and Toronto Maple Leafs, but would never again play another NHL game.

Cherry earned a number of minor-league titles in his career, winning the Calder Cup as AHL champion in Springfield in 1960, and again with Rochester in 1965, 1966 and 1968. He won the Presidents Cup as champion of the Western Hockey League with Vancouver in 1969, then retired prior to the 1969–70 season. He was back playing with Rochester in 1971–72, and took over as head coach later in the season. He was named coach of the year in the AHL in 1973–74 and was then hired to coach the Bruins.

Cherry coached Boston for five seasons, winning the Adams Division title four times and earning the Jack Adams Award as coach of the year in 1975–76. His teams, though, could never get past the Canadiens in the playoffs, losing twice to Montreal in the finals and once in a memorable semifinal in 1979. When his demand for a raise wasn't met, Cherry left Boston to become coach of the Colorado Rockies in 1979–80. After a dismal 19–48–13 season, he left coaching and soon moved into television, where he became an outspoken advocate of physical hockey and all things Canadian.

BILL CHRISTIAN belongs to one of the most prominent families in U.S. hockey history. His father, Ed Christian, helped build the arena that housed the

famed Warroad Lakers in Warroad, Minnesota. Bill and his brother, Roger, were both long-time stars of the team and members of the gold medal-winning 1960 U.S. Olympic hockey team. Bill's son Dave played for the 1980 "Miracle on Ice" gold medal team and went on to a long career in the NHL.

Bill Christian first got attention in hockey when he led his Warroad team to the finals of the second-ever Minnesota state youth tournament in 1952. Warroad was beaten by Eveleth, but Christian was named the tournament's most valuable player. The next year, he led Warroad High School to the finals of the state high school tournament.

After high school, he played one year for the University of Minnesota under coach John Mariucci before joining the 1957–58 U.S. national team that became the first American athletic club ever to play in the Soviet Union. Bill Christian also played for the U.S. national team in 1960, 1962, 1964 and 1965 and is best remembered for his contributions in 1960, when he scored two goals in a 3–2 win over the Soviet Union that all but clinched the gold medal at the Squaw Valley Olympic Games.

In addition to his international experience, Bill Christian was a long-time member of the Warroad Lakers and played for 23 years before retiring after the 1979–80 season. The team never had a losing record during that time, winning the Canadian intermediate title in 1964 and 1974 and the Manitoba senior hockey title in 1969 and 1970. With the Lakers, Bill played with his brother, Roger, and also with sons Dave and Eddie. In 1964, he and other members of the dynasty helped start a hockey stick company, Christian Brothers Inc. He was also a successful coach in youth hockey in Warroad.

Bill Christian was enshrined in the United States Hockey Hall of Fame in 1984. Roger Christian was inducted five years later.

ROGER CHRISTIAN The older brother of fellow U.S. Hockey Hall of Fame member Bill Christian, Roger Christian also had a lengthy career with the Warroad Lakers and representing his country in international hockey. He started playing high school hockey in Warroad, Minnesota in 1950, led the team in scoring in 1952 and helped it reach the finals of the state tournament in 1953. He was named all-Region twice during his high school career and to the all-State team once. Both he and Bill played with the 1958 U.S. national team that was the first American club ever to play in the Soviet Union; both were members of the gold medal-winning U.S. Olympic team in Squaw Valley, California, in 1960; and both played again with U.S. national teams in 1962, 1964 and 1965. Roger later played 18 years with the Warroad Lakers, who retired his uniform number (7) in 1974. He was elected to the U.S. Hockey Hall of Fame in 1989, five years after Bill.

DINO CICCARELLI Though Dino Ciccarelli had 72 goals and 70 assists for the London Knights of the Ontario Hockey Association in 1977–78, he went undrafted because of a serious knee injury the following season. The Minnesota North Stars signed him as a free agent in 1979 and he made his NHL debut with the club in 1980–81. Ciccarelli set a rookie record by scoring 14 goals in the playoffs that year as the North Stars reached the Stanley Cup finals. He has gone on to become one of the top goal scorers in NHL history. On February 3, 1998 he became just the ninth player to score 600 career goals in the National Hockey League.

In his first full season with the North Stars in 1981–82, Ciccarelli collected 55 goals and cracked the top 10 in scoring with 106 points. His 52 goals and 103 points in 1986–87 resulted in another top-10 finish, and Ciccarelli never fell below 37 goals in any full season in Minnesota prior to his trade to the Washington Capitals on March 7, 1989. Ciccarelli led Minnesota in goal-scoring five times and his total of 332 ranks behind only Brian Bellows (342) in the history of the North Stars franchise.

Ciccarelli led the Capitals with 41 goals and 79 points in 1989–90 and scored 41 again in his first season with the Detroit Red Wings in 1992–93. He was with the Red Wings when they reached the Stanley Cup finals in 1995 and was a member of the club that set an NHL record with 62 wins in 1995–96, but he was traded to the Tampa Bay Lightning on August 27, 1996. In his first season with Tampa Bay, Ciccarelli set a club record with 35 goals. He was dealt to the Florida Panthers on January 16, 1998.

KING CLANCY Francis Michael "King" Clancy entered the NHL as an 18-year-old in 1921–22, and he remained a part of the game until his death on November 8, 1986. His father also had been an outstanding athlete, and it was from him that he inherited his regal nickname. Clancy was among the smallest defensemen ever to play in the NHL, but he never backed down from his larger opponents.

Clancy played amateur hockey in his hometown of Ottawa before signing with the Senators in 1921–22. He and Frank Boucher were little-used spare players that season, but while Boucher left for Vancouver the following year, Clancy stayed in Ottawa to become a regular on defense alongside George Boucher after Eddie Gerard's retirement in 1923. Clancy helped Ottawa win the Stanley Cup in 1924 and in 1927, but the Senators played in the NHL's smallest market and the team was hit hard by the Depression. Many star players had to be sold after 1927, and the sale of King Clancy to the Toronto Maple Leafs for $35,000 (and players Art Smith and Eric Pettinger) before the

1930–31 season was then considered the biggest deal in hockey history.

Conn Smythe expected Clancy to be the spark his team needed to achieve greatness, and he was right. Clancy helped the Maple Leafs win the Stanley Cup in just his second season. The club won three Canadian Division titles and was on its way to a fourth when he retired early in 1936–37. Clancy had been a First or Second Team All-Star four years in a row from 1930–31 to 1933–34, and he consistently ranked among the top-scoring defensemen in the NHL.

After leaving Toronto, Clancy coached the Montreal Maroons for the first half of the 1937–38 season, then becoming a referee. He returned to the Maple Leafs to coach the team from 1953 to 1956 before becoming an assistant general manager under Punch Imlach. Clancy also served emergency stints behind the Leafs bench in 1966–67 and 1972–73 before settling into a role as the club's goodwill ambassador. He had been inducted as a member of the Hockey Hall of Fame in 1958.

DIT CLAPPER Aubrey "Dit" Clapper was the first man to play 20 seasons in the NHL, spending them all with the Boston Bruins between 1927–28 and 1946–47. He was one of the top-scoring right wingers in the game during his first 10 years, then one of the league's best defensemen over the final 10. He is the only player in NHL history to be named to the all-star team as a forward and a defenseman.

Clapper was only 13 years old when he played junior hockey in Oshawa and just 20 when he joined the Bruins. At 6'2" and 200 pounds, he was one of the biggest men of his era. He played on a line with Cooney Weiland and Dutch Gainor that quickly became Boston's best scoring unit, helping the Bruins to win the Stanley Cup in 1928–29. The trio then helped the team to rewrite the NHL record book when Boston went 38–5–1 in 1929–30, establishing the best single-season winning percentage in history. Clapper enjoyed his most productive season that year with 41 goals and 20 assists in 44 games, while Weiland topped the NHL with 43 goals and 30 assists. Clapper earned his first All-Star selection the following year when he was chosen to the Second Team. Another All-Star selection came in 1934–35 while playing on a line with Nels Stewart and Charlie Sands.

By the 1937–38 season, the Bruins had added star forwards like Bill Cowley, Milt Schmidt, Bobby Bauer and Woody Dumart to the roster, so coach Art Ross converted Clapper to defense. Paired with the great Eddie Shore, both players were chosen to the First All-Star Team in 1938–39 after the Bruins won the Stanley Cup. Clapper played with Flash Hollett the following year while adding another First Team All-Star selection. He then made it three in a row after another Stanley Cup win in 1940–41. He earned a Second Team berth in 1944–45, and he became a playing coach with the Bruins the following year.

On February 12, 1947, Dit Clapper retired as a player and was inducted immediately into the Hockey Hall of Fame. He continued to coach the Bruins until 1949. Clapper returned to hockey from business life to coach the Buffalo Bisons of the American Hockey League in 1959–60.

DONALD CLARK exhibited an aptitude for sports as a boy in Faribault, Minnesota, where he played high school baseball, hockey and football. He later played amateur baseball in the Southern Minnesota League and amateur hockey in the Minneapolis-St. Paul area. In October 1947, Clark founded the Minnesota Amateur Hockey Association with Bob Ridder and Everett "Buck" Riley and helped build it into the most successful organization of its kind in the United States. Clark served as president of the MAHA from 1954 to 1957 and was the organization's secretary-treasurer from 1949 to 1955 and again from 1958 until 1974.

Clark also had an active interest in the national aspects of hockey in the United States, and in 1958 he was the manager of the first U.S. national team to travel to the Soviet Union. He also began a lengthy term as vice president of the Amateur Hockey Association of the United States that year. In 1975, Clark was awarded the Lester Patrick Trophy for service to hockey in the United States and was inducted into the United States Hockey Hall of Fame as an administrator in 1978. He has also served as the Hall's president.

BOBBY CLARKE was diagnosed with diabetes at age 15, but despite the illness he became a junior hockey star in his hometown of Flin Flon, Manitoba and went on to a 15-year NHL playing career as the heart and soul of the Philadelphia Flyers. Clarke captained the Flyers Stanley Cup-winning teams of 1974 and 1975 and won the Hart Trophy as NHL MVP in 1972–73, 1974–75 and 1975–76. He was an NHL All-Star at center four years in a row between 1972–73 and 1975–76, twice each on the First and Second Teams. He was elected to the Hockey Hall of Fame in 1987.

Clarke led the Western Canada Hockey League in both assists and points with Flin Flon in 1967–68 and 1968–69 and was selected by the Flyers in the second round of the NHL Amateur Draft in 1969. His point totals increased steadily over his first three seasons, and in his fourth year he became the first player from an NHL expansion team to top 100 points, finishing second in the league with 104 points. He was named Flyers captain that season. Clarke remained among the top scorers in the NHL over the next five years, establishing a career high with 119 points in 1975–76 when he was runner-up to

Guy Lafleur for the Art Ross Trophy. Clarke's 89 assists in both 1974–75 and 1975–76 was a single-season record for a center until Wayne Gretzky broke it.

In addition to his offensive talent, Clarke was one of the NHL's best face-off men and an excellent two-way player who won the Selke Trophy as the NHL's best defensive forward in 1982–83. Other honors during Clarke's career include the Bill Masterton Trophy for perseverance and dedication to hockey in 1971–72 and the Lester Patrick Trophy for contributions to hockey in the United States in 1979–80. The trophy awarded to the leading scorer in the Western Hockey League is named in his honor.

Clarke retired as a player after the 1983–84 season as the leading scorer in Flyers history with 1,120 points on 358 goals and 852 assists. He was immediately named general manager in Philadelphia and oversaw the Flyers squads that made the Cup finals in 1985 and 1987. He then left to become g.m. and vice president of the Minnesota North Stars in 1990. In 1993–94, Clarke served as g.m. and vice president of the expansion Florida Panthers. He returned to Philadelphia as president and general manager on June 15, 1994. Clarke served as one of four general managers for Canada's victorious Canada Cup team in 1987 and was head g.m. of Canada's Olympic team in 1998.

JAMES CLAYPOOL was born in Hibbing, Minnesota, but attended prep school in Pennsylvania and played hockey at the University of Michigan in 1941–42 before he settled in Duluth, Minnesota, where he helped coordinate the building of neighborhood rinks and hockey programs while raising his family there. He became president of the Minnesota Amateur Hockey Association in 1957 and managed the 1960 United States Olympic hockey team that won a surprising gold medal at the Games in Squaw Valley, California. Then he went back to Duluth and renewed his involvement in youth hockey. In 1965, he managed the Duluth peewee team that won the national championship and during the 1970s he coordinated the construction of new indoor arenas to strengthen youth and high school hockey in his community. Claypool was inducted into the United States Hockey Hall of Fame as an administrator in 1995.

BILL CLEARY played on the silver medal-winning American Olympic team in 1956 and also represented the U.S. at the 1959 World Championships, then culminated his international career as the leading scorer on the gold medal-winning U.S. Olympic hockey team in 1960. He collected 14 points on seven goals and seven assists and scoring the first goal in a key 3–2 win over the Soviet Union in the second-last game that all but clinched the surprising gold medal victory in the tournament.

Cleary was a native of Cambridge, Massachusetts who gained hockey stardom during a standout career at Harvard. In his best season (1954–55), he set an NCAA single-season scoring record with 89 points and a Harvard record with 42 goals. He also set a school record with eight assists in a game and tied a record with a six-goal game. Cleary led Harvard to a 17–3–1 record that year as the Crimson team won both the Beanpot Tournament (a Boston area event involving Boston University, Boston College, Northeastern and Harvard) and the Ivy League championship and finished third at the NCAA hockey tournament. Cleary earned all-Ivy League, all-East and all-American honors that same season, won the John Tudor Cup as Harvard's most valuable player and was also named MVP in New England.

Cleary succeeded Cooney Weiland as head coach of the Harvard hockey team in March of 1971 – having handled the freshmen since 1968 and acted as Weiland's assistant in 1970 – and kept the position for the next 19 years, retiring after the 1989–90 season with a record of 324–201–22. During his tenure, Harvard reached the final four of the NCAA tournament seven times and played in the championship game three times, winning it all in 1988–89. Cleary also guided Harvard to 11 Ivy League crowns, four Beanpot championships and the Eastern Collegiate Athletic Conference tournament title in 1982–83 and 1986–87.

Bill Cleary was inducted into the United States Hockey Hall of Fame in 1976 and was joined by his brother Bob five years later.

BOB CLEARY Like his older brother Bill, Bob Cleary played prep school hockey at Belmont Hill before going on to a stellar career at Harvard.

Cleary led Belmont Hill to three consecutive Massachusetts private school championships while at the same time playing on the National junior champion on Cusick team in the Amateur Hockey Association of the United States in 1952–53 and 1953–54. When his Harvard career began, he set a freshman record with 77 points, then went on to the varsity team in 1955–56 and amassed 202 points on 100 goals and 102 assists over three seasons, topping the nation in scoring in both 1956–57 and 1957–58. In his senior year, Cleary served as team captain, led Harvard to a fourth-place finish at the NCAA hockey tournament for the second straight year, won his second consecutive Walter Brown Trophy as the outstanding player at an Eastern college and was selected as an all-American.

In 1959, Cleary played for the U.S. national team at the World Championships and in 1960 he was a late addition to the U.S. Olympic team. Cleary teamed with his brother Bill, and former Harvard teammate Bob McVey to form a high-scoring line that helped the Americans win a surprising

gold medal. Bob Cleary was inducted into the U.S. Hockey Hall of Fame in 1981, five years after his brother.

ODIE CLEGHORN was a strong stickhandler and impressive goal scorer who was one of few players to top 200 career goals during the era in which he played. While not quite possessing the fiery temper of his Hall of Fame brother Sprague, Odie was an aggressive player who was skilled in the art of stick-swinging and butt-ending. As a coach in the 1920s, he popularized the concept of changing lines on the fly.

The Cleghorn brothers both played with the Renfrew Millionaires during the 1910–11 National Hockey Association season and moved on to the Montreal Wanderers the following year. Odie was a high-scoring right winger and center, while Sprague was a skilled rushing defenseman. Neither player was with the team when it became a founding member of the NHL in 1917–18, as Sprague was out with a broken leg and Odie had a military exception that would have been voided if he played hockey.

Odie made his NHL debut with the Montreal Canadiens in 1918–19 and finished second in the league behind teammate Newsy Lalonde with 21 goals. He and his brother were reunited when Sprague joined the Canadiens in 1921–22, and both were members of the club's Stanley Cup-winning team of 1923–24. After one more season in Montreal, Sprague was sent to the Boston Bruins, while Odie joined the Pittsburgh Pirates.

Odie Cleghorn was both player and coach with the NHL's new Pittsburgh franchise. He was even forced to play a game in goal during the 1925–26 season when Roy Worters had pneumonia. (When Lester Patrick went in goal for the Rangers during the 1928 Stanley Cup final, it was Cleghorn who took over behind the New York bench.) After coaching the Pirates until 1928–29, Odie served as an NHL referee in the 1930s. He died on July 13, 1956, two days after the death of his brother Sprague.

SPRAGUE CLEGHORN was one of the game's greatest but roughest defensemen. He spent 17 seasons in either the National Hockey Association or the NHL as a star who often let his temper get the better of him.

After a year with the New York Crescents of the American Hockey Association, Sprague Cleghorn and his brother Odie joined the Renfrew Millionaires for the 1910–11 NHA season. Sprague started as a forward, but he moved back to team with Cyclone Taylor on the Renfrew defense. Soon, he was emulating Taylor's rushing style. The brothers joined the Montreal Wanderers for the 1911–12 season and remained there through 1916–17, Odie as a high-scoring right winger and Sprague as an offensive defenseman.

A broken leg kept Cleghorn off the ice during the NHL's inaugural season of 1917–18, but he was back in action the following year as a member of the Ottawa Senators. He joined an Ottawa defense that already featured Eddie Gerard and George Boucher, helping the team win the Stanley Cup in 1920. Cleghorn was with the Toronto St. Pats the following season, but he returned to Ottawa during the playoffs and helped them win another Stanley Cup title.

In 1921–22, Sprague joined his brother Odie with the Montreal Canadiens, where he was constantly involved in brawls with his former Ottawa teammates. His suspension after attacking Lionel Hitchman in the 1923 playoffs may have cost Montreal a chance at the Stanley Cup that season, though he did help the team win it all in 1924.

After one more year in Montreal, Cleghorn was sent to Boston, while his brother joined the Pittsburgh Pirates. Ironically, Cleghorn teamed with Lionel Hitchman on the Boston defense until the arrival of Eddie Shore. His final NHL season was 1927–28. Sprague Cleghorn died on July 11, 1956. His brother Odie died two days later. He was elected to the Hockey Hall of Fame in 1958.

REAL CLOUTIER was a high-scoring star with the Quebec Remparts of the Quebec Major Junior Hockey League who carried that success forward first to the World Hockey Association and then to the NHL as a member of the Quebec Nordiques. Cloutier recorded a hat trick in his first NHL game on October 10, 1979, tying a league record set by Alex Smart in 1942–43.

Cloutier collected 93 goals and 123 assists in his final junior season of 1973–74 and, after struggling as a rookie, had 60 goals and 54 assists in his second WHA season of 1975–76. A league scoring title came the following year when he had 141 points on 66 goals and 75 assists. Cloutier was second to Nordiques teammate Marc Tardif in league scoring with 129 points in 1977–78, then won a second scoring title in the WHA's final campaign of 1978–79. His 75 goals that season were the second-highest one-year total in league history behind Bobby Hull's record 77 goals in 1974–75. Cloutier ranks third all-time on the WHA career goal-scoring list (283) and is tied for fourth in total points (566).

While never reaching the lofty totals of his WHA days, Cloutier remained an effective scorer after Quebec entered the NHL in 1979–80. He had 42 goals and 47 assists in his first season and established personal NHL bests with 60 assists and 97 points in 1981–82. Dealt to the Buffalo Sabres on June 8, 1983, Cloutier ended his career after the 1984–85 season.

PAUL COFFEY has more goals, assists and points than any defenseman in the history of hockey and is one of the highest-scoring players at any position

ever to play in the NHL. He was the fourth player in NHL history to record 1,000 career assists and in 1996–97 he moved past Gordie Howe into second place behind Wayne Gretzky among the NHL's all-time assist leaders. Coffey is also one of the fastest skaters in the game.

Coffey was selected sixth overall by the Edmonton Oilers in the 1980 Entry Draft after an all-star season in the Ontario Hockey Association in 1979–80. He made his NHL debut in 1980–81 and by his second season of 1981–82, the Oilers had become the greatest offensive team in hockey history. Led by Wayne Gretzky's 92 goals and 120 assists, the Oilers scored a record 417 goals. Coffey collected 89 points to lead all NHL defensemen in scoring that year. His production increased each of the next two years and when Edmonton scored 446 goals in 1983–84, Coffey finished second to Gretzky in the NHL with 126 points. The Oilers won their first Stanley Cup title that season. Coffey had 121 points in 1984–85 and won the Norris Trophy for the first time as the league's best defenseman. The Oilers repeated as Stanley Cup champions that year.

Coffey earned his second Norris Trophy honor in 1985–86. He had a career-high 138 points that year (one short of Bobby Orr's record for defensemen) and scored 48 goals to surpass Orr's total of 46 from 1974–75. On March 14, 1986, Coffey tied Tom Bladon's record for defensemen of eight points in a single game with two goals and six assists. In 1987, Coffey won his third Stanley Cup title with the Oilers, but on November 24, 1987, he was dealt to Pittsburgh.

Now teaming with Mario Lemieux instead of Wayne Gretzky, Coffey maintained his status as the NHL's most gifted offensive defenseman by topping 100 points in both 1988–89 and 1989–90. In 1990–91, he helped the Penguins to win their first Stanley Cup championship but was traded to the Los Angeles Kings on February 19, 1992. Coffey was dealt to the Detroit Red Wings less than a year later where he won the Norris Trophy for the third time in 1994–95 after becoming the first defenseman in the history of the Red Wings hockey club to lead the team in scoring.

On the move again after a dispute with coach Scotty Bowman, Coffey was traded to the Hartford Whalers on October 9, 1996, then dealt to the Philadelphia Flyers on December 15, 1996. He was traded to the Chicago Blackhawks after the 1997–98 season.

NEIL COLVILLE With the great brother combination of Bill and Bun Cook winding down in New York, the Rangers unveiled new sibling scoring stars when Mac and Neil Colville joined the team. Combining with Alex Shibicky, the Bread Line would become one of the top-scoring trios in hockey, leading the Rangers to the Stanley Cup in 1940.

Neil Colville played junior hockey in his his hometown of Edmonton before joining the Rangers organization with the minor-league New York Crescents in 1934–35. He played briefly in the NHL the following season before becoming a regular in 1936–37. He cracked the top 10 in scoring for the first time in 1937–38, then again in 1938–39 when he was named to the Second All-Star Team. Colville earned another All-Star selection after the Rangers' Stanley Cup win of 1940, and he had a fourth straight finish among the top 10 in 1940–41. In 1941–42, he helped the Rangers post the best regular-season record in the NHL.

In 1942, Colville joined the Canadian armed forces, captaining the Ottawa Commandos to the Allan Cup in 1943 before serving as a navigator in the Royal Canadian Air Force. He was discharged in 1945. Colville returned to the Rangers, where he was converted into a defenseman and named team captain. He played four more seasons in New York; then, he spent some time with New Haven of the American Hockey League before coaching the Rangers in 1950–51 and part of 1951–52. He was elected to the Hockey Hall of Fame in 1967.

CHARLIE CONACHER was the best hockey player in one of Canada's greatest athletic families. He and his older brother Lionel are both Hall of Famers, while younger brother Roy was an NHL star as well. Charlie's son Peter, and Lionel's son Brian, also played in the NHL.

A member of the Toronto Marlboros Memorial Cup-winning team of 1928–29, Charlie Conacher entered the NHL with the Toronto Maple Leafs the following season. Playing on the famed Kid Line with Busher Jackson and Joe Primeau, Conacher quickly developed into the NHL's best right winger. He helped the Maple Leafs win the Stanley Cup in 1932, and he led or tied for the NHL lead in goal-scoring five times between 1930–31 and 1935–36. He led the league in points in 1933–34 and 1934–35, and he was either a First or Second Team All-Star every year from 1931–32 to 1935–36. In his nine seasons with Toronto, the Leafs won four Canadian Division titles and reached the Stanley Cup finals five times.

Known as "the Big Bomber," Conacher stood 6'1" and weighed about 200 pounds in his prime. He was as adept at making shifty moves around the net as he was at blasting a powerful wrist shot. He played a physical game, and injuries took their toll on him in his final years in Toronto. Conacher scored his 200th career goal with the Maple Leafs in 1937–38, but he was traded to the Detroit Red Wings for the 1938–39 season. He played two more years with the New York Americans before retiring in 1941 with 225 career goals.

Conacher turned to coaching after his playing days, guiding the Oshawa Generals to the Memorial Cup in 1944. He returned to the NHL as coach of the Chicago Black Hawks in 1947–48, but he retired to the business world after the 1949–50 season. Conacher was elected to the Hockey Hall of Fame in 1961.

LIONEL CONACHER was named Canada's male athlete of the half-century in 1950, also earning honors as Canada's greatest football player to that point. He had led the Toronto Argonauts to a Grey Cup victory in 1921, and he had played on Stanley Cup champions in 1934 and 1935. In addition, he was a star athlete in lacrosse, boxing and wrestling and a professional baseball player.

Conacher did not begin skating seriously until he was 16 years old, but he soon received pro offers from the Toronto St. Pats and Montreal Canadiens. He turned them all down, but he accepted an athletic scholarship to play football and study at Duquesne University in Pittsburgh. While there, he captained the Pittsburgh Yellow Jackets to the United States amateur hockey championship in 1924 and 1925. When Pittsburgh received an NHL franchise set to begin play for the 1925–26 season, Conacher turned pro as the Yellow Jackets became the Pittsburgh Pirates.

"The Big Train," as Conacher was known, was a lumbering skater who compensated for his lack of mobility by becoming an excellent shot-blocker. He was traded to the New York Americans during the 1926–27 season, improving as a defenseman by playing alongside Bullet Joe Simpson. Conacher served as a player-coach during the 1929–30 season in New York, but he was traded to the Montreal Maroons the following year. He joined the Chicago Black Hawks in 1933–34 and helped the team to win its first Stanley Cup championship while finishing runner-up to Aurel Joliat for the Hart Trophy. Traded back to the Maroons for the 1934–35 season, Conacher won another Stanley Cup title that year. He played two more seasons in Montreal, retiring from hockey after finishing runner-up for the Hart Trophy again in 1936–37. His son, Brian, would play later in the NHL.

Conacher was elected to the Ontario Legislature in 1937 and to the federal House of Commons in 1949, where he served until his death on May 26, 1954. He is a charter member of the Canadian Sports Hall of Fame (elected in 1955), the Canadian Football Hall of Fame (1963), the Canadian Lacrosse Hall of Fame (1966) and he was elected to the Hockey Hall of Fame in 1994. His brother Charlie had been elected to the Hockey Hall of Fame in 1961.

ROY CONACHER The younger brother of Hockey Hall of Famers Charlie and Lionel Conacher, Roy Conacher was a star player in his own right. He led the NHL with 26 goals in his rookie season of 1938–39 and helped the Boston Bruins win the Stanley Cup that year. He won another Stanley Cup title in Boston in 1940–41 but enlisted for military service with the Royal Canadian Air Force after the 1941–42 campaign.

Conacher returned to Boston after World War II to play four games in 1945–46 but was traded to the Detroit Red Wings prior to the start of the 1946–47 season. He led the Red Wings (and tied for seventh in the NHL) with 54 points that year, including a career-high 30 goals, but a contract dispute the following season resulted in Jack Adams trying to trade him to the New York Rangers. Conacher refused to report and announced his retirement. All was resolved two weeks later when he was dealt to the Chicago Black Hawks. Conacher had another excellent season in Chicago (where brother Charlie became coach during the year) and again cracked the top 10 scorers with 49 points even though the Black Hawks finished last in the NHL.

In 1948–49, Conacher played left wing on a line with Doug Bentley and Bill Mosienko and won the Art Ross Trophy as the NHL's scoring leader with 68 points. Bentley was second with 66 points, but once again Chicago missed the playoffs. Conacher led another weak Black Hawks team in scoring in 1949–50 and announced his retirement after the season. He was convinced to return for the 1950–51 campaign, but hung up his skates for good after playing just 12 games in 1951–52.

ALEX CONNELL set an NHL record that is not likely to be matched when he recorded shutouts in six straight games during the 1927–28 season, going unscored upon for a stretch of 446 minutes and nine seconds. His career goals-against average of 1.91 ties George Hainsworth for the lowest mark in NHL history.

Connell was known as "the Ottawa Fireman" during his career, partly because of his job with the Ottawa Fire Department and partly for his knack of putting out the fire of opposing marksmen. He starred in lacrosse and in baseball as a catcher while growing up in Ottawa. Connell did not get involved in hockey until being talked into playing goal while serving in the Canadian army in Kingston during World War I. After the war, he played amateur hockey in Ottawa, wearing a small black cap that would become his trademark.

By 1924–25, Connell had become so skilled in goal that the Ottawa Senators traded the great Clint Benedict to the Montreal Maroons in order to sign the local amateur to a professional contract. In 1925–26, he led the NHL with 15 shutouts and a 1.12 goals-against average. The following season, he helped the Senators to win the Stanley Cup.

When financial hardships forced the Senators to sell off players after 1927, Connell's great goaltending almost single-handedly kept the team competitive. When the Senators suspended operations in 1931–32, he joined the Detroit

Red Wings, finishing runner-up to Charlie Gardner for the Vezina Trophy. Connell was back in Ottawa in 1932–33, but he was hampered by injuries, missing almost all of the 1933–34 season.

When the Senators became the St. Louis Eagles in 1934–35, Tommy Gorman convinced Connell to join his Montreal Maroons hockey club. He helped the team to win the Stanley Cup that year. He didn't play in 1935–36, but he was back for a final season with the Maroons in 1936–37. He later coached junior hockey until 1949. Alex Connell was inducted into the Hockey Hall of Fame in 1958.

TONY CONROY began playing hockey in high school in St. Paul, Minnesota in the era when there were still seven players on a team. He played several positions between 1911 and 1914 and finally settled in as a rover or winger. He joined the St. Paul Athletic Club in 1914 and helped the team win the McNaughton Cup as U.S. amateur champions in 1917. After service in World War I, he returned to the Athletic Club and was one of the team's four players to make the 1920 U.S. team that finished second to Canada in the first Olympic hockey tournament. Conroy continued to play for the St. Paul team into the 1920s as they remained a strong contender for the national amateur title. Western champions in 1921–22 and 1922–23, they lost to Boston in the national finals both years.

Conroy became a member of the St. Paul Saints in 1925–26 and moved into the pros, turning down offers from NHL teams to play out his career in his hometown. Conroy was enshrined in the United States Hockey Hall of Fame in 1975.

BILL COOK was one of the top scorers in hockey during a 15-year professional career in Saskatoon and New York. He twice led his league in goals, he topped the assist list once, and he won a pair of scoring titles during four seasons with Saskatoon. Cook led the NHL in goals three times while winning two scoring titles in New York. Only Nels Stewart scored more goals than Bill Cook during his career.

Cook played amateur hockey in his hometown of Kingston, Ontario and in Sault Ste. Marie before signing professionally with the Saskatoon Sheiks of the Western Canada Hockey League in 1922–23. He played with legendary scoring star Newsy Lalonde on the Sheiks/Crescents, and he was joined in his final two seasons by brother Bun Cook.

When pro hockey collapsed in the west after the 1925–26 season, the Cook brothers were signed by Conn Smythe for the first New York Rangers team. Bill was named captain. Teamed with center Frank Boucher that first season, the Cook-Boucher-Cook combination became one of the top lines in NHL history. Bill was the triggerman among the slick passing trio, leading the NHL with 33 goals and 37 points in 44 games during the 1926–27 campaign. The Rangers won the Stanley Cup in 1928.

Cook tied Charlie Conacher for the NHL lead in goals with a career-high 34 in 1931–32, and he won his second scoring title in 1932–33 before the Rangers won their second Stanley Cup championship that year. He was named to the First All-Star Team at right wing in 1930–31, 1931–32 and 1932–33. He was a Second Team All-Star the following year. During the 1935–36 season, Rangers coach Lester Patrick broke up his aging forward line and moved Bill Cook back to defense. Still captain of the Rangers, he played his final NHL season in 1936–37. He was elected to the Hockey Hall of Fame in 1958, while his brother Bun was inducted in 1995.

BUN COOK Fred "Bun" Cook was a star in both amateur and professional hockey. He played in his hometown of Kingston, Ontario before helping the Sault Ste. Marie Greyhounds win the Allan Cup as Canadian amateur champions in 1923–24. The following season, he joined his brother Bill with the Saskatoon Crescents of the Western Canada Hockey League. When hockey in the west collapsed after the 1925–26 season, the Cook brothers were signed by Conn Smythe while he was assembling the first New York Rangers team.

The Cook brothers joined Frank Boucher in 1926–27 to become one of the top lines in NHL history. Bill was a more dangerous scorer, but Bun was also a productive offensive player who cracked the top 10 three times in nine NHL seasons. He was named to the Second All-Star Team in 1930–31, and he was a fan favorite at the Madison Square Garden while playing on Stanley Cup winners in 1928 and 1933.

Cook developed an arthritic condition that forced him out of the Rangers lineup midway through the 1935–36 season, but he recovered to play a final year with the Boston Bruins before a throat ailment led to his retirement after the 1936–37 campaign. He then became a coach with the Providence Reds of the American Hockey League in 1937, guiding the club to Calder Cup championships in 1938 and 1940. He moved on to the Cleveland Barons, where he won five league titles between 1945 and 1954. He later coached in the Eastern Professional Hockey League for two seasons before retiring in 1958. His brother Bill was elected to the Hockey Hall of Fame that year. Bun was enshrined in 1995.

LLOYD COOK scored more goals than any defenseman in the history of the Pacific Coast Hockey Association and once scored five in a single game on

February 1, 1916. He had broken in with the Vancouver Millionaires in 1914–15 and got the opportunity to learn from veterans Frank Patrick and Si Griffis. When Griffis broke his leg late in the season, Cook anchored the defense as Vancouver beat the Ottawa Senators in three straight games to become the first PCHA team to win the Stanley Cup.

When the Victoria Aristocrats temporarily became the Spokane Canaries for the 1916–17 season, Cook was sent south in a effort to strengthen the team. He returned to Vancouver the following year and teamed with Art Duncan on defense for most of the next seven years. During that time, Vancouver won four consecutive PCHA titles and Cook was selected as an all-star in 1920–21.

When Victoria and Vancouver joined the Western Canada Hockey League, Cook was among several western players who chose to sign instead with the NHL expansion team in Boston. He played just four games with the Bruins in 1924–25 and later concluded his career in the California Hockey League.

SHAYNE CORSON made his NHL debut when he played three games for the Montreal Canadiens in 1985–86. He played 55 games with the team the following season and earned a full-time spot on Montreal's NHL roster in 1987–88. He had a breakout year in 1988–89 when he scored 24 goals and led the club with 193 penalty minutes. He also helped the team to reach the Stanley Cup finals that season. The following year, Corson had 31 goals and led the Canadiens with 44 assists.

Corson was traded to the Edmonton Oilers on August 27, 1992 in the deal that brought Vincent Damphousse to Montreal. He ranked among the club's scoring leaders in each of his three years with the Oilers and was named team captain in 1994–95, but was traded to the St. Louis Blues on July 28, 1995. The Blues traded him back to Montreal on October 29, 1996.

In international play, Corson represented Canada at the World Junior Championships in 1985, when he won a gold medal, and in 1986, when he was named to the tournament all-star team after tying Joe Murphy for the scoring lead with 14 points in seven games. He also played for Team Canada at the 1991 Canada Cup and at the World Championships in 1993 and 1994, when Canada won its first world title since 1961. His excellent season with Montreal in 1997–98 earned him a spot on the Canadian Olympic team at Nagano.

ART COULTER An athlete of exceptional physical strength and endurance, Art Coulter joined the Chicago Black Hawks during the 1931–32 season. He teamed on defense with Taffy Abel to help Chicago win its first Stanley Cup title in 1934. He played with Marty Burke the following year, earning a berth on the Second All-Star Team.

Coulter was traded to the New York Rangers for Earl Seibert midway through the 1935–36 season, where he continued rank among the top defensive defenseman in the NHL. He succeeded Bill Cook as Rangers captain in 1937–38, and he was named to the Second All-Star Team again that season, an honor he would receive each of the next two years. Coulter helped New York to win the Stanley Cup in 1940 before playing two more seasons. He enlisted in the U.S. Coast Guard for World War II, ending his pro career. He was elected to the Hockey Hall of Fame in 1974.

YVAN COURNOYER Standing just 5'7" and weighing 178 pounds, Yvan Cournoyer was considered too small to play regularly in the NHL, but his blazing speed and puckhandling skill quickly convinced people otherwise. Known as "the Roadrunner," Cournoyer was a member of 10 Stanley Cup-winning teams in Montreal and captained the Canadiens from 1975–76 until his final season of 1978–79. He was elected to the Hockey Hall of Fame in 1982.

Cournoyer joined the NHL Canadiens roster in 1964–65 after playing with the Montreal Junior Canadiens and spending only seven games with Quebec of the American Hockey League. Used mainly on the power-play in his early years in the NHL, Cournoyer soon showed he could handle himself among bigger players. He scored 25 goals in 1966–67 and never fell below 24 over the next 11 years. Cournoyer topped 40 goals on four occasions, including a career-high 47 in 1971–72, and he had a career-best 87 points in 1968–69. He was named to the Second All-Star Team at right wing four times in five years between 1968–69 and 1972–73 and played on Team Canada in the 1972 Summit Series against the USSR. In the Stanley Cup finals against Chicago in 1973, Cournoyer tied a record with 12 points on six goals and six assists and won the Conn Smythe Trophy as playoff MVP.

A recurring back injury ended Cournoyer's career in 1978–79 and he retired with 863 points on 428 goals and 435 assists. He ranks behind only Maurice Richard, Guy Lafleur and Jean Beliveau among the Canadiens' all-time goal-scoring leaders and sits sixth in club history in both assists and points. His 64 goals and 63 assists in the postseason also rank him high among the Canadiens' all-time playoff leaders. Cournoyer totaled only 255 penalty minutes in his career, for an average of just 17 minutes per season.

BILL COWLEY was the greatest playmaker in hockey during his 13 years in the NHL, finishing among the top 10 in scoring seven times, leading the league in assists three times and winning one scoring title. These totals would have been even more impressive had he not been hampered by injuries so often during his career.

Cowley entered the NHL with the St. Louis Eagles during their lone season of 1934–35, and he was chosen by the Boston Bruins the following year in the draft of St. Louis players after the franchise folded. A slick stickhandler and terrific passer, Cowley quickly developed into a star in Boston. He earned the first of five All-Star selections (four to the First Team) in 1937–38. In 1939, he led all playoff performers in scoring when the Bruins won the Stanley Cup. Cowley earned the Hart Trophy in 1940–41 and the scoring title, and he led Boston to another Stanley Cup victory.

A broken jaw sidelined Cowley for much of the 1941–42 season, but he won the Hart Trophy again in 1942–43. In 1943–44, he was well on his way to smashing the record of 73 points in a single season. He had 71 in just 36 games when a knee injury, following a separated shoulder, kept him out for the final six weeks of the season. Cowley had another great year in 1944–45, but he missed much of the following season with a broken wrist. He retired after the 1946–47 campaign.

After his playing days, Cowley coached teams in Renfrew, Ontario and in Vancouver before opening and operating hotels in Ottawa and nearby Smiths Falls. In 1968, he was inducted into the Hockey Hall of Fame.

JOHN CRAWFORD was a powerful defenseman who could rush the puck as well as lay out solid bodychecks and was compared to a young Eddie Shore by Boston coach and general manager Art Ross during his early years with the Bruins. Crawford became a regular in Boston in 1938–39 and paired on defense with Flash Hollett for a Bruins team that won the Stanley Cup that season. Crawford played for another Stanley Cup champion in Boston in 1940–41 and was named to the Second All-Star Team in 1942–43.

In 1944–45 and 1945–46, Crawford teamed with Dit Clapper on the Bruins blue line and playing with the veteran player/coach improved his game to the point that Crawford was named a First Team All-Star in 1945–46. Crawford was one of few players who wore a helmet during this era, though for him it was as much a case of hiding his balding head as it was protecting it.

MARC CRAWFORD began his NHL coaching career with the Quebec Nordiques in 1994–95. He led the club to first place in the Northeast Division and second place overall in the NHL during that season, which was reduced to 48 games because of a labor dispute. He was rewarded with the Jack Adams Award as coach of the year. The Nordiques moved to Denver in 1995–96 and the Colorado Avalanche became the first team in NHL history to win the Stanley Cup in its first season in a new city. In February of 1998, Crawford coached Canada's team at the Nagano Olympics. He resigned as coach of the Avalanche after the 1997–98 season.

As a player, Crawford spent six years with the Vancouver Canucks from 1981–82 until 1986–87. He became coach and general manager of the junior Cornwall Royals of the Ontario Hockey League in 1988–89 and joined the Toronto Maple Leafs as coach of their St. John's affiliate in the American Hockey League two years later. Crawford's team reached the Calder Cup finals in his first season of 1991–92 and he was named coach of the year. He was with St. John's for three seasons before being hired by the Nordiques.

RUSTY CRAWFORD Russell "Rusty" Crawford had a lengthy career, playing until 1929–30 when he was 45 years old. He had began as an amateur in Verdun, Quebec for three seasons before going west to Prince Albert and Saskatoon, Saskatchewan. Crawford returned east and became a professional with the Quebec Bulldogs of the National Hockey Association in 1912–13, then playing 18 more years before retiring.

The Bulldogs were already Stanley Cup champions when Crawford was signed, and he helped them defend their title in the first of his five seasons there. When Quebec opted not to ice a team in the NHL's inaugural season of 1917–18, Crawford moved to the Ottawa Senators before joining Toronto later in the year and winning another Stanley Cup title.

Crawford spent one more season in Toronto before returning to Saskatchewan to play senior amateur hockey. When the Western Canada Hockey League was formed in 1921–22, he returned to the pro ranks with the Saskatoon Crescents. He later played with the Calgary Tigers and Vancouver Maroons until pro hockey collapsed in the West in 1926. He then joined Minneapolis of the American Hockey Association, continuing to play minor-league hockey there until 1929–30. Crawford was inducted into the Hockey Hall of Fame in 1962.

TERRY CRISP is one of only 13 men to date who have both played on and coached a Stanley Cup winner. He was a member of the Stanley Cup champion Philadelphia Flyers in 1974 and 1975 and coached the Calgary Flames to an NHL title in 1989.

Crisp was known for his hard work and defensive play during 11 seasons as a center in the NHL. He broke in with the Boston Bruins during the 1965–66 campaign, but did not become a regular in the NHL until being selected by the St. Louis Blues in the 1967 Expansion Draft. He again joined a first-year team in 1972 when he was picked by the New York Islanders, who traded him to the Flyers before the 1972–73 season was through.

It was with the Flyers where Crisp's coaching career began as an assistant

to Fred Shero from 1977 to 1979. He became a head coach with the Sault Ste. Marie Greyhounds of the Ontario Hockey League in 1979–80 and his six-year stint there ended with three consecutive league championships and coach of the year honors in 1982–83 and 1984–85. He spent the next two seasons coaching Calgary's top farm club in Moncton of the American Hockey League before moving up to the Flames in 1987–88. He won the Stanley Cup in just his second season, but was fired after the 1989–90 campaign.

Crisp served as an assistant coach with Canada's silver medal-winning team at the Albertville Olympics in 1992 and returned to the NHL when he was named head coach with the Tampa Bay Lightning in their first season of 1992–93. He was the longest-tenured coach in the NHL until being fired by the Lightning early in the 1997–98 season.

ROGER CROZIER enjoyed great success early in his NHL career and might have become one of the game's great goalies if not for injuries and a serious illness. Crozier suffered from pancreatitis, a condition that would keep him out of the lineup from time to time throughout his career.

Crozier made his debut with the Detroit Red Wings in 1963–64 and played 15 games for the injured Terry Sawchuk before replacing the future Hall of Famer the following year. He played all 70 games for Detroit in 1964–65 (making him the last NHL netminder to play in all of his team's games), won the Calder Trophy as rookie of the year, and earned a selection to the First All-Star Team. Pancreatitis kept Crozier out of action to begin the following year, but he later led the Red Wings to the Stanley Cup finals. Detroit lost the 1966 series to the Montreal Canadiens, but Crozier earned the Conn Smythe Trophy as playoff MVP.

When the Buffalo Sabres entered the NHL in 1970–71, Punch Imlach acquired Crozier and he shared the nets with Dave Dryden on the rapidly improving expansion team. In 1974–75, he teamed with Gerry Desjardins to lead the Sabres to the Stanley Cup final in just their fifth season. Buffalo lost to the Philadelphia Flyers.

Crozier spent one more season with the Sabres, then ended his playing career after three games with the Washington Capitals in 1976–77. He later worked in the Capitals front office, serving short stints as coach and general manager in 1981–82.

JOHN D'AMICO was the last man still active from the "Original Six" era when he worked his final NHL game on March 5, 1988. He had his first NHL assignment at the Boston Garden on October 12, 1964. D'Amico began his officiating career as a linesman, then worked briefly as a referee before returning to the lines.

D'Amico worked more than 1,700 games in his NHL career and appeared in the Stanley Cup finals over 20 times. He also handled seven NHL All-Star Games and was a linesman at the Canada Cup in 1976, 1981, 1984 and 1987. He saw further international duty in the 1979 Challenge Cup series and at Rendez-Vous '87. After his on-ice career, D'Amico went on to coach officials as a member of the NHL's Officiating Supervisory Staff. He was elected to the Hockey Hall of Fame in 1993.

CULLY DAHLSTROM Carl "Cully" Dahlstrom played high school hockey at Minneapolis South and played professionally in both Minneapolis and St. Paul in the American Hockey Association before joining the Chicago Black Hawks in 1937–38. Dahlstrom won the Calder Trophy as rookie of the year that season and although the Black Hawks barely made the playoffs, they came alive in the postseason to win the Stanley Cup with a roster heavy with American players.

Dahlstrom played an important part in Chicago's 1938 playoff rally. He scored the only goal (in overtime) in a 1–0 victory over the New York Americans in game two of the semifinals, which allowed Chicago to go on to win the best-of-three series. Later, he scored the first goal in a 4–1 victory over the Leafs in game four of the finals that got the Black Hawks the Cup.

Dahlstrom spent eight seasons in Chicago and enjoyed his most productive year in 1943–44 when he had 20 goals and 22 assists in the 50-game schedule. He retired after that campaign. In 1973, Dahlstrom was one of the charter members of the United States Hockey Hall of Fame.

JOE DALEY was a much traveled minor-league goaltender who saw some action in the NHL after expansion in 1967 and later became the winningest goalie in the history of the World Hockey Association. He posted 167 victories in seven WHA seasons and helped the Winnipeg Jets win the Avco Cup as league champions three times.

Daley played with the Pittsburgh Penguins, Buffalo Sabres and Detroit Red Wings between 1968 and 1972 before joining the Jets in 1972–73. He played without a mask that season and posted the league's second-best goals-against average with a mark of 2.89. His best season was 1975–76 when he went 41–17–1 and had a 2.84 average. In the playoffs that year, Daley had 10 wins and just one loss as the Jets won their first WHA title.

A member of the Jets throughout the entire history of the WHA, Daley helped the team win the Avco Cup again in each of the league's last two seasons, but retired before Winnipeg joined the NHL in 1979–80.

VINCENT DAMPHOUSSE was selected sixth overall by the Toronto Maple Leafs in the 1986 NHL Entry Draft after an all-star season with Laval of the Quebec Major Junior Hockey League in 1985–86. Damphousse played all 80 games as a rookie in Toronto in 1986–87 and finished sixth in scoring among first-year players with 46 points.

Damphousse improved his point production in each of his first four seasons in Toronto, reaching a high of 33 goals and 94 points in 1989–90. The following year, he slipped to 73 points, but the total was high enough to lead the Maple Leafs in scoring. Damphousse was traded to Edmonton in a multi-player deal on September 19, 1991, and went on to lead the Oilers in scoring that season. He was dealt to the Montreal Canadiens on August 27, 1992, and led his third different team in scoring for the third straight year with a career-high 97 points in 1992–93. He also led the Canadiens in playoff scoring with 23 points in 20 games as Montreal won the Stanley Cup.

Damphousse has continued to rank as one of Montreal's most productive scorers. He scored the first goal ever at the Molson Centre on March 16, 1996. He was a member of Team Canada at the World Cup of Hockey prior to the 1996–97 NHL season and succeeded Pierre Turgeon as captain in Montreal after Turgeon was traded on October 29, 1996.

LEO DANDURAND was one of the top sports entrepreneurs of his day. In addition to owning the Montreal Canadiens, he owned racehorses; he was a director of the Montreal Royals baseball team; he founded the Montreal Alouettes football team; and he owned restaurants, laundries, dry cleaners and a soft drink company.

Dandurand was born in Bourbonnais, Illinois, but he came to Canada in 1905, later serving as a referee in the National Hockey Association. He met Joseph Cattarinich during a real estate venture, and in 1921, Dandurand, Cattarinich and Louis Letourneau (the Three Musketeers of Sport) purchased the Montreal Canadiens for $11,000. Dandurand invited politicians, judges and business leaders to join the team's board of directors while building an NHL powerhouse that boasted such stars as Aurel Joliat and Howie Morenz, the greatest player in the game.

Dandurand was a hands-on owner who coached the team from 1921–22 to 1925–26 and again in 1934–35. The Canadiens won the Stanley Cup in 1924, 1930 and 1931, and when economic pressures during the Great Depression forced the sale of the team in 1935, the price had reached $165,000. Dandurand was elected to the Hockey Hall of Fame as a builder in 1963.

JACK DARRAGH was a native of Ottawa who grew up playing amateur hockey in Canada's capital. Turning professional, he played 13 years—his entire pro career— with the Senators. No player this century has spent more years in a Senators uniform.

Darragh joined the Senators for the 1910–11 season in the National Hockey Association, playing with high-scoring forwards Marty Walsh, Dubbie Kerr and Bruce Ridpath. In his first game on December 31, 1910, Darragh scored a goal against Georges Vezina, who was making his debut with the Montreal Canadiens that season. He went on to score 18 goals in 16 games that year, helping Ottawa to win the Stanley Cup.

While never leading the league in scoring, Darragh was always a productive player and a clutch performer. He played right wing on great forward lines with Skene Ronan and Punch Broadbent, Eddie Gerard and Angus Duford and Frank Nighbor and Cy Denneny. He scored in 10 consecutive games during the 1913–14 season, and he had five goals in a game on February 7, 1917.

Respected as a clean player, slick stickhandler and speedy skater, Darragh entered the NHL with the Senators when the league was formed in 1917–18, helping the team to win the Stanley Cup in 1920 and 1921 by scoring key playoff goals both years. He retired before the 1921–22 season, but he was back the following year to help Ottawa win another Stanley Cup title. Darragh saw action again during the 1923–24 season, but he died of peritonitis on June 25, 1924. He was elected to the Hockey Hall of Fame in 1962.

SCOTTY DAVIDSON Allan "Scotty" Davidson had a brief but brilliant hockey career before losing his life in Belgium during World War I. Davidson was born in Kingston, Ontario and learned the game under the coaching of James T. Sutherland, who often is called "the Father of Hockey."

A rugged, powerful youth, Davidson was a strong skater with a hard shot. He was a standout with the Kingston Frontenac juniors in 1909–10 and 1910–11 when the club won back-to-back Ontario Hockey Association titles. He then signed to play professionally in 1912 with one of the two new Toronto teams in the National Hockey Association. Davidson scored 19 goals in 20 games during the 1912–13 season and he had 23 goals the following year when the Blueshirts won the Stanley Cup.

Davidson enlisted for military service after World War I broke out in August of 1914. He was killed in action on June 6, 1915. He was elected to the Hockey Hall of Fame in 1950.

HAP DAY An outgoing personality and provocative sense of humor earned Clarence Day the nickname Happy or Hap. He had a 33-year association with the National Hockey League as a player, coach, referee and general manager.

Day played junior hockey in Midland, Ontario and senior hockey with the Hamilton Tigers before attending the University of Toronto to study pharmacy. Charles Querrie convinced him to play pro hockey while still in school and he signed with the Toronto St. Pats on December 13, 1924. During his first two seasons in the NHL, Day played left wing on a line with Jack Adams and Babe Dye. He was later converted into a defenseman.

When Conn Smythe purchased the St. Pats during the 1926–27 season, turning them into the Toronto Maple Leafs, Day and Ace Bailey were the two players he planned to build his new franchise around. Day was named the first captain of the Maple Leafs, holding that position until he left Toronto after the 1936–37 season. During his time with the Maple Leafs, Day anchored the defense with King Clancy and Red Horner. The team won its first Stanley Cup title in 1932, and it reached the finals three other times while winning three Canadian Division titles. Back on November 19, 1929, Day tied an NHL record for defenseman when he scored four goals in one game. He coached the West Toronto Nationals to the Memorial Cup while playing with the Leafs during the 1935–36 season.

Day played his final NHL season with the New York Americans in 1937–38. He spent the next two years as a referee before returning to Toronto as a highly successful coach. He guided the Leafs from 1940–41 to 1949–50, winning the Stanley Cup in 1942, 1945, 1947, 1948 and 1949. He became assistant general manager to Conn Smythe in 1950, and he was responsible for running the team until 1957, when he retired to enter business life. Day was elected to the Hockey Hall of Fame in 1961.

ALEX DELVECCHIO played 22 full seasons with the Detroit Red Wings and parts of two others before retiring on November 9, 1973. Only long-time teammate Gordie Howe has played more seasons in the NHL or taken part in more games than the 1,549 in which Delvecchio played. At the time of his retirement, Delvecchio's 825 assists and 1,281 points also ranked second to Howe. His 456 goals were sixth to that point in NHL history.

After a one-game trial during the 1950–51 season, Delvecchio joined the Red Wings to stay in 1951–52 and helped the team win the Stanley Cup that year. The following year, he replaced the departed Sid Abel on the Production Line between Howe and Ted Lindsay and was named to the Second All-Star Team at center. Delvecchio played on Stanley Cup winners again in 1954, then 1955, when he had seven goals and eight assists in 11 games. In 1958–59, Delvecchio was shifted to left wing on a line with Howe and Norm Ullman and earned another Second Team All-Star berth. He also won the Lady Byng Trophy, which he would win again in 1965–66 when he registered a career-high 31 goals.

Known as "Fats" because of his round face, Delvecchio was named captain of the Red Wings in 1962–63 and held the position until the time of his retirement. He was elected to the Hockey Hall of Fame in 1977.

JACQUES DEMERS' playing career ended at the age of 17 when he suffered a serious leg injury. He took a coaching job in a Junior B league in his hometown of Montreal in 1967–68 and led the Outremont Lions to three provincial titles in four years. Demers made his move into pro hockey in 1972–73 as the director of player personnel with the Chicago Cougars of the World Hockey Association, then coached the club the following year.

In 1975–76, Demers became coach and director of player personnel with the WHA's Indianapolis Racers, spending two seasons there before coaching the Cincinnati Stingers in 1977–78. He coached the Quebec Nordiques during the WHA's final season of 1978–79 and entered the NHL with Quebec the following year. He ran Quebec's American Hockey League affiliate in Fredericton the next two seasons, then returned to the NHL with the St. Louis Blues in 1983–84.

Demers spent three seasons in St. Louis, where he earned a reputation as a brilliant motivator who could get the most out of his players. In 1985–86, he led the Blues to within one game of the Stanley Cup finals, losing the seventh game of the Campbell Conference finals 2–1 to the Calgary Flames. On June 13, 1986, Demers signed on to coach the Detroit Red Wings. He won the Jack Adams Award with Detroit in both 1986–87 and 1987–88 to become the first man to be named coach of the year two years in a row.

After spending the 1990–91 and 1991–92 seasons as a radio broadcaster with the Nordiques, Demers returned to the NHL as coach of the Montreal Canadiens in 1992–93 and led team to its 24th Stanley Cup title that season. In 1994–95, the Canadiens missed the playoffs for the first time in 25 years and when Montreal started the 1995–96 season with five straight losses, Demers was fired. He remained in the organization as a scout until returning to coaching with the Tampa Bay Lightning on November 13, 1997.

CORB DENNENY is one of only seven players in NHL history to score six goals in a single game. He accomplished the feat with the Toronto St. Pats on January 26, 1921. His Hall of Fame brother Cy Denneny had a six-goal game with the Ottawa Senators later that season.

The Denneny brothers broke into the National Hockey Association (forerunner of the NHL) together with the Toronto Shamrocks in 1914–15 and moved to the Toronto Blueshirts the following year. Both went to Ottawa in

1916–17 but while Cy remained with the Senators, Corb was back in Toronto before the year was out. He was with the Torontos, or the Arenas as they are more commonly known, when they entered the NHL in 1917–18 and won the Stanley Cup. He later centered a line with future Hall of Famers Reg Noble and Babe Dye and won a second Stanley Cup title with the St. Pats in 1921–22.

Denneny was traded to the Vancouver Maroons for Jack Adams during the 1922–23 season, but was back in the NHL with the Hamilton Tigers the following year. Relegated to a substitute role, he did not score a goal all season. In 1924–25, Denneny joined the Saskatoon Crescents of the Western Canada Hockey League and regained his scoring touch while centering brothers Bill and Bun Cook.

When pro hockey collapsed in the west prior to the 1926–27 season, Denneny returned to Toronto. He saw some action with the Chicago Black Hawks the following year, then played minor-league hockey for three seasons before retiring in 1931.

CY DENNENY scored a career-high 36 goals in just 20 games for the Ottawa Senators during the first NHL season of 1917–18, finishing second to Joe Malone, who had 44 goals that year. It was the first of five times over a nine-year span that Denneny would be the runner-up in the NHL scoring race. He led the league with 22 goals and one assist in 1923–24.

Denneny was short and stocky and not a fast skater, but he possessed a hard, accurate shot. He scored more goals than any player in Senators history and only Newsy Lalonde and Joe Malone scored more among all players of his era. He had goals in 12 consecutive games during the 1917–18 season, and he scored six in one game on March 7, 1921.

Denneny and his brother Corb began their pro careers with the Toronto Shamrocks in 1914–15 before joining the Toronto Blueshirts the following year. Centered by Duke Keats, the trio formed the top-scoring line in the National Hockey Association. Denneny and Joe Malone battled all year to win the scoring title before both were beaten by Newsy Lalonde in a close race.

Prior to the 1916–17 season, Denneny was purchased by the Senators, and he was with Ottawa when the NHL was formed the following year. He helped the team win the Stanley Cup in 1920, 1921, 1923 and 1927, before leaving after the 1927–28 season to become a player-coach with the Boston Bruins. Denneny earned a fifth Stanley Cup championship in 1928–29. He then retired as a player and spent the next season as a referee. He coached junior and senior amateur teams in Ottawa in 1931–32 and the Senators in 1932–33 before retiring for good. He was elected to the Hockey Hall of Fame in 1959.

ERIC DESJARDINS was the first defenseman in NHL history to record a hat trick in the Stanley Cup finals when he did so in the Montreal Canadiens' 3–2 victory over the Los Angeles Kings in game two of the 1993 series. Montreal went on to win the Stanley Cup in five games.

Desjardins had made his NHL debut with Montreal in 1988–89 after a pair of all-star seasons with Granby of the Quebec Major Junior Hockey League. He won the Butch Bouchard Trophy as the top defenseman in the QMJHL in 1987–88 and quickly established himself as a top defenseman in the NHL as well, earning a spot on Team Canada at the 1991 Canada Cup.

During his seventh season with the Canadiens, Desjardins was traded to Flyers along with John LeClair on February 9, 1995. He has continued to rank among the league's best in Philadelphia. He was a member of the Canadian team at the World Cup of Hockey in 1996 and at the Nagano Olympics in 1998. Earlier in his career, Desjardins represented his country at the World Junior Championships in 1988, when he won a gold medal, and in 1989.

VIC DESJARDINS was a native of Sault Ste. Marie, Michigan who played hockey in Eveleth, Minnesota from 1922–23 until 1925–26, when the town was represented in the United States Amateur Hockey Association at a time when there were no American professional leagues and the USAHA represented the highest level of the game in the nation.

Though he stood only 5'9" and weighed just 160 pounds, Desjardins was a clever center with a knack for being in the right position for a shot on goal. He was also a capable defensive player. A solid goal scorer, Desjardins moved up to the pros with St. Paul of the American Hockey Association in 1926–27. He led the league in scoring with 20 goals and eight assists and was selected an all-American in 1927–28 and won another AHA scoring title with 25 goals and 10 assists in 45 games in 1929–30.

Desjardins' scoring prowess brought him to the Chicago Black Hawks in 1930–31, where he joined fellow Sault native Taffy Abel. The Black Hawks reached the Stanley Cup finals that season before losing to the Montreal Canadiens. Desjardins was with the New York Rangers the following year and again reached the Stanley Cup finals, only to be defeated by the Toronto Maple Leafs. He closed out his career with six more seasons in the minor leagues, mostly with Tulsa and Kansas City in the AHA, where he continued to rank among the league's top scorers. Desjardins was inducted into the United States Hockey Hall of Fame in 1974.

DICK DESMOND tended goal for Dartmouth College in an era in which the school was a collegiate hockey power in the East. He was instrumental in its

sharing the North American title with the University of Toronto in 1946–47 and reaching the finals of the NCAA's second national hockey tournament in 1949. He captained Dartmouth during the 1948–49 season, was selected as the MVP in the NCAA finals and was named all-Ivy League for the third consecutive year. His goals-against average in 60 games at Dartmouth was 2.98.

In 1950, Desmond allowed just 12 goals in seven games for the U.S. national team that won a silver medal at the World Championships in London. He was serving with the U.S. Air Force in 1952 when he was added to the roster of the American Olympic hockey team and again won a silver medal. Desmond was enshrined in the United States Hockey Hall of Fame in 1988.

FRANK DILIO gave many years of service to amateur hockey in Quebec. Hockey Hall of Famers Maurice Richard and Butch Bouchard, among many other stars, emerged from the junior ranks in Quebec during the time Dilio was associated with the game. A division in the Quebec Major Junior Hockey League is named in his honor.

Dilio's involvement in hockey began at St. Ann's Boys School in Montreal. He was secretary of their juvenile club in 1931 and later joined the Quebec Amateur Hockey Association as secretary before moving up to president in 1939. By 1943, Dilio had become registrar of the QAHA and added the duties of secretary in 1952. He held both positions until resigning in 1962. In 1963, he received the Canadian Amateur Hockey Association's Meritorious Award and was inducted into the Hockey Hall of Fame as a builder in 1964.

BOB DILL was a two-sport athlete who played baseball and hockey. He starred in both sports at Cretin High School in his native St. Paul, Minnesota, and after graduation spent the 1938–39 season with Miami in the little-known Tropical Hockey League. Dill played in Baltimore in 1940–41, and it was there that the stocky 5'8", 185-pound center was converted to defense.

Dill entered the pro ranks with Springfield of the American Hockey League in 1941–42. He was with the Buffalo Bisons (and the U.S. Coast Guard team) in 1942–43 and again in 1943–44 when the New York Rangers acquired him in January of 1944. Dill finished out the year in the NHL and played a full season with the Rangers in 1944–45.

Dill returned to Minnesota in 1945–46 and spent the next five years with the St. Paul Saints in the United States Hockey League. He left the pros after 1949–50 and spent the next season with the amateur St. Paul 7-Ups. In 1951–52, he was a player-coach with Springfield in the AHL. By this time, he had already served as a minor-league baseball manager for affiliates of the New York Giants, New York Yankees and Cincinnati Reds and played outfield with Minneapolis and Indianapolis in the American Association. His continuing involvement in hockey later saw him serve as a scout with the Minnesota North Stars. Dill was inducted into the United States Hockey Hall of Fame in 1979.

CECIL DILLON joined the New York Rangers in 1930–31 and became a regular at right wing on a line with Butch Keeling and Murray Murdoch in 1931–32. The line of Frank Boucher and Bill and Bun Cook was still the big line in New York at this time, but Dillon finished second behind Bill Cook in team scoring when the Rangers won the American Division but lost the Stanley Cup to the Toronto Maple Leafs in 1932. In 1933, Dillon led all playoff scorers with eight goals and 10 points as the Rangers beat the Maple Leafs to win the Stanley Cup.

With Boucher and the Cooks fading by 1935–36, Lester Patrick shuffled the Rangers line combinations and placed his son Lynn on a line with Dillon and Murray Murdoch. Dillon went on to lead the team in scoring that year and in each of the next two seasons as well. He was named to the NHL Second All-Star Team in 1936 and 1937 and to the First Team after the 1937–38 season.

Dillon spent a final year with the Rangers in 1938–39 and ended his NHL career with the Detroit Red Wings the following year. He then played two years in the American Hockey League before retiring.

MARCEL DIONNE Though he never played on a Stanley Cup winner in 18 seasons, Marcel Dionne was one of the greatest players in NHL history. At the time of his retirement in 1989, Dionne's 731 goals trailed only Gordie Howe and his 1,040 assists ranked behind only Howe and Wayne Gretzky. To date, his total of 1,771 points trails only Gretzky and Howe for third place in NHL history.

Dionne had an outstanding junior career with St. Catharines of the Ontario Hockey Association and was selected by the Detroit Red Wings in 1971 as the second pick in the Amateur Draft behind Guy Lafleur. Dionne set a rookie record with 77 points in 1971–72, but trailed both Ken Dryden and Richard Martin in voting for the Calder Trophy. By 1974–75, Dionne had emerged as one of the game's top scorers. He recorded 121 points that year to rank third in the NHL behind Bobby Orr and Phil Esposito, winning the Lady Byng Trophy for sportsmanlike conduct. It was an honor he would win again in 1979–80.

Dionne was acquired as a free agent by Los Angeles in 1975–76 and went on to star with the Kings for 12 seasons. In his second year in Los Angeles, Dionne topped 50 goals for the first of six times and his 122 points on 53 goals and 69 assists ranked second in the NHL behind Guy Lafleur's 136 points.

Dionne earned a berth on the First All-Star Team for that season and was a Second Team All-Star in 1978–79 when he set a career high with 59 goals. He again finished second in the scoring race that season with his 130 points just four less than Bryan Trottier.

Dionne centered the Triple Crown Line with Dave Taylor and Charlie Simmer in Los Angeles, and it was with this unit that he won his only scoring title in 1979–80. Dionne had 137 points that year to tie rookie Wayne Gretzky, but was awarded the Art Ross Trophy because he had 53 goals to Gretzky's 51. Dionne also edged Gretzky for the selection as center on the NHL's First All-Star Team that season, but was second behind Gretzky in both All-Star voting and points in 1980–81.

On March 10, 1987, Dionne was traded by Los Angeles to the New York Rangers, where he finished his career in 1988–89. He was elected to the Hockey Hall of Fame in 1992 and remains the Kings all-time leader in goals (550), assists (757) and points (1,307).

GORDIE DRILLON was playing in his hometown of Moncton, New Brunswick when he was discovered by the Maple Leafs and brought to Toronto to continue his amateur career. He was with the Leafs' American Hockey League farm club in Syracuse during the 1936–37 season when he got the call to Toronto to fill in for Charlie Conacher.

Standing six feet tall and weighing 185 pounds, Drillon was a big man, but he did not employ the same physical style as Conacher. Still, playing alongside Syl Apps, he would prove to be a more than adequate replacement for "the Big Bomber" as Toronto's top offensive threat. Drillon led the NHL in goals with 26, winning the scoring title with 52 points in 1937–38 (the last Leafs player to do so). He also won the Lady Byng Trophy that year, and he was named to the First All-Star Team at right wing. He was a First Team All-Star again the following year and a Second Team member in 1941–42.

Drillon led the Maple Leafs in goal-scoring and points four times during his six seasons in Toronto, helping the Leafs to reach the Stanley Cup finals three times, though he was benched in the 1942 finals when the Leafs rallied from a 3–0 game deficit to defeat the Detroit Red Wings. Drillon was sold to the Montreal Canadiens prior to the 1942–43 campaign, leading the Canadiens with a career-high 28 goals in what proved to be his final NHL season. In 1975, he was inducted into the Hockey Hall of Fame.

GRAHAM DRINKWATER won a junior hockey title with the Montreal Amateur Athletic Association in 1892–93, when the senior team earned the first Stanley Cup title. He also won hockey and football championships with McGill University in 1893 and 1894 before joining the Montreal Victorias hockey club in 1894–95 He had played briefly with the team two years before.

The Victorias won their first Stanley Cup title with Drinkwater in 1894–95, but they lost the Cup in a challenge match with the Winnipeg Victorias in February of 1896 before winning it back later in the year. The Montreal team retained the trophy through the next two seasons before Drinkwater was named team captain in 1898–99. The Montreal Victorias again defeated their Winnipeg counterparts in February of 1899, but the Stanley Cup was lost to the Montreal Shamrocks at season's end. Drinkwater was inducted into the Hockey Hall of Fame in 1950.

KEN DRYDEN was selected originally by the Boston Bruins in the 1964 Amateur Draft, but opted to attend Cornell University instead, becoming a three-time all-American between 1966 and 1969. Dryden played for the Canadian national team in 1969 before joining the Montreal Canadiens organization with their minor pro affiliate, Nova Scotia, in 1970–71.

Dryden played only six games in goal for the Canadiens after joining the team late in the 1970–71 season but then went on to star in the playoffs, taking part in all 20 games. He won the Conn Smythe Trophy after leading Montreal to a surprising Stanley Cup victory. Dryden was still considered a rookie the following season, which enabled him to win the Calder Trophy. He also earned a selection to the Second All-Star Team. Dryden shared goaltending duties with Tony Esposito on victorious Team Canada in the 1972 Summit Series against the Soviet Union, then played on another Stanley Cup winner in 1973. He also won the Vezina Trophy and was named to the First All-Star Team that year. While at the peak of his game, Dryden sat out the 1973–74 season in a contract dispute with the Canadiens, working as a legal clerk in order to obtain his law degree from McGill University.

Dryden returned to the Canadiens in 1974–75 and from 1976 until 1979 the Canadiens won four consecutive championships. During that time, Dryden either won or shared the Vezina Trophy each year while being named to the First All-Star Team. Although he was only 31 and had played just seven-plus seasons, Dryden retired in 1979. He had posted a record of 258–57–74 for a .758 winning percentage, easily the best in NHL goaltending history. He also had 46 shutouts and a 2.24 career goals-against average. It was expected that Dryden would enter law or politics, but instead he took his family to England and wrote a best-selling book called *The Game* based on his hockey experience. After returning to Canada in 1982, Dryden settled in Toronto where he served as Ontario Youth Commissioner, coordinating youth employment and training programs, from 1984 to 1986. He continued to write about hockey, the

workplace and education and hosted an acclaimed series of documentary television programs about hockey's role in Canadian culture.

On May 30, 1997, Dryden returned to active involvement in hockey when he was named president of the Toronto Maple Leafs, adding the duties of general manager three months later. He has been a member of the Hockey Hall of Fame since 1983.

STEVE DUCHESNE has been one of the NHL's best scoring defensemen throughout his career. He made his debut with the Los Angeles Kings in 1986–87 and was named to the All-Rookie Team that year along with fellow L.A. freshmen Luc Robitaille and Jimmy Carson. Duchesne led Kings defensemen in scoring all five seasons he was with the team but was traded to the Philadelphia Flyers on May 30, 1991.

After just one season with his new team, Duchesne was part of the package the Flyers traded to the Quebec Nordiques on June 30, 1992 for the rights to Eric Lindros. Duchesne established career highs with 62 assists and 82 points with Quebec in 1992–93, but was on the move again the following season when he was traded to the St. Louis Blues. Duchesne spent two years in St. Louis, then two season with the Ottawa Senators, where he scored the goal that clinched the club's first playoff berth in 1996–97. On August 25, 1997, the Senators traded Duchesne back to St. Louis. He returned to Los Angeles as a free agent following the 1997–98 season.

GEORGE DUDLEY was active in amateur hockey for more than 50 years. He first played the game in his hometown of Midland, Ontario, but began serving as an executive after obtaining his law degree in 1917. He was elected to the Canadian Amateur Hockey Association executive in 1925, served as its president from 1940 to 1942, became secretary in 1945 and later served as secretary manager. He was also president of the Ontario Hockey Association from 1934 to 1936.

Dudley was elected to the Hockey Hall of Fame as a builder in 1958, and remained active in sports administration until his death on May 8, 1960. At that time, he was treasurer of the OHA, president of the International Ice Hockey Federation and had been head of the hockey section of the 1960 Olympic Games.

DICK DUFF was a product of the Toronto Maple Leafs farm system, playing junior hockey at St. Michael's College and with the Toronto Marlboros before becoming a regular with the Maple Leafs in 1955–56. Though he had a slight build, Duff was aggressive and racked up 74 penalty minutes (a fairly high total in those days) as well as 18 goals in his rookie season.

Duff was at his best over the next three years, scoring 26, 26, and 29 goals. He would never again reach such high scoring totals but he was effective both offensively and as a penalty killer with Maple Leafs teams that won the Stanley Cup in 1961–62 and 1962–63. His production dropped off dramatically during the 1963–64 season and on February 22, 1964 he was one of five players traded to the New York Rangers in the deal that brought Andy Bathgate and Don McKenney to Toronto.

Duff was not happy in New York and on December 22, 1964 the Rangers shipped him to the Montreal Canadiens. He played on a line with Jean Beliveau and Yvon Cournoyer in Montreal that season and helped the Canadiens win the Stanley Cup. Duff played mostly with Cournoyer and Ralph Backstrom in 1965–66 and recaptured his earlier goal-scoring form with 21 goals. The Canadiens repeated as Stanley Cup champions that season. Duff played on his fifth and sixth Stanley Cup-winning teams in Montreal in 1967–68 (when he scored 25 goals) and 1968–69 but was sold to the Los Angeles Kings on January 23, 1970. The Kings traded him to the expansion Buffalo Sabres on December 1, 1970, and Duff ended his career after playing eight games with the Sabres during the 1971–72 season.

WOODY DUMART was the left winger on the Boston Bruins' famed Kraut Line of the 1930s and 1940s. Lifelong friends Dumart, Milt Schmidt and Bobby Bauer were a high-scoring trio who helped the Bruins win the Stanley Cup in 1939 and 1941. Dumart was the first of the three to arrive in the NHL when he played one game for the Bruins in 1935–36.

Dumart was considered one of the best two-way players in the NHL during his era and was used often to shadow some of the game's greatest players. Still, he managed to maintain an excellent scoring record and topped 20 goals on five occasions. In 1939–40, Schmidt, Dumart and Bauer finished 1–2–3 in the NHL scoring race and Dumart earned a berth on the Second All-Star Team, as he would again the following season. Early in the 1941–42 campaign, all three teammates enlisted in the Royal Canadian Air Force and were out of the NHL until 1945–46. Dumart picked up right were he had left off, and enjoyed his best season with 24 goals and 28 assists in 1946–47 when he earned his final selection to the Second All-Star Team.

The Kraut Line was broken up after the 1946–47 season by the retirement of Bobby Bauer, but Dumart continued to be an effective player for several more seasons. His numbers declined dramatically after the 1950–51 campaign and he retired after playing part of the 1954–55 season in the American Hockey League. In 1992, Dumart was elected to the Hockey Hall of Fame.

ART DUNCAN was with the Vancouver Millionaires of the Pacific Coast Hockey Association in 1915–16, but enlisted for military service in World War I the following year. He was a member of the 228th Battalion hockey team that began the 1916–17 season in the National Hockey Association before being sent overseas.

Returning from the Great War decorated with the Military Cross, Duncan resumed his hockey career with Vancouver in 1918–19. Lloyd Cook served as his defense partner and the two would help Vancouver win four consecutive PCHA championship titles before the pairing was broken up when Cook joined the Boston Bruins for the 1924–25 season. After a season with the Calgary Tigers in 1925–26, Duncan also moved on to the NHL when major-league pro hockey in the west collapsed.

Duncan began his NHL career in 1926–27 as a player-coach with the Detroit Cougars (who later became the Falcons, then Red Wings). Jack Adams replaced him as coach the following season and Duncan moved on to the Toronto St. Pats hockey club that had been bought by Conn Smythe and renamed the Maple Leafs. When Smythe purchased King Clancy and acquired Alex Levinsky to bolster his defense in 1930–31, Duncan retired to coach the club. He was replaced by Dick Irvin early in the 1931–32 season, the year the Maple Leafs won their first Stanley Cup.

THOMAS DUNDERDALE Though he actually grew up in Ottawa and Winnipeg, Tommy Dunderdale is the only man born in Australia to have been elected to the Hockey Hall of Fame. His 196 goals in the Pacific Coast Hockey Association rank second in league history behind the 203 scored by Mickey MacKay, and his 257 points are fourth on the PCHA's career list.

After playing junior hockey in Winnipeg, Dunderdale turned pro with the Montreal Shamrocks in 1909–10 when the team moved from the Canadian Hockey Association to the National Hockey Association. He was with the Quebec Bulldogs the following year before joining the Victoria Aristocrats for the inaugural PCHA season of 1911–12. The next year, he led the league in scoring with 24 goals and five assists. He tied Cyclone Taylor for the league lead with 24 goals again in 1913–14, scoring in all 15 games and being named to the PCHA all-star team at center.

Dunderdale played four years in Victoria, then three with the Portland Rosebuds, before returning to Victoria for five more seasons. He was on PCHA league champions with the Aristocrats in 1912–13 and 1913–14 and the Rosebuds in 1915–16, but he never was on a Stanley Cup champion. Victoria actually beat the Stanley Cup champion Quebec Bulldogs in a 1913 series, but the trophy was not on the line. The Aristocrats were defeated by the Toronto Blueshirts in a 1914 Cup challenge, and Portland lost to Montreal in 1916 when the Canadiens won their first Stanley Cup title.

Dunderdale won a second PCHA scoring title with 26 goals and seven assists for Victoria in 1920–21, but he soon was relegated to a backup role behind Frank Fredrickson. He wrapped up his career with the Saskatoon Crescents and Edmonton Eskimos of the Western Canada Hockey League in 1923–24. After his playing days, Dunderdale coached teams in Los Angeles, Edmonton and Winnipeg. He was elected to the Hockey Hall of Fame in 1974.

JIMMY DUNN was associated with a variety of sports over a lengthy administrative career in Winnipeg. Dunn held executive offices in baseball, softball, football, lacrosse, basketball, boxing and others, but he earned his greatest honors in hockey.

Dunn's involvement in hockey began after serving with distinction in World War I, when he became involved in several local leagues that became part of the Manitoba Amateur Hockey Association in 1927. In 1942, he became vice president of the MAHA, and three years later he began a six-year term as president. He later served as vice president and president of the Canadian Amateur Hockey Association.

Dunn retained an active interest in Manitoba hockey affairs, acting as convener of international tournaments in 1967 and 1968. He was also secretary-treasurer of the Manitoba Hockey Players Federation. Dunn was inducted into the Hockey Hall of Fame as a builder in 1968.

BILL DURNAN played only seven years in the NHL, but won the Vezina Trophy and was named to the First All-Star Team in goal on six occasions. Durnan was ambidextrous, able to use his stick or catch the puck equally well with either hand, but the pressure of the game's most difficult position forced his retirement in 1950. His six Vezina Trophy wins were the most in NHL history until Jacques Plante earned his seventh such honor in 1968–69.

Durnan was born in Toronto, but first came to attention playing goal with the Sudbury junior team that reached the Ontario Hockey Association finals in 1934. In 1940, he was a member of the Kirkland Lake Blue Devils when they won the Allan Cup. Durnan joined the Montreal Royals of the Quebec Senior Hockey League the following year and spent three seasons there before finally entering the NHL as a 28-year-old rookie with the Montreal Canadiens in 1943–44. The Canadiens featured the high-scoring Punch Line of Elmer Lach, Maurice Richard and Toe Blake that season, but much of the credit for Montreal winning its first Stanley Cup title in 13 years went to Durnan. His brilliant goaltending that season was rewarded with his first Vezina Trophy

and first All-Star selection. He won the dual honors again in each of the next three seasons as well, while helping the Canadiens win another Stanley Cup championship in 1946.

Turk Broda finally broke off Durnan's Vezina and All-Star run in 1947–48, but the Canadiens netminder was better than ever during the 1948–49 campaign. That year, he posted a career-best 2.10 goals-against average with 10 shutouts and set a modern NHL record when he went unscored upon for 309 minutes and 21 seconds, including a span of four consecutive shutouts. Durnan's numbers were almost as impressive in 1949–50, but he retired after that season. In 1963, he was elected to the Hockey Hall of Fame.

RED DUTTON Mervyn A. "Red" Dutton was one of the most penalized players in hockey during his career, but his toughness never was tested more severely than after being wounded at the battle of Vimy Ridge in World War I. Barely avoiding the amputation of his leg, he recovered and practiced seven hours a day in order to resume his career as a hockey player. The tough but talented defenseman was well-respected by opposing players, just as he would be later as an NHL executive.

Dutton began his professional career with the Calgary Tigers of the Western Canada Hockey League in its inaugural season of 1921–22. He played against the Montreal Canadiens when Calgary was defeated in the 1924 Stanley Cup finals, and he signed with the Montreal Maroons for the 1926–27 season after pro hockey in the west collapsed. He led the NHL in penalty minutes with the Maroons in 1928–29 and spent one more season in Montreal before being traded to the New York Americans for Lionel Conacher.

Dutton spent five seasons as a player with the Americans before being named playing coach in 1935–36. He promptly led the team to the playoffs for the first time in six seasons and became the full-time coach the following year. Dutton continued behind the bench until the franchise's final season as the Brooklyn Americans in 1941–42. He had been made responsible for the front-office management of the team and was the Americans' representative on the NHL Board of Governors. Dutton so impressed his fellow governors that he was persuaded to become NHL president upon the death of Frank Calder in 1943. He held the position until Clarence Campbell replaced him in 1946 and was inducted into the Hockey Hall of Fame in 1958.

BABE DYE was a superb stickhandler with a hard, accurate shot and was one of the best goal scorers of his era. In addition to his immense hockey skills, he played senior football while growing up in Toronto, and he was offered a $25,000 contract (a fabulous sum in those days) to play baseball for Connie Mack's Philadelphia Athletics in 1921. Dye did play minor-league baseball throughout much of his NHL career.

Dye entered the NHL with the Toronto St. Pats in 1919–20, but he found it difficult to break into the starting lineup that season. He began the next year with the Hamilton Tigers, but he was back in Toronto after just one game, leading the league with 35 goals that season. He ranked second in goals and third in points during the 1921–22 season. He led the St. Pats to the Stanley Cup with nine goals in the five-game final against the Vancouver Millionaires that spring, including four goals in a 5–1 Toronto victory in the deciding game. Dye then led the NHL in both goals and points in 1922–23 and 1924–25, with a career-high 38 goals in 29 games during the 1924–25 season. Twice between 1921 and 1925 he scored five goals in a game, and twice he had streaks of scoring in 11 consecutive games.

Dye joined the Chicago Black Hawks in 1926–27, enjoying one more good season before breaking a leg in training camp in 1927. The injury ended his baseball career and severely hampered the rest of his hockey career. His NHL playing days ended after the 1930–31 season, but he later served as a referee in the NHL and as a coach for the Chicago Shamrocks in the American Hockey Association. Dye was elected to the Hockey Hall of Fame in 1970.

ALAN EAGLESON His reputation has been damaged and he has been fined and jailed for embezzling from the player's pension fund and committing fraud in the organization of international hockey tournaments. Still, before all this came to light, Alan Eagleson's contributions to hockey were acknowledged in 1989 when he was inducted into the Hockey Hall of Fame as a builder. In 1998, he became the first Honoured Member to have his plaque removed from the Hall of Fame.

Eagleson graduated in law from the University of Toronto in 1957 and was a Conservative back-bench Member of Provincial Parliament in the Ontario government from 1963 to 1967. In the summer of 1966, he negotiated a contract for Bobby Orr with the Boston Bruins worth $75,000 over two years, at a time when the Bruins were offering the rookie $8,000 plus a $5,000 signing bonus. By June of 1967, at the urging of Orr's Boston teammates, Eagleson had organized the National Hockey League Players' Association.

The NHLPA was instrumental in increasing player salaries and eventually in creating a more stable relationship between players and management. As executive director of the NHLPA, Eagleson became one of the most powerful men in hockey, but his most visible connection to the game was in the international arena. Eagleson helped Hockey Canada president Charles Hay arrange the famous 1972 Summit Series between Canadian NHL pros and the

Soviet national team. The success of the 1972 series enabled Eagleson to assume a leadership role in the development of the Canada Cup, which was staged for the first time in 1976 and held again in 1981, 1984, 1987 and 1991. Eagleson stepped down as director of the NHLPA in December of 1991 after having survived attempts to oust him as leader of the union in June and August of 1989.

CHAUCER ELLIOTT Edwin "Chaucer" Elliott earned a reputation as an outstanding athlete and sportsman while excelling at many sports, including hockey, baseball and football. He played hockey and football at Queen's University in Kingston, played pro baseball in Toronto in 1903, and he later coached the Toronto Argonauts, Hamilton Tigers and Montreal Amateur Athletic Association football clubs. He played on a championship football team in 1899 before coaching Hamilton to the Canadian title in 1906.

Elliott became a hockey referee in 1903 and he was regarded as one of the best in Canada over the next 10 years before dying of cancer on March 13, 1913 at the age of 34. In 1961, along with Cooper Smeaton and Mickey Ion, he was one of the first three referees elected to the Hockey Hall of Fame.

PHIL ESPOSITO joined the Chicago Black Hawks during the 1963–64 season. Over the next three years, the stocky center proved himself to be both an effective scorer and playmaker, since his size made it difficult for defensemen to clear him out of the slot. On May 15, 1967, Esposito was the central figure in a six-player trade between the Black Hawks and the Bruins. In Boston, he combined with Bobby Orr to rewrite the NHL record book.

Esposito was runner-up behind former Chicago teammate Stan Mikita for the NHL scoring title in 1967–68, when he led the league with 49 assists. The following year, on March 2, 1969, he became the first player in NHL history to reach 100 points in a single season and ended the 1968–69 campaign with 126 points on 49 goals and 77 assists. In addition to winning the Art Ross Trophy as scoring champion for the first time, Esposito won the Hart Trophy as most valuable player. In 1969–70, he had 99 points and helped Boston to win its first Stanley Cup title in 29 years. The Bruins set an NHL record in 1970–71 with 57 wins and 121 points, and Esposito led the way by smashing Bobby Hull's single-season record of 58 goals with 76 goals in 78 games. He also collected 76 assists for 152 points, a total that remained an NHL record until surpassed by Wayne Gretzky in 1980–81. His goal-scoring record was broken by Gretzky one year later.

The Bruins were upset in the quarterfinals by the Montreal Canadiens in 1971, but Esposito won his second straight scoring title in 1971–72 and the Bruins recaptured the Stanley Cup. In September of 1972, he was the top scorer and inspirational leader of Team Canada in their hard-fought victory over the Soviet national team. By 1973–74, Esposito had won the Art Ross Trophy for the fifth time and was again rewarded with the Hart as MVP. In 1974–75, he was named to the all-star team for the eighth consecutive season, which included six straight selections to the First All-Star Team between 1968–69 and 1974–75.

On November 7, 1975, Esposito was again the central figure in a multi-player deal when the Bruins surprised the hockey world by trading him to the New York Rangers. His best days were behind him now, but Esposito still led the Rangers in scoring four years in a row and helped them reach the Stanley Cup finals in 1979. When he retired in 1981, Esposito's 717 goals and 1,590 points trailed only Gordie Howe's totals of 801 and 1,850 among the NHL's all-time leaders and his 873 assists were third all-time. He was elected to the Hockey Hall of Fame in 1984.

Esposito served as Rangers general manager (and briefly as coach) between 1986–87 and 1988–89. He helped to land an NHL expansion team in Tampa Bay during 1990 and 1991 and became the first general manager of the Lightning, who began play in the NHL in 1992–93.

TONY ESPOSITO Often referred to as Phil's kid brother when he broke into the NHL, Tony Esposito's skill as a goaltender very quickly earned him recognition in his own right. He had played three years of U.S. college hockey at Michigan Tech before making his NHL debut by playing 13 games for the Montreal Canadiens in 1968–69. He was then claimed by the Chicago Black Hawks in the Intra-League Draft in June of 1969. In 1969–70, Esposito set a modern NHL record with 15 shutouts to complement a 2.17 goals-against average. He won both the Calder and Vezina trophies that season and was selected to the First All-Star Team.

Esposito helped the Black Hawks reach the Stanley Cup finals in 1971, and in 1971–72 he posted a career-best 1.76 goals-against average to again win the Vezina Trophy and a berth on the First All-Star Team. He shared netminding duties with Ken Dryden on Team Canada in September of 1972 and played in the Stanley Cup finals again in 1973. Esposito was a Second Team All-Star that season, as he was in 1973–74 when he shared the Vezina Trophy with Bernie Parent of the Philadelphia Flyers.

Esposito remained the top goaltender in Chicago until 1982–83, earning All-Star honors for the final time in 1979–80 when he was selected to the First Team. When he retired after the 1983–84 season, Esposito's 423 victories trailed only Terry Sawchuk (447) and Jacques Plante (434) among the NHL's

all-time leaders and his 76 shutouts ranked seventh in history. He was elected to the Hockey Hall of Fame in 1988.

After his playing days, Esposito worked for the NHL Players' Association before becoming vice president and general manager of the Pittsburgh Penguins on April 14, 1988. Pittsburgh made the playoffs for the first time in seven years in 1988–89, but Esposito was fired in December of 1989. He joined brother Phil in the front office of the Tampa Bay Lightning when the franchise was granted officially in December of 1991, serving as director of hockey development and scouting.

DOUG EVERETT and Myles Lane are considered to be the best hockey players produced by Dartmouth College in the 1920s. Everett had been captain of the Colby Academy team for the 1921–22 season before enrolling at Dartmouth in the fall of 1922 and henceforth dazzled fans with his stickhandling, speed and hard shot. He was all-College in both his sophomore and junior years and was named by the *New York Herald Tribune* to one of the first all-American hockey teams.

After graduation in 1926, Everett had offers from the Boston Bruins, New York Rangers and Toronto Maple Leafs but declined and went into insurance in Concord, New Hampshire. He rose through the ranks to partner and chairman of the board of Morrill and Everett while he continued to play amateur hockey with the University Club of Boston. In 1932, he played with the U.S. Olympic hockey team that won a silver medal at the Lake Placid Games. Everett was enshrined in the United States Hockey Hall of Fame in 1974 and has a rink named in his honor in Concord.

ART FARRELL starred with Harry Trihey and Fred Scanlan on the Montreal Shamrocks at the turn of the century, helping the team to win the Canadian Amateur Hockey League title and the Stanley Cup in 1898–99 and 1899–1900. All three are in the Hockey Hall of Fame, and Farrell is credited as being one of the men responsible for shifting hockey from a game of individual stars to one that focused on teamwork. He wrote a hockey manual in 1899 that offers some of the first published records of the early rules of hockey.

Farrell scored 29 goals in 26 regular-season games during his four seasons with the Shamrocks, but he was at his best in Stanley Cup competition. He had two goals in a 6–2 victory over Queen's University in a one-game Stanley Cup challenge on March 14, 1899, and he had 10 goals in five games during two sets of challenges in 1900, including a pair of four-goal games. Farrell had five goals in one regular-season game on January 19, 1901. He was elected to the Hockey Hall of Fame in 1965.

BERNIE FEDERKO was the Blues' first choice (seventh overall) in the 1976 Amateur Draft and established himself as the franchise's best player during his time in St. Louis. His 13 seasons, 927 games, 352 goals, 721 assists, and 1,073 points were all Blues career records, though some have since been surpassed.

Federko was the first player in NHL history to record at least 50 assists for 10 consecutive seasons, achieving the feat between 1978–79 and 1987–88. He topped 100 points four times in his career and finished among the top 10 in scoring on five occasions. The Blues were consistently among the top teams in their division over Federko's tenure, but he was traded to Detroit on June 15, 1989 and finished his career with one season as a Red Wing.

SERGEI FEDOROV was the first European to win the Hart Trophy as the NHL's most valuable player when he captured the award in 1993–94. He was named to the First All-Star Team at center that year after finishing second to Wayne Gretzky for the NHL scoring title. He also won the Selke Trophy as the league's top defensive forward. Fedorov won the Selke Trophy again in 1995–96.

Fedorov was selected by the Detroit Red Wings in the 1989 Entry Draft and joined the NHL club in July of 1990 after leaving the Soviet national team en route to the Goodwill Games in Seattle. He led all rookies with 31 goals, 48 assists and 79 points in 1990–91 and earned a spot on the NHL All-Rookie Team while finishing runner-up to Ed Belfour in voting for the Calder Trophy. Fedorov's offensive production increased in each of the next two seasons leading up to his MVP campaign in 1993–94. He led the league in playoff scoring when the Red Wings reached the Stanley Cup finals in 1995 and led the club in postseason points when Detroit won the Cup in 1997. He returned from a lengthy holdout in 1997–98 to help the Red Wings repeat as Stanley Cup champions.

Despite his holdout through the first half of the 1997–98 season, Fedorov was a late addition to the Russian Olympic team in Nagano that won the silver medal. His previous international experience included winning a gold medal on the Soviet team at the 1989 World Junior Championships, when he centered a line with Pavel Bure and Alexander Mogilny, and further gold medals at the World Championships in 1989 and 1990. He was also a member of the Russian team at the World Cup of Hockey in 1996.

JOHN FERGUSON After winning the Stanley Cup five years in a row to close out the 1950s, the Montreal Canadiens had gone three years without a championship and general manager Frank Selke believed the missing ingredi-

ent was toughness. As a result, John Ferguson's contract was purchased from the Cleveland Barons of the American Hockey League after he scored 38 goals and led the league with 179 penalty minutes in 1962–63. In his eight seasons with Montreal, the Canadiens won the Stanley Cup five times.

Jean Beliveau has called Ferguson "the most formidable player of the decade, if not in the Canadiens' history." Ferguson himself says when he came to Montreal he "wanted to be the meanest, rottenest, most miserable cuss ever to play in the NHL." He consistently ranked among the league's penalty minute leaders, topping the NHL in 1966–67, but could also be an effective scorer with a career-high 29 goals in 1968–69. He refused to fraternize with opposition players during his career, even in summertime.

Ferguson retired after the Canadiens won the Stanley Cup in 1971 and was Harry Sinden's assistant coach with Team Canada in 1972. From 1976 to 1978, he was general manager of the New York Rangers before taking the same position with the Winnipeg Jets in the World Hockey Association's final season of 1978–79. The Jets won the Avco Cup that year and Ferguson remained with the club when Winnipeg entered the NHL in 1979, staying until 1989. He was in the Ottawa Senators' front office from 1992 to 1995 and became a scout with the San Jose Sharks in 1996.

VIACHESLAV FETISOV was recognized as one of the best defensemen in the world long before he made his debut in the National Hockey League with the New Jersey Devils in 1988–89. The long-time captain of the Central Red Army Team in Moscow had been an international star for years as a member of the Soviet national team.

Fetisov joined the Red Army in 1974–75 and got his first international exposure that year when the Soviets won gold at the European Junior Championships. The Soviets won the tournament again in 1976 and Fetisov was named the best defenseman. In 1977–78, he was a member of the gold medal-winning team at the World Junior Championships and was named to the tournament all-star team along with future NHLers Wayne Gretzky, Anton Stastny, Mats Naslund and Risto Siltanen. Fetisov also won his first World Championship that year as a member of the Soviet national team and was named to the First All-Star Team for the first of eight times in the Soviet National League.

Fetisov went on to play in 10 more World Championships and won six more gold medals. He was named the top defenseman at the tournament five times and was chosen for the all-star team on eight occasions. He also won gold medals at the Olympics in 1984 and 1988 and a silver medal in 1980 when the Russians lost the gold to the United States. Fetisov won the Golden Stick Award as the best player in Europe in 1983–84, 1985–86 and 1989–90. He was named the Soviet player of the year in 1981–82, 1985–86 and 1987–88 and was the top-scoring defenseman in the Soviet League in 1983–84 and from 1985–86 to 1987–88. Fetisov assisted on the Canada Cup-winning goal in 1981, was named to the Canada Cup all-star team in 1987 and represented Russia at the World Cup of Hockey in 1996. He also has received the Soviet Master of Sport award, a state honor comparable to induction into the Hockey Hall of Fame.

Fetisov was drafted by New Jersey back in 1983 but was not allowed to leave the Soviet Union for another six years. He made his NHL debut on October 5, 1989, and went on to play five seasons with the Devils. He sat out the beginning of the 1994–95 season before re-signing in New Jersey but was traded to the Detroit Red Wings on April 5, 1995. In 1996–97, Fetisov and former Red Army teammates Igor Larionov, Sergei Fedorov and Vladimir Konstantinov, plus fellow Russian Slava Kozlov, were part of the Detroit team that won the Stanley Cup for the first time since 1955. Fetisov organized the Stanley Cup's first visit to Russia that summer. In 1997–98 he helped the Red Wings repeat as champions.

FERN FLAMAN played 17 years in the NHL with the Boston Bruins and Toronto Maple Leafs. A tough, stay-at-home defenseman, he was known for his powerful bodychecks and his ability to clear the area in front of his team's goal. He led the NHL in penalty minutes with 150 in 1954–55 when he earned a selection to the Second All-Star Team. Flaman was also a Second Team All-Star in 1956–57 and 1957–58.

Flaman made a pair of one-game appearances with the Bruins before joining the NHL to stay in 1946–47. He was dealt to the Maple Leafs during the 1950–51 season and played for his only Stanley Cup winner that year. Toronto traded him back to Boston in 1954, and he was named captain of the team in 1955–56. Flaman remained Bruins captain until leaving the NHL after the 1960–61 season. He then became the playing coach with the Providence Reds of the American Hockey League, leading the team to the best record in the league in 1962–63. The following year, he added the third role of general manager before giving up his playing career. Flaman was coach and g.m. with the Los Angeles Blades of the Western Hockey League in 1966–67, then spent two seasons as coach of the Fort Worth Wings.

In 1970, Flaman became the head coach at Northeastern University and quickly built his team into a perennial power. He was selected as U.S. college coach of the year in 1982 and led Northeastern to the Hockey East title in 1989, his final season with the school. In 1990, Flaman was elected to the

Hockey Hall of Fame. From 1991 to 1995, he was a scout with the New Jersey Devils, Stanley Cup winners in 1995.

THEOREN FLEURY was selected by the Calgary Flames with the 166th pick in the 1987 Entry Draft. He topped 100 points in each of his last three seasons in junior hockey, leading the Western Hockey League with 160 points in 1987–88, but at just 5'6" and 160 pounds, he was thought to be too small to play in the NHL. He proved his critics wrong with his offensive skill and a competitive spirit.

Fleury helped the Salt Lake Golden Eagles win the Turner Cup as International Hockey League champions in 1987–88 and began the 1988–89 season with Salt Lake before joining the Flames midway through the season. Fleury helped Calgary to win the Stanley Cup that year, then scored 31 goals in his first full NHL season of 1989–90. In 1990–91, he became just the fifth player in Flames history to top 50 goals and 100 points in a single season. His 51 goals tied him for second-best in the NHL that year, and his 104 points ranked eighth, while his plus–minus total of +48 tied Marty McSorley for top spot in the NHL.

Between 1989–90 and 1993–94, Fleury topped 30 goals five years in a row and reached 100 points twice. He scored 29 goals in 47 games during the lockout-shortened season of 1994–95 and added 29 assists to finish sixth in the league in scoring and earn a spot on the Second All-Star Team. During the 1997–98 season, Fleury passed Joe Nieuwendyk as the all-time leading goal scorer in Flames history.

In addition to his success in the NHL, Fleury has starred in the international arena. He represented Canada at the World Junior Championships in 1987 and captained the team that won the junior title in 1988 while earning a spot on the tournament's all-star team. Fleury played for Team Canada at the World Championships in 1990 and was on the silver medal-winning team in 1991. He was a member of Team Canada at the 1991 Canada Cup, the 1996 World Cup of Hockey and the 1998 Nagano Olympics.

LOU FONTINATO added much-needed toughness to his team when he was called up to the New York Rangers in 1954–55. He played his first full season in the NHL the following year and became the first player in history to top 200 penalty minutes when he had 202 in 1955–56.

Fontinato consistently ranked among the league leaders in penalty minutes throughout his career and led the league twice in his first three seasons. But Fontinato was more than just a tough guy, he was also an effective defenseman. Still, he is perhaps best remembered for a fight he lost to Gordie Howe in February of 1959.

Prior to the 1961–62 campaign, the Rangers sent Fontinato to the Montreal Canadiens in exchange for Doug Harvey (who would serve as player-coach in New York) and he led the NHL in penalty minutes for a third time that season. His career came to a premature end the next year when he broke a bone in his back after crashing into the boards. Ironically, Fontinato's penalty record of 202 minutes was broken during his final season of 1962–63 when Howie Young of the Detroit Red Wings had 273 minutes in penalties.

ADAM FOOTE was selected by the Quebec Nordiques with the first choice in the second round of the 1989 Entry Draft. He returned to Sault Ste. Marie of the Ontario Hockey League for the next two seasons and was a First Team All-Star in 1990–91 before making his NHL debut in 1991–92. Foote was with Quebec for four seasons until the team moved to Denver and became the Colorado Avalanche.

Foote began to earn recognition as one of the NHL's best defensive defensemen when Colorado won the Stanley Cup in 1996, and his tough, physical play earned him a spot on Team Canada at the World Cup of Hockey in 1996. He was also a member of the Canadian Olympic team in Nagano in 1998.

JAKE FORBES Standing 5'6" and weighing only 140 pounds, Vernon "Jake" Forbes was an acrobatic goaltender who helped pave the way for other small netminders at a time when teams generally preferred a larger man who could take up more of the goal. A Toronto native who came up through the amateur ranks in his hometown, Forbes entered the NHL with the Toronto St. Pats during the 1919–20 season. He helped the St. Pats win the second half of the NHL schedule in 1920–21, though the team then lost the NHL championship in a playoff series against the Ottawa Senators, who had won the first half.

A contract dispute saw Forbes sit out the entire 1921–22 season and he was replaced by John Ross Roach who helped the St. Pats win the Stanley Cup that year. Forbes signed with the Hamilton Tigers in 1922–23 and endured two last-place seasons before the Tigers topped the NHL in 1924–25. Forbes posted a career-best 1.96 goals-against average that season, but a strike by the Hamilton players in the playoffs cost the Tigers a chance at the Stanley Cup and saw the team become the New York Americans the following year.

Forbes was the top goalie with the Americans for two seasons and in 1926–27 played every game in goal for his team for the fifth year in a row. However, he spent most of the 1927–28 season in the minors and after the Americans acquired Roy Worters in 1928–29 Forbes' NHL career was virtually over. He never played more than six games for the Americans.

season between 1928–29 and 1932–33, though he did continue playing in the minor leagues until 1935–36.

PETER FORSBERG was selected sixth overall by the Philadelphia Flyers in the first round of the 1991 NHL Entry Draft, but was sent to the Quebec Nordiques on June 30, 1992 as part of the deal that brought Eric Lindros to Philadelphia. Forsberg remained in his native Sweden, representing his country at the World Junior Championships, the World Championships and the Olympics before making his NHL debut in 1994–95. He set a tournament record with 31 points at the World Junior Championships in 1993 and scored the winning goal in a shootout when Sweden beat Canada for the gold medal at the 1994 Lillehammer Olympics.

Forsberg led all NHL rookies with 35 assists and 50 points in 1994–95 to win the Calder Trophy and earn a spot on the All-Rookie Team. In 1995–96, the Nordiques became the Colorado Avalanche and Forsberg led the club with 86 assists. His 116 points that season were just four behind Joe Sakic for the team lead and ranked fifth overall in the NHL. Forsberg was fifth again in playoff scoring as Colorado became the first NHL club to win the Stanley Cup in its first year in a new city. Injuries limited Forsberg to just 65 games in 1996–97, but he still collected 86 points. He was named to the First All-Star Team in 1997–98.

A national hero in his homeland, Forsberg was depicted on a Swedish postage stamp commemorating his Olympic gold medal-winning goal. He also played for Sweden at the World Cup of Hockey in 1996 and at the 1998 Olympics in Nagano. Forsberg's father coached the Swedish national team from 1995 to 1998.

FRANK FOYSTON began his hockey career in the east, but he became a scoring star in the west with the Seattle Metropolitans of the Pacific Coast Hockey Association. His 186 goals rank third behind Mickey MacKay and Tommy Dunderdale in PCHA history and his 247 points are fifth all-time. He played on four league champions in the coast league and a pair of Stanley Cup winners.

Foyston played amateur hockey in Barrie, Ontario and Toronto before turning pro with the Toronto Blueshirts for the 1912–13 season of the National Hockey Association. He helped the team win the Stanley Cup the following year, but he was one of several Blueshirts players lured to Seattle when the Metropolitans were formed for the 1915–16 season. His 36 goals in 1916–17 were third in the PCHA, and he then scored seven goals in four playoff games as the league champion Mets beat the Montreal Canadiens to become the first American-based team to win the Stanley Cup. He also starred against Montreal in 1919 with nine goals in five games before the Stanley Cup series was halted by the influenza epidemic.

After leading the PCHA in goals with 26 in 1919–20, Foyston was again a playoff star with six goals in five games as Seattle lost the Stanley Cup to the Ottawa Senators. He led the PCHA in goals with another 26 in 1920–21, and he scored five in a single game for the second time in his career during the 1921–22 season. He remained with Seattle through the 1923–24 campaign, joining the Victoria Cougars in the Western Canada Hockey League after the Metropolitans folded. Foyston won a third Stanley Cup title with Victoria in 1925.

When pro hockey in the west collapsed after the 1925–26 season, Foyston was one over several Victoria players to join the Detroit Cougars (later the Red Wings) in their first NHL season of 1926–27. He played two years in the NHL, followed by three minor-league seasons in Detroit, before retiring in 1930. Foyston was elected to the Hockey Hall of Fame in 1958.

EMILE FRANCIS had a lengthy playing career (mostly in the minor leagues), but it is his work as a coach, general manager and executive that made him one of the most respected individuals in the game. Francis played junior hockey in his hometown of North Battleford, Saskatchewan in the early 1940s and remained involved with the sport until stepping down as president of the Hartford Whalers after the 1992–93 season.

"The Cat," as Francis was known, played parts of six seasons in the NHL with the Chicago Black Hawks and New York Rangers between 1946–47 and 1951–52. He was the starting goalie in Chicago during the 1947–48 season and in a game against Detroit that season, he appeared in goal wearing a first baseman's glove. Red Wings general manager Jack Adams protested, but NHL president Clarence Campbell declared no rule had been broken and the modern goaltender's catching glove was born.

After retiring as a player in 1960, Francis began his coaching career in the organization with Guelph of the Ontario Hockey Association. He was [...] NHL club as assistant general manager in 1962 and took over [...] 1964–65. He served in that capacity until 1975–76 and [...] much of that time. He quickly built a struggling [...] teams in the NHL and led the Rangers to the [...] time in 22 years in 1972.

[...] joined the St. Louis Blues as executive vice pres- [...] He was promoted to president in 1977 and [...] ough the 1982–83 season. Francis was awarded the [...] or contributions to hockey in the United States in 1982

and also gained induction into the Hockey Hall of Fame as a builder that year. He was named president and general manager of Hartford in May of 1983, and spent his final 10 seasons in the NHL with the Whalers.

RON FRANCIS was chosen fourth overall by the Hartford Whalers in the 1981 Entry Draft and made his NHL debut on November 14, 1981 after beginning the year in Sault Ste. Marie. He has gone on to become one of the NHL's all-time leaders in assists and points.

Francis played 10 years in Hartford, leading the club in scoring on five occasions and in assists seven times. He was the team MVP on four occasions and is the franchise's all-time leader in goals (264), assists (557), points (821) and games played (714). Francis became captain of the Whalers in 1984–85 and continued to wear the "C" until the time of his trade to the Pittsburgh Penguins on March 4, 1991. The acquisition of Francis, along with Grant Jennings and Ulf Samuelsson, helped the Penguins to win their first Stanley Cup title in May of 1991. The following year, Pittsburgh repeated as champions and Francis led all playoff performers with 19 assists.

Surrounded by such offensive talents at Mario Lemieux and Jaromir Jagr, Francis finally earned recognition as one of the game's top players. He led the NHL in assists in 1994–95 and won both the Selke Trophy as best defensive forward and the Lady Byng Trophy for sportsmanlike conduct. In 1995–96, Francis established career highs when he tied Lemieux for the NHL lead with 92 assists and registered 119 points. Francis was the Lady Byng Trophy winner again in 1997–98. Following the season, he signed as free agent with the Carolina Hurricanes.

FRANK FREDRICKSON was considered the greatest amateur player in the world after captaining the Winnipeg Falcons to victory at the first Olympic hockey tournament in April of 1920. In December of that year, he signed a pro contract with Lester Patrick's Victoria Aristocrats (later the Cougars) and became a scoring star in the Pacific Coast Hockey Association.

Fredrickson was of Icelandic descent, as were most of his Falcons teammates, and the team had to overcome much prejudice while playing in Winnipeg. He first joined the Falcons senior team for the 1913–14 season, quickly establishing himself as the top player. He led the team to a league title in 1914–15, and in the following season he served as captain of the Falcons as well as his team at the University of Manitoba. Fredrickson enlisted for military duty with the 196th Western Universities Battalion in 1916, but he soon transferred to the 223rd Scandinavian Battalion along with several Falcons teammates. The 223rd iced a hockey team during the 1916–17 season before being sent overseas.

After serving as a pilot and flight instructor during World War I, Fredrickson returned to Winnipeg and helped re-form the Falcons for the 1919–20 hockey season. The team won its league title that year and advanced all the way to the Allan Cup finals where they defeated the University of Toronto to become Canada's amateur champions. The victory earned a trip to Antwerp for the Olympic hockey tournament, where the Falcons won a gold medal for Canada.

Fredrickson continued to excel after entering professional hockey and the Victoria team improved with him. By his third season (1922–23), he had led the team to the playoffs for the first time in 10 years by leading the league with 39 goals and 16 assists for a single-season PCHA record of 55 points. When Vancouver and Victoria joined the Western Canada Hockey League in 1924–25, Fredrickson helped the team win the league title and defeat the Montreal Canadiens for the Stanley Cup.

When pro hockey collapsed in the west, Fredrickson joined the NHL, where he played in Detroit, Boston and Pittsburgh. He coached the Pirates during the 1929–30 season. He continued coaching after retiring as a player, first in Winnipeg, then with Princeton University, with the Royal Canadian Air Force and at the University of British Columbia. Fredrickson was elected to the Hockey Hall of Fame in 1958.

ROBBIE FTOREK was a member of the United States national team and played at the Sapporo Olympics in 1972 when the Americans earned a surprising silver medal. He also represented the United States at the Canada Cup in 1976 and 1981.

Ftorek had two brief NHL trials with the Detroit Red Wings before becoming a star during five seasons in the World Hockey Association. Four times Ftorek finished among the top-five scorers in the WHA, establishing personal highs with 59 goals in 1977–78 and a league-leading 77 assists in 1978–79. His best season overall was 1976–77 when he won the Gordie Howe Trophy as the WHA's most valuable player with 41 goals and 72 assists for a career-high 117 points. Ftorek ranks among the top–10 in WHA history in both goals (216) and assists (307) and is fifth all-time in total points (523).

When four WHA teams joined the NHL in 1979–80, Ftorek returned to the league with the Quebec Nordiques. He also played with the New York Rangers before ending his playing days in New Haven of the American Hockey League. Ftorek also coached in New Haven prior to landing an NHL job in Los Angeles as the Kings' coach from 1987 to 1989. He was a head coach in Halifax in 1989–90 and an assistant with the Nordiques in 1990–91. Ftorek has

been a coach with the New Jersey Devils since 1991–92 and replaced Jacques Lemaire as head coach after the 1997–98 season. He was elected to the United States Hockey Hall of Fame in 1991.

GRANT FUHR was the Edmonton Oilers first-round draft choice (eighth overall) in 1981 after an all-star season with Victoria of the Western Hockey League. He made his NHL debut in 1982–83 and was a Second Team All-Star. Fuhr also finished second in the voting for the Vezina Trophy behind Billy Smith that year and received serious consideration for the Calder Trophy, which went to Dale Hawerchuk. He has gone on to become one of the winningest goaltenders in NHL history.

Fuhr's arrival in the NHL coincided with Edmonton's rise to power in the league and the Oilers' great scoring ability allowed him to set a record for goaltenders with 14 assists in 1983–84. Though his goals-against averages were often high behind such an offensive-minded team, Fuhr earned a reputation as a goalie who would not surrender the big goal. He was at his best in the playoffs, helping the Oilers to win the Stanley Cup in 1984, 1985, 1987 and 1988. The 1987–88 season also saw him win the Vezina Trophy and earn a selection to the First All-Star Team after leading the league in games played, wins, minutes and shutouts.

Fuhr missed the first 55 games of the 1990–91 season after being suspended by the NHL and was dealt to the Toronto Maple Leafs in a multi-player trade on September 19, 1991. With the emergence of Felix Potvin as a star in Toronto in 1992–93, Fuhr was dealt to the Buffalo Sabres on February 2, 1993 for Dave Andreychuk. Fuhr shared the Jennings Trophy with Dominik Hasek in Buffalo in 1993–94 but was sent to the Los Angeles Kings in a trade on February 14, 1995. His poor play in Los Angeles had many thinking his career was over, but he was signed by the Blues on July 14, 1995 and his career was revived.

The 1995–96 season saw Fuhr set an NHL record by playing in 79 games, including 76 in a row. He suffered a serious knee injury during the playoffs that year and once again it was thought his career might be over, but Fuhr returned to play 73 games in 1996–97 and 58 in 1997–98.

JAMES FULLERTON became the first full-time coach at Brown University in 1955–56. At first, he had difficulty building a roster at an Ivy League school known more for academics than athletics, but he was eventually able to build a strong hockey program. Brown won the Ivy League championship and reached the final four of the NCAA tournament in 1964–65, the most successful season in Brown hockey history, and Fullerton was rewarded with the Spencer Penrose Award as the NCAA coach of the year.

In 15 seasons at Brown, Fullerton's teams put up a 176–168–9 record and his outstanding ability was recognized four times with the Clark Hodder Award as the New England coach of the year. He was named to the U.S. Collegiate Hall of Fame in 1971 and to Brown University's Hall of Fame in 1974. Fullerton was also a member of the United States Olympic Committee from 1969 to 1972 and coached the American team at the World University Games in 1972.

As a player, Fullerton had been a star at Norwich University but turned down an offer to play professionally to take a coaching job at Norwood, a prep school in Lake Placid. He remained there for 24 years and also worked as a referee in professional, college and high school games in the Lake Placid area from 1933 to 1955. He served as vice president of the New England chapter of the Amateur Athletic Union referees and was referee-in-chief for the 1939 national amateur championships in Lake Placid.

After he took the job at Brown in 1955, Fullerton continued to show his organizational skills as a prominent force in the formation and development of the American Hockey Coaches Association, which he served as president. In 1992, he was enshrined in the United States Hockey Hall of Fame in the coaches category.

BILL GADSBY played his early hockey in Calgary and Edmonton before signing with the Chicago Black Hawks in 1946–47. He began the year with Kansas City of the United States Hockey League, but was promoted to the NHL where he would go on to play for 20 years. During that time, Gadsby was one of the hockey's best defenseman. He could rush the puck, was an excellent playmaker and was adept at blocking shots.

Gadsby spent eight years as one of the few bright spots on a weak team in Chicago. The Black Hawks finished in last place six times and made the playoffs only once during his time there, but Gadsby was named captain in 1952–53 and made the Second All-Star Team that season and the next. He was traded to the New York Rangers in November of 1954 and went on to enjoy the best years of his career. He was named to the all-star team in each of his first four full seasons in New York, including three selections to the First Team, and his 46 points (14 goals, 32 assists) in 1957–58 were the second-most ever scored by a defenseman to that point in NHL history (Babe Pratt had 57 in 1943–44). While he never won the Norris Trophy, Gadsby was runner-up behind Doug Harvey in 1955–56 and 1957–58 and finished second to Tom Johnson in 1958–59.

In 1960, Jack Adams worked out a trade that would have brought Gadsby to Detroit, but the Red Wings' Red Kelly refused to report to New York and the deal fell through. Adams finally acquired Gadsby in June of 1961, and the defenseman finally got a chance to play for a successful team. Though the Red Wings missed the playoffs in 1961–62, the team reached the Stanley Cup finals in three of the next four years. In 1964–65, the Red Wings finished in first place in the regular-season standings and Gadsby was named to the Second All-Star Team.

Gadsby retired after the 1965–66 season and became coach of the Edmonton Oil Kings in the Western Canada Junior Hockey League. He returned to the NHL as a coach with the Red Wings in 1968–69 and spent two games back of the Detroit bench the following year. He was inducted into the Hockey Hall of Fame in 1970.

BOB GAINEY was one of the greatest two-way performers in NHL history. He spent his entire 16-year playing career with the Montreal Canadiens, where he was a member of five Stanley Cup champions and captain of the team from 1981–82 until he retired after 1988–89. He was inducted into the Hockey Hall of Fame in 1992.

Beginning in 1977–78, Gainey won the Selke Trophy as the NHL's best defensive forward the first four years the honor was bestowed. In 1979, he earned the Conn Smythe Trophy as most valuable player in the playoffs after the Canadiens won their fourth consecutive Stanley Cup title. Gainey was also a key performer during the 1976 and 1981 Canada Cup tournaments and was described by Soviet coach Viktor Tikhonov as technically the world's best hockey player.

Upon his retirement from the NHL, Gainey spent a year as a playing coach in France. He then returned to the NHL in 1990–91 as coach of the Minnesota North Stars and led the team to the Stanley Cup finals that year. Gainey was named general manager in 1992 and served in the dual role through the club's move to Dallas in 1993 until January 8, 1996, when he relinquished his head coaching duties. His five-plus years behind the bench was the longest tenure of any coach in franchise history. Gainey served as assistant general manager for the Canadian Olympic team in 1998.

DON GALLINGER was a promising young player with the Boston Bruins who had his career ended by a gambling scandal in 1948. He had entered the NHL as a 17-year-old in 1942–43 and was proving himself to be an effective player even after many experienced NHLers returned from military service.

The NHL had been trying to clean up its image since Babe Pratt was suspended for gambling in 1945–46 and subsequent raids in Toronto broke up a hockey betting ring. In February of 1948, NHL president Clarence Campbell announced he had evidence that some players were wagering on games, though there were no suggestion that the outcomes had been fixed. On March 9, 1948, Campbell expelled Billy Taylor and Don Gallinger for life—though the ban would be lifted in 1970. Gallinger never played hockey again.

SERGE GAMBUCCI earned national recognition for his athletic prowess during his high school career in his hometown of Eveleth, Minnesota. He served in World War II, then attended St. Cloud Teachers College (now St. Cloud State University), where he captained the hockey team and was its top scorer for two seasons. He continued his hockey career as a top-level amateur player after college and was the playing coach and leading scorer for the Crookston Pirates in 1950–51 when they won the United States national amateur championship.

When his playing career was over, Gambucci turned to coaching and teaching, first at Cathedral High School in Crookston, Minnesota, then at Central High School in Grand Forks, North Dakota. His Grand Forks teams won 10 consecutive state championships between 1961 and 1970 and he finished his coaching career with the third-highest winning percentage in U.S. high school hockey history.

Serge Gambucci's lifetime achievements have seen him gain induction into the Grand Forks Central Athletic Hall of Fame, the Grand Forks Public School Teachers' Hall of Fame, the St. Cloud State University Athletic Hall of Fame and the North Dakota Coaches Association Hall of Fame. In 1996, he was enshrined in the coaches category of the United States Hockey Hall of Fame.

CHARLIE GARDINER Rated by most as the greatest goaltender of his day, and by many as the greatest of all-time, Charlie Gardiner was at the height of his career when tragedy cut his life short at the age of 29. Just two months prior to his death on June 14, 1934, he had posted a 1–0 shutout in overtime that had given the Chicago Black Hawks their first Stanley Cup victory.

Born in Scotland but raised in Winnipeg, Gardiner became a goaltender because he was a poor skater. He moved up quickly through the amateur ranks in Manitoba and turned pro with the Winnipeg Maroons of the American Hockey Association for the 1926–27 season. The following year, he joined Black Hawks and replaced veteran Hugh Lehman. Chicago was last in its division in each of Gardiner's first two years and the club's weak offensive record for futility with just 33 goals in 44 games in 1928–29. The would show only minimal improvement over the years, but Gardiner team successful. He earned his first of four consecutive All-St

(three to the First Team) after leading the league with 12 shutouts in 1930–31, and he won the Vezina Trophy for the first of two times in 1931–32.

Gardiner was at his finest in 1933–34, posting a career-best 1.63 goals-against average and leading the league with 10 shutouts. He won the Vezina Trophy for the second time and played for the NHL All-Stars in the Ace Bailey benefit game on February 14, 1934. He had been named captain of the Black Hawks that year and his brilliant goaltending led the weak offensive team to second place in the American Division. Though plagued by headaches throughout the season, Gardiner played all 48 regular-season games.

Playoff victories over the Montreal Canadiens and Montreal Maroons put the Black Hawks in the finals against the Detroit Red Wings, but Gardiner's headaches became so bad that he would slump over the crossbar to rest when the play was in the other end. Still, he made 40 saves in the 1–0 Stanley Cup-winning victory on April 10, 1934. Two months later, while at home in Winnipeg, Gardiner collapsed and died of a brain hemorrhage

HERB GARDINER did not play in the NHL until 1926–27 when he was 35 years old, but he promptly won the Hart Trophy as the player most valuable to his team. His hockey career began in his hometown of Winnipeg when he played for the Victorias in 1908, but Gardiner was soon out of the game after playing two seasons with the Northern Crown Bank in Winnipeg's Bankers League. He did not return to hockey until after he served in World War I.

Gardiner joined the Calgary Tigers in 1919 and was with that team when it entered the Western Canada Hockey League for its inaugural season of 1921–22. He played for the Calgary team that lost the Stanley Cup to the Montreal Canadiens in 1924 and joined that club in 1926–27 after pro hockey collapsed in the west. The big defenseman helped the Canadiens post the best defensive record in the NHL that season and was rewarded with the Hart Trophy.

Gardiner remained with the Canadiens until 1928–29 when he left the team to become a playing coach with the Chicago Black Hawks. He was back in Montreal for the playoffs that year, but was later sold to the Boston Bruins, who in turn sold him to the Philadelphia Arrows of the Canadian-American Hockey League. Gardiner remained in Philadelphia as a player, coach and general manager until 1949. He was inducted into the Hockey Hall of Fame in 1958.

JIMMY GARDNER learned his hockey while growing up in Montreal with fellow future Hall of Famer Dickie Boon. He and Boon were both members of the Montreal Amateur Athletic Association team that became known as "the Little Men of Iron" while winning the Stanley Cup in 1902, and both jumped to the Montreal Wanderers when that team was formed for the 1903–04 season.

Gardner played in the International (Pro) Hockey League (hockey's first professional circuit) from 1904–05 to 1906–07 before returning to Montreal with the Shamrocks. He rejoined the Wanderers in 1908–09 and he was with the club as both a player and a manager when the team was part of creating the National Hockey Association in 1909–10. The Wanderers won the Stanley Cup that season, but when the Pacific Coast Hockey Association was formed the following year, Gardner became a member of the New Westminster Royals. After two years on the coast, he returned to Montreal in 1913–14 and spent two seasons with the Canadiens, then retired to coach the team for two years.

Gardner shifted to officiating in the 1917–18 season, refereeing in the minors and then the Western Canada Hockey League in 1923–24. He returned to coaching in 1924–25 and he guided the Hamilton Tigers to a first-place finish in the NHL regular-season standings before the team was barred from the playoffs when a salary dispute triggered the NHL's first players strike. Gardner was elected to the Hockey Hall of Fame in 1962.

JOHN GARRISON's overtime goal gave the United States a 2–1 victory over Canada in Prague, Czechoslovakia in 1933 and brought the Americans their first world championship in hockey. The year before, Garrison had played defense for the U.S. Olympic hockey team that lost the gold medal to Canada because of a 2–1 loss at Lake Placid. Garrison also captained the U.S. team that won a bronze medal at the 1936 Winter Olympics and coached the American team that played at St. Moritz in 1948.

Prior to his international career, Garrison had been a school star. He played on the varsity team at the County Day School in West Newton, Massachusetts for six years before entering Harvard, where he played on the freshman team and then at center on the varsity team for three years. He received many pro-~~sional~~ offers after graduation from Harvard but chose a career in business ~~...~~ He continued to play amateur hockey and led several teams to the ~~...~~tes national title during the 1930s in addition to his international suc-~~...~~ was elected to the United States Hockey Hall of Fame in 1974.

~~...~~ a high school hockey star who went on to represent the ~~...~~lympics and also played university and senior ama-~~...~~dford High School team to the Massachusetts ~~...~~ and 1943–44 before military service in World ~~...~~key with the Needham (Massachusetts) Rockets. ~~...~~on-college players to make the 1948 U.S. Olympic ~~...~~ericans narrowly missed a bronze medal that year. ~~...~~ Garrity enrolled at Boston University and was soon

made captain of the freshman hockey team. On the varsity squad the following year, he broke the existing NCAA single-season record with 51 goals and had 33 assists as his school reached the 1950 NCAA tournament finals before losing to Colorado College. He was co-captain of the team in 1950–51 when the Terriers reached the final four of the NCAA tourney. Garrity was named an all-American and made the all-NCAA tournament teams in both 1949–50 and 1950–51. A hard-working student, Garrity graduated ahead of schedule in 1951 and played hockey with the Boston Olympics senior team in 1951–52.

Over the next 13 years, Garrity played senior hockey with various teams, notably in Brockton and Rockland, Massachusetts, where he won the Amateur Hockey Association of the United States national senior championship in 1958–59 and 1959–60 respectively. During this time, he also worked as a referee in high school, college and amateur hockey. He has coached high school and senior amateur hockey and served as an instructor at various Boston area hockey schools. Garrity was elected to the U.S. Hockey Hall of Fame in 1986.

MIKE GARTNER After an all-star season with Niagara Falls of the Ontario Hockey Association, Mike Gartner made his professional debut with the Cincinnati Stingers in the final World Hockey Association season of 1978–79. The following year, he entered the NHL with the Washington Capitals. Gartner established himself as one of the most consistent scorers in hockey history and on December 14, 1997 became only the fifth player ever to score 700 career goals. Previously, he had become just the sixth player in history to top 600 goals and 600 assists.

Though he has scored 50 goals just once in his career (1984–85), Gartner has topped 30 more than any other player in history and established a record by scoring 30 goals for 15 consecutive years between 1979–80 and 1993–94. He is one of the fastest skaters in the game.

Gartner spent his first 10 seasons with the Capitals, leading the team in goals on five occasions and in points four times. He was dealt to Minnesota at the NHL trade deadline on March 7, 1989, but did not even spend a full year with the North Stars before he was sent to the New York Rangers at the trade deadline on March 6, 1990. Gartner spent three full seasons with the Rangers, leading the club in goals each of those years, but was traded to the Toronto Maple Leafs at the trade deadline on March 21, 1994.

Gartner's consecutive 30-goal streak ended in Toronto during the lockout-shortened 1994–95 season, but he rebounded to lead the Maple Leafs with 35 goals in 1995–96. He was traded to the Phoenix Coyotes on June 22, 1996 in a cost-cutting move by the Maple Leafs and went on to top 30 for the 17th time in 1996–97. Though he has not played on a Stanley Cup winner, Gartner was a member of Team Canada for Canada Cup victories in 1984 and 1987. He also has been very active in the NHL Players' Association.

BERNIE GEOFFRION Bernie "Boom Boom" Geoffrion joined the Montreal Canadiens during the 1950–51 season and went on to become one of the top stars in the NHL. He had the misfortune of being a right winger in an era that boasted both Gordie Howe and Maurice Richard, and so was only named to three all-star teams, but his 393 career goals at the time of his retirement in 1968 then ranked fifth in NHL history. He was elected to the Hockey Hall of Fame in 1972.

Geoffrion played his first full season in Montreal in 1951–52 and led the Canadiens with 30 goals to win the Calder Trophy as rookie of the year. The following year, he played on his first Stanley Cup winner. In 1954–55, the late-season suspension of Rocket Richard allowed Geoffrion to win his first NHL scoring title. He was also named to the Second All-Star Team. Over the next five years, Geoffrion was a key contributor to the Montreal teams that won the Stanley Cup five consecutive times. His best season during that stretch was 1959–60, when he was again named to the Second All-Star Team.

Geoffrion enjoyed his greatest year in 1960–61 when he became just the second player in NHL history to score 50 goals in a season. He also collected 45 assists for a career-high 95 points (one short of the NHL record at the time) and won both the Art Ross and Hart trophies as well as a berth on the First All-Star Team. He retired after the 1963–64 season and became coach of the Quebec Aces, Montreal's farm club in the American Hockey League. He quit after two first-place seasons because the Canadiens did not hire him as coach and returned to the NHL as a player with the New York Rangers in 1966. He took over as coach of the Rangers in 1968–69, but had to give up the job for health reasons. Geoffrion was a scout with the Rangers over the next three years before returning to coaching with the expansion Atlanta Flames in 1972–73. He had good success in Atlanta over three seasons, but stepped down in 1974–75. He finally got his chance to coach the Canadiens in 1979–80, but was replaced after just 30 games because of health concerns.

DUKE GERAN Gerry "Duke" Geran was the first American player in the NHL. With the financially strapped Montreal Wanderers short on players during World War I, the Boston-area amateur was signed for the first NHL season of 1917–18. Geran dressed for all four games the Wanderers played that year (but only took part in one) before a fire destroyed the Montreal Arena on January 2, 1918 and the team withdrew from the NHL.

Geran was back in Boston for the next three years, then played hockey in

Paris, France in 1920–21 and led the league with an astounding 88 goals in just eight games. He returned to amateur hockey in Boston for the next three years before joining the Boston Bruins for 33 NHL games in 1925–26. Geran concluded his career the following season with the St. Paul Saints of the American Hockey Association.

EDDIE GERARD was a star in football, paddling, cricket, tennis and lacrosse, as well as hockey. Though they had been negotiating to sign him since as early as 1910, Gerard first joined the Ottawa Senators for the 1913–14 National Hockey Association season. He helped the team win the NHA title in 1915 before losing the Stanley Cup to the Vancouver Millionaires. Playing as a forward, he scored five goals in a game during the 1916–17 season. He switched to defense for the NHL's inaugural season of 1917–18, developing into one of the greats of the game.

Gerard played for his first Stanley Cup winner in 1920, and he became captain of the Senators the following season. He helped the team to win the Stanley Cup again in 1921, and he earned a third Stanley Cup championship while on loan to the Toronto St. Pats for the playoffs in 1922. He won yet another Stanley Cup title with Ottawa in 1923 before chronic asthma forced him to retire.

Gerard became coach of the Montreal Maroons when they joined the NHL in 1924–25, leading the team to a Stanley Cup victory the following year. He joined the New York Americans in 1931–32, but he was back in Montreal from 1932–33 to 1933–34. Gerard coached the St. Louis Eagles in 1934–35, but he was forced to quit halfway through the year. He died at age 47 on December 7, 1937. In 1945, he was one of 12 founding members elected to the Hockey Hall of Fame.

EDDIE GIACOMIN was not good enough to play Junior A hockey as a 15-year-old, and failed at a Detroit Red Wings tryout camp at age 18, yet he went on to become one of the top goaltenders in the NHL. He first began to attract attention with Washington of the Eastern Hockey League in 1959–60 and soon was playing with the Providence Reds of the American Hockey League. He finally got his chance at the NHL during the 1965–66 season.

The Rangers missed the playoffs for the fourth consecutive year in Giacomin's first season, but in 1966–67 he led the rebuilding club back to the postseason. Giacomin recorded a league-leading nine shutouts that year and was named to the First All-Star Team. He made the Second All-Star Team each of the next three years as the Rangers began to show rapid improvement after expansion. In 1970–71, Giacomin shared the New York net with Gilles Villemure and the two combined to win the Vezina Trophy. Giacomin posted a career-best 2.15 goals-against average that season and led the league with eight shutouts as he was again named a First Team All-Star.

Giacomin was a fan favorite in New York, making acrobatic saves and roaming far from his crease to play the puck. He was the club's all-time shutout leader, but the Rangers put him on waivers early in the 1975–76 season and he was claimed by the Detroit Red Wings on October 31, 1975. His first game as a Red Wing was against the Rangers in New York and Giacomin recorded a shutout. He played in Detroit until the 1977–78 season and was elected to the Hockey Hall of Fame in 1987.

JACK GIBSON John Liddell "Jack" Gibson was the founder of hockey's first professional circuit, the International (Pro) Hockey League, which operated with teams in Pittsburgh, Michigan and Sault Ste. Marie, Ontario from 1904 to 1907. The league featured some of the greatest talent of the day, including future Hall of Famers Cyclone Taylor, Newsy Lalonde and brothers Bruce and Hod Stuart.

Gibson was a star player in his own right, helping Berlin (now Kitchener) win Ontario's intermediate championship in 1897. His team was barred from the amateur Ontario Hockey Association after the players accepted $10 gold coins as a reward for a victory over rival Waterloo in January of 1898. Gibson later attended the Detroit College of Medicine, and in 1901, he began to operate a dental practice in Houghton, Michigan on the Upper Peninsula. At the urging of local reporter Merv Youngs, Gibson joined the Portage Lakers hockey team, quickly becoming its top star.

In 1903–04, the Portage Lakers played 26 games and won 24, outscoring their opposition 273–48. Doc Gibson was their leading scorer, and as more and more Canadian talent was lured to the area with the promise of being paid, he was instrumental in framing these players into hockey's first professional league in 1904–05. His team in Houghton was the class of the league, challenging the Ottawa Silver Seven for the Stanley Cup in 1905 and the Montreal Wanderers in 1906. Both challenges were refused. Soon, Canadian teams began offering comparable salaries to lure back their stars, and when an economic recession hit Michigan, the International (Pro) Hockey League folded after the 1906–07 season.

Gibson was inducted to the Hockey Hall of Fame in 1976, three years after being named as a founding member of the United States Hockey Hall of Fame.

ROD GILBERT overcame a broken back in junior hockey and more back surgery later in his career to become one of the best players in the NHL. He spent 15 full seasons with the Rangers and set 20 club scoring records. At the

time of his retirement in 1977, his 1,021 points on 406 goals and 615 assists were second only to Gordie Howe among right wingers in NHL history.

Gilbert was the most valuable player and scoring leader in the Ontario Hockey Association as a junior in Guelph in 1960–61, but fell on some debris on the ice during a playoff game and suffered a broken back which kept him out most of the 1961–62 season. He made the Rangers to stay in 1962–63, but after three seasons in the NHL the surgically-repaired vertebrae in his back had been damaged and a second operation was required. He missed half the season in 1965–66, but helped the Rangers to make the playoffs for the first time in five years in 1966–67. The following season, he was named to the Second All-Star Team.

Gilbert's best season came in 1971–72 when he had 43 goals and 54 assists and was named to the First All-Star Team. The G-A-G Line (Goal-A-Game) of Jean Ratelle, Vic Hadfield, and Gilbert finished third, fourth and fifth in the NHL scoring race behind Boston's Phil Esposito and Bobby Orr that year and led the Rangers to a berth in the Stanley Cup finals, where they lost in six games to the Bruins. In 1976, Gilbert won the Bill Masterton Trophy for perseverance and dedication to hockey. He was elected to the Hockey Hall of Fame in 1982.

BILLY GILMOUR was a member of a prominent Ottawa family that also sent brothers Dave and Suddy on to the famed Ottawa Silver Seven hockey club. Billy Gilmour was a right winger who joined the team in 1902–03, spending the next three years with Ottawa while also attending McGill University in Montreal.

Gilmour was with the Silver Seven during the period when they successfully defended their Stanley Cup title 10 times between 1903 and early 1906 before the Montreal Wanderers claimed the Cup with a playoff win to close out the 1906 season. He left the team after that year, but continued at McGill and joined the Montreal Victorias in 1907–08. The following season, Gilmour was back in Ottawa where he won another Stanley Cup title.

After the victory in 1909, Gilmour did not play hockey again (except for a brief period in 1910–11) until the 1915–16 season when he returned to Ottawa for two games. He scored a goal against Georges Vezina on January 15, 1916 before retiring for good after the season. In 1962, he was elected to the Hockey Hall of Fame.

DOUG GILMOUR was selected 134th overall by the St. Louis Blues in the 1982 NHL Entry Draft after helping the Cornwall Royals to win their second straight Memorial Cup championship. He was returned to junior hockey for the 1982–83 season and went on to lead the Ontario Hockey League with 177 points on 70 goals and 107 assists. He was named the league's most valuable player and selected to the first all-star team.

Despite his offensive prowess, Gilmour was considered a defensive specialist during his early years in St. Louis, but in his fourth season of 1986–87 he scored a career-high 42 goals and placed fifth in the NHL with 105 points. His play that year earned him a spot on Team Canada at the 1987 Canada Cup. In 1987–88, Gilmour set what was then a Blues record with 19 power play goals, but on September 6, 1988 he was traded to the Calgary Flames.

Gilmour helped Calgary to win its first Stanley Cup title in 1989, He then led the Flames with 64 assists in 1989–90 and was named co-captain in 1990–91. Gilmour was traded to Toronto on January 2, 1992 and he emerged as one of the top stars in the game during his time with the Maple Leafs. Gilmour established career highs and Toronto single-season records with 95 assists and 127 points in 1992–93 and led the Maple Leafs to the Campbell Conference finals. Gilmour won the Selke Trophy that year as the game's best defensive forward and finished runner-up to Mario Lemieux in voting for the Hart Trophy. In 1993–94, Gilmour's 111 points ranked fourth in the league and he again led the Maple Leafs to the conference finals.

Gilmour was named captain in Toronto for the 1994–95 season, but the team's fortunes began to sag. With the Maple Leafs slumping towards the bottom of the NHL standings in 1996–97, Gilmour was traded to the New Jersey Devils with Dave Ellett on February 25, 1997 for Jason Smith, Steve Sullivan and the rights to Alyn McCauley. After spending the 1997–98 season with New Jersey, Gilmour signed with the Chicago Blackhawks as a free agent.

PUD GLASS Frank "Pud" Glass joined the Montreal Wanderers in 1905, one year after the team was founded. He played on a line with team captain Cecil Blachford and future Hall of Famer Jack Marshall and helped the team defeat Ottawa for the championship of the Eastern Canada Amateur Hockey Association in 1906. The victory also gave the Wanderers the Stanley Cup.

Except for a loss to the Kenora Thistles in January of 1907 that was quickly avenged, the Wanderers beat all challengers for the Stanley Cup over the next three seasons. Glass had 18 goals in 12 games in 1908–09, including five in one game, but Ottawa ended the Wanderers championship reign that season.

The 1909–10 season saw the Wanderers play a key role in the formation of the National Hockey Association. Glass scored in 10 consecutive games during the 12-game season as the Wanderers won the NHA title and another Stanley Cup championship. He retired after spending the 1911–12 season with the Montreal Canadiens, then refereed in the NHA for several years.

MOOSE GOHEEN Francis Xavier "Moose" Goheen was a star in football and baseball, but it was hockey that brought him international acclaim as one of the first great players ever developed in the United States. Primarily a defenseman, he was known as "the only individual three-man rush in hockey" and as a prolific scorer. He was also one of the first players in the game to wear a helmet.

Goheen joined the St. Paul Athletic Club for the 1915–16 season, twice helping the team win the McNaughton Trophy (which was then symbolic of amateur hockey supremacy in the United States) before enlisting in the American army. He returned to Minnesota after World War I, helping St. Paul win the McNaughton Trophy again in 1920, and he was selected to play for his country at the first Olympic hockey tournament that year. The Americans registered one-sided victories against their European opponents, but they had to settle for a silver medal after a 2–0 loss to the Winnipeg Falcons, who represented Canada. Goheen was asked to play again at the 1924 Winter Olympics, but he declined the offer because of business commitments.

Goheen continued with the St. Paul Athletic club when it turned professional in 1926, playing with the team through 1932–33. During that time, the Boston Bruins claimed him and the Toronto Maple Leafs offered him a contract, but he preferred to remain at home with the Northern States Power Company. He was elected to the Hockey Hall of Fame in 1952. He then was selected as a charter member of the United States Hockey Hall of Fame in 1973. Goheen was honored by the Minnesota Hall of Fame in 1958 as the finest hockey player ever produced in the state.

BOB GOLDHAM joined the Toronto Maple Leafs during 1941–42 and was a member of the team that rallied from down three games to nothing to defeat the Detroit Red Wings for the Stanley Cup that spring. Goldham missed the next three seasons due to Word War II service in the Canadian Navy but was back with the Maple Leafs in 1945–46.

Injuries limited Goldham to just 11 games in Toronto in 1946–47 and he was with Pittsburgh of the American Hockey League to start the 1947–48 season before being included as one of the five players the Maple Leafs sent to the Chicago Black Hawks to acquire Max Bentley on November 4, 1947. Goldham finished the season in Chicago and spent the next two years with the Black Hawks. Though the team was weak, Goldham's skills improved while playing with Bill Gadsby.

On July 13, 1950, Goldham was traded to the Detroit Red Wings in a multiplayer deal. He spent the next six seasons in Detroit and in his first five years there the Red Wings finished in first place in the regular-season standings every year and won the Stanley Cup in 1952, 1954, and 1955. The 1954–55 season also saw Goldham named to the Second All-Star Team. He retired after the 1955–56 campaign.

Though he could rush the puck when the opportunity presented itself, Goldham was best known as a defensive defenseman and a skilled shot-blocker during his career. He later served as an analyst on Hockey Night in Canada telecasts during the 1960s and 1970s and campaigned for increased pension benefits for retired NHL players.

BOB GOODENOW joined the National Hockey League Players' Association as deputy executive director in September of 1990 and has been the NHLPA's executive director and general counsel since January 1992. Under his tenure, NHL players have experienced an unprecedented increase in salaries.

Prior to joining the NHLPA, Goodenow practiced law with two Detroit firms from 1985 to 1990. He concentrated his efforts on representing individual athletes, labor law and general business practices. Goodenow graduated from the University of Detroit Law School in 1979 after having previously graduated from Harvard in 1974. A hockey player at Harvard, he was named to the Eastern College Athletic Conference second all-star team in 1974.

EBBIE GOODFELLOW began his NHL career as a center, but earned greater fame after being converted to defense in his seventh season. Goodfellow was a native of Ottawa who was the leading scorer and all-star center with the Montagnards when they won the city championship of Ottawa in 1927–28. The following year, he was an all-star again with the Detroit Olympics of the Canadian Professional Hockey League before graduating to the NHL as a member of the Detroit Cougars (forerunner of the Red Wings).

Goodfellow had an impressive 17 goals and 17 assists in his rookie season, then led the American Division in scoring (and was second overall to Howie Morenz) with 25 goals and 23 assists in 1930–31. He led Detroit in scoring again in 1931–32, then helped the Red Wings win the American Division in 1933–34 before moving back to defense in 1935–36. Goodfellow was named to the Second All-Star Team that year after Detroit won its first Stanley Cup title. The Red Wings repeated as champions the following year, and Goodfellow was a First Team All-Star.

Goodfellow's last great season was 1939–40 when he won the Hart Trophy and was chosen along to the First All-Star Team. He was a player-coach during the latter years of his career, turning over the captaincy of the team to Sid Abel when he gave up his playing duties in 1942–43. Goodfellow was associated with his third and final Stanley Cup team that season. He coached the

Chicago Black Hawks from 1950 to 1952 before retiring to Florida. In 1963, he was inducted into the Hockey Hall of Fame.

PAUL GOODMAN With goaltender Mike Karakas nursing a broken toe, the Chicago Black scored a surprise 3–1 victory over the Toronto Maple Leafs in game one of the 1938 Stanley Cup final using Alfie Moore in goal. The journeyman netminder was ruled ineligible for the rest of the series and the Black Hawks were forced to go with an unproven farmhand in game two.

According to some reports, Paul Goodman of Wichita in the American Hockey Association was found in a movie house two and a half hours before game two. He had never even met Black Hawks coach Bill Stewart before he arrived at Maple Leaf Gardens. Though Goodman had posted a 1.77 goals-against average with a very weak Wichita club, he was not yet ready for the NHL and the Black Hawks were beaten 5–1. Karakas returned for game three wearing a steal-toed boot and Chicago went on to win the Stanley Cup three games to one.

Goodman was back in Wichita in 1938–39, but was called up to Chicago from Providence to replace Karakas during the 1939–40 season. The following year, he and Sam LoPresti shared the net in Chicago in what proved to be Goodman's final season.

MALCOLM GORDON A southerner from Baltimore, Maryland, Malcolm K. Gordon arrived as an outsider at St. Paul's School in Concord, New Hampshire in 1882 and went on to play a major role in the evolution of American hockey.

The sport had already been introduced to St. Paul's by Canadian teams prior to Gordon's arrival at the school, but he is considered the person who helped formalize the game by putting down on paper (in 1885) what is seen as the first set of rules for hockey in the United States. He became head coach at St. Paul's in 1888, and though play remained strictly intramural, Gordon first took the St. Paul's team to New York City in 1896 to play a squad of the school's alumni at the old St. Nicholas Rink.

Gordon's coaching career lasted until 1917, and during that time he developed many players for university teams in the eastern United States—most notable among them was the great Hobey Baker. Gordon also coached football and cricket at St. Paul's while maintaining a position as head of the history department. After World War I, he was in the real estate business until 1927, when he founded the Malcolm K. Gordon School at Garrison, New York. Headmaster until his retirement in 1952, he continued to teach at the school almost until the time of his death at the age of 96 on November 13, 1964. In 1973, Gordon was enshrined as a charter member in the coaches category of the United States Hockey Hall of Fame.

BUTCH GORING spent the better part of 11 seasons with the Los Angeles Kings between 1969–70 and 1979–80, earning a reputation as a hustler who played the game within the rules. He won the Lady Byng Trophy for sportsmanlike conduct in 1977–78 after scoring a career-high 37 goals and recording only one penalty during the season for the fourth time in his career.

Goring never had more than 16 penalty minutes in any one season, while scoring 20 goals or more 11 times including four consecutive 30-goal seasons. He is said to have used the same helmet he wore as a child throughout his entire NHL career.

Goring was traded to the New York Islanders on March 10, 1980 and his hustle and desire was credited with putting a talented team over the top. After four consecutive seasons of playoff disappointment, the Islanders won the Stanley Cup that spring and went on to win four championships in a row. Goring earned the Conn Smythe Trophy as playoff MVP in 1981.

The Islanders traded Goring to the Boston Bruins during the 1984–85 season and he retired at year's end. He coached the Bruins the following season but was fired early into the 1986–87 campaign. Afterwards, Goring continued to coach at the minor-league level.

TOMMY GORMAN was the youngest member of Canada's gold medal-winning lacrosse team as a 22-year-old at the London Olympics in 1908. He also was involved in harness racing, baseball and figure skating, and he was a sports writer and editor with the *Ottawa Citizen*, but his greatest fame came for his involvement in hockey. Gorman coached or managed seven Stanley Cup winners, three in Ottawa (1920, 1921 and 1923), two with the Montreal Canadiens (1944, 1946) and one each with the Chicago Black Hawks (1934) and Montreal Maroons (1935).

Gorman became associated with the Ottawa Senators in 1916–17 when they were still a part of the National Hockey Association, and he was one of the men responsible for the formation of the National Hockey League one year later. Gorman, Edgar Dey and Martin Rosenthal took over full ownership of the Senators in 1919 and established Ottawa as the NHL's first dynasty. Gorman sold his interest in the team to Frank Ahearn on January 24, 1925 and almost immediately signed as coach and general manager of the New York Americans. He remained with the team until 1928–29, then ran a race track in Mexico from 1929 to 1932.

Black Hawks owner Frederic McLaughlin brought Gorman back to the

NHL as the coach and general manager of his team in 1933–34, and though Chicago won its first Stanley Cup title that season, Gorman was fired. He had another Stanley Cup victory with the Montreal Maroons in 1934–35 and continued to coach that team until the franchise folded in 1938. In 1940, Gorman became general manager of the Montreal Canadiens and ran the team until the end of the 1945–46 season when he left the NHL to take over the Ottawa Auditorium. He also became president of the Ottawa Senators in the Quebec Senior Hockey League. The Senators won the Allan Cup in 1949, but Gorman was forced to fold the franchise in December because television broadcasts of NHL games had killed attendance in Ottawa. He then left hockey behind to operate the Connaught Park track that was the home of horse racing in the Ottawa area. He was elected to the Hockey Hall of Fame as a builder in 1963.

JOHNNY GOTTSELIG was born in Odessa, Russia, but raised in Winnipeg, Manitoba. He played on the Memorial Cup-winning Regina Pats in 1924–25 and later spent two seasons playing professionally with the American Hockey Association team in Winnipeg before being signed by the Chicago Black Hawks for the 1928–29 season.

Gottselig led the Black Hawks with 21 goals in 1929–30 and topped the team in both goals and points each of the next two years. Paul Thompson soon became the team's top offensive threat but Gottselig was still a key member of Chicago's first Stanley Cup-winning team in 1933–34. In 1934–35, he again led the Black Hawks in goals while playing on a line with Howie Morenz and Mush March. The slick stickhandler helped Chicago win the Stanley Cup again in 1938 and made the NHL Second All-Star Team in 1938–39 after leading the Black Hawks in goals (16), assists (23), and points (39), and ranking eighth in the NHL in scoring.

Gottselig remained with the Black Hawks until early in the 1940–41 season when he was named a player-coach with the team's American Hockey Association affiliate in Kansas City. With a shortage of players during World War II, Gottselig returned to Chicago in 1942–43. He played a final full season with the Black Hawks in 1943–44 and ended his playing career with one last game during the 1944–45 campaign.

In March of 1945, Gottselig replaced former teammate Paul Thompson as coach of the Black Hawks. He remained on the job until being replaced by Charlie Conacher in December of 1947, at which time Gottselig became assistant to Black Hawks president and general manager Bill Tobin. Gottselig later served as Chicago's director of public relations and as an analysts on Black Hawks radio broadcasts.

MICHEL GOULET With 548 career goals, Michel Goulet ranks among the NHL's all-time leaders and is topped by only Hall of Fame members Bobby Hull and John Bucyk as the most prolific left wingers in history. His 604 assists and 1,152 points also rank him among the NHL's best and he would have climbed even higher had his career not been ended by a serious head injury on March 16, 1994.

Goulet was a high-scoring junior prospect who began his career as an underage pro with the Birmingham Bulls of the World Hockey Association in the league's final season of 1978–79. He and fellow rookies Gaston Gingras, Craig Hartsburg, Rob Ramage, Pat Riggin and Rick Vaive were known as "the Baby Bulls" and all entered the NHL for the 1979–80 season. Goulet was a member of the Quebec Nordiques and helped them become one of the league's better teams. He established a career high with 57 goals in 1982–83 and topped 50 again in each of the next three seasons. He had over 100 points four times and finished among the top 10 in scoring on three occasions, including 1983–84 when he finished third with a career-high 121 points.

Goulet was traded to the Chicago Black Hawks on March 5, 1990 and, though he never again reached the lofty numbers he had attained in Quebec, he remained a productive player until his injury forced him to retire. Goulet became the director of player personnel with the Colorado Avalanche in 1996.

RON GRAHAME joined the Houston Aeros of the World Hockey Association out of the University of Denver in 1973–74 and went on to become one of the most successful goalies in the WHA. His 2.99 career goals-against average is the lowest in league history, while his 12 shutouts are tied for third all-time. Though he played just three complete seasons, Grahame's 102 wins rank him eighth in WHA history.

After seeing limited action with the Houston team that won the Avco Cup in his first season, Grahame was handed the top job in 1974–75 and promptly led the league with 33 victories and a 3.03 goals-against average. He earned the Ben Hatskin Trophy as the WHA's top goaltender and led the Aeros to a second consecutive league championship. His 39 victories during the 1975–76 season rank as the third-highest single-season total in league history, while his 2.74 average in 1976–77 was the second best ever in the WHA.

Grahame joined the Boston Bruins in 1977–78 and was the club's top goaltender during the regular season. He took a back seat to Gerry Cheevers in the playoffs and was traded to the Los Angeles Kings for a first-round draft choice prior to the 1978–79 campaign. (Boston used the pick to select Raymond Bourque.) Grahame was dealt to the Quebec Nordiques in 1980–81, which proved to be his final season.

MIKE GRANT In the early days of hockey, defensemen were known as point and cover point and were expected to stay in their own end to help protect the goalie at all times. The concept of a defenseman rushing the puck generally is credited to Lester Patrick or Art Ross, but Mike Grant was demonstrating high-speed end-to-end rushes with the Montreal Victorias as early as 1895. Patrick and Ross were boys in Montreal at the time, and they may have been inspired by Grant's heroics.

Mike Grant first attracted attention as an 11-year-old when he won speed-skating titles in three different age groups that ranged all the way up to 16. He was asked to try out for the Montreal Crystals hockey team, and he soon was captain of the junior squad. He led that team to a championship, earning two more titles as captain of the intermediate club before joining the Montreal Victorias in 1893–94. With that team, too, Grant quickly was named captain.

The Montreal Victorias won their first Stanley Cup title in 1895. The team lost a challenge to the Winnipeg Victorias in 1896 before quickly winning back the Cup, and they held on to it through the 1897–98 season. Grant remained with the club until 1900, when he spent a season with the Montreal Shamrocks. He then returned to the Victorias for a final year in 1901–02.

When he wasn't playing the game, Grant often served as a referee, and he continued in that capacity by officiating in Stanley Cup games until 1905. After retiring, he gave demonstrations and organized hockey exhibitions in the United States. Grant was elected to the Hockey Hall of Fame in 1950.

WALLY GRANT was a speedy forward who starred in high school hockey at Eveleth, Minnesota and then in the NCAA at the University of Michigan. He helped Eveleth High win the first Minnesota state high school tournament in 1945 when he scored the third and fourth goals as the Golden Bears rallied to beat Thief River Falls 4–3 in the championship game. Grant's 13 points in the tournament that year would remain one of the top five performances in state history for more than four decades.

Grant moved on to the University of Michigan in the fall of 1945 and participated in the first NCAA hockey tournament in 1948. Grant played on the Wolverines' well-known G-Line with Wally Gacek and Ted Greer and each of the three scored a goal in the third period as Michigan beat Dartmouth 8–4 to win the first NCAA title. In all, Grant played four seasons at Michigan between 1945–46 and 1949–50 (having missed a year after his freshman season to serve in the U.S. military) and took part in the NCAA tournament three times.

Grant worked for General Motors for 37 years and continued to support hockey at the University of Michigan through various alumni and booster clubs. He was enshrined in the United States Hockey Hall of Fame in 1994.

ADAM GRAVES joined Vic Hadfield as only the second player in New York Rangers history to score 50 goals in a season when he set a club record with 52 in 1993–94. Graves was named to the Second All-Star Team at left wing that season and also won the King Clancy Memorial Trophy for his humanitarian efforts.

The Rangers ended a 54-year jinx when they won the Stanley Cup in 1994, giving Graves his second Stanley Cup ring. He had won with the Edmonton Oilers in 1990. Earlier in his career, Graves won a gold medal with Team Canada at the World Junior Championships in 1988.

Graves was drafted by the Detroit Red Wings from the Windsor Spitfires of the Ontario Hockey League in 1986 but was returned to junior hockey. He was team captain in Windsor in 1987–88 and led all playoff scorers with 32 points as the Spitfires won the OHL championship. He also made his NHL debut that year. Graves split the 1988–89 season between Detroit and Adirondack of the American Hockey League and helped Adirondack to win the Calder Cup as AHL champions.

Detroit traded Graves to Edmonton on November 2, 1989, and after two seasons with the Oilers he signed with the Rangers on September 3, 1991. Graves had scored only 23 goals in 217 games in Edmonton and Detroit but scored 26 in his first year in New York and 36 in 1992–93. When the Rangers missed the playoffs that year, Graves served as captain of Team Canada at the 1993 World Championships.

SHORTY GREEN Wilfred "Shorty" Green is remembered best as captain of the Hamilton Tigers team that staged the first players strike in NHL history in 1925. He had been a star amateur player for several years before entering the National Hockey League.

Green played two seasons of intermediate hockey in his native Sudbury, Ontario before moving up to the senior team in 1914–15 and helping the squad win the Northern Ontario Hockey Association title. He was with the Sudbury Wolves until early in 1916 when he enlisted in the Canadian army. After being gassed at Passchendale in 1917, he returned home the following year. Green's hockey career continued when he joined the Hamilton Tigers amateur team that won the Allan Cup in 1919. Then, he returned to Sudbury. With brothers Shorty and Redvers "Red" Green in the lineup, the Wolves became a hockey powerhouse in the early 1920s. NHL teams began to show interest and the brothers turned pro with the Hamilton Tigers in 1923–24.

Placed on a line with future Hall of Famer Billy Burch, Red and Shorty Green helped to build a perennial NHL doormat into a first-place finisher by

1924–25. The NHL schedule had grown from 24 to 30 games that season and the Hamilton players announced that they were not willing take part in the playoffs unless they were each paid $200 for the extra games they had played. Club ownership refused and NHL president Frank Calder suspended the players.

The following season, the Hamilton franchise was sold, becoming the New York Americans. The Tigers players were all reinstated. Shorty Green scored the first goal at Madison Square Garden in a 3–1 loss to the Montreal Canadiens on December 19, 1925. He spent two seasons with the Americans before a serious knee injury sidelined him. He also coached the New York team in 1927–28. Green was elected to the Hockey Hall of Fame in 1962.

TED GREEN had been a top defenseman with the Boston Bruins for eight full seasons, earning a berth on the Second All-Star Team in 1968–69, before he suffered one of the most serious injuries in hockey history. Green's skull was fractured in a stick-swinging incident with Wayne Maki of the St. Louis Blues in a preseason game on September 21, 1969. He missed the entire 1969–70 season, but recovered to play nine more years of professional hockey.

Championships have followed Ted Green throughout his playing and coaching career, beginning in 1959 when he won the Memorial Cup with the Winnipeg Braves. Though he endured some of the worst years in NHL history with Boston in the 1960s, and his injury meant he did not take part in the Bruins' championship of 1970, he won the Stanley Cup with Boston in 1972. Green was one of the top NHL stars to jump to the rival World Hockey Association when he joined the New England Whalers and won the Avco Cup in the league's first season of 1972–73. He played for two more WHA championship teams after joining the Winnipeg Jets.

Green retired as a player during the 1978–79 season and became a coach, guiding the Carman Hornets to the 1979–80 Manitoba intermediate championship. He joined the Edmonton Oilers coaching staff in 1980–81 and was an assistant coach on five Stanley Cup-winning teams. He became Edmonton's head coach in 1991 and the assistant to Oilers president Glen Sather in 1993.

WAYNE GRETZKY learned to play hockey under the instruction of his father Walter on a backyard rink in his hometown of Brantford, Ontario. He grew up to become the most prolific scorer in the history of the NHL. Gretzky is the league's all-time leader in goals, assists and points, and since he recorded his 1,851st assist on October 26, 1997, his assist total exceeds the point total of every other player in history.

Gretzky was marked for stardom almost from the time he began to play organized hockey, particularly after the 1970–71 season when he collected 378 goals and 139 assists as an 11-year-old. He made his junior hockey debut in 1976–77 at age 15 and was a second team all-star as a 16-year-old with Sault Ste. Marie of the Ontario Hockey Association in 1977–78. It was in "the Soo" that season that Gretzky began to wear number 99.

Gretzky turned pro with the Indianapolis Racers of the World Hockey Association in 1978, but financial troubles saw him sent to the Edmonton Oilers after just eight games of the 1978–79 season. Gretzky finished third in the WHA behind Real Cloutier and Robbie Ftorek with 110 points (46 goals, 64 assists) that season, but few expected he would match those totals when he entered the NHL as an 18-year-old in 1979–80. Gretzky proved his critics wrong when he led the league with 86 assists and tied Marcel Dionne with 137 points, though Dionne received the Art Ross Trophy because his 53 goals were two more than Gretzky's 51. Gretzky did receive the Hart Trophy as most valuable player for the first of eight consecutive times that season (nine times in total).

Great as he was as a rookie, it was his second season of 1980–81 when Gretzky began to rewrite the NHL record book. His 109 assists that season broke Bobby Orr's record of 102 and his record 164 points broke Phil Esposito's record and brought him the first of seven consecutive Art Ross Trophy wins (10 in all). The next year, Gretzky shattered Esposito's record of 76 goals when he scored 92 times. With 120 assists and 212 points that season, Gretzky surpassed his own records. He would up those marks to 163 assists and 215 points in 1986–87. In addition to his own record-setting performances, Gretzky made the Oilers the best team in hockey as they won the Stanley Cup in 1984, 1985, 1987 and 1988.

On August 9, 1988, a stunned hockey public learned that Gretzky had been traded to the Los Angeles Kings. His arrival finally made hockey a hit in Southern California and helped to promote the game all across the United States. It was with the Kings against Edmonton on October 15, 1989 that Gretzky surpassed his childhood hero Gordie Howe as the NHL's all-time leading scorer with 1,851 points, and it was in Los Angeles on March 23, 1994 that Gretzky topped Howe with his 802nd goal. He also helped the Kings to reach the Stanley Cup finals in 1993.

With the Kings slumping in 1995–96, Gretzky was traded to the St. Louis Blues on February 27, 1996. Following that season, he signed with the New York Rangers on July 21, 1996. Though his production had tailed dramatically by this point, Gretzky tied Mario Lemieux for the NHL lead with 72 assists his first year in New York, 1996–97. He was fourth in the NHL with 90 points in 1997–98.

In addition to his record-breaking performances in the NHL, Gretzky has been a top star on the international stage. In 1978, he led Canada to a bronze medal at the World Junior Championships, leading the tournament in scoring, being named to the all-star team and being selected as the top forward. He later led the tournament in scoring when Canada won a bronze medal in the 1982 World Championship. Gretzky was also the scoring leader in the 1981, 1984, 1987 and 1991 Canada Cup tournaments. He represented his country at the World Cup of Hockey in 1996 and at the Nagano Olympics in 1998.

SI GRIFFIS was a member of the Rat Portage Thistles when the team challenged the Ottawa Silver Seven for the Stanley Cup in 1903 and 1905. An intelligent player and fast skater, Griffis was a rover with Rat Portage, but he had moved back to play defense by the time the town became known as Kenora and the team beat the Montreal Wanderers for the Stanley Cup in January of 1907.

Griffis retired from hockey after the Thistles lost the Stanley Cup in a return match against the Wanderers in March of 1907. Though the citizens of Kenora offered to build the American-born player a home in their town, he moved to Vancouver. Four years later, he signed a pro contract with Frank Patrick's Vancouver Millionaires for the inaugural 1911–12 season of the Pacific Hockey Hockey Association. He played all 60 minutes in his first game with Vancouver on January 5, 1912, recording three goals and two assists in an 8–3 win over the New Westminster Royals. Griffis was captain of the Millionaires when Vancouver became the first PCHA team to win the Stanley Cup in 1915, though he missed the playoff series against the Ottawa Senators because of a broken leg. The 1916–17 season would be his last as a full-time player, though he returned to the Vancouver lineup for parts of the next two seasons before retiring for good.

In addition to his hockey skill, Si Griffis was outstanding in many sports. He was a successful oarsman who helped his foursome win at the Canadian Henley Regatta in St. Catharines, Ontario in 1905. He was also a champion golfer and he became a great bowler later in life. He was elected to the Hockey Hall of Fame in 1950.

FRANK GRIFFITHS founded and developed Northwest Sports Enterprises Limited in 1974 and purchased the Vancouver Canucks on May 2 of that year under his company's auspices. He became a member of the NHL Board of Governors in 1974 and was appointed vice chairman and a member of the audit committee in 1979. In the latter capacity, he made a significant contribution to the NHL by helping several teams solidify their finances. Griffiths served on the board until 1987. He was elected to the Hockey Hall of Fame as a builder in 1993.

BEP GUIDOLIN Aldo "Bep" Guidolin is the youngest player in NHL history, joining the Boston Bruins as a 16-year-old in 1942–43. Wartime player shortages saw the Bruins go with several young rookies that season, and Guidolin played on a line with 17-year-old Don Gallinger and 20-year-old Bill Shill. With the Kraut Line of Milt Schmidt, Woody Dumart and Bobby Bauer all serving in the Royal Canadian Air Force, the Boston press dubbed this young threesome the Sprout Line.

Guidolin spent four seasons with the Bruins, though he missed the 1944–45 campaign for military service, and later played with the Chicago Black Hawks and Detroit Red Wings. He played several minor-league seasons after his NHL career ended in 1952 and later had his amateur status reinstated and won the Allan Cup with the Belleville McFarlands in 1958. His playing days ended in 1961.

In 1973, Guidolin returned to the NHL when he replaced Tom Johnson as Bruins coach. He lasted one more season before Boston hired Don Cherry, then became the first coach of the Kansas City Scouts when they entered the NHL in 1974–75.

VIC HADFIELD was the first 50-goal scorer in the history of the New York Rangers, reaching the milestone in 1971–72 while playing on a potent forward line with Jean Ratelle and Rod Gilbert. The trio was known as the G-A-G Line, an acronym for Goal-A-Game. The linemates were 3–4–5 in league scoring during the 1971–72 season behind Phil Esposito and Bobby Orr as the Rangers finished second to Boston in the regular-season standings. In the playoffs, the Rangers reached the Stanley Cup finals before losing to Boston.

Hadfield had joined the Rangers in 1961–62 and became a regular with New York in 1963–64 when he led the NHL with 151 penalty minutes. With a curved stick and hard slapshot, much was expected of him offensively but it was not until the entire team began to show dramatic improvement after expansion in 1967 that Hadfield became a scoring threat. He was named captain of the team in 1971 and responded with 50 goals, 56 assists and a spot on the Second All-Star Team. His great season earned him a position on Team Canada in 1972 but Hadfield was to be much-criticized for his decision to leave the team due to lack of playing time and return to the Rangers' training camp.

Hadfield's production declined over the next two years and he was traded to Pittsburgh before the 1974–75 season. He had two good years with the Penguins, but retired after playing only nine games in 1976–77.

GEORGE HAINSWORTH established an NHL record not likely to be broken when he recorded 22 shutouts during the 1928–29 season. He allowed

only 43 goals while playing in all of the Montreal Canadiens' 44 games that year, posting a 0.92 goals-against average. His career goals-against average of 1.91 is tied with Alex Connell for the lowest mark in NHL history.

Hainsworth was born in Toronto but played most of his amateur hockey in Berlin, Ontario (which later became Kitchener). He played on championship teams at the junior, intermediate and senior levels, including an Allan Cup winner in 1917–18, before finally turning professional with the Saskatoon Crescents of the Western Canada Hockey League in 1923–24. He spent three seasons out west, then joined the Montreal Canadiens in 1926–27 after Newsy Lalonde suggested him as a replacement for the late Georges Vezina. Hainsworth proved an immediate success in Montreal, winning the Vezina Trophy in each of his first three seasons while totaling 14, 13 and 22 shutouts and yearly goals-against averages of 1.47, 1.06 and 0.92.

Forward passing rules were modernized after the 1928–29 season, making it impossible for Hainsworth to post such stellar numbers again. Still, he helped the Canadiens win back-to-back Stanley Cup championships in 1930 and 1931. Before the 1933–34 season, Hainsworth was traded to Toronto for Lorne Chabot. He helped the Maple Leafs win two Canadian Division titles and reach the Stanley Cup finals twice in the next three years. He was replaced by Turk Broda midway through the 1936–37 season and returned to the Canadiens briefly before retiring. His 94 career shutouts were an NHL record until Terry Sawchuk surpassed the total in 1963–64. When his 10 shutouts in Saskatoon are included, his total of 104 shutouts is actually one more than Sawchuk's 103. Hainsworth was elected to the Hockey Hall of Fame in 1961.

GLENN HALL Known as "Mr. Goalie," Glenn Hall was one of the greatest netminders in NHL history, though the stress of NHL puckstopping often made him ill before games. Still, he set an incredible endurance record by playing 502 consecutive games from 1955 until a back injury sidelined him on November 8, 1963. Hall played 18 seasons in the NHL. With 84 career shutout, he is third on the NHL all-time list, trailing only Terry Sawchuk and George Hainsworth. He led the NHL in single-season shutouts six times.

Hall made brief appearances with the Red Wings in 1952–53 and 1954–55 before replacing Terry Sawchuk as Detroit's goaltender in 1955–56. He recorded a 2.12 goals-against average and led the league with 12 shutouts that season, while winning the Calder Trophy as rookie of the year. Hall was selected to the Second All-Star Team for the first of four times that year. He was a First Team All-Star for the first of six times in 1956–57, but Detroit then traded him to the Chicago Black Hawks, along with Ted Lindsay, for four players.

Hall spent the next 10 seasons in Chicago, where he earned eight all-star selections. In 1960–61, he helped the Black Hawks win their first Stanley Cup championship since 1938, and in 1966–67 he shared the Vezina Trophy with Denis DeJordy. Hall then became the first player selected by the St. Louis Blues in the 1967 Expansion Draft. He helped lead the Blues to the Stanley Cup finals in their first season of 1967–68 and won the Conn Smythe Trophy as playoff MVP despite losing to the Montreal Canadiens.

The following year, when Jacques Plante was brought out of retirement to team with Hall in the Blues net, the veteran goalie finally donned a mask for the first time in his career. Hall and Plante shared the Vezina Trophy in 1968–69 as St. Louis again reached the Stanley Cup finals before losing to Montreal. Hall remained with St. Louis until retiring after the 1970–71 season. In 1975, he was inducted into the Hockey Hall of Fame.

JOE HALL Though teammates would say later that his reputation for trouble was overrated, "Bad Joe" Hall was a star player over a lengthy career, but one who had a hard time controlling his temper. He was a member of the Montreal Canadiens when they played the Seattle Metropolitans for the Stanley Cup in 1919, but he died on April 5 of that year, four days after the series was canceled because of the Influenza epidemic.

Hall was born in England, raised in Winnipeg and Brandon, Manitoba, and he played in both of those cities at the start of his career in the Manitoba Hockey League. He joined the Portage Lakers in the International (Pro) Hockey League (hockey's first professional circuit) in 1905–06, but he returned to Brandon after one season. In January of 1907, he and Art Ross were added to the Kenora Thistles as they beat the Montreal Wanderers to win the Stanley Cup, though Hall did not see action in the two-game challenge.

The following year, Hall was expelled from the Manitoba league for rough play, and though the ban soon was lifted, he basically spent the rest of his career in the east. Hall was a member of the Montreal Shamrocks when that team left the Canadian Hockey Association for the National Hockey Association in 1909–10, but he was fined and suspended that year after punching referee Rod Kennedy during a fight with Frank Patrick of the Renfrew Millionaires. The following year, Hall joined the Quebec Bulldogs.

Moved back to defense in Quebec when the position was still known as point and cover point, Hall helped the Bulldogs to win the Stanley Cup in 1912. Teamed with Harry Mummery the following year, the two helped the Bulldogs to defend their title, anchoring the Quebec defense until the the NHL was formed in 1917–18. During that time, Hall had many memorable battles with Newsy Lalonde.

When Quebec chose not to operate a team in the NHL, Hall joined the Montreal Canadiens. Now a teammate of Lalonde's, he had to look for other opponents and found plenty of them. On January 28, 1918, he was fined and suspended after a stick-swinging incident with Toronto's Alf Skinner. Both players were charged with disorderly conduct by the Toronto police, but they were released with suspended sentences. Despite his temper, Joe Hall was considered the top defenseman of his day. He was elected to the Hockey Hall of Fame in 1961.

BILL HANLEY was born to Canadian parents in Ireland and grew up in Toronto. After serving with the Royal Canadian Navy in World War II, Hanley became involved in hockey as a part-time timekeeper for junior games at Maple Leaf Gardens and was soon handling NHL games as well. In 1947, he was asked by Ontario Hockey Association president George Panter to assist him as OHA business manager. Hanley agreed, and remained with the league as secretary-manager until retiring in 1974. In 1986, he was inducted into the Hockey Hall of Fame as a builder.

AUSTIE HARDING Francis Austin "Austie" Harding played four years of varsity hockey at the Noble and Greenough prep school in his native Boston before entering Harvard in the fall of 1935. He captained the freshman team before moving up to the varsity squad the following year. Harding led Harvard in scoring in 1936–37 and helped the school capture the Ivy League title that year. The team was a strong contender for Ivy League honors again in the next two seasons as Harding led the team in scoring in those years as well. He was team captain in his senior season of 1938–39, won the John Tudor Memorial Cup as Harvard's most valuable player and was also named an all-American. In the final game of his college career, Harding was on the ice for 58 of 60 minutes and had four goals and three assists in a 7–4 victory.

Harding attracted many pro scouts, but any dreams of a pro hockey career were put on hold by military service in World War II. After the war, Harding played amateur hockey with the Boston Athletic Association. He was inducted into the U.S. Hockey Hall of Fame in 1975.

NED HARKNESS was born in Ottawa, Ontario, but became a naturalized American citizen in 1949 and founded the varsity hockey program at the Rensselaer Polytechnic Institute in Troy, New York the following year. By 1954, Harkness had developed RPI into collegiate national champions as he coached the Engineers to a 5–4 overtime victory over Minnesota in the final game of the NCAA hockey tournament. In 1961 he coached RPI to the Eastern Collegiate Athletic Association championship. In 1963, Harkness became the hockey coach at Cornell. Under his guidance, the Big Red won NCAA titles in 1967 and 1970 and finished second at the NCAA tournament in 1969 and third in 1968. The 1967–68 season saw Harkness named national coach of the year. During his eight seasons at Cornell, the team won five Ivy League titles and four ECAC championships. His 1969–70 squad set an NCAA Division I hockey record with a perfect season of 29–0–0.

Harkness was appointed coach of the Detroit Red Wings in 1970–71, making him the first NCAA coach to go to the NHL. He spent just 38 games behind the bench, then replaced Sid Abel as Red Wings general manager, a post he maintained through the 1973–74 season. He then established a hockey program at Union College and University in Schenectady, New York and served as coach and rink director for the Skating Dutchmen until 1977. A year later, Harkness supervised the construction of the Civic Center in Glens Falls, New York and founded the American Hockey League's Adirondack Red Wings in 1979, with whom he served as general manager. He was named the AHL's executive of the year in 1980 and received the Daoust Golden Skate Award in 1986 for his contributions to the AHL.

Meanwhile, Harkness had been appointed president and chief executive officer of the U.S. Olympic Regional Development Authority in Lake Placid, New York in 1982. He is a member of the halls of fame for Cornell, New York State, Glens Falls and RPI and in 1994 became a member of the United States Hockey Hall of Fame in the coaches category.

FRED HARRIS Fred "Smokey" Harris was one of only three players to take part in each one of the Pacific Coast Hockey Association's 13 seasons, sharing that distinction with Bobby Rowe and Hugh Lehman. A fast skater and smooth stickhandler, Harris spent the first 12 seasons as a forward before moving back to defense.

Harris began with the Vancouver Millionaires in 1911–12, but was traded to Portland in 1914 when the Rosebuds became the first American team to enter a Canadian league that competed for the Stanley Cup. In 1915–16, he helped Portland win the PCHA championship. The Montreal Canadiens won their first Stanley Cup title that year when they beat Portland three games to two in a best of five playoff. Harris returned to Vancouver in 1918 and won three more PCHA titles, but never played for a Stanley Cup champion. He scored five goals in a game during the 1918–19 season and was named a PCHA all-star team.

In the final season of the PCHA, Harris was a member of the Seattle Metropolitans. When the team folded after the 1923–24 campaign, Vancouver and Victoria joined the Western Hockey League but Harris was one of several

western players who chose to sign instead with the NHL expansion team in Boston. He played just six games with the Bruins in 1924–25 and returned to Vancouver to finish the season. After five years in the minors, Harris was back in Boston for the 1930–31 season. He retired from hockey following a final minor-league campaign in 1931–32.

DOUG HARVEY was the best defenseman in hockey during his heyday and ranks with Bobby Orr and Eddie Shore among the greatest of all time. He could check, block shots, rush the puck, stickhandle and pass, but what made him truly unique was the way he could combine his skills to control the pace of the game. In addition to his hockey talent, Harvey played football and was good enough in baseball to be offered a pro contract by the old Boston Braves.

Harvey entered the NHL with the Canadiens in 1947–48 after a lengthy amateur career in his hometown of Montreal. By his fifth season in the NHL, it was apparent he was among the best in the game. He earned his first all-star selection in 1951–52 and would be chosen for 11 straight years. In 10 of those 11 years, Harvey was selected as a First Team All-Star, missing out only in 1958–59. He also won the Norris Trophy seven times in eight years between 1954–55 and 1961–62, again missing out in 1958–59 when the award went to teammate Tom Johnson. Harvey played on Stanley Cup winners in Montreal in 1953 and in every year from 1956 to 1960. In 1960–61, he was named to succeed the retired Maurice Richard as captain of the Canadiens, but it would be his final season in Montreal, as he became player-coach with the New York Rangers in 1961–62.

Harvey gave up his coaching role after one season in New York, but played with the Rangers for two more years, though much of his 1963–64 campaign was spent in the minors. Harvey spent the next three years playing minor-league hockey, returning to the NHL only briefly to play two games with the Detroit Red Wings in 1966–67. After expansion, Harvey signed with the St. Louis in time for the 1967–68 playoffs. He spent the 1968–69 season with the Blues before retiring. He was elected to the Hockey Hall of Fame in 1973.

DOMINIK HASEK became just the fifth goalie in NHL history to win the Hart Trophy (Roy Worters, 1929; Charlie Rayner, 1950; Al Rollins, 1954; Jacques Plante, 1962) after leading the Buffalo Sabres to a surprising first-place finish in the Northeast Division in 1996–97. Hasek also won the Vezina Trophy and was named to the First All-Star Team that year. His reputation as the best goalie in hockey was confirmed during the 1998 Olympics in Nagano, where Hasek was named the top goaltender after leading the Czech Republic to a surprising gold medal victory with upsets of the United States, Canada and Russia. He then went on to win the Hart Trophy for the second straight time and earned the Vezina Trophy once again. He also earned another selection to the First All-Star Team.

Hasek began his NHL career with the Chicago Blackhawks but saw most of his action with Indianapolis of the International Hockey League before being traded to Buffalo on August 7, 1992. By his second season with the Sabres, "the Dominator" had established himself as a star in the NHL as his 1.95 goals-against average was the first below 2.00 since Bernie Parent's 1.89 mark in 1973–74. Hasek also led the league with seven shutouts in 1993–94 as he won both the Vezina and Jennings trophies and was named to the First All-Star Team. Hasek was again a First Team All-Star and the Vezina Trophy winner in 1995–96 after leading the league with a 2.11 goals-against average and five shutouts. After just five seasons in Buffalo, Hasek had established himself as the Sabres' all-time leader in shutouts. He has played more games in the NHL that any other European-born goaltender.

Before his arrival in North America in 1990–91, Hasek had been a star goalie in his native Czechoslovakia. He was named the Czechoslovakian goaltender of the year five years in a row between 1985–86 and 1989–90 and was the player of the year in 1986–87, 1988–89 and 1989–90. On the international stage, Hasek was named the top goaltender and earned a silver medal at the World Junior Championships in 1983. He was a member of the Czech team at the Canada Cup as a 19-year-old in 1984 and was the starting goaltender in 1991. Hasek also represented the former Czechoslovakia at the World Championships several times and was named to the Czech Republic team for the World Cup of Hockey in 1996, but did not play.

DALE HAWERCHUK was a junior superstar who enjoyed immediate success in the NHL after being selected first overall by the Winnipeg Jets in the 1981 Entry Draft. He went on to collect 518 goals and 891 assists in a 16-year career, totals that rank among the highest in NHL history. His five assists in a single period on March 6, 1984 set an NHL record.

Hawerchuk had won back-to-back Memorial Cup championships with the Cornwall Royals in 1980 and 1981, earning numerous personal awards including Canadian major junior player of the year in 1981, before winning the Calder Trophy as NHL rookie of the year in 1981–82. His 103 points that season were the second-highest total by a rookie to that point in NHL history behind only Peter Stastny's 109 points the year before. Hawerchuk would go on to post five more 100-point seasons, ranking him among the top–10 in scoring four times including a third-place finish behind Wayne Gretzky and Jari Kurri with a career-high 130 points in 1984–85. Hawerchuk had seven seasons

with 40 goals or more, topping out with 53 in that same 1984–85 campaign. He was named to the NHL's Second All-Star Team that year.

On June 16, 1990, Hawerchuk was traded to Buffalo for Sabres defenseman Phil Housley. His offensive numbers were in decline, but Hawerchuk still managed to lead the team in scoring three of the five years he played in Buffalo. He joined the St. Louis Blues as a free agent in 1995 and scored his 500th career goal there on January 31, 1996 before being traded to Philadelphia on March 15 of that year. Hawerchuk ended his career after helping the Flyers to reach the Stanley Cup finals in 1996–97. He never played for a Stanley Cup champion but played strongly winning the Canada Cup with Team Canada in 1987 and 1991.

BILL HAY played junior hockey in Regina before attending Colorado College at a time when very few players made the NHL out of the NCAA. He is the son of Charles Hay, a member of the Hockey Hall of Fame in the builder's category who was instrumental in arranging the 1972 Summit Series between Team Canada and the Soviet Union.

Hay had been property of the Montreal Canadiens but he and Murray Balfour were sold to the Chicago Black Hawks prior to the 1959–60 season. A big man at 6'3" and over 190 pounds, Hay was an excellent skater and stick-handler who won the Calder Trophy in his rookie season. He centered Balfour and Bobby Hull with the Black Hawks and the threesome was soon known as the Million Dollar Line after a boast by Hawks owner James Norris that he wouldn't sell any of the three for $1 million. The trio helped Chicago win its first Stanley Cup title in 23 years in 1960–61 and Hay's playmaking skills helped Hull become just the third player in NHL history to score 50 goals in 1961–62.

Hay retired after the 1965–66 season but was convinced to rejoin the Black Hawks midway through the 1966–67 campaign. That year, Chicago finished atop the NHL regular-season standings for the first time in franchise history. Hay retired for good after the Black Hawks were upset by the Toronto Maple Leafs in the semifinals that spring.

CHARLES HAY As president of Hockey Canada, retired oil executive Charles Hay was instrumental in arranging the 1972 Summit Series between Team Canada and the Soviet Union. Hay worked diligently in order to overcome the reluctance of international hockey authorities to allow professionals to compete for Canada on the world stage.

Hockey Canada was formed in 1969 after an initial meeting in December of 1968 between representatives of the Canadian Amateur Hockey Association, the NHL and Canadian business and government leaders. The new group was established to organize and maintain a Canadian national team, but after the International Ice Hockey Federation backed away from a promise to let pro players take part in the 1970 World Championships, Canada withdrew from international competition. Hay continued to work for the inclusion of professional players at world events and his meetings with Soviet hockey officials cleared the way for the 1972 series between Canada's NHL pros and the national team of the USSR. His substantial contributions to international hockey were recognized in 1974 when he was elected to the Hockey Hall of Fame as a builder.

In his youth, Hay had been a goaltender with the University of Saskatoon team that lost the 1923 Allan Cup finals to the Toronto Granites. His son Bill played with the Chicago Black Hawks between 1959–60 and 1966–67.

GEORGE HAY was considered the best stickhandler in hockey when he played in the NHL, though he had enjoyed a long career by the time he got there. Hay was a member of the Winnipeg Monarchs in 1914–15 and 1915–16, where he first played with Dick Irvin. The two were teammates again with the Regina Vics in 1919–20 and 1920–21 before turning pro with the Regina Caps when the Western Canada Hockey League was formed in 1921–22.

Regina won the first WCHL title, but by 1925–26 the team had relocated and become the Portland Rosebuds. When pro hockey collapsed in the west after that year, Hay, Irvin and several other Portland players all joined the Chicago Black Hawks for that team's first NHL season. A shoulder injury limited his effectiveness in 1926–27, and Hay was dealt to the Detroit Cougars (later the Red Wings) the following year. He led the club in scoring in 1927–28, earning a place with an all-star team that was determined by the league's 10 coaches. Hay remained in Detroit, playing both in the NHL and the minor leagues, until 1933–34. He was elected to the Hockey Hall of Fame in 1958.

GEORGE HAYES was the first NHL official to be recognized as working more than 1,000 games, all but two of them as a linesman. In total, he handled 1,544 regular-season games, 149 more in the playoffs and 11 All-Star Games. Hayes began officiating in minor and high school hockey in 1936–37. He moved up to the Ontario Hockey Association in 1941–42, the American Hockey League in 1943–44 and on to the NHL in April of 1946.

At 6'3" and 220 pounds, Hayes commanded respect for both his size and his ability to maintain control. He continued to officiate in the NHL until 1964, when his career ended after a disagreement with the league over the need for an eye test. Hayes was inducted into the Hockey Hall of Fame in 1988.

ANDY HEBENTON never missed a game in his nine-year NHL career, playing 630 in a row over eight seasons with the New York Rangers and one year with the Boston Bruins. It was with Boston in 1963–64 that he broke Johnny Wilson's "ironman" record of 580 consecutive games. Hebenton's record stood until it was surpassed by Garry Unger in 1975. The current NHL "ironman" streak of 964 games is held by Doug Jarvis.

Amazingly, Hebenton's consecutive games streak stretches to 1,062 when his minor-league statistics are included as well. He never missed a game from March 8, 1952 with Victoria of the Pacific Coast Hockey League, through his NHL career, until October 18, 1967 with Portland of the Western Hockey. It was finally the death of his father that ended Hebenton's streak, as he returned home to attend the funeral. Amazingly, he had played 216 consecutive games in the minors before reaching the NHL, and 216 more minor-league games before the streak was stopped.

Hebenton was a right winger with good offensive numbers. He was a clean, two-way player, winning the Lady Byng Trophy for sportsmanlike conduct with the Rangers in 1956–57. He enjoyed his most productive NHL campaign two years later with 33 goals and 29 assists.

ANDERS HEDBERG The Winnipeg Jets of the World Hockey Association were the first North American team to actively pursue European talent. In 1974–75, the Jets unveiled Ulf Nilsson and Anders Hedberg among six new players. Hedberg and Nilsson teamed with Bobby Hull to form the most potent forward line in the WHA.

Converting Nilsson's slick passes, Hull set a pro hockey record with 77 goals in 1974–75. Hedberg had 53 goals and 47 assists that season and won the Lou Kaplan Trophy as rookie of the year. He and Nilsson both topped 100 points in each of the four years they spent in Winnipeg, with Hedberg never scoring less than 50 goals, including a career-high 70 in 1976–77. He ranks fifth all-time in WHA scoring with 236 goals in just four years and ninth in points with 458. Hedberg and Nilsson helped Winnipeg win the Avco Cup as WHA champion in 1975–76 and 1977–78.

The two Swedish superstars signed two-year contracts worth $1 million with the New York Rangers in 1978–79 and Hedberg went on to play seven seasons in the NHL. While unable to match his WHA totals, he never scored less than 20 goals in any full season and had 70-or-more points three times. After his playing days, Hedberg was a scout in Europe and was named an assistant general manager with the Toronto Maple Leafs in 1996.

PAUL HENDERSON scored the most famous goal in hockey history when he poked a rebound past Vladislav Tretiak with 34 seconds left in the final game to give Team Canada a victory over the Soviet Union in the 1972 Summit Series. Henderson scored the deciding goal in each of the last three games as Canada rallied to win the eight-game series 4–3–1.

Henderson was a graduate of the Red Wings' junior farm club in Hamilton who earned regular NHL duty with Detroit in 1964–65. He topped 20 goals in each of the next two seasons before being traded to the Toronto Maple Leafs with Norm Ullman and Floyd Smith in the deal that sent Frank Mahovlich to Detroit on March 3, 1968. Henderson was a solid performer in Toronto, scoring 30 goals in 1970–71 and establishing a career high with 38 the next year.

Unable to live up to the high expectations created by his national celebrity status, Henderson slumped during a 1972–73 season that was dogged by injury. Unhappy playing under owner Harold Ballard, he left the Maple Leafs for the Toronto Toros of the World Hockey Association in 1973–74 and remained with the team when it moved to Birmingham in 1976. After four WHA teams entered the NHL in 1979–80, Henderson returned to the league for a final season as a member of the Atlanta Flames.

JIM HENDY was hockey's first great statistician. Born in Barbados on May 6, 1905, but raised in Vancouver, Hendy first learned the sport while attending games as a boy in the Denman Street Arena, which had been built by Frank and Lester Patrick when they launched the Pacific Coast Hockey Association in 1911.

Hendy worked as a rancher and sailor as a young man before settling down as a telegraph operator and writer. All the while, he maintained his interest in hockey by compiling players' performances and personal statistics. This resulted in the publication of the first edition of *The Hockey Guide* in 1933. Hendy continued to produce the book annually through 1951, when the pressure of other work forced him to give it up. Hendy's records and rights were turned over to the NHL.

In addition to his statistical work, Hendy worked for the New York Rangers, where he was named head of publicity in 1940. He was later publicity boss for the American Hockey League before becoming president of the United States Hockey League in 1947. From 1949 to 1959, Hendy was general manager of the AHL's Cleveland Barons. He was inducted into the Hockey Hall of Fame as a builder in 1968.

CAMILLE HENRY won the Calder Trophy after scoring 24 goals for the New York Rangers during his rookie season of 1953–54. However, a scoring slump saw him sent to the minors in 1954–55 and he did not rejoin the Rangers

until the 1956–57 campaign. He returned to form during the 1957–58 season and led the Rangers with 32 goals while receiving just one minor penalty to earn both the Lady Byng Trophy and a selection to the Second All-Star Team.

At just 5'9" and 152 pounds, Henry was a slim and frail-looking player but "the Eel," as he was known, was a slick stickhandler and smooth skater with a hard, accurate shot. He again led the Rangers in goal-scoring with 37 in 1962–63 and 29 in 1963–64 and also served as captain during the 1963–64 and 1964–65 seasons. However, in the 11 years he played in New York the team only made the playoffs three times.

Henry was traded to the Chicago Black Hawks on February 4, 1965, but spent the all of the 1965–66 season in the minors. He did not play in 1966–67 but the Black Hawks traded him back to New York and he rejoined the Rangers during the 1967–68 season. He finished his NHL career with the St. Louis Blues.

RILEY HERN was a star goaltender who played on several championship teams at many levels of hockey throughout his career. He started playing in his hometown of St. Mary's with the local Ontario Hockey Association junior team, and he moved up through the intermediate and senior ranks before joining a team in London, Ontario. In 1903–04, Hern signed with the Portage Lakers team in Houghton, Michigan and played in the International (Pro) Hockey League (hockey's first professional circuit) until he moved to the Montreal Wanderers for the 1906–07 season.

Hern made Montreal his permanent home, helping the Wanderers to win the Stanley Cup in 1907, 1908 and 1910. Business concerns forced him to retire after the 1910–11 season, but he remained in the game as a goal judge and referee. He was a prominent member of the Rossmere Golf Club and St. Rose Boating Club in Montreal as well as several other sports organizations, and he served as president or director of many Montreal business organizations. Hern was elected to the Hockey Hall of Fame in 1962.

BOBBY HEWITSON was a star athlete in both football and lacrosse who later became a highly respected hockey official. He was inducted into the Hall of Fame as a referee in 1963. Hewitson led the Maitlands lacrosse team to a junior championship and quarterbacked the Capitals to a Canadian junior football title back in 1913 while starting a career in sportswriting around this time. He worked with the *Toronto Globe* and *Toronto Telegram*, from which he retired as sports editor in 1957.

Hewitson became a referee prior to 1920, officiating games in hockey, football and lacrosse. He was an NHL referee for 10 seasons, later becoming one of the original members of the Hot Stove League on hockey broadcasts. He was the first curator of both the Hockey Hall of Fame and Canada's Sports Hall of Fame located on the grounds of the Canadian National Exhibition in Toronto. Hewitson served as secretary of the Canadian Rugby Union for almost 25 years, and he was associated closely with horse racing.

FOSTER HEWITT's radio broadcasts from Maple Leaf Gardens helped make the Toronto team a national institution in Canada, and they made him as famous as the many superstars whose exploits he chronicled. Hewitt was a reporter with the *Toronto Star* when he broadcast his first hockey game from Toronto's Mutual Street Arena on March 22, 1923. He was hired by Conn Smythe to broadcast Maple Leaf games shortly after Smythe bought the team in February of 1927. His contribution to hockey as its pioneer of the airwaves was so great that Hewitt was inducted into the Hockey Hall of Fame as a builder in 1965.

Over his career, Hewitt called thousands of hockey games, first on radio and later on television. His trademark greeting of "Hello, Canada" and his excited call "He shoots, he scores!" became a regular feature of the game. In addition to NHL hockey, Hewitt covered World and Olympic championships, as well as the action in many other sports for listeners and viewers across Canada and the northeast United States. He became a successful businessman over the course of his broadcasting career, and he owned his own radio station in Toronto until he retired in 1981. His last great play-by-play assignment had been to call the action of the 1972 Canada-Russia Summit Series for Canadian television viewers.

WILLIAM A. HEWITT was secretary of the Ontario Hockey Association from 1903 to 1961, registrar and treasurer of the Canadian Amateur Hockey Association for 39 years and manager (or honorary manager) of Canada's gold medal-winning Olympic hockey teams of 1920, 1924 and 1928. He also spent 41 years in the newspaper business in Toronto, 32 as sports editor of the *Toronto Star*.

In addition to his many hockey duties, Hewitt helped form the Big Four football league (a forerunner of the Canadian Football League) in 1907, and he served terms as president and secretary of the Canadian Rugby Union. He acted as patrol judge at Toronto's Woodbine race track as early as 1905, and he was presiding steward at Ontario racetracks for 14 years. When Maple Leaf Gardens opened in 1931, Hewitt served as its first attractions manager. He was elected to the Hockey Hall of Fame as a builder in 1947. Son Foster Hewitt was elected in 1965.

BRYAN HEXTALL scored the winning goal in overtime when the New York Rangers defeated the Toronto Maple Leafs to capture the Stanley Cup in 1940. Hextall had enjoyed a breakthrough year that season, leading the NHL with 24 goals and earning a berth on the First All-Star Team. He would be a First Team All-Star again each of the next two years, leading the league with 26 goals in 1940–41 and topping the NHL with 56 points in 1941–42 when the Rangers finished in first place. He was named to the Second All-Star Team in 1942–43.

Hextall was born in Grenfell, Saskatchewan but grew up in Poplar Point, Manitoba and played on the juvenile provincial championship team there in 1929–30. He later played with the Winnipeg Monarchs and in Portage la Prairie before turning pro with the Vancouver Lions of the Western Hockey League in 1934–35. Vancouver won the WHL title the next year. Hextall joined the Philadelphia Ramblers in 1936–37 and became a regular with the Rangers the following season. By 1940–41, he was playing with Lynn Patrick and Phil Watson on one of the top forward lines in the NHL. Hextall continued to star with the Rangers until 1943–44 but was away from the game most of the next two years before returning to play two more seasons. His final year of 1948–49 was spent in the American Hockey League.

Hextall was well respected during his playing days and considered to be an excellent ambassador for the game. He was elected to the Hockey Hall of Fame in 1969. Sons Dennis and Bryan Jr. were NHL players, as is grandson Ron Hextall.

RON HEXTALL is the grandson of Hockey Hall of Famer Bryan Hextall and the son of NHL player Bryan Hextall Jr. He was a rookie sensation when he broke into the NHL with the Philadelphia Flyers in 1986–87, leading the league with 37 victories that season, winning the Vezina Trophy and finishing second to Luc Robitaille for the Calder Trophy. Hextall also was named to the First All-Star Team. In the playoffs, he helped the Flyers to reach the seventh game of the Stanley Cup finals before being defeated by the Edmonton Oilers and was rewarded with the Conn Smythe Trophy as playoff MVP.

Hextall played junior hockey in his hometown of Brandon, Manitoba and was a first team all-star and rookie of the year with Hershey of the American Hockey League in 1985–86 before entering the NHL. He spent his first six seasons with the Flyers, never quite living up to his rookie season and establishing a reputation as much for his violent temper as for his play. He was also known for his ability to shoot the puck and against the Boston Bruins on December 8, 1987, Hextall became the first NHL goaltender ever to score a goal by firing the puck into the opposition's net. He scored a second empty-net goal in the playoffs against the Washington Capitals on April 11, 1989.

Hextall was traded to the Quebec Nordiques on June 30, 1992 as part of the deal that brought Eric Lindros to Philadelphia. He played just one season in Quebec and was sent to the New York Islanders on June 20, 1993. Hextall established a career high with five shutouts during the 1993–94 season but was dealt back to Philadelphia on September 22, 1994.

Though often criticized for his tendency to give up soft goals, Hextall led the NHL with a 2.17 goals-against average for the Flyers in 1995–96 and equaled his career high with five shutouts in 1996–97. In the playoffs that year, he shared the net with Garth Snow as the Flyers reached the Stanley Cup finals before being swept by the Detroit Red Wings.

VIC HEYLIGER played high school hockey in his hometown of Concord, Massachusetts and prep school hockey at the Lawrence Academy in Groton, Connecticut before entering the University of Michigan in 1934. While at Michigan he was an all-American in 1935, 1936 and 1937 and scored what was then a school record of 116 goals. When he graduated, Heyliger played with the Chicago Black Hawks briefly in 1937–38 and 1943–44 and coached at the University of Illinois in between.

Heyliger attributed his development as a coach to the teachings of Bill Stewart and Paul Thompson, who coached him in Chicago, but he enjoyed his greatest success when he returned to his alma mater. He led Michigan to victory at the first NCAA hockey tournament in 1948 and guided the Wolverines to the national title again in 1951, 1952, 1953, 1955 and 1956. Among the top players coached by Heyliger at Michigan were John Matchefts and Willard Ikola, who helped lead the United States Olympic hockey team to a silver medal in 1956.

After his retirement from Michigan, Heyliger returned to coaching with the new hockey program at the United States Air Force Academy and helped organize the 1962 World Championships in Colorado Springs. He was invited to coach the West German national team for the 1962–63 season and later coached the American team at the 1966 World Championships. Heyliger remained active in coaching at the Air Force Academy until the end of the 1973–74 season and was inducted into the coaches section of the United States Hockey Hall of Fame in 1974.

AL HILL enjoyed the most productive debut of any rookie in NHL history when he collected five points in his first game on February 14, 1977. He had two goals and three assists as the Philadelphia Flyers beat the St. Louis Blues 6–4. Hill had begun the year at Springfield after earning an AHL contract during an impressive training camp in his first year out of junior hockey.

Despite his record-setting debut, Hill managed just one assist in eight more games with the Flyers that season. It would be four years before he earned full-time duty in the NHL, and he later spent more time in the minors for the Flyers, Edmonton Oilers, and Philadelphia again before his playing career ended in 1989.

MEL HILL "Sudden Death" Mel Hill earned his nickname when he scored three overtime goals for the Boston Bruins in a seven-game playoff victory over the New York Rangers in 1939. At the time, he was a little-known player in his first full year who had scored just 10 goals during the regular season.

Hill scored at 59:25 of overtime for a Boston victory in game one, had a goal at 8:24 of extra time in game two, then won the series for Boston in game seven after 48 minutes of overtime. In the finals against the Toronto Maple Leafs, Hill scored twice in regulation time during a five-game series that saw Boston win the Stanley Cup.

Though he never scored more than 18 goals in a single NHL season, and never had another overtime goal, Hill won a second Stanley Cup title with Boston in 1941, and a third with the Maple Leafs in 1945. To date, only Rocket Richard has equaled Hill's three overtime goals in one playoff year and no one else has ever duplicated the feat of three overtime goals in a single series.

KEN HITCHCOCK was named head coach of the Dallas Stars on January 8, 1996, taking over from Bob Gainey who gave up his coaching job to concentrate on his duties as general manager. In his first full season behind the bench in 1996–97, Hitchcock led Dallas to franchise records in wins (48) and points (104) as the club climbed from last in its division to first place. Both team records were broken in 1997–98 when Hitchcock's Stars went 49–22–11 for 109 points and won the Presidents' Trophy awarded to the NHL club finishing with the most points in the regular season. Hitchcock was nominated for the Jack Adams Award as NHL coach of the year.

Prior to his success in the NHL, Hitchcock had been a top coach at every level along the way. He posted a 575–69 mark in 10 seasons with Sherwood Park (an Edmonton suburb) and earned coach of the year honors in the Albert Minor Hockey Association in 1982–83 and 1983–84. The 1984–85 season saw Hitchcock join the Kamloops Blazers of the Western Hockey League, where he led his team to the West Division title five times in six years. He was also an assistant coach with the Canadian team that won the World Junior Championships in 1988. Hitchcock was the WHL coach of the year in 1986–87 and 1989–90 and was also named the top coach in Canadian major junior hockey in 1989–90 after leading Kamloops to the Memorial Cup tournament. His .693 winning percentage (291–125–15) in six years with the Blazers is the best in the history of the WHL.

Hitchcock served as an assistant coach with the Philadelphia Flyers from 1990–91 to 1992–93 before returning to head coaching duties with the Stars' International Hockey League farm club in Kalamazoo. He spent two-plus seasons in the IHL before being hired in Dallas.

LIONEL HITCHMAN teamed with Eddie Shore in Boston to give the Bruins one of hockey's greatest pair of defensemen. It was Hitchman's strong defensive style that allowed Shore the freedom to become such an outstanding offensive defenseman.

Hitchman began his professional career with the Ottawa Senators late in the 1922–23 season and played behind future Hall of Fame defensemen Eddie Gerard and George Boucher. In the playoffs that year, Hitchman lost several teeth when Sprague Cleghorn tested his toughness with a cross-check to the face, but he continued to play and later helped Ottawa win the Stanley Cup.

Art Ross acquired Hitchman for the Bruins during the team's premier season of 1924–25 and he later played alongside Cleghorn in Boston before being paired with Eddie Shore during the 1926–27 season. In 1927–28, Hitchman was named the first team captain in Bruins history, a position he held through the 1930–31 campaign. During that time, Boston emerged as an NHL power, winning the Stanley Cup in 1928–29 and posting a 38–5–1 record during the 1929–30 season.

Hitchman and Shore remained the top defensemen in Boston until 1933–34, when Hitchman began to see less playing time. He would retired at the end of that season.

CHARLIE HODGE spent 12 seasons in the Montreal Canadiens system, seeing only occasional action at the NHL level as an injury replacement for Jacques Plante, before finally arriving in the NHL to stay when Gump Worsley was hurt in 1963–64. Hodge played 62 games for the Canadiens that year and earned the Vezina Trophy as Montreal finished the regular season in first place. He was named to the Second All-Star Team that year, as he would be again in 1964–65 after helping the Canadiens win the Stanley Cup.

Hodge and Worsley shared the netminding duties in Montreal in 1965–66 and won the Vezina Trophy after the Canadiens had the NHL's best defensive record and again won the Stanley Cup. Hodge carried the bulk of the load in goal for the Canadiens during the 1966–67 season but Rogatien Vachon was called up late in the year and he and Worsley handled the playoffs. After the season, Hodge was selected by the Oakland Seals in the 1967 Expansion Draft.

Hodge was the starting goaltender on the worst team in the NHL in Oakland in 1966–67 but saw only limited duty over the next two years. He was then selected by Vancouver in the 1970 Expansion Draft and spent his final NHL campaign with the Canucks during their inaugural season of 1970–71.

KEN HODGE After breaking into the NHL with the Chicago Black Hawks, Ken Hodge was traded to the Boston Bruins with Phil Esposito and Fred Stanfield for Gilles Marotte, Pit Martin and Jack Norris on May 15, 1967. Hodge then developed into one of the NHL's top scorers as the Bruins became an NHL powerhouse. He played on Stanley Cup winners in 1969–70 and 1971–72 and starred on a line with Esposito and Wayne Cashman that was the most dangerous combination in the league.

Hodge made his first appearance among the NHL scoring leaders in 1968–69 when he had 90 points on 45 goals and 45 assists. He had 43 goals and 62 assists for 105 points in 1970–71 when the Bruins had a league-record 399 goals and Phil Esposito, Bobby Orr, John Bucyk and Hodge finished 1–2–3–4 in scoring. He scored 50 goals and equaled his 105 points with 55 assists as Esposito, Orr, Hodge, and Cashman finished 1–2–3–4 in scoring in 1973–74. Hodge was named to the First All-Star Team at right wing after both of his 105-point seasons.

The Bruins' big scoring line was broken up when Esposito was traded to the New York Rangers on November 7, 1975. On May 26, 1976, Hodge was also traded to New York but neither he nor Esposito produced points at the same rate they had in Boston. Hodge's NHL career ended during the 1977–78 season, though he played in the minor leagues until 1980. His son, Ken Hodge Jr., saw action in the NHL between 1988–89 and 1992–93.

FLASH HOLLETT William "Flash" Hollett set an NHL record for defensemen when he scored 20 goals for the Detroit Red Wings in 1944–45. The record lasted 23 years until Bobby Orr scored 21 goals in 1968–69.

Hollett began his NHL career as property of the Toronto Maple Leafs but spent most of his first season of 1933–34 on loan to the Ottawa Senators. He played the entire 1934–35 season alongside Hap Day on the Maple Leafs defense but was sold to the Boston Bruins the following year.

Playing with Eddie Shore and Dit Clapper in Boston, Hollett quickly developed into a talented rushing defenseman. He helped the Bruins win the Stanley Cup in 1939 and 1941 and tied Harry Cameron's 1921–22 record for a defenseman when he scored 19 goals in 1941–42. Hollett scored 19 goals again in 1942–43 and was named to the Second All-Star Team.

Despite his All-Star status, the Bruins dealt Hollett to Detroit during the 1943–44 season for the more rugged Pat Egan. The Red Wings paired Hollett with veteran defenseman Earl Siebert in 1944–45 and he responded with his record 20-goal season to earn a spot on the First All-Star Team. Injuries slowed him down in 1945–46 and he left the NHL after that season. He then had his amateur status reinstated and played senior hockey. He was a member of the Toronto Marlboros Allan Cup-winning team in his final season of 1949–50.

HAP HOLMES Harry "Hap" Holmes was an outstanding goaltender who played in the five top professional hockey leagues of his day over the course of a 16-year career. He turned pro with one of the two new Toronto franchises in the National Hockey Association in 1912–13, helping the Blueshirts win the Stanley Cup the following season. In 1915–16, Holmes was one of several Toronto players lured to the Pacific Coast Hockey Association's new team in Seattle. In 1916–17, he was a member of the Metropolitans team that became the first American Stanley Cup champions.

When the NHL was formed in 1917–18, Holmes returned east and helped the Torontos, or the Arenas as they are more commonly known, win the Stanley Cup that season. He was back in Seattle the following year, winning two more PCHA titles with the Mets, but a fourth Stanley Cup victory would have to wait.

Seattle folded after the 1923–24 season and Holmes joined the Victoria Cougars when they and the Vancouver Maroons entered the Western Canada Hockey League in 1924–25. Victoria emerged as the WCHL champion during the playoffs that year before defeating the Montreal Canadiens for the Stanley Cup. Holmes was still in Victoria the following season when the WCHL became the Western Hockey League.

After pro hockey collapsed in the west, Holmes was one of several Victoria players who were sold to the Detroit Cougars (later Red Wings) in that team's first NHL season of 1926–27. He played two years in Detroit and then retired. After his playing days, Holmes was instrumental in starting professional hockey in Cleveland. The American Hockey League perpetuates his memory through the Harry "Hap" Holmes Memorial Trophy, which is presented to the league's top goaltender. In 1972, Holmes was inducted into the Hockey Hall of Fame.

CHARLIE HOLT began his collegiate coaching career at Colby College in 1962. In 1968, he took over the head coaching job at the University of New Hampshire, where he enjoyed great success for 18 seasons. Under his leadership, New Hampshire qualified for the Eastern Collegiate Athletic Conference playoffs 14 times and reached the NCAA's final four in 1977, 1979 and 1982.

Holt accumulated 347 wins against only 232 losses in his career and won the Spencer Penrose Award as coach of the year three times. He was inducted into the coaches category of the United States Hockey Hall of Fame in 1997.

TOM HOOPER was a homegrown member of the Kenora Thistles team that won the Stanley Cup from the Montreal Wanderers in January of 1907 after unsuccessful challenges in 1903 and 1905 when the town was still known as Rat Portage. The Wanderers defeated the Thistles in a Stanley Cup rematch in March and Hooper joined the Montreal team the following year. He helped the Wanderers successfully defend the Stanley Cup against the Ottawa Vics in a challenge match in January of 1908 before finishing the season with the Montreal Amateur Athletic Association. He was elected to the Hockey Hall of Fame in 1962.

RED HORNER George Reginald "Red" Horner was an aggressive defenseman who led the NHL in penalties eight years in a row from 1932–33 to 1939–40. He set a league record that lasted for 20 seasons when he spent 167 minutes in the penalty box in 1935–36. Conn Smythe claimed that Horner's tough play made him the policeman for the club and gave other players more confidence on the ice. He was solid defensively in his own end and was also an effective rusher and fine playmaker.

Horner joined the Maple Leafs directly from the Toronto Marlboros in 1928–29 and spent his entire 12-year NHL career in Toronto. He was a key member of the Maple Leafs' first Stanley Cup-winning team in 1932. He helped Toronto win four Canadian Division titles and advance to the Stanley Cup finals on five more occasions before retiring after the 1939–40 season. He had been named captain of the Maple Leafs in 1938–39 and considered that the highest honor of his playing career. In 1965, Horner was inducted into the Hockey Hall of Fame.

TIM HORTON was a product of the Maple Leafs farm system who went on to play 18 full years in Toronto and 24 total seasons in the NHL. During much of that time, he was recognized as the strongest player in the game and one of the league's best defensemen. He could rush the puck effectively and had a powerful slapshot. He earned a reputation as a peacemaker over the course of his career, deterring opposition fighters with a grasp known as the "Horton Bear Hug."

Horton was a graduate of the Maple Leafs junior team at St. Michael's College who then spent the better part of three seasons with Toronto's Pittsburgh farm club in the American Hockey League before making the NHL to stay in 1952–53. He was a Second Team All-Star in his second season, but injuries hampered his effectiveness with a weak Toronto club over the next few years. In 1958–59, Horton was teamed with Allan Stanley and, along with Bob Baun and Carl Brewer, provided the solid defense that helped the Maple Leafs win the Stanley Cup in 1962, 1963 and 1964. Horton was a Second Team All-Star again in 1962–63 and earned First Team honors in 1963–64. He earned another selection to the Second All-Star Team when Toronto won the Stanley Cup again in 1966–67, and though the Maple Leafs declined rapidly after expansion, Horton was a First Team All-Star in both 1967–68 and 1968–69.

By 1969–70, Horton was 16 years older than any other Maple Leafs defenseman and his $80,000 salary made him the most expensive player on Toronto's roster. With the team struggling in last place, Horton was dealt to the New York Rangers on March 5, 1970. He spent the entire 1970–71 season with the Rangers, then played a year with the Pittsburgh Penguins. He was in his second season with the Buffalo Sabres when a tragic single-car accident ended his life on February 21, 1974. He was inducted into the Hockey Hall of Fame in 1977.

BRONCO HORVATH Joseph "Bronco" Horvath centered Johnny Bucyk and Vic Stasiuk on the Boston Bruins' famed Uke Line, so named for its players' Ukrainian heritage. Horvath had spent time with the New York Rangers and Montreal Canadiens, but it was not until he arrived in Boston in 1957 that his career blossomed.

The Uke Line combined for 174 points in 1957–58, as Horvath lead the Bruins with 30 goals and 66 points. He added five more goals in 12 playoff games as Boston advanced to the Stanley Cup finals before losing to Montreal. Horvath missed the first 25 games of the 1958–59 season because of a broken jaw, but returned to score 19 goals in just 45 games.

Horvath was at his best in 1959–60 when he battled Bobby Hull all season long for the NHL lead in goals and points. He tied "the Golden Jet" with 39 goals, but lost the Art Ross Trophy by a single point as he collected 41 assists to Hull's 42. Horvath was named to the NHL Second All-Star team behind Jean Beliveau at center that year.

After one more season with the Bruins, Horvath moved on to the Chicago Black Hawks in 1961–62 and split the following year between the New York Rangers and Toronto Maple Leafs before winding up in the minor leagues. Horvath continued playing minor-league hockey until 1969–70, interrupted only briefly by a return to the NHL with the Minnesota North Stars during the 1967–68 season.

PHIL HOUSLEY The highest-scoring U.S.-born defenseman in the history of the NHL, and just the fifth defenseman ever to top 1,000 points, Phil Housley

entered the league in 1982–83 after the Buffalo Sabres selected him directly out of high school with the sixth pick overall in the 1982 Entry Draft. He led all first-year defensemen in scoring that season and was named to the NHL All-Rookie Team.

Housley spent his first eight seasons with the Sabres, setting team records for a defenseman in goals, assists and points for both a single season and a career. On June 16, 1990, he was traded to the Winnipeg Jets in a package that brought Dale Hawerchuk to Buffalo. Housley was a finalist for the Norris Trophy with the Jets in 1991–92 and was named to the Second All-Star Team that year. He established career highs with 79 assists and 97 points in 1992–93. Housley has played since for the St. Louis Blues, Calgary Flames, New Jersey Devils and Washington Capitals.

In international competition, Housley represented the United States at the 1982 World Junior Championships and at the World Championships in 1982, 1986 and 1989. He also played at the Canada Cup in 1984 and 1987 and was a member of the team that beat Canada at the World Cup of Hockey in 1996.

GORDIE HOWE broke into the NHL with the Detroit Red Wings in 1946–47 and went on to star for 25 years, setting records that, at the time, seemed unbreakable. He had an effortless skating style and deceptive speed, combined with tremendous strength and a powerful shot. Howe retired after the 1970–71 season, but was back in the game two years later when he signed to play with sons Mark and Marty with the Houston Aeros of the World Hockey Association. After six years in the WHA, Howe returned to the NHL for a final season with the Hartford Whalers. When he finally retired after the 1979–80 campaign, Howe had 801 goals and 1,049 assists for 1,850 points in the NHL. Though those records have been broken, his 1,767 games over 26 NHL seasons are not likely to be surpassed.

Howe attended his first NHL training camp with the New York Rangers as a 15-year-old in 1943, but left the workouts in Winnipeg because he was homesick. The following year, he was invited to try out for the Red Wings, and in 1945–46 Howe was playing for Detroit's Omaha affiliate in the United States Hockey League. He was promoted to the Red Wings in 1946–47 and was teamed on a line with Sid Abel and Ted Lindsay. The high-scoring trio was dubbed the Production Line in 1948–49, and in 1949–50 Howe made his first appearance among the league scoring leaders when Lindsay, Abel and Howe finished 1–2–3 in the NHL. The Red Wings went on to win the Stanley Cup that year, though Howe was badly injured in the very first game of the play-offs. He recovered, and won his first scoring title in 1950–51. Howe would win the scoring title again in each of the next three years and eventually claimed the Art Ross Trophy six times. He also won the Hart Trophy on six occasions. While those totals have been surpassed, his record of 21 selections to NHL All-Star Team has not been beaten. Howe was picked to the First Team 12 times. He established a career high with 49 goals in 70 games in 1952–53, when the NHL was a tight defensive league, and when offenses exploded following expansion in 1967, the 41-year-old Howe had 103 points in 1968–69. He cracked the top 10 in scoring for the 21st consecutive year in 1969–70, but retired after injuries limited his effectiveness in 1970–71. He was inducted immediately into the Hockey Hall of Fame

Though he had not played in two years and was now 45, Howe was an instant success in the WHA, scoring 100 points in 1973–74 and helping Houston win the Avco Cup, which they won again the following year. In six seasons in the WHA with Houston and the New England Whalers, Howe collected 174 goals and 334 assists for 508 points to rank sixth in all-time WHA scoring. He returned to the NHL for a final season at age 51 and played all 80 games. For excellence and durability, his career will not be matched.

MARK HOWE The son of Gordie Howe, Mark Howe enjoyed a lengthy professional career of his own playing 22 seasons in the World Hockey Association and the NHL. He played junior hockey in Detroit and was a member of the U.S. Olympic hockey team that won a silver medal in 1972, though he spent most of the 1972–73 season playing with brother Marty as a member of the Toronto Marlboros of the Ontario Hockey Association. The following year, the Howe brothers turned pro and teamed with their father on a line with the Houston Aeros of the WHA.

Mark Howe had 38 goals and 41 assists for Houston in 1973–74, earning honors as a Second Team All-Star and rookie of the year and helping the Aeros win the Avco Cup, which they would win again the following year. The Howe clan joined the New England Whalers for the 1977–78 season and were with the team when it entered the NHL in 1979–80. A forward in the WHA, he now became one of the NHL's top defensemen. He joined the Flyers in 1982–83 and stabilized Philadelphia's defense over six seasons, helping the team reach the Stanley Cup finals in 1985 and 1987. His last four years in Philadelphia were hampered by a disc problem in his back.

In 1992, Howe signed as free agent with the Detroit Red Wings, the team on which his father had starred for 25 years. Injuries continued to limit his effectiveness and he retired in 1994–95. Howe never won the Stanley Cup in his playing career but was a scout for Detroit's championship team in 1996–97 and 1997–98.

SYD HOWE Like Gordie Howe (to whom he is not related), Syd Howe enjoyed a long NHL career starring with the Detroit Red Wings before retiring as the NHL's all-time scoring leader. His 528 points on 237 goals and 291 assists between 1929–30 and 1945–46 were 13 more than the great Nels Stewart and 61 more than the legendary Howie Morenz. Howe is also one of only seven players in history to score six goals in one NHL game, accomplishing the feat on February 3, 1944.

Howe grew up in Ottawa and starred in school leagues as well as in junior and senior hockey there before turning pro with the hometown Senators during the 1929–30 season. He also played with the Philadelphia Quakers, Toronto Maple Leafs and St. Louis Eagles before being sold to Detroit in February of 1935. There, he finally established himself as a star. Red Wings owner James D. Norris credited Howe's play with increasing the attendance and hockey interest in Detroit, and he helped the Red Wings win the Stanley Cup in 1936, 1937 and 1943.

Howe played center, wing and defense during his 17-year NHL career and continued to play hockey in Ottawa for parts of two seasons after leaving the NHL. He was elected to the Hockey Hall of Fame in 1965.

HARRY HOWELL enjoyed one of the longest playing careers in professional hockey history. He broke into the NHL in 1952–53 and continued playing through the 1975–76 season. When his 170 games in three World Hockey Association seasons are added to his 1,411 games over 21 years in the NHL, his total of 1,581 games becomes the highest of any defenseman in the game.

Howell began his NHL career with New York and proved so durable that he rarely missed any action over his first 16 years with the Rangers. His 1,160 games over 17 seasons are by far a team record. Howell spent most of his career with weak teams in New York and never played for a Stanley Cup winner, but was a First Team All-Star and Norris Trophy winner as a 35-year-old in 1966–67. His 12 goals and 40 points that season were both career highs.

Howell played with the Rangers until 1968–69 when he was sold to the Oakland (later California) Seals, where he played one-and-a-half seasons before being sold again to the Los Angeles Kings. He played in Los Angeles through the 1972–73 season, then jumped to the WHA. Howell was a playing coach with the New York-New Jersey franchise in 1973–74 and with the San Diego Mariners the following year. His final season of 1975–76 was spent with the Calgary Cowboys. He returned to the NHL as an assistant general manager with the Cleveland Barons in 1976–77 and was serving as the club's general manager when the it merged with the Minnesota North Stars in 1978. He served briefly as the coach of the North Stars in 1978–79. Howell was elected to the Hockey Hall of Fame in 1979.

BOBBY HULL began earning accolades as a sure NHL prospect as early as age 10. He progressed rapidly through the ranks in minor hockey and joined the Chicago Black Hawks as an 18-year-old in 1957–58. At the time of Hull's arrival, the Black Hawks had missed the playoffs four years in a row and in 11 of the last 12 seasons. Attendance was dismal and the franchise had been in danger of folding. Soon, Hull's scoring exploits were attracting huge crowds to the Chicago Stadium and in 1961 the Black Hawks were Stanley Cup champions. The team would continue to dominate the regular-season standings into the 1970s.

Hull had an impressive body build, with a muscular torso and powerful legs. His booming slapshot was powerful and accurate, and he was the fastest skater in the game. Combining those facts with his blonde, good looks, Hull was nicknamed "the Golden Jet." In 16 NHL seasons, he led the league in goals on seven occasions and in points three times. He first won the Art Ross Trophy in 1959–60 and won it again in 1961–62 when he became just the third player in NHL history (Maurice Richard and Bernie Geoffrion) to score 50 goals in a single season. His final scoring title came in 1965–66 when he set pre-expansion records with 54 goals and 97 points. He established a new NHL scoring record with 58 goals in 1968–69, when he also set a career high with 107 points. Hull had won the Hart Trophy as the NHL's most valuable player in both 1964–65 and 1965–66, and also earned the Lady Byng Trophy for sportsmanlike conduct in 1964–65.

By the end of the 1971–72 season, Bobby Hull's 604 goals ranked second only to Gordie Howe in NHL history. He also had 549 assists and 1,153 points and had been an All-Star on 12 occasions, including 10 selections to the First Team. But in June of 1972, Hull shocked the NHL establishment when he signed a 10-year deal worth $2.75 million with the Winnipeg Jets of the World Hockey Association. Though his signing led to his ban from Team Canada when it played the USSR later that year, it gave instant credibility to the fledgling league. Hull continued his high-scoring ways in the WHA, and in 1974–75 he established what was then a single-season professional hockey record with 77 goals. In his seven seasons in the WHA, Hull collected 303 goals and 335 assists for 638 points, totals that rank second, sixth and third respectively among the league's all-time leaders. He also played on Avco Cup champions in 1976, 1978 and 1979.

When Winnipeg became one of four WHA teams to enter the NHL in 1979–80, Hull returned to the league with the Jets. He ended his career playing with Gordie Howe on the Hartford Whalers later that season. In 1983, Hull

was elected to the Hockey Hall of Fame. His brother Dennis and son Brett also have starred in the NHL.

BRETT HULL As the son of Hockey Hall of Famer Bobby Hull, Brett Hull has followed in his famous father's footsteps to become one of the greatest goal scorers in the NHL. His 86 goals in 1990–91 rank as the third-highest single-season total in history behind Wayne Gretzky's 92 in 1981–82 and 87 in 1983–84. Hull scored his 500th career goal on December 22, 1996 to make him and Bobby the only father-son combination ever to reach the milestone.

Hull was chosen 117th overall by the Calgary Flames in the 1984 Entry Draft and spent the next two seasons at the University of Minnesota-Duluth. In 1986–87, he was named top rookie and selected to the first all-star team with Moncton of the American Hockey League. Hull got a chance to see regular duty with the Flames in 1987–88, but on March 7, 1988, he was traded to the St. Louis Blues.

In first full season with St. Louis, Hull had 41 goals and 43 assists. Teamed with Adam Oates in 1989–90, Hull was the top goal scorer in the NHL with 72 and earned a selection to the First All-Star Team at right wing. He also won the Lady Byng Trophy. With 86 goals and 45 assists in 1990–91, Hull's 131 points trailed only Wayne Gretzky and he was rewarded with the Hart Trophy as most valuable player. In 1991–92, Hull led the league for the third straight year with 70 goals and earned a third consecutive selection to the First All-Star Team. He topped 50 goals in each of the next two seasons as he surpassed Bernie Federko's total of 352 goals to become the leading goal scorer in Blues history. He upped his total in St. Louis to 527 goals before signing as a free agent with the Dallas Stars after the 1997–98 campaign.

Though he was born in Belleville, Ontario, Hull holds dual Canadian and U.S. citizenship and represented the U.S. at the World Championships in 1986. He also played for the U.S. in the 1991 Canada Cup. He was the tournament's top scorer when the Americans won the World Cup of Hockey in 1996. Hull was a member of the U.S. Olympic team at the Nagano Games in 1998.

DENNIS HULL joined his brother Bobby on the Chicago Black Hawks for the 1964–65 season after four years with the club's junior affiliate in St. Catharines of the Ontario Hockey Association. Though never a star on the level of his future Hall of Fame brother, Dennis was a productive NHL forward over a 14-year career.

Hull played his first full season for Chicago in 1966–67 and had his first 30-goal campaign in 1968–69. He established a career high with 40 goals in 1970–71 and helped the Black Hawks reach the Stanley Cup finals that season. He had another good year in 1971–72, but reached his peak after Bobby left Chicago for the World Hockey Association.

At his brother's insistence, Dennis accepted a spot on Team Canada for the 1972 Summit Series even though Bobby was not allowed to play and he scored twice in the four games in which he took part. During the regular season that followed, Hull set a career high with 90 points, then added 24 more in 16 playoff games as the Black Hawks advanced to the Stanley Cup finals, only to lose to the Montreal Canadiens as they did in 1971.

Hull remained with Chicago until 1976–77, when his production declined. He was traded to the Detroit Red Wings on December 2, 1977 and scored his 300th career goal during what proved to be his final season.

FRED HUME served terms as mayor in both New Westminster and Vancouver and was very active in sports in those British Columbia cities. He was a player, and later president, of the New Westminster Salmonbellies lacrosse team and president of the New Westminster soccer club that won three Canadian titles. He helped to form the Western Hockey League in 1952 and aided in the development of the New Westminster Royals hockey club. He was involved later with the Vancouver Canucks WHL franchise. The Fred Hume Trophy rewarded the most sportsmanlike player in the WHL from 1960–61 until the league's demise after the 1973–74 season. Hume had been inducted into the Hockey Hall of Fame as a builder in 1962.

In addition to his involvement in hockey, Hume was a dominant force in bringing the British Empire Games (later known as the Commonwealth Games) to Vancouver in 1954. His leadership brought professional baseball to Vancouver in 1955, and also saw the city host the Grey Cup game (Canada's football championship) for the first time that year.

DALE HUNTER When Dale Hunter collected his 1,000th career point on January 9, 1998, he became the first player in NHL history to achieve 1,000 points and 3,000 career penalty minutes. He is also the only player in history with more than 300 goals and over 3,000 penalty minutes. Hunter ranks second to Tiger Williams on the NHL's all-time penalty minute list, though he never has led the league in any one season.

Hunter entered the NHL with the Quebec Nordiques in 1980–81 and did not score less than 17 goals in any full season over seven years with the team. He established career highs with 79 points in 1983–84 and 28 goals in 1985–86. Hunter was traded to the Washington Capitals on June 13, 1987, and later matched his career highs in Washington in 1991–92 (goals) and 1992–93 (points). Brothers Dave and Mark also played in the NHL.

BOUSE HUTTON John Bower "Bouse" Hutton played at a time when goaltenders wore only skinny cricket pads for protection and used gloves and sticks that were not very different than those of other players. Still, he managed to produce goals-against averages that can be compared favorably to many goalies of a later era. He won his first major hockey championship in 1898–99 when he led his Ottawa team to the intermediate title in the Canadian Amateur Hockey League.

Hutton was the goaltender for the Ottawa Silver Seven when the team won the Stanley Cup in 1903 and 1904. He also played goal for the Ottawa Capitals lacrosse team and fullback with the Ottawa Rough Riders. In 1904, he became the only man in history to win Canadian titles in hockey, lacrosse and football in the same year. He retired from active competition after that season, but he continued to coach teams in Ottawa for several years. In 1962, Bouse Hutton was inducted into the Hockey Hall of Fame.

HARRY HYLAND was a Montreal native who played amateur hockey with several teams in that city before making his professional debut with the Montreal Shamrocks in 1908–09. He scored two goals in his first game playing in the Eastern Canada Hockey Association on January 2, 1909 as the Shamrocks beat Quebec 9–8. Joe Malone made his professional debut with Quebec's Bulldogs that same night.

Hyland led the Shamrocks with 18 goals in 11 games that season and continued to be a high-scoring right winger throughout his career. Though he would never lead his league in scoring, Hyland scored five goals in a game four times in his career. His eight goals for the Montreal Wanderers on January 25, 1913 stand as the second-highest single-game total in the history of the National Hockey Association. (Newsy Lalonde and Tommy Smith both had nine-goal games.)

Hyland had joined the NHA as a member of the Wanderers in the league's inaugural campaign of 1909–10, winning his only Stanley Cup title that season. He was also a member of the national champion Salmonbellies lacrosse team that year. Hyland joined the New Westminster Royals in the first season of the Pacific Coast Hockey Association in 1911–12, but he was back in Montreal the following year. He remained with the Wanderers until they joined the NHL in 1917–18, but he finished his career that season with the Ottawa Senators when the Wanderers withdrew from the league after fire destroyed the Montreal Arena. Hyland was elected to the Hockey Hall of Fame in 1962.

STEWART IGLEHART was the first man ever to represent the United States internationally in two different sports. He played many, but considered hockey his favorite. He was on the American team that beat Canada for the world championship in 1933 and also participated in the 1936 International Match in polo.

Born in Valparaiso, Chile, Iglehart was introduced to hockey by former Harvard great C.C. Pell while he was growing up in the Boston area. He went on to play at St. Paul's School (a breeding ground of U.S. hockey talent that had produced Hobey Baker), then went to Yale in 1928 and played varsity hockey from 1929–30 until 1931–32. Iglehart was considered one of the outstanding defensemen ever developed in college and was selected to both the 1932 and 1936 U.S. Olympic hockey teams but wasn't able to play either year due to conflicting responsibilities. But of course he did play internationally in 1933, and after that with the Crescent Athletic Club team that eventually became the New York Rovers, an amateur team that bred many future New York Rangers stars. Most hockey observers believed Iglehart could easily have moved up to the NHL, but he chose to stay in amateur hockey while pursuing a business career. He ended his playing days with the legendary St. Nicholas Hockey Club of New York City and was inducted into the U.S. Hockey Hall of Fame in 1975.

WILLARD IKOLA At the time of his induction into the United States Hockey Hall of Fame in the coaches category, Willard Ikola's teams at Edina High School had put up a record of 600–140–38, making him the winningest coach in the history of Minnesota high school sports. John Mariucci had convinced Edina to hire Ikola in the fall of 1958. His team went 4–9–5 that season, after which he never had a season under .500 and won eight state championships.

In his playing days, Ikola tended goal. As a freshman at Eveleth High School in 1946–47, his team was defeated in the semifinals of the Minnesota state tournament but over the next three seasons was never beaten as Eveleth won state championships in 1948, 1949 and 1950. Ikola then sat out his freshman year at the University of Michigan before leading the team to the NCAA tournament three years in a row. The Wolverines were national champions in 1952 and 1953 but were beaten in the semifinals in Ikola's senior year of 1953–54 by the eventual champions from Rensselaer Polytechnic Institute. While serving in the U.S. military in 1956, Ikola played for the silver medal-winning United States Olympic team in Cortina, Italy. He also played on the U.S. national team in 1957 and 1958.

PUNCH IMLACH George Imlach earned the nickname "Punch" while playing with the Toronto Goodyears, when he was knocked out in a game and swung punches at the team trainer upon being revived. Imlach played hockey in his hometown of Toronto with the Young Rangers, Goodyears and

Marlboros between 1935 and 1941, and later gained great fame as a successful coach and general manager with the Toronto Maple Leafs.

Imlach got into coaching while a member of the Quebec Aces, acting as a playing coach in 1949–50 and taking over behind the bench full-time the following year. By 1953–54, he had added the role of general manager with the Quebec Senior Hockey League team, and later became a co-owner. He spent the 1956–57 and 1957–58 seasons coaching the Springfield Indians of the American Hockey League before being named assistant general manager with the Toronto Maple Leafs in 1958–59. He was promoted quickly to general manager and promptly named himself to replace Billy Reay as the club's coach.

The Maple Leafs had been struggling before Imlach's arrival, but under his leadership they reached the playoffs in 10 of the next 11 seasons. Imlach was a determined, often stubborn man who demanded loyalty from his players. While not always popular, he did lead Toronto to Stanley Cup victories in 1962, 1963, 1964 and 1967. He retired after the 1969–70 season and spent the year as a syndicated columnist before returning to the NHL as the first coach and general manager of the Buffalo Sabres in 1970–71.

The Sabres quickly became a top team in the league under Imlach's guidance, making the playoffs in only their third season and reaching the Stanley Cup finals in 1975. He left Buffalo in December of 1978 and rejoined Toronto in July of 1979 as both coach and general manager. Continuing heart problems led to the termination of his Toronto contract after the 1981–82 season. Imlach was elected to the Hockey Hall of Fame in 1984.

MICKEY ION was a baseball player and lacrosse star who began refereeing amateur hockey games while playing professional lacrosse in Vancouver and New Westminster, British Columbia. Frank Patrick was impressed by his work and hired him as a referee for the Pacific Coast Hockey Association in 1912–13. Ion developed into the top referee in the PCHA and became responsible for selecting the league's all-star teams.

When professional hockey collapsed in the west after the 1925–26 season, Ion joined the NHL and became one of the top referees in that league over the next 15 years. King Clancy once described Ion as having "nothing but ice-water running through his veins," adding that he had learned the art of refereeing from Ion. In 1961, Mickey Ion, Cooper Smeaton and Chaucer Elliott became the first referees elected to the Hockey Hall of Fame.

DICK IRVIN James Dickenson Irvin was an outstanding hockey player over the course of his Hall of Fame career, and went on to become the winningest coach in hockey history before his total of 690 regular-season victories was surpassed by Scotty Bowman and Al Arbour. He had moved to Winnipeg as a boy in 1899 and it was there that his legendary career began.

Dick Irvin was a standout through church league and junior hockey with the Strathconas before moving up to the senior league Winnipeg Monarchs in 1912–13. He won the Allan Cup with the Monarchs in 1914–15, remaining with the team one more year before turning pro with the Portland Rosebuds of the Pacific Coast Hockey Association in 1916–17. Irvin finished fourth in the league with 35 goals that season and he then enlisted in the Canadian army.

After his military service, Irvin played hockey in Regina, entering the pro ranks again when the Regina Caps became part of the Western Canada Hockey League in 1921–22. The Caps won the WCHL title that season, but by 1925–26 the team relocated to Portland—the Oregon city had lost its PCHA franchise in 1918—and Irvin was a Rosebud once again. The league became known as the Western Hockey League that season and Irvin's 31 goals tied Bill Cook for the lead league. Pro hockey collapsed in the west after that year, and Irvin was one of several Portland players who wound up in the NHL as members of the original Chicago Black Hawks team.

Irvin was the first captain of the Black Hawks in 1926–27 and finished second in scoring in the NHL with 18 goals and 18 assists that year. Early in the 1927–28 campaign, he suffered a fractured skull, and though he returned to play one more season, he retired as a player in 1929. He began his coaching career with Chicago in 1930–31. Irvin then was hired by Conn Smythe shortly after the start of the 1931–32 season, leading the Maple Leafs to their first Stanley Cup victory that year. Irvin's Toronto teams reached the Stanley Cup finals six times in the next eight years, but they never won again, and he resigned after the 1939–40 season.

The Montreal Maroons had folded in 1938 and the Canadiens were on the verge of collapse themselves when Irvin arrived in Montreal in 1940–41. Under his guidance, the Canadiens returned to greatness. They won the Stanley Cup in 1944, 1946 and 1953, and the team he turned over to Toe Blake in 1955 was poised to win five consecutive championships. Irvin returned to Chicago for a final season in 1955–56. He died in 1957 and was elected to the Hockey Hall of Fame in 1958.

TOMMY IVAN Injuries cut short Tommy Ivan's playing career, but he went on to become one of the most successful coaches and general managers in NHL history. Ivan was brought into the Detroit Red Wings organization as a scout by Jack Adams and became coach of the club's United States Hockey League affiliate in Omaha in 1945–46, where he coached Gordie Howe. By 1946–47, Ivan was with Detroit's American Hockey League farm club in

Indianapolis. The following year, he was promoted to the NHL.

Ivan's Red Wings finished in first place in the regular-season standings in each of the six seasons he spent with the club from 1947–48 to 1953–54, and they won the Stanley Cup in 1950, 1952 and 1954. He left Detroit to become general manager of the Chicago Black Hawks in 1954–55, and though the team he inherited had missed the playoffs in seven of the last eight seasons, he rebuilt the franchise by designing a strong farm system. Ivan was one of the first NHL executives to tap into the U.S. college ranks for talent.

Under Ivan's leadership, the Black Hawks won the Stanley Cup for the first time in 23 years in 1960–61, and in 1966–67 the team finished first in the NHL standings for the first time in franchise history. The team remained a powerhouse well into the 1970s, and Ivan was inducted into the Hockey Hall of Fame as a builder in 1974. He remained the Black Hawks general manager until 1977, when he became a vice president (a position he continues to hold). Ivan also helped assemble players for the "Miracle on Ice" American gold medal team at the 1980 Lake Placid Olympics.

BUSHER JACKSON Harvey "Busher" Jackson played left wing on the Toronto Maple Leafs' famed Kid Line of the 1930s. He led the NHL in scoring when the Maple Leafs won their first Stanley Cup title in 1932 and was named a First Team All-Star that year. Jackson would go on to earn four more all-star selections, including three more berths on the First Team. During his time in Toronto, the Maple Leafs won four Canadian Division titles and reached the Stanley Cup finals on six occasions.

Jackson and Charlie Conacher both graduated to the Maple Leafs in 1929–30 after winning the Memorial Cup with the Toronto Marlboros the previous season. They were teamed on a line with slick center Joe Primeau that developed into one of the greatest forward units in NHL history. When Conacher began to slow down due to injuries and Primeau retired in 1936, Jackson played with his brother Art and Pep Kelly before teaming on another great Leafs line with Syl Apps and Gordie Drillon late in the 1936–37 season.

Handsome and fun-loving, Jackson was often at odds with Conn Smythe over his lackadaisical approach to the game. After he injured his shoulder against the Boston Bruins in the 1938–39 Stanley Cup finals, Smythe packaged Jackson as part of the deal that brought Sweeney Shriner to Toronto from the New York Americans. Jackson spent two years with the Americans and three seasons with the Bruins before retiring after the 1943–44 campaign. He was elected to the Hockey Hall of Fame in 1971.

JAROMIR JAGR was selected fifth overall by the Pittsburgh Penguins in the 1990 Entry Draft. He was named to the All-Rookie Team in 1990–91 and led all first-year players in the playoffs with 10 assists and 13 points to help the Penguins win their first Stanley Cup title. He finished fourth in playoff points when Pittsburgh repeated as Stanley Cup champions in 1992.

Jagr's offensive numbers improved in each of his first four years in the NHL and in his fifth season of 1994–95 he became the first European player to win the Art Ross Trophy. His 70 points actually tied Eric Lindros for the scoring lead in the abbreviated 48-game season, but Jagr won the Art Ross because he had scored more goals (32 to 29). Jagr was named to the First All-Star Team that season and was runner-up to Lindros in voting for the Hart Trophy as the NHL's most valuable player. In 1995–96, Jagr established career highs with 62 goals, 87 assists and 149 points. His goals and points ranked second in the NHL behind Penguins teammate Mario Lemieux that season, while his assists and points broke Mike Bossy's NHL record for a right winger. Jagr won the Art Ross Trophy outright in 1997–98. His 35 goals and 67 assists gave him 102 points and made him the only player in the NHL that season to top 100 and earned him a berth on the First All-Star Team.

Jagr played in his hometown of Kladno, Czechoslovakia before entering the NHL. He won a bronze medal with the Czechoslovakian team at the 1990 World Junior Championships and was named to the tournament all-star team, then earned another bronze medal at the World Championships that year. He played for Czechoslovakia again at the Canada Cup in 1991 and represented the Czech Republic at the World Championships in 1994. Jagr was also a member of the Czech Republic team at the World Cup of Hockey in 1996 and at the Nagano Olympics in 1998, where the Czechs were surprising gold medal winners.

DOUG JARVIS is the NHL's "ironman," playing 964 consecutive games in a streak that comprised his entire NHL playing career. Originally drafted by the Toronto Maple Leafs, he was traded to the Montreal Canadiens on June 26, 1975 and played his first game on October 8 of that year. The streak ended with the Hartford Whalers on October 10, 1987, when Jarvis moved into coach. He had passed Garry Unger's record of 914 consecutive games during the 1986–87 season.

Jarvis was an effective checker and penalty-killer who was a member of four Stanley Cup winners while in Montreal. Traded to the Washington Capitals prior to the 1982–83 season, he earned the Selke Trophy as the NHL's best defensive forward the following year. After becoming the NHL's new ironman in 1986–87, Jarvis was awarded the Masterton Trophy for perseverance and dedication to hockey. He is currently an assistant coach with the Dallas Stars.

BILL JENNINGS began his association with hockey in 1959 as the legal counsel for the Graham-Paige Corporation when it acquired controlling interest in Madison Square Garden Corporation, which in turn owned the New York Rangers. He took an active role in the direction of the hockey club and became president of the Rangers and the team's NHL governor in 1962. He still was holding both offices at the time of his induction into the Hockey Hall of Fame as a builder in 1975, and he was Rangers president until his death on August 17, 1981.

Throughout Jennings' association with the NHL, he was an ardent advocate of expansion and one of the principal architects of the growth of the game. He was also the originator of the Lester Patrick Trophy, which was donated to the NHL by the Rangers in 1966 to recognize outstanding contributions to hockey in the United States. Jennings himself won the award in 1971. He was instrumental in the founding of the Metropolitan Junior Hockey Association in the New York area in 1966. The NHL's William M. Jennings Trophy, awarded annually to the goaltender(s) for the team allowing the fewest goals, is named in his honor.

EDDIE JEREMIAH was a star schoolboy athlete in hockey, football and baseball when he went to Dartmouth College in 1926. In four years at Dartmouth, he earned two letters in football, two in baseball and three in hockey, then turned to professional hockey with New Haven of the Canadian-American Hockey League in 1930–31. The following year, Jeremiah played in the NHL with the New York Americans and Boston Bruins. He continued playing pro hockey with the Boston Cubs, New Haven and Philadelphia of the Can-Am league until 1933–34 and played a final season with Cleveland in the International-American Hockey League in 1934–35.

Jeremiah became the coach of the Boston Olympics in 1935–36 and guided the team to the National Amateur Athletic Union championship that season. A year later, Jeremiah returned to Dartmouth, where he served as coach (except for his time in the services in World War II) until his retirement in 1967.

In Jeremiah's first nine years back at Dartmouth, the team won the Pentagonal League championship seven times and went 46 games without a defeat (from December 23, 1941, until January 5, 1946). Jeremiah led Dartmouth to the NCAA hockey tournament in both 1948 and 1949 and won Ivy League titles in 1959 and 1960. He was elected to the United States Hockey Hall of Fame as a charter member in the coaches category in 1973.

BOB JOHNSON began skating as a four-year-old, and played amateur hockey in his hometown of Minneapolis, Minnesota. At the age of 13, he won a city championship as a first-year coach. He captained the team at Minneapolis Central High School in his senior year, then played college hockey at North Dakota and Minnesota.

In 1956, Johnson became head coach of Warroad High School in Warroad, Minnesota. After one season, he moved to Roosevelt High and won four city championships in six years. In 1963, Johnson took a position with Colorado College, then moved on to the University of Wisconsin in 1966. Johnson coached the Badgers for 15 years, winning NCAA titles in 1973, 1977 and 1981, and earning coach of the year honors in 1977. He also coached the U.S. national team from 1973 to 1976 and again in 1981, and took time off from Wisconsin in 1975–76 to coach the U.S. Olympic hockey team.

Johnson joined the NHL in 1982 as head coach of the Calgary Flames and spent five seasons with the club, leading Calgary to the Stanley Cup finals for the first time in 1986. He was executive director of USA Hockey over the next three years, supervising an unprecedented growth of amateur hockey in the United States. In 1990–91, Johnson returned to the NHL with the Pittsburgh Penguins and became just the second American-born coach to lead his team to the Stanley Cup (the first being Bill Stewart with the Chicago Black Hawks in 1938).

In September of 1991, Johnson was to coach the U.S. team at the Canada Cup, as he had in 1981 and 1984, but he was forced to relinquish the job due to ill health. He died on November 26, 1991. His gift for inspiring his players and everyone associated with him was recognized when he was named to the United States Hockey Hall of Fame in the coaches category in 1991 and inducted into the Hockey Hall of Fame as a builder in 1992.

CHING JOHNSON Ivan "Ching" Johnson and Clarence "Taffy" Abel were a formidable defensive pair in the early years of the New York Rangers before forward passing was permitted in the offensive zone. With his balding head and ever-present smile, Ching Johnson was a fan favorite over his 12-year NHL career, but his hard-hitting defensive style caused him to miss many games due to serious injuries, including a broken leg (1928–29) and a broken jaw (1929–30).

Johnson grew up in Winnipeg and played with the Winnipeg Monarchs after his military service in World War I. He moved to Eveleth, Minnesota and played three years there from 1920–21 to 1922–23 before joining the Minneapolis Millers for three more seasons. It was in Minneapolis that he first teamed with Taffy Abel, and both were signed by Conn Smythe when he was assembling the first New York Rangers team for the 1926–27 season. The two helped the Rangers to win the Stanley Cup in the team's second season, and Johnson continued to anchor the defense long after Abel was traded to the

Chicago Black Hawks in 1929. He was either a First or Second Team All-Star four years in a row from 1930–31 to 1933–34, and he took part in the Ace Bailey All-Star benefit game on February 14, 1934. He had also won a second Stanley Cup title in New York in 1933.

Injuries took their toll on Johnson and he was spending more time as a coach than a player by the 1936–37 campaign. Released by the Rangers after that season, he joined the rival New York Americans in 1937–38 before leaving the NHL at the age of 40. He played several more seasons in the minor leagues before finally retiring from the game for good. In 1958, Ching Johnson was inducted into the Hockey Hall of Fame.

MOOSE JOHNSON Ernie "Moose" Johnson stood 5'11" and weighed 185 pounds in a era of much smaller hockey players. He also employed the longest stick in hockey, and his full reach measured 99 inches. As a result, Johnson was one of the most effective defensemen of his era, though he actually began his career playing left wing.

Johnson started playing hockey in his hometown of Montreal around the turn of the century. By 1903–04, he was playing for the Montreal Amateur Athletic Association. He and teammate Ernie Russell joined the Montreal Wanderers in 1905–06, helping the team to defeat the Ottawa Silver Seven for the Stanley Cup that season. The Wanderers were Stanley Cup champions again in 1907, 1908 and 1910. It was in the 1909–10 season that Johnson became a defenseman after the Wanderers entered the National Hockey Association.

When the Pacific Coast Hockey Association was formed in 1911–12, Johnson joined the New Westminster Royals, helping the team win the first PCHA title. It was with the Royals in 1912 that the fans dubbed him "Moose" for the courage he showed in playing through injuries. He remained with the club for three seasons before the franchise moved to Portland, Oregon and became known as the Rosebuds. In 1915–16, he helped Portland win the PCHA title before losing to the Montreal Canadiens, as the latter won their first Stanley Cup title in franchise history.

After four years in Portland, the Rosebuds folded and Johnson joined the Victoria Aristocrats for the final four years of his career. Towards the close of the 1920–21 season, Johnson was presented with a trophy honoring him as the greatest defenseman in the PCHA. He had been named to the all-star team for 10 consecutive years. Johnson retired during the 1921–22 season, but he later came back to play minor-league hockey. He was named to the Hockey Hall of Fame in 1952.

TOM JOHNSON joined the Montreal Canadiens organization in 1947–48 but saw only brief action in the NHL until the 1950–51 season. He went on to become one of the best defensemen in the NHL. Johnson played with future Hall of Famers Doug Harvey, Butch Bouchard and Jacques Laperriere, along with many other great defensemen in Montreal, and coached Bobby Orr when he served behind the bench with the Boston Bruins. He was elected to the Hockey Hall of Fame in 1970.

Because of Doug Harvey, Johnson did not see a lot of time on the Canadiens power-play, but was the team leader in shorthand situations. He had speed and skill in the corners and was an excellent playmaker who was frequently used at center when his team needed a goal late in the game. Johnson was a Second Team All-Star on defense in 1955–56 and was named to the First All-Star Team in 1958–59. He also won the Norris Trophy that season. He was a member of the Canadiens Stanley Cup-winning team in 1953 and the Montreal teams that won five in a row between 1956 and 1960.

Johnson suffered a serious facial injury during the 1962–63 season, resulting in a fractured cheekbone and damage to the eye muscles that threatened his sight. The Canadiens left him unprotected due to his doubtful playing status and he was claimed by the Bruins for 1963–64. Johnson played two years in Boston, but during his second season, a skate severed nerves in his leg and he was forced to retire. Johnson then moved into the Bruins front office as assistant to the president and assistant general manager. In 1970–71, he took over from Harry Sinden as Bruins coach and led the team to the Stanley Cup in 1972. During the 1972–73 season, Johnson returned to his role as assistant general manager, which he held until May of 1989 when he was promoted to vice president. Johnson remains with the Bruins in that role.

VIRGIL JOHNSON was both a hockey star and quarterback of the football team at Minneapolis South High School. Though he stood just 5'9" and weighed only 165 pounds, he went on to a lengthy professional hockey career, mostly in the Twin Cities area.

Johnson was a member of the St. Paul Saints prior to making his NHL debut with the Chicago Black Hawks in 1937–38 when he was one of several Americans on that season's surprising Stanley Cup-winning team. He rejoined St. Paul before returning to Chicago in 1943–44 where he helped the Black Hawks reach the Stanley Cup finals again. He played briefly with Chicago in 1944–45, then spent two years with Minneapolis in the United States Hockey League before retiring from the pros after the 1946–47 season. He later played amateur hockey in Minneapolis and St. Paul and was enshrined in the United States Hockey Hall of Fame in 1974.

EDDIE JOHNSTON is the last man in NHL history to play every minute in goal for his team throughout an entire season, enduring 4,200 minutes of action over 70 games for the last-place Boston Bruins in 1962–63. Johnston was the top goaltender on some of the worst teams in NHL history before regularly sharing the net with Gerry Cheevers beginning in 1967–68.

With Bobby Orr anchoring the defense and combining with Phil Esposito to lead a potent offensive attack, the Bruins improved rapidly after NHL expansion. Johnson was now playing for an NHL powerhouse and helped the team win its first Stanley Cup title in 29 years in 1970. He had 30 wins and two ties against only six losses during Boston's record-setting season of 1970–71, then helped the team win another Stanley Cup championship in 1972.

After the 1972–73 campaign, Johnston was sent to the Toronto Maple Leafs to complete a deal that had seen the Bruins acquire Jacques Plante. He spent one year in Toronto, then three with the St. Louis Blues before they sold him to the Chicago Black Hawks during the 1977–78 campaign. That season would be Johnston's last. His 236 career victories and 32 shutouts rank him among the NHL's all-time leaders.

AUREL JOLIAT Known as "the Mighty Atom" or "the Little Giant" because of his diminutive size and determined play, Aurel Joliat stood just 5'6" and weighed less than 140 pounds during most of his 16-year NHL career. His stature and great skating skill made him difficult for opponents to check, and Joliat earned a reputation as the greatest left winger in hockey.

A football star until a broken leg led him to concentrate on hockey, Joliat's early ice experience came in his hometown of Ottawa and with Iroquois Falls of the Northern Ontario Hockey Association before he went west to Saskatchewan. Joliat was expected to join the Saskatoon Sheiks of the Western Canada Hockey League in 1922–23 but was instead sent to the Montreal Canadiens after Saskatoon bought Newsy Lalonde from the NHL team. He was an instant success in Montreal, and when the Canadiens signed Howie Morenz for the 1923–24 season, the two became a terrific tandem that led Montreal to a Stanley Cup title that year.

Morenz and Joliat were first teamed on a line with Billy Boucher, and later Art Gagnon, but the two were at their best when playing alongside Johnny Gagnon. This high-scoring combination led the Canadiens to back-to-back Stanley Cup victories in 1930 and 1931. Both Morenz and Joliat were named to the First All-Star Team in 1930–31 and Joliat subsequently earned three Second Team All-Star selections. He led the Canadiens in goal-scoring four years in a row between 1932–33 and 1935–36 and won the Hart Trophy in 1933–34. His 270 career goals equaled Morenz as the most scored by any NHL player during their era.

Though he was small, Joliat played an aggressive game and suffered numerous injuries throughout his career. He began seeing less ice time by the 1936–37 season and retired after the 1937–38 campaign. Joliat was elected to the Hockey Hall of Fame in 1947.

CHIEF JONES Joseph Jones and Joe Linder (a member of United States Hockey Hall of Fame) are the only two Americans known to have played in hockey's first professional league, the International (Pro) Hockey League of 1904 to 1907. Though the league had teams in Pittsburgh and northern Michigan's Upper Peninsula, it was stocked mainly by Canadian players who were paid to cross the border.

Chief Jones, as he was known, was a goaltender from St. Paul, Minnesota who was reportedly signed by the Portage Lake team of Houghton, Michigan during the 1902–03 season after they had difficulty scoring on him in a game against his St. Paul squad. Portage Lake's Jack Gibson did not officially form the International League until the 1904–05 season and by then Jones was playing in Sault Ste. Marie, Michigan.

Jones remained in the Michigan Soo for the three-year life span of the IPHL and played one more year there following the collapse of the league after the 1906–07 season. He then signed with Cobalt of the mining-rich Temiskaming Professional Hockey League in 1908–09. Jones suffered through a dismal year with the Silver Kings in 1909–10 when Cobalt was included in the inaugural season of the National Hockey Association (forerunner of the NHL), then signed with Waterloo of the Ontario Professional Hockey League when Cobalt was dropped from the NHA in 1910–11. Jones led Waterloo to the league's best defensive record as the team tied Galt atop the standings with a mark of 13–6–0. However, two of Waterloo's wins against Galt that season had resulted from technicalities and in a playoff to decide the league championship Jones' team was defeated 8–0 by Galt in what would be his final game.

HERB JORDAN was a high-scoring center who averaged better than two goal per game during his nine-year career but never won a scoring title or played for a Stanley Cup winner. Before Joe Malone became a star, Jordan was the Quebec Bulldogs' all-time leading scorer.

Jordan moved up to senior hockey in Quebec for the 1902–03 season and promptly led the team with 12 goals in seven games to finish third in scoring in the Canadian Amateur Hockey League. He improved to second behind future Hall of Famer Russell Bowie with 19 goals the following year, including eight in a single game. In subsequent seasons, Jordan would twice score six goals in a game and also have a pair of five-goal games.

In 1908–09, Jordan enjoyed his best season when he scored in all 12 games and had 30 goals to finish second in the Eastern Canada Hockey Association behind future Hall of Famer Marty Walsh of the Ottawa Senators. When Walsh refused to sign with Renfrew of the rival National Hockey Association for the 1909–10 season, M.J. and Ambrose O'Brien signed Jordan instead. Though he played only sparing over two seasons with Renfrew, Jordan remained there the rest of his life as a manager of O'Brien business interests.

CURTIS JOSEPH was not selected in the NHL Entry Draft but signed as a free agent with the St. Louis Blues on June 16, 1989 after an all-star season with the University of Wisconsin. He made his NHL debut on January 2, 1990 and picked up his first win on January 30. He went on to record 100 victories faster than any other goalie in Blues history (209 games).

Three times in his six seasons in St. Louis, Joseph finished among the leaders in voting for the Vezina Trophy. He finished as high as third in 1992–93 behind winner Ed Belfour and Tom Barrasso. On August 4, 1995, Joseph was traded to the Edmonton Oilers. After a contract holdout which saw him join Las Vegas of the International Hockey League, the Oilers traded Bill Ranford in order to make "Cujo" their number-one goaltender. In 1996–97, he helped the Oilers to reach the playoffs for the first time in five years. After spending three seaons with Edmonton, Joseph signed a lucrative four-year contract with the Toronto Maple Leafs on July 15, 1998.

In international hockey, Joseph won a silver medal with Team Canada at the 1996 World Championships and was named to the tournament's second all-star team. That experience helped him land one of the three goaltending positions for Canada at the 1996 World Cup of Hockey and at the 1998 Nagano Olympics.

GORDON JUCKES began his career in hockey as a child in Melville, Saskatchewan at about the same time he began apprenticing as a 10-year-old in the family's local newspaper business. He grew up to become both editor and publisher of the *Melville Advance* and president of the Melville Millionaires hockey team. Juckes was also president of the Saskatchewan Senior Hockey League.

Juckes enlisted in the Royal Canadian Artillery in World War II and rose to the rank of major before continuing his career in hockey management after the war. He became an executive member of the Saskatchewan Amateur Hockey Association in 1948–49, vice president in 1951–52 and president in 1953–54. In 1955, Juckes became a second vice president with the Canadian Amateur Hockey Association and was president by 1959. In 1960, he was appointed secretary-manager (later changed to executive director) of the CAHA and remained with the organization until retiring in 1978.

Juckes' contributions to hockey were rewarded with the United States Amateur Hockey Association diploma in 1962, the diploma of honor from the International Ice Hockey Federation in 1967, the CAHA Meritorious Award in 1976, plus lifetime membership in the Saskatchewan Amateur Hockey Association. At the time of his election to the Hockey Hall of Fame as a builder in 1979, Juckes was serving as a life member of the IIHF and sat on the boards of Hockey Canada and the Canadian Olympic Association.

NICK KAHLER was a popular athlete from the copper country in Michigan's Upper Peninsula who played amateur hockey both there and in Canada before joining the Duluth Curling Club hockey team in 1913–14. He later served as a player, coach and manager with the St. Paul Athletic Club, which won the McNaughton Cup as United States amateur hockey champions in 1916–17. Kahler continued with the Athletic Club until 1919–20 and was selected for the United States Olympic hockey team that year, but financial obligations made it impossible for him to travel to Belgium.

In 1920, Kahler launched the Minneapolis Millers in the United States Amateur Hockey Association. His team won the league title in 1924–25, but the rebirth of professional hockey in the U.S. brought on the demise of the Millers after the 1926–27 season. Kahler then coached the Augsburg College hockey team in 1927–28 and once again had a chance to represent the United States at the Olympics before a decision was made not to send a team to St. Moritz, Switzerland in 1928. Kahler later became owner of the Minnesota Millers professional team and saw them capture the American Hockey Association title in 1936–37.

In addition to his hockey interests, Kahler also founded the Golden Gloves boxing tournament in Minnesota and was inducted into the state's Sports Hall of Fame in 1962. He was inducted into the United States Hockey Hall of Fame as an administrator in 1980.

MIKE KARAKAS Though Lorne Chabot won the Vezina Trophy in 1934–35, the Chicago Black Hawks replaced him with Mike Karakas for the 1935–36 season. Karakas posted a 1.92 goals-against average in his rookie season and won the Calder Trophy but the team fell out of the playoffs the next year. In 1937–38, Chicago was only 14–25–9, but snuck into the postseason and caught fire. Karakas sparked the team to victories over the Montreal Canadiens and New York Americans, but missed the first two games of the Stanley Cup final against the Toronto Maple Leafs because of a broken toe.

Chicago split the first two games of the series with Alfie Moore and Paul Goodman in goal before Karakas returned with a steel-toed boot and led the Black Hawks to two straight wins and the Stanley Cup championship.

The Black Hawks missed the playoffs again in 1938–39 and Goodman replaced Karakas midway through the 1939–40 season. After some time in the minors, he finished the campaign with the Montreal Canadiens. Karakas was then back in the minors until he returned to Chicago in 1943–44. The following season, he was named to the NHL Second All-Star Team, but was back in the minors after one more year. Karakas was named as an original inductee into the United States Hockey Hall of Fame in 1973.

PAUL KARIYA One of the most popular young stars in the NHL, Paul Kariya made his debut with the Mighty Ducks of Anaheim during the 1994–95 season and finished third behind Peter Forsberg and Jim Carey in voting for the Calder Trophy. In 1995–96, he had 50 goals and 58 assists to finish seventh in the NHL with 108 points, earning a selection to the First All-Star Team at left wing while winning the Lady Byng Trophy. Kariya received both honors again in 1996–97 and finished runner-up to Dominik Hasek for the Hart Trophy after leading Anaheim to the playoffs for the first time in franchise history.

A fast skater with an excellent shot, Kariya was already a star before reaching the NHL. He was twice named the most valuable player in the British Columbia Junior Hockey League, adding Canadian Junior A player of the year honors in 1991–92. In 1992–93, he set several school and conference records at the University of Maine while leading the school to the NCAA championships and becoming the first freshman to win the Hobey Baker Award as the outstanding U.S. college player. He also had a chance to represent Canada twice in 1993, winning a gold medal at the World Junior Championships (where he was a tournament all-star) and playing at the 1993 World Championships.

Kariya was selected fourth overall by Anaheim at the 1993 NHL Entry Draft but chose to spend the 1993–94 season with the Canadian national team. He was the team's top scorer as Canada won a silver medal at the 1994 Lillehammer Olympics, then led the team in scoring again when Canada earned gold at the World Championships. That victory represented Canada's first world title since 1961. Kariya was with Team Canada again at the World Championships in 1996. He missed the World Cup of Hockey and the 1998 Olympics in Nagano due to injuries.

DUKE KEATS Gordon "Duke" Keats was born in Montreal, but he grew up in North Bay, playing hockey in Northern Ontario before joining the Toronto Blueshirts in 1915–16. He centered a line with brothers Corb and Cy Denneny that was the highest-scoring trio in the National Hockey Association that year.

Before the next season, Keats and several other pro hockey players enlisted for military duty with the 228th Battalion. He was supposed to play in the NHA with the army team in 1916–17, but Toronto owner Eddie Livingstone successfully appealed to have him play with the Blueshirts until the 228th went overseas, which it did in February of 1917.

After returning from military duty in World War I, Keats played amateur hockey in Edmonton, remaining with the Eskimos when the team turned pro and entered the Western Canada Hockey League in its inaugural season of 1921–22. Keats led the WCHL with 31 goals, 24 assists and 55 points that year—totals that would remain league highs throughout its five-year existence. He helped the Eskimos win the WCHL championship in 1922–23, but the team was beaten by the Ottawa Senators in the Stanley Cup finals.

Keats continued with Edmonton until pro hockey collapsed in the west after the 1925–26 season. His rights then were sold to the Boston Bruins. He played with Boston, Detroit and Chicago over two years in the NHL, but he left the Black Hawks early in the 1928–29 season after a dispute with owner Frederic McLaughlin. Keats joined Tulsa of the American Hockey Association that season, promptly winning the league scoring race. He returned to Edmonton in 1932–33, playing two seasons before retiring as a player, though he remained active in hockey in various capacities across western Canada for many years. Keats was inducted into the Hockey Hall of Fame in 1958.

MIKE KEENAN has been one of the NHL's most successful coaches, leading the Philadelphia Flyers, Chicago Blackhawks and New York Rangers to appearances in the Stanley Cup finals, winning it with the Rangers in 1994. Keenan also coached Team Canada to victory in both the 1987 and 1991 Canada Cup tournaments.

As a player, Keenan captained the St. Lawrence University hockey team, where he played from 1969–70 until 1971–72 while obtaining a Bachelor of Science degree in Physical Education. He won a Canadian collegiate championship at the University of Toronto in 1972–73 while obtaining his Master's degree in Education. Keenan's coaching career began with the Oshawa Legionaires of the Junior B Ontario Hockey Association in 1977–78 and he led the team to the Metro Toronto Junior B championship two years in a row. Keenan moved up to Junior A with the Peterborough Petes in 1979–80 and led that team to the Ontario Hockey League championship in his only season before turning pro with the Rochester Americans of the American Hockey League. Keenan spent three years in Rochester, capping his stay with a Calder

Cup championship in 1983. After coaching the University of Toronto to a Canadian collegiate championship in 1984, Keenan entered the NHL with the Philadelphia Flyers.

In his first season, Keenan earned the Jack Adams Award as coach of the year after the Flyers led the league with 113 points and reached the Stanley Cup finals. His teams won the Patrick Division in each of the next two seasons and reached the Stanley Cup finals again in 1987 but slumped to third place in 1987–88. Keenan was hired by the Chicago Blackhawks in June of 1988 and added the role of general manager two years later. He led the Blackhawks to the Stanley Cup finals in 1991 and won the Presidents' Trophy with 106 points in 1991–92. He was fired in November of 1992 and hired to coach the New York Rangers on April 17, 1993. Keenan's Rangers finished first in the NHL with 112 points in 1993–94 and went on to beat the Vancouver Canucks in a seven-game finals to win the Stanley Cup.

Keenan left the Rangers after just one season, and on July 18, 1994, he became coach and general manager of the St. Louis Blues. He was fired in January of 1997. On November 13, 1997, Keenan was hired to replace Tom Renney as coach of the Vancouver Canucks.

JACK KELLEY was an outstanding hockey player before he turned to coaching. He was named the top Boston schoolboy performer at Belmont High School in 1944–45 and attended Boston University (after military service with the U.S. Coast Guard), where he led the Terriers to the NCAA tournament finals in 1950 and 1951. In 1951–52, Kelley was named Boston University's most valuable player and was all-ECAC (Eastern College Athletic Conference).

Kelley began his coaching career at Weston High School, where he handled football, baseball and hockey. From 1955–56 to 1961–62, he coached Colby College before returning to Boston University in the fall of 1962. Over the next 10 years, Kelley led the Terriers to four NCAA tournaments and won national championships in 1971 and 1972.

When the World Hockey Association was formed, New England Whalers owner Howard Baldwin hired Kelley as his coach and general manager. Kelley led New England to the first WHA title in 1972–73 and the Whalers remained one of the top teams in the WHA throughout its seven-year existence.

When the Whalers entered the NHL in 1979–80, Kelley spent two seasons as the club's director of player operations. He later ran the Detroit Red Wings' American Hockey League affiliate at Adirondack for 11 seasons before rejoining Howard Baldwin with the Pittsburgh Penguins in March of 1993. He was named president of the Penguins three months later and continues to work in the Pittsburgh administration. Kelley was elected to the United States Hockey Hall of Fame in the coaches category in 1993.

SNOOKS KELLEY John "Snooks" Kelley was a hockey star at Cambridge Latin and Dean Academy before enrolling at Boston College. He was the top player on the Eagles in 1928–29, but the stock market crash of 1929 wiped out hockey as a varsity sport at the college before he graduated in 1930.

Kelley was a teacher at Cambridge Latin when he agreed to take a non-paying job as coach of the newly reinstated Boston College hockey team on January 8, 1933. He gave up playing with the Boston Hockey Club at that time and remained at his college for more than 40 years (with the exception of 1942 to 1946, when he served in the U.S. Navy).

Over the years, Kelley's Boston teams traveled more than 80,000 miles, both playing the game and promoting college hockey. The Eagles won the NCAA hockey tournament in 1949 and later won eight New England championships, eight Beanpot Tournament titles (a Boston area event involving Boston University, Boston College, Northeastern and Harvard) and made nine appearances in Eastern Collegiate Athletic Conference Division I playoffs. Kelley was named college hockey's coach of the year in 1959 and 1972, while 16 of his players won all-American honors and many played for the United States National and Olympic teams. Kelley was the first hockey coach in NCAA history to win more than 500 games.

Kelley steadfastly refused to recruit Canadian players for his teams at Boston College because he felt it would deprive American boys of a chance to develop their skills. He was enshrined in the coaches category of the United States Hockey Hall of Fame in 1974.

RED KELLY Leonard Patrick "Red" Kelly was a member of eight Stanley Cup winners, and he is the only NHL player with that many titles who did not skate for the Montreal Canadiens. Kelly won four Stanley Cup titles (1950, 1952, 1954 and 1955) with the Detroit Red Wings and four more (1962, 1963, 1964 and 1967) with the Toronto Maple Leafs. He was inducted into the Hockey Hall of Fame in 1969.

Kelly played junior hockey with the St. Michael's Majors in Toronto and entered the NHL with the Detroit Red Wings in 1947–48. In Kelly's second year, Detroit finished first in the NHL for the first of seven straight seasons, and by his third season of 1949–50 the Red Wings were Stanley Cup champions. Kelly was named to the Second All-Star Team on defense that year. He would be an All-Star for eight consecutive years (including six selections to the First All-Star Team), and win the Lady Byng Trophy in 1950–51, 1952–53

and 1953–54. He was also the first recipient of the Norris Trophy for the 1953–54 season. Kelly was an excellent checker who could rush the puck effectively, and he was used occasionally as a forward by the Red Wings. He was team captain in 1956–57 and 1957–58.

On February 4, 1960, it was announced that the Red Wings had traded Kelly to the Rangers, but the deal fell through when he refused to report. A few days later, he was sent to the Maple Leafs. Punch Imlach moved Kelly up to center in Toronto, where he continued to excel for seven seasons. Kelly played with Frank Mahovlich on his left wing and in 1960–61 he helped "the Big M" set what was then a Maple Leafs record with 48 goals. Kelly himself won the Lady Byng Trophy for a fourth time that season. In 1962, Kelly was convinced to enter politics and served three years as a Liberal member of the House of Commons in Ottawa, while still playing hockey with the Maple Leafs.

After Toronto won its fourth Stanley Cup championship of the decade in 1967, Kelly gave up playing to become coach of the expansion Los Angeles Kings. He led the team into the playoffs for two straight years, but had less success over the next three years as coach of the Pittsburgh Penguins. In 1973, Kelly returned to Toronto as coach of the Maple Leafs. He guided the team to four consecutive quarterfinal appearances, including three memorable matchups with the Philadelphia Flyers.

TEEDER KENNEDY Ted "Teeder" Kennedy was one of the greatest stars in the greatest era of the Toronto Maple Leafs. He played on Toronto teams that won the Stanley Cup five times in seven years between 1945 and 1951 and is to date the last Maple Leafs player to win the Hart Trophy, being chosen as MVP in his final full season of 1954–55. Kennedy had a scrambling skating style and a fierce competitive spirit that made him a fan favorite at Maple Leaf Gardens, where shouts of "Come o-n-n-n-n, Teeder!" became the battle cry.

Kennedy was originally property of the Montreal Canadiens and attended their training camp as a 16-year-old in 1941. The next year, the Maple Leafs traded the rights to Frank Eddolls to Montreal to obtain Kennedy and he became a regular in Toronto in 1943–44. He led the team in both goals and points in 1944–45 and starred in the playoffs when the Maple Leafs upset the Canadiens to win the Stanley Cup. Kennedy was again Toronto's leading scorer in 1946–47 and led the Maple Leafs past Montreal for the Stanley Cup. After another Stanley Cup victory in 1948, Kennedy succeeded Syl Apps as Maple Leafs captain in 1948–49 and led Toronto to a third consecutive Stanley Cup victory.

Individual honors finally began coming to Kennedy in 1949–50, when he was named to the Second All-Star Team. He was a Second Team All-Star again in 1950–51 when the Maple Leafs won yet another Stanley Cup title, and for a final time in 1953–54. Kennedy retired after his Hart Trophy-winning season of 1954–55, but made a comeback two years later to help bolster an injury-riddled Toronto lineup. He retired for good after the 1956–57 season and was elected to the Hockey Hall of Fame in 1966.

DAVE KEON was a product of St. Michael's College in Toronto who joined the Maple Leafs in 1960–61 and won the Calder Trophy as rookie of the year. An excellent skater and stickhandler, as well as an aggressive checker who played the game tough but clean, Keon went on to play in the NHL and World Hockey Association for 22 years as a top two-way center.

Following up on his fine rookie season, Keon won the Lady Byng Trophy and was a Second Team All-Star in 1961–62. He also helped the Leafs win the Stanley Cup that year. He won the Lady Byng Trophy again in 1962–63 after having recorded just two penalties over two seasons. His seven goals and five assists in 10 playoff games helped Toronto win another Stanley Cup title in 1963. The Maple Leafs made it three in a row in 1964, and when Toronto won again in 1967, Keon earned the Conn Smythe Trophy as playoff MVP. He succeeded George Armstrong as Maple Leafs captain in 1969–70 and enjoyed his best offensive season in 1970–71 when he had 38 goals and 38 assists. He was named again to the Second All-Star Team.

After 15 seasons with the Maple Leafs, Keon jumped to the World Hockey Association in 1975–76, spending the next four years with the Minnesota Fighting Saints, Indianapolis Racers and New England Whalers. He returned to the NHL in 1979–80 after the demise of the WHA and played with the Hartford Whalers until his retirement following the 1981–82 season. Keon was elected to the Hockey Hall of Fame in 1986.

DAVE KERR On March 14, 1938, goalie Dave Kerr of the New York Rangers was featured on the cover of *Time* magazine. He was nearing the end of a regular season that would see him lead the NHL with eight shutouts, post a 2.00 goals-against average, and earn a spot on the Second All-Star Team.

Kerr's NHL career began with the Montreal Maroons in 1930–31. He was signed after helping the Montreal Amateur Athletic Association win the Allan Cup the previous year, but didn't see regular action at the NHL level until 1933–34. That season, he played all 48 games for the Maroons and starred in a playoff victory over New York. When Tommy Gorman signed Alex Connell for the Maroons in 1934–35, Lester Patrick picked up Kerr for the Rangers.

Kerr spent seven seasons in New York and posted 40 shutouts, a club record that lasted until Ed Giacomin surpassed it in 1972–73. His best season was 1939–40, when he helped the Rangers win the Stanley Cup. He also led the

league again with eight shutouts that season, posted a league-leading and career-best 1.60 goals-against average, won the Vezina Trophy, and was named to the First All-Star Team. Kerr retired after the 1940–41 season and joined the Canadian armed forces.

DUBBIE KERR Albert "Dubbie" Kerr started his hockey career in his hometown of Brockville, Ontario before playing in Pittsburgh in 1907–08. He joined Toronto of the Ontario Professional Hockey League during the 1908–09 season, but jumped to the Ottawa Senators and became a star. Playing with future Hall of Famers Marty Walsh and Billy Gilmour, Kerr scored 20 goals in nine games as Ottawa won the Eastern Canada Hockey Association title and the Stanley Cup.

Kerr was one of several Senators players Renfrew tried to sign for the inaugural 1909–10 season of the National Hockey Association, but he turned them down. Injuries limited his playing time that year, but he was better than ever in 1910–11. Now playing with Walsh and Bruce Ridpath, Kerr scored in 12 consecutive games, including five in one game, and had 33 goals in 16 games to finish second behind Walsh in NHA scoring. Ottawa easily won the league championship and with it the Stanley Cup. Kerr, Ridpath, and Walsh had one, two, and three goals respectively in a 7–4 Stanley Cup challenge win over Galt. In another challenge against Port Arthur, Kerr and Ridpath again combined for three goals while Walsh scored 10 in a 13–4 victory.

Kerr retired after the 1911–12 season, but Lester Patrick lured him to Victoria of the Pacific Coast Hockey Association in 1913–14 and he was chosen the league's all-star left winger after leading the Aristocrats to the PCHA championship. He remained an effective scorer in the PCHA until 1920.

TIM KERR overcame numerous injuries and personal tragedy to become one of the top goal scorers in the NHL. Though injuries would eventually cut short his career and limit him to 370 goals, his goals-per-game ratio of .565 is one of the highest in league history. His 17 career hat tricks established a Philadelphia Flyers franchise record.

Kerr stood 6'3" and weighed 230 pounds and, as a result, took a physical pounding by defenseman around the opposition goal. Three knee injuries and a broken leg limited him to just 54 goals in his first three seasons before 1983–84 when he matched that total in just one year. Kerr scored 54 goals again the following season, then added 10 in 12 playoff games as the Flyers reached the Stanley Cup finals. He set a playoff record on April 13, 1985, when he scored four goals in a single period.

After two consecutive 54-goal seasons, Kerr upped his total to 58 in each of the next two years before more injuries began to limit his effectiveness. The Flyers let him go to the San Jose Sharks in the 1991 Expansion Draft, who then traded him to the New York Rangers. It was during the 1991–92 season that Kerr's wife Kathy died ten days after giving birth. He played with the Hartford Whalers in 1992–93 before injuries forced him to retire at the age of 32.

JOHN KILPATRICK General John Reed Kilpatrick served as president of the New York Rangers during the 1933–34 season and then from 1935 until 1960. He was elected as an NHL governor in 1936 and was an original director of the pension fund which was established in 1946. Kilpatrick liked to boast that he was New York's number-one hockey fan.

In his youth, Kilpatrick had been an outstanding athlete. He starred at both track and football while attending Yale University, earning all-American honors as an end in both 1909 and 1910. He is also the first to be credited with throwing an overhand forward pass in a game against Princeton in 1907. In 1955, Kilpatrick was elected to the College Football Hall of Fame. He was elected to the Hockey Hall of Fame as a builder in 1960. The General served in both World War I and World War II and received several decorations.

DAVE KING first came to prominence in Canada when he coached the national junior team to the World Junior Championship in 1982. From 1983–84 until 1991–92, King was vice president, general manager and coach of Canada's national team, guiding the club at both the World Championships and the Olympics. King's Olympic team won a silver medal in 1992 for Canada's first Olympic medal in hockey since a bronze back in 1968. He received the Order of Canada in 1992 and was inducted into the Canadian Olympic Hall of Fame in 1995.

King's coaching career began at the University of Saskatchewan in 1972–73. He later won Junior B provincial titles in 1975 and 1976 before joining the Saskatoon Blades of the Western Hockey League in 1976–77. In 1977–78, King coached Billings to the WHL title and was named coach of the year. He was back with the University of Saskatchewan from 1978–79 until 1982–83, leading the Huskies to three conference championships and a national title in 1983. He had been named Canadian collegiate coach of the year in 1979–80.

King entered the NHL with the Calgary Flames in 1992–93 and led the club to the Pacific Division title in 1993–94 and 1994–95. He spent the next two years as a consultant to the Japanese Ice Hockey Federation and the Nagano Olympic Games before returning to the NHL when he signed as an assistant coach with the Montreal Canadiens on May 26, 1997. King coached the Japanese team during the Nagano Olympics in 1998.

JACK KIRRANE learned to play hockey on a backyard rink flooded annually by his father, who was captain of the Brookline (Massachusetts) Fire Department. From there he progressed to Brookline High School, where he was all-Scholastic and MVP in the Eastern Schoolboy Hockey League. After high school, Kirrane joined the Boston Junior Olympics, and in 1948 he was named to the U.S. Olympic hockey team as a 17-year-old. It took another 12 years before he actually made it to the Olympics, however, to anchor the defense of the American team that stunned Canada and the Soviet Union to win gold at Squaw Valley in 1960. Kirrane also represented the United States at the World Championships in 1957 and 1963.

In addition to his international career, Kirrane played amateur hockey in the Boston area and in 1956–57 he was a member of the Wetzell Club of Brockton, Massachusetts that won the U.S. national senior amateur championship. Kirrane was enshrined in the United States Hockey Hall of Fame in 1987.

SEYMOUR KNOX III and his brother Northrup first applied for an NHL franchise for Buffalo in 1965 and continued to lobby the NHL after the city was passed over in the original NHL expansion of 1967. On December 2, 1969, the NHL announced it would add teams in Buffalo and Vancouver for the 1970–71 season.

Knox quickly assembled a first-rate organization under the guidance of coach and general manager Punch Imlach. The Sabres qualified for the postseason in only their third season and then reached the Stanley Cup finals in 1975. Knox was a long-time member of the NHL Board of Governors and was named director of the United States Hockey Hall of Fame in Eveleth, Minnesota in 1972. He was inducted into the Hockey Hall of Fame as a builder in 1993.

In addition to his involvement with the Sabres, Knox was very active in many charitable causes throughout the Greater Buffalo area. He was also the driving force behind the Buffalo Bandits of the Major Indoor Lacrosse League and the Buffalo Blizzard of the National Professional Soccer League.

SAKU KOIVU was the Montreal Canadiens' first choice (21st overall) in the 1993 NHL Entry Draft and ranked fourth in the league among rookie scorers after he joined the Canadiens in 1995–96. He was battling for the NHL scoring lead early in the 1996–97 season with 38 points in 30 games before a knee injury on December 7. Koivu had been the league's leading scorer in his final season in Finland (1994–95), when he also led TPS Turku to the championship. Previously, he had helped his TPS junior team to win the Finnish junior title in 1991–92.

Koivu was named to the Second All-Star Team at the 1993 World Junior Championships before playing for the Finnish national team at the World Championships. Koivu played in both tournaments again in 1994, winning a silver medal at the World Championships. He was also a member of Finland's bronze medal-winning team at the Olympics that year. In 1995, Koivu was named best forward as Finland won the World Championships. He was a member of the Finnish team at the World Cup of Hockey in 1996 and at the Nagano Olympics in 1998. His two goals and eight assists at the Olympics helped Finland earn a bronze medal and ranked him behind only teammate Teemu Selanne among the tournament scoring leaders.

OLAF KOLZIG emerged as a top goaltender during the 1997–98 season when his 33 wins, five shutouts and 2.20 goals-against average all ranked among the best in the game. "Ollie the Goalie" emerged as a star during the 1998 playoffs, leading the Washington Capitals to the Stanley Cup finals for the first time in franchise history. Along the way, Kolzig outperformed Dominik Hasek as the Caps eliminated the Buffalo Sabres to win the Eastern Conference championship.

Kolzig made his NHL debut with the Capitals in 1989–90, but spent most of his first seven seasons with the organization playing in the minor leagues. In 1994 he won the Jack Butterfield Trophy as the MVP of the Calder Cup playoffs for leading Portland to the American Hockey League championship. He finally got his chance to see regular duty in Washington in 1996–97 and earned the number-one job in 1997–98.

Born to German parents in Johannesburg, South Africa, Kolzig was raised in many different locales but grew up mostly in Toronto and Halifax. He represented Germany at the World Cup of Hockey in 1996 and played two games for the German team at the Nagano Olympics in 1998.

VLADIMIR KONSTANTINOV was recognized as one of the top defensemen in the NHL and helped the Detroit Red Wings to win the Stanley Cup in 1997 before tragedy struck. On June 13, 1997 — six days after Detroit's Stanley Cup victory — Konstantinov, Slava Fetisov and Red Wings trainer Sergei Mnatsakanov were all injured when a limousine in which they were traveling struck a tree. Konstantinov suffered massive head injuries that nearly cost him his life. His heroic efforts to recover served as an inspiration to his teammates throughout 1997–98 and Steve Yzerman passed the Stanley Cup to a wheelchair-bound Konstantinov after Detroit repeated as champions.

Prior to his arrival in the NHL, Konstantinov had played seven seasons with the Central Red Army team in Moscow, captaining both that team and the

Soviet national team with which he played at four World Championships. Konstantinov was drafted 221st overall by the Red Wings in 1989 and joined the team in 1991–92. He was named to the NHL All-Rookie Team that year and was a Second Team All-Star in 1995–96 after leading the league in plus–minus at +60.

UWE KRUPP played soccer as a youth and did not begin to play competitive hockey until his mid-teens. In 1983, he became just the fifth German player ever selected in the NHL Entry Draft when the Buffalo Sabres picked him 214th overall in the 11th round. He did not know of his selection until told by a German journalist several days after the draft.

Krupp played three more years in Germany and made his debut with Buffalo on October 29, 1986, just two hours after receiving clearance to play in the NHL from the International Ice Hockey Federation. At 6'6" (and 232 pounds), Krupp was the tallest player in NHL history at the time. He was named as one of the three stars in his first game, but was later sent to Rochester of the American Hockey League where he helped the team to win the Calder Cup championship that season. Krupp became a regular in Buffalo the following year and showed steady improvement each season. In 1990–91, he played in the All-Star Game and led all Sabres defensemen in scoring, but on October 25, 1991, he was traded to the New York Islanders as part of the deal that brought Pat LaFontaine to Buffalo.

Krupp played three seasons with the Islanders and helped the team reach the Wales Conference finals in 1992–93. He was traded to the Quebec Nordiques on June 28, 1994, and led Nordiques defensemen in scoring in 1994–95. When the team moved to Colorado in 1995–96, he missed virtually all of the season with a knee injury. Krupp returned for the final five games of the regular season and was a key contributor in Avalanche's playoff run, scoring the Stanley Cup-winning goal at 4:31 of the third overtime period as the Avalanche beat the Florida Panthers 1–0 to end a four-game sweep. He remained with Colorado through the 1997–98 season and then signed with the Detroit Red Wings as a free agent.

Internationally, Krupp played for the German national team at the World Championships in 1986 and 1990 and was a member of the German team at the World Cup of Hockey in 1996 and at the Nagano Olympics in 1998.

JARI KURRI surpassed Peter Stastny as the highest-scoring European player in the NHL on December 8, 1993. Four years later, on December 23, 1997, Kurri became just the eighth player in NHL history to score 600 career goals. Yet, even with his impressive offensive credentials, Kurri has been known as one of the best defensive forwards in the game.

Kurri played in his native Finland and was a member of the Finnish Olympic team in 1980 before being selected by the Edmonton Oilers in the 1980 Entry Draft. He made his NHL debut in 1980–81 and finished a distant second behind Wayne Gretzky on the Oilers in goals, assists and points that season. Teamed on a line at right wing with Gretzky, Kurri quickly developed into one of the league's best scorers and cracked the top 10 for the first time in 1982–83. He had 52 goals in 1983–84 to earn his first of three selections to Second All-Star Team and led all playoff performers with 14 goals that spring when the Oilers won their first Stanley Cup title.

The 1984–85 season saw Kurri establish career highs with 71 goals, 64 assists and 135 points to earn the first of two berths on the First All-Star Team. He also won the Lady Byng Trophy that year. In the playoffs, he tied a postseason record with 19 goals as the Oilers repeated as Stanley Cup champions. Kurri led the NHL with 68 goals in 1985–86 and was the top playoff goal scorer again in 1987 and 1988 as the Oilers won two more titles. He picked up his fifth Stanley Cup ring in 1990.

Kurri left the NHL after 10 seasons and played in Italy in 1990–91. That spring, he represented Finland at the World Championships in Helsinki, and though the Finns failed to reach the medal round, Kurri tied Mats Sundin for the tournament lead in scoring and was named to the all-star team.

On May 30, 1991, Kurri's rights were traded to the Los Angeles Kings in a three-way deal with Edmonton and the Philadelphia Flyers and he returned to the NHL for the 1991–92 season. Paired again with Wayne Gretzky, Kurri helped to lead Los Angeles to the Stanley Cup finals in 1993. He was traded to the New York Rangers on March 14, 1996 and played for the Mighty Ducks of Anaheim in 1996–97 before signing as a free agent with the Colorado Avalanche on July 11, 1997. In 1998, he once again represented Finland at the Olympics in Nagano and helped to win a bronze medal.

ELMER LACH centered Rocket Richard and Toe Blake on the Montreal Canadiens' famed Punch Line of the 1940s. Lach was a quick and intelligent player who was one of the greatest playmakers in hockey. He set up many goals for the high-scoring Richard and established an NHL record with 54 assists when the Rocket scored 50 goals in 50 games in 1944–45.

After playing amateur hockey in his home province of Saskatchewan, Lach joined the Canadiens in 1940–41. He was teamed with Blake and Richard in 1943–44 and made his first appearance among the NHL's top 10 scorers, which earned him a selection to the Second All-Star Team and helped the Canadiens win their first Stanley Cup title in 13 years. In 1944–45, Lach,

Richard and Blake finished 1–2–3 in the NHL scoring race and all three were named to the First All-Star Team. Lach also won the Hart Trophy that season. He earned another Second Team All-Star berth in 1945–46 as the Canadiens won the Stanley Cup for the second time in three years.

A broken cheekbone, then a fractured skull, limited Lach's playing time in 1946–47, but he earned the Art Ross Trophy (the first year it was awarded) after winning his second scoring title in 1947–48 and was again selected as a First Team All-Star. Serious injuries would limit Lach's playing time over much of the remaining six years of his career, but he earned a final selection to the First All-Star Team in 1951–52 and helped Montreal win another Stanley Cup championship in 1953. Lach's overtime goal in game five against the Boston Bruins gave the Canadiens a 1–0 win and a 4–1 series victory. He retired after playing one more season and was elected to the Hockey Hall of Fame in 1966.

ANDRE LACROIX played more games, collected more assists, and had more points than any player in the history of the World Hockey Association. He had enjoyed modest success in the NHL as a member of the Philadelphia Flyers between 1967 and 1971, but became an instant star with the Philadelphia Blazers in the inaugural WHA season of 1972–73.

Lacroix's 50 goals in the first WHA season more than doubled his best NHL total and his 74 assists that year gave him a league-leading 124 points. In addition to winning the W.D. Hunter Trophy as the scoring leader, Lacroix also earned the Gary Davidson Trophy as the WHA's first MVP.

Lacroix became the WHA's top playmaker, registering five of the league's all-time top–10 regular-season assist performances and leading the league twice. In 1974–75, he set a professional hockey record with 106 assists and added 41 goals to win a second scoring title with 147 points. Earlier that season, Lacroix had led Team Canada with six assists in eight games when a squad of WHA all-stars took on the Soviet Union.

A member of five WHA franchises during the league's seven-year existence, Lacroix played 551 games and ranks fourth all-time with 251 goals. His 574 assists are almost 200 more than runner-up J.C. Tremblay and his 798 points are 132 more than Marc Tardif and 160 more than Bobby Hull. When four WHA teams joined the NHL in 1979–80, Lacroix returned to the league with the Hartford Whalers and played one final season.

FRED LAKE Though he lost the sight in one eye in an accident in the International (Pro) Hockey League, Fred Lake later teamed with Hamby Shore to form a solid defensive pair for several seasons when defensemen were still known as point and cover point. The two played together in Winnipeg with the Strathconas in 1907–08 before both jumped to the Winnipeg Maple Leafs for an unsuccessful Stanley Cup challenge against the Montreal Wanderers later that season. Lake won the Stanley Cup after joining the Ottawa Senators for the 1908–09 season.

Shore joined his Manitoba teammate in Ottawa a year later, and he and Lake anchored the Senators defense in front of future Hall of Fame goaltender Percy LeSueur for four seasons, including the Stanley Cup campaign of 1910–11. The tandem was broken up when Lake went to the Toronto Ontarios for the 1914–15 season. He was back in Ottawa the following year when the Senators traded LeSueur to reacquire him, but played just two games.

GUY LAFLEUR With a combination of speed, style and scoring skill, Montreal Canadiens star Guy Lafleur was the most exciting player in the NHL during his prime. He was named to the First All-Star Team at right wing for six straight seasons between 1974–75 and 1979–80, won the Art Ross Trophy three years in a row from 1975–76 until 1977–78 and earned the Hart Trophy as the NHL's MVP in 1976–77 and 1977–78. He played on five Stanley Cup champions in Montreal, including four in a row between 1976 and 1979, winning the Conn Smythe Trophy as playoff MVP in 1977.

Lafleur idolized Jean Beliveau growing up and wore number 4 while starring with the Quebec Remparts of the Quebec Junior Hockey League. He capped his brilliant junior career with 130 goals and 79 assists and a Memorial Cup title in 1970–71 and was selected first overall by the Canadiens in the 1971 NHL Amateur Draft. Though his first-year statistics of 29 goals and 64 assists were impressive for a rookie, more had been expected of Lafleur, but "the Flower" did not truly blossom until his fourth season of 1974–75 when he had 53 goals and 66 assists. Lafleur went on to top 50 goals six years in a row (a record at the time), including a high of 60 in 1977–78. Lafleur become the youngest player in NHL history to score 400 goals and the youngest to reach 1,000 points. When he retired during the 1984–85 season, Lafleur's 518 goals ranked second in Canadiens history behind Maurice Richard and his 728 assists trailed only Jean Beliveau. His 1,246 points make Lafleur the leading scorer in the history of the storied franchise.

Lafleur was elected to the Hockey Hall of Fame in 1988 but decided to make a comeback for the 1988–89 season. He joined the New York Rangers that year, and on his first trip back to the Forum on February 4, 1988 he scored two goals. Lafleur spent the next two years with the Quebec Nordiques before retiring for good after the 1990–91 season. At the time, his 560 goals ranked seventh in NHL history and his 1,353 points were eighth. The Guy Lafleur

Trophy is awarded annually to the playoff MVP in the Quebec Major Junior Hockey League.

PAT LaFONTAINE was selected third overall by the New York Islanders in the 1983 NHL Entry Draft after a brilliant season with Verdun of the Quebec Major Junior Hockey League. LaFontaine led the QMJHL with 104 goals, 130 assists and 234 points, won the MVP award in the regular season and the playoffs, and was named the Canadian major junior player of the year.

LaFontaine spent the 1983–84 season with the United States national team and was the club's leading scorer at the Sarajevo Olympics before making his debut with the Islanders on February 29, 1984. He scored his first goal three nights later when he recorded a hat trick against the Toronto Maple Leafs. LaFontaine increased his scoring output in each of his first four NHL seasons, tying Mike Bossy for the Islanders lead with 38 goals in 1986–87. On April 18, 1987, LaFontaine scored at 8:47 of the fourth overtime period to give the Islanders a seven-game playoff series victory over the Washington Capitals in one of the longest games in NHL history.

The 1989–90 season saw LaFontaine join Mike Bossy and Bryan Trottier as the only players in Islanders history to score 50 goals. His 54 goals and 51 assists saw him crack the top 10 in scoring for the first time, but after just one more season LaFontaine was traded to the Buffalo Sabres in a multi-player deal on October 25, 1991. His 46 goals in 1991–92 led the Sabres and set a club record for centers, which he broke the following year when he scored 53 times. His career-high 95 assists and 148 assists that season saw him finish second behind Mario Lemieux in league scoring and earn a spot on the Second All-Star Team.

A serious knee injury sidelined LaFontaine for most of the 1993–94 season but he returned as team captain in 1994–95 and was awarded the Bill Masterton Trophy for perseverance and dedication to hockey. After another good season in 1995–96, LaFontaine missed most of 1996–97 after developing post-concussion syndrome. He was traded to the New York Rangers on September 29, 1997.

In addition to his Olympic experience in 1984, LaFontaine has represented the United States at the World Championships in 1989 and at the Canada Cup in 1987 and 1991. He was a member of the American team that beat Canada at the World Cup of Hockey in 1996 and also played for the U.S. Olympic team in Nagano in 1998.

NEWSY LALONDE Edouard Charles "Newsy" Lalonde was the greatest and most colorful hockey player of his era. Skilled as a scorer and a fighter, Lalonde was a tough customer who would not back down from any opponent, sometimes even clashing with teammates. Also a lacrosse star, Lalonde was named Canada's outstanding player of the half-century in that sport in 1950, the same year he was inducted into the Hockey Hall of Fame.

Lalonde earned his nickname when he worked in a newsprint plant as a boy in his hometown of Cornwall, Ontario. His hockey career also began in that city in 1904–05. Two years later, he was playing in hockey's first professional league as a member of the Sault Ste. Marie, Ontario team in the International (Pro) Hockey League. When the Ontario Professional Hockey League was formed in 1907–08, Lalonde joined the Toronto team, winning the scoring title with 29 goals in nine games. Toronto won the first OPHL title that year, but they lost a one-game Stanley Cup challenge to the Montreal Wanderers.

After a second season in the OPHL, Lalonde joined *les Canadiens* when the French-Canadian team was formed in Montreal for 1909–10, the inaugural season of the National Hockey Association. He was traded to the Renfrew Millionaires during the season, and ended the year as the league scoring leader. His nine goals for Renfrew on March 11, 1910, would remain a single-game high throughout the eight-year history of the NHA (though the mark was equaled by Tommy Smith).

Lalonde returned to the Canadiens in 1910–11, but he joined former Renfrew teammate Frank Patrick out west when he signed with the Vancouver Millionaires for 1911–12 in the new Pacific Coast Hockey Association. After leading the PCHA with 27 goals that year, he returned to Montreal again, winning another NHA scoring title in 1915–16 as the Canadiens won their first Stanley Cup title. He remained with the team through its entry into the NHL in 1917–18, and he went on to win NHL scoring titles in 1918–19 and 1920–21. He scored six goals in a single game on January 10, 1920. Lalonde also served as coach of the Canadiens during much of this time.

Lalonde remained with Montreal until after the 1921–22 season, when he fell out of favor with owner Leo Dandurand, who sent him to the Saskatoon Shieks of the Western Canada Hockey League in return for Aurel Joliat. Lalonde promptly led the WCHL with 30 goals as a player-coach in 1922–23. He returned to the NHL as a coach with the New York Americans in 1926–27, and he later coached the Ottawa Senators and Montreal Canadiens before retiring in 1935. He remained a lifelong fan of the Canadiens, continuing to attend games at the Forum until his death in 1971.

MYLES LANE was the first American collegiate player to jump directly to the NHL when he joined the New York Rangers after graduating from Dartmouth in 1928.

One of the best athletes ever produced at Dartmouth, he earned three letters in hockey and football respectively and another one in baseball between 1925 and 1928. He set a school record for most goals in a season by a defenseman when he scored 20 times in 1925–26, and his 50 goals in three seasons established a career mark. In football, he played halfback on the Dartmouth team that went 8–0 in 1925 and won the national championship. The team was 7–1 in 1927, with Lane accounting for 125 of Dartmouth's 280 points scored and being named all-American for his play.

Dealt to the Boston Bruins during the 1928–29 season, Lane wound up playing for a Stanley Cup champion that year. He played briefly with the Bruins in 1929–30 and again in 1933–34, but most of his pro career was spent with the Boston Cubs of the Canadian-American Hockey League. After his hockey career, Lane went into law and was one of America's most successful trial lawyers and an opponent of organized crime. He is a member of the National Football Foundation's Hall of Fame in New Brunswick, New Jersey, and became a charter member of the United States Hockey Hall of Fame in 1973.

DAVE LANGEVIN A four-time Stanley Cup champion with the New York Islanders, Dave Langevin first learned the game of hockey on the playgrounds of St. Paul, Minnesota. He played on two state independent championship teams and helped to compile a 28–1 record in his junior year at Hill High School. At the University of Minnesota-Duluth, he was a second team all-American in his final season of 1975–76. Drafted by the Islanders in 1974, Langevin instead turned pro with the Edmonton Oilers in the World Hockey Association in 1976–77.

When Edmonton entered the NHL for the 1979–80 season, Langevin was reclaimed by the Islanders and joined a Stanley Cup dynasty—NHL champions in all of his first three years although a knee injury suffered in Edmonton hampered him throughout his career. Told that he'd never play again before the Islanders' next title bid, Langevin missed much of the 1983 playoffs but returned to the lineup in time to help his team down the Oilers for their fourth Stanley Cup title in a row.

After six seasons with the Islanders, Langevin was picked up in the Waiver Draft by the Minnesota North Stars prior to the 1985–86 season. He was a member of the Los Angeles Kings the following year, then another knee injury ended his career at age 33. He has since coached high school, college and amateur hockey. Langevin was elected to the United States Hockey Hall of Fame in 1993.

JACQUES LAPERRIERE played in the Montreal Canadiens organization with the Montreal Junior Canadiens and the team's Eastern Professional Hockey League affiliate before reaching the NHL to stay in 1964–65. A big and mobile defenseman, Laperriere proved he was ready for the big time by winning the Calder Trophy as rookie of the year and earning a selection to the Second All-Star Team. Laperriere was a First Team All-Star in each of the next two seasons and also won the Norris Trophy as the league's best defenseman in 1965–66. He gained a final spot on the Second Team in 1969–70.

Laperriere had a reputation as a cool-headed player who was capable of controlling the pace of the game. He helped the Canadiens win the Stanley Cup six times during his 12 seasons in Montreal before a serious knee injury forced him to retire after the 1973–74 season. Laperriere remained active with the club following his retirement and was an assistant under six different head coaches for 16 years between 1981–82 and 1996–97. He was elected to the Hockey Hall of Fame in 1987. On June 24, 1997, Laperriere was hired to assist former Canadiens coach Pat Burns with the Boston Bruins.

GUY LAPOINTE established himself as one of the NHL's best defensemen over a 16-year career, playing on six Stanley Cup winners with the Montreal Canadiens during the 1970s. A native of Montreal, Lapointe joined the Junior Canadiens in 1967–68, turned pro the following season and reached the NHL to stay in 1970–71. He was elected to the Hockey Hall of Fame in 1993.

Lapointe was a member of "the Big Three" on the Canadiens defense with Serge Savard and Larry Robinson. He was a punishing checker who could join in the offensive rush, establishing career highs with 28 goals in 1974–75 and 76 points in 1976–77. Lapointe was elected to the First All-Star Team in 1972–73 and earned three consecutive berths on the Second Team from 1974–75 to 1976–77. He was traded to the St. Louis Blues on March 9, 1982, and finished his playing career with the Boston Bruins in 1983–84. Lapointe had been a member of Team Canada during the 1972 Summit Series with the Soviet Union and also at the 1976 Canada Cup.

Following his playing days, Lapointe became an assistant coach with the Quebec Nordiques. After just one year, he was named head coach and general manager of the Longueuil Chevaliers of the Quebec Major Junior Hockey League, where he remained for two years, winning a league title and a berth in the Memorial Cup tournament in 1986–87. He returned to the NHL as an assistant with Quebec again in 1987–88 and remained with the club for three years. He became a scout with the Calgary Flames in 1990 and was a member of the coaching staff there in 1995–96 and 1996–97 before he returned to scouting.

EDGAR LAPRADE was a long-time amateur star in Port Arthur, Ontario. He helped the Bearcats win the Allan Cup in 1939 and was named the most valu-

able player in the Thunder Bay Senior Hockey League in both 1938–39 and 1940–41. He did not turn pro until after World War II, signing with the New York Rangers for the 1945–46 season.

Laprade was a polished playmaker and effortless skater whose ability to backcheck and mastery of the poke check made him an excellent two-way player and effective penalty killer. Rangers teammates called him "Beaver" due to his work ethic and constant hustle. He was aggressive but clean and did not record a single penalty during his first NHL season, after which he won the Calder Trophy as rookie of the year. Twice more in his career Laprade would go through the entire season without a penalty, and in 1949–50 he won the Lady Byng Trophy. Laprade also led the Rangers with 22 goals and 44 points that year to win the team MVP award (after sharing it the previous year) and helped New York reach the Stanley Cup finals before losing to the Detroit Red Wings in double overtime in game seven.

Laprade missed half of 1950–51 after breaking his ankle in January, and retired after 1951–52. He returned for limited action when the Rangers ran into injury problems during the 1952–53 campaign and saw some action again the following season on a line with brothers Max and Doug Bentley. Laprade was back for a final season in 1954–55, but retired for good after suffering another injury. He was elected to the Hockey Hall of Fame in 1993.

IGOR LARIONOV centered the famous Soviet KLM line with Vladimir Krutov and Sergei Makarov during the 1980s. Larionov was a four-time all-star with the Central Red Army team in the Soviet National League between 1982–83 and 1987–88 and was the Soviet player of the year for the 1987–88 season. He was a member of the Soviet national team from 1981 to 1989, winning gold medals at the World Championships in 1982, 1983, 1986 and 1989, and at the Olympics in 1984 and 1988. He was also a member of the Soviet team that won the World Junior Championships in 1980 and the Canada Cup in 1981.

Larionov was selected 214th overall by the Vancouver Canucks in the 1985 NHL Entry Draft and finally was permitted to join the Canucks for the 1989–90 season. Vladimir Krutov also played for the Canucks that year (his only NHL season) and Sergei Makarov won the Calder Trophy as rookie of the year with the Calgary Flames. Larionov played three years in Vancouver and then spent the 1992–93 season in Switzerland before returning to the NHL with the San Jose Sharks in 1993–94. Makarov was a teammate for two seasons in San Jose.

On October 24, 1995, Larionov was traded to the Detroit Red Wings where he joined fellow Russians Sergei Fedorov, Slava Fetisov, Slava Kozlov and Vladimir Konstantinov. Larionov became an important part of the Detroit team that set an NHL record with 62 wins in 1995–96 and won the Stanley Cup for the first time in 42 years in 1997. He helped the Red Wings repeat as champions in 1998. Larionov was a member of the Russian team at the World Cup of Hockey in 1996 but was not part of the Russian Olympic team in Nagano in 1998.

REED LARSON A graduate of the youth hockey programs in his hometown of Minneapolis, Minnesota, Reed Larson went on to become a high school star and a collegiate hockey champion before launching a long NHL career. He was captain of the Detroit Red Wings in 1980–81 and 1981–82 and played in the Stanley Cup finals with the Boston Bruins in 1988. He also was a member of the American national team at the IIHF World Championships and the 1981 Canada Cup tournament.

A star defenseman at Roosevelt High School in Minneapolis, Larson was named all-City and all-State in both his junior and senior years. He went to the University of Minnesota in 1974 and helped the Golden Gophers win the 1974–75 Western Collegiate Hockey Association championship. The following season, he earned a berth on the WCHA first all-star team, then turned pro midway through his junior year when he signed with the Red Wings, who had selected him 22nd overall in the 1976 Amateur Draft.

In his first full season with Detroit in 1977–78, Larson led all Red Wings defensemen in scoring (60 points) and continued to do so for the next seven years. He topped 20 goals for five years in a row between 1979–80 and 1983–84, tying Denis Potvin for the second-longest such streak in the history of the NHL at the time, behind only Bobby Orr's record of seven straight 20-goal seasons. Larson's 451st career point on October 1, 1984 moved him past Red Kelly as the highest-scoring defenseman in the history of the Detroit Red Wings. He became just the fifth Red Wing ever to reach 500 career points on March 13, 1985. At the time, Larson was the highest-scoring U.S.-born player in NHL history.

After nine and a half seasons in Detroit, Larson was traded to Boston on March 10, 1986. He spent the next two full seasons with the Bruins, but then bounced around with the Edmonton Oilers, New York Islanders, Minnesota North Stars and Buffalo Sabres. Larson played most of his last three seasons in Italy before retiring after the 1991–92 campaign. He was inducted into the United States Hockey Hall of Fame in 1996.

JACK LAVIOLETTE was the man hired to run the new French-Canadian team in Montreal after Ambrose O'Brien secured financing for les Canadiens to take part in the inaugural National Hockey Association season of 1909–10. Laviolette later became one of only three athletes to be named to both the

Hockey Hall of Fame and the Canadian Sports Hall of Fame prior to 1970. It was his skill in lacrosse that earned him the latter honor.

Laviolette and Didier Pitre were teammates with the Montreal Nationals of the Federal Amateur Hockey League in 1903–04, and both spent the next three seasons playing in hockey's first professional league with the Sault Ste. Marie, Michigan franchise in the International (Pro) Hockey League. The two returned to Montreal with the Shamrocks in 1907–08, and when Laviolette took over the Canadiens in 1909, Pitre was the first player he signed. The two played defense together in 1909–10, but they later moved up to play on a forward line with Newsy Lalonde. Laviolette was known as "the Speed Merchant," and he, Lalonde and Pitre were the reason the Canadiens became known as "the Flying Frenchmen," a sobriquet that—off and on—has been applied to the team ever since.

Laviolette remained with the Canadiens for the rest of his career, helping the franchise win its first Stanley Cup title in 1915–16, then entering the NHL with the team in 1917–18. His playing days ended after that season when he lost a foot in a car accident but, amazingly, he came back to do some refereeing. Laviolette was inducted into the Hockey Hall of Fame in 1962.

DANNY LAWSON was a journeyman forward with three teams over five seasons in the NHL who emerged as a scoring star in the World Hockey Association. As a member of the Philadelphia Blazers, Lawson led the WHA with 61 goals in its inaugural season of 1972–73, a total that more than doubled his 28 goals in 219 career NHL games.

Without slick playmaker Andre Lacroix as a teammate in 1973–74, Lawson's production declined but he still managed to score 50 goals that season and had at least 30 goals in each of the next three years before retiring after the 1976–77 campaign. Though he played in only five of the league's seven seasons, Lawson's total of 218 goals ranks him eighth all-time in WHA history.

REGGIE LEACH grew up in poverty as one of 12 children raised by his paternal grandparents and was determined to improve his lot in life through hockey. Though the undisciplined habits he learned as a youth hurt him during his career, for a brief time Leach was one of the most dangerous goal scorers in the NHL.

A teammate of Bobby Clarke's as a junior in Flin Flon, Manitoba, Leach began his career with the Boston Bruins and California Golden Seals before the Philadelphia Flyers obtained him on Clarke's recommendation. Leach was acquired a week after Philadelphia's Stanley Cup victory in 1974 and he helped the team repeat as champions with 45 goals in 1974–75. The following season, Leach ended Phil Esposito's run of six-straight seasons as the NHL's leading goal scorer when he scored 61 goals. He added 19 goals in the postseason to set a playoff record, including five in one game against the Boston Bruins on May 6, 1976. The Flyers lost the Stanley Cup to the Montreal Canadiens that spring, but Leach earned the Conn Smythe Trophy to become just the third player in history to be named playoff MVP for a losing team (Roger Crozier and Glenn Hall).

Hounded by coach Fred Shero to improve his defense, Leach slumped over the next three seasons before rebounding to score 50 goals in 1979–80. He was waived by the Flyers after showing up late for practice during the 1981–82 season and finished out his NHL career the following season with the Detroit Red Wings.

AL LEADER was president of the Western Hockey League from its inception in 1952–53 until 1969. During that time, the league experienced periods of both financial and internal strain, but Leader's guidance eventually brought the WHL to a position of stability. He returned as president in June of 1974, but by then NHL expansion and the World Hockey Association had doomed the minor pro league and the WHL folded.

Though born in Manitoba, Leader's hockey career began as a 16-year-old in Saskatchewan. His first administrative post was as secretary of the Seattle City League in 1933. In the ensuing seven years, he played, coached and managed teams, while also serving as a referee. He organized a Defence Hockey League in 1940 during the Second World War, and from this he established contacts with pro hockey that led to his election as secretary-manager of the Pacific Coast Hockey League in 1944. By 1948, the PCHL had turned pro and Leader became its first president. (The Western Hockey League grew out of the PCHL in 1952–53). Leader, who had become a naturalized American citizen in 1933, was elected to the Hockey Hall of Fame as a builder in 1969.

ROBERT LeBEL played junior and senior hockey in his native Quebec and also played in New York State before helping to found the Interprovincial Senior League and serving as its first president from 1944 to 1947. He later served as president of the Quebec Amateur Hockey Association in 1955–56 and 1956–57 before becoming president of the Canadian Amateur Hockey Association from 1957–58 to 1958–59. LeBel was president of the International Ice Hockey Federation in 1960–61 and 1961–62. He was the first French-Canadian to hold the latter two offices.

In 1964, LeBel was named a life member of the both the QAHA and the CAHA and sat as CAHA's representative on the Hockey Hall of Fame's Governing Committee. LeBel was trustee of both the George T. Richardson Trophy (representative of the Eastern Canada junior championship) and the W.G. Hardy Trophy (Canadian intermediate championship), president of the Quebec Junior Hockey League and mayor of Chambly, Quebec. He was elected to the Hockey Hall of Fame as a builder in 1970. A division in the Quebec Major Junior Hockey League is named in his honor.

JOHN LeCLAIR When John LeClair scored 51 goals in 1997–98, he became the first American-born player ever to have three consecutive 50-goal seasons. LeClair has ranked among the top performers in the NHL since teaming with Eric Lindros after his trade to the Philadelphia Flyers on February 9, 1995.

LeClair was drafted out of high school by the Montreal Canadiens in 1987 and spent the next four years at the University of Vermont before making his NHL debut on March 9, 1991. He was the first Vermont native ever to reach the NHL. He became a regular with the Canadiens in 1992–93 and helped Montreal to win the Stanley Cup that season, but it was not until his arrival in Philadelphia that he became one of the NHL's top scorers.

Playing left wing alongside Eric Lindros and Mikael Renberg on the Legion of Doom line, LeClair and his linemates all cracked the top 10 in scoring in 1994–95. LeClair and Lindros were both named to the First All-Star Team. LeClair followed up with a 51-goal effort in 1995–96 and led the NHL in plus–minus at +44 in 1996–97. He was a Second Team All-Star in each of those seasons and returned to the First All-Star Team in 1997–98. LeClair was named to the all-star team at the World Cup of Hockey in 1996 after his six goals and 10 points ranked second in the tournament behind Brett Hull. He was also a member of the U.S. Olympic team in Nagano in 1998. LeClair had previously represented his country at the World Junior Championships in 1988 and 1989.

BRIAN LEETCH made his NHL debut with the New York Rangers on February 29, 1988 after competing for the United States at the Calgary Olympics. Leetch played his first full NHL season in 1988–89 and quickly established himself among the league's best defensemen. He led all rookies in assists and points that season and won the Calder Trophy. His 71 points was the second-highest total for a rookie defenseman behind Larry Murphy's 76 in 1980–81.

Leetch was selected ninth overall by the Rangers in the 1986 Entry Draft after two all-star seasons in high school hockey. He went on to become an all-American at Boston College in 1986–87 and was a finalist for the Hobey Baker Award after becoming the first freshman ever nominated for the top individual honor in U.S. college hockey. Leetch left the school after one season to join the U.S. national team and served as team captain at the Olympics.

Leetch established a Rangers record with 72 assists in 1990–91 and also set a team record with 88 points by a defenseman. He was named to the NHL Second All-Star Team. He broke both records with 80 assists and 102 points in 1991–92, won the Norris Trophy as best defenseman, and captured a place on the First All-Star Team. Injuries kept Leetch out for most of the 1992–93 season but he returned to star in 1993–94, particularly in the playoffs, where his 23 assists and 34 points led all scorers as the Rangers won the Cup for the first time since 1940. Leetch received the Conn Smythe Trophy as playoff MVP. On December 27, 1996, he surpassed Ron Greschner as the highest-scoring defenseman in Rangers history with his 611th point. He won the Norris Trophy for a second time and was selected again to the First All-Star Team in 1996–97.

In addition to his Olympic experience in 1988, Leetch represented the United States at the World Junior Championships in 1985, 1986 and 1987, winning a bronze medal in 1986 and being named to the tournament all-star team in 1987. He also played at the World Championships in 1987 and 1989 and at the Canada Cup in 1991. In 1996, Leetch was captain of the American team that beat Canada to win the World Cup of Hockey. In 1998, he returned to the Olympics as a member of the U.S. team in Nagano.

HUGH LEHMAN ranked among the best goalies in hockey over a career that spanned 25 years. He broke in with his hometown Pembroke team in 1903–04, and he helped the team win the Citizen Shield trophy as champions of the Ottawa Valley in 1905–06. The following year, Lehman was playing in hockey's first professional league as a member of the Sault Ste. Marie, Ontario team in the International (Pro) Hockey League.

Lehman was back in Pembroke in 1907–08, but when the Ontario Professional Hockey League was formed in 1908–09, he joined the team representing Berlin (now Kitchener). In January of 1910, Lehman was loaned to the defending OPHL champions from Galt when they took on the Ottawa Senators in a Stanley Cup challenge. He was back to play for the Stanley Cup again two months later after Berlin won the league title and challenged the Montreal Wanderers. Both of Lehman's teams were defeated.

When the Pacific Coast Hockey Association was formed in 1911–12, Lehman joined the franchise in New Westminster, helping the Royals to win the first PCHA championship. When the team moved to Portland, Oregon prior to the 1914–15 season, Lehman signed with the Vancouver Millionaires, winning another PCHA title. This time, he also won the Stanley Cup as the Millionaires defeated Ottawa in three straight games. Vancouver won PCHA championship honors again in 1917–18. They also were PCHA champions

from 1920–21 until 1923–24, but never won another Stanley Cup title.

Lehman remained with Vancouver through the team's entry into the Western Canada Hockey League, but when pro hockey collapsed in the west after the 1925–26 season, he became a member of the Chicago Black Hawks for their first NHL season of 1926–27. He played the final four games of his career with Chicago in 1927–28, then took over briefly as coach of the team. Lehman was inducted into the Hockey Hall of Fame in 1958.

JACQUES LEMAIRE

JACQUES LEMAIRE was considered to be very underrated by teammates and opponents during his 12-year career. Because of the tough competition at his position of center, Lemaire never achieved all-star status, but he was a key contributor to eight Stanley Cup champions during a career spent entirely with the Montreal Canadiens. He was inducted into the Hockey Hall of Fame in 1984.

Lemaire worked his way up through the Canadiens organization and arrived in the NHL in 1967–68. He scored 22 goals as a rookie and never fell below 20 during his entire career. An excellent two-way player, Lemaire established personal bests with 44 goals in 1972–73 and 61 assists and 97 points in 1977–78. He scored the Stanley Cup-winning goal in both 1977 and 1979 to become just the fifth player in NHL history at the time to achieve that double distinction. Lemaire retired following his second Cup-winning goal, which capped the Canadiens' fourth straight championship.

After leaving the NHL, Lemaire spent two years as a player-coach with the Sierre club in Switzerland before returning to North America in 1981. He was named the first head coach of the Quebec Major Junior Hockey League's expansion Longueuil Chevaliers prior to the 1982–83 season, and led the club to the QMJHL finals in its first year. On February 24, 1984, Lemaire succeeded Bob Berry as coach of Montreal Canadiens, but stepped down after the 1984–85 season. From 1985–86 to 1992–93, he served as assistant to the managing director in Montreal under Serge Savard, with the added title of director of hockey operations for the first three years.

On June 28, 1993, Lemaire was named head coach of the New Jersey Devils. He quickly built the team into one of the best in the NHL, leading the Devils to their first 100-point season in 1993–94 and earning the Jack Adams Award as coach of the year. The following season, he guided the club to its first Stanley Cup title. Lemaire remained the head coach in New Jersey until stepping down after the 1997–98 campaign.

MARIO LEMIEUX

MARIO LEMIEUX was described by Bobby Orr as being the most skilled player he ever had seen, but like Orr, Lemieux was forced to endure physical ailments that shortened his career. Lemieux was one of the most prolific and creative scorers in NHL history despite battling chronic back problems and Hodgkin's disease during the 12 years he played. When he decided to retire after the 1996–97 season, the traditional three-year waiting period was waived and Lemieux was elected immediately to the Hockey Hall of Fame.

Lemieux was a star from childhood and attracted great attention during the 1983–84 season when he set Quebec Major Junior Hockey League records with 133 goals and 282 points in 70 games. He led Laval to the Memorial Cup tournament that year and was named the Canadian major junior player of the year. He then was picked by the Pittsburgh Penguins with the first choice in the 1984 NHL Entry Draft. At the time, the Penguins were struggling at the gate and on the ice, but Lemieux would emerge Pittsburgh's hockey savior.

Lemieux scored his first goal on his first NHL shift in a game against the Boston Bruins on October 11, 1984. He went on to become just the third rookie in NHL history to score 100 points (Peter Stastny and Dale Hawerchuk) and won the Calder Trophy. He ranked among the NHL scoring leaders in both his second and third seasons, but it was not until he played alongside Wayne Gretzky and scored the series-winning goal at the Canada Cup in 1987 that Lemieux finally emerged as a true superstar. He won the Art Ross Trophy in 1987–88 with 168 points on 70 goals and 98 assists and was rewarded with the Hart Trophy. Wayne Gretzky had been injured that year, but Lemieux beat him outright in 1988–89 when he established career highs with 85 goals, 114 assists and 199 points.

Back injuries first sidelined Lemieux during the 1989–90 season, but he returned late in the 1990–91 campaign and led Pittsburgh to its first Stanley Cup title. He won the Conn Smythe Trophy as playoff MVP that year, as he would again when Pittsburgh made it two in a row in 1992. He also led the NHL in scoring once again that year. During the 1992–93 season, Lemieux was diagnosed with Hodgkin's disease (a form of cancer). Radiation treatments lasted from February 1 to March 2, when Lemieux immediately returned to the lineup. He went on to win the Art Ross Trophy for the fourth time and again was awarded the Hart Trophy.

Due to his many injuries and illnesses, Lemieux took the entire season off in 1994–95. He returned the following year and again won both the Hart and Art Ross trophies. He won his sixth scoring title during his final season of 1996–97. Lemieux retired with 613 goals, 881 assists and 1,494 points. His average of .823 goals-per-game is the best in NHL history and his 2.01 points-per-game is topped only by Wayne Gretzky.

PERCY LeSUEUR

PERCY LeSUEUR's career in hockey spanned 50 years as a player, coach, manager, columnist and broadcaster. He began playing as a right winger in his hometown of Quebec City, but he became a goalie while playing in Smiths Falls, Ontario. He attracted the attention of the Ottawa Silver Seven after they defeated his Smiths Falls team in a Stanley Cup challenge match in March of 1906, and they acquired his services a week later after losing a playoff game to the Montreal Wanderers 9–1.

"Peerless Percy," as he became known, played on Stanley Cup winners with the Ottawa Senators in 1909 and 1911. He was captain of the team for three years and was the Senators' only goaltender until 1912–13 when he began sharing the job with Clint Benedict. LeSueur coached the team for part of the 1913–14 season, but he was traded to the Toronto Shamrocks the following year. He played just one more year before joining the 48th Highlanders and seeing action in World War I.

LeSueur has been credited with inventing the gauntlet style of gloves worn by goaltenders of his era and for designing the goal nets used by the National Hockey Association and the NHL from 1912 to 1925. He served as a referee, then a coach, after his playing days, and he was the first manager of the Detroit Olympia when the building opened in 1927. He was also an original member of the Hot Stove League on radio broadcasts. LeSueur was elected to the Hockey Hall of Fame in 1961.

HERBIE LEWIS

HERBIE LEWIS was called "the Duke of Duluth" during four great years with the Duluth Hornets of the American Hockey Association. He later went on to star in the NHL with Detroit while the team was known as the Cougars, the Falcons and finally the Red Wings. Lewis had a reputation as a fast skater, an accurate passer and a sportsmanlike player.

Lewis played hockey in his hometown of Calgary before joining Duluth in 1924–25. He went on to become the chief drawing card and highest-paid player in the AHA before Jack Adams acquired him for Detroit in 1928–29. He led the team with 20 goals while playing on a line with Ebbie Goodfellow and Larry Aurie in 1929–30, and he later played on an outstanding line with Aurie and Cooney Weiland. Lewis led Detroit in both goals and points in 1932–33 and he and Aurie represented Detroit at the Ace Bailey All-Star benefit game on February 14, 1934.

Marty Barry was acquired by the Red Wings in 1935, and the combination of Lewis, Aurie and Barry helped Detroit win back-to-back Stanley Cup titles in 1936 and 1937. Lewis led the Red Wings in scoring again in 1937–38, but spent just one more year in the NHL, though he continued to play in the minor leagues before he retired. In 1989, Lewis was inducted into the Hockey Hall of Fame.

NICKLAS LIDSTROM

NICKLAS LIDSTROM played three seasons in the Swedish Elite League before joining the Detroit Red Wings for the 1991–92 season. He led all rookies in assists (49) and plus–minus (+36) that year and finished as the runner-up in voting for the Calder Trophy. He also earned a spot on the NHL All-Rookie Team. Lidstrom has gone on to become one of the top defensemen in the NHL and was a key contributor when Detroit won its first Stanley Cup title in 42 years in 1997. He helped the Red Wings repeat as champions the following year and was nominated for the Norris Trophy as the NHL's best defenseman in 1997–98 after leading all blueliners with 59 points (17 goals, 42 assists). He was also named to the First All-Star Team that year.

Lidstrom got his first international experience when he represented Sweden at the European Junior Championships in 1989. In 1990, he played at the World Junior Championships and in 1991 he was a member of the Swedish team that won the World Championship. He also played for Sweden at the Canada Cup in 1991 and at the World Championships again in 1994. Lidstrom competed at the World Cup of Hockey in 1996 and was a member of the Swedish Olympic team at Nagano in 1998.

PELLE LINDBERGH

PELLE LINDBERGH was a star goalie in Sweden from the time of his youth. He was the top goaltender on the Swedish national team by the time he was 20 and led his country to a bronze medal at the 1980 Winter Olympics in Lake Placid. His dream was to become the first great European goaltender in the NHL and he was well on his way to achieving it when he was killed in a car accident on November 10, 1985.

Lindbergh, who idolized Bernie Parent as a boy, was drafted by the Philadelphia Flyers in 1979 and joined the Maine Mariners of the American Hockey League the following year. In his first season, Lindbergh won the Hap Holmes Trophy as the AHL's top goaltender, was named rookie of the year, most valuable player, and was selected to the first all-star team. He joined the Flyers during the following season and became a regular in 1982–83, playing in the NHL All-Star Game and being named to the All-Rookie Team.

In 1984–85, Lindbergh led the league with 40 wins as the Flyers posted the NHL's best record. He also had the league's second-best save percentage and third-best goals-against average at 3.02 and was rewarded with the Vezina Trophy. In the playoffs, Lindbergh helped the Flyers reach the finals before losing the Stanley Cup to the Edmonton Oilers. He was off to a great start in 1985–86 with six wins in eight games at the time of his tragic death.

TREVOR LINDEN

TREVOR LINDEN After leading the Medicine Hat Tigers to back-to-back Memorial Cup championships and winning a gold medal with Team Canada at the World Junior Championships in 1988, Trevor Linden was selected second

overall by the Vancouver Canucks in the 1988 Entry Draft. He was the youngest player in the NHL during his rookie season of 1988–89 and set what was then a Canucks rookie record with 30 goals. Linden was the first Vancouver rookie to be named the team's most valuable player and finished second behind Brian Leetch in voting for the Calder Trophy.

In 1990–91, Linden led the Canucks in scoring after being named one of three team captains with Dan Quinn and Doug Lidster. In 1991–92, he became the sole captain (the youngest captain in the league) and again led the Canucks in scoring. His strong playoff performance in 1994 helped Vancouver reach the seventh game of the finals before losing the Stanley Cup to the New York Rangers. In 1995–96, he established a career high with 80 points on 33 goals and 47 assists. On February 27, 1996, Linden played in his 438th consecutive game to set a new Canucks record and was the NHL's reigning "ironman" before injuries limited him to just 49 games in 1996–97. However, after Mike Keenan was named coach of the Canucks during the 1997–98 season, Linden was traded to the New York Islanders on February 6, 1998.

In addition to representing Canada as a junior in 1988, Linden played at the World Championships in 1991 and was invited to training camp with Team Canada for the 1991 Canada Cup tournament. Linden played at the World Cup of Hockey in 1996 and was a member of the Canadian Olympic team at Nagano in 1998.

JOE LINDER is considered the first great American-born hockey player as both an amateur and professional player from 1905 until 1920 and a coach, manager and sponsor of the game in the region of Duluth, Minnesota and Superior, Wisconsin from 1920 until he died in 1948.

Linder starred in hockey, baseball and football during his high school years in Hancock, Michigan, and captained all three school sports teams every year of his high school career (1901 to 1905).

He played with the Calumet Miners in the International (Pro) Hockey League in 1905–06 and is one of only two known Americans (along with goaltender Joseph "Chief" Jones) to have played in this, the first professional hockey league. He spent only a year in the pro ranks, then played amateur hockey in Michigan's Upper Peninsula until 1911.

Linder moved to Duluth, Minnesota in 1912 and captained the Duluth team in the American Amateur Hockey Association until 1920. Their greatest triumph came on March 7, 1914 when Duluth beat the Winnipeg Victorias—the first victory ever by an American team over the Canadian club that had won the Stanley Cup back in 1896 and 1901 and the Allan Cup in 1911 and 1912.

In February of 1941, *Esquire* magazine said in a review of the American and Canadian hockey scene that "any list of the 30 best hockey players the whole world has had would have to include the American-born Linder." Joe Linder was enshrined in the U.S. Hockey Hall of Fame in 1975.

ERIC LINDROS At 6'4" and 236 pounds, Eric Lindros boasts a combination of strength and skill that has seen him become a superstar in the NHL—as had been projected for him since childhood.

After starring in Junior B hockey with St. Michael's in Toronto, Lindros was drafted by the Sault Ste. Marie Greyhounds of the Ontario Hockey League in 1989 but refused to report. He played instead with Compuware in Detroit until the Greyhounds traded his rights to the Oshawa Generals. Lindros finished the 1989–90 season in Oshawa and helped the team to win the Memorial Cup. He also played on Canada's gold medal-winning team at the World Junior Championships that year. In 1990–91, he led the OHL with 71 goals and 149 points, won another World Junior title, led the tournament in scoring and was named the Canadian major junior player of the year.

Lindros was selected first overall by the Quebec Nordiques in the 1991 NHL Entry Draft but refused to sign with the team he had asked not to choose him. Even though he was not under contract to an NHL club, the 18-year-old Lindros was asked to join Team Canada for the 1991 Canada Cup, and he picked up five points in eight games as Canada won the tournament. Instead of playing for Quebec, Lindros spent the 1991–92 season with the Canadian national team and helped Canada to win a silver medal at Albertville.

On June 30, 1992, the Philadelphia Flyers sent six players, two first-round draft choices and cash to Quebec to obtain the rights to Lindros, though it took the ruling of an arbitrator to determine that Quebec had not dealt Lindros' rights to the New York Rangers first. He finally made his NHL debut in 1992–93 and set a Flyers rookie record with 41 goals that season. His offensive production increased in 1993–94, and in 1994–95 he tied Jaromir Jagr for the NHL lead with 70 points in an abbreviated 48-game season. Jagr received the Art Ross Trophy because he had scored more goals, but Lindros earned the Hart Trophy as MVP and was named to the First All-Star Team. He was a Second Team All-Star in 1995–96 after establishing a career high with 115 points. Lindros led all playoff scorers with 26 points in 1997 as the Flyers reached the Stanley Cup finals before losing to the Detroit Red Wings.

In addition to his early international experience, Lindros represented Canada at the 1993 World Championships and at the World Cup of Hockey in 1996. In 1998, he was Canada's captain at the 1998 Nagano Olympics. His brother Brett played briefly with the New York Islanders before a head injury ended his career.

BERT LINDSAY The father of hockey legend Ted Lindsay, Bert Lindsay was a star in his own right. A goaltender, he played at McGill University in Montreal between 1902 and 1905 before embarking on an itinerant professional career. Lindsay was recruited to play goal for the Edmonton team that challenged the Montreal Wanderers for the Stanley Cup in December of 1908. Though stacked with other "ringers," including future Hall of Famers Lester Patrick, Didier Pitre and Tommy Phillips, Edmonton dropped the first game 7–3 and, despite their 7–6 victory in game two, lost the total-goal challenge series 13–10.

Following the unsuccessful Stanley Cup challenge, Lindsay spent the 1908–09 season in Renfrew and was the goalie for the Millionaires when M.J. and Ambrose O'Brien of Renfrew created the National Hockey Association for the 1909–10 season. After the 1910–11 campaign, Lindsay followed former teammate Lester Patrick to Victoria for the first season of the Pacific Coast Hockey Association. He was in goal when the Aristocrats won the PCHA title in 1912–13 and 1913–14, but never played for a Stanley Cup champion.

After a disappointing 1914–15 campaign, Lindsay left Victoria and returned to the NHA with the Montreal Wanderers. He was still with the club when it became a charter member of the NHL in 1917–18, but had his season cut short when the Wanderers disbanded following a fire in their home rink. The next year, Lindsay joined the Toronto Arenas after Hap Holmes left the defending Stanley Cup champions to return to the PCHA's Seattle Metropolitans. This team, too, did not survive to the end of the regular-season schedule and Lindsay retired.

TED LINDSAY was one of the toughest players in NHL history. Although small in stature at 5'8" and 160 pounds, "Terrible Ted" never was afraid to take on all comers, thus became one of the most dangerous fighters, as well as a top offensive threat, in the NHL. He was named as an All-Star at left wing nine times in his career, including eight selections to the First Team. Lindsay was an All-Star every year from 1947–48 to 1956–57 with the exception of 1954–55.

The son of former goaltender Bert Lindsay, Ted Lindsay became a star in junior hockey. He was a member of the St. Michael's College team that lost the Ontario junior finals to Oshawa in 1943–44, but then was added to the Generals roster in their successful bid to win the Memorial Cup. Lindsay turned pro with the Detroit Red Wings the following year and began his NHL career on a line with veterans Mud Bruneteau and Syd Howe. He was first teamed with Gordie Howe and Sid Abel during the 1946–47 season. The following year, Lindsay cracked the top 10 in scoring for the first time. It was during the 1948–49 season that the Abel-Lindsay-Howe combination was dubbed the Production Line, and that year the trio led the Red Wings to the first of seven consecutive first-place finishes. Lindsay led the NHL in scoring in 1949–50 and played on his first Stanley Cup winner that year. Detroit won the Cup again in 1952. Lindsay succeeded Abel as team captain in 1952–53 and led the Red Wings to Stanley Cup victories in 1954 and 1955.

On July 23, 1957, Lindsay was traded to the Chicago Black Hawks as punishment for his attempts to form a strong players union. Chicago had missed the playoffs four years in a row and in 10 of the last 11 seasons, but Lindsay helped to revitalize the franchise. He retired after the 1959–60 campaign, yet made a remarkable comeback with Detroit in 1964–65 and helped the Red Wings finish in first place. He retired for good after that season and was elected to the Hockey Hall of Fame in 1966. Lindsay later served as Red Wings general manager from 1976–77 to 1979–80, and also coached the team for the final nine games of the 1979–80 season and the first 20 games of 1980–81.

ED LITZENBERGER is the only player in the history of the NHL to win the Calder Trophy after being traded during his rookie season. Litzenberger came up through the Montreal Canadiens system and earned a regular spot with the team in 1954–55. However, he was dealt to Chicago midway through the season in an attempt to prop up the Black Hawks (who had been in danger of folding for several years). He wound up being named the top rookie after scoring 23 goals. Because of the trade, he also set what was then an NHL record for games played with 73 in a 70-game schedule.

Litzenberger slumped during his second full season but had 32 goals and 64 points to lead the Black Hawks and rank fifth in the NHL in scoring in 1956–57. Though Chicago missed the playoffs (for the tenth time in 11 years), Litzenberger was named to the Second All-Star Team at center that season. He went on to lead the Black Hawks, and rank among the league leaders, in scoring again each of the next two years. Litzenberger established career highs with 33 goals, 44 assists and 77 points in 1958–59 and led the team into the playoffs. He was also captain of the Black Hawks that year.

In January of 1960, Litzenberger was badly injured in a car accident that claimed the life of his wife. He overcame the tragedy to return to the Black Hawks late in the season and in 1960–61 he helped Chicago win its first Stanley Cup title in 23 years. The Black Hawks then traded him to the Detroit Red Wings, where he played only briefly before he was allowed to go to the Toronto Maple Leafs on waivers. With the Maple Leafs, Litzenberger won the Stanley Cup again in 1962 and 1963. He was also a member of Toronto's Stanley Cup-winning team in 1963–64, though he spent most of that season

with Rochester of the American Hockey League. Litzenberger spent the next two years with Toronto farm teams in Rochester and Victoria before retiring.

MIKE LIUT was a graduate of Bowling Green University who spent two seasons with the Cincinnati Stingers of the World Hockey Association before joining the St. Louis Blues for the 1979–80 season. The following year, he led the Blues to the second-best record in the league with a franchise-high 107 points and was runner-up to Wayne Gretzky in voting for the Hart Trophy. Liut was named to the First All-Star Team that year and beat Gretzky for the Lester B. Pearson Trophy, the MVP award voted on by the players.

Liut led all NHL goaltenders in games played in 1981–82 and 1982–83. He led the league in shutouts with four as a member of the Hartford Whalers in 1986–87 and posted the best goals-against average at 2.53 in 1989–90. He had been traded from Hartford to the Washington Capitals on March 6, 1990 and again led the league that season with four shutouts. Liut ended his career with the Capitals in 1991–92.

THOMAS LOCKHART enjoyed a long and illustrious association with amateur hockey in the United States, beginning in 1932 when he took over the organization and promotion of the sport at Madison Square Garden in New York. Previously, he had an active career as a boxer, cyclist and track star.

In 1933, Lockhart organized the Eastern Amateur Hockey League and became its president in 1935. Two years later, he formed the Amateur Hockey Association of the United States and served as its first president. AHAUS became responsible for administering to amateur hockey on a nationwide basis. Between 1932 and 1952, Lockhart also supervised the New York Metropolitan Amateur League while occasionally serving as coach and/or general manager of the New York Rovers of the EAHL. He was also business manager of the New York Rangers, a member of the United States Olympic Ice Hockey Committee and a delegate to the International Ice Hockey Federation. In addition, he was actively involved with the United States Amateur Athletic Union as vice president of its boxing committee.

Lockhart was elected to the Hockey Hall of Fame in the builder's category in 1965. In 1973, he was among the first group honored by induction into the United States Hockey Hall of Fame.

PAUL LOICQ began skating as a 16-year-old in 1906 and was selected to the national hockey team in his native Belgium three years later. He represented his country at the 1920 World Championships held in conjunction with the Olympic Games in Antwerp. Off the ice, he graduated from university as a lawyer and served with distinction in the Belgian army during World War I.

Loicq was elected president of the International Ice Hockey Federation in 1927 and held the office for 20 years. During that time, hockey's popularity increased rapidly across Europe, with both World and Olympic championships doing much to increase the game's international status. In 1961, Loicq was inducted into the Hockey Hall of Fame as a builder.

SAM LoPRESTI On March 4, 1941, the Boston Bruins fired a record 83 shots on goal in a game against the Chicago Black Hawks. Sam LoPresti made 80 saves but was still the loser in a 3–2 defeat. LoPresti had been summoned from Kansas City of the American Hockey Association earlier in the season to replace Paul Goodman in the Black Hawks goal.

After spending the 1941–42 season in Chicago, LoPresti joined the American army. He returned from World War II and played amateur hockey in his native Minnesota until 1951. In 1973, he became a charter member of the United States Hockey Hall of Fame. Son Pete LoPresti played in the NHL with the Minnesota North Stars and Edmonton Oilers between 1974–75 and 1980–81.

KEVIN LOWE was the first player ever selected by the Edmonton Oilers in the NHL Entry Draft when he was chosen 21st overall in 1979–80. He has gone on to play more games for the Oilers than any player in franchise history. Lowe was a high-scoring defenseman in the Quebec Junior Hockey League but became a defensive specialist on the offensive-minded Oilers.

Lowe was a member of Edmonton's five Stanley Cup-winning teams and was named the fifth captain in Oilers history in 1990–91. Like so many of his prominent teammates, Lowe wound up being traded by the Oilers when he was sent to the New York Rangers on December 11, 1992. Lowe picked up his sixth Stanley Cup ring when the Rangers ended their 54-year championship jinx in 1994.

After four seasons with the Rangers, Lowe returned to Edmonton when he signed as a free agent on September 28, 1997. He was credited with steadying a young Oilers defense as the team returned to the playoffs that season for the first time since 1992.

HARRY LUMLEY was signed as a 16-year-old by the Detroit Red Wings and made his NHL debut just two years later during the 1943–44 season. He played two games for Detroit that year and one period in goal as an injury replacement for the New York Rangers. The following year, he was once again recalled from Indianapolis and became the Red Wings' regular goaltender.

Known as "Apple Cheeks" for his ruddy complexion, Lumley spent five full seasons in Detroit. He helped the Red Wings win the Stanley Cup in 1950, but on July 13, 1950, he was sent to the Chicago Black Hawks to make room for Terry Sawchuk. His numbers suffered during two years with a weak Chicago team, but on September 11, 1952, Lumley was dealt to the Toronto Maple Leafs, where he enjoyed the best years of his career.

In his first season with the Maple Leafs, Lumley tied for the NHL lead with 10 shutouts. In 1953–54, he led the league with 13 shutouts, posted a 1.85 goals-against average, won the Vezina Trophy and was named to the First All-Star Team. His 13 shutouts were a modern NHL record until surpassed by Tony Esposito's 15 in 1969–70. Lumley had a 1.94 average for Toronto in 1954–55 and was selected as a First Team All-Star for the second year in a row.

After the 1955–56 season, Lumley was dropped from the Maple Leafs roster in favor of Ed Chadwick, but he returned to the NHL with the Boston Bruins during the 1957–58 campaign. He played three years in Boston and ended his hockey career after another minor-league campaign in 1960–61. Lumley retired to become a businessman in his hometown of Owen Sound, Ontario and remained active in sports through standardbred horse racing. He was elected to the Hockey Hall of Fame in 1980.

AL MacINNIS played on a Memorial Cup champion with the Kitchener Rangers in 1981 and then was selected 15th overall by the Calgary Flames in the 1981 Entry Draft. He played briefly in Calgary the next two seasons but spent most of his time in Kitchener, where he was named the top defenseman in the Ontario Hockey Association in 1981–82 and a first team all-star in both 1981–82 and 1982–83.

MacInnis spent his first full season in the NHL in 1984–85. His booming slapshot helped him become one of the top defensemen in the NHL. In 1985–86, he led the league with 15 assists in the playoffs as Calgary reached the Stanley Cup finals. In 1986–87, he was named to the Second All-Star Team. In 1988–89, MacInnis led all playoff performers with 24 assists and 31 points and won the Conn Smythe Trophy as the Flames won the Stanley Cup for the first time in franchise history.

MacInnis was named to the First All-Star Team in 1989–90 and again in 1990–91 when he became just the fourth defenseman in NHL history (Bobby Orr, Denis Potvin, Paul Coffey) to top 100 points in a season. He was a Second Team All-Star in 1993–94, but on July 4, 1994, MacInnis was traded to the St. Louis Blues for Phil Housley. He left Calgary as the Flames' all-time leader with 609 assists and 822 points.

In 1996, MacInnis was a member of Team Canada at the World Cup of Hockey and in 1998 he played for the Olympic team at Nagano. MacInnis had previously represented his country at the World Championships in 1990 and at the Canada Cup in 1991.

MICKEY MacKAY Duncan McMillan "Mickey" MacKay is the all-time leading scorer in the history of the Pacific Coast Hockey Association with 198 goals and 290 points. He played on six PCHA championship teams in Vancouver, helping the Millionaires to win the Stanley Cup in 1915.

"The Wee Scot," as MacKay often was called, played hockey with the Chesley Colts in his hometown of Chesley, Ontario before moving up to senior hockey in Edmonton and Grand Forks, British Columbia. He signed a professional contract with the Vancouver Millionaires in 1914–15, promptly leading the league with 33 goals. His 44 points that season were second in the PCHA behind teammate Cyclone Taylor's 45 as Vancouver won the league title and the Stanley Cup. MacKay was the all-star center in the PCHA that season. Though he was a great goal scorer, MacKay was known as an unselfish player throughout his career and he led the PCHA in assists in 1921–22.

A clean and gentlemanly player, MacKay had the misfortune of suffering a fractured jaw in the 1919 PCHA playoffs when he was cross-checked by Cully Wilson. Wilson was suspended from the league, while MacKay missed the entire 1919–20 season, playing amateur hockey in Calgary instead. He returned to Vancouver the following year to continue his high-scoring ways, leading the league with 27 goals in 1924–25 after Vancouver had joined the Western Canada Hockey League.

When pro hockey collapsed in the west following the 1925–26 campaign, MacKay joined the Chicago Black Hawks for their inaugural NHL season of 1926–27. He later played for the Pittsburgh Pirates and Boston Bruins, winning another Stanley Cup title with Boston in 1929 before retiring after the 1929–30 season. He was elected to the Hockey Hall of Fame in 1952.

RICK MacLEISH was the first player from an NHL expansion team to score 50 goals, reaching the milestone with the Philadelphia Flyers in 1972–73. He also had 50 assists that season, his first full year in the NHL. It was MacLeish's goal in game six of the 1974 finals that gave the Flyers a 1–0 win over Boston and made them the first expansion team to win the Stanley Cup. He was the NHL's leading scorer in the playoffs that year, and duplicated this feat when the Flyers won the Stanley Cup again in 1975.

FRANK MAHOVLICH was hailed as a superstar while playing junior hockey and he went on to record 533 goals and 570 assists during his NHL career.

He was also named to the all-star team on nine occasions (three First Team selections), yet "the Big M" was constantly criticized for not living up to expectations.

Mahovlich played his junior hockey at St. Michael's College and won the Red Tilson Memorial Trophy as the most valuable player in the Ontario Hockey Association in 1956–57. The following year, he joined the Toronto Maple Leafs and beat out Bobby Hull to win the Calder Trophy as rookie of the year. In 1960–61, Mahovlich established himself as one of the greatest goal scorers in hockey. He battled Bernie Geoffrion that season in a race to join Maurice Richard as the only 50-goal scorers to that point in NHL history. Mahovlich eventually fell two goals short, but his total of 48 was a Maple Leafs record until Rick Vaive scored 54 goals in 1981–82. Mahovlich led the Maple Leafs in goal-scoring every season from 1960–61 to 1965–66 and also led the team in points every year during that span except 1963–64.

He was the main offensive weapon on Toronto teams that won the Stanley Cup in 1962, 1963, 1964 and 1967, yet Mahovlich did not get along with coach and general manager Punch Imlach, who traded him to the Detroit Red Wings on March 3, 1968.

In Detroit, Mahovlich joined a roster that featured his brother Peter and was teamed on a line with Gordie Howe and Alex Delvecchio. He established a career high with 49 goals in 1968–69 and helped the 41-year-old Howe become just the third player in NHL history (Phil Esposito and Bobby Hull) to record 100 points in a season. Mahovlich was traded to the Canadiens on January 13, 1971 (where he rejoined his brother), and the moody superstar went on to enjoy his happiest times in Montreal. He helped the Canadiens win the Stanley Cup in 1971 and was a member of Team Canada in the 1972 Summit Series. During the 1972–73 season, Mahovlich became the eighth player in NHL history to record 1,000 points (February 1, 1973) and the fifth player to score 500 goals (March 21, 1973). He also played for his sixth Stanley Cup winner that season.

In 1974–75, Mahovlich returned to Toronto as a member of the Toros in the World Hockey Association. He spent two years with the Toros and two more with the Birmingham Bulls before retiring at the end of 1977–78. Mahovlich was elected to the Hockey Hall of Fame in 1981. In 1998 he was appointed to the Canadian Senate by Prime Minister Jean Chretien.

PETER MAHOVLICH set a Montreal Canadiens record with 82 assists in 1974–75 and with 35 goals that season he established a club record for points by a center with 117. The younger brother of Frank Mahovlich was selected second overall by the Detroit Red Wings in the 1963 Amateur Draft but didn't blossom as a player until after his trade to Montreal on June 6, 1969.

Mahovlich became a regular in Montreal in 1970–71, the year brother Frank joined the team, and was among the playoff leaders with 10 goals as the Canadiens won the Stanley Cup that spring. He was a member of Team Canada in the Summit Series with the Soviet Union in September of 1972 and was on a Stanley Cup winner again with Montreal in 1972–73. Mahovlich later helped the Canadiens win the Stanley Cup four years in a row from 1976 to 1979. Mahovlich centered the Canadiens' top line with wingers Guy Lafleur and Steve Shutt and finished in the top 10 in scoring in 1974–75 and 1975–76.

The Canadiens traded Mahovlich to the Pittsburgh Penguins in a deal for Pierre Larouche on November 29, 1977. He was dealt back to Detroit in 1979 and spent two seasons with the Red Wings before ending his career with Toledo of the International Hockey League in 1985–86.

KEN MALLEN was a great stickhandler and fast skater who was awarded a trophy in 1913 for beating future Hall of Famers Cyclone Taylor, Moose Johnson and Si Griffis in a series of speed races. He was a talented player who was given few opportunities in the east before he joined the Pacific Coast Hockey Association.

Mallen began his career in the Federal Amateur Hockey League, playing with Cornwall and the Montreal Wanderers in the league's first season of 1903–04. He spent the next three years with Calumet of the International (Pro) Hockey League (hockey's first professional circuit) before returning to the FAHL with Morrisburg in 1906–07. Mallen then bounced around for two years before joining the Ottawa Senators in 1909–10, where he saw little action. After a season as rover with the Quebec Bulldogs behind the forward line of Eddie Oatman, Jack McDonald and future Hall of Famer Joe Malone, Mallen joined the New Westminster Royals in 1911–12 and helped the team win the PCHA title in the league's first season.

After three years, the Royals moved to Portland, Oregon for the 1914–15 season but Mallen joined the Vancouver Millionaires instead. Playing right wing on a line with future Hall of Famers Frank Nighbor and Mickey MacKay, he helped Vancouver to win the league title and become the first PCHA team to win the Stanley Cup. Mallen was with the Victoria Aristocrats in 1915–16 and joined the team for its move south in 1916–17 when they became the Spokane Canaries. It would be his final season.

JOE MALONE was one of the most prolific players in hockey history and second only to Newsy Lalonde among the great goal scorers of his day. He led the NHL in scoring in its first season of 1917–18 with the astounding total of 44 goals in just 20 games played, and his seven goals on January 31, 1920, remain an NHL single-game record. Known as "Phantom Joe," he was a slick stickhandler, deceptive skater and a sportsmanlike player in an era noted for its rough play.

Malone made his professional debut with the Quebec Bulldogs in 1908–09, but he spent the next season with Waterloo of the Ontario Professional Hockey League after Quebec was excluded from the National Hockey Association. When the Bulldogs entered the NHA in 1910–11, Malone returned to Quebec, though he had yet to show much scoring promise. The breakthrough came the following season when he led the team with 21 goals as the Bulldogs won the NHA title and the Stanley Cup. In 1912–13, he led the NHA with 43 goals and scored nine in one game on March 8, 1913 during a Stanley Cup challenge series against Sydney, Nova Scotia. Malone earned a second NHA scoring title in 1916–17 when he tied Frank Nighbor for the league lead with 41 goals.

When the NHL was formed in 1917–18, Quebec chose not to operate its team and Malone joined the Montreal Canadiens. When the Bulldogs did enter the NHL in 1919–20, Malone returned to Quebec and won a second NHL scoring title with 39 goals in 24 games, even though his team was 4–20–0. He moved with the franchise to Hamilton for the next two years, but he returned to Montreal as a substitute player in 1922–23 and 1923–24 before retiring. In 1950, Joe Malone was elected to the Hockey Hall of Fame.

CESARE MANIAGO Between 1960–61 and 1966–67, Cesare Maniago played minor-league hockey in eight cities across North America. In brief NHL trials during this time period, he served as a backup to future Hall of Famers Johnny Bower in Toronto, Jacques Plante in Montreal, and Ed Giacomin in New York. Maniago played just 55 games in the NHL during that stretch, but allowed Bernie Geoffrion's record-tying 50th goal on March 16, 1961 and Bobby Hull's record-breaking 51st on March 12, 1966.

Maniago finally earned steady NHL employment after the Minnesota North Stars selected him in the 1967 Expansion Draft. He spent the next nine years with the club, sharing the net with Gump Worsley, another future Hall of Famer, in five of those seasons. Maniago concluded his career in 1978 after two seasons with the Vancouver Canucks.

SYLVIO MANTHA learned to play hockey in his hometown of Montreal, working his way up through the amateur ranks in the city prior to signing with the Canadiens for the 1923–24 season. Howie Morenz was also new to the team that year, and the two helped Montreal to win the Stanley Cup. Mantha played on five first-place teams during his 12 years with the Canadiens and three Stanley Cup champions.

Mantha had played forward as an amateur but was converted to defense during his first NHL season. He began to see more ice time with the Canadiens after Sprague Cleghorn was traded in 1925, and gained valuable experience in a defense pairing with Herb Gardiner. By the time the Canadiens won the Stanley Cup again in 1930, Mantha was among the best defensive defenseman in the game. He earned a Second Team All-Star selection in 1930–31 after Montreal won the Stanley Cup again. Another berth on the Second Team came the following year.

Mantha became a player-coach with the Canadiens in 1935–36, but the team had a poor finish that year and he moved on to Boston for a final season in 1936–37. For the next two years, he served as a linesman in the NHL and a referee in the American Hockey League. Mantha later coached amateur teams in Montreal for many years. He was elected to the Hockey Hall of Fame in 1960.

MUSH MARCH Though he stood just 5'5" and weighed only 154 pounds, Harold "Mush" March played 17 years with the Chicago Black Hawks between 1928–29 and 1944–45. Only Dit Clapper (who played 20 years with the Boston Bruins) spent more time in the NHL with one team during this era.

March played junior hockey in Regina, Saskatchewan before he joined the Black Hawks. He helped Chicago reach the Stanley Cup finals in his third season of 1930–31 and became a playoff hero three years later after being teamed on a line with Paul Thompson and Doc Romnes. March scored the series-winning goal to eliminate the Montreal Canadiens in the first round of the 1934 playoffs, then scored the game's only goal in a 1–0 overtime win over the Detroit Red Wings that gave the Black Hawks their first Stanley Cup championship. March was still starring on the club's top line with Thompson and Romnes when Chicago won the Stanley Cup again in 1938.

Despite the Stanley Cup victory, there were changes in Chicago in 1938–39 but even with the shakeup, March remained on the club's top line—only now he was playing with Johnny Gottselig and Cully Dahlstrom. Two years later, March was playing right wing alongside brothers Max and Doug Bentley.

Not until Bill Mosienko joined the team in 1941–42 was March's job as the Chicago's top right winger in jeopardy. When Mosienko became a regular in 1943–44, March was moved to the Black Hawks' second line. He responded with a career-high 37 points in his 16th season but suffered a serious knee injury in the playoffs which forced his retirement the following year.

JOHN MARIUCCI played hockey in high school in his native Eveleth, Minnesota before going on to star in both hockey and football at the University

of Minnesota. He was an all-American on the Golden Gophers hockey team that went undefeated in 1939–40. Mariucci turned pro the following season, playing first with Providence of the American Hockey League before being called up to the Chicago Black Hawks.

Mariucci was with the Black Hawks in 1940–41 and 1941–42 before his career was interrupted by military service. He returned to Chicago for 1945–46, and was named captain, a position he held for a year. He was captain of the Black Hawks again in his final NHL season of 1947–48. After four seasons of minor-league hockey, Mariucci returned to his alma mater as the hockey coach at the University of Minnesota in 1952–53.

As "the Godfather of Hockey in Minnesota," Mariucci encouraged the game at the high school level and recruited American players for his university team (which previously had been stocked mainly with Canadians). In his second season with the Gophers, he led the team to the NCAA finals. He remained coach at Minnesota until 1966–67, producing one dozen all-Americans and leading the United States Olympic hockey team to a silver medal in 1956.

After leaving the University of Minnesota, Mariucci returned to the NHL as an assistant general manager with the Minnesota North Stars from 1967 until 1974. He spent the next season as a scout with the North Stars before taking over the U.S. national team, which he coached from 1975–76 to 1977–78. He later returned to the North Stars as assistant g.m. from 1982 until his death on March 23, 1987.

Mariucci had been a firm believer that Americans could be as successful in hockey as Canadians, and time has proven him correct. He was a charter member of the United States Hockey Hall of Fame in 1973, won the Lester Patrick Trophy for his contributions to hockey in the United States in 1977 and was elected to the Hockey Hall of Fame as a builder in 1985.

JACK MARKS began his career in 1904–05 with Brockville of the Federal Amateur Hockey League and spent a second season with the club before showing up as a "ringer" brought in to bolster the New Glasgow, Nova Scotia Stanley Cup challenge team of 1906. Despite Marks' two goals in game one, the Montreal Wanderers scored an easy 10–3 victory and retained the Stanley Cup with a 7–2 win in game two.

Marks next surfaced in 1907–08 as a member of the Brantford franchise in the inaugural season of the Ontario Professional Hockey League, Canada's first outright professional circuit. When Toronto won the league championship, Marks got another chance at the Stanley Cup when he was added to that club. Again, he lost to the Montreal Wanderers.

After three seasons with Brantford, Marks joined the Quebec Bulldogs of the National Hockey Association in 1911–12. His first season there, Marks finally won the Stanley Cup, then made it two in a row as the Bulldogs won again in 1913. He was at his best in Quebec when playing right wing on a line with future Hall of Famers Joe Malone and Tommy Smith, providing passes for the two goal-scoring stars as well as handling most of the backchecking.

Quebec was a charter member of the NHL in 1917–18, but the Bulldogs did not operate a team that season and Marks joined the Montreal Wanderers. When that team withdrew after a fire destroyed its home arena, Marks moved on to Toronto where he saw limited action with that season's eventual Stanley Cup champion. When the Bulldogs resumed play in the 1919–20 season, Marks returned to Quebec and played the final game of his career there.

JACK MARSHALL Although he was a star athlete in football, soccer, lacrosse and baseball, it was in hockey that Jack Marshall earned his greatest fame. He played for five Stanley Cup champions over his lengthy career, beginning with the Winnipeg Victorias in 1901.

Marshall was only a part-time player with the Vics before joining the Montreal Amateur Athletic Association the following year. He helped them to win the Stanley Cup in 1902 by scoring the deciding goal in a 2–1 victory over his former Winnipeg team. It was in this game that the Montreal squad earned the nickname "the Little Men of Iron" for the tenacious way they hung on for victory. Marshall spent one more year with the AAA before becoming one of several players lured away when the Montreal Wanderers were formed in 1903–04. The player raid forced Wanderers president James Strachan to establish a new league in order to avoid reprisals. Marshall led the Federal Amateur Hockey League in scoring the next two years, tying the great Frank McGee with 17 goals in just eight games in 1904–05. He helped the Wanderers win the Stanley Cup in 1907.

Marshall also played with the Montreal Montagnards and Montreal Shamrocks, but he was back with the Wanderers when they joined the National Hockey Association in 1909–10. Now a defenseman (when the position was still known as point and cover point), he helped the team win the first National Hockey Association title and another Stanley Cup championship that season. Marshall remained with the Wanderers until 1912 when he joined the Toronto Blueshirts as a player-manager for that team's inaugural season of 1912–13. The following year, he led Toronto to a Stanley Cup championship, the fifth and final title of his career. Marshall returned to the Wanderers in 1915–16, playing two seasons before retiring. In 1965, he was elected to the Hockey Hall of Fame.

RICK MARTIN was selected fifth overall by the Buffalo Sabres in the 1971 Amateur Draft and made an immediate impression in the NHL by setting a rookie record with 44 goals in 1971–72. He finished runner-up to Ken Dryden in voting for the Calder Trophy that year.

Martin was the trigger man on the Sabres' famed French Connection line with Gilbert Perreault and Rene Robert. He had 52 goals in 1973–74 and 1974–75 and cracked the top 10 in NHL scoring both years. He also helped Buffalo reach the Stanley Cup finals in 1975 in just the franchise's fifth year of existence. He had 49 goals in 1975–76, but injuries during the next two seasons saw his production decline. Martin was traded to Los Angeles on March 10, 1981, but retired after playing just three games with the Kings the following season.

CAL MARVIN returned to his northern Minnesota hometown of Warroad after serving in the Marine Corps during World War II and helped establish a hockey program at the University of North Dakota in 1946. That same year, he also helped found the Warroad Lakers, a group that went on to become the most successful senior amateur hockey team in the United States. Marvin acted as both a player and a coach in the team's early years but was serving exclusively as coach by the mid-1950s.

Marvin took a year off from the Lakers in 1957–58 to coach the U.S. national team. He guided the squad to a fifth-place finish at the World Championships in Oslo, Norway and then the team became the first American athletic club to play in the Soviet Union. Marvin returned to Warroad the following year, but the international ties continued, as the Lakers would often face the U.S. national team in competition. Many of Marvin's players from Warroad have represented the United States at the Olympics, most notably brothers Bill and Roger Christian on the gold medal-winning team of 1960 and Bill's son, Dave, who played for the "Miracle on Ice" team in 1980. Marvin was also manager of the U.S. national team in 1965.

Marvin operated the Warroad Lakers through the 1996–97 season, but the continuing problem of trying to find suitable leagues to play in finally forced him to fold the club after that season. By then, the team's many achievements included its first title (United States National intermediate championship) in 1955; becoming the first U.S. amateur team to win a Canadian intermediate title in 1963; and winning the Allan Cup (the Stanley Cup of senior amateur hockey) three years in a row from 1993–94 until 1995–96. The Lakers were Allan Cup finalists in their last season of 1996–97.

Cal Marvin was elected to the United States Hockey Hall of Fame as an administrator in 1982. He is also a member of the Manitoba Sports Hall of Fame, the University of North Dakota Athletic Hall of Fame and the Warroad High School Athletic Hall of Fame.

CHARLES MASSON Though it is long forgotten today, Charles Masson was involved in one of the darkest incidents in hockey's history. The Ottawa Vics player was charged with manslaughter in connection with the death of Owen "Bud" McCourt, who died on March 7, 1907 as a result of injuries suffered during a game the night before.

In a Federal Amateur Hockey League game between Ottawa and Cornwall, Masson struck McCourt in the head with his hockey stick during a brawl. The Cornwall player left the ice cut and bleeding and was taken to the hospital after becoming unconscious. He died the next morning. A coroner's inquest deemed Masson responsible. The charge was to be murder, but was reduced to manslaughter.

Masson appeared before a judge and jury in Cornwall on April 10, 1907. Many witnesses were called, including teammates of both McCourt and Masson and referee Emmett Smith. Testimony indicated that McCourt had been hit by the stick of another Ottawa player before Masson's attack. Unable to determine which had been the fatal blow, the judge acquitted Masson on April 12. Cornwall had resigned from the Federal Amateur Hockey League following McCourt's death and this version of the league never operated again.

JOHN MATCHEFTS learned to skate at the age of five wearing a pair of figure skates that belonged to his older sister. By the age of 16 (in 1948), he was a high school star in Eveleth, Minnesota and was invited to play for the U.S. Olympic hockey team. High school league rules prevented his playing that year, but he did represent the U.S. at the World Championships in 1955 and won a silver medal with the American Olympic team in 1956.

Matchefts played on state championship teams at Eveleth High School in 1947, 1948 and 1949 while also starring in football and baseball. He was the first player named to the Minnesota all-State high school hockey team three times, then he helped the University of Michigan win the NCAA hockey tournament in 1951, 1952 and 1953. He was named to the all-tournament team and the all-American squad in 1951 and 1953 and was also captain of the Wolverines and MVP in the NCAA in 1953. Known as "the Fly" in his days at Michigan because of his speed, agility and maneuverability, Matchefts averaged two points per game, with 57 goals and 74 assists in his college career.

After his playing days, Matchefts spent 10 years as a high school coach in Eveleth and Thief River Falls, where he indoctrinated his young players in the passing patterns and team play he had witnessed among European teams and

guided teams from both schools to Minnesota state tournaments. Matchefts later coached at Colorado College from 1966 to 1971 and at the Air Force Academy from 1972 until 1986. He was coach of the year in the Western Collegiate Hockey Association in 1968. Matchefts has been a member of the United States Hockey Hall of Fame since 1991.

FRANK MATHERS was a member of the Toronto Maple Leafs for parts of three seasons between 1948–49 and 1951–52, but spent most of his time in the organization with the Maple Leafs' American Hockey League farm club in Pittsburgh, where he became one of the league's top defensemen. Mathers played on a Calder Cup winner as AHL champion in Pittsburgh in 1952 and 1955 and set a league record in 1955–56 when he was named to the all-star team for the fifth consecutive season.

Mathers joined the Hershey Bears in 1956–57 and became a player-coach the following season, leading the team to back-to-back Calder Cup titles in 1958 and 1959. His team lost in the finals in 1962 and the following season Mathers retired as a player to concentrate solely on coaching. His team reached the finals again in 1963 and 1965 before winning another championship in 1969. From 1973–74 until 1977–78, Mathers served as Hershey's general manager, adding the role of club president in 1978–79. The Bears won the Calder Cup again in 1974, 1980 and 1988 before he retired after the 1990–91 campaign.

For more than 40 years as a player, coach and executive, Frank Mathers helped shape and strengthen the American Hockey League. He earned the Lester Patrick Trophy for his contribution to hockey in the United States in 1987 and was inducted into the Hockey Hall of Fame as a builder in 1992.

STEAMER MAXWELL Fred Maxwell earned the nickname "Steamer" because of his tremendous speed as a skater. He was a rover during hockey's seven-man era, starring with the Winnipeg Monarchs and helping the team to win the Allan Cup in 1914–15. He played one more season with the club before becoming coach for two years.

Maxwell took over as coach of the Winnipeg Falcons, winning the Allan Cup with them in 1920, but he was unable to accompany the team to Antwerp, Belgium when it won the gold medal for Canada at the first Olympic hockey tournament. He remained with the Falcons until 1924–25. Maxwell then coached the Winnipeg Rangers to the Manitoba championship in 1925–26 before moving on to the Winnipeg Maroons of the American Hockey Association. He stayed with that professional club until the league terminated in 1927–28.

Returning to amateur hockey, Maxwell coached the Elmwood Millionaires to both junior and senior Manitoba championships in 1929–30. In 1935, he coached the Winnipeg Monarchs to victory in the World Championships at Davos, Switzerland. In addition to coaching, Maxwell was also a referee in both the pro and amateur ranks between 1910 and 1940. He was inducted into the Hockey Hall of Fame in 1962.

JOHN MAYASICH was considered one of the best amateur hockey players in the United States when he was added to a lineup of mostly college kids on the American Olympic hockey team in 1960. His muscle and hustle on the defense helped the United States pull off a stunning gold medal victory.

Mayasich had been a young star among stars in his native Eveleth, Minnesota on the Eveleth High School team that won 79 games in a row and four consecutive state championships between 1947–48 and 1950–51. He continued to stand out at the University of Minnesota and was all-American in 1952–53, 1953–54 and 1954–55. Mayasich was named to the NCAA all-tournament team in 1954 after leading the Gophers to the finals (where they were defeated by an exceptional team from Rensselaer Polytechnic Institute). He also led the Western Collegiate Hockey Association in scoring with 78 points in 1953–54 and 80 points the following year.

Mayasich began his international career with the United States Olympic hockey team in 1956 and earned a silver medal that year. Besides the transcendent 1960 Olympics, he represented America at the World Championships in 1958, 1961, 1962, 1966 and 1969. He had many offers to play professionally but stayed with the amateur Green Bay Bobcats after his collegiate career. Mayasich was elected to the United States Hockey Hall of Fame in 1976.

JACK McCARTAN had been an all-American twice at the University of Minnesota and played for the United States at the World Championships in 1959. Still, he was a late addition to the U.S. Olympic hockey team in 1960. Then it was his brilliant goaltending (like Jim Craig's at Lake Placid 20 years later) that was largely responsible for the surprising gold medal the U.S. team earned at Squaw Valley.

After the Olympics, McCartan appeared in four games with the New York Rangers, then spent most of the 1960–61 season with Kitchener-Waterloo in the Eastern Professional Hockey League, posting an impressive 2.79 goals-against average. McCartan did play eight games for the Rangers that season, but that was it for the NHL in a professional career that lasted until 1974–75.

McCartan led the EPHL with five shutouts for Kitchener-Waterloo in 1961–62, then spent most of the next nine years playing with San Francisco

and San Diego in the Western Hockey League. When the World Hockey Association was formed in 1972, he returned to his native Minnesota as a member of the Fighting Saints. McCartan saw action in 38 games during the 1972–73 season, but played just two games for Minnesota in each of the next two years before finally retiring. He was inducted into the United States Hockey Hall of Fame in 1983.

OWEN McCOURT Owen "Bud" McCourt was the first player in hockey history to die as the result of injuries suffered in a game. He passed away on March 7, 1907, the morning after he was struck on the head with a stick in a brawl during a Federal Amateur Hockey League game between Cornwall and the Ottawa Vics. Charles Masson was charged with manslaughter in McCourt's death, but was later acquitted.

Ironically, the fatal injury occurred in a game that need not have been played. Because McCourt had taken part in two games for the Montreal Shamrocks of the rival Eastern Canada Amateur Hockey Association earlier in the year, Ottawa protested its loss to Cornwall on February 15, 1907 and the game was ordered replayed on March 6. Clearly, McCourt's eligibility had been established, as he had already played three games before the protest, including one against the same Ottawa team. No subsequent protest was made when he took part in the replay of the game, which resulted in the tragedy.

Prior to his death, McCourt had been enjoying his most successful season. He had scored seven goals in one game and was tied for the league lead with 16 goals in eight games. After his death, Cornwall withdrew from the Federal Amateur Hockey League and this version of the league never operated again.

JACK McDONALD was a "ringer" from Quebec added to the team from New Glasgow, Nova Scotia that challenged the Montreal Wanderers for the Stanley Cup in December of 1906. Though he scored in both games, the Wanderers easily retained their trophy with 10–3 and 7–2 victories.

McDonald returned to Quebec for the 1906–07 season and spent the next three years with the team. When the club was abandoned after the National Hockey Association absorbed the Ottawa Senators and Montreal Shamrocks from the Canadian Hockey Association in 1909–10, McDonald, Joe Malone, and other Quebec players joined Waterloo of the Ontario Professional Hockey League. When Quebec entered the NHA in 1910–11, the players returned. A year later, they helped the Bulldogs win the NHA championship and the Stanley Cup. McDonald scored four goals in a 9–3 victory over Moncton in game one of a Stanley Cup challenge series and five goals in an 8–0 romp in game two.

After the Stanley Cup victory in 1912, every Quebec player was offered a contract by the rival Pacific Coast Hockey Association for the 1912–13 season. McDonald signed with the Vancouver Millionaires but returned to the NHA with the Toronto Ontarios the following year. The Ontarios won just four of 20 games, but McDonald had a career-high 26 goals to finish fourth in league scoring. He was back in Quebec for the 1914–15 season.

McDonald remained with the Bulldogs until the team entered the NHL in 1917–18. When Quebec chose not to operate a franchise that first season, he joined the Montreal Wanderers. His new team withdrew from the NHL after a fire destroyed its home arena and McDonald moved on to the Montreal Canadiens. He was back with the Bulldogs for the 1919–20 season and was later with the Canadiens and Toronto St. Pats before retiring after the 1921–22 campaign.

LANNY McDONALD was a high-scoring junior star with the Medicine Hat Tigers who was selected fourth overall by Toronto in the 1973 Amateur Draft. He jumped directly to the Maple Leafs roster in 1973–74 and soon developed into a fan favorite in Toronto. His bushy red mustache made him one of the most recognizable faces in the NHL, and his skill and sportsmanship made him one of the most popular players in the game over his 16-year career.

McDonald displayed little of his junior scoring touch during his first two years with Toronto, but in 1975–76 he collected 37 goals and 56 assists. In 1976–77, he had 44 goals and 90 points as both he and linemate Darryl Sittler cracked the top 10 NHL scorers. McDonald had 47 goals to rank among the scoring leaders again in 1977–78, and his overtime goal in the seventh game of the 1978 quarterfinals to beat the New York Islanders remains one of the Maple Leafs' greatest moments since their last Stanley Cup victory in 1967.

During his seventh season in Toronto, McDonald was dealt to the Colorado Rockies on December 29, 1979. He was named captain in Colorado in 1980–81 and retained the honor until his trade to the Calgary Flames during the 1981–82 season. In his first full year in Calgary (1982–83), McDonald established a career high with 66 goals (which, to date, remains a Flames record). He was co-captain in Calgary from 1982–83 until he retired after the 1988–89 campaign. That year, McDonald capped his career in style, scoring his 500th goal, collecting his 1,000th point and scoring the insurance goal in a 4–2 victory over the Montreal Canadiens that brought the Flames their first Stanley Cup championship. Since his retirement, McDonald has worked in the Flames front office.

Individual honors during McDonald's career included Second All-Star Team honors at right wing in 1976–77 and 1982–83. He won the Masterton Trophy in 1982–83 and the King Clancy Trophy in 1987–88 and was selected

as the NHL man of the year in 1988–89. His number 9 was the first number to be retired by the Flames, and in 1992 he became the first Calgary player ever inducted into the Hockey Hall of Fame. McDonald is involved with many children's charities, including the Special Olympics.

FRANK McGEE remains a legendary name in hockey more than 90 years after he last played the game and over 80 years since he was killed in action while serving in France during World War I. The scoring star with the Ottawa Silver Seven is remembered best for pouring in 14 goals during a single Stanley Cup playoff game as Ottawa defeated a team from Dawson City 23–2.

Though he had lost the sight in one eye prior to joining the Silver Seven, McGee helped Ottawa win the Stanley Cup for the first time in 1903 and successfully defend its title against 10 different challengers before losing to the Montreal Wanderers in 1906. McGee had 21 goals in eight Stanley Cup playoff games in 1904 and 18 in four games in 1905. He won the only scoring title of his brief career during the 1904–05 season, when he tied Jack Marshall for first place in the Federal Amateur Hockey League with 17 goals in six games. His best scoring season was 1905–06 when he potted 28 goals in just seven games, but he finished third in scoring in the Eastern Canada Amateur Hockey Association behind teammate Harry Smith and his great scoring rival Russell Bowie. It would be the final year of McGee's career.

In addition to his 14-goal game against Dawson City on January 16, 1905, McGee scored eight goals in a regular-season game against the Montreal Wanderers on March 3, 1906, and he had five goals in a game on seven occasions. He scored 71 goals in 23 regular-season games over four years and another 63 goals in 22 playoff contests. McGee was inducted into the Hall of Fame as one of its 12 original members in 1945.

BILLY McGIMSIE was a high-scoring member of the Kenora Thistles in 1907 when they became the team from the smallest town ever to win the Stanley Cup. McGimsie's family had moved to the town when he was one, and he played up through the ranks there in church, school and mercantile hockey. He was a member of the Thistles when Kenora, still known as Rat Portage, challenged the Ottawa Silver Seven unsuccessfully for the Stanley Cup in 1903 and 1905.

Kenora faced the Montreal Wanderers for the Stanley Cup in a two-game total-goals series in January of 1907. Following a 4–2 victory in game one, McGimsie scored a goal in the 8–6 victory in game two. He was not in the line-up for Kenora when the Wanderers defeated them in a Stanley Cup rematch in March of that year. He was elected to the Hockey Hall of Fame in 1962.

DON McKENNEY came up through the Bruins system, playing junior hockey with the Barrie Flyers of the Ontario Hockey Association and spending a year with the Hershey Bears of the American Hockey League before arriving in Boston in 1954–55. He quickly established himself as a good goal scorer and an excellent playmaking center who could also play solid defensive hockey.

McKenney led the Bruins, and ranked seventh in the NHL, with 60 points in 1956–57 and was a top-10 scorer again each of the next three years. He also helped the Bruins reach the Stanley Cup finals in both 1957 and 1958. McKenney led Boston with a career-high 32 goals in 1958–59 and led the NHL with a career-high 49 assists in 1959–60. He also won the Lady Byng Trophy that season.

McKenney captained the Bruins in 1961–62 and 1962–63 before Boston traded him to the New York Rangers for Dean Prentice in February of 1963. McKenney was then traded to the Toronto Maple Leafs along with Andy Bathgate in a blockbuster deal on February 22, 1964. He played on the only Stanley Cup winner of his career that year but his production dropped dramatically in 1964–65 and he spent part of the season with Rochester of the American Hockey League.

McKenney was picked up on waivers by the Red Wings after the 1964–65 season but spent most of the next two years in the minors. He was then selected by the Blues in the 1967 Expansion Draft and split the 1967–68 season between St. Louis and Kansas City of the Central Hockey League. McKenney retired after playing two more minor-league seasons.

FREDERIC McLAUGHLIN Major Frederic McLaughlin was commander of the Black Hawk regiment during World War I and he named the hockey team in his hometown of Chicago after that famed fighting unit. He was instrumental in the development of hockey in Chicago, helping to buy the Portland Rosebuds after the Western Hockey League collapsed in 1926 and using the players from that team to stock the Black Hawks roster for their first NHL season of 1926–27.

McLaughlin was the first president of the Black Hawks and soon purchased controlling interest in the club. He moved the team from the Chicago Coliseum to the Chicago Stadium in December of 1929, and league attendance records followed. Though he went through coaches at a rate of more than one per year, McLaughlin had built a Stanley Cup winner by 1934. Employing more U.S.-born players than any other NHL team, the Black Hawks won another Stanley Cup title in 1938.

McLaughlin died on December 17, 1944, but his estate continued to own the Black Hawks until the team was purchased by Arthur Wirtz and James D. Norris in 1952. In 1963, Major Frederic McLaughlin was inducted into the Hockey Hall of Fame as a builder.

DON McLEOD was a much-traveled minor-league goaltender who had brief trials with the Detroit Red Wings and Philadelphia Flyers in the early 1970s before becoming one of the top goaltenders in the World Hockey Association. Only Ernie Wakely saw more action in the WHA nets, and McLeod's 157 career wins and 11 shutouts both rank fourth in league history. He played with a large curve in his goalie stick and was adept at firing the puck the length of the ice to alleviate pressure.

"Smokey," as he was known, joined the Houston Aeros for the 1972–73 inaugural season of the WHA and helped the team with the Avco Cup the following year. The 1973–74 campaign was McLeod's best, earning him the Ben Hatskin Trophy as the league's top goaltender. He led the loop with 33 wins that year and his 2.56 goals-against average would remain the lowest single-season total in WHA history.

McLeod's performance with Houston earned him the role of backup to Gerry Cheevers when the WHA all-stars took on the Soviets prior to the 1974–75 season. He was with the Vancouver Blazers that year and again led the league with 33 wins, but suffered a league-leading 35 losses while playing in 72 of his team's 78 games. McLeod was also a member of the Calgary Cowboys, Edmonton Oilers and Quebec Nordiques before his career ended in 1977–78.

GEORGE McNAMARA was a big and rugged defenseman who often teamed with his brother Howard throughout his hockey career. The two, who were known as "the Dynamite Twins," had a brother named Harold who often played on teams with them.

The McNamara family moved to Sault Ste. Marie, Ontario when George was a boy, and he played with the local team in the International (Pro) Hockey League (the game's first professional circuit) in 1906–07. The following season, he became a member of the Montreal Shamrocks, where he was joined by brother Howard in 1908–09. In 1910–11, all three McNamara brothers were members of the Waterloo team in the Ontario Professional Hockey League. Howard and George played with Halifax of the Maritime Professional Hockey League in 1911–12.

When the National Hockey Association added two teams in Toronto for the 1912–13 season, the Dynamite Twins joined the Tecumsehs, who became known as the Ontarios the following year. Howard and George ensured the team had adequate defense, but a poor offense doomed them to last-place finishes both years. The Ontarios were bought by Eddie Livingstone prior to the 1914–15 season, and he renamed the team the Shamrocks. Livingstone signed Harold to join his brothers and the club improved to fifth in the six-team league. They might have reached fourth place if not for a game that had to be defaulted on February 3, 1915 when the three McNamara brothers returned to Sault Ste. Marie to attend their father's funeral.

George remained in Toronto after Howard left to join the Montreal Canadiens in 1915–16, but the two were teammates again when they enlisted with the Canadian army and played for the 228th Battalion team in the NHA before being sent overseas in February of 1917. George returned to Sault Ste. Marie after World War I to become a hockey coach. In 1924, he led the Sault Ste. Marie Greyhounds to the Allan Cup. He was elected to the Hockey Hall of Fame in 1958.

HOWIE MEEKER was a rookie sensation in 1946–47, scoring 27 goals for the Toronto Maple Leafs and winning the Calder Trophy. He set a record that year for a first year player when he had five goals in a game on January 18, 1947. To date, Meeker's mark has been matched only once (by Don Murdoch on October 12, 1976). He went on to spend eight years with the Maple Leafs and was the club's coach during the 1956–57 season. He was to become general manager the following year before losing his job in a front-office shuffle.

That Howie Meeker had an NHL career at all was an amazing feat, considering his legs had been badly injured by a grenade while serving in World War II. After lengthy rehabilitation, he returned to Canada and played senior hockey in Stratford in 1945–46 before joining the Maple Leafs. From 1951 until 1953, Meeker served as a Member of Parliament with the Conservative Party in Ottawa while also playing hockey in Toronto.

Long after his playing days, Meeker gained fame as a television analyst. He also operated hockey schools and wrote instructional hockey books .

MARK MESSIER Combining power, speed and skill, Mark Messier is also one of the great leaders in the NHL. He is a six-time Stanley Cup champion and has played more playoff games than anyone in NHL history. Messier also ranks fourth all-time in NHL scoring behind only Wayne Gretzky, Gordie Howe and Marcel Dionne.

After one season in the World Hockey Association, Messier was the Edmonton Oilers' second choice in the Entry Draft when they joined the NHL for the 1979–80 season. By his third NHL season he was a star, scoring 50 goals and being named to the First All-Star Team at left wing. Two 100-point

seasons followed and when the Oilers won their first Stanley Cup title in 1985, Messier earned the Conn Smythe Trophy as playoff MVP.

Now playing center on a second line behind Wayne Gretzky, Messier was in the shadow of "the Great One" on three more Oilers championships. When Gretzky was traded to the Los Angeles Kings on August 9, 1988, Messier responded to the challenge of becoming captain and team leader. He established career highs with 84 assists and 129 points in 1989–90, won the Hart Trophy and led the Oilers to a fifth Stanley Cup title.

After an injury-plagued 1990–91 campaign, Messier was traded on October 4, 1991 to the New York Rangers, who hoped his talent and leadership would end a Stanley Cup drought that dated back to 1940. Messier won the Hart Trophy again after leading the Rangers to a first-place finish in 1991–92. A Stanley Cup championship came two years later. Messier's inspirational words and play in the Eastern Conference finals against the New Jersey Devils that spring went a long way toward bringing the Stanley Cup back to New York for the first time in 54 years.

Messier remained with the Rangers until 1996–97, when he was reunited with Wayne Gretzky, but while he remained a top player, the team could not duplicate its Stanley Cup success. Messier then signed as a free agent with Vancouver before the 1997–98 season. Internationally, Messier played for Team Canada at the Canada Cup in 1984, 1987 and 1991 and at the World Cup of Hockey in 1996. The decision to omit him from Canada's 1998 Olympic team was very controversial.

STAN MIKITA came to Canada from Czechoslovakia with his aunt and uncle as a boy in 1948 and settled in St. Catharines, Ontario. He became a star junior player in his adopted hometown and went on to become one of the greatest players in NHL history over a 22-year career with the Chicago Black Hawks. Mikita and Bobby Hull helped change the Black Hawks from perennial losers into an NHL powerhouse. When he retired after the 1979–80 season, Mikita ranked second all-time behind Gordie Howe with 926 assists, sixth in goals with 541 and third with 1,467 points. His 1,394 games were fifth-most in NHL history to that point. He had been named to the NHL All-Star Team on eight occasions, including six selections as the First Team center.

Mikita joined the Black Hawks for a three-game trial in 1958–59 and became a regular the following season. In 1960–61, he helped Chicago win its first Stanley Cup title in 23 years. Though he was just 5'9" and weighed only 169 pounds, Mikita was prone to taking penalties early in his career, but was also an effective scorer, leading the NHL in points in both 1963–64 and 1964–65. As he gained more experience, Mikita's penalty totals dropped. In 1966–67 he became the first player in history to win the Hart Trophy, the Art Ross Trophy and the Lady Byng Trophy in the same season. His career-high 97 points that season also tied the single-season record for the pre-expansion era set by Bobby Hull just one year before. Mikita remained the top scorer in the NHL after expansion, recording a career-high 40 goals in 1967–68 and again winning the Hart, Art Ross and Lady Byng trophies. He continued to be an effective scorer into the mid 1970s before his totals finally began to decline.

Mikita's contributions to hockey in the United States were recognized in 1976 when he was awarded the Lester Patrick Trophy. He established the American Impaired Hearing Association in 1972–73 and continues to work for the children's charity. Mikita was elected to the Hockey Hall of Fame in 1983.

JAKE MILFORD John Calverley "Jake" Milford was an excellent junior hockey player who turned down pro offers from the Detroit Red Wings and New York Rangers to play hockey in England from 1934 until 1938. He was a member of the Wembley Canadians and the Wembley Monarchs. Milford returned to North America in 1938–39 and joined the Cleveland Barons in 1940–41, helping the team win the Calder Cup that year as American Hockey League champions.

After service in the Royal Canadian Air Force during World War II, Milford played with New Haven of the AHL in 1945–46 before joining the Dallas Texans of the United States Hockey League. In 1947–48, he became player-coach in Dallas. He then spent several seasons as a coach in amateur hockey before becoming a member of the New York Rangers organization as the general manager of their St. Paul affiliate in the Central Hockey League in 1957–58. Milford was either coach or g.m. with Rangers clubs in Brandon, St. Paul and Omaha until 1972–73, when he became a scout for New York. During eight years in the CHL, Milford's teams won four championships.

In the summer of 1973, Milford joined the Los Angeles Kings as assistant general manager and was promoted to the general manager's post on December 1, 1973. After a dispute with Kings owner Jack Kent Cooke, he quit the team and became g.m. of the Vancouver Canucks on May 31, 1977. Long noted as a shrewd judge of talent and an astute trader, Milford built the Canucks team that reached the Stanley Cup finals in 1982. He still was associated with the Canucks front office at the time of his death on December 24, 1984. That same year, he had been inducted into the Hockey Hall of Fame as a builder.

JOE MILLER After Lester Patrick's heroics in place of injured goalie Lorne Chabot in game two of the 1928 Stanley Cup finals, an agreement was reached with the Montreal Maroons for the New York Rangers to use New York

Americans goalie Joe Miller for the rest of the series.

After a 2–0 loss to the Maroons in game three, Miller posted a shutout of his own in game four and the best-of-five series was pushed to the limit. Miller was cut and suffered two black eyes in game five, but hung on for a 2–1 victory that gave the Rangers the Stanley Cup.

Before the next season, the Pittsburgh Pirates acquired Miller after failing to re-sign Roy Worters. He spent two seasons with the woeful Pittsburgh team and was with the Philadelphia Quakers in 1930–31 after the Pirates relocated. He spent the following season in the minor leagues and then retired.

MIKE MODANO was just the second American-born player to be selected first overall in the NHL Entry Draft when he was picked by the Minnesota North Stars in 1988. Five years earlier, the North Stars had made American Brian Lawton the number-one pick, but unlike Lawton, Modano has become a star in the NHL.

Modano was a high-scoring junior with the Prince Albert Raiders of the Western Hockey League and an all-star in his final season of 1988–89 despite missing 25 games with a broken wrist. He made his NHL debut when he played two playoff games for the North Stars that season and became a regular in Minnesota in 1989–90. His 75 points ranked second behind Sergei Makarov in rookie scoring. Modano finished as the runner-up behind Makarov in voting for the Calder Trophy. The following year, he helped the North Stars to reach the Stanley Cup finals with 20 points in 23 playoff games.

Modano led the North Stars in points in 1991–92 and in 1992–93. The team moved to Dallas in 1993–94 and Modano scored 50 goals that season, leading the Stars with 93 points. His 50 goals set a franchise record for centers and made him just the third player in Minnesota/Dallas history (Brian Bellows, Dino Ciccarelli) to score 50 in a season.

In international play, Modano represented the United States at the World Junior Championships in 1988 and 1989, finishing second behind fellow American Jeremy Roenick in scoring at the 1989 tournament. He played for the U.S. at the 1990 and 1993 World Championships and was tied for the team lead in scoring with Brett Hull at the 1991 Canada Cup. Modano was a member of the American team that beat Canada at the World Cup of Hockey in 1996 and played for the U.S. Olympic team in Nagano in 1998.

BILLY MOE employed a unique crouching method to check opposing players—he was called "the best blocking back in hockey"—and was one of only three American-born players in the NHL (along with Frank Brimsek and John Mariucci) when he played with the Rangers from 1944–45 until 1948–49.

Moe was born in Danvers, Massachusetts, but grew up in Minneapolis and first played hockey in local amateur leagues before moving on to the Eastern Hockey League, where he played with Atlantic City and Baltimore in 1939–40 and 1940–41. He turned pro when he signed with Philadelphia of the American Hockey League in 1941–42 and played the next two seasons with the Hershey Bears. He was named the AHL's most valuable player in 1943–44 and that attracted the attention of Lester Patrick, who acquired him for the Rangers.

Moe played five seasons in the NHL, then returned to Hershey for a couple of seasons (1949–50 and 1950–51) and played two more minor-league seasons before retiring after the 1952–53 campaign. Moe was enshrined in the United States Hockey Hall of Fame in 1974.

ALEXANDER MOGILNY joined the Central Red Army team as a 17-year-old in 1986–87 and played for the Soviet Union in the World Junior Championships in 1987, 1988 and 1989. He was selected as the top forward in the tournament when the Soviets won a silver medal in 1988 and was named to the second all-star team when the Soviet Union took the gold medal in 1989. That year, he played on a line with Pavel Bure and Sergei Fedorov. In 1988, Mogilny was the youngest Soviet hockey player ever to win an Olympic gold medal. In 1989, he won a gold medal at the World Championships.

Mogilny was selected by the Buffalo Sabres in the fifth round of the 1988 NHL Entry Draft and defected from the Soviet Union to join the team for the 1989–90 season. He scored a goal on his first shift 20 seconds into his first NHL game on October 5, 1989, but he finished the year with just 15 goals. Mogilny upped his offensive output in each of his next three seasons and established career highs in 1992–93 with 76 goals and 127 points, when he was named to the Second All-Star Team. Mogilny's 76 goals equaled the fifth-highest single-season total in NHL history and tied him with Teemu Selanne for the league lead that year.

Mogilny was named captain of the Sabres in place of an injured Pat LaFontaine during the 1993–94 season and led the team in scoring again during the abbreviated 1994–95 campaign. He was traded to the Vancouver Canucks on July 8, 1995 and scored 55 goals in 1995–96 to join Pavel Bure as the only Vancouver players in team history to top 50 goals. Mogilny played for the Russian team at the World Cup of Hockey in 1996 but was not part of the Russian Olympic team in Nagano in 1998.

DOUG MOHNS had one of the longest careers in NHL history, playing 1,394 games over 22 seasons. At the time of his retirement in 1975, only Gordie Howe, Alex Delvecchio, Tim Horton and Harry Howell had played

more games and his total remained in the top 10 for more than 20 years.

Mohns was a graduate of the Barrie Flyers who joined the Boston Bruins for the 1953–54 season and played both left wing and defense during his time in Boston. His most productive season was 1959–60 when he had 20 goals and 25 assists. The Bruins finished last in the NHL standings each of the next four seasons and Mohns was dealt to the Chicago Black Hawks on June 8, 1964.

The Black Hawks were a team on the rise when Mohns reached Chicago and he enjoyed the best years of his career there. Playing on a line with Stan Mikita and Ken Wharram, he topped 20 goals four years in a row including a high of 25 in 1966–67. He also had career highs with 35 assists and 60 points that season and joined teammates Mikita, Wharram, Bobby Hull and Phil Esposito among the NHL's top-10 scorers as Chicago finished in first place for the first time in team history.

Mohns' production began to decline after the 1968–69 season and Chicago traded him to the Minnesota North Stars on February 22, 1971. He later played for the Atlanta Flames and Washington Capitals before retiring after the 1974–75 campaign.

HARTLAND MOLSON The Honorable Senator Hartland Molson was president and later chairman of the board of both the Canadian Arena Company and the Montreal Canadiens hockey club from 1957 until 1968. During that time, the Canadiens were the greatest team in the NHL and Molson, as a member of the NHL finance committee, played a vital role in strengthening owner-player relations. He was also responsible for modernizing the Montreal Forum, which had been built in 1924. His father, Colonel Herbert Molson, had been one of the founders of the Canadian Arena Company, which had financed the Forum's original construction.

In his youth, Molson had been an excellent athlete. He was a member of the Kingston Frontenacs in 1926 and played with the Queen's University team that reached the Memorial Cup finals that year. He also played for the Royal Military College team that won the Canadian intermediate football title in 1927 and coached the Chamonix (France) Hockey Club in 1929

During World War II, Molson served with the Royal Canadian Air Force and was shot down during the Battle of Britain in 1940. He had risen to the rank of Group Captain and was awarded the Order of the British Empire when discharged in 1945. In 1955, he was appointed to the Canadian Senate. Senator Molson was elected to the Hockey Hall of Fame as a builder in 1973.

ANDY MOOG quietly became one of the most successful goaltenders in NHL history over his 18 year career. He was just the tenth man to win 300 games when he reached the milestone on March 18, 1994 and went on to post a record of 372–209–88. His .622 winning percentage is one of the highest ever recorded.

Moog entered the NHL with Edmonton in 1980–81 and made a name for himself in the playoffs that year when the Oilers swept the Montreal Canadiens in the opening round. He spent most of the 1981–82 season with Wichita of the Central Hockey League (earning honors as an all-star) before returning to Edmonton in 1982–83 to share the nets with Grant Fuhr. Moog was a member of Stanley Cup-winning teams with the Oilers in 1984, 1985 and 1987 before leaving the team in a dispute with Glen Sather in 1987–88. Moog joined the Canadian national team that season and played at the Calgary Olympics before Edmonton traded his rights to the Boston Bruins on March 8, 1988.

Moog remained in Boston through the 1992–93 season, enjoying his best year in 1989–90 when he and Rejean Lemelin shared the Jennings Trophy. Moog also helped the Bruins to reach the Stanley Cup finals that year, leading all playoff goalies with a pair of shutouts and a 2.11 goals-against average though Boston ultimately lost the Stanley Cup to the Oilers.

On June 20, 1993, Moog was traded to the Dallas Stars. In his first season with Dallas in 1993–94, he topped 20 wins for the fifth year in a row and the tenth time in his career but his win totals declined over the next two years despite good goals against averages. In 1996–97, he helped Dallas to win the Central Division with 28 victories and a career-best 2.15 average that ranked second in the NHL behind Martin Brodeur's 1.88. Despite Moog's excellent year, the Stars elected to sign Ed Belfour during the off-season and on July 17, 1997 Moog signed as a free agent with the Canadiens. He retired after playing one year in Montreal.

ALFIE MOORE was a long-time minor-leaguer who spent a portion of the 1936–37 season with the New York Americans before gaining fame as an emergency fill-in during the 1938 Stanley Cup finals. A Toronto native, Moore was summoned to play goal for the Chicago Black Hawks in the series opener against the Maple Leafs that year.

Chicago goalie Mike Karakas had broken his toe in the previous playoff round and the Black Hawks wanted to replace him with Dave Kerr of the New York Rangers. Conn Smythe refused and suggested Moore, who had spent the season with the Pittsburgh Hornets of the American Hockey League, but was back in Toronto working for a dry cleaning firm. When he got home from work and was told to report to Maple Leafs Gardens, Moore assumed Black Hawks coach Bill Stewart had come through with the tickets he had requested.

When Moore arrived before the game and was told he was needed in goal

because the Leafs wouldn't let Kerr play, he boldly informed Smythe that he'd win the game "even if I have to eat the puck." Gordie Drillon beat him on the Leafs' first shot, and Toronto was about to go up 2–0 when Moore threw his stick at Syl Apps. Instead of calling for a penalty shot, referee Mickey Ion merely blew the play dead. Moore settled down and Chicago scored a surprising 3–1 victory.

Though he was ruled ineligible for the rest of the series, Moore had started the Black Hawks en route to a four-game victory in the best-of-five series. The journeyman never played for Chicago again after the Stanley Cup victory and saw action in only three more NHL games (two with the Americans and one with Detroit Red Wings) over the final five years of his career.

DICKIE MOORE played on Memorial Cup champions with the Montreal Royals in 1948–49 and the Montreal Junior Canadiens in 1949–50 before joining the Montreal Canadiens midway through the 1951–52 NHL season. He saw part-time duty for three years before becoming a regular with the Canadiens in 1954–55. An excellent stickhandler and skater with a hard, accurate shot, Moore became one of the NHL's top offensive stars. He was handy with his elbows and fists and his aggressive play earned him the nickname "Digging Dickie."

Although plagued by injuries throughout his career, Moore managed to lead the NHL in scoring twice. He won his first title in 1957–58 despite playing the final three months of the season with a cast on his broken left wrist. In 1958–59, he established career highs with 41 goals and 55 assists for 96 points, breaking Gordie Howe's single-season record of 95 points set six years earlier. Moore's 96 points would prove to be the second-highest total of the pre-expansion era. (Both Bobby Hull and Stan Mikita would later total 97.) He was selected as a First Team All-Star at right wing both years in which he won the scoring title and was selected to the Second All-Star Team in 1960–61. Moore played on Stanley Cup champions in Montreal in 1953 and for five years in a row from 1956 to 1960.

Moore retired after the 1962–63 season, but made a comeback with the Toronto Maple Leafs in 1964–65. He retired again after that year, but returned to the NHL for a final appearance when he played 27 games with the St. Louis Blues in their first season of 1967–68. Moore was inducted into the Hockey Hall of Fame in 1974.

PADDY MORAN Patrick Joseph "Paddy" Moran had a lengthy playing career, but he retired from hockey one year before the NHL was formed. Though his yearly goals-against averages appear quite high by modern standards, Moran played in an era when goaltenders were required to remain standing at all times. He was at his best in the postseason when the Quebec Bulldogs were Stanley Cup champions in 1912 and 1913.

Moran was a native of Quebec City. He played junior hockey there with the Quebec Dominions and intermediate hockey with the Crescents, who were champions of Canada in 1900–01. The following year, he joined the Bulldogs. With the exception of 1909–10, when he played for both All-Montreal and Haileybury after Quebec was denied entry in the National Hockey Association, Moran remained with the Bulldogs until 1916–17. He was inducted into the Hockey Hall of Fame in 1958.

HOWIE MORENZ was voted Canada's outstanding hockey player of the half-century in 1950 and is considered to be the biggest star in the game during the colorful days of the 1920s and 1930s. His great skill helped sell the sport in the United States, where he was often called "the Babe Ruth of Hockey" because of his box office appeal. His many other nicknames came from his fabulous skating speed, as the Montreal star was often tagged with labels like "the Canadien Comet," "the Hurtling Habitant," "the Mitchell Meteor" and "the Stratford Streak."

Morenz was born in Mitchell, Ontario, but first attracted attention as a hockey star in nearby Stratford. Leo Dandurand signed him to his first professional contract for the 1923–24 season and Morenz immediately led the Montreal Canadiens to the Stanley Cup. In 1924–25 he had 27 goals in 30 games and finished second on the team in scoring behind linemate Aurel Joliat. Over the next seven seasons, no other player would lead the Canadiens in either goals or points. In both 1927–28 and 1930–31 he also was the NHL's top scorer, and in 1930 and 1931 led the Canadiens to back-to-back Stanley Cup championships. Morenz first won the Hart Trophy as the player most valuable to his team in 1927–28 and repeated as MVP in 1930–31 and 1931–32. When the first NHL All-Star Teams were selected in 1930–31, he was named to the First Team at center and repeated the honor the following year. A Second Team selection came in 1932–33.

An aggressive player throughout his career, injuries began to catch up with Morenz, and by 1933–34 his production had tailed off. He was traded to the Chicago Black Hawks prior to the 1934–35 season and dealt again to the New York Rangers during the 1935–36 campaign. With the Canadiens slumping both on the ice and at the box office, Morenz was brought back to Montreal for the 1936–37 season. Though no longer the star he had once been, the fans again flocked to see him, and the Canadiens were leading the league when Morenz suffered a broke leg during a game on January 28, 1937. He died on

March 8, 1937 while still in hospital. Over 10,000 fans attended a service at the Montreal Forum where his body lay in state, while thousands more lined the route of his funeral cortege. The NHL played its second All-Star Game to benefit the Morenz family on November 2, 1937. In 1945, he was one of the first 12 men inducted into the Hockey Hall of Fame.

BERNIE MORRIS was a goal-scoring star who helped bring the first Stanley Cup championship to the United States. He scored 14 goals in four games for the Seattle Metropolitans when they defeated the Montreal Canadiens to win the Stanley Cup in 1917. He is fourth all-time in goals (174) and third all-time in points (259) in the history of the Pacific Coast Hockey Association.

Morris entered the PCHA with the Victoria Aristocrats in 1914–15 but showed little promise. The following season, he was sent to Seattle when that city was granted a PCHA franchise and promptly led the league with 23 goals in 18 games. He scored a career-high 37 goals when the Mets won the league title the following season and his 17 assists gave him the league lead in points, though he had to settle for second place in the goal-scoring race behind Gordie Roberts who set a PCHA record with 43 goals that year.

Seattle's PCHA championship entitled them to host the Canadiens for the Stanley Cup in April of 1917. Morris scored three goals in an 8–4 loss in game one, then beat Georges Vezina twice more in a 6–1 Seattle victory in game two. He had another hat trick in game three, then poured in six goals as the Metropolitans won the series with a 9–1 romp in game four.

Bernie Morris remained in Seattle until he was traded to the Calgary Tigers of the Western Canadian Hockey League in 1923–24. He helped Calgary win the league title that year and was acquired by Boston the following season to try and help the floundering NHL expansion team. He spent just six games with the Bruins and finished the season with the Regina Capitals of the WCHL. Morris played minor-league hockey the next five years before retiring after the 1929–30 season.

KEN MORROW became the first player in hockey history to win an Olympic gold medal and the Stanley Cup in the same season in 1980, first with the U.S. team that produced the "Miracle on Ice" at Lake Placid in February and then with the New York Islanders in May. As if that weren't enough, he went on to play with four consecutive Stanley Cup-winning teams with the Islanders.

Morrow had been the first all-American player ever at Bowling Green State University and the Central Collegiate Hockey Association player of the year in 1978–79. At 6'4" and 210 pounds, he was a solid defensive defenseman who played 10 seasons in the NHL, all with the Islanders. Morrow was inducted into the United States Hockey Hall of Fame in 1995.

GUS MORTSON A tough defenseman, Gus Mortson was a strong skater who could rush the puck but was at his best playing a physical game. He led the NHL in penalty minutes with 133 in his rookie season of 1946–47 and went on to lead the league again in 1950–51, 1953–54 and 1956–57.

Mortson teamed almost exclusively with Jim Thomson during his six years on defense with the Toronto Maple Leafs but also paired occasionally with Bill Barilko and Garth Boesch. He played on Stanley Cup winners in Toronto in 1947, 1948, 1949 and 1951 and was named to the First All-Star Team in 1949–50.

Prior to the 1951–52 season, Mortson was traded to the Chicago Black Hawks as part of the deal that brought Harry Lumley to Toronto. Mortson played six years on a weak Chicago team that missed the playoffs five years in a row and served as captain from 1954–55 through 1956–57. He finished his NHL career with the Detroit Red Wings in 1958–59 but later played amateur hockey until 1966–67.

KENNY MOSDELL was a member of the Montreal Royals before making his NHL debut with the Brooklyn (formerly New York) Americans in 1941–42. When he played the final game of his NHL career with the Montreal Canadiens in the 1958–59 playoffs, Mosdell was the last member of the Americans ever to play in the NHL.

Mosdell joined the Montreal Canadiens in 1944–45 after military service with the Royal Canadian Air Force. He was a good checker and penalty killer and was a member of Stanley Cup-winning teams in Montreal in 1945–46 and 1952–53. Mosdell reached his peak offensively in the mid 1950s, scoring 22 goals in 1953–54 and earning a spot on the First All-Star Team at center. He netted 22 goals again in 1954–55 and was named to the Second Team All-Star.

Mosdell played with a third Stanley Cup winner in Montreal in 1955–56, but was sold to the Chicago Black Hawks after the season and played 25 games for them in 1956–57. Terms of the sale provided the Canadiens with the right to reacquire Mosdell and he was back with Montreal the following season though he spent most of the year in the minors. After another season in the minors in 1958–59, Mosdell was summoned to the Canadiens to replace an injured Jean Beliveau in a semifinal playoff series against the Black Hawks. His three games in that series were his last in the NHL, though he played one more season in the minors before retiring.

FRED MOSELEY played four years of varsity hockey at Noble and Greenough prep school in Boston before going to Harvard. He immediately made the freshman squad and went on to star at center on the varsity team for the next three years. Moseley won the John Tudor Cup as Harvard's most valuable player in 1934–35, then captained the team to its first official Ivy League title and was honored as an all-American in 1935–36. Moseley also played football and baseball at Harvard, but it was for hockey that he was named to the school's Hall of Fame. He continued to play amateur hockey with the St. Nicholas Club and Beaver Dam in the Winter Club League after his collegiate career came to an end. He was elected to the United States Hockey Hall of Fame in 1975.

BILL MOSIENKO of the Chicago Black Hawks set an NHL record when he scored three goals in 21 seconds on March 23, 1952 in a 7–6 victory over the New York Rangers on the final night of the season. Mosienko was a productive scorer and sportsmanlike player throughout his career, winning the Lady Byng Trophy in 1944–45. He also was named to the Second All-Star Team in 1944–45 and 1945–46. Mosienko may well have earned more All-Star selections had he not played right wing during the heyday of Rocket Richard and Gordie Howe.

Mosienko made his NHL debut with Chicago during the 1941–42 season and became a regular with the Black Hawks in 1943–44. He had 32 goals and 38 assists that season to rank among the top 10 in NHL scoring. In 1945–46, Black Hawks coach Johnny Gottselig put Mosienko together with brothers Max and Doug Bentley and the Pony Line was born. Though Mosienko was hurt for much of the 1945–46 season, the line combined for 179 points and was the top-scoring trio in 1946–47. Max Bentley led the NHL in scoring both seasons the line played together before he was traded to the Toronto Maple Leafs early in the 1947–48 campaign. That same year, Mosienko suffered a broken ankle in the All-Star Game and missed 30 games.

After the break up of the Pony Line, Mosienko played in combinations with Doug Bentley, Roy Conacher, Gus Bodnar, Gaye Stewart and Pete Babando. He remained with the Black Hawks for his entire 14-year NHL career and though the team was dismal during much of his time there, Mosienko was one of only a few players to score more than 250 goals during this era.

Following his departure from the NHL after the 1954–55 season, Mosienko helped establish the Winnipeg Warriors in his hometown and promptly led the team to the Western Hockey League title in its first season of 1955–56. The team then claimed the Edinburgh Cup by beating the champions of the Quebec Hockey League. Mosienko played with the Warriors until 1958–59 and coached the team in 1959–60. He was inducted into the Hockey Hall of Fame in 1965.

JOHN MUCKLER A journeyman minor-league player, John Muckler also served a long apprenticeship as a coach in the minor leagues and was affiliated with several NHL organizations before finally achieving glory with the Edmonton Oilers. As an assistant and co-coach with Glen Sather, Muckler was a key contributor to Edmonton's four Stanley Cup victories during the 1980s. He guided the Oilers to a fifth championship as head coach in 1990.

Muckler's coaching career began as a player-coach with the New York Rovers of the Eastern Hockey League in 1959–60. He moved to the Long Island Ducks in 1961–62 and remained with that club until 1965–66, winning the EHL championship and coach of the year honors in 1965. In 1966–67, Muckler was named director of player personnel for the New York Rangers and in 1967–68 he began a six-year association with the Minnesota North Stars as general manager of their minor-league affiliates. During this time, Muckler coached the North Stars briefly (in 1968–69) and was behind the bench with Memphis of the Central Hockey League (1967–68), and Cleveland and Jacksonville of the American Hockey League (1971–72, 1972–73).

In 1973–74, Muckler returned to the Rangers organization to coach their top farm club in Providence, leading the Reds to the Calder Cup as champions of the American Hockey League. He was named coach of the year that season. In 1978–79, Muckler was named coach of the year in the Central Hockey League and won the league title in his first year as coach and general manager of the Vancouver Canucks' Dallas farm team.

Muckler joined the Oilers organization in 1981–82 as coach of their CHL farm club in Wichita and was promoted to Glen Sather's staff the following year. He remained in Edmonton through the 1990–91 season, then signed with the Buffalo Sabres as director of hockey operations in the summer of 1991. He became head coach in December and added the role of general manager in 1993–94. Muckler gave up his coaching duties prior to the 1995–96 season. He was dismissed as Sabers g.m. following the 1996–97 season. Muckler returned to the Rangers again when he was hired to replace Colin Campbell as New York's head coach on February 19, 1998.

JOE MULLEN Though his single-season records for goals and points by an American-born player already had been surpassed, Joe Mullen was still the highest-scoring U.S. player in NHL history when he retired after the 1996–97 season. He was the first American to reach 1,000 career points (February 7, 1995) and the first to score 500 goals (March 14, 1997), retiring with 1,063 points on 502 goals and 561 assists.

Mullen starred at both Boston College and with Salt Lake City of the Central Hockey League before reaching the NHL with the St. Louis Blues. In

1981–82, he became the first player ever to score 20 goals in the minor leagues and in the NHL in the same season. Injuries slowed him down in 1982–83, but he established himself as a top NHL scorer with 41 goals in 1983–84.

Mullen was traded to the Calgary Flames on February 1, 1986 and went on to lead all playoff scorers with 12 goals that year as Calgary reached the Stanley Cup finals. In 1988–89, he established career highs with 51 goals, 59 assists and 110 points and again led all playoff scorers, this time with 16 goals, as the Flames won the Stanley Cup. At 32, Mullen was the second-oldest player (behind John Bucyk) ever to score 50 goals in a season. He was named to the First All-Star Team at right wing. He also won the Lady Byng Trophy that year, an award he had won previously in 1986–87.

On June 16, 1990, Mullen was acquired by the Pittsburgh Penguins and was a key contributor to Stanley Cup victories in 1991 and 1992. He remained with Pittsburgh through the 1994–95 campaign and was awarded the Lester Patrick Trophy for his contributions to hockey in the United States that year. Mullen played with the Boston Bruins in 1995–96 but returned to Pittsburgh for his final season of 1996–97. During his career, Mullen played for the United States team at Canada Cup tournaments in 1984, 1987 and 1991.

KIRK MULLER was chosen second overall behind Mario Lemieux by New Jersey in the 1984 NHL Entry Draft. He played junior with Kingston and Guelph of the OHL and was a member of the Canadian Olympic team in 1984 before making his NHL debut with the Devils in 1984–85.

Muller ranked among the top scorers in New Jersey in each of his first three seasons with the club. He was named team captain in 1987–88 and responded with career highs in goals (37) and assists (57) to lead the Devils with 94 points. He led New Jersey in scoring again in 1989–90, but his goal-scoring dropped off in 1990–91 and he was traded to the Montreal Canadiens on September 20, 1991.

Muller rebounded to score 36 goals his first season in Montreal and equaled career highs with 37 goals, 57 assists and 94 points in 1992–93. He also helped Montreal to win the Stanley Cup that season. Muller was named captain of the Canadiens in 1994–95 but was traded to the New York Islanders on April 5, 1995. On January 23, 1996, he was dealt to the Toronto Maple Leafs as part of a three-way deal involving the Ottawa Senators. Muller collected his 300th career goal with Toronto on February 18, 1996 and his 500th assist on April 6, but with the Maple Leafs fortunes on the decline in 1996–97, Muller was traded to the Florida Panthers on March 18, 1997.

HARRY MUMMERY was one of the largest players in the early days of professional hockey. He weighed in at 245 pounds in an era when players often weighed 100 pounds less. Though good-natured, his size made him an intimidating presence on defense and difficult for opponents to check when on a rush.

Mummery joined Quebec for the 1912–13 National Hockey Association season and was paired on defense with "Bad Joe" Hall, one of the roughest players of the day. The two helped the Bulldogs retain their NHA and Stanley Cup titles that season and remained together until Quebec traded Mummery to the Montreal Canadiens in 1916–17. He won another NHA title with Montreal that season, but the Canadiens lost the Stanley Cup to the Seattle Metropolitans, the first American team to win it. Mummery joined Toronto in 1917–18, the first season of the NHL, and helped that team win the Stanley Cup.

When the Bulldogs formed a team again for the NHL's third season, Mummery returned to Quebec. The team was weak, and the goaltending weaker, so Mummery (having made a brief appearance between the posts already during the year) was given a chance in net for the final two games of the season. He was beaten 11 times in an 11–6 loss to Ottawa, but got his revenge two nights later with a 10–4 win.

Mummery was with the Montreal Canadiens again in 1920–21 and set a career high with 15 goals in 24 games. The following season, he joined his transplanted Quebec teammates with the Hamilton Tigers. He saw limited action in 1922–23 and finished his career that season with the Saskatoon Crescents of the Western Canada Hockey League.

LARRY MURPHY set a record for rookie defensemen with 60 assists and 76 points in 1981–82 and was runner-up behind Peter Stastny for the Calder Trophy that year. He went on to become one of the highest-scoring defensemen in NHL history, becoming the fourth blueliner ever to record 1,000 career points (after Denis Potvin, Paul Coffey and Raymond Bourque) when he reached the milestone on March 27, 1996.

Murphy played his junior hockey with the Peterborough Petes of the Ontario Hockey Association, winning the Memorial Cup in 1978–79 and earning a berth on the OHA first all-star team in 1979–80. He was then selected fourth overall by the Los Angeles Kings in the 1980 Entry Draft. Murphy played three full seasons with the Kings before a trade to the Washington Capitals on October 18, 1983. He continued to rank among the best defensemen in the NHL during his time in Washington, setting a career high with 23 goals in 1986–87 and being named to the Second All-Star Team. The Capitals traded him to Minnesota on March 7, 1989, but he played only one full season as a North Star before being sent to the Pittsburgh Penguins on December 11, 1990.

Murphy was a key contributor to the success of the Penguins during his time

in Pittsburgh, helping the team win the Stanley Cup in 1991 and 1992 and earning berths on the Second All-Star Team in 1992–93 and 1994–95. On July 8, 1995, Murphy was traded to the Toronto Maple Leafs. With the Maple Leafs slumping and Murphy's offensive numbers in decline by 1996–97, Toronto fans were critical of the defenseman and he was traded to the Red Wings on March 18, 1997. In Detroit, he became an important contributor as the Red Wings won the Stanley Cup that year for the first time since 1955. He helped the Red Wings repeat as champions in 1998. In addition to his four Stanley Cup victories, Murphy was a member of Canada Cup-winning teams in 1987 and 1991.

MUZZ MURRAY Charles Uksila of the Portland Rosebuds became the first American-developed player to participate in the Stanley Cup finals in 1916. Hugh "Muzz" Murray was still only the second when he played for the Seattle Metropolitans of the Pacific Coast Hockey Association in the ill-fated 1919 series against the Montreal Canadiens that was halted due to a worldwide influenza epidemic before a winner could be determined. Murray appeared with Seattle in the finals again in 1920 (when the Mets were beaten by the Ottawa Senators) and played for Seattle in 1920–21, then closed out his professional career with the Calgary Tigers of the Western Canada Hockey League in 1921–22, though he came back to pro hockey briefly with the Tulsa Oilers of the American Hockey Association in 1931–32.

Murray's hockey career began in his native Sault Ste. Marie, Michigan, where he starred on local teams from 1911 until 1917 (at a time when this league was the highest level of hockey competition in the United States). In 1914–15, he captained Sault Ste. Marie to the Western Division title of the American Amateur Hockey Association before losing to Cleveland in the national finals. He was also named to the all-Western team that year.

Murray was known for his tough play and his scoring ability as well as a competitive spirit that made him a team leader. He continued to play hockey in Sault Ste. Marie until he was nearly 60 years old. His son, Hugh Jr.—also known as Muzz—shared goaltending duties with Frank Brimsek and Hub Nelson on the famed U.S. Coast Guard Cutters hockey team during World War II. Murray Sr. was enshrined in the United States Hockey Hall of Fame in 1987.

MATS NASLUND was selected in the second round of the 1979 Entry Draft and became the first European trained player to join the Montreal Canadiens when he made his debut in 1982–83. Small, speedy and smart, the Swedish import proved a popular addition to the Flying Frenchman and earned a spot on the NHL All-Rookie Team.

After a 42-goal season in 1984–85, Naslund became the first Montreal player since Guy Lafleur in 1979–80 to crack the top-10 in scoring when he collected 110 points on 43 goals and 67 assists in 1985–86. He led a rookie-laden team to a surprising Stanley Cup victory that spring, collecting three goals and four assists in a five-game victory over the Calgary Flames in the finals. Naslund was named to the NHL Second All-Star Team after the season.

Naslund played in the All Star Game in 1984 and 1986 before setting a record with five assists in the 1988 game. That season also saw him win the Lady Byng Trophy for sportsmanlike conduct. He returned to Europe following the 1989–90 campaign, but was back for a final appearance in the NHL with the Boston Bruins in 1994–95.

CAM NEELY was the NHL's best power forward during the late 1980s and early 1990s, combining toughness and strength with a deft scoring touch. His career was cut short by a rare thigh injury that left him susceptible to a variety of knee ailments.

Neely was selected ninth overall by the Vancouver Canucks in the 1983 Entry Draft but did not become a star until he was traded to the Boston Bruins for Barry Pederson on June 6, 1986. He was a Second Team All-Star after a 42-goal season in 1987–88 and again after scoring a career-high 55 goals in 1989–90. Neely joined Phil Esposito as the only Bruins players with back-to-back 50-goal seasons when he scored 51 in 1990–91 and earned another berth as a Second Team All-Star.

During the 1991 Prince of Wales Conference finals, Neely took a knee in the thigh from Ulf Samuelsson of the Pittsburgh Penguins and developed a condition called myositis ossificans whereby a portion of the thigh muscle turns to bone. The rare condition, as well as a series of knee injuries, dramatically limited his playing time over the next five seasons and forced him to retire prior to the 1996–97 campaign.

Neely's last great year came in 1993–94 when he scored 50 goals while playing in only 49 games. He actually scored his 50th goal in just his 44th game, matching Mario Lemieux for the second-fewest games ever needed to reach the milestone and trailing only Wayne Gretzky's 50 goals in 39 games in 1981–82.

Neely was honored with a fourth selection to the Second All-Star Team that year and won the Masterton Trophy for perseverence and dedication to hockey.

ROGER NEILSON has been a coach in the NHL since the 1977–78 season when he entered the league as head coach of the Toronto Maple Leafs. He had made his professional coaching debut one year earlier with the Dallas Blackhawks of the Central Hockey League after spending the previous 10 sea-

sons with the Peterborough Petes of the Ontario Hockey Association. Between 1966–67 and 1975–76, Neilson's Peterborough teams finished in third place or better on eight occasions and reached the Memorial Cup tournament after winning the OHA championship in 1972.

Neilson led the Maple Leafs to the semifinals in 1978 and pioneered the use of video as a teaching tool during his two years as coach in Toronto. He later coached the Buffalo Sabres (1979–80 to 1980–81) before taking over the Vancouver Canucks late in the 1981–82 season. Neilson led the Canucks on a surprising run to the Stanley Cup finals that year. He remained with the team until 1983–84 when he was fired and completed the year with the Los Angeles Kings. Neilson was then a co-coach with the Chicago Blackhawks from 1984–85 to 1986–87 before landing another head coaching job with the New York Rangers in 1989–90.

Neilson led the Rangers to a first-place finish in the Patrick Division in 1989–90 and first place overall in the NHL in 1991–92 when he was runner-up behind Pat Quinn for the Jack Adams Award as coach of the year. He was fired by the Rangers on January 4, 1993, but was hired by the expansion Florida Panthers on June 2, 1993. Neilson's defensive style proved a perfect fit with his Florida players and the Panthers set expansion records with 33 wins and 83 points in 1993–94. He was replaced in Florida after the 1994–95 season and was hired as an assistant coach in St. Louis in 1995–96. Neilson became a head coach again on March 9, 1998 when he was hired by the Philadelphia Flyers.

Since 1987, Neilson has held an off-season clinic at the University of Windsor that is attended by many amateur and professional coaches. He also has run a five-week international hockey camp since 1976. Since the summer of 1997, Neilson has held a hockey clinic for children at the Canada Centre in Metulla, Israel.

FRANCIS NELSON Sports editor of the *Toronto Globe* and an important person in the world of thoroughbred horse racing, Francis Nelson served as vice president of the Ontario Hockey Association from 1903 to 1905 under president John Ross Robertson. The following year, he was named OHA governor to the Amateur Athletic Union of Canada. Later, he was elected as a life member. In 1947, he was inducted into the Hockey Hall of Fame as a builder.

HUB NELSON Hubert "Hub" Nelson was a star goaltender of the 1930s who never got a chance to play in the NHL. He first played goal as a 12-year-old in his hometown of Minneapolis and later played on two championship teams (and was twice named all-City) in his high school career, then turned professional with the Minneapolis Millers in the Central Hockey League in 1930 and went on to a brilliant career in the CHL and the American Hockey Association.

Nelson routinely posted goals-against averages below 2.00 and consistently ranked as a league leader in both average and shutouts. The Rangers and Black Hawks made repeated efforts to buy Nelson while he was with the St. Louis Flyers of the AHA, but management wanted to keep him rather than give him an opportunity in the NHL. He did play with fellow American NHLers Frank Brimsek and John Mariucci on the powerhouse Coast Guard Cutters team during World War II, but Nelson chose to retire from hockey after his Coast Guard career and devoted his time to business interests in Minneapolis. He was inducted into the United States Hockey Hall of Fame in 1978.

ERIC NESTERENKO Because of his size, Eric Nesterenko was compared with Jean Beliveau early in his career with the Toronto Maple Leafs and his play suffered for it. He became a regular with the Maple Leafs in 1953–54 but Nesterenko was more concerned with furthering his education than with playing professional hockey. This led to a fallout with Maple Leafs management and he retired after the 1955–56 season.

Nesterenko was then sold to the Chicago Black Hawks, who agreed to let him play on a part-time basis while attending university. He played only weekend games for Chicago in 1956–57, but played the full season the following year on the Black Hawks' top line with Ed Litzenberger and Ted Lindsay and scored a career-high 20 goals. Over the next two years, Nesterenko commuted between Chicago and the University of Western Ontario in London. In 1960–61, was a member of the Black Hawks team that won the Stanley Cup for the first time in 23 years.

Nesterenko was an aggressive right winger and relentless checker who earned high penalty minute totals early in his career but was able to tone down the rough stuff in later years. He played with the Black Hawks until 1971–72, then spent some time with the Chicago Cougars of World Hockey Association in 1973–74 and played a final season of amateur hockey in Trail, British Columbia in 1975–76.

BERNIE NICHOLLS Just the fifth player in NHL history to score 70 goals (and still only one of eight ever to reach that level), Bernie Nicholls had 70 goals and 80 assists for the Los Angeles Kings in 1988–89. He also established personal highs that year with six assists and eight points in a game against the Toronto Maple Leafs on December 1, 1988.

Nicholls joined the Kings during the 1981–82 season and collected 32 points in just 22 games, including three hat tricks during a 10-game span. By 1983–84, he led the Kings with 95 points and the following year he reached 100 for the first time in his career. His 150-point season in 1988–89 ranked him fourth in the NHL, but on January 20, 1990, Nicholls was traded to the New York Rangers for Tomas Sandstrom and Tony Granato. He spent 1990–91 with the Rangers, but on October 4, 1991, he was traded to the Edmonton Oilers in the deal that brought Mark Messier to New York.

Nicholls went on to play with the New Jersey Devils, Chicago Blackhawks and San Jose Sharks. He was with the Devils on February 13, 1994 when he became the 39th player in NHL history to score 1,000 points. He was a Blackhawk in 1994–95 and led the team in scoring while becoming just the second Blackhawk ever (Bobby Hull, 1965–66) to record two four-goal games in one season. On October 20, 1996, Nicholls played his 1,000th NHL game as a member of San Jose and on January 30, 1997, he passed Hull on the NHL's all-time scoring list.

BILLY NICHOLSON was a star goaltender at the turn of the century with the Montreal Amateur Athletic Association, recording five shutouts in 27 league games over four seasons from 1899–1900 to 1902–03 in a era when shutouts were extremely rare. He was outstanding in Montreal's 1902 Stanley Cup challenge against the Winnipeg Victorias, recording a shutout in game two of the series and playing spectacularly in a 2–1 victory in the third and deciding game. The Montreal team earned the nickname "Little Men of Iron" for the tenacious way they hung on to beat Winnipeg.

In later years, the Little Men of Iron would be associated with the Montreal Wanderers after Nicholson and many of his teammates jumped to that franchise when it was formed in 1903–04. The goalie saw action with another Montreal club in 1907–08 when he led the league with the fewest goals allowed as a member of the Shamrocks. In the three seasons prior to his joining the Shamrocks, Nicholson had tended goal with the Calumet Miners of the International (Pro) Hockey League (hockey's first professional circuit).

From Montreal, Nicholson moved on to Haileybury for three years including the 1909–10 season when the northern Ontario town was included in the inaugural campaign of the National Hockey Association. Nicholson later played in the NHA with the Toronto Tecumsehs in 1912–13 before returning to the Wanderers in 1913–14. He then served as the rink manager in Haileybury for two years before being brought out of retirement by the Toronto Blueshirts in 1916–17 to replace future Hall of Famer Percy LeSueur who had enlisted with the army to serve in World War I.

SCOTT NIEDERMAYER was chosen third overall by the New Jersey Devils in the 1991 NHL Entry Draft. His brother Rob was the fifth pick in 1993 when he was drafted by the Florida Panthers. Scott was a star defenseman with Kamloops of the Western Hockey League, earning all-star honors in 1990–91 and in 1991–92. He also helped Kamloops to win the Memorial Cup in 1992 and was named tournament MVP.

Niedermayer made his NHL debut during the 1991–92 season. He became a regular the following year and was named to the All-Rookie Team. A swift skater and excellent puckhandler, Niedermayer led the Devils with a +19 rating in 1994–95. He was the team's top scoring defenseman in the playoffs as New Jersey won the Stanley Cup that season. In 1996, Niedermayer played for Team Canada at the World Cup of Hockey. He was a member of the Canadian Olympic team in Nagano in 1998.

JOE NIEUWENDYK joined Mike Bossy as just the second rookie in NHL history to top 50 goals when he scored 51 in 1987–88. He joined Bossy and Wayne Gretzky as the third player ever to score 50 goals in his first two NHL seasons after scoring another 51 in 1987–88.

Nieuwendyk was drafted by the Calgary Flames in 1985, but played two more seasons with Cornell in the NCAA (where he was an all-American both years) before making a brief NHL debut in 1986–87. Nieuwendyk followed up his pair of 51-goal efforts with back-to-back 45-goal seasons in 1989–90 and 1990–91 and went on to become the Flames career leader with 314 goals (since surpassed by Theoren Fleury) before he was traded to the Dallas Stars on December 19, 1995. He also served as captain in Calgary from 1991 to 1995.

Nieuwendyk won a silver medal with the Canadian team at the World Junior Championships in 1986 and played at the World Championships in 1990. He was named to Team Canada for the 1991 Canada Cup but was injured during training camp. In 1998, he was a member of the Canadian Olympic team that competed at Nagano.

FRANK NIGHBOR was the first recipient of two of the NHL's oldest individual honors, winning the Hart Trophy in 1923–24 and the Lady Byng Trophy the following year. The stylish center also won the Lady Byng Trophy in its second season, 1925–26. A great goal scorer and an excellent playmaker, Nighbor was an early exponent of the poke check, and fans of his day often would debate whether he was better on offense or defense.

"The Flying Dutchman" or "the Pembroke Peach," as Nighbor was known, played in his hometown of Pembroke and in Port Arthur, Ontario before turning pro with the Toronto Blueshirts of the National Hockey Association in 1912–13. He scored six goals in a game on February 15, 1913, finishing the

season fourth in the league with 25 goals in 19 games. The following year, Nighbor joined the Vancouver Millionaires of the Pacific Coast Hockey Association. In 1914–15, he played left wing on a line with Mickey MacKay and Cyclone Taylor as the high-scoring trio led Vancouver to a Stanley Cup victory over the Ottawa Senators. Nighbor was named the all-star left winger in the PCHA that season, but he returned to the NHA with the Senators in 1915–16. He remained in Ottawa for 15 years.

Nighbor tied Joe Malone for the scoring lead with 41 goals in the NHA's final season of 1916–17, but he slumped during the NHL's inaugural campaign of 1917–18 before finishing among the league scoring leaders each of the next three years. The Senators became the best team in the NHL during the 1920s, winning the Stanley Cup in 1920, 1921, 1923 and 1927. Despite the success, the small-market team was losing money and Nighbor was traded to the Toronto Maple Leafs during the 1929–30 season. It would be his last year in the NHL. He was elected to the Hockey Hall of Fame in 1947.

KENT NILSSON was a star in Sweden who came to North America in 1977 when he joined countrymen Ulf Nilsson and Anders Hedberg with the Winnipeg Jets of the World Hockey Association. His 107 points that year were fourth on the team behind the two other Swedes and Bobby Hull as the Jets won the Avco Cup. Kent's 107 points again in 1978–79 led the team that season as Winnipeg repeated as Avco Cup champions in the WHA's final year of existence.

When the Jets became one of four WHA teams to enter the NHL in 1979–80, Nilsson became property of the Atlanta Flames who had drafted him back in 1976. He had 40 goals and 53 assists that season and upped his totals to 49 and 82 after the Flames moved to Calgary the following season. Those 131 points in 1980–81 ranked him third in the NHL behind Wayne Gretzky and Marcel Dionne. Nilsson had another top–10 finish in 1982–83 when he had 104 points.

Nilsson was traded to the Minnesota North Stars on June 15, 1985, but was no longer producing points at the same pace and was dealt again, to the Edmonton Oilers, on March 2, 1987. Nilsson's 19 points in the playoffs that year ranked him among the leaders as Edmonton won the Stanley Cup. He spent the next seven season in Europe before making a final NHL appearance with the Oilers in 1994–95.

ULF NILSSON The Winnipeg Jets of the World Hockey Association were the first North American team to actively pursue European talent, unveiling Ulf Nilsson and Anders Hedberg among six new players in 1974–75. Hedberg and Nilsson played alongside Bobby Hull and formed the WHA's most productive forward line. Nilsson was a playmaking center who had 26 goals and 94 assists in his first WHA season. He helped Hull set a pro hockey record with 77 goals that year, while Hedberg scored 53 times and was named rookie of the year.

The two Swedes both topped 100 points in each of the four years they spent in Winnipeg. Nilsson was second in the league in assists his first two seasons and led the league the next two while recording the second-, third-, and fourth-highest single season totals in league history. He ranks fourth all-time in the WHA with 344 career assists. His 484 points rank eighth. Nilsson was named playoff MVP when the Jets won the Avco Cup in 1975–76 and helped Winnipeg win another league title in 1977–78.

The Swedish superstars joined the New York Rangers in 1978–79 when both signed two-year contracts worth $1 million, but injuries marred Nilsson's NHL career and he never played again after 1982–83. He was a member of the international NHL All-Star Team that played the Soviet Nationals in New York City in the three-game Challenge Cup series in February 1979.

REG NOBLE After a successful amateur career in the Ontario Hockey Association with teams in his hometown of Collingwood, Ontario and Toronto, Reg Noble began his professional career with the Toronto Blueshirts in the final National Hockey Association season of 1916–17. When Toronto was dropped from the league he finished the year with the Canadiens, but was ruled ineligible for the 1917 Stanley Cup series that Montreal would lose to the Seattle Metropolitans.

Noble was back in Toronto when new ownership took over the team for the NHL's first season of 1917–18. He finished third in the league with 30 goals in 20 games that year before helping the Torontos (who are more commonly known as the Arenas) win the Stanley Cup. Though he was fined and suspended several times by coach Charles Querrie for breaking training rules, Noble remained in Toronto until 1924–25, winning another Stanley Cup in 1922 after the team had become the St. Pats. Famous linemates for the left winger in Toronto include Corb Denneny and fellow future Hall of Famers Duke Keats, Babe Dye and Jack Adams.

Noble was traded to the Montreal Maroons shortly after they entered the NHL in 1924–25, playing center for the team that season. The next year, he was moved back to defense and helped the Maroons to win the Stanley Cup. After one more season in Montreal, Noble was traded to Detroit where he played for five years. Another trade brought him back to the Maroons during his final NHL season of 1932–33. He was inducted into the Hockey Hall of Fame in 1962.

BRUCE NORRIS took over the presidency of the Detroit Red Wings and the Olympia Stadium from his sister Marguerite Norris Riker in 1955. The Norris family had owned the Red Wings since 1932 and continued to do so until Bruce Norris sold the franchise to Mike Ilitch after the 1981–82 season. During his tenure, Norris financed a $2.5 million renovation of the Olympia for the 1965–66 season and served as the NHL's chairman of the board from 1966–67 to 1967–68 and again from 1972–73 to 1973–74. In 1979–80, Norris moved the Red Wings into Joe Louis Arena. In addition to hockey, he was president of the Norris Grain Company and raised cattle on his farm in Libertyville, Illinois. Norris was elected to the Hockey Hall of Fame as a builder in 1969.

JAMES NORRIS was born in St. Catharines, Ontario on December 10, 1879, but spent much of his early life in Montreal. There, he was a championship squash player and a good tennis player, and he gained his introduction to the game of hockey in that city. Later, he became a wealthy grain broker, establishing head offices in Chicago.

When the NHL awarded new franchises to New York, Detroit and Chicago in 1926, Norris hoped to land the Chicago club, but lost out to Major Frederic McLaughlin. He settled for the Chicago Shamrocks of the American Hockey League instead, purchasing that team in 1930. By the summer of 1932, Norris had his NHL franchise when he and his son James D. Norris bought the Detroit Olympia and the Falcons hockey team. The club was renamed the Detroit Red Wings and its new winged wheel logo was patterned after that of the Montreal Amateur Athletic Association. In 1933, the Norris family acquired the Chicago Stadium with Arthur Wirtz, and they would later own a majority interest in the Madison Square Garden Corporation, which owned the New York Rangers.

Under Norris ownership, Detroit won its first Stanley Cup title in 1936 and repeated as champions the following year. Norris was a firm believer in the maintenance of a strong farm system, and his financial support allowed Jack Adams to build an operation that brought Stanley Cup titles to Detroit again in 1943, 1950 and 1952. Norris passed away on December 4, 1952, but the organization continued to flourish under his children's leadership, winning the Stanley Cup again in 1954 and 1955.

After his death, the Norris family presented the NHL with the James Norris Memorial Trophy in 1953 to be awarded annually to the league's best defenseman. In 1958, James Norris was elected to the Hockey Hall of Fame as a builder. Son James D. Norris was inducted four years later.

JAMES D. NORRIS The father and son combination of James Norris and James D. Norris purchased the Detroit Olympia and Detroit Falcons in the summer of 1932 and changed the name of the hockey team to the Red Wings. Under Norris ownership, Detroit emerged as an NHL power, winning seven Stanley Cup titles between 1936 and 1955.

A year after they bought the Red Wings, the Norrises and Arthur Wirtz also acquired the Chicago Stadium, and on September 11, 1952, Wirtz and James D. Norris purchased the Black Hawks from the estate of Major Frederic McLaughlin. At the time, the Chicago team had missed the playoffs six years in a row, finishing in last place for three straight seasons. By developing a strong farm system as they had done in Detroit, Norris and Wirtz built the Black Hawks into Stanley Cup champions by 1961 and the team remained a power in the NHL for decades to come.

In addition to his hockey interests, James D. Norris was involved in boxing and promoted numerous championship fights. He also was active in horse racing. Norris was elected to the Hockey Hall of Fame as a builder in 1962, four years after his father had been inducted.

WILLIAM NORTHEY was president of the Montreal Amateur Athletic Association and a life member of the Canadian Amateur Hockey Association. He also was the manager of the Montreal Arena, and he later helped to supervise construction of the original Montreal Forum which opened in 1924. For many years, Northey was the managing director of that building.

When professional interests began to take over the Stanley Cup, it was Northey who prevailed upon Sir H. Montagu Allan to present the Allan Cup to recognize Canada's amateur champion. Northey also became the first trustee of the new trophy. He is credited with proposing the idea that the National Hockey Association eliminate the position of rover for the 1911–12 season. Northey was elected to the Hockey Hall of Fame as a builder in 1947.

BILL NYROP was an outstanding high school athlete who led Edina High School to the Minnesota state championship in 1969 and was named all-State that year. He enrolled at Notre Dame University in 1970 and played for four years and earned all-American honors there.

Nyrop was drafted by the Canadiens after his second year at Notre Dame and assigned to Nova Scotia in the American Hockey League in 1974. He was called up to Montreal during the 1975–76 season and helped the Canadiens win the Stanley Cup three years in a row. Nyrop then retired to pursue a law degree, but was persuaded to make a comeback with Minnesota in 1981–82. He ended his playing career in West Germany the following year.

After obtaining his law degree, Nyrop returned to hockey in 1992 as gen-

eral manager of Knoxville in the East Coast Hockey League. He later founded the West Palm Beach, Florida franchise in the Sunshine Hockey League. He became ill with cancer in August of 1995 and died on December 31 that same year. He was inducted into the United States Hockey Hall of Fame in 1997.

ADAM OATES played U.S. college hockey at Rensselaer Polytechnic Institute and was named to the NCAA all-American team in 1985. He signed as a free agent with the Detroit Red Wings on June 28, 1985 and split his first NHL season of 1985–86 between Detroit and Adirondack of the American Hockey League. Oates played three more years with the Red Wings but did not develop into a star until after his trade to the St. Louis Blues on June 15, 1989.

Oates centered Brett Hull on a line in St. Louis, and Hull led the NHL with 72 goals in 1989–90 while Oates finished tied for tenth in the league with 102 points. The following year, Hull scored 86 goals while Oates had 90 assists and 115 points to finish third in the NHL. The combination was broken up the following year, however, when Oates was traded to the Boston Bruins on February 7, 1992.

In Boston, Oates set career highs with 45 goals and a league-leading 97 assists to again finish third in the NHL scoring race with 142 points in 1992–93. He helped Cam Neely to score 50 goals in just 44 games in 1993–94 when his 112 points once again ranked third in the NHL. Oates cracked the top 10 for the sixth straight year in 1994–95.

With the Bruins slumping in 1996–97, Oates was sent to the Washington Capitals in a multi-player trade on March 1, 1997. During the 1997–98 season, Oates, Phil Housley and Dale Hunter all reached 1,000 points while playing for the Capitals. It marked the first time three teammates ever reached the milestone in the same year.

EDDIE OATMAN Though he never played in the NHL, Eddie Oatman was among the elite goal scorers of his era. He played on a line with Joe Malone and Jack McDonald for Waterloo of the Ontario Professional Hockey League in 1909–10 and accompanied them back to Quebec the following year when the Bulldogs were admitted into the National Hockey Association. The three helped Quebec win the Stanley Cup in 1912.

Every member of Quebec's championship team was offered a contract by the rival Pacific Coast Hockey Association for the 1912–13 season, and Oatman signed with the New Westminster Royals. The following year, he was named to the PCHA all-star team. New Westminster became the Portland Rosebuds for the 1914–15 season and a year later Oatman was an all-star again when his team took the PCHA championship. The Montreal Canadiens won their first Stanley Cup title that year when they beat Portland three games to two in a best-of-five playoff.

When the 228th Battalion secured a franchise in the NHA for the 1916–17 season, Oatman joined the roster. Portland had released him under the assumption he was going overseas but when the 228th was sent to Europe for military action in the First World War, Oatman was discharged from the army. The incident resulted in some bad publicity, but he was back in Portland the following season.

When the Rosebuds suspended operations, Oatman joined the Victoria Aristocrats and remained with the franchise until 1923, though he also saw action with the Vancouver Millionaires as an injury replacement when they lost the Stanley Cup to the Toronto St. Pats in 1922. Oatman was traded to the Calgary Tigers in 1923–24 and helped the team win the Western Canada Hockey League title, but was again denied a Stanley Cup championship when Calgary lost to the Montreal Canadiens. He remained in Calgary until pro hockey collapsed in the west after the 1925–26 season and then continued to play minor-league hockey until 1933–34, serving as a player-coach in his final two seasons. Oatman later coached in Yorkton, Prince Albert, and Saskatoon, Saskatchewan until 1940.

AMBROSE O'BRIEN was responsible for the creation of the National Hockey Association, forerunner of the NHL. As the man chosen by the hockey officials in his hometown of Renfrew, Ontario to get their team into the country's top hockey league, O'Brien joined with the Montreal Wanderers to form a new league after the Canadian Hockey Association refused to admit either club. The money the O'Briens spent to attract hockey's biggest stars to the NHA quickly established it as the game's most important hockey league.

Ambrose's father, M.J. O'Brien, already bankrolled hockey teams in the Ontario silver-mining towns of Cobalt and Haileybury, and these two teams also would be included in the NHA. The O'Briens financed a new French-Canadian team in Montreal that season, known as les Canadiens. Most of their efforts, however, went into buying the best available talent for the Renfrew Creamery Kings, and the lucrative contracts given to such players as Frank and Lester Patrick, Fred Whitcroft and Cyclone Taylor soon had people calling the team the Renfrew Millionaires.

Though the O'Briens fell short of their ultimate goal of bringing the Stanley Cup to Renfrew, they gave professional hockey an air of credibility it had not known previously. The O'Brien Trophy, awarded to champions of the National Hockey Association, was later adopted by the NHL. It currently resides in the Hockey Hall of Fame. O'Brien was inducted into the Hockey Hall of Fame as a builder in 1962.

BUDDY O'CONNOR Herbert William "Buddy" O'Connor moved up the hockey ranks in his hometown of Montreal, starring with the Montreal Royals before joining the Montreal Canadiens in 1941–42. At the time, O'Connor centered the Royals' Razzle Dazzle Line with wingers Pete Morin and Gerry Heffernan, and all three were signed by the Canadiens the same year. O'Connor stood just 5'7" and weighed only 145 pounds, but his smooth skating and deft stickhandling made him a star in the NHL.

O'Connor cracked the top 10 in scoring for the first time in 1942–43, and though he took a back seat behind the famed Punch Line of Elmer Lach, Rocket Richard and Toe Blake during much of his time with the Canadiens, he was a key contributor to Montreal's Stanley Cup-winning teams of 1944 and 1946. O'Connor was traded to the New York Rangers before the 1947–48 season and went on to have a career year with 24 goals and 36 assists for 60 points in 60 games. That season, he won both the Hart and Lady Byng trophies and was named to the Second All-Star Team.

On October 8, 1948, O'Connor and several Rangers teammates were injured in a car accident just prior to the campaign. O'Connor missed 14 games that season and his offensive numbers declined, but he starred in the playoffs the following year when the Rangers defeated the Canadiens in the semifinals before losing the Stanley Cup to the Detroit Red Wings in double overtime in the seventh game. O'Connor played one more year in the NHL, leaving the league after his tenth season in 1950–51. In 509 games, he had recorded just 34 penalty minutes. In 1988, O'Connor was inducted into the Hockey Hall of Fame.

HARRY OLIVER played hockey in his hometown of Selkirk, Manitoba before joining the Calgary Tigers in 1920–21. He was a member of that team when it joined the Western Canada Hockey League for its inaugural season of 1921–22 and helped Calgary reach the Stanley Cup finals against the Montreal Canadiens in 1924. Oliver was the Tigers career scoring leader with 90 goals and 48 assists over the five years before pro hockey collapsed in the west.

Oliver was sold to the Boston Bruins for the 1926–27 season and led his new club in scoring for three straight years, including 1928–29 when the Bruins won their first Stanley Cup championship. Boston was firmly established as an NHL powerhouse during Oliver's time with the team, but he was dealt to the New York Americans before the 1934–35 campaign and finished his career with three years there. His combined total of 217 goals between Calgary and the NHL made him one of the top scorers of his era. In 1967, Oliver was inducted into the Hockey Hall of Fame.

BERT OLMSTEAD broke into the NHL with Chicago, playing nine games for the Black Hawks in 1948–49. He went on to star with the Montreal Canadiens and Toronto Maple Leafs over a 13-year career, establishing a reputation as one of the game's best physical players. Olmstead was also a supreme motivator who could bring the best out in his teammates.

After playing his first full NHL season with Chicago in 1949–50, Olmstead was traded to the Detroit Red Wings during the 1950–51 season and then dealt again to Montreal. He proved a good fit at left wing on a line with Elmer Lach and Maurice Richard and was a key contributor to the Canadiens Stanley Cup-winning team of 1952–53, earning a selection to the Second All-Star Team. When Lach retired the following year, Olmstead played with Richard and Jean Beliveau. He was playing with Beliveau and Bernie Geoffrion in 1955–56 when he earned another Second Team All-Star selection and played on his second Stanley Cup winner. After helping the Canadiens win the Stanley Cup again in 1957 and 1958, Olmstead was acquired by the Toronto Maple Leafs for the 1958–59 season.

Olmstead played a major part in Punch Imlach's rebuilding process in Toronto, sometimes serving as an assistant coach as well as a player. He tied a career high with 18 goals in Toronto in 1960–61 and helped the Maple Leafs win the Stanley Cup for the first time in 11 years in 1962, his last year as a player. Olmstead got into coaching after his playing days and was the first coach of the expansion Oakland Seals in 1967–68. He was elected to the Hockey Hall of Fame in 1985.

EDDIE OLSON Though he never played in the NHL, Eddie Olson was a top American star of the 1950s. Olson was one of nine hockey-playing brothers from the town of Hancock in Michigan's Upper Peninsula and got his start in hockey with the Marquette Sentinels in his hometown.

When the United States entered World War II, Olson joined the famed Coast Guard Cutters hockey team that featured such American NHL stars as Frank Brimsek and John Mariucci. The Cutters played in the Eastern Amateur Hockey League and in 1942–43 Olson ranked sixth in league scoring with 57 points on 23 goals and 34 assists. He enjoyed another productive year in 1943–44, though the Cutters were not officially considered part of the EAHL that season. After the War, Olson spent the 1945–46 season with Oakland of the Pacific Coast Hockey League where his kick shot became a major offensive weapon. Originated by his brother Wesley, the shot would see Olson kick the blade of his stick to propel the puck forward.

Olson's greatest success in hockey came in the American Hockey League, first with St. Louis and then in Cleveland. Olson helped the Barons win the

Calder Cup championship in 1952–53 and 1953–54 and also captured many individual honors. He won the Les Cunningham Plaque as the AHL's most valuable player in 1952–53 and was named to the first all-star team at left wing after leading the league with 86 points. Olson was also a first team all-star in 1954–55 when he led the league with 41 goals and 88 points.

In 1955–56, Olson was a player-coach with the Victoria Cougars of the Western Hockey League, making him the first American to coach a professional team in Canada. He was elected to the United States Hockey Hall of Fame in 1977.

BRIAN O'NEILL was hired as the NHL's director of administration in 1966 and helped to oversee the Expansion Draft in 1967. He also prepared regular-season schedules. O'Neill was appointed executive director of the NHL in 1971 and executive vice president in 1977. Upon the retirement of Clarence Campbell as NHL president that year, O'Neill took over responsibility for player discipline. He administered the NHL's Montreal office and supervised NHL security.

O'Neill represented the NHL in negotiations with European national hockey federations and with the Canadian Hockey League. He directed the annual NHL Entry Draft and served on many league committees. He was named to the Hockey Hall of Fame's Board of Governors in 1980 and became chairman of the board in 1990. He stepped down from that post in 1992, when he also gave up his position with the NHL. O'Neill had been appointed as the trustee of the Stanley Cup in 1988. He was elected to the Hockey Hall of Fame as a builder in 1994.

CHRIS OSGOOD was selected by the Detroit Red Wings in the 1991 NHL Entry Draft after being named to the second all-star team in the Western Hockey League with Medicine Hat in 1990–91. He made his professional debut with Adirondack of the American Hockey League in 1992–93 and broke into the NHL in 1993–94.

Osgood played his first NHL game against Toronto on October 15, 1993 and earned his first victory eight days later against the Los Angeles Kings. His first two shutouts that year came in back-to-back games on February 24 and 26, 1994 and on April 20, 1994 he became the first Red Wings rookie goaltender since Terry Sawchuk to register a shutout in his first playoff game.

In 1994–95, Osgood was tied for second in the league with a .917 save percentage and finished fourth with a 2.26 goals-against average. The Red Wings set an NHL record with 62 wins in 1995–96 and Osgood led the league with 39 victories while setting club records with a 21-game unbeaten streak and 13-game winning streak. Osgood also joined Ron Hextall that season as the only goalies to that point in NHL history to score a legitimate goal when he fired the puck into an empty net on March 6, 1996. Osgood's 2.17 goals-against average that year was second-best in the NHL, just percentage points behind Ron Hextall, and he was selected to the Second All-Star Team.

Osgood and Mike Vernon shared the Jennings Trophy in 1995–96 and were runners-up behind Martin Brodeur and Mike Dunham of the New Jersey Devils in 1996–97. Osgood was the starting goaltender during the 1996–97 regular season but in the playoffs it was Vernon who led the Red Wings to their first Stanley Cup title in 42 years. Vernon was then traded during the off-season, reaffirming Osgood's status as the club's top netminder. Though shaky at times during the playoffs, he helped Detroit repeat as Stanley Cup champions in 1998.

GEORGE OWEN Jr. was born in Hamilton, Ontario, but grew up in Boston and learned his hockey there. He attended Newton High School and went on to Harvard in the fall of 1919. Owen captained the freshman hockey team and later served two seasons as captain of the varsity squad, a rare feat at Harvard. He played both center and defense during his collegiate hockey career and also starred in baseball and football. Owen was captain of the baseball team during his senior year.

Owen entered the brokerage business after graduation from Harvard but continued playing hockey with the Boston University Club. He was invited to join the United States Olympic team in 1924 but had to decline because of business obligations.

Owen's play remained so strong that he was signed by the Boston Bruins as a 26-year-old for the 1928–29 season. He was a member of the Bruins' first Stanley Cup-winning team that year and played for the record-setting 1929–30 squad that went 38–5–1. He was a defenseman for five seasons in Boston and was occasionally paired with Lionel Hitchman or the great Eddie Shore. Owen retired from hockey after the 1932–33 season. In 1973, he became a charter member in the United States Hockey Hall of Fame.

SANDIS OZOLINSH made his North American debut with the San Jose Sharks farm club in Kansas City in January of 1992 after playing the previous year-and-a-half in his native Riga, Latvia. Ozolinsh had been a member of the Soviet national junior team, winning a silver medal at the World Junior Championships in 1991 and a gold medal in 1992. He entered the NHL with the Sharks in 1992–93, joining former Riga teammate Arturs Irbe.

Ozolinsh led all Sharks defensemen in scoring his rookie season despite missing 47 games with injuries. He had 26 goals and 38 assists in 81 games in

1993–94 to again lead all Sharks defensemen and finished third overall on the team in scoring during the abbreviated 1994–95 season.

On October 26, 1995, San Jose traded Ozolinsh to the Colorado Avalanche for Owen Nolan, and he led all Avalanche defensemen in scoring in 1995–96. In the playoffs, he led all NHL defensemen with 19 points as Colorado won the Stanley Cup. He was named to the NHL First All-Star Team for the first time in 1996–97.

FRED PAGE spent a lifetime fostering the growth of hockey in Canada and around the world. He was a player, referee, coach and administrator in Port Arthur, Fort William and Thunder Bay, Ontario from the 1930s until the 1960s, and became an executive member of the Canadian Amateur Hockey Association in 1958.

Page served as second vice president of the CAHA from 1962 to 1964 and first vice president from 1964 to 1966. He helped lead European visits by the Port Arthur Bearcats in 1961–62 and the Lacombe (Alberta) Rockets in 1963–64. From 1964 until 1967, he was a member of the Canadian national team Committee. Beginning in 1966, Page represented the CAHA at meetings of the International Ice Hockey Federation and served as first vice president of the IIHF from 1968–69 until 1972. He was chairman and and sat on the hockey directorate for the 1972 Winter Olympics in Sapporo, Japan.

In 1973, Page helped to form the Pacific Coast Junior Hockey League and served as PCJHL president from 1975 until 1979, when the league amalgamated with the British Columbia Junior Hockey League. In 1981, he served as BCJHL president and became chairman of the board in 1983. In 1993, Page was inducted into the Hockey Hall of Fame as a builder.

ZIGMUND PALFFY led his team in either goals or points in each of the three seasons he spent in the Czech National League. He helped Dukla Trencin win a championship in 1991–92 and was the league's leading scorer in 1992–93. Internationally, Palffy won a bronze medal with the Czechoslovakian national junior team at the World Junior Championships in 1991 and played with the Czech team at the 1991 Canada Cup. An injury kept him out of the Albertville Olympics in 1992, but in 1994 he represented Slovakia at the Lillehammer Olympic Games and led all scorers with 10 points.

Palffy had spent most of the 1993–94 season with Salt Lake City of the International Hockey League, but in addition to playing at the Olympics that year, he made his NHL debut with the New York Islanders on January 6, 1994. He split the 1994–95 season between the Islanders and Denver of the International Hockey League and played his first full NHL season in 1995–96, when he led the Islanders with 43 goals and 77 points. That season, he joined Mike Bossy as the only players in Islanders history to record hat tricks in back-to-back games (March 3–5).

Palffy represented Slovakia at the World Championships and at the World Cup of Hockey in 1996 and cracked the top 10 in NHL scoring for the first time with 90 points in 1996–97. He was a top 10 scorer again with 87 points in 1997–98. Palffy was named to the Slovakian Olympic team at Nagano in 1998.

DING PALMER Winthrop "Ding" Palmer remains the leading goal scorer in the history of Yale University hockey after collecting 87 goals from 1927–28 to 1929–30. In his three seasons at Yale, the Elis posted a combined record of 45–6–2. The 1927–28 team was 13–4–0 (with Palmer's personal record accounting for an astounding 41 goals, including seven in a single game against New Hampshire) and improved to 15–1–1 the following year. The 1929–30 team has been called the greatest amateur hockey team in history. Palmer had 27 goals that year as the team went 17–1–1.

After Yale, Palmer played for the 1932 U.S. Olympic hockey team that lost the gold medal to Canada at Lake Placid, then for the American squad that defeated Canada 2–1 in Prague, Czechoslovakia to win the World Championships in 1933. Palmer was a charter member of the United States Hockey Hall of Fame in 1973.

BOB PARADISE starred in hockey, football and baseball at Cretin High School in his native St. Paul, Minnesota, earning all-State honors in both football and hockey. From there, he attended St. Mary's College, where he was an all-Conference performer in the Minnesota Intercollegiate Athletic Conference for four straight seasons, first as a center, then as a defenseman. It was as a defenseman that Paradise caught the eye of NHL scout and former Boston Bruins star Fern Flaman, but he turned down an offer to sign with Boston in 1965 so he could finish his education.

Paradise played for the United States Olympic hockey team in Grenoble in 1968 and for the U.S. national team at the IIHF World Championships in 1969 before finally making his NHL debut with the Minnesota North Stars during the 1971–72 season. He was sold to the expansion Atlanta Flames on June 6, 1972, but played only 18 games in Atlanta before being traded to the Pittsburgh Penguins. Known as a defensive defenseman, Paradise played with Pittsburgh, the Washington Capitals and then with Pittsburgh again before ending his NHL career after the 1978–79 season. He was elected to the United States Hockey Hall of Fame in 1989, joining his father in law, Bob Dill, who had been enshrined 10 years before.

BERNIE PARENT was a native of Montreal who grew up watching Jacques Plante play goal for the Canadiens on television. Like Plante, Parent became not only a star in the NHL, but one of the greatest goaltenders of all-time. His career ended prematurely in 1979 due to an eye injury.

Parent played his junior hockey with the Niagara Falls Flyers where he teamed with Doug Favell in 1964–65 to lead the team to a Memorial Cup championship. The following year, Parent turned pro and split the 1965–66 and 1966–67 campaigns between the Boston Bruins and their Oklahoma City farm club. In the Expansion Draft prior to the 1967–68 season, he was claimed by the Philadelphia Flyers. Parent was the top goalie in Philadelphia (with Favell as his backup) until he was traded to the Toronto Maple Leafs in February of 1971. In Toronto, he shared the net with his childhood idol, Plante.

Prior to the 1972–73 season, Parent became the first NHL player to sign with the World Hockey Association. He was to be a member of the Miami Screaming Eagles, but when the club withdrew prior to the WHA's first season he wound up playing with the Philadelphia Blazers. He was still in Philadelphia in 1973–74, only now he was back with the Flyers, who were ready to become both the toughest and most successful team in hockey.

Parent shared the Vezina Trophy with Tony Esposito in his first season back with the Flyers after leading the NHL with 12 shutouts and a 1.89 goals-against average. In the playoffs, he won the Conn Smythe Trophy after helping Philadelphia to become the first NHL expansion team to win the Stanley Cup. In 1974–75, Parent won the Vezina Trophy outright after leading the league with 12 shutouts and a 2.03 goals-against average. He also won his second consecutive selection as the Conn Smythe Trophy winner when the Flyers repeated as Stanley Cup champions.

Over the final four years of his career, both Parent and the Flyers continued to rate among the best in the NHL. He led the league in shutouts for a third time with seven in 1977–78, and when he was forced to retire the following year his 54 career shutouts placed him 14th in NHL history. His 270 victories also ranked him among the all-time leaders. Parent was elected to the Hockey Hall of Fame in 1984.

BRAD PARK was one of the top defenseman of his time, gaining seven selections to the all-star team in eight years between 1969–70 and 1977–78, including five berths on the First All-Star Team. He was also a member of Team Canada in 1972. Despite his obvious skill, Park never won the Norris Trophy but finished as runner-up to Bobby Orr four times in a five-year stretch from 1969–70 until 1973–74. He was also second in the voting behind Denis Potvin in 1975–76 and 1977–78.

Park developed into a junior standout with the Toronto Marlboros of the Ontario Hockey Association before entering the NHL with the New York Rangers during the 1968–69 season. Like Bobby Orr, Park would battle knee injuries throughout his career, undergoing five major operations and four arthroscopic surgeries. Still, he was able to play 60 games or more in all but four of his 17 NHL seasons. Park consistently ranked among the game's top-scoring defensemen and was especially effective on the power-play. He also played a more physical game than Orr. During his time in New York, the Rangers were one of the top teams in the NHL.

On November 7, 1975, Park was involved in one of the biggest trades in hockey history when he and Jean Ratelle, along with Joe Zanussi, were dealt to the Boston Bruins for Phil Esposito and Carol Vadnais. Park replaced Bobby Orr on the Bruins defense and was a key member on Boston teams that won four consecutive Adams Division titles and reached the Stanley Cup finals in 1977 and 1978. In August of 1983 he signed as a free agent with Detroit and finished his playing career with two seasons with the Red Wings. Park coached the Red Wings for part of the 1985–86 season. He was elected to the Hockey Hall of Fame in 1988.

CRAIG PATRICK is a member of the United States Hockey Hall of Fame as well as a member of one of hockey's most prominent families. He is the son of Hockey Hall of Famer Lynn Patrick and the grandson of hockey legend Lester Patrick. His uncle, Muzz Patrick, played in the NHL and was a long-time executive with the New York Rangers. Cousin Dick Patrick has been an executive with the Washington Capitals since 1982–83. Frank Patrick, Lester's brother, is also a member of the Hockey Hall of Fame.

Craig Patrick played hockey at the University of Denver and captained the Pioneers to the NCAA championship in 1969. He played for seval NHL clubs—the California Golden Seals, St. Louis Blues, Kansas City Scouts and Washington Capitals—from 1971–72 until 1978–79 and was a member of the United States team at the first Canada Cup tournament in 1976. Patrick got involved in hockey management when he served as an assistant coach and assistant general manager with the "Miracle on Ice" American team at the 1980 Lake Placid Olympics.

Like his father, uncle and grandfather before him, Patrick joined the New York Rangers organization when he signed as director of operations in 1980. On June 14, 1981, he became the youngest general manager in club history. He served as g.m. through the 1985–86 season, leading his team to the playoffs every year. He also coached the team during parts of the 1980–81 and 1984–85 seasons. Patrick then spent two years as director of athletics and recreation at

the University of Denver before becoming general manager of the Pittsburgh Penguins on December 5, 1989.

Patrick's work in Pittsburgh has seen him recognized as one of the best general managers in hockey. His acquisitions of Ron Francis, Ulf Samuelsson and Grant Jennings from the Hartford Whalers at the trade deadline in 1990–91 helped to bring the Penguins their first Stanley Cup title that year, and the deals he engineered to bring in Rick Tocchet, Ken Wregget and Kjell Samuelsson helped the team repeat as champions in 1992. The Penguins have remained one of the most successful teams in hockey during the 1990s and Patrick has become the longest-serving general manager in franchise history. Twice during his tenure he has taken over behind the bench, coaching the team briefly in 1989–90 and 1996–97.

FRANK PATRICK was a star player in his own right both before and after he and brother Lester Patrick formed the Pacific Coast Hockey Association in 1911–12. Both brothers served as players, coaches, managers and owners of PCHA franchises (Frank in Vancouver, Lester in Victoria) while Frank also served as league president. He was responsible for more than 20 changes to the way hockey was played that later became part of the NHL rule book.

Frank Patrick's hockey career began in Montreal, where he played with the Victorias, Westmount and McGill University, while his brother Lester starred with the Montreal Wanderers. The family later moved west to Nelson, British Columbia, where the brothers continued to play hockey. They returned east to join the Renfrew Millionaires when the National Hockey Association was formed in 1909–10. Frank played defense with Cyclone Taylor at Renfrew when the position was known as point and cover point, and the Patrick brothers formed a friendship with the star player that would last a lifetime. This led to his signing with Frank's Vancouver Millionaires in the PCHA's second season of 1912–13. Taylor's signing gave the fledgling league a major boost.

In order to form the Pacific Coast Hockey Association, the Patrick brothers used money from the sale of the family lumber business to build Canada's first artificial ice rinks in Vancouver and Victoria. They remained innovators throughout the history of the PCHA, adding blue lines to the ice, allowing forward passing, adopting assists as an official statistic and refining the modern playoff format. Meanwhile, Frank continued to star on the ice. His six goals in a game on March 6, 1912 is a record unmatched by any NHL defenseman, and he helped his Vancouver team to win the Stanley Cup in 1915.

In later years, Patrick was forced to concentrate more on his duties as league president than as a player, and when the PCHA was reduced to two teams after the 1923–24 season, Frank and Lester's Vancouver and Victoria franchises joined the Western Canada Hockey League. When pro hockey finally collapsed in the west after the 1925–26 season, Frank Patrick looked after the job of selling its players to NHL interests. He later served as managing director of the NHL (1933–34), as a coach with the Boston Bruins (1934–35, 1935–36) and as business manager of the Montreal Canadiens (1941–42). He was elected to the Hockey Hall of Fame as a builder in 1958.

LESTER PATRICK enjoyed one of the longest careers in hockey history, beginning as a player in 1903–04 and continuing as a coach, g.m., owner and NHL governor until his association with the New York Rangers ended in 1947, the same year he was inducted into the Hockey Hall of Fame.

Patrick learned to play hockey while growing up in Montreal, but he first came to prominence in 1903–04 as a rushing defenseman with a team from Brandon, Manitoba that unsuccessfully challenged the Ottawa Silver Seven for the Stanley Cup. After a season with Westmount in Montreal, Patrick joined the Montreal Wanderers in 1905–06, helping that team dethrone Ottawa as Stanley Cup champions. He played on another championship team with the Wanderers the following season before moving west to Nelson, British Columbia to work in the family lumber business. He continued to play hockey in Nelson on a team with his brother Frank, and he joined Edmonton in an unsuccessful Stanley Cup challenge against the Wanderers in December of 1908.

When the National Hockey Association was formed for the 1909–10 season, the Patrick brothers returned east as members of the Renfrew Millionaires. The brothers headed out west again after that season, and in 1911–12 they established the Pacific Coast Hockey Association. In order to form their league, the Patricks used money from the sale of the family lumber business to build Canada's first artificial ice rinks in Vancouver and Victoria. Both brothers served as players, coaches, managers and owners, Frank in Vancouver and Lester in Victoria. Lester remained active as a player until 1921–22, when he was forced to play two games in goal as an emergency replacement. He concentrated on his off-ice duties over the next three years, but he returned to play a complete season with Victoria in 1925–26. Hockey in the west collapsed after that season, and the Patricks sold the league's players to teams in the NHL.

In 1926–27, Lester Patrick joined the New York Rangers as coach and general manager, and he generally is credited with making pro hockey a success in the northeastern United States. He guided the Rangers to a Stanley Cup victory in 1928 (which included his famous emergency stint in goal) and again in 1933, and he was named to the NHL First All-Star Team as a coach six times in seven years between 1930–31 and 1937–38. He gave up coaching in 1939

while continuing as Rangers general manager until 1946. After leaving New York in 1947, he ran the minor-league Victoria Cougars of the Pacific Coast Hockey League until 1954. The Lester Patrick Trophy honoring contributions to hockey in the United States has been presented annually since 1966.

LYNN PATRICK Though he was the son of Lester Patrick, Lynn Patrick's youth was spent in a non-hockey environment. He was a star football and basketball player but did not play competitive hockey until joining a senior team in Montreal in 1933–34. His father feared being accused of nepotism and was reluctant to let Lynn join the Rangers, but did so the following year after other general managers began expressing interest.

Patrick showed modest success in his early years with the Rangers, but did play on a Stanley Cup winner in New York with his brother Muzz in 1940. Over the next three years, Lynn developed into one of the top players in the NHL. Playing on a line with Bryan Hextall and Phil Watson, Patrick led the league with 32 goals in 1941–42 and was named a First Team All-Star at left wing. The following year, he earned a Second Team selection after collecting a career-high 61 points. He missed the next two years due to military service before spending a final season with the Rangers in 1945–46. He then became a coach with New York's New Haven farm club in the American Hockey League.

Patrick returned to the NHL as coach of the Rangers during the 1947–48 season but quit the team after the 1949–50 Stanley Cup finals. He was to rejoin his father as the coach of Lester's Victoria club in the Pacific Coast Hockey League, but instead resurfaced in the NHL as the coach of the Boston Bruins in 1950–51. Patrick remained in that position until succeeding Art Ross as general manager in 1954–55, but left Boston after the 1965–66 season to become the first general manager of the St. Louis Blues. Patrick also coached the team briefly during the 1966–67 season before turning over that job to Scotty Bowman. He retired in 1977 as the Blues' senior vice president. In 1980, Lynn Patrick was inducted into the Hockey Hall of Fame.

MICHAEL PECA was a high-scoring center in junior hockey with the Ottawa 67's who has become one of the top defensive forwards in the NHL. Peca played briefly with the Vancouver Canucks in 1993–94 and 1994–95 before being dealt to Buffalo when the Sabres sent Alexander Mogilny to Vancouver. He scored the last goal at the Memorial Auditorium on April 14, 1996.

Peca earned the Selke Trophy in 1996–97 and was runner up (behind Jere Lehtinen) in 1997–98, as the Sabres enjoyed surprising success in both seasons. He became captain of the team in 1997–98. Before beginning his NHL career, Peca helped Team Canada win a gold medal at the World Junior Championships in 1994.

PETE PEETERS ranks among the top goaltenders of his day, leading the league in goals-against average twice during the 1980s. His eight shutouts for the Boston Bruins in 1982–83 was the best total of the decade, as was his 2.36 goals-against average that season.

Peeters entered the NHL with the Philadelphia Flyers, becoming the team's top goaltender in 1979–80 after earning the Hap Holmes Trophy and a second team all-star selection in the American Hockey League the previous season. He was undefeated over a stretch of 27 games early in the 1979–80 season as the Flyers set an NHL record with a 35-game unbeaten streak and finished first overall in the regular-season standings. Peeters spent two more years with Philadelphia before being dealt to Boston on June 9, 1982.

In his first year with the Bruins, Peeters led the league with 40 wins along with his eight shutouts and 2.36 average and his 31-game undefeated streak in 1982–83 is the second-longest in hockey history (Gerry Cheevers had a 32-game streak in 1971–72). He won the Vezina Trophy and was named to the First All-Star Team that year, but his numbers declined over the next few years and he was dealt to the Washington Capitals on November 14, 1985. Peeters led the league with a 2.78 goals-against average for Washington in 1987–88, but returned to Philadelphia in 1989 to finish his career.

GILBERT PERREAULT was the first draft pick in the history of the Buffalo Sabres, chosen first overall in the 1970 Amateur Draft. He went on to become the Sabres career leader in virtually every major category, including seasons (17), games (1,191), goals (512), assists (814) and points (1,326).

Before being drafted by Buffalo, Perreault was a scoring star with the Montreal Junior Canadiens in the Ontario Hockey Association. He led his team to the Memorial Cup title in 1969 and again in 1970, when he was named the OHA's most valuable player. Perreault's success continued during his first year with the Sabres, setting what were then rookie scoring records with 38 goals and 72 points to win the Calder Trophy. By 1972–73, Perreault was centering the French Connection line with Rene Robert and Richard Martin, and the high-scoring trio helped the Sabres reach the playoffs after only three seasons. Perreault won the Lady Byng Trophy that year.

In 1974–75, Perreault, Robert and Martin all cracked the top 10 in scoring as the Sabres won the Adams Division and reached the Stanley Cup finals in only their fifth season, losing to the Philadelphia Flyers. In 1975–76, Perreault established career highs with 44 goals, 69 assists and 113 points. He was named to the Second All-Star Team that season and in 1976–77.

When he retired on November 24, 1986, Perreault had led the Sabres in scoring 12 times and had owned seven of the team's top–10 single-season scoring performances. He ranked 12th in NHL history in goals, eighth in assists and seventh in points. Perreault was elected to the Hockey Hall of Fame in 1990.

TOMMY PHILLIPS was a native of Kenora, Ontario who starred with the hometown Thistles when they defeated the Montreal Wanderers in January of 1907 to make Kenora the smallest town ever to win the Stanley Cup. Phillips scored all four goals in a 4–2 victory on January 17, 1907, and added three more in the clinching 8–6 victory four nights later. He could skate, shoot and stickhandle, and he also was considered the best backchecker in the game.

Phillips played hockey as a boy in Kenora when the town was known as Rat Portage, but he came to prominence while attending McGill University and playing for the Montreal Amateur Athletic Association. He helped his Montreal team to defend the Stanley Cup in January and February of 1903 before losing it to Ottawa Silver Seven. He played for the Toronto Marlboros the following year when they unsuccessfully challenged Ottawa for the Stanley Cup.

By the 1904–05 season, Phillips was back home in Rat Portage as the leading scorer on the Thistles. He had five goals in a 9–3 victory over the Silver Seven in game one of a Stanley Cup challenge on March 7, 1905 before Ottawa rallied to win the best-of-three series. Phillips led the renamed Kenora Thistles to another Manitoba Hockey League title in 1905–06 before winning the Stanley Cup in 1907.

After the Thistles lost the Stanley Cup in a rematch with the Montreal Wanderers in March of 1907, Phillips joined the Ottawa Senators of the Eastern Canada Amateur Hockey Association. He scored 26 goals in 10 games during the 1907–08 season, including a pair of five-goal games and was generally regarded as the best player in hockey. Phillips was one of many "ringers" added to the Edmonton team that challenged the Montreal Wanderers for the Stanley Cup in December of 1908, but he broke his ankle in the first game and was never the same player afterwards.

Phillips played very little hockey over the next few years, but he signed with the Vancouver Millionaires in the inaugural season of the Pacific Coast Hockey Association. He was seventh in the league with 17 goals in 1911–12, but he retired from hockey at season's end. In 1945, he became one of the original 12 members inducted into the Hockey Hall of Fame.

ALLAN PICKARD Though originally from Exeter, Ontario, Allan Pickard was an important organizer and administrator of amateur hockey in Saskatchewan. He helped establish the Regina YMCA League during the 1920s, which grew into the Regina Parks League, one of the best-run minor hockey organizations in the country.

Pickard was a coach, executive and president of the Regina Aces in senior hockey during the late 1920s and became an executive member of the Saskatchewan Amateur Hockey Association in 1935–36. He was president of the SAHA in 1941–42 and 1942–43 and was also president of the Saskatchewan Senior Hockey League during the time it produced such stars as future Hall of Famers Elmer Lach and Max and Doug Bentley. Pickard was also president of the Western Canada Senior League and governor of Saskatchewan's Junior League and the Western Canada Junior League. He was president of the Canadian Amateur Hockey Association from 1947–48 to 1949–50. Pickard is a life member of both the SAHA and the CAHA and was inducted into the Hockey Hall of Fame as a builder in 1958.

PIERRE PILOTE was an aggressive defenseman who could play the body and rush the puck effectively. He was also a skilled playmaker who consistently ranked among the top-scoring defensemen of his day. His 59 points on 14 goals and 45 assists in 1964–65 were an NHL record for defensemen in the pre expansion era.

Pilote was a product of the Black Hawks system, playing junior hockey in St. Catharines, then joining Buffalo of the American Hockey League before making his debut in Chicago in 1955–56. He became a regular the following season and did not miss a game over his first five years. Beginning with the 1959–60 campaign, Pilote was chosen as an all-star eight years in a row, gaining three straight selections to the Second Team, then five to the First Team. He also won the Norris Trophy three years in a row from 1962–63 to 1964–65.

Pilote was a key member of Chicago's Stanley Cup-winning team of 1961 and served as Black Hawks captain from 1961–62 until 1967–68. He played his final season with the Toronto Maple Leafs in 1968–69. Pilote was elected to the Hockey Hall of Fame in 1975.

RUDY PILOUS coached championship teams in many different leagues over a much-traveled hockey career. He also was well traveled as a player, beginning in his hometown of Winnipeg, as well as Portage la Prairie, Selkirk, Manitoba, and Nelson, British Columbia in the 1920s and 1930s. He spent the 1936–37 season with the Richmond Hawks in England. He was a member of the New York Rovers (a Rangers farm club) in 1937–38 and was playing senior hockey in St. Catharines, Ontario the following year. In 1943, he established the St. Catharines Falcons junior team.

Pilous coached in St. Catharines from 1943–44 until 1945–46, then spent

the next four years with the Buffalo Bisons (American Hockey League), Houston Huskies (United States Hockey League), San Diego Skyhawks (Pacific Coast Hockey League) and Louisville Blades (USHL), winning championships with Houston in 1948 and in San Diego in 1949. In 1950, Pilous returned to St. Catharines (now known as the Teepees) and coached the team over eight successful seasons, winning the Memorial Cup in 1954.

Pilous entered the NHL as coach of the Chicago Black Hawks during the 1957–58 season and led the club to its first Stanley Cup title in 23 years in 1961. After the 1962–63 season, Pilous was replaced by Billy Reay. He became coach of the Denver Invaders of the Western Hockey League in 1963–64 and promptly led the team to a league championship. He later led the Victoria Maple Leafs to the WHL finals in 1965 and the Denver Spurs to the WHL finals in 1971. In 1973–74, Pilous signed on to assist player-coach Bobby Hull in running the Winnipeg Jets, and in 1976 and 1978 was general manager of the Jets teams that won the Avco Cup as champions of the World Hockey Association. In 1982, Pilous returned to St. Catharines as the general manager of the Toronto Maple Leafs American Hockey League affiliate in the city, serving until 1985–86. Pilous was inducted into the Hockey Hall of Fame in 1985.

DIDIER PITRE was the first man signed to play for *les Canadiens* when the new French-Canadian team formed for the National Hockey Association's inaugural season in 1909–10. He was a large man in an era of much smaller players and his powerful shot earned him the nickname "Cannonball." It was his skating speed, combined with that of Jack Laviolette and Newsy Lalonde, that would lead sportswriters to call the Canadiens "the Flying Frenchmen."

Pitre began his career as a defenseman when the position was known as point and cover point, and he joined the Montreal Nationals with Laviolette for the 1903–04 season. The two players spent the next three years with the Sault Ste. Marie, Michigan team in the International (Pro) Hockey League (hockey's first professional circuit) before returning to Montreal with the Shamrocks in 1907–08. Pitre was added as a "ringer" to the Edmonton squad that challenged the Montreal Wanderers for the Stanley Cup in December of 1908, and he also played in Renfrew before Laviolette signed him for the Canadiens in 1909. With the exception of the 1913–14 season, which he spent with the Vancouver Millionaires of the Pacific Coast Hockey Association, Pitre remained in Montreal until he retired from hockey in 1923.

Still a defenseman in his first two seasons with the Canadiens, Pitre was moved up to right wing in 1911–12, becoming one of the top scorers in the NHA. He had 30 goals in 20 games during the 1914–15 season. Pitre played on a forward line with Lalonde and Laviolette the following year that helped the Canadiens win their first Stanley Cup championship. Pitre and Lalonde both ranked among the scoring leaders when new teammate Joe Malone led the NHL with 44 goals in its first season of 1917–18. When Pitre retired after the 1922–23 season, he ranked second to Lalonde for the most career goals in a Canadiens uniform. In 1962, he was elected to the Hockey Hall of Fame.

JACQUES PLANTE was one of the most influential goaltenders in NHL history. He was one of the first netminders to roam from his crease, playing the puck for his defensemen and stopping dump-ins behind the net. More importantly, he was the first goalie to popularize the use of the mask as a standard piece of equipment. Plante was plagued with asthma throughout his career and missed 13 games during the 1957–58 season due to a sinus operation. He then began using a mask in practice. Canadiens management was opposed to him wearing it in games, but relented after Plante was badly cut by a shot from Andy Bathgate on November 1, 1959. The Canadiens went undefeated over the next 10 games and the goalie was permitted to wear his mask full-time.

Plante, a product of the Montreal Canadiens farm system, made brief but spectacular appearances with the Canadiens in 1952–53 and 1953–54 before becoming the club's regular goaltender in 1954–55. Plante was again impressive during his first full season with the Canadiens. From 1955–56 until 1959–60, he won the Vezina Trophy five years in a row while Montreal won the Stanley Cup five consecutive times. He was named to either the First or Second All-Star Team in each of those five seasons. In 1961–62, Plante won the Vezina Trophy for the sixth time and was again a First Team All-Star while becoming just the fourth goalie in NHL history (Roy Worters, Chuck Rayner and Al Rollins) to win the Hart Trophy.

Plante remained with Montreal through the 1962–63 season, but was traded to the New York Rangers for Gump Worsley on June 4, 1963. He retired after two seasons in New York, but was lured back to the game by the St. Louis Blues to share goaltending duties with Glenn Hall in 1968–69. The veteran duo shared the Vezina Trophy that year, allowing Plante to surpass Bill Durnan with his record seventh Vezina victory. In 1970–71, Plante was traded to the Toronto Maple Leafs, where he was named to the Second All-Star Team after producing a 1.88 goals-against average. Plante helped to groom Bernie Parent for stardom during his time in Toronto, but ended his NHL career with the Boston Bruins after a late-season trade in 1972–73. In 1974–75 he was back in action with the Edmonton Oilers of the World Hockey Association.

Jacques Plante was elected to the Hockey Hall of Fame in 1978. His lifetime NHL totals include 434 wins (ranking second to Terry Sawchuk's 447), 82 shutouts and a 2.38 goals-against average. His 14 shutouts in the playoffs are an NHL record. The Quebec Major Junior Hockey League rewards its top goaltenders with the Jacques Plante Trophy.

CONNIE PLEBAN John E. "Connie" Pleban launched his long hockey career in his native Minnesota, playing at Eveleth High School from 1930 to 1932 and then at Eveleth Junior College until 1934. He was a member of the Baby Ruth National Amateur Athletic Union champs in 1935 and a player-coach in Wisconsin with the Eagle River Falcons semi-pro team until 1938. Pleban returned to Eveleth as a player-coach with the semi-pro Rangers between 1938 and 1941, then spent two seasons as a player-coach in Michigan with the Marquette Sentinels before entering the service for World War II.

Pleban went back to Eveleth again after the war and in 1950 served as a player-coach on the United States national team that won a silver medal at the World Championships in London. He also helped build the U.S. Olympic hockey team that won a silver medal in Oslo in 1952. Pleban later coached the American team at the 1961 World Championships in Geneva and led the U.S. to a bronze medal at Colorado Springs a year later.

In addition to his international successes, Pleban began coaching at the University of Minnesota-Duluth in 1955. He led UMD's transition from small- to major-college status and in four years there his teams never lost a game in the Minnesota Intercollegiate Athletic Conference. Pleban also successfully lobbied the NCAA to permit bodychecking in all zones. As a resident of Duluth after his days at the university there, Pleban helped organize amateur teams and leagues through the 1960s and 1970s and was elected to the United States Hockey Hall of Fame in the coaches category in 1990.

BUD POILE Norman "Bud" Poile has played an integral part in the development of hockey as a player, coach, general manager and league executive. He played junior hockey in and around his hometown of Fort William, Ontario and signed his first pro contract with the Toronto Maple Leafs in 1942–43. He led the Leafs in playoff scoring that year, but left the team during the 1943–44 season for service in World War II.

Poile returned to Toronto late in the 1945–46 season and was a member of the Maple Leafs Stanley Cup-winning team of 1947. On November 4, 1947, he was one of five players Toronto traded to the Chicago Black Hawks to obtain Max Bentley. Poile later played with the Detroit Red Wings, New York Rangers and Boston Bruins before his NHL playing career ended after the 1949–50 season.

Poile became a playing coach with the Tulsa Oilers of the United States Hockey League in 1950–51 and joined the Edmonton Flyers of the Western Hockey League two years later. He led that team to a league championship in 1954–55, then gave up his playing duties to concentrate on coaching. He remained in Edmonton until 1960–61, also serving as general manager in 1957–58 and 1958–59. Poile joined the San Francisco Seals in 1962–63 and coached the team to three straight WHL championships. He was general manager of the Seals in 1965–66.

In 1966, Poile was hired as the first general manager of the Philadelphia Flyers and helped to assemble the team that entered the NHL in 1967–68. He left Philadelphia after the 1969–70 season to become g.m. of the Vancouver Canucks when they entered the NHL in 1970–71. After the 1972–73 season, he joined the World Hockey Association as vice president. He then served as commissioner of the minor pro Central Hockey League from 1976 until 1984. During the 1983–84 season, he also took on the top job with the International Hockey League. After the CHL suspended operations that year, he continued as IHL commissioner until 1988–89. That same year, the IHL began presenting the Poile Trophy to its playoff MVP and Poile himself was awarded the Lester Patrick Trophy for his contribution to hockey in the United States. In 1990, he was elected to the Hockey Hall of Fame as a builder.

SAM POLLOCK's devotion and single-mindedness of purpose made him stand out among the NHL general managers of his era. His astute judgement of players, his skill at negotiating trades and his dedication to the job allowed him to build championship teams at all levels of hockey, including nine Stanley Cup winners in 14 years as general manager of the Montreal Canadiens from 1964–65 to 1977–78. He was elected to the Hockey Hall of Fame in the builder's category in 1978.

Pollock became involved in hockey at an early age in his hometown of Montreal, and after six years of running minor hockey teams for the Canadiens, he was hired officially by the club in 1947. Three years later, he became director of player personnel, continuing in that capacity until 1964 when he was named vice president and general manager. His clever trades and shrewd draft choices ensured that Montreal carried on its tradition as the greatest franchise in hockey.

In addition to his nine Stanley Cup winners in Montreal, Pollock was coach and/or general manager of numerous other championship teams during his 30 years with the Canadiens organization: the Montreal Junior Canadiens (Memorial Cup, 1950), the Hull-Ottawa Junior Canadiens (Memorial Cup 1958), the Hull-Ottawa Canadiens (Eastern Pro League champs, 1961) and the Omaha Knights (Central Pro League champs, 1962). He also assembled Canada's team that won the first Canada Cup in 1976.

After retiring from hockey, Pollock was named chairman of Carena-Bancorp Equities Limited, and later joined John Labatt Limited as chairman in 1991. Through his association with Labatt, he became chairman of the board with the Toronto Blue Jays in 1995. Pollock continues to serve with the Blue Jays and on many other prominent boards across Canada.

DENIS POTVIN The New York Islanders drafted Denis Potvin first overall in the 1973 Amateur Draft to be the foundation for their developing team. By the time he retired after the 1987–88 season, Potvin had played for four Stanley Cup champions, been named to the all-star team seven times (including five selections to the First Team) and was the NHL's all-time leader in goals, assists and points by a defenseman. His number 5 was the first number ever retired by the Islanders.

Potvin was an Ottawa native who starred with the hometown 67's of the Ontario Hockey Association, setting a record for scoring by a defenseman with 123 points in his final junior year of 1972–73 that lasted until 1988–89. He won the Calder Trophy as rookie of the year for the Islanders in 1973–74 and was the runner-up behind Bobby Orr in Norris Trophy voting in 1974–75. He won the Norris Trophy after just his third season, and was named the NHL's top defenseman again in 1977–78 and 1978–79. Potvin established career highs during the 1978–79 season with 30 goals, 71 assists and 101 points.

In 1979–80, Potvin became captain of the Islanders and wore the "C" as his team won the Stanley Cup four years in a row. He continued to rank among the top players at his position, both offensively and defensively, after the Islanders Stanley Cup dynasty ended, and on April 4, 1987, Potvin became the first defenseman in NHL history to reach 1,000 career points. When he retired after the following season, Potvin had 1,052 points on 310 goals and 742 assists. He was elected to the Hockey Hall of Fame in 1990.

Potvin has worked as a television analyst since the end of his playing career and joined the broadcast crew of the Florida Panthers when the team entered the NHL in 1993–94. His brother Jean played in the NHL between 1970–71 and 1980–81.

FELIX POTVIN emerged as a star in the Quebec Major Junior Hockey League, leading the league in shutouts during each of the three seasons he played with Chicoutimi. He was named to the second all-star team in 1989–90 but was at his best during his final season of 1990–91. That year, Potvin was a first team all-star and the Canadian major junior goaltender of the year after leading Chicoutimi to the QMJHL title. He also made the Memorial Cup all-star team and won the Hap Emms Memorial Trophy as the top goaltender in the tournament. In addition, Potvin won a gold medal with Team Canada at the World Junior Championships that year.

Potvin had been chosen by the Toronto Maple Leafs in the 1990 Entry Draft and turned pro with the club's St. John's affiliate in 1991–92. That year, he won the Baz Bastien Memorial Trophy as the top goaltender in the American Hockey League, the Dudley "Red" Garrett Memorial Trophy as the AHL's top rookie and was named to the first all-star team. He made his NHL debut when he played four games for Toronto that season and his play with the Maple Leafs in 1992–93 was so solid that the team traded Grant Fuhr to the Buffalo Sabres. Potvin led the NHL with a 2.50 goals-against average in his rookie season and starred in the playoffs as the Maple Leafs reached the Campbell Conference Championship before losing to the Los Angeles Kings in seven games.

In his first full season with the Maple Leafs in 1993–94, Potvin tied Johnny Bower's club record with 34 victories and helped Toronto to reach the Conference finals for the second year in a row. While the club's fortunes have sagged since then, Potvin has gone on to become third all-time in Maple Leafs history behind Turk Broda and Bower in both games played and wins. He set a club record and led the league when he played 74 games in 1996–97. Potvin faced more shots that season than any goaltender in NHL history.

BABE PRATT Walter "Babe" Pratt was a star amateur player for several teams in his home province of Manitoba, as well as with the Kenora Thistles, before turning pro with the Philadelphia Ramblers of the Canadian-American Hockey League in 1935–36. Philadelphia was a New York Rangers farm club, and Pratt was promoted to the NHL roster in January of 1936. He joined a talented Rangers defense corps that included aging veteran Ching Johnson, whom Pratt replaced as a regular during the playoffs in 1937.

Pratt played six full seasons with the Rangers, helping the team to win the Stanley Cup in 1940 and finish in first place during the 1941–42 regular season. In November of 1942, Pratt was traded to the Toronto Maple Leafs, where he enjoyed the most productive seasons of his career. Pratt won the Hart Trophy and was named to the First All-Star Team in 1943–44 after establishing an NHL scoring record for defensemen with 57 points on 17 goals and 40 assists. He earned a Second Team All-Star selection the following season when he also helped the Maple Leafs to win the Stanley Cup.

On January 30, 1946, Pratt was at the center of controversy when it was announced he had been suspended from the NHL for betting on games involving teams other than his own. At an appeal, Pratt admitted he had gambled and promised he would not do so again. He was reinstated after missing nine games, but Conn Smythe later traded him to the Boston Bruins where he spent

his final NHL season in 1946–47. After a year in the American Hockey League, Pratt spent three seasons with New Westminster and one with Tacoma of the Pacific Coast Hockey League before retiring at the end of the 1951–52 campaign. He was elected to the Hockey Hall of Fame in 1966. Son Tracy Pratt spent 10 years in the NHL from 1967–68 to 1976–77.

DEAN PRENTICE A strong and aggressive left winger, Dean Prentice was called up to the New York Rangers from Guelph of the Ontario Hockey Association in 1952–53. He was placed on a line with former Guelph teammate Andy Bathgate for the 1954–55 season and went on to one of the longest careers in NHL history.

Prentice played 10 years in New York and led the Rangers with 24 goals in 1955–56 as the team made the playoffs for the first time in six seasons. His best year came in 1959–60 when he had 32 goals and 34 assists and was named to the Second All-Star Team.

Traded to the Boston Bruins during the 1962–63 season, Prentice was dealt again, joining the Red Wings in 1965–66. Reunited with Andy Bathgate in Detroit, and centered by Norm Ullman, Prentice helped lead the Red Wings to the Stanley Cup finals that season. Detroit's loss to the Montreal Canadiens that year would prove to be the the closest he ever came to winning a Stanley Cup championship.

Prentice remained with the Red Wings through the 1968–69 season and then enjoyed productive seasons with the Pittsburgh Penguins and Minnesota North Stars. He scored 26 goals as a 40-year-old in 1972–73 before retiring in 1974. He played 1,378 games in his 22-year career, totals that were topped by only Gordie Howe, Alex Delvecchio, and Tim Horton at the time.

JOE PRIMEAU was the center of the Toronto Maple Leafs' famed Kid Line of the 1930s and later became a successful coach. He is the only man in hockey history to guide teams that won the Memorial Cup, the Allan Cup and the Stanley Cup.

Primeau did not begin skating until he was 12 years old, but developed quickly as a hockey player and first began attracting attention at St. Michael's College in Toronto in 1923–24. He continued to play junior and senior hockey in Toronto before Conn Smythe signed him to a professional contract in 1927. Primeau made brief appearances with the Maple Leafs in 1927–28 and 1928–29, and finally made the NHL to stay in 1929–30 when he was teamed on a line with Busher Jackson and Charlie Conacher.

Although his linemates were more flashy, it was Primeau's steady work and strong two-way play that allowed Jackson and Conacher to become such great scorers. He led the NHL in assists in 1930–31, 1931–32 and 1933–34, and was runner-up in the league scoring race behind Jackson in 1931–32 and behind Conacher in 1933–34. "Gentleman Joe," as he was known, won the Lady Byng Trophy in 1931–32 and was named to the Second All-Star Team in 1933–34. He was a key contributor to the Maple Leafs' first Stanley Cup victory in 1932.

Primeau retired after the 1935–36 season to go into business. He operated a successful concrete company, but was back in hockey by 1938–39 as coach of the Toronto Marlboros senior team. He also coached the Toronto RCAF Hurricanes in 1942–43, before returning to St. Michael's and junior hockey in 1944–45. He guided the Majors to the Memorial Cup title that year, and again in 1946–47, then rejoined the Marlboros senior team and won the Allan Cup in 1949–50. The following year, Primeau was hired to replace Hap Day as coach of the Maple Leafs and promptly won the Stanley Cup. He was replaced by King Clancy behind the Leafs bench after his team missed the playoffs in 1952–53. In 1963, Joe Primeau was inducted into the Hockey Hall of Fame.

GOLDIE PRODGERS was a fast skater and tough checker who was equally skilled as a forward or defenseman throughout his career. Originally signed by Waterloo of the Ontario Professional Hockey League, Prodgers played forward because the team already had brothers Howard, Harold, and George McNamara on defense. His potential was recognized by the Quebec Bulldogs, who signed him for the 1911–12 National Hockey Association season and paired him on defense with "Bad Joe" Hall, one of the roughest players of the day. The two helped Quebec win the NHA title and the Stanley Cup that year.

After their Stanley Cup victory, every Quebec player was offered a contract by the rival Pacific Coast Hockey Association for the 1912–13 season. Prodgers signed with the Victoria Aristocrats and helped them win the PCHA title. When the leagues made peace the following year, Prodgers returned to the Bulldogs. In 1914–15, he joined the Montreal Wanderers and was paired on defense with another tough customer—Sprague Cleghorn. Moving again the following season, Prodgers signed with the Montreal Canadiens and scored the series-winning goal when the franchise won its first Stanley Cup championship in the spring of 1916.

Prodgers enlisted for military service and became a member of the 228th Battalion team that played in the NHA in 1916–17. The presence of George and Howard McNamara on the army team again forced Prodgers to become a forward and he scored 16 goals in just 12 games, including six in one game on January 6, 1917. Five weeks later, the military team was sent overseas.

Prodgers returned to hockey with the Toronto St. Patricks in 1919–20. The following season, he was one of several players sent to Hamilton in an attempt

to bolster the weak Tigers franchise. He spent four productive seasons in Hamilton, but retired after playing one game in 1924–25.

CHRIS PRONGER was a star in junior hockey. He was the Ontario Hockey League's top-scoring defenseman in 1991–92 and helped the Peterborough Petes to reach the Memorial Cup finals in 1993 when he was named Canadian major junior defenseman of the year. Pronger was selected second overall behind Alexander Daigle by the Hartford Whalers in the 1993 NHL Entry Draft and went on to be named Hartford's most valuable defenseman in 1993–94, earning a spot on the NHL All-Rookie Team.

Much was expected of the 6'5", 220-pound defenseman, but Pronger struggled during his second year in Hartford and was considered a disappointment in St. Louis in 1995–96 after the Blues acquired him in a trade for Brendan Shanahan. However, Pronger led the Blues in plus–minus at +15 in 1996–97 and was named team captain in 1997–98. He responded by earning a nomination for the Norris Trophy as the NHL's best defenseman. Pronger was a also member of the Canadian Olympic team in Nagano in 1998 and had previously represented his country at the World Junior Championships in 1993, where he won a gold medal.

MARCEL PRONOVOST A graceful skater and fine puck carrier, Marcel Pronovost played 21 years in the NHL, winning the Stanley Cup four times with the Detroit Red Wings and once with the Toronto Maple Leafs. He was a Second Team All-Star on defense in both the 1957–58 and 1958–59 seasons and was named to the First All-Star Team in each of the next two years. Pronovost was the seventh player in NHL history to play 1,000 games.

Pronovost made his NHL debut during the playoffs in 1950 after spending the 1949–50 campaign with Omaha of the United States Hockey League. He was called up to Detroit to fill in for Red Kelly on the Red Wings defense after Kelly was moved up to play forward in place of the injured Gordie Howe. Pronovost helped the Red Wings to win the Stanley Cup that year and earned a regular spot on the Detroit roster during the 1950–51 season. He played on Stanley Cup champions in Detroit again in 1952, 1954 and 1955. The respect he gained around the NHL was demonstrated before a game with the Canadiens at the Forum on March 1, 1960 when Montreal fans presented Pronovost with a new car. His Red Wings teammates gave him a diamond ring.

After his 16th season with the Red Wings, Pronovost was traded to Toronto as part of an eight-player deal on May 20, 1965. He helped the Maple Leafs to win the Stanley Cup in 1967 and played in Toronto until the 1969–70 season when he joined Tulsa of the Central Hockey League. Pronovost later coached the Tulsa team and was named CHL coach of the year in 1971–72. He was the coach of the Chicago Cougars during the first World Hockey Association season of 1972–73, and returned to the NHL as the coach of the Buffalo Sabres in 1977–78 and 1978–79. He also assisted Ted Lindsay as coach of the Red Wings for the last nine games of the 1979–80 season. Between 1975–76 and 1979–80, Pronovost spent time behind the bench with Hull of the Quebec Junior Hockey League. From 1991 to 1995, he was a scout with the New Jersey Devils, Stanley Cup winners in 1995. Pronovost was elected to the Hockey Hall of Fame in 1978.

CLAUDE PROVOST was an aggressive right winger and an excellent checker with surprising speed despite an awkward skating style. He was often employed by the Montreal Canadiens to shadow Bobby Hull during the 1960s and was one of few players capable of shutting down "the Golden Jet."

Toe Blake promoted Provost to the Canadiens in his first season as coach in in 1955–56 and his hustling style earning him a place on a star-studded Canadiens team that went on to win the Stanley Cup five years in a row. Though known mostly as a checker, Provost was also a capable offensive player whose scoring skills improved over the years. In 1961–62, he led the Canadiens with a career-high 33 goals and led the team again when he scored 27 in 1964–65. In addition, Provost established career highs with 37 assists and 64 points that season and was named to the First All-Star Team. The Canadiens were Stanley Cup champions in 1964–65 and Provost played on Stanley Cup winners again in 1966, 1968, and 1969, giving him nine championships in a 15-year career that ended after the 1969–70 season.

HARVEY PULFORD was a great all-around athlete who starred in virtually every sport he tried. His first title came at 13 when he was named the all-around sports champion in Ottawa's Model School. He continued winning honors until he was almost 50, including the Ottawa squash championship in 1922–23. He starred in football, lacrosse, boxing, paddling and rowing, but he earned his greatest fame in hockey as captain of the Ottawa Silver Seven, who won the Stanley Cup three years in a row, defeating 10 different challengers between 1903 and 1906.

Pulford joined the Ottawa Hockey Club in 1894, where he was a star defenseman until retiring in 1908. (During his time, the position was known as point and cover point). Not one to rush the puck, Pulford was solid checker who preferred to remain in his own end at virtually all times. He only scored eight goals, including playoff games, in his entire career, but he invariably was named to any all-star team selected by the sportswriters of his era.

In addition to his success in hockey, Pulford played football for the Ottawa Rough Riders when they won Canadian football titles in 1898, 1899 and 1900. He was a member of the Ottawa Capitals when they ruled Canadian lacrosse from 1897 to 1900. He was eastern Canada's light-heavyweight and heavyweight boxing champion from 1896 to 1898 and was the Canadian champion in double and single-blade paddling in 1898. He also won numerous national and international honors in rowing. In 1945, Pulford became one of the first 12 men inducted into the Hockey Hall of Fame.

FIDO PURPUR Clifford Joseph "Fido" Purpur began his NHL career in 1934–35 as a member of the St. Louis Eagles (formerly the Ottawa Senators). When the team folded after that season, Purpur spent the next six years with the St. Louis Flyers in the American Hockey Association. Purpur stood just 5'6" and weighed only 155 but became a fan favorite in St. Louis for his great speed and gutsy play. His best season with the Flyers was 1938–39 when he had 35 goals and 43 assists. He added three goals and three assists in seven playoff games that year as St. Louis won the Harry F. Sinclair Trophy as AHA champions.

Purpur returned to the NHL with the Chicago Black Hawks during the 1941–42 season. He spent time on a line with brothers Max and Doug Bentley but was also used by the Black Hawks to shadow a young Rocket Richard. Purpur and the Black Hawks faced Richard's Montreal Canadiens in the 1944 Stanley Cup finals but were beaten in four straight games. Purpur appeared in the Stanley Cup finals again in 1945 as a member of the Detroit Red Wings but lost the Cup that year to the Toronto Maple Leafs.

Purpur was back in St. Louis for the 1945–46 season and completed his professional career with St. Paul of the United States Hockey League in 1946–47. He later served as hockey coach at the University of North Dakota from 1949 until 1956 and his six sons all played amateur hockey. Purpur was elected to the United States Hockey Hall of Fame in 1974.

BILL QUACKENBUSH Though he was never a hard hitter, Bill Quackenbush was an effective checker who excelled at breaking up the rush. He collected just 95 penalty minutes in 14 NHL seasons and won the Lady Byng Trophy in 1948–49 when he went the entire year without a single penalty—a remarkable achievement for a defenseman. Quackenbush was also one of the best puck-carrying defensemen of his era. He was named to the all-star team five times in six years (including three selections to the First Team) between 1946–47 and 1952–53.

Quackenbush played junior hockey in Brantford, Ontario under coach Tommy Ivan, who would coach him later with the Detroit Red Wings. Detroit signed Quackenbush in 1942–43, but he played only 10 games with the Red Wings that year before breaking his wrist. The injury reduced his shooting power and so he became a playmaking specialist. His career total of 222 assists was surpassed by only Red Kelly among the defensemen of his day.

After seven seasons in Detroit, Quackenbush was traded to Boston, where he starred for another seven years. Brother Max joined him on the Bruins defense in 1950–51. He retired after the 1955–56 season and was elected to the Hockey Hall of Fame in 1976.

PAT QUINN was a defenseman in the NHL for nine seasons, but earned greater fame as a coach, general manager and team executive. He also holds a law degree from Widener University, Delaware School of Law.

Quinn was a member of the Edmonton Oil Kings' Memorial Cup-winning team of 1962–63 and turned pro the following season. He entered the NHL with the Toronto Maple Leafs in 1968–69 but did not see regular duty until after being selected by the Vancouver Canucks in the 1970 Expansion Draft. Quinn spent two years in Vancouver, then five with the Atlanta Flames, where he was team captain his final two seasons before retiring in 1977.

After his playing days, Quinn turned to coaching and was named head coach of the Philadelphia Flyers during the 1978–79 season. The following year, Quinn's team set a record with a 35-game unbeaten streak and topped the regular-season standings before losing the Stanley Cup to the New York Islanders. Quinn won the Jack Adams Award as coach of the year for the 1979–80 season, an honor he would win again with the Canucks in 1991–92.

Quinn was head coach of the Los Angeles Kings for three seasons before going to Vancouver in 1987–88 and becoming general manager after charges of tampering against the Canucks lead to a ruling that he could not become coach right away. He later became coach of the team, working behind the bench for three-and-a-half years and leading Vancouver to the seventh game of the Stanley Cup finals in 1994 before losing to the New York Rangers. Quinn was fired as Canucks president and general manager on November 4, 1997, but was hired as coach of the Maple Leafs on June 26, 1998.

BILL RANFORD made his NHL debut with Boston on March 29, 1986 after being called up from New Westminster of the Western Hockey League. He won his first three games to help Boston clinch a playoff spot and spent most of the 1986–87 season with the Bruins. He was with Maine of the American Hockey League in 1987–88 when the Bruins sent him to the Edmonton Oilers on March 8, 1988 as part of the package that brought Andy Moog to Boston.

Ranford emerged as the starting goaltender in Edmonton in 1989–90 and starred in the playoffs that year when the Oilers won the Stanley Cup. Ranford posted a 16–6 record while playing in all 22 Oilers postseason games and was rewarded with the Conn Smythe Trophy. He remained the top goaltender in Edmonton until Curtis Joseph was signed in 1995–96. He was traded back to Boston on January 11, 1996. On March 1, 1997, the Bruins traded him to the Washington Capitals with Adam Oates and Rick Tocchet for Jim Carey, Jason Allison, Anson Carter and draft choices. The next season the Capitals made it all the way to the Stanley Cup finals, but Ranford watched the entire playoff run from the bench. Olaf Kolzig had won the starting goaltender's job from him, and after the Capitals were swept by Detroit, Ranford was traded to the Tampa Bay Lightning.

In addition to his Stanley Cup victory with Edmonton in 1990, Ranford won the Canada Cup with Team Canada in 1991 and was a member of the 1994 Canadian team that won the World Championship for the first time since 1961. Ranford was named the outstanding goaltender at the 1994 tournament. He was also a member of Team Canada at the 1996 World Cup of Hockey.

FRANK RANKIN came from a prominent sports family in Stratford, Ontario. He was a rover in the era of seven-man hockey, helping his hometown team to win the Ontario Hockey Association junior championship three years in a row from 1906–07 to 1908–09. When department store owner John C. Eaton formed the Eaton Athletic Association in 1910, Rankin played rover and captained the Eaton's hockey team to the Ontario title in 1910–11 and 1911–12. Each year the team was defeated in the Allan Cup finals by the Winnipeg Victorias. Rankin was a member of the St. Michael's senior team in Toronto in 1912–13 and 1913–14 when the team reached the OHA finals, only to lose both times to the Toronto R&AA.

After his playing days, Rankin became a successful coach. In 1924, he directed the Toronto Granites to an Olympic gold medal. He was elected to the Hockey Hall of Fame in 1961.

JEAN RATELLE Like Jean Beliveau, Jean Ratelle was a star center who personified class, style and skill, both on and off the ice. He had played almost five pro seasons before making the NHL to stay, but wound up spending all or part of 21 years in the league. He retired after the 1980–81 campaign as the sixth-leading scorer in NHL history. He had collected 1,267 points on 491 goals and 776 assists while recording just 276 penalty minutes in 1,281 games.

Ratelle spent 15 seasons with the New York Rangers, usually playing alongside Rod Gilbert, who had been a teammate since youth. The Rangers famed G-A-G Line (Goal-A-Game) of Ratelle, Vic Hadfield and Gilbert was one of the game's most productive units, enjoying their best year in 1971–72 when they finished 3–4–5 in the NHL scoring race behind Phil Esposito and Bobby Orr and helped the Rangers to reach the Stanley Cup finals for the first time in 22 years. Ratelle established career highs with 46 goals, 63 assists and 109 points in 1971–72, though he missed the last part of the season with a broken ankle. He also won the Lady Byng Trophy that year and was named to the Second All-Star Team. In addition, Ratelle received the Lester B. Pearson Award as the players' choice for MVP.

On November 7, 1975, Ratelle was involved in one of the biggest trades in hockey history when he was sent to the Boston Bruins with Brad Park and Joe Zanussi for Phil Esposito and Carol Vadnais. Ratelle went on to win the Lady Byng Trophy for the second time that year, then led the Bruins with 61 assists and 94 points in 1976–77 and helped Boston to reach the Stanley Cup finals. Ratelle was also a key contributor to the Bruins team that made it to the Cup finals again in 1978. He continued to rank among the scoring leaders in Boston for two more years before his production finally declined in 1980–81. Ratelle was inducted into the Hockey Hall of Fame in 1985.

DONAT RAYMOND Senator Donat Raymond had a long association with professional hockey in Montreal. His first official connection to the game came in 1923 with the formation of the Canadian Arena Company, which built the Montreal Forum in 1924 and formed the Montreal Maroons to play in the building. The Montreal Canadiens became permanent tenants at the Forum in 1926–27.

The Maroons were a success on the ice, winning the Stanley Cup in 1926 and 1935, but the economic pressures of the Great Depression forced the team to fold after the 1937–38 season. By 1939–40, the Canadian Arena Company had taken over complete ownership of the Canadiens and Senator Raymond's financial support saved that club from a similar fate. Raymond remained president of the company until 1955 when he became chairman of the board, and held that position until his death on June 5, 1963. In 1958, Senator Donat Raymond was elected to the Hockey Hall of Fame as a builder.

CHUCK RAYNER Claude Earl "Chuck" Rayner played hockey in his home province of Saskatchewan prior to joining the Kenora Thistles, whom he backstopped to the Memorial Cup national junior finals, losing to the Oshawa Generals in 1939–40. The following season, Rayner turned pro and made his NHL debut with the New York Americans. He played with the team again when it was known as the Brooklyn Americans in its final season of 1941–42,

then joined the New York Rangers in 1945–46 after serving in the Royal Canadian Navy in World War II.

Rayner was an agile goalie who had the misfortune of playing with very weak teams during much of his career. Still, he was named to the Second All-Star Team three years in a row between 1948–49 and 1950–51. In 1949–50, Rayner became just the second goalie in history (Roy Worters) to win the Hart Trophy, as his solid netminding led the Rangers all the way to double overtime of the seventh game of the Stanley Cup finals before losing to the Detroit Red Wings.

Rayner enjoyed leaving his crease to handle the puck and once scored a goal while playing in a game during his navy days. Twice in games during the 1946–47 NHL season, he fired shots at the opposing goal in attempts to score. In a game against the Maple Leafs on February 19, 1950, Rayner rushed from his net after Toronto had pulled Turk Broda and fired a shot that just missed the empty cage. He was successful finally in scoring a goal for the Rangers on April 1, 1951 against a team of All-Stars from the Canadian Maritime provinces during a barnstorming tour. Rayner lost his starting job in the Rangers goal to Gump Worsley in 1952–53 and never played in the NHL again. He was elected to the Hockey Hall of Fame in 1973.

KEN REARDON was a star defenseman with the Montreal Canadiens who excelled at the rugged aspects of the game like bodychecking and blocking shots. His fearless style led to several injuries over the course of his career, but also made him a fan favorite in Montreal.

Reardon joined the Canadiens as a 19-year-old in 1940–41 and played two seasons before military service disrupted his career. He was a member of the Ottawa Commandos army team that won the Allan Cup in 1943 before he was sent overseas, then rejoined the Canadiens when he returned in 1945–46. Montreal won the Stanley Cup that season and Reardon was named to the Second All-Star Team. He would be an All-Star again in each of the final four seasons he played, including selections to the First Team in 1946–47 and 1949–50.

Reardon retired after the 1949–50 season and went on to a successful management career in the Canadiens organization. He was elected to the Hockey Hall of Fame in 1966.

BILLY REAY was a productive player with the Montreal Canadiens during the late 1940s and early 1950s, helping the team win the Stanley Cup in 1945–46 and 1952–53. He would gain much greater fame as a coach between 1957 and 1977, winning more games at the time than any man except Dick Irvin. Reay's 542 regular-season coaching victories are now the fourth-highest total in NHL history.

Reay began his NHL coaching career when he replaced Howie Meeker behind the Toronto Maple Leafs bench for the 1957–58 season. He was fired in December of the following year by general manager Punch Imlach, who installed himself as coach. Reay was back in the NHL with the Chicago Black Hawks in 1963–64 when he took over from Rudy Pilous.

Reay led Chicago to a first-place finish in the regular-season standings for the first time in franchise history in 1966–67 and coached some of the NHL's most productive offensive teams during the late 1960s and early 1970s. His Black Hawks won several West Division titles and reached the finals three times, but never won the Stanley Cup.

MARK RECCHI was selected by the Pittsburgh Penguins in the fourth round of the 1988 Entry Draft after an all-star season with Kamloops of the Western Hockey League. Recchi had 61 goals and a league-leading 93 assists in 1987–88, then led all WHL playoff performers with 21 assists and 31 points in 17 games.

Recchi made his NHL debut during the 1988–89 season but spent most of the year with Muskegon of the International Hockey League, where he helped the club to win the Turner Cup championship. He also was named to the second all-star team. Recchi began the 1989–90 season in Muskegon but was recalled by Pittsburgh on October 18, 1989, and went on to rank second among NHL rookies with 30 goals. His total of 67 points was the NHL's third-leading rookie mark that season. Recchi led the Penguins and was fourth in the NHL with 113 points in 1990–91, and his 34 points in the postseason ranked second behind Mario Lemieux as Pittsburgh won its first Stanley Cup championship.

The Penguins traded Recchi to the Philadelphia Flyers on February 19, 1992, and he finished the year with a combined 43 goals to earn a spot on the Second All-Star Team at right wing. In 1992–93, Recchi established career highs with 53 goals and 123 points to rank tenth in the NHL. He finished seventh with 107 points the following season.

On February 9, 1995, the Flyers traded Recchi to the Montreal Canadiens in a deal that brought them John LeClair and Eric Desjardins. Recchi led the Canadiens in goals and points during the 1994–95 season and has continued to rank among the team's top scorers. Internationally, Recchi won a gold medal with Team Canada at the World Junior Championships in 1988 and has played at the World Championships in 1990, 1993 and 1997, when he won another gold medal. He was a late addition to the Olympic team in Nagano in 1998.

MICKEY REDMOND was the first player in the history of the Detroit Red Wings to score 50 goals, breaking the team record of 49 shared by Gordie

Howe and Frank Mahovlich when he scored 52 in 1972–73. At the time, only six other players in hockey history had reached the 50-goal plateau. The following season, Redmond joined Bobby Hull and Phil Esposito as the only players with more than one 50-goal season when he scored 51.

A high-scoring junior star, Redmond's NHL career had begun with the Montreal Canadiens during the 1967–68 season. He was a member of Stanley Cup-winning teams in each of his first two seasons, but did not develop as a goal-scoring star until Montreal traded him to Detroit as part of a deal for Frank Mahovlich on January 13, 1971.

HENRI RICHARD Despite not possessing the fiery temper of his famous older brother Maurice, Henri Richard proved to be an aggressive player who could not be intimidated despite his small size. Standing just 5'7" and weighing only 160 pounds, many predicted Richard was too small to stay in the league, but he lasted 20 years and played for a record 11 Stanley Cup champions. He is the Canadiens all-time leader in games played, ranking eighth in goals and third in both assists and points behind Guy Lafleur and Jean Beliveau.

Richard joined the Montreal Canadiens in 1955–56 when his brother Maurice was at the peak of his fame. Though he did not possess the Rocket's brilliant goal-scoring ability, Henri proved to be a smoother skater and much better playmaker. "The Pocket Rocket" quickly became a fan favorite. Henri played for Stanley Cup winners in each of his first five seasons, and was establishing himself among the league's best offensive talents by his second year. In his third year, 1957–58, Richard led the NHL in assists and finished second overall in scoring behind teammate Dickie Moore. He was named to the First All-Star team at center and selections to the Second All-Star Team followed in 1958–59, 1960–61 and 1962–63. The 1962–63 season also saw Richard lead the league in assists for the second time.

Richard continued to star with the Canadiens throughout the 1960s, winning the Stanley Cup again in 1965, 1966, 1968 and 1969. A tenth Stanley Cup title came in 1971 when he scored the winning goal in the seventh game against the Chicago Black Hawks. In 1971–72, Richard was named to succeed Jean Beliveau as Canadiens captain, and he led the Canadiens to another Stanley Cup victory in 1973. He retired two years later and was inducted into the Hockey Hall of Fame in 1979.

MAURICE RICHARD For 18 seasons, Maurice Richard was the heart and soul of the Montreal Canadiens and the idol of hockey fans throughout Quebec. Nicknamed "the Rocket" by sportswriter Baz O'Meara because of his blazing speed, Richard was the first player in NHL history to score 50 goals in a season and the first to score 500 in his career. The Rocket was named to the NHL All-Star Team 14 years in a row from 1943–44 until 1956–57, with eight of those selections to the First Team. He played on eight Stanley Cup champions, including five in a row from 1956 to 1960, and though he never led the league in points, he was the NHL's top goal scorer five times. Richard played the game with a burning desire and his fiery temper often got him into trouble. After Richard was suspended for punching a linesman during a game, a riot broke out in Montreal four days later on March 17, 1955 that caused $500,000 worth of damage.

Richard was a native of Montreal who came up through the Canadiens system and broke into the NHL in 1942–43. He scored five goals in 16 games as a rookie before a broken ankle ended his season. Injuries would plague the Rocket throughout his career, but it would be years before they finally slowed him down.

In 1943–44 he was teamed with Toe Blake and Elmer Lach on the Punch Line and scored 32 goals in 46 games that season, then scored 12 goals in nine playoff games to lead the Canadiens to the Stanley Cup. In 1944–45, Richard scored 50 goals in 50 games to establish a single-season record that would last until Bobby Hull scored 54 goals in a 70-game season in 1965–66. Not until Wayne Gretzky scored 50 goals in 39 games in 1980–81 was Richard's goal-a-game pace surpassed. On December 28, 1944, Richard had five goals and three assists for a record eight points in one game. That mark was not surpassed until Darryl Sittler had 10 points in a game on February 7, 1976.

On November 8, 1952, Rocket Richard became the NHL's all-time leading goal scorer when he surpassed Nels Stewart with his 325th goal. He scored his 500th career goal on October 19, 1957. Injuries kept him out of a lot of action over his final three years and he retired after the 1959–60 season with 544 goals. Gordie Howe soon surpassed Rocket's total, as have many players since, but his 544 goals still remain the highest in Canadiens history. Richard had 26 games in his career when he scored three goals or more, more than any player in the six-team era. He was also the most prolific playoff scorer of his day with 82 goals in the postseason, and though that record has been surpassed, his six playoff overtime goals remain the most in NHL history. Rocket Richard was inducted into the Hockey Hall of Fame in 1961. Beginning in 1998–99, the NHL will award the Maurice Richard trophy to the league-leading goal scorer during the regular season.

GEORGE RICHARDSON was a member of a prominent sports family in Kingston, Ontario. He played with the 14th Regiment team in his hometown, losing the Ontario Hockey Association senior title to Stratford in 1906–07, but winning the championship the following year. In 1909, he was added to the

roster of the Queen's University hockey team, helping the school win an Allan Cup senior title.

Richardson entered the army during World War I and he was killed in action on February 9, 1916. Queen's University named its football stadium after him. In 1950, he was elected to the Hockey Hall of Fame.

STEPHANE RICHER and Guy Lafleur are the only two players in the history of the Montreal Canadiens to have more than one 50-goal season. Lafleur reached 50 six years in a row between 1974–75 and 1979–80, while Richer had 50 in 1987–88 and 51 in 1989–90. To date, he is the last Canadiens player to score 50 goals in a season.

Richer was rookie of the year in the Quebec Major Junior Hockey League in 1983–84 and a Second Team All-Star in 1984–85. He made his NHL debut with the Canadiens on January 15, 1985 and was a Stanley Cup winner in his first full season of 1985–86. Richer was the club's top goal scorer in three of the next five seasons but was traded to the New Jersey Devils on September 20, 1991. Richer led the Devils in goals in 1992–93 and was the club's top scorer in 1995 when New Jersey won the Stanley Cup. On August 22, 1996, the Devils traded Richer back to Montreal, but on January 15, 1998, the Canadiens dealt him to the Tampa Bay Lightning.

MIKE RICHTER was selected by the New York Rangers in the second round of the 1985 Entry Draft and played the next two seasons at the University of Wisconsin. In 1985–86, Richter was chosen freshman of the year in the Western Collegiate Hockey Association and in 1986–87 he was named a WCHA second team all-star. Richter was also a member of the U.S. national team in both 1986 and 1987. He spent the entire 1987–88 season with the U.S. national team, sharing netminding duties with Chris Terreri and playing at the Olympics in Calgary. Richter played for his country again in the 1991 Canada Cup and at the 1993 World Championships. In September of 1996, he starred in goal for the American team that beat Canada in the World Cup of Hockey. He also tended goal for the United States at the Nagano Olympics in 1998.

Richter made his professional debut after the Calgary Olympics when he joined the Colorado Rangers on March 1, 1988 and helped the team to win the West Division of the International Hockey League. Though he won the Lars-Erik Sjoberg award as the best Rangers rookie at training camp prior to the 1988–89 campaign, he spent the entire season in the IHL, leading the league with 57 games played. Richter then made his NHL debut when he played one game in the first round of the 1989 playoffs. He began the 1989–90 season with the Rangers, but was then sent to Flint of the IHL before returning to the NHL to stay on December 31, 1989.

Richter shared the Rangers goal with John Vanbiesbrouck from 1989–90 until 1992–93 and the two formed an effective combination. The tandem was broken up in June of 1993 when the Rangers traded Vanbiesbrouck to the Vancouver Canucks. Richter responded by leading the league with a career-high 42 victories as the Rangers topped the NHL standings in 1993–94. He then added 16 wins in the playoffs when New York won the Stanley Cup for the first time since 1942.

ROBERT RIDDER Born in New York City and educated at Harvard, Robert Ridder's involvement in hockey began in Minnesota in the 1940s with the Duluth Heralds. His association with the senior amateur team led to a belief that a state organization for all levels of amateur hockey was essential, so in October 1947, Ridder, Don Clark and Everett "Buck" Riley founded the Minnesota Amateur Hockey Association, an organization that would become the most successful of its kind in the United States. By 1952, Ridder's interest in hockey expanded into the international arena and he managed the United States Olympic team that won a silver medal behind Canada. He managed the team again in 1956 when it earned a silver medal behind the Soviet Union. When professional hockey came to Minnesota in the 1967–68 season, Ridder became one of nine original owners of the Minnesota North Stars. He was inducted into the United States Hockey Hall of Fame as an administrator in 1976.

BRUCE RIDPATH was a scoring star who may well have become a Hockey Hall of Famer like many of his teammates had an automobile accident not curtailed his career. He played alongside Newsy Lalonde at Toronto in the Ontario Professional Hockey League when that league was formed in 1907–08, helping the team to win the league title and scoring a goal in a 6–4 loss to the Montreal Wanderers in a one-game Stanley Cup challenge. Ridpath scored seven goals in a single league game on January 30, 1909.

Ridpath signed with the Ottawa Senators in 1909–10 and followed the team into the National Hockey Association. He played on a powerful forward line with Gordie Roberts and Marty Walsh and rover Bruce Stuart that season. Playing with Walsh, Dubbie Kerr and Jack Darragh the following year, Ridpath enjoyed his most productive season with 23 goals in 16 games and helped Ottawa win the NHA title and the Stanley Cup. He collected four goals in two games in Stanley Cup challenge victories over Galt and Port Arthur.

Ridpath was hit by a car in Toronto on November 2, 1911 and missed the entire 1911–12 season. Ottawa demanded $500 to release him to the new Toronto Blueshirts the following season, but he never played again. He

coached the team briefly that year before giving way to Jack Marshall who functioned as a player-coach.

BILL RILEY One of the greatest scorers in the history of NCAA hockey, Bill Riley played on the varsity team at Dartmouth in 1942–43 but had his collegiate career interrupted by military service in World War II and didn't resume competition until 1946–47. In four years of college hockey, he had 118 goals and 110 assists and was the leading scorer at Dartmouth in 1942–43, 1947–48 and 1948–49. He had five goals in a game twice in his career, one four-goal game and 10 hat tricks. Dartmouth compiled a 68–11–2 record during Riley's four years at the school and he was a major factor in the team's reaching the finals of the NCAA hockey tournament in its first two years (1948 and 1949), although Michigan and Boston College emerged as champions respectively.

Following his retirement as a player, Riley kept active in hockey as a referee. He was president of the New England Referees' Association in 1958 and commissioner of the New England Amateur Hockey League in 1971. Riley was elected to the United States Hockey Hall of Fame in 1977.

His brothers Joe and Jack were also college stars at Dartmouth. Jack was the coach of the U.S. gold medal-winning Olympic hockey team in 1960 and a long-time coach at the United States Military Academy. He joined Bill in the U.S. Hall of Fame in 1979.

JACK RILEY When Jack Riley coached an underdog American team to the United States' first gold medal in Olympic hockey in Squaw Valley, California in 1960, he was guiding a collection of mainly university players who stunned the hockey world with their victory. In those two respects, the 1960 team was much like the team that produced the "Miracle on Ice" 20 years later.

Riley himself had been a star player at Dartmouth before graduating in 1944 and played for the U.S. Olympic hockey team in 1948. In 1949, he was a player-coach on the American team that finished third at that year's world championships. He joined the coaching staff of the United States Military Academy hockey team in 1950 and became head coach in 1951. Except for the year with the Olympic team, he remained at Army until the 1985–86 season, when he turned his coaching job over to his son, Rob.

It was difficult to recruit top players due to the mandatory five-year military stint, but Riley had only six losing seasons in his 36 years at West Point. At the time of his retirement, his career total of 541 wins trailed only John McInnes of Michigan Tech in the history of NCAA hockey. Riley was inducted into the United States Hockey Hall of Fame in the coaches category in 1979. His brothers Joe and Bill Riley had also been players at Dartmouth, and Bill was elected to the U.S. Hall of Fame in 1977.

JOHN ROSS ROACH played amateur hockey in Toronto before signing with the St. Pats for the 1921–22 season. He helped the team to win the Stanley Cup that season and went on to play 13 more years in the NHL. Only 5'5" and 130 pounds, he has been described as a nervous type of goaltender, constantly in motion in front of his goal, clearing the ice and straightening his sweater.

Roach spent seven seasons in Toronto, including 1927–28 when Conn Smythe bought the St. Pats and renamed them the Maple Leafs, but was traded to the New York Rangers for Lorne Chabot prior to the 1928–29 campaign. That year, Roach established career bests with a 1.41 goals-against average and 13 shutouts. His shutout total was second only to George Hainsworth's record 22 that season and has been surpassed just five times in NHL history.

After four seasons with the Rangers, Roach moved on to Detroit in 1932–33 and helped the Red Wings tie the Boston Bruins for the best record in the league that season. Boston's Tiny Thompson won the Vezina Trophy that year, but Roach was selected to the First All-Star Team. He spent the next two years shuttling back and forth between Detroit and the minors before retiring. Roach's career total of 58 shutouts ranks 12th in NHL history.

GORDON ROBERTS was a high-scoring left winger who played professional hockey while obtaining a medical degree at McGill University in Montreal. Dr. Roberts continued to play for several seasons after opening a medical practice, and in 1916–17 he set a single-season record in the Pacific Coast Hockey Association with 43 goals in 23 games. Ottawa goalie Clint Benedict claimed Roberts' shots would curve simply because of his powerful wrist action.

Roberts entered professional hockey with the Ottawa Senators in 1909–10, scoring seven goals in two games as Ottawa successfully defended the Stanley Cup against a challenge from Edmonton in January of 1910. The Senators lost the Stanley Cup to the Montreal Wanderers by season's end, and Roberts joined the Montreal squad in 1910–11 when he entered McGill. He ranked among the leading scorers in the National Hockey Association every year from 1911–12 until his graduation from medical school in 1916.

Setting up a practice on the West Coast, Roberts joined the Vancouver Millionaires of the PCHA in 1916–17. When hospital duties took him to Seattle after his record-setting season, he joined the Metropolitans, recording another excellent year. Roberts did not play hockey in 1918–19, but he was back in Vancouver one year later to play a final season. In 1922, he returned to Ottawa for post-graduate work in medicine, and though the Senators tried

to sign him, he had retired from hockey for good. In 1971, Roberts was elected to the Hockey Hall of Fame.

EARL ROBERTSON Goalie Earl Robertson was the unlikely hero of the Detroit Red Wings' Stanley Cup championship in 1937. The long-time minor-leaguer was called up after Normie Smith injured his elbow in game three of Detroit's opening-round victory over the Montreal Canadiens. When Smith's elbow proved too sore for him to play against the New York Rangers in the Stanley Cup final, Robertson took over and led Detroit to a three-games-to-two victory with shutouts in the last two games.

The next season, Robertson signed with the New York Americans and remained with the franchise for the final five years of its existence. He shared the net with future Hall of Famer Chuck Rayner in 1940–41 and 1941–42 as the two goalies alternated between the Americans and the minor leagues in Springfield.

JOHN ROSS ROBERTSON was a rich and powerful member of Toronto society whose philanthropic efforts helped make the Hospital for Sick Children a world renowned medical facility. He founded the *Toronto Telegram* newspaper in 1867 and he later was elected to the Canadian House of Commons. In 1897, Robertson became an executive member of the Ontario Hockey Association. He was named vice president of the OHA in 1898 and became president on December 2, 1899. It was a position he would hold for six years. He donated three trophies to the OHA for annual competition, rewarding the champions of the junior, intermediate and senior divisions.

An outspoken opponent of professionalism in sports, Robertson stated in his first speech to the OHA that "a manly nation is always fond of manly sports. We want our boys to be strong, vigorous and self-reliant and we must encourage athletics. Sport should be pursued for its own sake." He was elected to the Hockey Hall of Fame as a builder in 1947.

CLAUDE ROBINSON grew up in Winnipeg, where he became an important member of the Winnipeg Victorias hockey club, first as a player and later as an executive. The Vics were winners of the Stanley Cup (1901) and the Allan Cup (1911 and 1912) during his time in the organization. In 1932, he managed the Winnipeg Hockey Club to a gold medal in the Winter Olympics at Lake Placid.

Robinson was the first man to suggest the formation of a national body to stage amateur hockey championships in Canada, and he became the first secretary when the Canadian Amateur Hockey Association was formed in 1914. He later was named a life member of the CAHA and was elected to the Hockey Hall of Fame as a builder in 1947.

LARRY ROBINSON's defensive prowess, combined with his ability to move the puck, made him one of the greatest defensemen in NHL history. He was part of "the Big Three" on the Montreal defense with Guy Lapointe and Serge Savard, helping the Canadiens win the Stanley Cup six times between 1973 and 1986. By the time he retired after the 1991–92 season, Robinson had set a record by playing in the playoffs for 20 consecutive years, and his 227 games played in the postseason were an NHL record, surpassed only by Mark Messier so far.

Known as "Big Bird," the 6'4", 225-pound Robinson played on his first Stanley Cup-winning team as a rookie in 1972–73 and was a major contributor to the Canadiens' four consecutive Stanley Cup titles between 1976 and 1979. His final Stanley Cup victory came in 1986. Robinson was also a member of Team Canada at the Canada Cup in 1976, 1981 and 1984. He won the Norris Trophy in 1976–77 and 1979–80 and was named to the NHL All Star team five years in a row between 1976–77 and 1980–81. Robinson earned three selections to the First Team during that time and garnered his final all-star selection in 1985–86 when he was named to the Second Team for the third time.

On July 25, 1989, Robinson signed with Los Angeles and spent his final three NHL seasons as a member of the Kings. He took a year off from the game after his retirement before joining the New Jersey Devils in 1993–94 as an assistant coach under former Canadiens teammate Jacques Lemaire. Robinson's influence made the Devils one of the NHL's best defensive teams and helped New Jersey to win the Stanley Cup in 1994–95. On July 26, 1995, Robinson was hired as the head coach in Los Angeles. He was inducted into the Hockey Hall of Fame the same year. Robinson guided the Kings back to the playoffs for the first time in five years in 1997–98 and finished as the runner-up to Pat Burns of the Boston Bruins for the Jack Adams Award as coach of the year.

LUC ROBITAILLE was selected by the Los Angeles Kings with the 171st pick in the 1994 NHL Entry Draft and played two more years with Hull of the Quebec Major Junior Hockey League before making his NHL debut. He was named to the QMJHL second all-star team in 1984–85 and to the first all-star team in 1985–86, when he was honored as the Canadian major junior player of the year.

Robitaille entered the NHL in 1986–87 and became the first rookie to lead the Kings in scoring. His 45 goals and 84 points also topped all first year players in the NHL, earning him the Calder Trophy and a place on the All Rookie Team with fellow Kings Jimmy Carson and Steve Duchesne. In addition,

Robitaille was named to the Second All-Star Team that season and would continue to be either a First or Second All-Star in each of the next six seasons.

Robitaille set an NHL record for left wingers (and established the third-longest streak in NHL history) by topping 40 goals eight years in a row. He first reached 50 in his second season of 1987–88 and established career highs with 62 goals and 125 points in 1992–93. Those marks also established NHL records for left wingers. Robitaille served as Kings captain in place of the injured Wayne Gretzky for the first 39 games of the 1992–93 season and helped Los Angeles to reach the Stanley Cup finals for the first time in team history that year. The Kings missed the playoffs in 1993–94 and Robitaille was selected to captain the Canadian team at the World Championships, where his winning goal in a shootout gave Team Canada its first world title since 1961.

On July 29, 1994, Robitaille was traded to Pittsburgh but spent just one year with the Penguins before being dealt to the New York Rangers on August 31, 1995. After two years with the Rangers, Robitaille was reacquired by Los Angeles on August 28, 1997.

MIKE RODDEN was a famed football coach and newspaper editor who was also an outstanding hockey referee. By his own count, Rodden officiated in 2,864 hockey games, 1,187 of them in the NHL during the 1920s and 1930s. He was inducted into the Hockey Hall of Fame as a referee in 1962.

Rodden had played hockey in his youth and was a coach in Toronto at De La Salle College, St. Mary's, the University of Toronto and with the St. Pats in the NHL in 1926–27. He also played baseball and lacrosse, but it was in football that Rodden gained his greatest acclaim. He is credited with coaching 27 championship teams at various levels of football in Ontario and led his team to the Grey Cup on five occasions. Rodden lost the Canadian championship game with the University of Toronto in 1920, Balmy Beach in 1924 and the Hamilton Tigers in 1927, before winning back-to-back titles with Hamilton in 1928 and 1929.

During his time as a football coach and hockey referee, Rodden also became the assistant sports editor with the *Toronto Globe* in 1918 and was promoted to sports editor in 1928. He remained on the job until 1936, and later became sports editor of the *Kingston Whig-Standard*, holding that position from 1944 until he retired in 1959. He was elected to the Hall of Fame in 1962.

JEREMY ROENICK led his Thayer Academy high school team to the Massachusetts state championships in 1987–88 and then was selected eighth overall by Chicago in the 1988 NHL Entry Draft. He began and ended the 1988–89 season with the Blackhawks, though he spent most of the year with Hull of the Quebec Major Junior Hockey League, where he was named to the Second All-Star Team. In his first full NHL season of 1989–90, Roenick ranked fourth among league rookies with 26 goals and third with 40 assists.

A fast and agile skater with excellent puckhandling skills, Roenick improved his offensive totals in 1990–91 and set a Blackhawks record for centers with 53 goals in 1991–92. His 24 power-play goals that year also set a team record. When Roenick scored 50 goals the following season, he joined Kevin Stevens as one of the first two American-born players to have back-to-back 50-goal seasons. He also joined Hockey Hall of Famer Bobby Hull as the only Chicago players to score 50 goals in two straight years. When he topped 100 points for the third year in a row in 1993–94, he became the first Blackhawks player ever to have three consecutive 100-point seasons.

Roenick spent two more years in Chicago, but a contract dispute led to his being traded to the Phoenix Coyotes on August 16, 1996. Because he was not yet under contract, Roenick chose not to play at the World Cup of Hockey that year. He had represented the United States at the World Junior Championships in 1989, when he led the tournament in scoring and was named to the first all-star team. Roenick also played for the American team at the World Championships in 1991 and at the 1991 Canada Cup. In 1998, he was a member of the U.S. Olympic team in Nagano.

AL ROLLINS After six seasons in the minor leagues, Al Rollins got his first chance in the NHL when Conn Smythe decided Toronto Maple Leafs goalie Turk Broda was too fat. Broda was ordered out of the lineup in November of 1949 and was replaced by Gil Mayer. For added insurance, Rollins was purchased from the Cleveland Barons of the American Hockey League. He got into two games for Toronto before the season was done.

Rollins was 6'2" and played a graceful, standup style. In 1950–51, he and Broda shared the Leafs net in a foreshadowing of the two-goal system that was then still more than 10 years away. The two gave the Leafs the best defensive record in the NHL by allowing one less goal than Terry Sawchuk did in all 70 games for the Detroit Red Wings. Rollins' 1.77 goals-against average was the best in the league as he earned the Vezina Trophy. In the playoffs, Rollins and Broda helped the Leafs to win the Stanley Cup.

In 1951–52, Rollins had the Toronto job to himself. He had another solid season, but was then traded to the Chicago Black Hawks for Harry Lumley on September 11, 1952. He helped Chicago reach the playoffs in 1952–53, but the team fell back into last place with only 12 victories in 1953–54. Rollins' exceptional play on such a poor team was rewarded with the Hart Trophy.

The stress of playing behind a weak defense kept Rollins out of action for

parts of the next two seasons, and he returned to the minors after the 1956–57 campaign. Rollins made a final NHL appearance with the New York Rangers in 1959–60.

DOC ROMNES Elwyn Nelson "Doc" Romnes spent 10 seasons in the NHL, mostly with the Chicago Black Hawks but also with the Toronto Maple Leafs and New York Americans. He was the first American player to win the Lady Byng Trophy for sportsmanlike conduct when he took the honor in 1935–36, and remained the only American to win the award until Joe Mullen 52 years later.

Romnes played high school hockey in his native White Bear Lake, Minnesota, as well as in St. Paul before turning professional with the St. Paul Saints of the American Hockey Association in 1928–29. He joined the Black Hawks during the 1930–31 season and helped them reach the Stanley Cup finals that year and win it in 1934 and 1938. During game two of the 1938 finals, the usually mild-mannered Romnes got involved in a fight with Leafs tough guy Red Horner and had his nose broken in five places. He played the third game of the series wearing a football helmet and a face guard. Ironically, Romnes and Horner became teammates in Toronto the following year. Romnes reached the Stanley Cup finals for the fourth time in his career with the Leafs in 1939, but Toronto was beaten by the Boston Bruins.

Romnes retired as a player after splitting the 1939–40 season between the New York Americans and Omaha of the AHA. He then coached at Michigan Tech University until 1945 and in 1945–46 guided the Kansas City Pla Mors to the United States Hockey League championship. He returned to collegiate coaching at the University of Minnesota in 1947 and stayed until 1952. In 1973, Doc Romnes became a charter member of the United States Hockey Hall of Fame.

SKENE RONAN Erskine "Skene" Ronan was a lightly regarded defenseman in the early years of his career who later became a star at center, but was always overshadowed by the future Hall of Famers he played with. Ronan played with Toronto of the Ontario Professional Hockey League in 1908–09 and though he saw some time at center that season when Newsy Lalonde was injured, he was back on defense with Art Ross in Haileybury in 1909–10; the inaugural season of the National Hockey Association. The following year, he played a few games at rover with the Renfrew Millionaires but still showed little offensive flair.

Renfrew dropped out of the NHA before the 1911–12 season and Ronan became a member of the Ottawa Senators. The team offered him as part of a plan to purchase fellow Renfrew refugee Cyclone Taylor from the Montreal Wanderers, but the trade never happened. The Senators kept Ronan and a new star was born.

With Marty Walsh slumping, Ottawa gave Ronan an opportunity to play center and he responded with a league-leading 35 goals in 18 games, including eight in one game against the Wanderers on February 14, 1912. (This was the second-highest single-game total in NHA history.) Ronan remained a productive player for two more seasons in Ottawa, but was sold to the Toronto Shamrocks in 1914–15 so the Senators could give Eddie Gerard more playing time. When the Shamrocks dropped out the following season, Ronan joined the Toronto Blueshirts but had to make way for Duke Keats and finished the year as a substitute with the Montreal Canadiens. Ronan scored the first goal in a 2–1 victory over the Portland Rosebuds in the final game of the 1916 Stanley Cup series that gave the Canadiens their first championship. He was out of hockey the next two years and retired for good after a brief comeback with the Ottawa Senators in the second NHL season of 1918–19.

DICK RONDEAU was a high school star at the Mount St. Charles Academy in Woonsocket, Rhode Island. In his senior season (1938–39), he was the leading scorer in his league with 27 goals and 11 assists as his school team posted a 21–2 record. They were proclaimed unofficial national champions and Rondeau was named as the center on the all-State team that year.

No longer eligible for high school hockey, Rondeau joined the Boston Junior Olympics in 1939–40. The Olympics played against major Eastern colleges and were runners-up in the national junior tournament that year. Rondeau was at this point recruited to play hockey at Dartmouth College by coach Eddie Jeremiah. After a solid season as a freshman, Rondeau centered a line with Jack Riley and Bill Harrison as Dartmouth won 21 games against only two losses and were proclaimed national champions for 1941–42. Rondeau led the nation in scoring that year with 45 goals and 32 assists.

At the time, Dartmouth was on a roll that would see them go undefeated in 46 games between December 23, 1941, and January 5, 1946. Rondeau captained the team in 1942–43 — and also took over as coach when Jeremiah joined the navy midseason — and again in 1943–44.

Rondeau had 103 goals and 73 assists during his college career and still holds numerous Dartmouth scoring records, including most goals in a season with 45; most hat tricks in a season and in a career; and most goals, assists and points in a game (12 goals and 11 assists in a 30–0 win over Middlebury on February 8, 1944).

After graduation, Rondeau entered the Marine Corps and played for San Diego in the Pacific Coast Hockey League while he was stationed in

California. A swimming accident ended his active playing career in 1945, but after the war he was involved as a coach at both Holy Cross and Providence College and as a linesman in the American Hockey League. Later, he was a minor official with the Central Hockey League and was active in youth hockey in Texas. Rondeau was inducted into the United States Hockey Hall of Fame in 1985.

ART ROSS was a defenseman throughout his career and a man who scored just one goal in three NHL games. It is ironic that he is remembered best today because he donated the trophy awarded to the NHL scoring leader, but Ross was an important player, coach, manager, inventor and strategist throughout a lifetime of service to hockey.

Ross learned to play the game while growing up in Montreal, and he was a member of the city's Westmount team in 1904–05 with childhood friends Frank and Lester Patrick. Like Lester, Ross was one of hockey's first rushing defensemen. He headed out west to Brandon, Manitoba the following season, and he was on loan to the Kenora Thistles when they defeated the Montreal Wanderers to win the Stanley Cup in January of 1907. A year later, Ross was a member of the Wanderers, playing for another Stanley Cup champion. While with the Wanderers in 1907–08 and 1908–09, he would show up occasionally on the roster of other teams as a "ringer" paid to play in important games.

In 1909–10, Ross was managing a new team called All-Montreal in the Canadian Hockey Association, but when the league lost a power struggle with the National Hockey Association, he joined the NHA's Haileybury Comets. The following year, Ross was back with the Wanderers. He criticized the salary cap imposed by owners in 1910–11 and he and Bruce Stuart were at the forefront of a plan to form a new players' league which never materialized. Ross fought for players' rights again in 1914 and in 1915, and his attempts to form another new league nearly brought him a suspension from all of organized hockey.

Ross played with the Ottawa Senators in 1914–15 and 1915–16, but he was back with the Wanderers in 1916–17. The team joined the NHL the following season, but it withdrew after a fire destroyed the Montreal Arena on January 2, 1918, and Ross retired as a player. He returned to the NHL as coach of the Hamilton Tigers in 1921–22. Next, he was hired as the coach and general manager of the Boston Bruins for their first season of 1924–25. Ross quickly built the team into a powerhouse, winning 10 division titles and the Stanley Cup three times by 1941. He coached the team on and off into the 1940s and served as the Bruins general manager until 1955. He also improved the design of the pucks and goal nets used in the NHL. The Art Ross net was in use until 1984, and his puck design has not been replaced. Ross was inducted into the Hockey Hall of Fame as one of its 12 original members in 1945.

LARRY ROSS graduated from Morgan Park High School in his hometown of Duluth, Minnesota in 1940 and joined the United States Navy. He played hockey on the Navy team in 1942–43 and later attended the University of Minnesota, where he was an all-American goaltender in 1950–51 and 1951–52.

After his university playing career, Ross became a highly successful high school coach in International Falls. His teams played in the Minnesota state tournament 13 times and won it six times. During the 1963–64, 1964–65 and 1965–66 seasons, Ross's Broncos went undefeated in 58 straight games. In all, his teams compiled a record of 566–169–21. His high school players would go on to swell the ranks of college hockey, with eight players later seeing Olympic action and 12 going on the play in the NHL. During his time in International Falls, Ross also started a hockey program at the nearby Rainy River Community College and ran both teams at the same time. From 1980 to 1984, he was a member of the scout staff of the Hartford Whalers, and after his retirement in 1985 he continued to serve on the coaching staffs of various hockey schools in Minnesota.

In 1983, Ross was named coach of the year by the Minnesota Hockey Coaches Association; in 1985, he was awarded the National High School Special Sports Award by the National High School Athletic Coaches Association; in 1988, he was the recipient of the John Mariucci College Award from the American College Hockey Coaches Association; and in 1988, Ross was inducted into the United States Hockey Hall of Fame in the coaches category.

P.D. ROSS When Governor-General Lord Stanley of Preston donated the Dominion Hockey Challenge Cup to honor Canada's hockey champion in 1893, Sheriff John Sweetland and Philip Dansken Ross were named as trustees. The new trophy soon would be known as the Stanley Cup, and no man had more to do with the important decisions regarding its development than P.D. Ross. He granted permissions and oversaw disputes during the Stanley Cup's early days as a challenge trophy and remained its trustee for 56 years. Shortly before he died in 1949, Ross delegated full authority of the Stanley Cup to the NHL.

Ross had been an impressive athlete as a young man. He was captain of the McGill University football team that played Harvard in 1876, introducing this new sport to the United States. He also played hockey for the Rideau Rebels, an Ottawa team that included the honorable Edward Stanley, whose father was

Governor-General of Canada. Ross was a member of several championship Canadian rowing crews, an avid golfer and a fine lacrosse player. In addition to his Stanley Cup duties, Ross was a trustee of the Minto Cup in lacrosse. He was inducted into the Hockey Hall of Fame as a builder in 1976.

BOBBY ROUSSEAU Bobby Rousseau was a member of Canada's silver medal-winning hockey team at the Squaw Valley Winter Olympics in 1960 and made his NHL debut with the Montreal Canadiens in 1960–61. A strong skater and good stickhandler with a hard slapshot, Rousseau scored 21 goals as a rookie in 1961–62 and won the Calder Trophy.

Considered an excellent checker by coach Toe Blake, Rousseau was used by the Canadiens to kill penalties but his offensive talent also saw him take part on the power-play. He scored five goals in a game against the Detroit Red Wings on February 1, 1964 and was named to the Second All-Star Team in 1965–66 after leading the Canadiens in both goals (30) and points (78) and tying Jean Beliveau and Stan Mikita for the NHL lead with 48 assists. He also helped the Canadiens win the Stanley Cup for the second year in a row that season.

Rousseau was a member of Stanley Cup-winning teams again in Montreal in 1968 and 1969, but was traded to the Minnesota North Stars on June 10, 1970. After a season with his new club, Rousseau was sent to the New York Rangers on May 25, 1971. He played two full seasons with the Rangers and retired after playing just eight games in 1974–75.

BOBBY ROWE began as a forward before moving to defense, and, as a result, enjoyed one of the longest careers in the early days of professional hockey. Rowe was with Renfrew of the Federal league in 1908–09 and became a member of the Renfrew Millionaires in the inaugural season of the National Hockey Association the following year. He was a teammate of Frank and Lester Patrick that season, and, after another year in Renfrew, Rowe followed the brothers out west when he signed with Lester's Victoria franchise in the new Pacific Coast Hockey Association for 1911–12. Rowe, Smokey Harris and Hugh Lehman would become the only three players to remain with the PCHA for its entire 13-year existence.

Rowe was more of a backchecker than a scorer as a forward with Victoria, and helped the club win the PCHA title in 1912–13 and 1913–14. Traded to the Seattle Metropolitans in 1916, he became a defenseman. In 1917, he helped Seattle become the first American franchise to win the Stanley Cup. Rowe was an all-star defenseman in the PCHA each of the next two seasons.

Bobby Rowe won two more PCHA titles in Seattle and remained with the Metropolitans until the franchise folded after the 1923–24 season. The Vancouver and Victoria PCHA clubs joined the Western Canada Hockey League, but Rowe was among several western players who chose to sign instead with the NHL expansion team in Boston. He played just four games with the Bruins in 1924–25, and concluded his career the following season by playing two games with the Portland Rosebuds of the Western Hockey League.

PATRICK ROY made his NHL debut with the Montreal Canadiens on February 23, 1985 and became a regular during the 1985–86 season. He was good enough during his first full season to earn a spot on the NHL All-Rookie Team, but it was during the playoffs that Roy first displayed how great he could be when he won 15 games and posted a 1.92 goals-against average to lead the Canadiens to a surprising Stanley Cup victory. Roy was rewarded with the Conn Smythe Trophy as playoff MVP.

Over the next six seasons, Roy established himself among the top goaltenders in the game. He shared the Jennings Trophy with Brian Hayward three years in a row between 1986–87 and 1988–89, won the Vezina Trophy in 1988–89, 1989–90 and 1991–92 and was named to either the First or Second All-Star Team five years in a row from 1986–87 to 1991–92. In 1992–93, Roy slumped to his highest goals-against average since his rookie season, but he avenged himself in the playoffs when he was absolutely brilliant in leading the Canadiens to another Stanley Cup title. He was 16–4 in the postseason, including 10 consecutive overtime victories, and had a 2.13 goals-against average as he once again received the Conn Smythe Trophy.

Roy established a career high in 1993–94 when he played in 68 games and posted a league-leading seven shutouts, but he had his first losing record when the Canadiens failed to make the playoffs in 1994–95. Mario Tremblay was brought in to coach the Canadiens early in the 1995–96 season and a clash between Roy and Tremblay resulted in the star goaltender being dealt to the Colorado Avalanche on December 6, 1995. On February 19, 1996, Roy recorded the 300th victory of his career when Colorado beat the Edmonton Oilers. He was just the 12th player in history to win 300 games and the second-youngest behind Terry Sawchuk. In the playoffs that year, Roy helped Colorado to win the Stanley Cup by leading all postseason goaltenders in games, wins, minutes and shutouts. He stopped 63 shots when the Avalanche capped a Stanley Cup sweep with a 1–0 triple-overtime victory over the Florida Panthers.

Though he consistently has been among the best in the game, Roy never was selected to play for his country in the Canada Cup and was overlooked again at the World Cup of Hockey in September of 1996. He finally was chosen to represent Canada at the 1998 Nagano Olympics.

BLAIR RUSSEL was an excellent player during the course of his hockey career with the Montreal Victorias. Though often overshadowed by his high-scoring teammate Russell Bowie, Russel was better defensively and effective as both a right winger and at center. Playing as an amateur throughout his career, he joined the Victorias in 1899, combining with Bowie to form the most potent scoring threat in hockey. When the Eastern Canada Amateur Hockey Association became a professional league in 1908–09, Russel refused all offers to play for pay with the Montreal Wanderers, retiring instead. He coached the Victorias in 1910 before settling into a successful business career in Montreal.

Russel scored 110 goals in 67 games over his eight-year career, including a high of seven goals in a game on January 2, 1904. He also had a six-goal game and a five-goal effort over the course of his career. His most productive season was 1906–07 when he had 25 goals in 10 games. In a vote conducted by daily newspapers in Montreal and Toronto, Russel was named to an all-star team along with such greats as Russell Bowie, Harvey Pulford, Frank McGee, Alf Smith and Billy Gilmour. All of those players are members of the Hockey Hall of Fame. Russel was inducted in 1965.

ERNIE RUSSELL was a fast skater and slick stickhandler who was among the greatest goal scorers of his era. He had eight goals in a game twice during his career, six-goal games on three occasions and four five-goal efforts. He once scored three goals or more in five consecutive games in 1907; in 1911–12, he had a streak of scoring at least one goal in 10 straight games.

Russell was captain of the Sterlings Juniors when they won the Canadian junior hockey championship in 1903. He also captained the Montreal Amateur Athletic Association football team to a junior title that year. He played hockey for the Montreal AAA in 1904–05, joining the Montreal Wanderers the following year. He helped the Wanderers win the Stanley Cup in 1906, 1907, 1908 and 1910, enjoying his best season in 1906–07 when he scored the astounding total of 42 goals in just nine games, adding 12 more goals in five playoff encounters.

Russell played with numerous future Hall of Famers during his years with the Wanderers including Lester Patrick, Hod Stuart, Harry Hyland, Jimmy Gardner and Gordie Roberts. He retired after 1913–14 and was elected to the Hockey Hall of Fame in 1965.

JACK RUTTAN was a legendary figure in Winnipeg hockey during a time when the city was one of the most important hockey centers in Canada. His playing career began with the Armstrong's Point team that won the juvenile championship of Winnipeg in 1905–06. He captured another juvenile title the following year as a member of the Winnipeg Rustler club.

In 1907–08, Ruttan played for the St. John's College team that won the Manitoba University Hockey League. After a second season with the college club, he joined the Manitoba Varsity team that won the 1909–10 championship of the Winnipeg Senior Hockey League. He played with the university team for two more seasons before joining the Winnipeg Hockey Club in 1912–13. This team claimed a national championship by winning the Allan Cup that season. Ruttan retired as a player after the Allan Cup victory, remaining active in Winnipeg for many years as a coach and referee. He was elected to the Hockey Hall of Fame in 1962.

GUNTHER SABETZKI The appointment of Dr. Gunther Sabetzki to the position of president of the International Ice Hockey Federation at the July 1975 Congress in Switzerland led to a declaration that professional players would be allowed to compete at the 1976 World Championships. This, in turn, allowed Canada to seek IIHF permission to stage the first Canada Cup tournament in 1976 and saw Canada make a full return to international hockey in 1977. Sabetzki also had been involved in planning the 1972 Summit Series between Canada and the Soviet Union.

Sabetzki had played hockey in his native Germany until the age of 20 and turned to the administrative side of the game in 1952 when he was named manager of the hockey association of the German province of Nordheim-Westfalen. Sabetzki was a founding member of the German Hockey Association in 1963 and organized the European Cup in 1965. He was elected to the IIHF Council in 1969 and succeeded Bunny Ahearne as president six years later. He stepped down from this position in 1994 and was elected to the Hockey Hall of Fame as a builder in 1995.

JOE SAKIC was a high-scoring junior center with the Swift Current Broncos, leading the Western Hockey League with 78 goals and 160 points in 1987–88 and being named Canadian major junior player of the year. He was selected by the Quebec Nordiques with the 15th choice in the 1988 NHL Entry Draft after Quebec had chosen Bryan Fogarty with the ninth pick.

Though the Nordiques only made the playoffs twice in Sakic's seven seasons in Quebec, he was able to establish himself as a star. He cracked the top 10 in scoring with 102 points in his second season of 1989–90 and was sixth in the NHL with 109 points in 1990–91. He was named captain of the Nordiques in 1992–93 and had 105 points that season as Quebec reached the playoffs for the first time in six years. The Nordiques missed the playoffs again

in 1993–94, but had an excellent season in 1994–95 when they finished the abbreviated 48-game season with the best record in the Eastern Conference. Sakic was the fourth-best scorer in the NHL that year.

The Nordiques moved to Denver and became the Colorado Avalanche in 1995–96. Sakic finished third in the NHL in scoring that season by establishing career highs with 51 goals, 69 assists and 120 points. He led all playoff performers with 18 goals and 34 points to earn the Conn Smythe Trophy as the Avalanche became the first team ever to win the Stanley Cup during its first year in a city.

In addition to his NHL success, Sakic has done well in the international arena. In 1988, he won a gold medal with Canada's team at the World Junior Championships and in 1991 he was the team's leading scorer when Canada earned a silver medal at the World Championships. Sakic was also a member of the gold medal-winning team in 1994, as Canada won the World Championship for the first time since 1961. He played on the Canadian team at the World Cup of Hockey in 1996 and at the Nagano Olympics in 1998.

BORJE SALMING was the first European player to become a star in the NHL. Signed by Toronto after the 1973 World Championships, the native of Kiruna, Sweden was forced to endure taunts and physical abuse from opponents after breaking into the NHL with the Maple Leafs in 1973–74, but went on to become one of the top defensemen in the league over 17 seasons. He was elected to the Hockey Hall of Fame in 1996.

Salming excelled at blocking shots, and was a strong skater who could rush the puck effectively and set up plays. He established a Maple Leafs record by being named to the NHL All-Star Team six times, earning the selections in six straight seasons from 1974–75 to 1979–80. He was a First Team All-Star in 1976–77 when he was runner-up to Larry Robinson in voting for the Norris Trophy. Salming was also second behind Robinson for the Norris Trophy in 1979–80.

In his early years in Toronto, the Maple Leafs were an improving team that seemed on the verge of becoming one of the NHL's best, but during the 1980s Salming was the star attraction on a dismal club. When he left Toronto after the 1988–89 season, he was the Maple Leafs all-time leader in goals, assists and points by a defenseman. He ranks first overall in franchise history with 620 assists and trails only Darryl Sittler and Dave Keon with 768 points. Salming played his final NHL season in 1989–90 as a member of the Detroit Red Wings.

Internationally, Salming played for Sweden at the World Championships in 1972 and 1973 and again in 1989. He played for his country at the Canada Cup in 1976, 1981 and 1991 and at the Olympics in 1992.

GLEN SATHER began his tenure with the Edmonton Oilers as a player in the World Hockey Association in 1976–77. On March 3, 1977, he assumed coaching duties and on June 15, 1979 (after the team entered the NHL) Sather was named president and general manager. He was coach and g.m. for the Oilers' first 10 NHL seasons and the architect of Edmonton's five Stanley Cup champions between 1984 and 1990.

In 842 regular-season games as coach of the Oilers, Sather's teams had a 464–268–110 record for a .616 winning percentage, and he was honored in 1985–86 with the Jack Adams Award as coach of the year. In the playoffs, Sather's Oilers won 89 of 126 games for a .706 winning percentage that is the best in NHL history. He coached the Oilers' first four Stanley Cup winners. Internationally, Sather coached Team Canada to victory in the 1984 Canada Cup and was part of the management team for the 1987 Canada Cup champions. He was also coach and general manager of the Canadian team that lost the World Cup of Hockey finals to the United States in 1996. Sather was elected to the Hockey Hall of Fame as a builder in 1997.

As a player, Sather was a member of the Edmonton Oil Kings in junior hockey before turning pro with the Detroit Red Wings' Memphis affiliate in the Central Professional Hockey League in 1964–65. He was drafted by the Bruins the following year and made his NHL debut with Boston in 1966–67. Sather also played with the Penguins, Rangers, Blues, Canadiens and North Stars over 10 years in the NHL.

DENIS SAVARD was a high-scoring junior star in Montreal who was passed over by the Canadiens for Doug Wickenheiser as the top choice in the 1980 Entry Draft. Savard was selected third overall by the Chicago Blackhawks and went on to become one of the top offensive stars in the NHL.

Savard was among the top 10 in scoring five times in his career, finishing as high as third on two occasions including 1987–88 when he had a career-high 131 points. He was one of the league's best playmakers but also had three straight years with more than 40 goals. Still, Savard earned only one All-Star selection, being named to the Second Team in 1982–83. As a center, he was overshadowed throughout his career by Wayne Gretzky, Mario Lemieux, Bryan Trottier and Dale Hawerchuk.

After 10 seasons with the Blackhawks, Savard was traded to Montreal for Chris Chelios on June 29, 1990. Under the Canadiens' tight defensive system, he no longer produced points as he had in Chicago but he earned a Stanley Cup ring in 1992–93. The following season, Savard signed with the Tampa Bay Lightning but was traded back to Chicago on April 6, 1995.

Savard's career ended with the Blackhawks after the 1996–97 season. He retired with 473 goals and 865 assists for 1,228 points, totals that rank him among the all-time leaders in NHL history.

SERGE SAVARD

SERGE SAVARD was a key member of teams that won eight Stanley Cup championships during the 15 seasons he played for the Montreal Canadiens. Savard was voted rookie of the year with Montreal's Central Professional Hockey League farm club in Houston in 1966–67 and joined the Canadiens to stay in 1967–68, playing for his first Stanley Cup winner that year. He then became the first defenseman to win the Conn Smythe Trophy as playoff MVP when Montreal repeated as champions in 1968–69.

Savard suffered a badly broken leg during both the 1970–71 and 1971–72 seasons, but recovered sufficiently to play with Team Canada against the Soviet Union in September of 1972 and contribute to another Stanley Cup winner in Montreal in 1973. He established career highs with 20 goals, 40 assists and 60 points in 1974–75, and was a key member of Montreal's "Big Three" on defense with Guy Lapointe and Larry Robinson when Montreal won the Stanley Cup four times in a row from 1976 until 1979. Savard was named to the Second All-Star Team for the 1978–79 season and also won the Bill Masterton Trophy that year for perseverance and dedication to hockey.

Savard retired after the 1980–81 season but was persuaded to join the Winnipeg Jets for the 1981–82 campaign. The club had missed the playoffs in each of its first two seasons in the NHL, but with Savard in the lineup the Jets showed a record 36-point improvement and qualified for the postseason for the first time. He retired for good after playing one more year, then returned to Montreal when he was named managing director of the Canadiens on April 28, 1983. He was elected to the Hockey Hall of Fame in 1986.

During his time in the executive suite of the Canadiens, Savard built teams that won the Adams Division title on four occasions and reached the Stanley Cup finals three times, winning in 1986 and 1993. He was fired early in 1995–96 after the Canadiens had failed to make the playoffs the previous season and had started the new campaign slowly.

TERRY SAWCHUK

TERRY SAWCHUK played more games, recorded more wins and posted more shutouts than any goalie in NHL history. He was an acrobatic netminder with lightning-fast reflexes who played out of a deep crouch, but his nervous temperament left him vulnerable to the stresses of hockey's most difficult position.

Sawchuk was rookie of the year in both the United States Hockey League (1947–48) and American Hockey League (1948–49) before arriving in the NHL for full-time duty with the Detroit Red Wings in 1950–51. He promptly posted a 1.98 goals-against average with 11 shutouts to earn the Calder Trophy as rookie of the year in the NHL, as well as a selection to the First All-Star Team. Sawchuk was an All-Star again in each of the next four seasons, winning the Vezina Trophy in 1951–52, 1952–53 and 1954–55. He played on Stanley Cup champions in 1952, 1954 and 1955. In the 1952 playoffs, Sawchuk helped Detroit win the Stanley Cup with eight straight victories in two playoff series while recording four shutouts and a 0.63 goals-against average — a modern record.

After five years in Detroit, Sawchuk had recorded 57 shutouts and had a goals-against average of less than 2.00, yet he was traded by Jack Adams to the Boston Bruins on June 3, 1955 to make room for Glenn Hall. Sawchuk battled illness during his second year in Boston, and by mid-January was overcome with stress-related depression. He left the team to recuperate and was traded back to Detroit on June 10, 1957. The Red Wings were no longer the powerhouse they had been, but Sawchuk continued to play well. He was a Second Team All-Star in 1958–59 and 1962–63, and in 1963–64 he surpassed George Hainsworth's all-time NHL record when he recorded his 95th career shutout. Sawchuk was traded to the Toronto Maple Leafs on June 10, 1964 where he teamed with Johnny Bower to form an excellent goaltending tandem. The two shared the Vezina Trophy for fewest goals against in 1964–65 and helped Toronto win the Stanley Cup in 1967. Sawchuk also recorded his 100th shutout that season.

In the Expansion Draft in June of 1967, Sawchuk was selected by the Los Angeles Kings. After a season in L.A., he was traded back to Detroit on October 15, 1968, where he saw limited action before being dealt to the New York Rangers the following season. Sawchuk was used sparingly by the Rangers in 1969–70 and died after the season in a household accident on May 31, 1970. In his 21-year career, Sawchuk had played 971 games with a record of 447–330–173, a 2.53 goals against average and 103 shutouts. The traditional three-year waiting period was waived and he was inducted into the Hockey Hall of Fame in 1971.

FRED SCANLAN

FRED SCANLAN was part of an outstanding forward line on the Montreal Shamrocks with Harry Trihey and Arthur Farrell. All three are members of the Hockey Hall of Fame. Though Trihey and Farrell scored more goals, Frank Selke recalled Scanlan as "the workhorse of the great Shamrocks forward line."

Scanlan joined the Shamrocks in 1897–98, and he helped the team to win the Stanley Cup in 1899 and 1900. After the 1900–01 season, he joined the Winnipeg Victorias, where he played two seasons before retiring. He was elected to the Hockey Hall of Fame in 1965.

MILT SCHMIDT

MILT SCHMIDT was the center and top scorer with the Boston Bruins famed Kraut Line of the 1930s and 1940s. Tough as well as talented, Schmidt was a strong skater and clever stickhandler. He was always dangerous around the net and would not give up the puck without a fight. Except for three years lost to military service in World War II, Schmidt was a Bruin as a player, coach, general manager and executive from midway through the 1936–37 season until 1973. He was elected to the Hockey Hall of Fame in 1961.

Schmidt played on his first Stanley Cup winner with Boston in 1939, then was a First Team All-Star and scoring champion in 1939–40 when he and linemates Woody Dumart and Bobby Bauer finished 1–2–3 in the league. Another Stanley Cup title followed in 1940–41 before military service took all three Bruins teammates away from the NHL midway through the 1941–42 season. Schmidt, Dumart and Bauer finished out the 1941–42 campaign with the Allan Cup-winning Ottawa RCAF team and later went overseas with the Royal Canadian Air Force.

Schmidt's play was not quite what it had been when he returned to Boston in 1945–46, but by 1946–47 he had regained his status as a First Team All-Star. He was named captain of the Bruins in 1950–51 and responded with a career-high 61 points. He also won the Hart Trophy and was named to the First All-Star Team that season. Schmidt was a Second Team All-Star in 1951–52. On Christmas Day in 1954, he retired as a player and immediately took over as coach of the Bruins. Schmidt remained on the job until 1960–61, leading the Bruins to the Stanley Cup finals in 1957 and 1958. Phil Watson took over in 1961–62, but Schmidt replaced Watson during the 1962–63 season and remained the team's coach until 1965–66. He became general manager in 1967 and remained in that position through the 1971–72 season. Schmidt was given an executive position in 1972–73, but left Boston after that year when the team refused to grant his request for a four-year contract.

After leaving Boston, Schmidt became the first general manager of the Washington Capitals. He also coached the team during parts of its first two seasons, 1974–75 and 1975–76.

SWEENEY SCHRINER

SWEENEY SCHRINER David "Sweeney" Schriner was born in Saratov, Russia, but grew up in Calgary and played all of his amateur hockey in the Alberta city. He turned pro with Syracuse of the International-American Hockey League in 1933–34 and entered the NHL with the New York Americans the following year.

Schriner was an instant success in the NHL, leading the Americans in scoring in 1934–35 and being named the league's rookie of the year. He led the NHL in scoring each of the next two years, earning a First Team All-Star berth at left wing in 1935–36 and a Second Team selection in 1936–37. Following two more excellent years with the Americans, Schriner was obtained by the Toronto Maple Leafs for Busher Jackson and three other players in a trade completed prior to the 1939–40 campaign.

Injuries hampered Schriner's effectiveness during his first year in Toronto, but he was again named to the Second All-Star Team in 1940–41. He helped Toronto win the Stanley Cup in 1941–42, scoring six goals in the playoffs including two in a 3–1 victory in game seven of the finals as Toronto rallied from a three-games-to-nothing deficit to defeat the Detroit Red Wings. Schriner was on another Stanley Cup winner in Toronto in 1944–45 and played his final NHL season in 1945–46. He was elected to the Hockey Hall of Fame in 1962.

DAVE SCHULTZ

DAVE SCHULTZ was the embodiment of the Philadelphia Flyers' "Broad Street Bullies" image. He was an intimidating player who coach Fred Shero said gave the rest of the team courage. He had not been a fighter during his junior career, but accepted the role in the minor leagues and soon after his arrival in 1972–73 became the NHL's penalty king while the Flyers became the league's most successful — and feared — franchise. Schultz's 472 minutes in penalties in 1974–75 remain an NHL single-season record but he was also an effective defensive player and scored a career-high 20 goals in 1973–74.

Schultz was traded by Philadelphia before the 1976–77 season and spent the final four years of his career with the Los Angeles Kings, Pittsburgh Penguins and Buffalo Sabres. Never completely comfortable in his enforcer role, Schultz wrote after his retirement that he resented having to fight Bobby Clarke's battles and criticized the Flyers' pack mentality.

CHARLES M. SCHULZ

CHARLES M. SCHULZ *Peanuts* cartoonist Charles M. Schulz was born in Minneapolis and raised in St. Paul, Minnesota. He attended St. Paul Saints and Minneapolis Millers games as a youngster in the 1930s and played hockey on a backyard rink built by his father, on frozen streets and in neighborhood school rinks. His love of the game in those formative years carried over into the cartoons he drew and followed him to California after his career led him there.

Schulz's five children learned to skate at the only arena in the Santa Rosa area. When it closed, Schulz's first wife, Joyce, convinced him to build the Redwood Empire Arena in 1969. He also arranged for skating instruction through local schools, with students bused to and from the rink.

With the support of his second wife, Jeannie, Schulz started a seniors hockey tournament at his arena in the early 1970s. From 12 teams at its start, the Snoopy Senior Hockey Tournament has grown into the largest seniors hockey event in the world. Schulz was honored for his contributions to hockey in the

United States with the Lester Patrick Trophy in 1981. In 1993, he was enshrined in the United States Hockey Hall of Fame as an administrator.

EARL SEIBERT is the son of Hall of Famer Oliver Seibert and was himself elected to the Hockey Hall of Fame in 1963. An outstanding defenseman over 15 years in the NHL, Seibert was an All-Star for 10 consecutive seasons between 1934–35 and 1943–44. He was selected to the First Team on four occasions.

Seibert began skating as a young boy and played amateur hockey in his hometown of Kitchener, Ontario. His speed, size and strength soon attracted professional offers and he joined the Springfield Indians of the Canadian-American Hockey League in 1929–30. Two years later, he entered the NHL with the New York Rangers. Playing with Ott Heller and Ching Johnson, Seibert quickly developed into a star and helped the Rangers to win the Stanley Cup in 1933.

The Rangers dealt Seibert to the Black Hawks for Art Coulter during the 1935–36 campaign and he played for a second Stanley Cup champion in Chicago in 1938. Seibert remained with the Black Hawks until a trade to the Detroit Red Wings during the 1944–45 season and retired after the 1945–46 campaign.

Standing 6'2" and weighing over 200 pounds, Seibert was an intimidating bodychecker during his career and an excellent shot-blocker. He was also an adept stickhandler. He and Oliver Seibert were the first father-son player combination ever elected to the Hockey Hall of Fame.

OLIVER SEIBERT was part of a prominent sports family in Berlin (now Kitchener), Ontario, where he once played on a team comprised entirely of family members. He is reputed to have beaten a horse in a one-mile race on the frozen Grand River, and it was claimed he could skate as fast backward as forward.

Seibert began his hockey career as a goaltender, but he switched to forward, starring there for many years. He had a brief stint in professional hockey with the International (Pro) Hockey League team in Sault Ste. Marie, Michigan, but he spent the majority of his career in his hometown. He was inducted into the Hockey Hall of Fame in 1961, two years before his son Earl was enshrined. The Seiberts were the first father-son combination to be elected to the Hall of Fame as players.

TEEMU SELANNE was drafted by the Winnipeg Jets tenth overall in 1988 but did not enter the NHL until 1992–93. "The Finnish Flash" was an immediate sensation, obliterating Mike Bossy's rookie record of 53 goals with 76 of his own. He also shattered Peter Stastny's NHL rookie mark of 109 points with 132. Selanne's 76 goals equaled the fifth best total in NHL history and tied Alexander Mogilny for the league lead that season. His 132 points ranked fifth in the league. Selanne easily won the Calder Trophy as rookie of the year and was named to the First All-Star Team at right wing. An achilles tendon injury limited Selanne to just 51 games in 1993–94, but he became the second-fastest player in NHL history to score 100 career goals when he reached the milestone in his 130th game. Mike Bossy had scored 100 goals in 129 games.

Selanne was traded to the Mighty Ducks of Anaheim in a multi-player deal on February 7, 1996, teaming with Paul Kariya to form an explosive offensive duo for the Ducks. Selanne was second in the NHL with 51 goals and 109 points in 1996–97 to earn another spot on the First All-Star Team and help Anaheim to reach the playoffs for the first time in just the team's fourth season. In 1997–98, he tied Peter Bondra of the Washington Capitals for the NHL lead with 52 goals.

Prior to his arrival in the NHL, Selanne had been a star in his native Finland. He was a Finnish all-star in both the 1990–91 and 1991–92 seasons and led the Finnish league with 39 goals in 44 games in 1991–92. Internationally, Selanne represented Finland at the World Junior Championships in 1989 and at the World Championships in 1991. He also played for Team Finland at the 1991 Canada Cup and was a member of the Finnish team at the 1992 Winter Olympics. Injuries kept Selanne from competing at the 1994 World Championships, but he represented his homeland again at the World Cup of Hockey in 1996 and at the Nagano Olympics in 1998, where he captured a bronze medal. Selanne was the top scorer at the Olympics with four goals and six assists in five games.

FRANK J. SELKE gave almost 60 years of service to hockey as a coach, manager and executive. He helped to build Stanley Cup and Memorial Cup champions in Toronto and Montreal and helped to establish a building for the Hockey Hall of Fame in 1961. He was also prominent in the construction of Maple Leaf Gardens, Cincinnati Gardens, the Rochester War Memorial arena and numerous other arenas.

Selke was only 14 when he became manager of the Iroquois Bantams in his hometown of Berlin (now Kitchener), Ontario and was running the Berlin Union Jacks when they lost to Conn Smythe's University of Toronto team in the Ontario Hockey Association junior playoffs in 1914 and 1915. Employment opportunities brought Selke to Toronto in 1918, and in 1919 he coached the University of Toronto Schools team to the first Memorial Cup

championship. Selke later organized the Toronto Ravinas, and Conn Smythe hired him in order to gain access to Ravinas players shortly after he purchased the Toronto St. Patricks and renamed them the Maple Leafs in February of 1927. While working with Smythe, Selke coached the Toronto Marlboros to the 1929 Memorial Cup and sent players like Red Horner, Charlie Conacher and Busher Jackson to the Maple Leafs.

Maple Leaf Gardens opened in November of 1931 and the Maple Leafs won their first Stanley Cup title in April of 1932. They continued to be an NHL powerhouse throughout the 1930s. When Conn Smythe left the team in 1942–43 to serve in World War II, he turned over operations to Selke, who guided the team to another title in 1945, but a dispute between the two when Smythe returned led to Selke's resignation in 1946. He then signed as general manager of the Montreal Canadiens. While operating that team, Selke oversaw an Allan Cup champion with the Montreal Royals senior team in 1947 and a Memorial Cup winner with the Royals junior team in 1949. He won his first Stanley Cup championship in Montreal in 1953 and assembled the team that won five straight Cup titles between 1956 and 1960. Selke retired in 1964 after 18 seasons with the Canadiens.

Selke was elected to the Hockey Hall of Fame as a builder in 1960. In 1977, the NHL Board of Governors honored him with the donation of the Frank J. Selke Trophy, presented annually to the league's top defensive forward. The Quebec Major Junior Hockey League presents its own Selke Trophy to its most sportsmanlike player.

BRENDAN SHANAHAN With a combination of goal-scoring skill, toughness and strong leadership qualities, Brendan Shanahan is one of the premier power forwards in the NHL. He was selected second overall by the New Jersey Devils behind Pierre Turgeon in the 1987 Entry Draft. Used mostly at center during his junior career with the London Knights, the Devils employed Shanahan at right wing during his rookie season of 1987–88. He struggled that year, but began to live up to expectations during the second half of the 1988–89 season and reached the 30-goal plateau for the first time in 1989–90.

Shanahan signed with the St. Louis Blues as a free agent on July 25, 1991 and scored 51 goals in 1992–93. The following year, he had 52 goals and led the Blues with 102 points to earn a spot on the NHL's First All-Star Team. Shanahan was second on St. Louis in scoring in 1994–95, but on July 25, 1995, he was traded to the Hartford Whalers for Chris Pronger. Shanahan was captain of the Whalers in 1995–96 and led the team with 44 goals and 78 points, but he was unhappy in Hartford and requested a trade. On October 9, 1996, he was dealt to the Detroit Red Wings.

Shanahan proved to be the spark a talented Detroit team needed to finally reach the top. He led the Red Wings with 46 goals and 87 points during the 1996–97 regular season and had a team-leading nine goals in the playoffs as Detroit won the Stanley Cup for the first time since 1955. His gritty play in the 1998 playoffs despite a back injury helped the Red Wings repeat as Stanley Cup champions.

In international hockey, Shanahan first represented Canada at the World Junior Championships in 1987 when he played for the team that was disqualified from the tournament because of a brawl with the Soviet team. In 1991, he was a member of Team Canada at the Canada Cup and in 1994 he helped Canada to win its first gold medal at the World Championships since 1961. Shanahan also played for the Canadian team at the World Cup of Hockey in 1996 and at the Nagano Olympics in 1998.

TIM SHEEHY was a high school star in International Falls who led his team to 59 consecutive victories and three straight Minnesota state championships between 1963–64 and 1965–66. Sheehy then turned down a chance to play major junior hockey in Canada in order to further his education.

Sheehy enrolled at Boston College in the fall of 1966. Freshman were not allowed to play varsity hockey at the time, but during the three seasons he did play he collected 185 points in just 80 games for a points-per-game average of 2.31 that remains a school record. He was an all-American in 1968–69 and 1969–70. Sheehy also played for the United States national team in 1969, 1970–71 and 1971–72. In 1972, he captained the American Olympic hockey team that won a surprising silver medal in Sapporo.

Sheehy signed his first professional contract with the New England Whalers after the World Hockey Association was formed for the 1972–73 season. He went on to play six WHA seasons with the Whalers, the Edmonton Oilers and the Birmingham Bulls before entering the NHL with the Detroit Red Wings during the 1977–78 season. His playing career ended in 1979–80 after a season split between the minors and the Hartford Whalers. Sheehy was elected to the United States Hockey Hall of Fame in 1997.

EDDIE SHORE Rivaled only by Doug Harvey and Bobby Orr as the greatest defenseman in hockey history, Eddie Shore actually began his professional career as a forward with the Regina Caps of the Western Canada Hockey League in 1924–25. He was converted to defense by the Edmonton Eskimos the following year, and entered the NHL with the Boston Bruins in 1926–27 after the collapse of pro hockey in the west.

Shore came to personify the rough and tumble game of hockey in the late

1920s and 1930s. A supremely talented player with a temper to match, he excelled at rushing the puck end-to-end and literally would knock down players who got in his way. His style resulted in high point totals and even higher penalty minutes, as he outscored all fellow defenseman during his era and trailed only Red Horner in terms of penalties.

When the NHL began selecting an All-Star Team in 1930–31, Shore was named eight times in the first nine years, missing out only in 1936–37 when he suffered a broken bone in his back. Seven of his eight selections were to the First All-Star Team. His is also the only defenseman in NHL history to win the Hart Trophy four times, being selected as the most valuable player in 1932–33, 1934–35, 1935–36 and 1937–38. Shore anchored the defense on Stanley Cup–winning teams in Boston in 1929 and 1939 and helped the Bruins finish first in the American Division eight times.

Anticipating retirement, Shore bought the Springfield Indians of the American Hockey League in 1939–40 and acted as a playing-owner that season. The Bruins arranged for him play home games only, but soon traded him to the New York Americans where his NHL career ended that season. Shore continued to operate his Springfield team until 1978, except for the years during World War II when he served as coach and general manager of the Buffalo Bisons of the AHL. He also owned teams in Fort Worth (in the United States Hockey League) and Oakland (in the Pacific Coast Hockey League) and briefly operated a team in New Haven. Shore was elected to the Hockey Hall of Fame in 1947.

HAMBY SHORE was a member of the last edition of the Ottawa Silver Seven when they were Stanley Cup champions in 1905. He was still playing in Ottawa as a member of the Senators when they were a part of the inaugural season of the NHL in 1917–18, but he died as a victim of the worldwide influenza epidemic later that year.

In addition to Ottawa, Shore also played in Manitoba, starring with the Strathconas in 1907–08 before joining the Winnipeg Maple Leafs for an unsuccessful Stanley Cup challenge against the Montreal Wanderers later that season. He returned to Ottawa to stay in the 1909–10 season that saw the Senators take part in the National Hockey Association's first season.

Shore and former Manitoba teammate Fred Lake anchored the Senators defense in front of future Hall of Fame goaltender Percy LeSueur for four seasons, including the Stanley Cup campaign of 1910–11. Shore's play declined after Lake left the team in 1913–14, but he was still a contributor to Ottawa's 1914–15 team that won the NHA title but lost the Stanley Cup to the Vancouver Millionaires of the Pacific Coast Hockey Association.

Shore's playing time began to decrease behind Art Ross in 1915–16 and he hoped to sign with the PCHA but the Senators wouldn't let him go. As a result, Shore was still with Ottawa when the team entered the NHL for what proved to be his final season.

STEVE SHUTT was a member of five Stanley Cup champions during his 13 years in Montreal. He was a minor contributor to Montreal's victory in his rookie season of 1972–73, but was one of the team's top offensive threats when the Canadiens won the Stanley Cup four years in a row from 1976 until 1979. Shutt's best season was 1976–77, when he led the NHL with 60 goals and finished third in the league with 105 points. His 60 goals that season were a record for left wingers that lasted until Luc Robitaille scored 63 in 1992–93.

Shutt was a star in junior hockey in his hometown of Toronto, playing on the Marlboros' top line with Dave Gardner and Billy Harris. Shutt scored 70 goals in 1970–71 and led the Ontario Hockey Association with 63 in 1971–72 before the Canadiens chose him fourth overall in the 1972 Amateur Draft. He played just six games in the minors, but was used sparingly in Montreal until 1974–75, when coach Scotty Bowman put him on a line with Guy Lafleur and Peter Mahovlich. Shutt scored 30 goals that year and 45 the next. His 60-goal season in 1976–77 earned him a selection to the First All-Star Team and his 49 goals the following year resulted in a spot on the Second Team.

On November 19, 1984, Shutt was acquired by Los Angeles. He finished out the 1984–85 season with the Kings, then announced his retirement. At the time, his 424 goals ranked 20th in NHL history. Shutt worked as a television commentator after his playing career and was elected to the Hockey Hall of Fame in 1993. He returned to Montreal as an assistant coach in 1993–94, but left the team after the 1996–97 season.

BABE SIEBERT Albert Charles "Babe" Siebert began his NHL career as a powerful left winger but later became an All-Star defenseman. He entered the NHL in 1925–26 when he and Nels Stewart were added to the Montreal Maroons to give the second-year team a more youthful outlook. The two promptly helped the team win the Stanley Cup.

Siebert's potential as a defenseman was recognized early by Maroons coach Eddie Gerard, who occasionally use him there until putting together the S-Line of Siebert, Stewart and Hooley Smith in 1929–30. The combination was one of the most dangerous in the NHL, with Stewart pouring in the goals while Smith and Siebert pounded the opposition with tough hits and strong backchecking. The S-Line was broken up dramatically after just three seasons when Stewart was traded to the Boston Bruins and Siebert was sent to the New

York Rangers in 1932–33. Lester Patrick immediately converted Siebert to defense, where he played alongside Ching Johnson and helped New York win the Stanley Cup that year. When Boston's Eddie Shore was suspended after the Ace Bailey incident in December of 1933, Art Ross acquired Siebert from the Rangers to solidify the Bruins defense.

Siebert remained in Boston until 1935–36, when he was selected to the First All-Star Team. He was then dealt to the Montreal Canadiens and named team captain for the 1936–37 season. The Canadiens were coming off a last-place finish, but Siebert shored up a weak defense and led the team to the top spot in the Canadian Division. He was rewarded with another First Team All-Star berth and the Hart Trophy. Siebert earned a First All-Star Team selection again after the 1937–38 season.

Following his third year in Montreal, it was announced that Siebert would take over as coach of the Canadiens in 1939–40, but he lost his life in a drowning accident on August 25, 1939. The NHL played its third All-Star Game to benefit the Siebert family on October 29, 1939. He was elected to the Hockey Hall of Fame in 1964.

CHARLIE SIMMER After NHL trials with the California Golden Seals and Cleveland Barons, and all-star seasons in the minor leagues, Charlie Simmer finally achieved stardom with the Los Angeles Kings as the left winger on the Triple Crown Line with Marcel Dionne and Dave Taylor.

Simmer scored goals in 13 consecutive games during the 1979–80 season for the longest streak in the NHL since 1921–22. He led the league with 56 goals that season even though his year was ended by injuries after 64 games. He earned a First Team All-Star selection, as he did in 1980–81 when he again scored 56 goals in a season cut short by injuries. That year, he had dueled Mike Bossy in an attempt to match Rocket Richard's feat of 50 goals in 50 games. Simmer fell one short with 49 goals and scored his 50th in 51 games while Bossy reached the 50–50 mark.

Still hampered by injuries in 1981–82, Simmer's production fell before he rebounded to score 44 goals in 1983–84. On October 24, 1985, he was dealt to the Boston Bruins, where his gritty performance and ability to overcome more injury problems earned him the Masterton Trophy for perseverance and dedication to hockey in 1986–87. The Penguins picked him up in 1987–88 and he spent his final NHL season in Pittsburgh. After a year in Europe, Simmer returned to North America and served as a player and assistant coach with San Diego of the International Hockey League.

BULLET JOE SIMPSON Harold Joseph Simpson earned the nickname "Bullet Joe" because of his speed as a skater. In his prime, he was called "the greatest living hockey player" by the legendary Newsy Lalonde. Simpson was a defenseman during his career, but he had several exceptional scoring seasons.

Simpson was a member of the Winnipeg Victorias in 1914–15 before enlisting in the Canadian army. He played hockey the following season with the 61st Battalion team that won the Allan Cup before it was sent overseas. In the army, he rose to the rank of lieutenant and he was wounded in battles at the Somme and Amiens before returning home with the Military Medal. He resumed his hockey career in his hometown of Selkirk, Manitoba before moving to Edmonton for 1920–21. He turned pro the following year when the Eskimos entered the Western Canada Hockey League.

The Eskimos finished first in the WCHL twice during Simpson's four-year tenure, reaching the Stanley Cup finals in 1923 before losing to the Ottawa Senators. The team received many offers for his services from the Vancouver Maroons and Ottawa Senators, but it sold him to the New York Americans prior to 1925–26. He spent six years as a player in the NHL, taking over as coach of the Americans from 1932–33 to 1934–35. He later coached minor-league teams in New Haven and Minneapolis, returning to the ice for a single game during the 1937–38 season of the American Hockey Association. Simpson was elected to the Hockey Hall of Fame in 1962.

HARRY SINDEN has been general manager of the Boston Bruins since 1972–73 and president of the club since 1989–90. He has been the driving force behind every aspect of the team, running both the business and hockey operations, and has been a key member of many league committees which bring policy and rule changes to the attention of the NHL Board of Governors. He was elected to the Hockey Hall of Fame as a builder in 1983.

Sinden never played in the NHL but was a star amateur player. He captained the Whitby Dunlops to the Allan Cup senior amateur championship in 1957 and 1959, and to the World Championship title in Oslo, Norway in 1958. He won an Olympic silver medal in 1960 when he was added to the roster of the Kitchener-Waterloo Dutchmen. In 1960–61, Sinden became affiliated with the Bruins organization as a member of the Kingston Frontenacs in the Eastern Professional Hockey League. He became player-coach at Kingston in 1961–62 and led the team to a league title in 1962–63. Sinden then served as player-coach for two years with the Minneapolis Bruins of the Central Pro League and won the CPHL title with the Oklahoma City Blazers in 1965–66.

In 1966–67, Sinden was promoted to head coach of the Boston Bruins and the following year led the team into the playoffs for the first time after an eight-year absence. In 1970, the Bruins were Stanley Cup champions for the

first time in 29 years. Sinden went into private business the next season, but was back in hockey in 1972 as coach of Team Canada for the Summit Series with the Soviet Union. He then returned to the Bruins as general manager. He went on to become the first general manager to oversee 1,000 wins, and he watched the Bruins stretch their consecutive playoff run to a North American pro sports record of 29 years before missing the postseason in 1996–97.

DARRYL SITTLER is the Toronto Maple Leafs all-time career leader with 389 goals and 916 points, and was the first player in Maple Leafs history to score 100 points in a season, reaching the century mark in 1975–76. Sittler set an NHL single-game record with 10 points on six goals on four assists on February 7, 1976, and tied a playoff record on April 22 of that year when he scored five goals in one game. In September of 1976, Sittler scored the winning goal in overtime in the final game against Czechoslovakia to give Team Canada a victory at the first Canada Cup tournament.

Sittler was a junior star with the London Knights of the Ontario Hockey Association before the Maple Leafs selected him eighth overall in the 1970 Amateur Draft. His numbers were unimpressive during his first two seasons, but in 1972–73, he had 29 goals and 77 points and did not fall below those totals until the last two seasons of his career. Sittler succeeded Dave Keon as captain of the Maple Leafs in 1975–76 and Toronto's fortunes rose over the next three seasons, culminating with a trip to the semifinals in 1978. Sittler established career highs with 45 goals and 72 assists in 1977–78 and his 117 points that season were a Maple Leafs record until Doug Gilmour had 127 in 1992–93.

The return of Punch Imlach as Maple Leafs general manager in 1979–80 led to dissension in the dressing room and resulted in Lanny McDonald being traded to the Colorado Rockies on December 29, 1979. Sittler resigned as captain in protest, and though he resumed the captaincy for the start of the 1980–81 season, he demanded a trade the following season and was dealt to the Philadelphia Flyers on January 20, 1982. Sittler remained with the Flyers through the 1983–84 season and spent his final year with the Detroit Red Wings in 1984–85. At the time of his retirement, Sittler's 1,121 points on 484 goals and 637 assists ranked 15th in NHL history. He was elected to the Hockey Hall of Fame in 1989.

Sittler returned to the Maple Leafs as an assistant to club president Cliff Fletcher on August 8, 1991. He continues to work with the team in marketing, community relations and alumni relations.

RAYMIE SKILTON was the second American ever to play in the NHL when he joined fellow Boston-area resident Duke Geran on the roster of the Montreal Wanderers for the second night of action in NHL history. Skilton was playing hockey for Boston Navy at the time and was a munitions expert stationed briefly in Montreal. When the Wanderers found themselves short one player for their game on December 22, 1917, Skilton was signed and lined up on defense. It would be the only game of his NHL career.

ALF SKINNER was the surprise star of Toronto's Stanley Cup championship in the NHL's inaugural season of 1917–18. He scored eight goals in the best-of-five final against the Vancouver Millionaires of the Pacific Coast Hockey Association to upstage more famous teammates Reg Noble, Harry Cameron and Corb Denneny, as well as high-scoring Vancouver stars Cyclone Taylor and Mickey MacKay.

Skinner had made his debut in the National Hockey Association in 1914–15 and played with the Toronto Shamrocks, Toronto Blueshirts and Montreal Wanderers over three years in the NHA. He became a member of the Torontos, more commonly known as the Arenas, in the NHL's first season. After Toronto won the NHL championship, Skinner scored seven goals in the first three games of the Stanley Cup series with Vancouver. His eighth goal came in the fifth and final game, when he tallied Toronto's initial score in a 2–1 victory.

Following the 1918–19 season, Skinner left Toronto for Vancouver. He had several productive seasons in the PCHA and four more trips to the Stanley Cup finals, but was never on another Cup champion.

When Vancouver and the Victoria Cougars joined the Western Canada Hockey League for the 1924–25 season, Skinner returned to the NHL and played for both the Boston Bruins and Montreal Maroons—the league's two new expansion teams. He joined another new NHL franchise when he played seven games with the Pittsburgh Pirates in 1925–26, then spent three seasons in the minor leagues before retiring.

TOD SLOAN won a Memorial Cup championship with the St. Michael's Majors in 1944–45 and won the Red Tilson Trophy as the Ontario Hockey Association's most valuable player in 1945–46. He then turned pro with the Toronto Maple Leafs' Pittsburgh farm club in the American Hockey League the following season. Sloan played one game with the Maple Leafs in 1947–48 and began the 1948–49 season in Toronto but was sent back to Pittsburgh.

Despite a slim build, Sloan was an aggressive player and racked up 105 penalty minutes during his first full season with Toronto in 1950–51. He was also a slick skater and good stickhandler who led the Maple Leafs with 31 goals that season and ranked eighth in the NHL with 56 points as Toronto won the Stanley Cup. Sloan led the Maple Leafs with 43 points in 1953–54 and

enjoyed his best season in 1955–56. He played on a line with George Armstrong and Dick Duff that year and had a team-leading 37 goals and 66 points. Sloan ranked fifth in the NHL in scoring and earned a berth on the Second All-Star Team.

Sloan played two more years with the Maple Leafs but injuries saw his scoring production decline. His involvement with the fledgling NHL Players' Association resulted in his being sold to the Black Hawks on June 4, 1958, and Sloan regained his form in Chicago. He had 27 goals in 1958–59 and 20 goals the following year, then helped the Black Hawks win their first Stanley Cup title since 1938 in 1960–61. Sloan left the NHL after that season and had his amateur status reinstated in order to join the Galt Terriers who won a silver medal at the World Championships in 1962.

ALEX SMART set a rookie record when he scored three goals in his first NHL game on January 14, 1943. His hat trick and one assist helped the Montreal Canadiens down the Chicago Black Hawks 5–1. Smart's record has only been duplicated once, by Real Cloutier of the Quebec Nordiques in 1979.

Smart was in his fifth season in the Quebec Senior Hockey League when he got the call to the NHL. He saw action in just seven more games with the Canadiens during the 1942–43 season, collecting two more goals and another assist, and never played in the NHL again. Smart's playing career ended in 1950 after seven more years in the QSHL.

COOPER SMEATON grew up in Montreal and played baseball, football, basketball and hockey with the Westmount Amateur Athletic Association. He had several offers to become a professional hockey player, but he remained an amateur. He also became an outstanding referee, handling many Allan Cup and Stanley Cup games over his career. Smeaton, Chaucer Elliott and Mickey Ion were the first referees elected to the Hockey Hall of Fame in 1961.

Smeaton refereed amateur hockey games before being appointed to the officiating staff of the National Hockey Association in 1913. His career was interrupted by military service, but he returned to referee in the NHL after World War I. In 1930–31, he coached the Philadelphia Quakers, refereeing again when the team withdrew from the league after that season. Smeaton was appointed head referee of the NHL, continuing until 1937 when he retired to devote more time to business. In 1946, he was appointed a trustee of the Stanley Cup by P.D. Ross. It was a position he held until his death on October 3, 1978.

ALF SMITH was the oldest of seven hockey-playing brothers from Ottawa, three of whom (Alf, Tommy and Harry) became top stars in the game. Alf was elected to the Hall of Fame in 1962; Tommy was honored in 1973. While not quite the scoring stars his brothers were, Alf still managed to lead the Amateur Hockey Association with 12 goals in eight games in 1896–97, though he was better known for his rough play and quick temper.

Smith played his early hockey with the Ottawa Electrics and Ottawa Capitals. He then spent a year in Pittsburgh before returning to his hometown in 1894–95. After playing two more years, he dropped out of hockey, but he made a comeback at age 30 after the Silver Seven won the Stanley Cup for the first time in 1903. Teaming on a forward line with Frank McGee and, later, his brother Harry, Smith helped the team defend its title over the next two seasons before losing to the Montreal Wanderers in 1906. Smith and his Ottawa teammate Harry "Rat" Westwick were added to the Kenora Thistles in March of 1907, but the new Stanley Cup champions were unable to defend their title when they too were beaten by the Montreal Wanderers.

Smith was back in Ottawa for the 1907–08 season. He spent the next year in Pittsburgh before returning to Ottawa as a coach. He guided the Ottawa Cliffsides hockey club to the first Allan Cup title in 1908, and he later coached the Ottawa Senators during the 1918–19 NHL season. Smith also served as a coach in Renfrew, North Bay and Moncton, New Brunswick.

BILLY SMITH was one of the top clutch goaltenders in NHL history. His netminding helped the New York Islanders win the Stanley Cup four years in a row from 1979–80 until 1982–83, though he was as well known for using his stick to punish opponents who crowded his crease. Smith was also the first NHL goaltender credited with scoring a goal when he was the last Islanders player to touch the puck before Rob Ramage scored in his own net during a 4–3 win over the Colorado Rockies on November 28, 1979. Smith was elected to the Hockey Hall of Fame in 1993.

Smith originally was drafted by the Los Angeles Kings in 1970 and led their Springfield farm club to the Calder Cup as American Hockey League champions in 1970–71. He spent five games with the Kings the following season and was then selected by the Islanders in the 1972 Expansion Draft. By 1974–75, Smith was a part of one of the league's best goaltending duos, sharing the Islanders net with Glenn "Chico" Resch, and the Islanders quickly became a force in the NHL. Though he split duties with Resch during the 1979–80 season, Smith was clearly the number-one goalie in the playoffs, taking part in 20 of 21 games as the Islanders won their first Stanley Cup title. Smith was a member of Team Canada at the 1981 Canada Cup, then won the Vezina Trophy and a selection to the First All-Star team in 1981–82. In 1982–83, he shared the Islanders net with Roland Melanson and the two combined to win the

Jennings Trophy. Smith was again number one in the postseason, winning the Conn Smythe Trophy as playoff MVP as the Islanders won their fourth consecutive Stanley Cup title.

Smith remained with the Islanders for the rest of his career, retiring after his 18th season in 1988–89. At the time, his 305 career victories ranked eighth in NHL history. Smith became the Islanders goaltending coach after his playing career, and his number 31 was retired on February 20, 1993. In 1993–94, Smith left the Islanders to become the goaltending coach of the Florida Panthers.

BOBBY SMITH enjoyed an outstanding junior career in his hometown of Ottawa, earning all-star honors in the Ontario Hockey Association in 1976–77 and 1977–78. The 1977–78 season also saw him beat Wayne Gretzky for the OHA scoring title and earn honors as Canadian major junior player of the year.

Smith was selected first overall by the Minnesota North Stars in the 1978 NHL Entry Draft and went on to win the Calder Trophy as rookie of the year in 1978–79 after leading the North Stars with 30 goals and 74 points. Smith would be Minnesota's top scorer in four of his first five years, helping the team reach the Stanley Cup finals in 1981 and recording career highs with 43 goals, 71 assists and 114 points in 1981–82. On October 28, 1983, he was traded to the Montreal Canadiens. Smith spent seven years in Montreal and helped the Canadiens win the Stanley Cup in 1985–86, scoring the Cup-winning goal in a 4–3 victory over the Calgary Flames in game five.

Smith was traded back to the North Stars on August 7, 1990 and finished out his playing career with three more years in Minnesota. He was a member of the North Stars team that reached the Stanley Cup finals in 1991, making him one of only three players (Neal Broten and Curt Giles) to play on both Minnesota teams that reached the finals. Smith retired after playing just 45 games in 1992–93. He had served as vice president of the NHL Players' Association between 1981 and 1990.

Following his playing career, Smith completed two degrees from the University of Minnesota, a Bachelor of Science and a Masters of Business Administration. On May 21, 1996, he was named the first executive vice president of hockey operations for the Phoenix Coyotes and became the Coyotes general manager during the 1996–97 season.

CLINT SMITH combined skill and sportsmanship in an NHL career that saw him set scoring records while accumulating just 24 penalty minutes in 11 seasons. He was the first player in history to win the Lady Byng Trophy with two different teams and was runner-up for the award on three other occasions.

Smith played his first full NHL season with the New York Rangers in 1937–38 and was runner-up for the Lady Byng Trophy after going the entire 48-game season without a penalty. He won the honor for the first time in 1938–39 after leading the Rangers in scoring with 41 points. Smith won the Stanley Cup with New York in 1940 and spent three more years with the Rangers before being sold to the Chicago Black Hawks prior to the 1943–44 season.

Playing on a line with Doug Bentley and Bill Mosienko, Smith enjoyed his most productive season with 72 points for Chicago in 1943–44 and set what was then an NHL record with 49 assists in a 50-game schedule. Smith and his linemates combined for a record 219 points that season, and Smith was again awarded the Lady Byng Trophy. He had two more excellent seasons in Chicago, including a career-high 26 goals in 1945–46, but his production tailed off in 1946–47. He left the NHL to become player-coach with the Tulsa Oilers of the United States Hockey League in 1947–48 and was named league MVP that season. The following year, he coached St. Paul to the USHL title. Smith was elected to the Hockey Hall of Fame in 1991.

DON SMITH was a scoring star who played alongside several future Hall of Famers but never won the Stanley Cup in his lengthy career. He began with Cornwall of the Federal Amateur Hockey League in 1904–05, and tied Bud McCourt for the league lead in scoring in 1906–07. Smith scored five goals against the Ottawa Vics in the game in which McCourt was killed by a high stick on March 6, 1907.

The FAHL collapsed after McCourt's death and Smith played with Portage la Prairie of the Manitoba Hockey League in 1907–08. He then spent a season in the Ontario Professional Hockey League before signing with the Montreal Shamrocks for the 1909–10 season, leading the club in scoring in the inaugural campaign of the National Hockey Association. His most productive season came the following year, when he had 26 goals in 16 games with the Renfrew.

When Renfrew withdrew from the NHA, Smith signed with the Victoria Aristocrats of the Pacific Coast Hockey Association in 1911–12 but returned to the NHA with the Montreal Canadiens the following year. He played on a line with Newsy Lalonde and Didier Pitre, and later centered Gordie Roberts and Harry Hyland after a trade to the Montreal Wanderers.

Smith left hockey after the 1915–16 season for military service in the First World War. When he returned from overseas, he made a brief comeback with the Canadiens during the 1919–20 NHL season.

FRANK SMITH On December 29, 1911, Frank Smith met with three other men in the basement of his home to form a new minor hockey league. The

league, first known as the Beaches Hockey League, eventually grew into the Metropolitan Toronto Hockey League. Smith was named its first secretary and he remained in that position until 1962. By then, the MTHL had grown into the biggest minor hockey organization in the world. Smith was honored with the top lifetime achievement awards by the MTHL, the Ontario Hockey Association and the Canadian Amateur Hockey Association. He was elected to the Hockey Hall of Fame as a builder in 1962.

GARY SMITH was known as "Suitcase" over a career that saw him play for teams in 13 different cities in 16 professional seasons. He saw brief action with the Toronto Maple Leafs in 1965–66 and 1966–67, before being selected by the California Seals in the 1967 Expansion Draft. Smith saw increased action in each of the next four years, setting an NHL single-season record for losses when he went 19–48–4 in 71 games with the Seals in 1970–71.

A trade to Chicago saw Smith back up Tony Esposito with the Black Hawks in 1971–72 and 1972–73 before moving on to the Vancouver Canucks, Minnesota North Stars and Washington Capitals. Smith played in the World Hockey Association in 1978–79 before returning to the NHL with the Winnipeg Jets for a final season in 1979–80.

HARRY SMITH Harold Henry "Harry" Smith was one of seven hockey-playing brothers, two of whom (Alf and Tommy) are members of the Hall of Fame. He showed plenty of the goal-scoring brilliance later demonstrated by Tommy, but discipline problems kept him from becoming a star.

Harry Smith joined his brother Alf on the Ottawa club that was in the last days of being known as the Silver Seven. Playing left wing during the season of 1905–06, Smith led the Eastern Canada Amateur Hockey Association in scoring with 31 goals in just eight games, topping even legendary teammate Frank McGee. He also had nine goals in three Stanley Cup challenge matches played during the season. In a postseason playoff with the Montreal Wanderers, Smith had the only goal in Ottawa's 9–1 loss, then had five goals in the second game of the total-goal series as Ottawa rallied to tie the round before losing the Stanley Cup by a final score of 12–10.

When Frank McGee retired, Smith took his place at center in 1906–07 and collected 23 goals in nine games. He left Ottawa the following season, playing in Winnipeg and Pittsburgh in 1907–08. Smith then joined the Montreal Wanderers and had five goals in one game and six in the series when the Wanderers defeated Edmonton in a two-game Stanley Cup challenge match in December of 1908. Smith would jump his contract three times during the 1908–09 season and spent the year playing in Pittsburgh, Toronto, and Haileybury as well as with the Wanderers.

Art Ross gave Smith a chance with the Haileybury team in the National Hockey Association's inaugural season of 1909–10, but he was overweight and unwilling to train. Smith had success with Waterloo of the Ontario Professional Hockey League in 1910–11 and also when he played in Schreiber, Ontario in 1911–12. He then put up good numbers with the NHA's Toronto Tecumsehs in 1912–13 but was dropped before that season was over. He was unsuccessful in a returned to Ottawa in 1913–14, but had 26 goals in 20 games in Halifax during what proved to be his final season.

HOOLEY SMITH Reginald Joseph "Hooley" Smith played amateur hockey in his hometown of Toronto and was a member of the Toronto Granite Club team that won the Allan Cup in 1922 and 1923. The team represented Canada in hockey at the first Winter Olympics in 1924 and easily won the gold medal.

Smith joined the Ottawa Senators in 1924–25 and developed a sweeping hook check that made him one of the NHL's most dangerous two-way forwards. He played right wing on a line with veterans Cy Denneny and Frank Nighbor, helping Ottawa finish first in the NHL standings in 1925–26, then contributing to a Stanley Cup win the following year. Smith was prone to taking foolish penalties in the early stages of his career, and an attack on Harry Oliver of the Boston Bruins during the 1927 Stanley Cup finals resulted in a suspension for the first month of the 1927–28 season. While he was suspended, the cash-strapped Senators sold him to the Montreal Maroons.

Smith first played with Nels Stewart and Jimmy Ward in Montreal before Babe Siebert was added at left wing in 1929–30, thus creating the S-Line. The trio proved to be one of the most dangerous lines in the NHL by combining Stewart's scoring skill with Smith and Siebert's aggressive checking. Smith remained with the Maroons after Stewart and Siebert were traded in 1932 and was made a center on a line with Jimmy Ward and Baldy Northcott. In 1934–35, he captained the Maroons to a Stanley Cup title and was named to the First All-Star Team the following year. His only previous All-Star selection had been to the Second Team in 1931–32.

When financial problems began to beset the Maroons, Smith was traded to Boston in 1936–37, but spent just one season with the Bruins before being dealt to the New York Americans. He saw some action at defense during his four-year stint in New York and retired in 1941. Smith was elected to the Hockey Hall of Fame in 1972.

SID SMITH joined the Toronto Maple Leafs in 1946–47, but while the Maple Leafs went on to win the Stanley Cup three years in a row, Smith spent most

of that time with the club's American Hockey League affiliate in Pittsburgh. After leading the AHL with 55 goals, 57, assists and 112 points in 1948–49, he was recalled to Toronto in time for the playoffs and starred on a line with Teeder Kennedy and Bill Ezinicki as the Maple Leafs won their third straight title that spring.

In his first full season in Toronto in 1949–50, Smith had 22 goals and led the Maple Leafs with 45 points. The following year, he had 30 goals and cracked the top 10 in the NHL with 51 points. Toronto won another Stanley Cup title that season and Smith was named to the Second All-Star Team at left wing. He ranked fifth in the NHL with 57 points in 1951–52 and led the Maple Leafs with 27 goals that year to earn another selection to the Second All-Star Team. He also won the Lady Byng Trophy.

Smith had the reputation of being a one-way player early in his career, but his defensive skills developed over the years. Still, he remained an offensive threat, leading the Maple Leafs in goals again in 1952–53 and 1953–54. In 1954–55, he led the Leafs for the fourth straight year with a career-high 33 goals and ranked eighth in the NHL with 54 points. Smith won the Lady Byng Trophy for a second time that season and was named to the First All-Star Team.

Following the retirement of Teeder Kennedy, Smith remained with the Maple Leafs in 1955–56 but scored just four goals in 55 games that year. He rebounded somewhat with 17 goals the following season but retired from the NHL early in the 1957–58 campaign. Smith then had his amateur status restored and was added to the roster of the Whitby Dunlops, who won the 1958 World Championship.

TOMMY SMITH was a member of a prominent Ottawa sports family who is joined by brother Alf in the Hockey Hall of Fame. He played in several cities across eastern Canada and in Pittsburgh, and he was among the highest-scoring players everywhere he went.

Smith played school and junior hockey in Ottawa, joining the Ottawa Vics of the Federal Amateur Hockey League in 1905–06. He also saw brief action with the Ottawa Silver Seven that season before turning professional in Pittsburgh, where he remained for three years. Smith was back in Canada with Brantford of the Ontario Professional Hockey League in 1908–09, promptly leading the league with 33 goals in 13 games. After joining the Cobalt Silver Kings for the first National Hockey Association season of 1909–10, he returned to the OPHL with Galt in 1910–11. Smith helped the team to win the league title, but Galt lost a Stanley Cup challenge to the Ottawa Senators on March 13, 1911. The next year, he was with Moncton of the Maritime Professional Hockey League. Smith led the team with an astounding 53 goals in 18 games before Moncton lost a Stanley Cup challenge to the Quebec Bulldogs. He finally won the Stanley Cup in 1913 after signing with Quebec.

Tommy Smith enjoyed great success playing next to Joe Malone with the Bulldogs. His 39 goals in 1912–13 were second in the NHA behind Malone's 43, and he followed it up by winning scoring titles each of the next two seasons. Except for a brief period with the Toronto Ontarios, Smith remained in Quebec until joining the Montreal Canadiens in 1916–17. He retired after that season, coaching for two years, but he later made a comeback that included 10 games with the Bulldogs during the NHL season of 1919–20.

Among Smith's many single-game scoring feats are a pair of nine-goal games, including one on the night of January 21, 1914 that tied Newsy Lalonde's NHA record. He also had one eight-goal game, a six-goal effort and five five-goal games. Smith was elected to the Hockey Hall of Fame in 1973.

CONN SMYTHE purchased the Toronto St. Patricks on February 14, 1927 and renamed the team the Toronto Maple Leafs. He chose the Maple Leaf name and emblem as a patriotic gesture because it had been the symbol of Canadian soldiers during World War I.

Smythe first came to prominence in hockey as the captain of the University of Toronto varsity team that won the Ontario junior championship in 1915. Later, he and most of his teammates enlisted for military service. Smythe returned to the University of Toronto after World War I and graduated in 1920. He then operated a sand and gravel company, but continued his involvement in hockey at U of T. Smythe coached the Varsity seniors to the Allan Cup in 1927, but was not on hand when the team won the gold medal at the Olympics in 1928.

While still coaching in Toronto, Smythe was hired by John Hammond in 1926 to assemble a team in New York after the Rangers were admitted into the NHL. Smythe signed relative unknowns like Lorne Chabot, Ching Johnson and Frank Boucher, among others, but was fired when he refused to acquire star Babe Dye, whom he did not think would fit in with his team approach. Smythe later used the money he was paid to leave New York to help finance his purchase of the St. Pats. (The team he built in New York won the Stanley Cup under Lester Patrick in 1928.)

Once established in Toronto, Smythe quickly went about building the Maple Leafs into a winner by adding such players as King Clancy, Joe Primeau, Charlie Conacher and Red Horner. He also hired Foster Hewitt to broadcast games and by 1931 had built Maple Leaf Gardens during the height of the Depression. The new arena brought respectability to pro hockey in Toronto, and the Leafs won their first Stanley Cup championship that season. Toronto was the best team in hockey during the 1930s, but after World War

II broke out, Smythe took a leave of absence from the Maple Leafs board and recruited a Sportsmen's Battery. He took it overseas, insisted on seeing combat duty himself and was badly wounded in July of 1944. He recovered and was running the Maple Leafs again by 1945.

Smythe remained in charge of the Maple Leafs until retiring in 1961. He already had been inducted into the Hockey Hall of Fame as a builder in 1958, and in 1964 Maple Leaf Gardens Limited donated the Conn Smythe Trophy to reward the most valuable player in the playoffs. Smythe also owned a successful horse-racing stable, winning the Queen's Plate in 1953 and 1967, and was very active in children's charities in Toronto.

ED SNIDER's sports career began in football, when he first came to Philadelphia as vice president of the National Football League's Eagles in 1964. He soon became involved in the effort to bring an NHL team to Philadelphia, and in 1966 the city was granted a franchise that would begin play with five other expansion teams in 1967–68. Snider continues to serve as chairman of the team.

Under Snider's leadership, the Flyers rose quickly to prominence, becoming the first expansion team to win the Stanley Cup in 1974 and repeating as champions in 1975. In the team's first 20 seasons, Philadelphia posted an 816–496–266 record for a .601 winning percentage that was second only to the Montreal Canadiens during that time.

As the founder of the Flyers, Snider was instrumental in building the Spectrum to house the team in 1967 and then the CoreStates Center in 1996–97. In 1974, he founded Spectacor, which oversees the operation of both the Flyers and their arenas. The group also developed the PRISM cable television network. In 1976, Snider created Hockey Central, an organization to promote and develop youth hockey in the Delaware Valley. In 1980, he won the Lester Patrick Trophy for his contributions to hockey in the United States. Snider was elected to the Hockey Hall of Fame as a builder in 1988.

LORD STANLEY OF PRESTON Frederick Arthur, Lord Stanley of Preston, was the son of a three-time Prime Minister of England and himself a British Member of Parliament. He sat in the House of Lords, and he served a short stint as the Secretary of State for the British colonies. In 1888, he was appointed Governor-General of Canada. Publicly shy and politically careful, Lord Stanley was an advocate of closer ties between Britain and its colonies.

The Governor-General enjoyed the winter sports he discovered in Canada and his sons became accomplished hockey players with the Rideau Rebels team in Ottawa. During his final year in office (1893), Lord Stanley donated the Dominion Hockey Challenge Cup to recognize Canada's hockey champion. The trophy quickly became known as the Stanley Cup. The original bowl was purchased in London at a cost of 10 guineas, about the equivalent of $50.

Originally an amateur trophy, the Dominion Hockey Challenge Cup did not belong to any one league; it was available by challenge to any team in Canada. By 1906, professional teams had begun to compete for it, and by 1910 the Stanley Cup had become the symbol of professional hockey supremacy in Canada. In 1914, a formalized playoff system was adopted by the National Hockey Association, the Pacific Coast Hockey Association and the Stanley Cup trustees, which was continued by the NHL, the PCHA and later the Western Canada Hockey League. American teams had begun competing for the Cup as early as 1916. After pro hockey collapsed in the west in 1926, the NHL became the only league to play for hockey's most prized trophy.

Lord Stanley and Sir H. Montagu Allan, who donated the Allan Cup, were elected to the Hockey Hall of Fame as builders in 1945 as part of the Hall's first inductions.

ALLAN STANLEY was overlooked behind star teammates and fellow great defensemen such as Doug Harvey, Red Kelly, Tim Horton and Harry Howell, but he played 1,244 games over a 21-year NHL career and was recognized eventually as one of the greats of the game. He never was noted for his skating speed, but his ability to anticipate the flow of the game meant he rarely was caught out of position.

Stanley joined the New York Rangers midway through the 1948–49 season, and though he remained with the team for most of the next five years, his laid-back style did not endear him to Rangers fans. He was traded to the Chicago Black Hawks for Bill Gadsby in November of 1954. Chicago sold him to the Bruins in October of 1956 and he had two good years in Boston before being traded to the Toronto Maple Leafs for Jim Morrison on October 8, 1958.

Teamed almost exclusively with Tim Horton, but also playing with Bob Baun, Carl Brewer and Marcel Pronovost, Stanley enjoyed the best years of his career in Toronto. He was named to the Second All-Star Team in 1959–60, 1960–61 and 1965–66, and helped the Maple Leafs win the Stanley Cup in 1962, 1963, 1964 and 1967. Stanley concluded his career with the Philadelphia Flyers in 1968–69. He was elected to the Hockey Hall of Fame in 1981.

BARNEY STANLEY played every position but goaltender during his hockey career, and he was also a playing coach for much of the time between 1919 and 1929. When the statistics of the Pacific Coast Hockey Association, Western Canada Hockey League and Western Hockey League are combined, Stanley

ranks seventh all-time with 143 goals and eighth all-time with 216 points.

Stanley played amateur hockey in his hometown of Paisley, Ontario, and out west in Edmonton before signing a pro contract with the Vancouver Millionaires during the 1914–15 season. He helped Vancouver become the first PCHA team to win the Stanley Cup that season, scoring four goals in a 12–3 win over the Ottawa Senators in the final game of the series. In 1916–17, he established a career high with 28 goals in 23 games.

After five years in Vancouver, Stanley returned to Edmonton as a player-coach with the Eskimos in 1919–20. The following year, he had the same role with the Calgary Tigers. He was a member of that team when the Western Canada Hockey League was formed in 1921–22. He spent the next two years as a player-coach with the WCHL's Regina Caps before returning to Edmonton in 1924–25 for two more seasons.

In 1926–27, Stanley joined the Winnipeg Maroons of the American Hockey Association as a player-coach before moving to the NHL's Chicago Black Hawks. His NHL stay was a short one, however, as he played just two games in Chicago while coaching the Black Hawks for 23 games. He was back in the AHA with Minneapolis for a final season as a player in 1928–29. He then returned to coaching with the Edmonton Pooler junior team for three seasons. Stanley was elected to the Hockey Hall of Fame in 1962.

PETER STASTNY Brothers Anton, Marian and Peter Stastny were star players in their homeland during the 1970s and members of the Czechoslovakian Olympic team that competed at Lake Placid in 1980. Anton was drafted by the Quebec Nordiques in 1979, and Peter was signed as a free agent after the two defected to North America. Both made their debuts with the Nordiques in 1980–81, with Marian joining them the following year.

All three Stastny brothers made an impact in Quebec as the Nordiques improved steadily, but only Peter emerged as an NHL superstar. He had been player of the year in Czechoslovakia in 1979–80 and followed up by winning the Calder Trophy as rookie of the year in the NHL. His 70 assists and 109 points in 1980–81 established rookie scoring records. Stastny had 100 points or more seven times in his career, including a high of 139 in 1981–82, and was in the top-10 in scoring on six occasions, finishing second behind Wayne Gretzky in 1982–83. He played in six All-Star Games but in an era dominated by centers like Gretzky and Mario Lemieux, Stastny never earned a postseason all-star selection.

On March 6, 1990, Stastny was traded to the New Jersey Devils but was no longer the same offensive threat. In 1993, he returned to Bratislava, which was now recognized as part of Slovakia, and played for the Slovakian Olympic team at Lillehammer in 1994. He returned to the NHL with the St. Louis Blues as a free agent late in the 1993–94 season and ended his playing days the following year. Stastny's was the all-time leading scorer among Europeans in the NHL until being surpassed by Jari Kurri on December 8, 1993. His 450 goals, 789 assists and 1,239 points rank among the all-time leaders in NHL history.

BILL STEWART became the first American born coach to lead his team to a Stanley Cup championship when he guided the Chicago Black Hawks to a surprising victory in 1938. (Bob Johnson is the only other American coach to win the Stanley Cup, and that wasn't until 1990–91 with the Pittsburgh Penguins.) The Black Hawks had barely qualified for the playoffs that year with a record of just 14–25–9 but came alive in the postseason to upset the Montreal Canadiens, New York Americans and Toronto Maple Leafs. The roster boasted several American players, including Mike Karakas, Cully Dahlstrom, Doc Romnes and Virgil Johnson who would later join Stewart in the United States Hockey Hall of Fame. U.S. Hall of Famer Vic Heyliger also played briefly with the 1937–38 Black Hawks. Despite his Stanley Cup success, Stewart was fired during the 1938–39 season.

Stewart's hockey career started in 1921 when he began officiating at games in the Boston area. By 1928, he was appointed a referee in the NHL. Except for his time coaching the Black Hawks, he held that position until 1941. Stewart was also a National League umpire from 1933 until 1954 and saw service in World Series games in 1933, 1937, 1948 and 1953. Stewart was enshrined in the coaches category of the United States Hockey Hall of Fame in 1982. His grandson, Paul Stewart, has been an NHL referee since 1987.

GAYE STEWART made his debut with the Toronto Maple Leafs in game five of the 1942 Stanley Cup finals as the Maple Leafs were rallying from down three games to nothing to defeat the Detroit Red Wings for the Stanley Cup. The following season, he won the Calder Trophy as rookie of the year after scoring 24 goals in a 48-game season.

After two years in the Canadian Navy, Stewart returned to Toronto in 1945–46. He led the NHL with 37 goals that year and finished second behind Max Bentley for the NHL scoring title to earn a berth on the First All-Star Team at left wing. In 1946–47, Stewart played on a line with Gus Bodnar and Bud Poile and helped the Maple Leafs win another Stanley Cup title. However, on November 4, 1947, Stewart, Bodnar, Poile, Bob Goldham and Ernie Dickens were traded to the Chicago Black Hawks for Max Bentley and Cy Thomas. Stewart went on to finish fourth in the NHL scoring race that season

with 56 points and was named to the Second All-Star Team even though Chicago finished last in the league.

Injuries limited Stewart's playing time during the 1948–49 season but he still scored 20 goals. After another good season in Chicago in 1949–50, Stewart was part of another big trade when he was dealt to the Detroit Red Wings as part of a nine-player swap. Stewart helped a powerful Red Wings team finish first in the regular-season standings in 1950–51 but he was then dealt to the New York Rangers.

After a decent season with the Rangers in 1951–52, Stewart was put on waivers and sold to the Montreal Canadiens early in the 1952–53 campaign but spent most of his time with the Quebec Aces. Stewart played with the Buffalo Bisons of the American Hockey League in 1953–54 and made his final NHL appearance that season when he was called up to Montreal for three playoff games. He retired after another year in Buffalo in 1954–55 and later worked as a referee in the NHL.

JACK STEWART John Sherratt "Black Jack" Stewart was effective at rushing the puck, but his forte was delivering punishing bodychecks. He was one of the hardest hitters in hockey. Stewart played junior in Portage la Prairie, Manitoba and signed professionally with the Detroit Red Wings organization in 1938. After a year-and-a-half in Pittsburgh of the American Hockey League, he was promoted to the NHL midway through the 1939–40 season and quickly established himself as a great defenseman.

Stewart played for a Stanley Cup champion in Detroit in 1942–43 and his performance that season was rewarded when he was named the Red Wings' most valuable player and selected to the First All-Star Team. After two years of service hockey during World War II, Stewart earned Second Team honors with Detroit again in 1945–46 and 1946–47, with two more selections to the First Team over the next two years. In 1949–50, Detroit won another Stanley Cup title, but prior to the 1950–51 campaign, Stewart was traded to the Chicago Black Hawks in an attempt to strengthen the failing franchise.

Stewart was named captain in Chicago but suffered a serious back injury during his first season, and it was feared his career might be over. He returned in 1951–52, but suffered a severe concussion that season and was given his unconditional release after doctors determined he should play no longer. The following year, he was a member of the Chatham Maroons of the Ontario Hockey Association senior league and served as a playing coach in Chatham in 1953–54. Stewart later coached in Windsor and Sault Ste. Marie and spent his final season in hockey as the coach of the Pittsburgh Hornets in the AHL in 1962–63. Stewart was elected to the Hockey Hall of Fame in 1964.

NELS STEWART was the most prolific scorer of his day, and his 324 career goals stood as an NHL record from the time of his retirement in 1940 until Maurice Richard scored his 325th on November 8, 1952. Stewart was an awkward skater who appeared slow-footed, but the deadly accuracy of his shot earned him the nickname "Old Poison."

Stewart was born in Montreal but raised in Toronto and played his amateur hockey there before joining Cleveland of the United States Amateur Hockey Association in 1920–21. He and Babe Siebert were signed by the Montreal Maroons for the team's second season of 1925–26 and the infusion of youthful talent helped the team win the Stanley Cup that year. Stewart had led the NHL in scoring with 34 goals and eight assists and was rewarded with the Hart Trophy.

In 1929–30, Stewart, Siebert and Hooley Smith were teamed to form the powerful S-Line. Stewart responded with a career-high 39 goals in 44 games and earned his second Hart Trophy win that year. During the next season, Stewart set an NHL record that still stands when he scored two goals in four seconds on January 3, 1931. (The record was equaled by Deron Quint of the Winnipeg Jets on December 15, 1995.)

The S-Line was one of the best in the NHL over three seasons, with Stewart providing most of the offense while Siebert and Smith took care of the backchecking. All three could be dangerous when the game got physical. The line was broken up when Stewart was dealt to the Boston Bruins prior to the 1932–33 season, but he continued to rank among the league's best scorers over the next three years. He was traded to the New York Americans in 1935–36 and remained there until retiring in 1939–40, except for 1936–37 when he was back in Boston for part of the year. Stewart was elected to the Hockey Hall of Fame in 1962.

KEVIN STEVENS and Jeremy Roenick became the first American-born players to score 50 goals in back-to-back seasons when they each reached the milestone in 1991–92 and 1992–93. Stevens' 55 goals during the 1992–93 season tied Jimmy Carson's 1987–88 record for the most goals ever scored by an American player in a single season.

Stevens was drafted by the Los Angeles Kings in 1983, but his rights were traded to the Pittsburgh Penguins later that year. Stevens spent the next four years at Boston College, serving as team captain in his senior season of 1986–87 and earning honors as a second team all-American. He played with the U.S. national team in 1987–88 and made his NHL debut with Pittsburgh on March 1, 1988 after playing at the Calgary Olympics. Stevens split the 1988–89 season between Pittsburgh and Muskegon of the International

Hockey League and became a regular with the Penguins the following year, scoring 29 goals and leading the club with 171 penalty minutes in 1989–90.

Stevens was named to the Second All-Star Team at left wing in 1990–91 after tying Mark Recchi for the Penguins lead with 40 goals. In the playoffs that year, Stevens led all scorers with 17 goals as Pittsburgh won its first Stanley Cup title. He had 54 goals in 1991–92 and set what was then a single-season record for both American-born players and left wingers with 123 points, finishing second to teammate Mario Lemieux in the scoring race. Stevens also became the first player in history to top 50 goals, 100 points and 200 penalty minutes in the same season. The Penguins repeated as Stanley Cup champions that year and Stevens was named to the First All-Star Team. He was a Second Team All-Star when he scored 55 goals in 1992–93, then joined Mario Lemieux as just the second player in Penguins history to top 40 goals four years in a row with 41 in 1993–94.

Because of injuries and the lockout, Stevens played only 27 games in 1994–95. He was traded to the Boston Bruins on August 25, 1995, but played poorly in Boston and was traded to the Los Angeles Kings for Rick Tocchet on January 25, 1996. The Kings traded Stevens to the New York Rangers for Luc Robitaille on August 28, 1997.

SCOTT STEVENS was chosen fifth overall by the Washington Capitals in the 1982 NHL Entry Draft. He earned a spot on the NHL's All-Rookie Team after the 1982–83 season and was third behind Dale Hawerchuk and Barry Pederson in voting for the Calder Trophy. Stevens has gone on to rank as one of the top defensemen in hockey.

Stevens spent eight years with Washington, establishing career highs with 21 goals (1984–85) and 61 assists (1988–89) and earning a spot on the First All-Star Team in 1987–88 in a season that saw him finish as runner-up to Raymond Bourque for the Norris Trophy. He signed as a free agent with the St. Louis Blues on July 16, 1990, and was named team captain for the 1990–91 season, but on September 3, 1991, he was awarded to the New Jersey Devils as compensation when St. Louis signed Devils free agent Brendan Shanahan.

Stevens was named to the Second All-Star Team in his first year with New Jersey and in 1992–93 he was named captain of the Devils. The 1993–94 season saw him record a career-high 78 points and earn another selection to the First All-Star Team. He also finished behind Raymond Bourque for the Norris Trophy again that year in an exceedingly close vote. In 1994–95, Stevens and the Devils were Stanley Cup champions. Since then, he has continued to anchor one of the best defenses in the NHL.

In addition to his Stanley Cup victory, Stevens won the Memorial Cup with the Kitchener Rangers in 1982, his last year of junior hockey. He won a Canada Cup title with Team Canada in 1991. He also represented Canada at the World Championships in 1983, 1985, 1987 and 1989, winning a bronze medal in 1983 and silver medals in 1987 and 1989. In 1996, Stevens played for Canada at the World Cup of Hockey and in 1998 he was a member of the Canadian Olympic team at Nagano.

RED STOREY Roy Alvin "Red" Storey played junior hockey in his hometown of Barrie, Ontario and one season in senior hockey with the Montreal Royals. He was also an excellent lacrosse and baseball player, but gained his greatest sports fame in football. As a member of the Toronto Argonauts, Storey came off the bench to score three touchdowns in the final 13 minutes of the 1938 Grey Cup during a 30–7 victory over the Winnipeg Blue Bombers. Unfortunately, a knee injury ended his football career in 1940.

Storey became a football referee in 1946 and continued until 1957, while officiating in lacrosse for 10 years. In addition, Storey began refereeing hockey games during this time, and in April of 1950 signed a contract to referee in the NHL. He was among the NHL's most colorful officials from 1951 until 1959 when he quit over a dispute with Clarence Campbell. By his own count, Storey refereed more than 2,000 hockey games at all levels. He was inducted into the Hockey Hall of Fame in 1967.

BRUCE STUART was capable of playing any of the forward positions in hockey, but he was at his best as a rover during the seven-man era. He played in his hometown of Ottawa and with the Quebec Bulldogs during four seasons in the Canadian Amateur Hockey League between 1898–99 and 1901–02. Bruce and his brother Hod were among the first Canadian players to sign professional contracts in the United States and Stuart enjoyed some of his most productive seasons between 1903–04 and 1906–07 with Pittsburgh and Portage Lakes in the International (Pro) Hockey League (the game's first pro circuit) before returning to Canada with the Montreal Wanderers.

Stuart helped the Wanderers win the Stanley Cup in 1907–08, but the promise of becoming team captain in Ottawa led him to the Senators the following year, and he led his new team to the Stanley Cup in 1908–09. Ottawa became a member of the National Hockey Association in 1909–10. It lost the Stanley Cup to the Wanderers that year before winning it back in 1911. Stuart, however, saw very little action for Ottawa that season. He had led an effort to form a new league after NHA owners threatened to impose a salary cap of $5,000 per team that year. He soon left the game to operate a shoe store in Ottawa rather than play hockey for reduced wages. In 1961, Bruce Stuart was

elected to the Hockey Hall of Fame. His brother Hod had been one of the 12 original members enshrined back in 1945.

HOD STUART was known as one of the best defenseman in hockey during his tragically brief career. He and his brother Bruce both played in their hometown of Ottawa and with the Quebec Bulldogs in the Canadian Amateur Hockey League. They then became two of the first Canadian players to sign professional contracts with teams in the United States.

Hod Stuart was a high-scoring defenseman with Pittsburgh, Portage Lakes and Calumet, Michigan, between 1902–03 and 1906–07—the days when the position was known as point and cover point. He left the International (Pro) Hockey League (the game's first professional circuit) midway through the 1906–07 campaign to join the Montreal Wanderers. In March of that year, he helped the Wanderers win back the Stanley Cup from the Kenora Thistles in a rematch of their January series. Stuart died just three months later in a diving accident on June 23, 1907. In 1945, he was one of the original 12 members elected to the Hockey Hall of Fame. His brother Bruce Stuart was inducted in 1961.

MATS SUNDIN was the first European player ever selected number one in the NHL Entry Draft when the Quebec Nordiques chose him in 1989. He played one more year in his native Sweden and represented his country at the 1990 World Junior Championships before making his NHL debut in 1990–91. Sundin scored his first goal in his first NHL game on October 4, 1990 and his 23 goals that year ranked fourth among all rookies. His 59 points tied Ken Hodge Jr. for second place behind Sergei Fedorov's 79.

Sundin improved his offensive numbers in 1991–92, and in 1992–93 he had 47 goals and led the Nordiques with 67 assists and 114 points as Quebec reached the playoffs for the first time in six years. Sundin had the longest scoring streak in the NHL that season when he recorded points in each of the Nordiques' first 30 games. He slumped to 32 goals and 85 points in 1993–94 and was traded to the Toronto Maple Leafs in a multi-player deal on June 28, 1994. Sundin replaced Doug Gilmour as the top offensive player in Toronto, and after Gilmour was traded during the 1996–97 season he replaced him as team captain in 1997–98.

Despite his own individual success, Sundin generally has played on weak teams during his NHL career. He has had much more success in international hockey, where he helped Sweden win back-to-back World Championships in 1991 and 1992. He also led the tournament in scoring when Sweden earned a bronze medal in 1994. Sundin represented Sweden at the Canada Cup in 1991 and at the World Cup of Hockey in 1996 and was named to the first all-star team in each of those tournaments. In 1998, he was a member of the Swedish team at the Nagano Olympics.

GARY SUTER won the Calder Trophy as rookie of the year with the Calgary Flames in 1985–86. His 68 points that season were then the second-highest total ever recorded by a first-year defenseman behind Larry Murphy's 76 in 1980–81. Brian Leetch topped Suter's total with 71 points in 1988–89.

Suter joined the Flames from the University of Wisconsin and quickly established himself among the top defensemen in the NHL. He was third in Norris Trophy voting behind Raymond Bourque and Scott Stevens in 1987–88 after establishing a career high with 91 points. He was named to the Second All-Star Team that year. Suter ranked seventh in Norris Trophy voting in 1988–89 and was a member of Calgary's first Stanley Cup-winning team that season, though a broken jaw forced him to miss most of the playoffs. He spent eight full seasons in Calgary and ranks among the Flames all-time leaders in games played (617), assists (437) and points (565).

Suter was traded to the Hartford Whalers on March 10, 1994 and then dealt to the Chicago Blackhawks the next day. He became the first Chicago defenseman to score a playoff hat trick in a game against the Toronto Maple Leafs on April 24, 1994. In 1995–96, he tied Raymond Bourque for the NHL lead in goals by a defenseman with 20. Suter played for the American team that beat Canada at the World Cup of Hockey in 1996 and was a member of the U.S. Olympic team in Nagano in 1998. He had previously represented the U.S. at the World Championships in 1985 and 1992 and at the Canada Cup in 1987 and 1991.

JAMES T. SUTHERLAND Captain James T. Sutherland coached the Kingston Frontenac Juniors to several championships while helping his hometown become a hockey hotbed in the years prior to World War I. Often known as "the Father of Hockey," Sutherland helped the game develop across eastern Ontario. He also moved up through the ranks of the Ontario Hockey Association to become president by 1915. He served in that office for two years and, after returning from military duty, he became president of the Canadian Amateur Hockey Association in 1919. He was honored as a life member in both the OHA and the CAHA. Sutherland was inducted into the Hockey Hall of Fame as a builder in 1947.

BRENT SUTTER was chosen 17th overall in the first round of the 1980 NHL Entry Draft by the New York Islanders, one year after the Islanders had made his brother Duane the 17th pick in 1979. Brent played three games for the Islanders in 1980–81 and joined the team to stay the following season. He

helped the Islanders to win their third straight Stanley Cup title in 1982 and their fourth in a row the following year. Duane had been a member of all four Islanders Stanley Cup winners.

Brent Sutter never scored less than 21 goals in 10 full seasons with the Islanders and established career highs with 40 goals, 62 assists and 102 points in 1984–85. He was named captain of the Islanders in 1987–88 and wore the "C" until the time of his trade to the Chicago Blackhawks on October 25, 1991. He topped 20 goals for the 12th straight season in Chicago in 1992–93. His offensive production dropped afterwards, but on February 5, 1995, he set a Blackhawks record for the fastest goal from the start of a game when he scored on the Vancouver Canucks after just eight seconds. The previous club record of nine seconds had been shared by Gus Bodnar and Bobby Hull.

In addition to his two Stanley Cup titles with the Islanders, Sutter was a Canada Cup winner with Team Canada in 1984, 1987 and 1991.

BRIAN SUTTER The first of the six Sutter brothers from Viking, Alberta to reach the NHL, Brian Sutter joined the St. Louis Blues during the 1976–77 season and went on to play for 11 more years. He served as team captain from 1979–80 until his retirement after the 1987–88 campaign and demonstrated a hard-nosed style of play throughout his career that would be the trademark of his family.

Sutter topped 30 goals five times in six seasons between 1978–79 and 1984–85, including a high of 46 in 1982–83. Injuries slowed him down in the later days of his playing career and he retired after the 1987–88 season. His 779 games played, 303 goals, 333 assists and 636 points continue to rank high among the Blues all-time leaders.

Upon his retirement, Sutter immediately was named as the new head coach of the Blues in 1988–89, guiding the club for four seasons. He led the team to the playoffs every year and exceeded Scotty Bowman's totals to become the Blues coach with the most wins with a record of 153–124–53. He won the Jack Adams Award as coach of the year in 1990–91 after leading the Blues to the second-best record in the league at 47–22–11 for 105 points.

In 1992–93, Sutter moved on to coach the Boston Bruins. He guided the club to its first 50-win season (51–26–7) in 10 years and finished second to Pat Burns in voting for the Jack Adams Award. Sutter's winning percentage in three seasons with the Bruins was .609. The club posted the third-best record in the NHL overall under his tenure. Still, he was fired by the Bruins after the 1994–95 season and remained out of hockey for two years before being named head coach of the Calgary Flames on July 3, 1997. The appointment made him the first Sutter ever to play or coach in the National Hockey League in his home province of Alberta.

DARRYL SUTTER was selected by the Chicago Black Hawks in the 11th round of the 1978 NHL Entry Draft and displayed the hustle, grit and determination that are synonymous with the Sutter name to become a solid NHL player. He was the American Hockey League rookie of the year with New Brunswick in 1979–80 and scored 40 goals as an NHL rookie in 1980–81.

Sutter played eight years with Chicago and was captain of the team for five seasons from 1982–83 until injuries forced him to retire after the 1986–87 campaign. He had 20 goals or more five times in his career and set a Black Hawks record in 1985 (since equaled by Jeremy Roenick in 1992) with 12 playoff goals. After his retirement, Sutter became an assistant coach in Chicago in 1987–88. He was the head coach of the Blackhawks' International Hockey League affiliate in Saginaw in 1988–89 and coached the Indianapolis Ice to the IHL Turner Cup championship the following year. In 1990–91, he returned to Chicago as an associate coach under Mike Keenan.

Sutter was named head coach of the Blackhawks in 1992–93 and led Chicago to first place in the NHL's overall standings that year with a record of 47–25–12 and 106 points. In three seasons as Blackhawks coach, Sutter posted a 110–80–26 record for a .569 winning percentage that is the second-best in franchise history behind Billy Reay's .589. He stepped down as coach after the 1994–95 season in order to spend more time with his family but remained associated with the Blackhawks as a consultant for special assignments over the next two years. On June 9, 1997, Sutter returned to the coaching ranks as the head coach of the San Jose Sharks.

ANATOLI TARASOV is generally regarded as the architect of Soviet domination of international amateur hockey. He and Arkady Chernyshev coached the Soviet Union to nine straight World and Olympic Championships between 1963 and 1972, including three straight Olympic gold medals, before Tarasov retired after the 1972 Games in Sapporo, Japan. He was inducted into the Hockey Hall of Fame as a builder in 1974.

Tarasov himself was a product of the Soviet hockey system, playing for teams in the late 1940s and early 1950s that paved the way for the first World Championship win by the USSR in 1954. After retiring as a player, he first coached the Soviet national team at the World Championships in 1958. Tarasov was a strong believer in conditioning and wrote many books on hockey. He also supervised the Soviet Golden Puck tournament for boys, in which more than one million youngsters were registered. In 1987, he served as a coaching consultant to the NHL's Vancouver Canucks.

MARC TARDIF was drafted second overall by the Montreal Canadiens in 1969 after they had selected his Montreal junior teammate Rejean Houle with the first pick. Both players quickly became regulars in the Canadiens lineup, but both jumped to the World Hockey Association in 1973–74. Tardif went on to become the leading goal scorer in league history.

In six season in the WHA, Tardif never scored less than 40 goals, including a high of 71 in 1975–76 when he added 77 assists for a league-record 148 points. In 1977–78, Tardif broke that record when he collected 154 points on 65 goals and 89 assists. In addition to his two scoring titles, Tardif won the Gordie Howe Trophy as most valuable player in each of those seasons. In between, he helped the Quebec Nordiques win the Avco Cup as WHA champions in 1976–77.

Tardif's career totals in the WHA include a league-record 316 goals (13 more than Bobby Hull) and 350 assists, which rank third in league history. His 666 total points are second-all time behind Andre Lacroix's total of 798. Tardif was also a member of the Team Canada squad of WHA all-stars that took on the Soviet Union in a series prior to the 1974–75 season.

When the Nordiques were among four teams admitted into the NHL for the 1979–80 season, Tardif returned to the league and played four more years.

BILLY TAYLOR's reputation was tarnished when he and Don Gallinger were suspended from the NHL for gambling on March 9, 1948. Before that, Taylor was known as a playmaking center who had cracked the top 10 in scoring three times in his five full NHL seasons. On March 16, 1947, he established a record (since equaled only by Wayne Gretzky) with seven assists in one game.

Taylor began his career with the Maple Leafs during the 1939–40 season and later lost two years to military service before returning to Toronto after World War II. He was traded to the Detroit Red Wings in 1946 and spent the 1947–48 season with the Boston Bruins and New York Rangers before being banned.

The NHL had been trying to clean up its image since Babe Pratt was suspended for gambling in 1945–46 and subsequent raids in Toronto broke up a hockey betting ring. In February of 1948, NHL president Clarence Campbell announced he had evidence some players were wagering on games, though there were no suggestion that games had been fixed. Taylor maintained he was never given a clear reason for the lifetime ban that followed.

Though he did play some amateur hockey in the early 1950s, Taylor remained virtually cut off from the game until he and Gallinger finally had their suspensions lifted in 1970.

CYCLONE TAYLOR Fred Taylor was nicknamed "Cyclone" for his matchless speed as a skater and the furious rushes he led from the defense during his time with the Ottawa Senators. Taylor was the greatest star of his day, and he helped give instant credibility to the new National Hockey Association in 1909–10. His decision to join the Pacific Coast Hockey Association did the same for that fledgling league when he signed there in 1912–13.

Taylor grew up in Listowel, Ontario and began his hockey career there. After refusing to join the Toronto Marlboros, he was banned from the Ontario Hockey Association, so he left home to play hockey in Portage la Prairie, Manitoba in 1905. Before the end of the 1905–06 season, he had signed a professional contract with the International (Pro) Hockey League team in Houghton, Michigan, becoming a star with the Portage Lakers in the game's first professional league. When the league collapsed, he signed with the Ottawa Senators for the 1907–08 season.

A forward until this point in his career, Taylor was moved to defense in Ottawa because his new linemates could not keep up with him. Playing a position then known as cover point, Taylor was free to use his blazing speed to lead individual rushes up the ice, knowing he could get back in time to help out in his own end. In 1908–09, he helped Ottawa to win the Stanley Cup. In the off-season that followed, Taylor was at the center of a fierce bidding war for his services that eventually led to his signing with the Renfrew Millionaires. His contract was reported to pay him $5,250 for the 12-game NHA season, and it was said to be the richest deal in North American sports. (Ty Cobb was making $6,500 with baseball's Detroit Tigers, but he had to play 154 games.)

When Renfrew dropped out of professional hockey after the 1910–11 season, Taylor sat out a year while the Senators and Montreal Wanderers fought over his rights. He then spurned both teams when he signed with former Renfrew teammate Frank Patrick's Vancouver Millionaires. Taylor became a forward again, playing center and rover, and the former defenseman developed into a scoring star who led the PCHA in goals three times and points five times. Though he played fewer games than anyone else ranked among the PCHA's all-time top–10 scorers, Taylor is the league's career leader in assists with 104. He ranks fifth overall with 159 goals and is second behind long-time teammate Mickey MacKay in points with 263. He also had seven goals in three games when Vancouver became the first team from the West Coast league to win the Stanley Cup in 1915. Cyclone Taylor was elected to the Hockey Hall of Fame in 1947.

DAVE TAYLOR was an all-American at Clarkson University but was still a relative unknown when the Los Angeles Kings selected him 210th overall in the 1975 Amateur Draft. A few seasons later, he was among the best right

wingers in the NHL while playing alongside Marcel Dionne and Charlie Simmer on the Triple Crown Line.

The best defensive player on a great offensive line, Taylor still collected plenty of points, establishing career highs with 47 goals and 112 points in 1980–81, and 67 assists the following season. He finished in the top 10 in NHL scoring on three occasions and played in five All-Star Games. Taylor earned a postseason All-Star selection to the Second Team in 1980–81.

Taylor was with the Kings throughout his entire 17-year playing career, helping Los Angeles reach the Stanley Cup finals in 1992–93. His number 18 was retired in 1995, joining Marcel Dionne and Rogie Vachon as the only Kings players so honored. He trails only Marcel Dionne on the Kings' all-time list of goals scored and points, and is third behind Dionne and Wayne Gretzky in all-time assists. Taylor's 431 goals, 638 assists, and 1,069 points also rank among the leaders in NHL history.

After his playing days, Taylor joined the Kings front office and was named vice president and general manager on April 22, 1997.

CLIFF THOMPSON coached at Eveleth High School from 1920 until his retirement in 1958, during which time his teams posted a record of 534–26–9. They won the state tournament in 1945, the first year it was held, and 78 games in a row in a four-year stretch between 1948 and 1951 (and the Minnesota state championship in each of those years). In addition, Thompson simultaneously guided the Eveleth Junior College team to 171 wins and only 28 losses.

Cliff Thompson's talent for player development sent a number of Eveleth and area players on to the NHL, foremost among them Frank Brimsek, Mike Karakas, Sam LoPresti and John Mariucci. Many others went on to college and international careers, such as John Matchefts and John Mayasich, who played for the U.S. Olympic team that won the gold medal in 1960. Thompson was named an honorary member of the American Hockey Coaches Association in 1957 and was a charter member of the United States Hockey Hall of Fame when he was enshrined in the coaches category in 1973.

PAUL THOMPSON The brother of Hockey Hall of Fame goaltender Tiny Thompson, Paul Thompson was a top left winger with the New York Rangers and Chicago Black Hawks during the 1920s and 1930s. He played junior hockey with the Calgary Canadians and was a Memorial Cup champion in 1925–26 before joining the Rangers for their first NHL season of 1926–27. The Rangers won the Stanley Cup the following year.

Thompson, Butch Keeling and Murray Murdoch formed a solid second line in New York behind the Rangers' top trio of Frank Boucher and brothers Bill and Bun Cook from 1928–29 until 1930–31. Prior to the 1931–32 campaign Thompson was dealt to the Chicago Black Hawks. In Chicago, he played on the club's top forward line for eight years with Mush March and Doc Romnes. Thompson led the team in scoring, and ranked among the top 10 in the NHL, six years in a row from 1932–33 until 1937–38. He also helped the Black Hawks win the Stanley Cup in 1934 and 1938, was named to the Second All-Star Team in 1935–36, and was a First Team All-Star in 1937–38 after collecting a career-high 22 goals and 44 points.

Thompson was named player-coach of the Black Hawks midway through the 1938–39 season, then retired as a player after the season to concentrate on his coaching duties. He guided the club to the Stanley Cup finals in 1944 but was replaced as coach by former teammate John Gottselig in March of 1945.

TINY THOMPSON In an era when most NHL goaltenders were quite small, Cecil "Tiny" Thompson actually stood 5'10" and weighed 180 pounds. His nickname came about because of the miniscule size of his goals-against averages. He posted a 1.15 average with 12 shutouts in his first NHL season of 1928–29 after joining the Boston Bruins with Cooney Weiland from the roster of the Minneapolis Millers. In the playoffs that year, he allowed just three goals in five games, including three shutouts, as Boston won its first Stanley Cup championship.

Forward passing rules were modernized in 1929–30, and Thompson's average rose to 2.19, though this was easily the best in the league. The Bruins' 38–5–1 record remains the NHL's highest winning percentage (.875) for one season. Thompson won the Vezina Trophy that season, then won it again in 1932–33, 1935–36 and 1937–38. He was named to the NHL First All-Star Team in 1935–36 and 1937–38 after claiming Second Team honors in 1930–31 and 1934–35. During his 10 years in Boston, the Bruins finished first in the American Division six times.

In 1938–39, the Bruins replaced Thompson with rookie Frank Brimsek and traded the veteran goalie to the Detroit Red Wings. He played two years in Detroit and ended his career after playing a single game with the Buffalo Bisons of the American Hockey League in 1940–41. Thompson's 2.08 goals-against average over 12 NHL seasons is among the best in history, and that mark dropped to 1.88 in playoff games. He was elected to the Hockey Hall of Fame in 1959. His brother Paul Thompson played with the New York Rangers and Chicago Black Hawks in the 1920s and 1930s.

JIMMY THOMSON was a product of the Toronto Maple Leafs system who became a regular in the NHL in 1946–47 and helped Toronto win the Stanley

Cup four times in his first five seasons. Thompson teamed with Gus Mortson on the Maple Leafs defense for six years and the two became business partners off the ice as well.

Thomson did not score a goal during six of the 11 full seasons he played in Toronto but was such a solid defensive defenseman that he was named to the Second All-Star Team in both 1950–51 and 1951–52. He was the Maple Leafs' captain during the 1956–57 season but his activities with the fledgling NHL Players' Association angered Conn Smythe who sold him to the Black Hawks after the season. Thompson played another year and then retired.

ESA TIKKANEN Though he played briefly in Canada as a teenager, it was in his native Finland where Esa Tikkanen developed into a star. He represented his homeland at the World Junior Championships in 1983, 1984 and 1985, earning a silver medal in 1984 and finishing second in the tournament in scoring in 1985. Tikkanen also played at his first World Championship in 1985.

Tikkanen had been drafted by the Edmonton Oilers in 1983 and joined the team for three games during the 1985 playoffs as the Oilers repeated as Stanley Cup champions. He split the 1985–86 season between Edmonton and Nova Scotia of the American Hockey League and played his first full year in the NHL in 1986–87. Able to produce points as well as hound opponents with his tight checking, Tikkanen helped Edmonton to win the Stanley Cup again in 1987, 1988 and 1990. He was runner-up for the Selke Trophy as the NHL's best defensive forward in 1989 and 1991.

Traded to the New York Rangers on March 17, 1993, Tikkanen joined several former Oilers such as Mark Messier and Kevin Lowe in helping the Rangers to win the Stanley Cup for the first time in 54 years in 1994. He was then traded to St. Louis on July 24, 1994, and was runner-up for the Selke Trophy for a third time with the Blues in 1994–95. Since then, Tikkanen has played for the New Jersey Devils, the Vancouver Canucks, the Rangers again, the Florida Panthers and the Washington Capitals. Tikkanen helped Washington to reach the Stanley Cup finals for the first time in 1998.

Tikkanen represented his country at the Canada Cup tournaments in 1987 and 1991 and was a member of Finland's team at the World Cup of Hockey in 1996. He also was named to the Finnish team for the Nagano Olympics in 1998.

KEITH TKACHUK was the first American-born player to lead the NHL in goals when he scored 52 in 1996–97. He was also the first player in the history of the Winnipeg Jets/Phoenix Coyotes franchise to have back-to-back 50 goal seasons, and he joined John LeClair that year as just the third and fourth American players (Kevin Stevens and Jeremy Roenick) to score 50 goals two years in a row. With 52 goals and 228 penalty minutes, Tkachuk joined Kevin Stevens, Brendan Shanahan and Gary Roberts as the only players ever to top 50 goals and 200 penalty minutes in the same season.

Tkachuk was drafted directly out of high school when Winnipeg selected him in the 1990 NHL Entry Draft. He spent the 1990–91 season at Boston University, where he was named to the Hockey East all-freshman team and helped BU to reach the NCAA finals. Tkachuk played with the U.S. national team in 1991–92 and joined the Jets that season after competing at the Albertville Olympics. He played his first full NHL season in 1992–93 and became Jets captain early in 1993–94. He was named to the Second All-Star Team in 1994–95 and had his first 50-goal season the following year.

In addition to his Olympic experience in 1992, Tkachuk represented the United States on a variety of Under–16 and Under–17 national teams and played at the World Junior Championships in 1991, where he tied Trent Klatt for the team lead with six goals in seven games. Tkachuk was named to the U.S. team at the 1994 World Championships but was unable to play. In 1996, he was a leader of the American team that beat Canada at the World Cup of Hockey. In 1998 he returned to the Olympics with the U.S. team at Nagano.

RICK TOCCHET With a good scoring touch and the ability to throw punishing bodychecks, Rick Tocchet has been one of the top power forwards in the NHL. Combining excellent offensive ability and tough physical play, he became the third player in NHL history (Pat Verbeek and Mike Foligno) to record 300 goals and 2,000 penalty minutes in his career.

Tocchet was chosen 121st overall by the Philadelphia Flyers in the 1983 Entry Draft but was returned to junior hockey for a final season with the Sault Ste. Marie Greyhounds. In 1983–84, he set an Ontario Hockey League playoff record with 22 goals and 36 points in 16 games. Tocchet joined the Flyers in 1984–85 and led the club with 181 penalty minutes in his rookie season. His penalty totals increased in each of the next three seasons, but so did his offensive production and in 1987–88, Tocchet became the third player in history (Dave Williams and Al Secord) to top 30 goals and 300 penalties minutes in one season. The following year, he was second on the Flyers in goals and points with 45 and 81.

Tocchet ranked as Philadelphia's all-time penalty minutes leader when he was traded to Pittsburgh on February 19, 1992. He helped the Penguins to repeat as Stanley Cup champions that year, then established career highs with 48 goals, 61 assists and 109 points in 1992–93. Tocchet spent one more season with Pittsburgh and then was traded to the Los Angeles Kings on July 29, 1994. He subsequently played with the Boston Bruins and Washington Capitals

before signing as a free agent with the Phoenix Coyotes on July 23, 1997.

In international hockey, Tocchet played for Team Canada in the 1987 and 1991 Canada Cup tournaments and at the 1991 World Championships.

BILL TORREY took the New York Islanders from expansion team to hockey dynasty through a combination of brilliant draft choices and astute trades. The team reached the playoffs in only its third season of 1974–75 and won the Stanley Cup for the first of four consecutive times in 1979–80.

Torrey entered the NHL as vice president of the expansion Oakland Seals in 1967. In 1972, he became the Islanders first employee when he accepted the job as general manager. Though the team was a dismal 12–60–6 in 1972–73, the Islanders reached the semifinals by 1974–75 and recorded 101 points in 1975–76. By this time, Torrey had drafted star players like Denis Potvin (1973) and Bryan Trottier (1974) and in 1977 selected Mike Bossy. These players, along with goalie Billy Smith, who was selected in the 1972 Expansion Draft, formed the nucleus of the Islanders Stanley Cup dynasty between 1980 and 1983.

From 1980 until 1989, Torrey served as Islanders president as well as general manager and then became the club's chairman of the board. He stepped down at the start of the 1992–93 season, but remained a consultant until joining the Florida Panthers as club president in April of 1993. That same year, Torrey was inducted into the Hockey Hall of Fame as a builder. His reputation was enhanced in Florida when the Panthers set expansion records with 33 wins, 83 points and a .494 winning percentage during the 1993–94 season, then reached the Stanley Cup finals in 1996 after just their third year in the NHL.

J.C. TREMBLAY became a regular with the Canadiens in 1961–62 and helped solidify the Montreal defense through the departures of future Hall of Famers Doug Harvey and Tom Johnson. Though lacking the notoriety of fellow Canadiens Jacques Laperriere and Serge Savard and other contemporaries such as Pierre Pilote and, later, Bobby Orr, Tremblay was one of the top defenseman in the NHL. It was considered a major coup when the Quebec Nordiques were able to sign him for the 1972–73 inaugural season of the World Hockey Association.

Tremblay immediately became the top player at his position in the WHA, leading the league with 75 assists the first season and winning the Dennis A Murphy Trophy as best defenseman, an honor he would win again two years later. Tremblay remained in Quebec through the WHA's entire seven-year existence and helped the Nordiques win the Avco Cup in 1976–77. He ranks second all-time in the WHA with 358 assists and collected more points (424) than any defenseman in league history.

VLADISLAV TRETIAK was the greatest goaltender ever produced by the Soviet Union and one of the very best netminders in hockey history. He first played the game at the age of 11 and by 15 was practicing with Moscow's Central Red Army Team. He joined the Red Army roster at 17 in 1968–69 and was a member of 13 Soviet League champions over the next 15 years. Tretiak was named as the goaltender on the first all-star team 14 straight seasons between 1970–71 and 1983–84.

Tretiak came to the attention of fans in North America with his brilliant play during the 1972 Summit Series between Team Canada and the Soviets. On New Year's Eve in 1975, he helped his Red Army Team earn a 3–3 tie with the Montreal Canadiens despite being outshot 38–13 in one of the greatest games ever played. He was named MVP when the Soviets won the Canada Cup in 1981 and won the Golden Stick award as the outstanding player in Europe three years in a row from 1981 to 1983. By the time he retired after the 1983–84 season, Tretiak had played for 10 World Champions with the Soviet national team and won Olympic gold medals in 1972, 1976 and 1984. In 98 World Championship games, he boasted a goals-against average of 1.92. He had a 1.74 mark in 19 Olympic games.

In 1989, Vladislav Tretiak was honored as the first Soviet-trained player elected to the Hockey Hall of Fame. He became the goaltender coach with the Chicago Blackhawks in 1990–91 and has remained a great ambassador for Russian hockey.

HARRY TRIHEY was the captain and top scorer with the Montreal Shamrocks when they were Stanley Cup champions in 1899 and 1900. A skilled stickhandler with a powerful shot, he played on a forward line that included fellow future Hall of Famers Art Farrell and Fred Scanlan. Trihey's 10 goals in a game on February 4, 1899 is a regular-season record among leagues that have competed for the Stanley Cup.

Trihey was an outstanding player in lacrosse and football, and he emerged as a scoring star on the ice by leading the Canadian Amateur Hockey League with 19 goals in seven games in 1898–99. The Shamrocks won the league title that season to claim the Stanley Cup from the Montreal Victorias, successfully defending it with a 6–2 victory over Queen's University. Trihey scored three goals in that game. The Shamrocks retained the Stanley Cup with a second CAHL championship the following season as Trihey again won the scoring title. He added seven goals in a three-game Stanley Cup series against the Winnipeg Victorias and five goals in a pair of wins over the Halifax Crescents.

Injuries limited his effectiveness the following season when the Shamrocks lost the Cup to the Winnipeg Victorias. Trihey retired when the 1900–01 campaign concluded.

After his playing days, Trihey served as secretary of the Canadian Amateur Hockey League, then becoming president. He was later an advisor to the Montreal Wanderers, and he remained associated with that club for several years. He also would serve as a referee in both league play and Stanley Cup games. In addition, Trihey operated a successful law practice in Montreal, and he was Lieutenant-Colonel of the 199th Battalion Irish Canadian Rangers during World War I. In 1950, he was elected to the Hockey Hall of Fame.

BRYAN TROTTIER was a member of six Stanley Cup champions during 18 seasons as a player in the NHL, winning four in a row with the New York Islanders between 1980 and 1983 and two straight with the Pittsburgh Penguins in 1991 and 1992. Trottier ended his career in 1993–94 as one of the highest-scoring players in hockey history and as one of the best two-way centers ever to play the game. He was elected to the Hockey Hall of Fame in 1997.

Trottier was selected by the New York Islanders in the second round of the 1974 Amateur Draft and entered the NHL in 1975–76 after an all-star season in his last year as a junior with Lethbridge in the Western Hockey League. He promptly set an NHL rookie scoring record with 95 points and won the Calder Trophy. In 1977–78, he led the league with 77 assists and finished second behind Guy Lafleur in the NHL scoring race. Trottier won the Art Ross Trophy the following season, collecting 134 points. He also won the Hart Trophy as most valuable player that season and earned his second straight selection to the First All-Star Team. In 1980, he earned the Conn Smythe Trophy as playoff MVP when the Islanders won their first Stanley Cup championship.

In addition to his four Stanley Cup titles, Trottier recorded over 100 points six times and more than 30 goals on 11 occasions in 13 years with the Islanders. He scored a career-high 50 goals in 1980–81 and was named to an NHL Second Team All-Star that year behind Wayne Gretzky. He was a Second Team All-Star again in 1983–84 when he had his last 100-point season.

On July 20, 1990, Trottier left the Islanders to sign as a free agent with Pittsburgh, where his leadership skills were credited with helping the talented Penguins develop into Stanley Cup champions. He retired after Pittsburgh's second Stanley Cup victory in 1992 and returned to the Islanders in a front-office job. Still feeling the desire to play, he went to back Pittsburgh for a final season in 1993–94, where he also acted as an assistant coach. At the time of his retirement, Trottier ranked 15th all-time with 524 goals, sixth in assists with 901 and sixth with 1,425 points.

HAL TRUMBLE took over the administration of the Amateur Hockey Association of the United States in 1970 when it was a part-time operation with a deficit of $18,000. By the time of his induction into the United States Hockey Hall of Fame in 1985, AHAUS was a full-time, professionally staffed organization with its own building in Colorado Springs, Colorado. Trumble's leadership saw AHAUS membership increase from 7,015 teams in 1971–72 to 11,543 in 1984–85 and the development of a complete program of coaching and clinics for referees. AHAUS (now known as USA Hockey) became the national governing body for hockey in the United States and the sport's exclusive members to the U.S. Olympic Committee and the International Ice Hockey Federation. And it was AHAUS that directed the 1980 U.S. Olympic hockey team toward the "Miracle on Ice" at Lake Placid.

Trumble learned to play hockey as a boy and played high school and senior amateur hockey in the 1950s. When his playing days ended, he became a referee, first in high schools, then at the college level and at last internationally. He refereed the gold and the bronze medal games at the 1968 Grenoble Olympics, and this range of experience led to an appointment as technical director of the International Ice Hockey Federation's Referees' Committee from 1972 to 1982. Trumble was also active as a team manager with the 1972 U.S. Olympic team that won a silver medal in Sapporo, Japan, and the 1983 U.S. national team that won the IIHF World Championships B Pool to earn a spot in the 1984 Sarajevo Olympics.

Through a long career in hockey, Trumble was also an international calibre umpire in both softball and baseball. He worked the Softball World Championship Tournament in 1959 and served as president of the National Council of Youth Sports Directors in 1980–81.

PIERRE TURGEON was selected first overall by the Buffalo Sabres in the 1987 NHL Entry Draft after an all-star season with Granby of the Quebec Major Junior Hockey League in 1986–87. Turgeon led the team in scoring for the second straight time that season with 154 points in 58 games and helped Granby to win a division title. Turgeon was also a member of the Canadian team that was disqualified after a brawl with the Soviet team at the 1987 World Junior Championships.

Turgeon's offensive totals were unimpressive during his rookie season of 1987–88, but he led the Sabres in both goals and points each of the next two years, including 1989–90, when his 106 points ranked seventh in the NHL. On October 25, 1991, Turgeon was traded to the New York Islanders in a multi-player deal that brought Pat LaFontaine to Buffalo. He went on to lead the

Islanders in scoring three years in a row. Turgeon's best season was 1992–93 when he set career highs with 58 goals, 74 assists and 132 points. He ranked sixth in the league in scoring that season and finished fifth in voting for the Hart Trophy while winning the Lady Byng Trophy.

Turgeon was traded to the Montreal Canadiens on April 5, 1995, and was named team captain on December 8, 1995. In that capacity, he received the torch from a long line of Canadiens captains during an elaborate ceremony to close the Montreal Forum on March 11, 1996. Turgeon led the Canadiens in scoring with 96 points that season but was traded to the St. Louis Blues on October 29, 1996, in a deal that brought Shayne Corson back to Montreal.

Brother Sylvain Turgeon also played in the NHL.

IAN TURNBULL set an NHL record for defensemen on February 2, 1977 when he scored five goals in the Toronto Maple Leafs' 9–1 win over the Detroit Red Wings. Turnbull's 22 goals that season is still a record for a Maple Leafs defenseman (tied by Al Iafrate in 1987–88), as are his 79 points. His 414 points in nine seasons with Toronto trail only Borje Salming (768) and Tim Horton (458) among Maple Leafs defenseman. His 112 goals are second only to Salming's 148.

Turnbull had been a high-scoring defenseman in junior hockey who entered the NHL with the Toronto Maple Leafs in 1973–74. He scored 20 goals in 1975–76 and went on to reach double figures seven years in a row. Turnbull was traded to the Los Angeles Kings on November 11, 1981 and finished out his career with the Pittsburgh Penguins in 1982–83.

LLOYD TURNER was born in Elmvale, Ontario and grew up to play and coach hockey in Sault Ste. Marie and Fort William before moving west to Calgary in 1909. There, he managed the Sherman Rink until it was destroyed by fire on February 24, 1915. After World War I, he took over operation of Calgary's Horseshoe Building from military authorities and converted it into the Victoria Arena. In March of 1919, the Montreal Canadiens played exhibition games in the Victoria Arena en route to Seattle for the ill-fated Stanley Cup series that was halted by the influenza epidemic.

In 1921, after a scandal in which Frank Patrick of the Pacific Coast Hockey Association claimed many players in Alberta's amateur Big Four League actually were being paid, Turner helped to form the professional Western Canada Hockey League. He was part-owner and general manager of the Calgary Tigers, who played and lost to the Montreal Canadiens for the Stanley Cup in 1924. Turner later moved to Minneapolis and Seattle, but came back to Calgary in 1931 and helped form the new Western Canada Hockey League in 1932–33. He also contributed to the revival of Allan Cup competition in amateur hockey during the 1930s and helped organize Alberta's Native groups into hockey tournament competition. Lloyd Turner was elected to the Hockey Hall of Fame as a builder in 1958.

WILLIAM THAYER TUTT is generally regarded as the father of the annual NCAA national hockey tournament. He was approached by a group of U.S. college coaches during the 1947–48 season and agreed to sponsor the first NCAA tournament and hold it at his family-owned venue in Colorado Springs. Tutt underwrote the costs of the event for its first 10 years until the NCAA hockey tournament became self-sufficient.

Turning his attention abroad, Tutt became the American representative to the International Ice Hockey Federation directorate in 1959. He personally financed the first tour in the United States of a visiting Soviet hockey team that year. He hosted the IIHF World Championships in Colorado Springs in 1962 and served as president of the IIHF from 1966–67 to 1968–69, later serving as vice president and council member. He also was active in the U.S. Olympic Committee and the U.S. Figure Skating Association. In June of 1972, Tutt succeeded long-time friend Tom Lockhart as president of the Amateur Hockey Association of the United States.

William Thayer Tutt was an original inductee into the United States Hockey Hall of Fame in 1973. In 1978, he received the Lester Patrick Trophy for his contributions to hockey in the United States and was elected to the Hockey Hall of Fame as a builder.

FRANK UDVARI came to Canada from Yugoslavia as a seven-year-old in 1931 and grew up in Kitchener, Ontario. Only three years after refereeing his first minor-league game, Udvari officiated his first NHL games in 1951–52 when he handled 12 games that season. Over 15 years, he worked 718 regular-season and 70 playoff games in the NHL. He was recognized as the top referee in the league over much of that time and was influential in helping many younger members of the NHL officiating staff. Udvari was elected to the Hockey Hall of Fame in 1973.

After working his last game in the 1966 Stanley Cup finals, Udvari was appointed supervisor of NHL officials. While in that capacity, he conducted officiating schools in Canada, the United States and Germany, and introduced the system of one referee and two linesmen to Finland in 1974. He also made a return to active duty at age 55 when he filled in briefly for an injured Dave Newell during a game between the New York Islanders and Atlanta Flames on December 30, 1978.

CHARLES UKSILA was the first player born, raised, and trained in the United States who ever played for the Stanley Cup. He did so in 1916 as a member of the Portland Rosebuds of the Pacific Coast Hockey Association. Portland was the first American-based team to play for the Stanley Cup that year but lost to the Montreal Canadiens, who became Stanley Cup champions for the first time. In 1914–15, Portland had become the first American team to play in a Canadian league after the PCHA franchise in New Westminster, British Columbia was transferred to Oregon's city of roses.

Uksila was a native of Calumet, Michigan who began his hockey career in Michigan's Upper Peninsula. He later played senior hockey in Detroit (1913–14) and in Portland (1914–15) before joining the pro ranks with the PCHA. Uksila spent a second season with the Rosebuds in 1917–18 and joined the Vancouver Millionaires the following season after the Portland franchise suspended operation. He served as a referee in the Vancouver Senior League in 1920–21 and was a referee in the American Hockey Association in 1930–31. Uksila also taught pro figure skating.

NORM ULLMAN was a high-scoring star in Edmonton who entered the NHL with the Detroit Red Wings in 1955–56. An excellent skater and stick-handler noted for his consistency and durability, Ullman shunned the spotlight during 20 years in the NHL but ranked among the game's best players.

Ullman played on a line with Gordie Howe and Ted Lindsay his second year in Detroit and helped the team to finish first overall that season. He then scored 23 goals in 1957–58 and fell below 20 only twice over the rest of his NHL career. Ullman led the Red Wings in goals in 1961, 1965 and 1966, leading the league with 42 in 1964–65 when his 83 points were just four behind Stan Mikita for the NHL scoring title. Ullman was a First Team All-Star that season and was named to the Second Team in 1966–67.

On March 3, 1968, Ullman, Paul Henderson and Floyd Smith were traded to the Toronto Maple Leafs in the deal that sent Frank Mahovlich to Detroit. Maple Leafs coach Punch Imlach, who had coached Jean Beliveau in senior hockey, called Ullman "the best center who ever played for me." He remained in Toronto through the 1974–75 season, then finished his career playing two seasons with the Edmonton Oilers of the World Hockey Association.

When he left the NHL, Ullman's career totals ranked eighth in goals (490), and fourth in assists (739) and points (1,229). He never played on a Stanley Cup winner. Ullman was inducted into the Hockey Hall of Fame in 1982.

GARRY UNGER broke Andy Hebenton's NHL record of 630 consecutive games played during the 1975–76 season and pushed his "ironman" streak to 914 games before injuries forced him out of the lineup on December 21, 1979. Unger's streak is now the second-longest in NHL history behind only the 964 consecutive games played by Doug Jarvis.

Unger broke into the NHL with the Toronto Maple Leafs during the 1967–68 season but was sent to the Detroit Red Wings as part of the package with Frank Mahovlich on March 8, 1968 in a trade that delivered Norm Ullman, Paul Henderson and Floyd Smith to Toronto. Unger scored 42 goals for Detroit during the 1969–70 season but was traded to the St. Louis Blues the following year. He never scored less than 30 goals in eight full seasons in St. Louis but was dealt to the Atlanta Flames prior to the 1979–80 seasons and it was there that his streak ended.

When the Flames moved to Calgary for the 1980–81 season, Unger was traded to the Los Angeles Kings but finished the year with the Edmonton Oilers. His final NHL season was 1982–83 but Unger played four years in Great Britain before retiring in 1987. He remains among the Blues career leaders in most offensive categories.

ROGIE VACHON was ridiculed as a "Junior B goalie" by Punch Imlach when the Montreal Canadiens started the rookie netminder against the Toronto Maple Leafs in the 1967 Stanley Cup final. Though the Leafs beat Vachon and the Canadiens that year, Rogie went on to become one of the winningest goaltenders in NHL history.

Following his debut in 1966–67, Vachon replaced Gump Worsley as the Canadiens' top goaltender. Worsley saw most of the postseason action when the Canadiens became Stanley Cup champions in 1967–68, but Vachon was the workhorse when the Canadiens won again in 1969. He held the top job in Montreal until Ken Dryden emerged as a star during the playoffs in 1971, and was traded to the Los Angeles Kings on November 4, 1971.

Vachon remained in Los Angeles through 1977–78, emerging as one of the league's top goalies while leading the Kings to respectability. He posted a career-best 2.24 goals-against average when the Kings set a franchise-record with 105 points in 1974–75 and was the goaltender when Team Canada won the first Canada Cup tournament in 1976.

In 1978, the Detroit Red Wings signed Vachon as a free-agent and were forced to give up Dale McCourt as compensation. McCourt went to court in an attempt to remain a Red Wing and later dropped his case when the Kings traded him back to Detroit. After two seasons with the Red Wings, Vachon was traded to the Boston Bruins, where he spent two more seasons before retiring. He had a lifetime goals-against average of 2.99 and his 355 career wins and 51 shutouts rank him among the NHL's all-time leaders.

Following his retirement, Vachon returned to Los Angeles to work in the Kings front office. He became general manager during the 1983–84 season and remained on at that position until 1991–92. He also served brief stints as coach in 1983–84 and 1987–88. On February 14, 1985, Vachon became the first player in Kings history to have his number (30) retired.

RICK VAIVE was named captain of the Toronto Maple Leafs in 1981–82 and went on to become the first player in franchise history to reach the 50-goal plateau when he scored 54 times that season. His total, to date, remains a franchise record. Vaive scored 51 goals in 1982–83 and had a third straight 50-goal year with 52 in 1983–84. He also established career highs with 41 assists and 93 points that season.

Vaive turned pro as a 19-year-old with the Birmingham Bulls of the World Hockey Association in 1978–79 and led the league in penalty minutes. He and fellow rookies Gaston Gingras, Michel Goulet, Craig Hartsburg, Rob Ramage and Pat Riggin were known as "the Baby Bulls" and all entered the NHL for the 1979–80 season. Vaive was with the Vancouver Canucks to start the year but he and Bill Derlago were traded to Toronto for Jerry Butler and Tiger Williams on February 18, 1980. Vaive spent the next seven seasons with the Maple Leafs and never scored less than 32 goals.

On February 23, 1986, Vaive was stripped of the Leafs captaincy after he skipped an early-morning practice. He spent one more season in Toronto but was then traded to the Chicago Blackhawks for Ed Olczyk on September 3, 1987. Vaive scored 43 goals in his first season in Chicago but was dealt to the Buffalo Sabres during the 1988–89 season. He had 441 goals when his NHL career ended in 1991–92 and has since been coaching in the minor leagues.

JOHN VANBIESBROUCK was undrafted out of midget hockey and had to sign as a walk-on with the Sault St. Marie Greyhounds of the Ontario Hockey League in 1980–81. He made his NHL debut with the New York Rangers just one year later and has gone on to become one of the winningest goaltenders in history. On December 27, 1997, Vanbiesbrouck became just the second American-born goaltender to post 300 victories in the NHL (two months after Tom Barrasso had become the first).

Vanbiesbrouck starred with the Rangers' Tulsa farm club in the Central Hockey League in 1983–84 and became a regular with the Rangers the following year. He won the Vezina Trophy and a selection to the First All-Star Team in just his second full season of 1985–86. Vanbiesbrouck shared the Rangers goal with Mike Richter from 1989–90 until 1992–93 and the two formed a fine combination. On June 20, 1993, Vanbiesbrouck was traded to the Vancouver Canucks and four days later he was selected by the Florida Panthers in the 1993 Expansion Draft.

Vanbiesbrouck's goaltending helped the Panthers to establish first-year records with 33 wins and 83 points as Florida just missed qualifying for the playoffs. His brilliant 1993–94 season saw him earn a spot on the Second All-Star Team and finish as runner-up to Dominik Hasek in voting for the Vezina Trophy. He also finished third behind Sergei Fedorov and Hasek for the Hart Trophy as the NHL's most valuable player. In 1995–96, Vanbiesbrouck's great play led the Panthers to the Stanley Cup finals in just their third season, and though the club was swept in the finals by the Colorado Avalanche he finished third behind Joe Sakic and Patrick Roy in voting for the Conn Smythe Trophy. Vanbiesbrouck remained with the Panthers through the 1997–98 season and then signed with the Philadelphia Flyers as a free agent.

Internationally, Vanbiesbrouck has represented the United States at the World Junior Championships in 1982 and 1983, the World Championships in 1985, 1987, 1989 and 1991, and the Canada Cup in 1984, 1987 and 1991. Injuries kept him out of the World Cup of Hockey in 1996 but he was a member of the U.S. Olympic team at Nagano in 1998.

MOOSE VASKO Elmer "Moose" Vasko was a product of the Chicago Black Hawks junior team in St. Catharines, where he played on a Memorial Cup champion in his first season of 1953–54. Vasko reached the NHL in 1956–57 and at 6'2" and 200 pounds he was one of the biggest players in the league. His size and strength made him a solid, and popular, defenseman.

The Black Hawks had missed the playoffs 10 times in 11 years when Vasko joined the team but with additions of other St. Catharines stars like Bobby Hull, Stan Mikita and coach Rudy Pilous, the Black Hawks returned to the playoffs in 1957–58 and were Stanley Cup champions by 1960–61. Vasko helped the Black Hawks reach the Stanley Cup finals again in 1962 and 1965 and was named to the Second All-Star Team in both 1962–63 and 1963–64.

Injuries limited Vasko's playing time in 1965–66 and he retired after that season but returned to the NHL in 1967–68 after being selected by the Minnesota North Stars in the 1967 Expansion Draft. Vasko played three seasons with the North Stars, though most of his final campaign of 1969–70 was spent with Salt Lake City of the Western Hockey League.

PAT VERBEEK In 1989–90, Pat Verbeek led the Hartford Whalers with 44 goals and 228 penalty minutes to become the first player player since Ted Lindsay in 1947–48 to lead his team in both categories. Verbeek repeated the feat in 1990–91, and during the 1993–94 season he joined Mike Foligno as the first

two players ever to reach career totals of 300 goals and 2,000 penalty minutes.

Verbeek's career began with the New Jersey Devils, playing six games in 1982–83 and becoming a regular the following season. In 1987–88, he set a Devils record with 46 goals. New Jersey traded him to Hartford on June 17, 1989 and he had back-to-back 40-goal seasons in his first two years with the Whalers. Verbeek became captain in Hartford in 1992–93 and continued to wear the "C" until he was traded to the New York Rangers on March 23, 1995. He reached the 40-goal plateau for the fourth time in his career with the Rangers in 1995–96 but signed as a free agent with the Dallas Stars on August 21, 1996.

In international hockey, Verbeek won a bronze medal at the World Junior Championships in 1983 and won a silver medal with Team Canada at the World Championships in 1989. In 1994, he was a member of the Canadian team that won the World Championship for the first time since 1961. Verbeek also represented his country at the World Cup of Hockey in 1996.

MIKE VERNON was a junior star with the Calgary Wranglers of the Western Hockey League, earning First Team All-Star honors in 1981–82 and 1982–83 and being named the top goaltender at the Memorial Cup tournament in 1983 while on loan to the champion Portland Winter Hawks. Vernon also made his NHL debut with the Calgary Flames during the 1982–83 season and went on to become the winningest goaltender (245 victories) in club history. When he won his 300th game with the Detroit Red Wings in 1996–97, Vernon became just the 13th goaltender in NHL history to reach the milestone.

Vernon took over as the top goaltender in Calgary midway through the 1985–86 season and led the Flames on a surprising run to the Cup finals that spring. In 1988–89, he starred as the Flames won the Stanley Cup for the first time. Vernon had posted a career-high 37 wins during the regular season that year and was named to the Second All-Star Team. In 1991, he won a silver medal as a member of Team Canada at the World Championships.

Vernon remained the number-one goaltender in Calgary through the 1993–94 season, but on June 29, 1994, he was traded to the Detroit Red Wings. In his first year with Detroit, Vernon helped the Red Wings to reach the Stanley Cup finals and in 1995–96 he and Chris Osgood shared the Jennings Trophy while the Red Wings set an NHL record with 62 wins. Vernon served as the backup to Osgood during the 1996–97 season, but coach Scotty Bowman decided to go with the veteran goaltender in the playoffs that spring and Vernon was brilliant in posting a 16–4 record with a 1.76 goals-against average. He earned the Conn Smythe Trophy as Detroit won the Stanley Cup for the first time in 42 years.

Despite his playoff heroics, the Red Wings sent Vernon to the San Jose Sharks on August 18, 1997. Many years earlier, Detroit had dealt away goaltender Harry Lumley after winning the Stanley Cup in 1950 and traded Terry Sawchuk following their victory in 1955.

GEORGES VEZINA played most of his career in an era when goaltenders were required to remain standing at all times. As a result, his statistics are not as impressive as many goaltenders of a later day, but he often is ranked among the greatest goalies of all-time. His legend is perpetuated by the Vezina Trophy, awarded annually to the top goaltender in the NHL.

Vezina began playing hockey in his hometown of Chicoutimi, Quebec and he became known as the "Chicoutimi Cucumber" for his ability to remain cool under pressure. He joined the Montreal Canadiens in 1910–11, never missing a regular-season or playoff game over the next 15 years. His 367-game streak ended on November 28, 1925, when chest pains forced him out of action. He never played again, and he died of tuberculosis on March 26, 1926. The ownership of the Montreal Canadiens donated the Vezina Trophy to honor his memory.

Over the course of his career, Vezina helped the Canadiens win either the National Hockey Association or NHL title on five occasions and the Stanley Cup in 1916 and 1924. He led the NHL in goals-against average in its first season of 1917–18 with a 3.93 mark, and he saw his numbers improve dramatically after 1922 when goaltenders were allowed to fall to the ice to make saves. In 1945, Vezina was one of the original 12 men elected to the Hockey Hall of Fame.

CARL VOSS As the first referee-in-chief of the National Hockey League from 1950 until 1965, Carl Voss made an enormous contribution to the development of referees and linesmen in professional hockey. He was responsible for assessing the work of officials in as many as 125 games per year and conducted hundreds of officiating schools. His job made him referee-in-chief over minor pro leagues that used NHL officials. He also was president of the United States Hockey League in 1949. In 1974, he was inducted into the Hockey Hall of Fame as a builder.

Voss already had an impressive sports legacy before becoming involved in refereeing. In 1923 and 1924, he was a member of the Queen's University football team from Kingston that won the Grey Cup as Canadian football champions. In 1926, he was a member of the Kingston Frontenacs hockey team and played for Queen's University, reaching the Memorial Cup finals. In February of 1927, he became the first player Conn Smythe signed after he bought the St. Patricks and renamed them the Toronto Maple Leafs.

Voss played briefly in Toronto, then starred with the Buffalo Bisons, win-

ning the International Hockey League scoring title and a league championship in 1932. He returned to the NHL in 1932–33 with the New York Rangers, but was traded to the Red Wings and went on to be named rookie of the year, the first time the NHL bestowed such an honor. He later played with the Ottawa Senators, St. Louis Eagles, New York Americans and Montreal Maroons before winding up with the Chicago Black Hawks, where he scored the Stanley Cup-winning goal in 1938.

FRED WAGHORN A referee in more than 2,000 hockey games and 1,500 lacrosse games over 50 years as an official, Fred C. Waghorn is responsible for some of the most important innovations in hockey. He is credited with initiating the system of dropping pucks for face-offs instead of placing them on the ice, and with implementing the use of a whistle rather than a handbell to stop play. Waghorn also instituted a rule stating the entire puck must cross the goal line for a goal to count. This was done after a game he officiated in 1900 in which a puck split in two, one half ending up in the net.

In addition to his contributions to the game as a referee, Waghorn was one of four men who organized the Beaches Hockey League in Toronto in 1911. This league grew into the Metropolitan Toronto Hockey League, the largest minor hockey organization in the world. Waghorn was inducted into the Hockey Hall of Fame as a builder in 1961.

ERNIE WAKELY saw more action than any other goaltender in the World Hockey Association. His 16 career shutouts are the top total in WHA history and his 164 wins rank third all-time, just three behind leader Joe Daley and one back of Richard Brodeur. Wakely's time in the WHA spanned the entire seven-year history of the league. He was a member of five different teams.

Wakely had begun his professional career in 1959–60 and had brief trials with the Montreal Canadiens in 1962–63 and 1968–69 before landing regular NHL duty with the St. Louis Blues in 1968–69. Wakely shared playing time with Jacques Plante and Glenn Hall in the St. Louis nets before eventually replacing the two future Hall of Famers. After a poor season in 1971–72, he left for the WHA.

JACK WALKER Though he was associated with hockey for more than 30 years, Jack Walker spent all but two years of his playing career in leagues that either predated or rivaled the NHL. He is credited with inventing the hook check, and he used this sweeping stick move to become one of the game's greatest defensive forwards.

Walker played his early hockey in Port Arthur, Ontario, winning four consecutive city championships and earning mention for his outstanding hook check when the Ottawa Senators beat Port Arthur in a Stanley Cup challenge in March of 1911. In 1912–13, he signed with the Toronto Blueshirts of the National Hockey Association. He actually spent most of the year with Moncton of the Maritime Professional Hockey League before returning to Toronto in 1913–14, where he helped the Blueshirts win a Stanley Cup title. After one more season in Toronto, Walker was one of several Blueshirts to join the PCHA's new team in Seattle in 1915–16. The following year, he helped the Metropolitans become the first American team to win the Stanley Cup.

Walker spent nine seasons in Seattle, where he helped the team to win four PCHA titles before it folded. He joined the Victoria Cougars in 1924–25 when they entered the Western Canada Hockey League and helped his new team to win the Stanley Cup. Pro hockey in the west collapsed after the 1925–26 season and Walker was one of several Victoria players sold to the Detroit Cougars (later the Red Wings) for that team's first NHL season in 1926–27.

After two years in Detroit, Walker returned to Seattle, playing minor-league hockey there for another two years. He then served as a player-coach in Hollywood and Oakland in the California Hockey League before retiring as a player to coach, manage and referee in the Pacific Coast Hockey League. Walker was inducted into the Hockey Hall of Fame in 1960.

MARTY WALSH was a native of Kingston, Ontario who first gained prominence in hockey with the Queen's University club that challenged the Ottawa Silver Seven for the Stanley Cup in February of 1906. He so impressed the Ottawa brass in a losing effort that they tried to acquire him when Frank McGee retired after the season.

Instead of joining Ottawa, Walsh signed with the Sault Ste. Marie, Ontario team in the International (Pro) Hockey League (hockey's first professional circuit), but he suffered a broken leg. After recovering, he signed with Ottawa for the 1907–08 season. Walsh led the Eastern Canada Hockey Association in scoring in 1908–09 as the Senators won the Stanley Cup. He was the league's top scorer again when Ottawa was part of the National Hockey Association in 1910–11. The team won another Stanley Cup title that season.

Walsh was known as a nimble and tricky skater who had a knack for being in the right position to take a shot. In a Stanley Cup challenge match on March 16, 1911, he scored 10 goals in a 13–4 victory over Port Arthur, the second-highest total in Stanley Cup history behind Frank McGee's 14 goals against Dawson City in 1905. Walsh's other single-game scoring feats include one seven-goal game, two six-goal games and a pair of five-goal efforts. He was elected to the Hockey Hall of Fame in 1962.

HARRY E. WATSON Harry "Moose" Watson was an amateur superstar who refused all offers to turn pro during his hockey career. Born in Newfoundland but raised mostly in Winnipeg, Watson was a high school star in that city before arriving in Toronto in 1915. He played junior hockey at St. Andrews College and with the Toronto Aura Lees in the Ontario Hockey Association before serving as a pilot in World War I. After service overseas, Watson played OHA senior hockey with the Toronto Dentals, moving on to the Toronto Granite Club in 1919–20.

The Granite Club won the John Ross Robertson Cup as OHA senior championship in 1920, 1922 and 1923, finishing runner-up in 1921 and adding the Allan Cup as Canadian amateur champions in 1922 and 1923. As Allan Cup champions, the Granites earned the right to represent Canada at the first Winter Olympics in 1924. Led by Watson's 36 goals in five games (including 13 in a 33–0 win over Switzerland), the Granites were easy gold medal winners at Chamonix, France.

Now considered the greatest amateur player in Canada, Watson was offered a $30,000 contract with the Montreal Maroons in 1925–26, but he turned it down, just as he had rejected previous offers from the Toronto St. Pats. He continued to play amateur hockey in Toronto, but he was soon more of a coach than a player. In 1931–32, he guided the Toronto National "Sea Fleas" club to the Allan Cup championship, retiring before the team earned a silver medal at the 1933 IIHF World Championships. Watson was elected to the Hockey Hall of Fame in 1962.

HARRY P. WATSON entered the NHL with the Brooklyn (formerly New York) Americans in 1941–42 and scored 10 goals as an 18-year-old rookie. When the team dropped out of the league after his first year, Watson was drafted by the Detroit Red Wings in 1942–43 and played for a Stanley Cup champion that year. He then joined the Royal Canadian Air Force and played two years of service hockey before returning to the NHL in 1945–46. He was traded to the Toronto Maple Leafs for Billy Taylor prior to the 1946–47 campaign.

At 6'1" and 203 pounds, Watson was a physical left winger who played the game aggressively but within the rules. He was a deceptively fast skater who was used to check the opposition's top scorers, but he had a good scoring touch of his own. He played on Stanley Cup winners his first three years in Toronto and led the Maple Leafs with a career-high 26 goals and 45 points in 1948–49. Watson won his fifth Stanley Cup title in 1951, assisting on Bill Barilko's famous winning goal. He was traded to the Chicago Black Hawks during the 1954–55 season and played his last two NHL seasons there.

At the time he left the NHL after the 1956–57 season, Watson's 236 career goals trailed only Maurice Richard, Gordie Howe and Ted Lindsay among active players. He had been runner-up to Bill Quackenbush for the Lady Byng Trophy in 1948–49 when he went the entire year without a penalty, and had played in seven All-Star Games. Watson was elected to the Hockey Hall of Fame in 1994.

PHIL WATSON played amateur hockey in his hometown of Montreal and was claimed by both the Canadiens and the New York Rangers as being on their negotiation list. The NHL governors awarded Watson to the Rangers and he made his debut with the club in 1935–36.

Watson first played on a line with Lynn Patrick and Cecil Dillon in New York, but in 1938–39 he was teamed with Bryan Hextall and Dutch Hiller. Watson finished among the top-10 scorers in the NHL that season and helped the Rangers win the Stanley Cup in 1939–40. Lynn Patrick join Hextall and Watson on the Rangers' top line in 1941–42 and that season Hextall led the NHL in scoring, while Patrick led the league in goals, and Watson in assists as the Rangers finished the regular season in first place. The team fell into last place in 1942–43 after several players were lost to military service and Watson was plagued by injuries.

Unable to gain a border crossing card because of wartime restrictions, a deal was worked out prior to the 1943–44 season to loan Watson to the Montreal Canadiens in exchange for two players. Though it was originally thought Watson would only be able to play in Toronto and Montreal, he was later cleared to play a full schedule and helped the Canadiens win the Stanley Cup that year.

Watson was back with the Rangers in 1944–45 and played with the team until 1947–48. He turned to coaching in 1948–49 and guided the New York Rovers of the Eastern Amateur Hockey League for three seasons, then coached the Quebec Citadelles from 1951–52 until 1953–54. He returned to the NHL as coach of the Rangers in 1955–56 and guided the team until he was replaced by Alf Pike in November of 1959. Watson later coached the Boston Bruins in 1961–62 and 1962–63.

DOUG WEIGHT made his NHL debut in the 1991 playoffs when he suited up with the New York Rangers for game six of the Patrick Division semifinals. He had spent the 1990–91 season with Lake Superior State, where he led the team to the Central Collegiate Hockey Association title and was rewarded as a CCHA first team all-star and an NCAA second team all-American.

Weight began the 1991–92 season with the Rangers and scored his first goal in the season-opener on October 3, 1991. He spent nine games with

Binghamton of the American Hockey League that year while recovering from an injury and was in the midst of his first full season in the NHL when he was traded to the Edmonton Oilers for Esa Tikkanen on March 17, 1993.

Weight has been the top scorer in Edmonton since the 1993–94 season and topped 100 points for the first time with 25 goals and 79 assists in 1995–96. He played for the American team that beat Canada at the World Cup of Hockey in 1996 and was a member of the U.S. Olympic team at Nagano in 1998. Weight had previously represented the United States at the World Championships in 1993 and 1994. In 1991, he finished one point ahead of Eric Lindros to rank as the leading scorer at the World Junior Championships.

COONEY WEILAND Ralph "Cooney" Weiland played 11 years in the NHL, winning the Stanley Cup in his first season of 1928–29 and in his last season of 1938–39. Standing just 5'7" and weighing only 150 pounds, Weiland was a slick stickhandler skilled at outmaneuvering opposition players.

Weiland played junior hockey in Seaforth and Owen Sound, Ontario, winning the Memorial Cup with the Owen Sound Grays in 1923–24. He played the next four years in Minnesota before he and Tiny Thompson joined the Boston Bruins directly from the roster of the Minneapolis Millers in 1928–29. The Bruins won their first Stanley Cup title that season. Weiland centered the Dynamite Line with wingers Dutch Gainor and Dit Clapper, and the high-scoring trio helped Boston rewrite the NHL record book after forward passing rules were modernized for the 1929–30 season. The Bruins went 38–5–1 that year, while Weiland obliterated Howie Morenz's mark of 51 points in a single season with 73 on 43 goals and 30 assists.

The Dynamite Line was broken up in 1932–33 when Weiland was traded to Ottawa. He promptly led the last-place club in scoring, but the cash-strapped Senators sold him to Detroit the following year. Weiland played on another great line with the Red Wings, centering Herbie Lewis and Larry Aurie. In 1934–35, he was named to the Second All-Star Team. Weiland returned to Boston the following year, where he spent four more seasons before retiring as a player after winning the Stanley Cup in 1939. He was immediately named coach of the Bruins and led them to another Stanley Cup title in 1941.

Weiland spent the next four seasons as coach of the American Hockey League's Hershey Bears, then guided the New Haven Ramblers in 1945–46. He became the head coach at Harvard University in 1950–51 and remained on the job for 21 years before retiring in 1971. That same year, Weiland was inducted into the Hockey Hall of Fame.

HARRY WESTWICK earned the nickname "Rat" because of his small stature and elusive style. A star player over a lengthy career in his hometown of Ottawa, Westwick was the rover on the Silver Seven team that first won the Stanley Cup in 1903. Ottawa successfully defeated 10 challengers before losing to the Montreal Wanderers in 1906. In addition to his hockey skill, he was also a fine lacrosse player with the Ottawa Capitals.

Westwick began his career as a goaltender before being converted to rover and playing his way up the hockey chain in Ottawa during the 1890s. He had his most productive season in 1904–05 when he scored 24 goals in 13 games, including the playoffs. In March of 1907, he and his Silver Seven teammate Alf Smith were added to the roster of the new Stanley Cup Kenora Thistles, but they could not help the team, as it lost the championship to the Montreal Wanderers. Westwick returned to Ottawa for one more season before he retired. In 1962, he was elected to the Hockey Hall of Fame.

KENNY WHARRAM bounced around between the Chicago Black Hawks and the minor leagues for six seasons before arriving in the NHL to stay in 1958–59. Small but speedy, the 5'9", 160-pounder had been a center in the minors but played right wing in the NHL.

In his first two full seasons with the Black Hawks, Wharram played with Stan Mikita and Bobby Hull or Eric Nesterenko but in 1960–61 coach Rudy Pilous teamed him with Mikita and Ab McDonald and the Scooter Line was born. The line helped the Black Hawks win the Stanley Cup for the first time since 1938 that season and remained together for three more years. In their final year together in 1963–64, Wharram scored a career-high 39 goals and won the Lady Byng Trophy. He was also named to the First All Star Team, as he would be again after scoring 31 goals in 1966–67.

Wharram played two more years with the Black Hawks but retired prior to the 1969–70 season after suffering a heart attack at training camp. Following a period of recovery, he returned to hockey as a coach at the amateur level.

FRED WHITCROFT first came to prominence in hockey while playing for the Peterborough team that won the Ontario Hockey Association junior championship in 1901. He played in Midland, Ontario in 1905, but he returned to Peterborough to captain the intermediate club that won the OHA championship the following year. A large man who could skate fast and stickhandle expertly, Whitcroft was a member of the Kenora Thistles when they won the Stanley Cup in 1907—though they were champions from only January to March, when they were beaten by the Montreal Wanderers in a rematch.

Whitcroft played in Edmonton in 1907–08, scoring a stunning 49 goals in just 16 games as the team won its league championship. In the Eskimos'

Stanley Cup challenge against the Montreal Wanderers in December of 1908, Whitcroft was the only member of the team not to be replaced by a "ringer." Edmonton was unsuccessful in its challenge, just as it would be in January of 1910 when the Eskimos took on the Ottawa Senators. Following that Stanley Cup series, Whitcroft signed with the Renfrew Millionaires for the first season of the NHA. After the 1909–10 campaign, he returned west to retire in Vancouver. Whitcroft traveled extensively in the ensuing years, visiting many exotic ports of call. He was elected to the Hockey Hall of Fame in 1962.

TIGER WILLIAMS Dave "Tiger" Williams is the NHL's all-time leader with 3,966 penalty minutes in his career. He could also be an effective offensive player who had at least 15 goals 10 times in 14 seasons. He reached 20 or more on four occasions, including a high of 35 in 1980–81 when he became the first player in the NHL to top 30 goals and 300 penalty minutes in the same season.

Williams was a fan favorite in Toronto during the late 1970s and was often employed at left wing alongside Darryl Sittler and Lanny McDonald on the Maple Leafs' top line. He was equally popular in Vancouver after his trade to the Canucks on February 18, 1980 and helped the team reach the Stanley Cup finals in 1982. Williams later saw action with the Detroit Red Wings, Los Angeles Kings and Hartford Whalers before ending his career in 1987–88.

TOMMY WILLIAMS joined the Boston Bruins during the 1961–62 season and became the first American to play regularly in the NHL since Frank Brimsek retired in 1950. Williams went on to play 13 years in the NHL, plus two years in the World Hockey Association, before retiring after the 1975–76 campaign.

Williams' father taught him how to play hockey while he was growing up in Duluth, Minnesota, and he was a high school star at Duluth Central. He joined the United States national team as an 18-year-old in 1958–59 and played at the World Championships in 1959, then on a line with brothers Bill and Roger Christian on the American team that surprised nearly everyone with an Olympic gold medal at Squaw Valley in 1960.

Although he had intended to play college hockey at the University of Minnesota after the Olympics, Williams was instead persuaded to try professional hockey. He joined the Boston Bruins' Kingston farm club in the Eastern Professional Hockey League in 1960–61 and was promoted from Kingston to Boston in January of 1962. On January 27, 1962, in just his second NHL game, Williams scored two goals in a 5–3 victory over the Chicago Black Hawks. He was projected to become the Bruins' first new scoring star since Don McKenney and delivered 23 goals in his first full season of 1962–63 but failed to reach such a total again in six more seasons with Boston.

Williams was traded to Minnesota on May 7, 1969 and established career highs with 52 assists and 67 points in 1969–70, but was dealt to the California Golden Seals on February 23, 1971. He was sold to the Boston Braves of the American Hockey League on March 5, 1972, but when the WHA was formed for the 1972–73 season, he signed on with the New England Whalers. After two seasons in the WHA, Williams returned to the NHL with the expansion Washington Capitals in 1974–75 and led the club with 22 goals, 36 assists and 58 points though the Caps posted a dismal 8–67–5 season. He retired after splitting the next season between Washington and the minors.

Tommy Williams entered the United States Hockey Hall of Fame in 1981. His brother, Warren Williams, played in the NHL with the St. Louis Blues and California Seals between 1973–74 and 1975–76.

CULLY WILSON Carol "Cully" Wilson was a tough but talented hockey player whose temper sometimes got the best of him. A cross-check that broke the jaw of Mickey MacKay late in the 1918–19 season resulted in Wilson being banned from the Pacific Coast Hockey Association.

Wilson's professional career had begun with the Toronto Blueshirts of the National Hockey Association in 1912–13 and he was a member of Toronto's first Stanley Cup champion in 1914. When the PCHA expanded to Seattle for the 1915–16 season, he and virtually all of his Toronto teammates were recruited to stock the team. Wilson spent four years with the Metropolitans, helping Seattle become the first American team to win the Stanley Cup in 1917. The Mets also won the PCHA title again in 1919, but the Stanley Cup series that year was halted by the worldwide influenza epidemic.

It was prior to the 1919–20 season that Wilson was banned from the PCHA, so he signed with the Toronto St. Pats of the NHL. He remained in the NHL for four seasons, playing with Toronto, the Montreal Canadiens, and Hamilton Tigers, before joining the Calgary Tigers of the Western Canada Hockey League in 1923–24. This resulted in his reinstatement into the PCHA, as the two leagues shared an interlocking schedule.

In his first season in Calgary, Wilson set what was then a pro hockey record with a hat trick in 61 seconds. He also helped the Tigers to win the WCHL championship but the team lost a Stanley Cup series to the Montreal Canadiens. Wilson spent two more years in Calgary, but when pro hockey collapsed in the west he joined the Chicago Black Hawks in 1926–27. He then played five years in the minors before retiring in 1932.

DOUG WILSON was noted for his booming slapshot and is the greatest offensive defenseman in the history of the Chicago Blackhawks. His 225 goals,

554 assists and 779 points are all career records for Blackhawks blueliners, and he also holds the single-season record in each of those categories. He led all Chicago defenseman in scoring 10 years in a row from 1981–82 to 1990–91.

Wilson won the Norris Trophy as the league's best defenseman in 1981–82 and was also selected to the First All-Star Team that season. He earned selections to the Second All-Star Team in 1984–85 and 1989–90. He played for Team Canada at the 1984 Canada Cup and took part in Rendez-Vous '87.

On September 6, 1991, Wilson was traded to the expansion San Jose Sharks and was named the team's first captain. He served in that capacity for two seasons before retiring after the 1992–93 campaign.

PHAT WILSON Gordon Allan "Phat" Wilson was a star amateur player who spurned numerous professional offers during a lengthy career that saw him develop into one of the finest defensemen of his era. He began playing hockey in his hometown of Port Arthur, Ontario, moving up the ranks to join the senior Port Arthur War Veterans in 1918. He remained with the team until 1920, when he left for Iroquois Falls and helped that team defeat the Sault Ste. Marie Greyhounds for the Northern Ontario Hockey Association championship.

Wilson was back in Port Arthur for the 1922–23 season, playing for the Bearcats team that won the Allan Cup as Canada's amateur champions in 1925, 1926 and 1929. In 1930, the Bearcats were western Canadian champions before losing to the Montreal Amateur Athletic Association in the Allan Cup finals. Wilson retired as a player after the 1931–32 season at the age of 37, but he remained as coach of the Bearcats. It was a position he held again in 1937–38 and 1939–40. In his youth, Wilson had also been a standout baseball player. He was elected to the Hockey Hall of Fame in 1962.

RON WILSON was born in Canada, but was raised in the United States and is an American citizen. As a player, he represented the United States on the U.S. national team in 1975, 1981, 1983 and 1987. He first coached the American squad at the 1994 World Championships and guided the United States to victory over Canada in the World Cup of Hockey in September of 1996. He also coached the U.S. team at the Nagano Olympics in 1998.

Wilson began his coaching career as an assistant with the Milwaukee Admirals of the International Hockey League in 1989–90 and spent the next three seasons as an assistant to Pat Quinn with the Vancouver Canucks. On June 30, 1993, Wilson was named the first coach of the Mighty Ducks of Anaheim and his first-year team equaled the Florida Panthers with an expansion-record 33 wins. After a poor season in 1994–95, the Mighty Ducks made a spirited run at the playoffs in 1995–96 and qualified for the postseason for the first time the following year. Wilson left the club after its fourth season and signed with the Washington Capitals on June 9, 1997. One year later, he had guided the Capitals to their first appearance in the Stanley Cup finals.

As a player, Wilson starred at Providence College between 1973–74 and 1976–77, earning all-American honors twice and four straight selections to the Hockey East all-star team. His best season was 1974–75 when he led the NCAA in scoring with 26 goals and 61 assists in just 27 games and was named Hockey East player of the year. Wilson was drafted by the Toronto Maple Leafs after that season and made his NHL debut in 1977–78, though most of his time with the Maple Leafs was spent in the minor leagues. Wilson played in Switzerland from 1980–81 until 1985–86 when he returned to the NHL with the Minnesota North Stars. He spent the rest of his career with Minnesota before retiring after the 1988–89 season.

Wilson's father Larry and his uncle John both played and coached in the NHL.

HAL WINKLER turned professional with the Edmonton Eskimos of the Western Canada Hockey League in 1921–22 after eight seasons of senior amateur hockey in Manitoba and Saskatchewan. He was considered one of the best goaltenders in the WCHL over three seasons with Edmonton and two with Calgary. He won a league title in 1922–23, but lost the Stanley Cup to the Ottawa Senators despite allowing only three goals in two games.

When professional hockey collapsed in the west, Winkler joined the New York Rangers for the 1926–27 season but was soon sold to the Boston Bruins. He helped Boston reach the Stanley Cup finals that year, where the Bruins were beaten by the Senators. In 1927–28, Winkler tied Ottawa's Alex Connell for the NHL lead with 15 shutouts.

The next year, the aging veteran was replaced by Tiny Thompson in the Bruins goal. Though he didn't play a single game for them during the 1928–29 season, Winkler was listed on the Stanley Cup as the team's "sub-goaltender" following their victory over the Rangers. He retired from hockey two years later after a minor-league season with the Boston Tigers.

RALPH WINSOR was a dominating figure in the early years of hockey at Harvard. He played for the school's team in 1901, was captain in 1902, then coached for the next 15 years. Harvard had a record of 124 wins and only 29 losses in the years Winsor coached, including undefeated seasons in a stretch from 1903 to 1906. Harvard also went undefeated in 1919 when Winsor served as assistant coach. But in all his years of coaching, it is said Winsor never accepted a payment and his modesty kept him from appearing in any team pictures.

Winsor was an innovator who is credited with advancing the development of modern sticks and skates and developing such tactics as backchecking and the shifting of defensemen from the traditional single-file alignment as point and cover point to the modern side-by-side pairing. In addition to his contributions at Harvard, Winsor also aided hockey at the high school level and at other colleges. In 1932, he coached the silver medal-winning U.S. Olympic team at Lake Placid. Winsor became a charter member of the U.S. Hockey Hall of Fame in 1973.

CODDY WINTERS Frank J. "Coddy" Winters was an ice polo player in his hometown of Duluth, Minnesota who took up hockey as it gained popularity, beginning in the era of seven-man hockey because it was considered the position where his blazing speed could be best put to use. Winters played in his hometown until his Duluth team played a series of games against a Cleveland all-star team in 1908. That summer, Winters himself moved to Ohio and played for various Cleveland amateur teams for the remainder of his hockey career. He spent the rest of his life in Cleveland and died there on November 17, 1944.

Winters had continued to play rover through the 1909, 1910 and 1911 seasons but was moved back to defense in 1912 and proved to be just as good at stopping the rush as he had been at carrying the puck. During a 17-year career in Cleveland, Winters played on championship teams in 1911–12, 1913–14 and 1921–22. He also coached at Case Tech during his playing days in Cleveland and made several trips to Philadelphia to coach the University of Pennsylvania team.

Throughout his career, Winters had many offers to turn professional but preferred to remain an amateur. Many in his day felt that Winters was equal in talent to Hobey Baker, who is widely regarded as one of the greatest American players in history. Like Baker, Winters became a charter member of the United States Hockey Hall of Fame in 1973.

ARTHUR WIRTZ was a native of Chicago and an associate of James Norris and James D. Norris when the father-son combination purchased Detroit's NHL franchise and the Olympia Stadium in the summer of 1932. The following year, the trio purchased the Chicago Stadium. The Norrises and Wirtz later acquired control of Madison Square Garden and the St. Louis Arena. In 1952, Wirtz and James D. Norris bought the Chicago Black Hawks.

The Black Hawks had missed the playoff six years in a row when Wirtz began his association with the team. By 1954, attendance had become so poor there were fears the franchise would fold, but the signing of Bobby Hull in 1957–58 helped save the team. Wirtz and Norris rebuilt the club into the 1961 Stanley Cup champion and the Black Hawks remained a league power for decades to come. Wirtz was also primarily responsible for persuading the NHL to expand to St. Louis in 1967, then sold the St. Louis Arena to the Salomon family who had been granted the Blues franchise.

Arthur Wirtz was elected to the Hockey Hall of Fame as a builder in 1971.

BILL WIRTZ became associated with the Chicago Black Hawks when his father, Arthur Wirtz, purchased the team with James D. Norris in 1952. The new ownership group soon built a floundering franchise on the verge of folding into a contender, winning the Stanley Cup in 1961. Bill Wirtz became club president in 1966 and saw the team finish the 1966–67 in first place, winning the regular-season title for the first time in franchise history. The Black Hawks continued to be a power in the NHL after expansion in 1967.

Wirtz joined the NHL Board of Governors in 1967, where he worked hard into the 1970s to make expansion work. His efforts resulted in him being elected chairman of the Board of Governors nine consecutive times during an 18-year stretch that ended when he stepped down after the 1991–92 season. During his tenure, the NHL continued to expand, including four teams from the World Hockey Association in 1979, and saw a huge increase in European players. Wirtz also changed the name of his club from Black Hawks to Blackhawks before the 1985–86 season after discovering that the name had been written as one word in the original charter.

Wirtz was elected to the Hockey Hall of Fame as a builder in 1976 and was awarded the Lester Patrick Trophy for contributions to hockey in the United States in 1978. (Both were honors also bestowed on his father.) He was elected to the United States Hockey Hall of Fame in 1985.

GUMP WORSLEY played professional hockey for 25 years, making stops in seven minor-league cities in four different leagues, eventually starring in the NHL with the New York Rangers, Montreal Canadiens and Minnesota North Stars. During all but his final season of 1973–74, he tended goal without wearing a mask. Lorne Worsley's nickname of "Gump" was acquired early in life because of his resemblance to a popular comic strip character.

Worsley began his long pro career with a brief stop in New Haven of the American Hockey League in 1949–50. The next year, he was with St. Paul, where he won the Charles Gardiner Memorial Trophy as rookie of the year in the United States Hockey League. Worsley was with Saskatoon in the Pacific Coast Hockey League in 1951–52, and joined the Rangers in 1952–53. He played 50 games in goal that season for a club that was easily the worst in the NHL, and was rewarded with the Calder Trophy as the NHL's top rookie. Still,

the Rangers replaced him with Johnny Bower the following season and Worsley was farmed out to Vancouver of the Western Hockey League.

From 1954–55 until 1962–63, Worsley was the top goaltender on generally weak teams in New York. On June 4, 1963, he was traded to the Montreal Canadiens in a multi-player deal for Jacques Plante, and his fortunes rose. Though he spent most of the 1963–64 and 1964–65 seasons with Quebec of the AHL, Worsley played on his first Stanley Cup champion in Montreal in 1965. The following season, he and Charlie Hodge shared the Vezina Trophy and helped the Canadiens win a second straight Stanley Cup title. Worsley was a Second Team All-Star that season and won First Team honors in 1967–68 after he and Rogie Vachon shared the Vezina Trophy in another Stanley Cup-winning season. Worsley had a 1.98 goals-against average and six shutouts that year, then went 11–0 in the playoffs.

Worsley was a member of a fourth Stanley Cup winner in Montreal in 1969, but the pressure of playing goal for the Canadiens got to him and he retired briefly during the 1969–70 season. He was sold to Minnesota on February 27, 1970 and played the final four years of his career there. Worsley retired for good after playing his 21st NHL season in 1973–74. His total of 860 games in goal is surpassed only by Terry Sawchuk and Jacques Plante. Worsley was elected to the Hockey Hall of Fame in 1980.

ROY WORTERS was one of the smallest goaltenders in NHL history. Known as "Shrimp," he stood just 5'3" and weighed only about 135 pounds. Still, he was one of the top goalies in an era of great netminders, despite playing on weak teams over most of his 12-year NHL career. He is credited with being the first goaltender to use the back of his stick blade to divert shots into the corner.

Worters played his early hockey in his hometown of Toronto, but was a member of the Pittsburgh Yellow Jackets when the team won back-to-back United States amateur championships in 1924 and 1925. After Pittsburgh was granted an NHL franchise in 1925–26, the Pirates signed practically the entire Yellow Jackets roster, and Worters turned pro.

Following his third year in Pittsburgh, Worters refused the contract offered him for 1928–29 and was suspended by NHL president Frank Calder. He soon was dealt to the New York Americans, where he posted a 1.15 goals-against average and 13 shutouts to lead the team into the playoffs after a last-place finish the year before. As a result, Worters became the first goaltender ever to win the Hart Trophy as the NHL's most valuable player. He won the Vezina Trophy in 1930–31 after leading the league with a 1.61 goals-against average and was named to the Second All-Star Team in 1931–32 and 1933–34.

Worters retired after the 1936–37 season, but remained active with the NHL Oldtimers' Association. He also worked on behalf of handicapped children. Roy Worters was inducted into the Hockey Hall of Fame in 1969.

LYLE WRIGHT was a Canadian from Winnipeg who came to Minneapolis in 1919 after serving in the Canadian Army during World War I. He played hockey himself for the next four years and then brought fellow Winnipegger Ching Johnson from Eveleth to Minneapolis to join the Minneapolis Millers in 1923–24. Wright managed the Millers from 1928 to 1931 and then became business manager of the Chicago Black Hawks. His stay in Chicago was brief, though, and he came back to work for the Minneapolis Arena until his death on May 24, 1963. Through his affiliation with the Arena, Wright was again associated with the Minneapolis Millers and also with the University of Minnesota in the early days of its hockey program. Wright was also involved with figure skating and the Ice Follies. He became a charter member of the United States Hockey Hall of Fame when he was inducted as an administrator in 1973.

KEN YACKEL was a member of the U.S. silver medal-winning hockey team at the 1952 Oslo Olympics and a star at both forward and defense for the University of Minnesota. He helped the Gophers reach the NCAA hockey's final four in 1953 and 1954 and also earned a selection to the all-tournament team and as all-American in 1954.

Yackel began his pro career with the Cleveland Barons in the American Hockey League in 1955–56. He also played in Saskatoon and his hometown of St. Paul, Minnesota, as well as in Providence en route to six games with the Boston Bruins in 1958–59. It would be his only NHL experience, but Yackel later went on to great success as a player-coach with the Minneapolis Millers in the International Hockey League.

In his first season in Minneapolis (1960–61), Yackel led the league in scoring with 114 points and coached the team to a regular-season championship, earning honors on the First All-Star Team both at left wing and as coach. He scored 50 goals the following season, and in 1962–63 he had 100 points and earned a selection to the Second All-Star Team, again at left wing and as coach.

After his playing career, Yackel coached the U.S. national team at the World Championships in 1965. In 1971, he returned to his alma mater late in the

hockey season to fill in as interim coach for the balance of the year. Later he was involved in the John Mariucci Inner City Hockey Starter Association, a program to encourage hockey among urban children in St. Paul. In 1986, Yackel was enshrined in the United States Hockey Hall of Fame.

STEVE YZERMAN was selected fourth overall by the Detroit Red Wings in the 1983 Entry Draft and made his NHL debut as an 18-year-old in 1983–84. He went on to play in the All-Star Game that year, setting a Red Wings record for goals (39) and points (87) by a rookie, finishing runner-up behind Tom Barrasso in voting for the Calder Trophy and earning a spot on the NHL All-Rookie Team.

Yzerman became the youngest captain in Red Wings history when he was named to the position as a 21-year-old in 1986–87 season. He went on to lead the team in scoring for seven straight years. In a six-year span between 1987–88 and 1992–93, Yzerman topped 100 points each season and had 50 goals or more five times. He established career highs and Red Wings single-season records with 65 goals, 90 assists and 155 points in 1988–89 when he finished third in the NHL in scoring behind Mario Lemieux and Wayne Gretzky. Yzerman was also third behind Lemieux and Gretzky in voting for the Hart Trophy that season, but received the Lester B. Pearson Award as the most outstanding player in voting by fellow NHLers. Yzerman was third in scoring again in 1989–90 with 127 points on 62 goals and 65 assists.

On February 24, 1993, Yzerman joined Gordie Howe and Alex Delvecchio as the only players in Red Wings history to record 1,000 career points. He currently is second behind Howe on the Red Wings' all-time scoring list. His 500th career goal came on January 17, 1996. Yzerman finally got a chance to raise the Stanley Cup in 1997 when the Red Wings won for the first time since 1955. He was a unanimous choice for the Conn Smythe Trophy as the most valuable player in the playoffs when Detroit made it two in a row in 1998. Yzerman was the leading scorer in the postseason with 24 points (six goals, 18 assists) and played outstanding two-way hockey.

In addition to his success in the NHL, Yzerman has also starred in the international arena. He won a bronze medal as a member of the Canadian team at the World Junior Championships in 1983 and played with Team Canada, first-place finishers at the 1984 Canada Cup tournament. He earned a silver medal with Team Canada at the IIHF World Championships in 1985 and 1989 and led all players in scoring at the 1990 World Championships. He also took part in the World Cup of Hockey in 1996 and was a member of the Canadian Olympic team in Nagano in 1998.

ALEXEI ZHAMNOV Prior to his arrival in the NHL, Alexei Zhamnov won a bronze medal as a member of the Soviet national team at the 1991 World Championships and also played at the 1991 Canada Cup. After the breakup of the Soviet Union, he won a gold medal with the Unified Team at the 1992 Albertville Olympics and represented Russia at the 1992 World Championships. Since entering the NHL, Zhamnov missed a chance to compete at the 1994 World Championships because of injuries but played for Russia again at the 1996 World Cup of Hockey and at the Nagano Olympics in 1998, where he won a silver medal.

Zhamnov broke into the NHL with the Winnipeg Jets in 1992–93 and placed fourth in the league among rookies with 72 points. He missed 23 games due to injuries in 1993–94, but still recorded 71 points and led the Jets with 45 assists. The following year, Zhamnov emerged as one of the top players in the NHL. He scored five goals in a game on April 1, 1995, and his 65 points on 30 goals and 35 assists ranked third in the league behind Jaromir Jagr and Eric Lindros during the abbreviated 48-game season. Zhamnov was named to the Second All-Star Team behind Lindros at center and was also the first Russian player ever to be nominated for the Lady Byng Trophy.

Zhamnov remained a member of the Jets through their last season in Winnipeg in 1995–96, but after the team moved to Phoenix he was traded to the Chicago Blackhawks on August 16, 1996, in a deal that brought Jeremy Roenick to the Coyotes.

JOHN A. ZIEGLER Jr. graduated from the University of Michigan in 1957 and began doing legal work for Bruce Norris, the Detroit Red Wings and the Detroit Olympia in 1959. He joined the NHL Board of Governors as an alternate governor for the Red Wings in 1966 and in September of 1977, he became the fourth NHL president in league history. He had played amateur hockey in the Detroit area from 1949 until 1969.

During his tenure as NHL president, Ziegler forged a strong working relationship with the NHL Players' Association and helped to negotiate the entry of four World Hockey Association teams into the NHL in 1979. He remained as president until the end of the 1991–92 season, when he was succeeded by Gil Stein. Ziegler was elected to the Hockey Hall of Fame as a builder in 1987.

Section 2

INTERNATIONAL BIOGRAPHICAL REGISTER

*S*OME OF THE PLAYERS AND GOALTENDERS *listed in this section also have additional entries in Section 1 of this chapter. Players with listings in both include North American stars who have had distinguished international hockey careers (e.g. Taffy Abel, Wayne Gretzky) or top European players who have had significant NHL careers (e.g. Borje Salming, Sergei Fedorov).*

Players are listed alphabetically by country. Due to political changes in Europe, many players have represented more than one country in their international hockey careers. IIHF-standard three-letter abbreviations are used to indicate the country each player has most recently represented in international competition as a player, coach or executive. Some players have represented more than one of these countries over the course of their careers. A list of IIHF country abbreviations is found on page 509.

AUSTRALIA

CHARLES COOPER His first international appearance took place in 1987 at the World and European Championships (Pool D)... The Australian team won the tournament... Finished the tournament with an amazing 18 goals and 24 assists for 42 points in seven games... Was second on the overall scoring list... Played forward for the Australian national team and took part in four other World Championships—Pool C in 1993, 1994 and 1995 and Pool D in 1997... Starred in 1995 tournament, collecting nine goals and six assists for 15 points in six games.

DAMIAN HOLLAND One of the best goalies in the history of Australian hockey... Made his debut on the international scene in 1989 at the World and European Championships (Pool C)... Saw action in five games... His second appearance, at the 1990 World Championships (Pool D) was very successful—he was named the best goaltender of the tournament... He earned the honor again two years later at the 1992 World Championships (Pool C)... Was the team's number-one goaltender at the World Championships (Pool C) in 1994 and 1995.

AUSTRIA

RICK CUNNINGHAM One of the best players in the history of Austrian hockey... He played in 83 games for the national team collecting 29 goals and 43 assists for 72 points... Starred at the World and European Championships in the late 1970s and 1980s... Was named the best defenseman of the tournament in 1979 (Pool B) and 1985 (Pool B)... Voted to the all-star team in 1979 (Pool B), 1981 (Pool C), 1982 (Pool B) and 1985 (Pool B).

Began his hockey career with HC Salzburg... Later played for Wiener EV, VSV Villach and EHC Lustenau... Spent nine seasons in the Austrian Bundesliga... Saw action in 296 games, collecting 224 goals and 373 assists for 597 points and 746 penalty minutes... He also played with the Ottawa Nationals and Toronto Toros in the World Hockey Association from 1972–73 to 1975–76.

DIETER KALT Played as a forward in 81 games for the Austrian national team... Scored 27 goals and added 12 assists for 39 points... From 1967 to 1972 he was the captain of the national team... Named coach of the Austrian national team in 1977... His son, Dieter Jr., is a member of the contemporary Austrian national team.

At the age of 14 he began to play for the juniors of Klagenfurter AC... In 1956, at 15, he made the seniors Klagenfurter AC team... Played for this club until 1970... Spent another two seasons with ATSE Graz... During his career he played on teams that won the national title 10 times... Scored 116 goals and 57 assists for 173 points... Coached Klagenfurter AC from 1974 to 1977... Under his coaching, the club won the national title in 1976 and 1977.

WERNER KERTH Became a member of the Austrian national team in 1986... Made his international debut at 1986 World and European Championships (Pool B)... Played at two Olympics and 10 World and European Championships, including Pool A appearances in 1995 and 1996... Had his best tournament in 1992 (Pool B), when he collected one goal and 11 assists for 12 points in seven games.

At the age of 16 he played on the same line with international star Alexander Yakushev while with the Kapfenberg club... He was the youngest player in the league... Later he became a three-time national champion with Klagenfurt and Innsbruck... Had a great season in 1992–93 with Graz, record-

ing 25 goals and 47 assists for 72 points in 52 games... Considered to be the leading player in Austria from 1988 to 1990... Nicknamed "Kertzky," to rhyme with Gretzky.

RUDOLF KILLIAS Named the head coach of the Swiss national team in 1974... Worked until 1977, leading the team to 32 wins in 68 games... Coached Swiss team at 1996 Olympics... Became the head coach of Austrian national team in 1980... During six seasons, his team won 46 games out of 81... Coached Austrian team at 1984 Olympics... In his career, coached at nine World and European Championships (Pools B and C).

Began his coaching career in the 1969–70 season with the Swiss club HC Ambri-Piotta... After a few seasons he coached the Swiss Nationals, he coached EHC Arosa in 1978–79... A few years later, in 1987, he began to coach in the Austrian league... From 1987 to 1989 he was the manager/coach of EV Innsbruck... In 1989, EV Innsbruck won the national Austrian title... Worked as a manager of SC Bern in Switzerland from 1989 to 1991... Led SC Bern to a championship title in 1991

RUDOLF KONIG Played for the Austrian national team from 1975 to 1989... Holds the Austrian record for appearances with the national team—156 games... Played at the 1976, 1984 and 1988 Olympics and at 10 World and European Championships... In 1978, starred at the Pool C tournament, collecting 14 goals and eight assists for 22 points in seven games... Had his best tournament in 1982 (Pool B)... Was first in scoring overall, named the best forward and voted to the all-star team.

He began his amazing career at the age of 16, with Klagenfurter AC... Won the national title with this club in his rookie season... Won a total of nine national titles, all with Klagenfurter AC... Retired in 1990... One of the best forwards in the history of Austrian hockey.

EDWARD LEBLER Made his debut with the Austrian national team in 1982 at the World and European Championships (Pool B)... Played at the 1984 and 1988 Olympics... Spent nine seasons with the national team (until 1990), ranking as one of the top-scoring forwards on the team.

Born in Canada, he made his first appearance in the Austrian league in 1981–82 with HC Salzburg... After one season, he joined the famous Klagenfurter AC... Played there until 1989 and was a member of teams that won the national title in 1985, 1986, 1987 and 1988... From 1989 to 1992 he played for EC Villach... In 1992 he became a national champion once again... Joined EK Zell am See in 1992.

MANFRED MUHR Became a member of the Austrian national team in 1988... Made his international debut at the 1988 Olympics... Saw action at two Olympics and eight World and European Championships... His most successful tournament was the 1992 World Championships (Pool B), where he collected four goals and six assists for 10 points in seven games.

Went to Canada at the age of 15 and played one year... Came back home and built very successful career in Austria... Won five national titles with Klagenfurt and Villach.

RICHARD NASHEIM Became an Austrian citizen in 1991 and was invited to the Austrian national team... He has played in every major international tournament since... Was second-best scorer overall and named to the all-star team at the Pool B World Championships in 1992... Played at one Olympics and seven World and European Championships.

Born in Regina, Saskatchewan... Began his hockey career in Canada... Moved to Austria and soon became one of the best players in the history of Austrian hockey... Played for Feldkirch... He was the Austrian League top scorer four times, most recently in 1992–93 when he had 46 goals and 57 assists for 103 points in 50 games for Feldkirch.

JOSEF PUSCHNIG Played at three Olympics and 11 World and European Championships... In 1972 (Pool C) and 1973 (Pool B) he was named to the all-star team of the tournament... In 1972 he was also named the best forward... In his career, he played in 123 games for the Austrian national team, collecting 50 goals and 54 assists for 104 points.

One of the legendary players of Austrian hockey... Began to play for Klagenfurter AC in 1963 at the age of 17... Spent his entire career with Klagenfurter AC... Played on 11 national championship teams... Saw action in 299 games, recording 190 goals and 296 assists for 486 points.

GERHARD PUSCHNIK He became a member of the Austrian national team in 1987... Played in the 1988 Calgary Olympics and the 1994 Lillehammer Games and at 10 IIHF World Championships... Was fifth overall in scoring at the Pool B World Championships in 1992, collecting eight goals and seven assists for 15 points in seven games.

Spent his entire career with Feldkirch, playing on teams that won the national title seven times... His most successful season was 1992–93 when he saw action in 50 games, recording 34 goals and 45 assists for 79 points to rank tenth in league scoring.

BRIAN STANKIEWICZ Became an Austrian citizen and started to play for the national team in 1982... Played at the Olympics in 1984, 1988 and 1994 and saw action at eight World and European Championships (mostly in Pool B)... Named the best goaltender of the World and European Championships (Pool B) in 1982 and 1991... In 1982 he was also named to the tournament all-star team.

Born in Toronto, Ontario... Began to play in Austria in 1980 with HC Salzburg... After two years with HC Salzburg, he played one season each with Wiener EV and WAT Stadlau... Played for EV Innsbruck beginning in 1984 and in 1993 joined EC Graz... He was on a national champion with EV Innsbruck in 1989... One of the best goalies in the history of Austrian hockey... Nicknamed "Hexer" which means "Magic Man."

KEN TYLER Was invited to work with the Austrian national team in 1991 and replaced Ludek Bukac, the famous Czech coach. Tyler's team won the Pool B World Championships in 1992 and was promoted to Pool A... Austrian national team was ninth at the Pool A World Championships in 1993... Coached the Austrian national team at the 1994 Olympics and at five World Championships.

Born in Toronto, Ontario... Worked as a head coach in Canada before arriving in Austria... Coached the teams of McGill University and the University of Windsor in the Canadian Inter-university Athletic Union... Later worked in Switzerland as a coach of Ajoie and Geneva.

WALTER ZNENAHLIK A member of the Austrian national team at 15 World and European Championships (Pool A three times) and at two Olympics... Played in 129 games, recording 49 goals and 29 assists for 78 points... Named to the all-star team of 1972 World and European Championships (Pool C)... After retiring, he coached Austrian national team... His son Peter is the member of the national team.

Spent 16 seasons in the Austrian league playing for Wiener EV, VEU Feldkirch, EC Kitzbuhel, WAT Stadlau and HC Salzburg... His teams won the national title three times... In his career he played in 282 games, collecting 56 goals and 104 assists for 160 points... After retiring he coached different Austrian clubs: WAT Stadlau (1972 to 1974 and 1981 to 1985), HC Salzburg (1976 to 78), Wiener EV (1978 to 1981 and 1988–89), EHC Lustenau (1985–86), UEC Modling (1986 to 1988), EC Graz (1989 to 1992).

BELARUS
see page 1859

BELGIUM

PAUL LOICQ began skating as a 16-year-old in 1906 and was selected to the national hockey team in his native Belgium three years later. He represented his country at the first World Championships held in conjunction with the 1920 Antwerp Olympics. Off the ice, Loicq had graduated from university as a lawyer and served with distinction in the Belgian army during World War I.

Loicq was elected president of the International Ice Hockey Federation in 1927 and held the office for 20 years. During that time, hockey's popularity increased rapidly across Europe, with both the World and Olympic championships doing much to increase the game's international status.

MIKE PELLEGRIMS One of the best Belgian players in the 1990s... He made his debut with the Belgian national team in 1989 at the World and European Championships (Pool D)... Helped his team gain a promotion to Pool C for the next year... Named the best defenseman of the tournament in 1990 and again in 1991... He also played for Belgian national team at the 1992 and 1993 World Championships (Pool C).

Joined French club SP Brest in 1994 after playing in Belgium... In 1995–96, he played on the championship team of France as a member of SP Brest... Recorded 14 goals and 22 assists for 36 points in 35 games that year... Joined the German club Adler Mannheim before 1996–97 season... Won the German national title with his new team.

WALTER STAPPAERTS A veteran forward of the Belgian national team who made his first appearance on the international scene in 1989 at the World and European Championships (Pool D)... Helped his team to be promoted to Pool C... Played five years in a row (from 1991 to 1995) in the Pool C World Championships... Named one of three best players in Belgium in 1991... Had his best performance at the World Championships in 1995, collecting three goals and six assists for nine points in six games.

LUC VAN WALLE One of the best Belgian goaltenders of the 1990s... He made his debut with the national team in 1991 at the World and European Championships (Pool C)... Named one of three best Belgian players of the tournament... Has played at every World Championship tournament since 1991 (Pools C and D)... Had his best performance in the 1994 World Championships (Pool C) when he allowed only 10 goals in four 4 games and had a goals-against average of 2.86.

TIM VOS A veteran defenseman of the Belgian national team, he made his debut on the international scene in 1989 at the World and European Championships (Pool D)... Belgium won the tournament that year and was promoted to Pool C... At the 1991 World and European Championships (Pool C), he was named one of three best players on his team... Has regularly played for the Belgian national team in throughout the 1990s... Had his best tournament in 1994 (Pool C), collecting four goals and two assists for six points in five games.

BULGARIA

VALENTIN DIMOV One of the best forwards in the history of Bulgarian hockey, he played 10 years for the Bulgarian national team... His first appearance was in 1981 at the World and European Championships (Pool C)... The rookie recorded four goals and three assists for seven points in seven games at that tournament and became a regular on the national team... He played for the national team until the 1991 World and European Championships (Pool C)... His best performance was in 1982, when he collected five goals and four assists for nine points in seven games.

BORIS MIHAILOV A veteran forward of the Bulgarian national team who made his first appearance on the international scene in 1985 at the World and European Championships (Pool C)... He quickly became a regular with Bulgarian national team and played for 13 years... Participated at tournaments of Pools B, C and D at the World and European Championships... Had his best performance in 1996 (Pool D), scoring four goals in five games.

KONSTANTIN MIHAILOV Considered one of the best goalies in the history of Bulgarian hockey... He began his career with the national team in 1985, playing at the World and European Championships (Pool C)... Played 13 seasons with the national team, participating in Pools B, C and D of the World and European Championships... The highlight of his career was in 1990 when he was named the best goaltender of the Pool C World and European Championships.

ATANAS TODOROV One of the best forwards in Bulgarian hockey during the 1970s and 1980s... He played at six World and European Championships (Pool C) in a row... Made his first appearance in 1978 and played for the national team until 1985... In 1982, had the best tournament of his career, collecting three goals and two assists for five points in seven games.

CANADA

GLENN ANDERSON After Canada's official return to international hockey at the World Championships in 1977, Father David Bauer was able to convince Hockey Canada to reinstitute the national team program for the still strictly amateur Olympic Games. Among the players who would compete for Canada at the 1980 Olympics was Glenn Anderson. The Canadian team finished sixth at the Lake Placid Games, and Anderson went on to an NHL career that would see him play on six Stanley Cup champions.

In addition to his NHL success, Anderson was also a member of Canadian teams that won the Canada Cup in 1984 and 1987. He also represented Canada at the World Championships in 1989 and 1992, winning a silver medal with the 1989 Team Canada squad.

GARY BEGG became a member of the Canadian national team when the program was established in 1963–64 to represent Canada in international events. A defensive defenseman, Begg was named to the tournament all-star team in 1966 when the Nats claimed their first World Championship medal, a bronze. He had also been a member of the team that finished fourth at the 1964 Innsbruck Olympics after a controversial change to the tie-breaking format and played with the fourth-place team at the 1965 World Championships. Later, Begg would add a bronze medal at the 1967 World Championships and conclude his international career with the Nats in 1969.

BRIAN BELLOWS first represented Canada when he played at the Canada Cup in 1984. He later played for his country at the World Championships in 1987, 1989 and 1990. He helped lead Canada to a silver medal at the 1989 event when he was named the best forward at the tournament after scoring eight goals and setting up six others for 14 points in 10 games.

Bellows had played 15 seasons in the NHL with the Minnesota North Stars, Montreal Canadiens (Stanley Cup champions in 1992–93), Tampa Bay Lightning and the Mighty Ducks of Anaheim before signing to play in Germany in 1997–98. After completing the season with the Berlin Capitals, he returned to the NHL late in the season as a member of the Washington Capitals.

ROB BLAKE After leading all NHL rookie defenseman in scoring with the Los Angeles Kings in 1990–91, Rob Blake was added to the Canadian roster for the 1991 World Championships and helped the team win a silver medal. In

1994, Blake was a member of the Team Canada squad that won the country's first World Championship title since 1961. He earned a second gold medal in 1997 when he collected two goals and two assists in 11 games and was named both a tournament all-star and best defenseman.

Blake was also named to Team Canada for the World Cup of Hockey in 1996, taking part in four games as Canada lost the World title to the United States. Blake was a member of the Canadian Olympic team in 1998, and though Canada finished out of the medals his strong play was recognized when he was named the top defenseman at the tournament.

CHARLIE BURNS was a member of the Whitby Dunlops in 1956–57 and helped the team win the Allan Cup that year. As winners of Canada's senior amateur championship, the Dunlops would represent the country at the 1958 World Championships. The Whitby team was strong at center with Burns, Bobby Attersley and Connie Broden and Canada outscored its opposition 78–4 in winning its first six games at the world tourney. A 4–2 win over the Soviet Union in the final game clinched the gold medal. Though his six points (three goals and three assists) in seven games ranked only sixth in scoring on the Canadian team, Burns' strong two-way play earned him the selection as the best forward at the World Championships that year. He joined the Detroit Red Wings in 1958–59 and went on to spend 11 years in the NHL with Detroit, Boston, Oakland, Pittsburgh and Minnesota.

MIKE BOSSY One of the most prolific goal scorers in NHL history, Mike Bossy also starred on the international level at the Canada Cup tournaments in 1981 and 1984. Though Canada was defeated 8–1 by the Soviet Union in the championship game in 1981, Bossy's eight goals led the tournament and his 11 points were just one behind Wayne Gretzky's total of 12. (Bryan Trottier, Guy Lafleur and Alexei Kasatonov also had 11 points that year.) Bossy was named a tournament all-star.

Bossy was back at the Canada Cup in 1984 and his overtime goal in the one-game semifinal with the Soviets that year gave Canada a 3–2 win and advanced the team to the finals where they beat Sweden in two-straight games. Bossy played on a line with New York Islanders teammates John Tonelli and Brent Sutter at that tournament. Tonelli was named the Canada Cup's Most Valuable Player.

ROGER BOURBONNAIS was a member of Father David Bauer's Canadian national team from the time of its inception in 1963–64 until it was disbanded in 1970. During that time Bourbonnais played at two Winter Olympic Games and at the World Championships four times. He won a bronze medal at the Grenoble Olympics in 1968, after having played for bronze medal-winning teams at the World Championships in 1966 and 1967. Bourbonnais was one of the top offensive talents on a Canadian squad that would continually struggle to score goals. He led the Nats with five assists at the 1964 Innsbruck Olympics and generally ranked among the club's top scorers at all major international events.

RAYMOND BOURQUE One of the greatest defenseman in NHL history, Raymond Bourque made his international debut at the 1981 Canada Cup. Canada was crushed 8–1 by the Soviet Union in the championship game that year. Bourque was back at the Canada Cup in 1984 when Team Canada defeated Sweden in the finals to regain its title. In 1987, Bourque's eight points (two goals and six assists) ranked sixth overall and first among defenseman as Canada again won the Canada Cup, this time defeating the Soviets in a thrilling three-game final. His exploits that year earned him a selection to the tournament all-star team.

In 1991, Bourque turned down an invitation to play in yet another Canada Cup tournament, as he would with the World Cup of Hockey in 1996 when he stated that he preferred to spend the time with his family. In 1998, Bourque once again represented Canada when he took part in the Olympic Games.

CARL BREWER Because of his stormy relationship with Toronto Maple Leafs coach and general manager Punch Imlach, Carl Brewer retired from the NHL after the 1964–65 season. He fought to regain his amateur status and joined the Canadian national team in 1966–67. Brewer finally provided the Nats with a defenseman who could be a creative passer out of his own end and helped give the team its strongest roster ever. He was named to the all-star team at the 1967 World Championships after Canada captured a bronze medal.

Brewer played hockey in Finland in 1966–67 and later returned to the NHL with the Detroit Red Wings in 1969–70. In 1976, He served as an assistant coach with the Finnish team at the first Canada Cup tournament.

KEN BRODERICK helped provide the Canadian national team with solid goaltending from 1963–64 until 1967–68, usually in tandem with either Seth Martin or Wayne Stephenson. He was a backup to Martin at the 1964 Innsbruck Olympics when a controversial change to the tie-breaking format dropped Canada into fourth place, but was the top goaltender ahead of Stephenson at Grenoble in 1968 when the Canadians earned an Olympic bronze medal.

In addition to his Olympic appearances, Broderick also tended goal for Canada at the World Championships in 1965 and 1966. Sharing duties with Martin in 1966, Broderick allowed just two goals in three games for a 0.66 goals-against average as the Canadian team took home a bronze medal. Following his stint with the national team, Broderick played briefly in the NHL with the Minnesota North Stars and Boston Bruins.

DENIS BRODEUR The father of star NHL goaltender Martin Brodeur (who represented Canada at the World Championships and the World Cup of Hockey in 1996, as well as the Olympics in 1998) Denis Brodeur earned a bronze medal with the Kitchener-Waterloo Dutchmen in 1956 when that team represented Canada at the Winter Olympics in Cortina d'Ampezzo, Italy.

Brodeur shared netminding duties with Keith Woodall at the 1956 Olympics, with both men posting 3–1 records in four games each. Brodeur registered a shutout in Canada's 4–0 win over Germany to open the competition and allowed just eight goals in his four games for a goals-against average of 2.00. Unfortunately, his 4–1 loss to the United States and Woodall's 2–0 loss to the Soviets in the final game doomed Canada to a third-place finish, the country's worst Olympic result to that point in history.

SEAN BURKE After serving as the backup goaltender with Canada's silver medal-winning squad at the 1986 World Junior Championships, Sean Burke moved on from the Toronto Marlboros of the Ontario Hockey League to join Canada's national team in 1986–87. The following season, he shared netminding duties with Andy Moog and played four games for Team Canada at the 1988 Calgary Olympics.

Burke earned a silver medal with Team Canada at the World Championships in 1989 and won a second silver in 1991. A contract dispute with the New Jersey Devils saw Burke once again join the Canadian national team for the 1991–92 season and win a silver medal at the Olympics after posting a 2.37 goals-against average in seven games. Burke finally earned gold in 1997 when his sparkling 2.17 goals-against average in 11 games helped Canada win the World Championship. Burke had been a member of Canada's Canada Cup-winning team of 1991, but had not seen any action.

BOBBY CLARKE was one of only five players (Phil Esposito, Paul Henderson, Yvan Cournoyer and Brad Park) to play all eight games for Team Canada at the historic 1972 Summit Series with the Soviet Union. Clarke's six points (two goals and four assists) ranked third on the team behind Esposito and Henderson.

Four years later, on January 11, 1976, Clarke led his Philadelphia Flyers to a 4–1 victory over the Central Red Army team in a game remembered for the Soviet team's decision to leave the ice in protest of the Flyers' tactics. It was the only game the Red Army team lost during its four-game "Super Series" tour. In September of that year, Clarke was a member of the Team Canada squad that won the inaugural Canada Cup tournament. His final international appearance came at the World Championships in 1982, helping Canada earn a bronze medal.

PAUL COFFEY The highest scoring defenseman in the history of the NHL has also enjoyed great success at the international level as Paul Coffey helped Canada win the Canada Cup in 1984, 1987 and 1991. Coffey was named to the all-star team at the 1984 event after finishing tied for second in tournament scoring with 11 points (three goals and eight assists), just one point behind Wayne Gretzky.

In addition to his three Canada Cup appearances, Coffey was a member of Team Canada at the World Cup of Hockey in 1996, collecting seven assists in eight games though Canada lost to the United States in the finals. Coffey also represented Canada at the World Championships in 1990.

GARY DINEEN was a top offensive talent in the early years of Father David Bauer's Canadian national team. On a team that generally struggled to put the puck in the net, Dineen led the team with nine points (three goals and six assists) in seven games at the 1964 Innsbruck Olympics and collected a team leading six goals and five assists in seven games at the 1965 World Championships. Unfortunately, Canada finished in fourth place at both tournaments. Dineen contributed a goal and four assists to Canada's bronze medal-winning performance at the 1967 IIHF World Championships and was also a member of the bronze medal-winning team at the 1968 Winter Olympics Olympics in Grenoble, France.

MARCEL DIONNE An NHL superstar on a team that rarely enjoyed playoff success, Marcel Dionne represented his country with distinction at four World Championships. Dionne was named the best forward at the tournament in 1978 after scoring nine goals and collecting 12 points in 10 games as Canada returned to the medal podium for the first time since 1967 with a third-place finish. Dionne played for Canada at the 1979 World Championships and earned a bronze medal again in 1983 and 1986.

Dionne was also a member of Team Canada at the first Canada Cup in 1976, collecting six points (a goal and five assists) in seven games as Canada won

the inaugural event. He had four goals in six games in 1981 when Canada lost the Canada Cup to the Soviet Union.

MURRAY DOWEY was the last member of the team added to the roster of the Royal Canadian Air Force (RCAF) Flyers. The goaltender was added as a replacement by Dick Ball after doctors discovered a lung condition that would prevent Ball from traveling to Europe for the 1948 Winter Olympics. Dowey was added to the Flyers from the roster of the Barker's Hockey Club in Toronto, which also provided Wally Halder and George Mara to the Canadian Olympic team.

Dowey recorded five shutouts in eight games for Canada at the 1948 St. Moritz Games and allowed only five goals in total. His excellent record was key to Canada claiming the gold medal, as the Flyers won the Olympic tournament because of a better goals average (69 for and five against) than Czechoslovakia (80 and 18) after the two teams finished with identical 7–0–1 records, including a scoreless tie against one another.

Dowey also became a part of Canadian Olympic trivia when he was penalized for throwing the puck forward (in violation of international rules) late in a 3–1 win over Sweden in the opening game of the 1948 tournament. Dowey was forced to spend the last eight seconds of the game in the penalty box—the only Canadian goaltender ever so punished—while defenseman Andre Laperriere used his stick and gloves to guard the net.

PHIL ESPOSITO Although Paul Henderson scored the series-winning goal for Team Canada in 1972, it was Phil Esposito who was both the club's top scorer and its emotional leader. Esposito had seven goals and six assists for 13 points in the eight-game summit with the Soviets. He scored the first goal for Team Canada just 30 seconds into game one at the Montreal Forum on September 2, 1972, but, like his teammates and the rest of Canadians, Esposito quickly learned that the Soviets would not be pushovers. His impassioned plea for fan support, and his disgust at the treatment the team had received, in a television interview after game four in Vancouver helped unite Team Canada for the final four games of the series in Moscow.

Four years after the historic 1972 Summit Series, Esposito was again a member of Team Canada at the inaugural Canada Cup. No longer the NHL's most dominant scorer, Esposito nonetheless managed four goals and three assists in seven games to rank among the team leaders as Canada won the tournament. Esposito made his final international appearance in 1977 when a Canadian team returned to the World Championships for the first time since launching a boycott of International Ice Hockey Federation events in 1970. Esposito had seven goals and three assists in 10 games and was selected as the best Canadian forward, but Canada could finish no better than fourth at the tournament.

THEOREN FLEURY was a member of the Canadian national junior team that was disqualified from the World Junior Championships in 1987 after brawling with the Soviet Union. He returned to the tournament the following year to captain Canada to a gold medal. Fleury had six goals and two assists in 1988 and was named to the tournament all-star team along with fellow Canadians Greg Hawgood and Jimmy Waite and future NHL stars Sergei Fedorov and Alexander Mogilny.

In 1990, Fleury represented Canada at the World Championships, where his 11 points (four goals and seven assists) ranked second on the team behind Steve Yzerman. Fleury returned to the World Championships in 1991 and helped Canada win a silver medal. In September of 1991, he was a member of the Canada Cup-winning Team Canada squad. In 1996, Fleury represented Canada at the World Cup of Hockey and in 1998 he was a member of the Canadian team at the Nagano Olympics.

FRANK FREDRICKSON was the captain of the Winnipeg Falcons, world hockey champions at the Olympics in 1920. Fredrickson was the tournament's leading scorer with 12 goals in just three games as the Canadian team swept to the gold medal.

Comprised mainly of players of Icelandic descent, the Falcons not only had to battle for respect in British-Protestant dominated Winnipeg they had to battle for a league in which to play. Both before and after World War I, Falcons players experienced prejudice, but by 1920 they had become Canada's darlings by winning the first Olympic hockey tournament.

The 1920 event was staged in Antwerp, Belgium in April in conjunction with the Olympic Games that were to be held in the city that summer. As Allan Cup (senior amateur) champions of Canada, the Falcons were sent overseas to represent their country. Not wishing to embarrass their outclassed European opponents by running up scores, the Falcons beat Czechoslovakia 15–0 in their opening game and then all but clinched the gold medal by defeating the United States 2–0 in game two. Frank Fredrickson's seven goals then paced the Falcons to a 12–1 victory over Sweden in their final game. Many years later, Fredrickson admitted that the Falcons had allowed Sweden to score their one goal simply because they had taken a liking to the team's players.

GRANT FUHR One of the winningest goalies in NHL history, Grant Fuhr

first showcased his talent on the international stage as one of three goaltenders (Pete Peeters and Reggie Lemelin) with Team Canada at the 1984 Canada Cup. In 1987, Fuhr played all nine games as the Canadians again won the Canada Cup this time beating the Russians in a thrilling three-game final. Though his 3.34 goals-against average was among the highest at the event, his record of 6–1–2 was the best and Fuhr was selected to the tournament all-star team. In 1989, Fuhr combined with Sean Burke in the Canadian goal to help lead Canada to a silver medal at the World Championships.

MIKE GARTNER's first international appearance for Canada came at the World Junior Championships in 1978 where Team Canada finished in third place behind the Soviets and Sweden. After entering the NHL in 1979–80, Gartner went on to appear at the World Championships for Canada three years in a row (1981 to 1983) as his NHL team (the Washington Capitals) struggled to qualify for the playoffs. His speed was an asset on the larger international ice surfaces and Gartner helped Canada win a bronze medal in 1982 and 1983. He was also a member of championship Canadian teams at the Canada Cup in 1984 and 1987.

WAYNE GRETZKY The most prolific scorer in NHL history, Wayne Gretzky has also been a major player on the international hockey stage. In 1978, he led Team Canada to a bronze medal behind the Soviets and Sweden at the World Junior Championships, leading the tournament with 17 points (eight goals and nine assists) in six games and being named both the best forward and the center on the all-star team. He also starred for Canada at the Canada Cup in 1981, 1984, 1987 and 1991, leading the tournament in scoring each year and being named to the all-star team when Canada won it all in 1984, 1987 and 1991. In 1987, Gretzky set up Mario Lemieux for the Canada Cup winning goal in the 6–5 deciding game of a thrilling three-game final series with the Soviets. This goal ranks among the greatest and most frequently replayed in Canada's international hockey history.

In 1996, Gretzky was a member of the Canadian team at the World Cup of Hockey and in 1998 he represented his country at the Olympic Games in Nagano. It was his dream to win a gold medal at the Olympics, but Canada came up short against the Czech Republic in the semifinals and had to settle for a disappointing fourth-place finish.

With his teams generally in the hunt for the Stanley Cup during his heyday, Wayne Gretzky has only represented Canada at the World Championships in 1982. That year he lead the tournament in scoring with 14 points (six goals and eight assists) and was named to the all star team as Canada earned a bronze medal.

WALLY HALDER The Royal Canadian Air Force (RCAF) Flyers began training to represent Canada at the 1948 Winter Olympics in October of 1947. However just 10 days before sailing for Europe on January 8, 1947 George Mara and Wally Halder of the Barker's Hockey Club in Toronto were added to the team, and the two were key contributor's to Canada's gold medal victory.

Halder scored the go-ahead goal in Canada's 3–1 win over Sweden to open the Olympics and went on to collect 21 goals and eight assists in eight games as the RCAF Flyers went 7–0–1 through the round robin tournament. He had five goals in a 21–1 rout of Italy and five more in a 12–3 romp over the United States. Halder later scored the opening goal in a 3–0 win over host Switzerland that clinched the gold medal. Only a scoreless tie with the Czechoslovakia team blemished Canada's otherwise perfect record at the Winter Olympics. The Czechoslovakian Olympic team also finished 7–0–1, but Canada claimed the gold medal thanks to a better goal differential of 69 for and only five against to Czechoslovakia's 80 and 18.

CRAIG HARTSBURG A solid, if unspectacular, defenseman throughout his NHL career, Craig Hartsburg also distinguished himself on the international stage. He was twice a member of Canada's national junior team, winning a silver medal in 1977 and a bronze in 1978. He was a member of the Canadian team that was beaten handily by the Soviets in the final game of the 1981 Canada Cup, but had a chance to redeem himself as a member of Team Canada's dramatic 1987 championship team.

In addition to the World Juniors and Canada Cup, Hartsburg also represented his country three times at the World Championships. He was a bronze medal winner with Team Canada in 1982 and 1983, and though Canada finished fourth at the 1987 World Championships Hartsburg's play was rewarded when he was named the tournament's best defenseman.

DALE HAWERCHUK Although Team Canada failed to reach the medal podium when Dale Hawerchuk was a member of the squad at the World Junior Championships in 1981, he would later earn a bronze medal at the World Championships in both 1982 and 1986. In 1989, Hawerchuk had four goals and eight assists four 12 points in 10 games as Canada captured a silver medal. His greatest international successes came at the Canada Cup, where the gifted offensive center was usually asked to take on a supporting role. Hawerchuk collected six points in nine games in Canada's thrilling victory in 1987 and had five points in nine games in the 1991 Canada Cup championship.

PAUL HENDERSON scored the most famous goal in Canadian hockey history on September 28, 1972. With 34 seconds remaining in the final game of the eight-game Summit Series against the Soviet Union, Henderson slipped the puck past Vladislav Tretiak for a 6–5 Team Canada victory and a 4–3–1 win in a series most Canadian players and fans had expected to sweep. Henderson had scored the winning goal in each of the last three games as Canada rallied to salvage the series and a country's national pride. His seven goals tied Phil Esposito and Alexander Yakushev for the lead in the historic eight-game event.

Henderson had been little more than an average hockey player during his NHL career, but his goal to win the 1972 series elevated him to a national hero. When he left the NHL for the World Hockey Association after the 1973–74 season he was an obvious choice for the Team Canada roster in the 1974 series between the Soviets and the WHA All-Stars. Henderson, Frank Mahovlich and Pat Stapleton were the only two players to play in both the 1972 and 1974 series. Henderson could contribute only two goals and one assist to the cause in 1974 (all in an 8–5 loss in game three) as the Soviets beat Canada 4–2–2 in the eight-game set.

W.A. HEWITT was secretary of the Ontario Hockey Association from 1903 to 1961 and registrar and treasurer of the Canadian Amateur Hockey Association for 39 years. He also spent 41 years in the newspaper business in Toronto, 32 as sports editor of the *Toronto Star*.

In 1920, Hewitt accompanied the Allan Cup-champion Winnipeg Falcons to Antwerp, Belgium for the first Olympic hockey tournament, which would later be considered the first World Championships. Surprised by the general lack of hockey knowledge he found in Europe, Hewitt convinced the directors of the International Ice Hockey Federation to adopt Canadian rules for the competition. The IIHF was so impressed by Hewitt and his proposal that they gave him the honor of refereeing the first Olympic game—an 8–0 win by Sweden over Belgium on April 23, 1920.

Having served as team secretary for the Falcons at the 1920 tournament, Hewitt later functioned as the general manager of the Toronto Granites when they won the first Winter Olympic hockey tournament in Chamonix, France in 1924. He also represented the Toronto Varsity Grads as manager at the 1928 Olympics in St. Moritz.

FRAN HUCK joined the Canadian national team in 1965–66 and was a member of the squad until the program was disbanded in 1970. He then went on to a professional career that saw him play briefly with the Montreal Canadiens and St. Louis Blues in the NHL and with the Winnipeg Jets and Minnesota Fighting Saints in the World Hockey Association.

Huck made his international debut with the Nats at the 1966 World Championships, leading the club with eight points on four goals and four assists. He helped Canada earn a bronze medal that year and was named to the tournament all-star team. Huck led Canada with 11 points (five goals and six assists) at the 1967 World Championships and earned another bronze medal. He again led Canada in scoring with the bronze medal-winning Olympic team in 1968, collecting four goals and five assists.

MARSHALL JOHNSTON was a member of the Canadian national team at four major international tournaments, the Winter Olympics in 1964 and 1968 and the World Championships in 1966 and 1967. Bronze medal winners in 1966 and 1967, Johnston helped Canada win Olympic bronze at Grenoble in 1968 when he led the team with six assists in seven games. Johnston's two goals at that tournament gave him eight points, ranking second on the squad behind Fran Huck's nine points.

Following his Olympic experience, Johnston joined the NHL's Minnesota North Stars, where he played sparingly over four seasons before earning regular duty with the California Golden Seals.

PAUL KARIYA had already established a sterling reputation in international hockey prior to his arrival in the NHL. A minor contributor to Canada's disappointing sixth-place squad at the 1992 World Junior Championships, Kariya collected two goals and a team-leading six assists in seven games as Canada rebounded to win the gold medal in 1993. He was rewarded for his play that year with a selection to the tournament all-star team. Kariya also played for Team Canada at the World Championships that season and had two goals and seven assists in eight games, although Canada finished out of the medals despite a 6–2 record.

A contract dispute with the Mighty Ducks of Anaheim (who had made him the fourth overall draft choice in 1993) resulted in Kariya joining Canada's national team in 1993–94. He was a member of Canada's silver medal-winning team at the Olympics that year but was stopped in a shootout in the final game that gave the gold medal to Sweden. Kariya later redeemed himself at the World Championships, leading Canada in scoring with five goals and seven assists as Team Canada defeated Finland in a shootout to win the world title for the first time since 1961. Kariya was second only to Mats Sundin in scoring at the 1994 World Championships and was named the tournament's best forward as well as an All-Star.

After joining the Mighty Ducks in 1994–95, Kariya again had the chance to represent Canada at the World Championships in 1996. Once again he was named the best forward and an All-Star although Team Canada could only manage a silver medal this year. Kariya was selected to the Canadian squad for the World Cup of Hockey in 1996 and the Nagano Olympics in 1998, but injuries kept him out of both tournaments.

GUY LAFLEUR had led the NHL in scoring for the first time with 125 points (56 goals and 69 assists) in 1975–76 and, as such, was named to the Canadian roster for the inaugural Canada Cup tournament in 1976. Lafleur picked up a goal and five assists in six games for Team Canada, who defeated Czechoslovakia to win the event. Lafleur was again a member of Team Canada in 1981, collecting two goals and nine assists for 11 points in seven games (good for a second-place tie in tournament scoring with Mike Bossy, Bryan Trottier and Alexei Kasatonov and only one point behind Wayne Gretzky). Lafleur had a goal and an assist during Canada's 7–3 victory over the Soviet Union in the preliminary round of the 1981 Canada Cup, but, like Wayne Gretzky, was completely shutdown by the Soviets during their 8–1 victory in the championship game.

In addition to his Canada Cup experience, Lafleur represented his country at the World Championships in 1981 where, in accordance with international rules, he was forced to wear a helmet for the first time since his junior days. Lafleur contributed only one goal in seven games to a fourth-place finish by Canada that year.

JEAN-PAUL LAMIRANDE An NHL player briefly in the 1940s and 1950s with the New York Rangers and Montreal Canadiens, defenseman J.P. Lamirande was playing with the Quebec Aces of the Quebec Hockey League in 1957–58 before applying to have his amateur status reinstated and joining the Whitby Dunlops. Lamirande was one of several reinforcements (including former NHL star Sid Smith) added to the roster of the defending Allan Cup champions who were preparing to represent Canada at the World Championships. The Canadian club ran up six lopsided victories before defeating the Soviet Union 4–2 in the final game to win the World Championship.

Lamirande was a member of the Belleville McFarlands in 1958–59 when he once again had the chance to represent Canada abroad. The McFarlands were perfect through seven games of the 1959 World Championships and knew they had already clinched the gold medal before they played Czechoslovakia (and lost 5–3) in the final game. Lamirande had helped anchor a Canadian defense that allowed only nine goals in eight games and recorded four shutouts. He was named the best defenseman at the tournament.

JAMIE MACOUN was a member of Team Canada at the World Championships in 1985, 1990 and 1991, winning a silver medal at the event in 1985 and 1991. Macoun was named the best defenseman at the 1991 World Championship tournament. In addition to his solid play in his own end, he had four goals in eight games at the World Championship that year, more than half the total of seven goals he had scored in 79 games with the Calgary Flames during the NHL season.

MARIO LEMIEUX Although he played in only three major tournaments, Mario Lemieux scored one of the greatest goals in Canadian international hockey history when he took a pass from Wayne Gretzky and rammed the puck past Sergei Mylnikov at 18:34 of the third period to give Team Canada a 6–5 victory in the third and deciding game of the 1987 Canada Cup finals. Lemieux's 11 goals in the tournament established a Canada Cup record and his 18 points ranked second to Gretzky's 21 in scoring that year as Lemieux earned a spot on the Canada Cup all-star team.

Lemieux's first appearance on international ice came at the World Junior Championships in 1983. He had five goals and five assists to rank second behind Dave Andreychuk in Canadian scoring as Team Canada claimed a bronze medal that year, but Lemieux's unhappy experiences at this tournament contributed as much as his many injuries to his decision to limit his international play over the years. Lemieux was a late addition to Canada's World Championship roster in 1985 and collected 10 points in nine games as Canada settled for a silver medal after dropping the final game of the tournament 3–1 to Czechoslovakia. Lemieux turned down pleas to join Team Canada at the World Championships in 1986 and 1987, but was one of the first to accept the invitation for the 1987 Canada Cup. His play at that tournament, and the dedication to the game he learned from Wayne Gretzky, is often credited with elevating Lemieux from simply another talented performer to one of the greatest players in hockey history.

VICTOR LINDQUIST scored what proved to be the gold medal-winning goal for Canada at the 1932 Winter Olympics when he put the puck past American Frankie Farrell after 7:12 of overtime for a 2–1 victory in the opening game of the tournament. Lindquist later added two more goals and six assists in a pair of wins over Poland (9–0 and 10–0) and Germany (4–1 and 5–0) before Canada clinched the Olympic gold medal in the four-team tournament with a 1–1 triple-overtime tie against the United States in the final game.

It had been the Winnipeg Hockey Club that represented Canada in Lake Placid in 1932, and in 1935 Olympic teammates Vic Lindquist, Roy Hinkle and Romeo Rivers were members of the Winnipeg Monarchs team that won the World Championship. Lindquist later become a prominent referee and officiate games at the 1962 and 1963 World Championships.

ERIC LINDROS played on two gold medal-winning teams at the World Junior Championships and was a member of Canada's 1991 Canada Cup-winning squad as an 18-year-old prior to signing with the NHL's Philadelphia Flyers. He contributed three goals and two assists in eight games that year as Canada beat the United States in the finals of the tournament.

Lindros was only a minor contributor to Canada's 1990 World Junior Championship, but collected six goals and 11 assists to finish second in scoring (behind Doug Weight) in 1991 and earned a spot on the tournament all-star team. Lindros was again a member of Canada's World Junior Team in 1992, captaining a squad that finished a disappointing sixth. He redeemed himself later in the year with the Canadian Olympic team, scoring five goals and adding six assists in eight games as Canada earned a silver medal in its best Olympic performance since 1960. The second-place finish was Canada's first trip to the medal podium since 1968.

In 1993, Lindros played for Team Canada at the World Championships and led the tournament in goals (11) and points (17) to earn accolades as an all-star and as best forward despite Canada's fourth-place finish. Lindros later represented his country at the World Cup of Hockey in 1996 and was captain of Canada's Olympic team at Nagano in 1998.

DON LOCKHART The Canadian Amateur Hockey Association had difficulty finding a team to represent Canada at the 1954 World Championships before finally selecting Toronto's East York Lyndhursts. The team was not of as high a caliber as the clubs usually sent to represent Canada, but had little trouble outscoring its opponents 57–5 in running up a perfect record through its first six games at the world tournament.

The netminder who had recorded a 0.83 goals-against average to that point for Canada was Don Lockhart. Lockhart would be named to the tournament all-star team and was also honored as the best goalie at the event despite allowing seven goals in a surprising 7–2 victory by the USSR in the final game. The loss dropped Canada into second place and gave the Soviets the World Championship the first time that they had entered the tournament.

AL MacINNIS After a season in which he would earn First Team All-Star honors in the NHL, Al MacInnis made his international hockey debut when he played for Team Canada at the 1990 World Championships. The following year, he was a member of the Canada Cup-winning Canadian squad. MacInnis was selected to represent his country once again at the World Cup of Hockey in 1996, but an injury kept him out of the tournament. In 1998, MacInnis played for Canada at the Nagano Olympics.

BARRY MacKENZIE had been a member of Father David Bauer's Memorial Cup winning St. Michael's College team in 1961 and joined Father Bauer's Canadian national team in 1964. He played at the Olympics that year and later represented Canada again at the World Championships in 1965, 1966, and 1967, earning a bronze medal in both 1966 and 1967. In 1968, MacKenzie earned another bronze medal at the Winter Games in Grenoble.

Like most of the Canadian national team's defenseman, MacKenzie never scored a lot of points but was solid in his own end. After his international experience he played one season of professional hockey and spent six games in the NHL with the Minnesota North Stars in 1968–69.

GEORGE MARA and Wally Halder were late additions to the Royal Canadian Air Force Flyers roster when the team represented Canada at the 1948 Winter Olympic Games in St. Moritz, Switzerland. The two members of the Barker's Hockey Club in Toronto would become the RCAF Flyers' main offensive contributors, as Halder had 21 goals and eight assists and Mara collected 17 goals and set up nine others as Canada won the gold medal. The RCAF Flyers claimed the Olympic gold because of a better goal average than Czechoslovakia after both nations finished the tournament 7–0–1 including a scoreless tie against each other.

Mara scored Canada's first goal at the Olympic tournament in a 3–1 win over Sweden in the opening game and went on to enjoy four-goal games in wins over the United States (12–1) and Austria (12–0). He had five goals in a 21–1 win over Italy and picked up an assist in the 3–0 win over Switzerland that clinched the gold medal in the final game.

SETH MARTIN was a longtime Canadian amateur star who would see NHL action with the St. Louis Blues in 1967–68. Martin was a member of the Trail Smoke Eaters when they became the last Canadian amateur team to win the World Championship in 1961. The Canadian Amateur Hockey Association had wanted to add a new goaltender to Trail's roster, but coach Bobby Kromm stuck with Martin and he allowed only six goals in the five games he played at the world event that year, posting a 1.28 goals-against average and being

named the tournament's best goalie. He was particularly brilliant in Trail's 5–1 win over the Soviet Union in the final game, clinching the World Championship for Canada. Trail returned to the World Championships in 1963, and while Martin was again named the tournament's best goalie the Canadian team fell to fourth place.

By 1964, Canada had developed a national team program and would use this team as its representative at international events. Martin became a member of the national team and played at the Innsbruck Olympics in 1964 and at the World Championships again in 1966 and 1967, often sharing goaltending duties with Ken Broderick. Martin was named to the tournament all-star team in 1966 and was once again selected as the best goalie that year. He was the last Canadian goaltender to be so honored until Bill Ranford in 1994.

GEORGE McAVOY Team captain George McAvoy was in his third year with the Penticton Vees, having already led them to a Western Canadian title in 1952–53, and the Allan Cup in 1953–54 before helping the small-town team from British Columbia win the World Championship in 1955. The win helped avenge the loss by Toronto's East York Lyndhursts the season before when the Soviet Union had become World Champions for the first time.

McAvoy anchored a Penticton defense that allowed only six goals in winning all eight games en route to the 1955 World Championship. The Canadian team clinched the victory with a 5–0 win over the Soviets in the tournament's final game. A tough defensive player who took care of his own end first, McAvoy contributed two goals to Canada's World Championship victory at the 1955 tournament including the final tally in the win over the Soviets.

JACK McLEOD was the top offensive star on the Trail Smoke Eaters when that club became the last Canadian amateur team to win the World Championship in 1961. A former professional who had spent parts of five seasons with the New York Rangers in the NHL, McLeod had had his amateur status reinstated and was playing with the Moose Jaw Canucks before being added to the Smoke Eaters roster.

Sweden was considered to have a legitimate chance of upsetting the Canadian team in the opening game of the IIHF World Championships in 1961, but McLeod's two goals led the Smokies to a 6–1 victory. He would go on to collect 10 goals as Trail went 6–0–1 during the tournament, including two goals in the 5–1 win over the Soviet Union that clinched the title for Trail in the final game.

In 1962, McLeod was added to the roster of the Galt Terriers for their appearance at the World Championships. This year, he collected 11 goals and six assists and was named to the tournament all-star team although the Canadian club finished a disappointing second behind Sweden in an event boycotted by the Soviets. McLeod had five goals and seven assists for Trail when the Smoke Eaters once again represented Canada at the World Championships in 1963, but the team could finish no better than fourth.

In 1965–66, Jack McLeod joined the Canadian national team program as the club's head coach. In an effort to add more offense to the lineup, he was also inserted onto the playing roster for the 1966 World Championships. McLeod collected four goals in seven games as Canada finished third that year. He later coached the Nats to a bronze medal finish at the 1967 World Championships and at the Winter Olympics in Grenoble, France in 1968.

MARK MESSIER One of the great team leaders in NHL history, Mark Messier is a six-time Stanley Cup champion who has also contributed to Canada Cup-winning Canadian squads in 1984, 1987 and 1991. He also won a silver medal with Team Canada at the 1989 World Championships. In 1996, Messier served as an alternate captain with the Canadian team at the World Cup of Hockey. The decision to leave him off the 1998 Olympic roster was one of the team's most controversial decisions.

MORRIS MOTT joined the Canadian national team in 1965–66 and helped the team win a bronze medal at the World Championships in both 1966 and 1967. At the Winter Olympics in Grenoble in 1968, Mott led the team with five goals in seven games as Canada earned another bronze medal. Four of Mott's goals came in an 11–0 win over East Germany that got the Canadians back on track after a 5–2 upset loss to Finland. Mott also represented Canada at the 1969 World Championships and was a member of the national team until the program was dismantled in 1970.

Following his stint with the Nats, Mott played hockey at Queen's University in Kingston, Ontario. He later spent three seasons in the NHL with the California Golden Seals and played two games with the Winnipeg Jets of the World Hockey Association in 1975–76. He spent most of that year playing hockey in Sweden. After his playing career, Mott became a history professor at Brandon University in Manitoba.

KIRK MULLER first represented Canada in international hockey at the World Junior Championships in 1984 and was later added to the Canadian national team, where it was hoped his goal-scoring ability would bolster Canada's chances at the Olympics that year in Sarajevo. The 18-year-old Muller contributed two goals in six games at the Olympics, but the low-scoring Canadian

squad was shut out in all three games that made up the medal round and wound up in fourth place.

Over the next five seasons, Muller would join Team Canada at the World Championships four times (1985, 1986, 1987 and 1989). He was a silver medal winner in 1985 and 1989 and earned a bronze in 1986. The 1989 tournament was Muller's best as he scored six goals and added four assists for 10 points in nine games.

TERRY O'MALLEY was an original member of Father David Bauer's Canadian national team program and was with the club from its inception in 1963–64 until it was dismantled in 1970. During six seasons, O'Malley played at four World Championships and two Olympic Games. The defensive defenseman was a member of bronze medal-winning teams at the World Championships in 1966 and 1967 and at the Grenoble Olympics in 1968.

When Canada returned to play in International Ice Hockey Federation events in 1977, Father Bauer was able to convince Hockey Canada to re-establish the national team program in order to comply with the rules of sending an amateur team to the 1980 Winter Olympics in Lake Placid. A surprise player surviving the final roster cut that year was 39-year-old Terry O'Malley who would play at the Olympics again 16 years after making his international debut at the Games in Innsbruck.

BOBBY ORR Injuries kept Bobby Orr out of the historic Canada-Russia Summit Series in 1972, but the eight-time Norris Trophy winner as the NHL's best defenseman would use the inaugural Canada Cup tournament to spotlight his many talents on the international stage. Orr was brilliant in this series, taking care of business in the defensive end and also tying fellow defenseman Denis Potvin for the Team Canada scoring lead with nine points (two goals and seven assists) as the Canadian squad won the tournament. Not only was Orr named an all-star on defense, but he was also named the Canada Cup's most valuable player. The tournament would prove to be Orr's swan song though, as continued problems with his knees limited him to just 26 games over the final three years of his NHL career.

WILF PAIEMENT was a member of the first Canadian team to play at the World Championships since the country's boycott of international events in 1970 when he took part in the tournament in 1977. Paiement had scored 41 goals for the Colorado Rockies in his third NHL season that year to earn a spot on the Team Canada roster. Though he collected five goals and five assists for 10 points in 10 games, Canada could finish no better than fourth.

Paiement returned to the World Championships in 1978 and had six goals and one assist to help Canada finish on the podium with a bronze medal. Canada slipped to fourth again at the 1979 event, but Paiement earned honors as the best forward that year even though his three goals and three assists represented his lowest point total in the three years he played in IIHF World Championship tournaments.

GILBERT PERREAULT was a member of Team Canada in the historic 1972 Summit Series, but was one of four players (along with Vic Hadfield, Rick Martin and Jocelyn Guevremont) who earned the scorn of Canadian fans by leaving the team in Moscow to return to training camp with their NHL teams. On January 4, 1976, Perreault led his NHL team—the Buffalo Sabres—to a 12–6 win over the Soviet Wings for the first of only two victories by NHL clubs in the eight-game "Super Series" involving the Wings and the Central Red Army.

In September of 1976, Perreault was again a member of Team Canada for the inaugural Canada Cup series. His eight points that year (four goals and four assists) tied him for second in Canadian scoring with Bobby Hull, just one point back of team leaders Bobby Orr and Denis Potvin. Perreault was also with Team Canada for the 1981 event, which was won by the Soviets who defeated Canada 8–1 in the final game.

YANIC PERREAULT A high-scoring player in both junior hockey and the minor leagues, Yanic Perreault played only 13 games in the NHL in three seasons in the Toronto Maple Leafs system. Traded to Los Angeles in 1994, he scored 25 goals for the Kings in 1995–96 and earned a selection to the Team Canada squad at the 1996 World Championships. Perreault had six goals and three assists in nine games to lead Canada to a silver medal and earn himself a selection as the tournament's best forward.

BILL RANFORD's brilliant goaltending in 1994 gave Canada its first World Championship since 1961, as he allowed just seven goals in six games for a 1.17 goals-against average and clinched the victory with a final save in a shootout win over Finland. Ranford also became the first Canadian to be named best goalie at the world tournament since Seth Martin back in 1966 and earned a spot on the all-star team.

Previous to the 1994 world title, Ranford had posted a 6–2 record and a 1.86 goals-against average at the World Championships in 1993, though Canada managed only a fourth-place finish that year. In 1991, Ranford allowed just 1.75 goals per 60 minutes to lead Team Canada to victory in the

Canada Cup. Later, Ranford would serve as a backup goaltender behind Curtis Joseph at the 1996 World Cup of Hockey.

LARRY ROBINSON A star defenseman who helped the Montreal Canadiens win the Stanley Cup six times and won the Norris Trophy twice as the NHL's best defenseman, Larry Robinson often found himself in more of a supporting role in international hockey and he played the part well. Robinson suited up for three Canada Cup tournaments, helping Canada win the inaugural event in 1976, and later helping to avenge 1981's loss to the Soviet Union with victory again in 1984. Robinson also represented Canada at the 1981 World Championships, where he was named both an all-star and the tournament's best defenseman despite Canada's fourth-place finish.

BRAD SCHLEGEL joined the Canadian national team in 1988–89 in an era in which NHL players were generally used to stock Canadian teams at the World Championships. Schlegel first played for Team Canada at the World Championships in 1991 and helped to earn a silver medal that year. In 1992, he captained the Canadian Olympic team to a silver medal at the Games in Albertville, France.

Schlegel entered the NHL with the Washington Capitals after the Olympics and was with the Calgary Flames in 1993–94 before rejoining the Canadian national team and helping Canada win another silver medal at the Olympics. Schlegel would continue his playing career in Germany and Austria after the Lillehammer Games but represented Canada one final time at the World Championships in 1985.

BRENDAN SHANAHAN's four goals tied Luc Robitaille for second spot on Team Canada behind Paul Kariya's five goals in 1994 as the Canadians won their first World Championship since 1961. Previously, the tenacious forward had been a Canada Cup champion in 1991. Shanahan had made his international debut back in 1987 as a member of the Canadian team disqualified from the World Junior Championships after brawling with the Soviet Union. In more recent years, Shanahan was a member of Team Canada at the World Cup of Hockey in 1996 and at the Nagano Olympics in 1998. Additional international action includes a brief appearance playing for Dusseldorf in Germany during the NHL labor dispute in 1994.

HARRY SINDEN The longtime general manager of the Boston Bruins, Harry Sinden never played in the NHL, but was an amateur star who helped the Whitby Dunlops win the Allan Cup as Canada's senior amateur champions in 1957 and 1959. In between, he led the Dunlops to the World Championship in 1958. Years later as a coach Sinden led Team Canada to a hard-fought victory over the Soviet Union in the historic 1972 Summit Series.

As captain of the Dunlops in the late 1950s, Sinden was the Whitby team's emotional leader. A defenseman, he collected four goals and three assists at the 1958 world tournament and stood on the podium as the Canadian national anthem was played after the event. The Dunlops were a perfect 7–0 on route to the world title, defeating the Soviet Union 4–2 to clinch the championship in their final game.

In 1960, Sinden and Whitby teammates Bob Attersley, Fred Etcher and George Samolenko were added to the roster of the Kitchener-Waterloo Dutchmen when they represented Canada at the Winter Olympics in Squaw Valley, California. Etcher, Attersley, and Samolenko ranked as the team's top three scorers, and Sinden added five goals and four assists while bolstering the defense as Canada earned a silver medal behind the surprising United States team that captured the country's first gold medal in Olympic hockey.

DARRYL SITTLER joined Paul Henderson on the honor roll of Canadian international goal-scoring heroes on September 15, 1976 when his overtime goal against Vladimir Dzurilla gave Team Canada a 5–4 win over Czechoslovakia and a sweep of the best-of-three final in the inaugural Canada Cup. Sittler's four goals in seven tournament games tied Gilbert Perreault and Phil Esposito for second place on the Canadian team behind Bobby Hull's five.

Darryl Sittler's only other international appearance came at the World Championships in 1983 when he scored three goals and was part of Canada's bronze medal-winning effort.

HARRY SMITH represented Canada at the World Championships three times, playing with the Trail Smoke Eaters in 1961 and 1963, and being added to the roster of the Galt Terriers in 1962. A defenseman, Smith was named to the World Championship all-star team at each of the three tournaments in which he played.

A native of Trail, as was virtually the entire Smoke Eaters roster, Smith helped solidify a Canadian defense that allowed only 11 goals in seven games at the 1961 World Championships and saw Seth Martin selected as the best goalie at the tournament. Smith also added two goals to the cause, including one in the 5–1 win over the Soviet Union in the final game, as Trail earned the last world title ever to be won by a Canadian amateur team. In 1962, Smith had five goals and seven assists at the World Championships, but Canada had to settle for a silver medal behind Sweden in a tournament boycotted by the

Soviet Union after the United States refused to grant entry visas for East Germany to compete at Colorado Springs.

Trail became the last Canadian club team to represent Canada at the World Championships in 1963. Though Smith was still an all-star and Seth Martin was once again named the best goalie, loses to Sweden and the Soviets to conclude the tournament saw the Smoke Eaters slide to fourth place. Canada would begin sending a national team to international events in 1964.

HOOLEY SMITH joined the Toronto Granites of the Ontario Hockey Association in 1921–22 and promptly helped the team win back-to-back Allan Cup championships in 1922 and 1923. As the top senior amateur club in Canada, the Granites were invited to represent Canada in hockey at the first Winter Olympic Games in 1924.

Smith, Bert McCaffery and Harry Watson were the Granites' top forwards and scored 18, 20 and 36 goals respectively in the 1924 Olympic tournament. In the preliminary round, Smith scored four goals in a 30–0 win over Czechoslovakia, four more in a 22–0 win over Sweden and five in a 33–0 win over Switzerland. In the semifinals, he scored four goals in a 19–2 win over Great Britain, then added a single goal in a 6–1 win over the United States in the gold medal game. Smith went on to enjoy a Hall of Fame career in the NHL, winning the Stanley Cup with the Ottawa Senators in 1927 and with the Montreal Maroons in 1935.

WAYNE STEPHENSON appeared in two IIHF World Championships and one Olympic Games hockey tournament with Father David Bauer's Canadian national team. He shared netminding duties with veteran Seth Martin at the 1967 World Championships, split the chores with Ken Broderick at the Olympics in 1968, and was the team's top goaltender ahead of Ken Dryden at the World Championships in 1969.

Stephenson was at his best internationally at the 1968 Grenoble Olympics, recording a 6–1 win over West Germany in the opening game and shutting out East Germany 11–0 to help get Canada back on track after a 5–2 loss to Finland in game two. In three games at the Olympics that year, Stevens recorded a 1.28 goals-against average and helped Canada win a bronze medal. He had also earned a bronze medal at the World Championships in 1967.

Following his stint with the national team, Stephenson joined the St. Louis Blues in 1971–72. He later spent five seasons with the Philadelphia Flyers and two years with the Washington Capitals.

SCOTT STEVENS One of the top defensemen in the NHL over a lengthy career, Scott Stevens has represented Canada in international play six times. He made his international debut at the World Championships in 1983, winning a bronze medal, and added a silver medal in both 1985 and 1989. Stevens was also with the Canadian team that finished fourth at the World Championships in 1987. He registered his first international tournament victory in 1991 when Team Canada defeated the United States in the finals of the Canada Cup. In 1996, Stevens was a member of the Canadian team that lost to the U.S. at the World Cup of Hockey. In 1998, he represented his country at the Olympic Games in Nagano.

BRENT SUTTER Leadership skills and a fierce determination, more than sheer ability, are the attributes of all six Sutter brothers who have played in the NHL. They are also the talents that saw Brent Sutter selected to the Team Canada roster at three successive Canada Cup tournaments. Sutter played on a line with fellow New York Islanders Mike Bossy and John Tonelli at the 1984 event and helped Canada avenge its 1981 tournament loss by sweeping Sweden in the finals. Sutter was also a key contributor to Canada's 1987 victory when the Soviets were defeated in a thrilling three game final. He added a third Canada Cup victory in 1991 when the Canadians beat the United States to win the tournament.

ADOLPHE TAMBELLINI Like most members of the 1961 Trail Smoke Eaters, Adolphe "Addy" Tambellini was employed by the Cominco Mining Company and was given seven weeks paid leave in order to prepare for and attend the World Championships in Switzerland. The youngest member of the 1961 team and a center with blazing speed, Tambellini was converted to left wing when Mike Legace was added to the Smoke Eaters roster. He scored two goals at the world tournament as Trail became the last Canadian amateur team to win the World Championship.

In 1963, Tambellini made his second international appearance when Trail once again earned the right to represent Canada at the World Championships. He had six goals and five assists that year and was named to the tournament all-star team though Trail could finish no better than fourth. It was the last time that a club team ever represented Canada at the World Championships. Tambellini's final appearance at the event came in 1967 when he earned a bronze medal as a member of the Canadian national team.

BILL WARWICK had many years of professional hockey behind him, including brief trials with the NHL's New York Rangers in 1942–43 and 1943–44 before having his amateur status reinstated and joining the Penticton Vees in

1952–53. In 1953–54 he set an all-time Okanagan Senior Hockey League record with 50 goals and had 95 points in just 58 games to win the league's most valuable player award. He also lead Penticton to the Allan Cup title that year. As defending Allan Cup national senior champions in 1955, Penticton had earned the right travel to Europe to represent Canada at the IIHF World Championships.

Combining tough physical play with a deft scoring touch, Bill Warwick, along with brothers Dick and Grant (Penticton's playing coach) led the Vees to the world title at the 1955 World tournament in Germany. Bill Warwick was the team's top scorer, collecting 13 goals as the Canadian team posted a perfect record of 8–0. He had six goals in a 12–1 win over the United States to open the tournament and scored two goals in the final game when Penticton beat the Soviets 5–0 to clinch the IIHF World Championship title. Warwick was named the best forward at the tournament.

DICK WARWICK The youngest of the three Warwick brothers, but the first to arrive in Penticton, Dick Warwick joined the Vees when the team was formed in 1951–52. He was joined by brothers Bill and Grant the following year and the three helped the team win the Allan Cup in 1953–54. As defending Allan Cup champions, Penticton was selected to represent Canada at the 1955 World Championships.

A prolific scorer and slick playmaker, Dick Warwick contributed six goals to the Penticton cause as the Vees claimed the world title with a perfect record of 8–0, including a 5–0 win over the Soviets to clinch the championship in the final game of the tournament. The win was sweet revenge for Canada hockey fans and organizers who had seen the Soviet national team claim the IIHF World Championship for the first time in 1954.

GRANT WARWICK After winning the Allan Cup with the Regina Abbotts in 1940–41, Grant Warwick embarked on an 11-year professional hockey career that included nine seasons in the NHL with the New York Rangers, Boston Bruins and Montreal Canadiens. He was the NHL's Calder Trophy winner as rookie of the year in 1941–42. Following his days as a pro, Warwick had his amateur status reinstated and joined his brothers Bill and Dick with the Penticton Vees in 1952–53. In 1953–54, he played for another Allan Cup winner in Penticton.

In 1955, the Vees represented Canada at the World Championships and Grant Warwick served as the team's playing coach. He scored six goals in eight games at the world tournament, including a tie-breaking goal late in the second game that led the Canadian team to a key 5–3 win over the gold medal contenders from Czechoslovakia. Following that victory Canada breezed to the World Championship with a perfect 8–0 record, including a convincing 5–0 win over the Soviet Union in the final game.

Penticton's win at the 1955 World Championships followed the Soviet Union's first victory the year before. When he was presented with the IIHF World Championship trophy, Grant Warwick declared that he was bringing it back to Canada where it belonged and would keep it there. When the International Ice Hockey Federation ordered Warwick to return the trophy in 1956, he had an exact replica made and sent it overseas instead. The original World Championship trophy would remain in Penticton where for many years it was displayed in a restaurant.

HARRY WATSON was one of several World War I veterans who joined the Toronto Granites of the Ontario Hockey Association when the team was formed for the 1919–20 season. The team quickly became a powerhouse in Canadian senior amateur hockey, winning back-to-back Allan Cup championships in 1922 and 1923. As the defending Allan Cup champs, the Granites earned the right to play for Canada at the first Winter Olympics in 1924.

The Granites proved much stronger than their European opponents and Watson collected 11 goals in a 30–0 win over Czechoslovakia, six in a 22–0 win over Sweden and 13 (still an Olympic record) in a 33–0 win over Switzerland. In the semifinals, he scored three goals in a 19–2 win over Great Britain, then added another hat trick in a 6–1 win over the United States in the gold medal game. In all, Watson scored 36 goals in five games as the Granites outscored the opposition 110–3. Watson turned down several offers to turn professional after the Olympics and remained an amateur throughout his Hall of Fame career.

STEVE YZERMAN made his international hockey debut at the World Junior Championships in 1983, when the Canadian team featuring Mario Lemieux recorded a third-place finish at the tournament. In 1984, a 19-year-old Yzerman was the youngest member of the Canadian team that beat Sweden in the finals of the Canada Cup.

Yzerman has gone on to represent Canada three times at the World Championships, winning a silver medal in 1985 and in 1989 when he was also named a tournament all-star. Yzerman led the World Championships in scoring with 20 points (10 goals and 10 assists) in 1990 and was named the best forward as well as a tournament all-star although Canada finished in fourth place. Yzerman also played for Team Canada at the World Cup of Hockey in 1996 and at the Nagano Olympics in 1998.

CHINA

ANFU WANG Forward... One of the best players in the history of Chinese hockey... Represented China at international tournaments in the 1980s and early 1990s... Named the best forward and to the all-star team at the World and European Championships in 1985 (Pool C)... Starred at this tournament and at the 1989 (Pool C) and 1991 (Pool C) tournaments... Recorded 17 points (1985), 15 points (1989) and 15 points (1991) respectively.

YONGJUN WANG Star goaltender of Chinese hockey... Played for the national team in the 1980s and early 1990s... Named the best goaltender of the World and European Championships in 1986 (Pool C) and 1991 (Pool C)... The tournament in 1991 was the highlight of his career... Played in seven games and registered a 3.00 goals-against average.

CROATIA
see page 1870

CZECHOSLOVAKIA, CZECH REPUBLIC AND SLOVAKIA

IIHF-standard three-letter abbreviations are used to indicate the country each player has most recently represented in international competition as a player, coach or executive. CZE – Czech Republic, SVK – Slovakia, TCH – Czechoslovakia.

SVK
PETER BONDRA Helped lead the Slovakian team to victory in the 1994 Olympic Qualifying Tournament... Led Slovak team in goal-scoring (with three) at the 1996 World Cup of Hockey... Played at the 1998 Olympics in Nagano.

Washington's eighth choice, 156th overall, in the 1990 NHL Entry Draft... Played two seasons for Kosice in Czechoslovakia... Named NHL Rookie of the Month in November 1990... Led all Caps rookies in scoring with 28 points in 1990–91... Led all Washington players in scoring with 85 points in 1992–93... Was named to the Wales Conference All-Star Team and scored a goal in the All-Star Game... On February 5, 1994, he tied Bengt Gustafsson's club record with five goals in a game against Tampa Bay... His four goals in a span of 4:12 set an NHL record... Was the first Capital, and just the tenth player in NHL history, to score four goals in one period... Scored twice in the final game of the 1994–95 season to claim the league goal-scoring crown with 34 in a 48-game season, becoming the first Washington player to lead the league in goals... In 1995–96, represented the Washington Capitals at the All-Star Game in Boston... Led Washington in goals scored with 52... In 1997–98, he led the NHL in goals (along with Anaheim's Teemu Selanne) with 52... Led the Capitals in scoring with 78 points in 76 games.

TCH
JIRI BUBLA first played for the Czechoslovakian national team at the World Championships in 1971 and was a member of the Czech team that beat the Soviet Union at the world tournament the following year. He represented his country at the World Championships through 1979, earning gold medals again in 1976 and 1977. Bubla was named a tournament all-star in 1978 and both an all-star and the best defenseman in 1979. He also played in the Olympics at Innsbruck in 1976 (silver medal) and at Lake Placid in 1980. Bubla was a member of the Czechoslovakian team that reached the finals of the first Canada Cup tournament in 1976.

Bubla was claimed by the Colorado Rockies in a Special Czechoslovakia NHL Entry Draft in 1981, but his rights were traded to the Vancouver Canucks. He made his NHL debut in Vancouver in 1981–82 and spent five seasons with the club.

CZE
LUDEK BUKAC Named assistant coach of the Czechoslovakian national team in 1979...Was named the head coach after the 1980 Lake Placid Olympics... His best achievements were the victories at the 1985 and 1996 World Championships... After spending six years with the Czechoslovakian national team, he was invited to coach the Austrian national team in 1986... In 1991 he started to coach the German national team... Came back to Czech Republic in 1994 and was named the head coach of the Czech team... One of the most respected coaches in Europe, Bukac coached at five Olympics, two Canada Cup tournaments, one World Cup of Hockey and 14 World and European Championships.

Began his hockey career in 1946 with the boys team of LTC Praha... Played until 1963 with four Prague teams: LTC, I.CLTK, Motorlet and Sparta, also with Dukla Jihlava... Spent 13 seasons in Czechoslovak League, recording 153 goals in 330 games... He played on national champions in 1947, 1948 and 1949 with LTC Praha... Saw action in 30 games with the Czechoslovakian national team, scoring 11 goals... Participated at the 1961 (silver) and 1963

(bronze) World Championships... After retirement as a player, he began to study the profession of hockey coach... To get experience, he was sent to the Oklahoma City Blazers (the Boston Bruins farm club) in 1965 and CSKA Moscow in 1966... Began his coaching career in 1967 with Sparta Praha... Coached Sparta, VSZ Kosice and Motor Ceske Budejovice until 1980.

CZE
PETR BRIZA Backup goaltender for Czechoslovakia at the 1987 Canada Cup, 1988 Olympics and 1989 World Championships but never saw action... Won a bronze medal at the 1990, 1992 and 1993 World Championships and the 1992 Albertville Olympics... Named the best goaltender and to the all-star team at the 1993 World Championships... From 1992 to 1994 played in all but one game for the national team at Albertville and Lillehammer Olympics and at the World Championships... Played two games for Czech Republic at the 1996 World Cup of Hockey.

Former Philadelphia Flyers goalie Pelle Lindbergh was one of his heroes... Led his club, Sparta Praha, to the Czechoslovakian title in 1990... Named MVP in the playoffs that year... Played two years in Finland with Lukko Rauma... Joined Landshut in Germany in 1993... His team finished second overall in the 1994–95 regular season and reached the finals in the playoffs... The only goalie in Czech hockey history to score a goal (1991 versus Steaua Bucharest from Romania)... Romanian goaltender was on the ice when goal was scored... In 1995–96, he backstopped Landshut to fourth place in the standings... Played all 55 games for Landshut in 1996–97 and reached the semifinals with his team.

TCH
JOSEF CERNY As a member of the Czechoslovakian national team he played at four Olympics and 12 World and European Championships between 1959 and 1972... Served as captain of the team for many years... Silver medalist at the World and European Championships in 1961, 1965, 1966, 1968 and 1971, bronze medalist in 1959, 1963, 1964, 1969 and 1970... Silver medalist at the 1968 Grenoble Olympics, bronze medalist at Innsbruck in 1964 and at the 1972 Sapporo Olympics.

Played 21 seasons in the Czechoslovak League... Started at the age of 18 in 1957 with Skoda Plzen... Spent the next 20 seasons with clubs from Brno (RH, ZKL, Zetor)... Has played the most number of games (686) in the history of Czechoslovak hockey... Scored 403 goals (second overall behind Milan Novy)... Played for the Czech national champion from 1960 to 1966... Twice (1963–64 and 1969–70) was the top league goal scorer... In 1978–79, was a playing coach of ATSE Graz (Austria)... Continued his coaching career in Austria with WAT Stadlau (1979 to 1982)... Came back to Czechoslovakia and coached ZVL Zilina (1982–83).

TCH
VLADIMIR DZURILLA One of the best goaltenders in the history of international hockey, Dzurilla made his debut with the Czechoslovakian national team at the 1963 World and European Championships... Saw action in three Olympics, 10 World and European Championships and the 1976 Canada Cup... World champion in 1972, 1976 and 1977, silver medalist in 1965, 1966 and 1968, bronze medalist in 1963, 1964, 1969 and 1970... Silver medalist at 1968 Grenoble Olympics, bronze medalist at the 1964 Innsbruck Games and the 1972 Sapporo Olympics... Finalist at the 1976 Canada Cup... Named the best goaltender of 1965 World and European Championships... Made the tournament all-star team in 1965 and 1969.

Began his great goaltending career in 1959 with Slovan Bratislava where he played until 1973... From 1973 to 1978 he played for Zetor Brno... Saw action in 571 games in 19 seasons in Czechoslovak League... Continued his career in Germany with in Augsburger AV (1978–79) and SC Riessersee (1979 to 1982)... Became a champion with SC Riessersee in 1980–81... Became a coach after retiring... From 1982 to 1985 he coached the juniors of Slovan Bratislava... Coached Zetor Brno in 1985–86 and 1989–90... Coached one season in Switzerland with EHC Olten (1986–87)... Worked in Germany with SC Riessersee (1987–88), Eintracht Frankfurt (1988–89), Nordhorn (1990–91), Klostersee (1991) and Straubing (1991 to 1993).

TCH
BOHUSLAV EBERMANN Left winger Bohuslav Ebermann was a member of the Czechoslovakian team that reached the final of the 1976 Canada Cup. He was a silver medalist at the 1976 Olympics as well and also participated in the 1980 Games in Lake Placid. He represented Czechoslovakia at six World Championship tournaments beginning in 1974, twice averaging a point per game or better. His team finished on the podium every time with a gold in 1977, four silver and one bronze medal.

SVK
JOZEF GOLONKA His outstanding international career began in 1959... Played at three Olympics and eight World and European Championships... Silver medalist with Czechoslovakian national team at the World and European Championships in 1965, 1966 and 1968, bronze medalist in 1964

and 1969... Silver medalist at the 1968 Grenoble Olympics, bronze medalist at the 1964 Innsbruck Olympics... Played in 134 games for the Czechoslovakian national team, scoring 82 goals... His international coaching career began with the Czechoslovakian national junior team (1979 to 1981)... Coached national B-team in 1981–82... Named the head coach of the Slovakian national team before the 1996–97 season.

Legendary forward who began his career in Bratislava... Played for Slovan Bratislava from 1955 to 1957 and 1959 to 1969... Also played for Dukla Jihlava from 1957 to 1959... Spent 14 seasons in the Czechoslovak League, played in 330 games and scored 298 goals... Best league goal scorer in 1960–61... Continued his career in Germany, where he played for SC Riessersee from 1969 to 1972... Came back to Czechoslovakia and played for Lokomotiv Bucina Zvolen (1972 to 1975)... Retired at the age of 37... Became the coach of SC Riessersee (1976 to 1979 and 1982–83)... Won the German national title with SC Riessersee in 1977–78... Coached Zetor Brno in 1979–80... Worked with German club Kolner EC from 1983 to 1985 winning the national title in 1983–84... From 1985 to 1988 coached his original club, Slovan Bratislava... Continued his coaching career with HC Davos (Switzerland) in 1988–89, with ECD Iserlohn (Germany) from 1989 to 1991 and with EHC 80 Nurnberg in 1991–92 and 1994–95.

TCH

KAREL GUT Played in three Olympics and nine World and European Championships from 1952 to 1960 as a member of the Czechoslovakian national team... Bronze medalist at the 1955, 1957 and 1959 World and European Championships... Named the tournament's best defenseman in 1955... Was the captain of the national team... Coached the national B-team and junior team from 1970 to 1972... Head coach of the Czechoslovakian national team from 1973 to 1980... Under his coaching the team won the World champions title in 1976 and 1977, got silver medals in 1974, 1975, 1978 and 1979 and an Olympic silver medal at Innsbruck in 1976.

Began his hockey career with the small-town team of LTC Uhrineves... Played defense... Was invited to ATK Praha and played there from 1949 to 1951... Later played for Tatra Smichov (1951 to 1953) and Spartak Sokolovo Praha (1953 to 1964)... Won the national championship in 1954... Saw action in 300 games in 14 seasons in the Czechoslovak League and scored 86 goals... Choose coaching career after retiring as a player... Coached Sparta Praha (1964 to 1967 and 1971 to 1973), German club EV Landshut (1967 to 1970 and 1980 to 1983)... EV Landshut won the German national title in 1969–70 and 1982–83.

SVK

OTO HASCAK A latecomer to the Czechoslovakian national team... Made his debut at the 1988 Calgary Olympics... Played at the 1989 and 1990 World and European Championships... Helped the Slovakian national team win an Olympic Qualification Tournament in Sheffield, England in 1993... Recorded one goal and three assists for four points in four games... As a member of the Slovakian national team, played at the 1994 Olympics and at the 1994 (Pool C), 1995 (Pool B) and 1996 (Pool A) World Championships... Saw action at the World Cup of Hockey in 1996.

Drafted by the Boston Bruins (seventh choice, 143rd overall) in the 1989 NHL Entry Draft... Spent seven seasons with Dukla Trencin as one of the best scorers on the team... Last two seasons with Dukla were the best in his career... In 1988–89 he finished in second place on the team's scoring list (behind Vladimir Ruzicka) and sixth overall in the Czech League with 50 points in 43 games... Was named to the all-star team at the end of the season... The next year he accumulated 56 points in 48 games and finished in fourth place among the league scoring leaders... Moved to Sweden and played three seasons with Sodertalje... Later played for Vastra Frolunda Goteborg of the Swedish League... Joined HC Petra Vsetin of the Czech Extraleague.

CZE

DOMINIK HASEK Starting goaltender for Czechoslovakia at the 1991 Canada Cup tournament... Played in the 1984 Canada Cup as a 19-year old... Named best goalie at the 1983 World Junior Championships as the Czechs finished second to the Soviet Union with a 5–1–1 record... Starred at 1998 Olympics in Nagano, allowing only six goals in six games as the Czech Republic won the gold medal... Named the best goaltender of the Olympic tournament.

Chicago's 11th choice, 199th overall, in the 1983 NHL Entry Draft... Played six seasons for Pardubice from 1981–82 to 1988–89 and one season for Dukla Jihlava in 1989–90... Czechoslovakian goaltender of the year in 1986, 1987, 1988, 1989, 1990... Player of the year in 1987, 1989, 1990... Named first team all-star in 1988, 1989, 1990... First runner up for the Hart Trophy in 1993–94 and the second runner up in 1994–95... Became the first European-trained goaltender to lead the NHL in goals-against average with a 1.95 mark in 1993–94... First goaltender to finish the regular season with an average below 2.00 since Bernie Parent in 1973–74... Led the NHL in goals-against average, and save percentage in both 1993–94 and 1994–95... Won Vezina Trophy in 1993–94, 1994–95 and 1996–97... Won Hart Trophy in 1996–97

(first goalie to win it since Jacques Plante in 1962) and again in 1997–98... Named to the NHL First All-Star Team in 1994, 1995, 1997 and 1998... In 1997–98, led the NHL in shutouts with 13.

CZE

IVAN HLINKA Played in 11 World Championships (1970 to 1979, 1981) and won the gold medal three times (1972, 1976 and 1977)... Named to the all-star team in 1978... He also won a bronze medal at 1972 Sapporo Olympics and a silver medal at the 1976 Innsbruck Games... Missed the 1980 Lake Placid Olympics due to a knee injury... Saw action in inaugural Canada Cup tournament in 1976... In his career, he recorded 132 goals in 256 games with the Czechoslovakian national team... Took the reins as a head coach of the national team in 1991 and worked until 1994... Under his coaching, the Czech national team got a bronze medal at the 1992 Albertville Olympics and won two World Championship bronze medals... Came back to coach the national team before 1997 World Championship and earned another bronze medal... His best achievement as a coach came with a gold medal at 1998 Olympics in Nagano.

A veteran of 16 seasons in the Czechoslovak League, Hlinka recorded 347 goals in 544 games... Played in the NHL for the Vancouver Canucks for two seasons; 1981–82 and 1982–83... He had 123 points (42 goals and 81 assists) in 137 games and was a key contributor to the 1981–82 edition of the Canucks which made it to the Stanley Cup finals—the first time the Canucks had played for the Stanley Cup in their history... Hlinka and Jiri Bubla were the first Czechoslovaks to play for the Canucks... The two had been selected in a special NHL draft for Czechoslovak players by Winnipeg and Colorado, but were signed by Vancouver when the Canucks learned that no formal agreement existed between the NHL and the Czechoslovak Hockey Federation... After finishing his NHL career, Hlinka played two seasons in Switzerland with Zug... Was named the coach of CHZ Litvinov in 1985.

TCH

JIRI HOLECEK His brilliant international career started in 1966 at the World and European Championships... Played at two Olympics and 10 World and European Championships from 1966 to 1978... World champion in 1972, 1976 and 1977, silver medalist in 1966, 1971, 1974, 1975 and 1978, bronze medalist in 1973... Winter Olympic silver medalist at Innsbruck in 1976, bronze medalist at Sapporo in 1972... Finalist of the 1976 Canada Cup... Named the best goaltender at the World and European Championships five times (1971, 1973, 1975, 1976 and 1978), voted to the all-star team five times (1971, 1972, 1973, 1976 and 1978).

One of the greatest goaltenders of all time, Holecek began his senior hockey career with Dukla Kosice (1963 to 1967)... Later he played for VSZ Kosice (1967 to 1973) and Sparta Praha (1973 to 1978)... Played 14 seasons in the Czechoslovak League and saw action in 488 games... Won the Golden Stick Award (best player of the year) in 1973–74... Continued his career in Germany, where he played for EHC Munchen 70 (1978 to 1980) and EHC Essen (1980–81)... After retiring, coached the Czechoslovak junior team and was a goaltending coach for the junior and senior national teams.

CZE

BOBBY HOLIK Won a bronze medal with the Czechoslovakian national junior team in the 1990 World Junior Championships... Named to tournament second all-star team... Won a bronze medal with Team Czechoslovakia at the 1990 World Championships... Played in the 1991 World Championships... Played for Czech Republic at the 1996 World Cup of Hockey.

Hartford's first draft choice in 1989 ...Father Jaroslav is a coach and former player, Uncle Jiri is one of the top goal scorers in Czech hockey history... Brother-in-law is former Calgary Flame Frantisek Musil... Skated on line with Mike Peluso and Randy McKay that played key role in 1995 playoffs as he won the Stanley Cup with the New Jersey Devils that year... In 1995–96, recorded 100th NHL assist and 200th point of his career... Led the Devils in scoring in 1997–98 with 29 goals and 36 assists for 65 points in 82 games.

TCH

JIRI HOLIK Never missed a major international tournament following his invitation to the Czechoslovakian national team in 1963–64 season... Played until 1977, participating in four Olympics and 14 World and European Championships... Also played at the 1976 Canada Cup... Saw action in 319 national team games (which is still a record)... Scored 132 goals in these games... World Champion in 1972, 1976 and 1977, silver medalist in 1965, 1966, 1968, 1971, 1974 and 1975, bronze medalist in 1964, 1969, 1970 and 1973... Olympic silver medalist at Innsbruck in 1976, bronze medalist at Sapporo in 1972... Finalist at the 1976 Canada Cup.

Had a lengthy career in the Czechoslovak League with Dukla Jihlava (1963 to 1978)... Played on teams that won the national title seven times... Saw action in 553 games in 15 seasons, scoring 283 goals... Played on the same line with his brother, Jaroslav... Continued his brilliant career in Germany with SB Rosenheim (1978 to 1980)... Later played in Austria for WAT Stadlau (1980–81) and Wiener EV (1984–85).

CZE

MILOSLAV HORAVA A national team veteran, Horava played for Czechoslovakia in four Olympic tournaments… He also played at the Canada Cup three times and at the World and European Championships on five occasions… His best achievement was a gold medal at the World Championships in 1985.

Began his hockey career in Kladno… Played for Poldi SONP Kladno from 1978 to 1983 and 1985 to 1989… Played for Dukla Jihlava from 1983 to 1985… Played on teams that won the Czechoslovak national title three times: 1980, 1984 and 1985… Horava played two full seasons for the New York Rangers (1989–90 and 1990–91), and left to play in the Swedish League after the Rangers traded him to Quebec… Originally drafted by Edmonton (eighth choice, 176th overall) in 1981 NHL Entry Draft, Horava was traded to the Rangers in an eight-player deal… After returning to Europe, he quickly became one of the best defensemen in the Swedish League… Was the top-scoring defenseman on MoDo Hockey Ornskoldsvik.

TCH

JIRI HRDINA Made his debut with the Czechoslovakian national team at the 1982 World and European Championships… In his career, he played at two Olympics, two Canada Cup tournaments and six World and European Championships… A world champion in 1985, a silver medalist at the World Championships in 1982 and 1983, a bronze medalist in 1987 and 1990, and an Olympic silver medalist at Sarajevo in 1984.

Began his hockey career in the town of Mlada Boleslav where he played for Autoskoda… Was invited to Sparta Praha in 1977… Played for Sparta until 1981… After spending two seasons with Dukla Trencin, came back to Sparta where he played until the end of the 1987–88 season… In his career, he played 389 games in the Czechoslovak League and scored 122 goals… Calgary's eighth choice, 159th overall, in the 1984 NHL Entry Draft… Signed a contract with the Flames right after 1988 Calgary Olympics… Played four full seasons in the NHL with Calgary and Pittsburgh collecting 45 goals and 85 assists for 130 points in 250 games… Three-time Stanley Cup champion: in 1989 (Calgary) and in 1991 and 1992 with Pittsburgh.

CZE

JAROMIR JAGR Won a bronze medal with the Czechoslovakian national junior team in 1990 at the World Junior Championships… Named to tournament all-star team… Won a bronze medal with Czechoslovakia at the 1990 World Championships… Played for Team Czechoslovakia in the 1991 Canada Cup… Played for Czech Republic in the 1994 World Championships… Scored one goal in three games for the Czechs at the 1996 World Cup of Hockey… Led the Czech Republic team to the 1998 Olympic gold medal in Nagano.

Pittsburgh's first choice, fifth overall in 1990 Entry Draft… Named to NHL All-Rookie Team in 1991… Led rookies in scoring during the 1991 playoffs when Pittsburgh won the Stanley Cup… Played in the 1992 NHL All-Star Game… Finished fourth in playoff scoring and had four game-winners in the 1992 playoffs when the Penguins repeated as Stanley Cup champions… Played in the 1993 NHL All-Star Game… Recorded a career-high six points in one game on November 16, 1993 versus Philadelphia… Voted to 1994 NHL All-Star Game but did not play due to injury… First European to win the Art Ross Trophy as NHL's top scorer in 1994–95… First player other than Wayne Gretzky or Mario Lemieux to win the scoring title since Marcel Dionne won in 1979–80… Named to NHL First All-Star Team in 1995… Runner-up for 1995 Hart Trophy, given to league's MVP… In 1995–96, finished second in the scoring race behind teammate Mario Lemieux… Named to First All-Star Team in 1995–96… Named to Second All-Star Team in 1996–97… Led the NHL in scoring in 1997–98 with 35 goals and 67 assists for 102 points in 77 games.

SVK

LUBOMIR KOLNIK A bronze medalist at the 1986 European Junior Championships (under 18) with the Czechoslovakian Junior Team… Made his debut with the national team at the 1991 World and European Championships… Played at the 1991 Canada Cup… Made his debut with the Slovakian national team at the Olympic Qualification Tournament in Sheffield, England in 1993 …Was the second-best scorer on the team with four goals and two assists for six points in four games… Has played in every tournament since the creation of Slovakian national team in 1993–94, including two Olympic Games and four World Championships… Also played at the 1996 World Cup of Hockey.

New Jersey's ninth choice in the 1990 draft, 116th overall… He had quickly become one of the leading scorers with Dukla Trencin… Played brilliantly in 1989–90 and 1990–91 season… Named to the all-star team in 1990–91…Next year he became a Czechoslovakian national champion with Dukla Trencin… Went to play in Finland in 1992–93… Became the best scorer overall in the Finnish Division 2 in 1992–93, collecting an amazing 84 points (46 goals and 38 assists) in 44 games with JoKP Joensuu… Played next year with Lukko Raumo of the top Finnish League… Came back to Slovakia before the 1994–95 season… Played with Dukla Trencin and Slovan Bratislava.

TCH

VLADIMIR KOSTKA One of the most respected coaches in the history of hockey… Named the coach of Czechoslovakian national team in 1957… Worked with the national team until 1973 (with few interruptions)… Coached the team at two Olympics and 11 World and European Championships… In 1972, under his coaching, the Czechoslovak team won the gold medal at the World Championships… The team had won a silver medal at the 1968 Grenoble Olympics and at the World Championship in 1961, 1965, 1966, 1968 and 1971, Bronze medals came at the World Championship in 1957, 1963, 1969, 1970 and 1973.

Began his hockey career in 1938… Played as center and a defenseman until 1954 with Sokol Konice, SK Konice, VS Brono, Slavia Brno, Banis Ostrava and VS Praha… Got into coaching after his playing career and as head coach of VS Praha until 1956.

CZE

FRANTISEK KUCERA Made his debut in a major international tournament in 1989 at the World and European Championships… Czechoslovakia won the bronze medal that year… In 1994, he played for the Czech Republic team at the World Championships… Made his comeback to the national team at the 1998 World Championships… Won another bronze medal with the team… Starred in the tournament… Named the best defenseman and chosen to the all-star team.

Began his hockey career with Sparta Praha… Made his debut in the Czechoslovak League at the age of 17… Played three seasons with Sparta and two seasons with Dukla Jihlava… Chicago's third choice, 77th overall, in the 1986 NHL Entry Draft… Signed with the Blackhawks before the 1990–91 season… Played seven NHL seasons with Chicago, Hartford, Vancouver and Philadelphia… Played in 354 games, collecting 21 goals and 75 assists for 96 points… Came back to HC Sparta Praha before the 1997–98 season.

TCH

JIRI LALA was part of the Czech national team's top line in the 1980s teamed with Igor Liba and either Dusan Pasek or Darius Rusnak. He played in the 1984 and 1988 Olympics and the 1981 and 1984 Canada Cup as well as in six World Championships. He was the top scorer for his club team, Motor Ceske Budejovice, in 1987–88 and then won similar honors in the German league with Eintracht Frankfurt in 1989–90 and 1990–91, Mannheimer ERC in 1992–93 and 1993–94 and Frankfurt in 1994–95 and 1996–97. He was also the top scorer in Great Britain with Ayr in 1996–97.

TCH

IGOR LIBA was a longtime member of VSZ Kosice both before and after his NHL appearance with the New York Rangers and Los Angeles Kings in 1988–89. He also represented Czechoslovakia at the World Junior Championships in 1979 and 1980 and was a member of the Czech national team from 1981–82 through 1987–88. During that time Liba played at five World Championships, winning a gold medal in 1985 in addition to two silvers and a bronze. He also earned a silver medal at the Sarajevo Olympics in 1984 and made a second Olympic appearance at Calgary four years later. He was a member of the Czech team at the Canada Cup tournaments in 1984 and 1987.

Following his brief NHL career, Liba returned to Europe, where he played in Switzerland, Italy and Austria as well as the Czech Republic and Slovakia. He again represented the Czech team at the Olympics and World Championships in 1992.

TCH

OLDRICH MACHAC After being invited to the Czechoslovakian national team in 1966–67 season, he never missed a major international tournament… Played at three Olympics, 12 World and European Championships and the 1976 Canada Cup… World Champion in 1972, 1976 and 1977, silver medalist in 1968, 1971, 1974, 1975 and 1978, bronze medalist in 1969, 1970 and 1973… Olympic silver medalist at Grenoble in 1968 and Innsbruck in 1976, bronze medalist at the 1972 Sapporo Games… Finalist at the 1976 Canada Cup… Always played in a defensive pair with Frantisek Pospisil on the national team… Named to the World Championship all-star team in 1972… Played in 293 games as a member of the Czechoslovakian national team and scored 37 goals.

His great career began in 1965, when the 19-year-old defenseman made his debut with Dukla Kosice… Played with Dukla until 1967… From 1967 to 1978 he played for ZKL (Zetor) Brno… Played in 490 games in the Czechoslovak League, scoring 108 goals… In 1978, he was invited to play for SB Rosenheim in Germany… Spent four seasons with the club… Played for a German national champion in his last season, 1981–82.

TCH

VLADIMIR MARTINEC His outstanding international career got started in 1970 at the World and European Championships in Stockholm, Sweden… Participated in three Olympics, 11 World and European Championships and one Canada Cup tournament… World Champion in 1972, 1976 and 1977, sil-

ver medalist in 1971, 1974, 1975, 1978 and 1979, bronze medalist in 1970, 1973 and 1981... Olympic silver medalist at Innsbruck in 1976, bronze medalist at Sapporo in 1972... Finalist at the 1976 Canada Cup... Played 289 games and scored 155 goals for the national team... Named to the all-star team of the World and European Championships three times: 1974, 1976 and 1977.

Spent almost his entire career with Tesla Pardubice, where he played from 1967 to 1978 and from 1979 to 1981... Played for Dukla Jihlava in 1978–79... Spent 14 seasons in Czechoslovak League, saw action in 539 games and scored 343 goals... Best scorer in 1978–79... Member of a national championship team in 1972–73... Won the Golden Stick Award (player of the year) four times: 1972–73, 1974–75, 1975–76 and 1978–79... Finished his great career in Germany with ESV Kaufbeuren (1981 to 1985)... After retiring, coached the juniors of Tesla Pardubice (1985 to 1987)... Named the head coach of Tesla Pardubice in 1988 and worked until 1991 when he accepted the invitation to coach in Germany, where he worked with ESV Kaufbeuren and Memmingen.

TCH
VACLAV NEDOMANSKY Had great career as a member of the Czechoslovakian national team... Played at two Olympics and 10 World and European Championships from 1965 to 1974... Played in 93 games in these tournaments and scored 78 goals ...World Champion in 1972, silver medalist in 1965, 1966, 1968, 1971 and 1974, bronze medalist in 1969, 1970 and 1973... Olympic silver medalist at Grenoble in 1968 and bronze medalist at Sapporo in 1972... Named best forward of the 1974 World and European Championships... Voted a tournament all-star in 1969, 1970 and 1974.

One of the best players in the history of Czech hockey, Nedomansky played 12 seasons for Slovan Bratislava of the Czechoslovak League... In 419 games, he scored 369 goals... Won the league goal-scoring crown four times: in 1966–67, 1970–71, 1971–72 and 1973–74... Played four season in the World Hockey Association with the Toronto Toros and Birmingham Bulls... In 252 WHA games, he collected 135 goals and 118 assists for 253 points... In 1977–78, signed with the NHL's Detroit Red Wings as a free agent... Spent six seasons in the NHL with Detroit, St.Louis and the New York Rangers... In 421 NHL games, he recorded 122 goals and 156 assists for 278 points... After finishing his playing career, Nedomansky coached the German club Schewenninger ERC (1987 to 1990) and Austrian club EV Innsbruck (1990–91).

CZE
PETR NEDVED Played for Team Canada at the 1994 Lillehammer Olympics after becoming a Canadian citizen... Won a silver medal... Played in three games for the Czech Republic at the 1996 World Cup of Hockey.

Vancouver's first choice, second overall, in the 1990 NHL Entry Draft... As a junior, named top rookie in the Western Hockey League and Canadian major junior rookie of the year in 1990... Led Vancouver with a plus–minus rating of +20 in 1992–93... Ranked second in the NHL in 1992–93 with a 25.5% shooting percentage... Set team record with a 15-game point-scoring streak during the 1992–93 season... Recorded 16 points in final 23 games of 1994–95... In 1995–96, finished second in the NHL in shooting percentage (22.1%)... Finished fourth in NHL in plus–minus (+37)... In 1996–97, finished fourth in Pittsburgh's scoring race behind Mario Lemieux, Jaromir Jagr and Ron Francis... A contract dispute with the Penguins saw him sit out the entire 1997–98 NHL season... Played briefly with Sparta Praha in the Czech Republic and with Las Vegas of the International Hockey League during his holdout.

TCH
MILAN NOVY Made his debut with the Czechoslovakian national team in 1975... Played seven seasons with the nationals... Participated in two Olympics, two Canada Cup tournaments and seven World and European Championships... World Champion in 1976 and 1977, silver medalist in 1975, 1978, 1979 and 1982, bronze medalist in 1981, Olympic silver medalist at Innsbruck in 1976, Canada Cup finalist in 1976... In 1976, he was named to the all-star team of two tournaments: the Canada Cup and the World and European Championships.

Spent the most of his career with Poldi SONP Kladno (1968 to 1972, 1974 to 1982 and 1986 to 1989)... Played for Dukla Jihlava from 1972 to 1974... Played for the Czechoslovak champion from 1974 to 1978 and in 1980... Won the Golden Stick Award (best player of the season) in 1976–77, 1980–81 and 1981–82... In 16 seasons in the Czechoslovak League, scored 474 goals (first overall) in 633 games... In 1982–83, he played for the Washington Capitals... In 73 NHL games, he collected 18 goals and 30 assists for 48 points... Came back to Europe and played for Swiss club Zurcher SC (1983 to 1985) and Austrian Wiener EV (1985–86).

SVK
ZIGMUND PALFFY Won a bronze medal with the Czechoslovakian national junior team at the 1991 World Junior Championships... Finished the junior tournament with 13 points, second on the team in scoring behind Martin

Rucinsky... Played for Czechoslovakia at the 1991 Canada Cup... Shoulder injury kept him out of the 1992 Albertville Olympics... Tops in assists (seven) and points (10) at the 1994 Lillehammer Olympics while playing for Slovakia... Also played in the 1996 World Championships and at the 1996 World Cup of Hockey.

New York Islanders second choice, 26th overall, in the 1991 NHL Entry Draft... Averaged a point a game and led his club in scoring in his first season in the Czech National League... Fourth leading scorer in the Czech League with Dukla Trencin in 1991–92... His team won the 1992 Czechoslovakian playoff championship... Led Czech League in points and assists in 1992–93... Made his NHL debut on January 7, 1994... Divided his playing time in 1994–95 between the Islanders and Denver of the International Hockey League... Improved steadily, finishing with 11 points in the final 15 games of the NHL season... Had big breakthrough season in 1995–96... His 17 power-play goals ranked eighth in NHL... Led the Islanders in goals (43), points (87), power-play goals (17), game-winning goals (6) and shots (257)... Joined Mike Bossy as only Islanders to record hat tricks in consecutive games... In 1997–98, led the Islanders in scoring with 45 goals and 42 assists for 87 points in 82 games.

SVK
DUSAN PASEK represented Czechoslovakia at the World Junior Championships in 1979 and 1980 before playing at the Canada Cup in 1981. He went on to represent Czechoslovakia at the Canada Cup again in 1984 and 1987 as well as at five World Championships and at the Olympics in Sarajevo in 1984 and Calgary in 1988.

Pasek spent one year in the NHL with the Minnesota North Stars in 1988–89 and played with the Kalamazoo Wings the following year before returning to his hometown of Bratislava in 1990–91. He also played in Italy and Finland over three seasons. In 1992, Pasek became general manager of the Slovak Ice Hockey Federation as well as the Slovan Bratislava team, moving up to vice president and then president in 1995. Slovakia won the Pool C World Championships in 1994, the Pool B title the following year and played at the World Cup of Hockey in 1996. Pasek was part of the executive of the Slovak team that played at Nagano in 1998. He was shot and killed shortly after the Olympics.

TCH
JAN PEKA Began to played for the Czechoslovakian national team when the nation was still known as Bohemia in 1913 and continued until 1936... Saw action in 76 international games... Played at two Olympics (1928 and 1936), six European Championships (1913 and 1925 to 1929) and eight World and European Championships (1920, 1928 and 1931 to 1936)... European champion in 1925, 1929 and 1933... Bronze medalist at the World Championships in 1920 and 1933.

One of the pioneers of hockey in Czechoslovakia... Began his career in Studentsky Hockey Cercle Karlin... Later played for AC Sparta Praha and the famous LTC Praha (1927 to 1936)... Played goaltender until the age of 42.

TCH
JAROSLAV PITNER His international coaching career got started in 1959 as a coach of the Czechoslovak junior team (until 1962)... From 1963 to 1965 coached the Czechoslovak B-team... Hired as a coach of the Czechoslovakian national team in 1966 and worked with Vladimir Kostka until 1973... Coached the team at two Olympics and seven World and European Championships... In 1972, under his coaching, the Czechoslovak team won the gold medal at the World Championships... The team also won an Olympic silver medal at Grenoble in 1968, a silver medal at the World Championships in 1968 and 1971 and bronze medal at the World Championships in 1969, 1970 and 1973.

Began his hockey career as a goaltender in 1947 with HC Zivonin... Later played for CSS Olomouc (until 1952)... From 1952 to 1955 he played for Kridla Vlasti, and from 1955 to 1958 for Moravia Olomouc... At the end of his career, became a playing assistant coach... In 1958 he was hired as a coach of Dukla Jihlava in the top Czechoslovak League... Worked at that position until 1982... Dukla Jihlava won eight national titles under his coaching (1967 to 1972, 1974 and 1982)... Later worked in Germany with VEB Selb (1982–83) and EV Landshut (1983 to 1985)... Coached Skoda Plzen from 1985 to 1987 and in 1990–91.

TCH
MICHAL PIVONKA caught the attention of NHL scouts at the 1983 European Junior Championships when he was named to the tournament all-star team. He represented Czechoslovakia at the World Junior Championships in 1984 and was named both an all-star and best forward at the 1985 event. That year, Pivonka also represented Czechoslovakia at the World Championships and won a gold medal. He played at both tournaments again in 1986. Pivonka entered the NHL with the Washington Capitals in 1986–87. After coming to North America, Pivonka played for Czechoslovakia at the Canada Cup in 1991.

TCH
FRANTISEK POSPISIL Played in three Olympics and 11 World and European Championships during his career with the Czechoslovakian national team... Also played at the 1976 Canada Cup... Was the captain of Czechoslovak team... World Champion in 1972, 1976 and 1977, silver medalist in 1968, 1971, 1974 and 1975, bronze medalist in 1969, 1970 and 1973... Olympic silver medalist at Grenoble in 1968 and Innsbruck in 1976, bronze medalist at Sapporo in 1972... Finalist at the 1976 Canada Cup... Played 262 games and scored 25 goals for the national team... Named best defenseman at the World and European Championships in 1972... Named to the all-star team of the World and European Championships three times: 1972, 1976 and 1977... Coached the Czechoslovak junior team from 1981 to 1985... From 1986 to 1988 he worked as an assistant coach of the national team.

One of the best defenseman in the history of international hockey, Pospisil began his career at 17 with Poldi SONP Kladno and played for this club his entire career, until 1978... Played for national championship teams from 1975 to 1978... Spent 17 seasons in Czechoslovak League, saw action in 622 games and scored 134 goals... Won the Golden Stick Award (player of the year) in 1970–71 and 1971–72... In 1978–79 he played in Germany for EV Landshut... Chose a coaching career after retiring as a player... Coached Poldi SONP Kladno (1979 to 1983), CHZ Litvinov (1983 to 1985)... Coached in Japan from 1990 to 1992.

CZE
MARTIN PROCHAZKA Participated at the 1990 European Junior Championships and at the 1991 and 1992 World Junior Championships... Won a bronze medal in both 1990 and 1991... Made his debut with the Czech Republic national team at the 1995 World Championships... A member of the gold medal-winning Czech Republic national team at the 1996 World Championships... Scored the winning goal in the final game versus Canada with just 19 seconds remaining... Played in the 1996 World Cup of Hockey... Starred at the 1997 World Championships, where he was the leading scorer with seven goals and seven assists in nine games and was named to the tournament all-star team ...Won bronze medal with Czech Republic Team that year... Helped the Czech Republic team capture the 1998 Olympic gold medal in Nagano.

Toronto's eighth choice, 135th overall, in 1991 draft... Began to play regularly in the Czechoslovakian League at the age of 17... Now a veteran of seven full seasons in the Czech Extraleague... Won a bronze medal with HC Kladno in the 1993–94 season... Named Czech player of the year in 1994–95, finishing second in scoring with 24 goals and 16 assists in 43 games... Played for Swedish club AIK Solna in 1996–97... Was second in scoring on the team with 16 goals and 23 assists for 39 points in 49 games... Made his NHL debut with Toronto Maple Leafs in 1997–98.

CZE
ROBERT REICHEL Brilliant junior career, usually playing on a line with Jaromir Jagr and Bobby Holik... Played in 1988 (gold) and 1989 (silver) European Junior Championships, 1988, 1989 (bronze) and 1990 (bronze) World Junior Championships... Led the European tournament in scoring in 1989 with 21 points (14 goals and seven in six games)... Led the Czechoslovakian junior team in scoring at the 1988 World Junior Championships as a 16-year old... Named best forward and was leading scorer (21 points in seven games) at the 1990 World Junior Championships... Won a bronze medal at senior World Championships in 1990 and 1992 and named to the all-star team in 1990... Became a World Champion as a member of Czech Republic national team in 1996 and was named to the tournament's first all-star team... Scored one goal in three games in the 1996 World Cup of Hockey... Won a bronze medal with Czech Republic team at the 1997 World Championships... Scored three goals in six games and became Olympic champion at Nagano in 1998.

Calgary's fourth choice, 70th overall, in the 1989 NHL Entry Draft... Won a bronze medal with Chemopetrol Litvinov in the 1989–90 season... Set a Czech league single-season scoring record with 83 points in 52 games in 1989–90... Named to the Czechoslovakian League all-star team that season... Played five seasons in the NHL with Calgary, recording back-to-back 40-goal seasons in 1992–93 and 1993–94... In 1995–96, was a top scorer in the DEL (German league) with Frankfurt (101 points in 46 games)... Was the second-leading scorer for the New York Islanders behind Zigmund Palffy in 1997–98 with 25 goals and 40 assists for 65 points in 82 games.

CZE
VLADIMIR RUZICKA Made his debut with the national team at 1983 World and European Championships... Played in every tournament for the national team until his NHL departure in the middle of 1989–90 season... Saw action at two Olympics, two Canada Cup tournaments and five World and European Championships... World Champion in 1985, silver medalist in 1983 and a bronze medalist in 1987 and 1989... He also earned a silver medal at the 1984 Sarajevo Olympics... Named to the all-star team at 1985 World and European Championships... Came back to the Czech national team for the 1997–98 sea-

son and helped them win an Olympic gold medal in Nagano.

Began his career in the Czechoslovak League at the age of 16 with CHZ Litvinov in 1979–80... Toronto's fifth choice, 73rd overall, in 1982 NHL Entry Draft... Played nine years with CHZ Litvinov and two seasons (1987 to 1989) with Dukla Trencin before joining the Edmonton Oilers... Played five years in the NHL with Edmonton, Boston and Ottawa... His best season was 1991–92 with the Bruins when he had 39 goals and 36 assists for 75 points in 77 games... In total, he played in 233 NHL games, collecting 82 goals and 85 assists for 167 points... After finishing his NHL career, came back to the Czech Republic and joined HC Slavia Praha.

CZE
BEDRICH SCERBAN Never played for the Czechoslovakian national junior team, but began to play for the national team in 1987... In eight years with the team, he never missed a major international tournament... Played at three Olympics, one Canada Cup and eight World and European Championships... Was the captain of the Czechoslovakian national team.

Began to play on a minor team in Jihlava... Scerban's idol growing up was 1960s-era Czechoslovakian player Jan Suchy, perhaps the best Czechoslovak defenseman ever... Joined Dukla Jihlava at 19 at the end of 1983–84 season and played seven full seasons with the team, winning national championships in 1985 and 1991... Scerban was the captain of his club... Following the championship 1990–91 season, Scerban inked a deal with Tappara Tampere of the Finnish League... A year later, his former coach with Dukla Jihlava, Stanislav Nevesely (who was also an assistant coach of the Czech national team) personally advised Tommy Sandlin, the coach of the Swedish club Brynas Gavle, to sign Scerban... In 1993, he became the only player in the history of Czechoslovakian hockey to win both a Czechoslovakian and a Swedish national championship after Brynas became champions of Sweden... Later, Screban came back to the Czech Republic and became a national champion again with HC Petra Vsetin.

TCH
BOHUSLAV STASTNY Left winger Bohuslav Stastny joined with Vladimir Martinec and Jiri Novak to form the top forward line for Tesla Pardubice and the Czech National team in the 1970s. He won the World Championship in 1972 and 1976 and also played in the 1976 Canada Cup and the 1976 Olympic Games in Innsbruck, Austria.

SVK
PETER STASTNY Starred on the Czechoslovakian national team which won the World and European Championships in 1976 and 1977... Silver medalist in 1978 and 1979... Played at the 1980 Lake Placid Olympics... Finalist with the Czech team at the 1976 Canada Cup... Became a Canadian citizen on April 2, 1984... Played for Team Canada at the 1984 Canada Cup... Joined the Slovakian national team before the 1993–94 season for an Olympic Qualification Tournament in Sheffield, England... Rejoined the team as a member of Slovan Bratislava in early November to play at Telehockeycup in Norway... Played at the 1994 Lillehammer Olympics and the 1995 World Championship (Pool B) as a member of Slovakian national team.

From 1973 to 1980 played for Slovan Bratislava of the Czechoslovak League... Won a Czechoslovakian League champion title in 1979 with Slovan Bratislava... A year after, he was named the player of the year of the Czechoslovakian League... Joined the Quebec Nordiques before the 1980–81 NHL season... Won the Calder Trophy as rookie of the Year after setting NHL records for most assists (70) and most points (109) by a rookie (Teemu Selanne broke his points record with 132 for the Winnipeg Jets in 1992–93)... Stastny's point totals in the 1980s topped only by Wayne Gretzky... Had 100 points or more in seven of 15 NHL seasons with Quebec, New Jersey and St. Louis... Played in the NHL All-Star Game in 1981, 1982, 1983, 1984, 1986 and 1988... Recorded 450 goals and 789 assists for 1,239 points in 977 regular season games... Added 33 goals and 72 assists for 105 points in 93 playoff games... Was the top-scoring European in NHL history until being surpassed by Jari Kurri.

TCH
KAREL STRAKA Played two seasons for the Czechoslovakian national team... The highlight of his career was the 1957 World and European Championships... Czecoslovak team finished third... Straka was named the best goaltender of the tournament... He saw action in four games and had a goals-against average of 1.25... In his career, he played seven games with the national team.

Began his hockey career in the town of Chomutov... In the 1950s, he played in the Czechoslovak League for Banik Chomutov (later team changed name to VTZ Chomutov)... Was one of the best goalies in the league... After retiring, coached the junior team of VTZ Chomutov.

CZE
ANTONIN STAVJANA The 1984–85 season was very memorable for Stavjana... He played at the Canada Cup and made his debut with the

Czechoslovakian national team at the World and European Championships in Prague at the age of 22... He was named to the second all-star team as the Czechoslovak team won the gold medal... A veteran of many international tournaments, Stavjana was later left off the national team for two seasons, but in 1992–93 Czech national team coach Ivan Hlinka returned Stavjana to the team... He is a veteran of two Olympics, two Canada Cup tournaments and eight World and European Championships... Won a gold medal at the 1996 World Championships.

At the age of 17 he became a regular with his native club, TJ Gottwaldov... His club was called TJ Gottwaldov prior to the political changes in Czechoslovakia in the fall of 1989, after that the name of the town was changed from Gottwaldov back to its original name of Zlin... Calgary's 11th choice, 247th overall, in the 1986 NHL Entry Draft... After spending nine seasons in the Czechoslovak League, he joined the Finnish club JoKP Joensuu before the 1990–91 season... Played two seasons in Finland and was invited to join the Swedish club HV 71 Jonkoping before the 1992–93 season... He later came back to the Czech Republic and became a national champion with HC Petra Vsetin.

TCH
JAN SUCHY His brilliant international career started at the 1965 World and European Championships... Played for the national team until 1974... Took part in one Olympics and eight World and European Championships... Silver medalist in 1965, 1966, 1968, 1971 and 1974, bronze medalist in 1969 and 1970... Olympic silver medalist at Grenoble in 1968... Named the best defenseman at the World and European Championships in 1969 and 1971 and named to the tournament all-star team three times: 1969, 1970 and 1971... Played in 160 games for the Czechoslovakian national team, scoring 44 goals.

Considered one of the best defenseman in the history of international hockey... Spent most of his career with Dukla Jihlava, from 1963 to 1979... In 16 seasons in the Czechoslovak League, played in 562 games and scored 162 goals... A member of teams that won the national title seven times... Named the best player of the year (Golden Stick Award) twice: 1968–69 and 1969–70... Continued his career in other European countries... Played in WAT Stadlau (Austria) from 1979 to 1981, ESV Kaufbeuren (Germany) in 1981–82, EV Landsberg (Germany) in 1982–83, UEC Modling (Austria) in 1983–84... Retired at the age of 40.

SVK
JULIUS SUPLER Began his international coaching career working with the Czechoslovakian national junior team (under 20)... By the end of the 1992–93 season, he was named the first coach of the Slovakian national team... Under his coaching, the Slovaks won the Qualification Tournament in Sheffield, England for the 1994 Lillehammer Olympics... Coached the Slovaks at the Lillehammer Games, the 1994 (Pool C), 1995 (Pool B) and 1996 (Pool A) World Championships... Won tournaments in 1994 and 1995.

Began his hockey career with LS Poprad and Liptovsky Mikulas of Czechoslovakian Division 2 in 1970... Next six seasons (and until 1976) he played in the Czechoslovakian League with Slovan Bratislava and VSZ Kosice... Began his coaching career as an assistant coach in PS Poprad in 1979–80... Worked in his native Poprad as an assistant coach until 1985 and later as a coach until 1987... Worked as a coach in Liptovsky Mikulas from 1987 to 1989... Named the coach of Dukla Trencin in 1989–90... Under his coaching Dukla Trencin got a silver medal in 1990, a bronze medal in 1991 and won the Czechoslovak national title in 1992... Named a coach of HC Kosice in 1992–93.

SVK
ROBERT SVEHLA Silver medal at the 1987 European Junior Championships playing for Czechoslovakia... An Olympian with Czechoslovakia at Albertville in 1992 and with Slovakia at Lillehammer in 1994 and Nagano in 1998... Won Olympic bronze in 1992... Also won bronze and was named best defenseman at the 1992 World Championships... Played in the 1996 World Cup of Hockey, recording three assists in three games.

Calgary's fourth choice, 78th overall, in the 1992 NHL Entry Draft... Spent three seasons playing in Sweden... Recalled from Malmo of Swedish Elite League on April 19, 1995... Played his first NHL game for the Florida Panthers against New Jersey one night later... Scored his first goal two nights later in a 4–2 win over Quebec... In 1995–96, his 49 assists set a single-season franchise record... Was third on Florida's scoring list and first among defensemen in 1997–98 with nine goals and 34 assists in 79 games.

CZE
ROMAN TUREK Czechoslovakia's top junior goalie in the late 1980s... Won three medals in junior international competitions: European gold in 1988 and World bronze in 1989 and 1990... All-star at the 1988 European Junior Championships... Named to the Czech national team roster for the 1993 World Championships, but didn't see any action... Backup to Petr Briza at the 1994 Lillehammer Olympics and the 1994 World Championships... Played well at the 1995 World Championships, earning all-star honors with a goals-against

average of 1.50... Played a key role as the Czechs won the 1996 World Championships... Played every minute in eight games, posting a goals-against average of 1.88... Named best goaltender and to the all-star team at the tournament... Played at the 1996 World Cup of Hockey.

Minnesota's sixth choice, 113th overall, in the 1990 NHL Entry Draft... Became a goalie because he was last in line at a youth hockey practice and only goaltending equipment was left... At 20 years old became a starter with his club, HC Ceske Budejovice... He was the only goalie in the Czech League who catches right... In 1991–92 HC Ceske Budejovice was relegated to the second division... Stayed with his club, despite invitations from other teams, and helped the team win promotion back to the top division... Won Golden Stick Award in 1993–94 as the best player of the Czech League... Spent the 1995–96 season in the German Hockey League with Nurnberg... Played in all but two games... Signed with the NHL's Dallas Stars in the summer of 1996.

TCH
VLADIMIR ZABRODSKY Played at two Olympics and six World and European Championships... World Champion in 1947 and 1949, bronze medalist in 1955... Silver medalist behind Canada at the 1948 St. Moritz Olympics... Voted to the all-star team at the 1954 World and European Championships... Played a total of 93 games for the national team and scored an amazing 158 goals.

Started his career in 1939 with LTC Praha where he played until 1949... From 1950 to 1960 he played for Spartak Sokolovo Praha... Was with Bohemians CKD Praha from 1963 to 1965... Spent 18 seasons in the Czechoslovak League (until the age of 42), played in 230 games and scored 306 goals... A member of teams that won the Czechoslovak national title six times... Won the goal-scoring title five times... In 1948, was a member of LTC Praha team which played the first international exhibition games in Moscow.

DENMARK

JESPER BROENG DUUS Made his first international appearance at the 1991 World and European Championships (Pool C)... Helped the Danish team to win the tournament that year and developed into one of the best defensemen on the team... Had his best career performance at the 1991 tournament, recording five goals in eight games... In the early 1990s, he played in Swedish League for Farjestads BK Karlstad.

HEINZ RIBE EHLERS One of the best players in the history of hockey in Denmark... A veteran forward with the national team, he starred at the end of 1980s and the beginning of the 1990s... The highlight of his career occurred at the 1987 World and European Championships (Pool C), where he was named the best forward and voted to the tournament all-star team... The Danish team finished second at the event that year... He also had great performance in the 1991 (Pool C) tournament, helping Denmark win the championship and be promoted to Pool B... Named the best forward of the tournament that year as well after recording an amazing 10 goals and 15 assists for 25 points in eight games... In the early 1990s he played for AIK Solna in Sweden.

BENT HANSEN Played in five World and European Championships during the late 1970s and 1980s... He made his debut in 1978 (Pool C) and had six goals and two assists for eight points in seven games... Helped the Danish national team to be promoted to Pool B of the World and European Championships... Had good tournament in 1981 (Pool C), recording four goals and five assist for five points in seven games.

EAST GERMANY
see page 1848

ESTONIA
see page 1859

FINLAND

MATTI HAGMAN As a member of the Finnish national team, he played at the 1976 Innsbruck Olympics and four World and European Championships... Also saw action at the Canada Cup tournament in 1976, 1981 and 1987... In total, played 104 games for the Finnish national team, collecting 21 goals and 42 assists for 63 points.

Began his senior career at the age of 17 with HIFK Helsinki... Played four seasons with the team... Boston's sixth choice, 104th overall, in 1975 NHL Amateur Draft... Signed with the Bruins before the 1976–77 season... Spent one and a half seasons with Boston before finishing the 1977–78 season with the Quebec Nordiques of the World Hockey Association... Came back to Finland and played two seasons with HIFK... From 1980 to 1982 he played in the NHL for the Edmonton Oilers... Came back to HIFK again and played until 1989 (in 1985–86 he played in Germany for EV Landshut)... Played on national title teams with HIFK in 1973–74, 1979–80 and 1982–83... From

1989 to 1991 he played for Reipas Lahti before spending his last season with HIFK... Played 513 games in the Finnish League, collecting 288 goals and 462 assists for 750 points.

RAIMO HELMINEN Played in the 1982 European Junior and 1983 World Junior Championships... Led all scorers at the 1984 World Junior Championships with 11 goals and 13 assists for 24 points in seven games... This single-tournament record stood until it was surpassed in 1993 by Sweden's Peter Forsberg... Along with winning a silver medal, he was named best forward at the 1984 World Juniors and was selected to the tournament all-star team... Saw action at four Olympics: 1984, 1988, 1992 and 1994, equalling the mark for most Olympic appearances by a Finnish hockey player... Won an Olympic silver medal at Calgary in 1988 and a bronze at Lillehammer in 1994... Won silver medal at the 1994 World Championships... Played in the 1987 Canada Cup and at five World Championships... Helped Finland win its first gold medal at the World Championships in 1995... In 1996–97, he played in his fourth consecutive World Championships with the Finnish national team... Saw action in three games in 1996 World Cup of Hockey, recording two assists... Helped Finnish national team capture a bronze medal at the 1998 Nagano Olympics.

New York Rangers second choice, 35th overall, in the 1984 NHL Entry Draft... Jumped to the NHL at the age of 21 and played with the Rangers, North Stars and Islanders... 40 points in 66 games as an NHL rookie with the Rangers... Started his hockey career in Finland with Ilves Tampere... Won a national Finnish title with Ilves in 1984–85... He finished the 1984–85 season as the league's third-leading scorer (21 goals and 36 assists in 36 games)... Named to the Finnish All-Star Team in 1987–88... After returning from the NHL, Helminen spent seven seasons in Sweden playing for Malmo, helping the club to Swedish national championships in 1992 and 1994... In 1995–96, was second in team scoring with Malmo (eight goals, 19 assists in 40 games played)... Came back to his original club, Ilves , in 1996–97 and had a great season, collecting 11 goals and 39 assists for 50 points in 49 games.

AARNE HONKAVAARA Finland's first hockey superstar, Aarne Honkavaara was the top scorer in the Finnish league six times from 1943–44 to 1951–52 as a member of Ilves Tampere. He was a member of the 1952 Finnish Olympic team and later coached the Finnish Nationals.

TIMO JUTILA Won two medals at the World Junior Championships, silver in 1981 and bronze in 1982... Played in the 1987 and 1991 Canada Cup tournaments... A veteran of three Olympics (1984, 1992 and 1994) and seven World Championships... Named to the World Championships All-Star Team in 1992 and 1994... Won an Olympic bronze medal in 1994... Helped Finland to its first gold medal and was named to the all-star team at the 1995 IIHF World Championships... He was also part of Finland's silver medal finsihes at the 1992 and 1994 World Championships... Leader in the dressing room, often serving as a captain of the Finnish national team... Captained the Finnish national team at the 1996 World Championships in Vienna, Austria... Played at the 1997 World Championships.

Buffalo's sixth choice, 68th overall, in the 1982 NHL Entry Draft... Signed with the Sabres in the summer of 1984, but played only 10 games in the NHL... Spent the major part of the 1984–85 season with the Rochester Americans of the American Hockey League... Began his senior career with Tappara Tampere... Won the Finnish national championship title five times, all with Tappara, in 1982, 1984, 1986, 1987 and 1988... Named to the Finnish League all-star team four times: 1987, 1988, 1993 and 1994... Named the best defenseman of the Finnish League in 1987... Starred in the 1988 Finnish League playoffs, finishing fourth in playoff scoring (six goals, six assists)... Joined Swedish club Lulea, the northernmost hockey team in the world, in 1988–89... Played four seasons in Sweden... Came back to play for Tappara in 1992... In 1995–96, he played his 16th season of elite division hockey and enjoyed the best season of his career, collecting 14 goals and 37 assists for 51 points in 49 games... Was seventh overall in the Finnish League in scoring, tops among defensemen... In 1996–97, played for Bern in Switzerland and won a champions title with his new team.

MATTI KEINONEN Played for the Finnish national team from 1962 to 1973... Participated in two Olympics and 10 World and European Championships... Was one of the best forwards on the team... He played in 196 games for the national team in his career... Scored 71 goals and had 49 assists for the total of 120 points.

Began his career in 1960 with Lukko Rauma... Played for Lukko from 1960 to 1965 and from 1968 to 1970... From 1965 to 1968 he played for RU-38 Pori... He later played for HJK Helsinki (1970 to 1973), Jokerit Helsinki (1973 to 1975), TPS Turku (1977 to 78)... In his career, he played 267 games in the Finnish League, collecting 186 goals and 125 assists for 311 points... Played for teams that won the national title twice: 1962–63 and 1966–67... After retiring, he began his coaching career... From 1982 to 1985 he coached TPS Turku... Later worked with Lukko Rauma.

VELI-PEKKA KETOLA Played at two Olympics and seven World and European Championships for Finland from 1968 to 1974... Participated at 1976 and 1981 Canada Cup tournaments... In his career with the national team, he played in 186 games, recording 60 goals and 45 assists for 105 points.

Made his first appearance in the Finnish League at 15 with Karhut Pori... Later played three full seasons with Karhut... The majority of the career spent with Assat Pori (1967 to 1969, 1970 to 1974 and 1977 to 1981)... Played one year (1969–70) with Jokerit Helsinki... A member of teams that won the national title three times: 1964–65, 1970–71 and 1977–78... In the Finnish League, he played in 401 games, recording 263 goals and 271 assists for 534 points... Spent three seasons with the Winnipeg Jets of the World Hockey Association (1974 to 1977)... The Jets won the AVCO Cup in 1975–76 WHA season... In 1981–82 played in the NHL with the Colorado Rockies.

MARKUS KETTERER Junior career highlighted by a brilliant performance at the 1987 World Junior Championships... Finns won gold and Ketterer was named best goaltender... Played in the 1991 Canada Cup... Stopped 42 shots in a 2–2 tie with Canada and made 36 saves in a 1–0 shutout of Czechoslovakia... Named the best goaltender of the 1991 World Championships with a goals-against average of 1.72... Won silver medal with the Finnish team at the 1992 World Championships... Named to the all-star team at this tournament... Played in the 1992 Albertville Olympics and six World Championships... Played in one game at the 1996 World Championships in Vienna, Austria.

Buffalo's sixth choice, 107th overall, in the 1992 NHL Entry Draft... Signed by the Sabres in 1993 but never played in the NHL, spending two seasons with Buffalo's farm club, the Rochester Americans of the American Hockey League... Won four consecutive Finnish League championships, in 1989, 1990 and 1991 with TPS Turku and in 1992 with Jokerit Helsinki... Named best goaltender in 1991–92... Left TPS after the 1990–91 season to return to his hometown team, Jokerit, whom he last played for in 1987–88... Grew up idolizing Soviet legend Vladislav Tretiak... In 1995–96, he played in Sweden after two years in North America... Spent his first year in Sweden's Elitserien playing for Farjestad Karlstad... His team finished third in the regular season and lost in the playoff semifinals to Lulea, the eventual 1995–96 Swedish champion... Became Swedish champion in 1996–97 with Farjestad.

SAKU KOIVU Played for Finland's national junior team in the 1993 World Junior Championships and was named to tournament second all-star team... Played for Team Finland at the 1993 World Championships... Played for the national junior team in 1994 World Junior Championships... Won silver medal with Finland at the 1994 World Championships, and was named to tournament all-star team... Won a bronze medal with Finland at the 1994 Lillehammer Olympics... Won a gold medal with Finland at the 1995 World Championship, named to the tournament all-star team and named best forward... Recorded one goal and three assists in four games during the 1996 World Cup of Hockey... Played at the 1997 World Championships in Finland... Finished second in scoring behind Teemu Selanne (two goals and eight assists for 10 points) at the 1998 Nagano Olympics... Won a bronze medal with the Finnish team.

Montreal's first choice, 21st overall, in the 1993 NHL Entry Draft ...Played on the first line for TPS Turku in the 1993 Finnish League playoffs, winning the championship... Coached by his father, Jukka, in Finland... Made his debut with the Montreal Canadiens on 1995–96 and finished fourth in voting for Calder Trophy, given to rookie of the year... Was third-leading scorer on the Montreal Canadiens roster in 1997–98 with 14 goals and 43 assists for 57 points in 69 games.

JARI KURRI Played for Finland in the 1987 Canada Cup... Named to tournament all-star team at the 1991 and 1994 IIHF World Championships... Won a silver medal with Finland at the 1994 World Championships... Scored one goal in four games of the 1996 World Cup of Hockey... In 1998, won a bronze medal with the Finnish team in at the Nagano Olympics.

Edmonton's third choice, 69th overall, in the 1980 NHL Entry Draft... Finished second in team scoring in 1981... Tied for ninth in the NHL scoring race in 1982–83... Played in the 1983 NHL All-Star Game... Runner-up in voting for 1983 Selke Trophy, given to NHL's best defensive forward... Led playoffs in goals in 1984 and helped Edmonton win the Stanley Cup... Named to Second All-Star Team in 1984... Became the third player in NHL history to record a 70-goal season in 1984–85... Tied record for most goals in one playoff year with 19 in 1985 as Edmonton repeated as Stanley Cup champions... Won the Lady Byng Trophy, given to player who best combines excellent play and gentlemanly conduct, in 1984–85... Named First Team All-Star in 1984–85... Led the NHL in goals with 68 in 1985–86... Named a Second Team All-Star in 1985–86... Finished second in NHL scoring behind teammate Wayne Gretzky in 1986–87 with 108 points... Named a First Team All-Star in 1986–87... Scored Stanley Cup-winning goal for Edmonton in 1987... Won fourth Stanley Cup with Edmonton in 1988... Named a Second Team All-Star in 1989... Won fifth Stanley Cup title with Edmonton in 1990... Played for the Milan Devils in Italy in 1990–91... Returned to the NHL with

the Los Angeles Kings in 1991–92... Scored 500th NHL goal versus Boston on October 17, 1992... Played 20 games in his native Finland with Jokerit during the 1994–95 season... Scored his 600th NHL goal with the Colorado Avalanche in 1997–98... Is the top-scoring European player in the history of the NHL.

JERE LEHTINEN Member of the Finnish national team that won gold in 1995 at the World Championships and was named to the tournament's all-star team... Assisted on the game-winning goal by Ville Peltonen in the gold medal game against Sweden... Along with linemates Peltonen and Saku Koivu, was on the ice for all four Finland goals in 4–1 win in final game... Played on Finland's 1994 Olympic team... Ranked fourth in tournament scoring (behind Peter Forsberg, Markus Naslund and David Vyborny) at the 1993 World Junior Championships with six goals and eight assists for 14 points in seven games)... Received the Seiko Award as one of the best three players on Team Finland during the 1993 World Juniors... Was a member of Team Finland that won the 1989 World Challenge Under–17 Championships... Recorded two goals and two assists in four games of the 1996 World Cup of Hockey... Won bronze medal at the 1998 Nagano Olympics, collecting four goals and two assists in six games with Finnish team.

Minnesota's third choice, 88th overall, in the 1992 NHL Entry Draft... Played for TPS in the Finnish League during the 1993–94 and 1994–95 seasons, winning the league title both years... In 1995–96, he made his debut in the NHL with the Dallas Stars... Named NHL rookie of the month for February... Finished seventh among rookies in assists with 22... Scored 23 goals in 72 games with Dallas in 1997–98.

JYRKI LUMME Won a silver medal with Finland at the the 1988 Winter Olympics in Calgary... Played for Finland at the 1990 IIHF World Championships... Ranked sixth in team scoring at the 1991 World tournament... Played for Team Finland at the 1991 Canada Cup... Member of the Finnish team at the 1996 World Championships... Played at the 1996 World Cup of Hockey... Won a bronze medal at the 1998 Olympics in Nagano.

Montreal's third choice, 57th overall, in the 1986 NHL Entry Draft... Boyhood idol was Risto Siltanen... Made his NHL debut with the Canadiens in 1989–90, but was later sent to Sherbrooke of the American Hockey League... Finished third in scoring among all rookie defensemen while splitting 1989–90 season between Montreal and Vancouver... Won the Walter "Babe" Pratt Award as the Vancouver Canucks' outstanding defenseman in 1991–92 after leading all Vancouver defensemen in scoring... Became fifth Canuck to win more than one Pratt Trophy when he led all Vancouver defensemen in scoring again in 1992–93... Career-high 55 points in 1993–94 was the sixth-highest total in history by a Canucks defenseman and just eight points off the record... Became Canucks' highest-scoring defensemen in postseason play during the 1994 playoffs as Vancouver reached the Stanley Cup finals... In 1995–96, led Canucks defensemen in goals (17), assists (37) and points (54)... Appeared in his 500th NHL game on March 12th, 1996... Finished the 1997–98 season as Vancouver's top scoring defenseman with nine goals and 21 assists for 30 points in 74 games.

PEKKA MARJAMAKI Had an outstanding career with the Finnish national team... Played for the nationals for 12 years... Participated at two Olympics and 10 World and European Championships... Named the best defenseman of 1975 World and European Championships... He played in 251 games for the Finnish national team in his career, recording 40 goals and 24 assists for 64 points... One of the best defenseman in the history of Finnish hockey.

A veteran of the Finnish League, Marjamaki spent almost his entire career with Tappara Tampere... He played for Tappara from 1964 to 1979 and from 1981 to 1984... From 1979 to 1981, he played in Sweden for HV 71 Jonkoping... In 18 seasons in the Finnish League, he played in 476 games, collecting 125 goals and 129 assists for 254 points... Played on teams that won the Finnish national title five times: 1974–75, 1976–77, 1978–79, 1981–82 and 1983–84.

JARMO MYLLYS Won a silver medal at the European Junior Championships (1983) and the World Junior Championships (1984)... Named best goaltender and an all-star at the 1983 European Junior Championships... Played in the 1985 World Junior Championships... Played for the Finnish national team at the 1987 Canada Cup... Played in the 1988 (silver) and 1994 (bronze) Olympics and in four World Championships... His strong play and 1.83 goals-against average at the 1988 Olympics in Calgary led the Finns to their first Olympic hockey medal... Named best goaltender at the 1995 World Championships as Finland won its first gold medal... Also won silver at the 1994 World Championships... Played for the Finnish national team at the 1996 World Cup of Hockey, the 1997 World Championships and the 1998 Nagano Olympics (won bronze medal).

Minnesota's ninth choice, 172nd overall, in the 1987 NHL Entry Draft... Prior to joining the North Stars, Myllys was Finnish national champion with Ilves Tampere in 1985... In 1987–88, while with Lukko, Myllys was named the best goaltender of the Finnish League and voted to the all-star team...

Spent four years in North America... First three years split between the North Stars and Kalamazoo in the International Hockey League... Named to the IHL second all-star team in 1990... Shared Kalamazoo's 1991 "Overall Excellence" Award with fellow goaltender Larry Dyck... Acquired from Minnesota by San Jose in the Dispersal Draft on May 30, 1991... After a year with the Sharks he returned home, playing for KooKoo Kouvola in the Finnish second division... Rejoined Lukko Rauma in 1993–94... Named to the 1994 Finnish all-star team... Joined Lulea in Sweden's Elitserien in 1994–95... In 1995–96, he played in all but one game during the regular season for his Swedish club, Lulea, helping his team finish first in the regular season and win the Swedish championship for the first time in club history... Played every minute in 13 playoff games... Reached playoff finals with Lulea in 1996–97.

MIKA NIEMINEN His first major international competition was the 1984 European Junior Championships where Finns finished fourth... Made his World Championships debut in 1991, compiling 11 points (five goals, six assists) and tying teammate Teemu Selanne and Soviet Valeri Kamensky for third place in the overall scoring race... First played at the World Championships in 1991... Won World Championship gold in 1995 and silver in 1992 and 1994... Centered a line with Jari Kurri on the right wing at the 1991 World Championships... Also teamed with Teemu Selanne at the 1992 Albertville Olympics... Won a bronze medal at the 1994 Lillehammer Olympics... Played in the 1996 World Cup of Hockey... Led Finnish team in scoring at the 1997 World Championships... Won a bronze medal in 1998 Olympics.

After growing up in Tampere, he went to Lahti to begin his professional career, playing for Kiekko-Reipas Lahti in the second division... After two years with Reipas, he was invited to Ilves Tampere of the Finnish League... Named rookie of the year in his first season with Ilves... Named to the all-star team in 1990... Won two medals with Ilves, bronze in 1989 and silver in 1990... Finished the 1990–91 season as the third-leading scorer in the Finnish League (20 goals, 42 assists in 44 games played)... Moved to Sweden in the summer of 1992 to play for Lulea and was the team's leading scorer for three seasons... Top scorer in the Swedish league in 1994–95 (18 goals, 31 assists in 38 games played)... In 1995–96, made his debut with Grasshopper Zurich in the Swiss Nationalliga-B... Finished the season as the club's best scorer (74 points in 36 games).

TEPPO NUMMINEN Was a member of Team Finland at the World Championships in 1987 and 1991... Had a goal and four assists for the silver medal-winning Finnish Olympic team at Calgary in 1988... Participated in the 1987 and 1991 Canada Cup tournaments... Was selected to represent Finland at the 1994 World Championships, but could not play due to injury... Member of the Finnish team at the 1996 World Championships... Played for Finland at the 1996 World Cup of Hockey... Named to the all-star team at the 1997 World Championships... Won bronze medal at the 1998 Olympics in Nagano.

Winnipeg's second choice, 29th overall, in the 1986 NHL Entry Draft... Childhood hero was Swedish tennis star Bjorn Borg... Played the 1984–85 season with Tappara in the Finnish Junior League... Promoted to Tappara's club in the Finnish elite division at age 17, playing three seasons... Made his NHL debut for the Jets on October 6, 1988, scoring a shorthanded, game-tying goal in a 2–2 tie with Vancouver... Played a second full season in 1991–92, becoming the only Jet to take part in all 80 games that year... A dislocated thumb cut short his 1993–94 campaign... Led Jets in plus–minus in 1994–95, with a +12 ranking... In 1997–98, led Phoenix Coyotes defensemen in scoring with 11 goals and 40 assists for 51 points in 82 games.

JANNE OJANEN The Finnish media gave Janne Ojanen the nickname of "Golden Boy" after winning gold medals at the 1986 European Junior Championships, the 1987 World Junior Championships and with his team in the Finnish League... European Junior all star in 1986... A veteran of the 1987 and 1991 Canada Cup tournaments, 1988 and 1994 Olympics and four World Championships... Missed the 1992 Albertville Olympics due to a wrist injury... Became a world champion in 1995 and won a silver medal in 1994... He scored one of the most important goals in Finnish hockey history when he scored the first goal in a 2–1 victory over the Soviet Union that brought Finland its first Olympic silver medal at Calgary in 1988... Played in the 1996 World Cup of Hockey and at the 1997 World Championships.

New Jersey's third choice, 45th overall, in the 1986 NHL Entry Draft... Joined the Devils organization in 1988–89... Played his first full NHL season for the Devils in 1989–90, collecting 17 goals and 13 assists for 30 points in 64 games... Came back to Finland in 1990, but rejoined the Devils prior to the 1992–93 season... Returned to Finland a year later... Began his hockey career with Tappara Tampere... Won national Finnish championship twice, both with Tappara in 1987 and 1988 during his first two regular seasons with the club... Named the Finnish rookie of the year in 1987... Third-leading scorer in the 1987 Finnish playoffs with 10 points in nine games... Returned from the NHL in 1993 and played three seasons in his native Tappara... Had 11 points in the 1994 playoffs... Finnish League's third-leading scorer in 1994–95... In 1995–96, he was the second-leading scorer in the Finnish League (20 goals, 44

assists in 45 games played) for Tappara… Next year, joined the Swedish Elite League, playing in Malmo.

LASSE OKSANEN A record holder for the most games played for the Finnish national team with 282… Holds second place on the all-time scoring list with 101 goals and 58 assists for 159 points… Had an amazing international career… Played 13 years for the national team… Participated in three Olympics, 13 World and European Championships and the 1976 Canada Cup… Captain of the team… In these major tournaments, he played in 124 games and scored 35 goals.

At the age of 18, Oksanen made his debut in the Finnish League with Ilves Tampere in 1960–61… Played almost his entire career with Ilves (1960 to 1975, 1977 to 1979 and 1980 to 1982)… Spent three years in Italy with HC Val Gardena (1975 to 1977) and HC Alleghe (1979–80)… His teams won the Finnish national title in 1961–62, 1965–66 and 1971–72… Played a total of 477 games in the Finnish League, recording 268 goals and 230 assists for 498 points.

ESA PELTONEN Outstanding international career… Participated at four Olympics, 11 World and European Championships and the 1976 Canada Cup… In these tournaments, he saw action in 109 games and scored 35 goals… In total, he played in 277 games for the Finnish national team (trailing only Lasse Oksanen in team history) and collected 93 goals and 49 assists for 142 points.

Started his career at 18 with Karpat Oulu in 1965–66… Played the next three seasons with Upon Pallo Lahti… Was invited to join HJK Helsinki in 1969 and played there for three seasons… Spent the next 11 seasons with HIFK Helsinki… His last season, 1983–84, played with Liekkoreipas Lahti… Played on national title-winning teams three times: 1973–74, 1979–80 and 1982–83… In the Finnish League, he played in 488 games and recorded 317 goals and 210 assists for 527 points.

REIJO RUOTSALAINEN represented Finland at the World Junior Championships from 1977 to 1979 and the the World Championships from 1978 to 1981. He was named best defenseman and a tournament all-star at the 1980 event.
From 1981–82 until 1989–90, Ruotsalainen played in the NHL with the New York Rangers, Edmonton Oilers and New Jersey Devils. He also spent time in both Finland and Sweden during those years, and represented his country again at the World Championships in 1985 and 1989, the Canada Cup in 1981 and 1987 and the 1988 Calgary Olympics. He has continued to play in Finland and Switzerland since 1990, though he remains on the NHL protected list of the Edmonton Oilers and was protected during the 1998 Expansion Draft. Ruotsalainen's father Reino coaches the Finnish national junior team.

CHRISTIAN RUUTTU Played in two World Junior Championships and won a silver medal in 1984… Played in the 1987 and 1991 Canada Cup tournaments… Led Finland in scoring at the 1991 Canada Cup with six points in six games… Played in eight World Championships, helping Finland win silver medals in 1992 and 1994… At the 1991 World Championships, he tied with Swede Mats Sundin as the tournament's leading goal scorer with seven goals… Scored one goal in four games in the 1996 World Cup of Hockey.

Buffalo's ninth choice, 134th overall, in the 1983 NHL Entry Draft… Signed with the Sabres prior to 1986–87 season… Played six years with the team… Had 60 points or more in his first four seasons with Buffalo… Played in the 1988 NHL All-Star Game… Played two and a half years with Chicago before being traded to Vancouver on March 10, 1995… Played in 621 games during his nine-year NHL career, recording 134 goals and 298 assists for 432 points… Returned to Europe and joined the Swedish club Vastra Frolunda prior to 1995–96 season… Started his hockey career in Assat Pori… Won two silver medals in the Finnish championships, with Assat Pori (1983–84) and with HIFK Helsinki (1985–86)… In 1983–84, at the age of 20, was the Finnish League's third-leading scorer with 60 points in 37 games… Was also third-leading scorer two years later with HIFK Helsinki… Named to the Finnish League all-star team in 1985–86… In 1995–96, spent his first season with Vastra Frolunda in Sweden… Helped the club to a second place finish in the regular season standings… Vastra Frolunda also reached the finals in the play-offs before losing to Lulea… Was seventh on the Swedish League's regular-season scoring list and led his club in scoring.

TEEMU SELANNE Played for Team Finland at the World Junior Championships in 1989… A member of Team Finland at the 1991 Canada Cup, scoring the game-winning goal in one of two Finnish wins… Played at the 1991 World Championships (team had 6–3–1 record) and at the 1992 Olympics for Finland… Selected to Team Finland for the 1994 World Championships but could not play because of injury… Led Finnish team in scoring at the 1996 World Cup of Hockey… Won a bronze medal at the 1998 Nagano Olympics and was top scorer of the tournament (four goals and six assists in five games).

Winnipeg's first choice, tenth overall, in the 1988 NHL Entry Draft…

Played five years with Jokerit in the Finnish League from 1987 to 1992… Was named to the Finnish All-Star team in 1991 and 1992… Tied for the NHL lead in goals with Alexander Mogilny and established a rookie record with 76 in 1992–93 and finished fifth in NHL scoring with 132 points, which also set rookie record (breaking Peter Stastny's mark of 109 points)… Scored his 100th goal in his 130th game, the second-fastest pace in NHL history (Mike Bossy, 129 games)… In his rookie season he represented Winnipeg at NHL All-Star Game… Sophomore season came to an end on January 26, 1994 when he suffered a severed achilles tendon in Winnipeg… His childhood hockey idols were Guy Lafleur, Jari Kurri and Wayne Gretzky… In 1997–98, while playing for Anaheim, tied for the NHL in goal-scoring along with Peter Bondra (Washington) with 52.

ARI SULANDER Made his debut with the Finnish national team at the 1993 World Championships… Was a backup goaltender… Also played backup role at the 1995, 1996 and 1997 World Championships… Starred 1997–98… Started the Nagano Olympics as a backup, but showed an excellent performance in the bronze medal game when Finland beat Canada 3–2… Named the best goaltender and to the second all-star team of the 1998 World Championship… Won silver medal with the Finnish team.

Spent his entire career with Jokerit Helsinki… Made his debut in the Finnish League in 1989–90… Won Finnish national title four times (1991–92, 1993–94, 1995–96 and 1996–97)… Won the European Champions Cup with Jokerit twice: in 1994–95 and 1995–96… Named to the all-star team of the tournament in 1994–95.

KARI TAKKO Won a silver medal as a member of the Finnish team at the 1979 European Junior Championships… Two years later he won another silver medal at the 1981 World Junior Championships… He won bronze at the 1982 World Juniors… Made his senior national team debut at the 1983 World Championships at the age of 20… Also played at the 1984 Sarajevo Olympics, the 1983, 1985 and 1991 World Championships and the 1987 Canada Cup… Played two games for Finland at the 1996 World Cup of Hockey.

Minnesota's fifth choice, 97th overall, in the 1984 NHL Entry Draft… Signed with the North Stars prior to the 1985–86 season… Spent the majority of his first season in North America with Springfield of the American Hockey League… Became a regular goaltender with the North Stars in 1986–87… Played four years in Minnesota before being traded to Edmonton in the middle of 1990–91 season… In six years in the NHL, he saw action in 142 games (37–71–14) with a goals-against average of 3.90… Came back to Finland in the summer of 1991 and rejoined his original club, Assat Pori… He had spent seven seasons with Assat before joining Minnesota… His last season before traveling to North America, 1984–85, saw him earn a berth on the Finnish all-star team and win the league's best goaltender award… Won four medals in the Finnish championships, all with Assat: silver in 1979, 1980 and 1984, bronze in 1995… Has remained with Assat since returning from North America… Named the best goaltender of the Finnish League in 1993–94… Played in all 48 games without being replaced.

ESA TIKKANEN Represented Finland at the 1983, 1984, and 1985 World Junior Championships… Earned a silver medal in 1984… second in tournament scoring behind teammate Esa Keskinen in 1985 with seven goals and 12 assists… Named to tournament's first all-star team… Played for Finland at the World Championships in 1985, 1989, 1993 and 1996… Played for the NHL All-Stars in Rendez-Vous '87… Member of Team Finland at the Canada Cup in 1987 and 1991… Won a bronze medal with the Finnish team at the Olympics in Nagano in 1998.

Edmonton's fourth choice, 80th overall, in the 1983 NHL Entry Draft… A member of four Stanley Cup champions in Edmonton (1985, 1987, 1988, and 1990)… Won a fifth Stanley Cup title with the Rangers in 1994… Has finished in the top three in voting for the Selke Trophy four times… Always wore #10 throughout his Finnish and NHL career… Made his NHL debut with the Oilers in the 1985 playoffs… Played his first full NHL season in 1986–87… His 78 points that year were fourth on the team and remain a career high (equaled once)… Was the fourth-leading playoff scorer in 1987–88… Set a new NHL record with two shorthanded goals just eight seconds apart versus Toronto on December 12, 1989… Led Edmonton in scoring with 69 points in 1990–91… Fractured shoulder limited him to just 40 games in 1991–92… Played his first game as a Ranger on March 17, 1993 versus his former Oiler teammates… In 1997–98, started the season with Florida Panthers and was traded to the Washington Capitals.

JORMA VALTONEN Played at three Olympics and nine World and European Championships from 1970 to 1984… Was 38 years old when he played for the national team for the final time… Named the best goaltender at the World and European Championships in 1972… In total, played in 232 games for the Finnish national team—fifth position on the all-time list… Played 65 games for Finland at major international tournaments.

One of the best Finnish goaltenders of all time, Valtonen began his career with TPS Turku… After two seasons (1964 to 1966), he spent one year with

RU–38 Pori and later played five seasons with Assat Pori... From 1972 to 1974 he played for Jokerit Helsinki before spending one season with FoPS Forssa... Played three years (1975 to 1978) in Italy with HC Val Gardena and HC Alleghe... Came back to Finland and played with TPS Turku (1978 to 1980 and 1981 to 1987)... He played in Germany with EHC 70 Munchen in 1980–81... Played on teams that won the national Finnish title in 1966–67, 1970–71 and 1972–73... Played in 525 games in the Finnish League.

HANNU VIRTA An all-star at the 1981 European Junior Championships... Won a bronze medal at the 1982 World Junior Championships... Saw action in the 1987 Canada Cup, 1994 Lillehammer Olympics and six World Championships... Tied Sweden's Anders Eldebrink as the top-scoring defensemen at the 1989 World Championships with eight points (three goals, five assists)... Finnish national team captain at the 1991 World Championships held in his hometown of Turku... Bronze medal at the 1994 Olympics, gold at the 1995 World Championships and silver at the 1994 World Championships... Played for the Finnish team at the 1996 World Cup of Hockey and the 1997 World Championships.

Buffalo's second choice, 38th overall, in the 1981 NHL Entry Draft... Joined the Sabres at the end of 1982–83 season for three games at the age of 19... He became a regular with the Sabres the next year... Played in 245 NHL games, recording 25 goals and 101 assists for 126 points... After spending four productive seasons with the Buffalo Sabres, returned to Finland in 1986 to serve his mandatory eight months of military service.

Began his hockey career with TPS Turku... Four-time Finnish champion, all with TPS (1989, 1990, 1991 and 1993), was silver medalist twice, both with TPS, in 1982 and 1994)... Long-time captain of TPS... Named rookie of the year in the Finnish League in 1981–82... Five-time member of the Finnish league all-star team (1987, 1989, 1990, 1991 and 1992)... Named Finland's best defenseman in 1987, 1989, 1990 and 1991... Played on European Champions Cup winner in 1993–94... In 1995–96, he played his second year with Grasshopper Zurich (along with Finland's Mika Nieminen) in the Swiss league's second division.

URPO YLONEN Had a brilliant international career... Made his debut with the Finnish national team at the 1963 World and European Championships... Played for the nationals until 1978... Participated at three Olympics and 10 World and European Championships... Named the best goaltender of 1970 World and European Championships... In total, he played in 188 games for the national team.

Spent his entire Finnish League career with the clubs from Turku... Played for TuTo Turku from 1965 to 1975 and for TPS Turku from 1975 to 1979... Won the national title with TPS in 1975–76... Played in 399 games in the Finnish league ...Continued his career in Germany with ERC Freiburg (1979 to 1983)... Retired at the age of 40.

FRANCE

STEPHANE BOTTERI One of the most experienced player in the history of the French national team, Botteri finished his career as the playing coach with CSG Morzine... Also worked as a skiing coach in Morzine... Became a French League champion in 1986–87 while with HC Mont Blanc... Named to the first all-star team the same season... Before joining CGS Morzine in October of 1992 he had played with Annecy, St.Gervais, Tours, Paris and Rouen... Second overall in all-time national team games played... Played for the national team from 1983 to 1994... Saw action at three Olympics and eight World and European Championships.

PHILIPPE BOZON Born in France... Spent his junior hockey career with St. Jean of the Quebec Major Junior Hockey League (1984 to 1987)... Named to the QMJHL second all-star team in 1985–86... Signed as a free agent with St. Louis Blues in the fall of 1985... Played in the minors with Peoria (International Hockey League)... Came back to France in 1987... Played five seasons in the French League with HC Mont Blanc, CSG Grenoble and HC Chamonix... Joined the St. Louis Blues after the 1992 Albertville Olympics... Played three years on the team... His total in the NHL is 144 games, 16 goals, 25 assists, 41 points.

Came back to France at the beginning of 1994–95 season and joined CSG Grenoble... Played the next two years in Switzerland national league with La Chaux-de-Fonds and HC Lausanne... Joined German Adler Mannheim before the 1996–97 season and later won the national title with the team... Has starred on the French national team from 1988 to date... Has played at three Olympics and eight World and European Championships... Named the best forward of the World and European Championships (Pool B) in 1991... Voted to the tournament all-star team in 1989 and 1991... Played for France at the 1998 Olympic Games in Nagano.

JACQUES LACARRIERE One of the best players in the history of French hockey... Defenseman... Starred in European hockey in the late 1920s and 1930s... Played at two Winter Olympic Games as a member of the French

Olympic team, 1928 (in St. Moritz, Switzerland) and 1936 (Garmisch-Partenkirchen, Germany).

KJELL LARSSON Born in Sweden... Before moving to France, the physical education teacher was a coach for instructors and junior coach of the Swedish Hockey Federation for 14 years... Arrived in France in 1986... Coached in Albertville, then signed a two-year contract with the national team... Made his French national team coaching debut at the 1987 World and European Championships (Pool B)... Coached France at three Olympics: 1988, 1992 and 1994... Also coached at four Pool B World and European Championships and three Pool A tournaments (1992 to 1994).

JEAN-PHILIPPE LEMOINE Began his career with CSG Grenoble in 1986–87... The next year he played in ASG Tours, but later came back to CSG Grenoble where he spent three seasons... Joined HC Rouen before the 1991–92 season... Won four national titles in a row with HC Rouen from 1992 to 1995... Joined SP Brest before the 1996–97 season and won the national title again that season... Since 1997 he has played in Germany for the Frankfurt Lions... A veteran defenseman with the French national team... Has missed only one tournament since 1985... Participated at three Olympics and 12 World and European Championships... Named the best defenseman and voted to the all-star team at 1986 World and European Championships (Pool B)... The captain of French national team... Played at the 1998 Olympics in Nagano, Japan.

FRANCK PAJONKOWSKI Three generations before, his family lived in Poland... Was the top scorer in France in 1990–91 while with HC Rouen, recording 28 goals and 42 assists for 70 points in 28 games... The next year (still with HC Rouen) was third in scoring with 29 goals and 10 assists for 39 points in 17 games... Was a French champion in 1991–92, 1992–93, 1993–94 and 1994–95 with HC Rouen... Before joining HC Rouen he played in Megeve and Paris... Spent 11 years with the national team from 1985 to 1996... Saw action at two Olympics and seven World and European Championships.

DENIS PEREZ A champion with Francais Volants Paris in 1983–84 and 1988–89... Later joined HC Rouen and won four national titles in a row from 1992 to 1995... A veteran defenseman on the French national team... His first appearance at the World and European Championships was in 1986 (Pool B)... Has played in every major tournament since... Saw action at four Olympics and 11 World and European Championships (Pool B five times, Pool A six times)... Played at the 1998 Nagano Olympics.

SERGE POUDRIER Born in Thetford Mines, Quebec, Canada... Came to France in 1986... Played in Anglet (1986 to 1989) at the beginning of his career, in Division 2... After spending two years with HC Bordeaux, he joined HC Rouen... A national champion with HC Rouen in 1991–92, 1992–93, 1993–94 and 1994–95... Played in Germany with Augsburger AV in 1996–97... Began his career with the French national team at the 1991 Pool B World and European Championships... Has seen action at three Olympics and six World and European Championships... Defenseman played at the 1998 Olympics in Nagano.

PIERRE POUSSE Best player in the French National League in 1992–93... Second time he won the award of the best player... Six brothers in the family (like the Sutter brothers) and all six play hockey... Went to play in Canada at a young age and later returned to France... Played with four French clubs prior to joining HC Amiens... Played for the French national team from 1989 to 1996... Saw action at two Olympics and seven World and European Championships.

ANTOINE RICHER Began his hockey career in Tours... Later played in Francais Volants Paris and HC Amiens... Was a captain of the national team and the first player who played more than 300 games with the national team... Played for the national team from 1982 to 1996... Saw action at three Olympics and 12 World and European Championships (Pool C three times, Pool B five times and Pool A four times)... One of the best players in the history of French hockey.

PETRI YLONEN Was the number-one goalie in France for many years... Born in Finland and married a French woman... Played two years with Briancon from 1987 to 1989... Joined HC Rouen before the 1989–90 season... A national champion with HC Rouen four straight times from 1991–92 to 1994–95... In 1991–92 he had the best goals-against average (3.16) in the French League while with Rouen HC... Had amazing 1.66 average in 1993–94... Joined the German club Augsburger EV before the 1996–97 season... A veteran of the French national team, Ylonen played in every major international tournament from 1991 to 1996... Saw action at two Winter Olympic Games and six IIHF World Championships including five tournaments appearances in Pool A.

GERMANY

IIHF-standard three-letter abbreviations are used to indicate the country each player has most recently represented in international competition as a player, coach or executive. Some players have represented more than one of these countries over the course of their careers. FRG – Federal Republic of Germany (West Germany), GDR – German Democratic Republic (East Germany), GER – Germany.

GER
THOMAS BRANDL One of Germany's most talented juniors of the late 1980s... Played at the 1986 and 1987 European Junior Championships as well as at three World Junior Championships (1987 Pool B, 1988 and 1989)... Helped his team to win the Pool B tournament in 1987, earning promotion to Pool A... A veteran of the German national team... Saw action at the 1992 and 1994 Olympics and five World Championships... In 1995–96, was a regular with the German national team but did not participate in the 1996 World Championships due to an injury... Scored one goal in four games at the 1996 World Cup of Hockey... Played for the German team at the 1998 Nagano Olympics.

Started his career in 1986–87 with Bad Tolz in the German second division recording 36 goals and 54 assists for 90 points in 40 games... At 18, joined Koln and spent nine seasons with the club... Two-time winner of the German championship (1988 and 1995)... Starred in the 1995 playoffs, collecting eight goals and 13 assists for 21 points in 15 games... Team leader... Physical player... Plays tough... Had his best season with Koln in 1995–96, recording 19 goals and 45 assists for 64 points in 44 games... Was second in scoring on Dusseldorf during the 1996–97 season.

GER
HELMUT DE RAAF Played nine years for the German national team... Participated in three Olympics and seven World and European Championships... Played in 114 games for the national team.

De Raaf began playing hockey at 13 when the local newspaper announced the town of Neuss, on the Rhine River, was building a new skating club... De Raaf was a soccer goalie and throughout childhood was too small to be out on the ice... Between age 16 and 18 grew seven inches... One of the most successful players in the history of German hockey... De Raaf ranked as Germany's number-one goalie for many years... He won four national titles with Kolner EC (1984 and 1986 to 1988) and five with Dusseldorfer EG (1990 to 1993 and 1996)... Played for Dusseldorfer EG (1981 to 1983 and 1988 to 1996) and Kolner EC (1983 to 1988)... He played in 699 games in 16 seasons in the Bundesliga.

GER
GEORG FRANZ Played in the 1983 European Junior Championships and 1983 and 1985 World Junior Championships... A regular with the German national team since 1985... A veteran of international competition... Played at the 1988 and 1994 Olympics and at seven World Championships... Missed 1992 Albertville Olympics due to the birth of his first child ...Was not able to play for the German national team at the 1996 World Championships due to an injury.

Spent his first professional season with Straubing in the German second division... At 18, he was brought up to play with Rosenheim and went on to win the national title twice (1985 and 1989)... An All-Star in 1988... Recovered from a career-threatening knee injury sustained in 1990... Joined Hedos Munchen in the summer of 1992... Won another German title with Munchen in 1993–94... Joined Landshut before the 1994–95 season... In 1995–96, he played in his 13th season in the German League and helped Landshut finish fourth in the regular-season standings... In 1996 and 1997, Landshut reached the playoff semifinals.

GER
KARL FRIESEN was born in Winnipeg and began his playing career in Manitoba before going on to a lengthy career in Germany spent mostly with Rosenheim. He played with Maine in the American Hockey League in 1985–86 and spent four games with the New Jersey Devils in 1986–87 before returning to Germany.

Friesen was a longtime member of the West German national team, who played at the World Championships six times between 1981 and 1989. He also represented West Germany at the Canada Cup in 1984 and at the Olympics in 1984 and 1988. In 1992, he played for the unified German team at the Albertville Olympics.

FRG
LORENZ FUNK Had a great international career... Played for the German national team from 1967 to 1989... Participated at two Olympics and 14 World and European Championships in Pools A and B... Won a bronze medal at 1976 Innsbruck Olympics... In his career, played in 225 games for the national team and scored 57 goals.

Played center... Played for EC Bad Tolz (1965 to 1973 and 1987–88), Berliner SC (1973 to 1982), SC Riessersee (1982–83) and Preussen Berlin (1983 to 1986)... Retired at 41... Played on a national champion in 1965–66, 1973–74 and 1975–76... Played 687 games in the German Bundesliga and scored 435 goals... Began his coaching career in 1986... Coached Preussen Berlin (1986–1988), EC Bad Tolz (1988 to 1990) and SV Bayreuth (1990–91).

GER
DIETER HEGEN One of Germany's leading international players... Played at 1979 and 1980 European Junior Championships... Saw action at the 1981 and 1982 World Junior Championships... Leading scorer at the 1981 World Juniors with eight goals and one assist for nine points in five games... Participated in the 1984 Canada Cup, five Olympic, 12 World Championships and the 1996 World Cup of Hockey.

Montreal's sixth choice, 46th overall, in the 1981 NHL Entry Draft... Living legend of German hockey... Started his career at 17 with Kaufbeuren, helping his club earn promotion to the German League from the second division... For more than 10 years he was a linemate of German superstar Gerd Truntschka... Seven-time German champion, 1987 and 1988 with Koln, 1990, 1991, 1992 and 1996 with Dusseldorf and 1994 with Hedos Munchen... Leading regular-season goal scorer in 1981 (54 goals), 1989 (35) and 1992 (41)... All-Star in 1981, 1984, 1985, 1989, 1990, 1991, 1992 and 1994... Best forward in 1981, 1990 and 1992... Player of the year in 1992... Nicknamed "Didi."

GER
JOSEF HEISS Played at the 1981 European Junior Championships and the 1981, 1982 and 1983 World Junior Championships... Joined the German national team after spending 10 years in the German League... Made his debut at the 1990 World Championships... Has seen action at the 1992, 1994 and 1998 Olympics and at eight World Championships... Played two games at the 1996 World Cup of Hockey.

Backup goaltender with league champion Riessersee Garmisch-Partenkirchen in 1980–81... After playing six years in his hometown, joined Dusseldorf in 1986 before moving on to Koln... Named best goaltender in 1988–89... Was instrumental in Koln's national title win in 1995 playoffs when he recorded three shutouts and posted a league-leading goals-against average of 1.93... Had another very good season with Koln in 1995–96... Finished the regular season with a 2.35 goals-against average (ranking second in the league behind Klaus Merk of the Berlin Capitals)... Finished fourth in goals-against average with 2.59 playing with Koln in the DEL in 1996–97.

GER
ULI HIEMER A veteran of three Olympics, nine World Championships and one Canada Cup tournament ...Played for the German national team from 1981 to 1995... Saw action in 159 international games, scoring 13 goals.

Played his first two season in the German Bundesliga with EV Fussen (1979 to 1981)... Joined Kolner EC in 1981 and played three seasons with that team... Drafted by the Colorado Rockies in the third round, 48th overall, of the 1981 NHL Entry Draft... He was second among New Jersey defensemen with 24 assists, third with 29 points, in his rookie NHL season of 1984–85... Established a Devils record for goals in game by defenseman, recording hat trick versus the Pittsburgh Penguins on October 31, 1984... First player of German origin to play regularly in the NHL... Played three years in the NHL (143 games, 19 goals and 54 assists for 73 points)... Came back to Germany in 1987...Joined Dusseldorfer EG...Won a national champion title with Kolner EC (1983–84) and five titles with Dusseldorfer EG (1990 to 1993 and 1996)... In 14 seasons in the Bundesliga, he played 697 games, scored 202 goals and added 364 assists for 566 points.

GER
GUSTAV JAENECKE Played for the German national team from 1927 to 1939... Saw action at three Olympics (winning a bronze in 1932) and at eight World Championships (silver in 1930, bronze in 1932 and 1934)... Played on gold medal-winning teams at the European Championships in 1930 and 1934, bronze medal winners in 1927, 1933, 1936, 1938 and 1939... Played a total of 82 international games and scored 43 goals.

One of the best German players in the pre-War era... Played for Berliner SC from 1924 to 1944 and won the national title 12 times... From 1946 to 1951 he played for SC Riessersee and won another three national titles for a record total of 15 national titles... Retired at the age of 43... Won the German title in tennis in 1932, and played five times at the Davis Cup.

GER
UDO KIESSLING Was a captain of the German national team... Played for the German national team from 1973 to 1992... Participated at five Olympics, 15 World and European Championships and the 1984 Canada Cup... Named to the World and European Championships all-star team in 1987... Won an Olympic bronze medal at Innsbruck in 1976... In total, he played 320 international games as a member of German team and scored 44 goals.

Considered one of the best defenseman in the history of German hockey... Spent 23 seasons in the Bundesliga... Played for SC Riessersee (1972–73), Augsburger EV (1973–74), EV Rosenheim (1974–75), Kolner EC (1976 to 1979 and 1982 to 1992), Dusseldorfer EG (1979 to 1982), EV Fussen (1982–83) and EV Landshut (1992 to 1996)... Won the national title six times, all with Kolner EC... Named player of the year three times... In his career in the Bundesliga, he played in 1,020 games, collecting 346 goals and 535 assists for 881 points... Played one NHL game with the Minnesota North Stars in 1981–82.

GER

UWE KRUPP Played for the German national team at the 1986 and 1990 World Championships... Wasn't able to play in the 1996 World Cup of Hockey due to injury... Saw action in two games at the 1998 Olympics in Nagano.

Buffalo's 13th choice, 214 overall, in the 1983 NHL Entry Draft... Played four years with Koln in West Germany's Elite League from 1982–83 through 1985–86 and was a German first team all-star in 1985–86 as well as being named as the league's top defenseman... Only the third player from Germany to be selected in the NHL draft... Played on the Calder Cup champion Rochester Americans of the American Hockey League in 1986–87... Led Quebec's defense in scoring in 1994–95 with 23 points (six goals and 17 assists)... In 1995–96, suffered a torn anterior cruciate ligament in the first game of the season and did not return to play until the last five games of the regular season... Played strongly in playoffs, appearing in all 22 of Colorado's games, totaling 16 points (four goals, 12 assists)... Scored the Stanley Cup-winning goal in overtime of game four versus the Florida Panthers.

GER

ERICH KUHNHACKL Outstanding international career... Played for the national team from 1973 to 1985... Participated in three Olympics and 10 World and European Championships... Bronze medalist at the 1976 Innsbruck Olympics... Named to the all-star team at the 1974 World and European Championships (Pool B)... Scored 131 goals (a Germany record) in 211 games for the national team... Coached the German junior team... Works as an assistant coach for the German national team.

One of the brightest starts in the history of German hockey... Played center... Played junior hockey in Czechoslovakia... Began playing in the German League in 1968... Was with EV Landshut from 1968 to 1976 (winning a champion in 1969–70), Kolner EC from 1976 to 1979 (champions in 1976–77 and 1978–79), returned to EV Landshut from 1979- to 1985 (champions in 1982–83) and played with EHC Olten in Switzerland in 1985–86... Came back to EV Landshut again and played there from 1986 to 1989... Retired at 39... Played in 773 games in the German Bundesliga and scored 725 goals... Named the player of the year three times... Won the scoring title seven times... Still holds Bundesliga records for goals in a season (83 in 1979–80), points in a season (155 in 1979–80), points in a career (1,431)... Coached EV Landshut from 1990 to 1992.

GER

FRANZ REINDL Played with the German national team from 1976 to 1986... Participated at three Olympics, one Canada Cup tournament and eight World and European Championships... Bronze medalist at the 1976 Innsbruck Olympics... Saw action in 131 international games with the national team and scored 38 goals... Named the assistant coach of the German team in 1991–92 season... Worked at two Olympics and three World Championships.

Played for SC Riessersee from 1972 to 1984 and for SB Rosenheim from 1984 to 1988... His teams were German national champion in 1977–78, 1980–81, 1984–85 and 1988–89... Played in 666 games in the German Bundesliga, scoring 423 goals... After retiring, coached SC Riessersee from 1988 to 1991.

FRG

ALOIS SCHLODER Captain of the German national team from 1971 to 1978... Played for the nationals for 12 years... Participated at three Olympics and 13 World and European Championships in Pools A and B... Bronze medalist at the 1976 Innsbruck Olympics... Named the best forward at the World and European Championships in 1969 (Pool B)... Played in 206 games for the German team and scored 87 goals.

A legendary veteran forward in German hockey... Spent 23 seasons in the Bundesliga all with the same club, EV Landshut (1963 to 1986)... Captain of the team from 1971 to 1986... Played on national title winner in 1969–70 and 1982–83... In 806 games, he scored 496 goals... In 1971–72 season was the top goal scorer in the league... Retired at 39.

GER

GERD TRUNTSCHKA A member of the German national team from 1979 to 1993... He was a long-time captain of the German national team... Truntschka played at four Olympics and nine World and European Championships... Named to the tournament all-star team at the World and European Championships in Vienna in 1987... Played at 1984 Canada Cup.

Truntschka is known as Germany's Wayne Gretzky... As a youth growing up in the Bavarian town of Landshut, Truntschka was also a noted soccer midfielder... Truntschka and Dieter Hegen formed the top scoring tandem in the German Bundesliga for a decade... In 1990, in a playoff game against Schwenningen, Truntschka had five goals and five assists... He played 19 seasons with EV Landshut (1975 to 1979), Kolner EC (1979 to 1989), Dusseldorfer EG (1989 to 1992) and Hedos Munchen (1992 to 1994) and recorded 477 goals and 943 assists for 1,420 points in 858 games...He played on national championship teams in 1984, 1986 to 1988, and 1990 to 1994.

FRG

XAVER UNSINN Played for the German national team at two Olympics and five World and European Championships... World silver medalist in 1953... Played a total of 72 games for the national team, scoring 24 goals... Named the head coach of the German team in 1963–64... In his career, he coached the national team at four Olympics, 10 World and European Championships and the 1984 Canada Cup... His biggest success came at the 1976 Innsbruck Olympics, where the Germans won a bronze medal.

As a player, Unsinn began his hockey career in 1946 with EV Fussen... Spent his entire career with EV Fussen and retired in 1960... He played on teams that won the national title eight times... From 1960 to 1962, he was a playing coach with ESV Kaufbeuren... Worked in ESV Kaufbeuren until 1966... Later coached Preussen Krefeld (1967–68), Augsburger EV (1968 to 1970), Dusseldorfer EG (1970 to 1972), Berliner SC (1972 to 1977), EV Rosenheim (1977–78) and the Swiss club SC Bern (1978 to 1981)... He coached three clubs that won the national title: Dusseldorfer EG (1971–72), Berliner SC (1973–74 and 1975–76) and SC Bern (1978–79).

GDR

JOACHIM ZIESCHE Played center and captained the East German national team... Played at the 1968 Olympics in Grenoble and at nine World and European Championships (Pool A eight times, Pool B once)... Played in 200 games for the East Germans... Worked as the assistant coach of GDR national team from 1978 to 1980 and was the head coach from 1981 to 1990.

One of the best players in the history of hockey in East Germany... Played 12 seasons with Dynamo Berlin (1958 to 1970)... After retiring, coached Dynamo Berlin from 1970 to 1989... In 1992–93 he coached SC Riessersee.

GREAT BRITAIN

JIMMY CHAPPELL One of the best forwards in the history of British hockey... Played center on the Earls Court team... Played for the Great Britain national team in the 1930s and 1940s... In 1936, won the "Triple Crown" with the national team, winning Olympic, World and European gold medals (all three titles were determined at the 1936 Olympics in Garmisch-Partenkirchen)... Played in six games and scored two goals at the tournament... Won the silver medal behind Canada at the 1937 and 1938 World Championships, thereby earning the European Championship both years... Came back to the national team after World War II and played at 1948 Olympics in St. Moritz.

GORDON DAILLEY Born in Calgary, Alberta... Played defense and left wing on the famous Wembley Lions team... Got a taste of international competition in 1935, winning the World bronze and European silver medals at the World and European Championships... A year later, was a member of Great Britain team that won the Olympic, World and European gold medals... Played defense in all seven games of the 1936 tournament at Garmisch-Partenkirchen... Won World silver and European gold at the 1937 and 1938 IIHF World and European Championship tournaments.

GERRY DAVEY Born in Port Arthur, Canada... Played right wing with Streatham... A superstar on the Great Britain national team... Joined the team in 1935 and won World bronze and European silver medals at the World and European Championships... In 1936, starred at Garmisch-Partenkirchen Olympics, scoring seven goals in six games... Britain became Olympic, World and European champions by winning the tournament... Won the silver medal behind Canada at 1937 and 1938 World Championships, thereby claiming the European Championship gold medal each year... Came back to the national team after World War II and played at the 1948 St. Moritz Olympics.

CARL ERHARDT One of only two members of the gold medal-winning 1936 British Olympic team who did not learn to play hockey in Canada... He learned his hockey in Germany and Switzerland where he went to school... Played for several British clubs, and was captain of Streatham's national championship team in 1934–35... First played for Great Britain in 1931 and captained the team in the 1934–35 World Championships... Captained British team at the 1936 Olympics in Garmisch-Partenkirchen... Was the oldest player at the event, turning 39 during the tournament... Britain's victory at Garmisch gave the team the "Triple Crown" of the Olympic, World and European Championships.

JIMMY FOSTER One of the best goaltenders in pre-War Europe... Played for the Richmond Hawks... Was the backbone of the Great Britain team at the 1936 Olympics in Garmisch-Partenkirchen... Played every minute of all seven games and allowed only three goals on 222 shots... Britain became Olympic, World and European champion by winning the tournament... Won the silver medal behind Canada at the 1937 and 1938 World Championships to become the European Champion in 1937 and 1938.

TONY HAND One of the best players in the modern era of British hockey... A forward, he played with the Murrayfield Racers and Sheffield Steelers and is the leading scorer in the history of the British League... In 15 seasons, he saw action in 525 games, recording 934 goals and 1,370 assists for 2,304 points... Played for the Great Britain national team from 1989 to 1994... Participated at six World and European Championships, starting in Pool D and finishing in Pool A... Played a total of 34 games in these tournaments, collecting 32 goals and 52 assists for 84 points... Named the best forward of the World and European Championships in 1989 (Pool D), 1990 (Pool D) and 1992 (Pool C).

ARCHIE STINCHCOMBE A left winger with Streatham, Stinchcombe played in six games with the British national team at 1936 Olympics in Garmisch-Partenkirchen... Won the "Triple Crown" of the Olympic, World and European gold medals by winning the tournament... Played in next two World and European Championships for Great Britain, earning the silver medal behind Canada in both 1937 and 1938 to claim the European Championship... Played for the national team again after the World War II at the 1948 Olympics in St. Moritz.

GREECE

SAVAS ADAMIDIS Starred at the 1995 World Championships (Pool C2) with the Greek national team... Played in all five games at the tournament... Named the best goaltender of 1992 World Championships (Pool C2).

HONG KONG

SUET-TUNG WU Made his debut with the Hong Kong national team at the 1987 World and European Championships (Pool D)... That was also the debut of the Hong Kong national team on the international scene... Played in all seven games of the tournament and scored one goal.

HUNGARY

JANOS ANCSIN A veteran of the national team and one of the best players in the history of Hungarian hockey... Began his career in 1981 at the World and European Championships (Pool C)... Played 17 seasons with the Hungarian national team and participated in 11 World and European Championships... Named to the all-star team at 1987 tournament (Pool C)... Had very good tournament in 1989 (Pool C) with 11 goals and four assists for 15 points in seven games.

TIBOR KISS A veteran of the Hungarian national team, he played in 10 World and European Championships (Pools B and C) from 1978 to 1994... Had his best tournaments in 1982 (Pool C), 1991 (Pool C) and 1993 (Pool C), where he collected seven points in each of the tournament... Scored six goals in eight games at the 1991 event.

GASPAR MENYHART One of the best players in Hungarian hockey in the 1970s and early 1980s... Starred at 1975 World and European Championships (Pool C) , where he collected four goals and five assist for nine points... Played on the national team until 1983... In his last tournament, the 1983 World and European Championships (Pool C), he recorded two goals and five assists for seven points in seven games.

ISRAEL

YEVGENY FELDMAN A member of the Israeli national hockey team since 1993... To date, has played in five straight World Championship events (Pools C and D)... In the last three years, he has become one of the best forwards on the team... Collected five goals and eight assists for 13 points in six games at the 1995 World Championships (Pool C)... In 1997 (Pool D), he recorded four goals and six assists for 10 points in five games.

YEVGENY GUSIN Began his hockey career in the former Soviet Union... Played for Khimik Voskresensk of the top Soviet League and the Soviet national junior team... Later played for Kristall Elektrostal (Division 2)... In 1991–92, played four games for Thunder Bay of the Colonial Hockey League... Began to play for the Israeli national team in 1993... To date, has played in five straight World Championships (Pools C and D)... Named the best goaltender at the 1996 World Championships (Pool D).

ITALY

JIM CORSI Born in Montreal, Quebec... Played at eight World and European Championships as a member of the Italian team from 1981 to 1990... Named best goaltender at the World and European Championships in 1986 (Pool B)... Chosen to the IIHF tournament all-star team in 1981 (Pool B) and 1987 (Pool B)... One of the best goaltenders in the history of Italian hockey... Played in 147 games for the Italian national team.

Played goaltender at Concordia University... In 1976–77 he played for Maine of North American Hockey League... Spent the next two seasons in the World Hockey Association with the Quebec Nordiques... Played in 63 WHA games with a goals-against average of 3.69... In 1979–80 he played in the NHL with the Edmonton Oilers (26 games, 3.65 average)... Finished the seasons in the Central Hockey League with Houston and Oklahoma City... Went to Italy... Played for HC Cortina and HC Varese.

DAVID DELFINO Born in Sommerville, Massachusetts... A member of the Italian national team since 1991... To date, has played at three Olympics and six World and European Championships... Voted to the all-star team in 1991 (Pool B World Championships)... Saw action at 1998 Olympics in Nagano.

A goaltender, he played college hockey at Lowell University (now the University of Massachusetts at Lowell)... He was undrafted after college, but was simultaneously offered a tryout with the Vancouver Canucks and contacted by the Italian League... He began to play for the HC Fassa Canazei team in the mountains of northern Italy in 1988–89... Played in Fassa four seasons before joining HC Alleghe... Won Alpenliga title with HC Alleghe in 1993... After five seasons with HC Alleghe, he joined Kolner Haie of the German League in 1997–98

BRYAN LEFLEY Born in Winnipeg, Manitoba... Moved to Italy and coached with HC Merano in 1985–86 and 1986–87... Won the Italian champions title with his club in 1986 ...Was promoted and worked as a head coach of the Italian national team in 1987–88... Went to Germany to coach Dusseldorfer EG for one year... In 1988–89 and 1989–90 he worked in Italy again, coaching AS Varese Hockey to the champions title in 1989... The next three seasons he was a coach of the Swiss club Ambri-Piotta... In the meantime, he was appointed head coach of the Italian national team while still being the coach in Ambri-Piotta... Replaced former Italian coach Gene Ubriaco after the 1992 Albertville Olympics where the Italian team finished last... Significantly improved the Italian team performance, as Italy finished ninth at the 1992 World Championships and made it to the quarterfinals the next year... Coached the Italian national team at the 1994 Lillehammer Olympics and at six World Championships.

Spent five seasons in the NHL with the New York Islanders, Kansas City Scouts and Colorado Rockies from 1972–73 to 1977–78... He had seven goals and 29 assists for 36 points in 228 games... Continued his hockey career in Germany with Dusseldorfer EG (1978–79 to 1979–80)... Played the next two seasons in Switzerland,with SC Bern... Began his coaching career in the Swiss national league, where he worked behind the bench of Zurcher SC in 1983–84 and EHC Basel in 1984–85.

BOB MANNO Born in Niagara Falls, Ontario... A veteran on the Italian national team, Manno played at the 1992 Albertville Olympics and at seven World and European Championships (Pool A in 1982 and Pool B in 1983, 1986, 1987, 1989, 1990 and 1991)... Named the best defenseman at the 1989 tournament... Chosen to the all-star team in 1986, 1989 and 1991.

Has had the best NHL career of any of his teammates throughout his career in Italy... He played defense with the Vancouver Canucks from 1976 through 1981, the Toronto Maple Leafs in 1981–82, went to Italy for a year (HC Merano and the national team) and returned to play for the Detroit Red Wings at left wing from 1983 to 1985... Played in the NHL All-Star Game in 1982... Manno returned to Italy after for 1985–86... His first year back he scored 115 points on 29 goals and 86 assists in 42 games with HC Merano.

ROBERT OBERRAUCH A member of the Italian national team since 1987, he has played in three Olympic Games and in nine World and European tournaments... Was the captain of the national team... Saw action at 1998 Olympics in Nagano.

One of the rare native Italians to have played in North America... Oberrauch toiled for one season in the Western Hockey League when he was 19 (1985–86)... He played for two teams in the WHL: Kamloops and Moose Jaw... Oberrauch was impressed by one of his teammates, forward Theo Fleury, now an NHL star with the Calgary Flames... Oberrauch started in the Italian League when he was 16 years old, the youngest player ever to play at that level in Italy... His team, HC Bolzano, has won seven championships in his 15 years there... He left the HC Bolzano team for one year to play for AC Milan Hockey in 1989–90, but returned.

GAETANO ORLANDO Born in Montreal, Quebec... One of Italy's few Italians with NHL experience, Orlando became perhaps the top player in the

Italian League and a primary force on the national team... A member of the national team since 1990... To date, has played at two Olympics and eight World and European Championships... Named the best forward in 1990 (Pool B) and voted to the all-star team in 1991 (Pool B)... Saw action at 1998 Olympics in Nagano.

Played for current New Jersey Devils general manager Lou Lamoriello at Providence College (1980 to 1984)... Before arriving in Italy, Orlando played for the Buffalo Sabres between 1984 and 1987, ringing up 44 points (18 goals and 26 assists) in 98 games... When his contract expired, he rejected the Sabres' new offer and was approached about playing in Italy... After playing for HC Bolzano for several years, Orlando joined AC Milan Hockey... Now is playing in Switzerland with SC Bern

MARTIN PAVLU Born in Plzen, Czechoslovakia but came to Italy in 1968 with his parents... A veteran of three Olympics and 12 World and European Championships and is still one of the leaders on the Italian national team... Began his career with the nationals in 1982... Captain of the Italian national team... Saw action at 1998 Nagano Olympics.

Has spent his entire career with HC Bolzano and quickly became one of the top players in Italy... His team won the Italian League national title from 1982 to 1985, in 1988, 1990, and from 1995 to 1997... His father, Jaroslav, is a professional hockey coach and coached HC Bolzano in its champion years of 1982 and 1983... Year by year Martin has led HC Bolzano in scoring and almost always ranks among the top 10 scorers in the Italian league overall.

LUCIO TOPATIGH Won the silver medal at the Italian under–16 ski jumping championships in 1978, but decided to make an early career switch to hockey... For two years during the summer (when he was 16 and 17), Topatigh saved up all of his money and paid his own way to hockey camps in Prague, Czechoslovakia... In 1986, he became a member of the Italian national team... Has participated in three Olympics and 10 World and European Championships... Saw action at 1998 Olympics in Nagano.

Named best rookie player in the Italian League when he played for HC Asiago in 1986... He was transferred to the HC Bolzano club, where he met a crucial figure in his career, Bolzano teammate Mark Pavelich, a star of the gold medal-winning 1980 United States Olympic hockey team from Lake Placid... Topatigh also credits the influence of Kent Nilsson and Mark Napier, who were teammates of his at various points of his career in Italy... He returned to HC Asiago in 1991... Joined AC Milan Hockey prior to the start of 1993–94 season... Came back to play for HC Bolzano.

BRUNO ZARRILLO Born in Winnipeg, Manitoba... Came to the Italian League at the age of 23, young for a North American to arrive in Italy... As a member of Italian national team he has played at three Olympics and seven World and European Championships... Saw action at 1998 Olympics in Nagano.

Moved to Italy and played for Latemar (Division 2) in 1988–89... Next year, he was invited to play for HC Bolzano... Played with American player Scott Young (now with Anaheim in the NHL) in Italy in 1991–92... He was second in the Italian League in scoring with 96 points (39 goals and 57 assists) in 36 games with HC Bolzano in 1990–91... HC Bolzano won national title in 1988, 1990, 1995, 1996 and 1997... At the beginning of 1996–97 season, joined Kolner Haie of German League.

JAPAN

YOSHIO HOSHINO A veteran forward of the Japanese national team, Hoshino played more than 10 seasons for the national team in the 1970s and 1980s... Saw action at the Olympics in 1972, 1976 and 1980... Had his most successful World and European Championship tournament in 1982 (Pool C)... Recorded seven goals and 15 assists for 22 points in seven games of that tournament... Named the best forward at the World and European Championships in 1982 (Pool C)... Helped his team to finish first and be promoted to Pool B.

TAKESHI IWAMOTO One of the best goaltenders in the history of Japanese hockey... Played for the national team in the late 1970s and 1980s... Saw action at the 1980 Lake Placid Olympics... Named the best goaltender and voted to the all-star team at the World and European Championships in 1978 (Pool B)... Named the best goaltender at the World and European Championships in 1982 (Pool C).

HIDEO KUROKAWA Forward... Played for the Japanese national team in the 1960s and 1970s... Saw action at the 1972 Olympics in Sapporo... Starred at the 1967 (Pool C), 1969 (Pool C) and 1970 (Pool B) World and European Championships... Scored 13, 12 and 11 goals at these tournaments... Named to the all-star team of the World and European Championships in 1970 (Pool B).

OSAMU WAKABAYASHI One of the best players in the history of hockey in Japan... A veteran of Olympic tournaments in 1972, 1976 and 1980... Named to the all-star team of the World and European Championships three

times: 1977 (Pool B), 1979 (Pool B) and 1982 (Pool C)... Named the best forward at the World and European Championships in 1979 (Pool B).

KAZAKHSTAN
see page 1859

LATVIA
see page 1859

LITHUANIA
see page 1859

NETHERLANDS

TONY COLLARD One of the best players in the history of Dutch hockey... Made his debut with the national team in 1981 when the Netherlands played at Pool A of the World and European Championships... Had great tournament in 1983 (Pool C), helping his team to be promoted to Pool B... Scored 22 goals and eight assists for 30 points in seven games that year and was named the best forward and voted to the tournament all-star team... Played in five World and European Championships... At his last tournament in 1989 (Pool C), he helped his team to win the title, recording nine goals and 14 assists for 23 points in seven games.

CORKY DE GRAAUW One of the best players in the history of Dutch hockey... He had his best tournament with the national team in the 1973 World and European Championships (Pool C), collecting 13 goals and nine assists for 22 points... Named the best forward at the tournament that year... Played at the 1980 Lake Placid Olympics, where he registered three goals and five assists for eight points in five games... Played in Pool A of the World and European Championships in 1981.

JACK DE HEER A veteran of the Dutch national team, he played more than 10 years at major competitions... Had his best tournament at the 1978 World and European Championships (Pool C), where he recorded an amazing 14 goals and 19 assists for 33 points in seven games... Named the best forward at the tournament that year... Named to the all-star team at the 1979 World and European Championships (Pool B)... Played at the 1980 Lake Placid Olympics, collecting three goals and three assists for six points in five games... Won the Pool C tournament with the Dutch team in 1978 and 1983.

GERRY GOBEL Considered one of the best goaltenders in the history of Dutch hockey... Played in the 1970s in both Pool B and C of the IIHF World and European Championships... Named the best goaltender at the World and European tournament three times: in 1972 (Pool C), 1974 (Pool B) and 1979 (Pool B)... Named to the all-star team in 1979 (Pool B).

LEO KOOPMANS Made his debut with the Dutch national team in 1978 at the World and European Championships (Pool C)... Helped his team win the tournament and be promoted to Pool B... Played in all five games during the Olympic tournament at Lake Placid in 1980... Played in five World and European Championships and had his best tournament in 1983 (Pool C), helping the team to win it with 13 goals and 10 assist for 23 points in seven games.

LARRY VAN WIEREN Played five years in a row for the Dutch national team... Made his debut in 1978 at the World and European Championships (Pool C)... The Netherlands won this tournament and was promoted to Pool B... Played at the 1980 Olympics in Lake Placid, collecting one goal and four assists for five points in five games... Named to the all-star team at the 1982 World and European Championships (Pool B).

NORTH KOREA

CHANG HO PAK Forward... Played a decade on the Peoples' Republic of Korea national team... Made his debut on the national team at the end of the 1980s... The highlight of his career was the 1993 World Championships (Pool C)... Although he played in only three games at the tournament, he recorded five goals and three assists for eight points.

NORWAY

ARNE BILLKVAM A veteran of three Olympics and seven World Championships... Made his debut with the Norwegian national team at the 1985 World Championships (Pool B).

For 14 years, Billkvam played for Norway's most respected club, Valerengen, which won the league championship six times... Billkvam grew up within walking distance of the rink in which Valerengen plays... His father-in-law, Knut Nybben Stenberg, was a star forward for Valerengen years ago... In the summer of 1992, Billkvam suddenly joined Furuset Oslo, the rival of Valerengen... Later played for Sparta Sarpsborg.

OLE ESKILD DAHLSTROM Saw action at two Olympics and seven World and European Championships ...Voted to the all-star team at the World and European Championships in 1989 (Pool B)... In the first game of the 1990 World and European Championships against the Soviet Union, Dahlstrom collided with Valery Kamensky (now with Quebec) at the red line and sustained a serious knee injury... A shoulder separation and an ankle injury impaired him in 1990–91 and prevented his participation in the World and European Championships (Pool B)

Selected by Minnesota in the 11th round (218th overall) of the 1990 NHL Entry Draft, he has been stalled by an unending string of injuries... When healthy, he is extremely creative who rivals Espen Knutsen as Norway's best young player... At the age of 17, recorded 26 goals and 38 assists for 64 points in 36 games with Furuset Oslo in 1987–88... Next season he joined Orebro in the Swedish Division 2 but did not succeed... Played for Furuset Oslo for five seasons... Joined Storhamar Hamar before the 1992–93 season.

AGE ELLINGSEN Made his debut with the Norwegian national team at the 1985 World and European Championships (Pool B)... A veteran of two Olympics and seven World and European Championships... Named the best defenseman of the World and European Championships in 1986 (Pool C) and 1987 (Pool B)... Voted to the all-star team at the World and European Championships in 1989 (Pool B).

Drafted by the Edmonton Oilers in the seventh round of the 1987 NHL Entry Draft... Was invited to the training camp once... Played for Storhamar Hamar in Norway.

GEIR HOFF Was the only Norwegian in the top 20 in scoring at the 1990 World and European Championships (Pool A)... A veteran of three Olympics and nine World and European Championships.

Began his career at 16 with Hasle/Loren Oslo... Later played for other Oslo-based clubs, Furuset and Valerengen, before joining Lillehammer in 1993–94... Spent 1984–85 season in Sweden with Vastra Frolunda Goteborg... Spent two seasons playing college hockey at Michigan State University in 1985–86 and 1986–87... In his first season at Michigan State, the Spartans won the NCAA championship... Named to Norwegian League all-star team in 1988 and 1991... Was the Golden Puck Award winner (best player in Norway) in 1990–91.

ROY JOHANSEN A veteran of three Olympics and seven World Championships... Made his debut with the Norwegian national team at the 1981 Pool B World and European Championships... Was a radio commentator at the 1990 World and European Championships... Scored the game-winning goal in a 1–0 win over France at the 1992 World Championships that helped Norway to stay in Pool A.

A veteran of Norwegian hockey... Began his career at the age of 16 in 1976–77... Has played 20 seasons in the league, 15 of them with Valerengen Oslo... Ranks among the leaders on all-time Norwegian scoring lists... Has played on seven Norwegian championship teams... Named the captain of Valerengen in 1991... His best year was 1987–88 when he recorded 31 goal and 43 assists for 74 points in 35 games with Valerengen to finish second in scoring in the Norwegian League.

ESPEN KNUTSEN Scored nine points for Norway at the 1990 World Junior Championships... Voted the star of the game for Norway in five of seven games at the 1991 World Junior Championships... Made his debut with the Norwegian national team at the 1994 Lillehammer Olympics... Has played at four World Championships for Norway since.

Selected in the tenth round (ninth choice, 204th overall) of the 1990 NHL Entry Draft by the Hartford Whalers... Knutsen grew up a few blocks from the Valerengen club rink, as his father was a dynamic scorer for the team... Knutsen's father was a part-time hairdresser who was slippery as a player so he was given the sobriquet "Soap"... Espen is nicknamed "Shampoo"... Played five years for Valerengen IF Oslo of the Norwegian League and three seasons with Djurgardens IF Stockholm of the Swedish League... Knutsen was traded to Anaheim in 1996... Played for the Mighty Ducks in the 1997–98 season.

ERIK KRISTIANSEN A veteran of four Olympics and 10 World and European Championships... Kristiansen's brother, Per Arne, played with him in at the Sarajevo Olympics in 1984... Erik began to play for the Norwegian national team in 1983 and never missed any major tournaments.

Scored over 30 goals five times in his career, including two seasons in which he registered 46 goals (in 36 games) for the Storhamar club in Hamar... Spent the 1987–88 season with Bjorkloven Umea in the Swedish League, otherwise he has spent his entire career with Storhamar Hamar, beginning with the 1978–79 season... Was named the best player in Norway (Golden Puck Award) in 1985... Also was named to Norwegian League all-star team in 1985 and 1987.

ORJAN LOVDAL A veteran of three Olympics and 10 World and European Championships... Made his debut with the Norwegian national team in

1981... Named the best forward of the World and European Championships in 1986 (Pool C) and 1989 (Pool B)... Voted to the all-star team at the World and European Championships in 1987 (Pool B) and 1989 (Pool B).

One of the brightest stars of Norwegian hockey... A two-time winner of the Golden Puck Award as the best player in Norway... Also a five-time all-star... Had his most successful campaign in 1985–86 when he scored 48 goals and added 60 assists for 108 points in just 36 games... Played for Stjernen Fredrikstad.

JIM MARTHINSEN Made his debut with the Norwegian national team at the 1980 Olympics in Lake Placid... A veteran of four Olympics and 13 World and European Championships... Named the best goalie at the 1987 Pool B World and European Championships... Voted to the all-star team at the World and European Championships in 1989 (Pool B).

The living legend of Norwegian hockey... Began his career later than the most Norwegian players... At 19 he started in goal for Valerengen Oslo... Played 19 seasons with Valerengen, excluding the 1988–89 and 1989–90 seasons when he played with Trondheim... Played on national championships teams seven times while with Valerengen... Was named the all-star goalie six times... Got the Golden Puck Award (best player in Norway) in 1989 and 1993... Holds the record for most games played in the Norwegian League.

PETTER SALSTEN Began on the Norwegian national team in 1986, two years before his older brother, Jorgen... Norway's franchise player... Was named the best defenseman and to the all-star team at the 1991 Pool B World and European Championships... He was the captain of the Norwegian national team... A veteran of three Olympics and 10 World and European Championships.

Began his career with Furuset Oslo in 1982–83... Furuset experienced financial problems and in 1990–91 and 1991–92 he played with AIK Solna of the Swedish League on the same blue line corps as Swedish legend and former Toronto Maple Leafs star Borje Salming... Later played for Storhamar Hamar in Norway ...Won the Golden Puck Award (given to the top player in the country) in 1988... Named to the Norwegian all-star team in 1988 and 1993... Petter is the younger, but more recognized of the two Salsten brothers.

ROBERT SCHISTAD A native Canadian (born in Wingham, Ontario)... Moved to Norway in 1986 and holds a Norwegian passport... Made his debut with the Norwegian national team at the 1991 Pool B World and European Championships... Has played at two Olympics and seven World and European Championships... The only Canadian on the Norwegian national team.

Played for the Viking club in Stavanger on the Atlantic coastline... Was named the all-star goalie in the Norwegian League in 1989–90... Played for Spektrum Flyers Oslo in 1995–96 and Czech club Sparta Praha in 1996–97... Joined Schwenninger Wild Wings (Germany) before 1997–98.

PETTER THORESEN A veteran of five Olympics and 10 World and European Championships... The top Norwegian scorer at the 1991 Pool B World and European Championships with eight points (five goals and three assists) in seven games... Made his debut with the national team at the 1980 Olympics in Lake Placid.

Began his career in 1978–79... Captain of the Valerengen Oslo club which won the 1992–93 Norwegian championship... He won four national titles with Valerengen... Later played for Storhamar Hamar.

NEW ZEALAND

JOHN DOWMAN Forward... Played in all three of New Zealand World Championship appearances: 1987 (Pool D), 1989 (Pool D) and 1995 (Pool C)... Had great tournament in 1987... Collected nine goals and two assists for 11 points in seven games... Always among the top scorers on the team.

POLAND

HENRYK BROMOWICZ Until 1950, had the name Henryk Brommer... Played for the Polish national team from 1946 to 1956... Saw action in 54 games, scored two goals... Played at the 1948, 1952 and 1956 Olympics and in total of four World and European Championships.

Defenseman... Began his career with Dab Katowice... From 1946 to 1960 played for Legia Warszawa (former name—CWKS Warszawa)... Won the national title eight times, from 1951 to 1957 and in 1959... Coached Legia Warszawa from 1961 to 1964.

MARIUSZ CZERKAWSKI Made his international debut in 1991 at age 19... Was the sixth-leading scorer at the 1991 World and European Championships (Pool B)... Played at the 1992 Albertville Olympics and at the 1992 World Championships.

The first Polish player ever drafted by an NHL team... Boston's fifth choice, 106th overall, in the 1991 NHL Entry Draft... As a junior, he became relatively well-grounded in the game after playing on GKS Tycht (1990–91)

which was coached by player-coach Henryk Gruth, one of the most respected hockey veterans in Poland... From 1991 to 1994, he played in Sweden, two seasons with Djurgardens IF Stockholm and one year with Hammarby IF (Division 2)... Signed a contract with the Boston Bruins at the end of the 1993–94 season... Has played with Edmonton and the New York Islanders.

ANDRZEJ FONFARA Played for the Polish national team from 1959 to 1970... Saw action in 98 international games, scored 54 goals... Was a captain of the team... Played at the 1964 Innsbruck Olympics and in eight World and European Championships... Starred at the 1963 (Pool B) tournament... Recorded nine goals and 11 assists for 20 points in six games.

Center... One of the best forwards in the history of Polish hockey... Played for GKS Katowice... Won the national title in 1962, 1965, 1968 and 1970.

BRONISLAW GOSZTYLA Played for the Polish national team from 1955 to 1966... Saw action in 114 international games and scored 41 goals... Was the captain of the team... Participated at the 1956 and 1964 Olympics and at a total of eight World and European Championships... Always was one of the top scorers on the national team.

Forward with KTH Krynica and Legia Warszawa... Won the Polish national title seven times: 1956, 1957, 1959, 1961, 1963, 1964 and 1967.

HENRYK GRUTH Made his debut with the Polish national team at 18 at the 1975 World and European Championships... Played 17 years on the national team... Captained the 1984, 1988 and 1992 Polish Olympic teams... Played at 14 World and European Championships from 1975 to 1992... Named to the all-star team at the World and European Championships in 1987 (Pool B)... Helped the Polish national team win the 1987 Pool B tournament and be promoted to Pool A... Named the assistant coach of the Polish national team before the 1995–96 season.

A living legend of the Polish hockey... The defenseman split his career between GKS Katowice and GKS Tychy... Began to play in the Polish League at the age of 17.

ADAM KOWALSKI Played for the Polish national team from 1932 to 1949... Saw action in 52 games and scored 22 goals... Played at the Olympics in 1932, 1936 and 1948... Also played at six World and European Championships.

Forward... Played 20 seasons for Cracovia Krakow from 1930 to 1950... Won the national title in 1937, 1946 and 1949... Was a referee after retiring.

LESZEK LEJCZYK Was named the Polish national team head coach in 1984... His first appearance on the international scene was a success, winning the 1985 World and European Championships in Pool B... His team also won the same tournament in 1987... Coached the team to a tenth-place finish at the 1988 Calgary Olympics... Also coached at the 1992 Olympics in Albertville... During his coaching career, the Polish national team played in Pool A three times: 1986, 1989 and 1992.

A Polish League player for 15 years... Played center for the Cracovia Krakow team from 1960 to 1963 and for LKS Lodz from 1963 to 1975... He studied law part time in his final years in the league... After retiring, he was a lawyer for five years but took a job as a coach in 1981 with LKS Lodz in the Polish League.

JERZY POTZ Played for the Polish national team from 1971 to 1979... Saw action in 204 games... Played at the 1972, 1976, 1980 and 1988 Olympics and at 10 World and European Championships.

One of the best defensemen in the history of Polish hockey... Began his career at 17 with LKS Lodz... Played for LKS from 1970 to 1982... From 1982 to 1989 played for the German club Eintracht Frankfurt... Played for Bad Nauheim in Germany in 1989–90... Joined German EC Kassel as a coach in 1991–92.

WALENTY ZIETARA Played for the Polish national team from 1970 to 1979... Played at the 1972 and 1976 Olympics and at seven World and European Championships... Named to the all-star team at the 1972 Pool B World event... Helped Poland win the tournament in 1972, earning promotion to Pool A.

A star forward in the 1970s... Played for Podhale Nowy Targ from 1965 to 1979... Won the national title 11 times with Podhale... Best scorer of the 1973–74 season (46 goals)... Named the Polish player of the year in 1971–72.

ROMANIA

GHEORGHE HUTAN Played for the Romanian national team for 17 seasons from 1977 to 1993, until the age of 39... Saw action at the 1980 Lake Placid Olympics... Named the best goaltender and to the all-star team at the World and European Championships in 1987 (Pool C)... Showed star performance at the 1991 World and European Championships (Pool C)... Played in eight games and registered a 3.01 goals-against average.

One of the best goalies in the history of Romanian hockey... Played for Dinamo Bucuresti.

VALERIAN NETEDU He and Gheorghe Hutan share the record for most times played on the National Romanian Team... Saw action at the 1976 and 1980 Olympics... Named the best goaltender at the World and European Championships in 1976 (Pool B)... Helped his team win the tournament that year and be promoted to Pool A... In 1977, played in all 10 games in Pool A... The highlight of his career was the game against Team USA... Netedu played brilliantly in a game won 5–4 by Romania.

Player for Steaua Bucuresti... One of the best goaltenders in Romanian hockey in the 1980s.

EDUARD PANA One of the best forwards in the history of Romanian hockey... Starred in the 1970s... Was the fifth-leading scorer overall at 1976 Innsbruck Olympics (playing in the tournament for seventh to 12th place)... Romanians won the group and Pana collected three goals and four assists for seven points... Also in 1976, Romania won the Pool B World and European Championships and was promoted to Pool A... Pana was the best scorer of the tournament, recording nine goals and six assists for 15 points in seven games... Played in all 10 games at the Pool A World and European Championships in 1977.

LASZLO SOLYOM Member of the Romanian national team for 12 years from 1977 to 1989... Played at the 1980 Lake Placid Olympics and at seven World and European Championships... Had his best performance in 1989 (Pool D)... Despite playing in only four games of the tournament, scored eight goals and assisted on five others for 13 points.

Forward... Played for Dinamo Bucuresti.

DORU TUREANU Made his debut with the Romanian national team at the 1975 World and European Championships (Pool B)... Later played at the 1976 and 1980 Olympics... Played forward and defense (at the end of his career)... Named the best forward at the World and European Championships in 1976 (Pool B)... Helped his team to win the tournament that year and be promoted to Pool A... Named the best defenseman at the World and European Championships in 1985 (Pool C)... The highlight of his career was the game against Team USA at the 1977 (Pool A) tournament... Scored two goals to help Romania win 5–4.

One of the best forwards and scorers in the history of Romanian hockey... Played for Dinamo Bucuresti in the 70s and 80s.

RUSSIA
see page 1859

SLOVAKIA
see page 1838

SLOVENIA
see page 1870

SOUTH AFRICA

ARN POTTER A veteran defenseman on the South African national team... Played at three World Championships (all Pool C) with the national team in the 1990s... His brother, Sean, also played on defense... Arn scored a goal in six games at the 1995 tournament... Named the best defenseman at the World Championships in 1992 (Pool C).

SOUTH KOREA

SANG-WON SEO A veteran forward of the Korean national team... Played in the 1990s in Pool C of the World and European Championships... Had his most successful tournament in 1995... Was one of the top scorers on the team... Collected seven goals and four assists for 11 points in six games.

EUI-SIK SHIM One of the top scorers of the Korean national team... Starred on the national team in the 1990s... Had his best performance at the 1995 World Championships (Pool C)... He scored five goals and had four assists for nine points in six games.

SPAIN

MIGUEL BALDRIS A star of Spanish hockey, he has played both forward and defense on the Spanish national team... Made his debut at the 1992 World Championships (Pool C) and was named the best forward of the tournament... Has played in every World Championship since... Began playing defense in 1994 and was named the best defenseman of the 1995 World Championships (Pool C)... Had great scoring numbers at this tournament, with two goals and six assists for eight points in six games.

GONZALO EGUILUZ An offensive defenseman of the Spanish national team who has played in every World Championship since joining the team in 1993 (Pool C)... Always one of the top scoring defenseman of the tournament... Had two great tournaments, in 1993 (Pool C) and 1994 (Pool C)... In 1993, he recorded four goals and three assists for seven points in six games... In 1994, he collected two goals and eight assists for 10 points in five games of the tournament.

IGNACIO SALEGUI One of the best scorers in the history of Spanish hockey... Made his debut on the international scene in 1989 at the World and European Championships (Pool D)... Never missed a tournament following the 1993 World Championships (Pool C)... Played in a total of six tournaments... Starred at the 1995 World Championships (Pool C), where he collected six goals and five assists for 11 points in six games.

SWEDEN

TOMMY ALBELIN A member of Team Sweden at the 1983 and 1984 World Junior Championships... Played with Tomas Sandstrom on the 1983 Junior team... Played for Sweden for four straight years at the World Championships beginning in 1985... Helped Sweden to a silver medal in 1986 and a gold medal at the 1987 World Championships... Played for Sweden in the 1987 and 1991 Canada Cup tournaments... Represented Sweden at the 1996 World Cup of Hockey, 1997 World Championships (silver medal) and 1998 Nagano Olympics.

Quebec's seventh choice, 152nd overall, in 1983 NHL draft, Albelin played five seasons with Djurgarden, Sweden from 1982–83 to 1986–87... Saw some action at left wing during the 1992–93 season with New Jersey... Was a member of the 1995 Stanley Cup champion Devils... In 1995–96, was acquired by the Calgary Flames from New Jersey as part of the five-player deal... Finished the 1997–98 season with two goals and 17 assists for 19 points in 69 games.

JONAS BERGQVIST One of Sweden's most distinguished international performers... Played in the 1987 and 1991 Canada Cup, the 1988 and 1994 Olympics and eight World Championships... Has a great collection of medals: gold at the 1987 and 1991 World Championships and 1994 Lillehammer Olympics, silver at the 1986, 1993 and 1995 Worlds and bronze at the 1988 Calgary Olympics and 1994 Worlds... One of only 11 members of Sweden's exclusive "Club-200" for the players who have played 200 or more games for the Swedish national team... Played at the 1996 World Championships in Vienna, and led the Swedish team with four goals... Scored one goal in four games in the 1996 World Cup of Hockey.

Calgary's sixth choice, 126th overall, in the 1988 NHL Entry Draft, he was signed by the Flames in 1989 and played 22 games during the 1989–90 season... Also played for the Flames' farm club in Salt Lake City... Played one season for Mannheim in Germany before returning to Sweden in 1991–92 to play for his original club, Leksands... Played 17 seasons, 15 of them for Leksand... Studied economics at Leksand University and has worked in public relations for a Swedish bank... His childhood hockey hero was Borje Salming... In 1995–96, led Leksand in scoring (16 goals, 14 assists in 37 games played).

LARS BJORN A member of the Swedish national team from 1950 to 1961... Played in 217 games for his country... Participated at three Olympics and 10 World and European Championships... Bronze Winter Olympic medalist in 1952... IIHF World Champion in 1953 and 1957, bronze medalist in 1952, 1954 and 1958... European Champion in 1952, 1953 and 1957... Named the best defenseman at the World and European Championships in 1954.

Began his career at 19... Played for Djurgardens IF Stockholm (1950 to 1967)... His team was Swedish national champion in 1950, 1954, 1955, and from 1958 to 1963... One of the best defensemen in the history of Swedish hockey.

CONNY EVENSSON Named the head coach of the Swedish national team before the 1990–91 season... Coached the team at the 1991 Canada Cup... Under his coaching, the Swedes won back-to-back World Championship titles in 1991 and 1992... Coached at the 1992 Albertville Olympics.

Played for Farjestads BK Karlstad as a playmaking center from 1965 to 1975... Was the team captain for five seasons... Later coached Farjestad to its first-ever national league championship title in 1980–81... Won another title with his club in 1985–86... Began coaching EHC Kloten in Switzerland in 1992... After two seasons came back to Sweden and coached Farjestad in 1994–95 and 1995–96.

PETER FORSBERG Ranked second in scoring at the 1992 World Junior Championships in Germany with three goals and eight assists in seven games, leading Sweden to a silver medal... Named the best forward at the 1993 World Junior Championships after setting a World Junior record with 31 points (seven goals and 24 assists) in just seven games... Was also named to the tournament all-star team after leading Sweden to a second-place finish behind

Canada... The line of Forsberg, Markus Naslund and Niklas Sundstrom set a World Junior record with 69 points in seven games in 1993... Is the all-time assists (32) and points (42) leader in World Junior history... Scored winning goal in shootout against Canada at Lillehammer in 1994 to give Sweden the country's first-ever Olympic gold medal... Recorded one goal and four assists in four games at both the 1996 World Cup of Hockey and the 1998 Nagano Olympics.

Philadelphia's first choice, sixth overall, in the 1991 NHL Entry Draft... Played six years for MoDo from 1989–90 through 1993–94... Had yet to play in North America when he was traded to Quebec as part of the mega-deal that brought Eric Lindros to Philadelphia... In 1994–95, he led all NHL rookies with 50 points (15 goals, 35 assists) and plus–minus (+17)... Ranked second in team scoring... Became the first player from Sweden to win the Calder Trophy as the NHL's rookie of the year... In 1995–96, he finished second to Joe Sakic in team scoring and fifth overall in the NHL with 116 points (30 goals and 86 assists) in 82 games... Won the Stanley Cup with the Colorado Avalanche in 1997... Led Colorado in scoring in both 1996–97 and 1997–98.

THOMAS GRADIN played junior hockey with MoDo from 1972–73 until 1975–76. During that time, he was a member of the Swedish junior national team at the three unofficial World Junior Championships staged in 1974, 1975 and 1976. He was named to the all-star team at the 1974 tournament and was selected best forward at the European Junior Championships that same year. Gradin went on to play for AIK Solna in the Swedish elite league in 1976–77 and 1977–78, representing his country at the World Championships in 1978.

Gradin was drafted by the Chicago Black Hawks in 1976 but his rights were traded to the Vancouver Canucks before he made his NHL debut in 1978–79. He became one of Vancouver's top players during his eight seasons with the Canucks. He also represented Sweden at the Canada Cup in 1981 and 1984. Gradin finished his NHL career with the Boston Bruins in 1986–87, then returned to Sweden were he played three more years with AIK Solna. He then coached MoDo for three years and made a brief return to action in 1996–97 when he played a pair of games for Vastra Frolunda.

BENGT-AKE GUSTAFSSON Became a member of the Swedish national team in 1978–79... Played in 117 games for Sweden... Participated at the 1992 Albertville Olympics and at five World and European Championships... World Champion in 1987 and 1991, silver medalist in 1981, bronze medalist in 1979... Played at the 1984 and 1987 Canada Cup tournaments... Sweden was a finalist in 1984.

Washington's seventh choice, 55th overall, in 1978 NHL Amateur Draft... Began his hockey career in his native town of Karlskoga... Later played for Farjestads BK Karlstad (1977 to 1979)... Joined the Capitals before the 1979–80 NHL season... Prior to that, played two playoff games with Edmonton (in the World Hockey Association) in the spring of 1979... Spent seven seasons with Washington before coming back to Sweden... His most successful NHL game occured on January 8, 1984 when he scored five goals against the Philadelphia Flyers, ironically all of them against countryman Pelle Lindbergh... In 1986–87, he played for Bofors IK Karlskoga (Swedish Division 2)... Returned to North America and played two more seasons with the Caps... Finished his NHL career with 196 goals and 359 assists for 555 points in 629 games... In 1989–90, he joined Farjestad in Sweden... Later successfully played for VEU Feldkirch in Austria.

LENNART HAGGROTH A member of the national team from 1961 to 1964... Played in 65 games for the Swedish national team... Participated at the 1964 Innsbruck Olympics and three World and European Championships... Olympic silver medalist in 1964... World and European Champion in 1962, silver medalist in 1963 and 1964... Named the best goaltender of the World and European Championships in 1962.

Played for Kiruna AIF (1958 to 1961) and Skelleftea AIK (1961 to 1966) of the Swedish League.

INGE HAMMARSTROM played with Brynas in the Swedish league from 1969–70 until 1972–73. He was also a member of the Swedish national team from 1971 to 1973, winning a silver medal (1972) and two bronze medals at the World Championships as well as playing at the 1972 Sapporo Olympics. He was drafted by the Toronto Maple Leafs in 1973 and made his NHL debut along with countryman and teammate Borje Salming in 1973–74. Hammarstrom played six years in the NHL with Toronto and St. Louis.

In the midst of his NHL career, Hammarstrom again represented Sweden at the inaugural Canada Cup tournament in 1976 and at the World Championships in 1979 where he earned another bronze medal. Returning to Brynas in 1979–80, Hammarstrom played for three more years and won a silver medal at the World Championships in 1981.

ANDERS HEDBERG Began to play for the Swedish national team in 1969 at age 18... Played in 100 games for Sweden... Participated at four World and European Championships... Silver medalist at the World Championships in 1970 and 1973, bronze medalist in 1972 and 1974... Played in both the 1976

and 1981 editions of the six-nation Canada Cup tournament.

Played for MoDo AIK Ornskoldsvik (1967 to 1972) and Djurgardens IF Stockholm (1972 to 1974)... Joined the Winnipeg Jets of the World Hockey Association before the 1974–75 season... Played four seasons with the Jets... Won AVCO Cup in 1976 and 1978... Played in 286 games with Winnipeg, recording 236 goals and 222 assists for 458 points (among the best totals in WHA history)... Signed as a free agent with the New York Rangers in 1978... In seven seasons with the Rangers, recorded 172 goals and 225 assists for 397 points in 465 games... Won the Bill Masterton Trophy in 1985.

GORAN HOGOSTA A top goaltender with Tunabro and Leksands from 1971–72 until 1976–77, Goran Hogosta also played for the Swedish national team at four consecutive World Championships from 1975 to 1978 and at the inaugural Canada Cup tournament in 1976. He won two bronze medals and a silver medal at the world event and was named both an all-star and best goalie at the 1977 tournament. Previously, Hogosta had been named best goalie at the European Junior Championships in 1973.

Hogosta spent three seasons in North America, playing one game with the New York Islanders in 1977–78 and 21 with the Quebec Nordiques in 1979–80, but spending the majority of his time in the minor leagues. He returned to Sweden in 1980–81 and spent eight seasons with Vastra Frolunda.

LEIF HOLMQVIST A member of the Swedish national team from 1962 to 1975... Played in 202 games for Sweden... Participated at the 1968 and 1972 Olympics and at nine World and European Championships... Silver medalist at the World Championships in 1967, 1969 and 1970, bronze medalist in 1965, 1971, 1972 and 1975... Named the best goaltender of the World and European Championships in 1969.

Played for Stromsbro IF (1958 to 1964) and AIK Solna (1964 to 1973 and 1974–75)... In 1973–74 played for the British professional club London Lions... Was a member of the Indianapolis Racers (World Hockey Association) in 1975–76... Nicknamed "Honken"... One of the best goalies in the history of Swedish hockey.

CALLE JOHANSSON Won gold and was an all-star at the 1985 European Junior Championships... Member of the Swedish team at the 1986 and 1987 World Junior Championships... Won a bronze medal in 1987... Named the outstanding defenseman of the tournament... Played for the Swedish team at the 1991 Canada Cup... Member of Sweden's gold medal teams at the 1991 and 1992 World Championships... Finished second on the Swedish team scoring list at the 1996 World Cup of Hockey (behind Mats Sundin)... Played at the 1998 Olympics in Nagano.

Buffalo's first choice, 14th overall, in the 1985 NHL Entry Draft... Boyhood idol was Borje Salming... Won a Swedish championship with Bjorkloven before making his NHL debut with the Sabres in 1987–88... Ranked second among NHL rookies in assists (38) and eighth in points (42)... Named to the 1987–88 All-Rookie Team... Has been with Washington since March of 1989... Established career highs in goals (14), assists (42), and points (56) in 1991–92... Led Caps defensemen in scoring in with 31 points in 46 games in 1994–95... Played five games for Kloten in Switzerland during the NHL lockout that year... In 1995–96, played in his 600th NHL game... Recorded his 300th point in a Capitals uniform... Wrist injury kept him out of the playoffs for the first time in his career... Finished 1997–98 regular season as third top scorer on the team... Recorded 15 goals and 20 assists for 35 points in 73 games.

SVEN JOHANSSON Played in 245 games for the Swedish national team from 1951 to 1966... Participated at the 1952, 1956, 1960 and 1964 Olympics and at 14 World and European Championships... Silver Olympic medalist at Innsbruck in 1964, bronze Olympic medalist at Oslo in 1952... World Champion in 1953, 1957 and 1962, silver medalist in 1963 and 1964, bronze medalist in 1952, 1954, 1958 and 1965... European Champion in 1952, 1953, 1957 and 1962... Named the best forward of the World and European Championships in 1957 and 1962... Voted to the all-star team of the World and European Championships in 1954.

Nicknamed "Tumba"... Played his entire career for Djurgardens IF Stockholm from 1948 to 1966... Swedish national champion in 1954, 1955 and from 1958 to 1963... One of the best players in the history of the game... Also played for the Swedish soccer national team.

TOMAS JONSSON Was already a member of the Swedish national team at age 19... Played in 200 games for Sweden... Participated at the 1980 and 1994 Olympics and at six World and European Championships... Olympic champion at Lillehammer in 1994, bronze medalist at Lake Placid in 1980... World Champion in 1991, silver medalist in 1981, 1986, 1990 and 1995, bronze medalist in 1979... Paired with 21-year-old offensive wunderkind Niklas Lindstrom (now with the Detroit Red Wings) in helping the Tre Kronor win the World Championship in 1991... Played at 1981 and 1987 Canada Cup tournaments.

New York Islanders' second choice, 25th overall, in the 1979 NHL Entry

Draft... Played for MoDo AIK Ornskoldsvik from 1977 to 1981... Swedish national champion in 1979... In 1981, joined the two-time defending Stanley Cup champion Islanders and won the Stanley Cup twice more with the team... Was traded to Edmonton for future considerations on February 15, 1989... Accumulated 85 goals and 259 assists for 344 points in 552 games over eight NHHL seasons... In 1989, he returned to Sweden, where he became the captain of Leksands IF.

NICKLAS LIDSTROM Member of Sweden's team at the 1988 European Junior and 1990 World Junior Championships... Member of Team Sweden at the 1991 Canada Cup... Played for Sweden on the gold medal-winning 1991 team that posted a 5–0–5 record at the World Championships... Also played on the 1994 team that captured bronze medal at Worlds... Played in the 1996 World Cup of Hockey and at the 1998 Nagano Olympics.

Detroit's third choice, 53rd overall, in the 1989 NHL Entry Draft... Played three seasons for Vasteras in the Swedish Elite League from 1989–90 to 1990–91... First runner-up to Pavel Bure for the 1991–92 Calder Trophy as NHL rookie of the year... Was first among NHL rookies in plus–minus and in assists and ranked third in scoring... Set club record for assists by a rookie defenseman with 49 and tied Reed Larson's rookie defenseman point mark with 60... Ranked second among defensemen in playoff scoring in 1994–95 with 16 points (Paul Coffey ranked first)... In 1995–96, he set a career high for points with 67 (17 goals, 50 assists)... Finished tied for sixth with Chicago's Gary Suter in points scored by a defenseman... Won the Stanley Cup with the Red Wings in 1997... Led the NHL in scoring among defensemen with 17 goals and 42 assists for 59 points in 80 games in 1997–98.

PELLE LINDBERGH was one of the top goaltenders in the world before his life was cut short in a tragic car accident in 1985. The Swedish netminder had been a member of the Philadelphia Flyers since 1981–82 and was coming off a season that had seen him win the Vezina Trophy in 1984–85. His childhood hero had been Flyers star Bernie Parent.

Lindbergh was just 20 years old when he represented Sweden at the Lake Placid Olympics in 1980. He had already established himself as a star by that time, having been named top goalie at the European Junior Championships in 1976 and 1977. He was also named best goalie and received an all-star selection at the World Junior Championships in 1979. He played for Sweden at the Canada Cup in 1981.

PETER LINDMARK Played in 174 games for the Swedish national team... Participated at the 1988 Calgary Olympics and at seven World and European Championships... Olympic bronze medalist in 1988... World Champion in 1987 and 1991, silver medalist in 1981 and 1986... Named the best goaltender of the World and European Championships in 1986... Voted to the all-star team at the World and European Championships in 1981 and 1986... Played at the 1981, 1984 and 1987 Canada Cup tournaments... A highlight of his career was an excellent performance when Sweden beat Team Canada 4–2 at the 1984 Canada Cup.

Played for Timra IK (1976 to 1984), Farjestads BK Karlstad (1984 to 1989)... A Swedish national champion in 1986 and 1988... Has been with Malmo IF since 1989–90 and won Swedish championships in 1992 and 1994.

CURT LINDSTROM Worked with the Swedish National Juniors in the early 1980s... Was named the assistant coach of the Swedish national team in a surprising move in the summer of 1984... Helped lead the Swedes to the finals (losing to Team Canada) at the 1984 Canada Cup... Named the head coach of the Swedish national team in 1985–86... His team played excellent hockey at the 1986 World and European Championships in Moscow, losing 3–2 to the powerful Soviet team in the decisive game and settling for a silver medal... Worked as an assistant coach of the national team to Tommy Sandlin for the next two season... The Swedes won the 1987 World Championship (their first since 1962)... In September of 1987 the team lost a semifinal to the Soviets at the Canada Cup after being ranked third in the round robin... The Swedish national team got a bronze medal at the Calgary Olympics in 1988... At the beginning of 1993–94, Lindstrom was named the head coach of the Finnish national team in another surprising move... He was the first Swedish coach to guide the Finnish national team... Worked in Finland until 1997... In 1995, the Finns won their first World Championship title.

Lindstrom played with Hammarby, Sodertalje and Huddinge (as a playing coach)... Started his coaching career at the age of 40, coaching Lidingo of Division 3 from 1980 to 1984... Later Lindstrom worked as a head coach with the Swiss club EHC Kloten (1988–89 to December of 1989), Germany's Hedos Munchen (1990–91 to October of 1991) and Sodertalje SK (Swedish Division 2) from January of 1992 to the end of the season.

HAKAN LOOB Played in 133 games for the Swedish national team... Participated at the 1992 and 1994 Olympics and at four World and European Championships... Olympic gold medalist at Lillehammer in 1994... Was instrumental in Sweden winning the 1987 and 1991 World Championships... Earned a silver medal in 1990... Finalist of the 1984 Canada Cup.

Began his career with Farjestads BK Karlstad (1979 to 1983)... Swedish national champion in 1981... Moved to North America in 1983 and became one of the more successful European players in the NHL... Recorded 193 goals and 236 assists for 429 points in 450 games during his six seasons with the Calgary Flames... Was named to the NHL's First All-Star Team in 1988... Returned to Sweden after the Flames won the Stanley Cup in 1989...Joined his former club, Farjestads BK Karlstad... Older brother, Peter, spent parts of the 1984–85 season with the Quebec Nordiques.

CURT LUNDMARK Coached the Swedish national B-team "Vikingarna" (while also coaching HV 71) from 1985 to 1989... Named an assistant coach to Conny Evensson of the Swedish national team in 1990... Helped Sweden win the gold medal at the 1991 and 1992 World Championships... Also worked with the team during the 1991 Canada Cup and the 1992 Albertville Olympics... Named the head coach of the Swedish national team prior to the 1992–93 season... His team lost the final game to Russia at the 1993 World Championships and got a silver medal... Later coached at the Lillehammer Olympics in 1994 and at the 1994 and 1995 World Championships.

Started his playing career in 1963 with the Swedish League club Skelleftea... Moved to Kiruna in order to fulfill his military service... Played in Kiruna for six years... Began his coaching career with Vasteras IK... Worked with the organization on different levels for 14 years... His real success came on the junior level, where he developed a lot of good players... He also coached HV 71 Jonkoping from 1985 to 89.

TORD LUNDSTROM Became a member of the Swedish national team in 1963 when he was just 18... Played in 200 games for Sweden until 1975... Participated at the 1968 and 1972 Olympics and at nine World and European Championships... Silver World Championship medalist in 1969, 1970 and 1973, bronze medalist in 1965, 1971, 1972 and 1975... Played at the 1976 Canada Cup... Was the captain of the Swedish national team for many years.

Played for Brynas IF Gavle from 1963 to 1973 and 1975 to 1979... Swedish national champion in 1964, 1966 to 1968, 1970 to 1972, 1976 and 1977... Captained the team... Played for Detroit Red Wings and in England with Detroit's farm club, the London Lions in 1973–74... After retiring as a player, he coached Brynas.

LARS-ERIK LUNDVALL Played in 190 games for the Swedish national team from 1954 to 1965... Participated at the 1956, 1960 and 1964 Olympics and at nine World and European Championships... Silver Olympic medalist in 1964... World Champion in 1957 and 1962, silver medalist in 1963 and 1964, bronze medalist in 1958... European Champion in 1957 and 1962.

Began his career with IFK Bofors Karlskoga (1950 to 1955)... Later played for Sodertalje SK (1955 to 1960) and Vastra Frolunda IF Goteborg (1960 to 1968)... Swedish national champion in 1956 and 1965... One of the best players in the history of Swedish hockey.

MATS NASLUND Played in 173 games for the Swedish national team... Participated at the 1980, 1992 and 1994 Olympics and at five World and European Championships... Olympic gold medalist at Lillehammer in 1994, bronze medalist at Lake Placid in 1980... World Champion in 1991, silver medalist in 1981, bronze medalist in 1979... Played at the 1984, 1987 and 1991 Canada Cup tournaments... Sweden was a finalist in 1984.

Began his career with Timra IK (1977–78)... Played for Brynas IF Gavle from 1978 to 1982... Swedish national champion in 1980... Joined the Montreal Canadiens in 1982... Was named to the NHL All-Rookie Team in 1982–83 ...In three of his eight NHL seasons with Montreal, Naslund led the Canadiens in goals and in four seasons he topped the team in points... Naslund's greatest season was in 1985–86 when he was named to the NHL Second All-Star Team and won the Stanley Cup with the Canadiens... In 1988, Naslund was awarded the Lady Byng Memorial Trophy... After finishing his NHL career, Naslund played one season in Switzerland with HC Lugano... He then returned to Sweden and played for Malmo IF... Helped Malmo win the Swedish championship in 1992... Came back to the NHL in 1994–95 and played for Boston... Tallied 251 goals and 383 assists for 634 points in 651 regular season games in his NHL career... Later came back to Brynas.

KENT NILSSON Nicknamed "Magic Man"... Played in 94 games for the Swedish national team... Participated at 1985 and 1989 World and European Championships... Played at the 1981, 1984 and 1987 Canada Cup tournaments... Sweden was a finalist in 1984.

Began his hockey career with Djurgardens IF Stockholm in 1975–76... Next season played for AIK Solna... Joined the Winnipeg Jets (World Hockey Association) in 1977–78 and played two seasons with the team... Winnipeg won the AVCO Cup in 1978... Made his debut in the NHL in 1979–80... Played eight seasons with Atlanta, Calgary, Minnesota and Edmonton... Won the Stanley Cup with the Oilers in 1987... Later played for HC Bolzano (Italy) and HC Lugano (Switzerland) in 1987–88, Djurgarden in 1988–89, Swiss club EHC Kloten from 1989 to 1992, back with Djurgarden in 1992–93, ATSE Graz (Austria) in 1993–94, Valerengens IF Oslo (Norway) and the Edmonton Oilers

in 1994–95... In his NHL career, played in 553 games, accumulating 264 goals and 422 assists for 686 points.

NILS NILSSON Played in 205 games for the Swedish national team from 1954 to 1967... Participated at the 1956, 1960 and 1964 Olympics and at 10 World and European Championships... Olympic silver medalist in 1964... World and European Champion in 1957 and 1962, silver medalist at the World Championships in 1963, 1964 and 1967... Bronze medalist in 1958 and 1965... Named the best forward at the World and European Championships in 1960... Voted to the all-star team at the World and European Championship tournament in 1962.

Began his brilliant career with Forshaga IF (1954 to 1962)... Later played for IK Gota and Leksands IF until 1969... Swedish national champion in 1969 with Leksand.

ULF NILSSON was one of the first Swedish players to become a superstar in North America after joining the Winnipeg Jets of the World Hockey Association with countryman Anders Hedberg in 1974–75. Both Hedberg and Nilsson ranked among the top scorers during each of their four seasons in the WHA and helped the Jets win the Avco Cup in 1976 and 1978. Nilsson was never able to duplicate his scoring feats during four NHL seasons with the New York Rangers.

Nilsson had played with AIK Solna in Sweden before joining the Jets and had represented his country at the World Championships in 1973 and 1974, winning a silver and a bronze medal. He later played for the Swedish team at the Canada Cup tournament in 1976 and 1981 and was a member of the NHL All-Star Team that took on the Soviet Union in the 1979 Challenge Cup.

BENGT OHLSON Began working with the Swedish junior national team in 1977... The team won a silver and two bronze medals at the World Junior Championships... Ohlson was promoted and became an assistant coach of the Swedish national team... He helped Tommy Sandlin at the 1980 Lake Placid Olympics where the Swedes finished third and was promoted to head coach... At the 1981 World and European Championships in Sweden, the hosts took silver... Ohlson worked as the head coach of the Swiss national team from 1982 to 1985... His best achievement was a second-place finish at the 1985 Pool B World Championships... He came back to Sweden and coached Swedish junior national team (under 18) in 1985–86 and the national B-team in 1986–87... Returned to Switzerland in 1987 and worked one season with Fribourg-Gotteron... Was invited to coach the Norwegian national team in 1991... Under his coaching the team kept its position in Pool A of the World Championships... Coached Norway at the 1992 Albertville Olympics and at the 1994 Games in Lillehammer.

Played for Leksands IF... After the retiring he started his coaching career as an assistant coach with Leksand... He took over as head coach in 1970 and remained with Leksand until 1977... Leksand won the Swedish national title three times in a row (1973, 1974 and 1975)... Swedish star Thomas Steen and former WHA and NHL players Christer Abrahamsson, Thommy Abrahamsson, Per-Olov Brasar and Dan Labraaten played under Ohlson.

CHRISTER OLSSON Played in 33 games for the Swedish national team... Starred at the World Championships in 1995... Named the best defenseman at the tournament... Helped Sweden win a silver medal.

Began his hockey career with Mora in Division 2... In 1992 was invited to Brynas IF Gavle and played there three seasons... Swedish national champion in 1993... St. Louis Blues' tenth choice, 275th overall, in the 1993 NHL Entry Draft... Split the 1995–96 season between St. Louis and its affiliate in Worcester (American Hockey League)... Played for the same teams next season before being traded to Ottawa.

RONALD PETTERSSON A member of "Tre Kronor" from 1954 to 1967... Played in 252 games for the Swedish national team... Played in every major international tournament from 1955 to 1967... Participated at the 1956, 1960 and 1964 Olympics and at 13 World and European Championships... Olympic silver medalist in 1964... World and European Champion in 1957 and 1962, silver medalist in 1963, 1964 and 1967, bronze medalist in 1958 and 1965... Coached the Swedish national team from 1974 to 1976... The Swedes got a bronze medal at the World Championships in 1975 and 1976... Coached the Norwegian national team from 1978 to 1981.

Began his career with Surahammars IF... From 1955 to 1960 played for Sodertalje SK, from 1960 to 1967 with Vastra Frolunda IF Goteborg... Played for the Swedish national champion in 1956 and 1965... Nicknamed "Sura-Pelle"... Considered one of the best players in the history of hockey... Began his coaching career in 1968... Coached the Swedish national junior team for five seasons.

MIKAEL RENBERG played two seasons with Pitea in the Swedish second division before moving up to Lulea in 1990–91. He represented Sweden at the World Junior Championships in 1992 and was named to the all-star team after Sweden won a silver medal at the World Championships in 1993.

Renberg was named to the NHL All-Rookie Team after collecting 38 goals and 44 assists for Philadelphia in 1993–94 and was a member of the Flyers' Legion of Doom line with Eric Lindros and John LeClair until injuries slowed him down during the 1995–96 season. He was a member of the Flyers team that reached the Stanley Cup finals in 1997 and represented Sweden at the Nagano Olympics in 1998.

THOMAS RUNDQVIST Captain of the Swedish national team for many years... Played in 267 games for Sweden—a record... Participated at the 1984, 1988 and 1992 Olympics and at eight World and European Championships... Olympic bronze medalist at Sarajevo in 1984 and Calgary in 1988... World Champion in 1987 and 1991, silver medalist in 1986, 1990 and 1993... Voted to the all-star team of the World and European Championships in 1991... Was a captain of the team in 1991... Played at 1987 Canada Cup.

Spent the major part of his career with Farjestads BK Karlstad (1979 to 1984 and 1985 to 1993)... Swedish national champion in 1981, 1986 and 1988... Played for the Montreal Canadiens in 1984–85 and spent most part of the seasons with the farm club in Sherbrooke... Joined the Austrian club VEU Feldkirch in 1993–94.

BORJE SALMING A legend of international hockey... Began to play for the Swedish national team in 1971... Played in 87 games for his country... Participated at 1992 Albertville Olympics and three World and European Championships... Silver medalist at the World Championships in 1973, bronze medalist in 1972... Voted to the tournament all-star team in 1973... Played at the 1976, 1981 and 1991 Canada Cup tournaments... Voted to the all-star team at the 1976 Canada Cup.

Played for Brynas IF Gavle from 1970 to 1973... Swedish national champion in 1971 and 1972... Joined the Toronto Maple Leafs in 1973–74 season... Played 17 seasons in the NHL (16 with Toronto, one with the Detroit Red Wings)... Accumulated 150 goals and 637 assists for 787 points in 1,148 games... Named to the NHL First All-Star Team in 1977... Named to the NHL Second All-Star Team in 1975, 1976, 1978, 1979 and 1980... Came back to Sweden in 1990 and played for AIK Solna.

TOMMY SALO Played at the 1991 World Junior Championships... Won an Olympic gold medal at Lillehammer in 1994... Sweden's first Olympic gold medal... Stopped five Canadian shooters in shoot-out to determine a winner in the final game... Won bronze at the 1994 World Championships... Played at the 1996 World Cup of Hockey, the 1997 World Championships and the 1998 Nagano Olympics... Won a silver medal at the 1997 Worlds... Named the best goaltender and voted to the tournament's all-star team.

New York Islanders' fifth choice, 118th, overall in the 1993 NHL Entry Draft... Led Swedish Elitserien with a goals-against average of 2.47 for Vasteras in 1992–93... First North American pro season was a great success as he earned the International Hockey League's 1994–95 top rookie, goalie and player honors with Denver... Led the IHL in games, wins, goals-against average, minutes and saves... Tied for first in shutouts... Joined the Islanders in April 1995... First NHL start April 11, 1995 versus Tampa Bay... First NHL win April 18, 1995 over. Quebec... Rejoined Denver for the end of IHL season and playoffs... Was in net for clinching game in second, third and fourth round of 1995 IHL playoffs... Won Turner Cup (IHL championship) in Denver... In 1995–96, he won a second consecutive Turner Cup title with Utah... In 1996–97, became the Islanders' number-one goalie... Finished the 1997–98 regular season with very respectable 2.64 goals-against average and .906 save percentage.

TOMMY SANDLIN Named the head coach of the Swedish national team before the 1978–79 season... Worked two seasons... Came back as a head coach in 1985... Worked until 1990... Under Sandlin's coaching, the Swedish national team won the World Championship in 1987, got World silver medals in 1986 and 1990 and a bronze in 1979... Won an Olympic bronze medal in 1980 and 1988... Coached at the 1987 Canada Cup.

Played from 1963 to 1968 but never saw action in the Swedish League... Retired in 1968 and began his coaching career... Coached Brynas IF Gavle from 1968 to 1977... Brynas won the champions title in 1970, 1971, 1972, 1976 and 1977... Coached MoDo AIK Ornskoldsvik from 1977 to 1982 (champions in 1979)... From 1982 to 1986, he worked with IF Bjorkloven Umea... He came back to coach Brynas in the 1990s.

TOMAS SANDSTROM Right winger Tomas Sandstrom was named best forward at the 1982 European Junior Championships where his Swedish team captured the gold medal. He played in the World Junior Championships in 1983, capturing similar individual honors. He began a productive NHL career in 1984–85 and has registered 40-or-more goals in 1986–87 with the Rangers and in 1990–91 with the Los Angeles Kings. He reached the Stanley Cup finals with Los Angeles in 1993 and was part of a Cup winner with Detroit in 1997. He played for Sweden at the World Championships in 1987 and 1989, at the 1991 Canada Cup, and at the 1998 Nagano Olympics.

ULF SAMUELSSON Hard-rock defenseman Ulf Samuelsson earned a gold medal and international honors early in his career when he was named to the tournament all-star team at the 1982 European Junior Championships. He represented Sweden at three World Junior Championships and made his debut at the World Championships in 1984–85. He played for the NHL All-Stars against the Soviet Nationals at Rendez-vous '87 and was a member of Team Sweden at the 1998 Olympics in Nagano. He played for Leksand in the Swedish league before joining the Hartford Whalers in 1984. He won back-to-back Stanley Cup titles with Pittsburgh in 1991 and 1992.

LARS-ERIK SJOBERG Began playing for the Swedish national team in 1964... Played in 140 games for his country... Captained the national team... Participated at the 1968 and 1972 Olympics and at six World and European Championships... Silver medalist at the World Championships in 1969, 1970 and 1973, bronze medalist in 1972 and 1974... Named the best defenseman and voted to the all-star team at the 1974 tournament... Played at the 1976 Canada Cup.

Played for Leksands IF (1963 to 1965 and 1967 to 1969), Djurgardens IF Stockholm (1965 to 1967) and Vastra Frolunda IF Goteborg (1969 to 1974)... Swedish national champion in 1969... Joined the Winnipeg Jets of the World Hockey Association in 1974 and played six years with the clubs (including one season in the NHL in 1979–80)... Was the first non-North American to captain the Jets... Winnipeg won the AVCO Cup as WHA champions in 1976, 1978 and 1979.

THOMAS STEEN Played in 75 games for the Swedish national team... Participated at three World and European Championships... Silver medalist in 1981 and 1986... Played at the Canada Cup tournament in 1981, 1984 and 1991... Sweden was a finalist in 1984.

Played for Leksands IF (1976 to 1980) and Farjestads BK Karlstad (1980–81)... Swedish national champion in 1981... Joined the Winnipeg Jets for the 1981–82 NHL season... Played 14 seasons with the Jets before retired after 1994–95... In his NHL career, he played in 950 games and recorded 264 goals and 553 assists for 817 points... His number 25 is retired... Resumed his hockey career at the end of 1995–96 season in Frankfurt, Germany... Played the next two full seasons in Germany with EHC Eisbaren Berlin.

ULF STERNER Played in 189 games for the Swedish national team from 1958 to 1973... Participated at the 1960 and 1964 Olympics and at 11 World and European Championships... Olympic silver medalist at Innsbruck in 1964... World Champion in 1962, silver medalist in 1963, 1964, 1967, 1969, 1970 and 1973, bronze medalist in 1971... Named the best forward at the World and European Championships in 1969... Voted to the tournament all-star team in 1962 and 1969.

Began his brilliant career with Forshaga IF... Played there until 1961... Later saw action with Vastra Frolunda IF Goteborg (1961 to 1964), Rogle BK Angelholm (1965 to 1967), again with Vastra Frolunda (1967 to 1969) and Farjestads BK Karlstad (1969 to 1973)... Finished his career with Vastra Frolunda (1974–1975)... In 1964–65 played four games with the New York Rangers, spending the major part of the season in the minors with Baltimore and St.Paul... Played for the British professional club London Lions in 1973–74.

ROLAND STOLTZ Played in 218 games for the Swedish national team from 1955 to 1968... Participated at the 1960, 1964 and 1968 Olympics and at 12 World and European Championships from 1957 to 1968... Never missed a tournament... Olympic silver medalist at Innsbruck in 1964,... World and European Champion in 1957 and 1962, silver medalist in 1963, 1964 and 1967, bronze medalist in 1958 and 1965... Named the best defenseman of the World and European Championships in 1963.

Began his junior career in Atlas Copco... Spent his entire career in the Swedish League with Djurgardens IF Stockholm (1956 to 1970)... He team was the Swedish national champion from 1958 to 1963.

ARNE STROMBERG One of the best coaches in the history of hockey... Head coach of the Swedish national team from 1961 to 1971... Coached the team at two Olympics and 10 World and European Championships... Under his coaching, the Swedes won the World title in 1962, silver medals in 1963, 1964, 1967, 1969 and 1970, bronze medals in 1965 and 1971 and an Olympic silver medal at Innsbruck in 1964.

Began his career at 17... Played defense for IF Skuru from 1937 to 1950... Began his coaching career in 1950... Worked 10 seasons with Djurgardens IF Stockholm and Vastra Frolunda IF Goteborg... From 1971 to 1980 coached Farjestads BK Karlstad... Later worked in Switzerland with SC Langnau and Switzerland's national team (1980–81)... Coached the Norwegian national team in 1981–82.

MATS SUNDIN Played at the European Junior Championships in 1988 and 1989... Member of Team Sweden at the 1990 World Juniors... Member of Swedish Team at 1991 World Championships, leading the team in goals

(seven) and points (12) as Sweden won the gold medal... Struck gold again with Sweden at the 1992 World Championships... Led team in points (eight), second in tournament in assists (six)... Selected to the first all-star team... Tournament scoring leader with 14 points (five goals and nine assists) at the 1994 World Championships... Won bronze medal... Led the Swedish team in scoring in the 1996 World Cup of Hockey... Scored three goals in four games at the 1998 Nagano Olympics.

Quebec's first choice, first overall, at the 1989 NHL Entry Draft... First European ever selected first overall in the NHL draft... Childhood hockey hero was Kent Nilsson... Scored in his first NHL game on October 4, 1990... Had a career-best seven-point game (five goals, two assists) versus Hartford on March 5, 1992... Had a point in each of Quebec's first 30 games to start the 1992–93 season (21 goals, 25 assists)... Went on to enjoy career highs that year in goals (47), assists (67) and points (114)... Finished 11th in NHL scoring... One of only two Quebec players to play all 84 games in 1993–94... Second in club goal-scoring in three of his four seasons in Quebec... Has led Toronto in scoring every year since being traded to the Maple Leafs in 1994... His 94 points in 1996–97 ranked seventh in the NHL... Named the Leafs captain prior to 1997–98 season... First European player to wear the "C" with the Toronto Maple Leafs.

LENNART SVEDBERG Played for the Swedish national team from 1961 to 1972... Took part in 125 games for his country... Participated at the 1968 Grenoble Olympics and at six World and European Championships... Silver medalist at the World Championships in 1969 and 1970, bronze medalist in 1965 and 1971... Named the best defenseman at the World and European Championships in 1970... Voted to the IIHF tournament all-star team in both 1969 and 1970.

One of the best defensemen in the history of the game... Began his career with Timra IK... Later played for Grums IK (1962–63), Brynas IF Gavle (1963 to 1967), Mora IK (1967 to 1969) and then back in Timra IK (1969 to 1972)... Swedish national champion in 1964... Played forward at the beginning of his career, but showed his real talent as defenseman.

SWITZERLAND

OLIVIER ANKEN A veteran of the Swiss national team... Saw action in 153 games with the team... Made his debut at the 1978 World and European Championships (Pool B)... Played at the 1988 Calgary Olympics and at nine World and European Championships... Named the best goaltender of the World and European Championships in 1985 (Pool B)... Named to the all-star team at the World and European Championships in 1985 (Pool B) and 1986 (Pool B).

One of the best goalies in the history of Swiss hockey... Played 550 games in the Swiss League, all with EHC Biel.

FERDINAND CATTINI Saw action at the 1936 and 1948 Olympics and at eight World and European Championships... Olympic bronze medalist at St. Moritz in 1948... Silver medalist at the World Championships in 1935, bronze medalist in 1937, 1939 and 1948... European champion in 1935 and 1939... Played in 107 games for the Swiss national team and scored 92 goals.

Nicknamed "Pic"... A member of legendary "ni-Sturm" ("ni-Line")with brother Hans Cattini and Richard "Bibi" Torriani... Played for HC Davos from 1932 to 1956... Won the Swiss national title 14 times... Coached HC Davos from 1952 to 1962

HANS CATTINI Saw action at the 1936 and 1948 Olympics and at eight World and European Championships... Olympic bronze medalist in 1948... Silver medalist at the World Championship in 1935, bronze medalist in 1937, 1939 and 1948 ...European champion in 1935 and 1939... Played in 111 games for the Swiss national team and scored 74 goals.

Played for HC Davos (1929–30 to 1947–48) and HC Lausanne (1947–48 to 1950–51)... A member of Switzerland's legendary "ni-Sturm" ("ni-Line") with brother Pic Cattini and Richard "Bibi" Torriani... His teams won 15 Swiss national titles.

MANUELE CELIO Made his debut with the Swiss national team at the 1987 World and European Championships... Has played in almost every major tournament since... Saw action at 1988 and 1992 Olympics and at eight World and European championships... Had his best tournament in 1996 (Pool B)... Scored four goals and added five assists for nine points in seven games .... His father, Guido, played for Ambri of the Swiss League and for the Swiss national team in the 1960s... His uncle and his younger brother also have played for Ambri-Piotta.

JORG EBERLE Member of the Swiss national team since 1982... Played at the 1988 and 1992 Olympics... Was a leading scorer of the Swiss team in 1988

with five goals and three assists for eight points in six games... Participated at 11 World and European Championships... Named best forward and to the all-star team at the World and European Championships in 1986 (Pool B)... Was a captain of the Swiss national team.

One of the top players in the history of Swiss hockey... Played for Herisau, HC Davos and HC Lugano... Captained the club.

EMIL HANDSCHIN Played in 133 games for the Swiss national team and scored 28 goals... Played at the 1948, 1952 and 1956 Olympics and at 10 World and European Championships... Bronze medalist at the 1948 Olympics in St. Moritz... Bronze medalist at the 1948, 1950, 1951 and 1953 World Championships... European champion in 1950.

Defenseman... Played for SC Bern, HC Davos and HC Basel.

JAKOB KOLLIKER A record holder for games played with Switzerland's national team with 213... Made his national team debut in 1973... A veteran of the 1976 and 1988 Winter Olympics and 12 World and European Championships... Named to the all-star team at the World and European Championships in 1981 (Pool B)... Named the assistant coach of the national team before the 1995–96 season.

Defenseman... Began his career in with EHC Biel in 1970 at the age of 17... Later played for Ambri-Piotta... Won Swisss national championship titles with ECH Biel in 1978, 1981 and 1983... He coached EHC Biel at the conclusion of his playing career.

ALFRED LUTHI A veteran forward with the Swiss national team... A member of the national team in the 1980s and early 1990s... Saw action at the 1988 and 1992 Olympics and at seven World and European Championships.

Began his career with HC Fribourg... Later played for EHC Biel and HC Lugano... Was one of the best centers in the Swiss National League... Always played on the line with Jorg Eberle, both as a member of HC Lugano and of the Swiss national team.

GEBHARD POLTERA Played in 108 games for the Swiss national team and scored 38 goals... Played at the 1948 and 1952 Olympics and at eight World and European Championships... Bronze medalist at the 1948 Olympics in St. Moritz... Bronze medalist at the 1950, 1951 and 1953 World Championships... Won gold as European champions in 1950... A member of one of Switzerland's top forward lines along with Ulrich Poltera and Hans-Martin Trepp.

Forward... Played for EHC Arosa (1940 to 1958)... Won the Swiss national title seven times in a row.

ULRICH POLTERA Played in 111 games for Switzerland's national team and scored 74 goals in international play... Played at the 1948 and 1952 Winter Olympic Games and at seven World and European Championship tournaments... Bronze medalist at the 1948 Olympics in St. Moritz... Bronze medalist at the 1950, 1951 and 1953 World Championships... European gold medal champion in 1950... A member of the famous Swiss line with Gebhard Poltera and Hans-Martin Trepp.

Forward... Played for EHC Arosa (1940 to 1958)... Won the Swiss national title seven times in a row.

RICHARD TORRIANI Participated at the 1928, 1936 and 1948 Olympics and at 11 World and European Championships... Olympic bronze medalist in 1928 and 1948... Silver medalist of the World Championships in 1935, bronze medalist in 1928, 1930, 1937, 1939 and 1948... European champion in 1935 and 1939... Played in 111 games for the Swiss national team and scored 86 goals... Coached the Swiss national team from 1952 to 1954... Coached Italian national team from 1955 to 1957.

Nicknamed "Bibi"... Played for EHC St.Moritz (1927–28), HC Davos (1928 to 1950) and one season with Zurcher SC... A member of legendary "ni-Sturm" ("ni-Line") with Ferdinand "Pic" Cattini and Hans Cattini... Played on teams that won the Swiss national title 18 times... After retiring, became a coach... Coached the German club SC Riessersee (1950 to 1952, 1954–55 and 1957 to 1962), and also Mannheimer ERC (Germany), and Swiss clubs HC Davos, EHC Visp, HC Basel and HC Lugano.

HANS-MARTIN TREPP Played in 94 games for the Swiss national team from 1946 to 1955 and scored 42 goals... Played at the 1948 and 1952 Olympics and at seven World and European Championships... Bronze medalist at the 1948 Olympics in St. Moritz... European champion in 1950... At the 1952 Olympic tournament in Oslo, he scored 11 goals in eight games... A member of the famous Swiss line with Gebhard Poltera and Ulrich Poltera.

Forward... Played for EHC Arosa (1939 to 1958)... Won the Swiss national championship on seven occasions... Top scorer of the Swiss League in 1955–56 and 1956–57.

USSR, RUSSIA,
COMMONWEALTH OF INDEPENDENT STATES,
FORMER SOVIET REPUBLICS

IIHF-standard three-letter abbreviations are used to indicate the country each player has most recently represented in international competition as a player, coach or executive. Some players have represented more than one of these countries over the course of their careers. BLR – Belarus, EST – Estonia, KAZ – Kazakhstan, LAT – Latvia, LIT – Lithuania, RUS – Russia, URS – Soviet Union, UKR – Ukraine.

URS

VENIAMIN ALEXANDROV Participated at the 1960, 1964 and 1968 Olympics and at 11 World and European Championships from 1957 to 1968... Never missed a tournament in these years... Olympic gold medalist at Innsbruck in 1964 and Grenoble in 1968... World Champion every year from 1963 to 1968... Voted to the all-star team at the World and European Championships in 1966 and 1967.

Spent his entire hockey career with CSKA Moscow of the Soviet League (1955 to 1969)... Won the Soviet national title 10 times... Played in 400 games and scored 351 goals... Member of an internationally famous line with Konstantin Loktev and Alexander Almetov... After retiring, he coached SKA Leningrad (1973–74)... Later worked as a coach in Bulgaria.

URS

ALEXANDER ALMETOV Participated at the 1960 and 1964 Olympics and at seven World and European Championships... Played internationally 1960 to 1967... Olympic gold medalist at Innsbruck in 1964... World Champion every year from 1963 to 1967... Voted to the IIHF's tournament all-star team in 1965 and 1967.

Spent his hockey career with CSKA Moscow of the Soviet League... Played from 1958 to 1967... Won the Soviet national title seven times... In his career, played in 220 league games and scored 212 goals... Member of an internationally famous line with Konstantin Loktev and Veniamin Alexandrov.

BLR

ALEXANDER ANDRIYEVSKY Played for the Soviet national junior team before the breakup of the Soviet Union and later became the star of the Belarus national team... In 1996, he was named the best forward and an all-star at the World Championships (Pool B) and also made the all-star team in 1997 (Pool B)... Played for the Belarus national team at the 1998 Olympics in Nagano, Japan.

Began his hockey career with Dynamo Minsk of the Soviet League... Joined Dynamo Moscow before the 1990–91 season... Played two years with Dynamo Moscow and won the national title both years... Chicago's 13th choice, 220th overall, in the 1991 NHL Entry Draft... Joined the Blackhawks organization in 1992... Played one game for the Blackhawks and spent most of the time with their farm club in Indianapolis... Scored 26 goals and had 25 assists for 51 points in 66 games in his first season with Indianapolis... Left North America after the 1993–94 season and joined the Finnish club HPK Hameenlinna in 1994–95.

LAT

HELMUT BALDERIS Nicknamed "Electric Train" for his speed... Participated at the 1980 Lake Placid Olympics and four World and European Championships... World Champion in 1978, 1979 and 1983 as a member of the Soviet national team... Named the best forward and voted to the tournament all-star team at the World and European Championships in 1977... Played at the 1976 Canada Cup... Coached the Latvian national team at the 1993 World Championships (Pool C).

Began his hockey career with Dynamo Riga... Played for Dynamo Riga from 1969 to 1977 and 1980 to 1985... Played for CSKA Moscow from 1977 to 1980... Won Soviet national titles three times... Scored 333 goals in 462 league games... Signed with the Minnesota North Stars and played in the 1989–90 season... Scored three goals and added six assists for nine points in 26 NHL games... Retired and coached in Japan.

LIT

DAINIUS BAUBA One of the best forward of the Lithuanian national team... Played at the World Championships in 1995 (Pool C) and 1996 (Pool D)... Named the best forward at the World Championships in 1996 (Pool D)... Had great scoring records in both tournaments... In 1995, he collected 13 goals and eight assists for 21 points in six games... In 1996, recorded 10 goals and six assists for 16 points in five games.

URS

VSEVOLOD BOBROV The first captain of the Soviet national team... Participated at the 1956 Olympics in Cortina d'Ampezzo and at four World and European Championships from 1954 to 1957... World Champion in 1954,

World and Olympic Champion 1956... Named the best forward at the World and European Championships in 1954... Considered one of the best hockey players of all time... Head coach of the Soviet national team from 1972 to 1974... Won the World Championship with the team in 1973 and 1974.

Began his hockey career with CDKA Moscow from 1946 to 1949... Played for VVS MVO Moscow from 1950 to 1953... Came back to CDSA Moscow (formerly CDKA) and played until 1957... Won the Soviet national title seven times... Played in 130 league games and scored 254 goals... Played in the historic games versus the Czechoslovakian club LTC Praha in 1948... Was a playing coach of VVS MVO in 1951 and 1952... Coached Moscow Spartak from 1964 to 1967 and won the national title in 1967.

RUS

PAVEL BURE Played on a line with Sergei Fedorov and Alexander Mogilny on the gold medal-winning Soviet team at the 1989 World Junior Championships... Selected as the tournament's best forward... Won a silver medal at the 1990 World Junior Championships... Silver medal again in 1991... Was a member of Soviet gold medal-winning team at the 1990 World Championships... Bronze medal in 1991... Didn't play at the 1996 World Cup of Hockey due an injury he sustained five days prior to Russia's first game of the tournament... Starred at 1998 Olympics, winning silver medal with the Russian team... Scored five goals in the semifinal game versus Finland and led the Olympics with nine goals... Named the best forward of the tournament.

Vancouver's fourth choice, 113th overall, in the 1989 NHL draft... Later ruled ineligible for the draft, then reinstated as Canucks property... Nicknamed "the Russian Rocket"... Became a regular with the Red Army team at age 17... Made his NHL debut on November 5, 1991... NHL rookie of the month for March/April 1992... Set Canucks club record for goals by a rookie (34)... First Canuck to win a major postseason award when he won the Calder Trophy... Became first Canuck to top 50 goals, 100 points in a season in 1992–93 when had 60 goals and 110 points... Second 60-goal season in 1993–94 made him the eighth player in NHL history to score 60 goals or more twice... Sixth-fastest player in NHL history to reach 100 career goals... Set a franchise record, and tied Brett Hull for NHL lead, with 25 power-play goals... Voted Canucks' most exciting player for the fourth year in a row in 1994–95... In 1995–96, a torn anterior cruciate ligament 15 games into the season sidelined him for the rest of the campaign... Led the Vancouver Canucks in scoring in 1997–98, with 51 goals and 39 assists for 90 points in 82 games.

RUS

VYACHESLAV BYKOV played center and represented the Soviet Union and Russia at nine World Championships beginning in 1983. He scored five-or-more goals in four consecutive tournaments beginning in 1985. He is a double gold medal winner (at the 1988 and 1992 Olympics) and represented the Soviet Union at the 1987 Canada Cup. Along with Andrei Khomutov, he was one of the first players given permission to play professionally outside the Soviet Union and has great success playing for Fribourg in Switzerland. He has been the top scorer in the Swiss league on four occasions in the 1990s.

URS

ARKADY CHERNYSHEV International coaching career began in 1948 when he coached the Moscow Selects team in three historic games versus LTC Praha of Czechoslovakia... Was named the head coach of the Soviet national team in its first official season of 1953–54... The Soviets won the gold medal in their first appearance at the World Championships in 1954... In two years, the team won Olympic gold in Cortina d'Ampezzo, Italy... Worked as a head coach of the Soviet national team until 1957 and later from 1961 to 1972... The Soviets made an incredible run, winning nine World champions titles in a row (1963 to 1971)... Under the coaching tandem of Chernyshev and Anatoli Tarasov, the Soviets also captured Olympic gold in 1964, 1968 and 1972.

Was a famous soccer player... Won the Soviet national title as a member of Dynamo Moscow soccer team in 1937 and 1940... Also played bandy with Dynamo Moscow... One of the pioneers of hockey in the Soviet Union... In 1946, scored the first goal of the first national championship of the Soviet Union... Was a forward and playing coach of Dynamo Moscow from 1946 to 1948... Scored four goals in 11 games... National champion in 1947, bronze medalist in 1948... Head coach of Dynamo Moscow from 1946 until 1974 — the longest tenure (28 seasons) in the history of the Soviet/Russian hockey... Under his coaching, Dynamo Moscow won the Soviet title in 1947 and 1954, silver medals in 1950, 1951, 1959, 1960, 1962, 1963, 1964, 1971 and 1972 and bronze medals in 1948, 1949, 1952, 1953, 1955, 1956, 1957, 1958, 1966, 1967, 1968, 1969 and 1974... Developed many superstars such as Alexander Maltsev, Valeri Vasiliev, Vitali Davydov and others.

RUS

IGOR DMITRIYEV As a coach, worked with the Soviet National Junior Teams of different ages... Led the Soviet junior team to a victory at the 1984 World Junior Championships... Named the assistant coach of the Soviet national team (worked with Viktor Tikhonov) in 1987... Worked at that posi-

tion until 1994... Coached the teams that won Olympic gold in at Calgary 1988 and Albertville in 1992 and won World championships in 1989 and 1990... Named the head coach of the Russian national team in 1996... Stopped working after one year due to illness.

Began his hockey career with Krylja Sovetov Moscow... Made his debut with the team in 1958 at the age of 17... Played center with Krylja Sovetov until 1974... Last 10 years was the captain of the team... Won the national title in 1974, got bronze medal in 1973... In 430 games with Krylja Sovetov scored 125 goals... Played in Austria, with Klagenfurt, from 1974 to 1976... Austrian national champion in 1976... Began his coaching career in 1976 with the juniors of Krylja Sovetov... Named the head coach of the senior team in 1983... Coached Krylja Sovetov until 1996... Under his coaching, the team won bronze medals in 1989, 1991 and 1993... Developed NHL players such as Sergei Nemchinov, Dmitri Mironov, Yuri Khmylev, Oleg Tverdovsky, Alexei Morozov, Dmitri Nabokov and others.

RUS
SERGEI FEDOROV Won a gold medal and had four goals and eight assists while playing on a line with Pavel Bure and Alexander Mogilny at 1989 World Junior Championships... Named to 1988 World Junior all-star team (five goals, seven assists in seven games)... Member of Team Russia at the 1991 Canada Cup... Won two World Championships gold medals with the Soviet national team, in 1989 (team was 10–0–0) and 1990 (8–1–1)... Led Russia in scoring with three goals and three assists in five games at the 1996 World Cup of Hockey... Earned a silver medal at the 1998 Olympics in Nagano.

Detroit's fourth choice, 74th overall, in the 1989 NHL Entry Draft... Played four seasons with the Central Red Army... Came to Detroit in 1990 after leaving the Soviet team prior to the Goodwill Games in Seattle... First runner-up behind Ed Belfour for the 1990–91 Calder Trophy... First runner-up to Guy Carbonneau for the 1991–92 Selke Trophy as the NHL's best defensive forward... Was the first European to win the Hart Trophy as NHL MVP (1993–94) after finishing second in scoring behind Wayne Gretzky with 120 points... Also won the Selke Trophy that year... In 1995–96, led the Red Wings in points with 107 (39 goals and 68 assists) and tied for eighth in the NHL... In 1996–97, he scored five goals in the game versus Washington on December 26, 1996... Won the Stanley Cup as a member of the Red Wings in 1997 and 1998.

RUS
VIACHESLAV FETISOV Won a gold medal at the 1975 and 1976 European Junior Championships... Named best defenseman at the 1976 European Junior Championships... Played in the 1978 World Junior Championships and was a member of the all-star team with future NHLers Wayne Gretzky, Anton Stastny, Mats Naslund and Risto Siltanen... Played for the Soviet Union at the 1980 Lake Placid Olympics, earning a silver medal... Won gold with the 1984 and 1988 Olympic teams... Performed in nine World Championships before leaving the Soviet Union, winning gold medals in 1978, 1981, 1982, 1983, 1986, 1989... Also won gold with the Soviets in 1990 after his first NHL season... Named the best defenseman at 1978, 1982, 1985, 1986 and 1989 World Championships... Named to World Championships all-star team in 1978, 1982, 1983, 1985, 1986, 1987, 1990 and 1991... Played on the Soviet Union's 1981 Canada Cup-winning team... Named to 1987 Canada Cup all-star team... Captain of the Russian team at the 1996 World Cup of Hockey.

New Jersey's sixth choice, 150th overall, in the 1983 NHL Entry Draft... Long-time captain of Central Red Army... Played with Red Army from 1974–75 to 1988–89... Named top defenseman in the Soviet League four times... Three-time Soviet player of the year... Earned Soviet Honored Master of Sport award, equivalent to the Hockey Hall of Fame... Three times was named winner of the Gold Stick Award as Europe's top player... In 1995–96, he tied his NHL career high for points with 42 (seven goals and 35 assists), matching his output from 1989–90, his first year... In 1997 and 1998, won the Stanley Cup with the Detroit Red Wings.

URS
ANATOLI FIRSOV Forward with brilliant skills and extremely hard slap-shot... Participated at the 1964, 1968 and 1972 Olympics and at eight IIHF World and European Championships from 1964 to 1972... Played in all tournaments during this span... Olympic gold medalist in 1964, 1968 and 1972... World Champion every year from 1964 to 1971... Named the best forward at the World and European Championships in 1967 and 1971... Voted to the all-star team at the World and European Championships on four occasions.

Began his hockey career with Spartak Moscow (1958 to 1961)... Played for CSKA Moscow of the Soviet League from 1961 to 1974... Played on the Soviet national champion nine times... Saw action in 474 league games and scored 344 goals... One of the best players in the history of hockey... After retiring, coached the junior team of CSKA Moscow.

LAT
ARTURS IRBE Member of the Soviet Team at the 1985 European Junior Championships... Named best goalie after allowing just five goals in five

games for a 1.00 goals-against average... Played at the 1989 and 1990 World and European Championships... Won two gold medals with the Soviet national team... Named the best goaltender of the World and European Championships in 1990... Played for the Latvian national team at the World Championships in 1996 (Pool B) and 1997 (Pool A).

Minnesota's 11th choice, 196th overall, in the 1989 NHL Entry Draft... Began his career with Dynamo Riga... Played four full seasons in the Soviet League... Won a silver medal with Dynamo Riga in 1987–88... Named the rookie of the year in 1987–88... From 1991–92 to 1995–96 played for the San Jose Sharks organization... Named to the International Hockey League First All-Star Team in 1991–92 while with Kansas City... Played in the NHL All-Star Game in 1994... Played with Dallas in 1996–97, Vancouver in 1997–98.

RUS
VALERI KAMENSKY Competed for the Soviet Union team that finished third in the 1985 World Junior Championships in Helsinki... Scored 13 points (seven goals, six assists) in seven games at the World Juniors to earn a spot on Second All-Star Team... Scored two goals and added one assist to earn first star in game two of Rendez-Vous '87... Member of the 1988 Soviet Union club that captured the Olympic gold medal in Calgary... Was captain of Red Army and of the Russian national team... Won a silver medal at the 1998 Olympics in Nagano.

Quebec's eighth choice, 129th overall, in the 1988 NHL Entry Draft... Played three years with Khimik from 1982–83 through 1984–85 and six years with CSKA in the Soviet National League from 1985–86 through 1990–91... Broke his leg in 1991–92 NHL preseason... Suffered a fractured wrist and broken ankle in separate incidents in 1992... Played his first NHL game in Minnesota on February 18, 1992 and scored his first NHL goal on six nights later... In 1995–96, he played on a line with Peter Forsberg and Claude Lemieux in Colorado, which combined for 107 goals (33% of the team total of 326) and 165 assists for 272 points... Scored the first goal in Colorado Avalanche history on October 6, 1995... Won a Stanley Cup title with Colorado in 1995–96... Finished second in scoring on Avalanche in 1997–98, collecting 26 goals and 40 assists for 66 points in 75 games.

URS
ALEXEI KASATONOV Participated at the 1980, 1984 and 1988 Olympics and at eight World and European Championships... Olympic gold medalist in Sarajevo in 1984 and Calgary in 1988, silver medalist at the Lake Placid Games in 1980... World Champion in 1981, 1982, 1983, 1986 and 1989... Named the best defenseman at the World and European Championships in 1983 ...Voted to the tournament all-star team in 1982, 1983, 1985, 1986 and 1991... Played with the Soviet team that won the 1981 Canada Cup... Voted to the all-star team at the 1981 Canada Cup tournament.

Began his hockey career with SKA Leningrad (1976 to 1978)... Played for CSKA Moscow of the Soviet League from 1978 to 89... Won the Soviet national title 11 times... In the second half of 1989–90 season, he joined the New Jersey Devils... Played seven NHL seasons with New Jersey, Anaheim, St. Louis and Boston... In 383 games, accumulated 38 goals and 122 assists for 160 points... Came back to Russia and played for HC CSKA in 1996–97.

RUS
DARIUS KASPARAITIS Played defense for Russia/CIS at both the 1992 World Junior Championships and World Championships. He won a junior gold medal and was named best defenseman in 1992. He also won a gold medal at the 1992 Winter Olympics and played for Russia at the 1992 World Championships, the 1996 World Championships and World Cup, and the 1998 Olympics. He made his NHL debut with the Islanders in 1992–93 after having played for Moscow Dynamo. He missed most of the 1994–95 season after undergoing reconstructive knee surgery. He was traded to the New York Islanders early in the 1996–97 season.

URS
VALERI KHARLAMOV Made his debut with the national team at the 1969 World and European Championships... Participated at the 1972, 1976 and 1980 Olympics and 11 World and European Championships from 1969 to 1980... Never missed a tournament... Olympic gold medalist in 1972 and 1976... World Champion eight times between 1969 and 1979... Named the best forward at the World and European Championships in 1976... Voted to the tournament all-star team in 1972, 1973 and 1976... Starred in the historic Canada–Russia Summit Series of 1972.

Began his hockey career with CSKA Moscow... Played for CSKA Moscow of the Soviet League from 1967 to 1981... A member of 11 Soviet national champions... One of the top scorers in the history of Soviet hockey... Played in 438 games and scored 293 goals... A ember of one of the best lines in the history of hockey along with Boris Mikhailov and Vladimir Petrov.

URS
VIKTOR KONOVALENKO One of the best goaltenders of all-time... Participated at the 1964 and 1968 Olympics and at nine World and European

Championships from 1961 to 1971… Olympic champion at Innsbruck in 1964 and at Grenoble in 1968… World Champion in 1963, 1964, 1965, 1966, 1967, 1968, 1970 and 1971… Voted to the all-star team at the World and European Championships in 1970… At the end of his career, played with Vladislav Tretiak on the national team and helped his development.

Began his hockey career in Gorky… Played for Torpedo Gorky of the Soviet League his entire career from 1956 to 1972… Won the silver medal in the Soviet League in 1961… Saw action in 450 league games… After retiring, coached the juniors of Torpedo Gorky.

EST

MIKHAIL KORSHUNOV Began to play for the Estonian national team following its creation in 1994 and has participated in every World Championship (Pool C) since… Had two outstanding tournaments, in 1994 and 1996… In 1994, he collected six goals and seven assists for 13 points in five games… He had 13 points on four goals and nine assists in seven games in 1996.

Began his hockey career with Krylja Sovetov Moscow… As a junior, he played on the same line as Sergei Priakin, the first Soviet player to signed with an NHL team (Calgary Flames, 1988–89)… Spent the majority of his career with Kreenholm Narva (divisions 2 and 3)… In 1991–92, he joined the Finnish club FoPS Forssa (Division 2)… In his first year in Finland, he recorded 33 goals and 35 assists for 68 points in 44 games.

BLR

ANDREI KOVALEV Played a few exhibition games for the Soviet national team and became a regular with Belarus national team at the 1995 World Championships (Pool C)… He was named the best forward of the tournament that year… Played for Belarus at the 1998 Nagano Olympics, recording one goal and three assists for four points in seven games.

Began his hockey career with Dynamo Minsk… In 1989, he joined Dynamo Moscow… Played two years with Dynamo Moscow and both years won the national title… Came back to Dynamo Minsk in 1991–92… Spent the second half of the season with New Haven of the International Hockey League… He was Washington's seventh choice, 114th overall, in the 1990 NHL Entry Draft… Spent the 1992–93 season with Greensboro of East Coast Hockey League, but returned to Europe the following year… Has spent the last five seasons playing in Germany, the last three with Krefeld Pinguine… In 1997–98, he was the top scorer on his club with 24 goals and 12 assists for 36 points in 47 games.

RUS

VYACHESLAV KOZLOV Member of the gold medal-winning Soviet Union team at the 1989 World Junior Championships… Finished tied for fourth in scoring with 11 points (four goals and seven assists) at the 1990 World Junior Championships in Helsinki as the Soviets placed second behind Canada… Rookie of the year in Soviet Elite League in 1989–90… Member of the Soviet team that won gold at the Goodwill Games in 1990… Played for the national team at the 1991 (bronze) and 1994 World Championships and in the 1991 Canada Cup… Played for the Russian team at the 1996 World Cup of Hockey.

Detroit's second choice, 45th overall, in the 1990 NHL Entry Draft… Auto accident in November 1991 limited him to 11 games with Central Red Army club that year… Assisted on a goal by Sergei Fedorov on his first shift in his first NHL game on March 12, 1992… Ranked third on Red Wings in scoring in 1993–94… In 1995–96, was the only Red Wing to play all 82 games in the regular season… Tied career high for points with 73 (36 goals, 37 assists)… Tied for fourth in team scoring and tied for second (with Steve Yzerman) in goals… Won the Stanley Cup in 1997 and 1998 with the Red Wings.

URS

VLADIMIR KRUTOV Participated at the 1980, 1984 and 1988 Olympics and at seven World and European Championships… Olympic gold medalist at Sarajevo in 1984 and Calgary in 1988, silver medalist at Lake Placid in 1980… World Champion in 1981, 1982, 1983, 1986 and 1989… Named the best forward at the World and European Championships in 1986 and 1987… Voted to the tournament all-star team in 1983, 1985, 1986 and 1987… Played for the Soviet team that won the 1981 Canada Cup… Voted to the all-star team at the 1987 Canada Cup tournament.

Began his hockey career with the juniors of CSKA… Played for CSKA Moscow of the Soviet League from 1978 to 1989… Won the Soviet national title 11 times… Played for the Vancouver Canucks in 1989–90… Recorded 11 goals and 23 assists for 34 points in 61 games… Played for Zurcher SC in the Swiss League from 1990 to 1992… Later played for Ostersunds IK in Sweden… In 1996–97 worked as the assistant coach of CSKA–2 Moscow.

URS

BORIS KULAGIN Named the assistant coach of the Soviet national team in the summer of 1972… Along with Vsevolod Bobrov as a head coach, coached the Soviets in the 1972 Summit Series versus Team Canada… Head coach of the Soviet national team from 1974 to 1977… The Soviets won Olympic gold at Innsbruck in 1976 and World Championship gold in 1975.

One of the pioneers of hockey in the former Soviet Union… Prior to that, had a good career in bandy and soccer… Was a member of hockey team VVS MVO Moscow from 1946 to 1948, played for Dzerzhinets Chelyabinsk in 1948–49… In 15 games scored two goals… Played in the first Soviet national championship in 1946–47… His hockey coaching career began in 1955 when he became a coach of the Army team in the city of Orenburg… Three years later, in 1958, he was appointed as a coach of SKA Kuibyshev, a farm club of CSKA Moscow… In 1961, he became the assistant coach of CSKA Moscow (Anatoli Tarasov was the head coach) and also coached the organization's junior team… In 1971, he got the coaching job which later made him famous—head coach of Krylja Sovetov Moscow… He assembled a team of young prospects and veteran players who were released from other clubs and, in 1974, won the national title… Under his coaching, the team also got bronze medal in 1973 and silver medal in 1975… Created and developed the line of line Yuri Lebedev, Vyacheslav Anisin and Alexander Bodunov… Coached Rodovre in Denmark to a national title in 1977–78… Coached Spartak Moscow from 1979 to 1984, winning silver medals in 1981 1982, 1983 and 1984 and a bronze medal in 1980.

RUS

IGOR LARIONOV Member of the 1980 Soviet Union national junior team that captured gold at the World Junior Championships… Named to 1980 World Junior tournament all-star team… Member of the Soviet Union's national team that won gold medals at both the 1984 and 1988 Winter Olympics and also earned gold at the 1983, 1986, and 1989 IIHF World Championships… Selected to the first team all-star at the 1983 and 1986 World Championships… Centered famous KLM line with Vladimir Krutov and Sergei Makarov… Led Soviets to an 8–1 win over Canada in the finals of the 1981 Canada Cup with two goals… Member of Soviet Union All-Stars that competed versus NHL All-Stars at Rendez-Vous '87… Recorded four assists in five games in the 1996 World Cup of Hockey playing for Team Russia.

Vancouver's 11th choice, 214th overall, in the 1985 NHL Entry Draft… Played 12 seasons in the Soviet National League from 1977–78 through 1988–89, totaling 437 points (207 goals, 230 assists) in 463 games… Earned Soviet player of the year Award in 1987–88 and was named to five All-Star Teams… Made his NHL debut with Vancouver in 1989–90… Led San Jose in plus–minus rating with a +20 in 1993–94… Nominated for the Bill Masterton Trophy in 1994–95… Traded to Detroit on October 24, 1995… Established NHL highs with 22 goals, 50 assists and 72 points that year… Won the Stanley Cup with the Red Wings in 1997 and 1998.

EST

IVAN LOGINOV Made his debut with the Estonian national team at the 1994 World Championships (Pool C)—the first tournament in which the team participated… He recorded nine goals and five assists for 14 points in five games in 1994 and has played at the event every year since… Starred at the 1996 World Championship (Pool C), collecting 12 goals and five assists for 17 points in seven games.

Began his hockey career with Kreenholm Narva of Division 2 of the former Soviet Union… Was a member of the Soviet national junior team… Made his debut with SKA St. Petersburg of the Soviet League at the end of 1992–93 season… In 1994–95 he played in Finland, for Kurra Nurmijarvi (Division 3)… Came back to SKA St. Petersburg before the start of 1996–97 season.

URS

KONSTANTIN LOKTEV Participated at the 1960 and 1964 Olympics and at eight World and European Championships from 1957 to 1966… Olympic gold medalist at Innsbruck in 1964… World Champion in 1964, 1965 and 1966 and was named best forward at the World and European Championships in 1966… Voted to the tournament all-star team in 1965 and 1966… Assistant coach of the Soviet national team from 1974 to 1977, helping the Soviets win the 1975 World Championships and a gold medal at the 1976 Innsbruck Olympics.

Began his hockey career with Spartak Moscow (1952–53) Later played for ODO Leningrad (1953–54)… Played for CSKA Moscow of the Soviet League from 1954 to 1966… Won the Soviet national title 10 times… In his career, played in 340 games and scored 213 goals… Member of an internationally famous line with Alexander Almetov and Veniamin Alexandrov… Head coach of CSKA Moscow from 1974 to 1977… Won the national title with the team in 1975 and 1977… Later worked in Poland.

URS

SERGEI MAKAROV An Olympic gold medalist at Sarajevo in 1984 and Calgary in 1988, silver medalist at Lake Placid in 1980… World Champion in 1978, 1979, 1981, 1982, 1983, 1986 and 1989… Named the best forward at the World and European Championships in 1979 and 1985… Voted to the tournament all-star team in 1979, 1981 to 1983, 1985 to 1987 and 1989… Played for the Canada Cup-winning Soviet team in 1981… Voted to the all-star team at the 1984 Canada Cup tournament… Assistant coach of the Russian team at 1996 World Cup of Hockey.

Began his hockey career with Traktor Chelyabinsk (1976 to 1978)… Played

for CSKA Moscow of the Soviet League from 1978 to 1989... Won the Soviet national title 11 straight times... In 519 league games, he scored 322 goals... Signed with the Calgary Flames in 1989... Won the Calder Trophy as the NHL's top rookie in 1989–90... Played six full NHL seasons with Calgary, San Jose and Dallas... Saw action in 424 games and recorded 134 goals and 250 assists for 384 points... In 1996–97 played five games with HC Fribourg-Gotteron in the Swiss League.

URS
ALEXANDER MALTSEV One of the best players in the history of hockey... Participated at the 1972, 1976 and 1980 Olympics and at 12 World and European Championships from 1969 to 1983... Olympic gold medalist at Sapporo in 1972 and Innsbruck in 1976, silver medalist at Lake Placid in 1980... World Champion in 1969, 1970, 1971, 1973, 1974, 1975, 1978, 1981 and 1983... Named the best forward at the World and European Championships in 1970, 1972 and 1981... Voted to the tournament all-star team in 1970, 1971, 1972, 1978 and 1981... Voted to the all-star team at 1976 Canada Cup... Starred with the Soviet Team in the 1972 Summit Series with Team Canada.

Began his hockey career with Olympia Kirovo-Chepetsk... Played for Dynamo Moscow of the Soviet League from 1967 to 1984... Won six silver and seven bronze medals in the Soviet League... Played in 530 games and scored 329 goals... Coached the juniors of Dynamo Moscow after retiring.

URS
BORIS MAYOROV Forward... Captain of the Soviet team... Participated at 1964 and 1968 Olympics and seven World and European Championships from 1961 to 1968... Olympic Champion in 1964 and 1968... World Champion in 1963, 1964, 1965, 1966, 1967 and 1968... Voted to the all-star team at the World and European Championships in 1961... Coached the national B-team... Assistant coach of the Soviet team at 1976 Canada Cup.

Spent his entire hockey career with Spartak Moscow (1956 to 1969)... Won Soviet national title three times... Was the captain of the team... Member of the famous line Yevgeny Mayorov—Vyacheslav Starshinov—Boris Mayorov... Scored 255 goals in 400 games... Coached Spartak Moscow from 1969 to 1971 and 1985 to 1989... Worked in Finland, with Jokerit Helsinki.

RUS
BORIS MIKHAILOV Captain of the Soviet team for many years... Participated at the 1972, 1976 and 1980 Olympics and at 11 World and European Championships from 1969 to 1980... Olympic gold medalist at Sapporo in 1972 and Innsbruck in 1976, silver medalist at Lake Placid in 1980... World Champion in 1969, 1970, 1971, 1973, 1974, 1975, 1978 and 1979... Named the best forward at the World and European Championships and voted to the tournament all-star team in 1973 and 1979... A star player with the Soviet Team in the 1972 Summit Series with Team Canada... Named the head coach of the Russian team before 1992–93 season... Worked at three World Championships, winning a gold medal in 1993... Coached the Russian team at the 1996 World Cup of Hockey... Assistant coach at 1997 IIHF World Championships.

Began his hockey career with Energiya Saratov (1962 to 1965)... Later played for Lokomotov Moscow (1965 to 1967)... Played for CSKA Moscow of the Soviet League from 1967 to 1981... Won the Soviet national title 11 times... Captained the team for many years... The top scorer in the history of Soviet hockey... Played in 572 games and scored 427 goals... Member of one of the best lines in the history of hockey with Vladimir Petrov and Valeri Kharlamov... Coached SKA Leningrad (later SKA St.Petersburg) from 1981 to 1984 and from 1992 to 1998... Worked as the assistant coach of CSKA from 1984 to 1991... Coached in Switzerland in 1991–92 with HC Rapperswil-Jona.

RUS
ALEXANDER MOGILNY Played for the Soviet Union in the World Junior Championships in 1987, 1988 and 1989... Won silver medal in 1988 and gold in 1989... Selected as the best forward at the 1988 tournament... Named to the second all-star team in 1989... Played on a line with Sergei Fedorov and Pavel Bure at the 1989 tournament... Youngest Soviet hockey player ever to win an Olympic gold medal at the 1988 Calgary Games... Member of the Soviet Team at the 1989 World Championships... Scored two goals and four assists in five games at the 1996 World Cup of Hockey.

Buffalo's fourth choice, 89th overall, in the 1988 NHL Entry Draft... Joined the Central Red Army team at the age of 17... Played three seasons before arriving in North America in May 1989... Scored for the Sabres on the first shift of his first NHL game, 20 seconds after the opening face-off on October 5, 1989... Was fourth on the Sabres in scoring in 1990–91 and tied for the team lead in plus–minus at +14... Tied an NHL record on December 21, 1991, scoring a goal against Toronto just five seconds into the game... Set a Sabres record, and tied Teemu Selanne for the NHL lead, with 76 goals in 1992–93... Holds Sabres single season records for goals, shots, game-winning goals and hat tricks... Injuries slowed him down over the next two seasons...

In 1995–96, he led the Vancouver Canucks in goals (55), assists (52) and points (107) and finished seventh in scoring in the NHL... Had three hat tricks, including a club record three goals in 2:25 on December 23rd.... Finished third in scoring on Canucks roster in 1997–98 despite playing in only 51 games.

RUS
SERGEI NEMCHINOV Won a gold medal with the Soviet Union Junior Team at the 1983 and 1984 World Junior Championships... Played for the runner-up Soviet Union squad in the 1987 Canada Cup... Played for Soviet Union in Rendez-Vous '87... Won gold medal with the Soviet Union at the 1989 and 1990 World Championships... Won gold medal with Soviet Union at the 1990 Goodwill Games... Won bronze medal with Soviet Union at the 1991 World Championships... Played on the first line along with Alexander Mogilny and Sergei Fedorov in the 1996 World Cup of Hockey... Won silver medal at the 1998 Olympics in Nagano.

New York Rangers' 13th choice, 244th overall, in the 1990 NHL Entry Draft... Became the first Russian-born player to play for Rangers in 1991–92... Finished fourth in rookie goal-scoring with 30 goals in 1991–92... Recorded league's fifth-highest shooting percentage (24.2%)... Won the 1994 Stanley Cup with Rangers... Traded to the Vancouver Canucks at the end of 1996–97 season... Signed with the New York Islanders before 1997–98 season.

LAT
SANDIS OZOLINSH Played for the Soviet Union at the 1991–92 Four Nations Cup Under–20 tournament and was named best defenseman... Played for the Latvian national team at the 1998 World Championships.

San Jose's third choice, 30th overall, in the 1991 NHL Entry Draft... Began his career with Dynamo Riga... Played two years in the Soviet League... Moved to North America in the middle of the 1991–92 season... Played for Kansas City of the International Hockey League... Became a regular on defense with the San Jose Sharks in 1992–93... Traded to Colorado at the beginning of 1995–96 season... Won Stanley Cup with the Avalanche in 1996... Made the NHL First All-Star Team in 1996–97... Played in the NHL All-Star Game in 1994, 1997 and 1998.

URS
VLADIMIR PETROV Participated at the 1972, 1976 and 1980 Olympics and at 11 World and European Championships from 1969 to 1981... Olympic gold medalist in Sapporo in 1972 and Innsbruck in 1976, silver medalist at Lake Placid in 1980... World Champion in 1969, 1970, 1971, 1973, 1974, 1975, 1978, 1979 and 1981... Voted to the all-star team at the World and European Championships in 1973, 1977 and 1979... Starred for the Soviet Union in the 1972 Summit Series against Team Canada.

Began his hockey career with Krylja Sovetov Moscow (1965 to 1967)... Played for CSKA Moscow of the Soviet League from 1967 to 1981... Was with SKA Leningrad from 1981 to 1983... Won the Soviet national title 11 times... One of the top scorers in the history of Soviet hockey... Played in 553 games and scored 370 goals... Member of one of the best lines in the history of hockey with Boris Mikhailov and Valeri Kharlamov.

URS
NIKOLAI PUCHKOV Participated at two Olympics and at seven World and European Championships... Olympic gold medalist at Cortina d'Ampezzo in 1956, bronze medalist at Squaw Valley in 1960... World Champion in 1954... Named the best goaltender at the World and European Championships in 1959... One of the best goaltender in the history of Soviet hockey... Assistant coach of the silver medal-winning Soviet team at the 1972 World and European Championships.

Began his hockey career with VVS MVO Moscow from 1949 to 1953... Played for CSKA Moscow of the Soviet League from 1953 to 1962... In 1962–63 played for SKA Leningrad... Won the Soviet national title nine times... Saw action in 220 league games... From 1963 to 1973, 1974 to 1977 and 1978 to 1980 worked as a head coach of SKA Leningrad... The team won a bronze medal in the Soviet League in 1971... Later worked in Kiruna, Sweden.

URS
ALEXANDER RAGULIN Participated at the 1964, 1968 and 1972 Olympics and at 12 World and European Championships from 1961 to 1973... A three-time Olympic gold medalist... World Champion in nine years in a row from 1963 to 1971 and again in 1973... Named the best defenseman at the World and European Championships in 1966 and 1967... Voted to the tournament all-star team in 1963, 1965, 1966 and 1967... Was a member of the Soviet team in the Summit Series with Team Canada in 1972.

Began his hockey career with Khimik Voskresensk (1957 to 1962)... Played for CSKA Moscow of the Soviet League from 1962 to 1973... Won the Soviet national title nine times... Played in 427 games and scored 60 goals... One of the best defensemen in the history of hockey... After retiring, coached the juniors of CSKA.

BLR

RUSLAN SALEI Made his debut for the Belarus national team at the age of 20 at the World Championships (Pool C) in 1994... Played at the tournament the next year as well... He was the best defenseman on the Belarus team at the 1998 Olympics in Nagano, Japan.

Made his debut with Dynamo Minsk at the age of 18 in 1992–93 season and became a regular with the team the following year... After playing two full seasons in Minsk, he joined the Las Vegas Thunder of the International Hockey League... In 1995–96, he played in 76 games for Las Vegas, collecting seven goals and 23 assists... Drafted by Anaheim after that season (first choice, ninth overall, in the 1996 Entry Draft)... Played 30 games with Mighty Ducks in his first season in the NHL... Became a regular in 1996–97, playing in 66 games and recording five goals and 10 assists.

KAZ

KONSTANTIN SHAFRANOV Made his debut with the Kazakhstan national team at the 1993 World Championships (Pool C)... Participated at the 1998 Olympics in Nagano.

Drafted by St. Louis (tenth choice, 229th overall) in the 1996 NHL Entry Draft... Began his hockey career in Ust-Kamenogorsk... Played in the Soviet League for Torpedo Ust-Kamenogorsk from 1989–90 to 1993–94... In 1993–94, had a short stint (four games) with Detroit of the Colonial Hockey League... In 1994–95 and 1995–96 played for Metallurg Magnitogorsk... Joined Fort Wayne of the International Hockey League at the beginning of 1995–96 season... Had a very successful season, recording 46 goals and 28 assists for 74 points in 74 games... Won the Garry F. Longman Memorial Trophy as the top rookie of IHL... Started the1996–97 season with St.Louis (five games), but spent the major part of the season with the farm club in Worcester (American Hockey League).

UKR

VALERI SHIRYAEV Played for the Soviet national team... World and European Champion in 1989 with the Soviets... Played for Ukrainian national team at the 1994 and 1995 World Championships (Pool C)... Named the best defenseman at the Pool C tournament in 1995.

Began his hockey career in Togliatti... At the age of 17 was invited to join Sokol Kiev (1980–81)... Played for Sokol until 1991... Bronze medalist of the Soviet League in 1984–85 with Sokol Kiev... In 1991–92, he joined the Swiss club ECH Biel-Bienne and, after two seasons, was invited to join another Swiss club, HC La Chaux-de-Fonds (Nationalliga B)... Played two seasons there, helping his team earn a promotion to Nationalliga A... Joined HC Davos in 1996–97.

UKR

YURI SHUNDROV Played a few exhibition games with the Soviet national team... Played for the Ukrainian national team at the World Championships in 1995 and 1997 (at the age of 41).

Goaltender... Began his career with Dizelist Penza... Invited to Sokol Kiev in 1978... Played for Sokol until 1991... Bronze medalist of the Soviet League in 1984–85 with Sokol Kiev... Later played for Khimik Voskresensk... After one season in Slovenia, came back to Sokol... Joined Khimik before the 1997–98 season.

URS

NIKOLAI SOLOGUBOV Participated at the 1956 and 1960 Olympics and at eight World and European Championships... Olympic gold medalist at Cortina d'Ampezzo in 1956... World Champion in 1954 and 1963... Was one of the best defensemen of his time... Named the best defenseman at the World and European Championships in 1956, 1957 and 1960.

Began his hockey career with SKA Khabarovsk... Played for CSKA Moscow of the Soviet League from 1949 to 1964... In 1964–65 played for SKA MVO Kalinin ...Won the Soviet national title nine times... Saw action in 350 games, scored 128 goals... Played in a defensive pairing with Ivan Tregubov.

URS

VYACHESLAV STARSHINOV One of the best players in the history of Soviet hockey... Participated at the 1964 and 1968 Olympics and at 10 World and European Championships from 1961 to 1971...

Two-time Olympic gold medalist... World Champion nine years in a row from 1963 to 1971... Named the best forward at the World and European Championships in 1965.

Began his hockey career with Spartak Moscow... Played for Spartak of the Soviet League from 1957 to 1972, 1974–75 and 1978–79... Won the Soviet national title three times... Scored 405 goals in 540 games... Was a captain of the team... Member of a famous line Yevgeny Mayorov and Boris Mayorov... Coached Spartak Moscow from 1972 to 1974... Playing coach with Oji Seishi in Japan from 1976 to 78.

UKR

ANATOLI STEPANISCHEV Played a few exhibition games with the Soviet national team... Played at four straight World Championships (Pool C) for the Ukrainian national team from 1993 to 1996... Named the best forward and voted to the all-star team at the 1996 tournament.

Began his career with Dizelist Penza... Joined Sokol Kiev in 1981... Played until 1990... Bronze medalist of the Soviet League in 1984–85 with Sokol Kiev... Later played for Neftekhimik Nizhnekamsk of the Russian League.

URS

ANATOLI TARASOV Had great success on the international scene as the coach of the Soviet national team... Worked with the team from 1958 to 1960... Under his coaching the team won three European titles and a bronze and two silver medals at the World Championships... His most successful years were 1962 to 1972 when he and Arkady Chernyshev coached the Soviet national team together... This tandem led the Soviet team to three consecutive Olympic titles (1964, 1968 and 1972), nine straight World Championship titles from 1963 to 1971 and eight European titles in a row... In 1974 was inducted to the Hockey Hall of Fame in the builders category.

Played as forward with VVS MVO Moscow in 1946–47 and CDKA Moscow (later CDSA Moscow) from 1947 to 1953 as a playing coach... National champion in 1948, 1949 and 1950, silver medalist in 1952 and 1953... In 100 games, he scored 106 goals... Saw action in the historic games versus the Czechoslovakian club LTC Praha in 1948... Worked as a head coach with the famous CSKA Moscow from 1947 to 1960 and 1961 to 1975... Under his coaching guidance, the team won the Soviet national title from 1948 to 1950, in 1955, 1956, 1958 to 1960, 1963 to 1966, 1968, 1970 to 1973 and 1975... Wrote many books on the tactics and skills in Soviet hockey... Considered one of the best coaches in the history of hockey and the father of Soviet Hockey.

URS

MIKHAIL TATARINOV Defenseman... Played at the 1990 World and European Championships and won both titles with the Soviet team... Scored three goals and added eight assists for 11 points in 10 games... Named the best defenseman at the World and European Championships in 1990... Voted to the tournament all-star team.

Began his hockey career with Yermak Angarsk... Played for Sokol Kiev of the Soviet League from 1983 to 1986... Played for Dynamo Moscow from 1986 to 1990... Won Soviet national title in 1990... Signed with the Washington Capitals in the middle of the 1990–91 season... Played three seasons in the NHL with Washington, Quebec and Boston... Saw action in 161 games and accumulated 21 goals and 48 assists for 69 points.

RUS

VIKTOR TIKHONOV As a player, he saw action in a few exhibition games for the Soviet national team... It is was as a coach that he enjoyed considerable success... Worked as the head coach of the Soviet national B-team from 1974 to 1976... Coached the Soviets at first Canada Cup tournament in 1976... Was head coach of the Soviet/Russian national team from 1977 to 1994... His teams won gold medals at the Olympics in 1984, 1988 and 1992... His teams won gold medals at the World Championships in 1978, 1979, 1981, 1982, 1983, 1986, 1989 and 1990... Also won the Canada Cup in 1981.

Began his hockey career with VVS MVO Moscow... Played as a defenseman from 1949 to 1953... Next 10 seasons played for Dynamo Moscow... Played on Soviet national champions in 1951, 1952, 1953 and 1954, silver medalists in 1959, 1960, 1962 and 1963, bronze medalists in 1955, 1956, 1957 and 1958... Played in 296 games, scored 35 goals... After retiring, worked as an assistant coach with Dynamo Moscow... In 1971 named the head coach of Dynamo Riga... In two seasons, Dynamo Riga made huge strides from the second division to the sixth best team in the country... Named the head coach of CSKA Moscow in 1977... CSKA Moscow won 13 national titles in a row from 1977–78 to 1988–89... Under his coaching, CSKA Moscow also won 13 straight European Champions Cup titles... Was instrumental in creating legendary "Green Unit" of Viacheslav Fetisov, Alexei Kasatonov, Sergei Makarov, Igor Larionov and Vladimir Krutov... Introduced to Soviet hockey the strategy of playing four forward lines.

URS

IVAN TREGUBOV Participated at the 1956 Olympics in Cortina d'Ampezzo and at six World and European Championships... World and Olympic Champion in 1956... Named best defenseman at the World and European Championships in 1958 and 1961... Had the nickname "Ivan the Terrible"... One of the best defensemen of his era.

Began his hockey career with ODO Khabarovsk (1950 to 1952)... Played for CSKA Moscow of the Soviet League from 1952 to 1962... Continued his career with SKA Kuibyshev (1962 to 1964) and Khimik Voskresensk (1964–65)... Won the Soviet national title six times... Played in 283 league games and scored 60 goals... Played in a defensive pairing with Nikolai Sologubov.

URS

VLADISLAV TRETIAK Considered one of the finest goaltenders in the history of hockey... Came to prominence in North America after starring in the historic 1972 Summit Series between Team Canada and the Soviet Union... Participated at the 1972, 1976, 1980 and 1984 Olympics and at 13 World and European Championships from 1970 to 1984... Played in all international tournaments during his career... Olympic gold medalist in 1972, 1976 and 1984, silver medalist at Lake Placid in 1980... World Champion in 1970, 1971, 1973, 1974, 1975, 1978, 1979, 1981, 1982 and 1983... Named the best goaltender at the World and European Championships in 1974, 1979, 1981 and 1983... Voted to the tournament all-star team in 1975, 1979 and 1983... Voted to the all-star team and named the tournament MVP after the Soviets won the 1981 Canada Cup.

Made his debut in the Soviet League at age 17... Played for CSKA Moscow of the Soviet League from 1969 to 1984... Won the Soviet national title 13 times, from 1970 to 1973, 1975 and from 1977 to 1984... Played in 482 games in the Soviet League... Began working as as a goaltending coach for the NHL's Chicago Blackhawks after retiring.

BLR

VLADIMIR TSYPLAKOV Made his debut with the Belarus national team at the 1998 Nagano Olympics... In five games, he collected a goal and an assist for two points.

Started to play for Dynamo Minsk of the Soviet League at 19... Spent four seasons with that club and came to North America before the 1992–93 season... Split his first year between Detroit of the Colonial Hockey League and Indianapolis of the International Hockey League... Spent two excellent seasons with the Fort Wayne Komets of IHL... Drafted by Los Angeles in 1995 Entry Draft (fourth choice, 59th overall)... His performance had steadily improved during his years with the Kings and he had his best season in 1997–98... Finished the season as the third-leading scorer on the team with 18 goals and 34 assists for 52 points in 73 games.

EST

EDUARD VALIULLIN One of the best players on the Estonian national team, he began to play internationally in 1994 at the World Championships (Pool C)... Named the best forward at that tournament after collecting 10 goals and nine assists for 19 points in five games... Also starred at the event in 1995 when he was voted to the tournament all-star team.

Began his hockey career with the Estonian club Tallex Tallinn (Division 3)... In 1988–89, he joined Sokol Kiev of the top Soviet League... Played four years for Sokol Kiev... In 1992–93, he joined the Finnish club SaiPa Lappeenranta (Division 2)... Later played for IkVi Tampere and Titaanit Kotka (Division 3).

URS

VALERI VASILIEV A captain of the Soviet national team... Participated at the 1972, 1976 and 1980 Olympics and 11 World and European Championships from 1970 to 1982... Double Olympic gold medalist (1972 and 1976)... World Champion in 1970, 1973, 1974, 1975, 1978, 1979, 1981 and 1982... Named the best defenseman at the World and European Championships in 1973, 1977 and 1979... Voted to the tournament all-star team in 1974, 1975, 1977, 1979 and 1981... A member of the Soviet Canada Cup-winning team in 1981... Had been a member of the Soviet team at the historic 1972 Summit Series with Team Canada.

Began his hockey career with Torpedo Gorky... Shifted to Moscow-based Dynamo in the top division of the Soviet Union's national league from 1967 to 1984 where he won won six silver and seven bronze medals... Played in 619 games and scored 71 goals... Coached Dynamo Moscow's junior clubs from 1984 to 1989... Worked in Germany as the coach of EC Ratingen (1990) and Bad Reichenhall (1991)... In 1996–97, he became an assistant coach of Spartak Moscow.

URS

ALEXANDER YAKUSHEV Participated at the 1972 and 1976 Olympics and at 10 World and European Championships from 1967 to 1979... Two-time Olympic gold medalist... World Champion in 1967, 1969, 1970, 1973, 1974, 1975 and 1979... Named the best forward at the World and European Championships in 1975... Voted to the tournament all-star team in 1974... Was the top scorer for the Soviet team with 11 points (seven goals and four assists) in the historic eight-game Summit Series between team Canada and the USSR in 1972.

Began his hockey career with Spartak Moscow... Played for Spartak in the Soviet Union's national league from 1966 to 1980... Won the Soviet national title three times... One of the top scorers in the history of Soviet hockey... Played in 568 games and scored 339 goals... Played in Austria for SV Kapfenberg for two seasons (1980 to 1982)... Worked as an assistant coach with Spartak from 1983 to 1985 and 1987 to 1989... Was head coach of Spartak Moscow from 1989 to 1993... Went on to coach HC Ambri-Piotta in Switzerland's national league.

RUS

ALEXEI YASHIN Won a gold medal with the CIS (Commonwealth of Independent States) national junior team at the 1992 World Junior Championships... Played for the Russian national junior team at the 1993 World Junior Championships... Also won a gold medal with Russia at the 1993 World Championships... Played for Russia in the 1994, 1996 and 1997 World Championships... Played in the 1996 World Cup of Hockey... Won a silver medal at Nagano in 1998... Was the second-leading scorer on the Russian team (behind Pavel Bure) with three goals and three assists.

Ottawa's first choice, second overall, in the 1992 NHL Entry Draft... NHL rookie of the month in November 1993... Played in the 1994 NHL All-Star Game and scored the game-winning goal... Named Senators team MVP as a rookie... Led NHL rookies in assists (49) and finished second in points (79)... Led Ottawa in scoring with 44 points (21 goals, 23 assists) in 48 games in 1994–95... Led Ottawa Senators to the playoffs for the first time in 1996–97... Led the team in scoring in 1997–98 with 33 goals and 39 assists for 72 points in 82 games.

KAZ

VITALI YEREMEYEV Has played regularly for the Kazakhstan national team since 1994... Named the best goaltender of the World Championships four times: in 1994 (Pool C), 1995 (Pool C), 1996 (Pool C) and 1997 (Pool B)... Voted to the all-star team in 1995 (Pool C) and 1996 (Pool C)... Participated at the 1998 Olympics in Nagano.

New York Rangers' 11th choice, 209th overall, in the 1994 NHL Entry Draft... Began his career in Ust-Kamenogorsk... Played for Torpedo Ust-Kamenogorsk in 1993–94... Was invited to CSKA Moscow and played three seasons there... Joined Torpedo Yaroslavl before the 1997–98 season... Before the breakup of the Soviet Union, played regularly for the Soviet junior teams of all ages.

UKR

RAMIL YULDASHEV Saw action with the Ukrainian national team at the 1993, 1994 and 1995 World Championships (Pool C)... Named the best forward at the 1993 tournament... Was one of the top scorers in 1993 (15 goals and seven assists for 22 points in seven games) and in 1994 (12 goals and two assists for 14 points in six games).

Played for Salavat Yulayev Ufa from 1978 to 1984... Joined Sokol Kiev in 1984–85... Played for Sokol until 1991... Bronze medalist of the Soviet League in 1984–85 with Sokol Kiev... Top scorer of the Soviet League in 1990–91... Joined the Swiss club EHC Biel-Bienne in 1991... Played three seasons in Switzerland.

RUS

DIMITRI YUSHKEVICH Won a gold medal at the 1992 Albertville Olympics... Member of the Russian national team at the 1992, 1993, 1994 and 1998 World Championships... Won a gold medal in 1993 and was named best defenseman at the tournament... Saw action at the 1996 World Cup of Hockey as a member of the Russian national team... Played at the 1998 Olympics in Nagano, Japan.

Philadelphia's sixth choice, 122nd overall, in the 1991 NHL Entry Draft... Hockey hero is Vladislav Tretiak... Captured Soviet National League title in his only season with Moscow Dynamo in 1991–92... Played three seasons with Torpedo Yaroslavl prior to that... Made his NHL debut October 6, 1992... Was third among Flyers defensemen in assists and points in his rookie season... Returned to Russia for a brief time during the NHL labor dispute in 1994–95 and played 10 games for Torpedo Yaroslavl... Second among Flyers defensemen in scoring that season... Led all Philadelphia defensemen with three power-play goals... In 1995–96, picked up his first point as a Maple Leaf with an assist on Octiber 21st... In 1997–98, he played in 72 games with Toronto and recorded 12 assists.

RUS

ALEXEI ZHAMNOV Center Alexei Zhamnov recorded seven points for the Soviet national junior team at the 1990 World Junior Championships. He won a bronze medal at the 1991 World Championships and played for the Soviets in the 1991 Canada Cup. He won a gold medal with the Unified Team at the 1992 Albertville Olympics and a silver with Russia in Nagano in 1998. He also played in the World Cup of Hockey in 1996. Dynamo Moscow was his Soviet club team before he was drafted 77th overall by Winnipeg in the 1990 NHL Entry Draft. He played four seasons with Winnipeg before being traded to Chicago and set an NHL personal best with 73 points in 1997–98.

RUS

ALEXEI ZHITNIK Played for the Unified Team at the 1992 Albertville Olympics, winning a gold medal... Named assistant captain of Team Russia at the 1994 World Championships... Played for Russia in three World Championships (1992, 1994 and 1996) Was named best defenseman at the 1996 tournament... Played at the World Cup of Hockey in 1996... Played all six games at the 1998 Olympics in Nagano, registering two assists.

Los Angeles' fourth round choice, 81st overall, in the 1991 NHL Entry Draft... Played three years for Sokol Kiev and the Central Red Army Team in the Soviet Elite League from 1989–90 through 1991–92 before joining Los Angeles for the 1992–93 season... Posted the second highest point total by a rookie defenseman in franchise history in 1992–93 with 48 points (12 goals, 36 assists)... Point total was also second-highest among rookie defensemen in the NHL... Scored a goal on his first shot as a Sabre, February 15, 1995... In 1997–98 season, was second in scoring on the Sabres with 15 goals and 30 assists for 45 points in 78 games.

LAT

SERGEI ZHOLTOK As a junior, played for the Soviet national team at the European Junior Championships... Selected as a tournament all-star after collecting six goals and four assists four 10 points in six games... Made his debut with the Latvian national team at the 1994 World Championships... Had six goals in four games... Had three goals and three assists in five games for Latvia at the 1997 World Championships.

Boston's second choice, 55th overall, in the 1992 NHL Entry Draft... Played two seasons for Dynamo Riga in the Soviet League... In three years with the Bruins organization spent most of the times with Providence of American Hockey League... Played for the Las Vegas Thunder (International Hockey League) in 1995–96... Scored 51 goals and had 50 assists for 101 points in 82 games... Signed as a free agent with Ottawa before the 1996–97 season.

RUS

SERGEI ZUBOV Won a silver medal with the Soviet Union national junior team at the 1988 European Junior Championships... Won a gold medal with the Soviet Union at the 1989 World Junior Championships... Won a silver medal with the Soviet Union at the 1990 World Junior Championships and was named to tournament's second all-star team... Won a gold medal with the CIS team (Commonwealth of Independent States) at the 1992 Albertville Olympics... Played at the 1996 World Cup of Hockey.

New York Rangers' sixth choice, 85th overall, in the 1990 NHL Entry Draft... Led New York in scoring, placing second in league scoring among defensemen, with 89 points in 1993–94... Led NHL defensemen with 77 assists... Was the first defenseman to lead his team in scoring while playing for a regular-season champion... Placed fourth in team scoring in the 1994 playoffs when the Rangers won the Stanley Cup... Finished ninth in league scoring among defensemen in 1994–95... In 1995–96, finished eighth in league scoring among defensemen despite missing 18 games... One of two NHL defensemen to average more than one point per game... Traded to the Dallas Stars before the 1996–97 season... Had excellent 1997–98 season, finishing third in scoring among league defensemen with 10 goals and 47 assists for 57 points in 73 games as Dallas posted the NHL's best record.

LIT

DAINIUS ZUBRUS Philadelphia's first choice, 15th overall, in the 1996 NHL Entry Draft... Born and began his career in Elektrenai, same Lithuanian town where Darius Kasparaitis grew up... Played Junior A hockey in Ontario (for Pembroke and Caledon) in 1995–96... Spent the entire 1996–97 season with the Flyers... As a rookie, played in 68 games and collected eight goals and 13 assists for 21 points... Added five goals and four assists for nine points in 19 playoff games... Played in the Stanley Cup finals in 1997.

UKRAINE
see page 1859

USA

TAFFY ABEL For much of his career with the New York Rangers and Chicago Black Hawks, Clarence "Taffy" Abel was the only American-born player in the NHL. A native of Sault Ste. Marie, Michigan, Abel began his hockey career in his hometown, but also played amateur hockey in Minnesota. He was a member of the United States Olympic hockey team at the first Winter Games in Chamonix, France in 1924 and won a silver medal. The Americans were nearly as dominant as the Canadian club that year, and lost only to Canada (6–1 in the gold medal game) after running roughshod over their European opponents.

Abel was signed by the New York Rangers when they entered the NHL in 1926–27 and helped the team win the Stanley Cup in 1928. In his final NHL season of 1933–34, he helped the Chicago Black Hawks win the Stanley Cup.

TONY AMONTE starred at Boston University and signed his first professional contract with the New York Rangers on April 2, 1991—two days after BU lost the NCAA championship to Michigan in triple overtime. He scored 35 goals as an NHL rookie in 1991–92 and was a finalist for the Calder Trophy that went to Pavel Bure that year.

In international play, Amonte represented the United States team at the World Junior Championships in 1989 and 1990 and at the World

Championships in 1991 and 1993. In 1996, he scored the series-winning goal in game three as the United States beat Canada at the World Cup of Hockey. He was also a member of the U.S. Olympic team at Nagano in 1998.

HERB BROOKS gained fame as coach of the "Miracle on Ice" United States Olympic hockey team that defeated the Soviet Union at the Lake Placid Olympics in 1980 and went on to win the gold medal. He had been the last player cut from the 1960 United States Olympic squad that had won the gold medal in hockey at Squaw Valley in 1960. Brooks did later played on the U.S. Olympic team in 1964 and 1968 and on the U.S. national team in 1962, 1965, 1967, and 1970, earning a bronze medal at the World Championships in 1962 and helping the Americans win the B Pool in 1970.

Brooks was a collegiate player at the University of Minnesota from 1955 to 1959. He became coach at the school in 1972 and transformed the last-place Gophers into NCAA champions by 1974. Brooks led Minnesota to the NCAA title again in 1976 and 1979 before going on to guide the U.S. gold medal team. (He had also coached the Americans at the World Championships in 1959.) There was immediate speculation after Lake Placid that Brooks would coach the New York Rangers, but he wound up in Switzerland for a year before joining his former Olympic assistant Craig Patrick in New York. Brooks later coached the Minnesota North Stars and the New Jersey Devils. In 1995, he joined Craig Patrick again as a scout with the Pittsburgh Penguins. Brooks coached the Olympic hockey team from France at the Nagano Games in 1998.

AARON BROTEN The middle of the three Broten brothers who played in the NHL, Aaron Broten represented the United States at the World Championships in 1981, 1982, 1985, 1986 and 1987. He also played at the Canada Cup in 1984 and 1987, teaming with brother Neal (a member of the 1980 gold medal-winning American team) at the 1984 event. Broten played 12 years in the NHL and was the first member of the New Jersey Devils to top 200 assists and 300 points in franchise history.

NEAL BROTEN was a member of the "Miracle on Ice" U.S. Olympic hockey team that won the gold medal in Lake Placid in 1980, collecting a goal and six assists in eight games. He went on to become the highest scoring American-born player in the history of the NHL until being surpassed by Joe Mullen. Broten added a Stanley Cup victory to his Olympic gold medal as a member of the New Jersey Devils in 1994–95.

In addition to his Olympic experience, Broten represented the United States at the Canada Cup tournament in 1981 and 1984, playing with brother Aaron at the 1984 event. He made is final international appearance with the U.S. team at the World Championships in 1990.

CHRIS CHELIOS has been one of the game's dominant defenseman for much of the 1980s and 1990s. He became the first American-born player to win the Norris Trophy as the NHL's best defenseman when he received the award as a member of the Montreal Canadiens in 1988–89. Chelios was also the Norris Trophy winner with the Chicago Blackhawks in 1992–93 and 1995–96.

Internationally, Chelios represented the United States at the World Junior Championships in 1982 and played for the U.S. National and Olympic teams in 1983–84. He was a member of American squad at the Canada Cup in 1984, 1987 and 1991. He was named an all-star at the 1991 tournament and was selected as an all-star again in 1996 when he was a key contributor to the U.S. team that beat Canada at the World Cup of Hockey. Chelios also played for the U.S. Olympic team in Nagano in 1998.

KEITH CHRISTIANSEN was one of the top offensive players on the United States national team and represented his country at the World Championships in 1969, 1970 and 1971. He had five goals and five assists for the U.S. squad that won the B Pool tournament in 1970. In 1972, he was a member of the American team that won a surprising silver medal at the Winter Olympics in Sapporo. He went on to play two seasons with the Minnesota Fighting Saints in the World Hockey Association.

BILL CHRISTIAN is a member of one of the most prominent families in United States hockey history. Father Ed Christian helped build the Warroad Arena that housed the famed Warroad Lakers in Warroad, Minnesota, while sons Bill and Roger were both long-time stars of the team and members of the gold medal-winning 1960 United States Olympic hockey team. Bill son's Dave played for the 1980 "Miracle on Ice" gold medal team and went on to a long NHL career.

Bill Christian first came to prominence in youth and high school hockey in Warroad, and after a year at the University of Minnesota he joined the 1957–58 United States national team that became the first American athletic team ever to play in the Soviet Union. Christian also played for the U.S. national team in 1960, 1962, 1964, and 1965. He is best remembered for his contributions in 1960 when he scored two goals in a crucial win 3–2 win over the Soviet Union that all but clinched the gold medal for the American team at the Squaw Valley Olympics. He earned a bronze medal at the World Championships in 1962.

DAVE CHRISTIAN The son of Bill Christian, a legendary American amateur hockey star who played with the 1960 gold medal-winning U.S. Olympic team, Dave Christian added to the family's rich hockey legacy by winning a gold medal with the "Miracle on Ice" team in 1980. He would go on to score 340 goals for five NHL teams over a 15-year career.

Christian was a forward who was converted to defense for the U.S. Olympic team because coach Herb Brooks thought he was smart enough and talented enough to handle the switch. Christian led the American team with eight assists en route to the gold medal at the Lake Placid Games. In addition to his Olympic experience, Christian represented the United States at the Canada Cup tournament in 1981, 1984 and 1991. He also played at the World Championships in 1981 and 1989.

GORDON CHRISTIAN A brother of the more famous Bill and Roger Christian, Gordon Christian preceded the two onto the United States national team, first representing his country at the World Championships in 1955. He collected five goals in six games for the American team that earned a silver medal behind the Soviet Union at the 1956 Winter Olympics in Cortina d'Ampezzo, Italy. In 1958, Gordon Christian and his brothers were members of the U.S. national team that became the first American sports team ever to play in the Soviet Union.

ROGER CHRISTIAN The older brother of Bill Christian, Roger Christian also had a lengthy career with the Warroad Lakers and representing the United States in international hockey. Both he and Bill and brother Gordon played with the 1958 U.S. national team that was the first American club ever to play in the Soviet Union and both were members of the gold medal-winning U.S. Olympic team in Squaw Valley, California in 1960. The Christians earned bronze medals with the United States team at the 1962 World Championships and were also members of the U.S. national team in 1964 and 1965.

Roger Christian started playing high school hockey in Warroad, Minnesota in 1950, led the team in scoring in 1952, and helped the team reach the finals of the state tournament in 1953. He later played 18 years with the Warroad Lakers, who retired his uniform number 7 in 1974.

BILL CLEARY was the leading scorer on the gold medal-winning United States Olympic hockey team at Squaw Valley, California in 1960. He had 14 points on seven goals and seven assists and scored the first goal in a key 3–2 win over the Soviet Union in the second-last game of the tournament that all but clinched the surprising gold medal victory. Cleary had previously played on the silver medal-winning Olympic team in 1956 and also represented the United States at the 1959 World Championships when he was named the best forward at the tournament. His brother Bob also played on both the 1959 and 1960 U.S. teams.

Cleary was a native of Cambridge, Massachusetts who gained hockey stardom during a standout career at Harvard University. His greatest season was 1954–55 when he set an NCAA single-season scoring record with 89 points and a Harvard record with 42 goals. Cleary led Harvard to an Ivy League title and a third-place finish at the NCAA hockey tournament that year.

BOB CLEARY Like his older brother Bill, Bob Cleary played prep school hockey at Belmont Hill before going on to a stellar career at Harvard University. He topped the NCAA in scoring in both 1956–57 and 1957–58. Cleary served as team captain in 1957–58 and was selected as an all-American that season.

In 1959, Cleary played for the United States national team at the World Championships and in 1960 he was a late addition to the U.S. Olympic team. Cleary teamed with his brother Bill and former Harvard teammate Bob McVey to form a high-scoring line that helped the Americans win a surprising gold medal in Squaw Valley, California.

PAUL COPPO led the United States national team in scoring with nine goals and 16 points when the Americans earned a bronze medal at the 1962 World Championships in Colorado Springs, Colorado. The Soviet Union boycotted the event that year after American officials refused to grant entry visas to the East German squad.

Coppo was a member of the U.S. team at the 1964 Winter Olympics in Innsbruck, collecting seven points in seven games that year. He later represented his country again at the World Championships again in 1965 and 1969.

GERRY COSBY In 1933, Gerry Cosby tended goal on the American team that won the gold medal at the World Championships. The United States beat Canada 2–1 in the final game to earn its first world title. In 1936, Cosby shared goaltending duties with Thomas Moone at the Winter Olympics in Garmisch-Partenkirchen, Germany. He allowed just a single goal in five games played as the Americans claimed a bronze medal behind Great Britain and Canada. Cosby would later operate a popular sporting goods business in New York City.

JIM CRAIG The backbone of the 1980 "Miracle on Ice" U.S. Olympic team, Jim Craig played every game at Lake Placid, earning a 6–0–1 record and a

2.14 goals-against average. He was spectacular in the key 4–3 win over the Soviet Union, making 36 saves as the U.S. team was outshot 39–16. Television coverage of Jim Craig wrapped in the stars-and-stripes while searching the stands for his father after the American victory is one of the enduring images of the Lake Placid Games.

Craig was signed by the NHL's Atlanta Flames shortly after the Olympics and played with the Boston Bruins in 1980–81. He would later see brief action with the Minnesota North Stars. Craig returned to the U.S. national team in 1982–83 and was named the all-star goaltender when the Americans won the B Pool World Championships in 1983. Prior to his Olympic experience, Craig had represented the United States at the World Championships in 1979.

JOHN CUNNIFF An all-American at Boston College, John Cunniff became a member of the United States national team in 1966–67 and represented his country at the 1967 World Championships and at the 1968 Grenoble Winter Olympics. Cunniff then embarked on a seven-year professional career that saw him spend two years with the New England Whalers of the World Hockey Association. He later returned to the World Championships with the U.S. team in 1975.

A head coach in the NHL with the Hartford Whalers (1981–82) and New Jersey Devils (1989 to 1991), Cunniff continued his international ties after getting involved in coaching. He was an assistant coach with Team USA at the 1981 Canada Cup, with the U.S. national junior team in 1989–90 and 1990–91, and with the American team at the World Championships in 1991, 1992 and 1993. He was an associate coach of the 1994 U.S. Olympic team in Lillehammer and an assistant coach with the American squad that beat Canada to win the World Cup of Hockey in 1996. He was again an assistant to head coach Ron Wilson at the 1998 Nagano Olympics.

MIKE CURRAN was a member of the United States national team in 1969, 1970, and 1971, playing at the World Championships each of those years. In 1970, the U.S. won the title at the B Pool tournament. Despite his international experience, Curran had to battle to earn the number-one job with the U.S. Olympic team in 1972. His goaltending in Sapporo that year was a key reason why the Americans won a surprising gold medal. Curran was particularly brilliant in a 51-save performance in a 5–1 U.S. victory over Czechoslovakia.

Curran was signed by the Minnesota Fighting Saints for the inaugural World Hockey Association season of 1972–73 and played in the WHA until 1977. He also represented the United States internationally again at the World Championships in 1976 and 1977 and shared the American goal with Pete LoPresti and Cap Raeder at the inaugural Canada Cup tournament in 1976.

CLARK DONATELLI represented the United States at the World Junior Championships in 1984 and 1985 and at the World Championships in 1985, 1986 and 1987 while playing hockey at Boston University. In 1987–88, he joined the U.S. national team and played at the Olympics in Calgary in 1988. Donatelli turned professional in 1988–89 and made began his career in the NHL with the Minnesota North Stars in 1989–90. He rejoined the U.S. national team for the 1991–92 season and played at the Albertville Olympics in 1992. After the Olympics, Donatelli signed with the Boston Bruins. He retired after the 1995–96 season having spent the majority of his professional career in the International Hockey League.

MIKE ERUZIONE A Boston University player who had represented the United States at the World Championships in 1975 and 1976, Mike Eruzione gained everlasting fame when he scored the winning goal against the Soviet Union for the United States team at Lake Placid in 1980. Eruzione's goal midway through the third period gave the U.S. a 4–3 win over the Soviets. Two days later, the Americans completed the "Miracle on Ice" with a win over Finland to clinch the Olympic title.

As captain of the team, Eruzione accepted the gold medal on behalf of his teammates and then called them all up to the podium to join him as the American national anthem was played. He retired after winning the gold, believing nothing could equal the Olympic triumph. Eruzione later served as a consultant for the television movie "Miracle on Ice" and is now a member of the Boston University hockey coaching staff and director of development for BU Athletics. He has also been a longtime television hockey analyst in the United States.

ROBBIE FTOREK was a member of the United States national team and played at the Sapporo Olympics in 1972 when the Americans earned a surprising silver medal. The Americans success that year was completely unexpected, as the U.S. had already been relegated to the B Pool of the World Championships due to poor performances in previous years. Ftorek was also a member of the B Pool World Championship team in 1972 and was named to the tournament all-star team.

Ftorek had become a star in the World Hockey Association by the time he represented the United States at the inaugural Canada Cup tournament in 1976. He was playing in the NHL in 1981 when he made his final international appearance at that year's Canada Cup.

GARY GAMBUCCI After starring at the University of Minnesota, Gary Gambucci joined the United States national team for the 1968–69 season and spent three years with the club. He played at the World Championships in 1969, 1970 and 1971, helping the Americans win the B Pool title in 1970. His 10 goals, eight assists and 18 points all ranked second at the tournament that year as Gambucci earned a spot on the all-star team.

Gambucci entered the NHL with Minnesota in 1971–72, but spent most of his time in the minors over four seasons in the North Stars organization. He later played with the Minnesota Fighting Saints of the World Hockey Association and represented the United States internationally for a final time at the World Championships in 1976.

TONY GRANATO After four years of college hockey with the University of Wisconsin, and having represented the United States at the World Junior Championships in 1983 and 1984, Tony Granato joined the U.S. national team in 1987–88. He played at the 1988 Olympics and made his professional debut in the International Hockey League following the Calgary Games.

Granato broke into the NHL with the New York Rangers in 1988–89 and has gone on to play with the Los Angeles Kings and San Jose Sharks. In addition to his Olympic experience he represented the United States at the World Championships four years in a row from 1985 to 1988. Granato was also a member of the U.S. team that lost in the finals of the 1991 Canada Cup.

DERIAN HATCHER is an intimidating physical presence on the Dallas Stars defense and can also be an offensive threat. Hatcher led all U.S. defensemen with three goals at the World Cup of Hockey in 1996 as the Americans defeated Canada to win the tournament. He also played for the U.S. team at the Olympic Games in Nagano in 1998. Previously, Hatcher had represented his country at the 1993 World Championships.

KEVIN HATCHER is a high-scoring blueliner in the NHL who holds the Washington Capitals record for goals by a defenseman with 34 in 1992–93. He first represented the United States in international hockey at the World Junior Championships in 1984. He would later play for his country at the Canada Cup in 1987 and 1991 and was a member of the American team that beat the Canadians in the finals of the World Cup of Hockey in 1996. Hatcher was also a member of the U.S. Olympic team at Nagano in 1998.

PHIL HOUSLEY The highest-scoring U.S.-born defenseman in the history of the NHL, and just the fifth defenseman ever to top 1,000 points, Phil Housley entered the league in 1982–83 after the Buffalo Sabres selected him directly out of high school with the sixth pick overall in the 1982 Entry Draft. Housley has since played for the St. Louis Blues, Calgary Flames, New Jersey Devils and Washington Capitals.

In international competition, Housley represented the United States at the 1982 World Junior Championships and at the World Championships in 1982, 1986, and 1989. He also played at the Canada Cup in 1984 and 1987 and was a member of the American team that beat Canada at the World Cup of Hockey in 1996.

BRETT HULL As the son of Hockey Hall of Famer Bobby Hull, Brett Hull has followed in his famous father's footsteps as one of the greatest goal scorers in the NHL. The 86-goal effort he recorded in 1990–91 ranks as one the highest single-season totals in NHL history, trailing only Wayne Gretzky's 92 goals in 1981–82 and his 87 in 1983–84. Hull scored his 500th career goal on December 22, 1996 to make him and Bobby the only father-son combination ever to each reach the milestone.

Though he was born in Belleville, Ontario, Hull holds dual Canadian and U.S. citizenship and represented the United States at the World Championships in 1986, where he collected seven goals and four assists in 10 games. He also played for the U.S. in the 1991 Canada Cup (tying for the team lead in scoring with Mike Modano with nine points) and was selected as an all-star after leading the tournament in scoring with seven goals and four assists in seven games when the Americans beat Canada in the World Cup of Hockey in 1996. Hull was also a member of the U.S. Olympic hockey team at the Nagano Games in 1998.

WILLARD IKOLA A legend among the United States high school coaching ranks, Willard Ikola was a star goaltender before moving behind the bench. He led his Eveleth High School team to three straight undefeated seasons and three straight state championships from 1948 to 1950. He later won NCAA championships with the University of Michigan in 1952 and 1953.

Ikola was serving with the U.S. Army in Europe in 1956 when he was added to the roster of the American team at the Olympics in Cortina d'Ampezzo, Italy. He played three games in goal for the U.S. at the tournament, including a key 4–1 win over Canada in which he made 38 saves to all but eliminate the Canadians from gold medal contention. The United States settled for the silver medal in 1956 after a 4–0 loss to the gold medal-winning Soviet Union. Ikola also represented the United States at the World Championships in 1958.

MARK JOHNSON The son of University of Wisconsin coach "Badger" Bob Johnson (who also coached Calgary and Pittsburgh in the NHL), Mark Johnson was the American team's most valuable player and the leading scorer at the 1980 Lake Placid Olympics. Johnson had five goals and six assists for 11 points for the "Miracle on Ice" gold medal winners, including two goals in the 4–3 victory over the Soviet Union. American coach Herb Brooks called Johnson "the man who makes us go" and his teammates nicknamed him "Magic" because of his smooth moves.

Johnson signed with the Pittsburgh Penguins shortly after the Olympics and went on to play 11 NHL seasons with Pittsburgh, Hartford, St. Louis and New Jersey. He would also represent the United States again at the World Championships in 1981, 1982, 1985, 1986, 1987 and 1990. When his NHL career ended after the 1989–90 season, Johnson spent a year playing with Milano in Italy.

Prior to his Olympic experience, Johnson had played for the U.S. at the World Championships in 1978 and 1979 while being coached by his father at the University of Wisconsin. When Johnson was a high school senior in 1976, his father had added him to the roster of Team USA for its pre-Olympic tour. Though he held his own against more experienced players, Bob Johnson elected to keep his son out of the Olympics because he felt there would be too much pressure on him at a very young age.

PAUL JOHNSON was already an experienced international player, having represented the United States at the World Championships in 1958 and 1959, when he was named to the United States Olympic team in 1960. A powerful skater and talented offensive threat, Johnson contributed five goals and three assists, including the game winner in a key 2–1 victory over Canada, as the U.S. earned a surprising gold medal at Squaw Valley, California. Johnson also played for his country at the 1961 World Championships and was again a member of the U.S. team at the Innsbruck Olympics in 1964.

PAT LaFONTAINE spent the 1983–84 season with the United States national team and was the club's leading scorer at the 1984 Sarajevo Olympics before making his NHL debut with the New York Islanders on February 29, 1984. He's gone on to be a scoring star with the Islanders, Buffalo Sabres and New York Rangers.

In addition to his Olympic experience in 1984, LaFontaine has represented the United States at the World Championships in 1989 and at the Canada Cup in 1987 and 1991. He was a member of the American team that beat Canada at the World Cup of Hockey in 1996 and also played for the U.S. Olympic team in Nagano in 1998.

ROD LANGWAY was a star defensive defenseman over a 15-year NHL career spent with the Montreal Canadiens and Washington Capitals, winning the Norris Trophy as the NHL's best blueliner in 1982–83 and 1983–84. Internationally, Langway represented the United States at the Canada Cup in 1981, 1984 and 1987 and was named to the tournament all-star team in 1984. He also played at the World Championships in 1982.

JOHN LeCLAIR Played for the United States national junior team at the 1988 and 1989 World Junior Championships. He recorded 10 points for Team USA en route to a first-place finish in the inaugural World Cup of Hockey in 1996 and was a member of the 1998 U.S. Olympic team.

LeClair is the only native of Vermont ever to play in NHL. He won the Stanley Cup with Montreal in 1993 and reached the finals with Philadelphia in 1997. He is a three-time 50-goal scorer in the NHL with the Flyers and was named to the NHL First All-Star Team in 1995 and 1998 and to the Second All-Star Team in 1996 and 1997 at left wing.

BRIAN LEETCH made his NHL debut with the New York Rangers on February 29, 1988 after competing for the United States at the Calgary Olympics. He had been an all-American at Boston College in 1986–87 and was a finalist for the Hobey Baker Award after becoming the first freshman ever nominated for the top individual honor in U.S. College hockey. Leetch left the school after one season to join the U.S. national team and served as team captain at the Olympics.

In addition to his Olympic experience in 1988, Leetch represented the United States at the World Junior Championships in 1985, 1986 and 1987, winning a bronze medal in 1986 and being named to the tournament all-star team in 1987. He also played at the World Championships in 1987 and 1989 and at the Canada Cup in 1991. In 1996, Leetch was a captain of the American team that beat Canada at the World Cup of Hockey. In 1998, he returned to the Olympics as a member of the U.S. team in Nagano.

LEN LILYHOLM was a member of the United States national team who played at the World Championships in 1966 and 1967. In 1968, he was a member of the team that played at the Grenoble Olympics. In 1970, he starred for the U.S. team that won the B Pool at the World Championships, leading the tournament with 12 assists and 20 points. Lilyholm and the Americans were back in the A Pool at the World Championships in 1971. In 1972, he played

professionally with the Minnesota Fighting Saints of the World Hockey Association. He made his final international appearance with the American team that won the B Pool World Championship in 1974.

JOHN MAYASICH was considered one of the best amateur hockey players in the United States when he was added to a lineup made up mostly of college kids on the American Olympic hockey team in 1960. His added muscle and hustle on the U.S. defense, plus his booming slapshot, helped the team pull off a stunning gold medal victory.

Mayasich began his international career with the United States Olympic hockey team in 1956 and earned a silver medal that year. His three goals in a 4–1 win over Canada all but ensured the American's second-place finish In addition to his Olympic experience, Mayasich also represented America at the World Championships in 1958, 1961, 1962, 1966, and 1969, earning a bronze medal in 1962 as well as a selection to the tournament all-star team. He had many offers to turn professional during his career, but instead played with the amateur Green Bay Bobcats after his starring days in high school and university in Minnesota.

JACK McCARTAN had been an all-American twice at the University of Minnesota and had played for the United States at the World Championships in 1959. Still, he was only a late addition to the U.S. Olympic hockey team in 1960, on loan from the U.S. Army. Like Jim Craig at Lake Placid in 1980, it was McCartan who was most responsible for the surprising gold medal victory with his brilliant goaltending at Squaw Valley.

McCartan was at his best in the Americans' surprising 2–1 win over Canada during the medal round. He made 38 saves, including 20 in the second period, in a loss that Harry Sinden of the Kitchener-Waterloo Dutchmen referred to as "shocking to us." McCartan was also stellar two days later in preserving the Americans' first win over the Soviet Union. The 3–2 victory all but clinched the gold medal for the United States, who made it official with a 9–4 win over Czechoslovakia in the final game.

After the Olympics, McCartan appeared in four games with the New York Rangers. He played eight games for the Rangers in 1960–61, but would never again play in the NHL in a professional career that lasted until 1974–75.

DICK MEREDITH, John Mayasich and Bob Cleary were members of the United States team at both the 1956 and 1960 Olympics. Meredith had two goals for the American silver medal-winning team at Cortina d'Ampezzo in 1956 and two goals and two assists for the surprising gold medal winners at Squaw Valley in 1960. In between his Olympic experiences, Meredith represented the United States at the World Championships in 1958 and 1959.

BOB MILLER was a member of the United States national team in 1975–76 and played at the Innsbruck Olympics in 1976. He was also drafted by the Boston Bruins that year and made his NHL debut in 1977–78. Miller spent parts of six seasons in the NHL with Boston, Los Angeles and the Colorado Rockies and also played in Finland and Switzerland in the mid 1980s. In addition to his Olympic experience, Miller represented the United States at the World Championships in 1977, 1981, 1982 and 1985. He also played for Team USA at the Canada Cup tournament in 1981.

MIKE MODANO was just the second American-born player ever to be selected first overall in the NHL Entry Draft when he was picked by the Minnesota North Stars in 1988. Five years earlier, the North Stars had made American Brian Lawton the number-one pick. Modano has gone on to star in both Minnesota and with the Dallas Stars.

In international play, Modano represented the United States at the World Junior Championships in 1988 and 1989, finishing second behind fellow American Jeremy Roenick in scoring at the 1989 tournament with 15 points (six goals and nine assists). He played for the U.S. at the 1990 and 1993 World Championships and was tied for the team lead in scoring with Brett Hull (nine points) at the 1991 Canada Cup. Modano was a member of the American team that beat Canada at the World Cup of Hockey in 1996 and played for the U.S. Olympic team in Nagano in 1998.

KEN MORROW became the first player in hockey history to win an Olympic gold medal and the Stanley Cup in the same season, winning with the "Miracle on Ice" United States hockey team at Lake Placid in February of 1980 and then with the New York Islanders in May. His solid positional play anchored the American defense and helped make Jim Craig's brilliant play possible. Morrow went on to play with four consecutive Stanley Cup-winning teams with the Islanders.

At 6'4" and 210 pounds, Morrow was a defensive defenseman who went on to play10 seasons in the NHL, all with the Islanders. Previously, he had become the first All-American player ever chosen at Bowling Green University in 1978–79.

JOE MULLEN Though his NHL single-season records for goals and points by an American-born player had already been surpassed, Joe Mullen was still

the highest-scoring U.S. player in NHL history (with 502 goals and 1,063 points) when he retired after the 1996–97 season. He was the first American to reach 1,000 career points (February 7, 1995) and the first to score 500 goals (March 14, 1997). During his career, Mullen played for the United States at Canada Cup tournaments in 1984, 1987 and 1991. The 1991 American team reached the finals before being defeated for the title by the Canadians.

LOU NANNE Born in Sault Ste. Marie, Ontario, Lou Nanne played minor-league hockey there with Phil Esposito. He later became a naturalized American citizen and starred at the University of Minnesota where he became the first defenseman to win the Western Collegiate Hockey Association scoring title in 1962–63. In 1967–68, Nanne joined the United States national team and captained the squad at the 1968 Olympic Games at Grenoble.

Nanne began his NHL career with the North Stars after the Olympics and remained with Minnesota as a player through the 1977–78 season, representing the United States again at the World Championships in 1976 and 1977 and at the inaugural Canada Cup tournament in 1976. After his playing days, Nanne served as coach, and later general manager and president of the North Stars. In 1981 and 1984, he was general manager of the American team at the Canada Cup.

ED OLCYZK was a member of the United States national team in 1983–84 and collected seven points (two goals and five assists) in six games for the Americans at the 1984 Olympics in Sarajevo. He was selected by the Chicago Blackhawks with the third overall pick in the 1984 Entry Draft and began his NHL career in 1984–85. Olcyzk would continue to be a key offensive threat for the United States at various international events, playing for his country in the Canada Cup tournament in 1984, 1987 and 1991 and at the World Championships in 1986, 1987, 1989 and 1993.

JOEL OTTO A solid two-way center over the course of his NHL career, Joel Otto represented the United States at the World Championships in 1985 and 1990. He also played for Team USA at the Canada Cup in 1987 and was co-captain of the team that reached the finals of the 1991 event. In 1996, he was a member of the American team that defeated Canada at the World Cup of Hockey. Otto also played at the Nagano Olympics in 1998.

WINTHROP PALMER "Ding" Palmer is the leading goal scorer in the history of Yale University hockey, collecting 87 goals from 1927–28 to 1929–30. In his three seasons at Yale, the Elis posted a combined record of 45–6–2. He scored an astounding 41 goals in 17 games in 1927–28, including seven in a single game against New Hampshire.

After leaving Yale, Palmer played for the 1932 U.S. Olympic hockey team that lost the gold medal to Canada thanks to a 2–1 loss in the opening game at Lake Placid. In 1933, he played for the American squad that defeated Canada 2–1 in Prague, Czechoslovakia to win the World Championship for the United States for the first time.

CRAIG PATRICK built the Pittsburgh Penguins into Stanley Cup champions in 1991 and 1992 and is a member of one of hockey's most prominent families. He is the son of Hockey Hall of Famer Lynn Patrick and the grandson of hockey legend Lester Patrick. His uncle, Muzz Patrick, played in the NHL and was longtime executive with the New York Rangers. Cousin Dick Patrick has been an executive with the Washington Capitals since 1982–83. Frank Patrick is also a member of the Hockey Hall of Fame.

Craig Patrick played hockey at the University of Denver and captained the Pioneers to the NCAA championship in 1968–69. He played in the NHL with the California Golden Seals, St. Louis Blues, Kansas City Scouts, and Washington Capitals from 1971–72 until 1978–79 and was a member of the United States team at the first Canada Cup in 1976. Patrick also represented the United States at the World Championships in 1970 (B Pool champions), 1971 and 1979. He is best known in international hockey circles, however, as the assistant coach and assistant general manager with the "Miracle on Ice" American hockey team at the 1980 Lake Placid Olympics.

MARK PAVELICH played with Buzz Schneider and John Harrington on the Conehead Line (named after the *Saturday Night Live* characters) on the 1980 "Miracle on Ice" gold medal-winning team at Lake Placid. Pavelich joined the U.S. national team from the University of Minnesota-Duluth and contributed a goal and seven assists to the Olympic effort.

Pavelich played with Lugano in Switzerland in 1980–81 and represented the United States again that season when he joined the American team at the 1981 World Championships. He entered the NHL with the New York Rangers in 1981–82 and played five seasons before joining the Minnesota North Stars in 1986–87. Pavelich then spent two years playing in Switzerland and Italy and later returned to the NHL with the San Jose Sharks for two games in 1991–92.

MIKE RAMSEY The youngest player on the 1980 "Miracle on Ice" team, Mike Ramsey was only 18 years old when he joined the United States national team in 1979–80. He joined the Buffalo Sabres after the gold medal victory

at Lake Placid and went on to play 18 years in the NHL with Buffalo, Pittsburgh and Detroit. In 1997–98, Ramsey became an assistant coach with the Sabres.

In addition to his Olympic experience, Ramsey represented the United States at the World Championships in 1982. He also played for the American squad at the Canada Cup tournament in 1984 and 1987.

MIKE RICHTER was selected by the New York Rangers in the second round of the 1985 NHL Entry Draft and played the next two seasons at the University of Wisconsin. Richter played for the U.S. team at the World Junior Championships in 1985 and 1986 and at the World Championships in both 1986 and 1987. He spent the entire 1987–88 season with the national team, sharing netminding duties with Chris Terreri and playing at the Olympics in Calgary. He made his NHL debut in the playoffs one year later.

Richter later played for his country again in the 1991 Canada Cup and at the 1993 World Championships. In September of 1996, he was the number-one goalie for the American team at the World Cup of Hockey where his brilliant play led the United States to a two-games-to-one victory over Canada in the finals. Richter allowed just 15 goals in six games for a 2.43 goals-against average and was not just named to the World Cup all-star team but was also named the tournament's most valuable player. Richter tended goal for the United States at the Nagano Olympics in 1998.

ROBERT RIDDER Though born in New York City and educated at Harvard University, Robert Ridder's involvement in hockey began in Minnesota in the 1940s with the Duluth Heralds. In October of 1947, Ridder, Don Clark, and Everett "Buck" Riley founded the Minnesota Amateur Hockey Association. By 1952, Ridder's interest in hockey had expanded to the international arena and that year he managed the United States Olympic team. The American squad won a silver medal behind Canada that year and Ridder managed the team again in 1956 when it earned a silver medal behind the Soviet Union.

DON RIGAZIO tended goal for the American team at the World Championships in 1955. At the Olympics in Cortina d'Ampezzo in 1956 and at the World Championships in 1958, he shared U.S. netminding duties with Willard Ikola. Rigazio allowed just seven goals in the four games he played at the 1956 Olympics, posting a 1.75 goals-against average that helped the Americans claim the silver medal behind the Soviet Union, which was making its first appearance in Olympic hockey that year.

JACK RILEY coached an underdog American team to the United States' first gold medal in Olympic hockey at Squaw Valley, California in 1960. Like the 1980 "Miracle on Ice team," the 1960 U.S. squad was mainly a collection of university players who stunned the hockey world with their victory. Riley himself had been a star player at Dartmouth before graduating in 1944 and played for the U.S. Olympic team in 1948. In 1949, he was a player coach on the American team that finished third at that year's World Championships.

Riley joined the coaching staff of the United States Military Academy hockey team in 1950 and became head coach in 1951. Except for his year with the Olympic team, Riley remained at Army through the 1985–86 season.

DON ROSS was a mainstay on the United States national team during the 1960s, representing his country at the 1964 Innsbruck Olympics and at the 1968 Grenoble Games. He also played for his country at the World Championships in 1966 and 1967. Later, he helped the Americans win the B Pool World Championship in 1970 and was named to the all-star team on defense along with fellow American George Konik who was also named the best defenseman at the event. Ross played for the American team at the World Championships again in 1971.

JOE SACCO was a member of the United States team at the World Junior Championships in 1989 while playing hockey at Boston University. He represented the United States at the World Championships while still playing with BU in 1990 and played at the tournament again in 1991 after having made his NHL debut with the Toronto Maple Leafs.

Sacco joined the U.S. national team in 1991–92 and played at both the 1992 Albertville Olympics and the 1992 World Championships. Sacco was playing in the NHL with the Mighty Ducks of Anaheim when he represented the United States again at the World Championships in 1994 and 1996. He won a bronze at the 1996 tournament as the U.S. earned its first World Championship medal since a third-place finish in 1962.

BUZZ SCHNEIDER was the only member of the 1980 United States "Miracle on Ice Team" who had played in the 1976 Innsbruck Olympics. He had also represented his country when the Americans won the B Pool World Championship in 1974. Schneider had been at the A Pool World Championships in 1975, 1976 and 1977 and would be again in 1982.

Schneider played with Mark Pavelich and John Harrington on the Conehead Line (named after the *Saturday Night Live* characters) on the 1980 Olympic team. The oldest player on the U.S. squad, the 25-year-old Schneider

has been called the unsung hero of the team by assistant coach and general manager Craig Patrick. Schneider contributed five goals and three assists to the gold medal effort.

KEVIN STEVENS and Jeremy Roenick became the first American-born players to score 50 goals in back-to-back NHL seasons when they each reached the milestone in 1991–92 and 1992–93. Stevens' 55 goals during the 1992–93 seasons tied Jimmy Carson's 1987–88 record for the most goals ever scored by an American player in a single season.

Stevens played with the U.S. national team in 1987–88 and made his NHL debut with the Pittsburgh Penguins on March 1, 1988 after playing at the Calgary Olympics. He would later represent the United States at the World Championships in 1987, 1990 and 1996. He earned a bronze medal at the 1996 tournament when the Americans returned to the podium for the first time in A Pool competition since 1962.

LARRY STORDAHL represented the United States at the World Championships in 1966 and later played for the American team at the 1968 Winter Olympics in Grenoble, France. In 1969, he was a member of the U.S. squad that finished last at the World Championships and was relegated to the B Pool. He helped the Americans gain a measure of revenge in 1970 when his five goals and five assists ranked him among the scoring leaders and helped the U.S. win the B Pool World Championship.

GARY SUTER won the Calder Trophy as the NHL rookie of the year with the Calgary Flames in 1985–86. His 68 points that season were then the second-highest total ever recorded by a first-year defenseman behind Larry Murphy's 76 in 1980–81. Fellow American Brian Leetch has since topped Suter's total with 71 points in 1988–89.

Suter played for the U.S. team that beat Canada at the World Cup of Hockey in 1996 and was a member of the U.S. Olympic team in Nagano in 1998. He had previously represented the United States at the World Championships in 1985 and 1992 and at the Canada Cup in 1987 and 1991.

CHRIS TERRERI was an all-American goalie at Providence College when he first represented the United States at the World Championships in 1985. He also played for the U.S. at the tournament while still with Providence in 1986 and returned in 1987 after making his NHL debut with the New Jersey Devils.

Following his first professional season, Terreri chose to hone his skills with the U.S. national team in 1987–88, sharing the net with Mike Richter that year and playing at the 1988 Calgary Olympics. It would not be until the World Championships in 1997 that Terreri once again had the chance to represent the United States in international play.

ALLAN VAN enjoyed one of the longest careers in United States national team history. He first represented his country internationally at the 1938 World Championships and made his last appearance with the silver medal-winning team that finished behind only Canada at the 1952 Oslo Olympics. Van also appeared at the 1939 World Championships (where the Americans finished second behind Canada) and returned to international competition following World War II as a member of the bronze medal-winning U.S. team at the 1949 World Championships. Van also played at the 1950 World Championships, where the Americans once again finished second behind their Canadian rivals.

JOHN VANBIESBROUCK On December 27, 1997, John Vanbiesbrouck became just the second American-born goaltender to post 300 victories in the NHL (two months after Tom Barrasso had become the first). Internationally, Vanbiesbrouck first represented the United States at the World Junior Championships in 1982 and 1983. He also played for his country at the World Championships in 1985, 1987, 1989, and 1991.

Vanbiesbrouck was a member of the United States Canada Cup team in 1987 and 1991. In 1991, he shared netminder duties with Rangers teammate Mike Richter as the U.S. reached the final before being swept by Canada in two straight games. Injuries kept Vanbiesbrouck out of the World Cup of Hockey in 1996, but he was a member of the U.S. Olympic hockey team at Nagano in 1998.

JIM WARDEN tended goal for the United States at the World Championships in 1975. In 1976, he was a member of the U.S. team at the Innsbruck Olympics. Warden represented his country again in 1978 and 1979, playing at the World Championships both years.

CARL WETZEL was a journeyman minor-leaguer who had appeared in two NHL games with the Detroit Red Wings in 1964–65 before joining the United States national team in 1966–67. Wetzel appeared with the U.S. team at the 1967 World Championships and was named a tournament all-star and the best goalie despite the Americans' fifth-place finish.

Wetzel made a final NHL appearance when he played five games with the Minnesota North Stars in 1967–68. He returned to the U.S. national team in 1969–70 and helped the Americans win the B Pool World Championship.

After playing for the U.S. national team again in 1970–71, Wetzel spent the 1971–72 season with Kitzbuhel in Austria before playing the final game of his career with the Minnesota Fighting Saints of the World Hockey Association in 1972–73.

RON WILSON Although he was born in Canada, Ron Wilson was raised in the United States and became an American citizen. As a player, he represented the United States on the national team in 1975, 1981, 1983, and 1987. He helped the Americans win the B Pool World Championship in 1983 and was named to the tournament all-star team. Wilson first coached the American squad at the 1994 World Championships and guided the United States to victory over Canada in the World Cup of Hockey in September of 1996. He also coached the U.S. team at the Nagano Olympics in 1998.

As a player, Wilson starred at Providence University between 1973–74 and 1976–77, earning All-American honors twice. He made his NHL debut in 1977–78, though most of his time with the Toronto Maple Leafs was spent in the minor leagues. Wilson played in Switzerland from 1980–81 until 1985–86 when he returned to the NHL with the Minnesota North Stars. He spent the rest of his career with Minnesota before retiring after the 1988–89 season.

SCOTT YOUNG is one of only 10 players to have represented the United States three times at the World Junior Championships. He played at the tournament in 1985, 1986 and 1987, winning a bronze medal in 1986 and being named to the tournament all-star team in 1987 after scoring seven goals in seven games. Young also played at the World Championships that year.

Young was a member of the U.S. national team in 1987–88 and collected two goals and six assists at the 1988 Calgary Olympics before making his NHL debut with the Hartford Whalers. He represented the United States at the World Championships again in 1989 and rejoined the national team in 1991–92, playing at the Albertville Olympics. Young also had 22 goals in 18 games playing with Bolzano in Italy that season.

After returning to the NHL with the Quebec Nordiques for two seasons, Young once again played for the United States at the 1994 World Championships and then spent most of the 1994–95 season in Germany. Back in the NHL, Young earned a Stanley Cup ring with the Colorado Avalanche in June of 1996 and was a member of the United States team that defeated Canada in the World Cup of Hockey in September of that year.

WEST GERMANY
see page 1848

YUGOSLAVIA, CROATIA AND SLOVENIA

IIHF-standard three-letter abbreviations are used to indicate the country each player has most recently represented in international competition as a player, coach or executive. Some players have represented more than one of these countries over the course of their careers. CRO – Croatia, SLO – Slovenia, YUG – Yugoslavia.

YUG

MUSTAFA BESIC One of the best forwards in Yugoslavian hockey... In the 1980s, was one of the top scorers on the national team... Played at the 1980 Olympics in Lake Placid... Named the best forward at the World and European Championships in 1989 (Pool C)... Named to the all-star team at the World and European Championships in 1987 (Pool C).

CRO

GENNADY GORBACHEV Born in the former Soviet Union... Began his hockey career in Moscow with Krylja Sovetov and later played in the top Soviet League with Krylja Sovetov Moscow, Izhstal Izhevsk and Torpedo Togliatti (Division 2)... After finishing his career in Russia, he accepted the invitation to play hockey in Croatia... Became a Croatian citizen and was

invited to play for the national team in 1995... Had a brilliant performance at the 1995 World Championships (Pool C2) when the Croatian team won the tournament... He was the best scorer on his team at that event and second overall with 12 goals and five assists in six games... Named best forward of the tournament... Played for Croatia in two other World Championships.

SLO

GORAZD HITI Began playing for the Yugoslavian national team in 1969... Played at the 1972, 1976 and 1984 Olympics... Retired in the 1980s... Named the best forward at the World and European Championships in 1974 (Pool B)... Named to the all-star team at the World and European Championships in 1973 (Pool B) and 1974 (Pool B).

A superstar forward of Yugoslavian hockey for many years... Played for Jesenice and Olimpija Ljubljana... National champion from 1966 to 1970, and in 1972, 1975 and 1976.

SLO

RUDI HITI Began playing for the Yugoslavian Nation Team in 1965... Saw action at the 1972 Olympics... Retired in the 1980s... Named to the all-star team of the World and European Championships four straight times from 1971 to 1974 (all Pool B)... Named the head coach of the Slovenian national team in its first season of existence in 1992–93.

A superstar center of Yugoslavian hockey for many years... Played for Jesenice and Olimpija Ljubljana... His teams were national champions from 1964 to 1970, and in 1972 and 1975... Later played for HC Alleghe in Italy.

CRO

DRAGUTIN LJUBIC Became a member of the Croatian national team in 1994... Played at four World Championships (Pool C three times and Pool D once)... Starred at the 1995 Pool C2 tournament, helping his team to win it... Had an excellent goals-against average of 2.73 in six games and was named the best goaltender at the tournament.

SLO

DOMINIK LOMOVSEK Goaltender... Played for the Yugoslavian national team in the 1980s and early 1990s... Participated at the 1984 Olympics in Sarajevo, Yugoslavia... Played 12 seasons on the international level... Played for the Slovenian national team in its first international appearance: the 1993 (Pool C) World Championships... Saw action in four games that year and allowed only four goals against for a 1.81 average... Named the best goaltender at the World and European Championships in 1985 (Pool C) and 1989 (Pool C)... Named to the all-star team in 1985 (Pool C).

YUG

ZVONKO SUVAK Had great career with the Yugoslavian national team in the late 1970s and 1980s as one of the top scorers on the team... Played for the national team 10 seasons, beginning in 1979... Top scorer of 1979 (Pool C) World and European Championships with 21 goals and four assists for 25 points in seven games... Named to the all-star team at the World and European Championships in 1982 (Pool C).

SLO

TOMAZ VNUK Forward... A veteran of the Slovenian national team... Played at its first major international tournament, the 1993 World Championships (Pool C)... Has never missed a tournament since... Starred in 1993, collecting 10 goals and four assists for 14 points in seven games.

SLO

NIK ZUPANCIC Played for the Yugoslavian national team at the 1989 (Pool C) World and European Championships... In 1993, he played for the Slovenian national team at its first international competition, the World Championships (Pool C)... Has never missed a tournament since... In 1993, recorded nine goals and nine assists for 18 points in seven games... Named to the all-star team of the World Championships in 1996 (Pool C).

Section 3

WOMEN'S HOCKEY
BIOGRAPHICAL REGISTER

CANADA

CASSIE CAMPBELL was Canada's top-scoring defenseman at the 1997 Women's World Championships with two goals and six assists for the gold medal winners and was named to the tournament all-star team. She was also a member of Canada's Women's World Championship team in 1994. Campbell had a goal and two assists at the 1998 Nagano Olympics when Canada settled for a silver medal behind the United States. Campbell was the sportwoman of the year at Guelph University in 1996.

NANCY DROLET scored three goals, including the game winner in over-time, when Canada beat the United States in the gold medal game at the 1997 Women's World Championships. She was also a member of Canada's championship teams in 1994 and 1992 and represented her country at the Pacific Rim Championship in 1996. Drolet also played on the Canadian team that won a silver medal at the 1998 Olympic Games in Nagano. She is an all-round athlete and a top-class softball player.

DANIELLE GOYETTE Though her father died shortly before the Olympics, Danielle Goyette was Canada's leading scorer with nine points in Nagano and led the tournament with eight goals. She had the lone Canadian goal in the gold medal game. A great skater with an accurate shot, Goyette led Canada in scoring with 10 points (three goals and seven assists) at the 1992 World Championships and was an all-star at the 1994 tournament when she again led Canada with nine goals and 12 points. Goyette was a member of a third World Champion squad in 1997. She has also represented Canada at the Pacific Rim Championship in both 1995 and 1996, scoring the winning goal in a shootout with the Americans at the 1995 event.

GERALDINE HEANEY The best offensive defenseman on Canada's team, Geraldine Heaney was a member of the World Championship squads in 1990, 1992, 1994 and 1997. In both 1992 and 1994 she was named best defenseman at the Women's World Championships, an honor that she also garnered at the Pacific Rim Championship in 1996. Heaney collected six points to rank fourth in scoring for the Canadian team at the Winter Olympics in Nagano in 1998.

A fitness fanatic and an all-around athlete, Heaney is considered one of the top female in-line hockey players in the world. She has also been invited to try out for Northern Ireland's national women's soccer team.

ANGELA JAMES A legendary name among Canadian women's hockey, the decision to leave Angela James off the roster of the 1998 Olympic team was as controversial as the decision to leave Mark Messier off the men's team. James had been a member of Canada's champion teams at each of the previous four Women's World Championships.

James was Canada's leading scorer with 11 goals at the 1990 Women's World Championships and was an All-Star forward at the 1992 event. She had also been a top Canadian scoring threat at the 1994 and 1997 World tournaments and represented her country at the Pacific Championship in 1996.

KAREN NYSTROM A speedy right winger with a hard, accurate shot, Karen Nystrom was a member of Canada's IIHF Women's World Championship teams in 1992, 1994 and 1997. She also played for Canada at the Nagano Olympics in 1998. She was the top scorer in the Central Ontario Hockey League for three seasons.

An excellent soccer player in addition to her hockey skills, Nystrom was her high school's MVP in both sports from grade 9 through grade 13. She is also a five-time Ontario Cup winner in soccer.

LESLIE REDDON played on Ontario championship teams in each of her four seasons at the University of Toronto and was the first women every to play on the men's hockey team at the University of New Brunswick. She was the top goalie on the 1997 Canadian Women's World Championship team after sharing the job with Manon Rheaume in 1994. Reddon and Rheaume again shared netminding duties for Canada in Nagano in 1998.

MANON RHEAUME Perhaps the most famous female hockey player in the world, Manon Rheaume was the first woman to play with an NHL team when she saw action in a 1992 preseason game for the Tampa Bay Lightning. She has since played for a variety of men's minor-league teams.

Rheaume first appeared with Canada's National Women's Team in 1992.

She was named to the all-star team when Canada won the Women's World Championship in 1992 and 1994, but was cut from the team prior to the 1997 World Championships. An aggressive goaltender who can handle the puck well, Rheaume regained her spot on the national team and played well at the 1998 Olympics in Nagano.

FRANCE ST. LOUIS The oldest player on Canada's women's team at the 1998 Nagano Olympics, 39-year-old France St. Louis was a veteran of Canada's Women's World Championship teams of 1990, 1992, 1994 and 1997. She was the top scorer in the Quebec Senior Hockey League as a 38-year-old in 1996–97, but is noted as an outstanding defensive center who excels at winning face-offs. She was Quebec's female athlete of the decade in hockey and lacrosse for 1980 to 1990 and the athlete of the year in 1986.

VICKY SUNOHARA was a star player with Northeastern University and represented Canada at the first official Women's World Championships in 1990, collecting six goals and three assists in five games. She did not play with the national team again until 1997. Sunohara was a member of the Canadian women's team at the 1998 Olympics, where she attracted much attention due to the fact that her grandparents were born in Nagano.

HAYLEY WICKENHEISER A physically dominant player who is also an excellent passer, 19-year-old Hayley Wickenheiser's six assists led the women's Olympic tournament in Nagano in 1998. Her eight points ranked her second on her team, one point behind Danielle Goyette, and tied her for third at the Olympics. The Philadelphia Flyers offered her an invitation to work out at the team's rookie camp in 1998.

Wickenheiser first joined the Canadian Women's national team as a 15-year-old in 1994 and was part of championship wins in both 1994 and 1997. Her four goals and five assists at the 1997 tournament ranked second in scoring and earned her a spot on the all-star team. She has also represented Canada at the Pacific Rim Championship in 1995 and 1996. Growing up in Shaunavon, Saskatchewan, Wickenheiser consistently rated as the best player on boys teams in older age groups. As a 12-year-old in 1991, she scored the winning goal in the gold medal game in the 17-and-under girls division at the Canada Summer Games. Four years later she was a pitcher and shortstop with Canada's team at the 1995 World Junior Softball Championship. She is the fourth cousin of former NHL player Doug Wickenheiser.

STACY WILSON A veteran of Canada's Women's World Championship teams in 1990, 1992, 1994 and 1997, Stacy Wilson served as a team captain with tremendous leadership skills. In the national championship in 1997, Wilson had a medal she received as MVP of a game cut into 20 pieces in order to share it with her teammates. Her five assists at the Olympics in 1998 ranked her second on the Canadian team behind Hayley Wickenheiser and tied her for second overall in the tournament, though Canada had to settle for a silver medal behind the United States.

CHINA

HONG DANG was a member of the team from China that finished fifth at the Women's World Championships in 1992. She also played for the Chinese teams that finished fourth at the world event behind Canada, the United States and Finland in 1994 and 1997. Dang represented China at the Nagano Olympics in 1998 as a member of the team that finished fourth once again behind the U.S., Canada and Finland.

HONG GUO was a member of the Chinese national team at the Women's World Championships in 1992 and 1994. She emerged as one of the top goaltenders in women's hockey at the Pacific Rim Championship, helping China earn a bronze medal in 1995 and being named the best goalie at the event when China earned another bronze medal in 1996. Her stellar goaltending at the Nagano Olympics led China to the bronze medal game against Finland, though the Chinese team had to settle for fourth place after a 4–1 loss to the Finns.

WEI GUO scored three goals for China at the Nagano Olympics in 1998, tying for the lead on a team that finished fourth behind the United States, Canada and Finland. Guo had previously been a member of the Chinese teams that finished fourth behind Canada, the U.S. and Finland at the Women's World Championships in 1994 and 1997. She first played at the world tourney in 1992, when China finished fifth.

HONGMEI LIU had two goals and three assists in five games to tie for top spot in scoring on the Chinese team at the Nagano Olympics in 1998. China finished fourth at that tournament behind the United States, Canada and China.

Liu first appeared on the international arena at the Women's World Championships in 1992 and had eight goals and three assists to lead China to a fourth-place finish at the world tourney in 1994. China again finished fourth in 1997. Liu was a member of the Chinese team that earned a bronze medal behind the United States and Canada at the Pacific Championship in 1995.

DENMARK

KATJA MOESGAARD was a member of the Danish team the first time Denmark appeared at the Women's World Championships in 1992. In 1995, she collected four goals and four assists in four games for Denmark in the B Pool of the European Women's Championships.

FINLAND

SARI FISK played for Finland when the team won the European Women's Championship in 1991, collecting 10 goals and two assists for a Finnish team that outscored its opposition 71–0. In 1992, she won a bronze medal with Finland at the Women's World Championships and would win bronze again in 1994 and 1997. She was third on the team in scoring with six points (two goals and four assists) in six games when Finland once again earned a bronze medal, this time at the Olympics, in 1998. Fisk was also a member of the Finnish team that won the European Women's Championship in 1995.

MARIANNE IHALAINEN A veteran of the Finnish National Women's Team, Marianne Ihalainen was a member of the teams from Finland that won the bronze medal at the Women's World Championships in 1990, 1992, 1994 and 1997. She was also a member of the Finnish team that claimed the bronze medal at the Nagano

SARI KROOKS was a member of the Finnish team that came in third behind Canada and the United States at the Women's World Championships in 1990, 1992, 1994, and 1997. She played with the Olympic team from Finland that recorded a third-place finish behind the United States and Canada at the Nagano Olympics in 1998. Krooks also played for the Finnish teams that won the European Women's Championship in 1989 and 1995. She was named to the tournament all-star team in 1995 after collecting six goals and eight assists in five games.

MARIKA LEHTIMAKI is a veteran of women's hockey in Finland, helping the Finnish team win the European Women's Championship in 1993, 1995 and 1996. She also played for third-place teams from Finland at the Women's World Championships in 1990, 1992 and 1994. Though she missed the World Championships in 1997, Lehtimaki was again a member of the Finnish team when Finland earned a bronze medal at the Nagano Olympics in 1998.

RIIKKA NIEMINEN One of the top offensive talents in women's hockey, Finland's Riikka Nieminen led the Olympic tournament in scoring with 12 points, and was second behind Canada's Danielle Goyette with seven goals, in Nagano in 1998. Nieminen led Finland to a bronze medal that year after having played with Finnish teams that had placed third at the Women's World Championships in 1990, 1992, 1994 and 1997. She was named a tournament all-star in 1992, 1994 and 1997 and was also named the best forward in 1994 after collecting 13 points (four goals and nine assists) in five games. Nieminen had nine goals and 14 assists in five games in 1995 when she led Finland to a gold medal in the European Women's Championship. She had also earned gold at the European event in 1989.

GERMANY

MAREN VALENTI played for West Germany at the first official Women's World Championships in 1990. She had three goals and two assists on a low-scoring team that finished in fourth place at the European Women's Championships in 1993. In 1994, she played for the German team at the Women's World Championships. In 1995 she had four goals and three assists on a German team that scored only 11 goals at the European Championships.

NETHERLANDS

SASKIA ADMIRAAL played for Holland in the B Pool of the European World Championships in 1995. She had two goals and three assists for five points in four games at the tournament.

NORWAY

MARIANNE DAHLSTROM In 1989, Marianne Dahlstrom had nine points (three goals and six assists) in five games as Norway turned in a fourth-place performance at the European Women's Championships. Dahlstrom also represented Norway at the Women's World Championships in 1992, 1994 and 1997.

INGER LISE FAGERNES was a top-scoring player for Norwegian teams that managed sixth-place finishes at the Women's Worlds in 1990, 1992 and 1994. When she was kept off the scoreboard in five games at the 1997 event, Norway fell into eighth (last) place. Fagernes was a member of the Norwegian team that finished fourth at the European Women's Championships in 1991 and that won a bronze medal at the European tourney in 1993.

RUSSIA

YEKATERINA PASHKEVICH collected five goals and 14 assists in just four games for Russia while playing in the B Pool of the European World Championships in 1995. In 1996, she had six goals in five games and was a tournament all-star as Russia earned a silver medal behind Sweden in the A Pool of the European World Championships. The performance earned Russia a spot in the 1997 Women's World Championships, where Pashkevich collected three goals for a Russian team that finished sixth.

TATJANA TSAREVA had eight goals and four assists in just four games for Russia in the B Pool of the European Women's World Championships in 1995. In 1997, she was a member of the first Russian team to make an appearance at the Women's World Championships.

SWITZERLAND

RAMONA FHURER was a member of the Swiss National Women's Team at the Women's World Championships in 1994 and 1997.

RUTH KUNZLE represented Switzerland at the Women's World Championships in 1992, 1994 and 1997.

EDITH NIEDERHAUSER is a veteran of the Swiss National Women's Team, representing Switzerland at the Women's World Championships in 1990, 1992, 1994 and 1997. Niederhauser had four goals and three assists to lead the Swiss team to a fifth place finish in 1990, the country's best result at the world event.

PATRICIA SAUTTER played for Switzerland's National Women's Team at the Women's World Championships in 1994 and 1997. Though Switzerland surrendered 27 goals in five games at the 1997 event, Sautter's outstanding goaltending earned her a spot on the tournament all-star team. She earned a shutout in a 1–0 victory over Norway that lifted Switzerland to a seventh-place finish that year.

SWEDEN

LOTTA ALMBLAD was a member of the Swedish National Women's Team at the Women's World Championships in 1992, 1994, and 1997. She also represented Sweden at the Nagano Olympics in 1998. Almblad was a member of the Swedish team that ranked second to Finland at the 1995 Women's World Championships and played for the team that won the European tourney in 1996.

GUNILLA ANDERSSON A veteran of the Swedish National Women's Team, Gunilla Anderson has represented Sweden at the Women's World Championships in 1992, 1994 and 1997. She also played at the Nagano Olympics in 1998. Anderson was named the best defenseman after helping Sweden finish second behind Finland at the European Women's Championships in 1995.

KRISTINA BERGSTRAND represented Sweden at the European Women's Championships in 1989 and 1991. In 1991 she was named to the tournament all-star team and also picked as the best forward after tallying eight goals and 12 assists for 20 points in just five games. Sweden finished second behind Finland that year. Bergstrand has also represented Sweden at the Women's World Championships in 1990, 1992, 1994 and 1997. The Swedish veteran also played at the Nagano Olympics in 1998.

CAMILLA KEMPE played for Sweden at the Women's World Championships in 1990, 1992, 1994 and 1997, collecting five goals in five games at the event in both 1990 and 1992. She was also a member of the Swedish team that came in second behind Finland at the European Women's Championships in 1993.

USA

LISA MILLER-BROWN was the only married member of the gold medal-winning United States National Women's Team at the Nagano Olympics in 1998. She was married in August of 1995 and left the next day for the U.S. National Women's Team training camp. In 1996, she gave up her job as head coach of the women's team at Princeton University in order to train full time for the national team.

Miller-Brown is considered one of the American team's strongest players and is a determined forechecker who anchored the team's penalty-killing unit. In addition to her Olympic experience, she played with the U.S. team that finished second behind Canada at the Women's World Championships in 1990, 1992, 1994 and 1997. She also took part in the Pacific Championship in 1995.

KARYN BYE was the United States' top scorer with five goals in six games on the gold medal-winning women's team at the 1998 Nagano Olympics. She is considered to have one of the hardest shots in women's hockey and is a good skater with excellent puck control who has averaged a goal per game in international competition.

Bye played high school hockey on the boys team in River Falls, Wisconsin before going on to play women's university hockey at New Hampshire. As a member of the United States National Women's Team, she has appeared at the Women's World Championships in 1992, 1994, and 1997 where the Americans finished second behind Canada every year. Bye was named to the tournament all-star team in 1994. She has also represented the United States at the Pacific Rim Championship in 1995 and 1996.

COLLEEN COYNE The top defensive defenseman on the United States National Women's Team, Colleen Coyne helped the U.S. record the lowest team goals-against average (1.33) en route to winning the gold medal over Canada at the Nagano Olympics in 1998. Coyne had previously been a member of the U.S. teams that had lost the Women's World Championship to Canada in 1992, 1994 and 1997.

In addition to her international experience, Coyne starred in women's university hockey at New Hampshire. She was also an all-American in lacrosse in 1989 and was the assistant coach with the women's hockey team in 1993–94 while continuing her studies.

CAMMI GRANATO One of only two American players (along with Lisa Miller-Brown) to appear in each of the first four Women's World Championships, Cammi Granato's 27 goals and 44 points in 20 games make her the leading scorer in the history of the tournament through 1997. After losing to Canada in 1990, 1992, 1994 and 1997, Granato captained the United States team to a gold medal victory at the 1998 Olympic Games in Nagano. Her four goals and four assists at the Olympics ranked her in a four-way tie for top spot on the American squad.

The brother of NHL player Tony Granato, Cammie Granato has done more than any other player to popularize women's hockey in the United States. She has been named both the best forward and a member of the tournament all-star team at the Women's World Championships in 1992 and 1997 and has also represented the United States at the Pacific Championship in 1995 and 1996.

SHELLEY LOONEY was one of the American team's top scorers with four goals in six games as the United States won the gold medal in women's hockey at the 1998 Nagano Olympics. Her goal at 10:57 of the second period in the gold medal game against Canada gave the Americans a 2–0 lead and proved to be the game winner in a 3–1 victory.

A tough competitor and all-around player who is solid both offensively and defensively, Looney suffered a broken jaw at the World Championships in 1997 after blocking a shot in overtime in the gold medal game eventually won by Canada. Previously, Looney had played for the U.S. team that was beaten by Canada for the World Championship in 1992 and 1994. She also represented her country at the Pacific Rim Championship in 1995.

TARA MOUNSEY Although she was the third-youngest player on the United States National Women's Team at the 1998 Nagano Olympics, 19-year-old Tara Mounsey was considered the team's top defenseman and possible the best all-around talent. A slick skater with a booming shot, Mounsey's six points (two goals and four assists) in six games topped all American defenseman at the Olympics and ranked her sixth overall in scoring for the gold medal winners.

Dubbed "the Bobby Orr of Women's Hockey," Mounsey starred on a boys high school team in Concord, New Hampshire before going on to play women's hockey at Brown University. Prior to the Olympics, she had represented the United States at the Women's World Championships in 1997.

ERIN WHITTEN Fourteen months after Canadian goaltender Manon Rheaume broke the gender barrier by appearing in a 1992 Tampa Bay Lightning NHL exhibition game, American Erin Whitten began playing with the Toledo Storm of the East Coast Hockey League. On October 30, 1993, Whitten became the first female goaltender to record a victory in a professional game.

A high school star on the boys team in her hometown of Glens Falls, New York, Whitten developed into an elite goaltender during four seasons of women's university hockey at New Hampshire. She was the top goaltender on the United States National Women's Team, appearing at the Women's World Championships in 1992, 1994 and 1997 where the team finished second behind Canada every year. In 1994, Whitten was named the best goalie at the tournament.

HOCKEY HALL OF FAME AND UNITED STATES HOCKEY HALL OF FAME MEMBERS

HOCKEY HALL OF FAME

PLAYERS

Abel, Sid
* Adams, Jack
Apps, Syl
Armstrong, George
* Bailey, Ace
* Bain, Dan
* Baker, Hobey
Barber, Bill
* Barry, Marty
Bathgate, Andy
* Bauer, Bobby
Beliveau, Jean
* Benedict, Clint
* Bentley, Doug
* Bentley, Max
* Blake, Hector "Toe"
Boivin, Leo
* Boon, Dickie
Bossy, Mike
Bouchard, Emile "Butch"
* Boucher, Frank
* Boucher, George
Bower, Johnny
* Bowie, Russell
Brimsek, Frank
* Broadbent, Harry "Punch"
* Broda, Walter "Turk"
Bucyk, John
* Burch, Billy
* Cameron, Harry
Cheevers, Gerry
* Clancy, Francis "King"
* Clapper, Aubrey "Dit"
Clarke, Bobby
* Cleghorn, Sprague
* Colville, Neil
* Conacher, Charlie
* Conacher, Lionel
* Connell, Alex
* Cook, Fred "Bun"
* Cook, Bill
Coulter, Art
Cournoyer, Yvan
* Cowley, Bill
* Crawford, Rusty
* Darragh, Jack
* Davidson, Scotty
* Day, Clarence "Hap"
Delvecchio, Alex
* Denneny, Cy
Dionne, Marcel
* Drillon, Gordie
* Drinkwater, Charles Graham
Dryden, Ken
Dumart, Woody
* Dunderdale, Thomas
* Durnan, Bill
* Dutton, Mervyn "Red"
* Dye, Cecil "Babe"
Esposito, Tony
Esposito, Phil
* Farrell, Arthur
Flaman, Fern
* Foyston, Frank
* Fredrickson, Frank
Gadsby, Bill
Gainey, Bob
* Gardiner, Charlie
* Gardiner, Herb
* Gardner, Jimmy
Geoffrion, Bernie "Boom Boom"
* Gerard, Eddie
Giacomin, Eddie
Gilbert, Rod
* Gilmour, Billy
* Goheen, Frank X. "Moose"
* Goodfellow, Ebbie
* Grant, Mike
* Green, Wilfred "Shorty"
* Griffis, Si
* Hainsworth, George
Hall, Glenn

* Hall, Joe
* Harvey, Doug
* Hay, George
* Hern, Riley
* Hextall, Bryan Sr.
* Holmes, Harry "Hap"
* Hooper, Tom
Horner, Reginald "Red"
* Horton, Tim
Howe, Gordie
* Howe, Syd
Howell, Harry
Hull, Bobby
* Hutton, Bouse
* Hyland, Harry
* Irvin, Dick
* Jackson, Harvey "Busher"
* Johnson, Ernie "Moose"
* Johnson, Ivan "Ching"
Johnson, Tom
* Joliat, Aurel
* Keats, Gordon "Duke"
Kelly, Leonard "Red"
Kennedy, Teeder
Keon, Dave
Lach, Elmer
Lafleur, Guy
* Lalonde, Edouard "Newsy"
Laperriere, Jacques
Lapointe, Guy
Laprade, Edgar
* Laviolette, Jack
* Lehman, Hugh
Lemaire, Jacques
Lemieux, Mario
* LeSueur, Percy
* Lewis, Herbie
Lindsay, Ted
Lumley, Harry
* MacKay, Duncan "Mickey"
Mahovlich, Frank
* Malone, Joe
* Mantha, Sylvio
* Marshall, Jack
* Maxwell, Fred "Steamer"
McDonald, Lanny
* McGee, Frank
* McGimsie, Billy
* McNamara, George
Mikita, Stan
Moore, Dickie
* Moran, Paddy
* Morenz, Howie
* Mosienko, Billy
* Nighbor, Frank
* Noble, Reg
* O'Connor, Herbert "Buddy"
* Oliver, Harry
Olmstead, Bert
Orr, Bobby
Parent, Bernie
Park, Brad
* Patrick, Lynn
* Patrick, Lester
Perreault, Gilbert
* Phillips, Tommy
Pilote, Pierre
* Pitre, Didier
* Plante, Jacques
Potvin, Denis
* Pratt, Walter "Babe"
* Primeau, Joe
Pronovost, Marcel
Pulford, Bob
* Pulford, Harvey
Quackenbush, Bill
* Rankin, Frank
Ratelle, Jean
Rayner, Chuck
Reardon, Kenny
Richard, Henri
Richard, Maurice "Rocket"
* Richardson, George
* Roberts, Gordon
Robinson, Larry

* Ross, Art
* Russel, Blair
* Russell, Ernie
* Ruttan, Jack
Salming, Borje
Savard, Serge
* Sawchuk, Terry
* Scanlan, Fred
Schmidt, Milt
* Schriner, David "Sweeney"
* Seibert, Earl
* Seibert, Oliver
* Shore, Eddie
Shutt, Steve
* Siebert, Albert "Babe"
* Simpson, Harold "Bullet Joe"
Sittler, Darryl
Smith, Alf
Smith, Clint
* Smith, Reginald "Hooley"
* Smith, Tommy
Smith, Billy
* Stanley, Allan
* Stanley, Barney
* Stewart, John "Black Jack"
* Stewart, Nels
* Stuart, Bruce
* Stuart, Hod
* Taylor, Fred "Cyclone"
* Thompson, Cecil "Tiny"
Tretiak, Vladislav
Trottier, Bryan
* Trihey, Harry
Ullman, Norm
* Vezina, Georges
* Walker, Jack
* Walsh, Marty
* Watson, Harry E.
* Watson, Harry
* Weiland, Ralph "Cooney"
* Westwick, Harry
* Whitcroft, Fred
* Wilson, Gordon "Phat"
Worsley, Lorne "Gump"
* Worters, Roy

BUILDERS

Adams, Charles
* Adams, Weston W.
* Aheam, Frank
* Ahearne, J.F. "Bunny"
* Allan, Sir Montagu
Allen, Keith
Arbour, Al
* Ballard, Harold
* Bauer, Father David
* Bickell, John Paris
Bowman, Scott
* Brown, George V.
* Brown, Walter A.
* Buckland, Frank
Butterfield, Jack
* Calder, Frank
* Campbell, Angus
* Campbell, Clarence
* Cattarinich, Joseph
* Dandurand, J.V. "Leo"
* Dilio, Frank
* Dudley, George
* Dunn, Jimmy
Francis, Emile
* Gibson, J.L. "Doc"
* Gorman, Tommy
* Griffiths, Frank A.
* Hanley, William
* Hay, Charles
* Hendy, Jim
* Hewitt, Foster
* Hewitt, W.A.
* Hume, Fred
* Imlach, George "Punch"
Ivan, Tommy
* Jennings, Bill
* Johnson, Bob
* Juckes, Gordon

* Kilpatrick, Gen. John Reed
* Knox, Seymour III
* Leader, Al
LeBel, Robert
* Lockhart, Thomas
* Loicq, Paul
* Mariucci, John
Mathers, Frank
* McLaughlin, Major Frederic
* Milford, Jake
Molson, Hon. Hartland
* Nelson, Francis
* Norris, Bruce A.
* Norris, James Sr.
* Norris, James
* Northey, William
* O'Brien, Ambrose
O'Neill, Brian
* Page, Fred
* Patrick, Frank
* Pickard, Allan
* Pilous, Rudy
Poile, Norman "Bud"
Pollock, Sam
* Raymond, Sen. Donat
* Robertson, John Ross
* Robinson, Claude
* Ross, Philip D.
Sabetzki, Gunther
Sather, Glen
* Selke, Frank J.
Sinden, Harry
* Smith, Frank
* Smythe, Conn
Snider, Ed
* Stanley of Preston, Lord
* Sutherland, James T.
* Tarasov, Anatoli
Torrey, Bill
* Turner, Lloyd
* Tutt, William Thayer
* Voss, Carl
* Waghorn, Fred
* Wirtz, Arthur
Wirtz, Bill
Ziegler, John A. Jr.

REFEREES/LINESMEN

Armstrong, Neil
Ashley, John
Chadwick, Bill
D'Amico, John
* Elliott, Chaucer
* Hayes, George
* Hewitson, Bobby
* Ion, Mickey
Pavelich, Matt
* Rodden, Mike
* Smeaton, Cooper
Storey, Roy "Red"
Udvari, Frank

UNITED STATES HOCKEY HALL OF FAME

PLAYERS

* Abel, Clarence Taffy
* Baker, Hobey
Bartholome, Earl
* Bessone, Peter
Blake, Bob
Boucha, Henry
* Brimsek, Frank
Cavanagh, Joe
* Chaisson, Ray
* Chase, John
Christian, Roger
Christian, Bill
Cleary, Bob
Cleary, Bill
* Conroy, Tony
Dahlstrom, Carl "Cully"
* Desjardins, Victor
* Desmond, Richard

* Dill, Bob
* Everett, Doug
Ftorek, Robbie
* Garrison, John
Garrity, Jack
* Goheen, Frank X. "Moose"
Grant, Wally
* Harding, Austie
* Iglehart, Stewart
* Johnson, Virgil
* Karakas, Mike
Kirrane, Jack
* Lane, Myles
Langevin, Dave
Larson, Reed
* Linder, Joseph
* LoPresti, Sam
* Mariucci, John
Matchefts, John
Mayasich, John
McCartan, Jack
Moe, Billy
Morrow, Ken
* Moseley, Fred
* Murray, Muzz
* Nelson, Hub
* Nyrop, Bill
Olson, Eddie
* Owen, Jr., George
* Palmer, Winthrop "Ding"
Paradise, Robert
Purpur, Clifford "Fido"
Riley, Bill
* Romnes, Elwin "Doc"
Rondeau, Dick
Sheehy, Tim
* Williams, Tommy
* Winters, Coddy
* Yackel, Ken

COACHES

* Almquist, Oscar
Bessone, Amo
Brooks, Herb
Ceglarski, Len
* Fullerton, James
Gambucci, Sergio
* Gordon, Malcolm
Harkness, Ned
Heyliger, Vic
Holt, Charlie
Ikola, Willard
* Jeremiah, Eddie
* Johnson, Bob
* Kelley, John "Snooks"
Kelley, Jack
Patrick, Craig
Pleban, Connie
Riley, Jack
* Ross, Larry
* Thompson, Cliff
* Stewart, Bill
* Winsor, Ralph

ADMINISTRATORS

* Brown, George V.
* Brown, Walter A.
Bush, Walter
Clark, Donald
Claypool, James
* Gibson, J.C. "Doc"
* Jennings, Bill
* Kahler, Nick
* Lockhart, Tommy
Marvin, Cal
Ridder, Bob
Schulz, Charles M.
Trumble, Hal
* Tutt, William Thayer
Wirtz, Bill
* Wright, Lyle

REFEREE

Chadwick, Bill

* Deceased

NOTES ON CONTRIBTORS AND ACKNOWLEDGMENTS

CONTRIBUTORS

Kevin Allen has been *USA Today*'s hockey beat writer since 1986. He is the author of *USA Hockey: A Celebration of a Great Tradition* and *Shootin' and Smilin'*, a biography of Brett Hull. He is a member of the Professional Hockey Writers Association and the Hockey Hall of Fame Selection Committee.

Ron Andrews works for The Sports Network in Toronto. He was a longtime statistician for the NHL, helping to modernize the way in which the league handled its statistics.

Ted Barris is the author of *Playing Overtime: A Celebration of Oldtimers' Hockey*.

Pavel Barta is a noted hockey journalist in the Czech Republic. For the last decade he has covered hockey for *Gol* magazine, the largest sports weekly in the Czech Republic.

Mike Board covers the Calgary Flames for the *Calgary Herald*.

Ron Boileau is the president of the British Columbia Junior Hockey League and a member of the Society for International Hockey Research.

Frank Bonello played with the Whitby Dunlops, Allan Cup and IIHF World Champions. He later coached the Toronto Marlboros junior club. He is the director of the NHL's Central Scouting Service.

Paul Bontje is a Toronto-based freelance researcher who has specialized in the intricacies of the NHL Amateur and Entry drafts.

Bob Borgen produces Los Angeles Kings television broadcasts for Fox Sports West. He is a member of the Society for International Hockey Research.

Tim Campbell covers hockey and other sports for the *Winnipeg Free Press*. He covered the Winnipeg Jets when that franchise was located in Manitoba.

Cammy Clark is a hockey columnist who covers the Mighty Ducks of Anaheim and the Los Angeles Kings for the *Orange County Register*.

Donald M. Clark is a member, as well as the past president, of the United States Hockey Hall of Fame. He is a co-founder of the Minnesota Amateur Hockey Association and was vice president of the Amateur Hockey Association of the United States. He is a recipient of the Lester Patrick Trophy for service to American hockey.

Pat Conway (contributing statistician) provided much of the biographical information used in *Total Hockey*. Mr Conway collected telephone books from numerous communities in Canada and the United States and painstakingly phoned or wrote to all the former players he could find. He passed away in 1994.

Dan Diamond (editor) designed the *NHL Official Guide & Record Book* in 1984 and has edited numerous books about the sport including the *Official NHL 75th Anniversary Book*. He has asked Gordie Howe for his autograph in four different decades.

Ralph Dinger (managing editor) is an experienced researcher and editor who has specialized in goaltending records. He is managing editor of the *NHL Official Guide & Record Book*.

Phil Drackett played, coached and managed professional ice hockey in Britain and is the author of several sports books, including *Flashing Blades*, a history of British ice hockey. He edited the hockey magazine *Ice Hockey World*, first published in 1935, and was the first man elected to honorary life membership of the British Ice Hockey Writers Association.

Alex Dubiel (contributing statistician) is a musician and data base manager who has developed computer programs vital to updating *Total Hockey*'s statistical data.

Bob Duff is a hockey historian whose detailed statistical research has uncovered much information about the early years of the NHL. He covers the Detroit Red Wings for the *Windsor Star* and was the research editor for *The Hockey Encyclopedia* in 1983. He is a member of the Society for International Hockey Research.

Milt Dunnell is one of Canada's most distinguished sports editors and writers, having covered hockey and a wide range of sporting topics for the *Toronto Star* for more than half a century. He is a recipient of the Hockey Hall of Fame's Elmer Ferguson Memorial Award for writing.

James Duplacey (managing editor) is a former curator of the Hockey Hall of Fame. He is the author of the Hockey Superstars series of children's books and frequently consulted on matters of hockey history by broadcasters and journalists.

Jack Falla floods his backyard rink near Boston. He is a former staffer with *Sports Illustrated*, for whom he wrote the instructional book *Sports Illustrated Hockey: Learn to Play the Modern Way*. He has also worked for the NHL

Ivan Filippov lives and works in Vancouver and Prague. His company, Bynamics Corporation, exports North American hockey-related products into the Czech Republic.

Stan and Shirley Fischler operate the Fischler Hockey Service in New York. Stan has authored some 70 books about hockey, many in collaboration with Shirley, including *The Hockey Encyclopedia* in 1983. He also works as a commentator on telecasts of New York Islanders and New Jersey Devils games and is a contributor to *The Hockey News*.

Bill Fitsell is a freelance writer and founding president of the Society for International Hockey Research. He has been a longtime contributor to the *Kingston Whig-Standard* in his home town of Kingston, Ontario.

Ernie Fitzsimmons (consulting statistician) is one of hockey's leading statistical historians. He has worked as the statistician for the Fredericton Canadiens of the American Hockey League. He is a member of the Society for International Hockey Research.

Bruce Garrioch covers the Ottawa Senators hockey club for the *Ottawa Sun*.

Denis Gibbons specializes in international and Olympic hockey history. He did statistical work for CBS on network television coverage of hockey from the Nagano Olympic Games and has also worked for *The Hockey News*. He is a member of the Society for International Hockey Research

Roger Godin is a former director of the United States Hockey Hall of Fame. His hockey specialty is the history of the American game, particularly at the collegiate level. He is a member of the Society for International Hockey Research and lives in Bel Air, Maryland.

Glen R. Goodhand is an ordained minister with an avid interest in hockey history. He has contributed columns to newspapers in the Beaverton, Ontario area and is a founding member of the Society for International Hockey Research.

Jeff Gordon has covered hockey for the *St. Louis Post-Dispatch* since 1986. His work has appeared in *The Hockey News*, *The Sporting News*, *Inside Sports*, *Hockey Digest*, *Rinkside*, *Power Play* and *Hockey Stars*.

Chrys Goyens co-wrote *Lions in Winter*, a history of the Montreal Canadiens, and *My Life in Hockey* with Jean Beliveau. He is also the author of children's books about the Toronto Maple Leafs and Montreal Canadiens. He was part of the editorial team that produced *The Montreal Forum: 1924–1996*.

Stu Hackel is a life-long hockey fan who writes about hockey for *The Village Voice* in New York. He is a former editor of *Goal Magazine*.

John Halligan is a longtime public relations executive for both the New York Rangers and the NHL.

Billy Harris is a former member of the Toronto Maple Leafs who coached in the World Hockey Association and in Europe. An avid photographer, many of his pictures appeared in his book *The Glory Years* about the Maple Leafs of the 1960s.

Martin Harris (contributing statistician) is Britain's foremost hockey historian. He is a former council member of the British Ice Hockey Association and a member of the Society for International Hockey Research.

Tom Hoffarth has covered the media (radio, television, computers etc.) for the *Los Angeles Daily News* for the past six years. He has written for several different Los Angeles-area newspapers over the past 20 years.

William Humber is a member of both the Society for International Hockey Research and the Society for American Baseball Research. He is a sports historian who has written several books and/or articles about baseball in Canada, hockey and soccer.

Douglas Hunter is a freelance writer, editor and graphic designer. He is the author of two books about yacht racing as well as the hockey books *War Games*, *Open Ice: The Tim Horton Story* and *A Breed Apart: An Illustrated History of Goaltending*.

Dick Irvin is a longtime Montreal-based broadcaster whose first book, the biographical *Now Back to You Dick*, was released in 1988. The son of legendary coach Dick Irvin Sr., he has also written about coaches and goaltenders. His most recent book is *Tough Calls: NHL Referees and Linesmen Tell Their Story*.

Marina Joukova (contributing statistician) worked for the Soviet Hockey Federation as a statistician in the late 1980s. She was responsible for one of the first projects that computerized Soviet hockey statistics.

Brian Kendall is the author of *100 Great Moments In Hockey* and *Shutout: The Legend of Terry Sawchuk*.

Paul Kitchen is a longtime member of the Society for International Hockey Research who has served as the organization's president in recent years.

Jeff Z. Klein is a staff editor with *The New York Times Magazine*. From 1990 through 1995 he was a sports editor at *The Village Voice*. He has written several books about hockey, many in collaboration with Karl-Eric Reif. His short story entitled "Now I Can Die in Peace" appeared in the fiction anthology *Original Six*.

Steve Knowles is the information coordinator for the public relations department of the Edmonton Oilers. He is also involved in university hockey in Western Canada.

Igor Kuperman (international editor) began compiling hockey statistics in his native Moscow. He worked as a sports journalist in the Soviet Union before coming to North America in 1991. He works in the hockey operations department of the Phoenix Coyotes.

Eero Lehti is the manager of youth hockey programs for the Finnish Ice Hockey Association.

Al Mason (contributing statistician) played Junior A hockey and later coached in the Metropolitan Toronto Hockey League. Since 1985, he has scouted for Ontario Hockey League teams. He is a longtime collector of hockey and baseball statistical books.

Gary Mason is the sports editor and a columnist with the *Vancouver Sun*. He covers the Vancouver Canucks.

William Martin is an attorney in Chicago and co-author of *The Crime of the Century*. He is a member of the Society for International Hockey Research.

Brian McFarlane has worked as a commentator on "Hockey Night in Canada," NBC and CBS. He is a recipient of the Foster Hewitt Memorial Award for broadcasting and has written more than 30 books about hockey. He is a member of the Society for International Hockey Research and operates his own hockey museum.

Ross McKeon covers the San Jose Sharks for the *San Francisco Examiner*.

Gary Meagher (senior contributing editor) has worked with the National Hockey League since 1981. He is currently vice president, public relations and media services.

Scott Morrison is the sports editor of the *Toronto Sun*. He is also a columnist with the newspaper and the author of *Fire on Ice* about Eric Lindros and *The Day Canada Stood Still* about the 1972 Canada–Russia series.

Morris Mott is a former member of the Canadian national hockey team. He is currently a professor of history at Brandon University in Brandon, Manitoba. He is a member of the Society for International Hockey Research.

Don Munro was the longtime president of Munro Games, makers of table-top hockey games into the 1970s. His father, Don Munro Sr., invented the first table-top hockey game during the Great Depression.

Harry Neale was a member of the 1956 Memorial Cup champion Toronto Marlboros. He later became a coach in the World Hockey Association and a coach and general manager in the NHL before turning to broadcasting. Currently, he is the lead analyst for Toronto Maple Leafs and CBC telecasts.

Roger Neilson became a head coach with his seventh NHL team when he took over the Philadelphia Flyers during the 1997–98 season. He enters 1998–99 ranked 11th in all-time NHL games coached. He led the Vancouver Canucks to the Stanley Cup finals in 1982 and the New York Rangers to the Presidents' Trophy in 1992.

Don O'Hanley is a former American Hockey League statistician and publicist and an expert on the history of New York-area hockey. He is a member of the Society for International Hockey Research

Frank Orr is a recipient of the Hockey Hall of Fame's Elmer Ferguson Memorial Award for writing. Retired now, he was a longtime columnist for the *Toronto Star*. He is the author of several books about hockey.

Mark Paddock is a former arts columnist who now works as a freelance hockey journalist and editor. A graduate of King's College in Halifax, he resides in St. John's Newfoundland. He is the co-author of *The NHL: Today's Stars, Tomorrow's Legends*.

John Pasternak (data management) developed the data base of player and goaltender statistics for *Total Hockey* and the *NHL Official Guide & Record Book*. He lives and works in Hillsburgh, Ontario.

John Paton (contributing statistician) is a retired banker who traveled to numerous communities in Ontario to research and compile detailed statistical histories of Ontario Hockey Association junior and senior leagues.

Arthur Pincus (senior editorial consultant) is a veteran sports editor who has worked for the *New York Times* and *Washington Post*. He was hired as the NHL's vice president of public relations in 1993.

Andrew Podnieks is a hockey historian and photographer and a former creative writing teacher. His is the author of *Canada's Olympic Hockey Teams: The Complete History 1920-1998* and *Portraits of the Game*, as well as *The Blue & White Book* and several other books about hockey.

Thomas D. Picard is an avid compiler of hockey statistics. He lives in Seven Sisters Falls, Manitoba.

Tom Ratschunas is the leading hockey statistician in Europe. He edited the *IIHF International Hockey Guide* during the 1970s and 1980s. He provides statistical services to many European hockey leagues and IIHF competitions.

Rob Raven is an avid collector of table-top hockey games. He is active on the collectables circuit, where he is known as "the Table Hockey Kid."

Jim Regan is a former school teacher who played collegiate hockey in New Brunswick.

Karl-Eric Reif has worked for 15 years as a sportswriter, columnist and cartoonist for *The Village Voice*, *The American*, *The Hockey*

News and other publications. He has co-authored several books about hockey with Jeff Z. Klein.

Stewart Roberts (contributing statistician) is a freelance journalist specializing in hockey. He has been editor/publisher of the British hockey yearbook *The Ice Hockey Annual* since 1976 and is a former publicity officer of the British Ice Hockey Association.

John Sanful is an avid enthusiast of Russian athletic and political history from Czarist Russia to post-Soviet times. He has published the book *Russian Revolution: Exodus to the NHL* and co-authored the upcoming *Mo: The Mike Modano Story*. He runs his own company, Little Odessa Productions.

David Spaner has worked as a feature writer, reporter and editor for numerous publications. He is currently employed at the *Vancouver Province*.

Jan Stark is the editor of the Swedish hockey annual *Årets Ishockey*. He has covered the game since 1973 and is one of the founding members of the Swedish Professional Icehockey Writers Association, as well as the Swedish Icehockey Historical and Statistical Society.

Ed Sweeney is a hockey researcher and historian in his native Winnipeg who is in the process of completing *The History of Manitoba Hockey, the First Fifty Years. Volume One*. He is the curator of the Manitoba Hockey Hall of Fame, a director of the Manitoba Hockey Foundation and a member of the Society for International Hockey Research.

Chris Tredree works with the NHL public relations department in Toronto.

Dr. Garth Vaughan is the author of *The Puck Starts Here: The origins of Canada's great winter game, Ice Hockey*. He is keenly interested in the history of Windsor, Nova Scotia and actively involved in the Windsor Hockey Heritage Centre. He is a member of the Society for International Hockey Research.

Michel Vigneault is a hockey researcher and author specializing in French Canadian sports history in Montreal and Quebec. He is a member of the Society for International Hockey Research.

Gordon Wade (contributing statistician) has been Britain's senior hockey statistician since 1982. He is the statistician for Britain's ice hockey Superleague and for Rupert Murdoch's British cable TV channel SkySport.

Tim Wharnsby is a columnist and sports editor with the *Toronto Sun*. He traveled to Nagano to cover the 1998 Winter Olympics.

Peter Wilton is a Toronto-based journalist who specializes in medical issues and Canadian history. In addition to his published work, he is a guest correspondent for CBC radio.

Eric Zweig (managing editor) is the author of the historical novel *Hockey Night in the Dominion of Canada*. He has written about sports history for several Canadian media outlets including *The Globe and Mail*, *The Beaver* and CBC Radio.

REFERENCES

Authors names follow book titles where appropriate:

NHL Entry Draft Book, NHL Official Guide and Record Book, NHL Guide, NHL Playoff Fact Guide, NHL Official Rule Book, NHL Year in Review, The Hockey News, The Sporting News, media guides from NHL teams, minor pro and junior leagues, *The Trail of the Stanley Cup* (Charles Coleman), *The Blue & White Book, The Red Wing Book* and *Canada's Olympic Hockey Teams: The Complete History 1920-1998* (Andrew Podnieks), *Canada on Ice* (Robert Kirk), *The College Hockey Guide, The Hockey Encyclopedia* (Stan and Shirley Fischler with Bob Duff), *Mackie's Hockey Atlas* (Roy W. Mackie), *The (Annotated) Rules of Hockey* (James Duplacey), *USA Hockey* (Kevin Allen) *United States Hockey Hall of Fame* souvenir book and *World Hockey Association 1972–1979* (Scott Adam Surgent).

PHOTO CREDITS

Interior photo credits – Harold Barkley – 621; Bruce Bennett Studios, 49; Collection of Dan Diamond and Associates, 441, 557; Hockey Hall of Fame, 1; Hockey Hall of Fame – Imperial Oil Turofsky Collection, 373;

ACKNOWLEDGMENTS

Thanks to the following contributors:

Copy Editors – David Coates, Lloyd Davis, Mark Paddock, Sheila Wawanash, Jonathan Zweig.

Jim Anderson (IHL), Don Andrews, Joe Bertagna, Mike A. Boland, Bruce Bennett, Tim Bryant (IHL), Paul R. Carroll Jr., Bruce Delventhal, Denis Demers (QMJHL), Gene Dupras, Krister Eriksson, Jeff Fanter (ECAC), Donald Guay, Peter Fillman, Marlene Fitzsimmons, Rob Fitzsimmons, Mel Foster, Pierre Genest, Dan Hamill, Lloyd Hamshaw (WHL), C. David Johnson, Lori Kessel (UHL), Robert Kirk, Gunter Klein, Marina Klein, Len Kotylo, Zhenia Kuperman, Eric Lavigne, Ron Leger, W.D. Lighthall, Roy W. Mackie, John MacKinnon (CHA), Sam Malkin, Al Mason, Carol McLaughlin, Mike Leonetti, Herb Morrell (OHL), John D. Painter (NCAA), Gary J. Pearce, Todd Radom, Valentina Riazanova, Dennis M. Riggin, Jason Rothwell (ECHL), Ed Saunders (Hockey East), Doug Spencer (WCHA), Prof. Bill Spray, Matt Steinke (CHL), William C.G. Swift Jr., David Talbot, Natalia Taran, Tony Techko, Garry Toffoli, Sammy Wallace (WCHL), Jeff Weiss (CCHA), Brenda Whiteway, William Wolper (AHL), Scott Woods (IHL).

Many persons over many years have contributed to the compilation and maintenance of the historical records of the National Hockey League. Our thanks to these current and former NHL employees and executives for their best efforts:

Susan Aglietti, Ron Andrews, Mark Atcheson, Rhonda Barber, Mario Carangi, Jocelyne Comeau, Luc Coulombe, Linda Delisi, Lise Desjardins, Susan Elliott, Benny Ercolani, Jane Freer, Gail Glenister, Jim Gregory, Mike Griffin, Dave Griffiths, Gerry Helper, Greg Inglis, Norm Jewison, David Keon, Dan Leary, Roger Leblond, Belinda Lerner, Bryan Lewis, Duane Lewis, Garry Lovegrove, Preston Lovegrove, Ken McKenzie, Gary Meagher, NHL Central Registry, Joel Nixon, Brian O'Neill, Carol Randall, Jackie Rinaldi, Carole Robertson, Michelle Romanin, Kelley Rossett, Madeline Supino, Chris Tredree, Hilda Turrif

Special thanks to the many persons who have contributed information, advice and/or hard work...

• the media relations departments of NHL, minor professional and junior clubs. Similar thanks to the sports information staffers from NCAA and CIAU hockey programs who helped fill in data gaps.

• our colleagues at the Hockey Hall of Fame in Toronto: Craig Campbell, Jeff Davis, Jeff Denomme, Phil Pritchard, Marilyn Robbins, Jane Rodney; and Paulette Laakkonen at the U.S. Hockey Hall of Fame in Eveleth, Minnesota;

• the Total Sports support team in Kingston, New York: Donna Harris, Mike Montella, Robbie Walters and Connie Neuhauser;

• Frank Daniels III, George Schlukbier, Petra Weishaupt and Will York at Total Sports in Raleigh, North Carolina;

• Maidie Oliveau

• John Martin and Cheryl Smith of Worldsport Properties, publishers of the *NHL Yearbook* magazine;

• Chris Whalen, Joe Fonseca and Marshall Hoare of Stafford Graphics, Toronto;

• Peter Bird, consulting typographic designer, of Starkey & Henricks, New York;

• Promotion, distribution and sales staffs at Andrews McMeel Publishing in Kansas City and at the Canadian Manda Group in Toronto;

• Staff and crews at Moore Data Management Services, *Total Hockey*'s printer in Scarborough, Ontario;

A particular tip of the approved helmet-and-visor—and an extended metaphor—is proferred to John Thorn, publisher at Total Sports, who gave us a double-Olympic-size rink to perform upon; to Arthur Pincus, Gary Meagher and David McConnachie of the NHL who flooded the ice and sang the national anthems before the game; to Benny Ercolani, Greg Inglis and David Keon of NHL public relations who sharpened our skates just so; and to David Pietrusza of Total Sports and Peggy Goddard and f-stop Fitzgerald of Balliett & Fitzgerald who drove the Zamboni that smoothed the surface. To honor such a superb team, it's *Total Hockey*'s responsibility and pleasure to put the biscuit in the basket. End of hockey metaphor.

LEAGUE AND INTERNATIONAL EVENT ABBREVIATIONS

LEAGUES

AAHL	All-American Hockey League
ACHL	Atlantic Coast Hockey League
ACSHL	Atlantic Coast Senior Hockey League
AHA	American Hockey Association
AHL	American Hockey League
AIAA	Atlantic Intercollegiate Athletic Association
AJHL	Alberta Junior Hockey Leagues
Alpenliga	Alpenliga (Europe)
ASHL	Alberta Senior Hockey Leagues
AUAA	Atlantic University Athletic Association
Austria	Austrian Hockey League
BCJHL	British Columbia Junior Hockey League
BHL	Boundary Hockey League
Big 4	Alberta Big 4 Hockey League 1919, 1920
Big 4	Maritime Senior Big 4 1946 to 1951
Big 6	Manitoba Big 6 Hockey League
Britain	British Ice Hockey League
CAHA	Canadian Amateur Hockey Association
CAHL	Canadian Amateur Hockey League
CAHL	Central Alberta Senior Hockey League
Cal-Pro	California Hockey League
Can-Am	Canadian-American Hockey League
Can-Pro	Canadian Professional Hockey League
CASH	Central Amateur Senior Hockey League
CBSHL	Cape Breton Senior Hockey Leagues
CCAU	Canadian Colleges Athletic Union
CCHA	Central Collegiate Hockey Association
Cgy-Jr.	Calgary and District Junior Hockey Leagues
Cgy-Sr.	Calgary and District Senior Hockey Leagues
CHA	Canadian Hockey Association
CHL	Central Hockey League 1925 to 1941
CHL	Central Professional Hockey League 1963 to 1985
CHL	Central Hockey League 1992 to date
CIAU	Canadian Interuniversity Athletic Union
CIHU	Canadian Intercollegiate Hockey Union
CIS	Commonwealth of Independent States
City Jr.	City and District Junior Hockey Leagues
City Sr.	City and District Senior Hockey Leagues
ColHL	Colonial Hockey League
CWUAA	Canadian Western University Athletic Association
CWUAA	Canadian Western University Athletic Association
Czech.	Czech Republic Extraleague
ECAC	Eastern College Athletic Conference
ECAHA *	Eastern Canada Amateur Hockey Association
ECHA	Eastern Canada Hockey Association
ECHA	Eastern Collegiate Hockey Association 1991 to date
ECHL	Eastern Canada Professional Hockey League 1914–15
ECHL	East Coast Hockey League
ECSHL	Eastern Canada Senior Hockey League
Edm-Jr.	Edmonton and District Junior Hockey Leagues
Edm-Sr.	Edmonton and District Senior Hockey Leagues
EHL	Eastern Hockey League
EOHL	Eastern Ontario Senior Hockey League
EPHL	Eastern Professional Hockey League
EuroHL	European Hockey League
EXHIB	Team played Exhibition Season only
F'ton-Jr.	Fredericton and District Junior Hockey Leagues
F'ton-Sr.	Fredericton and District Senior Hockey Leagues
FAHL	Federal Amateur Hockey League
Finland	Finnish National League
France	French National Hockey Association
Germany	Bundesliga/Deutsche Eishockey Liga
GPAC	Great Plains Athletic Conference
H.E.	Hockey East
H.S.	Canadian and American High School
Hfx-Jr.	Halifax and District Junior Hockey Leagues
Hfx-Sr.	Halifax and District Senior Hockey Leagues
IAHL	International-American Hockey League
IHL	International Hockey League 1945 to date
IHL *	International Professional Hockey League 1904 to 1907
Inter-Sr.	Intermediate Hockey Leagues
Italy	Italian National Hockey Association
Ivy	Ivy Collegiate Hockey Division
Jr. A	Junior A Hockey League
Jr. B	Junior B Hockey Division
Juvenile	Canadian Juvenile Hockey Division
Kootenay	British Columbia-Kootenay Hockey League
MHL Sr. *	Manitoba Professional Hockey League 1907 to 1909

MHL Sr.	Manitoba Senior Hockey Leagues 1909 to date
MIAA	Maritime Intercollegiate Athletic Union
MIHL	Maritime Independant Hockey League
MJHL	Manitoba Junior Hockey League
MMHL	Maritime Major Hockey League
MOHL	Michigan-Ontario Hockey League
MPHL *	Maritime Professional Hockey League
MSHL	Maritime Senior Hockey League
MTHL	Metro Toronto Hockey League
Mtl-Jr.	Montreal and District Junior Hockey Leagues
Mtl-Sr.	Montreal and District Senior Hockey Leagues
MWJHL	Mid-West Junior Hockey League
NAHL	North American Hockey League
Nat-Team	National Teams
NBIHL	New Brunswick Intermediate Hockey League
NBJHL	New Brunswick Junior Hockey Leagues
NBSHL	New Brunswick Senior Hockey Leagues
NCAA	National Collegiate Athletic Association
NCHA	Northern Collegiate Hockey Association
NEHL	North East Hockey League
NESHL	New England Senior Hockey League
Nfld.	Newfoundland Senior Hockey Leagues
NHA *	National Hockey Association
NHL *	National Hockey League
NMHL	Northern Michigan Hockey League
NNBSL	North Shore New Brunswick Sr. Hockey League
NOHA	Northern Ontario Hockey Association
NOHL	Northern Ontario Hockey League
NSHL	Northern Saskatchewan Hockey League
NSSHL	Nova Scotia Senior Hockey League
NWHL	North West Hockey League
NYJHL	New York Junior Hockey Leagues
NYOHL	New York-Ontario Senior Hockey League
OHA	Ontario Hockey Association Junior A
OHA Sr.	Ontario Hockey Association Senior A
OHL	Ontario Hockey League
OJHL	Ontario Junior Hockey Leagues
OPHL *	Ontario Professional Hockey League 1909 to 1911
OPHL	Ontario Professional Hockey League 1930–31
OQAA	Ontario-Quebec Athletic Association
OSHL	Okanogan Senior Hockey League
OSIAA	Ottawa-St. Lawrence Intercolleg. Athletic Assoc.
Ott-Jr.	Ottawa and District Junior Hockey Leagues
Ott-Sr.	Ottawa and District Senior Hockey Leagues
OUAA	Ontario University Athletic Association
OVSHL	Ottawa Valley Senior Hockey League
PCHA *	Pacific Coast Hockey Association
PCHL	Pacific Coast Hockey League
PEI Jr.	Prince Edward Island Junior Hockey Leagues
PEI Sr.	Prince Edward Island Senior Hockey Leagues
PHL	Pacific Hockey League
PrHL	Prairie Hockey League
QCHL	Quebec City Senior Hockey League
QHL	Quebec Hockey League
QJHL	Quebec Junior Hockey Leagues
QMJHL	Quebec Major Junior Hockey League
QPHL	Quebec Provincial Hockey League
QSHL	Quebec Senior Hockey League
QUAA	Quebec University Athletic Association
RCHL	Regina City Senior Hockey league
RMJHL	Rocky Mountain Junior Hockey League
RMSHL	Rocky Mountain Senior Hockey League
Scotland	Scottish Hockey League
SHL	Southern Hockey League 1973 to 1976
SHL	Southern Hockey League 1995 to 1997
SIHL	Senior Intercollegiate Hockey League
SJHL	Saskatchewan Junior Hockey League
Slovak	Slovak Republic Extraleague
SLSHL	St. Lawrence Senior Hockey League
SSHL	Saskatchewan Senior Hockey League
SunHL	Sunshine Hockey League
Sweden	Swedish Elite Hockey League
Switz.	Swiss National League
TBJHL	Thunder Bay Junior Hockey League
TBSHL	Thunder Bay Senior Hockey League
Tem-Pro	Temiskaming Professional Hockey League
Tier II	Tier II Hockey Division
Tor-Jr.	Toronto and District Junior Hockey Leagues
Tor-Sr.	Toronto and District Senior Hockey Leagues
Tri-State	Tri-State Senior Hockey League
UHL	United Hockey League
USAHA	United States Amateur Hockey Association

USHL	United States (Pro) Hockey League 1945 to 1951
USHL	United States (Sr.) Hockey League 1960 to 1970
USHL	United States (Jr.) Hockey League 1977 to date
USSR	Union of Soviet Socialist Republics
Van-Jr.	Vancouver and District Junior Hockey Leagues
Van-Sr.	Vancouver and District Senior Hockey Leagues
WCHA	Western Collegiate Hockey Association
WCHL *	Western Canada Hockey League 1921 to 1925
WCHL	West Coast Hockey League 1995 to date
WCIAA	Western Canada Intercollegiate Athletic Assoc.
WCIAU	Western Canada Intercollegiate Athletic Union
WCJHL	Western Canadian Junior Hockey Leagues
WCSHL	Western Canada Senior Hockey League
WHA *	World Hockey Association
WHL *	Western Hockey League 1925–26
WHL	Western Hockey League 1951 to 1975
WHL	Western Canada Major Junior Hockey League 1977 to date
WIHA	Western Intercollegiate Hockey Association USA
WIHL	Western International Hockey League
WOHL	Western Ontario Senior Hockey League
WPHL	Western Pennsylvania Hockey League 1903, 1907, 1908
WPHL	Western Professional Hockey League 1995 to date

* Indicates major league. See Chapter 68, page 642, The Rival Big Leagues; Chapter 70, page 646, Using the Pre-Expansion Player Register; and Chapter 72, page 823, Using the Modern Player register.

INTERNATIONAL EVENTS

C Cup	Canada Cup 1976, 1981, 1984, 1987, 1991
ChalCup	NHL–Soviet Challenge Cup 1979
D Cup	NHL–Sweden Dagens Nyheter Cup
EJC-A	IIHF European Junior Championships, Pool A
FrTour	NHL–Soviet Friendship Tour
Olympics	Winter Olympic Games 1924 to 1998
RV'87	Rendez-Vouz '87
Summit	Canada–Soviet Summit Series 1972 and 1974
SuperS	NHL-Soviet Super Series
W Cup	World Cup of Hockey 1996
WC-A	IIHF World Championships, Pool A
WC-B	IIHF World Championships, Pool B
WC-C	IIHF World Championships, Pool C
WC-C1	IIHF World Championships, Pool C, Group 1
WC-C2	IIHF World Championships, Pool C, Group 2
WC-D	IIHF World Championships, Pool D
WEC	IIHF World and European Championships
WEC-A	IIHF World and European Championships, Pool A
WEC-B	IIHF World and European Championships, Pool B
WEC-C	IIHF World and European Championships, Pool C
WEC-D	IIHF World and European Championships, Pool D
WJC-A	IIHF World Junior Championships, Pool A
WJC-B	IIHF World Junior Championships, Pool B
WJC-C	IIHF World Junior Championships, Pool C
WJC-C1	IIHF World Junior Championships, Pool C, Group 1
WJC-C2	IIHF World Junior Championships, Pool C, Group 2
WJC-D	IIHF World Junior Championships, Pool D

ACCURACY AND COMPREHENSIVENESS

remain *Total Hockey*'s top priorities.

We appreciate clarification and comments from our readers.

Please direct these to:

Total Hockey
194 Dovercourt Road
Toronto, Ontario
Canada M6J 3C8

e-mail ddiam48@aol.com

All readers who correct errors or contribute in other ways will be acknowledged in future editions.

Your involvement makes a better book.